CW00693702

Income Tax Regulations

Including Proposed Regulations

As of May 5, 2019

Volume 6

Proposed Regulations and Preambles

Wolters Kluwer Editorial Staff Publication

ISBN 978-0-8080-4783-4 (Set)
ISBN 978-0-8080-5228-9 (Volume 1)
ISBN 978-0-8080-5229-6 (Volume 2)
ISBN 978-0-8080-5231-9 (Volume 3)
ISBN 978-0-8080-5232-6 (Volume 4)
ISBN 978-0-8080-5233-3 (Volume 5)
ISBN 978-0-8080-5234-0 (Volume 6)

2700 Lake Cook Road
Riverwoods, IL 60015
800 344 3734
CCHCPELink.com

Printed in the United States of America

Certified Sourcing
www.sfiprogram.org
SFI-01681

CONTENTS

TABLE OF CONTENTS

INDEX
PROPOSED REGULATIONS UNDER THE 1986 CODE

[References are to Reg. § numbers.]

[Index to Final and Temporary Regulations Begins on Page 19,003.]

A

T

U

V

W

[The next page is 73,031.]

List of Proposed Regulations—2019

Under the Administrative Procedure Act, most changes in regulations must be issued in proposed form, and interested parties are given, generally, 30 days after the date of publication of the Notice of Proposed Rulemaking in the Federal Register within which to file objections or suggestions. Sometime thereafter, the regulations are issued in permanent form. Proposed income tax regulations under the 1986 Code are included in this list.

1986 Code Sec.	Regs. Section	Date Proposed[1]	Date Adopted[2]	Paragraph (¶)
2	1.2-1, 1.2-2	1/19/17	. . . .	49,737
3	1.3-1	1/19/17	. . . .	49,737
21	1.21-1	1/19/17	. . . .	49,737
25	1.25-1—1.25-8	5/8/85	. . . .	49,054
	1.25-4	9/3/85	. . . .	49,059
25A	1.25A-0—1.25A-2, 1.25A-5	8/2/16	. . . .	49,709
32	1.32-2	1/19/17	. . . .	49,737
36B	1.36B-2	7/8/16	. . . .	49,704
	1.36B-2	10/29/18	. . . .	49,774
	1.36B-6	5/3/13	. . . .	49,574
	1.36B-6	9/1/15	. . . .	49,664
	1.36B-2—1.36B-4	7/28/14	. . . .	49,624
40	1.40-1, 1.40-2	7/29/08	. . . .	49,389
40A	1.40A-1	7/29/08	. . . .	49,389
41	1.41-0, 1.41-6	12/13/13	. . . .	49,599
42	1.42-1	6/22/87	. . . .	49,080
	1.42-2	2/15/18	TD 9849, 3/11/19	49,755
	1.42-5	2/25/16	. . . .	49,687
	1.42-10	3/3/16	. . . .	49,689
45D	1.45D-1	8/11/08	. . . .	49,393
46	1.46-11	2/15/18	TD 9849, 3/11/19	49,755
48	1.48-9	1/26/82	. . . .	49,020
	1.48-12	8/8/18	. . . .	49,765
50	1.50-1	7/22/16	. . . .	49,707
56	1.56(g)-1	12/30/92	. . . .	49,130
	1.56-1, 1.56(g)-1, 1.56A-1—1.56A-5	2/15/18	TD 9849, 3/11/19	49,755
59A	1.59A-1—1.59A-10	12/21/18	. . . .	49,783
61	1.61-6, 1.61-7	4/8/86	. . . .	49,070
	1.61-16	2/3/78	. . . .	49,007
	1.61-21	10/9/92	. . . .	49,132
	1.61-2T, 1.61-21	2/15/18	TD 9849, 3/11/19	49,755
62	1.62-1	3/28/88	. . . .	49,092
63	1.63-1—1.63-3	1/19/17	. . . .	49,737

[1] Date published in the *Federal Register*.
[2] Date filed with the *Federal Register*.

1986 Code Sec.	Regs. Section	Date Proposed[1]	Date Adopted[2]	Paragraph (¶)
	1.63-3	9/19/17	. . . .	49,744
66	1.66-4, 1.66-5	8/13/13	. . . .	49,580
	1.66-0—1.66-5	11/20/15	. . . .	49,674
67	1.67-1, 1.67-2	3/28/88	. . . .	49,092
	1.67-3T	9/30/91	. . . .	49,124
	1.67-3T	9/3/92	. . . .	49,131
71	1.71-1	8/31/84	. . . .	49,041
72	1.72-4, 1.72-13	4/30/75	. . . .	49,003
	1.72-6	10/18/06	. . . .	49,280
	1.72(e)-1	2/4/86	. . . .	49,066
	1.72-15, 1.72-17A, 1.72-18	2/15/18	TD 9849, 3/11/19	49,755
74	1.74-1, 1.74-2	1/9/89	. . . .	49,110
78	1.78-1	2/15/18	TD 9849, 3/11/19	49,755
	1.78-1	12/7/18	. . . .	49,781
79	1.79-4	2/4/86	. . . .	49,066
83	1.83-3, 1.83-6	5/24/05	. . . .	49,242
101	1.101-2	4/30/75	. . . .	49,003
	1.101-5, 1.101-6	2/15/18	TD 9849, 3/11/19	49,755
	1.101-8	12/15/92	. . . .	49,134
	1.101-1, 1.101-6	3/25/19	. . . .	49,789
102	1.102-1	1/9/89	. . . .	49,110
103	5f.103-1	11/15/82	. . . .	49,021
	5f.103-1	12/19/86	. . . .	49,073
	5f.103-1	9/19/17	. . . .	49,744
	5f.103-2	9/28/17	TD 9845, 12/28/18	49,746
	5c.103-1—5c.103-3, 5f.103-3	2/15/18	TD 9849, 3/11/19	49,755
	1.103-8	8/22/84	. . . .	49,038
	1.103-8	11/7/85	. . . .	49,062
	1.103-10	2/21/86	. . . .	49,067
	1.103-10	2/21/86	. . . .	49,068
103A	6a.103A-1—6a.103A-3	7/1/81	. . . .	49,017
	6a.103A-1, 6a.103A-2	11/10/81	. . . .	49,019
	6a.103A-2	5/8/85	. . . .	49,054
	6a.103A-2	4/8/86	. . . .	49,070
105	1.105-11	2/25/83	. . . .	49,025
	7.105-1, 7.105-2	2/15/18	TD 9849, 3/11/19	49,755
106	1.106-1	6/15/87	. . . .	49,078
117	1.117-0—1.117-6	6/9/88	. . . .	49,100
120	1.120-1, 1.120-2	4/29/80	. . . .	49,011
122	1.122-1	4/30/75	. . . .	49,003
125	1.125-0—1.125-3	8/6/07	. . . .	49,315
	1.125-5—1.125-7	8/6/07	. . . .	49,315
126	16A.126-0—16A.126-2	5/21/81	. . . .	49,016
132	1.132-1	2/15/18	TD 9849, 3/11/19	49,755
133	1.133-1	2/4/86	. . . .	49,066
147	1.147(f)-1	9/28/17	TD 9845, 12/28/18	49,746
148	1.148-0, 1.148-1, 1.148-11	6/12/18	TD 9854, 4/8/19	49,761

[1] Date published in the *Federal Register*.

[2] Date filed with the *Federal Register*.

1986 Code Sec.	Regs. Section	Date Proposed[1]	Date Adopted[2]	Paragraph (¶)
	1.148-1A—1.148-6A, 1.148-9A, 1.148-10A	2/15/18	TD 9849, 3/11/19	49,755
149	1.149(d)-1A	2/15/18	TD 9849, 3/11/19	49,755
150	1.150-1	4/10/02	. . . .	49,187
	1.150-3	12/28/18	. . . .	49,786
	1.150-1A	2/15/18	TD 9849, 3/11/19	49,755
151	1.151-1—1.151-4	1/19/17	. . . .	49,737
152	1.152-2	11/30/00	. . . .	49,176
	1.152-0—1.152-5	1/19/17	. . . .	49,737
162	1.162-10	2/4/86	. . . .	49,066
	1.162-20	11/25/80	. . . .	49,014
	1.162-25T	1/7/85	. . . .	49,051
	1.162-25T	11/1/85	. . . .	49,061
	1.162-25T	2/15/18	TD 9849, 3/11/19	49,755
	1.162-30	2/26/04	. . . .	49,216
	1.162-31	6/10/16	. . . .	49,701
	1.162(l)-1	7/28/14	. . . .	49,624
163	5f.163-1	11/15/82	. . . .	49,021
	5f.163-1	4/8/86	. . . .	49,070
	5f.163-1	9/19/17	. . . .	49,744
	1.163-4	4/8/86	. . . .	49,070
	1.163-5, 1.163-5T	9/19/17	. . . .	49,744
	1.163-5T	5/19/88	. . . .	49,097
	1.163-5T	5/19/88	. . . .	49,098
	1.163-6	5/8/85	. . . .	49,054
	1.163-8	7/2/87	. . . .	49,081
	1.163-9, 1.163-10	12/22/87	. . . .	49,087
	1.163(j)-0—1.163(j)-10	6/13/91	Withdrawn, 11/26/2018	49,121
	1.163(j)-0—1.163(j)-11	12/28/18	. . . .	49,780
165	1.165-11	10/14/16	. . . .	49,716
	1.165-12	9/19/17	. . . .	49,744
	1.165-13T	2/15/18	TD 9849, 3/11/19	49,755
166	1.166-4	12/19/83	. . . .	49,030
	1.166-4	2/15/18	TD 9849, 3/11/19	49,755
167	1.167(a)-5	7/18/88	. . . .	49,105
	1.167(a)-11	2/16/84	. . . .	49,032
	1.167(a)-13	3/15/94	. . . .	49,144
	1.167(a)-14	8/8/18	. . . .	49,765
	1.167(n)-0—1.167(n)-7	5/31/02	. . . .	49,190
168	1.168-1—1.168-6	2/16/84	. . . .	49,032
	1.168(b)-1, 1.168(d)-1, 1.168(i)-4, 1.168(i)-6, 1.168(k)-0	8/8/18	. . . .	49,765
	1.168(j)-1	7/2/85	. . . .	49,055

[1] Date published in the *Federal Register*.
[2] Date filed with the *Federal Register*.

1986 Code Sec.	Regs. Section	Date Proposed[1]	Date Adopted[2]	Paragraph (¶)
	1.168(f)(8)-1, 1.168(f)(8)-1T, 5c.168(f)(8)-1—5c.168(f)(8)-11, 5f.168(f)(8)-1	2/15/18	TD 9849, 3/11/19	49,755
169	1.169-3	8/8/18	. . . .	49,765
170A	1.170A-1, 1.170A-13	8/27/18	. . . .	49,768
172	1.172(h)-0—1.172(h)-5	9/17/12	. . . .	49,548
178	1.178-1	2/16/84	. . . .	49,032
	1.178-2, 1.178-3	2/15/18	TD 9849, 3/11/19	49,755
179	1.179-4, 1.179-6	8/8/18	. . . .	49,765
179B	1.179B-1	6/27/08	. . . .	49,376
183	1.183-1	8/7/80	. . . .	49,013
197	1.197-1	3/15/94	. . . .	49,144
	1.197-2	12/19/17	. . . .	49,738
199	1.199-0—1.199-4, 1.199-6, 1.199-8	8/27/15	. . . .	49,661
199A	1.199A-0—1.199A-6	8/9/18	TD 9847, 2/4/19	49,766
	1.199A-0, 1.199A-3, 1.199A-6	2/8/19	. . . .	49,787
212	1.212-1	8/7/80	. . . .	49,013
	1.212-1	2/26/04	. . . .	49,216
215	1.215-1	8/31/84	. . . .	49,041
219	1.219-1—1.219-3	7/14/81	. . . .	49,018
	1.219(a)-1—1.219(a)-6	1/23/84	. . . .	49,031
220	1.220-1	7/14/81	. . . .	49,018
245A	1.245A(e)-1	12/28/18	. . . .	49,785
249	1.249-1	4/8/86	. . . .	49,070
250	1.250-0, 1.250-1, 1.250(a)-1, 1.250(b)-1—1.250(b)-6	3/6/19	. . . .	49,788
262	1.262-1	8/7/80	. . . .	49,013
263	1.263(g)-1—1.263(g)-5	1/18/01	. . . .	49,181
263A	1.263A-0, 1.263A-1, 1.263A-2	9/5/12	TD 9843, 11/19/18	49,546
	1.263A-9	12/28/18	. . . .	49,780
265	1.265-2	5/7/04	. . . .	49,219
267	1.267(a)-2	11/30/84	. . . .	49,048
269A	1.269A-1	3/31/83	. . . .	49,026
	1.267A-1—1.267A-7	12/28/18	. . . .	49,785
274	1.274-1, 1.274-3, 1.274-8	1/9/89	. . . .	49,110
	1.274-5T, 1.274-6T	11/1/85	. . . .	49,061
	1.274-6T	2/15/18	TD 9849, 3/11/19	49,755
275	51.2, 51.11	7/28/14	. . . .	49,625
280A	1.280A-1—1.280A-3	8/7/80	. . . .	49,013
	1.280A-1—1.280A-3	7/21/83	. . . .	49,028
280F	1.280F-1—1.280F-5	10/24/84	. . . .	49,045
	1.280F-1, 1.280F-3, 1.280F-5	11/1/85	. . . .	49,061
280H	1.280H-0T, 1.280H-1T	5/27/88	. . . .	49,099
301	1.301-2	1/19/09	Withdrawn, 3/28/19	49,413

[1] Date published in the *Federal Register*.

[2] Date filed with the *Federal Register*.

1986 Code Sec.	Regs. Section	Date Proposed[1]	Date Adopted[2]	Paragraph (¶)
	1.301-1	3/26/19	. . . .	49,792
302	1.302-2, 1.302-5	1/19/09	Withdrawn, 3/28/19	49,413
304	1.304-1—1.304-3, 1.304-5	1/19/09	Withdrawn, 3/28/19	49,413
305	1.305-1, 1.305-3, 1.305-7	4/13/16	. . . .	49,695
312	1.312-10	11/15/00	. . . .	49,175
	1.312-15	8/8/18	. . . .	49,765
337	1.337(d)-7	6/8/16	. . . .	49,700
	1.337(d)-3	3/25/19	. . . .	49,790
	1.337(d)-7	3/26/19	. . . .	49,791
351	1.351-1	12/23/14	. . . .	49,635
	1.351-2	1/19/09	Withdrawn, 3/28/19	49,413
354	1.354-1	1/19/09	Withdrawn, 3/28/19	49,413
355	1.355-0, 1.355-1, 1.355-3	5/8/07	. . . .	49,297
	1.355-0, 1.355-2, 1.355-8, 1.355-9	7/15/16	. . . .	49,706
	1.355-0, 1.355-8	12/19/16	. . . .	49,728
	1.355-1	1/19/09	Withdrawn, 3/28/19	49,413
356	1.356-1	1/19/09	Withdrawn, 3/28/19	49,413
	1.356-1	3/26/19	. . . .	49,792
358	1.358-1, 1.358-2, 1.358-6	1/19/09	Withdrawn, 3/28/19	49,413
361	1.361-1	12/23/14	. . . .	49,635
367	1.367(a)-1, 1.367(a)-6, 1.367(d)-1	5/16/86	. . . .	49,071
	1.367(a)-1T	1/16/90	. . . .	49,115
	1.367(b)-5, 1.367(b)-8, 1.367(e)-1	11/15/00	. . . .	49,175
	1.367(a)-9	2/11/09	. . . .	49,415
368	1.368-1	1/19/09	Withdrawn, 3/28/19	49,413
	1.368-1	12/19/11	Withdrawn, 4/1/19	49,513
	1.368-2	3/26/19	. . . .	49,792
381	1.381(c)(11)-1	2/15/18	TD 9849, 3/11/19	49,755
	1.381(c)(4)-1	10/15/18	. . . .	49,771
	1.381(c)(20)-1	12/28/18	. . . .	49,780
382	1.382-2T	8/11/87	. . . .	49,083
	1.382-1, 1.382-2, 1.382-5, 1.382-6	12/28/18	. . . .	49,780
	1.382-7	10/15/18	. . . .	49,771
	1.382-2T	9/20/89	. . . .	49,112
383	1.383-1	12/21/18	. . . .	49,783
385	1.383-0, 1.383-1	12/28/18	. . . .	49,780
385	1.385-3, 1.385-4	10/21/16	. . . .	49,717

[1] Date published in the *Federal Register*.

[2] Date filed with the *Federal Register*.

1986 Code Sec.	Regs. Section	Date Proposed[1]	Date Adopted[2]	Paragraph (¶)
	1.385-1, 1.385-2, 1.385-3	9/24/18	. . . .	49,770
401	1.401(a)-1, 1.401(a)-3	11/10/04	. . . .	49,228
	1.401(a)-1	1/27/16	. . . .	49,678
	1.401(a)-13, 1.401(a)-20	10/9/08	. . . .	49,401
	1.401-1, 1.401-4, 1.401-10—1.401-13, 1.401(e)-1—1.401(e)-6, 1.401(f)-1, 11.402(e)(4)(A)-1, 11.402(e)(4)(B)-1	2/15/18	TD 9849, 3/11/19	49,755
	1.401(k)-1, 1.401(k)-3, 1.401(k)-6, 1.401(m)-3	11/14/18	. . . .	49,778
402	1.402(a)-1, 1.402(e)-2, 1.402(e)-3	4/30/75	. . . .	49,003
	1.402(a)-1, 1.402(e)-2, 1.402(e)-14	5/31/79	. . . .	49,008
	1.402(a)-1, 1.402(e)-1	2/15/18	TD 9849, 3/11/19	49,755
	1.402(a)(5)-1	2/4/86	. . . .	49,066
	1.402(f)-1	10/9/08	. . . .	49,401
403	1.403(a)-1, 1.403(a)-2	4/30/75	. . . .	49,003
	1.403(a)-1	2/15/18	TD 9849, 3/11/19	49,755
	1.403(a)-2	5/31/79	. . . .	49,008
404	1.404(a)-1, 1.404(b)-1, 1.404(d)-1,1.404(k)-1	2/4/86	. . . .	49,066
	1.404(a)-1,1.404(a)-2A —1.404(a)-10, 1.404(a)(8)-1T, 1.404(e)-1A	2/15/18	TD 9849, 3/11/19	49,755
	1.404(h)-1	7/14/81	. . . .	49,018
	1.404(k)-2	8/24/05	. . . .	49,247
404A	1.404A-0—1.404A-7	5/7/93	. . . .	49,142
408	1.408-2—1.408-4, 1.408-6—1.408-9	7/14/81	. . . .	49,018
	1.408-2, 1.408-3, 1.408-10	1/23/84	. . . .	49,031
	1.408-5	11/16/84	. . . .	49,047
409A	1.409A-0, 1.409A-4	12/8/08	. . . .	49,406
	1.409A-0—1.409A-4, 1.409A-6	6/22/16	. . . .	49,702
410	1.410(a)-3, 1.410(a)-8, 1.410(a)-9	1/6/88	. . . .	49,088
	1.410(a)-4A	4/8/88	. . . .	49,093
	1.410(a)-1, 1.410(b)-0, 1.410(b)-1	2/15/18	TD 9849, 3/11/19	49,755
411	1.411(a)-1, 1.411(a)-7, 1.411(b)-2, 1.411(c)-1	4/11/88	. . . .	49,093
	1.411(a)-1, 1.411(a)-5, 1.411(a)-9, 1.411(d)-2, 1.411(d)-5	2/15/18	TD 9849, 3/11/19	49,755
	1.411(a)-3, 1.411(a)-4, 1.411(a)-8	1/6/88	. . . .	49,088
	1.411(a)-11	10/9/08	. . . .	49,401

[1] Date published in the *Federal Register*.
[2] Date filed with the *Federal Register*.

1986 Code Sec.	Regs. Section	Date Proposed[1]	Date Adopted[2]	Paragraph (¶)
	1.411(b)-1	6/18/08	. . . .	49,374
	1.411(c)-1	12/22/95	. . . .	49,151
	1.411(d)-1	4/9/80	. . . .	49,010
	1.411(d)-1	6/12/80	. . . .	49,012
412	1.412(a)-1, 1.412(b)-1, 1.412(b)-4, 1.412(c)(2)-2,1.412(c)(4)-1—1.412(c)(10)-1, 1.412(g)-1	12/1/82	. . . .	49,022
	1.412(b)-5, 1.412(c)(1)-3T, 1.412(l)(7)-1	2/15/18	TD 9849, 3/11/19	49,755
413	1.413-1, 1.413-2	12/1/82	. . . .	49,022
414	1.414(m)-1—1.414(m)-4	2/25/83	. . . .	49,025
	1.414(o)-1	8/27/87	. . . .	49,084
	1.414(q)-1	2/19/88	. . . .	49,089
415	1.415(c)-2	11/15/13	. . . .	49,593
416	1.416-1	2/15/18	TD 9849, 3/11/19	49,755
417	1.417(e)-1	10/9/08	. . . .	49,401
	1.417(e)-1	11/25/16	. . . .	49,722
419	1.419-1	2/4/86	. . . .	49,066
419A	1.419A-1	2/4/86	. . . .	49,066
	1.419A-2	7/3/85	. . . .	49,056
432	1.432(a)-1, 1.432(b)-1	3/18/08	. . . .	49,357
442	1.442-1	1/5/93	. . . .	49,139
444	1.444-0T—1.444-3T	5/27/88	. . . .	49,099
446	1.446-1	1/28/99	. . . .	49,169
	1.446-2	12/22/92	. . . .	49,136
	1.446-3	7/10/91	. . . .	49,123
	1.446-3	2/26/04	. . . .	49,216
	1.446-3	9/16/11	. . . .	49,493
	1.446-3	5/8/15	. . . .	49,647
	1.446-3	12/28/18	. . . .	49,780
	1.446-4	12/19/2017	. . . .	49,753
448	1.448-1T	6/16/87	. . . .	49,079
451	1.451-1, 1.451-2	4/8/86	. . . .	49,070
	1.451-5	10/15/18	. . . .	49,771
453	1.453-1	5/3/84	. . . .	49,034
	1.453-4—1.453-6, 1.453-10	2/15/18	TD 9849, 3/11/19	49,755
	15A.453-0, 15A.453-1	2/4/81	. . . .	49,015
453A	1.453A-0—1.453A-2	2/15/18	TD 9849, 3/11/19	49,755
453B	1.453B-1	12/23/14	. . . .	49,635
454	1.454-1	4/8/86	. . . .	49,070
457	1.457-1, 1.457-2, 1.457-4, 1.457-6, 1.457-7, 1.457-9—1.457-13	6/22/16	. . . .	49,703
460	1.460-3, 1.460-4, 1.460-5, 1.460-6	8/4/08	. . . .	49,390

[1] Date published in the *Federal Register*.

[2] Date filed with the *Federal Register*.

1986 Code Sec.	Regs. Section	Date Proposed[1]	Date Adopted[2]	Paragraph (¶)
465	1.465-1—1.465-7, 1.465-9—1.465-13, 1.465-22—1.465-26, 1.465-38, 1.465-39, 1.465-41—1.465-45, 1.465-66—1.465-69, 1.465-75—1.465-79, 1.465-95	6/5/79	. . . .	49,009
468A	1.468A-1, 1.468A-5	12/29/16	. . . .	49,730
469	1.469-1T, 1.469-2T, 1.469-3T, 1.469-5T	2/24/88	. . . .	49,090
	1.469-0, 1.469-5, 1.469-5T, 1.469-9	11/28/11	. . . .	49,509
	1.469-9, 1.469-11	12/28/18	. . . .	49,780
471	1.471-12	1/28/99	. . . .	49,169
472	1.472-2	2/10/83	. . . .	49,024
475	1.475(a)-1, 1.475(a)-2, 1.475(b)-3	1/4/95	. . . .	49,145
	1.475(c)-1, 1.475(c)-2, 1.475(e)-1, 1.475(f)-1,1.475(f)-2, 1.475(g)-1	1/28/99	. . . .	49,169
	1.475(g)-2	3/6/98	. . . .	49,165
	1.475-0, 1.475(b)-4	2/15/18	TD 9849, 3/11/19	49,755
482	1.482-0—1.482-2, 1.482-8	3/6/98	. . . .	49,165
	1.482-1	9/16/15	. . . .	49,667
501	1.501(a)-1, 1.501(c)(3)-1	7/2/14	. . . .	49,619
	1.501(c)(4)-1	11/29/13	. . . .	49,595
	1.501(c)(9)-2	8/7/92	. . . .	49,129
	1.501(c)(20)-1	4/29/80	. . . .	49,011
	1.501(c)(17)-1, 1.501(c)(18)-1, 1.501(k)-1	2/15/18	TD 9849, 3/11/19	49,755
503	1.503(c)-1, 1.503(e)-4	2/15/18	TD 9849, 3/11/19	49,755
505	1.505(c)-1	2/4/86	. . . .	49,066
506	1.506-1	7/12/16	. . . .	49,705
508	1.508-1	7/2/14	. . . .	49,619
509	1.509(a)-4	2/9/16	. . . .	49,682
511	1.511-2	6/22/15	. . . .	49,654
512	1.512(a)-5	2/6/14	. . . .	49,609
	1.512(b)-1	9/16/11	. . . .	49,493
513	1.513-1	6/22/15	. . . .	49,654
514	1.514(c)-2	11/23/16	. . . .	49,721
527	1.527-3	8/28/79	. . . .	49,009A
529	1.529-0—1.529-6	8/24/98	. . . .	49,167
529A	1.529A-0—1.529A-7	6/22/15	. . . .	49,654
563	1.563-3	1/5/93	. . . .	49,139
581	1.581-2	12/19/83	. . . .	49,030
582	1.582-1	4/8/86	. . . .	49,070
591	1.591-1	12/19/83	. . . .	49,030
593	1.593-1—1.593-11	12/19/83	. . . .	49,030

[1] Date published in the *Federal Register*.

[2] Date filed with the *Federal Register*.

1986 Code Sec.	Regs. Section	Date Proposed[1]	Date Adopted[2]	Paragraph (¶)
	1.593-1—1.593-8, 1.593-10, 1.593-11	2/15/18	TD 9849, 3/11/19	49,755
612	1.612-3	2/8/00	....	49,172
617	1.617-4	11/3/14	....	49,633
636	1.636-1	4/8/86	....	49,070
641	1.641(c)-1	4/19/19	....	49,796
642	1.642(c)-1, 1.642(c)-2	5/5/88	....	49,096
	1.642(c)-3	8/27/18	....	49,768
643	1.643(d)-1	2/15/18	TD 9849, 3/11/19	49,755
	1.643(f)-1	8/9/18	TD 9847, 2/4/19	49,766
652	1.652(b)-1	4/30/75	....	49,003
664	1.664-1	12/19/75	....	49,004
665	1.665(f)-1A, 1.665(g)-1A	2/15/18	TD 9849, 3/11/19	49,755
667	1.667(a)-1A	2/15/18	TD 9849, 3/11/19	49,755
671	1.671-1, 1.671-2	9/27/96	....	49,154
702	1.702-3	12/23/87	....	49,086
704	1.704-1	5/24/05	....	49,242
	1.704-1	2/4/16	....	49,680
	1.704-1	10/5/16	....	49,714
	1.704-1	12/7/16	....	49,725
	1.704-1	8/9/18	....	49,767
	1.704-1, 1.704-3	11/3/14	....	49,633
	1.704-1, 1.704-3	1/19/17	....	49,738
	1.704-1, 1.704-3	8/8/18	....	49,765
	1.704-3, 1.704-4	8/22/07	....	49,318
	1.704-3, 1.704-4	1/16/14	....	49,604
	7.704-1	2/15/18	TD 9849, 3/11/19	49,755
705	1.705-1	8/9/18	....	49,767
	1.706-4	8/9/18	....	49,767
706	1.706-2	11/30/84	....	49,048
	1.706-3	5/24/05	....	49,242
	1.706-0, 1.706-2, 1.706-2T, 1.706-3, 1.706-4	8/3/15	....	49,658
707	1.707-0, 1.707-5, 1.707-9	10/5/16	....	49,714
	1.707-1	5/24/05	....	49,242
	1.707-0, 1.707-1, 1.707-2, 1.707-9	7/23/15	....	49,657
	1.707-5, 1.707-5T, 1.707-9, 1.707-9T	7/18/18	....	49,762
721	1.721-1	5/24/05	....	49,242
	1.721-1	12/23/14	....	49,655
	1.721(c)-1—1.721(c)-7	1/19/17	....	49,738
732	1.732-1	11/3/14	....	49,633
	1.732-2	1/16/14	....	49,604
734	1.734-1, 1.734-2	1/16/14	....	49,604
736	1.736-1	11/3/14	....	49,633
	1.736-1	7/23/15	....	49,657
737	1.737-1, 1.737-2, 1.737-5	8/22/07	....	49,318

[1] Date published in the *Federal Register*.

[2] Date filed with the *Federal Register*.

1986 Code Sec.	Regs. Section	Date Proposed[1]	Date Adopted[2]	Paragraph (¶)
	1.737-1	1/16/14	. . . .	49,604
743	1.743-1	1/16/14	. . . .	49,604
	1.743-1	8/8/18	. . . .	49,765
751	1.751-1	11/3/14	. . . .	49,633
752	1.752-0, 1.752-2, 1.752-4, 1.752-5	12/16/13	. . . .	49,600
	1.752-0, 1.752-2	10/5/16	. . . .	49,714
	1.752-2	10/21/16	. . . .	49,717
754	1.754-1	10/12/17	. . . .	49,749
755	1.755-1	1/16/14	. . . .	49,604
	1.755-1	11/3/14	. . . .	49,633
761	1.761-1	5/24/05	. . . .	49,242
	1.761-3	2/5/13	. . . .	49,564
801	1.801-4	1/2/97	. . . .	49,156
802	1.802-2—1.802-5, 1.802(b)-1	2/15/18	TD 9849, 3/11/19	49,755
803	1.803-1—1.803-7	2/15/18	TD 9849, 3/11/19	49,755
806	1.806-1, 1.806-2	2/15/18	TD 9849, 3/11/19	49,755
809	1.809-1—1.809-3, 1.809-5, 1.809-7, 1.809-8	2/15/18	TD 9849, 3/11/19	49,755
810	1.810-1, 1.810-2, 1.810-4	2/15/18	TD 9849, 3/11/19	49,755
815	1.815-5	2/15/18	TD 9849, 3/11/19	49,755
818	1.818-3	4/8/86	. . . .	49,070
822	1.822-1—1.822-3, 1.822-4, 1.822-8, 1.822-12	2/15/18	TD 9849, 3/11/19	49,755
831	1.831-2, 1.831-4	2/15/18	TD 9849, 3/11/19	49,755
832	1.832-7T	2/15/18	TD 9849, 3/11/19	49,755
846	1.846-0, 1.846-1, 1.846-2, 1.846-2T, 1.846-3, 1.846-4, 1.846-4T	11/7/16	. . . .	49,776
851	1.851-2	9/28/16	. . . .	49,713
856	5.856-1	2/15/18	TD 9849, 3/11/19	49,755
860C	1.860C-2	12/28/18	. . . .	49,780
860D	1.860D-1	9/19/17	. . . .	49,744
860F	1.860F-4	9/30/91	. . . .	49,124
860G	1.860G-3	4/13/16	. . . .	49,695
861	1.861-2	4/8/86	. . . .	49,070
	1.861-3	4/13/16	. . . .	49,695
	1.861-4	10/17/07	. . . .	49,327
	1.861-8—1.861-12, 1.861-14	9/14/88	. . . .	49,109
	1.861-8—1.861-14, 1.861-17	12/7/18	. . . .	49,781
	1.861-9T	2/15/18	TD 9849, 3/11/19	49,755
	1.861-9T, 1.861-13T	8/2/89	. . . .	49,111
	1.861-12	1/19/09	Withdrawn, 3/28/19	49,413
	1.861-18	10/15/18	. . . .	49,771
863	1.863-3, 1.863-7	3/6/98	. . . .	49,165
	1.863-3A	9/14/88	. . . .	49,109
	1.863-7	9/16/11	. . . .	49,493

[1] Date published in the *Federal Register*.
[2] Date filed with the *Federal Register*.

1986 Code Sec.	Regs. Section	Date Proposed[1]	Date Adopted[2]	Paragraph (¶)
864	1.864-4, 1.864-6	3/6/98	. . . .	49,165
	1.864-8	6/14/88	. . . .	49,101
	1.864(b)-1	6/12/98	. . . .	49,166
	1.864(c)(8)-1	12/27/18	. . . .	49,784
871	1.871-14	9/19/17	. . . .	49,744
	1.871-1	2/15/18	TD 9849, 3/11/19	49,755
	1.871-15	1/24/17	. . . .	49,740
881	1.881-3	9/19/17	. . . .	49,744
882	1.882-5	3/8/96	. . . .	49,152
	1.882-5	12/28/18	. . . .	49,780
884	1.884-1	3/8/96	. . . .	49,152
	1.884-2T, 1.884-3T	9/2/88	. . . .	49,106
892	1.892-1—1.892-7	6/27/88	. . . .	49,103
	1.892-4, 1.892-5	11/3/11	. . . .	49,503
894	1.894-1	3/6/98	. . . .	49,165
897	1.897-4A, 1.897-5—1.897-9	5/5/88	. . . .	49,095
	1.897-7, 1.897-7T	12/27/18	. . . .	49,784
898	1.898-0—1.898-4	1/5/93	. . . .	49,139
	1.898-4	6/13/01	. . . .	49,139
901	1.901-2	3/30/07	. . . .	49,293
	1.901(j)-1	12/7/18	. . . .	49,781
	1.901(m)-1—1.901(m)-8	12/7/16	. . . .	49,725
902	1.902-3	2/15/18	TD 9849, 3/11/19	49,755
	1.902-1, 1.902-3	3/26/19	. . . .	49,792
904	1.904-4, 1.904(g)-3	6/25/12	. . . .	49,542
	1.904-1—1.904-6, 1.904(b)-3, 1.904(f)-12	12/7/18	. . . .	49,781
	1.904-5	7/13/99	. . . .	49,170
905	1.905-3, 1.905-4, 1.905-5	6/23/88	. . . .	49,102
	1.905-3, 1.905-4, 1.905-5	11/7/07	. . . .	49,329
921	1.921-1T	2/3/87	. . . .	49,074
	1.921-1T, 1.921-2, 1.921-3T	2/15/18	TD 9849, 3/11/19	49,755
	1.921-3T	2/15/18	. . . .	49,755
922	1.923-1	2/15/18	TD 9849, 3/11/19	49,755
923	1.923-1T	2/15/18	TD 9849, 3/11/19	49,755
924	1.924(a)-1T, 1.924(c)-1, 1.924(d)-1, 1.924(e)-1	2/15/18	TD 9849, 3/11/19	49,755
925	1.925(a)-1, 1.925(a)-1T, 1.925(b)-1T	2/15/18	TD 9849, 3/11/19	49,755
926	1.926(a)-1, 1.926(a)-1T	2/15/18	TD 9849, 3/11/19	49,755
927	1.927(a)-1, 1.927(d)-2	3/3/87	. . . .	49,075
	1.927(b)-1T, 1.927(d)-1, 1.927(e)-1, 1.927(e)-2T, 1.927(f)-1	2/15/18	TD 9849, 3/11/19	49,755
936	1.936-2, 1.936-3, 1.936-3A, 7.936-1	1/21/86	. . . .	49,065
	1.936-10	5/13/91	. . . .	49,120
937	1.937-1	8/27/15	. . . .	49,662

[1] Date published in the *Federal Register*.
[2] Date filed with the *Federal Register*.

1986 Code Sec.	Regs. Section	Date Proposed[1]	Date Adopted[2]	Paragraph (¶)
951	1.951-2	2/15/18	TD 9849, 3/11/19	49,755
	1.951-1	10/10/18	. . . .	48,769
951A	1.951A-0—1.951A-7	10/10/18	. . . .	49,769
952	1.952-1	12/7/18	. . . .	49,781
953	1.953-0—1.953-7	4/17/91	. . . .	49,119
954	1.954-0—1.954-2, 1.954-9	7/13/99	. . . .	49,170
	1.954-1	12/7/18	. . . .	49,781
	1.954-1T	4/17/91	. . . .	49,119
	1.954-2	9/16/11	. . . .	49,493
	1.954-0, 1.954-2	12/19/2017	. . . .	49,753
956	1.956-1, 1.956-2	6/14/88	. . . .	49,101
	1.956-1	11/5/18	. . . .	49,775
	1.956-2	5/8/15	. . . .	49,647
	1.956-4	11/3/16	. . . .	49,720
959	1.959-1—1.959-4	8/29/06	. . . .	49,277
960	1.960-1—1.960-7	12/7/18	. . . .	49,781
961	1.961-1—1.961-4	8/29/06	. . . .	49,277
962	1.962-1, 1.962-2, 1.962-4	2/15/18	TD 9849, 3/11/19	49,755
	1.962-1, 1.962-2	8/2/18	TD 9846, 2/4/19	49,764
	1.962-1	3/6/19	. . . .	49,788
964	1.964-1	4/17/91	. . . .	49,119
	1.964-4	2/15/18	TD 9849, 3/11/19	49,755
	1.964-1	11/4/11	. . . .	49,504
965	1.965-0—1.965-9	5/2/18	TD 9846, 2/4/19	49,764
	1.965-5, 1.965-7	12/7/18	. . . .	49,781
986	1.986(c)-1	5/2/18	TD 9846, 2/4/19	49,764
987	1.987-1—1.987-4, 1.987-6, 1.987-8, 1.987-12	12/8/16	. . . .	49,726
988	1.988-1	3/17/92	. . . .	49,125
	1.988-1	9/16/11	. . . .	49,493
	1.988-2	3/17/92	. . . .	49,125
	1.988-4	3/6/98	. . . .	49,165
	1.988-5	3/17/92	. . . .	49,125
	1.988-7	12/19/2017	. . . .	49,753
991	1.991-1	2/3/87	. . . .	49,074
992	1.992-1, 1.992-2	2/3/87	. . . .	49,074
993	1.993-1	4/8/86	. . . .	49,070
995	1.995-2, 1.995-2A, 1.995-8, 1.995(f)-1	2/3/87	. . . .	49,074
	1.995-4	11/3/14	. . . .	49,633
996	1.996-1, 1.996-9	2/3/87	. . . .	49,074
999	1.999-1	2/24/77	. . . .	49,006
1001	1.1001-1	10/18/06	. . . .	49,280
	1.1001-3	12/28/18	. . . .	49,786
1002	1.1002-1	1/19/09	Withdrawn, 3/28/19	49,413
1012	1.1012-2	4/8/86	. . . .	49,070
1014	1.1014-10	3/4/16	. . . .	49,690

[1] Date published in the *Federal Register*.

[2] Date filed with the *Federal Register*.

1986 Code Sec.	Regs. Section	Date Proposed[1]	Date Adopted[2]	Paragraph (¶)
1016	1.1016-2	1/19/09	Withdrawn, 3/28/19	49,413
	1.1016-3, 1.1016-4	2/16/84	. . . .	49,032
	1.1016-5	4/8/86	. . . .	49,070
1031	1.1031(d)-1	7/18/88	. . . .	49,105
1037	1.1037-1	4/8/86	. . . .	49,070
1038	1.1038-1	2/15/18	TD 9849, 3/11/19	49,755
1041	1.1041-1	8/31/84	. . . .	49,041
1042	1.1042-1	2/4/86	. . . .	49,066
	1.1042-1T	7/10/03	. . . .	49,208
1058	1.1058-1, 1.1058-2	7/26/83	. . . .	49,029
1092	1.1092(b)-1, 1.1092(b)-2, 1.1092(b)-5	1/24/85	. . . .	49,052
	1.1092(b)-3, 1.1092(b)-4	1/24/85	. . . .	49,053
	1.1092(d)-2	5/2/95	. . . .	49,148
1223	1.1223-2	7/26/83	. . . .	49,029
	1.1223-1	2/15/18	TD 9849, 3/11/19	49,755
1231	1.1231-1	11/3/14	. . . .	49,633
1232	1.1232-1—1.1232-3A	4/8/86	. . . .	49,070
	1.1232-1, 1.1232-2, 1.1232-4	2/15/18	TD 9849, 3/11/19	49,755
1234	1.1234-3	2/5/13	. . . .	49,564
1234A	1.1234A-1	2/26/04	. . . .	49,216
1245	1.1245-1, 1.1245-2, 1.1245-4	11/3/14	. . . .	49,633
1248	1.1248-1	4/17/91	. . . .	49,119
	1.1248-1	11/3/14	. . . .	49,633
1250	1.1250-1	11/3/14	. . . .	49,633
1252	1.1252-2	11/3/14	. . . .	49,633
1254	1.1254-5	11/3/14	. . . .	49,633
1255	16A.1255-1, 16A.1255-2	5/21/81	. . . .	49,016
1256	1.1256(b)-1, 1.1256(g)-1	9/16/11	. . . .	49,493
1271	1.1271-0	8/25/04	. . . .	49,226
1275	1.1275-2	8/25/04	. . . .	49,226
	1.1275-1	9/24/18	. . . .	49,770
1287	1.1287-1	9/19/17	. . . .	49,744
1291	1.1291-0	4/28/95	. . . .	49,147
	1.1291-1—1.1291-7	4/1/92	. . . .	49,126
1293	1.1293-1	4/1/92	. . . .	49,126
	1.1293-2	12/24/96	. . . .	49,155
1294	1.1294-1	3/2/88	. . . .	49,091
1295	1.1295-1	4/1/92	. . . .	49,126
	1.1295-2	12/24/96	. . . .	49,155
1296	1.1296-4	1/2/98	. . . .	49,164
	1.1296-4, 1.1296-6	4/28/95	. . . .	49,147
1297	1.1297-4	9/27/96	. . . .	49,154
	1.1297-4	4/24/15	. . . .	49,645
1361	18.0	1/26/83	. . . .	49,023
	1.1361-5	3/6/15	. . . .	49,640
	1.1361-1	4/19/19	. . . .	49,796

[1] Date published in the *Federal Register*.
[2] Date filed with the *Federal Register*.

1986 Code Sec.	Regs. Section	Date Proposed[1]	Date Adopted[2]	Paragraph (¶)
1362	1.1362-3	3/6/15	. . . .	49,640
1374	1.1374-10	1/19/09	Withdrawn, 3/28/19	49,413
1379	18.1379-1, 18.1379-2	1/26/83	. . . .	49,023
1400Z	1.1400Z-2(a)-1, 1.1400Z-2(c)-1, 1.1400Z-2(d)-1, 1.1400Z-2(e)-1	10/29/18	. . . .	49,773
	1.1400Z2(a)-1— 1.1400Z2(d)-1, 1.1400Z2(f)-1, 1.1400Z2(g)-1	5/1/19	. . . .	49,795
1402	1.1402(a)-2	1/13/97	. . . .	49,157
	1.1402(g)-1	2/15/18	TD 9849, 3/11/19	49,755
1411	1.1411-0, 1.1411-3, 1.1411-4, 1.1411-7	12/2/13	. . . .	49,594
1441	1.1441-1	10/14/97	. . . .	49,160
	1.1441-1, 1.1441-3—1.1441-7	3/6/14	. . . .	49,612
	1.1441-1, 1.1441-6	12/18/18	. . . .	49,782
	1.1441-1, 1.1441-2, 1.1441-6, 1.1441-7	1/6/17	. . . .	49,733
	1.1441-3	10/14/97	. . . .	49,161
	1.1441-3	10/17/07	. . . .	49,326
1445	1.1445-10, 1.1445-11	5/5/88	. . . .	49,095
1446	1.1446-3	7/20/17	. . . .	49,743
1461	1.1461-2	4/13/16	. . . .	49,695
	1.1461-1, 1.1461-2	12/18/18	. . . .	49,782
1471	1.1471-2	4/13/16	. . . .	49,695
	1.1471-1, 1.1471-3, 1.1471-4	1/6/17	. . . .	49,732
	1.1471-1—1.1471-5	12/18/18	. . . .	49,782
	1.1471-5	1/6/17	TD 9852, 3/21/19	49,732
1472	1.1472-1	1/6/17	TD 9852, 3/21/19	49,732
1473	1.1473-1	4/13/16	. . . .	49,695
	1.1473-1	12/18/18	. . . .	49,782
1474	1.1474-1	1/6/17	. . . .	49,732
	1.1474-1, 1.1474-2	12/18/18	. . . .	49,782
1502	1.1502-1, 1.1502-5, 1.1502-33,1.1502-55	12/30/92	. . . .	49,138
	1.1502-2	12/30/92	withdrawn, 12/13/18	49,138
	1.1502-2, 1.1502-4, 1.1502-43, 1.1502-47, 1.1502-59A, 1.1502-100	12/21/18	. . . .	49,783
	1.1502-11, 1.1502-12	6/11/15	. . . .	49,650
	1.1502-12	8/29/06	. . . .	49,277
	1.1502-12, 1.1502-13, 1.1502-50	3/6/19	. . . .	49,788
	1.1502-13	5/7/04	. . . .	49,219
	1.1502-13	1/16/14	. . . .	49,604

[1] Date published in the *Federal Register*.

[2] Date filed with the *Federal Register*.

1986 Code Sec.	Regs. Section	Date Proposed[1]	Date Adopted[2]	Paragraph (¶)
	1.1502-13	3/6/15	....	49,640
	1.1502-13, 1.1502-21, 1.1502-36, 1.1502-79, 1.1502-90, 1.1502-91, 1.1502-95, 1.1502-98, 1.1502-99	12/28/18	....	49,780
	1.1502-21	5/31/02	....	49,189
	1.1502-21	6/23/10	....	49,450
	1.1502-21, 1.1502-72	9/17/12	....	49,548
	1.1502-21, 1.1502-22, 1.1502-28	3/6/15	....	49,640
	1.1502-21, 1.1502-21A, 1.1502-22, 1.1502-22A, 1.1502-23A,1.1502-24	6/11/15	....	49,650
	1.1502-32	8/29/06	....	49,277
	1.1502-76	3/6/15	....	49,640
	1.1502-80	11/14/01	....	49,183
	1.1502-80	3/18/04	....	49,217
	1.1502-81	3/18/87	....	49,076
	1.1502-91	10/24/11	....	49,499
	1.1502-12, 1.1502-13, 1.1502-32, 1.1502-51	10/10/18	....	48,769
1503	1.1503(d)-1, 1.1503(d)-3, 1.1503(d)-6, 1.1503(d)-7, 1.1503(d)-8	12/28/18	....	49,785
1504	1.1504-4	12/28/18	....	49,780
1552	1.1552-1	12/30/92	....	49,138
3401	31.3401(a)-1T	1/7/85	....	49,051
3406	31.3406(b)(3)-2	12/17/09	....	49,439
3501	31.3501(a)-1	1/7/85	....	49,051
	31.3501(a)-1T	2/15/18	TD 9849, 3/11/19	49,755
3508	31.3508-1	1/7/86	....	49,064
3509	31.3509-1	1/7/86	....	49,064
3511	31.3511-1	5/6/16	....	49,697
4701	46.4701-1	9/19/17	....	49,744
4941	53.4941(d)-2	8/20/85	....	49,057
4963	53.4963-1	11/7/18	TD 9855, 4/5/19	49,777
4971	54.4971-1—54.4971-3	12/1/82	....	49,022
4972	54.4972-1	2/15/18	TD 9849, 3/11/19	49,755
4973	54.4973-1	7/14/81	....	49,018
4974	54.4974-1	7/14/81	....	49,018
4976	54.4976-1T	2/4/86	....	49,066
4977	54.4977-1T	1/7/85	....	49,051
4978	54.4978-1T	2/4/86	....	49,066
4981	55.4981-1, 55.4981-2	2/15/18	TD 9849, 3/11/19	49,755
5000A	1.5000A-2	6/10/16	....	49,701
	1.5000A-3	7/8/16	....	49,704
6011	53.6011-1	11/7/18	TD 9855, 4/5/19	49,777
	54.6011-1T	4/3/87	....	49,077

[1] Date published in the *Federal Register*.
[2] Date filed with the *Federal Register*.

1986 Code Sec.	Regs. Section	Date Proposed[1]	Date Adopted[2]	Paragraph (¶)
	1.6011-2	2/3/87	. . . .	49,074
	1.6011-4	9/26/07	. . . .	49,322
	301.6011-2	6/22/15	. . . .	49,654
	301.6011-2	5/31/18	. . . .	49,760
	301.6011-6	9/14/10	. . . .	49,462
	301.6011-8	9/9/13	. . . .	49,587
	301.6011-9	9/9/13	. . . .	49,588
6012	1.6012-6	7/20/17	. . . .	49,743
	1.6012-2, 1.6012-4	2/15/18	TD 9849, 3/11/19	49,755
6013	1.6013-1	1/19/17	. . . .	49,737
6015	1.6015-0, 1.6015-5, 1.6015-9	8/13/13	. . . .	49,580
	1.6015-0—1.6015-9	11/20/15	. . . .	49,674
6031	1.6031(b)-1, 1.6031(c)-1	9/6/88	. . . .	49,107
	1.6031(a)-1	7/20/17	. . . .	49,743
6033	1.6033-2	11/25/80	. . . .	49,014
	1.6033-2	7/20/17	. . . .	49,743
6035	1.6035-1	3/4/16	. . . .	49,690
	1.6035-1	2/15/18	TD 9849, 3/11/19	49,755
6038	1.6038-2, 1.6038-5	10/10/18	. . . .	48,769
	1.6038-2, 1.6038-3	12/28/18	. . . .	49,785
	1.6038-2, 1.6038-3	3/6/19	. . . .	49,788
6038A	1.6038A-1, 1.6038A-2, 1.6038A-4	12/21/18	. . . .	49,783
	1.6038A-2	12/28/18	. . . .	49,785
	1.6038A-2	3/6/19	. . . .	49,788
6038B	1.6038B-1T	5/16/86	. . . .	49,071
	1.6038B-2	1/19/17	. . . .	49,738
6038C	1.6038C-1	12/10/90	. . . .	49,118
6041	1.6041-2, 1.6041-6	7/20/17	. . . .	49,743
6041A	1.6041A-1	1/7/86	. . . .	49,064
6043	1.6043-4T	5/24/05	. . . .	49,239
6045	1.6045-1	4/8/86	. . . .	49,070
	1.6045-1	9/19/17	. . . .	49,744
	1.6045-1	10/17/18	. . . .	49,772
6045B	1.6045B-1	4/13/16	. . . .	49,695
6046	1.6046-1	4/17/91	. . . .	49,119
6048	301.6048-1	2/15/18	TD 9849, 3/11/19	49,755
	404.6048-1	2/15/18	TD 9849, 3/11/19	49,755
6049	1.6049-4—1.6049-6	4/8/86	. . . .	49,070
	1.6049-5	12/17/86	. . . .	49,072
	1.6049-5	9/19/17	. . . .	49,744
	1.6049-7	9/30/91	. . . .	49,124
6050H	1.6050H-1, 1.6050H-1T, 1.6050H-2	2/15/18	TD 9849, 3/11/19	49,755
6050J	1.6050J-1T	8/31/84	. . . .	49,040
6050K	1.6050K-1	11/3/14	. . . .	49,633
6050S	1.6050S-1, 1.6050S-2	8/2/16	. . . .	49,709
6050Y	1.6050Y-1—1.6050Y-4	3/25/19	. . . .	49,789

[1] Date published in the *Federal Register*.

[2] Date filed with the *Federal Register*.

1986 Code Sec.	Regs. Section	Date Proposed[1]	Date Adopted[2]	Paragraph (¶)
6051	31.6051-1—31.6051-3	9/20/17	. . . .	49,745
6052	1.6052-2	9/20/17	. . . .	49,745
6055	1.6055-1	8/2/16	. . . .	49,708
	1.6055-2	6/10/16	. . . .	49,701
6056	301.6056-2	6/10/16	. . . .	49,701
6057	301.6057-1, 301.6057-2	6/21/12	. . . .	49,539
6071	53.6071-1	11/7/18	TD 9855, 4/5/19	49,777
	301.6071-2	9/14/10	. . . .	49,462
	31.6071(a)-1	7/20/17	. . . .	49,743
	1.6071-1	2/15/18	TD 9849, 3/11/19	49,755
6072	1.6072-2	7/20/17	. . . .	49,743
	1.6072-4	2/15/18	TD 9849, 3/11/19	49,755
6081	1.6081-11	6/21/12	. . . .	49,539
	1.6081-1—1.6081-3, 1.6081-5, 1.6081-6, 1.6081-9	7/20/17	. . . .	49,743
6091	1.6091-1	2/15/18	TD 9849, 3/11/19	49,755
6096	301.6096-2	2/15/18	TD 9849, 3/11/19	49,755
6103	301.6103(j)(1)-1	12/9/16	. . . .	49,727
	301.6103(n)-1	3/13/18	. . . .	49,758
6104	301.6104(c)-1	3/15/11	. . . .	49,475
6109	1.6109-2	2/15/12	. . . .	49,524
	301.6109-3	1/19/17	. . . .	49,737
	301.6109-4	9/20/17	. . . .	49,745
6111	301.6111-1	8/15/84	. . . .	49,036
	301.6111-1	10/31/84	. . . .	49,046
	301.6111-1	3/4/86	. . . .	49,069
	301.6111-3	9/26/07	. . . .	49,322
6164	1.6164-4, 1.6164-8	3/26/84	. . . .	49,033
6221	301.6221(a)-1	8/9/18	TD 9844, 12/21/18	49,767
6222	301.6222-1	8/9/18	TD 9844, 12/21/18	49,767
6225	301.6225-4	8/9/18	. . . .	49,767
	301.6225-1—301.6225-3	8/9/18	TD 9844, 12/21/18	49,767
6226	301.6226-4	8/9/18	. . . .	49,767
	301.6226-1—301.6226-3	8/9/18	TD 9844, 12/21/18	49,767
6227	301.6227-1—301.6227-3	8/9/18	TD 9844, 12/21/18	49,767
6231	301.6231-1	8/9/18	TD 9844, 12/21/18	49,767
6232	301.6232-1	8/9/18	TD 9844, 12/21/18	49,767
6233	301.6233(a)-1, 301.6233(b)-1	8/9/18	TD 9844, 12/21/18	49,767
6234	301.6234-1	8/9/18	TD 9844, 12/21/18	49,767
6235	301.6235-1	8/9/18	TD 9844, 12/21/18	49,767
6241	301.6241-1—301.6241-8	8/9/18	TD 9844, 12/21/18	49,767
6402	301.6402-7	6/11/15	. . . .	49,650
6501	301.6501(o)-1—301.6501(o)-3	2/15/18	TD 9849, 3/11/19	49,755
6511	301.6511(d)-7, 301.6511(g)-1	2/15/18	TD 9849, 3/11/19	49,755
6601	301.6601-1	10/9/84	. . . .	49,044
6611	301.6611-1	10/9/84	. . . .	49,044

[1] Date published in the *Federal Register*.

[2] Date filed with the *Federal Register*.

1986 Code Sec.	Regs. Section	Date Proposed[1]	Date Adopted[2]	Paragraph (¶)
6621	301.6621-2	12/28/84	. . . .	49,049
6652	301.6652-4	1/23/84	. . . .	49,031
6655	1.6655-0, 1.6655-2, 1.6655-6	10/15/18	. . . .	49,771
	1.6655-5	12/21/18	. . . .	49,783
6662	1.6662-8	3/4/16	. . . .	49,690
6689	301.6689-1	6/23/88	. . . .	49,102
	301.6689-1	11/7/07	. . . .	49,329
6693	301.6693-1	7/14/81	. . . .	49,018
6707A	301.6707A-1	8/28/15	TD 9853, 3/25/19	49,663
6708	301.6708-1	8/29/84	. . . .	49,039
6709	1.6709-1T	5/8/85	. . . .	49,054
6721	301.6721-1	3/4/16	. . . .	49,690
	301.6721-0, 301.6721-1	10/17/18	. . . .	49,772
	301.6721-1	5/31/18	. . . .	49,760
6722	301.6722-1	3/4/16	. . . .	49,690
	301.6722-1	10/17/18	. . . .	49,772
6723	301.6723-1A	2/15/18	TD 9849, 3/11/19	49,755
6724	301.6724-1	7/9/03	. . . .	49,206
	301.6724-1	8/2/16	. . . .	49,708
	301.6724-1	8/2/16	. . . .	49,709
	301.6724-1	10/17/18	. . . .	49,772
7519	1.7519-0T—1.7519-3T	5/27/88	. . . .	49,099
7602	301.7602-1	3/28/18	. . . .	49,759
7611	301.7611-1	8/5/09	. . . .	49,426
7701	301.7701-1	9/14/10	. . . .	49,462
	305.7701-1	5/7/84	. . . .	49,035
	301.7701-2	5/4/16	. . . .	49,696
	301.7701-3	12/28/18	. . . .	49,785
	301.7701-17	2/4/86	. . . .	49,066
	301.7701(b)-7	4/27/92	. . . .	49,127
7702	1.7702-1	7/5/91	. . . .	49,122
	1.7702-2, 1.7702A-1	12/15/92	. . . .	49,134
7705	301.7705-1, 301.7705-2	5/6/16	. . . .	49,697
7871	305.7871-1	5/7/84	. . . .	49,035
7872	1.7872-1—1.7872-14	8/20/85	. . . .	49,057
	1.7872-4	4/8/86	. . . .	49,070
....	300.3	10/13/16	. . . .	49,715
	300.0, 300.5, 300.6, 300.10—300.13	11/19/18	. . . .	49,779
	301.9100-3	4/17/08	. . . .	49,363
9801	54.9801-1, 54.9801-2, 54.9801-4—54.9801-7	12/30/04	. . . .	49,234
	54.9801-2	6/10/16	. . . .	49,701
	54.9801–2	10/29/18	. . . .	49,774
9802	54.9802-3	10/7/09	. . . .	49,435
	54.9802-4	10/29/18	. . . .	49,774
9815	54.9815-2711	10/29/18	. . . .	49,774
9831	54.9831-1	12/30/04	. . . .	49,234
	54.9831-1	6/10/16	. . . .	49,701
	54.9831-1	10/29/18	. . . .	49,774
Procedural Rules	601.106	9/20/93	. . . .	49,143

[The next page is 73,601.]

[1] Date published in the *Federal Register*.
[2] Date filed with the *Federal Register*.

DETERMINATION OF TAX LIABILITY

Dependency Exemption: Authorized Placement Agency: Definition

Dependency Exemption: Authorized Placement Agency: Definition.—Amendments to Reg. §§1.2-1 and 1.2-2, relating to the definition of an authorized placement agency for purposes of a dependency exemption for a child placed for adoption that were issued prior to the changes made to the law by the Working Families Tax Relief Act of 2004, are proposed (published in the Federal Register on January 19, 2017) (REG-137604-07).

Par. 2. Section 1.2-1 is revised to read as follows:

§1.2-1. Returns of surviving spouse and head of household.—(a) *In general.*—Tax is determined under section 1(a) for a return of a surviving spouse, as defined in section 2(a) and §1.2-2(a). Tax is determined under section 1(b) for a return of a head of household, as defined in section 2(b) and §1.2-2(b).

(b) *Death of a spouse.*—If married taxpayers have different taxable years solely because of the death of either spouse, the taxable year of the deceased spouse is deemed to end on the last day of the surviving spouse's taxable year for purposes of determining their eligibility to file a joint return for that year. For rules relating to filing a joint return in the year a spouse dies, see section 6013 and the related regulations.

(c) *Tax tables.*—For rules on the use of the tax tables that apply to individuals, see section 3 and the related regulations.

(d) *Change in rates.*—For the treatment of taxable years during which a change in the tax rates occurs, see section 15.

(e) *Applicability date.*—This section applies to taxable years beginning after the date these regulations are published as final regulations in the **Federal Register**.

Par. 3. Section 1.2-2 is revised to read as follows:

§1.2-2. Definitions and special rules.—(a) *Surviving spouse.*—(1) *In general.*—If a taxpayer is eligible to file a joint return under section 6013 (without applying section 6013(a)(3)) for the taxable year in which the taxpayer's spouse dies, the taxpayer qualifies as a surviving spouse for each of the two taxable years immediately following the year of the spouse's death if the taxpayer—

(i) Has not remarried before the close of the taxable year; and

(ii) Maintains as the taxpayer's home a household that is for the taxable year the principal place of abode of a son or daughter (including by adoption), stepson, or stepdaughter who is a member of the taxpayer's household and who is a dependent of the taxpayer within the meaning of paragraph (a)(2) of this section.

(2) *Dependent.*—An individual is a dependent of a taxpayer for purposes of this paragraph (a) if the taxpayer may claim a deduction under section 151 for the individual, without applying sections 152(b)(1), (b)(2), and (d)(1)(B).

(b) *Head of household.*—(1) *In general.*—A taxpayer qualifies as a head of household if the taxpayer is not married at the end of the taxable year, is not a surviving spouse, as defined in paragraph (a) of this section, and either—

(i) Maintains as the taxpayer's home a household that is for more than one-half of the taxable year the principal place of abode of a qualifying child or dependent of the taxpayer, within the meaning of paragraph (b)(2) of this section, who is a member of the taxpayer's household during that period; or

(ii) Maintains a household, whether or not the taxpayer's home, that is for the taxable year the principal place of abode of a parent of the taxpayer, within the meaning of paragraph (b)(3) of this section.

(2) *Qualifying child or dependent.*—(i) *Qualifying child.*—An individual is a qualifying child for purposes of this paragraph (b) if the individual is a qualifying child of the taxpayer as defined in section 152(c) and the related regulations, determined without applying section 152(e). However, if the individual is married at the end of the taxpayer's taxable year, the individual is not a qualifying child for purposes of this section if the individual is not the taxpayer's dependent because of the limitations of section 152(b)(2) (relating to an individual filing a joint return with his or her spouse) or 152(b)(3) (relating to individuals who are citizens or nationals of other countries).

(ii) *Dependent.*—An individual is a dependent for purposes of this paragraph (b) if the individual is the taxpayer's dependent, within the meaning of section 152 without applying sections 152(d)(2)(H) (relating to an individual qualifying as a member of the household) and 152(d)(3) (relating to the special rule for multiple support agreements) for whom the taxpayer may claim a deduction under section 151.

(3) *Parent.*—An individual is a parent of the taxpayer for purposes of this paragraph (b) if the individual is the taxpayer's father or mother, including a father or mother who legally adopted the taxpayer, and is the taxpayer's dependent within the meaning of section 152 without applying section 152(d)(3), relating to the special rule for multiple support agreements, for whom the taxpayer may claim a deduction under section 151.

(4) *Limitation.*—An individual may qualify only one taxpayer as a head of household for taxable years beginning in the same calendar year.

(5) *Marital status.*—For purposes of this paragraph (b), the marital status of a taxpayer is determined at the end of the taxpayer's taxable year. A taxpayer is considered not married if the taxpayer is legally separated from the taxpayer's spouse under a decree of divorce or separate maintenance, if at any time during the taxable year the taxpayer's spouse is a nonresident alien, or if the provisions of section 7703(b) are satisfied. A taxpayer is considered married if the taxpayer's spouse, other than a spouse who is a nonresident alien, dies during the taxable year.

(6) *Nonresident alien.*—A taxpayer does not qualify as a head of household if the tax-

payer is a nonresident alien, as defined in section 7701(b)(1)(B), at any time during the taxable year.

(c) *Member of the household.*—An individual is a member of a taxpayer's household if the individual and the taxpayer reside in the same living quarters and the taxpayer maintains the household, in part, for the benefit of the individual. An individual is a member of a taxpayer's household despite a temporary absence due to special circumstances. An individual is not treated as a member of the taxpayer's household if, at any time during the taxable year of the taxpayer, the relationship between the individual and the taxpayer violates local law. See §1.152-4(c)(2) for rules relating to temporary absences.

(d) *Maintaining a household.*—(1) *In general.*—A taxpayer maintains a household only if during the taxable year the taxpayer pays more than one-half of the cost of operating the household for the mutual benefit of the residents. These expenses include property taxes, mortgage interest, rent, utility charges, upkeep and repairs, property insurance, and food consumed on the premises. A taxpayer may treat a home's fair market rental value as a cost of maintaining a household, instead of the sum of payments for property taxes, mortgage interest, and property insurance. Expenses of maintaining a household do not include—

(i) The cost of clothing, education, medical treatment, vacations, life insurance, and transportation;

(ii) The value of services performed in the household by the taxpayer or any other person qualifying the taxpayer as a head of household or as a surviving spouse; or

(iii) An expense paid or reimbursed by any other person.

(2) *Proration of costs.*—In determining whether a taxpayer pays more than one-half of the cost of maintaining a household that is the principal place of abode of a qualifying child or dependent for less than a taxable year, the cost for the entire taxable year is prorated on the basis of the number of calendar months the qualifying child or dependent resides in the household. A period of less than a calendar month is treated as a full calendar month. Thus, for example, if the cost of maintaining a household for a taxable year is $30,000, and a taxpayer shares a principal place of abode with a qualifying child or dependent from May 20 to December 31, the taxpayer must furnish more than $10,000 (8/12 of $30,000 × 50 percent) in maintaining the household from May 1 to December 31 to satisfy the requirements of this paragraph (d).

(3) *New household.*—If a new household is established during the taxpayer's taxable year (for example, if spouses separate and one moves out of the family home with the child), the cost of maintaining the new household for the year is the cost of maintaining that household beginning with the date the new household is established. If one spouse and the child remain in the family home and the other parent moves out of the home, the cost of maintaining the household for the year is the cost of maintaining the household beginning with the date the other spouse moves out.

(4) *Birth, death, adoption, or placement.*—If an individual is a member of a household for less than a taxable year as a result of the individual's birth, death, adoption, or placement with a taxpayer for adoption or in foster care during that year, the requirement that the individual be a member of the household for more than one-half of the taxable year is satisfied if the individual is a member of the household for more than one-half of the period after the individual's birth, adoption, or placement for adoption or in foster care or before the individual's death.

(5) *Shared residence.*—(i) *In general.*—If two or more taxpayers not filing a joint return reside in the same living quarters, each taxpayer may be treated as maintaining a separate household if each provides more than one-half of the cost of maintaining the separate household. For this purpose, two households in the same living quarters are not considered separate households if any individual in one household is the spouse of any individual in the other household, or if any individual in one household may claim, or would have priority under the tiebreaker rules in section 152(c)(4) to claim, any individual in the other household as a dependent.

(ii) *Examples.*—The following examples illustrate the rules in this paragraph (d)(5). In each example, assume that if a taxpayer may be treated as residing in a separate household, that taxpayer provides more than one-half of the cost of maintaining that household.

Example 1. Two sisters and their respective children reside in the same living quarters. Neither sister may claim the other sister as a dependent. Each sister pays more than one-half of the expenses for herself and her children, and each sister claims each of her own children as a dependent. Because neither sister may claim the other sister as a dependent, and because neither sister would have priority to claim any of the other sister's children as a qualifying child under the tiebreaker rules of section 152(c)(4), each sister is treated as maintaining a separate household.

Example 2. A and B, an unmarried couple, have two children together (C1 and C2) and all four individuals live in the same living quarters for the entire tax year. Both A and B contribute to paying the expenses of the couple and the two children. A has higher adjusted gross income than B. Each parent files a tax return. Under the tiebreaker rules in section 152(c)(4), the parent with the higher adjusted gross income (in this case, A) would have priority to claim each child as a qualifying child if both claimed the child. As a result, B may not be treated as maintaining a separate household with either child or both children. Therefore, if B may be claimed as A's dependent, then all four individuals are members of the same household. However, if B may not be claimed as A's dependent, B may be treated as maintaining a separate household consisting solely of B, even if B claims one of the children as a dependent on B's return.

Example 3. The facts are the same as in *Example 2* of this paragraph (d)(5)(ii) except that A and B do not have any children together; C1 is the child of A and C2 is the child of B. Neither A nor B may claim the other as a dependent, and each parent pays more than one-half of the expenses for himself or herself and his or her child. Because neither A nor B may claim the other adult or the other adult's child as a dependent, each adult is treated as maintaining a separate household.

Example 4. Grandparent, Parent, and Child live together and Child meets the definition of a qualifying child for both Parent and Grandparent. Both Parent and Grandparent pay their respective expenses, and both contribute to paying Child's expenses. Neither Parent nor Grandparent may claim the other as a dependent. Under the tiebreaker rules of section 152(c)(4), Parent would have priority over Grandparent to claim Child as a qualifying child. Therefore, Grandparent may not be treated as maintaining a household for Grandparent and Child separate from the household of Parent. However, Parent may be treated as maintaining a household for Parent and Child separate from the household of Grandparent.

(e) *Special rules for maintaining a household.*—(1) *Principal place of abode.*—For purposes of this section, the term *principal place of abode* has the same meaning as in section 152 and § 1.152-4(c).

(2) *Part-year residence.*—If, during the taxable year, an individual who may qualify a taxpayer as head of household is born or dies, is adopted or lawfully placed for adoption with the taxpayer, is an eligible foster child, or is a missing child, whether the taxpayer maintained a household that is the principal place of abode of the individual for the required period is determined under § 1.152-4(d) and (e).

(3) *Change of location.*—A taxpayer may maintain a household even though the physical location of the household changes.

(f) *Certain married individuals living apart.*—An individual who is considered not married under section 7703(b) also is considered not married for all purposes of part I of subchapter A of chapter 1 of the Code.

(g) *Applicability date.*—This section applies to taxable years beginning after the date these regulations are published as final regulations in the **Federal Register**.

Dependency Exemption: Authorized Placement Agency: Definition

Dependency Exemption: Authorized Placement Agency: Definition.—Amendments to Reg. §§1.3-1, relating to the definition of an authorized placement agency for purposes of a dependency exemption for a child placed for adoption that were issued prior to the changes made to the law by the Working Families Tax Relief Act of 2004, are proposed (published in the Federal Register on January 19, 2017) (REG-137604-07).

Par. 4. Section 1.3-1 is revised to read as follows:

§ 1.3-1. Tax tables for individuals.—(a) *In general.*—Except as otherwise provided in paragraph (b) of this section, in lieu of the tax imposed by section 1, an individual who does not itemize deductions for the taxable year and whose taxable income for the taxable year does not exceed the ceiling amount as defined in paragraph (c) of this section, must determine his or her tax liability under the prescribed tax tables in tax forms and publications of the Internal Revenue Service. The individual must use the appropriate tax rate category under the tax tables. The tax imposed under section 3 and this section shall be treated as tax imposed by section 1.

(b) *Exceptions.*—Section 3 and this section do not apply to (1) an individual making a return for a period of fewer than 12 months as a result of a change in annual accounting period, or (2) an estate or trust.

(c) *Ceiling amount defined.*—The ceiling amount means the highest amount of taxable income for which a tax amount is determined in the tax tables for the tax rate category in which the taxpayer falls.

(d) *Special rule for surviving spouse.*—A taxpayer filing as a surviving spouse uses the same tax rate category as a taxpayer filing a joint return.

(e) *Applicability date.*—This section applies to taxable years beginning after the date these regulations are published as final regulations in the **Federal Register**.

Dependency Exemption: Authorized Placement Agency: Definition

Dependency Exemption: Authorized Placement Agency: Definition.—Amendments to Reg. § 1.21-1, relating to the definition of an authorized placement agency for purposes of a dependency exemption for a child placed for adoption that were issued prior to the changes made to the law by the Working Families Tax Relief Act of 2004, are proposed (published in the Federal Register on January 19, 2017) (REG-137604-07).

Par. 5. Section 1.21-1 is amended by revising paragraph (a)(1), removing paragraph (h), redesignating paragraphs (j), (k), and (l) as paragraphs (h), (j), and (k), and revising newly redesignated paragraph (k) to read as follows:

§ 1.21-1. Expenses for household and dependent care services necessary for gainful employment.—(a) *In general.*—(1) Section 21 allows a credit to a taxpayer against the tax imposed by chapter 1 for employment-related expenses for household services and care (as defined in paragraph (d) of this section) of a qualifying individual (as defined in paragraph (b) of this section). The purpose of the expenses must be to enable the taxpayer to be gainfully employed (as defined in paragraph (c) of this section). For taxable years beginning after December 31, 2004, a qualifying individual must have the same principal place of abode (as defined by paragraph (g) of this section) as the taxpayer for more than one-half of the taxable year.

* * *

(k) *Applicability date.*—(1) *In general.*—Except as provide in paragraph (k)(2) of this section, this section and §§ 1.21-2 through 1.21-4 apply to taxable years ending after August 14, 2007.

(2) *Exception.*—Paragraph (a)(1) of this section applies to taxable years beginning after the date these regulations are published as final regulations in the **Federal Register**.

Mortgage Credit Certificates: Issuance: Penalties

Mortgage Credit Certificates: Issuance: Penalties.—Temporary Reg. §§1.25-1T—1.25-4T, relating to the issuance of mortgage credit certificates, are also proposed as final and, when adopted, would become Reg. §§1.25-1—1.25-4 (published in the Federal Register on May 8, 1985).

§1.25-1. Credit for interest paid on certain home mortgages.
§1.25-2. Amount of credit.
§1.25-3. Qualified mortgage credit certificate.
§1.25-4. Qualified mortgage credit certificate program.

Mortgage Credit Certificates: Information

Mortgage Credit Certificates: Information Reporting.—An amendment to Temporary Reg. §1.25-4T, dealing with information reporting and policy statement requirements, is also proposed to be finalized (published in the Federal Register on September 3, 1985).

§1.25-4. Qualified mortgage credit certificate program.

Mortgage Credit Certificates: Issuance

Mortgage Credit Certificates: Issuance: Penalties.—Temporary Reg. §§1.25-5T—1.25-8T, relating to the issuance of mortgage credit certificates, are also proposed as final and, when adopted, would become Reg. §§1.25-5—1.25-8 (published in the Federal Register on May 8, 1985).

§1.25-5. Limitation on aggregate amount of mortgage credit certificates.
§1.25-6. Form of qualified mortgage credit certificate.
§1.25-7. Public notice.
§1.25-8. Reporting requirements.

Qualified Tuition: Related Expenses: Reporting

Qualified Tuition: Related Expenses: Reporting.—Amendments to Reg. §§1.25A-0—1.25A-2 and 1.25A-5, revising the rules for reporting qualified tuition and related expenses under section 6050S on a Form 1098-T, "Tuition Statement," and conforming the regulations to changes made to section 6050S by the Protecting Americans from Tax Hikes Act of 2015, are proposed (published in the Federal Register on August 2, 2016) (corrected September 26, 2016) (REG-131418-14).

Par. 2. Section 1.25A-0 is amended by:

1. Revising the entry for §1.25A-1(e)(1) introductory text.
2. Adding entries for §1.25A-1(e)(1), (2), and (3).
3. Revising the entries for §1.25A-1(f) introductory text and (f)(2).
4. Adding entries for §1.25A-1(f)(3) and (4).
5. Revising the entries for §1.25A-1(g) and (h).
6. Adding an entry for §1.25A-1(i).
7. Revising the entries for §§1.25A-2(d)(3), (4), (5), and (6).
8. Adding entries for §§1.25A-2(d)(7) and (e).
9. Revising the entry for §1.25A-5(f)(6).
10. Adding entries for §§1.25A-5(f)(7) and (g).

The revisions and additions read as follows:

§1.25A-0. Table of Contents.

* * *

§1.25A-1. Calculation of Education Tax Credit and General Eligibility Requirements.

* * *

(e) Identification requirements.

(1) In general.

(2) Additional identification requirements for the American Opportunity Tax Credit.

(i) TIN must be issued on or before the due date of the original return.

(ii) Return must include the eligible educational institution's employer identification number (EIN).

(3) Applicability dates.

(f) Statement requirement.

* * *

(2) Exceptions.

(3) Transition rule.

(4) Applicability date.

(g) Claiming the credit in the case of a dependent.

(h) Married taxpayers.

(i) Nonresident alien taxpayers and dependents.

§1.25A-2. Definitions.

* * *

(d) * * *

(3) Course materials for the American Opportunity Tax Credit for taxable years beginning after December 31, 2008.

(4) Personal expenses.

(5) Treatment of a comprehensive or bundled fee.

(6) Hobby courses.

(7) Examples.

(e) Applicability date.

* * *

§1.25A-5. Special Rules Relating to Characterization and Timing of Payments.

* * *

(f) * * *

(6) Treatment of refunds where qualified tuition and related expenses paid in two taxable years for the same academic period.

(7) Examples.

(g) Applicability date.

Par. 3. Section 1.25A-1 is amended by:
1. Revising paragraph (e).
2. Redesignating paragraphs (f), (g), and (h) as paragraphs (g), (h), and (i), respectively.
3. Adding a new paragraph (f).
4. In newly redesignated paragraph (g)(2), removing the language "(f)" and adding "(g)" in its place.

The revisions and additions read as follows:

§1.25A-1. Calculation of education tax credit and general eligibility requirements.

* * *

(e) *Identification requirements.*—(1) *In general.*—No education tax credit is allowed unless a taxpayer includes on the federal income tax return claiming the credit the name and the taxpayer identification number (TIN) of the student for whom the credit is claimed. For rules relating to assessment for an omission of a correct taxpayer identification number, see section 6213(b) and (g)(2)(J).

(2) *Additional identification requirements for the American Opportunity Tax Credit (AOTC).*—(i) *TIN must be issued on or before the due date of the original return.*—For any federal income tax return (including an amended return) filed after December 18, 2015, no AOTC is allowed unless the TIN of the student and the TIN for the taxpayer claiming the credit are issued on or before the due date, or the extended due date if the extension request is timely filed, for filing the return for the taxable year for which the credit is claimed.

(ii) *Return must include the eligible educational institution's employer identification number (EIN).*—For taxable years beginning after December 31, 2015, no AOTC is allowed unless the taxpayer includes the EIN of each eligible educational institution to which qualified tuition and related expenses were paid.

(3) *Applicability dates.*—(i) Except as provided in paragraphs (e)(3)(ii) and (iii) of this section, this paragraph (e) applies on or after December 26, 2002.

(ii) Paragraph (e)(2)(i) of this section applies to federal income tax returns (including amended returns) filed after December 18, 2015.

(iii) Paragraph (e)(2)(ii) of this section applies to taxable years beginning after December 31, 2015.

(f) *Statement requirement.*—(1) *In general.*—Except as provided in paragraph (f)(2) of this section, for taxable years beginning after June 29, 2015, no education tax credit is allowed unless the taxpayer (or the taxpayer's dependent) receives a statement furnished by an eligible educational institution, as defined in §1.25A-2(b), containing all of the information required under §1.6050S-1(b)(2). The amount of qualified tuition and related expenses reported on the statement furnished by an eligible educational institution may not reflect the total amount of the qualified tuition and related expenses paid during the taxable year for which a taxpayer may claim an education tax credit. A taxpayer that substantiates payment of qualified tuition and related expenses that are not reported on Form 1098-T, "Tuition Statement", may include those expenses in computing the amount of the education tax credit allowable for the taxable year.

(2) *Exceptions.*—Paragraph (f)(1) of this section does not apply—

(i) If the taxpayer or the taxpayer's dependent:

(A) Has not received such a statement from an eligible educational institution required to furnish such statement under section 6050S and the regulations thereunder as of January 31 of the year following the taxable year to which the education tax credit relates or the date the return is filed claiming the education tax credit, whichever is later;

(B) Has requested, in the manner prescribed in forms, instructions, or in other published guidance, the eligible educational institution to furnish the Form 1098-T after January 31 of the year following the taxable year to which the education tax credit relates but on or before the date the return is filed claiming the education tax credit; and

(C) Has cooperated fully with the eligible educational institution's efforts to obtain information necessary to furnish the statement;

(ii) If the eligible educational institution is not required to furnish a statement to the student under section 6050S and the regulations thereunder; or

(iii) As otherwise provided in published guidance of general applicability, see §601.601(d)(2) of this chapter.

(3) *Applicability date.*—Paragraph (f) of this section applies to credits claimed for taxable years beginning after June 29, 2015.

* * *

Par. 4. Section 1.25A-2 is amended by:
1. Revising paragraphs (d)(2)(i) and (ii).
2. In paragraph (d)(2)(iii), removing the language "(d)(3)" and adding "(d)(4)" in its place.

3. Redesignating paragraphs (d)(3), (4), (5), and (6) as paragraphs (d)(4), (5), (6), and (7), respectively.

4. Adding a new paragraph (d)(3).

5. In newly redesignated paragraph (d)(5), by removing the language "(d)(3)" and adding "(d)(4)" in its place.

6. In newly redesignated paragraph (d)(7), revising *Example 2*, redesignating *Examples 3, 4, 5*, and 6, as *Examples 4, 5, 6*, and *7*, and adding a new *Example 3*.

7. Adding paragraph (e).

The revisions and additions read as follows:

§1.25A-2. Definitions.

* * *

(d) * * *

(2) *Required fees.*—(i) *In general.*—Except as provided in paragraphs (d)(3) and (4) of this section, the test for determining whether any fee is a qualified tuition and related expense is whether the fee is required to be paid to the eligible educational institution as a condition of the student's enrollment or attendance at the institution.

(ii) *Books, supplies, and equipment.*—For taxable years beginning before January 1, 2009, for purposes of the Hope Scholarship Credit, and for taxable years beginning after December 31, 1997, for purposes of the Lifetime Learning Credit, qualified tuition and related expenses include fees for books, supplies, and equipment used in a course of study only if the fees must be paid to the eligible educational institution for the enrollment or attendance of the student at the institution. For taxable years beginning after December 31, 2008, see paragraph (d)(3) of this section for rules relating to books, supplies and equipment for purposes of the American Opportunity Tax Credit.

* * *

(3) *Course materials for the American Opportunity Tax Credit for taxable years beginning after December 31, 2008.*—For taxable years beginning after December 31, 2008, the term "qualified tuition and related expenses" for purposes of the American Opportunity Tax Credit under section 25A(i) includes the amount paid for course materials (such as books, supplies, and equipment) required for enrollment or attendance at an eligible educational institution. For this purpose, "required for enrollment or attendance" means that the course materials are needed for meaningful attendance or enrollment in a course of study, regardless of whether the course materials are purchased from the institution.

* * *

(7) * * *

Example 2. First-year students attending College W during 2008 are required to obtain books and other materials used in its mandatory first-year curriculum. The books and other reading materials are not required to be purchased from College W and may be borrowed from other students or purchased from off-campus bookstores, as well as from College W's bookstore. College W bills students for any books and materials purchased from College W's bookstore. The expenses paid for the first-year books and materials purchased at College W's bookstore are not qualified tuition and related expenses because under §1.25A-2(d)(2)(ii) the books and materials are not required to be purchased from College W for enrollment or attendance at the institution. In addition, expenses paid for the first-year books and materials borrowed from other students or purchased from vendors other than College W's bookstore are also not qualified tuition and related expenses because under §1.25A-2(d)(2)(ii) the books and materials are not required to be purchased from College W for enrollment or attendance at the institution.

Example 3. Assume the same facts as *Example 2*, except that the books and materials are required for first-year students attending College W during 2009. Because the expenses are paid with respect to enrollment or attendance after 2008, §1.25A-1(d)(3) applies rather than §1.25A-1(d)(2)(ii), if the taxpayer claims the American Opportunity Tax Credit under section 25A(i). Under §1.25A-1(d)(3), expenses for books and other course materials are qualified tuition and related expenses for purposes of the American Opportunity Tax Credit if they are needed for meaningful attendance in the student's course of study at College W. Accordingly, if the taxpayer claims the American Opportunity Tax Credit for 2009, the expenses paid for the first-year books and materials are qualified tuition and related expenses. However, if the taxpayer claims the Lifetime Learning Credit for 2009 under section 25A(c), §1.25A-2(d)(2)(ii) applies rather than §1.25A-1(d)(3). Accordingly, if the taxpayer claims the Lifetime Learning Credit, the expenses paid for the first-year books and materials purchased at College W's bookstore are not qualified tuition and related expenses because under §1.25A-2(d)(2)(ii) the books and materials are not required to be purchased from College W for enrollment or attendance at the institution.

* * *

(e) *Applicability date.*—(1) Except as provided in paragraph (e)(2) of this section, this section applies on or after December 26, 2002.

(2) Paragraphs (d)(2)(i), (d)(2)(ii), (d)(3), and *Examples 2* and *3* of paragraph (d)(7) of this section apply to qualified tuition and related expenses paid, and education furnished in academic periods beginning, on or after the date of publication of the Treasury decision adopting these rules as final regulations in the **Federal Register**. However, taxpayers may apply paragraphs (d)(2)(i), (d)(2)(ii), (d)(3), and *Examples 2* and *3* of paragraph (d)(7) of this section for taxable years beginning after December 31, 2008, for which the period of limitations on filing a claim for credit or refund under section 6511 has not expired.

Par. 5. Section 1.25A-5 is amended by:

1. In paragraph (e)(2)(ii), revising the *Example*.

2. Redesignating paragraph (f)(6) as paragraph (f)(7).

3. Adding a new paragraph (f)(6).

4. In newly redesignated paragraph (f)(7), adding *Example 4*.
5. Adding paragraph (g).
The revisions and additions read as follows:

§1.25A-5. Special rules relating to characterization and timing of payments.

* * *

(e) * * *

(2) * * *

(ii) * * *

Example. In December 2016, Taxpayer A, a calendar year taxpayer who is not a dependent of another taxpayer under section 151, receives a bill from College Z for $5,000 for qualified tuition and related expenses to attend College Z for the 2017 spring semester, which begins in January 2017. This is the first semester that Taxpayer A will attend College Z. On December 15, 2016, Taxpayer A pays College Z $1,000 in qualified tuition and related expenses for the 2017 spring semester. On February 15, 2017, Taxpayer A pays College Z the remaining $4,000 due for qualified tuition and related expenses for the 2017 spring semester. In August 2017, Taxpayer A receives a bill from College Z for $7,000 for qualified tuition and related expenses to attend College Z for the 2017 fall semester, which begins in September 2017. Taxpayer A pays the entire $7,000 on September 1, 2017. In December 2017, Taxpayer A receives a bill from College Z for $7,000 for qualified tuition and related expenses to attend for the 2018 spring semester. Taxpayer A pays $1,000 of the 2018 spring semester bill on December 15, 2017 and $6,000 of that bill in February 15, 2018. Taxpayer A does not enroll in an eligible educational institution for the 2018 fall semester or the 2019 spring semester. Taxpayer A may claim an education tax credit on Taxpayer A's 2016 Form 1040 with respect to the $1,000 taxpayer paid to College Z on December 15, 2016 for the 2017 spring semester. On Taxpayer A's 2017 Form 1040, Taxpayer A may claim an education credit with respect to the $12,000 Taxpayer A paid to College Z during 2017 ($4,000 paid on February 15, 2017 for the 2017 spring semester, $7,000 paid on September 1, 2017, for the 2017 fall semester, and $1,000 paid on December 15, 2017, for the 2018 spring semester). On Taxpayer A's 2018 Form 1040, Taxpayer A may claim an education credit with respect to the $6,000 taxpayer paid to College Z on February 15, 2018.

* * *

(f) * * *

(6) *Treatment of refunds where qualified tuition and related expenses paid in two taxable years for the same academic period*.—If a taxpayer or someone other than the taxpayer—

(i) Pays qualified tuition and related expenses in one taxable year (prior taxable year) for a student's enrollment or attendance at an eligible educational institution during an academic period beginning in the first three months of the taxpayer's next taxable year (subsequent taxable year);

(ii) Pays qualified tuition and related expenses in the subsequent taxable year for the academic period beginning in the first three months of the subsequent taxable year; and

(iii) Receives a refund of qualified tuition and related expenses during the subsequent taxable year for the academic period beginning in the first three months of the subsequent taxable year (including an amount treated as a refund under paragraph (f)(4) or (5) of this section), the taxpayer may allocate the refund in any proportion to qualified tuition and related expenses paid in the prior taxable year under paragraph (f)(2) or (3) of this section or the subsequent taxable year under paragraph (f)(1) of this section, except that the amount of the refund allocated to a taxable year may not exceed the qualified tuition and related expenses paid during the taxable year with respect to the academic period beginning in the subsequent taxable year. The sum of the amounts allocated to each taxable year cannot exceed the amount of the refund.

(7) * * *

Example 4. In December 2016, Taxpayer D, a calendar year taxpayer who is not a dependent of another taxpayer under section 151, receives a bill from University X for $2,000 for qualified tuition and related expenses to attend University X as a full-time student for the 2017 spring semester, which begins in January 2017. In December 2016, D pays $500 of qualified tuition and related expenses for the 2017 spring semester. In January 2017, D pays an additional $1,500 of qualified tuition and related expenses for the 2017 spring semester. Early in the 2017 spring semester, D withdraws from several courses and no longer qualifies as a full-time student. As a result of D's change in status from a full-time student to a part-time student, D receives a $750 refund from University X on February 16, 2017. D has no other qualified tuition and related expenses for 2017. Under paragraph (f)(6) of this section, D may allocate all, or a portion, of the $750 refund to reduce the $1,500 of qualified tuition and related expenses paid in 2017 or D may also allocate a portion of the $750 refund, up to $500, to reduce the qualified tuition and related expenses paid in 2016 and allocate the remainder of the refund to reduce the qualified tuition and related expenses paid in 2017.

(g) *Applicability date*.—(1) Except as provided in paragraph (g)(2) of this section, this section applies on or after December 26, 2002.

(2) Paragraphs (e)(2)(ii), (f)(6), and *Example 4* in paragraph (f)(7) of this section apply to qualified tuition and related expenses paid and education furnished in academic periods beginning on or after the date of publication of the Treasury decision adopting these rules as final regulations in the **Federal Register**. However, taxpayers may apply paragraphs (e)(2)(ii), (f)(6), and *Example 4* in paragraph (f)(7) of this section in taxable years for which the limitation on filing a claim for credit or refund under section 6511 has not expired.

Dependency Exemption: Authorized Placement Agency: Definition

Dependency Exemption: Authorized Placement Agency: Definition.—Amendments to Reg. §1.32-2, relating to the definition of an authorized placement agency for purposes of a dependency exemption for a child placed for adoption that were issued prior to the changes made to the law by

the Working Families Tax Relief Act of 2004, are proposed (published in the Federal Register on January 19, 2017) (REG-137604-07).

Par. 6. Section 1.32-2 is amended by revising the section heading, adding paragraph (c)(3), and revising paragraph (e) to read as follows:

§ 1.32-2. Earned income credit.

* * *

(c) * * *

(3) *Qualifying child.*—(i) *In general.*—For purposes of this section, a qualifying child of the taxpayer is a qualifying child as defined in section 152(c), determined without applying sections 152(c)(1)(D) and 152(e).

(ii) *Application of tie-breaker rules.*—For purposes of determining whether a taxpayer is an eligible individual under section 32(c)(1)(A), if an individual meets the definition of a qualifying child under paragraph (c)(3)(i) of this section for more than one taxpayer and the individual is treated as the qualifying child of a taxpayer under the tiebreaker rules of section 152(c)(4) and the related regulations, then that taxpayer may be an eligible individual under section 32(c)(1)(A)(i) and may claim the earned income credit for a taxpayer with a qualifying child if all other requirements of section 32 are satisfied. If an individual meets the definition of a qualifying child under paragraph (c)(3)(i) of this section for more than one taxpayer and the individual is not treated as the qualifying child of a taxpayer under the tiebreaker rules of section 152(c)(4) and the related regulations, then the individual also is not treated as a qualifying child of that taxpayer in the taxable year for purposes of section 32(c)(1)(A). Thus, that taxpayer may be an eligible individual under section 32(c)(1)(A)(ii) and may claim the earned income credit for a taxpayer without a qualifying child if all other requirements are satisfied.

(iii) *Examples.*—The following examples illustrate the rules of this paragraph (c). In each example, the taxpayer uses the calendar year as the taxpayer's taxable year and, except to the extent indicated, each taxpayer meets the requirements to claim the benefits(s) described in the example.

Example 1. Child, Parent, and Grandparent share the same principal place of abode for the taxable year. Child meets the definition of a qualifying child under paragraph (c)(3)(i) of this section for both Parent and Grandparent (and for no other person) for the taxable year. Parent claims the earned income credit with Child as Parent's qualifying child. Under the tiebreaker rules of section 152(c)(4)(A) and the related regulations, Child is treated as the qualifying child of Parent and is not treated as the qualifying child of Grandparent. Under section 32(c)(1) and paragraph (c)(3)(ii) of this section, Parent is an eligible individual under section 32(c)(1)(A)(i) who may claim the earned income credit for a taxpayer with a qualifying child, and Grandparent is an eligible individual under section 32(c)(1)(A)(ii) who may claim the earned income credit for a taxpayer without a qualifying child.

Example 2. The facts are the same as in *Example 1* of this paragraph (c)(3)(iii), except that Grandparent, rather than Parent, claims Child as a qualifying child, and Grandparent's adjusted gross income is higher than Parent's adjusted gross income. Under the tiebreaker rules of section 152(c)(4)(C) and the related regulations, Child is treated as the qualifying child of Grandparent and is not treated as the qualifying child of Parent. Under section 32(c)(1) and paragraph (c)(3)(ii) of this section, Grandparent is an eligible individual under section 32(c)(1)(A)(i) who may claim the earned income credit for a taxpayer with a qualifying child, and Parent is an eligible individual under section 32(c)(1)(A)(ii) who may claim the earned income credit for a taxpayer without a qualifying child.

* * *

(e) *Applicability date.*—(1) *In general.*—Except as provided in paragraph (e)(2) of this section, this section applies to taxable years beginning after March 5, 2003.

(2) *Exception.*—Paragraph (c)(3) of this section applies to taxable years beginning after the date these regulations are published as final regulations in the **Federal Register.**

Premium Tax Credit: Individual Shared Responsibility

Premium Tax Credit: Individual Shared Responsibility.—Amendments to Reg. §1.36B-2, relating to the health insurance premium tax credit (premium tax credit) and the individual shared responsibility provision, are proposed (published in the Federal Register on July 8, 2016) (corrected September 14, 2016) (REG-109086-15).

Par. 4. Section 1.36B-2 is amended by:

6. Adding new paragraphs (c)(3)(v)(A)(7)

§ 1.36B-2. Eligibility for premium tax credit.

* * *

(c) * * *

(3) * * *

(v) * * *

(A) * * *

(*7*) *Opt-out arrangements.*—(*i*) *In general.*—Except as otherwise provided in this paragraph (c)(3)(v)(A)(*7*), the amount of an opt-out payment made available to an employee under an opt-out arrangement increases the employee's required contribution for purposes of determining the affordability of the eligible employer-sponsored plan to which the opt-out arrangement relates, regardless of whether the employee enrolls in the eligible employer-sponsored plan or declines to enroll in that coverage and is paid the opt-out payment.

(*ii*) *Eligible opt-out arrangements.*—The amount of an opt-out payment made available to an employee under an eligible opt-out arrangement does not increase the employee's required contribution for purposes of determining the affordability of the eligible employer-sponsored plan to which the eligible opt-out arrangement relates, regardless of whether the employee enrolls in the eligible employer-sponsored plan or is paid the opt-out payment.

(iii) Definitions.—The following definitions apply for purposes of this paragraph (c)(3)(v)(A)(*7*):

(A) Opt-out payment.—The term *opt-out payment* means a payment that is available only if an employee declines coverage, including waiving coverage in which the employee would otherwise be enrolled, under an eligible employer-sponsored plan and that is not permitted to be used to pay for coverage under the eligible employer-sponsored plan. An amount provided as an employer contribution to a cafeteria plan that is permitted to be used by the employee to purchase minimum essential coverage is not an opt-out payment, whether or not the employee may receive the amount as a taxable benefit. See paragraph (c)(3)(v)(A)(*6*) of this section for the treatment of employer contributions to a cafeteria plan.

(B) Opt-out arrangement.—The term *opt-out arrangement* means the arrangement under which an opt-out payment is made available.

(C) Eligible opt-out arrangement.—The term *eligible opt-out arrangement* means an arrangement under which an employee's right to receive an opt-out payment is conditioned on the employee providing reasonable evidence that the employee and all other individuals for whom the employee reasonably expects to claim a personal exemption deduction for the taxable year or years that begin or end in or with the employer's plan year to which the opt-out arrangement applies (employee's expected tax family) have or will have minimum essential coverage (other than coverage in the individual market, whether or not obtained through the Marketplace) during the period of coverage to which the opt-out arrangement applies. For this purpose, reasonable evidence of alternative coverage may include the employee's attestation that the employee and all other members of the employee's expected tax family have or will have minimum essential coverage (other than coverage in the individual market, whether or not obtained through the Marketplace) for the relevant period. Regardless of the evidence of alternative coverage required under the arrangement, to be an eligible opt-out arrangement, the arrangement must provide that the opt-out payment will not be made, and the employer in fact must not make the payment, if the employer knows or has reason to know that the employee or any other member of the employee's expected tax family does not have or will not have the alternative coverage. The arrangement must also require that the evidence of the alternative coverage be provided no less frequently than every plan year to which the eligible opt-out arrangement applies, and that it must be provided no earlier than a reasonable period of time before the commencement of the period of coverage to which the eligible opt-out arrangement applies. If the reasonable evidence (such as an attestation) is obtained as part of the regular annual open enrollment period that occurs within a few months before the commencement of the next plan year of employer-sponsored coverage, it will qualify as being provided no earlier than a reasonable period of time before commencement of the applicable period of coverage. An eligible opt-out arrangement is also permitted to require evidence of alternative coverage to be provided at a later date, such as after the plan year starts, which would enable the employer to require evidence that the employee and all other members of the employee's expected tax family have already obtained the alternative coverage. Nothing in this rule prohibits an employer from requiring reasonable evidence of alternative coverage other than an attestation in order for an employee to qualify for an opt-out payment under an eligible opt-out arrangement. Further, provided that the reasonable evidence requirement is met, the amount of an opt-out payment made available under an eligible opt-out arrangement continues to be excluded from the employee's required contribution for the remainder of the period of coverage to which the opt-out payment originally applied even if the alternative coverage subsequently terminates for the employee or for any other member of the employee's expected tax family, regardless of whether the opt-out payment is required to be adjusted or terminated due to the loss of alternative coverage, and regardless of whether the employee is required to provide notice of the loss of alternative coverage to the employer.

(iv) Examples.—The following examples illustrate the provisions of this paragraph (c)(3)(v)(A)(*7*). In each example, the eligible employer-sponsored plan's plan year is the calendar year.

Example 1. Taxpayer B is an employee of Employer X, which offers its employees coverage under an eligible employer-sponsored plan that requires B to contribute $3,000 for self-only coverage. X also makes available to B a payment of $500 if B declines to enroll in the eligible employer-sponsored plan. Therefore, the $500 opt-out payment made available to B under the opt-out arrangement increases B's required contribution under X's eligible employer-sponsored plan from $3,000 to $3,500, regardless of whether B enrolls in the eligible employer-sponsored plan or declines to enroll and is paid the opt-out payment.

Example 2. The facts are the same as in *Example 1,* except that availability of the $500 opt-out payment is conditioned not only on B declining to enroll in X's eligible employer-sponsored plan but also on B providing reasonable evidence no earlier than the regular annual open enrollment period for the next plan year that B and all other members of B's expected tax family are or will be enrolled in minimum essential coverage through another source (other than coverage in the individual market, whether or not obtained through the Marketplace). B's expected tax family consists of B and B's spouse, C, who is an employee of Employer Y. During the regular annual open enrollment period for the upcoming plan year, B declines coverage under X's eligible employer-sponsored plan and provides X with reasonable evidence that B and C will be enrolled in Y's employer-sponsored plan, which is minimum essential coverage. The opt-out arrangement provided by X is an eligible opt-out arrangement, and, therefore, the $500 opt-out payment made available to B does not increase B's required contribution under X's eligible employer-sponsored plan. B's required contribution for self-only coverage under X's eligible employer-sponsored plan is $3,000.

Example 3. The facts are the same as in *Example 2,* except that B and C have two children that B expects to claim as dependents for the taxable year that coincides with the upcoming plan year. During the regular annual open enrollment period for the upcoming plan year, B declines coverage under X's eligible employer-sponsored plan and provides X with reasonable evidence that B and C will be enrolled in Y's employer-sponsored plan, which is minimum essential coverage. However, B does not provide reasonable evidence that B's children will be enrolled in minimum essential coverage (other than coverage in the individual market, whether or not obtained through the Marketplace); therefore, X determines B is not eligible for the opt-out payment, and B does not receive it. The $500 opt-out payment made available under the opt-out arrangement does not increase B's required contribution under X's eligible employer-sponsored plan because the opt-out arrangement provided by X is an eligible opt-out arrangement. B's required contribution for self-only coverage under X's eligible employer-sponsored plan is $3,000.

Example 4. Taxpayer D is married and is employed by Employer Z, which offers its employees coverage under an eligible employer-sponsored plan that requires D to contribute $2,000 for self-only coverage. Z also makes available to D a payment of $300 if D declines to enroll in the eligible employer-sponsored plan and provides reasonable evidence no earlier than the regular annual open enrollment period for the next plan year that D is or will be enrolled in minimum essential coverage through another source (other than coverage in the individual market, whether or not obtained through the Marketplace); the opt-out arrangement is not conditioned on whether the other members of D's expected tax family have other coverage. This opt-out arrangement is not an eligible opt-out arrangement because it does not condition the right to receive the opt-out payment on D providing reasonable evidence that D and the other members of D's expected tax family have (or will have) minimum essential coverage (other than coverage in the individual market, whether or not obtained through the Marketplace). Therefore, the $300 opt-out payment made available to D under the opt-out arrangement increases D's required contribution under Z's eligible employer-sponsored plan. D's required contribution for self-only coverage under Z's eligible employer-sponsored plan is $2,300.

* * *

Insurance Coverage: Health Reimbursement Arrangements

Insurance Coverage: Health Reimbursement Arrangements.—Amendments to Reg. §1.36B-2, regarding health reimbursement arrangements (HRAs) and other account-based group health plans, are proposed (published in the Federal Register on October 29, 2018) (REG-136724-17).

Par. 2. Section 1.36B-2 is amended by:

a. Redesignating paragraph (c)(3)(i) as paragraph (c)(3)(i)(A) and revising the subject heading of newly designated paragraph (c)(3)(i)(A).

b. Adding a new paragraph (c)(3)(i) subject heading and paragraph (c)(3)(i)(B).

c. Adding a sentence at the end of paragraphs (c)(3)(ii) and (c)(3)(v)(A)(*1*) and (2).

d. Revising paragraphs (c)(3)(v)(A)(3) and (5).

e. Adding a sentence at the end of paragraph (c)(3)(vi).

f. Adding paragraph (c)(5).

g. Revising paragraph (e)(1).

h. Adding paragraph (e)(3).

The revisions and additions read as follows:

§1.36B-2. Eligibility for premium tax credit.

* * *

(c) * * *

(3) * * *

(i) *In general.*—(A) *Plans other than health reimbursement arrangements (HRAs) or other account-based group health plans described in paragraph (c)(3)(i)(B) of this section.*—* * *

(B) *HRAs and other account-based group health plans integrated with individual health insurance coverage.*—An employee who is offered an HRA or other account-based group health plan that would be integrated with individual health insurance coverage, within the meaning of §§54.9802-4 and 54.9815-2711(d)(4) of this chapter, if the individual enrolls in individual health insurance coverage, and an individual who is offered the HRA or other account-based group health plan because of a relationship to the employee (a related HRA individual), are eligible for minimum essential coverage under an eligible employer-sponsored plan for any month for which the HRA or other account-based group health plan is offered if the HRA or other account-based group health plan is affordable for the month under paragraph (c)(5) of this section or if the employee does not opt out of and waive future reimbursements from the HRA or other account-based group health plan. An HRA or other account-based group health plan described in this paragraph (c)(3)(i)(B) that is affordable for a month under paragraph (c)(5) of this section is treated as providing minimum value for the month. For purposes of paragraphs (c)(3) and (5) of this section, the definitions under §54.9815-2711(d)(6) of this chapter apply.

(ii) * * * The plan year for an HRA or other account-based group health plan described in paragraph (c)(3)(i)(B) of this section is the plan's 12-month coverage period (or the remainder of the 12-month coverage period for a newly eligible individual or an individual who enrolls during a special enrollment period).

* * *

(v) * * *

(A) * * *

(*1*) * * * See paragraph (c)(5) of this section for rules for when an HRA or other account-based group health plan described in paragraph (c)(3)(i)(B) of this section is affordable for an employee for a month.

(*2*) * * * See paragraph (c)(5) of this section for rules for when an HRA or other account-based group health plan described in paragraph (c)(3)(i)(B) of this section is affordable for a related HRA individual for a month.

(3) *Employee safe harbor.*—An eligible employer-sponsored plan is not affordable for an employee or a related individual for a plan year if, when the employee or a related individual enrolls in a qualified health plan for a period coinciding with the plan year (in whole or in part), an Exchange determines that the eligible employer-sponsored plan is not affordable for that plan year. This paragraph (c)(3)(v)(A)(3) does not apply to a determination made as part of the redetermination process described in 45 CFR 155.335 unless the individual receiving an Exchange redetermination notification affirmatively responds and provides current information on affordability. This paragraph (c)(3)(v)(A)(3) does not apply for an individual who, with intentional or reckless disregard for the facts, provides incorrect information to an Exchange concerning the portion of the annual premium for coverage for the employee or related individual under the plan. A reckless disregard of the facts occurs if the taxpayer makes little or no effort to determine whether the information provided to the Exchange is accurate under circumstances that demonstrate a substantial deviation from the standard of conduct a reasonable person would observe. A disregard of the facts is intentional if the taxpayer knows that the information provided to the Exchange is inaccurate. See paragraph (c)(5) of this section for an employee safe harbor that applies when an Exchange determines that an HRA or other account-based group health plan described in paragraph (c)(3)(i)(B) of this section is not affordable for an employee or a related HRA individual for the period of enrollment in a qualified health plan.

* * *

(5) *Employer contributions to HRAs integrated with eligible employer-sponsored plans.*—Amounts newly made available for the current plan year under an HRA that an employee may use to pay premiums, or may use to pay cost-sharing or benefits not covered by the primary plan in addition to premiums, reduce the employee's required contribution if the HRA would be integrated, within the meaning of §54.9815-2711(d)(2) of this chapter, with an eligible employer-sponsored plan for an employee enrolled in the plan. The eligible employer-sponsored plan and the HRA must be offered by the same employer. Employer contributions to an HRA described in this paragraph (c)(3)(v)(A)(5) reduce an employee's required contribution only to the extent the amount of the annual contribution is required under the terms of the plan or otherwise determinable within a reasonable time before the employee must decide whether to enroll in the eligible employer-sponsored plan.

* * *

(vi) * * * An HRA or other account-based group health plan described in paragraph (c)(3)(i)(B) of this section that is affordable for a month under paragraph (c)(5) of this section is treated as providing minimum value for the month.

* * *

(5) *Affordable HRA or other account-based group health plan.*—(i) *In general.*—Except as otherwise provided in this paragraph (c)(5), an HRA or other account-based group health plan described in paragraph (c)(3)(i)(B) of this section is affordable for a month if the employee's required HRA contribution (as defined in paragraph (c)(5)(ii) of this section) for the month does not exceed 1/12 of the product of the employee's household income for the taxable year and the required contribution percentage (as defined in paragraph (c)(3)(v)(C) of this section).

(ii) *Required HRA contribution.*—An employee's required HRA contribution is the excess of—

(A) The monthly premium for the lowest cost silver plan for self-only coverage of the employee offered in the Exchange for the rating area in which the employee resides, over

(B) The monthly self-only HRA or other account-based group health plan amount (or the monthly maximum amount available to the employee under the HRA or other account-based group health plan if the HRA or other account-based group health plan provides for reimbursements up to a single dollar amount regardless of whether an employee has self-only or other-than-self-only coverage).

(iii) *Monthly amount.*—For purposes of paragraph (c)(5)(ii) of this section, the monthly self-only HRA or other account-based group health plan amount is the self-only HRA or other account-based group health plan amount newly made available under the HRA for the plan year, divided by the number of months in the plan year the HRA or other account-based group health plan is available to the employee. The monthly maximum amount newly made available to the employee under the HRA or other account-based group health plan is the maximum amount newly-made available for the plan year to the employee under the plan, divided by the number of months in the plan year the HRA or other account-based group health plan is available to the employee.

(iv) *Employee safe harbor.*—An HRA or other account-based group health plan described in paragraph (c)(3)(i)(B) of this section is not affordable for a month for an employee or a related HRA individual if, when the employee or related HRA individual enrolls in a qualified health plan for a period coinciding with the period the HRA or other account-based group health plan is available to the employee or related HRA individual (in whole or in part), an Exchange determines that the HRA or other account-based group health plan is not affordable for the period of enrollment in the qualified health plan. This paragraph (c)(5)(iv) does not apply to a determination made as part of the redetermination process described in 45 CFR 155.335 unless the individual receiving an Exchange redetermination notification affirmatively responds and provides current information on affordability. This paragraph (c)(5)(iv) does not apply for an individual who, with intentional or reckless disregard for the facts, provides incorrect information to an Exchange concerning the relevant HRA or other account-based group health plan amount offered by the employee's employer. A reckless disregard of the facts occurs if the taxpayer makes little or no effort to determine whether the information provided to the Exchange is accurate under circumstances that demonstrate a substantial deviation from the standard of conduct a reasonable person would observe. A disregard of the facts is intentional if the taxpayer knows that the information provided to the Exchange is inaccurate.

(v) *Amounts used for affordability determination.*—Only amounts that are newly made available for the plan year of the HRA or other account-based group health plan described in paragraph (c)(3)(i)(B) of this section and determinable within a reasonable time before the beginning of the plan year of the HRA or other account-based health plan are considered in determining whether an HRA or other account-based group health plan described in paragraph (c)(3)(i)(B) of this section is affordable. Amounts made available for a prior plan year that carry over to the current plan year are not taken into account for purposes of this paragraph (c)(5).

(vi) *Affordability for part-year period.*—Affordability under this paragraph (c)(5) is determined separately for each employment period that is less than a full calendar year or for the portions of the plan year of an employer's HRA or other account-based group health plan that fall in different taxable years of an applicable taxpayer. An HRA or other account-based group health plan described in paragraph (c)(3)(i)(B) of this section is affordable for a part-year period if the employee's annualized required HRA contribution for the part-year period does not exceed the required contribution percentage of the applicable taxpayer's household income for the taxable year. The employee's annualized required HRA contribution is the employee's required HRA contribution for the part-year period times a fraction, the numerator of which is 12 and the denominator of which is the number of months in the part-year period during the applicable taxpayer's taxable year. Only full calendar months are included in the computation under this paragraph (c)(5)(vi).

(vii) *Related individual not allowed as a personal exemption deduction.*—A related HRA individual is treated as ineligible for minimum essential coverage under an HRA or other account-based group health plan described in paragraph (c)(3)(i)(B) of this section for months that the employee opted out of and waived future reimbursements from the HRA or other account-based group health plan and the employee is not allowed a personal exemption deduction under section 151 for the related HRA individual.

(viii) *Post-employment coverage.*—An individual who is offered an HRA or other account-based group health plan described in paragraph (c)(3)(i)(B) of this section, for months after an employee terminates employment with the employer offering the HRA or other account-based group health plan, is eligible for minimum essential coverage under the HRA or other account-based group health plan for months after termination of employment only if the employee does not forfeit or opt out of and waive future reimbursements from the HRA or other account-based group health plan for months after termination of employment.

(ix) *Examples.*—The following examples illustrate the provisions of this paragraph (c)(5). The required contribution percentage is defined in paragraph (c)(3)(v)(C) of this section and is updated annually. Because the required contribution percentage for 2020 has not yet been determined, the examples assume a required contribution percentage for 2020 of 9.86%.

(A) *Example 1. Determination of affordability.* (1) In 2020 Taxpayer A is single, has no dependents, and has household income of $28,000. A is an employee of Employer X for all of 2020. X offers its employees an HRA described in paragraph (c)(3)(i)(B) of this section that reimburses $2,400 of medical care expenses for single employees with no children (the self-only HRA amount) and $4,000 for employees with a spouse or children for the medical expenses of the employees and their family members. A enrolls in a qualified health plan through the Exchange in the rating area in which A resides and remains enrolled for all of 2020. The monthly premium for the lowest cost silver plan for self-only coverage of A that is offered in the Exchange for the rating area in which A resides is $500.

(2) A's required HRA contribution, as defined in paragraph (c)(5)(ii) of this section, is $300, the excess of $500 (the monthly premium for the lowest cost silver plan for self-only coverage of A) over $200 (1/12 of the self-only HRA amount provided by Employer X to its employees). In addition, 1/12 of the product of 9.86 percent and A's household income is $230 ($28,000 x .0986 = $2,761; $2,761/12 = $230). Because A's required HRA contribution of $300 exceeds $230 (1/12 of the product of 9.86 percent and A's household income), the HRA is unaffordable for A for each month of 2020 under paragraph (c)(5) of this section. If A opts out of and waives future reimbursements from the HRA, A is not eligible for minimum essential coverage under the HRA for each month of 2020 under paragraph (c)(3)(i)(B) of this section.

(B) *Example 2. Determination of affordability for a related HRA individual.* (1) In 2020 Taxpayer B is married and has one child who is a dependent of B for 2020. B has household income of $28,000. B is an employee of Employer X for all of 2020. X offers its employees an HRA described in paragraph (c)(3)(i)(B) of this section that reimburses $3,600 of medical care expenses for single employees with no children (the self-only HRA amount) and $5,000 for employees with a spouse or children for the medical expenses of the employees and their family members. B, B's spouse, and B's child enroll in a qualified health plan through the Exchange in the rating area in which B resides and they remain enrolled for all of 2020. No advance credit payments are made for their coverage. The monthly premium for the lowest cost silver plan for self-only coverage of B that is offered in the Exchange for the rating area in which B resides is $500.

(2) B's required HRA contribution, as defined in paragraph (c)(5)(ii) of this section, is $200, the excess of $500 (the monthly premium for the lowest cost silver plan for self-only coverage for B) over $300 (1/12 of the self-only HRA amount provided by Employer X to its employees). In addition, 1/12 of the product of 9.86 percent and B's household income for 2020 is $230 ($28,000 x .0986 = $2,761; $2,761/12 = $230). Because B's required HRA contribution of $200 does not exceed $230 (1/12 of the product of 9.86 percent and B's household income for 2020), the HRA is affordable for B under paragraph (c)(5) of this section, and B is eligible for minimum essential coverage under an eligible employer-sponsored plan for each month of 2020 under paragraph (c)(3)(i)(B) of this section. In addition,

B's spouse and child are also eligible for minimum essential coverage under an eligible employer-sponsored plan for each month of 2020 under paragraph (c)(3)(i)(B) of this section.

(C) *Example 3. Exchange determines that HRA is unaffordable.* (*1*) The facts are the same as in *Example 2*, except that B, when enrolling in Exchange coverage for B's family, received a determination by the Exchange that the HRA was unaffordable, because B believed B's household income would be lower than it turned out to be. Consequently, advance credit payments were made for their 2020 coverage.

(*2*) Under paragraph (c)(5)(iv) of this section, the HRA is considered unaffordable for B, B's spouse, and B's child for each month of 2020 provided that B did not, with intentional or reckless disregard for the facts, provide incorrect information to the Exchange concerning the HRA or B's household income.

(D) *Example 4. Affordability determined for part of a taxable year (part-year period).* (*1*) Taxpayer C is an employee of Employer X. C's household income for 2020 is $28,000. X offers its employees an HRA described in paragraph (c)(3)(i)(B) of this section that reimburses medical care expenses of $3,600 for single employees without children (the self-only HRA amount) and $5,000 to employees with a spouse or children for the medical expenses of the employees and their family members. X's HRA plan year is September 1 to August 31 and C is first eligible to participate in the HRA for the period beginning September 1, 2020. C enrolls in a qualified health plan through the Exchange in the rating area in which C resides for all of 2020. The monthly premium for the lowest cost silver plan for self-only coverage of C that is offered in the Exchange for the rating area in which C resides for 2020 is $500.

(*2*) Under paragraph (c)(3)(vi) of this section, the affordability of the HRA is determined separately for the period September 1 through December 31, 2020, and for the period January 1 through August 31, 2021. C's required HRA contribution, as defined in paragraph (c)(5)(ii) of this section, for the period September 1 through December 31, 2020, is $200, the excess of $500 (the monthly premium for the lowest cost silver plan for self-only coverage for C) over $300 (1/12 of the self-only HRA amount provided by X to its employees). In addition, 1/12 of the product of 9.86 percent and C's household income is $230 ($28,000 x .0986 = $2,761; $2,677/12 = $230). Because C's required HRA contribution of $200 does not exceed $230, the HRA is affordable for C for each month in the period September 1 through December 31, 2020, under paragraph (c)(5) of this section. Affordability for the period January 1 through August 31, 2021, is determined using C's 2021 household income and required HRA contribution.

(E) *Example 5. Carryover amounts ignored in determining affordability.* (*1*) Taxpayer D is an employee of Employer X for all of 2020 and 2021. D is single. For each of 2020 and 2021, X offers its employees an HRA described in paragraph (c)(3)(i)(B) of this section that provides reimbursement for medical care expenses of $2,400 to single employees with no children (the self-only HRA amount) and $4,000 to employees with a spouse or children for the medical expenses of the employees and their family members. Under the terms of the HRA, amounts that an employee does not use in a calendar year may be carried over and used in the next calendar year. In 2020, D used only $1,500 of her $2,400 maximum reimbursement and the unused $900 is carried over and may be used by D in 2021.

(*2*) Under paragraph (c)(5)(v) of this section, only the $2,400 self-only HRA amount offered to D for 2021 is considered in determining whether D's HRA is affordable. The $900 carryover amount is not considered in determining the affordability of the HRA.

* * *

(e) * * *

(1) Except as provided in paragraphs (e)(2) and (3) of this section, this section applies to taxable years ending after December 31, 2013.

* * *

(3) Paragraphs (c)(3)(i)(B) and (c)(5) of this section, and the last sentences at the end of paragraphs (c)(3)(ii), (c)(3)(v)(A)(*1*), (c)(3)(v)(A)(2), (c)(3)(v)(A)(3), and (c)(3)(vi) of this section apply to taxable years beginning on or after January 1, 2020.

Health Insurance Premium Tax Credit: Employer-Sponsored Plans: Minimum Value

Health Insurance Premium Tax Credit: Employer-Sponsored Plans: Minimum Value.—Reg. §1.36B-6, affecting individuals who enroll in qualified health plans through Affordable Insurance Exchanges and claim the health insurance premium tax credit and providing guidance on determining whether health coverage under an eligible employer-sponsored plan provides minimum value, is proposed (published in the Federal Register on May 3, 2013) (REG-125398-12). Reg. §1.36B-6(a) and (g), as proposed on May 3, 2013, were withdrawn and replaced on September 1, 2015 (REG-143800-14). Portions of proposed Reg. §1.36B-6 were adopted by T.D. 9745 on December 16, 2015; the remaining proposed amendments are below.

☐ Par. 6. Section 1.36B-6 is added [amended] to read as follows:

§1.36B-6. Minimum value.—(a) * * *

(2) The plan provides substantial coverage of inpatient hospital services and physician services.

(b) *MV standard population.*—The MV standard population is a standard population developed and described through summary statistics by the Department of Health and Human Services (HHS). The MV standard population is based on the population covered by typical self-insured group health plans.

(c) *MV percentage.*—(1) *In general.*—An eligible employer-sponsored plan's MV percentage is—

(i) The plan's anticipated covered medical spending for benefits provided under a particular essential health benefits (EHB) benchmark plan described in 45 CFR 156.110

(EHB coverage) for the MV standard population based on the plan's cost-sharing provisions;

(ii) Divided by the total anticipated allowed charges for EHB coverage provided to the MV standard population; and

(iii) Expressed as a percentage.

(2) * * *

(3) * * *

(4) * * *

(5) *Expected spending adjustments for health savings accounts and health reimbursement arrangements.*—The amount taken into account under paragraph (c)(3) or (c)(4) of this section is the amount of expected spending for health care costs in a benefit year.

(d) *Methods for determining MV.*—An eligible employer-sponsored plan may use one of the following methods to determine whether the plan provides MV—

(1) The MV Calculator made available by HHS and IRS, with adjustments permitted by paragraph (e) of this section;

(2) One of the safe harbors established by HHS and IRS and described in published guidance, see § 601.601(d) of this chapter;

(3) Actuarial certification, as described in paragraph (f) of this section, if an eligible employer-sponsored plan has nonstandard features that are not compatible with the MV Calculator and may materially affect the MV percentage; or

(4) For plans in the small group market, conformance with the requirements for a level of metal coverage defined at 45 CFR 156.140(b) (bronze, silver, gold, or platinum).

(e) *Scope of essential health benefits and adjustment for benefits not included in MV Calculator.*—An eligible employer-sponsored plan may include in calculating its MV percentage all benefits included in any EHB benchmark (as defined in 45 CFR part 156). An MV percentage that is calculated using the MV Calculator may be adjusted based on an actuarial analysis that complies with the requirements of paragraph (f) of this section to the extent of the value of these benefits that are outside the parameters of the MV Calculator.

(f) *Actuarial certification.*—(1) *In general.*—An actuarial certification under paragraph (d)(3) of this section must satisfy the requirements of this paragraph (f).

(2) *Membership in American Academy of Actuaries.*—The actuary must be a member of the American Academy of Actuaries.

(3) *Actuarial analysis.*—The actuary's analysis must be performed in accordance with generally accepted actuarial principles and methodologies and specific standards that may be provided in published guidance, see § 601.601(d) of this chapter.

(4) *Use of MV Calculator.*—The actuary must use the MV Calculator to determine the plan's MV percentage for coverage the plan provides that is measurable by the MV Calculator. The actuary may perform an actuarial analysis of the plan's EHB coverage for the MV standard population for benefits not measured by the MV Calculator to determine the effect of nonstandard features that are not compatible with the MV Calculator. The actuary may certify the plan's MV percentage based on the MV percentage that results from use of the MV Calculator and the actuarial analysis of the plan's coverage that is not measured by the MV calculator.

(g) * * *

(2) *Exception.*—Paragraph (a)(2) of this section applies for plan years beginning after November 3, 2014.

Excise Taxes: Taxable Fuel: Returns: Definitions

Excise Taxes: Taxable Fuel: Returns: Definitions.—Reg. §§ 1.40-2 and 1.40A-1 and amendments to Reg. § 1.40-1, relating to credits and payments for alcohol mixtures, biodiesel mixtures, renewable diesel mixtures, alternative fuel mixtures, and alternative fuel sold for use or used as a fuel and relating to the definition of gasoline and diesel fuel, are proposed (published in the Federal Register on July 29, 2008) (REG-155087-05).

Par. 2. Section 1.40-1 is revised to read as follows:

§ 1.40-1. Alcohol used as a fuel.—For the definition of "alcohol" for purposes of the credits allowed by section 40, see § 48.6426-1(c) of this chapter.

Par. 3. Sections 1.40-2 is added to read as follows:

§ 1.40-2. Small ethanol producer credit.—(a) *In general.*—Section 40 provides a small ethanol producer credit for each gallon of qualified ethanol production of an eligible small ethanol producer. Section 40(b)(4)(B) defines "qualified ethanol production". Section 40(g)(1) defines "eligible small ethanol producer". Section 40(g)(5) provides authority to prescribe such regulations as may be necessary to prevent the credit from directly or indirectly benefiting any person with a direct or indirect productive capacity of more than 60 million gallons of alcohol during the taxable year. A person has produced ethanol if the person has title to the ethanol immediately after it is created.

(b) *Qualified ethanol production.*—Section 40(b)(4)(B) limits qualified ethanol production to ethanol that is produced by an eligible small ethanol producer. Ethanol is "produced" for this purpose only when a feedstock other than ethanol is transformed into ethanol.

(c) *Denial of credit for ethanol produced at certain facilities.*—The person at whose facilities ethanol is produced is treated for purposes of section 40(g)(5) as an indirect beneficiary of any credit allowed with respect to the ethanol. Accordingly, the small ethanol producer credit is not allowed with respect to ethanol that is produced at the facilities of a contract manufacturer or other person if such contract manufacturer or other person has a direct or indirect productive capacity of more than 60 million gallons of alcohol during the taxable year. Similarly, if the manufacturer does not have a productive capacity of more than 60 million gallons but more than 15 million gallons of ethanol is produced at the manufacturer's facilities during the taxable year, the small ethanol producer credit is allowed with respect to only the first 15 million gallons of ethanol produced at the facilities during the taxable year.

(d) *Examples*.—The following examples illustrate the application of this section:

Example 1. X purchases hydrous ethanol and processes it into anhydrous ethanol. X is not the producer of the ethanol because X does not transform a feedstock other than ethanol into ethanol.

Example 2. Y arranges with contract manufacturer Z to produce 10 million gallons of ethanol. Y is not related to Z. Y provides the raw materials and retains title to them and to the finished ethanol. Z has the capacity to produce 100 million gallons of alcohol per year. The small producer credit is not allowed with respect to the 10 million gallons of ethanol because it is produced at the facilities of a contract manufacturer that has a productive capacity of more than 60 million gallons of alcohol during the taxable year.

(e) *Effective/applicability date*.—This section is applicable on and after the date of publication of these regulations in the **Federal Register** as final regulations. [Reg. § 1.40-2.]

Par. 3. Sections 1.40A-1 is added to read as follows:

§ 1.40A-1. Biodiesel.—(a) *In general*.—Rules similar to the rules of § 1.40-2 apply for purposes of the small agri-biodiesel producer credit allowed by section 40A.

(b) *Definitions*.—For the definitions of "biodiesel" and "renewable diese" for purposes of the credits allowed by section 40A, see § 48.6426-1(b) of this chapter.

(c) *Effective/applicability date*.—This section is applicable on and after the date of publication of these regulations in the **Federal Register** as final regulations. [Reg. § 1.40A-1.]

Qualified Research Expenditures (QREs): Credit for Increasing Research Activities: Intra-Group Gross Receipts

Qualified Research Expenditures (QREs): Credit for Increasing Research Activities: Intra-Group Gross Receipts.—Amendments to Reg. § 1.41-0, relating to the treatment of qualified research expenditures (QREs) and gross receipts resulting from transactions between members of a controlled group of corporations or a group of trades or businesses under common control (intra-group transactions) for purposes of determining the credit under section 41 for increasing research activities (research credit), are proposed (published in the Federal Register on December 13, 2013) (REG-159420-04).

☐ Par. 2. In § 1.41-0, the table of contents is amended by:

1. Revising the section heading for § 1.41-6 and the entries for § 1.41-6 (i), (i)(1), (i)(2), (i)(3), (i)(4), and (i)(5).
2. Adding a new entry for § 1.41-6(i)(6).
3. Adding a new entry for § 1.41-6(j)(4).

The addition reads as follows:

§ 1.41-0. Table of contents.

* * *

§ 1.41-6 Controlled groups.

* * *

(i) Transactions between controlled group members.

(1) In general.

(2) Exception for certain amounts received from foreign corporate controlled group members.

(3) In-house research expenses.

(4) Contract research expenses.

(5) Payment for supplies.

(6) Consistency requirement.

(j) * * *

* * *

(4) Intra-group transactions.

* * *

Credit: Research Activities: Internal-Use Software Exclusion

Credit: Research Activities: Internal-Use Software Exclusion.—Amendments to Reg. § 1.41-4, relating to the computation of the research credit under Code Sec. 41(c), the definition of qualified research under Code Sec. 41(d), and when computer software is excepted from the internal-use software exclusion contained in Code Sec. 41(d)(4)(E), are proposed (published in the Federal Register on December 26, 2001) (REG-112991-01) (corrected March 19, 2002). These proposed regulations have been designed to lay to rest many of the disputes that arose after T.D. 8930 was published. *Note:* Proposed amendments to Reg. § 1.41-0 and portions of the proposed amendments to Reg. § 1.41-4 were adopted by T.D. 9104 on December 30, 2003; however, proposed Reg. § 1.41-4(c)(6), pertaining to internal use computer software, was specifically not adopted.

☐ Par. 4. Section 1.41-4 is revised to read as follows [see *Note*, above]:

§ 1.41-4. Qualified research for expenditures paid or incurred in taxable years ending on or after December 26, 2001.

* * *

(c) * * *

(6) *Internal use software for taxable years beginning on or after December 31, 1985*.—(i) *General rule*.—Research with respect to computer software that is developed by (or for the benefit of) the taxpayer primarily for the taxpayer's internal use is eligible for the research credit only if the software satisfies the requirements of paragraph (c)(6)(ii) of this section.

(ii) *Requirements*.—The requirements of this paragraph (c)(6)(ii) are—

(A) The software satisfies the requirements of section 41(d)(1);

(B) The software is not otherwise excluded under section 41(d)(4) (otHer than section 41(d)(4)(E)); and

(C) One of the following conditions is met—

(1) The taxpayer develops the software for use in an activity that constitutes qualified research (other than the development of the internal-use software itself);

(2) The taxpayer develops the software for use in a production process that satisfies the requirements of section 41(d)(1);

(3) The taxpayer develops the software for use in providing computer services to customers; or

(4) The software satisfies the high threshold of innovation test of paragraph (c)(6)(vi) of this section.

(iii) *Computer software and hardware developed as a single product.*—This paragraph (c)(6) does not apply to the development costs of a new or improved package of computer software and hardware developed together by the taxpayer as a single product (or to the costs to modify an acquired computer software and hardware package), of which the software is an integral part, that is used directly by the taxpayer in providing services in its trade or business to customers. In these cases, eligibility for the research credit is to be determined by examining the combined software-hardware product as a single product.

(iv) *Primarily for internal use.*—Unless computer software is developed to be commercially sold, leased, licensed, or otherwise marketed, for separately stated consideration to unrelated third parties, computer software is presumed developed by (or for the benefit of) the taxpayer primarily for the taxpayer's internal use. For example, the computer software may serve general and administrative functions of the taxpayer, or may be used in providing a noncomputer service. General and administrative functions include, but are not limited to, functions such as payroll, bookkeeping, financial management, financial reporting, personnel management, sales and marketing, fixed asset accounting, inventory management and cost accounting. Computer software that is developed to be commercially sold, leased, licensed, or otherwise marketed, for separately stated consideration to unrelated third parties is not developed primarily for the taxpayer's internal use. The requirements of this paragraph (c)(6) apply to computer software that is developed primarily for the taxpayer's internal use even though the taxpayer subsequently sells, leases, licenses, or otherwise markets the computer software for separately stated consideration to unrelated third parties.

(v) *Software used in the provisions of services.*—(A) *Computer services.*—For purposes of this section, a computer service is a service offered by a taxpayer to customers who conduct business with the taxpayer primarily for the use of the taxpayer's computer or software technology. A taxpayer does not provide a computer service merely because customers interact with the taxpayer's software.

(B) *Noncomputer services.*—For purposes of this section, a noncomputer service is a service offered by a taxpayer to customers who conduct business with the taxpayer primarily to obtain a service other than a computer service, even if such other service is enabled, supported, or facilitated by computer or software technology.

(vi) *High threshold of innovation test.*—Computer software satisfies this paragraph (c)(6)(vi) only if the taxpayer can establish that—

(A) The software is innovative in that the software is intended to be unique or novel and is intended to differ in a significant and inventive way from prior software implementations or methods;

(B) The software development involves significant economic risk in that the taxpayer commits substantial resources to the development and there is substantial uncertainty, because of technical risk, that such resources would be recovered within a reasonable period; and

(C) The software is not commercially available for use by the taxpayer in that the software cannot be purchased, leased, or licensed and used for the intended purpose without modifications that would satisfy the requirements of paragraphs (c)(6)(vi)(A) and (B) of this section.

(vii) *Application of high threshold of innovation test.*—The costs of developing internal use software are eligible for the research credit only if the software satisfies the high threshold of innovation test of paragraph (c)(6)(vi) of this section. This test takes into account only the results attributable to the development of the new or improved software independent of the effect of any modifications to related hardware or other software.

(viii) *Illustrations.*—The following examples illustrate provisions contained in this paragraph (c)(6) of this section. No inference should be drawn from these examples concerning the application of section 41(d)(1) and paragraph (a) of this section to these facts. The examples are as follows:

Example 1. (i) *Facts.* X, an insurance company, has increased its number of insurance policies in force. In recent years, regulatory and financial accounting rules for computing actuarial reserves on these insurance policies have changed several times. In order to compute actuarial reserves in a more timely and cost-effective manner, X undertakes to create an improved reserve valuation software that will generate data for regulatory and financial accounting purposes.

(ii) *Conclusion.* The improved reserve valuation software created by X is internal use software because the software is not developed to be commercially sold, leased, licensed, or otherwise marketed, for separately stated consideration to unrelated third parties. The improved reserve valuation software was developed by X to serve X's general and administrative functions. X's costs of developing the reserve valuation software are eligible for the research credit only if the software satisfies the high threshold of innovation test of paragraph (c)(6)(vi) of this section.

Example 2. (i) *Facts.* Assume the same facts as in *Example 1.* Also assume that in order to create the improved reserve valuation software, X purchases updated hardware with a new operating system to build the new software system. Several other insurance companies using the same updated hardware and new operating system have in place software systems that can handle the volume of transactions that X seeks to handle, provide reserve computations within a similar time frame, and accommodate the most current regulatory and financial accounting requirements.

(ii) *Conclusion*. X's reserve valuation software system is internal use software that does not satisfy the high threshold of innovation test of paragraph (c)(6)(vi) of this section. The software is not intended to be unique or novel in that it is intended to be merely comparable to software developed by other insurance companies. The software does not differ in a significant or inventive way from prior software implementations because X's reserve valuation software system was developed using the same technologies and methods that were employed by other insurance companies. Further, X's reserve valuation software is not excluded from the application of paragraph (c)(6) of this section by the rule of paragraph (c)(6)(iii) of this section.

Example 3. (i) *Facts*. In 1986, X, a large regional bank with hundreds of branch offices, maintained separate software systems for each of its customer's accounts, including checking, deposit, loan, lease, and trust. X determined that improved customer service could be achieved by redesigning its disparate systems into one customer-centric system. X also determined that commercially available database management systems did not meet all of the critical requirements of the proposed system. Specifically, available relational database management systems were well suited for the proposed system's data modeling requirements but not the data integrity and transaction throughput (transactions-per-second) requirements. Rather than waiting several years for vendor offerings to mature and become viable for its purpose, X decided to embark upon the project utilizing older technology that satisfied the data integrity and transaction throughput requirements but that was severely challenged with respect to the data modeling capabilities. X commits substantial resources to this project and, because of technical risk, X cannot determine if it will recover its resources in a reasonable period. Early in the course of the project, industry analysts observed that the project appeared highly ambitious and risky. The limitations of the technology X was attempting to utilize required that X develop a new database architecture that could accommodate transaction volumes unheard-of in the industry. X was unable to successfully develop the system and X abandoned the project.

(ii) *Conclusion*. X intended to develop a computer software system primarily for X's internal use because X did not intend to commercially sell, lease, license, or otherwise market the software, for separately stated consideration to unrelated third parties, and X intended to use the software in providing noncomputer services to its customers. X's software development activities satisfy the high threshold of innovation test of paragraph (c)(6)(vi) of this section because the system was intended to be innovative in that it was intended to be novel and it was intended to differ in a significant and inventive way from prior software implementations. In addition, X's development activities involved significant economic risk in that X committed substantial resources to the development and there was substantial uncertainty, because of technical risk, that such resources would be recovered within a reasonable period. Finally, at the time X undertook the development of the system, software meeting X's requirements was not commercially available for use by X.

Example 4. (i) *Facts*. X wishes to improve upon its capabilities in the area of insurance fraud prevention, detection and control. X believes that it can exceed the capabilities of current commercial offerings in this area by developing and applying pattern matching algorithms that are not implemented in current vendor offerings. X has determined that many insurance fraud perpetrators can evade detection because its current system relies too heavily on exact matches and scrubbed data. Because a computer software system that will accomplish these objectives is not commercially available, X undertakes to develop and implement advanced pattern matching algorithms that would significantly improve upon the capabilities currently available from vendors. X commits substantial resources to the development of the software system and cannot determine, because of technical risk, if it will recover its investment within a reasonable period.

(ii) *Conclusion*. X's computer software system is developed primarily for X's internal use because X did not intend to sell, lease, license or otherwise market the software, for separately stated consideration to unrelated third parties. X's software development activities satisfy the high threshold of innovation test of paragraph (c)(6)(vi) of this section because the software system is innovative in that it was intended to be novel and it was intended to differ in a significant and inventive way from prior software implementations. In addition, X's development activities involved significant economic risk in that X committed substantial resources to the development and there was substantial uncertainty, because of technical risk, that such resources would be recovered within a reasonable period. Finally, at the time X undertook the development of the software, software satisfying X's requirements was not commercially available for use by X.

Example 5. (i) *Facts*. X is engaged in the business of designing, manufacturing, and selling widgets. X delivers its widgets in the same manner and time as its competitors. To improve customer service, X undertakes to develop computer software that will monitor the progress of the manufacture and delivery of X's widgets to enable X's customers to track their widget orders from origination to delivery, whether by air, land or ship. In addition, at the request of a customer, X will be able to intercept and return or reroute packages prior to delivery. At the time X undertakes its software development activities, X is uncertain whether it can develop the real-time communication software necessary to achieve its objective. None of X's competitors have a comparable tracking system. X commits substantial resources to the development of the system and, because of technical risk, X cannot determine if it will recover its investment within a reasonable period.

(ii) *Conclusion*. X's computer software is developed primarily for X's internal use because the software is not developed to be commercially sold, leased, licensed, or otherwise marketed, for separately stated consideration to unrelated third parties. X's computer software was developed to be used by X in providing noncomputer services to its customers. X's software satisfies the high threshold of innovation test of paragraph (c)(6)(vi) of this section because, at the time the research is undertaken, X's software is designed to provide a new tracking capability that is novel in that none of X's competitors have such a capability. Further, the new capability differs in a significant and inventive way from prior software implementations. In addition, X's development activities involved significant economic risk in that X committed substantial resources to the development and there was substantial uncertainty, because of technical risk, that such resources would be recovered within a reasonable period. Finally, at the time X undertook the development of the software, software satisfying X's requirements was not commercially available for use by X.

Example 6. (i) *Facts*. X, a multinational chemical manufacturer with different business and financial systems in each of its divisions, undertakes a software development project aimed at integrating the majority of the functional areas of its major software systems into a single enterprise resource management system supporting centralized financial systems, inventory, and management reporting. This project involves the detailed analysis of X's (as well as each of X's divisions') legacy systems to understand the actual current business processes and data requirements. X also has to develop programs to fill in the gaps between the software features and X's system requirements. X hires Y, a systems consulting firm to assist with this development effort. Y has experience in developing similar systems. X, working jointly with Y, evaluates its needs, establishes goals for the new system, re-engineers the business processes that will be made concurrently with the implementation of the new system, and chooses and purchases a software system upon which to base its enterprise-wide system.

(ii) *Conclusion*. X's enterprise-wide computer software is developed primarily for internal use because the software is not developed to be commercially sold, leased, licensed, or otherwise marketed, for separately stated consideration to unrelated third parties. X's computer software was developed to be used by X to serve X's general and administrative functions. However, the development of X's enterprise management system does not satisfy the high threshold of innovation test of paragraph (c)(6)(vi) of this section because the system that X is seeking to develop is not intended to be unique or novel. Further, the software does not differ in a significant or inventive way from software implemented by other manufacturers.

Example 7. (i) *Facts*. X, a financial services company specializing in commercial mortgages, decides to support its ongoing expansion by upgrading its information technology infrastructure. In order to accommodate its expanding efforts to acquire and maintain corporate borrowers and draw securitized loan investors, X builds a scalable and modular enterprise network to run its latest business applications, including web-based portfolio access for investors and staff, document imaging for customer service personnel, desktop access to information services for in-house securities traders and multimedia on-line training and corporate information delivery for all company personnel. As a result, X is able to access market information faster and function more efficiently and effectively than before. The new network is based on a faster local area network technology which is better able to meet the higher bandwidth requirements of X's current multimedia applications.

(ii) *Conclusion*. X's software is developed primarily for X's internal use because the software is not developed to be commercially sold, leased, licensed, or otherwise marketed, for separately stated consideration to unrelated third parties. X's software development activities do not meet the high threshold of innovation test of paragraph (c)(6)(vi) of this section because the system is not intended to be unique or novel. Further, the software does not differ in a significant or inventive way from other existing software implementations.

Example 8. (i) *Facts*. X, a corporation, undertook a software project to rewrite a legacy mainframe application using an object-oriented programming language, and to move the new application off the mainframe to a client/server environment. Both the object-oriented language and client/server technologies were new to X. This project was undertaken to develop a more maintainable application, and to be able to implement new features more quickly. X had to perform a detailed analysis of the old legacy application in order to determine the requirements of the rewritten application. To accomplish this task, X had to train the legacy mainframe programmers in the new object-oriented and client/server technologies that they would have to utilize. Several of X's competitors had successfully implemented similar systems using object-oriented programming language and client/server technologies.

(ii) *Conclusion*. X's software is developed primarily for internal use because the software is not developed to be commercially sold, leased, licensed, or otherwise marketed, for separately stated consideration to unrelated third parties. X's activities to rewrite a legacy mainframe application using an object-oriented programming language, and to move the application from X's mainframe to a client/server environment do not satisfy the high threshold of innovation test of paragraph (c)(6)(vi) of this section. The software developed is not intended to be either unique or novel and is not intended to differ in a significant and inventive way from prior software implementations or methods.

Example 9. (i) *Facts*. X, a retail and distribution company, wants to upgrade its warehouse management software. Therefore, X performs an analysis of the warehouse management products and vendors in the marketplace. X selects vendor V's software and, in turn, develops the software interfaces between X's legacy systems and V's warehouse management software in order to integrate the new warehouse management system with X's financial and inventory systems. The development of these interfaces requires a detailed understanding of all the input and output fields and their data formats, and how they map from the old system to the new system and vice-versa. Once X develops the interfaces, X has to perform extensive testing and validation work to ensure that the interfaces work correctly and accurately.

(ii) *Conclusion*. X's software is developed primarily for internal use because the software is not developed to be commercially sold, leased, licensed, or otherwise marketed, for separately stated consideration to unrelated third parties. X's software development activities do not satisfy the high threshold of innovation test of paragraph (c)(6)(vi) of this section because the software development does not involve significant economic risk in that there is no substantial uncertainty, because of technical risk, that such resources will be recovered within a reasonable period.

Example 10. (i) *Facts*. X, a credit card company, knows that its customers are not comfortable with purchasing products over the Internet because they feel the Web is not secure. X decides to build a payment system that provides customers with a single use, automatically generated, short-term time-based, transaction number. This single-use transaction number has a short expiration period that is just long enough to allow a merchant to process and fill the customer's order. Thus, when a customer wishes to make a purchase over the Internet, the customer requests X to generate automatically a single-use transaction number that merchant systems will accept as a legitimate card number. All purchases using single-use transaction numbers are automatically linked back to the customer's credit card account. X commits substantial resources to the development of the system and X cannot determine, because of technical risk, if it will recover its investment within a reasonable period. At the time of this project, nothing exists in the market that has these capabilities.

(ii) *Conclusion*. X's software is developed primarily for internal use because the software is not developed to be commercially sold, leased, licensed, or otherwise marketed, for separately stated consideration to unrelated third parties. X's computer software is developed primarily for X's internal use because it was intended to be used by X in providing noncomputer services to its customers. X's software satisfies the high threshold of innovation test of paragraph (c)(6)(vi) of this section because the system is a novel way to solve the security issue of making purchases over the Internet. Further, because of the secure payment capability, the software differs in a significant and inventive way from prior software implementations. In addition, X's development activities involved significant economic risk in that X committed substantial resources to the development and there was substantial uncertainty, because of technical risk, that such resources would be recovered within a reasonable period. Finally, at the time X undertook the development of the software, software satisfying X's requirements was not commercially available for use by X.

Example 11. (i) *Facts*. X, a corporation, wants to expand its internal computing power, and is aware that its PCs and workstations are idle at night, on the weekends, and for a significant part of any business day. Because the corporate computations that X needs to make could be done on workstations as well as PCs, X develops a screen-saver like application that runs on employee computers. When employees' computers have been idle for an amount of time set by each employee, the "screen-saver" starts to execute. However, instead of displaying moving lines, like the typical screen-saver, X's application goes back to a central server to get a new job to execute. This job will execute on the idle employee's computer until it has either finished, or the employee resumes working on his computer. X wants to ensure that it can manage all of the computation jobs distributed across its thousands of PCs and workstations. In addition, X wants to ensure that the additional load on its network caused by downloading the jobs and uploading the results, as well as in monitoring and managing the jobs, does not adversely impact the corporate computing infrastructure. At the time X undertook this software development project, X was uncertain, because of technical risk, it could develop a server application that could schedule and distribute the jobs across thousands of PCs and workstations, as well as handle all the error conditions that occur on a user's machine. Also, at the time X undertook this project, there was no commercial application available with such a capability.

(ii) *Conclusion*. X's computer software is developed primarily for internal use because the software is not developed to be commercially sold, leased, licensed, or otherwise marketed, for separately stated consideration to unrelated third parties. X's computer software was developed to be used by X to serve X's general and administrative functions. X's software satisfies the high threshold of innovation test of paragraph (c)(6)(vi) of this section because making use of idle corporate computing resources through what is ostensibly a screen-saver, was a novel approach to solving X's need for more computer intensive processing time. In addition, X's software development involves significant economic risk in that there was substantial uncertainty, because of technical risk, that the server application that schedules and distributes the jobs across thousands of PCs and workstations, as well as handles all the error conditions that can occur on a user's machine, amounts to developing a new operating system with new capabilities. Finally, at the time X undertook the development of the software, software satisfying X's requirements was not commercially available for use by X.

Example 12. (i) *Facts*. (A) X, a corporation, wants to protect its internal documents without building a large public key infrastructure. In addition, X needs to implement a new highly secure encryption algorithm that has a "back-door" such that X can decrypt and read any document, even when the employee is on vacation or leaves the company. X wants to develop a new encryption algorithm that is both secure, easy to use, and difficult to break. Current commercial encryption/decryption products are too slow for high-level secure encryption processing. Furthermore, no commercial product exists that provides the capability of having a secure back-door key to decrypt files when the owner is unavailable.

(B) The development of the encryption/decryption software requires specialized knowledge of cryptography and computational methods. Due to the secret nature of X's work, the encryption algorithm has to be unbreakable, yet recoverable should the employee forget his key. X commits substantial resources to the development of the system and, because of technical risk, cannot estimate whether it will recover its investment within a reasonable period.

(ii) *Conclusion*. X's back-door file encryption software is developed primarily for internal use because the software is not developed to be commercially sold, leased, licensed, or otherwise marketed, for separately stated consideration to unrelated third parties. X's back-door file encryption software was developed to be used by X to serve X's general and administrative functions. X's encryption software satisfies the high threshold of innovation test of paragraph (c)(6)(vi) of this section because, at the time the research is undertaken, X's software is designed to provide encryption and back-door decryption capabilities that are unique in that no other product has these capabilities, which indicates the software encryption system differs in a significant way from prior software implementations. Further, the encryption and back-door decryption capabilities indicate that the software differs in a significant and inventive way from prior software implementations. In addition, X's development activities involved significant economic risk in that X committed substantial resources to the development and there was substantial uncertainty, because of technical risk, that such resources would be recovered within a reasonable period. Finally, at the time X undertook the development of the software, software satisfying X's requirements was not commercially available for use by X.

Example 13. (i) *Facts*. X, a large regional telephone company, is experiencing rapidly increasing customer demand. X would like to determine whether evolutionary algorithms such as genetic algorithms may improve its ability to design cost-effective networks and extend existing networks. X would also like to determine whether such adaptive algorithms may be used to optimize the routing of call traffic across existing networks in order to use efficiently the resources available without causing congestion. X first explores the use of evolutionary algorithms for the call routing task, because X determines that this type of complex, unpredictable problem is most appropriate for an adaptive algorithm solution. X develops and tests genetic algorithms until it determines that it has developed a software system it can test on a pilot basis on its existing networks. X commits substantial resources to the project, and cannot predict, because of technical risk, whether it will recover its resources within a reasonable period. Finally, at the time X undertook the development of the software, software satisfying X's requirements was not commercially available for use by X.

(ii) *Conclusion*. X's software is developed primarily for internal use because the software is not developed to be commercially sold, leased, licensed, or otherwise marketed, for separately stated consideration to unrelated third parties. X's computer software is intended to be used by X in providing noncomputer services to its customers. X's software satisfies the high threshold of innovation test of paragraph (c)(6)(vi) of this section because the software is intended to be novel and is intended to differ in a significant and inventive way from other existing software implementations. In addition, X's development activities involved significant economic risk in that X committed substantial resources to the development and there was substantial uncertainty, because of technical risk, that such resources would be recovered within a reasonable period. Finally, at the time X undertook the development of the software, software satisfying X's requirements was not commercially available.

(ix) *Effective date*.—This paragraph (c)(6) is applicable for taxable years beginning after December 31, 1985.

* * *

Qualified Research Expenditures (QREs): Credit for Increasing Research Activities: Intra-Group Gross Receipts

Qualified Research Expenditures (QREs): Credit for Increasing Research Activities: Intra-Group Gross Receipts.—Amendments to Reg. §1.41-6, relating to the treatment of qualified research expenditures (QREs) and gross receipts resulting from transactions between members of a controlled group of corporations or a group of trades or businesses under common control (intra-group transactions) for purposes of determining the credit under section 41 for increasing research activities (research credit), are proposed (published in the Federal Register on December 13, 2013) (REG-159420-04).

☐ Par. 3. Section 1.41-6 is amended by:

1. Revising the section heading.
2. Revising paragraph (i)(1).
3. Removing paragraph (i)(4).
4. Redesignating paragraphs (i)(2) and (3) as paragraphs (i)(3) and (4), respectively.
5. Adding new paragraph (i)(2).
6. Adding new paragraph (i)(6).
7. Revising the first sentence of paragraph (j)(1).
8. Adding new paragraph (j)(4).

The revisions and additions read as follows:

§1.41-6. Controlled groups.

* * *

(i) *Transactions between controlled group members*.—(1) *In general—Treatment of transactions*.—Except as otherwise provided in this paragraph, all activities giving rise to amounts included in gross receipts under §1.41-3(c) (transactions) between members of a controlled group as defined in paragraph (a)(3) of this section (intra-group transactions) are generally disregarded in determining the QREs and gross receipts of a member for purposes of the research credit.

(2) *Exception for certain amounts received from foreign corporate controlled group member.*—(i) *In general.*—Notwithstanding paragraph (i)(1) of this section, gross receipts (within the meaning of § 1.41-3(c)) from an intra-group transaction are taken into account if—

(A) A foreign corporate controlled group member engages in a transaction with a party outside of the group (an external transaction) involving the same or a modified version of tangible or intangible property or a service that was previously the subject of one or more intra-group transactions (an internal transaction); and

(B) The external transaction does not give rise to gross receipts that are effectively connected with a trade or business within the United States, the Commonwealth of Puerto Rico, or any possession of the United States.

(ii) *Timing of inclusion.*—The amount described as taken into account in computing gross receipts in paragraph (i)(2)(i) of this section is taken into account in the year a foreign corporate controlled group member engages in the external transaction described in paragraph (i)(2)(i)(B) of this section.

(iii) *Multiple intra-group transactions.*—If there is more than one internal transaction, then only the last internal transaction giving rise to gross receipts (within the meaning of section 1.41-3(c)) is taken into account in the research credit computation pursuant to paragraph (i)(2)(i) of this section.

(iv) *Examples.*—The following examples illustrate the principles of paragraph (i)(2) of this section.

Example 1. Domestic Controlled Group Member Includes in Gross Receipts Proceeds From Intra-group Sale. D and F are members of the same controlled group. D is a domestic corporation. F is a foreign corporation that is organized under the laws of Country. F does not conduct a trade or business within the United States, Puerto Rico, or any U.S. possession. In Year 1, D sells Product to F for $8x. In Year 2, F sells Product to F's unrelated customer for $10x. Because the Product that F sells outside the group is the same Product that was the subject of an internal transaction (i.e., the sale from D to F), and the $10x that F receives upon sale of Product outside the group is not effectively connected with a trade or business within the United States, the Commonwealth of Puerto Rico, or any possession of the United States, the $8x that D receives from F is included in D's gross receipts for purposes of computing the amount of the group credit. The $8x of gross receipts is taken into account in Year 2, the year of the external transaction. See paragraph (i)(2) of this section. The $10x that F receives from F's customer is excluded from gross receipts under section 41(c)(7) because it is not effectively connected with the conduct of a trade or business within the United States, the Commonwealth of Puerto Rico, or any possession of the United States.

Example 2. Domestic Controlled Group Member Includes in Gross Receipts Amounts Received For Intra-group Transfer of License. Assume the same facts as in *Example 1*, except in Year 1, D licenses intellectual property (license) to F for $8x. F owns similar intellectual property that it plans to license to a customer together with the license it received from D. In Year 2, F licenses its intellectual property and sublicenses D's intellectual property to F's unrelated customer for $20x. Because the intellectual property that F sublicenses outside the group is the same intellectual property that was the subject of an internal transaction (i.e., the license from D to F), and the $20x that F receives for the license and sublicense of intellectual property outside the group is not effectively connected with a trade or business within the United States, the Commonwealth of Puerto Rico, or any possession of the United States, the $8x that D receives from F is included in D's gross receipts for purposes of computing the amount of the group credit. The $8x of gross receipts is taken into account in Year 2, the year of the external transaction. See paragraph (i)(2) of this section. The $20x that F receives from F's customer is excluded from gross receipts under section 41(c)(7) because it is not effectively connected with the conduct of a trade or business within the United States, the Commonwealth of Puerto Rico, or any possession of the United States.

Example 3. Domestic Controlled Group Member Includes in Gross Receipts Proceeds From Intra-group Sale Following Multiple Internal Transactions. D, F1, and F2 are members of the same controlled group. D is a domestic corporation. F1 and F2 are foreign corporations that are organized under the laws of Country. F1 and F2 do not conduct a trade or business within the United States, Puerto Rico, or any U.S. possession. In Year 1, D sells Product to F1 for $8x. In Year 2, F1 sells Product to F2 for $9x, and F2 sells Product to F2's unrelated customer for $10x. Both D's sale to F1 and F1's sale to F2 are internal transactions involving Product that precede F2's external transaction involving Product. The $10x that F2 receives upon sale of Product outside the group is not effectively connected with a trade or business within the United States, the Commonwealth of Puerto Rico, or any possession of the United States. Accordingly, the group will include gross receipts from an internal transaction in its research credit computation pursuant to paragraph (i)(2)(i) of this section. Because F1's sale of Product to F2 does not produce gross receipts that are effectively connected with the conduct of a trade or business within the United States, the Commonwealth of Puerto Rico, or any possession of the United States, those gross receipts are not taken into account even though that sale is the most recent internal transaction preceding the external transaction. See section 41(c)(7) and paragraph (i)(2)(i) of this section. Therefore, D will include $8x of gross receipts in its research credit computation in Year 2, the year of the external transaction, because the transfer from D to F1 is the last internal transaction giving rise to includible gross receipts. See paragraph (i)(2)(iii) of this section.

Example 4. Foreign Partnership Controlled Group Member Includes in Gross Receipts Proceeds From Intra-group Sale. Assume the same facts as in *Example 3*, except that F1 is a foreign partnership for federal income tax purposes and is part of the controlled group (within the meaning of § 1.41-6(a)(3)(ii)) that includes D and F2. Both D's sale to F1 and F1's sale to F2 are internal transactions involving Product that precede F2's external transaction involving Product. The $10x that F2 receives upon sale of Product outside the group is not effectively connected with a trade or business within the United States, the Commonwealth of Puerto Rico, or any possession of the United States. Accordingly, the group will include gross receipts from an internal transaction in its research credit computation pursuant to paragraph (i)(2)(i) of this section. F1's sale to F2 is the most recent internal transaction preceding the external transaction giving rise to gross receipts (see paragraph (i)(2)(iii)). The gross receipts from F1's sale to F2 are not excluded under section 41(c)(7) and paragraph (i)(2)(i) of this section because F1 is a partnership. Therefore, F1 will include $9x of gross receipts in its research credit computation in Year 2 because the transfer from F1 to F2 is the last internal transaction giving rise to gross receipts. See paragraph (i)(2)(iii) of this section.

Example 5. Domestic Controlled Group Member Includes in Gross Receipts Proceeds From Intra-group Sale Following Multiple Internal Transactions that Include a Section 721 Exchange. Assume the same facts as *Example 3*, except that in an exchange meeting the requirements of section 721(a), F2 transfers Product to PRS, a partnership that is not part of the controlled group within the meaning of § 1.41-6(a)(3)(ii). Both D's sale to F1 and F1's sale to F2 are internal transactions involving Product that precede F2's transfer of Product to PRS. The exchange engaged in by F2 does not give rise to gross receipts that are effectively connected with a trade or business within the United States, the Commonwealth of Puerto Rico, or any possession of the United States. Because F1's sale of Product to F2 does not produce gross receipts that are effectively connected with the conduct of a trade or business within the United States, the Commonwealth of Puerto Rico, or any possession of the United States, those gross receipts are not taken into account even though that sale is the most recent internal transaction preceding the external transaction. See section 41(c)(7) and paragraph (i)(2)(i) of this section. Therefore, D will include $8x of gross receipts in its research credit computation in Year 2, the year of the external transaction, because the transfer from D to F1 is the last internal transaction giving rise to includible gross receipts. See paragraphs (i)(2)(i) and (i)(2)(iii) of this section.

* * *

(6) *Consistency requirement.*—In computing the research credit for taxable years beginning on or after the date of publication of these regulations as final regulations in the **Federal Register**, QREs and gross receipts taken into account in computing a taxpayer's fixed-base percentage and a taxpayer's base amount must be determined on a basis consistent with the definition of QREs and gross receipts for the credit year, without regard to the law in effect for the taxable years taken into account in computing the fixed-base percentage or the base amount. This consistency requirement applies even if the period for filing a claim for credit or refund has expired for any taxable year taken into account in computing the fixed-base percentage or the base amount.

(j) *Effective/applicability dates.*—(1) *In general.*—Except as otherwise provided in this paragraph (j), these regulations apply to taxable years ending on or after May 24, 2005.

* * *

(4) *Intra-group transactions.*—Paragraphs (i)(1) and (2) of this section apply to taxable years beginning on or after the date of publication of these regulations as final regulations in the **Federal Register**.

Low-Income Housing Credit

Low-Income Housing Credit.—Temporary Reg. § 1.42-1T, relating to the low-income housing credit, is also proposed as a final regulation and, when adopted, would become Reg. § 1.42-1 (published in the Federal Register on June 22, 1987).

§ 1.42-1. Limitation on low-income housing credit allowed with respect to qualified low-income buildings receiving housing credit allocations from a State or local housing credit agency.

Business Related Credits: New Markets Tax Credit

Business Related Credits: New Markets Tax Credit.—Amendments to Reg. § 1.45D-1, revising and clarifying certain rules relating to recapture of the new markets tax credit and affecting certain taxpayers claiming the new markets tax credit, are proposed (published in the Federal Register on August 11, 2008) (REG-149404-07).

Par. 2. Section 1.45D-1 is amended by:

1. Redesignating the paragraph (a) entries for paragraphs (e)(4), (e)(5), (e)(6), and (e)(7) as paragraphs (e)(5), (e)(6), (e)(7), and (e)(8), respectively, adding a new entry for paragraph (e)(4), and revising the entry for paragraph (h)(2).

3. Revising paragraph (d)(6)(i).

4. Revising paragraph (e)(3)(iii) introductory text.

5. Redesignating paragraphs (e)(3)(iii)(B), (e)(3)(iii)(C), (e)(3)(iii)(D), and (e)(3)(iii)(E) as paragraphs (e)(3)(iii)(C), (e)(3)(iii)(D), (e)(3)(iii)(E), and (e)(3)(iii)(F), respectively, and adding new paragraph (e)(3)(iii)(B).

6. Revising newly-designated paragraph (e)(3)(iii)(D).

7. Redesignating paragraphs (e)(4), (e)(5), (e)(6), and (e)(7) as paragraphs (e)(5), (e)(6), (e)(7), and (e)(8), respectively, and adding new paragraph (e)(4).

8. Revising the heading for paragraph (h)(2) and adding a sentence at the end of the paragraph.

The additions and revisions read as follows:

§ 1.45D-1. New markets tax credit.

(a) * * *

(e) * * *

(4) Section 708(b)(1)(B) termination.

* * *

(h) * * *

(2) Exception for certain provisions.

* * *

(d) * * *

(6) * * *

(i) * * * Except as provided in paragraph (d)(6)(ii) of this section, an entity is treated as a qualified active low-income community business for the duration of the qualified community development entity's (CDE's) investment in the entity if the CDE reasonably expects, at the time the CDE makes the capital or equity investment in, or loan to, the entity, that the entity will satisfy the requirements to be a qualified active low-income community business under paragraphs (d)(4)(i) and (d)(5) of this section (including, if applicable, portions of business under paragraph (d)(4)(iii) of this section) throughout the entire period of the investment or loan. A CDE may rely on this paragraph (d)(6)(i) to treat an entity as a qualified active low-income community business even if the CDE's investment in or loan to the entity is made through other CDEs under paragraph (d)(1)(iv)(A) of this section.

(e) * * *

(3) * * *

(iii) *Capital interest in a partnership.*—In the case of an equity investment that is a capital interest in a CDE that is a partnership for Federal tax purposes, a pro rata cash distribution by the CDE to its partners based on each partner's capital interest in the CDE during the taxable year will not be treated as a redemption for purposes of paragraph (e)(2)(iii) of this section if the distribution does not exceed the sum of the CDE's "operating income" for the taxable year and the CDE's undistributed "operating income" (if any) for the prior taxable year. For purposes of this paragraph (e)(3)(iii), § 1.704-1(b)(1)(vii) applies to treat an allocation to a partner of its share of partnership net or "bottom line" taxable income or loss as an allocation to such partner of the same share of each item of income, gain, loss, and deduction that is taken into account in computing the partner's net or "bottom line" taxable income or loss. In addition, a nonpro rata "de minimis" cash distribution by a CDE to a partner or partners during the taxable year will not be treated as a redemption. A non-pro rata "de minimis" cash distribution may not exceed the lesser of 5 percent of the CDE's "operating income" for that taxable year or 10 percent of the partner's capital interest in the CDE. For purposes of this paragraph (e)(3)(iii), with respect to any taxable year, "operating income" is the sum of:

* * *

(B) Tax-exempt income under section 103;

* * *

(D) Deductions under sections 167 and 168, including the additional first-year depreciation under section 168(k), and any other depreciation and amortization deductions under the Code;

* * *

(e) * * *

(4) *Section 708(b)(1)(B) termination.* A termination under section 708(b)(1)(B) of a CDE that is a partnership is not a recapture event.

* * *

(h) * * *

(2) *Exception for certain provisions.*—* * * Paragraph (d)(6)(i) of this section as it relates to a CDE's investment under paragraph (d)(1)(iv)(A), paragraph (e)(3)(iii) of this section as it relates to the distribution of undistributed "operating income" for the prior taxable year and to the application of § 1.704-1(b)(1)(vii), paragraph (e)(3)(iii)(B) of this section, paragraph (e)(3)(iii)(D) of this section as it relates to any other depreciation and amortization deductions under the Code, and paragraph (e)(4) of this section apply to taxable years ending on or after the date of publication of the Treasury decision adopting these rules as final regulation in the **Federal Register**.

Energy Credits: Subsidized Borrowings

Energy Credits: Subsidized Borrowings.—Reproduced below is the text of proposed amendments of Reg. § 1.48-9, relating to the rule which reduces the energy credit where energy property is financed by subsidized energy financing or tax-exempt industrial development bonds (published in the Federal Register on January 26, 1982).

☐ The proposed amendments to the Income Tax Regulations (26 CFR Part 1) are as follows: Section 1.48-9 is amended by adding a new paragraph (o) to read as follows:

§ 1.48-9. Definition of energy property.—

* * *

(o) *Energy property financed by subsidized energy financing or industrial development bonds.*—(1) *In general.*—(i) This paragraph (o) prescribes rules—

(A) For reducing the qualified investment for purposes of the energy credit. See section 48(1)(11) as amended by section 223(c)(1) of the Crude Oil Windfall Profit Tax Act of 1980 (P.L. 96-223) and paragraph (o)(2) of this section.

(B) For reducing the energy credit percentage. See section 48(1)(11) as amended by section 221(b)(2) of that Act and paragraph (o)(6) of this section.

(ii) For effective dates, see paragraph (o)(8) of this section.

(2) *General rule.*—For purposes of the energy credit, qualified investment in any energy property (determined without this paragraph (o)) is reduced by the amount of subsidized borrowed funds used to finance in whole or in part the energy property. Funds borrowed are subsidized if they are directly or indirectly attributable to the proceeds of exempt IDB's or subsidized energy financing.

(3) *Exempt IDB defined.*—For purposes of this paragraph (c), an exempt IDB is an industrial development bond (within the meaning of section 103(b)(2)) with respect to which the interest paid is excluded from gross income under section 103.

(4) *Subsidized energy financing.*—(i) Funds are attributable to subsidized energy financing if the source of the funds for financing (other than exempt IDB's) is provided directly or indirectly (such as in association with, or through the facilities of, a bank or other lender) by, or through, a

government agency under a program a principal purpose of which is to provide (or assist in providing) financing for projects designed to conserve or produce energy. For purposes of this paragraph (o), a government agency is a State or local governmental unit referred to in § 1.103-1(a) or the Federal government.

(ii) Subsidized energy financing does not include a grant includible in gross income under section 61, a nontaxable government grant, or a credit against State or local taxes. Loan guarantees, price guarantees, purchase commitments, price support loans, and similar arrangements are not considered subsidized energy financing unless the arrangement is essentially subsidized borrowing under subdivision (i) of this subparagraph (4).

(iii) The following examples illustrate this subparagraph (4).

Example (1). A law in State A requires, as part of its Statewide energy program, that public utilities in the State provide low-interest loans to business enterprises for the purchase of energy property. The utilities are able to make these low-interest loans available to the enterprises by charging a 2 percent surcharge on each utility service bill. The funds from the surcharge are kept separate in an escrow account. This type of low interest loan is not subsidized energy financing and will not reduce the qualified investment of any energy property purchased with these funds.

Example (2). Assume the same facts as in example (1) except that, in lieu of the surcharge, the utilities receive money from the State for the express purpose of providing energy loans. Any low-interest loans made from these funds will be considered subsidized energy financing.

Example (3). State B allows a tax credit to a financial institution which makes low interest loans to corporations for the purpose of acquiring energy devices. The financial institution receives a credit each year in the amount of the excess of the interest that would have been paid at market rates and the actual interest paid on such loans. The State B tax credit arrangement is an interest subsidy. Thus, any low-interest loans pursuant to this credit arrangement is considered subsidized energy financing.

Example (4). State C wishes to encourage the production of synthetic fuels. As an inducement to Corporation X to build a synthetic fuel production plant, C enters into a contract with X guaranteeing X a certain price for the first 1,000 barrels of daily production. Before the plant is operational and pursuant to the price guarantee commitment, X receives an interest free advance of $10,000. Since the advance of funds is essentially a subsidized energy loan, it is considered to be subsidized energy financing.

(5) *Allocation of proceeds.*—(i) For purposes of the general rule, this subparagraph (5) sets forth the manner of determining the amount of subsidized borrowed funds that are considered used to finance energy property.

(ii) If borrowings attributable to subsidized energy financing are used to finance a facility, the entire amount of the borrowings are considered used to finance the energy property included in that facility and thus is applied directly to reduce the qualified investment in the energy property.

(iii)(A) If borrowings attributable to the proceeds of exempt IDB's are used to finance a facility, the borrowings reduce the qualified investment in that energy property. The amount of those borrowings considered used to finance energy property included in that facility equals the amount of the borrowings multiplied by a fraction. The numerator of the fraction is the qualified investment in the energy property before the reduction and the denominator is the total cost of that facility.

(B) If borrowings are attributable to the proceeds of exempt IDB's the exempt status of which is derived solely under section 103(b)(4), and the proceeds of such borrowings are used solely to finance the type of property or facility described in section 103(b)(4) from which the issue derives its tax-exempt status, then the facility referred to in paragraph (o)(5)(iii)(A) of this section is the property or facility from which the issue derives its tax-exempt status.

(iv) If both borrowings attributable to subsidized energy financing and borrowings attributable to exempt IDB financing are used to finance a facility, the total amount of subsidized energy financing is first applied directly to reduce the qualified investment (determined without this subdivision (iv)) in the energy property included in the facility. Then, paragraph (o)(5)(iii) of this section is applied to the exempt IDB financing by reducing both the numerator and the denominator of the fraction by the same total amount.

(v) The following examples illustrate this subparagraph (5).

Example (1). In 1983, Corporation X builds a facility costing $10,000. The facility includes energy property having a useful life of 7 years and the qualified investment (before reduction) is $8,000. X receives in 1983 a $6,000 energy loan from the Department of Energy for this facility at a subsidized rate of interest. The qualified investment for the energy property is reduced by $6,000 to $2,000. See paragraph (o)(5)(ii) of this section.

Example (2). Assume the same facts as in example (1) except that the $6,000 is borrowed from a fund established by a local government unit from the proceeds of exempt IDB's. The qualified investment in the energy property is reduced by $4,800 (i.e., $6,000 × $8,000/$10,000). Thus, the qualified investment is reduced from $8,000 to $3,200. See paragraph (o)(5)(iii)(A) of this section.

Example (3). Assume the same facts as in example (1) except that the total $6,000 borrowed to finance the property is from two sources. $2,000 is a subsidized energy loan and $4,000 is attributable to the proceeds of exempt IDB's. First, the qualified investment in the energy property of $8,000 is reduced by the subsidized energy loan of $2,000 to $6,000. For purposes of allocating the proceeds from exempt IDB's, the numerator and denominator of the fraction in example (2) are both reduced by this $2,000 from $8,000/$10,000 to $6,000/$8,000. Thus, the amount attributed to the proceeds of exempt IDB's is $3,000 (i.e., $4,000 × $6,000/$8,000), and the qualified investment for the energy property is $3,000, i.e., $6,000 − $3,000. See paragraph (o)(5)(iv) of this section.

Example (4). (a) In 1983, Corporation Y constructs a coal gasification project having an estimated useful life of 20 years and consisting of a gasifier and air pollution control equipment. The total cost of the project is $60 million, allocable to various types of property as follows:

($000,000 omitted)

	Gasifier	Pollution control equipment
Energy property	$30	$10
Other	10	10
	$40	$20

(b) Y finances construction of the project with subsidized financing ($10 million) and conventional financing ($36 million). Y also receives proceeds of $14 million from an issue of exempt IDB's, the exempt status of which is derived solely under section 103(b)(4)(F). Y uses the proceeds of the exempt IDB's solely to provide the pollution control equipment.

(c) Qualified investment for the energy credit is determined as follows:

	Energy property	
	Gasifier	Pollution control equipment
1. Cost	$30	$ 10
2. Allocation of subsidized energy financing ($10) to energy property		
(a) $10 × 30/40	7.5	
(b) $10 × 10/40		2.5
3. Remainder after applying paragraph (o)(5)(ii) of this section	$22.5	$ 7.5
4. Allocation of proceeds ($14) of IDB exempt solely under section 103(b)(4):		
(a) Fraction of cost of pollution control equipment that is energy property		10/20
(b) Reduce numerator and denominator of fraction by line 2(b)		7.5/17.5
(c) Multiply by proceeds		$ 14
(d) Allocated proceeds (line (b) × (c))		$ 6
5. Qualified investment for energy credit after applying paragraph (o)(5)(i)— (iv) of this section (line 3—line 4(d))	$22.5	$ 1.5

(6) *One-half exempt IDB rule for certain periods.*—For periods beginning on or after October 1, 1978, to which the general rule of paragraph (o)(2) of this section does not apply, the energy percentage for property is one-half of the energy percentage determined under section 46(a)(2)(C) if any funds borrowed to finance the facility of which the energy property is a part are directly or indirectly attributable to the proceeds of exempt IDB's. For explanation of the effective date of this subparagraph (6), see paragraph (o)(8) of this section.

(7) *Add-on equipment rule.*—(i) Energy property is not considered to be financed with subsidized borrowings solely because it is installed in an existing facility which has been previously so financed.

(ii) The facts and circumstances determine if energy property installed in connection with existing property is a separate unit or installed pursuant to a design, plan, or as a component of a larger property (such as a project or facility).

(iii) The following example illustrates this subparagraph (7).

Example. In 1981, corporation X finances its energy facility with the proceeds of exempt IDB's. The facility meets all air pollution laws and regulations in existence, or anticipated, when it is placed in service. In 1982, a new State regulation requires the installation of additional air pollution control equipment which is alternative energy property under section 48(l)(3)(A)(vi). X receives subsidized energy financing and installs the added equipment pursuant to the new regulation. The added air pollution control equipment is a separate unit. Therefore, the subsidized energy loan for the facility is not imputed to the qualified investment in this new separate unit.

(8) *Effective dates.*—(i) The general rule in paragraph (o)(2) of this section applies to early application property for periods after December 31, 1979. Early application property is defined in paragraph (o)(9) of this section. For other property, it applies to periods after December 31, 1982.

(ii) Notwithstanding paragraph (o)(8)(i) of this section, funds attributable under paragraph (o)(4) of this section to subsidized energy financing made before January 1, 1980, shall not be taken into account for purposes of reducing qualified investment under the general rule of paragraph (o)(2) of this section. See section 223(c)(2)(D) of P.L. 96-223. Subsidized energy financing is considered made before January 1, 1980, if it meets the requirements of §1.167(j)-4(c) (applied without reference to any dates therein).

(iii) The one-half-exempt IDB rule in paragraph (o)(6) of this section applies for periods beginning after October 1, 1978, to which the general rule of paragraph (o)(2) of this section does not apply.

(iv) For purposes of this subparagraph (8), whether qualified investment (without any reduction under this paragraph (o)) falls within a period is determined under section 48(m). If under section 48(m) this qualified investment for energy property is allocable to more than one period, the portion of subsidized borrowings used to finance the property (as determined under paragraph (o)(5) of this section) is ratably apportioned to this qualified investment for each period in proportion to this qualified investment for each period.

(v) The following examples illustrate this subparagraph (8).

Example (1). (a) Corporation Z begins building on February 1, 1980, a facility costing $100,000, $75,000 of which is solar energy property which generates electricity. The energy property has a useful life of seven years. The facility is completed in 1983. Z spent $45,000 for the energy property for the period ending on December 31, 1982, and $30,000 for periods after that date. In connection with this facility, Z receives a loan of $10,000 attributable to subsidized energy financing made in January 1980.

(b) The subsidized energy financing is allocated between the two periods in proportion to the amount of basis of energy property attributable to each period. Thus, $6,000 of the subsidized financing is allocated to the period before 1983 (*i.e.*, $10,000 × $45,000/$75,000) and $4,000 is allocated to the period after 1982 (*i.e.*, $10,000 × $30,000/$75,000). See paragraph (o)(8)(iv) of this section.

(c) The $6,000 of subsidized energy financing attributable to the period before 1983 does not reduce qualified investment in energy property (other than early application property) because the general rule in paragraph (o)(2) of this section does not apply. However, the qualified investment of $30,000 for the period after 1982 is reduced by $4,000 to $26,000.

Example (2). Assume the same facts as in example (1) except that the energy property is early application property. The general rule in paragraph (o)(2) of this section applies and the total amount of subsidized energy financing ($10,000) is subtracted from the total qualified investment. Thus, the qualified investment for the energy credit is reduced from $75,000 to $65,000.

Example (3). (a) Assume the same facts as in example (1) except that the $10,000 loan was attributable to the proceeds of exempt IDB financing. Exempt IDB financing allocated to pre-1983 periods does not reduce the qualified investment. Instead, the energy percentage is reduced by one-half from 15 percent to 7½ percent and applied against the qualified investment allocable to such periods, *i.e.*, $45,000. See section 46(a)(2)(C).

(b) The amount of exempt IDB financing attributable to qualified investment in energy property is $7,500 (*i.e.*, $10,000 × $75,000/$100,000). The portion of that amount attributable to periods after 1982 is $3,000 (*i.e.*, $7,500 × $30,000/$75,000). Accordingly, the qualified investment for the energy property attributable to periods after 1982 is reduced from $30,000 by $3,000 to $27,000. See paragraph (o)(8)(iv) of this section.

Example (4). Assume the same facts in example (3) except that the energy property is early application property. The general rule in paragraph (o)(2) of this section applies to the entire energy property, and the total amount of the proceeds of exempt IDB's is multiplied by the fraction in paragraph (o)(5)(iii) of this section. Thus, the qualified investment of $75,000 is reduced by $7,500 (*i.e.*, $10,000 × $75,000/$100,000) to $67,500.

(9) *Early application property*.—(i) Early application property is—

(A) Qualified hydroelectric generating property (described in section 48(1)(2)(A)(vii)),

(B) Cogeneration equipment (described in section 48(1)(2)(A)(viii)),

(C) Qualified intercity buses (described in section 48(1)(2)(A)(ix)),

(D) Ocean thermal property (described in section 48(1)(3)(A)(ix)), or

(E) Expanded energy property.

(ii) Expanded energy property is—

(A) Property that is included for the first time as alternative energy property under clause (iii) or (v) of section 48(1)(3)(A) by reason of the amendments thereto by section 222(b)(1) and (2) of the Crude Oil Windfall Profit Tax Act of 1980 (Pub. L. 96-223, 94 Stat. 229),

(B) Solar or wind energy property that provides solar process heat referred to in section 49(1)(4)(C),

(C) Modifications to alumina electrolytic cells referred to in section 48(1)(5)(L), and

(D) Property described in the last sentence of section 48(1)(3)(A) (relating to storage equipment for refuse-derived fuel).

Qualified Property: Additional First Year Depreciation Deduction

Qualified Property: Additional First Year Depreciation Deduction.—Amendments to Reg. §1.48-12, providing guidance regarding the additional first year depreciation deduction under section 168(k) of the Internal Revenue Code (Code), are proposed (published in the Federal Register on August 8, 2018) (REG-104397-18).

Par. 2. Section 1.48-12 is amended by:

1. In the last sentence in paragraph (a)(2)(i), removing "The last sentence" and adding "The next to last sentence" in its place;
2. Adding two sentences at the end of paragraph (a)(2)(i); and
3. Adding a sentence to the end of paragraph (c)(8)(i).

The additions read as follows:

§1.48-12. Qualified rehabilitated building; expenditures incurred after December 31, 1981.—(a) * * *

(2) * * *

(i) * * * The last sentence of paragraph (c)(8)(i) of this section applies to qualified rehabilitation expenditures that are qualified property under section 168(k)(2) and placed in service by a taxpayer during or after the taxpayer's taxable year that includes the date of publication of a Treasury decision adopting these rules as final regulations in the **Federal Register**. However, a taxpayer may rely on the last sentence in paragraph (c)(8)(i) of this section in these proposed regulations for qualified rehabilitation expenditures that are qualified property under section

168(k)(2) and acquired and placed in service after September 27, 2017, by the taxpayer during taxable years ending on or after September 28, 2017, and ending before the taxpayer's taxable year that includes the date of publication of a Treasury decision adopting these rules as final regulations in the **Federal Register**.

* * *

(c) * * *

(8) * * *

(i) * * * Further, see § 1.168(k)-2(f)(9) if the qualified rehabilitation expenditures are qualified property under section 168(k), as amended by the Tax Cuts and Jobs Act, Public Law 115-97 (131 Stat. 2054 (December 22, 2017)).

* * *

Income Inclusion Rule: Lessee Having Acquired Investment Credit Property

Income Inclusion Rule: Lessee Having Acquired Investment Credit Property.—Amendments to Reg. § 1.50-1, relating to the income inclusion rules under section 50(d)(5) of the Internal Revenue Code (Code) that are applicable to a lessee of investment credit property when a lessor of such property elects to treat the lessee as having acquired the property, are proposed. (published in the Federal Register on July 22, 2016) (REG-102516-15).

§ 1.50-1. Lessee's income inclusion following election of lessor of investment credit property to treat lessee as acquirer.—[The text of proposed amendment to § 1.50-1 is the same as the text of § 1.50-1T(a) through (f) as added by T.D. 9776].

Consolidated Returns: AMT

Consolidated Returns: Alternative Minimum Tax.—Reproduced below is the text of a proposed amendment to Reg. § 1.56(g)-1, relating to the computation of the alternative minimum tax by consolidated groups (published in the Federal Register on December 30, 1992).

☐ Par. 2. Section 1.56(g)-1 is amended by revising paragraph (n) to read as follows:

§ 1.56(g)-1. Adjusted current earnings.

* * *

(n) *Adjustment for adjusted current earnings of consolidated groups.*—For consolidated return years for which the due date of the income tax return (without regard to extensions) is on or after [the date that is sixty days after final regulations are filed with the Federal Register], the rules of § 1.1502-55(b)(3) apply in computing the adjustment for adjusted current earnings of a consolidated group.

* * *

Base Erosion and Anti-Abuse Tax: Guidance

Base Erosion and Anti-Abuse Tax: Guidance.—Reg. §§ 1.59A-1—1.59A-10, regarding the tax on base erosion payments of taxpayers with substantial gross receipts and reporting requirements thereunder, are proposed (published in the Federal Register on December 21, 2018) (REG-104259-18).

Par. 2. Sections 1.59A-1 through 1.59A-10 are added to read as follows:

§ 1.59A-1. Base erosion and anti-abuse tax.—(a) *Purpose.*—This section and §§ 1.59A-2 through 1.59A-10 (collectively, the "section 59A regulations") provide rules under section 59A to determine the amount of the base erosion and anti-abuse tax. Paragraph (b) of this section provides definitions applicable to the section 59A regulations. Section 1.59A-2 provides rules regarding how to determine whether a taxpayer is an applicable taxpayer. Section 1.59A-3 provides rules regarding base erosion payments and base erosion tax benefits. Section 1.59A-4 provides rules for calculating modified taxable income. Section 1.59A-5 provides rules for calculating the base erosion minimum tax amount. Section 1.59A-6 provides rules relating to qualified derivative payments. Section 1.59A-7 provides rules regarding application of section 59A to partnerships. Section 1.59A-8 is reserved for rules regarding the application of section 59A to certain expatriated entities. Section 1.59A-9 provides an anti-abuse rule to prevent avoidance of section 59A. Finally, § 1.59A-10 provides the applicability date for the section 59A regulations.

(b) *Definitions.*—For purposes of this section and §§ 1.59A-2 through 1.59A-10, the following terms have the meanings described in this paragraph (b).

(1) *Aggregate group.*—The term *aggregate group* means the group of corporations determined by—

(i) Identifying a controlled group of corporations as defined in section 1563(a), except that the phrase "more than 50 percent" is substituted for "at least 80 percent" each place it appears in section 1563(a)(1) and the determination is made without regard to sections 1563(a)(4) and (e)(3)(C), and

(ii) Once the controlled group of corporations is determined, excluding foreign corporations except with regard to income that is, or is treated as, effectively connected with the conduct of a trade or business in the United States under an applicable provision of the Internal Revenue Code or regulations published under 26 CFR chapter I. Notwithstanding the foregoing, if a foreign corporation determines its net taxable income under an applicable income tax treaty of the United States, it is excluded from the controlled group of corporations except with regard to income taken into account in determining its net taxable income.

(2) *Applicable section 38 credits.*—The term *applicable section 38 credits* means the credits allowed under section 38 for the taxable year that are properly allocable to—

(i) The low-income housing credit determined under section 42(a),

(ii) The renewable electricity production credit determined under section 45(a), and

(iii) The investment credit determined under section 46, but only to the extent properly allocable to the energy credit determined under section 48.

(3) *Applicable taxpayer*.—The term *applicable taxpayer* means a taxpayer that meets the requirements set forth in § 1.59A-2(b).

(4) *Bank*.—The term *bank* means an entity defined in section 581.

(5) *Base erosion and anti-abuse tax rate*.—The term *base erosion and anti-abuse tax rate* means the percentage that the taxpayer applies to its modified taxable income for the taxable year to calculate its base erosion minimum tax amount. See § 1.59A-5(c) for the base erosion and anti-abuse tax rate applicable to the relevant taxable year.

(6) *Business interest expense*.—The term *business interest expense*, with respect to a taxpayer and a taxable year, has the meaning provided in § 1.163(j)-1(b)(2).

(7) *Deduction*.—The term *deduction* means any deduction allowable under chapter 1 of subtitle A of the Internal Revenue Code.

(8) *Disallowed business interest expense carryforward*.—The term *disallowed business interest expense carryforward* has the meaning provided in § 1.163(j)-1(b)(9).

(9) *Domestic related business interest expense*.—The term *domestic related business interest expense* for any taxable year is the taxpayer's business interest expense paid or accrued to a related party that is not a foreign related party.

(10) *Foreign person*.—The term *foreign person* means any person who is not a United States person. For purposes of the preceding sentence, a United States person has the meaning provided in section 7701(a)(30), except that any individual who is a citizen of any possession of the United States (but not otherwise a citizen of the United States) and who is not a resident of the United States is not a United States person. See § 1.59A-7(b) for rules applicable to partnerships.

(11) *Foreign related business interest expense*.—The term *foreign related business interest expense* for any taxable year is the taxpayer's business interest expense paid or accrued to a foreign related party.

(12) *Foreign related party*.—The term *foreign related party* means a foreign person, as defined in paragraph (b)(10) of this section, that is a related party, as defined in paragraph (b)(17) of this section, with respect to the taxpayer. In addition, for purposes of § 1.59A-3(b)(4)(v)(B), a foreign related party also includes the foreign corporation's home office or a foreign branch of the foreign corporation. See § 1.59A-7(c) for rules applicable to partnerships.

(13) *Gross receipts*.—The term *gross receipts* has the meaning provided in § 1.448-1T(f)(2)(iv).

(14) *Member of an aggregate group*.—The term *member of an aggregate group* means a corporation that is included in an aggregate group, as defined in paragraph (b)(1) of this section.

(15) *Registered securities dealer*.—The term *registered securities dealer* means any dealer as defined in section 3(a)(5) of the Securities Exchange Act of 1934 that is registered, or required to be registered, under section 15 of the Securities Exchange Act of 1934.

(16) *Regular tax liability*.—The term *regular tax liability* has the meaning provided in section 26(b).

(17) *Related party*.—(i) *In general*.—A *related party*, with respect to an applicable taxpayer, is—

(A) Any 25-percent owner of the taxpayer;

(B) Any person who is related (within the meaning of section 267(b) or 707(b)(1)) to the taxpayer or any 25-percent owner of the taxpayer; or

(C) A controlled taxpayer within the meaning of § 1.482-1(i)(5) together with, or with respect to, the taxpayer.

(ii) *25-percent owner*.—With respect to any corporation, a *25-percent owner* means any person who owns at least 25 percent of—

(A) The total voting power of all classes of stock of the corporation entitled to vote; or

(B) The total value of all classes of stock of the corporation.

(iii) *Application of Section 318*.—section 318 applies for purposes of paragraphs (b)(17)(i) and (ii) of this section, except that—

(A) "10 percent" is substituted for "50 percent" in section 318(a)(2)(C); and

(B) Section 318(a)(3)(A) through (C) are not applied so as to consider a United States person as owning stock that is owned by a person who is not a United States person.

(18) *TLAC long-term debt required amount*.—The term *TLAC long-term debt required amount* means the specified minimum amount of debt that is required pursuant to 12 CFR 252.162(a).

(19) *TLAC securities amount*.—The term *TLAC securities amount* is the sum of the adjusted issue prices (as determined for purposes of § 1.1275-1(b)) of all TLAC securities issued and outstanding by the taxpayer.

(20) *TLAC security*.—The term *TLAC security* means an eligible internal debt security, as defined in 12 CFR 252.161.

(21) *Unrelated business interest expense*.—The term *unrelated business interest expense* for any taxable year is the taxpayer's business interest expense paid or accrued to a party that is not a related party. [Reg. § 1.59A-1.]

§ 1.59A-2. Applicable taxpayer.—(a) *Scope*.—This section provides rules for determining whether a taxpayer is an applicable taxpayer. Paragraph (b) of this section defines an applicable taxpayer. Paragraph (c) of this section provides rules for determining whether a taxpayer is an applicable taxpayer by reference to the aggregate group of which the taxpayer is a member. Paragraph (d) of this section provides rules regarding the gross receipts test. Paragraph (e) of this section provides rules regarding the base erosion percentage calculation. Paragraph (f) of this section provides examples illustrating the rules of this section.

(b) *Applicable taxpayer*.—For purposes of section 59A, a taxpayer is an applicable taxpayer with respect to any taxable year if the taxpayer—

(1) Is a corporation, but not a regulated investment company, a real estate investment trust, or an S corporation;

(2) Satisfies the gross receipts test of paragraph (d) of this section; and

(3) Satisfies the base erosion percentage test of paragraph (e) of this section.

(c) *Aggregation rules.*—A taxpayer that is a member of an aggregate group determines its gross receipts and its base erosion percentage on the basis of the aggregate group as of the end of the taxpayer's taxable year. For these purposes, transactions that occur between members of the taxpayer's aggregate group that were members of the aggregate group as of the time of the transaction are not taken into account. In the case of a foreign corporation that is a member of an aggregate group, only transactions that relate to income effectively connected with, or treated as effectively connected with, the conduct of a trade or business in the United States are disregarded for this purpose. In the case of a foreign corporation that is a member of an aggregate group and that determines its net taxable income under an applicable income tax treaty of the United States, only transactions that are taken into account in determining its net taxable income are disregarded for this purpose.

(d) *Gross receipts test.*—(1) *Amount of gross receipts.*—A taxpayer, or the aggregate group of which the taxpayer is a member, satisfies the gross receipts test if it has average annual gross receipts of at least $500,000,000 for the three-taxable-year period ending with the preceding taxable year.

(2) *Period for measuring gross receipts for an aggregate group.*—(i) *Calendar year taxpayers that are members of an aggregate group.*—In the case of a corporation that has a calendar year and that is a member of an aggregate group, the corporation applies the gross receipts test in paragraph (d)(1) of this section on the basis of the gross receipts of the aggregate group for the three-calendar-year period ending with the preceding calendar year, without regard to the taxable year of any other member of the aggregate group.

(ii) *Fiscal year taxpayers that are members of an aggregate group.*—In the case of a corporation that has a fiscal year and that is a member of an aggregate group, the corporation applies the gross receipts test in paragraph (d)(1) of this section on the basis of the gross receipts of the aggregate group for the three-fiscal-year period ending with the preceding fiscal year of the corporation, without regard to the taxable year of any other member of the aggregate group.

(3) *Gross receipts of foreign corporations.*—With respect to any foreign corporation, only gross receipts that are taken into account in determining income that is effectively connected with the conduct of a trade or business within the United States are taken into account for purposes of paragraph (d)(1) of this section. In the case of a foreign corporation that is a member of an aggregate group and that determines its net taxable income under an applicable income tax treaty of the United States, the foreign corporation includes only gross receipts that are attributable to transactions taken into account in determining its net taxable income.

(4) *Gross receipts of an insurance company.*—For any corporation that is subject to tax under subchapter L or any corporation that would be subject to tax under subchapter L if that corporation were a domestic corporation, gross receipts are reduced by return premiums, but are not reduced by any reinsurance premiums paid or accrued.

(5) *Gross receipts from partnerships.*—See § 1.59A-7(b)(5)(ii).

(6) *Taxpayer not in existence for entire three-year period.*—If a taxpayer was not in existence for the entire three-year period referred to in paragraph (d)(1) of this section, the taxpayer determines a gross receipts average for the period that it was in existence, taking into account paragraph (d)(7) of this section.

(7) *Treatment of short taxable year.*—If a taxpayer has a taxable year of fewer than 12 months (a short period), gross receipts are annualized by multiplying the gross receipts for the short period by 365 and dividing the result by the number of days in the short period.

(8) *Treatment of predecessors.*—For purposes of determining gross receipts under this paragraph (d), any reference to a taxpayer includes a reference to any predecessor of the taxpayer. For this purpose, a predecessor includes the distributor or transferor corporation in a transaction described in section 381(a) in which the taxpayer is the acquiring corporation.

(9) *Reductions in gross receipts.*—Gross receipts for any taxable year are reduced by returns and allowances made during that taxable year.

(10) *Gross receipts of consolidated groups.*—For purposes of section 59A, the gross receipts of a consolidated group are determined by aggregating the gross receipts of all of the members of the consolidated group. See § 1.1502-59A(b).

(e) *Base erosion percentage test.*—(1) *In general.*—A taxpayer, or the aggregate group of which the taxpayer is a member, satisfies the base erosion percentage test if its base erosion percentage is three percent or higher.

(2) *Base erosion percentage test for banks and registered securities dealers.*—(i) *In general.*—A taxpayer that is a member of an affiliated group (as defined in section 1504(a)(1)) that includes a bank (as defined in § 1.59A-1(b)(4)) or a registered securities dealer (as defined in section § 1.59A-1(b)(15)) satisfies the base erosion percentage test if its base erosion percentage is two percent or higher.

(ii) *Aggregate groups.*—An aggregate group of which a taxpayer is a member and that includes a bank or a registered securities dealer that is a member of an affiliated group (as defined in section 1504(a)(1)) will be subject to the base erosion percentage threshold described in paragraph (e)(2)(i) of this section.

(iii) *De minimis exception for banking and registered securities dealer activities.*—An aggregate group that includes a bank or a registered securities dealer that is a member of an affiliated group (as defined in section 1504(a)(1)) is not treated as including a bank or registered securities dealer for purposes of paragraph (e)(2)(i) of this section for a taxable year, if, in that taxable year, the total gross receipts of the aggregate group attributable to the bank or the registered securities dealer represent less than two percent of the total gross receipts of the aggregate group, as determined under paragraph (d) of this section. When there is no aggregate group, a consolidated group that includes a bank or a registered securities dealer is not treated as including a bank or registered securities dealer for purposes of paragraph (e)(2)(i) of this section for a taxable year, if, in that taxable year, the total gross receipts of the consolidated group attributable to the bank or the registered securities dealer represent less than two percent of the total gross receipts of the consolidated group, as determined under paragraph (d) of this section.

(3) *Computation of base erosion percentage.*—(i) *In general.*—The taxpayer's base erosion percentage for any taxable year is determined by dividing—

(A) The aggregate amount of the taxpayer's (or in the case of a taxpayer that is a member of an aggregate group, the aggregate group's) base erosion tax benefits (as defined in § 1.59A-3(c)(1)) for the taxable year, by

(B) The sum of—

(1) The aggregate amount of the deductions (including deductions for base erosion tax benefits described in § 1.59A-3(c)(1)(i) and base erosion tax benefits described in § 1.59A-3(c)(1)(ii)) allowable to the taxpayer (or in the case of a taxpayer that is a member of an aggregate group, any member of the aggregate group) under chapter 1 of Subtitle A for the taxable year;

(2) The base erosion tax benefits described in § 1.59A-3(c)(1)(iii) with respect to any premiums or other consideration paid or accrued by the taxpayer (or in the case of a taxpayer that is a member of an aggregate group, any member of the aggregate group) to a foreign related party for any reinsurance payment taken into account under sections 803(a)(1)(B) or 832(b)(4)(A) for the taxable year; and

(3) Any amount paid or accrued by the taxpayer (or in the case of a taxpayer that is a member of an aggregate group, any member of the aggregate group) resulting in a reduction of gross receipts described in § 1.59A-3(c)(1)(iv) for the taxable year.

(ii) *Certain items not taken into account in denominator.*—Except as provided in paragraph (e)(3)(viii) of this section, the amount under paragraph (e)(3)(i)(B) of this section is determined by not taking into account—

(A) Any deduction allowed under section 172, 245A, or 250 for the taxable year;

(B) Any deduction for amounts paid or accrued for services to which the exception described in § 1.59A-3(b)(3)(i) applies;

(C) Any deduction for qualified derivative payments that are not treated as base erosion payments by reason of § 1.59A-3(b)(3)(ii);

(D) Any exchange loss within the meaning of § 1.988-2 from a section 988 transaction as described in § 1.988-1(a)(1);

(E) Any deduction for amounts paid or accrued to foreign related parties with respect to TLAC securities that are not treated as base erosion payments by reason of § 1.59A-3(b)(3)(v); and

(F) Any deduction not allowed in determining taxable income from the taxable year.

(iii) *Effect of treaties on base erosion percentage determination.*—In computing the base erosion percentage, the amount of the base erosion tax benefit with respect to a base erosion payment on which tax is imposed by section 871 or 881 and with respect to which tax has been deducted and withheld under section 1441 or 1442 is equal to the gross amount of the base erosion tax benefit before the application of the applicable treaty multiplied by a fraction equal to—

(A) The rate of tax imposed without regard to the treaty, reduced by the rate of tax imposed under the treaty; over

(B) The rate of tax imposed without regard to the treaty.

(iv) *Amounts paid or accrued between members of a consolidated group.*—See § 1.1502-59A(b).

(v) *Deductions and base erosion tax benefits from partnerships.*—See § 1.59A-7(b).

(vi) *Mark-to-market positions.*—For any position with respect to which the taxpayer (or in the case of a taxpayer that is a member of an aggregate group, a member of the aggregate group) applies a mark-to-market method of accounting for federal income tax purposes, the taxpayer must determine its gain or loss with respect to that position for any taxable year by combining all items of income, gain, loss, or deduction arising with respect to the position during the taxable year, regardless of how each item arises (including from a payment, accrual, or mark) for purposes of paragraph (e)(3) of this section. See paragraph (f)(1) of this section (*Example 1*) for an illustration of this rule. For purposes of section 59A, a taxpayer computes its losses resulting from positions subject to a mark-to-market regime under the Internal Revenue Code based on a single mark for the taxable year on the earlier of the last business day of the taxpayer's taxable year and the disposition (whether by sale, offset, exercise, termination, expiration, maturity, or other means) of the position, regardless of how frequently a taxpayer marks to market for other purposes. See § 1.59A-3(b)(2)(iii) for the application of this rule for purposes of determining the amount of base erosion payments.

(vii) *Computing the base erosion percentage when members of an aggregate group have different taxable years.*—(A) *Calendar year taxpayers that are members of an aggregate group.*—In the case of a taxpayer that has a calendar year and that is a member of an aggregate group, the taxpayer applies the base erosion percentage in paragraph (e)(1) or (2) of this section (and determines the base erosion percentage used in § 1.59A-4(b)(2)(ii)) on the basis of the base erosion percentage for the calendar year in the manner set forth in paragraph (e)(3) of this section, without regard to the taxable year of any other member of the aggregate group. See paragraph (f)(2) of this section (*Example 2*) for an illustration of this rule. For purposes of applying paragraph (e)(3)(vi) of this section, all members of the aggregate group are treated as having a calendar year.

(B) *Fiscal year taxpayers that are members of an aggregate group.*—In the case of a taxpayer that has a fiscal year and that is a member of an aggregate group, the taxpayer applies the base erosion percentage test in paragraph (e)(1) or (2) of this section (and determines the base erosion percentage used in § 1.59A-4(b)(2)(ii)) on the basis of the base erosion percentage for its fiscal year in the manner set forth in paragraph (e)(3) of this section, without regard to the taxable year of any other member of the aggregate group. See paragraph (f)(2) of this section (*Example 2*) for an illustration of this rule. For purposes of applying paragraph (e)(3)(vi) of this section, all members of the aggregate group are treated as having the taxpayer's fiscal year.

(C) *Transition rule for aggregate group members with different taxable years.*—For purposes of this paragraph (e)(3)(vii), if the taxpayer has a different taxable year than another member of the taxpayer's aggregate group, each taxpayer that is a member of the aggregate group determines the availability of the exception in § 1.59A-3(b)(3)(vi) (amounts paid or accrued in taxable years beginning before January 1, 2018) by using the taxpayer's taxable year for all members of the taxpayer's aggregate group.

(viii) *Certain payments that qualify for the effectively connected income exception and another base erosion payment exception.*—Subject to paragraph (c) of this section (transactions that occur between members of the taxpayer's aggregate group), a payment that qualifies for the effectively connected income exception described in § 1.59A-3(b)(3)(iii) and either the service cost method exception described in § 1.59A-3(b)(3)(i), the qualified derivative payment exception described in § 1.59A-3(b)(3)(ii), or the TLAC exception described in § 1.59A-3(b)(3)(v) is not subject to paragraph (e)(3)(ii)(B), (C), or (E) of this section and those amounts are included in the denominator of the base erosion percentage if the foreign related party who received the payment is not a member of the aggregate group.

(f) *Examples.*—The following examples illustrate the rules of this section.

(1) *Example 1: Mark-to-market.* (i) *Facts.* (A) Foreign Parent (FP) is a foreign corporation that owns all of the stock of domestic corporation (DC) and foreign corporation (FC). FP and FC are foreign related parties of DC under § 1.59A-1(b)(12) but not members of the aggregate group. DC is a registered securities dealer that does not hold any securities for investment. On January 1 of year 1, DC enters into two interest rate swaps for a term of two years, one with unrelated Customer A as the counterparty (position A) and one with unrelated Customer B as the counterparty (position B). Each of the swaps provides for semiannual periodic payments to be made or received on June 30 and December 31. No party makes any payment to any other party upon initiation of either of the swaps (that is, they are entered into at-the-money). DC is required to mark-to-market positions A and B for federal income tax purposes. DC is a calendar year taxpayer.

(B) For position A in year 1, DC makes a payment of $150 on June 30, and receives a payment of $50 on December 31. There are no other payments in year 1. On December 31, position A has a value to DC of $110 (that is, position A is in-the-money by $110).

(C) For position B in year 1, DC receives a payment of $120 on June 30, and makes a payment of $30 on December 31. There are no other payments in year 1. On December 31, position B has a value to DC of ($130) (that is, position B is out-of-the-money by $130).

(ii) *Analysis.* (A) With respect to position A, based on the total amount of payments made and received in year 1, DC has a net deduction of $100. In addition, DC has a mark-to-market gain of $110. As described in paragraph (e)(3)(vi) of this section, the mark-to-market gain of $110 is combined with the net deduction of $100 resulting from the payments. Therefore, with respect to position A, DC has a gain of $10, and thus has no deduction in year 1 for purposes of section 59A.

(B) With respect to position B, based on the total amount of payments made and received in year 1, DC has net income of $90. In addition, DC has a mark-to-market loss of $130. As described in paragraph (e)(3)(vi) of this section, the mark-to-market loss of $130 is combined with the net income of $90 resulting from the payments. Therefore, with respect to position B, DC has a loss of $40, and thus has a $40 deduction in year 1 for purposes of section 59A.

(2) *Example 2: Determining gross receipts test and base erosion percentage when aggregate group members have different taxable years.* (i) *Facts.* Foreign Parent (FP) is a foreign corporation that owns all of the stock of a domestic corporation that uses a calendar year (DC1) and a domestic corporation that uses a fiscal year ending on January 31 (DC2). FP does not have income effectively connected with the conduct of a trade or business within the United States. DC2 is a member of DC1's aggregate group, and DC1 is a member of DC2's aggregate group.

(ii) *Analysis.* (A) For DC1's tax return filed for the calendar year ending December 31, 2026, DC1 determines its gross receipts based on gross receipts of DC1 and DC2 for the calendar years ending December 31, 2023, December 31, 2024, and December 31, 2025. Further, DC1 determines its base erosion percentage for the calendar year ending December 31, 2026, on the basis of transactions of DC1 and DC2 for the calendar year ending December 31, 2026.

(B) For DC2's tax return filed for the fiscal year ending January 31, 2027, DC2 determines its gross receipts based on gross receipts of DC2 and DC1 for the fiscal years ending January 31, 2024, January 31, 2025, and January 31, 2026. Further, DC2 determines its base erosion percentage for the fiscal year ending January 31, 2027, on the basis of transactions of DC2 and DC1 for the fiscal year ending January 31, 2027. [Reg. § 1.59A-2.]

§ 1.59A-3. Base erosion payments and base erosion tax benefits.—(a) *Scope.*—This section provides definitions and related rules regarding base erosion payments and base erosion tax benefits. Paragraph (b) of this section provides definitions and rules regarding base erosion payments. Paragraph (c) of this section provides rules for determining the amount of base erosion tax benefits. Paragraph (d) of this section provides examples illustrating the rules described in this section.

(b) *Base erosion payments.*—(1) *In general.*—Except as provided in paragraph (b)(3) of this section, a *base erosion payment* means—

(i) Any amount paid or accrued by the taxpayer to a foreign related party of the taxpayer and with respect to which a deduction is allowable under chapter 1 of subtitle A of the Internal Revenue Code;

(ii) Any amount paid or accrued by the taxpayer to a foreign related party of the taxpayer in connection with the acquisition of property by the taxpayer from the foreign related party if the character of the property is subject to the allowance for depreciation (or amortization in lieu of depreciation);

(iii) Any premium or other consideration paid or accrued by the taxpayer to a foreign related party of the taxpayer for any reinsurance payments that are taken into account under section 803(a)(1)(B) or 832(b)(4)(A); or

(iv) Any amount paid or accrued by the taxpayer that results in a reduction of the gross receipts of the taxpayer if the amount paid or accrued is with respect to—

(A) A surrogate foreign corporation, as defined in section 59A(d)(4)(C)(i), that is a related party of the taxpayer (but only if the corporation first became a surrogate foreign corporation after November 9, 2017); or

(B) A foreign person that is a member of the same expanded affiliated group, as defined in section 59A(d)(4)(C)(ii), as the surrogate foreign corporation.

(2) *Operating rules.*—(i) *Amounts paid or accrued in cash and other consideration.*—For purposes of paragraph (b)(1) of this section, an amount paid or accrued includes an amount paid or accrued using any form of consideration, including cash, property, stock, or the assumption of a liability.

(ii) *Transactions providing for net payments.*—Except as otherwise provided in paragraph (b)(2)(iii) of this section or as permitted by the Internal Revenue Code or the regulations, the amount of any base erosion payment is determined on a gross basis, regardless of any contractual or legal right to make or receive payments on a net basis. For this purpose, a right to make or receive payments on a net basis permits the parties to a transaction or series of transactions to settle obligations by offsetting any amounts to be paid by one party against amounts owed by that party to the other party. For example, any premium or other consideration paid or accrued by a taxpayer to a foreign related party for any reinsurance payments is not reduced by or netted against other amounts owed to the taxpayer from the foreign related party or by reserve adjustments or other returns.

(iii) *Amounts paid or accrued with respect to mark-to-market position.*—For any transaction with respect to which the taxpayer applies the mark-to-market method of accounting for federal income tax purposes, the rules set forth in § 1.59A-2(e)(3)(vi) apply to determine the amount of base erosion payment.

(iv) *Coordination among categories of base erosion payments.*—A payment that does not satisfy the criteria of one category of base erosion payment may be a base erosion payment described in one of the other categories.

(v) *Certain domestic passthrough entities.*—(A) *In general.*—If an applicable taxpayer pays or accrues an amount that would be a base erosion payment except for the fact that the payment is made to a specified domestic passthrough, then the applicable taxpayer will be treated as making a base erosion payment to each specified foreign related party for purposes of section 59A and §§ 1.59A-2 through 1.59A-10. This rule has no effect on the taxation of the specified domestic passthrough under subchapter J or subchapter M of the Code (as applicable).

(B) *Amount of base erosion payment.*—The amount of the base erosion payment is equal to the lesser of the amount paid or accrued by the applicable taxpayer to or for the benefit of the specified domestic passthrough and the amount of the deduction allowed under section 561, 651 or 661 to the specified domestic passthrough with respect to amounts paid, credited, distributed, deemed distributed or required to be distributed to a specified foreign related party.

(C) *Specified domestic passthrough.*—For purposes of this paragraph (b)(2)(v), specified domestic passthrough means:

(1) A domestic trust that is not a grantor trust under subpart E of subchapter J of Chapter 1 of the Code ("domestic trust") and which domestic trust is allowed a deduction under section 651 or section 661 with respect to amounts paid, credited, or required to be distributed to a specified foreign related party;

(2) A real estate investment trust (as defined in § 1.856-1(a)) that pays, or is deemed to pay, a dividend to a specified foreign related party for which a deduction is allowed under section 561; or

(3) A regulated investment company (as defined in § 1.851-1(a)) that pays, or is deemed to pay, a dividend to a specified foreign related party for which a deduction is allowed under section 561.

(D) *Specified foreign related party.*—For purposes of this paragraph (b)(2)(v), specified foreign related party means, with respect to a specified domestic passthrough, any foreign related party of an applicable taxpayer that is a direct or indirect beneficiary or shareholder of the specified domestic passthrough.

(vi) *Transfers of property to related taxpayers.*—If a taxpayer owns property of a character subject to the allowance for depreciation (or amortization in lieu of depreciation) with respect to which paragraph (c)(1)(ii) of this section applies, and the taxpayer sells, exchanges, or otherwise transfers the property to another taxpayer that is a member of an aggregate group that includes the taxpayer, any deduction for depreciation (or amortization in lieu of deprecation) by the transferee taxpayer remains subject to paragraph (c)(1)(ii) of this section to the same extent the amounts would have been so subject in the hands of the transferor. See paragraph (d)(7) of this section (*Example 7*) for an illustration of this rule.

(3) *Exceptions to base erosion payment.*—Paragraph (b)(1) of this section does not apply to the types of payments or accruals described in paragraphs (b)(3)(i) through (vii) of this section.

(i) *Certain services cost method amounts.*—(A) *In general.*—Amounts paid or accrued by a taxpayer to a foreign related party for services that meet the requirements in paragraph (b)(3)(i)(B) of this section, but only to the extent of the total services cost of those services. Thus, any amount paid or accrued to a foreign related party in excess of the total services cost of services eligible for the services cost method exception (the mark-up component) remains a base erosion payment. For this purpose, services are an activity as defined in § 1.482-9(l)(2) performed by a foreign related party (the renderer) that provides a benefit as defined in § 1.482-9(l)(3) to the taxpayer (the recipient).

(B) *Eligibility for the services cost method exception.*—To be eligible for the services cost method exception, all of the requirements of § 1.482-9(b) must be satisfied, except that:

(1) The requirements of § 1.482-9(b)(5) do not apply for purposes of de-

termining eligibility for the service cost method exception in this section; and

(2) Adequate books and records must be maintained as described in paragraph (b)(3)(i)(C) of this section, instead of as described in §1.482-9(b)(6).

(C) *Adequate books and records.*—Permanent books of account and records must be maintained for as long as the costs with respect to the services are incurred by the renderer. The books and records must be adequate to permit verification by the Commissioner of the amount charged for the services and the total services costs incurred by the renderer, including a description of the services in question, identification of the renderer and the recipient of the services, calculation of the amount of profit mark-up (if any) paid for the services, and sufficient documentation to allow verification of the methods used to allocate and apportion the costs to the services in question in accordance with §1.482-9(k).

(D) *Total services cost.*—For purposes of this section, total services cost has the same meaning as total services costs in §1.482-9(j).

(ii) *Qualified derivative payments.*—Any qualified derivative payment as described in §1.59A-6.

(iii) *Effectively connected income.*—(A) *In general.*—Amounts paid or accrued to a foreign related party that are subject to federal income taxation as income that is, or is treated as, effectively connected with the conduct of a trade or business in the United States under an applicable provision of the Internal Revenue Code or regulations. This paragraph (b)(3)(iii) applies only if the taxpayer receives a withholding certificate on which the foreign related party claims an exemption from withholding under section 1441 or 1442 because the amounts are effectively connected income.

(B) *Application to certain treaty residents.*—Notwithstanding paragraph (b)(3)(iii)(A) of this section, if a foreign related party determines its net taxable income under an applicable income tax treaty, amounts paid or accrued to the foreign related party taken into account in determining its net taxable income.

(iv) *Exchange loss on a section 988 transaction.*—Any exchange loss within the meaning of §1.988-2 from a section 988 transaction described in §1.988-1(a)(1) that is an allowable deduction and that results from a payment or accrual by the taxpayer to a foreign related party of the taxpayer.

(v) *Amounts paid or accrued with respect to TLAC securities.*—(A) *In general.*—Except as provided in paragraph (b)(3)(v)(B) of this section, amounts paid or accrued to foreign related parties with respect to TLAC securities.

(B) *Limitation on exclusion for TLAC securities.*—The amount excluded under paragraph (b)(3)(v)(A) of this section is no greater than the product of the scaling ratio and amounts paid or accrued to foreign related parties with respect to TLAC securities for which a deduction is allowed.

(C) *Scaling ratio.*—For purposes of this paragraph (b)(3)(v), the scaling ratio for a taxable year of a taxpayer is a fraction the numerator of which is the average TLAC long-term debt required amount and the denominator of which is the average TLAC securities amount. The scaling ratio may in no event be greater than one.

(D) *Average TLAC securities amount.*—The average TLAC securities amount for a taxable year is the average of the TLAC securities amounts for the year, computed at regular time intervals in accordance with this paragraph. The TLAC securities amounts used in calculating the average TLAC securities amount is computed on a monthly basis.

(E) *Average TLAC long-term debt required amount.*—The average TLAC long-term debt required amount for a taxable year is the average of the TLAC long-term debt required amounts, computed on a monthly basis.

(vi) *Amounts paid or accrued in taxable years beginning before January 1, 2018.*—Any amount paid or accrued in taxable years beginning before January 1, 2018.

(vii) *Business interest carried forward from taxable years beginning before January 1, 2018.*—Any disallowed business interest described in section 163(j)(2) that is carried forward from a taxable year beginning before January 1, 2018.

(4) *Rules for determining the amount of certain base erosion payments.*—The following rules apply in determining the deductible amount that is a base erosion payment.

(i) *Interest expense allocable to a foreign corporation's effectively connected income.*—(A) *Method described in §1.882-5(b) through (d).*—A foreign corporation that has interest expense allocable under section 882(c) to income that is, or is treated as, effectively connected with the conduct of a trade or business within the United States applying the method described in §1.882-5(b) through (d) has base erosion payments under paragraph (b)(1)(i) of this section for the taxable year equal to the sum of—

(1) The interest expense on a liability described in §1.882-5(a)(1)(ii)(A) or (B) (direct allocations) or interest expense on U.S.-booked liabilities, as described in §1.882-5(d)(2), that is paid or accrued by the foreign corporation to a foreign related party; and

(2) The interest expense on U.S.-connected liabilities in excess of U.S.-booked liabilities (hereafter, excess U.S.-connected liabilities), as described in §1.882-5(d)(5), multiplied by a fraction, the numerator of which is the foreign corporation's average worldwide liabilities due to a foreign related party, and the denominator of which is the foreign corporation's average total worldwide liabilities. For purposes of this fraction, any liability that is a U.S.-booked liability or is subject to a direct allocation is excluded from both the numerator and the denominator of the fraction.

(B) *Separate currency pools method.*—A foreign corporation that has interest expense allocable under section 882(c) to income that is, or is treated as, effectively connected with the conduct of a trade or business within the United States applying the separate currency pools method described in §1.882-5(e) has a base erosion payment under paragraph (b)(1)(i) of this section for the taxable year equal to the sum of—

(1) The interest expense on a liability described in §1.882-5(a)(1)(ii)(A) or (B) (direct allocations) that is paid or accrued by the foreign corporation to a foreign related party; and

(2) The interest expense attributable to each currency pool, as described in §1.882-5(e)(1)(iii), multiplied by a fraction equal to the foreign corporation's average worldwide liabilities denominated in that currency and that is due to a foreign related party over the foreign corporation's average total worldwide liabilities denominated in that currency. For purposes of this fraction, any liability that has a direct allocation is excluded from both the numerator and the denominator.

(C) *U.S.-booked liabilities in excess of U.S.-connected liabilities.*—A foreign corporation that is computing its interest expense under the method described in §1.882-5(b) through (d) and that has U.S.-booked liabilities in excess of U.S.-connected liabilities must apply the scaling ratio pro-rata to all interest expense consistent with §1.882-5(d)(4) for purposes of determining the amount of allocable interest expense that is a base erosion payment.

(D) *Liability reduction election.*—A foreign corporation that elects to reduce its liabilities under §1.884-1(e)(3) must reduce its liabilities on a pro-rata basis, consistent with the requirements under §1.884-1(e)(3)(iii), for purposes of determining the amount of allocable interest expense that is a base erosion payment.

(ii) *Other deductions allowed with respect to effectively connected income.*—A deduction allowed under §1.882-4 for an amount paid or accrued by the foreign corporation to a foreign related party (including a deduction for an amount apportioned in part to effectively connected income and in part to income that is not effectively connected income) is treated as a base erosion payment under paragraph (b)(1) of this section.

(iii) *Depreciable property.*—Any amount paid or accrued by the foreign corporation to a foreign related party of the taxpayer in connection with the acquisition of property by the foreign corporation from the foreign related party if the character of the property is subject to the allowance for depreciation (or amortization in lieu of depreciation) is a base erosion payment to the extent the property so acquired is used, or held for use, in the conduct of a trade or business within the United States.

(iv) *Coordination with ECI exception.*—For purposes of this paragraph (b)(4), amounts paid or accrued to a foreign related party treated as effectively connected income (or, in the case of foreign related party that determines net taxable income under an applicable income tax treaty, such amounts that are taken into account in determining net taxable income) are not treated as paid to a foreign related party. Additionally, for purposes of paragraph (b)(4)(i)(A)(*2*) or (b)(4)(i)(B)(*2*) of this section, a liability with interest paid or accrued to a foreign related party that is treated as effectively connected income (or, in the case of foreign related party that determines net taxable income under an applicable income tax treaty, interest taken into account in determining net taxable income) is treated as a liability not due to a foreign related party.

(v) *Coordination with certain tax treaties.*—(A) *Allocable expenses.*—If a foreign corporation elects to determine its taxable income pursuant to business profits provisions of an income tax treaty rather than provisions of the Internal Revenue Code, or the regulations published under 26 CFR chapter I, for determining effectively connected income, and the foreign corporation does not apply §§1.882-5 and 1.861-8 to allocate interest and other deductions, then in applying paragraphs (b)(4)(i) and (ii) of this section, the foreign corporation must determine whether each allowable deduction attributed to the permanent establishment in its determination of business profits is a base erosion payment under paragraph (b)(1) of this section.

(B) *Internal dealings under certain income tax treaties.*—If, pursuant to the terms of an applicable income tax treaty, a foreign corporation determines the profits attributable to a permanent establishment based on the assets used, risks assumed, and functions performed by the permanent establishment, then any deduction attributable to any amount paid or accrued (or treated as paid or accrued) by the permanent establishment to the foreign corporation's home office or to another branch of the foreign corporation (an "internal dealing") is a base erosion payment to the extent such payment or accrual is described under paragraph (b)(1) of this section.

(vi) *Business interest expense arising in taxable years beginning after December 31, 2017.*—Any disallowed business interest expense described in section 163(j)(2) that resulted from a payment or accrual to a foreign related party that first arose in a taxable year beginning after December 31, 2017, is treated as a base erosion payment under paragraph (b)(1)(i) of this section in the year that the business interest expense initially arose. See paragraph (c)(4) of this section for rules that apply when business interest expense is limited under section 163(j)(1) in order to determine whether the disallowed business interest is attributed to business interest expense paid to a person that is not a related party, a foreign related party, or a domestic related party.

(c) *Base erosion tax benefit.*—(1) *In general.*—Except as provided in paragraph (c)(2) of this section, a base erosion tax benefit means:

(i) In the case of a base erosion payment described in paragraph (b)(1)(i) of this section, any deduction that is allowed under chapter 1 of subtitle A of the Internal Revenue Code for the taxable year with respect to that base erosion payment;

(ii) In the case of a base erosion payment described in paragraph (b)(1)(ii) of this section, any deduction allowed under chapter 1 of subtitle A of the Internal Revenue Code for the taxable year for depreciation (or amortization in lieu of depreciation) with respect to the property acquired with that payment;

(iii) In the case of a base erosion payment described in paragraph (b)(1)(iii) of this section, any reduction under section 803(a)(1)(B) in the gross amount of premiums and other consideration on insurance and annuity contracts for premiums and other consideration arising out of indemnity insurance, or any deduction under section 832(b)(4)(A) from the amount of gross premiums written on insurance contracts during the taxable year for premiums paid for reinsurance; or

(iv) In the case of a base erosion payment described in paragraph (b)(1)(iv) of this section, any reduction in gross receipts with respect to the payment in computing gross income of the taxpayer for the taxable year for purposes of chapter 1 of subtitle A of the Internal Revenue Code.

(2) *Withholding tax exception to base erosion tax benefit.*—Except as provided in paragraph (c)(3) of this section, any base erosion tax benefit attributable to any base erosion payment is not taken into account as a base erosion tax benefit if tax is imposed on that payment under section 871 or 881, and the tax has been deducted and withheld under section 1441 or 1442.

(3) *Effect of treaty on base erosion tax benefit.*—If any treaty between the United States and any foreign country reduces the rate of tax imposed by section 871 or 881, the amount of base erosion tax benefit that is not taken into account under paragraph (c)(2) of this section is equal to the amount of the base erosion tax benefit before the application of paragraph (c)(2) of this section multiplied by a fraction of—

(i) The rate of tax imposed without regard to the treaty, reduced by the rate of tax imposed under the treaty; over

(ii) The rate of tax imposed without regard to the treaty.

(4) *Application of section 163(j) to base erosion payments.*—(i) *Classification of payments or accruals of business interest expense based on the payee.*—The following rules apply for corporations and partnerships:

(A) *Classification of payments or accruals of business interest expense of a corporation.*—For purposes of this section, in the year that business interest expense of a corporation is paid or accrued the business interest expense is classified as foreign related business interest expense, domestic related business interest expense, or unrelated business interest expense.

(B) *Classification of payments or accruals of business interest expense by a partnership.*—For purposes of this section, in the year that business interest expense of a partnership is paid or accrued, the business interest expense that is allocated to a partner is classified separately with respect to each partner in the partnership as foreign related business interest expense, domestic related business interest expense, or unrelated business interest expense.

(C) *Classification of payments or accruals of business interest expense that is subject to the exception for effectively connected income.*—For purposes of paragraph (c)(4)(i)(A) and (B) of this section, business interest expense paid or accrued to a foreign related party to which the exception in paragraph (b)(3)(iii) of this section (effectively connected income) applies is classified as domestic related business interest expense.

(ii) *Ordering rules for business interest expense that is limited under section 163(j)(1) to determine which classifications of business interest expense are deducted and which classifications of business interest expense are carried forward.*—(A) *In general.*—Section 163(j) and the regulations published under 26 CFR chapter I provide a limitation on the amount of business interest expense allowed as a deduction in a taxable year by a corporation or a partner in a partnership. In the case of a corporation with a disallowed business interest expense carryforward, the regulations under section 163(j) determine the ordering of the business interest expense deduction that is allowed on a year-by-year basis by reference first to business interest expense incurred in the current taxable year and then to disallowed business interest expense carryforwards from prior years. To determine the amount of base erosion tax benefit under paragraph (c)(1) of this section, this paragraph (c)(4)(ii) sets forth ordering rules that determine the amount of the deduction of business interest expense allowed under section 163(j) that is classified as paid or accrued to a foreign related party for purposes of paragraph (c)(1)(i) of this section. This paragraph (c)(4)(ii) also sets forth similar ordering rules that apply to disallowed business interest expense carryforwards for which a deduction is permitted under section 163(j) in a later year.

(B) *Ordering rules for treating business interest expense deduction and disallowed business interest expense carryforwards as foreign related business interest expense, domestic related business interest expense, and unrelated business interest expense.*—(*1*) *General ordering rule for allocating business interest expense deduction between classifications.*—For purposes of paragraph (c)(1) of this section, if a deduction for business interest expense is not subject to the limitation under section 163(j)(1) in a taxable year, the deduction is treated first as foreign related business interest expense and domestic related business interest expense (on a pro-rata basis), and second as unrelated business interest expense. The same principle applies to business interest expense of a partnership that is deductible at the partner level under §1.163(j)-6(f).

(*2*) *Ordering of business interest expense incurred by a corporation.*—If a corporation's business interest expense deduction allowed for any taxable year is attributable to business interest expense paid or accrued in that taxable year and to disallowed business interest expense carryforwards from prior taxable years, the ordering of business interest expense deduction provided in paragraph (c)(4)(ii)(B)(*1*) of this section among the classifications described therein applies separately for the carryforward amount from each taxable year, following the ordering set forth in §1.163(j)-5(b)(2). Corresponding adjustments to the classification of disallowed business interest expense carryforwards are made consistent with this year-by-year approach. For purposes of section 59A and this section, an acquiring corporation in a transaction described in section 381(a) will succeed to and take into account the classification of any disallowed business interest expense carryforward. See §1.381(c)(20)-1.

(*3*) *Ordering of business interest expense incurred by a partnership and allocated to a corporate partner.*—For a corporate partner in a partnership that is allocated a business interest expense deduction under §1.163(j)-6(f), the ordering rule provided in paragraph (c)(4)(ii)(B)(*1*) of this section applies separately to the corporate partner's allocated business interest expense deduction from the partnership; that deduction is not comingled with the business interest expense deduction addressed in paragraph (c)(4)(ii)(B)(*1*) or (*2*) of this section or the corporate partner's items from any other partnership. Similarly, when a corporate partner in a partnership is allocated excess business interest expense from a partnership under the rules set forth in §1.163(j)-6(f) and the excess interest expense becomes deductible to the corporate partner, that partner applies the ordering rule provided in paragraph (c)(4)(ii)(B)(*1*) of this section separately to that excess interest expense on a year-by-year basis. Corresponding adjustments to the classification of disallowed business interest expense carryforwards are made consistent with this year-by-year and partnership-by-partnership approach.

(d) *Examples*.—The following examples illustrate the application of this section. For purposes of all the examples, assume that the taxpayer is an applicable taxpayer and all payments apply to a taxable year beginning after December 31, 2017.

(1) *Example 1: Determining a base erosion payment*. (i) *Facts*. FP is a foreign corporation that owns all of the stock of FC, a foreign corporation, and DC, a domestic corporation. FP has a trade or business in the United States with effectively connected income (USTB). DC owns FDE, a foreign disregarded entity. DC pays interest to FDE and FC. FDE pays interest to USTB. All interest paid by DC to FC and by FDE to USTB is deductible by DC in the current year for regular income tax purposes. FDE also acquires depreciable property from FP during the taxable year. FP's income from the sale of the depreciable property is not effectively connected with the conduct of FP's trade or business in the United States. DC and FP (based only on the activities of USTB) are applicable taxpayers under § 1.59A-2(b).

(ii) *Analysis*. The payment of interest by DC to FC is a base erosion payment under paragraph (b)(1)(i) of this section because the payment is made to a foreign related party and the interest payment is deductible. The payment of interest by DC to FDE is not a base erosion payment because the transaction is not a payment to a foreign person and the transaction is not a deductible payment. With respect to the payment of interest by FDE to USTB, if FP's USTB treats the payment of interest by FDE to USTB as income that is effectively connected with the conduct of a trade or business in the United States pursuant to section 864 or as profits attributable to a U.S. permanent establishment of a tax treaty resident, and if DC receives a withholding certificate from FP with respect to the payment, then the exception in paragraph (b)(3)(iii) of this section applies. Accordingly, the payment from DC, through FDE, to USTB is not a base erosion payment even though the payment is to the USTB of FP, a foreign related party. The acquisition of depreciable property by DC, through FDE, is a base erosion payment under paragraph (b)(1)(ii) of this section because there is a payment to a foreign related party in connection with the acquisition by the taxpayer of property of a character subject to the allowance for depreciation and the exception in paragraph (b)(3)(iii) of this section does not apply because FP's income from the sale of the depreciable property is not effectively connected with the conduct of FP's trade or business in the United States. See § 1.59A-2 for the application of the aggregation rule with respect to DC and FP's USTB.

(2) *Example 2: Interest allocable under § 1.882-5*. (i) *Facts*. FC, a foreign corporation, has income that is effectively connected with the conduct of a trade or business within the United States. FC determines its interest expense under the three-step process described in §§ 1.882-5(b) through (d) with a total interest expense of $125x. The total interest expense is comprised of interest expense of $100x on U.S.-booked liabilities ($60x paid to a foreign related party and $40x paid to unrelated persons) and $25x of interest on excess U.S.-connected liabilities. FC has average total liabilities (that are not U.S.-booked liabilities) of $10,000x and of that number $2000x are liabilities held by a foreign related party. FC is an applicable taxpayer with respect to its effectively connected income. Assume all of the interest expense is deductible in the current taxable year and that none of the interest is subject to the effectively connected income exception in paragraph (b)(3)(iii) of this section.

(ii) *Analysis*. Under paragraph (b)(4)(i) of this section, the total amount of interest expense determined under § 1.882-5 that is a base erosion payment is $65x ($60x + 5x). FC has $60x of interest on U.S.-booked liabilities that is paid to a foreign related party and that is treated as a base erosion payment under paragraph (b)(4)(i)(A)(*1*) of this section. Additionally, $5x of the $25x of interest on excess U.S.-connected liabilities is treated as a base erosion payment under paragraph (b)(4)(i)(A)(2) of this section ($25x * ($2000x / $10,000x)).

(3) *Example 3: Interaction with section 163(j)*. (i) *Facts*. Foreign Parent (FP) is a foreign corporation that owns all of the stock of DC, a domestic corporation that is an applicable taxpayer. In Year 1, DC has adjusted taxable income, as defined in section 163(j)(8), of $1000x and pays the following amounts of business interest expense: $420x that is paid to unrelated Bank, and $360x that is paid to FP. DC does not earn any business interest income or incur any floor plan financing interest expense in Year 1. None of the exceptions in paragraph (b)(3) of this section apply, and the interest is not subject to withholding.

(ii) *Analysis*— (A) *Classification of business interest*. In Year 1, DC is only permitted to deduct $300x of business interest expense under section 163(j)(1) ($1000x x 30%). Paragraph (c)(4)(ii)(B) of this section provides that for purposes of paragraph (c)(1) of this section the deduction is treated first as foreign related business interest expense and domestic related business interest expense (here, only FP); and second as unrelated business interest expense (Bank). As a result, the $300x of business interest expense that is permitted under section 163(j)(1) is treated entirely as the business interest paid to the related foreign party, FP. All of DC's $300x deductible interest is treated as an add-back to modified taxable income in the Year 1 taxable year for purposes of § 1.59A-4(b)(2)(i).

(B) *Ordering rules for business interest expense carryforward*. Under section 163(j)(2), the $480x of disallowed business interest ($420x + $360x - $300x) is carried forward to the subsequent year. Under paragraph (c)(4)(ii)(B)(*1*) and (*2*) of this section, the interest carryforward is correspondingly treated first as unrelated business interest expense, and second pro-rata as foreign related business interest expense and domestic related business interest expense. As a result, $420x of the $480x business interest expense carryforward is treated first as business interest expense paid to Bank and the remaining $60x of the $480x business interest expense carryforward is treated as interest paid to FP and as an add-back to modified taxable income.

(4) *Example 4: Interaction with section 163(j); carryforward*. (i) *Facts*. The facts are the same as in paragraph (d)(3) of this section (the facts in *Example 3*), except that in addition, in Year 2, DC has adjusted taxable income of $250x, and pays the following amounts of business interest expense: $50x that is paid to unrelated Bank, and $45x that is paid to FP. DC does not earn any business interest income or incur any floor plan financing interest expense in Year 2. None of the exceptions in paragraph (b)(3) of this section apply.

(ii) *Analysis*— (A) *Classification of business interest*. In Year 2, for purposes of section 163(j)(1), DC is treated as having paid or accrued total business interest of $575x, consisting of $95x business interest expense actually paid in Year 2 and $480x of business interest expense that is carried forward from Year 1. DC is permitted to deduct $75x of business interest expense in Year 2 under the limitation in section 163(j)(1) ($250x x 30%). Section 1.163(j)-5(b)(2) provides that, for purposes of section 163(j), the allowable business interest expense is first attributed to amounts paid or accrued in the current year, and then attributed to amounts carried over from earlier years on a first-in-first-out basis from the earliest year. Accordingly, the $75x of deductible business interest expense is deducted entirely from the $95x business interest expense incurred in Year 2 for section 163(j) purposes. Because DC's business interest expense deduction is limited under section 163(j)(1) and because DC's total business interest expense is attributable to more than one taxable year, paragraph (c)(4)(ii)(B)(*2*) of this section provides that the ordering rule in paragraph (c)(4)(ii)(B)(*1*) of this section is applied separately to each annual amount of section 163(j) disallowed business interest expense carryforward. With respect to the Year 2 layer, which is deducted first, paragraph (c)(4)(ii)(B) of this section provides that, for purposes of paragraph (c)(1) of this section, the Year 2 $75x deduction is treated first as foreign related business interest expense and domestic related business interest expense (here, only FP, $45x); and second as unrelated business interest expense (Bank, $30x). Consequentially, all of the $45x deduction of business interest expense that was paid to FP in Year 2 is treated as a base erosion tax benefit and an add-back to modified taxable income for the Year 2 taxable year for purposes of § 1.59A-4(b)(2)(i).

(B) *Ordering rules for business interest expense carryforward*. The disallowed business interest expense carryforward of $20x from Year 2 is correspondingly treated first as interest paid to Bank under paragraph (c)(4)(i) of this section. The disallowed business interest expense carryforward of $480x from the Year 1 layer that is also not allowed as a deduction in Year 2 remains treated as $420x paid to Bank and $60 paid to FP.

(5) *Example 5: Interaction with section 163(j); carryforward*. (i) *Facts*. The facts are the same as in paragraph (d)(4) of this section (the facts in *Example 4*), except that in addition, in Year 3, DC has adjusted taxable income of $4000x and pays no business interest expense. DC does not earn any business interest income or incur any floor plan financing interest expense in Year 3.

(ii) *Analysis*. In Year 3, DC is treated as having paid or accrued total business interest expense of $500x, consisting of $480x of business interest expense that is carried forward from Year 1 and $20x of business interest expense that is carried forward from Year 2 for purposes of section 163(j)(1). DC is permitted to deduct $1200x of business interest expense in Year 3 under the limitation in section 163(j)(1) ($4000x x 30%). For purposes of section 163(j), DC is treated as first deducting the business interest expense from Year 1 then the business interest expense from Year 2. See § 1.163(j)-5(b)(2). Because none of DC's $500x business interest expense is limited under section 163(j), the stacking rule in paragraph (c)(4)(ii) of this section for allowed and disallowed business interest expense does not apply. For purposes of § 1.59A-4(b)(2)(i), DC's add-back to modified taxable income is $60x determined by the classifications in paragraph (c)(4)(i)(A) of this section ($60x treated as paid to FP from Year 1).

(6) *Example 6: Interaction with section 163(j); partnership*. (i) *Facts*. The facts are the same as in paragraph (d)(4) of this section (the facts in *Example 4*), except that in addition, in Year 2, DC forms a domestic partnership (PRS) with Y, a domestic corporation that is not related to DC within the meaning of § 1.59A-1(b)(17). DC and Y are equal partners in partnership PRS. In Year 2, PRS has ATI of $100x and $48x of business interest expense. $12x of PRS's business interest expense is paid to Bank, and $36x of PRS's business interest expense is paid to FP. PRS allocates the items comprising its $100x of ATI $50x to DC and $50x to Y. PRS allocates its $48x of business interest expense $24x to DC and $24x to Y. DC classifies its $24x of business interest expense as $6x unrelated business interest expense (Bank) and $18x as foreign related business interest expense (FP) under paragraph (c)(4)(i)(B) of this section. Y classifies its $24x of business interest expense as entirely unrelated business interest expense of Y (Bank and FP) under paragraph (c)(4)(i)(B) of this section. None of the exceptions in paragraph (b)(3) of this section apply.

(ii) *Partnership level analysis*. In Year 2, PRS's section 163(j) limit is 30 percent of its ATI, or $30x ($100x x 30 percent). Thus, PRS has $30x of deductible business interest expense and $18x of excess business interest expense ($48x - $30x). The $30x of deductible business interest expense is includible in PRS's non-separately stated income or loss, and is not subject to further limitation under section 163(j) at the partners' level.

(iii) *Partner level allocations analysis*. Pursuant to § 1.163(j)-6(f)(2), DC and Y are each allocated $15x of deductible business interest expense and $9x of excess business interest expense. At the end of Year 2, DC and Y each have $9x of excess business interest expense from PRS, which under § 1.163(j)-6 is not treated as paid or accrued by the partner until such partner is allocated excess taxable income or excess business interest income from PRS in a succeeding year. Pursuant to § 1.163(j)-6(e), DC and Y, in computing their limit under section 163(j), do not increase any of their section 163(j) items by any of PRS's section 163(j) items.

(iv) *Partner level allocations for determining base erosion tax benefits*. The $15x of deductible business interest expense allocated to DC is treated first as foreign related business interest expense (FP) under paragraph (c)(4)(ii)(B) of this section. DC's excess business interest expense from PRS of $9x is classified first as the unrelated business interest expense with respect to Bank ($6x) and then as the remaining portion of the business interest expense paid to FP ($3x, or $18x - $15x). Under paragraph (c)(4)(ii)(B)(*3*) of this section, these classifications of the PRS items apply irrespective of the classifications of DC's own interest expense as set forth in paragraph (d)(4) of this section (*Example* 4).

(v) *Computation of modified taxable income*. For Year 2, DC is treated as having incurred base erosion tax benefits of $60x, consisting of the $15x base erosion tax benefit with respect to its interest in PRS that is computed in paragraph (d)(6)(iii) of this section (*Example* 6) and $45x that is computed in paragraph (d)(4) of this section (*Example* 4).

(7) *Example 7: Transfers of property to related taxpayers*. (i) *Facts*. FP is a foreign corporation that owns all of the stock of DC1 and DC2, both domestic corporations. DC1 and DC2 are both members of the same aggregate group but are not members of the same consolidated tax group under section 1502. In Year 1, FP sells depreciable property to DC1. On the first day of the Year 2 tax year, DC1 sells the depreciable property to DC2.

(ii) *Analysis*— (A) *Year 1*. The acquisition of depreciable property by DC1 from FP is a base erosion payment under paragraph (b)(1)(ii) of this section because there is a payment to a foreign related party in connection with the acquisition by the taxpayer of property of a character subject to the allowance for depreciation.

(B) *Year* 2. The acquisition of the depreciable property in Year 2 by DC2 is not itself a base erosion payment because DC2 did not acquire the property from a foreign related party. However, under paragraph (b)(2)(vi) of this section any depreciation expense taken by DC2 on the property acquired from DC1 is a base erosion payment and a base erosion tax benefit under paragraph (c)(1)(ii) of this section because the acquisition of the depreciable property was a base erosion payment by DC1 and the property was sold to a member of the aggregate group; therefore, the depreciation expense continues as a base erosion tax benefit to DC2 as it would have been to DC1 if it continued to own the property. [Reg. § 1.59A-3.]

§ 1.59A-4. Modified taxable income.—(a) *Scope*.—Paragraph (b)(1) of this section provides rules for computing modified taxable income. Paragraph (b)(2) of this section provides rules addressing how base erosion tax benefits and net operating losses affect modified taxable income. Paragraph (b)(3) of this section provides a rule for a holder of a residual interest in a REMIC. Paragraph (c) of this section provides examples illustrating the rules described in this section.

(b) *Computation of modified taxable income*.—(1) *In general*.—The term *modified taxable income* means a taxpayer's taxable income, as defined in section 63(a), determined with the additions described in paragraph (b)(2) of this section. Notwithstanding the foregoing, the taxpayer's taxable income may not be reduced to an amount less than zero as a result of a net operating loss deduction allowed under section 172. See paragraphs (c)(1) and (2) of this section (*Examples 1* and *2*).

(2) *Modifications to taxable income*.—The amounts described in this paragraph (b)(2) are added back to a taxpayer's taxable income to determine its modified taxable income.

(i) *Base erosion tax benefits*.—The amount of any base erosion tax benefit as defined in § 1.59A-3(c)(1).

(ii) *Certain net operating loss deductions*.—The base erosion percentage, as described in § 1.59A-2(e)(3), of any net operating loss deduction allowed to the taxpayer under section 172 for the taxable year. For purposes of determining modified taxable income, the net operating loss deduction allowed does not exceed taxable income before taking into account the net operating loss deduction. See paragraph (c)(1) and (2) of this section (*Examples 1* and 2). The base erosion percentage for the taxable year that the net operating loss arose is used to determine the addition under this paragraph (b)(2)(ii). For a net operating loss that arose in a taxable year beginning before January 1, 2018, the base erosion percentage for the taxable year is zero.

(3) *Rule for holders of a residual interest in a REMIC*.—For purposes of paragraph (b)(1) of this section, the limitation in section 860E(a)(1) is not taken into account for determining the taxable income amount that is used to compute modified taxable income for the taxable year.

(c) *Examples*.—The following examples illustrate the rules of paragraph (b) of this section.

(1) *Example 1: Current year loss*. (i) *Facts*. A domestic corporation (DC) is an applicable taxpayer that has a calendar taxable year. In 2020, DC has gross income of $100x, a deduction of $80x that is not a base erosion tax benefit, and a deduction of $70x that is a base erosion tax benefit. In addition, DC has a net operating loss carryforward to 2020 of $400x that arose in 2016.

(ii) *Analysis*. DC's starting point for computing modified taxable income is $(50x), computed as gross income of $100x, less a deduction of $80x (non-base erosion tax benefit) and a deduction of $70x (base erosion tax benefit). Under paragraph (b)(2)(ii) of this section, DC's starting point for computing modified taxable income does not take into account the $400x net operating loss carryforward because the allowable deductions for 2020, not counting the NOL deduction, exceed the gross income for 2020. DC's modified taxable income for 2020 is $20x, computed as $(50x) + $70x base erosion tax benefit.

(2) *Example 2: Net operating loss deduction*. (i) *Facts*. The facts are the same as in paragraph (c)(1)(i) of this section (the facts in *Example 1*), except that DC's gross income in 2020 is $500x.

(ii) *Analysis*. DC's starting point for computing modified taxable income is $0x, computed as gross income of $500x, less: a deduction of $80x (non-base erosion tax benefit), a deduction of $70x (base erosion tax benefit), and a net operating loss deduction of $350x (which is the amount of taxable income before taking into account the net operating loss deduction, as provided in paragraph (b)(2)(ii) of this section ($500x - $150x)). DC's modified taxable income for 2020 is $70x, computed as $0x + $70x base erosion tax benefit. DC's modified taxable income is not increased as a result of the $350x net operating loss deduction in 2020 because the base erosion percentage of the net operating loss that arose in 2016 is zero under paragraph (b)(2)(ii) of this section. [Reg. § 1.59A-4.]

§ 1.59A-5. Base erosion minimum tax amount.—(a) *Scope.*—Paragraph (b) of this section provides rules regarding the calculation of the base erosion minimum tax amount. Paragraph (c) of this section describes the base erosion and anti-abuse tax rate applicable to the taxable year.

(b) *In general.*—With respect to any applicable taxpayer, the base erosion minimum tax amount for any taxable year is, the excess (if any) of—

(1) An amount equal to the base erosion and anti-abuse tax rate multiplied by the modified taxable income of the taxpayer for the taxable year, over

(2) An amount equal to the regular tax liability as defined in § 1.59A-1(b)(16) of the taxpayer for the taxable year, reduced (but not below zero) by the excess (if any) of-

(i) The credits allowed under chapter 1 of subtitle A of the Code against regular tax liability over

(ii) The sum of the credits described in paragraph (b)(3) of this section.

(3) *Credits that do not reduce regular tax liability.*—The sum of the following credits are used in paragraph (b)(2)(ii) of this section to limit the amount by which the credits allowed under chapter 1 of subtitle A of the Internal Revenue Code reduce regular tax liability—

(i) *Taxable years beginning on or before December 31, 2025.*—For any taxable year beginning on or before December 31, 2025—

(A) The credit allowed under section 38 for the taxable year that is properly allocable to the research credit determined under section 41(a);

(B) The portion of the applicable section 38 credits not in excess of 80 percent of the lesser of the amount of those applicable section 38 credits or the base erosion minimum tax amount (determined without regard to this paragraph (b)(3)(i)(B)); and

(C) Any credits allowed under sections 33 and 37.

(ii) *Taxable years beginning after December 31, 2025.*—For any taxable year beginning after December 31, 2025, any credits allowed under sections 33 and 37.

(c) *Base erosion and anti-abuse tax rate.*—(1) *In general.*—For purposes of calculating the base erosion minimum tax amount, the base erosion and anti-abuse tax rate is—

(i) *Calendar year 2018.*—For taxable years beginning in calendar year 2018, five percent.

(ii) *Calendar years 2019 through 2025.*—For taxable years beginning after December 31, 2018, through taxable years beginning before January 1, 2026, 10 percent.

(iii) *Calendar years after 2025.*—For taxable years beginning after December 31, 2025, 12.5 percent.

(2) *Increased rate for banks and registered securities dealers.*—In the case of a taxpayer that is a member of an affiliated group (as defined in section 1504(a)(1)) that includes a bank or a registered securities dealer, the percentage otherwise in effect under paragraph (c)(1) of this section is increased by one percentage point.

(3) *Application of section 15.*—Section 15 does not apply to any taxable year that includes January 1, 2018. See § 1.15-1(d). For a taxpayer using a taxable year other than the calendar year, section 15 applies to any taxable year beginning after January 1, 2018. [Reg. § 1.59A-5.]

§ 1.59A-6. Qualified derivative payment.—(a) *Scope.*—This section provides additional guidance regarding qualified derivative payments. Paragraph (b) of this section defines the term qualified derivative payment. Paragraph (c) of this section provides guidance on certain payments that are not treated as qualified derivative payments. Paragraph (d) defines the term derivative for purposes of section 59A. Paragraph (e) of this section provides an example illustrating the rules of this section.

(b) *Qualified derivative payment.*—(1) *In general.*—A *qualified derivative payment* means any payment made by a taxpayer to a foreign related party pursuant to a derivative with respect to which the taxpayer—

(i) Recognizes gain or loss as if the derivative were sold for its fair market value on the last business day of the taxable year (and any additional times as required by the Internal Revenue Code or the taxpayer's method of accounting);

(ii) Treats any gain or loss so recognized as ordinary; and

(iii) Treats the character of all items of income, deduction, gain, or loss with respect to a payment pursuant to the derivative as ordinary.

(2) *Reporting requirements.*—(i) *In general.*—No payment is a qualified derivative payment under paragraph (b)(1) of this section for any taxable year unless the taxpayer reports the information required in § 1.6038A-2(b)(7)(ix) for the taxable year.

(ii) *Failure to satisfy the reporting requirement.*—If a taxpayer fails to satisfy the reporting requirement described in paragraph (b)(2)(i) of this section with respect to any payments, those payments will not be eligible for the qualified derivative payment exception described in § 1.59A-3(b)(3)(ii). A taxpayer's failure to report a payment as a qualified derivative payment does not impact the eligibility of any other payment which the taxpayer properly reported under paragraph (b)(2)(i) of this section from being a qualified derivative payment.

(3) *Amount of any qualified derivative payment.*—The amount of any qualified derivative payment excluded from the denominator of the base erosion percentage as provided in § 1.59A-2(e)(3)(ii)(C) is determined as provided in § 1.59A-2(e)(3)(vi).

(c) *Exceptions for payments otherwise treated as base erosion payments.*—A payment does not constitute a qualified derivative payment if—

(1) The payment would be treated as a base erosion payment if it were not made pursuant to a derivative, including any interest, royalty, or service payment; or

(2) In the case of a contract that has derivative and nonderivative components, the payment is properly allocable to the nonderivative component.

(d) *Derivative defined.*—(1) *In general.*—For purposes of this section, the term *derivative* means any contract (including any option, forward contract, futures contract, short position, swap, or similar contract) the value of which, or any payment or other transfer with respect to which, is (directly or indirectly) determined by reference to one or more of the following:

(i) Any share of stock in a corporation;

(ii) Any evidence of indebtedness;

(iii) Any commodity that is actively traded;

(iv) Any currency; or

(v) Any rate, price, amount, index, formula, or algorithm.

(2) *Exceptions.*—The following contracts are not treated as derivatives for purposes of section 59A.

(i) *Direct interest.*—A derivative contract does not include a direct interest in any item described in paragraph (d)(1)(i) through (v) of this section.

(ii) *Insurance contracts.*—A derivative contract does not include any insurance, annuity, or endowment contract issued by an insurance company to which subchapter L applies (or issued by any foreign corporation to which the subchapter would apply if the foreign corporation were a domestic corporation).

(iii) *Securities lending and sale-repurchase transactions.*—A derivative contract does not include any securities lending transaction, sale-repurchase transaction, or substantially similar transaction. Securities lending transaction and sale-repurchase transaction have the same meaning as provided in §1.861-2(a)(7).

(3) *American depository receipts.*—For purposes of section 59A, American depository receipts (or any similar instruments) with respect to shares of stock in a foreign corporation are treated as shares of stock in that foreign corporation.

(e) *Example.*—The following example illustrates the rules of this section.

(1) *Facts.* Domestic Corporation (DC) is a dealer in securities within the meaning of section 475. On February 1, 2019, DC enters into a contract (Interest Rate Swap) with Foreign Parent (FP), a foreign related party, for a term of five years. Under the Interest Rate Swap, DC is obligated to make a payment to FP each month, beginning March 1, 2019, in an amount equal to a variable rate determined by reference to the prime rate, as determined on the first business day of the immediately preceding month, multiplied by a notional principal amount of $50 million. Under the Interest Rate Swap, FP is obligated to make a payment to DC each month, beginning March 1, 2019, in an amount equal to 5% multiplied by the same notional principal amount. The Interest Rate Swap satisfies the definition of a notional principal contract under §1.446-3(c). DC recognizes gain or loss on the Interest Rate Swap pursuant to section 475. DC reports the information required to be reported for the taxable year under §1.6038A-2(b)(7)(ix).

(2) *Analysis.* The Interest Rate Swap is a derivative as described in paragraph (d) of this section because it is a contract that references the prime rate and a fixed rate for determining the amount of payments. The exceptions described in paragraph (c) of this section do not apply to the Interest Rate Swap. Because DC recognizes ordinary gain or loss on the Interest Rate Swap pursuant to section 475(d)(3), it satisfies the condition in paragraph (b)(1)(ii) of this section. Because DC satisfies the requirement relating to the information required to be reported under paragraph (b)(2) of this section, any payment to FP with respect to the Interest Rate Swap will be a qualified derivative payment. Therefore, under §1.59A-3(b)(3)(ii), the payments to FP are not base erosion payments. [Reg. §1.59A-6.]

§1.59A-7. Application of base erosion and anti-abuse tax to partnerships.—(a) *Scope.*—This section provides rules regarding how partnerships and their partners are treated for purposes of section 59A. Paragraph (b) of this section provides the general application of an aggregate approach to partnerships for purposes of section 59A, including specific rules addressing the application of section 59A to amounts paid or accrued by a partnership to a related party, rules addressing the application of section 59A to amounts paid or accrued to a partnership from a related party, and other operating rules. Paragraph (c) of this section provides rules for determining whether a party is a foreign related party.

(b) *Application of section 59A to a partnership.*—(1) *In general.*—Except as otherwise provided in this section, section 59A is applied at the partner level in the manner described in this section. The provisions of section 59A must be interpreted in a manner consistent with this approach.

(2) *Payment made by a partnership.*—Except as provided in paragraph (b)(4) of this section, for purposes of determining whether a payment or accrual by a partnership is a base erosion payment, any amount paid or accrued by a partnership is treated as paid or accrued by each partner based on the partner's distributive share of items of deduction (or other amounts that could be base erosion tax benefits) with respect to that amount (as determined under section 704).

(3) *Payment received by a partnership.*—For purposes of determining whether a payment or accrual to a partnership is a base erosion payment of the payor, any amount paid or accrued to a partnership is treated as paid or accrued to each partner based on the partner's distributive share of the income or gain with respect to that amount (as determined under section 704).

(4) *Exception for base erosion tax benefits of certain partners.*—(i) *In general.*—For purposes of determining a partner's amount of base erosion tax benefits, a partner does not take into account its distributive share of any partnership amount of base erosion tax benefits for the taxable year if—

(A) The partner's interest in the partnership represents less than ten percent of the capital and profits of the partnership at all times during the taxable year;

(B) The partner is allocated less than ten percent of each partnership item of income, gain, loss, deduction, and credit for the taxable year; and

(C) The partner's interest in the partnership has a fair market value of less than $25 million on the last day of the partner's taxable year, determined using a reasonable method.

(ii) *Attribution.*—For purposes of paragraph (b)(4)(i) of this section, a partner's interest in a partnership or partnership item is determined by adding the interests of the partner and any related party of the partner (as determined under section 59A), taking into account any interest owned directly, indirectly, or through constructive ownership (applying the section 318 rules as modified by section 59A (except section 318(a)(3)(A) through (C) will also apply so as to consider a United States person as owning stock that is owned by a person who is not a United States person), but excluding any interest to the extent already taken into account).

(5) *Other relevant items.*—(i) *In general.*—For purposes of section 59A, subject to paragraph (b)(4) of this section, each partner is treated as owning its share of the partnership items determined under section 704, including the assets of the partnership, using a reasonable method with respect to the assets. For items that are allocated to the partners, the partner is treated as owning its distributive share (including of deductions and base erosion tax benefits). For items that are not allocated to the partners, the partner is treated as owning an interest proportionate with the partner's distributive share of partnership income.

(ii) *Gross receipts.*—(A) *In general.*—For purposes of section 59A, each partner in the partnership includes a share of partnership gross receipts in proportion to the partner's distributive share (as determined under section 704) of items of gross income that were taken into account by the partnership under section 703.

(B) *Foreign corporation.*—A foreign corporation takes into account a share of gross receipts only with regard to receipts that produce income that is effectively connected with the conduct of a trade or business within the United States. In the case of a foreign corporation that determines its net taxable income under an applicable income tax treaty, the foreign corporation takes into account its share of gross receipts only with regard to such gross receipts that are taken into account in determining its net taxable income.

(iii) *Registered securities dealers.*—If a partnership, or a branch of the partnership, is a registered securities dealer, each partner is treated as a registered securities dealer unless the partner's interest in the registered securities dealer would satisfy the criteria for the exception in paragraph (b)(4) of this section. For purposes of applying the de minimis exception in §1.59A-2(e)(2)(iii), the partner takes into account its distributive share of the relevant partnership items.

(iv) *Application of sections 163(j) and 59A(c)(3) to partners of partnerships.*—See §1.59A-3(c)(4).

(6) *Tiered partnerships.*—If the partner of a partnership is a partnership, then paragraphs (b) and (c) of this section are applied again at the level of the partner, applying this paragraph successively until the partner is not a partnership. Paragraph (b)(4) of this section is only applied at the level where the partner is not itself a partnership.

(c) *Foreign related party.*—With respect to any person that owns an interest in a partnership, the related party determination in section 59A(g) applies at the partner level. [Reg. §1.59A-7.]

§1.59A-8. Application of base erosion and anti-abuse tax to certain expatriated entities.—[Reserved]

[Reg. §1.59A-8.]

§1.59A-9. Anti-abuse and recharacterization rules.—(a) *Scope.*—This section provides rules for recharacterizing certain transactions according to their substance for purposes of applying section 59A and the section 59A regulations. Paragraph (b) of this section provides specific anti-abuse rules. Paragraph (c) of this section provides examples illustrating the rules of paragraph (b) of this section.

(b) *Anti-abuse rules.*—(1) *Transactions involving unrelated persons, conduits, or intermediaries.*—If a taxpayer pays or accrues an amount to one or more intermediaries (including an intermediary unrelated to the taxpayer) that would have been a base erosion payment if paid or accrued to a foreign related party, and one or more of the intermediaries makes (directly or indirectly) corresponding payments to or for the benefit of a foreign related party as part of a transaction (or series of transactions), plan or arrangement that has as a principal purpose avoiding a base erosion payment (or reducing the amount of a base erosion payment), the role of the intermediary or intermediaries is disregarded as a conduit, or the amount paid or accrued to the intermediary is treated as a base erosion payment, as appropriate.

(2) *Transactions to increase the amount of deductions taken into account in the denominator of the base erosion percentage computation.*—A transaction (or component of a transaction or series of transactions), plan or arrangement that has a principal purpose of increasing the deductions taken into account for purposes of §1.59A-2(e)(3)(i)(B) (the denominator of the base erosion percentage computation) is disregarded for purposes of §1.59A-2(e)(3).

(3) *Transactions to avoid the application of rules applicable to banks and registered securities dealers.*—A transaction (or series of transactions), plan or arrangement that occurs among related parties that has a principal purpose of avoiding the rules applicable to certain banks and registered securities dealers in §1.59A-2(e)(2) (base erosion percentage test for banks and registered securities dealers) or §1.59A-5(c)(2) (increased base erosion and anti-abuse tax rate for banks and registered securities dealers) is not taken into account for purposes of §1.59A-2(e)(2) or §1.59A-5(c)(2).

(c) *Examples.*—The following examples illustrate the application of paragraph (b) of this section. For purposes of all of the examples, assume that FP, a foreign corporation, owns all the stock of DC, a domestic corporation and an applicable taxpayer and that none of the foreign corporations are subject to federal income taxation with respect to income that is, or is treated as, effectively connected with the conduct of a trade or business in the United States under an applicable provision of the Internal Revenue Code or regulations thereunder. Also assume that all payments occur in a taxable year beginning after December 31, 2017.

(1) *Example 1: Substitution of payments that are not base erosion payments for payments that otherwise would be base erosion payments through a conduit or intermediary.* (i) *Facts.* FP owns Property 1 with a fair market value of $95x, which FP in-

tends to transfer to DC. A payment from DC to FP for Property 1 would be a base erosion payment. Corp A is a domestic corporation that is not a related party with respect to DC. As part of a plan with a principal purpose of avoiding a base erosion payment, FP enters into an arrangement with Corp A to transfer Property 1 to Corp A in exchange for $95x. Pursuant to the same plan, Corp A transfers Property 1 to DC in exchange for $100x. Property 1 is subject to the allowance for depreciation (or amortization in lieu of depreciation) in the hands of DC.

(ii) *Analysis*. The arrangement between FP, DC, and Corp A is deemed to result in a $95x base erosion payment under paragraph (b)(1) of this section because DC's payment to Corp A would have been a base erosion payment if paid to a foreign related person, and Corp A makes a corresponding payment to FP as part of the series of transactions that has as a principal purpose avoiding a base erosion payment.

(2) *Example 2: Alternative transaction to base erosion payment*. (i) *Facts*. The facts are the same as in paragraph (c)(1)(i) of this section (the facts in *Example 1*), except that DC does not purchase Property 1 from FP or Corp A. Instead, DC purchases Property 2 from Corp B, a domestic corporation that is not a related party with respect to DC and that originally produced or acquired Property 2 for Corp B's own account. Property 2 is substantially similar to Property 1, and DC uses Property 2 in substantially the same manner that DC would have used Property 1.

(ii) *Analysis*. Paragraph (b)(1) of this section does not apply to the transaction between DC and Corp B because Corp B does not make a corresponding payment to or for the benefit of FP as part of a transaction, plan or arrangement.

(3) *Example 3: Alternative financing source*. (i) *Facts*. On Date 1, FP loaned $200x to DC in exchange for Note A. DC pays or accrues interest annually on Note A, and the payment or accrual is a base erosion payment within the meaning of § 1.59A-3(b)(1)(i). On Date 2, DC borrows $200x from Bank, a corporation that is not a related party with respect to DC, in exchange for Note B. The terms of Note B are substantially similar to the terms of Note A. DC uses the proceeds from Note B to repay Note A.

(ii) *Analysis*. Paragraph (b)(1) of this section does not apply to the transaction between DC and Bank because Bank does not make a corresponding payment to or for the benefit of FP as part of the series of transactions.

(4) *Example 4: Alternative financing source that is a conduit*. (i) *Facts*. The facts are the same as in paragraph (c)(3)(i) of this section (the facts in *Example 3*) except that in addition, with a principal purpose of avoiding a base erosion payment, and as part of the same plan or arrangement as the Note B transaction, FP deposits $250x with Bank. The difference between the interest rate paid by Bank to FP on FP's deposit and the interest rate paid by DC to Bank is less than one percentage point. The interest rate charged by Bank to DC would have differed absent the deposit by FP.

(ii) *Analysis*. The transactions between FP, DC, and Bank are deemed to result in a base erosion payment under paragraph (b)(1) of this section because DC's payment to Bank would have been a base erosion payment if paid to a foreign related person, and Bank makes a corresponding payment to FP as part of the series of transactions that has as a principal purpose avoiding a base erosion payment. See Rev. Rul. 87-89, 1987-2 C.B. 195, Situation 3.

(5) *Example 5: Transactions to increase the amount of deductions taken into account in the denominator of the base erosion percentage computation*. (i) *Facts*. With a principal purpose of increasing the deductions taken into account by DC for purposes of § 1.59A-2(e)(3)(i)(B), DC enters into a long position with respect to Asset with Financial Institution 1 and simultaneously enters into a short position with respect to Asset with Financial Institution 2. Financial Institution 1 and Financial Institution 2 are not related to DC and are not related to each other.

(ii) *Analysis*. Paragraph (b)(2) of this section applies and the transactions between DC and Financial Institution 1 and DC and Financial Institution 2. These transactions are not taken into account for purposes of § 1.59A-2(e)(3)(i)(B) because the transactions have a principal purpose of increasing the deductions taken into account for purposes of § 1.59A-2(e)(3)(i)(B). [Reg. § 1.59A-9.]

§ 1.59A-10. Applicability date.—Sections 1.59A-1 through 1.59A-9 apply to taxable years beginning after December 31, 2017. [Reg. § 1.59A-10.]

COMPUTATION OF TAXABLE INCOME

Imputed Interest: OID: Safe Haven Rates

Imputed Interest: Original Issue Discount: Safe Haven Interest Rates.—Reproduced below are the texts of proposed amendments of Reg §§ 1.61-6 and 1.61-7, relating to (1) the tax treatment of debt instruments issued after July 1, 1982, that contain original issue discount, (2) the imputation of and the accounting for interest with respect to sales and exchanges of property occurring after December 31, 1984, and (3) safe haven interest rates for loans or advances between commonly controlled taxpayers and safe haven leases between such taxpayers (published in the Federal Register on April 8, 1986).

□ Par. 2. Paragraph (c)(3) of § 1.61-6 is revised to read as follows:

§ 1.61-6. Gains derived from dealings in property.

* * *

(c) *Character of recognized gain.*—* * *

(3) Amounts received on retirement or sale or exchange of debt instruments, section 1271;

* * *

□ Par. 3. In paragraph (d) of § 1.61-7, the third sentence is amended by removing the phrase "section 1232" and adding in its place the phrase "section 1271".

§1.61-7. Interest.

Compensation Reduction Plans

Gross Income: Deferred: Compensation Reduction Plans or Arrangements.—Reproduced below is the text of proposed Reg. §1.61-16, relating to amounts payment of which are deferred under compensation reduction plans or arrangements (published in the Federal Register on February 3, 1978).

☐ 26 CFR Part 1 is amended by adding a new §1.61-16 immediately after §1.61-15. The new section reads as follows:

§1.61-16. Amounts payments of which are deferred under certain compensation reduction plans or arrangements.—(a) *In general.*—Except as otherwise provided in paragraph (b) of this section, if under a plan or arrangement (other than a plan or arrangement described in sections 401(a), 403(a) or (b), or 405(a)) payment of an amount of a taxpayer's basic or regular compensation fixed by contract, statute, or otherwise (or supplements to such compensation, such as bonuses, or increases in such compensation) is, at the taxpayer's individual option, deferred to a taxable year later than that in which such amount would have been payable but for his exercise of such option, the amount shall be treated as received by the taxpayer in such earlier taxable year. For purposes of this paragraph, it is immaterial that the taxpayer's rights in the amount payment of which is so deferred become forfeitable by reason of his exercise of the option to defer payment.

(b) *Exception.*—Paragraph (a) of this section shall not apply to an amount payment of which is deferred as described in paragraph (a) under a plan or arrangement in existence on February 3, 1978, if such amount would have been payable, but for the taxpayer's exercise of the option, at any time prior to [date 30 days following publication of this section as a Treasury Decision]. For purposes of this paragraph, a plan or arrangement in existence on February 3, 1978, which is significantly amended after such date will be treated as a new plan as of the date of such amendment. Examples of significant amendments would be extension of coverage to an additional class of taxpayers or an increase in the maximum percentage of compensation subject to the taxpayer's option.

Fringe Benefits: Employer-Provided Vehicle and Fuel: Lease Valuation Rule

Fringe Benefits: Employer-Provided Vehicle and Fuel: Lease Valuation Rule.—Reproduced below is the text of a proposed amendment to Reg. §1.61-21, relating to the valuation of an employee's personal use of employer-provided fuel when an employer-provided automobile is valued pursuant to the automobile lease valuation rule (published in the Federal Register on October 9, 1992).

☐ Par. 2. Section 1.61-21 is amended by revising paragraphs (d)(3)(ii)(A), (B), and (D) as follows:

§1.61-21. Taxation of fringe benefits.

* * *

(d) * * *

(3) * * *

(ii) *Fuel excluded.*—(A) *In general.*—The Annual Lease Values do not include the fair market value of fuel provided by the employer, whether fuel is provided in kind or its cost is reimbursed by or charged to the employer. Thus, if an employer provides fuel for the employee's personal use, the fuel must be valued separately for inclusion in income.

(B) *Valuation of fuel provided in kind.*—Fuel provided in kind may be valued at fair market value based on all the facts and circumstances or, in the alternative, may be valued at 5.5 cents per mile for all miles driven by the employee in calendar years 1989 through 1992. For subsequent calendar years, the applicable cents-per-mile rate is the amount specified in the annual Revenue Procedure concerning the optional standard mileage rates used in computing deductible costs of operating a passenger automobile for business. However, fuel provided in kind may not be valued at the alternative cents-per-mile rate for miles driven outside the United States, Canada, or Mexico.

* * *

(D) *Additional methods available to employers with fleets of at least 20 automobiles.*—(*1*) *Fleet-average cents-per-mile fuel cost.*—If an employer with a fleet of at least 20 automobiles (regardless of whether the requirements of paragraph (d)(5)(v)(D) of this section are met) reimburses employees for the cost of fuel or allows employees to charge the employer for the cost of fuel, the fair market value of fuel provided to those automobiles may be determined by reference to the employer's fleet-average cents-per-mile fuel cost. The fleet-average cents-per-mile fuel cost is equal to the fleet-average per-gallon fuel cost divided by the fleet-average miles-per-gallon rate. The averages described in the preceding sentence must be determined by averaging the per-gallon fuel costs and miles-per-gallon rates of a representative sample of the automobiles in the fleet equal to the greater of ten percent of the automobiles in the fleet or 20 automobiles for a representative period, such as a two-month period.

(*2*) *Alternative cents-per-mile method.*—In lieu of determining the fleet-average cents-per-mile fuel cost under paragraph (d)(3)(ii)(D)(*1*) of this section, an employer with a fleet of at least 20 automobiles may value the fuel provided for these automobiles by reference to the cents-per-mile rate set forth in paragraph (d)(3)(ii)(B) of this section (regardless of whether the requirements of paragraph (d)(5)(v)(D) of this section are met).

* * *

Individual Retirement Plans: Simplified Employee Pensions

Individual Retirement Plans: Simplified Employee Pensions.—Reproduced below is the text of proposed amendment of Reg. §1.62-1, relating to individual retirement plans and simplified employee pensions (published in the Federal Register on July 14, 1981).

□ Par. 1. Section 1.62-1 is amended by revising paragraph (c)(13) to read as follows:

§1.62-1. Adjusted gross income.

* * *

(c) * * *

(13) Deductions allowed by sections 219 and 220 for contributions to an individual retirement account described in section 408(a), for an individual retirement annuity described in section 408(b), or for a retirement bond described in section 409;

* * *

Dependency Exemption: Authorized Placement Agency: Definition

Dependency Exemption: Authorized Placement Agency: Definition.—Reg. §1.63-3 and amendments to Reg. §§1.63-1 and 1.63-2, relating to the definition of an authorized placement agency for purposes of a dependency exemption for a child placed for adoption that were issued prior to the changes made to the law by the Working Families Tax Relief Act of 2004, are proposed (published in the Federal Register on January 19, 2017) (REG-137604-07).

Par. 7. Section 1.63-1 is amended by:

1. Removing the language "the zero bracket amount and" from the section heading.
2. Removing the language "section 63(g)" and replacing it with the language "section 63(e)" in paragraph (a).

§1.63-1. Change of treatment with respect to the zero bracket amount and itemized deductions.

Par. 8. Section 1.63-2 is revised to read as follows:

§1.63-2. Standard deduction.—The standard deduction means the sum of the basic standard deduction and the additional standard deduction.

Par. 9. Section 1.63-3 is added to read as follows:

§1.63-3. Additional standard deduction for the aged and blind.—(a) *In general.*—A taxpayer who, at the end of the taxable year, has attained age 65 or is blind is entitled to an additional standard deduction amount. The additional standard deduction amount is the sum of the amounts to which the taxpayer is entitled under paragraphs (b) and (c) of this section. If an individual meets the requirements for both the additional amount for the aged and the additional amount for the blind, the taxpayer is entitled to both additional amounts.

(b) *Additional amount for the aged.*—(1) *Aged taxpayer or spouse.*—A taxpayer is entitled to an additional amount under section 63(f)(1) if the taxpayer has attained age 65 before the end of the taxable year. If spouses file a joint return, each spouse who has attained age 65 before the end of the taxable year for which the spouses file the joint return is entitled to an additional amount. A married taxpayer who files a separate return is entitled to an additional amount for the taxpayer's spouse if the spouse has attained age 65 before the end of the taxable year and, for the calendar year in which the taxable year of the taxpayer begins, the spouse has no gross income and is not the dependent of another taxpayer. The taxpayer is not entitled to an additional amount if the spouse dies before attaining age 65, even though the spouse would have attained age 65 before the end of the taxpayer's taxable year.

(2) *Age determined.*—For purposes of section 63(f) and this paragraph (b), a taxpayer's age is determined as of the last day of the taxpayer's taxable year. A person attains the age of 65 on the first moment of the day preceding his or her sixty-fifth birthday.

(c) *Additional amount for the blind.*—(1) *Blind taxpayer or spouse.*—A taxpayer is entitled to an additional amount under section 63(f)(2) if the taxpayer is blind at the end of the taxable year. If spouses file a joint return, each spouse who is blind at the end of the taxable year for which the spouses file the joint return is entitled to an additional amount. A married taxpayer who files a separate return is entitled to an additional amount for the taxpayer's spouse if the spouse is blind and, for the calendar year in which the taxable year of the taxpayer begins, the spouse has no gross income and is not the dependent of another taxpayer. If the spouse dies during the taxable year, the date of death is the time for determining the spouse's blindness.

(2) *Blindness determined.*—A taxpayer who claims an additional amount allowed by section 63(f)(2) for the blind must maintain in the taxpayer's records a statement from a physician skilled in the diseases of the eye or a registered optometrist stating that the physician or optometrist has examined the person for whom the additional amount is claimed and, in the opinion of the physician or optometrist, the person's central visual acuity did not exceed 20/200 in the better eye with correcting lenses, or the person's visual acuity was accompanied by a limitation in the field of vision such that the widest diameter of the visual field subtends an angle no greater than 20 degrees. The statement must provide that the physician or optometrist examined the person in the taxpayer's taxable year for which the amount is claimed, or that the physician or optometrist examined the person in an earlier

year and that the visual impairment is irreversible.

(d) *Applicability date.*—This section and §§1.63-1(a) and 1.63-2 apply to taxable years beginning after the date these regulations are published as final regulations in the **Federal Register**. [Reg. §1.63-3.]

Taxable Income: Relief from Joint and Several Liability

Taxable Income: Relief from Joint and Several Liability.—Amendments to Reg. §§1.66-1—1.66-5, relating to relief from joint and several liability under section 6015 of the Internal Revenue Code and reflecting changes in the law made by the Tax Relief and Health Care Act of 2006 as well as changes in the law arising from litigation, are proposed (published in the Federal Register on November 20, 2015) (REG-134219-08).

Par. 2. Section 1.66-1 is amended by adding paragraph (d) to read as follows:

§1.66-1. Treatment of community income.

* * *

(d) *Effective/applicability date.*—This section is applicable beginning July 10, 2003.

Par. 3. Section 1.66-2 is amended by adding paragraph (e) to read as follows:

§1.66-2. Treatment of community income where spouses live apart.

* * *

(e) *Effective/applicability date.*—This section is applicable beginning July 10, 2003.

Par. 4. Section 1.66-3 is amended by adding paragraph (d) to read as follows:

§1.66-3. Denial of the Federal income tax benefits resulting from the operation of community property law where spouses not notified.

* * *

(d) *Effective/applicability date.*—This section is applicable beginning July 10, 2003.

Par. 5. Section 1.66-4 is amended by:

1. The last sentence of paragraphs (a)(3) and (b) are revised.
2. Paragraph (l) is added and reserved.
3. Paragraph (m) is added.

The revisions and additions read as follows:

§1.66-4. Request for relief from the Federal income tax liability resulting from the operation of community property law.—(a) * * *

(3) * * * Factors relevant to whether it would be inequitable to hold a requesting spouse liable, more specifically described under the applicable administrative procedure issued under section 66(c) (Rev. Proc. 2013-34 (2013-2 CB 397) (See §601.601(d)(2) of this chapter), or other applicable guidance published by the Secretary), are to be considered in making a determination under this paragraph (a).

(b) * * * Factors relevant to whether it would be inequitable to hold a requesting spouse liable, more specifically described under the applicable administrative procedure issues under section 66(c) (Rev. Proc. 2013-34 (2013-2 CB 397) (See §601.601(d)(2) of this chapter), or other applicable guidance published by the Secretary), are to be considered in making a determination under this paragraph (b).

* * *

(l) [Reserved]

(m) *Effective/applicability date.*—This section is applicable beginning July 10, 2003, except that paragraphs (a)(3) and (b) of this section will be applicable on the date of publication of a Treasury Decision adopting these rules as final regulations in the **Federal Register**.

Par. 6. Section 1.66-5 is removed.

§1.66-5. Effective date.

Tax Liability: Relief from Joint and Several Liability

Tax Liability: Relief from Joint and Several Liability.—Amendments to Reg. §§1.66-4 and 1.66-5, providing guidance to taxpayers on when and how to request relief under sections 66 and 6015, are proposed (published in the Federal Register on August 13, 2013) (REG-132251-11).

☐ Par. 2 In §1.66-4, paragraph (j)(2)(ii) is revised to read as follows:

§1.66-4. Request for relief from the Federal income tax liability resulting from the operation of community property law.

* * *

(j) * * *

(2) * * *

(ii) *Equitable relief.*—The earliest time for submitting a request for equitable relief from the Federal income tax liability resulting from the operation of community property law under paragraph (b) of this section is the date the requesting spouse receives notification of an audit or a letter or notice from the IRS stating that there may be an outstanding liability with regard to that year (as described in paragraph (j)(2)(iii) of this section). A request for equitable relief from the Federal income tax liability resulting from the operation of community property law under paragraph (b) of this section for a liability that is properly reported but unpaid is properly submitted with the requesting spouse's individual Federal income tax return, or after the requesting spouse's individual Federal income tax return is filed. To request equitable relief under § 1.66-4, a requesting spouse must file Form 8857, "Request for Innocent Spouse Relief," or other similar statement with the IRS within the period of limitation on collection of tax in section 6502 or within the period of limitation on credit or refund of tax in section 6511, as applicable to the tax liability. If a requesting spouse files a request for equitable relief under § 1.66-4 within the period of limitation on collection of tax, the IRS will consider the request for equitable relief, but the requesting spouse will be eligible for a credit or refund of tax only if the limitation period for credit or refund of tax is open when the request is filed (assuming all other requirements are met, including the limit on amount of credit or refund prescribed in section 6511(b)(2)). Alternatively, if a requesting spouse files a request for equitable relief after the period of limitation on collection of tax has expired but while the limitation period on credit or refund of tax remains open, the IRS will consider the request for equitable relief insofar as tax was paid by or collected from the requesting spouse, and the requesting spouse will be eligible for a potential credit or refund of tax. If neither the section 6502 nor section 6511 limitation period is open when a requesting spouse files a request for equitable relief, the IRS will not consider the request for equitable relief.

* * *

□ Par. 3. Section 1.66-5 is revised to read as follows:

§ 1.66-5. Effective/applicability date.—Except for § 1.66-4(j)(2)(ii), sections 1.66-1 through 1.66-4 are applicable on July 10, 2003. Section 1.66-4(j)(2)(ii) applies to any request for relief filed on or after July 25, 2011 (the date that Notice 2011-70, 2011-32 IRB, was issued to the public).

Itemized Deductions

Itemized Deductions: Two-Percent Floor.—Temporary Reg. §§ 1.67-1T and 1.67-2T, relating to the two-percent floor on miscellaneous itemized deductions, are also proposed as final regulations and, when adopted, would become Reg. §§ 1.67-1 and 1.67-2 (published in the Federal Register on March 28, 1988).

§ 1.67-1. 2-percent floor on miscellaneous itemized deductions.

§ 1.67-2. Treatment of pass-through entities.

REMICs: Reporting Information: Extension of Time

REMICs: Reporting Information: Extension of Time.—Reproduced below is the text of a proposed amendment to Temporary Reg. § 1.67-3T, relating to real estate mortgage investment conduits (published in the Federal Register on September 30, 1991).

□ Par. 2. Section 1.67-3T is amended by revising the last sentence of paragraph (f)(2)(ii)(A) to read as follows:

§ 1.67-3T. Allocation of expenses by real estate mortgage investment conduits (Temporary).

* * *

(f) * * *

(2) * * *

(ii) * * *

(A) * * * The separate statement provided in a separate mailing must be furnished to each pass-through interest holder no later than the 41st day following the close of the calendar year.

* * *

REMICs: Reporting Requirements: Allocable Investment Expenses

REMICs: Reporting Requirements: Allocable Investment Expenses.—Temporary Reg. § 1.67-3T(a) through (e), relating to reporting requirements with respect to real estate mortgage investment conduits (REMICs), is also proposed as final (published in the Federal Register on September 3, 1992).

§ 1.67-3. Allocation of expenses by real estate mortgage investment conduits.

Transfers Between Spouses

Transfers: Alimony, Separate Maintenance, and Dependency Exemption.—Temporary Reg. § 1.71-1T, relating to the treatment of transfers of property between spouses and former spouses, the tax treatments of alimony and separate maintenance payments, and the dependency exemption in the case of a child of divorced parents, is also proposed as a final regulation and, when adopted, would become Reg. § 1.71-1 (published in the Federal Register on August 31, 1984).

§ 1.71-1. Alimony and separate maintenance payments.

Exclusion Ratio

Exclusion Ratio.—Reproduced below is the text of a proposed amendment of Reg. §1.72-4, relating to the exclusion ratio (published in the Federal Register on April 30, 1975).

§1.72-4. Exclusion ratio.—(a) *General rule.*—(1)(i) To determine the proportionate part of the total amount received each year as an annuity which is excludable from the gross income of a recipient in the taxable year of receipt (other than amounts received under (A) certain employee annuities described in section 72(d) and §1.72-13, or (B) certain annuities described in section 72(n) and §1.122-1), an exclusion ratio is to be determined for each contract. In general, this ratio is determined by dividing the investment in the contract as found under §1.72-6 by the expected return under such contract as found under §1.72-5. Where a single consideration is given for a particular contract which provides for two or more annuity elements, an exclusion ratio shall be determined for the contract as a whole by dividing the investment in such contract by the aggregate of the expected returns under all the annuity elements provided thereunder. However, where the provisions of paragraph (b)(3) of §1.72-2 apply to payments received under such a contract, see paragraph (b)(3) of §1.72-6.

* * *

Annuity Contracts: Exchanges of Property

Annuity Contracts: Exchanges of Property.—Amendments to Reg. §1.72-6, providing guidance on the taxation of the exchange of property for an annuity contract, are proposed (published in the Federal Register on October 18, 2006) (REG-141901-05).

☐ Par. 2. In §1.72-6, paragraph (e) is added to read as follows:

§1.72-6. Investment in the contract.

* * *

(e) *Certain annuity contracts received in exchange for property.*—(1) *In general.*—If an annuity contract is received in an exchange subject to §1.1001-1(j), the aggregate amount of premiums or other consideration paid for the contract equals the amount realized attributable to the annuity contract, determined according to §1.1001-1(j).

(2) *Effective date.*—(i) *In general.*—Except as provided in paragraph (e)(2)(ii), this paragraph (e) is applicable for annuity contracts received after October 18, 2006, in an exchange subject to §1.1001-1(j).

(ii) This paragraph (e) is applicable for annuity contracts received after April 18, 2007, in an exchange subject to §1.1001-1(j) if the following conditions are met—

(A) The issuer of the annuity contract is an individual;

(B) The obligations under the annuity contract are not secured, either directly or indirectly; and

(C) The property transferred in exchange for the annuity contract is not subsequently sold or otherwise disposed of by the transferee during the two-year period beginning on the date of the exchange. For purposes of this provision, a disposition includes without limitation a transfer to a trust (whether a grantor trust, a revocable trust, or any other trust) or to any other entity even if solely owned by the transferor.

Exclusion Ratio: Special Rule

Exclusion Ratio.—Reproduced below is the text of a proposed amendment of Reg. §1.72-13, relating to the exclusion ratio (published in the Federal Register on April 30, 1975).

☐ Section 1.72-13(e)(3) is amended by deleting "72(o)" and inserting in lieu thereof "72(n)". As amended §1.72-13(e)(3) reads as follows:

§1.72-13. Special rule for employee contributions recoverable in three years.—

* * *

(e) *Inapplicability of section 72(d) and this section.*—Section 72(d) and this section do not apply to: * * *

(3) Amounts paid to an annuitant under chapter 73 of title 10 of the United States Code with respect to which section 72(n) and §1.122-1 apply.

Employee Trusts: Effective Dates

Employee Trusts: Tax Reform Act of 1984: Effective Dates.—Temporary Reg. §1.72(e)-1T is also proposed as a final regulation and, when adopted, would become Reg. §1.72(e)-1 (published in the Federal Register on February 4, 1986).

§1.72(e)-1. Treatment of distributions where substantially all contributions are employee contributions.

Prizes and Awards

Exclusions: Prizes and Awards: Employee Achievement Awards.—Reproduced below are the texts of proposed Reg. §1.74-2 and a proposed amendment of Reg. §1.74-1, relating to prizes and awards and employee achievement awards (published in the Federal Register on January 9, 1989).

☐ Paragraph 1. The authority for Part 1 continues to read in part:

Authority: 26 U.S.C. 7805. * * *

☐ Par. 2. Section 1.74-1 is amended as follows:

(a) Paragraph (a)(1) is amended by

(1) Removing the phrase "subsection (b)" and adding the phrase "subsections (b) and (c)" in its place, and

(2) Removing the word "any" in the last sentence and adding the word "most" in its place.

(b) Paragraph (b) is amended by

(1) Removing the word "and" from the first sentence, and

(2) Removing "award" at the end of the first sentence and adding the language set forth below in its place.

(c) Paragraph (c) is removed and new paragraphs (c), (d), (e), (f), and (g) are added directly following paragraph (b) to read as set forth below.

§1.74-1. Prizes and awards.—* * *

(b) *Exclusion from gross income* . . . award; and (4) the payor transfers the prize or award (and the prize or award is, in fact, transferred) to one or more governmental units or organizations described in paragraph (1) or (2) of section 170(c) pursuant to a designation by the recipient. Accordingly, awards such as the Nobel prize and the Pulitzer prize will qualify for the exclusion if the award is transferred by the payor to one or more qualifying organizations pursuant to a qualified designation by the recipient.

(c) *Designation by recipient*.—(1) *In general*.—To qualify for the exclusion under this section, the recipient must make a qualifying designation, in writing, within 45 days of the date the prize or award is granted (see paragraph (e)(3) of this section for a definition of "granted"). A qualifying designation is required to indicate only that a designation is being made. The document does not need to state on its face that the organization(s) are entities described in paragraph (1) and/or (2) of section 170(c) to result in a qualified designation. Furthermore, it is not necessary that the document do more than identify a class of entities from which the payor may select a recipient. However, designation of a specific nonqualified donee organization or designation of a class of recipients that may include nonqualified donee organizations is not a qualified designation. The following example illustrates the application of this section:

A distinguished ophthalmologist, S, is awarded the Nobel prize for medicine. S may designate that the prize money be given to a particular university that is described in section 170(c)(1), or to any university that is described in that section. However, S cannot designate that the award be given to a donee that is not described in section 170(c)(1), such as a foreign medical school. Selection of such a donee or inclusion of such a donee on a list of possible donees on S's designation would disqualify the designation.

(2) *Prizes and awards granted before 60 days after date of publication of final regulations*.—In the case of prizes and awards granted before 60 days after date of publication of final regulations, a qualifying designation may be made at any time prior to 105 days after date of publication of final regulations.

(d) *Transferred by payor*.—An exclusion will not be available under this section unless the designated items or amounts are transferred by the payor to one or more qualified donee organizations. The provisions of this paragraph shall not be satisfied unless the items or amounts are transferred by the payor to one or more qualifying donee organizations no later than the due date of the return (without regard to extensions) for the taxable year in which the items or amounts would otherwise be includible in the recipient's gross income. A transfer may be accomplished by any method that results in the receipt of the items or amounts by one or more qualified donee organizations from the payor and does not involve a disqualifying use of the items or amounts. Delivery of items or amounts by a person associated with a payor (*e.g.*, a contractual agent, licensee, or other representative of the payor) will satisfy the requirements of this section so long as the items or amounts are received by, or on behalf of, one or more qualified donee organizations. Possession of a prize or an award by any person before a designation is made will not result in the disallowance of an exclusion unless a disqualifying use of the items or amounts is made before the items or amounts are returned to the payor for transfer to one or more qualified donee organizations (see paragraph (e)(2) of this section for a definition of "disqualifying use"). Accordingly, transfer of an item or amount to a nonqualified donee organization will not result in an ineffective transfer under this section if the item or amount is timely returned to the payor by the nonqualified donee organization before a disqualifying use of the item or amount is made and the item or amount is then transferred to a qualifying organization.

(e) *Definitions*.—(1) For purposes of this section, "qualified donee organizations" means entities defined in section 170(c)(1) or (2) of the Code.

(2) For purposes of this section, the term "disqualifying use" means, in the case of cash or other intangibles, spending, depositing, investing or otherwise using the prize or award so as to enure to the benefit of the recipient or any person other than the grantor or an entity described in section 170 (c)(1) or (2). In the case of tangible items, the term "disqualifying use" means physical possession of the item for more than a brief period of time by any person other than the grantor or an entity described in section 170(c)(1) or (2). Thus, physical possession by the recipient or a person associated with the recipient may constitute a disqualifying use if the item is kept for more than a brief period of time. For example, receipt of an unexpected tangible award at a ceremony that otherwise comports with the requirements of this section will not constitute a disqualifying use unless the recipient fails to return the item to the payor as soon as practicable after receipt.

(3) For purposes of this section, an item will be considered "granted" when it is subject to the recipient's dominion and control to such an extent that it otherwise would be includible in the recipient's gross income.

(f) *Charitable deduction not allowable.*—Neither the payor nor the recipient will be allowed a charitable deduction for the value of any prize or award that is excluded under this section.

(g) *Qualified scholarships.*—See section 117 and the regulations thereunder for provisions relating to qualified scholarships.

☐ Par. 3. New section 1.74-2 is added to immediately follow section 1.74-1 as set forth below.

§ 1.74-2. Special exclusion for certain employee achievement awards.—(a) *General rule.*—(1) Section 74(c) provides an exclusion from gross income for the value of an employee achievement award (as defined in section 274(j)) received by an employee if the cost to the employer of the award does not exceed the amount allowable as a deduction to the employer for the cost of the award. Thus, where the cost to the employer of an employee achievement award is fully deductible after considering the limitation under section 274(j), the value representing the employer's cost of the award is excludable from the employee's gross income.

(2) Where the cost of an award to the employer is so disproportionate to the fair market value of the award that there is a significant likelihood that the award was given as disguised compensation, no portion of the award will qualify as an employee achievement award excludable under the provisions of this section (see also § 1.274-8(c)(1) and (4)).

(b) *Excess deduction award.*—Where the cost to the employer of an employee achievement award exceeds the amount allowable as a deduction to the employer, the recipient must include in gross income an amount which is the greater of (1) the excess of such cost over the amount that is allowable as a deduction (but not to exceed the fair market value of the award) or (2) the excess of the fair market value of the award over the amount allowable as a deduction to the employer.

(c) *Examples.*—The operation of this section may be illustrated by the following examples:

Example (1). An employer makes a qualifying length of service award to an employee in the form of a television set. Assume that the deduction limitation under § 274(j)(2) applicable to the award is $400. Assume also that the cost of the television set to the employer was $350, and that the fair market value of the television set is $475. The amount excludable is $475 (the full fair market value of the television set). This is true even though the fair market value exceeds both the cost of the television set to the employer and the $400 deduction allowable to the employer for nonqualified plan awards under section 274(j)(2)(A).

Example (2). Assume the same facts as in example (1) except that the fair market value of the television set is $900. Under these circumstances, the fair market value of the television set is so disproportionate to the cost of the item to the employer that the item will be considered payment of disguised compensation. As a result, no portion of the award will qualify as an employee achievement award. Since no portion of the award is excludable by the employee, the employer must report the full fair market value of the award as compensation on the employee's Form W-2.

Example (3). An employer makes a qualifying safety achievement award to an employee in the form of a pearl necklace. Assume that the deduction limitation under section 274(j) is $400. Assume also that the cost of the necklace to the employer is $425 and that the fair market value of the necklace is $475. The amount includible by the employee in gross income is the greater of (a) $25 (the difference between the cost of the item ($425) and the employer's deductible amount of $400) or (b) $75 (the amount by which the fair market value of the award ($475) exceeds the employer's deductible amount of $400). Accordingly, $75 is the amount includible in the employee's gross income. The remaining portion of the fair market value of the award (*i.e.,* the $400 amount allowable as a deduction to the employer) is not included in the gross income of the employee. If the cost of the pearl necklace to the employer was $500 instead of $425, then $100 would be includible in the employee's gross income because the excess of the cost of the award over $400 (*i.e.,* $100) is greater than the excess of the fair market value of the award over $400 (*i.e.,* $75). The employer must report the $75, which is includible in the employee's gross income, as compensation on the employee's Form W-2.

Example (4). An employer invites its employees to attend a party it is sponsoring to benefit a charity. In order to encourage the employees to attend the party and to make contributions to the charity, the employer promises to match the employees' contributions and also provide expensive prizes to be awarded to contributing employees selected at random. Each employee receiving a prize must include the full fair market value of the prize in gross income because the prizes are not qualifying achievement awards under section 274(j) or de minimis fringe benefits under section 132(e). Since the prizes are not excludable, the employer must report the full fair market value of the prize as compensation on the employee's Form W-2.

(d) *Special rules.*—(1) The exclusion provided by this section shall not be available for any award made by a sole proprietorship to the sole proprietor.

(2) In the case of an employer exempt from taxation under Subtitle A of the Code, any reference in this section to the amount allowable as a deduction to the employer shall be treated as a reference to the amount which would be allowable as a deduction to the employer if the employer were not exempt from taxation under Subtitle A of the Code.

(e) *Exclusion for certain de minimis fringe benefits.*—Nothing contained in this section shall preclude the exclusion of the value of an employee award that is otherwise qualified for exclusion under section 132(e). [Reg. § 1.74-2.]

Determination of the Foreign Tax Credit: Guidance

Determination of the Foreign Tax Credit: Guidance.—Amendments to Reg. §1.78-1, relating to the determination of the foreign tax credit under the Internal Revenue Code, including changes made by the Tax Cuts and Jobs Act, are proposed (published in the Federal Register on December 7, 2018) (REG-105600-18).

Par. 2. Section 1.78-1 is revised to read as follows:

§1.78-1. Gross up for deemed paid foreign tax credit.—(a) *Taxes deemed paid by certain domestic corporations treated as a dividend.*—If a domestic corporation chooses to have the benefits of the foreign tax credit under section 901 for any taxable year, an amount that is equal to the foreign income taxes deemed to be paid by the corporation for the year under section 960 (in the case of section 960(d), determined without regard to the phrase "80 percent of" in section 960(d)(1)) is, to the extent provided by this section, treated as a dividend (a *section 78 dividend*) received by the domestic corporation from the foreign corporation. A section 78 dividend is treated as a dividend for all purposes of the Code, except that it is not treated as a dividend for purposes of section 245 or 245A, and does not increase the earnings and profits of the domestic corporation or decrease the earnings and profits of the foreign corporation. Any reduction under section 907(a) of the foreign income taxes deemed paid with respect to combined foreign oil and gas income does not affect the amount treated as a section 78 dividend. *See* §1.907(a)-1(e)(3). Similarly, any reduction under section 901(e) of the foreign income taxes deemed paid with respect to foreign mineral income does not affect the amount treated as a section 78 dividend. *See* §1.901-3(a)(2)(i), (b)(2)(i)(b), and (d), *Example 8*. Any reduction under section 6038(c)(1)(B) in the foreign taxes paid or accrued by a foreign corporation is taken into account in determining foreign taxes deemed paid and the amount treated as a section 78 dividend. See, for example, §1.6038-2(k)(5), *Example 1*. To the extent provided in the Code, section 78 does not apply to any tax not allowed as a credit. See, for example, sections 901(j)(3), 901(k)(7), 901(l)(4), 901(m)(6), and 908(b). For rules on determining the source of a section 78 dividend in computing the limitation on the foreign tax credit under section 904, see §§1.861-3(a)(3), 1.862-1(a)(1)(ii), and 1.904-5(m)(6). For rules on assigning a section 78 dividend to a separate category, see §1.904-4(o).

(b) *Date on which section 78 dividend is received.*—A section 78 dividend is considered received by a domestic corporation on the date on which—

(1) The corporation includes in gross income under section 951(a)(1)(A) the amounts by reason of which there are deemed paid under section 960(a) the foreign income taxes that give rise to that section 78 dividend, notwithstanding that the foreign income taxes may be carried back or carried over to another taxable year and deemed to be paid or accrued in such other taxable year under section 904(c); or

(2) The corporation includes in gross income under section 951A(a) the amounts by reason of which there are deemed paid under section 960(d) the foreign income taxes that give rise to that section 78 dividend.

(c) *Applicability date.*—This section applies to taxable years of foreign corporations that begin after December 31, 2017, and to taxable years of United States shareholders in which or with which such taxable years of foreign corporations end. The second sentence of paragraph (a) of this section also applies to section 78 dividends that are received after December 31, 2017, by reason of taxes deemed paid under section 960(a) with respect to a taxable year of a foreign corporation beginning before January 1, 2018.

Employee Trusts: Effective Dates

Employee Trusts: Tax Reform Act of 1984: Effective Date.—Temporary Reg. §1.79-4T is also proposed as a final regulation and, when adopted, would become Reg. §1.79-4 (published in the Federal Register on February 4, 1986).

§1.79-4. Questions and answers relating to the nondiscrimination requirements for group-term life insurance.

Partnerships: Equity for Services

Partnerships: Equity for Services.—Amendments to Reg. §1.83-3, providing that the transfer of a partnership interest in connection with the performance of services is subject to Code Sec. 83 and providing rules for coordinating Code Sec. 83 with partnership taxation principles, are proposed (published in the Federal Register on May 24, 2005) (REG-105346-03).

☐ Par. 2. Section 1.83-3 is amended as follows:

1. Paragraph (e) is amended by adding two new sentences after the first sentence.
2. Paragraph (l) is added.

The revision and addition read as follows:

§1.83-3. Meaning and use of certain terms.

* * *

(e) *Property.*—* * * Accordingly, property includes a partnership interest. The previous sentence is effective for transfers on or after the date final regulations are published in the Federal Register. * * *

* * *

(l) *Special rules for the transfer of a partnership interest.*—(1) Subject to such additional conditions, rules, and procedures that the Commissioner may prescribe in regulations, revenue rulings, notices, or other guidance published in the Internal Revenue Bulletin (see

§ 601.601(d)(2)(ii)(*b*) of this chapter), a partnership and all of its partners may elect a safe harbor under which the fair market value of a partnership interest that is transferred in connection with the performance of services is treated as being equal to the liquidation value of that interest for transfers on or after the date final regulations are published in the **Federal Register** if the following conditions are satisfied:

(i) The partnership must prepare a document, executed by a partner who has responsibility for Federal income tax reporting by the partnership, stating that the partnership is electing, on behalf of the partnership and each of its partners, to have the safe harbor apply irrevocably as of the stated effective date with respect to all partnership interests transferred in connection with the performance of services while the safe harbor election remains in effect and attach the document to the tax return for the partnership for the taxable year that includes the effective date of the election.

(ii) Except as provided in paragraph (l)(1)(iii) of this section, the partnership agreement must contain provisions that are legally binding on all of the partners stating that—

(A) The partnership is authorized and directed to elect the safe harbor; and

(B) The partnership and each of its partners (including any person to whom a partnership interest is transferred in connection with the performance of services) agrees to comply with all requirements of the safe harbor with respect to all partnership interests transferred in connection with the performance of services while the election remains effective.

(iii) If the partnership agreement does not contain the provisions described in paragraph (l)(1)(ii) of this section, or the provisions are not legally binding on all of the partners of the partnership, then each partner in a partnership that transfers a partnership interest in connection with the performance of services must execute a document containing provisions that are legally binding on that partner stating that—

(A) The partnership is authorized and directed to elect the safe harbor; and

(B) The partner agrees to comply with all requirements of the safe harbor with respect to all partnership interests transferred in connection with the performance of services while the election remains effective.

(2) The specified effective date of the safe harbor election may not be prior to the date that the safe harbor election is executed. The partnership must retain such records as may be necessary to indicate that an effective election has been made and remains in effect, including a copy of the partnership's election statement under this paragraph (l), and, if applicable, the original of each document submitted to the partnership by a partner under this paragraph (l). If the partnership is unable to produce a record of a particular document, the election will be treated as not made, generally resulting in termination of the election. The safe harbor election also may be terminated by the partnership preparing a document, executed by a partner who has responsibility for Federal income tax reporting by the partnership, which states that the partnership, on behalf of the partnership and each of its partners, is revoking the safe harbor election on the stated effective date, and attaching the document to the tax return for the partnership for the taxable year that includes the effective date of the revocation.

Partnerships: Equity for Services

Partnerships: Equity for Services.—Amendments to Reg. § 1.83-6, providing that the transfer of a partnership interest in connection with the performance of services is subject to Code Sec. 83 and providing rules for coordinating Code Sec. 83 with partnership taxation principles, are proposed (published in the Federal Register on May 24, 2005) (REG-105346-03).

☐ Par. 3. Section 1.83-6 is amended by revising the first sentence of paragraph (b) to read as follows:

§ 1.83-6. Deduction by employer.

* * *

(b) *Recognition of gain or loss.*—Except as provided in section 721 and section 1032, at the time of a transfer of property in connection with the performance of services the transferor recognizes gain to the extent that the transferor receives an amount that exceeds the transferor's basis in the property. * * *

* * *

Life Insurance Contracts: Information Reporting

Life Insurance Contracts: Information Reporting.—Amendments to Reg. § 1.101-1, providing guidance on new information reporting obligations under section 6050Y related to reportable policy sales of life insurance contracts and payments of reportable death benefits, are proposed (published in the Federal Register on March 25, 2019) (REG-103083-18).

Par. 2. Section 1.101-1 is amended by:

1. Removing the second and third sentences in paragraph (a)(1) and adding a sentence at the end of the paragraph.

2. Revising paragraphs (b)(1) through (3).

3. Removing paragraphs (b)(4) and (5).

Adding paragraphs (c) through (g).

The revisions and additions read as follows:

§ 1.101-1. Exclusion from gross income of proceeds of life insurance contracts payable by reason of death.—(a)(1) * * * If the life insurance contract is an employer-owned life insurance contract within the definition of section 101(j)(3), the amount to be excluded from gross income may be affected by the provisions of section 101(j).

* * *

(b) * * *

(1) *Transfer of an interest in a life insurance contract for valuable consideration.*—(i) *In general.*—In the case of a transfer of an interest in a life insurance contract for valuable consideration, including a reportable policy sale for valuable consideration, the amount of the proceeds attributable to the interest that is excludable from gross income under section 101(a)(1) is limited under section 101(a)(2) to the sum of the actual value of the consideration for the transfer paid by the transferee and the premiums and other amounts subsequently paid by the transferee with respect to the interest. For exceptions to this general rule for certain transfers for valuable consideration that are not reportable policy sales, see paragraph (b)(1)(ii) of this section. The application of section 101(d), (f) or (j), which is not addressed in paragraph (b) of this section, may further limit the amount of the proceeds excludable from gross income.

(ii) *Exceptions.*—(A) *Exception for carryover basis transfers.*—The limitation described in paragraph (b)(1)(i) of this section does not apply to the transfer of an interest in a life insurance contract for valuable consideration if each of the following requirements are satisfied. First, the transfer is not a reportable policy sale. Second, the basis of the interest, for the purpose of determining gain or loss with respect to the transferee, is determinable in whole or in part by reference to the basis of the interest in the hands of the transferor (see section 101(a)(2)(A)). Third, paragraph (b)(1)(ii)(B) of this section does not apply. In the case of a transfer described in this paragraph (b)(1)(ii)(A), the amount of the proceeds attributable to the interest that is excludable from gross income under section 101(a)(1) is limited to the sum of the amount that would have been excludable by the transferor if the transfer had not occurred and the premiums and other amounts subsequently paid by the transferee. The preceding sentence applies without regard to whether the interest previously has been transferred and the nature of any prior transfer of the interest.

(B) *Exception for transfers to certain persons.*—*(1) In general.*—The limitation described in paragraph (b)(1)(i) of this section does not apply to the transfer of an interest in a life insurance contract for valuable consideration if both of the following requirements are satisfied. First, the transfer is not a reportable policy sale and the interest was not previously transferred for valuable consideration in a reportable policy sale. Second, the interest is transferred to the insured, a partner of the insured, a partnership in which the insured is a partner, or a corporation in which the insured is a shareholder or officer (see section 101(a)(2)(B)).

(2) Transfers to certain persons subsequent to a reportable policy sale.—If a transfer of an interest in a life insurance contract would be described in paragraph (b)(1)(ii)(B)(*1*) of this section, but for the fact that the interest was previously transferred for valuable consideration in a reportable policy sale (whether in the immediately preceding transfer or an earlier transfer), then the amount of the proceeds attributable to the interest that is excludable from gross income under section 101(a)(1) is limited to the sum of—

(i) The higher of the amount that would have been excludable by the transferor if the transfer had not occurred or the actual value of the consideration for the transfer paid by the transferee; and

(ii) The premiums and other amounts subsequently paid by the transferee.

(2) *Other transfers.*—(i) *Gratuitous transfer of an interest in a life insurance contract.*—To the extent that a transfer of an interest in a life insurance contract is gratuitous, including a reportable policy sale that is not for valuable consideration, the amount of the proceeds attributable to the interest that is excludable from gross income under section 101(a)(1) is limited to the sum of the amount of the proceeds attributable to the gratuitously transferred interest that would have been excludable by the transferor if the transfer had not occurred and the premiums and other amounts subsequently paid by the transferee.

(ii) *Partial transfers.*—When only part of an interest in a life insurance contract is transferred, the transferor's exclusion is ratably apportioned among the several parts. If multiple parts of an interest are transferred, the transfer of each part is treated as a separate transaction, with each transaction subject to the rule under paragraph (b) of this section that is appropriate to the type of transfer involved.

(iii) *Bargain sales.*—When the transfer of an interest in a life insurance contract is in part a sale and in part a gratuitous transfer, the transfer of each part is treated as a separate transaction for purposes of determining the amount of the proceeds attributable to the interest that is excludable from gross income under section 101(a)(1). Each separate transaction is subject to the rule under paragraph (b) of this section that is appropriate to the type of transfer involved.

(3) *Determination of amounts paid by the transferee.*—For purposes of paragraphs (b)(1) and (2) of this section, in determining the amounts, if any, of consideration paid by the transferee for the transfer of an interest in a life insurance contract and premiums and other amounts subsequently paid by the transferee with respect to that interest, the amounts paid by the transferee are reduced, but not below zero, by amounts received by the transferee under the life insurance contract that are not received as an annuity, to the extent excludable from gross income under section 72(e).

(c) *Reportable policy sale.*—(1) *In general.*—Except as provided in paragraph (c)(2) of this section, a reportable policy sale for purposes of this section and section 6050Y is any direct or indirect acquisition of an interest in a life insurance contract if the acquirer has, at the time of the acquisition, no substantial family, business, or financial relationship with the insured apart from the acquirer's interest in the life insurance contract.

(2) *Exceptions.*—None of the following transactions is a reportable policy sale:

(i) A transfer of an interest in a life insurance contract between entities with the same beneficial owners, if the ownership interest of each beneficial owner in the transferor entity does not vary by more than a 20 percent ownership interest from that beneficial owner's ownership interest in the transferee entity. In a series of transfers, the prior sentence is applied by comparing the beneficial owners' ownership interest in the first transferor entity and the last transferee entity. For purposes of this paragraph (c)(2)(i), each beneficial owner of a trust is deemed to have an ownership interest determined by the broadest possible exercise of a trustee's discretion in that beneficial owner's favor. *Example 10* in paragraph (g)(10) of this section provides an illustration of the application of this paragraph (c)(2)(i).

(ii) A transfer between corporations that are members of an affiliated group (as defined in section 1504(a)) that files a consolidated U.S. income tax return for the taxable year in which the transfer occurs.

(iii) The indirect acquisition of an interest in a life insurance contract by a person if—

(A) The partnership, trust, or other entity that directly holds the interest in the life insurance contract acquired that interest in a reportable policy sale reported in compliance with section 6050Y(a) and § 1.6050Y-2; or

(B) Immediately before the acquisition, no more than 50 percent of the gross value of the assets (as determined under paragraph (f)(4) of this section) of the partnership, trust, or other entity that directly holds the interest in the life insurance contract consists of life insurance contracts, and with respect to that partnership, trust, or other entity, the person indirectly acquiring the interest in the contract (acquirer) and his or her family members own, in the aggregate—

(1) With respect to an S corporation, stock possessing 5 percent or less of the total combined voting power of all classes of stock entitled to vote and 5 percent or less of the total value of shares of all classes of stock of the S corporation;

(2) With respect to a trust or decedent's estate, 5 percent or less of the corpus and 5 percent or less of the annual income (taking into account, for the purpose of determining any person's ownership interest, the maximum amount of income and corpus that could be distributed to or held for the benefit of that person); or

(3) With respect to a partnership or other entity that is not a corporation or a trust, 5 percent or less of the capital interest and 5 percent or less of the profits interest.

(d) *Substantial relationship.*—(1) *Substantial family relationship.*—For purposes of this section, a substantial family relationship means the relationship between an individual and any family member of that individual as defined in paragraph (f)(3) of this section. In addition, a substantial family relationship exists between an individual and his or her former spouse with regard to the transfer of an interest in a life insurance contract to (or in trust for the benefit of) that former spouse incident to divorce. A substantial family relationship also exists between the insured and a partnership, trust, or other entity if all of the beneficial owners of that partnership, trust, or other entity have a substantial family relationship with the insured. For example, a substantial family relationship exists between the insured and an entity that acquires an interest in a life insurance contract on the insured's life if the insured is the sole beneficial owner of the entity or each beneficial owner of the entity is either the insured or a family member of the insured.

(2) *Substantial business relationship.*—For purposes of this section, a substantial business relationship between the insured and the acquirer exists in each of the following situations:

(i) The insured is a key person (as defined in section 264) of, or materially participates (within the meaning of section 469) in, an active trade or business as an owner, employee, or contractor, and at least 80% of that trade or business is owned (directly or indirectly, through one or more partnerships, trusts, or other entities) by the acquirer or the beneficial owners of the acquirer.

(ii) The acquirer acquires an active trade or business and acquires the interest in the life insurance contract either as part of that acquisition or from a person owning significant property leased to the acquired trade or business or life insurance policies held to facilitate the succession of the ownership of the business if—

(A) The insured—

(1) Is an employee within the meaning of section 101(j)(5)(A) of the acquired trade or business immediately preceding the acquisition; or

(2) Was a director, highly compensated employee, or highly compensated individual within the meaning of section 101(j)(2)(A)(ii) of the acquired trade or business, and the acquirer, immediately after the acquisition, has ongoing financial obligations to the insured with respect to the insured's employment by the trade or business (for example, the life insurance contract is maintained by the acquirer to fund current or future retirement, pension, or survivorship obligations based on the insured's relationship with the entity or to fund a buy-out of the insured's interest in the acquired trade or business); and

(B) The acquirer either carries on the acquired trade or business or uses a significant portion of the acquired business assets in an active trade or business that does not include investing in interests in life insurance contracts.

(3) *Substantial financial relationship.*—For purposes of this section, a substantial financial relationship between the insured and the acquirer exists in each of the following situations:

(i) The acquirer (directly or indirectly, through one or more partnerships, trusts, or other entities of which it is a beneficial owner) has, or the beneficial owners of the acquirer have, a common investment (other than the interest in the life insurance contract) with the insured and a buy-out of the insured's interest in the common investment by the co-investor(s) after the insured's death is reasonably foreseeable.

(ii) The acquirer maintains the life insurance contract on the life of the insured to provide funds to purchase assets or satisfy liabilities following the death of the insured.

(iii) The acquirer is an organization described in sections 170(c), 2055(a), and 2522(a) that previously received financial support in a substantial amount or significant volunteer support from the insured.

(4) *Special rules.*—Paragraphs (d)(4)(i) and (ii) of this section apply for purposes of determining whether a substantial business relationship exists under paragraph (d)(2) of this section and for purposes of determining whether a substantial financial relationship exists under paragraph (d)(3) of this section.

(i) *Indirect acquisitions.*—The acquirer in an indirect acquisition of an interest in a life insurance contract is deemed to have a substantial business or financial relationship with the insured if the direct holder of the interest in the life insurance contract has a substantial business or financial relationship with the insured immediately before and after the date the acquirer acquires its interest.

(ii) *Acquisitions by certain persons.*—The sole fact that an acquirer is a partner of the insured, a partnership in which the insured is a partner, or a corporation in which the insured is a shareholder or officer, is not sufficient to establish a substantial business or financial relationship with the insured. In addition, an acquirer need not be a partner of the insured, a partnership in which the insured is a partner, or a corporation in which the insured is a shareholder or officer to have a substantial business or financial relationship with the insured.

(e) *Interest in a life insurance contract.*—(1) *Definition.*—For purposes of this section and section 6050Y, the term *interest in a life insurance contract* means the interest held by any person that has taken title to or possession of the life insurance contract (also referred to as a life insurance policy), in whole or part, for state law purposes, including any person that has taken title or possession as nominee for another person, and the interest held by any person that has an enforceable right to receive all or a part of the proceeds of a life insurance contract or to any other economic benefits of the policy as described in § 20.2042-1(c)(2) of this chapter, such as the enforceable right to designate a contract beneficiary. Any person named as the owner in the life insurance contract generally is the owner (or an owner) of the contract and holds an interest in the contract.

(2) *Transfer of an interest in a life insurance contract.*—For purposes of this section and section 6050Y, the term *transfer of an interest in a life insurance contract* means the transfer of any interest in the life insurance contract, including any transfer of title to, possession of, or legal or beneficial ownership of the life insurance contract itself. The creation of an enforceable right to receive all or a part of the proceeds of a life insurance contract constitutes the transfer of an interest in the life insurance contract. The following events are not a transfer of an interest in a life insurance contract: the revocable designation of a beneficiary of the policy proceeds (until the designation becomes irrevocable other than by reason of the death of the insured); the pledging or assignment of a policy as collateral security; and the issuance of a life insurance contract to a policyholder, other than the issuance of a policy in an exchange pursuant to section 1035.

(3) *Acquisition of an interest in a life insurance contract.*—For purposes of this section and section 6050Y, the acquisition of an interest in a life insurance contract may be direct or indirect.

(i) *Direct acquisition of an interest in a life insurance contract.*—For purposes of this section and section 6050Y, the transfer of an interest in a life insurance contract results in the direct acquisition of the interest by the transferee (acquirer).

(ii) *Indirect acquisition of an interest in a life insurance contract.*—For purposes of this section and section 6050Y, an indirect acquisition of an interest in a life insurance contract occurs when a person (acquirer) becomes a beneficial owner of a partnership, trust, or other entity that holds (whether directly or indirectly) the interest in the life insurance contract. For purposes of this paragraph (e)(3)(ii), the term *other entity* does not include a C corporation, unless more than 50 percent of the gross value of the assets of the C corporation consists of life insurance contracts (as determined under paragraph (f)(4) of this section) immediately before the indirect acquisition.

(f) *Definitions.*—The following definitions apply for purposes of this section:

(1) *Beneficial owner.*—A beneficial owner of a partnership, trust or other entity is an individual or C corporation with an ownership interest in that entity. The interest may be held directly or indirectly, through one or more other partnerships, trusts, or other entities. For instance, an individual that directly owns an interest in a partnership (P1), which directly owns an interest in another partnership (P2), is an indirect beneficial owner of P2 and any assets or other entities owned by P2 directly or indirectly. For purposes of this paragraph (f)(1), the beneficial owners of a trust include those who may receive current distributions of trust income or corpus and those who could receive distributions if the trust were to terminate currently.

(2) *C corporation.*—The term *C corporation* has the meaning given to it in section 1361(a)(2).

(3) *Family member.*—With respect to any individual, the term *family member* refers to any person described in paragraphs (f)(3)(i) through (vii) of this section. For purposes of this paragraph (f)(3), full effect is given to a legal adoption, and a step-child is deemed to be a descendant. The family members of an individual include:

(i) The individual;

(ii) The individual's spouse or a person with whom the individual is in a registered domestic partnership, civil union, or other similar relationship established under state law;

(iii) Any parent, grandparent, or great-grandparent of the individual or of the person described in paragraph (f)(3)(ii) of this section and any spouse of such parent, grandparent, or great-grandparent, or person with whom the parent, grandparent, or great-grandparent is in a registered domestic partnership, civil union, or other similar relationship established under state law;

(iv) Any lineal descendant of the individual or of any person described in paragraph (f)(3)(ii) or (iii) of this section;

(v) Any spouse of a lineal descendant described in paragraph (f)(3)(iv) of this section and any person with whom such a lineal descendant is in a registered domestic partnership, civil union, or other similar relationship established under state law;

(vi) Any lineal descendant of a person described in paragraph (f)(3)(v) of this section; and

(vii) Any trust established and maintained for the primary benefit of the individual or one or more persons described in paragraph (f)(3)(i) through (vi) of this section.

(4) *Gross value of assets.*—(i) *Determination of gross value of assets.*—Except as otherwise provided in paragraph (f)(4)(ii) and (iii) of this section, for purposes of paragraphs (c)(2)(iii)(B) and (e)(3)(ii) of this section, the term *gross value of*

assets means, with respect to any entity, the fair market value of the entity's assets.

(ii) *Determination of gross value of assets of publicly traded entity.*—For purposes of determining the gross value of assets of an entity that is publicly traded, if the entity's annual Form 10-K filed with the United States Securities and Exchange Commission (or equivalent annual filing if the entity is publicly traded in a non-U.S. jurisdiction) for the period immediately preceding a person's acquisition of an ownership interest in the entity does not contain information demonstrating that more than 50 percent of the gross value of the entity's assets consist of life insurance contracts, that person may assume that no more than 50 percent of the gross value of the entity's assets consist of life insurance contracts, unless that person has actual knowledge or reason to know that more than 50 percent of the gross value of the entity's assets consist of life insurance contracts.

(iii) *Safe harbor definition of gross value of assets.*—An entity may choose to determine the gross value of all the entity's assets for purposes of this section using the following alternative definition of *gross value of assets*:

(A) In the case of assets that are life insurance policies or annuity or endowment contracts that have cash values, the cash surrender value as defined in section 7702(f)(2)(A); and

(B) In the case of assets not described in paragraph (f)(4)(iii)(A) of this section, the adjusted bases (within the meaning of section 1016) of such assets.

(5) *Transfer for valuable consideration.*—A transfer for valuable consideration means any transfer of an interest in a life insurance contract for cash or other consideration reducible to a money value.

(g) *Examples.*—The application of this section is illustrated by the following examples, all of which assume that the transferee did not receive any amounts under the life insurance contract other than the amounts described in the examples:

(1) *Example 1.* A is the initial policyholder of a $100,000 insurance policy on A's life. A sells the policy to B, A's child, for $6,000, its fair market value. B is not a partner in a partnership in which A is a partner. B receives the proceeds of $100,000 upon the death of A. Because the transfer to B was for valuable consideration, and none of the exceptions in paragraph (b)(1)(ii) of this section applies, the amount of the proceeds B may exclude from B's gross income under this section is limited under paragraph (b)(1)(i) of this section to $6,000 plus any premiums and other amounts paid by B subsequent to the transfer.

(2) *Example 2.* The facts are the same as in *Example 1* in paragraph (g)(1) of this section except that, before A's death, B gratuitously transfers the policy back to A. A's estate receives the proceeds of $100,000 on A's death. Because the transfer from B to A is a gratuitous transfer, the amount of the proceeds A's estate may exclude from gross income under this section is limited under paragraph (b)(2)(i) of this section to the sum of the amount B could have excluded had the transfer back to A not occurred ($6,000 plus any premiums and other amounts paid by B subsequent to the transfer to B, as described in *Example 1* in paragraph (g)(1) of this section) plus any premiums and other amounts paid by A subsequent to the transfer to A.

(3) *Example 3.* The facts are the same as in *Example 1* in paragraph (g)(1) of this section except that, before A's death, B sells the policy back to A for its fair market value. A's estate receives the proceeds of $100,000 on A's death. The transfer from A to B is not a reportable policy sale because the acquirer B has a substantial family relationship with the insured A. The transfer from B to A is also not a reportable policy sale because the acquirer A has a substantial family relationship with the insured A. Accordingly, paragraph (b)(1)(ii)(B)(*1*) of this section applies to the transfer to A. The amount of the proceeds A's estate may exclude from gross income is not limited by paragraph (b) of this section.

(4) *Example 4.* A is the initial policyholder of a $100,000 insurance policy on A's life. A transfers the policy for $6,000, its fair market value, to an individual, C, who does not have a substantial family, business, or financial relationship with A. The transfer from A to C is a reportable policy sale. C receives the proceeds of $100,000 on A's death. The amount of the proceeds C may exclude from C's gross income under this section is limited under paragraph (b)(1)(i) of this section to $6,000 plus any premiums and other amounts paid by C subsequent to the transfer.

(5) *Example 5.* The facts are the same as in *Example 4* in paragraph (g)(4) of this section, except that before A's death, C transfers the policy back to A for $8,000, its fair market value. A's estate receives the proceeds of $100,000 on A's death. The transfer from C to A is not a reportable policy sale because the acquirer A has a substantial family relationship with the insured A. Because that transfer follows a reportable policy sale (the transfer from A to C), the amount of the proceeds that A's estate may exclude from gross income under this section is limited by paragraph (b)(1)(ii)(B)(2) of this section to the sum of—

(i) The higher of the amount C could have excluded had the transfer back to A not occurred ($6,000 plus any premiums and other amounts paid by C subsequent to the transfer to C, as described in *Example 4* in paragraph (g)(4) of this section) or the actual value of the consideration for that transfer paid by A ($8,000); and

(ii) Any premiums and other amounts paid by A subsequent to the transfer to A.

(6) *Example 6.* The facts are the same as in *Example 4* in paragraph (g)(4) of this section, except that before A's death, C gratuitously transfers the policy to A. A's estate receives the proceeds of $100,000 on A's death. Because the transfer from C to A was gratuitous, the amount of the proceeds A's estate may exclude from gross income is limited under paragraph (b)(2)(i) of this section to the sum of the amount C could have excluded had the transfer back to A not occurred ($6,000 plus any premiums and other amounts paid by C subsequent to the transfer to C, as described in *Example 4* in paragraph (g)(4) of this section), plus any premiums and other amounts paid by A subsequent to the transfer back to A.

(7) *Example 7.* A is the initial policyholder of a $100,000 insurance policy on A's life. A contributes the policy to Corporation X in exchange for stock. Corporation X's basis in the policy is

determinable in whole or in part by reference to A's basis in the policy. Corporation X conducts an active trade or business that it wholly owns, and A materially participates in that active trade or business as an employee of Corporation X. Corporation X receives the proceeds of $100,000 on A's death. A's contribution of the policy to Corporation X is not a reportable policy sale because Corporation X has a substantial business relationship with A under paragraph (d)(2)(i) of this section. Accordingly, under paragraph (b)(1)(ii)(B)(*1*) of this section, Corporation X may exclude the full amount of the proceeds from gross income because Corporation X's exclusion is not limited by paragraph (b) of this section.

(8) *Example 8*. The facts are the same as in *Example 7* in paragraph (g)(7) of this section, except that Corporation X transfers its active trade or business and the policy on A's life to Corporation Y in a tax-free reorganization at a time when A is still employed by Corporation X, but is no longer a shareholder of Corporation X. Corporation Y's basis in the policy is determinable in whole or in part by reference to Corporation X's basis in the property, and Corporation Y carries on the trade or business acquired from Corporation X. Corporation Y receives the proceeds of $100,000 on A's death. The transfer from Corporation X to Corporation Y is not a reportable policy sale because Corporation Y has a substantial business relationship with A under paragraph (d)(2)(ii) of this section. The amount of the proceeds that Corporation Y may exclude from gross income is limited under paragraph (b)(1)(ii)(A) of this section to the sum of the amount that would have been excludable by Corporation X had the transfer to Corporation Y not occurred (the full amount of the proceeds, as described in *Example 7* in paragraph (g)(7) of this section), plus any premiums and other amounts paid by Corporation Y subsequent to the transfer. Accordingly, Corporation Y may exclude the full amount of the proceeds from gross income.

(9) *Example 9*. A is the initial policyholder of a $100,000 insurance policy on A's life. A contributes the policy to a C corporation, Corporation W, in exchange for stock. Before and after the acquisition, A and A's family members own less than 5% of the total combined voting power of all classes of Corporation W stock entitled to vote and less than 5% of the total value of all classes of Corporation W stock. Corporation W's basis in the policy is determinable in whole or in part by reference to A's basis in the property. However, no substantial family, business, or financial relationship exists between A and Corporation W. Corporation W receives the proceeds of $100,000 on A's death. A's contribution of the policy to Corporation W is a reportable policy sale. Under paragraph (b)(1)(i) of this section, the amount of the proceeds Corporation W may exclude from gross income is limited to the actual value of the stock exchanged for the policy, plus any premiums and other amounts paid by Corporation W subsequent to the transfer.

(10) *Example 10*. Partnership X and Partnership Y are owned by individuals A, B, and C. A holds 40% of the capital and profits interest of Partnership X and 20% of the capital and profits interest of Partnership Y. B holds 35% of the capital and profits interest of Partnership X and 40% of the capital and profits interest of Partnership Y. C holds 25% of the capital and profits interest of Partnership X and 40% of the capital and profits interest of Partnership Y. Partnership X is the initial policyholder of a $100,000 insurance policy on the life of A. Partnership Y purchases the policy from Partnership X. Under paragraph (c)(2)(i) of this section, this transfer is not a reportable policy sale because the ownership interest of each beneficial owner in Partnership X does not vary from that owner's interest in Partnership Y by more than a 20% ownership interest. A's ownership varies by a 20% interest, B's ownership varies by a 5% interest, and C's ownership varies by a 15% interest.

(11) *Example 11*. Partnership X conducts an active trade or business and is the initial policyholder of a $100,000 insurance policy on the life of its full-time employee, A. A materially participates in Partnership X's active trade or business in A's capacity as an employee. Individual B acquires a 10% profits interest in Partnership X in exchange for a cash payment of $1,000,000. Under paragraphs (d)(1) through (3) of this section, B does not have a substantial family, business, or financial relationship with A. Under paragraph (d)(4)(i) of this section, B is deemed to have a substantial business relationship with A because, under paragraph (d)(2)(i) of this section, Partnership X (the direct policyholder) has a substantial business relationship with A. Accordingly, although the acquisition of the 10% partnership interest by B is an indirect acquisition of a 10% interest in the insurance policy covering A's life, the acquisition is not a reportable policy sale.

(12) *Example 12*. The facts are the same as in *Example 11* in paragraph (g)(11) of this section, except that A is no longer an employee of Partnership X when B acquires the profits interest in Partnership X, and Partnership X does not have any ongoing financial obligations to A. Also, B acquires only a 5% partnership interest in exchange for a cash payment of $500,000. Partnership X does not own an interest in any other life insurance policies, and the gross value of its assets is $10 million. Although neither Partnership X nor B has a substantial family, business, or financial relationship with A at the time of B's indirect acquisition of an interest in the policy covering A's life, because B's profits interest in Partnership X does not exceed 5%, and because no more than 50% of Partnership X's asset value consists of life insurance contracts, the exception in paragraph (c)(2)(iii)(B) of this section applies, and B's indirect acquisition of an interest in the policy covering A's life is not a reportable policy sale.

Employee Death Benefits

Employee Death Benefits.—Reproduced below is the text of a proposed amendment of Reg. §1.101-2, relating to employees' death benefits (published in the Federal Register on April 30, 1975).

□ Paragraph (d) of §1.101-2 is amended by revising subparagraph (3)(i) and example (2) of subparagraph (3)(ii) to read as follows:

§1.101-2. Employees' death benefits.

* * *

(d) *Nonforfeitable rights.*—* * *

(3)(i) Notwithstanding the rule stated in paragraph (d)(1) of this section and illustrated in paragraph (d)(2) of this section, the exclusion from gross income provided by section 101(b) applies to a lump sum distribution (as defined in section 402(e)(4)(A) and the regulations thereunder) with respect to which the deceased employee possessed, immediately before his death, a nonforfeitable right to receive the amounts while living (see section 101(b)(2)(B) (i) and (ii)). See paragraph (d)(4) of this section relating to the exclusion of amounts which are received under annuity contracts purchased by certain exempt organizations and with respect to which the deceased employee possessed, immediately before his death, a nonforfeitable right to receive the amounts while living.

(ii) The application of the provisions of paragraph (d)(3)(i) of this section may be illustrated by the following examples:

* * *

Example (2). The trustee of the X Corporation noncontributory, "qualified," profit-sharing plan is required under the provisions of the plan to pay to the beneficiary of B, an employee of the X Corporation who died on July 1, 1974, the benefit due on account of the death of B. The provisions of the profit-sharing plan give each participating employee, in case of termination of employment, a 10 percent vested interest in the amount accumulated in his account for each of the first 10 years of participation in the plan, but, in case of death, the entire balance to the credit of the participant's account is to be paid to his beneficiary. At the time of B's death, he had been a participant for five years. The accumulation in his account was $8,000, and the amount which would have been distributable to him in the event of termination of employment was $4,000 (50 percent of $8,000). After his death, $8,000 is paid to his beneficiary in a lump sum. (It may be noted that these are the same facts as in example (5) of subparagraph (2) of this paragraph except that the employee has been a participant for five years instead of three and the plan is a "qualified" plan.) It is immaterial that the employee had a nonforfeitable right to $4,000, because the payment of the $8,000 to the beneficiary is the payment of a lump sum distribution to which subdivision (i) of this subparagraph applies. Assuming no other death benefits are involved, the beneficiary may exclude $5,000 of the $8,000 payment from gross income.

Example (3). The fact are the same as in example (2) except that the beneficiary is entitled to receive only the $4,000 to which the employee had a nonforfeitable right and elects, 30 days after B's death, to receive it over a period of ten years. Because the distribution is not a lump sum distribution and because B's interest is nonforfeitable, no exclusion from gross income is allowable with respect to the $4,000.

Example (4). The X Corporation instituted a trust, forming part of a "qualified" profit-sharing plan for its employees, the cost thereof being borne entirely by the corporation. The plan provides, in part, that if an employee leaves the employ of the corporation, either voluntarily or involuntarily, before retirement, 10 percent of the account balance provided for the employee in the trust fund will be paid to the employee for each of the first 10 years of service. The plan further provides that if an employee dies before reaching retirement age, his beneficiary will receive a percentage of the account balance provided for the employee in the trust fund, on the same basis as shown in the preceding sentence. A, an employee of the X Corporation for 5 years, died before attaining retirement age while in the employ of the corporation. At the time of his death, $15,000 was the account balance provided for him in the trust fund. His beneficiary receives $7,500 in a lump sum, an amount equal to 50 percent of the account balance provided for A's retirement. The beneficiary may exclude from gross income (assuming no other death benefits are involved) $5,000 of the $7,500, since the latter amount constitutes a lump sum distribution to which subdivision (i) of this subparagraph applies.

Life Insurance Contracts: Information Reporting

Life Insurance Contracts: Information Reporting.—Amendments to Reg. §1.101-6, providing guidance on new information reporting obligations under section 6050Y related to reportable policy sales of life insurance contracts and payments of reportable death benefits, are proposed (published in the Federal Register on March 25, 2019) (REG-103083-18).

Par. 3. Section 1.101-6 is amended by revising paragraph (b) to read as follows:

§1.101-6. Effective date.

* * *

(b) Notwithstanding paragraph (a) of this section, for purposes of section 6050Y, §1.101-1(b), (c), (d), (e), (f), and (g) apply to reportable policy sales made after December 31, 2017, and to reportable death benefits paid after December 31, 2017. For any other purpose, §1.101-1(b), (c), (d), (e), (f), and (g) apply to transfers of life insurance contracts, or interests therein, made after the date the Treasury decision adopting these regulations as final regulations is published in the **Federal Register**.

Life Insurance Contracts: Qualified Accelerated Death Benefits

Life Insurance Contracts: Qualified Accelerated Death Benefits.—Reproduced below is the text of proposed Reg. §1.101-8, relating to the definition of a life insurance contract for federal tax purposes and the tax treatment of amounts received as qualified accelerated death benefits (published in the Federal Register on December 15, 1992).

☐ Par. 2. Section 1.101-8 is added to read as follows:

§1.101-8. Amounts paid with respect to terminally ill individuals.—For purposes of section 101(a), a qualified accelerated death benefit (as defined in §1.7702-2(d)), received on or after [date on which final regulations are published in the Federal Register], is treated as an amount paid by reason of the death of the insured. [Reg. §1.101-8.]

Prizes and Awards

Exclusions: Prizes and Awards: Employee Achievement Awards.—Reproduced below is the text of a proposed amendment of Reg. §1.102-1, relating to prizes and awards and employee achievement awards (published in the Federal Register on January 9, 1989).

☐ Par. 4. Section 1.102-1 is amended as follows:

(a) The last sentence of paragraph (a) is removed.

(b) A new paragraph (f) is added immediately following paragraph (e) to read as follows.

§1.102-1. Gifts and inheritances.

* * *

(f) *Exclusions.*—(1) *In general.*—Section 102 does not apply to prizes and awards (including employee achievement awards) (see section 74); certain de minimis fringe benefits (see section 132); any amount transferred by or for an employer to, or for the benefit of, an employee (see section 102(c)); or to qualified scholarships (see section 117).

(2) *Employer/Employee transfers.*—For purposes of section 102(c), extraordinary transfers to the natural objects of an employer's bounty will not be considered transfers to, or for the benefit of, an employee if the employee can show that the transfer was not made in recognition of the employee's employment. Accordingly, section 102(c) shall not apply to amounts transferred between related parties (*e.g.*, father and son) if the purpose of the transfer can be substantially attributed to the familial relationship of the parties and not to the circumstances of their employment.

Registration Requirements: Debt Obligations: Interest Deduction

Obligations of the United States: Registration Requirement: Deduction of Interest.—The text of Temporary Reg. §5f.103-1, relating to registration requirements with respect to debt obligations, has also been proposed as a final regulation and, when adopted, would become Reg. §1.103-8(a)(7) (published in the Federal Register on November 15, 1982). *NOTE: Code Sec. 103 has been amended to remove special exempt bond issue rules and provide similar rules in Code Secs. 141-150. This proposed regulation was issued under Code Sec. 103 as it read before amendment.*

§5f.103-1. Obligations issued after December 31, 1982, required to be in registered form (temporary).

Debt Obligations: Registration Requirements: Withholding

Registration-Required Obligations: Withholding.—An amendment to Temporary Reg. §5f.103-1, relating to the definition of the term "registration-required" with respect to certain types of obligations and to the repeal of the 30 percent withholding tax on certain types of interest, is also proposed as final (published in the Federal Register on December 19, 1986). *NOTE: Code Sec. 103 has been amended to remove special exempt bond issue rules and provide similar rules in Code Secs. 141-150. This proposed amendment was issued under Code Sec. 103 as it read before amendment.*

§5f.103-1. Obligations issued after December 31, 1982, required to be in registered form (temporary).

Definition of Registered Form: Guidance

Definition of Registered Form: Guidance.—Amendments to Reg. §5f.103-1, providing guidance on the definitions of registration-required obligation and registered form, including guidance on the issuance of pass-through certificates and participation interests in registered form, are proposed (published in the Federal Register on September 19, 2017) (REG-125374-16).

Par. 13. Section 5f.103-1(d) is amended by revising the paragraph heading and adding two sentences at the end of the paragraph to read as follows:

§5f.103-1. Obligations issued after December 31, 1982, required to be in registered form.

* * *

(d) *Applicability date.*—* * * For the purpose of determining whether bonds satisfy the requirements of section 149(a), this section applies to bonds issued prior to the date 90 days after the publication of the Treasury decision adopting these rules as final regulations in the **Federal Register**, and §1.149(a)-1 of this chapter applies to bonds issued on or after the date 90 days after the publication of the Treasury decision adopting these rules as final regulations in the **Federal Register**. For all other purposes, see §1.163-5(a)(2) and (b) of this chapter for obligations issued after March 18, 2012.

* * *

Industrial Development Bonds for Water Facilities

Industrial Development Bonds: Issuance to Finance Certain Water Facilities.—Reproduced below is the text of a proposed amendment of Reg. §1.103-8, relating to the income tax exemption

for interest on industrial development bonds issued to finance certain water facilities (published in the Federal Register on August 22, 1984). ***NOTE: Code Sec. 103 has been amended to remove special exempt bond issue rules and provide similar rules in Code Secs. 141-150. This proposed amendment was issued under Code Sec. 103 as it read before amendment.***

□ Section 1.103-8 (relating to exemption for interest on bonds to finance certain exempt facilities) is amended by revising paragraph (h) thereof. The revised provisions read as follows:

§1.103-8. Interest on bonds to finance certain exempt facilities.

* * *

(h) *Water facilities.*—(1) *General rule for obligations issued after November 6, 1978.*—Section 103(b)(4)(G) provides that section 103(b)(1) shall not apply to any obligation issued after November 6, 1978, by (or on behalf of) a State or local governmental unit which is issued as part of an issue substantially all of the proceeds of which are to be used to provide facilities for the furnishing of water for any purpose if certain requirements are met. In order to qualify under section 103(b)(4)(G) and this paragraph as an exempt facility, the facility must satisfy the requirements established by subparagraph (3) of this paragraph.

(2) *Facilities for the furnishing of water defined.*—For purposes of section 103(b)(4)(G) and this paragraph, the term "facilities for the furnishing of water" means those components of a system for the distribution of water to customers that are necessary for the collection, treatment, and distribution of water to a service area, and other functionally related and subordinate components as defined in §1.103-8(a)(3). For a component to come within this definition, it must be part of a system which, when viewed as a whole, is for the distribution of water to customers. A system or component does not come within this definition if it is a production facility that merely uses water in the production process (*e.g.*, a cooling pond, or equipment using water internally within a manufacturing plant). For example, an extension of a pipeline to carry water to a single industrial user from a qualified system is a qualified component because the system as a whole qualifies, but the internal water facilities of a private plant would not be a qualified component. In general, a series of dams will not constitute a single system, but each will constitute a separate system. Components of a dam or reservoir used to generate electric energy, such as generators and turbines, will not qualify as facilities for the furnishing of water (of course they may qualify as components for the local furnishing of electric energy under section 103(b)(4)(E) or as components used in hydroelectric generating facilities qualifying under section 103(b)(4)(H)). However, a reservoir or dam does not necessarily fail to qualify as facilities for the furnishing of water solely because one use of the water is to produce electricity if at least 90 percent of the water is available for other purposes, such as irrigation and domestic consumption, in addition to producing electricity.

(3) *Additional requirements.*—(i) The facility must make its water available to members of the general public. For this purpose, the general public includes electric utility, industrial, agricultural, and commercial users. In order to make its water available to the general public, a facility must make available to residential users within its service area, municipal water districts within its service area, or any combination thereof, at least 25 percent of its capacity (which must be a considerable quantity in absolute terms). Except with respect to residential users and municipal water districts, a water facility is not required to make available water to all segments of the general public in order to qualify under this subdivision (i). For example, if an industrial user agrees to "take or pay for" the entire capacity of a reservoir (but is guaranteed only 25 to 75 percent of the capacity), the facility will comply with this subdivision (i), provided the remainder of the water will be made available to residential users or municipal water districts within the service area. However, a facility is not considered to make water available to the general public merely because it is available for swimming, water skiing, and other recreational activities. A water facility is not required to make its water available to the general public immediately after its construction in order to qualify under this subdivision (i); it is sufficient that the facility is available to serve the general public. For example, if a pipeline is built to serve a sparsely inhabited region which lacks water, the pipeline meets the requirement of this subdivision (i) if it will serve the general public that the new source of water reasonably may be expected to cause to move into the region.

(ii) The facility must be operated either by—

(A) A governmental unit, within the meaning of §1.103-7(b)(2), or the United States government or an agency or instrumentality thereof, or

(B) A regulated public water utility whose rates for the furnishing or sale of the water are required to be established or approved by a State or political subdivision thereof, by an agency or instrumentality of the United States, or by a public service or public utility commission or other similar body of any State or political subdivision thereof.

A governmental unit or a regulated public water utility is considered to operate a facility only if it has responsibility and control over the repairs and maintenance of the facility. For example, if an industrial user leases the facility on a long-term basis, and it either controls the maintenance and repair of the facility, or bears these costs, then the facility fails to meet the requirement that it be operated by a governmental unit or a regulated public water utility.

* * *

Tax Exempt Status of Industrial Development Bonds

Nontaxables: Government Obligations: Tax-Exempt Industrial Development Bonds.—Reproduced below is the text of a proposed amendment of Reg. §1.103-8, relating to the definition of low or moderate income made by the Tax Reform Act of 1984 (published in the Federal Register on November 7, 1985). ***NOTE: Code Sec. 103 has been amended to remove special exempt bond issue***

rules and provide similar rules in Code Secs. 141-150. This proposed amendment was issued under Code Sec. 103 as it read before amendment.

Par. 2. Section 1.103-8 is amended by revising paragraph (b)(1), (b)(3) and paragraph (b)(4)(i) and (ii), by adding a new paragraph (b)(4)(v), by revising paragraph (b)(5), paragraph (b)(7)(ii), and paragraph (b)(8)(v), by revising *Example (3)* of paragraph (b)(9), and by adding new *Example (12)* and *Example (13)* to follow *Example (11)* of paragraph (b)(9). These revised and added provisions read as follows:

§1.103-8. Interest on bonds to finance certain exempt facilities.

* * *

(b) *Residential rental property.*—(1) *General rule for obligations issued after April 24, 1979.*—Section 103(b)(1) shall not apply to any obligation which is issued after April 24, 1979, and is part of an issue substantially all of the proceeds of which are to be used to provide a residential rental project in which 20 percent or more of the units in the project that are to be provided with the proceeds of the issue (other than those units to be provided with an insubstantial amount of the proceeds of the issue as permitted under paragraph (a)(3) of this section) are to be occupied by individuals or families of low or moderate income (as defined in paragraph (b)(8)(v) of this section). See paragraph (b)(4)(v) with respect to mixed-use projects. In the case of a targeted area project, the minimum percentage is 15 percent. See generally §1.103-7 for rules relating to refunding issues.

* * *

(3) *Transitional rule.*—For purposes of this section, obligations issued after April 24, 1979, may be treated as issued before April 25, 1979, if the transitional requirements of section 1104 of the Mortgage Subsidy Bond Tax Act of 1980 (94 Stat. 2670), as amended by section 614 of the Tax Reform Act of 1984 (98 Stat. 914), are satisfied.

(4) *Residential rental project.*—(i) *In general.*—A residential rental project is a building or structure, together with any facilities functionally related and subordinate thereto, containing one or more similarly constructed units that—

(a) Are not used on a transient basis, and

(b) Satisfy the requirements of paragraph (b)(5)(i) of this section and are available to members of the general public in accordance with the requirements of paragraph (a)(2) of this section.

Although a residential rental project may include other property, such as commercial office space, special rules apply to such mixed-use projects (see paragraph (b)(4)(v)). Hotels, motels, dormitories, fraternity and sorority houses, rooming houses, hospitals, nursing homes, sanitariums, and rest homes are not residential rental projects (but, with respect to obligations issued prior to January 1, 1986, only if such facilities are for use on a transient basis). In addition, trailer parks and courts for use on a transient basis are not residential rental projects.

(ii) *Multiple buildings and partial use of buildings.*—*(a)* Proximate buildings or structures that have similarly constructed units are treated as part of the same project if they are owned for Federal tax purposes by the same person and they are financed pursuant to a common plan.

(b) Buildings or structures are proximate if they are located on a single tract of land. The term "tract" means any parcel or parcels of land that either are contiguous or are contiguous except for the interposition of a road, street, stream or similar property. Parcels are contiguous if their boundaries meet at one or more points.

(c) Similarly constructed units located in a single building and financed pursuant to a common plan of financing are treated as part of the same project.

(d) A common plan of financing exists if, for example, all such buildings or similarly constructed units are provided by the same issue or several issues subject to a common indenture.

* * *

(v) *Mixed-use projects.*—*(a)* For purposes of this paragraph (b), a mixed-use project is a building or structure, together with any facilities functionally related and subordinate thereto, containing—

(1) One or more similarly constructed units rented or available for rental that, in the aggregate, meet the low or moderate income occupancy requirement of paragraph (b)(5)(ii), and

(2) Other property the use of which is unrelated to such units, *e.g.*, commercial office space, owner-occupied residences, and units that, in the aggregate, do not meet the low or moderate income occupancy requirement of paragraph (b)(5)(ii) ("nonqualifying property").

(b) For purposes of determining whether, in the case of a mixed-use project, substantially all of the proceeds of the issue are to be used to provide a residential rental project, only the proceeds to be used to provide the units described in paragraph (b)(4)(v)*(a)(1)* and the other portions of the project allocable to such units are treated as being used to provide a residential rental project. Other portions of the project allocable to such units include—

(1) The allocable portion of property benefitting both such units and the nonqualifying property (*e.g.*, common elements), and

(2) All property benefitting only such units (*e.g.*, recreational facilities used only by occupants of the units described in paragraph (b)(4)(v)*(a)(1)*).

(c) In determining whether, in the case of a mixed-use project, substantially all of the proceeds of an issue are to be used to provide a residential rental project, the cost of property that will benefit, directly or indirectly, both the units described in paragraph (b)(4)(v)*(a)(1)* and the nonqualifying property must be allocated between such units and the nonqualifying property. For example, in the case of a mixed-use project part of which is to be used for commercial purposes, the cost of the building's foundation must be allocated between the commercial portion of the building and the units described in paragraph (b)(4)(v)*(a)(1)*. The allocation of the cost of such common elements may be made according to any reasonable method that properly reflects the proportionate benefit to be derived, directly or indirectly, by the units described in paragraph (b)(4)(v)*(a)(1)* and the

nonqualifying property. Allocating the cost of such common elements based on the ratio of the total floor space in the building or structure that is to be used for nonqualifying property to all other floor space in the building or structure is, generally, a reasonable method; however, in the case of any common elements with respect to which an allocation according to this method does not reasonably reflect the relative benefits to be derived, directly or indirectly, by the units described in paragraph (b)(4)(v)(*a*)(*1*) and the nonqualifying property, the allocation may not be made according to this method. For example, this method would not be a reasonable method for making the allocation in the case of a residential rental project one-half of the floor space of which is used for shopping space where three-fourths of the parking lot for the building will be used to serve the shopping space and the balance of the parking lot will be used to serve tenants of the units described in paragraph (b)(4)(v)(*a*)(*1*); the cost of constructing the parking lot must be allocated based on the proportion of the parking lot to be used, directly or indirectly, by the tenants of the units described in paragraph (b)(4)(v)(*a*)(*1*) and by the owners and tenants of the nonqualifying portion of the project.

(5) *Requirements must be continuously satisfied.*—(i) *Rental requirement.*—Once available for occupancy, each unit (as defined in paragraph (b)(8)(i) of this section) in a residential rental project that was provided with the proceeds of an issue described in section 103(b)(4)(A) (other than those units provided with an insubstantial amount of the proceeds of the issue as permitted under paragraph (a)(3) of this section) must be rented or available for rental on a continuous basis for the longer of—

(*a*) The remaining term of the obligation, or

(*b*) The qualified project period (as defined in paragraph (b)(7) of this section).

(ii) *Low or moderate income occupancy requirement.*—Individuals or families of low or moderate income must occupy that percentage of completed units in the project that were provided with the proceeds of an issue described in section 103(b)(4)(A) (other than those units provided with an insubstantial amount of the proceeds of the issue as permitted under paragraph (a)(3) of this section) applicable to the project under paragraph (b)(1) of this section continuously during the qualified project period. For this purpose, a unit occupied by an individual or family who at the commencement of the occupancy is of low or moderate income is treated as occupied by an individual or family of low or moderate income even though the individual or family ceases to be of low or moderate income during the period of their occupancy. Moreover, such unit is treated as occupied by an individual or family of low or moderate income until reoccupied, other than for a temporary period not in excess of 31 days, at which time a redetermination of whether the unit is occupied by an individual or family of low or moderate income shall be made.

* * *

(7) *Qualified project period.*—* * *

(ii) For obligations issued after September 3, 1982, a period beginning on the later of the first day on which at least 10 percent of the units in the project that are provided with the proceeds of the issue are first occupied or the date of issue of an obligation described in section 103(b)(4)(A) and this paragraph and ending on the later of the date—

(*a*) Which is 10 years after the date on which at least 50 percent of the units in the project that are provided with the proceeds of the issue are first occupied,

(*b*) Which is a qualified number of days after the date on which any of the units in the project that are provided with the proceeds of the issue are first occupied, or

(*c*) On which any assistance provided with respect to the project under section 8 of the United States Housing Act of 1937 terminates. For purposes of this paragraph (b)(7)(ii), the term "qualified number of days" means 50 percent of the total number of days comprising the term of the obligation with the longest maturity in the issue used to provide the project. In the case of a refunding of such an issue, the longest maturity is equal to the sum of the period the prior issue was outstanding and the longest term of any refunding obligations.

(8) *Other definitions.*—* * *

(v) *Low or moderate income.*—Individuals and families of low or moderate income shall be determined in a manner consistent with determinations of lower income families under section 8 of the United States Housing Act of 1937, as amended, except that the percentage of median gross income that qualifies as low or moderate income shall be 80 percent of the median gross income for the area with adjustments for smaller and larger families. Therefore, occupants of a unit are considered individuals or families of low or moderate income only if their adjusted income (computed in the manner prescribed in § 1.167(k)-3(b)(3)) does not exceed 80 percent of the median gross income for the area with adjustments for smaller and larger families. With respect to obligations issued prior to January 1, 1986, determinations of low or moderate income shall be made in accordance with the requirements of this paragraph (b)(8)(v) except that median gross income for the area need not be adjusted for family size. Notwithstanding the foregoing, the occupants of a unit shall not be considered to be of low or moderate income if all the occupants are students (as defined in section 151(e)(4)), no one of whom is entitled to file a joint return under section 6013. The method of determining low or moderate income in effect on the date of issue will be determinative for such issue even if such method is subsequently changed. In the event programs under section 8(f) of the Housing Act of 1937, as amended, are terminated prior to the date of issue, the applicable method shall be that in effect immediately prior to the date of such termination.

(9) *Examples.*—* * *

Example (3). The facts are the same as in example (1), except that the proceeds of the obligation are provided to N, a cooperative housing corporation. N uses the proceeds to finance the construction of a portion of a cooperative housing project. The balance of the project is financed with the proceeds of a note that is not described in section 103(a). Shares in the cooperative carrying the rights to occupy the units in the portion of the project financed with the proceeds of the obligation issued by City X will be sold to shareholders who will rent the units to other persons. The balance of the shares in the cooperative, carrying the rights to occupy more than half of the space in the project, will be sold to individuals who will occupy the units themselves. The project is a residential rental project within the meaning of section 103(b)(4)(A) and this paragraph (b).

* * *

Example (12). In July 1985, County X issues a $10 million issue of industrial development bonds to be used to finance the construction of a building to be owned by Corporation W. Corporation W will construct a 10 story building. The first 2 floors of the building will be made available for commercial use. The remaining 8 floors will consist of similarly constructed units that will be made available as residences on a rental basis to members of the general public. Corporation W uses substantially all of the proceeds of the issue to finance the 8 floors of the building to be made available as rental units, the portions of the building benefitting, directly or indirectly, only the rental units, and the portions of the building benefitting, directly or indirectly, both the rental units and the commercial space that are properly allocable to the rental units. The remainder of the building is financed other than with the proceeds of an obligation described in section 103(a). Corporation W will make 20 percent of the rental units available to low or moderate income individuals, and all of the other requirements of this section are met. The obligations are used to provide a residential rental project within the meaning of section 103(b)(4)(A) and this section, and the obligations are described in section 103(a).

Example (13). The facts are the same as in example (12), except that Corporation W uses the proceeds of the issue to finance the entire building including the 2 floors to be available for commercial use. The cost of the 2 floors available for commercial use, including those portions of the building that benefit both the commercial space and the rental units that are properly allocable to the commercial space, is $2 million. Under paragraph (b)(4)(v) of this section, the building is a residential rental project. However, substantially all of the proceeds of the issue are not used to provide a residential rental project since, in making this determination, proceeds used to provide nonqualifying property are treated as not used to provide a residential rental project. Therefore, the obligations are not described in section 103(b)(4)(A) and this paragraph (b).

* * *

Industrial Development Bonds: Small Issues

Interest Received: Governmental Obligations: Industrial Development Bonds: Principal User.—Reproduced below is the text of a proposed amendment of Reg. §1.103-10, which would define the term "principal user" for purposes of Code Sec. 103(b)(6), (15) (published in the Federal Register on February 21, 1986). ***NOTE: Code Sec. 103 has been amended to remove special exempt bond issue rules and provide similar rules in Code Secs. 141-150. This proposed amendment was issued under Code Sec. 103 as it read before amendment.***

☐ Par. 2. Section 1.103-10 is amended by adding a new sentence after the second sentence of paragraph (b)(2)(i); by deleting "*(e)*" and adding "*(f)*" in lieu thereof in the first sentence of paragraph (b)(2)(iv) and by adding a new subdivision *(f)* at the end of subdivision (iv) thereof; by adding two new sentences after the first sentence of paragraph (d)(1); by revising paragraph (d)(2)(ii); by adding two new sentences at the end of paragraph (d)(2); by revising the first sentence of paragraph (g); and by adding a new paragraph (h). The revised and added provisions read as follows:

§1.103-10. Exemption for certain small issues of industrial development bonds.

* * *

(b) *Small issue exemption.*—* * *

(2) *$10 million or less.*—(i) * * * All capital expenditures described in paragraph (b)(2)(ii) with respect to each principal user and each related person must be aggregated with the issue of obligations in question for purposes of determining whether the $10 million limitation of section 103(b)(6)(D) is exceeded. * * *

(iv) * * *

(f) A capital expenditure with respect to a facility other than the bond-financed facility ("other facility") is an excluded expenditure if the principal user of the other facility does not become a principal user of the facility financed by the proceeds of the issue in question ("bond-financed facility") until after the last day of the test period described in paragraph (i)(3)(ii) of this section. In addition, a capital expenditure with respect to an "other facility" becomes an excluded expenditure on and after the date the principal user of the other facility ceases to use the bond-financed facility; if, however, the issue financing the bond-financed facility lost its tax-exempt status on or before that date, this sentence will not apply to restore its tax-exempt status. * * *

* * *

(d) *Certain prior issues taken into account.*—(1) *In general.*—* * * Thus, the outstanding face amount of all prior issues specified in paragraph (d)(2) with respect to each principal user and each related person and taken into account under this paragraph (d)(1) must be aggregated with the issue of obligations in question for purposes of determining whether the $1 million limitation of section 103(b)(6)(A) or the $10 million limitation of section 103(b)(6)(D) has been exceeded with respect to the issue in question. The outstanding face amount of the prior exempt small issue is the principal amount outstanding at the time of issuance of the subsequent exempt small issue. * * *

(2) *Prior issues specified.*—* * *

(ii) The principal user of the facilities described in paragraph (d)(2)(i) of this section is the same person or two or more related persons (as defined in section 103(b)(6)(C) and in paragraph (e) of this section) at any time on or after the date of issue of the subsequent issue but before the expiration of the test period described in paragraph (i)(3)(ii) of this section with respect to the subsequent issue.

The loss of tax exemption with respect to the interest on the subsequent issue shall be effective on the date of issue of the subsequent issue. For purposes of this paragraph (d), when a person ceases to use a facility financed by either the prior issue or the subsequent issue, the prior issue will no longer be taken into account under paragraph (d)(1) with respect to the subsequent issue; if, however, the subsequent issue loses its tax-exempt status on or before the date the person ceases to use either of the facilities described in this subparagraph, this paragraph will not apply to restore the tax-exempt status of the subsequent issue. * * *

* * *

(g) *Examples.*—The application of the rules contained in section 103(b)(6) and in paragraphs (a) through (f) of this section are illustrated by the following examples: * * *

* * *

(h) *Rules relating to principal users.*—(1) *Definition of principal user.*—For purposes of section 103(b)(6) and § 1.103-10, the term "principal user" means a person who is a principal owner, a principal lessee, a principal output purchaser, or an "other" principal user. The term "principal user" also includes a person who is related to another person who is a principal user under section 103(b)(6)(C) and paragraph (e) of this section, unless the other person ceased to use the facility before the two persons became related. For purposes of this paragraph (h)—

(i) *Principal owner.*—A principal owner is a person who at any time holds more than a 10-percent ownership interest (by value) in the facility or, if no person holds more than a 10-percent ownership interest, then the person (or persons in the case of multiple equal owners) who holds the largest ownership interest in the facility. A person is treated as holding an ownership interest if such person is an owner for Federal income tax purposes generally. Thus, for example, where a facility constructed on land subject to a ground lease has an economic useful life less than the noncancellable portion of the term of the ground lease, the ground lessor shall not, merely by reason of that reversionary interest, be treated as the principal user of the facility before the ground lease expires.

(ii) *Principal lessee.*—A principal lessee is a person who at any time leases more than 10 percent of the facility (disregarding portions used by the lessee under a short-term lease). The portion of a facility leased to a lessee is generally determined by reference to its fair rental value. A short-term lease is one which has a term of one year or less, taking into account all options to renew and reasonably anticipated renewals.

(iii) *Principal output purchaser.*—A principal output purchaser is any person who purchases output of an electric or thermal energy, gas, water, or other similar facility, unless the total output purchased by such person during each one-year period beginning with the date the facility is placed in service is 10 percent or less of the facility's output during each such period.

(iv) *Other principal user.*—An "other" principal user is a person who enjoys a use of the facility (other than a short-term use) in a degree comparable to the enjoyment of a principal owner or a principal lessee, taking into account all the relevant facts and circumstances, such as the person's participation in control over use of the facility or its remote or proximate geographic location. For example, a party to a contract who would be treated as a lessee using more than 10 percent of a facility on a long-term basis but for the special rules of section 7701(e)(3) and (5) (relating to service contracts for certain energy and water facilities and low-income housing) is an "other" principal user. A short-term use means use that is comparable to use under a short-term lease.

(2) *Operating rules.*—(i) In determining whether a person is a principal user of a facility, it is irrelevant where in a chain of use such person's use occurs. For example, where a sublessee subleases more than 10 percent of a facility from a lessee, both the lessee and the sublessee are principal lessees.

(ii) In determining whether a person owns or uses more than 10 percent of a facility or whether he uses it for more than one year, the person is treated as owning or using the facility to the extent that any person related to such person under section 103(b)(6)(C) and paragraph (e) of this section owns or uses the facility. For purposes of the preceding sentence, the term "use" includes use pursuant to an output purchase arrangement.

(iii) Co-owners or co-lessees who are collectively treated as a partnership subject to subchapter K under section 761(a) are not treated as principal users merely by reason of their ownership of partnership interests; such ownership is, however, taken into account in determining whether persons are related under section 103(b)(6)(C) and paragraph (e) of this section.

(iv) For purposes of this section, a principal user of a facility is treated as ceasing to use the facility when he ceases to own, lease, purchase the output of, or otherwise use the facility, as the case may be. A person who is a principal user of a facility because he is related to another person who is a principal user is treated as ceasing to use the facility when the other person ceases to use the facility or when the two persons cease to be related. A principal user who ceases to use a facility continues to be a principal user. See, however, paragraph (b)(2)(iv)(*f*) of this section (relating to excluded expenditures), paragraph (d)(2) (relating to prior issues), and paragraph (h)(1) (defining principal user), which may apply when a principal user ceases to use a facility.

(3) *Special rule for exempt persons.*—If an exempt person, as defined in section 103(b)(3) and § 1.103-7(b)(2), is a principal user of a facility financed with an issue of obligations described in section 103(b)(6), the following amounts must be aggregated with the issue in determining whether the $1 million limit of section 103(b)(6)(A) or the $10 million limit of section 103(b)(6)(D) has been exceeded:

(i) The outstanding face amount of any prior exempt small issue of industrial development bonds described in paragraph (d) of this section that financed a facility of which the exempt person is a principal user,

(ii) For purposes of the $10 million limitation, capital expenditures described in paragraph (b)(2)(ii) of this section paid or incurred with respect to other facilities used by the exempt person in an unrelated trade or business (within the meaning of section 513 and § 1.513-1) and of which the exempt person is a principal user, and

(iii) Any section 103(b)(6)(D) capital expenditures paid or incurred with respect to the facility financed by the issue in question.

(4) *Examples.*—The application of the rules of section 103(b)(6) and this paragraph (h) is illustrated by the following examples:

Example (1). On September 1, 1986, City L, after making the section 103(b)(6)(D) election, issues $8 million of obligations to finance the costs of acquiring a newly constructed warehouse within City L, owned by Corporation Z, a non-exempt person, which thus is a principal user of the warehouse. Beginning on September 1, 1986, the entire warehouse is leased to Corporation Y, an unrelated non-exempt person, for a 2-year term; thus, Y is also a principal user of the warehouse. On June 30, 1988, Y ceases to lease the warehouse. On October 1, 1988, Y incurs $20 million of capital expenditures in connection with its purchase of an office building in City L. Although Y continues to be a principal user of the warehouse under paragraph (h)(2)(iv) of this section, Y's capital expenditures after the date it ceases to use the warehouse are excluded expenditures under paragraph (b)(2)(iv)(*f*) of this section. Accordingly, the $20 million Y incurred with respect to the office building is not taken into account for purposes of determining whether the $10 million limitation of section 103(b)(6)(D) has been exceeded.

Example (2). The facts are the same as in Example (1), except that on October 1, 1985, City L issued an exempt small issue to finance acquisition of a newly constructed office building in the amount of $5 million, of which $4 million is outstanding on September 1, 1986. On December 1, 1988, Corporation Z leases 15 percent (by fair rental value) of the office building financed by the 1985 issue for a 2-year term. Thus, beginning on December 1, 1988, Z is a principal user of the office building. On December 1, 1988, Z still owns the warehouse financed by the 1986 issue. Because Z became a principal user of the office building before the end of the 3-year test period described in paragraph (i)(3)(ii) of this section with respect to the 1986 issue, the $4 million outstanding amount of the 1985 issue must be aggregated with the $8 million 1986 issue for purposes of determining whether the 1986 issue has exceeded the $10 million limitation of section 103(b)(6)(D). Because the sum of the two issues ($4 million of the prior 1985 issue outstanding on September 1, 1986, and the $8 million subsequent issue issued on September 1, 1986) exceeds $10 million, the interest on the 1986 issue ceases to be tax-exempt on September 1, 1986. Had Z's lease begun after September 1, 1989, the two issues would not have to be aggregated.

Example (3). On June 1, 1985, City O issues $15 million of its obligations to finance an expansion of a hospital owned by H, an organization described in section 501(c)(3) exempt from taxation under section 501(a). None of the proceeds of the issue will be used by H in an unrelated trade or business or in the trade or business of non-exempt persons. On November 1, 1986, City O, after making the section 103(b)(6)(D) election, issues $5 million of its obligations to construct a medical office building which will be owned by H for Federal income tax purposes and which will be entirely leased (for terms in excess of one year) to physicians, none of whom will lease over 10 percent of the building by value. On July 1, 1987, H incurs a $500,000 capital expenditure for permanent improvements to the medical office building. In addition, on August 1, 1987, W, a non-exempt person related to H, incurs a $1 million capital expenditure with respect to a facility that W owns within City O and uses in its trade or business. For purposes of determining whether the $10 million limitation of section 103(b)(6)(D) has been exceeded with respect to the November 1, 1986, issue for the medical office building, H must take into account the $5 million issue, the $500,000 of capital expenditures made with respect to the medical office building, and W's $1 million capital expenditure. Because the sum of these amounts is less than $10 million, interest on the issue does not cease to be tax-exempt. H is not required to take into account the June 1, 1985, issue financing the hospital expansion because that issue is not an exempt small issue as defined in section 103(b)(6) (see paragraph (h)(3)(i) of this section) and because the cost of the facility financed by the June 1, 1985, issue is neither a section 103(b)(6)(D) capital expenditure with respect to the medical office building owned by H (see paragraph (h)(3)(iii) of this section) nor a section 103(b)(6)(D) capital expenditure for a separate facility used by H in an unrelated trade or business (see paragraph (h)(3)(ii) of this section).

* * *

Industrial Development Bonds: Limitations

Interest Received: Governmental Obligations: Limitation on Beneficiaries.—Reproduced below is the text of a proposed amendment of Reg. §1.103-10, relating to industrial development bonds and the beneficiaries of such bond issues (published in the Federal Register on February 21, 1986). ***NOTE: Code Sec. 103 has been amended to remove special exempt bond issue rules and provide similar rules in Code Secs. 141-150. This proposed amendment was issued under Code Sec. 103 as it read before amendment.***

☐ Par. 2. Section 1.103-10 is revised by adding a new paragraph (i) immediately following paragraph (h) therein. The new paragraph reads as follows:

§1.103-10. Exemption for certain small issues of industrial development bonds.

* * *

(i) *$40 million limitation for beneficiaries of small issues of industrial development bonds.*—(1) *General rule.*—Section 103(b)(6) and §1.103-10(a) do not apply to an issue of obligations ("issue in question") if—

(i) The portion of the aggregate authorized face amount of the issue in question allocated to any test-period beneficiary as defined in paragraph (i)(3) of this section, of the issue, plus

(ii) The portion of the outstanding principal amount of prior bonds, as defined in paragraph (i)(2) of this section, allocated—

(*a*) To the test-period beneficiary described in paragraph (i)(1)(i) of this section, or

(*b*) To a person who at any time during the test period of the issue in question is related to such beneficiary,

exceeds $40 million. If interest on the issue in question would, but for this paragraph and section 103(b)(15), be exempt from Federal income taxation solely because of section 103(b)(6), the issue is treated as an issue of obligations not described in section 103(a) on and after the date of issuance. For purposes of this paragraph (i), the aggregate authorized face amount of the issue in question and the outstanding principal amount of a prior bond shall be determined without regard to section 103(b)(6)(B) or (D) (requiring certain amounts of prior issues or capital expenditures to be taken into account in determining the aggregate face amount of the issue in question or of the prior bond).

(2) *Prior bonds.*—For purposes of this paragraph (i), "prior bonds" means prior or simultaneous issues of industrial development bonds described in paragraph (4), (5), or (6) of section 103(b) the interest on which is exempt from tax pursuant to section 103(a), including such bonds issued before January 1, 1984. For purposes of paragraph (i)(1)(ii) of this section, "outstanding principal amount of prior bonds" means the principal amount that is outstanding at the time of issuance of the issue in question, not including the amount to be redeemed from the proceeds of the issue in question. Thus, the outstanding principal amount of prior bonds does not include the portion of the original face amount that has been discharged, nor does it include any amount to be issued in the future.

(3) *Test-period beneficiary.*—(i) *In general.*—For purposes of this paragraph (i), a "test-period beneficiary" of the issue in question or of an issue of prior bonds means any person who at any time during the test period for the issue is a principal user, as defined in paragraph (h)(1) of this section, of a facility financed by the proceeds of the issue, including a person who is related to a principal user. For purposes of the preceding sentence, a person shall be treated as related to a principal user only if that person is related to such user within the meaning of section 103(b)(6)(C) and paragraph (e) of this section at any time during the test period, and such user has not ceased to use the facility before the persons became related. See paragraph (h)(2)(iv) of this section for circumstances in which a person will be treated as ceasing to use a facility. A test-period beneficiary does not cease to be a test-period beneficiary if he ceases to use the facility; the portion of the issue allocated to the test-period beneficiary continues to be so allocated until the issue is no longer outstanding.

(ii) *Test period.*—The "test period" for an issue means the 3-year period beginning on the later of the date the facility financed by the proceeds of the issue is placed in service or the date of issue of such issue. A facility shall be considered as being placed in service at the time the facility is placed in a condition or state of readiness and availability for a specifically assigned function. If separate facilities are financed by an issue and the facilities are placed in service at different times, there shall be separate test periods for the portions of the issue financing each separate facility. If a single facility (consisting of separately depreciable items of property) is placed in service in stages, then the entire facility will be deemed placed in service when its last portion is placed in service.

(4) *Allocation of issue.*—(i) *In general.*—The portion of the amount of an issue allocated to a test-period beneficiary is the highest percent of the facility financed by proceeds of the issue that the beneficiary owned or used on a regular basis during the test period. For example, a person that owns the entire facility shall be allocated 100 percent of the issue; a person that leases 90 percent of a facility for two years of the test period and leases 35 percent for the third year shall be allocated 90 percent of the issue.

(ii) *Portion allocable to lessee and output purchaser.*—The portion of a facility used by a lessee is generally determined by reference to its fair rental value. The portion of a facility used by a principal output purchaser, as defined in paragraph (h)(1)(iii) of this section, is the highest portion of the facility's total output purchased by such purchaser during any of the three years of the test period.

(iii) *Portion allocable to related person.*—The portion of an issue allocable to a person who is a test-period beneficiary because he is related to a principal user is the same portion allocated to such principal user.

(iv) *Double allocation.*—The total amount of an issue allocated to test-period beneficiaries may exceed 100 percent of its outstanding face amount, such as when one test-period beneficiary is an owner and another person leases the facility for over a year. However, if a beneficiary is the owner of all or a portion of a facility that is leased to or otherwise used by such beneficiary or by a related person, then the portion of the issue the proceeds of which were used to finance the facility is allocated only once to the beneficiary. For example, if Corporation X owns an undivided 50 percent of a facility while related Corporation Y is the lessee of 60 percent of the facility, the portion of the issue financing the facility allocable to X is 80 percent (50 percent plus 30 percent), because one-half of the 60-percent portion used by Y (30 percent) is considered attributable to the portion owned by X.

(v) *Allocation of remainder of issue to owners.*—If the portion of an issue allocated to all test-period beneficiaries of the bond-financed facility (other than related persons) is less than 100 percent, the remainder shall be allocated to test-period beneficiaries who are owners of the facility in proportion to the amount of the issue otherwise allocable to such persons by reason of their ownership interests during the test period.

(vi) *Bond redeemed before person becomes principal user.*—If all or some of the outstanding principal amount of the issue in question or of prior bonds is redeemed other than from the proceeds of a refunding issue described in section 103(a) either before or as soon as reasonably practicable after a person becomes a test-period beneficiary with respect to the issue in question, but in no event later than 180 days after the date such person becomes a test-period beneficiary, then the amount of the issue so redeemed will not be allocated to such person (or to a related person) in determining whether the issue in question exceeds the $40 million limitation. With respect to obligations that are issued after August 20, 1986, paragraph (i)(4)(vi) shall not apply if the terms of the issue provide for a delay in redemption a principal purpose of which is to benefit from the 180-day period referred to therein. In the case of a person who becomes a test-period beneficiary before February 21, 1986, bonds redeemed before August 20, 1986, shall be considered redeemed as soon as reasonably practicable for purposes of the first sentence of this paragraph (i)(4)(vi) and the 180-day limitation referred to therein shall not apply.

(5) *Treatment of certain successors as test-period beneficiaries.*—If a corporation, partnership, or other entity which is a test-period beneficiary with respect to one or more issues transfers substantially all of its properties to another person (or to two or more related persons within the meaning of section 103(b)(6)(C)), or if a corporation acquires the assets of a test-period beneficiary in a transaction described in section 381(a), the transferee shall be treated as a test-period beneficiary with respect to such issues and shall be allocated the portion of such issues that were allocated to the transferor prior to the transfer. The preceding sentence shall not apply to the extent that it would result in double allocation of an issue, such as in the case of a transfer to a related person. This paragraph (i)(5) shall apply regardless of whether gain is required to be recognized by the transferor for Federal income tax purposes and regardless of whether the transferor remains in existence after the transfer. If the transferor remains in existence after the transfer, this paragraph (i)(5) shall not relieve the transferor of its allocation of any issue. This paragraph (i)(5) shall apply only for purposes of determining the tax exemption of issues of which the transferee becomes the test-period beneficiary after the transfer described herein.

(6) *Examples.*—The application of section 103(b)(15) and this paragraph (i) may be illustrated by the following examples:

Example (1). On September 1, 1986, City M issues a $9 million obligation to finance acquisition of a newly constructed shopping center that is placed in service on September 1, 1986, and is owned and managed by Corporation X. Half of the shopping center (determined by fair rental value) is leased for a term exceeding 1 year to Corporation Y. X owns 60 percent of the shares of Y. The other half of the shopping center (also determined by fair rental value) is leased in equal shares for a term exceeding 1 year to A and B, two unrelated corporations. As of September 1, 1986, $30 million of prior issues of obligations are outstanding and are allocable to X as a test-period beneficiary under the rules of §1.103-10(i)(4). As of that date there is no prior issue of obligations outstanding and allocable to Y, A, or B as test-period beneficiaries. Because X owns 100 percent of the shopping center, 100 percent of the 1986 issue ($9 million) is allocated to X. Therefore, for purposes of determining whether the 1986 issue exceeds the $40 million limitation of section 103(b)(15), the $30 million of outstanding prior issues must be added to the $9 million 1986 issue. Because Y leases 50 percent of the shopping center, 50 percent of the 1986 issue ($4.5 million) is allocated to Y. Although Y is related to X under section 103(b)(15)(E), the $4.5 million of the 1986 issue that is allocated to Y is not added to the $39 million allocated to X under paragraph (i)(4)(iv) of this section since such amount has already been allocated to X as owner of the shopping center. Because A and B each leases 25 percent of the shopping center, each is allocated 25 percent ($2.25 million) of the 1986 issue.

Example (2). The facts are the same as in *Example (1)* except that A owns a 60-percent interest in an airport hotel described in §1.103-8(e)(2)(ii)(*d*) and, because of such ownership interest, is allocated $15 million of prior outstanding obligations described in section 103(b)(4)(D). In addition, County N issues $25 million of obligations described in section 103(b)(4)(E) on October 1, 1986, to finance construction of a solid-waste disposal facility that will be owned by C, A's wholly-owned subsidiary corporation. In this case, with respect to the September 1, 1986, issue, A is allocated the $15 million prior issue that is outstanding with respect to A's share of the airport hotel bond and the $2.25 million that is A's allocable share of the September 1, 1986, issue for a total of $17.25 million. Because the solid-waste disposal facility bonds had not yet been issued when the September 1, 1986, obligation was issued, no portion of the $25 million of obligations to finance C's solid-waste disposal facility will be treated as part of A's allocable obligations with respect to the September 1, 1986, issue even though A and C are related persons. In addition, even though A and C are related persons and even though on the date of issue of the solid-waste disposal bonds C will be allocated more than $40 million of outstanding obligations for purposes of section 103(b)(15) (including A's $17.25 million of outstanding prior obligations), the $40 million limitation of section 103(b)(15) does not render the interest on the October 1, 1986, bonds taxable since the October 1, 1986, issue qualifies for tax exemption under section 103(b)(4), and the $40 million limitation of section 103(b)(15) does not apply to render taxable bonds issued under section 103(b)(4).

Example (3). On October 1, 1986, City K issues an $8 million issue of obligations exempt under section 103(b)(6) to finance acquisition of a newly-constructed manufacturing plant owned by Corporation L. On October 1, 1986, Corporation M has $35 million of prior outstanding obligations allocable to it under section 103(b)(15). On October 1, 1986, L has no prior outstanding obligations allocable to itself. On April 1, 1988, M acquires 100 percent of the stock of L, which still owns the plant financed by the 1986 issue. Since M and L became related to each other during the 3-year test period of the 1986 issue and L had not ceased to use the facility, the $8 million issue is allocated to M under section 103 (b)(15). This allocation causes the 1986 issue to exceed the $40 million limitation of section 103(b)(15) and the interest upon the issue to become taxable on and after October 1, 1986. However, if at least $3 million of the 1986 issue or of other issues allocated to M are redeemed as soon as reasonably practicable, and no later than 180 days after M's acquisition of L's stock, then the 1986 issue would not exceed the $40 million limitation.

Example (4). The facts are the same as in *Example (3)*, except the October 1, 1986, bonds were issued on January 1, 1985, the plant acquired with the proceeds of the issue was placed in service on January 1, 1985, and M had $39 million of prior outstanding obligations allocable to it on January 1, 1985. Because M and L became related to each other after the test period for the January 1, 1985, issue ended, M is not a test-period beneficiary, and the January 1, 1985, issue does not exceed the $40 million limitation of section 103(b)(15). However, if either M or L subsequently becomes a test-period beneficiary of an issue of obligations, then the outstanding principal amount of the January 1, 1985, issue and of the other issues allocable to M would be taken into account in applying the $40 million limitation to that issue.

Mortgage Subsidy Bonds

Interest on Mortgage Subsidy Bonds: Exemption.—Temporary Reg. §§6a.103A-1—6a.103A-3, relating to the exemption of interest on mortgage subsidy bonds, are also proposed as final regulations (published in the Federal Register on July 1, 1981). *NOTE: Code Sec. 103A has been repealed. Similar exempt bond issue rules have been provided in Code Secs. 141-150. These proposed regulations were issued under Code Sec. 103A as it read before amendment.*

§6a.103A-1. Interest on mortgage subsidy bonds.

§6a.103A-2. Qualified mortgage bond.

§6a.103A-3. Qualified veteran's mortgage bonds.

Mortgage Subsidy Bonds: Interest Exemption

Interest on Mortgage Subsidy Bonds: Exemption.—Amendments to Temporary Reg. §§6a.103A-1 and 6a.103A-2, relating to mortgage subsidy bonds, are also proposed as final regulations (published in the Federal Register on November 10, 1981). *NOTE: Code Sec. 103A has been repealed. Similar exempt bond issue rules have been provided in Code Secs. 141-150. These proposed regulations were issued under Code Sec. 103A as it read before amendment.*

§6a.103A-1. Interest on mortgage subsidy bonds.

§6a.103A-2. Qualified mortgage bond.

Mortgage Credit Certificates: Qualified Mortgage Bond

Mortgage Credit Certificates Issuance: Penalties.—An amendment to Temporary Reg. §6a.103A-2, relating to the issuance of mortgage credit certificates, is also proposed as final (published in the Federal Register on May 8, 1985). *NOTE: Code Sec. 103A has been repealed. Similar exempt bond issue rules have been provided in Code Secs. 141-150. This proposed amendment was issued under Code Sec. 103A as it read before amendment.*

§6a.103A-2. Qualified mortgage bond.

Imputed Interest: OID: Safe Haven Interest Rates

Imputed Interest: Original Issue Discount: Safe Haven Interest Rates.—Reproduced below is the text of a proposed amendment of Temporary Reg. §6a.103A-2, relating to (1) the tax treatment of debt instruments issued after July 1, 1982, that contain original issue discount, (2) the imputation of and the accounting for interest with respect to sales and exchanges of property occurring after December 31, 1984, and (3) safe haven interest rates for loans or advances between commonly controlled taxpayers and safe haven leases between such taxpayers (published in the Federal Register on April 8, 1986). *NOTE: Code Sec. 103A has been repealed. Similar exempt bond issue rules have been provided in Code Secs. 141-150. This proposed amendment was issued under Code Sec. 103A as it read before amendment.*

□ Par. 41. Paragraph (i)(2)(vi)(B) of §6a.103A-2 is amended by removing the phrase "section 1232(b)(2)" and adding in its place the phrase "section 1273(b)".

§6a.103A-2. Qualified mortgage bond.

Affiliated Service Groups

Employees' Trusts: Affiliated Service Groups.—Reproduced below is the text of a proposed amendment of Reg. §1.105-11, which prescribes rules for determining whether two or more separate service organizations constitute an affiliated group and which detail how certain requirements are satisfied by a qualified retirement plan maintained by a member of an affiliated service group (published in the Federal Register on February 28, 1983).

□ Paragraph 1. Paragraph (f) of section 1.105-11 is amended by striking out "section 414(b) and (c)" and inserting in lieu thereof "section 414(b), (c) or (m),"

§1.105-11. Self-insured medical reimbursement plan.

Sickness and Disability Payments: Group Health Plan

Business Expenses: Sickness and Disability Payments: Group Health Plan.—Reproduced below is the text of a proposed amendment of Reg. §1.106-1, relating to the requirement that a group health plan offer continuation coverage to people who would otherwise lose coverage as a result of certain events (published in the Federal Register on June 15, 1987).

☐ Par. 2. Section 1.106-1 is amended by redesignating the existing text as paragraph (a), revising the first sentence of paragraph (a), and adding a new paragraph (b). The revised and added provisions read as follows:

§1.106-1. Contributions by employer to accident and health plans.—(a) Except as set forth in paragraph (b) of this section, the gross income of an employee does not include contributions which his employer makes to an accident or health plan for compensation (through insurance or otherwise) to the employee for personal injuries or sickness incurred by him, his spouse, or his dependents, as defined in section 152. * * *

(b) In situations involving group health plans that do not comply with section 162(k), the exclusion described in paragraph (a) of this section is not available to highly compensated employees (as defined in section 414(q)). See §1.162-26 (regarding continuation coverage requirements of group health plans).

* * *

Scholarships

Exclusions: Scholarships: Payment for Services.—Reproduced below are the texts of proposed Reg. §§1.117-0 and 1.117-6 and proposed amendments of Reg. §§1.117-1—1.117-5, relating to the exclusion from gross income of qualified scholarships (published in the Federal Register on June 9, 1988).

☐ Par. 2. A new §1.117-0 is added to read as follows:

§1.117-0. Outline of regulations pertaining to scholarships and fellowship grants.—(a) *§1.117-1.*—Exclusion of amounts received as a scholarship or fellowship grant in taxable years beginning before 1987, but only in the case of scholarships and fellowships granted before August 17, 1986.

(b) *§1.117-2.*—Limitations applicable to taxable years beginning before 1987, but only in the case of scholarships and fellowships granted before August 17, 1986.

(c) *§1.117-3.*—Definitions applicable to taxable years beginning before 1987, but only in the case of scholarships and fellowships granted before August 17, 1986.

(d) *§1.117-4.*—Items not considered as scholarships or fellowship grants in taxable years beginning before 1987, but only in the case of scholarships and fellowships granted before August 17, 1986.

(e) *§1.117-5.*—Federal grants requiring future service as a federal employee pertaining to taxable years beginning before 1987, but only in the case of scholarships and fellowships granted before August 17, 1986.

(f) *§1.117-6.*—Qualified scholarships. [Reg. §1.117-0.]

☐ Par. 3. Section 1.117-1 is amended by revising the heading to read as set forth below, inserting "and before August 17, 1986," after "July 28, 1956," in the first sentence of paragraph (b)(2)(i), and adding a new paragraph (c) to read as follows:

§1.117-1. Exclusion of amounts received as a scholarship or fellowship grant in taxable years beginning before 1987, but only in the case of scholarships and fellowships granted before August 17, 1986.

* * *

(c) *Special rule; termination date; cross reference.*—For purposes of this section, all references to section 117 within this section are to section 117 as in effect prior to its amendment by the Tax Reform Act of 1986, unless otherwise indicated. This section does not apply to amounts granted after August 16, 1986, except to the extent that amounts granted after August 16, 1986, and before January 1, 1987, and received prior to January 1, 1987, are attributable to expenditures incurred before January 1, 1987. See §1.117-6(f) for rules relating to when a scholarship or fellowship is granted for purposes of section 117 as amended by the 1986 Act.

☐ Par. 4. Section 1.117-2 is amended by revising the heading to read as set forth below, inserting "and before August 17, 1986," after "December 31, 1961," in the first sentence of paragraph (b)(1)(iii), and adding a new paragraph (c) to read as follows:

§1.117-2. Limitations applicable to taxable years beginning before 1987, but only in the case of scholarships and fellowships granted before August 17, 1986.—

* * *

(c) *Special rule; termination date; cross reference.*—For purposes of this section, all references to section 117 within this section are to section 117 as in effect prior to its amendment by the Tax Reform Act of 1986, unless otherwise indicated. This section does not apply to amounts granted after August 16, 1986, except to the extent that amounts granted after August 16, 1986, and before January 1, 1987, and received prior to January 1, 1987, are attributable to expenditures incurred before January 1, 1987. See §1.117-6(f) for rules relating to when a scholarship or fellowship is granted for purposes of section 117 as amended by the 1986 Act.

☐ Par. 5. Section 1.117-3 is amended by revising the heading to read as set forth below, inserting "of the Internal Revenue Code of 1954" after "151(e)(4)" in the first sentence of paragraph (b), inserting "of the Internal Revenue Code of 1954" after "151(e)(4)" in the last sentence of paragraph (b), and adding a new paragraph (f) to read as follows:

§1.117-3. Definitions applicable to taxable years beginning before 1987, but only in the case of scholarships and fellowships granted before August 17, 1986.—

* * *

(f) *Special rule; termination date; cross reference.*—For purposes of this section, all references to section 117 within this section are to section 117 as in effect prior to its amendment by the Tax Reform Act of 1986, unless otherwise indicated. This section does not apply to amounts granted after August 16, 1986, except to the extent that amounts granted after August 16, 1986, and before January 1, 1987, and received prior to January 1, 1987, are attributable to expenditures incurred before January 1, 1987. See §1.117-6(f) for rules relating to when a scholarship or fellowship is granted for purposes of section 117 as amended by the 1986 Act.

☐ Par. 6. Section 1.117-4 is amended as follows: 1. the heading is revised as set forth below; 2. the first sentence is revised by inserting "(a) *Applicability.*" before "The"; 3. paragraphs (a), (b), and (c) are redesignated as paragraphs (1), (2), and (3); 4. paragraphs (1) and (2) of paragraph (3) as redesignated are redesignated as paragraphs (i) and (ii); 5. the second sentence of paragraph (3)(ii) as redesignated is amended by removing "subparagraph (1)" and adding in its place "subparagraph (i)"; and 6. a new paragraph (b) is added to read as set forth below.

§1.117-4. Items not considered as scholarships or fellowship grants in taxable years beginning before 1987, but only in the case of scholarships and fellowships granted before August 17, 1986.—

* * *

(b) *Special rule; termination date; cross reference.*—For purposes of this section, all references to section 117 within this section are to section 117 as in effect prior to its amendment by the Tax Reform Act of 1986, unless otherwise indicated. This section does not apply to amounts granted after August 16, 1986, except to the extent that amounts granted after August 16, 1986, and before January 1, 1987, and received prior to January 1, 1987, are attributable to expenditures incurred before January 1, 1987. See §1.117-6(f) for rules relating to when a scholarship or fellowship is granted for purposes of section 117 as amended by the 1986 Act.

☐ Par. 7. Section 1.117-5 is amended by revising the heading to read as set forth below, adding a second sentence to paragraph (f), and adding a new paragraph (g) to read as follows:

§1.117-5. Federal grants requiring future service as a federal employee pertaining to taxable years beginning before 1987, but only in the case of scholarships and fellowships granted before August 17, 1986.—

* * *

(f) *Effective date.*—* * * This section does not apply to amounts granted after August 16, 1986, except to the extent that amounts granted after August 16, 1986, and before January 1, 1987, and received prior to January 1, 1987, are attributable to expenditures incurred before January 1, 1987.

(g) *Special rule; cross reference.*—For purposes of this section, all references to section 117 within this section are to section 117 as in effect prior to its amendment by the Tax Reform Act of 1986, unless otherwise indicated. See §1.117-6(f) for rules relating to when a scholarship or fellowship is granted for purposes of section 117 as amended by the 1986 Act.

☐ Par. 8. A new §1.117-6 is added to read as follows:

§1.117-6. Qualified scholarships.—

(a) *Outline of provisions.*

(b) Exclusion of qualified scholarships.

(c) Definitions.

(1) Qualified scholarship.

(2) Qualified tuition and related expenses.

(3) Scholarship or fellowship grant.

(i) In general.

(ii) Items not considered as scholarships or fellowship grants.

(4) Candidate for a degree.

(5) Educational organization.

(6) Examples.

(d) Inclusion of qualified scholarships and qualified tuition reductions representing payment for services.

(1) In general.

(2) Payment for services.

(3) Determination of amount of scholarship or fellowship grant representing payment for services.

(4) Characterization of scholarship or fellowship grants representing payment for services for purposes of the reporting and withholding requirements.

(5) Examples.

(e) Recordkeeping requirements.

(f) Effective date.

(1) In general.

(2) When a scholarship or fellowship is granted.

(3) Scholarships or fellowships granted before August 17, 1986.

(i) In general.

(ii) Amounts received in subsequent academic periods that were not initially described as fixed cash amounts or readily determinable amounts.

(iii) Examples.

(4) Expenditures incurred before January 1, 1987.

(g) Reporting and withholding requirements.

(h) Characterization of scholarship or fellowship grants exceeding amounts permitted to be excluded from gross income for purposes of the standard deduction and filing requirements for dependents.

(b) *Exclusion of qualified scholarships.*—(1) Gross income does not include any amount received as a qualified scholarship by an individual who is a candidate for a degree at an educational organization described in section 170(b)(1)(A)(ii), subject to the rules set forth in paragraph (d) of this section. Generally, any amount of a scholarship or fellowship grant that is not excludable under section 117 is includable in the gross income of the recipient for the taxable year in which such amount is received, notwithstanding the provisions of section 102 (relating to exclusion from gross income of gifts). However, see section 127 and the regulations thereunder for rules permitting an exclusion from gross income for certain educational assistance payments. See also section 162 and the regulations thereunder for the deductibility as a trade or business expense of the educational expenses of an individual who is not a candidate for a degree.

(2) If the amount of a scholarship or fellowship grant eligible to be excluded as a qualified scholarship under this paragraph cannot be determined when the grant is received because expenditures for qualified tuition and related expenses have not yet been incurred, then that portion of any amount received as a scholarship or fellowship grant that is not used for qualified tuition and related expenses within the academic period to which the scholarship or fellowship grant applies must be included in the gross income of the recipient for the taxable year in which such academic period ends.

(c) *Definitions.*—(1) *Qualified scholarship.*—For purposes of this section, a qualified scholarship is any amount received by an individual as a scholarship or fellowship grant (as defined in paragraph (c)(3) of this section), to the extent the individual establishes that, in accordance with the conditions of the grant, such amount was used for qualified tuition and related expenses (as defined in paragraph (c)(2) of this section). To be considered a qualified scholarship, the terms of the scholarship or fellowship grant need not expressly require that the amounts received be used for tuition and related expenses. However, to the extent that the terms of the grant specify that any portion of the grant cannot be used for tuition and related expenses or designate any portion of the grant for purposes other than tuition and related expenses (such as for room and board, or for a meal allowance), such amounts are not amounts received as a qualified scholarship. See paragraph (e) of this section for rules relating to recordkeeping requirements for establishing amounts used for qualified tuition and related expenses.

(2) *Qualified tuition and related expenses.*—For purposes of this section, qualified tuition and related expenses are—

(i) Tuition and fees required for the enrollment or attendance of a student at an educational organization described in section 170(b)(1)(A)(ii); and

(ii) Fees, books, supplies, and equipment required for courses of instruction at such an educational organization.

In order to be treated as related expenses under this section, the fees, books, supplies, and equipment must be required of all students in the particular course of instruction. Incidental expenses are not considered related expenses. Incidental expenses include expenses incurred for room and board, travel, research, clerical help, and equipment and other expenses that are not required for either enrollment or attendance at an educational organization, or in a course of instruction at such educational organization. See paragraph (c)(6), Example (1) of this section.

(3) *Scholarship or fellowship grant.*—(i) *In general.*—Generally, a scholarship or fellowship grant is a cash amount paid or allowed to, or for the benefit of, an individual to aid such individual in the pursuit of study or research. A scholarship or fellowship grant also may be in the form of a reduction in the amount owed by the recipient to an educational organization for tuition, room and board, or any other fee. A scholarship or fellowship grant may be funded by a governmental agency, college or university, charitable organization, business, or any other source. To be considered a scholarship or fellowship grant for purposes of this section, any amount received need not be formally designated as a scholarship. For example, an "allowance" is treated as a scholarship if it meets the definition set forth in this paragraph. However, a scholarship or fellowship grant does not include any amount provided by an individual to aid a relative, friend, or other individual in the pursuit of study or research if the grantor is motivated by family or philanthropic considerations.

(ii) *Items not considered as scholarships or fellowship grants.*—The following payments or allowances are not considered to be amounts received as a scholarship or fellowship grant for purposes of section 117:

(A) Educational and training allowances to a veteran pursuant to section 400 of the Servicemen's Readjustment Act of 1944 (58 Stat. 287) or pursuant to 38 U.S.C. 1631 (formerly section 231 of the Veterans' Readjustment Assistance Act of 1952).

(B) Tuition and subsistence allowances to members of the Armed Forces of the United States who are students at an educational institution operated by the United States or approved by the United States for their education and training, such as the United States Naval Academy and the United States Military Academy.

(4) *Candidate for a degree.*—For purposes of this section, a candidate for a degree is—

(i) A primary or secondary school student;

(ii) An undergraduate or graduate student at a college or university who is pursuing studies or conducting research to meet the requirement for an academic or professional degree; or

(iii) A full-time or part-time student at an educational organization described in section 170(b)(1)(A)(ii) that—

(A) Provides an educational program that is acceptable for full credit towards a bachelor's or higher degree, or offers a program of training to prepare students for gainful employment in a recognized occupation, and

(B) Is authorized under Federal or State law to provide such a program and is accredited by a nationally recognized accreditation agency.

The student may pursue studies or conduct research at an educational organization other than the one conferring the degree provided that such study or research meets the requirements of the educational organization granting the degree. See paragraph (c)(6), Examples (2) and (3) of this section.

(5) *Educational organization.*—For purposes of this section, an educational organization is an organization described under section 170(b)(1)(A)(ii) and the regulations thereunder. An educational organization is described in section 170(b)(1)(A)(ii) if it has as its primary function the presentation of formal instruction, and it normally maintains a regular faculty and curriculum and normally has a regularly enrolled body of pupils or students in attendance at the place where its educational activities are regularly carried on. See paragraph (c)(6), Example (4) of this section.

(6) *Examples.*—The provisions of this paragraph may be illustrated by the following examples:

Example (1). On September 1, 1987, A receives a scholarship from University U for academic year 1987-1988. A is enrolled in a writing course at U. Suggested supplies for the writing course in which A is enrolled include a word processor, but students in the course are not required to obtain a word processor. Any amount used for suggested supplies is not an amount used for qualified tuition and related expenses for purposes of this section. Thus, A may not include the cost of a word processor in determining the amount received by A as a qualified scholarship.

Example (2). B is a scholarship student during academic year 1987-1988 at Technical School V located in State W. B is enrolled in a program to train individuals to become data processors. V is authorized by State W to provide this program and is accredited by an appropriate accreditation agency. B is a candidate for a degree for purposes of this section. Thus, B may exclude from gross income any amount received as a qualified scholarship, subject to the rules set forth in paragraph (d) of this section.

Example (3). C holds a Ph.D. in chemistry. On January 31, 1988, Foundation X awards C a fellowship. During 1988 C pursues chemistry research at Research Foundation Y, supported by the fellowship grant from X. C is not an employee of either foundation. C is not a candidate for a degree for purposes of this section. Thus, the fellowship grant from X must be included in C's gross income.

Example (4). On July 1, 1987, D receives a $500 scholarship to take a correspondence course from School Z. D receives and returns all lessons to Z through the mail. No students are in attendance at Z's place of business. D is not attending an educational organization described in section 170(b)(1)(A)(ii) for purposes of this section. Thus, the $500 scholarship must be included in D's gross income.

(d) *Inclusion of qualified scholarships and qualified tuition reductions representing payment for services.*—(1) *In general.*—The exclusion from gross income under this section does not apply to that portion of any amount received as a qualified scholarship or qualified tuition reduction (as defined under section 117(d)) that represents payment for teaching, research, or other services by the student required as a condition to receiving the qualified scholarship or qualified tuition reduction, regardless of whether all candidates for the degree are required to perform such services. The provisions of this paragraph (d) apply not only to cash amounts received in return for such services, but also to amounts by which the tuition or related expenses of the person who performs services are reduced, whether or not pursuant to a tuition reduction plan described in section 117(d).

(2) *Payment for services.*—For purposes of this section, a scholarship or fellowship grant represents payment for services when the grantor requires the recipient to perform services in return for the granting of the scholarship or fellowship. A requirement that the recipient pursue studies, research, or other activities primarily for the benefit of the grantor is treated as a requirement to perform services. A requirement that a recipient furnish periodic reports to the grantor for the purpose of keeping the grantor informed as to the general progress of the individual, however, does not constitute the performance of services. A scholarship or fellowship grant conditioned upon either past, present, or future teaching, research, or other services by the recipient represents payment for services under this section. See paragraph (d)(5), Examples (1), (2), (3) and (4) of this section.

(3) *Determination of amount of scholarship or fellowship grant representing payment for services.*—If only a portion of a scholarship or fellowship grant represents payment for services, the grantor must determine the amount of the scholarship or fellowship grant (including any reduction in tuition or related expenses) to be allocated to payment for services. Factors to be taken into account in making this allocation include, but are not limited to, compensation paid by—

(i) The grantor for similar services performed by students with qualifications comparable to those of the scholarship recipient, but who do not receive scholarship or fellowship grants;

(ii) The grantor for similar services performed by full-time or part-time employees of the grantor who are not students; and

(iii) Educational organizations, other than the grantor of the scholarship or fellowship, for similar services performed either by students or other employees.

If the recipient includes in gross income the amount allocated by the grantor to payment for services and such amount represents reasonable compensation for those services, then any additional amount of a scholarship or fellowship grant received from the same grantor that meets the requirements of paragraph (b) of this section is excludable from gross income. See paragraph (d)(5), Examples (5) and (6) of this section.

(4) *Characterization of scholarship or fellowship grants representing payment for services for purposes of the reporting and withholding requirements.*—Any amount of a scholarship or fellowship grant that represents payment for services (as defined in paragraph (d)(2) of this section) is considered wages for purposes of sections 3401 and 3402 (relating to withholding for income taxes), section 6041 (relating to returns of information), and section 6051 (relating

to reporting wages of employees). The application of sections 3101 and 3111 (relating to the Federal Insurance Contributions Act (FICA)), or section 3301 (relating to the Federal Unemployment Tax Act (FUTA)) depends upon the nature of the employment and the status of the organization. See sections 3121(b), 3306(c), and the regulations thereunder.

(5) *Examples.*—The provisions of this paragraph may be illustrated by the following examples:

Example (1). On November 15, 1987, A receives a $5,000 qualified scholarship (as defined in paragraph (c)(1) of this section) for academic year 1988-1989 under a federal program requiring A's future service as a federal employee. The $5,000 scholarship represents payment for services for purposes of this section. Thus, the $5,000 must be included in A's gross income as wages.

Example (2). B receives a $10,000 scholarship from V Corporation on June 4, 1987, for academic year 1987-1988. As a condition to receiving the scholarship, B agrees to work for V after graduation. B has no previous relationship with V. The $10,000 scholarship represents payment for future services for purposes of this section. Thus, the $10,000 scholarship must be included in B's gross income as wages.

Example (3). On March 15, 1987, C is awarded a fellowship for academic year 1987-1988 to pursue a research project the nature of which is determined by the grantor, University W. C must submit a paper to W that describes the research results. The paper does not fulfill any course requirements. Under the terms of the grant, W may publish C's results, or otherwise use the results of C's research. C is treated as performing services for W. Thus, C's fellowship from W represents payment for services and must be included in C's gross income as wages.

Example (4). On September 27, 1987, D receives a qualified scholarship (as defined in paragraph (c)(1) of this section) from University X for academic year 1987-1988. As a condition to receiving the scholarship, D performs services as a teaching assistant for X. Such services are required of all candidates for a degree at X. The amount of D's scholarship from X is equal to the compensation paid by X to teaching assistants who are part-time employees and not students at X. D's scholarship from X represents payment for services. Thus, the entire amount of D's scholarship from X must be included in D's gross income as wages.

Example (5). On June 11, 1987, E receives a $6,000 scholarship for academic year 1987-1988 from University Y. As a condition to receiving the scholarship, E performs services as a researcher for Y. Other researchers who are not scholarship recipients receive $2,000 for similar services for the year. Therefore, Y allocates $2,000 of the scholarship amount to compensation for services performed by E. Thus, the portion of the scholarship that represents payment for services, $2,000, must be included in E's gross income as wages. However, if E establishes expenditures of $4,000 for qualified tuition and related expenses (as defined in paragraph (c)(2) of this section), then $4,000 of E's scholarship is excludable from E's gross income as a qualified scholarship.

Example (6). During 1987 F is employed as a research assistant to a faculty member at University Z. F receives a salary from Z that represents reasonable compensation for the position of research assistant. In addition to salary, F receives from Z a qualified tuition reduction (as defined in section 117(d)) to be used to enroll in an undergraduate course at Z. F includes the salary in gross income. Thus, the qualified tuition reduction does not represent payment for services and therefore, is not includable in F's gross income.

(e) *Recordkeeping requirements.*—In order to be eligible to exclude from gross income any amount received as a qualified scholarship (as defined in paragraph (c)(1) of this section), the recipient must maintain records that establish amounts used for qualified tuition and related expenses (as defined in paragraph (c)(2) of this section) as well as the total amount of qualified tuition and related expenses. Such amounts may be established by providing to the Service, upon request, copies of relevant bills, receipts, cancelled checks, or other documentation or records that clearly reflect the use of the money. The recipient must also submit, upon request, documentation that establishes receipt of the grant, notification date of the grant, and the conditions and requirements of the particular grant. Subject to the rules set forth in paragraph (d) of this section, qualified scholarship amounts are excludable without the need to trace particular grant dollars to particular expenditures for qualified tuition and related expenses.

(f) *Effective date.*—(1) *In general.*—The rules of this section generally apply to taxable years beginning on or after January 1, 1987. However, section 117, as in effect prior to its amendment by the Tax Reform Act of 1986 (1986 Act), continues to apply to scholarships and fellowships granted before August 17, 1986, whenever received. In addition, section 117, as in effect prior to its amendment by the 1986 Act, applies in the case of scholarships and fellowships granted after August 16, 1986, and before January 1, 1987, to the extent of any amount received prior to January 1, 1987, that is attributable to expenditures incurred before January 1, 1987.

(2) *When a scholarship or fellowship is granted.*—For purposes of this section, a scholarship or fellowship is granted when the grantor either notifies the recipient of the award or notifies an organization or institution acting on behalf of a specified recipient of the award to be provided to such recipient. If the notification is sent by mail, notification occurs as of the date the notice is postmarked. If evidence of a postmark does not exist, the date on the award letter is treated as the notification date.

(3) *Scholarships or fellowships granted before August 17, 1986.*—(i) *In general.*—For purposes of this section, a scholarship or fellowship is considered granted before August 17, 1986, to the extent that, in a notice of award made before that date, the grantor made a firm commitment to provide the recipient with a fixed cash amount or a readily determinable amount. A notice of award is treated as containing a firm commitment even if the scholarship or fellowship grant is subject to a condition that the recipient remain in good standing or maintain a specific grade point average. In addition, a requirement that the recipient file a financial statement on an an-

nual basis to show continuing financial need is not treated as a requirement to reapply to the grantor. If a scholarship or fellowship, initially awarded before August 17, 1986, is granted for a period exceeding one academic period (for example, a semester), amounts received in subsequent academic periods are treated as granted before August 17, 1986, only if—

(A) The amount awarded for the first academic period is described in the original notice of award as a fixed cash amount or readily determinable amount;

(B) The original notice of award contains a firm commitment by the grantor to provide the scholarship or fellowship grant for more than one academic period; and

(C) The recipient is not required to reapply to the grantor in order to receive the scholarship or fellowship grant in future academic periods.

Scholarship or fellowship amounts treated as granted before August 17, 1986, must be applied against qualified tuition and related expenses before any amount of a scholarship or fellowship treated as granted after August 16, 1986, may be eligible for exclusion as a qualified scholarship.

(ii) *Amounts received in subsequent academic periods that were not initially described as fixed cash amounts or readily determinable amounts.*—If the notice of award of a scholarship or fellowship grant satisfies the requirements of paragraph (f)(3)(i) of this section but does not describe the amount to be received in subsequent academic periods as either a fixed cash amount or readily determinable amount, then the amount received in each subsequent academic period that is treated as granted before August 17, 1986, may not exceed the amount granted for the initial academic period. To the extent that any amount received in a subsequent academic period, under the same notice of award, exceeds the amount received in the initial academic period, the excess amount is treated as a scholarship or fellowship granted after August 16, 1986.

(iii) *Examples.*—The provisions of this paragraph may be illustrated by the following examples:

Example (1). On January 7, 1985, A receives a notice of award under a federal program of a $500 scholarship for the academic period Spring 1985. A receives the $500 in February 1988. For purposes of this section the $500 scholarship is granted before August 17, 1986, and thus is subject to section 117 prior to its amendment by the 1986 Act.

Example (2). On May 7, 1986, B receives a notice of award of a scholarship in the amount of $4,000 annually for four years. The total amount of this scholarship is a fixed cash amount. Thus, $16,000, the total amount of the scholarship for all four years, is subject to section 117 prior to its amendment by the 1986 Act.

Example (3). On May 7, 1986, C is notified of the award of the Y scholarship that will pay for C's tuition, room, and board for four years. The total amount of the Y scholarship is readily determinable. Thus, the total amount of the Y scholarship for all four years is subject to section 117 prior to its amendment by the 1986 Act.

Example (4). On May 7, 1986, D is notified that she is the recipient of a scholarship to attend University Z. The scholarship is not conditioned upon the performance of services by D. The notice provides that Z will award scholarship funds for four years and specifies that D will receive $5,000 during the first year. D is not required to reapply in order to receive scholarship funds during years 2 through 4. However, the notice does not specify the scholarship funds to be received in years 2 through 4. The $5,000 received in year 1 is treated as granted before August 17, 1986, because this amount is a fixed cash amount described in the notice of award. In addition, because Z has made a specific commitment to provide scholarship funds during years 2 through 4 without requiring D to reapply for the scholarship, an amount from Z not exceeding $5,000 per year is treated as granted before August 17, 1986, during years 2 through 4. Thus, if D receives $4,000 from Z in year 2, the entire $4,000 is treated as granted before August 17, 1986. If, in year 3, D receives $6,000 from Z, only $5,000 of the amount received is treated as granted before August 17, 1986. The additional $1,000 received in year 3 is treated as granted after August 16, 1986. Whether this additional $1,000 is excludable from D's gross income depends upon the amount of qualified tuition and related expenses (as defined in paragraph (c)(2) of this section) incurred by D in year 3. Thus, if D's qualified tuition and related expenses for year 3 are $6,000, the entire $6,000 is excludable from D's gross income.

Example (5). Assume the same facts as in Example (4) except that D's qualified tuition and related expenses in year 3 are $5,500. D excludes the $5,000 that is treated as granted before August 17, 1986. However, this $5,000 must be applied against the total qualified tuition and related expenses of $5,500 owed by D for year 3 before any amount received from a scholarship or fellowship granted after August 16, 1986, may be excluded. The additional $1,000 received by D that is treated as granted after August 16, 1986, is excludable to the extent of $500, the amount by which qualified tuition and related expenses exceed the amount that is treated as granted before August 17, 1986. The remaining $500 scholarship amount must be included in D's gross income.

Example (6). Assume the same facts as in Example (4) except that D's qualified tuition and related expenses for year 3 are $5,000. The amount of D's qualified tuition and related expenses for year 3 is equal to the scholarship amount from Z treated as granted before August 17, 1986. Thus, no part of the $1,000 treated as granted after August 16, 1986, is excludable from D's gross income.

(4) *Expenditures incurred before January 1, 1987.*—In the case of scholarships and fellowships granted after August 16, 1986, and before January 1, 1987, amounts received prior to January 1, 1987, that are attributable to expenditures incurred prior to January 1, 1987, are subject to section 117 as in effect prior to its amendment by the 1986 Act. For purposes of this section, an expenditure is incurred when it becomes properly due and payable by the recipient. However, expenditures relating to an academic period beginning after December 31, 1986, paid by the recipient before January 1, 1987, prior to the time when the recipient is billed for such expenditures, are not treated as expenditures incurred

before January 1, 1987. Thus, if in December 1986 an educational organization billed a scholarship recipient for expenses relating to the academic period beginning in January 1987, and the recipient used scholarship amounts received prior to January 1, 1987, to pay the expenses on January 5, 1987, the scholarship amounts used to pay such expenses are considered attributable to expenditures incurred prior to January 1, 1987. If, however, on December 31, 1986, a scholarship recipient used scholarship amounts to pay expenses relating to the academic period beginning in January 1987, before the recipient was billed for such expenses, the amounts used are not treated as attributable to expenditures incurred before January 1, 1987.

(g) *Reporting and withholding requirements.*—For return of information requirements, see sections 6041, 6051, and the regulations thereunder. For withholding from scholarships or fellowship grants representing payment for services, see sections 3401, 3402, and the regulations thereunder. For withholding from scholarships or fellowship grants of nonresident aliens, see section 1441 and the regulations thereunder. For the application of FICA, see sections 3101 and 3111. For the application of FUTA, see section 3301.

(h) *Characterization of scholarship or fellowship grants exceeding amounts permitted to be excluded from gross income for purposes of the standard deduction and filing requirements for dependents.*—For purposes of section 63(c)(5) (relating to the standard deduction for dependents) and section 6012(a)(1)(C)(i) (relating to dependents required to make returns of income), any amount of a scholarship or fellowship grant in excess of the amount permitted to be excluded from gross income under paragraph (b) of this section is considered earned income. For example, on June 11, 1987, A, a student who has no other earned or unearned income for the year and can be claimed as a dependent on another taxpayer's return of tax, receives a $1,000 scholarship for room and board. The $1,000 must be included in A's gross income because it is not a qualified scholarship under paragraph (b) of this section. However, for purposes of sections 63(c)(5) and 6012(a)(1)(C)(i), the $1,000 is earned income. Accordingly, A is not required to file a return of tax for 1987 because A's gross income ($1,000) does not exceed A's standard deduction ($1,000) and A has no unearned income. [Reg. § 1.117-6.]

Qualified Group Legal Services Plans

Qualified Group Legal Services Plans.—Reproduced below are the texts of proposed Reg. §§ 1.120-1 and 1.120-2, relating to qualified group legal services plans (published in the Federal Register on April 29, 1980).

☐ Par. 2. New §§ 1.120-1 and 1.120-2 are added to the appropriate place:

§ 1.120-1. Amounts received under a qualified group legal services plan.—(a) *Exclusion from gross income.*—The gross income of an employee, or the employee's spouse or dependent, does not include—

(1) Amounts contributed by an employer on behalf of the employee, spouse or dependent under a qualified group legal services plan described in § 1.120-2,

(2) The value of legal services provided the employee, spouse or dependent under the plan, or

(3) Amounts paid to the employee, spouse or dependent under the plan as reimbursement for the cost of personal legal services provided to the employee, spouse or dependent.

(b) *Definitions.*—For rules relating to the meaning of the terms "employee," "employer," "spouse," and "dependent" see paragraph (d)(3) and (4) and paragraph (i) of § 1.120-2.

(c) *Effective date.*—This section is effective with respect to employer contributions made on behalf of, and legal services provided to, an employee, spouse or dependent on or after the first day of the period of plan qualification (as determined under § 1.120-3(d)) and in taxable years of the employee, spouse or dependent beginning after December 31, 1976, and ending before January 1, 1982. [Reg. § 1.120-1.]

§ 1.120-2. Qualified group legal services plan.—(a) *In general.*—In general, a qualified group legal services plan is a plan established and maintained by an employer under which the employer provides employees, or their spouses or dependents, personal legal services by prepaying, or providing in advance for, all or part of the legal fees for the services. To be a qualified plan, the plan must satisfy the requirements described in paragraphs (b) through (h) of this section and be recognized as a qualified plan by the Internal Revenue Service. Section 1.120-3 provides rules under which a plan must apply to the Internal Revenue Service for recognition as a qualified plan.

(b) *Separate written plan.*—The plan must be a separate written plan of the employer. For purposes of this section—

(1) *Plan.*—The term "plan" implies a permanent as distinguished from a temporary program. Thus, although the employer may reserve the right to change or terminate the plan, and to discontinue contributions thereunder, the abandonment of the plan for any reason other than a business necessity soon after it has taken effect will be evidence that the plan from its inception was not a *bona fide* plan for the benefit of employees generally (see paragraph (d) of this section). Such evidence will be given special weight if, for example, a plan is abandoned soon after extensive benefits are provided to persons with respect to whom discrimination in plan benefits is prohibited (see paragraph (e) of this section).

(2) *Separate plan.*—The requirement that the plan be a separate plan means that the plan may not provide benefits which are not personal legal services within the meaning of paragraph (c) of this section. For example, the requirement for a separate plan is not satisfied if personal legal services are provided under an employee benefit plan that also provides pension, disability, life insurance, medical or other such nonlegal benefits. The requirement for a separate plan does not, however, preclude a single plan from being adopted by more than one employer.

(c) *Personal legal services.*—(1) *In general.*—In general, benefits under the plan must consist of, or be provided with respect to, only personal legal services that are specified in the plan. The plan must specifically prohibit a diversion or use of any funds of the plan for purposes other than the providing of personal legal services for the participants. In general, a personal legal service is a legal service (within the meaning of subparagraph (3) of this paragraph) provided to a participant employee, spouse or dependent which is not directly connected with or pertaining to—

(i) A trade or business of the employee, spouse or dependent,

(ii) The management, conservation or preservation of property held by the employee, spouse or dependent for the production of income, or

(iii) The production or collection of income by the employee, spouse or dependent.

(2) *Certain personal legal services.*—Notwithstanding subparagraph (1)(ii) and (iii) of this paragraph, the following (if legal services within the meaning of subparagraph (3)) are considered personal legal services—

(i) A legal service provided to a participant with respect to securing, increasing or collecting alimony under a decree of divorce (or payments in lieu of alimony) or the division or redivision of community property under the community property laws of a State,

(ii) A legal service provided to a participant as heir or legatee of a decedent, or as beneficiary under a testamentary trust, in protecting or asserting rights to property of a decedent, or

(iii) A legal service provided to a participant with respect to the participant's claim for damages, other than compensatory damages, for personal injury.

(3) *Legal services.*—(i) *Services of a lawyer.*—In general, a legal service is a service performed by a lawyer if the performing of the service constitutes the practice of law.

(ii) *Services of a person not a lawyer.*—A legal service may include a service performed by a person who is not a lawyer, if the service is performed under the direction or control of a lawyer, in connection with a legal service (within the meaning of subdivision (i)) performed by the lawyer, and the fee for the service is included in the legal fee of the lawyer. Examples of services to which this subdivision (ii) may apply are the services of an accountant, a researcher, a paralegal, a law clerk, an investigator or a searcher of title to real property.

(iii) *Court fees.*—Amounts payable to a court in connection with the presentation, litigation or appeal from a matter before a court is considered the cost of a legal service. For example, benefits under the plan may be provided with respect to a court filing fee, a fee for service of summons or other process, the cost of a transcript of trial or the posting of bail bond.

(iv) *Other fees or charges.*—An amount payable to a competent governmental authority (for example, the United States, a State or any subdivision thereof) is considered the cost of a legal service, if the amount is payable with respect to the filing or registration of a legal document (for example, a deed or will). However, any amount payable directly or indirectly to a governmental authority is not the cost of a legal service, if the amount is in the nature of a tax. For example, although a plan may provide for payment of an amount payable to a county for the filing or registration of a deed to real property, a plan may not provide for payment of an amount in the nature of a tax on the transfer of title to real property.

(4) *Limited initial consultation.*—A plan is not other than a qualified plan merely because, in connection with providing personal legal services, the plan provides a specified "limited initial consultation" benefit without restricting the benefit to personal legal services. An "initial consultation" is a consultation, the purpose of which is to determine whether a plan participant is in need of a personal legal service and, if so, whether the required personal legal service may be provided under the plan. An initial consultation must not include document preparation or review, or representation of the participant. An initial consultation benefit is "limited", if under the plan it is limited either in time (*e. g.*, no more than 4 hours of initial consultation during any year) or number (*e. g.*, no more than 4 initial consultations during any year).

(d) *Exclusive benefit.*—(1) *In general.*—The plan must benefit only employees of the employer, including individuals who are employees within the meaning of paragraph (i)(1) of this section, or the spouses or dependents of employees.

(2) *Plans to which more than one employer contributes.*—In the case of a plan to which more than one employer contributes, in determining whether the plan is for the exclusive benefit of an employer's employees, or their spouses or dependents, the employees of any employer who maintains the plan are considered the employees of each employer who maintains the plan.

(3) *Spouses of employees.*—In general, for purposes of determining whether a plan is for the exclusive benefit of an employer's employees, or their spouses or dependents, the determination of whether an individual is a spouse of an employee is made at the time the legal services are provided to the individual. The term "spouse" includes a surviving spouse of a deceased employee. Although, in general, the term "spouse" does not include a person legally separated from an employee under a decree of divorce or separate maintenance, a legal service provided to an employee's former spouse after the issuing of a decree of divorce, annulment or separate maintenance from the employee is considered a service provided to the spouse of an employee, if the service relates to the divorce, annulment or separation. For purposes of this section and § 1.120-1, the term "spouse" includes an individual to whom benefits may be provided under this subparagraph.

(4) *Dependents of employees.*—For purposes of determining whether a plan is for the exclusive benefit of an employer's employees, or their spouses or dependents, benefits provided to the following individuals are considered benefits provided to a dependent of an employee:

(i) An individual who is a dependent of an employee within the meaning of section 152 for the taxable year of the employee within which the legal services are provided to the individual;

(ii) An individual who is described in paragraph (h)(2) of this section (relating to certain surviving dependents) at the time the legal services are provided to the individual; or

(iii) An individual who is a dependent of an employee within the meaning of section 152 for the taxable year of the employee ending on the date of the employee's death, under age 21 on the date of the employee's death, and under age 21 at the time the legal services are provided to the individual.

For purposes of this section and §1.120-1, the term "dependent" means an individual to whom benefits may be provided under this subparagraph.

(5) *Estates of employees.*—A plan is for the exclusive benefit of the employer's employees, or their spouses or dependents, notwithstanding that the plan provides benefits to the personal representative of a deceased employee, or spouse or dependent, with respect to the estate of the deceased.

(e) *Prohibited discrimination.*—(1) *In general.*—The plan must benefit the employer's employees generally. Among those benefited may be employees who are officers, shareholders, self-employed or highly compensated. A plan is not for the benefit of employees generally, however, if the plan discriminates in favor of employees described in the preceding sentence, or their spouses or dependents, in eligibility requirements (see subparagraph (2) of this paragraph) or in contributions or benefits (see subparagraph (3) of this paragraph).

(2) *Eligibility to participate.*—A plan need not provide benefits for all employees (or their spouses or dependents). A plan must, however, benefit those employees (or their spouses or dependents) who qualify under a classification of employees set up by the employer which is found by the Internal Revenue Service not to discriminate in favor of employees who are officers, shareholders, self-employed or highly compensated, or their spouses or dependents. In general, this determination shall be made by applying the same standards as are applied under section 410(b)(1)(B) (relating to qualified pension, profit-sharing and stock bonus plans), without regard to section 401(a)(5). For purposes of making this determination, there shall be excluded from consideration employees not covered by the plan who are included in a unit of employees covered by an agreement which the Secretary of Labor finds to be a collective bargaining agreement between employee representatives and one or more employers, if the Internal Revenue Service finds that group legal services plan benefits were the subject of good faith bargaining between the employee representatives and the employer or employers. For purposes of determining whether such bargaining occurred, it is not material that the employees are not covered by another plan or that the employer's present plan was not considered in the bargaining.

(3) *Contributions and benefits.*—(i) *In general.*—Employer contributions under the plan or benefits provided under the plan must not discriminate in favor of employees who are officers, shareholders, self-employed or highly compensated, or their spouses or dependents, as against other employees, or their spouses or dependents, covered by the plan. This does not mean that contributions or benefits may not vary. Variations in contributions or benefits may be provided so long as the plan, viewed as a whole for the benefit of employees in general, with all its attendant circumstances, does not discriminate in favor of those with respect to whom discrimination is prohibited. Thus, contributions or benefits which vary by reason of a formula which takes into account years of service with the employer, or other factors, are not prohibited unless those factors discriminate in favor of employees who are officers, shareholders, self-employed or highly compensated, or their spouses or dependents. Under this subparagraph (3), if a plan covers employees who are highly compensated, and benefits under the plan uniformly increase as compensation increases, the plan is not a qualified plan.

(ii) *Relative utilization of plan benefits.*—Not only must a plan not discriminate on its face in employer contributions or plan benefits in favor of employees who are officers, shareholders, self-employed or highly compensated, or their spouses or dependents, the plan also must not discriminate in favor of such employees, or their spouses or dependents, in actual operation. Accordingly, the extent to which such employees, or their spouses or dependents, as a group, utilize plan benefits must be compared to the extent to which all other employees, or their spouses or dependents, as a group, utilize plan benefits. A plan is not other than a qualified plan for a plan year merely because, relative to their number, those employees, or their spouses or dependents, with respect to whom discrimination is prohibited utilize plan benefits to a greater extent than do other employees, or their spouses or dependents. However, a persistent pattern of greater relative utilization of plan benefits by the group of employees who are officers, shareholders, self-employed or highly compensated, or their spouses or dependents, may be evidence that the plan discriminates in favor of such employees and is not for the benefit of employees generally. Such evidence will be considered, together with all other pertinent facts and circumstances, to determine whether the plan improperly discriminates in actual operation.

(f) *Contribution limitation.*—(1) *In general.*—Under section 120(c)(3), a plan is a qualified plan for a plan year only if no more than 25% of the amount contributed by the employer under the plan for the plan year is contributed on behalf of the limitation class described in subparagraph (2). A plan satisfies the requirements of section 120(c)(3) for a plan year (as determined under the plan) if either—

(i) The plan satisfies the requirements of subparagraph (3), or

(ii) The percentage determined under subparagraph (4) is 25% or less, and the plan is not other than a qualified plan by reason of subparagraph (5).

(2) *Limitation class.*—The limitation class consists of—

(i) *Shareholders.*—Individuals who, on any day of the plan year, own more than 5% of the total number of shares of outstanding stock of the employer, or

(ii) *Owners.*—In the case of an employer's trade or business which is not incorporated, individuals who on any day of the plan year, own more than 5% of the capital or profits interest in the employer, and

(iii) *Spouses and dependents.*—Individuals who are spouses or dependents of shareholders or owners described in subdivisions (i) and (ii).

For purposes of determining stock ownership, the attribution rules described in paragraph (i)(4) of this section apply. The regulations prescribed under section 414(c) are applicable in determining an individual's interest in the capital or profits of an unincorporated trade or business.

(3) *Disregarding allocation rules.*—(i) *Plans providing legal services directly.*—If a plan is one under which legal services are provided directly to a participant, the plan will satisfy the requirements of section 120(c)(3), without regard to the allocation rules described in subparagraphs (4) and (5) of this paragraph, if the plan satisfies the following requirement. The plan must provide and be operated so that no legal service may be provided to a member of the limitation class if to provide the service would cause the fair market value of legal services provided to date during the plan year to members of the limitation class to exceed 25% of the fair market value of the legal services provided under the plan to date during the plan year.

(ii) *Plans providing reimbursement for the cost of legal services.*—If a plan is one under which a participant is reimbursed for the cost of legal services, the plan will satisfy the requirements of section 120(c)(3), without regard to the allocation rules described in subparagraphs (4) and (5) of this paragraph, if the plan satisfies the following requirement. The plan must provide and be operated so that no amount may be paid to a member of the limitation class if the payment would cause amounts paid to date during the plan year to members of the limitation class to exceed 25% of the amounts paid under the plan to date during the plan year.

(iii) *Limitation class; special rule.*—For purposes of this subparagraph (3), an individual is a member of the limitation class only if the individual is a member (within the meaning of subparagraph (2)) on or before the date on which the determination described in subdivision (ii) or (iii) is required to be made.

(iv) *Example.*—The provisions of subdivision (iii) of this subparagraph may be illustrated by the following example:

Example. (A) Plan X is a qualified group legal services plan under which plan participants are reimbursed for the cost of personal legal services specified in the plan. The plan includes a provision satisfying the requirements of subdivision (ii) of this subparagraph. The plan year is the calendar year.

(B) A, an individual, is a participant in Plan X. On March 18, 1981, A is paid an amount under the plan. On June 21, 1981, A purchases shares of stock of the employer maintaining the plan. As a result of the purchase A owns more than 5% of the total number of shares of outstanding stock of the employer. Accordingly, under subparagraph (2) of this paragraph, A is a member of the limitation class for the plan year 1981. On August 14, 1981, A sells the shares of stock purchased on June 21, 1981, and no longer owns more than 5% of the total number of shares of outstanding stock of the employer. On October 9, 1981, A is paid an additional amount under the plan.

(C) For purposes of the determination required by subdivision (ii) of this subparagraph, if the determination is made for a date after March 17, 1981, and before June 21, 1981, the amount paid to A on March 18, 1981, is not considered an amount paid to a member of the limitation class. If the determination is made for a date after June 20, 1981, the amount paid to A on March 18, 1981, is considered an amount paid to a member of the limitation class. With respect to a determination made for a date after October 8, 1981, the amount paid to A on October 9, 1981, is considered an amount paid to a member of the limitation class.

(4) *Contribution allocation.*—(i) *Equal benefits.*—In general, if under a plan the same benefits are made available to each participant, the percentage of the amount contributed by the employer for a plan year that is considered contributed on behalf of the limitation class is equal to the number of participants who are members of the limitation class at any time during the plan year, divided by the number of individuals who are participants in the plan at any time during the plan year.

(ii) *Unequal benefits.*—In general, if under the plan different benefits are made available to different participants or different classes of participants, the percentage of the amount contributed by the employer for a plan year that is considered contributed on behalf of the limitation class is equal to the fair market value (as of the first day of the plan year) of those benefits available under the plan to participants who are members of the limitation class at any time during the plan year, divided by the fair market value (as of the first day of the plan year) of those benefits available under the plan to all individuals who are participants in the plan at any time during the plan year.

(iii) *Individual premiums.*—Notwithstanding subdivision (i) or (ii) of this subparagraph, if benefits are provided under the plan in exchange for the employer's prepayment or payment of a premium, and the amount of the prepayment or premium is determined by taking into account the circumstances of individual participants or classes of participants, the percentage of the amount contributed by the employer for a plan year that is considered contributed on behalf of the limitation class is equal to the sum of the prepayments or premiums paid for the plan year on behalf of participants who are members of the limitation class at any time during the plan year, divided by the sum of the prepayments or premiums paid for the plan year. A prepayment or premium is paid for the plan year if it is paid with respect to legal services provided or made available during the plan year. This subdivision (iii) will apply if, for example, equal benefits are provided each participant under the plan in exchange for the employer's payment of a premium with respect to each participant employee, and the amount of the premium varies, taking into account the employee's income level, the number and ages of the employee's dependents or other such factors.

(5) *Relative utilization of plan benefits.*—(i) *Application.*—The extent to which members of the limitation class, as a class, utilize plan benefits shall be taken into account in determining the percentage of amounts contributed by the employer that is considered contributed on be-

half of the limitation class. The rules described in this subparagraph (5) are in addition to those described in subparagraph (4) of this paragraph, and a plan may be other than a qualified plan by reason of the application of this subparagraph (5), notwithstanding that the percentage determined under subparagraph (4) is 25% or less.

(ii) *Computation.*—Under this subparagraph (5), if during any three successive plan years, benefits paid to or with respect to the limitation class (as determined for each plan year) exceed 25% of all benefits paid under the plan during the three years, the plan is not a qualified plan for the next succeeding plan year.

(iii) *Reapplication for recognition as a qualified plan.*—A plan that is not a qualified plan for a plan year by reason of this subparagraph (5), may reapply under § 1.120-3 for recognition as a qualified plan for any plan year following the first plan year for which it is not a qualified plan. A plan so reapplying will be recognized as a qualified plan for any plan year for which recognition is sought only if the plan is a qualified plan under this subparagraph (5) for the first plan year for which such recognition is sought and otherwise satisfies the requirements of section 120 and this section.

(g) *Employer contributions.*—(1) *In general.*—Employer contributions under the plan may be made only—

(i) To insurance companies, or to organizations or persons that provide personal legal services, or indemnification against the cost of personal legal services, in exchange for a prepayment or payment of a premium,

(ii) To organizations or trusts described in section 501(c)(20),

(iii) To organizations described in section 501(c) that are permitted by that section to receive payments from an employer for support of a qualified group legal services plan, except that the organization shall pay or credit the contribution to an organization or trust described in section 501(c)(20),

(iv) As prepayment to providers of legal services under the plan, or

(v) A combination of the above.

(2) *Prepayment required.*—For purposes of subparagraph (1)(i) and (iv), employer contributions are considered prepayments or premiums only if a contribution made with respect to benefits reasonably anticipated to be provided under the plan during any month is made on or before the tenth day of the month.

(h) *Employee contributions.*—(1) *In general.*—A plan is not a qualified plan if it permits participants to contribute under the plan other than as described in subparagraphs (2) and (3) of this paragraph.

(2) *Certain separated employees and surviving spouses and dependents.*—A plan will not be other than a qualified plan merely because the plan allows—

(i) A separated former employee,

(ii) A surviving spouse of a deceased employee, or

(iii) An individual who is a dependent of an employee within the meaning of section 152 for the taxable year of the employee ending on the date of the death of the employee,

to elect to continue as a participant under the plan on a self-contributory basis for a period not to exceed one year after the separation or death.

(3) *Certain employee contributions in lieu of employer contributions.*—This subparagraph (3) applies with respect to a plan that—

(i) Is maintained pursuant to an agreement that the Secretary of Labor finds to be a collective bargaining agreement between employee representatives and one or more employers, and

(ii) Provides that an employer is required to contribute (or contribute in full) on behalf of a participant employee only if the employee completes a minimum number of hours of service with the employer within a stated period ending on or before the date the contribution is otherwise required to be made by the employer.

Such a plan is not other than a qualified plan merely because it permits a participant employee to contribute under the plan an amount not required to be contributed by the employer because the employee fails to complete the minimum number of hours. However, no amount may be contributed by an employee under this subparagraph (3) unless employer contributions on behalf of participant employees are required to be made monthly or more often, and at least one employer contribution is made on behalf of the employee under the plan before the contribution by the employee is made under the plan. In addition, a plan shall not be a qualified plan for a plan year by reason of this subparagraph (3), if amounts contributed by employees under this subparagraph (3) during the plan year exceed 5% of the total amount contributed under the plan during the plan year.

(i) *Definitions.*—For purposes of this section, § 1.120-1 and § 1.120-3—

(1) *Employee.*—The term "employee" includes—

(i) A retired, disabled or laid-off employee,

(ii) A present employee who is on leave, as, for example, in the Armed Forces of the United States,

(iii) An individual who is self-employed within the meaning of section 401 (c)(1), or

(iv) A separated former employee who is covered by the plan by reason of paragraph (h)(2)(i) of this section (relating to employee contributions).

(2) *Employer.*—An individual who owns the entire interest in an unincorporated trade or business is treated as his or her own employer. A partnership is treated as the employer of each partner who is an employee within the meaning of section 401(c)(1).

(3) *Officer.*—An officer is an individual who is an officer within the meaning of regulations prescribed under section 414(c).

(4) *Shareholder.*—The term "shareholder" includes an individual who is a shareholder as determined by the attribution rules under section 1563(d) and (e), without regard to § 1563(e)(3)(C).

(5) *Highly compensated.*—The term "highly compensated" has the same meaning as it does for purposes of section 410(b)(1)(B). [Reg. § 1.120-2.]

Reduced Retirement Pay

Reduced Retirement Pay: Uniformed Services: Applicable Rules.—Reproduced below is the text of a proposed amendment of Reg. §1.122-1, relating to the applicable rules regarding reduced uniformed services retirement pay (published in the Federal Register on April 30, 1975).

□ Section 1.122-1 is amended by deleting "72(o)" each place it appears and inserting in lieu thereof "72(n)". As amended, §1.122-1(b)(2)(ii) and examples (2) and (3) of §1.122-(d) read as follows:

§1.122-1. Applicable rules relating to certain reduced uniformed services retirement pay.

* * *

(b) *Rule applicable after December 31, 1965.*— * * *

(2) * * *

(ii) Upon the death of a member or former member of the uniformed services, where the "consideration for the contract" (as described in paragraph (b)(2)(iii) of this section) has not been excluded in whole or in part from gross income under section 122(b) and (b)(2)(i) of this section, the survivor of such member who is receiving an annuity under chapter 73 of title 10 of the United States Code shall, after December 31, 1965, exclude from gross income under section 72(n) and this subdivision such annuity payments received after December 31, 1965, until there has been so excluded annuity payments equalling the portion of the "consideration for the contract" not previously excluded under paragraph (b)(2)(i) of this section.

* * *

(d) *Examples.*—The rules discussed in paragraph (a) of this section may be illustrated by the following examples:

* * *

Example (2). Assume the facts in Example (1) except that A retires on disability resulting from active service and his disability is rated at 40 percent. The entire amount of disability retirement pay, prior to and including 1966, is excludable from gross income under sections 104(a)(4) and 105(d), and in 1966, section 122(a). Assume further that A attains retirement age on December 31, 1966, dies on January 1, 1967, and his widow then begins receiving a survivor annuity under the Retired Serviceman's Family Protection Plan (10 U.S.C. 1431). A's widow may exclude from gross income in 1967 and 1968 under section 72(n) and paragraph (b)(2)(ii) of this section, the $1,800 of "consideration for the contract" i.e., the reductions in 1963, 1964, and 1965 to provide the survivor annuity. Thus, A's widow will exclude all of the survivor annuity she receives in 1967 ($1,350) and $450 of the $1,350 annuity received in 1968. In addition, if A had not attained retirement age at the time of his death, his widow would, under section 101 and paragraph (a)(2) of §1.101-2, exclude up to $5,000 subject to the limitations of paragraph (b)(2)(ii) of this section.

Example (3). Assume, in the previous example, that A dies on January 1, 1965, and his widow then begins receiving a survivor annuity. Assume further that A's widow is entitled to exclude under section 72(b) $1,000 of the $1,350 she received in 1965. Under section 72(n) and paragraph (b)(2)(ii) of this section, A's widow for 1966 will exclude the $200 remaining consideration for the contract ($1,200 – $1,000) and will include $1,150 of the survivor annuity in gross income.

* * *

Employee Benefits: Cafeteria Plans

Employee Benefits: Cafeteria Plans.—Reg. §§1.125-0, 1.125-1, 1.125-2, 1.125-5, 1.125-6 and 1.125-7, providing guidance on cafeteria plans, are proposed (published in the Federal Register on August 6, 2007) (REG-142695-05).

□ Par. 2. Sections 1.125-0, 1.125-1 and 1.125-2 are added to read as follows:

§1.125-0. Table of contents.—This section lists captions contained in §§1.125-1, 1.125-2, 1.125-5, 1.125-6 and §1.125-7.

§1.125-1 Cafeteria plans; general rules.

(a) Definitions.

(b) General rules.

(c) Written plan requirements.

(d) Plan year requirements.

(e) Grace period.

(f) Run-out period.

(g) Employee for purpose of Section 125.

(h) After-tax employee contributions.

(i) Prohibited taxable benefits.

(j) Coordination with other rules.

(k) Group-term life insurance.

(l) COBRA premiums.

(m) Payment or reimbursement of employees' individual accident and health insurance premiums.

(n) Section 105 rules for accident and health plan offered through a cafeteria plan.

(o) Prohibition against deferred compensation.

(p) Benefits relating to more than one year.

(q) Nonqualified benefits.

(r) Employer contributions to a cafeteria plan.

(s) Effective/applicability date.

§1.125-2 Cafeteria plans; elections.

(a) Rules relating to making elections and revoking elections.

(b) Automatic elections.

(d) Election rules for salary reduction contributions to HSAs.

(d) Optional election for new employees.

(e) Effective/applicability date.

§1.125-5 Flexible spending arrangements.

(a) Definition of flexible spending arrangement.

(b) Flex-credits allowed.

(c) Use-or-lose rule.

(d) Uniform coverage rules applicable to health FSAs.

(e) Required period of coverage for a health FSA, dependent care FSA and adoption assistance FSA.

(f) Coverage on a month-by-month or expense-by-expense basis prohibited.

(g) FSA administrative practices.

(h) Qualified benefits permitted to be offered through a FSA.

(i) Section 129 rules for dependent care assistance program offered through a cafeteria plan.

(j) Section 137 rules for adoption assistance program offered through a cafeteria plan.

(k) FSAs and the rules governing the tax-favored treatment of employer-provided health benefits.

(l) Section 105(h) requirements.

(m) HSA-compatible FSAs- limited-purpose health FSAs and post-deductible health FSAs.

(n) Qualified HSA distributions.

(o) FSA experience gains or forfeitures.

(p) Effective/applicability date.

§ 1.125-6 Substantiation of expenses for all cafeteria plans.

(a) Cafeteria plan payments and reimbursements.

(b) Rules for claims substantiation for cafeteria plans.

(c) Debit cards - overview.

(d) Mandatory rules for all debit cards usable to pay or reimburse medical expenses.

(e) Substantiation of expenses incurred at medical care providers and certain other stores with Drug Stores and Pharmacies merchant category code.

(f) Inventory information approval system.

(g) Debit cards used to pay or reimburse dependent care assistance.

(h) Effective/applicability date.

§ 1.125-7 Cafeteria plan nondiscrimination rules.

(a) Definitions.

(b) Nondiscrimination as to eligibility.

(c) Nondiscrimination as to contributions and benefits.

(d) Key employees.

(e) Section 125(g)(2) safe harbor for cafeteria plans providing health benefits.

(f) Safe harbor test for premium-only-plans.

(g) Permissive disaggregation for nondiscrimination testing.

(h) Optional aggregation of plans for nondiscrimination testing.

(i) Employees of certain controlled groups.

(j) Time to perform nondiscrimination testing.

(k) Discrimination in actual operation prohibited.

(l) Anti-abuse rule.

(m) Tax treatment of benefits in a cafeteria plan.

(n) Employer contributions to employees' Health Savings Accounts.

(o) Effective/applicability date.

[Reg. § 1.125-0.]

§ 1.125-1. Cafeteria plans; general rules.—(a) *Definitions.*—The definitions set forth in this paragraph (a) apply for purposes of section 125 and the regulations.

(1) The term *cafeteria plan* means a separate written plan that complies with the requirements of section 125 and the regulations, that is maintained by an employer for the benefit of its employees and that is operated in compliance with the requirements of section 125 and the regulations. All participants in a cafeteria plan must be employees. A cafeteria plan must offer at least one permitted taxable benefit (as defined in paragraph (a)(2) of this section) and at least one qualified benefit (as defined in paragraph (a)(3) of this section). A cafeteria plan must not provide for deferral of compensation (except as specifically permitted in paragraph (o) of this section).

(2) The term *permitted taxable benefit* means cash and certain other taxable benefits treated as cash for purposes of section 125. For purposes of section 125, *cash* means cash compensation (including salary reduction), payments for annual leave, sick leave, or other paid time off and severance pay. A distribution from a trust described in section 401(a) is not cash for purposes of section 125. *Other taxable benefits treated as cash* for purposes of section 125 are:

(i) Property;

(ii) Benefits attributable to employer contributions that are currently taxable to the employee upon receipt by the employee; and

(iii) Benefits purchased with after-tax employee contributions, as described in paragraph (h) of this section.

(3) *Qualified benefit.*—Except as otherwise provided in section 125(f) and paragraph (q) of this section, the term *qualified benefit* means any benefit attributable to employer contributions to the extent that such benefit is not currently taxable to the employee by reason of an express provision of the Internal Revenue Code (Code) and which does not defer compensation (except as provided in paragraph (o) of this section). The following benefits are qualified benefits that may be offered under a cafeteria plan and are excludible from employees' gross income when provided in accordance with the applicable provisions of the Code—

(A) Group-term life insurance on the life of an employee in an amount that is less than or equal to the $50,000 excludible from gross income under section 79(a), but not combined with any permanent benefit within the meaning of § 1.79-0;

(B) An accident and health plan excludible from gross income under section 105 or 106, including self-insured medical reimbursement plans (such as health FSAs described in § 1.125-5);

(C) Premiums for COBRA continuation coverage (if excludible under section 106) under the accident and health plan of the employer sponsoring the cafeteria plan or premiums for COBRA continuation coverage of an employee of the employer sponsoring the cafeteria plan under an accident and health plan sponsored by a different employer;

(D) An accidental death and dismemberment insurance policy (section 106);

(E) Long-term or short-term disability coverage (section 106);

(F) Dependent care assistance program (section 129);

(G) Adoption assistance (section 137);

(H) A qualified cash or deferred arrangement that is part of a profit-sharing plan or stock bonus plan, as described in paragraph (o)(3) of this section (section 401(k));

(I) Certain plans maintained by educational organizations (section 125(d)(2)(C) and paragraph (o)(3)(iii) of this section); and

(J) Contributions to Health Savings Accounts (HSAs) (sections 223 and 125(d)(2)(D)).

(4) *Dependent.*—The term *dependent* generally means a dependent as defined in section

152. However, the definition of dependent is modified to conform with the underlying Code section for the qualified benefit. For example, for purposes of a benefit under section 105, the term dependent means a dependent as defined in section 152, determined without regard to section 152(b)(1), (b)(2) or (d)(1)(B).

(5) *Premium-only-plan.*—A *premium-only-plan* is a cafeteria plan that offers as its sole benefit an election between cash (for example, salary) and payment of the employee share of the employer-provided accident and health insurance premium (excludible from the employee's gross income under section 106).

(b) *General rules.*—(1) *Cafeteria plans.*—Section 125 is the exclusive means by which an employer can offer employees an election between taxable and nontaxable benefits without the election itself resulting in inclusion in gross income by the employees. Section 125 provides that cash (including certain taxable benefits) offered to an employee through a nondiscriminatory cafeteria plan is not includible in the employee's gross income merely because the employee has the opportunity to choose among cash and qualified benefits (within the meaning of section 125(e)) through the cafeteria plan. Section 125(a), (d)(1). However, if a plan offering an employee an election between taxable benefits (including cash) and nontaxable qualified benefits does not meet the section 125 requirements, the election between taxable and nontaxable benefits results in gross income to the employee, regardless of what benefit is elected and when the election is made. An employee who has an election among nontaxable benefits and taxable benefits (including cash) that is not through a cafeteria plan that satisfies section 125 must include in gross income the value of the taxable benefit with the greatest value that the employee could have elected to receive, even if the employee elects to receive only the nontaxable benefits offered. The amount of the taxable benefit is includible in the employee's income in the year in which the employee would have actually received the taxable benefit if the employee had elected such benefit. This is the result even if the employee's election between the nontaxable benefits and taxable benefits is made prior to the year in which the employee would actually have received the taxable benefits. See paragraph (q) in § 1.125-1 for nonqualified benefits.

(2) *Nondiscrimination rules for qualified benefits.*—Accident and health plan coverage, group-term life insurance coverage, and benefits under a dependent care assistance program or adoption assistance program do not fail to be qualified benefits under a cafeteria plan merely because they are includible in gross income because of applicable nondiscrimination requirements (for example, sections 79(d), 105(h),129(d), 137(c)(2)). See also § § 1.105-11(k) and 1.125-7.

(3) *Examples.*—The following examples illustrate the rules of paragraph (b)(1) of this section.

Example 1. Distributions from qualified pension plan used for health insurance premiums. (i) Employer A maintains a qualified section 401(a) retirement plan for employees. Employer A also provides accident and health insurance (as described in section 106) for employees and former employees, their spouses and dependents. The health insurance premiums are partially paid through a cafeteria plan. None of Employer A's employees are public safety officers. Employer A's health plan allows former employees to elect to have distributions from the qualified retirement plan applied to pay for the health insurance premiums through the cafeteria plan.

(ii) Amounts distributed from the qualified retirement plan which the former employees elect to have applied to pay health insurance premiums through the cafeteria plan are includible in their gross income. The same result occurs if distributions from the qualified retirement plan are applied directly to reimburse section 213(d) medical care expenses incurred by a former employee or his or her spouse or dependents. These distributions are includible in their income, and are not cash for purposes of section 125. The plan is not a cafeteria plan with respect to former employees.

Example 2. Severance pay used to pay COBRA premiums. Employer B maintains a cafeteria plan, which offers employees an election between cash and employer-provided accident and health insurance (excludible from employees' gross income under section 106). Employer B pays terminating employees severance pay. The cafeteria plan also allows a terminating employee to elect between receiving severance pay and using the severance pay to pay the COBRA premiums for the accident and health insurance. These provisions in the cafeteria plan are consistent with the requirements in section 125.

(4) *Election by participants.*—(i) *In general.*—A cafeteria plan must offer participants the opportunity to elect between at least one permitted taxable benefit and at least one qualified benefit. For example, if employees are given the opportunity to elect only among two or more nontaxable benefits, the plan is not a cafeteria plan. Similarly, a plan that only offers the election among salary, permitted taxable benefits, paid time off or other taxable benefits is not a cafeteria plan. See section 125(a), (d). See § 1.125-2 for rules on elections.

(ii) *Premium-only-plan.*—A cafeteria plan may be a premium-only-plan.

(iii) *Examples.*—The following examples illustrate the rules of paragraph (b)(4)(i) of this section.

Example 1. No election. Employer C covers all its employees under its accident and health plan (excludible from employees' gross income under section 106). Coverage is mandatory (that is, employees have no election between cash and the Employer C's accident and health plan). This plan is not a cafeteria plan, because the plan offers employees no election between taxable and nontaxable benefits. The accident and health coverage is excludible from employees' gross income

Example 2. Election between cash and at least one qualified benefit. Employer D offers its employees a plan with an election between cash and an employer-provided accident and health plan (excludible from employees' gross income under section 106). If the plan also satisfies all the other requirements of section 125, the plan is a cafeteria plan because it offers an election between at least one taxable benefit and at least one nontaxable qualified benefit.

Example 3. Election between employer flex-credits and qualified benefits. Employer E offers its employees an election between an employer flex-credit (as defined in paragraph (b) in §1.125-5) and qualified benefits. If an employee does not elect to apply the entire employer flex-credit to qualified benefits, the employee will receive no cash or other taxable benefit for the unused employer flex-credit. The plan is not a cafeteria plan because it does not offer an election between at least one taxable benefit and at least one nontaxable qualified benefit.

Example 4. No election between cash and qualified benefits for certain employees. (i) Employer F maintains a calendar year plan offering employer-provided accident and health insurance coverage which includes employee-only and family coverage options.

(ii) The plan provides for an automatic enrollment process when a new employee is hired, or during the annual election period under the plan: only employees who certify that they have other health coverage are permitted to elect to receive cash. Employees who cannot certify are covered by the accident and health insurance on a mandatory basis. Employer F does not otherwise request or collect information from employees regarding other health coverage as part of the enrollment process. If the employee has a spouse or child, the employee can elect between cash and family coverage.

(iii) When an employee is hired, the employee receives a notice explaining the plan's automatic enrollment process. The notice includes the salary reduction amounts for employee-only coverage and family coverage, procedures for certifying whether the employee has other health coverage, elections for family coverage, information on the time by which a certification or election must be made, and the period for which a certification or election will be effective. The notice is also given to each current employee before the beginning of each plan year, (except that the notice for a current employee includes a description of the employee's existing coverage, if any).

(iv) For a new employee, an election to receive cash or to have family coverage is effective if made when the employee is hired. For a current employee, an election is effective if made prior to the start of each calendar year or under any other circumstances permitted under §1.125-4. An election for any prior year carries over to the next succeeding plan year unless changed. Certification that the employee has other health coverage must be made annually.

(v) Contributions used to purchase employer-provided accident and health coverage under section 125 are not includible in an employee's gross income if the employee can elect cash. Section 125 does not apply to the employee-only coverage of an employee who cannot certify that he or she has other health coverage and, therefore, does not have the ability to elect cash in lieu of health coverage.

(5) *No deferred compensation.*—Except as provided in paragraph (o) of this section, in order for a plan to be a cafeteria plan, the qualified benefits and the permitted taxable benefits offered through the cafeteria plan must not defer compensation. For example, a cafeteria plan may not provide for retirement health benefits for current employees beyond the current plan year or group-term life insurance with a permanent benefit, as defined under §1.79-0.

(c) *Written plan requirements.*—(1) *General rule.*—A cafeteria plan must contain in writing the information described in this paragraph (c), and depending on the qualified benefits offered in the plan, may also be required to contain additional information described in paragraphs (c)(2) and (c)(3) of this section. The cafeteria plan must be adopted and effective on or before the first day of the cafeteria plan year to which it relates. The terms of the plan must apply uniformly to all participants. The cafeteria plan document may be comprised of multiple documents. The written cafeteria plan must contain all of the following information—

(i) A specific description of each of the benefits available through the plan, including the periods during which the benefits are provided (the periods of coverage);

(ii) The plan's rules governing participation, and specifically requiring that all participants in the plan be employees;

(iii) The procedures governing employees' elections under the plan, including the period when elections may be made, the periods with respect to which elections are effective, and providing that elections are irrevocable, except to the extent that the optional change in status rules in §1.125-4 are included in the cafeteria plan;

(iv) The manner in which employer contributions may be made under the plan, (for example, through an employee's salary reduction election or by nonelective employer contributions (that is, flex-credits, as defined in paragraph (b) in §1.125-5) or both);

(v) The maximum amount of employer contributions available to any employee through the plan, by stating:

(A) The maximum amount of elective contributions (i.e., salary reduction) available to any employee through the plan, expressed as a maximum dollar amount or a maximum percentage of compensation or the method for determining the maximum dollar amount; and

(B) For contributions to section 401(k) plans, the maximum amount of elective contributions available to any employee through the plan, expressed as a maximum dollar amount or maximum percentage of compensation that may be contributed as elective contributions through the plan by employees.

(vi) The plan year of the cafeteria plan;

(vii) If the plan offers paid time off, the required ordering rule for use of nonelective and elective paid time off in paragraph (o)(4) of this section;

(viii) If the plan includes flexible spending arrangements (as defined in §1.125-5(a)), the plan's provisions complying with any additional requirements for those FSAs (for example, the uniform coverage rule and the use-or-lose rules in paragraphs (d) and (c) in §1.125-5);

(ix) If the plan includes a grace period, the plan's provisions complying with paragraph (e) of this section; and

(x) If the plan includes distributions from a health FSA to employees' HSAs, the plan's provisions complying with paragraph (n) in §1.125-5.

(2) *Additional requirements under sections 105(h), 129, and 137.*—A written plan is required for self-insured medical reimbursement plans

(§1.105-11(b)(1)(i)), dependent care assistance programs (section 129(d)(1)), and adoption assistance (section 137(c)). Any of these plans or programs offered through a cafeteria plan that satisfies the written plan requirement in this paragraph (c) for the benefits under these plans and programs also satisfies the written plan requirements in §1.105-11(b)(1)(i), section 129(d)(1), and section 137(c) (whichever is applicable). Alternatively, a self-insured medical reimbursement plan, a dependent care assistance program, or an adoption assistance program is permitted to satisfy the requirements in §1.105-11(b)(1)(i), section 129(d)(1), or section 137(c) (whichever is applicable) through a separate written plan, and not as part of the written cafeteria plan.

(3) *Additional requirements under section 401(k).*—See §1.401(k)-1(e)(7) for additional requirements that must be satisfied in the written plan if the plan offers deferrals into a section 401(k) plan.

(4) *Cross-reference allowed.*—In describing the benefits available through the cafeteria plan, the written cafeteria plan need not be self-contained. For example, the written cafeteria plan may incorporate by reference benefits offered through other *separate written plans*, such as a section 401(k) plan, or coverage under a dependent care assistance program (section 129), without describing in full the benefits established through these other plans. But, for example, if the cafeteria plan offers different maximum levels of coverage for dependent care assistance programs, the descriptions in the separate written plan must specify the available maximums.

(5) *Amendments to cafeteria plan.*—Any amendment to the cafeteria plan must be in writing. A cafeteria plan is permitted to be amended at any time during a plan year. However, the amendment is only permitted to be effective for periods after the later of the adoption date or effective date of the amendment. For an amendment adding a new benefit, the cafeteria plan must pay or reimburse only those expenses for new benefits incurred after the later of the amendment's adoption date or effective date.

(6) *Failure to satisfy written plan requirements.*—If there is no written cafeteria plan, or if the written plan fails to satisfy any of the requirements in this paragraph (c) (including cross-referenced requirements), the plan is not a cafeteria plan and an employee's election between taxable and nontaxable benefits results in gross income to the employee.

(7) *Operational failure.*—(i) *In general.*—If the cafeteria plan fails to operate according to its written plan or otherwise fails to operate in compliance with section 125 and the regulations, the plan is not a cafeteria plan and employees' elections between taxable and nontaxable benefits result in gross income to the employees.

(ii) *Failure to operate according to written cafeteria plan or section 125.*—Examples of failures resulting in section 125 not applying to a plan include the following—

(A) Paying or reimbursing expenses for qualified benefits incurred before the later of the adoption date or effective date of the cafeteria plan, before the beginning of a period of coverage or before the later of the date of adoption or effective date of a plan amendment adding a new benefit;

(B) Offering benefits other than permitted taxable benefits and qualified benefits;

(C) Operating to defer compensation (except as permitted in paragraph (o) of this section);

(D) Failing to comply with the uniform coverage rule in paragraph (d) in §1.125-5;

(E) Failing to comply with the use-or-lose rule in paragraph (c) in §1.125-5;

(F) Allowing employees to revoke elections or make new elections, except as provided in §1.125-4 and paragraph (a) in §1.125-2;

(G) Failing to comply with the substantiation requirements of §1.125-6;

(H) Paying or reimbursing expenses in an FSA other than expenses expressly permitted in paragraph (h) in §1.125-5;

(I) Allocating experience gains other than as expressly permitted in paragraph (o) in §1.125-5;

(J) Failing to comply with the grace period rules in paragraph (e) of this section; or

(K) Failing to comply with the qualified HSA distribution rules in paragraph (n) in §1.125-5.

(d) *Plan year requirements.*—(1) *Twelve consecutive months.*—The plan year must be specified in the cafeteria plan. The plan year of a cafeteria plan must be twelve consecutive months, unless a short plan year is allowed under this paragraph (d). A plan year is permitted to begin on any day of any calendar month and must end on the preceding day in the immediately following year (for example, a plan year that begins on October 15, 2007, must end on October 14, 2008). A calendar year plan year is a period of twelve consecutive months beginning on January 1 and ending on December 31 of the same calendar year. A plan year specified in the cafeteria plan is effective for the first plan year of a cafeteria plan and for all subsequent plan years, unless changed as provided in paragraph (d)(2) of this section.

(2) *Changing plan year.*—The plan year is permitted to be changed only for a valid business purpose. A change in the plan year is not permitted if a principal purpose of the change in plan year is to circumvent the rules of section 125 or these regulations. If a change in plan year does not satisfy this subparagraph, the attempt to change the plan year is ineffective and the plan year of the cafeteria plan remains the same.

(3) *Short plan year.*—A short plan year of less than twelve consecutive months is permitted for a valid business purpose.

(4) *Examples.*—The following examples illustrate the rules in paragraph (d) of this section:

Example 1. Employer with calendar year. Employer G, with a calendar taxable year, first establishes a cafeteria plan effective July 1, 2009. The cafeteria plan specifies a calendar plan year. The first cafeteria plan year is the period beginning on July 1, 2009, and ending on December 31, 2009. Employer G has a business purpose for a short first cafeteria plan year.

Example 2. Employer changes insurance carrier. Employer H establishes a cafeteria plan effective January 1, 2009, with a calendar year plan year. The cafeteria plan offers an accident and health plan through Insurer X. In March 2010, Employer H contracts to provide accident and health insurance through another insurance company, Y. Y's accident and health insurance is offered on a July 1-June 30 benefit year. Effective July 1, 2010, Employer H amends the plan to change to a July 1-June 30 plan year. Employer H has a business purpose for changing the cafeteria plan year and for the short plan year ending June 30, 2010.

(5) *Significance of plan year.*—The plan year generally is the coverage period for benefits provided through the cafeteria plan to which annual elections for these benefits apply. Benefits elected pursuant to the employee's election for a plan year generally may not be carried forward to subsequent plan years. However, see the grace period rule in paragraph (e) of this section.

(e) *Grace period.*—(1) *In general.*—A cafeteria plan may, at the employer's option, include a grace period of up to the fifteenth day of the third month immediately following the end of each plan year. If a cafeteria plan provides for a grace period, an employee who has unused benefits or contributions relating to a qualified benefit (for example, health flexible spending arrangement (health FSA) or dependent care assistance) from the immediately preceding plan year, and who incurs expenses for that same qualified benefit during the grace period, may be paid or reimbursed for those expenses from the unused benefits or contributions as if the expenses had been incurred in the immediately preceding plan year. A grace period is available for all qualified benefits described in paragraph (a)(3) of this section, except that the grace period does not apply to paid time off and elective contributions under a section 401(k) plan. The effect of the grace period is that the employee may have as long as 14 months and 15 days (that is, the 12 months in the current cafeteria plan year plus the grace period) to use the benefits or contributions for a plan year before those amounts are *forfeited* under the *use-or-lose* rule in paragraph (c) in §1.125-5. If the grace period is added to a cafeteria plan through an amendment, all requirements in paragraph (c) of this section must be satisfied.

(2) *Grace period optional features.*—A grace period provision may contain any or all of the following—

(i) The grace period may apply to some qualified benefits described in paragraph (a)(3) of this section, but not to others;

(ii) The grace period provision may limit the amount of unused benefits or contributions available during the grace period. The limit must be uniform and apply to all participants. However, the limit must not be based on a percentage of the amount of the unused benefits or contributions remaining at the end of the immediately prior plan year;

(iii) The last day of the grace period may be sooner than the fifteenth day of the third month immediately following the end of the plan year (that is, the grace period may be shorter than two and one half months);

(iv) The grace period provision is permitted to treat expenses for qualified benefits incurred during the grace period either as expenses incurred during the immediately preceding plan year or as expenses incurred during the current plan year (for example, the plan may first apply the unused contributions or benefits from the immediately preceding year to pay or reimburse grace period expenses and then, when the unused contributions and benefits from the prior year are exhausted, the grace period expenses may be paid from current year contributions and benefits.); and

(v) The grace period provision may permit the employer to defer the allocation of expenses described in paragraph (e)(2)(iv) of this section until after the end of the grace period.

(3) *Grace period requirements.*—A grace period must satisfy the requirements in paragraph (c) of this section and all of the following requirements:

(i) The grace period provisions in the cafeteria plan (including optional provisions in paragraph (e)(2) of this section) must apply uniformly to all participants in the cafeteria plan, determined as of the last day of the plan year. Participants in the cafeteria plan through COBRA and participants who were participants as of the last day of the plan year but terminate during the grace period are participants for purposes of the grace period. See §54.4980B-2, Q & A-8 of this chapter;

(ii) The grace period provision in the cafeteria plan must state that unused benefits or contributions relating to a particular qualified benefit may only be used to pay or reimburse expenses incurred with respect to the same qualified benefit. For example, unused amounts elected to pay or reimburse medical expenses in a health FSA may not be used to pay or reimburse dependent care expenses incurred during the grace period; and

(iii) The grace period provision in the cafeteria plan must state that to the extent any unused benefits or contributions from the immediately preceding plan year exceed the expenses for the qualified benefit incurred during the grace period, those remaining unused benefits or contributions may not be carried forward to any subsequent period (including any subsequent plan year), cannot be cashed-out and must be forfeited under the use-or-lose rule. See paragraph (c) in §1.125-5

(4) *Examples.*—The following examples illustrate the rules in this paragraph (e).

Example 1. Expenses incurred during grace period and immediately following plan year. (i) Employer I's calendar year cafeteria plan includes a grace period allowing all participants to apply unused benefits or contributions remaining at the end of the plan year to qualified benefits incurred during the grace period immediately following that plan year. The grace period for the plan year ending December 31, 2009, ends on March 15, 2010.

(ii) Employee X timely elected salary reduction of $1,000 for a health FSA for the plan year ending December 31, 2009. As of December 31, 2009, X has $200 remaining unused in his health FSA. X timely elected salary reduction for a health FSA of $1,500 for the plan year ending December 31, 2010.

(iii) During the grace period from January 1 through March 15, 2010, X incurs $300 of unreimbursed medical expenses (as defined in section 213(d)). The unused $200 from the plan year ending December 31, 2009, is applied to pay or reimburse $200 of X's $300 of medical expenses incurred during the grace period. Therefore, as of March 16, 2010, X has no unused benefits or contributions remaining for the plan year ending December 31, 2009.

(iv) The remaining $100 of medical expenses incurred between January 1 and March 15, 2010, is paid or reimbursed from X's health FSA for the plan year ending December 31, 2010. As of March 16, 2010, X has $1,400 remaining in the health FSA for the plan year ending December 31, 2010.

Example 2. Unused benefits exceed expenses incurred during grace period. Same facts as *Example 1*, except that X incurs $150 of section 213(d) medical expenses during the grace period (January 1 through March 15, 2010). As of March 16, 2010, X has $50 of unused benefits or contributions remaining for the plan year ending December 31, 2009. The unused $50 cannot be cashed-out, converted to any other taxable or nontaxable benefit, or used in any other plan year (including the plan year ending December 31, 2009). The unused $50 is subject to the use-or-lose rule in paragraph (c) in §1.125-5 and is forfeited. As of March 16, 2010, X has the entire $1,500 elected in the health FSA for the plan year ending December 31, 2010.

Example 3. Terminated participants. (i) Employer J's cafeteria plan includes a grace period allowing all participants to apply unused benefits or contributions remaining at the end of the plan year to qualified benefits incurred during the grace period immediately following that plan year. For the plan year ending on December 31, 2009, the grace period ends March 15, 2010.

(ii) Employees A, B, C, and D each timely elected $1,200 salary reduction for a health FSA for the plan year ending December 31, 2009. Employees A and B terminated employment on September 15, 2009. Each has $500 of unused benefits or contributions in the health FSA.

(iii) Employee A elected COBRA for the health FSA. Employee A is a participant in the cafeteria plan as of December 31, 2009, the last day of the 2009 plan year. Employee A has $500 of unused benefits or contributions available during the grace period for the 2009 plan year (ending March 15, 2010).

(iv) Employee B did not elect COBRA for the health FSA. Employee B is not a participant in the cafeteria plan as of December 31, 2009. The grace period does not apply to Employee B.

(v) Employee C has $500 of unused benefits in his health FSA as of December 31, 2009, and terminated employment on January 15, 2010. Employee C is a participant in the cafeteria plan as of December 31, 2009 and has $500 of unused benefits or contributions available during the grace period ending March 15, 2010, even though he terminated employment on January 15, 2010.

(vi) Employee D continues to work for Employer H throughout 2009 and 2010, also has $500 of unused benefits or contributions in his health FSA as of December 31, 2009, but made no health FSA election for 2010. Employee D is a participant in the cafeteria plan as of December 31, 2009 and has $500 of unused benefits or contributions available during the grace period ending March 15, 2010, even though he is not a participant in a health FSA for the 2010 plan year.

(f) *Run-out period.*—A cafeteria plan is permitted to contain a run-out period as designated by the employer. A run-out period is a period after the end of the plan year (or grace period) during which a participant can submit a claim for reimbursement for a qualified benefit incurred during the plan year (or grace period). Thus, a plan is also permitted to provide a deadline on or after the end of the plan year (or grace period) for submitting a claim for reimbursement for the plan year. Any run-out period must be provided on a uniform and consistent basis with respect to all participants.

(g) *Employee for purposes of section 125.*—(1) *Current employees, former employees.*—The term employee includes any current or former employee (including any laid-off employee or retired employee) of the employer. See paragraph (g)(3) of this section concerning limits on participation by former employees. Specifically, the term *employee* includes the following—

(i) Common law employee;

(ii) Leased employee described in section 414(n);

(iii) Full-time life insurance salesman (as defined in section 7701(a)(20)); and

(iv) A current employee or former employee described in paragraphs (g)(1)(i) through (iii) of this section.

(2) *Self-employed individual not an employee.*—(i) *In general.*—The term *employee* does not include a self-employed individual or a 2-percent shareholder of an S corporation, as defined in paragraph (g)(2)(ii) of this subsection. For example, a sole proprietor, a partner in a partnership, or a director solely serving on a corporation's board of directors (and not otherwise providing services to the corporation as an employee) is not an employee for purposes of section 125, and thus is not permitted to participate in a cafeteria plan. However, a sole proprietor may sponsor a cafeteria plan covering the sole proprietor's employees (but not the sole proprietor). Similarly, a partnership or S corporation may sponsor a cafeteria plan covering employees (but not a partner or 2-percent shareholder of an S corporation).

(ii) *Two percent shareholder of an S corporation.*—A 2-percent shareholder of an S corporation has the meaning set forth in section 1372(b).

(iii) *Certain dual status individuals.*—If an individual is an employee of an employer and also provides services to that employer as an independent contractor or director (for example, an individual is both a director and an employee of a C corp), the individual is eligible to participate in that employer's cafeteria plan solely in his or her capacity as an employee. This rule does not apply to partners or to 2-percent shareholders of an S corporation.

(iv) *Examples.*—The following examples illustrate the rules in paragraphs (g)(2)(ii) and (g)(2)(iii) of this section:

Example 1. Two-percent shareholders of an S corporation. (i) Employer K, an S corporation, maintains a cafeteria plan for its employees (other than 2-percent shareholders of an S corporation). Employer K's taxable year and the plan year are the calendar year. On January 1, 2009, individual Z owns 5 percent of the outstanding stock in Employer K. Y, who owns no stock in Employer K, is married to Z. Y and Z are employees of Employer K. Z is a 2-percent shareholder in Employer K (as defined in section 1372(b)). Y is also a 2-percent shareholder in Employer K by operation of the attribution rules in section 318(a)(1)(A)(i).

(ii) On July 15, 2009, Z sells all his stock in Employer K to an unrelated third party, and ceases to be a 2-percent shareholder. Y and Z continue to work as employees of Employer K during the entire 2009 calendar year. Y and Z are ineligible to participate in Employer K's cafeteria plan for the 2009 plan year.

Example 2. Director and employee. T is an employee and also a director of Employer L, a C corp that sponsors a cafeteria plan. The cafeteria plan allows only employees of Employer L to participate in the cafeteria plan. T's annual compensation as an employee is $50,000; T is also paid $3,000 annually in director's fees. T makes a timely election to salary reduce $5,000 from his employee compensation for dependent care benefits. T makes no election with respect to his compensation as a director. T may participate in the cafeteria plan in his capacity as an employee of Employer L.

(3) *Limits on participation by former employees.*—Although former employees are treated as employees, a cafeteria plan may not be established or maintained predominantly for the benefit of former employees of the employer. Such a plan is not a cafeteria plan.

(4) *No participation by the spouse or dependent of an employee.*—(i) *Benefits allowed to participant's spouse or dependents but not participation.*—The spouse or dependents of employees may not be participants in a cafeteria plan unless they are also employees. However, a cafeteria plan may provide benefits to spouses and dependents of participants. For example, although an employee's spouse may benefit from the employee's election of accident and health insurance coverage or of coverage through a dependent care assistance program, the spouse may not participate in a cafeteria plan (that is, the spouse may not be given the opportunity to elect or purchase benefits offered by the plan).

(ii) *Certain elections after employee's death.*—An employee's spouse is not a participant in a cafeteria plan merely because the spouse has the right, upon the death of the employee, to elect among various settlement options or to elect among permissible distribution options with respect to the deceased employee's benefits through a section 401(k) plan, Health Savings Account, or certain group-term life insurance offered through the cafeteria plan. See §54.4980B-2, Q & A 8 and §54.4980B-4, Q & A-1 of this chapter on COBRA rights of a participant's spouse or dependents.

(5) *Employees of certain controlled groups.*—All employees who are treated as employed by a single employer under section 414(b), (c), (m), or (o) are treated as employed by a single employer for purposes of section 125. Section 125(g)(4); section 414(t).

(h) *After-tax employee contributions.*—(1) *Certain after-tax employee contributions treated as cash.*—In addition to the cash benefits described in paragraph (a)(2) of this section, in general, a benefit is treated as cash for purposes of section 125 if the benefit does not defer compensation (except as provided in paragraph (o) of this section) and an employee who receives the benefit purchases such benefit with after-tax employee contributions or is treated, for all purposes under the Code (including, for example, reporting and withholding purposes), as receiving, at the time that the benefit is received, cash compensation equal to the full value of the benefit at that time and then purchasing the benefit with after-tax employee contributions. Thus, for example, long-term disability coverage is treated as cash for purposes of section 125 if the cafeteria plan provides that an employee may purchase the coverage through the cafeteria plan with after-tax employee contributions or provides that the employee receiving such coverage is treated as having received cash compensation equal to the value of the coverage and then as having purchased the coverage with after-tax employee contributions. Also, for example, a cafeteria plan may offer employees the opportunity to purchase, with after-tax employee contributions, group-term life insurance on the life of an employee (providing no permanent benefits), an accident and health plan, or a dependent care assistance program.

(2) *Accident and health coverage purchased for someone other than the employee's spouse or dependents with after-tax employee contributions.*—If the requirements of section 106 are satisfied, employer-provided accident and health coverage for an employee and his or her spouse or dependents is excludible from the employee's gross income. The fair market value of coverage for any other individual, provided with respect to the employee, is includible in the employee's gross income. §1.106-1; §1.61-21(a)(4), and §1.61-21(b)(1). A cafeteria plan is permitted to allow employees to elect accident and health coverage for an individual who is not the spouse or dependent of the employee as a taxable benefit.

(3) *Example.*—The following example illustrates the rules of this paragraph (h):

Example. Accident and health plan coverage for individuals who are not a spouse or dependent of an employee. (i) Employee C participates in Employer M's cafeteria plan. Employee C timely elects salary reduction for employer-provided accident and health coverage for himself and for accident and health coverage for his former spouse. C's former spouse is not C's dependent. A former spouse is not a spouse as defined in section 152.

(ii) The fair market value of the coverage for the former spouse is $1,000. Employee C has $1,000 includible in gross income for the accident and health coverage of his former spouse, because the section 106 exclusion applies only to employer-provided accident and health coverage for the employee or the employee's spouse or dependents.

(iii) No payments or reimbursements received under the accident and health coverage result in gross income to Employee C or to the former spouse. The result is the same if the $1,000 for coverage of C's former spouse is paid from C's after-tax income outside the cafeteria plan.

(i) *Prohibited taxable benefits.*—Any taxable benefit not described in paragraph (a)(2) of this section and not treated as cash for purposes of section 125 in paragraph (h) of this section is not permitted to be included in a cafeteria plan. A plan that offers taxable benefits other than the taxable benefits described in paragraph (a)(2) and (h) of this section is not a cafeteria plan.

(j) *Coordination with other rules.*—(1) *In general.*—If a benefit is excludible from an employee's gross income when provided separately, the benefit is excludible from gross income when provided through a cafeteria plan. Thus, a qualified benefit is excludible from gross income if both the rules under section 125 and the specific rules providing for the exclusion of the benefit from gross income are satisfied. For example, if the nondiscrimination rules for specific qualified benefits (for example, sections 79(d), 105(h), 129(d)(2), 137(c)(2)) are not satisfied, those qualified benefits are includible in gross income. Thus, if $50,000 in group-term life insurance is offered through a cafeteria plan, the nondiscrimination rules in section 79(d) must be satisfied in order to exclude the coverage from gross income.

(2) *Section 125 nondiscrimination rules.*—Qualified benefits are includible in the gross income of highly compensated participants or key employees if the nondiscrimination rules of section 125 are not satisfied. See § 1.125-7.

(3) *Taxable benefits.*—If a benefit that is includible in gross income when offered separately is offered through a cafeteria plan, the benefit continues to be includible in gross income.

(k) *Group-term life insurance.*—(1) *In general.*—In addition to offering up to $50,000 in group-term life insurance coverage excludible under section 79(a), a cafeteria plan may offer coverage in excess of that amount. The cost of coverage in excess of $50,000 in group-term life insurance coverage provided under a policy or policies carried directly or indirectly by one or more employers (taking into account all coverage provided both through a cafeteria plan and outside a cafeteria plan) is includible in an employee's gross income. Group-term life insurance combined with permanent benefits, within the meaning of § 1.79-0, is a prohibited benefit in a cafeteria plan.

(2) *Determining cost of insurance includible in employee's gross income.*—(i) *In general.*—If the aggregate group-term life insurance coverage on the life of the employee (under policies carried directly or indirectly by the employer) exceeds $50,000, all or a portion of the insurance is provided through a cafeteria plan, and the group-term life insurance is provided through a plan that meets the nondiscrimination rules of section 79(d), the amount includible in an employee's gross income is determined under paragraphs (k)(2)(i)(A) through (C) of this section. For each employee—

(A) The entire amount of salary reduction and employer flex-credits through a cafeteria plan for group-term life insurance coverage on the life of the employee is excludible from the employee's gross income, regardless of the amount of employer-provided group-term life insurance on the employee's life (that is, whether or not the coverage provided to the employee both through the cafeteria plan and outside the cafeteria plan exceeds $50,000);

(B) The cost of the group-term life insurance in excess of $50,000 of coverage is includible in the employee's gross income. The amount includible in the employee's income is determined using the rules of § 1.79-3 and Table I (*Uniform Premiums for $1,000 of Group-Term Life Insurance Protection*). See subparagraph (C) of this paragraph (k)(2)(i) for determining the amount paid by the employee for purposes of reducing the Table I amount includible in income under § 1.79-3.

(C) In determining the amount paid by the employee toward the purchase of the group-term life insurance for purposes of § 1.79-3, only an employee's after-tax contributions are treated as an amount paid by the employee.

(ii) *Examples.*—The rules in this paragraph (k) are illustrated by the following examples, in which the group-term life insurance coverage satisfies the nondiscrimination rules in section 79(d), provides no permanent benefits, is for a 12-month period, is the only group-term life insurance coverage provided under a policy carried directly or indirectly by the employer, and applies Table I (*Uniform Premiums for $1,000 of Group-Term Life Insurance Protection) effective July 1, 1999:*

Example 1. Excess group-term life insurance coverage provided through salary reduction in a cafeteria plan. (i) Employer N provides group-term life insurance coverage to its employees only through its cafeteria plan. Employer N's cafeteria plan allows employees to elect salary reduction for group-term life insurance. Employee B, age 42, elected salary reduction of $200 for $150,000 of group-term life insurance. None of the group-term life insurance is paid through after-tax employee contributions.

(ii) B's $200 of salary reduction for group-term life insurance is excludible from B's gross income under paragraph (k)(2)(i)(A).

(iii) B has a total of $150,000 of group-term life insurance. The group-term life insurance in excess of the dollar limitation of section 79 is $100,000 (150,000 – 50,000).

(iv) The Table I cost is $120 for $100,000 of group-term life insurance for an individual between ages 40 to 44. The Table I cost of $120 is reduced by zero (because B paid no portion of the group-term life insurance with after-tax employee contributions), under paragraphs (k)(2)(i)(A)-(B) of this section.

(v) The amount includible in B's gross income for the $100,000 of excess group-term life insurance is $120.

Example 2. Excess group-term life insurance coverage provided through salary reduction in a cafeteria plan where employee purchases a portion of group-term life insurance coverage with after-tax contributions. (i) Same facts as *Example 1*, except that B elected salary reduction of $100 and makes an after-tax contribution of $100 toward the purchase of group-term life insurance coverage.

(ii) B's $100 of salary reduction for group-term life insurance is excludible from B's gross income, under paragraph (k)(2)(i)(A) of this section.

(iii) B has a total of $150,000 of group-term life insurance. The group-term life insurance in excess of the dollar limitation of section 79 is $100,000 (150,000 – 50,000).

(iv) The Table I cost is $120 for $100,000 of group-term life insurance for an individual between ages 40 to 44, under (k)(2)(i)(B). The Table I cost of $120 is reduced by $100 (because B paid $100 for the group-term life insurance with after-tax employee contributions), under paragraphs (k)(2)(i)(B) and (k)(2)(i)(C) of this section.

(v) The amount includible in B's gross income for the $100,000 of excess group-term life insurance coverage is $20.

Example 3. Excess group-term life insurance coverage provided through salary reduction in a cafeteria plan and outside a cafeteria plan. (i) Same facts as *Example 1* except that Employer N also provides (at no cost to employees) group-term life insurance coverage equal to each employee's annual salary. Employee B's annual salary is $150,000. B has $150,000 of group-term life insurance directly from Employer N, and also $150,000 coverage through Employer N's cafeteria plan.

(ii) B's $200 of salary reduction for group-term life insurance is excludible from B's gross income, under paragraph (k)(2)(i)(A) of this section.

(iii) B has a total of $300,000 of group-term life insurance. The group-term life insurance in excess of the dollar limitation of section 79 is $250,000 (300,000 – 50,000).

(iv) The Table I cost is $300 for $250,000 of group-term life insurance for an individual between ages 40 to 44. The Table I cost of $300 is reduced by zero (because B paid no portion of the group-term life insurance with after-tax employee contributions), under paragraphs (k)(2)(i)(B) and (k)(2)(i)(C) of this section.

(v) The amount includible in B's gross income for the $250,000 of excess group-term life insurance is $300.

Example 4. Excess group-term life insurance coverage provided through salary reduction in a cafeteria plan and outside a cafeteria plan. (i) Same facts as *Example 3* except that Employee C's annual salary is $30,000. C has $30,000 of group-term life insurance coverage provided directly from Employer N, and elects an additional $30,000 of coverage for $40 through Employer N's cafeteria plan. C is 42 years old.

(ii) C's $40 of salary reduction for group-term life insurance is excludible from C's gross income, under paragraph (k)(2)(i)(A) of this section.

(iii) C has a total of $60,000 of group-term life insurance. The group-term life insurance in excess of the dollar limitation of section 79 is $10,000 (60,000 – 50,000).

(iv) The Table I cost is $12 for $10,000 of group-term life insurance for an individual between ages 40 to 44. The Table I cost of $12 is reduced by zero (because C paid no portion of the group-term life insurance with after-tax employee contributions), under paragraphs (k)(2)(i)(B) and (k)(2)(i)(C) of this section.

(v) The amount includible in C's gross income for the $10,000 of excess group-term life insurance coverage is $12.

(l) *COBRA premiums.*—(1) *Paying COBRA premiums through a cafeteria plan.*—Under § 1.125-4(c)(3)(iv), COBRA premiums for an employer-provided group health plan are qualified benefits if:

(i) The premiums are excludible from an employee's income under section 106; or

(ii) The premiums are for the accident and health plan of the employer sponsoring the cafeteria plan, even if the fair market value of the premiums is includible in an employee's gross income. See also paragraph (e)(2) in § 1.125-5 and § 54.4980B-2, Q & A-8 of this chapter for COBRA rules for health FSAs.

(2) *Example.*—The following example illustrates the rules of this paragraph (l):

Example. COBRA premiums. (i) Employer O maintains a cafeteria plan for full-time employees, offering an election between cash and employer-provided accident and health insurance and other qualified benefits. Employees A, B, and C participate in the cafeteria plan. On July 1, 2009, Employee A has a qualifying event (as defined in § 54.4980B-4 of this chapter).

(ii) Employee A was a full-time employee and became a part-time employee and for that reason, is no longer covered by Employer O's accident and health plan. Under § 1.125-4(f)(3)(ii), Employee A changes her election to salary reduce to pay her COBRA premiums.

(iii) Employee B previously worked for another employer, quit and elected COBRA. Employee B begins work for Employer O on July 1, 2009, and becomes eligible to participate in Employer O's cafeteria plan on July 1, 2009, but will not be eligible to participate in Employer O's accident and health plan until October 1, 2009. Employee B elects to salary reduce to pay COBRA premiums for coverage under the accident and health plan sponsored by B's former employer.

(iv) Employee C and C's spouse are covered by Employer O's accident and health plan until July 1, 2009, when C's divorce from her spouse became final. C continues to be covered by the accident and health plan. On July 1, 2009, C requests to pay COBRA premiums for her former spouse (who is not C's dependent (as defined in section 152)) with after-tax employee contributions.

(v) Salary reduction elections for COBRA premiums for Employees A and B are qualified benefits for purposes of section 125 and are excludible from the gross income of Employees A and B. Employer O allows A and B to salary reduce for these COBRA premiums.

(vi) Employer O allows C to pay for COBRA premiums for C's former spouse, with after-tax employee contributions because although accident and health coverage for C's former spouse is permitted in a cafeteria plan, the premiums are includible in C's gross income.

(vii) The operation of Employer O's cafeteria plan satisfies the requirements of this paragraph (l).

(m) *Payment or reimbursement of employees' individual accident and health insurance premiums.*—(1) *In general.*—The payment or reimbursement of employees' substantiated individual health insurance premiums is excludible from employees' gross income under section 106 and is a qualified benefit for purposes of section 125.

(2) *Example.*—The following example illustrates the rule of this paragraph (m):

Example. Payment or reimbursement of premiums. (i) Employer P's cafeteria plan offers the following benefits for employees who are covered by an individual health insurance policy. The employee substantiates the expenses for the premiums for the policy (as required in paragraph (b)(2) in § 1.125-6) before any payments or reimbursements to the employee for premiums are made. The payments or reimbursements are made in the following ways:

(ii) The cafeteria plan reimburses each employee directly for the amount of the employee's substantiated health insurance premium;

(iii) The cafeteria plan issues the employee a check payable to the health insurance company for the amount of the employee's health insurance premium, which the employee is obligated to tender to the insurance company;

(iv) The cafeteria plan issues a check in the same manner as (iii), except that the check is payable jointly to the employee and the insurance company; or

(v) Under these circumstances, the individual health insurance policies are accident and health plans as defined in § 1.106-1. This benefit is a qualified benefit under section 125.

(n) *Section 105 rules for accident and health plan offered through a cafeteria plan.*—(1) *General rule.*—In order for an accident and health plan to be a qualified benefit that is excludible from gross income if elected through a cafeteria plan, the cafeteria plan must satisfy section 125 and the accident and health plan must satisfy section 105(b) and (h).

(2) *Section 105(b) requirements in general.*—Section 105(b) provides an exclusion from gross income for amounts paid to an employee from an employer-funded accident and health plan specifically to reimburse the employee for certain expenses for medical care (as defined in section 213(d)) incurred by the employee or the employee's spouse or dependents during the period for which the benefit is provided to the employee (that is, when the employee is covered by the accident and health plan).

(o) *Prohibition against deferred compensation.*—(1) *In general.*—Any plan that offers a benefit that defers compensation (except as provided in this paragraph (o)) is not a cafeteria plan. See section 125(d)(2)(A). A plan that permits employees to carry over unused elective contributions, after-tax contributions, or plan benefits from one plan year to another (except as provided in paragraphs (e), (o)(3) and (4) and (p) of this section) defers compensation. This is the case regardless of how the contributions or benefits are used by the employee in the subsequent plan year (for example, whether they are automatically or electively converted into another taxable or nontaxable benefit in the subsequent plan year or used to provide additional benefits of the same type). Similarly, a cafeteria plan also defers compensation if the plan permits employees to use contributions for one plan year to purchase a benefit that will be provided in a subsequent plan year (for example, life, health or disability if these benefits have a savings or investment feature, such as whole life insurance). See also Q & A-5 in § 1.125-3, prohibiting deferring compensation from one cafeteria plan year to a subsequent cafeteria plan year. See paragraph (e) of this section for grace period rules. A plan does not defer compensation merely because it allocates experience gains (or forfeitures) among participants in compliance with paragraph (o) in § 1.125-5.

(2) *Effect if a plan includes a benefit that defers the receipt of compensation or a plan operates to defer compensation.*—If a plan violates paragraph (o)(1) of this section, the availability of an election between taxable and nontaxable benefits under such a plan results in gross income to the employees.

(3) *Cash or deferred arrangements that may be offered in a cafeteria plan.*—(i) *In general.*—A cafeteria plan may offer the benefits set forth in this paragraph (o)(3), even though these benefits defer compensation.

(ii) *Elective contributions to a section 401(k) plan.*—A cafeteria plan may permit a covered employee to elect to have the employer, on behalf of the employee, pay amounts as contributions to a trust that is part of a profit-sharing or stock bonus plan or rural cooperative plan (within the meaning of section 401(k)(7)), which includes a qualified cash or deferred arrangement (as defined in section 401(k)(2)). In addition, after-tax employee contributions under a qualified plan subject to section 401(m) are permitted through a cafeteria plan. The right to make such contributions does not cause a plan to fail to be a cafeteria plan merely because, under the qualified plan, employer matching contributions (as defined in section 401(m)(4)(A)) are made with respect to elective or after-tax employee contributions.

(iii) *Additional permitted deferred compensation arrangements.*—A plan maintained by an educational organization described in section 170(b)(1)(A)(ii) to the extent of amounts which a covered employee may elect to have the employer pay as contributions for post-retirement group life insurance is permitted through a cafeteria plan, if—

(A) All contributions for such insurance must be made before retirement; and

(B) Such life insurance does not have a cash surrender value at any time.

(iv) *Contributions to HSAs.*—Contributions to covered employees' HSAs as defined in section 223 (but not contributions to Archer MSAs).

(4) *Paid time off.*—(i) *In general.*—A cafeteria plan is permitted to include elective paid time off (that is, vacation days, sick days or personal days) as a permitted taxable benefit through the plan by permitting employees to receive more paid time off than the employer otherwise provides to the employees on a nonelective basis, but only if the inclusion of elective paid time off through the plan does not operate to permit the deferral of compensation. In addition, a plan that only offers the choice of cash or paid time off is not a cafeteria plan and is not subject to the rules of section 125. In order to avoid deferral of compensation, the cafeteria plan must preclude any employee from using the paid time off or receiving cash, in a subsequent plan year, for any portion of such paid time off remaining unused as of the end of the plan year. (See paragraph (o)(4)(iii) of this section for the deadline to cash out unused elective paid time off.) For example, a plan that offers employees the opportunity to purchase paid time off (or to receive cash or other benefits through the plan in lieu of paid time off) is not a cafeteria plan if employees who purchase the paid time off for a plan year are allowed to use any unused paid time off in a subsequent plan year. This is the case even though the plan does not permit the employee to convert, in any subsequent plan year, the unused paid time off into any other benefit.

(ii) *Ordering of elective and nonelective paid time off.*—In determining whether a plan providing paid time off operates to permit the deferral of compensation, a cafeteria plan must provide that employees are deemed to use paid time off in the following order:

(A) *Nonelective paid time off.*—Nonelective paid time off (that is, paid time off with respect to which the employee has no election) is used first;

(B) *Elective paid time off.*—Elective paid time off is used after all nonelective paid time off is used.

(iii) *Cashing out or forfeiture of unused elective paid time off, in general.*—The cafeteria plan must provide that all unused elective paid time off (determined as of the last day of the plan year) must either be paid in cash (within the time specified in this paragraph (o)(4)) or be forfeited. This provision must apply uniformly to all participants in the cafeteria plan.

(A) *Cash out of unused elective paid time off.*—A plan does not operate to permit the deferral of compensation merely because the plan provides that an employee who has not used all elective paid time off for a plan year receives in cash the value of such unused paid time off. The employee must receive the cash on or before the last day of the cafeteria plan's plan year to which the elective contributions used to purchase the unused elective paid time off relate.

(B) *Forfeiture of unused elective paid time off.*—If the cafeteria plan provides for forfeiture of unused elective paid time off, the forfeiture must be effective on the last day of the plan year to which the elective contributions relate.

(iv) *No grace period for paid time off.*—The grace period described in paragraph (e) of this section does not apply to paid time off.

(v) *Examples.*—The following examples illustrate the rules of this paragraph (o)(4):

Example 1. Plan cashes out unused elective paid time off on or before the last day of the plan year. (i) Employer Q provides employees with two weeks of paid time off for each calendar year. Employer Q's human resources policy (that is, outside the cafeteria plan), permits employees to carry over one nonelective week of paid time off to the next year. Employer Q maintains a calendar year cafeteria plan that permits the employee to purchase, with elective contributions, an additional week of paid time off.

(ii) For the 2009 plan year, Employee A (with a calendar tax year), timely elects to purchase one additional week of paid time off. During 2009, Employee A uses only two weeks of paid time off. Employee A is deemed to have used two weeks of nonelective paid time off and zero weeks of elective paid time off.

(iii) Pursuant to the cafeteria plan, the plan pays Employee A the value of the unused elective paid time off week in cash on December 31, 2009. Employer Q includes this amount on the 2009 Form W-2 for Employee A. This amount is included in Employee A's gross income in 2009. The cafeteria plan's terms and operations do not violate the prohibition against deferring compensation.

Example 2. Unused nonelective paid time off carried over to next plan year. (i) Same facts as *Example 1*, except that Employee A uses only one week of paid time off during the year. Pursuant to the cafeteria plan, Employee A is deemed to have used one nonelective week, and having retained one nonelective week and one elective week of paid time off. Employee A receives in cash the value of the unused elective paid time off on December 31, 2009. Employer Q includes this amount on the 2009 Form W-2 for Employee A. Employee A must report this amount as gross income in 2009.

(ii) Pursuant to Employer Q's human resources policy, Employee A is permitted to carry over the one nonelective week of paid time off to the next year. Nonelective paid time off is not part of the cafeteria plan (that is, neither Employer Q nor the cafeteria plan permit employees to exchange nonelective paid time off for other benefits).

(iii) The cafeteria plan's terms and operations do not violate the prohibition against deferring compensation.

Example 3. Forfeiture of unused elective paid time off. Same facts as *Example 2*, except that pursuant to the cafeteria plan, Employee A forfeits the remaining one week of elective paid time off. The cafeteria plan's terms and operations do not violate the prohibition against deferring compensation.

Example 4. Unused elective paid time off carried over to next plan year. Same facts as *Example 1*, except that Employee A uses only two weeks of paid time off during the 2009 plan year, and, under the terms of the cafeteria plan, Employee A is treated as having used the two nonelective weeks and as having retained the one elective week. The one remaining week (that is, the elective week) is carried over to the next plan year (or the value thereof used for any other purpose in the next plan year). The plan operates to permit deferring compensation and is not a cafeteria plan.

Example 5. Paid time off exchanged for accident and health insurance premiums. Employer R provides employees with four weeks of paid time off for a year. Employer R's calendar year cafeteria plan permits employees to exchange up to one week of paid time off to pay the employee's share of accident and health insurance premiums. For the 2009 plan year, Employee B (with a calendar tax year), timely elects to exchange one week of paid time off (valued at $769) to pay accident and health insurance premiums for 2009. The $769 is excludible from Employee B's gross income under section 106. The cafeteria plan's terms and operations do not violate the prohibition against deferring compensation.

(p) *Benefits relating to more than one year.*—(1) *Benefits in an accident and health insurance policy relating to more than one year.*—Consistent with section 125(d), an accident and health insurance policy may include certain benefits, as set forth in this paragraph (p)(1), without violating the prohibition against deferred compensation.

(i) *Permitted benefits.*—The following features or benefits of insurance policies do not defer compensation—

(A) Credit toward the deductible for unreimbursed covered expenses incurred in prior periods;

(B) Reasonable lifetime maximum limit on benefits;

(C) Level premiums;

(D) Premium waiver during disability;

(E) Guaranteed policy renewability of coverage, without further evidence of insurability (but not guaranty of the amount of premium upon renewal);

(F) Coverage for a specified accidental injury;

(G) Coverage for a specified disease or illness, including payments at initial diagnosis of the specified disease or illness, and progressive payments of a set amount per month following the initial diagnosis (sometimes referred to as progressive diagnosis payments); and

(H) Payment of a fixed amount per day (or other period) of hospitalization.

(ii) *Requirements of permitted benefits.*—All benefits described in paragraph (p)(1)(i) of this section must in addition satisfy all of the following requirements—

(A) No part of any benefit is used in one plan year to purchase a benefit in a subsequent plan year;

(B) The policies remain in force only so long as premiums are timely paid on a current basis, and, irrespective of the amount of premiums paid in prior plan years, if the current premiums are not paid, all coverage for new diseases or illnesses lapses. See paragraph (p)(1)(i)(D), allowing premium waiver during disability;

(C) There is no investment fund or cash value to rely upon for payment of premiums; and

(D) No part of any premium is held in a separate account for any participant or beneficiary, or otherwise segregated from the assets of the insurance company.

(2) *Benefits under a long-term disability policy relating to more than one year.*—A long-term disability policy paying disability benefits over more than one year does not violate the prohibition against deferring compensation.

(3) *Reasonable premium rebates or policy dividends.*—Reasonable premium rebates or policy dividends paid with respect to benefits provided through a cafeteria plan do not constitute impermissible deferred compensation if such rebates or dividends are paid before the close of the 12-month period immediately following the cafeteria plan year to which such rebates and dividends relate.

(4) *Mandatory two-year election for vision or dental insurance.*—When a cafeteria plan offers vision or dental insurance that requires a mandatory two-year coverage period, but not longer (sometimes referred to as a "two-year lock-in"), the mandatory two-year coverage period does not result in deferred compensation in violation of section 125(d)(2), provided both of the following requirements are satisfied—

(i) The premiums for each plan year are paid no less frequently than annually; and

(ii) In no event does a cafeteria plan use salary reduction or flex-credits relating to the first year of a two-year election to apply to vision or dental insurance for the second year of the two-year election.

(5) *Using salary reduction amounts from one plan year to pay accident and health insurance premiums for the first month of the immediately following plan year.*—(i) *In general.*—Salary reduction amounts from the last month of one plan year of a cafeteria plan may be applied to pay accident and health insurance premiums for insurance during the first month of the immediately following plan year, if done on a uniform and consistent basis with respect to all participants (based on the usual payroll interval for each group of participants).

(ii) *Example.*—The following example illustrates the rules in this paragraph (p)(5):

Example. Salary reduction payments in December of calendar plan year to pay accident and health insurance premiums for January. Employer S maintains a calendar year cafeteria plan. The cafeteria plan offers employees a salary reduction election for accident and health insurance. The plan provides that employees' salary reduction amounts for the last pay period in December are applied to pay accident and health insurance premiums for the immediately following January. All employees are paid bi-weekly. For the plan year ending December 31, 2009, Employee C elects salary reduction of $3,250 for accident and health coverage. For the last pay period in December 2009, $125 (3,250/26) is applied to the accident and health insurance premium for January 2010. This plan provision does not violate the prohibition against deferring compensation.

(q) *Nonqualified benefits.*—(1) *In general.*—The following benefits are nonqualified benefits that are not permitted to be offered in a cafeteria plan—

(i) Scholarships described in section 117;

(ii) Employer-provided meals and lodging described in section 119;

(iii) Educational assistance described in section 127;

(iv) Fringe benefits described in section 132;

(v) Long-term care insurance, or any product which is advertised, marketed or offered as long-term care insurance;

(vi) Long-term care services (but see paragraph (q)(3) of this section);

(vii) Group-term life insurance on the life of any individual other than an employee (whether includible or excludible from the employee's gross income);

(viii) Health reimbursement arrangements (HRAs) that provide reimbursements up to a maximum dollar amount for a coverage period and that all or any unused amount at the end of a coverage period is carried forward to increase the maximum reimbursement amount in subsequent coverage periods;

(ix) Contributions to Archer MSAs (section 220); and

(x) Elective deferrals to a section 403(b) plan.

(2) *Nonqualified benefits not permitted in a cafeteria plan.*—The benefits described in this paragraph (q) are not qualified benefits or taxable benefits or cash for purposes of section 125 and thus may not be offered in a cafeteria plan regardless of whether any such benefit is purchased with after-tax employee contributions or on any other basis. A plan that offers a nonqualified benefit is not a cafeteria plan. Employees' elections between taxable and nontaxable benefits through such plan result in gross income to the participants for any benefit elected. See section 125(f). See paragraph (q)(3) of this section for special rule on long-term care insurance purchased through an HSA.

(3) *Long-term care insurance or services purchased through an HSA.*—Although long-term care insurance is not a qualified benefit and may not be offered in a cafeteria plan, a cafeteria plan is permitted to offer an HSA as a qualified benefit, and funds from the HSA may be used to pay

eligible long-term care premiums on a qualified long-term care insurance contract or for qualified long-term care services.

(r) *Employer contributions to a cafeteria plan.*—(1) *Salary reduction-in general.*—The term *employer contributions* means amounts that are not currently available (after taking section 125 into account) to the employee but are specified in the cafeteria plan as amounts that an employee may use for the purpose of electing benefits through the plan. A plan may provide that employer contributions may be made, in whole or in part, pursuant to employees' elections to reduce their compensation or to forgo increases in compensation and to have such amounts contributed, as employer contributions, by the employer on their behalf. See also § 1.125-5 (flexible spending arrangements). Also, a cafeteria plan is permitted to require employees to elect to pay the employees' share of any qualified benefit through salary reduction and not with after-tax employee contributions. A cafeteria plan is also permitted to pay reasonable cafeteria plan administrative fees through salary reduction amounts, and these salary reduction amounts are excludible from an employee's gross income.

(2) *Salary reduction as employer contribution.*—Salary reduction contributions are employer contributions. An employee's salary reduction election is an election to receive a contribution by the employer in lieu of salary or other compensation that is not currently available to the employee as of the effective date of the election and that does not subsequently become currently available to the employee.

(3) *Employer flex-credits.*—A cafeteria plan may also provide that the employer contributions will or may be made on behalf of employees equal to (or up to) specified amounts (or specified percentages of compensation) and that such nonelective contributions are available to employees for the election of benefits through the plan.

(4) *Elective contributions to a section 401(k) plan.*—See § 1.401(k)-1 for general rules relating to contributions to section 401(k) plans.

(s) *Effective/applicability date.*—It is proposed that these regulations apply on and after plan years beginning on or after January 1, 2009, except that the rule in paragraph (k)(2)(i)(B) of this section is effective as of the date the proposed regulations are published in the **Federal Register**. [Reg. § 1.125-1.]

§ 1.125-2. Cafeteria plans; elections.—(a) *Rules relating to making and revoking elections.*—(1) *Elections in general.*—A plan is not a cafeteria plan unless the plan provides in writing that employees are permitted to make elections among the permitted taxable benefits and qualified benefits offered through the plan for the plan year (and grace period, if applicable). All elections must be irrevocable by the date described in paragraph (a)(2) of this section except as provided in paragraph (a)(4) of this section. An election is not irrevocable if, after the earlier of the dates specified in paragraph (a)(2) of this section, employees have the right to revoke their elections of qualified benefits and instead receive the taxable benefits for such period, without regard to whether the employees actually revoke their elections.

(2) *Timing of elections.*—In order for employees to exclude qualified benefits from employees' gross income, benefit elections in a cafeteria plan must be made before the earlier of—

(i) The date when taxable benefits are currently available; or

(ii) The first day of the plan year (or other coverage period).

(3) *Benefit currently available to an employee—in general.*—Cash or another taxable benefit is currently available to the employee if it has been paid to the employee or if the employee is able currently to receive the cash or other taxable benefit at the employee's discretion. However, cash or another taxable benefit is not currently available to an employee if there is a significant limitation or restriction on the employee's right to receive the benefit currently. Similarly, a benefit is not currently available as of a date if the employee may under no circumstances receive the benefit before a particular time in the future. The determination of whether a benefit is currently available to an employee does not depend on whether it has been constructively received by the employee for purposes of section 451.

(4) *Exceptions to rule on making and revoking elections.*—If a cafeteria plan incorporates the change in status rules in § 1.125-4, to the extent provided in those rules, an employee who experiences a change in status (as defined in § 1.125-4) is permitted to revoke an existing election and to make a new election with respect to the remaining portion of the period of coverage, but only with respect to cash or other taxable benefits that are not yet currently available. See paragraph (c)(1) of this section for a special rule for changing elections prospectively for HSA contributions and paragraph (r)(4) in § 1.125-1 for section 401(k) elections. Also, only an employee of the employer sponsoring a cafeteria plan is allowed to make, revoke or change elections in the employer's cafeteria plan. The employee's spouse, dependent or any other individual other than the employee may not make, revoke or change elections under the plan.

(5) *Elections not required on written paper documents.*—A cafeteria plan does not fail to meet the requirements of section 125 merely because it permits employees to use electronic media for such transactions. The safe harbor in § 1.401(a)-21 applies to electronic elections, revocations and changes in elections under section 125.

(6) *Examples.*—The following examples illustrate the rules in this paragraph (a):

Example 1. Election not revocable during plan year. Employer A's cafeteria plan offers each employee the opportunity to elect, for a plan year, between $5,000 cash for the plan year and a dependent care assistance program of up to $5,000 of dependent care expenses incurred by the employee during the plan year. The cafeteria plan requires employees to elect between these benefits before the beginning of the plan year. After the year has commenced, employees are prohibited from revoking their elections. The cafeteria plan allows revocation of elections based on changes in status (as described in § 1.125-4). Employees who elected the dependent care assistance program do not include the $5,000 cash in gross income. The cafeteria plan satisfies the requirements in this paragraph (a).

Example 2. Election revocable during plan year. Same facts as *Example 1* except that Employer A's cafeteria plan allows employees to revoke their elections for dependent care assistance at any time during the plan year and receive the unused amount of dependent care assistance as cash. The cafeteria plan fails to satisfy the requirements in this paragraph (a), and is not a cafeteria plan. All employees are treated as having received the $5,000 in cash even if they do not revoke their elections. The same result occurs even though the cash is not payable until the end of the plan year.

(b) *Automatic elections.*—(1) *In general.*—For new employees or current employees who fail to timely elect between permitted taxable benefits and qualified benefits, a cafeteria plan is permitted, but is not required, to provide default elections for one or more qualified benefits (for example, an election made for any prior year is deemed to be continued for every succeeding plan year, unless changed).

(2) *Example.*—The following example illustrates the rules in this paragraph (b):

Example. Automatic elections for accident and health insurance.

(i) Employer B maintains a calendar year cafeteria plan. The cafeteria plan offers accident and health insurance with an option for employee-only or family coverage. All employees are eligible to participate in the cafeteria plan immediately upon hire.

(ii) The cafeteria plan provides for an automatic enrollment process: each new employee and each current employee is automatically enrolled in employee-only coverage under the accident and health insurance plan, and the employee's salary is reduced to pay the employee's share of the accident and health insurance premium, unless the employee affirmatively elects cash. Alternatively, if the employee has a spouse or child, the employee can elect family coverage.

(iii) When an employee is hired, the employee receives a notice explaining the automatic enrollment process and the employee's right to decline coverage and have no salary reduction. The notice includes the salary reduction amounts for employee-only coverage and family coverage, procedures for exercising the right to decline coverage, information on the time by which an election must be made, and the period for which an election is effective. The notice is also given to each current employee before the beginning of each subsequent plan year, except that the notice for a current employee includes a description of the employee's existing coverage, if any.

(iv) For a new employee, an election to receive cash or to have family coverage rather than employee-only coverage is effective if made when the employee is hired. For a current employee, an election is effective if made prior to the start of each calendar year or under any other circumstances permitted under § 1.125-4. An election made for any prior year is deemed to be continued for every succeeding plan year, unless changed.

(v) Contributions used to purchase accident and health insurance through a cafeteria plan are not includible in the gross income of the employee solely because the plan provides for automatic enrollment as a default election whereby the employee's salary is reduced each year to pay for a portion of the accident and health insurance through the plan (unless the employee affirmatively elects cash).

(c) *Election rules for salary reduction contributions to HSAs.*—(1) *Prospective elections and changes in salary reduction elections allowed.*—Contributions may be made to an HSA through a cafeteria plan. A cafeteria plan offering HSA contributions through salary reduction may permit employees to make prospective salary reduction elections or change or revoke salary reduction elections for HSA contributions (for example, to increase or decrease salary reduction elections for HSA contributions) at any time during the plan year, effective before salary becomes currently available. If a cafeteria plan offers HSA contributions as a qualified benefit, the plan must—

(i) Specifically describe the HSA contribution benefit;

(ii) Allow a participant to prospectively change his or her salary reduction election for HSA contributions on a monthly basis (or more frequently); and

(iii) Allow a participant who becomes ineligible to make HSA contributions to prospectively revoke his or her salary reduction election for HSA contributions.

(2) *Example.*—The following example illustrates the rules in this paragraph (c):

Example. Prospective HSA salary reduction elections. (i) A cafeteria plan with a calendar plan year allows employees to make salary reduction elections for HSA contributions through the plan. The cafeteria plan permits employees to prospectively make, change or revoke salary contribution elections for HSA contributions, limited to one election, change or revocation per month.

(ii) Employee M participates in the cafeteria plan. Before salary becomes currently available to M, M makes the following elections. On January 2, 2009, M elects to contribute $100 for each pay period to an HSA, effective January 3, 2009. On March 15, 2009, M elects to reduce the HSA contribution to $35 per pay period, effective April 1, 2009. On May 1, 2009, M elects to discontinue all HSA contributions, effective May 15, 2009. The cafeteria plan implements all of Employee M's elections,

(iii) The cafeteria plan's operation is consistent with the section 125 election, change and revocation rules for HSA contributions.

(d) *Optional election for new employees.*—A cafeteria plan may provide new employees 30 days after their hire date to make elections between cash and qualified benefits. The election is effective as of the employee's hire date. However, salary reduction amounts used to pay for such an election must be from compensation not yet currently available on the date of the election. The written cafeteria plan must provide that any employee who terminates employment and is rehired within 30 days after terminating employment (or who returns to employment following an unpaid leave of absence of less than 30 days) is not a new employee eligible for the election in this paragraph (d).

(e) *Effective/applicability date.*—It is proposed that these regulations apply on and after plan years beginning on or after January 1, 2009. [Reg. § 1.125-2.]

☐ Par. 3. Sections 1.125-5, 1.125-6 and 1.125-7 are added to read as follows:

§1.125-5. Flexible spending arrangements.—(a) *Definition of flexible spending arrangement.*—(1) *In general.*—An FSA generally is a benefit program that provides employees with coverage which reimburses specified, incurred expenses (subject to reimbursement maximums and any other reasonable conditions). An expense for qualified benefits must not be reimbursed from the FSA unless it is incurred during a period of coverage. See paragraph (e) of this section. After an expense for a qualified benefit has been incurred, the expense must first be substantiated before the expense is reimbursed. See paragraphs (a) through (f) in §1.125-6.

(2) *Maximum amount of reimbursement.*—The maximum amount of reimbursement that is reasonably available to an employee for a period of coverage must not be substantially in excess of the total salary reduction and employer flex-credit for such participant's coverage. A maximum amount of reimbursement is not substantially in excess of the total salary reduction and employer flex-credit if such maximum amount is less than 500 percent of the combined salary reduction and employer flex-credit. A single FSA may provide participants with different levels of coverage and maximum amounts of reimbursement. See paragraph (r) in §1.125-1 and paragraphs (b) and (d) in this section for the definition of salary reduction, employer flex-credit, and uniform coverage rule.

(b) *Flex-credits allowed.*—(1) *In general.*—An FSA in a cafeteria plan must include an election between cash or taxable benefits (including salary reduction) and one or more qualified benefits, and may include, in addition, "employer flex-credits." For this purpose, flex-credits are non-elective employer contributions that the employer makes for every employee eligible to participate in the employer's cafeteria plan, to be used at the employee's election only for one or more qualified benefits (but not as cash or a taxable benefit). See §1.125-1 for definitions of qualified benefits, cash and taxable benefits.

(2) *Example.*—The following example illustrates the rules in this paragraph (b):

Example. Flex-credit. Contribution to health FSA for employees electing employer-provided accident and health plan. Employer A maintains a cafeteria plan offering employees an election between cash or taxable benefits and premiums for employer-provided accident and health insurance or coverage through an HMO. The plan also provides an employer contribution of $200 to the health FSA of every employee who elects accident and health insurance or HMO coverage. In addition, these employees may elect to reduce their salary to make additional contributions to their health FSAs. The benefits offered in this cafeteria plan are consistent with the requirements of section 125 and this paragraph (b).

(c) *Use-or-lose rule.*—(1) *In general.*—An FSA may not defer compensation. No contribution or benefit from an FSA may be carried over to any subsequent plan year or period of coverage. See paragraph (k)(3) in this section for specific exceptions. Unused benefits or contributions remaining at the end of the plan year (or at the end of a grace period, if applicable) are forfeited.

(2) *Example.*—The following example illustrates the rules in this paragraph (c):

Example. Use-or-lose rule. (i) Employer B maintains a calendar year cafeteria plan, offering an election between cash and a health FSA. The cafeteria plan has no grace period.

(ii) Employee A plans to have eye surgery in 2009. For the 2009 plan year, Employee A timely elects salary reduction of $3,000 for a health FSA. During the 2009 plan year, Employee A learns that she cannot have eye surgery performed, but incurs other section 213(d) medical expenses totaling $1,200. As of December 31, 2009, she has $1,800 of unused benefits and contributions in the health FSA. Consistent with the rules in this paragraph (c), she forfeits $1,800.

(d) *Uniform coverage rules applicable to health FSAs.*—(1) *Uniform coverage throughout coverage period- in general.*—The maximum amount of reimbursement from a health FSA must be available at all times during the period of coverage (properly reduced as of any particular time for prior reimbursements for the same period of coverage). Thus, the maximum amount of reimbursement at any particular time during the period of coverage cannot relate to the amount that has been contributed to the FSA at any particular time prior to the end of the plan year. Similarly, the payment schedule for the required amount for coverage under a health FSA may not be based on the rate or amount of covered claims incurred during the coverage period. Employees' salary reduction payments must not be accelerated based on employees' incurred claims and reimbursements.

(2) *Reimbursement available at all times.*—Reimbursement is deemed to be available at all times if it is paid at least monthly or when the total amount of the claims to be submitted is at least a specified, reasonable minimum amount (for example, $50).

(3) *Terminated participants.*—When an employee ceases to be a participant, the cafeteria plan must pay the former participant any amount the former participant previously paid for coverage or benefits to the extent the previously paid amount relates to the period from the date the employee ceases to be a participant through the end of that plan year. See paragraph (e)(2) in this section for COBRA elections for health FSAs.

(4) *Example.*—The following example illustrates the rules in this paragraph (d):

Example. Uniform coverage. (i) Employer C maintains a calendar year cafeteria plan, offering an election between cash and a health FSA. The cafeteria plan prohibits accelerating employees' salary reduction payments based on employees' incurred claims and reimbursements.

(ii) For the 2009 plan year, Employee N timely elects salary reduction of $3,000 for a health FSA. Employee N pays the $3,000 salary reduction amount through salary reduction of $250 per month throughout the coverage period. Employee N is eligible to receive the maximum amount of reimbursement of $3,000 at all times throughout the coverage period (reduced by prior reimbursements).

(iii) N incurs $2,500 of section 213(d) medical expenses in January, 2009. The full $2,500 is reimbursed although Employee N has made only one salary reduction payment of $250. N incurs $500 in medical expenses in February,

2009. The remaining $500 of the $3,000 is reimbursed. After Employee N submits a claim for reimbursement and substantiates the medical expenses, the cafeteria plan reimburses N for the $2,500 and $500 medical expenses. Employer C's cafeteria plan satisfies the uniform coverage rule.

(5) *No uniform coverage rule for FSAs for dependent care assistance or adoption assistance.*—The uniform coverage rule applies only to health FSAs and does not apply to FSAs for dependent care assistance or adoption assistance. See paragraphs (i) and (j) of this section for the rules for FSAs for dependent care assistance and adoption assistance.

(e) *Required period of coverage for a health FSA, dependent care FSA and adoption assistance FSA.*—(1) *Twelve-month period of coverage—in general.*—An FSA's period of coverage must be 12 months. However, in the case of a short plan year, the period of coverage is the entire short plan year. See paragraph (d) in § 1.125-1 for rules on plan years and changing plan years.

(2) *COBRA elections for health FSAs.*—For the application of the health care continuation rules of section 4980B of the Code to health FSAs, see Q & A-2 in § 54.4980B-2 of this chapter.

(3) *Separate period of coverage permitted for each qualified benefit offered through FSA.*—Dependent care assistance, adoption assistance, and a health FSA are each permitted to have a separate period of coverage, which may be different from the plan year of the cafeteria plan.

(f) *Coverage on a month-by-month or expense-by-expense basis prohibited.*—In order for reimbursements from an accident and health plan to qualify for the section 105(b) exclusion, an employer-funded accident and health plan offered through a cafeteria plan may not operate in a manner that enables employees to purchase the accident and health plan coverage only for periods when employees expect to incur medical care expenses. Thus, for example, if a cafeteria plan permits employees to receive accident and health plan coverage on a month-by-month or an expense-by-expense basis, reimbursements from the accident and health plan fail to qualify for the section 105(b) exclusion. If, however, the period of coverage under an accident and health plan offered through a cafeteria plan is twelve months and the cafeteria plan does not permit an employee to elect specific amounts of coverage, reimbursement, or salary reduction for less than twelve months, the cafeteria plan does not operate to enable participants to purchase coverage only for periods during which medical care will be incurred. See § 1.125-4 and paragraph (a) in § 1.125-2 regarding the revocation of elections during a period of coverage on account of changes in family status.

(g) *FSA administrative practices.*—(1) *Limiting health FSA enrollment to employees who participate in the employer's accident and health plan.*—At the employer's option, a cafeteria plan is permitted to provide that only those employees who participate in one or more specified employer-provided accident and health plans may participate in a health FSA. See § 1.125-7 for nondiscrimination rules.

(2) *Interval for employees' salary reduction contributions.*—The cafeteria plan is permitted to specify any interval for employees' salary reduction contributions. The interval specified in the plan must be uniform for all participants.

(h) *Qualified benefits permitted to be offered through an FSA.*—Dependent care assistance (section 129), adoption assistance (section 137) and a medical reimbursement arrangement (section 105(b)) are permitted to be offered through an FSA in a cafeteria plan.

(i) *Section 129 rules for dependent care assistance program offered through a cafeteria plan.*—(1) *General rule.*—In order for dependent care assistance to be a qualified benefit that is excludible from gross income if elected through a cafeteria plan, the cafeteria plan must satisfy section 125 and the dependent care assistance must satisfy section 129.

(2) *Dependent care assistance in general.*—Section 129(a) provides an employee with an exclusion from gross income both for an employer-funded dependent care assistance program and for amounts paid or incurred by the employer for dependent care assistance provided to the employee, if the amounts are paid or incurred through a dependent care assistance program. See paragraph (a)(4) in § 1.125-6 on when dependent care expenses are incurred.

(3) *Reimbursement exclusively for dependent care assistance.*—A dependent care assistance program may not provide reimbursements other than for dependent care expenses; in particular, if an employee has dependent care expenses less than the amount specified by salary reduction, the plan may not provide other taxable or nontaxable benefits for any portion of the specified amount not used for the reimbursement of dependent care expenses. Thus, if an employee has elected coverage under the dependent care assistance program and the period of coverage has commenced, the employee must not have the right to receive amounts from the program other than as reimbursements for dependent care expenses. This is the case regardless of whether coverage under the program is purchased with contributions made at the employer's discretion, at the employee's discretion, or pursuant to a collective bargaining agreement. Arrangements formally outside of the cafeteria plan providing for the adjustment of an employee's compensation or an employee's receipt of any other benefits on the basis of the assistance or reimbursements received by the employee are considered in determining whether a dependent care benefit is a dependent care assistance program under section 129.

(j) *Section 137 rules for adoption assistance program offered through a cafeteria plan.*—(1) *General rule.*—In order for adoption assistance to be a qualified benefit that is excludible from gross income if elected through a cafeteria plan, the cafeteria plan must satisfy section 125 and the adoption assistance must satisfy section 137.

(2) *Adoption assistance in general.*—Section 137(a) provides an employee with an exclusion from gross income for amounts paid or expenses incurred by the employer for qualified adoption expenses in connection with an employee's adoption of a child, if the amounts are paid or incurred through an adoption assistance program. Certain limits on amount of expenses and employee's income apply.

(3) *Reimbursement exclusively for adoption assistance.*—Rules and requirements similar to the rules and requirements in paragraph (i)(3) of this section for dependent care assistance apply to adoption assistance.

(k) *FSAs and the rules governing the tax-favored treatment of employer-provided health benefits.*—(1) *Medical expenses.*—Health plans that are flexible spending arrangements, as defined in paragraph (a)(1) of this section, must conform to the generally applicable rules under sections 105 and 106 in order for the coverage and reimbursements under such plans to qualify for tax-favored treatment under such sections. Thus, health FSAs must qualify as accident and health plans. See paragraph (n) in §1.125-1. A health FSA is only permitted to reimburse medical expenses as defined in section 213(d). Thus, for example, a health FSA is not permitted to reimburse dependent care expenses.

(2) *Limiting payment or reimbursement to certain section 213(d) medical expenses.*—A health FSA is permitted to limit payment or reimbursement to only certain section 213(d) medical expenses (except health insurance, long-term care services or insurance). See paragraph (q) in §1.125-1. For example, a health FSA in a cafeteria plan is permitted to provide in the written plan that the plan reimburses all section 213(d) medical expenses allowed to be paid or reimbursed under a cafeteria plan except over-the-counter drugs.

(3) *Application of prohibition against deferred compensation to medical expenses.*—(i) *Certain advance payments for orthodontia permitted.*—A cafeteria plan is permitted, but is not required to, reimburse employees for orthodontia services before the services are provided but only to the extent that the employee has actually made the payments in advance of the orthodontia services in order to receive the services. These orthodontia services are deemed to be incurred when the employee makes the advance payment. Reimbursing advance payments does not violate the prohibition against deferring compensation.

(ii) *Example.*—The following example illustrates the rules in paragraph (k)(3):

Example. Advance payment to orthodontist. Employer D sponsors a calendar year cafeteria plan which offers a health FSA. Employee K elects to salary reduce $3,000 for a health FSA for the 2009 plan year. Employee K's dependent requires orthodontic treatment. K's accident and health insurance does not cover orthodontia. The orthodontist, following the normal practice, charges $3,000, all due in 2009, for treatment, to begin in 2009 and end in 2010. K pays the $3,000 in 2009. In 2009, Employer D's cafeteria plan may reimburse $3,000 to K, without violating the prohibition against deferring compensation in section 125(d)(2).

(iii) *Reimbursements for durable medical equipment.*—A health FSA in a cafeteria plan that reimburses employees for equipment (described in section 213(d)) with a useful life extending beyond the period of coverage during which the expense is incurred does not provide deferred compensation. For example, a health FSA is permitted to reimburse the cost of a wheelchair for an employee.

(4) *No reimbursement of premiums for accident and health insurance or long-term care insurance or services.*—A health FSA is not permitted to treat employees' premium payments for other health coverage as reimbursable expenses. Thus, for example, a health FSA is not permitted to reimburse employees for payments for other health plan coverage, including premiums for COBRA coverage, accidental death and dismemberment insurance, long-term disability or short-term disability insurance or for health coverage under a plan maintained by the employer of the employee or the employer of the employee's spouse or dependent. Also, a health FSA is not permitted to reimburse expenses for long-term care insurance premiums or for long-term care services for the employee or employee's spouse or dependent. See paragraph (q) in §1.125-1 for nonqualified benefits

(l) *Section 105(h) requirements.*—Section 105(h) applies to health FSAs. Section 105(h) provides that the exclusion provided by section 105(b) is not available with respect to certain amounts received by a highly compensated individual (as defined in section 105(h)(5)) from a discriminatory self-insured medical reimbursement plan, which includes health FSAs. See §1.105-11. For purposes of section 105(h), coverage by a self-insured accident and health plan offered through a cafeteria plan is an optional benefit (even if only one level and type of coverage is offered) and, for purposes of the optional benefit rule in §1.105-11(c)(3)(i), employer contributions are treated as employee contributions to the extent that taxable benefits are offered by the plan.

(m) *HSA-compatible FSAs-limited-purpose health FSAs and post-deductible health FSAs.*—(1) *In general.—Limited-purpose health FSAs* and *post-deductible health FSAs* which satisfy all the requirements of section 125 are permitted to be offered through a cafeteria plan.

(2) *HSA-compatible FSAs.*—Section 223(a) allows a deduction for certain contributions to a "Health Savings Account" (HSA) (as defined in section 223(d)). An *eligible individual* (as defined in section 223(c)(1)) may contribute to an HSA. An eligible individual must be covered under a "high deductible health plan" (HDHP) and not, while covered under an HDHP, under any health plan which is not an HDHP. A general purpose health FSA is not an HDHP and an individual covered by a general purpose health FSA is not eligible to contribute to an HSA. However, an individual covered by an HDHP (and who otherwise satisfies section 223(c)(1)) does not fail to be an eligible individual merely because the individual is also covered by a limited-purpose health FSA or post-deductible health FSA (as defined in this paragraph (m)) or a combination of a limited-purpose health FSA and a post-deductible health FSA.

(3) *Limited-purpose health FSA.*—A limited-purpose health FSA is a health FSA described in the cafeteria plan that only pays or reimburses permitted coverage benefits (as defined in section 223(c)(2)(C)), such as vision care, dental care or preventive care (as defined for purposes of section 223(c)(2)(C)). See paragraph (k) in this section.

(4) *Post-deductible health FSA.*—(i) *In general.*—A post-deductible health FSA is a health FSA described in the cafeteria plan that only pays or reimburses medical expenses (as defined in section 213(d)) for preventive care or medical expenses incurred after the minimum annual HDHP deductible under section 223(c)(2)(A)(i) is satisfied. See paragraph (k) in this section. No medical expenses incurred before the annual HDHP deductible is satisfied may be reimbursed by a post-deductible FSA, regardless of whether

the HDHP covers the expense or whether the deductible is later satisfied. For example, even if chiropractic care is not covered under the HDHP, expenses for chiropractic care incurred before the HDHP deductible is satisfied are not reimbursable at any time by a post-deductible health FSA.

(ii) *HDHP and health FSA deductibles.*—The deductible for a post-deductible health FSA need not be the same amount as the deductible for the HDHP, but in no event may the post-deductible health FSA or other coverage provide benefits before the minimum annual HDHP deductible under section 223(c)(2)(A)(i) is satisfied (other than benefits permitted under a limited-purpose health FSA). In addition, although the deductibles of the HDHP and the other coverage may be satisfied independently by separate expenses, no benefits may be paid before the minimum annual deductible under section 223(c)(2)(A)(i) has been satisfied. An individual covered by a post-deductible health FSA (if otherwise an eligible individual) is an eligible individual for the purpose of contributing to the HSA.

(5) *Combination of limited-purpose health FSA and post-deductible health FSA.*—An FSA is a combination of a limited-purpose health FSA and post-deductible health FSA if each of the benefits and reimbursements provided under the FSA are permitted under either a limited-purpose health FSA or post-deductible health FSA. For example, before the HDHP deductible is satisfied, a combination limited-purpose and post-deductible health FSA may reimburse only preventive, vision or dental expenses. A combination limited-purpose and post-deductible health FSA may also reimburse any medical expense that may otherwise be paid by an FSA (that is, no insurance premiums or long-term care benefits) that is incurred after the HDHP deductible is satisfied.

(6) *Substantiation.*—The substantiation rules in this section apply to limited-purpose health FSAs and to post-deductible health FSAs. In addition to providing third-party substantiation of medical expenses, a participant in a post-deductible health FSA must provide information from an independent third party that the HDHP deductible has been satisfied. A participant in a limited-purpose health FSA must provide information from an independent third-party that the medical expenses are for vision care, dental care or preventive care.

(7) *Plan amendments.*—See paragraph (c) in §1.125-1 on the required effective date for amendments adopting or changing limited-purpose, post-deductible or combination limited-purpose and post-deductible health FSAs.

(n) *Qualified HSA distributions.*—(1) *In general.*—A health FSA in a cafeteria plan is permitted to offer employees the right to elect qualified HSA distributions described in section 106(e). No qualified HSA distribution may be made in a plan year unless the employer amends the health FSA written plan with respect to all employees, effective by the last day of the plan year, to allow a qualified HSA distribution satisfying all the requirements in this paragraph (n). See also section 106(e)(5)(B). In addition, a distribution with respect to an employee is not a qualified HSA distribution unless all of the following the requirements are satisfied—

(i) No qualified HSA distribution has been previously made on behalf of the employee from this health FSA;

(ii) The employee elects to have the employer make a qualified HSA distribution from the health FSA to the HSA of the employee;

(iii) The distribution does not exceed the lesser of the balance of the health FSA on—

(A) September 21, 2006; or

(B) The date of the distribution;

(iv) For purposes of this paragraph (n)(1), balances as of any date are determined on a cash basis, without taking into account expenses incurred but not reimbursed as of a date, and applying the uniform coverage rule in paragraph (d) in this section;

(v) The distribution is made no later than December 31, 2011; and

(vi) The employer makes the distribution directly to the trustee of the employee's HSA.

(2) *Taxation of qualified HSA distributions.*—A qualified HSA distribution from the health FSA covering the participant to his or her HSA is a rollover to the HSA (as defined in section 223(f)(5)) and thus is generally not includible in gross income. However, if the participant is not an eligible individual (as defined in section 223(c)(1)) at any time during a testing period following the qualified HSA distribution, the amount of the distribution is includible in the participant's gross income and he or she is also subject to an additional 10 percent tax (with certain exceptions). Section 106(e)(3).

(3) *No effect on health FSA elections, coverage, use-or-lose rule.*—A qualified HSA distribution does not alter an employee's irrevocable election under paragraph (a) of §1.125-2, or constitute a change in status under §1.125-4(a). If a qualified HSA distribution is made to an employee's HSA, even if the balance in a health FSA is reduced to zero, the employee's health FSA coverage continues to the end of the plan year. Unused benefits and contributions remaining at the end of a plan year (or at the end of a grace period, if applicable) must be forfeited.

(o) *FSA experience gains or forfeitures.*—(1) *Experience gains in general.*—An FSA experience gain (sometimes referred to as forfeitures in the use-or-lose rule in paragraph (c) in this section) with respect to a plan year (plus any grace period following the end of a plan year described in paragraph (e) in §1.125-1), equals the amount of the employer contributions, including salary reduction contributions, and after-tax employee contributions to the FSA minus the FSA's total claims reimbursements for the year. Experience gains (or forfeitures) may be—

(i) Retained by the employer maintaining the cafeteria plan; or

(ii) If not retained by the employer, may be used only in one or more of the following ways—

(A) To reduce required salary reduction amounts for the immediately following plan year, on a reasonable and uniform basis, as described in paragraph (o)(2) of this section;

(B) Returned to the employees on a reasonable and uniform basis, as described in paragraph (o)(2) of this section; or

(C) To defray expenses to administer the cafeteria plan.

(2) *Allocating experience gains among employees on reasonable and uniform basis.*—If not retained by the employer or used to defray expenses of administering the plan, the experience gains must be allocated among employees on a reasonable and uniform basis. It is permissible to allocate these amounts based on the different coverage levels of employees under the FSA. Experience gains allocated in compliance with this paragraph (o) are not a deferral of the receipt of compensation. However, in no case may the experience gains be allocated among employees based (directly or indirectly) on their individual claims experience. Experience gains may not be used as contributions directly or indirectly to any deferred compensation benefit plan.

(3) *Example.*—The following example illustrates the rules in this paragraph (o):

Example. Allocating experience gains. (i) Employer L maintains a cafeteria plan for its 1,200 employees, who may elect one of several different annual coverage levels under a health FSA in $100 increments from $500 to $2,000.

(ii) For the 2009 plan year, 1,000 employees elect levels of coverage under the health FSA. For the 2009 plan year, the health FSA has an experience gain of $5,000.

(iii) The $5,000 may be allocated to all participants for the plan year on a per capita basis weighted to reflect the participants' elected levels of coverage.

(iv) Alternatively, the $5,000 may be used to reduce the required salary reduction amount under the health FSA for all 2009 participants (for example, a $500 health FSA for the next year is priced at $480) or to reimburse claims incurred above the elective limit in 2010 as long as such reimbursements are made on a reasonable and uniform level.

(p) *Effective/applicability date.*—It is proposed that these regulations apply on and after plan years beginning on or after January 1, 2009. [Reg. § 1.125-5.]

§ 1.125-6. Substantiation of expenses for all cafeteria plans.—(a) *Cafeteria plan payments and reimbursements.*—(1) *In general.*—A cafeteria plan may pay or reimburse only those substantiated expenses for qualified benefits incurred on or after the later of the effective date of the cafeteria plan and the date the employee is enrolled in the plan. This requirement applies to all qualified benefits offered through the cafeteria plan. See paragraph (b) of this section for substantiation rules.

(2) *Expenses incurred.*—(i) *Employees' medical expenses must be incurred during the period of coverage.*—In order for reimbursements to be excludible from gross income under section 105(b), the medical expenses reimbursed by an accident and health plan elected through a cafeteria plan must be incurred during the period when the participant is covered by the accident and health plan. A participant's period of coverage includes COBRA coverage. See § 54.4980B-2 of this chapter. Medical expenses incurred before the later of the effective date of the plan and the date the employee is enrolled in the plan are not incurred during the period for which the employee is covered by the plan. However, the actual reimbursement of covered medical care expenses may be made after the applicable period of coverage.

(ii) *When medical expenses are incurred.*—For purposes of this rule, medical expenses are incurred when the employee (or the employee's spouse or dependents) is provided with the medical care that gives rise to the medical expenses, and not when the employee is formally billed, charged for, or pays for the medical care.

(iii) *Example.*—The following example illustrates the rules in this paragraph (a)(2):

Example. Medical expenses incurred after termination. (i) Employer E maintains a cafeteria plan with a calendar year plan year. The cafeteria plan provides that participation terminates when an individual ceases to be an employee of Employer E, unless the former employee elects to continue to participate in the health FSA under the COBRA rules in § 54.4980B- 2 of this chapter. Employee G timely elects to salary reduce $1,200 to participate in a health FSA for the 2009 plan year. As of June 30, 2009, Employee G has contributed $600 toward the health FSA, but incurred no medical expenses. On June 30, 2009, Employee G terminates employment and does not continue participation under COBRA. On July 15, 2009, G incurs a section 213(d) medical expense of $500.

(ii) Under the rules in paragraph (a)(2) of this section, the cafeteria plan is prohibited from reimbursing any portion of the $500 medical expense because, at the time the medical expense is incurred, G is not a participant in the cafeteria plan.

(3) *Section 105(b) requirements for reimbursement of medical expenses through a cafeteria plan.*—(i) *In general.*—In order for medical care reimbursements paid to an employee through a cafeteria plan to be excludible under section 105(b), the reimbursements must be paid pursuant to an employer-funded *accident and health plan*, as defined in section 105(e) and §§ 1.105-2 and 1.105-5.

(ii) *Reimbursement exclusively for section 213(d) medical expenses.*—A cafeteria plan benefit through which an employee receives reimbursements of medical expenses is excludable under section 105(b) only if reimbursements from the plan are made specifically to reimburse the employee for medical expenses (as defined in section 213(d)) incurred by the employee or the employee's spouse or dependents during the period of coverage. Amounts paid to an employee as reimbursement are not paid specifically to reimburse the employee for medical expenses if the plan provides that the employee is entitled, or operates in a manner that entitles the employee, to receive the amounts, in the form of cash (for example, routine payment of salary) or any other taxable or nontaxable benefit irrespective of whether the employee (or the employee's spouse or dependents) incurs medical expenses during the period of coverage. This rule applies even if the employee will not receive such amounts until the end or after the end of the period. A plan under which employees (or their spouses and dependents) will receive reimbursement for medical expenses up to a specified amount and, if they incur no medical expenses, will receive cash or any other benefit in lieu of the reimbursements is not a benefit qualifying for the exclusion under sections 106 and 105(b). See § 1.105-2. This is the case without regard to whether the benefit was purchased with contributions made at the employer's discretion, at the employee's discretion (for example, by salary reduction election), or pursuant to a collective bargaining agreement.

(iii) *Other arrangements*.—Arrangements formally outside of the cafeteria plan that adjust an employee's compensation or an employee's receipt of any other benefits on the basis of the expenses incurred or reimbursements the employee receives are considered in determining whether the reimbursements are through a plan eligible for the exclusions under sections 106 and 105(b).

(4) *Reimbursements of dependent care expenses*.—(i) *Dependent care expenses must be incurred*.—In order to satisfy section 129, dependent care expenses may not be reimbursed before the expenses are incurred. For purposes of this rule, dependent care expenses are incurred when the care is provided and not when the employee is formally billed, charged for, or pays for the dependent care.

(ii) *Dependent care provided during the period of coverage*.—In order for dependent care assistance to be provided through a dependent care assistance program eligible for the section 129 exclusion, the care must be provided to or on behalf of the employee during the period for which the employee is covered by the program. For example, if for a plan year, an employee elects a dependent care assistance program providing for reimbursement of dependent care expenses, only reimbursements for dependent care expenses incurred during that plan year are provided from a dependent care assistance program within the scope of section 129. Also, for purposes of this rule, expenses incurred before the later of the program's effective date and the date the employee is enrolled in the program are not incurred during the period when the employee is covered by the program. Similarly, if the dependent care assistance program furnishes the dependent care in-kind (for example, through an employer-maintained child care facility), only dependent care provided during the plan year of coverage is provided through a dependent care assistance program within the meaning of section 129. See also § 1.125-5 for FSA rules.

(iii) *Period of coverage*.—In order for dependent care assistance through a cafeteria plan to be provided through a dependent care assistance program eligible for the section 129 exclusion, the plan may not operate in a manner that enables employees to purchase dependent care assistance only for periods during which the employees expect to receive dependent care assistance. If the period of coverage for a dependent care assistance program offered through a cafeteria plan is twelve months (or, in the case of a short plan year, at least equal to the short plan year) and the plan does not permit an employee to elect specific amounts of coverage, reimbursement, or salary reduction for less than twelve months, the plan is deemed not to operate to enable employees to purchase coverage only for periods when dependent care assistance will be received. See paragraph (a) in § 1.125-2 and § 1.125-4 regarding the revocation of elections during the period of coverage on account of changes in family status. See paragraph (e) in this section for required period of coverage for dependent care assistance.

(iv) *Examples*.—The following examples illustrate the rules in paragraphs (a)(4)(i)-(iii) of this section:

Example 1. Initial non-refundable fee for child care. (i) Employer F maintains a calendar year cafeteria plan, offering employees an election between cash and qualified benefits, including dependent care assistance. Employee M has a one-year old dependent child. Employee M timely elected $5,000 of dependent care assistance for 2009. During the entire 2009 plan year, Employee M satisfies all the requirements in section 129 for dependent care assistance.

(ii) On February 1, 2009, Employee M pays an initial non-refundable fee of $500 to a licensed child care center (unrelated to Employer F or to Employee M), to reserve a space at the child care center for M's child. The child care center's monthly charges for child care are $1,200. When the child care center first begins to care for M's child, the $500 non-refundable fee is applied toward the first month's charges for child care.

(iii) On March 1, 2009, the child care center begins caring for Employee M's child, and continues to care for the child through December 31, 2009. On March 1, 2009, M pays the child care center $700 (the balance of the $1,200 in charges for child care to be provided in March 2009). On April 1, 2009, M pays the child care center $1,200 for the child care to be provided in April 2009.

(iv) Dependent care expenses are incurred when the services are provided. For dependent care services provided in March 2009, the $500 nonrefundable fee paid on February 1, 2009, and the $700 paid on March 1, 2009 may be reimbursed on or after the later of the date when substantiated or April 1, 2009. For dependent care services provided in April 2009, the $1,200 paid on April 1, 2009 may be reimbursed on or after the later of the date when substantiated or May 1, 2009.

Example 2. Non-refundable fee forfeited. Same facts as *Example 1*, except that the child care center never cared for M's child (who was instead cared for at Employer F's onsite child care facility). Because the child care center never provided child care services to Employee M's child, the $500 non-refundable fee is not reimbursable.

(v) *Optional spend-down provision*.—At the employer's option, the written cafeteria plan may provide that dependent care expenses incurred after the date an employee ceases participation in the cafeteria plan (for example, after termination) and through the last day of that plan year (or grace period immediately after that plan year) may be reimbursed from unused benefits, if all of the requirements of section 129 are satisfied.

(vi) *Example*.—The following example illustrates the rules in paragraph (a)(4)(v) of this section:

Example. Terminated employee's post-termination dependent care expenses. (i) For calendar year 2009, Employee X elects $5,000 salary reduction for dependent care assistance through Employer G's cafeteria plan. X works for Employer G from January 1 through June 30, 2009, when X terminates employment. As of June 30, 2009, X had paid $2,500 in salary reduction and had incurred and was reimbursed for $2,000 of dependent care expenses.

(ii) X does not work again until October 1, 2009, when X begins work for Employer H. X was employed by Employer H from October 1, 2009 through December 31, 2009. During this period, X also incurred $500 of dependent care expenses. During all the periods of employment in 2009, X satisfied all requirements in section 129 for excluding payments for dependent care assistance from gross income.

(iii) Employer G's cafeteria plan allows terminated employees to "spend down" unused salary reduction amounts for dependent care assistance, if all requirements of section 129 are satisfied. After X's claim for $500 of dependent care expenses is substantiated, Employer G's cafeteria plan reimburses X for $500 (the remaining balance) of dependent care expenses incurred during X's employment for Employer H between October 1, 2009 and December 31, 2009. Employer G's cafeteria plan and operation are consistent with section 125.

(b) *Rules for claims substantiation for cafeteria plans.*—(1) *Substantiation required before reimbursing expenses for qualified benefits.*—This paragraph (b) sets forth the substantiation requirements that a cafeteria plan must satisfy before paying or reimbursing any expense for a qualified benefit.

(2) *All claims must be substantiated.*—As a precondition of payment or reimbursement of expenses for qualified benefits, a cafeteria plan must require substantiation in accordance with this section. Substantiating only a percentage of claims, or substantiating only claims above a certain dollar amount, fails to comply with the substantiation requirements in § 1.125-1 and this section.

(3) *Substantiation by independent third-party.*—(i) *In general.*—All expenses must be substantiated by information from a third-party that is independent of the employee and the employee's spouse and dependents. The independent third-party must provide information describing the service or product, the date of the service or sale, and the amount. Self-substantiation or self-certification of an expense by an employee does not satisfy the substantiation requirements of this paragraph (b). The specific requirements in sections 105(b), 129, and 137 must also be satisfied as a condition of reimbursing expenses for qualified benefits. For example, a health FSA does not satisfy the requirements of section 105(b) if it reimburses employees for expenses where the employees only submit information describing medical expenses, the amount of the expenses and the date of the expenses but fail to provide a statement from an independent third-party (either automatically or subsequent to the transaction) verifying the expenses. Under § 1.105-2, all amounts paid under a plan that permits self-substantiation or self-certification are includible in gross income, including amounts reimbursed for medical expenses, whether or not substantiated. See paragraph (m) in § 1.125-5 for additional substantiation rules for limited-purpose and post-deductible health FSAs.

(ii) *Rules for substantiation of health FSA claims using an explanation of benefits provided by an insurance company.*—(A) *Written statement from an independent third-party.*—If the employer is provided with information from an independent third-party (such as an "*explanation of benefits*" (*EOB*) from an insurance company) indicating the date of the section 213(d) medical care and the employee's responsibility for payment for that medical care (that is, coinsurance payments and amounts below the plan's deductible), and the employee certifies that any expense paid through the health FSA has not been reimbursed and that the employee will not seek reimbursement from any other plan covering health benefits, the claim is fully substantiated without the need for submission of a receipt by the employee or further review.

(B) *Example.*—The following example illustrates the rules in this paragraph (b)(3):

Example.Explanation of benefits. (i) During the plan year ending December 31, 2009, Employee Q is a participant in the health FSA sponsored by Employer J and is enrolled in Employer J's accident and health plan.

(ii) On March 1, 2009, Q visits a physician's office for medical care as defined in section 213(d). The charge for the physician's services is $150. Under the plan, Q is responsible for 20 percent of the charge for the physician's services (that is, $30). Q has sufficient FSA coverage for the $30 claim.

(iii) Employer J has coordinated with the accident and health plan so that Employer J or its agent automatically receives an EOB from the plan indicating that Q is responsible for payment of 20 percent of the $150 charged by the physician. Because Employer J has received a statement from an independent third-party that Q has incurred a medical expense, the date the expense was incurred, and the amount of the expense, the claim is substantiated without the need for J to submit additional information regarding the expense. Employer J's FSA reimburses Q the $30 medical expense without requiring Q to submit a receipt or a statement from the physician. The substantiation rules in paragraph (b) in this section are satisfied.

(4) *Advance reimbursement of expenses for qualified benefits prohibited.*—Reimbursing expenses before the expense has been incurred or before the expense is substantiated fails to satisfy the substantiation requirements in § 1.105-2, § 1.125-1 and this section.

(5) *Purported loan from employer to employee.*—In determining whether, under all the facts and circumstances, employees are being reimbursed for unsubstantiated claims, special scrutiny will be given to other arrangements such as employer-to-employee loans based on actual or projected employee claims.

(6) *Debit cards.*—For purposes of this section, a *debit card* is a debit card, credit card, or stored value card. See also paragraphs (c) through (g) of this section for additional rules on payments or reimbursements made through debit cards.

(c) *Debit cards-overview.*—(1) *Mandatory rules for all debit cards usable to pay or reimburse medical expenses.*—Paragraph (d) of this section sets forth the mandatory procedures for debit cards to substantiate section 213(d) medical expenses. These rules apply to all debit cards used to pay or reimburse medical expenses. Paragraph (e) of this section sets forth additional substantiation rules that may be used for medical expenses incurred at medical care providers and certain stores with the Drug Stores and Pharmacies merchant category code. Paragraph

(f) in this section sets forth the requirements for an inventory information approval system which must be used to substantiate medical expenses incurred at merchants or service providers that are not medical care providers or certain stores with the Drug Stores and Pharmacies merchant category code and that may be used for medical expenses incurred at all merchants.

(2) *Debit cards used for dependent care assistance.*—Paragraph (g) of this section sets forth additional rules for debit cards usable for reimbursing dependent care expenses.

(3) *Additional guidance.*—The Commissioner may prescribe additional guidance of general applicability, published in the Internal Revenue Bulletin (see § 601.601(d)(2)(ii)(*b*) of this chapter), to provide additional rules for debit cards.

(d) *Mandatory rules for all debit cards usable to pay or reimburse medical expenses.*—A health FSA paying or reimbursing section 213(d) medical expenses through a debit card must satisfy all of the following requirements—

(1) Before any employee participating in a health FSA receives the debit card, the employee agrees in writing that he or she will only use the card to pay for medical expenses (as defined in section 213(d)) of the employee or his or her spouse or dependents, that he or she will not use the debit card for any medical expense that has already been reimbursed, that he or she will not seek reimbursement under any other health plan for any expense paid for with a debit card, and that he or she will acquire and retain sufficient documentation (including invoices and receipts) for any expense paid with the debit card.

(2) The debit card includes a statement providing that the agreements described in paragraph (d)(1) of this section are reaffirmed each time the employee uses the card.

(3) The amount available through the debit card equals the amount elected by the employee for the health FSA for the cafeteria plan year, and is reduced by amounts paid or reimbursed for section 213(d) medical expenses incurred during the plan year.

(4) The debit card is automatically cancelled when the employee ceases to participate in the health FSA.

(5) The employer limits use of the debit card to—

(i) Physicians, dentists, vision care offices, hospitals, other medical care providers (as identified by the merchant category code);

(ii) Stores with the merchant category code for Drugstores and Pharmacies if, on a location by location basis, 90 percent of the store's gross receipts during the prior taxable year consisted of items which qualify as expenses for medical care described in section 213(d); and

(iii) Stores that have implemented the inventory information approval system under paragraph (f).

(6) The employer substantiates claims based on payments to medical care providers and stores described in paragraphs (d)(5)(i) and (ii) of this section in accordance with either paragraph (e) or paragraph (f) of this section.

(7) The employer follows all of the following correction procedures for any improper payments using the debit card—

(i) Until the amount of the improper payment is recovered, the debit card must be deactivated and the employee must request payments or reimbursements of medical expenses from the health FSA through other methods (for example, by submitting receipts or invoices from a merchant or service provider showing the employee incurred a section 213(d) medical expense);

(ii) The employer demands that the employee repay the cafeteria plan an amount equal to the improper payment;

(iii) If, after the demand for repayment of improper payment (as described in paragraph (d)(7)(ii) of this section), the employee fails to repay the amount of the improper charge, the employer withholds the amount of the improper charge from the employee's pay or other compensation, to the full extent allowed by applicable law;

(iv) If any portion of the improper payment remains outstanding after attempts to recover the amount (as described in paragraph (d)(7)(ii) and (iii) of this section), the employer applies a claims substitution or offset to resolve improper payments, such as a reimbursement for a later substantiated expense claim is reduced by the amount of the improper payment. So, for example, if an employee has received an improper payment of $200 and subsequently submits a substantiated claim for $250 incurred during the same coverage period, a reimbursement for $50 is made; and

(v) If, after applying all the procedures described in paragraph (d)(7)(ii) through (iv) of this section, the employee remains indebted to the employer for improper payments, the employer, consistent with its business practice, treats the improper payment as it would any other business indebtedness.

(e) *Substantiation of expenses incurred at medical care providers and certain other stores with Drug Stores and Pharmacies merchant category code.*—(1) *In general.*—A health FSA paying or reimbursing section 213(d) medical expenses through a debit card is permitted to comply with the substantiation provisions of this paragraph (e), instead of complying with the provisions of paragraph (f), for medical expenses incurred at providers described in paragraph (e)(2) of this section.

(2) *Medical care providers and certain other stores with Drug Stores and Pharmacies merchant category code.*—Medical expenses may be substantiated using the methods described in paragraph (e)(3) of this section if incurred at physicians, pharmacies, dentists, vision care offices, hospitals, other medical care providers (as identified by the merchant category code) and at stores with the Drug Stores and Pharmacies merchant category code, if, on a store location-by-location basis, 90 percent of the store's gross receipts during the prior taxable year consisted of items which qualify as expenses for medical care described in section 213(d).

(3) *Claims substantiation for copayment matches, certain recurring medical expenses and real-time substantiation.*—If all of the requirements in this paragraph (e)(3) are satisfied, copayment matches, certain recurring medical expenses and medical expenses substantiated in real-time are substantiated without the need for submission of receipts or further review.

(i) *Matching copayments-multiples of five or fewer.*—If an employer's accident or health plan covering the employee (or the employee's spouse or dependents) has copayments in specific dollar amounts, and the dollar amount of the transaction at a medical care provider equals an exact multiple of not more than five times the dollar amount of the copayment for the specific service (for example, pharmacy benefit copayment, copayment for a physician's office visit) under the accident or health plan covering the specific employee-cardholder, then the charge is fully substantiated without the need for submission of a receipt or further review.

(A) *Tiered copayments.*—If a health plan has multiple copayments for the same benefit, (for example, tiered copayments for a pharmacy benefit), exact matches of multiples or combinations of up to five copayments are similarly fully substantiated without the need for submission of a receipt or further review.

(B) *Copayment match must be exact multiple.*—If the dollar amount of the transaction is not an exact multiple of the copayment (or an exact match of a multiple or combination of different copayments for a benefit in the case of multiple copayments), the transaction must be treated as conditional pending confirmation of the charge, even if the amount is less than five times the copayment.

(C) *No match for multiple of six or more times copayment.*—If the dollar amount of the transaction at a medical care provider equals a multiple of six or more times the dollar amount of the copayment for the specific service, the transaction must be treated as conditional pending confirmation of the charge by the submission of additional third-party information. See paragraph (d) of this section. In the case of a plan with multiple copayments for the same benefit, if the dollar amount of the transaction exceeds five times the maximum copayment for the benefit, the transaction must also be treated as conditional pending confirmation of the charge by the submission of additional third-party information. In these cases, the employer must require that additional third-party information, such as merchant or service provider receipts, be submitted for review and substantiation, and the third-party information must satisfy the requirements in paragraph (b)(3) of this section.

(D) *Independent verification of copayment required.*—The copayment schedule required under the accident or health plan must be independently verified by the employer. Statements or other representations by the employee are not sufficient. Self-substantiation or self-certification of an employee's copayment in connection with copayment matching procedures through debit cards or otherwise does not constitute substantiation. If a plan's copayment matching system relies on an employee to provide a copayment amount without verification of the amount, claims have not been substantiated, and all amounts paid from the plan are included in gross income, including amounts paid for medical care whether or not substantiated. See paragraph (b) in this section.

(4) *Certain recurring medical expenses.*—Automatic payment or reimbursement satisfies the substantiation rules in this paragraph (e) for payment of recurring expenses that match expenses previously approved as to amount, medical care provider and time period (for example, for an employee who refills a prescription drug on a regular basis at the same provider and in the same amount). The payment is substantiated without the need for submission of a receipt or further review.

(5) *Real-time substantiation.*—If a third party that is independent of the employee and the employee's spouse and dependents (for example, medical care provider, merchant, or pharmacy benefit manager) provides, at the time and point of sale, information to verify to the employer (including electronically by email, the internet, intranet or telephone) that the charge is for a section 213(d) medical expense, the expense is substantiated without the need for further review.

(6) *Substantiation requirements for all other medical expenses paid or reimbursed through a health FSA debit card.*—All other charges to the debit card (other than substantiated copayments, recurring medical expenses or real-time substantiation, or charges substantiated through the inventory information approval system described in paragraph (f) of this section) must be treated as conditional, pending substantiation of the charge through additional independent third-party information describing the goods or services, the date of the service or sale and the amount of the transaction. All such debit card payments must be substantiated, regardless of the amount of the payment.

(f) *Inventory information approval system.*—(1) *In general.*—An inventory information approval system that complies with this paragraph (f) may be used to substantiate payments made using a debit card, including payments at merchants and service providers that are not described in paragraph (e)(2) of this section. Debit card transactions using this system are fully substantiated without the need for submission of a receipt by the employee or further review.

(2) *Operation of inventory information approval system.*—An inventory information approval system must operate in the manner described in this paragraph (f)(2).

(i) When an employee uses the card, the payment card processor's or participating merchant's system collects information about the items purchased using the inventory control information (for example, *stock keeping units* (SKUs)). The system compares the inventory control information for the items purchased against a list of items, the purchase of which qualifies as expenses for medical care under section 213(d) (including nonprescription medications).

(ii) The section 213(d) medical expenses are totaled and the merchant's or payment card processor's system approves the use of the card only for the amount of the section 213(d) medical expenses eligible for coverage under the health FSA (taking into consideration the uniform coverage rule in paragraph (d) of § 1.125-5);

(iii) If the transaction is only partially approved, the employee is required to tender additional amounts, resulting in a split-tender transaction. For example, if, after matching inventory information, it is determined that all items purchased are section 213(d) medical expenses, the entire transaction is approved, subject to the coverage limitations of the health FSA;

(iv) If, after matching inventory information, it is determined that only some of the items purchased are section 213(d) medical expenses, the transaction is approved only as to the section 213(d) medical expenses. In this case, the merchant or service-provider must request additional payment from the employee for the items that do not satisfy the definition of medical care under section 213(d);

(v) The merchant or service-provider must also request additional payment from the employee if the employee does not have sufficient health FSA coverage to purchase the section 213(d) medical items;

(vi) Any attempt to use the card at non-participating merchants or service-providers must fail.

(3) *Employer's responsibility for ensuring inventory information approval system's compliance with §1.105-2, §1.125-1, §1.125-6 and recordkeeping requirements.*—An employer that uses the inventory information approval system must ensure that the inventory information approval system complies with the requirements in §§1.105-2, 1.125-1, and §1.125-6 for substantiating, paying or reimbursing section 213(d) medical expenses and with the recordkeeping requirements in section 6001.

(g) *Debit cards used to pay or reimburse dependent care assistance.*—(1) *In general.*—An employer may use a debit card to provide benefits under its dependent care assistance program (including a dependent care assistance FSA). However, dependent care expenses may not be reimbursed before the expenses are incurred. See paragraph (a)(4) in this section. Thus, if a dependent care provider requires payment before the dependent care services are provided, the expenses cannot be reimbursed at the time of payment through use of a debit card or otherwise.

(2) *Reimbursing dependent care assistance through a debit card.*—An employer offering a dependent care assistance FSA may adopt the following method to provide reimbursements for dependent care expenses through a debit card—

(i) At the beginning of the plan year or upon enrollment in the dependent care assistance program, the employee pays initial expenses to the dependent care provider and substantiates the initial expenses by submitting to the employer or plan administrator a statement from the dependent care provider substantiating the dates and amounts for the services provided.

(ii) After the employer or plan administrator receives the substantiation (but not before the date the services are provided as indicated by the statement provided by the dependent care provider), the plan makes available through the debit card an amount equal to the lesser of—

(A) The previously incurred and substantiated expense; or

(B) The employee's total salary reduction amount to date.

(iii) The card may be used to pay for subsequently incurred dependent care expenses.

(iv) The amount available through the card may be increased in the amount of any additional dependent care expenses only after the additional expenses have been incurred.

(3) *Substantiating recurring dependent care expenses.*—Card transactions that collect information matching expenses previously substantiated and approved as to dependent care provider and time period may be treated as substantiated without further review if the transaction is for an amount equal to or less than the previously substantiated expenses. Similarly, dependent care expenses previously substantiated and approved through nonelectronic methods may also be treated as substantiated without further review. In both cases, if there is an increase in previously substantiated amounts or a change in the dependent care provider, the employee must submit a statement or receipt from the dependent care provider substantiating the claimed expenses before amounts relating to the increased amounts or new providers may be added to the card.

(4) *Example.*—The following example illustrates the rules in this paragraph (g):

Example. Recurring dependent care expenses. (i) Employer K sponsors a dependent care assistance FSA through its cafeteria plan. Salary reduction amounts for participating employees are made on a weekly payroll basis, which are available for dependent care coverage on a weekly basis. As a result, the amount of available dependent care coverage equals the employee's salary reduction amount minus claims previously paid from the plan. Employer K has adopted a payment card program for its dependent care FSA.

(ii) For the plan year ending December 31, 2009, Employee F is a participant in the dependent care FSA and elected $5,000 of dependent care coverage. Employer K reduces F's salary by $96.15 on a weekly basis to pay for coverage under the dependent care FSA.

(iii) At the beginning of the 2009 plan year, F is issued a debit card with a balance of zero. F's childcare provider, ABC Daycare Center, requires a $250 advance payment at the beginning of the week for dependent care services that will be provided during the week. The dependent care services provided for F by ABC qualify for reimbursement under section 129. However, because as of the beginning of the plan year, no services have yet been provided, F cannot be reimbursed for any of the amounts until the end of the first week of the plan year (that is, the week ending January 5, 2009), after the services have been provided.

(iv) F submits a claim for reimbursement that includes a statement from ABC with a description of the services, the amount of the services, and the dates of the services. Employer K increases the balance of F's payment card to $96.15 after the services have been provided (i.e., the lesser of F's salary reduction to date or the incurred dependent care expenses). F uses the card to pay ABC $96.15 on the first day of the next week (January 8, 2009) and pays ABC the remaining balance due for that week ($153.85) by check.

(v) To the extent that this card transaction and each subsequent transaction is with ABC and is for an amount equal to or less than the previously substantiated amount, the charges are fully substantiated without the need for the submission by F of a statement from the provider or further review by the employer. However, the subsequent amount is not made available on the card until the end of the week when the services have been provided. Employer K's dependent care debit card satisfies the substantiation requirements of this paragraph (g).

(h) *Effective/applicability date.*—It is proposed that these regulations apply on and after plan years beginning on or after January 1, 2009. However, the effective dates for the previously issued guidance on debit cards, which is incorporated in this section, remain applicable. [Reg. § 1.125-6.]

§ 1.125-7. Cafeteria plan nondiscrimination rules.—(a) *Definitions.*—(1) *In general.*—The definitions set forth in this paragraph (a) apply for purposes of section 125(b), (c), (e) and (g) and this section.

(2) *Compensation.*—The term *compensation* means compensation as defined in section 415(c)(3).

(3) *Highly compensated individual.*—(i) *In general.*—The term *highly compensated individual* means an individual who is—

(A) An officer;

(B) A five percent shareholder (as defined in paragraph (a)(8) of this section); or

(C) Highly compensated.

(ii) *Spouse or dependent.*—A spouse or a dependent of any highly compensated individual described in (a)(3)(i) of this section is a highly compensated individual. Section 125(e).

(4) *Highly compensated participant.*—The term *highly compensated participant* means a highly compensated individual who is eligible to participate in the cafeteria plan.

(5) *Nonhighly compensated individual.*—The term *nonhighly compensated individual* means an individual who is not a highly compensated individual.

(6) *Nonhighly compensated participant.*—The term *nonhighly compensated participant* means a participant who is not a highly compensated participant.

(7) *Officer.*—The term *officer* means any individual or participant who for the preceding plan year (or the current plan year in the case of the first year of employment) was an officer. Whether an individual is an *officer* is determined based on all the facts and circumstances, including the source of the individual's authority, the term for which he or she is elected or appointed, and the nature and extent of his or her duties. Generally, the term officer means an administrative executive who is in regular and continued service. The term officer implies continuity of service and excludes individuals performing services in connection with a special and single transaction. An individual who merely has the title of an officer but not the authority of an officer, is not an officer. Similarly, an individual without the title of an officer but who has the authority of an officer is an officer. Sole proprietorships, partnerships, associations, trusts and labor organizations also may have officers. See §§ 301.7701-1 through -3

(8) *Five percent shareholder.*—A *five percent shareholder* is an individual who in either the preceding plan year or current plan year owns more than five percent of the voting power or value of all classes of stock of the employer, determined without attribution.

(9) *Highly compensated.*—The term *highly compensated* means any individual or participant who for the preceding plan year (or the current plan year in the case of the first year of employment) had compensation from the employer in excess of the compensation amount specified in section 414(q)(1)(B), and, if elected by the employer, was also in the top-paid group of employees (determined by reference to section 414(q)(3)) for such preceding plan year (or for the current plan year in the case of the first year of employment).

(10) *Key employee.*—A *key employee* is a participant who is a key employee within the meaning of section 416(i)(1) at any time during the preceding plan year. A key employee covered by a collective bargaining agreement is a key employee.

(11) *Collectively bargained plan.*—A *collectively bargained plan* is a plan or the portion of a plan maintained under an agreement which is a collective bargaining agreement between employee representatives and one or more employers, if there is evidence that cafeteria plan benefits were the subject of good faith bargaining between such employee representatives and such employer or employers.

(12) *Year of employment.*—For purposes of section 125(g)(3)(B)(i), a *year of employment* is determined by reference to the elapsed time method of crediting service. See § 1.410(a)-7.

(13) *Premium-only-plan.*—A premium-only-plan is described in paragraph (a)(5) in § 1.125-1.

(14) *Statutory nontaxable benefits.*—*Statutory nontaxable benefits* are qualified benefits that are excluded from gross income (for example, an employer-provided accident and health plan excludible under section 106 or a dependent care assistance program excludible under section 129). Statutory nontaxable benefits also include group-term life insurance on the life of an employee includible in the employee's gross income solely because the coverage exceeds the limit in section 79(a).

(15) *Total benefits.*—*Total benefits* are qualified benefits and permitted taxable benefits.

(b) *Nondiscrimination as to eligibility.*—(1) *In general.*—A cafeteria plan must not discriminate in favor of highly compensated individuals as to eligibility to participate for that plan year. A cafeteria plan does not discriminate in favor of highly compensated individuals if the plan benefits a group of employees who qualify under a reasonable classification established by the employer, as defined in § 1.410(b)-4(b), and the group of employees included in the classification satisfies the safe harbor percentage test or the unsafe harbor percentage component of the facts and circumstances test in § 1.410(b)-4(c). (In applying the § 1.410(b)-4 test, substitute highly compensated individual for highly compensated employee and substitute nonhighly compensated individual for nonhighly compensated employee).

(2) *Deadline for participation in cafeteria plan.*—Any employee who has completed three years of employment (and who satisfies any conditions for participation in the cafeteria plan that are not related to completion of a requisite length of employment) must be permitted to elect to participate in the cafeteria plan no later than the first day of the first plan year beginning after the date the employee completed three years of employment (unless the employee sepa-

rates from service before the first day of that plan year).

(3) *The safe harbor percentage test.*—(i) *In general.*—For purposes of the safe harbor percentage test and the unsafe harbor percentage component of the facts and circumstances test, if the cafeteria plan provides that only employees who have completed three years of employment are permitted to participate in the plan, employees who have not completed three years of employment may be excluded from consideration. However, if the cafeteria plan provides that employees are allowed to participate before completing three years of employment, all employees with less than three years of employment must be included in applying the safe harbor percentage test and the unsafe harbor percentage component of the facts and circumstances test. See paragraph (g) of this section for a permissive disaggregation rule.

(ii) *Employees excluded from consideration.*—In addition, for purposes of the safe harbor percentage test and the unsafe harbor percentage component of the facts and circumstances test, the following employees are excluded from consideration —

(A) Employees (except key employees) covered by a collectively bargained plan as defined in paragraph (a)(11) of this section;

(B) Employees who are nonresident aliens and receive no earned income (within the meaning of section 911(d)(2)) from the employer which constitutes income from sources within the United States (within the meaning of section 861(a)(3)); and

(C) Employees participating in the cafeteria plan under a COBRA continuation provision.

(iv) *Examples.*—The following examples illustrate the rules in paragraph (b) of this section:

Example 1. Same qualified benefit for same salary reduction amount. Employer A has one employer-provided accident and health insurance plan. The cost to participants electing the accident and health plan is $10,000 per year for single coverage. All employees have the same opportunity to salary reduce $10,000 for accident and health plan. The cafeteria plan satisfies the eligibility test.

Example 2. Same qualified benefit for unequal salary reduction amounts. Same facts as *Example 1* except the cafeteria plan offers nonhighly compensated employees the election to salary reduce $10,000 to pay premiums for single coverage. The cafeteria plan provides an $8,000 employer flex-credit to highly compensated employees to pay a portion of the premium, and provides an election to them to salary reduce $2,000 to pay the balance of the premium. The cafeteria plan fails the eligibility test.

Example 3. Accident and health plans of unequal value. Employer B's cafeteria plan offers two employer-provided accident and health insurance plans: Plan X, available only to highly compensated participants, is a low-deductible plan. Plan Y, available only to nonhighly compensated participants, is a high deductible plan (as defined in section 223(c)(2)). The annual premium for single coverage under Plan X is $15,000 per year, and $8,000 per year for Plan Y. Employer B's cafeteria plan provides that highly compensated participants may elect salary reduction of $15,000 for coverage under Plan X, and that nonhighly compensated participants may elect salary reduction of $8,000 for coverage under Plan Y. The cafeteria plan fails the eligibility test.

Example 4. Accident and health plans of unequal value for unequal salary reduction amounts. Same facts as *Example 3*, except that the amount of salary reduction for highly compensated participants to elect Plan X is $8,000. The cafeteria plan fails the eligibility test.

(c) *Nondiscrimination as to contributions and benefits.*—(1) *In general.*—A cafeteria plan must not discriminate in favor of highly compensated participants as to contributions and benefits for a plan year.

(2) *Benefit availability and benefit election.*—A cafeteria plan does not discriminate with respect to contributions and benefits if either qualified benefits and total benefits, or employer contributions allocable to statutory nontaxable benefits and employer contributions allocable to total benefits, do not discriminate in favor of highly compensated participants. A cafeteria plan must satisfy this paragraph (c) with respect to both benefit availability and benefit utilization. Thus, a plan must give each similarly situated participant a uniform opportunity to elect qualified benefits, and the actual election of qualified benefits through the plan must not be disproportionate by highly compensated participants (while other participants elect permitted taxable benefits). Qualified benefits are disproportionately elected by highly compensated participants if the aggregate qualified benefits elected by highly compensated participants, measured as a percentage of the aggregate compensation of highly compensated participants, exceed the aggregate qualified benefits elected by nonhighly compensated participants measured as a percentage of the aggregate compensation of nonhighly compensated participants. A plan must also give each similarly situated participant a uniform election with respect to employer contributions, and the actual election with respect to employer contributions for qualified benefits through the plan must not be disproportionate by highly compensated participants (while other participants elect to receive employer contributions as permitted taxable benefits). Employer contributions are disproportionately utilized by highly compensated participants if the aggregate contributions utilized by highly compensated participants, measured as a percentage of the aggregate compensation of highly compensated participants, exceed the aggregate contributions utilized by nonhighly compensated participants measured as a percentage of the aggregate compensation of nonhighly compensated participants.

(3) *Example.*—The following example illustrates the rules in paragraph (c) of this section:

Example. Contributions and benefits test. Employer C's cafeteria plan satisfies the eligibility test in paragraph (b) of this section. Highly compensated participants in the cafeteria plan elect aggregate qualified benefits equaling 5 percent of aggregate compensation; nonhighly compensated participants elect aggregate qualified benefits equaling 10 percent of aggregate compensation. Employer C's cafeteria plan passes the contribution and benefits test.

(d) *Key employees.*—(1) *In general.*—If for any plan year, the statutory nontaxable benefits provided to key employees exceed 25 percent of the aggregate of statutory nontaxable benefits provided for all employees through the cafeteria plan, each key employee includes in gross income an amount equaling the maximum taxable benefits that he or she could have elected for the plan year. However, see safe harbor for premium-only-plans in paragraph (f) of this section.

(2) *Example.*—The following example illustrates the rules in paragraph (d) of this section:

Example. (i) *Key employee concentration test.* Employer D's cafeteria plan offers all employees an election between taxable benefits and qualified benefits. The cafeteria plan satisfies the eligibility test in paragraph (b) of this section. Employer D has two key employees and four nonhighly compensated employees. The key employees each elect $2,000 of qualified benefits. Each nonhighly compensated employee also elects $2,000 of qualified benefits. The qualified benefits are statutory nontaxable benefits.

(ii) Key employees receive $4,000 of statutory nontaxable benefits and nonhighly compensated employees receive $8,000 of statutory nontaxable benefits, for a total of $12,000. Key employees receive 33 percent of statutory nontaxable benefits (4,000/12,000). Because the cafeteria plan provides more than 25 percent of the aggregate of statutory nontaxable benefits to key employees, the plan fails the key employee concentration test.

(e) *Safe harbor for cafeteria plans providing health benefits.*—(1) *In general.*—A cafeteria plan that provides health benefits is not treated as discriminatory as to benefits and contributions if:

(i) Contributions under the plan on behalf of each participant include an amount which equals 100 percent of the cost of the health benefit coverage under the plan of the majority of the highly compensated participants similarly situated, or equals or exceeds 75 percent of the cost of the health benefit coverage of the participant (similarly situated) having the highest cost health benefit coverage under the plan, and

(ii) Contributions or benefits under the plan in excess of those described in paragraph (e)(1)(i) of this section bear a uniform relationship to compensation.

(2) *Similarly situated.*—In determining which participants are similarly situated, reasonable differences in plan benefits may be taken into account (for example, variations in plan benefits offered to employees working in different geographical locations or to employees with family coverage versus employee-only coverage).

(3) *Health benefits.*— Health benefits for purposes of this rule are limited to major medical coverage and exclude dental coverage and health FSAs.

(4) *Example.*—The following example illustrates the rules in paragraph (e) of this section:

Example. (i) All 10 of Employer E's employees are eligible to elect between permitted taxable benefits and salary reduction of $8,000 per plan year for self-only coverage in the major medical health plan provided by Employer E. All 10 employees elect $8,000 salary reduction for the major medical plan.

(ii) The cafeteria plan satisfies the section 125(g)(2) safe harbor for cafeteria plans providing health benefits.

(f) *Safe harbor test for premium-only-plans.*—(1) *In general.*—A premium-only-plan (as defined in paragraph (a)(13) of this section) is deemed to satisfy the nondiscrimination rules in section 125(c) and this section for a plan year if, for that plan year, the plan satisfies the safe harbor percentage test for eligibility in paragraph (b)(3) of this section.

(2) *Example.*—The following example illustrates the rules in paragraph (f) of this section:

Example. Premium-only-plan. (i) Employer F's cafeteria plan is a premium-only-plan (as defined in paragraph (a)(13) of this section). The written cafeteria plan offers one employer-provided accident and health plan and offers all employees the election to salary reduce same amount or same percentage of the premium for self-only or family coverage. All key employees and all highly compensated employees elect salary reduction for the accident and health plan, but only 20 percent of nonhighly compensated employees elect the accident and health plan.

(ii) The premium-only-plan satisfies the nondiscrimination rules in section 125(b) and (c) and this section.

(g) *Permissive disaggregation for nondiscrimination testing.*—(1) *General rule.*—If a cafeteria plan benefits employees who have not completed three years of employment, the cafeteria plan is permitted to test for nondiscrimination under this section as if the plan were two separate plans—

(i) One plan benefiting the employees who completed one day of employment but less than three years of employment; and

(ii) Another plan benefiting the employees who have completed three years of employment.

(2) *Disaggregated plans tested separately for eligibility test and contributions and benefits test.*—If a cafeteria plan is disaggregated into two separate plans for purposes of nondiscrimination testing, the two separate plans must be tested separately for both the nondiscrimination as to eligibility test in paragraph (b) of this section and the nondiscrimination as to contributions and benefits test in paragraph (c) of this section.

(h) *Optional aggregation of plans for nondiscrimination testing.*—An employer who sponsors more than one cafeteria plan is permitted to aggregate two or more of the cafeteria plans for purposes of nondiscrimination testing. If two or more cafeteria plans are aggregated into a combined plan for this purpose, the combined plan must satisfy the nondiscrimination as to eligibility test in paragraph (b) of this section and the nondiscrimination as to contributions and benefits test in paragraph (c) of this section, as though the combined plan were a single plan. Thus, for example, in order to satisfy the benefit availability and benefit election requirements in paragraph (c)(2) of this section, the combined plan must give each similarly situated participant a uniform opportunity to elect qualified benefits and the actual election of qualified benefits by highly compensated participants must not be disproportionate. However, if a principal purpose of the aggregation is to manipulate the nondiscrimination testing requirements or to otherwise discriminate in favor of highly compensated individuals or participants, the plans will not be permitted to be aggregated for nondiscrimination testing.

(i) *Employees of certain controlled groups.*—All employees who are treated as employed by a single employer under section 414(b), (c), (m), or (o) are treated as employed by a single employer for purposes of section 125. Section 125(g)(4); section 414(t).

(j) *Time to perform nondiscrimination testing.*—(1) *In general.*—Nondiscrimination testing must be performed as of the last day of the plan year, taking into account all non-excludable employees (or former employees) who were employees on any day during the plan year.

(2) The following example illustrates the rules in paragraph (j) of this section:

Example. When to perform discrimination testing. (i) Employer H employs three employees and maintains a calendar year cafeteria plan. During the 2009 plan year, Employee J was an employee the entire calendar year, Employee K was an employee from May 1, through August 31, 2009, and Employee L worked from January 1, 2009 to April 15, 2009, when he retired.

(ii) Nondiscrimination testing for the 2009 plan year must be performed on December 31, 2009, taking into account employees J, K, and L's compensation in the preceding year.

(k) *Discrimination in actual operation prohibited.*—In addition to not discriminating as to either benefit availability or benefit utilization, a cafeteria plan must not discriminate in favor of highly compensated participants in actual operation. For example, a plan may be discriminatory in actual operation if the duration of the plan (or of a particular nontaxable benefit offered through the plan) is for a period during which only highly compensated participants utilize the plan (or the benefit). See also the key employee concentration test in section 125(b)(2).

(l) *Anti-abuse rule.*—(1) *Interpretation.*—The provisions of this section must be interpreted in a reasonable manner consistent with the purpose of preventing discrimination in favor of highly compensated individuals, highly compensated participants and key employees.

(2) *Change in plan testing procedures.*—A plan will not be treated as satisfying the requirements of this section if there are repeated changes to plan testing procedures or plan provisions that have the effect of manipulating the nondiscrimination testing requirements of this section, if a principal purpose of the changes was to achieve this result.

(m) *Tax treatment of benefits in a cafeteria plan.*—(1) *Nondiscriminatory cafeteria plan.*—A participant in a nondiscriminatory cafeteria plan (including a highly compensated participant or key employee) who elects qualified benefits is not treated as having received taxable benefits offered through the plan, and thus the qualified benefits elected by the employee are not includible in the employee's gross income merely because of the availability of taxable benefits. But see paragraph (j) in §1.125-1 on nondiscrimination rules for sections 79(d), 105(h), 129(d), and 137(c)(2), and limitations on exclusion.

(2) *Discriminatory cafeteria plan.*—A highly compensated participant or key employee participating in a discriminatory cafeteria plan must include in gross income (in the participant's taxable year within which ends the plan year with respect to which an election was or could have been made) the value of the taxable benefit with the greatest value that the employee could have elected to receive, even if the employee elects to receive only the nontaxable benefits offered.

(n) *Employer contributions to employees' Health Savings Accounts.*—If an employer contributes to employees' Health Savings Accounts (HSAs) through a cafeteria plan (as defined in §54.4980G-5 of this chapter) those contributions are subject to the nondiscrimination rules in section 125 and this section and are not subject to the comparability rules in section 4980G. See §§ 54.4980G-0 through 54.4980G-5 of this chapter.

(o) *Effective/applicability date.*—It is proposed that these regulations apply on and after plan years beginning on or after January 1, 2009. [Reg. §1.125-7.]

Cost-Sharing Payments: Conservation Payments

Cost-Sharing Payments: Conservation Payments: Exclusions: Recapture.—Temporary Reg. §§16A.126-0—16A.126-2, relating to cost-sharing payments, are also proposed as final regulations (published in the Federal Register on May 21, 1981).

§16A.126-0. Effective dates.

§16A.126-1. Certain cost sharing payments—In general.

§16A.126-2. Section 126 elections.

Employee Trusts: Effective Dates

Employee Trusts: Tax Reform Act of 1984: Effective Dates.—Temporary Reg. §1.133-1T is also proposed as a final regulation and, when adopted, would become Reg. §1.133-1 (published in the Federal Register on February 4, 1986).

§1.133-1. Questions and answers relating to interest on certain loans used to acquire employer securities.

Definition of Registered Form: Guidance

Definition of Registered Form: Guidance.—Reg. §1.149(a)-1, providing guidance on the definitions of registration-required obligation and registered form, including guidance on the issuance of pass-through certificates and participation interests in registered form, is proposed (published in the Federal Register on September 19, 2017) (REG-125374-16).

Par. 2. Section 1.149(a)-1 is added to read as follows:

§1.149(a)-1. Obligations required to be in registered form.—(a) *General rule.*—Interest on a registration-required bond shall not be exempt from tax notwithstanding section 103(a) or any other provision of law, exclusive of any treaty obligation of the United States, unless the bond is issued in registered form (as defined in §1.163-5(b)). For this purpose, registration-required bond has the same meaning as registration-required obligation in §1.163-5(a)(2).

(b) *Applicability date.*—This section applies to bonds issued on or after the date 90 days after the publication of the Treasury decision adopting these rules as final regulations in the **Federal Register**. For bonds issued before the date 90 days after the publication of the Treasury decision adopting these rules as final regulations in the **Federal Register**, see §5f.103-1 of this chapter. [Reg. §1.149(a)-1.]

Tax-Exempt Bonds: State and Local Governments: Refunding Issue: Definition

Tax-Exempt Bonds: State and Local Governments: Refunding Issue: Definition.—Amendments to Reg. §1.150-1, relating to the definition of refunding issue applicable to tax-exempt bonds issued by States and local governments, are proposed (published in the Federal Register on April 10, 2002) (REG-165706-01).

☐ Par. 2. Section 1.150-1 is amended as follows:

1. Paragraph (a)(2)(iii) is added.
2. Paragraphs (d)(2)(ii) and (d)(2)(v) are revised.

The added and revised provisions read as follows:

§1.150-1. Definitions.—(a) * * *

(2) * * *

(iii) *Special effective date for paragraphs (d)(2)(ii) and (d)(2)(v).*—Paragraphs (d)(2)(ii) and (d)(2)(v) of this section apply to bonds sold on or after the date of publication of final regulations in the Federal Register, and may be applied by issuers in whole, but not in part, to any issue that is sold on or after April 10, 2002.

* * *

(d) * * *

(2) * * *

(ii) *Certain issues with different obligors.*—(A) *In general.*—An issue is not a refunding issue to the extent that the obligor (as defined in paragraph (d)(2)(ii)(B) of this section) of one issue is neither the obligor of the other issue nor a related party with respect to the obligor of the other issue. The determination of whether persons are related for this purpose is generally made immediately before the issuance of the refinancing issue. This paragraph (d)(2)(ii)(A) does not apply to any issue that is issued in connection with a transaction to which section 381(a) applies.

(B) *Definition of obligor.*—The obligor of an issue means the actual issuer of the issue, except that the obligor of the portion of an issue properly allocable to an investment in a purpose investment means the conduit borrower under that purpose investment. The obligor of an issue used to finance qualified mortgage loans, qualified student loans, or similar program investments (as defined in §1.148-1) does not include the ultimate recipient of the loan (e.g., the homeowner, the student).

(C) *Certain integrated transactions.*—If, within six months before or after a person assumes (including taking subject to) obligations of an unrelated party in connection with an acquisition transaction (other than a transaction to which section 381(a) applies), the assumed issue is refinanced, the refinancing issue is not a refunding issue. An acquisition transaction is a transaction in which a person acquires from an unrelated party—

(1) Assets (other than an equity interest in an entity);

(2) Stock of a corporation with respect to which a valid election under section 338 is made; or

(3) Control of a governmental unit or a 501(c)(3) organization through the acquisition of stock, membership interests or otherwise.

(D) *Special rule for affiliated persons.*—Paragraphs (d)(2)(ii)(A) and (C) of this section do not apply to any issue that is issued in connection with a transaction between affiliated persons (as defined in paragraph (d)(2)(ii)(E) of this section), unless—

(1) The refinanced issue is redeemed on the earliest date on which it may be redeemed (or otherwise within 90 days after the date of issuance of the refinancing issue); and

(2) The refinancing issue is treated for all purposes of sections 103 and 141 through 150 as financing the assets that were financed with the refinanced issue.

(E) *Affiliated persons.*—For purposes of paragraph (d)(2)(ii)(D) of this section, persons are affiliated persons if—

(1) At any time during the six months prior to the transaction, more than 5 percent of the voting power of the governing body of either person is in the aggregate vested in the other person and its directors, officers, owners, and employees; or

(2) During the one-year period beginning six months prior to the transaction, the composition of the governing body of the acquiring person (or any person that controls the acquiring person) is modified or established to reflect (directly or indirectly) representation of the interests of the acquired person or the person

from whom assets are acquired (or there is an agreement, understanding, or arrangement relating to such a modification or establishment during that one-year period).

(F) *Reverse acquisitions*.—Notwithstanding any other provision of this paragraph (d)(2)(ii), a refinancing issue is a refunding issue if the obligor of the refinanced issue (or any person that is related to the obligor of the refinanced issue immediately before the transaction) has or obtains in the transaction the right to appoint the majority of the members of the governing body of the obligor of the refinancing issue (or any person that controls the obligor of the refinancing issue). See paragraph (d)(2)(v) *Example* 2 of this section.

* * *

(v) *Examples*.—The provisions of this paragraph (d)(2) are illustrated by the following examples:

Example 1. Consolidation of 501(c)(3) hospital organizations. (i) A and B are unrelated hospital organizations described in section 501(c)(3). A has assets with a fair market value of $175 million, and is the obligor of outstanding tax-exempt bonds in the amount of $75 million. B has assets with a fair market value of $145 million, and is the obligor of outstanding tax-exempt bonds in the amount of $50 million. In response to significant competitive pressures in the healthcare industry, and for other substantial business reasons, A and B agree to consolidate their operations. To accomplish the consolidation, A and B form a new 501(c)(3) hospital organization, C. A and B each appoint one-half of the members of the initial governing body of C. Subsequent to the initial appointments, C's governing body is self-perpetuating. On December 29, 2003, State Y issues bonds with sale proceeds of $129 million and lends the entire sale proceeds to C. The 2003 bonds are collectively secured by revenues of A, B and C. Simultaneously with the issuance of the 2003 bonds, C acquires the sole membership interest in each of A and B. C's ownership of these membership interests entitles C to exercise exclusive control over the assets and operations of A and B. C uses the $129 million of sale proceeds of the 2003 bonds to defease the $75 million of bonds on which A was the obligor, and the $50 million of bonds on which B was the obligor. All of the defeased bonds will be redeemed on the first date on which they may be redeemed. In addition, C treats the 2003 bonds as financing the same assets as the defeased bonds. The 2003 bonds do not constitute a refunding issue because the obligor of the 2003 bonds (C) is neither the obligor of the defeased bonds nor a related party with respect to the obligors of those bonds immediately before the issuance of the 2003 bonds. In addition, the requirements of paragraph (d)(2)(ii)(D) of this section have been satisfied.

(ii) The facts are the same as in paragraph (i) of this *Example 1*, except that C acquires the membership interests in A and B subject to the obligations of A and B on their respective bonds, and the 2003 bonds are sold within six months after the acquisition by C of the membership interests. The 2003 bonds do not constitute a refunding issue.

Example 2. Reverse acquisition. D and E are unrelated hospital organizations described in section 501(c)(3). D has assets with a fair market value of $225 million, and is the obligor of outstanding tax-exempt bonds in the amount of $100 million. E has assets with a fair market value of $100 million. D and E agree to consolidate their operations. On May 18, 2004, Authority Z issues bonds with sale proceeds of $103 million and lends the entire sale proceeds to E. Simultaneously with the issuance of the 2004 bonds, E acquires the sole membership interest in D. In addition, D obtains the right to appoint the majority of the members of the governing body of E. E uses the $103 million of sale proceeds of the 2004 bonds to defease the bonds of which D was the obligor. All of the defeased bonds will be redeemed on the first date on which they may be redeemed. In addition, E treats the 2004 bonds as financing the same assets as the defeased bonds. The 2004 bonds constitute a refunding issue because the obligor of the defeased bonds (D) obtains in the transaction the right to appoint the majority of the members of the governing body of the obligor of the 2004 bonds (E). See paragraph (d)(2)(ii)(F) of this section.

Example 3. Relinquishment of control. The facts are the same as in *Example 2*, except that D does not obtain the right, directly or indirectly, to appoint any member of the governing body of E. Rather, E obtains the right both to approve and to remove without cause each member of the governing body of D. In addition, prior to being acquired by E, D experiences financial difficulties as a result of mismanagement. Thus, as part of E's acquisition of D, all of the former members of D's governing body resign their positions and are replaced with persons appointed by E. The 2004 bonds do not constitute a refunding issue.

* * *

State and Local Governments: Tax-Exempt Bonds

State and Local Governments: Tax-Exempt Bonds.—Reg. §1.150-3, addressing when tax-exempt bonds are treated as retired for purposes of section 103 and sections 141 through 150 of the Internal Revenue Code, is proposed (published in the Federal Register on December 31, 2018) (REG-141739-08).

Par. 2. Section 1.150-3 is added to read as follows:

§1.150-3. Retirement standards for state and local bonds.—(a) *General purpose and scope.*—This section provides rules to determine when a tax-exempt bond is retired for purposes of sections 103 and 141 through 150.

(b) *General rules for retirement of a tax-exempt bond.*—Except as otherwise provided in paragraph (c) of this section, a tax-exempt bond is retired when:

(1) A significant modification of the bond occurs under §1.1001-3;

(2) The issuer or its agent acquires the bond in a manner that liquidates or extinguishes the bondholder's investment in the bond; or

(3) The bond is otherwise redeemed (for example, redeemed at maturity).

(c) *Exceptions to retirement of a tax-exempt bond.*—(1) *Qualified tender right does not result in a modification.*—In applying §1.1001-3 to a qualified tender bond for purposes of paragraph (b)(1) of this section, both the existence and exercise of a qualified tender right are disregarded. Thus, a change in the interest rate mode made in connection with the exercise of a qualified tender right generally is not a modification because the change occurs by operation of the terms of the bond and the holder's resulting right to put the bond to the issuer or its agent does not prevent the issuer's option from being a unilateral option.

(2) *Acquisition pursuant to a qualified tender right.*—Acquisition of a qualified tender bond by the issuer or its agent does not result in retirement of the bond under paragraph (b)(2) of this section if the acquisition is pursuant to the operation of a qualified tender right and neither the issuer nor its agent continues to hold the bond after the close of the 90-day period beginning on the date of the tender.

(3) *Acquisition of a tax-exempt bond by a guarantor or liquidity facility provider.*—Acquisition of a tax-exempt bond by a guarantor or liquidity facility provider acting on the issuer's behalf does not result in retirement of the bond under paragraph (b)(2) of this section if the acquisition is pursuant to the terms of the guarantee or liquidity facility and the guarantor or liquidity facility provider is not a related party (as defined in §1.150-11(b)) to the issuer.

(d) *Effect of retirement.*—If a bond is retired pursuant to paragraph (b)(1) of this section (that is, in a transaction treated as an exchange of the bond for a bond with modified terms), the bond is treated as a new bond issued at the time of the modification as determined under §1.1001-3. If the issuer or its agent resells a bond retired pursuant to paragraph (b)(2) of this section, the bond is treated as a new bond issued on the date of resale. In both cases, the rules of §1.150-1(d) apply to determine if the new bond is part of a refunding issue.

(e) *Definitions.*—For purposes of this section, the following definitions apply:

(1) *Issuer* means the State or local governmental unit (as defined in §1.103-1) that actually issues the tax-exempt bond and any related party (as defined in §1.150-1(b)) to the actual issuer (as distinguished, for example, from a conduit borrower that is not a related party to the actual issuer).

(2) *Qualified tender bond* means a tax-exempt bond that, pursuant to the terms of its governing contract, has all of the features described in this paragraph (e)(2). During each authorized interest rate mode, the bond bears interest at a fixed interest rate, a qualified floating rate under §1.1275-5(b), or an objective rate for a tax-exempt bond under §1.1275-5(c)(5). Interest on the bond is unconditionally payable at periodic intervals of no more than one year. The bond has a stated maturity date that is not later than 40 years after the issue date of the bond. The bond includes a qualified tender right.

(3) *Qualified tender right* means a right or obligation of a holder of the bond to tender the bond for purchase as described in this paragraph (e)(3). The purchaser under the tender may be the issuer, its agent, or another party. The tender right is available on at least one date before the stated maturity date. For each such tender, the purchase price of the bond is equal to par (plus any accrued interest). Following each such tender, the issuer or its remarketing agent either redeems the bond or uses reasonable best efforts to resell the bond within the 90-day period beginning on the date of the tender. Upon any such resale, the purchase price of the bond is equal to par (plus any accrued interest).

(f) *Applicability date.*—This section applies to events and actions taken with respect to bonds that occur on or after the date that is 90 days after the date of publication of the Treasury decision adopting these rules as final regulations in the **Federal Register**. [Reg. §1.150-3.]

Dependency Exemption: Authorized Placement Agency: Definition

Dependency Exemption: Authorized Placement Agency: Definition.—Amendments to Reg. §§1.151-1—1.151-4, relating to the definition of an authorized placement agency for purposes of a dependency exemption for a child placed for adoption that were issued prior to the changes made to the law by the Working Families Tax Relief Act of 2004, are proposed (published in the Federal Register on January 19, 2017) (REG-137604-07).

Par. 10. Section 1.151-1 is amended by revising paragraphs (a)(1), (c), and (d) to read as follows:

§1.151-1. Deductions for personal exemptions.—(a) * * *

(1) In computing taxable income, an individual is allowed a deduction for the exemptions for an individual taxpayer and spouse (the personal exemptions) and the exemption for a dependent of the taxpayer.

* * *

(c) *Additional exemption for dependent.*—Section 151(c) allows a taxpayer an exemption for each individual who is a dependent (as defined in section 152) of the taxpayer for the taxable year. See §§1.152-1 through 1.152-5 for rules relating to dependents.

(d) *Applicability date.*—Paragraphs (a)(1) and (c) of this section apply to taxable years beginning after the date these regulations are published as final regulations in the **Federal Register**.

Par. 11. Sections 1.151-2, 1.151-3, and 1.151-4 are removed.

§1.151-2. Additional exemptions for dependents.

§1.151-3. Definitions.

§1.151-4. Amount of deduction for each exemption under section 151.

Dependency Exemption: Authorized Placement Agency: Definition

Dependency Exemption: Authorized Placement Agency: Definition.—Reg. §§1.152-0 and 1.152-4 and amendments to Reg. §§1.152-1—1.152-5, relating to the definition of an authorized placement agency for purposes of a dependency exemption for a child placed for adoption that were issued prior to the changes made to the law by the Working Families Tax Relief Act of 2004, are proposed (published in the Federal Register on January 19, 2017) (REG-137604-07).

Par. 12. Section 1.152-0 is added under the undesignated center heading Deductions for Personal Exemptions to read as follows:

§1.152-0. Table of contents.—This section lists the captions contained in §1.152-1 through §1.152-5.

Par. 13. Section 1.152-1 is revised to read as follows:

§ 1.152-1. General rules for dependents.—(a) *In general.*—(1) *Dependent defined.*—Except as provided in section 152(b) and paragraph (a)(2) of this section, the term *dependent* means a qualifying child as described in § 1.152-2 or a qualifying relative as described in § 1.152-3. In general, an individual may be treated as the dependent of only one taxpayer for taxable years beginning in the same calendar year.

(2) *Exceptions.*—(i) *Dependents ineligible.*—If an individual is a dependent of a taxpayer for a taxable year of the taxpayer, the individual is treated as having no dependents for purposes of section 152 and the related regulations in the individual's taxable year beginning in the calendar year in which that taxable year of the taxpayer begins. For purposes of this paragraph (a)(2)(i), an individual is not a dependent of a person if that person is not required to file an income tax return under section 6012 and either does not file an income tax return or files an income tax return solely to claim a refund of estimated or withheld taxes.

(ii) *Married dependents.*—An individual is not treated as a dependent of a taxpayer for a taxable year of the taxpayer if the individual files a joint return, other than solely to claim a refund of estimated or withheld taxes, with the individual's spouse under section 6013 for the taxable year beginning in the calendar year in which that taxable year of the taxpayer begins.

(iii) *Citizens or nationals of other countries.*—An individual who is not a citizen or national of the United States is not treated as a dependent of a taxpayer unless the individual is a resident, as defined in section 7701(b), of the United States or of a country contiguous to the United States (Canada or Mexico). This limitation, however, does not apply to an adopted child, as defined in section 152(f)(1)(B) and paragraph (b)(1)(ii) of this section, if the taxpayer is a citizen or national of the United States and the child has the same principal place of abode as the taxpayer and is a member of the taxpayer's household, within the meaning of §§ 1.152-4(c) and 1.2-2(c), respectively, for the taxpayer's taxable year. See § 1.152-4(d)(2) for rules relating to residence for a portion of a taxable year. A taxpayer and the child have the same principal place of abode for the taxpayer's taxable year if the taxpayer and child have the same principal place of abode for the entire portion of the taxable year following the placement of the child with the taxpayer.

(b) *Definitions.*—The following definitions apply for purposes of section 152 and the related regulations.

(1) *Child.*—(i) *In general.*—The term *child* means a son, daughter, stepson, or stepdaughter, or an eligible foster child, within the meaning of paragraph (b)(1)(iii) of this section, of the taxpayer.

(ii) *Adopted child.*—In determining whether an individual bears any of the relationships described in paragraph (b)(1)(i) of this section, § 1.152-2(b), or § 1.152-3(b), a legally adopted child of a person, or a child who is lawfully placed with a person for legal adoption by that person, is treated as a child by blood of that person. A child lawfully placed with a person for legal adoption by that person includes a child placed for legal adoption by a parent, an authorized placement agency, or any other person(s) authorized by law to place a child for legal adoption.

(iii) *Eligible foster child.*—The term *eligible foster child* means a child who is placed with a person by an authorized placement agency or by judgment, decree, or other order of any court of competent jurisdiction.

(iv) *Authorized placement agency.*—The term *authorized placement agency* means a State, the District of Columbia, a possession of the United States, a foreign country, an Indian Tribal Government (ITG) (as defined in section 7701(a)(40)), or an agency or organization that is authorized by a State, the District of Columbia, a possession of the United States, a foreign country, an ITG, or a political subdivision of any of the foregoing, to place children for legal adoption or in foster care.

(2) *Student.*—The term *student* means an individual who, for some part of each of five calendar months, whether or not consecutive, during the calendar year in which the taxable year of the taxpayer begins, either is a full-time student at an educational organization, as defined in section 170(b)(1)(A)(ii), or is pursuing a full-time course of institutional on-farm training under the supervision of an accredited agent of an educational organization or of a State or political subdivision of a State. A full-time student is one who is enrolled for the number of hours or courses that the educational organization considers full-time attendance.

(3) *Brother and sister.*—The terms *brother* and *sister* include a brother or sister by half blood.

(4) *Parent.*—The term *parent* refers to a biological or adoptive parent of an individual. It does not include a stepparent who has not adopted the individual.

(c) *Applicability date.*—This section, and §§ 1.152-2, 1.152-3, and 1.152-4 apply to taxable years beginning after the date these regulations are published as final regulations in the **Federal Register**.

Par. 14. Section 1.152-2 is revised to read as follows:

§1.152-2. Qualifying child.—(a) *In general.*—The term *qualifying child* of a taxpayer for a taxable year means an individual who satisfies the tests described in paragraphs (b), (c), (d), (e), and (f) of this section. If an individual satisfies the definition of a qualifying child for more than one taxpayer, then the tiebreaker rules in paragraph (g) of this section apply. See, however, section 152(e) and §1.152-5 for a special rule for a child of divorced or separated parents or parents who live apart.

(b) *Qualifying child relationship test.*—The individual must bear one of the following relationships to the taxpayer—

(1) A child of the taxpayer or descendant of such a child; or

(2) A brother, sister, stepbrother, or stepsister of the taxpayer, or a descendant of any of these relatives.

(c) *Residency test.*—The individual must have the same principal place of abode as the taxpayer for more than one-half of the taxable year. Generally, an individual has the same principal place of abode as the taxpayer for more than one-half of the taxable year if the individual resides with the taxpayer for more than one-half of the taxable year. See §1.152-4(c) for rules relating to principal place of abode and temporary absence and for determining whether an individual resides with the taxpayer for more than one-half of the taxable year.

(d) *Age test.*—(1) *In general.*—The individual must be younger than the taxpayer claiming the individual as a qualifying child and must not have attained the age of 19, or age 24 if the individual is a student within the meaning of §1.152-1(b)(2), as of the end of the calendar year in which the taxpayer's taxable year begins. For purposes of this section, an individual attains an age on the anniversary of the individual's birth.

(2) *Disabled individual.*—This age requirement is treated as satisfied if the individual is permanently and totally disabled, as defined in section 22(e)(3), at any time during the calendar year.

(e) *Qualifying child support test.*—The individual must not provide more than one-half of the individual's own support for the calendar year in which the taxpayer's taxable year begins. See §1.152-4(a) for rules relating to the definition and sources of an individual's support.

(f) *Joint return test.*—The individual must not file a joint return, other than solely to claim a refund of estimated or withheld taxes, under section 6013 with the individual's spouse for the taxable year beginning in the calendar year in which the taxpayer's taxable year begins.

(g) *Child who is eligible to be claimed as a qualifying child by more than one taxpayer.*—(1) *In general.*—Under section 152(c)(4), if an individual satisfies the definition of a qualifying child for two or more taxpayers (eligible taxpayers) for a taxable year beginning in the same calendar year, the following rules apply.

(i) *More than one eligible parent.*—If more than one eligible taxpayer is a parent of the individual (eligible parent), any one of the eligible parents may claim the individual as a qualifying child. However, if more than one eligible parent claims the individual as a qualifying child, and those eligible parents do not file a joint return with each other, the individual is treated as the qualifying child of the eligible parent claiming the individual with whom the individual resides for the longest period of time during the taxable year as determined under §1.152-4(c)(3). If the individual resides for the same amount of time during the taxable year with each eligible parent claiming the child, the individual is treated as the qualifying child of the eligible parent with the highest adjusted gross income who claims the individual.

(ii) *Eligible parent not claiming.*—If at least one eligible taxpayer is a parent of the individual, but no eligible parent claims the individual as a qualifying child, the individual may be treated as the qualifying child of another eligible taxpayer only if that taxpayer's adjusted gross income exceeds both the adjusted gross income of each eligible parent of the individual and the adjusted gross income of each other eligible taxpayer, if any.

(iii) *One eligible parent and other eligible taxpayer(s).*—Except as provided in paragraph (g)(1)(i) or (ii) of this section, if there are two or more eligible taxpayers, only one of whom is the parent of the individual, the individual is treated as the qualifying child of the eligible parent.

(iv) *No eligible parent.*—If no eligible taxpayer is a parent of the individual, the individual is treated as the qualifying child of the eligible taxpayer with the highest adjusted gross income for the taxable year.

(2) *Determination of adjusted gross income of a person who files a joint return.*—For purposes of section 152 and the related regulations, the adjusted gross income of each person who files a joint return is the total adjusted gross income shown on the joint return.

(3) *Coordination with other provisions.*—Except to the extent that section 152(e) and §1.152-5 apply, if more than one taxpayer may claim a child as a qualifying child, the child is treated as the qualifying child of only one taxpayer for purposes of head of household filing status under section 2(b), the child and dependent care credit under section 21, the child tax credit under section 24, the earned income credit under section 32, the exclusion from income for dependent care assistance under section 129, and the dependency exemption under section 151. Thus, the taxpayer claiming the individual as a qualifying child under any one of these sections is the only taxpayer who may claim any credit or exemption under these other sections for that same individual for a taxable year beginning in the same calendar year as the taxpayer's taxable year. If section 152(e) applies, however, the noncustodial parent may claim the child as a qualifying child for purposes of the dependency exemption and the child tax credit, and another person may claim the child for purposes of one or more of these other provisions. See §1.152-5 for rules under section 152(e).

(4) *Examples.*—The following examples illustrate the rules in this paragraph (g). In the examples, each taxpayer uses the calendar year as the taxpayer's taxable year, the child is a qualifying child (as described in section 152(c) and this section) of each taxpayer, and, except to the extent indicated, each taxpayer meets the requirements to claim the benefit(s) described in the example.

Example 1. (i) A and B, parents of Child, are married to each other. A, B, and Child share the same principal place of abode for the first 8 months of the year. Thus, both parents satisfy the qualifying child residency test of paragraph (c) of this section. For the last 4 months of the year, the parents live apart from each other, and B and Child share the same principal place of abode. Section 152(e), relating to divorced or separated parents, does not apply. The parents file as married filing separately for the taxable year, and both parents claim Child as a qualifying child.

(ii) Under paragraph (g)(1)(i) of this section, Child is treated as a qualifying child of B for all purposes, because Child resided with B for the longer period of time during the taxable year. Because section 152(e) does not apply, Child may not be treated as a qualifying child of A for any purpose.

Example 2. (i) The facts are the same as in *Example 1* of this paragraph (g)(4), except that B does not claim Child as a qualifying child.

(ii) Because A and B are not both claiming the same child as a qualifying child, under paragraph (g)(1)(i) of this section, Child is treated as a qualifying child of A.

Example 3. (i) Child, Child's parent (D), and Grandparent share the same principal place of abode. D is not married and is not a qualifying child or dependent of Grandparent, and Grandparent is not D's dependent. Section 152(e), relating to divorced or separated parents, does not apply. Under paragraph (a) of this section, Child meets the definition of a qualifying child of both D and Grandparent. D claims Child as a qualifying child for purposes of the child and dependent care credit under section 21, the earned income credit under section 32, and the dependency exemption under section 151. Grandparent claims Child as a qualifying child for purposes of head of household filing status under section 2(b).

(ii) Under paragraph (g)(1)(iii) of this section, Child is treated as the qualifying child of D for all purposes, because D is eligible to claim and claims Child as D's qualifying child. Because D is eligible to claim and claims Child as D's qualifying child, under paragraph (g)(3) of this section, Child may not be treated as a qualifying child of Grandparent for any purpose. Grandparent erroneously claimed Child as Grandparent's qualifying child for purposes of head of household filing status under section 2(b). If D had not claimed Child as D's qualifying child for any purpose, under paragraph (g)(1)(ii) of this section, Grandparent could have claimed Child as Grandparent's qualifying child if Grandparent's adjusted gross income (AGI) exceeded D's AGI. In that situation, under paragraph (g)(3) of this section, Grandparent could have claimed Child as Grandparent's qualifying child for purposes of any of the child-related tax benefits, provided that Grandparent had met the requirements of those sections.

Example 4. (i) The facts are the same as in *Example 3* of this paragraph (g)(4), except that Child's parents, D and E, are married to each other and share the same principal place of abode with Child and Grandparent for the entire taxable year. Under paragraph (a) of this section, Child meets the definition of a qualifying child of both parents and Grandparent. D and E file a joint return for the taxable year and do not claim Child as a qualifying child for any purpose.

(ii) Because D or E may claim Child as a qualifying child but neither claims Child as a qualifying child for any purpose, under paragraph (g)(1)(ii) of this section, Grandparent may claim Child as a qualifying child if Grandparent's AGI exceeds the total AGI reported on the joint return of D and E.

Example 5. (i) The facts are the same as in *Example 4* of this paragraph (g)(4), except that D and E are divorced from each other, E moved into a separate residence during that year and is the noncustodial parent, and section 152(e), relating to divorced or separated parents, applies. E attaches to E's return a Form 8332 on which D agrees to release D's claim to a dependency exemption for Child and E claims Child as a qualifying child for purposes of the dependency exemption and the child tax credit.

(ii) Under paragraph (g)(3) of this section, Child is treated as a qualifying child of E for purposes of the dependency exemption and the child tax credit. Child may be treated as a qualifying child of D for purposes of the earned income credit. If D claims Child as a qualifying child for purposes of the earned income credit, under paragraph (g)(1)(iii) of this section, Child may not be treated as a qualifying child of Grandparent for any purpose.

Example 6. (i) F and G, parents of two children, are married to each other. F, G, and both children share the same principal place of abode for the entire taxable year. F and G file as married filing separately for the taxable year. F claims the older child as a qualifying child for purposes of the child tax credit, dependency exemption, and the child and dependent care credit. G claims the younger child as a qualifying child for purposes of the same three tax benefits.

(ii) The older child is treated as a qualifying child of F and the younger child is treated as a qualifying child of G. The tiebreaker rule of paragraph (g)(1)(i) of this section does not apply because F and G are not claiming the same child as a qualifying child.

Par. 15. Section 1.152-3 is revised to read as follows:

§1.152-3. Qualifying relative.—(a) *In general.*—The term *qualifying relative* of a taxpayer for a taxable year means an individual who satisfies the tests described in paragraphs (b), (c), (d), and (e) of this section. See, however, section 152(e) and §1.152-5 for a special rule for a child of divorced or separated parents or parents who live apart.

(b) *Qualifying relative relationship test.*—The individual must bear one of the following relationships to the taxpayer:

(1) A child or descendant of a child;

(2) A brother, sister, stepbrother, or stepsister;

(3) A father or mother, or an ancestor of either;

(4) A stepfather or stepmother;

(5) A niece or nephew;

(6) An aunt or uncle;

(7) A son-in-law, daughter-in-law, father-in-law, mother-in-law, brother-in-law, or sister-in-law; or

(8) An individual (other than one who at any time during the taxable year was the taxpayer's spouse, determined without regard to section 7703) who for the taxable year of the taxpayer has the same principal place of abode as the taxpayer and is a member of the taxpayer's household. See § 1.2-2(c) for the definition of a member of the household, and § 1.152-4(c) for rules relating to the meaning of principal place of abode and the meaning of temporary absence.

(c) *Gross income test.*—(1) *In general.*—The individual's gross income for the calendar year in which the taxable year begins must be less than the exemption amount as defined in section 151(d).

(2) *Income of disabled or handicapped individuals.*—For purposes of paragraph (c)(1) of this section, the gross income of an individual who is permanently and totally disabled, as defined in section 22(e)(3), at any time during the taxable year does not include income for services performed by the individual at a sheltered workshop, as defined in section 152(d)(4)(B), if—

(i) The principal reason for the individual's presence at the workshop is the availability of medical care there; and

(ii) The individual's income arises solely from activities at the workshop that are incident to the medical care.

(d) *Qualifying relative support test.*—(1) *In general.*—The individual must receive over one-half of the individual's support from the taxpayer for the calendar year in which the taxpayer's taxable year begins. See § 1.152-4(a) for rules relating to support.

(2) *Certain income of taxpayer's spouse.*—A payment to a spouse that is includible in the payee spouse's gross income under section 71 (relating to alimony and separate maintenance payments) or section 682 (relating to income of an estate or trust in the case of divorce) is not treated as a payment by the payor spouse for the support of any dependent.

(3) *Support from stepparent.*—Any support provided to or for the benefit of an individual by a stepparent of the individual is treated as support provided by the individual's parent who is married to the stepparent.

(4) *Multiple support agreements.*—If more than one-half of an individual's support is provided by two or more persons together, a taxpayer is treated as having contributed over one-half of the support of that individual for the calendar year if—

(i) No one person contributes more than one-half of the individual's support;

(ii) Each member of the group that collectively contributes more than one-half of the support of the individual would have been entitled to claim the individual as a dependent for a taxable year beginning in that calendar year but for the fact that the group member alone did not contribute more than one-half of the individual's support;

(iii) The taxpayer claiming the individual as a qualifying relative contributes more than 10 percent of the individual's support; and

(iv) Each other group member who contributes more than 10 percent of the support of the individual furnishes to the taxpayer claiming the individual as a dependent a written declaration that the other person will not claim the individual as a dependent for any taxable year beginning in that calendar year.

(e) *Not a qualifying child test.*—(1) *In general.*—The individual must not be a qualifying child of the taxpayer or of any other taxpayer for any taxable year beginning in the calendar year in which the taxpayer's taxable year begins. An individual is not a qualifying child of a person, however, if that person is not required to file an income tax return under section 6012, and either does not file an income tax return or files an income tax return solely to claim a refund of estimated or withheld taxes.

(2) *Examples.*—The following examples illustrate the rules in this paragraph (e). In each example, each taxpayer uses the calendar year as the taxpayer's taxable year, and except to the extent otherwise indicated, each taxpayer meets the requirements to claim the benefits described in the example.

Example 1. For the taxable year, B provides more than one-half of the support of an unrelated friend, C, and C's 3-year-old child, D, who are members of B's household. No taxpayer other than C is eligible to claim D as a qualifying child. C has no gross income, is not required by section 6012 to file a Federal income tax return, and does not file a Federal income tax return for the taxable year. Under paragraph (e)(1) of this section, because C does not have a filing requirement and does not file an income tax return, D is not treated as a qualifying child of C, and B may claim both C and D as B's qualifying relatives.

Example 2. The facts are the same as in *Example 1* of this paragraph (e)(2) except that C has earned income of $1,500 during the taxable year, had income tax withheld from C's wages, and is not required by section 6012 to file an income tax return. C files an income tax return solely to obtain a refund of withheld taxes and does not claim the earned income credit under section 32. Under paragraph (e)(1) of this section, because C does not have a filing requirement and files only to obtain a refund of withheld taxes, D is not treated as a qualifying child of C, and B may claim both C and D as B's qualifying relatives.

Example 3. The facts are the same as in *Example 2* of this paragraph (e)(2) except that C's earned income is more than the amount of the dependency exemption for that year. C files an income tax return for the taxable year to obtain a refund of withheld taxes and claims the earned income credit. Because C filed an income tax return to obtain the earned income credit and not solely to obtain a refund of withheld taxes, D is a qualifying child of a taxpayer (C), and B may not claim D as a qualifying relative. B also may not claim C as a qualifying relative because C fails the gross income test under paragraph (c) of this section.

Par. 16. Redesignate § 1.152-4 as § 1.152-5, and add a new § 1.152-4 to read as follows:

§ 1.152-4. Rules for a qualifying child and a qualifying relative.—(a) *Support.*—(1) *In general.*—The term *support* includes food, shelter, clothing, medical and dental care, education, and similar items. Support does not include an individual's Federal, State, and local income taxes paid from the individual's own income or assets, Social Security and Medicare taxes under section 3101 paid from the individual's own income, life insurance premiums, or funeral expenses. In determining whether an individual provided more than one-half of the individual's own support for purposes of § 1.152-2(e), or whether a taxpayer provided more than one-half of an individual's support for purposes of § 1.152-3(d), the amount of support provided by the individual, or the taxpayer, is compared to the total amount of the individual's support from all sources. For these purposes, except as otherwise provided in this paragraph (a), the amount of an individual's total support is the amount of support from all sources, and includes support the individual provides and amounts that are excludable from gross income. Generally, the amount of an item of support is the amount of expense paid or incurred to furnish the item of support. If the item of support furnished is property or a benefit, such as lodging, however, the amount of the item of support is the fair market value of the item.

(2) *Payments made during the year for unpaid or future support.*—For purposes of determining the amount of support provided in a calendar year, an amount paid in a calendar year after the calendar year in which the liability is incurred is treated as paid in the year of payment. An amount paid in a calendar year before due, whether or not made in the form of a lump sum payment in settlement of a person's liability for support, is treated as support paid during the calendar year of payment rather than the calendar year when payment is due. A payment of a liability from amounts set aside in trust in a prior year is treated as made in the year in which the liability is paid.

(3) *Governmental payments.*—(i) *Governmental payments as support.*—(A) *In general.*—Except as provided in paragraph (a)(3)(iii) of this section, governmental payments and subsidies for an item of support are support provided by a third party, the government.

(B) *Examples.*—Payments of Temporary Assistance for Needy Families (42 U.S.C. 601-619), low-income housing assistance (42 U.S.C. 1437f), Supplemental Nutrition Assistance Program benefits (7 U.S.C. chapter 51), Supplemental Security Income payments (42 U.S.C. 1381-1383f), foster care maintenance payments, and adoption assistance payments are governmental payments and subsidies for an item of support as described in paragraph (a)(3)(i)(A) of this section.

(ii) *Governmental payments based on a taxpayer's contributions.*—(A) *In general.*—Except as provided in paragraph (a)(3)(iii) of this section, governmental payments based on a taxpayer's earnings and contributions into the Social Security system are support provided by the individual for whose benefit the payments are made to the extent those payments are used for that individual's support.

(B) *Examples.*—Social Security old age benefits under section 202(b) of Title II of the Social Security Act (SSA) (42 U.S.C. 402) are governmental payments based on a taxpayer's earnings and contributions into the Social Security system as described in paragraph (a)(3)(ii)(A) of this section. Similarly, Social Security survivor and disability insurance benefits paid under section 202(d) of the SSA to, or for the benefit of, the child of a deceased or disabled parent are treated as support provided by the child to the extent those payments are used for the child's support.

(iii) *Payments used for support of another individual.*—Governmental payments and subsidies described in paragraph (a)(3)(i) of this section and governmental payments described in paragraph (a)(3)(ii) of this section that are used by the recipient or other intended beneficiary to support another person are support of that person provided by the recipient or other intended beneficiary, rather than support provided by a third party, the government.

(4) *Medical insurance.*—Medical insurance premiums, including Part A Basic Medicare premiums, if any, under Title XVIII of the Social Security Act (42 U.S.C. 1395c to 1395i-5), Part B Supplemental Medicare premiums under Title XVIII of the Social Security Act (42 U.S.C. 1395j to 1395w-6), Part C Medicare + Choice Program premiums under Title XVIII of the Social Security Act (42 U.S.C. 1395w-21 to 1395w-29), and Part D Voluntary Prescription Drug Benefit Medicare premiums under Title XVIII of the Social Security Act (42 U.S.C. 1395w-101 to 1395w-154), are treated as support. Medical insurance proceeds, including benefits received under Medicare Part A, Part B, Part C, and Part D, are not treated as items of support and are disregarded in determining the amount of the individual's support. Services provided to an individual under the medical and dental care provisions of the Armed Forces Act (10 U.S.C. chapter 55) are not treated as support and are disregarded in determining the amount of the individual's support.

(5) *Medical care payments from personal injury claim.*—Payments for the medical care of an injured individual from a third party, including a third party's insurance company, in satisfaction of a legal claim for the personal injury of the individual are not treated as items of support and are disregarded in determining the amount of the individual's support.

(6) *Scholarships.*—Amounts a student who is the child of the taxpayer receives as a scholarship for study at an educational organization described in section 170(b)(1)(A)(ii) are not treated as an item of support and are disregarded in determining the amount of the student's support.

(b) *Relationship test.*—(1) *Joint return.*—A taxpayer may satisfy the relationship test described in § 1.152-2(b) (relating to a qualifying child) or in § 1.152-3(b) (relating to a qualifying relative) if a described relationship exists between an individual and the taxpayer claiming that individual as a qualifying child or qualifying relative, even though the taxpayer files a joint return with his or her spouse who does not have a described relationship with the individual.

(2) *Divorce or death of spouse*.—If the relationship between the taxpayer and an individual claimed by that taxpayer as a dependent results from a marriage, the taxpayer's qualifying relationship with the individual continues after the termination of the marriage by divorce or death.

(c) *Principal place of abode*.—(1) *In general*.—The term *principal place of abode* of a person means the primary or main home or dwelling where the person resides. A person's principal place of abode need not be the same physical location throughout the taxable year and may be temporary lodging such as a homeless shelter or relief housing resulting from displacement caused by a natural disaster.

(2) *Temporary absence*.—The taxpayer and an individual have the same principal place of abode despite a temporary absence by either person because of special circumstances. An absence is temporary if the person would have resided at the place of abode but for the absence and, under the facts and circumstances, it is reasonable to assume that the person will return to reside at the place of abode. An individual who does not reside with the taxpayer because of a temporary absence is treated as residing with the taxpayer. For example, a nonpermanent failure to occupy the abode by reason of illness, education, business, vacation, military service, institutionalized care for a child who is totally and permanently disabled (as defined in section 22(e)(3)), or incarceration may be treated as a temporary absence because of special circumstances. If an infant must remain in a hospital for a period of time after birth and would have resided with the taxpayer during that period but for the hospitalization, the infant is treated as having the same principal place of abode as the taxpayer during the period of hospitalization.

(3) *Residing with taxpayer for more than one-half of the taxable year*.—(i) *In general*.—An individual has the same principal place of abode as the taxpayer for more than one-half of the taxable year if the individual resides with the taxpayer for at least 183 nights during the taxpayer's taxable year, or 184 nights if the taxable year includes a leap day.

(ii) *Nights of residence*.—(A) *Nights counted*.—For purposes of determining whether an individual resides with the taxpayer for more than one-half of the taxable year, an individual resides with a taxpayer for a night if the individual sleeps

(1) At the taxpayer's principal place of abode, whether or not the taxpayer is present; or

(2) In the company of the taxpayer when the individual does not sleep at the taxpayer's principal place of abode (for example, when the taxpayer and the individual are on vacation).

(B) *Night straddling two taxable years*.—If an individual resides with a taxpayer for a night that extends over two taxable years, that night is allocated to the taxable year in which the night begins.

(C) *Exception for a parent who works at night*.—If, in a calendar year, because of a taxpayer's nighttime work schedule, an individual resides for at least 183 days, or 184 days if the taxable year includes a leap day, but not nights with the taxpayer, the individual is treated as residing with the taxpayer for more than one-half of the taxable year.

(D) *Absences*.—An individual who does not reside with a taxpayer for a night because of a temporary absence as described in paragraph (c)(2) of this section is treated as residing with the taxpayer for that night if the individual would have resided with the taxpayer for that night but for the absence.

(4) *Examples*.—The following examples illustrate the rules of this paragraph (c). In each example, each taxpayer uses the calendar taxable year, and section 152(e) does not apply.

Example 1. B and C are the divorced parents of Child. In 2015, Child sleeps at B's principal place of abode for 210 nights and at C's principal place of abode for 155 nights. Under paragraph (c)(3) of this section, Child resides with B for at least 183 nights during 2015 and has the same principal place of abode as B for more than one-half of 2015.

Example 2. D and E are the divorced parents of Child, and Grandparent is E's parent. In 2015, Child resides with D for 140 nights, with E for 135 nights, and with Grandparent for the last 90 nights of the year. None of these periods is a temporary absence. Under paragraph (c)(3) of this section, Child does not have the same principal place of abode as D, E, or Grandparent for more than one-half of 2015.

Example 3. The facts are the same as in *Example 2* of this paragraph (c)(4), except that, for the 90-day period that Child lives with Grandparent, E is temporarily absent on military service. Child would have lived with E if E had not been absent during that period. Under paragraphs (c)(2) and (c)(3)(ii)(D) of this section, Child is treated as residing with E for 225 nights in 2015 and, therefore, Child has the same principal place of abode as E for more than one-half of 2015.

Example 4. The facts are the same as in *Example 2* of this paragraph (c)(4), except that, for the last 90 days of the year Child, who is 18, moves into Child's own apartment and begins full-time employment. Because Child's absence is not temporary, under paragraph (c)(2) of this section, Child is not treated as residing with D or E for the 90 nights. Under paragraph (c) of this section, Child does not have the same principal place of abode as D or E for more than one-half of 2015.

Example 5. F and G are the divorced parents of Child. In 2015, Child sleeps at F's principal place of abode for 170 nights and at G's principal place of abode for 170 nights. Child spends 25 nights of the year away from F and G at a summer camp. Child would have spent those nights with F if Child had not gone to summer camp. Under paragraphs (c)(2) and (c)(3)(ii)(D) of this section, Child is treated as residing with F for 195 nights and, therefore, Child has the same principal place of abode as F for more than one-half of 2015.

Example 6. H and J are the divorced parents of Child. In 2015, Child sleeps at H's principal place of abode for 180 nights and at J's principal place of abode for 180 nights. For 5 nights during that year, Child sleeps at Grandparent's abode or at the house of a friend. Child would have spent all 5 nights at H's house if Child had not slept at Grandparent's or a friend's house. Under paragraphs (c)(2) and (c)(3)(ii)(D) of this section, Child is treated as residing with H for 185 nights and, therefore, Child has the same principal place of abode as H for more than one-half of 2015.

(d) *Residence for a portion of a taxable year because of special circumstances.*—(1) *Individual who is born or dies during the year.*—If an individual is born or dies during a taxpayer's taxable year, the residency test for a qualifying child is treated as met if the taxpayer and the individual have the same principal place of abode for more than one-half of the portion of the taxable year during which the individual is alive. If an individual is born or dies during a taxpayer's taxable year, the relationship test for a qualifying relative who is a member of the taxpayer's household is treated as met if the taxpayer and the individual have the same principal place of abode for the entire portion of the taxable year during which the individual is alive.

(2) *Adopted child or foster child.*—If, during a taxpayer's taxable year, the taxpayer adopts a child, a child is lawfully placed with a taxpayer for legal adoption by that taxpayer, or an eligible foster child is placed with a taxpayer, the residency test for a qualifying child and the residency requirement under § 1.152-1(a)(2)(iii) for a child who is not a citizen or national of the United States are treated as met if the taxpayer and the child have the same principal place of abode for more than one-half of the portion of the taxable year as required for a qualifying child, or for the entire taxable year as required for a noncitizen, following the placement of the child with the taxpayer.

(e) *Missing child.*—(1) *Qualifying child.*—A child of the taxpayer who is presumed by law enforcement authorities to have been kidnapped by someone who is not a member of the family of either the child or the taxpayer, and who had for the taxable year in which the kidnapping occurred the same principal place of abode as the taxpayer for more than one-half of the portion of the taxable year before the date of the kidnapping, is treated as meeting the residency test for a qualifying child, as described in § 1.152-2(c), of the taxpayer for all taxable years ending during the period that the child is missing. Also, the child is treated as meeting the residency test in the year of the child's return if the child has the same principal place of abode as the taxpayer for more than one-half of the portion of the taxable year following the date of the child's return.

(2) *Qualifying relative.*—A child of the taxpayer who is presumed by law enforcement authorities to have been kidnapped by someone who is not a member of the family of either the child or the taxpayer, and who was a qualifying relative of the taxpayer for the portion of the taxable year before the date of the kidnapping, is treated as a qualifying relative, as described in section 152(d) and § 1.152-3, of the taxpayer for all taxable years ending during the period that the child is missing. Also, the child is treated as a qualifying relative of the taxpayer in the year of the child's return if the child is a qualifying relative of the taxpayer for the portion of the taxable year following the date of the child's return.

(3) *Age limitation.*—The special rules provided in this paragraph (e) cease to apply as of the first taxable year of the taxpayer beginning after the calendar year in which there is a determination that the child is dead or, if earlier, in which the child would have attained age 18.

(4) *Application.*—This paragraph (e) applies solely for purposes of determining surviving spouse or head of household filing status under section 2, the child tax credit under section 24, the earned income credit under section 32, and the dependency exemption under section 151.

Par. 17. In newly redesignated § 1.152-5, paragraphs (e)(2), (e)(3)(iii), and (h) are revised to read as follows:

§ 1.152-5. Special rule for a child of divorced or separated parents or parents who live apart.

* * *

(e) * * *

(2) *Attachment to return.*—(i) *In general.*—A noncustodial parent must attach a copy of the written declaration to the parent's original or amended return for each taxable year for which the noncustodial parent claims an exemption for the child. A noncustodial parent may submit a copy of the written declaration to the IRS during an examination to substantiate a claim to a dependency exemption for a child. A copy of a written declaration attached to an amended return, or provided during an examination, will not meet the requirement of this paragraph (e) if the custodial parent signed the written declaration after the custodial parent filed a return claiming a dependency exemption for the child for the year at issue, and the custodial parent has not filed an amended return to remove that claim to a dependency exemption for the child.

(ii) *Examples.*—The following examples illustrate the rules of this paragraph (e).

Example 1. Custodial parent (CP) files her 2015 return on March 1, 2016, and claims a dependency exemption for Child. At noncustodial parent's (NCP) request, CP signs a Form 8332 for the 2015 tax year on April 15, 2016. On April 15, NCP files his return claiming a dependency exemption for Child and attaches the signed Form 8332 to his return. Under section 152(e) and paragraph (b) of this section, NCP is allowed a dependency exemption for Child for 2015, and CP is not allowed a dependency exemption for Child for that year.

Example 2. The facts are the same as in *Example 1* of this paragraph (e)(2)(ii), except NCP files on April 15, 2016, a request for an extension to file his tax return because he does not have a signed Form 8332. CP signs the Form 8332 for the 2015 tax year in August of 2016, and NCP files his return a week later. NCP claims a dependency exemption for Child and attaches the signed Form 8332 to his return. Under section 152(e) and paragraph (b) of this section, NCP is allowed a dependency exemption for Child for 2015, and CP is not allowed a dependency exemption for Child for that year.

Example 3. CP files his 2015 return on March 1, 2016, and claims a dependency exemption for Child. NCP files her return on April 15, 2016, and does not claim a dependency exemption for Child, even though her divorce decree allocates the dependency exemption for Child to her. CP signs a Form 8332 for the 2015 tax year in August of 2016, and NCP files an amended return a week later and attaches the signed Form 8332 to her amended return claiming a dependency exemption for Child. Under paragraph (e)(2) of this section, NCP is not allowed a dependency exemption for Child for 2015 if CP has not amended his return to remove a claim to the dependency exemption for Child for that year.

(3) * * *

(iii) *Attachment to return.*—The parent revoking the written declaration must attach a copy of the revocation to the parent's original or amended return for each taxable year for which the parent claims a child as a dependent as a result of the revocation. The parent revoking the written declaration must keep a copy of the revocation and evidence of delivery of the notice to the other parent, or of the reasonable efforts to provide actual notice. A parent may submit a copy of a revocation to the IRS during an examination to substantiate a claim to a dependency exemption for the child.

* * *

(h) *Applicability date.*—(1) *In general.*—Except as provided in paragraph (h)(2) of this section, this section applies to taxable years beginning after July 2, 2008.

(2) *Exception.*—Paragraphs (e)(2) and (e)(3)(iii) of this section apply to taxable years beginning after the date these regulations are published as final regulations in the **Federal Register**.

Employee Trusts: Effective Dates

Employee Trusts: Tax Reform Act of 1984: Effective Dates.—Temporary Reg. § 1.162-10T is also proposed as a final regulation and, when adopted, would become Reg. § 1.162-10 (published in the Federal Register on February 4, 1986).

§ 1.162-10. Certain employee benefits.

Expenditures Incurred in Attempts to Influence Legislation

Business Expenses: Private Foundations, Excise Taxes: Expenditures Incurred in Attempts to Influence Legislation.—Reproduced below is the text of a proposed amendment of Reg. § 1.162-20, relating to the treatment, for federal income tax purposes, of expenditures incurred in attempts to influence legislation (published in the Federal Register on November 25, 1980).

§ 1.162-20. Expenditures attributable to lobbying, political campaigns, attempts to influence legislation, etc., and certain advertising.—(a) *In general.*—(1) *Scope of section.*—This section contains rules governing the deductibility or nondeductibility of expenditures for lobbying purposes, for the promotion or defeat of legislation, for political campaign purposes (including the support of or opposition to any candidate for public office) or for carrying on propaganda (including advertising) related to any of the foregoing purposes. This section also deals with expenditures for institutional or "good will" advertising.

(2) *Institutional or "good will" advertising.*—Expenditures for institutional or "good will" advertising which keeps the taxpayer's name before the public are generally deductible as ordinary and necessary business expenses provided the expenditures are related to the patronage the taxpayer reasonably expects in the future. For example, a deduction will ordinarily be allowed for the cost of advertising which keeps the taxpayer's name before the public in connection with encouraging contributions to such organizations as the Red Cross, the purchase of United States Savings Bonds, or participation in similar causes. In like fashion, expenditures for advertising which presents views on economic, financial, social, or other such issues, but which does not attempt to influence the public with respect to legislative matters (see paragraph (c)(4) of this section) or involve any of the other activities specified in paragraph (c) of this section for which a deduction is not allowable, are deductible if they otherwise meet the requirements of the regulations under section 162.

(b) *Taxable years beginning before January 1, 1963.*—For rules with respect to taxable years beginning before January 1, 1963, see 26 CFR 1.162-20(b) (Rev. as of April 1, 1980).

(c) *Taxable years beginning after December 31, 1962.*—(1) *In general.*—For taxable years beginning after December 31, 1962, certain types of expenses incurred with respect to legislative matters are deductible under section 162(a) if they otherwise meet the requirements of the regulations under section 162. These deductible expenses are described in subparagraph (2) of this paragraph. All other expenditures for lobbying purposes, for the promotion or defeat of legislation, for political campaign purposes (including the support of or opposition to any candidate for public office), or for carrying on propaganda (including advertising) relating to any of the foregoing purposes (see subparagraph (4) of this paragraph) are not deductible from gross income for such taxable years. For the disallowance of deductions for bad debts and worthless securities of a political party, see § 1.271-1. For the disallowance of deductions for certain indirect political contributions, such as the cost of certain advertising and the cost of admission to certain dinners, programs, and inaugural events, see § 1.276-1.

* * *

(3) *Deductibility of dues and other payments to an organization.*—If part of the activities of an organization, such as a labor union or a trade association, consists of one or more of the activities to which this paragraph relates (legislative matters, political campaigns, etc.) exclusive of any activity constituting an appearance or communication with respect to legislation or proposed legislation of direct interest to the organization (see subparagraph (2)(ii)(*b*)(*1*)), a deduction will be allowed only for such portion of the dues or other payments to the organization as the taxpayer can clearly establish is attrib-

utable to activities to which this paragraph does not relate and to any activity constituting an appearance or communication with respect to legislation or proposed legislation of direct interest to the organization. In no event shall a deduction be allowed for that portion of a special assessment or similar payment (including an increase in dues) made to any organization for any activity to which this paragraph relates if the activity does not constitute an appearance or communication with respect to legislation or proposed legislation of direct interest to the organization. If an organization pays or incurs expenses allocable to legislative activities which meet the tests of subdivisions (i) and (ii) of subparagraph (2) of this paragraph (appearances or communications with respect to legislation or proposed legislation of direct interest to the organization) on behalf of its members, the dues paid by a taxpayer are deductible to the extent used for such activities. Dues paid by a taxpayer will be considered to be used for such an activity, and thus deductible, although the legislation or proposed legislation involved is not of direct interest to the taxpayer, if, pursuant to the provisions of subparagraph (2)(ii)(*b*)(*1*) of this paragraph, the legislation or proposed legislation is of direct interest to the organization, as such, or is of direct interest to one or more members of the organization. For other provisions relating to the deductibility of dues and other payments to an organization, such as a labor union or trade association, see paragraph (c) of § 1.162-15. For requirement that an organization furnish to members and contributors a statement about expenditures, see § 1.6033-2(k). This subparagraph applies to expenditures made after 1980. For corresponding rules for expenditures made before 1981, see 26 CFR § 1.162-20(c)(3) (Rev. as of April 1, 1980).

(4) *Limitations with respect to legislative matters.*—(i) *In general.*—No deduction shall be allowed under section 162(a) for any amount paid or incurred (whether by way of contribution, gift, or otherwise) in connection with any attempt (including what is commonly referred to as a grassroots campaign) to influence the general public, or any segment thereof, with respect to legislative matters. A communication shall be considered an attempt to influence the general public, or a segment thereof, with respect to legislative matters if, and only if, the communication satisfies all of the following three tests:

(A) It pertains to legislation being considered by, or likely in the immediate future to be proposed to, a legislative body, or seeks or opposes legislation;

(B) It reflects a view with respect to the desirability of legislation (for this purpose, a communication that pertains to legislation but expresses no explicit view on the legislation shall be deemed to reflect a view on legislation if the communication is selectively disseminated to persons likely to share a common view of the legislation); and

(C) It is communicated in a form and distributed in a manner so as to reach individuals as members of the general public, that is, as voters or constituents, as opposed to a communication designed for academic, scientific, or similar purposes. A communication may meet this test even if it reaches the public only indirectly as in a news release submitted to the media. No portion of an expenditure in connection with an advertisement is deductible if any part of the advertisement constitutes an attempt to influence the general public with respect to legislative matters.

(ii) *Definitions.*—For purposes of this subparagraph—

(A) The term "legislation" includes action by the Congress, any state legislature, any local council, or similar legislative body, or by the public in a referendum, initiative, constitutional amendment, or similar procedure. The term "legislation" includes a proposed treaty required to be submitted by the President to the Senate for its advice and consent from the time the President's representative begins to negotiate its position with the prospective parties to the proposed treaty.

(B) The term "action" includes the introduction, amendment, enactment, defeat, or repeal of Acts, bills, resolutions, or similar items.

(C) The term "legislative body" does not include executive, judicial, or administrative bodies.

(D) The term "administrative bodies" includes school boards, housing authorities, sewer and water districts, zoning boards, and other similar Federal, State, or local special purpose bodies, whether elective or appointive.

(iii) *Examples.*—The provisions of this subparagraph relating to attempts to influence the public with respect to legislative matters may be illustrated by the following examples:

Example (1). Several major businesses in State W place in local newspapers an advertisement asserting that lack of new capital is hurting the state's economy. The advertisement recommends that residents either invest more in local businesses or increase their savings so that funds will be available to others interested in making investments. Although the advertisement expresses a view with respect to a general problem that might receive legislative attention and is distributed in a manner so as to reach many individuals, it does not constitute an attempt to influence the public with respect to legislative matters because it pertains to private conduct rather than legislation.

Example (2). Assume the same facts as in example (1), except that the advertisement, although not expressly calling for legislative action, also asserts that particular kinds of state tax incentives (which could not be implemented without legislation) would substantially increase capital formation. Thus, the advertisement is seeking action by the legislature and, at least in part, is addressed to individuals as voters or constituents rather than as potential investors. The advertisement reflects a view with respect to the desirability of the legislation. The advertisement constitutes an attempt to influence the public with respect to a legislative matter, and no portion of any expenditures in connection with the advertisement may be deducted.

Example (3). There is pending in the legislature of State X a proposal to amend certain laws concerning voting in state elections. As a public service, M, a manufacturer in State X, places in local newspapers an advertisement that explains both the current voting laws and the proposed amendments. The advertisement takes no position on the merits of the proposal. Under these circumstances, the advertisement does not reflect a view with respect to the desirability of the proposal and does not constitute an attempt to influence the general public with respect to the proposal.

Example (4). The legislature of State Y is considering a proposal to prohibit hunting on land owned by the state. Hunters in State Y are generally opposed to the measure. N, a manufacturer of hunting equipment, prepares a pamphlet that outlines the proposal and its effects but expresses no view on its merits. N arranges for distribution of the pamphlet to customers of stores in State Y that specialize in hunting equipment. The pamphlet pertains to legislation and is deemed to reflect a view with respect to the desirability of the legislation by reason of its selective distribution to an audience likely to oppose the prohibition on hunting. The information is communicated in a form and distributed in a manner so as to reach individuals as voters or constituents. Expenditures in connection with the preparation and distribution of the pamphlet are nondeductible.

Example (5). The legislature in State Z is considering a proposal to require pharmaceutical firms to test the safety of their products through certain laboratory procedures. P, a pharmaceutical firm in State Z, prepares a detailed report on the usefulness of the tests that would be required under the proposal. The report concludes that the tests specified in the proposal are poorly designed. P distributes copies of the report to university professors in the field of health science without suggesting that the recipients make any attempt to influence the public with respect to the proposal. Although the report pertains to legislation and implies that the legislative proposal under consideration should not be enacted, the form of the report and its limited distribution indicate that copies were furnished to the recipients as scholars in the field rather than as members of the general public, that is, as voters or constituents. The expenditures for the report, therefore, are not expenditures in connection with an attempt to influence the public with respect to the proposal.

Example (6). Assume the same facts as in example (5) except that, instead of distributing copies of the report to university professors, P distributes to various civic groups leaflets summarizing the conclusions and recommendations of the report. The information is communicated in a form and distributed in a manner so as to reach individuals as voters or constituents. Expenditures in connection with the report and the leaflet are nondeductible.

Example (7). Corporation Q pays for the radio broadcast of an advertisement that refers to a current controversy and urges citizens to "become involved". The advertisement does not discuss the merits of any legislative proposal, but it does offer a free booklet which analyzes and takes positions on various legislative proposals relating to the controversy. Expenditures in connection with the advertisement and the booklet are nondeductible because together they constitute an attempt by Q to influence the public with respect to this legislative matter.

Example (8). Corporation R makes the services of B, one of its executives, available to S, a trade association of which R is a member. B works for several weeks to assist S to develop materials designed to influence public opinion on legislation. In performing this work, B uses office space and clerical assistance provided by R. R pays full salary and benefits to B during this period and receives no reimbursement from S for these payments or for the other facilities and assistance provided. All expenditures of R, including the allocable office expenses, that are attributable to this assignment are nondeductible because B was engaged in an attempt to influence the public on legislative matters.

* * *

Fringe Benefits: Taxability

Fringe Benefits: Taxability.—Reg. §1.162-25T, relating to the treatment of taxable and nontaxable fringe benefits, is proposed (published in the Federal Register on January 7, 1985) (LR-216-84).

§1.162-25T. Deductions with respect to noncash fringe benefits.

Substantiation: Travel, Entertainment, Gifts, Listed Property, Etc.

Business Expenses: Substantiation: Recordkeeping Requirements: Listed Property.—An amendment to Temporary Reg. §1.162-25T, relating to the requirement that any deduction or credit with respect to certain business-related expenses be substantiated with adequate or sufficient evidence to corroborate a taxpayer's own statement and to the limitations on cost recovery deductions and the investment tax credit for listed property, is also proposed as final (published in the Federal Register on November 6, 1985).

§1.162-25T. Deductions with respect to noncash fringe benefits.

Notional Principal Contracts: Contingent Nonperiodic Payments

Notional Principal Contracts: Contingent Nonperiodic Payments.—Reg. §1.162-30, relating to the inclusion into income or deduction of a contingent nonperiodic payment provided for under a notional principal contract, is proposed (published in the Federal Register on February 26, 2004) (REG-166012-02).

☐ Par. 2. Section 1.162-30 is added to read as follows:

§1.162-30. Notional principal contract payments.—(a) *In general.*—Amounts taken into account by a taxpayer pursuant to §1.446-3(d)(1) (including mark-to-market deductions) with respect to a notional principal contract as defined in §1.446-3(c)(1)(i), are deductible as ordinary and necessary business expenses. However, this section will not apply to any amount representing interest expense on the deemed loan component of a significant nonperiodic payment as described in §1.446-3(g)(4). For any loss arising from a termination payment as defined in §1.446-3(h)(1), see section 1234A and the regulations thereunder. For the timing of deductions with respect to notional principal contracts, see §1.446-3.

(b) *Effective date.*—Paragraph (a) of this section is applicable to notional principal contracts entered into on or after 30 days after the date a Treasury decision based on these proposed regulations is published in the Federal Register. [Reg. §1.162-30.]

Expatriate Health Plans: Issuers: Excepted Benefits

Expatriate Health Plans: Issuers: Excepted Benefits.—Amendments to Reg. §1.162-31, relating to the rules for expatriate health plans, expatriate health plan issuers, and qualified expatriates under the Expatriate Health Coverage Clarification Act of 2014 (EHCCA), are proposed (published in the Federal Register on June 10, 2016) (REG-135702-15).

2. Section 1.162-31 is amended by adding paragraph (b)(5)(v) to read as follows:

§1.162-31. The $500,000 deduction limitation for remuneration provided by certain health insurance providers.

* * *

(b) * * *

(5) * * *

(v) *Expatriate health plan coverage.* For purposes of this section, amounts received in payment for expatriate health plan coverage, as defined in §54.9831-1(f)(3), are not premiums.

* * *

Registration Requirements with Respect to Debt Obligations

Obligations of the United States: Registration Requirements: Deduction of Interest.—The text of Temporary Reg. §5f.163-1, relating to registration requirements with respect to debt obligations, has also been proposed as a final regulation and, when adopted, would become Reg. §1.163-5 (published in the Federal Register on November 15, 1982).

§5f.163-1. Denial of interest deduction on certain obligations issued after December 31, 1982, unless issued in registered form.

Imputed Interest: OID: Safe Haven Interest Rates

Reproduced below is the text of a proposed amendment to Temporary Reg. §5f.163-1, relating to (1) the tax treatment of debt instruments issued after July 1, 1982, that contain original issue discount, (2) the imputation of and the accounting for interest with respect to sales and exchanges of property occurring after December 31, 1984, and (3) safe haven interest rates for loans or advances between commonly controlled taxpayers and safe haven leases between such taxpayers (published in the Federal Register on April 8, 1986).

§5f.163-1. Denial of interest deduction on certain obligations issued after December 31, 1982, unless issued in registered form.

☐ Par. 39. Paragraph (f) of §5f.163-1 is amended by removing the word "1232(d)" from each place that it appears and adding in its place the word "1287", and by removing the phrase "section 1232B" from each place that it appears and adding in its place the phrase "section 1286".

* * *

Definition of Registered Form: Guidance

Definition of Registered Form: Guidance.—Amendments to Reg. §5f.163-1, providing guidance on the definitions of registration-required obligation and registered form, including guidance on the issuance of pass-through certificates and participation interests in registered form, are proposed (published in the Federal Register on September 19, 2017) (REG-125374-16).

Par. 14. Section 5f.163-1(d) is amended by revising the paragraph heading and adding a sentence at the end of the paragraph to read as follows:

§5f.163-1. Denial of interest deduction on certain obligations issued after December 31, 1982, unless issued in registered form.

* * *

(d) *Applicability date.*—* * * For obligations issued after March 18, 2012, see §1.163-5 of this chapter.

* * *

Imputed Interest: OID: Safe Haven Leases

Imputed Interest: Original Issue Discount: Safe Haven Interest Rates.—Reproduced below is the text of a proposed amendment to Reg. §1.163-4, relating to (1) the tax treatment of debt instruments issued after July 1, 1982, that contain original issue discount, (2) the imputation of and the accounting for interest with respect to sales and exchanges of property occurring after December 31, 1984, and (3) safe haven interest rates for loans or advances between commonly controlled taxpayers and safe haven leases between such taxpayers (published in the Federal Register on April 8, 1986).

§1.163-4. Deduction for original issue discount on certain obligations issued after May 27, 1969.

☐ Par. 4. Section 1.163-4 is amended as follows:

1. The heading is revised by adding a comma and the phrase "and before July 2, 1982" after the word "1969".

2. In paragraph (a)(1), the second sentence is amended by removing the phrase "section 1232(b)(1)" and adding in its place the phrase "section 1273(a)(1)", and the second sentence is further amended by removing the phrase "the second sentence thereof" in parenthetical and adding in its place the phrase "section 1273(a)(3)".

3. Paragraph (b) is amended by removing the phrase "section 1232(b)(1)" from each place that it appears in the paragraph and adding its place the phrase "section 1273(a)(1)", by removing the phrase "the second sentence thereof" from each place it appears in the paragraph and adding in its place the phrase "section 1273(a)(3)", and by removing the phrase "section 1232(a)(3)(A)" from *Example (4)* and adding in its place the phrase "section 1271(a)(3)(A)".

4. Paragraph (d) is amended by adding the phrase "and before July 2, 1982," after the word "1969," each place that it appears.

Pass-Through Certificates: Registration: Sanctions

Interest Paid: Pass-Through Certificates: Registration Requirements.—Temporary Reg. §1.163-5T, relating to registration requirements with respect to certain debt obligations and sanctions on issuers of registration-required obligations not in registered form, is also proposed as a final regulation and, when adopted, would become Reg. §1.163-5 (published in the Federal Register on May 19, 1988).

§1.163-5. Denial of interest deduction on certain obligations issued after December 31, 1982, unless issued in registered form.

Pass-Through Certificates: Registration: Transfers

Interest Paid: Pass-Through Certificates: Registration Requirements.—Reproduced below is the text of a proposed amendment of Temporary Reg. §1.163-5T, relating to registration requirements with respect to certain debt obligations and sanctions on issuers of registration-required obligations not in registered form (published in the Federal Register on May 19, 1988).

☐ Par. 2. Paragraph (d)(7) is added immediately after paragraph (d)(6) of §1.163-5T. The added paragraph reads as follows:

§1.163-5T. Denial of interest deduction on certain obligations issued after December 31, 1982, unless issued in registered form (temporary).

(d) *Pass-through certificates.*

* * *

(7)(i) For purposes of section 4701, any person who holds a registration-required obligation that is in registered form within the meaning of §5f.103-1(c)(1) and transfers the obligation through a method not described in §5f.103-1(c)(1) is considered to have issued the obligation so transferred on the date of the transfer in the principal amount of the obligation received by the transferee. Such person is therefore liable for any excise tax under section 4701 that may be imposed. This paragraph (d)(7) applies to transfers of obligations occurring after August 17, 1988.

(ii) The provisions of this paragraph (d)(7) may be illustrated by the following examples:

Example (1). X, a corporation, holds a registration required obligation in registered form in the principal amount of 10x with a maturity date of December 31, 1999. X transfers the obligation through a method not described in §5f.103-1(c)(1) on June 30, 1990. For purposes of section 4701, X is considered to have issued an obligation on June 30, 1990 in the principal amount of 10x with a maturity date of December 31, 1999. Because X has issued a registration required obligation not in registered form, X is liable for the tax imposed by section 4701 in an amount computed with reference to the principal amount of 10x and the period beginning on June 30, 1990 and ending on December 31, 1999.

Example (2). X, a corporation, holds a registration required obligation in registered form as nominee of Y, a corporation. The principal amount of the obligation is 10x and the maturity date of the obligation is December 31, 1999. On June 30, 1990, X issued a bearer receipt to Y for the obligation. For purposes of section 4701, X is considered to have issued an obligation on June 1990 in the principal amount of 10x with a maturity date of December 31, 1999. Because X has issued a registration-required obligation not in registered form, X is liable for the tax imposed by section 4701 in an amount computed with reference to the principal amount of 10x and the period beginning June 30, 1990 and ending December 31, 1999.

Example (3). The facts are the same as in *Example* (1) except that X transfers 5x of the 10x obligation held by X. X is considered to have issued an obligation on June 30, 1990 in the principal amount of 5x with a maturity date of December 31, 1999. Because X has issued a registration required obligation not in registered form, X is liable for the tax imposed by section 4701 in an amount computed with reference to the principal amount of 5x and the period beginning on June 30, 1990 and ending on December 31, 1999.

Example (4). The facts are the same as in *Example* (1) except that X is a natural person. X is considered to have issued an obligation on June 30, 1990 in the principal amount of 10x with a maturity date of December 31, 1999. Because X is a natural person, the obligation is not a registration required obligation and, therefore, X is not subject to the tax imposed under section 4701.

Definition of Registered Form: Guidance

Definition of Registered Form: Guidance.—Amendments to Reg. §§1.163-5 and 1.163-5T, providing guidance on the definitions of registration-required obligation and registered form, including guidance on the issuance of pass-through certificates and participation interests in registered form, are proposed (published in the Federal Register on September 19, 2017) (REG-125374-16).

Par. 3. Section 1.163-5 is amended by revising the section heading and adding paragraphs (a), (b), and (c)(3)(iii) to read as follows:

§1.163-5. Denial of interest deduction on certain obligations unless issued in registered form.—(a) *Denial of deduction.*—(1) *In general.*—No deduction shall be allowed a taxpayer under section 163 for interest paid or accrued on a registration-required obligation (as defined in section 163(f) and paragraph (a)(2) of this section) unless such obligation is issued in registered form (as defined in paragraph (b) of this section). An obligation that is not in registered form under paragraph (b) of this section is an obligation in bearer form.

(2) *Registration-required obligation.*—(i) *In general.*—The term *registration-required obligation* means any obligation (including a pass-through certificate or participation interest described in paragraph (a)(3) of this section and a regular interest in a REMIC described in paragraph (a)(4) of this section) other than—

(A) An obligation issued by a natural person;

(B) An obligation not of a type offered to the public (as described in paragraph (a)(2)(ii) of this section); or

(C) An obligation that has a maturity at the date of issue of not more than 1 year.

(ii) *Obligation not of a type offered to the public.*—For purposes of section 163(f)(2)(A)(ii) and paragraph (a)(2)(i)(B) of this section, an obligation is not of a type offered to the public unless the obligation is traded on an established market as determined under §1.1273-2(f) without regard to §1.1273-2(f)(6).

(3) *Pass-through certificates and participation interests.*—(i) *Pass-through certificate.*—(A) *In general.*—A pass-through certificate is considered to be a registration-required obligation if the pass-through certificate is described in paragraph (a)(2)(i) of this section without regard to whether any obligation held by the entity to which the pass-through certificate relates is described in paragraph (a)(2)(i) of this section.

(B) *Definition of pass-through certificate.*—For purposes of paragraph (a) of this section, a *pass-through certificate* is an instrument evidencing an interest in a grantor trust under Subpart E of Part I of Subchapter J of the Code, or a similar fund, that principally holds debt instruments. For purposes of this paragraph (a)(3)(i)(B), a similar fund includes an entity that, under §§301.7701-1 through 301.7701-3 of this chapter, is disregarded as an entity separate from its owner or classified as a partnership for federal tax purposes, without regard to whether the fund has the power to vary the assets in the fund or the sequence of payments made to holders. In addition, for purposes of this paragraph (a)(3)(i)(B), a similar fund does not include a business entity that is classified as a corporation under §301.7701-2 of this chapter.

(ii) *Participation interest.*—A participation interest that evidences ownership of some or all of one or more obligations and that is treated as conveying ownership of a specified portion of the obligation or obligations (and not ownership of an entity treated as created under §301.7701-1(a)(2) of this chapter) is considered to be a registration-required obligation if the participation interest is described in paragraph (a)(2)(i) of this section without regard to whether any obligation to which the participation interest relates is described in paragraph (a)(2)(i) of this section.

(iii) *Treatment of obligation held by a trust or fund.*—An obligation held by a trust or a fund in which ownership interests are represented by pass-through certificates is considered to be in registered form or to be a registration-required obligation if the obligation held by the trust or fund is in registered form (as defined in paragraph (b) of this section) or is a registration-required obligation described in paragraph (a)(2)(i) of this section, without regard to whether the pass-through certificates are so considered.

(iv) *Examples.*—The application of paragraph (a)(3) of this section may be illustrated by the following examples:

Example 1. Fund, a partnership under the laws of the state in which it is organized, acquires a pool of student loans. The student loans are issued by natural persons and, therefore, are not registration-required obligations as described in paragraph (a)(2)(i) of this section. Fund contributes the student loans to Trust, a business trust under the laws of the state in which Trust is organized. Trust has the power to vary the investments in Trust, and is not treated as a trust of which the grantor is the owner under Subpart E of Part I of Subchapter J of the Code. Trust issues certificates evidencing an interest in Trust. The certificates issued by Trust are offered to the public. The certificates issued by Trust are pass-through certificates (as described in paragraph (a)(3)(i)(B) of this section) and are described in paragraph (a)(2)(i) of this section, and thus, are registration-required obligations described in paragraph (a)(2)(i) of this section, even though the student loans held by Trust are not registration-required obligations.

Example 2. Partnership U purchases a building from Partnership V. Partnership U makes a cash down payment and issues a note secured by a mortgage in the building to Partnership V for the remaining purchase price of the building. The note is not a registration-required obligation described in paragraph (a)(2)(i) of this section because it is not an obligation of a type offered to the public. Partnership V offers participations in the underlying note to the public. Under the terms of the participation, each participant will own an interest in the note that will entitle the participant to a specified portion of the interest and principal generated by the note. The participation is a participation interest described in paragraph (a)(3)(ii) of this section and is described in paragraph (a)(2)(i) of this section, and, thus, is a registration-required obligation described in paragraph (a)(2)(i) of this section, even though the underlying note is not a registration-required obligation.

(4) *REMICs*.—(i) *Regular interest in a REMIC*.—A regular interest in a REMIC, as defined in sections 860D and 860G and the regulations thereunder, is considered to be a registration-required obligation if the regular interest is described in paragraph (a)(2)(i) of this section, without regard to whether one or more of the obligations held by the REMIC to which the regular interest relates is described in paragraph (a)(2)(i) of this section.

(ii) *Treatment of obligation held by a REMIC*.—An obligation described in paragraph (a)(2)(i) of this section and held by a REMIC is treated as a registration-required obligation regardless of whether the regular interests in the REMIC are so treated.

(5) *Applicability date*.—(i) *In general*.—Except as otherwise provided in paragraphs (a)(5)(ii) and (iii) of this section, paragraph (a) of this section applies to obligations issued after March 18, 2012. For obligations issued on or before March 18, 2012, see §5f.163-1 of this chapter.

(ii) *Obligations not of a type offered to the public*.—Paragraph (a)(2)(ii) of this section applies to obligations issued after the date of publication of a Treasury decision adopting these rules as final regulations in the **Federal Register**.

(iii) *Pass-through certificates, participation interests, and regular interests in REMICs*.—Paragraph (a) of this section applies to pass-through certificates, participation interests, and regular interests in REMICs issued after the date of publication of a Treasury decision adopting these rules as final regulations in the **Federal Register**. For pass-through certificates or regular interests in REMICs issued on or before the date of publication of a Treasury decision adopting these rules as final regulations in the **Federal Register**, see §1.163-5T.

(b) *Registered form*.—(1) *General rule*.—Except as provided in paragraph (b)(4) of this section, an obligation is in registered form if a transfer of the right to receive both principal and any stated interest on the obligation may be effected only—

(i) By surrender of the old obligation and either the reissuance of the old obligation to the new holder or the issuance of a new obligation to the new holder;

(ii) Through a book entry system (as described in paragraph (b)(2) of this section) maintained by the issuer of the obligation (or its agent) or by a clearing organization (as defined in paragraph (b)(3) of this section); or

(iii) Through both of the methods described in paragraphs (b)(1)(i) and (ii) of this section.

(2) *Book entry system*.—(i) *In general*.—An obligation will be considered transferable through a book entry system, including a dematerialized book entry system, if ownership of the obligation or an interest in the obligation is required to be recorded in an electronic or physical register maintained by the issuer of the obligation (or its agent) or by a clearing organization (as defined in paragraph (b)(3) of this section).

(ii) *Book entry system maintained by clearing organization that effectively immobilizes a bearer form obligation*.—An obligation represented by one or more physical certificates in bearer form will be considered to be in registered form if the physical certificates are effectively immobilized. A physical certificate is effectively immobilized only if—

(A) The physical certificate is issued to and held by a clearing organization (as defined in paragraph (b)(3) of this section) for the benefit of purchasers of interests in the obligation under arrangements that prohibit the transfer of the physical certificate except to a successor clearing organization subject to terms that effectively immobilize the physical certificate, as provided in paragraph (b)(2)(ii) of this section, in the hands of the successor clearing organization; and

(B) Ownership of the obligation or an interest in the obligation is transferable only through a book entry system (as described in paragraph (b)(2)(i) of this section) maintained by the clearing organization (as defined in paragraph (b)(3) of this section).

(3) *Definition of clearing organization*.—For purposes of paragraph (b) of this section, *clearing organization* means an entity that is in the business of holding obligations for or reflecting the ownership interests of member organizations and transferring obligations among such member organizations by credit or debit to the account of a member organization without the necessity of physical delivery of the obligation.

(4) *Temporal limitations on registered form*.—(i) *In general*.—Except as provided in paragraphs (b)(4)(ii) and (iii) of this section, an obligation is not considered to be in registered form as of a particular time if the obligation may be transferred at that time or at a time or times on or before the maturity of the obligation by any means not described in paragraph (b)(1) of this section.

(ii) *Events that permit issuance of physical certificates in bearer form*.—(A) *In general*.—An obligation transferrable through a dematerialized book entry system is not in bearer form pursuant to paragraph (b)(4)(i) of this section solely because a holder of the obligation (or an interest therein) has a right to obtain a physical certificate in bearer form upon the occurrence of one or both of the following events—

(1) A termination of business without a successor by the clearing organization that maintains the book entry system; or

(2) The issuance of physical securities at the issuer's request upon a change in tax law that would be adverse to the issuer but for the issuance of physical securities in bearer form.

(B) *Treatment upon issuance of physical certificate in bearer form*.—Upon the occurrence of one or both of the events described in paragraph (b)(4)(ii)(A) of this section, any obligation with respect to which a holder, or a group of holders acting collectively, may obtain a physical certificate in bearer form will no longer be in registered form, regardless of whether a physical certificate in bearer form has actually been issued.

(iii) *Obligations in registered form until maturity*.—An obligation that as of a particular time is not considered to be in registered form because the obligation may be transferred at a time or times before the maturity of the obligation by a means not described in paragraph (b)(1) of this section and that during the period beginning at a later time and ending at maturity may be transferred only by a means described in paragraph (b)(1) of this section is considered to be in registered form during the period beginning at that later time.

(5) *Examples.*—The application of paragraph (b) of this section may be illustrated by the following examples:

Example 1. X issues an obligation that is a registration-required obligation as described in paragraph (a)(2)(i) of this section. At issuance, X issues the obligation in the purchaser's name evidencing the purchaser's ownership of the principal and interest under the obligation. The purchaser may transfer the obligation only by surrendering the obligation to X and by X issuing a new instrument to the new holder. X's obligation is issued in registered form under paragraph (b)(1) of this section.

Example 2. Corporation A issues US$500 million of debt (the Note) evidenced by a physical certificate that is registered in the name of ABC, a clearing organization (as defined in paragraph (b)(3) of this section). Under the terms of the Note, Corporation A must maintain an electronic register identifying the owners of interests in the Note, and a transfer of the right to receive either principal or any stated interest on such ownership interests may be effected only through a change to the electronic register. Pursuant to an agreement with Corporation A, ABC takes custody of the physical certificate evidencing the Note and receives all principal and interest on the Note from Corporation A. Independently of its agreement with Corporation A, ABC maintains electronic records of its members' ownership interests in the Note and distributes principal and interest to members' accounts in accordance with those interests. ABC's members, in turn, maintain electronic records of their customers' ownership interests in the Note and similarly distribute principal and interest to their customers' accounts. Corporation A's electronic register identifies ABC as the sole owner of the Note. Corporation A does not record transfers of ownership interests in the Note to or among ABC's members, and ABC does not record transfers of ownership interests in the Note to or among its members' customers. Corporation A's electronic register is a book entry system as described in paragraph (b)(2)(i) of this section, and the Note is in registered form under paragraph (b)(1) of this section.

Example 3. The facts are the same as in *Example 2* of paragraph (b)(5) of this section, except that, instead of maintaining an electronic register, Corporation A issues a global bearer certificate (Certificate) to ABC pursuant to an agreement that prohibits the transfer of Certificate except to a successor clearing organization subject to terms that effectively immobilize Certificate, as provided in paragraph (b)(2)(ii) of this section, in the hands of the successor clearing organization. Further, holders of interests in Certificate may only obtain physical bearer certificates upon cessation of ABC's operations without a successor or, at Corporation A's request, upon a change in tax law that would be adverse to Corporation A but for the issuance of physical bearer certificates. Because ownership of interests in Certificate may be transferred only through a dematerialized book entry system maintained by ABC, and because the circumstances under which definitive bearer certificates may be issued to holders of interests in Certificate are limited to the circumstances described in paragraph (b)(4)(ii)(A) of this section, Certificate is an immobilized bearer form obligation described in paragraph (b)(2)(ii) of this section and is accordingly in registered form under paragraph (b)(2)(ii) of this section.

Example 4. The facts are the same as in *Example 3* of paragraph (b)(5) of this section, except that purchasers of interests in Certificate have the right to obtain definitive bearer certificates upon request at any time until maturity of Certificate. Because the circumstances under which definitive bearer obligations may be issued to holders of interests in Certificate are not limited to the circumstances described in paragraph (b)(4)(ii)(A) of this section, Certificate is not considered to be issued in registered form under paragraph (b)(4)(i) of this section.

Example 5. Bank makes a loan to borrower secured by real property (Loan). Participations in Loan are traded on an established market. The participations are participation interests described in paragraph (a)(3)(ii) of this section and are accordingly registration-required obligations described in paragraph (a)(2)(i) of this section. Bank remains the registered owner of Loan and maintains an electronic book entry system that identifies participants. Participation interests may be transferred only by surrender of the old participation interest and reissuance of the participation interest in the name of the new participant, or by transfer of the participation interest from the name of the old participant to the name of the new participant in the book entry system of Bank. Bank's book entry system is described in paragraph (b)(2)(i) of this section, and, accordingly, under paragraph (b)(1)(iii) of this section, the participation interests are in registered form.

(6) *Applicability date.*—Paragraph (b) of this section applies to obligations issued after March 18, 2012. Taxpayers may apply the rules in section 3 of Notice 2012-20, 2012-13 IRB 574, for obligations issued prior to the date of publication of the Treasury decision adopting these rules as final regulations in the **Federal Register**. For obligations issued on or before March 18, 2012, see § 5f.103-1 of this chapter.

(c) * * *

(3) * * *

(iii) *Applicability to obligations issued after March 18, 2012.*—For purposes of section 163(f), paragraph (c) of this section does not apply to obligations issued after March 18, 2012. However, for purposes of determining whether an obligation is described in section 4701(b)(1)(B) or whether the exception in section 6049 from information reporting of interest or original discount with respect to obligations that have an original term of 183 days or less applies, paragraph (c) of this section continues to apply to obligations issued after March 18, 2012. See §§ 1.4701-1(b)(3) and 1.6049-5(b)(10).

Par. 4. Section 1.163-5T is amended by adding paragraph (f) to read as follows:

§1.163-5T. Denial of interest deduction on certain obligations issued after December 31, 1982, unless issued in registered form (temporary).

* * *

(f) *Applicability date*.—This section applies to obligations to which §5f.163-1 of this chapter applies. See §5f.163-1(d) of this chapter.

Mortgage Credit Certificates

Mortgage Credit Certificates: Issuance: Penalties.—Temporary Reg. §1.163-6T, relating to the issuance of mortgage credit certificates, is also proposed as final and when adopted, would become Reg. §1.163-6 (published in the Federal Register on May 8, 1985).

§1.163-6. Reduction of deduction where section 25 credit taken.

Interest Paid: Allocation

Interest Paid or Payable: Allocation.—Temporary Reg. §1.163-8T, relating to the allocation of interest expense among a taxpayer's expenditures, is also proposed as a final regulation and, when adopted, would become Reg. §1.163-8 (Published in the Federal Register on July 12, 1987).

§1.163-8. Allocation of interest expense among expenditures.

Personal Interest: Qualified Residence Interest

Personal Interest: Paid or Accrued: Qualified Residence Interest.—Temporary Reg. §§1.163-9T, and 1.163-10T, relating to the treatment of personal interest and the treatment and determination of qualified residence interest, are also proposed as final regulations and, when adopted, would become Reg. §§1.163-9 and 1.163-10 (published in the Federal Register on December 22, 1987).

§1.163-9. Personal interest.

§1.163-10. Qualified residence interest.

Deduction for Business Interest Expense: Limitation

Deduction for Business Interest Expense: Limitation.—Reg. §§1.163(j)-0—1.163(j)-11, regarding the limitation on the deduction for business interest expense after the enactment of recent tax legislation, are proposed (published in the Federal Register on December 28, 2018) (REG-106089-18).

Par. 2. Section 1.163(j)-0 is added to read as follows:

§1.163(j)-0. Table of contents.—This section lists the table of contents for §§1.163(j)-1 through 1.163(j)-11.

§1.163(j)-5 General rules governing disallowed business interest expense carryforwards for C corporations.

(a) Scope and definitions.

(1) Scope.

(2) Definitions.

(i) Current-year business interest expense.

(ii) Allocable share of the consolidated group's remaining section 163(j) limitation.

(iii) Consolidated group's remaining section 163(j) limitation.

(iv) Remaining current-year interest ratio.

(b) Treatment of disallowed business interest expense carryforwards.

(1) In general.

(2) Deduction of business interest expense.

(3) Consolidated groups.

(i) In general.

(ii) Deduction of business interest expense.

(A) General rule.

(B) Section 163(j) limitation is equal to or exceeds the current-year business interest expense and disallowed business interest expense carryforwards from prior taxable years.

(C) Current-year business interest expense and disallowed business interest expense carryforwards exceed section 163(j) limitation.

(iii) Departure from group.

(iv) Example.

(c) Disallowed business interest expense carryforwards in transactions to which section 381(a) applies.

(d) Limitations on disallowed business interest expense carryforwards from separate return limitation years.

(1) General rule.

(2) Deduction of disallowed business interest expense carryforwards arising in a SRLY.

(3) Examples.

(e) Application of section 382.

(1) Pre-change loss.

(2) Loss corporation.

(3) Ordering rules for utilization of pre-change losses and for absorption of the section 382 limitation.

(4) Disallowed business interest expense from the pre-change period in the year of a testing date.

(f) Overlap of SRLY limitation with section 382.

(g) Additional limitations.

(h) Applicability date.

§1.163(j)-6 Application of the business interest deduction limitation to partnerships and subchapter S corporations.

(a) Overview.

(b) Definitions.

(1) Section 163(j) items.

(2) Partner basis items.

(3) Remedial items.

(4) Excess business interest income.

(5) Deductible business interest expense.

(6) Section 163(j) excess items.

(7) Non-excepted assets.

(8) Excepted assets.

(c) Character of business interest expense.

(d) Adjusted taxable income of the partnership.

(1) Modification of adjusted taxable income for partnerships.

(2) Section 734(b), partner basis items, and remedial items.

(e) Adjusted taxable income and business interest income of partners.

(1) Modification of adjusted taxable income for partners.

(2) Partner basis items and remedial items.

(3) Disposition of partnership interests.

(4) Double counting of business interest income and floor plan financing interest expense prohibited.

(f) Allocation and determination of section 163(j) excess items made in the same manner as nonseparately stated taxable income or loss of the partnership.

(1) Overview.

(i) In general.

(ii) Relevance solely for purposes of section 163(j).

(2) Steps for allocating deductible business interest expense and section 163(j) excess items.

(i) Partnership-level calculation required by section 163(j)(4)(A).

(ii) Determination of each partner's relevant section 163(j) items.

(iii) Partner-level comparison of business interest income and business interest expense.

(iv) Matching partnership and aggregate partner excess business interest income.

(v) Remaining business interest expense determination.

(vi) Determination of final allocable ATI.

(A) Positive allocable ATI.

(B) Negative allocable ATI.

(C) Final allocable ATI.

(vii) Partner-level comparison of thirty percent of adjusted taxable income and remaining business interest expense.

(viii) Partner priority right to ATI capacity excess determination.

(ix) Matching partnership and aggregate partner excess taxable income.

(x) Matching partnership and aggregate partner excess business interest expense.

(xi) Final section 163(j) excess item and deductible business interest expense allocation.

(g) Carryforwards.

(1) In general.

(2) Treatment of excess of business interest expense allocated to partners.

(3) Excess taxable income and excess business interest income ordering rule.

(h) Basis adjustments.

(1) Section 704(d) ordering.

(2) Excess business interest expense basis adjustments.

(3) Basis adjustments upon disposition of partnership interest.

(i) Complete disposition of partnership interest.

(ii) Partial disposition of partnership interest.

(i) [Reserved]

(j) Investment items.

(k) [Reserved]

(l) S corporations.

(i) General rule.
(ii) Permissible methodologies for allocating asset basis between or among two or more trades or businesses.
(iii) Special rules.
(A) Consistent allocation methodologies.
(1) In general.
(2) Consent to change allocation methodology.
(B) De minimis exceptions.
(1) De minimis amount of gross income from trades or businesses.
(2) De minimis amount of asset basis allocable to a trade or business.
(C) Allocations of excepted regulated utility trades or businesses.
(1) In general.
(2) Permissible method for allocating asset basis for utility trades or businesses.
(3) De minimis rule for excepted utility trades or businesses.
(4) Example.
(4) Disallowed business interest expense carryforwards; floor plan financing interest expense.
(5) Additional rules relating to basis.
(i) Calculation of adjusted basis.
(A) Non-depreciable property other than land.
(B) Depreciable property other than inherently permanent structures.
(C) Special rule for land and inherently permanent structures.
(D) Depreciable or amortizable intangible property and depreciable income forecast method property.
(E) Assets not yet used in a trade or business.
(F) Trusts established to fund specific liabilities.
(G) Inherently permanent structure.
(ii) Partnership interests; stock in non-consolidated domestic corporations.
(A) Partnership interests.
(1) Calculation of asset basis.
(2) Allocation of asset basis.
(i) In general.
(ii) De minimis rule.
(iii) Partnership assets not properly allocable to a trade or business.
(iv) Inapplicability of partnership look-through rule.
(B) Stock in non-consolidated domestic corporations.
(1) In general.
(2) Domestic non-consolidated C corporations.
(i) Allocation of asset basis.
(ii) De minimis rule.
(iii) Inapplicability of corporate look-through rule.
(3) S corporations.
(i) Calculation of asset basis.
(ii) Allocation of asset basis.
(iii) De minimis rule.
(iv) Inapplicability of S corporation look-through rule.
(C) Stock in CFCs.
(D) Inapplicability of look-through rule to partnerships or non-consolidated corporations to which the small business exemption applies.
(E) Tiered entities.
(iii) Cash and cash equivalents and customer receivables.
(iv) Deemed asset sale.
(v) Other adjustments.
(6) Determination dates; determination periods; reporting requirements.
(i) Definitions.
(ii) Application of look-through rules.
(iii) Reporting requirements.
(A) Books and records.
(B) Information statement.
(iv) Failure to file statement.
(7) Ownership threshold for look-through rules.
(i) Corporations.
(A) Asset basis.
(B) Dividends.
(ii) Partnerships.
(iii) Inapplicability of look-through rule.
(8) Anti-abuse rule.
(d) Direct allocations.
(1) In general.
(2) Financial services entities.
(3) Assets used in more than one trade or business.
(4) Adjustments to basis of assets to account for direct allocations.
(5) Example.
(e) Examples.
(f) Applicability date.

§1.163(j)-11 Transition rules.

(a) Application of section 163(j) limitation if a corporation joins a consolidated group with a taxable year beginning before January 1, 2018.
(1) In general.
(2) Example.
(b) Treatment of disallowed disqualified interest.
(1) In general.
(2) Earnings and profits.
(3) Disallowed disqualified interest of members of an affiliated group.
(i) Scope.
(ii) Allocation of disallowed disqualified interest to members of the affiliated group.
(A) In general.
(B) Definitions.
(1) Allocable share of the affiliated group's disallowed disqualified interest.
(2) Disallowed disqualified interest ratio.
(3) Exempt related person interest expense.
(iii) Treatment of carryforwards.
(4) Application of section 382.
(i) Ownership change occurring before the date the Treasury decision adopting these regulations as final regulations is published in the **Federal Register**.
(A) Pre-change loss.
(B) Loss corporation.
(ii) Ownership change occurring on or after the date the Treasury decision adopting these regulations as final regulations is published in the **Federal Register**.
(A) Pre-change loss.
(B) Loss corporation.
(iii) Definitions.

(5) [Reserved]

(6) Treatment of excess limitation from taxable years beginning before January 1, 2018.

(7) Example.

(c) Applicability date.

[Reg. § 1.163(j)-0.]

Par. 3. Sections 1.163(j)-1 through 1.163(j)-11 are added to read as follows:

§ 1.163(j)-1. Definitions.—(a) *In general.*—This section defines terms used in the section 163(j) regulations. For purposes of the rules sets forth in §§ 1.163(j)-2 through 1.163(j)-11, additional definitions for certain terms are provided in those sections.

(b) *Definitions.*—(1) *Adjusted taxable income.*—The term *adjusted taxable income* (ATI) means the taxable income of the taxpayer for the taxable year, with the adjustments in this paragraph (b).

(i) *Additions.*—The amounts of the following items (if any) are added to taxable income to determine ATI —

(A) Any business interest expense;

(B) Any net operating loss deduction under section 172;

(C) Any deduction under section 199A;

(D) For taxable years beginning before January 1, 2022, any deduction for depreciation under section 167, section 168, or section 168 of the Internal Revenue Code of 1954 (former section 168);

(E) For taxable years beginning before January 1, 2022, any deduction for the amortization of intangibles (for example, under section 167 or 197) and other amortized expenditures (for example, under section 195(b)(1)(B), 248, or 1245(a)(2)(C));

(F) For taxable years beginning before January 1, 2022, any deduction for depletion under section 611;

(G) Any deduction for a capital loss carryback or carryover; and

(H) Any deduction or loss that is not properly allocable to a non-excepted trade or business (for rules governing the allocation of items to an excepted trade or business, see §§ 1.163(j)-1(b)(38) and 1.163(j)-10).

(ii) *Subtractions.*—The amounts of the following items (if any) are subtracted from taxable income to determine ATI—

(A) Any business interest income;

(B) Any floor plan financing interest expense for the taxable year;

(C) With respect to the sale or other disposition of property, the lesser of:

(1) Any gain recognized on the sale or other disposition of such property; and

(2) Any depreciation, amortization, or depletion deductions for the taxable years beginning after December 31, 2017, and before January 1, 2022, with respect to such property;

(D) With respect to the sale or other disposition of stock of a member of a consolidated group that includes the selling member, the investment adjustments, as defined under § 1.1502-32, with respect to such stock that are attributable to deductions described in paragraph (b)(1)(ii)(C) of this section;

(E) With respect to the sale or other disposition of an interest in a partnership, the taxpayer's distributive share of deductions described in paragraph (b)(1)(ii)(C) of this section with respect to property held by the partnership at the time of such sale or other disposition to the extent such deductions were allowable under section 704(d); and

(F) Any income or gain that is not properly allocable to a non-excepted trade or business (for rules governing the allocation of items to an excepted trade or business, see §§ 1.163(j)-1(b)(38) and 1.163(j)-10)).

(iii) *Depreciation, amortization, or depletion expenses capitalized to inventory under section 263A.*—Depreciation, amortization, or depletion expense that is capitalized to inventory under section 263A is not a depreciation, amortization, or depletion deduction for purposes of this paragraph (b)(1).

(iv) *Other adjustments.*—ATI is computed with the other adjustments provided in §§ 1.163(j)-2 through 1.163(j)-11.

(v) *Additional rules relating to adjusted taxable income in other sections.*—(A) For rules governing the ATI of C corporations, see §§ 1.163(j)-4(b)(2) and (3) and 1.163(j)-10(a)(2)(ii).

(B) For rules governing the ATI of RICs and REITs, see § 1.163(j)-4(b)(4).

(C) For rules governing the ATI of tax-exempt corporations, see § 1.163(j)-4(b)(5).

(D) For rules governing the ATI of consolidated groups, see § 1.163(j)-4(d)(2)(iv) and (v).

(E) For rules governing the ATI of partnerships, see § 1.163(j)-6(d).

(F) For rules governing the ATI of partners, see § 1.163(j)-6(e).

(G) For rules governing partnership basis adjustments impacting ATI, see § 1.163(j)-6(h)(2).

(H) For rules governing the ATI of S corporations, see § 1.163(j)-6(l)(3).

(I) For rules governing the ATI of S corporation shareholders, see § 1.163(j)-6(l)(4).

(J) For rules governing the ATI of applicable CFCs and certain CFC group members, as defined in § 1.163(j)-7(f), see § 1.163(j)-7(c).

(K) For rules governing the ATI of United States shareholders of applicable CFCs, including the treatment of inclusions under sections 78, 951(a), and 951A(a), see § 1.163(j)-7(d).

(L) For rules governing the ATI of specified foreign persons, as defined in § 1.163(j)-8(g)(7), with effectively connected income, see § 1.163(j)-8(b)(2).

(M) For rules governing the ATI of specified foreign partners, as defined in § 1.163(j)-8(g)(6), other than applicable CFCs, as defined in § 1.163(j)-8(g)(1), see § 1.163(j)-8(c)(1).

(N) For rules governing the ATI of certain beneficiaries of trusts and estates, see § 1.163(j)-2(f).

(2) *Business interest expense.*—(i) *In general.*—The term *business interest expense* means interest expense that is properly allocable to a non-excepted trade or business or that is floor plan financing interest expense. Business interest expense also includes disallowed business interest expense carryforwards (as defined in paragraph (b)(9) of this section). For the treatment of investment interest, see section 163(d); and for the treatment of personal interest, see section 163(h).

(ii) *Special rules.*—For special rules for defining business interest expense in certain circumstances, see §§1.163(j)-3(b)(2) (regarding disallowed interest expense), 1.163(j)-4(b) (regarding C corporations) and (d)(2)(iii) (regarding consolidated groups), and 1.163(j)-8(b)(3) (regarding foreign persons engaged in a U.S. trade or business).

(3) *Business interest income.*—(i) *In general.*—The term *business interest income* means interest income which is properly allocable to a non-excepted trade or business. For the treatment of investment income, see section 163(d).

(ii) *Special rules.*—For special rules defining business interest income in certain circumstances, see §§1.163(j)-4(b) (regarding C corporations) and (d)(2)(iii) (regarding consolidated groups) and 1.163(j)-8(b)(4) (regarding foreign persons engaged in a U.S. trade or business).

(4) *C corporation.*—The term *C corporation* has the meaning provided in section 1361(a)(2).

(5) *Cleared swap.*—The term *cleared swap* means a swap that is cleared by a derivatives clearing organization, as such term is defined in section 1a of the Commodity Exchange Act (7 U.S.C. 1a), or by a clearing agency, as such term is defined in section 3 of the Securities Exchange Act of 1934 (15 U.S.C. 78c), that is registered as a derivatives clearing organization under the Commodity Exchange Act or as a clearing agency under the Securities Exchange Act of 1934, respectively, if the derivatives clearing organization or clearing agency requires the parties to the swap to post and collect margin or collateral.

(6) *Consolidated group.*—The term *consolidated group* has the meaning provided in §1.1502-1(h).

(7) *Consolidated return year.*—The term *consolidated return year* has the meaning provided in §1.1502-1(d).

(8) *Disallowed business interest expense.*—The term *disallowed business interest expense* means the amount of business interest expense for a taxable year in excess of the amount allowed as a deduction for the taxable year under section 163(j)(1) and §1.163(j)-2(b).

(9) *Disallowed business interest expense carryforward.*—The term *disallowed business interest expense carryforward* means any business interest expense described in §1.163(j)-2(c).

(10) *Disallowed disqualified interest.*—The term *disallowed disqualified interest* means interest expense, including carryforwards, for which a deduction was disallowed under old section 163(j) (as defined in paragraph (b)(26) of this section) in the taxpayer's last taxable year beginning before January 1, 2018, and that was carried forward pursuant to old section 163(j).

(11) *Electing farming business.*—The term *electing farming business* means a trade or business that makes an election as provided in §1.163(j)-9 or other published guidance and that is—

(i) A farming business, as defined in section 263A(e)(4) or §1.263A-4(a)(4); or

(ii) Any trade or business of a specified agricultural or horticultural cooperative, as defined in section 199A(g)(4).

(12) *Electing real property trade or business.*—The term *electing real property trade or business* means a trade or business that makes an election as provided in §1.163(j)-9 or other published guidance and that is described in—

(i) Section 469(c)(7)(C) and §1.469-9(b)(2); or

(ii) Section 1.163(j)-9(g).

(13) *Excepted regulated utility trade or business.*—(i) *In general.*—The term *excepted regulated utility trade or business* means a trade or business—

(A) That furnishes or sells:

(1) Electrical energy, water, or sewage disposal services;

(2) Gas or steam through a local distribution system; or

(3) Transportation of gas or steam by pipeline; and

(B) To the extent that the rates for the furnishing or sale of the items in paragraph (b)(13)(i)(A) of this section—

(1) Have been established or approved by a State or political subdivision thereof, by any agency or instrumentality of the United States, or by a public service or public utility commission or other similar body of any State or political subdivision thereof and are determined on a cost of service and rate of return basis; or

(2) Have been established or approved by the governing or ratemaking body of an electric cooperative.

(ii) *Excepted and non-excepted utility trades or businesses.*—If a taxpayer is engaged in both an excepted trade or business and a non-excepted trade or business described in this paragraph (b)(13), the taxpayer must allocate items between the trades or businesses. See §§1.163(j)-1(b)(38) and 1.163(j)-10(c)(3)(iii)(C). Some trades or businesses with de minimis furnishing or sales of items described in paragraph (b)(13)(i)(A) of this section that are not sold pursuant to rates determined on a cost of service and rate of return basis as required in paragraph (b)(13)(i)(B)*(1)* of this section, or by the governing or ratemaking body of an electric cooperative as required in paragraph (b)(13)(i)(B)*(2)* of this section are treated as excepted trades or businesses. See §1.163(j)-10(c)(3)(iii)(C)(3).

(14) *Excess business interest expense.*—The term *excess business interest expense* means, with respect to a partnership, the amount of disallowed business interest expense of the partnership for a taxable year under section §1.163(j)-2(b), except as provided in §1.163(j)-6(h)(2).

(15) *Excess taxable income.*—With respect to any partnership or S corporation, the term *excess taxable income* means the amount which bears the same ratio to the partnership's ATI as—

(i) The excess (if any) of—

(A) The amount determined for the partnership or S corporation under section 163(j)(1)(B); over

(B) The amount (if any) by which the business interest expense of the partnership, reduced by the floor plan financing interest expense, exceeds the business interest income of the partnership or S corporation; bears to

(ii) The amount determined for the partnership or S corporation under section 163(j)(1)(B).

(16) *Floor plan financing indebtedness.*—The term floor plan financing indebtedness means indebtedness—

(i) Used to finance the acquisition of motor vehicles held for sale or lease; and

(ii) Secured by the inventory so acquired.

(17) *Floor plan financing interest expense.*—The term *floor plan financing interest expense* means interest paid or accrued on floor plan financing indebtedness. For purposes of the section 163(j) regulations, all floor plan financing interest expense is treated as business interest expense. See paragraph (b)(2) of this section.

(18) *Group.*—The term *group* has the meaning provided in § 1.1502-1(a).

(19) *Intercompany transaction.*—The term *intercompany transaction* has the meaning provided in § 1.1502-13(b)(1)(i).

(20) *Interest.*—The term *interest* means any amount described in paragraph (b)(20)(i), (ii), (iii), or (iv) of this section.

(i) *In general.*—Interest is an amount paid, received, or accrued as compensation for the use or forbearance of money under the terms of an instrument or contractual arrangement, including a series of transactions, that is treated as a debt instrument for purposes of section 1275(a) and § 1.1275-1(d), and not treated as stock under § 1.385-3, or an amount that is treated as interest under other provisions of the Internal Revenue Code (Code) or the regulations thereunder. Thus, for example, interest includes—

(A) Original issue discount (OID), as adjusted by the holder for any acquisition premium or amortizable bond premium;

(B) Qualified stated interest, as adjusted by the holder for any amortizable bond premium or by the issuer for any bond issuance premium;

(C) Acquisition discount;

(D) Amounts treated as taxable OID under section 1286 (relating to stripped bonds and stripped coupons);

(E) Accrued market discount on a market discount bond to the extent includible in income by the holder under either section 1276(a) or 1278(b);

(F) OID includible in income by a holder that has made an election under § 1.1272-3 to treat all interest on a debt instrument as OID;

(G) OID on a synthetic debt instrument arising from an integrated transaction under § 1.1275-6;

(H) Repurchase premium to the extent deductible by the issuer under § 1.163-7(c);

(I) Deferred payments treated as interest under section 483;

(J) Amounts treated as interest under a section 467 rental agreement;

(K) Amounts treated as interest under section 988;

(L) Forgone interest under section 7872;

(M) De minimis OID taken into account by the issuer;

(N) Amounts paid or received in connection with a sale-repurchase agreement treated as indebtedness under Federal tax principles; in the case of a sale-repurchase agreement relating to tax-exempt bonds, however, the amount is not tax-exempt interest;

(O) Redeemable ground rent treated as interest under section 163(c); and

(P) Amounts treated as interest under section 636.

(ii) *Swaps with significant nonperiodic payments.*—(A) *Non-cleared swaps.*—A swap other than a cleared swap with significant nonperiodic payments is treated as two separate transactions consisting of an on-market, level payment swap and a loan. The loan must be accounted for by the parties to the contract independently of the swap. The time value component associated with the loan, determined in accordance with § 1.446-3(f)(2)(iii)(A), is recognized as interest expense to the payor and interest income to the recipient.

(B) [Reserved]

(iii) *Other amounts treated as interest.*—(A) *Treatment of premium.*—*(1) Issuer.*—If a debt instrument is issued at a premium within the meaning of § 1.163-13, any ordinary income under § 1.163-13(d)(4) is treated as interest income of the issuer.

(2) Holder.—If a taxable debt instrument is acquired at a premium within the meaning of § 1.171-1 and the holder elects to amortize the premium, any amount otherwise deductible under section 171(a)(1) as a bond premium deduction under § 1.171-2(a)(4)(i)(A) or (C) is treated as interest expense of the holder.

(B) *Treatment of ordinary income or loss on certain debt instruments.*—If an issuer of a contingent payment debt instrument subject to § 1.1275-4(b), a nonfunctional currency contingent payment debt instrument subject to § 1.988-6, or an inflation-indexed debt instrument subject to § 1.1275-7 recognizes ordinary income on the debt instrument in accordance with the rules in § 1.1275-4(b), § 1.988-6(b)(2), or § 1.1275-7(f), whichever is applicable, the ordinary income is treated as interest income of the issuer. If a holder of a contingent payment debt instrument subject to § 1.1275-4(b), a nonfunctional currency contingent payment debt instrument subject to § 1.988-6, or an inflation-indexed debt instrument subject to § 1.1275-7 recognizes an ordinary loss on the debt instrument in accordance with the rules in § 1.1275-4(b), § 1.988-6(b)(2), or § 1.1275-7(f), whichever is applicable, the ordinary loss is treated as interest expense of the holder.

(C) *Substitute interest payments.*—A substitute interest payment described in § 1.861-2(a)(7) is treated as interest expense to the payor or interest income to the recipient; in the case of a sale-repurchase agreement or a securities lending transaction relating to tax-exempt bonds, however, the recipient of a substitute payment does not receive tax-exempt interest income.

(D) *Section 1258 gain.*—Any gain treated as ordinary gain under section 1258 is treated as interest income.

(E) *Amounts affecting a taxpayer's effective cost of borrowing.*—Income, deduction, gain, or loss from a derivative, as defined in section 59A(h)(4)(A), that alters a taxpayer's effective cost of borrowing with respect to a liability of the taxpayer is treated as an adjustment to interest expense of the taxpayer. For example, a taxpayer that is obligated to pay interest at a floating rate on a note and enters into an interest rate swap that entitles the taxpayer to receive an amount that is equal to or that closely approximates the interest rate on the note in exchange for a fixed amount is, in effect, paying interest expense at a fixed rate by entering into the interest rate swap. Income, deduction, gain, or loss from the swap is treated as an adjustment to interest expense. Similarly, any gain or loss resulting from a termination or other disposition of the swap is an adjustment to interest expense, with the timing of gain or loss subject to the rules of § 1.446-4.

(F) *Yield adjustments.*—Income, deduction, gain, or loss from a derivative, as defined in section 59A(h)(4)(A), that alters a taxpayer's effective yield with respect to a debt instrument held by the taxpayer is treated as an adjustment to interest income by the taxpayer.

(G) *Certain amounts labeled as fees.*—*(1) Commitment fees.*—Any fees in respect of a lender commitment to provide financing are treated as interest if any portion of such financing is actually provided.

(2) [Reserved]

(H) *Debt issuance costs.*—Any debt issuance costs subject to § 1.446-5 are treated as interest expense of the issuer.

(I) *Guaranteed payments.*—Any guaranteed payments for the use of capital under section 707(c) are treated as interest.

(J) *Factoring income.*—The excess of the amount that a taxpayer collects on a factored receivable (or realizes upon the sale or other disposition of the factored receivable) over the amount paid for the factored receivable by the taxpayer is treated as interest income. For purposes of this paragraph (b)(20)(iii)(J), the term *factored receivable* includes any account receivable or other evidence of indebtedness, whether or not issued at a discount and whether or not bearing stated interest, arising out of the disposition of property or the performance of services by any person, if such account receivable or evidence of indebtedness is acquired by a person other than the person who disposed of the property or provided the services that gave rise to the account receivable or evidence of indebtedness.

(iv) *Anti-avoidance rule for amounts predominantly associated with the time value of money.*—Any expense or loss, to the extent deductible, incurred by a taxpayer in a transaction or series of integrated or related transactions in which the taxpayer secures the use of funds for a period of time is treated as interest expense of the taxpayer if such expense or loss is predominantly incurred in consideration of the time value of money.

(v) *Examples.*—The examples in this paragraph (b)(20)(v) illustrate the application of paragraphs (b)(20)(i) through (iv) of this section. Unless otherwise indicated, assume the following: A, B, C, D, and Bank are domestic C corporations that are publicly traded; the exemption for certain small businesses in § 1.163(j)-2(d) does not apply; A is not engaged in an excepted trade or business; and all amounts of interest expense are deductible except for the potential application of section 163(j).

(A) *Example 1*—*(1) Facts.* *(i)* A is a calendar year taxpayer that is engaged in a manufacturing business. In January 2019, A, which has an investment-grade credit rating, enters into the following transactions (the transactions): Bank transfers a portfolio of U.S. Treasury bonds (the Treasury portfolio) to A; A agrees to pay Bank an amount equivalent to any interest paid on the Treasury portfolio during the transactions and a fee for lending the Treasury portfolio to A; A agrees to return to Bank securities that are substantially identical to the Treasury portfolio upon request, regardless of any value increases or decreases in the market value of the Treasury portfolio; A rehypothecates the Treasury portfolio in exchange for cash, which A uses to purchase a portfolio of corporate bonds (the debt portfolio); and the transactions remain in place for the duration of the 2019 calendar year until Bank delivers a notice to A recalling the Treasury portfolio 5 business days before December 31, 2019.

(ii) The obligations undertaken with respect to the transactions are not collateralized. Assume that the transactions do not result in a sale-repurchase agreement treated as indebtedness under Federal tax principles. During the course of the transactions, the debt portfolio generates $70x of interest income. The Treasury portfolio generates $60x of interest income during the course of the transactions and A pays $60x to Bank under its obligation to pay amounts equivalent to the interest paid on the Treasury portfolio.

(2) Analysis. The transactions involving Bank and A are transactions described in paragraph (b)(20)(iii)(C) of this section. Consequently, the $60x of substitute interest payments that A paid to Bank in 2019 is treated as interest expense for purposes of section 163(j). In addition, the $70x of interest income generated by the debt portfolio is interest income to A.

(B) *Example 2*—*(1) Facts.* A is a calendar year taxpayer that is engaged in a manufacturing business. In early 2019, A enters into the following transactions:

(i) A enters into a loan obligation in which A borrows Japanese yen from Bank in an amount equivalent to $2000x with an interest rate of 1 percent (at the time of the loan, the U.S. dollar equivalent interest rate on a loan of $2,000x is 5 percent); and

(ii) A enters into a foreign currency swap transaction (FX Swap) with Bank with a notional principal amount of $2000x under which A receives Japanese yen at 1 percent multiplied by the amount of Japanese yen borrowed from Bank (which for 2019 equals $20x) and pays U.S. dollars at 5 percent multiplied by a notional amount of $2000x ($100x per year). The FX Swap is not integrated with the loan obligation under § 1.988-5.

(2) Analysis. The FX Swap alters A's cost of borrowing within the meaning of paragraph (b)(20)(iii)(E) of this section. As a result, for purposes of section 163(j), the $100x paid by A to Bank on the FX Swap is treated by A as interest expense and the $20x paid by Bank to A on the FX Swap is treated by A as a reduction of interest expense.

(C) *Example 3*—*(1) Facts.* A borrows from B two ounces of gold at a time when the spot price for gold is $500x per ounce. A agrees to return the two ounces of gold in six months. A sells the two ounces of gold to C for $1,000x. A then enters into a contract with D to purchase two ounces of gold six months in the future for

$1,013x. In exchange for the use of $1,000x in cash, A has sustained a loss of $13x on related transactions.

(2) *Analysis.* A has obtained the use of $1,000x and, in a series of related transactions, created a loss of $13x predominantly associated with the time value of money. As a result, for purposes of section 163(j), the loss of $13x is treated as interest expense under paragraph (b)(20)(iv) of this section.

(21) *Interest expense.*—The term *interest expense* means interest that is paid or accrued, or treated as paid or accrued, for the taxable year.

(22) *Interest income.*—The term *interest income* means interest that is included in gross income for the taxable year.

(23) *Inventory.*—The term *inventory* means property held for sale or for lease, or both, by a taxpayer in the ordinary course of its trade or business.

(24) *Member.*—The term *member* has the meaning provided in § 1.1502-1(b).

(25) *Motor vehicle.*—The term *motor vehicle* means a motor vehicle as defined in section 163(j)(9)(C).

(26) *Old section 163(j).*—The term *old section 163(j)* means section 163(j) immediately prior to its amendment by Public Law 115-97, 131 Stat. 2054 (2017).

(27) *Real estate investment trust.*—The term *real estate investment trust* (REIT) has the meaning provided in section 856.

(28) *Real property.*—The term *real property* includes—

(i) Real property as defined in § 1.469-9(b)(2); and

(ii) Any direct or indirect right, including a license or other contractual right, to share in the appreciation in value of, or the gross or net proceeds or profits generated by, an interest in real property, including net proceeds or profits associated with tolls, rents or other similar fees.

(29) *Regulated investment company.*—The term *regulated investment company* (RIC) has the meaning provided in section 851.

(30) *S corporation.*—The term *S corporation* has the meaning provided in section 1361(a)(1).

(31) *Section 163(j) limitation.*—The term *section 163(j) limitation* means the limit on the amount of business interest expense that a taxpayer may deduct in a taxable year under section 163(j) and § 1.163(j)-2(b).

(32) *Section 163(j) regulations.*—The term *section 163(j) regulations* means this section and §§ 1.163(j)-2 through 1.163(j)-11.

(33) *Separate return limitation year.*—The term *separate return limitation year* (SRLY) has the meaning provided in § 1.1502-1(f).

(34) *Separate return year.*—The term *separate return year* has the meaning provided in § 1.1502-1(e).

(35) *Separate taxable income.*—The term *separate taxable income* has the meaning provided in § 1.1502-12.

(36) *Tax-exempt corporation.*—The term *tax-exempt corporation* means any corporation subject to tax under section 511.

(37) *Taxable income.*—(i) *In general.*—The term *taxable income*, with respect to a taxpayer and a taxable year, has the meaning provided in section 63, but for this purpose computed without regard to the application of section 163(j) and the section 163(j) regulations.

(ii) *General rules to coordinate the application of sections 163(j) and 250.*—If for a taxable year a taxpayer is allowed a deduction under section 250(a)(1) that is properly allocable to a non-excepted trade or business, then taxable income for the taxable year is determined without regard to the limitation in section 250(a)(2). For this purpose, the amount of the deduction allowed under section 250(a)(1), without regard to the limitation in section 250(a)(2), is determined without regard to the application of section 163(j) and the section 163(j) regulations.

(iii) [Reserved]

(iv) *Special rules for defining taxable income.*—(A) For special rules defining the taxable income of a RIC or REIT, see § 1.163(j)-4(b)(4)(ii).

(B) For special rules defining the taxable income of consolidated groups, see § 1.163(j)-4(d)(2)(iv).

(C) For special rules defining the taxable income of a partnership, see § 1.163(j)-6(d)(1).

(D) For special rules defining the taxable income of an S corporation, see § 1.163(j)-6(l)(3).

(E) For special rules defining the taxable income of certain controlled foreign corporations, see § 1.163(j)-7(c)(1).

(38) *Trade or business.*—(i) *In general.*—The term *trade or business* means a trade or business within the meaning of section 162.

(ii) *Excepted trade or business.*—The term *excepted trade or business* means a trade or business that is described in paragraphs (b)(38)(ii)(A) through (D) of this section. For additional rules related to excepted trades or businesses, including elections made under section 163(j)(7)(B) and (C), see § 1.163(j)-9.

(A) The trade or business of performing services as an employee.

(B) Any electing real property trade or business.

(C) Any electing farming business.

(D) Any excepted regulated utility trade or business.

(iii) *Non-excepted trade or business.*—The term *non-excepted trade or business* means any trade or business that is not an excepted trade or business.

(39) *Unadjusted basis.*—The term *unadjusted basis* means the basis as determined under section 1012 or other applicable sections of chapter 1 of subtitle A of the Code, including subchapters O (relating to gain or loss on dispositions of property), C (relating to corporate distributions and adjustments), K (relating to partners and partnerships), and P (relating to capital gains and losses) of the Code. Unadjusted basis is determined without regard to any adjustments described in section 1016(a)(2) or (3), to any adjustments for tax credits claimed by the taxpayer (for example, under section 50(c)), or to any adjustments for any portion of the basis for which the taxpayer has elected to treat as an expense (for example, under section 179, 179B, or 179C).

(c) *Applicability date.*—This section applies to taxable years ending after the date the Treasury decision adopting these regulations as final regulations is published in the **Federal Register**.

However, taxpayers and their related parties, within the meaning of sections 267(b) and 707(b)(1), may apply the rules of this section to a taxable year beginning after December 31, 2017, so long as the taxpayers and their related parties consistently apply the rules of the section 163(j) regulations, and if applicable, §§1.263A-9, 1.381(c)(20)-1, 1.382-6, 1.383-1, 1.469-9, 1.882-5, 1.1502-13, 1.1502-21, 1.1502-36, 1.1502-79, 1.1502-91 through 1.1502-99, (to the extent they effectuate the rules of §§1.382-6 and 1.383-1), and 1.1504-4 to those taxable years. [Reg. §1.163(j)-1.]

§1.163(j)-2. Deduction for business interest expense limited.—(a) *Overview.*—This section provides general rules regarding the section 163(j) limitation. Paragraph (b) of this section provides rules regarding the basic computation of the section 163(j) limitation. Paragraph (c) of this section provides rules for disallowed business interest expense carryforwards. Paragraph (d) of this section provides rules regarding the small business exemption from the section 163(j) limitation. Paragraph (e) of this section provides rules regarding real estate mortgage investment conduits (REMICs). Paragraph (f) of this section provides examples illustrating the application of this section. Paragraph (g) of this section provides an anti-avoidance rule.

(b) *General rule.*—Except as otherwise provided in this section or in §§1.163(j)-3 through 1.163(j)-11, the amount allowed as a deduction for business interest expense for the taxable year cannot exceed the sum of—

(1) The taxpayer's business interest income for the taxable year;

(2) 30 percent of the taxpayer's ATI for the taxable year, or zero if the taxpayer's ATI for the taxable year is less than zero; and

(3) The taxpayer's floor plan financing interest expense for the taxable year.

(c) *Disallowed business interest expense carryforward.*—(1) *In general.*—Under section 163(j)(2), any business interest expense disallowed under paragraph (b) of this section, or any disallowed disqualified interest that is properly allocable to a non-excepted trade or business under §1.163(j)-10, is carried forward to the succeeding taxable year as business interest expense that is subject to paragraph (b) of this section in such succeeding taxable year (a disallowed business interest expense carryforward).

(2) *Coordination with small business exemption.*—If disallowed business interest expense is carried forward under the rules of paragraph (c)(1) of this section to a taxable year in which the small business exemption in paragraph (d) of this section applies to the taxpayer, then the general rule in paragraph (b) of this section does not apply to limit the deduction of the disallowed business interest expense carryforward in that taxable year.

(3) *Cross-references.*—(i) For special rules regarding disallowed business interest expense carryforwards for taxpayers that are C corporations, including members of a consolidated group, see §1.163(j)-5.

(ii) For special rules regarding disallowed business interest expense carryforwards of S corporations, see §§1.163(j)-5(b)(2) and 1.163(j)-6(l)(5).

(iii) For special rules regarding disallowed business interest expense carryforwards from partnerships, see §1.163(j)-6.

(iv) For special rules regarding disallowed business interest expense carryforwards from partnerships engaged in a U.S. trade or business, see §1.163(j)-8(c)(2).

(d) *Small business exemption.*—(1) *Exemption.*—The general rule in paragraph (b) of this section does not apply to any taxpayer, other than a tax shelter as defined in section 448(d)(3), in any taxable year if the taxpayer meets the gross receipts test of section 448(c) and the regulations thereunder for the taxable year.

(2) *Application of the gross receipts test.*—(i) *In general.*—In the case of any taxpayer that is not a corporation or a partnership, and except as provided in paragraphs (d)(2)(ii), (iii), and (iv) of this section, the gross receipts test and aggregation rules of section 448(c) and the regulations thereunder are applied in the same manner as if such taxpayer were a corporation or partnership.

(ii) *Gross receipts of individuals.*—Except as provided in paragraph (d)(2)(iii) of this section regarding partnership and S corporation interests and when the aggregation rules of section 448(c) apply, an individual taxpayer's gross receipts include all items specified as gross receipts in regulations under section 448(c), whether or not derived in the ordinary course of the taxpayer's trade or business. For purposes of section 163(j), an individual taxpayer's gross receipts do not include inherently personal amounts, including, but not limited to, personal injury awards or settlements with respect to an injury of the individual taxpayer, disability benefits, Social Security benefits received by the taxpayer during the taxable year, and wages received as an employee that are reported on Form W-2.

(iii) *Partners and S corporation shareholders.*—Except when the aggregation rules of section 448(c) apply, each partner in a partnership includes a share of partnership gross receipts in proportion to such partner's distributive share (as determined under section 704) of items of gross income that were taken into account by the partnership under section 703. Additionally, each shareholder in an S corporation includes a pro rata share of S corporation gross receipts.

(iv) *Tax-exempt organizations.*—For purposes of section 163(j), the gross receipts of an organization subject to tax under section 511 includes only gross receipts taken into account in determining its unrelated business taxable income.

(e) *REMICs.*—For the treatment of interest expense by a REMIC as defined in section 860D, see §1.860C-2(b)(2)(ii).

(f) *Calculation of ATI with respect to certain beneficiaries.*—The ATI of a trust or estate beneficiary is reduced by any income (including any distributable net income) received from the trust or estate by the beneficiary to the extent such income supported a deduction for business interest expense under section 163(j)(1)(B) or §1.163(j)-2(b)(2) in computing the trust or estate's taxable income.

(g) *Examples.*—The examples of this paragraph (g) illustrate the application of section 163(j) and the provisions of this section. Unless otherwise indicated, assume the following: X and Y are domestic C corporations; C and D are U.S. resident individuals not subject to any foreign income tax; PRS is a domestic partnership with partners who are all individuals; all taxpayers use a calendar taxable year; the exemption for certain small businesses in section 163(j)(3) and paragraph (d) of this section does not apply; and the interest expense would be deductible but for section 163(j).

(1) *Example 1: Limitation on business interest expense deduction*—(i) *Facts*. During its taxable year ending December 31, 2019, X has ATI of $100x. X has business interest expense of $50x, which includes $10x of floor plan financing interest expense, and business interest income of $20x.

(ii) *Analysis*. X's section 163(j) limitation is $60x, which is the sum of its business interest income ($20x), plus 30 percent of its ATI ($100x x 30 percent = $30x), plus its floor plan financing interest expense ($10x). See § 1.163(j)-2(b). Because X's business interest expense ($50x) does not exceed X's section 163(j) limitation ($60x), X can deduct all $50x of its business interest expense for the 2019 taxable year.

(2) *Example 2: Carryforward of business interest expense*—(i) *Facts*. The facts are the same as in *Example 1* in paragraph (g)(1)(i) of this section, except that X has $80x of business interest expense, which includes $10x of floor plan financing interest expense.

(ii) *Analysis*. As in *Example 1* in paragraph (g)(1)(ii) of this section, X's section 163(j) limitation is $60x. Because X's business interest expense ($80x) exceeds X's section 163(j) limitation ($60x), X may only deduct $60x of its business interest expense for the 2019 taxable year, and the remaining $20x of its business interest expense will be carried forward to the succeeding taxable year as a disallowed business interest expense carryforward. See § 1.163(j)-2(c).

(3) *Example 3: ATI computation*—(i) *Facts*. During the 2019 taxable year, Y has taxable income of $30x (without regard to the application of section 163(j)), which includes the following: $20x of business interest income; $50x of business interest expense, which includes $10x of floor plan financing interest expense; $25x of net operating loss deduction under section 172; and $15x of depreciation deduction under section 167.

(ii) *Analysis*. (A) For purposes of determining the section 163(j) limitation, Y's ATI is $90x, calculated as follows:

Table 1 to paragraph (g)(3)(ii)(A)

Taxable income:	$30x
Less:	
Floor plan financing interest	10x
Business interest income	*20x*
	0x

(B) Plus:

Table 1 to paragraph (g)(3)(ii)(B)

Business interest expense	$50x
Net operating loss deduction	25x
Depreciation deduction	*15x*
ATI	$90x

(4) *Example 4: Floor plan financing interest expense*—(i) *Facts*. C is the sole proprietor of an automobile dealership that uses a cash method of accounting. In the 2019 taxable year, C paid $30x of interest on a loan that was obtained to purchase sedans for sale by the dealership. The indebtedness is secured by the sedans purchased with the loan proceeds. In addition, C paid $20x of interest on a loan, secured by the dealership's office equipment, which C obtained to purchase convertibles for sale by the dealership.

(ii) *Analysis*. For the purpose of calculating C's section 163(j) limitation, only the $30x of interest paid on the loan to purchase the sedans is floor plan financing interest expense. The $20x paid on the loan to purchase the convertibles is not floor plan financing interest expense for purposes of section 163(j) because the indebtedness was not secured by the inventory of convertibles. However, because under § 1.163(j)-10 the interest paid on the loan to purchase the convertibles is properly allocable to C's dealership trade or business, and because floor plan financing interest expense is also business interest expense, C has $50x of business interest expense for the 2019 taxable year.

(5) *Example 5: Interest not properly allocable to non-excepted trade or business*—(i) *Facts*. The facts are the same as in *Example 4* in paragraph (g)(4)(i) of this section, except that the $20x of interest C pays is on acquisition indebtedness obtained to purchase C's personal residence and not to purchase convertibles for C's dealership trade or business.

(ii) *Analysis*. Because the $20x of interest expense is not properly allocable to a non-excepted trade or business, and therefore is not business interest expense as defined in § 1.163(j)-1(b)(2), C's only business interest expense is the $30x that C pays on the loan used to purchase sedans for sale in C's dealership trade or business. C deducts the $20x of interest related to his residence under the rules of section 163(h), without regard to section 163(j).

(6) *Example 6: Small business exemption*—(i) *Facts*. During the 2019 taxable year, D, the sole proprietor of a trade or business reported on Schedule C, has interest expense properly allocable to that trade or business. D also earns gross income from providing services as an employee that is reported on a Form W-2. Under section 448(c) and the regulations thereunder, D has average annual gross receipts of $21 million, including $1 million of wages in each of the three prior taxable years and $2 million of income from investments not related to a trade or business in each of the three prior taxable years. Also, in each of the three prior taxable years, D received $5 million in periodic payments of compensatory damages awarded in a personal injury lawsuit.

(ii) *Analysis*. Section 163(j) does not apply to D for the taxable year, because D qualifies for the small business exemption under § 1.163(j)-2(d). The wages that D receives as an employee and the compensatory damages that D received from D's personal injury lawsuit are not gross receipts, as provided in § 1.163(j)-2(d)(2)(ii). D may deduct all of its business interest expense for the 2019 taxable year without regard to section 163(j).

(7) *Example 7: Aggregation of gross receipts*—(i) *Facts*. X and Y are domestic C corporations under common control, within the meaning of section 52(a) and § 1.52-1(b). X's only trade or

business is a farming business described in §1.263A-4(a)(4). During the taxable year ending December 31, 2019, X has average annual gross receipts under section 448(c) of $6 million. During the same taxable year, Y has average annual gross receipts under section 448(c) of $21 million.

(ii) *Analysis*. Because X and Y are under common control, they must aggregate gross receipts for purposes of section 448(c) and the small business exemption in §1.163(j)-2(d). See section 448(c)(2). Therefore, X and Y are both considered to have $27 million in average annual gross receipts for 2019. X and Y must separately apply section 163(j) to determine any limitation on the deduction for business interest expense. Assuming X otherwise meets the requirements in §1.163(j)-9 in 2019, X may elect for its farming business to be an excepted trade or business.

(h) *Anti-avoidance rule*.—Arrangements entered into with a principal purpose of avoiding the rules of section 163(j) or the section 163(j) regulations, including the use of multiple entities to avoid the gross receipts test of section 448(c), may be disregarded or recharacterized by the Commissioner of the IRS to the extent necessary to carry out the purposes of section 163(j).

(i) *Applicability date*.—This section applies to taxable years ending after the date the Treasury decision adopting these regulations as final regulations is published in the **Federal Register**. However, taxpayers and their related parties, within the meaning of sections 267(b) and 707(b)(1), may apply the rules of this section to a taxable year beginning after December 31, 2017, so long as the taxpayers and their related parties consistently apply the rules of the section 163(j) regulations, and if applicable, §§1.263A-9, 1.381(c)(20)-1, 1.382-6, 1.383-1, 1.469-9, 1.882-5, 1.1502-13, 1.1502-21, 1.1502-36, 1.1502-79, 1.1502-91 through 1.1502-99, (to the extent they effectuate the rules of §§1.382-6 and 1.383-1), and 1.1504-4 to those taxable years. [Reg. §1.163(j)-2.]

§1.163(j)-3. Relationship of business interest deduction limitation to other provisions affecting interest.—(a) *Overview*.—This section contains rules regarding the relationship between section 163(j) and certain other provisions of the Code. Paragraph (b) of this section provides the general rules concerning the relationship between section 163(j) and certain other provisions of the Code. Paragraph (c) of this section provides examples illustrating the application of this section. For rules regarding the relationship between sections 163(j) and 704(d), see §1.163(j)-6(h)(1) and (2).

(b) *Coordination of section 163(j) with certain other provisions*.—(1) *In general*.—Section 163(j) and the section 163(j) regulations generally apply only to business interest expense that would be deductible in the current taxable year without regard to section 163(j). Except as otherwise provided in this section, section 163(j) applies after the application of provisions that subject interest expense to disallowance, deferral, capitalization, or other limitation. For the rules that must be applied in determining whether excess business interest is paid or accrued by a partner, see section 163(j)(4)(B)(ii) and §1.163(j)-6.

(2) *Disallowed interest provisions*.—For purposes of section 163(j), business interest expense does not include interest expense that is permanently disallowed as a deduction under another provision of the Code, such as in section 163(e)(5)(A)(i), (f), (l), or (m), or section 264(a), 265, 267A, or 279.

(3) *Deferred interest provisions*.—Other than sections 461(l), 465, and 469, Code provisions that defer the deductibility of interest expense, such as section 163(e)(3) and (e)(5)(A)(ii), 267(a)(2) and (3), 1277, or 1282, apply before the application of section 163(j). For purposes other than sections 465 and 469, interest expense is taken into account for section 163(j) purposes in the taxable year when it is no longer deferred under another section of the Code.

(4) *At risk rules, passive activity loss provisions, and limitation on excess business losses of noncorporate taxpayers*.—Section 163(j) applies before the application of sections 461(l), 465, and 469.

(5) *Capitalized interest expenses under sections 263A and 263(g)*.—Sections 263A and 263(g) apply before the application of section 163(j). Capitalized interest expense under those sections is not treated as business interest expense for purposes of section 163(j). For ordering rules that determine whether interest expense is capitalized under section 263A(f), see the regulations under section 263A(f), including §1.263A-9(g).

(6) *Reductions under section 246A*.—Section 246A applies before section 163(j). Any reduction in the dividends received deduction under section 246A reduces the amount of business interest expense taken into account under section 163(j).

(7) *Section 381*.—Disallowed business interest expense carryforwards are items to which an acquiring corporation succeeds under section 381(a). See section 381(c)(20), and §§1.163(j)-5(c) and 1.381(c)(20)-1.

(8) *Section 382*.—For rules governing the interaction of sections 163(j) and 382, see section 382(d)(3) and (k)(1), §§1.163(j)-5(e) and 1.163(j)-11(b), the regulations under sections 382 and 383, and §§1.1502-91 through 1.1502-99.

(9) *Other types of interest provisions*.—Except as otherwise provided in the section 163(j) regulations, provisions that characterize interest expense as something other than business interest expense under section 163(j), such as section 163(d), govern the treatment of that interest expense, and such interest expense will not be treated as business interest expense for any purpose under section 163(j).

(10) [Reserved]

(c) *Examples*.—The examples of this paragraph (c) illustrate the application of section 163(j) and the provisions of this section. Unless otherwise indicated, assume the following: X and Y are domestic C corporations with a calendar taxable year; D is a U.S. resident individual not subject to any foreign income tax; none of the taxpayers have floor plan financing interest expense; and the exemption for small businesses in §1.163(j)-2(d) does not apply.

(1) *Example 1: Disallowed interest expense*—(i) *Facts*. In 2019, X has $30x of interest expense. Of X's interest expense, $10x is permanently disallowed under section 265. X's business interest income is $3x and X's ATI is $90x.

(ii) *Analysis*. Under paragraph (b)(2) of this section, the $10x interest expense that is permanently disallowed under section 265 cannot be taken into consideration for purposes of section

163(j) in the 2019 taxable year. X's section 163(j) limitation, or the amount of business interest expense that X may deduct is limited to $30x under § 1.163(j)-2(b), determined by adding X's business interest income ($3x) and 30 percent of X's 2018 ATI ($27x). Therefore, in the 2019 taxable year, none of the $20x of X's deduction for its business interest expense is disallowed under section 163(j).

(2) *Example 2: Deferred interest expense*—(i) *Facts*. In 2019, Y has no business interest income, $120x of ATI, and $70x of interest expense. Of Y's interest expense, $30x is not currently deductible under section 267(a)(2). Assume that the $30x expense will be allowed as a deduction under section 267(a)(2) in 2020.

(ii) *Analysis*. Under paragraph (b)(3) of this section, section 267(a)(2) is applied before section 163(j). Accordingly, $30x of Y's interest expense cannot be taken into consideration for purposes of section 163(j) in 2019 because it is not currently deductible under section 267(a)(2). Accordingly, in 2019, if the interest expense is properly allocable to a non-excepted trade or business, Y will have $4x of disallowed business interest expense because the $40x of business interest expense in 2019 ($70x - $30x) exceeds 30 percent of its ATI for the taxable year ($36x). The $30x of interest expense not allowed as a deduction in the 2019 taxable year under section 267(a)(2) will be taken into account in determining the business interest expense deduction under section 163(j) in 2020, the taxable year in which it is allowed as a deduction under section 267(a)(2), if it is allocable to a trade or business. Additionally, the $4x of disallowed business interest expense in 2019 will be carried forward to 2020 as a disallowed business interest expense carryforward. See § 1.163(j)-2(c).

(3) *Example 3: Passive activity loss*—(i) *Facts*. D is engaged in a rental activity treated as a passive activity within the meaning of section 469. For tax year 2019, D receives $200x of rental income and incurs $300x of expenses all properly allocable to the rental activity, consisting of $150x of interest expense, $60x of maintenance expenses, and $90x of depreciation expense. D's ATI is $400x.

(ii) *Analysis*. Under paragraph (b)(4) of this section, section 163(j) is applied before the section 469 passive loss rules apply. D's section 163(j) limitation is $120x, determined by adding to D's business interest income ($0), floor plan financing ($0), and 30 percent of D's ATI ($120x). See § 1.163(j)-2(b). Because D's business interest expense of $150x exceeds D's section 163(j) limitation for 2019, $30x of D's business interest expense is disallowed under section 163(j) and will be carried forward as a disallowed business interest expense carryforward. See § 1.163(j)-2(c). Because the section 163(j) limitation is applied before the limitation under section 469, only $120x of the business interest expense allowable under section 163(j) is included in determining D's passive activity loss limitation for the 2019 tax year under section 469. The $30x of disallowed business interest expense is not an allowable deduction under section 163(j) and, therefore, is not a deduction under section 469 in the current taxable year. See § 1.469-2(d)(8).

(4) *Example 4: Passive activity loss by taxpayer that also participates in a non-passive activity*—(i) *Facts*. For 2019, D has no business interest income and ATI of $1,000x, entirely attributable to a passive activity within the meaning of section 469. D has business interest expense of $1,000x, $900x of which is properly allocable to a passive activity and $100x of which is properly allocable to a non-passive activity in which D materially participates. D has other business deductions that are not subject to section 469 of $600x, and a section 469 passive loss from the previous year of $250x.

(ii) *Analysis*. Under paragraph (b)(4) of this section, section 163(j) is applied before the section 469 passive loss rules apply. D's section 163(j) limitation is $300x, determined by adding D's business interest income ($0), floor plan financing ($0), and 30 percent of D's ATI ($300x)). Next, applying the limitation under section 469 to the $300x business interest expense deduction allowable under sections 163(a) and (j), $270x (a proportionate amount of the $300x (0.90 x $300x)) is business interest expense included in determining D's passive activity loss limitation under section 469, and $30x (a proportionate amount of the $300x (0.10 x $300)) is business interest expense not included in determining D's passive activity loss limitation under section 469. Because D's interest expense of $1,000x exceeds 30 percent of its ATI for 2019, $700x of D's interest expense is disallowed under section 163(j) and will be carried forward as a disallowed business interest expense carryforward. Section 469 does not apply to any portion of the $700x disallowed business interest expense because that business interest expense is not an allowable deduction under section 163(j) and, therefore, is not an allowable deduction under section 469 in the current taxable year. See § 1.469-2(d)(8).

(d) *Applicability date*.—The provisions of this section apply to taxable years ending after the date the Treasury decision adopting these regulations as final regulations is published in the **Federal Register**. However, taxpayers and their related parties, within the meaning of sections 267(b) and 707(b)(1), may apply the rules of this section to a taxable year beginning after December 31, 2017, so long as the taxpayers and their related parties consistently apply the rules of the section 163(j) regulations, and if applicable, § § 1.263A-9, 1.381(c)(20)-1, 1.382-6, 1.383-1, 1.469-9, 1.882-5, 1.1502-13, 1.1502-21, 1.1502-36, 1.1502-79, 1.1502-91 through 1.1502-99 (to the extent they effectuate the rules of § § 1.382-6 and 1.383-1), and 1.1504-4 to those taxable years. [Reg. § 1.163(j)-3.]

§ 1.163(j)-4. General rules applicable to C corporations (including REITs, RICs, and members of consolidated groups) and tax-exempt corporations.—(a) *Scope*.—This section provides certain rules regarding the computation of items of income and expense under section 163(j) for taxpayers that are C corporations (including members of a consolidated group, REITs, and RICs) and tax-exempt corporations. Paragraph (b) of this section provides rules regarding the characterization of items of income, gain, deduction, or loss. Paragraph (c) of this section provides rules regarding adjustments to earnings and profits. Paragraph (d) of this section provides special rules applicable to members of a consolidated group. Paragraph (e) of this section provides cross-references to other rules within the 163(j) regulations that may be applicable to C corporations.

(b) *Characterization of items of income, gain, deduction, or loss.*—(1) *Interest expense and interest income.*—Solely for purposes of section 163(j), all interest expense of a taxpayer that is a C corporation is treated as properly allocable to a trade or business. Similarly, solely for purposes of section 163(j), all interest income of a taxpayer that is a C corporation is treated as properly allocable to a trade or business. For rules governing the allocation of interest expense and interest income between excepted and non-excepted trades or businesses, see § 1.163(j)-10.

(2) *Adjusted taxable income.*—Solely for purposes of section 163(j), all items of income, gain, deduction, or loss of a taxpayer that is a C corporation are treated as properly allocable to a trade or business. For rules governing the allocation of tax items between excepted and non-excepted trades or businesses, see § 1.163(j)-10.

(3) *Investment interest, investment income, and investment expenses of a partnership with a C corporation partner.*—(i) *Characterization as expense or income properly allocable to a trade or business.*—For purposes of section 163(j), any investment interest, within the meaning of section 163(d), that a partnership pays or accrues and that is allocated to a C corporation partner is treated by the C corporation as interest expense that is properly allocable to a trade or business of that partner. Similarly, for purposes of section 163(j), except as provided in § 1.163(j)-7(d)(1)(ii), any investment income or investment expenses, within the meaning of section 163(d), that a partnership receives, pays, or accrues and that is allocated to a C corporation partner is treated by the C corporation as properly allocable to a trade or business of that partner.

(ii) *Impact of characterization on partnership.*—The characterization of a partner's investment interest, investment income, or investment expenses pursuant to paragraph (b)(3)(i) of this section will not affect the characterization of these items as investment interest, investment income, or investment expenses at the partnership level.

(iii) *Investment interest expense and investment interest income of a partnership not treated as excess business interest expense or excess taxable income of a C corporation partner.*—Investment interest expense of a partnership that is treated as business interest expense by a C corporation partner is not treated as excess business interest expense. Investment interest income of a partnership that is treated as business interest income by a C corporation partner is not treated as excess taxable income. For rules governing excess business interest expense and excess taxable income, see § 1.163(j)-6.

(4) *Application to RICs and REITs.*—(i) *In general.*—Except as otherwise provided in paragraphs (b)(4)(ii) and (iii) of this section, the rules in this paragraph (b) apply to RICs and REITs.

(ii) *Taxable income for purposes of calculating the adjusted taxable income of RICs and REITs.*—The taxable income of a RIC or REIT for purposes of calculating adjusted taxable income (ATI) is the taxable income of the corporation, without any adjustment that would be made under section 852(b)(2) or 857(b)(2) to compute investment company taxable income or real estate investment trust taxable income, respectively. For example, the taxable income of a RIC or REIT is not reduced by the deduction for dividends paid, but is reduced by the dividends received deduction (DRD) and the other deductions described in sections 852(b)(2)(C) and 857(b)(2)(A), taking into account § 1.163(j)-1(b)(37)(ii). See paragraph (b)(4)(iii) of this section for an adjustment to adjusted taxable income in respect of these items.

(iii) *Other adjustments to adjusted taxable income for RICs and REITs.*—In the case of a taxpayer that, for a taxable year, is a RIC to which section 852(b) applies or a REIT to which section 857(b) applies, the taxpayer's ATI for the taxable year is increased by the amounts of any deductions described in section 852(b)(2)(C) or 857(b)(2)(A), taking into account § 1.163(j)-1(b)(37)(ii).

(5) *Application to tax-exempt corporations.*—The rules in this paragraph (b) apply to a corporation that is subject to the unrelated business income tax under section 511 only with respect to that corporation's items of income, gain, deduction, or loss that are taken into account in computing the corporation's unrelated business taxable income, as defined in section 512.

(6) *Examples.*—The principles of this paragraph (b) are illustrated by the following examples. For purposes of the examples in this paragraph (b)(6), T is a taxable domestic C corporation whose taxable year ends on December 31; T is neither a consolidated group member nor a RIC or a REIT; neither T nor PS1, a domestic partnership, owns at least 80 percent of the stock of any corporation; neither T nor PS1 qualifies for the small business exemption in § 1.163(j)-2(d) or is engaged in an excepted trade or business; T has no floor plan financing expense; all interest expense is deductible except for the potential application of section 163(j); and the facts set forth the only corporate or partnership activity.

(i) *Example 1: C corporation items properly allocable to a trade or business*—(A) *Facts.* In taxable year 2019, T's taxable income (without regard to the application of section 163(j)) is $320x. This amount is comprised of the following tax items: $1,000x of revenue from inventory sales; $500x of ordinary and necessary business expenses (excluding interest and depreciation); $200x of interest expense; $50x of interest income; $50x of depreciation deductions under section 168; and a $20x gain on the sale of stock.

(B) *Analysis.* For purposes of section 163(j), each of T's tax items is treated as properly allocable to a trade or business. Thus, T's ATI for the 2019 taxable year is $520x ($320x of taxable income + $200x business interest expense - $50x business interest income + $50x depreciation deductions = $520x), and its section 163(j) limitation for the 2019 taxable year is $206x ($50x of business interest income + 30 percent of its ATI (30 percent x $520x) = $206x). As a result, all $200x of T's interest expense is deductible in the 2019 taxable year under section 163(j).

(C) *Taxable year beginning in 2022.* The facts are the same as in *Example 1* in paragraph (b)(6)(i)(A) of this section, except that the taxable year is 2022 and therefore depreciation deductions are not added back to ATI under § 1.163(j)-1(b)(1)(i)(E). As a result, T's ATI for 2022 is $470x ($320x of taxable income + $200x business interest expense - $50x business interest income = $470x), and its section 163(j) limitation for the 2022 taxable year is $191x ($50x of business interest income + 30 percent of its ATI (30 percent x $470x) = $191x). As a result, T may only deduct $191x of its business interest expense for the taxable year, and the remaining $9x will be carried forward to the 2023 taxable year as a disallowed business interest expense carryforward. See § 1.163(j)-2(c).

(ii) *Example 2: C corporation partner*—(A) *Facts*. T and individual A each own a 50 percent interest in PS1, a general partnership. PS1 borrows funds from a third party (Loan 1) and uses those funds to buy stock in publicly-traded corporation X. PS1's only activities are holding X stock (and receiving dividends) and making payments on Loan 1. In the 2019 taxable year, PS1 receives $150x in dividends and pays $100x in interest on Loan 1.

(B) *Analysis*. For purposes of section 163(d) and (j), PS1 has investment interest expense of $100x and investment income of $150x, and PS1 has no interest expense or interest income that is properly allocable to a trade or business. PS1 allocates its investment interest expense and investment income to its two partners pursuant to § 1.163(j)-6(j). Pursuant to paragraph (b)(3) of this section, T's allocable share of PS1's investment interest expense is treated as a business interest expense of T, and T's allocable share of PS1's investment income is treated as properly allocable to a trade or business of T. This business interest expense is not treated as excess business interest expense, and this income is not treated as excess taxable income. See paragraph (b)(3)(iii) of this section. T's treatment of its allocable share of PS1's investment interest expense and investment income as business interest expense and income properly allocable to a trade or business, respectively, does not affect the character of these items at the PS1 level and does not affect the character of A's allocable share of PS1's investment interest and investment income.

(C) *Partnership engaged in a trade or business*. The facts are the same as in *Example 2* in paragraph (b)(6)(ii)(A) of this section, except that PS1 also is engaged in Business 1, and PS1 borrows funds from a third party to finance Business 1 (Loan 2). In 2019, Business 1 earns $150x of net income (excluding interest expense and depreciation), and PS1 pays $100x of interest on Loan 2. For purposes of § 1.163-8T, the interest paid on Loan 2 is allocated to a trade or business (and is therefore not treated as investment interest expense under section 163(d)). As a result, PS1 has investment interest expense of $100x (attributable to Loan 1), business interest expense of $100x (attributable to Loan 2), $150x of investment income, and $150x of income from Business 1. PS1's ATI is $150x (its net income from Business 1 excluding interest and depreciation), and its section 163(j) limitation is $45x (30 percent x $150x). Pursuant to § 1.163(j)-6, PS1 has $55x of excess business interest expense ($100x - $45x), half of which ($27.5x) is allocable to T. Additionally, pursuant to paragraph (b)(3)(i) of this section, T's allocable share of PS1's investment interest expense ($50x) is treated as a business interest expense of T for purposes of section 163(j), and T's allocable share of PS1's investment income ($75x) is treated as properly allocable to a trade or business of T. Therefore, with respect to T's interest in PS1, T is treated as having $50x of business interest expense that is not treated as excess business interest expense, $75x of income that is properly allocable to a trade or business, and $27.5x of excess business interest expense.

(c) *Effect on earnings and profits*.—(1) *In general*.—In the case of a taxpayer that is a C corporation, except as otherwise provided in paragraph (c)(2) of this section, the disallowance and carryforward of a deduction for the taxpayer's business interest expense under § 1.163(j)-2 will not affect whether or when the business interest expense reduces the taxpayer's earnings and profits.

(2) *Special rule for RICs and REITs*.—In the case of a taxpayer that is a RIC or a REIT for the taxable year in which a deduction for the taxpayer's business interest expense is disallowed under § 1.163(j)-2(b), or in which the RIC or REIT is allocated any excess business interest expense from a partnership under section 163(j)(4)(B)(i) and § 1.163(j)-6, the taxpayer's earnings and profits are adjusted in the taxable year or years in which the business interest expense is deductible or, if earlier, in the first taxable year for which the taxpayer no longer is a RIC or a REIT.

(3) *Special rule for partners that are C corporations*.—If a taxpayer that is a C corporation is allocated any excess business interest expense from a partnership under section 163(j)(4)(B)(i) and § 1.163(j)-6, and if any amount of the excess business interest expense has not yet been treated as business interest expense by the taxpayer at the time of the taxpayer's disposition of all or substantially all of its interest in the partnership, then the taxpayer must increase its earnings and profits by that amount immediately prior to its disposition of the partnership interest.

(4) *Examples*.—The principles of this paragraph (c) are illustrated by the following examples. For purposes of the examples in this paragraph (c)(4), except as otherwise provided in the examples, X is a taxable domestic C corporation whose taxable year ends on December 31; X is not a member of a consolidated group; X does not qualify for the small business exemption under § 1.163(j)-2(d); X is not engaged in an excepted trade or business; X has no floor plan financing indebtedness; all interest expense is deductible except for the potential application of section 163(j); X has no accumulated earnings and profits at the beginning of the 2019 taxable year; and the facts set forth the only corporate activity.

(i) *Example 1: Earnings and profits of a taxable domestic C corporation other than a RIC or a REIT*—(A) *Facts*. X is a corporation that does not intend to qualify as a RIC or a REIT for its 2019 taxable year. In that year, X has taxable income (without regard to the application of section 163(j)) of $0, which includes $100x of gross income and $100x of interest expense on a loan from an unrelated third party. X also makes a $100x distribution to its shareholders that year.

(B) *Analysis*. The $100x of interest expense is business interest expense for purposes of section 163(j) (see paragraph (b)(1) of this section). X's ATI in the 2019 taxable year is $100x ($0 of taxable income computed without regard to $100x of business interest expense). Thus, X may deduct $30x of its $100x of business interest expense in the 2019 taxable year under

§ 1.163(j)-2(b) (30 percent x $100x), and X may carry forward the remainder ($70x) to X's 2020 taxable year as a disallowed business interest expense carryforward under § 1.163(j)-2(c). Although X may not currently deduct all $100x of its business interest expense in the 2019 taxable year, X must reduce its earnings and profits in that taxable year by the full amount of its business interest expense ($100x) in that taxable year. As a result, no portion of X's distribution of $100x to its shareholders in the 2019 taxable year is a dividend within the meaning of section 316(a).

(ii) *Example 2: RIC adjusted taxable income and earnings and profits*—(A) *Facts.* X is a corporation that intends to qualify as a RIC for its 2019 taxable year. In that taxable year, X's only items are $100x of interest income, $50x of dividend income from C corporations that only issue common stock and in which X has less than a twenty percent interest (by vote and value), $10x of net capital gain, and $125x of interest expense. None of the dividends are received on debt financed portfolio stock under section 246A. The DRD determined under section 243(a) with respect to X's $50x of dividend income is $25x. X pays $42x in dividends to its shareholders, meeting the requirements of section 562 during X's 2019 taxable year, including $10x that X reports as capital gain dividends in written statements furnished to X's shareholders.

(B) *Analysis.* (*1*) Under paragraph (b) of this section, all of X's interest expense is considered business interest expense, all of X's interest income is considered business interest income, and all of X's other income is considered to be properly allocable to a trade or business. Under paragraph (b)(4)(ii) of this section, prior to the application of section 163(j), X's taxable income is $10x ($100x business interest income + $50x dividend income + $10x net capital gain - $125x business interest expense - $25x DRD = $10x). Under paragraph (b)(4)(iii) of this section, X's ATI is increased by the DRD. As such, X's ATI for the 2019 taxable year is $60x ($10x taxable income + $125x business interest expense - $100x business interest income + $25x DRD = $60x).

(*2*) X may deduct $118x of its $125x of business interest expense in the 2019 taxable year under section 163(j)(1) ($100x business interest income + (30 percent x $60x of ATI) = $118x), and X may carry forward the remainder ($7x) to X's taxable year ending December 31, 2020. See § 1.163(j)-2(b) and (c).

(*3*) After the application of section 163(j), X has taxable income of $17x ($100x interest income + $50x dividend income + $10x capital gain - $25x DRD - $118x allowable interest expense = $17x) for the 2019 taxable year. X will have investment company taxable income (ICTI) in the amount of $0 ($17x taxable income - $10x capital gain + $25x DRD - $32x dividends paid deduction for ordinary dividends = 0). The excess of X's net capital gain ($10x) over X's dividends paid deduction determined with reference to capital gain dividends ($10x) is also $0.

(*4*) Under paragraph (c)(2) of this section, X will not reduce its earnings and profits by the amount of interest expense disallowed as a deduction in the 2019 taxable year under section 163(j). Thus, X has current earnings and profits in the amount of $42x ($100x interest income + $50x dividend income + $10x capital gain - $118x allowable business interest expense = $42x) before giving effect to dividends paid during the 2019 taxable year.

(iii) *Example 3: Carryforward of disallowed interest expense*—(A) *Facts.* The facts are the same as the facts in *Example 2* in paragraph (c)(4)(ii)(A) of this section for the 2019 taxable year. In addition, X has $50x of interest income and $20x of interest expense for the 2020 taxable year.

(B) *Analysis.* Under paragraph (b) of this section, all of X's interest expense is considered business interest expense, all of X's interest income is considered business interest income, and all of X's other income is considered to be properly allocable to a trade or business. Because X's $50x of business interest income exceeds the $20x of business interest expense from the 2020 taxable year and the $7x of disallowed business interest expense carryforward from the 2019 taxable year, X may deduct $27x of business interest expense in the 2020 taxable year. Under paragraph (c)(2) of this section, X must reduce its current earnings and profits for the 2020 taxable year by the full amount of the deductible business interest expense ($27x).

(iv) *Example 4: REIT adjusted taxable income and earnings and profits*—(A) *Facts.* X is a corporation that intends to qualify as a REIT for its 2019 taxable year. X is not engaged in an excepted trade or business and is not engaged in a trade or business that is eligible to make any election under section 163(j)(7). In that year, X's only items are $100x of mortgage interest income, $30x of dividend income from C corporations that only issue common stock and in which X has less than a ten percent interest (by vote and value) in each C corporation, $10x of net capital gain from the sale of mortgages on real property that is not property described in section 1221(a)(1), and $125x of interest expense. None of the dividends are received on debt financed portfolio stock under section 246A. The DRD determined under section 243(a) with respect to X's $30x of dividend income is $15x. X pays $28x in dividends meeting the requirements of section 562 during X's 2019 taxable year, including $10x that X properly designates as capital gain dividends under section 857(b)(3)(B).

(B) *Analysis.* (*1*) Under paragraph (b) of this section, all of X's interest expense is considered business interest expense, all of X's interest income is considered business interest income, and all of X's other income is considered to be properly allocable to a trade or business. Under paragraph (b)(4)(ii) of this section, prior to the application of section 163(j), X's taxable income is $0 ($100x business interest income + $30x dividend income + $10x net capital gain - $125x business interest expense - $15x DRD = $0). Under paragraph (b)(4)(iii) of this section, X's ATI is increased by the DRD. As such, X's ATI for the 2019 taxable year is $40x ($0 taxable income + $125x business interest expense - $100x business interest income + $15x DRD = $40x).

(*2*) X may deduct $112x of its $125x of business interest expense in the 2019 taxable year under section 163(j)(1) ($100x business interest income + (30 percent x $40x of ATI) = $112x), and X may carry forward the remainder of its business interest expense ($13x) to X's 2020 taxable year.

(*3*) After the application of section 163(j), X has taxable income of $13x ($100x business interest income + $30x dividend income + $10x capital gain - $15x DRD - $112x allowable business interest expense = $13x) for the 2019 taxable year. X will have real estate investment trust taxable income (REITTI) in the amount of $0 ($13x taxable income + $15x of DRD - $28x dividends paid deduction = $0).

(4) Under paragraph (c)(2) of this section, X will not reduce earnings and profits by the amount of business interest expense disallowed as a deduction in the 2019 taxable year. Thus, X has current earnings and profits in the amount of $28x ($100x business interest income + $30x dividend income + $10x capital gain - $112x allowable business interest expense = $28x) before giving effect to dividends paid during X's 2019 taxable year.

(v) *Example 5: Carryforward of disallowed interest expense*—(A) *Facts*. The facts are the same as in *Example 4* in paragraph (c)(4)(iv)(A) of this section for the 2019 taxable year. In addition, X has $50x of mortgage interest income and $20x of interest expense for the 2020 taxable year. X has no other tax items for the 2020 taxable year.

(B) *Analysis*. Because X's $50x of business interest income exceeds the $20x of business interest expense from the 2020 taxable year and the $13x of disallowed business interest expense carryforwards from the 2019 taxable year, X may deduct $33x of business interest expense in 2020. Under paragraph (c)(2) of this section, X must reduce its current earnings and profits for 2020 by the full amount of the deductible interest expense ($33x).

(d) *Special rules for consolidated groups*.—(1) *Scope*.—This paragraph (d) provides certain rules applicable to members of a consolidated group. For all members of a consolidated group for a consolidated return year, the computations required by section 163(j) and the section 163(j) regulations are made in accordance with the rules of this paragraph (d) unless otherwise provided elsewhere in the section 163(j) regulations. For rules governing the carryforward of disallowed business interest expense, including rules governing the treatment of disallowed business interest expense carryforwards when members enter or leave a group, see § 1.163(j)-5.

(2) *Calculation of the section 163(j) limitation for members of a consolidated group*.—(i) *In general*.—A consolidated group has a single section 163(j) limitation, the absorption of which is governed by § 1.163(j)-5(b)(3)(ii).

(ii) *Interest*.—For purposes of determining whether amounts, other than amounts in respect of intercompany obligations, as defined in § 1.1502-13(g)(2)(ii), intercompany items, as defined in § 1.1502-13(b)(2), or corresponding items, as defined in § 1.1502-13(b)(3), are treated as interest within the meaning of § 1.163(j)-1(b)(20), all members of a consolidated group are treated as a single taxpayer.

(iii) *Calculation of business interest expense and business interest income for a consolidated group*.—For purposes of calculating the section 163(j) limitation for a consolidated group, the consolidated group's current-year business interest expense (as defined in § 1.163(j)-5(a)(2)(i)) and business interest income, respectively, are the sum of each member's current-year business interest expense and business interest income, including amounts treated as business interest expense and business interest income under paragraph (b)(3) of this section.

(iv) *Calculation of adjusted taxable income*.—For purposes of calculating the ATI for a consolidated group, the relevant taxable income is the consolidated group's consolidated taxable income, determined under § 1.1502-11 without regard to any carryforwards or disallowances under section 163(j). Additionally, if for a taxable year a member of a consolidated group is allowed a deduction under section 250(a)(1) that is properly allocable to a non-excepted trade or business, then, for purposes of calculating ATI, consolidated taxable income for the taxable year is determined as if the deduction were not subject to the limitation in section 250(a)(2). For this purpose, the amount of the deduction allowed under section 250(a)(1) is determined without regard to the application of section 163(j) and the section 163(j) regulations. Further, for purposes of calculating the ATI of the group, intercompany items and corresponding items are disregarded to the extent that they offset in amount. Thus, for example, certain portions of the intercompany items and corresponding items of a group member engaged in a non-excepted trade or business will not be included in ATI to the extent that the counterparties to the relevant intercompany transactions are engaged in one or more excepted trades or businesses.

(v) *Treatment of intercompany obligations*.—For purposes of determining a member's business interest expense and business interest income, and for purposes of calculating the consolidated group's ATI, all intercompany obligations, as defined in § 1.1502-13(g)(2)(ii), are disregarded. Therefore, interest expense and interest income from intercompany obligations are not treated as business interest expense and business interest income.

(3) *Investment adjustments*.—For rules governing investment adjustments within a consolidated group, see § 1.1502-32(b).

(4) *Ownership of partnership interests by members of a consolidated group*.—(i) *Dispositions of partnership interests*.—The transfer of a partnership interest in an intercompany transaction that does not result in the termination of the partnership is treated as a disposition for purposes of the basis adjustment rule in section 163(j)(4)(B)(iii)(II), regardless of whether the transfer is one in which gain or loss is recognized. See § 1.1502-13 for rules applicable to the redetermination of attributes of group members. A change in status of a member (becoming or ceasing to be a member) is not treated as a disposition for purposes of section 163(j)(4)(B)(iii)(II).

(ii) *Basis adjustments under § 1.1502-32*.—A member's allocation of excess business interest expense from a partnership and the resulting decrease in basis in the partnership interest under section 163(j)(4)(B) is not a noncapital, nondeductible expense for purposes of § 1.1502-32(b)(3)(iii). Additionally, an increase in a member's basis in a partnership interest under section 163(j)(4)(B)(iii)(II) to reflect excess business interest expense not deducted by the consolidated group is not tax-exempt income for purposes of § 1.1502-32(b)(3)(ii). Investment adjustments are made under § 1.1502-32(b)(3)(i) when the excess business interest expense from the partnership is absorbed by the consolidated group. See § 1.1502-32(b).

(iii) [Reserved]

(5) *Examples*.—The principles of this paragraph (d) are illustrated by the following examples (see also § 1.1502-13(c)(7)(ii)(R) and (S)). For purposes of the examples in this paragraph (d)(5), S is a member of the calendar-year consolidated group of which P is the common parent; the P group does not qualify for the small business exemption in § 1.163(j)-2(d); no member of the P group is engaged in an excepted trade or business; all interest expense is deductible except for the potential application of section 163(j); and the facts set forth the only corporate activity.

(i) *Example 1: Calculation of the section 163(j) limitation*—(A) *Facts*. In the 2019 taxable year, P has $50x of separate taxable income after taking into account $65x of interest paid on a loan from a third party (without regard to any disallowance under section 163(j)) and $35x of depreciation deductions under section 168. In turn, S has $40x of separate taxable income in the 2019 taxable year after taking into account $10x of depreciation deductions under section 168. S has no interest expense in the 2019 taxable year. The P group's consolidated taxable income for the 2019 taxable year is $90x, determined under § 1.1502-11 without regard to any disallowance under section 163(j).

(B) *Analysis*. As provided in paragraph (b)(1) of this section, P's interest expense is treated as business interest expense for purposes of section 163(j). If P and S were to apply the section 163(j) limitation on a separate-entity basis, then P's ATI would be $150x ($50x + $65x + $35x = $150x), its section 163(j) limitation would be $45x (30 percent x $150x = $45x), and a deduction for $20x of its $65x of business interest expense would be disallowed in the 2019 taxable year under section 163(j). However, as provided in paragraph (d)(2) of this section, the P group computes a single section 163(j) limitation, and that computation begins with the P group's consolidated taxable income (as determined prior to the application of section 163(j)), or $90x. The P group's ATI is $200x ($50x + $40x + $65x + $35x + $10x = $200x). Thus, the P group's section 163(j) limitation for the 2019 taxable year is $60x (30 percent x $200x = $60x). As a result, all but $5x of the P group's business interest expense is deductible in the 2019 taxable year. P carries over the $5x of disallowed business interest expense to the succeeding taxable year.

(ii) *Example 2: Intercompany obligations*—(A) *Facts*. On January 1, 2019, G, a corporation unrelated to P and S, lends P $100x in exchange for a note that accrues interest at a 10 percent annual rate. A month later, P lends $100x to S in exchange for a note that accrues interest at a 12 percent annual rate. In 2019, P accrues and pays $10x of interest to G on P's note, and S accrues and pays $12x of interest to P on S's note. For that year, the P group's only other items of income, gain, deduction, and loss are $40x of income earned by S from the sale of inventory, and a $30x deductible expense arising from P's payment of tort liability claims.

(B) *Analysis*. As provided in paragraph (d)(2)(v) of this section, the intercompany obligation between P and S is disregarded in determining P and S's business interest expense and business interest income and in determining the P group's ATI. For purposes of section 163(j), P has $10x of business interest expense and a $30x deduction for the payment of tort liability claims, and S has $40x of income. The P group's ATI is $10x ($40x - $30x = $10x), and its section 163(j) limitation is $3x (30 percent x $10x = $3x). The P group may deduct $3x of its business interest expense in the 2019 taxable year. A deduction for P's remaining $7x of business interest expense is disallowed in the 2019 taxable year, and this amount is carried forward to the 2020 taxable year.

(e) *Cross-references*.—For rules governing the treatment of disallowed business interest expense carryforwards for C corporations, see § 1.163(j)-5. For rules governing the application of section 163(j) to a C corporation or a consolidated group engaged in both excepted and non-excepted trades or businesses, see § 1.163(j)-10.

(f) *Applicability date*.—The provisions of this section apply to taxable years ending after the date the Treasury decision adopting these regulations as final regulations is published in the **Federal Register**. However, taxpayers and their related parties, within the meaning of sections 267(b) and 707(b)(1), may apply the rules of this section to a taxable year beginning after December 31, 2017, so long as the taxpayers and their related parties consistently apply the rules of the section 163(j) regulations, and if applicable, §§ 1.263A-9, 1.381(c)(20)-1, 1.382-6, 1.383-1, 1.469-9, 1.882-5, 1.1502-13, 1.1502-21, 1.1502-36, 1.1502-79, 1.1502-91 through 1.1502-99 (to the extent they effectuate the rules of §§ 1.382-6 and 1.383-1), and 1.1504-4 to those taxable years. [Reg. § 1.163(j)-4.]

§ 1.163(j)-5. General rules governing disallowed business interest expense carryforwards for C corporations.—(a) *Scope and definitions*.—(1) *Scope*.—This section provides certain rules regarding disallowed business interest expense carryforwards for taxpayers that are C corporations, including members of a consolidated group. Paragraph (b) of this section provides rules regarding the treatment of disallowed business interest expense carryforwards. Paragraph (c) of this section provides cross-references to other rules regarding disallowed business interest expense carryforwards in transactions to which section 381(a) applies. Paragraph (d) of this section provides rules regarding limitations on disallowed business interest expense carryforwards from separate return limitation years (SRLYs). Paragraph (e) of this section provides cross-references to other rules regarding the application of section 382 to disallowed business interest expense carryforwards. Paragraph (f) of this section provides rules regarding the overlap of the SRLY limitation with section 382.

(2) *Definitions*.—(i) *Current-year business interest expense*.—The term *current-year business interest expense* means business interest expense (as defined in § 1.163(j)-1(b)(2)) that would be deductible in the current taxable year without regard to section 163(j) and that is not a disallowed business interest expense carryforward (as defined in § 1.163(j)-1(b)(9)) from a prior taxable year.

(ii) *Allocable share of the consolidated group's remaining section 163(j) limitation*.—The term *allocable share of the consolidated group's remaining section 163(j) limitation* means, with respect to any member of a consolidated group, the product of the consolidated group's remaining section 163(j) limitation and the member's remaining current-year interest ratio.

(iii) *Consolidated group's remaining section 163(j) limitation.*—The term *consolidated group's remaining section 163(j) limitation* means the amount of the consolidated group's section 163(j) limitation calculated pursuant to § 1.163(j)-4(d)(2), reduced by the amount of interest deducted by members of the consolidated group pursuant to paragraph (b)(3)(ii)(C)(2) of this section.

(iv) *Remaining current-year interest ratio.*—The term *remaining current-year interest ratio* means, with respect to any member of a consolidated group for a particular taxable year, the ratio of the remaining current-year business interest expense of the member after applying the rule in paragraph (b)(3)(ii)(C)(2) of this section, to the sum of the amounts of remaining current-year business interest expense for all members of the consolidated group after applying the rule in paragraph (b)(3)(ii)(C)(2) of this section.

(b) *Treatment of disallowed business interest expense carryforwards.*—(1) *In general.*—The amount of any business interest expense of a C corporation not allowed as a deduction for any taxable year as a result of the limitation under section 163(j)(1) and § 1.163(j)-2(b) is carried forward to the succeeding taxable year as a disallowed business interest expense carryforward under section 163(j)(2) and § 1.163(j)-2(c).

(2) *Deduction of business interest expense.*—For a taxpayer that is a C corporation, current-year business interest expense is deducted in the current taxable year before any disallowed business interest expense carryforwards from a prior taxable year are deducted in that year. Disallowed business interest expense carryforwards are deducted in the order of the taxable years in which they arose, beginning with the earliest taxable year, subject to certain limitations (for example, the limitation under section 382). For purposes of section 163(j), disallowed disqualified interest is treated as carried forward from the taxable year in which a deduction was disallowed under old section 163(j).

(3) *Consolidated groups.*—(i) *In general.*—A consolidated group's disallowed business interest expense carryforwards for the current consolidated return year (the current year) are the carryforwards from the group's prior consolidated return years plus any carryforwards from separate return years.

(ii) *Deduction of business interest expense.*—(A) *General rule.*—All current-year business interest expense of members of a consolidated group is deducted in the current year before any disallowed business interest expense carryforwards from prior taxable years are deducted in the current year. Disallowed business interest expense carryforwards from prior taxable years are deducted in the order of the taxable years in which they arose, beginning with the earliest taxable year, subject to the limitations described in this section.

(B) *Section 163(j) limitation is equal to or exceeds the current-year business interest expense and disallowed business interest expense carryforwards from prior taxable years.*—If a consolidated group's section 163(j) limitation for the current year is equal to or exceeds the aggregate amount of its members' current-year business interest expense and disallowed business interest expense carryforwards from prior taxable years that are available for deduction, then none of the current-year business interest expense or disallowed business interest expense carryforwards will be subject to disallowance in the current year under section 163(j). However, a deduction for the members' business interest expense may be subject to limitation under other provisions of the Code or the regulations promulgated thereunder (see, for example, paragraphs (c), (d), (e), and (f) of this section).

(C) *Current-year business interest expense and disallowed business interest expense carryforwards exceed section 163(j) limitation.*—If the aggregate amount of members' current-year business interest expense and disallowed business interest expense carryforwards from prior taxable years exceeds the consolidated group's section 163(j) limitation for the current year, then the following rules apply in the order provided.

(1) The group first determines whether its section 163(j) limitation for the current year equals or exceeds the aggregate amount of the members' current-year business interest expense.

(i) If the group's section 163(j) limitation for the current year equals or exceeds the aggregate amount of the members' current-year business interest expense, then no amount of the group's current-year business interest expense will be subject to disallowance in the current year under section 163(j). Once the group has taken into account its members' current-year business interest expense, the group applies the rules of paragraph (b)(3)(ii)(C)(*4*) of this section.

(ii) If the aggregate amount of members' current-year business interest expense exceeds the group's section 163(j) limitation for the current year, then the group applies the rule in paragraph (b)(3)(ii)(C)(*2*) of this section.

(2) If this paragraph (b)(3)(ii)(C)(*2*) applies (see paragraph (b)(3)(ii)(C)(*1*)(*ii*) of this section), then each member with current-year business interest expense and with current-year business interest income or floor plan financing interest deducts current-year business interest expense in an amount that does not exceed the sum of the member's business interest income and floor plan financing interest expense for the current year.

(3) After applying the rule in paragraph (b)(3)(ii)(C)(*2*) of this section, if the group has any section 163(j) limitation remaining for the current year, then each member with remaining current-year business interest expense deducts a portion of its expense based on its allocable share of the consolidated group's remaining section 163(j) limitation.

(4) If this paragraph (b)(3)(ii)(C)(*4*) applies (see paragraph (b)(3)(ii)(C)(*1*)(*i*) of this section), and if the group has any section 163(j) limitation remaining for the current year after applying the rules in paragraph (b)(3)(ii)(C)(*1*) of this section, then disallowed business interest expense carryforwards permitted to be deducted in the current year will be deducted in the order of the taxable years in which they arose, beginning with the earliest taxable year. Disallowed business interest expense carryforwards from taxable years ending on the same date that are available to offset consolidated taxable income for the current year generally will be deducted

on a pro rata basis, under the principles of paragraph (b)(3)(ii)(C)(*3*) of this section. For example, assume that P and S are the only members of a consolidated group with a section 163(j) limitation for the current year (Year 2) of $200x; the amount of current-year business interest expense deducted in Year 2 is $100x; and P and S, respectively, have $140x and $60x of disallowed business interest expense carryforwards from Year 1 that are not subject to limitation under paragraph (c), (d), or (e) of this section. Under these facts, P would be allowed to deduct $70x of its carryforwards from Year 1 ($100x x ($140x / ($60x + $140x)) = $70x), and S would be allowed to deduct $30x of its carryforwards from Year 1 ($100x x ($60x / ($60x + $140x)) = $30x). But see § 1.383-1(d)(1)(ii), providing that, if losses subject to and not subject to the section 382 limitation are carried from the same taxable year, losses subject to the limitation are deducted before losses not subject to the limitation.

(*5*) Each member with remaining business interest expense after applying the rules of this paragraph (b)(3)(ii), taking into account the limitations in paragraphs (c), (d), (e), and (f) of this section, will carry the expense forward to the succeeding taxable year as a disallowed business interest expense carryforward under section 163(j)(2) and § 1.163(j)-2(c).

(iii) *Departure from group*.—If a corporation ceases to be a member during a consolidated return year, the corporation's current-year business interest expense from the taxable period ending on the day of the corporation's change in status as a member, as well as the corporation's disallowed business interest expense carryforwards from prior taxable years that are available to offset consolidated taxable income in the consolidated return year, are first made available for deduction during that consolidated return year. See § 1.1502-76(b)(1)(i); see also § 1.1502-36(d) (regarding reductions of deferred deductions on the transfer of loss shares of subsidiary stock). Only the amount that is neither deducted by the group in that consolidated return year nor otherwise reduced under the Code or regulations may be carried to the corporation's first separate return year after its change in status.

(iv) *Example: Deduction of interest expense*—(A) *Facts*. (*1*) P wholly owns A, which is a member of the consolidated group of which P is the common parent. P and A each borrow money from Z, an unrelated third party. The business interest expense of P and A in Years 1, 2, and 3, and the P group's section 163(j) limitation for those years, are as follows:

Table 1 to paragraph (b)(3)(iv)(A)(*1*)

Year	P's business interest expense	A's business interest expense	P group's section 163(j) limitation
1	$150x	$50x	$100x
2	60x	90x	120x
3	25x	50x	185x

(*2*) P and A have neither business interest income nor floor plan financing interest expense in Years 1, 2, and 3. Additionally, the P group is neither eligible for the small business exemption in § 1.163(j)-2(d) nor engaged in an excepted trade or business within the meaning of § 1.163(j)-1(b)(38)(ii).

(B) *Analysis*—(*1*) *Year 1*. In Year 1, the aggregate amount of the P group members' current-year business interest expense ($150x + $50x) exceeds the P group's section 163(j) limitation ($100x). As a result, the rules of paragraph (b)(3)(ii)(C) of this section apply. Because the P group members' current-year business interest expense exceeds the group's section 163(j) limitation for Year 1, P and A must apply the rule in paragraph (b)(3)(ii)(C)(*2*) of this section. Pursuant to paragraph (b)(3)(ii)(C)(2) of this section, each of P and A must deduct its current-year business interest expense to the extent of its business interest income and floor plan financing interest expense. Neither P nor A has business interest income or floor plan financing interest expense in Year 1. Next, pursuant to paragraph (b)(3)(ii)(C)(*3*) of this section, each of P and A must deduct a portion of its current-year business interest expense based on its allocable share of the consolidated group's remaining section 163(j) limitation ($100x). P's allocable share is $75x ($100x x ($150x / $200x) = $75x), and A's allocable share is $25x ($100x x ($50x / $200x) = $25x). Accordingly, in Year 1, P deducts $75x of its current-year business interest expense, and A deducts $25x of its current-year business interest expense. P has a disallowed business interest expense carryforward from Year 1 of $75x ($150x - $75x = $75x), and A has a disallowed business interest expense carryforward from Year 1 of $25x ($50x - $25x = $25x).

(*2*) *Year 2*. In Year 2, the aggregate amount of the P group members' current-year business interest expense ($60x + $90x) and disallowed business interest expense carryforwards ($75x + $25x) exceeds the P group's section 163(j) limitation ($120x). As a result, the rules of paragraph (b)(3)(ii)(C) of this section apply. Because the P group members' current-year business interest expense exceeds the group's section 163(j) limitation for Year 2, P and A must apply the rule in paragraph (b)(3)(ii)(C)(*2*) of this section. Pursuant to paragraph (b)(3)(ii)(C)(2) of this section, each of P and A must deduct its current-year business interest expense to the extent of its business interest income and floor plan financing interest expense. Neither P nor A has business interest income or floor plan financing interest expense in Year 2. Next, pursuant to paragraph (b)(3)(ii)(C)(*3*) of this section, each of P and A must deduct a portion of its current-year business interest expense based on its allocable share of the consolidated group's remaining section 163(j) limitation ($120x). P's allocable share is $48x (($120x x ($60x / $150x)) = $48x), and A's allocable share is $72x (($120x x ($90x / $150x)) = $72x). Accordingly, in Year 2, P deducts $48x of current-year business interest expense, and A deducts $72x of current-year business interest expense. P has a disallowed business interest expense carryforward from Year 2 of $12x ($60x - $48x = $12x), and A has a disallowed business interest expense carryforward from Year 2 of $18x ($90x - $72x = $18x). Additionally, because the P group has no section 163(j) limitation remaining after deducting current-year business interest expense in Year 2, the full amount of P and A's disallowed business interest expense carryforwards from Year 1 ($75x and $25x, respectively) also are carried forward to Year 3. As a result, at the beginning of Year 3, P and A's respective disallowed business interest expense carryforwards are as follows:

Table 1 to paragraph (b)(3)(iv)(B)(2)

	Year 1 disallowed business interest expense carryforwards	Year 2 disallowed business interest expense carryforwards	Total disallowed business interest expense carryforwards
P	$75x	$12x	$87x
A	*25x*	*18x*	*43x*
Total	100x	30x	130x

(*3*) *Year 3.* In Year 3, the aggregate amount of the P group members' current-year business interest expense ($25x + $50x = $75x) and disallowed business interest expense carryforwards ($130x) exceeds the P group's section 163(j) limitation ($185x). As a result, the rules of paragraph (b)(3)(ii)(C) of this section apply. Because the P group's section 163(j) limitation for Year 3 equals or exceeds the P group members' current-year business interest expense, no amount of the members' current-year business interest expense will be subject to disallowance under section 163(j) (see paragraph (b)(3)(ii)(C)(*1*) of this section). After each of P and A deducts its current-year business interest expense, the P group has $110x of section 163(j) limitation remaining for Year 3 ($185x - $25x - $50x = $110x). Next, pursuant to paragraph (b)(3)(ii)(C)(*4*) of this section, $110x of disallowed business interest expense carryforwards are deducted on a pro rata basis, beginning with carryforwards from Year 1. Because the total amount of carryforwards from Year 1 ($100x) is less than the section 163(j) limitation remaining after the deduction of Year 3 business interest expense ($110x), all of the Year 1 carryforwards are deducted in Year 3. After current-year business interest expense and Year 1 carryforwards are deducted, the P group's remaining section 163(j) limitation in Year 3 is $10x. Because the Year 2 carryforwards ($30x) exceed the remaining section 163(j) limitation ($10x), under paragraph (b)(3)(ii)(C)(*4*) of this section, each of P and A will deduct a portion of its Year 2 carryforwards based on its allocable share of the consolidated group's remaining section 163(j) limitation. P's allocable share is $4x (($10x x ($12x / $30x)) = $4x), and A's allocable share is $6x (($10x x ($18x / $30x)) = $6x). Accordingly, P and A may deduct $4x and $6x, respectively, of their Year 2 carryforwards. For Year 4, P and A have $8x and $12x of disallowed business interest expense carryforwards from Year 2, respectively.

(c) *Disallowed business interest expense carryforwards in transactions to which section 381(a) applies.*—For rules governing the application of section 381(c)(20) to disallowed business interest expense carryforwards, including limitations on an acquiring corporation's use of the disallowed business interest expense carryforwards of the transferor or distributor corporation in the acquiring corporation's first taxable year ending after the date of distribution or transfer, see § 1.381(c)(20)-1.

(d) *Limitations on disallowed business interest expense carryforwards from separate return limitation years.*—(1) *General rule.*—Except as provided in paragraph (f) of this section (relating to an overlap with section 382), the disallowed business interest expense carryforwards of a member arising in a separate return limitation year (or SRLY (see § 1.1502-1(f))) that are included in the consolidated group's business interest expense deduction for any taxable year under paragraph (b) of this section may not exceed the group's section 163(j) limitation for that year, determined by reference only to the member's items of income, gain, deduction, and loss for that year (section 163(j) SRLY limitation). For purposes of this paragraph (d), the SRLY subgroup principles of § 1.1502-21(c)(2) apply with appropriate adjustments.

(2) *Deduction of disallowed business interest expense carryforwards arising in a SRLY.*—Notwithstanding paragraph (d)(1) of this section, disallowed business interest expense carryforwards of a member arising in a SRLY are available for deduction by the consolidated group in the current year only to the extent the group has any remaining section 163(j) limitation for the current year after the deduction of current-year business interest expense and disallowed business interest expense carryforwards from earlier taxable years that are permitted to be deducted in the current year (see paragraph (b)(3)(ii)(A) of this section), and only to the extent the section 163(j) SRLY limitation for the current year exceeds the amount of the member's business interest expense already deducted by the group in that year under paragraph (b)(3)(ii) of this section. SRLY-limited disallowed business interest expense carryforwards are deducted on a pro rata basis (under the principles of paragraph (b)(3)(ii)(C)(*3*) of this section) with non-SRLY limited disallowed business interest expense carryforwards from taxable years ending on the same date.

(3) *Examples.*—The principles of this paragraph (d) are illustrated by the following examples. For purposes of the examples in this paragraph (d)(3), unless otherwise stated, P, R, S, and T are taxable domestic C corporations that are not regulated investment companies (RICs) or real estate investment trusts (REITs) and that file their tax returns on a calendar-year basis; none of P, R, S, or T qualifies for the small business exemption under section 163(j)(3) or is engaged in an excepted trade or business; all interest expense is deductible except for the po-

tential application of section 163(j); and the facts set forth the only corporate activity.

(i) *Example 1: Determination of SRLY limitation*—(A) *Facts.* Individual A owns P. In 2019, A forms T, which pays or accrues a $100x business interest expense for which a deduction is disallowed under section 163(j) and that is carried forward to 2020. P does not pay or accrue business interest expense in 2019, and P has no disallowed business interest expense carryforwards from prior taxable years. At the close of 2019, P acquires all of the stock of T, which joins with P in filing a consolidated return beginning in 2020. Neither P nor T pays or accrues business interest expense in 2020, and the P group has a section 163(j) limitation of $300x in that year. This limitation would be $70x if determined by reference solely to T's items for 2020.

(B) *Analysis.* T's $100x of disallowed business interest expense carryforwards from 2019 arose in a SRLY. P's acquisition of T was not an ownership change as defined by section 382(g); thus, T's disallowed business interest expense carryforwards are subject to the SRLY limitation in paragraph (d)(1) of this section. The section 163(j) SRLY limitation for 2020 is the P group's section 163(j) limitation, determined by reference solely to T's items for 2020 ($70x). See paragraph (d)(1) of this section. Thus, $70x of T's disallowed business interest expense carryforwards are available to be deducted by the P group in 2020, and the remaining $30x of T's disallowed business interest expense carryforwards are carried forward to 2021.

(C) *Section 163(j) limitation of $0.* The facts are the same as in paragraph (A) of this *Example 1*, except that the section 163(j) SRLY limitation for 2020 (computed by reference solely to T's items for that year) is $0. Because the amount of T's disallowed business interest expense carryforwards that may be deducted by the P group in 2020 may not exceed the section 163(j) SRLY limitation for that year, none of T's carryforwards from 2019 may be deducted by the P group in 2020.

(ii) *Example 2: Deduction of disallowed business interest expense carryforwards arising in a SRLY*—(A) *Facts.* P and S are the only members of a consolidated group. P has neither current-year business interest expense nor disallowed business interest expense carryforwards. S has $100x of disallowed business interest expense carryforwards that arose in a SRLY and $150x of current-year business interest. The section 163(j) SRLY limitation for the current year (computed by reference solely to S's items for that year) is $200x. Assume that the P group's section 163(j) limitation for the current year would permit all of S's current-year business interest expense and disallowed business interest expense carryforwards to be deducted in the current year but for the rules of this paragraph (d).

(B) *Analysis.* Under paragraph (d)(1) of this section, the section 163(j) SRLY limitation for the current year of $200x (computed by reference solely to S's items for that year) exceeds the amount of S's business interest expense taken into account by the P group in the current year under paragraph (b)(3)(ii) of this section ($150x) by $50x. Thus, $50x of S's disallowed business interest expense carryforwards that arose in a SRLY may be taken into account by the P group in the current year.

(e) *Application of section 382.*—(1) *Pre-change loss.*—For rules governing the treatment of a disallowed business interest expense as a pre-change loss for purposes of section 382, see §§1.382-2(a) and 1.382-6. For rules governing the application of section 382 to disallowed disqualified interest carryforwards, see §1.163(j)-11(b)(4).

(2) *Loss corporation.*—For rules governing when a disallowed business interest expense causes a corporation to be a loss corporation within the meaning of section 382(k)(1), see §1.382-2(a). For the application of section 382 to disallowed disqualified interest carryforwards, see §1.163(j)-11(b)(4).

(3) *Ordering rules for utilization of pre-change losses and for absorption of the section 382 limitation.*—For ordering rules for the utilization of disallowed business interest expense, net operating losses, and other pre-change losses, and for the absorption of the section 382 limitation, see §1.383-1(d).

(4) *Disallowed business interest expense from the pre-change period in the year of a testing date.*—For rules governing the treatment of disallowed business interest expense from the pre-change period (within the meaning of §1.382-6(g)(2)) in the year of a testing date, see §1.382-2.

(f) *Overlap of SRLY limitation with section 382.*—The limitation provided in paragraph (d) of this section does not apply to disallowed business interest expense carryforwards when the application of paragraph (d) of this section results in an overlap with the application of section 382. For purposes of applying this paragraph (f), the principles of §1.1502-21(g) apply with appropriate adjustments.

(g) *Additional limitations.*—Additional rules provided under the Code or regulations also apply to limit the use of disallowed business interest expense carryforwards. For rules governing the relationship between section 163(j) and other provisions affecting the deductibility of interest, see §1.163(j)-3.

(h) *Applicability date.*—This section applies to taxable years ending after the date the Treasury decision adopting these regulations as final regulations is published in the **Federal Register**. However, taxpayers and their related parties, within the meaning of sections 267(b) and 707(b)(1), may apply the rules of this section to a taxable year beginning after December 31, 2017, so long as the taxpayers and their related parties consistently apply the rules of the section 163(j) regulations, and if applicable, §§1.263A-9, 1.381(c)(20)-1, 1.382-6, 1.383-1, 1.469-9, 1.882-5, 1.1502-13, 1.1502-21, 1.1502-36, 1.1502-79, 1.1502-91 through 1.1502-99 (to the extent they effectuate the rules of §§1.382-6 and 1.383-1), and 1.1504-4 to those taxable years. [Reg. §1.163(j)-5.]

§1.163(j)-6. Application of the business interest deduction limitation to partnerships and subchapter S corporations.—(a) *Overview.*—If a deduction for business interest expense of a partnership or S corporation is subject to limitation under section 163(j), section 163(j)(4) provides that the section 163(j) limitation applies at the partnership or S corporation level and any deduction for business interest expense within the meaning of section 163(j) is taken into account in determining the nonseparately stated taxable income or loss of the partnership or S corporation. Once a partnership or S corporation determines its business interest expense, business interest income, ATI, and floor plan financing interest expense, the partnership or S corporation calculates its section 163(j) limitation by applying the rules of §1.163(j)-2(b) and this section. Paragraph (b) of this section provides definitions used in this section. Paragraph (c) of this section provides rules regarding the character of a partnership's deductible business interest expense and excess business interest expense. Paragraph (d) of this section provides rules regarding the calculation of a partnership's ATI and floor plan financing interest expense. Paragraph (e) of this section provides rules regarding a partner's ATI and business interest income. Paragraph (f) of this section provides an eleven-step computation necessary for properly allocating a partnership's deductible business interest expense and section 163(j) excess items to its partners. Paragraph (g) of this section applies carryforward rules at the partner level if a partnership has excess business interest expense, as defined in §1.163(j)-1(b)(14). Paragraph (h) of this section provides basis adjustment rules and paragraph (j) of this section provides rules regarding investment items of a partnership. Paragraph (l) of this section provides rules regarding S corporations. Paragraph (m) of this section provides rules for partnerships and S corporations not subject to section 163(j). Paragraph (o) of this section provides examples illustrating the rules of this section. Paragraph (p) provides the applicability date of the rules in this section.

(b) *Definitions.*—In addition to the definitions contained in §1.163(j)-1, the following definitions apply for purposes of this section.

(1) *Section 163(j) items.*—The term *section 163(j) items* means the partnership or S corporation's business interest expense, business interest income, and items comprising ATI, as defined in §1.163(j)-1(b)(1).

(2) *Partner basis items.*—The term *partner basis items* means any items of income, gain, loss, or deduction resulting from either an adjustment to the basis of partnership property used in a non-excepted trade or business made pursuant to section 743(b) or the operation of section 704(c)(1)(C)(i) with respect to such property. Partner basis items also include section 743(b) basis adjustments used to increase or decrease a partner's share of partnership gain or loss on the sale of partnership property used in a non-excepted trade or business (as described in §1.743-1(j)(3)(i)) and amounts resulting from the operation of section 704(c)(1)(C)(i) used to decrease a partner's share of partnership gain or increase a partner's share of partnership loss on the sale of such property.

(3) *Remedial items.*—The term *remedial items* means any allocation to a partner of remedial items of income, gain, loss, or deduction pursuant to section 704(c) and §1.704-3(d).

(4) *Excess business interest income.*—The term *excess business interest income* means the amount by which a partnership's or S corporation's business interest income exceeds its business interest expense in a taxable year.

(5) *Deductible business interest expense.*—The term *deductible business interest expense* means the amount of a partnership's or S corporation's business interest expense that is deductible under section 163(j) in the current taxable year following the application of the limitation contained in §1.163(j)-2(b).

(6) *Section 163(j) excess items.*—The term *section 163(j) excess items* means the partnership's excess business interest expense, excess taxable income, and excess business interest income.

(7) *Non-excepted assets.*—The term *non-excepted assets* means assets from a trade or business other than assets from an excepted regulated utility trade or business, electing farming business, or electing real property trade or business, as such terms are defined in §1.163(j)-1.

(8) *Excepted assets.*—The term *excepted assets* means assets from an excepted regulated utility trade or business, electing farming business, or electing real property trade or business, as such terms are defined in §1.163(j)-1.

(c) *Character of business interest expense.*—If a partnership has deductible business interest expense, such deductible business interest expense is not subject to any additional application of section 163(j) at the partner-level because it is taken into account in determining the non-separately stated taxable income or loss of the partnership. For all other purposes of the Code, however, deductible business interest expense and excess business interest expense retain their character as business interest expense at the partner-level. For example, for purposes of section 469, such business interest expense retains its character as either passive or non-passive in the hands of the partner. Additionally, for purposes of section 469, deductible business interest expense and excess business interest expense from a partnership remain interest derived from a trade or business in the hands of a partner even if the partner does not materially participate in the partnership's trade or business activity. For additional rules regarding the interaction between sections 465, 469, and 163(j), see §1.163(j)-3.

(d) *Adjusted taxable income of the partnership.*—(1) *Modification of adjusted taxable income for partnerships.*—The ATI of the partnership generally is determined in accordance with §1.163(j)-1(b)(1). For purposes of computing the partnership's ATI, the taxable income of the partnership is determined under section 703(a) and includes any items described in section 703(a)(1) to the extent such items are otherwise included under §1.163(j)-1(b)(1).

(2) *Section 734(b), partner basis items, and remedial items.*—A partnership takes into account items resulting from adjustments made to the basis of its property pursuant to section 734(b) for purposes of calculating its ATI pursuant to §1.163(j)-1(b)(1). However, partner basis items and remedial items are not taken into account in determining a partnership's ATI under §1.163(j)-1(b)(1). Instead, partner basis items and remedial items are taken into account by the partner in determining the partner's ATI pursuant to §1.163(j)-1(b)(1). See *Example 8* in paragraph (o)(8) of this section.

(e) *Adjusted taxable income and business interest income of partners.*—(1) *Modification of adjusted taxable income for partners.*—The ATI of a partner in a partnership generally is determined in accordance with §1.163(j)-1(b)(1) without regard to such partner's distributive share of any items of income, gain, deduction, or loss of such partnership, and is increased by such partner's distributive share of such partnership's excess taxable income determined under paragraph (f) of this section. For rules regarding corporate partners, see § 1.163(j)-4(b)(3).

(2) *Partner basis items and remedial items.*—Partner basis items and remedial items are taken into account as items derived directly by the partner in determining the partner's ATI for purposes of the partner's section 163(j) limitation. If a partner is allocated remedial items, such partner's ATI is increased or decreased by the amount of such items. Additionally, to the extent a partner is allocated partner basis items, such partner's ATI is increased or decreased by the amount of such item. See *Example 8* in paragraph (o)(8) of this section.

(3) *Disposition of partnership interests.*—If a partner recognizes gain or loss upon the disposition of interests in a partnership, and the partnership in which the interest is being disposed owns only non-excepted trade or business assets, the gain or loss on the disposition of the partnership interest is included in the partner's ATI. For dispositions of interests in partnerships that own:

(i) Non-excepted assets and excepted assets; or

(ii) Investment assets; or

(iii) Both. See § 1.163(j)-10(b)(4)(ii).

(4) *Double counting of business interest income and floor plan financing interest expense prohibited.*—For purposes of calculating a partner's section 163(j) limitation, the partner does not include—

(i) Business interest income from a partnership that is subject to section 163(j) except to the extent it is allocated excess business interest income from that partnership pursuant to paragraph (f)(2) of this section; and

(ii) The partner's allocable share of the partnership's floor plan financing interest expense because such floor plan financing interest expense has already been taken into account by the partnership in determining its nonseparately stated taxable income or loss for purposes of section 163(j).

(f) *Allocation and determination of section 163(j) excess items made in the same manner as nonseparately stated taxable income or loss of the partnership.*—(1) *Overview.*—(i) *In general.*—The purpose of this section is to provide guidance regarding how a partnership must allocate its deductible business interest expense and section 163(j) excess items, if any, among its partners. For purposes of section 163(j)(4) and this section, allocations and determinations of deductible business interest expense and section 163(j) excess items are considered made in the same manner as the nonseparately stated taxable income or loss of the partnership if, and only if, such allocations and determinations are made in accordance with the eleven-step computation set forth in paragraphs (f)(2)(i) through (xi) of this section. A partnership first determines its section 163(j) limitation, total amount of deductible business interest expense, and section 163(j) excess items under paragraph (f)(2)(i) of this section. The partnership then applies paragraphs (f)(2)(ii) through (xi) of this section, in that order, to determine how those items of the partnership are allocated among its partners. At the conclusion of the eleven-step computation set forth in paragraphs (f)(2)(i) through (xi) of this section, the total amount of deductible business interest expense and section 163(j) excess items allocated to each partner will equal the partnership's total amount of deductible business interest expense and section 163(j) excess items.

(ii) *Relevance solely for purposes of section 163(j).*—No rule set forth in paragraph (f)(2) of this section prohibits a partnership from making an allocation to a partner of any item of partnership income, gain, loss, or deduction that is otherwise permitted under section 704 and the regulations thereunder. Accordingly, any calculations in paragraphs (f)(2)(i) through (xi) of this section are solely for the purpose of determining each partner's deductible business interest expense and section 163(j) excess items, and do not otherwise affect any other provision under the Code, such as section 704(b). Additionally, floor plan financing interest expense is not allocated in accordance with paragraph (f)(2) of this section. Instead, floor plan financing interest expense of a partnership is allocated to its partners under section 704(b) and is taken into account as a nonseparately stated item of loss for purposes of section 163(j).

(2) *Steps for allocating deductible business interest expense and section 163(j) excess items.*—(i) *Partnership-level calculation required by section 163(j)(4)(A).*—First, a partnership must determine its section 163(j) limitation pursuant to § 1.163(j)-2(b). This calculation determines a partnership's total amounts of excess business interest income, excess taxable income, excess business interest expense (that is, the partnership's section 163(j) excess items), and deductible business interest expense under section 163(j) for a taxable year.

(ii) *Determination of each partner's relevant section 163(j) items.*—Second, a partnership must determine each partner's allocable share of each section 163(j) item under section 704(b) and the regulations thereunder including any allocations under section 704(c), other than remedial items as defined in paragraph (b)(3) of this section. Only section 163(j) items that were actually taken into account in the partnership's section 163(j) calculation under paragraph (f)(2)(i) of this section are taken into account for purposes of this paragraph (f)(2)(ii). Partner basis items, allocations of investment income and expense, remedial items, and amounts determined for the partner under § 1.163(j)-8T are not taken into account for purposes of this paragraph (f)(2)(ii). For purposes of paragraphs (f)(2)(ii) through (xi) of this section, the term *allocable ATI* means a partner's distributive share of the partnership's ATI (i.e., a partner's distributive share of gross income and gain items comprising ATI less such partner's distributive share of gross loss and deduction items comprising ATI), the term *allocable business interest income* means a partner's distributive share of the partnership's business interest income, and the term *allocable business interest expense* means a partner's distributive share of the partnership's business interest expense that is not floor plan financing interest expense.

(iii) *Partner-level comparison of business interest income and business interest expense.*—Third, a partnership must compare each partner's allocable business interest income to such partner's allocable business interest expense. Paragraphs (f)(2)(iii) through (v) of this section determine how a partnership must allocate its excess business interest income among its partners, as well as the amount of each partner's allocable business interest expense that is not deductible business interest expense after taking the partnership's business interest income into account. To the extent a partner's allocable business interest income exceeds its allocable business interest expense, the partner has an *allocable business interest income excess*. The aggregate of all the partners' allocable business interest income excess amounts is the *total allocable business interest income excess*. To the extent a partner's allocable business interest expense exceeds its allocable business interest income, the partner has an *allocable business interest income deficit*. The aggregate of all the partners' allocable business interest income deficit amounts is the *total allocable business interest income deficit*. These amounts are required to perform calculations in paragraphs (f)(2)(iv) and (v) of this section, which appropriately reallocate allocable business interest income excess to partners with allocable business interest income deficits in order to reconcile the partner-level calculation under paragraph (f)(2)(iii) of this section with the partnership-level result under paragraph (f)(2)(i) of this section.

(iv) *Matching partnership and aggregate partner excess business interest income.*—Fourth, a partnership must determine each partner's final allocable business interest income excess. A partner's *final allocable business interest income excess* is determined by reducing, but not below zero, such partner's allocable business interest income excess (if any) by the partner's step four adjustment amount. A partner's *step four adjustment amount* is the product of the total allocable business interest income deficit and the ratio of such partner's allocable business interest income excess to the total allocable business interest income excess. The rules of this paragraph (f)(2)(iv) ensure that, following the application of paragraph (f)(2)(xi) of this section, the aggregate of all the partners' allocations of excess business interest income equals the total amount of the partnership's excess business interest income as determined in paragraph (f)(2)(i) of this section.

(v) *Remaining business interest expense determination.*—Fifth, a partnership must determine each partner's remaining business interest expense. A partner's *remaining business interest expense* is calculated by reducing, but not below zero, such partner's allocable business interest income deficit (if any) by such partner's step five adjustment amount. A partner's *step five adjustment amount* is the product of the total allocable business interest income excess and the ratio of such partner's allocable business interest income deficit to the total allocable business interest income deficit. Generally, a partner's remaining business interest expense is a partner's allocable business interest income deficit adjusted to reflect a reallocation of allocable business interest income excess from other partners. Determining a partner's remaining business interest expense is necessary to perform an ATI calculation that begins in paragraph (f)(2)(vii) of this section.

(vi) *Determination of final allocable ATI.*—Sixth, a partnership must determine each partner's final allocable ATI. Paragraphs (f)(2)(vi) through (x) of this section determine how a partnership must allocate its excess taxable income and excess business interest expense among its partners.

(A) *Positive allocable ATI.*—To the extent a partner's income and gain items comprising its allocable ATI exceed its deduction and loss items comprising its allocable ATI, the partner has *positive allocable ATI*. The aggregate of all the partners' positive allocable ATI amounts is the *total positive allocable ATI*.

(B) *Negative allocable ATI.*—To the extent a partner's deduction and loss items comprising its allocable ATI exceed its income and gain items comprising its allocable ATI, the partner has negative allocable ATI. The aggregate of all the partners' negative allocable ATI amounts is the *total negative allocable ATI*.

(C) *Final allocable ATI.*—Any partner with a negative allocable ATI, or an allocable ATI of $0, has a positive allocable ATI of $0. Any partner with a positive allocable ATI of $0 has a final allocable ATI of $0. The final allocable ATI of any partner with a positive allocable ATI greater than $0 is such partner's positive allocable ATI reduced, but not below zero, by the partner's step six adjustment amount. A partner's *step six adjustment amount* is the product of the total negative allocable ATI and the ratio of such partner's positive allocable ATI to the total positive allocable ATI. The total of the partners' final allocable ATI amounts must equal the partnership's ATI amount used to compute its section 163(j) limitation pursuant to § 1.163(j)-2(b).

(vii) *Partner-level comparison of thirty percent of adjusted taxable income and remaining business interest expense.*—Seventh, a partnership must compare each partner's ATI capacity to such partner's remaining business interest expense as determined under paragraph (f)(2)(v) of this section. A partner's *ATI capacity* is the amount that is thirty percent of such partner's final allocable ATI as determined under paragraph (f)(2)(vi) of this section. A partner's final allocable ATI is grossed down to thirty percent prior to being compared to its remaining business interest expense in this calculation to parallel the partnership's adjustment to its ATI under section 163(j)(1)(B). To the extent a partner's ATI capacity exceeds its remaining business interest expense, the partner has an *ATI capacity excess*. The aggregate of all the partners' ATI capacity excess amounts is the *total ATI capacity excess*. To the extent a partner's remaining business interest expense exceeds its ATI capacity, the partner has an *ATI capacity deficit*. The aggregate of all the partners' ATI capacity deficit amounts is the *total ATI capacity deficit*. These amounts (which may be subject to adjustment under paragraph (f)(2)(viii) of this section) are required to perform calculations in paragraphs (f)(2)(ix) and (x) of this section, which appropriately reallocate ATI capacity excess to partners with ATI capacity deficits in order to reconcile the partner-level calculation under paragraph (f)(2)(vii) of this section with the partnership-level result under paragraph (f)(2)(i) of this section.

(viii) *Partner priority right to ATI capacity excess determination.*—(A) Eighth, the partnership must determine whether it is required to make any adjustments described in this paragraph (f)(2)(viii) and, if it is, make such adjustments. The rules of this paragraph (f)(2)(viii) are necessary to account for adjustments made to a partner's allocable ATI in paragraph (f)(2)(vi) of this section to ensure that the partners who had a negative allocable ATI do not inappropriately benefit under the rules of paragraphs (f)(2)(ix) through (xi) of this section to the detriment of the partners who had positive allocable ATI. The partnership must perform the calculations and make the necessary adjustments described under paragraphs (f)(2)(viii)(B) and (C) or paragraph (f)(2)(viii)(D) of this section if, and only if, there is—

(1) An excess business interest expense amount greater than $0 under paragraph (f)(2)(i) of this section;

(2) A total negative allocable ATI amount greater than $0 under paragraph (f)(2)(vi) of this section; and

(3) A total ATI capacity excess amount greater than $0 under paragraph (f)(2)(vii) of this section.

(B) A partnership must determine each partner's priority amount and usable priority amount. A partner's *priority amount* is thirty percent of the amount by which a partner's positive allocable ATI under paragraph (f)(2)(vi)(A) of this section exceeds such partner's final allocable ATI under paragraph (f)(2)(vi)(C) of this section. However, only partners with an ATI capacity deficit as determined under paragraph (f)(2)(vii) of this section can have a priority amount greater than $0. The aggregate of all the partners' priority amounts is the *total priority amount*. A partner's *usable priority amount* is the lesser of such partner's priority amount and such partner's ATI capacity deficit as determined under paragraph (f)(2)(vii) of this section. The aggregate of all the partners' usable priority amounts is the *total usable priority amount*. If the total ATI capacity excess amount, as determined under paragraph (f)(2)(vii) of this section, is greater than or equal to the total usable priority amount, then the partnership must perform the adjustments described in paragraph (f)(2)(viii)(C) of this section. If the total usable priority amount is greater than the total ATI capacity excess amount, as determined under paragraph (f)(2)(vii) of this section, then the partnership must perform the adjustments described in paragraph (f)(2)(viii)(D) of this section.

(C) For purposes of paragraph (f)(2)(ix) of this section, each partner's final ATI capacity excess amount is $0. For purposes of paragraph (f)(2)(x) of this section, the following terms have the following meanings for each partner:

(1) Each partner's *ATI capacity deficit* is such partner's ATI capacity deficit as determined under paragraph (f)(2)(vii) of this section reduced by such partner's usable priority amount.

(2) The *total ATI capacity deficit* is the total ATI capacity deficit as determined under paragraph (f)(2)(vii) of this section reduced by the total usable priority amount.

(3) The *total ATI capacity excess* is the total ATI capacity excess as determined under paragraph (f)(2)(vii) of this section reduced by the total usable priority amount.

(D) Any partner with a priority amount greater than $0 is a *priority partner*. Any partner that is not a priority partner is a *non-priority partner*. For purposes of paragraph (f)(2)(ix) of this section, each partner's final ATI capacity excess amount is $0. For purposes of paragraph (f)(2)(x) of this section, each non-priority partner's final ATI capacity deficit amount is such partner's ATI capacity deficit as determined under paragraph (f)(2)(vii) of this section. For purposes of paragraph (f)(2)(x) of this section, the following terms have the following meanings for priority partners.

(1) Each priority partner must determine its step eight excess share. A partner's *step eight excess share* is the product of the total ATI capacity excess as determined under paragraph (f)(2)(vii) of this section and the ratio of the partner's priority amount to the total priority amount.

(2) To the extent a priority partner's step eight excess share exceeds its ATI capacity deficit as determined under paragraph (f)(2)(vii) of this section, such excess amount is the priority partner's *ATI capacity excess* for purposes of paragraph (f)(2)(x) of this section. The *total ATI capacity excess* is the aggregate of the priority partners' ATI capacity excess amounts as determined under this paragraph (f)(2)(viii)(D)(*2*).

(3) To the extent a priority partner's ATI capacity deficit as determined under paragraph (f)(2)(vii) of this section exceeds its step eight excess share, such excess amount is the priority partner's *ATI capacity deficit* for purposes of paragraph (f)(2)(x) of this section. The *total ATI capacity deficit* is the aggregate of the priority partners' ATI capacity deficit amounts as determined under this paragraph (f)(2)(viii)(D)(*3*).

(ix) *Matching partnership and aggregate partner excess taxable income.*—Ninth, a partnership must determine each partner's final ATI capacity excess. A partner's *final ATI capacity excess* amount is determined by reducing, but not below zero, such partner's ATI capacity excess (if any) by the partner's step nine adjustment amount. A partner's *step nine adjustment amount* is the product of the total ATI capacity deficit and the ratio of such partner's ATI capacity excess to the total ATI capacity excess. The rules of this paragraph (f)(2)(ix) ensure that, following the application of paragraph (f)(2)(xi) of this section, the aggregate of all the partners' allocations of excess taxable income equals the total amount of the partnership's excess taxable income as determined in paragraph (f)(2)(i) of this section.

(x) *Matching partnership and aggregate partner excess business interest expense.*—Tenth, a partnership must determine each partner's final ATI capacity deficit. A partner's *final ATI capacity deficit* amount is determined by reducing, but not below zero, such partner's ATI capacity deficit (if any) by the partner's step ten adjustment amount. A partner's *step ten adjustment amount* is the product of the total ATI capacity excess and the ratio of such partner's ATI capacity deficit to the total ATI capacity deficit. Generally, a partner's final ATI capacity deficit is a partner's ATI capacity deficit adjusted to reflect a reallocation of ATI capacity excess from other partners. The rules of this paragraph (f)(2)(x) ensure that, following the application of paragraph (f)(2)(xi) of this section, the aggregate of all the partners' allocations of excess business interest expense equals the total amount of the partnership's excess business interest expense as determined in paragraph (f)(2)(i) of this section.

(xi) *Final section 163(j) excess item and deductible business interest expense allocation.*—Eleventh, a partnership must allocate section 163(j) excess items and deductible business interest expense to its partners. Excess business interest income calculated under paragraph (f)(2)(i) of this section, if any, is allocated dollar for dollar by the partnership to its partners with final allocable business interest income excess amounts. Excess business interest expense calculated under paragraph (f)(2)(i) of this section, if any, is allocated dollar for dollar to partners with final ATI capacity deficit amounts. After grossing up each partner's final ATI capacity excess amount by ten-thirds, excess taxable income calculated under paragraph (f)(2)(i) of this section, if any, is allocated dollar for dollar to partners with final ATI capacity excess amounts. A partner's allocable business interest expense is deductible business interest expense to the extent it exceeds such partner's share of excess business interest expense. See paragraphs (o)(11) through (15) of this section.

(g) *Carryforwards.*—(1) *In general.*—The amount of any business interest expense not allowed as a deduction to a partnership by reason of § 1.163(j)-2(b) and paragraph (f)(2) of this section for any taxable year is—

(i) Not treated as business interest expense of the partnership in the succeeding taxable year; and

(ii) Subject to paragraph (g)(2) of this section, treated as excess business interest expense which is allocated to each partner pursuant to paragraph (f)(2) of this section.

(2) *Treatment of excess business interest expense allocated to partners.*—If a partner is allocated excess business interest expense from a partnership under paragraph (f)(2) of this section for any taxable year —

(i) Solely for purposes of section 163(j), such excess business interest expense is treated as business interest expense paid or accrued by the partner in the next succeeding taxable year in which the partner is allocated excess taxable income or excess business interest income from such partnership, but only to the extent of such excess taxable income or excess business interest income; and

(ii) Any portion of such excess business interest expense remaining after the application of paragraph (g)(2)(i) of this section is excess business interest expense that is subject to the limitations of paragraph (g)(2)(i) of this section in succeeding years, unless paragraph (m)(3) of this section applies. See paragraphs (o)(1) through (10) of this section.

(3) *Excess taxable income and excess business interest income ordering rule.*—In the event a partner has excess business interest expense from a prior taxable year and is allocated excess taxable income or excess business interest income from the same partnership in a succeeding taxable year, the partner must treat, for purposes of section 163(j), the excess business interest expense as business interest expense paid or accrued by the partner in an amount equal to the partner's share of the partnership's excess taxable income or excess business interest income in such succeeding taxable year. See paragraphs (o)(2) through (10) of this section.

(h) *Basis adjustments.*—(1) *Section 704(d) ordering.*—Deductible business interest expense and excess business interest expense are subject to section 704(d). If a partner is subject to a limitation on loss under section 704(d) and a partner is allocated losses from a partnership in a taxable year, § 1.704-1(d)(2) requires that the limitation on losses under section 704(d) be apportioned amongst these losses based on the character of each loss (each grouping of loses based on character being a "section 704(d) loss class"). If there are multiple section 704(d) loss classes in a given year, § 1.704-1(d)(2) requires the partner to apportion the limitation on losses under section 704(d) to each section 704(d) loss class proportionately. For purposes of applying this proportionate rule, any deductible business interest expense (whether allocated to the partner in the current taxable year or suspended under section 704(d) in a prior taxable year), any excess business interest expense allocated to the partner in the current taxable year, and any excess business interest expense from a prior taxable year that was suspended under section 704(d) ("negative section 163(j) expense") shall comprise the same section 704(d) loss class. Once the partner determines the amount of limitation on losses apportioned to this section 704(d) loss class, any deductible business interest expense is taken into account before any excess business interest expense or negative section 163(j) expense. See paragraph (o)(9) of this section.

(2) *Excess business interest expense basis adjustments.*—The adjusted basis of a partner in a partnership interest is reduced, but not below zero, by the amount of excess business interest expense allocated to the partner pursuant to paragraph (f)(2) of this section. Negative section 163(j) expense is not treated as excess business interest expense in any subsequent year until such negative section 163(j) expense is no longer suspended under section 704(d). Therefore, negative section 163(j) expense does not affect, and is not affected by, any allocation of excess taxable income to the partner. Accordingly, any excess taxable income allocated to a partner from a partnership while the partner still has negative section 163(j) expense will be included in the partner's ATI. However, once the negative section 163(j) expense is no longer suspended under section 704(d), it becomes excess business interest expense, which is subject to the general rules in paragraph (g) of this section. See paragraph (o)(10) of this section.

(3) *Basis adjustments upon disposition of partnership interest.*—(i) *Complete disposition of partnership interest.*—If a partner disposes of all or substantially all of a partnership interest (whether by sale, exchange, or redemption), the adjusted basis of the partnership interest is increased immediately before the disposition by the amount of the excess (if any) of the amount of the basis reduction under paragraph (h)(2) of this section over the portion of any excess business interest expense allocated to the partner under paragraph (f)(2) of this section which has previously been treated under paragraph (g) of this section as business interest expense pair or accrued by the partner, regardless of whether the disposition was a result of a taxable or nontaxable transaction. Therefore, the adjusted basis of a partner in a partnership interest is not increased by any negative section 163(j) expense upon the disposition of a partnership interest. No deduction under section 163(j) is allowed to

the transferor or transferee under chapter 1 of subtitle A of the Code for any excess business interest expense resulting in a basis increase under this section or any negative section 163(j) expense.

(ii) *Partial disposition of partnership interest.*—If a partner disposes of less than substantially all of its interest in a partnership (whether by sale, exchange, or redemption), a partner shall not increase its basis in its partnership interest by the amount of any excess business interest expense that has not yet been treated as business interest expense paid or accrued by the partner in accordance with paragraph (g) of this section. Any such excess business interest expense shall remain excess business interest expense of the transferor partner until such time as the transferor partner is allocated an appropriate amount of excess taxable income or excess business interest income from the partnership or the partner disposes of its partnership interest in accordance with paragraph (h)(2)(i) of this section. Additionally, any negative section 163(j) expense shall remain negative section 163(j) expense of the transferor partner until such negative section 163(j) expense is no longer suspended under section 704(d).

(i) [Reserved]

(j) *Investment items.*—Any item of a partnership's income, gain, deduction, or loss that is investment interest income or expense pursuant to § 1.163-8T is allocated to each partner in accordance with section 704(b) and the regulations thereunder and the effect of such allocation for purposes of section 163 is determined at the partner-level. See § 1.163(j)-4(b)(3), section 163(d), and § 1.163-8T.

(k) [Reserved]

(l) *S corporations.*—(1) *In general.*—In the case of any S corporation, the section 163(j) limitation is applied at the S corporation level, and any deduction allowed for business interest expense is taken into account in determining the nonseparately stated taxable income or loss of the S corporation. An S corporation determines its section 163(j) limitation in the same manner as set forth in § 1.163(j)-2(b). Allocations of excess taxable income and excess business interest income are made in accordance with the shareholders' respective pro rata interests in the S corporation pursuant to section 1366(a)(1) after determining the S corporation's section 163(j) limitation pursuant to § 1.163(j)-2(b).

(2) *Character of deductible business interest expense.*—If an S corporation has deductible business interest expense, such deductible business interest expense is not subject to any additional application of section 163(j) at the shareholder-level because such deductible business interest expense is taken into account in determining the nonseparately stated taxable income or loss of the S corporation. For all other purposes of the Code, however, deductible business interest expense retains its character as business interest expense at the shareholder-level. For example, for purposes of section 469, such deductible business interest expense retains its character as either passive or non-passive in the hands of the shareholder. Additionally, for purposes of section 469, deductible business interest expense from an S corporation remains interest derived from a trade or business in the hands of a shareholder even if the shareholder does not materially participate in the S corporation's trade or business activity. For additional rules regarding the interaction between sections 465, 469, and 163(j), see § 1.163(j)-3.

(3) *Adjusted taxable income of an S corporation.*—The ATI of an S corporation generally is determined in accordance with § 1.163(j)-1(b)(1). For purposes of computing the S corporation's ATI, the taxable income of the S corporation is determined under section 1363(b) and includes—

(i) Any item described in section 1363(b)(1); and

(ii) Any item described in § 1.163(j)-1(b)(1), to the extent such item is consistent with subchapter S of the Code.

(4) *Adjusted taxable income and business interest income of S corporation shareholders.*—(i) *Adjusted taxable income of S corporation shareholders.*—The ATI of an S corporation shareholder is determined in accordance with § 1.163(j)-1(b)(1) without regard to such shareholder's distributive share of any items of income, gain, deduction, or loss of such S corporation, and is increased by such shareholder's distributive share of such S corporation's excess taxable income, as defined in § 1.163(j)-1(b)(15).

(ii) *Disposition of S corporation stock.*—If a shareholder of an S corporation recognizes gain or loss upon the disposition of stock of the S corporation, and the corporation in which the stock is being disposed only owns non-excepted trade or business assets, the gain or loss on the disposition of the stock is included in the shareholder's ATI. For dispositions of stock of S corporations that own:

(A) Non-excepted assets and excepted assets; or

(B) Investment assets; or

(C) Both. See § 1.163(j)-10(b)(4)(ii).

(iii) *Double counting of business interest income and floor plan financing interest expense prohibited.*—For purposes of calculating an S corporation shareholder's section 163(j) limitation, the shareholder does not include—

(A) Business interest income from an S corporation that is subject to section 163(j) except to the extent it is allocated excess business interest income from that S corporation pursuant to paragraph (l)(1) of this section; and

(B) The shareholder's share of the S corporation's floor plan financing interest expense because such floor plan financing interest expense has already been taken into account by the S corporation in determining its nonseparately stated taxable income or loss for purposes of section 163(j).

(5) *Carryforwards.*—The amount of any business interest expense not allowed as a deduction for any taxable year by reason of the limitation contained in § 1.163(j)-2(b) is carried forward in the succeeding taxable year as a disallowed business interest expense carryforward under the rules set forth in § 1.163(j)-2(c) (whether to an S corporation or C corporation taxable year). S corporations are subject to:

(i) The same ordering rules as a C corporation that is not a member of a consolidated group; and

(ii) The limitation under section 382. See § 1.163(j)-5(b)(2) and (e).

(6) *Basis adjustments and disallowed business interest expense carryforwards.*—An S corporation shareholder's adjusted basis in its S corporation stock is reduced, but not below zero, when a disallowed business interest expense carryforward becomes deductible under section 163(j).

(7) *Accumulated adjustment accounts.*—The accumulated adjustment account of an S corporation is adjusted to take into account business interest expense in the year in which the S corporation treats such business interest expense as deductible under the section 163(j) limitation. See section 1368(e)(1).

(8) *Termination of qualified subchapter S subsidiary election.*—If a corporation's qualified subchapter S subsidiary election terminates and any disallowed business interest expense carryforward is attributable to the activities of the qualified subchapter S subsidiary at the time of termination, such disallowed business interest expense carryforward remains with the parent S corporation and no portion of these items is allocable to the former qualified subchapter S subsidiary.

(9) *Investment items.*—Any item of an S corporation's income, gain, deduction, or loss that is investment interest income or expense pursuant to § 1.163-8T is allocated to each shareholder in accordance with the shareholders' pro rata interests in the S corporation pursuant to section 1366(a)(1). See section 163(d), § 1.163-8T.

(m) *Partnerships and S corporations not subject to section 163(j).*—(1) *Partnerships and S corporations not subject to section 163(j) by reason of the small business exemption.*—If a partnership or S corporation is not subject to section 163(j) by reason of § 1.163(j)-2(d) (exempt entity), the exempt entity does not calculate the section 163(j) limitation under § 1.163(j)-2 and these regulations. Because an exempt entity is not subject to section 163(j)(4), it does not take its deduction for business interest expense into account in determining its non-separately stated taxable income or loss within the meaning of section 163(j)(4)(A)(i) and retains its character as business interest expense. See § 1.163(j)-6(c). Thus, if a partner or S corporation shareholder is allocated business interest expense from an exempt entity, that allocated business interest expense will be subject to the partner's or S corporation shareholder's section 163(j) limitations. Additionally, contrary to the general rule in § 1.163(j)-6(e)(1), a partner or S corporation shareholder includes items of income, gain, loss, or deduction of such exempt entity when calculating its ATI. Finally, business interest income of such exempt entity is included in the partner's or S corporation shareholder's section 163(j) limitation regardless of the exempt entity's business interest expense amount.

(2) *Partnerships and S corporations not subject to section 163(j) by reason of an excepted trade or business.*—To the extent a partnership or S corporation is not subject to section 163(j) because it has an excepted trade or business as defined in § 1.163(j)-1(b)(38)(ii) (excepted entity), the entity does not apply its section 163(j) limitation under § 1.163(j)-2 and this section with respect to the business interest expense that is allocable to such excepted trade or business. If a partner or S corporation shareholder is allocated any section 163(j) item that is allocable to the partnership's or S corporation's excepted trade or business (excepted 163(j) items), such excepted 163(j) items are excluded from the partner or shareholder's section 163(j) deduction calculation. See § 1.163(j)-10(c) (regarding the allocation of items between excepted and non-excepted trades or businesses).

(3) *Partnerships that allocated excess business interest expense prior to becoming not subject to section 163(j).*—If a partnership allocates excess business interest expense to one or more of its partners, and in a succeeding taxable year becomes not subject to the requirements of section 163(j), the excess business interest expense from the prior taxable years is treated as paid or accrued by the partner in such succeeding taxable year. See paragraphs (o)(6) and (7) of this section.

(4) *S corporations with disallowed business interest expense carryforwards prior to becoming not subject to section 163(j).*—If an S corporation has a disallowed business interest expense carryforward for a taxable year, and in the succeeding taxable year becomes not subject to the requirements of section 163(j), then such disallowed business interest expense carryforward—

(i) Continues to be carried forward at the S corporation level;

(ii) Is no longer subject to the section 163(j) limitation; and

(iii) Is taken into account in determining the nonseparately stated taxable income or loss of the S corporation.

(n) [Reserved]

(o) *Examples.*—The examples in this paragraph illustrate the provisions of section 163(j) as applied to partnerships and subchapter S corporations. For purposes of these examples, each partnership is subject to the provisions of section 163(j), was created or organized in the United States, and is a calendar year taxpayer. Unless stated otherwise, all partners are subject to the provisions of section 163(j), are not subject to a limitation under section 704(d) or 1366(d), have no tax items other than those listed in the example, are U.S. citizens, and are calendar year taxpayers. The phrase "section 163(j) limit" shall equal the maximum potential deduction allowed under section 163(j)(1). Unless stated otherwise, business interest expense means business interest expense that is not floor plan financing interest expense. With respect to partnerships, all allocations are in accordance with section 704(b) and the regulations thereunder.

(1) *Example 1*—(i) *Facts.* X and Y are equal partners in partnership PRS. In Year 1, PRS has $100 of ATI and $40 of business interest expense. PRS allocates the items comprising its $100 of ATI $50 to X and $50 to Y. PRS allocates its $40 of business interest expense $20 to X and $20 to Y. X has $100 of ATI and $20 of business interest expense from its sole proprietorship. Y has $0 of ATI and $20 of business interest expense from its sole proprietorship.

(ii) *Partnership-level.* In Year 1, PRS's section 163(j) limit is 30 percent of its ATI, or $30 ($100 x 30 percent). Thus, PRS has $30 of deductible business interest expense and $10 of excess business interest expense. Such $30 of deductible business interest expense is includable in PRS's non-separately stated income or loss, and is not subject to further limitation under section 163(j) at the partners' level.

(iii) *Partner-level allocations.* Pursuant to § 1.163(j)-6(f)(2), X and Y are each allocated $15 of deductible business interest expense and $5 of excess business interest expense. At the end of Year 1, X and Y each have $5 of excess business interest expense from PRS, which is not treated as paid or accrued by the partner until such partner is allocated excess taxable income or excess business interest income from PRS in a succeeding taxable year. Pursuant to § 1.163(j)-6(e)(1), X and Y, in computing their limit under section 163(j), do not increase any of their section 163(j) items by any of PRS's section 163(j) items. X and Y each increase their outside basis in PRS by $30 ($50 - $20).

(iv) *Partner-level computations.* X, in computing its limit under section 163(j), has $100 of ATI and $20 of business interest expense from its sole proprietorship. X's section 163(j) limit is $30 ($100 x 30 percent). Thus, X's $20 of business interest expense is deductible business interest expense. Y, in computing its limit under section 163(j), has $20 of business interest expense from its sole proprietorship. Y's section 163(j) limit is $0 ($0 x 30 percent). Thus, Y's $20 of business interest expense is not allowed as a deduction and is treated as business interest expense paid or accrued by Y in Year 2.

(2) *Example 2*—(i) *Facts.* The facts are the same as in *Example 1* in paragraph (o)(1)(i) of this section. In Year 2, PRS has $200 of ATI, $0 of business interest income, and $30 of business interest expense. PRS allocates the items comprising its $200 of ATI $100 to X and $100 to Y. PRS allocates its $30 of business interest expense $15 to X and $15 to Y. X has $100 of ATI and $20 of business interest expense from its sole proprietorship. Y has $0 of ATI and $20 of business interest expense from its sole proprietorship.

(ii) *Partnership-level.* In Year 2, PRS's section 163(j) limit is 30 percent of its ATI plus its business interest income, or $60 ($200 x 30 percent). Thus, PRS has $100 of excess taxable income, $30 of deductible business interest expense, and $0 of excess business interest expense. Such $30 of deductible business interest expense is includable in PRS's non-separately stated income or loss, and is not subject to further limitation under section 163(j) at the partners' level.

(iii) *Partner-level allocations.* Pursuant to § 1.163(j)-6(f)(2), X and Y are each allocated $50 of excess taxable income, $15 of deductible business interest expense, and $0 of excess business interest expense. As a result, X and Y each increase their ATI by $50. Because X and Y are each allocated $50 of excess taxable income from PRS, and excess business interest expense from a partnership is treated as paid or accrued by a partner to the extent excess taxable income and excess business interest income are allocated from such partnership to a partner, X and Y each treat $5 of excess business interest expense (the carryforward from Year 1) as paid or accrued in Year 2. X and Y each increase their outside basis in PRS by $85 ($100 - $15).

(iv) *Partner-level computations.* X, in computing its limit under section 163(j), has $150 of ATI ($100 from its sole proprietorship, plus $50 excess taxable income) and $25 of business interest expense ($20 from its sole proprietorship, plus $5 excess business interest expense treated as paid or accrued in Year 2). X's section 163(j) limit is $45 ($150 x 30 percent). Thus, X's $25 of business interest expense is deductible business interest expense. At the end of Year 2, X has $0 of excess business interest expense from PRS ($5 from Year 1, less $5 treated as paid or accrued in Year 2). Y, in computing its limit under section 163(j), has $50 of ATI ($0 from its sole proprietorship, plus $50 excess taxable income) and $45 of business interest expense ($20 from its sole proprietorship, plus $20 disallowed business interest expense from Year 1, plus $5 excess business interest expense treated as paid or accrued in Year 2). Y's section 163(j) limit is $15 ($50 x 30 percent). Thus, $15 of Y's business interest expense is deductible business interest expense. The $30 of Y's business interest expense not allowed as a deduction ($45 business interest expense, less $15 section 163(j) limit) is treated as business interest expense paid or accrued by Y in Year 3. At the end of Year 2, Y has $0 of excess business interest expense from PRS ($5 from Year 1, less $5 treated as paid or accrued in Year 2).

(3) *Example 3*—(i) *Facts.* The facts are the same as in *Example 1* in paragraph (o)(1)(i) of this section. In Year 2, PRS has $0 of ATI, $60 of business interest income, and $40 of business interest expense. PRS allocates its $60 of business interest income $30 to X and $30 to Y. PRS allocates its $40 of business interest expense $20 to X and $20 to Y. X has $100 of ATI and $20 of business interest expense from its sole proprietorship. Y has $0 of ATI and $20 of business interest expense from its sole proprietorship.

(ii) *Partnership-level.* In Year 2, PRS's section 163(j) limit is 30 percent of its ATI plus its business interest income, or $60 (($0 x 30 percent) + $60). Thus, PRS has $20 of excess business interest income, $0 of excess taxable income, $40 of deductible business interest expense, and $0 of excess business interest expense. Such $40 of deductible business interest expense is includable in PRS's non-separately stated income or loss, and is not subject to further limitation under section 163(j) at the partners' level.

(iii) *Partner-level allocations.* Pursuant to § 1.163(j)-6(f)(2), X and Y are each allocated $10 of excess business interest income, and $20 of deductible business interest expense. As a result, X and Y each increase their business interest income by $10. Because X and Y are each allocated $10 of excess business interest income from PRS, and excess business interest expense from a partnership is treated as paid or accrued by a partner to the extent excess taxable income and excess business interest income are allocated from such partnership to a partner, X and Y each treat $5 of excess business interest expense (the carryforward from Year 1) as paid or accrued in Year 2. X and Y each increase their outside basis in PRS by $10 ($30 - $20).

(iv) *Partner-level computations.* X, in computing its limit under section 163(j), has $100 of ATI (from its sole proprietorship), $10 of business interest income (from the allocation of $10 of excess business interest income from PRS), and $25 of business interest expense ($20 from its sole proprietorship, plus $5 excess business interest expense treated as paid or accrued in Year 2). X's section 163(j) limit is $40 (($100 x 30 percent) + $10). Thus, X's $25 of business interest expense is deductible business interest expense. At the end of Year 2, X has $0 of excess business interest expense from PRS ($5 from Year 1, less $5 treated as paid or accrued in Year 2). Y, in computing its limit under section 163(j), has $0 of ATI (from its sole proprietorship), $10 of business interest income, and $45 of business interest expense ($20 from its sole proprietorship, plus $20 disallowed business interest expense from Year 1, plus $5 excess business interest expense treated as paid or accrued in Year 2). Y's section 163(j) limit is $10 (($0 x 30 percent) + $10). Thus, $10 of Y's business interest expense is deductible business interest expense. The $35 of Y's business interest expense not allowed as a deduction ($45 business interest expense, less $10 section 163(j) limit) is treated as business interest expense paid or accrued by Y in Year 3. At the end of Year 2, Y has $0 of excess business interest expense from PRS ($5 from Year 1, less $5 treated as paid or accrued in Year 2).

(4) *Example 4*—(i) *Facts*. The facts are the same as in *Example 1* in paragraph (o)(1)(i) of this section. In Year 2, PRS has $100 of ATI, $60 of business interest income, and $40 of business interest expense. PRS allocates the items comprising its $100 of ATI $50 to X and $50 to Y. PRS allocates its $60 of business interest income $30 to X and $30 to Y. PRS allocates its $40 of business interest expense $20 to X and $20 to Y. X has $100 of ATI and $20 of business interest expense from its sole proprietorship. Y has $0 of ATI and $20 of business interest expense from its sole proprietorship.

(ii) *Partnership-level*. In Year 2, PRS's section 163(j) limit is 30 percent of its ATI plus its business interest income, or $90 (($100 x 30 percent)) + $60). Thus, PRS has $20 of excess business interest income, $100 of excess taxable income, $40 of deductible business interest expense, and $0 of excess business interest expense. Such $40 of deductible business interest expense is includable in PRS's non-separately stated income or loss, and is not subject to further limitation under section 163(j) at the partners' level.

(iii) *Partner-level allocations*. Pursuant to § 1.163(j)-6(f)(2), X and Y are each allocated $10 of excess business interest income, $50 of excess taxable income, and $20 of deductible business interest expense. As a result, X and Y each increase their business interest income by $10 and ATI by $50. Because X and Y are each allocated $10 of excess business interest income and $50 of excess taxable income from PRS, and excess business interest expense from a partnership is treated as paid or accrued by a partner to the extent excess taxable income and excess business interest income are allocated from such partnership to a partner, X and Y each treat $5 of excess business interest expense (the carryforward from Year 1) as paid or accrued in Year 2. X and Y each increase their outside basis in PRS by $60 ($80 - $20).

(iv) *Partner-level computations*. X, in computing its limit under section 163(j), has $150 of ATI ($100 from its sole proprietorship, plus $50 excess taxable income), $10 of business interest income, and $25 of business interest expense ($20 from its sole proprietorship, plus $5 excess business interest expense treated as paid or accrued in Year 2). X's section 163(j) limit is $55 (($150 x 30 percent) + $10). Thus, $25 of X's business interest expense is deductible business interest expense. At the end of Year 2, X has $0 of excess business interest expense from PRS ($5 from Year 1, less $5 treated as paid or accrued in Year 2). Y, in computing its limit under section 163(j), has $50 of ATI ($0 from its sole proprietorship, plus $50 excess taxable income), $10 of business interest income, and $45 of business interest expense ($20 from its sole proprietorship, plus $20 disallowed business interest expense from Year 1, plus $5 excess business interest expense treated as paid or accrued in Year 2). Y's section 163(j) limit is $25 (($50 x 30 percent) + $10). Thus, $25 of Y's business interest expense is deductible business interest expense. Y's $20 of business interest expense not allowed as a deduction ($45 business interest expense, less $25 section 163(j) limit) is treated as business interest expense paid or accrued by Y in Year 3. At the end of Year 2, Y has $0 of excess business interest expense from PRS ($5 from Year 1, less $5 treated as paid or accrued in Year 2).

(5) *Example 5*—(i) *Facts*. The facts are the same as in *Example 1* in paragraph (o)(1)(i) of this section. In Year 2, PRS has $100 of ATI, $11.20 of business interest income, and $40 of business interest expense. PRS allocates the items comprising its $100 of ATI $50 to X and $50 to Y. PRS allocates its $11.20 of business interest income $5.60 to X and $5.60 to Y. PRS allocates its $40 of business interest expense $20 to X and $20 to Y. X has $100 of ATI and $20 of business interest expense from its sole proprietorship. Y has $0 of ATI and $20 of business interest expense from its sole proprietorship.

(ii) *Partnership-level*. In Year 2, PRS's section 163(j) limit is 30 percent of its ATI plus its business interest income, or $41.20 (($100 x 30 percent) + $11.20). Thus, PRS has $0 of excess business interest income, $4 of excess taxable income, and $40 of deductible business interest expense. Such $40 of deductible business interest expense is includable in PRS's non-separately stated income or loss, and is not subject to further limitation under section 163(j) at the partners' level.

(iii) *Partner-level allocations*. Pursuant to § 1.163(j)-6(f)(2), X and Y are each allocated $2 of excess taxable income, $20 of deductible business interest expense, and $0 of excess business interest expense. As a result, X and Y each increase their ATI by $2. Because X and Y are each allocated $2 of excess taxable income from PRS, and excess business interest expense from a partnership is treated as paid or accrued by a partner to the extent excess taxable income and excess business interest income are allocated from such partnership to a partner, X and Y each treat $2 of excess business interest expense (a portion of the carryforward from Year 1) as paid or accrued in Year 2. X and Y each increase their outside basis in PRS by $35.60 ($55.60 - $20).

(iv) *Partner-level computations*. X, in computing its limit under section 163(j), has $102 of ATI ($100 from its sole proprietorship, plus $2 excess taxable income), $0 of business interest income, and $22 of business interest expense ($20 from its sole proprietorship, plus $2 excess business interest expense treated as paid or accrued). X's section 163(j) limit is $30.60 ($102 x 30 percent). Thus, X's $22 of business interest expense is deductible business interest expense. At the end of Year 2, X has $3 of excess business interest expense from PRS ($5 from Year 1, less $2 treated as paid or accrued in Year 2). Y, in computing its limit under section 163(j), has $2 of ATI ($0 from its sole proprietorship, plus $2 excess taxable income), $0 of business interest income, and $42 of business interest expense ($20 from its sole proprietorship, plus $20 disallowed business interest expense from Year 1, plus $2 excess business interest expense treated as paid or accrued in Year 2). Y's section 163(j) limit is $0.60 ($2 x 30 percent). Thus, $0.60 of Y's business interest expense is deductible business interest expense. Y's $41.40 of business interest expense not allowed as a deduction ($42 business interest expense, less $0.60 section 163(j) limit) is treated as business interest expense paid or accrued by Y in Year 3. At the end of Year 2, Y has $3 of excess business interest expense from PRS ($5 from Year 1, less $2 treated as paid or accrued in Year 2).

(6) *Example 6*—(i) *Facts*. The facts are the same as in *Example 5* in paragraph (o)(5)(i) of this section, except in Year 2 Y becomes not subject to section 163(j) under section 163(j)(3).

(ii) *Partnership-level*. Same analysis as *Example 5* in paragraph (o)(5)(ii) of this section.

(iii) *Partner-level allocations*. Same analysis as *Example 5* in paragraph (o)(5)(iii) of this section.

(iv) *Partner-level computations*. For X, same analysis as *Example 5* in paragraph (o)(5)(iv) of this section. Y is not subject to section 163(j) under section 163(j)(3). Thus, all $42 of business interest expense ($20 from its sole proprietorship, plus $20 disallowed business interest expense from Year 1, plus $2 excess business interest expense treated as paid or accrued in Year 2) is not subject to limitation under §1.163(j)-2(d). At the end of Year 2, Y has $3 of excess business interest expense from PRS ($5 from Year 1, less $2 treated as paid or accrued in Year 2).

(7) *Example 7*—(i) *Facts*. The facts are the same as in *Example 5* in paragraph (o)(5)(i) of this section, except in Year 2 PRS and Y become not subject to section 163(j) under section 163(j)(3).

(ii) *Partnership-level*. In Year 2, PRS becomes not subject to section 163(j)(4) by reason of section 163(j)(3). As a result, none of PRS's $30 of business interest expense is subject to limitation at the partnership level.

(iii) *Partner-level allocations*. Because section 163(j) does not apply, PRS's $30 of business interest expense is not taken into account in determining its non-separately stated taxable income or loss. Thus, PRS's $30 of business interest expense retains its character as business interest expense for purposes of section 163(j), and is potentially subject to limitation at the partners' level. As a result, X and Y each increase their business interest expense by $15. Further, because PRS is not subject to section 163(j)(4) by reason of section 163(j)(3), the provision requiring each partner of the partnership to determine their ATI without regard to such partner's distributive share of any items of income, gain, deduction, or loss of such partnership (section 163(j)(4)(ii)(I)) is no longer applicable under §1.163(j)-6(m)(1). As a result, X and Y each increase their ATI by $100. Further, because PRS is not subject to section 163(j)(4) by reason of section 163(j)(3), the excess business interest expense from Year 1 is treated as paid or accrued by the partners pursuant to §1.163(j)-6(m)(3). As a result, X and Y each treat their $5 of excess business interest expense from Year 1 as paid or accrued in Year 2, and increase their business interest expense by $5.

(iv) *Partner-level computations*. X, in computing its limit under section 163(j), has $200 of ATI ($100 from its sole proprietorship, plus $100 ATI from PRS) and $40 of business interest expense ($20 from its sole proprietorship, plus $15 from PRS, plus $5 of excess business interest expense treated as paid or accrued in Year 2). X's section 163(j) limit is $60 ($200 x 30 percent). Thus, $40 of X's business interest expense is deductible business interest expense. Y is not subject to section 163(j) under section 163(j)(3). As a result, Y's business interest expense is not subject to limitation under section 163(j). Thus, all $60 of Y's business interest expense ($20 from its sole proprietorship, plus $20 disallowed from year 1, plus $15 from PRS from year 2, plus $5 of excess business interest expense treated as paid or accrued in Year 2) is not subject to limitation under section 163(j).

(8) *Example 8*—(i) *Facts*. In Year 1, X, Y, and Z formed partnership PRS. Upon formation, X and Y each contributed $100, and Z contributed non-excepted and non-depreciable trade or business property with a basis of $0 and fair market value of $100 (Blackacre). PRS allocates all items pro rata between its partners. Immediately after the formation of PRS, Z sold all of its interest in PRS to A for $100 (assume the interest sale is respected for U.S. federal income tax purposes). In connection with the interest transfer, PRS made a valid election under section 754. Therefore, after the interest sale, A had a $100 positive section 743(b) adjustment in Blackacre. In Year 1, PRS had $0 of ATI, $15 of business interest expense, and $0 of business interest income. Pursuant to §1.163(j)-6(f)(2), PRS allocated each of the partners $5 of excess business interest expense. In Year 2, PRS sells Blackacre for $100 which generated $100 of ATI. The sale of Blackacre was PRS's only item of income in Year 2. In accordance with section 704(c), PRS allocates all $100 of gain resulting from the sale of Blackacre to A. Additionally, PRS has $15 of business interest expense, all of which it allocates to X. A has $50 of ATI and $20 of business interest expense from its sole proprietorship.

(ii) *Partnership-level*. In Year 2, PRS's section 163(j) limit is 30 percent of its ATI, or $30 ($100 x 30 percent). Thus, PRS has $15 of deductible business interest expense and $50 of excess taxable income. Such $15 of deductible business interest expense is includable in PRS's non-separately stated income or loss, and is not subject to further limitation under section 163(j) at X's level.

(iii) *Partner-level allocations*. Pursuant to §1.163(j)-6(f)(2), X is allocated $15 of deductible business interest expense and X's outside basis in PRS is reduced by $15. A is allocated $50 of excess taxable income and, as a result, A increases its ATI by $50. Because A is allocated $50 of excess taxable income, and excess business interest expense from a partnership is treated as paid or accrued by a partner to the extent excess taxable income and excess business interest income are allocated from such partnership to a partner, A treats $5 of excess business interest expense (the carryforward from Year 1) as paid or accrued in Year 2. PRS's $100 of gain allocated to A in Year 2 is fully reduced by A's $100 section 743(b) adjustment. Therefore, at the end of Year 2, there is no change to A's outside basis in PRS.

(iv) *Partner-level*. A, in computing its limit under section 163(j), has $0 of ATI ($50 from its sole proprietorship, plus $50 excess taxable income, less $100 ATI reduction as a result of A's section 743(b) adjustment under § 1.163(j)-6(e)(2)) and $25 of business interest expense ($20 from its sole proprietorship, plus $5 excess business interest expense treated as paid or accrued in Year 2). A's section 163(j) limit is $0 ($0 x 30 percent). Thus, all $25 of A's business interest expense is not allowed as a deduction and is treated as business interest expense paid or accrued by A in Year 3.

(9) *Example 9*—(i) *Facts*. X and Y are equal partners in partnership PRS. At the beginning of Year 1, X and Y each have an outside basis in PRS of $5. In Year 1, PRS has $0 of ATI, $20 of business interest income, and $40 of business interest expense. PRS allocates its $20 of business interest income $10 to X and $10 to Y. PRS allocates $40 of business interest expense $20 to X and $20 to Y. X has $100 of ATI and $20 of business interest expense from its sole proprietorship. Y has $0 of ATI and $20 of business interest expense from its sole proprietorship.

(ii) *Partnership-level*. In Year 1, PRS's section 163(j) limit is 30 percent of its ATI plus its business interest income, or $20 (($0 x 30 percent) + $20). Thus, PRS has $0 of excess business interest income, $0 of excess taxable income, $20 of deductible business interest expense, and $20 of excess business interest expense. Such $20 of deductible business interest expense is includable in non-separately stated income or loss of PRS, and not subject to further limitation under section 163(j) by the partners.

(iii) *Partner-level allocations*. Pursuant to § 1.163(j)-6(f)(2), X and Y are each allocated $10 of deductible business interest expense and $10 of excess business interest expense. After adjusting each partners respective basis for business interest income under section 705(a)(1)(A), pursuant to § 1.163(j)-6(h)(1), X and Y each take their $10 of deductible business interest expense into account when reducing their outside basis in PRS before taking the $10 of excess business interest expense into account. Following each partner's reduction in outside basis due to the $10 of deductible business interest expense, each partner has $5 of outside basis remaining in PRS. Pursuant to § 1.163(j)-6(h)(2), each partner has $5 of excess business interest expense and $5 of negative section 163(j) expense. In sum, at the end of Year 1, X and Y each have $5 of excess business interest expense from PRS which reduces each partner's outside basis to $0 (and is not treated as paid or accrued by the partners until such partner is allocated excess taxable income or excess business interest income from PRS in a succeeding taxable year), and $5 of negative section 163(j) expense (which is suspended under section 704(d) and not treated as excess business interest expense of the partners until such time as the negative section 163(j) expense is no longer subject to a limitation under section 704(d)).

(iv) *Partner-level computations*. X, in computing its limit under section 163(j), has $100 of ATI (from its sole proprietorship) and $20 of business interest expense (from its sole proprietorship). X's section 163(j) limit is $30 ($100 x 30 percent). Thus, $20 of X's business interest expense is deductible business interest expense. Y, in computing its limit under section 163(j), has $20 of business interest expense (from its sole proprietorship). Y's section 163(j) limit is $0 ($0 x 30 percent). Thus, $20 of Y's business interest expense is not allowed as a deduction in Year 1, and is treated as business interest expense paid or accrued by Y in Year 2.

(10) *Example 10*—(i) *Facts*. The facts are the same as in *Example 9* in paragraph (o)(9)(i) of this section. In Year 2, PRS has $20 of gross income that is taken into account in determining PRS's ATI (i.e., properly allocable to a trade or business), $30 of gross deductions from an investment activity, and $0 of business interest expense. PRS allocates the items comprising its $20 of ATI $10 to X and $10 to Y. PRS allocates the items comprising its $30 of gross deductions $15 to X and $15 to Y. X has $100 of ATI and $20 of business interest expense from its sole proprietorship. Y has $0 of ATI and $20 of business interest expense from its sole proprietorship.

(ii) *Partnership-level*. In Year 2, PRS's section 163(j) limit is 30 percent of its ATI plus its business interest income, or $6 ($20 x 30 percent). Because PRS has no business interest expense, all $20 of its ATI is excess taxable income.

(iii) *Partner-level allocations*. Pursuant to § 1.163(j)-6(f)(2), X and Y are each allocated $10 of excess taxable income. Because X and Y are each allocated $10 of excess taxable income from PRS, X and Y each increase their ATI by $10. Pursuant to § 1.704-(1)(d)(2), each partner's limitation on losses under section 704(d) must be allocated to its distributive share of each such loss. Thus, each partner reduces its adjusted basis of $10 (attributable to the allocation of items comprising PRS's ATI in Year 2) by $7.50 of gross deductions from Year 2 ($10 x ($15 of total gross deductions from Year 2 / $20 of total losses disallowed)), and $2.50 of excess business interest expense that was carried over as negative section 163(j) expense from Year 1 ($10 x ($5 of negative section 163(j) expense treated as excess business interest expense solely for the purposes of section 704(d) / $20 of total losses disallowed)). Following the application of section 704(d), each partner has $7.50 of excess business interest expense from PRS ($5 excess business interest expense from Year 1, plus $2.50 of excess business interest expense that was formerly negative section 163(j) expense carried over from Year 1). Excess business interest expense from a partnership is treated as paid or accrued by a partner to the extent excess taxable income and excess business interest income are allocated from such partnership to the partner. As a result, X and Y each treat $7.50 of excess business interest expense as paid or accrued in Year 2.

(iv) *Partner-level computations*. X, in computing its limit under section 163(j), has $110 of ATI ($100 from its sole proprietorship, plus $10 excess taxable income) and $27.50 of business interest expense ($20 from its sole proprietorship, plus $7.50 excess business interest expense treated as paid or accrued in Year 2). X's section 163(j) limit is $33 ($110 x 30 percent). Thus, $27.50 of X's business interest expense is deductible business interest expense. At the end of Year 2, X has $0 of excess business interest expense from PRS ($5 from Year 1, plus $2.50 treated as excess business interest expense in Year 2, less $7.50 treated as paid or accrued in Year 2), and $2.50 of negative section 163(j) expense from PRS. Y, in computing its limit under section 163(j), has $10 of ATI ($0 from its sole proprietorship, plus $10 excess taxable income) and $47.50 of business interest expense ($20 from its sole proprietorship, plus $20 disallowed business interest expense from Year 1, plus $7.50 excess business interest expense treated as paid or accrued in Year 2). Y's section 163(j) limit is $3 ($10 x 30 percent). Thus, $3 of Y's business interest expense is deductible business interest expense. The $44.50 of Y's business interest expense not allowed as a deduction ($47.50 business interest expense, less $3 section 163(j) limit) is treated as business interest expense paid or accrued by Y in Year 3. At the end of Year 2, Y has $0 of excess business interest expense from PRS ($5 from Year 1, plus $2.50 treated as excess business interest expense in Year 2, less $7.50 treated as paid or accrued in Year 2), and $2.50 of negative section 163(j) expense from PRS.

(11) *Example 11: Facts.* A (an individual) and B (a corporation) own all of the interests in partnership PRS. In Year 1, PRS has $100 of ATI, $10 of investment interest income, $20 of business interest income (BII), $60 of business interest expense (BIE), and $10 of floor plan financing interest expense. PRS's ATI consists of $100 of gross income and $0 of gross deductions. PRS allocates its items comprising ATI $100 to A and $0 to B. PRS allocates its business interest income $10 to A and $10 to B. PRS allocates its business interest expense $30 to A and $30 to B. PRS allocates all $10 of its investment interest income and all $10 of its floor plan financing interest expense to B. A has ATI from a sole proprietorship, unrelated to PRS, in the amount of $300.

(i) First, PRS determines its limitation pursuant to § 1.163(j)-2. PRS's section 163(j) limit is 30 percent of its ATI plus its business interest income, or $50 (($100 x 30 percent) + $20). Thus, PRS has $0 of excess business interest income (EBII), $0 of excess taxable income, $50 of deductible business interest expense, and $10 of excess business interest expense. PRS takes its $10 of floor plan financing into account in determining its nonseparately stated taxable income or loss.

(ii) Second, PRS determines each partner's allocable share of section 163(j) items used in its own section 163(j) calculation. B's $10 of investment interest income is not included in B's allocable business interest income amount because the $10 of investment interest income was not taken into account in PRS's section 163(j) calculation. B's $10 of floor plan financing interest expense is not included in B's allocable business interest expense. The $300 of ATI from A's sole proprietorship is not included in A's allocable ATI amount because the $300 was not taken into account in PRS's section 163(j) calculation.

Table 1 to paragraph (o)(11)(ii)

	A	B	Total
Allocable ATI	$100	$0	$100
Allocable BII	$10	$10	$20
Allocable BIE	$30	$30	$60

(iii) Third, PRS compares each partner's allocable business interest income to such partner's allocable business interest expense. Because each partner's allocable business interest expense exceeds its allocable business interest income by $20 ($30 - $10), each partner has an allocable business interest income deficit of $20. Thus, the total allocable business interest income deficit is $40 ($20 + $20). No partner has allocable business interest income excess because no partner has allocable business interest income in excess of its allocable business interest expense. Thus, the total allocable business interest income excess is $0.

Table 1 to paragraph (o)(11)(iii)

	A	B	Total
Allocable BII	$10	$10	N/A
Allocable BIE	$30	$30	N/A
If allocable BII exceeds allocable BIE, then such amount = Allocable BII excess	$0	$0	$0
If allocable BIE exceeds allocable BII, then such amount = Allocable BII deficit	$20	$20	$40

(iv) Fourth, PRS determines each partner's final allocable business interest income excess. Because no partner had any allocable business interest income excess, each partner has final allocable business interest income excess of $0.

(v) Fifth, PRS determines each partner's remaining business interest expense. PRS determines A's remaining business interest expense by reducing, but not below $0, A's allocable business interest income deficit ($20) by the product of the total allocable business interest income excess ($0) and the ratio of A's allocable business interest income deficit to the total business interest income deficit ($20/$40). Therefore, A's allocable business interest income deficit of $20 is reduced by $0 ($0 x 50 percent). As a result, A's remaining business interest expense is $20. PRS determines B's remaining business interest expense by reducing, but not below $0, B's allocable business interest income deficit ($20) by the product of the total allocable business interest income excess ($0) and the ratio of B's allocable business interest income deficit to the total business interest income deficit ($20/$40). Therefore, B's allocable business interest income deficit of $20 is reduced by $0 ($0 x 50 percent). As a result, B's remaining business interest expense is $20.

Table 1 to paragraph (o)(11)(v)

	A	B	Total
Allocable BII deficit	$20	$20	$40
Less: (Total allocable BII excess) x (Allocable BII deficit / Total allocable BII deficit)	$0	$0	N/A
= Remaining BIE	$20	$20	$40

(vi) Sixth, PRS determines each partner's final allocable ATI. Any partner with a negative allocable ATI, or an allocable ATI of $0, has a positive allocable ATI of $0. Therefore, B has a positive allocable ATI of $0. Because A's allocable ATI is comprised of $100 of income and gain and $0 of deduction and loss, A has positive allocable ATI of $100. Thus, the total positive allocable ATI is $100 ($100 + $0). PRS determines A's final allocable ATI by reducing, but not below $0, A's positive allocable ATI ($100) by the product of total negative allocable ATI ($0) and the ratio of A's positive allocable ATI to the total positive allocable ATI ($100/$100). Therefore, A's positive allocable ATI is reduced by $0 ($0 x 100 percent). As a result, A's final allocable ATI is $100. Because B has a positive allocable ATI of $0, B's final allocable ATI is $0.

Table 1 to paragraph (o)(11)(vi)

	A	B	Total
Allocable ATI	$100	$0	$100
If deduction and loss items comprising allocable ATI exceed income and gain items comprising allocable ATI, then such excess amount = Negative allocable ATI	$0	$0	$0
If income and gain items comprising allocable ATI equal or exceed deduction and loss items comprising allocable ATI, then such amount = Positive allocable ATI	$100	$0	$100

Table 2 to paragraph (o)(11)(vi)

	A	B	Total
Positive allocable ATI	$100	$0	$100
Less: (Total negative allocable ATI) x (Positive allocable ATI / Total positive allocable ATI)	$0	$0	N/A
= Final allocable ATI	$100	$0	$100

(vii) Seventh, PRS compares each partner's ATI capacity (ATIC) amount to such partner's remaining business interest expense. A's ATIC amount is $30 ($100 x 30 percent) and B's ATIC amount is $0 ($0 x 30 percent). Because A's ATIC amount exceeds its remaining business interest expense by $10 ($30 - $20), A has an ATIC excess of $10. B does not have any ATIC excess. Thus, the total ATIC excess is $10 ($10 + $0). A does not have any ATIC deficit. Because B's remaining business interest expense exceeds its ATIC amount by $20 ($20 - $0), B has an ATIC deficit of $20. Thus, the total ATIC deficit is $20 ($0 + $20).

Table 1 to paragraph (o)(11)(vii)

	A	B	Total
ATIC (Final allocable ATI x 30 percent)	$30	$0	N/A
Remaining BIE	$20	$20	N/A
If ATIC exceeds remaining BIE, then such excess = ATIC excess	$10	$0	$10
If remaining BIE exceeds ATIC, then such excess = ATIC deficit	$0	$20	$20

(viii)(A) Eighth, PRS must perform the calculations and make the necessary adjustments described under paragraph (f)(2)(viii) of this section if, and only if, PRS has:

(*1*) An excess business interest expense greater than $0 under paragraph (f)(2)(i) of this section;

(*2*) A total negative allocable ATI greater than $0 under paragraph (f)(2)(vi) of this section; and

(*3*) A total ATIC excess amount greater than $0 under paragraph (f)(2)(vii) of this section.

(B) Because PRS does not meet all three requirements in paragraph (o)(11)(viii)(A) of this section, PRS does not perform the calculations or adjustments described in paragraph (f)(2)(viii) of this section. In sum, the correct amounts to be used in paragraphs (o)(11)(ix) and (x) of this section are as follows.

Table 1 to paragraph (o)(11)(viii)(B)

	A	B	Total
ATIC excess	$10	$0	$10
ATIC deficit	$0	$20	$20

(ix) Ninth, PRS determines each partner's final ATIC excess amount. Because A has an ATIC excess, PRS must determine A's final ATIC excess amount. A's final ATIC excess amount is A's ATIC excess ($10), reduced, but not below $0, by the product of the total ATIC deficit ($20) and the ratio of A's ATIC excess to the total ATIC excess ($10/$10). Therefore, A has $0 of final ATIC excess ($10 — ($20 x 100 percent)).

Table 1 to paragraph (o)(11)(ix)

	A	B	Total
ATIC excess	$10	$0	N/A
Less: (Total ATIC deficit) x (ATIC excess / Total ATIC excess)	$20	$0	N/A
= Final ATIC excess	$0	$0	$0

(x) Tenth, PRS determines each partner's final ATIC deficit amount. Because B has an ATIC deficit, PRS must determine B's final ATIC deficit amount. B's final ATIC deficit amount is B's ATIC deficit ($20), reduced, but not below $0, by the product of the total ATIC excess ($10) and the ratio of B's ATIC deficit to the total ATIC deficit ($20/$20). Therefore, B has $10 of final ATIC deficit ($20 — ($10 x 100 percent)).

Table 1 to paragraph (o)(11)(x)

	A	B	Total
ATIC deficit	$0	$20	N/A
Less: (Total ATIC excess) x (ATIC deficit / Total ATIC deficit)	$0	$10	N/A
= Final ATIC deficit	$0	$10	$10

(xi) Eleventh, PRS allocates deductible business interest expense and section 163(j) excess items to the partners. Pursuant to paragraph (f)(2)(i) of this section, PRS has $10 of excess business interest expense. PRS allocates the excess business interest expense dollar for dollar to the partners with final ATIC deficits amounts. Thus, PRS allocates all $10 of its excess business interest expense to B. A partner's allocable business interest expense is deductible business interest expense to the extent it exceeds such partner's share of excess business interest expense. Therefore, A has deductible business interest expense of $30 ($30 - $0) and B has deductible business interest expense of $20 ($30 - $10).

Table 1 to paragraph (o)(11)(xi)

	A	B	Total
Deductible BIE	$30	$20	$50
EBIE allocated	$0	$10	$10
ETI allocated	$0	$0	$0
EBII allocated	$0	$0	$0

(12) *Example 12: Facts.* A, B, and C own all of the interests in partnership PRS. In Year 1, PRS has $150 of ATI, $10 of business interest income, and $40 of business interest expense. PRS's ATI consists of $200 of gross income and $50 of gross deductions. PRS allocates its items comprising ATI ($50) to A, $200 to B, and $0 to C. PRS allocates its business interest income $0 to A, $0 to B, and $10 to C. PRS allocates its business interest expense $30 to A, $10 to B, and $0 to C.

(i) First, PRS determines its limitation pursuant to § 1.163(j)-2. PRS's section 163(j) limit is 30 percent of its ATI plus its business interest income, or $55 (($150 x 30 percent) + $10). Thus, PRS has $0 of excess business interest income, $50 of excess taxable income, $40 of deductible business interest expense, and $0 of excess business interest expense.

(ii) Second, PRS determines each partner's allocable share of section 163(j) items used in its own section 163(j) calculation.

Table 1 to paragraph (o)(12)(ii)

	A	B	C	Total
Allocable ATI	($50)	$200	$0	$150
Allocable BII	$0	$0	$10	$10
Allocable BIE	$30	$10	$0	$40

(iii) Third, PRS compares each partner's allocable business interest income to such partner's allocable business interest expense. Because A's allocable business interest expense exceeds its allocable business interest income by $30 ($30 - $0), A has an allocable business interest income deficit of $30. Because B's allocable business interest expense exceeds its allocable business interest income by $10 ($10 - $0), B has an allocable business interest income deficit of $10. C does not have any allocable business interest income deficit. Thus, the total allocable business interest income deficit is $40 ($30 + $10 + $0). A and B do not have any allocable business interest income excess. Because C's allocable business interest income exceeds its allocable business interest expense by $10 ($10 - $0), C has an allocable business interest income excess of $10. Thus, the total allocable business interest income excess is $10 ($0 + $0 + $10).

Table 1 to paragraph (o)(12)(iii)

	A	B	C	Total
Allocable BII	$0	$0	$10	N/A
Allocable BIE	$30	$10	$0	N/A
If allocable BII exceeds allocable BIE, then such amount = Allocable BII excess	$0	$0	$10	$10
If allocable BIE exceeds allocable BII, then such amount = Allocable BII deficit	$30	$10	$0	$40

(iv) Fourth, PRS determines each partner's final allocable business interest income excess. Because A and B do not have any allocable business interest income excess, each partner has final allocable business interest income excess of $0. PRS determines C's final allocable business interest income excess by reducing, but not below $0, C's allocable business interest income excess ($10) by the product of the total allocable business interest income deficit ($40) and the ratio of C's allocable business interest income excess to the total allocable business interest income excess ($10/$10). Therefore, C's allocable business interest income excess of $10 is reduced by $10 ($40 x 100 percent). As a result, C's allocable business interest income excess is $0.

Table 1 to paragraph (o)(12)(iv)

	A	B	C	Total
Allocable BII excess	$0	$0	$10	N/A
Less: (Total allocable BII deficit) x (Allocable BII excess / Total allocable BII excess)	$0	$0	$40	N/A
= Final Allocable BII Excess	$0	$0	$0	$10

(v) Fifth, PRS determines each partner's remaining business interest expense. PRS determines A's remaining business interest expense by reducing, but not below $0, A's allocable business interest income deficit ($30) by the product of the total allocable business interest income excess ($10) and the ratio of A's allocable business interest income deficit to the total business interest income deficit ($30/$40). Therefore, A's allocable business interest income deficit of $30 is reduced by $7.50 ($10 x 75 percent). As a result, A's remaining business interest expense is $22.50. PRS determines B's remaining business interest expense by reducing, but not below $0, B's allocable business interest income deficit ($10) by the product of the total allocable business interest income excess ($10) and the ratio of B's allocable business interest income deficit to the total business interest income deficit ($10/$40). Therefore, B's allocable business interest income deficit of $10 is reduced by $2.50 ($10 x 25 percent). As a result, B's remaining business interest expense is $7.50. Because C does not have any allocable business interest income deficit, C's remaining business interest expense is $0.

Table 1 to paragraph (o)(12)(v)

	A	B	C	Total
Allocable BII deficit	$30	$10	$0	$40
Less: (Total allocable BII excess) x (Allocable BII deficit / Total allocable BII deficit)	$7.50	$2.50	$0	N/A
= Remaining BIE	$22.50	$7.50	$0	N/A

(vi) Sixth, PRS determines each partner's final allocable ATI. Because A's allocable ATI is comprised of $50 of items of deduction and loss and $0 of income and gain, A has negative allocable ATI of $50. A is the only partner with negative allocable ATI. Thus, the total negative allocable ATI amount is $50. Any partner with a negative allocable ATI, or an allocable ATI of $0, has a positive allocable ATI of $0. Therefore, A and C have a positive allocable ATI of $0. Because B's allocable ATI is comprised of $200 of items of income and gain and $0 of deduction and loss, B has positive allocable ATI of $200. Thus, the total positive allocable ATI is $200 ($0 + $200 + $0). PRS determines B's final allocable ATI by reducing, but not below $0, B's positive allocable ATI ($200) by the product of total negative allocable ATI ($50) and the ratio of B's positive allocable ATI to the total positive allocable ATI ($200/$200). Therefore, B's positive allocable ATI is reduced by $50 ($50 x 100 percent). As a result, B's final allocable ATI is $150.

Table 1 to paragraph (o)(12)(vi)

	A	B	C	Total
Allocable ATI	($50)	$200	$0	$150
If deduction and loss items comprising allocable ATI exceed income and gain items comprising allocable ATI, then such excess amount = Negative allocable ATI	$50	$0	$0	$50
If income and gain items comprising allocable ATI equal or exceed deduction and loss items comprising allocable ATI, then such amount = Positive allocable ATI	$0	$200	$0	$200

Table 2 to paragraph (o)(12)(vi)

	A	B	C	Total
Positive allocable ATI	$0	$200	$0	$200
Less: (Total negative allocable ATI) x (Positive allocable ATI / Total positive allocable ATI)	$0	$50	$0	N/A
= Final allocable ATI	$0	$150	$0	$150

(vii) Seventh, PRS compares each partner's ATI capacity (ATIC) amount to such partner's remaining business interest expense. A's ATIC amount is $0 ($0 x 30 percent), B's ATIC amount is $45 ($150 x 30 percent), and C's ATIC amount is $0 ($0 x 30 percent). A does not have any ATIC excess. Because B's ATIC amount exceeds its remaining business interest expense by $37.50 ($45 - $7.50), B has an ATIC excess amount of $37.50. C does not have any ATIC excess. Thus, the total ATIC excess amount is $37.50 ($0 + $37.50 + $0). Because A's remaining business interest expense exceeds its ATIC amount by $22.50 ($22.50 - $0), A has an ATIC deficit of $22.50. B and C do not have any ATIC deficit. Thus, the total ATIC deficit is $22.50 ($22.50 + $0 + $0).

Table 1 to paragraph (o)(12)(vii)

	A	B	C	Total
ATIC (Final allocable ATI x 30 percent)	$0	$45	$0	N/A
Remaining BIE	$22.50	$7.50	$0	N/A
If ATIC exceeds remaining BIE, then such excess = ATIC excess	$0	$37.50	$0	$37.50
If remaining BIE exceeds ATIC, then such excess = ATIC deficit	$22.50	$0	$0	$22.50

(viii)(A) Eighth, PRS must perform the calculations and make the necessary adjustments described under paragraph (f)(2)(viii) of this section if, and only if, PRS has:

(*1*) An excess business interest expense greater than $0 under paragraph (f)(2)(i) of this section;

(*2*) A total negative allocable ATI greater than $0 under paragraph (f)(2)(vi) of this section; and

(*3*) A total ATIC excess amount greater than $0 under paragraph (f)(2)(vii) of this section.

(B) Because PRS does not meet all three requirements in paragraph (o)(12)(viii)(A) of this section, PRS does not perform the calculations or adjustments described in paragraph (f)(2)(viii) of this section. In sum, the correct amounts to be used in paragraphs (o)(12)(ix) and (x) of this section are as follows.

Table 1 to paragraph (o)(12)(viii)(B)

	A	B	C	Total
ATIC excess	$0	$37.50	$0	$37.50
ATIC deficit	$22.50	$0	$0	$22.50

(ix) Ninth, PRS determines each partner's final ATIC excess amount. Because B has ATIC excess, PRS must determine B's final ATIC excess amount. B's final ATIC excess amount is B's ATIC excess ($37.50), reduced, but not below $0, by the product of the total ATIC deficit ($22.50) and the ratio of B's ATIC excess to the total ATIC excess ($37.50/$37.50). Therefore, B has $15 of final ATIC excess ($37.50 — ($22.50 x 100 percent)).

Table 1 to paragraph (o)(12)(ix)

	A	B	C	Total
ATIC excess	$0	$37.50	$0	N/A
Less: (Total ATIC deficit) x (ATIC excess / Total ATIC excess)	$0	$22.50	$0	N/A
= Final ATIC excess	$0	$15	$0	$15

(x) Tenth, PRS determines each partner's final ATIC deficit amount. Because A has an ATIC deficit, PRS must determine A's final ATIC deficit amount. A's final ATIC deficit amount is A's ATIC deficit ($22.50), reduced, but not below $0, by the product of the total ATIC excess ($37.50) and the ratio of A's ATIC deficit to the total ATIC deficit ($22.50/$22.50). Therefore, A has $0 of final ATIC deficit ($22.50 — ($37.50 x 100 percent)).

Table 1 to paragraph (o)(12)(x)

	A	B	C	Total
ATIC deficit	$22.50	$0	$0	N/A
Less: (Total ATIC excess) x (ATIC deficit / Total ATIC deficit)	$37.50	$0	$0	N/A
= Final ATIC deficit	$0	$0	$0	$0

(xi) Eleventh, PRS allocates deductible business interest expense and section 163(j) excess items to the partners. Pursuant to paragraph (f)(2)(i) of this section, PRS has $50 of excess taxable income and $40 of deductible business interest expense. After grossing up each partner's final ATIC excess amounts by ten-thirds, excess taxable income is allocated dollar for dollar to partners with final ATIC excess amounts. Thus, PRS allocates its excess taxable income (ETI) $50 to B. A partner's allocable business interest expense is deductible business interest expense to the extent it exceeds such partner's share of excess business interest expense (EBIE). Therefore, A has deductible business interest expense of $30 ($30 - $0), B has deductible business interest expense of $10 ($10 - $0), and C has deductible business interest expense of $0 ($0 - $0).

Table 1 to paragraph (o)(12)(xi)

	A	B	C	Total
Deductible BIE	$30	$10	$0	$40
EBIE allocated	$0	$0	$0	$0
ETI allocated	$0	$50	$0	$50
EBII allocated	$0	$0	$0	$0

(13) *Example 13: Facts.* A, B, and C own all of the interests in partnership PRS. In Year 1, PRS has $100 of ATI, $0 of business interest income, and $50 of business interest expense. PRS's ATI consists of $200 of gross income and $100 of gross deductions. PRS allocates its items comprising ATI $100 to A, $100 to B, and ($100) to C. PRS allocates its business interest expense $0 to A, $25 to B, and $25 to C.

(i) First, PRS determines its limitation pursuant to §1.163(j)-2. PRS's section 163(j) limit is 30 percent of its ATI plus its business interest income, or $30 ($100 x 30 percent). Thus, PRS has $30 of deductible business interest expense and $20 of excess business interest expense.

(ii) Second, PRS determines each partner's allocable share of section 163(j) items used in its own section 163(j) calculation.

Table 1 to paragraph (o)(13)(ii)

	A	B	C	Total
Allocable ATI	$100	$100	($100)	$100

Table 1 to paragraph (o)(13)(ii)

	A	B	C	Total
Allocable BII	$0	$0	$0	$0
Allocable BIE	$0	$25	$25	$50

(iii) Third, PRS compares each partner's allocable business interest income to such partner's allocable business interest expense. No partner has allocable business interest income. Consequently, each partner's allocable business interest income deficit is equal to such partner's allocable business interest expense. Thus, A's allocable business interest income deficit is $0, B's allocable business interest income deficit is $25, and C's allocable business interest income deficit is $25. The total allocable business interest income deficit is $50 ($0 + $25 + $25). No partner has allocable business interest income excess because no partner has allocable business interest income in excess of its allocable business interest expense. Thus, the total allocable business interest income excess is $0.

Table 1 to paragraph (o)(13)(iii)

	A	B	C	Total
Allocable BII	$0	$0	$0	N/A
Allocable BIE	$0	$25	$25	N/A
If allocable BII exceeds allocable BIE, then such amount = Allocable BII excess	$0	$0	$0	$0
If allocable BIE exceeds allocable BII, then such amount = Allocable BII deficit	$0	$25	$25	$50

(iv) Fourth, PRS determines each partner's final allocable business interest income excess. Because no partner had any allocable business interest income excess, each partner has final allocable business interest income excess of $0.

(v) Fifth, PRS determines each partner's remaining business interest expense. Because no partner has any allocable business interest income excess, each partner's remaining business interest expense equals its allocable business interest income deficit. Thus, A's remaining business interest expense is $0, B's remaining business interest expense is $25, and C's remaining business interest expense is $25.

Table 1 to paragraph (o)(13)(v)

	A	B	C	Total
Allocable BII deficit	$0	$25	$25	$50
Less: (Total allocable BII excess) x (Allocable BII deficit / Total allocable BII deficit)	$0	$0	$0	N/A
= Remaining BIE	$0	$25	$25	N/A

(vi) Sixth, PRS determines each partner's final allocable ATI. Because C's allocable ATI is comprised of $100 of items of deduction and loss and $0 of income and gain, C has negative allocable ATI of $100. C is the only partner with negative allocable ATI. Thus, the total negative allocable ATI amount is $100. Any partner with a negative allocable ATI, or an allocable ATI of $0, has a positive allocable ATI of $0. Therefore, C has a positive allocable ATI of $0. Because A's allocable ATI is comprised of $100 of items of income and gain and $0 of deduction and loss, A has positive allocable ATI of $100. Because B's allocable ATI is comprised of $100 of items of income and gain and $0 of deduction and loss, B has positive allocable ATI of $100. Thus, the total positive allocable ATI is $200 ($100 + $100 + $0). PRS determines A's final allocable ATI by reducing, but not below $0, A's positive allocable ATI ($100) by the product of total negative allocable ATI ($100) and the ratio of A's positive allocable ATI to the total positive allocable ATI ($100/$200). Therefore, A's positive allocable ATI is reduced by $50 ($100 x 50 percent). As a result, A's final allocable ATI is $50. PRS determines B's final allocable ATI by reducing, but not below $0, B's positive allocable ATI ($100) by the product of total negative allocable ATI ($100) and the ratio of B's positive allocable ATI to the total positive allocable ATI ($100/$200). Therefore, B's positive allocable ATI is reduced by $50 ($100 x 50 percent). As a result, B's final allocable ATI is $50. Because C has a positive allocable ATI of $0, C's final allocable ATI is $0.

Table 1 to paragraph (o)(13)(vi)

	A	B	C	Total
Allocable ATI	$100	$100	($100)	$100
If deduction and loss items comprising allocable ATI exceed income and gain items comprising allocable ATI, then such excess amount = Negative allocable ATI	$0	$0	$100	$100

Table 1 to paragraph (o)(13)(vi)

	A	B	C	Total
If income and gain items comprising allocable ATI equal or exceed deduction and loss items comprising allocable ATI, then such amount = Positive allocable ATI	$100	$100	$0	$200

Table 2 to paragraph (o)(13)(vi)

	A	B	C	Total
Positive allocable ATI	$100	$100	$0	$200
Less: (Total negative allocable ATI) x (Positive allocable ATI / Total positive allocable ATI)	$50	$50	$0	N/A
= Final allocable ATI	$50	$50	$0	$100

(vii) Seventh, PRS compares each partner's ATI capacity (ATIC) amount to such partner's remaining business interest expense. A's ATIC amount is $15 ($50 x 30 percent), B's ATIC amount is $15 ($50 x 30 percent), and C's ATIC amount is $0 ($0 x 30 percent). Because A's ATIC amount exceeds its remaining business interest expense by $15 ($15 - $0), A has an ATIC excess of $15. B and C do not have any ATIC excess. Thus, the total ATIC excess is $15 ($15 + $0 + $0). A does not have any ATIC deficit. Because B's remaining business interest expense exceeds its ATIC amount by $10 ($25 - $15), B has an ATIC deficit of $10. Because C's remaining business interest expense exceeds its ATIC amount by $25 ($25 - $0), C has an ATIC deficit of $25. Thus, the total ATIC deficit is $35 ($0 + $10 + $25).

Table 1 to paragraph (o)(13)(vii)

	A	B	C	Total
ATIC (Final allocable ATI x 30 percent)	$15	$15	$0	N/A
Remaining BIE	$0	$25	$25	N/A
If ATIC exceeds remaining BIE, then such excess = ATIC excess	$15	$0	$0	$15
If remaining BIE exceeds ATIC, then such excess = ATIC deficit	$0	$10	$25	$35

(viii)(A) Eighth, PRS must perform the calculations and make the necessary adjustments described under paragraph (f)(2)(viii) of this section if, and only if, PRS has:

(*1*) An excess business interest expense greater than $0 under paragraph (f)(2)(i) of this section;

(*2*) A total negative allocable ATI greater than $0 under paragraph (f)(2)(vi) of this section; and

(*3*) A total ATIC excess greater than $0 under paragraph (f)(2)(vii) of this section. Because PRS satisfies each of these three requirements, PRS must perform the calculations and make the necessary adjustments described under paragraph (f)(2)(viii)(B) and (C) or (D) of this section.

(B) PRS must determine each partner's priority amount and usable priority amount. Only partners with an ATIC deficit under paragraph (f)(2)(vii) of this section can have a priority amount greater than $0. Thus, only partners B and C can have a priority amount greater than $0. PRS determines a partner's priority amount as thirty percent of the amount by which such partner's allocable positive ATI exceeds its final allocable ATI. Therefore, A's priority amount is $0, B's priority amount is $15 (($100 - $50) x 30 percent), and C's priority amount is $0 (($0 - $0) x 30 percent). Thus, the total priority amount is $15 ($0 + $15 + $0). Next, PRS must determine each partner's usable priority amount. Each partner's usable priority amount is the lesser of such partner's priority amount or ATIC deficit. Thus, A has a usable priority amount of $0, B has a usable priority amount of $10, and C has a usable priority amount of $0. As a result, the total usable priority amount is $10 ($0 + $10 + $0). Because the total ATIC excess under paragraph (f)(2)(vii) of this section ($15) is greater than the total usable priority amount ($10), PRS must perform the adjustments described in paragraph (f)(2)(viii)(C) of this section.

Table 1 to paragraph (o)(13)(viii)(B)

	A	B	C	Total
(Positive allocable ATI - Final allocable ATI)	$0	$50	$0	N/A
Multiplied by 30 percent	30 percent	30 percent	30 percent	N/A
= Priority amount	$0	$15	$0	$15

Table 2 to paragraph (o)(13)(viii)(B)

	A	B	C	Total
Priority amount	$0	$15	$0	N/A
ATIC deficit	$0	$10	$25	N/A
Lesser of priority amount or ATIC deficit = Usable priority amount	$0	$10	$0	$10

(C) For purposes of paragraph (f)(2)(ix) of this section, each partner's final ATIC excess is $0. For purposes of paragraph (f)(2)(x) of this section, the following terms shall have the following meanings. Each partner's ATIC deficit is such partner's ATIC deficit as determined pursuant to paragraph (f)(2)(vii) of this section reduced by such partner's usable priority amount. Thus, A's ATIC deficit is $0 ($0 - $0), B's ATIC deficit is $0 ($10 - $10), and C's ATIC deficit is $25 ($25 - $0). The total ATIC deficit is the total ATIC deficit determined pursuant to paragraph (f)(2)(vii) ($35) reduced by the total usable priority amount ($10). Thus, the total ATIC deficit is $25 ($35 - $10). The total ATIC excess is the total ATIC excess determined pursuant to paragraph (f)(2)(vii) of this section ($15) reduced by the total usable priority amount ($10). Thus, the total ATIC excess is $5 ($15 - $5).

Table 1 to paragraph (o)(13)(viii)(C)

	A	B	C	Total
ATIC deficit	$0	$10	$25	N/A
Less: Usable priority amount	$0	$10	$0	N/A
= ATIC deficit for purposes of paragraph (f)(2)(x) of this section	$0	$0	$25	$25

(D) In light of the fact that the total ATIC excess was greater than the total usable priority amount under paragraph (f)(2)(viii)(B) of this section, paragraph (f)(2)(viii)(D) of this section does not apply. In sum, the correct amounts to be used in paragraph (f)(2)(x) of this section are as follows.

Table 1 to paragraph (o)(13)(viii)(C)

	A	B	C	Total
ATIC excess	$5	$0	$0	$5
ATIC deficit	$0	$0	$25	$25

(ix) Ninth, PRS determines each partner's final ATIC excess amount. Pursuant to paragraph (f)(2)(viii)(C) of this section, each partner's final ATIC excess amount is $0.

(x) Tenth, PRS determines each partner's final ATIC deficit amount. Because C has an ATIC deficit, PRS must determine C's final ATIC deficit amount. C's final ATIC deficit amount is C's ATIC deficit ($25), reduced, but not below $0, by the product of the total ATIC excess ($5) and the ratio of C's ATIC deficit to the total ATIC deficit ($25/$25). Therefore, C has $20 of final ATIC deficit ($25 — ($5 x 100 percent)).

Table 1 to paragraph (o)(13)(x)

	A	B	C	Total
ATIC deficit	$0	$0	$25	N/A
Less: (Total ATIC excess) x (ATIC deficit / Total ATIC deficit)	$0	$0	$5	N/A
= Final ATIC deficit	$0	$0	$20	$20

(xi) Eleventh, PRS allocates deductible business interest expense and section 163(j) excess items to the partners. Pursuant to paragraph (f)(2)(i) of this section, PRS has $20 of excess business interest expense. PRS allocates the excess business interest expense dollar for dollar to the partners with final ATIC deficits. Thus, PRS allocates its excess business interest expense $20 to C. A partner's allocable business interest expense is deductible business interest expense to the extent it exceeds such partner's share of excess business interest expense. Therefore, A has deductible business interest expense of $0 ($0 - $0), B has deductible business interest expense of $25 ($25 - $0), and C has deductible business interest expense of $5 ($25 - $20).

Table 1 to paragraph (o)(13)(xi)

	A	B	C	Total
Deductible BIE	$0	$25	$5	$30

Table 1 to paragraph (o)(13)(xi)

	A	B	C	Total
EBIE allocated	$0	$0	$20	$20
ETI allocated	$0	$0	$0	$0
EBII allocated	$0	$0	$0	$0

(14) *Example 14: Facts*. A, B, C, and D own all of the interests in partnership PRS. In Year 1, PRS has $200 of ATI, $0 of business interest income, and $140 of business interest expense. PRS's ATI consists of $600 of gross income and $400 of gross deductions. PRS allocates its items comprising ATI $100 to A, $100 to B, $400 to C, and ($400) to D. PRS allocates its business interest expense $0 to A, $40 to B, $60 to C, and $40 to D.

(i) First, PRS determines its limitation pursuant to § 1.163(j)-2. PRS's section 163(j) limit is 30 percent of its ATI plus its business interest income, or $60 ($200 x 30 percent). Thus, PRS has $60 of deductible business interest expense and $80 of excess business interest expense.

(ii) Second, PRS determines each partner's allocable share of section 163(j) items used in its own section 163(j) calculation.

Table 1 to paragraph (o)(14)(ii)

	A	B	C	D	Total
Allocable ATI	$100	$100	$400	($400)	$200
Allocable BII	$0	$0	$0	$0	$0
Allocable BIE	$0	$40	$60	$40	$140

(iii) Third, PRS compares each partner's allocable business interest income to such partner's allocable business interest expense. No partner has allocable business interest income. Consequently, each partner's allocable business interest income deficit is equal to such partner's allocable business interest expense. Thus, A's allocable business interest income deficit is $0, B's allocable business interest income deficit is $40, C's allocable business interest income deficit is $60, and D's allocable business interest income deficit is $40. The total allocable business interest income deficit is $140 ($0 + $40 + $60 + $40). No partner has allocable business interest income excess because no partner has allocable business interest income in excess of its allocable business interest expense. Thus, the total allocable business interest income excess is $0.

Table 1 to paragraph (o)(14)(iii)

	A	B	C	D	Total
Allocable BII	$0	$0	$0	$0	N/A
Allocable BIE	$0	$40	$60	$40	N/A
If allocable BII exceeds allocable BIE, then such amount = Allocable BII excess	$0	$0	$0	$0	$0
If allocable BIE exceeds allocable BII, then such amount = Allocable BII deficit	$0	$40	$60	$40	$140

(iv) Fourth, PRS determines each partner's final allocable business interest income excess. Because no partner has any allocable business interest income excess, each partner has final allocable business interest income excess of $0.

(v) Fifth, PRS determines each partner's remaining business interest expense. Because no partner has any allocable business interest income excess, each partner's remaining business interest expense equals its allocable business interest income deficit. Thus, A's remaining business interest expense is $0, B's remaining business interest expense is $40, C's remaining business interest expense is $60, and D's remaining business interest expense is $40.

Table 1 to paragraph (o)(14)(v)

	A	B	C	D	Total
Allocable BII deficit	$0	$40	$60	$40	$140
Less: (Total allocable BII excess) x (Allocable BII deficit / Total allocable BII deficit)	$0	$0	$0	$0	N/A
= Remaining BIE	$0	$40	$60	$40	N/A

(vi) Sixth, PRS determines each partner's final allocable ATI. Because D's allocable ATI is comprised of $400 of items of deduction and loss and $0 of income and gain, D has negative allocable ATI of $400. D is the only partner with negative allocable ATI. Thus, the total negative allocable ATI amount is $400. Any partner with a negative allocable ATI, or an allocable ATI of $0, has a positive allocable ATI of $0. Therefore, D has a positive allocable ATI of $0. PRS determines A's final allocable ATI by reducing, but not below $0, A's positive allocable ATI ($100) by the product of total negative allocable ATI ($400) and the ratio of A's positive allocable ATI to the total positive allocable ATI ($100/$600). Therefore, A's positive allocable ATI is reduced by $66.67 ($400 x 16.67 percent). As a result, A's final allocable ATI is $33.33. PRS determines B's final allocable ATI by reducing, but not below $0, B's positive allocable ATI ($100) by the product of total negative allocable ATI ($400) and the ratio of B's positive allocable ATI to the total positive allocable ATI ($100/$600). Therefore, B's positive allocable ATI is reduced by $66.67 ($400 x 16.67 percent). As a result, B's final allocable ATI is $33.33. PRS determines C's final allocable ATI by reducing, but not below $0, C's positive allocable ATI ($400) by the product of total negative allocable ATI ($400) and the ratio of C's positive allocable ATI to the total positive allocable ATI ($400/$600). Therefore, C's positive allocable ATI is reduced by $266.67 ($400 x 66.67 percent). As a result, C's final allocable ATI is $133.33. Because D has a positive allocable ATI of $0, D's final allocable ATI is $0.

Table 1 to paragraph (o)(14)(vi)

	A	B	C	D	Total
Allocable ATI	$100	$100	$400	($400)	$200
If deduction and loss items comprising allocable ATI exceed income and gain items comprising allocable ATI, then such excess amount = Negative allocable ATI	$0	$0	$0	$400	$400
If income and gain items comprising allocable ATI equal or exceed deduction and loss items comprising allocable ATI, then such amount = Positive allocable ATI	$100	$100	$400	$0	$600

Table 2 to paragraph (o)(14)(vi)

	A	B	C	D	Total
Positive allocable ATI	$100	$100	$400	$0	$600
Less: (Total negative allocable ATI) x (Positive allocable ATI / Total positive allocable ATI)	$66.67	$66.67	$266.67	$0	N/A
= Final allocable ATI	$33.33	$33.33	$133.33	$0	$200

(vii) Seventh, PRS compares each partner's ATI capacity (ATIC) amount to such partner's remaining business interest expense. A's ATIC amount is $10 ($33.33 x 30 percent), B's ATIC amount is $10 ($33.33 x 30 percent), C's ATIC amount is $40 ($133.33 x 30 percent), and D's ATIC amount is $0 ($0 x 30 percent). Because A's ATIC amount exceeds its remaining business interest expense by $10 ($10 - $0), A has an ATIC excess of $10. B, C, and D do not have any ATIC excess. Thus, the total ATIC excess is $10 ($10 + $0 + $0 + $0). A does not have any ATIC deficit. Because B's remaining business interest expense exceeds its ATIC amount by $30 ($40 - $10), B has an ATIC deficit of $30. Because C's remaining business interest expense exceeds its ATIC amount by $20 ($60 - $40), C has an ATIC deficit of $20. Because D's remaining business interest expense exceeds its ATIC amount by $40 ($40 - $0), D has an ATIC deficit of $40. Thus, the total ATIC deficit is $90 ($0 + $30 + $20 + $40).

Table 1 to paragraph (o)(14)(vii)

	A	B	C	D	Total
ATIC (Final allocable ATI x 30 percent)	$10	$10	$40	$0	N/A
Remaining BIE	$0	$40	$60	$40	N/A
If ATIC exceeds remaining BIE, then such excess = ATIC excess	$10	$0	$0	$0	$10
If remaining BIE exceeds ATIC, then such excess = ATIC deficit	$0	$30	$20	$40	$90

(viii)(A) Eighth, PRS must perform the calculations and make the necessary adjustments described under paragraph (f)(2)(viii) of this section if, and only if, PRS has (1) an excess business interest expense greater than $0 under paragraph (f)(2)(i) of this section, (2) a total negative allocable ATI greater than $0 under paragraph (f)(2)(vi) of this section, and (3) a total ATIC excess amount greater than $0 under paragraph (f)(2)(vii) of this section. Because PRS satisfies each of these three requirements, PRS must perform the calculations and make the necessary adjustments described under paragraphs (f)(2)(viii)(B) and (C) or paragraph (f)(2)(viii)(D) of this section.

(B) PRS must determine each partner's priority amount and usable priority amount. Only partners with an ATIC deficit under paragraph (f)(2)(vii) of this section can have a priority amount greater than $0. Thus, only partners B, C, and D can have a priority amount greater than $0. PRS determines a partner's priority amount as thirty percent of the amount by which such partner's allocable positive ATI exceeds its final allocable ATI. Therefore, B's priority amount is $20 (($100 - $33.33) x 30 percent), C's priority amount is $80 (($400 - $133.33) x 30 percent), and D's priority amount is $0 (($0 - $0) x 30 percent). Thus, the total priority amount is $100 ($0 + $20 + $80 + $0). Next, PRS must determine each partner's usable priority amount. Each partner's usable priority amount is the lesser of such partner's priority amount or ATIC deficit. Thus, A has a usable priority amount of $0, B has a usable priority amount of $20, C has a usable priority amount of $20, and D has a usable priority amount of $0. As a result, the total usable priority amount is $40 ($0 + $20 + $20 + $0). Because the total usable priority amount ($40) is greater than the total ATIC excess under paragraph (f)(2)(vii) ($10), PRS must perform the adjustments described in paragraph (f)(2)(viii)(D) of this section.

Table 1 to paragraph (o)(14)(viii)(B)

	A	B	C	D	Total
(Positive allocable ATI - Final allocable ATI)	$0	$66.67	$266.67	$0	N/A
Multiplied by 30 percent	30 percent	30 percent	30 percent	30 percent	N/A
= Priority amount	$0	$20	$80	$0	$100

Table 2 to paragraph (o)(14)(viii)(B)

	A	B	C	D	Total
Priority amount	$0	$20	$80	$0	N/A
ATIC deficit	$0	$30	$20	$40	N/A
Lesser of priority amount or ATIC deficit = Usable priority amount	$0	$20	$20	$0	$40

(C) In light of the fact that the total usable priority amount is greater than the total ATIC excess under paragraph (f)(2)(viii)(B) of this section, paragraph (f)(2)(viii)(C) of this section does not apply.

(D)(*1*) Because B and C are the only partners with priority amounts greater than $0, B and C are priority partners, while A and D are non-priority partners. For purposes of paragraph (f)(2)(ix) of this section, each partner's final ATIC excess amount is $0. For purposes of paragraph (f)(2)(x) of this section, each non-priority partner's final ATIC deficit amount is such partner's ATIC deficit determined pursuant to paragraph (f)(2)(vii) of this section. Therefore, A has a final ATIC deficit of $0 and D has a final ATIC deficit of $40. Additionally, for purposes of paragraph (f)(2)(x) of this section, PRS must determine each priority partner's step eight excess share. A priority partner's step eight excess share is the product of the total ATIC excess and the ratio of the partner's priority amount to the total priority amount. Thus, B's step eight excess share is $2 ($10 x ($20/$100)) and C's step eight excess share is $8 ($10 x ($80/$100)). To the extent a priority partner's step eight excess share exceeds its ATIC deficit, the excess shall be the partner's ATIC excess for purposes of paragraph (f)(2)(x) of this section. Thus, B and C each have an ATIC excess of $0, resulting in a total ATIC excess is $0. To the extent a priority partner's ATIC deficit exceeds its step eight excess share, the excess shall be the partner's ATIC deficit for purposes of paragraph (f)(2)(x) of this section. Because B's ATIC deficit ($30) exceeds its step eight excess share ($2), B's ATIC deficit for purposes of paragraph (f)(2)(x) of this section is $28 ($30 - $2). Because C's ATIC deficit ($20) exceeds its step eight excess share ($8), C's ATIC deficit for purposes of paragraph (f)(2)(x) of this section is $12 ($20 - $8). Thus, the total ATIC deficit is $40 ($28 + $12).

Table 1 to paragraph (o)(14)(viii)(D)(*1*)

	A	B	C	D	Total
Non-priority partners ATIC deficit in paragraph (f)(2)(vii) = Final ATIC deficit for purposes of paragraph (f)(2)(x) of this section	$0	N/A	N/A	$40	N/A

Table 2 to paragraph (o)(14)(viii)(D)(*1*)

	A	B	C	D	Total
Priority partners step eight excess share = (Total ATIC excess) x (Priority / Total priority)	N/A	$2	$8	N/A	N/A

Table 2 to paragraph (o)(14)(viii)(D)(*1*)

	A	B	C	D	Total
ATIC deficit	N/A	$30	$20	N/A	N/A
If step eight excess share exceeds ATIC deficit, then such excess = ATIC excess for purposes of paragraph (f)(2)(x) of this section	N/A	$0	$0	N/A	$0
If ATIC deficit exceeds step eight excess share, then such excess = ATIC deficit for purposes of paragraph (f)(2)(x) of this section	N/A	$28	$12	N/A	$40

(2) In sum, the correct amounts to be used in paragraph (f)(2)(x) of this section are as follows:

Table 1 to paragraph (o)(14)(viii)(D)(2)

	A	B	C	D	Total
ATIC excess	$0	$0	$0	$0	$0
ATIC deficit	$0	$28	$12	$0	$40
Non-priority partner final ATIC deficit	$0	$0	$0	$40	N/A

(ix) Ninth, PRS determines each partner's final ATIC excess amount. Pursuant to paragraph (f)(2)(viii)(D) of this section, each priority and non-priority partner's final ATIC excess amount is $0.

(x) Tenth, PRS determines each partner's final ATIC deficit amount. Because B has an ATIC deficit, PRS must determine B's final ATIC deficit amount. B's final ATIC deficit amount is B's ATIC deficit ($28), reduced, but not below $0, by the product of the total ATIC excess ($0) and the ratio of B's ATIC deficit to the total ATIC deficit ($28/$40). Therefore, B has $28 of final ATIC deficit ($28 — ($0 x 70 percent)). Because C has an ATIC deficit, PRS must determine C's final ATIC deficit amount. C's final ATIC deficit amount is C's ATIC deficit ($12), reduced, but not below $0, by the product of the total ATIC excess ($0) and the ratio of C's ATIC deficit to the total ATIC deficit ($12/$40). Therefore, C has $12 of final ATIC deficit ($12 — ($0 x 30 percent)). Pursuant to paragraph (f)(2)(viii)(D) of this section, D's final ATIC deficit amount is $40.

Table 2 to paragraph (o)(14)(x)

	A	B	C	D	Total
ATIC deficit	N/A	$28	$12	N/A	N/A
Less: (Total ATIC excess) x (ATIC deficit / Total ATIC deficit)	N/A	$0	$0	N/A	N/A
= Final ATIC deficit	$0	$28	$12	$40	$80

(xi) Eleventh, PRS allocates deductible business interest expense and section 163(j) excess items to the partners. Pursuant to paragraph (f)(2)(i) of this section, PRS has $80 of excess business interest expense. PRS allocates the excess business interest expense dollar for dollar to the partners with final ATIC deficits. Thus, PRS allocates its excess business interest expense $28 to B, $12 to C, and $40 to D. A partner's allocable business interest expense is deductible business interest expense to the extent it exceeds such partner's share of excess business interest expense. Therefore, A has deductible business interest expense of $0 ($0 - $0), B has deductible business interest expense of $12 ($40 - $28), C has deductible business interest expense of $48 ($60 - $12), and D has deductible business interest expense of $0 ($40 - $40).

Table 1 to paragraph (o)(14)(xi)

	A	B	C	D	Total
Deductible BIE	$0	$12	$48	$0	$60
EBIE allocated	$0	$28	$12	$40	$80
ETI allocated	$0	$0	$0	$0	$0
EBII allocated	$0	$0	$0	$0	$0

(15) *Example 15: Facts*. A, B, C, and D own all of the interests in partnership PRS. In Year 1, PRS has $200 of ATI, $0 of business interest income, and $150 of business interest expense. PRS's ATI consists of $500 of gross income and $300 of gross deductions. PRS allocates its items comprising ATI $50 to A, $50 to B, $400 to C, and ($300) to D. PRS allocates its business interest expense $0 to A, $50 to B, $50 to C, and $50 to D.

(i) First, PRS determines its limitation pursuant to § 1.163(j)-2. PRS's section 163(j) limit is 30 percent of its ATI plus its business interest income, or $60 ($200 x 30 percent). Thus, PRS has $60 of deductible business interest expense, and $90 of excess business interest expense.

(ii) Second, PRS determines each partner's allocable share of section 163(j) items used in its own section 163(j) calculation.

Table 1 to paragraph (o)(15)(ii)

	A	B	C	D	Total
Allocable ATI	$50	$50	$400	($300)	$200
Allocable BII	$0	$0	$0	$0	$0
Allocable BIE	$0	$50	$50	$50	$150

(iii) Third, PRS compares each partner's allocable business interest income to such partner's allocable business interest expense. No partner has allocable business interest income. Consequently, each partner's allocable business interest income deficit is equal to such partner's allocable business interest expense. Thus, A's allocable business interest income deficit is $0, B's allocable business interest income deficit is $50, C's allocable business interest income deficit is $50, and D's allocable business interest income deficit is $50. The total allocable business interest income deficit is $150 ($0 + $50 + $50 + $50). No partner has allocable business interest income excess because no partner has allocable business interest income in excess of its allocable business interest expense. Thus, the total allocable business interest income excess is $0.

Table 1 to paragraph (o)(15)(iii)

	A	B	C	D	Total
Allocable BII	$0	$0	$0	$0	N/A
Allocable BIE	$0	$50	$50	$50	N/A
If allocable BII exceeds allocable BIE, then such amount = Allocable BII excess	$0	$0	$0	$0	$0
If allocable BIE exceeds allocable BII, then such amount = Allocable BII deficit	$0	$50	$50	$50	$150

(iv) Fourth, PRS determines each partner's final allocable business interest income excess. Because no partner has any allocable business interest income excess, each partner has final allocable business interest income excess of $0.

(v) Fifth, PRS determines each partner's remaining business interest expense. Because no partner has any allocable business interest income excess, each partner's remaining business interest expense equals its allocable business interest income deficit. Thus, A's remaining business interest expense is $0, B's remaining business interest expense is $50, C's remaining business interest expense is $50, and D's remaining business interest expense is $50.

Table 1 to paragraph (o)(15)(v)

	A	B	C	D	Total
Allocable BII deficit	$0	$50	$50	$50	$150
Less: (Total allocable BII excess) x (Allocable BII deficit / Total allocable BII deficit)	$0	$0	$0	$0	N/A
= Remaining BIE	$0	$50	$50	$50	N/A

(vi) Sixth, PRS determines each partner's final allocable ATI. Because D's allocable ATI is comprised of $300 of items of deduction and loss and $0 of income and gain, D has negative allocable ATI of $300. D is the only partner with negative allocable ATI. Thus, the total negative allocable ATI amount is $300. Any partner with a negative allocable ATI, or an allocable ATI of $0, has a positive allocable ATI of $0. Therefore, D has a positive allocable ATI of $0. PRS determines A's final allocable ATI by reducing, but not below $0, A's positive allocable ATI ($50) by the product of total negative allocable ATI ($300) and the ratio of A's positive allocable ATI to the total positive allocable ATI ($50/$500). Therefore, A's positive allocable ATI is reduced by $30 ($300 x 10 percent). As a result, A's final allocable ATI is $20. PRS determines B's final allocable ATI by reducing, but not below $0, B's positive allocable ATI ($50) by the product of total negative allocable ATI ($300) and the ratio of B's positive allocable ATI to the total positive allocable ATI ($50/$500). Therefore, B's positive allocable ATI is reduced by $30 ($300 x 10 percent). As a result, B's final allocable ATI is $20. PRS determines C's final allocable ATI by reducing, but not below $0, C's positive allocable ATI ($400) by the product of total negative allocable ATI ($300) and the ratio of C's positive allocable ATI to the total positive allocable ATI ($400/$500). Therefore, C's positive allocable ATI is reduced by $240 ($300 x 80 percent). As a result, C's final allocable ATI is $160. Because D has a positive allocable ATI of $0, D's final allocable ATI is $0.

Table 1 to paragraph (o)(15)(vi)

	A	B	C	D	Total
Allocable ATI	$50	$50	$400	($300)	$200
If deduction and loss items comprising allocable ATI exceed income and gain items comprising allocable ATI, then such excess amount = Negative allocable ATI	$0	$0	$0	$300	$300
If income and gain items comprising allocable ATI equal or exceed deduction and loss items comprising allocable ATI, then such amount = Positive allocable ATI	$50	$50	$400	$0	$500

Table 2 to paragraph (o)(15)(vi)

	A	B	C	D	Total
Positive allocable ATI	$50	$50	$400	$0	$500
Less: (Total negative allocable ATI) x (Positive allocable ATI / Total positive allocable ATI)	$30	$30	$240	$0	N/A
= Final allocable ATI	$20	$20	$160	$0	$200

(vii) Seventh, PRS compares each partner's ATI capacity (ATIC) amount to such partner's remaining business interest expense. A's ATIC amount is $6 ($20 x 30 percent), B's ATIC amount is $6 ($20 x 30 percent), C's ATIC amount is $48 ($160 x 30 percent), and D's ATIC amount is $0 ($0 x 30 percent). Because A's ATIC amount exceeds its remaining business interest expense by $6 ($6 - $0), A has an ATIC excess of $6. B, C, and D do not have any ATIC excess. Thus, the total ATIC excess amount is $6 ($6 + $0 + $0 + $0). A does not have any ATIC deficit. Because B's remaining business interest expense exceeds its ATIC amount by $44 ($50 - $6), B has an ATIC deficit of $44. Because C's remaining business interest expense exceeds its ATIC amount by $2 ($50 - $48), C has an ATIC deficit of $2. Because D's remaining business interest expense exceeds its ATIC amount by $50 ($50 - $0), D has an ATIC deficit of $50. Thus, the total ATIC deficit is $96 ($0 + $44 + $2 + $50).

Table 1 to paragraph (o)(15)(vii)

	A	B	C	D	Total
ATIC (Final allocable ATI x 30 percent)	$6	$6	$48	$0	N/A
Remaining BIE	$0	$50	$50	$50	N/A
If ATIC exceeds remaining BIE, then such excess = ATIC excess	$6	$0	$0	$0	$6
If remaining BIE exceeds ATIC, then such excess = ATIC deficit	$0	$44	$2	$50	$96

(viii)(A) Eighth, PRS must perform the calculations and make the necessary adjustments described under paragraph (f)(2)(viii) of this section if, and only if, PRS has:

(*1*) An excess business interest expense greater than $0 under paragraph (f)(2)(i) of this section;

(*2*) A total negative allocable ATI greater than $0 under paragraph (f)(2)(vi) of this section; and

(*3*) A total ATIC excess amount greater than $0 under paragraph (f)(2)(vii) of this section. Because PRS satisfies each of these three requirements, PRS must perform the calculations and make the necessary adjustments described under paragraph (f)(2)(viii) of this section.

(B) PRS must determine each partner's priority amount and usable priority amount. Only partners with an ATIC deficit under paragraph (f)(2)(vii) of this section of this section can have a priority amount greater than $0. Thus, only partners B, C, and D can have a priority amount greater than $0. PRS determines a partner's priority amount as thirty percent of the amount by which such partner's allocable positive ATI exceeds its final allocable ATI. Therefore, B's priority amount is $9 (($50 - $20) x 30 percent), C's priority amount is $72 (($400 - $160) x 30 percent), and D's priority amount is $0 (($0 - $0) x 30 percent). Thus, the total priority amount is $81 ($0 + $9 + $72 + $0). Next, PRS must determine each partner's usable priority amount. Each partner's usable priority amount is the lesser of such partner's priority amount or ATIC deficit. Thus, B has a usable priority amount of $9, C has a usable priority amount of $2, and D has a usable priority amount of $0. As a result, the total usable priority amount is $11 ($0 + $9 + $2 + $0). Because the total usable priority amount ($11) is greater than the total ATIC excess ($6) under paragraph (f)(2)(vii) of this section, PRS must perform the adjustments described in paragraph (f)(2)(viii)(D) of this section.

Table 1 to paragraph (o)(15)(viii)(B)

	A	B	C	D	Total
(Positive allocable ATI - Final allocable ATI)	$0	$30	$240	$0	N/A
Multiplied by 30 percent	30 percent	30 percent	30 percent	30 percent	N/A
= Priority amount	$0	$9	$72	$0	$81

Table 2 to paragraph (o)(15)(viii)(B)

	A	B	C	D	Total
Priority amount	$0	$9	$72	$0	N/A
ATIC deficit	$0	$44	$2	$50	N/A
Lesser of priority amount or ATIC deficit = Usable priority amount	$0	$9	$2	$0	$11

(C) In light of the fact that the total usable priority amount is greater than the total ATIC excess under paragraph (f)(2)(viii)(B) of this section, paragraph (f)(2)(viii)(C) of this section does not apply.

(D)(*1*) Because B and C are the only partners with priority amounts greater than $0, B and C are priority partners, while A and D are non-priority partners. For purposes of paragraph (f)(2)(ix) of this section, each partner's final ATIC excess amount is $0. For purposes of paragraph (f)(2)(x) of this section, each non-priority partner's final ATIC deficit amount is such partner's ATIC deficit determined pursuant to paragraph (f)(2)(vii) of this section. Therefore, A has a final ATIC deficit of $0 and D has a final ATIC deficit of $50. Additionally, for purposes of paragraph (f)(2)(x) of this section, PRS must determine each priority partner's step eight excess share. A priority partner's step eight excess share is the product of the total ATIC excess and the ratio of the partner's priority amount to the total priority amount. Thus, B's step eight excess share is $0.67 ($6 x ($9/$81)) and C's step eight excess share is $5.33 ($6 x ($72/$81)). To the extent a priority partner's step eight excess share exceeds its ATIC deficit, the excess shall be the partner's ATIC excess for purposes of paragraph (f)(2)(x) of this section. B's step eight excess share does not exceed its ATIC deficit. Because C's step eight excess share ($5.33) exceeds its ATIC deficit ($2), C's ATIC excess for purposes of paragraph (f)(2)(x) of this section is $3.33 ($5.33 - $2). Thus, the total ATIC excess for purposes of paragraph (f)(2)(x) of this section is $3.33 ($0 + $3.33). To the extent a priority partner's ATIC deficit exceeds its step eight excess share, the excess shall be the partner's ATIC deficit for purposes of paragraph (f)(2)(x) of this section. Because B's ATIC deficit ($44) exceeds its step eight excess share ($0.67), B's ATIC deficit for purposes of paragraph (f)(2)(x) of this section is $43.33 ($44 - $0.67). C's ATIC deficit does not exceed its step eight excess share. Thus, the total ATIC deficit for purposes of paragraph (f)(2)(x) of this section is $43.33 ($43.33 + $0).

Table 1 to paragraph (o)(15)(viii)(D)(*1*)

	A	B	C	D	Total
Non-priority partners ATIC deficit in paragraph (f)(2)(vii) = Final ATIC deficit for purposes of paragraph (f)(2)(x) of this section	$0	N/A	N/A	$50	N/A

Table 2 to paragraph (o)(15)(viii)(D)(*1*)

	A	B	C	D	Total
Priority partners step eight excess share = (Total ATIC excess) x (Priority / Total priority)	N/A	$0.67	$5.33	N/A	N/A
ATIC deficit	N/A	$44	$2	N/A	N/A
If step eight excess share exceeds ATIC deficit, then such excess = ATIC excess for purposes of paragraph (f)(2)(x) of this section	N/A	$0	$3.33	N/A	$3.33
If ATIC deficit exceeds step eight excess share, then such excess = ATIC deficit for purposes of paragraph (f)(2)(x) of this section	N/A	$43.33	$0	N/A	$43.33

(2) In sum, the correct amounts to be used in paragraph (f)(2)(x) of this section are as follows.

Table 1 to paragraph (o)(15)(viii)(D)(2)

	A	B	C	D	Total
ATIC excess	$0	$0	$3.33	$0	$3.33
ATIC deficit	$0	$43.33	$0	$0	$43.33
Non-priority partner final ATIC deficit	$0	$0	$0	$50	N/A

(ix) Ninth, PRS determines each partner's final ATIC excess amount. Pursuant to paragraph (f)(2)(viii)(D) of this section, each priority and non-priority partner's final ATIC excess amount is $0.

(x) Tenth, PRS determines each partner's final ATIC deficit amount. Because B has an ATIC deficit, PRS must determine B's final ATIC deficit amount. B's final ATIC deficit amount is B's ATIC deficit ($43.33), reduced, but not below $0, by the product of the total ATIC excess ($3.33) and the ratio of B's ATIC deficit to the total ATIC deficit ($43.33/$43.33). Therefore, B has $40 of final ATIC deficit ($43.33 — ($3.33 x 100 percent)). Pursuant to paragraph (f)(2)(viii)(D) of this section, D's final ATIC deficit amount is $40.

Table 1 to paragraph (o)(15)(x)

	A	B	C	D	Total
ATIC deficit	$0	$43.33	$0	N/A	N/A
Less: (Total ATIC excess) x (ATIC deficit / Total ATIC deficit)	$0	$3.33	$0	N/A	N/A
= Final ATIC deficit	$0	$40	$0	$50	$90

(xi) Eleventh, PRS allocates deductible business interest expense and section 163(j) excess items to the partners. Pursuant to paragraph (f)(2)(i) of this section, PRS has $90 of excess business interest expense. PRS allocates the excess business interest expense dollar for dollar to the partners with final ATIC deficits. Thus, PRS allocates its excess business interest expense $40 to B and $50 to D. A partner's allocable business interest expense is deductible business interest expense to the extent it exceeds such partner's share of excess business interest expense. Therefore, A has deductible business interest expense of $0 ($0 - $0), B has deductible business interest expense of $10 ($50 - $40), C has deductible business interest expense of $50 ($50 - $0), and D has deductible business interest expense of $0 ($50 - $50).

Table 1 to paragraph (o)(15)(xi)

	A	B	C	D	Total
Deductible BIE	$0	$10	$50	$0	$60
EBIE allocated	$0	$40	$0	$50	$90
ETI allocated	$0	$0	$0	$0	$0
EBII allocated	$0	$0	$0	$0	$0

(16) *Example 16*—(i) *Facts.* A and B are equal shareholders in X, a subchapter S corporation. In Year 1, X has $100 of ATI and $40 of business interest expense. A has $100 of ATI and $20 of business interest expense from its sole proprietorship. B has $0 of ATI and $20 of business interest expense from its sole proprietorship.

(ii) *S corporation-level.* In Year 1, X's section 163(j) limit is 30 percent of its ATI, or $30 ($100 x 30 percent). Thus, X has $30 of deductible business interest expense and $10 of disallowed business interest expense. Such $30 of deductible business interest expense is includable in X's non-separately stated income or loss, and is not subject to further limitation under section 163(j). X carries forward the $10 of disallowed business interest expense to Year 2 as a disallowed business interest expense carryforward under § 1.163(j)-2(c). X may not currently deduct all $40 of its business interest expense in Year 1. X only reduces its accumulated adjustments account in Year 1 by the $30 of deductible business interest expense in Year 1 under § 1.163(j)-6(l)(7).

(iii) *Shareholder allocations.* A and B are each allocated $35 of nonseparately stated taxable income ($50 items of income or gain, less $15 of deductible business interest expense) from X. A and B do not reduce their basis in X by the $10 of disallowed business interest expense.

(iv) *Shareholder-level computations.* A, in computing its limit under section 163(j), has $100 of ATI and $20 of business interest expense from its sole proprietorship. A's section 163(j) limit is $30 ($100 x 30 percent). Thus, A's $20 of business interest expense is deductible business interest expense. B, in computing its limit under section 163(j), has $20 of business interest expense from its sole proprietorship. B's section 163(j) limit is $0 ($0 x 30 percent). Thus, B's $20 of business interest expense is not allowed as a deduction and is treated as business interest expense paid or accrued by B in Year 2.

(17) *Example 17*—(i) *Facts.* The facts are the same as in *Example 16* in paragraph (o)(16) of this section. In Year 2, X has $233.33 of ATI, $0 of business interest income, and $30 of business interest expense. A has $100 of ATI and $20 of

business interest expense from its sole proprietorship. B has $0 of ATI and $20 of business interest expense from its sole proprietorship.

(ii) *S corporation-level.* In Year 2, X's section 163(j) limit is 30 percent of its ATI plus its business interest income, or $70 ($233.33 x 30 percent). Because X's section 163(j) limit exceeds X's $40 of business interest expense ($30 from Year 2, plus the $10 disallowed business interest expense carryforwards from Year 1), X may deduct all $40 of business interest expense in Year 2. Such $40 of deductible business interest expense is includable in X's non-separately stated income or loss, and is not subject to further limitation under section 163(j). Pursuant to § 1.163(j)-6(l)(7), X must reduce its accumulated adjustments account by $40. Additionally, X has $100 of excess taxable income under § 1.163(j)-1(b)(15).

(iii) *Shareholder allocations.* A and B are each allocated $96.67 of nonseparately stated taxable income ($116.67 items of income or gain, less $20 of deductible business interest expense) from X. Additionally, A and B are each allocated $50 of excess taxable income under § 1.163(j)-6(l)(4). As a result, A and B each increase their ATI by $50.

(iv) *Shareholder-level computations.* A, in computing its limit under section 163(j), has $150 of ATI ($100 from its sole proprietorship, plus $50 excess taxable income) and $20 of business interest expense (from its sole proprietorship). A's section 163(j) limit is $45 ($150 x 30 percent). Thus, A's $20 of business interest expense is deductible business interest expense. B, in computing its limit under section 163(j), has $50 of ATI ($0 from its sole proprietorship, plus $50 excess taxable income) and $40 of business interest expense ($20 from its sole proprietorship, plus $20 disallowed business interest expense from its sole proprietorship in Year 1). B's section 163(j) limit is $15 ($50 x 30 percent). Thus, $15 of B's business interest expense is deductible business interest expense. The $25 of B's business interest expense not allowed as a deduction ($40 business interest expense, less $15 section 163(j) limit) is treated as business interest expense paid or accrued by B in Year 3.

(p) *Applicability date.*—This section applies to taxable years ending after the date the Treasury decision adopting these regulations as final regulations is published in the **Federal Register**. However, taxpayers and their related parties, within the meaning of sections 267(b) and 707(b)(1), may apply the rules of this section to a taxable year beginning after December 31, 2017, so long as the taxpayers and their related parties consistently apply the rules of the section 163(j) regulations, and if applicable, §§ 1.263A-9, 1.381(c)(20)-1, 1.382-6, 1.383-1, 1.469-9, 1.882-5, 1.1502-13, 1.1502-21, 1.1502-36, 1.1502-79, 1.1502-91 through 1.1502-99 (to the extent they effectuate the rules of §§ 1.382-6 and 1.383-1), and 1.1504-4 to those taxable years. [Reg. § 1.163(j)-6.]

§ 1.163(j)-7. Application of the business interest deduction limitation to foreign corporations and United States shareholders.—(a) *Overview.*—This section provides rules for the application of section 163(j) to foreign corporations with shareholders that are United States persons. Paragraph (b) of this section provides rules regarding the application of section 163(j) to certain controlled foreign corporations. Paragraph (c) of this section provides rules concerning the computation of adjusted taxable income (ATI) of certain controlled foreign corporations. Paragraph (d) of this section provides rules concerning the computation of ATI of a United States shareholder of certain controlled foreign corporations (CFC). Paragraph (e) of this section provides a rule regarding the effect of section 163(j) on the earnings and profits of foreign corporations. Paragraph (f) of this section provides definitions that apply for purposes of this section. Paragraph (g) of this section provides examples illustrating the application of this section. Paragraph (h) of this section provides dates of applicability.

(b) *Application of section 163(j) to an applicable CFC and certain partnerships.*—(1) *Scope.*—This paragraph (b) provides rules regarding the application of section 163(j) to an applicable CFC and certain partnerships. Paragraph (b)(2) of this section describes the general application of section 163(j) to an applicable CFC and certain partnerships in which an applicable CFC is a partner. Paragraph (b)(3) of this section provides an election to use an alternative method for computing the deduction for business interest expense of a member of a CFC group. Paragraph (b)(4) of this section treats certain partnerships as members of a CFC group for purposes of this paragraph (b). Paragraph (b)(5) of this section provides the rules regarding an election to apply paragraph (b)(3) of this section.

(2) *General application of section 163(j) to an applicable CFC and a partnership with at least one partner that is an applicable CFC.*—Except as otherwise provided in this paragraph (b) or in the section 163(j) regulations, section 163(j) and the section 163(j) regulations apply to determine the deductibility of an applicable CFC's business interest expense for purposes of computing its taxable income in the same manner as those provisions apply to determine the deductibility of a domestic C corporation's business interest expense for purposes of computing its taxable income. Furthermore, if an applicable CFC is a partner in a partnership, except as otherwise provided in this paragraph (b) or in the section 163(j) regulations, section 163(j) and the section 163(j) regulations apply to the partnership in the same manner as those provisions would apply if the applicable CFC were a domestic C corporation. If an applicable CFC has income that is, or is treated as, effectively connected with the conduct of a trade or business in the United States or if a partnership is engaged in a trade or business conducted in the United States, see also §§ 1.163(j)-8(d) and 1.882-5 for additional rules concerning the deduction for interest.

(3) *Alternative approach for computing the deduction for business interest expense.*—If a CFC group election is properly made and in effect with respect to a specified taxable year of a CFC group member of a CFC group, then—

(i) The portion of the CFC group member's business interest expense that is subject to the general rule under § 1.163(j)-2(b) is the amount equal to the CFC group member's allocable share of the CFC group's applicable net business interest expense, or, in the case in which the CFC group member is also a member of a financial services subgroup, the allocable share of the applicable subgroup net business interest expense; and

(ii) The limitation provided in § 1.163(j)-2(b) is applied without regard to § 1.163(j)-2(b)(1) and (3).

(4) *Treatment of certain partnerships as a CFC group member.*—(i) *General rule.*—If one or more CFC group members of the same CFC group, in the aggregate, own more than 80 percent of the interests in the capital or profits in a partnership, then, except as provided in paragraph (b)(4)(ii) of this section, the partnership is treated as a CFC group member. If there is a financial services subgroup with respect to the CFC group, this paragraph (b)(4) will apply only if all of the CFC group members described in the preceding sentence are financial services subgroup members or none of them are financial services subgroup members. If a partnership is treated as a CFC group member, then an interest in the partnership is treated as stock for purposes of applying this section.

(ii) *Exception for certain partnerships engaged in a United States trade or business.*—Notwithstanding paragraph (b)(4)(i) of this section, a partnership is not treated as a CFC group member if the partnership is engaged in a trade or business in the United States, directly or indirectly through another passthrough entity, and one or more partners has income that is effectively connected with the conduct of a trade or business in the United States, including any income that is treated as effectively connected income under an applicable provision of the Code or regulations, and at least one of the partners is not exempt from U.S. tax by reason of a U.S. income tax treaty. Notwithstanding the preceding sentence, a partnership that, without regard to this paragraph (b)(4)(ii), would be treated as a CFC group member under paragraph (b)(4)(i) of this section, is treated as a CFC group member solely for purposes of determining if another entity is a CFC group member with respect to the CFC group.

(5) *CFC group election.*—(i) *Manner of making a CFC group election.*—Subject to paragraph (b)(5)(ii) of this section, a CFC group election is made by applying paragraph (b)(3) of this section for purposes of computing the amount of a CFC group member's deduction for business interest expense. Except as otherwise provided in publications, forms, instructions, or other guidance, a separate statement or form evidencing the election need not be filed.

(ii) *Consistency requirement.*—An election under paragraph (b)(5)(i) of this section is not effective unless all CFC group members of the CFC group make the election. If an entity becomes a CFC group member of a CFC group for which a CFC group election is in effect, the entity must make the CFC group election.

(iii) *Duration of a CFC group election.*—A CFC group election is irrevocable. If an entity ceases to be a CFC group member of a CFC group for which a CFC group election is in effect, the election terminates solely with respect to such entity. If a CFC group ceases to exist, a CFC group election terminates with respect to all CFC group members of the CFC group.

(c) *Rules concerning the computation of adjusted taxable income of an applicable CFC and certain CFC group members.*—(1) *Computation of taxable income.*—For purposes of computing taxable income of an applicable CFC for a taxable year, the applicable CFC's gross income and allowable deductions are determined under the principles of § 1.952-2 or the rules of section 882 for determining taxable income that is effectively connected with the conduct of a trade or business in the United States, as applicable.

(2) *Treatment of certain dividends.*—For purposes of computing the ATI of an applicable CFC for a taxable year, any dividend included in gross income that is received from a related person, within the meaning of section 954(d)(3), with respect to the distributee is subtracted from taxable income.

(3) *Treatment of CFC excess taxable income.*—(i) *In general.*—If a CFC group election is in effect for a specified taxable year of a CFC group member and if the CFC group member (*upper-tier member*) directly owns stock in one or more other CFC group members (*lower-tier member*), then, for purposes of computing ATI of the upper-tier member for the specified taxable year, there is added to taxable income the sum of the products of the following amounts with respect to each lower-tier member—

(A) The CFC excess taxable income (if any) of the lower-tier member for the lower-tier member's specified taxable year; and

(B) The percentage (by value) of the stock of the lower-tier member that is directly owned by the upper-tier member on the last day of the lower-tier member's specified taxable year.

(ii) *Ordering rules.*—For purposes of applying paragraph (c)(3)(i) of this section, if a CFC group member is an upper-tier member with respect to a CFC group member and a lower-tier member with respect to another CFC group member, paragraph (c)(3)(i) of this section is applied starting with the lowest-tier CFC group member in the chain of ownership. If an upper-tier member is a partner in a lower-tier member that is a partnership, which is an entity that does not have CFC excess taxable income but that may have excess taxable income (as defined in § 1.163(j)-1(b)(15)), see § 1.163(j)-6(f) for determining the upper-tier member's share of the lower-tier member's excess taxable income (if any).

(d) *Rules concerning the computation of adjusted taxable income of a United States shareholder.*—(1) *In general.*—(i) *Treatment of gross income inclusions that are properly allocable to a non-excepted trade or business.*—If for a taxable year a United States shareholder with respect to one or more applicable CFCs includes amounts in gross income under section 78, 951(a), or 951A(a) that are properly allocable to a non-excepted trade or business (each amount, a *specified deemed inclusion* and such amounts, collectively *specified deemed inclusions*), then, for purposes of computing ATI of the United States shareholder, there is subtracted from taxable income an amount equal to the specified deemed inclusions, reduced by the portion of the deduction allowed under section 250(a)(1), without regard to the taxable income limitation of section 250(a)(2), by reason of the specified deemed inclusions (such a deduction, a *specified section 250 deduction*). For rules concerning inclusions under sections 78, 951(a), and 951A(a) and deductions allowable under section 250 that are not properly allocable to a non-excepted trade or business, see § 1.163(j)-1(b)(1)(ii)(F) and (b)(1)(i)(H), respectively.

(ii) *Treatment of deemed inclusions of a domestic partnership that are not allocable to any trade or business*.—If a United States shareholder that is a domestic partnership includes amounts in gross income under section 951(a) or 951A(a) that are not properly allocable to trade or business of the domestic partnership, then, notwithstanding § 1.163(j)-4(b)(3), to the extent a C corporation partner, including an indirect partner in the case of tiered partnerships, takes such amounts into account as a distributive share in accordance with section 702 and § 1.702-1(a)(8)(ii), the C corporation partner may not treat such amounts as properly allocable to a trade or business of the C corporation partner.

(2) *Additional rule after application of paragraph (d)(1) of this section for a United States shareholder of a CFC group member with a CFC group election in effect*.—(i) *In general*.—Subject to paragraph (d)(3) of this section, if for a taxable year, a United States shareholder owns directly, or indirectly through one or more foreign pass-through entities, stock of one or more CFC group members of a CFC group for which a CFC group election is in effect for the specified taxable year of each CFC group member that ends with or within the taxable year of the United States shareholder, then, for purposes of computing ATI of the United States shareholder, in addition to the subtraction described in paragraph (d)(1) of this section, there is added to taxable income the amount equal to the sum of the amounts of eligible CFC group ETI, as defined in paragraph (d)(2)(ii) of this section, with respect to each specified highest-tier member of the United States shareholder, but not in excess of the amount of the CFC group inclusions, as defined in paragraph (d)(2)(iii) of this section, of the United States shareholder for the taxable year. For purposes of this paragraph (d)(2)(i), members of a consolidated group are treated as a single United States shareholder.

(ii) *Eligible CFC group ETI*.—The term *eligible CFC group ETI* means, with respect to a specified highest-tier member and a specified taxable year, the amount equal to the product of the following three amounts—

(A) The specified highest-tier member's CFC excess taxable income for the specified taxable year, taking into account the application of paragraph (c)(3) of this section;

(B) The specified highest-tier member's specified ETI ratio for the specified taxable year; and

(C) The percentage, by value, of the stock of the specified highest-tier member that is owned directly, or indirectly through one or more foreign passthrough entities, by the United States shareholder on the last day of the specified taxable year.

(iii) *CFC group inclusions*.—The term *CFC group inclusions* means, with respect to a United States shareholder and a taxable year, the amounts of the specified deemed inclusions subtracted from taxable income under paragraph (d)(1)(i) of this section that are with respect to CFC group members, other than amounts included in gross income by reason of section 78, reduced by the portion of any specified section 250 deduction described in paragraph (d)(1)(i) of this section that is allowable by reason of such specified deemed inclusions.

(3) *Special rules if a domestic partnership is a United States shareholder of a CFC group member with a CFC group election in effect*.—Paragraph (d)(2) of this section does not apply with respect to a United States shareholder described in paragraph (d)(2) of this section that is a domestic partnership (such a partnership, a *U.S. shareholder partnership*). If a U.S. shareholder partnership has a domestic C corporation partner, including an indirect partner in the case of tiered partnerships, (such a partner, a *U.S. corporate partner*), then, for purposes of computing ATI of the U.S. corporate partner, paragraph (d)(2) of this section is applied by treating the U.S. shareholder partnership, and in case of tiered partnerships, any tiered partnership that is a domestic partnership, as if it were a foreign partnership and by making the following modifications—

(i) The term "U.S. corporate partner" is substituted for the term "United States shareholder" each place it appears in paragraph (d)(2) of this section; and

(ii) If a U.S. shareholder partnership includes an amount in gross income under section 951(a) or 951(A) with respect to a CFC group member, then to the extent the amount is taken into account by a U.S. corporate partner as a distributive share in accordance with section 702 and § 1.702-1(a)(8)(ii), such amount is treated as a specified deemed inclusion of the U.S. corporate partner with respect to the CFC group member for purposes of applying paragraph (d)(2)(iii) of this section.

(4) *Inclusions under section 951A(a)*.—For purposes of applying paragraph (d) of this section, the portion of a United States shareholder's inclusion under section 951A(a) treated as being with respect to a CFC group member is determined under section 951A(f)(2) and § 1.951A-6(b)(2).

(e) *Effect on earnings and profits*.—In the case of a foreign corporation, the disallowance and carryforward of a deduction for the corporation's business interest expense under § 1.163(j)-2 will not affect whether and when such business interest expense reduces the corporation's earnings and profits. Thus, for example, if a United States person has elected under section 1295 to treat a passive foreign investment company (as defined in section 1297) (PFIC) as a qualified electing fund, then the disallowance and carryforward of a deduction for the PFIC's business interest expense under § 1.163(j)-2 will not affect whether or when such business interest expense reduces the PFIC's earnings and profits. Similarly, the disallowance and carryforward of a deduction for an applicable CFC's business interest expense will not affect the earnings and profits limitation for subpart F income under section 952(c). See also § 1.163(j)-4(c).

(f) *Definitions*.—The following definitions apply for purposes of this section.

(1) *Allocable share*.—(i) *General rule*.—The term *allocable share* means, with respect to a CFC group member of a CFC group and a specified taxable year, the amount equal to the product of the CFC group's applicable net business interest expense (multiplicand), if any, and a fraction, the numerator of which is equal to the amount of the CFC group member's net business interest expense, and the denominator of which is equal to the sum of the amounts of the net business interest expense of each CFC group member.

(ii) *Special rule if there is a financial services subgroup.*—If there is a financial services subgroup with respect to a CFC group, then paragraph (f)(1)(i) of this section is applied with the following modifications—

(A) With respect to a CFC group member that is also a financial services subgroup member—

(1) The multiplicand is equal to the amount of the applicable subgroup net business interest expense; and

(2) The denominator of the fraction is determined by replacing the term "CFC group member" with the term "financial services subgroup member."

(B) With respect to a CFC group member this is not a financial services subgroup member—

(1) The multiplicand is reduced by the amount of the applicable subgroup net business interest expense; and

(2) The denominator of the fraction is reduced by the sum of the amounts of the net business interest expense of each financial services subgroup member.

(2) *Applicable CFC.*—The term *applicable CFC* means a controlled foreign corporation described in section 957, but only if the foreign corporation has at least one United States shareholder that owns, within the meaning of section 958(a), stock of the foreign corporation.

(3) *Applicable net business interest expense.*—The term *applicable net business interest expense* means, with respect to a CFC group and a majority U.S. shareholder taxable year, the excess, if any, of the sum of the amounts of the business interest expense of each CFC group member for the specified taxable year, over the sum of the amounts of the business interest income of each CFC group member for the specified taxable year.

(4) *Applicable subgroup net business interest expense.*—The term *applicable subgroup net business interest expense* means, with respect to a financial services subgroup of a CFC group and a majority U.S. shareholder taxable year, the excess, if any, of the sum of the amounts of the business interest expense of each financial services subgroup member for the specified taxable year, over the sum of the amounts of the business interest income of each financial services subgroup member for the specified taxable year.

(5) *CFC excess taxable income.*—(i) *In general.*—The term *CFC excess taxable income* means, with respect to a CFC group member, other than a partnership described in paragraph (b)(4)(i) of this section, and a specified taxable year, the amount which bears the same ratio to the CFC group member's ATI, as—

(A) The excess (if any) of—

(1) The amount determined for the CFC group member under § 1.163(j)-2(b)(2); over

(2) The CFC group member's allocable share of either the applicable net business interest expense or the applicable subgroup net business interest expense, as applicable; bears to

(B) The amount determined for the CFC group member under § 1.163(j)-2(b)(2).

(ii) *CFC group member is a partnership.*—If a CFC group member is a partnership, see § 1.163(j)-1(b)(15) for determining the extent to which the partnership has excess taxable income. For rules concerning a partner's share of a partnership's excess taxable income, see § 1.163(j)-6(f).

(6) *CFC group.*—(i) *In general.*—The term *CFC group* means two or more applicable CFCs if 80 percent or more of the total value of shares of all classes of stock of each applicable CFC is owned, within the meaning of section 958(a), either by a single United States shareholder or by multiple U.S. shareholders that are related persons, within the meaning of section 267(b) or 707(b)(1), (each a *related United States shareholder* and collectively *related United States shareholders*), provided the stock of each applicable CFC is owned in the same proportion by each related United States shareholder.

(ii) *Aggregation rules.*—The following rules apply for the purpose of applying paragraph (f)(6)(i) of this section—

(A) Members of a consolidated group and individuals described in section 318(a)(1)(A)(i) who file a joint tax return are treated as a single person; and

(B) If a single United States person, as defined in section 957(c), taking into account the application of paragraph (f)(6)(ii)(A) of this section, owns, directly or indirectly through one or more passthrough entities, more than 80 percent of the interests in a pass-through entity that is a United States shareholder that owns, within the meaning of section 958(a), stock in an applicable CFC, then that United States person is treated as owning the stock of the applicable CFC that is owned by the passthrough entity. For purposes of applying the 80-percent threshold described in the preceding sentence, if the pass-through entity is a partnership, then the 80-percent threshold is satisfied if the United States person owns at least 80 percent of the interests in the capital or the profits of the partnership, and if the passthrough entity is not a partnership, then the 80-percent threshold is satisfied if the United States person owns at least 80 percent of the value of all interests of the passthrough entity.

(7) *CFC group election.*—The term *CFC group election* means an election to apply paragraph (b)(3) of this section.

(8) *CFC group member.*—The term *CFC group member* means, with respect to a CFC group, an entity included in the CFC group. An entity that has, including through ownership of an interest in a passthrough entity, income which is effectively connected with a trade or business conducted in the United States, including any income that is treated as effectively connected income under an applicable provision of the Code or regulations, and not exempt from U.S. tax by reason of a U.S. income tax treaty is not treated as a member of a CFC group, other than solely for purposes of determining if another entity is a CFC group member with respect to the CFC group.

(9) *Financial services subgroup.*—The term *financial services subgroup* means, with respect to a CFC group, a group comprised of each CFC group member of the CFC group that is an eligible controlled foreign corporation (as defined in section 954(h)(2)(A)), a qualified insurance company (as defined in section 953(e)(3)), or eligible for the dealer exception in computing foreign personal holding company income (as described in section 954(c)(2)(C)).

(10) *Financial services subgroup member.*—The term *financial services subgroup member* means, with respect to a financial services subgroup of a CFC group, a CFC group member that is also a member of the financial services subgroup.

(11) *Majority U.S. shareholder taxable year.*—The term *majority U.S. shareholder taxable year* means, with respect to a CFC group, one of the following taxable years, applied sequentially—

(i) If there is a single United States shareholder of the CFC group for purposes of paragraph (f)(6)(i) of this section, then the taxable year of the United States shareholder;

(ii) If paragraph (f)(11)(i) of this section does not apply and a related United States shareholder owns, within the meaning of section 958(a), more stock of the members of the CFC group, by value, than is owned, within the meaning of section 958(a), by any other related United States shareholder, then the taxable year of the first-mentioned related United States shareholder;

(iii) If paragraphs (f)(11)(i) and (ii) of this section do not apply and if one or more related United States shareholders with the same taxable year, in aggregate, own, within the meaning of section 958(a), more stock of the members of the CFC group (by value) than is, in aggregate, owned, within the meaning of section 958(a), by other related United States shareholders with the same taxable year, then the taxable year of the first-mentioned related United States shareholders; and

(iv) If paragraphs (f)(11)(i), (ii), and (iii) of this section do not apply, then the calendar year.

(12) *Net business interest expense.*—The term *net business interest expense* means, with respect to a CFC group member of a CFC group and a specified taxable year, the excess, if any, of the amount of the CFC group member's business interest expense over the amount of the CFC group member's business interest income, in each case determined without regard to section 163(j) and the section 163(j) regulations.

(13) *Passthrough entity.*—The term *passthrough entity* means a partnership, S corporation, or any other entity (domestic or foreign) that is not a corporation if all items of income and deduction of the entity are included in the income of its owners or beneficiaries. An *interest in a passthrough entity* means an interest in the capital or profits of the entity or stock of an S corporation, as applicable.

(14) *Specified ETI ratio.*—(i) *In general.*—The term *specified ETI ratio* means, with respect to a specified highest-tier member of a CFC group and a specified taxable year, the ratio computed as a fraction (expressed as a percentage), the numerator of which is the sum of the amounts described in paragraph (f)(14)(iii) of this section with respect to each CFC group member described in paragraph (f)(14)(ii) of this section, and the denominator of which is the sum of the amounts described in paragraph (f)(14)(iv) of this section with respect to each CFC group member described in paragraph (f)(14)(ii) of this section that has amounts included in the numerator. The specified ETI ratio may not exceed 100 percent. If the numerator and the denominator of the fraction are not both greater than zero, the specified ETI ratio is treated as being equal to zero.

(ii) *Includable CFC group members.*—For purposes of applying paragraph (f)(14)(i) of this section, a CFC group member is described in this paragraph (f)(14)(ii) if—

(A) The CFC group member is the specified highest-tier member or a specified lower-tier member with respect to the specified highest-tier member; and

(B) The CFC group member has CFC excess taxable income without regard to paragraph (c)(3) of this section.

(iii) *Numerator.*—For purposes of applying (f)(14)(i) of this section, the amount described in this paragraph (f)(14)(iii) is, with respect to a CFC group member and a specified taxable year, the sum of the amounts included in gross income under sections 951(a) and 951A(a) of each United States shareholder with respect to the CFC group member for the taxable years of the United States shareholders in which or with which the specified taxable year of the CFC group member ends. For purposes of this paragraph (f)(14)(iii), the portion of a United States shareholder's inclusion under section 951A(a) treated as being with respect to a CFC group member is determined under section 951A(f)(2) and § 1.951A-6(b)(2).

(iv) *Denominator.*—For purposes of applying (f)(14)(i) of this section, the amount described in this paragraph (f)(14)(iv) is, with respect to a CFC group member and a specified taxable year, the taxable income of the CFC group member for the specified taxable year.

(15) *Specified highest-tier member.*—The term *specified highest-tier member* means, with respect to a CFC group, a CFC group member in which a United States shareholder owns directly, or indirectly through one or more foreign passthrough entities, stock of the CFC group member.

(16) *Specified lower-tier member.*—The term *specified lower-tier member* means, with respect to a specified highest-tier member of a CFC group, a CFC group member in which the specified highest-tier member owns stock directly or indirectly through a chain of ownership.

(17) *Specified taxable year.*—The term *specified taxable year* means, with respect to a CFC group member of a CFC group, the taxable year that ends with or within a majority U.S. shareholder year.

(18) *United States shareholder.*—The term *United States shareholder* has the meaning provided in section 951(b).

(g) *Examples.*—The following examples illustrate the application of this section. For each example, unless otherwise stated, the referenced business interest expense is deductible but for the application of section 163(j), no exemptions from the application of section 163(j) are available, none of the business interest expense is floor plan financing interest expense, and no foreign corporation has income that is effectively connected with a trade or business conducted in the United States or is an entity described in paragraph (f)(9) of this section (regarding entities that provide certain types of financial services).

(1) *Example 1: Computation of section 163(j) limitation of CFC group members*—(i) *Facts.* USP, a domestic C corporation, wholly owns US1 and US2, each of which is a domestic C corporation.

USP, US1, and US2 are members of a consolidated group of which USP is the common parent (USP group). US1 wholly owns CFC1, a foreign corporation, and US2 wholly owns CFC2 and CFC3, each of which is a foreign corporation. The USP group has a calendar year taxable year. For U.S. tax purposes, CFC1, CFC2, and CFC3 each have a fiscal taxable year ending on November 30. CFC1 has an outstanding loan of $1,000x from a third-party (CFC1 note). CFC1 has a receivable of $500x from each of CFC2 and CFC3 (CFC2 note and CFC3 note, respectively). Interest on all debt is paid and accrued annually on November 30. During the taxable year ending November 30, 2019, CFC1 has business interest expense of $90x attributable to CFC1 note and business interest income of $100x attributable to CFC2 note and CFC3 note, and CFC2 and CFC3 each have $50x of business interest expense attributable to CFC2 note and CFC3 note, respectively. Assume that each of CFC1, CFC2, and CFC3 has ATI of $100x computed on a separate company basis for the taxable year ending November 30, 2019. The USP group has no business interest expense.

(ii) *Analysis*—(A) *Determination of CFC group*. US1 owns (within the meaning of section 958(a)) all of the stock of CFC1, and US2 owns (within the meaning of section 958(a)) all of the stock of each of CFC2 and CFC3. Under paragraph (f)(2) of this section, each of CFC1, CFC2, and CFC3 is an applicable CFC. Under paragraph (f)(6)(ii)(A) of this section, because US1 and US2 are members of a consolidated group, US1 and US2 are treated as a single person for purposes determining a CFC group under paragraph (f)(6)(i) of this section. Therefore, because 80 percent or more of the stock of each of CFC1, CFC2, and CFC3 is owned (within the meaning of section 958(a)) by a single United States shareholder, under paragraph (f)(6)(i) of this section, CFC1, CFC2, and CFC3 are members of a CFC group (USP CFC group).

(B) *CFC group election is made*. Assume a CFC group election is properly made. Under paragraph (f)(11)(i) of this section, because there is a single United States shareholder of the USP CFC group with a calendar taxable year, the majority U.S. shareholder taxable year with respect to the USP CFC group ends on December 31, 2019. Under paragraph (f)(17) of this section, the specified taxable year of each of CFC1, CFC2, and CFC3 is November 30, 2019, which is the taxable year that ends with or within the majority U.S. shareholder taxable year ending on December 31, 2019. Under paragraph (f)(3) of this section, the applicable net business interest expense of the USP CFC group is $90x. The $90x is the excess of $190x, which is the sum of the amounts of the business interest expense of each of CFC1, CFC2, and CFC3 ($90x, $50x, and $50x, respectively), over $100x, which is the sum of the amounts of the business interest income of each of CFC1, CFC2, and CFC3 ($100x, $0, and $0, respectively). Under paragraph (f)(12) of this section, CFC1 has $0 of net business interest expense ($90x business interest expense does not exceed $100x of business interest income), and CFC2 and CFC3 each have $50x of net business interest expense (each has $50x business interest expense and $0 business interest income). Because CFC2 and CFC3 each has net business interest expense, under paragraph (f)(1) of this section, each has an allocable share of the applicable net business interest expense of the USP CFC group. The allocable share of each of CFC2 and CFC3 is $45x, computed as $90x (the applicable net business interest expense) multiplied by the fraction equal to $50x / $100x (the net business interest expense of the member and the sum of the amounts of net business interest expense of all members, respectively). Under paragraph (b)(3)(i) of this section, none of CFC1's $90x of business interest expense and $45x of each of CFC2's and CFC3's $50x of business interest expense is subject to the general rule under § 1.163(j)-2(b) (and $5x of each of CFC2's and CFC3's business interest expense is not subject to limitation under § 1.163(j)-2(b)), and, under paragraph (b)(3)(ii) of this section, the general rule under § 1.163(j)-2(b), as applied to CFC2 and CFC3, is computed without regard to § 1.163(j)-2(b)(1) and (3). Thus, under § 1.163(j)-2(b), CFC2's limitation is $30x ($100x ATI computed on a separate company basis x 30 percent). The amount of CFC2's business interest expense subject to limitation under paragraph (b)(3) of this section, $45x, exceeds CFC2's limitation under § 1.163(j)-2(b), $30x. Accordingly, $35x ($5x not subject to limitation + $30x) of CFC2's business interest expense is deductible, and under § 1.163(j)-2(c), the remaining $15x of business interest expense is not deductible and will be carried forward as a disallowed business interest expense carryforward. The analysis for CFC3 is the same as for CFC2. Because the USP group has no business interest expense, the application of paragraph (d) of this section is not relevant.

(C) *CFC group election is not made*. Instead, assume a CFC group election is not made. In this case, each of CFC1, CFC2, and CFC3 must compute its interest deduction limitation under § 1.163(j)-2(b), without regard to paragraph (b)(3) of this section. CFC1's business interest expense of $90x is deductible because it has business interest income of $100x. CFC2's business interest expense limitation is $30x ($100x ATI computed on a separate company basis x 30 percent). Accordingly, $30x of CFC2's business interest expense is deductible, and under § 1.163(j)-2(c), the remaining $20x of business interest expense is disallowed business interest expense and will be carried forward as a disallowed business interest expense carryforward. The analysis for CFC3 is the same as for CFC2.

(2) *Example 2: Computation and allocation of CFC excess taxable income*—(i) *Facts*. USP, a domestic C corporation, wholly owns CFC1, a foreign corporation. CFC1 wholly owns CFC2, a foreign corporation, and CFC2 wholly owns each of CFC3 and CFC4, both of which are foreign corporations (CFC1, CFC2, CFC3, and CFC4, collectively, the USP CFC group). All entities have a calendar year for U.S. tax purposes. For Year 1, assume the following additional facts: Prior to the application of section 163(j), CFC1 has no items of income, gain, deduction, or loss; CFC2 has a taxable loss of $5x (including $5x of business interest expense); CFC3 has taxable income of $85x (including $15x of business interest expense); CFC4 has $60x of taxable income (including $40x of business interest expense); a CFC group election is in effect for the CFC group; there is no intercompany debt between any CFC group member; 50 percent of CFC3's items of

income and gain are subpart F income (as defined in section 952), and 50 percent of CFC3's items of deduction and loss are properly allocable to subpart F income, and with respect to the remaining portion of CFC3's items of income, gain, deduction, and loss, no portion is taken into account in computing tested income (as defined in section 951A(c)(2)(A)) or tested loss (as defined in section 951A(c)(2)(B)) of CFC3; CFC4's items of income and gain are all tested income, and CFC4's items of deduction are all properly allocable to such income; no portion of CFC2's items of income, gain, deduction, or loss is taken into account in computing tested income or tested loss; no CFC group member has qualified business asset investment (as defined in section 951A(d)); for purposes of computing ATI, there are no subtractions or additions to taxable income described in § 1.163(j)-1(b)(1) with respect to any CFC group member of the USP CFC group other than for business interest expense; for simplicity, no foreign income taxes are paid by any CFC group member of the USP CFC group; in addition to the inclusions in gross income under sections 951(a)(1) and 951A(a) with respect to the CFC group members of the USP CFC group, USP has business interest expense of $20x.

(ii) *Analysis*—(A) *Application of section 163(j) to CFC group members of the USP CFC group; computation of USP CFC group's applicable net business interest expense.* Under paragraph (f)(3) of this section, the USP CFC group's applicable net business interest expense is $60x ($0 + $5x + $15x + $40x with respect to CFC1, CFC2, CFC3, and CFC4, respectively). Because there is no debt between the CFC group members of the USP CFC group, under paragraph (b)(3) of this section, each of the CFC group members allocable share of the $60x is equal to its separate company business interest expense. In particular, CFC1's allocable share of the USP CFC group's applicable net interest expense is zero, CFC2's allocable share is $5x, CFC3's allocable share is $15x, and CFC4's allocable share is $40x.

(B) *Application of section 163(j) to CFC4.* Under § 1.163(j)-1(b)(1), CFC4's ATI is $100x ($60x taxable income + $40x business interest expense). Under § 1.163(j)-2(b), CFC4's limitation is $30x ($100x ATI computed on a separate company basis x 30 percent). The amount of CFC4's business interest expense subject to limitation, $40x, exceeds CFC4's limitation, $30x. Accordingly, under § 1.163(j)-2(c), $10x of business interest expense is not deductible and will be carried forward as a disallowed business interest expense carryforward. Because $10x of business interest expense is not currently deductible, CFC4's tested income is $70x ($60x taxable income prior to application of section 163(j), increased by $10x of disallowed business interest expense).

(C) *Application of section 163(j) to CFC3.* Under § 1.163(j)-1(b)(1), CFC3's ATI is $100x ($85x taxable income + 15x business interest expense). Under § 1.163(j)-2(b), CFC3's limitation is $30x ($100x ATI computed on a separate company basis x 30 percent). Because the amount of CFC3's business interest expense subject to limitation, $15x, does not exceed CFC3's limitation, $30x, all of CFC3's business interest expense is currently deductible. Accordingly, CFC3's subpart F income is $42.50x ($85x taxable income x 50 percent). Furthermore, CFC3 has CFC excess taxable income of $50x ($100x x ($15x / $30x)).

(D) *Application of section 163(j) to CFC2.* Under § 1.163(j)-1(b)(1), taking into account the application of paragraph (c)(3) of this section, CFC2's ATI is $50x (($5x) taxable loss + $5x business interest expense + $50x (100 percent x $50x of CFC3's excess taxable income)). Under § 1.163(j)-2(b), CFC2's limitation is $15x ($50x ATI x 30 percent). Because the amount of CFC2's business interest expense subject to limitation, $5x, does not exceed CFC2's limitation, $15x, all of CFC2's business interest expense is currently deductible. Furthermore, CFC2 has CFC excess taxable income of $33.33x ($50x x ($10x / $15x)).

(E) *Application of section 163(j) to CFC1.* Under § 1.163(j)-1(b)(1), taking into account the application of paragraph (c)(3) of this section, CFC1's ATI is $33.33x ($0 taxable income + $33.33x (100 percent x $33.33x of CFC2's excess taxable income)). CFC1 has no business interest expense subject to limitation and therefore CFC1 has CFC excess taxable income of $33.33x.

(F) *Application of section 163(j) to USP.* Under section 951(a)(1), USP includes $42.50x in gross income with respect to CFC3. Under section 951A(a), USP includes $70x in gross income, all of which is allocable to CFC4 under section 951A(f)(2), and under section 250(a)(1)(B), USP is allowed a deduction of $35x. Thus, the amount of USP's CFC group inclusions is $77.50x ($42.50 + $70x - $35x), and USP's taxable income prior to the application of section 163(j) is $57.50x ($77.50x - $20x business interest expense). Under § 1.163(j)-1(b)(1), taking into account the application of paragraph (d)(2) of this section, USP's ATI is $16.67x. USP's ATI, $16.67x, is equal to $57.50x of taxable income + $20x of business interest expense - $77.50x of CFC group inclusions + $16.67x of eligible CFC group ETI. The eligible CFC group ETI, $16.67x, is determined as $33.33x (CFC1's excess taxable income) x 50 percent (CFC1's specified ETI ratio) x 100 percent (percentage of stock of CFC1 owned directly by USP)). Under paragraph (f)(14) of this section, the specified ETI ratio of CFC1 is 50 percent ($42.50x / $85x). The numerator of the fraction, $42.50x, is equal to the amount of USP's gross income inclusion under section 951(a) with respect to CFC3. The denominator of the fraction, $85x, is equal to the amount of the taxable income of CFC3. The numerator and the denominator of the fraction do not include amounts with respect to CFC1, CFC2, and CFC4, because none of them has CFC excess taxable income without regard to the application of paragraph (c)(3) of this section. Furthermore, USP includes no amounts in gross income under section 951(a) or 951A(a) with respect to CFC1 or CFC2. Under § 1.163(j)-2(b), USP's section 163(j) limitation is $5x ($16.67x ATI x 30 percent). The amount of USP's business interest expense, $20x, exceeds USP's section 163(j) limitation, $5x. Accordingly, under § 1.163(j)-2(c), $15x of business interest expense is not deductible and is carried forward as a disallowed business interest expense carryforward.

(h) *Applicability date.*—This section applies to a taxable year of a foreign corporation ending after the date the Treasury decision adopting these regulations as final regulations is published in the **Federal Register** and to a taxable year of a shareholder of the foreign corporation ending with or within the taxable year of the foreign corporation. However, a foreign corporation and its shareholders and their related parties, within the meaning of sections 267(b) and 707(b)(1), may apply this section to a taxable year of the foreign corporation beginning after December 31, 2017, and to a taxable year of a shareholder of the foreign corporation ending with or within the taxable year of the foreign corporation, if the foreign corporation and its shareholders and their related parties consistently apply all of the section 163(j) regulations, and if applicable, §§1.263A-9, 1.381(c)(20)-1, 1.382-6, 1.383-1, 1.469-9, 1.882-5, 1.1502-13, 1.1502-21, 1.1502-36, 1.1502-79, 1.1502-91 through 1.1502-99 (to the extent they effectuate the rules of §§1.382-6 and 1.383-1), and 1.1504-4 to those taxable years. [Reg. §1.163(j)-7.]

§1.163(j)-8. Application of the business interest deduction limitation to foreign persons with effectively connected income.—(a) *Overview*.—This section provides rules concerning the application of section 163(j) to foreign persons engaged in a trade or business in the United States. Paragraph (b) of this section modifies the application of section 163(j) for specified foreign persons with effectively connected taxable income. Paragraph (c) of this section modifies the application of section 163(j) for specified foreign partners in a partnership engaged in a trade or business in the United States. Paragraph (d) of this section provides rules for certain controlled foreign corporations with effectively connected taxable income. Paragraph (e) of this section coordinates the application of section 163(j) and §1.882-5. Paragraph (f) of this section provides a coordination rule for determining effectively connected earnings and profits for purposes of the branch profits tax under section 884. Paragraph (g) of this section provides definitions that apply for purposes of this section. Paragraph (h) of this section provides examples that illustrate the application of this section. Paragraph (i) of this section provides dates of applicability.

(b) *Application of section 163(j) and the section 163(j) regulations to specified foreign persons with effectively connected taxable income*.—(1) *In general*.—If a taxpayer is a specified foreign person, then the modifications described in this paragraph (b) are made to the application of section 163(j) and the section 163(j) regulations. If a specified foreign person is also a specified foreign partner, then the modifications described in this paragraph (b) are subject to the partner-level modifications described in paragraph (c) of this section.

(2) *Modification of adjusted taxable income*.—ATI for a specified foreign person for a taxable year means the specified foreign person's effectively connected taxable income for the taxable year, adjusted for the items described in §1.163(j)-1(b)(1)(i) through (iv) that are taken into account in determining effectively connected taxable income.

(3) *Modification of business interest expense*.—(i) *General rule*.—Business interest expense for a specified foreign person means interest described in §1.163(j)-1(b)(2) that is determined under §1.882-5, in the case of a foreign corporation, or under §1.861-9T(d)(2), in the case of a non-resident alien individual, and allocable to income which is effectively connected taxable income.

(ii) *Exclusion of certain business interest expense of a specified foreign partner*.—If a foreign corporation is a specified foreign partner in a partnership engaged in a trade or business in the United States, then, for purposes of paragraph (b)(3)(i) of this section, business interest expense excludes the portion of interest expense determined under §1.882-5 that is attributable to interest on U.S. booked liabilities of the partnership determined under §1.882-5(d)(2)(vii).

(4) *Modification of business interest income*.—The business interest income of a specified foreign person means interest described in §1.163(j)-1(b)(3) that is effectively connected taxable income.

(5) *Modification of floor plan financing interest expense*.—The floor plan financing interest expense of a specified foreign person means interest described §1.163(j)-1(b)(17) that is allocable to income which is effectively connected taxable income.

(6) *Modification of allocation of interest expense and interest income that is properly allocable to a trade or business*.—For purposes of §1.163(j)-10(c), a specified foreign person's interest expense and interest income that is properly allocable to a trade or business is only allocated to the specified foreign person's excepted or non-excepted trades or business that have effectively connected taxable income. If the specified foreign person is also a specified foreign partner, this rule only applies to the trades or business not in the partnership.

(c) *Partner-level modifications to §1.163(j)-6 for partnerships engaged in a U.S. trade or business*.—(1) *Modification related to a partnership's excess taxable income*.—If for a taxable year a specified foreign partner, other than an applicable CFC, has allocable excess taxable income with respect to a partnership, then, for purposes of computing the specified foreign partner's ATI for the taxable year, the excess, if any, of the amount of the allocable excess taxable income over the amount of the specified excess taxable income is subtracted from ATI.

(2) *Modification related to a partnership's excess business interest expense*.—If for a taxable year a specified foreign partner, other than an applicable CFC, has allocable excess business interest expense with respect to a partnership, then, for purposes of determining the specified foreign partner's business interest expense for a succeeding taxable year, the amount of the allocable excess business interest expense treated as disallowed business interest expense carryforward under §1.163(j)-6(f) is determined by taking into account only the portion of allocable excess business interest expense that is specified excess business interest expense and such excess business interest expense is limited to the portion of allocable excess taxable income for the succeeding taxable year that is specified excess taxable income.

(3) *Modification related to a partnership's excess business interest income*.—If for a taxable year a specified foreign partner, other than an applicable CFC, has allocable excess business interest income (as defined in §1.163(j)-6(b)(4)) with respect to a partnership, then, for purposes of determining the specified foreign partner's section

163(j) limitation, the amount of allocable excess business interest income that can be used by the specified foreign partner cannot exceed the amount of ECI excess business interest income.

(d) *An applicable CFC with effectively connected taxable income.*—If an applicable CFC has effectively connected taxable income for a taxable year in which the applicable CFC has disallowed business interest expense, then a portion of the disallowed business interest expense is treated as being with respect to the applicable CFC's interest expense determined under § 1.882-5. That portion is equal to the amount of the applicable CFC's disallowed business interest expense multiplied by a fraction, the numerator of which is the applicable CFC's effectively connected taxable income for the taxable year, adjusted for the items described in § 1.163(j)-1(b)(1)(i) through (iv) that are taken into account in determining effectively connected taxable income, and the denominator of which is the applicable CFC's ATI for the taxable year. However, in no case will such portion exceed the amount of interest expense determined under § 1.882-5. See also § 1.163(j)-7(b)(2) (concerning the general application of section 163(j) to an applicable CFC).

(e) *Coordination of section 163(j) and § 1.882-5.*—(1) *General rules.*—(i) *Ordering rule.*—A foreign corporation first determines its interest expense under § 1.882-5 and then determines the amount of disallowed business interest expense.

(ii) *Treatment of disallowed business interest expense carryforward.*—If a foreign corporation has a disallowed business interest expense carryforward from a taxable year, then such carryforward is not taken into account for purposes of determining interest expense under § 1.882-5 in the succeeding taxable year.

(iii) *Treatment of allocable excess business interest expense.*—If a foreign corporation has allocable excess business interest expense from a taxable year that is treated under § 1.163(j)-6(g)(2) as disallowed business interest expense carryforward, such interest is not taken into account for purposes of determining interest expense under § 1.882-5 in the succeeding taxable year.

(iv) *Scaling ratio.*—If a foreign corporation determines its interest expense under the method described in § 1.882-5(b) through (d) and has U.S. booked liabilities in excess of U.S. connected liabilities, the foreign corporation must apply the scaling ratio (as defined in § 1.882-5(d)(4)(ii)) pro rata to all interest expense paid or accrued by the foreign corporation consistent with § 1.882-5(d)(4)(i), including for purposes of paragraph (b)(3)(ii) of this section.

(2) *Amount of interest determined under § 1.882-5 that is disallowed business interest expense.*—(i) *Foreign corporation is not a specified foreign partner.*—If a foreign corporation is not a specified foreign partner for a taxable year, then the amount of the foreign corporation's interest expense determined under § 1.882-5 for which a deduction is disallowed for the taxable year is either—

(A) The amount of disallowed business interest expense computed under § 1.163(j)-2(b) with respect to business interest expense described in paragraph (b)(3)(i) of this section, in the case of a foreign corporation that is not an applicable CFC; or

(B) The amount of disallowed business interest expense determined under paragraph (d) of this section, in the case of an applicable CFC.

(ii) *Foreign corporation is a specified foreign partner.*—If a foreign corporation is a specified foreign partner with respect to one or more partnerships engaged in a trade or business in the United States for a taxable year, then the portion of the foreign corporation's business interest expense determined under § 1.882-5 for which a deduction is disallowed for the taxable year is equal to the sum of the following amounts—

(A) Either—

(*1*) The amount described in paragraph (e)(2)(i)(A) of this section, in the case of a foreign corporation that is not an applicable CFC; or

(*2*) The amount described in paragraph (e)(2)(i)(B) of this section, in the case of an applicable CFC; and

(B) With respect to each partnership that has excess business interest expense for the taxable year that ends with or within the foreign corporation's taxable year, the amount of the foreign corporation's specified excess business interest expense.

(f) *Coordination with branch profits tax.*—(1) *Effect on effectively connected earnings and profits.*—The disallowance and carryforward of business interest expense under § 1.163(j)-2(b) and (c) will not affect when such business interest expense reduces the effectively connected earnings and profits of a foreign corporation, as defined in § 1.884-1(f).

(2) *Effect on U.S. net equity.*—The disallowance and carryforward of business interest expense under § 1.163(j)-2(b) and (c) will not affect the computation of the U.S. net equity of a foreign corporation, as defined in § 1.884-1(c).

(g) *Definitions.*—The following definitions apply for purposes of this section.

(1) *Applicable CFC.*—The term *applicable CFC* means a foreign corporation described in section 957, but only if the foreign corporation has at least one United States shareholder that owns, within the meaning of section 958(a), stock of the foreign corporation.

(2) *ECI excess business interest income.*—The term *ECI excess business interest income* means, with respect to a specified foreign partner and a partnership, the excess, if any, of the specified foreign partner's allocable business interest income (as defined in § 1.163(j)-6(f)(2)(ii)) over its allocable business interest expense (as defined in § 1.163(j)-6(f)(2)(ii)), but, for purposes of determining a specified foreign partner's allocable business interest income and allocable business interest expense, taking into account only the portion of the partnership's business interest income determined under paragraph (b)(4) of this section as if the partnership were a specified foreign person, over the business interest expense on the U.S. booked liabilities of the partnership as determined under § 1.882-5(d)(2)(vii).

(3) *Effectively connected taxable income.*—The term *effectively connected taxable income* means taxable income of a person that is, or is treated as. effectively connected with the conduct of a trade business in the United States under an applicable provision of the Code or

regulations or, if an income tax treaty applies, business profits attributable to a U.S. permanent establishment of a tax treaty resident eligible for benefits under an income tax treaty between the United States and the treaty country.

(4) *Specified excess business interest expense*.—The term *specified excess business interest expense* means, with respect to a specified foreign partner and a partnership, the amount determined by multiplying the specified foreign partner's allocable excess business interest expense (as determined under § 1.163(j)-6(f)) by the partnership's specified ratio for the taxable year.

(5) *Specified excess taxable income*.—The term *specified excess taxable income* means, with respect to a specified foreign partner and a partnership, the amount determined by multiplying the amount of the specified foreign partner's allocable excess taxable income (as determined under § 1.163(j)-6(f)) by the amount of the partnership's specified ratio for the taxable year.

(6) *Specified foreign partner*.—The term *specified foreign partner* means, with respect to a partnership that is engaged in a U.S. trade or business, a partner that is a specified foreign person or an applicable CFC.

(7) *Specified foreign person*.—The term *specified foreign person* means a nonresident alien individual, as defined in section 7701(b) and the regulations thereunder, or a foreign corporation other than an applicable CFC.

(8) *Specified ratio*.—The term *specified ratio* means, with respect to a partnership, a fraction (expressed as a percentage), the numerator of which is the ATI for the partnership determined under paragraph (b)(2) of this section as if the partnership were a specified foreign person, and the denominator of which is the ATI for the partnership determined under § 1.163(j)-6(d).

(h) *Examples*.—The following examples illustrate the application of this section. For all examples, assume that all referenced interest expense is deductible but for the application of section 163(j), the small business exemption under § 1.163(j)-2(d) is not available, no party is engaged in an excepted trade or business, and no business interest expense is floor plan financing interest expense.

(1) *Example 1: Limitation on business interest deduction of a foreign corporation*—(i) *Facts*. FC, a foreign corporation that is not an applicable CFC, has $100x of gross income that is effectively connected income. FC has $60x of other income which is not effectively connected income. FC has total expenses of $100x. Assume that under § 1.882-5, FC has $30x of interest expense allocable to income which is effectively connected income. Under section 882(c) and the regulations thereunder, FC has $40x of other expenses properly allocated and apportioned to income which is effectively connected taxable income. FC does not have any business interest income.

(ii) *Analysis*. FC is a specified foreign person under paragraph (g)(7) of this section. Under paragraph (e)(2) of this section, the amount of FC's interest expense determined under § 1.882-5 that is disallowed is the disallowed business interest expense computed under § 1.163(j)-2(b) with respect to interest expense described in paragraph (b)(3) of this section. Under § 1.163(j)-4(b)(1), all interest paid or accrued by FC is properly allocable to a trade or business and therefore under paragraph (b)(3) of this section, FC has business interest expense of $30x. FC has $30x of effectively connected taxable income described in paragraph (g)(3) of this section ($100x - $30x - $40x). Under paragraph (b)(2) of this section, FC has ATI of $60x, determined as $30x of effectively connected taxable income, increased by $30x of business interest expense. Accordingly, FC's section 163(j) limitation is $18x ($60x x 30 percent). Because FC's business interest expense ($30x) exceeds the section 163(j) limitation ($18x), FC may only deduct $18x of business interest expense. Under § 1.163(j)-2(c), the remaining $12x is disallowed business interest expense carryforward and under paragraph (e)(1)(ii) of this section, the $12x is not taken into account for purposes of applying § 1.882-5 in the succeeding taxable year.

(2) *Example 2: Use of a disallowed business interest expense carryforward*—(i) *Facts*. The facts are the same as in *Example 1* in paragraph (h)(1)(i) of this section except that FC has $300x of gross income which is all effectively connected income. Furthermore assume that FC has a disallowed business interest expense carryforward of $25x from the prior taxable year.

(ii) *Analysis*. Under paragraph (e)(1)(ii) of this section, FC's $25x of disallowed business interest expense carryforward is not taken into account for purposes of determining FC's interest under § 1.882-5. Therefore, FC has $30x of business interest expense determined under § 1.882-5. Under paragraph (g)(3) of this section, FC has effectively connected taxable income of $205x ($300x gross income - $55x interest expense ($30x + $25x) - $40x other expenses). Under paragraph (b)(2) of this section, FC has ATI of $260x, determined as $205x of effectively connected taxable income, increased by $55x of business interest expense. Accordingly, FC's section 163(j) limitation is $78x ($260x x 30 percent). Under paragraph (b)(3) of this section, FC has business interest expense of $55x ($30x + $25x disallowed interest carryforward) for the taxable year. Because FC's business interest expense ($55x) does not exceed the section 163(j) limitation ($78x), FC may deduct all $55x of business interest expense.

(3) *Example 3: Foreign corporation is engaged in a U.S. trade or business and a specified foreign partner in a partnership engaged in a U.S. trade or business*—(i) *Facts*. FC, a foreign corporation that is not an applicable CFC, owns a 50-percent interest in ABC, a foreign partnership that is engaged in a trade or business in the United States. ABC has two lines of businesses, Business A and Business B. Business A produces $120x of taxable income (including interest expense) and Business B produces $80x of taxable income. FC is allocated 50 percent of all items of income and expense of Business A and Business B. Business A has business interest expense of $20x on $400x of liabilities but has no business interest income. Business B does not have any business interest expense or business interest income. With respect to FC, only Business A produces effectively connected income. FC has an outside basis of $500x in the ABC partnership for purposes of § 1.882-5(b), step 1. All of the liabilities of Business A are U.S. booked liabilities for purposes of § 1.882-5(d). In addition to owning a 50-percent interest in ABC, FC conducts a separate business that is engaged in a trade or business in the United States (Business X). Business X has effec-

tively connected taxable income of $50x, U.S. assets with an adjusted basis of $300x, U.S. booked liabilities of $160x, and interest on U.S. booked liabilities of $15x. FC computes its interest expense under the three-step method described in § 1.882-5(b) through (d) and uses the fixed ratio of 50 percent for purposes of § 1.882-5(c), step 2. Assume the interest rate on excess U.S. connected liabilities is 5 percent. For the taxable year, FC has total interest expense of 500x for purposes of § 1.882-5(a)(3).

(ii) *Analysis*—(A) *Application of section 163(j) to ABC*. Under § 1.163(j)-6(a), ABC computes a section 163(j) limitation at the partnership level. Under § 1.163(j)-6(d), ABC has ATI of $220x, determined as $200x of taxable income ($120x from Business A + $80x from Business B), increased by $20x of business interest expense of Business A. Under § 1.163(j)-2(b), ABC's section 163(j) limitation is $66x ($220x x 30 percent). Because ABC's business interest expense ($20x) does not exceed the section 163(j) limitation ($66x), ABC can deduct all of its business interest expense for the taxable year. Under § 1.163(j)-1(b)(15), ABC has excess taxable income of $153.33x ($220x x ($46x/$66x)). Under § 1.163(j)-6(f), FC is allocated 50 percent of the $153.33x of ABC's excess taxable income, or $76.67x of allocable excess taxable income, but, under paragraph (c)(1) of this section, the amount by which the allocable excess taxable income exceeds FC's specified excess taxable income (as defined in paragraph (g)(5) of this section) is a subtraction from FC's ATI. Under paragraph (g)(5) of this section, FC's specified excess taxable income is $48.79x, which is equal to the product of $76.67x and ABC's specified ratio of 63.64 percent. Under paragraph (g)(8) of this section, ABC's specified ratio of 63.64 percent is determined as $140x / $220x (where the numerator of $140x is the ATI of ABC determined under paragraph (b)(2) of this section as if ABC were a specified foreign person ($120x taxable income of Business A, increased by $20x of business interest expense), and the denominator of $220x is the ATI of ABC under § 1.163(j)-6(d)). FC's allocable excess taxable income ($76.67x) exceeds its specified excess taxable income ($48.79x) by $27.88x.

(B) *Application of § 1.882-5 to FC*. FC is a specified foreign partner under paragraph (g)(6) of this section. Under paragraph (e)(1) of this section, FC first determines its interest expense under § 1.882-5 and then determines its disallowed business interest expense. Under § 1.882-5(b), step 1, FC has U.S. assets of $800x ($500x (FC's basis in its interest in ABC) + $300x (FC's basis in Business X assets)). Under § 1.882-5(c), step 2, applying the 50-percent safe harbor in § 1.882-5 for a non-banking business, FC has U.S. connected liabilities of $400x ($800x x 50 percent). Under § 1.882-5(d), step 3, FC has U.S. booked liabilities of $360x ($200x (50-percent share of Business A liabilities of ABC of $400x) + $160x (Business X liabilities) and interest on U.S. booked liabilities of $25x ($10x (50-percent share of $20x interest expense of Business A) + $15x (interest expense of Business X)). FC has excess U.S. connected liabilities of $40x ($400x – $360x) and interest on such excess liabilities of $2x ($40x x 5 percent). FC's interest expense determined under § 1.882-5 is $27x ($25x + $2x).

(C) *Application of section 163(j) to FC*. Under paragraph (e)(2)(ii) of this section, the amount of business interest expense that is disallowed for FC is equal to only the amount of interest described in paragraph (b)(3) of this section that is disallowed because there is no specified excess business interest expense with respect to ABC. Under paragraph (b)(3) of this section, FC's business interest expense (at the corporate level) is $17x, the amount determined under § 1.882-5 ($27x) less the amount of interest on U.S. booked liabilities from ABC determined under § 1.882-5(d)(2)(vii) ($10x), which was subject to the section 163(j) limitation at the ABC partnership level. Under § 1.163(j)-6(e)(1), FC's ATI is determined under § 1.163(j)-1(b)(1) without regard to FC's distributive share of any items of income, gain, deduction, or loss of ABC. Under paragraph (b)(2) of this section, taking into account the application of paragraph (c)(1) of this section, FC's ATI is $115.77x ($50x effectively connected taxable income with respect to Business X, + $17x (business interest expense under § 1.882-5 of 27x less the amount of interest on U.S. booked liabilities from ABC determined under § 1.882-5(d)(2)(vii) of $10x) + $76.65x (excess taxable income from ABC) - $27.88x (amount excess taxable income exceeds specified excess taxable income)). FC's section 163(j) limitation is $34.73x ($115.77x x 30 percent). Because FC's business interest expense ($17x) is less than FC's section 163(j) limitation ($34.73x) and all of its share of ABC's interest is deductible, FC may deduct all $27x of interest determined under § 1.882-5.

(4) *Example 4: Scaleback of interest expense under § 1.882-5*—(i) *Facts*. Assume the same facts in *Example 3* in paragraph (h)(3)(i) of this section except that Business X has U.S. booked liabilities of $300x and interest on U.S. booked liabilities of $20x.

(ii) *Analysis*—(A) *Application of section 163(j) to ABC*. The analysis is the same as *Example 3* in paragraph (h)(3)(ii)(A) of this section.

(B) *Application of § 1.882-5 to FC*. Under § 1.882-5(b), step 1, FC has U.S. assets of $800x ($500x (FC's basis in its interest in ABC) + $300x (FC's basis in Business X assets)). Under § 1.882-5(c), step 2, applying the 50-percent safe harbor in § 1.882-5 for a non-banking business, FC has U.S. connected liabilities of $400x ($800x x 50 percent). Under § 1.882-5(d), step 3, FC has U.S. booked liabilities of $500x ($200x (50-percent share of Business A liabilities of ABC of $400x) + $300x (Business X liabilities) and interest on U.S. booked liabilities of $30x ($10x (50-percent share of $20x interest expense of Business A) + $20x (interest expense of Business X)). FC has excess U.S. booked liabilities of $100x ($500x – $400x) and the interest expense on U.S. booked liabilities must be reduced by the scaling ratio as provided in § 1.882-5(d)(4). FC's interest expense determined under § 1.882-5 is $24x ($30x x (400/500 scaling ratio)).

(C) *Application of section 163(j) to FC*. Under paragraph (b)(3) of this section, FC's business interest expense is $16x, the amount determined under § 1.882-5 ($24x) less the amount of interest on U.S. booked liabilities from ABC determined under § 1.882-5(d)(2)(vii) after applying the scaling ratio ($8x, determined as interest expense of Business A of $10x x scaling ratio of 400/500), which was subject to the section 163(j) limitation at the ABC partnership level. Under §1.163(j)-6(e)(1), FC's ATI is determined under §1.163(j)-1(b)(1) without regard to FC's distributive share of any items of income, gain, deduction, or loss of ABC. Under paragraph (b)(2) of this section, taking into account the application of paragraph (c)(1) of this section, FC's ATI is $114.79x ($50x effectively connected taxable income with respect to Business X + $16x (business interest expense under §1.882-5 of 24x less the amount of interest on U.S. booked liabilities from ABC determined under §1.882-5(d)(2)(vii), after applying the scaleback, of $8x) + $76.67x (excess taxable income from ABC) - $27.88x (amount excess taxable income exceeds specified excess taxable income)). FC's section 163(j) limitation is $34.44x ($114.79x x 30 percent). Because FC's business interest expense ($16x) is less than FC's section 163(j) limitation ($34.44x) and all of ABC's interest is deductible, FC may deduct all $24x of interest determined under §1.882-5.

(5) *Example 5: Separate currency pools method*—(i) *Facts*. Assume the same facts in *Example 3* in paragraph (h)(3)(i) of this section except that FC does not conduct Business X; the value of FC's interest in ABC for purposes of §1.882-5(e)(i), step 1, is $1,000x; and FC computes its interest expense under the separate currency pools method in §1.882-5(e) and for purposes of applying such method, the prescribed interest rate is 5 percent.

(ii) *Analysis*—(A) *Application of section 163(j) to ABC*. The analysis is the same as in *Example 3* in paragraph (h)(1)(ii)(A) of this section.

(B) *Application of §1.882-5 to FC*. Under §1.882-5(e)(i), step 1, FC has U.S. assets of $1,000x (FC's basis in its partnership interest in ABC). Under §1.882-5(e)(1)(ii), step 2, FC has U.S. connected liabilities of $500x ($1,000x x 50 percent) applying the 50 percent safe harbor for non-banking business. Under §1.882-5(e)(1)(iii), step 3, the interest expense under §1.882-5 is $25x ($500x x 5 percent).

(C) *Application of section 163(j) to FC*. Under paragraph (b)(3) of this section, FC's business interest expense is $15x, the amount determined under §1.882-5 ($25x) less the amount of interest on U.S. booked liabilities from ABC determined under §1.882-5(d)(2)(vii) of $10x, which was subject to the section 163(j) limitation at the ABC partnership level. Under §1.163(j)-6(e)(1), FC's ATI is determined under §1.163(j)-1(b)(1) without regard to FC's distributive share of any items of income, gain, deduction, or loss of ABC. Under paragraph (b)(2) of this section, taking into account the application of paragraph (c)(1) of this section, FC's ATI is $48.79x ($76.67x (excess taxable income from ABC) — $27.88x (amount excess taxable income exceeds specified excess taxable income)). FC's section 163(j) limitation is $14.64x ($48.79x x 30 percent). Because FC's business interest expense ($15x) exceeds the 163(j) limitation ($14.64x), FC may only deduct $14.64x of its business interest expense. Under §1.163(j)-2(c), the remaining $0.36x is disallowed business interest expense carryforward and under paragraph (e)(1)(ii) of this section, the $0.36x is not taken into account for purposes of applying §1.882-5 in the succeeding taxable year. Accordingly, FC may deduct 24.64x of the $25x interest determined under §1.882-5.

(6) *Example 6: Specified foreign partner with excess business interest expense*—(i) *Facts - Year 1*. FC, a foreign corporation that is not an applicable CFC, owns a 50-percent interest in XYZ, a foreign partnership that is engaged in a trade or business in the United States. XYZ has two lines of businesses, Business S and Business T. Business S produces $50x of taxable income (including interest expense), and Business T produces $40x of taxable income (including interest expense). FC is allocated 50 percent of all items of income and expenses of Business S and Business T. Business S has business interest expense of $30x on $500x of liabilities but has no business interest income. Business T has business interest expense of $50x on $500x of liabilities but has no business interest income. With respect to FC, only Business S produces effectively connected income. FC has an adjusted basis of $500x in XYZ for purposes of §1.882-5(b), step 1. All of the liabilities of Business S are U.S. booked liabilities for purposes of §1.882-5(d). FC computes its interest expense under the three-step method described in §1.882-5(b) through (d) and uses the fixed ratio of 50 percent for purposes of §1.882-5(c), step 2.

(ii) *Analysis with respect to Year* 1—(A) *Application of section 163(j) to XYZ*. Under §1.163(j)-6(a), XYZ computes a section 163(j) limitation at the partnership-level. Under §1.163(j)-6(d), XYZ has ATI of $170x, determined as $90x of taxable income ($50x from Business S + $40x from Business T), increased by $80x of business interest expense ($30x from Business S + $50x from Business T). Under §1.163(j)-2(b), XYZ's section 163(j) limitation is $51x ($170x x 30 percent). Because XYZ's business interest expense ($80x) exceeds the section 163(j) limitation ($51x), XYZ may only deduct $51x of business interest expense and $29x is disallowed under section 163(j). Under §1.163(j)-6(f), FC is allocated $14.5x of excess business interest expense (50 percent x $29x). Under paragraph (c)(2) of this section, the amount of allocable business interest expense that can be used by FC is equal to the amount of specified excess business interest, and the amount of such interest that is treated as paid or accrued by FC in the succeeding taxable year is limited to the amount of FC's specified excess taxable income allocated to FC in the succeeding taxable year.

(B) *Application of §1.882-5 to FC*. FC is a specified foreign partner under paragraph (g)(6) of this section. Under paragraph (e)(1) of this section, FC first determines its interest expense under §1.882-5 and then determines its disallowed business interest expense. Under §1.882-5(b), step 1, FC has U.S. assets of $500x (FC's adjusted basis in its interest in XYZ). Under §1.882-5(c), step 2, applying the 50-percent fixed ratio in §1.882-5 for a non-banking business, FC has U.S. connected liabilities of $250x ($500x x 50 percent). Under §1.882-5(d), step 3, FC has U.S. booked liabilities of $250x ($500x x 50-percent share of Business S liabilities of XYZ) and interest on U.S. booked liabilities of $15x (50 percent share of $30x interest expense of Business S). Because FC has U.S. connected liabilities equal to its U.S. booked liabilities, its interest expense under §1.882-5 is $15x (the amount of interest expense on its U.S. booked liabilities).

(C) *Application of section 163(j) to FC*. Under paragraph (e)(2)(ii) of this section, the amount of business interest expense that is disallowed for

FC is equal to the sum of the amount of interest described in paragraph (b)(3) of this section that is disallowed plus the amount of FC's specified excess business interest expense. FC's business interest expense (at the corporate level) under paragraph (b)(3) of this section is $0, the amount determined under § 1.882-5 ($15x) less the amount of interest on U.S. booked liabilities from XYZ determined under § 1.882-5(d)(2)(vii) ($15x), which was subject to the section 163(j) limitation at the XYZ partnership level. Because FC (at the corporate level) has no business interest expense, there is no business interest expense subject to the section 163(j) limitation. However, because FC has excess business interest expense with respect to XYZ, a deduction for a portion of the $15x of interest on U.S. booked liabilities from XYZ determined under § 1.882-5(d)(2)(vii) will be disallowed for the taxable year. The amount of such interest that is limited is equal to the amount of the FC's specified excess business interest expense determined under paragraph (g)(4) of this section. The specified excess business interest expense is $6.82x, determined by multiplying FC's distributive share of excess business interest expense ($14.5x) by XYZ's specified ratio of 47.06 percent, determined under paragraph (g)(8) of this section. The specified ratio of 47.06 percent is determined by dividing $80x ATI determined under paragraph (b)(2) of the section as if XYZ were a specified foreign person (determined as $50x taxable income from Business S + $30x business interest expense from Business S) by $170x of XYZ ATI. FC may only deduct $8.18x ($15x - $6.82x) of business interest expense. Under § 1.163(j)-2(c), the remaining $6.82x is disallowed business interest expense carryforward and under paragraph (e)(1)(ii) of this section, the $6.82x is not taken into account for purposes of applying § 1.882-5 in the succeeding taxable year.

(iii) *Facts - Year 2*. During Year 2, Business S produces $170x of taxable income (including interest expense) and Business T produces $150x (including interest expense) of taxable income. Business S has business interest expense of $30x on $500x of liabilities but has no business interest income. Business T has business interest expense of $50x on $500x of liabilities but no business interest income. With respect to FC, only Business S produces effectively connected taxable income. FC has an adjusted basis of $600x in XYZ for purposes of § 1.882-5(b), step 1. All of the liabilities of Business S are U.S. booked liabilities for purposes of § 1.882-5(d). FC computes its interest expense under the three-step method described in § 1.882-5(b) through (d) and uses the fixed ratio of 50 percent for purposes of § 1.882-5(c), step 2. The interest rate on excess U.S. connected liabilities is 5 percent. For the taxable year, FC has total interest expense of $1,000x for purposes of § 1.882-5(a)(3).

(iv) *Analysis with respect to Year 2*—(A) *Application of section 163(j) to XYZ*. Under § 1.163(j)-6(a), XYZ computes a section 163(j) limitation at the partnership-level. Under § 1.163(j)-6(d), XYZ has ATI of $400x, determined as $320x of taxable income ($170x from Business S + $150x from Business T), increased by $80x of business interest expense ($30x from Business S + $50x from Business T). Under § 1.163(j)-2(b), XYZ's section 163(j) limitation is $120x ($400x x 30 percent). Because XYZ's business interest expense ($80x) does not exceed the section 163(j) limitation ($120x), XYZ can deduct all of its business interest expense for the taxable year. Under § 1.163(j)-1(b)(15), XYZ has excess taxable income of $133.30x ($400x x ($40x/$120x)). Under § 1.163(j)-6(f), FC is allocated 50 percent of the $133.33x of XYZ's excess taxable income, or $66.66x of allocable excess taxable income, but, under paragraph (c)(1) of this section, the amount by which the allocable excess taxable income exceeds FC's specified excess taxable income (as defined in paragraph (g)(5) of this section) is a subtraction from FC's ATI. Under paragraph (g)(5) of this section, FC's specified excess taxable income is $33.33x, which is equal to the product of FC's allocable excess taxable income of $66.66x and XYZ's specified ratio of 50 percent. Under paragraph (g)(8) of this section, XYZ's specified ratio of 50 percent is determined as $200x / $400x (where the numerator of $200x is the ATI of XYZ determined under paragraph (b)(2) of this section as if XYZ were a specified foreign person ($170x taxable income of Business S, increased by $30x of business interest expense), and the denominator of $400x is the ATI of XYZ under § 1.163(j)-6(d)). FC's allocable excess taxable income ($66.66x) exceeds its specified excess taxable income ($33.33x) by $33.33x.

(B) *Treatment of excess business interest expense from Year 1*. In Year 1, XYZ had disallowed business interest expense of $29x and under § 1.163(j)-6(f), FC's allocable excess business interest expense was $14.50x. Under paragraph (c)(2) of this section, FC may use its allocable excess business interest expense in a succeeding taxable year only to the extent of its specified excess business interest expense, which, in this case, was determined to be $6.82x, and, with respect to Year 2, the amount of specified excess business interest expense treated as paid or accrued by FC is limited to FC's specified excess taxable income ($33.33x). Thus, FC can treat the entire $6.82x as business interest expense paid or accrued in Year 2.

(C) *Application of § 1.882-5 to FC*. Under § 1.882-5(b), step 1, FC has U.S. assets of $600x (FC's adjusted basis in its interest in XYZ). Under § 1.882-5(c), step 2, applying the 50 percent fixed ratio in § 1.882-5 for a non-banking business, FC has U.S. connected liabilities of $300x ($600x x 50 percent). Under § 1.882-5(d), step 3, FC has U.S. booked liabilities of $250x ($500x x 50-percent share of Business S liabilities of XYZ) and interest on U.S. booked liabilities of $15x (50 percent share of $30x interest expense of Business S). FC has excess U.S. connected liabilities of $50x ($300x – $250x) and interest on such excess liabilities of $2.5x ($50x x 5 percent). FC's interest expense determined under § 1.882-5 is $17.5x ($15x + $2.5x).

(D) *Application of section 163(j) to FC*. Under paragraph (e)(2)(ii) of this section, the amount of business interest expense that is disallowed for FC is equal to only the amount of interest described in paragraph (b)(3) of this section that is disallowed because there is no excess business interest expense with respect to XYZ. FC's business interest expense (at the corporate level) under paragraphs (b)(3) and (e)(1) of this section is $9.32x, determined as the sum of $2.50x (the amount determined under § 1.882-5 ($17.50x) less the amount of interest on U.S. booked liabilities from XYZ determined under

§ 1.882-5(d)(2)(vii) ($15x) that is excluded under paragraph (b)(3)(ii) of this section) + $6.82x (allocable business interest expense from Year 1 treated as paid or accrued in Year 2). Under § 1.163(j)-6(e)(1), FC's ATI is determined under § 1.163(j)-1(b)(1) without regard to FC's distributive share of any items of income, gain, deduction, or loss of XYZ. Under paragraph (b)(2) of this section, taking into account the application of paragraph (c)(1) of this section, FC's ATI is $33.33x, determined as $66.66x (excess taxable income from XYZ) — $33.33x (amount excess taxable income exceeds specified excess taxable income). FC's section 163(j) limitation is $10x ($33.33x x 30 percent). Because FC's business interest expense (at the corporate level) of $9.32x is less than FC's section 163(j) limitation of $10x, FC may deduct all $9.32x of business interest expense ($2.50x from Year 2 and $6.82x from Year 1). Because all of XYZ's business interest expense is deductible, FC may also deduct the $15x of business interest expense on U.S. booked liabilities of XYZ for Year 2.

(7) *Example 7: Coordination of section 163(j) and branch profits tax*—(i) *Facts*. FC, a foreign corporation that is not an applicable CFC, uses cash that is treated as a U.S. asset under § 1.884-1(d) in order to pay interest described in paragraph (b)(3) of this section for which a deduction for such interest is disallowed under § 1.163(j)-2(b).

(ii) *Analysis*. Assuming that FC's U.S. assets otherwise remain constant during the year, the U.S. assets of FC will have decreased by the amount of cash used to pay the interest expense, and the U.S. net equity of FC will be computed accordingly.

(i) *Applicability date*.—This section applies to taxable years ending after the date the Treasury decision adopting these regulations as final regulations is published in the **Federal Register**. However, taxpayers and their related parties, within the meaning of sections 267(b) and 707(b)(1), may apply this section to a taxable year beginning after December 31, 2017, if the taxpayers and their related parties consistently apply all of the section 163(j) regulations, and if applicable, § § 1.263A-9, 1.381(c)(20)-1, 1.382-6, 1.383-1, 1.469-9, 1.882-5, 1.1502-13, 1.1502-21, 1.1502-36, 1.1502-79, 1.1502-91 through 1.1502-99 (to the extent they effectuate the rules of § § 1.382-6 and 1.383-1), and 1.1504-4 to those taxable years. [Reg. § 1.163(j)-8.]

§ 1.163(j)-9. Elections for excepted trades or businesses; safe harbor for certain REITs.—(a) *Overview*.—This section provides rules and procedures for making an election under section 163(j)(7)(B) to be an electing real property trade or business, as defined in § 1.163(j)-1(b)(12), and an election under section 163(j)(7)(C) to be an electing farming business, as defined in § 1.163(j)-1(b)(11).

(b) *Scope and effect of election*.—(1) *In general*.—An election under this section is made with respect to each eligible trade or business of the taxpayer and applies only to such trade or business for which the election is made. An election under this section applies to the taxable year in which the election is made and to all subsequent taxable years, except as otherwise provided in this section.

(2) *Irrevocability*.—An election under this section is irrevocable.

(c) *Time and manner of making election*.—(1) *In general*.—Subject to paragraph (e) of this section, a taxpayer makes an election under this section by attaching an election statement to the taxpayer's timely filed original Federal income tax return, including extensions. A taxpayer may make elections for multiple trades or businesses on a single election statement.

(2) *Election statement contents*.—The election statement should be titled "Section 1.163(j)-9 Election" and must contain the following information for each trade or business:

(i) The taxpayer's name;

(ii) The taxpayer's address;

(iii) The taxpayer's social security number (SSN) or employer identification number (EIN);

(iv) A description of the taxpayer's electing trade or business, including the principal business activity code; and

(v) A statement that the taxpayer is making an election under section 163(j)(7)(B) or (C), as applicable.

(3) *Consolidated group's trade or business*.—For a consolidated group's trade or business, the election under this section is made by the agent for the group, as defined in § 1.1502-77, on behalf of itself and members of the consolidated group. Only the name and taxpayer identification number (TIN) of the agent for the group, as defined in § 1.1502-77, must be provided on the election statement.

(4) *Partnership's trade or business*.—An election for a partnership must be made on the partnership's return with respect to any trade or business that the partnership conducts. An election by a partnership does not apply to a trade or business conducted by a partner outside the partnership.

(d) *Termination of election*.—(1) *In general*.—An election under this section automatically terminates if a taxpayer ceases to engage in the electing trade or business. A taxpayer is considered to cease to engage in an electing trade or business if the taxpayer sells or transfers substantially all of the assets of the electing trade or business to an acquirer that is not a related party in a taxable asset transfer. A taxpayer is also considered to cease to engage in an electing trade or business if the taxpayer terminates its existence for Federal income tax purposes or ceases operation of the electing trade or business, except to the extent that such termination or cessation results in the sale or transfer of substantially all of the assets of the electing trade or business to an acquirer that is a related party, or in a transaction that is not a taxable asset transfer.

(2) *Taxable asset transfer defined*.—For purposes of this paragraph (d), the term taxable asset transfer means a transfer in which the acquirer's basis or adjusted basis in the assets is not determined, directly or indirectly, in whole or in part, by reference to the transferor's basis in the assets.

(3) *Related party defined*.—For purposes of this paragraph (d), the term *related party* means any person who bears a relationship to the taxpayer which is described section 267(b) or 707(b)(1).

(4) *Anti-abuse rule*.—If, within 60 months of a sale or transfer of assets described in para-

graph (d)(1) of this section, the taxpayer or a related party reacquires substantially all of the assets that were used in the taxpayer's prior electing trade or business, or substantially similar assets, and resumes conducting such prior electing trade or business, the taxpayer's previously terminated election under this section is reinstated and is effective on the date the prior electing trade or business is reacquired.

(e) *Additional guidance.*—The rules and procedures regarding the time and manner of making an election under this section and the election statement contents in paragraph (c) of this section may be modified through other guidance (see §§601.601(d) and 601.602 of this chapter). Additional situations in which an election may terminate under paragraph (d) of this section may be provided through guidance published in the **Federal Register** or in the Internal Revenue Bulletin (see §601.601(d) of this chapter).

(f) *Examples.*—The examples of this paragraph (f) illustrate the application of this section. Unless otherwise indicated, assume the following: X and Y are domestic C corporations; D and E are U.S. resident individuals not subject to any foreign income tax; and the exemption for certain small businesses in §1.163(j)-2(d) does not apply.

(1) *Example 1: Scope of election*—(i) *Facts.* During her taxable year ending December 31, 2019, D, a sole proprietor, owned and operated a dairy farm and a tree farm as separate farming businesses described in section 263A(e)(4). D filed its original Federal income tax return for the 2019 taxable year on August 1, 2020, and included with the return an election statement meeting the requirements of paragraph (c)(2) of this section. The election statement identified D's dairy farm business as an electing trade or business under this section. On March 1, 2021, D sold some but not all or substantially all of the assets from her dairy farm business to her neighbor, E, who is unrelated to D. After the sale, D continued to operate the dairy farm trade or business.

(ii) *Analysis.* D's election under this section was properly made and is effective for the 2019 taxable year and subsequent years. D's dairy farm business is an excepted trade or business because D made the election with her timely filed Federal income tax return. D's tree farm business is a non-excepted trade or business. The sale of some but not all or substantially all of the assets from D's dairy farm business has no impact on D's election under this section.

(2) *Example 2: Cessation of entire trade or business*—(i) *Facts.* X has a real property trade or business for which X made an election under this section by attaching an election statement to A's 2019 Federal income tax return. On March 1, 2020, X sold all of the assets used in its real property trade or business to Y, an unrelated party, and ceased to engage in the electing trade or business. On June 1, 2027, X started a new real property trade or business that was substantially similar to X's prior electing trade or business.

(ii) *Analysis.* X's election under this section terminated on March 1, 2020, under paragraph (d)(1) of this section. X may choose whether to make an election under this section for X's new real property trade or business that A started in 2027.

(3) *Example 3: Anti-abuse rule*—(i) *Facts.* The same facts are the same as in *Example 2* in paragraph (f)(2)(i) of this section, except that X restarted her previous real property trade or business on February 1, 2021, when X reacquired substantially all of the assets that X had sold on March 1, 2020.

(ii) *Analysis.* X's election under this section terminated on March, 1, 2020, under paragraph (d)(1) of this section. On February 1, 2021, X's election was reinstated under paragraph (d)(4) of this section. X's new real property trade or business is treated as a resumption of X's prior electing trade or business and is therefore treated as an electing real property trade or business.

(4) *Example 4: Trade or business continuing after acquisition*—(i) *Facts.* X has a farming business for which X made an election under this section by attaching an election statement to X's timely filed 2019 Federal income tax return. Y, unrelated to X, also has a farming business, but Y has not made an election under this section. On July 1, 2020, X transferred all of its assets to Y in a transaction described in section 368(a)(1)(D) (a "D reorganization"). After the transfer, Y continues to operate the farming trade or business acquired from X.

(ii) *Analysis.* Under paragraph (d)(1) of this section, Y is subject to X's election under this section for the trade or business that uses X's assets because the sale or transfer was not in a taxable transaction. Y cannot revoke X's election, but X's election has no effect on Y's existing farming business for which Y has not made an election under this section.

(5) *Example 5: Trade or business merged after acquisition*—(i) *Facts.* The facts are the same as in *Example 4* in paragraph (f)(4)(i) of this section, except that Y uses the assets acquired from X in a trade or business that is neither a farming business (as defined in section 263A(e)(4) or §1.263A-4(a)(4)) nor a trade or business of a specified agricultural or horticultural cooperative (as defined in section 199A(g)(4)).

(ii) *Analysis.* Y is not subject to X's election for Y's farming business because the farming trade or business ceased to exist after the acquisition.

(g) *Safe harbor for REITs.*—(1) *In general.*—If a REIT holds real property, as defined in §1.856-10, interests in partnerships holding real property, as defined in §1.856-10, or shares in other REITs holding real property, as defined in §1.856-10, the REIT is eligible to make the election described in paragraph (b)(1) of this section to be an electing real property trade or business for purposes of sections 163(j)(7)(B) and 168(g)(1)(F) for all or part of its assets. The portion of the REIT's assets eligible for this election is determined under paragraph (g)(2) or (3) of this section.

(2) *REITs that do not significantly invest in real property financing assets.*—If a REIT makes an election described in paragraph (g)(1) of this section and the value of the REIT's real property financing assets, as defined in paragraphs (g)(5) and (6) of this section, at the close of the taxable year is 10 percent or less of the value of the REIT's total assets at the close of the taxable year, as determined under section 856(c)(4)(A), then all of the REIT's assets are treated as assets of an excepted trade or business.

(3) *REITs that significantly invest in real property financing assets.*—If a REIT makes an election described in paragraph (g)(1) of this section and the value of the REIT's real property financing assets, as defined in paragraphs (g)(5) and (6) of this section, at the close of the taxable year is more than 10 percent of the value of the REIT's total assets at the close of the taxable year, as determined under section 856(c)(4)(A), then for allocation of interest expense, interest income, and other items of expense and gross income to excepted and non-excepted trades or businesses, the REIT must apply the rules set forth in § 1.163(j)-10 as modified by paragraph (g)(4) of this section.

(4) *REIT real property assets, interests in partnerships, and shares in other REITs.*—(i) *Real property assets.*—Assets held by a REIT described in paragraph (g)(3) of this section that meet the definition of real property under § 1.856-10 are treated as assets of an excepted trade or business.

(ii) *Partnership interests.*—If a REIT described in paragraph (g)(3) of this section holds an interest in a partnership, in applying the partnership look-through rule described in § 1.163(j)-10(c)(5)(ii)(A)(*2*), the REIT treats assets of the partnership that meet the definition of real property under § 1.856-10 as assets of an excepted trade or business. This application of the definition of real property under § 1.856-10 does not affect the characterization of the partnership's assets at the partnership level or for any non-REIT partner.

(iii) *Shares in other REITs.*—If a REIT (shareholder REIT) described in paragraph (g)(3) of this section holds an interest in another REIT, then for purposes of applying the allocation rules in § 1.163(j)-10, the partnership look-through rule described in § 1.163(j)-10(c)(5)(ii)(A)(*2*) applies to the assets of the other REIT (as if the other REIT were a partnership) in determining the extent to which shareholder REIT's adjusted basis in the shares of the other REIT is allocable to an excepted or non-excepted trade or business of shareholder REIT. However, no portion of the adjusted basis of shareholder REIT's shares in the other REIT is allocated to a non-excepted trade or business if all of the other REIT's assets are treated as assets of an excepted trade or business under paragraph (g)(2) of this section. If shareholder REIT does not receive from the other REIT the information necessary to determine whether and the extent that the assets of the other REIT are investments in real property financing assets, then shareholder REIT's shares in the other REIT are treated as assets of a non-excepted trade or business under § 1.163(j)-10(c).

(5) *Value of shares in other REITs.*—If a REIT (shareholder REIT) holds shares in another REIT, then for purposes of applying the value tests under paragraphs (g)(2) and (3) of this section, the value of shareholder REIT's real property financing assets includes the portion of the value of shareholder REIT's shares in the other REIT that is attributable to the other REIT's investments in real property financing assets. However, no portion of the value of shareholder REIT's shares in the other REIT is included in the value of shareholder REIT's real property financing assets if all of the other REIT's assets are treated as assets of an excepted trade or business under paragraph (g)(2) of this section. If shareholder REIT does not receive from the other REIT the information necessary to determine whether and the extent that the assets of the other REIT are investments in real property financing assets, then shareholder REIT's shares in the other REIT are treated as real property financing assets for purposes of paragraphs (g)(2) and (3) of this section.

(6) *Real property financing assets.*—For purposes of this paragraph (g), *real property financing assets* include interests, including participation interests, in the following: mortgages, deeds of trust, and installment land contracts; mortgage pass-thru certificates guaranteed by Government National Mortgage Association (GNMA), Federal National Mortgage Association (FNMA), Federal Home Loan Mortgage Corporation (FHLMC), or Canada Mortgage and Housing Corporation (CMHC); REMIC regular interests; other interests in investment trusts classified as trusts under § 301.7701-4(c) of this chapter that represent undivided beneficial ownership in a pool of obligations principally secured by interests in real property and related assets that would be permitted investments if the investment trust were a REMIC; obligations secured by manufactured housing treated as single family residences under section 25(e)(10), without regard to the treatment of the obligations or the properties under state law; and debt instruments issued by publicly offered REITs.

(h) *Special anti-abuse rule for certain real property trades or businesses.*—(1) *In general.* Except as provided in paragraph (h)(2) of this section, a real property trade or business does not constitute a trade or business eligible for an election described in paragraph (b)(1) of this section to be an electing real property trade or business if at least 80 percent, determined by fair market value, of the business's real property is leased, whether or not the arrangement is pursuant to a written lease or pursuant to a service contract or another agreement that is not denominated as a lease, to a trade or business under common control with the real property trade or business. For purposes of this paragraph (h), two trades or businesses are under common control if 50 percent of the direct and indirect ownership of both businesses are held by related parties within the meaning of sections 267(b) and 707(b).

(2) *Exception for certain REITs.*—The special anti-abuse rule in paragraph (h)(1) does not apply to REITs that lease qualified lodging facilities, as defined in section 856(d)(9)(D), and qualified health care properties, as defined in section 856(e)(6)(D).

(i) *Applicability date.*—This section applies to taxable years ending after the date the Treasury decision adopting these regulations as final regulations is published in the **Federal Register**. However, taxpayers and their related parties, within the meaning of sections 267(b) and 707(b)(1), may apply the rules of this section to a taxable year beginning after December 31, 2017, so long as the taxpayers and their related parties consistently apply the rules of the section 163(j) regulations, and if applicable, §§ 1.263A-9, 1.381(c)(20)-1, 1.382-6, 1.383-1, 1.469-9, 1.882-5, 1.1502-13, 1.1502-21, 1.1502-36, 1.1502-79, 1.1502-91 through 1.1502-99 (to the extent they effectuate the rules of §§ 1.382-6 and 1.383-1), and 1.1504-4 to those taxable years. [Reg. §1.163(j)-9.]

§1.163(j)-10. Allocation of interest expense, interest income, and other items of expense and gross income to an excepted trade or business.—(a) *Overview.*—(1) *In general.*—(i) *Purposes.*—This section provides the exclusive rules for allocating tax items that are properly allocable to a trade or business between excepted trades or businesses and non-excepted trades or businesses for purposes of section 163(j). The amount of a taxpayer's interest expense that is properly allocable to excepted trades or businesses is not subject to limitation under section 163(j). The amount of a taxpayer's other items of income, gain, deduction, or loss, including interest income, that is properly allocable to excepted trades or businesses is excluded from the calculation of the taxpayer's section 163(j) limitation. See section 163(j)(6) and (j)(8)(A)(i); see also §1.163(j)-1(b)(1)(i)(H), (b)(1)(ii)(F), and (b)(3). The general method of allocation set forth in paragraph (c) of this section is based on the approach that money is fungible and that interest expense is attributable to all activities and property, regardless of any specific purpose for incurring an obligation on which interest is paid. In no event may the amount of interest expense allocated under this section exceed the amount of interest paid or accrued, or treated as paid or accrued, by the taxpayer within the taxable year.

(ii) *Application of section.*—The amount of a taxpayer's tax items properly allocable to a trade or business, other than interest expense and interest income, that is properly allocable to excepted trades or businesses for purposes of section 163(j) is determined as set forth in paragraph (b) of this section. The amount of a taxpayer's interest expense and interest income that is properly allocable to excepted trades or businesses for purposes of section 163(j) generally is determined as set forth in paragraph (c) of this section, except as otherwise provided in paragraph (d) of this section. For purposes of this section, a taxpayer's activities are not treated as a trade or business if those activities do not involve the provision of services or products to a person other than the taxpayer. For example, if a taxpayer engaged in a manufacturing trade or business has in-house legal personnel that provide legal services solely to the taxpayer, the taxpayer is not treated as also engaged in the trade or business of providing legal services.

(2) *Coordination with other rules.*—(i) *In general.*—The rules of this section apply after a taxpayer has determined whether any interest expense or interest income paid, received, or accrued is properly allocable to a trade or business. Similarly, the rules of this section apply to other tax items after a taxpayer has determined whether those items are properly allocable to a trade or business. For instance, a taxpayer must apply §1.163-8T to determine which items of interest expense are investment interest under section 163(d) before applying the rules in paragraph (c) of this section to allocate interest expense between excepted and non-excepted trades or businesses. After determining whether its tax items are properly allocable to a trade or business, a taxpayer that is engaged in both excepted and non-excepted trades or businesses must apply the rules of this section to determine the amount of interest expense that is business interest expense subject to limitation under section 163(j) and to determine which items are included or excluded in computing its section 163(j) limitation.

(ii) *Treatment of investment interest, investment income, and investment expenses of a partnership with a C corporation or tax-exempt corporation as a partner.*—For rules governing the treatment of investment interest, investment income, and investment expenses of a partnership with a C corporation or tax-exempt corporation as a partner, see §§1.163(j)-4(b)(3) and 1.163(j)-6(j).

(3) *Application of allocation rules to foreign corporations and foreign partnerships.*—The rules of this section apply to foreign corporations and foreign partnerships. See §§1.163(j)-7 and 1.163(j)-8.

(4) *Application of allocation rules to members of a consolidated group.*—(i) *In general.*—As provided in §1.163(j)-4(d), the computations required by section 163(j) and the section 163(j) regulations generally are made for a consolidated group on a consolidated basis. In this regard, for purposes of applying the allocation rules of this section, all members of a consolidated group are treated as one corporation. Therefore, the rules of this section apply to the activities conducted by the group as if those activities were conducted by a single corporation. For example, the group (rather than a particular member) is treated as engaged in excepted or non-excepted trades or businesses. In the case of intercompany obligations, within the meaning of §1.1502-13(g)(2)(ii), for purposes of allocating asset basis between excepted and non-excepted trades or businesses, the obligation of the member borrower is not considered an asset of the creditor member. Similarly, intercompany transactions, within the meaning of §1.1502-13(b)(1)(i), are disregarded for purposes of this section, as are the resulting offsetting items, and property is not treated as used in a trade or business to the extent the use of such property in that trade or business derives from an intercompany transaction. Further, stock of a group member that is owned by another member of the same group is not treated as an asset for purposes of this section, and the transfer of any amount of member stock to a non-member is treated by the group as a transfer of the member's assets proportionate to the amount of member stock transferred. Additionally, stock of a corporation that is not a group member is treated as owned by the group.

(ii) *Application of excepted business percentage to members of a consolidated group.*—After a consolidated group has determined the percentage of the group's interest expense allocable to excepted trades or businesses for the taxable year (and thus not subject to limitation under section 163(j)), this exempt percentage is applied to the interest paid or accrued by each member during the taxable year to any lender that is not a group member. Therefore, except to the extent paragraph (d) of this section (providing rules for certain qualified nonrecourse indebtedness) applies, an identical percentage of the interest paid or accrued by each member of the group to any lender that is not a group member will be treated as allocable to excepted trades or businesses, regardless of whether any particular member actually engaged in an excepted trade or business.

(iii) *Basis in assets transferred in an intercompany transaction.*—For purposes of allocating interest expense and interest income under paragraph (c) of this section, the basis of property does not include any gain or loss realized with respect to the property by another member in an intercompany transaction, as defined in § 1.1502-13(b), whether or not the gain or loss is deferred.

(5) *Tax-exempt organizations.*—For organizations subject to tax under section 511, section 512 and the regulations thereunder determine the rules for allocating all income and expenses among multiple trades or businesses.

(6) [Reserved]

(7) *Examples.*—The following examples illustrate the principles of this paragraph (a).

(i) *Example 1: Items properly allocable to a trade or business*—(A) *Facts.* Individual T operates Business X, a non-excepted trade or business, as a sole proprietor. In Year 1, T pays or accrues $40x of interest expense and receives $100x of gross income with respect to Business X that is not eligible for a section 199A deduction. T borrows money to buy a car for personal use, and T pays or accrues $20x of interest expense with respect to the car loan. T also invests in corporate bonds, and, in Year 1, T receives $50x of interest income on those bonds.

(B) *Analysis.* Under paragraphs (a)(1) and (2) of this section, T must determine which items of income and expense, including items of interest income and interest expense, are properly allocable to a trade or business. T's $100x of gross income and T's $40x of interest expense with respect to Business X are properly allocable to a trade or business. However, the interest expense on T's car loan is personal interest within the meaning of section 163(h)(2) rather than interest properly allocable to a trade or business. Similarly, T's interest income from corporate bonds is not properly allocable to a trade or business because it is interest from investment activity. See section 163(d)(4)(B).

(ii) *Example 2: Intercompany transaction*—(A) *Facts.* S is a member of a consolidated group of which P is the common parent. P conducts an electing real property trade or business (Business X), and S conducts a non-excepted trade or business (Business Y). P leases Building V (which P owns) to S for use in Business Y.

(B) *Analysis.* Under paragraph (a)(4)(i) of this section, a consolidated group is treated as a single corporation for purposes of applying the allocation rules of this section, and the consolidated group (rather than a particular member of the group) is treated as engaged in excepted and non-excepted trades or businesses. Thus, intercompany transactions are disregarded for purposes of this section. As a result, the lease of Building V by P to S is disregarded. Moreover, because Building V is used in Business Y, basis in this asset is allocated to Business Y rather than Business X for purposes of these allocation rules, regardless of which member (P or S) owns the building.

(b) *Allocation of tax items other than interest expense and interest income.*—(1) *In general.*—For purposes of calculating ATI, tax items other than interest expense and interest income are allocated to a particular trade or business in the manner described in this paragraph (b). It is not necessary to allocate items under this paragraph (b) for purposes of calculating ATI if all of the taxpayer's items subject to allocation under this paragraph (b) are allocable to excepted trades or businesses, or if all of those items are allocable to non-excepted trades or businesses.

(2) *Gross income other than dividends and interest income.*—A taxpayer's gross income other than dividends and interest income is allocated to the trade or business that generated the gross income.

(3) *Dividends.*—(i) *Look-through rule.*—If a taxpayer receives a dividend, within the meaning of section 316, that is not investment income, within the meaning of section 163(d), and if the taxpayer looks through to the assets of the payor corporation under paragraph (c)(5)(ii) of this section for the taxable year, then, solely for purposes of allocating amounts received as a dividend during the taxable year to excepted or non-excepted trades or businesses under this paragraph (b), the dividend income is treated as allocable to excepted or non-excepted trades or businesses based upon the relative amounts of the payor corporation's adjusted basis in the assets used in its trades or businesses, determined pursuant to paragraph (c) of this section. If at least 90 percent of the payor corporation's adjusted basis in its assets during the taxable year, determined pursuant to paragraph (c) of this section, is allocable to either excepted trades or businesses or to non-excepted trades or businesses, all of the taxpayer's dividend income from the payor corporation for the taxable year is treated as allocable to either excepted or non-excepted trades or businesses, respectively.

(ii) *Inapplicability of the look-through rule.*—If a taxpayer receives a dividend that is not investment income, within the meaning of section 163(d), and if the taxpayer does not look through to the assets of the payor corporation under paragraph (c)(5)(ii) of this section for the taxable year, then the taxpayer must treat the dividend as allocable to a non-excepted trade or business.

(4) *Gain or loss from the disposition of non-consolidated C corporation stock, partnership interests, or S corporation stock.*—(i) *Non-consolidated C corporations.*—If a taxpayer recognizes gain or loss upon the disposition of stock in a non-consolidated C corporation that is not property held for investment, within the meaning of section 163(d)(5), and if the taxpayer looks through to the assets of the C corporation under paragraph (c)(5)(ii) of this section for the taxable year, then the taxpayer must allocate gain or loss from the disposition of stock to excepted or non-excepted trades or businesses based upon the relative amounts of the corporation's adjusted basis in the assets used in its trades or businesses, determined pursuant to paragraph (c) of this section. However, if a taxpayer recognizes gain or loss upon the disposition of stock in a non-consolidated C corporation that is not property held for investment, within the meaning of section 163(d)(5), and if the taxpayer does not look through to the assets of the C corporation under paragraph (c)(5)(ii) of this section for the taxable year, then the taxpayer must treat the gain or loss from the disposition of stock as allocable to a non-excepted trade or business. For rules governing the transfer of stock of a member of a consolidated group, see paragraph (a)(4)(i) of this section.

(ii) *Partnerships and S corporations.*—(A) If a taxpayer recognizes gain or loss upon the disposition of interests in a partnership or stock in an S corporation that owns:

(1) Non-excepted assets and excepted assets;

(2) Investment assets; or

(3) Both;

(B) The taxpayer determines a proportionate share of the amount properly allocable to a non-excepted trade or business in accordance with the allocation rules set forth in paragraph (c)(5)(ii)(A) or (c)(5)(ii)(B)(3) of this section, as appropriate, and includes such proportionate share of gain or loss in the taxpayer's ATI. This rule also applies to tiered passthrough entities, as defined in §1.163(j)-7(f)(13), by looking through each passthrough entity tier (for example, an S corporation that is the partner of the highest-tier partnership would look through each lower-tier partnership), subject to paragraph (c)(5)(ii)(D) of this section. With respect to a partner that is a C corporation or tax-exempt corporation, a partnership's investment assets are taken into account and treated as non-excepted trade or business assets.

(5) *Expenses, losses, and other deductions.*—(i) *Expenses, losses, and other deductions that are definitely related to a trade or business.*—Expenses (other than interest expense), losses, and other deductions (collectively, *deductions* for purposes of this paragraph (b)(5)) that are definitely related to a trade or business are allocable to the trade or business to which they relate. A deduction is considered definitely related to a trade or business if the item giving rise to the deduction is incurred as a result of, or incident to, an activity of the trade or business or in connection with property used in the trade or business (see §1.861-8(b)(2)). If a deduction is definitely related to one or more excepted trades or businesses and one or more non-excepted trades or businesses, the deduction is apportioned between the excepted and non-excepted trades or businesses based upon the relative amounts of the taxpayer's adjusted basis in the assets used in those trades or businesses, as determined under paragraph (c) of this section.

(ii) *Other deductions.*—Deductions that are not described in paragraph (b)(5)(i) of this section are ratably apportioned to all gross income.

(6) *Treatment of certain investment items of a partnership with a C corporation partner.*—Any investment income or investment expenses that a partnership receives, pays, or accrues and that is treated as properly allocable to a trade or business of a C corporation partner under §1.163(j)-4(b)(3)(i) is treated as properly allocable to a non-excepted trade or business of the C corporation partner.

(7) *Example: Allocation of income and expense.*—The following example illustrates the principles of this paragraph (b):

(i) *Facts.* T conducts an electing real property trade or business (Business Y), which is an excepted trade or business. T also operates a lumber yard (Business Z), which is a non-excepted trade or business. In Year 1, T receives $100x of gross rental income from real property leasing activities. T also pays or accrues $60x of expenses in connection with its real property leasing activities and $20x of legal services performed on behalf of both Business Y and Business Z. T receives $60x of gross income from lumber yard customers and pays or accrues $50x of expenses related to the lumber yard business. For purposes of expense allocations under paragraphs (b) and (c) of this section, T has $240x of adjusted basis in its Business Y assets and $80x of adjusted basis in its Business Z assets.

(ii) *Analysis.* Under paragraph (b)(2) of this section, for Year 1, $100x of rental income is allocated to Business Y, and $60x of income from lumber yard customers is allocated to Business Z. Under paragraph (b)(5)(i) of this section, $60x of expenses paid or accrued in connection with real property leasing activities are allocated to Business Y, and $50x of expenses related to the lumber yard are allocated to Business Z. The $20x of remaining expenses for legal services performed on behalf of both Business Y and Business Z are allocated according to the relative amounts of T's basis in the assets used in each business. The total amount of T's basis in the assets used in Businesses Y and Z is $320x, of which 75 percent ($240x / $320x) is used in Business Y and 25 percent ($80x / $320x) is used in Business Z. Accordingly, $15x of the expenses for legal services are allocated to Business Y and $5x are allocated to Business Z.

(c) *Allocating interest expense and interest income that is properly allocable to a trade or business.*—(1) *General rule.*—(i) *In general.*—Except as otherwise provided in this section, the amount of a taxpayer's interest expense and interest income that is properly allocable to a trade or business is allocated to the taxpayer's excepted or non-excepted trades or businesses for purposes of section 163(j) based upon the relative amounts of the taxpayer's adjusted basis in the assets, as determined under paragraph (c)(5) of this section, used in its excepted or non-excepted trades or businesses. The taxpayer must determine the adjusted basis in its assets as of the close of each determination date, as defined in paragraph (c)(6) of this section, in the taxable year and average those amounts to determine the relative amounts of asset basis for its excepted and non-excepted trades or businesses for that year. It is not necessary to allocate interest expense or interest income under this paragraph (c) for purposes of determining a taxpayer's business interest expense and business interest income if all of the taxpayer's interest income and expense is allocable to excepted trades or businesses (in which case the taxpayer is not subject to the section 163(j) limitation) or if all of the taxpayer's interest income and expense is allocable to non-excepted trades or businesses.

(ii) *De minimis exception.*—If 90 percent or more of the taxpayer's basis in its assets for the taxable year is allocable to either excepted or non-excepted trades or businesses pursuant to this paragraph (c), then all of the taxpayer's interest expense and interest income for that year that is properly allocable to a trade or business is treated as allocable to either excepted or non-excepted trades or businesses, respectively.

(2) *Example.*—The following example illustrates the principles of paragraph (c)(1) of this section: T is a calendar-year C corporation engaged in an electing real property trade or business, the business of selling wine, and the business of selling hand-carved wooden furni-

ture. In Year 1, T has $100x of interest expense that is deductible except for the potential application of section 163(j). Based upon determinations made on the determination dates of March 31, June 30, September 30, and December 31, T's average adjusted basis in the assets used in the electing real property trade or business (an excepted trade or business) in Year 1 is $800x, and T's total average adjusted basis in the assets used in the other two businesses in Year 1 is $200x. Thus, $80x (($800x / ($800x + $200x)) x $100x) of T's interest expense for Year 1 is allocable to T's electing real property trade or business and is not business interest expense subject to limitation under section 163(j). The remaining $20x of T's interest expense is business interest expense for Year 1 that is subject to limitation under section 163(j).

(3) *Asset used in more than one trade or business.*—(i) *General rule.*—If an asset is used in more than one trade or business during a determination period, as defined in paragraph (c)(6) of this section, the taxpayer's adjusted basis in the asset is allocated to each trade or business using the permissible methodology under this paragraph (c)(3) that most reasonably reflects the use of the asset in each trade or business during that determination period. An allocation methodology most reasonably reflects the use of the asset in each trade or business if it most properly reflects the proportionate benefit derived from the use of the asset in each trade or business. If none of the permissible methodologies set forth in paragraph (c)(3)(ii) of this section reasonably reflects the use of the asset in each trade or business, the taxpayer's basis in the asset is not taken into account for purposes of this paragraph (c).

(ii) *Permissible methodologies for allocating asset basis between or among two or more trades or businesses.*—Subject to the special rules in paragraphs (c)(3)(iii) and (c)(5) of this section, a taxpayer's basis in an asset used in two or more trades or businesses during a determination period may be allocated to those trades or businesses based upon—

(A) The relative amounts of gross income that an asset generates, has generated, or may reasonably be expected to generate, within the meaning of § 1.861-9T(g)(3), with respect to the trades or businesses;

(B) If the asset is land or an inherently permanent structure, the relative amounts of physical space used by the trades or businesses; or

(C) If the trades or businesses generate the same unit of output, the relative amounts of output of those trades or businesses (for example, if an asset is used in two trades or businesses, one of which is an excepted regulated utility trade or business, and the other of which is a non-excepted regulated utility trade or business, the taxpayer may allocate basis in the asset based upon the relative amounts of kilowatt-hours generated by each trade or business).

(iii) *Special rules.*—(A) *Consistent allocation methodologies.*—*(1) In general.*—Except as otherwise provided in paragraph (c)(3)(iii)(A)(*2*) of this section, a taxpayer may not vary its allocation methodology from one determination period to the next within a taxable year or from one taxable year to the next.

(2) Consent to change allocation methodology.—If a taxpayer determines that a different allocation methodology properly reflects the proportionate benefit derived from the use of assets in its trades or businesses, the taxpayer may change its method of allocation under paragraphs (c)(3)(i) and (ii) of this section with the consent of the Commissioner. To obtain consent, a taxpayer must submit a request for a letter ruling under the applicable administrative procedures, and consent only will be granted in extraordinary circumstances.

(B) *De minimis exceptions.*—*(1) De minimis amount of gross income from trades or businesses.*—If at least 90 percent of gross income that an asset generates, has generated, or may reasonably be expected to generate, within the meaning of § 1.861-9T(g)(3), during a determination period is with respect to either excepted trades or businesses or non-excepted trades or businesses, the taxpayer's entire basis in the asset for the determination period must be allocated to either excepted or non-excepted trades or businesses, respectively.

(2) De minimis amount of asset basis allocable to a trade or business.—If 90 percent or more of the taxpayer's basis in an asset would be allocated to either excepted trades or businesses or non-excepted trades or businesses during a determination period pursuant to this paragraph (c)(3), the taxpayer's entire basis in the asset for the determination period must be allocated to either excepted or non-excepted trades or businesses, respectively.

(C) *Allocations of excepted regulated utility trades or businesses.*—*(1) In general.*—Except as provided in the de minimis rule in paragraph (c)(3)(iii)(C)(*3*) of this section, if a taxpayer is engaged in the trade or business of the furnishing or sale of items described in § 1.163(j)-1(b)(13)(i)(A), the taxpayer is engaged in an excepted regulated utility trade or business only to the extent the rates for the items furnished and sold are described in § 1.163(j)-1(b)(13)(i)(B). Thus, for example, electricity sold at market rates rather than on a cost of service and rate of return basis must be treated as electricity sold by a non-excepted regulated utility trade or business. The taxpayer must allocate under this paragraph (c) the basis of assets used in the utility trade or business between its excepted and non-excepted trades or businesses.

(2) Permissible method for allocating asset basis for utility trades or businesses.—In the case of a utility trade or business described in paragraph (c)(3)(iii)(C)(*1*) of this section, and except as provided in the de minimis rule in paragraph (c)(3)(iii)(C)(*3*) of this section, the method described in paragraph (c)(3)(ii)(C) of this section is the only permissible method for allocating the taxpayer's basis in assets used in the trade or business between the taxpayer's excepted and non-excepted trades or businesses of selling or furnishing the items described in § 1.163(j)-1(b)(13)(i)(A).

(3) De minimis rule for excepted utility trades or businesses.—If a taxpayer is engaged in a utility trade or business described in paragraph (c)(3)(iii)(C)(*1*) of this section, and if more than 90 percent of the items described in § 1.163(j)-1(b)(13)(i)(A) are furnished or sold at rates determined in the manner described in

§ 1.163(j)-1(b)(13)(i)(B), the taxpayer's entire trade or business is an excepted regulated utility trade or business, and paragraph (c)(3)(iii)(C)(*2*) of this section does not apply.

(4) Example.—The following example illustrates the principles of this paragraph (c)(3)(iii)(C):

(i) *Facts.* X, a C corporation, is engaged in the trade or business of generating electrical energy. During each determination period in the taxable year, 80 percent of the kilowatts generated in the electricity generation trade or business is sold at rates established by a public utility commission on a rate of return basis. The remaining 20 percent of the kilowatts is sold on the wholesale markets at rates not established on a rate of return basis or by the governing or ratemaking body of an electric cooperative. None of the assets used in X's utility generation trade or business are used in any other trade or business.

(ii) *Analysis.* For purposes of section 163(j), under paragraph (c)(3)(iii)(C)(*1*) of this section, 80 percent of X's electricity generation business is an excepted regulated utility trade or business, and the remaining 20 percent of X's business is a non-excepted utility trade or business. Under paragraph (c)(3)(iii)(C)(*2*) of this section, X must allocate 80 percent of the basis of the assets used in its utility business to excepted trades or business and the remaining 20 percent of the basis in its assets to non-excepted trades or businesses.

(4) *Disallowed business interest expense carryforwards; floor plan financing interest expense.*—Disallowed business interest expense carryforwards (which were treated as allocable to a non-excepted trade or business in a prior taxable year) are not re-allocated between non-excepted and excepted trades or businesses in a succeeding taxable year. Instead, the carryforwards continue to be treated as allocable to a non-excepted trade or business. Floor plan financing interest expense also is not subject to allocation between excepted and non-excepted trades or businesses (see § 1.163(j)-1(b)(17)) and is always treated as allocable to non-excepted trades or businesses.

(5) *Additional rules relating to basis.*—(i) *Calculation of adjusted basis.*—(A) *Non-depreciable property other than land.*—Except as otherwise provided in paragraph (c)(5)(i)(E) of this section, for purposes of this section, the adjusted basis of an asset other than land with respect to which no deduction is allowable under section 167, section 168 of the Internal Revenue Code of 1954 (former section 168), or section 197, as applicable, is the adjusted basis of the asset for determining gain or loss from the sale or other disposition of that asset as provided in § 1.1011-1. Self-created intangible assets are not taken into account for purposes of this paragraph (c).

(B) *Depreciable property other than inherently permanent structures.*—For purposes of this section, the adjusted basis of any tangible asset with respect to which a deduction is allowable under section 167, other than inherently permanent structures, is determined by using the alternative depreciation system under section 168(g) before any application of the additional first-year depreciation deduction (for example, under section 168(k) or (m)), and the adjusted basis of any tangible asset with respect to which a deduction is allowable under former section 168, other than inherently permanent structures, is determined by using the taxpayer's method of computing depreciation for the asset under former section 168. The depreciation deduction with respect to the property described in this paragraph (c)(5)(i)(B) is allocated ratably to each day during the period in the taxable year to which the depreciation relates.

(C) *Special rule for land and inherently permanent structures.*—Except as otherwise provided in paragraph (c)(5)(i)(E) of this section, for purposes of this section, the adjusted basis of any asset that is land, including nondepreciable improvements to land, or an inherently permanent structure is its unadjusted basis.

(D) *Depreciable or amortizable intangible property and depreciable income forecast method property.*—For purposes of this section, the adjusted basis of any intangible asset with respect to which a deduction is allowable under section 167 or 197, as applicable, is determined in accordance with section 167 or 197, as applicable, and the adjusted basis of any asset described in section 167(g)(6) for which the deduction allowable under section 167 is determined by the taxpayer under section 167(g), is determined in accordance with section 167(g). The depreciation or amortization deduction with respect to the property described in this paragraph (c)(5)(i)(D) is allocated ratably to each day during the period in the taxable year to which the depreciation or amortization relates.

(E) *Assets not yet used in a trade or business.*—Assets that have been acquired or that are under development but that are not yet used in a trade or business are not taken into account for purposes of this paragraph (c). For example, construction works in progress (such as buildings, airplanes, or ships) are not taken into account for purposes of this paragraph (c). Similarly, land acquired by a taxpayer for construction of a building by the taxpayer to be used in a trade or business is not taken into account for purposes of this paragraph (c) until the building is placed in service. This rule does not apply to interests in a partnership or stock in a corporation.

(F) *Trusts established to fund specific liabilities.*—Trusts required by law to fund specific liabilities (for example, pension trusts and plant decommissioning trusts) are not taken into account for purposes of this paragraph (c).

(G) *Inherently permanent structure.*—For purposes of this section, the term *inherently permanent structure* has the meaning provided in § 1.856-10(d)(2).

(ii) *Partnership interests; stock in non-consolidated domestic corporations.*—(A) *Partnership interests.*—(*1*) *Calculation of asset basis.*—For purposes of this section, a partner's interest in a partnership is treated as an asset of the partner. For these purposes, the partner's adjusted basis in a partnership interest is reduced, but not below zero, by the partner's share of partnership liabilities, as determined under section 752, and is further reduced as provided in paragraph (c)(5)(ii)(A)(*2*)(*iii*) of this section.

(2) Allocation of asset basis.—*(i) In general.*—For purposes of determining the extent to which a partner's adjusted basis in its partnership interest is allocable to an excepted or non-

excepted trade or business, the partner may look through to such partner's share of the partnership's basis in the partnership's assets, taking into account any adjustments under sections 734(b) and 743(b), and adjusted to the extent required under paragraph (d)(4) of this section, except as otherwise provided in paragraph (c)(5)(ii)(D) of this section. For purposes of the preceding sentence, such partner's share of partnership assets is determined using a reasonable method taking into account special allocations under section 704(b). Notwithstanding paragraph (c)(7) of this section, if a partner's direct and indirect interest in a partnership is greater than or equal to 80 percent of the partnership's capital or profits, the partner must apply the rules in this paragraph (c)(5)(ii)(A) to look through to the partnership's basis in the partnership's assets.

(ii) De minimis rule.—If, after applying paragraph (c)(5)(ii)(A)(2)(*iii*) of this section, at least 90 percent of a partner's share of a partnership's basis in its assets (including adjustments under sections 734(b) and 743(b)) is allocable to either excepted trades or businesses or non-excepted trades or businesses, without regard to assets not properly allocable to a trade or business, the partner's entire basis in its partnership interest is treated as allocable to either excepted or non-excepted trades or businesses, respectively. For purposes of the preceding sentence, such partner's share of partnership assets is determined using a reasonable method taking into account special allocations under section 704(b).

(iii) Partnership assets not properly allocable to a trade or business.—For purposes of applying paragraphs (c)(5)(ii)(A)(2)(*i*) and (*ii*) of this section with respect to a partner that is a C corporation or tax-exempt corporation, such partner's share of a partnership's assets that are not properly allocable to a trade or business is treated as properly allocable to an excepted or non-excepted trade or business with respect to such partner in the same manner that such assets would be treated if held directly by such partner. With respect to a partner other than a C corporation or tax-exempt corporation, a partnership's assets that are not properly allocable to a trade or business are treated as neither excepted nor non-excepted trade or business assets, and such partner's adjusted basis in its partnership interest is reduced by that partner's share of the partnership's asset basis with respect to those assets. For purposes of this paragraph (c)(5)(ii)(A)(2)(*iii*), such partner's share of a partnership's assets is determined under a reasonable method taking into account special allocations under section 704(b).

(iv) Inapplicability of partnership look-through rule.—If a partner, other than a C corporation or a tax-exempt corporation, chooses not to look through to the partnership's basis in the partnership's assets under paragraph (c)(5)(ii)(A)(2)(*i*) of this section or is precluded by paragraph (c)(5)(ii)(D) of this section from applying such partnership look-through rule, the partner generally will treat its basis in the partnership interest as either an asset held for investment or a non-excepted trade or business asset as determined under section 163(d). If a partner that is a C corporation or a tax-exempt corporation chooses not to look through to the partnership's basis in the partnership's assets under paragraph (c)(5)(ii)(A)(2)(*i*) of this section or is precluded by paragraph (c)(5)(ii)(D) of this section from applying such partnership look-through rule, the taxpayer must treat its entire basis in the partnership interest as allocable to a non-excepted trade or business.

(B) *Stock in non-consolidated domestic corporations.*—*(1) In general.*—For purposes of this section, if a taxpayer owns stock in a domestic C corporation that is not a member of the taxpayer's consolidated group, or if the taxpayer owns stock in an S corporation, the stock is treated as an asset of the taxpayer.

(2) Domestic non-consolidated C corporations.—*(i) Allocation of asset basis.*—If a shareholder satisfies the minimum ownership threshold in paragraph (c)(7) of this section, then, for purposes of determining the extent to which the shareholder's basis in its stock in the domestic non-consolidated C corporation is allocable to an excepted or non-excepted trade or business, the shareholder must look through to the corporation's basis in the corporation's assets, adjusted to the extent required under paragraph (d)(4) of this section, except as otherwise provided in paragraph (c)(5)(ii)(D) of this section.

(ii) De minimis rule.—If at least 90 percent of the domestic non-consolidated C corporation's basis in the corporation's assets is allocable to either excepted trades or businesses or non-excepted trades or businesses, the shareholder's entire interest in the corporation's stock is treated as allocable to either excepted or non-excepted trades or businesses, respectively.

(iii) Inapplicability of corporate look-through rule.—If a shareholder other than a C corporation or a tax-exempt corporation does not satisfy the minimum ownership threshold in paragraph (c)(7) of this section or is precluded by paragraph (c)(5)(ii)(D) of this section from applying the corporation look-through rule of paragraph (c)(5)(ii)(B)(2)(*i*) of this section, the shareholder generally will treat its entire basis in the corporation's stock as an asset held for investment. If a shareholder that is a C corporation or a tax-exempt corporation does not satisfy the minimum ownership threshold in paragraph (c)(7) of this section or is precluded by paragraph (c)(5)(ii)(D) of this section from applying the corporation look-through rule of paragraph (c)(5)(ii)(B)(2)(*i*) of this section, the shareholder must treat its entire basis in the corporation's stock as allocable to a non-excepted trade or business.

(3) S corporations.—*(i) Calculation of asset basis.*—For purposes of this section, a shareholder's share of stock in an S corporation is treated as an asset of the shareholder. Additionally, for these purposes, the shareholder's adjusted basis in a share of S corporation stock is adjusted to take into account the modifications in paragraph (c)(5)(i)(A) of this section with respect to the assets of the S corporation (for example, a shareholder's adjusted basis in its S corporation stock is increased by the shareholder's share of depreciation with respect to an inherently permanent structure owned by the S corporation).

(ii) Allocation of asset basis.—For purposes of determining the extent to which a shareholder's basis in its stock of an S corpora-

tion is allocable to an excepted or non-excepted trade or business, the shareholder may look through to such shareholder's share of the S corporation's basis in the S corporation's assets, allocated on a pro rata basis, adjusted to the extent required under paragraph (d)(4) of this section, except as otherwise provided in paragraph (c)(5)(ii)(D) of this section. Notwithstanding paragraph (c)(7) of this section, if a shareholder's direct and indirect interest in an S corporation is greater than or equal to 80 percent of the S corporation's stock by vote and value, the shareholder must apply the rules in this paragraph (c)(5)(ii)(B)(*3*) to look through to the S corporation's basis in the S corporation's assets.

(iii) De minimis rule.—If at least 90 percent of a shareholder's share of an S corporation's basis in its assets is allocable to either excepted trades or businesses or non-excepted trades or businesses, the shareholder's entire basis in its S corporation stock is treated as allocable to either excepted or non-excepted trades or businesses, respectively.

(iv) Inapplicability of S corporation look-through rule.—If a shareholder chooses not to look through to the S corporation's basis in the S corporation's assets under paragraph (c)(5)(ii)(B)(*3*)(*ii*) of this section or is precluded by paragraph (c)(5)(ii)(D) of this section from applying such S corporation look-through rule, the shareholder generally will treat its basis in the S corporation stock as either an asset held for investment or a non-excepted trade or business asset as determined under section 163(d).

(C) *Stock in CFCs.*—The rules applicable to domestic non-consolidated C corporations in paragraph (c)(5)(ii)(B) of this section also apply to CFCs.

(D) *Inapplicability of look-through rule to partnerships or non-consolidated corporations to which the small business exemption applies.*—A taxpayer may not apply the look-through rules in paragraphs (b)(3) and (c)(5)(ii)(A), (B), and (C) of this section to a partnership, S corporation, or non-consolidated corporation that is eligible for the small business exemption under section 163(j)(3) and § 1.163(j)-2(d)(1).

(E) *Tiered entities.*—If a taxpayer applies the look-through rules of this paragraph (c)(5)(ii), the taxpayer must do so for all lower-tier entities with respect to which the taxpayer satisfies, directly or indirectly, the minimum ownership threshold in paragraph (c)(7) of this section, subject to the limitation in paragraph (c)(5)(ii)(D) of this section, beginning with the lowest-tier entity.

(iii) *Cash and cash equivalents and customer receivables.*—Except as otherwise provided in paragraph (d)(2) of this section, a taxpayer's basis in its cash and cash equivalents and customer receivables is not taken into account for purposes of this paragraph (c). This rule also applies to a lower-tier entity if a taxpayer looks through to the assets of that entity under paragraph (c)(5)(ii) of this section. For purposes of this paragraph (c)(5)(iii), the term *cash and cash equivalents* includes cash, foreign currency, commercial paper, any interest in an investment company registered under the Investment Company Act of 1940 (1940 Act) and regulated as a money market fund under 17 CFR 270.2a-7 (Rule 2a-7 under the 1940 Act), any obligation of a government, and any derivative that is substantially secured by an obligation of a government, or any similar asset. For purposes of this paragraph (c)(5)(iii), a *derivative* is a derivative described in section 59A(h)(4)(A), without regard to section 59A(h)(4)(C). For purposes of this paragraph (c)(5)(iii), the term *government* means the United States or any agency or instrumentality of the United States; a State or any political subdivision thereof, including the District of Columbia and any possession or territory of the United States, within the meaning of section 103 and § 1.103-1; or any foreign government, any political subdivision of a foreign government, or any wholly owned agency or instrumentality of any one of the foregoing within the meaning of § 1.1471-6(b).

(iv) *Deemed asset sale.*—Solely for purposes of determining the amount of basis allocable to excepted and non-excepted trades or businesses under this section, an election under section 336, 338, or 754, as applicable, is deemed to have been made for any acquisition of corporate stock or partnership interests with respect to which the taxpayer demonstrates to the satisfaction of the Commissioner, in the information statement required by paragraph (c)(6)(iii)(B) of this section, that the taxpayer was eligible to make an election but was actually or effectively precluded from doing so by a regulatory agency with respect to an excepted regulated utility trade or business. Any additional basis taken into account under this rule is reduced ratably over a 15-year period beginning with the month of the acquisition and is not subject to the anti-abuse rule in paragraph (c)(8) of this section.

(v) *Other adjustments.*—The Commissioner may make appropriate adjustments to prevent a taxpayer from intentionally and artificially increasing its basis in assets attributable to an excepted trade or business.

(6) *Determination dates; determination periods; reporting requirements.*—(i) *Definitions.*—For purposes of this section, the term *determination date* means the last day of each quarter of the taxpayer's taxable year (and the last day of the taxpayer's taxable year, if the taxpayer has a short taxable year), and the term *determination period* means the period beginning the day after one determination date and ending on the next determination date.

(ii) *Application of look-through rules.*—If a taxpayer that applies the look-through rules of paragraph (c)(5)(ii) of this section has a different taxable year than the partnership or non-consolidated corporation to which the taxpayer is applying those rules, then, for purposes of this paragraph (c)(6), the taxpayer must use the most recent quarterly figures from the partnership or non-consolidated corporation. For example, assume that PS1 is a partnership with a May 31 taxable year, and that C (a calendar-year C corporation) is a partner whose ownership interest satisfies the ownership threshold in paragraph (c)(7) of this section. PS1's determination dates are February 28, May 31, August 31, and November 30. In turn, C's determination dates are March 31, June 30, September 30, and December 31. If C looks through to PS1's basis in its assets under paragraph (c)(5)(ii) of this section, then, for purposes of determining the amount of C's asset basis that is attributable to its excepted and non-excepted businesses on March 31, C must use PS1's asset basis calculations for February 28.

(iii) *Reporting requirements.*—(A) *Books and records.*—A taxpayer must maintain books of account and other records and data as necessary to substantiate the taxpayer's use of an asset in an excepted trade or business and to substantiate the adjustments to asset basis for purposes of applying paragraph (c) of this section. One indication demonstrating that a particular asset is used in a particular trade or business is if the taxpayer maintains separate books and records for all of its excepted and non-excepted trades or businesses, and can show the asset in the books and records of a particular excepted or non-excepted trade or business. For rules governing record retention, see § 1.6001-1.

(B) *Information statement.*—Except as otherwise provided in publications, forms, instructions, or other guidance, each taxpayer that is making an allocation under this paragraph (c) must prepare a statement containing the information described in this paragraph (c)(6)(iii) and must attach the statement to its timely filed Federal income tax return for the taxable year. The statement, which must be titled "Section 163(j) Asset Basis Calculations," must include the following information:

(1) The taxpayer's adjusted basis in the assets used in its excepted and non-excepted businesses, determined on a quarterly basis as set forth in this section, including detailed information for the different groups of assets identified in paragraphs (c)(5)(i), (c)(5)(ii), and (d) of this section;

(2) The determination dates on which asset basis was measured during the taxable year;

(3) The names and taxpayer identification numbers (TINs) of all entities for which basis information is being provided, including partnerships and corporations if the taxpayer that owns an interest in a partnership or corporation looks through to the partnership's or corporation's basis in the partnership's or corporation's assets under paragraph (c)(5)(ii) of this section. If the taxpayer is a member of a consolidated group, the name and TIN of the agent for the group, as defined in § 1.1502-77, must be provided, but the taxpayer need not provide the names and TINs of all other consolidated group members;

(4) Asset basis information for corporations or partnerships if the taxpayer looks through to the corporation's or partnership's basis in the corporation's or partnership's assets under paragraph (c)(5)(ii) of this section; and

(5) A summary of the method or methods used to determine asset basis in property used in both excepted and non-excepted businesses, as well as information regarding any deemed sale under paragraph (c)(5)(iv) of this section.

(iv) *Failure to file statement.*—If a taxpayer fails to file the statement described in paragraph (c)(6)(iii) of this section or files a statement that does not comply with the requirements of paragraph (c)(6)(iii) of this section, the Commissioner may treat the taxpayer as if all of its interest expense is properly allocable to a non-excepted trade or business, unless the taxpayer shows that there was reasonable cause for failing to comply with, and the taxpayer acted in good faith with respect to, the requirements of paragraph (c)(6)(iii) of this section, taking into account all pertinent facts and circumstances.

(7) *Ownership threshold for look-through rules.*—(i) *Corporations.*—(A) *Asset basis.*—A shareholder must look through to the assets of a non-consolidated domestic C corporation or a CFC under paragraph (c)(5)(ii) of this section for purposes of allocating the shareholder's basis in its stock in the corporation between excepted and non-excepted trades or businesses if the shareholder's direct and indirect interest in the corporation satisfies the ownership requirements of section 1504(a)(2). A shareholder may look through to the assets of an S corporation under paragraph (c)(5)(ii) of this section for purposes of allocating the shareholder's basis in its stock in the S corporation between excepted and non-excepted trades or businesses regardless of the shareholder's direct and indirect interest in the S corporation.

(B) *Dividends.*—A shareholder must look through to the activities of a non-consolidated domestic C corporation or a CFC under paragraph (b)(3) of this section if the shareholder's direct and indirect interest in the corporation satisfies the ownership requirements of section 1504(a)(2). A shareholder may look through to the activities of an S corporation under paragraph (b)(3) of this section regardless of the shareholder's direct and indirect interest in the S corporation.

(ii) *Partnerships.*—A partner may look through to the assets of a partnership under paragraph (c)(5)(ii) of this section for purposes of allocating the partner's basis in its partnership interest between excepted and non-excepted trades or businesses regardless of the partner's direct and indirect interest in the partnership.

(iii) *Inapplicability of look-through rule.*—For circumstances in which a taxpayer that satisfies the ownership threshold in this paragraph (c)(7) may not apply the look-through rules in paragraphs (b)(3) and (c)(5)(ii) of this section, see paragraph (c)(5)(ii)(D) of this section.

(8) *Anti-abuse rule.*—If a principal purpose for the acquisition, disposition, or change in use of an asset was to artificially shift the amount of basis allocable to excepted or non-excepted trades or businesses on a determination date, the additional basis or change in use will not be taken into account for purposes of this section. For example, if an asset is used in a non-excepted trade or business for most of the taxable year, and if the taxpayer begins using the asset in an excepted trade or business towards the end of the year with a principal purpose of shifting the amount of basis in the asset that is allocable to the excepted trade or business, the change in use is disregarded for purposes of this section. A purpose may be a principal purpose even though it is outweighed by other purposes (taken together or separately). In determining whether a taxpayer has a principal purpose described in this paragraph (c)(8), factors to be considered include, for example, the following: the business purpose for the acquisition, disposition, or change in use; the length of time the asset was used in a trade or business; whether the asset was acquired from a related person; and whether the taxpayer's aggregate basis in its assets increased or decreased temporarily on or around a determination date. A principal purpose is presumed to be present in any case in

which the acquisition, disposition, or change in use lacks a substantial business purpose and increases the taxpayer's basis in assets used in its excepted trades or businesses by more than 10 percent during the taxable year.

(d) *Direct allocations.*—(1) *In general.*—For purposes of this section, a taxpayer with qualified nonrecourse indebtedness, within the meaning of § 1.861-10T(b), must directly allocate interest expense from the indebtedness to the taxpayer's assets in the manner and to the extent provided in § 1.861-10T(b).

(2) *Financial services entities.*—For purposes of this section, a taxpayer that is engaged in the trade or business of banking, within the meaning of section 581, insurance, financing, or a similar business that derives active financing income as described in § 1.904-4(e)(2) (an active financing business) must directly allocate interest expense and interest income from that business to the taxpayer's assets used in that business. The special rule for cash and cash equivalents in paragraph (c)(5)(iii) of this section does not apply to an entity that qualifies as a financial services entity as described in § 1.904-4(e)(3).

(3) *Assets used in more than one trade or business.*—If an asset is used in more than one trade or business, the taxpayer must apply the rules in paragraph (c)(3) of this section to determine the extent to which interest that is directly allocated under this paragraph (d) is allocable to excepted or non-excepted trades or businesses.

(4) *Adjustments to basis of assets to account for direct allocations.*—In determining the amount of a taxpayer's basis in the assets used in its excepted and non-excepted trades or businesses for purposes of paragraph (c) of this section, adjustments must be made to reflect direct allocations under this paragraph (d). These adjustments consist of reductions in the amount of the taxpayer's basis in its assets for purposes of paragraph (c) of this section to reflect assets to which interest expense is directly allocated under this paragraph (d). These adjustments must be made before the taxpayer averages the adjusted basis in its assets as determined on each determination date during the taxable year.

(5) *Example: Direct allocation of interest expense.*—(i) *Facts.* T conducts an electing real property trade or business (Business X) and operates a retail store that is a non-excepted trade or business (Business Y). In Year 1, T issues Note A to a third party in exchange for $1,000x for the purpose of acquiring Building B. Note A is qualified nonrecourse indebtedness (within the meaning of § 1.861-10T(b)) secured by Building B. T then uses those funds to acquire Building B for $1,200x, and T uses Building B in Business X. During Year 1, T pays $500x of interest, of which $100x is interest payments on Note A. For Year 1, T's basis in its assets used in Business X (as determined under paragraph (c) of this section) is $3,600x (excluding cash and cash equivalents), and T's basis in its assets used in Business Y (as determined under paragraph (c) of this section) is $800x (excluding cash and cash equivalents). Each of Business X and Business Y also has $100x of cash and cash equivalents.

(ii) *Analysis.* Because Note A is qualified nonrecourse indebtedness that is secured by Building B, in allocating interest expense between Businesses X and Y, T first must directly allocate the $100x of interest expense it paid with respect to Note A to Business X in accordance with paragraph (d)(1) of this section. Thereafter, T must allocate the remaining $400x of interest expense between Businesses X and Y under paragraph (c) of this section. After excluding T's $1,200x cost basis in Building B (see paragraph (d)(4) of this section), and without regard to T's $200x of cash and cash equivalents (see paragraph (c)(5)(iv) of this section), T's basis in assets used in Businesses X and Y is $2,400x and $800x (75 percent and 25 percent), respectively. Thus, $300x of the remaining $400x of interest expense would be allocated to Business X, and $100x would be allocated to Business Y.

(e) *Examples.*—The examples in this paragraph (e) illustrate the principles of this section. For purposes of these examples, assume that no taxpayer is eligible for the small business exemption under section 163(j)(3) and § 1.163(j)-2(d), no taxpayer has floor plan financing interest expense, and no taxpayer has qualified nonrecourse indebtedness within the meaning of § 1.861-10T(b).

(1) *Example 1: Interest allocation within a consolidated group*—(i) *Facts.* S is a member of a consolidated group of which P is the common parent. P conducts an electing real property trade or business (Business X), and S conducts a non-excepted trade or business (Business Y). In Year 1, P pays or accrues (without regard to section 163(j)) $35x of interest expense and receives $10x of interest income, and S pays or accrues (without regard to section 163(j)) $115x of interest expense and receives $5x of interest income (for a total of $150x of interest expense and $15x of interest income). For purposes of this example, assume that, pursuant to paragraph (c) of this section, $30x of the P group's interest expense and $3x of the P group's interest income is allocable to Business X, and the remaining $120x of interest expense and $12x of interest income is allocable to Business Y.

(ii) *Analysis.* Under paragraph (a)(4) of this section, 20 percent of the P group's Year 1 interest expense ($30x / $150x) and interest income ($3x / $15x) is allocable to an excepted trade or business. Thus, $7x ($35x x 20 percent) of P's interest expense and $2x ($10x x 20 percent) of P's interest income is allocable to an excepted trade or business. The remaining $28x of P's interest expense is business interest expense subject to limitation under section 163(j), and the remaining $8x of P's interest income is business interest income that increases the group's section 163(j) limitation. In turn, $23x ($115x x 20 percent) of S's interest expense and $1x ($5x x 20 percent) of S's interest income is allocable to an excepted trade or business. The remaining $92x of S's interest expense is business interest expense subject to limitation under section 163(j), and the remaining $4x of S's interest income is business interest income that increases the group's section 163(j) limitation.

(2) *Example 2: Interest allocation within a consolidated group with assets used in more than one trade or business*—(i) *Facts.* S is a member of a consolidated group of which P is the common parent. P conducts an electing real property trade or business (Business X), and S conducts a non-excepted trade or business (Business Y). In Year 1, P pays or accrues (without regard to section 163(j)) $50x of interest expense, and S

pays or accrues $100x of interest expense (without regard to section 163(j)). P leases 40 percent of space in Building V (which P owns) to S for use in Business Y, and P leases the remaining 60 percent of space in Building V to third parties. For purposes of allocating interest expense under paragraph (c) of this section, the P group's basis in its assets (excluding Building V) used in Businesses X and Y is $180x and $620x, respectively. The P group's basis in Building V for purposes of allocating interest expense under paragraph (c) of this section is $200x.

(ii) *Analysis*. Under paragraph (c)(3)(ii) of this section, the P group's basis in Building V ($200x) is allocated to excepted and non-excepted trades or businesses in accordance with the use of space by Business Y (40 percent) and Business X (the remainder, or 60 percent). Accordingly, $120x of the basis in Building V is allocated to excepted trades or businesses (60 percent x $200x), and $80x is allocated to non-excepted trades or businesses (40 percent x $200x). After allocating the basis in Building V, the P group's total basis in the assets used in excepted and non-excepted trades or businesses is $300x and $700x, respectively. Under paragraphs (a)(4) and (c) of this section, 30 percent ($300x / $1000x) of the P group's Year 1 interest expense is properly allocable to an excepted trade or business. Thus, $15x ($50x x 30 percent) of P's interest expense is properly allocable to an excepted trade or business, and the remaining $35x of P's interest expense is business interest expense subject to limitation under section 163(j). In turn, $30x ($100x x 30 percent) of S's interest expense is properly allocable to an excepted trade or business, and the remaining $70x of S's interest expense is business interest expense subject to limitation under section 163(j).

(3) *Example 3: Application of look-through rules*—(i) *Facts*. (A) A and B are unrelated individual taxpayers. A owns 100 percent of the stock of Corp 1, a calendar-year domestic C corporation. The basis of A's stock in Corp 1 is $500x. Corp 1 owns 10 percent of the interests in PS1 (a domestic partnership), and B owns the remaining 90 percent. Corp 1's basis in its PS1 interests is $25x, and B's basis in its PS1 interests is $225x. PS1 owns 100 percent of the stock of Corp 2, a calendar-year domestic C corporation. PS1 has a basis of $1000x in its Corp 2 stock.

(B) In 2020, Corp 1 was engaged solely in a non-excepted trade or business. That same year, PS1's only activity was holding Corp 2 stock. In turn, Corp 2 was engaged in both an electing farming business and a non-excepted trade or business. Under the allocation rules in paragraph (c) of this section, 50 percent of Corp 2's asset basis in 2020 was allocable to the electing farming business. The remaining 50 percent was allocable to the non-excepted trade or business.

(C) Individuals A and B each paid or accrued (without regard to section 163(j)) $150x of interest expense allocable to a trade or business under §1.163-8T (along with personal interest and investment interest). A's trade or business was an excepted trade or business, and B's trade or business was a non-excepted trade or business. A's basis in the assets used in its trade or business was $100x, and B's basis in the assets used in its trade or business was $112.5x.

(ii) *Analysis*. (A) As provided in paragraph (c)(5)(ii)(E) of this section, if a taxpayer applies the look-through rules of paragraph (c)(5)(ii) of this section, the taxpayer must begin with the lowest-tier entity to which it is eligible to apply the look-through rules. A directly owns 100 percent of the stock of Corp 1; thus, A satisfies the 80 percent minimum ownership threshold with respect to Corp 1. A also owns 10 percent of the interests in PS1. There is no minimum ownership threshold for partnerships; thus, A may apply the look-through rules to PS1. However, A does not directly or indirectly own at least 80 percent of the stock of Corp 2; thus, A may not look through its indirect interest in Corp 2. In turn, B directly owns 90 percent of the interests in PS1, and B indirectly owns at least 80 percent of the stock of Corp 2. Thus, B may apply the look-through rules to both PS1 and Corp 2.

(B) From A's perspective, PS1 is not engaged in a trade or business for purposes of section 163(j); instead, PS1 is merely holding its Corp 2 stock as an investment. Under paragraph (c)(5)(ii)(A)(2) of this section, if a partnership is not engaged in a trade or business, then its C corporation partner must treat its entire basis in the partnership interest as allocable to a non-excepted trade or business. Thus, for purposes of A's application of the look-through rules, Corp 1's entire basis in its PS1 interest ($25x) is allocable to a non-excepted trade or business. Corp 1's basis in its other assets also is allocable to a non-excepted trade or business (the only trade or business in which Corp 1 is engaged). Thus, under paragraph (c) of this section, A's $500x basis in its Corp 1 stock is allocable entirely to a non-excepted trade or business. A's $100x basis in its other business assets is allocable to an excepted trade or business. Thus, 5/6 (or $125x) of A's $150x of interest expense is properly allocable to a non-excepted trade or business and is business interest expense subject to limitation under section 163(j), and the remaining $25x of A's $150x of interest expense is allocable to an excepted trade or business and is not subject to limitation under section 163(j).

(C) From B's perspective, PS1 must look through its stock in Corp 2 to determine the extent to which PS1's basis in the stock is allocable to an excepted or non-excepted trade or business. Half of Corp 2's basis in its assets is allocable to an excepted trade or business, and the other half is allocable to a non-excepted trade or business. Thus, from B's perspective, $500x of PS1's basis in its Corp 2 stock (PS1's only asset) is allocable to an excepted trade or business, and the other half is allocable to a non-excepted trade or business. B's basis in its PS1 interests is $225x. Applying the look-through rules to B's PS1 interests, $112.5x of B's basis in its PS1 interests is allocable to an excepted trade or business, and $112.5x of B's basis in its PS1 interests is allocable to a non-excepted trade or business. Since B's basis in the assets used in its non-excepted trade or business also was $112.5x, two-thirds of B's interest expense ($100x) is properly allocable to a non-excepted trade or business and is business interest expense subject to limitation under section 163(j), and one-third of B's interest expense ($50x) is allocable to an excepted trade or business and is not subject to limitation under section 163(j).

(4) *Example 4: Excepted and non-excepted trades or businesses in a consolidated group*—(i) *Facts*. P is the common parent of a consolidated

group of which A and B are the only other members. A conducts an electing real property trade or business (Business X), and B conducts a non-excepted trade or business (Business Y). In Year 1, A pays or accrues (without regard to section 163(j)) $50x of interest expense and earns $70x of gross income in the conduct of Business X, and B pays or accrues (without regard to section 163(j)) $100x of interest expense and earns $150x of gross income in the conduct of Business Y. B owns Building V, which it uses in Business Y. For purposes of allocating the P group's Year 1 business interest expense between excepted and non-excepted trades or businesses under paragraph (c) of this section, the P group's basis in its assets (other than Building V) used in Businesses X and Y is $180x and $620x, respectively, and the P group's basis in Building V is $200x. At the end of Year 1, B sells Building V to a third party and realizes a gain of $60x in addition to the $150x of gross income B earned that year from the conduct of Business Y.

(ii) *Analysis.* (A) Under paragraphs (a)(4) and (c) of this section, the P group's basis in its assets used in its trades or businesses is allocated between the P group's excepted trade or business (Business X) and its non-excepted trade or business (Business Y) as though these trades or businesses were conducted by a single corporation. Under paragraph (c) of this section, the P group's basis in its assets used in Businesses X and Y is $180x and $820x, respectively. Accordingly, 18 percent ($180x / $1,000x) of the P group's total interest expense ($150x) is properly allocable to an excepted trade or business ($27x), and the remaining 82 percent of the P group's total interest expense is business interest expense properly allocable to a non-excepted trade or business ($123x).

(B) To determine the P group's section 163(j) limitation, paragraph (a) of this section requires that certain items of income and deduction be allocated to the excepted and non-excepted trades or businesses of the P group as though these trades or businesses were conducted by a single corporation. In Year 1, the P group's excepted trade or business (Business X) has gross income of $70x, and the P group's non-excepted trade or business (Business Y) has gross income of $150x. Because Building V was used exclusively in Business Y, the $60x of gain from the sale of Building V in Year 1 is attributed to Business Y under paragraph (b)(2) of this section. The P group's section 163(j) limitation is $63x (30 percent x $210x), which allows the P group to deduct $63x of its $123x of business interest expense allocated to the P group's non-excepted trades or businesses. The group's $27x of interest expense that is allocable to excepted trades or businesses may be deducted without limitation under section 163(j).

(iii) *Intercompany transaction.* The facts are the same as in *Example 4* in paragraph (e)(4)(i) of this section, except that A owns Building V and leases it to B in Year 1 for $20x for use in Business Y, and A sells Building V to a third party for a $60 gain at the end of Year 1. Under paragraphs (a)(4) and (c) of this section, all members of the P group are treated as a single corporation. As a result, the P group's basis in its assets used in its trades or businesses is allocated between the P group's excepted trade or business (Business X) and its non-excepted trade or business (Business Y) as though these trades or businesses were conducted by a single corporation. A lease between two divisions of a single corporation would produce no rental income or expense. Thus, the $20x of rent paid by B to A does not affect the P group's ATI. Moreover, under paragraph (c) of this section, Building V is an asset used in the P group's non-excepted trade or business (Business Y). Accordingly, although A owns Building V, the basis in Building V is added to the P group's basis in assets used in Business Y for purposes of allocating interest expense under paragraph (c) of this section. In the same vein, when A sells Building V to a third party at a gain of $60x, the gain is included in the P group's ATI because Building V was used in a non-excepted trade or business of the P group (Business Y) prior to its sale.

(5) *Example 5: Captive activities*—(i) *Facts.* S and T are members of a consolidated group of which P is the common parent. P conducts an electing real property trade or business (Business X), S conducts a non-excepted trade or business (Business Y), and T provides transportation services to Businesses X and Y but does not have any customers outside of the P group. For Year 1, T provides transportation services using a single bus with a basis of $120x.

(ii) *Analysis.* Under paragraph (a)(4) of this section, activities conducted by a consolidated group are treated as though those activities were conducted by a single corporation. Because the activities of T are limited to providing intercompany transportation services, T does not conduct a trade or business for purposes of section 163(j). Under paragraph (c)(3) of this section, business interest expense is allocated to excepted and non-excepted trades or businesses based on the relative basis of the assets used in those businesses. The basis in T's only asset, a bus, is therefore allocated between Business X and Business Y according to the use of T's bus by these businesses. Business X uses one-third of T's services, and Business Y uses two-thirds of T's services. Thus, $40x of the basis of T's bus is allocated to Business X, and $80x of the basis of T's bus is allocated to Business Y.

(f) *Applicability date.*—This section applies to taxable years ending after the date the Treasury decision adopting these regulations as final regulations is published in the **Federal Register**. However, taxpayers and their related parties, within the meaning of sections 267(b) and 707(b)(1), may apply the rules of this section to a taxable year beginning after December 31, 2017, so long as the taxpayers and their related parties consistently apply the rules of the section 163(j) regulations, and if applicable, §§1.263A-9, 1.381(c)(20)-1, 1.382-6, 1.383-1, 1.469-9, 1.882-5, 1.1502-13, 1.1502-21, 1.1502-36, 1.1502-79, 1.1502-91 through 1.1502-99 (to the extent they effectuate the rules of §§1.382-6 and 1.383-1), and 1.1504-4 to those taxable years. [Reg. §1.163(j)-10.]

§1.163(j)-11. Transition rules.—(a) *Application of section 163(j) limitation if a corporation joins a consolidated group with a taxable year beginning before January 1, 2018.*—(1) *In general.*—If a corporation (S) joins a consolidated group whose taxable year began before January 1, 2018, and if S is subject to the section 163(j) limitation at the time of its change in status, then section 163(j) will apply to S's short taxable year that ends on the day of S's change in status, but section 163(j) will not apply to S's short taxable year that begins the next day (when S is a member of the acquiring consolidated group). Any business interest expense paid or accrued (without regard to section 163(j)) by S in its short taxable year ending on the day of S's change in status for which a deduction is disallowed under section 163(j) will be carried forward to the acquiring group's first taxable year beginning after December 31, 2017. Those disallowed business interest expense carryforwards may be subject to limitation under other provisions of these regulations (see, for example, § 1.163(j)-5(c), (d), (e), and (f)).

(2) *Example.*—Acquiring Group is a consolidated group with a fiscal year end of November 30; Target is a stand-alone calendar-year C corporation. On May 31, 2018, Acquiring Group acquires Target in a transaction that is not an ownership change for purposes of section 382. Acquiring Group is not subject to the section 163(j) limitation during its taxable year beginning December 1, 2017. As a result of the acquisition, Target has a short taxable year beginning January 1, 2018 and ending May 31, 2018. Target is subject to the section 163(j) limitation during this short taxable year. However, Target (as a member of Acquiring Group) is not subject to the section 163(j) limitation during Acquiring Group's taxable year ending November 30, 2018. Any disallowed business interest expense carryforwards from Target's taxable year ending May 31, 2018, will not be available for use in Acquiring Group's taxable year ending November 30, 2018. However, that disallowed business interest expense is carried forward to Acquiring Group's taxable year beginning December 1, 2018, and can be deducted by the group, subject to the separate return limitation year (SRLY) limitation. See § 1.163(j)-5(d).

(b) *Treatment of disallowed disqualified interest.*—(1) *In general.*—Disallowed disqualified interest is carried forward to the taxpayer's first taxable year beginning after December 31, 2017, and is subject to disallowance as a disallowed business interest expense carryforward under section 163(j) and § 1.163(j)-2, except to the extent the interest is properly allocable to an excepted trade or business under § 1.163(j)-10. See § 1.163(j)-10(a)(6).

(2) *Earnings and profits.*—A taxpayer may not reduce its earnings and profits in a taxable year beginning after December 31, 2017, to reflect any disallowed disqualified interest carryforwards to the extent the payment or accrual of the disallowed disqualified interest reduced the earnings and profits of the taxpayer in a prior taxable year.

(3) *Disallowed disqualified interest of members of an affiliated group.*—(i) *Scope.*—This paragraph (b)(3)(i) applies to corporations that were treated as a single taxpayer under old section 163(j)(6)(C) and that had disallowed disqualified interest.

(ii) *Allocation of disallowed disqualified interest to members of the affiliated group.*—(A) *In general.*—Each member of the affiliated group is allocated its allocable share of the affiliated group's disallowed disqualified interest as provided in paragraph (b)(3)(ii)(B) of this section.

(B) *Definitions.*—The following definitions apply for purposes of paragraph (b)(3)(ii) of this section.

(1) Allocable share of the affiliated group's disallowed disqualified interest.—The term *allocable share of the affiliated group's disallowed disqualified interest* means, with respect to any member of an affiliated group for the member's last taxable year beginning before January 1, 2018, the product of the total amount of the disallowed disqualified interest of all members of the affiliated group under old section 163(j)(6)(C) and the member's disallowed disqualified interest ratio.

(2) Disallowed disqualified interest ratio.—The term *disallowed disqualified interest ratio* means, with respect to any member of an affiliated group for the member's last taxable year beginning before January 1, 2018, the ratio of the exempt related person interest expense of the member for the last taxable year beginning before January 1, 2018, to the sum of the amounts of exempt related person interest expense for all members of the affiliated group.

(3) Exempt related person interest expense.—The term *exempt related person interest expense* means interest expense that is, or is treated as, paid or accrued by a domestic C corporation, or by a foreign corporation with income, gain, or loss that is effectively connected, or treated as effectively connected, with the conduct of a trade or business in the United States, to—

(i) Any person related to the taxpayer, within the meaning of sections 267(b) or 707(b)(1), applying the constructive ownership and attribution rules of section 267(c), if no U.S. tax is imposed with respect to the interest under subtitle A of the Internal Revenue Code, determined without regard to net operating losses or net operating loss carryovers, and taking into account any applicable treaty obligation of the United States. For this purpose, interest that is subject to a reduced rate of tax under any treaty obligation of the United States applicable to the recipient is treated as in part subject to the statutory tax rate under sections 871 or 881 and in part not subject to tax, based on the proportion that the rate of tax under the treaty bears to the statutory tax rate. Thus, for purposes of section 163(j), if the statutory tax rate is 30 percent, and pursuant to a treaty U.S. tax is instead limited to a rate of 10 percent, two-thirds of the interest is considered interest not subject to U.S. tax under subtitle A of the Internal Revenue Code;

(ii) A person that is not related to the taxpayer, within the meaning of sections 267(b) or 707(b)(1), applying the constructive ownership and attribution rules of section 267(c), with respect to indebtedness on which there is a disqualified guarantee, within the meaning of paragraph (6)(D) of old section 163(j), of such indebtedness, and no gross basis U.S. tax is imposed with respect to the interest. For purposes of this paragraph (b)(3)(ii)(B)(3)(*ii*), a *gross basis U.S. tax* means any tax imposed by this subtitle A of the Internal Revenue Code that is determined by reference to the gross amount of any item of income without any reduction for any deduction allowed by subtitle A of the Internal Revenue Code. Interest that is subject to a gross basis U.S. tax that is eligible for a reduced rate of tax under any treaty obligation of the United States applicable to the recipient is treated as, in

part, subject to the statutory tax rate under sections 871 or 881 and, in part, not subject to a gross basis U.S. tax, based on the proportion that the rate of tax under the treaty bears to the statutory tax rate. Thus, for purposes of section 163(j), if the statutory tax rate is 30 percent, and pursuant to a treaty U.S. tax is instead limited to a rate of 10 percent, two-thirds of the interest is considered interest not subject to a gross basis U.S. tax under subtitle A of the Internal Revenue Code; or

(iii) A REIT, directly or indirectly, to the extent that the domestic C corporation, or a foreign corporation with income, gain, or loss that is effectively connected, or treated as effectively connected, with the conduct of a trade or business in the United States, is a taxable REIT subsidiary, as defined in section 856(l), with respect to the REIT.

(iii) *Treatment of carryforwards.*—The amount of disallowed disqualified interest allocated to a taxpayer pursuant to paragraph (b)(3)(ii) of this section is treated in the same manner as described in paragraph (b)(1) of this section.

(4) *Application of section 382.*—(i) *Ownership change occurring before the date the Treasury decision adopting these regulations as final regulations is published in the* **Federal Register**.—(A) *Pre-change loss.*—For purposes of section 382(d)(3), unless the rules of § 1.382-2(a)(7) apply, disallowed disqualified interest is not a pre-change loss under § 1.382-2(a) subject to a section 382 limitation with regard to an ownership change on a change date occurring before the date the Treasury decision adopting these regulations as final regulations is published in the **Federal Register**. But see section 382(h)(6)(B) (regarding built-in deduction items).

(B) *Loss corporation.*—For purposes of section 382(k)(1), unless the rules of § 1.382-2(a)(7) apply, disallowed disqualified interest is not a carryforward of disallowed interest described in section 381(c)(20) with regard to an ownership change on a change date occurring before the date the Treasury decision adopting these regulations as final regulations is published in the **Federal Register**. But see section 382(h)(6) (regarding built-in deductions).

(ii) *Ownership change occurring on or after the date the Treasury decision adopting these regulations as final regulations is published in the* **Federal Register**.—(A) *Pre-change loss.*—For rules governing the treatment of disallowed disqualified interest as a pre-change loss for purposes of section 382 with regard to an ownership change on a change date occurring on or after the date the Treasury decision adopting these regulations as final regulations is published in the **Federal Register**, see §§ 1.382-2(a)(2) and 1.382-6(c)(3).

(B) *Loss corporation.*—For rules governing when disallowed disqualified interest causes a corporation to be a loss corporation with regard to an ownership change occurring on or after the date the Treasury decision adopting these regulations as final regulations is published in the **Federal Register**, see § 1.382-2(a)(1)(i)(A).

(iii) *Definitions.*—For purposes of this paragraph (b)(4), the terms *ownership change* and *change date* have the meanings provided in section 382 and the regulations thereunder.

(5) [Reserved]

(6) *Treatment of excess limitation from taxable years beginning before January 1, 2018.*—No amount of excess limitation under old section 163(j)(2)(B) may be carried forward to taxable years beginning after December 31, 2017.

(7) *Example: Members of an affiliated group.*—(i) *Facts.* A, B, and C are calendar-year domestic C corporations that are members of an affiliated group (within the meaning of section 1504(a)) that was treated as a single taxpayer under old section 163(j)(6)(C) and the proposed regulations thereunder (see formerly proposed § 1.163(j)-5). For the taxable year ending December 31, 2017, the separately determined amounts of exempt related person interest expense of A, B, and C were $0, $600x, and $150x, respectively (for a total of $750x). The affiliated group has $200x of disallowed disqualified interest in that year.

(ii) *Analysis.* The affiliated group's disallowed disqualified interest expense for the 2017 taxable year ($200x) is allocated among A, B, and C based on the ratio of each member's exempt related person interest expense to the group's exempt related person interest expense. Because A has no exempt related person interest expense, no disallowed disqualified interest is allocated to A. Disallowed disqualified interest of $160x is allocated to B (($600x / $750x) x $200x), and disallowed disqualified interest of $40x is allocated to C (($150x / $750x) x $200x). Thus, B and C have $160x and $40x, respectively, of disallowed disqualified interest that is carried forward to the first taxable year beginning after December 31, 2017. No excess limitation that was allocated to A, B, or C under old section 163(j) will carry forward to the first taxable year beginning after December 31, 2017.

(iii) *Carryforward of disallowed disqualified interest to 2018 taxable year.* The facts are the same as in the *Example* in paragraph (b)(7)(i) of this section, except that, for the taxable year ending December 31, 2018, A, B, and C are members of a consolidated group that has a section 163(j) limitation of $140x, current-year business interest expense (as defined in § 1.163(j)-5(a)(2)(i)) of $80x, and no excepted trade or business. Under paragraph (b)(1) of this section, disallowed disqualified interest is carried to the taxpayer's first taxable year beginning after December 31, 2017, and is subject to disallowance under section 163(j) and § 1.163(j)-2. Under § 1.163(j)-5(b)(3)(ii)(D)(*1*), a consolidated group that has section 163(j) limitation remaining for the current year after deducting all current-year business interest expense deducts each member's disallowed disqualified interest carryforwards from prior taxable years, starting with the earliest taxable year, on a pro rata basis (subject to certain limitations). In accordance with paragraph (b)(1) of this section, the rule in § 1.163(j)-5(b)(3)(ii)(D)(*1*) applies to disallowed disqualified interest carried forward to the taxpayer's first taxable year beginning after December 31, 2017. Accordingly, after deducting $80x of current-year business interest expense in 2018, the group may deduct $60x of its $200x disallowed disqualified interest carryforwards. Under paragraph (b)(3) of this section, B has $160x of disallowed disqualified interest carryforwards, and C has $40x of disallowed disqualified interest carryforwards. Thus, $48x (($160x / $200x) x

$60x) of B's disallowed disqualified interest carryforwards, and $12x (($40x / $200x) x $60x) of C's disallowed disqualified interest carryforwards, are deducted by the consolidated group in the 2018 taxable year.

(c) *Applicability date.*—This section applies to taxable years ending after the date the Treasury decision adopting these regulations as final regulations is published in the **Federal Register**. However, taxpayers and their related parties, within the meaning of sections 267(b) and 707(b)(1), may apply the rules of this section to a taxable year beginning after December 31, 2017, so long as the taxpayers and their related parties consistently apply the rules of the section 163(j) regulations, and if applicable, §§1.263A-9, 1.381(c)(20)-1, 1.382-6, 1.383-1, 1.469-9, 1.882-5, 1.1502-13, 1.1502-21, 1.1502-36, 1.1502-79, 1.1502-91 through 1.1502-99 (to the extent they effectuate the rules of §§1.382-6 and 1.383-1), and 1.1504-4 to those taxable years. [Reg. §1.163(j)-11.]

Disaster Loss Deduction: Election

Disaster Loss Deduction: Election.—Amendments to Reg. §1.165-11, relating to the election to take a disaster loss in the preceding year, are proposed (published in the Federal Register on October 14, 2016) (REG-150992-13).

2. Section 1.165-11 is amended by:

a. Removing and reserving paragraphs (a) through (e) and

b. Adding reserved paragraphs (f) through (i).

The revisions and additions read as follows:

§1.165-11. Election in respect of losses attributable to a disaster.—(a) through (i) [*Reserved*].—[The text of proposed §1.165-11(a) through (i) is the same as the text of §1.165-11T(a) through (i) as added by T.D. 9789].

Definition of Registered Form: Guidance

Definition of Registered Form: Guidance.—Amendments to Reg. §1.165-12, providing guidance on the definitions of registration-required obligation and registered form, including guidance on the issuance of pass-through certificates and participation interests in registered form, are proposed (published in the Federal Register on September 19, 2017) (REG-125374-16).

Par. 5. Section 1.165-12 is amended by:

1. Revising paragraph (a).
2. Redesignating paragraphs (b)(1) and (2) as (b)(2) and (3), respectively.
3. Adding a new paragraph (b)(1).
4. Revising the paragraph heading and first sentence of newly redesignated paragraph (b)(2).
5. Redesignating paragraph (d) as paragraph (d)(1).
6. Revising the paragraph heading and the first sentence of newly redesignated paragraph (d)(1).
7. Adding a new paragraph heading for paragraph (d).
8. Adding paragraph (d)(2).

The revisions and additions read as follows:

§1.165-12. Denial of deduction for losses on registration-required obligations not in registered form.—(a) *In general.*—Except as provided in paragraph (c) of this section, nothing in section 165(a) and the regulations thereunder, or in any other provision of law, shall be construed to provide a deduction for any loss sustained on any registration-required obligation held after December 31, 1982, unless the obligation is in registered form or the issuance of the obligation was subject to tax under section 4701. The term *registration-required obligation* has the meaning given to that term in section 163(f)(2) and §1.163-5(a)(2)(i). For purposes of this section, the term *holder* means the person that would be denied a loss deduction under section 165(j)(1) or denied capital gain treatment under section 1287(a). For purposes of this section, the term *United States* means the United States and its possessions within the meaning of §1.163-5(c)(2)(iv).

(b) *Registered form.*—(1) *Obligations issued after March 18, 2012.*—With respect to obligations issued after March 18, 2012, the term *registered form* has the meaning given that term in §1.163-5(b).

(2) *Obligations issued after September 21, 1984 and on or before March 18, 2012.*—With respect to any obligation originally issued after September 21, 1984, and on or before March 18, 2012, the term *registered form* has the meaning given that term in §5f.103-1 of this chapter. * * *

* * *

(d) *Applicability date.*—(1) *In general.*—Except as provided in paragraph (d)(2) of this section, these regulations apply generally to obligations issued after January 20, 1987. * * *

(2) *Obligations issued after March 18, 2012.*—Paragraph (a) of this section applies to obligations issued after March 18, 2012. For the rules that apply to obligations issued on or before March 18, 2012, see §1.165-12 as contained in 26 CFR part 1, revised as of the date of the most recent annual revision.

Minimum Addition to Reserves for Losses: Mutual Savings Banks

Minimum Addition to Reserves for Losses: Mutual Savings Banks.—Reproduced below is the text of a proposed amendment of Reg. §1.166-4, relating to the minimum addition to reserves for losses on loans of mutual savings banks and other organizations (published in the Federal Register on December 19, 1983).

☐ Paragraph 1. Paragraph (d)(3) of §1.166-4 is amended by removing "§§1.593-1 through 1.593-11" and inserting "§§1.593-1 through 1.593-8" in lieu thereof.

§1.166-4. Reserve for bad debts.

Allocation Rules

Gains and Losses: Asset Acquisitions: Allocation Rules.—Temporary Reg. §1.167(a)-5T, relating to allocation rules for certain asset acquisitions under Code Sec. 1060, is also proposed as a final regulation and, when adopted, would become Reg. §1.167(a)-5 (published in the Federal Register on July 18, 1988).

§1.167(a)-5. Apportionment of basis.

Accelerated Cost Recovery System

Accelerated Cost Recovery System.—Reproduced below is the text of a proposed amendment of Reg. §1.167(a)-11, relating to the Accelerated Cost Recovery System for recovering capital costs of eligible property (published in the Federal Register on February 16, 1984).

§1.167(a)-11. Depreciation based on class lives and asset depreciation ranges for property placed in service after December 31, 1970.— (a) *In general.*—(1) *Summary.*—This section does not apply with respect to recovery property (within the meaning of section 168 and the regulations thereunder) placed in service after December 31, 1980. * * *

* * *

(d) *Special rules for salvage, repairs and retirements.*—* * *

(2) *Treatment of repairs.*—(i) *In general.*—(*a*) *Treatment of repair expenditures.*—* * *

(*b*) *Property placed in service after December 31, 1980.*—This paragraph (d)(2) does not apply to any expenditures with respect to property first placed in service after December 31, 1980, but may apply to expenditures paid or incurred after such date with respect to property first placed in service before January 1, 1981. Expenditures with respect to property first placed in service after December 31, 1980, shall be treated as capital expenditures or as deductible expenses for the taxable year in which paid or incurred in accordance with the general rules provided in sections 162, 212, and 263. Property is considered first placed in service for purposes of this paragraph (d)(2)(i)(*b*) under the rules of paragraph (e)(1)(i) and (ii) of this section.

(ii) *Election of repair allowance.*—* * * For taxable years ending after December 31, 1980, and before February 16, 1984, notwithstanding paragraph (f)(1) of this section, the taxpayer may elect (in the original return or in an amended return) to apply this section and the asset guideline class repair allowance described in paragraph (d)(2)(iii) of this section on or before the later of the due date (including extensions) of the taxpayer's tax return for the taxable year or November 16, 1984.

* * *

(viii) *Treatment of property improvements and excluded additions.*—* * *

(*d*) Paragraph (d)(2)(viii)(*a*), (*b*), and (*c*) of this section does not apply to a property improvement, excluded addition, or part thereof considered first placed in service by the taxpayer after December 31, 1980. Such property improvement, excluded addition, or part thereof shall generally be treated as a separate item of recovery property (as defined in section 168(c)(1)), and shall be assigned to the appropriate class of recovery property in accordance with section 168(c)(2). See §1.168-2(e)(2). For taxable years ending after December 31, 1980, notwithstanding the succeeding sentence, for purposes of this paragraph (d)(2)(viii)(*d*), a property improvement, excluded addition, or part thereof is considered first placed in service under the rules provided in paragraph (e)(1)(i) and (ii) of this section and not under the rules provided in paragraph (e)(1)(iii) and (iv) of this section. * * *

* * *

Deductions: Elections: Depreciation: Intangible Property

Deductions: Elections: Depreciation: Intangible Property.—Temporary Reg. §1.167(a)-13T, relating to the procedures for making elections under the intangibles provisions of the Omnibus Budget Reconciliation Act of 1993 (P.L. 103-66), is also proposed as a final regulation and, when adopted, would become Reg. §1.167(a)-13 (published in the Federal Register on March 15, 1994).

☐ Par. 2. Section 1.167(a)-13 is added to read as follows:

§1.167(a)-13. Certain elections for intangible property.—For rules applying the elections under sections 13261(g)(2) and (3) of the Omnibus Budget Reconciliation Act of 1993 to intangible property described in section 167(f), see §1.197-1. [Reg. §1.167(a)-13.]

Qualified Property: Additional First Year Depreciation Deduction

Qualified Property: Additional First Year Depreciation Deduction.—Amendments to Reg. §1.167(a)-14, providing guidance regarding the additional first year depreciation deduction under section 168(k) of the Internal Revenue Code (Code), are proposed (published in the Federal Register on August 8, 2018) (REG-104397-18).

Par. 3. Section 1.167(a)-14 is amended by:

1. In the third sentence in paragraph (b)(1), removing "under section 168(k)(2) or §1.168(k)-1," and adding "under section 168(k)(2) and §1.168(k)-1 or 1.168(k)-2, as applicable," in its place;

2. In the last sentence in paragraph (e)(3), removing "and before 2010"; and
3. Adding two sentences at the end of paragraph (e)(3).
The addition reads as follows:

§1.167(a)-14. Treatment of certain intangible property excluded from section 197.

* * *

(e) * * *

(3) * * * The language "or §1.168(k)-2, as applicable," in the third sentence in paragraph (b)(1) of this section applies to computer software that is qualified property under section 168(k)(2) and placed in service by a taxpayer during or after the taxpayer's taxable year that includes the date of publication of a Treasury decision adopting these rules as final regulations in the **Federal Register**. However, a taxpayer may rely on the language "or §1.168(k)-2, as applicable," in the third sentence in paragraph (b)(1) of this section in these proposed regulations for computer software that is qualified property under section 168(k)(2) and acquired and placed in service after September 27, 2017, by the taxpayer during taxable years ending on or after September 28, 2017, and ending before the taxpayer's taxable year that includes the date of publication of a Treasury decision adopting these rules as final regulations in the **Federal Register**.

Depreciation: Income Forecast Method: Guidance on Cost Recovery

Depreciation: Income Forecast Method: Guidance on Cost Recovery.—Reg. §§1.167(n)-0—1.167(n)-7, relating to deductions available to taxpayers using the income forecast method of depreciation under Code Sec. 167(g), are proposed (published in the Federal Register on May 31, 2002) (REG-103823-99) (corrected August 6, 2002).

☐ Par. 2. Sections 1.167(n)-0 through 1.167(n)-7 are added to read as follows:

§1.167(n)-0. Outline of regulation sections for section 167(g).—This section lists the major captions contained in §1.167(n)-1 through §1.167(n)-7.

§1.167(n)-1. Income forecast method.

(a) Overview.
(b) Method of accounting.
(1) In general.
(2) Election of the income forecast method.

§1.167(n)-2. Basis.

(a) Depreciable basis.
(1) In general.
(2) Timing of basis determinations and redeterminations.
(3) Separate Property.
(b) Basis redeterminations.
(c) Unrecovered depreciable basis.
(d) Example.

§1.167(n)-3. Income from the property.

(a) Current year income.
(1) In general.
(2) Special rule for advance payments.
(b) Forecasted total income.
(c) Revised forecasted total income.
(d) Special rules.
(1) Disposition of the property.
(2) Syndication income from television series.
(3) Apportionment of income in certain circumstances.
(4) Examples.

§1.167(n)-4. Computation of depreciation using the income forecast method.

(a) Computation of depreciation allowance.
(b) Revised computation.
(1) Change in estimated income.
(2) Requirement to use the revised computation.
(c) Basis redeterminations.
(1) Calculation of depreciation allowance.
(2) Example.
(d) Special rules.
(1) Final year depreciation.
(2) Certain basis redeterminations.
(3) Disposition of property.
(4) Separate property.
(e) Examples.

§1.167(n)-5. Property for which the income forecast method may be used.

(a) In general.
(b) Specific exclusions.
(c) Costs treated as separate property.
(1) Costs giving rise to a significant increase in income.
(2) Significant increase in income.
(3) Special rule for costs paid or incurred after the end of the final year.
(4) Time separate property is placed in service.
(5) Examples.
(d) Aggregations treated as a single income forecast property.
(1) Multiple episodes of a television series produced in the same taxable year.
(2) Multiple episodes of a television series produced in more than one taxable year.
(3) Multiple interests acquired pursuant to a single contract.
(4) Videocassettes and DVDs.

§1.167(n)-6. Look-back method.

(a) Application of the look-back method.
(b) Operation of the look-back method.
(1) In general.
(2) Property-by-property application.
(c) Recalculation of depreciation allowances.
(1) Computation.
(2) Revised forecasted total income from the property.
(3) Special rule for basis redeterminations.
(d) Hypothetical overpayment or underpayment of tax.
(1) In general.
(2) Hypothetical overpayment or underpayment, actual recomputation.
(3) Hypothetical overpayment or underpayment, simplified method.
(4) Definitions.

(e) Recomputation year.

(1) In general.

(2) Look-back method inapplicable in certain de minimis cases.

(f) De minimis basis exception.

(g) Treatment of look-back interest.

(1) In general.

(2) Additional interest due on interest only after tax liability due.

(3) Timing of look-back interest.

(4) Statute of limitations; compounding of interest on look-back interest.

(h) Example.

§1.167(n)-7. Effective date.

[Reg. §1.167(n)-0.]

§1.167(n)-1. Income forecast method.—(a) *Overview.*—This section and §§1.167(n)-2 through 1.167(n)-7 provide rules for computing depreciation allowances under section 167 for property depreciated using the income forecast method. Because the income forecast method is only appropriate for property with unique income earning characteristics, only property specified in §1.167(n)-5 may be depreciated under the income forecast method. A taxpayer using the income forecast method generally computes depreciation allowances each year based upon the ratio of current year income to forecasted total income from the property as described in §1.167(n)-4. Current year income and forecasted total income are determined in accordance with the provisions of §1.167(n)-3. In addition, a taxpayer must determine depreciable basis for income forecast property in accordance with the basis rules of §1.167(n)-2. Property depreciated under the income forecast method generally is subject to the look-back rules of §1.167(n)-6 whereby taxpayers must determine the amount of interest owed on any hypothetical underpayment of tax, or due on any hypothetical overpayment of tax, attributable to the use of estimated income in the computation of income forecast depreciation. Under these rules, look-back computations must be performed in specified recomputation years, which are generally the 3rd and 10th taxable years after the taxable year that the property is placed in service.

(b) *Method of accounting.*—(1) *In general.*—The computation of depreciation under the income forecast method is elected on a property-by-property basis, and is a method of accounting under section 446 that may not be changed without the consent of the Commissioner. However, a change in forecasted total income in accordance with the rules of §1.167(n)-4 is not a change in method of accounting requiring the Commissioner's consent.

(2) *Election of the income forecast method.*—A taxpayer elects the income forecast method by computing allowances for depreciation for the eligible property in accordance with the provisions of this section and §§1.167(n)-2 through §1.167(n)-6. See §1.167(n)-5 for rules regarding eligible property. [Reg. §1.167(n)-1.]

§1.167(n)-2. Basis.—(a) *Depreciable basis.*—(1) *In general.*—The basis upon which the allowance for depreciation is computed with respect to income forecast property is the basis of the income forecast property for purposes of section 1011 without regard to the adjustments described in section 1016(a)(2) and (3).

(2) *Timing of basis determinations and redeterminations.*—Costs paid or incurred in or after the taxable year in which the income forecast property is placed in service are taken into account in accordance with a taxpayer's method of accounting in redetermining the basis of income forecast property in the taxable year paid or incurred (i.e., when all events have occurred that establish the fact of the liability, the amount of the liability can be determined with reasonable accuracy, and economic performance has occurred with respect to the liability). See §§1.446-1(c)(1)(i) and (ii), 1.461-1(a)(1) and (2), and 1.263A-1(c). Accordingly, contingent payments may not be included in the basis of income forecast property when the property is placed in service, but are included in the basis of income forecast property in the taxable year in which they are paid or incurred, even if the forecasted total income used in the computation of income forecast depreciation allowances is sufficient to indicate that the contingency will be satisfied.

(3) *Separate property.*—Certain amounts paid or incurred in taxable years after income forecast property is placed in service are treated as separate property for purposes of computing depreciation allowances under the income forecast method. See §1.167(n)-5(c).

(b) *Basis redeterminations.*—If an amount required to be capitalized into the basis of income forecast property is paid or incurred after the income forecast property is placed in service, and if the amount required to be capitalized is not treated as separate property in accordance with §1.167(n)-5(c), the basis of the income forecast property is redetermined and the amount required to be capitalized is the basis redetermination amount. The redetermined basis of the income forecast property is the depreciable basis of the income forecast property increased by the basis redetermination amount. In the year basis is redetermined (and in subsequent taxable years), the redetermined basis must be used to determine depreciation under the income forecast method. An additional allowance for depreciation under the income forecast method is allowed in the taxable year the basis of certain income forecast property is redetermined. See §1.167(n)-4(c).

(c) *Unrecovered depreciable basis.*—For any taxable year, the unrecovered depreciable basis of an income forecast property is the depreciable basis of the property less the adjustments described in section 1016(a)(2) and (3).

(d) *Example.*—The provisions of §1.167(n)-2 are illustrated by the following example:

(i) *Studio* contracts with *Actor* to star in a motion picture film to be produced by *Studio.* Both *Studio* and *Actor* are calendar year taxpayers; *Studio* is an accrual basis taxpayer and *Actor* is a cash basis taxpayer. As compensation for *Actor's* services, the contract guarantees *Actor* a payment of five percent of the gross income from the film, beginning after the film has earned a total gross income (net of distribution costs) of $ 100x. *Studio* estimates that the film will earn a total gross income of $160x by the end of the 10th taxable year following the taxable year that the film is placed in service. The film is placed in service and earns $ 65x of gross income in year one, $ 30x in year two, and $ 25x in year three. Because the income from the film does not exceed $100x in either year one or year two, *Studio* pays nothing under the contract to *Actor* in years one and two. In year three, the cumulative income from the film reaches $120x, which exceeds the $100x threshold by $20x. Based on this excess, *Studio* calculates that it owes *Actor* $ 1x, calculated by multiplying $20x by *Actor'* s contractual percentage of five percent. *Studio* pays $1x to *Actor* 20 days after the end of year three.

(ii) *Studio* may not include the $1x paid to *Actor* in the basis of the film in years one or two because *Studio* does not have a fixed liability to pay *Actor* any amount under the contract in years one and two. Furthermore, while *Studio* does have a fixed liability to pay *Actor* $1x in year three, the requirements of section 404 are not met in year three and *Studio* thus may not include the $1x in the basis of the film in year three. In year four, when section 404 is satisfied, *Studio* incurs the $1x in accordance with § 1.263A-1(c) and increases its basis in the film. The $1x is treated as a basis redetermination amount under § 1.167(n)-2(b) in year four.

[Reg. § 1.167(n)-2.]

§ 1.167(n)-3. Income from the property.— (a) *Current year income.*—(1) *In general.*—Current year income is the income from an income forecast property for the current year (less the distribution costs of the income forecast property for such year), determined in accordance with the taxpayer's method of accounting. All income earned in connection with the income forecast property is included in current year income, except as provided in paragraph (d) of this section. In the case of a film, television show, or similar property, such income includes, but is not limited to—

(i) Income from foreign and domestic theatrical, television, and other releases and syndications;

(ii) Income from releases, sales, rentals, and syndications of video tape, DVD, and other media; and

(iii) Incidental income associated with the property, such as income from the financial exploitation of characters, designs, titles, scripts, and scores, but only to the extent that such incidental income is earned in connection with the ultimate use of such items by, or the ultimate sale of merchandise to, persons who are not related to the taxpayer (within the meaning of section 267(b)).

(2) *Special rule for advance payments.*—In the year that income forecast property is placed in service, current year income for an income forecast property includes income included in gross income for any prior taxable year in connection with the property. This paragraph applies separately to any cost treated as separate property under § 1.167(n)-5(c).

(b) *Forecasted total income.*—Forecasted total income is the sum of current year income for the year that income forecast property is placed in service, plus all income from the income forecast property that the taxpayer reasonably believes will be includible in current year income in subsequent taxable years (as adjusted for distribution costs) up to and including the 10thtaxable year after the year in which the income forecast property is placed in service. Forecasted total income is based on the conditions known to exist at the end of the taxable year for which the income forecast property is placed in service.

(c) *Revised forecasted total income.*—If information is discovered in a taxable year following the year in which income forecast property is placed in service that indicates that forecasted total income is inaccurate, a taxpayer must compute revised forecasted total income for the taxable year. Revised forecasted total income is based on the conditions known to exist at the end of the taxable year for which the revised forecast is being made. Revised forecasted total income for the taxable year is the sum of current year income for the taxable year and all prior taxable years, plus all income from the income forecast property that the taxpayer reasonably believes will be includible in current year income in taxable years after the current taxable year up to and including the 10th taxable year after the year in which the income forecast property is placed in service. Where a taxpayer computes revised forecasted total income in accordance with this § 1.167(n)-3(c), see § 1.167(n)-4(b) for the computation of the allowance for income forecast depreciation.

(d) *Special rules.*—(1) *Disposition of the property.*—In computing the depreciation allowance for an income forecast property, income from the sale or other disposition of income forecast property is not included in current year income. However, if the income forecast property is disposed of prior to the end of the 10th taxable year following the taxable year in which the property is placed in service, income from the sale or other disposition of income forecast property is taken into account in calculating revised forecasted total income both for purposes of calculating the allowance for depreciation in the year of disposition and for purposes of applying look-back. See § 1.167(n)-4(d)(3) and § 1.167(n)-6(c)(2).

(2) *Syndication income from television series.*—(i) In the case of a television series produced for distribution on television networks, current year income and forecasted total income (or, if applicable, revised forecasted total income) used in the computation of the depreciation allowance for such property under § 1.167(n)-4 need not include income from syndication of the television series before the earlier of—

(A) The fourth taxable year beginning after the date the first episode in the series is placed in service; or

(B) The earliest taxable year in which the taxpayer has an arrangement relating to the syndication of the series.

(ii) For purposes of this paragraph (d)(2), an arrangement relating to syndication of a series of television shows means any arrangement other than the first run exhibition agreement. For example, an arrangement for exhibition of a television series by individual television stations is an arrangement for syndication if it results in an exhibition of one or more episodes of the series beginning after one or more episodes of the series have been exhibited on a television network. A first run exhibition agreement is an agreement under which any episode (including a pilot episode) of a television series is first placed in service within a particular market.

(3) *Apportionment of income in certain circumstances.*—When income from a particular source relates to more than one income forecast property the taxpayer must make a reasonable allocation of the income among those properties

based on all relevant factors. Situations where allocation is necessary include income generated by a syndication arrangement involving more than one income forecast property, incidental income described in paragraph (a)(1)(iii) of this section that relates to more than one motion picture, and income associated with income forecast property when expenditures relating to the property have given rise to separate property as defined in §1.167(n)-5(c). For example, when a taxpayer sells or licenses merchandise that features the likeness of a character that has appeared in more than one film, relevant factors might include merchandise sales figures prior to the release of the subsequent film, specific identification of certain merchandise with one particular film, and the taxpayer's prior experience with similar situations.

(4) *Examples.*—The provisions of this section are illustrated by the following examples:

Example 1. C produces a motion picture film featuring the adventures of a fictional character. C sells merchandise using the character's image, enters into licensing agreements with unrelated parties for the use of the image, and uses the image to promote a ride at an amusement park that is wholly owned by C. Pursuant to paragraph (a)(1) of this section, income from the sales of merchandise by C to consumers and income from the licensing agreements are included in current year income. No portion of the admission fees for the amusement park is included in current year income because the amusement part is wholly owned by C.

Example 2. Assume the same facts as in *Example 1.* C forecasts that the cumulative amount of current year income it will earn (net of distribution costs) from the year it places the motion picture film in service through the end of the 7th taxable year thereafter to be $345x. C also forecasts that the motion picture film will earn current year income of $155x from the beginning of the 8th taxable year through the end of the 10th taxable year after the year the income forecast property is placed in service. C anticipates the sale of the motion picture film at the end of the 7th taxable year after the year the property is placed in service and in fact sells the motion picture film for $200x on the last day of the 7th taxable year after the year the property is placed in service. C's computations of forecasted total income must reflect the fact that C forecasts that $500x will be earned by the motion picture film through the end of the 10th taxable year after the year the property is placed in service ($345x from the year the film is placed in service through the end of the 7th taxable year after the taxable year that the property was placed in service, plus $155x C forecasts from the beginning of the 8th taxable year through the end of the 10th taxable year after the year the property is placed in service). Even though C only expects to earn $345x prior to the sale of the film, C may not use $345x as forecasted total income in computing its depreciation allowance under the income forecast method. Similarly, C may not use the combination of the amounts it expects to earn prior to the sale ($345x) plus the anticipated sales proceeds ($200x) or $545x as forecasted total income, except when computing its depreciation allowance for the 7th taxable year after the year in which the income forecast property was placed in service and for purposes of computing look-back interest.

[Reg. §1.167(n)-3.]

§1.167(n)-4. Computation of depreciation using the income forecast method.—(a) *Computation of depreciation allowance.*—Generally, the depreciation allowance for an income forecast property for a given taxable year is computed by multiplying the depreciable or redetermined basis of the property (as defined in §1.167(n)-2) by a fraction, the numerator of which is current year income (as defined in §1.167(n)-3(a)) and the denominator of which is forecasted total income (as defined in §1.167(n)-3(b)).

(b) *Revised computation.*—(1) *Change in estimated income.*—The depreciation allowance for an income forecast property for any taxable year following the year in which income forecast property is placed in service may be computed using the computation provided in this paragraph (b)(1) if revised forecasted total income differs from forecasted total income. Thus, for example, a taxpayer using the income forecast method for a motion picture may revise upward the forecast of total income from the motion picture (to arrive at revised forecasted total income) in a taxable year wherein the taxpayer discovers that the motion picture is more popular than originally expected, and may thereafter use the revised computation to compute the allowance for income forecast depreciation for the motion picture. Under the revised computation, the unrecovered depreciable basis of the income forecast property (as defined in §1.167(n)-2(c)) is multiplied by a fraction, the numerator of which is current year income and the denominator of which is obtained by subtracting from revised forecasted total income the amounts of current year income from prior taxable years.

(2) *Requirement to use the revised computation.*—The revised computation described in paragraph (b)(1) of this section must be used in any taxable year following the year in which income forecast property is placed in service if forecasted total income (as defined in §1.167(n)-3(b)) (or, if applicable, revised forecasted total income (as defined in §1.167(n)-3(c)) in the immediately preceding taxable year is either—

(i) Less than 90 percent of revised forecasted total income for the taxable year; or

(ii) Greater than 110 percent of revised forecasted total income for the taxable year.

(c) *Basis redeterminations.*—(1) *Calculation of depreciation allowance.*—An additional depreciation allowance is available under this paragraph in the taxable year that basis is redetermined under §1.167(n)-2(b) when that taxable year is subsequent to the taxable year in which income forecast property is placed in service, but prior to the 10th taxable year following the taxable year in which the property is placed in service. The additional depreciation allowance is that portion of the basis redetermination amount that would have been recovered through depreciation allowances in prior taxable years if the basis redetermination amount had been included in depreciable basis in the taxable year that the property was placed in service. This §1.167(n)-4(c) does not apply to property treated as a single income forecast property pursuant to §1.167(n)-5(d)(1) through (4).

(2) *Example.*—The provisions of paragraph (c)(1) of this section are illustrated by the following example:

Example. *D*, an accrual basis movie producer, enters into a contract with *E*, an author, under which *D* will make a film based on *E*'s book. *E* performs no services for *D*, but merely permits *D* to use the book as a basis for *D*'s film. *D* pays *E* a fixed dollar amount upon entry into the agreement and promises to pay *E* a contingent payment of five percent of *D*'s income from the film, beginning after the film has earned $100,000 (net of distribution costs). *D* estimates that forecasted total income from the film will be $200,000. The film earns $65,000 of current year income in year one, $30,000 in year two, and $25,000 in year three. *D* takes allowances for depreciation in year one ($65,000 divided by $200,000, multiplied by the basis of the film) and year two ($30,000 divided by $200,000, multiplied by the basis of the film). In year three, *D*'s liability to *E* becomes fixed and *D* pays *E* $1,000. The $1,000 incurred by *D* is a basis redetermination amount that increases the basis of the film for purposes of computing *D*'s depreciation allowance for the film for year three. In addition to the year three allowance based on current year income ($25,000 divided by $200,000 multiplied by the basis of the film, which includes for year three the $1,000 basis redetermination amount), *D* is entitled to an additional allowance for depreciation for year three under paragraph (c)(1). This additional allowance is $475, the sum of the allowance of $325 that would have been allowed in year one ($65,000 divided by $200,000, multiplied by the $1,000 payment to *E*) and the allowance of $150 that would have been allowed in year two ($30,000 divided by $200,000, multiplied by $1,000) if the $1,000 had been included in basis in the year that the film was placed in service.

(d) *Special rules.*—(1) *Final year depreciation.*—Except as provided in paragraphs (d)(2) and (3) of this section, a taxpayer may deduct as a depreciation allowance the remaining depreciable basis of income forecast property depreciated under the income forecast method in the earlier of—

(i) The year in which the taxpayer reasonably believes, based on the conditions known to exist at the end of the taxable year, that no income from the income forecast property will be included in current year income in any subsequent taxable year up to and including the 10th taxable year following the taxable year the income forecast property is placed in service; or

(ii) The 10th taxable year following the taxable year the income forecast property is placed in service.

(2) *Certain basis redeterminations.*—A taxpayer may deduct as a depreciation allowance the amount of any basis redetermination that occurs in a taxable year in which the taxpayer reasonably believes, based on the conditions known to exist at the end of the taxable year, that no income from the income forecast property will be included in current year income in any subsequent taxable year. In addition, a taxpayer may deduct as a depreciation allowance the amount of any basis redetermination that occurs in a taxable year following a taxable year in which a deduction is allowable under paragraph (d)(1) of this section.

(3) *Disposition of property.*—Paragraph (d)(1) of this section does not apply to income forecast property that is sold or otherwise disposed of before the end of the 10th taxable year following the taxable year that the property is placed in service. In the case of such a disposition, the allowance for depreciation in the year of disposition is calculated by multiplying the depreciable basis (or, if applicable, the redetermined basis) of the property by a fraction, the numerator of which is current year income and the denominator of which is the sum of the amount realized on the disposition of the property plus all amounts included in current year income in the year of disposition and in taxable years prior to the year of disposition.

(4) *Separate property.*—The deductions provided in paragraphs (d)(1) and (2) of this section apply separately to property that is treated as separate property under § 1.167(n)-5(c).

(e) *Examples.*—The provisions of this section are illustrated by the following examples:

Example 1. *F* places in service income forecast property with a depreciable basis of $100x, and estimates that forecasted total income from the property will be $200x. In taxable year one, current year income is $80x. The depreciation allowance for year one is $40x, computed by multiplying the depreciable basis of the property of $100x by the fraction obtained by dividing current year income of $80x by forecasted total income of $200x.

Example 2. Assume the same facts as in *Example 1.* In year two, *F*'s current year income is $40x. In addition, *F* computes revised forecasted total income to be $176x. *F* is required to compute its depreciation allowance for this property using the revised computation of paragraph (b)(1) of this section because forecasted total income in year one of $200x is greater than 110 percent of revised forecasted total income in year two (110 percent of $176x = $193.6x). The depreciation allowance for taxable year two computed under the revised computation is $25x, computed by multiplying the unrecovered depreciable basis of $60x by the fraction obtained by dividing current year income of $40x by $96x (revised forecasted total income of $176x less current year income from prior taxable years of $80x).

Example 3. Assume the same facts as in *Example 2.* Because F used the revised computation in year two, the revised computation applies in year three. In year three, *F*'s current year income is $32x. The depreciation allowance for year three computed under the revised computation is $20x, computed by multiplying the unrecovered depreciable basis of $60x by the fraction obtained by dividing current year income of $32x by $96x (revised forecasted total income of $176x less current year income from taxable years prior to the change in estimate taxable year of $80x).

[Reg. § 1.167(n)-4.]

§ 1.167(n)-5. Property for which the income forecast method may be used.—(a) *In general.*—The depreciation allowance under § 1.167(n)-4 may be computed under the income forecast method only with respect to eligible property. Eligible property is limited to an interest (including interests involving limited rights in property) in the following property—

(1) Property described in section 168(f)(3) and (4);

(2) Copyrights;

(3) Books;

(4) Patents;

(5) Theatrical productions; and

(6) Other property as designated in published guidance by the Commissioner.

(b) *Specific exclusions.*—The income forecast method does not apply to any amortizable section 197 intangible (as defined in section 197(c) and § 1.197-2(d)).

(c) *Costs treated as separate property.*—(1) *Costs giving rise to a significant increase in income.*—(i) *In general.*—For purposes of § 1.167(n)-1 through § 1.167(n)-6, any amount paid or incurred after the income forecast property is placed in service must be treated as a separate property if the cost is significant and gives rise to an increase in income that is significant and that was not included in either forecasted total income or revised forecasted total income in a prior taxable year.

(ii) *Exception for de minimis amounts.*—For purposes of this paragraph, a cost that is less than the lesser of 5 percent of the depreciable basis (as of the date the amount is paid or incurred) of the income forecast property to which the amount relates or $100,000 is not significant. Such a cost is therefore not treated as separate property but is instead treated as a basis redetermination amount in accordance with § 1.167(n)-2(b).

(2) *Significant increase in income.*—For purposes of this paragraph, whether an increase in income is significant is determined by comparing the amount that would be considered revised forecasted total income from the amounts treated as separate property to the most recent estimate of forecasted total income or revised forecasted total income used in calculating an allowance for depreciation with respect to the income forecast property.

(3) *Special rule for costs paid or incurred after the end of the final year.*—For purposes of § 1.167(n)-1 through § 1.167(n)-6, any amount paid or incurred with respect to an income forecast property in a taxable year following the year in which the taxpayer claims a depreciation allowance in accordance with the final year depreciation rules of § 1.167(n)-4(d)(1) is treated as a basis redetermination amount under § 1.167(n)-2(b) provided the amount is not expected to give rise to a significant increase in current year income in any taxable year.

(4) *Time separate property is placed in service.*—Separate property is treated as placed in service in the year the amount giving rise to the property is paid or incurred.

(5) *Examples.*—The provisions of this paragraph (c) are illustrated in the following examples:

Example 1. G releases a film in 2001 and begins to recover the depreciable basis in the film using the income forecast method in the year 2001. In 2003, the film is re-edited and restored, and director's commentary is added in order to prepare the film for release on DVD. The total cost of preparing the film for the DVD release exceeds both 5 percent of the depreciable basis of the film and $100,000. G did not anticipate the income from the DVD market, and did not include any DVD release income in the income projections for the film in prior years. If G anticipates that the additional DVD release income will be significant in relation to the forecasted total income used in calculating an allowance for depreciation for 2002 (the previous taxable year), the additional amount gives rise to separate property and must be recovered over the forecasted total income from the DVD. If not, G must treat the additional amounts as additions to basis under § 1.167(n)-2(b).

Example 2. G releases a film in 2001 and recovers the depreciable basis in the film using the income forecast method in the years 2001 through 2011. In 2018, the film is re-edited and restored, and director's commentary is added in order to prepare the film for release on a newly discovered technology. If G anticipates that the additional new technology release income will be significant in relation to the revised forecasted total income used in calculating an allowance for depreciation for 2011 (the last taxable year for which an allowance was claimed), the cost of preparing the release gives rise to separate property and must be recovered over the forecasted total income from the new technology release. If not, G may deduct the cost in 2018, the year paid or incurred.

(d) *Aggregations treated as a single income forecast property.*—Taxpayers must apply the income forecast method on a property-by-property basis, unless one of the aggregation rules provided in paragraphs (d)(1) through (4) of this section applies. If a taxpayer applies one of the aggregation rules provided in paragraphs (d)(1) through (4) of this section, costs incurred in taxable years after the initial income forecast property is placed in service are treated as basis redeterminations under § 1.167(n)-2; however, the additional allowance for depreciation provided in § 1.167(n)-4(c)(1) does not apply. The application of the provisions of paragraphs (d)(1) through (d)(4) is a method of accounting that may not be changed without the consent of the Commissioner. Permissible aggregations are limited to the following:

(1) *Multiple episodes of a television series produced in the same taxable year.*—The producer of a television series may treat multiple episodes of a single television series produced in the same taxable year as a single unit of property for purposes of the income forecast method.

(2) *Multiple episodes of a television series produced in more than one taxable year.*—The producer of a television series may treat multiple episodes of a single television series that are produced as a single season of episodes and placed in service over a period not in excess of twelve consecutive calendar months as a single unit of property for purposes of the income forecast method notwithstanding that the twelve-month period may span more than one taxable year.

(3) *Multiple interests acquired pursuant to a single contract.*—Multiple interests in specifically identified income forecast properties acquired for broadcast pursuant to a single contract may be treated as a single unit of property for purposes of the income forecast method.

(4) *Videocassettes and DVDs.*—The purchaser or licensee of videocassettes and DVDs for rental to the public may treat multiple copies of the same title purchased or licensed in the

same taxable year as a single unit of property for purposes of the income forecast method. [Reg. §1.167(n)-5.]

§1.167(n)-6. Look-back method.—(a) *Application of the look-back method.*—If a taxpayer claims a depreciation deduction under the income forecast method for any eligible income forecast property, such taxpayer is required to pay (or is entitled to receive) interest computed as described in this paragraph for any year to which the look-back method applies (a recomputation year). The look-back method generally must be applied when income forecast property is disposed of or ceases to generate income. Further, the look-back method generally applies in the 3rd and 10th taxable years following the year in which income forecast property is placed in service. Under the look-back method, taxpayers must pay interest on deductions accelerated by the underestimation of either forecasted total income or revised forecasted total income from income forecast property. Conversely, taxpayers are entitled to receive interest on deductions delayed by the overestimation of either forecasted total income or revised forecasted total income from income forecast property. If either forecasted total income or revised forecasted total income are overestimated or underestimated, interest may arise from basis redeterminations. The computation of adjusted tax liability as part of the look-back method is hypothetical; application of the look-back method does not require a taxpayer to adjust tax liability as reported on the taxpayer's tax returns, on an amended return, or as adjusted on examination for prior years.

(b) *Operation of the look-back method.*—(1) *In general.*—Under the look-back method, a taxpayer must perform a series of computations to determine look-back interest that the taxpayer is either required to pay or entitled to receive. As specified in paragraph (c) of this section, a taxpayer must first recompute depreciation allowances using revised forecasted total income rather than forecasted total income from income forecast property for the recomputation year (as defined in paragraph (e) of this section) and each prior year. These recomputed depreciation amounts are then used to determine a hypothetical tax liability that would have arisen had the taxpayer used revised forecasted total income rather than forecasted total income in determining depreciation allowances. The hypothetical tax liability is compared to the taxpayer's prior tax liability and interest is calculated in accordance with paragraph (d) of this section on the resulting hypothetical overpayments or underpayments of tax for each year. Reporting requirements and special rules for the resulting amounts of interest are specified in paragraph (g) of this section.

(2) *Property-by-property application.*—Except as provided in this section, the look-back method applies to each property for which the income forecast method is used. Aggregations properly treated as a single income forecast property pursuant to §1.167(n)-5(d) are treated as a single property for purposes of applying the look-back method.

(c) *Recalculation of depreciation allowances.*—(1) *Computation.*—Under the look-back method, a taxpayer must compute the depreciation allowances for each income forecast property subject to the look-back method that would have been allowable under §1.167(n)-1 through §1.167(n)-5 for prior taxable years if the computation of the amounts so allowable had been made using revised forecasted total income as calculated at the end of the recomputation year.

(2) *Revised forecasted total income from the property.*—(i) *In general.*—Except as provided in this paragraph (c)(2), revised forecasted total income is determined in accordance with §1.167(n)-3(c).

(ii) *Syndication income from television-series.*—Income excluded from forecasted total income (or, if appropriate revised forecasted total income) in any prior taxable year pursuant to §1.167(n)-3(d)(2) is excluded from revised forecasted total income for purposes of this section for that year.

(iii) *Disposition of income forecast property.*—For purposes of this section, income from the disposition of property must be taken into account in determining the amount of revised forecasted total income. Thus, when income forecast property is disposed of prior to the end of the 10th taxable year following the taxable year the property is placed in service, revised forecasted total income from the property for the year of disposition is deemed to be the sum of the amount realized on the disposition of the property plus all amounts included in current year income in the year of disposition and in taxable years prior to the year of disposition.

(3) *Special rule for basis redeterminations.*—For purposes of the look-back calculation, any amount that is not treated as a separate property under §1.167(n)-5(c) that is paid or incurred with respect to income forecast property after the property is placed in service is taken into account by discounting (using the Federal mid-term rate determined under section 1274(d) as of the time the cost is paid or incurred) the amount to its value as of the date the property is placed in service. The taxpayer may elect for the recomputation year with respect to any income forecast property to have the preceding sentence not apply to the property by taking the amount into account in the year that the amount was paid or incurred in the same manner as it was taken into account under §1.167(n)-2.

(d) *Hypothetical overpayment or underpayment of tax.*—(1) *In general.*—(i) *Years for which a hypothetical overpayment or underpayment must be computed.*—After recalculating depreciation allowances in accordance with paragraph (c) of this section, a taxpayer must calculate a hypothetical overpayment or underpayment of tax for each prior taxable year for which income tax liability is affected by the change in depreciation allowances. A redetermination of income tax liability is required for every tax year for which the income tax liability would have been affected by a change in the allowance for income forecast depreciation in any year. For example, if the change in depreciation allowance results in a net operating loss carryforward that affects income tax liability in a subsequent taxable year, income tax liability must be recomputed for such subsequent year.

(ii) *Methods of determining a hypothetical overpayment or underpayment.*—Generally, the calculation of the hypothetical overpayment or underpayment of tax must be made under the method described in paragraph (d)(2) of this section. Certain taxpayers are required to use the simplified method contained in paragraph (d)(3) of this section.

(iii) *Cumulative determination of hypothetical income tax liability.*—The redetermination of income tax liability in any prior taxable year for which income tax liability is affected by the change in depreciation allowances must take into account all previous applications of the look-back calculation. Thus, for example, in computing the amount of a hypothetical overpayment or underpayment of tax for a prior taxable year for which income tax liability is affected by the change in depreciation allowances, the hypothetical income tax liability is compared to the hypothetical income tax liability for that year determined as of the previous application of the look-back method.

(2) *Hypothetical overpayment or underpayment, actual recomputation.*—(i) *Computation of change in income tax liability.*—The hypothetical overpayment or underpayment is calculated first by redetermining the tax liability for each prior taxable year (either as originally reported, or as subsequently adjusted on examination or by amended return) using depreciation allowances calculated in paragraph (c) of this section for each prior taxable year in which depreciation allowances were determined under the income forecast method for the income forecast property (affected year). These recomputed depreciation allowances are then substituted for the depreciation allowances allowed (or allowable) for each affected year (whether originally reported, or as subsequently adjusted on examination or by amended return) and a revised taxable income is computed. A hypothetical income tax liability is then computed for each affected year using revised taxable income for that year. The hypothetical income tax liability for any affected year must be computed by taking into account all applicable additions to tax, credits, and net operating loss carrybacks and carryforwards. The tax, if any, imposed under section 55 (relating to alternative minimum tax) must be taken into account. Hypothetical income tax liability for each affected year is then compared to the tax liability determined as of the latest of the following dates—

(A) The original due date of the return (including extensions);

(B) The date of a subsequently amended or adjusted return; or

(C) The date of the previous application of the look-back method, in which case the hypothetical income tax liability for the affected year used in the most recent previous application of the look-back method (previous hypothetical tax liability) is used.

(ii) *Determination of interest.*—Once the hypothetical overpayment or underpayment for each year is computed, the adjusted overpayment rate under section 460(b)(7), compounded daily, is applied to the overpayment or underpayment determined under paragraph (d)(2)(i) of this section for the period beginning with the due date of the return (determined without regard to extensions) for the year in which either an overpayment or underpayment arises, and ending on the earlier of the due date of the return (determined without regard to extensions) for the redetermination year, or the first date by which both the income tax return for the filing year is filed and the tax for that year has been paid in full. The amounts of interest on overpayments are then netted against interest on underpayments to arrive at look-back interest that must be paid by the taxpayer or that the taxpayer is entitled to receive.

(iii) *Changes in the amount of a loss or credit carryback or carryforward.*—If a recomputation of income forecast depreciation results in an increase or decrease to a net operating loss carryback (but not a carryforward), the interest a taxpayer is entitled to receive or required to pay must be computed on the decrease or increase in tax attributable to the change to the carryback only from the due date (not including extensions) of the return for the prior taxable year that generated the carryback and not from the due date of the return for the prior taxable year in which the carryback was absorbed. In the case of a change in the amount of a carryforward as a result of applying the look-back method, interest is computed from the due date of the return for the years in which the carryforward was absorbed.

(iv) *Changes in the amount of income tax liability that generated a subsequent refund.*—If the hypothetical income tax liability for any affected year is less than the amount of the affected year tax liability (as reported on the taxpayer's original return, as subsequently adjusted on examination, as adjusted by amended return, or as redetermined by the last previous application of the look-back method), and any portion of the affected year tax liability was refunded as a result of a loss or credit carryback arising in a year subsequent to the affected year, the look-back method applies as follows to properly reflect the time period of the use of the tax overpayment. To the extent the amount of refund because of the carryback exceeds the hypothetical income tax liability for the affected year, the taxpayer is entitled to receive interest only until the due date (not including extensions) of the return for the year in which the carryback arose.

(v) *Example.*—The provisions of this paragraph (d)(2) are illustrated by the following example:

Example. Upon the cessation of income from an income forecast property in 2003, the taxpayer computes a hypothetical income tax liability for 2001 under the look-back method. This computation results in a hypothetical income tax liability ($1,200x) that is less than the actual income tax liability the taxpayer originally reported ($1,500x). In addition, the taxpayer had already received a refund of some or all of the actual 2001 income tax liability by carrying back a net operating loss (NOL) that arose in 2002. The time period over which interest would be computed on the hypothetical overpayment of $300x for 2001 would depend on the amount of the refund generated by the carryback, as illustrated by the following three alternative situations:

(i) If the amount refunded because of the NOL is $1,500x, interest is credited to the taxpayer on the entire hypothetical overpayment of $300x from the due date of the 2001 return, when the hypothetical overpayment occurred, until the due date of the 2002 return, when the taxpayer received a refund for the entire amount of the 2001 tax, including the hypothetical overpayment.

(ii) If the amount refunded because of the NOL is $1,000x, interest is credited to the taxpayer on the entire amount of the hypothetical overpayment of $300x from the due date of the 2001 return, when the hypothetical overpayment occurred, until the due date of the 2003 return. In this situation interest is credited until the due date of the return for the recomputation year, rather than the due date of the return for the year in which the carryback arose, because the amount refunded was less than the hypothetical income tax liability of $1,200x. Therefore, no portion of the hypothetical overpayment is treated as having been refunded to the taxpayer before the recomputation year.

(iii) If the amount refunded because of the NOL is $1,300x, interest is credited to the taxpayer on $100x ($1,300x-$1,200x) from the due date of the 2001 return until the due date of the 2002 return because only this portion of the total hypothetical overpayment is treated as having been refunded to the taxpayer before the recomputation year. However, the taxpayer did not receive a refund for the remaining $200x of the overpayment at that time and, therefore, is credited with interest on $200x through the due date of the tax return for 2003, the recomputation year.

(3) *Hypothetical overpayment or underpayment, simplified method.*—(i) *Introduction.*—This paragraph provides a simplified method for calculating look-back interest. A pass-through entity that is not a closely held pass-through entity is required to apply the simplified method at the entity level with respect to income forecast property and the owners of the entity do not calculate look-back interest for the property. Under the simplified method, a taxpayer calculates the hypothetical underpayments or overpayments of tax for a prior year based on an assumed marginal tax rate.

(ii) *Operation of the simplified method.*—Under the simplified method, depreciation allowances for income forecast property are first recomputed in accordance with the procedures contained in paragraph (c) of this section. These recomputed depreciation allowances are then compared with depreciation allowances allowed (or allowable) for each prior taxable year (whether originally reported, as subsequently adjusted on examination or by amended return, or as recomputed in the most recent previous application of the look-back method) to arrive at changes in depreciation allowances for the income forecast property. When multiple properties are subject to the look-back method in any given affected year, the changes in depreciation allowances attributable to each income forecast property determined in accordance with paragraph (c) of this section for each such year are cumulated or netted against one another to arrive at a net change in income forecast depreciation for purposes of computing the hypothetical overpayment or underpayment attributable to the year. The hypothetical underpayment or overpayment of tax for each affected year is then determined by multiplying the applicable regular tax rate (as defined in paragraph (d)(3)(iv) of this section) by the increase or decrease in depreciation allowances.

(iii) *Determination of interest.*—Interest is credited to the taxpayer on the net overpayment and is charged to the taxpayer on the net underpayment for each affected year by applying the adjusted overpayment rate under section 460(b)(7), compounded daily, to the overpayment or underpayment determined under paragraph (d)(3)(ii) of this section for the period beginning with the due date of the return (determined without regard to extensions) for the affected year, and ending on the earlier of the due date of the return (determined without regard to extensions) for the recomputation year, or the first date by which both the income tax return for the recomputation year is filed and the tax for that year has been paid in full. The resulting amounts of interest are then netted to arrive at look-back interest that must be paid by the taxpayer or that the taxpayer is entitled to receive.

(iv) *Applicable tax rate.*—For purposes of determining hypothetical underpayments or overpayments of tax under the simplified method, the applicable regular rate is generally the highest rate of tax in effect for corporations under section 11. However, the applicable regular tax rate is the highest rate of tax imposed on individuals under section 1 if, at all times during all affected years, more than 50 percent of the interests in the entity were held by individuals directly or through 1 or more pass-through entities. The highest rate of tax imposed on individuals is determined without regard to any additional tax imposed for the purpose of phasing out multiple tax brackets or exemptions.

(4) *Definitions.*—(i) *Pass-through entity.*—For purposes of this section, a pass-through entity is either a partnership, an S corporation, an estate or a trust.

(ii) *Closely-held pass-through entity.*—A closely-held pass-through entity is a pass-through entity that, at any time during any year for which allowances for depreciation are recomputed, 50 percent or more (by value) of the beneficial interests in that entity are held (directly or indirectly) by or for 5 or fewer persons. For this purpose, the term *person* has the same meaning as in section 7701(a)(1), except that a pass-through entity is not treated as a person. In addition, the constructive ownership rules of section 1563(e) apply by substituting the term *beneficial interest* for the term *stock* and by substituting the term *pass-through entity* for the term *corporation* used in that section, as appropriate, for purposes of determining whether a beneficial interest in a pass-through entity is indirectly owned by any person.

(e) *Recomputation year.*—(1) *In general.*—Except as provided in this paragraph (e), the term *recomputation year* means, with respect to any income forecast property—

(i) The earlier of—

(A) The year the income from the income forecast property ceases with respect to the taxpayer (and with respect to any person who would be treated as a single taxpayer with the taxpayer under rules similar to those in section 41(f)(1)); or

(B) The 3rd taxable year beginning after the taxable year in which the income forecast property was placed in service; and

(ii) The earlier of—

(A) The year the income from the income forecast property ceases with respect to the taxpayer (and with respect to any person who would be treated as a single taxpayer with the taxpayer under rules similar to those in section 41(f)(1)); or

(B) The 10th taxable year following the taxable year the income forecast property is placed in service.

(2) *Look-back method inapplicable in certain de minimis cases.*—(i) *De minimis difference between actual and forecasted income.*—A taxable year described in paragraph (e)(1) of this section is not a recomputation year if forecasted total income (as defined in § 1.167(n)-3(b)) or, where applicable, revised forecasted total income (as defined in § 1.167(n)-3(c)), for each preceding taxable years is—

(A) Greater than 90 percent of revised forecasted total income for the taxable year that would otherwise be a recomputation year; and

(B) Less than 110 percent of revised forecasted total income for the taxable year that would otherwise be a recomputation year.

(ii) *Application of the de minimis rule where the look-back method was previously applied.*—For purposes of applying paragraph (e)(2)(i) of this section in any taxable year after a taxable year in which the look-back method has previously been applied, revised forecasted total income for the year the look-back method was applied, forecasted total income for the year the income forecast property was placed in service, and revised forecasted total income for all taxable years preceding the taxable year in which the look-back method was previously applied are deemed to be equal to the amount of revised forecasted total income that was used for purposes of applying the look-back method in the most recent taxable year for which the look-back method was applied.

(f) *De minimis basis exception.*—The look-back method does not apply to any income forecast property with an adjusted basis, determined in accordance with section 1011 but without regard to the adjustments described in section 1016(a)(2) and (3), as of the close of any year that would otherwise be a recomputation year of $100,000 or less.

(g) *Treatment of look-back interest.*—(1) *In general.*—The amount of interest a taxpayer is required to pay is treated as an income tax under Subtitle A of the Internal Revenue Code, but only for purposes of Subtitle F of the Internal Revenue Code (other than sections 6654 and 6655), which addresses tax procedure and administration. Thus, a taxpayer that fails to report look-back interest when due is subject to any penalties under Subtitle F of the Internal Revenue Code applicable to a failure to report and pay a tax liability. However, look-back interest to be paid is treated as interest arising from an underpayment of tax under Subtitle A of the Internal Revenue Code, even though it is treated as an income tax liability for penalty purposes. Thus, look-back interest required to be paid by an individual, or by a pass-through entity on behalf of an individual owner (or beneficiary) under the simplified method, is personal interest and, therefore, is not deductible in accordance with § 1.163-9T(b)(2). Interest received under the look-back method is treated as taxable interest income for all purposes, and is not treated as a reduction in tax liability. The determination of whether interest computed under the look-back method is treated as income tax under Subtitle A of the Internal Revenue Code is determined on a net basis for each recomputation year. Thus, if a taxpayer computes both hypothetical overpayments of tax and hypothetical underpayments of tax for years prior to any given recomputation year, the taxpayer has an increase in tax only if the total interest computed on underpayments for all prior taxable years for which income tax liability is affected by the application of the look-back method exceeds the total interest computed on overpayments for such years, taking into account all income forecast property for which the look-back method is required. Interest determined at the entity level under the simplified method is allocated among the owners (or beneficiaries) for reporting purposes in the same manner that interest income and interest expense are allocated to owners (or beneficiaries) and subject to the allocation rules applicable to such entities.

(2) *Additional interest due on interest only after tax liability due.*—For each recomputation year, taxpayers are required to file a Form 8866, "Interest Computation Under the Look-back Method for Property Depreciated Under the Income Forecast Method," at the time the return for that recomputation year is filed to report the interest a taxpayer is required to pay or entitled to receive under the look-back method. Even if the taxpayer has received an extension to file its income tax return for the recomputation year, look-back interest is computed with respect to the hypothetical increase (or decrease) in the tax liability determined under the look-back method only until the initial due date of that return (without regard to the extension). Interest is charged, unless the taxpayer otherwise has a refund that fully offsets the amount of interest due, (or credited) with respect to the amount of look-back interest due (or to be refunded) under the look-back method from the initial due date of the return through the date the return is filed. No interest is charged (or credited) after the due date of the return with respect to the amount of the hypothetical increases (or decreases) in tax liability determined under the look-back method.

(3) *Timing of look-back interest.*—For purposes of determining taxable income under Subtitle A of the Internal Revenue Code, any amount refunded to the taxpayer as a result of the application of the look-back method is includible in gross income in accordance with the taxpayer's method of accounting for interest income. Any amount required to be paid is taken into account as interest expense arising from an underpayment of income tax in the tax year it is properly taken into account under the taxpayer's method of accounting for interest expense.

(4) *Statute of limitations; compounding of interest on look-back interest.*—For guidance on the statute of limitations applicable to the assessment and collection of look-back interest owed by a taxpayer, see sections 6501 and 6502. A taxpayer's claim for credit or refund of look-back interest *previously paid by or collected from a taxpayer* is a claim for credit or refund of an overpayment of tax and is subject to the statute of limitations provided in section 6511. A taxpayer's claim for look-back interest (or interest payable on look-back interest) that is not attributable to an amount previously paid or collected from a taxpayer is a general claim against the

federal government. For guidance on the statute of limitations that applies to general claims against the federal government, see 28 U.S.C. 2401 and 2501. For guidance applicable to the compounding of interest when the look-back interest is not paid, see sections 6601 to 6622.

(h) *Example.*—The provisions of this section are illustrated by the following example:

Example. (i) *H*, a calendar year corporation, creates a motion picture at a cost of $60x. *H* completes the motion picture in 2001 and begins exhibition of the film that same year. Assume that $60x is greater than $100,000. In 2001, *H* anticipates that it will earn $200x from the motion picture (net of distribution costs). *H* therefore uses this amount as Forecasted Total Income when computing depreciation allowances for the motion picture.

(ii) *H* earns current year income of $80x in 2001, $60x in 2002, and $40x in 2003. During the period from 2001 to 2004, one of the actors who appeared in *H*'s film became more popular, and this increase in the actor's popularity increased the demand for *H*'s film. In 2004, therefore, *H* revised its forecast of income from the film upward to $240x. *H* earns $20x in 2004 from the motion picture and $10x in 2005.

(iii) Based on these facts, *H*'s allowances for depreciation for the motion picture for 2001 would be $24x, computed by multiplying the depreciable basis of the motion picture of $60x by current year income of $80x divided by forecasted total income of $200x under §1.167(n)-4(a). Similarly, *H*'s allowances for depreciation for the motion picture for 2002 would be $18x, computed by multiplying the depreciable basis of the motion picture of $60x by current year income of $60x divided by forecasted total income of $200x, and *H*'s allowances for depreciation for the motion picture for 2003 would be $12x, computed by multiplying the depreciable basis of the motion picture of $60x by current year income of $40x divided by forecasted total income of $200x.

(iv) In 2004, *H* determines revised forecasted total income of $240x in accordance with §1.167(n)-3(c). Because revised forecasted total income in 2004 of $240x is greater than 110 percent of forecasted total income used in computing the allowance for depreciation in the immediately preceding year (110 percent of $200x equals $220x), *H* is required under §1.167(n)-4(b)(2) to compute the allowance for depreciation in 2004 and thereafter using the revised computation. *H* first computes its unrecovered depreciable basis in the motion picture under §1.167(n)-2(c) of $6x by subtracting from the depreciable basis of $60x the depreciation allowances for 2001, 2002, and 2003 of $24x, $18x, and $12x. *H* then multiplies the unrecovered depreciable basis of $6x by the current year income for 2004 of $20x divided by $60x (revised forecasted total income $240x less current year income for all years prior to 2004 ($80x + $60x + $40x or $180x), resulting in a depreciation allowance for 2004 of $2x.

(v) In 2005, *H* is required to use the revised computation because *H* used it in 2004. Thus, *H* multiplies the unrecovered depreciable basis of $6x times current year income for 2005 of $10x divided by $60x (revised forecasted total income as computed in 2004), resulting in a depreciation allowance for 2005 of $1x.

(vi) Thus, *H*'s allowances for depreciation may be summarized as follows:

Year	*Current Year Income*	*Forecasted Total Income*	*Revised Forecasted Total Income*	*Depreciable Basis*	*Unrecovered Depreciable Basis*	*Depreciation Allowance*
2001	80x	200x		60x		24x
2002	60x	200x		60x		18x
2003	40x	200x		60x		12x
2004	20x		240x		6x	2x
2005	10x		240x		6x	1x

(vii) Under paragraph (e)(l)(i)(B) of this section, 2004 is a recomputation year (because 2004 is the third taxable year after the year in which the motion picture was placed in service) unless a de minimis rule applies. The de minimis rule in paragraph (e)(2) of this section does not apply in 2004 because forecasted total income of $200x used in the computation of income forecast depreciation in 2001, 2002 and 2003 is not greater than 90 percent of year 2004 revised forecasted total income of $240x (90 percent of $240x = $216x). Thus, *H* must apply the look-back method for 2004.

(viii) If *H* sells the motion picture in 2006 for $25x prior to earning any current year income from the motion picture, *H* would not be entitled to any allowance for depreciation in 2006. (The special rule of §1.167(n)-3(d)(l) precludes *H* from including income from the sale of the motion picture in current year income, *H* has no other current year income, and §1.167(n)-4(d)(3) precludes the use of the final year depreciation rule of §1.167(n)-4(d)(1)). Under paragraph (e)(1)(ii)(A) of this section, 2006 is a recomputation year (because in 2006 the income from the property to *H* ceases) unless a de minimis rule applies.

(ix) To determine whether the de minimis rule applies, *H* is required to determine revised forecasted total income for 2006. Under paragraph (c)(2) of this section, revised forecasted total income for 2006 is deemed to be the sum of current year income for the years 2001—2006 of $210x ($80x + $60x + $40x + $20x + $10x + $0x) plus the amount realized from the sale of the motion picture of $25x or $235x. Revised forecasted total income for 2005 is $240x, and pursuant to paragraph (e)(2)(ii) of this section, revised forecasted total income for the years 2001—2004 is deemed (for purposes of determining whether 2006 is a recomputation year) to be the amount of revised forecasted total income used in the 2004 application of the look-back method of $240x. Because $240x is greater than $212x (90 percent of $235x) and less than $259x (110 percent of $235x), the de minimis rule applies and *H* is not required to apply the look-back method in 2006.

[Reg. § 1.167(n)-6.]

§ 1.167(n)-7. Effective date.—The regulations under § 1.167(n)-1 through § 1.167(n)-6 are applicable for property placed in service on or after the date that final regulations are published in the Federal Register. [Reg. § 1.167(n)-7.]

Accelerated Cost Recovery System

Accelerated Cost Recovery System.—Reproduced below are the texts of proposed Reg. §§ 1.168-1—1.168-4, 1.168-5(b)—(f) and 1.168-6, relating to the Accelerated Cost Recovery System for recovering capital costs of eligible property (published in the Federal Register on February 16, 1984). Proposed Reg. § 1.168-5(a) was adopted by T.D. 8116 on 12/23/86. Proposed Reg. § 1.168-2(n) was withdrawn by REG-209682-94 on 1/29/98.

□ Par. 2. New §§ 1.168-1 through 1.168-6 are added. The new sections read as follows:

§ 1.168-1. Accelerated Cost Recovery System; in general.—(a) *Cost recovery deduction allowed.*—Section 168 of the Internal Revenue Code of 1954 provides a system for determining cost recovery deductions for recovery property, the Accelerated Cost Recovery System ("ACRS"). The deduction allowable under section 168 is deemed to constitute the reasonable allowance for depreciation allowed as a deduction under section 167(a). Operating rules regarding determination of the allowable cost recovery deduction are provided in § 1.168-2. The definition of recovery property and the classification of recovery property into recovery categories of 3, 5, 10, and 15 years are provided in § 1.168-3. ACRS must be applied with respect to recovery property placed in service after December 31, 1980, except for certain property which does not qualify under section 168 or which may be excluded from ACRS; § 1.168-4 provides rules regarding such exclusions and non-qualifications. Special rules regarding ACRS are provided in § 1.168-5. Rules relating to the recognition of gain or loss on dispositions are provided in § 1.168-6.

(b) *Cross references.*—See § 1.167(a)-11(d)(2) regarding the election after 1980 of the repair allowance for certain property. See § 1.178-1 regarding the availability of ACRS deductions for, or the amortization of, improvements on leased property. See § 1.1016-3(a)(3) regarding the basis adjustment for the amount allowable where no ACRS deduction is claimed. [Reg. § 1.168-1.]

§ 1.168-2. Amount of deduction for recovery property.—(a) *Computation of recovery allowance.*—(1) *General rule.*—Except as otherwise provided in section 168 and the regulations thereunder, the recovery allowance for any taxable year equals the aggregate amount determined by multiplying the unadjusted basis (as defined in § 1.168-2(d)) of recovery property (as defined in § 1.168-3) by the appropriate applicable percentage provided in paragraph (b) of this section. For purposes of determining the recovery allowance, salvage value shall be disregarded.

(2) *No allowance in year of disposition.*—Except for 15-year real property and except as otherwise provided in § 1.168-5, no recovery allowance shall be allowed in the year of disposition of recovery property.

(3) *Proration of allowance in year of disposition of 15-year real property.*—In the taxable year in which 15-year real property is disposed of, the recovery allowance shall be determined by multiplying the allowance (determined without regard to this subparagraph) by a fraction, the numerator of which equals the number of months in the taxable year that the property is in service in the taxpayer's trade or business or for the production of income and the denominator of which is 12. In the case of 15-year real property that is disposed of in the first recovery year, the denominator shall equal the number of months in the taxpayer's taxable year after the recovery property was placed in service by the taxpayer (including the month the property was placed in service). If the recovery allowance for the taxable year is limited by reason of the short taxable year rules of section 168(f)(5) and paragraph (f) of this section (*e.g.*, if the taxpayer dies, or if the taxpayer is a corporation which becomes a member, or ceases being a member, of an affiliated group of corporations filing a consolidated return), then the denominator shall equal the number of months in the taxpayer's taxable year. For purposes of this subparagraph, 15-year real property shall be treated as disposed of as of the last day of the month preceding the month in which it is withdrawn from service.

(b) *Applicable percentage.*—(1) *Property other than 15-year real property.*—The applicable percentage for recovery property, other than 15-year real property, is as follows:

If the recovery year is:	*And the class of property is:*			
	3-year	*5-year*	*10-year*	*15-year Public Utility*
	The applicable percentage is:			
1	25	15	8	5
2	38	22	14	10
3	37	21	12	9
4		21	10	8
5		21	10	7
6			10	7
7			9	6
8			9	6
9			9	6
10			9	6
11				6

If the recovery year is:	*3-year*	*5-year*	*10-year*	*15-year Public Utility*
	The applicable percentage is:			
12				6
13				6
14				6
15				6

(2) *15-year real property*.—(i) The applicable percentage for 15-year real property, other than low-income housing is as follows:

If the recovery year is:	*And the month in the 1st recovery year the property is placed in service is:*											
	1	*2*	*3*	*4*	*5*	*6*	*7*	*8*	*9*	*10*	*11*	*12*
	The applicable percentage is:											
1	12	11	10	9	8	7	6	5	4	3	2	1
2	10	10	11	11	11	11	11	11	11	11	11	12
3	9	9	9	9	10	10	10	10	10	10	10	10
4	8	8	8	8	8	8	9	9	9	9	9	9
5	7	7	7	7	7	7	8	8	8	8	8	8
6	6	6	6	6	7	7	7	7	7	7	7	7
7	6	6	6	6	6	6	6	6	6	6	6	6
8	6	6	6	6	6	6	5	6	6	6	6	6
9	6	6	6	6	5	6	5	5	5	6	6	6
10	5	6	5	6	5	5	5	5	5	5	6	5
11	5	5	5	5	5	5	5	5	5	5	5	5
12	5	5	5	5	5	5	5	5	5	5	5	5
13	5	5	5	5	5	5	5	5	5	5	5	5
14	5	5	5	5	5	5	5	5	5	5	5	5
15	5	5	5	5	5	5	5	5	5	5	5	5
16	—	—	1	1	2	2	3	3	4	4	4	5

(ii) The applicable percentage for 15-year real property that is low-income housing is as follows:

If the recovery year is:	*And the month in the 1st recovery year the property is placed in service is:*											
	1	*2*	*3*	*4*	*5*	*6*	*7*	*8*	*9*	*10*	*11*	*12*
	The applicable percentage is:											
1	13	12	11	10	9	8	7	6	4	3	2	1
2	12	12	12	12	12	12	12	13	13	13	13	13
3	10	10	10	10	11	11	11	11	11	11	11	11
4	9	9	9	9	9	9	9	9	10	10	10	10
5	8	8	8	8	8	8	8	8	8	8	8	9
6	7	7	7	7	7	7	7	7	7	7	7	7
7	6	6	6	6	6	6	6	6	6	6	6	6
8	5	5	5	5	5	5	5	5	5	5	6	6
9	5	5	5	5	5	5	5	5	5	5	5	5
10	5	5	5	5	5	5	5	5	5	5	5	5
11	4	5	5	5	5	5	5	5	5	5	5	5
12	4	4	4	5	4	5	5	5	5	5	5	5
13	4	4	4	4	4	4	5	4	5	5	5	5
14	4	4	4	4	4	4	4	4	4	5	4	4
15	4	4	4	4	4	4	4	4	4	4	4	4
16	—	—	1	1	2	2	2	3	3	3	4	4

(iii) For purposes of this section, the term "low-income housing" means property described in clause (i), (ii), (iii), or (iv) of section 1250(a)(1)(B).

(iv) For purposes of this subparagraph (2), 15-year real property placed in service on or after the first day of a month shall be treated as placed in service in that month.

(c) *Election of optional recovery percentage*.—(1) *Straight line method*.—Except as provided by section 168(f)(2) and § 1.168-2(g) (relating to property used predominantly outside the United States), in lieu of using the applicable percentages prescribed in section 168(b)(1) and (2) and § 1.168-2(b), the taxpayer may elect (in accordance with § 1.168-5(e)), for recovery property placed in service during the taxable year, to determine the recovery allowance by using the straight line method over one of the recovery periods elected by the taxpayer and set forth in the following table:

Class of property	*Recovery periods*
3-year property	3, 5, or 12 years
5-year property	5, 12, or 25 years
10-year property	10, 25, or 35 years
15-year real property	15, 35, or 45 years
15-year public utility property	15, 35, or 45 years

Such election is irrevocable without the consent of the Commissioner. See subparagraph (4) of this paragraph for tables containing the applicable percentages to be used in computing the recovery allowance.

(2) *Election for property other than 15-year real property.*—Except in the case of 15-year real property, a single recovery period must be elected under this paragraph for all recovery property which is in the same recovery class and which is placed in service in the same taxable year. A different recovery period may be elected (or the tables provided in section 168(b)(1) and §1.168-2(b)(1) may be used) for recovery property in different recovery classes placed in service during the same taxable year, or for recovery property placed in service in different taxable years, whether or not in the same recovery class.

(3) *Election for 15-year real property.*—In the case of 15-year real property, the election provided in paragraph (c)(1) may be made separately with respect to each property.

(4) *Applicable percentage.*—(i) For property other than 15-year real property—

If the recovery year is:	*And the period elected is:*							
	3	*5*	*10*	*12*	*15*	*25*	*35*	*45*
	The applicable percentage is:							
1	17	10	5	4	3	2	1	1.1
2	33	20	10	9	7	4	3	2.3
3	33	20	10	9	7	4	3	2.3
4	17	20	10	9	7	4	3	2.3
5		20	10	9	7	4	3	2.3
6		10	10	8	7	4	3	2.3
7			10	8	7	4	3	2.3
8			10	8	7	4	3	2.3
9			10	8	7	4	3	2.3
10			10	8	7	4	3	2.3
11			5	8	7	4	3	2.3
12				8	6	4	3	2.2
13				4	6	4	3	2.2
14					6	4	3	2.2
15					6	4	3	2.2
16					3	4	3	2.2
17						4	3	2.2
18						4	3	2.2
19						4	3	2.2
20						4	3	2.2
21						4	3	2.2
22						4	3	2.2
23						4	3	2.2
24						4	3	2.2
25						4	3	2.2
26						2	3	2.2
27							3	2.2
28							3	2.2
29							3	2.2
30							3	2.2
31							3	2.2
32							2	2.2
33							2	2.2
34							2	2.2
35							2	2.2
36							1	2.2
37								2.2
38								2.2
39								2.2
40								2.2
41								2.2
42								2.2
43								2.2
44								2.2
45								2.2
46								1.1

(ii) For 15-year real property—

(A) For which a 15-year period is elected—

If the recovery year is:	And the month in the 1st recovery year that the property is placed in service is:						
	1	2-3	4	5-6	7-8	9-10	11-12
	The applicable percentage is:						
1	7	6	5	4	3	2	1
2	7	7	7	7	7	7	7
3	7	7	7	7	7	7	7
4	7	7	7	7	7	7	7
5	7	7	7	7	7	7	7
6	7	7	7	7	7	7	7
7	7	7	7	7	7	7	7
8	7	7	7	7	7	7	7
9	7	7	7	7	7	7	7
10	7	7	7	7	7	7	7
11	6	6	6	6	6	6	6
12	6	6	6	6	6	6	6
13	6	6	6	6	6	6	6
14	6	6	6	6	6	6	6
15	6	6	6	6	6	6	6
16		1	2	3	4	6	6

(B) For which a 35-year period is elected—

If the recovery year is:	And the month in the 1st recovery year that the property is placed in service is:		
	1-2	3-6	7-12
	The applicable percentage is:		
1	3	2	1
2	3	3	3
3	3	3	3
4	3	3	3
5	3	3	3
6	3	3	3
7	3	3	3
8	3	3	3
9	3	3	3
10	3	3	3
11	3	3	3
12	3	3	3
13	3	3	3
14	3	3	3
15	3	3	3
16	3	3	3
17	3	3	3
18	3	3	3
19	3	3	3
20	3	3	3
21	3	3	3
22	3	3	3
23	3	3	3
24	3	3	3
25	3	3	3
26	3	3	3
27	3	3	3
28	3	3	3
29	3	3	3
30	3	3	3
31	2	2	2
32	2	2	2
33	2	2	2
34	2	2	2
35	2	2	2
36		1	2

(C) For which a 45-year period is elected—

If the recovery year is:	*And the month in the 1st recovery year that the property is placed in service is:*											
	1	*2*	*3*	*4*	*5*	*6*	*7*	*8*	*9*	*10*	*11*	*12*
	The applicable percentage is:											
1	2.3	2.0	1.9	1.7	1.5	1.3	1.2	.9	.7	.6	.4	.2
2	2.3	2.3	2.3	2.3	2.3	2.3	2.3	2.3	2.3	2.3	2.3	2.3
3	2.3	2.3	2.3	2.3	2.3	2.3	2.3	2.3	2.3	2.3	2.3	2.3
4	2.3	2.3	2.3	2.3	2.3	2.3	2.3	2.3	2.3	2.3	2.3	2.3
5	2.3	2.3	2.3	2.3	2.3	2.3	2.3	2.3	2.3	2.3	2.3	2.3
6	2.3	2.3	2.3	2.3	2.3	2.3	2.3	2.3	2.3	2.3	2.3	2.3
7	2.3	2.3	2.3	2.3	2.3	2.3	2.3	2.3	2.3	2.3	2.3	2.3
8	2.3	2.3	2.3	2.3	2.3	2.3	2.3	2.3	2.3	2.3	2.3	2.3
9	2.3	2.3	2.3	2.3	2.3	2.3	2.3	2.3	2.3	2.3	2.3	2.3
10	2.3	2.3	2.3	2.3	2.3	2.3	2.3	2.3	2.3	2.3	2.3	2.3
11	2.2	2.2	2.2	2.2	2.2	2.2	2.2	2.2	2.2	2.2	2.2	2.2
12	2.2	2.2	2.2	2.2	2.2	2.2	2.2	2.2	2.2	2.2	2.2	2.2
13	2.2	2.2	2.2	2.2	2.2	2.2	2.2	2.2	2.2	2.2	2.2	2.2
14	2.2	2.2	2.2	2.2	2.2	2.2	2.2	2.2	2.2	2.2	2.2	2.2
15	2.2	2.2	2.2	2.2	2.2	2.2	2.2	2.2	2.2	2.2	2.2	2.2
16	2.2	2.2	2.2	2.2	2.2	2.2	2.2	2.2	2.2	2.2	2.2	2.2
17	2.2	2.2	2.2	2.2	2.2	2.2	2.2	2.2	2.2	2.2	2.2	2.2
18	2.2	2.2	2.2	2.2	2.2	2.2	2.2	2.2	2.2	2.2	2.2	2.2
19	2.2	2.2	2.2	2.2	2.2	2.2	2.2	2.2	2.2	2.2	2.2	2.2
20	2.2	2.2	2.2	2.2	2.2	2.2	2.2	2.2	2.2	2.2	2.2	2.2
21	2.2	2.2	2.2	2.2	2.2	2.2	2.2	2.2	2.2	2.2	2.2	2.2
22	2.2	2.2	2.2	2.2	2.2	2.2	2.2	2.2	2.2	2.2	2.2	2.2
23	2.2	2.2	2.2	2.2	2.2	2.2	2.2	2.2	2.2	2.2	2.2	2.2
24	2.2	2.2	2.2	2.2	2.2	2.2	2.2	2.2	2.2	2.2	2.2	2.2
25	2.2	2.2	2.2	2.2	2.2	2.2	2.2	2.2	2.2	2.2	2.2	2.2
26	2.2	2.2	2.2	2.2	2.2	2.2	2.2	2.2	2.2	2.2	2.2	2.2
27	2.2	2.2	2.2	2.2	2.2	2.2	2.2	2.2	2.2	2.2	2.2	2.2
28	2.2	2.2	2.2	2.2	2.2	2.2	2.2	2.2	2.2	2.2	2.2	2.2
29	2.2	2.2	2.2	2.2	2.2	2.2	2.2	2.2	2.2	2.2	2.2	2.2
30	2.2	2.2	2.2	2.2	2.2	2.2	2.2	2.2	2.2	2.2	2.2	2.2
31	2.2	2.2	2.2	2.2	2.2	2.2	2.2	2.2	2.2	2.2	2.2	2.2
32	2.2	2.2	2.2	2.2	2.2	2.2	2.2	2.2	2.2	2.2	2.2	2.2
33	2.2	2.2	2.2	2.2	2.2	2.2	2.2	2.2	2.2	2.2	2.2	2.2
34	2.2	2.2	2.2	2.2	2.2	2.2	2.2	2.2	2.2	2.2	2.2	2.2
35	2.2	2.2	2.2	2.2	2.2	2.2	2.2	2.2	2.2	2.2	2.2	2.2
36	2.2	2.2	2.2	2.2	2.2	2.2	2.2	2.2	2.2	2.2	2.2	2.2
37	2.2	2.2	2.2	2.2	2.2	2.2	2.2	2.2	2.2	2.2	2.2	2.2
38	2.2	2.2	2.2	2.2	2.2	2.2	2.2	2.2	2.2	2.2	2.2	2.2
39	2.2	2.2	2.2	2.2	2.2	2.2	2.2	2.2	2.2	2.2	2.2	2.2
40	2.2	2.2	2.2	2.2	2.2	2.2	2.2	2.2	2.2	2.2	2.2	2.2
41	2.2	2.2	2.2	2.2	2.2	2.2	2.2	2.2	2.2	2.2	2.2	2.2
42	2.2	2.2	2.2	2.2	2.2	2.2	2.2	2.2	2.2	2.2	2.2	2.2
43	2.2	2.2	2.2	2.2	2.2	2.2	2.2	2.2	2.2	2.2	2.2	2.2
44	2.2	2.2	2.2	2.2	2.2	2.2	2.2	2.2	2.2	2.2	2.2	2.2
45	2.2	2.2	2.2	2.2	2.2	2.2	2.2	2.2	2.2	2.2	2.2	2.2
46		.3	.4	.6	.8	1.0	1.1	1.4	1.6	1.7	1.9	2.1

(iii) For purposes of this paragraph, 15-year real property that is placed in service on or after the first day of a month shall be treated as placed in service in that month.

(5) *Property financed with the proceeds of industrial development bonds.*—If, in accordance with section 168(f)(12) and § 1.168-2(m), the recovery allowance for property financed with the proceeds of an industrial development bond (as described in section 103(b)) is determined using the straight line method, then an election as provided in section 168(b)(3) and this paragraph shall be deemed to have been made with respect to such property.

(d) *Unadjusted basis.*—(1) *Computation.*—Except as provided in paragraph (j)(6)(ii) of this section (relating to change of status), the unadjusted basis of recovery property is equal to the difference between—

(i) The basis of the property for purposes of determining gain under sections 1011 through 1024 but without regard to any adjustments to basis described in section 1016(a)(2) and (3), and

(ii) Any portion of the basis for which the taxpayer properly elects amortization in lieu of cost recovery (*e.g.*, under section 167(k)) or treatment as an expense under section 179.

The unadjusted basis of recovery property shall be first taken into account under this section for the taxable year in which the property is placed in service (as defined in paragraph (l)(2) of this § 1.168-2) as recovery property.

(2) *Reductions in basis.*—(i) If an investment tax credit is determined under section 46(a)(2) with respect to recovery property, then, unless the taxpayer makes an election provided under section 48(q)(4), for purposes of this section the unadjusted basis shall be reduced by 50 percent of the amount of the credit so determined. In the case of a credit determined under section 46(a)(2) for any qualified rehabilitation

expenditure made in connection with a qualified rehabilitated building (other than a certified historic structure), the unadjusted basis shall be reduced by 100 percent of the amount of the credit so determined. See section 48(q) and the regulations thereunder. For rules relating to the treatment of such basis adjustment upon the disposition of an asset from a mass asset account, see § 1.168-2(h)(4).

(ii) Subject to the rules of other applicable provisions of the Code (*e.g.*, section 280A), for recovery property which is used in the taxpayer's trade or business (or for the production of income) as well as in a personal or tax-exempt activity throughout a taxable year, the unadjusted basis shall be determined by multiplying the unadjusted basis (determined without regard to this subdivision) by a fraction, the numerator of which equals the taxpayer's use of the property during the taxable year in his trade or business (or for the production of income) and the denominator of which equals the taxpayer's total use of the property during the taxable year. For property converted from personal or tax-exempt use to use in the taxpayer's trade or business (or for the production of income), or for property devoted to increased use in the taxpayer's trade or business (or for the production of income), see § 1.168-2(j).

Example. In 1981, A, a calendar year taxpayer, purchases a car for $10,000 to be used in his business as well as for his personal enjoyment. During 1981, A drives the car a total of 20,000 miles of which 8,000 miles (*i.e.*, 40 percent) is in the course of A's business. During 1982, A drives the car a total of 30,000 miles of which 21,000 miles (*i.e.*, 70 percent) is in the course of A's business. During 1983, A drives the car a total of 10,000 miles of which 3,000 miles (*i.e.*, 30 percent) is in the course of A's business. The optional straight line method provided under § 1.168-2(c) is not elected. Thus, A's recovery allowance in 1981 equals $1,000 (*i.e.*, ($10,000 × .40) × .25), in 1982 equals $2,660 (*i.e.*, ($10,000 × .70) × .38) and in 1983 equals $1,110 (*i.e.*, ($10,000 × .30) × .37). If A continues to use the car in his business after 1983, additional recovery may be allowed. See § 1.168-2(j).

(3) *Redeterminations.*—(i) For the taxable year (and subsequent taxable years) in which the unadjusted basis of recovery property is redetermined (*e.g.*, due to contingent purchase price or discharge of indebtedness), the recovery allowance shall be the amount determined by multiplying the redetermined adjusted basis by the redetermined applicable percentage. For purposes of this subparagraph, the redetermination adjusted basis is the unadjusted basis reduced by the recovery allowance previously allowed or allowable to the taxpayer with respect to the property and adjusted to reflect the redetermination. The redetermined applicable percentage is the percentage determined by dividing the applicable percentage otherwise provided in paragraph (b), (c), (g), or (m) of § 1.168-2 for the recovery year by an amount equal to the unrecovered percentage (*i.e.*, 100 percent minus the applicable percentage for recovery years prior to the year in which the basis is redetermined). Thus, the increase or decrease in basis shall be accounted for over the remaining recovery years beginning with the recovery year in which the basis is redetermined.

(ii) The following examples illustrate the provisions of this subparagraph (3):

Example (1). On July 15, 1984, A places in service 5-year recovery property with an unadjusted basis of $100,000. In order to purchase the property, A borrowed $80,000 from B. On December 1, 1984, B forgives $10,000 of the indebtedness. A makes the election provided in section 108(d)(4). The recovery allowance for the property in 1984 is $15,000. Under section 1017(a), as of January 1, 1985, the adjusted basis of the property is $75,000. In 1985 the recovery allowance is $19,411.77 (*i.e.*, .22/(1.00 − .15) × ($100,000 − ($10,000 + $15,000))). In 1986, 1987, and 1988 the recovery allowance is $18,529.41 in each year (*i.e.*, .21/(1.00 − .15) × ($100,000 − ($10,000 + $15,000))).

Example (2). On July 15, 1984, C purchases and places in service 5-year recovery property with an unadjusted basis of $100,000. In addition to the $100,000, C agrees to pay the seller 25 percent of the gross profits from the operation of the property in the first year. On July 15, 1985, C pays to the seller an additional $10,000. The recovery allowance for the property in 1984 is $15,000. In 1985 the recovery allowance is $24,588.23 (*i.e.*, .22/(1.00 − .15) × ($100,000 + ($10,000 − $15,000))). In 1986, 1987, and 1988 the recovery allowance is $23,470.59 in each year (*i.e.*, .21/(1.00 − .15) × ($100,000 + ($10,000 − $15,000))).

(e) *Components and improvements.*—(1) *Component cost recovery not permitted.*—In general, the unadjusted basis of structural components (as defined in § 1.48-1(e)(2)) of a building must be recovered as a whole. Thus, the same recovery period and method must be used for all structural components, and such components must be recovered as constituent parts of the building of which they are a part. The recovery period for a component begins on the later of the first day of the month in which the component is placed in service as recovery property or the first day of the month in which the building of which the component is a part is placed in service as recovery property. See subparagraph (3) of this paragraph for the treatment of components of a building which is made available in stages.

(2) *Treatment of amounts added to capital account.*—(i) Sections 162, 212, and 263 provide rules for the treatment of certain expenditures for the repair, maintenance, rehabilitation, or improvement of property. An expenditure which is treated as a capital expenditure under such sections (after application of the repair allowance rules of § 1.167(a)-11(d)(2)) is treated as the purchase of recovery property if the improvement for which the expenditure is made is placed in service after December 31, 1980. The recovery of such expenditure shall begin when the improvement is placed in service. See subparagraph (3) of this paragraph for the treatment of a building which is made available in stages.

(ii) For capital expenditures (which are section 1250 class property) made with respect to an improvement of a building which is recovery property, the taxpayer must use the same recovery period and method as are used with respect to the building, unless the improvement qualifies as a substantial improvement. See subparagraph (4) of this paragraph. If capital expenditures (which are section 1250 class property) are made with respect to improvements of a building which is not recovery property under section 168(e) and §1.168-4, then the taxpayer may select any applicable recovery period and method for the recovery of the first of such expenditures. The recovery period and method so selected shall apply to each subsequent expenditure (unless the improvement qualifies as a substantial improvement).

(iii) A capital expenditure made with respect to the improvement of property, other than a building, is assigned to the same recovery class (as defined in §1.168-3(b)) as the property of which the improvement is a part. For such an expenditure, the taxpayer need not use the same recovery period and method as are used with respect to the property of which the improvement is a part.

(3) *Recovery for a building which is made available in stages.*—This subparagraph (3) (and not subparagraphs (1) and (2) of this paragraph) applies to a building which is made available in stages. For purposes of this section, a building shall be considered placed in service (and, therefore, recovery will begin) only when a significant portion is made available for use in a finished condition (*e.g.*, when a certificate of occupancy is issued with respect to such portion). If less than the entire building is made available, then the unadjusted basis which is taken into account under this section shall be that amount of the unadjusted basis of the building (including capital expenditures for any components) as is properly allocable to the portion made available. If another portion of the building is subsequently made available, then that amount of the unadjusted basis (including capital expenditures for any components) as is properly allocable to the ensuing portion shall be taken into account under this section when such portion becomes available. The taxpayer must use the same recovery period and method for all portions of the building.

(4) *Substantial improvements.*—(i) A substantial improvement to a building shall be treated as a separate building. Thus, the taxpayer may use a different period and method for computing the recovery allowance for the substantial improvement than are used for computing the allowance for the building.

(ii) An improvement is a substantial improvement if—

(A) Over 24 consecutive months the aggregate expenditures properly chargeable to the capital account for a building equal at least 25 percent of the adjusted basis of the building (disregarding adjustments provided in section 1016(a)(2) and (3)) as of the day on which the first expenditure is made, and

(B) All expenditures for the improvement are made 3 or more years after the building is placed in service by the taxpayer.

For purposes of the preceding sentence, a building acquired in a transaction to which section 1031 or 1033 applies is considered placed in service when the building that was replaced was placed in service. Similarly, a building acquired in a transaction to which section 168(f)(10)(A) applies is deemed placed in service by the transferee when such building was placed in service by the transferor. An expenditure which is allocated to a 24-month period shall not be allocated to another 24-month period. For example, an expenditure may not be part of one substantial improvement when considered together with an expenditure incurred 15 months earlier and also be part of another substantial improvement when combined with an expenditure incurred 10 months later.

(iii) It is possible that an improvement will not be part of a substantial improvement in the taxable year in which the improvement is placed in service but will become part of a substantial improvement in a subsequent taxable year. In such case, if the taxpayer uses a different method and recovery period with respect to the substantial improvement, then the tax return filed for the taxable year in which the first improvement is placed in service shall be amended accordingly.

(5) *Examples.*—The provisions of this paragraph may be illustrated by the following examples:

Example (1). In 1985, A spends $10,000 to improve machinery used in his trade or business. The $10,000 is added to capital account under the principles of sections 162, 212, and 263. The machinery would be 5-year property if placed in service after 1980. The $10,000 expenditure is treated as the purchase of 5-year recovery property, placed in service in 1985. Any election made by A with respect to the underlying machinery will not affect the recovery allowance for the improvement.

Example (2). B, a calendar year taxpayer, begins constructing a 10-story office building in 1982. All floors will have approximately the same amount of usable floor space. By 1983, B has paid or incurred $10 million for the building's shell (and other items not directly related to any specific portion of the building), $4 million for work with respect to the first three floors, and $5 million for work directly related to other floors (including installation of components). In March 1983, B receives a certificate of occupancy for the first three floors and begins offering the floors for rental to tenants. The building is considered placed in service in March 1983. No deduction is allowable under this section with respect to the building for 1982. No election is made under §1.168-2(c) to use the optional recovery percentages. B's recovery for 1983 is the properly allocable unadjusted basis times the applicable percentage (10 percent). The properly allocable unadjusted basis is $7 million, consisting of the amount of unadjusted basis directly related to the portion of the building which is made available for use ($4 million), plus that amount of the unadjusted basis which is not directly related to any specific portion of the building ($10 million) properly allocable to the portion which is made available for use (*i.e.*, 3 floors/10 floors equals 30 percent or $3 million). No deduction is allowable in 1983 for the $5 million paid or incurred for work directly related to portions of the building not made available for use. B will recover the $7 million unadjusted basis over the 15-year recovery period, beginning in March 1983.

Example (3). The facts are the same as in example (2) except that, in January 1984, B receives a certificate of occupancy for the remaining seven floors and begins offering them for rental to tenants. B has spent an additional $7 million to complete the building as of the date on which the remaining seven floors are offered for rental. In January 1984, B takes into account as unadjusted basis the $12 million not previously taken into account, plus the $7 million of later expenditures. B will recover the $19 million unadjusted basis over a 15-year recovery period beginning in January 1984. B may not use a different recovery period and method for such amount than were used for the amount taken into account in March 1983.

Example (4). The facts are the same as in examples (2) and (3) except that in 1990 B spends $1 million, which is added to capital account to rehabilitate certain portions of the building. The $1 million is treated as the purchase by B of 15-year real property in 1990. B must use the same recovery period and method with respect to that improvement as were used for the underlying building. The improvement has a 15-year recovery period, and the recovery begins when the improvement is placed in service.

Example (5). In 1983 C spends $1 million, which is added to capital account, to rehabilitate certain portions of a building placed in service by C in 1975. The $1 million is treated as the purchase by C of 15-year real property in 1983. C may use any applicable recovery period and method with respect to such expenditure, and the recovery begins when the improvement is placed in service. The recovery period and method selected with respect to such expenditure, however, will apply to all ensuing capital expenditures made by C with respect to the building, unless an expenditure qualifies as part of a substantial improvement. The result in this example would be the same if the building were placed in service by C after 1980, but did not qualify as recovery property by reason of the provisions of section 168(e)(4) and § 1.168-4(d).

(f) *Short taxable years.*—(1) *General rule.*—For any recovery year in which there are less than 12 months (hereinafter in this section referred to as a "short taxable year"), the recovery allowance shall be determined by multiplying the deduction which would have been allowable if the recovery year were not a short taxable year by a fraction the numerator of which equals the number of months and part-months in the short taxable year and the denominator of which is 12. This paragraph shall not apply to 15-year real property for the year the property is placed in service or disposed of.

(2) *Subsequent years' allowance.*—Recovery allowances for years in a recovery period following a short taxable year shall be determined in accordance with paragraph (a), (c), (g), or (m) of this section without reference to the short taxable year.

(3) *Unrecovered allowance.*—In the taxable year following the last year in the recovery period, a recovery allowance is permitted to the extent of any unrecovered allowance. If the optional recovery percentages are elected under § 1.168-2(c) or (g)(3) and the short taxable year is the last recovery year, then the unrecovered allowance shall be allowed in the year following the short taxable year. The term "unrecovered allowance" means the difference between—

(i) The recovery allowance properly allowed for the short taxable year, and

(ii) The recovery allowance which would have been allowable if such year were not a short taxable year.

In no event shall the recovery allowance for any taxable year following the last year in the recovery period be greater than what the recovery allowance would be for the last year in the recovery period assuming that such year consists of 12 months. Any amount in excess of such recovery allowance for the last year in the recovery period shall be taken into account in the following taxable year or years in the same manner as provided in this subparagraph (3).

(4) *When a taxable year begins.*—For purposes of this section, a taxable year of a person placing property in service does not include any month prior to the month in which the person begins engaging in a trade or business or holding recovery or depreciable property for the production of income. For purposes of applying the preceding sentence to an employee, an employee is not considered engaged in a trade or business by virtue of his employment except that, for purposes of applying this section to recovery property used for purposes of employment, the taxable year includes any month during which a person is engaged in trade or business as an employee. In addition, if a person engages in a small amount of trade or business activity for the purpose of obtaining a disproportionately large recovery allowance for assets for the taxable year in which they are placed in service, and if placing those assets in service represents a substantial increase in the person's level of business activity, then for purposes of the recovery allowance for such assets the person will not be treated as beginning a trade or business until the increased amount of business activity begins. For property held for the production of income, the principle of the preceding sentence also applies.

(5) *Successive short taxable years.*—In applying the rule of subparagraph (1) of this paragraph, no month shall be taken into account more than once. Thus, if a taxpayer has successive short taxable years, with one taxable year ending and the following taxable year beginning in the same calendar month, then the recovery year which is ending shall not include the month in which the taxable year terminates.

(6) *Examples.*—The following examples illustrate the application of this paragraph:

Example (1). On October 10, 1983, A and B enter into an agreement to form a partnership (P), for the purpose of leasing sailboats. The partnership adopts a calendar year as its taxable year pursuant to § 1.706-1(b)(1). On November 5, 1983, P purchases four sailboats for a total of $20,000 and places the sailboats in service immediately. For purposes of section 168, P's taxable year begins on November 5, 1983. Sailboats are 5-year recovery property as defined in section 168(c)(2). No straight line election is made under § 1.168-2(c). The recovery allowance for the sailboats in 1983, a short taxable year, is $500 (*i.e.,* .15 × $20,000 × 2/12). In 1984, the recovery allowance is $4,400 (.22 × $20,000). In 1985, 1986, and 1987, the recovery allowance is $4,200 annually (.21 × $20,000). In 1988, the taxable year following the last year in the recovery period, the unrecovered allowance equal to $2,500 may be deducted by A and B.

Example (2). In November 1984, Corporation L is incorporated and places in service two race horses which it acquired for a total of $18,500. The corporation adopts a calendar year as its taxable year. For purposes of section 168, the race horses are 3-year recovery property. No straight line election is made under § 1.168-2(c).

In 1984, the recovery allowance permitted to L for the race horses is $770.83 (*i.e.,* (.25 × $18,500) × 2/12). At the close of business on June 30, 1985, all of the stock of L is acquired by Corporation M. M elects in accordance with section 1501 to file a consolidated return with respect to M and L. M's taxable year begins on July 1. By reason of becoming included in the consolidated return, under § 1.1502-76 L's second taxable year ending June 30, 1985, is also a short taxable year containing 6 months. In the second taxable year, L is permitted a recovery allowance equal to $3,515 (*i.e.,* .38 × $18,500 × 6/12). In the third taxable year ending June 30, 1986, L is entitled to a recovery allowance of $6,845 (*i.e.,* .37 × $18,500). Thus, the unrecovered allowance as of July 1, 1986, equals $7,369.17. Since the unrecovered allowance exceeds the recovery allowance for the third recovery year (the last year in the recovery period), the recovery allowance for the taxable year ending June 30, 1987, equals the allowance for such year, $6,845. The recovery allowance in the taxable year ending June 30, 1988, equals $524.17, the remaining unrecovered allowance.

Example (3). On August 1, 1984, Partnership M is formed and places in service a warehouse which will be leased to an unrelated person. M acquires the warehouse for $250,000. M adopts a calendar year as its taxable year pursuant to § 1.706-1(b)(1). In 1984, M has a short taxable year within the meaning of § 1.168-2(f)(1). Since the property is 15-year real property, however, the recovery allowance is computed as though 1984 were a full taxable year. Because the recovery property would have been placed in service in the eighth month of M's normal taxable year, the recovery property is deemed placed in service in the eighth month of the first recovery year. The recovery allowance in 1984 is $12,500 (*i.e.,* .05 × $250,000).

Example (4). In July 1983, D, who has been an employee of Corporation N since 1982, purchases an automobile for use in the performance of his employment for N. On June 5, 1984, D purchases a truck for use in another business. D begins the new business on June 5, 1984. In 1984, D holds no other depreciable or recovery property for the production of income. D does not have a short taxable year for the automobile purchased in 1983 since the automobile is used by D in his trade or business as an employee. Since an employee is not considered engaged in a trade or business by virtue of employment, however, for purposes of determining when a taxable year begins with respect to property not used in the trade or business of employment, D has a short taxable year in 1984 for the truck purchased in that year. The recovery allowance permitted D in 1984 with respect to the truck must be adjusted in accordance with the provisions of § 1.168-2(f).

Example (5). A has been actively engaged in the trade or business of selling used cars since 1981. On July 1, 1983, A accepts employment with Corporation M and on that same date purchases a truck for $10,000 for use in the performance of his employment for M. A does not have a short taxable year for the truck because the taxable year of a person placing property in service includes all months during which that person is engaged in a trade or business.

Example (6). In 1983, C graduates from college and on July 1, 1983, is employed by N. On that same day, C purchases an automobile for $10,000 for use in the performance of his employment for N. C has a short taxable year for the automobile purchased in 1983. Although, for recovery property used for purposes of employment, the taxable year includes any month during which a person is an employee, C does not begin that trade or business until July. In addition, C is engaged in no other trade or business (and does not hold any depreciable or recovery property for the production of income) during the taxable year. The recovery allowance permitted C in 1983 with respect to the automobile must be adjusted in accordance with the provisions of § 1.168-2(f).

Example (7). Corporation X, a calendar year taxpayer, has been in the trade or business of selling household appliances since 1979. On July 1, 1983, X purchases a restaurant. On that same day, X purchases restaurant equipment for use in its new business. X does not have a short taxable year for the restaurant equipment because the taxable year of a person placing property in service includes all months during which that person is engaged in a trade or business.

(g) *Special rules for property used predominantly outside the United States.*—(1) *General rule.*—(i) In lieu of the deduction allowed under paragraphs (a) and (c) of this § 1.168-2, except as provided in subparagraphs (3) and (4) of this paragraph, and except as otherwise provided in section 168 and the regulations thereunder, the recovery allowance for recovery property used predominantly outside the United States (as described in § 1.168-2(g)(5)) during the taxable year equals the aggregate amount determined by multiplying the unadjusted basis (as defined in § 1.168-2(d)) of such recovery property by the applicable percentage provided in paragraph (g)(2) of this section. For purposes of determining the recovery allowance, salvage value shall be disregarded.

(ii) The recovery period for recovery property used predominantly outside the United States, other than 15-year real property, shall be the present class life. For recovery property (other than 15-year real property) which is not assigned a present class life, the recovery period shall be 12 years. For 15-year real property used predominantly outside the United States, the recovery period shall be 35 years.

(iii) Except for 15-year real property and except as otherwise provided in § 1.168-5, no recovery allowance shall be allowed in the year of disposition of recovery property described in this paragraph.

(iv) For purposes of this paragraph, rules similar to the rules of paragraph (e) of this section shall apply.

(2) *Applicable percentages.*—(i) For property other than 15-year real property—

If the recovery year is:	And the recovery period is:								
	2.5	3	3.5	4	5	6	6.5	7	7.5	8
	The applicable percentage is:									
1	40	33	29	25	20	17	15	14	13	13
2	48	45	41	38	32	28	26	25	23	22
3	12	15	17	19	19	18	18	17	17	16

If the recovery year is:	And the recovery period is: 2.5	3	3.5	4	5	6	6.5	7	7.5	8
	The applicable percentage is:									
4		7	13	12	12	12	13	13	13	12
5				6	12	10	10	9	9	9
6					5	10	9	9	9	8
7						5	9	9	8	8
8								4	8	8
9										4

If the recovery year is:	And the recovery period is: 8.5	9	9.5	10	10.5	11	11.5	12	12.5	13
	The applicable percentage is:									
1	12	11	11	10	10	9	9	8	8	8
2	21	20	19	18	17	17	16	15	15	14
3	16	15	15	14	14	13	13	13	12	12
4	12	12	12	12	11	11	11	11	10	10
5	9	9	9	9	9	9	9	9	9	9
6	8	8	7	7	7	7	7	7	7	7
7	8	7	7	7	7	7	6	6	6	6
8	7	7	7	7	7	6	6	6	6	6
9	7	7	7	7	6	6	6	6	6	5
10		4	6	6	6	6	6	6	6	5
11				3	6	6	6	5	5	5
12						3	5	5	5	5
13								3	5	5
14										3

If the recovery year is:	And the recovery period is: 13.5	14	15	16	16.5	17	18	19	20	22
	The applicable percentage is:									
1	7	7	7	6	6	6	6	5	5	5
2	14	13	12	12	11	11	10	10	10	9
3	12	11	11	10	10	10	9	9	9	8
4	10	10	9	9	9	9	8	8	8	7
5	8	8	8	8	8	8	7	7	7	6
6	7	7	7	7	7	7	7	6	6	6
7	6	6	6	6	6	6	6	6	6	5
8	6	5	5	5	5	5	5	5	5	5
9	5	5	5	5	5	5	5	5	4	4
10	5	5	5	5	5	4	4	4	4	4
11	5	5	5	5	4	4	4	4	4	4
12	5	5	5	4	4	4	4	4	4	4
13	5	5	5	4	4	4	4	4	4	4
14	5	5	4	4	4	4	4	4	4	3
15		3	4	4	4	4	4	4	3	3
16			2	4	4	4	4	4	3	3
17				2	4	3	4	3	3	3
18						2	3	3	3	3
19							2	3	3	3
20								2	3	3
21									2	3
22										3
23										2

If the recovery year is:	And the recovery period is: 25	26.5	28	30	35	45	50
	The applicable percentage is:						
1	4	4	4	3	3	2	2
2	8	7	7	6	6	4	4
3	7	7	6	6	5	4	4
4	6	6	6	6	5	4	4
5	6	6	6	5	5	4	3
6	6	5	5	5	4	4	3
7	5	5	5	5	4	3	3
8	5	5	4	4	4	3	3
9	4	4	4	4	4	3	3
10	4	4	4	4	3	3	3
11	4	4	4	3	3	3	3
12	3	3	3	3	3	3	3
13	3	3	3	3	3	3	2
14	3	3	3	3	3	3	2
15	3	3	3	3	3	2	2
16	3	3	3	3	3	2	2
17	3	3	3	3	2	2	2
18	3	3	3	3	2	2	2
19	3	3	3	3	2	2	2
20	3	3	3	3	2	2	2
21	3	3	3	3	2	2	2
22	3	3	2	2	2	2	2

If the recovery year is:	*And the recovery period is:* 25	26.5	28	30	35	45	50
	The applicable percentage is:						
23	3	3	2	2	2	2	2
24	2	2	2	2	2	2	2
25	2	2	2	2	2	2	2
26	1	2	2	2	2	2	2
27		1	2	2	2	2	2
28			2	2	2	2	2
29			1	2	2	2	2
30				2	2	2	2
31				1	2	2	2
32					2	2	2
33					2	2	2
34					2	2	2
35					2	2	2
36					1	2	1
37						1	1
38						1	1
39						1	1
40						1	1
41						1	1
42						1	1
43						1	1
44						1	1
45						1	1
46						1	1
47							1
48							1
49							1
50							1
51							1

(ii) For 15-year real property—

If the recovery year is	*And the month in the 1st recovery year in which the property is placed in service is:* 1	2,3	4,5,6	7,8	9,10,11,12
	The applicable percentage is:				
1	4	4	3	2	1
2	4	4	4	4	4
3	4	4	4	4	4
4	4	4	4	4	4
5	4	4	4	4	4
6	3	3	3	4	4
7	3	3	3	3	3
8	3	3	3	3	3
9	3	3	3	3	3
10	3	3	3	3	3
11	3	3	3	3	3
12	3	3	3	3	3
13	3	3	3	3	3
14	3	3	3	3	3
15	3	3	3	3	3
16	3	3	3	3	3
17	3	3	3	3	3
18	3	3	3	3	3
19	3	3	3	3	3
20	3	3	3	3	3
21	3	3	3	3	3
22	3	3	3	3	3
23	3	3	3	3	3
24	3	3	3	3	3
25	3	2	3	2	3
26	2	2	2	2	2
27	2	2	2	2	2
28	2	2	2	2	2
29	2	2	2	2	2
30	2	2	2	2	2
31	2	2	2	2	2
32	2	2	2	2	2
33	2	2	2	2	2
34	2	2	2	2	2
35	2	2	2	2	2
36		1	1	2	2

(3) *Election of optional recovery percentage method.*—(i) In lieu of the applicable percentage provided by subparagraphs (1) and (2), the taxpayer may elect (in accordance with § 1.168-5(e)), for recovery property used predominantly outside the United States that is placed in service during the taxable year, to determine the recovery allowance by using the straight line method over one of the recovery periods elected by the taxpayer and set forth in the following table:

CLASS OF PROPERTY	RECOVERY PERIOD
3-year property	5 or 12 years or present class life
5-year property	12 or 25 years or present class life
10-year property	25 or 35 years or present class life
15-year real property	35 or 45 years
15-year public utility property	35 or 45 years or present class life

Such election is irrevocable without the consent of the Commissioner. See subdivision (iv) of this subparagraph for tables containing the applicable percentages to be used in computing the recovery allowance.

(ii) Except in the case of 15-year real property, a single recovery period must be elected under this subparagraph for all recovery property placed in service in the same taxable year which is in the same recovery class and which has the same present class life. For property other than 15-year real property the recovery period elected may not be shorter than the present class life (or, if none, 12 years). A different recovery period may be elected (or the tables provided in subparagraph (2) may be used) for recovery property in different recovery classes, or with different present class lives, placed in service during the taxable year, or for recovery property placed in service in a different taxable year, whether or not in the same recovery class or with the same present class life.

(iii) In the case of 15-year real property, the election provided by this subparagraph may be made separately with respect to each property.

(iv)(A) For property other than 15-year real property—

If the recovery year is:	*And the period elected is:* 2.5	3	3.5	4	5	6	6.5	7	7.5
	The applicable percentage is:								
1	20	17	14	13	10	8	8	8	7
2	40	33	29	25	20	17	16	14	14
3	40	33	29	25	20	17	16	14	14
4		17	28	25	20	17	15	14	13
5				12	20	17	15	14	13
6					10	17	15	14	13
7						7	15	14	13
8								8	13

If the recovery year is:	*And the period elected is:* 8	8.5	9	9.5	10	10.5	11	11.5	12
	The applicable percentage is:								
1	6	6	6	5	5	5	5	4	4
2	13	12	11	11	10	10	9	9	9
3	13	12	11	11	10	10	9	9	9
4	13	12	11	11	10	10	9	9	9
5	13	12	11	11	10	10	9	9	9
6	12	12	11	11	10	10	9	9	8
7	12	12	11	10	10	9	9	9	8
8	12	11	11	10	10	9	9	9	8
9	6	11	11	10	10	9	9	9	8
10			6	10	10	9	9	8	8
11					5	9	9	8	8
12							5	8	8
13									4

If the recovery year is:	*And the period elected is:* 12.5	13	13.5	14	15	16	16.5	17	18
	The applicable percentage is:								
1	4	4	4	4	3	3	3	3	3
2	8	8	8	8	7	7	7	6	6
3	8	8	8	7	7	7	6	6	6
4	8	8	8	7	7	7	6	6	6
5	8	8	8	7	7	7	6	6	6
6	8	8	8	7	7	6	6	6	6
7	8	8	7	7	7	6	6	6	6
8	8	8	7	7	7	6	6	6	6
9	8	8	7	7	7	6	6	6	6
10	8	8	7	7	7	6	6	6	6
11	8	7	7	7	7	6	6	6	6
12	8	7	7	7	6	6	6	6	5
13	8	7	7	7	6	6	6	6	5
14		3	7	7	6	6	6	6	5
15				4	6	6	6	6	5
16					3	6	6	6	5
17						3	6	5	5
18								2	5
19									2

If the recovery year is:	And the period elected is: 19	20	22	25	26.5	28	30	35
	The applicable percentage is:							
1	3	3	2	2	2	2	2	1
2	6	5	5	4	4	4	4	3
3	6	5	5	4	4	4	4	3
4	6	5	5	4	4	4	4	3
5	6	5	5	4	4	4	4	3
6	6	5	5	4	4	4	4	3
7	5	5	5	4	4	4	4	3
8	5	5	5	4	4	4	4	3
9	5	5	5	4	4	4	4	3
10	5	5	5	4	4	4	4	3
11	5	5	5	4	4	4	3	3
12	5	5	5	4	4	4	3	3
13	5	5	5	4	4	4	3	3
14	5	5	4	4	4	4	3	3
15	5	5	4	4	4	4	3	3
16	5	5	4	4	4	4	3	3
17	5	5	4	4	4	3	3	3
18	5	5	4	4	4	3	3	3
19	5	5	4	4	4	3	3	3
20	2	5	4	4	4	3	3	3
21		2	4	4	4	3	3	3
22			4	4	3	3	3	3
23			2	4	3	3	3	3
24				4	3	3	3	3
25				4	3	3	3	3
26				2	3	3	3	3
27					3	3	3	3
28						3	3	3
29						2	3	3
30							3	3
31							2	3
32								2
33								2
34								2
35								2
36								1

If the recovery year is:	And the period elected is: 45	50
	The applicable percentage is:	
1	1.1	1
2	2.3	2
3	2.3	2
4	2.3	2
5	2.3	2
6	2.3	2
7	2.3	2
8	2.3	2
9	2.3	2
10	2.3	2
11	2.3	2
12	2.2	2
13	2.2	2
14	2.2	2
15	2.2	2
16	2.2	2
17	2.2	2
18	2.2	2
19	2.2	2
20	2.2	2
21	2.2	2
22	2.2	2
23	2.2	2
24	2.2	2
25	2.2	2
26	2.2	2
27	2.2	2
28	2.2	2
29	2.2	2
30	2.2	2
31	2.2	2
32	2.2	2
33	2.2	2
34	2.2	2
35	2.2	2
36	2.2	2
37	2.2	2

If the recovery year is:	And the period elected is: 45	50
	The applicable percentage is:	
38	2.2	2
39	2.2	2
40	2.2	2
41	2.2	2
42	2.2	2
43	2.2	2
44	2.2	2
45	2.2	2
46	1.1	2
47		2
48		2
49		2
50		2
51		1

(B) *For 15-year real property.—(1)* If a 35-year period is elected—

If the recovery year is:	And the month in the 1st recovery year the property is placed in service is: 1-2	3-6	7-12
		The applicable percentage is:	
1	3	2	1
2	3	3	3
3	3	3	3
4	3	3	3
5	3	3	3
6	3	3	3
7	3	3	3
8	3	3	3
9	3	3	3
10	3	3	3
11	3	3	3
12	3	3	3
13	3	3	3
14	3	3	3
15	3	3	3
16	3	3	3
17	3	3	3
18	3	3	3
19	3	3	3
20	3	3	3
21	3	3	3
22	3	3	3
23	3	3	3
24	3	3	3
25	3	3	3
26	3	3	3
27	3	3	3
28	3	3	3
29	3	3	3
30	3	3	3
31	2	2	2
32	2	2	2
33	2	2	2
34	2	2	2
35	2	2	2
36		1	2

(2) If a 45-year period is elected—

If the recovery year is:	And the month in the 1st recovery year the property is placed in service is: 1	2	3	4	5	6	7	8	9	10	11	12
						The applicable percentage is:						
1	2.3	2.0	1.9	1.7	1.5	1.3	1.2	.9	.7	.6	.4	.2
2	2.3	2.3	2.3	2.3	2.3	2.3	2.3	2.3	2.3	2.3	2.3	2.3
3	2.3	2.3	2.3	2.3	2.3	2.3	2.3	2.3	2.3	2.3	2.3	2.3
4	2.3	2.3	2.3	2.3	2.3	2.3	2.3	2.3	2.3	2.3	2.3	2.3
5	2.3	2.3	2.3	2.3	2.3	2.3	2.3	2.3	2.3	2.3	2.3	2.3
6	2.3	2.3	2.3	2.3	2.3	2.3	2.3	2.3	2.3	2.3	2.3	2.3
7	2.3	2.3	2.3	2.3	2.3	2.3	2.3	2.3	2.3	2.3	2.3	2.3
8	2.3	2.3	2.3	2.3	2.3	2.3	2.3	2.3	2.3	2.3	2.3	2.3
9	2.3	2.3	2.3	2.3	2.3	2.3	2.3	2.3	2.3	2.3	2.3	2.3
10	2.3	2.3	2.3	2.3	2.3	2.3	2.3	2.3	2.3	2.3	2.3	2.3
11	2.2	2.2	2.2	2.2	2.2	2.2	2.2	2.2	2.2	2.2	2.2	2.2
12	2.2	2.2	2.2	2.2	2.2	2.2	2.2	2.2	2.2	2.2	2.2	2.2
13	2.2	2.2	2.2	2.2	2.2	2.2	2.2	2.2	2.2	2.2	2.2	2.2
14	2.2	2.2	2.2	2.2	2.2	2.2	2.2	2.2	2.2	2.2	2.2	2.2
15	2.2	2.2	2.2	2.2	2.2	2.2	2.2	2.2	2.2	2.2	2.2	2.2

If the recovery year is:	*And the month in the 1st recovery year the property is placed in s ervice is:*											
	1	2	3	4	5	6	7	8	9	10	11	12
	The applicable percentage is:											
16	2.2	2.2	2.2	2.2	2.2	2.2	2.2	2.2	2.2	2.2	2.2	2.2
17	2.2	2.2	2.2	2.2	2.2	2.2	2.2	2.2	2.2	2.2	2.2	2.2
18	2.2	2.2	2.2	2.2	2.2	2.2	2.2	2.2	2.2	2.2	2.2	2.2
19	2.2	2.2	2.2	2.2	2.2	2.2	2.2	2.2	2.2	2.2	2.2	2.2
20	2.2	2.2	2.2	2.2	2.2	2.2	2.2	2.2	2.2	2.2	2.2	2.2
21	2.2	2.2	2.2	2.2	2.2	2.2	2.2	2.2	2.2	2.2	2.2	2.2
22	2.2	2.2	2.2	2.2	2.2	2.2	2.2	2.2	2.2	2.2	2.2	2.2
23	2.2	2.2	2.2	2.2	2.2	2.2	2.2	2.2	2.2	2.2	2.2	2.2
24	2.2	2.2	2.2	2.2	2.2	2.2	2.2	2.2	2.2	2.2	2.2	2.2
25	2.2	2.2	2.2	2.2	2.2	2.2	2.2	2.2	2.2	2.2	2.2	2.2
26	2.2	2.2	2.2	2.2	2.2	2.2	2.2	2.2	2.2	2.2	2.2	2.2
27	2.2	2.2	2.2	2.2	2.2	2.2	2.2	2.2	2.2	2.2	2.2	2.2
28	2.2	2.2	2.2	2.2	2.2	2.2	2.2	2.2	2.2	2.2	2.2	2.2
29	2.2	2.2	2.2	2.2	2.2	2.2	2.2	2.2	2.2	2.2	2.2	2.2
30	2.2	2.2	2.2	2.2	2.2	2.2	2.2	2.2	2.2	2.2	2.2	2.2
31	2.2	2.2	2.2	2.2	2.2	2.2	2.2	2.2	2.2	2.2	2.2	2.2
32	2.2	2.2	2.2	2.2	2.2	2.2	2.2	2.2	2.2	2.2	2.2	2.2
33	2.2	2.2	2.2	2.2	2.2	2.2	2.2	2.2	2.2	2.2	2.2	2.2
34	2.2	2.2	2.2	2.2	2.2	2.2	2.2	2.2	2.2	2.2	2.2	2.2
35	2.2	2.2	2.2	2.2	2.2	2.2	2.2	2.2	2.2	2.2	2.2	2.2
36	2.2	2.2	2.2	2.2	2.2	2.2	2.2	2.2	2.2	2.2	2.2	2.2
37	2.2	2.2	2.2	2.2	2.2	2.2	2.2	2.2	2.2	2.2	2.2	2.2
38	2.2	2.2	2.2	2.2	2.2	2.2	2.2	2.2	2.2	2.2	2.2	2.2
39	2.2	2.2	2.2	2.2	2.2	2.2	2.2	2.2	2.2	2.2	2.2	2.2
40	2.2	2.2	2.2	2.2	2.2	2.2	2.2	2.2	2.2	2.2	2.2	2.2
41	2.2	2.2	2.2	2.2	2.2	2.2	2.2	2.2	2.2	2.2	2.2	2.2
42	2.2	2.2	2.2	2.2	2.2	2.2	2.2	2.2	2.2	2.2	2.2	2.2
43	2.2	2.2	2.2	2.2	2.2	2.2	2.2	2.2	2.2	2.2	2.2	2.2
44	2.2	2.2	2.2	2.2	2.2	2.2	2.2	2.2	2.2	2.2	2.2	2.2
45	2.2	2.2	2.2	2.2	2.2	2.2	2.2	2.2	2.2	2.2	2.2	2.2
46		.3	.4	.6	.8	1.0	1.1	1.4	1.6	1.7	1.9	2.1

(4) *Rules for year of disposition and placement in service of 15-year real property.*—(i) In the taxable year in which 15-year real property is disposed of, the recovery allowance shall be determined by multiplying the allowance (determined without regard to this subdivision) by a fraction, the numerator of which equals the number of months in the taxable year that the property is in service in the taxpayer's trade or business or for the production of income and the denominator of which is 12. In the case of 15-year real property that is disposed of during the first recovery year, the denominator shall equal the number of months in the taxpayer's taxable year after the property was placed in service by the taxpayer (including the month the property was placed in service). If the recovery allowance for the taxable year is limited by reason of the short taxable year rules of section 168(f)(5) and paragraph (f) of this section (*e.g.*, if the taxpayer dies, or if the taxpayer is a corporation which becomes a member, or ceases being a member, of an affiliated group of corporations filing a consolidated return), then the denominator shall equal the number of months in the taxpayer's taxable year.

(ii) For purposes of this paragraph—

(A) 15-year real property that is placed in service on or after the first day of a month shall be treated as placed in service in that month; and

(B) 15-year real property that is disposed of during the recovery year shall be treated as disposed of as of the last day of the month preceding the month in which it is withdrawn from service.

(5) *Determination of whether property is used predominantly outside the United States.*—(i) The determination of whether property is used predominantly outside the United States (as defined in section 7701(a)(9)) during the taxable year shall be made by comparing the period in such year during which the property is physically located outside of the United States with the period during which the property is physically located within the United States. If the property is physically located outside the United States during more than 50 percent of the taxable year, such property shall be considered used predominantly outside the United States during the year. If property is placed in service after the first day of the taxable year, the determination of whether such property is physically located outside the United States during more than 50 percent of the taxable year shall be made with respect to the period beginning on the date on which the property is placed in service and ending on the last day of such taxable year.

(ii) This paragraph applies whether recovery property is used predominantly outside the United States by the owner or by the lessee of the property. For recovery property which is leased, the determination of whether such property is physically located outside the United States during the taxable year shall be made with respect to the taxable year of the lessor.

(iii) For purposes of this §1.168-2(g), the following property is not "property used predominantly outside the United States":

(A) Any aircraft which is registered by the Administrator of the Federal Aviation Agency, and which (*1*) is operated, whether on a scheduled or nonscheduled basis, to and from the United States, or (*2*) is operated under contract with the United States, provided that the use of the aircraft under the contract constitutes its principal use outside the United States during the taxable year. The term "to and from the United States" shall not exclude an aircraft which makes flights from one point in a foreign country to another such point, as long as such aircraft returns to the United States with some degree of frequency;

(B) Rolling stock which is used within and without the United States and which is (*1*) of a domestic railroad corporation subject to part I of the Interstate Commerce Act or (*2*) of a United States person (other than a corporation subject to part I of the Interstate Commerce Act) but only if the rolling stock is not leased to one or more foreign persons for periods totaling more than 12 months in any 24-month period. For purposes of this subdivision (iii)(B), the term "rolling stock" means locomotives, freight and passenger train cars, floating equipment, and miscellaneous transportation equipment on wheels, the expenditures for which are of the type chargeable to the equipment investment accounts in the uniform system of accounts for railroad companies prescribed by the Interstate Commerce Commission.

(C) Any vessel documented under the laws of the United States which is operated in the foreign or domestic commerce of the United States. A vessel is documented under the laws of the United States if it is registered, enrolled, or licensed under the laws of the United States by the Commandant, United States Coast Guard. Vessels operated in the foreign or domestic commerce of the United States include those documented for use in foreign trade, coast-wise trade, or fisheries;

(D) Any motor vehicle of a United States person (as defined in section 7701(a)(30)) which is operated to and from the United States with some degree of frequency;

(E) Any container of a United States person which is used in the transportation of property to and from the United States;

(F) Any property (other than a vessel or an aircraft) of a United States person which is used for the purpose of exploring for, developing, removing, or transporting resources from the Outer Continental Shelf (within the meaning of section 2 of the Outer Continental Shelf Lands Act, as amended and supplemented, 43 U.S.C. section 1331), *e.g.*, offshore drilling equipment;

(G) Any property which (*1*) is owned by a domestic corporation (other than a corporation which has an election in effect under section 936 or which is entitled to the benefits of section 934(b)), by a United States citizen (other than a citizen entitled to the benefits of section 931, 932, 933, or 934(c)), or by a domestic partnership, all of whose partners are domestic corporations (none of which has an election in effect under section 936 or is entitled to the benefits of section 934(b)) or United States citizens (none of whom is entitled to the benefits of section 931, 932, 933, or 934(c)), and (*2*) which is used predominantly in a possession of the United States during the taxable year by such a corporation, citizen, or partnership, or by a corporation created or organized in, or under the law of, a possession of the United States. The determination of whether property is used predominantly in a possession of the United States during the taxable year shall be made under principles similar to those described in subdivision (i) of this subparagraph. For example, if a machine is placed in service in a possession of the United States on July 1, 1981, by a calendar year taxpayer and if it is physically located in such a possession during more than 50 percent of the period beginning on July 1, 1981, and ending on December 31, 1981, then such machine shall be considered used predominantly in a possession of the United States during the taxable year 1981;

(H) Any communications satellite (as defined in section 103(3) of the Communications Satellite Act of 1962, 47 U.S.C. section 702(3)), or any interest therein, of a United States person;

(I) Any cable, or any interest therein, of a domestic corporation engaged in furnishing telephone service to which section 46(c)(3)(B)(iii) applies (or of a wholly owned domestic subsidiary of such corporation), if such cable is part of a submarine cable system which constitutes part of a communications link exclusively between the United States and one or more foreign countries;

(J) Any property (other than a vessel or an aircraft) of a United States person which is used in international or territorial waters within the northern portion of the Western Hemisphere for the purpose of exploring for, developing, removing, or transporting resources from ocean waters or deposits under such waters. The term "northern portion of the Western Hemisphere" means the area lying west of the 30th meridian west of Greenwich, east of the international dateline, and north of the Equator, but not including any foreign country which is a country of South America; and

(K) Any property described in section 48(l)(3)(A)(ix) which is owned by a United States person and which is used in international or territorial waters to generate energy for use in the United States.

(h) *Mass asset accounts*.—(1) *In general*.—In accordance with the provisions of § 1.168-5(e), a taxpayer may elect to account for mass assets (as defined in § 1.168-2(h)(2)) in the same mass asset account, as though such assets were a single asset. If such treatment is elected, the taxpayer, upon disposition of an asset in the account, shall include as ordinary income (as defined in section 64) all proceeds realized to the extent of the unadjusted basis in the account (as defined in paragraph (d) of this section), less any amounts previously so included, and shall include as capital gain any excess, unless gain on such disposition is not recognized under another provision of the Code. With respect to the recovery allowance, the account shall be treated as though the asset were not disposed of.

(2) *Definition*.—For purposes of this section, the term "mass assets" means a mass or group of individual items of recovery property (i) not necessarily homogenous, (ii) each of which is minor in value relative to the total value of such mass or group, (iii) numerous in quantity, (iv) usually accounted for only on a total dollar or quantity basis, (v) with respect to which separate identification is impracticable, (vi) with the same present class life, and (vii) placed in service in the same taxable year.

(3) *Election*.—The election under this paragraph shall be made for the taxable year in which the assets in the account are placed in service. The election shall apply, with respect to the account, throughout the applicable recovery period and for all subsequent taxable years. The taxpayer is not bound by such election with respect to assets placed in service in other taxable years, or with respect to other assets placed in service in the same taxable year, which may properly be included in another mass asset ac-

count (*e.g.*, assets with a different present class life).

(4) *Recovery of an increase in basis.*—To the extent that § 1.168-2(d)(2)(i) (relating to reductions in basis) applies, if as a result of early disposition of an asset in a mass asset account (determined in accordance with the provision of subparagraph (5) of this paragraph), the investment tax credit is recaptured (in accordance with section 47 and the regulations thereunder), then the basis of the account shall be increased by an amount equal to one-half of the amount of the recapture. Such increase shall be treated in a manner similar to § 1.168-2(d)(3), relating to redeterminations. For purposes of subparagraph (1) of this paragraph, such increase will be taken into account as unadjusted basis in determining the inclusion of proceeds as ordinary income.

(5) *Identification of dispositions for purposes of basis increase.*—For purposes of subparagraph (4) of this paragraph, disposition of assets from a mass asset account shall be determined by the use of an appropriate mortality dispersion table. If the taxpayer adopts recordkeeping practices consistent with his prior practices and consonant with good accounting and engineering practices, and supplies such reasonable information as may be required by the Commissioner, the mortality dispersion table may be based upon an acceptable sampling of the taxpayer's actual experience or other acceptable statistical or engineering techniques. Alternatively, the taxpayer may use the following standard mortality dispersion table:

STANDARD MORTALITY DISPERSION TABLE
PERCENTAGE OF BASIS OF MASS ASSET ACCOUNT CONSIDERED DISPOSED OF EACH 12-MONTH PERIOD AFTER THE ACCOUNT IS PLACED IN SERVICE

Present Class Life	*1st (1)*	*2nd (2)*	*3rd (3)*	*4th (4)*	*5th (5)*	*6th (6)*	*7th (7)*	*8th (8)*	*9th (9)*	*10th (10)*
2.5	3.59	23.84	45.14	23.84	3.59	...	...	...	...	...
3.0	2.28	13.59	34.13	34.13	13.59	2.28	...	...	...	...
3.5	1.62	8.23	23.51	33.28	23.51	8.23	1.62	...	...	...
4.0	1.22	5.46	15.98	27.34	27.34	15.98	5.46	1.22	...	...
5.0	.82	2.77	7.92	15.91	22.58	22.58	15.91	7.92	2.77	.82
6.0	.62	1.66	4.40	9.19	14.98	19.15	19.15	14.98	9.19	4.40
6.5	.55	1.33	3.38	7.25	12.00	16.39	18.20	16.39	12.00	7.25
7.0	.51	1.11	2.74	5.49	9.64	13.87	16.64	16.64	13.87	9.64
7.5	.47	.92	2.20	4.49	7.79	11.55	14.65	15.86	14.65	11.55
8.0	.44	.78	1.85	3.61	6.46	9.52	12.91	14.43	14.43	12.91
8.5	.40	.70	1.52	2.97	5.16	8.19	10.87	13.05	14.28	13.05
9.0	.38	.61	1.29	2.47	4.43	6.69	9.27	11.93	12.93	12.93
9.5	.37	.52	1.13	2.07	3.69	5.57	8.13	10.44	11.72	12.72
10 and 10.5	.35	.47	.97	1.80	3.09	4.83	6.90	9.01	10.79	11.79
11 and 11.5	.32	.39	.75	1.35	2.24	3.64	5.10	6.82	8.51	10.24
12 and 12.5	.30	.32	.60	1.06	1.73	2.67	3.88	5.31	6.79	8.19
13 and 13.5	.28	.27	.49	.84	1.34	2.04	3.12	4.13	5.37	6.63
14	.27	.24	.40	.71	1.06	1.68	2.32	3.17	4.38	5.26
15	.26	.21	.35	.57	.89	1.31	1.89	2.60	3.43	4.36
16 and 16.5	.25	.18	.29	.49	.75	1.10	1.48	2.13	2.83	3.83
17	.24	.16	.28	.42	.60	.92	1.30	1.67	2.34	2.82
18	.23	.15	.24	.37	.51	.78	1.08	1.39	1.93	2.50
19	.23	.14	.20	.32	.47	.66	.92	1.15	1.61	2.08
20-24	.22	.13	.19	.28	.40	.57	.77	1.03	1.36	1.73
25-29	.20	.09	.12	.18	.23	.31	.41	.53	.67	.85
30-50	.19	.07	.09	.12	.15	.20	.25	.32	.40	.49

Present Class Life	*11th (11)*	*12th (12)*	*13th (13)*	*14th (14)*	*15th (15)*	*16th (16)*	*17th (17)*	*18th (18)*	*19th (19)*	*20th (20)*
2.5	...	...	...	...	...	...	...	...	...	...
3.0	...	...	...	...	...	...	...	...	...	...
3.5	...	...	...	...	...	...	...	...	...	...
4.0	...	...	...	...	...	...	...	...	...	...
5.0	...	...	...	...	...	...	...	...	...	...
6.0	1.66	.62	...	...	...	...	...	...	...	...
6.5	3.38	1.33	.55	...	...	...	...	...	...	...
7.0	5.49	2.74	1.11	.51	...	...	...	...	...	...
7.5	7.70	4.49	2.20	.92	.47	...	...	...	...	...
8.0	9.52	6.46	3.61	1.85	.78	.44	...	...	...	...
8.5	10.87	8.19	5.16	2.97	1.52	.70	.40	...	...	...
9.0	11.93	9.27	6.69	4.43	2.47	1.29	.61	.38	...	...
9.5	11.72	10.44	8.13	5.57	3.69	2.07	1.13	.52	.37	...
10 and 10.5	11.79	10.79	9.01	6.90	4.83	3.09	1.80	.97	.47	.35
11 and 11.5	10.64	10.64	10.24	8.51	6.82	5.10	3.64	2.24	1.35	.75
12 and 12.5	9.28	9.87	9.87	9.28	8.19	6.79	5.31	3.88	2.67	1.73
13 and 13.5	7.77	8.62	9.10	9.10	8.62	7.77	6.63	5.37	4.13	3.12
14	6.62	7.25	8.32	8.32	8.32	8.32	7.25	6.62	5.26	4.38
15	5.32	6.23	7.04	7.61	7.93	7.93	7.61	7.04	6.23	5.32

Present Class Life	*11th (11)*	*12th (12)*	*13th (13)*	*14th (14)*	*15th (15)*	*16th (16)*	*17th (17)*	*18th (18)*	*19th (19)*	*20th (20)*
16 and 16.5	4.22	5.30	6.11	6.80	6.89	7.54	7.54	6.89	6.80	6.11
17	3.71	4.48	4.94	5.93	6.51	6.54	7.14	7.14	6.54	6.51
18	3.12	3.57	4.46	4.81	5.71	6.19	6.21	6.75	6.75	6.21
19	2.60	2.97	3.76	4.37	4.96	5.48	5.53	6.19	6.36	6.36
20-24	2.17	2.66	3.18	3.72	4.25	4.76	5.22	5.57	5.83	5.96
25-29	1.06	1.29	1.55	1.85	2.18	2.50	2.84	3.19	3.54	3.84
30-50	.59	.72	.87	1.02	1.20	1.40	1.60	1.83	2.86	2.30

Present Class Life	*21st (21)*	*22nd (22)*	*23rd (23)*	*24th (24)*	*25th (25)*	*26th (26)*	*27th (27)*	*28th (28)*	*29th (29)*	*30th (30)*
2.5	...	...	...	...	...	...	...	...	...	...
3.0	...	...	...	...	...	...	...	...	...	...
3.5	...	...	...	...	...	...	...	...	...	...
4.0	...	...	...	...	...	...	...	...	...	...
5.0	...	...	...	...	...	...	...	...	...	...
6.0	...	...	...	...	...	...	...	...	...	...
6.5	...	...	...	...	...	...	...	...	...	...
7.0	...	...	...	...	...	...	...	...	...	...
7.5	...	...	...	...	...	...	...	...	...	...
8.0	...	...	...	...	...	...	...	...	...	...
8.5	...	...	...	...	...	...	...	...	...	...
9.0	...	...	...	...	...	...	...	...	...	...
9.5	...	...	...	...	...	...	...	...	...	...
10 and 10.5	...	...	...	...	...	...	...	...	...	...
11 and 11.5	.39	.32	...	...	...	...	...	...	...	...
12 and 12.5	1.06	.60	.32	.30	...	...	...	...	...	...
13 and 13.5	2.04	1.34	.84	.49	.27	.28	...	...	...	...
14	3.17	2.32	1.68	1.06	.71	.40	.24	.27	...	...
15	4.36	3.43	2.60	1.89	1.31	.89	.57	.35	.21	.26
16 and 16.5	5.30	4.22	3.83	2.83	2.13	1.48	1.10	.75	.49	.29
17	5.93	4.94	4.48	3.71	2.82	2.34	1.67	1.30	.92	.60
18	6.19	5.71	4.81	4.46	3.57	3.12	2.50	1.93	1.39	1.08
19	6.19	5.53	5.48	4.96	4.37	3.76	2.97	2.60	2.08	1.61
20-24	5.96	5.83	5.57	5.22	4.76	4.25	3.72	3.18	2.66	2.17
25-29	4.13	4.38	4.58	4.70	4.78	4.78	4.70	4.58	4.38	4.13
30-50	2.54	2.78	3.01	3.23	3.42	3.61	3.75	3.86	3.95	3.98

For purposes of applying the standard mortality dispersion table, all assets in a mass asset account placed in service during a taxable year are considered to be placed in service on the same day. If the taxpayer uses the standard mortality dispersion table for a taxable year, such table must be used for all subsequent taxable years unless the taxpayer obtains the consent of the Commissioner.

(6) *Transitional rule.*—Unless the taxpayer establishes to the contrary (by statistical methods or otherwise), all proceeds realized upon the disposition of assets from one or more mass asset accounts shall be considered realized with respect to accounts placed in service by the taxpayer after December 31, 1980.

(i) [Reserved]

(j) *Changes in use.*—(1) *Conversion from personal use or use in tax-exempt activity.*—If property which was previously used by the taxpayer for personal purposes or in a tax-exempt activity is converted to use in a trade or business or for the production of income during the taxable year, then the recovery allowance for the taxable year (and subsequent taxable years) shall be determined as though the property were placed in service by the taxpayer as recovery property on the date on which the conversion occurs. Thus, the recovery allowance shall be determined by multiplying the unadjusted basis (as provided in subparagraph (6)(ii) of this paragraph) by the applicable percentage.

(2) *Increased business use of property.*—If a taxpayer uses property in a trade or business (or for the production of income) and for personal (or tax-exempt) purposes during a recovery period, and increases the business (or income-producing) use of such property after the recovery for that period is completed, then a recovery allowance shall continue to be allowed with respect to such property. The amount of the allowance shall be determined as though, to the extent of the increase in business (or income-producing) use, the property were placed in service by the taxpayer as recovery property at the beginning of the taxable year in which such increased use occurs. Thus, the recovery allowance for the taxable year shall be determined first by multiplying the unadjusted basis (as provided in subparagraph (6)(ii) of this paragraph) by the applicable percentage, and then by the excess of the percentage of the business (or income-producing) use during the taxable year over the average of such use during the prior recovery period (or periods). The combined recovery under this subparagraph and subparagraph (1) shall not exceed the original cost of the property. See Example (2) of subparagraph (7) of this paragraph.

(3) *Domestic property changing recovery classes.*—(i) When the class of recovery property not used predominantly outside the United States changes during the taxable year, and the property continues to be used as recovery property by the taxpayer (*e.g.*, when property ceases to be used predominantly in connection with research and experimentation) the following rules apply:

(A) If the change results in the property's being assigned to a class with a shorter recovery period, then the recovery allowance for the taxable year in which the change occurs (and subsequent taxable years) shall be determined as though the property were placed in service as recovery property in the year of the change. Thus, the recovery allowance shall be determined by multiplying the unadjusted basis (as provided in subparagraph (6)(ii) of this paragraph) by the applicable percentage. Alternatively, the taxpayer may continue to treat the property as though the change had not occurred.

(B) If the change results in the property's being assigned to a class with a longer recovery period, then the recovery allowance for the taxable year of the change (and subsequent taxable years) shall be determined as though the property had originally been assigned to that longer recovery class. Proper adjustment shall be made under the principles of §1.168-2(d)(3) (relating to redeterminations) to account for the deductions allowable to the taxpayer with respect to the property prior to the year of the change in excess of those which would have been allowable had the taxpayer used the applicable percentages for the longer recovery class for those years.

(4) *Foreign property.*—(i) If recovery property ceases being used predominantly outside the United States during a taxable year, and the property continues to be used as recovery property by the taxpayer, then the recovery allowance for the taxable year (and subsequent taxable years) shall be determined as though the property were placed in service as recovery property in the year of the cessation. Thus, the recovery allowance shall be determined by multiplying the unadjusted basis (as provided in subparagraph (6)(ii) of this paragraph) by the applicable percentage. Alternatively, the taxpayer may continue to treat the property as though the cessation had not occurred. See §§1.168-5(e)(5) and 1.1016-3(a)(3)(iii) and (iv).

(ii) If the recovery property begins to be used by the taxpayer predominantly outside the United States during a taxable year after having been used otherwise by the taxpayer as recovery property in the previous taxable year, then the recovery allowance for the taxable year in which the change occurs (and subsequent years) shall be determined as though the property had originally been placed in service by the taxpayer as recovery property used predominantly outside the United States. Proper adjustment shall be made under the principles of §1.168-2(d)(3) to account for the difference between the deductions allowable with respect to the property prior to the year of the change and those which would have been allowable had the taxpayer used the applicable percentages for property used predominantly outside the United States for those years.

(5) *Low income housing.*—If 15-year real property begins or ceases to be low income housing (as defined in §1.168-2(b)(2) (iii)) during a taxable year, then the recovery allowance for the taxable year in which the change occurs (and subsequent taxable years) shall be determined under the principles of paragraph (j)(3)(i)(B) and (4) (ii) of this section.

(6) *Special rules.*—(i) For purposes of this paragraph, if, prior to a change in status, the taxpayer used the optional applicable percentages (under paragraph (c) or (g)(3) of this section) with respect to recovery property, then similar optional percentages shall be used with respect to the property after the change.

(ii) For purposes of subparagraphs (1) and (2) of this paragraph, the unadjusted basis shall be the lesser of the fair market value or the adjusted basis of the property (taking into account the adjustments described in section 1016(a)(3)) at the time of the conversion to use in the taxpayer's trade or business (or for the production of income), or at the beginning of the taxable year in which the increase in business (or income-producing) use occurs, as the case may be. For purposes of subparagraphs (3)(i)(A) and (4)(i) of this paragraph, the unadjusted basis shall be the adjusted basis of the property (taking into account the adjustments described in section 1016(a)(2) and (3)) at the beginning of the year in which the change or cessation occurs.

(7) *Examples.*—The following examples illustrate the application of this paragraph:

Example (1). A, a calendar year taxpayer, purchases a house in 1981 which he occupies as his principal residence. In June 1985, A ceases to occupy the house and converts it to rental property. Under paragraph (j)(1) of this section, for purposes of determining the recovery allowance, A is deemed to have placed the house in service as recovery property in June 1985. A does not elect to compute the recovery allowance by use of the optional recovery method provided in §1.168-2(c). Thus, A's recovery allowance under section 168 for 1985 is determined by multiplying the unadjusted basis of the property by .07. Under paragraph (j)(6)(ii) of this section, the unadjusted basis is the lesser of the property's basis or its fair market value in June 1985. See also section 280A and the regulations thereunder.

Example (2). In 1981, B (a calendar year taxpayer) purchases an automobile for $10,000. In taxable years 1981 through 1983, B's business use of the automobile is 60 percent of his total use. B does not elect use of the optional percentages provided in §1.168-2(c). The fair market value of the automobile at the beginning of 1984 is $7,500. In 1984, B's business use of the automobile is 70 percent of the total. B's allowable deduction for 1984 is $187.50, computed as follows: $7,500 (lesser of basis or fair market value) × .25 (applicable percentage) × .10 (increase in the percentage business use in 1984 (70 percent) over the average business use during 1981-1983 (60 percent)). In 1985, B's business use of the automobile is 50 percent of the total. B is entitled to no recovery allowance with respect to the automobile for 1985 since B's business use of the automobile in that year does not exceed the average business use during 1981-1983 (60 percent). In 1986, B's business use of the automobile is 75 percent of the total. B's allowable deduction for 1986 is $416.25 computed as follows: $7,500 (lesser of basis or fair market value in 1984) × .37 (applicable percentage) × .15 (increase in the percentage business use in 1986 (75 percent) over the average business use during 1981-1983 (60 percent)).

Example (3). In 1981 C, a calendar year taxpayer, purchases for $20,000 and places in service section 1245 class property used predominantly in connection with research and experimentation. C does not elect to compute the recovery allowance by use of the optional method as provided in § 1.168-2(c). In 1981 C's allowable deduction is $5,000 (*i.e.*, .25 × $20,000). In 1982 C continues to use the property as recovery property, but not predominantly in connection with research and experimentation. As a result, in 1982 the property is treated as 5-year property. C's recovery allowance for 1982 (and subsequent taxable years) is determined as though C had placed the property in service in 1981 as 5-year property. The excess recovery allowance allowed in 1981 is accounted for in accordance with § 1.168-2(d)(3). Thus, the difference between the recovery allowance which would have been allowed had the applicable percentage for 5-year property been used (*i.e.*, .15 × $20,000 = $3,000) and the recovery allowance allowed in 1981 (*i.e.*, .25 × $20,000 = $5,000) equals $2,000 and is accounted for as follows:

Unadjusted basis × applicable percentage for second recovery year ($20,000.00 × .22)	$4,400.00
Excess allowance × applicable percentage for second recovery year ÷ the sum of the remaining unused applicable percentages (($2,000.00 × .22)/.85)	– 517.65
Difference—allowable deduction for 1982	$3,882.35

Example (4). In 1981 D, a calendar year taxpayer, places in service 5-year recovery property with an unadjusted basis of $100,000 and a present class life of 8 years. D uses the property predominantly outside the United States in 1981, 1982, and 1983. D does not elect to compute the recovery allowance by use of the optional method as provided in § 1.168-2(g)(3). In 1984 D uses the property as recovery property but not predominantly outside the United States. D's allowable deduction for 1984 (and subsequent taxable years) is determined as though D placed the property in service in 1984 as recovery property not used predominantly outside the United States. The basis of the property is deemed to be the adjusted basis in 1984. Thus, D's allowable deduction for 1984 is $7,350 (*i.e.*, .15 × $49,000 (basis)) and for 1985 is $10,780 (*i.e.*, .22 × $49,000 (basis)). If D elected to use the optional method based on the present class life, D would use the optional percentages based on a 5-year recovery period. Alternatively, D may continue to treat the property as though it continued to be used predominantly outside the United States. If so treated D's allowable deductions for 1984 and 1985 would be $12,000 (*i.e.*, .12 × $100,000) and $9,000 (.09 × $100,000), respectively.

Example (5). The facts are the same as in example (4) except that the recovery property is not used predominantly outside the United States for 1981 through 1983. In 1984, however, D begins using the property predominantly outside the United States. D's allowable deduction for 1984 is determined as though D placed the property in service in 1981 as property used predominantly outside the United States. Additionally, D accounts for the difference between the recovery allowance for 1981 through 1983 ($58,000) and the allowance which would have been allowable for those years had the applicable percentages for property used predominantly outside the United States been used ($51,000) in accordance with § 1.168-2(d)(3). Thus, the recovery allowance in 1984 is $10,285.71, determined as follows:

Unadjusted basis × applicable percentage for 4th recovery year for property with an 8-year present class life ($100,000.00 × .12)	$12,000.00
Excess recovery from 1981 through 1983 × applicable percentage for 4th recovery year ÷ the sum of the remaining unused applicable percentages (($7,000.00 × .12)/.49)	– 1,714.29
Difference	$10,285.71

If, for 1981 through 1983, D elected to use the optional method based on a 5-year recovery period, then the allowable deduction for 1984 and subsequent taxable years would be determined using the optional percentages over the 8-year present class life.

(k) *Ratable inclusion rule.*—(1) *General rule.*—In general, the recovery allowance provided by section 168 and this section shall be considered as accruing ratably over the taxable year. Thus, for example, the distributive share of the recovery allowance for each partner in a partnership in which a partner's partnership interest varies so as to be subject to section 706(c)(2)(B) shall be determined by allocating to each partner a pro rata share of such allowance for the entire taxable year of the partnership. This paragraph does not apply, however, in determining the recovery allowance for the taxable year in which 15-year real property is placed in service or disposed of.

(2) *Example.*—The provisions of this subparagraph are illustrated by the following example:

Example. In 1978 A and B each acquire 50 percent interests in partnership P which is in the business of renting and managing beach resort property. On December 1, 1983, C and D each acquire from the partnership 25 percent interests in the partnership. On December 15, 1983, the partnership acquires for rental and places in service two sailboats (5-year recovery property) for $10,000 each. No election is made to use the optional recovery percentages provided by § 1.168-2(c). The recovery allowance for P for the sailboats in 1983 equals $3,000 (*i.e.*, .15 × $20,000). The recovery allowance, however, must be allocated pro rata over the taxable year. As such, the distributive share of the recovery allowance for A and B is $1,437.50 each. The distributive share of the recovery allowance for C and D is $62.50 each.

(l) *Definitions.*—For purposes of section 168 and §§ 1.168-1 through 1.168-6—

(1) *Disposition.*—The term "disposition" means the permanent withdrawal of property from use in the taxpayer's trade or business or use for the production of income. Withdrawal may be made in several ways, including sale, exchange, retirement, abandonment, or destruction. A disposition does not include a transfer of property by gift or by reason of the death of the

taxpayer. See §1.168-5(f)(3) and (4). A disposition also does not include the retirement of a structural component of 15-year real property. The manner of disposition (*e.g.*, ordinary retirement, abnormal retirement) is not a consideration. For rules relating to nonrecognition transactions see section 168(f)(7) and (10)) and the regulations thereunder. For rules relating to the recognition of gain or loss on dispositions, see §1.168-6.

(2) *Placed in service.*—The term "placed in service" means the time that property is first placed by the taxpayer in a condition or state of readiness and availability for a specifically assigned function, whether for use in a trade or business, for the production of income, in a tax-exempt activity, or in a personal activity. In the case of a building which is intended to house machinery and equipment, such readiness and availability shall be determined without regard to whether the machinery or equipment which the building houses, or is intended to house, has been placed in service. However, in an appropriate case, as, for example, where the building is essentially an item of machinery or equipment, or the use of the building is so closely related to the use of the machinery or equipment that it clearly can be expected to be replaced or retired when the property it initially houses is replaced or retired, the determination of readiness or availability of the building shall be made by taking into account the readiness and availability of such machinery or equipment. For a building which becomes available for use in separate stages, see paragraph (e)(3) of this section.

(3) *Recovery year.*—The term "recovery year" means the taxable year during which recovery property is placed in service by the taxpayer and each subsequent taxable year for which a deduction is allowable to the taxpayer under this section with respect to such property.

(4) *Recovery period.*—The term "recovery period" means the actual period of years assigned, or elected by the taxpayer, for the computation under this section of the recovery allowance with respect to the unadjusted basis of the recovery property (*e.g.*, 3 years, 5 years, 12 years, present class life). The recovery period does not include any year after the end of the period assigned or elected, even though under paragraph (c), (g)(3), or (m) of this section a year following the recovery period may be a recovery year (as defined in subparagraph (3)).

(m) *Limitation on property financed with proceeds of industrial development bonds.*—[Reserved]

(n) [Withdrawn.]

[Reg. §1.168-2.]

§1.168-3. Recovery property.—(a) *Recovery property.*—(1) *In general.*—Except as provided in §1.168-4, "recovery property" to which ACRS applies means tangible property of a character subject to the allowance for depreciation which is—

(i) Used in a trade or business, or

(ii) Held for the production of income.

Property is considered recovery property only if such property would have been depreciable under section 167. Thus, ACRS applies only to that part of the property which is subject to wear and tear, to decay or decline from natural causes, to exhaustion, and to obsolescence. ACRS does not apply to inventories or stock in trade, works of art, or to land apart from the improvements or physical development added to it. ACRS does not apply to natural resources which are subject to the allowance for depletion provided in section 611. No deduction shall be allowed under ACRS for automobiles or other vehicles used solely for pleasure, for a building used by the taxpayer solely as his residence, or for furniture or furnishings therein, personal effects, or clothing; but properties and costumes used exclusively in a business, such as a theatrical business, may be recovery property. For rules regarding the recovery allowance for property which is used partly for business and partly for personal purposes, or which is converted from personal to business use, see §§1.168-2(d)(2)(ii) and 1.168-2(j)(1) and (2).

(2) *Intangible property.*—[Reserved]

(3) *Boilers fueled by oil or gas.*—The term "recovery property" includes property described in section 167(p), relating to boilers fueled by oil or gas, if such property otherwise qualifies as "recovery property" under section 168 and subparagraph (1) of this paragraph.

(b) *Classes of recovery property.*—Each item of recovery property shall be assigned to one of the following classes of property:

(1) 3-year property,

(2) 5-year property,

(3) 10-year property,

(4) 15-year real property, or

(5) 15-year public utility property.

Any property which is treated as included in a class of property by reason of paragraph (c)(1), (2), (3), (4), or (5) of this §1.168-3 shall not be treated as property included in any other class.

(c) *3-, 5-, 10-, and 15-year recovery property; definitions.*—(1) *3-year property.*—The following recovery property is included in the 3-year class:

(i) Section 1245 class property (as defined in paragraph (c)(6) of this §1.168-3) with a present class life (as defined in paragraph (c)(8)) of 4 years or less,

(ii) Section 1245 class property predominantly used in connection with research and experimentation (as described in section 174 and §1.174-2(a)). Property is used in connection with research and experimentation if the property is used (A) by its owner to conduct research and experimentation in its owner's trade or business, (B) by its owner to conduct research and experimentation for another person, (C) by a lessee to conduct research and experimentation in its trade or business, or (D) by the lessee to conduct research and experimentation for another person, and

(iii) Any race horse which is more than 2 years old at the time the horse is placed in service and any other horse which is more than 12 years old at the time the horse is placed in service. A horse is more than 2 (or 12) years old after 24 (or 144) months after its actual birthdate. Examples of 3-year recovery property are automobiles and light-duty trucks.

(2) *5-year property.*—The following recovery property is included in the 5-year class: Section 1245 class property which is not 3-year property (as defined in paragraph (c)(1)), or 10-year property (as defined in paragraph (c)(3)), or 15-year public utility property (as defined in paragraph (c)(5) and (10)). Included in the 5-year recovery property class are horses which are not included in the 3-year recovery property class,

property which, prior to January 1, 1981, may have been depreciated under the retirement-replacement-betterment method (subject to the provisions of § 1.168-5(a)), single-purpose agricultural and horticultural structures, and storage facilities (other than buildings and their structural components) used in connection with the distribution of petroleum or any of its primary products. Primary products of petroleum are products described in § 1.993-3(g)(3)(i).

(3) *10-year property.*—The following recovery property is included in the 10-year class:

(i) Public utility property with a present class life of more than 18 years but not more than 25 years, other than section 1250 class property (as defined in paragraph (c)(7)) or 3-year property,

(ii) Section 1250 class property with a present class life of 12.5 years or less,

(iii) Railroad tank cars,

(iv) Manufactured homes (as defined in 42 U.S.C. section 5402(6)) which are section 1250 class property used as dwelling units, and

(v) Qualified coal utilization property (as defined in paragraph (c)(9)) which would otherwise be 15-year public utility property.

A building (and its structural components, if any) is not treated as having a present class life of 12.5 years or less if, in its original use (as defined in paragraph (c)(11) of this § 1.168-3), the building (and its structural components, if any) does not have a present class life of 12.5 years or less. Thus, for example, a theme park structure is considered 10-year property only if the original use of such structure is as a theme park structure.

(4) *15-year real property.*—Fifteen-year real property is section 1250 class property which does not have a present class life of 12.5 years or less (including section 1250 class property which does not have a present class life). Examples of 15-year real property are office buildings and elevators and escalators.

(5) *15-year public utility property.*—Fifteen-year public utility property is public utlity property, other than section 1250 class property or 3-year property, with a present class life of more than 25 years. Examples of 15-year public utility property are: most property in electric utility steam production plants, gas utility manufactured gas production plants, water utility property, and telephone distribution plants.

(6) *Section 1245 class property defined.*—For purposes of section 168 and §§ 1.168-1 through 1.168-6, section 1245 class property is tangible property described in section 1245(a)(3) (other than subparagraphs (C) and (D)). See § 1.168-4 for exclusion of certain "section 1245 class property" from recovery property.

(7) *Section 1250 class property defined.*—For purposes of section 168 and §§ 1.168-1 through 1.168-6, section 1250 class property is property described in section 1250(c) and property described in section 1245(a)(3)(C). See § 1.168-4 for exclusion of certain "section 1250 class property" from recovery property.

(8) *Present class life defined.*—(i) For purposes of section 168 and §§ 1.168-1 through 1.168-6, present class life is the asset depreciation range (ADR) class life ("midpoint" or "asset guideline period") (if any) applicable with respect to the property as of January 1, 1981, published in Rev. Proc. 83-35. No changes will be made to the classes or class lives which are set forth in Rev. Proc. 83-35.

(ii) The application of subdivision (i) may be illustrated by the following example:

Example. X purchases a light-duty truck to be used in his trade or business. The ADR midpoint life of this asset as of January 1, 1981, determined under Rev. Proc. 83-35 is 4 years. Since this truck is section 1245 class property with a present class life of 4 years or less, it is 3-year recovery property under section 168.

(9) *Qualified coal utilization property.*—See section 168(g)(8) for the definition of "qualified coal utilization property".

(10) *Public utility property.*—(i) For purposes of section 168 and §§ 1.168-1 through 1.168-6, the term "public utility property" means property used predominantly in the trade or business of the furnishing or sale of—

(A) Electrical energy, water, or sewage disposal services,

(B) Gas or steam through a local distribution system,

(C) Telephone services, or other communication services if furnished or sold by the Communications Satellite Corporation for purposes authorized by the Communications Satellite Act of 1962 (47 U.S.C. section 701), or

(D) Transportation of gas or steam by pipeline, if the rates for such furnishing or sale, as the case may be, are regulated, *i.e.*, are established or approved by a State (including the District of Columbia) or political subdivision thereof, by any agency or instrumentality of the United States, or by a public service or public utility commission or other similar body of any State or political subdivision thereof. A taxpayer's rates are "regulated" if they are established or approved on a rate-of-return basis. Rates regulated on a rate-of-return basis are an authorization to collect revenues that cover the taxpayer's cost of providing goods or services, including a fair return on the taxpayer's investment in providing such goods or services, where the taxpayer's costs and investment are determined by use of a uniform system of accounts prescribed by the regulatory body. A taxpayer's rates are not "regulated" if they are established or approved on the basis of maintaining competition within an industry, insuring adequate service to customers of an industry, insuring adequate security for loans, or charging "reasonable" rates within an industry since the taxpayer is not authorized to collect revenues based on the taxpayer's cost of providing goods or services. Rates are considered to be "established or approved" if a schedule of rates is filed with a regulatory body that has the power to approve such rates, even though the regulatory body takes no action on the filed schedule or generally leaves undisturbed rates filed by the taxpayer.

(ii) Public utility property includes property which is leased to others by a taxpayer, where the leasing of such property is part of the lessor's public utility activity, as described in subdivision (i). Public utility property also includes property leased to a person who uses such property predominantly in a public utility activity, as described in subdivision (i).

(11) *"Original use".*—The term "original use" means the first use to which the property is put, whether or not such use corresponds to the

use of such property by the taxpayer. [Reg. § 1.168-3.]

§ 1.168-4. Exclusions from ACRS.—(a) *Property placed in service by the taxpayer before January 1, 1981.*—ACRS does not apply with respect to property placed in service by the taxpayer before January 1, 1981. See § 1.168-2(l)(2) for when property is placed in service. As provided in paragraph (d) of this section, ACRS does not apply with respect to property placed in service before January 1, 1981, which is transferred in certain "churning" transactions. If property is excluded from ACRS, the provisions of section 167 (and related provisions) apply in determining the allowable depreciation deduction with respect to such property.

(b) *Property amortized or depreciated other than in terms of years.*—(1) *Depreciation.*—If—

(i) Property can properly be depreciated under a method not expressed in a term of years (such as unit-of-production) which, before January 1, 1981, was a recognized method within the particular industry for the type of property in question, and

(ii) The taxpayer properly elects such treatment for such property in accordance with section 168(f)(4) and § 1.168-5(e) for the first taxable year for which an ACRS deduction would (but for this election) be allowable with respect to such property in the hands of the taxpayer,

then such property shall be entirely excluded from ACRS so long as it remains in the hands of such taxpayer. A taxpayer may elect to apply a depreciation method not expressed in a term of years (and thereby exclude the property from ACRS) with respect to some or all property within the same recovery class and placed in service in the same taxable year.

(2) *Amortization.*—If—

(i) The basis of a recovery property may be amortized, in lieu of being depreciated, under any section of the Code (such as section 167(k), relating to expenditures to rehabilitate low-income rental housing, or section 169, relating to pollution control facilities), and

(ii) The taxpayer properly elects to amortize such property in accordance with the relevant amortization provision,

then the amount subject to such amortization shall be excluded from the property's unadjusted basis as defined in section 168(d)(1)(A) and § 1.168-2(d). A taxpayer may elect amortization with respect to one property (or a portion thereof) and apply ACRS with respect to other property (or the remaining portion) within the same recovery class and placed in service in the same taxable year.

(c) *Special rule for public utility property.*—[Reserved]

(d) *Anti-churning rules for certain transactions in property placed in service before 1981.*—(1) *In general.*—To be eligible for ACRS, property must be placed in service by the taxpayer after 1980. The anti-churning rules of section 168(e)(4) and this paragraph (d) are designed generally to deny ACRS to property in service before 1981 in the absence of a significant change in ownership or use.

(2) *Section 1245 class property.*—(i) *In general.*—Section 1245 class property, as defined in section 168(g)(3) and § 1.168-3(c)(6), acquired by the taxpayer after December 31, 1980, will not qualify for ACRS if—

(A) The property was owned or used at any time during 1980 by the taxpayer or a related person,

(B) The property is acquired from a person who owned such property at any time during 1980, and, as part of the transaction, the user of the property does not change,

(C) The property is leased by the taxpayer for more than 3 months to a person (or a person related to such person) who owned or used such property at any time during 1980, or

(D) The property is acquired in a transaction in which the user of such property does not change, and the property does not qualify for ACRS in the hands of the person from whom the property is so acquired due to subdivisions (B) and (C) of this paragraph (d)(2)(i).

See section 168(e)(4)(D) and subparagraph (6) of this paragraph (d) for definition of the term "related person". See subparagraph (3) of this paragraph (d) for the treatment of the acquisition of section 1245 class property acquired incidental to the acquisition of section 1250 class property. See subparagraph (4) of this paragraph (d) for other special rules.

(ii) *Change in user.*—For purposes of subdivision (i) of this paragraph (d)(2), the user of a section 1245 class property shall not be considered to have changed as part of a transaction if the property is physically used, for more than 3 months after its transfer, by the same person (or a related person) who used such property before the transfer, or if such person, pursuant to a plan, resumes use of the property after the transfer. If the former owner (or a related person) continues to operate section 1245 class property through an arrangement such as a management contract for more than 3 months after the transfer, then all facts and circumstances will be taken into account in determining whether the user of the property has changed as part of such transaction for purposes of section 168(e)(4)(A) and subdivision (i) of this paragraph (d)(2). Among the factors which would indicate that the user of section 1245 property has changed in such case are—

(A) The arrangement in question is a customary commercial practice,

(B) The transaction in question has been arranged at arm's length, and

(C) The new owner has assumed all benefits and burdens of ownership. For purposes of this subdivision (ii)(C), the former owner will not be considered to have retained any benefits and burdens of ownership solely by reason of receiving contingent payments if such payments—

(1) Represent the real value of services rendered,

(2) Are reasonable in amount, and

(3) Are ordinary and customary in both nature and amount within the industry and region for the transaction in question.

(3) *Section 1250 class property.*—A section 1250 class property, as defined in section 168(g)(4) and § 1.168-3(c)(7), acquired by the taxpayer after December 31, 1980, will not qualify for ACRS if—

(i) The property was owned at any time during 1980 by the taxpayer or a related person,

(ii) The property is leased by the taxpayer for more than 3 months to a person (or a person related to such person) who owned such property at any time during 1980, or

(iii) The property is acquired in an exchange described in section 1031 (relating to exchange of property held for productive use or investment), section 1033 (relating to involuntary conversions), section 1038 (relating to certain reacquisitions of real property), or section 1039 (relating to certain sales of low-income housing projects), to the extent that the basis of such property includes an amount representing the adjusted basis of other property owned by the taxpayer or a related person at any time during 1980. The excess of the basis of the property acquired over the adjusted basis of such other property shall be considered a separate item of property, eligible for ACRS, provided that the exchange is not otherwise treated as a "churning" transaction under section 168(e)(4) and this paragraph. Property which does not qualify for ACRS under this subdivision shall be considered, for purposes of this section, as owned by the taxpayer during 1980.

See section 168(e)(4)(D) and subparagraph (6) of this paragraph (d) for definition of the term "related person". If, in a transaction, section 1245 class property is acquired incidental to the acquisition of section 1250 class property, then the rules of section 168(e)(4)(B) and this subparagraph shall apply with respect to the section 1245 property acquired in such transaction instead of the rules of section 168(e)(4)(A) and paragraph (d)(2) of this section. The preceding sentence will not apply in transactions where section 1245 property constitutes a significant portion of the property acquired.

(4) *Special rules.*—(i) *Property under construction during 1980.*—For purposes of paragraph (d)(2) and (3) of this section, a taxpayer shall not be deemed to own property under construction during 1980 until it is placed in service, as described in § 1.168-2(1)(2).

(ii) *Entire property excluded.*—Except as provided in paragraph (d)(3)(iii) of this section (relating to excess basis in substituted basis transactions), subdivision (iii) of this paragraph (d)(4) (relating to the lease of a portion of section 1250 class property), and paragraph (d)(6)(ii)(C) of this section (relating to transactions between persons related by reason of the application of § 1.267(b)-1(b)), if property is acquired in a transaction described in paragraph (d)(2) or (3) of this section, the entire property shall be excluded from ACRS.

(iii) *Lease of portion of section 1250 class property.*—Paragraph (d)(3)(ii) of this section (relating to the lease of section 1250 class property) shall apply only with respect to that portion of the property (determined on a fair market value basis) that is leased to the person (or to a person related to such person) who owned the property during 1980. The portion of the property excluded from ACRS shall not exceed the portion of the property which was owned by the lessee (or a person related to the lessee) during 1980.

(iv) *Undivided interests.*—Subject to the provisions of paragraph (d)(7) of this section (relating to avoidance), if an undivided interest in property is acquired, and the resulting arrangement is not a partnership for tax purposes, then such interest shall be treated as a separate item of property for purposes of paragraph (d)(2) and (3) of this section.

(v) *Acquisition by or lease to 1980 owner or user.*—If recovery property is acquired by, or leased to, its 1980 owner (or, in the case of section 1245 class property, its 1980 owner or user), or a related person, then the property shall cease to qualify for ACRS.

(vi) *Sale-leaseback of disqualified property.*—If property which does not qualify for ACRS under this section becomes the subject of a sale-leaseback transaction, then the property shall not become ACRS property by virtue of that transaction.

(5) *Certain nonrecognition transactions.*—(i) *In general.*—With respect to property placed in service by the transferor or distributor before January 1, 1981, and which is acquired by the taxpayer after December 31, 1980, in a nonrecognition transaction described in section 168(e)(4)(C) and in subdivision (ii) of this paragraph (d)(5), ACRS shall not apply to the extent that the property's basis in the hands of the taxpayer is determined by reference to its basis in the hands of the transferor or distributor. In such a transaction, the taxpayer shall be treated as the transferor or distributor for purposes of computing the depreciation allowance under section 167 with respect to so much of the basis of the acquired property in the hands of the taxpayer as does not exceed its adjusted basis in the hands of the transferor or distributor. However, the taxpayer shall treat the portion of the basis of the acquired property which exceeds the adjusted basis in the hands of the transferor or distributor as a separate item of property, eligible for ACRS, provided that sale or exchange of such property by the transferor or distributor to the taxpayer would not be treated as a "churning" transaction under section 168(e)(4) and this paragraph.

(ii) *Nonrecognition transactions affected.*—Subdivision (i) of this paragraph (d)(5) applies to transactions described in any of the following provisions:

(A) Section 332 (relating to distributions in complete liquidation of an 80 percent or more controlled subsidiary corporation) except where the basis of the assets distributed is determined under section 334(b)(2) (as in effect on August 31, 1982);

(B) Section 351 (relating to transfer to a corporation controlled by transferor);

(C) Section 361 (relating to exchanges pursuant to certain corporate reorganizations);

(D) Section 371(a) (relating to exchanges pursuant to certain receivership and bankruptcy proceedings);

(E) Section 374(a) (relating to exchanges pursuant to certain railroad reorganizations);

(F) Section 721 (relating to transfers to a partnership in exchange for a partnership interest); and

(G) Section 731 (relating to distributions by a partnership to a partner).

A distribution of property by a partnership to a partner in liquidation of the partner's interest in the partnership (where the basis of the distributed property to the partner is determined under section 732(b)) is not a transaction described in section 168(e)(4)(C) and this subdivision (ii) since, in such case, the basis of the property is determined by reference to the partner's adjusted basis in his interest in the partnership and not by reference to the basis of the property in the hands of the partnership. However, such distribution may be described in paragraph (d)(2) or (3) of this section.

(iii) *Successive application.*—Property which does not qualify for ACRS by reason of its acquisition in a nonrecognition transaction will not qualify for ACRS if it is subsequently transferred in another nonrecognition transaction. The preceding sentence shall apply to the extent that the basis of the property in the hands of the transferee does not exceed the basis that does not qualify for ACRS in the hands of the transferor.

(6) *Related person defined.*—(i) *In general.*—For purposes of this paragraph (d) except as provided in section 168(e)(4)(E) and in subparagraph (11) of this paragraph (d), persons are related if—

(A) They bear a relationship specified in section 267(b) or section 707(b)(1) and the regulations thereunder, or

(B) They are engaged in trades or businesses under common control (as defined by subsections (a) and (b) of section 52 and the regulations thereunder).

For purposes of applying section 267(b) and 707(b)(1) with respect to this paragraph (d)(6), "10 percent" shall be substituted for "50 percent".

(ii) *Special rules.*—(A) In general, persons are related if they are related either immediately before or immediately after the taxpayer's acquisition of the property in question. When a partnership's acquisition of property results from the termination of another partnership under section 708(b)(1)(B), whether the acquiring partnership is related to such other partnership shall be determined by comparing the ownership of the acquiring partnership immediately after the acquisition with that of the terminated partnership as it existed immediately before the event resulting in such termination occurs. Similarly, when the acquisition of property by a partner results from the termination of a partnership under section 708(b)(1)(A), whether the acquiring person is related to the partnership shall be determined immediately before the event resulting in such termination occurs.

(B) If a person would be related to a corporation, partnership, or trust which owned (or, in the case of section 1245 class property, owned or used) property during 1980 but for the fact that such corporation, partnership, or trust is no longer in existence when the taxpayer acquires such property, then, for purposes of this subparagraph (6), such corporation, partnership, or trust is deemed to be in existence when the taxpayer acquires such property. Similarly, when a taxpayer leases property to a newly-created corporation, partnership, or trust, and a person who owned (or, in the case of section 1245 class property, owned or used) such property during 1980 would be related to the lessee but for the fact that such corporation, partnership, or trust is not in existence when the taxpayer acquires such property, then, for purposes of this subparagraph (6), such corporation, partnership, or trust is deemed to be in existence when the taxpayer acquires such property.

(C) If persons are related by reason of the application of § 1.267(b)-1(b), then only a portion of the property shall be excluded from ACRS, consistent with the principles of § 1.267(b)-1(b). See, however, paragraph (d)(7) of this section (relating to avoidance).

(D) If persons are not considered to be engaged in trades or businesses under common control (as defined by subsections (a) and (b) of section 52 and the regulations thereunder), but are considered to be related persons by substituting "10 percent" for "50 percent" within the provisions of section 267(b) or 707(b)(1), then such persons are considered to be related persons for purposes of this subparagraph (6).

(7) *Avoidance purpose indicated.*—Property acquired by the taxpayer after December 31, 1980, does not qualify for ACRS if it is acquired in a transaction one of whose principal purposes is to avoid the operation of the effective date rule of section 168(e)(1) and the "anti-churning" rules of section 168(e)(4), and the rules of this section. A transaction will be presumed to have a principal purpose of avoidance if it does not effect a significant change in ownership or use of property in service before 1981 commensurate with that otherwise required for ACRS to apply. Among the circumstances in which a principal avoidance purpose may be indicated, and in which the property involved in the transfer may therefore be ineligible for ACRS, are—

(i) The same person owns (other than as a nominee), directly or indirectly, more than a 10 percent interest in the taxpayer (or the taxpayer's lessee) and in a person who owned (or, in the case of section 1245 class property, owned or used) the property during 1980;

(ii) There is a mere change in form of the ownership of property owned by a person during 1980 (such as from a partnership to undivided interests);

(iii) The taxpayer (or the taxpayer's lessee) and a person who owned (or, in the case of section 1245 class property, owned or used) the property during 1980 are engaged in trades or businesses under common control within the meaning of section 52(a) and (b) and the regulations thereunder, substituting a 25 percent test for the 50 percent tests of § 1.52-1, or there is a similar 25 percent common ownership in the property (or in a leasehold of the property) and in a person who owned (or, in the case of section 1245 class property, owned or used) the property during 1980;

(iv) The taxpayer (or the taxpayer's lessee) is related during 1980 to the person who owned (or, in the case of section 1245 class property, owned or used) the property during 1980;

(v) Section 1250 class property is operated by a person who owned such property during 1980 (or by a related person) under a management contract and, had such property been section 1245 class property instead of section 1250 class property, the user would be considered not to have changed as part of the transaction (see § 1.168-4(d)(2)(ii));

(vi) The taxpayer leases section 1250 class property to a person and, through one or more subleases, the property is leased to a person who owned such property during 1980 (or to a related person); or

(vii) Section 1245 class property is acquired in an exchange described in section 1031, relating to exchange of property held for productive use or investment, to the extent that the basis of such property includes an amount representing the adjusted basis of other property owed by the taxpayer or a related person at any time during 1980. In the case of property which does not qualify for ACRS under this subdivision, rules similar to those of paragraph (d)(3)(iii) of this section shall apply.

In general, the avoidance intent indicated in subdivisions (i) through (vii) may be rebutted by evidence of an overriding business purpose (or purposes) for the transaction. However, even if the taxpayer demonstrates an overriding business purpose (or purposes) for the transaction, the property will not qualify for ACRS if the Internal Revenue Service establishes that one of the principal purposes of the transaction is to avoid the operation of the effective date rule of section 168(e)(1) and the "anti-churning" rules of section 168(e)(4), and the rules of this section.

(8) *Adjustment to basis of partnership property.*—ACRS shall not apply with respect to any adjustment to the basis of partnership property made under section 734(b) (relating to the optional adjustment to the basis of undistributed partnership property) or section 743(b) (relating to the optional adjustment to the basis of partnership property) if the partnership property itself does not qualify for ACRS because of section 168(e) and this section. If a partnership has property which qualifies for ACRS, see § 1.168-2(n) for the application of ACRS to the adjustments, pursuant to section 734(b) or 743(b), to the basis of such property.

(9) *Acquisitions by reason of death.*—Property acquired by the taxpayer after December 31, 1980, by reason of death, for which the basis is determined under section 1014(a), is eligible for ACRS.

(10) *Reduction in unadjusted basis.*—The unadjusted basis of property for purposes of section 168(d)(1) and § 1.168-2(d) shall be reduced to the extent that such property does not qualify for ACRS due to the application of this paragraph (d). The basis not taken into account for ACRS purposes pursuant to the preceding sentence shall be taken into account by the taxpayer for purposes of other provisions of the Code.

(11) *Certain corporate transactions.*—For purposes of section 168(e)(4) and § 1.168-4(d)(6), a corporation is not related to a distributee (or, in the case of a transaction described in section 338, the new target corporation) if—

(i) Such corporation is a distributing corporation in a transaction to which section 334(b)(2)(B) (as in effect on August 31, 1982) applies, or is a target corporation for which an election under section 338 is made, and at least 80 percent of the stock of such corporation (as described in section 334(b)(2)(B) or 338(d)(3)) is acquired by purchase after December 31, 1980, or

(ii) Such corporation is a distributing corporation in a complete liquidation to which section 331(a) applies, or a partial liquidation to which section 331(a) (as in effect on August 31, 1982) applies, or to which section 302(b)(4) applies, and the distributee (or a related person) by himself or together with one or more persons acquires the amount of stock specified in subdivision (i) of this paragraph (d)(11) by purchase after December 31, 1980.

(e) *Examples.*—The application of this section may be illustrated by the following examples:

Example (1). In 1978 A buys a house which he uses as his family residence. In 1983, A's family moves out, and A converts the house into rental property. A may not use ACRS with respect to the property because he placed it in service before 1981. A must depreciate the property in accordance with section 167 and the regulations thereunder, subject to the other applicable provisions of the Code.

Example (2). In 1982 X Corp. purchases and places in service two major pieces of manufacturing equipment. One is newly constructed, while the other is a used machine expected to produce only 5,000 additional units. X elects to depreciate the used machine under the unit-of-production method. Such method was properly used within X's industry before 1981. Assuming that X has met the requirements of section 168(f)(4) and § 1.168-5(e), the used machine will not be recovery property as defined in section 168(c)(1) and § 1.168-3(a). X will apply ACRS with respect to the new machine even though it properly elected to apply the unit-of-production method with respect to the used machine.

Example (3). On November 15, 1984, B, a calendar year taxpayer, places in service a 10-unit apartment building for individuals and families of low income under section 8 of the United States Housing Act of 1937. B acquired the building for $100,000 and has incurred an additional $100,000 of expenditures for its rehabilitation, which B elects to amortize under section 167(k). In 1984, B is entitled to an allowance under ACRS of $2,000 (*i.e.*, .02 × $100,000). The $100,000 which B amortizes under section 167(k) is not included in the unadjusted basis and therefore is not recovered under the provisions of ACRS.

Example (4). C is an individual engaged in the trucking business. On February 1, 1983, C purchases a new truck from a dealer. As is his normal business practice, C financed the transaction partly by trading in a truck C had used in his business for the previous 3 years. Although this transaction is described in section 1031, it does not have as one of its principal purposes avoidance of the rules of section 168(e)(1) and (4). C therefore will use ACRS with respect to the entire unadjusted basis of the truck purchased in 1983, including cash paid, indebtedness incurred, and the amount attributable to the adjusted basis of the used truck traded in.

Example (5). On June 1, 1983, in a transaction described in section 1031, Corporation M exchanges a corporate jet, acquired before 1981, for a very similar corporate jet owned and also acquired before 1981 by unrelated Corporation N. There is no significant difference to M or N in the use of the jet acquired from that of the jet exchanged, and the operations of each corporation do not change significantly as a result of the transaction. These facts and circumstances indicate that one of the principal purposes of this transaction is to avoid the principles of paragraphs (1) and (4) of section 168(e). Thus, absent evidence of an overriding business purpose (or purposes) for the transaction, neither of the jets will be treated as recovery property. Further, even if an overriding business purpose (or purposes) for the transaction is (or are) demonstrated, the property will not be eligible for ACRS if the Internal Revenue Service establishes that one of the principal purposes of the transaction is to avoid the principles of paragraphs (1) and (4) of section 168(e). The result in this example would be the same if, after the exchange, M or N sold the acquired property and leased it back, or sold the property to a related person.

Example (6). Z Corp., owner and largest occupant of the Z Building since 1965, sells this building to an institutional investor, M Corp., on May 1, 1983. After this sale, 25 percent of the Z Building is leased to Z until May 1, 1985. Because 25 percent of the Z Building is leased for more than 3 months by Z, which owned the building during 1980, M may not take ACRS deductions with respect to this 25 percent portion. Such portion must be depreciated in accordance with section 167. However, ACRS will apply with respect to the portion of the Z Building which is not leased by Z for more than 3 months after the above-described sale. If Z had leased the building only until July 31, 1983, then M Corp. would apply ACRS with respect to the entire building.

Example (7). During 1980 O Corp. undertakes construction of a department store which becomes available for its assigned business function on April 1, 1981. For purposes of section 168(e)(4)(B), O is not treated as owning the department store building under construction until it placed it in service on April 1, 1981. Accordingly, ACRS will apply with respect to the building, beginning on the day it is placed in service.

Example (8). On June 1, 1983, P Corp. sells an undivided 70 percent interest in a building it has owned since March 1, 1980, to Q Corp. which is not related to P. R Corp., which is not related to P, has occupied the building as a tenant since June 1980 and will continue to occupy it after this sale. P and Q will own the building as tenants-in-common. Q, but not P, will take ACRS deductions with respect to its portion of the building. The fact that the user of the building did not change will not affect this result. However, if P and Q had formed a partnership which owned the building after the sale, no portion of the building would qualify for ACRS because the taxpayer acquiring the property after 1980 (the partnership) would be related under section 168(e)(4)(D) to a person (P) which owned the building in 1980.

Example (9). On January 1, 1984, D, a 20 percent partner in Partnership W, sells his entire partnership interest to E for $400,000. Partnership W has one asset, a building it placed in service before 1981. D's adjusted basis in his partnership interest, allocable entirely to the building, is $200,000 when it is sold. A valid election under section 754 is in effect with respect to the sale of the partnership interest. Accordingly, Partnership W makes an adjustment pursuant to section 743(b) to increase the basis of the building with respect to E from $200,000 to $400,000. Under the provisions of § 1.168-4(d)(8) no portion of the increase in the basis of the partnership property with respect to E is eligible for ACRS because the partnership property itself does not qualify for ACRS due to the provisions of section 168(e)(1) and § 1.168-4(a).

Example (10). In 1983, F, an individual, sells a piece of business equipment he placed in service in 1980 to X, a partnership in which F owns a 20 percent interest. No portion of such equipment will qualify for ACRS since it was acquired after 1980 by the taxpayer (Partnership X) and was owned during 1980 by a related person (partner P). The result in this example would not be changed if F owned no interest in X in 1980.

Example (11). G, an individual, has owned an apartment building containing furnished apartments since 1979. On June 1, 1983, G sells the building and its furnishings to unrelated Partnership Y. The furniture was purchased by G before 1981. Most of these apartments will continue to be occupied by the same tenants who occupied them before the sale. For purposes of section 168(e)(4)(I) and § 1.168-4(d)(3), the furniture is acquired incidental to the acquisition of the building. Therefore, ACRS will apply with respect to the furniture, notwithstanding that many of the tenants who use the furniture do not change as part of the transaction.

Example (12). On June 1, 1983, Partnership Z purchases a factory which has been leased by Corporation S, an unrelated person, since 1979. Corporation S continues to use this factory for more than 3 months after the sale. The pre-1981 section 1245 class property transferred in this transaction, such as machinery and equipment, represents a significant portion of the unadjusted basis of the property purchased by Z. Since the unadjusted basis of such section 1245 class property is significant in relation to the factory's unadjusted basis, for purposes of section 168(e)(4)(I) and § 1.168-4(d)(3), the machinery and equipment are not acquired incidental to the acquisition of the factory. Since the user of such machinery and equipment does not change as part of the transaction, Partnership Z may not use ACRS with respect to such section 1245 class property. However, Z will use ACRS with respect to the factory and the other section 1250 class property acquired.

Example (13). Partnership W, in which Partner E holds a 25 percent interest, has as its sole asset an office building it placed in service in 1980. On May 1, 1983, E dies, and his partnership interest, whose basis is determined under section 1014, passes to his daughter, D. ACRS is not available with respect to any increase in the basis of the partnership property with respect to D, because the partnership property itself does not qualify for ACRS due to the provisions of section 168(e)(1) and § 1.168-4(a).

Example (14). On July 1, 1983, Corporation X sells a building it had owned in 1980 to Corporation Y, an unrelated person. X retains an option to repurchase this building within 5 years. This building qualifies as recovery property in Y's hands, and Y will take ACRS deductions under section 168 with respect to it. On July 1, 1985, X exercises its option and repurchases the building. When X repurchases the building, it ceases to be recovery property because the taxpayer (X) owned the building during 1980. X may not take ACRS deductions with respect to the repurchased building. Instead, X must depreciate it under section 167 and the regulations thereunder.

Example (15). F, an individual, sells his business (including section 1245 class property owned in 1980) to G, on August 1, 1983. Under their arrangement, F continues to manage the business for G, using the same equipment he had previously used. F receives as compensation for managing the business a fixed salary plus 5 percent of the gross profits. The arrangement follows customary commercial practice and was negotiated by F and G at arm's length. In addition, the amounts received (including the 5 percent of gross profits) represent the real value of the services rendered by F and are reasonable in amount. Further, receipt of 5 percent of gross profits under these circumstances is an ordinary and customary feature in the sale of a business in the industry and region in question. This arrangement results in a sufficient change in the ownership and use of the equipment that G will recover the cost of such equipment under ACRS.

Example (16). Individuals J and K each own a 50 percent interest in Partnership X, whose only asset is a building placed in service before 1981. On August 1, 1983, H, an individual, purchases a 25 percent interest each from J and K. Partnership X is deemed under section 708(b)(1)(B) to have terminated when H purchases the 50 percent interest. The building is not eligible for ACRS because the taxpayer acquiring the property after 1980 (the new partnership formed by H, J, and K) is related to the person who owned the property during 1980 (the old partnership), since J and K own more than a 10 percent interest in each of the two partnerships.

Example (17). In 1980, individual A owns all of the stock of Corporation T, which in turn owns depreciable property. In 1982, A sells the stock of T to unrelated Corporation V. Shortly thereafter, T sells some of the depreciable property it owned in 1980 to A. Under section 168(e)(4)(D), the property is not owned during 1980 by a person related to the taxpayer (A) since A is not related to the 1980 owner (T) when A acquires the property. However, an avoidance purpose is indicated under § 1.168-4(d)(7)(iv) since A was related in 1980 to the 1980 owner (T). Also, A broke the relationship with T shortly before acquiring the property. Accordingly, A may not use ACRS with respect to the property acquired, unless he can demonstrate an overriding business purpose (or purposes) for the transaction. Further, even if an overriding business purpose (or purposes) for the transaction is (or are) demonstrated, the property will not be eligible for ACRS if the Internal Revenue Service establishes that one of the principal purposes of the transaction is to avoid the principles of paragraphs (1) and (4) of section 168(e).

Example (18). In 1980, individual B owns all of the stock of Corporations X and Y. In 1980, X owns depreciable property. In 1981, X liquidates. In 1982, B sells to Y property owned by X in 1980. Y may not use ACRS with respect to the acquired property. Since the taxpayer (Y) would be related to the 1980 owner (X) but for the fact that X is no longer in existence when Y acquires the property, then, under § 1.168-4(d)(6)(ii)(B), X is considered to be in existence for purposes of determining whether the property was owned (or used) by a related person during 1980.

Example (19). In 1980, individual C owns all of the stock of Corporation M, which in turn owns all of the stock of Corporation N. In 1980, N owns depreciable property. In 1981, N distributes such 1980 property to M. In 1982, M sells the N stock to an unrelated person. In 1983, M distributes to C the property it received from N. Under section 168(e)(4)(D), the property is not owned during 1980 by a person related to the taxpayer (C), since C is not related to the 1980 owner (N) when C acquires the property. However, under § 1.168-4(d)(7)(iv) an avoidance purpose is indicated since the taxpayer (C) is related in 1980 to the 1980 owner (N). Also, upon acquisition, C is related to the person from whom the property is acquired (M). Therfore, C may not use ACRS with respect to the property unless he demonstrates an overriding business purpose (or purposes) for the transaction. Further, even if an overriding business purpose (or purposes) for the transaction is (or are) demonstrated, the property will not be eligible for ACRS if the Internal Revenue Service establishes that one of the principal purposes of the transaction is to avoid the principles of paragraphs (1) and (4) of section 168(e).

Example (20). D owns 20 percent of Corporation X and a 20 percent interest in Partnership P. X owns depreciable property in 1980. In 1981, X sells the property to P. Under § 1.267(b)-1(b), the sale is considered as occurring between X and the members of the partnership (including D) separately. Accordingly, under the principles of § 1.267(b)-1(b), 20 percent of the unadjusted basis of the property is excluded from ACRS. In addition, under § 1.168-4(d)(7)(i) an avoidance purpose is indicated since D owns more than a 10 percent interest in the taxpayer (P) and the person who owned the property during 1980 (X). Therefore, ACRS is not available with respect to the remainder of the unadjusted basis of the property unless an overriding business purpose (or purposes) for the transaction is (or are) demonstrated. Further, even if an overriding business purpose (or purposes) for the transaction is (or are) demonstrated, the property will not be eligible for ACRS if the Internal Revenue Service establishes that one of the principal purposes of the transaction is to avoid the principles of paragraphs (1) and (4) of section 168(e).

Example (21). In 1980, E leases section 1245 class property to F. In 1982, at the termination of the lease, F purchases the property from E and continues to use it for more than 3 months after the sale. F is not entitled to use ACRS with respect to the property since, as part of the transaction, the user of the property did not change. The result in this example would be the same if, instead of selling the property to F, E sold the property to G, subject to F's lease, with F's use continuing for more than 3 months after the sale.

Example (22). In 1980, H and I each own section 1245 class property which they use in their respective businesses. In 1981, H and I swap titles to the property, with the parties continuing to use the same property as before the exchange. Neither H nor I is entitled to use ACRS with respect to the acquired property, since the user of the property does not change as part of the transaction.

Example (23). A owns section 1250 class property in 1980. In 1981, A sells the property to B who leases it back to A. B later sells the property to C, subject to A's lease. ACRS is not available with respect to the property in the hands of C since the taxpayer (C) leases the property to a person who owned it during 1980 (A).

Example (24). D owns section 1250 class property in 1980. In 1981, D transfers the property to E (an unrelated person) in exchange for property of a like kind in a transaction described in section 1031. Subsequently, D sells to and leases back from F the property acquired from E. Under § 1.168-4(d)(3)(iii), the property acquired from E is considered to have been owned by D in 1980. Therefore, ACRS is not available with respect to such property in the hands of F since the taxpayer (F) leases the property to a person who owned it during 1980 (D). The result in this example would be the same if, instead of selling the property to F, D sold it to G (regardless of whether G leased it back to D), a person related to D under section 168(e)(4)(D) and §1.168-4(d)(6).

Example (25). In 1980, Corporation X places in service section 1245 class property. In 1981, X merges into Corporation Y in a transaction described in section 368(a)(1)(A). Subsequently, Y sells to and leases back from Z the 1980 section 1245 class property acquired from X in the merger. Under §1.168-4(d)(4)(vi), ACRS is not available with respect to the property in the hands of Z. [Reg. §1.168-4.]

§1.168-5. Special rules.

* * *

(b) *Transferee bound by transferor's period and method in certain transactions.*—(1) *In general.*—In the case of recovery property which is transferred in a transaction described in section 168(f)(10)(B) and subparagraph (2) of this §1.168-5(b), the transferee shall be treated as the transferor for purposes of computing the recovery allowance under section 168(a) and §1.168-2 with respect to so much of the basis of such property in the hands of the transferee as does not exceed its adjusted basis (determined before the application of the section 48(q)(2) adjustment, if any) in the hands of the transferor immediately before the transfer.

(2) *Transactions covered.*—The provisions of subparagraph (1) of this paragraph (b) apply to the following transactions:

(i) A transaction described in—

(A) Section 332 (relating to distributions in complete liquidation of an 80 percent or more controlled subsidiary corporation) except where the basis of the assets distributed is determined under section 334(b)(2) (as in effect on August 31, 1982);

(B) Section 351 (relating to transfer to a corporation controlled by transferor);

(C) Section 361 (relating to exchanges pursuant to certain corporate reorganizations);

(D) Section 371(a) (relating to exchanges pursuant to certain receivership and bankruptcy proceedings);

(E) Section 374(a) (relating to exchanges pursuant to certain railroad reorganizations);

(F) Section 721 (relating to transfers to a partnership in exchange for a partnership interest); and

(G) Section 731 (relating to distributions by a partnership to a partner);

(ii) An acquisition (other than one described in subdivision (i) of this paragraph (2)) from a related person (as defined in section 168(e)(4)(D) and §1.168-4(d)(6)). Property acquired from a decedent is not property acquired in a transaction included in this subdivision (ii); and

(iii) An acquisition followed by a leaseback to the person from whom the property is acquired. A leaseback does not exist for purposes of this subdivision (iii) if the former owner in turn subleases the property to another person.

(3) *Transactions excluded.*—The provisions of section 168(f)(10)(A) and paragraph (b)(1) of this section do not apply—

(i) To recovery property which is transferred within 12 months after the property is placed in service by the transferor. The exception of this subdivision (i) shall not apply in the case of a transaction also described in section 168(f)(7) (*i.e.*, a transaction in which gain or loss is not recognized in whole or in part); or

(ii) To any transaction described in section 168(e)(4) and §1.168-4(d).

(4) *Allowable deduction when transferor and transferee are calendar year taxpayers or have the same fiscal year.*—When the transferor and transferee are calendar year taxpayers or when both the transferee and transferor have the same fiscal year—

(i) *Allowable deduction in year of transfer.*—The allowable deduction for the recovery year in which the property is transferred shall be prorated between the transferor and the transferee on a monthly basis. For property other than 15-year real property, the transferor's deduction for such year is the deduction allowable to the transferor (determined without regard to this subdivision) multiplied by a fraction, the numerator of which is the number of months in the transferor's taxable year before the month in which the transfer occurs, and the denominator of which is the total number of months in the transferor's taxable year. The remaining portion of the transferor's allowable deduction for the taxable year of the transfer (determined without regard to this subdivision) shall be allocated to the transferee. For property transferred in a transaction described in section 332, 361, 371(a), 374(a), or 731, the two preceding sentences shall be applied by disregarding that the taxable year of the transferor may end on the date of the transfer. In the case of 15-year real property, the transferor's deduction for the year of the transfer is the deduction allowable to the transferor under the disposition rules of §1.168-2(a)(3) or (g)(4) (as the case may be). The remaining portion of the transferor's allowable deduction for the taxable year of the transfer (determined as if the transfer had not occurred) shall be allocated to the transferee. See subdivision (ii) of this paragraph (4) for a special rule applicable to certain nonrecognition transactions.

(ii) *Special rule for certain nonrecognition transactions occurring as of the close of business on the last day of any calendar month.*—For purposes of this paragraph (b), in the case of a transaction described in section 168(f)(10(B)(i) and paragraph (b)(2)(i) of this section, if the transfer occurs as of the close of business on the last day of any calendar month, such transfer is deemed to occur on the first day of the next calendar month.

(iii) *Transferee's allowable deduction for a taxable year subsequent to the year of transfer.*—The allowable deduction to the transferee for taxable years subsequent to the year of transfer shall be determined as if the cost of the property were being recovered in the transferor's hands (*i.e.*, by multiplying the transferor's applicable recovery percentage for the current recovery year by the transferor's unadjusted basis in the transferred property).

Thus, for example, A, a calendar year taxpayer, purchases for $30,000 and places in service

15-year real property (other than low income housing) on February 15, 1981, and transfers the property to partnership B, a calendar year partnership, on March 15, 1981, in a transaction described in section 721. A does not elect to use the optional recovery percentages provided in § 1.168-2(c). For 1981, A's allowable deduction is $300 (*i.e.*, $30,000 × .11 × 1/11). B's allowable deductions for 1981 and 1982 are $3,000 (*i.e.*, $3,300 – $300) and $3,000 (*i.e.*, .10 × $30,000), respectively.

(5) *Allowable deduction when transferor and transferee have different taxable years.*—When the transferor and the transferee have different taxable years—

(i) *Transferor's allowable deduction.*—The allowable deduction to the transferor for any taxable year in which the property is transferred shall be determined as under paragraph (b)(4)(i) and (ii) of this section.

(ii) *Transferee's allowable deduction.*—In computing the transferee's allowable deduction for the year of transfer and for subsequent taxable years, the property shall similarly be treated as if its cost were being recovered by the transferor. However, the allowable deduction for any taxable year shall be allocated to the transferee based on the transferee's taxable year.

Thus, for example, B, a calendar year taxpayer, purchases for $30,000 and places in service 15-year real property (other than low income housing) on February 15, 1981. B's allowable deduction for 1981 is $3,300 (*i.e.*, .11 × $30,000). B transfers the property to C on March 15, 1982. C's taxable year is a fiscal year ending June 30. For 1982, B's allowable deduction is $500 (*i.e.*, $30,000 × .10 × 2/12). For fiscal year 1982, C's allowable deduction is $1,000 (*i.e.*, the remainder of B's 1982 deduction ($2,500), allocated to the period March 1 through June 30, 1982 (4 months/10 months)). For fiscal year 1983, C's allowable deduction is $2,850 (*i.e.*, the remainder of B's allowable 1982 deduction ($1,500), plus $1,350 which is B's allowable 1983 deduction of $2,700 ($30,000 × .09) allocated to the period January 1 through June 30, 1983 (*i.e.*, $2,700 × 6 months/12 months).

(6) *Transferee's basis lower than transferor's.*—If the adjusted basis of the property in the hands of the transferee is lower than the adjusted basis of the property in the hands of the transferor immediately before the transfer, see § 1.168-2 (d) (3) for rules relating to redeterminations of basis.

(7) *Portion of basis in hands of transferee which exceeds transferor's adjusted basis.*—The transferee shall treat as newly purchased ACRS property that portion of the basis of the property in the hands of the transferee that exceeds the adjusted basis (determined before the application of the section 48 (q) (2) adjustment, if any) of the property in the hands of the transferor immediately before the transfer. Thus, such excess shall be treated as recovery property placed in service by the transferee in the year of the transfer. The transferee may choose any applicable recovery period and recovery method with respect to such excess and need not use the transferor's recovery period and recovery method.

(8) *Examples.*—The application of this paragraph (b) may be illustrated by the following examples:

Example (1). In 1981, A, a calendar year taxpayer, purchases for $12,000 and places in service 3-year recovery property. Under section 168 (b) (1) and § 1.168-2 (b) (1), the recovery allowances for the first and second recovery years are $3,000 (*i.e.*, .25 × $12,000) and $4,560 (*i.e.*, .38 × $12,000), respectively. On February 15, 1983, A transfers the property to M Corporation, a calendar year taxpayer, in exchange for M's stock and $2,000 cash in a transaction described in section 351. A's recovery allowance for 1983 is $370 (*i.e.*, (1/12 × .37) × $12,000). A's adjusted basis immediately before the exchange is $4,070 (*i.e.*, $12,000 – $7,930). Assume A recognizes gain of $2,000 on the transaction. The basis attributable to the property under section 362 is determined to be $6,070 in the hands of M Corporation. Under the provisions of section 168 (f) (10) (A) and this paragraph (b), M, the transferee, is treated the same as A, the transferor, with respect to $4,070, which is so much of M's basis as does not exceed A's adjusted basis. However, in computing the deduction allowable with respect to such basis, A's unadjusted basis ($12,000) is used. Thus, in the third recovery year, M may deduct $4,070 (*i.e.*, (11/12 × .37) × $12,000) under section 168 (f) (10) (A) and § 1.168-5 (b) (1) and (4). The remaining $2,000 of basis in the property is treated as newly purchased ACRS property placed in service in 1983. M may choose any applicable recovery period and recovery method with respect to such $2,000 and need not use A's recovery period and recovery method.

Example (2). In 1983, B, a calendar year taxpayer, purchases for $12,000 and places in service 5-year recovery property. Under section 46, B's investment tax credit for such property is $1,200. Under section 48 (q) (1) and § 1.168-2 (d) (2), B reduces his basis of $600 (*i.e.*, .50 × $1,200). Therefore, B's unadjusted basis for purposes of section 168 is $11,400 (*i.e.*, $12,000 – $600). Under section 168 (b) (1) and § 1.168-2 (b) (1), the recovery allowances for the first and second recovery years are $1,710 (*i.e.*, .15 × $11,400) and $2,508 (*i.e.*, .22 × $11,400), respectively. On February 15, 1985, B sells the property for $13,000 to C, a related party (as defined in section 168 (e) (4) (D) and § 1.168-4 (d)(6)) who is a calendar year taxpayer. B's recovery allowance for 1985 is $199.50 (*i.e.*, (1/12 × .21) × $11,400). B's adjusted basis (determined without regard to the section 48 (q) (2) adjustment), immediately before the sale is $6,982.50 (*i.e.*, $11,400 – $4,417.50). The basis of the property under section 1012 is $13,000 in C's hands. Under the provisions of section 168 (f) (10) (A) and this paragraph (b), C, the transferee, is treated the same as B, the transferor, with respect to $6,982.50, which is so much of C's basis as does not exceed B's adjusted basis. However, in computing the deduction allowable with respect to such basis, B's unadjusted basis ($11,400) is used. Thus, in the third recovery year, C may deduct $2,194.50 (*i.e.*, (11/12 × .21) × $11,400) under section 168 (f) (10) (A) and § 1.168-5 (b) (1) and (4). In the fourth and fifth recovery years, C may deduct $2,394 (*i.e.*, .21 × $11,400) each year. The remaining basis of $6,017.50 (*i.e.*, $13,000 – $6,982.50) in property is treated as newly purchased ACRS property placed in service in 1985. C may choose any applicable period and recovery method with respect to such amount and need not use B's recovery period and recovery method.

Example (3). In 1981, D, a calendar year taxpayer, purchases for $12,000 and places in service 5-year recovery property. Under section 168 (b) (1) and §1.168-2 (b) (1), the recovery allowances for the first and second recovery years are $1,800 (*i.e.,* .15 × $12,000) and $2,640 (*i.e.,* .22 × $12,000), respectively. On March 15, 1983, D transfers the property to N Corporation, a taxpayer having a fiscal year ending June 30, in exchange for N's stock and $2,000 cash in a transaction described in section 351. D's recovery allowance for 1983 is $420 (*i.e.,* (2/12 × .21) × $12,000). D's adjusted basis in the property immediately before the exchange is $7,140 (*i.e.,* $12,000 – $4,860). Assume D recognizes gain of $2,000 on the transaction. The basis attributable to the property under section 362 is determined to be $9,140 in the hands of N Corporation. Under the provisions of section 168(f) (10) (A) and this paragraph (b), N, the transferee, is treated the same as D, the transferor, with respect to $7,140, which is so much of N's basis as does not exceed D's adjusted basis. However, in computing the deduction allowable with respect to such basis, D's unadjusted basis ($12,000) is used. Thus, for fiscal year 1983, N Corporation's allowable deduction with respect to the carryover basis is $840 (*i.e.,* (4/12 × .21) × $12,000). For fiscal years 1984 and 1985, N Corporation's allowable deduction is $2,520 (*i.e.,* [(6/12 × .21) + (6/12 × .21)] × $12,000). For fiscal year 1986, N Corporation's allowable deduction is $1,260 (*i.e.,* (6/12 × .21) × $12,000). The remaining $2,000 of basis in the property is treated as newly purchased ACRS property. N may choose any applicable recovery period and recovery method with respect to such basis and need not use D's recovery period and recovery method. N elects to use the optional recovery percentage based on a 5-year recovery period with respect to the $2,000 of basis which is treated as newly purchased ACRS property. For fiscal years 1983, 1984, 1985, 1986, 1987, and 1988, N's recovery allowance with respect to such $2,000 basis are $200, $400, $400, $400, $400, and $200, respectively. If N's fiscal year ending June 30, 1983, were a short taxable year, the provisions of §1.168-2(f) would apply with respect to the $2,000 considered newly purchased ACRS property, but not with respect to N's basis carried over from D.

Example (4). On May 1, 1981, E, a calendar year taxpayer, purchases for $100,000 and places in service 5-year recovery property. On April 1, 1982, E sells the property for $100,000 to F who leases it back to E. Under the provisions of paragraph (b) (3), section 168 (f) (10) (A) and §1.168-5 (b) (1) do not apply. Thus, F may choose any applicable recovery period and recovery method with respect to its unadjusted basis of $100,000, with recovery beginning in 1982.

Example (5). Assume the same facts as in example (4) except that the property is sold to F and leased back to E on June 15, 1982. Assume further that F's fiscal year ends on July 31, 1982. For 1981, E's allowable deduction is $15,000 (*i.e.,* .15 × $100,000), and for 1982 is $9,166.67 (*i.e.,* $100,000 × .22 × 5/12). E's adjusted basis in the property immediately before the transfer is $75,833.33 (*i.e.,* $100,000 – $24,166.67). Under the provisions of section 168(f)(10)(A) and this paragraph (b), F, the transferee, is treated the same as E, the transferor, with respect to $75,833.33 which is so much of F's basis as does not exceed E's adjusted basis. However, in computing the deduction allowable with respect to such basis, E's unadjusted basis ($100,000) is used. Thus, for the fiscal year ending July 31, 1982, F's allowable deduction with respect to the carryover basis is $3,666.66 (*i.e.,* 2/12 × .22 × $100,000). For fiscal year 1983, F's allowable deduction is $21,416.67 (*i.e.,* (5/12 × .22 × $100,000) + (7/12 × .21 × $100,000)). For fiscal years 1984 and 1985, F's allowable deductions are $21,000 (*i.e.,* (.21 × 5/12 × $100,000) + (.21 × 7/12 × $100,000)). For the fiscal year ending July 31, 1986, F's allowable deduction is $8,750 (*i.e.,* 5/12 × .21 × $100,000). The remaining $24,166.67 of basis is treated as newly-purchased property, placed in service by F in 1981. F may choose any applicable recovery period and method for such amount and need not use E's recovery period and method.

Example (6). On January 1, 1981, G, a calendar year taxpayer, purchases for $1 million and places in service 15-year real property (other than low income housing). On July 15, 1988, G sells the property to H for $1.5 million, who leases it back to G. H's taxable year is a fiscal year ending September 30. G does not elect use of the optional percentages provided by §1.168-2(c). For 1988, G's allowable deduction is $30,000 (*i.e.,* .06 × $1,000,000 × 6/12). H is treated the same as G with respect to $390,000, which is so much of the basis of the property in the hands of H as does not exceed its adjusted basis to G immediately before the transfer (*i.e.,* $1,000,000 – $610,000). H's allowable deduction for its fiscal year ending September 30, 1988, with respect to such basis is $15,000 (*i.e.,* the remainder of G's allowable deduction for 1988 ($30,000) allocated to the period July 1 through September 30, 1988 (3 months/6 months)). For H's fiscal year ending September 30, 1989, H's allowable deduction is $60,000 (*i.e.,* the remainder of G's allowable 1988 deduction ($15,000) plus G's allowable 1989 deduction ($60,000) allocated to the period January 1 through September 30, 1989 (9 months/12 months) or $45,000). For H's fiscal year ending September 30, 1990, H's allowable deduction is $52,500 (*i.e.,* the remainder of G's allowable deduction for 1989 ($15,000), plus G's allowable deduction for 1990 ($50,000), allocated to the period January 1 through September 30, 1990 (9 months/12 months), or $37,500). For H's fiscal year ending September 30, 1996, H is entitled to G's allowable deduction for 1995 ($50,000), allocated to the period October 1 through December 31, 1995 (3 months/12 months), or $12,500. The amount of H's basis in excess of G's adjusted basis (*i.e.,* $1,500,000 less $390,000, or $1,110,000) is treated as newly purchased ACRS property placed in service by H on July 15, 1988. H may use any applicable recovery period and method with respect to such basis. Thus, assuming H does not elect the optional percentages provided by §1.168-2(c), H has an additional allowable deduction for its year ending September 30, 1988, of $33,300 (*i.e.,* .03 × $1,110,000). For its fiscal year ending September 30, 1989, H's allowable deduction with respect to such basis is $122,100 (*i.e.,* .11 × $1,110,000).

Example (7). On January 1, 1981, partnership P, a calendar year taxpayer, purchases for $1,000,000 and places in service 15-year real property (other than low income housing) which is the only asset of the partnership. At no time does the partnership have an election under section 754 in effect. P is owned equally by partners A, B, and C. On April 18, 1985, individual D purchases the interests of B and C for $1,500,000, thereby terminating the partnership under section 708(b)(1)(B). The deduction allowable with respect to the property for 1985 prior to the termination is $17,500 (*i.e.*, $1,000,000 × .07 × 3/12). The partnership's adjusted basis in the property immediately before the termination is $592,500 (*i.e.*, $1,000,000 − $407,500). Under the provisions of section 168(f)(10)(A) and § 1.168-5(b)(1), the new partnership which is created by A and D is treated the same as the old partnership with respect to $592,500, which is so much of the adjusted basis of the property to the new partnership as does not exceed its adjusted basis to the old partnership. However, in computing the allowable deduction with respect to such basis the old partnership's unadjusted basis ($1,000,000) is used. Thus, for 1985, the deduction allowable to the new partnership with respect to such basis is $52,500 (*i.e.*, $1,000,000 × .07 × 9/12) and for 1986 is $60,000 (*i.e.*, $1,000,000 × .06). This result would be the same if D purchased a 95 percent interest in the partnership. Recovery of such basis will be completed in 1995. The new partnership's basis in the property in excess of that of the old partnership is taken into account under ACRS as if it were newly-purchased recovery property placed in service in 1985. Any applicable period and method may be used with respect to such basis.

Example (8). In 1981, Corporation X, a calendar year taxpayer, purchases for $100,000 and places in service 5-year recovery property. Under section 168(b)(1) and § 1.168-2(b)(1), X's recovery allowance for 1981 is $15,000. On March 15, 1982, X merges into Corporation Y in a transaction described in section 368(a)(1)(A) solely in exchange for Y stock. Y's taxable year is a fiscal year ending August 31. X's recovery allowance for 1982 is $3,666.66 (*i.e.*, 2/12 × .22 × $100,000). Under section 362, Y's basis in the property is the same as the property's adjusted basis in the hands of X immediately before the transfer. Therefore, for fiscal year 1982, Y's allowable deduction is $11,000 which is the remainder of X's allowable deduction for 1982, $18,333.34 (*i.e.*, $22,000 − $3,666.66) allocated to the period March 1, 1982, through August 31, 1982 (*i.e.*, 6 months/10 months). For fiscal year 1983, Y's allowable deduction is $21,333.34 which is the remainder of X's allowable deduction for 1982 ($7,333.34) plus the deduction which would be allowable to X in 1983 (*i.e.*, $100,000 × .21, or $21,000) allocated to the period January 1 through August 31, 1983 (*i.e.*, $21,000 × 8 months/12 months or $14,000). In computing the deductions allowable to X and Y, the fact that X's taxable year ends on the date of the merger is disregarded.

(c) *Recovery property reacquired by the taxpayer.*—(1) *In general.*—Recovery property which is disposed of and then reacquired by the taxpayer shall be treated (for purposes of computing the allowable deduction under section 168(a) and § 1.168-2) as if such property had not been disposed of by the taxpayer. This paragraph (c)(1) generally applies only to so much of the taxpayer's adjusted basis in the reacquired property as does not exceed his adjusted basis at the time he disposed of the property.

(2) *Taxpayers to whom provisions apply.*—The provisions of section 168(f)(10)(C) and paragraph (c)(1) of this section apply only to a taxpayer who, at the time of the disposition of the property, anticipates a reacquisition of the same property.

(3) *Exceptions.*—Section 168(f)(10)(C) and paragraph (c)(1) of this section shall not apply—

(i) To recovery property which is disposed of during the same taxable year that the property is placed in service by the taxpayer, or

(ii) To any transaction described in section 168(e)(4) and § 1.168-4(d).

(4) *Taxpayer resumes prior recovery.*—For purposes of paragraph (c)(1) of this § 1.168-5, the reacquiring taxpayer shall resume the recovery under § 1.168-2 applicable at the time of the disposition. For example, if the taxpayer originally uses a 3-year recovery period and the applicable percentages prescribed in section 168(b)(1) and § 1.168-2(b)(1), in the year of reacquisition the recovery allowance is computed by applying the applicable percentage for the year of disposition to the original unadjusted basis (*i.e.*, the unadjusted basis at the time the taxpayer originally placed the recovery property in service).

(5) *Portion of unadjusted basis in reacquired property which exceeds taxpayer's adjusted basis at the time of disposition.*—That part of the unadjusted basis in the reacquired property which exceeds the taxpayer's adjusted basis in the property at the time of disposition shall be treated generally as newly purchased ACRS property. For property other than a building, any appropriate recovery period and method may be used with respect to such excess. For a building, the taxpayer must use the same recovery period and method with respect to such excess as are used for the building, unless such excess would qualify as a substantial improvement under § 1.168-2(e)(4) if paid or incurred by the taxpayer for an improvement if he had continued to own the building.

(6) *Unadjusted basis in reacquired property lower than taxpayer's adjusted basis at time of disposition.*—If the unadjusted basis in the reacquired property is lower than the taxpayer's adjusted basis in the property at the time of disposition, see § 1.168-2(d)(3) for rules relating to redetermination of basis.

(7) *Examples.*—The provisions of this paragraph may be illustrated by the following examples:

Example (1). In 1981 A, a calendar year taxpayer, purchases for $6,000 and places in service 3-year recovery property. A does not elect an optional recovery percentage under § 1.168-2(c). Under section 168(b)(1) and § 1.168-2(b)(1), A's recovery allowance for 1981 is $1,500 (*i.e.*, .25 × $6,000). A wants to change his method of cost recovery from the use of the accelerated percentages to the use of the optional straight line percentages. To effectuate this change, A sells the property to B in 1982 for $7,000 anticipating that B will sell the property back to A. B does not elect to use an optional recovery percentage. B's recovery deduction for 1982 is $1,750 (*i.e.*, .25 × $7,000). In 1983 A reacquires the property from B for $9,000. With respect to that portion of A's unadjusted basis in the reacquired property which does not exceed the adjusted basis at the time of disposition (*i.e.*, $4,500), A's recovery allowance for 1983 is determined as if A had not disposed of the property, that is, by applying the percentage (38 percent) applicable for the second recovery year (*i.e.*, 1982, the year of disposition) to the original unadjusted basis ($6,000). Thus, A's allowable deduction is $2,280 (*i.e.*, .38 × $6,000). That portion of the unadjusted basis in the reacquired property which exceeds A's adjusted basis at the time of disposition (*i.e.*, $4,500) is treated as newly purchased ACRS property placed in service in 1983. A may use any appropriate recovery period and method for such excess. Thus, if A uses the tables under § 1.168-2(b)(1), A's recovery allowance for 1983 also includes $1,125 (*i.e.*, .25 × $4,500). A's recovery allowances for 1984 are $2,220 (*i.e.*, .37 × $6,000) plus $1,710 (*i.e.*, .38 × $4,500). A's recovery allowance for 1985 is $1,665 (*i.e.*, .37 × $4,500).

Example (2). In 1981 C, a calendar year taxpayer, purchases for $15,000 and places in service 3-year recovery property and elects under § 1.168-2(c) the optional 5-year recovery period using the straight line method. Under § 1.168-2(c)(4), C's recovery allowance for 1981 is $1,500 (*i.e.*, .10 × $15,000). C wants to change his method of cost recovery from the use of the optional straight line percentages to the use of the accelerated percentages. Consent to change is not granted to C under section 168(f)(4). Therefore, C tries to effectuate this change by selling the property to D in 1982 for $16,000 anticipating that D will sell the property back to C. D does not elect to use the optional recovery percentages. D's recovery allowance for 1982 is $4,000 (*i.e.*, .25 × $16,000). In 1983, C reacquires the property from D for $17,000. With respect to that portion of C's unadjusted basis in the reacquired property that does not exceed the adjusted basis at the time of disposition (*i.e.*, $13,500), C must use the option recovery percentages originally elected. C's recovery allowances for 1983, 1984, 1985, 1986, and 1987 are determined as if C had not disposed of the property, that is, by applying the applicable percentages beginning in the second recovery year to the original unadjusted basis ($15,000). Thus, C's allowable deductions are $3,000, $3,000, $3,000, $3,000, and $1,500, respectively. With respect to that portion of the unadjusted basis in the reacquired property which exceeds C's adjusted basis at the time of disposition (*i.e.*, $3,500), C may use any appropriate recovery period and method. Cost recovery for this portion of the reacquired property begins in 1983 as if C placed the property in service in that year.

Example (3). On February 15, 1981, E, a calendar year taxpayer, purchases for $30,000 and places in service 15-year real property (other than low income housing) and does not elect the optional straight line percentages under § 1.168-2(c). Under § 1.168-2(b)(2), E's recovery allowance for 1981 is $3,000 (*i.e.*, .11 × $30,000). E wants to change his method of cost recovery from the use of the accelerated percentages to the use of the optional straight line percentages. To effectuate this change, E sells the property to F on February 15, 1983, anticipating that F will sell the property back to E. E's recovery allowance for 1982 is $3,000 (*i.e.*, .10 × $30,000) and for 1983 is $225 (*i.e.*, .09 × 1/12 × $30,000). In 1985 E reacquires the property from F for $28,000. With respect to that portion of E's unadjusted basis in the reacquired property which does not exceed the adjusted basis at the time of disposition (*i.e.*, $23,475) E's recovery allowance for 1985 is determined as if E had not disposed of the property, that is, by applying the percentage (9 percent) applicable for the third recovery year to the original unadjusted basis ($30,000). The recovery for the year of reacquisition must be adjusted to reflect the number of months the property is used by the taxpayer in that year as recovery property. Thus, if E reacquired the property in July, E's recovery allowance for 1985 would be $1,350 (*i.e*, .09 × 6/12 × $30,000). The unrecovered allowance for the third recovery year, $1,125 ($30,000 × .09 × 5/12), must be recovered in the year following the last recovery year. With respect to that portion of the unadjusted basis in the reacquired property which exceeds E's adjusted basis at the time of disposition (*i.e.*, $4,525), E may not elect an optional recovery period. Cost recovery for this portion of the reacquired property will begin in 1985. Thus, if the reacquisition occurred in July, E's allowable deduction for 1985 with respect to this portion would be $271.50 (*i.e.*, .06 × $4,525).

(d) *Treatment of leasehold improvements.*—(1) *In general.*—Capital expenditures made by a lessee for the erection of buildings or the construction of other permanent improvements on leased property are recoverable through ACRS deductions or amortization deductions. If the recovery period of such improvements in the hands of the taxpayer is equal to or shorter than the remaining period of the lease, the allowances shall take the form of ACRS deductions under section 168. If, on the other hand, the recovery period of such property in the hands of the taxpayer would be longer than the remaining period of such lease, the allowances shall take the form of annual deductions from gross income in an amount equal to the unrecovered cost of such capital expenditures divided by the number of years remaining on the term of the lease. Such deductions shall be in lieu of ACRS deductions. See section 162 and the regulations thereunder.

(2) *Determination of recovery period.*—For purposes of determining whether the recovery period is longer than the lease term, an election of an optional recovery period under section 168(b)(3) or (f)(2)(C) shall be taken into account.

(3) *Determination of the effect given to lease renewal options; related lessee and lessor.*—Section 178 governs the effect to be given renewal options in determining whether the recovery period of the improvements exceeds the remaining period of the lease. Section 178 also provides rules for determining the period of a lease when the lessee and lessor are related. In making any determination under section 178, the "recovery period" of the improvement shall be taken into account in lieu of its useful life. See § 1.178-1.

(4) *Improvements made by lessor.*—If a lessor makes an improvement to the leased property, the cost of the improvement must be recovered under the general provisions of section 168. The provisions of 168(f)(6) and this paragraph (d) do not apply to improvements made by the lessor.

(5) *Example.*—The application of this paragraph may be illustrated by the following example:

Example. In 1981, A leases B's land for a term of 99 years. The lease provisions do not include any options to renew the lease. In 2034, A places in service 15-year real property which he built on the leased premises. Since the remaining term of the lease (46 years) is longer than any recovery period which A could select under section 168 (*i.e.,* 15, 35, or 45 years), A must recover the costs of the improvement under section 168.

(e) *Manner and time for making election.*—(1) *Elections to which this paragraph applies.*—The rules in this paragraph apply to the following elections provided under section 168:

(i) Section 168(b)(3)(A) and (B)(i) and § 1.168-2(c)(1) and (2), relating to election of optional recovery percentage with respect to property in the same recovery class (*i.e.,* all 3-year recovery property);

(ii) Section 168(b)(3)(A) and (B)(ii) and § 1.168-2(c)(1) and (3), relating to election of optional recovery percentage on a property-by-property basis for 15-year real property;

(iii) Section 168(d)(2)(A) and § 1.168-2(h), relating to election to account for mass assets in the same mass asset account and to include in income all proceeds realized on disposition;

(iv) Section 168(e)(2) and § 1.168-4(b), relating to election to exclude property from ACRS by use of a method of depreciation not expressed in a term of years;

(v) Section 168(f)(2)(C)(i) and (ii)(I) and § 1.168-2(g)(3)(i) and (ii), relating to election of optional recovery percentage for property used predominantly outside the United States in the same recovery class and with the same present class life (*e.g.,* 3-year recovery property with a present class life of 4 years); and

(vi) Section 168(f)(2)(C)(i) and (ii)(II) and § 1.168-2(g)(3)(i) and (iii), relating to election of optional recovery percentage on a property-by-property basis for 15-year real property used predominantly outside the United States.

Use by a taxpayer of a method of cost recovery described in section 168(b)(1) and (2) and § 1.168-2(b)(1) and (2) or section 168(f)(2)(A) and (B) and § 1.168-2(g)(1) and (2) (relating to the use of the accelerated percentages) is not an election for purposes of section 168 and this paragraph (e). Thus, no consent will be granted to change from such a method to another method described in section 168. The provisions of section 168(f)(4) and this paragraph (e) do not apply to elections which must be made under another section of the Code. Thus, for example, if a taxpayer wants to amortize property under section 167(k), the rules under section 167(k) apply with respect to such election and the revocation of such election.

(2) *Time for making elections.*—Except as provided in subparagraph (4) or (5), the elections specified in subparagraph (1) of this paragraph (e) shall be made on the taxpayer's income tax return filed for the taxable year in which the property is placed in service as recovery property (as defined in § 1.168-3(a)) by the taxpayer. If the taxpayer does not file a timely return (taking into account extensions of the time for filing) for such taxable year, the election shall be made at the time the taxpayer files his first return for such year. The election may be made on a return, as amended, filed within the time prescribed by law (including extensions) for filing the return for such taxable year. A separate election may be made for each corporation which is a member of an affiliated group (as defined in section 1504) and which joins in the making of a consolidated return in accordance with section 1502 and the regulations thereunder. See § 1.1502-77.

(3) *Manner of making elections.*—Except as provided in subparagraph (5), Form 4562 is provided for making an election under this paragraph and for submitting the information required. The taxpayer must specify in the election—

(i) The name of the taxpayer;

(ii) The taxpayer's identification number;

(iii) The year the recovery property was placed in service (or, in the case of 15-year real property, the month the property was placed in service);

(iv) The unadjusted basis of the recovery property; and

(v) Such other information as may be required.

An election will not be rendered invalid so long as there is substantial compliance, in good faith, with the requirements of this subparagraph (3).

(4) *Special rule for qualified rehabilitated buildings.*—In the case of any qualified rehabilitated building (as defined in section 48(g)(1)), an election under section 168(b)(3) and § 1.168-2(c) (relating to election of optional recovery percentage) may be made at any time before the date 3 years after the building was placed in service by the taxpayer.

(5) *Special rule for foreign taxpayers.*—(i) *Foreign corporations subject to section 964.*—In the case of a foreign corporation whose earnings and profits are determined under section 964, the elections specified in subparagraph (1) of this paragraph (e) shall be made at the time and in the manner provided in § 1.964-1(c). Except as provided in the regulations under section 952 and section 1248, any election made under this subdivision (i) shall apply with respect to the recovery property affected by the election from the taxable year in which such property is placed in service. Such election may be revoked only as provided in § 1.964-1(c)(7) and subparagraph (9) of this paragraph.

(ii) *Foreign taxpayers other than corporations subject to section 964.*—In the case of a foreign taxpayer other than a corporation described in subdivision (i) of this subparagraph (5), the elections specified in subparagraph (1) of this paragraph (e) shall be made at the time and in the manner provided in subparagraphs (2) and (3) of this paragraph, except that the election shall be made on the taxpayer's income tax return for the later of the taxable year in which the property is placed in service as recovery property by the taxpayer or the first taxable year in which the taxpayer is subject to United States tax. Any election made under this subdivision (ii) shall apply with respect to the recovery property affected by the election from the taxable year in which such property is placed in service. Such election may be revoked only as provided in subparagraph (9) of this paragraph. No election may be made under this subdivision (ii) by a taxpayer who was required to, but did not make the election at the time and in the manner prescribed under subdivision (i). For purposes of this subdivision (ii)—

(A) "Foreign taxpayer" means a taxpayer that is not a United States person as defined in section 7701(a)(30), and

(B) "United States tax" means tax under subtitle A of the Code (relating to income taxes) other than sections 871(a)(1) and 881 thereof.

(6) *Failure to elect optional recovery percentages.*—If a taxpayer does not elect to use the optional recovery percentages within the time and in the manner prescribed in subparagraphs (2), (3), (4), and (5) (or is not considered to have elected under § 1.168-2(c)(5)), the amount allowable under section 168 must be determined under section 168(b)(1) or (2) (or under section 168(f)(2)(A) or (B), where applicable) for the year in which the recovery property is placed in service and for all subsequent recovery years. Thus, no election to use such optional percentages may be made by the taxpayer in any other manner (*e.g.*, through a request under section 446(e) to change the taxpayer's method of accounting).

(7) *Individuals, partnerships, trusts, estates, and corporations.*—Except as provided in subparagraph (8) of this paragraph with respect to transactions to which section 168(f)(10)(A) and (B) applies, and subject to other applicable provisions of the Code and regulations, if recovery property is placed in service by an individual, trust, estate, partnership, or corporation, an election under this paragraph shall be made by the individual, trust, estate, partnership, or corporation placing such property in service.

(8) *Transactions to which section 168(f)(10)(A) and (B) applies.*—In a transaction to which section 168(f)(10)(A) and (B) and paragraph (b) of this § 1.168-5 apply, the transferee is bound by the transferor's election (or nonelection) under this paragraph with respect to the property so acquired. The rule of the preceding sentence shall apply with respect to so much of the basis of the property in the hands of the transferee as does not exceed the adjusted basis of the property in the hands of the transferor immediately before the transfer.

(9) *Revocation of election.*—An election under this paragraph, once made, may be revoked only with the consent of the Commissioner. Such consent will be granted only in extraordinary circumstances. Requests for consent must be filed with the Commissioner of Internal Revenue, Washington, D.C. 20224.

(f) *Treatment of certain nonrecognition transactions.*—(1) *Section 1033 transactions.*—(i) *Allowable deduction for section 1033 converted property.*—For any taxable year in which a transaction described in section 1033 occurs, the full year's allowable deduction shall be prorated on a monthly basis under the principles of paragraph (b)(4)(i) of this section. Thus, for example, on March 3, 1981, A, a calendar year taxpayer, purchases for $25,000 and places in service 3-year recovery property. On August 14, 1981, the property is converted. A's 1981 allowable deduction for the converted property is $3,645.83 (*i.e.*, $25,000 × .25 × 7/12). If the property were 15-year real property (other than low income housing) A's 1981 allowable deduction for the converted property would be $1,250 (*i.e.*, $25,000 × .10 × 5/10).

(ii) *Allowable deduction for section 1033 replacement property in year of replacement and subsequent taxable years.*—(A) Replacement property acquired in a transaction to which section 1033 applies, which qualifies as recovery property, shall be treated the same as the converted property. Thus, the replacement property shall be recovered over the remaining recovery period using the same recovery method as the converted property. The preceding sentence applies only with respect to so much of the basis (as determined under section 1033(b)) in the replacement property as does not exceed the adjusted basis in the converted property. Any excess of the unadjusted basis of the replacement property over the adjusted basis of the converted property shall be treated as newly purchased ACRS property. Any excess of the adjusted basis of the converted property over the unadjusted basis of the replacement property shall be recovered under the principles of § 1.168-2(d)(3) (relating to redeterminations).

(B) The allowable deduction for the replacement property in the year of replacement (whether such replacement year is the same as the year of conversion or a later year) shall be based on the number of months the replacement property is in service as recovery property during the replacement year.

(1) If the number of months in the conversion year after the property is converted (including the month of conversion) is greater than or equal to the number of months the replacement property is in service during the replacement year, the allowable deduction for the replacement year shall equal—

$$(a/b \times c) \times d$$

where

a = number of months replacement property is in service as recovery property during replacement year,

b = 12 or, in the case of 15-year real property converted in the first recovery year, the number of months in the taxpayer's taxable year after the converted property was placed in service by the taxpayer (including the month the property was placed in service),

c = applicable recovery percentage for converted property in year of conversion, and

d = unadjusted basis of converted property.

An allowance is permitted to the extent of any unrecovered allowance in the taxable year following the final recovery year. The term "unrecovered allowance" means the difference between—

(i) The sum of recovery allowances for the year of the conversion and the year of the replacement, and

(ii) The recovery allowance which would have been allowable in the year of conversion had such conversion not occurred.

In a year following the year of replacement, the allowable deduction shall be computed by multiplying the applicable recovery percentage for the next recovery year to the unadjusted basis of the converted property.

(2) If the number of months in the conversion year after the property is converted (including the month of conversion) is less than the number of months the replacement property is in service during the replacement year, the

allowable deduction for the replacement year shall equal—

$$[(a/b \times c) + (d/12 \times e)] \times f$$

where

a = number of months in conversion year after the property is converted (including the month of conversion),

b = 12 or, in the case of 15-year real property converted in the first recovery year, the number of months in the taxpayer's taxable year after the converted property was placed in service by the taxpayer (including the month the property was placed in service),

c = applicable recovery percentage for converted property in the year of conversion,

d = number of months replacement property is in service as recovery property during replacement year minus a,

e = applicable recovery percentage for the next recovery year, and

f = unadjusted basis of converted property.

An allowance is permitted to the extent of any unrecovered allowance in the taxable year following the final recovery year. The term "unrecovered allowance" means the difference between—

(i) The sum of the recovery allowances for the year of conversion and the year of replacement, and

(ii) The sum of the recovery allowances which would have been allowable in the year of conversion and the next recovery year had such conversion not occurred.

In a year following the year of replacement, the allowable deduction shall be computed by multiplying the unadjusted basis of the converted property by the applicable recovery percentage for the second recovery year after the year of conversion.

(iii) *Examples.*—The provisions of paragraph (f)(1)(i) and (ii) may be illustrated by the following examples:

Example (1). On January 1, 1981, A, a calendar year taxpayer, purchases for $40,000 and places in service recovery property which is 15-year real property (other than low income housing). Under section 168(b)(2) and § 1.168-2(b)(2), the allowable deductions for the first and second recovery years are $4,800 (*i.e.*, .12 × $40,000) and $4,000 (*i.e.*, .10 × $40,000). On March 3, 1983, A's property is involuntarily converted. Under the provisions of subdivision (i), A's 1983 allowable deduction for the converted property is $600 (*i.e.*, 2/12 × .09 × $40,000). On May 15, 1984, A acquires replacement property. A's unadjusted basis in the replacement property is the same as his adjusted basis in the converted property (*i.e.*, $30,600). Under the provisions of subdivision (ii), the replacement property is treated the same as the converted property with respect to such $30,600 of basis. However, in computing the allowable deduction with respect to such basis, A's unadjusted basis in the converted property ($40,000) is used. Thus, A's allowable deduction for 1984 is $2,400 (*i.e.*, 8/12 × .09 × $40,000). Under the provisions of subdivision (ii)(B)(*1*), the unrecovered allowance is $600 (*i.e.*, $3,600 – $3,000), and it must be recovered in the taxable year following the final recovery year, that is, in the taxable year following the fifteenth recovery year. A's allowable deduction for 1985 is $3,200 (*i.e.*, .08 × $40,000).

Example (2). Assume the same facts as in example (1) except that A acquires the replacement property on January 1, 1984. A's allowable deduction for 1984 is $3,533.33 (*i.e.*, [(10/12 × .09) = (2/12 × .08)] × $40,000). Under the provisions of subdivision (ii)(B)(2), the unrecovered allowance is $2,666.67 (*i.e.*, $6,800 – $4,133.33), and it must be recovered in the taxable year following the final recovery year, that is, in the taxable year following the fifteenth recovery year. A's allowance deduction for 1985 is $2,800 (*i.e.*, .07 × $40,000).

Example (3). Assume the same facts as in example (1) except that A acquires the replacement property on the same day as the conversion (March 3, 1983). A's allowable deduction for 1983 for the converted property is $600 (*i.e.*, (2/12 × .09) × $40,000). A's allowable deduction for 1983 for the replacement property is $3,000 (*i.e.*, (10/12 × .09) × $40,000). A's allowable deduction for 1984 is $3,200 (*i.e.*, $40,000 × .08).

Example (4). On February 3, 1981, B, a calendar year taxpayer, purchases for $100,000 and places in service recovery property which is 15-year real property (other than low income housing). On June 25, 1981, B's property is involuntarily converted. On that same day B acquires replacement property with the same basis as the converted property. B's allowable deduction for 1981 for the converted property is $4,000 (*i.e.*, 4/11 × .11 × $100,000). B's allowable deduction for 1981 for the replacement property is $7,000 (*i.e.*, 7/11 × .11 × $100,000). B's allowable deduction for 1982 is $10,000 (*i.e.*, $100,000 × .10).

(2) *Section 1031 transactions.*—(i) *Allowable deductions.*—In a transaction to which section 1031 applies, the allowable deduction for the exchanged and acquired properties shall be determined under the principles of subparagraph (1) of this paragraph. Similarly, any excess of the unadjusted basis of the acquired property over the adjusted basis of the exchanged property shall be treated as newly purchased ACRS property, and any excess of the adjusted basis of the exchanged property over the unadjusted basis of the acquired property shall be recovered under the principles of § 1.168-2(d)(3) (relating to redeterminations).

(ii) *Examples.*—The provisions of paragraph (f)(2)(i) may be illustrated by the following examples:

Example (1). In 1981 A, a calendar year taxpayer, purchases for $12,000 and places in service recovery property which is 3-year recovery property. Under section 168(b)(1) and § 1.168-2(b)(1), the allowable deductions for the first and second recovery years are $3,000 (*i.e.*, .25 × $12,000) and $4,560 (*i.e.*, .38 × $12,000), respectively. On March 3, 1983, A exchanges this property and $1,000 cash for property of a "like kind." A's 1983 allowable deduction for the exchanged property is $740 (*i.e.*, 2/12 × .37 × $12,000). A's basis in the acquired property is $4,700. The acquired property is treated the same as the exchanged property with respect to $3,700, which is so much of the basis in the acquired property as does not exceed the adajusted basis in the exchanged property. However, in computing the allowable deduction with respect to such basis, A's unadjusted basis in the exchanged property ($12,000) is used. Therefore, A's 1983 allowable deduction for the acquired property with respect to the substituted basis is $3,700 (*i.e.,* 10/12 × .37 × $12,000). The remaining $1,000 of basis in the acquired property is treated as newly purchased ACRS property placed in service in 1983. A may choose any applicable recovery period and recovery method for such basis and need not use the same recovery period and recovery method used for the exchanged property. If A uses the tables provided in section 168(b)(1) and § 1.168-2(b)(1), for 1983, 1984, and 1985, A is entitled to additional allowable deductions of $250, $380, and $370, respectively.

Example (2). On February 8, 1981, B, a calendar year taxpayer, purchases for $80,000 and places in service 15-year real property (other than low income housing). Under the provisions of section 168(b)(2) and § 1.168-2(b)(2), the allowable deduction for 1981 is $8,800 (*i.e.,* .11 × $80,000). On March 3, 1982, B exchanges this property and $20,000 cash for property of a "like kind." B's 1982 allowable deduction for the exchanged property is $1,333.33 (*i.e.,* 2/12 × .10 × $80,000). B's basis in the acquired property is $89,866.67. The acquired property is treated the same as the exchanged property with respect to $69,866.67, which is so much of the basis in the acquired property as does not exceed the adjusted basis in the exchanged property. However, in computing the allowable deduction with respect to such basis, B's unadjusted basis in the exchanged property ($80,000) is used. Therefore, B's 1982 and 1983 allowable deductions for the acquired property with respect to the substituted basis are $6,666.66 (*i.e.,* 10/12 × .10 × $80,000) and $7,200 (*i.e.,* .09 × $80,000), respectively. The remaining $20,000 of basis in the acquired property is treated as newly purchased ACRS property placed in service in March 1982. B may choose any applicable recovery period and recovery method for this basis and need not use the same period and method used for the exchanged property. If B uses the tables prescribed in § 1.168-2(b)(2), B's 1982 allowable deduction for this basis is $2,000 (*i.e.,* $20,000 × .10).

(3) *Transfers of property by gift.*—(i) *Allowable deductions.*—With respect to recovery property which is transferred by gift (where the donee's basis is determined under section 1015), the allowable deduction for the taxable year of the gift shall be apportioned between the donor and donee under the principles of paragraphs (b) (including paragraph (b)(4)(ii)) and (f)(1) of this section, and the donee shall be treated as the donor for subsequent taxable years to the extent that the donee's basis is carried over from the donor. That portion of the donee's basis (as determined under section 1015) in the property that exceeds the donor's adjusted basis immediately preceding the gift shall be treated as newly purchased ACRS property. The donee may choose any applicable recovery period and recovery method with respect to such excess and need not use the donor's recovery period and recovery method.

(ii) *Example.*—The provisions of paragraph (f)(3)(i) may be illustrated by the following example:

Example. In 1981 A, a calendar year taxpayer, purchases for $12,000 and places in service 5-year recovery property. Under section 168(b)(1) and § 1.168-2(b)(1), the allowable deduction for 1981 is $1,800 (*i.e.,* .15 × $12,000). On March 15, 1982, A transfers the property by gift to B (another calendar year taxpayer) who continues to use it as recovery property. A's 1982 allowable deduction is $440 (i.e., 2/12 × .22 × $12,000). Under section 1015, B's basis in the property is determined to be $11,000. In the hands of B, the donee, the property is treated the same as in the hands of the donor with respect to $9,760, which is so much of the carryover basis as does not exceed the donor's adjusted basis in the property immediately preceding the gift. However, in computing the allowable deduction with respect to such basis, the donor's unadjusted basis ($12,000) is used. Therefore, B's 1982 allowable deduction with respect to such basis is $2,200 (*i.e.,* 10/12 × .22 × $12,000). The remaining $1,240 (*i.e.,* $11,000 – $9,760) of basis is treated as newly purchased ACRS property. B may choose any applicable recovery period and recovery method for such basis and need not use the donor's recovery period and recovery method.

(4) *Transfers of property by reason of death.*—Where recovery property is transferred by reason of the death of the taxpayer, the allowable deduction for the taxpayer's taxable year which ends upon his death shall be governed by the rules applicable to short taxable years. See § 1.168-2(f). [Reg. § 1.168-5.]

§ 1.168-6. Gain or loss on dispositions.—(a) *General rule.*—Except as provided in § 1.168-2(h) (relating to mass assets), where recovery property is disposed of during a taxable year, the following rules shall apply:

(1) If the asset is disposed of by sale or exchange, gain or loss shall be recognized as provided under the applicable provisions of the Code.

(2) If the asset is disposed of by physical abandonment, loss shall be recognized in the amount of the adjusted basis of the asset at the time of the abandonment. For a loss to qualify for recognition under this subparagraph (2), the taxpayer must intend to discard the asset irrevocably so that he will neither use the asset again, nor retrieve it for sale, exchange, or other disposition.

(3) If the asset is disposed of other than by sale or exchange or physical abandonment (as, for example, where the asset is transferred to a supplies or scrap account), gain shall not be recognized. Loss shall be recognized in the amount of the excess of the adjusted basis of the asset over its fair market value at the time of the disposition. No loss shall be recognized upon the conversion of property to personal use.

(b) *Definitions.*—(1) See § 1.168-2(l)(1) for the definition of "disposition," which excludes the retirement of a structural component of 15-year real property. Thus, no loss shall be recognized on such retirement, and the unadjusted basis of the property under § 1.168-2(d) shall not be reduced. For example, if a taxpayer replaces the roof on 15-year real property, no loss is recognized upon the retirement of the replaced roof, and the unadjusted basis of the property continues to be recovered over the remaining period. For determination of the deductions allowable under section 168 with respect to the expenditures paid or incurred to replace the roof, see § 1.168-2(e).

(2) The adjusted basis of an asset at the time of its disposition is its unadjusted basis, as provided in § 1.168-2, adjusted as prescribed in § 1.1011-1. [Reg. § 1.168-6.]

Qualified Property: Additional First Year Depreciation Deduction

Qualified Property: Additional First Year Depreciation Deduction.—Amendments to Reg. §§1.168(b)-1 and 1.168(d)-1, providing guidance regarding the additional first year depreciation deduction under section 168(k) of the Internal Revenue Code (Code), are proposed (published in the Federal Register on August 8, 2018) (REG-104397-18).

Par. 4. Section 1.168(b)-1 is amended by adding paragraph (a)(5) and revising paragraph (b) to read as follows:

§1.168(b)-1. Definitions.—(a) * * *

(5) *Qualified improvement property.*—(i) Is any improvement that is section 1250 property to an interior portion of a building, as defined in §1.48-1(e)(1), that is nonresidential real property, as defined in section 168(e)(2)(B), if the improvement is placed in service by the taxpayer after the date the building was first placed in service by any person and if—

(A) For purposes of section 168(e)(6), the improvement is placed in service by the taxpayer after December 31, 2017;

(B) For purposes of section 168(k)(3) as in effect on the day before amendment by section 13204(a)(4)(B) of the Tax Cuts and Jobs Act, Public Law 115-97 (131 Stat. 2054 (December 22, 2017)) ("Act"), the improvement is acquired by the taxpayer before September 28, 2017, the improvement is placed in service by the taxpayer before January 1, 2018, and the improvement meets the original use requirement in section 168(k)(2)(A)(ii) as in effect on the day before amendment by section 13201(c)(1) of the Act; or

(C) For purposes of section 168(k)(3) as in effect on the day before amendment by section 13204(a)(4)(B) of the Act, the improvement is acquired by the taxpayer after September 27, 2017; the improvement is placed in service by the taxpayer after September 27, 2017, and before January 1, 2018; and the improvement meets the requirements in section 168(k)(2)(A)(ii) as amended by section 13201(c)(1) of the Act; and

(ii) Does not include any qualified improvement for which an expenditure is attributable to—

(A) The enlargement, as defined in §1.48-12(c)(10), of the building;

(B) Any elevator or escalator, as defined in §1.48-1(m)(2); or

(C) The internal structural framework, as defined in §1.48-12(b)(3)(iii), of the building.

(b) *Effective date.*—(1) *In general.*—Except as provided in paragraph (b)(2) of this section, this section is applicable on or after February 27, 2004.

(2) *Application of paragraph (a)(5) of this section.*—(i) *In general.*—Except as provided in paragraph (b)(2)(ii) of this section, paragraph (a)(5) of this section is applicable on or after the date of publication of a Treasury decision adopting these rules as final regulations in the **Federal Register**.

(ii) *Early application of paragraph (a)(5) of this section.*—A taxpayer may rely on the provisions of paragraph (a)(5) of this section in these proposed regulations for the taxpayer's taxable years ending on or after September 28, 2017, and ending before the taxpayer's taxable year that includes the date of publication of a Treasury decision adopting these rules as final regulations in the **Federal Register**.

Par. 5. Section 1.168(d)-1 is amended by:

1. Adding a sentence at the end of paragraph (b)(3)(ii);
2. Adding a sentence at the end of paragraph (b)(7)(ii); and
3. Adding two sentences at the end of paragraph (d)(2).

The additions read as follows:

§1.168(d)-1. Applicable conventions—half-year and mid-quarter conventions.

* * *

(b) * * *

(3) * * *

(ii) * * * Further, see §1.168(k)-2(f)(1) for rules relating to qualified property under section 168(k), as amended by the Tax Cuts and Jobs Act, Public Law 115-97 (131 Stat. 2054 (December 22, 2017)), that is placed in service by the taxpayer in the same taxable year in which either a partnership is terminated as a result of a technical termination under section 708(b)(1)(B) or the property is transferred in a transaction described in section 168(i)(7).

* * *

(7) * * *

(ii) * * * However, see §1.168(k)-2(f)(1)(iii) for a special rule regarding the allocation of the additional first year depreciation deduction in the case of certain contributions of property to a partnership under section 721.

* * *

(d) * * *

(2) * * * The last sentences in paragraphs (b)(3)(ii) and (b)(7)(ii) of this section apply to qualified property under section 168(k)(2) placed in service by a taxpayer during or after the taxpayer's taxable year that includes the date of publication of a Treasury decision adopting these rules as final regulations in the **Federal Register**. However, a taxpayer may rely on the last sentences in paragraphs (b)(3)(ii) and (b)(7)(ii) of this section in these proposed regulations for qualified property under section 168(k)(2) acquired and placed in service after September 27, 2017, by the taxpayer during taxable years ending on or after September 28, 2017, and ending before the taxpayer's taxable year that includes the date of publication of a Treasury decision adopting these rules as final regulations in the **Federal Register**.

* * *

Tax-Exempt Entity Leasing

Accelerated Cost Recovery System: Tax-Exempt Entity Leasing.—Temporary Reg. § 1.168(j)-1T, regarding tax-exempt entity leasing is also proposed as a final regulations and, when adopted, would become Reg. § 1.168(j)-1 (published in the Federal Register on July 2, 1985).

§ 1.168(j)-1. Questions and answers concerning tax-exempt entity leasing rules.

Qualified Property: Additional First Year Depreciation Deduction

Qualified Property: Additional First Year Depreciation Deduction.—Amendments to Reg. §§ 1.168(i)-4 and 1.168(i)-6, providing guidance regarding the additional first year depreciation deduction under section 168(k) of the Internal Revenue Code (Code), are proposed (published in the Federal Register on August 8, 2018) (REG-104397-18).

Par. 6. Section 1.168(i)-4 is amended by:

1. In the penultimate sentence in paragraph (b)(1), removing "§§ 1.168(k)-1T(f)(6)(iii) and 1.1400L(b)-1T(f)(6)" and adding "§ 1.168(k)-1(f)(6)(iii) or 1.168(k)-2(f)(6)(iii), as applicable, and § 1.1400L(b)-1(f)(6)" in its place;

2. In the fifth sentence in paragraph (c), removing "§§ 1.168(k)-1T(f)(6)(ii) and 1.1400L(b)-1T(f)(6)" and adding "§ 1.168(k)-1(f)(6)(ii) or 1.168(k)-2(f)(6)(ii), as applicable, and § 1.1400L(b)-1(f)(6)" in its place;

3. In the second sentence in paragraph (d)(3)(i)(C), removing "§§ 1.168(k)-1T(f)(6)(iv) and 1.400L(b)-1T(f)(6)" and adding "§ 1.168(k)-1(f)(6)(iv) or 1.168(k)-2(f)(6)(iv), as applicable, and § 1.400L(b)-1(f)(6)" in its place;

4. In the last sentence in paragraph (d)(4)(i), removing "§§ 1.168(k)-1T(f)(6)(iv) and 1.1400L(b)-1T(f)(6)" and adding "§ 1.168(k)-1(f)(6)(iv) or 1.168(k)-2(f)(6)(iv), as applicable, and § 1.400L(b)-1(f)(6)" in its place;

5. Revising the first sentence in paragraph (g)(1); and

6. Redesignating paragraph (g)(2) as paragraph (g)(3) and adding new paragraph (g)(2).

The addition and revision read as follows:

§ 1.168(i)-4. Changes in use.

* * *

(g) * * *

(1) * * * Except as provided in paragraph (g)(2) of this section, this section applies to any change in the use of MACRS property in a taxable year ending on or after June 17, 2004. * * *

(2) *Qualified property under section 168(k) acquired and placed in service after September 27, 2017.*—The language "or § 1.168(k)-2(f)(6)(iii), as applicable" in paragraph (b)(1) of this section, the language "or § 1.168(k)-2(f)(6)(ii), as applicable" in paragraph (c) of this section, and the language "or § 1.168(k)-2(f)(6)(iv), as applicable" in paragraphs (d)(3)(i)(C) and (d)(4)(i) of this section applies to any change in use of MACRS property, which is qualified property under section 168(k)(2), by a taxpayer during or after the taxpayer's taxable year that includes the date of publication of a Treasury decision adopting these rules as final regulations in the **Federal Register**. However, a taxpayer may rely on the language "or § 1.168(k)-2(f)(6)(iii), as applicable" in paragraph (b)(1) of this section, the language "or § 1.168(k)-2(f)(6)(ii), as applicable" in paragraph (c) of this section, and the language "or § 1.168(k)-2(f)(6)(iv), as applicable" in paragraphs (d)(3)(i)(C) and (d)(4)(i) of this section in these proposed regulations for any change in use of MACRS property, which is qualified property under section 168(k)(2) and acquired and placed in service after September 27, 2017, by the taxpayer during taxable years ending on or after September 28, 2017, and ending before the taxpayer's taxable year that includes the date of publication of a Treasury decision adopting these rules as final regulations in the **Federal Register**.

* * *

Par. 7. Section 1.168(i)-6 is amended by:

1. In paragraph (d)(3)(ii)(B), removing "1.168(k)-1(f)(5) or § 1.1400L(b)-1(f)(5)" wherever it appears and adding "1.168(k)-1(f)(5), 1.168(k)-2(f)(5), or 1.1400L(b)-1(f)(5)" in its place;

2. In paragraph (d)(3)(ii)(E), removing "1.168(k)-1(f)(5) or § 1.1400L(b)-1(f)(5)" and adding "1.168(k)-1(f)(5), 1.168(k)-2(f)(5), or 1.1400L(b)-1(f)(5)" in its place;

3. Adding a sentence at the end of paragraph (d)(4);

4. Adding a sentence at the end of paragraph (h); and

5. Adding paragraph (k)(4).

The additions read as follows:

§ 1.168(i)-6. Like-kind exchanges and involuntary conversions.

* * *

(d) * * *

(4) * * * Further, see § 1.168(k)-2(f)(5)(iv) for replacement MACRS property that is qualified property under section 168(k), as amended by the Tax Cuts and Jobs Act, Public Law 115-97 (131 Stat. 2054 (December 22, 2017)).

* * *

(h) * * * Further, see § 1.168(k)-2(f)(5) for qualified property under section 168(k), as amended by the Tax Cuts and Jobs Act, Public Law 115-97 (131 Stat. 2054 (December 22, 2017)).

* * *

(k) * * *

(4) *Qualified property under section 168(k) acquired and placed in service after September 27, 2017.*—The language "1.168(k)-2(f)(5)," in paragraphs (d)(3)(ii)(B) and (E) of this section

and the last sentences in paragraphs (d)(4) and (h) of this section apply to a like-kind exchange or an involuntary conversion of MACRS property, which is qualified property under section 168(k)(2), for which the time of replacement occurs on or after the date of publication of a Treasury decision adopting these rules as final regulations in the **Federal Register**. However, a taxpayer may rely on the language "1.168(k)-2(f)(5)," in paragraphs (d)(3)(ii)(B) and (E) of this section and the last sentences in paragraphs (d)(4) and (h) of this section in these proposed regulations for a like-kind exchange or an involuntary conversion of MACRS property, which is qualified property under section 168(k)(2), for which the time of replacement occurs on or after September 28, 2017, and occurs before the date of publication of a Treasury decision adopting these rules as final regulations in the **Federal Register**.

Qualified Property: Additional First Year Depreciation Deduction

Qualified Property: Additional First Year Depreciation Deduction.—Amendments to Reg. §1.168(k)-0, providing guidance regarding the additional first year depreciation deduction under section 168(k) of the Internal Revenue Code (Code), are proposed (published in the Federal Register on August 8, 2018) (REG-104397-18).

Par. 8. Section 1.168(k)-0 is amended by revising the introductory text and adding an entry for §1.168(k)-2 in numerical order to the table of contents to read as follows:

§1.168(k)-0. Table of contents.—This section lists the major paragraphs contained in §§1.168(k)-1 and 1.168(k)-2.

* * *

Qualified Property: Additional First Year Depreciation Deduction

Qualified Property: Additional First Year Depreciation Deduction.—Reg. §1.168(k)-2, providing guidance regarding the additional first year depreciation deduction under section 168(k) of the Internal Revenue Code (Code), is proposed (published in the Federal Register on August 8, 2018) (REG-104397-18).

Par. 9. Section 1.168(k)-2 is added to read as follows:

§1.168(k)-2. Additional first year depreciation deduction for property acquired and placed in service after September 27, 2017.—(a) *Scope and definitions.*—(1) *Scope.*—This section provides rules for determining the additional first year depreciation deduction allowable under section 168(k) for qualified property acquired and placed in service after September 27, 2017.

(2) *Definitions.*—For purposes of this section—

(i) *Act* is the Tax Cuts and Jobs Act, Public Law 115-97 (131 Stat. 2054 (December 22, 2017)); and

(ii) *Applicable percentage* is the percentage provided in section 168(k)(6).

(b) *Qualified property.*—(1) *In general.*—Qualified property is depreciable property, as defined in §1.168(b)-1(a)(1), that meets all the following requirements in the first taxable year in which the property is subject to depreciation by the taxpayer whether or not depreciation deductions for the property are allowable:

(i) The requirements in §1.168(k)-2(b)(2) (description of qualified property);

(ii) The requirements in §1.168(k)-2(b)(3) (original use or used property acquisition requirements);

(iii) The requirements in §1.168(k)-2(b)(4) (placed-in-service date); and

(iv) The requirements in §1.168(k)-2(b)(5) (acquisition of property).

(2) *Description of qualified property.*—(i) *In general.*—Depreciable property will meet the requirements of this paragraph (b)(2) if the property is—

(A) MACRS property, as defined in §1.168(b)-1(a)(2), that has a recovery period of 20 years or less. For purposes of this paragraph (b)(2)(i)(A) and section 168(k)(2)(A)(i)(I), the recovery period is determined in accordance with section 168(c) regardless of any election made by the taxpayer under section 168(g)(7). This paragraph (b)(2)(i)(A) includes the following MACRS property that is acquired by the taxpayer after September 27, 2017, and placed in service by the taxpayer after September 27, 2017, and before January 1, 2018:

(1) Qualified leasehold improvement property as defined in section 168(e)(6) as in effect on the day before amendment by section 13204(a)(1) of the Act;

(2) Qualified restaurant property, as defined in section 168(e)(7) as in effect on the day before amendment by section 13204(a)(1) of the Act, that is qualified improvement property as defined in § 1.168(b)-1(a)(5)(i)(C) and (a)(5)(ii); and

(3) Qualified retail improvement property as defined in section 168(e)(8) as in effect on the day before amendment by section 13204(a)(1) of the Act;

(B) Computer software as defined in, and depreciated under, section 167(f)(1) and the regulations under section 167(f)(1);

(C) Water utility property as defined in section 168(e)(5) and depreciated under section 168;

(D) Qualified improvement property as defined in § 1.168(b)-1(a)(5)(i)(C) and (a)(5)(ii) and depreciated under section 168;

(E) Qualified film or television production, as defined in section 181(d) and § 1.181-3, for which a deduction would have been allowable under section 181 without regard to section 181(a)(2) and (g), or section 168(k);

(F) Qualified live theatrical production, as defined in section 181(e), for which a deduction would have been allowable under section 181 without regard to section 181(a)(2) and (g), or section 168(k); or

(G) A specified plant, as defined in section 168(k)(5)(B), for which the taxpayer has properly made an election to apply section 168(k)(5) for the taxable year in which the specified plant is planted, or grafted to a plant that has already been planted, by the taxpayer in the ordinary course of the taxpayer's farming business, as defined in section 263A(e)(4) (for further guidance, see paragraph (e) of this section).

(ii) *Property not eligible for additional first year depreciation deduction.*—Depreciable property will not meet the requirements of this paragraph (b)(2) if the property is—

(A) Described in section 168(f) (for example, automobiles for which the taxpayer uses the optional business standard mileage rate);

(B) Required to be depreciated under the alternative depreciation system of section 168(g) pursuant to section 168(g)(1)(A), (B), (C), (D), (F), or (G), or other provisions of the Internal Revenue Code (for example, property described in section 263A(e)(2)(A) if the taxpayer or any related person, as defined in section 263A(e)(2)(B), has made an election under section 263A(d)(3), or property described in section 280F(b)(1));

(C) Included in any class of property for which the taxpayer elects not to deduct the additional first year depreciation (for further guidance, see paragraph (e) of this section);

(D) A specified plant that is placed in service by the taxpayer during the taxable year and for which the taxpayer made an election to apply section 168(k)(5) for a prior taxable year;

(E) Included in any class of property for which the taxpayer elects to apply section 168(k)(4). This paragraph (b)(2)(ii)(E) applies to property placed in service in any taxable year beginning before January 1, 2018;

(F) Described in section 168(k)(9)(A) and placed in service in any taxable year beginning after December 31, 2017; or

(G) Described in section 168(k)(9)(B) and placed in service in any taxable year beginning after December 31, 2017.

(3) *Original use or used property acquisition requirements.*—(i) *In general.*—Depreciable property will meet the requirements of this paragraph (b)(3) if the property meets the original use requirements in paragraph (b)(3)(ii) of this section or if the property meets the used property acquisition requirements in paragraph (b)(3)(iii) of this section.

(ii) *Original use.*—(A) *In general.*—Depreciable property will meet the requirements of this paragraph (b)(3)(ii) if the original use of the property commences with the taxpayer. Except as provided in paragraphs (b)(3)(ii)(B) and (C) of this section, original use means the first use to which the property is put, whether or not that use corresponds to the use of the property by the taxpayer. Additional capital expenditures incurred by a taxpayer to recondition or rebuild property acquired or owned by the taxpayer satisfy the original use requirement. However, the cost of reconditioned or rebuilt property does not satisfy the original use requirement (but may satisfy the used property acquisition requirements in paragraph (b)(3)(iii) of this section). The question of whether property is reconditioned or rebuilt property is a question of fact. For purposes of this paragraph (b)(3)(ii)(A), property that contains used parts will not be treated as reconditioned or rebuilt if the cost of the used parts is not more than 20 percent of the total cost of the property, whether acquired or self-constructed.

(B) *Conversion to business or income-producing use.*—*(1) Personal use to business or income-producing use.*—If a taxpayer initially acquires new property for personal use and subsequently uses the property in the taxpayer's trade or business or for the taxpayer's production of income, the taxpayer is considered the original user of the property. If a person initially acquires new property for personal use and a taxpayer subsequently acquires the property from the person for use in the taxpayer's trade or business or for the taxpayer's production of income, the taxpayer is not considered the original user of the property.

(2) Inventory to business or income-producing use.—If a taxpayer initially acquires new property and holds the property primarily for sale to customers in the ordinary course of the taxpayer's business and subsequently withdraws the property from inventory and uses the property primarily in the taxpayer's trade or business or primarily for the taxpayer's production of income, the taxpayer is considered the original user of the property. If a person initially acquires new property and holds the property primarily for sale to customers in the ordinary course of the person's business and a taxpayer subsequently acquires the property from the per-

son for use primarily in the taxpayer's trade or business or primarily for the taxpayer's production of income, the taxpayer is considered the original user of the property. For purposes of this paragraph (b)(3)(ii)(B)(*2*), the original use of the property by the taxpayer commences on the date on which the taxpayer uses the property primarily in the taxpayer's trade or business or primarily for the taxpayer's production of income.

(C) *Fractional interests in property.*—If, in the ordinary course of its business, a taxpayer sells fractional interests in new property to third parties unrelated to the taxpayer, each first fractional owner of the property is considered as the original user of its proportionate share of the property. Furthermore, if the taxpayer uses the property before all of the fractional interests of the property are sold but the property continues to be held primarily for sale by the taxpayer, the original use of any fractional interest sold to a third party unrelated to the taxpayer subsequent to the taxpayer's use of the property begins with the first purchaser of that fractional interest. For purposes of this paragraph (b)(3)(ii)(C), persons are not related if they do not have a relationship described in section 267(b) or 707(b) and the regulations under section 267(b) or 707(b).

(iii) *Used property acquisition requirements.*—(A) *In general.*—Depreciable property will meet the requirements of this paragraph (b)(3)(iii) if the acquisition of the used property meets the following requirements:

(*1*) Such property was not used by the taxpayer or a predecessor at any time prior to such acquisition;

(*2*) The acquisition of such property meets the requirements of section 179(d)(2)(A), (B), and (C), and § 1.179-4(c)(1)(ii), (iii), and (iv), or 1.179-4(c)(2) (property is acquired by purchase); and

(*3*) The acquisition of such property meets the requirements of section 179(d)(3) and § 1.179-4(d) (cost of property) (for further guidance regarding like-kind exchanges and involuntary conversions, see paragraph (f)(5) of this section).

(B) *Property was not used by the taxpayer at any time prior to acquisition.*—(*1*) *In general.*—Solely for purposes of paragraph (b)(3)(iii)(A)(*1*) of this section, the property is treated as used by the taxpayer or a predecessor at any time prior to acquisition by the taxpayer or predecessor if the taxpayer or the predecessor had a depreciable interest in the property at any time prior to such acquisition, whether or not the taxpayer or the predecessor claimed depreciation deductions for the property. If a lessee has a depreciable interest in the improvements made to leased property and subsequently the lessee acquires the leased property of which the improvements are a part, the unadjusted depreciable basis, as defined in § 1.168(b)-1(a)(3), of the acquired property that is eligible for the additional first year depreciation deduction, assuming all other requirements are met, must not include the unadjusted depreciable basis attributable to the improvements.

(*2*) *Taxpayer has a depreciable interest in a portion of the property.*—If a taxpayer initially acquires a depreciable interest in a portion of the property and subsequently acquires a depreciable interest in an additional portion of the same property, such additional depreciable interest is not treated as used by the taxpayer at any time prior to its acquisition by the taxpayer. This paragraph (b)(3)(iii)(B)(*2*) does not apply if the taxpayer or a predecessor previously had a depreciable interest in the subsequently acquired additional portion. For purposes of this paragraph (b)(3)(iii)(B)(*2*), a portion of the property is considered to be the percentage interest in the property. If a taxpayer holds a depreciable interest in a portion of the property, sells that portion or a part of that portion, and subsequently acquires a depreciable interest in another portion of the same property, the taxpayer will be treated as previously having a depreciable interest in the property up to the amount of the portion for which the taxpayer held a depreciable interest in the property before the sale.

(*3*) *Application to members of a consolidated group.*—(*i*) *Same consolidated group.*—Solely for purposes of applying paragraph (b)(3)(iii)(A)(*1*) of this section, if a member of a consolidated group, as defined in § 1.1502-1(h), acquires depreciable property in which the consolidated group had a depreciable interest at any time prior to the member's acquisition of the property, the member will be treated as having a depreciable interest in the property prior to the acquisition. For purposes of this paragraph (b)(3)(iii)(B)(*3*)(*i*), a consolidated group will be treated as having a depreciable interest in property during the time any current or previous member of the group had a depreciable interest in the property while a member of the group.

(*ii*) *Certain acquisitions pursuant to a series of related transactions.*—Solely for purposes of applying paragraph (b)(3)(iii)(A)(*1*) of this section, if a series of related transactions includes one or more transactions in which property is acquired by a member of a consolidated group and one or more transactions in which a corporation that had a depreciable interest in the property becomes a member of the group, the member that acquires the property will be treated as having a depreciable interest in the property prior to the time of its acquisition.

(*iii*) *Time for testing membership.*—Solely for purposes of applying paragraph (b)(3)(iii)(B)(*3*)(*i*) and (*ii*) of this section, if a series of related transactions includes one or more transactions in which property is acquired by a member of a consolidated group and one or more transactions in which the transferee of the property ceases to be a member of a consolidated group, whether the taxpayer is a member of a consolidated group is tested immediately after the last transaction in the series.

(C) *Special rules for a series of related transactions.*—Solely for purposes of section 168(k)(2)(E)(ii) and paragraph (b)(3)(iii)(A) of this section, in the case of a series of related transactions (for example, a series of related transactions including the transfer of a partnership interest, the transfer of partnership assets, or the disposition of property and the disposition, directly or indirectly, of the transferor or transferee of the property)—

(*1*) The property is treated as directly transferred from the original transferor to the ultimate transferee; and

(*2*) The relation between the original transferor and the ultimate transferee is tested immediately after the last transaction in the series.

(iv) *Application to partnerships.*—(A) *Section 704(c) remedial allocations.*—Remedial allocations under section 704(c) do not satisfy the requirements of paragraph (b)(3) of this section. See § 1.704-3(d)(2).

(B) *Basis determined under section 732.*—Any basis of distributed property determined under section 732 does not satisfy the requirements of paragraph (b)(3) of this section.

(C) *Section 734(b) adjustments.*—Any increase in basis of depreciable property under section 734(b) does not satisfy the requirements of paragraph (b)(3) of this section.

(D) *Section 743(b) adjustments.*—*(1) In general.*—For purposes of determining whether the transfer of a partnership interest meets the requirements of paragraph (b)(3)(iii)(A) of this section, each partner is treated as having a depreciable interest in the partner's proportionate share of partnership property. Any increase in basis of depreciable property under section 743(b) satisfies the requirements of paragraph (b)(3)(iii)(A) of this section if—

(i) At any time prior to the transfer of the partnership interest that gave rise to such basis increase, neither the transferee partner nor a predecessor of the transferee partner had any depreciable interest in the portion of the property deemed acquired to which the section 743(b) adjustment is allocated under section 755 and the regulations under section 755; and

(ii) The transfer of the partnership interest that gave rise to such basis increase satisfies the requirements of paragraphs (b)(3)(iii)(A)(*2*) and (*3*) of this section.

(2) Relatedness tested at partner level.—Solely for purposes of paragraph (b)(3)(iv)(D)(*1*)(*ii*) of this section, whether the parties are related or unrelated is determined by comparing the transferor and the transferee of the transferred partnership interest.

(v) *Syndication transaction.*—If a lessor has a depreciable interest in the property and the lessor and any predecessor did not previously have a depreciable interest in the property, and the property is sold by the lessor or any subsequent purchaser within three months after the date the property was originally placed in service by the lessor (or, in the case of multiple units of property subject to the same lease, within three months after the date the final unit is placed in service, so long as the period between the time the first unit is placed in service and the time the last unit is placed in service does not exceed 12 months), and the user of the property after the last sale during the three-month period remains the same as when the property was originally placed in service by the lessor, the purchaser of the property in the last sale during the three-month period is considered the taxpayer that acquired the property for purposes of applying paragraphs (b)(3)(ii) and (iii) of this section.

(vi) *Examples.*—The application of this paragraph (b)(3) is illustrated by the following examples. Unless the facts specifically indicate otherwise, assume that the parties are not related within the meaning of section 179(d)(2)(A) or (B) and § 1.179-4(c), no corporation is a member of a consolidated or controlled group, and the parties do not have predecessors:

Example 1. (i) On August 1, 2018, *A* buys a new machine for $35,000 from an unrelated party for use in *A*'s trade or business. On July 1, 2020, *B* buys that machine from *A* for $20,000 for use in *B*'s trade or business. On October 1, 2020, *B* makes a $5,000 capital expenditure to recondition the machine. *B* did not have any depreciable interest in the machine before *B* acquired it on July 1, 2020.

(ii) *A*'s purchase price of $35,000 satisfies the original use requirement of paragraph (b)(3)(ii) of this section and, assuming all other requirements are met, qualifies for the additional first year depreciation deduction.

(iii) *B*'s purchase price of $20,000 does not satisfy the original use requirement of paragraph (b)(3)(ii) of this section, but it does satisfy the used property acquisition requirements of paragraph (b)(3)(iii) of this section. Assuming all other requirements are met, the $20,000 purchase price qualifies for the additional first year depreciation deduction. Further, *B*'s $5,000 expenditure satisfies the original use requirement of paragraph (b)(3)(ii) of this section and, assuming all other requirements are met, qualifies for the additional first year depreciation deduction, regardless of whether the $5,000 is added to the basis of the machine or is capitalized as a separate asset.

Example 2. *C*, an automobile dealer, uses some of its automobiles as demonstrators in order to show them to prospective customers. The automobiles that are used as demonstrators by *C* are held by *C* primarily for sale to customers in the ordinary course of its business. On November 1, 2017, *D* buys from *C* an automobile that was previously used as a demonstrator by *C*. *D* will use the automobile solely for business purposes. The use of the automobile by *C* as a demonstrator does not constitute a "use" for purposes of the original use requirement and, therefore, *D* will be considered the original user of the automobile for purposes of paragraph (b)(3)(ii) of this section. Assuming all other requirements are met, *D*'s purchase price of the automobile qualifies for the additional first year depreciation deduction for *D*, subject to any limitation under section 280F.

Example 3. On April 1, 2015, *E* acquires a horse to be used in *E*'s thoroughbred racing business. On October 1, 2018, *F* buys the horse from *E* and will use the horse in *F*'s horse breeding business. *F* did not have any depreciable interest in the horse before *F* acquired it on October 1, 2018. The use of the horse by *E* in its racing business prevents *F* from satisfying the original use requirement of paragraph (b)(3)(ii) of this section. However, *F*'s acquisition of the horse satisfies the used property acquisition requirements of paragraph (b)(3)(iii) of this section. Assuming all other requirements are met, *F*'s purchase price of the horse qualifies for the additional first year depreciation deduction for *F*.

Example 4. In the ordinary course of its business, *G* sells fractional interests in its aircraft to unrelated parties. *G* holds out for sale eight equal fractional interests in an aircraft. On October 1, 2017, *G* sells five of the eight fractional interests in the aircraft to *H* and *H* begins to use its proportionate share of the aircraft immediately upon purchase. On February 1, 2018, *G* sells to *I* the remaining unsold 3/8 fractional interests in the aircraft. *H* is considered the original user as to its 5/8 fractional interest in the aircraft and *I* is considered the original user as to its 3/8 fractional interest in the aircraft. Thus, assuming all other requirements are met, *H*'s purchase price for its 5/8 fractional interest in the aircraft qualifies for the additional first year depreciation deduction and *I*'s purchase price for its 3/8 fractional interest in the aircraft qualifies for the additional first year depreciation deduction.

Example 5. On September 1, 2017, *J*, an equipment dealer, buys new tractors that are held by *J* primarily for sale to customers in the ordinary course of its business. On October 15, 2017, *J* withdraws the tractors from inventory and begins to use the tractors primarily for producing rental income. The holding of the tractors by *J* as inventory does not constitute a "use" for purposes of the original use requirement and, therefore, the original use of the tractors commences with *J* on October 15, 2017, for purposes of paragraph (b)(3)(ii) of this section. However, the tractors are not eligible for the 100-percent additional first year depreciation deduction because *J* acquired the tractors before September 28, 2017.

Example 6. *K* is in the trade or business of leasing equipment to others. During 2016, *K* buys a new machine (Machine #1) and then leases it to *L* for use in *L*'s trade or business. The lease between *K* and *L* for Machine #1 is a true lease for federal income tax purposes. During 2018, *L* enters into a written binding contract with *K* to buy Machine #1 at its fair market value on May 15, 2018. *L* did not have any depreciable interest in Machine #1 before *L* acquired it on May 15, 2018. As a result, *L*'s acquisition of Machine #1 satisfies the used property acquisition requirements of paragraph (b)(3)(iii) of this section. Assuming all other requirements are met, *L*'s purchase price of Machine #1 qualifies for the additional first year depreciation deduction for *L*.

Example 7. The facts are the same as in *Example 6* of this paragraph (b)(3)(vi), except that *K* and *L* are related parties within the meaning of section 179(d)(2)(A) or (B) and § 1.179-4(c). As a result, *L*'s acquisition of Machine #1 does not satisfy the used property acquisition requirements of paragraph (b)(3)(iii) of this section. Thus, Machine #1 is not eligible for the additional first year depreciation deduction for *L*.

Example 8. The facts are the same as in *Example 6* of this paragraph (b)(3)(vi), except *L* incurred capital expenditures of $5,000 to improve Machine #1 on September 5, 2017, and has a depreciable interest in such improvements. *L*'s purchase price of $5,000 for the improvements to Machine #1 satisfies the original use requirement of § 1.168(k)-1(b)(3)(i) and, assuming all other requirements are met, qualifies for the 50-percent additional first year depreciation deduction. Because *L* had a depreciable interest only in the improvements to Machine #1, *L*'s acquisition of Machine #1, excluding *L*'s improvements to such machine, satisfies the used property acquisition requirements of paragraph (b)(3)(iii) of this section. Assuming all other requirements are met, *L*'s unadjusted depreciable basis of Machine #1, excluding the amount of such unadjusted depreciable basis attributable to *L*'s improvements to Machine #1, qualifies for the 100-percent additional first year depreciation deduction.

Example 9. During 2016, *M* and *N* purchased used equipment for use in their trades or businesses and each own a 50 percent interest in such equipment. Prior to this acquisition, *M* and *N* did not have any depreciable interest in the equipment. Assume this ownership arrangement is not a partnership. During 2018, *N* enters into a written binding contract with *M* to buy *M*'s interest in the equipment. Pursuant to paragraph (b)(3)(iii)(B)(*2*) of this section, *N* is not treated as using *M*'s interest in the equipment prior to N's acquisition of *M*'s interest. As a result, *N* s acquisition of *M*'s interest in the equipment satisfies the used property acquisition requirements of paragraph (b)(3)(iii) of this section. Assuming all other requirements are met, *N*'s purchase price of *M*'s interest in the equipment qualifies for the additional first year depreciation deduction for *N*.

Example 10. The facts are the same as in *Example 9* of this paragraph (b)(3)(vi), except *N* had a 100 percent depreciable interest in the equipment prior to 2016 and *M* purchased from *N* a 50 percent interest in the equipment during 2016. As a result, N's acquisition of *M*'s interest in the equipment during 2018 does not satisfy the used property acquisition requirements of paragraphs (b)(3)(iii)(A)(*1*) and (b)(3)(iii)(B)(*1*) of this section. Paragraph (b)(3)(iii)(B)(*2*) of this section does not apply because *N* initially acquired a 100 percent depreciable interest in the equipment. Accordingly, *N*'s purchase price of *M*'s interest in the equipment during 2018 does not qualify for the additional first year depreciation deduction for *N*.

Example 11. The facts are the same as in *Example 9* of this paragraph (b)(3)(vi), except during 2018, *M* also enters into a written binding contract with *N* to buy *N*'s interest in the equipment. Pursuant to paragraph (b)(3)(iii)(B)(*2*) of this section, both *M* and *N* are treated as previously having a depreciable interest in a 50-percent portion of the equipment. Accordingly, the acquisition by *M* of *N*'s 50-percent interest and the acquisition by *N* of *M*'s 50-percent interest in the equipment during 2018 do not qualify for the additional first year depreciation deduction.

Example 12. *O* and *P* form an equal partnership, *OP*, in 2018. *O* contributes cash to *OP*, and *P* contributes equipment to *OP*. *OP*'s basis in the equipment contributed by *P* is determined under section 723. Because *OP*'s basis in such equipment is determined in whole or in part by reference to *P*'s adjusted basis in such equipment, *OP*'s acquisition of such equipment does not satisfy section 179(d)(2)(C) and § 1.179-4(c)(1)(iv) and, thus, does not satisfy the used property acquisition requirements of paragraph (b)(3)(iii) of this section. Accordingly, *OP*'s acquisition of such equipment is not eligible for the additional first year depreciation deduction.

Example 13. *Q*, *R*, and *S* form an equal partnership, *QRS*, in 2019. Each partner contributes $100, which *QRS* uses to purchase a retail motor fuels outlet for $300. Assume this retail motor fuels outlet is *QRS*' only property and is qualified property under section 168(k)(2)(A)(i). *QRS* makes an election not to deduct the additional first year depreciation for all qualified property placed in service during 2019. *QRS* has a section 754 election in effect. *QRS* claimed depreciation of $15 for the retail motor fuels outlet for 2019. During 2020, when the retail motor fuels outlet's fair market value is $600, *Q* sells all of his partnership interest to *T* in a fully taxable transaction for $200. *T* never previously had a depreciable interest in the retail motor fuels outlet. *T* takes an outside basis of $200 in the partnership interest previously owned by *Q*. *T*'s share of the partnership's previously taxed capital is $95. Accordingly, *T*'s section 743(b) adjustment is $105 and is allocated entirely to the retail motor fuels outlet under section 755. Assuming all other requirements are met, *T*'s section 743(b) adjustment qualifies for the additional first year depreciation deduction.

Example 14. The facts are the same as in *Example 13* of this paragraph (b)(3)(vi), except that *Q* sells his partnership interest to *U*, a related person within the meaning of section 179(d)(2)(A) or (B) and § 1.179-4(c). *U*'s section 743(b) adjustment does not qualify for the additional first year depreciation deduction.

Example 15. The facts are the same as in *Example 13* of this paragraph (b)(3)(vi), except that *Q* dies and his partnership interest is transferred to *V*. *V* takes a basis in *Q*'s partnership interest under section 1014. As a result, section 179(d)(2)(C)(ii) and § 1.179-4(c)(1)(iv) are not satisfied, and *V*'s section 743(b) adjustment does not qualify for the additional first year depreciation deduction.

Example 16. The facts are the same as in *Example 13* of this paragraph (b)(3)(vi), except that *QRS* purchased the retail motor fuels outlet from *T* prior to *T* purchasing *Q*'s partnership interest in *QRS*. *T* had a depreciable interest in such retail motor fuels outlet. Because *T* had a depreciable interest in the retail motor fuels outlet before *T* acquired its interest in *QRS*, *T*'s section 743(b) adjustment does not qualify for the additional first year depreciation deduction.

Example 17. In November 2017, AA Corporation purchases a used drill press costing $10,000 and is granted a trade-in allowance of $2,000 on its old drill press. The used drill press is qualified property under section 168(k)(2)(A)(i). The old drill press had a basis of $1,200. Under sections 1012 and 1031(d), the basis of the used drill press is $9,200 ($1,200 basis of old drill press plus cash expended of $8,000). Only $8,000 of the basis of the used drill press satisfies the requirements of section 179(d)(3) and § 1.179-4(d) and, thus, satisfies the used property acquisition requirement of paragraph (b)(3)(iii) of this section. The remaining $1,200 of the basis of the used drill press does not satisfy the requirements of section 179(d)(3) and § 1.179-4(d) because it is determined by reference to the old drill press. Accordingly, assuming all other requirements are met, only $8,000 of the basis of the used drill press is eligible for the additional first year depreciation deduction.

Example 18. In a series of related transactions, a father sells a machine to an unrelated party who sells the machine to the father's daughter for use in the daughter's trade or business. Pursuant to paragraph (b)(3)(iii)(C) of this section, the transfers of the machine are treated as a direct transfer from the father to his daughter and the time to test whether the parties are related is immediately after the last transaction in the series. Because the father and the daughter are related parties within the meaning of section 179(d)(2)(A) and § 1.179-4(c)(ii), the daughter's acquisition of the machine does not satisfy the used property acquisition requirements of paragraph (b)(3)(iii) of this section. Further, because the transfers of the machine are treated as a direct transfer from the father to his daughter, the unrelated party's acquisition of the machine is not eligible for the additional first year depreciation deduction.

Example 19. Parent owns all of the stock of B Corporation and C Corporation. Parent, B Corporation, and C Corporation are all members of the Parent consolidated group. C Corporation has a depreciable interest in Equipment #1. During 2018, C Corporation sells Equipment #1 to B Corporation. Prior to this acquisition, B Corporation never had a depreciable interest in Equipment #1. B Corporation's acquisition of Equipment #1 does not satisfy the used property acquisition requirements of paragraph (b)(3)(iii) of this section for two reasons. First, B Corporation and C Corporation are related parties within the meaning of section 179(d)(2)(B) and § 1.179-4(c)(2)(iii). Second, pursuant to paragraph (b)(3)(iii)(B)(*3*)(*i*) of this section, B Corporation is treated as previously having a depreciable interest in Equipment #1 because B Corporation is a member of the Parent consolidated group and C Corporation, while a member of the Parent consolidated group, had a depreciable interest in Equipment #1. Accordingly, B Corporation's acquisition of Equipment #1 is not eligible for the additional first year depreciation deduction.

Example 20. (i) Parent owns all of the stock of D Corporation and E Corporation. Parent, D Corporation, and E Corporation are all members of the Parent consolidated group. D Corporation has a depreciable interest in Equipment #2. No other members of the Parent consolidated group ever had a depreciable interest in Equipment #2. During 2018, D Corporation sells Equipment #2 to *BA*, a person not related, within the meaning of section 179(d)(2)(A) or (B) and § 1.179-4(c), to any member of the Parent consolidated group. In an unrelated transaction during 2019, E Corporation acquires Equipment #2 from *BA* or another person not related to any member of the Parent consolidated group within the meaning of section 179(d)(2)(A) or (B) and § 1.179-4(c).

(ii) Pursuant to paragraph (b)(3)(iii)(B)(*3*)(*i*) of this section, E Corporation is treated as previously having a depreciable interest in Equipment #2 because E Corporation is a member of the Parent consolidated group, and D Corporation, while a member of the Parent consolidated group, had a depreciable interest in Equipment #2. As a result, E Corporation's acquisition of Equipment #2 does not satisfy the used property acquisition requirements of paragraph (b)(3)(iii) of this section. Thus, E Corporation's acquisition of Equipment #2 is not eligible for the additional first year depreciation deduction. The results would be the same if D Corporation had ceased to be a member of the Parent consolidated group prior to E Corporation's acquisition of Equipment #2.

Example 21. (i) Parent owns all of the stock of F Corporation and G Corporation. Parent, F Corporation, and G Corporation are all members of the Parent consolidated group. G Corporation has a depreciable interest in Equipment #3. No other members of the Parent consolidated group ever had a depreciable interest in Equipment #3. X Corporation is the common parent of a consolidated group and is not related, within the meaning of section 179(d)(2)(A) or (B) and § 1.179-4(c), to any member of the Parent consolidated group. No member of the X consolidated group ever had a depreciable interest in Equipment #3. In a series of related transactions, G Corporation sells Equipment #3 to F Corporation, and Parent sells all of the stock of F Corporation to X Corporation.

(ii) F Corporation was a member of the Parent consolidated group at the time it acquired Equipment #3 from G Corporation, another member of the group. Paragraph (b)(3)(iii)(B)(*3*)(*i*) of this section generally treats each member of a consolidated group as having a depreciable interest in property during the time any member of the group had a depreciable interest in such property while a member of the group. Nevertheless, because there is a series of related transactions that includes the acquisition of Equipment #3 and a transaction in which F Corporation, the transferee of the property, leaves the Parent consolidated group and joins the X consolidated group, the time to test whether F Corporation is a member of the Parent consolidated group for purposes of paragraph (b)(3)(iii)(B)(*3*)(*i*) of this section is met is immediately after the last transaction in the series, that is, the sale of the F Corporation stock to X Corporation. See paragraph (b)(3)(iii)(B)(*3*)(*iii*) of this section. Accordingly, because F Corporation is not a member of the Parent consolidated group after the last transaction of the series, F Corporation is not treated as previously having a depreciable interest in Equipment #3 by virtue of G Corporation's depreciable interest in Equipment #3 under paragraph (b)(3)(iii)(B)(*3*)(*i*) of this section.

(iii) After the sale of the F Corporation stock to X Corporation, F Corporation is a member of the X consolidated group. Because no member of the X consolidated group previously had a depreciable interest in Equipment #3, F Corporation is not treated as previously having a depreciable interest in Equipment #3 under paragraph (b)(3)(iii)(B)(*3*)(*i*) of this section.

(iv) Because relatedness is tested after F Corporation leaves the Parent consolidated group, F Corporation and G Corporation are not related within the meaning of section 179(d)(2)(A) or (B) and § 1.179-4(c). Accordingly, F Corporation's acquisition of Equipment #3 satisfies the used property acquisition requirements of paragraph (b)(3)(iii)(A)(*1*) of this section and, assuming all other requirements are met, F Corporation's acquisition of Equipment #3 is eligible for the additional first year depreciation deduction.

Example 22. (i) H Corporation, which is not a member of a consolidated group, has a depreciable interest in Equipment #4. Parent owns all the stock of I Corporation, and Parent and I Corporation are members of the Parent consolidated group. No member of the Parent consolidated group ever had a depreciable interest in Equipment #4. Neither Parent nor I Corporation is related to H Corporation within the meaning of section 179(d)(2)(A) or (B) and § 1.179-4(c). During 2018, H Corporation sells Equipment #4 to a person not related to H Corporation, Parent, or I Corporation within the meaning of section 179(d)(2)(A) or (B) and § 1.179-4(c). In a series of related transactions, during 2019, Parent acquires all of the stock of H Corporation, and I Corporation purchases Equipment #4 from an unrelated person.

(ii) In a series of related transactions, H Corporation became a member of the Parent consolidated group, and I Corporation, also a member of the Parent consolidated group, acquired Equipment #4. Because H Corporation previously had a depreciable interest in Equipment #4, pursuant to paragraph (b)(3)(iii)(B)(*3*)(*ii*) of this section, I Corporation is treated as having a depreciable interest in Equipment #4. As a result, I Corporation's acquisition of Equipment #4 does not satisfy the used property acquisition requirements of paragraph (b)(3)(iii) of this section. Accordingly, I Corporation's acquisition of Equipment #4 is not eligible for the additional first year depreciation deduction.

Example 23. (i) J Corporation, K Corporation, and L Corporation are unrelated parties within the meaning of section 179(d)(2)(A) or (B) and § 1.179-4(c). None of J Corporation, K Corporation, and L Corporation is a member of a consolidated group. J Corporation has a depreciable interest in Equipment #5. During 2018, J Corporation sells Equipment #5 to K Corporation. During 2020, J Corporation merges into L Corporation in a transaction described in section 368(a)(1)(A). In 2021, L Corporation acquires Equipment #5 from K Corporation.

(ii) Because J Corporation is the predecessor of L Corporation and J Corporation previously had a depreciable interest in Equipment #5, L Corporation's acquisition of Equipment #5 does not satisfy paragraphs (b)(3)(iii)(A)(*1*) and (b)(3)(iii)(B)(*1*) of this section and, thus, does not satisfy the used property acquisition requirements of paragraph (b)(3)(iii) of this section. Accordingly, L Corporation's acquisition of Equipment #5 is not eligible for the additional first year depreciation deduction.

Example 24. (i) M Corporation acquires and places in service a used airplane on March 26, 2018. Prior to this acquisition, M Corporation never had a depreciable interest in this airplane. On March 26, 2018, M Corporation also leases the used airplane to N Corporation, an airline company. On May 27, 2018, M Corporation sells to O Corporation the used airplane subject to the lease with N Corporation. M Corporation and O Corporation are related parties within the meaning of section 179(d)(2)(A) or (B) and § 1.179-4(c). As of May 27, 2018, N Corporation is still the lessee of the used airplane. Prior to this acquisition, O Corporation never had a depreciable interest in the used airplane. O Corporation is a calendar-year taxpayer.

(ii) The sale transaction of May 27, 2018, satisfies the requirements of paragraph (b)(3)(v) of this section. As a result, O Corporation is considered the taxpayer that acquired the used airplane for purposes of applying the used property acquisition requirements in paragraph (b)(3)(iii) of this section. In applying these rules, the fact that M Corporation and O Corporation are related parties is not taken into account because O Corporation, not M Corporation, is treated as acquiring the used airplane. Further, pursuant to paragraph (b)(4)(iv) of this section, the used airplane is treated as originally placed in service by O Corporation on May 27, 2018. Because O Corporation never had a depreciable interest in the used airplane and assuming all other requirements are met, O Corporation's purchase price of the used airplane qualifies for the 100-percent additional first year depreciation deduction for O Corporation.

Example 25. (i) The facts are the same as in *Example 24* of this paragraph (b)(3)(vi). Additionally, on September 5, 2018, O Corporation sells to P Corporation the used airplane subject to the lease with N Corporation. Prior to this acquisition, P Corporation never had a depreciable interest in the used airplane.

(ii) Because O Corporation, a calendar-year taxpayer, placed in service and disposed of the used airplane during 2018, the used airplane is not eligible for the additional first year depreciation deduction for O Corporation pursuant to paragraph (f)(1)(i) of this section.

(iii) Because P Corporation never had a depreciable interest in the used airplane and assuming all other requirements are met, P Corporation's purchase price of the used airplane qualifies for the 100-percent additional first year depreciation deduction for P Corporation.

(4) *Placed-in-service date.*—(i) *In general.*—Depreciable property will meet the requirements of this paragraph (b)(4) if the property is placed in service by the taxpayer for use in its trade or business or for production of income after September 27, 2017; and, except as provided in paragraphs (b)(2)(i)(A) and (D) of this section, before January 1, 2027, or, in the case of property described in section 168(k)(2)(B) or (C), before January 1, 2028.

(ii) *Specified plant.*—If the taxpayer has properly made an election to apply section 168(k)(5) for a specified plant, the requirements of this paragraph (b)(4) are satisfied only if the specified plant is planted before January 1, 2027, or is grafted before January 1, 2027, to a plant that has already been planted, by the taxpayer in the ordinary course of the taxpayer's farming business, as defined in section 263A(e)(4).

(iii) *Qualified film, television, or live theatrical production.*—(A) For purposes of this paragraph (b)(4), a qualified film or television production is treated as placed in service at the time of initial release or broadcast as defined under §1.181-1(a)(7).

(B) For purposes of this paragraph (b)(4), a qualified live theatrical production is treated as placed in service at the time of the initial live staged performance. Solely for purposes of this paragraph, the term *initial live staged performance* means the first commercial exhibition of a production to an audience. However, the term *initial live staged performance* does not include limited exhibition, prior to commercial exhibition to general audiences, if the limited exhibition is primarily for purposes of publicity, determining the need for further production activity, or raising funds for the completion of production. For example, an initial live staged performance does not include a preview of the production if the preview is primarily to determine the need for further production activity.

(iv) *Syndication transaction.*—If a lessor has a depreciable interest in the property and the lessor and any predecessor did not previously have a depreciable interest in the property, and the property is sold by the lessor or any subsequent purchaser within three months after the date the property was originally placed in service by the lessor (or, in the case of multiple units of property subject to the same lease, within three months after the date the final unit is placed in service, so long as the period between the time the first unit is placed in service and the time the last unit is placed in service does not exceed 12 months), and the user of the property after the last sale during this three-month period remains the same as when the property was originally placed in service by the lessor, the property is treated as originally placed in service by the purchaser of the property in the last sale during the three-month period but not earlier than the date of the last sale.

(v) *Technical termination of a partnership.*—For purposes of this paragraph (b)(4), in the case of a technical termination of a partnership under section 708(b)(1)(B) occurring in a taxable year beginning before January 1, 2018, qualified property placed in service by the terminated partnership during the taxable year of termination is treated as originally placed in service by the new partnership on the date the qualified property is contributed by the terminated partnership to the new partnership.

(vi) *Section 168(i)(7) transactions.*—For purposes of this paragraph (b)(4), if qualified property is transferred in a transaction described in section 168(i)(7) in the same taxable year that the qualified property is placed in service by the transferor, the transferred property is treated as originally placed in service on the date the transferor placed in service the qualified property. In the case of multiple transfers of qualified property in multiple transactions described in section 168(i)(7) in the same taxable year, the placed-in-service date of the transferred property is deemed to be the date on which the first transferor placed in service the qualified property.

(5) *Acquisition of property.*—(i) *In general.*—This paragraph (b)(5) provides rules for the acquisition requirements in section 13201(h) of the Act. These rules apply to all property, including self-constructed property or property described in section 168(k)(2)(B) or (C).

(ii) *Acquisition date.*—Except as provided in paragraph (b)(5)(vi) of this section, depreciable property will meet the requirements of this paragraph (b)(5) if the property is acquired by the taxpayer after September 27, 2017, or is acquired by the taxpayer pursuant to a written binding contract entered into by the taxpayer after September 27, 2017. Property that is manufactured, constructed, or produced for the taxpayer by another person under a written binding contract that is entered into prior to the manufacture, construction, or production of the property for use by the taxpayer in its trade or business or for its production of income is acquired pursuant to a written binding contract. If a taxpayer acquired the property pursuant to a written binding contract and such contract states the date on which the contract was entered into and a closing date, delivery date, or other similar date, the date on which the contract was entered into is the date the taxpayer acquired the property. See paragraph (b)(5)(v) of this section for when a qualified film, television, or live theatrical production is treated as acquired for purposes of this paragraph (b)(5).

(iii) *Definition of binding contract.*—(A) *In general.*—A contract is binding only if it is enforceable under State law against the taxpayer or a predecessor, and does not limit damages to a specified amount (for example, by use of a liquidated damages provision). For this purpose, a contractual provision that limits damages to an amount equal to at least 5 percent of the total contract price will not be treated as limiting damages to a specified amount. In determining whether a contract limits damages, the fact that there may be little or no damages because the contract price does not significantly differ from fair market value will not be taken into account. For example, if a taxpayer entered into an irrevocable written contract to purchase an asset for $100 and the contract did not contain a provision for liquidated damages, the contract is considered binding notwithstanding the fact that the asset had a fair market value of $99 and under local law the seller would only recover the difference in the event the purchaser failed to perform. If the contract provided for a full refund of the purchase price in lieu of any damages allowable by law in the event of breach or cancellation, the contract is not considered binding.

(B) *Conditions.*—A contract is binding even if subject to a condition, as long as the condition is not within the control of either party or a predecessor. A contract will continue to be binding if the parties make insubstantial changes in its terms and conditions or if any term is to be determined by a standard beyond the control of either party. A contract that imposes significant obligations on the taxpayer or a predecessor will be treated as binding notwithstanding the fact that certain terms remain to be negotiated by the parties to the contract.

(C) *Options.*—An option to either acquire or sell property is not a binding contract.

(D) *Letter of intent.*—A letter of intent for an acquisition is not a binding contract.

(E) *Supply agreements.*—A binding contract does not include a supply or similar agreement if the amount and design specifications of the property to be purchased have not been specified. The contract will not be a binding contract for the property to be purchased until both the amount and the design specifications are specified. For example, if the provisions of a supply or similar agreement state the design specifications of the property to be purchased, a purchase order under the agreement for a specific number of assets is treated as a binding contract.

(F) *Components.*—A binding contract to acquire one or more components of a larger property will not be treated as a binding contract to acquire the larger property. If a binding contract to acquire the component does not satisfy the requirements of this paragraph (b)(5), the component does not qualify for the additional first year depreciation deduction.

(iv) *Self-constructed property.*—(A) *In general.*—If a taxpayer manufactures, constructs, or produces property for use by the taxpayer in its trade or business or for its production of income, the acquisition rules in paragraph (b)(5)(ii) of this section are treated as met for the property if the taxpayer begins manufacturing, constructing, or producing the property after September 27, 2017. This paragraph (b)(5)(iv) does not apply to property that is manufactured, constructed, or produced for the taxpayer by another person under a written binding contract that is entered into prior to the manufacture, construction, or production of the property for use by the taxpayer in its trade or business or for its production of income (for further guidance, see paragraphs (b)(5)(ii) and (iii) of this section).

(B) *When does manufacture, construction, or production begin.*—(*1*) *In general.*—For purposes of paragraph (b)(5)(iv)(A) of this section, manufacture, construction, or production of property begins when physical work of a significant nature begins. Physical work does not include preliminary activities such as planning or designing, securing financing, exploring, or researching. The determination of when physical work of a significant nature begins depends on the facts and circumstances. For example, if the taxpayer constructs a retail motor fuels outlet on-site for use by the taxpayer in its trade or business, construction begins when physical work of a significant nature commences at the site by the taxpayer; that is, when work begins on the excavation for footings, pouring the pads for the outlet, or the driving of foundation pilings into the ground. Preliminary work, such as clearing a site, test drilling to determine soil condition, or excavation to change the contour of the land (as distinguished from excavation for footings) does not constitute the beginning of construction. However, if the taxpayer assembles a retail motor fuels outlet on-site from modular units manufactured off-site by the taxpayer and delivered to the site where the outlet will be used, manufacturing begins when physical work of a significant nature commences at the off-site location by the taxpayer.

(*2*) *Safe harbor.*—For purposes of paragraph (b)(5)(iv)(B)(*1*) of this section, a taxpayer may choose to determine when physical work of a significant nature begins in accordance with this paragraph (b)(5)(iv)(B)(*2*). Physical work of a significant nature will be considered to begin at the time the taxpayer incurs (in the case of an accrual basis taxpayer) or pays (in the case of a cash basis taxpayer) more than 10 percent of the total cost of the property (excluding the cost of any land and preliminary activities such as planning or designing, securing financing, exploring, or researching). A taxpayer chooses to apply this paragraph (b)(5)(iv)(B)(*2*) by filing a federal income tax return for the placed-in-service year of the property that determines when physical work of a significant nature begins consistent with this paragraph (b)(5)(iv)(B)(*2*).

(C) *Components of self-constructed property.*—(*1*) *Acquired components.*—If a binding contract, as defined in paragraph (b)(5)(iii) of this section, to acquire a component does not satisfy the requirements of paragraph (b)(5)(ii) of this section, the component does not qualify for the additional first year depreciation deduction. A binding contract described in the preceding sentence to acquire one or more components of a larger self-constructed property will not preclude the larger self-constructed property from satisfying the acquisition rules in paragraph (b)(5)(iv)(A) of this section. Accordingly, the unadjusted depreciable basis of the larger self-constructed property that is eligible for the additional first year depreciation deduction, assuming all other requirements are met, must not include the unadjusted depreciable basis of any component that does not satisfy the requirements of paragraph (b)(5)(ii) of this section. If the manufacture, construction, or production of the larger self-constructed property begins before September 28, 2017, the larger self-constructed property and any acquired components related to the larger self-constructed property do not qualify for the additional first year depreciation deduction under this section.

(2) Self-constructed components.—If the manufacture, construction, or production of a component by the taxpayer does not satisfy the requirements of this paragraph (b)(5)(iv), the component does not qualify for the additional first year depreciation deduction. However, if the manufacture, construction, or production of a component does not satisfy the requirements of this paragraph (b)(5)(iv), but the manufacture, construction, or production of the larger self-constructed property satisfies the requirements of this paragraph (b)(5)(iv), the larger self-constructed property qualifies for the additional first year depreciation deduction, assuming all other requirements are met, even though the component does not qualify for the additional first year depreciation deduction. Accordingly, the unadjusted depreciable basis of the larger self-constructed property that is eligible for the additional first year depreciation deduction, assuming all other requirements are met, must not include the unadjusted depreciable basis of any component that does not qualify for the additional first year depreciation deduction. If the manufacture, construction, or production of the larger self-constructed property began before September 28, 2017, the larger self-constructed property and any self-constructed components related to the larger self-constructed property do not qualify for the additional first year depreciation deduction under this section.

(v) *Qualified film, television, or live theatrical production*.—(A) For purposes of section 13201(h)(1)(A) of the Act, a qualified film or television production is treated as acquired on the date principal photography commences.

(B) For purposes of section 13201(h)(1)(A) of the Act, a qualified live theatrical production is treated as acquired on the date when all of the necessary elements for producing the live theatrical production are secured. These elements may include a script, financing, actors, set, scenic and costume designs, advertising agents, music, and lighting.

(vi) *Specified plant*.—If the taxpayer has properly made an election to apply section 168(k)(5) for a specified plant, the requirements of this paragraph (b)(5) are satisfied if the specified plant is planted after September 27, 2017, or is grafted after September 27, 2017, to a plant that has already been planted, by the taxpayer in the ordinary course of the taxpayer's farming business, as defined in section 263A(e)(4).

(vii) *Examples*.—The application of this paragraph (b)(5) is illustrated by the following examples. Unless the facts specifically indicate otherwise, assume that the parties are not related within the meaning of section 179(d)(2)(A) or (B) and §1.179-4(c), and the parties do not have predecessors:

Example 1. On September 1, 2017, *BB*, a corporation, entered into a written agreement with *CC*, a manufacturer, to purchase 20 new lamps for $100 each within the next two years. Although the agreement specifies the number of lamps to be purchased, the agreement does not specify the design of the lamps to be purchased. Accordingly, the agreement is not a binding contract pursuant to paragraph (b)(5)(iii)(E) of this section.

Example 2. The facts are the same as in *Example 1* of this paragraph (b)(5)(vii). On December 1, 2017, *BB* placed a purchase order with *CC* to purchase 20 new model XPC5 lamps for $100 each for a total amount of $2,000. Because the agreement specifies the number of lamps to be purchased and the purchase order specifies the design of the lamps to be purchased, the purchase order placed by *BB* with *CC* on December 1, 2017, is a binding contract pursuant to paragraph (b)(5)(iii)(E) of this section. Accordingly, assuming all other requirements are met, the cost of the 20 lamps qualifies for the 100-percent additional first year depreciation deduction.

Example 3. The facts are the same as in *Example 1* of this paragraph (b)(5)(vii), except that the written agreement between *BB* and *CC* is to purchase 100 model XPC5 lamps for $100 each within the next two years. Because this agreement specifies the amount and design of the lamps to be purchased, the agreement is a binding contract pursuant to paragraph (b)(5)(iii)(E) of this section. However, because the agreement was entered into before September 28, 2017, no lamp acquired by *BB* under this contract qualifies for the 100-percent additional first year depreciation deduction.

Example 4. On September 1, 2017, *DD* began constructing a retail motor fuels outlet for its own use. On November 1, 2018, *DD* ceases construction of the retail motor fuels outlet prior to its completion. Between September 1, 2017, and November 1, 2018, *DD* incurred $3,000,000 of expenditures for the construction of the retail motor fuels outlet. On May 1, 2019, *DD* resumed construction of the retail motor fuels outlet and completed its construction on August 31, 2019. Between May 1, 2019, and August 31, 2019, *DD* incurred another $1,600,000 of expenditures to complete the construction of the retail motor fuels outlet and, on September 1, 2019, *DD* placed the retail motor fuels outlet in service. None of *DD*'s total expenditures of $4,600,000 qualify for the 100-percent additional first year depreciation deduction because, pursuant to paragraph (b)(5)(iv)(A) of this section, *DD* began constructing the retail motor fuels outlet before September 28, 2017.

Example 5. The facts are the same as in *Example 4* of this paragraph (b)(5)(vii) except that *DD* began constructing the retail motor fuels outlet for its own use on October 1, 2017, and *DD* incurred the $3,000,000 between October 1, 2017, and November 1, 2018. *DD*'s total expenditures of $4,600,000 qualify for the 100-percent additional first year depreciation deduction because, pursuant to paragraph (b)(5)(iv)(A) of this section, *DD* began constructing the retail motor fuels outlet after September 27, 2017, and *DD* placed the retail motor fuels outlet in service on September 1, 2019. Accordingly, assuming all other requirements are met, the additional first year depreciation deduction for the retail motor fuels outlet will be $4,600,000, computed as $4,600,000 multiplied by 100 percent.

Example 6. On August 15, 2017, *EE* entered into a written binding contract with *FF* to manufacture an aircraft described in section 168(k)(2)(C) for use in *EE*'s trade or business. *FF* begins to manufacture the aircraft on October 1, 2017. *EE* places the aircraft in service on March 1, 2018. Pursuant to paragraph (b)(5)(ii) of this section, the aircraft is acquired by *EE* pursuant to a written binding contract. Because *EE* entered into such contract before September 28, 2017, the aircraft does not qualify for the 100-percent additional first year depreciation deduction.

Example 7. On June 1, 2017, *HH* entered into a written binding contract to acquire a new component part of property that is being constructed by *HH* for its own use in its trade or business. *HH* commenced construction of the property in November 2017, and placed the property in service in November 2018. Because *HH* entered into a written binding contract to acquire a component part prior to September 28, 2017, pursuant to paragraphs (b)(5)(ii) and (b)(5)(iv)(C)(*1*) of this section, the component part does not qualify for the 100-percent additional first year depreciation deduction. However, pursuant to paragraphs (b)(5)(iv)(A) and (b)(5)(iv)(C)(*1*) of this section, the property constructed by *HH* will qualify for the 100-percent additional first year depreciation deduction, because construction of the property began after September 27, 2017, assuming all other requirements are met. Accordingly, the unadjusted depreciable basis of the property that is eligible for the 100-percent additional first year depreciation deduction must not include the unadjusted depreciable basis of the component part.

Example 8. The facts are the same as in *Example 7* of this paragraph (b)(5)(vii) except that *HH* entered into the written binding contract to acquire the new component part on September 30, 2017, and *HH* commenced construction of the property on August 1, 2017. Pursuant to paragraphs (b)(5)(iv)(A) and (C) of this section, neither the property constructed by *HH* nor the component part will qualify for the 100-percent additional first year depreciation deduction, because *HH* began construction of the property prior to September 28, 2017.

Example 9. On September 1, 2017, *II* acquired and placed in service equipment. On October 15, 2017, *II* sells the equipment to *JJ* and leases the property back from *JJ* in a sale-leaseback transaction. Pursuant to paragraph (b)(5)(ii) of this section, *II*'s cost of the equipment does not qualify for the 100-percent additional first year depreciation deduction because *II* acquired the equipment prior to September 28, 2017. However, *JJ* acquired used equipment from an unrelated party after September 27, 2017, and, assuming all other requirements are met, *JJ*'s cost of the used equipment does qualify for the 100-percent additional first year depreciation deduction for *JJ*.

Example 10. On July 1, 2017, *KK* began constructing property for its own use in its trade or business. *KK* placed this property in service on September 15, 2017. On October 15, 2017, *KK* sells the property to *LL* and leases the property back from *LL* in a sale-leaseback transaction. Pursuant to paragraph (b)(5)(iv) of this section, *KK*'s cost of the property does not qualify for the 100-percent additional first year depreciation deduction because construction began prior to September 28, 2017. However, *LL* acquired used property from an unrelated party after September 27, 2017, and, assuming all other requirements are met, *LL*'s cost of the used property does qualify for the 100-percent additional first year depreciation deduction for *LL*.

(c) *Property described in section 168(k)(2)(B) or (C).*—(1) *In general.*—Property described in section 168(k)(2)(B) or (C) will meet the acquisition requirements of section 168(k)(2)(B)(i)(III) or (k)(2)(C)(i) if the property is acquired by the taxpayer before January 1, 2027, or acquired by the taxpayer pursuant to a written binding contract that is entered into before January 1, 2027. Property described in section 168(k)(2)(B) or (C) also must meet the acquisition requirement in section 13201(h)(1)(A) of the Act (for further guidance, see paragraph (b)(5) of this section).

(2) *Definition of binding contract.*—For purposes of this paragraph (c), the rules in paragraph (b)(5)(iii) of this section for a binding contract apply.

(3) *Self-constructed property.*—(i) *In general.*—If a taxpayer manufactures, constructs, or produces property for use by the taxpayer in its trade or business or for its production of income, the acquisition rules in paragraph (c)(1) of this section are treated as met for the property if the taxpayer begins manufacturing, constructing, or producing the property before January 1, 2027. Property that is manufactured, constructed, or produced for the taxpayer by another person under a written binding contract, as defined in paragraph (b)(5)(iii) of this section, that is entered into prior to the manufacture, construction, or production of the property for use by the taxpayer in its trade or business or for its production of income is considered to be manufactured, constructed, or produced by the taxpayer. If a taxpayer enters into a written binding contract, as defined in paragraph (b)(5)(iii) of this section, before January 1, 2027, with another person to manufacture, construct, or produce property described in section 168(k)(2)(B) or (C) and the manufacture, construction, or production of this property begins after December 31, 2026, the acquisition rule in paragraph (c)(1) of this section is met.

(ii) *When does manufacture, construction, or production begin.*—(A) *In general.*—For purposes of this paragraph (c)(3), manufacture, construction, or production of property begins when physical work of a significant nature begins. Physical work does not include preliminary activities such as planning or designing, securing financing, exploring, or researching. The determination of when physical work of a significant nature begins depends on the facts and circumstances. For example, if a retail motor fuels outlet is to be constructed on-site, construction begins when physical work of a significant nature commences at the site; that is, when work begins on the excavation for footings, pouring the pads for the outlet, or the driving of foundation pilings into the ground. Preliminary work, such as clearing a site, test drilling to determine soil condition, or excavation to change the contour of the land (as distinguished from excavation for footings) does not constitute the beginning of construction. However, if a retail motor fuels outlet is to be assembled on-site from modular units manufactured off-site and delivered to the site where the outlet will be used, manufacturing begins when physical work of a significant nature commences at the off-site location.

(B) *Safe harbor*.—For purposes of paragraph (c)(3)(ii)(A) of this section, a taxpayer may choose to determine when physical work of a significant nature begins in accordance with this paragraph (c)(3)(ii)(B). Physical work of a significant nature will be considered to begin at the time the taxpayer incurs (in the case of an accrual basis taxpayer) or pays (in the case of a cash basis taxpayer) more than 10 percent of the total cost of the property (excluding the cost of any land and preliminary activities such as planning or designing, securing financing, exploring, or researching). When property is manufactured, constructed, or produced for the taxpayer by another person, this safe harbor test must be satisfied by the taxpayer. For example, if a retail motor fuels outlet is to be constructed for an accrual basis taxpayer by another person for the total cost of $200,000 (excluding the cost of any land and preliminary activities such as planning or designing, securing financing, exploring, or researching), construction is deemed to begin for purposes of this paragraph (c)(3)(ii)(B) when the taxpayer has incurred more than 10 percent (more than $20,000) of the total cost of the property. A taxpayer chooses to apply this paragraph (c)(3)(ii)(B) by filing a federal income tax return for the placed-in-service year of the property that determines when physical work of a significant nature begins consistent with this paragraph (c)(3)(ii)(B).

(iii) *Components of self-constructed property*.—(A) *Acquired components*.—If a binding contract, as defined in paragraph (b)(5)(iii) of this section, to acquire a component does not satisfy the requirements of paragraph (c)(1) of this section, the component does not qualify for the additional first year depreciation deduction. A binding contract described in the preceding sentence to acquire one or more components of a larger self-constructed property will not preclude the larger self-constructed property from satisfying the acquisition rules in paragraph (c)(3)(i) of this section. Accordingly, the unadjusted depreciable basis of the larger self-constructed property that is eligible for the additional first year depreciation deduction, assuming all other requirements are met, must not include the unadjusted depreciable basis of any component that does not satisfy the requirements of paragraph (c)(1) of this section. If a binding contract to acquire the component is entered into before January 1, 2027, but the manufacture, construction, or production of the larger self-constructed property does not begin before January 1, 2027, the component qualifies for the additional first year depreciation deduction, assuming all other requirements are met, but the larger self-constructed property does not.

(B) *Self-constructed components*.—If the manufacture, construction, or production of a component by the taxpayer does not satisfy the requirements of paragraph (c)(3)(i) of this section, the component does not qualify for the additional first year depreciation deduction. However, if the manufacture, construction, or production of a component does not satisfy the requirements of paragraph (c)(3)(i) of this section, but the manufacture, construction, or production of the larger self-constructed property satisfies the requirements of paragraph (c)(3)(i) of this section, the larger self-constructed property qualifies for the additional first year depreciation deduction, assuming all other requirements are met, even though the component does not qualify for the additional first year depreciation deduction. Accordingly, the unadjusted depreciable basis of the larger self-constructed property that is eligible for the additional first year depreciation deduction, assuming all other requirements are met, must not include the unadjusted depreciable basis of any component that does not qualify for the additional first year depreciation deduction. If the manufacture, construction, or production of a component begins before January 1, 2027, but the manufacture, construction, or production of the larger self-constructed property does not begin before January 1, 2027, the component qualifies for the additional first year depreciation deduction, assuming all other requirements are met, but the larger self-constructed property does not.

(iv) *Examples*.—The application of this paragraph (c) is illustrated by the following examples:

Example 1. On June 1, 2017, *MM* decided to construct property described in section 168(k)(2)(B) for its own use. However, one of the component parts of the property had to be manufactured by another person for *MM*. On August 15, 2017, *MM* entered into a written binding contract with *NN* to acquire this component part of the property for $100,000. The manufacture of the component part commenced on September 1, 2018, and *MM* received the completed component part on February 1, 2020. The cost of this component part is 9 percent of the total cost of the property to be constructed by *MM*. *MM* began constructing the property described in section 168(k)(2)(B) on January 15, 2020, and placed this property, including all component parts, in service on November 1, 2021. Pursuant to paragraphs (b)(5)(iv)(C)(*1*) and (c)(1) of this section, the component part of $100,000 manufactured by *NN* for *MM* is not eligible for the 100-percent additional first year depreciation deduction because the written binding contract to acquire such component part was entered into before September 28, 2017. However, pursuant to paragraph (c)(3)(i) of this section, the cost of the property described in section 168(k)(2)(B), excluding the cost of the component part of $100,000 manufactured by *NN* for *MM*, is eligible for the 100-percent additional first year depreciation deduction, assuming all other requirements are met, because construction of the property began after September 27, 2017, and before January 1, 2027, and the property described in section 168(k)(2)(B) was placed in service by *MM* before January 1, 2028.

Example 2. On June 1, 2026, *OO* decided to construct property described in section 168(k)(2)(B) for its own use. However, one of the component parts of the property had to be manufactured by another person for *OO*. On August 15, 2026, *OO* entered into a written binding contract with *PP* to acquire this component part of the property for $100,000. The manufacture of the component part commenced on September 1, 2026, and *OO* received the completed component part on February 1, 2027. The cost of this component part is 9 percent of the total cost of the property to be constructed by *OO*. *OO* began constructing the property described in section 168(k)(2)(B) on January 15, 2027, and placed this property, including all component parts, in service on November 1, 2027. Pursuant to paragraph (c)(3)(iii)(B) of this section, the self-constructed component part of $100,000 manufactured by *PP* for *OO* is eligible for the additional first year depreciation deduction, assuming all other requirements are met, because the manufacturing of the component part began before January 1, 2027, and the property described in section 168(k)(2)(B), the larger self-constructed property, was placed in service by *OO* before January 1, 2028. However, pursuant to paragraph (c)(3)(i) of this section, the cost of the property described in section 168(k)(2)(B), excluding the cost of the self-constructed component part of $100,000 manufactured by *PP* for *OO*, is not eligible for the additional first year depreciation deduction because construction of the property began after December 31, 2026.

Example 3. On December 1, 2026, *QQ* entered into a written binding contract, as defined in paragraph (b)(5)(iii) of this section, with *RR* to manufacture an aircraft described in section 168(k)(2)(C) for use in *QQ*'s trade or business. *RR* begins to manufacture the aircraft on February 1, 2027. *QQ* places the aircraft in service on August 1, 2027. Pursuant to paragraph (c)(3)(i) of this section, the aircraft meets the requirements of paragraph (c)(1) of this section because the aircraft was acquired by *QQ* pursuant to a written binding contract entered into before January 1, 2027. Further, the aircraft was placed in service by *QQ* before January 1, 2028. Thus, assuming all other requirements are met, *QQ*'s cost of the aircraft is eligible for the additional first year depreciation deduction.

(d) *Computation of depreciation deduction for qualified property.*—(1) *Additional first year depreciation deduction.*—(i) *Allowable taxable year.*—The additional first year depreciation deduction is allowable—

(A) Except as provided in paragraph (d)(1)(i)(B) or (f) of this section, in the taxable year in which the qualified property is placed in service by the taxpayer for use in its trade or business or for the production of income; or

(B) In the taxable year in which the specified plant is planted, or grafted to a plant that has already been planted, by the taxpayer in the ordinary course of the taxpayer's farming business, as defined in section 263A(e)(4), if the taxpayer properly made the election to apply section 168(k)(5) (for further guidance, see paragraph (e) of this section).

(ii) *Computation.*—Except as provided in paragraph (f)(5) of this section, the allowable additional first year depreciation deduction for qualified property is determined by multiplying the unadjusted depreciable basis, as defined in § 1.168(b)-1(a)(3), of the qualified property by the applicable percentage. Except as provided in paragraph (f)(1) of this section, the additional first year depreciation deduction is not affected by a taxable year of less than 12 months. See paragraph (f)(1) of this section for qualified property placed in service or planted or grafted, as applicable, and disposed of during the same taxable year. See paragraph (f)(5) of this section for qualified property acquired in a like-kind exchange or as a result of an involuntary conversion.

(iii) *Property described in section 168(k)(2)(B).*—For purposes of paragraph (d)(1)(ii) of this section, the unadjusted depreciable basis, as defined in § 1.168(b)-1(a)(3), of qualified property described in section 168(k)(2)(B) is limited to the property's unadjusted depreciable basis attributable to the property's manufacture, construction, or production before January 1, 2027.

(iv) *Alternative minimum tax.*—(A) *In general.*—The additional first year depreciation deduction is allowable for alternative minimum tax purposes—

(1) Except as provided in paragraph (d)(1)(iv)(A)*(2)* of this section, in the taxable year in which the qualified property is placed in service by the taxpayer; or

(2) In the taxable year in which a specified plant is planted by the taxpayer, or grafted by the taxpayer to a plant that was previously planted, if the taxpayer properly made the election to apply section 168(k)(5) (for further guidance, see paragraph (e) of this section).

(B) *Special rules.*—In general, the additional first year depreciation deduction for alternative minimum tax purposes is based on the unadjusted depreciable basis of the property for alternative minimum tax purposes. However, see paragraph (f)(5)(iii)(E) of this section for qualified property acquired in a like-kind exchange or as a result of an involuntary conversion.

(2) *Otherwise allowable depreciation deduction.*—(i) *In general.*—Before determining the amount otherwise allowable as a depreciation deduction for the qualified property for the placed-in-service year and any subsequent taxable year, the taxpayer must determine the remaining adjusted depreciable basis of the qualified property. This remaining adjusted depreciable basis is equal to the unadjusted depreciable basis, as defined in § 1.168(b)-1(a)(3), of the qualified property reduced by the amount of the additional first year depreciation allowed or allowable, whichever is greater. The remaining adjusted depreciable basis of the qualified property is then depreciated using the applicable depreciation provisions under the Internal Revenue Code for the qualified property. The remaining adjusted depreciable basis of the qualified property that is MACRS property is also the basis to which the annual depreciation rates in the optional depreciation tables apply (for further guidance, see section 8 of Rev. Proc. 87-57 (1987-2 C.B. 687) and § 601.601(d)(2)(ii)(*b*) of this chapter). The depreciation deduction allowable for the remaining adjusted depreciable basis of the qualified property is affected by a taxable year of less than 12 months.

(ii) *Alternative minimum tax.*—For alternative minimum tax purposes, the depreciation deduction allowable for the remaining adjusted depreciable basis of the qualified property is based on the remaining adjusted depreciable basis for alternative minimum tax purposes. The remaining adjusted depreciable basis of the qualified property for alternative minimum tax purposes is depreciated using the same depreciation method, recovery period (or useful life in the case of computer software), and convention that apply to the qualified property for regular tax purposes.

(3) *Examples.*—This paragraph (d) is illustrated by the following examples:

Example 1. On March 1, 2023, *SS*, a calendar-year taxpayer, purchased and placed in service qualified property that costs $1 million and is 5-year property under section 168(e). *SS* depreciates its 5-year property placed in service in 2023 using the optional depreciation table that corresponds with the general depreciation system, the 200-percent declining balance method, a 5-year recovery period, and the half-year convention. For 2023, *SS* is allowed an 80-percent additional first year depreciation deduction of $800,000 (the unadjusted depreciable basis of $1 million multiplied by 0.80). Next, *SS* must reduce the unadjusted depreciable basis of $1 million by the additional first year depreciation deduction of $800,000 to determine the remaining adjusted depreciable basis of $200,000. Then, *SS'* depreciation deduction allowable in 2023 for the remaining adjusted depreciable basis of $200,000 is $40,000 (the remaining adjusted depreciable basis of $200,000 multiplied by the annual depreciation rate of 0.20 for recovery year 1).

Example 2. On June 1, 2023, *TT*, a calendar-year taxpayer, purchased and placed in service qualified property that costs $1,500,000. The property qualifies for the expensing election under section 179 and is 5-year property under section 168(e). *TT* did not purchase any other section 179 property in 2023. *TT* makes the election under section 179 for the property and depreciates its 5-year property placed in service in 2023 using the optional depreciation table that corresponds with the general depreciation system, the 200-percent declining balance method, a 5-year recovery period, and the half-year convention. Assume the maximum section 179 deduction for 2023 is $1,000,000. For 2023, *TT* is first allowed a $1,000,000 deduction under section 179. Next, *TT* must reduce the cost of $1,500,000 by the section 179 deduction of $1,000,000 to determine the unadjusted depreciable basis of $500,000. Then, for 2023, *TT* is allowed an 80-percent additional first year depreciation deduction of $400,000 (the unadjusted depreciable basis of $500,000 multiplied by 0.80). Next, *TT* must reduce the unadjusted depreciable basis of $500,000 by the additional first year depreciation deduction of $400,000 to determine the remaining adjusted depreciable basis of $100,000. Then, *TT*'s depreciation deduction allowable in 2023 for the remaining adjusted depreciable basis of $100,000 is $20,000 (the remaining adjusted depreciable basis of $100,000 multiplied by the annual depreciation rate of 0.20 for recovery year 1).

(e) *Elections under section 168(k).*—(1) *Election not to deduct additional first year depreciation.*—(i) *In general.*—A taxpayer may make an election not to deduct the additional first year depreciation for any class of property that is qualified property placed in service during the taxable year. If this election is made, the election applies to all qualified property that is in the same class of property and placed in service in the same taxable year, and no additional first year depreciation deduction is allowable for the property placed in service during the taxable year in the class of property, except as provided in § 1.743-1(j)(4)(i)(B)(*1*).

(ii) *Definition of class of property.*—For purposes of this paragraph (e)(1), the term *class of property* means:

(A) Except for the property described in paragraphs (e)(1)(ii)(B) and (D), and (e)(2) of this section, each class of property described in section 168(e) (for example, 5-year property);

(B) Water utility property as defined in section 168(e)(5) and depreciated under section 168;

(C) Computer software as defined in, and depreciated under, section 167(f)(1) and the regulations under section 167(f)(1);

(D) Qualified improvement property as defined in § 1.168(b)-1(a)(5)(i)(C) and (a)(5)(ii), and depreciated under section 168;

(E) Each separate production, as defined in § 1.181-3(b), of a qualified film or television production;

(F) Each separate production, as defined in section 181(e)(2), of a qualified live theatrical production; or

(G) A partner's basis adjustment in partnership assets under section 743(b) for each class of property described in paragraphs (e)(1)(ii)(A) through (F), and (e)(2) of this section (for further guidance, see § 1.743-1(j)(4)(i)(B)(*1*)).

(iii) *Time and manner for making election.*—(A) *Time for making election.*—Any election specified in paragraph (e)(1)(i) of this section must be made by the due date, including extensions, of the Federal tax return for the taxable year in which the qualified property is placed in service by the taxpayer.

(B) *Manner of making election.*—Any election specified in paragraph (e)(1)(i) of this section must be made in the manner prescribed on Form 4562, "Depreciation and Amortization," and its instructions. The election is made separately by each person owning qualified property (for example, for each member of a consolidated group by the common parent of the group, by the partnership (including basis adjustments in the partnership assets under section 743(b)), or by the S corporation). If Form 4562 is revised or renumbered, any reference in this section to that form shall be treated as a reference to the revised or renumbered form.

(iv) *Failure to make election.*—If a taxpayer does not make the election specified in paragraph (e)(1)(i) of this section within the time and in the manner prescribed in paragraph (e)(1)(iii) of this section, the amount of depreciation allowable for that property under section 167(f)(1) or 168, as applicable, must be determined for the placed-in-service year and for all subsequent taxable years by taking into account the additional first year depreciation deduction. Thus, any election specified in paragraph (e)(1)(i) of this section shall not be made by the taxpayer in any other manner (for example, the election cannot be made through a request under section 446(e) to change the taxpayer's method of accounting).

(2) *Election to apply section 168(k)(5) for specified plants.*—(i) *In general.*—A taxpayer may make an election to apply section 168(k)(5) to one or more specified plants that are planted, or grafted to a plant that has already been planted, by the taxpayer in the ordinary course of the taxpayer's farming business, as defined in section 263A(e)(4). If this election is made for a specified plant, such plant is not treated as qualified property under section 168(k) and this section in its placed-in-service year.

(ii) *Time and manner for making election.*—(A) *Time for making election.*—Any election specified in paragraph (e)(2)(i) of this section must be made by the due date, including extensions, of the Federal tax return for the taxable year in which the taxpayer planted or grafted the specified plant to which the election applies.

(B) *Manner of making election.*—Any election specified in paragraph (e)(2)(i) of this section must be made in the manner prescribed on Form 4562, "Depreciation and Amortization," and its instructions. The election is made separately by each person owning specified plants (for example, for each member of a consolidated group by the common parent of the group, by the partnership, or by the S corporation). If Form 4562 is revised or renumbered, any reference in this section to that form shall be treated as a reference to the revised or renumbered form.

(iii) *Failure to make election.*—If a taxpayer does not make the election specified in paragraph (e)(2)(i) of this section for a specified plant within the time and in the manner prescribed in paragraph (e)(2)(ii) of this section, the specified plant is treated as qualified property under section 168(k), assuming all requirements are met, in the taxable year in which such plant is placed in service by the taxpayer. Thus, any election specified in paragraph (e)(2)(i) of this section shall not be made by the taxpayer in any other manner (for example, the election cannot be made through a request under section 446(e) to change the taxpayer's method of accounting).

(3) *Election for qualified property placed in service during the 2017 taxable year.*—(i) *In general.*—A taxpayer may make an election to deduct 50 percent, instead of 100 percent, additional first year depreciation for all qualified property acquired after September 27, 2017, by the taxpayer and placed in service by the taxpayer during its taxable year that includes September 28, 2017. If a taxpayer makes an election to apply section 168(k)(5) for its taxable year that includes September 28, 2017, the taxpayer also may make an election to deduct 50 percent, instead of 100 percent, additional first year depreciation for all specified plants that are planted, or grafted to a plant that has already been planted, after September 27, 2017, by the taxpayer in the ordinary course of the taxpayer's farming business during such taxable year.

(ii) *Time and manner for making election.*—(A) *Time for making election.*—Any election specified in paragraph (e)(3)(i) of this section must be made by the due date, including extensions, of the Federal tax return for the taxpayer's taxable year that includes September 28, 2017.

(B) *Manner of making election.*—Any election specified in paragraph (e)(3)(i) of this section must be made in the manner prescribed on the 2017 Form 4562, "Depreciation and Amortization," and its instructions. The election is made separately by each person owning qualified property (for example, for each member of a consolidated group by the common parent of the group, by the partnership, or by the S corporation).

(iii) *Failure to make election.*—If a taxpayer does not make the election specified in paragraph (e)(3)(i) of this section within the time and in the manner prescribed in paragraph (e)(3)(ii) of this section, the amount of depreciation allowable for qualified property under section 167(f)(1) or 168, as applicable, acquired and placed in service, or planted or grafted, as applicable, by the taxpayer after September 27, 2017, must be determined for the taxable year that includes September 28, 2017, and for all subsequent taxable years by taking into account the 100-percent additional first year depreciation deduction, unless the taxpayer makes the election specified in paragraph (e)(1)(i) of this section within the time and in the manner prescribed in paragraph (e)(1)(iii) of this section for the class of property in which the qualified property is included. Thus, any election specified in paragraph (e)(3)(i) of this section shall not be made by the taxpayer in any other manner (for example, the election cannot be made through a request under section 446(e) to change the taxpayer's method of accounting).

(4) *Alternative minimum tax.*—If a taxpayer makes an election specified in paragraph (e)(1) of this section for a class of property or in paragraph (e)(2) of this section for a specified plant, the depreciation adjustments under section 56 and the regulations under section 56 do not apply to the property or specified plant, as applicable, to which that election applies for purposes of computing the taxpayer's alternative minimum taxable income. If a taxpayer makes an election specified in paragraph (e)(3) of this section for all qualified property, see paragraphs (d)(1)(iv) and (d)(2)(ii) of this section.

(5) *Revocation of election.*—(i) *In general.*—Except as provided in paragraph (e)(5)(ii) of this section, an election specified in this paragraph (e), once made, may be revoked only by filing a request for a private letter ruling and obtaining the Commissioner of Internal Revenue's written consent to revoke the election. The Commissioner may grant a request to revoke the election if the taxpayer acted reasonably and in good faith, and the revocation will not prejudice the interests of the Government. See generally § 301.9100-3 of this chapter. An election specified in this paragraph (e)may not be revoked through a request under section 446(e) to change the taxpayer's method of accounting.

(ii) *Automatic 6-month extension.*—If a taxpayer made an election specified in this paragraph (e), an automatic extension of 6 months from the due date of the taxpayer's Federal tax return, excluding extensions, for the placed-in-service year or the taxable year in which the specified plant is planted or grafted, as applicable, is granted to revoke that election, provided the taxpayer timely filed the taxpayer's Federal tax return for the placed-in-service year or the taxable year in which the specified plant is planted or grafted, as applicable, and, within this 6-month extension period, the taxpayer, and all taxpayers whose tax liability would be affected by the election, file an amended Federal tax return for the placed-in-service year or the taxable year in which the specified plant is planted or grafted, as applicable, in a manner that is consistent with the revocation of the election.

(f) *Special rules.*—(1) *Property placed in service and disposed of in the same taxable year.*—(i) *In general.*—Except as provided in paragraphs (f)(1)(ii) and (iii) of this section, the additional first year depreciation deduction is not allowed for qualified property placed in service or planted or grafted, as applicable, and disposed of during the same taxable year. Also if qualified property is placed in service and disposed of during the same taxable year and then reacquired and again placed in service in a subsequent taxable year, the additional first year depreciation deduction is not allowable for the property in the subsequent taxable year.

(ii) *Technical termination of a partnership.*—In the case of a technical termination of a partnership under section 708(b)(1)(B) in a taxable year beginning before January 1, 2018, the additional first year depreciation deduction is allowable for any qualified property placed in service or planted or grafted, as applicable, by the terminated partnership during the taxable year of termination and contributed by the terminated partnership to the new partnership. The allowable additional first year depreciation deduction for the qualified property shall not be claimed by the terminated partnership but instead shall be claimed by the new partnership for the new partnership's taxable year in which the qualified property was contributed by the terminated partnership to the new partnership. However, if qualified property is both placed in service or planted or grafted, as applicable, and contributed to a new partnership in a transaction described in section 708(b)(1)(B) by the terminated partnership during the taxable year of termination, and if such property is disposed of by the new partnership in the same taxable year the new partnership received such property from the terminated partnership, then no additional first year depreciation deduction is allowable to either partnership.

(iii) *Section 168(i)(7) transactions.*—If any qualified property is transferred in a transaction described in section 168(i)(7) in the same taxable year that the qualified property is placed in service or planted or grafted, as applicable, by the transferor, the additional first year depreciation deduction is allowable for the qualified property. The allowable additional first year depreciation deduction for the qualified property for the transferor's taxable year in which the property is placed in service or planted or grafted, as applicable, is allocated between the transferor and the transferee on a monthly basis. This allocation shall be made in accordance with the rules in § 1.168(d)-1(b)(7)(ii) for allocating the depreciation deduction between the transferor and the transferee. However, solely for purposes of this section, if the qualified property is transferred in a section 721(a) transaction to a partnership that has as a partner a person, other than the transferor, who previously had a depreciable interest in the qualified property, in the same taxable year that the qualified property is placed in service or planted or grafted, as applicable, by the transferor, the allowable additional first year depreciation deduction is allocated entirely to the transferor, and not to the partnership. Additionally, if qualified property is both placed in service or planted or grafted, as applicable, and transferred in a transaction described in section 168(i)(7) by the transferor during the same taxable year, and if such property is disposed of by the transferee, other than by a transaction described in section 168(i)(7), during the same taxable year the transferee received such property from the transferor, then no additional first year depreciation deduction is allowable to either party.

(iv) *Examples.*—The application of this paragraph (f)(1) is illustrated by the following examples:

Example 1. *UU* and *VV* are equal partners in *Partnership JL*, a general partnership. *Partnership JL* is a calendar-year taxpayer. On October 1, 2017, *Partnership JL* purchased and placed in service qualified property at a cost of $30,000. On November 1, 2017, *UU* sells its entire 50 percent interest to *WW* in a transfer that terminates the partnership under section 708(b)(1)(B). As a result, terminated *Partnership JL* is deemed to have contributed the qualified property to new *Partnership JL*. Pursuant to paragraph (f)(1)(ii) of this section, new *Partnership JL*, not terminated *Partnership JL*, is eligible to claim the 100-percent additional first year depreciation deduction allowable for the qualified property for the taxable year 2017, assuming all other requirements are met.

Example 2. On January 5, 2018, *XX* purchased and placed in service qualified property for a total amount of $9,000. On August 20, 2018, *XX* transferred this qualified property to *Partnership BC* in a transaction described in section 721(a). No other partner of *Partnership BC* has ever had a depreciable interest in the qualified property. *XX* and *Partnership BC* are calendar-year taxpayers. Because the transaction between *XX* and *Partnership BC* is a transaction described in section 168(i)(7), pursuant to paragraph (f)(1)(iii) of this section, the 100-percent additional first year depreciation deduction allowable for the qualified property is allocated between *XX* and *Partnership BC* in accordance with the rules in § 1.168(d)-1(b)(7)(ii) for allocating the depreciation deduction between the transferor and the transferee. Accordingly, the 100-percent additional first year depreciation deduction allowable of $9,000 for the qualified property for 2018 is allocated between *XX* and *Partnership BC* based on the number of months that *XX* and *Partnership BC* held the qualified property in service during 2018. Thus, because the qualified property was held in service by *XX* for 7 of 12 months, which includes the month in which *XX* placed the qualified property in service but does not include the month in which the qualified property was transferred, *XX* is allocated $5,250 ($^7/_{12}$ × $9,000 additional first year depreciation deduction). *Partnership BC* is allocated $3,750, the remaining $^5/_{12}$ of the $9,000 additional first year depreciation deduction allowable for the qualified property.

(2) *Redetermination of basis.*—If the unadjusted depreciable basis, as defined in § 1.168(b)-1(a)(3), of qualified property is redetermined (for example, due to contingent purchase price or discharge of indebtedness) before January 1, 2027, or in the case of property described in section 168(k)(2)(B) or (C), is redetermined before January 1, 2028, the additional first year depreciation deduction allowable for the qualified property is redetermined as follows:

(i) *Increase in basis.*—For the taxable year in which an increase in basis of qualified property occurs, the taxpayer shall claim an additional first year depreciation deduction for qualified property by multiplying the amount of the increase in basis for this property by the applicable percentage for the taxable year in which the underlying property was placed in service by the taxpayer. For purposes of this paragraph (f)(2)(i), the additional first year depreciation deduction applies to the increase in basis only if the underlying property is qualified property. To determine the amount otherwise allowable as a depreciation deduction for the increase in basis of qualified property, the amount of the increase in basis of the qualified property must be reduced by the additional first year depreciation deduction allowed or allowable, whichever is greater, for the increase in basis and the remaining increase in basis of—

(A) Qualified property, except for computer software described in paragraph (b)(2)(i)(B) of this section, is depreciated over the recovery period of the qualified property remaining as of the beginning of the taxable year in which the increase in basis occurs, and using the same depreciation method and convention applicable to the qualified property that applies for the taxable year in which the increase in basis occurs; and

(B) Computer software, as defined in paragraph (b)(2)(i)(B) of this section, that is qualified property is depreciated ratably over the remainder of the 36-month period, the useful life under section 167(f)(1), as of the beginning of the first day of the month in which the increase in basis occurs.

(ii) *Decrease in basis.*—For the taxable year in which a decrease in basis of qualified property occurs, the taxpayer shall reduce the total amount otherwise allowable as a depreciation deduction for all of the taxpayer's depreciable property by the excess additional first year depreciation deduction previously claimed for the qualified property. If, for such taxable year, the excess additional first year depreciation deduction exceeds the total amount otherwise allowable as a depreciation deduction for all of the taxpayer's depreciable property, the taxpayer shall take into account a negative depreciation deduction in computing taxable income. The excess additional first year depreciation deduction for qualified property is determined by multiplying the amount of the decrease in basis for this property by the applicable percentage for the taxable year in which the underlying property was placed in service by the taxpayer. For purposes of this paragraph (f)(2)(ii), the additional first year depreciation deduction applies to the decrease in basis only if the underlying property is qualified property. Also, if the taxpayer establishes by adequate records or other sufficient evidence that the taxpayer claimed less than the additional first year depreciation deduction allowable for the qualified property before the decrease in basis, or if the taxpayer claimed more than the additional first year depreciation deduction allowable for the qualified property before the decrease in basis, the excess additional first year depreciation deduction is determined by multiplying the amount of the decrease in basis by the additional first year depreciation deduction percentage actually claimed by the taxpayer for the qualified property before the decrease in basis. To determine the amount to reduce the total amount otherwise allowable as a depreciation deduction for all of the taxpayer's depreciable property for the excess depreciation previously claimed, other than the additional first year depreciation deduction, resulting from the decrease in basis of the qualified property, the amount of the decrease in basis of the qualified property must be adjusted by the excess additional first year depreciation deduction that reduced the total amount otherwise allowable as a depreciation deduction, as determined under this paragraph (f)(2)(ii), and the remaining decrease in basis of—

(A) Qualified property, except for computer software described in paragraph (b)(2)(i)(B) of this section, reduces the amount otherwise allowable as a depreciation deduction over the recovery period of the qualified property remaining as of the beginning of the taxable year in which the decrease in basis occurs, and using the same depreciation method and convention of the qualified property that applies in the taxable year in which the decrease in basis occurs. If, for any taxable year, the reduction to the amount otherwise allowable as a depreciation deduction, as determined under this paragraph (f)(2)(ii)(A), exceeds the total amount otherwise allowable as a depreciation deduction for all of the taxpayer's depreciable property, the taxpayer shall take into account a negative depreciation deduction in computing taxable income; and

(B) Computer software, as defined in paragraph (b)(2)(i)(B) of this section, that is qualified property reduces the amount otherwise allowable as a depreciation deduction over the remainder of the 36-month period, the useful life under section 167(f)(1), as of the beginning of the first day of the month in which the decrease in basis occurs. If, for any taxable year, the reduction to the amount otherwise allowable as a depreciation deduction, as determined under this paragraph (f)(2)(ii)(B), exceeds the total amount otherwise allowable as a depreciation deduction for all of the taxpayer's depreciable property, the taxpayer shall take into account a negative depreciation deduction in computing taxable income.

(iii) *Definitions.*—Except as otherwise expressly provided by the Internal Revenue Code (for example, section 1017(a)), the regulations under the Internal Revenue Code, or other guidance published in the Internal Revenue Bulletin for purposes of this paragraph (f)(2)—

(A) An increase in basis occurs in the taxable year an amount is taken into account under section 461; and

(B) A decrease in basis occurs in the taxable year an amount would be taken into account under section 451.

(iv) *Examples.*—The application of this paragraph (f)(2) is illustrated by the following examples:

Example 1. (i) On May 15, 2023, *YY*, a cash-basis taxpayer, purchased and placed in service qualified property that is 5-year property at a cost of $200,000. In addition to the $200,000, *YY* agrees to pay the seller 25 percent of the gross profits from the operation of the property in 2023. On May 15, 2024, *YY* paid to the seller an additional $10,000. *YY* depreciates the 5-year property placed in service in 2023 using the optional depreciation table that corresponds with the general depreciation system, the 200-percent declining balance method, a 5-year recovery period, and the half-year convention.

(ii) For 2023, *YY* is allowed an 80-percent additional first year depreciation deduction of $160,000 (the unadjusted depreciable basis of $200,000 multiplied by 0.80). In addition, *YY*'s depreciation deduction for 2023 for the remaining adjusted depreciable basis of $40,000 (the unadjusted depreciable basis of $200,000 reduced by the additional first year depreciation deduction of $160,000) is $8,000 (the remaining adjusted depreciable basis of $40,000 multiplied by the annual depreciation rate of 0.20 for recovery year 1).

(iii) For 2024, *YY*'s depreciation deduction for the remaining adjusted depreciable basis of $40,000 is $12,800 (the remaining adjusted depreciable basis of $40,000 multiplied by the annual depreciation rate of 0.32 for recovery year 2). In addition, pursuant to paragraph (f)(2)(i) of this section, *YY* is allowed an additional first year depreciation deduction for 2024 for the $10,000 increase in basis of the qualified property. Consequently, *YY* is allowed an additional first year depreciation deduction of $8,000 (the increase in basis of $10,000 multiplied by 0.80, the applicable percentage for 2023). Also, *YY* is allowed a depreciation deduction for 2024 attributable to the remaining increase in basis of $2,000 (the increase in basis of $10,000 reduced by the additional first year depreciation deduction of $8,000). The depreciation deduction allowable for 2024 attributable to the remaining increase in basis of $2,000 is $889 (the remaining increase in basis of $2,000 multiplied by 0.4444, which is equal to 1/remaining recovery period of 4.5 years at January 1, 2024, multiplied by 2). Accordingly, for 2024, *YY*'s total depreciation deduction allowable for the qualified property is $21,689 ($12,800 plus $8,000 plus $889).

Example 2. (i) On May 15, 2023, *ZZ*, a calendar-year taxpayer, purchased and placed in service qualified property that is 5-year property at a cost of $400,000. To purchase the property, *ZZ* borrowed $250,000 from Bank1. On May 15, 2024, Bank1 forgives $50,000 of the indebtedness. *ZZ* makes the election provided in section 108(b)(5) to apply any portion of the reduction under section 1017 to the basis of the depreciable property of the taxpayer. *ZZ* depreciates the 5-year property placed in service in 2023 using the optional depreciation table that corresponds with the general depreciation system, the 200-percent declining balance method, a 5-year recovery period, and the half-year convention.

(ii) For 2023, *ZZ* is allowed an 80-percent additional first year depreciation deduction of $320,000 (the unadjusted depreciable basis of $400,000 multiplied by 0.80). In addition, *ZZ*'s depreciation deduction allowable for 2023 for the remaining adjusted depreciable basis of $80,000 (the unadjusted depreciable basis of $400,000 reduced by the additional first year depreciation deduction of $320,000) is $16,000 (the remaining adjusted depreciable basis of $80,000 multiplied by the annual depreciation rate of 0.20 for recovery year 1).

(iii) For 2024, *ZZ*'s deduction for the remaining adjusted depreciable basis of $80,000 is $25,600 (the remaining adjusted depreciable basis of $80,000 multiplied by the annual depreciation rate 0.32 for recovery year 2). Although Bank1 forgave the indebtedness in 2024, the basis of the property is reduced on January 1, 2025, pursuant to sections 108(b)(5) and 1017(a) under which basis is reduced at the beginning of the taxable year following the taxable year in which the discharge of indebtedness occurs.

(iv) For 2025, *ZZ*'s deduction for the remaining adjusted depreciable basis of $80,000 is $15,360 (the remaining adjusted depreciable basis of $80,000 multiplied by the annual depreciation rate 0.192 for recovery year 3). However, pursuant to paragraph (f)(2)(ii) of this section, *ZZ* must reduce the amount otherwise allowable as a depreciation deduction for 2025 by the excess depreciation previously claimed for the $50,000 decrease in basis of the qualified property. Consequently, *ZZ* must reduce the amount of depreciation otherwise allowable for 2025 by the excess additional first year depreciation of $40,000 (the decrease in basis of $50,000 multiplied by 0.80, the applicable percentage for 2023). Also, *ZZ* must reduce the amount of depreciation otherwise allowable for 2025 by the excess depreciation attributable to the remaining decrease in basis of $10,000 (the decrease in basis of $50,000 reduced by the excess additional first year depreciation of $40,000). The reduction in the amount of depreciation otherwise allowable for 2025 for the remaining decrease in basis of $10,000 is $5,714 (the remaining decrease in basis of $10,000 multiplied by 0.5714, which is equal to (1/remaining recovery period of 3.5 years at January 1, 2025) multiplied by 2). Accordingly, assuming the qualified property is the only depreciable property owned by *ZZ*, for 2025, *ZZ* has a negative depreciation deduction for the qualified property of $30,354 ($15,360 minus $40,000 minus $5,714).

(3) *Sections 1245 and 1250 depreciation recapture.*—For purposes of section 1245 and the regulations under section 1245, the additional first year depreciation deduction is an amount allowed or allowable for depreciation. Further, for purposes of section 1250(b) and the regulations under section 1250(b), the additional first year depreciation deduction is not a straight line method.

(4) *Coordination with section 169.*—The additional first year depreciation deduction is allowable in the placed-in-service year of a certified pollution control facility, as defined in § 1.169-2(a), that is qualified property even if the taxpayer makes the election to amortize the certified pollution control facility under section 169 and the regulations under section 169 in the certified pollution control facility's placed-in-service year.

(5) *Like-kind exchanges and involuntary conversions.*—(i) *Scope.*—The rules of this paragraph (f)(5) apply to replacement MACRS property or replacement computer software that is qualified property at the time of replacement provided the time of replacement is after September 27, 2017, and before January 1, 2027; or, in the case of replacement MACRS property or replacement computer software that is qualified property described in section 168(k)(2)(B) or (C), the time of replacement is after September 27, 2017, and before January 1, 2028.

(ii) *Definitions.*—For purposes of this paragraph (f)(5), the following definitions apply:

(A) *Replacement MACRS property* has the same meaning as that term is defined in § 1.168(i)-6(b)(1).

(B) *Relinquished MACRS property* has the same meaning as that term is defined in § 1.168(i)-6(b)(2).

(C) *Replacement computer software* is computer software, as defined in paragraph (b)(2)(i)(B) of this section, in the hands of the acquiring taxpayer that is acquired for other computer software in a like-kind exchange or in an involuntary conversion.

(D) *Relinquished computer software* is computer software that is transferred by the taxpayer in a like-kind exchange or in an involuntary conversion.

(E) *Time of disposition* has the same meaning as that term is defined in §1.168(i)-6(b)(3) for relinquished MACRS property. For relinquished computer software, *time of disposition* is when the disposition of the relinquished computer software takes place under the convention determined under §1.167(a)-14(b).

(F) Except as provided in paragraph (f)(5)(iv) of this section, the *time of replacement* has the same meaning as that term is defined in §1.168(i)-6(b)(4) for replacement MACRS property. For replacement computer software, the *time of replacement* is, except as provided in paragraph (f)(5)(iv) of this section, the later of—

(1) When the replacement computer software is placed in service under the convention determined under §1.167(a)-14(b); or

(2) The time of disposition of the relinquished property.

(G) *Exchanged basis* has the same meaning as that term is defined in §1.168(i)-6(b)(7) for MACRS property, as defined in §1.168(b)-1(a)(2). For computer software, the *exchanged basis* is determined after the amortization deductions for the year of disposition are determined under §1.167(a)-14(b) and is the lesser of—

(1) The basis in the replacement computer software, as determined under section 1031(d) and the regulations under section 1031(d), or section 1033(b) and the regulations under section 1033(b); or

(2) The adjusted depreciable basis of the relinquished computer software.

(H) *Excess basis* has the same meaning as that term is defined in §1.168(i)-6(b)(8) for replacement MACRS property. For replacement computer software, the *excess basis* is any excess of the basis in the replacement computer software, as determined under section 1031(d) and the regulations under section 1031(d), or section 1033(b) and the regulations under section 1033(b), over the exchanged basis as determined under paragraph (f)(5)(ii)(G) of this section.

(I) *Remaining exchanged basis* is the exchanged basis as determined under paragraph (f)(5)(ii)(G) of this section reduced by—

(1) The percentage of such basis attributable to the taxpayer's use of property for the taxable year other than in the taxpayer's trade or business or for the production of income; and

(2) Any adjustments to basis provided by other provisions of the Code and the regulations under the Code (including section 1016(a)(2) and (3)) for periods prior to the disposition of the relinquished property.

(J) *Remaining excess basis* is the excess basis as determined under paragraph (f)(5)(ii)(H) of this section reduced by—

(1) The percentage of such basis attributable to the taxpayer's use of property for the taxable year other than in the taxpayer's trade or business or for the production of income;

(2) Any portion of the basis the taxpayer properly elects to treat as an expense under section 179 or 179C; and

(3) Any adjustments to basis provided by other provisions of the Code and the regulations under the Code.

(K) *Year of disposition* has the same meaning as that term is defined in §1.168(i)-6(b)(5).

(L) *Year of replacement* has the same meaning as that term is defined in §1.168(i)-6(b)(6).

(M) *Like-kind exchange* has the same meaning as that term is defined in §1.168(i)-6(b)(11).

(N) *Involuntary conversion* has the same meaning as that term is defined in §1.168(i)-6(b)(12).

(iii) *Computation.*—(A) *In general.*—If the replacement MACRS property or the replacement computer software, as applicable, meets the original use requirement in paragraph (b)(3)(ii) of this section and all other requirements of section 168(k) and this section, the remaining exchanged basis for the year of replacement and the remaining excess basis, if any, for the year of replacement for the replacement MACRS property or the replacement computer software, as applicable, are eligible for the additional first year depreciation deduction. If the replacement MACRS property or the replacement computer software, as applicable, meets the used property acquisition requirements in paragraph (b)(3)(iii) of this section and all other requirements of section 168(k) and this section, only the remaining excess basis for the year of replacement for the replacement MACRS property or the replacement computer software, as applicable, is eligible for the additional first year depreciation deduction. See paragraph (b)(3)(iii)(A)(3) of this section. The additional first year depreciation deduction applies to the remaining exchanged basis and any remaining excess basis, as applicable, of the replacement MACRS property or the replacement computer software, as applicable, if the time of replacement is after September 27, 2017, and before January 1, 2027; or, in the case of replacement MACRS property or replacement computer software, as applicable, described in section 168(k)(2)(B) or (C), the time of replacement is after September 27, 2017, and before January 1, 2028. The additional first year depreciation deduction is computed separately for the remaining exchanged basis and any remaining excess basis, as applicable.

(B) *Year of disposition and year of replacement.*—The additional first year depreciation deduction is allowable for the replacement MACRS property or replacement computer software in the year of replacement. However, the additional first year depreciation deduction is not allowable for the relinquished MACRS property or the relinquished computer software, as applicable, if the relinquished MACRS property or the relinquished computer software, as applicable, is placed in service and disposed of in a like-kind exchange or in an involuntary conversion in the same taxable year.

(C) *Property described in section 168(k)(2)(B).*—For purposes of paragraph (f)(5)(iii)(A) of this section, the total of the remaining exchanged basis and the remaining excess basis, if any, of the replacement MACRS property that is qualified property described in section 168(k)(2)(B) and meets the original use requirement in paragraph (b)(3)(ii) of this section is limited to the total of the property's remaining exchanged basis and remaining excess basis, if any, attributable to the property's manufacture, construction, or production after September 27, 2017, and before January 1, 2027. For purposes of paragraph (f)(5)(iii)(A) of this section, the remaining excess basis, if any, of the replacement MACRS property that is qualified property described in section 168(k)(2)(B) and meets the used property acquisition requirements in paragraph (b)(3)(iii) of this section is limited to the property's remaining excess basis, if any, attributable to the property's manufacture, construction, or production after September 27, 2017, and before January 1, 2027.

(D) *Effect of §1.168(i)-6(i)(1) election.*—If a taxpayer properly makes the election under §1.168(i)-6(i)(1) not to apply §1.168(i)-6 for any MACRS property, as defined in §1.168(b)-1(a)(2), involved in a like-kind exchange or involuntary conversion and either of the following:

(1) The replacement MACRS property meets the original use requirement in paragraph (b)(3)(ii) of this section and all other requirements of section 168(k) and this section, the total of the exchanged basis, as defined in §1.168(i)-6(b)(7), and the excess basis, as defined in §1.168(i)-6(b)(8), if any, in the replacement MACRS property is eligible for the additional first year depreciation deduction; or

(2) The replacement MACRS property meets the used property acquisition requirements in paragraph (b)(3)(iii) of this section and all other requirements of section 168(k) and this section, only the excess basis, as defined in §1.168(i)-6(b)(8), if any, in the replacement MACRS property is eligible for the additional first year depreciation deduction.

(E) *Alternative minimum tax.*—The additional first year depreciation deduction is allowed for alternative minimum tax purposes for the year of replacement of replacement MACRS property or replacement computer software, as applicable, that is qualified property. If the replacement MACRS property or the replacement computer software, as applicable, meets the original use requirement in paragraph (b)(3)(ii) of this section and all other requirements of section 168(k) and this section, the additional first year depreciation deduction for alternative minimum tax purposes is based on the remaining exchanged basis and the remaining excess basis, if any, of the replacement MACRS property or the replacement computer software, as applicable, for alternative minimum tax purposes. If the replacement MACRS property or the replacement computer software, as applicable, meets the used property acquisition requirements in paragraph (b)(3)(iii) of this section and all other requirements of section 168(k) and this section, the additional first year depreciation deduction for alternative minimum tax purposes is based on the remaining excess basis, if any, of the replacement MACRS property or the replacement computer software, as applicable, for alternative minimum tax purposes.

(iv) *Replacement MACRS property or replacement computer software that is acquired and placed in service before disposition of relinquished MACRS property or relinquished computer software.*—If, in an involuntary conversion, a taxpayer acquires and places in service the replacement MACRS property or the replacement computer software, as applicable, before the time of disposition of the involuntarily converted MACRS property or the involuntarily converted computer software, as applicable; and the time of disposition of the involuntarily converted MACRS property or the involuntarily converted computer software, as applicable, is after December 31, 2026, or, in the case of property described in service 168(k)(2)(B) or (C), after December 31, 2027, then—

(A) The time of replacement for purposes of this paragraph (f)(5) is when the replacement MACRS property or replacement computer software, as applicable, is placed in service by the taxpayer, provided the threat or imminence of requisition or condemnation of the involuntarily converted MACRS property or involuntarily converted computer software, as applicable, existed before January 1, 2027, or, in the case of property described in section 168(k)(2)(B) or (C), existed before January 1, 2028; and

(B) The taxpayer depreciates the replacement MACRS property or replacement computer software, as applicable, in accordance with paragraph (d) of this section. However, at the time of disposition of the involuntarily converted MACRS property, the taxpayer determines the exchanged basis, as defined in §1.168(i)-6(b)(7), and the excess basis, as defined in §1.168(i)-6(b)(8), of the replacement MACRS property and begins to depreciate the depreciable exchanged basis, as defined in §1.168(i)-6(b)(9), of the replacement MACRS property in accordance with §1.168(i)-6(c). The depreciable excess basis, as defined in §1.168(i)-6(b)(10), of the replacement MACRS property continues to be depreciated by the taxpayer in accordance with the first sentence of this paragraph (f)(5)(iv)(B). Further, in the year of disposition of the involuntarily converted MACRS property, the taxpayer must include in taxable income the excess of the depreciation deductions allowable, including the additional first year depreciation deduction allowable, on the unadjusted depreciable basis of the replacement MACRS property over the additional first year depreciation deduction that would have been allowable to the taxpayer on the remaining exchanged basis of the replacement MACRS property at the time of replacement, as defined in paragraph (f)(5)(v)(A) of this section, plus the depreciation deductions that would have been allowable, including the additional first year depreciation deduction allowable, to the taxpayer on the depreciable excess basis of the replacement MACRS property from the date the replacement MACRS property was placed in service by the taxpayer, taking into account the applicable convention, to the time of disposition of the involuntarily converted MACRS property. Similar rules apply to replacement computer software.

(v) *Examples.*—The application of this paragraph (f)(5) is illustrated by the following examples:

Example 1. (i) In April 2016, *CSK*, a calendar-year corporation, acquired for $200,000 and placed in service Canopy V1, a gas station canopy. Canopy V1 is qualified property under section 168(k)(2), as in effect on the day before amendment by the Act, and is 5-year property under section 168(e). *CSK* depreciated Canopy V1 under the general depreciation system of section 168(a) by using the 200-percent declining balance method of depreciation, a 5-year recovery period, and the half-year convention. *CSK* elected to use the optional depreciation tables to compute the depreciation allowance for Canopy V1. In November 2017, Canopy V1 was destroyed in a fire and was no longer usable in *CSK*'s business. In December 2017, in an involuntary conversion, *CSK* acquired and placed in service Canopy W1 with all of the $160,000 of insurance proceeds *CSK* received due to the loss of Canopy V1. Canopy W1 is qualified property under section 168(k)(2) and this section, and is 5-year property under section 168(e). Canopy W1 also meets the original use requirement in paragraph (b)(3)(ii) of this section. *CSK* did not make the election under § 1.168(i)-6(i)(1).

(ii) For 2016, *CSK* is allowed a 50-percent additional first year depreciation deduction of $100,000 for Canopy V1 (the unadjusted depreciable basis of $200,000 multiplied by 0.50), and a regular MACRS depreciation deduction of $20,000 for Canopy V1 (the remaining adjusted depreciable basis of $100,000 multiplied by the annual depreciation rate of 0.20 for recovery year 1).

(iii) For 2017, *CSK* is allowed a regular MACRS depreciation deduction of $16,000 for Canopy V1 (the remaining adjusted depreciable basis of $100,000 multiplied by the annual depreciation rate of 0.32 for recovery year 2 × 1/2 year).

(iv) Pursuant to paragraph (f)(5)(iii)(A) of this section, the additional first year depreciation deduction allowable for Canopy W1 for 2017 equals $64,000 (100 percent of Canopy W1's remaining exchanged basis at the time of replacement of $64,000 (Canopy V1's remaining adjusted depreciable basis of $100,000 minus 2016 regular MACRS depreciation deduction of $20,000 minus 2017 regular MACRS depreciation deduction of $16,000)).

Example 2. (i) The facts are the same as in *Example 1* of this paragraph (f)(5)(v), except *CSK* elected not to deduct the additional first year depreciation for 5-year property placed in service in 2016. *CSK* deducted the additional first year depreciation for 5-year property placed in service in 2017.

(ii) For 2016, *CSK* is allowed a regular MACRS depreciation deduction of $40,000 for Canopy V1 (the unadjusted depreciable basis of $200,000 multiplied by the annual depreciation rate of 0.20 for recovery year 1).

(iii) For 2017, *CSK* is allowed a regular MACRS depreciation deduction of $32,000 for Canopy V1 (the unadjusted depreciable basis of $200,000 multiplied by the annual depreciation rate of 0.32 for recovery year 2 × 1/2 year).

(iv) Pursuant to paragraph (f)(5)(iii)(A) of this section, the additional first year depreciation deduction allowable for Canopy W1 for 2017 equals $128,000 (100 percent of Canopy W1's remaining exchanged basis at the time of replacement of $128,000 (Canopy V1's unadjusted depreciable basis of $200,000 minus 2016 regular MACRS depreciation deduction of $40,000 minus 2017 regular MACRS depreciation deduction of $32,000)).

Example 3. The facts are the same as in *Example 1* of this paragraph (f)(5)(v), except Canopy W1 meets the used property acquisition requirements in paragraph (b)(3)(iii) of this section. Because the remaining excess basis of Canopy W1 is zero, *CSK* is not allowed any additional first year depreciation for Canopy W1 pursuant to paragraph (f)(5)(iii)(A) of this section.

Example 4. (i) In December 2016, *AB*, a calendar-year corporation, acquired for $10,000 and placed in service Computer X2. Computer X2 is qualified property under section 168(k)(2), as in effect on the day before amendment by the Act, and is 5-year property under section 168(e). *AB* depreciated Computer X2 under the general depreciation system of section 168(a) by using the 200-percent declining balance method of depreciation, a 5-year recovery period, and the half-year convention. *AB* elected to use the optional depreciation tables to compute the depreciation allowance for Computer X2. In November 2017, *AB* acquired Computer Y2 by exchanging Computer X2 and $1,000 cash in a like-kind exchange. Computer Y2 is qualified property under section 168(k)(2) and this section, and is 5-year property under section 168(e). Computer Y2 also meets the original use requirement in paragraph (b)(3)(ii) of this section. *AB* did not make the election under § 1.168(i)-6(i)(1).

(ii) For 2016, *AB* is allowed a 50-percent additional first year depreciation deduction of $5,000 for Computer X2 (unadjusted basis of $10,000 multiplied by 0.50), and a regular MACRS depreciation deduction of $1,000 for Computer X2 (the remaining adjusted depreciable basis of $5,000 multiplied by the annual depreciation rate of 0.20 for recovery year 1).

(iii) For 2017, *AB* is allowed a regular MACRS depreciation deduction of $800 for Computer X2 (the remaining adjusted depreciable basis of $5,000 multiplied by the annual depreciation rate of 0.32 for recovery year 2 × 1/2 year).

(iv) Pursuant to paragraph (f)(5)(iii)(A) of this section, the 100-percent additional first year depreciation deduction for Computer Y2 for 2017 is allowable for the remaining exchanged basis at the time of replacement of $3,200 (Computer X2's unadjusted depreciable basis of $10,000 minus additional first year depreciation deduction allowable of $5,000 minus the 2016 regular MACRS depreciation deduction of $1,000 minus the 2017 regular MACRS depreciation deduction of $800) and for the remaining excess basis at the time of replacement of $1,000 (cash paid for Computer Y2). Thus, the 100-percent additional first year depreciation deduction allowable for Computer Y2 totals $4,200 for 2017.

Example 5. (i) In July 2017, *BC*, a calendar-year corporation, acquired for $20,000 and placed in service Equipment X3. Equipment X3 is qualified property under section 168(k)(2), as in effect on the day before amendment by the Act, and is 5-year property under section 168(e). *BC* depreciated Equipment X3 under the general depreciation system of section 168(a) by using the 200-percent declining balance method of depreciation, a 5-year recovery period, and the half-year convention. *BC* elected to use the optional depreciation tables to compute the depreciation allowance for Equipment X3. In December 2017, *BC* acquired Equipment Y3 by exchanging Equipment X3 and $5,000 cash in a like-kind exchange. Equipment Y3 is qualified property under section 168(k)(2) and this section, and is 5-year property under section 168(e). Equipment Y3 also meets the used property acquisition requirements in paragraph (b)(3)(iii) of this section. *BC* did not make the election under § 1.168(i)-6(i)(1).

(ii) Pursuant to § 1.168(k)-1(f)(5)(iii)(B), no additional first year depreciation deduction is allowable for Equipment X3 and, pursuant to § 1.168(d)-1(b)(3)(ii), no regular depreciation deduction is allowable for Equipment X3, for 2017.

(iii) Pursuant to paragraph (f)(5)(iii)(A) of this section, no additional first year depreciation deduction is allowable for Equipment Y3's remaining exchanged basis at the time of replacement of $20,000 (Equipment X3's unadjusted depreciable basis of $20,000). However, pursuant to paragraph (f)(5)(iii)(A) of this section, the 100-percent additional first year depreciation deduction is allowable for Equipment Y3's remaining excess basis at the time of replacement of $5,000 (cash paid for Equipment Y3). Thus, the 100-percent additional first year depreciation deduction allowable for Equipment Y3 is $5,000 for 2017.

Example 6. (i) The facts are the same as in *Example 5* of this paragraph (f)(5)(v), except *BC* properly makes the election under § 1.168(i)-6(i)(1) not to apply § 1.168(i)-6 to Equipment X3 and Equipment Y3.

(ii) Pursuant to § 1.168(k)-1(f)(5)(iii)(B), no additional first year depreciation deduction is allowable for Equipment X3 and, pursuant to § 1.168(d)-1(b)(3)(ii), no regular depreciation deduction is allowable for Equipment X3, for 2017.

(iii) Pursuant to § 1.168(i)-6(i)(1), *BC* is treated as placing Equipment Y3 in service in December 2017 with a basis of $25,000 (the total of the exchanged basis of $20,000 and the excess basis of $5,000). However, pursuant to paragraph (f)(5)(iii)(D)(2) of this section, the 100-percent additional first year depreciation deduction is allowable only for Equipment Y3's excess basis at the time of replacement of $5,000 (cash paid for Equipment Y3). Thus, the 100-percent additional first year depreciation deduction allowable for Equipment Y3 is $5,000 for 2017.

(6) *Change in use.*—(i) *Change in use of depreciable property.*—The determination of whether the use of depreciable property changes is made in accordance with section 168(i)(5) and § 1.168(i)-4.

(ii) *Conversion to personal use.*—If qualified property is converted from business or income-producing use to personal use in the same taxable year in which the property is placed in service by a taxpayer, the additional first year depreciation deduction is not allowable for the property.

(iii) *Conversion to business or income-producing use.*—(A) *During the same taxable year.*—If, during the same taxable year, property is acquired by a taxpayer for personal use and is converted by the taxpayer from personal use to business or income-producing use, the additional first year depreciation deduction is allowable for the property in the taxable year the property is converted to business or income-producing use, assuming all of the requirements in paragraph (b) of this section are met. See paragraph (b)(3)(ii) of this section relating to the original use rules for a conversion of property to business or income-producing use.

(B) *Subsequent to the acquisition year.*—If property is acquired by a taxpayer for personal use and, during a subsequent taxable year, is converted by the taxpayer from personal use to business or income-producing use, the additional first year depreciation deduction is allowable for the property in the taxable year the property is converted to business or income-producing use, assuming all of the requirements in paragraph (b) of this section are met. For purposes of paragraphs (b)(4) and (5) of this section, the property must be acquired by the taxpayer for personal use after September 27, 2017, and converted by the taxpayer from personal use to business or income-producing use by January 1, 2027. See paragraph (b)(3)(ii) of this section relating to the original use rules for a conversion of property to business or income-producing use.

(iv) *Depreciable property changes use subsequent to the placed-in-service year.*—(A) If the use of qualified property changes in the hands of the same taxpayer subsequent to the taxable year the qualified property is placed in service and, as a result of the change in use, the property is no longer qualified property, the additional first year depreciation deduction allowable for the qualified property is not redetermined.

(B) If depreciable property is not qualified property in the taxable year the property is placed in service by the taxpayer, the additional first year depreciation deduction is not allowable for the property even if a change in the use of the property subsequent to the taxable year the property is placed in service results in the property being qualified property in the taxable year of the change in use.

(v) *Examples.*—The application of this paragraph (f)(6) is illustrated by the following examples:

Example 1. (i) On January 1, 2019, *FFF*, a calendar year corporation, purchased and placed in service several new computers at a total cost of $100,000. *FFF* used these computers within the United States for 3 months in 2019 and then moved and used the computers outside the United States for the remainder of 2019. On January 1, 2020, *FFF* permanently returns the computers to the United States for use in its business.

(ii) For 2019, the computers are considered as used predominantly outside the United States in 2019 pursuant to § 1.48-1(g)(1)(i). As a result, the computers are required to be depreciated under the alternative depreciation system of section 168(g). Pursuant to paragraph (b)(2)(ii)(B) of this section, the computers are not qualified property in 2019, the placed-in-service year. Thus, pursuant to paragraph (f)(6)(iv)(B) of this section, no additional first year depreciation deduction is allowed for these computers, regardless of the fact that the computers are permanently returned to the United States in 2020.

Example 2. (i) On February 8, 2023, GGG, a calendar year corporation, purchased and placed in service new equipment at a cost of $1,000,000 for use in its California plant. The equipment is 5-year property under section 168(e) and is qualified property under section 168(k). *GGG* depreciates its 5-year property placed in service in 2023 using the optional depreciation table that corresponds with the general depreciation system, the 200-percent declining balance method, a 5-year recovery period, and the half-year convention. On June 4, 2024, due to changes in GGG's business circumstances, *GGG* permanently moves the equipment to its plant in Mexico.

(ii) For 2023, *GGG* is allowed an 80-percent additional first year depreciation deduction of $800,000 (the adjusted depreciable basis of $1,000,000 multiplied by 0.80). In addition, *GGG's* depreciation deduction allowable in 2023 for the remaining adjusted depreciable basis of $200,000 (the unadjusted depreciable basis of $1,000,000 reduced by the additional first year depreciation deduction of $800,000) is $40,000 (the remaining adjusted depreciable basis of $200,000 multiplied by the annual depreciation rate of 0.20 for recovery year 1).

(iii) For 2024, the equipment is considered as used predominantly outside the United States pursuant to § 1.48-1(g)(1)(i). As a result of this change in use, the adjusted depreciable basis of $160,000 for the equipment is required to be depreciated under the alternative depreciation system of section 168(g) beginning in 2024. However, the additional first year depreciation deduction of $800,000 allowed for the equipment in 2023 is not redetermined.

(7) *Earnings and profits.*—The additional first year depreciation deduction is not allowable for purposes of computing earnings and profits.

(8) *Limitation of amount of depreciation for certain passenger automobiles.*—For a passenger automobile as defined in section 280F(d)(5), the limitation under section 280F(a)(1)(A)(i) is increased by $8,000 for qualified property acquired and placed in service by a taxpayer after September 27, 2017.

(9) *Coordination with section 47.*—(i) *In general.*—If qualified rehabilitation expenditures, as defined in section 47(c)(2) and § 1.48-12(c), incurred by a taxpayer with respect to a qualified rehabilitated building, as defined in section 47(c)(1) and § 1.48-12(b), are qualified property, the taxpayer may claim the rehabilitation credit provided by section 47(a), provided the requirements of section 47 are met—

(A) With respect to the portion of the basis of the qualified rehabilitated building that is attributable to the qualified rehabilitation expenditures if the taxpayer makes the applicable election under paragraph (e)(1)(i) of this section not to deduct any additional first year depreciation for the class of property that includes the qualified rehabilitation expenditures; or

(B) With respect to the portion of the remaining rehabilitated basis of the qualified rehabilitated building that is attributable to the qualified rehabilitation expenditures if the taxpayer claims the additional first year depreciation deduction on the unadjusted depreciable basis, as defined in § 1.168(b)-1(a)(3) but before the reduction in basis for the amount of the rehabilitation credit, of the qualified rehabilitation expenditures; and the taxpayer depreciates the remaining adjusted depreciable basis, as defined in paragraph (d)(2)(i) of this section, of such expenditures using straight line cost recovery in accordance with section 47(c)(2)(B)(i) and § 1.48-12(c)(7)(i). For purposes of this paragraph (f)(9)(i)(B), the remaining rehabilitated basis is equal to the unadjusted depreciable basis, as defined in § 1.168(b)-1(a)(3) but before the reduction in basis for the amount of the rehabilitation credit, of the qualified rehabilitation expenditures that are qualified property reduced by the additional first year depreciation allowed or allowable, whichever is greater.

(ii) *Example.*—The application of this paragraph (f)(9) is illustrated by the following example:

Example. (i) Between February 8, 2023, and June 4, 2023, *JM*, a calendar-year taxpayer, incurred qualified rehabilitation expenditures of $200,000 with respect to a qualified rehabilitated building that is nonresidential real property under section 168(e). These qualified rehabilitation expenditures are qualified property and qualify for the 20-percent rehabilitation credit under section 47(a)(1). *JM's* basis in the qualified rehabilitated building is zero before incurring the qualified rehabilitation expenditures and *JM* placed the qualified rehabilitated building in service in July 2023. *JM* depreciates its nonresidential real property placed in service in 2023 under the general depreciation system of section 168(a) by using the straight line method of depreciation, a 39-year recovery period, and the mid-month convention. *JM* elected to use the optional depreciation tables to compute the depreciation allowance for its depreciable property placed in service in 2023. Further, for 2023, *JM* did not make any election under paragraph (e) of this section.

(ii) Because *JM* did not make any election under paragraph (e) of this section, *JM* is allowed an 80-percent additional first year depreciation deduction of $160,000 for the qualified rehabilitation expenditures for 2023 (the unadjusted depreciable basis of $200,000 (before reduction in basis for the rehabilitation credit) multiplied by 0.80). *JM* also is allowed to claim a rehabilitation credit of $8,000 for the remaining rehabilitated basis of $40,000 (the unadjusted depreciable basis (before reduction in basis for the rehabilitation credit) of $200,000 less the additional first year depreciation deduction of $160,000, multiplied by 0.20 to calculate the rehabilitation credit). For 2023, the ratable share of the rehabilitation credit of $8,000 is $1,600. Further, *JM's* depreciation deduction for 2023 for the remaining adjusted depreciable basis of $32,000 (the unadjusted depreciable basis (before reduction in basis for the rehabilitation credit) of $200,000 less the additional first year depreciation deduction of $160,000 less the rehabilitation credit of $8,000) is $376.64 (the remaining adjusted depreciable basis of $32,000 multiplied by the depreciation rate of 0.01177 for recovery year 1, placed in service in month 7).

(10) *Coordination with section 514(a)(3).*—The additional first year depreciation deduction is not allowable for purposes of section 514(a)(3).

(g) *Applicability dates.*—(1) *In general.*—Except as provided in paragraph (g)(2) of this section, the rules of this section apply to—

(i) Qualified property under section 168(k)(2) that is placed in service by the taxpayer during or after the taxpayer's taxable year that includes the date of publication of a Treasury decision adopting these rules as final regulations in the **Federal Register**; and

(ii) A specified plant for which the taxpayer properly made an election to apply section 168(k)(5) and that is planted, or grafted to a plant that was previously planted, by the taxpayer during or after the taxpayer's taxable year that includes the date of publication of a Treasury decision adopting these rules as final regulations in the **Federal Register**.

(2) *Early application*.—A taxpayer may rely on the provisions of this section in these proposed regulations for—

(i) Qualified property under section 168(k)(2) acquired and placed in service after September 27, 2017, by the taxpayer during taxable years ending on or after September 28, 2017, and ending before the taxpayer's taxable year that includes the date of publication of a Treasury decision adopting these rules as final regulations in the **Federal Register**; and

(ii) A specified plant for which the taxpayer properly made an election to apply section 168(k)(5) and that is planted, or grafted to a plant that was previously planted, after September 27, 2017, by the taxpayer during taxable years ending on or after September 28, 2017, and ending before the taxpayer's taxable year that includes the date of publication of a Treasury decision adopting these rules as final regulations in the **Federal Register**. [Reg. § 1.168(k)-2.]

Qualified Property: Additional First Year Depreciation Deduction

Qualified Property: Additional First Year Depreciation Deduction.—Amendments to Reg. § 1.169-3, providing guidance regarding the additional first year depreciation deduction under section 168(k) of the Internal Revenue Code (Code), are proposed (published in the Federal Register on August 8, 2018) (REG-104397-18).

Par. 10. Section 1.169-3 is amended by adding a sentence at the end of paragraph (a) and adding two sentences at the end of paragraph (g) to read as follows:

§ 1.169-3. Amortizable basis.—(a) * * * Further, before computing the amortization deduction allowable under section 169, the adjusted basis for purposes of determining gain for a facility that is acquired and placed in service after September 27, 2017, and that is qualified property under section 168(k), as amended by the Tax Cuts and Jobs Act, Public Law 115-97 (131 Stat. 2054 (December 22, 2017)) (the "Act"), or § 1.168(k)-2, must be reduced by the amount of the additional first year depreciation deduction allowed or allowable, whichever is greater, under section 168(k), as amended by the Act.

* * *

(g) * * * The last sentence of paragraph (a) of this section applies to a certified pollution control facility that is qualified property under section 168(k)(2) and placed in service by a taxpayer during or after the taxpayer's taxable year that includes the date of publication of a Treasury decision adopting these rules as final regulations in the **Federal Register**. However, a taxpayer may rely on the last sentence in paragraph (a) of this section in these proposed regulations for a certified pollution control facility that is qualified property under section 168(k)(2) and acquired and placed in service after September 27, 2017, by the taxpayer during taxable years ending on or after September 28, 2017, and ending before the taxpayer's taxable year that includes the date of publication of a Treasury decision adopting these rules as final regulations in the **Federal Register**.

Charitable Contribution Deductions: State or Local Tax Credits

Charitable Contribution Deductions: State or Local Tax Credits.—Amendments to Reg. §§ 1.170A-1 and 1.170A-13, providing rules governing the availability of charitable contribution deductions under section 170 when a taxpayer receives or expects to receive a corresponding state or local tax credit, are proposed (published in the Federal Register on August 27, 2018) (REG-112176-18).

Par. 2. Section 1.170A-1 is amended by redesignating paragraphs (h)(3) through (h)(5) as paragraphs (h)(4) through (h)(6), and adding a new paragraph (h)(3) to read as follows:

§ 1.170A-1. Charitable, etc., contributions and gifts; allowance of deduction.

* * *

(h) * * *

(3) *Payments resulting in state or local tax benefits*.—(i) *State or local tax credits*.—Except as provided in paragraph (h)(3)(v) of this section, if a taxpayer makes a payment or transfers property to or for the use of an entity listed in section 170(c), the amount of the taxpayer's charitable contribution deduction under section 170(a) is reduced by the amount of any state or local tax credit that the taxpayer receives or expects to receive in consideration for the taxpayer's payment or transfer.

(ii) *State or local tax deductions*.—(A) *In general*.—If a taxpayer makes a payment or transfers property to or for the use of an entity listed in section 170(c), and the taxpayer receives or expects to receive a state or local tax deduction that does not exceed the amount of the taxpayer's payment or the fair market value of the property transferred by the taxpayer to such entity, the taxpayer is not required to reduce its charitable contribution deduction under section 170(a) on account of such state or local tax deduction.

(B) *Excess state or local tax deductions*.—If the taxpayer receives or expects to receive a state or local tax deduction that exceeds the amount of the taxpayer's payment or the fair market value of the property transferred, the taxpayer's charitable contribution deduction under section 170 is reduced.

(iii) *In consideration for*.—For purposes of paragraph (h)(3)(i) of this section, the term *in consideration for* shall have the meaning set forth in § 1.170A-13(f)(6), except that the state or local tax credit need not be provided by the donee organization.

(iv) *Amount of reduction*.—For purposes of paragraph (h)(3)(i) of this section, the amount of any state or local tax credit is the maximum credit allowable that corresponds to the amount of the taxpayer's payment or transfer to the entity listed in section 170(c).

(v) *State or local tax*.—For purposes of paragraph (h)(3) of this section, the term *state or local tax* means a tax imposed by a State, a possession of the United States, or by a political subdivision of any of the foregoing, or by the District of Columbia.

(vi) *Exception*.—Paragraph (h)(3)(i) of this section shall not apply to any payment or transfer of property if the amount of the state or local tax credit received or expected to be received by the taxpayer does not exceed 15 percent of the taxpayer's payment, or 15 percent of the fair market value of the property transferred by the taxpayer.

(vii) *Examples*.—The following examples illustrate the provisions of this paragraph (h)(3). The examples in paragraph (h)(6) of this section are not illustrative for purposes of this paragraph (h)(3).

Example 1. A, an individual, makes a payment of $1,000 to X, an entity listed in section 170(c). In exchange for the payment, A receives or expects to receive a state tax credit of 70% of the amount of A's payment to X. Under paragraph (h)(3)(i) of this section, A's charitable contribution deduction is reduced by $700 (70% x $1,000). This reduction occurs regardless of whether A is able to claim the state tax credit in that year. Thus, A's charitable contribution deduction for the $1,000 payment to X may not exceed $300.

Example 2. B, an individual, transfers a painting to Y, an entity listed in section 170(c). At the time of the transfer, the painting has a fair market value of $100,000. In exchange for the painting, B receives or expects to receive a state tax credit equal to 10% of the fair market value of the painting. Under paragraph (h)(3)(vi) of this section, B is not required to apply the general rule of paragraph (h)(3)(i) of this section because the amount of the tax credit received or expected to be received by B does not exceed 15% of the fair market value of the property transferred to Y. Accordingly, the amount of B's charitable contribution deduction for the transfer of the painting is not reduced under paragraph (h)(3)(i) of this section.

Example 3. C, an individual, makes a payment of $1,000 to Z, an entity listed in section 170(c). In exchange for the payment, under state M law, C is entitled to receive a state tax deduction equal to the amount paid by C to Z. Under paragraph (h)(3)(ii)(A) of this section, C is not required to reduce its charitable contribution deduction under section 170(a) on account of the state tax deduction.

(viii) *Effective/applicability date*.—This paragraph (h)(3) applies to amounts paid or property transferred by a taxpayer after August 27, 2018.

* * *

Par. 3. Section 1.170A-13(f)(7) is amended by removing the cross-reference "§1.170A-1(h)(4)" and adding in its place "§1.170A-1(h)(5)".

§1.170A-13. Recordkeeping and return requirements for deductions for charitable contributions.

Application of Section 172(h): Regulations: Consolidated Groups

Application of Section 172(h): Regulations: Consolidated Groups.—Reg. §§1.172(h)-0—1.172(h)-5, providing guidance regarding the treatment of corporate equity reduction transactions (CERTs), including the treatment of multiple step plans for the acquisition of stock and CERTs involving members of a consolidated group, are proposed (published in the Federal Register on September 17, 2012) (REG-140668-07) (corrected October 23, 2012).

☐ Par. 2. Sections 1.172(h)-0 through 1.172(h)-5 are added to read as follows:

§1.172(h)-0. Table of Contents.—This section lists the paragraphs contained in §§1.172(h)-1 through 1.172(h)-5.

§1.172(h)-1. Existence of CERT and loss limitation years.—(a) *In general.*—If there is a corporate equity reduction transaction (CERT) and an applicable corporation has a corporate equity reduction interest loss (CERIL) for any loss limitation year, section 172(b)(1)(E) and (h), this section, §§1.172(h)-2 through 1.172(h)-5, and §1.1502-72 (collectively, the *CERT rules*) limit the amount of net operating loss that can be carried back to any taxable year preceding the taxable year in which the CERT occurs. This section provides rules regarding the determination of whether a CERT has occurred and whether a taxable year constitutes a loss limitation year. See §1.172(h)-2 for rules regarding the computation of a CERIL.

(b) *Applicable corporation.*—(1) *In general.*—The CERT rules apply only to applicable corporations. The term *applicable corporation* means a C corporation that acquires stock, or the stock of which is acquired, in a major stock acquisition (MSA), a C corporation making distributions with respect to, or redeeming, its stock in connection with an excess distribution (ED), or a C corporation that is a successor of any corporation described in this paragraph (b)(1). For special rules regarding the definition of an applicable corporation with regard to members that join and leave a consolidated group, see §1.1502-72(a) and (b).

(2) *Predecessor and successor.*—For purposes of the CERT rules, the term *predecessor* means a transferor or distributor of assets to a transferee or distributee (the successor) in a transaction to which section 381(a) applies. A corporation is a successor to its predecessor, and to all predecessors of that predecessor. If an applicable corporation transfers or distributes its assets to a successor, the successor is treated as an applicable corporation in the successor's taxable year during which the transfer or distribution occurs and any subsequent years.

(c) *CERT defined.*—(1) *In general.*—A CERT can be an MSA or an ED.

(2) *MSA defined.*—An *MSA* is the acquisition by a corporation pursuant to a plan of such corporation (or any group of persons acting in concert with such corporation) of stock in another corporation representing 50 percent or more (by vote or value) of the stock in such other corporation.

(3) *ED defined.*—An *ED* is any excess of the aggregate distributions made during a taxable year by a corporation with respect to its stock, over the greater of—

(i) 150 percent of the average of such distributions (the three-year distribution average) during the three taxable years immediately preceding such taxable year (the distribution lookback period); or

(ii) 10 percent of the fair market value of the stock of such corporation as of the beginning of such taxable year. For purposes of testing a potential ED, distributions include redemptions.

(d) *Transactions tested as CERTs.*—(1) *Tax-free transactions.*—A transaction may constitute a CERT and must be tested under the CERT rules regardless of whether gain or loss is recognized by any party. For example, a distribution that qualifies for tax-free treatment under section 355 is tested as a potential ED (or part of a potential ED). Likewise, the acquisition by a corporation of 50 percent or more of the stock of another corporation in a transaction meeting the requirements of section 351, section 368(a)(1)(A) and (a)(2)(E), or section 368(a)(1)(B) constitutes an MSA.

(2) *Multiple step plan of acquisition.*—Solely for purposes of determining whether an MSA has occurred and determining the consequences of an MSA, all steps of an integrated plan (including redemptions and other distributions) are tested as a single potential MSA. If an integrated plan qualifies as an MSA and includes one or

more distributions, then, for purposes of applying the CERT rules, the distributions are treated solely as a part of the MSA, regardless of whether such distributions would otherwise constitute an ED (or would so qualify in conjunction with other distributions). Any distributions during the year that are not part of the integrated plan qualifying as an MSA are tested as a potential ED.

(3) *Examples.*—The following examples illustrate the rules of this paragraph (d). For purposes of these examples, unless otherwise stated, assume that all entities are domestic C corporations that do not join in the filing of a consolidated return and that the entities have no history of paying dividends or otherwise making distributions:

Example 1. Spin-off. Distributing corporation (D) distributes stock of controlled corporation (C) to its shareholders in a transaction that satisfies the requirements of section 355. There is no taxable "boot" associated with the distribution. Pursuant to paragraph (d)(1) of this section, D's distribution of C stock is tested as a potential ED (in conjunction with any other distributions by D during the same taxable year). The same result would obtain if D distributes boot to its shareholders in addition to C stock.

Example 2. Bootstrap acquisition. (i) *Facts.* T is a publicly-traded, widely-held corporation with a single class of stock outstanding with a fair market value of $100. The following steps occur as part of an integrated plan. Corporation A acquires 10 percent of the outstanding stock of T for $10. A forms a new corporation, S, with a contribution of $25. S obtains a loan of $65 from an unrelated lender, and then merges with and into T, with T surviving. In the merger, all shareholders of T except A receive cash in exchange for their shares, and as a consequence, A owns all of the outstanding stock of T. As a result of the merger, T becomes liable for S's $65 loan. Assume that the $90 cash payment from T to the T shareholders should be treated as a redemption to the extent of the $65 loan assumed by T, and as a stock acquisition by A to the extent of the remaining $25.

(ii) *Analysis.* A's direct acquisition of 10 percent of T's outstanding stock and the steps culminating with the merger are part of an integrated plan. Therefore, the multiple steps are tested together as a potential MSA. Because the steps of the integrated plan resulted in A's acquisition of 100 percent of T, the transaction is treated as a single MSA. Furthermore, because the $65 redemption is part of an MSA, it is treated solely as part of the MSA and is not tested as a potential ED. See paragraph (d)(2) of this section.

(e) *Loss limitation years.*—The taxable year in which a CERT occurs and each of the two succeeding taxable years constitute loss limitation years with regard to the CERT. See §1.172(h)-4(b) (addressing loss limitation years of successors) and §1.1502-72(a)(3) (addressing loss limitation years of consolidated groups and former members of consolidated groups).

(f) *Computation of three-year distribution average relevant to a potential ED.*—(1) *Integrated plan.*—Section 172(h)(3)(C)(ii)(I) and paragraph (c)(3) of this section treat as an ED the excess of distributions in a taxable year over the taxpayer's average distributions (three-year distribution average) made in the three taxable years preceding the taxable year in which a potential ED occurs (distribution lookback period). The computation of a taxpayer's three-year distribution average under this paragraph (f) excludes any distribution during the distribution lookback period that is treated as part of an integrated plan qualifying as an MSA pursuant to paragraph (d)(2) of this section. See §1.1502-72(f)(2) and (3) for rules relating to distributions (including intercompany distributions) made during a consolidated return year.

(2) *Short taxable year.*—For purposes of computing the three-year distribution average under this paragraph (f), if the year of the potential ED is less than a full 12-month year, the distribution history with regard to any year of the taxpayer during a distribution lookback period (distribution lookback period year) equals the amount of distributions made during the distribution lookback period year multiplied by a fraction, the numerator of which equals the number of days in the short taxable year of the potential ED, and the denominator of which equals the number of days in the distribution lookback period year. The value of the fraction may not exceed 100 percent. No distributions are deemed made (in excess of amounts actually distributed) in a distribution lookback period year that is shorter than the year of the potential ED.

(g) *Effective/applicability date.*—This section is applicable to CERTs occurring on or after the date of publication of the Treasury decision adopting these rules as final regulations in the **Federal Register**. This section is also applicable to the deconsolidation of a member from, or the acquisition of a corporation by, a consolidated group that occurs on or after the date of publication of the Treasury decision adopting these rules as final regulations in the **Federal Register**. However, in each case, this section does not apply to any CERT, deconsolidation, or acquisition occurring pursuant to a written agreement that is binding before the date of publication of the Treasury decision adopting these rules as final regulations in the **Federal Register**. [Reg. §1.172(h)-1.]

§1.172(h)-2. Computation of a CERIL.—(a) *In general.*—(1) *Scope.*—The portion of a net operating loss (NOL) that is treated as a corporate equity reduction interest loss (CERIL) (as defined in paragraph (a)(2) of this section) cannot be carried back to a taxable year preceding the taxable year in which the corporate equity reduction transaction (CERT) occurs. This section provides rules for computing allocable interest deductions necessary to compute a CERIL for purposes of applying section 172(b)(1)(E) and (h), §§1.172(h)-1 through 1.172(h)-5, and §1.1502-72 (the CERT rules).

(2) *CERIL defined.*—A *CERIL* means, with respect to any loss limitation year, the excess (if any) of the NOL for such taxable year over the NOL for such taxable year determined without regard to any allocable interest deductions otherwise taken into account in computing such loss.

(b) *Computation of allocable interest deductions.*—(1) *In general.*—*Allocable interest deductions* are deductions allowed for interest on the portion of indebtedness allocable to a CERT. Except as provided in section 172(h)(2)(E) (relating to adjustments for certain unforeseeable events), indebtedness is allocated to a CERT in the manner prescribed in section 263A(f)(2)(A), without regard to clause (i) thereof (relating to traced debt). Generally, interest deductions are allocable to a CERT if the interest expense could have been avoided if the CERT had not been undertaken (for example, if the amount of CERT costs (as defined in paragraph (b)(3)) had instead been used to pay down debt). See section 263A(f)(2)(A)(ii) and § 1.263A-9(a)(1). For purposes of applying the avoided cost rules of section 263A(f)(2)(A)(ii), all CERT costs are treated as if they were cash expenditures.

(2) *Operating rules.*—This section provides a method for identifying the pool of costs to be treated as arising from a CERT (CERT costs). The interest allocable to those CERT costs is then computed under the principles of the avoided cost rules under section 263A(f)(2)(A) (without regard to paragraph (i) thereof) and the regulations thereunder, but substituting "CERT costs" or "accumulated CERT costs" (as defined in paragraph (b)(4)) for "production expenditures" or "accumulated production expenditures," where those terms appear. In addition, for purposes of applying the avoided cost rules to compute interest allocable to a CERT, the "production period" is treated as beginning on the first date of the taxable year in which the CERT occurs (year of the CERT) on which there are accumulated CERT costs. Because the principles of section 263A(f)(2)(A)(i) are inapplicable to CERT computations, the principles of § 1.263A-9(b) (relating to traced debt) are also inapplicable. Instead, accumulated CERT costs are treated in their entirety as expenditures allocable to non-traced debt as that term is defined under § 1.263A-9(c)(5), and interest allocable to a CERT is calculated without tracing debt under the provisions of § 1.263A-9(d)(1). Limitations apply to the amount of interest allocable to a CERT. See, for example, section 172(h)(2)(C)(ii) and § 1.172(h)-3 (generally relating to three-year average interest history)..

(3) *CERT costs defined.*—(i) *Major stock acquisition.*—CERT costs with regard to a major stock acquisition (MSA) include the fair market value of the stock acquired, whether that stock is acquired in exchange for cash, for stock of the acquirer, or for other property. In addition, CERT costs include the fair market value of any distributions to shareholders that are treated as part of the MSA under § 1.172(h)-1(d)(2). CERT costs also include the sum of amounts paid or incurred to facilitate any step of the MSA to the extent that those amounts are required to be capitalized under section 263(a), and any amounts disallowed under section 162(k). See also § 1.1502-72(a)(4) for additional rules regarding CERT costs in the case of a reverse acquisition.

(ii) *Excess distribution.*—CERT costs with regard to an excess distribution (ED) include the fair market value of any distributions to shareholders during the year of the CERT. CERT costs also include the sum of amounts paid or incurred to facilitate the distributions to the extent that those amounts are required to be capitalized under section 263(a), and any amounts disallowed under section 162(k). To the extent that neither section 263(a) nor section 162(k) applies or if only section 162(k) applies to a distribution included in an ED, additional CERT costs associated with the distribution are determined under the principles of § 1.263(a)-4(e) (relating to the capitalization of certain costs incurred to acquire or create intangibles), applied as if the distribution were a transaction within the scope of § 1.263(a)-4.

(iii) *Borrowing costs included in CERT costs.*—For purposes of identifying CERT costs with regard to an MSA or ED under this paragraph (b)(3), the determination of whether costs facilitate an MSA or ED is made without regard to §§ 1.263(a)-5(c)(1) and 1.263(a)-4(e)(1)(iv) (excluding borrowing costs). Therefore, certain costs of debt financing are included in CERT costs.

(4) *Accumulated CERT costs.*—(i) *Major stock acquisition.*—Except as otherwise provided in this paragraph (b)(4), accumulated CERT costs with regard to an MSA as of a particular date are the total CERT costs described in paragraph (b)(3) of this section that have been taken into account as of that date under the applicable corporation's method of accounting. For example, CERT costs incurred in the taxable year after the year of the CERT are not included in accumulated CERT costs in the year of the CERT, but are included in accumulated CERT costs during the taxable year in which they are incurred and in any succeeding loss limitation year. Similarly, CERT costs include costs incurred after the date on which a CERT occurs if the CERT consists of multiple steps. See § 1.172(h)-5(a).

(ii) *Excess distribution.*—Except as provided otherwise in this paragraph (b)(4), accumulated CERT costs as of a particular date with regard to an ED are the total CERT costs described in paragraph (b)(3) of this section that have been taken into account as of that date under the applicable corporation's method of accounting, multiplied by a fraction, the numerator of which equals the amount of distributions constituting an ED during the year of the CERT pursuant to § 1.172(h)-1(c)(3), and the denominator of which equals the total amount of distributions made during the year of the CERT. CERT costs include costs incurred after date on which a CERT occurs if the CERT consists of multiple steps. See § 1.172(h)-5(a).

(iii) *CERT costs incurred in a year prior to a CERT year.*—CERT costs incurred in a year prior to the year of the CERT are treated as incurred on the first day of the year of the CERT.

(iv) *Year constitutes loss limitation year with regard to multiple CERTs.*—If a single taxable year constitutes a loss limitation year with regard to more than one CERT, the accumulated CERT costs on any particular date during that year include accumulated CERT costs under this paragraph (b)(4) with regard to all such CERTs. See § 1.172(h)-3(d) for rules regarding computation of a CERIL if a year constitutes a loss limitation year with regard to multiple CERTs.

(5) *No netting of interest income and deductions.*—Allocable interest deductions under paragraph (b)(1) of this section are the deductions allowed for interest on any indebtedness allocable to a CERT. Allocable interest deductions are not netted against a taxpayer's interest income.

(6) *Certain unforeseeable events.*—[Reserved].

(7) *Examples.*—The following examples illustrate the rules of this paragraph (b). Unless otherwise provided, assume that all entities are

domestic C corporations that do not join in the filing of consolidated returns and are accrual method taxpayers. Assume that all applicable corporations have substantial NOLs in their loss limitation years:

Example 1. CERT costs in MSA. (i) *Facts.* On February 1, Year 5, Corporation A begins investigating the possible acquisition of Corporation T. On March 1, Year 5, A enters into an exclusivity agreement with T. On July 1, Year 5, A engages in an MSA when it acquires all of the stock of T in exchange for cash. A incurs costs for services rendered by its outside counsel and an investment banker. A's outside counsel and the investment banker conduct due diligence on T, determine the value of T, negotiate and structure the transaction with T, draft the purchase agreement, secure shareholder approval, and prepare SEC filings. In addition, the investment banker arranges borrowings to fund both the stock acquisition and A's operations. A also pays a bonus to one of its corporate officers, who negotiated the acquisition of T. Before and after the acquisition is consummated, A incurs costs to relocate personnel and equipment, and to integrate records and information systems.

(ii) *Analysis.* The CERT costs taken into account by A in computing interest allocable to the CERT include the fair market value of the T stock. See paragraph (b)(3)(i) of this section. The costs incurred on or after the date of the exclusivity agreement, March 1, Year 5, (but not before) to conduct due diligence are also included in A's CERT costs. See paragraph (b)(3)(i) of this section and § 1.263(a)-5(e)(1). A's CERT costs also include all amounts incurred to determine the value of T, negotiate and structure the transaction with T, draft the purchase agreement, secure shareholder approval, and prepare SEC filings. See § 1.263(a)-5(e)(2). In addition, A's CERT costs include borrowing costs that facilitate the CERT. See paragraph (b)(3)(iii) of this section. A's CERT costs do not include any portion of the bonus paid to the corporate officer or the costs incurred to relocate personnel and equipment, and to integrate records and information systems. See § 1.263(a)-5(c)(6) and (d).

Example 2. CERT costs in ED. (i) *Facts.* X corporation is a calendar-year taxpayer. On July 1, Year 5, X makes a distribution of $80,000 to its shareholders, $60,000 of which constitutes an ED. X makes no other distributions during Year 5. At previous regular quarterly board of directors meetings, the directors discussed the July 1, Year 5 distribution. On March 30, Year 5, X incurs $2,500 in borrowing costs that constitute CERT costs under paragraph (b)(3)(iii) of this section. In addition, on March 30 and April 15, Year 5, X incurs $500 and $3,000, respectively, for work performed by its outside counsel which facilitates the ED under the principles of § 1.263(a)-4(e). During Year 5, X pays its directors for attendance at the regular quarterly board of directors meetings. No additional CERT costs are incurred in Years 6 and 7.

(ii) *CERT costs.* X's CERT costs include the fair market value of all distributions made during the year of the CERT ($80,000), as well as the $2,500 of borrowing costs. See paragraph (b)(3)(ii) and (iii) of this section. In addition, under the principles of § 1.263(a)-4(e), X's CERT costs include the costs incurred for work performed by A's outside counsel related to the ED. See paragraph (b)(3)(ii) of this section and § 1.263(a)-4(e)(1)(i). X's CERT costs do not include amounts paid to X's board of directors to attend the regular board of directors meetings. See § 1.263(a)-4(e)(4)(ii)(B).

(iii) *Accumulated CERT costs.* Under paragraph (b)(4)(ii) of this section, X's accumulated CERT costs as of a particular date with regard to its ED are the total CERT costs that have been taken into account as of that date multiplied by a fraction the numerator of which equals the amount of distributions constituting ED during the year of the CERT, and the denominator of which equals the total amount of distributions made during the year of the CERT. Here $60,000 is divided by $80,000, which equals 3/4. The CERT occurs during X's Year 5, and that year is a loss limitation year with regard to the CERT. X's accumulated CERT costs on March 30, Year 5 are $2,250 (3,000 x 3/4). X's accumulated CERT costs are $4,500 (6,000 x 3/4) on April 15, Year 5 and $64,500 (86,000 x 3/4) on July 1, Year 5. X's Years 6 and 7 are also loss limitation years. Because no additional CERT costs are incurred in Years 6 and 7, throughout those years, X's accumulated CERT costs are $64,500.

Example 3. Accumulated CERT costs in an MSA. (i) *All CERT costs incurred in year of CERT.* X corporation is a calendar-year taxpayer. On March 1, Year 5, X acquires all of the stock of unrelated corporation T in an MSA. X's loss limitation years are calendar Years 5, 6, and 7. During Year 5, X incurs the following CERT costs: $4,000 on January 30; $50,000 on March 1; and $9,000 on March 15. During Year 5, X's accumulated CERT costs are: $4,000 as of January 30; $54,000 as of March 1; and $63,000 as of March 15. See paragraph (b)(4)(i) of this section. No additional CERT costs are incurred in Years 6 and 7. As a result, throughout Years 6 and 7, X's accumulated CERT costs are $63,000.

(ii) *Portion of CERT costs incurred prior to year of CERT.* The facts are the same as in paragraph (i) of this *Example 3*, except during Year 4, X incurs $2,000 of CERT costs. During Year 5, X's accumulated CERT costs are: $2,000 as of January 1 (reflecting costs incurred during Year 4); $6,000 as of January 30; $56,000 as of March 1; and $65,000 as of March 15. See paragraph (b)(4)(i) and (iii) of this section. X is treated as having no accumulated CERT costs during Year 4.

(c) *Effective/applicability date.*—This section is applicable to CERTs occurring on or after the date of publication of the Treasury decision adopting these rules as final regulations in the **Federal Register**. This section is also applicable to the deconsolidation of a member from, or the acquisition of a corporation by, a consolidated group that occurs on or after the date of publication of the Treasury decision adopting these rules as final regulations in the **Federal Register**. However, in each case, this section does not apply to any CERT, deconsolidation, or acquisition occurring pursuant to a written agreement that is binding before the date of publication of the Treasury decision adopting these rules as final regulations in the **Federal Register**. [Reg. § 1.172(h)-2.]

§ 1.172(h)-3. Limitation on allocable interest deductions.—(a) *General rule.*—The amount of allocable interest deductions (determined under § 1.172(h)-2(b)) for any loss limitation year is limited to the excess (if any) of the amount allowable as a deduction for interest paid or accrued by the taxpayer during the loss limitation year, over the average of interest paid or accrued by the taxpayer (the three-year average) for the three taxable years preceding the taxable year in which the corporate equity reduction transaction (CERT) occurred (the lookback period). This section provides additional rules for computing the three-year average relevant to any loss limitation year for purposes of applying section 172(b)(1)(E) and (h), §§1.172(h)-1 through 1.172(h)-5, and §1.1502-72 (the CERT rules).

(b) *Three-year average for a short loss limitation year.*—(1) *General rule.*—For purposes of computing the three-year average if the relevant loss limitation year is less than a full 12-month year, the interest paid or accrued with regard to any year of the taxpayer during a lookback period (lookback period year) equals the amount of interest treated as paid or accrued multiplied by a fraction, the numerator of which equals the number of days in the short loss limitation year, and the denominator of which equals the number of days in the lookback period year. The value of the fraction may not exceed 100 percent. Zero interest is deemed paid or accrued (in excess of amounts actually paid or accrued) in a lookback period year that is shorter than the loss limitation year.

(2) *Example.*—The following example illustrates the short loss limitation year rule of this paragraph (b):

Example. (i) *Facts.* T, a domestic C corporation, was organized on July 1, Year 1. T's first taxable year is a short taxable year, which includes July 1 through December 31, Year 1 (184 days). T's next two taxable years are full calendar years: Calendar Year 2 and Calendar Year 3. T's Year 4 ends on September 30 as a result of a change in accounting period. T engages in a CERT during its taxable Year 4, which includes January 1, Year 4, through September 30, Year 4 (273 days). T's next two taxable periods are full 12-month fiscal years ending on September 30, Year 5, and September 30, Year 6.

(ii) *Year 4 analysis.* T's taxable Year 4 is a short loss limitation year. Therefore, in computing its three-year average applicable to loss limitation Year 4, T multiplies its interest treated as paid or accrued during each of the three years of the lookback period by the fraction specified in paragraph (b)(1) of this section. The pertinent fraction with regard to Year 1 of the lookback period is 273/184 (number of days in short loss limitation year divided by the number of days in the lookback period year). However, under paragraph (b)(1) of this section, the value of the fraction cannot exceed 100 percent. As a result, T includes in the computation of its three-year average its actual interest paid or accrued in Year 1. As to Years 2 and 3, T includes in the computation of its three-year average its actual interest paid or accrued in each of those years, multiplied by a fraction equal to 273/365.

(iii) *Year 5 and 6 analysis.* Because T's taxable Years 5 and 6 are full 12- month loss limitation years, T includes in the computation of its three-year average applicable to those loss limitation years its actual interest paid or accrued in each year of the lookback period, without adjustment.

(c) *Computation of interest paid or accrued by corporation with incomplete lookback period.*—(1) *Lookback period for corporation not in existence.*—If an applicable corporation was not in existence for three taxable years preceding the taxable year in which the CERT occurred (the lookback period), for purposes of determining the limitation on allocable interest deductions under section 172(h)(2)(C) and paragraph (a) of this section, the applicable corporation's lookback period is deemed to have additional 12-month periods that end on the calendar date that is one day prior to the date of the corporation's organization. See §1.172(h)-4(c)(2)(i)(B) (regarding determination of lookback period for successor applicable corporations not in existence on date of CERT) and §1.1502-72(d)(4)(ii) (regarding consolidated groups not in existence during the entire lookback period).

(2) *Interest history of corporation not in existence.*—If an applicable corporation was not in existence for the entire lookback period, it is treated as having paid or accrued zero interest during periods deemed to exist under paragraph (c)(1) of this section in computing any three-year average. However, if the applicable corporation is a successor corporation pursuant to §1.172(h)-1(b)(2), the computation of any three-year average for the successor includes interest paid or accrued by any predecessor during the lookback period. See §1.172(h)-4(c)(2)(ii)(A).

(3) *Example.*—The following example illustrates the rules of this paragraph (c):

Example. Corporation not in existence for entire lookback period. C is a domestic C corporation that does not join in the filing of a consolidated return and maintains a calendar taxable year. C is formed on October 1, Year 3, and engages in a CERT during Year 5. For purposes of computing any CERIL related to the CERT, paragraph (a) of this section requires that C must measure its interest deductions for the lookback period. However, C was not in existence for three taxable years preceding the year in which the CERT occurred. Rather, C was in existence for one full calendar taxable year (Year 4) and one short taxable year (October 1 through December 31, Year 3). Pursuant to paragraph (c)(1) of this section, C's lookback period is deemed to include an additional taxable period (October 1, Year 2, through September 30, Year 3). Further, in computing any three-year average, C is treated as having paid or accrued zero interest during the deemed additional period. See paragraph (c)(2) of this section.

(d) *Computation of a CERIL if single year constitutes loss limitation year with regard to multiple CERTs.*—(1) *Single CERIL computation.*—This paragraph (d) applies if a taxable year constitutes a loss limitation year of the taxpayer with regard to more than one CERT. In that case, a single corporate equity reduction interest loss (CERIL) is computed under section 172(h)(1) and §1.172(h)-2(a)(2) for that year. This computation takes into account accumulated CERT costs for every CERT, determined under §1.172(h)-2(b)(4)(iv) for the loss limitation year.

(2) *Limitation on allocable interest deductions.*—In computing the single CERIL under this paragraph (d), section 172(h)(2)(C) and paragraph (a) of this section are applied a single time to limit the cumulative amount of interest allocable to all of the CERTs to the excess (if any) of the

amount allowable as a deduction for interest paid or accrued by the taxpayer during the loss limitation year over the three-year average for the lookback period. The limitation is not applied separately with respect to interest allocable to a particular CERT.

(3) *Computation of three-year average if CERTs have different lookback periods.*—(i) *In general.*—If the lookback periods (as defined in paragraph (a) of this section or in § 1.1502-72(d)(4)) relevant to all of the CERTs pertinent to a loss limitation year are not identical, a cumulative three-year average is computed by applying the rules of paragraph (d)(3)(ii) of this section. The cumulative threeyear average is treated as the three-year average relevant to the loss limitation year, and is applied to determine the limitation on the amount of interest allocable to all of the CERTs under section 172(h)(2)(C) and paragraph (a) of this section.

(ii) *Cumulative three-year average.*—The cumulative three-year average applicable to any loss limitation year is computed under this paragraph (d)(3)(ii). With regard to each lookback period relevant to a loss limitation year, a modified three-year average is computed. The modified three-year average is the threeyear average relevant to a particular lookback period (determined under section 172(h)(2)(C) and this section) multiplied by a fraction, the numerator of which equals the accumulated CERT costs as of the close of the loss limitation year that are attributable to the particular CERT or CERTs to which the three-year average corresponds, and the denominator of which equals the total accumulated CERT costs as of the close of the loss limitation year that are attributable to all CERTs relevant to the loss limitation year. See § 1.172(h)-2(b)(4) defining accumulated CERT costs. The sum of all modified three-year averages is the cumulative three-year average for that year.

(4) *Allocation of a CERIL among CERTS.*—After the computation of the single CERIL for a loss limitation year that is attributable to all CERTs, the total CERIL is allocated to particular CERTs, if CERILs attributable to different CERTs are subject to different limitations on carryback. See section 172(b)(1)(E)(i) and § 1.172(h)-5(b) (regarding prohibition on carrybacks). For purposes of this allocation, the CERT costs attributable to each particular CERT are identified. The total CERIL is then attributed to each CERT by multiplying the total CERIL by a fraction, the numerator of which equals the accumulated CERT costs as of the close of the loss limitation year that are attributable to a particular CERT, and the denominator of which equals the total accumulated CERT costs as of the close of the loss limitation year that are attributable to all CERTs relevant to the loss limitation year. See § 1.172(h)-2(b)(4) defining accumulated CERT costs.

(5) *Examples.*—The following examples illustrate the rules of this paragraph (d). Unless otherwise provided, assume that all entities are domestic C corporations that do not join in the filing of consolidated returns and that maintain calendar taxable years. Assume that all applicable corporations have substantial net operating losses in their loss limitation years:

Example 1. Multiple CERTs with identical lookback period. (i) *Facts.* Corporation A maintains a calendar taxable year. A engages in two separate CERTs during its taxable Year 4. The lookback period for both CERTs is January 1, Year 1, through December 31, Year 3. The total amount of interest deductions allocable to CERT 1 and CERT 2 (before application of section 172(h)(2)(C) and paragraph (a) of this section) is $50. A's total interest expense during Year 4 was $150, and its three-year average interest for the lookback period was $120.

(ii) *Analysis.* Year 4 constitutes a loss limitation year with regard to both CERT 1 and CERT 2. A single CERIL is computed with regard to Year 4, and the limitation on allocable interest under section 172(h)(2)(C) and paragraph (a) of this section is applied a single time. See paragraphs (d)(1) and (2) of this section. The limitation under section 172(h)(2)(C) and paragraph (a) of this section is applied to the cumulative amount of interest allocable to the two CERTs ($50). See paragraph (d)(2) of this section. The limitation under section 172(h)(2)(C) and paragraph (a) of this section equals the excess of the amount of interest allowable in Year 4 ($150) over the three-year average ($120), or $30. Therefore, the CERIL is limited to $30.

Example 2. Multiple CERTs with different lookback periods. (i) *Facts.* Corporation A maintains a calendar taxable year. A engages in CERT 1 during its taxable Year 4. The lookback period relevant to CERT 1 is January 1, Year 1, through December 31, Year 3. A also engages in CERT 2 during its taxable Year 5. The lookback period relevant to CERT 2 is January 1, Year 2, through December 31, Year 4. The total amount of interest deductions allocable to CERT 1 and CERT 2 (before application of section 172(h)(2)(C) and paragraph (a) of this section) during taxable Year 5 is $50. A's total interest expense during Year 5 is $126. A's three-year average interest that is relevant to loss limitation Year 5 for the CERT 1 lookback period is $100, and its three-year average interest that is relevant to loss limitation Year 5 for the CERT 2 lookback period is $110. A's accumulated CERT costs attributable to CERT 1 are $400. A's accumulated CERT costs attributable to CERT 2 are $600.

(ii) *Cumulative three-year average.* Year 5 is a loss limitation year with regard to both CERT 1 and CERT 2. A single CERIL is computed with regard to Year 5, and the limitation on allocable interest under section 172(h)(2)(C) and paragraph (a) of this section is applied a single time. See paragraph (d)(1) and (2) of this section. The limitation under section 172(h)(2)(C) and paragraph (a) of this section is applied to the cumulative amount of interest allocable to the two CERTs ($50). See paragraph (d)(2) of this section. Because Year 5 constitutes a loss limitation year with regard to CERTs with different lookback periods, the relevant three-year average applied under section 172(h)(2)(C) and paragraph (a) of this section is the cumulative three-year average, which is the sum of all modified three-year averages. See paragraph (d)(3)(ii) of this section. The modified three-year average with regard to CERT 1 is the three-year average for CERT 1 multiplied by $400/$1,000 (accumulated CERT costs attributable to CERT 1 divided by the total accumulated CERT costs attributable to CERTs 1 and 2), or 2/5. Therefore, the modified three-year average with regard to CERT 1 is $40 (100 × 2/5). The modified three-year average with regard to CERT 2 is the three-year average for CERT 2 multiplied by $600/$1,000 (accumulated CERT costs attributable to CERT 2 divided by the total accumulated CERT costs attributable to CERTs 1 and 2), or 3/5. Therefore, the modified three-year average with regard to CERT 2 is $66 (110 × 3/5). Thus, the cumulative threeyear average interest for Year 5 is $106 ($40 + $66). See paragraph (d)(3) of this section. The limitation under section 172(h)(2)(C) and paragraph (a) of this section equals the excess of the amount of interest allowable in Year 5 ($126) over the cumulative three-year average interest ($106), or $20. Therefore, the CERIL for Year 5 is limited to $20.

(iii) *Allocation of a CERIL to different CERTs*. Because Year 5 constitutes a loss limitation year with regard to more than one CERT, and a CERIL associated with each CERT is subject to different limitations on carryback, the total CERIL must be allocated between CERT 1 and CERT 2. See paragraph (d)(4) of this section. The portion of the total CERIL allocated to CERT 1 is the total CERIL multiplied by $400/$1,000 (accumulated CERT costs attributable to CERT 1 divided by the total accumulated CERT costs attributable to CERTs 1 and 2), or 2/5. Therefore, the portion of the total CERIL allocated to CERT 1 is $8 ($20 × 2/5). The portion of the total CERIL allocated to CERT 2 is the total CERIL multiplied by $600/$1,000 (accumulated CERT costs attributable to CERT 2 divided by the total accumulated CERT costs attributable to CERTs 1 and 2), or 3/5. Therefore, the portion of the total CERIL allocated to CERT 2 is $12 ($20 × 3/5). See paragraph (d)(4) of this section. See also section 172(b)(1)(E)(i) and § 1.172(h)-5(b)(1) for rules regarding the prohibition on carryback of a CERIL.

Example 3. CERTs of multiple corporations with identical lookback period. (i) *Facts*. Corporation T maintains a taxable year ending on June 30. On August 31, Year 5, T engages in CERT 1. Unrelated P is the parent of a group that maintains a calendar taxable year. On October 31, Year 5, P acquires all the stock of T in an MSA (CERT 2). T is first included in the P group on November 1, Year 5. For its calendar Year 5, the P group is treated as an applicable corporation with respect to CERT 1 and CERT 2. See § 1.1502-72(a)(2)(iv)(A). The P group's lookback period for both CERTs is January 1, Year 2, through December 31, Year 4. The total CERIL of the group in Year 5 is $80. The P group's accumulated CERT costs attributable to CERT 1 are $500. The P group's accumulated CERT costs attributable to CERT 2 are $1,500. The P group has a consolidated net operating loss (CNOL) in Year 5, a portion of which is allocable to T under § 1.1502-21(b)(2)(iv)(B).

(ii) *Allocation of a CERIL to different CERTs*. Year 5 constitutes a loss limitation year with regard to two CERTs that share a common lookback period. However, the CERIL associated with the different CERTs is subject to different limitations on carryback under § 1.172(h)-5(b)(1) (some CNOL will be carried back to the group's consolidated return years and some will be carried back to T's separate return years). Therefore, the total CERIL must be allocated between CERT 1 and CERT 2. The portion of the total CERIL allocated to CERT 1 is the total CERIL multiplied by $500/$2,000 (accumulated CERT costs attributable to CERT 1 divided by the total accumulated CERT costs attributable to CERTs 1 and 2), or 1/4. See paragraph (d)(4) of this section. Therefore, the portion of the total CERIL allocated to CERT 1 is $20 ($80 x 1/4). The portion of the total CERIL allocated to CERT 2 is the total CERIL multiplied by $1,500/$2,000 (accumulated CERT costs attributable to CERT 2 divided by the total accumulated CERT costs attributable to CERTs 1 and 2), or 3/4. Therefore, the portion of the total CERIL allocated to CERT 2 is $60 ($80 × 3/4).

(e) *Effective/applicability date*.—This section is applicable to CERTs occurring on or after the date of publication of the Treasury decision adopting these rules as final regulations in the **Federal Register**. This section is also applicable to the deconsolidation of a member from, or the acquisition of a corporation by, a consolidated group that occurs on or after the date of publication of the Treasury decision adopting these rules as final regulations in the **Federal Register**. However, in each case, this section does not apply to any CERT, deconsolidation, or acquisition occurring pursuant to a written agreement that is binding before the date of publication of the Treasury decision adopting these rules as final regulations in the **Federal Register**. [Reg. § 1.172(h)-3.]

§ 1.172(h)-4. Special rules for predecessors and successors.—(a) *Scope*.—This section provides guidance with regard to the application of section 172(b)(1)(E) and (h), §§ 1.172(h)-1 through 1.172(h)-5, and § 1.1502-72 (the CERT rules) to predecessors and successors (as defined in § 1.172(h)-1(b)(2)).

(b) *Loss limitation years*.—(1) *In general*.—This paragraph (b)(1) applies to identify loss limitation years of a successor. The taxable year in which a corporate equity reduction transaction (CERT) actually occurs is a loss limitation year. See § 1.172(h)-1(e). Any taxable year of a successor (potential loss limitation year) of any applicable corporation is a loss limitation year with regard to the CERT if, under the carryover rules of sections 172(b)(1)(A)(ii) and 381(c)(1), the potential loss limitation year constitutes the first or second taxable year following the taxable year of the corporation that actually engaged in the CERT which includes the date on which the CERT occurred. See § 1.172(h)-5(a) (defining date on which CERT occurs in multiple-step transaction); but see § 1.1502-72(a)(3) (defining loss limitation years of consolidated groups and corporations that were previously members of a consolidated group).

(2) *Example*.—The following example illustrates the rules of this paragraph (b):

Example. Loss limitation years of successor. T is a domestic C corporation that maintains a calendar taxable year and does not join in the filing of a consolidated return. On March 31, Year 6, T engages in a CERT. On June 30, Year 6, T merges into Corporation A, a calendar-year taxpayer, in a transaction to which section 381(a) applies. T's taxable Year 6 ends on the date of the merger, and A succeeds to T's tax attributes. See section 381(a) and (b)(1). T's only loss limitation year with respect to the Year 6 CERT is its short taxable year ending June 30, Year 6. See section 172(b)(1)(E)(ii) and § 1.172(h)-1(e). Following the merger, A is the successor to T, and A is treated as an applicable corporation with regard to the Year 6 CERT. See § 1.172(h)-1(b)(2). A's calendar

Years 6 and 7 are the second and third loss limitation years with regard to the Year 6 CERT. See section 172(b)(1)(E)(ii) and paragraph (b)(1) of this section.

(c) *Computation of a CERIL.*—(1) *CERT costs.*—For purposes of computing any corporate equity reduction interest loss (CERIL) under section 172(h)(1) and §1.172(h)-2(a)(2), any CERT costs incurred (or treated as incurred under this paragraph (c)) by a predecessor are attributed to the successor. However, such costs are treated as having been incurred by the successor only for purposes of applying the avoided cost rules of section 263A(f)(2)(A) to any measurement date (as defined in §1.263A-9(f)(2)) after the date of the section 381(a) transaction.

(2) *Limitation on allocable interest deductions.*—(i) *Lookback period.*—(A) *In general.*—The *lookback period* with regard to a CERT is the three taxable years preceding the taxable year in which the CERT occurs. See §1.172(h)-3(a). The lookback period that is relevant to the calculation of any CERIL of a successor (successor's lookback period) is the three years preceding the taxable year of the successor that includes the date on which the CERT occurred. See §1.172(h)-5(a) (defining the date on which a CERT occurs if the CERT consists of multiple steps) and §1.172(h)-3(c) (regarding corporations with insufficient lookback periods).

(B) *Successor not in existence on date of CERT.*—If a successor was not in existence on the date on which the CERT occurred, for purposes of determining the lookback period, the successor is deemed to have additional 12-month periods that end on the calendar date that is one day prior to the date of the corporation's organization. The successor is deemed to have a sufficient number of such additional periods such that the successor is treated as having a year that includes the date on which the CERT occurred and as having three years (the lookback period) immediately preceding the deemed year that includes the date of the CERT. See §1.172(h)-3(c)(1) regarding lookback period for corporation lacking three-year history.

(ii) *Computation of three-year average.*—(A) *In general.*—Except as otherwise provided in this paragraph (c)(2)(ii), for purposes of determining any three-year average of a successor under section 172(h)(2)(C)(ii) and §1.172(h)-3, the interest paid or accrued by a successor includes interest paid or accrued by all corporations that are its predecessors as of the end of the successor's taxable year. If the dates of any taxable year of a predecessor do not precisely correspond to the dates of a taxable year of the successor, the interest paid or accrued by the predecessor is apportioned equally to each date of the predecessor's taxable year. The successor is treated as having paid or accrued in any year during the lookback period all predecessor interest that is apportioned to a date within that lookback period year.

(B) *Year of successor transaction.*—In computing the three-year average that is relevant to the taxable year of a successor that includes the date of the section 381(a) transaction that resulted in successor status, the successor includes only a pro rata portion of the predecessor's amount of interest paid or accrued during the successor's lookback period. The pro rata amount equals the predecessor's interest treated as paid or accrued for the dates of the successor's lookback period, multiplied by a fraction, the numerator of which equals the number of days in the loss limitation year of the successor that follow the date of the transaction that resulted in successor status, and the denominator of which equals the number of days in the successor's loss limitation year. The predecessor's amount of interest treated as paid or accrued that is subject to proration under this paragraph (c)(2)(ii)(B) is the interest history of the predecessor that would otherwise be fully combined with the interest history of the successor under paragraph (c)(2)(ii)(A) of this section.

(3) *Examples.*—The following examples illustrate the rules of this paragraph (c). Unless otherwise provided, assume that all entities are domestic C corporations that do not join in the filing of consolidated returns and that maintain calendar taxable years. Assume that all applicable corporations have substantial net operating losses in their loss limitation years:

Example 1. Predecessor corporation engages in CERT. (i) *Facts.* Corporation X is a calendar-year taxpayer. On February 1, Year 5, X engages in a CERT. On August 1, Year 5, X merges into unrelated corporation Y in a transaction to which section 381(a) applies. Y is a calendar-year taxpayer and all of its taxable years are full calendar years. All of X's taxable years prior to the year of the merger are full calendar years.

(ii) *Analysis.* X's only loss limitation year is its short year ending August 1, Year 5. X's lookback period relevant to the Year 5 CERT includes X's calendar Years 2, 3, and 4. See paragraph (c)(2)(i)(A) of this section; see also §1.172(h)-3(b)(1) (computation of three-year average for a short loss limitation year). Following the merger, Y is the successor to X, and Y is treated as an applicable corporation with regard to the Year 5 CERT. See §1.172(h)-1(b)(2). Because Y's calendar Year 5 follows a single loss limitation year of X with regard to the same CERT, Y's calendar Years 5 and 6 are loss limitation years with regard to the Year 5 CERT. See paragraph (b)(1) of this section and §1.381(c)(1)-1(e)(3). Y's lookback period for the Year 5 CERT is its calendar Years 2, 3, and 4. See paragraph (c)(2)(i)(A) of this section. The computations of Y's three-year averages relevant to its loss limitation Years 5 and 6 include interest paid or accrued by Y and by all of Y's predecessors, including X, during the lookback period. See paragraph (c)(2)(ii)(A) of this section. However, because Year 5 is Y's taxable year that includes the date of the section 381(a) transaction that resulted in Y's successor status, for purposes of computing Y's three-year average for Y's loss limitation Year 5, Y includes only a pro rata portion of X's amount of interest paid or accrued. In the proration, X's amount of interest paid or accrued during the three-year lookback period is multiplied by 151/365 (the number of days in Y's loss limitation Year 5 that follow the date of the section 381(a) transaction that resulted in Y's successor status, divided by the number of days in Y's loss limitation Year 5). See paragraph (c)(2)(ii)(B) of this section.

(iii) *Predecessor and successor have different taxable years.* The facts are the same as in paragraph (i) of this *Example 1*, except that X maintained a taxable year ending June 30 before its merger into Y. X's full taxable year ending June

30, Year 5, and its short year ending August 1, Year 5, are its loss limitation years with regard to its February 1, Year 5 CERT. See section 172(b)(1)(E)(ii) and §1.172(h)-1(e). Following the merger of X into Y, Y is a successor to X and is treated as an applicable corporation with regard to the Year 5 CERT. Y's calendar Year 5 is the third loss limitation year with regard to the CERT. See paragraph (b)(1) of this section. Y's lookback period is Y's three taxable years preceding Y's taxable year that includes the date of the CERT, which are Years 2, 3, and 4. Further, because the dates of X's taxable years do not precisely correspond to the dates of Y's taxable years, X's interest paid or accrued is apportioned equally to each date within each of X's taxable years. Y is treated as having paid or accrued in any year during the lookback period all of X's interest that is so apportioned. See paragraph (c)(2)(ii)(A) of this section. However, because Y's taxable Year 5 includes the date of the section 381(a) transaction that resulted in Y's successor status, for purposes of computing Y's three-year average for loss limitation Year 5, Y includes only a pro rata portion of X's interest history. See paragraphs (c)(2)(ii)(B) of this section.

Example 2. Successor corporation not in existence for entire lookback period. (i) *Facts*. Corporation A is formed on October 1, Year 3, and thereafter maintains a calendar taxable year. Immediately after A is formed in Year 3, a second corporation, T, merges into A in a transaction that meets the requirements of section 368(a)(1)(A). During Year 5, A engages in a CERT.

(ii) *Analysis*. A's loss limitation years are its calendar Years 5, 6, and 7. See section 172(b)(1)(E)(ii). For purposes of computing any CERIL related to the Year 5 CERT, section 172(h)(2)(C)(ii) and §1.172(h)-3 require that A measure its interest deductions for the three years preceding the taxable year of the CERT (three-year average). However, A is in existence for only two taxable years before the year in which the CERT occurs. Therefore, pursuant to §1.172(h)-3(c)(1), A is deemed to have an additional taxable period (October 1, Year 2, through September 30, Year 3). Further, in computing the three-year average, A is treated as having paid or accrued zero interest during the deemed year. See §1.172(h)-3(c)(2). However, because T is the predecessor of A, the computation of A's three-year average relevant to its loss limitation Year 5 includes interest paid or accrued by T during the lookback period (October 1,Year 2, through December 31, Year 4). See paragraph (c)(2)(ii)(A) of this section and §1.172(h)-3(c)(2). Because T merges into A in a year prior to any loss limitation year, there is no proration of T's interest history under paragraph (c)(2)(ii)(B) of this section.

(d) *Three-year distribution average*.—For purposes of determining any three-year distribution average of a successor under section 172(h)(3)(C)(ii)(I) and §1.172(h)-1(c)(3), the distributions made by a successor include distributions made by all corporations that are its predecessors as of the end of the successor's taxable year. If the dates of any taxable year of a predecessor do not correspond to the dates of a taxable year of the successor, the distributions made by the predecessor are apportioned equally to each date of the predecessor's taxable year. The successor is treated as having made in its taxable years all predecessor distributions that are apportioned to a date within those taxable years.

(e) *Effective/applicability date*.—This section is applicable to CERTs occurring on or after the date of publication of the Treasury decision adopting these rules as final regulations in the **Federal Register**. This section is also applicable to the deconsolidation of a member from, or the acquisition of a corporation by, a consolidated group that occurs on or after the date of publication of the Treasury decision adopting these rules as final regulations in the **Federal Register**. However, in each case, this section does not apply to any CERT, deconsolidation, or acquisition occurring pursuant to a written agreement that is binding before the date of publication of the Treasury decision adopting these rules as final regulations in the **Federal Register**. [Reg. §1.172(h)-4.]

§1.172(h)-5. Operating rules.—(a) *Date on which CERT occurs in a multi-step transaction*.—For purposes of applying section 172(b)(1)(E) and (h), §§1.172(h)-1 through 1.172(h)-4, and this section, and §1.1502-72 (the CERT rules), if a corporate equity reduction transaction (CERT) consists of multiple steps, the date on which the CERT occurs is the earliest date on which the requirements for CERT status are satisfied. For example, if multiple distributions are made in a single year, an excess distribution (ED) is treated as occurring on the earliest date on which the amount of distributions satisfies the greater of the two thresholds contained in section 172(h)(3)(C)(ii) and §1.172(h)-1(c)(3). A major stock acquisition (MSA) is treated as occurring on the earliest date on which at least 50 percent of the stock of a corporation is acquired, subject to the provisions of section 172(h)(3)(B) and §1.172(h)-1(c)(2).

(b) *Prohibition on carryback*.—(1) *In general*.—No corporate equity reduction interest loss (CERIL) attributable to a CERT may be carried back under section 172 or §1.1502-21(b) to any taxable year (including a consolidated return year) that includes solely dates that precede the date on which the CERT occurred. In addition, if a corporation becomes a member of a consolidated group as a result of a CERT, no CERIL allocable to that CERT may be carried back under section 172 or §1.1502-21(b) to the taxable year of the acquired corporation that includes the date on which the CERT occurred, or to any preceding taxable year. See §1.172(h)-3(d)(4) regarding allocation of a CERIL among CERTs, and §1.1502-21(b)(2)(iv)(C)(1) for the apportionment of a CERIL among consolidated group members.

(2) *Example*.—The following example illustrates the rules of this paragraph (b):

Example. Prohibition on carryback. (i) *Facts*. T corporation maintains a taxable year ending June 30. X corporation is the parent of a group that maintains a calendar taxable year. On March 31, Year 5, the X group acquires all of the T stock in a CERT, and T is first included in the X group on April 1, Year 5. During its consolidated return Year 5, the X group has a consolidated net operating loss (CNOL), a portion of which constitutes a CERIL, pursuant to section 172(h)(1) and §1.172(h)-2(a)(2). Part of the CERIL is apportioned to T, pursuant to § 1.1502-21(b)(2)(iv)(C)(1).

(ii) *Analysis*. On the date of the acquisition, both the X group and T constitute applicable corporations with regard to the Year 5 CERT. See section 172(b)(1)(E)(iii)(I) and § 1.172(h)-1(b). T's short taxable year ending on March 31, Year 5, was T's taxable year in which the CERT occurred. The X group's year in which the CERT occurred was its consolidated return Year 5. Section 172(b)(1)(E)(i) and paragraph (b) of this section prohibit the carryback of a CERIL to years preceding the taxable year in which the CERT occurs. Pursuant to paragraph (b)(1) of this section, no portion of a CERIL relating to the X group CNOL can be carried back to any taxable year that includes solely dates that precede the date on which the CERT occurred. As a result, no portion of the CERIL can be carried back to the X group's Year 4, or any preceding year. Moreover, because T becomes a member of the X group as a result of the CERT, no portion of the CERIL can be carried back to T's short taxable year ending March 31, Year 5, or any preceding taxable year. See paragraph (b)(1) of this section.

(c) *Stock issuances and computation of three-year distribution average*.—(1) *In general*.—In determining whether an ED has occurred, aggregate distributions made during a taxable year are reduced by the aggregate amount of stock issued by the applicable corporation during the year in which the potential ED occurred in exchange for money or property other than stock of the applicable corporation. Similarly, the computation of any three-year distribution average under section 172(h)(3)(C)(ii)(I) and § 1.172(h)-1(f) is reduced by the average of the stock issuances described in section 172(h)(3)(E)(ii) and this paragraph (c)(1) during the three years of the distribution lookback period (threeyear stock issuance average).

(2) *Example*.—The following example illustrates the rules of this paragraph (c):

Example. (i) *Facts*. C is a corporation that maintains a calendar taxable year. During Year 5, C makes a large distribution to its shareholders. During taxable Years 2, 3, and 4, C distributes an average of $100,000 per year. In addition, during taxable Year 2, C issued stock in exchange for $90,000 cash. During taxable Year 3, C issued stock in exchange for $15,000 cash. C issued no stock during taxable Year 4.

(ii) *Analysis*. C must test its Year 5 distribution as a potential ED. C's three-year distribution average without respect to any stock issued during the distribution lookback period is $100,000. C's three-year distribution average is reduced by the average of the stock issued by the corporation in exchange for money or property other than stock in C during the years of the distribution lookback period (three-year stock issuance average). See paragraph (c)(1) of this section. C's three-year stock issuance average is $35,000 [($90,000 + $15,000 + 0)/3]. Therefore, T's three-year distribution average is $65,000 ($100,000 - $35,000).

(d) *Computation of the alternative minimum tax net operating loss deduction*.—The CERT rules governing the carryback of net operating losses following a CERT also apply to the carryback of an alternative minimum tax net operating loss.

(e) *Effective/applicability date*.—This section is applicable to CERTs occurring on or after the date of publication of the Treasury decision adopting these rules as final regulations in the **Federal Register**. This section is also applicable to the deconsolidation of a member from, or the acquisition of a corporation by, a consolidated group that occurs on or after the date of publication of the Treasury decision adopting these rules as final regulations in the **Federal Register**. However, in each case, this section does not apply to any CERT, deconsolidation, or acquisition occurring pursuant to a written agreement that is binding before the date of publication of the Treasury decision adopting these rules as final regulations in the **Federal Register**. [Reg. § 1.172(h)-5.]

Accelerated Cost Recovery System

Accelerated Cost Recovery System.—Reproduced below is the text of a proposed amendment of Reg. § 1.178-1, relating to the Accelerated Cost Recovery System for recovering capital costs of eligible property (published in the Federal Register on February 16, 1984).

☐ Par. 3. Section 1.178-1 is amended as follows:

1. Paragraph (a) is amended by removing the term "section 167 or 611" and inserting "section 167, 168, or 611" in its place.

2. Paragraph (b)(1)(i) and (3) is amended by removing the term "estimated useful life" in each of the three places it appears and removing the term "section 167" in the one place it appears and by inserting "estimated useful life or, in the case of recovery property (as defined in section 168), the recovery period (including, where applicable, any optional recovery period under section 168(b)(3) or (f)(2)(C))" and by inserting "section 167 or 168", respectively, in its place.

3. Paragraph (b)(2) is amended by removing the term "(or depreciation)" and by inserting "(or depreciation under section 167 or accelerated cost recovery under section 168)" in lieu thereof.

4. Paragraph (d)(1)(i) is amended by removing the term "remaining estimated useful life" and by inserting "remaining estimated useful life or, in the case of recovery property (as defined in section 168), the recovery period (including, where applicable, any optional recovery period under section 168(b)(3) or (f)(2)(C))" in its place.

5. Paragraph (b)(6) is amended by adding two examples immediately after example (5), which read as follows:

§ 1.178-1. Depreciation or amortization of improvements on leased property and cost of acquiring a lease.

* * *

(b) *Determination of amount of deduction*.— * * *

(6) * * *

Example (6). Lessee C, a calendar year taxpayer, constructs a building on land leased from lessor D. The construction is completed and the building is placed in service on January 1, 1984, at which time C has 8 years remaining on the lease with no options to renew. On January 1, 1988, D grants C an option to renew the lease for a 10-year period. As of January 1, 1988, the date the renewal option is granted, section 178(a) and paragraph (b)(1) of this section become applicable, since the portion of the term of the lease remaining upon completion of the building (8 years) is less than 60 percent of any recovery period applicable to the building (60 percent of the shortest recovery period (15 years) is 9 years). As of the January 1, 1988, the term of the lease shall be treated as including the remaining portion of the original lease (4 years) and the 10-year renewal, or 14 years, unless C can establish that, as of the close of 1988, it is more probable that the lease will not be renewed than that it will be. In such case, since the term of the lease as of January 1, 1988 (14 years), is less than the ACRS recovery period, a deduction is not allowed under section 168 with respect to such building.

Example (7). The facts are the same as in example (6), except that the option to renew is for 15 years. If, as of the close of 1988, C cannot establish that it is more probable that the lease will not be renewed than that it will be, the term of the lease as of January 1, 1988, will be 19 years. Since the term of the lease would be longer than the ACRS recovery period (unless a 35- or 45-year optional recovery period were desired), the provisions of section 168 will be applicable with respect to this building. For purposes of section 168, C is considered as having placed the building in service on January 1, 1988, with a 15-year recovery period extending from that time. C's unadjusted basis for purposes of section 168 is the adjusted basis in the building as of January 1, 1988.

* * *

Qualified Property: Additional First Year Depreciation Deduction

Qualified Property: Additional First Year Depreciation Deduction.—Amendments to Reg. §§1.179-4 and 1.179-6, providing guidance regarding the additional first year depreciation deduction under section 168(k) of the Internal Revenue Code (Code), are proposed (published in the Federal Register on August 8, 2018) (REG-104397-18).

Par. 11. Section 1.179-4 is amended by revising paragraph (c)(2) to read as follows:

§1.179-4. Definitions.

* * *

(c) * * *

(2) Property deemed to have been acquired by a new target corporation as a result of a section 338 election (relating to certain stock purchases treated as asset acquisitions) or a section 336(e) election (relating to certain stock dispositions treated as asset transfers) will be considered acquired by purchase.

* * *

Par. 12. Section 1.179-6 is amended by revising the first sentence in paragraph (a) and adding paragraph (e) to read as follows:

§1.179-6. Effective/applicability dates.—(a) * * * Except as provided in paragraphs (b), (c), (d), and (e) of this section, the provisions of §§1.179-1 through 1.179-5 apply for property placed in service by the taxpayer in taxable years ending after January 25, 1993. * * *

* * *

(e) *Application of §1.179-4(c)(2)*.—(1) *In general*.—Except as provided in paragraph (e)(2) of this section, the provisions of §1.179-4(c)(2) relating to section 336(e) are applicable on or after the date of publication of a Treasury decision adopting these rules as final regulations in the **Federal Register**.

(2) *Early application*.—A taxpayer may rely on the provisions of §1.179-4(c)(2) relating to section 336(e) in these proposed regulations for the taxpayer's taxable years ending on or after September 28, 2017, and ending before the date of publication of a Treasury decision adopting these rules as final regulations in the **Federal Register**.

Capital Costs: Deduction: EPA Sulfur Regulations

Capital Costs: Deduction: EPA Sulfur Regulations.—Reg. §1.179B-1, relating to the deduction for qualified capital costs paid or incurred by a small business refiner to comply with the highway diesel fuel sulfur control requirements of the Environmental Protection Agency (EPA), is proposed (published in the Federal Register on June 27, 2008) (REG-143453-05).

□ Par. 2. Section 1.179B-1 is added to read as follows:

§1.179B-1. Deduction for capital costs incurred in complying with Environmental Protection Agency sulfur regulations.

[The text of this proposed §1.179B-1 is the same as the text of §1.179B-1T as added by T.D. 9404].

Business Use or Rental of Dwelling Unit

Business Use or Rental of Dwelling Unit.—Reproduced below is the text of a proposed amendment of Reg. §1.183-1, relating to the deductibility of expenses in connection with the business use, or the rental of others, of a dwelling unit that the taxpayer is deemed to have used for personal purposes during the taxable year (published in the Federal Register on August 7, 1980).

☐ Paragraph 1. Section 1.183-1 is amended by adding at the end thereof the following new paragraph:

§1.183-1. Activities not engaged in for profit.

* * *

(g) *Coordination with section 280A.*—If section 280A(a) (relating to disallowance of deductions for certain expenses with respect to the use of a dwelling unit used as a residence) applies with respect to any dwelling unit (or portion thereof) for the taxable year—

(1) Section 183 and this section shall not apply to that unit (or portion thereof) for that year, but

(2) That year shall be taken into account as a taxable year for purposes of applying section 183(d).

See section 280A and the regulations thereunder for definitions and rules relating to use of dwelling units. Note that the limitations of section 280A(e) and §1.280A-3(c) applies in any case where an individual or an electing small business corporation uses a dwelling unit for personal purposes on any day during the taxable year.

* * *

Deductions: Elections: Depreciation: Intangible Property

Deductions: Elections: Depreciation: Intangible Property.—Temporary Reg. §1.197-1T, relating to the procedures for making elections under the intangibles provisions of the Omnibus Budget Reconciliation Act of 1993 (P.L. 103-66), is also proposed as a final regulation and, when adopted, would become Reg. §1.197-1 (published in the Federal Register on March 15, 1994).

☐ Par 3. Section 1.197-1 is added to read as follows:

§1.197-1. Certain elections for intangible property.—[The text of this proposed section is the same as the text of Temporary Reg. §1.197-1T as added by T.D. 8528.]

U.S. Persons: Partnerships with Foreign Partners: Transfers of Appreciated Property

U.S. Persons: Partnerships with Foreign Partners: Transfers of Appreciated Property.—Amendments to Reg. §1.197-2, addressing transfers of appreciated property by U.S. persons to partnerships with foreign partners related to the transferor, are proposed (published in the Federal Register on January 19, 2017) (REG-127203-15).

Par. 2. Section 1.197-2 is amended by adding paragraphs (h)(12)(vii)(C) and (l)(5) to read as follows:

§1.197-2. Amortization of goodwill and certain other intangibles.

* * *

(h) * * *

(12) * * *

(vii) * * *

(C) [The text of proposed §1.197-2(h)(12)(vii)(C) is the same as the text of §1.197-2T(h)(12)(vii)(C) as added by T.D. 9814].

* * *

(l) * * *

(5) [The text of proposed §1.197-2(l)(5) is the same as the text of §1.197-2T(l)(5) as added by T.D. 9814].

* * *

Domestic Production Activities: Deduction Regulations: Allocation of W- 2 Wages: Acquisition or Disposition

Domestic Production Activities: Deduction Regulations: Allocation of W- 2 Wages: Acquisition or Disposition.—Amendments to Reg. §§1.199-0—1.199-4, 1.199-6 and 1.199-8, involving the domestic production activities deduction under section 199 of the Internal Revenue Code and providing guidance to taxpayers on the amendments made to section 199 by the Energy Improvement and Extension Act of 2008 and the Tax Extenders and Alternative Minimum Tax Relief Act of 2008, involving oil related qualified production activities income and qualified films, and the American Taxpayer Relief Act of 2012, involving activities in Puerto Rico, are proposed (published in the Federal Register on August 27, 2015) (REG-136459-09).

Par. 2. Section 1.199-0 is amended by:

1. Adding entries in the table of contents for §1.199-1(f).

2. Revising the entry in the table of contents for §1.199-2(c) and adding entries for §1.199-2(c)(1), (2), and (3).

3. Adding an entry in the table of contents for §1.199-2(f).

4. Redesignating the entry in the table of contents for §1.199-3(h) as the entry for §1.199-3(h)(1), adding introductory text for §1.199-3(h), and adding an entry for §1.199-3(h)(2).

5. Redesignating the entry in the table of contents for §1.199-3(i)(9) as the entry for §1.199-3(i)(10) and adding introductory text and entries in the table of contents for §1.199-3(i)(9).

6. Redesignating the entry in the table of contents for §1.199-3(k)(10) as the entry for §1.199-3(k)(11) and adding an entry for §1.199-3(k)(10).

7. Adding entries in the table of contents for §1.199-4(b)(2)(iii).

8. Revising the introductory text in the table of contents for §1.199-8(i) and adding the entries for §1.199-8(i)(10) and (i)(11).

§1.199-0. Table of contents.

* * *

Par. 3. Section 1.199-1 is amended by adding paragraph (f) to read as follows:

§1.199-1. Income attributable to domestic production activities.

* * *

(f) *Oil related qualified production activity income (Oil related QPAI).*—(1) *In general.*—(i) *Oil related QPAI.*—Oil related QPAI for any taxable year is an amount equal to the excess (if any) of the taxpayer's DPGR (as defined in §1.199-3) derived from the production, refining or processing of oil, gas, or any primary product thereof (oil related DPGR) over the sum of:

(A) The CGS that is allocable to such receipts; and

(B) Other expenses, losses, or deductions (other than the deduction allowed under this section) that are properly allocable to such receipts. See §§1.199-3 and 1.199-4.

(ii) *Special rule for oil related DPGR.*—Oil related DPGR does not include gross receipts derived from the transportation or distribution of oil, gas, or any primary product thereof. However, to the extent that a taxpayer treats gross receipts derived from transportation or distribution of oil, gas, or any primary product thereof as DPGR under paragraph (d)(3)(i) of this section or under §1.199-3(i)(4)(i)(B), then the taxpayer must treat those gross receipts as oil related DGPR.

(iii) *Definition of oil.*—The term *oil* includes oil recovered from both conventional and non-conventional recovery methods, including crude oil, shale oil, and oil recovered from tar/oil sands.

(iv) *Primary product from oil or gas.*—A primary product from oil or gas is, for purposes of this paragraph:

(A) *Primary product from oil.*—The term *primary product from oil* means all products derived from the destructive distillation of oil, including:

(1) Volatile products;

(2) Light oils such as motor fuel and kerosene;

(3) Distillates such as naphtha;

(4) Lubricating oils;

(5) Greases and waxes; and

(6) Residues such as fuel oil.

(B) *Primary product from gas.*—The term *primary product from gas* means all gas and associated hydrocarbon components from gas wells or oil wells, whether recovered at the lease or upon further processing, including:

(1) Natural gas;

(2) Condensates;

(3) Liquefied petroleum gases such as ethane, propane, and butane; and

(4) Liquid products such as natural gasoline.

(C) *Primary products and changing technology.*—The primary products from oil or gas described in paragraphs (f)(1)(iv)(A) and (B) of this section are not intended to represent either the only primary products from oil or gas, or the only processes from which primary products may be derived under existing and future technologies.

(D) *Non-primary products.*—Examples of non-primary products include, but are not limited to, petrochemicals, medicinal products, insecticides, and alcohols.

(2) *Cost allocation methods for determining oil related QPAI.*—(i) *Section 861 method.*—A taxpayer that uses the section 861 method to determine deductions that are allocated and apportioned to gross income attributable to DPGR must use the section 861 method to determine deductions that are allocated and apportioned to gross income attributable to oil related DPGR. See § 1.199-4(d).

(ii) *Simplified deduction method.*—A taxpayer that uses the simplified deduction method to apportion deductions between DPGR and non-DPGR must determine the portion of deductions allocable to oil related DPGR by multiplying the deductions allocable to DPGR by the ratio of oil related DPGR divided by DPGR from all activities. See § 1.199-4(e).

(iii) *Small business simplified overall method.*—A taxpayer that uses the small business simplified overall method to apportion total costs (CGS and deductions) between DPGR and non-DPGR must determine the portion of total costs allocable to DPGR that are allocable to oil related DPGR by multiplying the total costs allocable to DPGR by the ratio of oil related DPGR divided by DPGR from all activities. See § 1.199-4(f).

Par. 4. Section 1.199-2 is amended by revising paragraph (c), adding a sentence at the end of paragraph (e)(1), and adding paragraph (f) to read as follows:

§ 1.199-2. Wage limitation.

* * *

(c) [The text of the proposed amendments to § 1.199-2(c) is the same as the text of § 1.199-2T(c) as added by T.D. 9731].

* * *

(e) * * *

(1) * * * In the case of a qualified film (as defined in § 1.199-3(k)) for taxable years beginning after 2007, the term *W-2 wages* includes compensation for services (as defined in § 1.199-3(k)(4)) performed in the United States by actors, production personnel, directors, and producers (as defined in § 1.199-3(k)(1)).

* * *

(f) *Commonwealth of Puerto Rico.*—In the case of a taxpayer described in § 1.199-3(h)(2), the determination of W-2 wages of such taxpayer shall be made without regard to any exclusion under section 3401(a)(8) for remuneration paid for services performed in the Commonwealth of Puerto Rico. This paragraph (f) only applies as provided in section 199(d)(8).

Par. 5. Section 1.199-3 is amended by:

1. In paragraph (d)(4):

a. Redesignating *Example 6, Example 7, Example 8, Example 9, Example 10, Example 11*, and *Example 12* as *Example 7, Example 8, Example 9, Example 10, Example 11, Example 12*, and *Example 13*, respectively;

b. In newly-designated *Example 10*, removing the language "*Example 8*" and adding "*Example 9*" in its place; and

c. Adding *Example 6* and *Example 14*.

2. Revising the last sentence in paragraphs (e)(1) and (3).

3. In paragraph (e)(5):

a. Revising the third sentence in *Example 1*, the second sentence in *Example 4*, and *Example 5*.

b. Adding *Example 9*.

4. Revising the last sentence in paragraph (f)(1).

5. Revising *Example 1*, removing *Example 2*, and redesignating *Example 3* as *Example 2* in paragraph (f)(4).

6. Removing the second and third sentences in paragraph (g)(1).

7. Revising paragraph (g)(4)(i).

8. Redesignating paragraph (h) as paragraph (h)(1), adding paragraph (h) heading and adding paragraph (h)(2).

9. Revising paragraph (i)(3).

10. Removing *Example 3*; redesignating *Example 5* as *Example 3*; and revising *Example 4* in paragraph (i)(5)(iii).

11. In paragraph (i)(6)(iv)(D)(2), removing the language "§ 1.199-3T(i)(8)" and adding "§ 1.199-3(i)(8)" in its place.

12. Redesignating paragraph (i)(9) as paragraph (i)(10) and adding paragraph (i)(9).

13. Adding three sentences after the first sentence in paragraph (k)(1), revising paragraph (k)(2)(ii) introductory text, and adding a sentence at the end of paragraph (k)(3)(i).

14. Removing the first, second, and fifth sentences in paragraph (k)(3)(ii).

15. Adding one sentence at the end of paragraph (k)(6).

16. Adding two sentences before the last sentence in paragraph (k)(7)(i).

17. Revising the last sentence in paragraph (k)(8).

18. Redesignating paragraph (k)(10) as paragraph (k)(11) and adding paragraph (k)(10).

19. In newly redesignated paragraph (k)(11):

a. Revising *Example 3*;

b. Removing *Example 4*; redesignating *Example 5* and *Example 6* as *Example 4* and *Example 5*, respectively; and adding *Example 6, Example 7, Example 8, Example 9, Example 10*, and *Example 11*; and

c. Revising the third sentence in newly redesignated *Example 4*.

20. Adding one sentence at the end of paragraph (m)(2)(i).
21. Revising paragraph (m)(5).
The revisions and additions read as follows:

§1.199-3. Domestic production gross receipts.

* * *

(d) * * *

(4) * * *

Example 6. The facts are the same as *Example 3* except that R offers three-car sets together with a coupon for a car wash for sale to customers in the normal course of R's business. The gross receipts attributable to the car wash do not qualify as DPGR because a car wash is a service, assuming the de minimis exception under paragraph (i)(4)(i)(B)(6) of this section does not apply. In determining R's DPGR, under paragraph (d)(2)(i) of this section, the three-car set is an item if the gross receipts derived from the sale of the three-car sets without the car wash qualify as DPGR under this section.

* * *

Example 14. Z is engaged in the trade or business of construction under NAICS code 23 on a regular and ongoing basis. Z purchases a piece of property that has two buildings located on it. Z performs construction activities in connection with a project to substantially renovate building 1. Building 2 is not substantially renovated and together building 1 and building 2 are not substantially renovated, as defined under paragraph (m)(5) of this section. Z later sells building 1 and building 2 together in the normal course of Z's business. Z can use any reasonable method to determine what construction activities constitute an item under paragraph (d)(2)(iii) of this section. Z's method is not reasonable if Z treats the gross receipts derived from the sale of building 1 and building 2 as DPGR. This is because Z's construction activities would not have substantially renovated buildings 1 and 2 if they were considered together as one item. Z's method is reasonable if it treats the construction activities with respect to building 1 as the item under paragraph (d)(2)(iii) of this section because the proceeds from the sale of building 1 constitute DPGR.

(e) * * *

(1) * * * Pursuant to paragraph (f)(1) of this section, the taxpayer must be the party engaged in the MPGE of the QPP during the period the MPGE activity occurs in order for gross receipts derived from the MPGE of QPP to qualify as DPGR.

* * *

(3) * * * Notwithstanding paragraph (i)(4)(i)(B)(4) of this section, if the taxpayer installs QPP MPGE by the taxpayer, then the portion of the installing activity that relates to the QPP is an MPGE activity.

* * *

(5) * * *

Example 1. * * * A stores the agricultural products.* * *

* * *

Example 4. * * * Y engages in the reconstruction and refurbishment activity and installation of the parts.* * *

Example 5. The following activities are performed by Z as part of the MPGE of the QPP: materials analysis and selection, subcontractor inspections and qualifications, testing of component parts, assisting customers in their review and approval of the QPP, routine production inspections, product documentation, diagnosis and correction of system failure, and packaging for shipment to customers. Because Z MPGE the QPP, these activities performed by Z are part of the MPGE of the QPP. If Z did not MPGE the QPP, then these activities, such as testing of component parts, performed by Z are not the MPGE of QPP.

* * *

Example 9. X is in the business of selling gift baskets containing various products that are packaged together. X purchases the baskets and the products included within the baskets from unrelated third parties. X plans where and how the products should be arranged into the baskets. On an assembly line in a gift basket production facility, X arranges the products into the baskets according to that plan, sometimes relabeling the products before placing them into the baskets. X engages in no other activity besides packaging, repackaging, labeling, or minor assembly with respect to the gift baskets. Therefore, X is not considered to have engaged in the MPGE of QPP under paragraph (e)(2) of this section.

* * *

(f) * * *

(1) * * * If a qualifying activity under paragraph (e)(1), (k)(1), or (l)(1) of this section is performed under a contract, then the party to the contract that is the taxpayer for purposes of this paragraph (f) during the period in which the qualifying activity occurs is the party performing the qualifying activity.

* * *

(4) * * *

Example 1. X designs machines that it sells to customers. X contracts with Y, an unrelated person, for the manufacture of the machines. The contract between X and Y is a fixed-price contract. To manufacture the machines, Y purchases components and raw materials. Y tests the purchased components. Y manufactures the raw materials into additional components and Y physically performs the assembly of the components into machines. Y oversees and directs the activities under which the machines are manufactured by its employees. X also has employees onsite during the manufacturing for quality control. Y packages the finished machines and ships them to X's customers. Pursuant to paragraph (f)(1) of this section, Y is the taxpayer during the period the manufacturing of the machines occurs and, as a result, Y is treated as the manufacturer of the machines.

* * *

(g) * * *

(4) * * *

(i) *Contract with an unrelated person.*—If a taxpayer enters into a contract with an unrelated person pursuant to which the unrelated person is required to MPGE QPP within the United States for the taxpayer, the taxpayer is not considered to have engaged in the MPGE of that QPP pursuant to paragraph (f)(1) of this section, and therefore, for purposes of making any determination under this paragraph (g), the

MPGE or production activities or direct labor and overhead of the unrelated person under the contract are only attributed to the unrelated person.

* * *

(h) *United States.*—* * *

(2) *Commonwealth of Puerto Rico.*—The term *United States* includes the Commonwealth of Puerto Rico in the case of any taxpayer with gross receipts for any taxable year from sources within the Commonwealth of Puerto Rico, if all of such receipts are taxable under section 1 or 11 for such taxable year. This paragraph (h)(2) only applies as provided in section 199(d)(8).

(i) * * *

(3) *Hedging transactions.*—(i) *In general.*—For purposes of this section, provided that the risk being hedged relates to property described in section 1221(a)(1) giving rise to DPGR or relates to property described in section 1221(a)(8) consumed in an activity giving rise to DPGR, and provided that the transaction is a hedging transaction within the meaning of section 1221(b)(2)(A) and § 1.1221-2(b) and is properly identified as a hedging transaction in accordance with § 1.1221-2(f), then—

(A) In the case of a hedge of purchases of property described in section 1221(a)(1), income, deduction, gain, or loss on the hedging transaction must be taken into account in determining CGS;

(B) In the case of a hedge of sales of property described in section 1221(a)(1), income, deduction, gain, or loss on the hedging transaction must be taken into account in determining DPGR; and

(C) In the case of a hedge of purchases of property described in section 1221(a)(8), income, deduction, gain, or loss on the hedging transaction must be taken into account in determining DPGR.

(ii) *Effect of identification and nonidentification.*—The principles of § 1.1221-2(g) apply to a taxpayer that identifies or fails to identify a transaction as a hedging transaction, except that the consequence of identifying as a hedging transaction a transaction that is not in fact a hedging transaction described in paragraph (i)(3)(i) of this section, or of failing to identify a transaction that the taxpayer has no reasonable grounds for treating as other than a hedging transaction described in paragraph (i)(3)(i) of this section, is that deduction or loss (but not income or gain) from the transaction is taken into account under paragraph (i)(3) of this section.

(iii) *Other rules.*—See § 1.1221-2(e) for rules applicable to hedging by members of a consolidated group and § 1.446-4 for rules regarding the timing of income, deductions, gains or losses with respect to hedging transactions.

* * *

(5) * * *

(iii) * * *

Example 4. X produces a live television program that is a qualified film. In 2010, X broadcasts the television program on its station and distributes the program through the Internet. The television program contains product placements and advertising for which X received compensation in 2010. Because the methods and means of distributing a qualified film under paragraph (k)(1) of this section do not affect the availability of the deduction under section 199 for taxable years beginning after 2007, pursuant to paragraph (i)(5)(ii) of this section, all of X's product placement and advertising gross receipts for the program are treated as derived from the distribution of the qualified film.

* * *

(9) *Partnerships and S corporations engaging in production of qualified films.*—(i) *In general.*—For taxable years beginning after 2007, in the case of each partner of a partnership or shareholder of an S corporation who owns (directly or indirectly) at least 20 percent of the capital interests in such partnership or the stock of such S corporation, such partner or shareholder shall be treated as having engaged directly in any qualified film produced by such partnership or S corporation, and such partnership or S corporation shall be treated as having engaged directly in any qualified film produced by such partner or shareholder.

(ii) *No double attribution.*—When a partnership or S corporation is treated as having engaged directly in any qualified film produced by a partner or shareholder, any other partners of the partnership or shareholders of the S corporation who did not participate directly in the production of the qualified film are treated as not having engaged directly in the production of the qualified film at the partner or shareholder level. When a partner or shareholder is treated as having engaged directly in any qualified film produced by a partnership or S corporation, any other partnerships or S corporations in which that partner or shareholder owns an interest (excluding the partnership or S corporation that produced the film), are treated as not having engaged directly in the production of the qualified film at the partnership or S corporation level.

(iii) *Timing of attribution.*—A partner or shareholder is treated as having engaged directly in any qualified film produced by the partnership or S corporation, regardless of when the qualified film was produced by the partnership or S corporation, during any period that the partner or shareholder owns (directly or indirectly) at least 20 percent of the capital interests in the partnership or stock of the S corporation (attribution period). During any period that a partner or shareholder owns less than a 20 percent of the capital interests in such partnership or the stock of such S corporation, that partner or shareholder is not treated as having engaged directly in the qualified film produced by the partnership or S corporation for purposes of this paragraph (i)(9). A partnership or S corporation is treated as having engaged directly in a qualified film produced by a partner or shareholder during any period the partner or shareholder owns (directly or indirectly) at least 20 percent of the capital interests in such partnership or the stock of S corporation (attribution period). During any period that the partner or shareholder owns less than 20 percent of the capital interests in such partnership or stock of such S corporation, the partnership or S corporation is not treated as having engaged directly in the qualified film produced by the partner or shareholder for purposes of this paragraph (i)(9). The attribution period under this paragraph (i)(9) may be shorter or longer than a taxpayer's taxable year, depending on the length of the attribution period.

(iv) *Examples*.—The following examples illustrate an application of this paragraph (i)(9). Assume that all taxpayers are calendar year taxpayers.

Example 1. In 2010, Studio A and Studio B form an S corporation in which each is a 50-percent shareholder to produce a qualified film. Studio A owns the rights to distribute the film domestically and Studio B owns the rights to distribute the film outside of the United States. The production activities of the S corporation are attributed to each shareholder, and thus each shareholder's revenue from the distribution of the qualified film is treated as DPGR during the attribution period because Studio A and Studio B are treated as having directly engaged in any film that was produced by the S corporation.

Example 2. The facts are the same as *Example 1* except that, in 2011, after the S corporation's production of the qualified film, Studio C becomes a shareholder that owns at least 20 percent of the stock of the S corporation. Studio C is treated as having directly engaged in any film that was produced by the S corporation during the attribution period, as defined in paragraph (i)(9)(iii) of this section.

Example 3. In 2010, Studio A and Studio B form a partnership in which each is a 50-percent partner to distribute a qualified film. Studio A produced the film and contributes it to the partnership and Studio B contributes cash to the partnership. The production activities of Studio A are attributed to the partnership, and thus the partnership's revenue from the distribution of the qualified film is treated as DPGR during the attribution period, as defined in paragraph (i)(9)(iii) of this section, because the partnership is treated as having directly engaged in any film that was produced by Studio A.

Example 4. The facts are the same as *Example 3* except that Studio B receives a distribution of the rights to license an intangible associated with the qualified film produced by Studio A. Any receipts derived from the licensing of the intangible by Studio B are non-DPGR because Studio A's production activities are attributed to the partnership, and are not further attributed to Studio B.

Example 5. The facts are the same as *Example 3* except that, at some point in 2011, Studio A owns less than a 20-percent capital interest in the partnership. During the period that Studio A owns less than a 20-percent capital interest in the partnership between Studio A and Studio B, the partnership is not treated as directly engaging in the production of a qualified film. Therefore, any future receipts the partnership derives from the film after the end of the attribution period, as defined in paragraph (i)(9)(iii) of this section, are non-DPGR. Studio A, however, is still treated as having engaged directly in the production of the qualified film.

* * *

(k) * * *

(1) * * * For taxable years beginning after 2007, the term *qualified film* includes any copyrights, trademarks, or other intangibles with respect to such film (intangibles). For purposes of this paragraph (k), other intangibles include rights associated with the exploitation of a qualified film, such as endorsement rights, video game rights, merchandising rights, and other similar rights. See paragraph (k)(10) of this section for a special rule for disposition of promotional films.* * *

(2) * * *

(ii) *Film produced by a taxpayer*.—Except for intangibles under paragraph (k)(1) of this section, if a taxpayer produces a film and the film is affixed to tangible personal property (for example, a DVD), then for purposes of this section—

* * *

(3) * * *

(i) * * * For taxable years beginning after 2007, the methods and means of distributing a qualified film shall not affect the availability of the deduction under section 199.

* * *

(6) * * * Production activities do not include transmission or distribution activities with respect to a film, including the transmission of a film by electronic signal and the activities facilitating such transmission (such as formatting that enables the film to be transmitted).

(7) * * *

(i) * * * Paragraph (g)(3)(ii) of this section includes all costs paid or incurred by a taxpayer, whether or not capitalized or required to be capitalized under section 263A, to produce a live or delayed television program, and also includes any lease, rental, or license fees paid by a taxpayer for all or any portion of a film, or films produced by a third party that taxpayer uses in its film. License fees for films produced by third parties are not included in the direct labor and overhead to produce the film for purposes of applying paragraph (g)(3) of this section. * * *

* * *

(8) * * * If one party performs a production activity pursuant to a contract with another party, then only the party that is considered the taxpayer pursuant to paragraph (f)(1) of this section during the period in which the production activity occurs is treated as engaging in the production activity.

* * *

(10) *Special rule for disposition of promotional films and products or services promoted in promotional films*.—A promotional film is a film produced to promote a taxpayer's particular product or service and the term includes, but is not limited to, commercials, infomercials, advertising films, and sponsored films. A product or service is promoted in a promotional film if the product or service appears in, is described during, or is in a similar way alluded to by such film. If a promotional film meets the requirements to be treated as a qualified film produced by the taxpayer, then a taxpayer derives gross receipts from the lease, rental, license, sale, exchange, or other disposition of a qualified film, including any copyrights, trademarks, or other intangibles when the promotional film's disposition is distinct (separate and apart) from the disposition of the promoted product or service. Gross receipts are not derived from the disposition of a qualified film, including any copyrights, trademarks, or other intangibles when gross receipts are derived from a disposition of the promoted product or service.

(11) * * *

Example 3. X produces live television programs that are qualified films. X shows the programs on its own television station. X sells advertising time slots to advertisers for the television programs. Because the methods and means of distributing a qualified film under paragraph (k)(1) of this section do not affect the availability of the deduction under section 199 for taxable years beginning after 2007, the advertising income X receives from advertisers is derived from the lease, rental, license, sale, exchange, or other disposition of the qualified films and is DPGR.

Example 4. * * * Y is considered the taxpayer performing the qualifying activities pursuant to paragraph (f)(1) of this section with respect to the DVDs during the MPGE and duplication process. * * *

* * *

Example 6. X produced a qualified film and licenses the trademark of Character A, a character in the qualified film, to Y for reproduction of the Character A image onto t-shirts. Y sells the t-shirts with Character A's likeness to customers, and pays X a royalty, based on sales of the t-shirts. X's qualified film only includes intangibles with respect to the qualified film in taxable years beginning after 2007, including the trademark of Character A. Accordingly, any gross receipts derived from the license of the trademark of Character A to Y occurring in a taxable year beginning before 2008 are non-DPGR, and any gross receipts derived from the license of the trademark of Character A occurring in a taxable year beginning after 2007 are DPGR (assuming all other requirements of this section are met). The royalties X derives from Y occurring in a taxable year beginning before 2008 are non-DPGR because the royalties are derived from an intangible (which is not within the definition of a qualified film under paragraph (k)(1) of this section for taxable years beginning before 2008).

Example 7. Y, a media company, acquires all of the intangible rights to Book A, which was written and published in 2008, and all of the intangible rights associated with a qualified film that is based on Book A. The qualified film based on Book A is produced in 2009 by Y. Y owns the copyright and trademark to Character B, the lead character in Book A and the qualified film based on Book A. Y licenses Character B's copyright and trademark to Z for $50,000,000. For 2009, without taking into account the payment from Z, Y derives 40 percent of its gross receipts from the qualified film based on Book A, and 60 percent from Book A. Z's payment is attributable to both Book A and the qualified film based on Book A. Therefore, Y must allocate Z's payment, and only the gross receipts derived from licensing the intangible rights associated with the qualified film based on Book A, or 40 percent, are DPGR.

Example 8. Z produces a commercial in the United States that features Z's shirts, shoes, and other athletic equipment that all have Z's trademarked logo affixed (promoted products). Z's commercial is a qualified film produced by Z. Z sells the shirts, shoes, and athletic equipment to customers at retail establishments. Z's gross receipts are derived from the disposition of the promoted products and are not derived from the disposition of Z's qualified film, including any copyrights, trademarks, or other intangibles with respect to Z's qualified film.

Example 9. X produces a commercial in the United States that features X's services (promoted services). X's commercial is a qualified film produced by X. The commercial includes Character A developed to promote X's services. Gross receipts that X derives from providing the promoted services are not derived from the disposition of X's qualified film, including any copyrights, trademarks, or other intangibles with respect to X's qualified film. X also licenses the right to reproduce Character A developed to promote X's services to Y so that Y can produce t-shirts featuring Character A. This license is distinct (separate and apart) from a disposition of the promoted services and the gross receipts are derived from the license of an intangible with respect to X's qualified film produced by X. X's gross receipts derived from the license to reproduce Character A are DPGR.

Example 10. Y produces a qualified film in the United States. Y purchases DVDs and affixes the qualified film to the DVDs. Y purchases gift baskets and sells individual gift baskets that contain a DVD with the affixed qualified film in its retail stores in the normal course of Y's business. Under § 1.199-3(k)(2)(ii)(A), Y may treat the DVD as part of the qualified film produced by taxpayer, but Y cannot treat the gift baskets as part of the qualified film produced by taxpayer. The gross receipts that Y derives from the sale of the DVD are DPGR derived from a qualified film, but the gross receipts that Y derives from the sale of the gift baskets are non-DPGR.

Example 11. The facts are the same as in *Example 10* except that the individual gift baskets that Y sells also contain boxes of popcorn and candy manufactured by Y within the United States. Under § 1.199-3(k)(2)(ii)(A), Y cannot treat the gift baskets including the boxes of popcorn and candy manufactured by Y as part of the qualified film produced by taxpayer. Gross receipts from the sale of the DVD are still treated as DPGR derived from a qualified film. Y must separately determine whether the gross receipts from the tangible personal property it sells qualify as DPGR. Thus, Y must determine whether the gift basket, including the boxes of popcorn and candy but excluding the qualified film, is an item for purposes of § 1.199-3(d)(1)(i).

* * *

(m) * * *

(2) * * *

(i) * * * A taxpayer whose engagement in the activity is primarily limited to approving or authorizing invoices or payments is not considered engaged in a construction activity as a general contractor or in any other capacity.

* * *

(5) *Definition of substantial renovation.*—The term *substantial renovation* means activities the costs of which would be required to be capitalized by the taxpayer as an improvement under § 1.263(a)-3, other than an amount described in § 1.263(a)-3(k)(1)(i) through (iii). If not otherwise defined under § 1.263(a)-3, the unit of property for purposes of § 1.263(a)-3 is the real property, as defined in paragraph (m)(3) of this section, to which the activities relate.

* * *

Par. 6. Section 1.199-4 is amended by adding a sentence after the seventh sentence in paragraph (b)(1) and adding paragraph (b)(2)(iii) to read as follows:

§1.199-4. Costs allocable to domestic production gross receipts.

* * *

(b) * * *

(1) * * * In the case of a long-term contract accounted for under the percentage-of-completion method described in §1.460-4(b) (PCM), or the completed-contract method described in §1.460-4(d) (CCM), CGS for purposes of this section includes the allocable contract costs described in §1.460-5(b) (in the case of a contract accounted for under PCM) or §1.460-5(d) (in the case of a contract accounted for under CCM). * * *

(2) * * *

(iii) *Cost of goods sold associated with activities undertaken in an earlier taxable year.*—(A) *In general.*—A taxpayer must allocate CGS between DPGR and non-DPGR under the rules provided in paragraphs (b)(2)(i) and (ii) of this section, regardless of whether certain costs included in CGS can be associated with activities undertaken in an earlier taxable year (including a year prior to the effective date of section 199). A taxpayer may not segregate CGS into component costs and allocate those component costs between DPGR and non-DPGR.

(B) *Example.*—The following example illustrates an application of paragraph (b)(2)(iii)(A) of this section:

Example. During the 2009 taxable year, X manufactured and sold Product A. All of the gross receipts from sales recognized by X in 2009 were from the sale of Product A and qualified as DPGR. Employee 1 was involved in X's production process until he retired in 2003. In 2009, X paid $30 directly from its general assets for Employee 1's medical expenses pursuant to an unfunded, self-insured plan for retired X employees. For purposes of computing X's 2009 taxable income, X capitalized those medical costs to inventory under section 263A. In 2009, the CGS for a unit of Product A was $100 (including the applicable portion of the $30 paid for Employee 1's medical costs that was allocated to cost of goods sold under X's allocation method for additional section 263A costs). X has information readily available to specifically identify CGS allocable to DPGR and can identify that amount without undue burden and expense because all of X's gross receipts from sales in 2009 are attributable to the sale of Product A and qualify as DPGR. The inventory cost of each unit of Product A sold in 2009, including the applicable portion of retiree medical costs, is related to X's gross receipts from the sale of Product A in 2009. X may not segregate the 2009 CGS by separately allocating the retiree medical costs, which are components of CGS, to DPGR and non-DPGR. Thus, even though the retiree medical costs can be associated with activities undertaken in prior years, $100 of inventory cost of each unit of Product A sold in 2009, including the applicable portion of the retiree medical expense cost component, is allocable to DPGR in 2009.

* * *

Par. 7. Section 1.199-6 is amended by adding *Example 4* to paragraph (m) to read as follows:

§1.199-6. Agricultural and horticultural cooperatives.

* * *

(m) * * *

Example 4. (i) The facts are the same as *Example 1* except that Cooperative X's payments of $370,000 for its members' corn qualify as per-unit retain allocations paid in money within the meaning of section 1388(f) and Cooperative X reports the per-unit retain allocations paid in money on Form 1099-PATR.

(ii) Cooperative X is a cooperative described in paragraph (f) of this section. Accordingly, this section applies to Cooperative X and its patrons and all of Cooperative X's gross receipts from the sale of its patrons' corn qualify as domestic production gross receipts (as defined in §1.199-3(a)). Cooperative X's QPAI is $1,370,000. Cooperative X's section 199 deduction for its taxable year 2007 is $82,200 (.06 X $1,370,000). Because this amount is more than 50% of Cooperative X's W-2 wages (.5 X $130,000 = $65,000), the entire amount is not allowed as a section 199 deduction, but is instead subject to the wage limitation section 199(b), and also remains subject to the rules of section 199(d)(3) and this section.

Par. 8. Section 1.199-8 is amended by revising the heading of paragraph (i) and adding paragraphs (i)(10) and (11) to read as follows:

§1.199-8. Other rules.

* * *

(i) *Effective/applicability dates.*—* * *

* * *

(10) [The text of the proposed amendments to §1.199-8(i)(10) is the same as the text of §1.199-8T(i)(10) as added by T.D. 9731].

(11) *Energy Improvement and Extension Act of the 2008, Tax Extenders and Alternative Minimum Tax Relief Act of 2008, Tax Relief, Unemployment Insurance Reauthorization, and Job Creation Act of 2010, and other provisions.* Section 1.199-1(f); the last sentence in §1.199-2(e)(1) and paragraph (f); §1.199-3(d)(4) *Example 6* and *Example 14*, the last sentence in paragraph (e)(1), the last sentence in paragraph (e)(3), the third sentence in paragraph (e)(5) *Example 1*, the second sentence in paragraph (e)(5) *Example 4*, paragraph (e)(5) *Example 5* and *Example 9*, the last sentence in paragraph (f)(1), paragraph (f)(4) *Example 1*, paragraph (g)(4)(i), paragraphs (h)(2), (i)(3), (i)(5) *Example 4*, and (i)(9), the second, third, and fourth sentences in paragraph (k)(1), paragraph (k)(2)(ii), the second sentence in paragraph (k)(3)(i), the last sentence in paragraph (k)(6), the second sentence from the last sentence in paragraph (k)(7)(i), the last sentence in paragraph (k)(8), paragraph (k)(10), the third sentence in paragraph (k)(11) *Example 4*, paragraph (k)(11) *Example 3*, *Example 6*, *Example 7*, *Example 8*, *Example 9*, *Example 10*, and *Example 11*, the last sentence in paragraph (m)(2)(i), paragraph (m)(5); the eighth sentence in §1.199-4(b)(1) and paragraph (b)(2)(iii); and

§1.199-6(m) *Example 4* apply to taxable years beginning on or after the date the final regulations are published in the **Federal Register**.

Qualified Business Income: Deduction

Qualified Business Income: Deduction.—Amendments to Reg. §1.199A-0, concerning the deduction for qualified business income under section 199A of the Internal Revenue Code, are proposed (published in the Federal Register on February 8, 2019) (REG-134652-18).

Par. 2. Section 1.199A-0 is amended by:

1. Adding entries for §1.199A-3(b)(1)(iv)(A) and (B).

2. Adding entries for §1.199A-3(d), (d)(1) and (2), (d)(2)(i) through (iii), (d)(2)(iii)(A) and (B), (d)(3), (d)(3)(i) through (v), (d)(4), (d)(4)(i) and (ii), and (d)(5) and (6).

3. Adding entries for §1.199A-6(d)(3)(iii) and (v).

The additions read as follows:

§1.199A-0. Table of contents.

* * *

* * *

Qualified Business Income: Deduction

Qualified Business Income: Deduction.—Amendments to Reg. §1.199A-3, concerning the deduction for qualified business income under section 199A of the Internal Revenue Code, are proposed (published in the Federal Register on February 8, 2019) (REG-134652-18).

Par. 3. Section 1.199A-3 is amended by revising paragraph (b)(1)(iv) and adding paragraph (d) to read as follows:

§1.199A-3. Qualified business income, qualified REIT dividends, and qualified PTP income.

* * *

(b) ***

(1) * * *

(iv) *Previously disallowed losses.*—(A) *In general.*—Previously disallowed losses or deductions (including losses disallowed under sections 465, 469, 704(d), and 1366(d)) allowed in the taxable year generally are taken into account for purposes of computing QBI to the extent the disallowed loss or deduction is otherwise allowed by section 199A and this section. These losses shall be used, for purposes of section 199A and these regulations, in order from the oldest to the most recent on a first-in, first-out (FIFO) basis and shall be treated as losses from a separate trade or business. To the extent such losses relate to a PTP, they must be treated as a loss from a separate PTP in the taxable year the losses are taken into account. However, losses or deductions that were disallowed, suspended, limited, or carried over from taxable years ending before January 1, 2018 (including under sections 465, 469, 704(d), and 1366(d)), are not taken into account in a later taxable year for purposes of computing QBI.

(B) *Attributes of disallowed loss determined in year loss is incurred.*—Whether a disallowed loss or deduction is attributable to a trade or business, and otherwise meets the requirements of this section is determined in the year the loss is incurred. Whether a disallowed loss or deduction is attributable to a specified service trade or business (including whether an individual has taxable income under the threshold amount, within the phase-in range, or in excess of the phase-in range) also is determined in the year the loss is incurred. To the extent a loss is partially disallowed, QBI in the year of disallowance must be reduced proportionately.

* * *

(d) *Section 199A dividends paid by a regulated investment company.*—(1) *In general.*—If section 852(b) applies to a regulated investment company (RIC) for a taxable year, the RIC may pay section 199A dividends, as defined in this paragraph (d).

(2) *Definition of section 199A dividend.*—(i) *In general.*—Except as provided in paragraph (d)(2)(ii) of this section, a section 199A dividend is any dividend or part of such a dividend that a RIC pays to its shareholders and reports as a section 199A dividend in written statements furnished to its shareholders.

(ii) *Reduction in the case of excess reported amounts.*—If the aggregate reported amount with respect to the RIC for any taxable year exceeds the RIC's qualified REIT dividend income for the taxable year, then a section 199A dividend is equal to—

(A) The reported section 199A dividend amount, reduced by;

(B) The excess reported amount that is allocable to that reported section 199A dividend amount.

(iii) *Allocation of excess reported amount.*—(A) *In general.*—Except as provided in paragraph (d)(2)(iii)(B) of this section, the excess reported amount (if any) that is allocable to the reported section 199A dividend amount is that portion of the excess reported amount that bears the same ratio to the excess reported amount as the reported section 199A dividend amount bears to the aggregate reported amount.

(B) *Special rule for noncalendar-year RICs.*—In the case of any taxable year that does not begin and end in the same calendar year, if the post-December reported amount equals or exceeds the excess reported amount for that taxable year, paragraph (d)(2)(iii)(A) of this section is applied by substituting "post-December reported amount" for "aggregate reported amount," and no excess reported amount is allocated to any dividend paid on or before December 31 of that taxable year.

(3) *Definitions.*—For purposes of paragraph (d) of this section—

(i) *Reported section 199A dividend amount.*—The term *reported section 199A dividend amount* means the amount of a dividend distribution reported to the RIC's shareholders under paragraph (d)(2)(i) of this section as a section 199A dividend.

(ii) *Excess reported amount.*—The term *excess reported amount* means the excess of the aggregate reported amount over the RIC's qualified REIT dividend income for the taxable year.

(iii) *Aggregate reported amount.*—The term *aggregate reported amount* means the aggregate amount of dividends reported by the RIC under paragraph (d)(2)(i) of this section as section 199A dividends for the taxable year (including section 199A dividends paid after the close of the taxable year and described in section 855).

(iv) *Post-December reported amount.*—The term *post-December reported amount* means the aggregate reported amount determined by taking into account only dividends paid after December 31 of the taxable year.

(v) *Qualified REIT dividend income.*—The term *qualified REIT dividend income* means, with respect to a taxable year of a RIC, the excess of the amount of qualified REIT dividends, as defined in §1.199A-3(c)(2), includible in the RIC's taxable income for the taxable year over the amount of the RIC's deductions that are properly allocable to such income.

(4) *Treatment of section 199A dividends by shareholders.*—(i) *In general.*—For purposes of section 199A and the regulations under section 199A, a section 199A dividend is treated by a taxpayer that receives the section 199A dividend as a qualified REIT dividend.

(ii) *Holding period.*—Paragraph (d)(4)(i) does not apply to any dividend received with respect to a share of RIC stock—

(A) That is held by the shareholder for 45 days or less (taking into account the principles of section 246(c)(3) and (4)) during the 91-day period beginning on the date which is 45 days before the date on which the share becomes ex-dividend with respect to such dividend; or

(B) To the extent that the shareholder is under an obligation (whether pursuant to a short sale or otherwise) to make related payments with respect to positions in substantially similar or related property.

(5) *Example.*—The following example illustrates the provisions of this paragraph (d).

(i) Example. (A) X is a corporation that has elected to be a RIC. For its taxable year ending March 31, 2019, X has $25,000x of net long-term capital gain, $60,000x of qualified dividend income, $25,000x of taxable interest income, $15,000x of net short-term capital gain, and $25,000x of qualified REIT dividends. X has $15,000x of deductible expenses, of which $3,000x is allocable to the qualified REIT dividends. On December 31, 2018, X pays a single dividend of $100,000x on December 31, and reports $20,000x of the dividend as a section 199A dividend in written statements to its shareholders. On March 31, 2019, X pays a dividend of $35,000x, and reports $5,000x of the dividend as a section 199A dividend in written statements to its shareholders.

(B) X's qualified REIT dividend income under paragraph (d)(3)(v) of this section is $22,000x, which is the excess of X's $25,000x of qualified REIT dividends over $3,000x in allocable expenses. The reported section 199A dividend amounts for the December 31, 2018, and March 31, 2019, distributions are $20,000x and $5,000x, respectively. For the taxable year ending March 31, 2019, the aggregate reported amount of section 199A dividends is $25,000x, and the excess reported amount under paragraph (d)(3)(ii) of this section is $3,000x. Because X is a noncalendar-year RIC and the post-December reported amount of $5,000x exceeds the excess reported amount of $3,000x, the entire excess reported amount is allocated under paragraphs (d)(2)(iii)(A) and (B) of this section to the reported section 199A dividend amount for the March 31, 2019, distribution. No portion of the excess reported amount is allocated to the reported section 199A dividend amount for the December 31, 2018, distribution. Thus, the section 199A dividend on March 31, 2019, is $2,000x, which is the reported section 199A dividend amount of $5,000x reduced by the $3,000x of allocable excess reported amount. The section 199A dividend on December 31, 2018, is the $20,000x that X reports as a section 199A dividend.

(C) Shareholder A, a United States person, receives a dividend from X of $100x on December 31, 2018, of which $20x is reported as a section 199A dividend. If A meets the holding period requirements in paragraph (d)(4)(ii) of this section with respect to the stock of X, A treats $20x of the dividend from X as a qualified

REIT dividend for purposes of section 199A for A's 2018 taxable year.

(D) A receives a dividend from X of $35x on March 31, 2019, of which $5x is reported as a section 199A dividend. If A meets the holding period requirements in paragraph (d)(4)(ii) of this section with respect to the stock of X, A may only treat $2x of the dividend from X as a section 199A dividend for A's 2019 taxable year.

(6) *Applicability date.*—The provisions of paragraph (d) of this section apply to taxable years ending after the date the Treasury decision adopting these regulations as final regulations is published in the Federal Register. However, taxpayers may rely on the rules of this section until the date the Treasury decision adopting these regulations as final regulations is published in the Federal Register.

* * *

Qualified Business Income: Deduction

Qualified Business Income: Deduction.—Amendments to Reg. §1.199A-6, concerning the deduction for qualified business income under section 199A of the Internal Revenue Code, are proposed (published in the Federal Register on February 8, 2019) (REG-134652-18).

Par. 4. Section 1.199A-6 is amended by adding paragraphs (d)(3)(iii) and (v) to read as follows:

§1.199A-6. Relevant passthrough entities (RPEs), publicly traded partnerships (PTPs), trusts, and estates.

* * *

(d) ***

(3) ***

(iii) *Separate shares.*—In the case of a trust described in section 663(c) with substantially separate and independent shares for multiple beneficiaries, such trust will be treated as a single trust for purposes of determining whether the taxable income of the trust exceeds the threshold amount.

* * *

(v) *Charitable remainder trusts.*—A charitable remainder trust described in section 664 is not entitled to and does not calculate a section 199A deduction and the threshold amount described in section 199A(e)(2) does not apply to the trust. However, any taxable recipient of a unitrust or annuity amount from the trust must determine and apply the recipient's own threshold amount for purposes of section 199A taking into account any annuity or unitrust amounts received from the trust. A recipient of a unitrust or annuity amount from a trust may take into account QBI, qualified REIT dividends, or qualified PTP income for purposes of determining the recipient's section 199A deduction for the taxable year to the extent that the unitrust or annuity amount distributed to such recipient consists of such section 199A items under §1.664-1(d). For example, if a charitable remainder trust has investment income of $500, qualified dividend income of $200, and qualified REIT dividends of $1,000, and distributes $1,000 to the recipient, the trust would be treated as having income in two classes within the category of income described in §1.664-1(d)(1)(i)(*a*)(*1*), for purposes of §1.664-1(d)(1)(ii)(*b*). Because the annuity amount first carries out income in the class subject to the highest income tax rate, the entire annuity payment comes from the class with the investment income and qualified REIT dividends. Thus, the charitable remainder trust would be treated as distributing a proportionate amount of the investment income ($500/(1,000+500)*1,000 = $333) and qualified REIT dividends ($1000/(1,000+500)*1000 = $667) because the investment income and qualified REIT dividends are taxed at the same rate and within the same class, which is higher than the rate of tax for the qualified dividend income which is in a separate class. The charitable remainder trust in this example would not be treated as distributing any of the qualified dividend income until it distributed all of the investment income and qualified REIT dividends (more than $1,500 in total) to the recipient. To the extent that a trust is treated as distributing QBI, qualified REIT dividends, or qualified PTP income to more than one unitrust or annuity recipient in the taxable year, the distribution of such income will be treated as made to the recipients proportionately, based on their respective shares of the total of QBI, qualified REIT dividends, or qualified PTP income distributed for that year. The trust allocates and reports any W-2 wages or UBIA of qualified property to the taxable recipient of the annuity or unitrust interest based on each recipient's share of the trust's total QBI (whether or not distributed) for that taxable year. Accordingly, if 10 percent of the QBI of a charitable remainder trust is distributed to the recipient and 90 percent of the QBI is retained by the trust, 10 percent of the W-2 wages and UBIA of qualified property is allocated and reported to the recipient and 90 percent of the W-2 wages and UBIA of qualified property is treated as retained by the trust. However, any W-2 wages retained by the trust do not carry over to subsequent taxable years for section 199A purposes. Any QBI, qualified REIT dividends, or qualified PTP income of the trust that is unrelated business taxable income is subject to excise tax and that tax must be allocated to the corpus of the trust under §1.664-1(c).

* * *

Itemized Deductions for Individuals

Business Use or Rental of Dwelling Unit.—Reproduced below is the text of a proposed amendment of Reg. §1.212-1, relating to the deductibility of expenses in connection with the business use, or the rental to others, of a dwelling unit that the taxpayer is deemed to have used for personal purposes during the taxable year (published in the Federal Register on August 7, 1980).

☐ Par. 2. Paragraph (h) of §1.212-1 is amended by adding at the end thereof a new sentence to read as follows:

§1.212-1. Nontrade or nonbusiness expenses.—

* * *

(h) * * * But see section 280A and the regulations thereunder.

* * *

Notional Principal Contracts: Contingent Nonperiodic Payments

Notional Principal Contracts: Contingent Nonperiodic Payments.—Amendments to Reg. §1.212-1, relating to the inclusion into income or deduction of a contingent nonperiodic payment provided for under a notional principal contract, are proposed (published in the Federal Register on February 26, 2004) (REG-166012-02).

☐ Par. 3. In §1.212-1, paragraph (q) is added to read as follows:

§1.212-1. Nontrade or nonbusiness expenses.

* * *

(q) *Notional principal contract payments.*—(1) Amounts taken into account by an individual pursuant to §1.446-3(d)(1) (including mark-to-market deductions) with respect to a notional principal contract as defined in §1.446-3(c)(1)(i), are ordinary and necessary, and are deductible to the extent these amounts are paid or incurred in connection with the production or collection of income. However, this section will not apply to any amount representing interest expense on the deemed loan component of a significant nonperiodic payment as described in §1.446-3(g)(4). For any loss arising from a termination payment as defined in §1.446-3(h)(1), see section 1234A and the regulations thereunder. For the timing of deductions with respect to notional principal contracts, see §1.446-3.

(2) *Effective date.*—Paragraph (q) of this section is applicable to notional principal contracts entered into on or after 30 days after the date a Treasury decision based on these proposed regulations is published in the Federal Register.

Transfers Between Spouses

Transfers: Alimony, Separate Maintenance, and Dependency Exemption.—Temporary Reg. §1.215-1T, relating to the treatment of transfers of property between spouses and former spouses, the tax treatments of alimony and separate maintenance payments, and the dependency exemption in the case of a child of divorced parents, is also proposed as a final regulation and, when adopted, would become Reg. §1.215-1 (published in the Federal Register on August 31, 1984).

§1.215-1. Alimony, etc., payments.

IRAs: SEPs: Deduction

Individual Retirement Plans: Simplified Employee Pensions.—Reproduced below are the texts of proposed Reg. §1.219-3 and proposed amendments of Reg. §§1.219-1 and 1.219-2, relating to individual retirement plans and simplified employee pensions (published in the Federal Register on July 14, 1981).

☐ Par. 2. Section 1.219-1 is revised by adding: (1) a new subdivision (iv) to paragraph (b)(2), and (2) new paragraphs (d) and (e) to read as follows:

§1.219-1. Deduction for retirement savings.—

* * *

(b) *Limitations and restrictions.*—* * *

(2) *Restrictions.*—* * *

(iv) *Alternative deduction.*—No deduction is allowed under subsection (a) for the taxable year if the individual claims the deduction allowed by section 220 (relating to retirement savings for certain married individuals) for the taxable year.

* * *

(d) *Time when contributions deemed made.*—(1) *Taxable years beginning before January 1, 1978.*—For taxable years beginning before January 1, 1977, a taxpayer must make a contribution to an individual retirement plan during a taxable year in order to receive a deduction for such taxable year. For taxable years beginning after December 31, 1976, and before January 1, 1978, a taxpayer shall be deemed to have made a contribution on the last day of the preceding taxable year if the contribution is made on account of such taxable year and is made not later than 45 days after the end of such taxable year. A contribution made not later than 45 days after the end of a taxable year shall be treated as made on account of such taxable year if the individual specifies in writing to the trustee, insurance company, or custodian that the amounts contributed are for such taxable year.

(2) *Taxable years beginning after December 31, 1977.*—For taxable years beginning after December 31, 1977, a taxpayer shall be deemed to have made a contribution on the last day of the preceding taxable year if the contribution is made on account of such taxable year and is made not later than the time prescribed by law for filing the return for such taxable year (including extensions thereof). A contribution made not later than the time prescribed by law for filing the return for a taxable year (including extensions thereof) shall be treated as made on account of such taxable year if it is irrevocably specified in writing to the trustee, insurance company, or custodian that the amounts contributed are for such taxable year.

(3) *Time when individual retirement plan must be established.*—For purposes of this paragraph, an individual retirement plan need not be established until the contribution is made.

(4) *Year of inclusion in income.*—Any amount paid by an employer to an individual retirement account, for an individual retirement annuity or for an individual retirement bond (including an individual retirement account or individual retirement annuity maintained as part

of a simplified employee pension plan) shall be included in the gross income of the employee for the taxable year for which the contribution is made.

(e) *Excess contributions treated as contribution made during subsequent year for which there is an unused limitation.*—(1) *In general.*—If for the taxable year the maximum amount allowable as a deduction under this section exceeds the amount contributed, then the taxpayer, whether or not a deduction is actually claimed, shall be treated as having made an additional contribution for the taxable year in an amount equal to the lesser of—

(i) The amount of such excess, or

(ii) The amount of the excess contributions for such taxable year (determined under section 4973(b)(2) without regard to subparagraph (C) thereof).

(2) *Amount contributed.*—For purposes of this paragraph, the amount contributed—

(i) Shall be determined without regard to this paragraph, and

(ii) Shall not include any rollover contribution.

(3) *Special rule where excess deduction was allowed for closed year.*—Proper reduction shall be made in the amount allowable as a deduction by reason of this paragraph for any amount allowed as a deduction under this section or section 220 for a prior taxable year for which the period for assessing a deficiency has expired if the amount so allowed exceeds the amount which should have been allowed for such prior taxable year.

(4) *Effective date.*—(i) This paragraph shall apply to the determination of deductions for taxable years beginning after December 31, 1975.

(ii) If, but for this subdivision, an amount would be allowable as a deduction by reason of section 219(c)(5) for a taxable year beginning before January 1, 1978, such amount shall be allowable only for the taxpayer's first taxable year beginning in 1978.

(5) *Examples.*—The provisions of this paragraph may be illustrated by the following examples. (Assume in each example, unless otherwise stated, that B is less than age 70½ and is not covered by a simplified employee pension or a plan described in section 219(b)(2).)

Example (1). (i) B, a calendar-year taxpayer, earns $8,000 in compensation includible in gross income for 1979. On December 1, 1979, B establishes an individual retirement account (IRA) and contributes $1,500 to the account. B does not withdraw any money from the IRA after the initial contribution. Under section 219(b)(l), the maximum amount that B can deduct for 1979 is 15% of $8,000 or $1,200. B has an excess contribution for 1979 of $300.

(ii) For 1980, B has compensation includible in gross income of $12,000. B makes a $1,000 contribution to his IRA for 1980.

(iii) Although B made only a $1,000 contribution to his IRA for 1980, under the rules contained in this paragraph, B is treated as having made an additional contribution of $300 for 1980 and will be allowed to deduct $1,300 as his 1980 IRA contribution.

Example (2). (i) For 1979, the facts are the same as in *Example (1).*

(ii) For 1980, B has compensation includible in gross income of $12,000. B makes a $1,500 contribution to his IRA for 1980.

(iii) B will be allowed a $1,500 deduction for 1980 (the amount of his contribution). B will not be allowed a deduction for the $300 excess contribution made in 1979 because the maximum amount allowable for 1980 does not exceed the amount contributed.

Example (3). (i) For 1979, the facts are the same as in *Example (1).*

(ii) For 1980, B has compensation includible in gross income of $12,000. B makes a $1,400 contribution to his IRA for 1980.

(iii) For 1980, B will be allowed to deduct his contribution of $1,400 and $100 of the excess contribution made for 1979. He will not be allowed to deduct the remaining $200 of the excess contribution made for 1979 because that would make his deduction for 1980 more than $1,500, his allowable deduction for 1980.

(iv) For 1981, B has compensation includible in gross income of $15,000. B makes a $1,300 contribution to his IRA for 1981.

(v) B will be allowed to deduct the remaining $200 and his $1,300 contribution for 1981.

Example (4). (i) For 1979, the facts are the same as in *Example (1).*

(ii) For 1980, B has compensation includible in gross income of $12,000. B makes a $1,000 contribution to his IRA for 1980. B is allowed to deduct the $300 excess contribution for 1980 but fails to do so on his return. Consequently, B deducts only $1,000 for 1980.

(iii) Under no circumstances will B be allowed to deduct the $300 excess contribution made for 1979 for any taxable year after 1980 because B is treated as having made the contribution for 1980.

Example (5). (i) For 1979, the facts are the same as in *Example (1).*

(ii) For 1980, B has compensation includible in gross income of $15,000 and is an active participant in a plan described in section 219(b)(2)(A).

(iii) B will not be allowed to deduct for 1980 the $300 excess contribution for 1979 because the maximum amount allowable as a deduction under sections 219(b)(1) and 219(b)(2) is $0.

□ Par. 3. Section 1.219-2 is amended by: (1) revising the first sentence of paragraph (b)(1); (2) renumbering paragraph (b)(2), (3), and (4) as paragraph (b)(3), (4) and (5), respectively, and adding a new paragraph (b)(2) before the renumbered paragraph (b)(3), (4) and (5); (3) revising paragraph (f) and (4) adding new examples (3), (4) and (5) after *Example (2)* in paragraph (h). These revised and added provisions read as follows:

§1.219-2. Definition of active participant.—

* * *

(b) *Defined benefit plans.*—(1) *In general.*—Except as provided in subparagraphs (2), (3), (4) and (5) of this paragraph, an individual is an active participant in a defined benefit plan if for any portion of the plan year ending with or within such individual's taxable year he is not excluded under the eligibility provisions of the plan. * * *

(2) *Special rule for offset plans.*—For taxable years beginning after December 31, 1980, an individual who satisfies the eligibility requirements of a plan under which benefits are offset by Social Security or Railroad Retirement benefits is not considered an active participant by virtue of participation in such plan for a particular plan year if such individual's compensation for the calendar year during which such plan year ends does not exceed the offset plan's breakpoint compensation amount for such plan year. Breakpoint compensation is the maximum compensation determined for the plan for a plan year that any participant could earn and have a projected benefit from the offset plan of $0. For purposes of determining the projected plan benefit, the following assumptions are made: plan participation begins at age 25 and maximum credited service is earned for participation from age 25 to age 65 regardless of the participant's actual participation; plan benefits, including the offset, are based on W-2 earnings from the employer for such calendar year regardless of the definition of compensation on which plan benefits are based; and the projected Social Security Primary Insurance Amount (PIA) is computed under a formula that the Commissioner may, from time to time, prescribe for this purpose.

* * *

(f) *Certain individuals not active participants.*—(1) *Election out of plan.*—For purposes of this section, an individual who elects pursuant to the plan not to participate in the plan will be considered to be ineligible for participation for the period to which the election applies. In the case of a defined benefit plan, such an election shall be effective no earlier than the first plan year commencing after the date of the election.

(2) *Members of reserve components.*—A member of a reserve component of the armed forces (as defined in section 261(a) of Title 10 of the United States Code) is not considered to be an active participant in a plan described in section 219(b)(2)(A)(iv) for a taxable year solely because he is a member of a reserve component unless he has served in excess of 90 days on active duty (other than military duty for training) during the year.

(3) *Volunteer firefighters.*—An individual whose participation in a plan described in section 219(b)(2)(A)(iv) is based solely upon his activity as a volunteer firefighter and whose accrued benefit as of the beginning of the taxable year is not more than an annual benefit of $1,800 (when expressed as a single life annuity commencing at age 65) is not considered to be an active participant in such a plan for the taxable year.

* * *

(h) *Examples.*—* * *

Example (3). (i) For plan year X the annual projected Social Security PIA is determined as follows:

*Compensation Range**	*PIA Formula**
$0 to $1,626	PIA = $1,464
$1,627 to $2,160 . . .	PIA = .90 (compensation)
$2,161 to $13,020 . .	PIA = .32 (compensation) + $1,253
$13,021 to $22,900 .	PIA = .15 (compensation) + $3,466
$22,901 and over . .	PIA = $6,901

* These numbers are for illustrative purposes only.

(ii) V is a defined benefit plan which provides a normal retirement benefit of 1.5% of high five-year average earnings excluding overtime pay, minus 2% of Social Security PIA, the difference multiplied by years of plan participation up to a maximum of 30 years. V provides that individuals commence plan participation on their date of employment. Normal retirement age is 62. V's breakpoint compensation for the plan year ending in year X can be determined as follows:

I. Determine V's projected benefit:

An individual credited with 40 years of service (from age 25 to 65) would have a projected benefit of:

(30) (1.5% (compensation) – 2% (PIA))

or

45% (compensation) – 60% (PIA).

Note that in the determination of the projected benefit, the normal retirement age is assumed to be age 65 rather than the actual normal retirement age of 62, the participant is assumed to have 40 years of credited service, and the plan definition of compensation is assumed to be the same as is used to compute the Social Security benefit.

II. Determine V's formula compensation changepoints. The formula compensation changepoints are amounts where the projected benefit formula, expressed in terms of compensation, changes:

Since V's benefit formula applies uniformly to all compensation, the compensation changepoints are determined by the PIA portion only, and are

a. $1,626
b. 2,160
c. 13,020
d. 22,900

III. Determine which of the formula compensation changepoints first produces a projected benefit greater than 0. This can be done by testing the projected benefit for compensation amounts equal to V's compensation changepoints:

a. Formula compensation changepoint equal to $1,626.

i. Projected benefit = 45% × 1,626 – 60% × 1,464 = 0

V's compensation breakpoint, therefore, exceeds $1,626.

b. Formula compensation changepoint equal to $2,160.

i. Projected benefit = 45% × 2,160 – 60% × (.90 × 2,160) = 0

V's compensation breakpoint, therefore, exceeds $2,160.

c. Formula compensation changepoint equal to $13,020.

i. Projected benefit = 45% × 13,020 – 60% × (.32 × 13,020 + 1,253) = 2,607.

V's compensation breakpoint is, therefore, in the compensation range $2,161 to $13,020.

IV. Determine V's compensation breakpoint within the $2,161 to $13,020 compensation range.

V's compensation breakpoint can be determined by finding the greatest compensation that will result in a projected benefit of 0 for this compensation range:

a. 45% × compensation – 60% × (.32 × compensation + 1,253) = 0

b. Eliminate the parentheses in equation a by multiplying each of the terms within the parentheses by – 60%. 45% × compensation – 19.2% × compensation – 751.80 = 0.

c. Add 751.80 to both sides of equation in b and combine the first two terms. 25.8% × compensation = 751.80.

d. Dividing both sides of the equation in c by 25.8%, V's breakpoint compensation for 1979 = $2,914.

V. Therefore, individuals whose W-2 earnings from the employer do not exceed $2,914 in year X are not considered active participants by virtue of participating in Plan V.

Example (4). For year X the annual projected Social Security PIA is determined as in *Example (3).*

T is a defined benefit plan which provides a normal retirement benefit equal to 20% of final average earnings plus 10% of such earnings in excess of $2,000 minus 45% of PIA, the net result reduced pro rata for participation less than 15 years. Participation commences upon attainment of age 20. Normal retirement age is 65.

I. Determine T's projected benefit for year X.

An individual credited with 40 years of service (from age 25 to 65) would have a projected benefit of:

20% of compensation plus 10% of compensation in excess of $2,000, if any

minus

45% of PIA

II. Determine T's formula compensation changepoints.

$2,000 is a formula compensation changepoint, in addition to the four PIA changepoints, since T's benefit formula changes at this compensation amount. The five formula compensation changepoints are:

a. $1,626
b. 2,000
c. 2,160
d. 13,020
e. 22,900

III. Determine which of T's formula compensation changepoints first produces a projected benefit greater than 0.

a. Compensation changepoint equal to $1,626

i. Projected benefit = 20% × 1,626 + 10% × 0 – 45% × 1,424 = 0

[T]'s compensation breakpoint, therefore, exceeds $1,626.

b. Compensation changepoint equal to $2,000

i. Projected benefit = 20% × 2,000 + 10% × 0 – 45% × (.90 × 2,000) = 0.

T's compensation breakpoint, therefore, exceeds $2,000.

c. Compensation changepoint equal to $2,160

i. Projected benefit = 20% × 2,160 + 10% × (2,160 – 2,000) – 45% × (.90 × 2,160) = 0.

T's compensation breakpoint, therefore, exceeds $2,160.

d. Compensation changepoint equal to $13,020

i. Projected benefit = 20% × 13,020 + 10% (13,020 – 2,000) – 45% × (.32 × 13,020 + 1,253) = 1,267.

T's compensation breakpoint is, therefore, in the compensation range $2,160 to $13,020.

IV. Determine T's breakpoint compensation within the $2,160 to $13,020 range.

T's compensation breakpoint can be determined by finding the greatest compensation that will result in a projected benefit of 0 for this range:

a. 20% × comp. + 10% × (comp. – 2,000) – 45% × (.32 × comp. + 1,253) = 0.

b. Eliminating both parentheses in equation a. by multiplying each of the terms within by the appropriate percentage.

20% × comp. + 10% × comp. – 200 – 14.4% × comp. – 563.85 = 0.

c. Add 763.85 to both sides of equation and combine remaining terms in equation b.

15.6% × comp. = 763.85.

d. Dividing each side of equation c. by 15.6%, T's breakpoint compensation for year X = $4,896.

V. Therefore, individuals whose W-2 earnings do not exceed $4,896 in year X are not considered active participants by virtue of participating in Plan T.

Example (5). Assume the same facts as *Example (4),* except that T also provides a minimum monthly benefit of $100 for participants with 15 or more years of plan participation. There is no compensation amount which will produce a projected benefit of $0. Therefore, all individuals who satisfy T's eligibility requirements are considered active participants.

☐ Par. 4. There are added after § 1.219-2 the following new sections:

§ 1.219-3. Limitation on simplified employee pension deductions.—(a) *General rule.*—(1) *In general.*—Under section 219(b)(7), if an employer contribution is made on behalf of an employee to a simplified employee pension described in section 408(k), the limitations of this section, and not section 219(b)(1) and § 1.219-1(b)(1), shall apply for purposes of computing the maximum allowable deduction for that individual employee. The other rules of section 219 and §§ 1.219-1 and 1.219-2 apply for purposes of computing an individual's deduction except as modified by this section.

(2) *Employer limitation.*—The maximum deduction limitation under section 219(a) for an employee with respect to an employer contribution to the employee's simplified employee pension under that employer's arrangement cannot exceed an amount equal to the lesser of—

(i) 15 percent of the employee's compensation from that employer (determined without regard to the employer contribution to the simplified employee pension) includible in the employee's gross income for the taxable year, or

(ii) The amount contributed by that employer to the employee's simplified employee pension and included in gross income (but not in excess of $7,500).

(3) *Special rules.*—(i) *Compensation.*—Compensation referred to in paragraph (a)(2)(i) has the same meaning as under § 1.219-1(c)(1) except that it includes only the compensation from the employer making the contribution to the simplified employee pension. Thus, if an in-

dividual earns $50,000 from employer A and $20,000 from employer B and employer B contributes $4,000 to a simplified employee pension on behalf of the individual, the maximum amount the individual will be able to deduct under section 219(b)(7) is 15 percent of $20,000, or $3,000.

(ii) *Special rule for officers, shareholders, and owner-employees.*—In the case of an employee who is an officer, shareholder, or owner-employee described in section 408(k)(3) with respect to a particular employer, the $7,500 amount referred to in paragraph (a)(2)(ii) shall be reduced by the amount of tax taken into account with respect to such individual under section 408(k)(3)(D).

(iii) *More than one employer arrangement.*—Except as provided in paragraph (c), below, the maximum deduction under paragraph (a)(2) for an individual who receives simplified employee pension contributions under two or more employers' simplified employee pension arrangements cannot exceed the sum of the maximum deduction limitations computed separately for that individual under each such employer's arrangement.

(iv) *Section 408 rules.*—Under section 408(j), for purposes of applying the $7,500 limitations under section 408(a)(1), (b), (b)(2)(B) and (d)(5) (§1.408-2(b)(1), §1.408-3(b)(2) and §1.408-4(h)(3)(i), respectively), the $7,500 limitations shall be applied separately with respect to each employer's contributions to an individual's simplified employee pension.

(b) *Limitations not applicable to SEP contributions*—

(1) *Active participant.*—The limitations on coverage by certain other plans in section 219(b)(2) and §1.219-1(b)(2)(i) shall not apply with respect to the employer contribution to a simplified employee pension. Thus, an employee is allowed a deduction for an employer's contribution to a simplified employee pension even though he is an active participant in an employer's qualified plan.

(2) *Contributions to simplified employee pensions after age 70 1/2.*—The denial of deductions for contributions after age 70 1/2 contained in section 219(b)(3) and §1.219-1(b)(2)(ii) shall not apply with respect to the employer contribution to a simplified employee pension.

(c) *Multiple employer, etc. limitations.*—(1) *Section 414(b) and (c) employers.*—In the case of a controlled group of employers within the meaning of section 414(b) or (c), the maximum deduction limitation for an employee under paragraph (a)(2) shall be computed by treating such employers as one employer maintaining a single simplified pension arrangement and by treating the compensation of that employee from such employers as if from one employer. Thus, for example, for a particular employee the 15 percent limitation on compensation would be determined with regard to the compensation from all employers within such group. Further, the maximum deduction with respect to such group could not exceed $7,500.

(2) *Self-employed individuals.*—In the case of an employee who is a self-employed individual within the meaning of section 401(c)(1) with respect to more than one trade or business, the maximum deduction limitation for such an employee under paragraph (a)(2) shall not exceed the lesser of the sum of such limitation applied separately with respect to the simplified employee pension arrangement of each trade or business or such limitation determined by treating such trades or businesses as if they constituted a single employer.

(d) *Additional deduction for employee contributions.*—If the maximum allowable deduction for an individual employee determined under paragraph (a) for employer contributions to that individual's simplified employee pensions is less than $1,500, the individual shall be entitled to an additional deduction for contributions to individual retirement programs maintained on his behalf. The additional deduction shall equal the excess, if any, of the section 219(b)(1) and §1.219-1(b)(1) maximum deduction limitation over the maximum deduction limitation determined under paragraph (a). For purpose of determining the compensation limit of section 219(b)(1), employer simplified employee pension contributions shall not be taken into account. Thus, for example, if $1,000 is deductible by individual A for employer contributions under a simplified employee pension arrangement and A's compensation, not including the $1,000 SEP contribution, is $10,000, than A would be entitled to an additional deduction of $500.

(e) *Examples.*—The provisions of this section may be illustrated by the following examples:

Example (1). Corporation X is a calendar-year, cash basis taxpayer. It adopts a simplified employee pension agreement in 1980 and wishes to contribute the maximum amount on behalf of each employee for 1980. Individual E is a calendar-year taxpayer who is employed solely by Corporation X in 1980. Beginning in June, 1980, Corporation X pays $100 each month into a simplified employee pension maintained on behalf of E. X makes a total payment to E's simplified employee pension during the year of $700. E's other compensation from X for the year totals $15,000. The maximum amount which E will be allowed to deduct as a simplified employee pension contribution is 15% of $15,000, or $2,250. Therefore, X may make an additional contribution for 1980 to E's simplified employee pension of $1,550. X makes this additional contribution to E's simplified employee pension in February of 1981. E's total compensation for 1980 includible in gross income is $15,000 + $2,250 or $17,250.

Example (2). (i) Corporation G is a calendar-year taxpayer which does not maintain an integrated plan as defined in section 408(k)(3)(E). It adopts a simplified employee pension agreement for 1980. It wishes to contribute 15% of compensation on behalf of each employee reduced by its tax under section 3111(a). The corporation has 4 employees, A, B, C, and D. D is a shareholder. The compensation for these employees for 1980 is as follows:

A =$10,000
B = 20,000
C = 30,000
D = 60,000

(ii) The amount of money which the corporation will be allowed to contribute on behalf of each employee under this allocation formula and the amount of the employer contribution each employee will be allowed to deduct is set forth in the following table:

Employee	Compensation	Lesser of $7500 or 15% of Comp.	3111(a)[1] Tax	SEP[2] Contribution	Sec. 219(b)(7) deduction
A	$10,000	$1,500	$508.00	$992.00	$992.00
B	20,000	3,000	1,016.00	1,984.00	1,984.00
C	30,000	4,500	1,315.72	3,184.28	3,184.28
D	60,000	7,500	1,315.72	6,184.28	6,184.28

[1] The section 3111(a) tax is computed by multiplying compensation up to the taxable wage base ($25,900 for 1980) by the tax rate (5.08% for 1980).

[2] Simplified Employee Pension

Example (3). Corporations A and B are calendar year taxpayers. Corporations A and B are not members of a controlled group of employers within the meaning of section 414(b) or (c). Individual M is employed full-time by Corporation A and part-time by Corporation B. Corporation A adopts a simplified employee pension agreement for calendar year 1980 and agrees to contribute 15% of compensation for each participant. M is a participant under Corporation A's simplified employee pension agreement and earns $15,000 for 1980 from Corporation A before A's contribution to his simplified employee pension. M also earns $5,000 as a part-time employee of Corporation B for 1980. Corporation A contributes $2,500 to M's simplified employee pension. The maximum amount that M will be allowed to deduct under section 219(b)(7) for 1980 is 15% of $15,000 or $2,250. The remaining $250 is an excess contribution because M cannot consider the compensation earned from Corporation B under § 1.219-3(a)(3)(i).

Example (4). Individual P is employed by Corporation H and Corporation O. Corporation H and O are not members of a controlled group of employers within the meaning of section 414(b) or (c). Both Corporation H and Corporation O maintain a simplified employee pension arrangement and contribute 15 percent of compensation on behalf of each employee. P earns $50,000 from Corporation H and $60,000 from Corporation O. Corporation H and O each contributes $7,500 under its simplified employee pension arrangement to an individual retirement account maintained on behalf of P. P will be allowed to deduct $15,000 for employer contributions to simplified employee pensions because each employer has a simplified employee pension arrangement and the SEP contributions by Corporation H and O do not exceed the applicable $7,500-15 percent limitation. [Reg. § 1.219-3.]

IRAs: SEPs: Qualified Voluntary Employee Contributions

Individual Retirement Plans: Simplified Employee Pensions: Qualified Voluntary Employee Contributions.—Reproduced below are the texts of proposed Reg. §§ 1.219(a)-1—1.219(a)-6, relating to individual retirement plans, simplified employee pensions and qualified voluntary employee contributions (published in the Federal Register on January 23, 1984).

☐ Paragraph 1. There are added after proposed § 1.219-3, 46 Fed. Reg. 36202 (1981), the following new sections 1.219(a)-1 through 1.219(a)-6:

§ 1.219(a)-1. Deduction for contributions to individual retirement plans and employer plans under the Economic Recovery Tax Act of 1981.—(a) *In general.*—Under section 219, as amended by the Economic Recovery Tax Act of 1981, an individual is allowed a deduction from gross income for amounts paid on his behalf to an individual retirement plan or to certain employer retirement plans. The following is a table of contents for the rules for deductions on behalf of individuals to individual retirement plans or employer plans.

§ 1.219(a)-2: Individual retirement plans.

§ 1.219(a)-3: Spousal individual retirement accounts.

§ 1.219(a)-4: Simplified employee pensions.

§ 1.219(a)-5: Employer plans.

§ 1.219(a)-6: Divorced individuals.

(b) *Definitions.*—The following is a list of terms and their definitions to be used for purposes of this section and §§ 1.219(a)-2 through 1.219(a)-6:

(1) *Individual retirement plan.*—The term "individual retirement plan" means an individual retirement account described in section 408(a), an individual retirement annuity described in section 408(b), and a retirement bond described in section 409.

(2) *Simplified employee pension.*—The term "simplified employee pension" has the meaning set forth in § 1.408-7(a).

(3) *Compensation.*—The term "compensation" means wages, salaries, professional fees, or other amounts derived from or received for personal service actually rendered (including, but not limited to, commissions paid salesmen, compensation for services on the basis of a percentage of profits, commissions on insurance premiums, tips, and bonuses), but does not include amounts derived from or received as earnings or profits from property (including, but not limited to, interest and dividends) or amounts not includible in gross income such as amounts excluded under section 911. Compensation includes earned income, as defined in section 401(c)(2), reduced by amounts deductible under sections 404 and 405. Compensation does not include amounts received as deferred compensation, including any pension or annuity payment. Compensation does not include unemployment compensation within the meaning of section 85(c).

(4) *Qualified voluntary employee contribution.*—The term "qualified voluntary employee contribution" means any employee contribution which is not a mandatory contribution within the meaning of section 411(c)(2)(C) made by an

individual as an employee under a qualified employer plan or government plan, which plan allows an employee to make such contributions, and which the individual has not designated as a contribution other than a qualified voluntary employee contribution. Thus, if employee contributions are required as a condition of plan participation, they are mandatory contributions within the meaning of section 411(c)(2)(C) and cannot be treated as qualified voluntary employee contributions.

(5) *Qualified retirement contribution.*—The term "qualified retirement contribution" means any amount paid in cash for the taxable year by or on behalf of an individual for his benefit to an individual retirement plan and any qualified voluntary employee contribution paid in cash by the individual for the taxable year.

(6) *Deductible employee contribution.*—The term "deductible employee contribution" means any qualified voluntary employee contribution made after December 31, 1981, in a taxable year beginning after such date and allowable as a deduction under section 219(a) for such taxable year.

(7) *Qualified employer plan.*—The term "qualified employer plan" means—

(i) A plan described in section 401(a) which includes a trust exempt from tax under section 501(a),

(ii) An annuity plan described in section 403(a),

(iii) A qualified bond purchase plan described in section 405(a), and

(iv) A plan under which amounts are contributed by an individual's employer for an annuity contract described in section 403(b).

(8) *Government plan.*—The term "government plan" means any retirement plan, whether or not qualified, established and maintained for its employees by the United States, by a State or political subdivision thereof, or by an agency or instrumentality of any of the foregoing.

(c) *Effective date.*—This section and §§1.219(a)-2 through 1.219(a)-6 are effective for taxable years of individuals beginning after December 31, 1981. [Reg. §1.219(a)-1.]

§1.219(a)-2. Deduction for contributions to individual retirement plans under the Economic Recovery Tax Act of 1981.—(a) *In general.*—Subject to the limitations and restrictions of paragraph (b) and the special rules of paragraph (c)(3) of this section, there shall be allowed a deduction under section 62 from gross income of amounts paid for the taxable year of an individual by or on behalf of such individual to an individual retirement plan. The deduction described in the preceding sentence shall be allowed only to the individual on whose behalf such individual retirement plan is maintained and only in the case of a contribution of cash. No deduction is allowable under this section for a contribution of property other than cash. In the case of a retirement bond, no deduction is allowed if the bond is redeemed within 12 months of its issue date.

(b) *Limitations and restrictions.*—(1) *Maximum deduction.*—The amount allowable as a deduction for contributions to an individual retirement plan to an individual for any taxable year cannot exceed the lesser of—

(i) $2,000, or

(ii) An amount equal to the compensation includible in the individual's gross income for the taxable year,

reduced by the amount of the individual's qualified voluntary employee contributions for the taxable year.

(2) *Contributions after age 70 1/2.*—No deduction is allowable for contributions to an individual retirement plan to an individual for the taxable year of the individual if he has attained the age of 70 1/2 before the close of such taxable year.

(3) *Rollover contributions.*—No deduction is allowable under §1.219(a)-2(a) for any taxable year of an individual with respect to a rollover contribution described in section 402(a)(5), 402(a)(7), 403(a)(4), 403(b)(8), 405(d)(3), 408(d)(3), or 409(b)(3)(C).

(4) *Amounts contributed under endowment contracts.*—(i) For any taxable year, no deduction is allowable under §1.219(a)-2(a) for amounts paid under an endowment contract described in §1.408-3(e) which is allowable under subdivision (ii) of this subparagraph to the cost of life insurance.

(ii) For any taxable year, the cost of current life insurance protection under an endowment contract described in paragraph (b)(4)(i) of this section is the product of the net premium cost, as determined by the Commissioner, and the excess, if any, of the death benefit payable under the contract during the policy year beginning in the taxable year over the cash value of the contract at the end of such policy year.

(c) *Special rules.*—(1) *Separate deduction for each individual.*—The maximum deduction allowable for contributions to an individual retirement plan is computed separately for each individual. Thus, if a husband and wife each has compensation of $15,000 for the taxable year, the maximum amount allowable as a deduction on their joint return is $4,000. See §1.219(a)-3 for the maximum deduction for a spousal individual retirement plan when one spouse has no compensation.

(2) *Community property.*—Section 219 is to be applied without regard to any community property laws. Thus, if, for example, a husband and wife, live in a community property jurisdiction, the husband has compensation of $30,000 for the taxable year, and the wife has no compensation for the taxable year, then the maximum amount allowable as a deduction for contributions to an individual retirement plan, other than a spousal individual retirement plan, is $2,000.

(3) *Employer contributions.*—For purposes of this chapter, any amount paid by an employer to an individual retirement plan of an employee (other than a self-employed individual who is an employee within the meaning of section 401(c)(1)) constitutes the payment of compensation to the employee. The payment is includible in the employee's gross income, whether or not a deduction for such payment is allowable under section 219 to this employee. An employer will be entitled to a deduction for compensation paid to an employee for amounts the employer contributes on the employee's behalf to an individual retirement plan if such deduction is otherwise allowable under section 162. See §1.404(h)-1 for certain limitations on this deduc-

tion in the case of employer contributions to a simplified employee pension.

(4) *Year of inclusion in income.*—Any amount paid by an employer to an individual retirement plan (including an individual retirement account or individual retirement annuity maintained as part of a simplified employee pension arrangement) shall be included in the gross income of the employee for the taxable year for which the contribution was made.

(5) *Time when contributions deemed made.*—A taxpayer shall be deemed to have made a contribution on the last day of the preceding taxable year if the contribution is made on account of the taxable year which includes such last day and is made not later than the time prescribed by law for filing the return for such taxable year (including extensions thereof). A contribution made not later than the time prescribed by law for filing the return for a taxable year (including extensions thereof) shall be treated as made on account of such taxable year if it is irrevocably specified in writing to the trustee, insurance company, or custodian that the amounts contributed are for such taxable year.

(d) *Excess contributions treated as contribution made during subsequent year for which there is an unused limitation.*—(1) *In general.*—This paragraph sets forth rules for the possible deduction of excess contributions made to an individual retirement plan for the taxable years following the taxable year of the excess contribution. If for a taxable year subsequent to the taxable year for which the excess contribution was made, the maximum amount allowable as a deduction for contributions to an individual retirement plan exceeds the amount contributed, then the taxpayer, whether or not a deduction is actually claimed, shall be treated as having made an additional contribution for the taxable year in an amount equal to the lesser of—

(i) The amount of such excess, or

(ii) The amount of the excess contributions for such taxable year (determined under section 4973(b)(2) without regard to subparagraph (C) thereof).

(2) *Amount contributed.*—For purposes of this paragraph, the amount contributed—

(i) Shall be determined without regard to this paragraph, and

(ii) Shall not include any rollover contribution.

(3) *Special rule where excess deduction was allowed for closed year.*—Proper reduction shall be made in the amount allowable as a deduction by reason of this paragraph for any amount allowed as a deduction for contributions to an individual retirement plan for a prior taxable year for which the period for assessing a deficiency has expired if the amount so allowed exceeds the amount which should have been allowed for such prior taxable year.

(4) *Excise tax consequences.*—See section 4973 and the regulations thereunder for the excise tax applicable to excess contributions made to individual retirement plans.

(5) *Examples.*—The provisions of this paragraph may be illustrated by the following examples. (Assume in each example, unless otherwise stated, that T is less than age $70^1/2$ and is not married.)

Example (1). (i) T, a calendar-year taxpayer, earns $1,500 in compensation includible in gross income for 1982. On December 1, 1982, T establishes an individual retirement account (IRA) and contributes $2,000 to the account. T does not withdraw any money from the IRA after the initial contribution. Under section 219(b)(1), the maximum amount that T can deduct for 1982 is $1,500. T has an excess contribution for 1982 of $500.

(ii) For 1983, T has compensation includible in gross income of $12,000. T makes a $1,000 contribution to his IRA for 1983.

(iii) Although T made only a $1,000 contribution to his IRA for 1983, under the rules contained in this paragraph, T is treated as having made an additional contribution of $500 for 1983 and will be allowed to deduct $1,500 as his 1983 IRA contribution.

Example (2). (i) For 1982, the facts are the same as in *Example (1).*

(ii) For 1983, T has compensation includible in gross income of $12,000. T makes a $2,000 contribution to his IRA for 1983.

(iii) T will be allowed a $2,000 deduction for 1983 (the amount of his contribution). T will not be allowed a deduction for the $500 excess contribution made in 1982 because the maximum amount allowable for 1983 does not exceed the amount contributed.

Example (3). (i) For 1982, the facts are the same as in *Example (1).*

(ii) For 1983, T has compensation includible in gross income of $12,000. T makes a $1,800 contribution to his IRA for 1983.

(iii) For 1983, T will be allowed to deduct his contribution of $1,800 and $200 of the excess contribution made for 1982. He will not be allowed to deduct the remaining $300 of the excess contribution made for 1982 because his deduction for 1983 would then exceed $2,000, his allowable deduction for 1983.

(iv) For 1984, T has compensation includible in gross income of $15,000. T makes a $1,300 contribution to his IRA for 1984.

(v) T will be allowed to deduct both his $1,300 contribution for 1984 and the remaining $300 contribution made for 1982.

Example (4). (i) For 1982, the facts are the same as in *Example (1).*

(ii) For 1983, T has compensation includible in gross income of $12,000. T makes a $1,000 contribution to his IRA for 1983. T is allowed to deduct the $500 excess contribution for 1983 but fails to do so on his return. Consequently, T deducts only $1,000 for 1983.

(iii) Under no circumstances will T be allowed to deduct the $500 excess contribution made for 1982 for any taxable year after 1983 because T is treated as having made the contribution for 1983.

Example (5). (i) For 1982, the facts are the same as in *Example (1).*

(ii) For 1983, T has no compensation includible in gross income.

(iii) T will not be allowed to deduct for 1983 the $500 excess contribution for 1982 because the maximum amount allowable as a deduction under section 219(b)(1) is $0. [Reg. § 1.219(a)-2.]

§ 1.219(a)-3. Deduction for retirement savings for certain married individuals.—(a) *In general.*—Subject to the limitations and restrictions of paragraphs (c) and (d) and the special rules of paragraph (e) of this section, there shall be allowed a deduction under section 62 from gross income of amounts paid for the taxable year of an individual by or on behalf of such individual for the benefit of his spouse to an individual retirement plan. The amounts contributed to an individual retirement plan by or on behalf of an individual for the benefit of his spouse shall be deductible only by such individual and only in the case of a contribution of cash. No deduction is allowable under this section for a contribution of property other than cash. In the case of an individual retirement bond, no deduction is allowed if the bond is redeemed within 12 months of its issue date.

(b) *Definition of compensation.*—For purposes of this section, the term "compensation" has the meaning set forth in § 1.219(a)-1(b)(3).

(c) *Maximum deduction.*—The amount allowable as a deduction under this section to an individual for any taxable year may not exceed the smallest of—

(1) $2,000,

(2) An amount equal to the compensation includible in the individual's gross income for the taxable year less the amount allowed as a deduction under section 219(a) (determined without regard to contributions to a simplified employee pension allowed under section 219(b)(2)), § 1.219(a)-2 and § 1.219(a)-5 for the taxable year, or

(3) $2,250 less the amount allowed as a deduction under section 219(a) (determined without regard to contributions to a simplified employee pension allowed under section 219(b)(2)), § 1.219(a)-2 and § 1.219(a)-5 for the taxable year.

(d) *Limitations and restrictions.*—(1) *Requirement to file joint return.*—No deduction is allowable under this section for a taxable year unless the individual and his spouse file a joint return under section 6013 for the taxable year.

(2) *Employed spouses.*—No deduction is allowable under this section if the spouse of the individual has any compensation for the taxable year of such spouse ending with or within the taxable year of the individual. For purposes of this subparagraph, compensation has the meaning set forth in § 1.219(a)-1(b)(3), except that compensation shall include amounts excluded under section 911.

(3) *Contributions after age 70 1/2.*—No deduction is allowable under this section with respect to any payment which is made for a taxable year of an individual if the individual for whose benefit the individual retirement plan is maintained has attained age 70 1/2 before the close of such taxable year.

(4) *Recontributed amounts.*—No deduction is allowable under this section for any taxable year of an individual with respect to a rollover contribution described in section 402(a)(5), 402(a)(7), 403(a)(4), 403(b)(8), 405(d)(3), 408(d)(3), or 409(b)(3)(C).

(5) *Amounts contributed under endowment contracts.*—The rules for endowment contracts under this section are the same as the provisions for such contracts under § 1.219(a)-2(b)(4).

(e) *Special rules.*—(1) *Community property.*—This section is to be applied without regard to any community property laws.

(2) *Time when contributions deemed made.*—The time when contributions are deemed made is determined under section 219(f)(3). See § 1.219(a)-2(c)(5). [Reg. § 1.219(a)-3.]

§ 1.219(a)-4. Deduction for contributions to simplified employee pensions.—(a) *General rule.*—(1) *In general.*—Under section 219(b)(2), if an employer contribution is made on behalf of an employee to a simplified employee pension described in section 408(k), the limitations of this section, and not section 219(b)(1) and § 1.219(a)-2, shall apply for purposes of computing the maximum allowable deduction with respect to that contribution for that individual employee.

(2) *Employer limitation.*—The maximum deduction under section 219(b)(2) for an employee with respect to an employer contribution to the employee's simplified employee pension under that employer's arrangement cannot exceed an amount equal to the lesser of—

(i) 15 percent of the employee's compensation from that employer (determined without regard to the employer contribution to the simplified employee pension) includible in the employee's gross income for the taxable year, or

(ii) The amount contributed by that employer to the employee's simplified employee pension and included in gross income (but not in excess of $15,000).

(3) *Special rules.*—(i) *Compensation.*—Compensation referred to in paragraph (a)(2)(i) has the same meaning as under § 1.219(a)-1(b)(3) except that it includes only the compensation from the employer making the contribution to the simplified employee pension. Thus, if an individual earns $50,000 from employer A and $20,000 from employer B and employer B contributes $4,000 to a simplified employee pension on behalf of the individual, the maximum amount the individual will be able to deduct under section 219(b)(2) is 15 percent of $20,000, or $3,000.

(ii) *Special rule for officers, shareholders, and owner-employees.*—In the case of an employee who is an officer, shareholder, or owner-employee described in section 408(k)(3) with respect to a particular employer, the $15,000 amount referred to in paragraph (a)(2)(ii) shall be reduced by the amount of tax taken into account with respect to such individual under section 408(k)(3)(D).

(iii) *More than one employer arrangement.*—Except as provided in paragraph (c), below, the maximum deduction under paragraph (a)(2) for an individual who receives simplified employee pension contributions under two or more employers' simplified employee pension arrangements cannot exceed the sum of the maximum deduction limitations computed separately for that individual under each such employer's arrangement.

(iv) *Section 408 rules.*—Under section 408(j), the limitations under section 408(a)(1) and (b)(2)(B) (§ 1.408-2(b)(1) and § 1.408-3(b)(2)), shall be applied separately with respect to each employer's contributions to an individual's simplified employee pension.

(4) *Additional deduction for individual retirement plan and qualified voluntary employee contribution.*—The deduction under this paragraph is in addition to any deduction allowed under section

219(a) to the individual for qualified retirement contributions.

(b) *Contributions to simplified employee pensions after age 70 1/2.*—The denial of deductions for contributions after age 70 1/2 contained in section 219(d)(1) and § 1.219(a)-2(b)(2) shall not apply with respect to employer contributions to a simplified employee pension.

(c) *Multiple employer, etc. limitations.*—(1) *Section 414(b), (c) and (m) employers.*—In the case of a controlled group of employers within the meaning of section 414(b) or (c) or employers aggregated under section 414(m), the maximum deduction limitation for an employee under paragraph (a)(2) shall be computed by treating such employers as one employer maintaining a single simplified employee pension arrangement and by treating the compensation of that employee from such employers as if from one employer. Thus, for example, for a particular employee the 15 percent limitation on compensation would be determined with regard to the compensation from all employers within such group. Further, the maximum deduction with respect to contributions made by employers included within such group could not exceed $15,000.

(2) *Self-employed individuals.*—In the case of an employee who is a self-employed individual within the meaning of section 401(c)(1) with respect to more than one trade or business, the maximum deduction limitation for such an employee under paragraph (a)(2) shall not exceed the lesser of the sum of such limitation applied separately with respect to the simplified employee pension arrangement of each trade or business or such limitation determined by treating such trades or businesses as if they constituted a single employer.

(d) *Examples.*—The provisions of this section may be illustrated by the following examples:

Example (1). Corporation X is a calendar-year, cash basis taxpayer. It adopts a simplified employee pension agreement in 1982 and wishes to contribute the maximum amount on behalf of each employee for 1982. Individual E is a calendar-year taxpayer who is employed solely by Corporation X in 1982. Beginning in June, 1982, Corporation X pays $100 each month into a simplified employee pension maintained on behalf of E. X makes a total payment to E's simplified employee pension during the year of $700. E's other compensation from X for the year totals $15,000. The maximum amount which E will be allowed to deduct as a simplified employee pension contribution is 15% of $15,000, or $2,250. Therefore, X may make an additional contribution for 1982 to E's simplified employee pension in February of 1983. E's total compensation includible in gross income for 1982 is $15,000 + $2,250 or $17,250.

Example (2). (i) Corporation G is a calendar-year taxpayer which adopts a simplified employee pension agreement for 1982. It does not maintain an integrated plan as defined in section 408(k)(3)(E). It wishes to contribute 15% of compensation on behalf of each employee reduced by its tax under section 3111(a). The corporation has 4 employees, A, B, C, and D. D is a shareholder. The compensation for these employees for 1982 is as follows:

A = $10,000

B = 20,000

C = 30,000

D = 120,000

(ii) The amount of money which the corporation will be allowed to contribute on behalf of each employee under this allocation formula and the amount of the employer contribution each employee will be allowed to deduct is set forth in the following table:

Employee	Compensation	Lesser of $15,000 or 15% of Comp.	3111(a)[1] Tax	SEP Contribution[2]	Sec. 219(b)(2) deduction
A	$10,000	$1,500	$540.00	$960.00	$960.00
B	20,000	3,000	1,080.00	1,920.00	1,920.00
C	30,000	4,500	1,620.00	2,880.00	2,880.00
D	120,000	15,000	1,749.60	13,250.40	13,250.40

[1] The section 3111(a) tax is computed by multiplying compensation up to the taxable wage base ($32,400 for 1982) by the tax rate (5.40% for 1982).

[2] Simplified Employee Pension.

Example (3). Corporations A and B are calendar year taxpayers. Corporations A and B are not aggregated employers under section 414(b), (c) or (m). Individual M is employed full-time by Corporation A and part-time by Corporation B. Corporation A adopts a simplified employee pension agreement for calendar year 1982 and agrees to contribute 15% of compensation for each participant. M is a participant under Corporation A's simplified employee pension agreement and earns $15,000 for 1982 from Corporation A before A's contribution to his simplified employee pension. M also earns $5,000 as a part-time employee of Corporation B for 1982. Corporation A contributes $2,500 to M's simplified employee pension. The maximum amount that M will be allowed to deduct under section 219(b)(2) for 1982 is 15% of $15,000 or $2,250. In addition, M would be allowed to deduct the remaining $250 under section 219(a) for qualified retirement contributions.

Example (4). Individual P is employed by Corporation H and Corporation O. Corporations H and O are not aggregated employers under section 414(b), (c) or (m). Both Corporation H and Corporation O maintain a simplified employee pension arrangement and contribute 15 percent of compensation on behalf of each employee, up to a maximum of 5,000. P earns $100,000 from Corporation H and $120,000 from Corporation O. Corporation H and O each contribute $15,000 under its simplified employee pension arrangement to an individual retirement account maintained on behalf of P. P will be allowed to deduct $30,000 for employer contributions to simplified employee pensions because each employer has a simplified employee pension arrangement and the SEP contributions by Corporation H and O do not exceed the applicable $15,000-15 percent limitation with respect to compensation received from each employer. In addition, P would be allowed to deduct $2,000 under section 219(a) for qualified retirement contributions. [Reg. §1.219(a)-4.]

§1.219(a)-5. Deduction for employee contributions to employer plans.—(a) *Deduction allowed.*—In the case of an individual, there is allowed as a deduction amounts contributed in cash to a qualified employer plan or government plan (as defined, respectively, in paragraphs (b)(7) and (b)(8) of §1.219(a)-1) and designated as qualified voluntary employee contributions. If an employee transfers an amount of cash from one account in a plan to the qualified voluntary employee contribution account, such transfer is a distribution for purposes of sections 72, 402 and 403, and the amounts are considered recontributed as qualified voluntary employee contributions. No deduction will be allowed for a contribution of property other than cash.

(b) *Limitations.*—(1) *Maximum amount of deduction.*—The amount allowable as a deduction under paragraph (a) to any individual for any taxable year shall not exceed the lesser of $2,000 or an amount equal to the compensation (from the employer who maintains the plan) includible in the individual's gross income for such taxable year.

(2) *Contributions after age 70 ½.*—No deduction is allowable for contributions under paragraph (a) to an individual for the taxable year of the individual if he has attained the age of 70½ before the close of such taxable year.

(3) *Rollover contributions.*—No deduction is allowable under paragraph (a) for any taxable year of an individual with respect to a rollover contribution described in section 402(a)(5), 402(a)(7), 403(a)(4), 403(b)(8), 405(d)(3), 408(d)(3), or 409(b)(3)(C).

(c) *Rules for plans accepting qualified voluntary employee contributions.*—(1) *Plan provision, etc.*—(i) No plan may receive qualified voluntary employee contributions unless the plan document provides for acceptance of voluntary contributions. No plan may receive qualified voluntary employee contributions unless either the plan document provides for acceptance of qualified voluntary employee contributions or the employer or the plan administrator manifests an intent to accept such contributions. Such intention must be communicated to the employees. Any manner of communication that satisfies §1.7476-2(c)(1) shall satisfy the requirements of this subparagraph.

(ii) If the plan document provides for the acceptance of voluntary contributions, but does not specifically provide for acceptance of qualified voluntary employee contributions, the plan qualification limitation on voluntary contributions (the limit of 10 percent of the employee's cumulative compensation less prior voluntary contributions) would apply to both qualified voluntary employee contributions and other voluntary contributions. On the other hand, if the plan document provides for acceptance of both qualified voluntary employee contributions and other voluntary contributions, the plan qualification limitation on voluntary contributions would apply only to the contributions other than the qualified voluntary employee contributions.

(2) *Plans accepting only qualified voluntary employee contributions.*—A qualified pension plan or stock bonus plan may be established that provides only for qualified voluntary employee contributions. Similarly, a government plan may be established that provides only for qualified voluntary employee contributions. A plan that provides only for qualified voluntary employee contributions would not satisfy the qualification requirements for a profit-sharing plan.

(3) *Recordkeeping provisions.*—Separate accounting for qualified voluntary employee contributions that are deductible under this section is not required as a condition for receiving qualified voluntary employee contributions. However, failure to properly account for such contributions may result in adverse tax consequences to employees upon subsequent plan distributions and reporting and recordkeeping penalties for employers. See section 72(o) for rules for accounting for such contributions.

(4) *Status as employee.*—An amount will not be considered as a qualified voluntary employee contribution on behalf of an individual unless the individual is an employee of the employer at some time during the calendar year for which the voluntary contribution is made. See section 415(c) concerning the effect of a nondeductible voluntary employee contribution on plan qualification.

(5) *Contribution before receipt of compensation.*—A plan may allow an individual to make a qualified voluntary employee contribution greater than the amount he has received in compensation from the employer at the time the contribution is made. However, see paragraph (f) of this section.

(d) *Designations, procedures, etc.*—(1) *Plan procedures.*—(i) A plan which accepts qualified voluntary employee contributions may adopt procedures by which an employee can designate the character of the employee's voluntary contributions as either qualified voluntary employee contributions or other employee contributions. Such procedures may, but need not, be in the plan document.

(ii) In the absence of such plan procedures, all voluntary employee contributions shall be deemed to be qualified voluntary employee contributions unless the employee notifies the employer that the contributions are not qualified voluntary employee contributions. Such notification must be received by April 15 following the calendar year for which such contributions were made. If such notification is not received, contributions are deemed to be qualified voluntary employee contributions for the prior year.

(2) *Characterization procedures, etc.*—(i) The plan procedures may allow an employee to elect whether or not an employee contribution is to be treated as a qualified voluntary employee contribution or as other voluntary contributions. This election can be required either prior to or after the contribution is made. If a contribution may be treated under such procedures as a qualified voluntary employee contribution or other voluntary contribution for a calendar year and the employee has not by April 15 of the subsequent calendar year designated the character of the contribution, the contribution must be treated as a qualified voluntary

employee contribution for the calendar year. An employer may allow the election to be irrevocable or revocable. A procedure allowing revocable elections may limit the time within which an election may be revoked. The revocation of an election after April 15 following the calendar year for which the contribution was made is deemed to be ineffective in changing the character of employee contributions.

(ii) For purposes of this section, if the plan procedures allow employees to make contributions on account of the immediately preceding calendar year, a taxpayer shall be deemed to have made a qualified voluntary employee contribution to such plan on the last day of the preceding calendar year if the contribution is on account of such year and is made by April 15 of the calendar year or such earlier time as provided by the plan procedure.

(e) *Nondiscrimination requirements.*—(1) *General rule.*—Plans subject to the nondiscrimination requirements of section 401(a)(4) which accept qualified voluntary employee contributions must permit such contributions in a nondiscriminatory manner in order to satisfy section 401(a)(4). If a plan permits participants to make qualified voluntary employee contributions, the opportunity to make such contributions must be reasonably available to a nondiscriminatory group of employees. The availability standard will be satisfied if a nondiscriminatory group of employees is eligible to make qualified voluntary employee contributions under the terms of the plan and if a nondiscriminatory group of employees actually has the opportunity to make qualified voluntary employee contributions when plan restrictions are taken into account.

(2) *Eligible employees.*—A nondiscriminatory group of employees is eligible to make qualified voluntary employee contribution under the terms of the plan if the group either meets the percentage requirements of section 410(b)(1)(A) or comprises a classification of employees that does not discriminate in favor of employees who are officers, shareholders, or highly compensated, as provided in section 410(b)(1)(B).

(3) *Plan restrictions.*—In some cases, an employee may not be permitted to make qualified voluntary employee contributions until a plan restriction (such as making a certain level of mandatory employee contributions) is satisfied. In this case, it is necessary to determine whether a nondiscriminatory group of employees actually has the opportunity to make qualified voluntary employee contributions. For this purpose, only employees who have satisfied the plan restriction will be considered to have the opportunity to make deductible contributions. Thus, for example, if a plan requires an employee to make mandatory contributions of 6 percent of compensation in order to make qualified voluntary employee contributions and if only a small percentage of employees make the 6 percent mandatory contributions, then the group of employees who have the opportunity to make qualified voluntary employee contributions may not satisfy either test under section 410(b). A similar rule is applicable to integrated plans: employees who are not permitted to make qualified voluntary employee contributions to such a plan because they earn less than the integration level amount will be considered as employees who do not have the opportunity to make qualified voluntary employee contributions.

(4) *Permissible contributions.*—If the availability standards are met, and if the qualified voluntary employee contributions permitted are not higher, as a percentage of compensation, for officers, shareholders or highly compensated employees than for other participants, the qualified voluntary employee contribution feature will meet the requirement that contributions or benefits not discriminate in favor of employees who are officers, shareholders, or highly compensated. This is so because the contributions are made by the employee, not the employer.

(5) *Acceptable contributions.*—A plan may accept qualified voluntary employee contributions in an amount less than the maximum deduction allowable to an individual.

(f) *Excess qualified voluntary employee contributions.*—Voluntary employee contributions which exceed the amount allowable as a deduction under paragraph (b) of this section will be treated as nondeductible voluntary employee contributions to the plan. See § 1.415-6(b)(8).

(g) *Reports.*—(1) *Requirements.*—Each employer who maintains a plan which accepts qualified voluntary employee contributions must furnish to each employee—

(i) A report showing the amount of qualified voluntary employee contributions the employee made for the calendar year, and

(ii) A report showing the amount of withdrawals made by the employee of qualified voluntary employee contributions during the calendar year.

(2) *Times.*—(i) The report required by paragraph (g)(1)(i) of this section must be furnished by the later of January 31 following the year for which the contribution was made or the time the contribution is made.

(ii) The report required by paragraph (g)(1)(ii) of this section must be furnished by January 31 following the year of withdrawal.

(3) *Authority for additional reports.*—The Commissioner may require additional reports to be given to individuals or to be filed with the Service. Such reports shall be furnished at the time and in the manner that the Commissioner specifies.

(4) *Authority to modify reporting requirements.*—The Commissioner may, in his discretion, modify the reporting requirements of this paragraph. Such modification may include: the matters to be reported, the forms to be used for the reports, the time when the reports must be filed or furnished, who must receive the reports, the substitution of the plan administrator for the employer as the person required to file or furnish the reports, and the deletion of some or all of the reporting requirements. The Commissioner may, in his discretion, relieve employers from making the reports required by section 219(f)(4) and this paragraph (g). This discretion includes the ability to relieve categories of employers (but not individual employers) from furnishing or filing any report required by section 219(f)(4) and this paragraph (g).

(5) *Effective date.*—This paragraph shall apply to reports for calendar years after 1982. [Reg. § 1.219(a)-5.]

§ 1.219(a)-6. Alternative deduction for divorced individuals.—(a) *In general.*—a divorced individual may use the provisions of this section rather than § 1.219(a)-2 in computing the maximum amount he may deduct as a contribution to an individual retirement plan. A divorced individual is not required to use the provisions of this section; he may use the provisions of § 1.219(a)-2 in computing the maximum amount he may deduct as a contribution to an individual retirement plan.

(b) *Individuals who may use this section.*—An individual may compute the deduction for a contribution to an individual retirement plan under this section if—

(1) An individual retirement plan was established for the benefit of the individual at least five years before the beginning of the calendar year in which the decree of divorce or spearate maintenance was issued, and

(2) For at least three of the former spouse's most recent five taxable years ending before the taxable year in which the decree was issued, such former spouse was allowed a deduction under section 219(c) (or the corresponding provisions of prior law) for contributions to such individual retirement plan.

(c) *Limitations.*—(1) *Amount of deduction.*—An individual who computes his deduction for contributions to an individual retirement plan under this section may deduct the smallest of—

(i) The amount contributed to the individual retirement plan for the taxable year,

(ii) $1,125, or

(iii) The sum of the amount of compensation includible in the individual's gross income for the taxable year and any qualifying alimony received by the individual during the taxable year.

(2) *Contributions after age 70 1/2.*—No deduction is allowable for contributions to an individual retirement plan to an individual for the taxable year of the individual if he has attained the age of 70 1/2 before the close of such taxable year.

(3) *Rollover contributions.*—No deduction is allowable under this section for any taxable year of an individual with respect to a rollover contribution described in section 402(a)(5), 402(a)(7), 403(a)(4), 403(b)(8), 405(d)(3), 408(d)(3), or 409(b)(3)(C).

(d) *Qualifying alimony.*—For purposes of this section, the term "qualifying alimony" means amounts includible in the individual's gross income under section 71(a)(1) (relating to a decree of divorce or separate maintenance). [Reg. § 1.219(a)-6.]

* * *

IRAs: SEPs: Married Individuals

Individual Retirement Plans: Simplified Employee Pensions.—Reproduced below is the text of proposed Reg. § 1.220-1, relating to individual retirement plans and simplified employee pensions (published in the Federal Register on July 14, 1981).

§ 1.220-1. Deduction for retirement savings for certain married individuals.—(a) *In general.*—Subject to the limitations and restrictions of paragraphs (c), (d) and (e) and the special rules of paragraph (f) of this section, there shall be allowed a deduction under section 62 from gross income of amounts paid for the taxable year of an individual by or on behalf of such individual for the benefit of himself and his spouse to an individual retirement account described in section 408(a), for an individual retirement annuity described in section 408(b), or for an individual retirement bond described in section 409. The amounts contributed to an individual retirement account, for an individual retirement annuity, or for an individual retirement bond by or on behalf of an individual for the benefit of himself and his spouse shall be deductible only by such individual. The first sentence of this paragraph shall apply only in the case of a contribution of cash; a contribution of property other than cash is not allowable as a deduction. In the case of an individual retirement bond, a deduction will not be allowed if the bond is redeemed within 12 months of its issue date.

(b) *Definitions.*—(1) *Compensation.*—For purposes of this section, the term "compensation" has the meaning set forth in § 1.219-1(c)(1).

(2) *Active participant.*—For purposes of this section, the term "active participant" has the meaning set forth in § 1.219-2.

(3) *Individual retirement subaccount.*—For purposes of this section, the term individual retirement subaccount is that part of an individual retirement account maintained for the exclusive benefit of the individual or the individual's spouse and which meets the following requirements:

(i) The individual or spouse for whom the subaccount is maintained has exclusive control over the subaccount after deposits have been made,

(ii) The subaccount, by itself, meets the requirements of section 408(a), except that it is not a separate trust,

(iii) The trustee or custodian maintains records indicating the ownership of the funds, and

(iv) The individual and spouse do not jointly own the individual retirement account of which the subaccount is a part.

(c) *Types of funding arrangements permitted.*—The deduction under paragraph (a) of this section shall be allowed only if one of the following types of funding arrangements is used:

(1) A separate individual retirement account, individual retirement annuity, or individual retirement bond is established or purchased for the benefit of the individual and a separate individual retirement account, individual retirement annuity or individual retirement bond is established or purchased for the individual's spouse.

(2) A single individual retirement account described in section 408 (a) is established or purchased and such account has an individual retirement subaccount for the benefit of the individual and an individual retirement subaccount for the benefit of the spouse. The single individual retirement account cannot be owned jointly by the husband and wife.

(3) An individual retirement account described in section 408(c) is maintained by an

employer or employee association and such account has arrangements described in subparagraphs (1) or (2).

(d) *Maximum deduction.*—The amount allowable as a deduction under section 220(a) to an individual for any taxable year may not exceed—

(1) Twice the amount paid (including prior excess contributions) to the account, subaccount, annuity, or for the bond, established for the individual or for the spouse to or for which the lesser amount was paid for the taxable year,

(2) An amount equal to 15 percent of the compensation includible in the individual's gross income for the taxable year, or

(3) $1,750 whichever is the smallest amount.

(e) *Limitations and restrictions.*—(1) *Alternative deduction.*—No deduction is allowable under section 220(a) for the taxable year if the individual claims the deduction allowed by section 219(a) for the taxable year.

(2) *Individual or spouse covered by certain other plans.*—No deduction is allowable under section 220(a) to an individual for the taxable year if for any part of such year—

(i) He or his spouse was an active participant (as defined in § 1.219-2), or

(ii) Amounts were contributed by his employer, or his spouse's employer, on the individual's or spouse's behalf for an annuity contract described in section 403(b) (whether or not his, or his spouse's, rights in such contract are nonforfeitable).

(3) *Contributions after age 70 1/2.*—No deduction is allowable under section 220(a) with respect to any payment which is made for a taxable year of an individual if either the individual or his spouse has attained age 70 1/2 before the close of such taxable year.

(4) *Recontributed amounts.*—No deduction is allowable under section 220(a) for any taxable year of an individual with respect to a rollover contribution described in section 402(a)(5), 402(a)(7), 403(a)(4), 403(b)(8), 408(d)(3), or 409(b)(3)(C).

(5) *Amounts contributed under endowment contracts.*—The rules for endowment contracts under section 220 are the same as the provisions for such contracts under § 1.219-1(b)(3).

(6) *Employed spouses.*—No deduction is allowable under section 220(a) if the spouse of the individual has any compensation (as defined in § 1.219-1(c)(1) determined without regard to section 911) for the taxable year of such spouse ending with or within the taxable year of the individual.

(f) *Special rules.*—(1) *Community property.*—Section 220 is to be applied without regard to any community property laws.

(2) *Time when contributions deemed made.*—The time when contributions are deemed made is determined in the same manner as under section 219(c)(3). See § 1.219-1(d).

(g) *Excess contributions treated as contribution made during subsequent year for which there is an unused limitation.*—(1) *In general.*—If for the taxable year the maximum amount allowable as a deduction under this section exceeds the amount contributed, then the taxpayer, whether or not a deduction is actually claimed, shall be treated as having made an additional contribution for the taxable year in an amount equal to the lesser of—

(i) The amount of such excess, or

(ii) The amount of the excess contributions for such taxable year (determined under section 4973(b)(2) without regard to subparagraph (C) thereof).

For purposes of computing the maximum deduction under section 220(b)(1), the excess contribution for a previous year shall be treated as made for the current year.

(2) *Amount contributed.*—For purposes of this paragraph, the amount contributed—

(i) Shall be determined without regard to this paragraph, and

(ii) Shall not include any rollover contribution.

(3) *Special rule where excess contribution was allowed for closed year.*—Proper reduction shall be made in the amount allowable as a deduction by reason of this paragraph for any amount allowed as a deduction under this section or section 219 for a prior taxable year for which the period for assessing a deficiency has expired if the amount so allowed exceeds the amount which should have been allowed for such prior taxable year.

(4) *Examples.*—The provisions of this paragraph may be illustrated by the following examples:

Example (1). (i) H, a calendar-year taxpayer, earns $10,000 in compensation includible in gross income for 1979. H is married to W, also a calendar-year taxpayer, who has no compensation for 1979. For 1979, neither H nor W is covered by certain other plans within the meaning of section 220(b)(3). On November 24, 1979, H establishes an individual retirement account (IRA) for himself and an individual retirement account for W. H contributes $850 to each account. Neither H nor W withdraws any money from either account after the initial contribution. Under section 220(b)(1) the maximum amount that H can deduct for 1979 is 15 percent of the compensation includible in his gross income or $1,500. H has made an excess contribution of $200 for 1979.

(ii) For 1980, H has compensation includible in gross income of $12,000. W has no compensation for 1980. For 1980, neither H nor W is covered by certain other plans within the meaning of section 220(b)(3). No contributions are made to the IRA of H or W for 1980.

(iii) Although H made no contributions to either his or W's IRA for 1980, under the rules contained in this paragraph, H is treated as having made an additional contribution of $100 to his IRA and $100 to W's IRA for 1980 and will be allowed to deduct $200 as his 1980 IRA contribution.

Example (2). (i) For 1979, the facts are the same as in *Example (1).*

(ii) For 1980, H has compensation of $15,000 includible in gross income and is not covered by any other plans within the meaning of section 219(b)(2). W also goes to work in 1980 and has compensation of $6,000, but is not covered by certain other plans within the meaning of section 219(b)(2). H will not be treated as having made a deductible contribution of a previous year's excess contribution within the meaning of section 220(c)(6) because W has compensation for 1980. However, both H and W now meet the deduction standards of section 219 and each will be treated as having made a deductible contribution of $100 to their separate IRA's for 1980 under section 219(c)(5).

Example (3). (i) For 1979, the facts are the same as in *Example (1).*

(ii) For 1980, H has compensation of $15,000 includible in gross income and is covered by certain other plans within the meaning of section 220(b)(3). W has no compensation for 1980 and is not covered by certain other plans within the meaning of section 220(b)(3). H will not be treated as having made a deductible contribution of a previous year's excess contribution within the meaning of section 219(c)(5) or 220(c)(6) because H is covered by other plans for 1980 and has no allowable deduction under section 219 or 220.

(iii) W will not be treated as having made a deductible contribution of a previous year's excess contribution within the meaning of section 219(c)(5) because W has no compensation for 1980 and thus no allowable deduction under section 219.

(h) *Effective date.*—(1) This section is effective for taxable years beginning after December 31, 1976.

(2) If, but for this subparagraph, an amount would be allowable as a deduction by reason of section 220(c)(6) and paragraph (g) for a taxable year beginning before January 1, 1978, such amount shall be allowable only for the taxpayer's first taxable year beginning in 1978. [Reg. § 1.220-1]

Hybrid Arrangements: Rules

Hybrid Arrangements: Rules.—Reg. § 1.245A(e)-1, implementing sections 245A(e) and 267A of the Internal Revenue Code regarding hybrid dividends and certain amounts paid or accrued in hybrid transactions or with hybrid entities, is proposed (published in the Federal Register on December 28, 2018) (REG-104352-18).

Par. 2. Section 1.245A(e)-1 is added to read as follows:

§ 1.245A(e)-1. Special rules for hybrid dividends.—(a) *Overview.*—This section provides rules for hybrid dividends. Paragraph (b) of this section disallows the deduction under section 245A(a) for a hybrid dividend received by a United States shareholder from a CFC. Paragraph (c) of this section provides a rule for hybrid dividends of tiered corporations. Paragraph (d) of this section sets forth rules regarding a hybrid deduction account. Paragraph (e) of this section provides an anti-avoidance rule. Paragraph (f) of this section provides definitions. Paragraph (g) of this section illustrates the application of the rules of this section through examples. Paragraph (h) of this section provides the applicability date.

(b) *Hybrid dividends received by United States shareholders.*—(1) *In general.*—If a United States shareholder receives a hybrid dividend, then—

(i) The United States shareholder is not allowed a deduction under section 245A(a) for the hybrid dividend; and

(ii) The rules of section 245A(d) (disallowance of foreign tax credits and deductions) apply to the hybrid dividend.

(2) *Definition of hybrid dividend.*—The term *hybrid dividend* means an amount received by a United States shareholder from a CFC for which but for section 245A(e) and this section the United States shareholder would be allowed a deduction under section 245A(a), to the extent of the sum of the United States shareholder's hybrid deduction accounts (as described in paragraph (d) of this section) with respect to each share of stock of the CFC, determined at the close of the CFC's taxable year (or in accordance with paragraph (d)(5) of this section, as applicable). No other amount received by a United States shareholder from a CFC is a hybrid dividend for purposes of section 245A.

(3) *Special rule for certain dividends attributable to earnings of lower-tier foreign corporations.*—This paragraph (b)(3) applies if a domestic corporation sells or exchanges stock of a foreign corporation and, pursuant to section 1248, the gain recognized on the sale or exchange is included in gross income as a dividend. In such a case, for purposes of this section—

(i) To the extent that earnings and profits of a lower-tier CFC gave rise to the dividend under section 1248(c)(2), those earnings and profits are treated as distributed as a dividend by the lower-tier CFC directly to the domestic corporation under the principles of § 1.1248-1(d); and

(ii) To the extent the domestic corporation indirectly owns (within the meaning of section 958(a)(2)) shares of stock of the lower-tier CFC, the hybrid deduction accounts with respect to those shares are treated as hybrid deduction accounts of the domestic corporation. Thus, for example, if a domestic corporation sells or exchanges all the stock of an upper-tier CFC and under this paragraph (b)(3) there is considered to be a dividend paid directly by the lower-tier CFC to the domestic corporation, then the dividend is generally a hybrid dividend to the extent of the sum of the upper-tier CFC's hybrid deduction accounts with respect to stock of the lower-tier CFC.

(4) *Ordering rule.*—Amounts received by a United States shareholder from a CFC are subject to the rules of section 245A(e) and this section based on the order in which they are received. Thus, for example, if on different days during a CFC's taxable year a United States shareholder receives dividends from the CFC, then the rules of section 245A(e) and this section apply first to the dividend received on the earliest date (based on the sum of the United States shareholder's hybrid deduction accounts with respect to each share of stock of the CFC), and then to the dividend received on the next earliest date (based on the remaining sum).

(c) *Hybrid dividends of tiered corporations.*—(1) *In general.*—If a CFC (the *receiving CFC*) receives a tiered hybrid dividend from another CFC, and a domestic corporation is a United States shareholder with respect to both CFCs, then, notwithstanding any other provision of the Code—

(i) The tiered hybrid dividend is treated for purposes of section 951(a)(1)(A) as subpart F income of the receiving CFC for the taxable year of the CFC in which the tiered hybrid dividend is received;

(ii) The United States shareholder must include in gross income an amount equal to its pro rata share (determined in the same manner as under section 951(a)(2)) of the subpart F income described in paragraph (c)(1)(i) of this section; and

(iii) The rules of section 245A(d) (disallowance of foreign tax credit, including for taxes that would have been deemed paid under section 960(a) or (b), and deductions) apply to the amount included under paragraph (c)(1)(ii) of this section in the United States shareholder's gross income.

(2) *Definition of tiered hybrid dividend.*—The term *tiered hybrid dividend* means an amount received by a receiving CFC from another CFC to the extent that the amount would be a hybrid dividend under paragraph (b)(2) of this section if, for purposes of section 245A and the regulations under section 245A as contained in 26 CFR part 1 (except for section 245A(e)(2) and this paragraph (c)), the receiving CFC were a domestic corporation. A tiered hybrid dividend does not include an amount described in section 959(b). No other amount received by a receiving CFC from another CFC is a tiered hybrid dividend for purposes of section 245A.

(3) *Special rule for certain dividends attributable to earnings of lower-tier foreign corporations.*—This paragraph (c)(3) applies if a CFC sells or exchanges stock of a foreign corporation and pursuant to section 964(e)(1) the gain recognized on the sale or exchange is included in gross income as a dividend. In such a case, rules similar to the rules of paragraph (b)(3) of this section apply.

(4) *Interaction with rules under section 964(e).*—To the extent a dividend described in section 964(e)(1) (gain on certain stock sales by CFCs treated as dividends) is a tiered hybrid dividend, the rules of section 964(e)(4) do not apply and, therefore, the United States shareholder is not allowed a deduction under section 245A(a) for the amount included in gross income under paragraph (c)(1)(ii) of this section.

(d) *Hybrid deduction accounts.*—(1) *In general.*—A specified owner of a share of CFC stock must maintain a hybrid deduction account with respect to the share. The hybrid deduction account with respect to the share must reflect the amount of hybrid deductions of the CFC allocated to the share (as determined under paragraphs (d)(2) and (3) of this section), and must be maintained in accordance with the rules of paragraphs (d)(4) through (6) of this section.

(2) *Hybrid deductions.*—(i) *In general.*—The term *hybrid deduction* of a CFC means a deduction or other tax benefit (such as an exemption, exclusion, or credit, to the extent equivalent to a deduction) for which the requirements of paragraphs (d)(2)(i)(A) and (B) of this section are both satisfied.

(A) The deduction or other tax benefit is allowed to the CFC (or a person related to the CFC) under a relevant foreign tax law.

(B) The deduction or other tax benefit relates to or results from an amount paid, accrued, or distributed with respect to an instrument issued by the CFC and treated as stock for U.S. tax purposes. Examples of such a deduction or other tax benefit include an interest deduction, a dividends paid deduction, and a deduction with respect to equity (such as a notional interest deduction). *See* paragraph (g)(1) of this section. However, a deduction or other tax benefit relating to or resulting from a distribution by the CFC with respect to an instrument treated as stock for purposes of the relevant foreign tax law is considered a hybrid deduction only to the extent it has the effect of causing the earnings that funded the distribution to not be included in income (determined under the principles of § 1.267A-3(a)) or otherwise subject to tax under the CFC's tax law. Thus, for example, a refund to a shareholder of a CFC (including through a credit), upon a distribution by the CFC to the shareholder, of taxes paid by the CFC on the earnings that funded the distribution results in a hybrid deduction of the CFC, but only to the extent that the shareholder, if a tax resident of the CFC's country, does not include the distribution in income under the CFC's tax law or, if not a tax resident of the CFC's country, is not subject to withholding tax (as defined in section 901(k)(1)(B)) on the distribution under the CFC's tax law. *See* paragraph (g)(2) of this section.

(ii) *Application limited to items allowed in taxable years beginning after December 31, 2017.*—A deduction or other tax benefit allowed to a CFC (or a person related to the CFC) under a relevant foreign tax law is taken into account for purposes of this section only if it was allowed with respect to a taxable year under the relevant foreign tax law beginning after December 31, 2017.

(3) *Allocating hybrid deductions to shares.*—A hybrid deduction is allocated to a share of stock of a CFC to the extent that the hybrid deduction (or amount equivalent to a deduction) relates to an amount paid, accrued, or distributed by the CFC with respect to the share. However, in the case of a hybrid deduction that is a deduction with respect to equity (such as a notional interest deduction), the deduction is allocated to a share of stock of a CFC based on the product of—

(i) The amount of the deduction allowed for all of the equity of the CFC; and

(ii) A fraction, the numerator of which is the value of the share and the denominator of which is the value of all of the stock of the CFC.

(4) *Maintenance of hybrid deduction accounts.*—(i) *In general.*—A specified owner's hybrid deduction account with respect to a share of stock of a CFC is, as of the close of the taxable year of the CFC, adjusted pursuant to the following rules.

(A) First, the account is increased by the amount of hybrid deductions of the CFC allocable to the share for the taxable year.

(B) Second, the account is decreased by the amount of hybrid deductions in the account that gave rise to a hybrid dividend or tiered hybrid dividend during the taxable year. If a specified owner has more than one hybrid deduction account with respect to its stock of the CFC, then a pro rata amount in each hybrid deduction account is considered to have given rise to the hybrid dividend or tiered hybrid dividend, based on the amounts in the accounts before applying this paragraph (d)(4)(i)(B).

(ii) *Acquisition of account.*—(A) *In general.*—The following rules apply when a person (the *acquirer*) acquires a share of stock of a CFC from another person (the *transferor*).

(1) In the case of an acquirer that is a specified owner of the share immediately after the acquisition, the transferor's hybrid deduction account, if any, with respect to the share becomes the hybrid deduction account of the acquirer.

(2) In the case of an acquirer that is not a specified owner of the share immediately after the acquisition, the transferor's hybrid deduction account, if any, is eliminated and accordingly is not thereafter taken into account by any person.

(B) *Additional rules.*—The following rules apply in addition to the rules of paragraph (d)(4)(ii)(A) of this section.

(1) Certain section 354 or 356 exchanges.—The following rules apply when a shareholder of a CFC (the CFC, the *target CFC;* the shareholder, the *exchanging shareholder*) exchanges stock of the target CFC for stock of another CFC (the *acquiring CFC*) pursuant to an exchange described in section 354 or 356 that occurs in connection with a transaction described in section 381(a)(2) in which the target CFC is the transferor corporation.

(i) In the case of an exchanging shareholder that is a specified owner of one or more shares of stock of the acquiring CFC immediately after the exchange, the exchanging shareholder's hybrid deduction accounts with respect to the shares of stock of the target CFC that it exchanges are attributed to the shares of stock of the acquiring CFC that it receives in the exchange.

(ii) In the case of an exchanging shareholder that is not a specified owner of one or more shares of stock of the acquiring CFC immediately after the exchange, the exchanging shareholder's hybrid deduction accounts with respect to its shares of stock of the target CFC are eliminated and accordingly are not thereafter taken into account by any person.

(2) Section 332 liquidations.—If a CFC is a distributor corporation in a transaction described in section 381(a)(1) (the *distributing CFC*) in which a controlled foreign corporation is the acquiring corporation (the *distributee CFC*), then each hybrid account with respect to a share of stock of the distributee CFC is increased pro rata by the sum of the hybrid accounts with respect to shares of stock of the distributing CFC.

(3) Recapitalizations.—If a shareholder of a CFC exchanges stock of the CFC pursuant to a reorganization described in section 368(a)(1)(E) or a transaction to which section 1036 applies, then the shareholder's hybrid deduction accounts with respect to the stock of the CFC that it exchanges are attributed to the shares of stock of the CFC that it receives in the exchange.

(5) *Determinations and adjustments made on transfer date in certain cases.*—This paragraph (d)(5) applies if on a date other than the date that is the last day of the CFC's taxable year a United States shareholder of the CFC or an upper-tier CFC with respect to the CFC directly or indirectly transfers a share of stock of the CFC, and, during the taxable year, but on or before the transfer date, the United States shareholder or upper-tier CFC receives an amount from the CFC that is subject to the rules of section 245A(e) and this section. In such a case, as to the United States shareholder or upper-tier CFC and the United States shareholder's or upper-tier CFC's hybrid deduction accounts with respect to each share of stock of the CFC (regardless of whether such share is transferred), the determinations and adjustments under this section that would otherwise be made at the close of the CFC's taxable year are made at the close of the date of the transfer. Thus, for example, if a United States shareholder of a CFC exchanges stock of the CFC in an exchange described in § 1.367(b)-4(b)(1)(i) and is required to include in income as a deemed dividend the section 1248 amount attributable to the stock exchanged, the sum of the United States shareholder's hybrid deduction accounts with respect to each share of stock of the CFC is determined, and the accounts are adjusted, as of the close of the date of the exchange. For this purpose, the principles of § 1.1502-76(b)(2)(ii) apply to determine amounts in hybrid deduction accounts at the close of the date of the transfer.

(6) *Effects of CFC functional currency.*—(i) *Maintenance of the hybrid deduction account.*—A hybrid deduction account with respect to a share of CFC stock must be maintained in the functional currency (within the meaning of section 985) of the CFC. Thus, for example, the amount of a hybrid deduction and the adjustments described in paragraphs (d)(4)(i)(A) and (B) of this section are determined based on the functional currency of the CFC. In addition, for purposes of this section, the amount of a deduction or other tax benefit allowed to a CFC (or a person related to the CFC) is determined taking into account foreign currency gain or loss recognized with respect to such deduction or other tax benefit under a provision of foreign tax law comparable to section 988 (treatment of certain foreign currency transactions).

(ii) *Determination of amount of hybrid dividend.*—This paragraph (d)(6)(ii) applies if a CFC's functional currency is other than the functional currency of a United States shareholder or upper-tier CFC that receives an amount from the CFC that is subject to the rules of section 245A(e) and this section. In such a case, the sum of the United States shareholder's or upper-tier CFC's hybrid deduction accounts with respect to each share of stock of the CFC is, for purposes of determining the extent that a dividend is a hybrid dividend or tiered hybrid dividend, translated into the functional currency of the United States shareholder or upper-tier CFC based on the spot rate (within the meaning of § 1.988-1(d)) as of the date of the dividend.

(e) *Anti-avoidance rule.*—Appropriate adjustments are made pursuant to this section, including adjustments that would disregard the transaction or arrangement, if a transaction or arrangement is undertaken with a principal purpose of avoiding the purposes of this section. For example, if a specified owner of a share of CFC stock transfers the share to another person, and a principal purpose of the transfer is to shift the hybrid deduction account with respect to the share to the other person or to cause the hybrid deduction account to be eliminated, then for purposes of this section the shifting or elimination of the hybrid deduction account is disregarded as to the transferor. As another example, if a transaction or arrangement is undertaken to affirmatively fail to satisfy the holding period requirement under section 246(c)(5) with a principal purpose of avoiding the tiered hybrid dividend rules described in paragraph (c) of this section, the transaction or arrangement is disregarded for purposes of this section.

(f) *Definitions.*—The following definitions apply for purposes of this section.

(1) The term *controlled foreign corporation* (or *CFC*) has the meaning provided in section 957.

(2) The term *person* has the meaning provided in section 7701(a)(1).

(3) The term *related* has the meaning provided in this paragraph (f)(3). A person is related to a CFC if the person is a related person within the meaning of section 954(d)(3).

(4) The term *relevant foreign tax law* means, with respect to a CFC, any regime of any foreign country or possession of the United States that imposes an income, war profits, or excess profits tax with respect to income of the CFC, other than a foreign anti-deferral regime under which a person that owns an interest in the CFC is liable to tax. Thus, the term includes any regime of a foreign country or possession of the United States that imposes income, war profits, or excess profits tax under which—

(i) The CFC is liable to tax as a resident;

(ii) The CFC has a branch that gives rise to a taxable presence in the foreign country or possession of the United States; or

(iii) A person related to the CFC is liable to tax as a resident, provided that under such person's tax law the person is allowed a deduction for amounts paid or accrued by the CFC (because, for example, the CFC is fiscally transparent under the person's tax law).

(5) The term *specified owner* means, with respect to a share of stock of a CFC, a person for which the requirements of paragraphs (f)(5)(i) and (ii) of this section are satisfied.

(i) The person is a domestic corporation that is a United States shareholder of the CFC, or is an upper-tier CFC that would be a United States shareholder of the CFC were the upper-tier CFC a domestic corporation.

(ii) The person owns the share directly or indirectly through a partnership, trust, or estate. Thus, for example, if a domestic corporation directly owns all the shares of stock of an upper-tier CFC and the upper-tier CFC directly owns all the shares of stock of another CFC, the domestic corporation is the specified owner with respect to each share of stock of the upper-tier CFC and the upper-tier CFC is the specified owner with respect to each share of stock of the other CFC.

(6) The term *United States shareholder* has the meaning provided in section 951(b).

(g) *Examples.*—This paragraph (g) provides examples that illustrate the application of this section. For purposes of the examples in this paragraph (g), unless otherwise indicated, the following facts are presumed. US1 is a domestic corporation. FX and FZ are CFCs formed at the beginning of year 1. FX is a tax resident of Country X and FZ is a tax resident of Country Z. US1 is a United States shareholder with respect to FX and FZ. No distributed amounts are attributable to amounts which are, or have been, included in the gross income of a United States shareholder under section 951(a). All instruments are treated as stock for U.S. tax purposes.

(1) *Example 1. Hybrid dividend resulting from hybrid instrument*—(i) *Facts.* US1 holds both shares of stock of FX, which have an equal value. One share is treated as indebtedness for Country X tax purposes ("Share A"), and the other is treated as equity for Country X tax purposes ("Share B"). During year 1, under Country X tax law, FX accrues $80x of interest to US1 with respect to Share A and is allowed a deduction for the amount (the "Hybrid Instrument Deduction"). During year 2, FX distributes $30x to US1 with respect to each of Share A and Share B. For U.S. tax purposes, each of the $30x distributions is treated as a dividend for which, but for section 245A(e) and this section, US1 would be allowed a deduction under section 245A(a). For Country X tax purposes, the $30x distribution with respect to Share A represents a payment of interest for which a deduction was already allowed (and thus FX is not allowed an additional deduction for the amount), and the $30x distribution with respect to Share B is treated as a dividend (for which no deduction is allowed).

(ii) *Analysis.* The entire $30x of each dividend received by US1 from FX during year 2 is a hybrid dividend, because the sum of US1's hybrid deduction accounts with respect to each of its shares of FX stock at the end of year 2 ($80x) is at least equal to the amount of the dividends ($60x). *See* paragraph (b)(2) of this section. This is the case for the $30x dividend with respect to Share B even though there are no hybrid deductions allocated to Share B. *See id.* As a result, US1 is not allowed a deduction under section 245A(a) for the entire $60x of hybrid dividends and the rules of section 245A(d) (disallowance of foreign tax credits and deductions) apply. *See* paragraph (b)(1) of this section. Paragraphs (g)(1)(ii)(A) through (D) of this section describe the determinations under this section.

(A) At the end of year 1, US1's hybrid deduction accounts with respect to Share A and Share B are $80x and $0, respectively, calculated as follows.

(*1*) The $80x Hybrid Instrument Deduction allowed to FX under Country X tax law (a relevant foreign tax law) is a hybrid deduction of FX, because the deduction is allowed to FX and relates to or results from an amount accrued with respect to an instrument issued by FX and treated as stock for U.S. tax purposes. *See* paragraph (d)(2)(i) of this section. Thus, FX's hybrid deductions for year 1 are $80x.

(*2*) The entire $80x Hybrid Instrument Deduction is allocated to Share A, because the deduction was accrued with respect to Share A. *See* paragraph (d)(3) of this section. As there are no additional hybrid deductions of FX for year 1, there are no additional hybrid deductions to allocate to either Share A or Share B. Thus, there are no hybrid deductions allocated to Share B.

(*3*) At the end of year 1, US1's hybrid deduction account with respect to Share A is increased by $80x (the amount of hybrid deductions allocated to Share A). *See* paragraph (d)(4)(i)(A) of this section. Because FX did not pay any dividends with respect to either Share A or Share B during year 1 (and therefore did not pay any hybrid dividends or tiered hybrid dividends), no further adjustments are made. *See* paragraph (d)(4)(i)(B) of this section. Therefore, at the end of year 1, US1's hybrid deduction accounts with respect to Share A and Share B are $80x and $0, respectively.

(B) At the end of year 2, and before the adjustments described in paragraph (d)(4)(i)(B) of this section, US1's hybrid deduction accounts with respect to Share A and Share B remain $80x and $0, respectively. This is because there are no hybrid deductions of FX for year 2. *See* paragraph (d)(4)(i)(A) of this section.

(C) Because at the end of year 2 (and before the adjustments described in paragraph (d)(4)(i)(B) of this section) the sum of US1's hybrid deduction accounts with respect to Share A and Share B ($80x, calculated as $80x plus $0) is at least equal to the aggregate $60x of year 2 dividends, the entire $60x dividend is a hybrid dividend. *See* paragraph (b)(2) of this section.

(D) At the end of year 2, US1's hybrid deduction account with respect to Share A is decreased by $60x, the amount of the hybrid deductions in the account that gave rise to a hybrid dividend or tiered hybrid dividend during year 2. *See* paragraph (d)(4)(i)(B) of this section. Because there are no hybrid deductions in the hybrid deduction account with respect to Share B, no adjustments with respect to that account are made under paragraph (d)(4)(i)(B) of this section. Therefore, at the end of year 2 and taking into account the adjustments under paragraph (d)(4)(i)(B) of this section, US1's hybrid deduction account with respect to Share A is $20x ($80x less $60x) and with respect to Share B is $0.

(iii) *Alternative facts – notional interest deductions.* The facts are the same as in paragraph (g)(1)(i) of this section, except that for each of year 1 and year 2 FX is allowed $10x of notional interest deductions with respect to its equity, Share B, under Country X tax law (the "NIDs"). In addition, during year 2, FX distributes $47.5x (rather than $30x) to US1 with respect to each of Share A and Share B. For U.S. tax purposes, each of the $47.5x distributions is treated as a dividend for which, but for section 245A(e) and this section, US1 would be allowed a deduction under section 245A(a). For Country X tax purposes, the $47.5x distribution with respect to Share A represents a payment of interest for which a deduction was already allowed (and thus FX is not allowed an additional deduction for the amount), and the $47.5x distribution with respect to Share B is treated as a dividend (for which no deduction is allowed). The entire $47.5x of each dividend received by US1 from FX during year 2 is a hybrid dividend, because the sum of US1's hybrid deduction accounts with respect to each of its shares of FX stock at the end of year 2 ($80x plus $20x, or $100x) is at least equal to the amount of the dividends ($95x). *See* paragraph (b)(2) of this section. As a result, US1 is not allowed a deduction under section 245A(a) for the $95x hybrid dividend and the rules of section 245A(d) (disallowance of foreign tax credits and deductions) apply. *See* paragraph (b)(1) of this section. Paragraphs (g)(1)(iii)(A) through (D) of this section describe the determinations under this section.

(A) The $10x of NIDs allowed to FX under Country X tax law in year 1 are hybrid deductions of FX for year 1. *See* paragraph (d)(2)(i) of this section. The $10x of NIDs is allocated equally to each of Share A and Share B, because the hybrid deduction is with respect to equity and the shares have an equal value. *See* paragraph (d)(3) of this section. Thus, $5x of the NIDs is allocated to each of Share A and Share B for year 1. For the reasons described in paragraph (g)(1)(ii)(A) of this section, the entire $80x Hybrid Instrument Deduction is allocated to Share A. Therefore, at the end of year 1, US1's hybrid deduction accounts with respect to Share A and Share B are $85x and $5x, respectively.

(B) Similarly, the $10x of NIDs allowed to FX under Country X tax law in year 2 are hybrid deductions of FX for year 2, and $5x of the NIDs is allocated to each of Share A and Share B for year 2. *See* paragraphs (d)(2)(i) and (d)(3) of this section. Thus, at the end of year 2 (and before the adjustments described in paragraph (d)(4)(i)(B) of this section), US1's hybrid deduction account with respect to Share A is $90x ($85x plus $5x) and with respect to Share B is $10x ($5x plus $5x). *See* paragraph (d)(4)(i) of this section.

(C) Because at the end of year 2 (and before the adjustments described in paragraph (d)(4)(i)(B) of this section) the sum of US1's hybrid deduction accounts with respect to Share A and Share B ($100x, calculated as $90x plus $10x) is at least equal to the aggregate $95x of year 2 dividends, the entire $95x of dividends are hybrid dividends. *See* paragraph (b)(2) of this section.

(D) At the end of year 2, US1's hybrid deduction accounts with respect to Share A and Share B are decreased by the amount of hybrid deductions in the accounts that gave rise to a hybrid dividend or tiered hybrid dividend during year 2. *See* paragraph (d)(4)(i)(B) of this section. A total of $95x of hybrid deductions in the accounts gave rise to a hybrid dividend during year 2. For the hybrid deduction account with respect to Share A, $85.5x in the account is considered to have given rise to a hybrid deduction (calculated as $95x multiplied by $90x/$100x). *See id.* For the hybrid deduction account with respect to Share B, $9.5x in the account is considered to have given rise to a hybrid deduction (calculated as $95x multiplied by $10x/$100x). *See id.* Thus, following these adjustments, at the end of year 2, US1's hybrid deduction account with respect to Share A is $4.5x ($90x less $85.5x) and with respect to Share B is $0.5x ($10x less $9.5x).

(iv) *Alternative facts – deduction in branch country*—(A) *Facts.* The facts are the same as in paragraph (g)(1)(i) of this section, except that for Country X tax purposes Share A is treated as equity (and thus the Hybrid Instrument Deduction does not exist and under Country X tax law FX is not allowed a deduction for the $30x distributed in year 2 with respect to Share A). However, FX has a branch in Country Z that gives rise to a taxable presence under Country Z tax law, and for Country Z tax purposes Share A is treated as indebtedness and Share B is treated as equity. Also, during year 1, for Country Z tax purposes, FX accrues $80x of interest to US1 with respect to Share A and is allowed an $80x interest deduction with respect to its Country Z branch income. Moreover, for Country Z tax purposes, the $30x distribution with respect to Share A in year 2 represents a payment of interest for which a deduction was already allowed (and thus FX is not allowed an additional deduction for the amount), and the $30x distribution with respect to Share B in year 2 is treated as a dividend (for which no deduction is allowed).

(B) *Analysis*. The $80x interest deduction allowed to FX under Country Z tax law (a relevant foreign tax law) with respect to its Country Z branch income is a hybrid deduction of FX for year 1. *See* paragraphs (d)(2)(i) and (f)(4) of this section. For reasons similar to those discussed in paragraph (g)(1)(ii) of this section, at the end of year 2 (and before the adjustments described in paragraph (d)(4)(i)(B) of this section), US1's hybrid deduction accounts with respect to Share A and Share B are $80x and $0, respectively, and the sum of the accounts is $80x. Accordingly, the entire $60x of the year 2 dividend is a hybrid dividend. *See* paragraph (b)(2) of this section. Further, for the reasons described in paragraph (g)(1)(ii)(D) of this section, at the end of year 2 and taking into account the adjustments under paragraph (d)(4)(i)(B) of this section, US1's hybrid deduction account with respect to Share A is $20x ($80x less $60x) and with respect to Share B is $0.

(2) *Example 2. Tiered hybrid dividend rule; tax benefit equivalent to a deduction*—(i) *Facts*. US1 holds all the stock of FX, and FX holds all 100 shares of stock of FZ (the "FZ shares"), which have an equal value. The FZ shares are treated as equity for Country Z tax purposes. During year 2, FZ distributes $10x to FX with respect to each of the FZ shares, for a total of $1,000x. The $1,000x is treated as a dividend for U.S. and Country Z tax purposes, and is not deductible for Country Z tax purposes. If FX were a domestic corporation, then, but for section 245A(e) and this section, FX would be allowed a deduction under section 245A(a) for the $1,000x. Under Country Z tax law, 75% of the corporate income tax paid by a Country Z corporation with respect to a dividend distribution is refunded to the corporation's shareholders (regardless of where such shareholders are tax residents) upon a dividend distribution by the corporation. The corporate tax rate in Country Z is 20%. With respect to FZ's distributions, FX is allowed a refundable tax credit of $187.5x. The $187.5x refundable tax credit is calculated as $1,250x (the amount of pre-tax earnings that funded the distribution, determined as $1,000x (the amount of the distribution) divided by 0.8 (the percentage of pre-tax earnings that a Country Z corporation retains after paying Country Z corporate tax)) multiplied by 0.2 (the Country Z corporate tax rate) multiplied by 0.75 (the percentage of the Country Z tax credit). Under Country Z tax law, FX is not subject to Country Z withholding tax (or any other tax) with respect to the $1,000x dividend distribution.

(ii) *Analysis*. $937.5x of the $1,000x of dividends received by FX from FZ during year 2 is a tiered hybrid dividend, because the sum of FX's hybrid deduction accounts with respect to each of its shares of FZ stock at the end of year 2 is $937.5x. *See* paragraphs (b)(2) and (c)(2) of this section. As a result, the $937.5x tiered hybrid dividend is treated for purposes of section 951(a)(1)(A) as subpart F income of FX and US1 must include in gross income its pro rata share of such subpart F income, which is $937.5x. *See* paragraph (c)(1) of this section. In addition, the rules of section 245A(d) (disallowance of foreign tax credits and deductions) apply with respect to US1's inclusion. *Id*. Paragraphs (g)(2)(ii)(A) through (C) of this section describe the determinations under this section. The characterization of the FZ stock for Country X tax purposes (or for purposes of any other foreign tax law) does not affect this analysis.

(A) The $187.5x refundable tax credit allowed to FX under Country Z tax law (a relevant foreign tax law) is equivalent to a $937.5x deduction, calculated as $187.5x (the amount of the credit) divided by 0.2 (the Country Z corporate tax rate). The $937.5x is a hybrid deduction of FZ because it is allowed to FX (a person related to FZ), it relates to or results from amounts distributed with respect to instruments issued by FZ and treated as stock for U.S. tax purposes, and it has the effect of causing the earnings that funded the distributions to not be included in income under Country Z tax law. *See* paragraph (d)(2)(i) of this section. $9.375x of the hybrid deduction is allocated to each of the FZ shares, calculated as $937.5x (the amount of the hybrid deduction) multiplied by 1/100 (the value of each FZ share relative to the value of all the FZ shares). *See* paragraph (d)(3) of this section. The result would be the same if FX were instead a tax resident of Country Z (and not Country X) and under Country Z tax law FX were to not include the $1,000x in income (because, for example, Country Z tax law provides Country Z resident corporations a 100% exclusion or dividends received deduction with respect to dividends received from a resident corporation). *See* paragraph (d)(2)(i) of this section.

(B) Thus, at the end of year 2, and before the adjustments described in paragraph (d)(4)(i)(B) of this section, the sum of FX's hybrid deduction accounts with respect to each of its shares of FZ stock is $937.5x, calculated as $9.375x (the amount in each account) multiplied by 100 (the number of accounts). *See* paragraph (d)(4)(i) of this section. Accordingly, $937.5x of the $1,000x dividend received by FX from FZ during year 2 is a tiered hybrid dividend. *See* paragraphs (b)(2) and (c)(2) of this section.

(C) Lastly, at the end of year 2, each of FX's hybrid deduction accounts with respect to its shares of FZ is decreased by the $9.375x in the account that gave rise to a hybrid dividend or tiered hybrid dividend during year 2. *See* paragraph (d)(4)(i)(B) of this section. Thus, following these adjustments, at the end of year 2, each of FX's hybrid deduction accounts with respect to its shares of FZ stock is $0, calculated as $9.375x (the amount in the account before the adjustments described in paragraph (d)(4)(i)(B) of this section) less $9.375x (the adjustment described in paragraph (d)(4)(i)(B) of this section with respect to the account).

(iii) *Alternative facts – imputation system that taxes shareholders*. The facts are the same as in paragraph (g)(2)(i) of this section, except that under Country Z tax law the $1,000 dividend to FX is subject to a 30% gross basis withholding tax, or $300x, and the $187.5x refundable tax credit is applied against and reduces the withholding tax to $112.5x. The $187.5x refundable tax credit provided to FX is not a hybrid deduction because FX was subject to Country Z withholding tax of $300x on the $1,000x dividend (such withholding tax being greater than the $187.5x credit). *See* paragraph (d)(2)(i) of this section.

(h) *Applicability date.*—This section applies to distributions made after December 31, 2017. [Reg. § 1.245A(e)-1.]

Imputed Interest: Original Issue Discount

Imputed Interest: Original Issue Discount: Safe Haven Interest Rates.—Reproduced below is the text of a proposed amendment of Reg. § 1.249-1, relating to (1) the tax treatment of debt instruments issued after July 1, 1982, that contain original issue discount, (2) the imputation of and the accounting for interest with respect to sales and exchanges of property occurring after December 31, 1984, and (3) safe haven interest rates for loans or advances between commonly controlled taxpayers and safe haven leases between such taxpayers (published in the Federal Register on April 8, 1986).

□ Par. 6. Section 1.249-1 is amended as follows:

1. In paragraph (c)(2) by removing the phrase "section 1232(b)" and adding in its place the phrase "sections 1273(b) and 1274", and by removing the phrase "§ § 1.163-3 and 1.163-4," and adding in its place the phrase "§ § 1.163-3, 1.163-4, and 1.163-7."

2. In paragraph (d)(2), the first sentence, by removing the phrase "§ § 1.163-3 and 1.163-4," and adding in its place the phrase "§ § 1.163-3, 1.163-4, and 1.163-7."

3. In paragraph (f)(2), the second sentence, by removing the phrase "§ § 1.163-3(c) and 1.163-4(c)," and adding in its place the phrase "§ § 1.163-3(c), 1.163-4(c), and 1.163-7(f)."

§ 1.249-1. Limitation on deduction of bond premium on repurchase.

Foreign-Derived Intangible Income: Global Intangible Low-Taxed Income: Deduction

Foreign-Derived Intangible Income: Global Intangible Low-Taxed Income: Deduction.—Reg. § § 1.250-0, 1.250-1 and 1.250(a)-1 through 1.250(b)-6, providing guidance to determine the amount of the deduction for foreign-derived intangible income and global intangible low-taxed income, are proposed (published in the Federal Register on March 6, 2019) (corrected April 11, 2019) (corrected April 12, 2019) (REG-104464-18).

Par. 2. Sections 1.250-0, 1.250-1, and 1.250(a)-1 through 1.250(b)-6 are added to read as follows:

§ 1.250-0. Table of contents.—This section lists the table of contents for § § 1.250-1 through 1.250(b)-6.

(g) Determination of foreign-derived intangible income for tax-exempt corporations.

§1.250(b)-2 Qualified business asset investment.

(a) Scope.

(b) Definition of qualified business asset investment.

(c) Specified tangible property.

(1) In general.

(2) Tangible property.

(d) Dual use property.

(1) In general.

(2) Dual use ratio.

(3) Example.

(e) Determination of adjusted basis of specified tangible property.

(1) In general.

(2) Effect of change in law.

(3) Specified tangible property placed in service before enactment of section 250.

(f) Special rules for short taxable years.

(1) In general.

(2) Determination of quarter closes.

(3) Reduction of qualified business asset investment.

(4) Example.

(g) Partnership property.

(1) In general.

(2) Definitions related to partnership QBAI.

(i) In general.

(ii) Partnership QBAI ratio.

(iii) Partnership specified tangible property.

(3) Determination of adjusted basis.

(4) Example.

(h) Anti-avoidance rule for certain transfers of property.

(1) In general.

(2) Rule for structured arrangements.

(3) Per se rules for certain transactions.

(4) Definitions related to anti-avoidance rule.

(i) Disqualified period.

(ii) FDII-eligible related party.

(iii) Specified related party.

(iv) Transfer.

(5) Examples.

§1.250(b)-3 FDDEI transactions.

(a) Scope.

(b) Definitions.

(1) FDII filing date.

(2) Foreign person.

(3) General property.

(4) Intangible property.

(5) Recipient.

(6) Renderer.

(7) Sale.

(8) Seller.

(9) United States.

(10) United States person.

(11) United States territory.

(c) Foreign military sales.

(d) Reliability of documentation.

(e) Transactions with multiple elements.

(f) Treatment of certain loss transactions.

(1) In general.

(2) Example.

(g) Treatment of partnerships.

(1) In general.

(2) Examples.

§1.250(b)-4 FDDEI sales.

(a) Scope.

(b) Definition of FDDEI sale.

(c) Foreign person.

(1) In general.

(2) Documentation of status as a foreign person.

(i) In general.

(ii) Special rules.

(A) Special rule for small businesses.

(B) Special rule for small transactions.

(d) Foreign use for general property.

(1) In general.

(2) Determination of foreign use.

(i) In general.

(ii) Determination of domestic use.

(iii) Determination of manufacture, assembly, or other processing.

(A) In general.

(B) Property subject to a physical and material change.

(C) Property incorporated into second product as a component.

(iv) Determination of foreign use for transportation property.

(3) Documentation of foreign use of general property.

(i) In general.

(ii) Special rules.

(A) Special rule for small businesses.

(B) Special rule for small transactions.

(iii) Sales of fungible mass of general property.

(4) Examples.

(e) Foreign use for intangible property.

(1) In general.

(2) Determination of foreign use.

(i) In general.

(ii) Sales in exchange for periodic payments.

(iii) Sales in exchange for a lump sum.

(3) Documentation of foreign use of intangible property.

(i) Documentation for sales for periodic payments.

(ii) Certain sales to foreign unrelated parties

(iii) Documentation for sales in exchange for a lump sum.

(4) Examples.

(f) Special rule for certain financial instruments.

§1.250(b)-5 FDDEI services.

(a) Scope.

(b) Definition of FDDEI service.

(c) Definitions.

(1) Benefit.

(2) Business recipient.

(3) Consumer.

(4) General service.

(5) Property service.

(6) Proximate service.

(7) Transportation service.

(d) General services provided to consumers.

(1) In general.

(2) Location of consumer.

(3) Documentation of location of consumer.

(i) In general.

(ii) Special rules

(A) Special rule for small businesses.

(B) Special rule for small transactions.

(e) General services provided to business recipients.

(1) In general.

(2) Location of business recipient.

(i) In general.

(A) Determination of business operations that benefit from the service.

(B) Determination of amount of benefit conferred on operations outside the United States.

(ii) Location of business recipient's operations.

(3) Documentation of location of business recipient.

(i) In general.

(ii) Special rules.

(A) Special rule for small businesses.

(B) Special rule for small transactions.

(4) Related parties.

(5) Examples.

(f) Proximate services.

(g) Property services.

(h) Transportation services.

§ 1.250(b)-6 Related party transactions.

(a) Scope.

(b) Definitions.

(1) Foreign related party.

(2) Foreign unrelated party.

(3) Related party sale.

(4) Related party service.

(5) Unrelated party transaction.

(c) Related party sales.

(1) In general.

(i) Sale of property in an unrelated party transaction.

(ii) Use of property in an unrelated party transaction.

(2) Treatment of foreign related party as seller or renderer.

(3) Transactions between a foreign related party and other foreign related parties.

(4) Example.

(d) Related party services.

(1) In general.

(2) Substantially similar services.

(3) Location of recipient of services provided by related party.

(4) Examples.

[Reg. § 1.250-0.]

§ 1.250-1. Introduction.—(a) *Overview.*—Sections 1.250(a)-1 through 1.250(b)-6 provide rules to determine a domestic corporation's section 250 deduction. Section 1.250(a)-1 provides rules to determine the amount of a domestic corporation's deduction for foreign-derived intangible income and global intangible low-taxed income. Section 1.250(b)-1 provides general rules and definitions regarding the computation of foreign-derived intangible income. Section 1.250(b)-2 provides rules for determining a domestic corporation's qualified business asset investment. Section 1.250(b)-3 provides general rules and definitions regarding the determination of gross foreign-derived deduction eligible income. Section 1.250(b)-4 provides rules regarding the determination of gross foreign-derived deduction eligible income from the sale of property. Section 1.250(b)-5 provides rules regarding the determination of gross foreign-derived deduction eligible income from the provision of a service. Section 1.250(b)-6 provides rules regarding the sale of property or provision of a service to a related party.

(b) *Applicability dates.*—Sections 1.250(a)-1 through 1.250(b)-6 apply to taxable years ending on or after March 4, 2019. However, for taxable years beginning on or before March 4, 2019, taxpayers may use any reasonable documentation maintained in the ordinary course of the taxpayer's business that establishes that a recipient is a foreign person, property is for a foreign use (within the meaning of § 1.250(b)-4(d) and (e)), or a recipient of a general service is located outside the United States (within the meaning of § 1.250(b)-5(d)(2) and (e)(2)), as applicable, in lieu of the documentation required in §§ 1.250(b)-4(c)(2), (d)(3), and (e)(3) and 1.250(b)-5(d)(3) and (e)(3), provided that such documentation meets the reliability requirements described in § 1.250(b)-3(d). [Reg. § 1.250-1.]

§ 1.250(a)-1. Deduction for foreign-derived intangible income and global intangible low-taxed income.—(a) *Scope.*—This section provides rules for determining the amount of a domestic corporation's deduction for foreign-derived intangible income and global intangible low-taxed income. Paragraph (b) of this section provides general rules for determining the amount of the deduction. Paragraph (c) of this section provides definitions relevant for determining the amount of the deduction. Paragraph (d) of this section provides reporting requirements for a domestic corporation claiming the deduction. Paragraph (e) of this section provides a rule for determining the amount of the deduction of a member of a consolidated group. Paragraph (f) of this section provides examples illustrating the application of this section.

(b) *Allowance of deduction.*—(1) *In general.*—A domestic corporation is allowed a deduction for any taxable year equal to the sum of—

(i) 37.5 percent of its foreign-derived intangible income for the year; and

(ii) 50 percent of—

(A) Its global intangible low-taxed income for the year; and

(B) The amount treated as a dividend received by the corporation under section 78 which is attributable to its global intangible low-taxed income for the year.

(2) *Taxable income limitation.*—In the case of a domestic corporation with a section 250(a)(2) amount for a taxable year, for purposes of applying paragraph (b)(1) of this section for the year—

(i) The corporation's foreign-derived intangible income for the year (if any) is reduced (but not below zero) by an amount that bears the same ratio to the corporation's section 250(a)(2) amount that the corporation's foreign-derived intangible income for the year bears to the sum of the corporation's foreign-derived intangible income and global intangible low-taxed income for the year; and

(ii) The corporation's global intangible low-taxed income for the year (if any) is reduced (but not below zero) by the excess of the corporation's section 250(a)(2) amount over the amount of the reduction described in paragraph (b)(2)(i) of this section.

(3) *Reduction in deduction for taxable years after 2025.*—For any taxable year of a domestic corporation beginning after December 31, 2025, paragraph (b)(1) of this section applies by substituting—

(i) 21.875 percent for 37.5 percent in paragraph (b)(1)(i) of this section; and

(ii) 37.5 percent for 50 percent in paragraph (b)(1)(ii) of this section.

(4) *Treatment under section 4940.*—For purposes of section 4940(c)(3)(A), a deduction under section 250(a) is not treated as an ordinary and necessary expense paid or incurred for the production or collection of gross investment income.

(c) *Definitions.*—The following definitions apply for purposes of this section.

(1) *Domestic corporation.*—The term *domestic corporation* has the meaning set forth in section 7701(a), but does not include a regulated investment company (as defined in section 851), a real estate investment trust (as defined in section 856), or an S corporation (as defined in section 1361).

(2) *Foreign-derived intangible income.*—The term *foreign-derived intangible income* has the meaning set forth in § 1.250(b)-1(b).

(3) *Global intangible low-taxed income.*—The term *global intangible low-taxed income* means, with respect to a domestic corporation for a taxable year, the sum of the corporation's GILTI inclusion amount under § 1.951A-1(c) for the taxable year and the corporation's distributive share of any U.S. shareholder partnership's GILTI inclusion amount under § 1.951A-5(b)(2).

(4) *Section 250(a)(2) amount.*—The term *section 250(a)(2) amount* means, with respect to a domestic corporation for a taxable year, the excess (if any) of the sum of the corporation's foreign-derived intangible income and global intangible low-taxed income (determined without regard to section 250(a)(2) and paragraph (b)(2) of this section), over the corporation's taxable income determined with regard to all items of income, deduction, or loss, except for the deduction allowed under section 250 and this section. Therefore, for example, a domestic corporation's taxable income under the previous sentence is determined taking into account the application of sections 163(j) and 172(a). For a corporation that is subject to the unrelated business income tax under section 511, taxable income is determined only by reference to that corporation's unrelated business taxable income defined under section 512.

(d) *Reporting requirement.*—Each domestic corporation (or individual making an election under section 962) that claims a deduction under section 250 for a taxable year must make an annual return on Form 8993, "Section 250 Deduction for Foreign-Derived Intangible Income (FDII) and Global Intangible Low-Taxed Income (GILTI)" (or any successor form) for such year, setting forth the information, in such form and manner, as Form 8993 (or any successor form) or its instructions prescribe. Returns on Form 8993 (or any successor form) for a taxable year must be filed with the domestic corporation's (or in the case of a section 962 election, the individual's) income tax return on or before the due date (taking into account extensions) for filing the corporation's (or in the case of a section 962 election, the individual's) income tax return.

(e) *Determination of deduction for consolidated groups.*—A member of a consolidated group (as defined in § 1.1502-1(h)) determines its deduction under section 250(a) and this section under the rules provided in § 1.1502-50(b).

(f) *Examples.*—The following examples illustrate the application of this section. For purposes of the examples, it is assumed that DC is a domestic corporation that is not a member of a consolidated group and the taxable year of DC begins after 2017 and before 2026.

(1) *Example 1: Application of the taxable income limitation*—(i) *Facts.* For the taxable year, without regard to section 250(a)(2) and paragraph (b)(2) of this section, DC has foreign-derived intangible income of $100x and global intangible low-taxed income of $300x. DC's taxable income (without regard to section 250(a) and this section) is $300x.

(ii) *Analysis.* DC has a section 250(a)(2) amount of $100x, which is equal to the excess of the sum of DC's foreign-derived intangible income and global intangible low-taxed income of $400x ($100x + $300x) over its taxable income of $300x. As a result, DC's foreign-derived intangible income and global intangible low-taxed income are reduced, in the aggregate, by $100x under section 250(a)(2) and paragraph (b)(2) of this section for purposes of calculating DC's deduction allowed under section 250(a)(1) and paragraph (b)(1) of this section. DC's foreign-derived intangible income is reduced by $25x, the amount that bears the same ratio to the section 250(a)(2) amount ($100x) as DC's foreign-derived intangible income ($100x) bears to the sum of DC's foreign-derived intangible income and global intangible low-taxed income ($400x). DC's global intangible low-taxed income is reduced by $75x, which is the remainder of the section 250(a)(2) amount ($100x - $25x). Therefore, for purposes of calculating its deduction under section 250(a)(1) and paragraph (b)(1) of this section, DC's foreign-derived intangible income is $75x ($100x - $25x) and its global intangible low-taxed income is $225x ($300x - $75x). Accordingly, DC is allowed a deduction for the taxable year under section 250(a)(1) and paragraph (b)(1) of this section of $140.63x ($75x x 0.375 + $225x x 0.50).

(2) *Example 2: Interaction of sections 163(j), 172, and 250*—(i) *Facts.* For the taxable year, DC has gross DEI (as defined in § 1.250(b)-1(c)(14)) and gross FDDEI (as defined in § 1.250(b)-1(c)(15)) of $300x. DC has no income for the taxable year other than income included in gross DEI. DC also has a net operating loss carryover to the taxable year under section 172(b) of $130x and business interest (as defined in section 163(j)(5), without regard to any carryforwards described in section 163(j)(2)) of $100x. Under § 1.250(b)-1(d)(2), all of DC's interest expense is allocable to gross FDDEI and the net operating loss carryover, to the extent absorbed in the taxable year, is allocable to gross FDDEI. DC has no other allowable deductions, qualified business asset investment (as defined in § 1.250(b)-2(b)), or global intangible low-taxed income for the taxable year. DC has no floor plan financing interest (as defined in section 163(j)(9)) for the taxable year and no business interest income (as defined in section 163(j)(6)) for the taxable year.

(ii) *Analysis*—(A) *Calculation of tentative section 250 deduction for purposes of section 163(j).*

First, for purposes of applying section 163(j), the amount of the deduction allowed to DC under section 250(a)(1) is determined without regard to the application of section 163(j) and the section 163(j) regulations, without regard to section 172, and without regard to section 250(a)(2) and paragraph (b)(2) of this section (*tentative section 250 deduction*). See § 1.163(j)-1(b)(37)(ii); see also § 1.250(b)-1(d)(2)(ii). Therefore, solely for purposes of calculating DC's tentative section 250 deduction, DC's allowable deductions under § 1.250(b)-1(d)(2)(ii) for computing its foreign-derived intangible income are $100x, the amount of its business interest before the application of section 163(j). DC's deduction eligible income (as defined in § 1.250(b)-1(c)(2)) is $200x, the excess of its gross DEI (as defined in § 1.250(b)-1(c)(14)) of $300x, over its deductions properly allocable to gross DEI of $100x. DC's foreign-derived deduction eligible income (as defined in § 1.250(b)-1(c)(12)) is also $200x, the excess of its gross FDDEI of $300x over its deductions properly allocable to gross FDDEI of $100x. DC's foreign-derived ratio (as defined in § 1.250(b)-1(c)(13)) is 100%, which is the ratio of DC's foreign-derived deduction eligible income of $200x to DC's deduction eligible income of $200x. DC's deemed intangible income (as defined § 1.250(b)-1(c)(3)) is $200x, the excess of its deduction eligible income of $200x over its qualified business asset investment of $0. Therefore, DC's foreign-derived intangible income for purposes of the tentative section 250 deduction is $200x, which is equal to DC's deemed intangible income of $200x multiplied by its foreign-derived ratio of 100%. Accordingly, DC's tentative section 250 deduction is $75x ($200x x 0.375).

(B) *Calculation of disallowance under section 163(j)(1).* Second, the amount of DC's business interest deduction allowed under section 163(j) is determined taking into account the tentative section 250 deduction, but without regard to section 172(a). See section 163(j)(8)(A)(iii). Under section 163(j)(1) and § 1.163(j)-2(b), DC's deduction for business interest is limited to 30% of adjusted taxable income plus the amount of any business interest income for the taxable year and the amount of any floor plan financing interest for the taxable year. In this case, DC has no business interest income or floor plan financing interest for the taxable year and therefore DC's deduction for business interest is limited to 30% of DC's adjusted taxable income for the taxable year. DC's adjusted taxable income is equal to DC's taxable income with the relevant adjustments set forth under section 163(j)(8) and the regulations under section 163(j). For this purpose, DC's taxable income is computed without regard to DC's business interest and the amount of any net operating loss deduction under section 172, but taking into account the tentative section 250 deduction. Taking into account the tentative section 250 deduction, DC's adjusted taxable income is $225x ($300x - $75x). Therefore, the amount of DC's allowable deduction for business interest is $67.5x ($225x x 0.30) and the remaining $32.5x of DC's business interest expense will be carried forward to the succeeding taxable year.

(C) *Calculation of net operating loss deduction under section 172(a).* Third, the amount of DC's net operating loss deduction under section 172(a) is determined taking into account section 163(j), but without regard to section 250(a) and paragraph (b)(1) of this section. See § 1.250(b)-1(d)(2)(ii). Under section 172(a)(2), the amount of DC's net operating loss deduction is limited to 80% of taxable income. Taking into account the allowable deduction for business interest (but not its deduction allowed under section 250(a)), DC's taxable income is $232.5x ($300x - $67.5x), and its taxable income limitation under section 172(a)(2) is $186x ($232.5x x 0.80). DC is entitled to a net operating loss deduction equal to its entire net operating loss carryover of $130x, because such amount is less than $186x.

(D) *Calculation of FDII.* Fourth, the amount of DC's foreign-derived intangible income is determined, taking into account the deductions allowed after the application of sections 163(j) and 172(a). DC's allowable deductions under § 1.250(b)-1(d)(2)(ii) for computing its foreign-derived intangible income are $197.5x, which is equal to its allowed deduction for business interest of $67.5x plus its net operating loss deduction of $130x. Accordingly, DC's deduction eligible income (as defined in § 1.250(b)-1(c)(2)) is $102.5x, the excess of its gross DEI (as defined in § 1.250(b)-1(c)(14)) of $300x, over its deductions properly allocable to gross DEI of $197.5x. DC's foreign-derived deduction eligible income (as defined in § 1.250(b)-1(c)(12)) is also $102.5x, the excess of its gross FDDEI of $300x, over its deductions properly allocable to gross FDDEI of $197.5x. DC's foreign-derived ratio (as defined in § 1.250(b)-1(c)(13)) is 100%, which is the ratio of DC's foreign-derived deduction eligible income of $102.5x to DC's deduction eligible income of $102.5x. DC's deemed intangible income (as defined in § 1.250(b)-1(c)(3)) is $102.5x, the excess of its deduction eligible income of $102.5x over its qualified business asset investment of $0. Accordingly, DC's foreign-derived intangible income before application of section 250(a)(2) and paragraph (b)(2) of this section is $102.5x, which is equal to DC's deemed intangible income of $102.5x multiplied by its foreign-derived ratio of 100%.

(E) *Calculation of section 250 deduction.* Finally, the amount of DC's deduction under section 250 is determined after the application of section 250(a)(2), which is applied taking into account DC's business interest allowed under section 163(j) and its net operating loss deduction under section 172(a). DC's taxable income for purposes of section 250(a)(2) and paragraph (b)(2) of this section is $102.5x, which is $300x of gross income minus $197.5x, which is equal to its deduction for business interest of $67.5x plus its net operating loss deduction of $130x. DC does not have a section 250(a)(2) amount (as defined in paragraph (c)(4) of this section) for the year because DC's foreign-derived intangible income of $102.5x, determined without regard to section 250(a)(2) and paragraph (b)(2) of this section, does not exceed DC's taxable income of $102.5x. Therefore, the amount of DC's foreign-derived intangible income is not reduced under section 250(a)(2) and paragraph (b)(2) of this section. Accordingly, for the taxable year, DC is allowed a deduction under section 250(a)(1) and paragraph (b)(1) of this section of $38.44x ($102.5x x 0.375). [Reg. § 1.250(a)-1.]

§ 1.250(b)-1. Computation of foreign-derived intangible income (FDII).—(a) *Scope.*—This section provides rules for computing foreign-derived intangible income. Paragraph (b) of this section defines foreign-derived intangible income. Paragraph (c) of this section provides definitions that are relevant for computing foreign-derived intangible income. Paragraph (d) of this section provides rules for computing gross income and allocating and apportioning deductions for purposes of computing deduction eligible income and foreign-derived deduction eligible income. Paragraph (e) of this section provides rules for computing the deduction eligible income and foreign-derived deduction eligible income of a domestic corporate partner. Paragraph (f) of this section provides a rule for computing the foreign-derived intangible income of a member of a consolidated group. Paragraph (g) of this section provides a rule for computing the foreign-derived intangible income of a tax-exempt corporation.

(b) *Definition of foreign-derived intangible income.*—Subject to the provisions of this section, the term *foreign-derived intangible income* means, with respect to a domestic corporation for a taxable year, the corporation's deemed intangible income for the year multiplied by the corporation's foreign-derived ratio for the year.

(c) *Definitions.*—This paragraph (c) provides definitions that apply for purposes of this section and § § 1.250(b)-2 through 1.250(b)-6.

(1) *Controlled foreign corporation.*—The term *controlled foreign corporation* has the meaning set forth in section 957(a).

(2) *Deduction eligible income.*—The term *deduction eligible income* means, with respect to a domestic corporation for a taxable year, the excess (if any) of the corporation's gross DEI for the year, over the deductions properly allocable to gross DEI for the year, as determined under paragraph (d)(2) of this section.

(3) *Deemed intangible income.*—The term *deemed intangible income* means, with respect to a domestic corporation for a taxable year, the excess (if any) of the corporation's deduction eligible income for the year, over the corporation's deemed tangible income return for the year.

(4) *Deemed tangible income return.*—The term *deemed tangible income return* means, with respect to a domestic corporation and a taxable year, 10 percent of the corporation's qualified business asset investment for the year.

(5) *Dividend.*—The term *dividend* has the meaning set forth in section 316, and includes any amount treated as a dividend under any other provision of subtitle A of the Internal Revenue Code or the regulations thereunder (for example, under section 78, 356(a)(2), 367(b), or 1248).

(6) *Domestic corporation.*—The term *domestic corporation* has the meaning set forth in § 1.250(a)-1(c)(1).

(7) *Domestic oil and gas extraction income.*—The term *domestic oil and gas extraction income* means income described in section 907(c)(1), substituting "within the United States" for "without the United States."

(8) *FDDEI sale.*—The term *FDDEI sale* has the meaning set forth in § 1.250(b)-4(b).

(9) *FDDEI service.*—The term *FDDEI service* has the meaning set forth in § 1.250(b)-5(b).

(10) *FDDEI transaction.*—The term *FDDEI transaction* means a FDDEI sale or a FDDEI service.

(11) *Foreign branch income.*—The term *foreign branch income* means gross income attributable to a foreign branch of a domestic corporation or a partnership under § 1.904-4(f)(2), except that the term also includes any income or gain that would not be treated as gross income attributable to a foreign branch under § 1.904-4(f) but that arises from the direct or indirect sale (as defined in § 1.250(b)-3(b)(7)) of any asset (other than stock) that produces gross income attributable to a foreign branch, including by reason of the sale of a disregarded entity or interest in a partnership. See also § 1.904-4(f)(2)(v) (providing that if a principal purpose of recording or failing to record an item of gross income on the books and records of a foreign branch is the avoidance of the purposes of section 250 (in connection with section 250(b)(3)(A)(i)(VI)), the item must be attributed to one or more foreign branches of the foreign branch owner in a manner that reflects the substance of the transaction).

(12) *Foreign-derived deduction eligible income.*—The term *foreign-derived deduction eligible income* means, with respect to a domestic corporation for a taxable year, the excess (if any) of the corporation's gross FDDEI for the year, over the deductions properly allocable to gross FDDEI for the year, as determined under paragraph (d)(2) of this section.

(13) *Foreign-derived ratio.*—The term *foreign-derived ratio* means, with respect to a domestic corporation for a taxable year, the ratio (not to exceed one) of the corporation's foreign-derived deduction eligible income for the year to the corporation's deduction eligible income for the year. If a domestic corporation has no foreign-derived deduction eligible income for a taxable year, the corporation's foreign-derived ratio is zero for the year.

(14) *Gross DEI.*—The term *gross DEI* means, with respect to a domestic corporation or a partnership for a taxable year, the gross income of the corporation or partnership for the year determined without regard to the following items of gross income—

(i) Amounts included in gross income under section 951(a)(1);

(ii) Global intangible low-taxed income (as defined in § 1.250(a)-1(c)(3));

(iii) Financial services income (as defined in section 904(d)(2)(D) and § 1.904-4(e)(1)(ii));

(iv) Dividends received from a controlled foreign corporation with respect to which the corporation or partnership is a United States shareholder;

(v) Domestic oil and gas extraction income; and

(vi) Foreign branch income.

(15) *Gross FDDEI.*—The term *gross FDDEI* means, with respect to a domestic corporation or a partnership for a taxable year, the portion of the gross DEI of the corporation or partnership for the year which is derived from all of its FDDEI transactions.

(16) *Gross non-FDDEI.*—The term *gross non-FDDEI* means, with respect to a domestic corporation for a taxable year, the portion of the corporation's gross DEI that is not included in gross FDDEI.

(17) *Modified affiliated group.*—(i) *In general.*—The term *modified affiliated group* means an

affiliated group as defined in section 1504(a) determined by substituting "more than 50 percent" for "at least 80 percent" each place it appears, and without regard to section 1504(b)(2) and (3).

(ii) *Special rule for noncorporate entities.*—Any person (other than a corporation) that is controlled by one or more members of a modified affiliated group (including one or more persons treated as a member or members of a modified affiliated group by reason of this paragraph (c)(17)(ii)) or that controls any such member is treated as a member of the modified affiliated group.

(iii) *Definition of control.*—For purposes of paragraph (c)(17)(ii) of this section, the term *control* has the meaning set forth in section 954(d)(3).

(18) *Qualified business asset investment.*—The term *qualified business asset investment* has the meaning set forth in § 1.250(b)-2(b).

(19) *Related party.*—The term *related party* means, with respect to any person, any member of a modified affiliated group that includes such person.

(20) *United States shareholder.*—The term *United States shareholder* has the meaning set forth in section 951(b) and § 1.951-1(g).

(d) *Treatment of cost of goods sold and allocation and apportionment of deductions.*—(1) *Cost of goods sold for determining gross DEI and gross FDDEI.*—For purposes of determining the gross income included in gross DEI and gross FDDEI of a domestic corporation or a partnership, the cost of goods sold of the corporation or partnership is attributed to gross receipts with respect to gross DEI or gross FDDEI under any reasonable method. Cost of goods sold must be attributed to gross receipts with respect to gross DEI or gross FDDEI regardless of whether certain costs included in cost of goods sold can be associated with activities undertaken in an earlier taxable year (including a year before the effective date of section 250). A domestic corporation or partnership may not segregate cost of goods sold with respect to a particular product into component costs and attribute those component costs disproportionately to gross receipts with respect to amounts excluded from gross DEI or gross FDDEI, as applicable.

(2) *Deductions properly allocable to gross DEI and gross FDDEI.*—(i) *In general.*—For purposes of determining a domestic corporation's deductions that are properly allocable to gross DEI and gross FDDEI, the corporation's deductions are allocated and apportioned to gross DEI and gross FDDEI under the rules of §§ 1.861-8 through 1.861-14T and 1.861-17 by treating section 250(b) as an operative section described in § 1.861-8(f). In allocating and apportioning deductions under §§ 1.861-8 through 1.861-14T and 1.861-17, gross FDDEI and gross non-FDDEI are treated as separate statutory groupings. The deductions allocated and apportioned to gross DEI equal the sum of the deductions allocated and apportioned to gross FDDEI and gross non-FDDEI. All items of gross income described in paragraphs (c)(14)(i) through (vi) of this section are in the residual grouping. For purposes of this paragraph (d)(2)(i), research and experimental expenditures are allocated and apportioned in accordance with § 1.861-17 without taking into account the exclusive apportionment rule of § 1.861-17(b).

(ii) *Determination of deductions to allocate.*—All deductions allowed to a domestic corporation are allocated and apportioned to gross DEI and gross FDDEI for a taxable year under paragraph (d)(2)(i) of this section, other than the deduction allowed under section 250(a) and § 1.250(a)-1(b). For this purpose, the amount of the net operating loss deduction under section 172(a) is determined without regard to section 250. See also § 1.163(j)-1(b)(37)(ii) (for purposes of determining the limitation under section 163(j)(1), the deduction under section 250(a)(1) is determined without regard to the application of section 163(j) and the section 163(j) regulations and without regard to the taxable income limitation of section 250(a)(2) and § 1.250(a)-1(b)(2)).

(3) *Examples.*—The following example illustrates the application of this paragraph (d).

(i) *Presumed facts.*—The following facts are assumed for purposes of the examples—

(A) DC is a domestic corporation that is not a member of a consolidated group.

(B) All sales and services are provided to persons that are not related parties.

(C) All sales and services to foreign persons qualify as FDDEI transactions.

(ii) *Examples.*—(A) *Example 1: Allocation of deductions*—(*1*) *Facts.* For a taxable year, DC manufactures products A and B in the United States. DC sells products A and B and provides services associated with products A and B to United States and foreign persons. DC's qualified business asset investment for the taxable year is $1,000x. DC has $300x of deductible interest expense allowed under section 163. DC has assets with a tax book value of $2,500x. The tax book value of DC's assets used to produce products A and B and services is split evenly between assets that produce gross FDDEI and assets that produce gross non-FDDEI. DC has $840x of supportive deductions, as defined in § 1.861-8(b)(3), attributable to general and administrative expenses incurred for the purpose of generating the class of gross income that consists of gross DEI. DC apportions the $840x of deductions on the basis of gross income in accordance with § 1.861-8T(c)(1). For purposes of determining gross FDDEI and gross DEI under paragraph (d)(1) of this section, DC attributes $200x of cost of goods sold to Product A and $400x of cost of goods sold to Product B, and then attributes the cost of goods sold for each product ratably between the gross receipts of such product sold to foreign persons and the gross receipts of such product sold to United States persons. The manner in which DC attributes the cost of goods sold is a reasonable method. DC has no other items of income, loss, or deduction. For the taxable year, DC has the following income tax items relevant to the determination of its foreign-derived intangible income:

Table 1 To Paragraph (d)(3)(ii)(A)(*1*)

	Product A	Product B	Services	Total
Gross receipts from U.S. persons	$200x	$800x	$100x	$1,100x

Table 1 To Paragraph (d)(3)(ii)(A)(*1*)

	Product A	Product B	Services	Total
Gross receipts from foreign persons	$200x	$800x	$100x	$1,100x
Total gross receipts	$400x	$1,600x	$200x	$2,200x
Cost of goods sold for gross receipts from U.S. persons	$100x	$200x	$0	$300x
Cost of goods sold for gross receipts from foreign persons	$100x	$200x	$0	$300x
Total cost of goods sold	$200x	$400x	$0	$600x
Gross income	$200x	$1,200x	$200x	$1,600x
Tax book value of assets used to produce products/services	$500x	$500x	$1,500x	$2,500x

(2) *Analysis*—(*i*) *Determination of gross FDDEI and gross non-FDDEI.* Because DC does not have any income described in section 250(b)(3)(A)(i)(I) through (VI) and paragraphs (c)(14)(i) through (vi) of this section, none of its gross income is excluded from gross DEI. DC's gross DEI is $1,600x ($2,200x total gross receipts less $600x total cost of goods sold). DC's gross FDDEI is $800x ($1,100x of gross receipts from foreign persons minus attributable cost of goods sold of $300x).

(*ii*) *Determination of foreign-derived deduction eligible income.* To calculate its foreign-derived deduction eligible income, DC must determine the amount of its deductions that are allocated and apportioned to gross FDDEI and then subtract those amounts from gross FDDEI. DC's interest deduction of $300x is allocated and apportioned to gross FDDEI on the basis of the average total value of DC's assets in each grouping. DC has assets with a tax book value of $2,500x split evenly between assets that produce gross FDDEI and assets that produce gross non-FDDEI. Accordingly, an interest expense deduction of $150x is apportioned to DC's gross FDDEI. With respect to DC's supportive deductions of $840x that are related to DC's gross DEI, DC apportions such deductions between gross FDDEI and gross non-FDDEI on the basis of gross income. Accordingly, supportive deductions of $420x are apportioned to DC's gross FDDEI. Thus, DC's foreign-derived deduction eligible income is $230x, which is equal to its gross FDDEI of $800x less $150x of interest expense deduction and $420x of supportive deductions.

(*iii*) *Determination of deemed intangible income.* DC's deemed tangible income return is $100x, which is equal to 10% of its qualified business asset investment of $1,000x. DC's deduction eligible income is $460x, which is equal to its gross DEI of $1,600x less $300x of interest expense deductions and $840x of supportive deductions. Therefore, DC's deemed intangible income is $360x, which is equal to the excess of its deduction eligible income of $460x over its deemed tangible income return of $100x.

(*iv*) *Determination of foreign-derived intangible income.* DC's foreign-derived ratio is 50%, which is the ratio of DC's foreign-derived deduction eligible income of $230x to DC's deduction eligible income of $460x. Therefore, DC's foreign-derived intangible income is $180x, which is equal to DC's deemed intangible income of $360x multiplied by its foreign-derived ratio of 50%.

(B) *Example 2: Allocation of deductions with respect to a partnership*—(*1*) *Facts*—(*i*) *DC's operations.* DC is engaged in the production and sale of products consisting of two separate product groups in three-digit Standard Industrial Classification (SIC) Industry Groups, hereafter referred to as Group AAA and Group BBB. All of the gross income of DC is included in gross DEI. DC incurs $250x of research and experimental (R&E) expenditures in the United States that are deductible under section 174. None of the R&E is legally mandated as described in § 1.861-17(a)(4) and none is included in cost of goods sold. For purposes of determining gross FDDEI and gross DEI under paragraph (d)(1) of this section, DC attributes $210x of cost of goods sold to Group AAA products and $900x of cost of goods sold to Group BBB products, and then attributes the cost of goods sold with respect to each such product group ratably between the gross receipts with respect to such product group sold to foreign persons and the gross receipts with respect to such product group not sold to foreign persons. The manner in which DC attributes the cost of goods sold is a reasonable method. For the taxable year, DC has the following income tax items relevant to the determination of its foreign-derived intangible income:

Table 2 To Paragraph (d)(3)(ii)(B)(*1*)(*i*)

	Group AAA Products	Group BBB Products	Total
Gross receipts from U.S. persons	$200x	$800x	$1,000x
Gross receipts from foreign persons	$100x	$400x	$500x
Total gross receipts	$300x	$1,200x	$1,500x
Cost of goods sold for gross receipts from U.S. persons	$140x	$600x	$750x
Cost of goods sold for gross receipts from foreign persons	$70x	$300x	$370x
Total cost of goods sold	$210x	$900x	$1,110x

Table 2 To Paragraph (d)(3)(ii)(B)(*1*)(i)

	Group AAA Products	Group BBB Products	Total
Gross income	$90x	$300x	$390x
R&E deductions	$40x	$210x	$250x

(*ii*) *PRS's operations.* In addition to its own operations, DC is a partner in PRS, a partnership that also produces products described in SIC Group AAA. DC is allocated 50% of all income, gain, loss, and deductions of PRS. During the taxable year, PRS sells Group AAA products solely to foreign persons, and all of its gross income is included in gross DEI. PRS has $400 of gross receipts from sales of Group AAA products for the taxable year and incurs $100x of research and experimental (R&E) expenditures in the United States that are deductible under section 174. None of the R&E is legally mandated as described in § 1.861-17(a)(4) and none is included in cost of goods sold. For purposes of determining gross FDDEI and gross DEI under paragraph (d)(1) of this section, PRS attributes $200x of cost of goods sold to Group AAA products, and then attributes the cost of goods sold with respect to such product group ratably between the gross receipts with respect to such product group sold to foreign persons and the gross receipts with respect to such product group not sold to foreign persons. The manner in which PRS attributes the cost of goods sold is a reasonable method. DC's distributive share of PRS taxable items is $100x of gross income and $50x of R&E deductions, and DC's share of PRS's gross receipts from sales of Group AAA products for the taxable year is $200x under § 1.861-17(f)(3).

(*iii*) *Election to use sales method to allocate and apportion R&E.* DC has elected to use the sales method to apportion its R&E deductions under § 1.861-17. Neither DC nor PRS licenses or sells its intangible property to controlled or uncontrolled corporations in a manner that necessitates including the sales by such corporations for purposes of apportioning DC's R&E deductions.

(2) *Analysis*—(*i*) *Determination of gross DEI and gross FDDEI.* Under paragraph (e)(*1*) of this section, DC's gross DEI, gross FDDEI, and deductions allocable to those amounts include its distributive share of gross DEI, gross FDDEI, and deductions of PRS. Thus, DC's gross DEI for the year is $490x ($390x attributable to DC and $100x attributable to DC's interest in PRS). DC's gross income from sales of Group AAA products to foreign persons is $30x ($100x of gross receipts minus attributable cost of goods sold of $70x). DC's gross income from sales of Group BBB products to foreign persons is $100x ($400x of gross receipts minus attributable cost of goods sold of $300x). DC's gross FDDEI for the year is $230x ($30x from DC's sale of Group AAA products plus $100x from DC's sale of Group BBB products plus DC's distributive share of PRS's gross FDDEI of $100x).

(*ii*) *Allocation and apportionment of R&E deductions.* To determine foreign-derived deduction eligible income, DC must allocate and apportion its R&E expense of $300x ($250x incurred directly by DC and $50x incurred indirectly through DC's interest in PRS). In accordance with § 1.861-17, R&E expenses are first allocated to a class of gross income related to a three-digit SIC group code. DC's R&E expenses related to products in Group AAA are $90x ($40x incurred directly by DC and $50x incurred indirectly through DC's interest in PRS) and its expenses related to Group BBB are $210x. None of those expenses were legally mandated by a particular country and therefore do not require the allocation of R&E expense solely to income arising from that jurisdiction. The exclusive apportionment rule in § 1.861-17(b) does not apply for purposes of apportioning R&E to gross DEI and gross FDDEI. See paragraph (d)(2)(i) of this section. Accordingly, all R&E expense attributable to a particular SIC group code is apportioned on the basis of the amounts of sales within that SIC group code. Total sales within Group AAA were $500x ($300x directly by DC and $200x attributable to DC's interest in PRS), $300x of which were made to foreign persons ($100x directly by DC and $200x attributable to DC's interest in PRS). Therefore, the $90x of R&E expense related to Group AAA is apportioned $54x to gross FDDEI ($90x x $300x/$500x) and $36x to gross non-FDDEI ($90x x $200x/$500x). Total sales within Group BBB were $1,200x, $400x of which were made to foreign persons. Therefore, the $210x of R&E expense related to products in Group BBB is apportioned $70x to gross FDDEI ($210x x $400x/$1,200x) and $140x to gross non-FDDEI ($210x x $800x/$1,200x). Accordingly, DC's foreign-derived deduction eligible income for the tax year is $106x ($230x gross FDDEI minus $124x of R&E ($54x + $70x) allocated and apportioned to gross FDDEI).

(e) *Domestic corporate partners.*—(1) *In general.*—A domestic corporation's deduction eligible income and foreign-derived deduction eligible income for a taxable year are determined taking into account the corporation's share of gross DEI, gross FDDEI, and deductions of any partnership (whether domestic or foreign) in which the corporation is a direct or indirect partner. For purposes of the preceding sentence, a domestic corporation's share of each such item of a partnership is determined in accordance with the corporation's distributive share of the underlying items of income, gain, deduction, and loss of the partnership that comprise such amounts. See § 1.250(b)-2(g) for rules calculating the increase to a domestic corporation's qualified business asset investment by the corporation's share of partnership QBAI.

(2) *Reporting requirement for partnership with domestic corporate partners.*—A partnership that has one or more direct or indirect partners that are domestic corporations and that is required to file a return under section 6031 must furnish to each such partner on or with such partner's Schedule K-1 (Form 1065 or any successor form) by the due date (including extensions) for furnishing Schedule K-1 the partner's share of the partnership's gross DEI, gross FDDEI, deductions that are definitely related to the partnership's gross DEI and gross FDDEI, and partnership QBAI (as determined under § 1.250(b)-2(g)) for each taxable year in which the

partnership has gross DEI, gross FDDEI, deductions that are definitely related to the partnership's gross DEI or gross FDDEI, or partnership specified tangible property (as defined in § 1.250(b)-2(g)(2)(iii)).

(3) *Examples*.—The following examples illustrate the application of this paragraph (e).

(i) *Presumed facts*.—The following facts are assumed for purposes of the examples—

(A) DC, a domestic corporation, is a partner in PRS, a partnership.

(B) FP and FP2 are foreign persons.

(C) FC is a foreign corporation.

(D) The allocations under PRS's partnership agreement satisfy the requirements of section 704.

(E) No partner of PRS is a related party of DC.

(F) DC, PRS, and FC all use the calendar year as their taxable year.

(G) PRS has no items of income, loss, or deduction for its taxable year, except the items of income described.

(ii) *Examples*.—(A) *Example 1: Sale by partnership to foreign person*—(*1*) *Facts*. Under the terms of the partnership agreement, DC is allocated 50% of all income, gain, loss, and deductions of PRS. For the taxable year, PRS recognizes $20x of gross income on the sale of general property (as defined in § 1.250(b)-3(b)(3)) to FP, a foreign person (as determined under § 1.250(b)-4(c)), for a foreign use (as determined under § 1.250(b)-4(d)). The gross income recognized on the sale of property is not described in section 250(b)(3)(A)(I) through (VI) or paragraphs (c)(14)(i) through (vi) of this section.

(*2*) *Analysis*. PRS's sale of property to FP is a FDDEI sale as described in § 1.250(b)-4(b). Therefore, the gross income derived from the sale ($20x) is included in PRS's gross DEI and gross FDDEI, and DC's share of PRS's gross DEI and gross FDDEI ($10x) is included in DC's gross DEI and gross FDDEI for the taxable year.

(B) *Example 2: Sale by partnership to foreign person attributable to foreign branch*—(*1*) *Facts*. The facts are the same as in paragraph (e)(3)(ii)(A)(*1*) of this section (the facts in *Example 1*), except the income from the sale of property to FP is attributable to a foreign branch of PRS.

(*2*) *Analysis*. PRS's sale of property to FP is excluded from PRS's gross DEI under section 250(b)(3)(A)(VI) and paragraph (c)(14)(vi) of this section. Accordingly, DC's share of PRS's gross income of $10x from the sale is not included in DC's gross DEI or gross FDDEI for the taxable year.

(C) *Example 3: Partnership with a loss in gross FDDEI*—(*1*) *Facts*. The facts are the same as in paragraph (e)(3)(ii)(A)(*1*) of this section (the facts in *Example 1*), except that in the same taxable year, PRS also sells property to FP2, a foreign person (as determined under § 1.250(b)-4(c)), for a foreign use (as determined under § 1.250(b)-4(d)). After taking into account both sales, PRS has a gross loss of $30x.

(*2*) *Analysis*. Both the sale of property to FP and the sale of property to FP2 are FDDEI sales because each sale is described in § 1.250(b)-4(b). DC's share of PRS's gross loss ($15x) from the sales is included in DC's gross DEI and gross FDDEI.

(D) *Example 4: Sale by partnership to foreign related party of the partnership*—(*1*) *Facts*. Under the terms of the partnership agreement, DC has 25% of the capital and profits interest in the partnership and is allocated 25% of all income, gain, loss, and deductions of PRS. PRS owns 100% of the single class of stock of FC. In the taxable year, PRS has $20x of gain on the sale of general property (as defined in § 1.250(b)-3(b)(3)) to FC, and FC makes a material physical change to the property within the meaning of § 1.250(b)-4(d)(2)(iii) outside the United States before selling the property to customers in the United States. PRS satisfies the documentation requirement of § 1.250(b)-4(d)(3) with respect to the sale.

(*2*) *Analysis*. The sale of property by PRS to FC is described in § 1.250(b)-4(b) without regard to the application of § 1.250(b)-6, since the sale is to a foreign person (as determined under § 1.250(b)-4(c)) for a foreign use (as determined under § 1.250(b)-4(d)). However, FC is a foreign related party of PRS within the meaning of section 250(b)(5)(D) and § 1.250(b)-6(b)(1), because FC and PRS are members of a modified affiliated group within the meaning of paragraph (c)(17) of this section. Therefore, the sale by PRS to FC is a related party sale within the meaning of § 1.250(b)-6(b)(3). Under section 250(b)(5)(C)(i) and § 1.250(b)-6(c), because FC did not sell the property, or use the property in connection with other property sold or the provision of a service, to a foreign unrelated party before the property was subject to a domestic use, the sale by PRS to FC is not a FDDEI sale. See § 1.250(b)-6(c)(1). Accordingly, the gain from the sale ($20x) is included in PRS's gross DEI but not its gross FDDEI, and DC's share of PRS's gain ($5x) is included in DC's gross DEI but not gross FDDEI. This is the result notwithstanding that FC is not a related party of DC because FC and DC are not members of a modified affiliated group within the meaning of paragraph (c)(17) of this section.

(f) *Determination of foreign-derived intangible income for consolidated groups*.—A member of a consolidated group (as defined in § 1.1502-1(h)) determines its foreign-derived intangible income under the rules provided in § 1.1502-50.

(g) *Determination of foreign-derived intangible income for tax-exempt corporations*.—The foreign-derived intangible income of a corporation that is subject to the unrelated business income tax under section 511 is determined only by reference to that corporation's items of income, gain, deduction, or loss, and adjusted bases in property, that are taken into account in computing the corporation's unrelated business taxable income (as defined in section 512). For example, if a corporation that is subject to the unrelated business income tax under section 511 has tangible property used in the production of both unrelated business income and gross income that is not unrelated business income, only the portion of the basis of such property taken into account in computing the corporation's unrelated business taxable income is taken into account in determining the corporation's qualified business asset investment. Similarly, if a corporation that is subject to the unrelated business income tax under section 511 has tangible property that is used in both the production of gross DEI and the production of gross income that is not gross DEI, only the corporation's unrelated business income is taken into account in determining the corporation's dual use ratio with respect to such property under § 1.250(b)-2(d)(2). [Reg. § 1.250(b)-1.]

§ 1.250(b)-2. Qualified business asset investment.—(a) *Scope.*—This section provides general rules for determining the qualified business asset investment of a domestic corporation for purposes of determining its deemed tangible income return under § 1.250(b)-1(c)(4). Paragraph (b) of this section defines qualified business asset investment. Paragraph (c) of this section defines tangible property and specified tangible property. Paragraph (d) of this section provides rules for determining the portion of property that is specified tangible property when the property is used in the production of both gross DEI and gross income that is not gross DEI. Paragraph (e) of this section provides rules for determining the adjusted basis of specified tangible property. Paragraph (f) of this section provides rules for determining qualified business asset investment of a domestic corporation with a short taxable year. Paragraph (g) of this section provides rules for increasing the qualified business asset investment of a domestic corporation by reason of property owned through a partnership. Paragraph (h) of this section provides an anti-avoidance rule that disregards certain transfers when determining the qualified business asset investment of a domestic corporation.

(b) *Definition of qualified business asset investment.*—The term *qualified business asset investment* means the average of a domestic corporation's aggregate adjusted bases as of the close of each quarter of a domestic corporation's taxable year in specified tangible property that is used in a trade or business of the domestic corporation and is of a type with respect to which a deduction is allowable under section 167. See paragraph (f) of this section for rules relating to the qualified business asset investment of a domestic corporation with a short taxable year.

(c) *Specified tangible property.*—(1) *In general.*—The term *specified tangible property* means, subject to paragraph (d) of this section, tangible property used in the production of gross DEI.

(2) *Tangible property.*—For purposes of paragraph (c)(1) of this section, the term *tangible property* means property for which the depreciation deduction provided by section 167(a) is eligible to be determined under section 168 without regard to section 168(f)(1), (2), or (5) and the date placed in service.

(d) *Dual use property.*—(1) *In general.*—In the case of tangible property (as defined in paragraph (c)(2) of this section) of a domestic corporation that is used in both the production of gross DEI and the production of gross income that is not gross DEI in a domestic corporation's taxable year, the portion of the adjusted basis in the property treated as adjusted basis in specified tangible property for the domestic corporation's taxable year is determined by multiplying the average of the domestic corporation's adjusted basis in the property by the dual use ratio with respect to the property for the domestic corporation's taxable year.

(2) *Dual use ratio.*—The term *dual use ratio* means, with respect to specified tangible property—

(i) In the case of specified tangible property that produces directly identifiable income for a domestic corporation's taxable year, the ratio of the gross DEI produced by the property for the taxable year to the total amount of gross income produced by the property for the taxable year.

(ii) In the case of specified tangible property that does not produce directly identifiable income for a domestic corporation's taxable year, the ratio of the gross DEI of the domestic corporation for the taxable year to the total amount of gross income of the domestic corporation for the taxable year.

(3) *Example.*—The following example illustrates the application of this paragraph (d).

(i) *Facts.* DC, a domestic corporation, owns a machine that produces both gross DEI and domestic oil and gas extraction income. For the taxable year, the machine produces gross DEI of $750x and domestic oil and gas extraction income of $250x. The average adjusted basis of the machine for the taxable year in the hands of DC is $4,000x. DC also owns an office building for its administrative functions with an average adjusted basis for the taxable year of $10,000x. The office building does not produce directly identifiable income. DC has no other specified tangible property. For the taxable year, DC's gross DEI is $2,000x and its gross income is $5,000x.

(ii) *Analysis.* The machine and office building are both property for which the depreciation deduction provided by section 167(a) are eligible to be determined under section 168. Therefore, under paragraph (c)(2) of this section, the machine and office building are tangible property. The machine and office building are used in both the production of gross income that is included in gross DEI and gross income that is not included in gross DEI, because domestic oil and gas extraction income is an item of gross income excluded from gross DEI under section 250(b)(3)(A)(i)(V) and § 1.250(b)-1(c)(14)(v). Therefore, under paragraph (d)(1) of this section, the portion of the basis in the machine treated as basis in specified tangible property is equal to DC's average basis in the machine for the year ($4,000x), multiplied by the dual use ratio under paragraph (d)(2)(i) of this section (0.75), which is the proportion that the gross DEI produced by the property ($750x) bears to the total gross income produced with respect to the property ($1,000x). Accordingly, $3,000x ($4,000x x 0.75) of DC's adjusted basis in the machine is taken into account in determining DC's qualified business asset investment. Under paragraph (d)(1) of this section, the portion of the basis in the office building treated as basis in specified tangible property is equal to DC's average basis in the office building for the year ($10,000x), multiplied by the dual use ratio under paragraph (d)(2)(ii) of this section (0.40), which is the ratio of DC's gross DEI for the taxable year ($2,000x) to DC's total gross income for the taxable year ($5,000x). Accordingly, $4,000x ($10,000x x 0.40) of DC's adjusted basis in the office building is taken into account in determining DC's qualified business asset investment under paragraph (b) of this section. Accordingly, DC's total qualified business asset investment is $7,000x ($3,000x + $4,000x).

(e) *Determination of adjusted basis of specified tangible property.*—(1) *In general.*—The adjusted basis in specified tangible property is determined by using the alternative depreciation system under section 168(g), and by allocating the depreciation deduction with respect to such property for the domestic corporation's taxable year ratably to each day during the period in the taxable year to which such depreciation relates.

(2) *Effect of change in law*.—The determination of adjusted basis for purposes of paragraph (b) of this section is made without regard to any provision of law enacted after December 22, 2017, unless such later enacted law specifically and directly amends the definition of qualified business asset investment under section 250 or section 951A.

(3) *Specified tangible property placed in service before enactment of section 250*.—The adjusted basis in property placed in service before December 22, 2017, is determined using the alternative depreciation system under section 168(g), as if this system had applied from the date that the property was placed in service.

(f) *Special rules for short taxable years*.—(1) *In general*.—In the case of a domestic corporation that has a taxable year that is less than twelve months (a *short taxable year*), the rules for determining the qualified business asset investment of the domestic corporation under this section are modified as provided in paragraphs (f)(2) and (3) of this section with respect to the taxable year.

(2) *Determination of quarter closes*.—For purposes of determining quarter closes, in computing the qualified business asset investment of a domestic corporation for a short taxable year, the quarters of the domestic corporation for purposes of this section are the full quarters beginning and ending within the short taxable year (if any), determining quarter length as if the domestic corporation did not have a short taxable year, plus one or more short quarters (if any).

(3) *Reduction of qualified business asset investment*.—The qualified business asset investment of a domestic corporation for a short taxable year is the sum of—

(i) The sum of the domestic corporation's aggregate adjusted bases in specified tangible property as of the close of each full quarter (if any) in the domestic corporation's taxable year divided by four; plus

(ii) The domestic corporation's aggregate adjusted bases in specified tangible property as of the close of each short quarter (if any) in the domestic corporation's taxable year multiplied by the sum of the number of days in each short quarter divided by 365.

(4) *Example*.—The following example illustrates the application of this paragraph (f).

(i) *Facts*. A, an individual, owns all of the stock of DC, a domestic corporation. A owns DC from the beginning of the taxable year. On July 15 of the taxable year, A sells DC to USP, a domestic corporation that is unrelated to A. DC becomes a member of the consolidated group of which USP is the common parent and as a result, under § 1.1502-76(b)(2)(ii), DC's taxable year is treated as ending on July 15. USP and DC both use the calendar year as their taxable year. DC's aggregate adjusted bases in specified tangible property for the taxable year are $250x as of March 31, $300x as of June 30, $275x as of July 15, $500x as of September 30, and $450x as of December 31.

(ii) *Analysis*—(A) *Determination of short taxable years and quarters*. DC has two short taxable years during the taxable year. The first short taxable year is from January 1 to July 15, with two full quarters (January 1-March 31 and April 1-June 30) and one short quarter (July 1-July 15). The second taxable year is from July 16 to December 31, with one short quarter (July 16-September 30) and one full quarter (October 1-December 31).

(B) *Calculation of qualified business asset investment for the first short taxable year*. Under paragraph (f)(2) of this section, for the first short taxable year, DC has three quarter closes (March 31, June 30, and July 15). Under paragraph (f)(3) of this section, the qualified business asset investment of DC for the first short taxable year is $148.80x, the sum of $137.50x (($250x + $300x)/4) attributable to the two full quarters and $11.30x ($275x x 15/365) attributable to the short quarter.

(C) *Calculation of qualified business asset investment for the second short taxable year*. Under paragraph (f)(2) of this section, for the second short taxable year, DC has two quarter closes (September 30 and December 31). Under paragraph (f)(3) of this section, the qualified business asset investment of DC for the second short taxable year is $217.98x, the sum of $112.50x ($450x/4) attributable to the one full quarter and $105.48x ($500x x 77/365) attributable to the short quarter.

(g) *Partnership property*.—(1) *In general*.—For purposes of paragraph (b) of this section, if a domestic corporation holds an interest in one or more partnerships as of the close of the domestic corporation's taxable year, the qualified business asset investment of the domestic corporation for its taxable year is increased by the sum of the domestic corporation's partnership QBAI with respect to each partnership for the domestic corporation's taxable year.

(2) *Definitions related to partnership QBAI*.—(i) *In general*.—The term *partnership QBAI* means the sum of the domestic corporation's share of the partnership's adjusted basis in partnership specified tangible property as of the close of a partnership taxable year that ends with or within a domestic corporation's taxable year. A domestic corporation's share of the partnership's adjusted basis in partnership specified tangible property is determined separately with respect to each partnership specified tangible property of the partnership by multiplying the partnership's adjusted basis in the property by the partnership QBAI ratio with respect to the property. If the partnership's taxable year is less than twelve months, the principles of paragraph (f) of this section apply in determining a domestic corporation's partnership QBAI with respect to the partnership.

(ii) *Partnership QBAI ratio*.—The term *partnership QBAI ratio* means, with respect to partnership specified tangible property—

(A) In the case of partnership specified tangible property that produces directly identifiable income for a partnership taxable year, the ratio of the domestic corporation's distributive share of the gross income produced by the property for the partnership taxable year that is included in the gross DEI of the domestic corporation for its taxable year to the total gross income produced by the property for the partnership taxable year.

(B) In the case of partnership specified tangible property that does not produce directly identifiable income for a partnership taxable year, the ratio of the domestic corporation's distributive share of the gross income of the partnership for the partnership taxable year that is included in the gross DEI of the domestic corporation for its taxable year to the total amount of gross income of the partnership for the partnership taxable year.

(iii) *Partnership specified tangible property*.—The term *partnership specified tangible property* means tangible property (as defined in paragraph (c)(2) of this section) of a partnership that is—

(A) Used in the trade or business of the partnership;

(B) Of a type with respect to which a deduction is allowable under section 167; and

(C) Used in the production of gross DEI.

(3) *Determination of adjusted basis*.—For purposes of this paragraph (g), a partnership's adjusted basis in partnership specified tangible property is determined based on the average of the partnership's adjusted basis in the property as of the close of each quarter in the partnership taxable year. The principles of paragraphs (e) and (h) of this section apply for purposes of determining a partnership's adjusted basis in partnership specified tangible property and the portion of such adjusted basis taken into account in determining a domestic corporation's partnership QBAI.

(4) *Example*.—The following example illustrates the rules of this paragraph (g).

(i) *Facts*. DC, a domestic corporation, is a partner in PRS. Both DC and PRS use the calendar year as their taxable year. PRS owns two assets, Asset A and Asset B, both of which are tangible property used in PRS's trade or business that it depreciates under section 168. Asset A and Asset B are used solely in the production of gross DEI. The average of PRS's adjusted basis as of the close of each quarter of PRS's taxable year in Asset A is $100x, and the average of PRS's adjusted basis as of the close of each quarter of PRS's taxable year in Asset B is $50x. Asset A produces $10x of directly identifiable gross income for the taxable year, and Asset B produces $50x of directly identifiable gross income for the taxable year. DC's distributive share of the gross income from Asset A is $8x and its distributive share of the gross income from Asset B is $10x. DC's entire distributive share of income from Asset A and Asset B is included in DC's gross DEI for the taxable year. See § 1.250(b)-1(e)(1). DC's distributive share satisfies the requirements of section 704(b).

(ii) *Analysis*. Each of Asset A and Asset B is partnership specified tangible property because each is tangible property, of a type with respect to which a deduction is allowable under section 167, used in PRS's trade or business, and used in the production of gross DEI. DC's partnership QBAI ratio for Asset A is 80%, the ratio of DC's distributive share of the gross income from Asset A for the taxable year that is included in DC's gross DEI ($8x) to the total gross income produced by Asset A for the taxable year ($10x). DC's partnership QBAI ratio for Asset B is 20%, the ratio of DC's distributive share of the gross income from Asset B for the taxable year that is included in DC's gross DEI ($10x) to the total gross income produced by Asset B for the taxable year ($50x). DC's share of the average of PRS's adjusted basis of Asset A is $80x, PRS's adjusted basis in Asset A of $100x multiplied by DC's partnership QBAI ratio for Asset A of 80%. DC's share of the average of PRS's adjusted basis of Asset B is $10x, PRS's adjusted basis in Asset B of $50x multiplied by DC's partnership QBAI ratio for Asset B of 20%. Therefore, DC's partnership QBAI with respect to PRS is $90x ($80x + $10x). Accordingly, under paragraph (g)(1) of this section, DC increases its qualified business asset investment for the taxable year by $90x.

(h) *Anti-avoidance rule for certain transfers of property*.—(1) *In general*.—If, with a principal purpose of decreasing the amount of its deemed tangible income return, a domestic corporation transfers specified tangible property (*transferred property*) to a specified related party of the domestic corporation and, within the disqualified period, the domestic corporation or an FDII-eligible related party of the domestic corporation leases the same or substantially similar property from any specified related party, then, solely for purposes of determining the qualified business asset investment of the domestic corporation under paragraph (b) of this section, the domestic corporation is treated as owning the transferred property from the later of the beginning of the term of the lease or date of the transfer of the property until the earlier of the end of the term of the lease or the end of the recovery period of the property.

(2) *Rule for structured arrangements*.—For purposes of paragraph (h)(1) of this section, a transfer of specified tangible property to a person that is not a related party or lease of property from a person that is not a related party is treated as a transfer to or lease from a specified related party if the transfer or lease is pursuant to a structured arrangement. A structured arrangement exists only if either paragraph (h)(2)(i) or (ii) of this section is satisfied.

(i) The reduction in the domestic corporation's deemed tangible income return is a material factor in the pricing of the arrangement with the transferee.

(ii) Based on all the facts and circumstances, the reduction in the domestic corporation's deemed tangible income return is a principal purpose of the arrangement. Facts and circumstances that indicate the reduction in the domestic corporation's deemed tangible income return is a principal purpose of the arrangement include—

(A) Marketing the arrangement as tax-advantaged where some or all of the tax advantage derives from the reduction in the domestic corporation's deemed tangible income return;

(B) Primarily marketing the arrangement to domestic corporations which earn foreign-derived deduction eligible income;

(C) Features that alter the terms of the arrangement, including the return, in the event the reduction in the domestic corporation's deemed tangible income return is no longer relevant; or

(D) A below-market return absent the tax effects or benefits resulting from the reduction in the domestic corporation's deemed tangible income return.

(3) *Per se rules for certain transactions*.—For purposes of paragraph (h)(1) of this section, a transfer of property by a domestic corporation to

a specified related party (including a party deemed to be a specified related party under paragraph (h)(2) of this section) followed by a lease of the same or substantially similar property by the domestic corporation or an FDII-eligible related party from a specified related party (including a party deemed to be a specified related party under paragraph (h)(2) of this section) is treated per se as occurring pursuant to a principal purpose of decreasing the amount of the domestic corporation's deemed tangible income return if both the transfer and the lease occur within a six-month period.

(4) *Definitions related to anti-avoidance rule.*—The following definitions apply for purpose of this paragraph (h).

(i) *Disqualified period.*—The term *disqualified period* means, with respect to a transfer, the period beginning one year before the date of the transfer and ending the earlier of the end of the remaining recovery period (under the system described in section 951A(d)(3)(A)) of the property or one year after the date of the transfer.

(ii) *FDII-eligible related party.*—The term *FDII-eligible related party* means, with respect to a domestic corporation, a member of the same consolidated group as the domestic corporation or a partnership with respect to which at least 80 percent of the interests in partnership capital and profits are owned, directly or indirectly, by the domestic corporation or one or more members of the consolidated group that includes the domestic corporation.

(iii) *Specified related party.*—The term *specified related party* means, with respect to a domestic corporation, a related party (as defined in § 1.250(b)-1(c)(19)) other than an FDII-eligible related party.

(iv) *Transfer.*—The term *transfer* means any disposition, exchange, contribution, or distribution of property, and includes an indirect transfer. For example, a transfer of an interest in a partnership is treated as a transfer of the assets of the partnership. In addition, if paragraph (h)(1) of this section applies to treat a domestic corporation as owning specified tangible property by reason of a lease of the property, the termination or lapse of the lease of the property is treated as a transfer of the property by the domestic corporation to the lessor.

(5) *Examples.*—The following examples illustrate the application of this paragraph (h).

(i) *Example 1: Sale-leaseback with a related party*—(A) *Facts.* DC, a domestic corporation, owns Asset A, which is specified tangible property. DC also owns all the single class of stock of DS, a domestic corporation, and FS1 and FS2, each a controlled foreign corporation. DC and DS are members of the same consolidated group. On January 1, Year 1, DC sells Asset A to FS1. At the time of the sale, Asset A had a remaining recovery period of 10 years under the alternative depreciation system. On February 1, Year 1, FS2 leases Asset B, which is substantially similar to Asset A, to DS for a five-year term ending on January 31, Year 6.

(B) *Analysis.* Because DC transfers specified tangible property (Asset A), to a specified related party of DC (FS1), and, within a six month period (January 1, Year 1 to February 1, Year 1), an FDII-eligible related party of DC (DS) leases a substantially similar property (Asset B), DC's transfer of Asset A and lease of Asset B are treated as per se occurring pursuant to a principal purpose of decreasing the amount of its deemed tangible income return. Accordingly, for purposes of determining DC's qualified business asset investment, DC is treated as owning Asset A from February 1, Year 1, the later of the date of the transfer of Asset A (January 1, Year 1) and the beginning of the term of the lease of Asset B (February 1, Year 1), until January 31, Year 6, the earlier of the end of the term of the lease of Asset B (January 31, Year 6) or the remaining recovery period of Asset A (December 31, Year 10).

(ii) *Example 2: Sale-leaseback with a related party; lapse of initial lease*—(A) *Facts.* The facts are the same as in paragraph (h)(5)(i)(A) of this section (the facts in *Example 1*). In addition, DS allows the lease of Asset B to expire on February 1, Year 6. On June 1, Year 6, DS and FS2 renew the lease for a five-year term ending on May 31, Year 11.

(B) *Analysis.* Because DC is treated as owning Asset A under paragraph (h)(1) of this section, the lapse of the lease of Asset B is treated as a transfer of Asset A to FS2 on February 1, Year 6, under paragraph (h)(4)(iv) of this section. Further, because DC is deemed to transfer specified tangible property (Asset A) to a specified related party (FS2) upon the lapse of the lease, and within a six month period (February 1, Year 6 to June 1, Year 6), an FDII-eligible related party of DC (DS) leases a substantially similar property (Asset B), DC's deemed transfer of Asset A under paragraph (h)(4)(iv) of this section and lease of Asset B are treated as per se occurring pursuant to a principal purpose of decreasing the amount of its deemed tangible income return. Accordingly, for purposes of determining DC's qualified business asset investment, DC is treated as owning Asset A from June 1, Year 6, the later of the date of the deemed transfer of Asset A (February 1, Year 6) and the beginning of the term of the lease of Asset B (June 1, Year 6), until December 31, Year 10, the earlier of the end of the term of the lease of Asset B (May 31, Year 11) or the remaining recovery period of Asset A (December 31, Year 10). [Reg. § 1.250(b)-2.]

§ 1.250(b)-3. FDDEI transactions.—(a) *Scope.*—This section provides rules related to the determination of whether a sale of property or provision of a service is a FDDEI transaction. Paragraph (b) of this section provides definitions related to the determination of whether a sale of property or provision of a service is a FDDEI transaction. Paragraph (c) of this section provides rules regarding a sale of property or provision of a service to a foreign government or an international organization. Paragraph (d) of this section provides rules for determining the reliability of documentation. Paragraph (e) of this section provides a rule for characterizing a transaction with both sales and services elements. Paragraph (f) of this section provides a rule for treating certain loss transactions as FDDEI transactions. Paragraph (g) of this section provides a rule for determining whether a sale of property or provision of a service to a partnership is a FDDEI transaction.

(b) *Definitions.*—This paragraph (b) provides definitions that apply for purposes of this section and § § 1.250(b)-4 through 1.250(b)-6.

(1) *FDII filing date.*—The term *FDII filing date* means, with respect to a sale of property by

a seller or provision of a service by a renderer, the date, including extensions, by which the seller or renderer is required to file an income tax return (or in the case of a seller or renderer that is a partnership, a return of partnership income) for the taxable year in which the gross income from the sale of property or provision of a service is included in the gross income of the seller or renderer.

(2) *Foreign person.*—The term *foreign person* means a person that is not a United States person, and includes a foreign government or an international organization.

(3) *General property.*—The term *general property* means any property other than—

(i) Intangible property;

(ii) A security (as defined in section 475(c)(2)); or

(iii) A commodity (as defined in section 475(e)(2)(B) through (D)).

(4) *Intangible property.*—The term *intangible property* has the meaning set forth in section 367(d)(4).

(5) *Recipient.*—The term *recipient* means a person that purchases property or services from a seller or renderer.

(6) *Renderer.*—The term *renderer* means a person that provides a service to a recipient.

(7) *Sale.*—The term *sale* means any sale, lease, license, exchange, or disposition of property, and includes any transfer of property in which gain or income is recognized under section 367.

(8) *Seller.*—The term *seller* means a person that sells property to a recipient.

(9) *United States.*—The term *United States* has the meaning set forth in section 7701(a)(9), as expanded by section 638(1) with respect to mines, oil and gas wells, and other natural deposits.

(10) *United States person.*—The term *United States person* has the meaning set forth in section 7701(a)(30), except that the term does not include an individual that is a bona fide resident of a United States territory within the meaning of section 937(a).

(11) *United States territory.*—The term *United States territory* means American Samoa, Guam, the Northern Mariana Islands, Puerto Rico, or the U.S. Virgin Islands.

(c) *Foreign military sales.*—For purposes of determining whether a sale of property or a provision of a service is a FDDEI transaction, if a sale of property or a provision of a service is made to the United States or an instrumentality thereof pursuant to 22 U.S.C. 2751 et seq. under which the United States or an instrumentality thereof purchases the property or service for resale or on-service, on commercial terms, to a foreign government or agency or instrumentality thereof, and the contract between the seller or renderer and the United States or an instrumentality thereof provides that the sale or service is purchased for resale or on-service to such foreign government or agency or instrumentality thereof, then the sale of property or provision of a service is treated as a sale of property or a provision of a service to the foreign government.

(d) *Reliability of documentation.*—For purposes of the documentation requirements described in §§1.250(b)-4 through 1.250(b)-6, documentation is reliable only if each of the requirements described in paragraphs (d)(1) through (3) of this section is satisfied.

(1) As of the FDII filing date, the seller or renderer does not know and does not have reason to know that the documentation is unreliable or incorrect. For this purpose, a seller or renderer has reason to know that documentation is unreliable or incorrect if its knowledge of all the relevant facts or statements contained in the documentation is such that a reasonably prudent person in the position of the seller or renderer would question the accuracy or reliability of the documentation.

(2) The documentation is obtained by the seller or renderer by the FDII filing date with respect to the sale or service.

(3) The documentation is obtained no earlier than one year before the date of the sale or service.

(e) *Transactions with multiple elements.*—If a transaction includes both a sale component and a service component, the transaction is classified according to the overall predominant character of the transaction for purposes of determining whether the transaction is subject to §1.250(b)-4 or §1.250(b)-5.

(f) *Treatment of certain loss transactions.*—(1) *In general.*—If a seller knows or has reason to know that property is sold to a foreign person for a foreign use (within the meaning of §1.250(b)-4(d)(2) or (e)(2)) or a renderer knows or has reason to know that a general service (as defined in §1.250(b)-5(c)(4)) is provided to a person located outside the United States (within the meaning of §1.250(b)-5(d)(2) or (e)(2)), but the seller or renderer does not satisfy the documentation requirements described in §1.250(b)-4(c)(2), (d)(3), or (e)(3) or §1.250(b)-5(d)(3) or (e)(3), as applicable, the transaction is deemed to be a FDDEI transaction with respect to a domestic corporation if not treating the transaction as a FDDEI transaction would increase the amount of the corporation's foreign-derived deduction eligible income for the taxable year relative to its foreign-derived deduction eligible income that would be determined if the transaction were treated as a FDDEI transaction. If a seller or renderer engages in more than one transaction described in the preceding sentence in a taxable year, the previous sentence applies by comparing the corporation's foreign-derived deduction eligible income if each such transaction were not treated as a FDDEI transaction to its foreign-derived deduction eligible income if each such transaction were treated as a FDDEI transaction.

(2) *Example.*—The following example illustrates the application of this paragraph (f).

(i) *Facts.* During a taxable year, DC, a domestic corporation, manufactures products A and B in the United States. DC sells product A for $200x and product B for $800x. DC knows or has reason to know that all of its sales of product A and product B are to foreign persons for a foreign use. DC establishes that its sales of product B are to foreign persons for a foreign use but does not obtain documentation establishing that any sales of product A are to foreign person for a foreign use. DC's cost of goods sold is $450x. For purposes of determining gross FDDEI, under §1.250(b)-1(d)(1) DC attributes $250x of cost of goods sold to product A and $200x of cost of goods sold to product B, and then attributes the cost of goods sold for each product ratably between the gross receipts of such product sold to foreign persons and the gross receipts of such product not sold to foreign persons. The manner in which DC attributes the cost of goods sold is a reasonable method. DC has no other items of income, loss, or deduction.

Table 1 to paragraph (f)(2)(i)

	Product A	Product B	Total
Gross receipts	$200x	$800x	$1,000x
Cost of Goods Sold	$250x	$200x	$450x
Gross Income (Loss)	($50x)	$600x	$550x

(ii) *Analysis.* By not treating the sales of product A as FDDEI sales, the amount of DC's foreign-derived deduction eligible income would increase by $50x relative to its foreign-derived deduction eligible income if the sales of product A were treated as FDDEI sales. Accordingly, because DC knows or has reason to know that its sales of product A are to foreign persons for a foreign use, the sales of product A constitute FDDEI sales under paragraph (f)(1) of this section, and thus the $50x loss from the sale of product A is included in DC's gross FDDEI.

(g) *Treatment of partnerships.*—(1) *In general.*—For purposes of determining whether a sale of property to or by a partnership or a provision of a service to or by a partnership is a FDDEI transaction, a partnership is treated as a person. Accordingly, for example, a partnership may be a seller, renderer, recipient, or related party, including a foreign related party (as defined in § 1.250(b)-6(b)(1)).

(2) *Examples.*—The following examples illustrate the application of this paragraph (g).

(i) *Example 1: Domestic partner sale to foreign partnership with a foreign branch*-(A) *Facts.* DC, a domestic corporation, is a partner in PRS, a foreign partnership. DC and PRS are not related parties. PRS has a foreign branch within the meaning of § 1.904-4(f)(3)(iii). DC and PRS both use the calendar year as their taxable year. For the taxable year, DC recognizes $20x of gain on the sale of general property to PRS for a foreign use (as determined under § 1.250(b)-4(d)). During the same taxable year, PRS recognizes an additional $20x of gain on the sale of the property to a foreign person for a foreign use (as determined under § 1.250(b)-4(d)). PRS's income on the sale of the property is attributable to its foreign branch.

(B) *Analysis.* DC's sale of property to PRS, a foreign partnership, is a FDDEI sale because it is a sale to a foreign person for a foreign use. Therefore, DC's gain of $20x on the sale to PRS is included in DC's gross DEI and gross FDDEI. However, PRS's gain of $20x is not included in the gross DEI or gross FDDEI of PRS because the gain is foreign branch income within the meaning of § 1.250(b)-1(c)(11). Accordingly, none of PRS's gain on the sale of property is included in DC's gross DEI or gross FDDEI under § 1.250(b)-1(e)(1).

(ii) *Example 2: Domestic partner sale to domestic partnership without a foreign branch*—(A) *Facts.* The facts are the same as in paragraph (g)(2)(i)(A) of this section (the facts in *Example 1*), except PRS is a domestic partnership that does not have a foreign branch within the meaning of § 1.904-4(f)(3)(iii).

(B) *Analysis.* DC's sale of property to PRS, a domestic partnership, is not a FDDEI sale because the sale is to a United States person. Therefore, the gross income from DC's sale to PRS is included in DC's gross DEI, but is not included in its gross FDDEI. However, PRS's subsequent sale is a FDDEI sale, and therefore the gain of $20x is included in the gross DEI and gross FDDEI of PRS. Accordingly, DC includes its distributive share of PRS's gain from the sale in determining DC's gross DEI and gross FDDEI for the taxable year under § 1.250(b)-1(e)(1). [Reg. § 1.250(b)-3.]

§ 1.250(b)-4. FDDEI sales.—(a) *Scope.*—This section provides rules for determining whether a sale of property is a FDDEI sale. Paragraph (b) of this section defines a FDDEI sale. Paragraph (c) of this section provides rules for determining whether a recipient is a foreign person. Paragraph (d) of this section provides rules for determining whether general property is sold for a foreign use. Paragraph (e) of this section provides rules for determining whether intangible property is sold for a foreign use. Paragraph (f) of this section provides a special rule for the sale of certain financial instruments.

(b) *Definition of FDDEI sale.*—Except as provided in § 1.250(b)-6(c), the term *FDDEI sale* means a sale of general property or intangible property to a foreign person (as determined under paragraph (c) of this section) for a foreign use (as determined under paragraphs (d) and (e) of this section).

(c) *Foreign person.*—(1) *In general.*—A recipient is a foreign person for purposes of paragraph (b) of this section only if the seller establishes that the recipient is a foreign person by obtaining the documentation described in paragraph (c)(2) of this section (which meets the reliability requirements described in § 1.250(b)-3(d)) and, as of the FDII filing date, the seller does not know or have reason to know that the recipient is not a foreign person.

(2) *Documentation of status as a foreign person.*—(i) *In general.*—Except as provided in paragraph (c)(2)(ii) of this section, a seller establishes the status of a recipient as a foreign person by obtaining one or more of the following types of documentation with respect to the person—

(A) A written statement by the recipient that the recipient is a foreign person;

(B) With respect to a recipient that is an entity, documentation that establishes that the entity is organized or created under the laws of a foreign jurisdiction;

(C) With respect to an individual, any valid identification issued by a foreign government or an agency thereof that is typically used for identification purposes;

(D) Documents filed with a government or an agency or instrumentality thereof that provide the foreign jurisdiction of organization or residence of an entity (for example, a publicly traded corporation's annual report filed with the U.S. Securities and Exchange Commission that includes the jurisdiction of organization or residence of foreign subsidiaries of the corporation); or

(E) Any other forms of documentation as prescribed by the Secretary in forms, instructions, or other guidance.

(ii) *Special rules.*—(A) *Special rule for small businesses.*—A seller that receives less than $10,000,000 in gross receipts during a prior taxable year establishes the status of any recipient as a foreign person for a taxable year if the seller's shipping address for the recipient is outside the United States. If the seller's prior taxable year was less than 12 months (a short period), gross receipts are annualized by multiplying the gross receipts for the short period by 365 and dividing the result by the number of days in the short period.

(B) *Special rule for small transactions.*—A seller that receives less than $5,000 in gross receipts during a taxable year from a recipient establishes the status of such recipient as a foreign person for such taxable year if the seller's shipping address for the recipient is outside the United States.

(d) *Foreign use for general property.*—(1) *In general.*—The sale of general property is for a foreign use only if the seller establishes that the property is for a foreign use within the meaning of paragraph (d)(2) of this section by obtaining the documentation described in paragraph (d)(3) of this section (which meets the reliability requirements described in § 1.250(b)-3(d)) and, as of the FDII filing date, the seller does not know or have reason to know that the property is not for a foreign use within the meaning of paragraph (d)(2) of this section.

(2) *Determination of foreign use.*—(i) *In general.*—Except as provided in paragraph (d)(2)(iv) of this section, the sale of general property is for a foreign use if—

(A) The property is not subject to a domestic use within three years of the date of delivery; or

(B) The property is subject to manufacture, assembly, or other processing outside the United States before the property is subject to a domestic use.

(ii) *Determination of domestic use.*—General property is subject to domestic use if—

(A) The property is subject to any use, consumption, or disposition within the United States; or

(B) The property is subject to manufacture, assembly, or other processing within the United States.

(iii) *Determination of manufacture, assembly, or other processing.*—(A) *In general.*—General property is subject to manufacture, assembly, or other processing only if the property is physically and materially changed (as described in paragraph (d)(2)(iii)(B) of this section) or the property is incorporated as a component into a second product (as described in paragraph (d)(2)(iii)(C) of this section).

(B) *Property subject to a physical and material change.*—For purposes of paragraph (d)(2)(iii)(A) of this section, the determination of whether general property is subject to a physical and material change is made based on all the relevant facts and circumstances. However, general property is not considered subject to physical and material change if it is subject only to minor assembly, packaging, or labeling.

(C) *Property incorporated into second product as a component.*—For purposes of paragraph (d)(2)(iii)(A) of this section, general property is treated as a component incorporated into a second product only if the fair market value of such property when it is delivered to the recipient constitutes no more than 20 percent of the fair market value of the second product, determined when the second product is completed. For purposes of the preceding sentence, all general property that is sold by the seller and incorporated into the second product is treated as a single item of property.

(iv) *Determination of foreign use for transportation property.*—In the case of aircraft, railroad rolling stock, vessel, motor vehicle, or similar property that provides a mode of transportation and is capable of traveling internationally (*international transportation property*), such property is for a foreign use only if, during the three year period from the date of delivery, the property is located outside the United States more than 50 percent of the time and more than 50 percent of the miles traversed in the use of the property are traversed outside the United States. For purposes of the preceding sentence, international transportation property is deemed to be within the United States at all times during which it is engaged in transport between any two points within the United States, except where the transport constitutes uninterrupted international air transportation within the meaning of section 4262(c)(3) and the regulations under that section (relating to tax on air transportation of persons).

(3) *Documentation of foreign use of general property.*—(i) *In general.*—Except as provided in paragraphs (d)(3)(ii) and (iii) of this section, a seller establishes that general property, or a portion of a particular class of fungible general property, is for a foreign use only if the seller obtains one or more of the following types of documentation with respect to the sale—

(A) A written statement from the recipient or a related party of the recipient that the recipient's use or intended use of the property is for a foreign use (within the meaning of paragraph (d)(2) of this section);

(B) A binding contract between the seller and the recipient which provides that the recipient's use or intended use of the property is for a foreign use (within the meaning of paragraph (d)(2) of this section);

(C) Except in the case of international transportation property, documentation of shipment of the general property (including both property located within the United States or outside the United States, such as in a warehouse, storage facility, or assembly site located outside United States) to a location outside the United States (for example, a copy of the export bill of lading issued by the carrier which delivered the property, or a copy of the certificate of lading for the property executed by a customs officer of the country to which the property is delivered); or

(D) Any other forms of documentation as prescribed by the Secretary in forms, instructions, or other guidance.

(ii) *Special rules.*—(A) *Special rule for small businesses.*—A seller that receives less than $10,000,000 in gross receipts during the prior taxable year establishes that the sale of general property in a taxable year to any recipient is for a foreign use for the taxable year if the seller's shipping address for the recipient is outside the United States. If the seller's prior taxable year was a short period, gross receipts are annualized by multiplying the gross receipts for the short period by 365 and dividing the result by the number of days in the short period.

(B) *Special rule for small transactions.*—A seller that receives less than $5,000 in gross receipts during a taxable year from a recipient establishes that the sale of general property to the recipient is for a foreign use for the taxable year if the seller's shipping address for the recipient is outside the United States.

(iii) *Sales of fungible mass of general property.*—In the case of sales of multiple items of general property, which because of their fungible nature cannot reasonably be specifically traced to the location of use (*fungible mass*), as an alternative to obtaining the documentation described in paragraphs (d)(3)(i)(A) through (D) of this section, a seller may establish that a portion of the fungible mass is for a foreign use through market research, including statistical sampling, economic modeling and other similar methods indicating that the property will be subject to a foreign use. If, under the preceding sentence, the seller establishes that 90 percent or more of a fungible mass is for a foreign use, then the entire fungible mass is for a foreign use. If, under the first sentence of this paragraph (d)(3)(iii), the seller does not establish that 10 percent or more of the sale of a fungible mass is for a foreign use, then no portion of the fungible mass is for a foreign use.

(4) *Examples.*—The following examples illustrate the application of this paragraph (d).

(i) *Presumed facts.*—The following facts are assumed for purposes of the examples—

(A) DC is a domestic corporation.

(B) FP is a foreign person that is a foreign unrelated party (as defined in § 1.250(b)-6(b)(2)) with respect to DC, and DC obtains documentation establishing that FP is a foreign person.

(C) Any documentation obtained meets the reliability requirements described in § 1.250(b)-3(d).

(D) The treatment of any sale as a FDDEI sale would not reduce DC's foreign-derived deduction eligible income for the year.

(ii) *Examples.*—(A) *Example 1: Manufacturing outside the United States*—(*1*) *Facts.* DC sells general property for $18x to FP for manufacture outside the United States and obtains documentation of shipment of the property to a location outside the United States. DC does not know or have reason to know that the property will be subject to a domestic use before manufacture, but DC knows or has reason to know that the property will be subject to a domestic use after manufacture and within three years of delivery to FP. FP will incorporate the property into a second product outside the United States that FP will sell to a United States person for $100x. The property is not physically or materially changed in the process of its incorporation into the second product.

(*2*) *Analysis.* Because the fair market value of the general property FP purchases from DC and incorporates into the second product does not exceed 20% of the fair market value of the second product, the general property FP purchases from DC is a component, and therefore the property is treated as subject to manufacture, assembly, or other processing outside the United States. See paragraphs (d)(2)(iii)(A) and (B) of this section. As a result, notwithstanding that DC knows or has reason to know that the property will be subject to a domestic use within three years of delivery, DC does not know or have reason to know that its sale of general property to FP is not for a foreign use. See paragraph (d)(2)(i)(B) of this section. Accordingly, DC's sale of property to FP is for a foreign use under paragraph (d)(2) of this section, and the sale is a FDDEI sale.

(B) *Example 2: Manufacturing outside the United States*—(*1*) *Facts.* The facts are the same as in paragraph (d)(2)(iv)(A)(*1*) of this section (the facts in *Example 1*), except FP purchases the general property from DC for $25x.

(*2*) *Analysis.* Because the fair market value of the general property FP purchases from DC and incorporates into the second product exceeds 20% of the fair market value of the second product, the general property is not treated as a component of the second product. Because the property is also not subject to a physical and material change in the process of incorporation into the second product, the property is not subject to manufacture, assembly, or other processing outside the United States. As a result, because DC knows or has reason to know that FP will sell the second product, which includes the property, for domestic use, DC knows or has reason to know that its sale of general property to FP is not for a foreign use. Accordingly, DC's sale of the property to FP is not for a foreign use under paragraph (d)(2) of this section, and the sale is not a FDDEI sale.

(C) *Example 3: Sale of a fungible mass of products*—(*1*) *Facts.* DC and persons other than DC sell multiple units of fungible general property to FP during the taxable year. DC obtains documentation of shipment of the property to a location outside the United States, but it knows or has reason to know that some portion of the property will be resold back to customers in the United States. DC also engages in reliable market research that determines that approximately 25% of the fungible general property FP sold during the taxable year is for domestic use.

(*2*) *Analysis.* Notwithstanding that the documentation of shipment meets the reliability requirements of § 1.250(b)-3(d), DC knows or has reason to know that certain units of the property are not for a foreign use. See paragraphs (d)(1) and (2) of this section. However, DC can establish foreign use of a portion of the fungible property through its market research. See paragraphs (d)(1) and (d)(3)(iii) of this section. Based on its market research, DC knows that approximately 25% of the total units of fungible general property that FP purchased from all persons in the taxable year is sold by FP for domestic use. Accordingly, DC satisfies the test for a foreign use under paragraph (d)(2) of this section with respect to 75% of its sales of the property to FP.

(e) *Foreign use for intangible property.*—(1) *In general.*—A sale of intangible property is for a foreign use only to the extent the seller establishes that the sale is for a foreign use within the meaning of paragraph (e)(2) of this section by obtaining documentation described in paragraph (e)(3) of this section (which meets the reliability requirements described in § 1.250(b)-3(d)) and, as of the FDII filing date, the seller does not know or have reason to know that the portion of the sale of the intangible property for which the seller establishes foreign use is not for a foreign use within the meaning of paragraph (e)(2) of this section.

(2) *Determination of foreign use.*—(i) *In general.*—A sale of intangible property is for a foreign use only to the extent that the intangible property generates revenue from exploitation outside the United States. A sale of intangible property rights providing for exploitation both within the United States and outside the United States is for a foreign use in proportion to the revenue generated from exploitation of the intangible property outside the United States over the total revenue generated from the exploitation of the intangible property. For intangible property used in the development, manufacture, sale, or distribution of a product, the intangible property is treated as exploited at the location of the end user when the product is sold to the end user. Paragraphs (e)(2)(ii) and (iii) of this section provide rules for how and when to determine revenue from exploitation with respect to different types of sales of intangible property.

(ii) *Sales in exchange for periodic payments.*—In the case of a sale of intangible property to a foreign person in exchange for periodic payments, the extent to which the sale is for a foreign use is determined on an annual basis based on the actual revenue earned by the recipient for the taxable year in which a periodic payment is received.

(iii) *Sales in exchange for a lump sum.*—In the case of a sale of intangible property to a foreign person for a lump sum, the extent to which the sale is for a foreign use is determined based on the ratio of the total net present value of revenue the seller would have reasonably expected to earn from the exploitation of the intangible property outside the United States to the total net present value of revenue the seller would have reasonably expected to earn from the exploitation of the intangible property.

(3) *Documentation of foreign use of intangible property.*—(i) *Documentation for sales for periodic payments.*—Except as provided in paragraph (e)(3)(ii) of this section, a seller establishes the extent to which a sale of intangible property described in paragraph (e)(2)(ii) of this section is for a foreign use by obtaining one or more of the following types of documentation with respect to the sale—

(A) A written statement from the recipient providing the amount of the annual revenue from sales or sublicenses of the intangible property or sales of products with respect to which the intangible property is used that is generated as a result of exploitation of the intangible property outside the United States and the total amount of revenue from such sales or sublicenses worldwide;

(B) A binding contract for the sale of the intangible property that provides that the intangible property can be exploited solely outside the United States;

(C) Audited financial statements or annual reports of the recipient stating the amount of annual revenue earned within the United States and outside the United States from sales of products with respect to which the intangible property is used;

(D) Any statements or documents used by the seller and the recipient to determine the amount of payment due for exploitation of the intangible property if those statements or documents provide reliable data on revenue earned within the United States and outside the United States; or

(E) Any other forms of documentation as prescribed by the Secretary in forms, instructions, or other guidance.

(ii) *Certain sales to foreign unrelated parties.*—In the case of a sale of intangible property described in paragraph (e)(2)(ii) of this section that are not contingent on revenue or profit to a foreign unrelated party (as defined in § 1.250(b)-6(b)(2)), where the seller is unable to obtain the documentation described in paragraph (e)(3)(i) of this section without undue burden, a seller establishes the extent to which the sale of intangible property is for a foreign use using the principles of paragraph (e)(3)(iii) of this section, except that the seller must make reasonable projections on an annual basis.

(iii) *Documentation for sales in exchange for a lump sum.*—A seller establishes the extent to which a sale of intangible property described in paragraph (e)(2)(iii) of this section is for a foreign use through documentation containing reasonable projections of the amount and location of revenue that the seller would have reasonably expected to earn from exploiting the intangible property. To be considered reasonable, the projections must be consistent with the financial data and projections used by the seller to determine the price it sold the intangible property to the foreign person.

(4) *Examples.*—The following examples illustrate the application of this paragraph (e).

(i) *Presumed facts.*—The following facts are assumed for purposes of the examples—

(A) DC is a domestic corporation.

(B) Except as otherwise provided, FP and FP2 are foreign persons that are foreign unrelated parties (as defined in § 1.250(b)-6(b)(2)) with respect to DC.

(C) Any documentation obtained meets the reliability requirements described in § 1.250(b)-3(d).

(D) All of DC's income is deduction eligible income.

(E) The treatment of any sale as a FDDEI sale would not reduce DC's foreign-derived deduction eligible income for the year.

(ii) *Examples.*—(A) *Example 1: License of worldwide rights with documentation*—(*1*) *Facts.* DC licenses to FP worldwide rights to the copyright to composition A in exchange for annual royalties of $60x. FP sells composition A to customers through digital downloads from servers. In the taxable year, FP earns $100x in revenue from sales of copies of composition A to customers, of which $60x is from customers located in the United States and the remaining $40x is from customers located outside the United States. FP provides DC with records showing the amount of revenue earned in the taxable year from sales of composition A to establish the royalties owed to DC. These records also provide DC with the amount of revenue earned from sales of composition A in different countries, including the United States.

(2) *Analysis*. Based on the information provided, DC has obtained documentation establishing that 40% ($40x/$100x) of the revenue generated by the copyright during the taxable year is earned outside the United States. Accordingly, a portion of DC's license to FP is for a foreign use under paragraph (e)(2) of this section and therefore such portion is a FDDEI sale. The $24x of royalty (0.40 x $60x) derived with respect to such portion is included in DC's gross FDDEI for the taxable year.

(B) *Example 2: License of worldwide rights without documentation*—(1) *Facts*. The facts are the same as in paragraph (e)(4)(ii)(A)(1) of this section (the facts in *Example 1*), except FP does not provide DC with data showing how much revenue was earned from sales in different countries.

(2) *Analysis*. DC has not obtained documentation establishing the amount of revenue FP earned from sales of composition A outside the United States. Accordingly, DC's license of the copyright is not for a foreign use under paragraph (e)(2) of this section and is not a FDDEI sale.

(C) *Example 3: Sale of patent rights protected in the United States and other countries; documentation through financial projections*—(1) *Facts*. DC owns a patent for an active pharmaceutical ingredient ("API") approved for treatment of disease A ("indication A") in the United States and in Countries A, B, and C. The patent is registered in the United States and in Countries A, B, and C. DC sells to FP all of its patent rights to the API for indication A for a lump sum payment of $1,000x. DC has no basis in the patent rights. To determine the sales price for the patent rights, DC projected that the net present value of the revenue it would earn from selling a pharmaceutical product incorporating the API for indication A was $5,000x, with 15% of the revenue earned from sales within the United States and 85% of the revenue earned from sales outside the United States.

(2) *Analysis*. Based on the financial projections DC used to determine the sales price, DC has obtained documentation establishing that 85% of the revenue that will be generated by the patent rights will be outside the United States. Accordingly, a portion of DC's sale to FP is for a foreign use under paragraph (e)(2) of this section and such portion is a FDDEI sale. The $850x (85% x $1,000x) of gain derived with respect to such portion is included in DC's gross FDDEI for the taxable year.

(D) *Example 4: Limited use license of copyrighted computer software; documentation through public filing*—(1) *Facts*. DC provides FP with a limited use license to copyrighted computer software in exchange for an annual fee of $100x. The limited use license restricts FP's use of the computer software to 100 of FP's employees. The limited use license prohibits FP from using the computer software in any way other than as an end-user, which includes prohibiting sublicensing, selling, reverse engineering, or modifying the computer software. FP's annual report for the taxable year indicates that all of FP's employees are physically located outside the United States.

(2) *Analysis*. The software licensed to FP is exploited where its employees that use the software are located. The revenue DC earns from the limited use license to FP is based on the number of FP's employees allowed to use the computer software as end-users. Based on FP's annual report for the taxable year, DC has obtained documentation establishing that all the revenue generated for the use of the copyrighted computer software is earned outside the United States for the taxable year. Accordingly, DC's license to FP is for a foreign use and therefore a FDDEI sale. The entire $100x of the license fee is included in DC's gross FDDEI for the taxable year.

(E) *Example 5: Limited use license of copyrighted computer software; documentation through public filing*—(1) *Facts*. The facts are the same as in paragraph (e)(4)(ii)(D)(*1*) of this section (the facts in *Example 4*), except that FP's annual report for the taxable year indicates that FP has offices both within and outside the United States, and that 50% of FP's revenue is earned within the United States.

(2) *Analysis*. Based on FP's annual report for the taxable year, DC has obtained documentation establishing that 50% of the revenue generated from the use of the copyrighted computer software is outside the United States for the taxable year. Accordingly, a portion of DC's license to FP is for a foreign use and therefore such portion is a FDDEI sale. The $50x of license fee derived with respect to such portion is included in DC's gross FDDEI for the taxable year.

(F) *Example 6: Deemed sale in exchange for contingent payments under section 367(d)*—(1) *Facts*. DC owns 100% of the stock of FP, a foreign related party (as defined in § 1.250(b)-6(b)(1)) with respect to DC. FP manufactures and sells product A. For the taxable year, DC contributes to FP exclusive worldwide rights to patents, trademarks, knowhow, customer lists, and goodwill and going concern value (collectively, intangible property) related to product A in an exchange described in section 351. As a result, DC is required to report an annual income inclusion on its Federal income tax return based on the productivity, use, or disposition of the contributed intangible property under section 367(d). DC includes a percentage of FP's revenue in its gross income under section 367(d) each year. In the current taxable year, FP earns $1,000x of revenue from sales of product A. Based on FP's sales records for the taxable year, $300x of its revenue is earned from sales of product A to customers within the United States, and $700x of its revenue is earned from sales of product A to customers outside the United States.

(2) *Analysis*. DC's deemed sale of the intangible property to FP in exchange for payments contingent upon the productivity, use, or disposition of the intangible property related to product A under section 367(d) is a sale for purposes of section 250 and this section. See § 1.250(b)-3(b)(7). Based on FP's sales records, DC has obtained documentation that 70% ($700/$1,000x) of the revenue generated by the intangible property is generated outside the United States in the taxable year. Accordingly,

for the taxable year, 70% of DC's deemed sale to FP is for a foreign use, and 70% of DC's income inclusion under section 367(d) derived with respect to such portion is included in DC's gross FDDEI for the taxable year.

(f) *Special rule for certain financial instruments.*—The sale of a security (as defined in section 475(c)(2)) or a commodity (as defined in section 475(e)(2)(B) through (D)) is not a FDDEI sale. [Reg. § 1.250(b)-4.]

§ 1.250(b)-5. FDDEI services.—(a) *Scope.*—This section provides rules for determining whether a provision of a service is a FDDEI service. Paragraph (b) of this section defines a FDDEI service. Paragraph (c) of this section provides definitions relevant for determining whether a provision of a service is a FDDEI service. Paragraph (d) of this section provides rules for determining whether a general service is provided to a consumer located outside the United States. Paragraph (e) of this section provides rules for determining whether a general service is provided to a business recipient located outside the United States. Paragraph (f) of this section provides rules for determining whether a proximate service is provided to a recipient located outside the United States. Paragraph (g) of this section provides rules for determining whether a service is provided with respect to property located outside the United States. Paragraph (h) of this section provides rules for determining whether a transportation service is provided to a recipient, or with respect to property, located outside the United States.

(b) *Definition of FDDEI service.*—Except as provided in § 1.250(b)-6(d), the term *FDDEI service* means a provision of a service described in one of paragraphs (b)(1) through (5) of this section. If only a portion of a service is treated as provided to a person, or with respect to property, outside the United States, the provision of the service is a FDDEI service only to the extent of the gross income derived with respect to such portion.

(1) The provision of a general service to a consumer located outside the United States (as determined under paragraph (d) of this section).

(2) The provision of a general service to a business recipient located outside the United States (as determined under paragraph (e) of this section).

(3) The provision of a proximate service to a recipient located outside the United States (as determined under paragraph (f) of this section).

(4) The provision of a property service with respect to tangible property located outside the United States (as determined under paragraph (g) of this section).

(5) The provision of a transportation service to a recipient, or with respect to property, located outside the United States (as determined under paragraph (h) of this section).

(c) *Definitions.*—This paragraph (c) provides definitions that apply for purposes of this section and § 1.250(b)-6.

(1) *Benefit.*—The term *benefit* has the meaning set forth in § 1.482-9(l)(3).

(2) *Business recipient.*—The term *business recipient* means a recipient other than a consumer.

(3) *Consumer.*—The term *consumer* means a recipient that is an individual that purchases a general service for personal use.

(4) *General service.*—The term *general service* means any service other than a property service, proximate service, or transportation service.

(5) *Property service.*—The term *property service* means a service, other than a transportation service, provided with respect to tangible property, but only if substantially all of the service is performed at the location of the property and results in physical manipulation of the property such as through assembly, maintenance, or repair. Substantially all of a service is performed at the location of property if the renderer spends more than 80 percent of the time providing the service at or near the location of the property.

(6) *Proximate service.*—The term *proximate service* means a service, other than a property service or a transportation service, provided to a recipient, but only if substantially all of the service is performed in the physical presence of the recipient or, in the case of a business recipient, its employees. Substantially all of a service is performed in the physical presence of the recipient or its employees if the renderer spends more than 80 percent of the time providing the service in the physical presence of the recipient or its employees.

(7) *Transportation service.*—The term *transportation service* means a service to transport a person or property using aircraft, railroad rolling stock, vessel, motor vehicle, or any similar mode of transportation.

(d) *General services provided to consumers.*—(1) *In general.*—A general service is provided to a consumer located outside the United States only if the renderer establishes that the consumer is located outside the United States by obtaining the documentation described in paragraph (d)(3) of this section (which meets the reliability requirements described in § 1.250(b)-3(d)) and, as of the FDII filing date, the renderer does not know or have reason to know that the consumer is located within the United States (as determined under paragraph (d)(2) of this section) when the service is provided.

(2) *Location of consumer.*—For purposes of paragraph (d)(1) of this section, the consumer of a general service is located where the consumer resides when the service is provided.

(3) *Documentation of location of consumer.*—(i) *In general.*—Except as provided in paragraph (d)(3)(ii) of this section, a renderer establishes that a consumer is located outside the United States only if the renderer obtains one or more of the following types of documentation with respect to the consumer—

(A) A written statement by the consumer indicating that the consumer resides outside the United States when the service is provided;

(B) Any valid identification issued by a foreign government or an agency thereof that is typically used for identification purposes; or

(C) Any other forms of documentation as prescribed by the Secretary in forms, instructions, or other guidance.

(ii) *Special rules.*—(A) *Special rule for small businesses.*—A renderer that receives less than $10,000,000 in gross receipts during the prior taxable year establishes that any consumer of a service provided in the taxable year is located outside the United States if the renderer's billing address for the consumer is outside of the United States. If a renderer has a prior taxable year of fewer than 12 months (a short period), gross receipts are annualized by multiplying the gross receipts for the short period by 365 and dividing the result by the number of days in the short period.

(B) *Special rule for small transactions.*—A renderer that receives less than $5,000 in gross receipts during a taxable year from a consumer establishes that such consumer is located outside the United States for such taxable year if the renderer's billing address for the consumer is outside the United States.

(e) *General services provided to business recipients.*—(1) *In general.*—A general service is provided to a business recipient located outside the United States only to the extent that the renderer establishes that the service is provided to a business recipient located outside the United States (as determined under paragraph (e)(2) of this section) by obtaining the documentation described in paragraph (e)(3) of this section (which meets the reliability requirements described in § 1.250(b)-3(d)) and, as of the FDII filing date, the renderer does not know or have reason to know that the portion of the service which the seller establishes is provided to a business recipient located outside the United States is provided to a business recipient that is located within the United States when the service is provided.

(2) *Location of business recipient.*—(i) *In general.*—A service is provided to a business recipient located outside of the United States to the extent that the gross income derived by the renderer from such service is allocated to the business recipient's operations outside the United States under the rules in paragraphs (e)(2)(i)(A) and (B) of this section. A service is provided to a business recipient located within the United States to the extent that a service is not provided to a business recipient located outside the United States.

(A) *Determination of business operations that benefit from the service.*—If the renderer provides a service that provides a benefit to the operations of the business recipient in specific locations, gross income of the renderer is allocated to a business recipient's operations outside the United States to the extent that the benefit of the service is conferred on operations of the business recipient that are located outside the United States. However, if the renderer is unable to obtain reliable information regarding the specific locations of the operations of the business recipient to which a benefit is conferred, or if the renderer provides a service that does not provide a benefit to specific locations of the business recipient's operations but rather will generally confer a benefit on all locations of the business recipient's operations, gross income of the renderer is allocated ratably to all of the business recipient's operations at the time the service is provided.

(B) *Determination of amount of benefit conferred on operations outside the United States.*—The amount of the benefit conferred on a business recipient's operations located outside the United States is determined under any method that is reasonable under the circumstances. In determining whether a method is reasonable, the principles of § 1.482-9(k) apply, treating the business recipient's operations in different locations as if they were "recipients" and treating the renderer's gross income as if they were "costs" as those terms are used in § 1.482-9(k). Reasonable methods may include, for example, allocations based on time spent or costs incurred by the renderer or gross receipts, revenue, profits, or assets of the business recipient.

(ii) *Location of business recipient's operations.*—For purposes of this paragraph (e), a business recipient is treated as having operations in any location where it maintains an office or other fixed place of business.

(3) *Documentation of location of business recipient.*—(i) *In general.*—A renderer establishes that a business recipient is located outside the United States only if the renderer obtains one or more of the types of documentation described in paragraphs (e)(3)(i)(A) through (E) of this section. The documentation must also support the renderer's allocation of income described in paragraph (e)(2)(i) of this section.

(A) A written statement from the business recipient that specifies the locations of the operations of the business recipient that benefit from the service.

(B) A binding contract that specifies the locations of the operations of the business recipient that benefit from the service.

(C) Documentation obtained in the ordinary course of the provision of the service that specifies the locations of the operations of the business recipient that benefit from the service.

(D) Publicly available information that establishes the locations of the operations of the business recipient.

(E) Any other forms of documentation as prescribed by the Secretary in forms, instructions, or other guidance.

(ii) *Special rules.*—(A) *Special rule for small businesses.*—A renderer that receives less than $10,000,000 in gross receipts during a prior taxable year establishes that a business recipient of a service provided in a taxable year is located outside the United States if the renderer's billing address for the business recipient is outside of the United States. If the renderer's prior taxable year is less than 12 months (a short period), gross receipts are annualized by multiplying the gross receipts for the short period by 365 and dividing the result by the number of days in the short period.

(B) *Special rule for small transactions.*—A renderer that receives less than $5,000 in gross receipts during a taxable year from services provided to a business recipient in such taxable year establishes that such business recipient is located outside the United States if the renderer's billing address for the business recipient is outside the United States.

(4) *Related parties.*—For purposes of this paragraph (e), a reference to a business recipient includes a reference to any related party of the business recipient.

(5) *Examples.*—The following examples illustrate the application of this paragraph (e).

(i) *Presumed facts.*—The following facts are assumed for purposes of the examples—

(A) DC is a domestic corporation.

(B) A and R are not related parties of DC.

(C) Any documentation obtained meets the reliability requirements described in §1.250(b)-3(d).

(D) The treatment of any service as a FDDEI service would not reduce DC's foreign-derived deduction eligible income for the year.

(ii) *Examples.*—(A) *Example 1: Service that benefits specific aspects of the business recipient's business*—(1) *Facts.* For the taxable year, DC provides a marketing service to R, a company that operates restaurants within and outside of the United States, in exchange for $150x. Publicly available information indicates that 50% of the revenue earned by R and its related parties is from customers located outside of the United States. However, the marketing service that DC provides relates specifically to a single chain of restaurants that R operates. Sales information that R provides to DC indicates that 70% of the revenue of the restaurant chain is from locations within the United States and 30% of the revenue is from locations outside the United States.

(2) *Analysis.* R is located outside the United States in part under paragraph (e)(2)(i) of this section because DC's services benefit both R's operations within the United States and its operations outside the United States. Under paragraph (e)(2)(i) of this section, the portion of the service provided by DC that is treated as provided to a person located outside the United States is determined by the amount of DC's gross income from the service that is allocated to R's operations outside the United States. Because DC provides a service that provides a benefit to R's operations in specific locations, and reliable information about the specific locations of the operations that receive a benefit is available, DC must determine R's location based on information relating specifically to R's business operations that benefits from DC's service. See paragraph (e)(2)(i)(A) of this section. In this case, allocation of DC's gross income based on the revenue of the business recipient is a reasonable method. See paragraph (e)(2)(i)(B) of this section. Therefore, 30% of the provision of the marketing service is treated as the provision of a service to a person located outside the United States and a FDDEI service under paragraph (b)(2) of this section. Accordingly, $45x ($150x × 0.30) of DC's gross income from the provision of the marketing service is included in DC's gross FDDEI for the taxable year.

(B) *Example 2: Service that benefits the business recipient's operations generally*—(1) *Facts.* The facts are the same as in paragraph (e)(5)(ii)(A)(1) of this section (the facts in *Example 1*), except that DC provides an information technology service to R that benefits R's entire business.

(2) *Analysis.* Because the service that DC provides relate to R's entire business, DC may rely on publicly available information indicating that 50% of R's operations are outside of the United States. See paragraph (e)(2)(i)(A) of this section. Therefore, 50% of the provision of the information technology service is treated as a service to a person located outside the United States and a FDDEI service under paragraph (b)(2) of this section. Accordingly, $75x ($150x x 0.50) of DC's gross income from the provision of the information technology service is included in DC's gross FDDEI for the taxable year.

(C) *Example 3: No reliable information about which operations benefit from the service*—(1) *Facts.* The facts are the same as in paragraph (e)(5)(ii)(A) (1) of this section (the facts in *Example 1*), except that no information is available to DC about the specific chain of restaurants for which the service is provided.

(2) *Analysis.* Because the only information available to DC relates to R's entire business, DC may rely on publicly available information indicating that 50% of R's operations are outside of the United States to determine the portion of the service treated as provided to a person located outside the United States. See paragraph (e)(2)(i)(A) of this section. Therefore, 50% of the provision of the marketing service is treated as a service to a person located outside the United States and a FDDEI service under paragraph (b)(2) of this section. Accordingly, $75x ($150x x 0.50) of DC's gross income from the provision of the marketing service is included in DC's gross FDDEI for the taxable year.

(D) *Example 4: Service provided to a domestic intermediary*—(1) *Facts.* A, a domestic corporation that operates solely in the United States, enters into a services agreement with R, a company that operates solely outside the United States. Under the agreement, A agrees to perform a consulting service for R. A hires DC to provide a service to A that A will use in the provision of a consulting service to R.

(2) *Analysis.* A is located within the United States because the service that DC provides A confers a benefit solely to A's operations within the United States. R is located outside the United States because the service that A provides to R confers a benefit solely to R's operations outside the United States. See paragraph (e)(2)(i) of this section. Because DC provides a service to A, a person located within the United States, DC's provision of the service to A is not a FDDEI service under paragraph (b)(2) of this section, even though the service is used by A in providing a service to R, a person located outside the United States. See also section 250(b)(5)(B)(ii). However, A's provision of the consulting service to R may be a FDDEI service, in which case A's gross income from the provision of such service would be included in A's gross FDDEI.

(f) *Proximate services.*—A proximate service is provided with respect to a recipient located outside the United States if the proximate service is performed outside the United States. In the case of a proximate service performed partly within the United States and partly outside of the United States, a proportionate amount of the service is treated as provided to a recipient located outside the United States corresponding to the portion of time the renderer spends providing the service outside of the United States.

(g) *Property services.*—A property service is provided with respect to tangible property located outside the United States only if the property is located outside the United States for the duration of the period the service is performed.

(h) *Transportation services.*—Except as provided in this paragraph (h), a transportation service is provided to a recipient, or with respect to property, located outside the United States only if both the origin and the destination of the service are outside of the United States. However, in the case of a transportation service provided to a recipient, or with respect to property, where either the origin or the destination of the service is outside of the United States, but not both, then 50 percent of the transportation service is considered provided to a recipient, or with respect to property, located outside the United States. [Reg. §1.250(b)-5.]

§1.250(b)-6. Related party transactions.—(a) *Scope.*—This section provides additional rules for determining whether a sale of property or a provision of a service to a related party is a FDDEI transaction. Paragraph (b) of this section provides additional definitions relevant for determining whether a sale of property or a provision of a service to a related party is a FDDEI transaction. Paragraph (c) of this section provides additional rules for determining whether a sale of general property to a foreign related party is a FDDEI sale. Paragraph (d) of this section provides additional rules for determining whether the provision of a general service to a business recipient that is a related party is a FDDEI service.

(b) *Definitions.*—This paragraph (b) provides definitions that apply for purposes of this section.

(1) *Foreign related party.*—The term *foreign related party* means, with respect to a seller or renderer, any foreign person that is a related party of the seller or renderer.

(2) *Foreign unrelated party.*—The term *foreign unrelated party* means, with respect to a seller, a foreign person that is not a related party of the seller.

(3) *Related party sale.*—The term *related party sale* means a sale of general property to a foreign related party that satisfies the requirements described in §1.250(b)-4(b) without regard to paragraph (c) of this section. See §1.250(b)-1(e)(3)(ii)(D) *(Example 4)* for an illustration of a related party sale in the case of a seller that is a partnership.

(4) *Related party service.*—The term *related party service* means a provision of a general service to a business recipient that is a related party of the renderer and that is described in §1.250(b)-5(b)(2) without regard to paragraph (d) of this section.

(5) *Unrelated party transaction.*—The term *unrelated party transaction* means, with respect to property purchased in a related party sale from a seller—

(i) A sale of the property by a foreign related party to a foreign unrelated party with respect to the seller;

(ii) A sale of property by a foreign related party to a foreign unrelated party with respect to the seller if the property sold in the related party sale is a component of the property sold to the foreign unrelated party;

(iii) A sale of property by a foreign related party to a foreign unrelated party with respect to the seller, other than a sale described in paragraph (b)(5)(ii) of this section, if the property sold in the related party sale is used in connection with the property sold to the foreign unrelated party; or

(iv) A provision of a service by a foreign related party to a foreign unrelated party with respect to the seller, if the property sold in the related party sale was used in connection with the provision of the service.

(c) *Related party sales.*—(1) *In general.*—A related party sale is a FDDEI sale only if the requirements described in either paragraph (c)(1)(i) or (ii) of this section are satisfied with respect to the related party sale. Section 250(b)(5)(C)(i) and this paragraph (c) does not apply to determine whether a sale of intangible property to a foreign related party is a FDDEI sale.

(i) *Sale of property in an unrelated party transaction.*—A related party sale is a FDDEI sale if an unrelated party transaction described in paragraph (b)(5)(i) or (ii) of this section occurs with respect to the property purchased in the related party sale, such unrelated party transaction is described in §1.250(b)-4(b), and, except as provided in this paragraph (c)(1)(i), the unrelated party transaction occurs on or before the FDII filing date. In the case of an unrelated party transaction that occurs after the FDII filing date with respect to a related party sale, a taxpayer may file an amended return for the taxable year in which the related party sale occurred, within the period of limitations provided by section 6511, claiming the related party sale as a FDDEI sale for purposes of determining the taxpayer's foreign-derived intangible income for that taxable year.

(ii) *Use of property in an unrelated party transaction.*—A related party sale is a FDDEI sale if, as of the FDII filing date, the seller in the related party sale reasonably expects that one or more unrelated party transactions described in paragraph (b)(5)(iii) or (iv) of this section will occur with respect to the property purchased in the related party sale, such unrelated party transaction or transactions would be described in §1.250(b)-4(b) or §1.250(b)-5(b) without regard to the documentation rules in §1.250(b)-4 or §1.250(b)-5, and more than 80 percent of the revenue earned by the foreign related party with respect to the property will be earned from such unrelated party transaction or transactions.

(2) *Treatment of foreign related party as seller or renderer.*—For purposes of determining whether a sale of property or provision of a service by a foreign related party is, or would be, described in §1.250(b)-4 or §1.250(b)-5 (except for purposes of obtaining documentation), the foreign related party that sells the property or provides the service is treated as a seller or renderer, as applicable, and the foreign unrelated party is treated as the recipient. In the case of an unrelated party transaction described in paragraph (b)(5)(i) or (ii) of this section, the seller in the related party sale must obtain the documentation required in §1.250(b)-4.

(3) *Transactions between a foreign related party and other foreign related parties.*—All foreign related parties of the seller are treated as if they were a single foreign related party for purposes of applying paragraphs (c)(1) and (2) of this section. Accordingly, if a foreign related party sells or uses property purchased in a related party sale in a transaction with a second foreign related party of the seller, transactions between the second foreign related party and unrelated parties may be treated as an unrelated party transaction for purposes of applying paragraph (c)(1) of this section to a related party sale.

(4) *Example.*—The following example illustrates the application of paragraph (c) of this section.

(i) *Facts.* DC, a domestic corporation, sells a machine to FC, a foreign related party of DC in a transaction described in § 1.250(b)-4(b) (without regard to § 1.250(b)-6(c)). FC uses the machine solely to manufacture product A. As of the FDII filing date for the taxable year, FC reasonably expects that more than 80% of future revenue from sales of product A will be from sales that would be described in § 1.250(b)-4(b) without regard to the documentation requirements of § 1.250(b)-4(c) and (d).

(ii) *Analysis.* The sale by DC to FC is a related party sale. Because FC uses the machine to make product A, but the machine is not a component of product A, FC's sale of product A is an unrelated party transaction described in paragraph (b)(5)(iii) of this section. Therefore, DC's sale of the machine is only a FDDEI sale if the requirements of paragraph (c)(1)(ii) of this section are satisfied. Because DC reasonably expects that more than 80% of the revenue from future sales of product A will be from unrelated party transactions that would be described in § 1.250(b)-4(b), DC's sale of the machine to FC is a FDDEI sale.

(d) *Related party services.*—(1) *In general.*—Except as provided in this paragraph (d)(1), a related party service is a FDDEI service only if the related party service is not substantially similar to a service provided by the related party to a person located within the United States. However, if a related party service is substantially similar to a service provided (in whole or in part) by the related party to a person located in the United States solely by reason of paragraph (d)(2)(ii) of this section, the amount of gross income from the related party service attributable to a FDDEI service is equal to the gross income from the related party service multiplied by a fraction, the numerator of which is the sum of the benefits conferred by the related party service to persons not located within the United States and the denominator of which is the sum of all benefits conferred by the related party service. Section 250(b)(5)(C)(ii) and this paragraph (d)(1) apply only to a general service provided to a business recipient and are not applicable with respect to any other service provided to a foreign related party.

(2) *Substantially similar services.*—A related party service is substantially similar to a service provided by the related party to a person located within the United States only if the related party service is used by the related party to provide a service to a person located within the United States and either—

(i) 60 percent or more of the benefits conferred by the related party service are to persons located within the United States; or

(ii) 60 percent or more of the price paid by persons located within the United States for the service provided by the related party is attributable to the related party service.

(3) *Location of recipient of services provided by related party.*—For purposes of paragraph (d) of this section, the location of a consumer or business recipient with respect to a related party service is determined under the principles of § 1.250(b)-5(d)(2) and (e)(2), respectively.

(4) *Examples.*—The following examples illustrate the application of this paragraph (d).

(i) *Presumed facts.*—The following facts are assumed for purposes of the examples—

(A) DC is a domestic corporation.

(B) FC is a foreign corporation and a foreign related party of DC that operates solely outside the United States.

(C) The service DC provides to FC is a general service provided to a business recipient located outside the United States as described in § 1.250(b)-5(b)(2) without regard to the application of paragraph (d) of this section.

(D) The benefits conferred by DC's service to FC's customers are not indirect or remote within the meaning of § 1.482-9(l)(3)(ii).

(ii) *Examples.*—(A) *Example 1: Services that are substantially similar services under paragraph (d)(2)(i) of this section*—(*1*) *Facts.* FC enters into a services agreement with R, a company that operates restaurant chains within and outside the United States. Under the agreement, FC agrees to furnish a design for the renovation of a chain of restaurants that R owns, which design will include architectural plans. FC hires DC to provide an architectural service to FC that FC will use in the provision of its design service to R. The architectural service that DC provides to FC will serve no other purpose than to enable FC to provide its service to R. The architectural service will benefit solely R's operations within the United States. FC pays an arm's length price of $50x to DC for the architectural service and DC recognizes $50x of gross income from the service. FC incurs additional costs to add additional design elements to the plans and charges R a total of $100x for its service.

(*2*) *Analysis.* The service that DC provides to FC is used in the provision of a service to R. R is treated as entirely located within the United States under paragraph (d)(3) of this section and the principles of § 1.250(b)-5(e)(2) because only its U.S. operations benefit from the service provided by DC. Because FC uses DC's architectural service to provide its design service to R, and the architectural service that DC provides to FC will serve no purpose other than to enable FC to provide its service to R, 100% of the benefits conferred by DC's architectural service are to R, a person located within the United States. Therefore, the service provided by DC to FC is substantially similar to the service provided by FC to R under paragraph (d)(2)(i) of this section. Accordingly, DC's provision of the architectural service to FC is not a FDDEI service under paragraph (d)(1) of this section and DC's gross income from the architectural service ($50x) is not included in its gross FDDEI.

(B) *Example 2: Services that are substantially similar services under paragraph (d)(2)(ii) of this section*—(*1*) *Facts.* The facts are the same as paragraph (d)(4)(ii)(A)(*1*) (the facts in *Example 1*), except that FC pays an arm's length price of $75x to DC for the architectural service, DC recognizes $75x of gross income from the service, and 90% of the benefits of DC's architectural service are conferred on R's operations outside the United States.

(*2*) *Analysis*—(*i*) *Analysis under paragraph (d)(2)(i) of this section.* R is treated as located within the United States with respect to DC's architectural service under paragraph (d)(3) of this section to the extent of the benefits conferred on its operations within the United States by the architectural service. See § 1.250(b)-5(e)(2). Because 90% of the benefits of DC's architectural service are conferred on R's operations outside the United States, only 10% of the benefits of DC's architectural service are treated as conferred on persons located within the United States under paragraph (d)(3) of this section. Therefore, the architectural service provided by DC to FC is not substantially similar to the design service provided by FC to persons located within the United States under paragraph (d)(2)(i) of this section.

(*ii*) *Analysis under paragraph (d)(2)(ii) of this section.* Because 10% of the benefits of FC's architectural design services are conferred on R's operations within the United States, $10x of the amount paid by R for FC's services (10% x $100) is treated as paid by persons located within the United States. Similarly, because 10% of the benefits of DC's architectural services are conferred on R's operations within the United States, of the $10x paid with respect to R's operations within the United States, $7.5x (10% × $75x) is attributable to DC's architectural service. Accordingly, because 75% ($7.5x/$10x) of the price paid by R to FC for the design service is attributable to the architectural service provided by DC to FC, and R is a person located within the United States under paragraph (d)(3) of this section and the principles of § 1.250(b)-5(e)(2), the architectural service provided by DC to FC is substantially similar to the design service provided by FC to persons located within the United States under paragraph (d)(2)(ii) of this section.

(*iii*) *Application of paragraph (d)(1) of this section.* Because DC's architectural service is substantially similar to FC's design service provided to R, a person located in the United States, solely by reason of paragraph (d)(2)(ii) of this section, the amount of gross income from DC's architectural service included in its gross FDDEI is $67.5x, which is equal to DC's gross income from the architectural service ($75x) multiplied by 90%, which is the percentage of the benefits of DC's architectural service that are conferred on R's operations outside the United States. [Reg. § 1.250(b)-6.]

Business Use or Rental of Dwelling Unit

Business Use or Rental of Dwelling Unit.—Reproduced below is the text of a proposed amendment of § 1.262-1, relating to the deductibility of expenses in connection with the business use, or the rental to others, of a dwelling unit that the taxpayer is deemed to have used for personal purposes during the taxable year (published in the Federal Register on August 7, 1980).

* * *

☐ Par. 3. Paragraph (b)(3) of § 1.262-1 is amended to read as follows:

§ 1.262-1. Personal, living and family expenses.—

* * *

(b) *Examples of personal, living, and family expenses.*—* * *

(3) Expenses and maintaining a household, including amounts paid for rent, water, utilities, domestic service, and the like are not deductible. For rules relating to expenses incurred in connection with dwelling units used for both business purposes and personal purposes, see section 280A and the regulations thereunder.

* * *

Straddles: Capitalization of Interest: Carrying Charges: Personal Property

Straddles: Capitalization of Interest: Carrying Charges: Personal Property.—Reg. §§ 1.263(g)-1—1.263(g)-5, clarifying what constitutes interest and carrying charges and when interest and carrying charges are properly allocable to personal property that is part of a straddle and clarifying that a taxpayer's obligation under a debt instrument can be a position in personal property that is part of a straddle, are proposed (published in the Federal Register on January 18, 2001) (REG-105801-00) (corrected April 2, 2001).

☐ Par. 2. Sections 1.263(g)-1, 1.263(g)-2, 1.263(g)-3, 1.263(g)-4, and 1.263(g)-5 are added to read as follows:

§ 1.263(g)-1. Treatment of interest and carrying charges in the case of straddles; in general.—(a) Under section 263(g), no deduction is allowed for interest and carrying charges allocable to personal property that is part of a straddle (as defined in section 1092(c)). The purpose of section 263(g) is to coordinate the character and the timing of items of income and loss attributable to a taxpayer's positions that are part of a straddle. In order to prevent payments or accruals related to a straddle transaction from giving rise to recognition of deductions or losses before related income is recognized and to prevent the items of loss and income from having different character, no deduction is allowed for interest and carrying charges properly allocable to personal property that is part of a straddle. Rather, such amounts are chargeable to the capital account of the personal property to which the interest and carrying charges are properly allocable.

(b) Section 263(g) does not apply if none of the taxpayer's positions that are part of the straddle are personal property. Section 263(g) also does not apply to hedging transactions as defined in section 1256(e) (see section 263(g)(3)) or to securities to which the mark-to-market accounting method provided by section 475 applies (see section 475(d)(1)).

(c) Section 1.263(g)-2 provides a definition of personal property for purposes of section 263(g) and §§ 1.263(g)-1 through 1.263(g)-5. Section 1.263(g)-3 provides a definition of interest and carrying charges for purposes of section 263(g), section 1092, §§ 1.263(g)-1 through 1.263(g)-5, and § 1.1092(b)-4T. Section 1.263(g)-4 provides a set of allocation rules governing the capitalization of amounts to which section 263(g) applies. [Reg. §1.263(g)-1.]

§1.263(g)-2. Personal property to which interest and carrying charges may properly be allocable.—(a) *Definition of personal property.*—For purposes of section 263(g) and of §§1.263(g)-1 through 1.263(g)-5, *personal property* means property, whether or not actively traded, that is not real property. For purposes of the preceding sentence, a position in personal property may itself be property. In general, however, a position in personal property is not property of a taxpayer unless the position confers or may confer substantial rights on the taxpayer.

(1) *Application to certain financial instruments.*—Personal property includes a stockholder's ownership of common stock, a holder's ownership of a debt instrument, and either party's position in a forward contract or in a conventional swap agreement. Personal property does not include a position that imposes obligations but does not confer substantial rights on the taxpayer. Therefore, the obligor's position in a debt instrument generally is not personal property, even though the obligor may have typical rights of a debtor, such as the right to prepay the debt. However, the obligor on a debt instrument has a position in any personal property underlying the debt instrument. See §1.1092(d)-1(d).

(2) *Options.*—For the purposes of applying this section, a put option or call option imposes obligations but does not confer substantial rights on the grantor, whether or not the option is cash-settled.

(b) *Example.*—The following example illustrates the rules stated in paragraph (a) of this section:

Example. (i) *Facts. A* purchases 100 ounces of gold at a cost of $\$x$. *A* transfers the 100 ounces of gold to a trust that issues multiple classes of trust certificates and is treated as a partnership for tax purposes. In return, *A* receives two trust certificates that are not personal property of a type that is actively traded within the meaning of section 1092(d)(1). One certificate entitles *A* to a payment on termination of the trust at the end of four years equal to the value of the 100 ounces of gold up to a maximum value of $\$(x + y)$. The other certificate entitles *A* to a payment equal to the amount by which the value of 100 ounces of gold exceeds $\$(x + y)$ on termination of the trust. *A* sells the second certificate and keeps the first certificate.

(ii) *Analysis.* The trust certificate retained by *A* is property that is not real property. In addition, ownership of the trust certificate confers certain substantial rights on *A*. Therefore, although the trust certificate is not personal property of a type that is actively traded, *A*'s interest in the trust certificate is personal property for purposes of section 263(g).

[Reg. §1.263(g)-2.]

§1.263(g)-3. Interest and carrying charges properly allocable to personal property that is part of a straddle.—(a) *In general.*—For purposes of section 263(g), section 1092, §§1.263(g)-1 through 1.263(g)-5, and §1.1092(b)-4T, *interest and carrying charges properly allocable to personal property that is part of a straddle* means the excess of interest and carrying charges (as defined in paragraph (b) of this section) over the allowable income offsets (as defined in paragraph (e) of this section).

(b) *Interest and carrying charges.*—Interest and carrying charges are otherwise deductible amounts paid or accrued with respect to indebtedness or other financing incurred or continued to purchase or carry personal property that is part of a straddle and otherwise deductible amounts paid or incurred to carry personal property that is part of a straddle. As provided in section 263(g)(2), interest includes any amount paid or incurred in connection with personal property used in a short sale. Interest and carrying charges include—

(1) Otherwise deductible payments or accruals (including interest and original issue discount) on indebtedness or other financing issued or continued to purchase or carry personal property that is part of a straddle;

(2) Otherwise deductible fees or expenses paid or incurred in connection with acquiring or holding personal property that is part of a straddle including, but not limited to, fees or expenses incurred to purchase, insure, store, maintain or transport the personal property; and

(3) Other otherwise deductible payments or accruals on financial instruments that are part of a straddle or that carry part of a straddle.

(c) *Indebtedness or other financing incurred or continued to purchase or carry personal property that is part of a straddle.*—For purposes of paragraph (b)(1) of this section, indebtedness or other financing that is incurred or continued to purchase or carry personal property that is part of a straddle includes—

(1) Indebtedness or other financing the proceeds of which are used directly or indirectly to purchase or carry personal property that is part of the straddle;

(2) Indebtedness or other financing that is secured directly or indirectly by personal property that is part of the straddle; and

(3) Indebtedness or other financing the payments on which are determined by reference to payments with respect to the personal property or the value of, or change in value of, the personal property.

(d) *Financial instruments that are part of a straddle or that carry part of a straddle.*—For purposes of paragraph (b)(3), financial instruments that are part of a straddle or that carry part of a straddle include—

(1) A financial instrument that is part of the straddle;

(2) A financial instrument that is issued in connection with the creation or acquisition of a position in personal property if that position is part of the straddle;

(3) A financial instrument that is sold or marketed as part of an arrangement that involves a taxpayer's position in personal property that is part of the straddle and that is purported to result in either economic realization of all or part of the appreciation in an asset without simultaneous recognition of taxable income or a current tax deduction (for interest, carrying charges, payments on a notional principal contract, or otherwise) reflecting a payment or expense that is economically offset by an increase in value that is not concurrently recognized for tax purposes or has a different tax character (for example, an interest payment that is economically offset by an increase in value that may result in a capital gain in a later tax period); and

(4) Any other financial instrument if the totality of the facts and circumstances support a reasonable inference that the issuance, purchase, or continuation of the financial instrument by the taxpayer was intended to purchase or carry personal property that is part of the straddle.

(e) *Allowable income offsets.*—The allowable income offsets are:

(1) The amount of interest (including original issue discount) includible in gross income for the taxable year with respect to such personal property;

(2) Any amount treated as ordinary income under section 1271(a)(3)(A), 1278, or 1281(a) with respect to such personal property for the taxable year;

(3) The excess of any dividends includible in gross income with respect to such property for the taxable year over the amount of any deductions allowable with respect to such dividends under section 243, 244, or 245;

(4) Any amount that is a payment with respect to a security loan (within the meaning of section 512(a)(5)) includible in income with respect to the personal property for the taxable year; and

(5) Any amount that is a receipt or accrual includible in income for the taxable year with respect to a financial instrument described in § 1.263(g)-3(d) to the extent the financial instrument is entered into to purchase or carry the personal property. [Reg. § 1.263(g)-3.]

§ 1.263(g)-4. Rules for allocating amounts to personal property that is part of a straddle.—(a) *Allocation rules.*—(1) Interest and carrying charges paid or accrued on indebtedness or other financing issued or continued to purchase or carry personal property that is part of a straddle are allocated, in the order listed—

(i) To personal property that is part of the straddle purchased, directly or indirectly, with the proceeds of the indebtedness or other financing;

(ii) To personal property that is part of the straddle and directly or indirectly secures the indebtedness or other financing; or

(iii) If all or a portion of such interest and carrying charges are determined by reference to the value or change in value of personal property, to such personal property.

(2) Fees and expenses described in § 1.263(g)-3(b)(2) are allocated to the personal property, the acquisition or holding of which resulted in the fees and expenses being paid or incurred.

(3) In all other cases, interest and carrying charges are allocated to personal property that is part of a straddle in the manner that under all the facts and circumstances is most appropriate.

(b) *Coordination with other provisions.*—In the case of a short sale, section 263(g) applies after section 263(h). See sections 263(g)(4)(A) and (h)(6). In case of an obligation to which section 1277 (dealing with deferral of interest deduction allocable to accrued market discount) or 1282 (dealing with deferral of interest deduction allocable to certain accruals on short-term indebtedness) applies, section 263(g) applies after section 1277 and section 1282. See section 263(g)(4)(B). Capitalization under section 263(g) applies before loss deferral under section 1092.

(c) *Examples.*—The following examples illustrate the rules stated in §§ 1.263(g)-2, 1.263(g)-3, and 1.263(g)-4.

Example 1. Cash and Carry Silver.

(i) *Facts.* On January 1, 2002, *A* borrows $*x* at 6% interest and uses the proceeds to purchase *y* ounces of silver from *B*. At approximately the same time, *A* enters into a forward contract with C to deliver *y* ounces of silver to C in one year.

(ii) *Analysis.* The *y* ounces of silver and the forward contract to deliver *y* ounces of silver in one year are offsetting positions with respect to the same personal property and therefore constitute a straddle. See sections 1092(c)(1), (c)(3)(A)(i). The proceeds of the debt instrument were used to purchase personal property that is part of the straddle. Consequently, *A*'s interest payments are interest and carrying charges properly allocable to personal property that is part of a straddle. See § 1.263(g)-3(b)(1) & (c)(1). Under § 1.263(g)-4(a)(1)(i), the interest payments must be charged to the capital account for the *y* ounces of silver purchased by *A* with the proceeds of the borrowing.

Example 2. Additional indebtedness issued to carry personal property.

(i) *Facts.* The facts are the same as for Example 1 except that during the year 2002, the market price of silver increases and *A* is required to post variation margin as security for its obligation to deliver *y* ounces of silver to *C*. *A* incurs additional indebtedness to obtain funds necessary to meet *A*'s variation margin requirement.

(ii) *Analysis.* The additional indebtedness is incurred to continue to carry *A*'s holding of *y* ounces of silver. Consequently, *A*'s interest payments on the additional indebtedness are interest and carrying charges properly allocable to personal property that is part of a straddle and must be charged to the capital account for the *y* ounces of silver.

Example 3. Contingent payment debt instrument.

(i) *Facts.* On January 1, 2002, *D* enters into a contract to deliver *x* barrels of fuel oil to *E* on July 1, 2004, at an aggregate price equal to $*y*. Soon afterward, *D* issues a contingent payment debt instrument to *F* with a principal amount of $*z* and a 2-year term that pays interest quarterly at a rate determined at the beginning of each quarter equal to the greater of zero and the London Interbank Offered Rate (LIBOR) adjusted by an index that varies inversely with changes in the price of fuel oil (so that the interest rate increases as the price of fuel oil decreases and vice versa). The change in the aggregate amount of interest paid on the $*z* of debt due to the functioning of the index approximates the concurrent aggregate change in value of *x* barrels of fuel oil and, thus, the value of *D*'s interest in the forward contract.

(ii) *Analysis.* The debt instrument and the forward contract are offsetting positions with respect to the same personal property and constitute a straddle. See section 1092(c)(1), (c)(3)(A)(i). When issued, the debt instrument is a position in personal property that is part of a straddle. See § 1.1092(d)-1(d). Consequently, *D*'s interest payments are interest and carrying charges properly allocable to personal property that is part of a straddle and must be allocated to the capital account for the forward contract for the delivery of *x* barrels of fuel oil to *E*. See

§§1.263(g)-3(b)(1), (b)(3), (c)(3), and (d)(1) and -4(a)(1)(iii).

Example 4. Financial instrument issued to carry personal property that is part of a straddle.

(i) *Facts.* The facts are the same as for Example 3 except that *D* also enters into a two-year interest rate swap under which *D* receives LIBOR times a notional principal amount equal to $z and pays 7% times $z.

(ii) *Analysis.* Because of the relationship between the two-year debt instrument issued by *D* and the interest rate swap, the interest rate swap is a financial instrument that carries personal property that is part of a straddle. See §1.263(g)-3(d)(4). Net payments made by *D* under the interest rate swap are chargeable to the capital account for the forward contract for the delivery of *x* barrels of fuel oil to *E*. Similarly, net payments received by *D* under the interest rate swap are allowable offsets. See §1.263(g)-3(e)(5).

Example 5. Contingent payment debt instrument with embedded short position.

(i) *Facts.* On January 1, 1998, *G* purchases 100,000 shares of the common stock of *XYZ* corporation (which is publicly traded). On January 1, 2002, the 100,000 shares of *XYZ* corporation common stock were worth $*x* per share. On that date, *G* issued a contingent payment debt instrument for $100,000*x*. The terms of the debt instrument provided that the holders would receive an annual payment of $2,000*x* on December 31 of each year up to and including the maturity date of December 31, 2007. On the maturity date, the holders would also receive a payment of $100,000*x* plus an additional amount, if the price of an *XYZ* share exceeded $1.2*x* on such date, equal to 100,000 times three-quarters of the amount of such excess per share. Thus, *G*'s aggregate payments on the debt instrument varied directly with the increase in value in the *XYZ* shares.

(ii) *Analysis.* The debt instrument is a position in *XYZ* stock. See §1.1092(d)-1(d). The *XYZ* stock is personal property within the meaning of section 1092(d)(3)(B) because the debt instrument is a position with respect to substantially similar or related property (other than stock) within the meaning of section 1092(d)(3)(B)(i)(II). See §1.1092(d)-2(c). The debt instrument and the *XYZ* shares are offsetting positions with respect to the same personal property and constitute a straddle. See sections 1092(c)(1), (c)(3)(A)(i). Consequently, *G*'s interest payments are interest and carrying charges properly allocable to personal property that is part of a straddle, see §§1.263(g)-3(b)(1), (b)(3), (c)(3), and (d)(1), and must be allocated to the capital account for the *XYZ* common stock, see §1.263(g)-4(a)(1)(iii) and (a)(3).

Example 6. Straddle including partnership interest.

(i) *Facts.* H borrows money from *I* to purchase 100 ounces of gold at a cost of $*u*. *H* transfers the 100 ounces of gold and $*v* to a newly created trust that issues multiple classes of trust certificates and is treated as a partnership for tax purposes. In return, H receives two trust certificates. One certificate entitles the holder to a payment on termination of the trust at the end of four years equal to the value of the 100 ounces of gold up to a maximum value of $(*u* + *w*). The other certificate entitles the holder to a payment equal to the amount by which the value of 100 ounces of gold exceeds $(*u* + *w*) on termination of the trust. *H* sells the second certificate and keeps the first certificate. *H* also enters into a forward contract to sell 100 ounces of gold for $1.12*u* per ounce on a date two years after creation of the trust. The trust uses part of the $*v* and similar cash contributions from other investors to pay costs of storing the gold held by the trust and allocates *H*'s share of the expenses to *H*.

(ii) *Analysis.* The trust certificate retained by *H* and the forward contract entered into by *H* are personal property for the purposes of section 263(g). See §1.263(g)-2(a). They are also offsetting positions and constitute a straddle. Section 1092(c)(1). The borrowing from *I* is an indebtedness incurred to purchase personal property that is part of a straddle. See §§1.263(g)-3(b)(1) and (c)(1). Similarly, the gold storage expenses are expenses incurred due to the taxpayer's holding personal property that is part of a straddle. See §1.263(g)-3(b)(2). Therefore both the interest on the borrowing and the gold storage expenses must be allocated to the capital account for the partnership interest represented by the retained trust certificate. See §1.263(g)-4(a)(1)(i) and (a)(2).

Example 7. Equity Swap.

(i) *Facts.* On January 1, 1998, *J* purchases 100,000 shares of the common stock of *XYZ* corporation (which is publicly traded). On December 31, 2001, the 100,000 shares of *XYZ* corporation common stock were worth $*x* per share. On that date, *J* entered into a NPC with *K*. The terms of the NPC provided that *K* would receive an annual payment on December 31 of each year equal to 100,000 times any appreciation in the value of a share of *XYZ* corporation stock above its price at the end of trading on December 31 of the preceding year and 100,000 times the dividends paid during the year on each share of *XYZ* corporation stock. In return, on December 31 of each year, *J* would receive an amount equal to LIBOR times the value of 100,000 *XYZ* shares at the end of trading on December 31 of the preceding year plus 100,000 times the amount of any decrease in the value of a share of *XYZ* corporation stock below its price at the end of trading on December 31 of the preceding year. Payments between *J* and *K* would be netted and continue up to and including the maturity date of the NPC on December 31, 2008. Thus, *J*'s aggregate payments on the NPC varied directly with the increase in value in the *XYZ* shares.

(ii) *Analysis.* The NPC is a position in *XYZ* stock. See §1.1092(d)-2(c). The *XYZ* stock is personal property within the meaning of section 1092(d)(3)(B) because the NPC is a position with respect to substantially similar or related property (other than stock) within the meaning of section 1092(b)(3)(B)(i)(II). See §1.1092(d)-2(a)(1)(ii). The NPC and the *XYZ* shares are offsetting positions with respect to the same personal property and constitute a straddle. See sections 1092(c)(1), (c)(3)(A)(i). Consequently, *J*'s payments are interest and carrying charges properly allocable to personal property that is part of a straddle. See §§1.263(g)-3(b)(3) and (d)(1). Therefore, they should be allocated to the personal property that is part of the straddle in the manner that is most appropriate under all the facts and circumstances. In this case, because these payments are incurred to carry the *XYZ* shares, they should be allocated to the capital account for the *XYZ* common stock. See § 1.263(g)-4(a)(3).

[Reg. § 1.263(g)-4.]

§ 1.263(g)-5. Effective dates.—Sections 1.263(g)-1, 1.263(g)-2, 1.263(g)-3, and 1.263(g)-4 apply to interest and carrying charges properly allocable to personal property that are paid, incurred, or accrued after the date these regulations are adopted as final regulations by publication in the Federal Register for a straddle established on or after January 17, 2001. [Reg. § 1.263(g)-5.]

Deduction for Business Interest Expense: Limitation

Deduction for Business Interest Expense: Limitation.—Amendments to Reg. § 1.263A-9, regarding the limitation on the deduction for business interest expense after the enactment of recent tax legislation, are proposed (published in the Federal Register on December 28, 2018) (REG-106089-18).

Par. 4. Section 1.263A-9 is amended by revising the first and third sentences of paragraph (g)(1)(i) to read as follows:

§ 1.263A-9. The avoided cost method.

* * *

(g) * * *

(1) * * *

(i) Interest must be capitalized under section 263A(f) before the application of section 163(d) (regarding the investment interest limitation), section 163(j) (regarding the limitation on business interest expense), section 266 (regarding the election to capitalize carrying charges), section 469 (regarding the limitation on passive losses), and section 861 (regarding the allocation of interest to United States sources). * * * However, in applying section 263A(f) with respect to the excess expenditure amount, the taxpayer must capitalize all interest that is neither investment interest under section 163(d), business interest expense under section 163(j), nor passive interest under section 469 before capitalizing any interest that is either investment interest, business interest expense, or passive interest. * * *

* * *

Consolidated Returns: Intercompany Obligations: Disallowance of Interest Expense Deductions

Consolidated Returns: Intercompany Obligations: Disallowance of Interest Expense Deductions.—Amendments to Reg. § 1.265-2, affecting corporations filing consolidated returns by providing special rules for the treatment of certain intercompany transactions involving interest on intercompany obligations, are proposed (published in the Federal Register on May 7, 2004) (REG-128590-03).

☐ Par. 2. In § 1.265-2, paragraph (c) is added to read as follows:

§ 1.265-2. Interest relating to tax-exempt income.

* * *

(c) *Special rule for consolidated groups.*—(1) *Treatment of intercompany obligations.*—(i) *Direct tracing to nonmember indebtedness.*—If a member of a consolidated group incurs or continues indebtedness to a nonmember, that indebtedness is directly traceable to all or a portion of an intercompany obligation (as defined in § 1.1502-13(g)(2)(ii)) extended to a member of the group (B) by another member of the group (S), and section 265(a)(2) applies to disallow a deduction for all or a portion of B's interest expense incurred with respect to the intercompany obligation, then § 1.1502-13(c)(6)(i) will not apply to exclude an amount of S's interest income with respect to the intercompany obligation that equals the amount of B's disallowed interest deduction.

(ii) *Limitation.*—The amount of interest income to which § 1.1502-13(c)(6)(i) will not apply as a result of the application of paragraph (c)(1)(i) of this section cannot exceed the interest expense on the portion of the indebtedness to the nonmember that is directly traceable to the intercompany obligation.

(2) *Examples.*—The rules of this paragraph (c) are illustrated by the following examples. For purposes of these examples, unless otherwise stated, P and S are members of a consolidated group of which P is the common parent. P owns all of the outstanding stock of S. The taxable year of the P group is the calendar year and all members of the P group use the accrual method of accounting. L is a bank unrelated to any member of the consolidated group. All obligations are on the same terms and conditions, remain outstanding at the end of the applicable year, and provide for payments of interest on December 31 of each year that are greater than the appropriate applicable Federal rate (AFR). The examples are as follows:

Example 1. (i) *Facts.* On January 1, 2005, P borrows $100x from L and lends the entire $100x of borrowed proceeds to S. S uses the $100x of borrowed proceeds to purchase tax-exempt securities. P's indebtedness to L is directly traceable to the intercompany obligation between P and S. In addition, there is direct evidence that the proceeds of S's intercompany obligation to P were used to fund S's purchase or carrying of tax-exempt obligations. During the 2005 taxable year, P incurs $10x of interest expense on its loan from L, and S incurs $10x of interest expense on its loan from P. Under section 265(a)(2), the entire $10x of S's interest expense on the intercompany obligation to P is disallowed as a deduction.

(ii) *Analysis.* Because section 265(a)(2) permanently and explicitly disallows $10x of S's interest expense, ordinarily $10x of P's interest income on the intercompany obligation would be redetermined to be excluded from P's gross income under § 1.1502-13(c)(6)(i). However, under this paragraph (c), § 1.1502-13(c)(6)(i) will not apply to exclude P's interest income with respect to the intercompany obligation in an amount that equals S's disallowed interest deduction with respect to the intercompany obligation. Accordingly, § 1.1502-13(c)(6)(i) will not apply to exclude P's $10x of interest income on the intercompany obligation and P must include in income $10x of interest income from the intercompany obligation.

Example 2. (i) *Facts.* The facts are the same as in Example 1, except that P incurs only $8x of interest expense on its loan from L.

(ii) *Analysis.* Section 1.1502-13(c)(6)(i) will apply to exclude only a portion of P's $10x of interest income on the intercompany obligation. Under paragraph (c)(1)(ii) of this section, the amount of P's interest income that § 1.1502-13(c)(6)(i) will not apply to exclude is $8x, the total interest expense incurred by P on its indebtedness to L. Consequently, P must include in income $8x of interest income from the intercompany obligation and § 1.1502-13(c)(6)(i) will apply to exclude $2x of interest income from the intercompany obligation.

(3) *Effective date.*—The provisions of this section shall apply to taxable years beginning on or after the date these regulations are published as final regulations in the Federal Register.

Deductions and Losses Between Related Taxpayers

Deductions: Losses: Interest: Transactions Between Related Taxpayers.—Temporary Reg. § 1.267(a)-2T, relating to deductions, timing of deductions and losses in transactions between certain related taxpayers, is also proposed as a final regulation and, when adopted, would become Reg. § 1.267(a)-2 (published in the Federal Register on November 30, 1984).

§ 1.267(a)-2. Temporary regulations; questions and answers arising under the Tax Reform Act of 1984.

Hybrid Arrangements: Rules

Hybrid Arrangements: Rules.—Reg. §§ 1.267A-1—1.267A-7, implementing sections 245A(e) and 267A of the Internal Revenue Code regarding hybrid dividends and certain amounts paid or accrued in hybrid transactions or with hybrid entities, are proposed (published in the Federal Register on December 28, 2018) (REG-104352-18).

Par. 3. Sections 1.267A-1 through 1.267A-7 are added to read as follows:

§ 1.267A-1. Disallowance of certain interest and royalty deductions.—(a) *Scope.*—This section and §§ 1.267A-2 through 1.267A-5 provide rules regarding when a deduction for any interest or royalty paid or accrued is disallowed under section 267A. Section 1.267A-2 describes hybrid and branch arrangements. Section 1.267A-3 provides rules for determining income inclusions and provides that certain amounts are not amounts for which a deduction is disallowed. Section 1.267A-4 provides an imported mismatch rule. Section 1.267A-5 sets forth definitions and special rules that apply for purposes of section 267A. Section 1.267A-6 illustrates the application of section 267A through examples. Section 1.267A-7 provides applicability dates.

(b) *Disallowance of deduction.*—This paragraph (b) sets forth the exclusive circumstances in which a deduction is disallowed under section 267A. Except as provided in paragraph (c) of this section, a specified party's deduction for any interest or royalty paid or accrued (the amount paid or accrued with respect to the specified party, a *specified payment*) is disallowed under section 267A to the extent that the specified payment is described in this paragraph (b). *See also* § 1.267A-5(b)(5) (treating structured payments as specified payments). A specified payment is described in this paragraph (b) to the extent that it is—

(1) A disqualified hybrid amount, as described in § 1.267A-2 (hybrid and branch arrangements);

(2) A disqualified imported mismatch amount, as described in § 1.267A-4 (payments offset by a hybrid deduction); or

(3) A specified payment for which the requirements of the anti-avoidance rule of § 1.267A-5(b)(6) are satisfied.

(c) *De minimis exception.*—Paragraph (b) of this section does not apply to a specified party for a taxable year in which the sum of the specified party's interest and royalty deductions (determined without regard to this section) is less than $50,000. For purposes of this paragraph (c), specified parties that are related (within the meaning of § 1.267A-5(a)(14)) are treated as a single specified party. [Reg. § 1.267A-1.]

§ 1.267A-2. Hybrid and branch arrangements.—(a) *Payments pursuant to hybrid transactions.*—(1) *In general.*—If a specified payment is made pursuant to a hybrid transaction, then, subject to § 1.267A-3(b) (amounts included or includible in income), the payment is a disqualified hybrid amount to the extent that—

(i) A specified recipient of the payment does not include the payment in income, as determined under § 1.267A-3(a) (to such extent, a *no-inclusion*); and

(ii) The specified recipient's no-inclusion is a result of the payment being made pursuant to the hybrid transaction. For this purpose, the specified recipient's no-inclusion is a result of the specified payment being made pursuant to the hybrid transaction to the extent that the no-inclusion would not occur were the specified recipient's tax law to treat the payment as interest or a royalty, as applicable. *See* § 1.267A-6(c)(1) and (2).

(2) *Definition of hybrid transaction.*—The term *hybrid transaction* means any transaction, series of transactions, agreement, or instrument one or more payments with respect to which are treated as interest or royalties for U.S. tax purposes but are not so treated for purposes of the tax law of a specified recipient of the payment. Examples of a hybrid transaction include an instrument a payment with respect to which is treated as interest for U.S. tax purposes but, for

purposes of a specified recipient's tax law, is treated as a distribution with respect to equity or a return of principal. In addition, a specified payment is deemed to be made pursuant to a hybrid transaction if the taxable year in which a specified recipient recognizes the payment under its tax law ends more than 36 months after the end of the taxable year in which the specified party would be allowed a deduction for the payment under U.S. tax law. *See also* § 1.267A-6(c)(8). Further, a specified payment is not considered made pursuant to a hybrid transaction if the payment is a disregarded payment, as described in paragraph (b)(2) of this section.

(3) *Payments pursuant to securities lending transactions, sale-repurchase transactions, or similar transactions.*—This paragraph (a)(3) applies if a specified payment is made pursuant to a repo transaction and is not regarded under a foreign tax law but another amount connected to the payment (the *connected amount*) is regarded under such foreign tax law. For this purpose, a *repo transaction* means a transaction one or more payments with respect to which are treated as interest (as defined in § 1.267A-5(a)(12)) or a structured payment (as defined in § 1.267A-5(b)(5)(ii)) for U.S. tax purposes and that is a securities lending transaction or sale-repurchase transaction (including as described in § 1.861-2(a)(7)), or other similar transaction or series of related transactions in which legal title to property is transferred and the property (or similar property, such as securities of the same class and issue) is reacquired or expected to be reacquired. For example, this paragraph (a)(3) applies if a specified payment arising from characterizing a repo transaction of stock in accordance with its substance (that is, characterizing the specified payment as interest) is not regarded as such under a foreign tax law but an amount consistent with the form of the transaction (such as a dividend) is regarded under such foreign tax law. When this paragraph (a)(3) applies, the determination of the identity of a specified recipient of the specified payment under the foreign tax law is made with respect to the connected amount. In addition, if the specified recipient includes the connected amount in income (as determined under § 1.267A-3(a), by treating the connected amount as the specified payment), then the amount of the specified recipient's no-inclusion with respect to the specified payment is correspondingly reduced. *See* § 1.267A-6(c)(2). Further, the principles of this paragraph (a)(3) apply to cases similar to repo transactions in which a foreign tax law does not characterize the transaction in accordance with its substance.

(b) *Disregarded payments.*—(1) *In general.*—Subject to § 1.267A-3(b) (amounts included or includible in income), the excess (if any) of the sum of a specified party's disregarded payments for a taxable year over its dual inclusion income for the taxable year is a disqualified hybrid amount. *See* § 1.267A-6(c)(3) and (4).

(2) *Definition of disregarded payment.*—The term *disregarded payment* means a specified payment to the extent that, under the tax law of a tax resident or taxable branch to which the payment is made, the payment is not regarded (for example, because under such tax law it is a disregarded transaction involving a single taxpayer or between group members) and, were the payment to be regarded (and treated as interest or a royalty, as applicable) under such tax law, the tax resident or taxable branch would include the payment in income, as determined under § 1.267A-3(a). In addition, a disregarded payment includes a specified payment that, under the tax law of a tax resident or taxable branch to which the payment is made, is a payment that gives rise to a deduction or similar offset allowed to the tax resident or taxable branch (or group of entities that include the tax resident or taxable branch) under a foreign consolidation, fiscal unity, group relief, loss sharing, or any similar regime. Moreover, a disregarded payment does not include a deemed branch payment, or a specified payment pursuant to a repo transaction or similar transaction described in paragraph (a)(3) of this section.

(3) *Definition of dual inclusion income.*—With respect to a specified party, the term *dual inclusion income* means the excess, if any, of—

(i) The sum of the specified party's items of income or gain for U.S. tax purposes, to the extent the items of income or gain are included in the income of the tax resident or taxable branch to which the disregarded payments are made, as determined under § 1.267A-3(a) (by treating the items of income or gain as the specified payment); over

(ii) The sum of the specified party's items of deduction or loss for U.S. tax purposes (other than deductions for disregarded payments), to the extent the items of deduction or loss are allowable (or have been or will be allowable during a taxable year that ends no more than 36 months after the end of the specified party's taxable year) under the tax law of the tax resident or taxable branch to which the disregarded payments are made.

(4) *Payments made indirectly to a tax resident or taxable branch.*—A specified payment made to an entity an interest of which is directly or indirectly (determined under the rules of section 958(a) without regard to whether an intermediate entity is foreign or domestic) owned by a tax resident or taxable branch is considered made to the tax resident or taxable branch to the extent that, under the tax law of the tax resident or taxable branch, the entity to which the payment is made is fiscally transparent (and all intermediate entities, if any, are also fiscally transparent).

(c) *Deemed branch payments.*—(1) *In general.*—If a specified payment is a deemed branch payment, then the payment is a disqualified hybrid amount if the tax law of the home office provides an exclusion or exemption for income attributable to the branch. *See* § 1.267A-6(c)(4).

(2) *Definition of deemed branch payment.*—The term *deemed branch payment* means, with respect to a U.S. taxable branch that is a U.S. permanent establishment of a treaty resident eligible for benefits under an income tax treaty between the United States and the treaty country, any amount of interest or royalties allowable as a deduction in computing the business profits of the U.S. permanent establishment, to the extent the amount is deemed paid to the home office (or other branch of the home office) and is not regarded (or otherwise taken into account) under the home office's tax law (or the other branch's tax law). A deemed branch payment may be otherwise taken into account for this purpose if, for example, under the home office's

tax law a corresponding amount of interest or royalties is allocated and attributable to the U.S. permanent establishment and is therefore not deductible.

(d) *Payments to reverse hybrids.*—(1) *In general.*—If a specified payment is made to a reverse hybrid, then, subject to §1.267A-3(b) (amounts included or includible in income), the payment is a disqualified hybrid amount to the extent that—

(i) An investor of the reverse hybrid does not include the payment in income, as determined under §1.267A-3(a) (to such extent, a *no-inclusion*); and

(ii) The investor's no-inclusion is a result of the payment being made to the reverse hybrid. For this purpose, the investor's no-inclusion is a result of the specified payment being made to the reverse hybrid to the extent that the no-inclusion would not occur were the investor's tax law to treat the reverse hybrid as fiscally transparent (and treat the payment as interest or a royalty, as applicable). *See* §1.267A-6(c)(5).

(2) *Definition of reverse hybrid.*—The term *reverse hybrid* means an entity (regardless of whether domestic or foreign) that is fiscally transparent under the tax law of the country in which it is created, organized, or otherwise established but not fiscally transparent under the tax law of an investor of the entity.

(3) *Payments made indirectly to a reverse hybrid.*—A specified payment made to an entity an interest of which is directly or indirectly (determined under the rules of section 958(a) without regard to whether an intermediate entity is foreign or domestic) owned by a reverse hybrid is considered made to the reverse hybrid to the extent that, under the tax law of an investor of the reverse hybrid, the entity to which the payment is made is fiscally transparent (and all intermediate entities, if any, are also fiscally transparent).

(e) *Branch mismatch payments.*—(1) *In general.*—If a specified payment is a branch mismatch payment, then, subject to §1.267A-3(b) (amounts included or includible in income), the payment is a disqualified hybrid amount to the extent that—

(i) A home office, the tax law of which treats the payment as income attributable to a branch of the home office, does not include the payment in income, as determined under §1.267A-3(a) (to such extent, a *no-inclusion*); and

(ii) The home office's no-inclusion is a result of the payment being a branch mismatch payment. For this purpose, the home office's no-inclusion is a result of the specified payment being a branch mismatch payment to the extent that the no-inclusion would not occur were the home office's tax law to treat the payment as income that is not attributable a branch of the home office (and treat the payment as interest or a royalty, as applicable). *See* §1.267A-6(c)(6).

(2) *Definition of branch mismatch payment.*—The term *branch mismatch payment* means a specified payment for which the following requirements are satisfied:

(i) Under a home office's tax law, the payment is treated as income attributable to a branch of the home office; and

(ii) Either—

(A) The branch is not a taxable branch; or

(B) Under the branch's tax law, the payment is not treated as income attributable to the branch.

(f) *Relatedness or structured arrangement limitation.*—A specified recipient, a tax resident or taxable branch to which a specified payment is made, an investor, or a home office is taken into account for purposes of paragraphs (a), (b), (d), and (e) of this section, respectively, only if the specified recipient, the tax resident or taxable branch, the investor, or the home office, as applicable, is related (as defined in §1.267A-5(a)(14)) to the specified party or is a party to a structured arrangement (as defined in §1.267A-5(a)(20)) pursuant to which the specified payment is made. [Reg. §1.267A-2.]

§1.267A-3. Income inclusions and amounts not treated as disqualified hybrid amounts.—(a) *Income inclusions.*—(1) *General rule.*—For purposes of section 267A, a tax resident or taxable branch includes in income a specified payment to the extent that, under the tax law of the tax resident or taxable branch—

(i) It includes (or it will include during a taxable year that ends no more than 36 months after the end of the specified party's taxable year) the payment in its income or tax base at the full marginal rate imposed on ordinary income; and

(ii) The payment is not reduced or offset by an exemption, exclusion, deduction, credit (other than for withholding tax imposed on the payment), or other similar relief particular to such type of payment. Examples of such reductions or offsets include a participation exemption, a dividends received deduction, a deduction or exclusion with respect to a particular category of income (such as income attributable to a branch, or royalties under a patent box regime), and a credit for underlying taxes paid by a corporation from which a dividend is received. A specified payment is not considered reduced or offset by a deduction or other similar relief particular to the type of payment if it is offset by a generally applicable deduction or other tax attribute, such as a deduction for depreciation or a net operating loss. For this purpose, a deduction may be treated as being generally applicable even if it is arises from a transaction related to the specified payment (for example, if the deduction and payment are in connection with a back-to-back financing arrangement).

(2) *Coordination with foreign hybrid mismatch rules.*—Whether a tax resident or taxable branch includes in income a specified payment is determined without regard to any defensive or secondary rule contained in hybrid mismatch rules, if any, under the tax law of the tax resident or taxable branch. For this purpose, a defensive or secondary rule means a provision of hybrid mismatch rules that requires a tax resident or taxable branch to include an amount in income if a deduction for the amount is not disallowed under applicable tax law.

(3) *Inclusions with respect to reverse hybrids.*—With respect to a tax resident or taxable branch that is an investor of a reverse hybrid, whether the investor includes in income a specified payment made to the reverse hybrid is determined without regard to a distribution from the reverse hybrid (or right to a distribution from the reverse hybrid triggered by the payment).

(4) *De minimis inclusions and deemed full inclusions.*—A preferential rate, exemption, exclusion, deduction, credit, or similar relief particular to a type of payment that reduces or offsets 90 percent or more of the payment is considered to reduce or offset 100 percent of the payment. In addition, a preferential rate, exemption, exclusion, deduction, credit, or similar relief particular to a type of payment that reduces or offsets 10 percent or less of the payment is considered to reduce or offset none of the payment.

(b) *Certain amounts not treated as disqualified hybrid amounts to extent included or includible in income.*—(1) *In general.*—A specified payment, to the extent that but for this paragraph (b) it would be a disqualified hybrid amount (such amount, a *tentative disqualified hybrid amount*), is reduced under the rules of paragraphs (b)(2) through (4) of this section, as applicable. The tentative disqualified hybrid amount, as reduced under such rules, is the disqualified hybrid amount. *See* §1.267A-6(c)(3) and (7).

(2) *Included in income of United States tax resident or U.S. taxable branch.*—A tentative disqualified hybrid amount is reduced to the extent that a specified recipient that is a tax resident of the United States or a U.S. taxable branch takes the tentative disqualified hybrid amount into account in its gross income.

(3) *Includible in income under section 951(a)(1).*—A tentative disqualified hybrid amount is reduced to the extent that the tentative disqualified hybrid amount is received by a CFC and includible under section 951(a)(1) (determined without regard to properly allocable deductions of the CFC and qualified deficits under section 952(c)(1)(B)) in the gross income of a United States shareholder of the CFC. However, the tentative disqualified hybrid amount is reduced only if the United States shareholder is a tax resident of the United States or, if the United States shareholder is not a tax resident of the United States, then only to the extent that a tax resident of the United States would take into account the amount includible under section 951(a)(1) in the gross income of the United States shareholder.

(4) *Includible in income under section 951A(a).*—A tentative disqualified hybrid amount is reduced to the extent that the tentative disqualified hybrid amount increases a United States shareholder's pro rata share of tested income (within the meaning of section 951A(c)(2)(A)) with respect to a CFC, reduces the shareholder's pro rata share of tested loss (within the meaning of section 951A(c)(2)(B)) of the CFC, or both. However, the tentative disqualified hybrid amount is reduced only if the United States shareholder is a tax resident of the United States or, if the United States shareholder is not a tax resident of the United States, then only to the extent that a tax resident of the United States would take into account the amount that increases the United States shareholder's pro rata share of tested income with respect to the CFC, reduces the shareholder's pro rata share of tested loss of the CFC, or both. [Reg. §1.267A-3.]

§1.267A-4. Disqualified imported mismatch amounts.—(a) *Disqualified imported mismatch amounts.*—A specified payment (to the extent not a disqualified hybrid amount, as described in §1.267A-2) is a disqualified imported mismatch amount to the extent that, under the set-off rules of paragraph (c) of this section, the income attributable to the payment is directly or indirectly offset by a hybrid deduction incurred by a tax resident or taxable branch that is related to the specified party (or that is a party to a structured arrangement pursuant to which the payment is made). For purposes of this section, any specified payment (to the extent not a disqualified hybrid amount) is referred to as an *imported mismatch payment;* the specified party is referred to as an *imported mismatch payer;* and a tax resident or taxable branch that includes the imported mismatch payment in income (or a tax resident or taxable branch the tax law of which otherwise prevents the imported mismatch payment from being a disqualified hybrid amount, for example, because under such tax law the tax resident's no-inclusion is not a result of hybridity) is referred to as the *imported mismatch payee. See* §1.267A-6(c)(8), (9), and (10).

(b) *Hybrid deduction.*—A hybrid deduction means, with respect to a tax resident or taxable branch that is not a specified party, a deduction allowed to the tax resident or taxable branch under its tax law for an amount paid or accrued that is interest (including an amount that would be a structured payment under the principles of §1.267A-5(b)(5)(ii)) or royalty under such tax law (regardless of whether or how such amounts would be recognized under U.S. law), to the extent that a deduction for the amount would be disallowed if such tax law contained rules substantially similar to those under §§1.267A-1 through 1.267A-3 and 1.267A-5. In addition, with respect to a tax resident that is not a specified party, a hybrid deduction includes a deduction allowed to the tax resident with respect to equity, such as a notional interest deduction. Further, a hybrid deduction for a particular accounting period includes a loss carryover from another accounting period, to the extent that a hybrid deduction incurred in an accounting period beginning on or after December 20, 2018 comprises the loss carryover.

(c) *Set-off rules.*—(1) *In general.*—In the order described in paragraph (c)(2) of this section, a hybrid deduction directly or indirectly offsets the income attributable to an imported mismatch payment to the extent that, under paragraph (c)(3) of this section, the payment directly or indirectly funds the hybrid deduction.

(2) *Ordering rules.*—The following ordering rules apply for purposes of determining the extent that a hybrid deduction directly or indirectly offsets income attributable to imported mismatch payments.

(i) First, the hybrid deduction offsets income attributable to a factually-related imported mismatch payment that directly or indirectly funds the hybrid deduction. For this purpose, a *factually-related imported mismatch payment* means an imported mismatch payment that is made pursuant to a transaction, agreement, or instrument entered into pursuant to the same plan or series of related transactions that includes the transaction, agreement, or instrument pursuant to which the hybrid deduction is incurred.

(ii) Second, to the extent remaining, the hybrid deduction offsets income attributable to an imported mismatch payment (other than a factually-related imported mismatch payment) that directly funds the hybrid deduction.

(iii) Third, to the extent remaining, the hybrid deduction offsets income attributable to an imported mismatch payment (other than a factually-related imported mismatch payment) that indirectly funds the hybrid deduction.

(3) *Funding rules.*—The following funding rules apply for purposes of determining the extent that an imported mismatch payment directly or indirectly funds a hybrid deduction.

(i) The imported mismatch payment directly funds a hybrid deduction to the extent that the imported mismatch payee incurs the deduction.

(ii) The imported mismatch payment indirectly funds a hybrid deduction to the extent that the imported mismatch payee is allocated the deduction.

(iii) The imported mismatch payee is allocated a hybrid deduction to the extent that the imported mismatch payee directly or indirectly makes a funded taxable payment to the tax resident or taxable branch that incurs the hybrid deduction.

(iv) An imported mismatch payee indirectly makes a funded taxable payment to the tax resident or taxable branch that incurs a hybrid deduction to the extent that a chain of funded taxable payments exists connecting the imported mismatch payee, each intermediary tax resident or taxable branch, and the tax resident or taxable branch that incurs the hybrid deduction.

(v) The term *funded taxable payment* means, with respect to a tax resident or taxable branch that is not a specified party, a deductible amount paid or accrued by the tax resident or taxable branch under its tax law, other than an amount that gives rise to a hybrid deduction. However, a funded taxable payment does not include an amount deemed to be an imported mismatch payment pursuant to paragraph (f) of this section.

(vi) If, with respect to a tax resident or taxable branch that is not a specified party, a deduction or loss that is not incurred by the tax resident or taxable branch is directly or indirectly made available to offset income of the tax resident or taxable branch under its tax law, then, for purposes of this paragraph (c), the tax resident or taxable branch to which the deduction or loss is made available and the tax resident or branch that incurs the deduction or loss are treated as a single tax resident or taxable branch. For example, if a deduction or loss of one tax resident is made available to offset income of another tax resident under a tax consolidation, fiscal unity, group relief, loss sharing, or any similar regime, then the tax residents are treated as a single tax resident for purposes of paragraph (c) of this section.

(d) *Calculations based on aggregate amounts during accounting period.*—For purposes of this section, amounts are determined on an accounting period basis. Thus, for example, the amount of imported mismatch payments made by an imported mismatch payer to a particular imported mismatch payee is equal to the aggregate amount of all such payments made by the payer during the accounting period.

(e) *Pro rata adjustments.*—Amounts are allocated on a pro rata basis if there would otherwise be more than one permissible manner in which to allocate the amounts. Thus, for example, if multiple imported mismatch payers make an imported mismatch payment to a particular imported mismatch payee, the amount of such payments exceeds the hybrid deduction incurred by the payee, and the payments are not factually-related imported mismatch payments, then a pro rata portion of each payer's payment is considered to directly fund the hybrid deduction. *See* § 1.267A-6(c)(9).

(f) *Certain amounts deemed to be imported mismatch payments for certain purposes.*—For purposes of determining the extent that income attributable to an imported mismatch payment is directly or indirectly offset by a hybrid deduction, an amount paid or accrued by a tax resident or taxable branch that is not a specified party is deemed to be an imported mismatch payment (and such tax resident or taxable branch and a specified recipient of the amount, determined under § 1.267A-5(a)(19), by treating the amount as the specified payment, are deemed to be an imported mismatch payer and an imported mismatch payee, respectively) to the extent that—

(1) The tax law of such tax resident or taxable branch contains hybrid mismatch rules; and

(2) Under a provision of the hybrid mismatch rules substantially similar to this section, the tax resident or taxable branch is denied a deduction for all or a portion of the amount. *See* § 1.267A-6(c)(10). [Reg. § 1.267A-4.]

§ 1.267A-5. Definitions and special rules.—(a) *Definitions.*—For purposes of §§ 1.267A-1 through 1.267A-7 the following definitions apply.

(1) The term *accounting period* means a taxable year, or a period of similar length over which, under a provision of hybrid mismatch rules substantially similar to § 1.267A-4, computations similar to those under that section are made under a foreign tax law.

(2) The term *branch* means a taxable presence of a tax resident in a country other than its country of residence under either the tax resident's tax law or such other country's tax law.

(3) The term *branch mismatch payment* has the meaning provided in § 1.267A-2(e)(2).

(4) The term *controlled foreign corporation* (or *CFC*) has the meaning provided in section 957.

(5) The term *deemed branch payment* has the meaning provided in § 1.267A-2(c)(2).

(6) The term *disregarded payment* has the meaning provided in § 1.267A-2(b)(2).

(7) The term *entity* means any person (as described in section 7701(a)(1), including an entity that under §§ 301.7701-1 through 301.7701-3 of this chapter is disregarded as an entity separate from its owner) other than an individual.

(8) The term *fiscally transparent* means, with respect to an entity, fiscally transparent with respect to an item of income as determined under the principles of § 1.894-1(d)(3)(ii) and (iii), without regard to whether a tax resident (either the entity or interest holder in the entity) that derives the item of income is a resident of a country that has an income tax treaty with the United States.

(9) The term *home office* means a tax resident that has a branch.

(10) The term *hybrid mismatch rules* means rules, regulations, or other tax guidance substan-

tially similar to section 267A, and includes rules the purpose of which is to neutralize the deduction/no-inclusion outcome of hybrid and branch mismatch arrangements. Examples of such rules would include rules based on, or substantially similar to, the recommendations contained in OECD/G-20, *Neutralising the Effects of Hybrid Mismatch Arrangements, Action 2: 2015 Final Report* (October 2015), and OECD/G-20, *Neutralising the Effects of Branch Mismatch Arrangements, Action 2: Inclusive Framework on BEPS* (July 2017).

(11) The term *hybrid transaction* has the meaning provided in § 1.267A-2(a)(2).

(12) The term *interest* means any amount described in paragraph (a)(12)(i) or (ii) of this section (as adjusted by amounts described in paragraph (a)(12)(iii) of this section) that is paid or accrued, or treated as paid or accrued, for the taxable year or that is otherwise designated as interest expense in paragraph (a)(12)(i) or (ii) of this section (as adjusted by amounts described in paragraph (a)(12)(iii) of this section).

(i) *In general.*—Interest is an amount paid, received, or accrued as compensation for the use or forbearance of money under the terms of an instrument or contractual arrangement, including a series of transactions, that is treated as a debt instrument for purposes of section 1275(a) and § 1.1275-1(d), and not treated as stock under § 1.385-3, or an amount that is treated as interest under other provisions of the Internal Revenue Code (Code) or the regulations under 26 CFR part 1. Thus, for example, interest includes—

(A) Original issue discount (OID);

(B) Qualified stated interest, as adjusted by the issuer for any bond issuance premium;

(C) OID on a synthetic debt instrument arising from an integrated transaction under § 1.1275-6;

(D) Repurchase premium to the extent deductible by the issuer under § 1.163-7(c);

(E) Deferred payments treated as interest under section 483;

(F) Amounts treated as interest under a section 467 rental agreement;

(G) Forgone interest under section 7872;

(H) De minimis OID taken into account by the issuer;

(I) Amounts paid or received in connection with a sale-repurchase agreement treated as indebtedness under Federal tax principles; in the case of a sale-repurchase agreement relating to tax-exempt bonds, however, the amount is not tax-exempt interest;

(J) Redeemable ground rent treated as interest under section 163(c); and

(K) Amounts treated as interest under section 636.

(ii) *Swaps with significant nonperiodic payments.*—(A) *Non-cleared swaps.*—A swap that is not a cleared swap and that has significant nonperiodic payments is treated as two separate transactions consisting of an on-market, level payment swap and a loan. The loan must be accounted for by the parties to the contract independently of the swap. The time value component associated with the loan, determined in accordance with § 1.446-3(f)(2)(iii)(A), is recognized as interest expense to the payor.

(B) [Reserved]

(C) *Definition of cleared swap.*—The term *cleared swap* means a swap that is cleared by a derivatives clearing organization, as such term is defined in section 1a of the Commodity Exchange Act (7 U.S.C. 1a), or by a clearing agency, as such term is defined in section 3 of the Securities Exchange Act of 1934 (15 U.S.C. 78c), that is registered as a derivatives clearing organization under the Commodity Exchange Act or as a clearing agency under the Securities Exchange Act of 1934, respectively, if the derivatives clearing organization or clearing agency requires the parties to the swap to post and collect margin or collateral.

(iii) *Amounts affecting the effective cost of borrowing that adjust the amount of interest expense.*—Income, deduction, gain, or loss from a derivative, as defined in section 59A(h)(4)(A), that alters a person's effective cost of borrowing with respect to a liability of the person is treated as an adjustment to interest expense of the person. For example, a person that is obligated to pay interest at a floating rate on a note and enters into an interest rate swap that entitles the person to receive an amount that is equal to or that closely approximates the interest rate on the note in exchange for a fixed amount is, in effect, paying interest expense at a fixed rate by entering into the interest rate swap. Income, deduction, gain, or loss from the swap is treated as an adjustment to interest expense. Similarly, any gain or loss resulting from a termination or other disposition of the swap is an adjustment to interest expense, with the timing of gain or loss subject to the rules of § 1.446-4.

(13) The term *investor* means, with respect to an entity, any tax resident or taxable branch that directly or indirectly (determined under the rules of section 958(a) without regard to whether an intermediate entity is foreign or domestic) owns an interest in the entity.

(14) The term *related* has the meaning provided in this paragraph (a)(14). A tax resident or taxable branch is related to a specified party if the tax resident or taxable branch is a related person within the meaning of section 954(d)(3), determined by treating the specified party as the "controlled foreign corporation" referred to in that section and the tax resident or taxable branch as the "person" referred to in that section. In addition, for these purposes, a tax resident that under §§ 301.7701-1 through 301.7701-3 of this chapter is disregarded as an entity separate from its owner for U.S. tax purposes, as well as a taxable branch, is treated as a corporation. Further, for these purposes neither section 318(a)(3), nor § 1.958-2(d) or the principles thereof, applies to attribute stock or other interests to a tax resident, taxable branch, or specified party.

(15) The term *reverse hybrid* has the meaning provided in § 1.267A-2(d)(2).

(16) The term *royalty* includes amounts paid or accrued as consideration for the use of, or the right to use—

(i) Any copyright, including any copyright of any literary, artistic, scientific or other work (including cinematographic films and software);

(ii) Any patent, trademark, design or model, plan, secret formula or process, or other similar property (including goodwill); or

(iii) Any information concerning industrial, commercial or scientific experience, but does not include—

(A) Amounts paid or accrued for after-sales services;

(B) Amounts paid or accrued for services rendered by a seller to the purchaser under a warranty;

(C) Amounts paid or accrued for pure technical assistance; or

(D) Amounts paid or accrued for an opinion given by an engineer, lawyer or accountant.

(17) The term *specified party* means a tax resident of the United States, a CFC (other than a CFC with respect to which there is not a United States shareholder that owns (within the meaning of section 958(a)) at least ten percent (by vote or value) of the stock of the CFC), and a U.S. taxable branch. Thus, an entity that is fiscally transparent for U.S. tax purposes is not a specified party, though an owner of the entity may be a specified party. For example, in the case of a payment by a partnership, a domestic corporation or a CFC that is a partner of the partnership is a specified party whose deduction for its allocable share of the payment is subject to disallowance under section 267A.

(18) The term *specified payment* has the meaning provided in § 1.267A-1(b).

(19) The term *specified recipient* means, with respect to a specified payment, any tax resident that derives the payment under its tax law or any taxable branch to which the payment is attributable under its tax law. The principles of § 1.894-1(d)(1) apply for purposes of determining whether a tax resident derives a specified payment under its tax law, without regard to whether the tax resident is a resident of a country that has an income tax treaty with the United States. There may be more than one specified recipient with respect to a specified payment.

(20) The term *structured arrangement* means an arrangement with respect to which one or more specified payments would be a disqualified hybrid amount (or a disqualified imported mismatch amount) if the specified payment were analyzed without regard to the relatedness limitation in § 1.267A-2(f) (or without regard to the language "that is related to the specified party" in § 1.267A-4(a)) (either such outcome, a *hybrid mismatch*), provided that either paragraph (a)(20)(i) or (ii) of this section is satisfied. A *party to a structured arrangement* means a tax resident or taxable branch that participates in the structured arrangement. For this purpose, an entity's participation in a structured arrangement is imputed to its investors.

(i) The hybrid mismatch is priced into the terms of the arrangement.

(ii) Based on all the facts and circumstances, the hybrid mismatch is a principal purpose of the arrangement. Facts and circumstances that indicate the hybrid mismatch is a principal purpose of the arrangement include—

(A) Marketing the arrangement as tax-advantaged where some or all of the tax advantage derives from the hybrid mismatch;

(B) Primarily marketing the arrangement to tax residents of a country the tax law of which enables the hybrid mismatch;

(C) Features that alter the terms of the arrangement, including the return, in the event the hybrid mismatch is no longer available; or

(D) A below-market return absent the tax effects or benefits resulting from the hybrid mismatch.

(21) The term *tax law* of a country includes statutes, regulations, administrative or judicial rulings, and treaties of the country. When used with respect to a tax resident or branch, tax law refers to—

(i) In the case of a tax resident, the tax law of the country or countries where the tax resident is resident; and

(ii) In the case of a branch, the tax law of the country where the branch is located.

(22) The term *taxable branch* means a branch that has a taxable presence under its tax law.

(23) The term *tax resident* means either of the following:

(i) A body corporate or other entity or body of persons liable to tax under the tax law of a country as a resident. For this purpose, a body corporate or other entity or body of persons may be considered liable to tax under the tax law of a country as a resident even though such tax law does not impose a corporate income tax. A body corporate or other entity or body of persons may be a tax resident of more than one country.

(ii) An individual liable to tax under the tax law of a country as a resident. An individual may be a tax resident of more than one country.

(24) The term *United States shareholder* has the meaning provided in section 951(b).

(25) The term *U.S. taxable branch* means a trade or business carried on in the United States by a tax resident of another country, except that if an income tax treaty applies, the term means a permanent establishment of a tax treaty resident eligible for benefits under an income tax treaty between the United States and the treaty country. Thus, for example, a U.S. taxable branch includes a U.S. trade or business of a foreign corporation taxable under section 882(a) or a U.S. permanent establishment of a tax treaty resident.

(b) *Special rules*.—For purposes of §§ 1.267A-1 through 1.267A-7, the following special rules apply.

(1) *Coordination with other provisions*.—Except as otherwise provided in the Code or in regulations under 26 CFR part 1, section 267A applies to a specified payment after the application of any other applicable provisions of the Code and regulations under 26 CFR part 1. Thus, the determination of whether a deduction for a specified payment is disallowed under section 267A is made with respect to the taxable year for which a deduction for the payment would otherwise be allowed for U.S. tax purposes. See, for example, sections 163(e)(3) and 267(a)(3) for rules that may defer the taxable year for which a deduction is allowed. *See also* § 1.882-5(a)(5) (providing that provisions that disallow interest expense apply after the application of § 1.882-5). In addition, provisions that characterize amounts paid or accrued as something other than interest or royalty, such as § 1.894-1(d)(2), govern the treatment of such amounts and therefore such

amounts would not be treated as specified payments.

(2) *Foreign currency gain or loss.*—Except as set forth in this paragraph (b)(2), section 988 gain or loss is not taken into account under section 267A. Foreign currency gain or loss recognized with respect to a specified payment is taken into account under section 267A to the extent that a deduction for the specified payment is disallowed under section 267A, provided that the foreign currency gain or loss is described in § 1.988-2(b)(4) (relating to exchange gain or loss recognized by the issuer of a debt instrument with respect to accrued interest) or § 1.988-2(c) (relating to items of expense or gross income or receipts which are to be paid after the date accrued). If a deduction for a specified payment is disallowed under section 267A, then a proportionate amount of foreign currency loss under section 988 with respect to the specified payment is also disallowed, and a proportionate amount of foreign currency gain under section 988 with respect to the specified payment reduces the amount of the disallowance. For this purpose, the proportionate amount is the amount of the foreign currency gain or loss under section 988 with respect to the specified payment multiplied by the amount of the specified payment for which a deduction is disallowed under section 267A.

(3) *U.S. taxable branch payments.*—(i) *Amounts considered paid or accrued by a U.S. taxable branch.*—For purposes of section 267A, a U.S. taxable branch is considered to pay or accrue an amount of interest or royalty equal to—

(A) The amount of interest or royalty allocable to effectively connected income of the U.S. taxable branch under section 873(a) or 882(c)(1), as applicable; or

(B) In the case of a U.S. taxable branch that is a U.S. permanent establishment of a treaty resident eligible for benefits under an income tax treaty between the United States and the treaty country, the amount of interest or royalty deductible in computing the business profits attributable to the U.S. permanent establishment, if such amounts differ from the amounts allocable under paragraph (b)(3)(i)(A) of this section.

(ii) *Treatment of U.S. taxable branch payments.*—(A) *Interest.*—Interest considered paid or accrued by a U.S. taxable branch of a foreign corporation under paragraph (b)(3)(i) of this section is treated as a payment directly to the person to which the interest is payable, to the extent it is paid or accrued with respect to a liability described in § 1.882-5(a)(1)(ii)(A) (resulting in directly allocable interest) or with respect to a U.S. booked liability, as defined in § 1.882-5(d)(2). If the amount of interest allocable to the U.S. taxable branch exceeds the interest paid or accrued on its U.S. booked liabilities, the excess amount is treated as paid or accrued by the U.S. taxable branch on a pro-rata basis to the same persons and pursuant to the same terms that the home office paid or accrued interest for purposes of the calculations described in paragraph (b)(3)(i) of this section, excluding any interest treated as already paid directly by the branch.

(B) *Royalties.*—Royalties considered paid or accrued by a U.S. taxable branch under paragraph (b)(3)(i) of this section are treated solely for purposes of section 267A as paid or accrued on a pro-rata basis by the U.S. taxable branch to the same persons and pursuant to the same terms that the home office paid or accrued such royalties.

(C) *Permanent establishments and interbranch payments.*—If a U.S. taxable branch is a permanent establishment in the United States, rules analogous to the rules in paragraphs (b)(3)(ii)(A) and (B) of this section apply with respect to interest and royalties allowed in computing the business profits of a treaty resident eligible for treaty benefits. This paragraph (b)(3)(ii)(C) does not apply to interbranch interest or royalty payments allowed as deduction under certain U.S. income tax treaties (as described in § 1.267A-2(c)(2)).

(4) *Effect on earnings and profits.*—The disallowance of a deduction under section 267A does not affect whether or when the amount paid or accrued that gave rise to the deduction reduces earnings and profits of a corporation.

(5) *Application to structured payments.*—(i) *In general.*—For purposes of section 267A and the regulations under section 267A as contained in 26 CFR part 1, a structured payment (as defined in paragraph (b)(5)(ii) of this section) is treated as a specified payment.

(ii) *Structured payment.*—A structured payment means any amount described in paragraphs (b)(5)(ii)(A) or (B) of this section (as adjusted by amounts described in paragraph (b)(5)(ii)(C) of this section).

(A) *Certain payments related to the time value of money (structured interest amounts).*—*(1) Substitute interest payments.*—A substitute interest payment described in § 1.861-2(a)(7).

(2) Certain amounts labeled as fees.—*(i) Commitment fees.*—Any fees in respect of a lender commitment to provide financing if any portion of such financing is actually provided.

(ii) [Reserved]

(3) Debt issuance costs.—Any debt issuance costs subject to § 1.446-5.

(4) Guaranteed payments.—Any guaranteed payments for the use of capital under section 707(c).

(B) *Amounts predominately associated with the time value of money.*—Any expense or loss, to the extent deductible, incurred by a person in a transaction or series of integrated or related transactions in which the person secures the use of funds for a period of time, if such expense or loss is predominately incurred in consideration of the time value of money.

(C) *Adjustment for amounts affecting the effective cost of funds.*—Income, deduction, gain, or loss from a derivative, as defined in section 59A(h)(4)(A), that alters a person's effective cost of funds with respect to a structured payment described in paragraph (b)(5)(ii)(A) or (B) of this section is treated as an adjustment to the structured payment of the person.

(6) *Anti-avoidance rule.*—A specified party's deduction for a specified payment is disallowed to the extent that both of the following requirements are satisfied:

(i) The payment (or income attributable to the payment) is not included in the income of a tax resident or taxable branch, as determined under § 1.267A-3(a) (but without regard to the de minimis and full inclusion rules in § 1.267A-3(a)(3)).

(ii) A principal purpose of the plan or arrangement is to avoid the purposes of the regulations under section 267A. [Reg. §1.267A-5.]

§1.267A-6. Examples.—(a) *Scope.*—This section provides examples that illustrate the application of §§1.267A-1 through 1.267A-5.

(b) *Presumed facts.*—For purposes of the examples in this section, unless otherwise indicated, the following facts are presumed:

(1) US1, US2, and US3 are domestic corporations that are tax residents solely of the United States.

(2) FW, FX, and FZ are bodies corporate established in, and tax residents of, Country W, Country X, and Country Z, respectively. They are not fiscally transparent under the tax law of any country.

(3) Under the tax law of each country, interest and royalty payments are deductible.

(4) The tax law of each country provides a 100 percent participation exemption for dividends received from non-resident corporations.

(5) The tax law of each country, other than the United States, provides an exemption for income attributable to a branch.

(6) Except as provided in paragraphs (b)(4) and (5) of this section, all amounts derived (determined under the principles of §1.894-1(d)(1)) by a tax resident, or attributable to a taxable branch, are included in income, as determined under §1.267A-3(a).

(7) Only the tax law of the United States contains hybrid mismatch rules.

(c) *Examples.*—(1) *Example 1. Payment pursuant to a hybrid financial instrument*—(i) *Facts.* FX holds all the interests of US1. FX holds an instrument issued by US1 that is treated as equity for Country X tax purposes and indebtedness for U.S. tax purposes (the FX-US1 instrument). On date 1, US1 pays $50x to FX pursuant to the instrument. The amount is treated as an excludible dividend for Country X tax purposes (by reason of the Country X participation exemption) and as interest for U.S. tax purposes.

(ii) *Analysis.* US1 is a specified party and thus a deduction for its $50x specified payment is subject to disallowance under section 267A. As described in paragraphs (c)(1)(ii)(A) through (C) of this section, the entire $50x payment is a disqualified hybrid amount under the hybrid transaction rule of §1.267A-2(a) and, as a result, a deduction for the payment is disallowed under §1.267A-1(b)(1).

(A) US1's payment is made pursuant to a hybrid transaction because a payment with respect to the FX-US1 instrument is treated as interest for U.S. tax purposes but not for purposes of Country X tax law (the tax law of FX, a specified recipient that is related to US1). *See* §1.267A-2(a)(2) and (f). Therefore, §1.267A-2(a) applies to the payment.

(B) For US1's payment to be a disqualified hybrid amount under §1.267A-2(a), a no-inclusion must occur with respect to FX. *See* §1.267A-2(a)(1)(i). As a consequence of the Country X participation exemption, FX includes $0 of the payment in income and therefore a $50x no-inclusion occurs with respect to FX. *See* §1.267A-3(a)(1). The result is the same regardless of whether, under the Country X participation exemption, the $50x payment is simply excluded from FX's taxable income or, instead, is reduced or offset by other means, such as a $50x dividends received deduction. *See id.*

(C) Pursuant to §1.267A-2(a)(1)(ii), FX's $50x no-inclusion gives rise to a disqualified hybrid amount to the extent that it is a result of US1's payment being made pursuant to the hybrid transaction. FX's $50x no-inclusion is a result of the payment being made pursuant to the hybrid transaction because, were the payment to be treated as interest for Country X tax purposes, FX would include $50x in income and, consequently, the no-inclusion would not occur.

(iii) *Alternative facts – multiple specified recipients.* The facts are the same as in paragraph (c)(1)(i) of this section, except that FX holds all the interests of FZ, which is fiscally transparent for Country X tax purposes, and FZ holds all of the interests of US1. Moreover, the FX-US1 instrument is held by FZ (rather than by FX) and US1 makes its $50x payment to FZ (rather than to FX); the payment is derived by FZ under its tax law and by FX under its tax law and, accordingly, both FZ and FX are specified recipients of the payment. Further, the payment is treated as interest for Country Z tax purposes and FZ includes it in income. For the reasons described in paragraph (c)(1)(ii) of this section, FX's no-inclusion causes the payment to be a disqualified hybrid amount. FZ's inclusion in income (regardless of whether Country Z has a low or high tax rate) does not affect the result, because the hybrid transaction rule of §1.267A-2(a) applies if any no-inclusion occurs with respect to a specified recipient of the payment as a result of the payment being made pursuant to the hybrid transaction.

(iv) *Alternative facts – preferential rate.* The facts are the same as in paragraph (c)(1)(i) of this section, except that for Country X tax purposes US1's payment is treated as a dividend subject to a 4% tax rate, whereas the marginal rate imposed on ordinary income is 20%. FX includes $10x of the payment in income, calculated as $50x multiplied by 0.2 (.04, the rate at which the particular type of payment (a dividend for Country X tax purposes) is subject to tax in Country X, divided by 0.2, the marginal tax rate imposed on ordinary income). *See* §1.267A-3(a)(1). Thus, a $40x no-inclusion occurs with respect to FX ($50x less $10x). The $40x no-inclusion is a result of the payment being made pursuant to the hybrid transaction because, were the payment to be treated as interest for Country X tax purposes, FX would include the entire $50x in income at the full marginal rate imposed on ordinary income (20%) and, consequently, the no-inclusion would not occur. Accordingly, $40x of US1's payment is a disqualified hybrid amount.

(v) *Alternative facts – no-inclusion not the result of hybridity.* The facts are the same as in paragraph (c)(1)(i) of this section, except that Country X has a pure territorial regime (that is, Country X only taxes income with a domestic source). Although US1's payment is pursuant to a hybrid transaction and a $50x no-inclusion occurs with respect to FX, FX's no-inclusion is not a result of the payment being made pursuant to the hybrid transaction. This is because if Country X tax law were to treat the payment as interest, FX would include $0 in income and, consequently, the $50x no-inclusion would still occur. Accordingly, US1's payment is not a disqualified hybrid amount. *See* §1.267A-2(a)(1)(ii). The result would be the same if Country X instead did not impose a corporate income tax.

(2) *Example 2. Payment pursuant to a repo transaction*—(i) *Facts*. FX holds all the interests of US1, and US1 holds all the interests of US2. On date 1, US1 and FX enter into a sale and repurchase transaction. Pursuant to the transaction, US1 transfers shares of preferred stock of US2 to FX in return for $1,000x paid from FX to US1, subject to a binding commitment of US1 to reacquire those shares on date 3 for an agreed price, which represents a repayment of the $1,000x plus a financing or time value of money return reduced by the amount of any distributions paid with respect to the preferred stock between dates 1 and 3 that are retained by FX. On date 2, US2 pays a $100x dividend on its preferred stock to FX. For Country X tax purposes, FX is treated as owning the US2 preferred stock and therefore is the beneficial owner of the dividend. For U.S. tax purposes, the transaction is treated as a loan from FX to US1 that is secured by the US2 preferred stock. Thus, for U.S. tax purposes, US1 is treated as owning the US2 preferred stock and is the beneficial owner of the dividend. In addition, for U.S. tax purposes, US1 is treated as paying $100x of interest to FX (an amount corresponding to the $100x dividend paid by US2 to FX). Further, the marginal tax rate imposed on ordinary income under Country X tax law is 25%. Moreover, instead of a participation exemption, Country X tax law provides its tax residents a credit for underlying foreign taxes paid by a non-resident corporation from which a dividend is received; with respect to the $100x dividend received by FX from US2, the credit is $10x.

(ii) *Analysis*. US1 is a specified party and thus a deduction for its $100x specified payment is subject to disallowance under section 267A. As described in paragraphs (c)(2)(ii)(A) through (D) of this section, $40x of the payment is a disqualified hybrid amount under the hybrid transaction rule of § 1.267A-2(a) and, as a result, $40x of the deduction is disallowed under § 1.267A-1(b)(1).

(A) Although US1's $100x interest payment is not regarded under Country X tax law, a connected amount (US2's dividend payment) is regarded and derived by FX under such tax law. Thus, FX is considered a specified recipient with respect to US1's interest payment. *See* § 1.267A-2(a)(3).

(B) US1's payment is made pursuant to a hybrid transaction because a payment with respect to the sale and repurchase transaction is treated as interest for U.S. tax purposes but not for purposes of Country X tax law (the tax law of FX, a specified recipient that is related to US1), which does not regard the payment. *See* § 1.267A-2(a)(2) and (f). Therefore, § 1.267A-2(a) applies to the payment.

(C) For US1's payment to be a disqualified hybrid amount under § 1.267A-2(a), a no-inclusion must occur with respect to FX. *See* § 1.267A-2(a)(1)(i). As a consequence of Country X tax law not regarding US1's payment, FX includes $0 of the payment in income and therefore a $100x no-inclusion occurs with respect to FX. *See* § 1.267A-3(a). However, FX includes $60x of a connected amount (US2's dividend payment) in income, calculated as $100x (the amount of the dividend) less $40x (the portion of the connected amount that is not included in Country X due to the foreign tax credit, determined by dividing the amount of the credit, $10x, by 0.25, the tax rate in Country X). *See id.* Pursuant to § 1.267A-2(a)(3), FX's inclusion in income with respect to the connected amount correspondingly reduces the amount of its no-inclusion with respect to US1's payment. Therefore, for purposes of § 1.267A-2(a), FX's no-inclusion with respect to US1's payment is considered to be $40x ($100x less $60x). *See* § 1.267A-2(a)(3).

(D) Pursuant to § 1.267A-2(a)(1)(ii), FX's $40x no-inclusion gives rise to a disqualified hybrid amount to the extent that FX's no-inclusion is a result of US1's payment being made pursuant to the hybrid transaction. FX's $40x no-inclusion is a result of US1's payment being made pursuant to the hybrid transaction because, were the sale and repurchase transaction to be treated as a loan from FX to US1 for Country X tax purposes, FX would include US1's $100x interest payment in income (because it would not be entitled to a foreign tax credit) and, consequently, the no-inclusion would not occur.

(iii) *Alternative facts – structured arrangement*. The facts are the same as in paragraph (c)(2)(i) of this section, except that FX is a bank that is unrelated to US1. In addition, the sale and repurchase transaction is a structured arrangement and FX is a party to the structured arrangement. The result is the same as in paragraph (c)(2)(ii) of this section. That is, even though FX is not related to US1, it is taken into account with respect to the determinations under § 1.267A-2(a) because it is a party to a structured arrangement pursuant to which the payment is made. *See* § 1.267A-2(f).

(3) *Example 3. Disregarded payment*—(i) *Facts*. FX holds all the interests of US1. For Country X tax purposes, US1 is a disregarded entity of FX. During taxable year 1, US1 pays $100x to FX pursuant to a debt instrument. The amount is treated as interest for U.S. tax purposes but is disregarded for Country X tax purposes as a transaction involving a single taxpayer. During taxable year 1, US1's only other items of income, gain, deduction, or loss are $125x of gross income and a $60x item of deductible expense. The $125x item of gross income is included in FX's income, and the $60x item of deductible expense is allowable for Country X tax purposes.

(ii) *Analysis*. US1 is a specified party and thus a deduction for its $100x specified payment is subject to disallowance under section 267A. As described in paragraphs (c)(3)(ii)(A) and (B) of this section, $35x of the payment is a disqualified hybrid amount under the disregarded payment rule of § 1.267A-2(b) and, as a result, $35x of the deduction is disallowed under § 1.267A-1(b)(1).

(A) US1's $100x payment is not regarded under the tax law of Country X (the tax law of FX, a related tax resident to which the payment is made) because under such tax law the payment is a disregarded transaction involving a single taxpayer. *See* § 1.267A-2(b)(2) and (f). In addition, were the tax law of Country X to regard the payment (and treat it as interest), FX would include it in income. Therefore, the payment is a disregarded payment to which § 1.267A-2(b) applies. *See* § 1.267A-2(b)(2).

(B) Under § 1.267A-2(b)(1), the excess (if any) of US1's disregarded payments for taxable year 1 ($100x) over its dual inclusion income for the taxable year is a disqualified hybrid amount. US1's dual inclusion income for taxable year 1 is

$65x, calculated as $125x (the amount of US1's gross income that is included in FX's income) less $60x (the amount of US1's deductible expenses, other than deductions for disregarded payments, that are allowable for Country X tax purposes). *See* § 1.267A-2(b)(3). Therefore, $35x is a disqualified hybrid amount ($100x less $65x). *See* § 1.267A-2(b)(1).

(iii) *Alternative facts – non-dual inclusion income arising from hybrid transaction*. The facts are the same as in paragraph (c)(3)(i) of this section, except that US1 holds all the interests of FZ (a CFC) and US1's only item of income, gain, deduction, or loss during taxable year 1 (other than the $100x payment to FX) is $80x paid to US1 by FZ pursuant to an instrument treated as indebtedness for U.S. tax purposes and equity for Country X tax purposes (the US1-FZ instrument). In addition, the $80x is treated as interest for U.S. tax purposes and an excludible dividend for Country X tax purposes (by reason of the Country X participation exemption). Paragraphs (c)(3)(iii)(A) and (B) of this section describe the extent to which the specified payments by FZ and US1, each of which is a specified party, are disqualified hybrid amounts.

(A) The hybrid transaction rule of § 1.267A-2(a) applies to FZ's payment because such payment is made pursuant to a hybrid transaction, as a payment with respect to the US1-FZ instrument is treated as interest for U.S. tax purposes but not for purposes of Country X's tax law (the tax law of FX, a specified recipient that is related to FZ). As a consequence of the Country X participation exemption, an $80x no-inclusion occurs with respect to FX, and such no-inclusion is a result of the payment being made pursuant to the hybrid transaction. Thus, but for § 1.267A-3(b), the entire $80x of FZ's payment would be a disqualified hybrid amount. However, because US1 (a tax resident of the United States that is also a specified recipient of the payment) takes the entire $80x payment into account in its gross income, no portion of the payment is a disqualified hybrid amount. *See* § 1.267A-3(b)(2).

(B) The disregarded payment rule of § 1.267A-2(b) applies to US1's $100x payment to FX, for the reasons described in paragraph (c)(3)(ii)(A) of this section. In addition, US1's dual inclusion income for taxable year 1 is $0 because, as a result of the Country X participation exemption, no portion of FZ's $80x payment to US1 (which is derived by FX under its tax law) is included in FX's income. *See* §§ 1.267A-2(b)(3) and 1.267A-3(a). Therefore, the entire $100x payment from US1 to FX is a disqualified hybrid amount, calculated as $100x (the amount of the payment) less $0 (the amount of dual inclusion income). *See* § 1.267A-2(b)(1).

(4) *Example 4. Payment allocable to a U.S. taxable branch*—(i) *Facts*. FX1 and FX2 are foreign corporations that are bodies corporate established in and tax residents of Country X. FX1 holds all the interests of FX2, and FX1 and FX2 file a consolidated return under Country X tax law. FX2 has a U.S. taxable branch ("USB"). During taxable year 1, FX2 pays $50x to FX1 pursuant to an instrument (the "FX1-FX2 instrument"). The amount paid pursuant to the instrument is treated as interest for U.S. tax purposes but, as a consequence of the Country X consolidation regime, is treated as a disregarded transaction between group members for Country X tax purposes. Also during taxable year 1, FX2 pays $100x of interest to an unrelated bank that is not a party to a structured arrangement (the instrument pursuant to which the payment is made, the "bank-FX2 instrument"). FX2's only other item of income, gain, deduction, or loss for taxable year 1 is $200x of gross income. Under Country X tax law, the $200x of gross income is attributable to USB, but is not included in FX's income because Country X tax law exempts income attributable to a branch. Under U.S. tax law, the $200x of gross income is effectively connected income of USB. Further, under section 882, $75x of interest is, for taxable year 1, allocable to USB's effectively connected income. USB has neither liabilities that are directly allocable to it, as described in § 1.882-5(a)(1)(ii)(A), nor booked liabilities, as defined in § 1.882-5(d)(2).

(ii) *Analysis*. USB is a specified party and thus any interest or royalty allowable as a deduction in determining its effectively connected income is subject to disallowance under section 267A. Pursuant to § 1.267A-5(b)(3)(i)(A), USB is treated as paying $75x of interest, and such interest is thus a specified payment. Of that $75x, $25x is treated as paid to FX1, calculated as $75x (the interest allocable to USB under section 882) multiplied by 1/3 ($50x, FX2's payment to FX1, divided by $150x, the total interest paid by FX2). *See* § 1.267A-5(b)(3)(ii)(A). As described in paragraphs (c)(4)(ii)(A) and (B) of this section, the $25x of the specified payment treated as paid by USB to FX1 is a disqualified hybrid amount under the disregarded payment rule of § 1.267A-2(b) and, as a result, a deduction for that amount is disallowed under § 1.267A-1(b)(1).

(A) USB's $25x payment to FX1 is not regarded under the tax law of Country X (the tax law of FX1, a related tax resident to which the payment is made) because under such tax law the payment is a disregarded transaction between group members. *See* § 1.267A-2(b)(2) and (f). In addition, were the tax law of Country X to regard the payment (and treat it as interest), FX1 would include it in income. Therefore, the payment is a disregarded payment to which § 1.267A-2(b) applies. *See* § 1.267A-2(b)(2).

(B) Under § 1.267A-2(b)(1), the excess (if any) of USB's disregarded payments for taxable year 1 ($25x) over its dual inclusion income for the taxable year is a disqualified hybrid amount. USB's dual inclusion income for taxable year 1 is $0. This is because, as a result of the Country X exemption for income attributable to a branch, no portion of USB's $200x item of gross income is included in FX2's income. *See* § 1.267A-2(b)(3). Therefore, the entire $25x of the specified payment treated as paid by USB to FX1 is a disqualified hybrid amount, calculated as $25x (the amount of the payment) less $0 (the amount of dual inclusion income). *See* § 1.267A-2(b)(1).

(iii) *Alternative facts – deemed branch payment*. The facts are the same as in paragraph (c)(4)(i) of this section, except that FX2 does not pay any amounts during taxable year 1 (thus, it does not pay the $50x to FX1 or the $100x to the bank). However, under an income tax treaty between the United States and Country X, USB is a U.S. permanent establishment and, for taxable year 1, $25x of royalties is allowable as a deduction in computing the business profits of USB and is deemed paid to FX2. Under Country X tax law, the $25x is not regarded. Accordingly, the $25x is a specified payment that is a deemed branch payment. *See* §§1.267A-2(c)(2) and 1.267A-5(b)(3)(i)(B). The entire $25x is a disqualified hybrid amount for which a deduction is disallowed because the tax law of Country X provides an exclusion or exemption for income attributable to a branch. *See* §1.267A-2(c)(1).

(5) *Example 5. Payment to a reverse hybrid*—(i) *Facts*. FX holds all the interests of US1 and FY, and FY holds all the interests of FV. FY is an entity established in Country Y, and FV is an entity established in Country V. FY is fiscally transparent for Country Y tax purposes but is not fiscally transparent for Country X tax purposes. FV is fiscally transparent for Country X tax purposes. On date 1, US1 pays $100x to FY. The amount is treated as interest for U.S. tax purposes and Country X tax purposes.

(ii) *Analysis*. US1 is a specified party and thus a deduction for its $100x specified payment is subject to disallowance under section 267A. As described in paragraphs (c)(5)(ii)(A) through (C) of this section, the entire $100x payment is a disqualified hybrid amount under the reverse hybrid rule of §1.267A-2(d) and, as a result, a deduction for the payment is disallowed under §1.267A-1(b)(1).

(A) US1's payment is made to a reverse hybrid because FY is fiscally transparent under the tax law of Country Y (the tax law of the country in which it is established) but is not fiscally transparent under the tax law of Country X (the tax law of FX, an investor that is related to US1). *See* §1.267A-2(d)(2) and (f). Therefore, §1.267A-2(d) applies to the payment. The result would be the same if the payment were instead made to FV. *See* §1.267A-2(d)(3).

(B) For US1's payment to be a disqualified hybrid amount under §1.267A-2(d), a no-inclusion must occur with respect to FX. *See* §1.267A-2(d)(1)(i). Because FX does not derive the $100x payment under Country X tax law (as FY is not fiscally transparent under such tax law), FX includes $0 of the payment in income and therefore a $100x no-inclusion occurs with respect to FX. *See* §1.267A-3(a).

(C) Pursuant to §1.267A-2(d)(1)(ii), FX's $100x no-inclusion gives rise to a disqualified hybrid amount to the extent that it is a result of US1's payment being made to the reverse hybrid. FX's $100x no-inclusion is a result of the payment being made to the reverse hybrid because, were FY to be treated as fiscally transparent for Country X tax purposes, FX would include $100x in income and, consequently, the no-inclusion would not occur. The result would be the same if Country X tax law instead viewed US1's payment as a dividend, rather than interest. *See* §1.267A-2(d)(1)(ii).

(iii) *Alternative facts – inclusion under anti-deferral regime*. The facts are the same as in paragraph (c)(5)(i) of this section, except that, under a Country X anti-deferral regime, FX includes in its income $100x attributable to the $100x payment received by FY. If under the rules of §1.267A-3(a) FX includes the entire attributed amount in income (that is, if FX includes the amount in its income at the full marginal rate imposed on ordinary income and the amount is not reduced or offset by certain relief particular to the amount), then a no-inclusion does not occur with respect to FX. As a result, in such a case, no portion of US1's payment would be a disqualified hybrid amount under §1.267A-2(d).

(iv) *Alternative facts – multiple investors*. The facts are the same as in paragraph (c)(5)(i) of this section, except that FX holds all the interests of FZ, which is fiscally transparent for Country X tax purposes; FZ holds all the interests of FY, which is fiscally transparent for Country Z tax purposes; and FZ includes the $100x payment in income. Thus, each of FZ and FX is an investor of FY, as each directly or indirectly holds an interest of FY. *See* §1.267A-5(a)(13). A no-inclusion does not occur with respect to FZ, but a $100x no-inclusion occurs with respect to FX. FX's no-inclusion is a result of the payment being made to the reverse hybrid because, were FY to be treated as fiscally transparent for Country X tax purposes, then FX would include $100x in income (as FZ is fiscally transparent for Country X tax purposes). Accordingly, FX's no-inclusion is a result of US1's payment being made to the reverse hybrid and, consequently, the entire $100x payment is a disqualified hybrid amount.

(v) *Alternative facts – portion of no-inclusion not the result of hybridity*. The facts are the same as in paragraph (c)(5)(i) of this section, except that the $100x is viewed as a royalty for U.S. tax purposes and Country X tax purposes, and Country X tax law contains a patent box regime that provides an 80% deduction with respect to certain royalty income. If the payment would qualify for the Country X patent box deduction were FY to be treated as fiscally transparent for Country X tax purposes, then only $20x of FX's $100x no-inclusion would be the result of the payment being paid to a reverse hybrid, calculated as $100x (the no-inclusion with respect to FX that actually occurs) less $80x (the no-inclusion with respect to FX that would occur if FY were to be treated as fiscally transparent for Country X tax purposes). *See* §1.267A-3(a). Accordingly, in such a case, only $20x of US1's payment would be a disqualified hybrid amount.

(6) *Example 6. Branch mismatch payment*—(i) *Facts*. FX holds all the interests of US1 and FZ. FZ owns BB, a Country B branch that gives rise to a taxable presence in Country B under Country Z tax law but not under Country B tax law. On date 1, US1 pays $50x to FZ. The amount is treated as a royalty for U.S. tax purposes and Country Z tax purposes. Under Country Z tax law, the amount is treated as income attributable to BB and, as a consequence of County Z tax law exempting income attributable to a branch, is excluded from FZ's income.

(ii) *Analysis*. US1 is a specified party and thus a deduction for its $50x specified payment is subject to disallowance under section 267A. As described in paragraphs (c)(6)(ii)(A) through (C) of this section, the entire $50x payment is a disqualified hybrid amount under the branch mismatch rule of §1.267A-2(e) and, as a result, a deduction for the payment is disallowed under §1.267A-1(b)(1).

(A) US1's payment is a branch mismatch payment because under Country Z tax law (the tax law of FZ, a home office that is related to US1) the payment is treated as income attributable to BB, and BB is not a taxable branch (that is, under Country B tax law, BB does not give rise to a taxable presence). *See* §1.267A-2(e)(2) and (f). Therefore, § 1.267A-2(e) applies to the payment. The result would be the same if instead BB were a taxable branch and, under Country B tax law, US1's payment were treated as income attributable to FZ and not BB. *See* § 1.267A-2(e)(2).

(B) For US1's payment to be a disqualified hybrid amount under § 1.267A-2(e), a no-inclusion must occur with respect to FZ. See § 1.267A-2(e)(1)(i). As a consequence of the Country Z branch exemption, FZ includes $0 of the payment in income and therefore a $50x no-inclusion occurs with respect to FZ. *See* § 1.267A-3(a).

(C) Pursuant to § 1.267A-2(e)(1)(ii), FZ's $50x no-inclusion gives rise to a disqualified hybrid amount to the extent that it is a result of US1's payment being a branch mismatch payment. FZ's $50x no-inclusion is a result of the payment being a branch mismatch payment because, were the payment to not be treated as income attributable to BB for Country Z tax purposes, FZ would include $50x in income and, consequently, the no-inclusion would not occur.

(7) *Example 7. Reduction of disqualified hybrid amount for certain amounts includible in income*—(i) *Facts.* US1 and FW hold 60% and 40%, respectively, of the interests of FX, and FX holds all the interests of FZ. Each of FX and FZ is a *CFC*. FX holds an instrument issued by FZ that it is treated as equity for Country X tax purposes and as indebtedness for U.S. tax purposes (the FX-FZ instrument). On date 1, FZ pays $100x to FX pursuant to the FX-FZ instrument. The amount is treated as a dividend for Country X tax purposes and as interest for U.S. tax purposes. In addition, pursuant to section 954(c)(6), the amount is not foreign personal holding company income of FX. Further, under section 951A, the payment is included in FX's tested income. Lastly, Country X tax law provides an 80% participation exemption for dividends received from nonresident corporations and, as a result of such participation exemption, FX includes $20x of FZ's payment in income.

(ii) *Analysis.* FZ, a CFC, is a specified party and thus a deduction for its $100x specified payment is subject to disallowance under section 267A. But for § 1.267A-3(b), $80x of FZ's payment would be a disqualified hybrid amount (such amount, a "tentative disqualified hybrid amount"). *See* §§ 1.267A-2(a) and 1.267A-3(b)(1). Pursuant to § 1.267A-3(b), the tentative disqualified hybrid amount is reduced by $48x. *See* § 1.267A-3(b)(4). The $48x is the tentative disqualified hybrid amount to the extent that it increases US1's pro rata share of tested income with respect to FX under section 951A (calculated as $80x multiplied by 60%). *See id.* Accordingly, $32x of FZ's payment ($80x less $48x) is a disqualified hybrid amount under § 1.267A-2(a) and, as a result, $32x of the deduction is disallowed under § 1.267A-1(b)(1).

(iii) *Alternative facts – United States shareholder not a tax resident of the United States.* The facts are the same as in paragraph (c)(7)(i) of this section, except that US1 is a domestic partnership, 90% of the interests of which are held by US2 and the remaining 10% of which are held by a foreign individual that is a nonresident alien (as defined in section 7701(b)(1)(B)). As is the case in paragraph (c)(7)(ii) of this section, $48x of the $80x tentative disqualified hybrid amount increases US1's pro rata share of the tested income of FX. However, US1 is not a tax resident of the United States. Thus, the $48x reduces the tentative disqualified hybrid amount only to the extent that the $48x would be taken into account by a tax resident of the United States. *See* § 1.267A-3(b)(4). US2 (a tax resident of the United States) would take into account $43.2x of such amount (calculated as $48x multiplied by 90%). Thus, $36.8x of FZ's payment ($80x less $43.2x) is a disqualified hybrid amount under § 1.267A-2(a). *See id.*

(8) *Example 8. Imported mismatch rule – direct offset*—(i) *Facts.* FX holds all the interests of FW, and FW holds all the interests of US1. FX holds an instrument issued by FW that is treated as equity for Country X tax purposes and indebtedness for Country W tax purposes (the FX-FW instrument). FW holds an instrument issued by US1 that is treated as indebtedness for Country W and U.S. tax purposes (the FW-US1 instrument). In accounting period 1, FW pays $100x to FX pursuant to the FX-FW instrument. The amount is treated as an excludible dividend for Country X tax purposes (by reason of the Country X participation exemption) and as interest for Country W tax purposes. Also in accounting period 1, US1 pays $100x to FW pursuant to the FW-US1 instrument. The amount is treated as interest for Country W and U.S. tax purposes and is included in FW's income. The FX-FW instrument was not entered into pursuant to the same plan or series of related transactions pursuant to which the FW-US1 instrument was entered into.

(ii) *Analysis.* US1 is a specified party and thus a deduction for its $100x specified payment is subject to disallowance under section 267A. The $100x payment is not a disqualified hybrid amount. In addition, FW's $100x deduction is a hybrid deduction because it is a deduction allowed to FW that results from an amount paid that is interest under Country W tax law, and were Country X law to have rules substantially similar to those under §§ 1.267A-1 through 1.267A-3 and 1.267A-5, a deduction for the payment would be disallowed (because under such rules the payment would be pursuant to a hybrid transaction and FX's no-inclusion would be a result of the hybrid transaction). *See* §§ 1.267A-2(a) and 1.267A-4(b). Under § 1.267A-4(a), US1's payment is an imported mismatch payment, US1 is an imported mismatch payer, and FW (the tax resident that includes the imported mismatch payment in income) is an imported mismatch payee. The imported mismatch payment is a disqualified imported mismatch amount to the extent that the income attributable to the payment is directly or indirectly offset by the hybrid deduction incurred by FX (a tax resident that is related to US1). *See* § 1.267A-4(a). Under § 1.267A-4(c)(1), the $100x hybrid deduction directly or indirectly offsets the income attributable to US1's imported mismatch payment to the extent that the payment directly or indirectly funds the hybrid deduction. The entire $100x of US1's payment directly funds the hybrid deduction because FW (the imported mismatch payee) incurs at least that amount of the hybrid deduction. *See* § 1.267A-4(c)(3)(i). Accordingly, the entire $100x payment is a disqualified imported mismatch amount under § 1.267A-4(a) and, as a result, a deduction for the payment is disallowed under § 1.267A-1(b)(2).

(iii) *Alternative facts – long-term deferral.* The facts are the same as in paragraph (c)(8)(i) of this section, except that the FX-FW instrument is treated as indebtedness for Country X and Country W tax purposes, and FW does not pay any amounts pursuant to the instrument during accounting period 1. In addition, under Country W tax law, FW is allowed to deduct interest under the FX-FW instrument as it accrues, whereas under Country X tax law FX does not recognize income under the FX-FW instrument until interest is paid. Further, FW accrues $100x of interest during accounting period 1, and FW will not pay such amount to FX for more than 36 months after the end of the accounting period. The results are the same as in paragraph (c)(8)(ii) of this section. That is, FW's $100x deduction is a hybrid deduction, *see* §§1.267A-2(a), 1.267A-3(a), and 1.267A-4(b), and the income attributable to US1's $100x imported mismatch payment is offset by the hybrid deduction for the reasons described in paragraph (c)(8)(ii) of this section. As a result, a deduction for the payment is disallowed under §1.267A-1(b)(2).

(iv) *Alternative facts – notional interest deduction.* The facts are the same as in paragraph (c)(8)(i) of this section, except that the FX-FW instrument does not exist and thus FW does not pay any amounts to FX during accounting period 1. However, during accounting period 1, FW is allowed a $100x notional interest deduction with respect to its equity under Country W tax law. Pursuant to §1.267A-4(b), FW's notional interest deduction is a hybrid deduction. The results are the same as in paragraph (c)(8)(ii) of this section. That is, the income attributable to US1's $100x imported mismatch payment is offset by FW's hybrid deduction for the reasons described in paragraph (c)(8)(ii) of this section. As a result, a deduction for the payment is disallowed under §1.267A-1(b)(2).

(v) *Alternative facts – foreign hybrid mismatch rules prevent hybrid deduction.* The facts are the same as in paragraph (c)(8)(i) of this section, except that the tax law of Country W contains hybrid mismatch rules and under such rules FW is not allowed a deduction for the $100x that it pays to FX on the FX-FW instrument. The $100x paid by FW therefore does not give rise to a hybrid deduction. *See* §1.267A-4(b). Accordingly, because the income attributable to US1's payment is not directly or indirectly offset by a hybrid deduction, the payment is not a disqualified imported mismatch amount. Therefore, a deduction for the payment is not disallowed under §1.267A-2(b)(2).

(9) *Example 9. Imported mismatch rule – indirect offsets and pro rata allocations*—(i) *Facts.* FX holds all the interests of FZ, and FZ holds all the interests of US1 and US2. FX has a Country B branch that, for Country X and Country B tax purposes, gives rise to a taxable presence in Country B and is therefore a taxable branch ("BB"). Under the Country B-Country X income tax treaty, BB is a permanent establishment entitled to deduct expenses properly attributable to BB for purposes of computing its business profits under the treaty. BB is deemed to pay a royalty to FX for the right to use intangibles developed by FX equal to cost plus y%. The deemed royalty is a deductible expense properly attributable to BB under the Country B-Country X income tax treaty. For Country X tax purposes, any transactions between BB and X are disregarded. The deemed royalty amount is equal to $80x during accounting period 1. In addition, an instrument issued by FZ to FX is properly reflected as an asset on the books and records of BB (the FX-FZ instrument). The FX-FZ instrument is treated as indebtedness for Country X, Country Z, and Country B tax purposes. In accounting period 1, FZ pays $80x pursuant to the FX-FZ instrument; the amount is treated as interest for Country X, Country Z, and Country B tax purposes, and is treated as income attributable to BB for Country X and Country B tax purposes (but, for Country X tax purposes, is excluded from FX's income as a consequence of the Country X exemption for income attributable to a branch). Further, in accounting period 1, US1 and US2 pay $60x and $40x, respectively, to FZ pursuant to instruments that are treated as indebtedness for Country Z and U.S. tax purposes; the amounts are treated as interest for Country Z and U.S. tax purposes and are included in FZ's income for Country Z tax purposes. Lastly, neither the instrument pursuant to which US1 pays the $60x nor the instrument pursuant to which US2 pays the $40x was entered into pursuant to a plan or series of related transactions that includes the transaction or agreement giving rise to BB's deduction for the deemed royalty.

(ii) *Analysis.* US1 and US2 are specified parties and thus deductions for their specified payments are subject to disallowance under section 267A. Neither of the payments is a disqualified hybrid amount. In addition, BB's $80x deduction for the deemed royalty is a hybrid deduction because it is a deduction allowed to BB that results from an amount paid that is treated as a royalty under Country B tax law (regardless of whether a royalty deduction would be allowed under U.S. law), and were Country B tax law to have rules substantially similar to those under §§1.267A-1 through 1.267A-3 and 1.267A-5, a deduction for the payment would be disallowed because under such rules the payment would be a deemed branch payment and Country X has an exclusion for income attributable to a branch. *See* §§1.267A-2(c) and 1.267A-4(b). Under §1.267A-4(a), each of US1's and US2's payments is an imported mismatch payment, US1 and US2 are imported mismatch payers, and FZ (the tax resident that includes the imported mismatch payments in income) is an imported mismatch payee. The imported mismatch payments are disqualified imported mismatch amounts to the extent that the income attributable to the payments is directly or indirectly offset by the hybrid deduction incurred by BB (a taxable branch that is related to US1 and US2). *See* §1.267A-4(a). Under §1.267A-4(c)(1), the $80x hybrid deduction directly or indirectly offsets the income attributable to the imported mismatch payments to the extent that the payments directly or indirectly fund the hybrid deduction. Paragraphs (c)(9)(ii)(A) and (B) of this section describe the extent to which the imported mismatch payments directly or indirectly fund the hybrid deduction.

(A) Neither US1's nor US2's payment directly funds the hybrid deduction because FZ (the imported mismatch payee) did not incur the hybrid deduction. *See* §1.267A-4(c)(3)(i). To determine the extent to which the payments indirectly fund the hybrid deduction, the amount of the hybrid deduction that is allocated to FZ must be determined. *See* § 1.267A-4(c)(3)(ii). FZ is allocated the hybrid deduction to the extent that it directly or indirectly makes a funded taxable payment to BB (the taxable branch that incurs the hybrid deduction). *See* § 1.267A-4(c)(3)(iii). The $80x that FZ pays pursuant to the FX-FZ instrument is a funded taxable payment of FZ to BB. *See* § 1.267A-4(c)(3)(v). Therefore, because FZ makes a funded taxable payment to BB that is at least equal to the amount of the hybrid deduction, FZ is allocated the entire amount of the hybrid deduction. *See* § 1.267A-4(c)(3)(iii).

(B) But for US2's imported mismatch payment, the entire $60x of US1's imported mismatch payment would indirectly fund the hybrid deduction because FZ is allocated at least that amount of the hybrid deduction. *See* § 1.267A-4(c)(3)(ii). Similarly, but for US1's imported mismatch payment, the entire $40x of US2's imported mismatch payment would indirectly fund the hybrid deduction because FZ is allocated at least that amount of the hybrid deduction. *See id.* However, because the sum of US1's and US2's imported mismatch payments to FZ ($100x) exceeds the hybrid deduction allocated to FZ ($80x), pro rata adjustments must be made. *See* § 1.267A-4(e). Thus, $48x of US1's imported mismatch payment is considered to indirectly fund the hybrid deduction, calculated as $80x (the amount of the hybrid deduction) multiplied by 60% ($60x, the amount of US1's imported mismatch payment to FZ, divided by $100x, the sum of the imported mismatch payments that US1 and US2 make to FZ). Similarly, $32x of US2's imported mismatch payment is considered to indirectly fund the hybrid deduction, calculated as $80x (the amount of the hybrid deduction) multiplied by 40% ($40x, the amount of US2's imported mismatch payment to FZ, divided by $100x, the sum of the imported mismatch payments that US1 and US2 make to FZ). Accordingly, $48x of US1's imported mismatch payment, and $32x of US2's imported mismatch payment, is a disqualified imported mismatch amount under § 1.267A-4(a) and, as a result, a deduction for such amounts is disallowed under § 1.267A-1(b)(2).

(iii) *Alternative facts – loss made available through foreign group relief regime*. The facts are the same as in paragraph (c)(9)(i) of this section, except that FZ holds all the interests in FZ2, a body corporate that is a tax resident of Country Z, FZ2 (rather than FZ) holds all the interests of US1 and US2, and US1 and US2 make their respective $60x and $40x payments to FZ2 (rather than to FZ). Further, in accounting period 1, a $10x loss of FZ is made available to offset income of FZ2 through a Country Z foreign group relief regime. Pursuant to § 1.267A-4(c)(3)(vi), FZ and FZ2 are treated as a single tax resident for purposes of § 1.267A-4(c) because a loss that is not incurred by FZ2 (FZ's $10x loss) is made available to offset income of FZ2 under the Country Z group relief regime. Accordingly, the results are the same as in paragraph (c)(9)(ii) of this section. That is, by treating FZ and FZ2 as a single tax resident for purposes of § 1.267A-4(c), BB's hybrid deduction offsets the income attributable to US1's and US2's imported mismatch payments to the same extent as described in paragraph (c)(9)(ii) of this section.

(10) *Example 10. Imported mismatch rule – ordering rules and rule deeming certain payments to be imported mismatch payments*—(i) *Facts*. FX holds all the interests of FW, and FW holds all the interests of US1, US2, and FZ. FZ holds all the interests of US3. FX advances money to FW pursuant to an instrument that is treated as equity for Country X tax purposes and indebtedness for Country W tax purposes (the FX-FW instrument). In a transaction that is pursuant to the same plan pursuant to which the FX-FW instrument is entered into, FW advances money to US1 pursuant to an instrument that is treated as indebtedness for Country W and U.S. tax purposes (the FW-US1 instrument). In accounting period 1, FW pays $125x to FX pursuant to the FX-FW instrument; the amount is treated as an excludible dividend for Country X tax purposes (by reason of the Country X participation exemption regime) and as deductible interest for Country W tax purposes. Also in accounting period 1, US1 pays $50x to FW pursuant to the FW-US1 instrument; US2 pays $50x to FW pursuant to an instrument treated as indebtedness for Country W and U.S. tax purposes (the FW-US2 instrument); US3 pays $50x to FZ pursuant to an instrument treated as indebtedness for Country Z and U.S. tax purposes (the FZ-US3 instrument); and FZ pays $50x to FW pursuant to an instrument treated as indebtedness for Country W and Country Z tax purposes (FW-FZ instrument). The amounts paid by US1, US2, US3, and FZ are treated as interest for purposes of the relevant tax laws and are included in the respective specified recipient's income. Lastly, neither the FW-US2 instrument, the FW-FZ instrument, nor the FZ-US3 instrument was entered into pursuant to a plan or series of related transactions that includes the transaction pursuant to which the FX-FW instrument was entered into.

(ii) *Analysis*. US1, US2, and US3 are specified parties (but FZ is not a specified party, see § 1.267A-5(a)(17)) and thus deductions for US1's, US2's, and US3's specified payments are subject to disallowance under section 267A. None of the specified payments is a disqualified hybrid amount. Under § 1.267A-4(a), each of the payments is thus an imported mismatch payment, US1, US2, and US3 are imported mismatch payers, and FW and FZ (the tax residents that include the imported mismatch payments in income) are imported mismatch payees. The imported mismatch payments are disqualified imported mismatch amounts to the extent that the income attributable to the payments is directly or indirectly offset by FW's $125x hybrid deduction. *See* § 1.267A-4(a) and (b). Under § 1.267A-4(c)(1), the $125x hybrid deduction directly or indirectly offsets the income attributable to the imported mismatch payments to the extent that the payments directly or indirectly fund the hybrid deduction. Paragraphs (c)(10)(ii)(A) through (C) of this section describe the extent to which the imported mismatch payments directly or indirectly fund the hybrid deduction and are therefore disqualified hybrid amounts for which a deduction is disallowed under § 1.267A-1(b)(2).

(A) First, the $125x hybrid deduction offsets the income attributable to US1's imported mismatch payment, a factually-related imported mismatch payment that directly funds the hybrid deduction. *See* § 1.267A-4(c)(2)(i). The entire

$50x of US1's payment directly funds the hybrid deduction because FW (the imported mismatch payee) incurs at least that amount of the hybrid deduction. *See* § 1.267A-4(c)(3)(i). Accordingly, the entire $50x of the payment is a disqualified imported mismatch amount under § 1.267A-4(a).

(B) Second, the remaining $75x hybrid deduction offsets the income attributable to US2's imported mismatch payment, a factually-unrelated imported mismatch payment that directly funds the remaining hybrid deduction. § 1.267A-4(c)(2)(ii). The entire $50x of US2's payment directly funds the remaining hybrid deduction because FW (the imported mismatch payee) incurs at least that amount of the remaining hybrid deduction. *See* § 1.267A-4(c)(3)(i). Accordingly, the entire $50x of the payment is a disqualified imported mismatch amount under § 1.267A-4(a).

(C) Third, the $25x remaining hybrid deduction offsets the income attributable to US3's imported mismatch payment, a factually-unrelated imported mismatch payment that indirectly funds the remaining hybrid deduction. *See* § 1.267A-4(c)(2)(iii). The imported mismatch payment indirectly funds the remaining hybrid deduction to the extent that FZ (the imported mismatch payee) is allocated the remaining hybrid deduction. § 1.267A-4(c)(3)(ii). FZ is allocated the remaining hybrid deduction to the extent that it directly or indirectly makes a funded taxable payment to FW (the tax resident that incurs the hybrid deduction). § 1.267A-4(c)(3)(iii). The $50x that FZ pays to FW pursuant to the FW-FZ instrument is a funded taxable payment of FZ to FW. § 1.267A-4(c)(3)(v). Therefore, because FZ makes a funded taxable payment to FW that is at least equal to the amount of the remaining hybrid deduction, FZ is allocated the remaining hybrid deduction. § 1.267A-4(c)(3)(iii). Accordingly, $25x of US3's payment indirectly funds the $25x remaining hybrid deduction and, consequently, $25x of US3's payment is a disqualified imported mismatch amount under § 1.267A-4(a).

(iii) *Alternative facts – amount deemed to be an imported mismatch payment.* The facts are the same as in paragraph (c)(10)(i) of this section, except that US1 is not a domestic corporation but instead is a body corporate that is only a tax resident of Country E (hereinafter, "FE") (thus, for purposes of this paragraph (c)(10)(iii), the FW-US1 instrument is instead issued by FE and is the "FW-FE instrument"). In addition, the tax law of Country E contains hybrid mismatch rules and, under a provision of such rules substantially similar to § 1.267A-4, FE is denied a deduction for the $50x it pays to FW under the FW-FE instrument. Pursuant to § 1.267A-4(f), the $50x that FE pays to FW pursuant to the FW-FE instrument is deemed to be an imported mismatch payment for purposes of determining the extent to which the income attributable to US2's and US3's imported mismatch payments is offset by FW's hybrid deduction. The results are the same as in paragraphs (c)(10)(ii)(B) and (C) of this section. That is, by treating the $50x that FE pays to FW as an imported mismatch payment, FW's hybrid deduction offsets the income attributable to US2's and US3's imported mismatch payments to the same extent as described in paragraphs (c)(10)(ii)(B) and (C) of this section.

(iv) *Alternative facts – amount deemed to be an imported mismatch payment not treated as a funded taxable payment.* The facts are the same as in paragraph (c)(10)(i) of this section, except that FZ holds its interests of US3 indirectly through FE, a body corporate that is only a tax resident of Country E (hereinafter, "FE"), and US3 makes its $50x payment to FE (rather than to FZ); US3's $50x payment is treated as interest for Country E tax purposes and FE includes the payment in income. In addition, during accounting period 1, FE pays $50x of interest to FZ pursuant to an instrument and such amount is included in FZ's income. Further, the tax law of Country E contains hybrid mismatch rules and, under a provision of such rules substantially similar to § 1.267A-4, FE is denied a deduction for $25x of the $50x it pays to FZ, because under such provision $25x of the income attributable to FE's payment is considered offset against $25x of FW's hybrid deduction. With respect to US1 and US2, the results are the same as described in paragraphs (c)(10)(ii)(A) and (B) of this section. However, no portion of US3's payment is a disqualified imported mismatch amount. This is because the $50x that FE pays to FZ is not considered to be a funded taxable payment, because under a provision of Country E's hybrid mismatch rules that is substantially similar to § 1.267A-4, FE is denied a deduction for a portion of the $50x. *See* § 1.267A-4(c)(3)(v) and (f). Therefore, there is no chain of funded taxable payments connecting US3 (the imported mismatch payer) and FW (the tax resident that incurs the hybrid deduction); as a result, US3's payment does not indirectly fund the hybrid deduction. *See* § 1.267A-4(c)(3)(ii) through (iv). [Reg. § 1.267A-6.]

§ 1.267A-7. Applicability dates.—(a) *General rule.*—Except as provided in paragraph (b) of this section, §§ 1.267A-1 through 1.267A-6 apply to taxable years beginning after December 31, 2017.

(b) *Special rules.*—Sections 1.267A-2(b), (c), (e), 1.267A-4, and 1.267A-5(b)(5) apply to taxable years beginning on or after December 20, 2018. In addition, § 1.267A-5(a)(20) (defining structured arrangement), as well as the portions of §§ 1.267A-1 through 1.267A-3 that relate to structured arrangements and that are not otherwise described in this paragraph (b), apply to taxable years beginning on or after December 20, 2018. [Reg. § 1.267A-7.]

Personal Service Corporations

Personal Service Corporations: Allocation of Income and Deductions.—Reproduced below is the text of proposed Reg. § 1.269A-1, relating to the reallocation of income, deductions, credits, and exclusions between a personal service corporation and its employee-owners if the corporation was formed or availed of primarily to evade or avoid Federal income taxes (published in the Federal Register on March 31, 1983).

□ The Income Tax Regulations (26 CFR Part 1) are proposed to be amended by adding the new § 1.269A-1, in the appropriate place:

§1.269A-1. Personal service corporations.—(a) *In general.*—Section 269A permits the Internal Revenue Service to reallocate income and tax benefits between personal service corporations and their employee-owners to prevent evasion or avoidance of Federal income taxes or to reflect clearly the income of the personal service corporation or any of its employee-owners, if:

(1) Substantially all of the services of the personal service corporation are performed for or on behalf of one other entity, and

(2) The principal purpose for which the corporation was formed or availed of is the evasion or avoidance of Federal income tax. Such purpose is evidenced when use of the corporation either reduces the income of any employee-owner, or secures for any employee-owner one or more tax benefits which would not otherwise be available.

(b) *Definitions.*—For purposes of section 269A and the regulations thereunder, the following definitions will apply:

(1) *Personal service corporation.*—The term "personal service corporation" means a corporation the principal activity of which is the performance of personal services that are substantially performed by employee-owners.

(2) *Employee-owner.*—The term "employee-owner" means an employee who owns, directly or indirectly, on any day of the corporation's taxable year, more than 10 percent of the outstanding stock of the personal service corporation. Section 318 will apply to determine indirect stock ownership, except that "5 percent" is to be substituted for "50 percent" in section 318(a)(2)(C).

(3) *Entity.*—The term "entity" means a corporation, partnership, or other entity. All persons related to such entity will be treated as one entity. A related person is a related person within the meaning of section 103(b)(6)(C).

(4) *Not otherwise be available.*—The term "not otherwise be available" refers to any tax benefit that would not be available to an employee-owner had such employee-owner performed the personal services in an individual capacity.

(5) *Qualified employer plan.*—The term "qualified employer plan" means a qualified employer plan as defined in section 219(e)(3).

(6) *Tax benefits.*—The term "tax benefits" means any expense, deduction, credit, exclusion or other allowance which would not otherwise be available. The term includes, but is not limited to: multiple surtax exemptions being claimed by the owners of a single integrated business operation conducted through multiple corporate entities, accumulation of income by the corporation, the corporate dividends received deduction under section 243, deferral of income of an employee-owner through the use of a corporation with a fiscal year or accounting method differing from that of such employee-owner, the use of multiple classes of stock to deflect income to taxpayers in lower tax brackets, group-term life insurance (section 79), certain accident and health plans (section 105 and 106), certain employee death benefits (section 101), meals and lodging furnished for the convenience of the employer (section 119), and qualified transportation expenses (section 124). Except as otherwise provided in paragraph (d)(2)(ii) of this section, the term "tax benefits" does not include contributions to a qualified employer plan.

(c) *Safe harbor.*—In general, a personal service corporation will be deemed not to have been formed or availed of for the principal purpose of avoiding or evading Federal income taxes if the Federal income tax liability of no employee-owner is reduced in a 12 month period by more than the lesser of (1) $2,500 or (2) 10 percent of the Federal income tax liability of the employee-owner that would have resulted in that 12 month period had the employee-owner performed the personal services in an individual capacity. For purposes of the computation required by this paragraph, any current corporate tax liability incurred for that 12 month period by the personal service corporation will be considered to be the tax liability of the employee-owners in proportion to the employee-owners' stock holdings in the personal service corporation.

(d) *Special rules relating to qualified employer plans.*—(1) *In general.*—Contributions to, and benefits under, qualified employer plans will not be taken into account in determining the presence or absence of a principal purpose of the personal service corporation for purposes of paragraph (c) of this section, except as provided in this paragraph.

(2) *Taxable years beginning before January 1, 1984.*—For taxable years beginning before January 1, 1984.

(i) *Corporations in existence on or before September 3, 1982.*—For corporations in existence on or before September 3, 1982, the general rule provided in paragraph (d)(1) of this section will apply unless:

(A) The corporation adopts a new qualified employer plan after September 3, 1982 that has a plan year differing from either the taxable year of the corporation or the calendar year; or

(B) The corporation changes the plan year of an existing qualified employer plan, or its taxable year, after September 3, 1982, in a manner that would extend the period during which section 416 (relating to restrictions on "top heavy" plans), or section 269A (if this (B) did not apply) would be inapplicable to such corporation.

If (A) or (B) applies, the corporation will be treated as a corporation formed after September 3, 1982 for purposes of this paragraph.

(ii) *Corporations formed after September 3, 1982.*—For corporations formed after September 3, 1982, contributions to, and benefits under, a qualified employer plan that are in excess of those that would have been available to an employee-owner performing the personal services in an individual capacity are to be taken into account in determining the principal purpose of the personal service corporation and will be considered to be tax benefits.

(e) *Effective dates.*—(1) *In general.*—In general, section 269A and this section are effective for taxable years of personal service corporations beginning after December 31, 1982. Taxable years of employee-owners generally are not considered for purposes of this paragraph.

(2) *Exceptions.*—If a personal service corporation changes its taxable year or qualified employer plan year after September 3, 1982, in a

manner that would delay the effective date of section 416 (relating to restrictions on top-heavy plans), or section 269A (but for this (2)), section 269A will be applied to the corporation and its employee-owners on the earlier of the first day of the first taxable year of the corporation or any of its employee-owners beginning after December 31, 1982.

(f) *Effect on section 269A on other sections.*—Nothing in section 269A or the regulations thereunder, including the safe harbor provided in paragraph (c) of this section, precludes application with respect to personal service corporations or their employee-owners of any other Code section (*e.g.*, sections 61 or 482) or tax law principle (*e.g.*, assignment of income doctrine) to reallocate or reapportion income, deductions, credits, etc., so as to reflect the true earner of income. [Reg. § 1.269A-1.]

Prizes and Awards

Exclusions: Prizes and Awards: Employee Achievement Awards.—Reproduced below are the texts of proposed amendments to Reg. §§ 1.274-1 and 1.274-3, relating to prizes and awards and employee achievement awards (published in the Federal Register on January 9, 1989).

□ Par. 5. Section 1.274-1 is amended by removing everything after the word "business" in the last sentence of paragraph (d) and adding in its place "activity, see § 1.274-6"; revising paragraph (e) and adding paragraph (f) to read as follows:

§ 1.274-1. Disallowance of certain entertainment, gift and travel expenses.—* * * (e) treatment of personal portion of entertainment facility, see § 1.274-7, and (f) employee achievement awards, see § 1.274-8.

□ Par. 6. Section 1.274-3 is amended as follows:

§ 1.274-3. Disallowance of deduction for gifts.

(a) The last sentence of paragraph (b)(1) is amended by substituting "subsections (b) and (c) of section 74" for "section 74(b)".

(b) The language "recipient, or" at the end of paragraph (b)(2)(ii) is replaced by the language "recipient".

(c) Subdivisions (iii) and (iv) of paragraph (b)(2) are removed.

(d) The first, second, and fourth sentences of the flush material immediately following subdivision (iv) are removed and the last sentence is amended by substituting "sections 61, 74, 102, and 132" for "sections 61, 74, and 102".

(e) Paragraph (d) is removed and paragraphs (e), (f), and (g) are redesignated as paragraphs (d), (e), and (f).

Substantiation: Travel, Entertainment, Gifts, Listed Property, Etc.

Business Expenses: Substantiation: Recordkeeping Requirements: Listed Property.—Temporary Reg. §§ 1.274-5T and 1.274-6T, relating to the requirement that any deduction or credit with respect to certain business-related expenses be substantiated with adequate or sufficient evidence to corroborate a taxpayer's own statement and to the limitations on cost recovery deductions and the investment tax credit for listed property, are proposed (published in the Federal Register on November 6, 1985) (LR-145-84). Portions of Reg. § 1.274-5T were adopted by T.D. 8864 on January 21, 2000.

§ 1.274-5. Substantiation requirements.

§ 1.274-6. Substantiation with respect to certain types of listed property for taxable years beginning after 1985.

Prizes and Awards

Exclusions: Prizes and Awards: Employee Achievement Awards.—Reproduced below is the text of proposed Reg. § 1.274-8 relating to prizes and awards and employee achievement awards (published in the Federal Register on January 9, 1989).

□ Par. 7. Section 1.274-8 is redesignated as § 1.274-9 and a new § 1.274-8 is added immediately following § 1.274-7 to read as set forth below.

§ 1.274-8. Disallowance of certain employee achievement award expenses.—(a) *In general.*—No deduction is allowable under section 162 or 212 for any portion of the cost of an employee achievement award (as defined in section 274(j)(3)(A)) in excess of the deduction limitations of section 274(j)(2).

(b) *Deduction limitations.*—The deduction for the cost of an employee achievement award made by an employer to an employee: (1) which is not a qualified plan award, when added to the cost to the employer for all other employee achievement awards made to such employee during the taxable year which are not qualified plan awards, shall not exceed $400, and (2) which is a qualified plan award, when added to the cost to the employer for all other employee achievement awards made to such employee during the taxable year (including employee achievement awards which are not qualified plan awards), shall not exceed $1,600. Thus, the $1,600 limitation is the maximum amount that may be deducted by an employer for all employee achievement awards granted to any one employee during the taxable year.

(c) *Definitions.*—(1) *Employee achievement award.*—The term "employee achievement award", for purposes of this section, means an item of tangible personal property that is transferred to an employee by reason of the employee's length of service or safety achievement. The item must be awarded as part of a meaningful presentation, and under conditions and circumstances that do not create a significant likelihood of the payment of disguised compensation. For purposes of section 274(j), an award made by a sole proprietorship to the sole proprietor is not an award made to an employee.

(2) *Tangible personal property.*—For purposes of this section, the term "tangible personal property" does not include cash or a certificate (other than a nonnegotiable certificate conferring only the right to receive tangible personal property). If a certificate entitles an employee to receive a reduction of the balance due on his account with the issuer of the certificate, the certificate is a negotiable certificate and is not tangible personal property for purposes of this section. Other items that will not be considered to be items of tangible personal property include vacations, meals, lodging, tickets to theater and sporting events, and stocks, bonds, and other securities.

(3) *Meaningful presentation.*—Whether an award is presented as part of a meaningful presentation is determined by a facts and circumstances test. While the presentation need not be elaborate, it must be a ceremonious observance emphasizing the recipient's achievement in the area of safety or length of service.

(4) *Disguised compensation.*—An award will be considered disguised compensation if the conditions and circumstances surrounding the award create a significant likelihood that it is payment of compensation. Examples include the making of employee achievement awards at the time of annual salary adjustments or as a substitute for a prior program of awarding cash bonuses, the providing of employee achievement awards in a manner that discriminates in favor of highly paid employees, or, with respect to awards the cost of which would otherwise be fully deductible by the employer under the deduction limitations of section 274(j)(2), the making of an employee achievement award the cost of which to the employer is grossly disproportionate to the fair market value of the item.

(5) *Qualified plan awards.*—(i) *In general.*—Except as provided in paragraph (c)(5)(ii) of this section, the term "qualified plan award" means an employee achievement award that is presented pursuant to an established written plan or program that does not discriminate in terms of eligibility or benefits in favor of highly compensated employees. See section 414(q) of the Code for the definition of highly compensated employees. Whether an award plan is established shall be determined from all the facts and circumstances of the particular case, including the frequency and timing of any changes to the plan. Whether or not an award plan is discriminatory shall be determined from all the facts and circumstances of the particular case. An award plan may fail to qualify because it is discriminatory in its actual operation even though the written provisions of the award plan are nondiscriminatory.

(ii) *Items not treated as qualified plan awards.*—No award presented by an employer during the taxable year will be considered a qualified plan award if the average cost of all employee achievement awards presented during the taxable year by the taxpayer under any plan described in paragraph (c)(5)(i) of this section exceeds $400. The average cost of employee achievement awards shall be computed by dividing (A) the sum of the costs to the employer for all employee achievement awards (without regard to the deductibility of those costs) by (B) the total number of employee achievement awards presented. For purposes of the preceding sentence, employee achievement awards of nominal value shall not be taken into account in the computation of average cost. An employee achievement award that costs the employer $50 or less shall be considered to be an employee achievement award of nominal value.

(d) *Special rules.*—(1) *Partnership.*—Where employee achievement awards are made by a partnership, the deduction limitations of section 274(j)(2) shall apply to the partnership as well as to each member thereof.

(2) *Length of service awards.*—An item shall not be treated as having been provided for length of service achievement if the item is presented for less than 5 years employment with the taxpayer or if the award recipient received a length of service achievement award (other than an award excludable under section 132(e)(1)) during that year or any of the prior 4 calendar years. An award presented upon the occasion of a recipient's retirement is a length of service award subject to the rules of this section. However, under appropriate circumstances, a traditional retirement award will be treated as a de minimis fringe. For example, assume that an employer provides a gold watch to each employee who completes 25 years of service with the employer. The value of the gold watch is excluded from gross income as a de minimis fringe. However, if the employer provides a gold watch to an employee who has not completed lengthy service with the employer or on an occasion other than retirement, the value of the watch is not excludable from gross income under section 132(e).

(3) *Safety achievement awards.*—(i) *In general.*—An item shall not be treated as having been provided for safety achievement if—

(A) During the taxable year, employee achievement awards (other than awards excludable under section 132(e)(1)) for safety achievement have previously been awarded by the taxpayer to more than 10 percent of the eligible employees of the taxpayer, or

(B) Such item is awarded to a manager, administrator, clerical employee, or other professional employee.

(ii) *"Eligible employee" defined.*—An eligible employee is one not described in paragraph (d)(3)(i)(B) of this section and who has worked in a full-time capacity for the taxpayer for a minimum of one year immediately preceding the date on which the safety achievement award is presented.

(iii) *Special rules.*—Where safety achievement awards are presented to more than 10 percent of the taxpayer's eligible employees, only those awards presented to eligible employees before 10 percent of the taxpayer's eligible employees are exceeded shall be treated as having been provided for safety achievement. Where the only safety achievement awards presented by an employer consist of items that are presented at one time during the calendar year, then, if safety achievement awards are presented to more than 10 percent of the taxpayer's eligible employees, the taxpayer may deduct an amount equal to the product of the cost of the item (subject to the applicable deduction limitation) and 10 percent of the taxpayer's eligible employees. Except as provided in the preceding sentence, no award shall be treated as having been provided for safety achievement except to the extent that it can be reasonably demonstrated that that award was made before the 10 percent limitation was exceeded. [Reg. §1.274-8.]

Business Use or Rental of Dwelling Unit

Business Use or Rental of Dwelling Unit.—Reproduced below are the texts of proposed Reg. §§1.280A-1—1.280A-3, relating to the deductibility of expenses in connection with the business use, or the rental to others, of a dwelling unit that the taxpayer is deemed to have used for personal purposes during the taxable year (published in the Federal Register on August 7, 1980, with amendments published in the Federal Register on July 21, 1983; Reg. §1.280A-2(b)(2) and (3) were withdrawn on May 20, 1994).

§1.280A-1. Limitations on deductions with respect to a dwelling unit which is used by the taxpayer during the taxable year as a residence.—(a) *General rule.*—In the case of an individual, a partnership, a trust, an estate, or an electing small business corporation (as defined in section 1371 (b)), no deductions which would otherwise be allowable under chapter 1 of the Code shall be allowed with respect to the use of a dwelling unit used by such person during the taxable year as a residence except as provided in section 280A and in §§1.280A-1 through 1.280A-3. The requirements imposed by section 280A are in addition to the requirements imposed by other provisions of the Code. If a deduction is claimed for an item attributable to a dwelling unit used by the taxpayer during the taxable year as a residence, the taxpayer must first establish that it is otherwise allowable as a deduction under chapter 1 of the Code before the provisions of section 280A become applicable. Section 1.280A-2 sets forth the rules relating to the deductibility of expenses attributable to the business use of a dwelling unit used as a residence. Section 1.280A-3 sets forth the rules relating to the deductibility of expenses attributable to the rental of a dwelling unit used as a residence. Note that the allocation rule of section 280A(e) and §1.280A-3(c) applies to expenses attributable to any dwelling unit used by the taxpayer for personal purposes on any day during the taxable year, whether or not the taxpayer is treated as using the unit as a residence.

(b) *Deductions allowable without regard to any connection with a trade or business or an income-producing activity.*—Deductions which are allowable without regard to any connection with a trade or business or an income-producing activity are allowed with respect to the use of dwelling units. Such deductions include the deduction for interest under section 163, the deduction for taxes under section 164, and the deduction for casualty losses under section 165.

(c) *Dwelling unit.*—(1) *In general.*—For purposes of this section and §§1.280A-2 and 1.280A-3, the term "dwelling unit" includes a house, apartment, condominium, mobile home, boat, or similar property, which provides basic living accommodations such as sleeping space, toilet, and cooking facilities. A single structure may contain more than one dwelling unit. For example, each apartment in an apartment building is a separate dwelling unit. Similarly, if the basement of a house contains basic living accommodations, the basement constitutes a separate dwelling unit. All structures and other property appurtenant to a dwelling unit which do not themselves constitute dwelling units are considered part of the unit. For example, an individual who rents to another person space in a garage which is appurtenant to a house which the individual owns and occupies may claim deductions with respect to that rental activity only to the extent allowed under section 280A, paragraph (b) of this section, and §1.280A-3.

(2) *Exception.*—Notwithstanding the provisions of paragraph (c)(1) of this section, the term "dwelling unit" does not include any unit or portion of a unit which is used exclusively as a hotel, motel, inn, or similar establishment. Property is so used only if it is regularly available for occupancy by paying customers and only if no person having an interest in the property is deemed under the rules of this section to have used the unit (or the portion of the unit) as a residence during the taxable year. Thus, this exception may apply to a portion of a home used to furnish lodging to tourists or to long-term boarders such as students. This exception may also apply to a unit entered in a rental pool (see 1.280A-3 (e)) if the owner of the unit does not use it as a residence during the taxable year.

(d) *Use as a residence.*—(1) *In general.*—For purposes of this section and §§1.280A-2 and 1.280A-3, a taxpayer uses a dwelling unit during the taxable year as a residence if the taxpayer uses the unit for personal purposes for a number of days which exceeds the greater of—

(i) 14 days, or

(ii) 10 percent of the number of days during the year for which the unit is rented at a fair rental.

For purposes of this determination, a unit shall not be treated as rented at fair rental for any day on which it is used for personal purposes.

(2) *Examples.*—The provisions of this paragraph (e) may be illustrated by the following examples:

Example (1). B owns a boat suitable for overnight use. B is deemed, under paragraph (d) of this section, to have used the boat for personal purposes for 16 days during B's taxable year. B rents the boat at fair rental for 163 days during B's taxable year. B is not deemed to have used the boat for personal purposes on any of the 163 days for which it is rented at fair rental. Since the number of days on which B used the boat for personal purposes does not exceed 16.3 (10 percent of 163, the number of days on which the boat is treated as rented at a fair rental for purposes of this determination), B has not used the boat as a residence for the taxable year.

Example (2). Assume the same facts as in example (1) of this subparagraph, except that 5 of the 16 days on which B is deemed to have used the boat for personal purposes were included in the 163 days on which the boat was rented at fair rental. On those 5 days the boat is not treated as rented at a fair rental for purposes of this paragraph. Since the number of days on which B used the boat for personal purposes exceeds 15.8 (10 percent of 158, the number of days on which the boat is treated as rented at a fair rental for purposes of this determination), B has used the boat as a residence for the taxable year.

(e) *Personal use of dwelling unit.*—(1) *General rule.*—For purposes of this section and §§1.280A-2 and 1.280A-3, a taxpayer shall be deemed to have used a dwelling unit for personal purposes on any day on which, for any part of the day, any portion of the unit is used—

(i) For personal purposes by the taxpayer or any other person who has an interest in the unit;

(ii) By brother or sister (whether by the whole or half blood), spouse, ancestor, or lineal descendant of the taxpayer or of any other person who has an interest in the unit;

(iii) By any individual who uses the unit under an arrangement which enables the taxpayer to use some other dwelling unit for any period of time, whether or not a rental is charged for the use of the other unit and regardless of the length of time that the taxpayer uses the other unit; or

(iv) By any individual, other than an employee with respect to whose use section 119 (relating to meals or lodging furnished for the convenience of the employer) applies, unless for such day the dwelling unit is rented for a rental which, under the facts and circumstances, is fair rental.

For purposes of this paragraph, a person is considered to have an interest in a dwelling unit if that person holds any interest in the unit (other than a security interest or an interest under a lease for a fair rental) even if there are no immediate rights to possession and enjoyment under the interest.

(2) *Rental at fair rental to other persons for use as principal residence.*—Notwithstanding paragraph (e) (1) of this section, a taxpayer shall not be treated as using a dwelling unit for personal purposes by reason of a rental arrangement for any day on which the taxpayer rents the dwelling unit at a fair rental to any person for use as that person's principal residence. If a taxpayer actually makes personal use of a unit on any such day, however, that personal use is taken into account because it arises other than "by reason of a rental arrangement." For purposes of the preceding sentence, a brief visit during which the taxpayer is a guest of the occupant of the unit shall not be considered personal use by the taxpayer. For the meaning of the term "principal residence," see section 1034 and §1.1034-1 (c) (3).

(3) *Rental to persons having interest in the unit.*—(i) *In general.*—Paragraph (e) (2) of this section shall apply in the case of a rental of a unit to a person who has an interest in the unit only if the rental is pursuant to a shared equity financing agreement.

(ii) *Shared equity financing agreement.*—A shared equity financing agreement is any written agreement under which—

(A) Two or more persons acquire qualified ownership interests in the dwelling unit, and

(B) A person (or persons) holding one or more of the interests is—

(1) Entitled to occupy the dwelling unit for use as a principal residence, and

(2) Required to pay rent to one or more persons holding a qualified ownership interest in the unit.

(iii) *Fair rental.*—For purposes of this paragraph (e)(3), the determination whether a unit is rented at a fair rental (within the meaning of paragraph (g) of this section) shall be made in light of all the facts and circumstances that existed at the time the agreement was entered into. The totality of rights and obligations of all parties under the agreement is taken into account in determining fair rental.

(iv) *Qualified ownership interest.*—For purposes of this paragraph (e)(3), the term "qualified ownership interest" means an undivided interest for more than 50 years in the entire dwelling unit and appurtenant land being acquired in the transaction to which the shared equity financing agreement relates.

(v) *Not necessary that all owners charge fair rental.*—A shared equity financing arrangement may exist even if one or more of the owners does not charge the occupant fair rental for use of the unit. Paragraph (e)(2) of this section, however, applies only to those owners who do charge fair rental.

(4) *Special rule for "qualified rental period".*—For purposes of determining whether section 280A(c)(5) and §1.280A-3(d) limit deductions for expenses allocable to a "qualified rental period," a taxpayer shall not be considered to have used the rented unit for personal purposes on any day during the taxable year before or after a "qualified rental period" described in paragraph (e)(4)(i) of this section, or before a "qualified rental period" described in paragraph (e)(4)(ii) of this section, if the rented unit was the principal residence of the taxpayer with respect to that day. The use of the unit for personal purposes shall, however, be taken into account for all other purposes of section 280A. A "qualified rental period" is a consecutive period of—

(i) 12 or more months which begins or ends during the taxable year, or

(ii) less than 12 months which begins in the taxable year and at the end of which the rented unit is sold or exchanged, and for which the unit is rented, or is held for rental, at a fair rental. For the meaning of the term "principal residence," see section 1034 and §1.1034-1(c)(3).

(5) *Dwelling units in which a partnership, a trust, an estate, or an electing small business corporation has an interest.*—(i) *In general.*—This paragraph (e)(5) sets out special rules for purposes of applying paragraph (e)(1) and (2) of this section to a dwelling unit in which a partnership, a trust,

an estate, an electing small business corporation (as defined in section 1371(b), as it read before the enactment of the Subchapter S Revision Act of 1982), or an S corporation (as defined in section 1361(a)) has an interest. For purposes of this paragraph (e)(5), these entities shall be referred to as pass-through entities, and any partner, beneficiary, or shareholder that owns an interest in such an entity shall be referred to as beneficial owner of the entity.

(ii) *Personal use under paragraph (e)(1).*—For purposes of paragraph (e)(1) of this section, a pass-through entity shall be considered to have made personal use of a dwelling unit on any day on which any beneficial owner of the entity would be considered to have made personal use of the unit. Personal use under the preceding sentence shall be determined as if each beneficial owner had an interest in the unit. Thus, for example, personal use by a sister of a partner is considered personal use by the partnership.

(iii) *Personal use under paragraph (e)(2).*—(A) *In general.*—For purposes of applying the second sentence of paragraph (e)(2) of this section to a dwelling unit in which a pass-through entity has an interest, actual personal use by any beneficial owner of that pass-through entity shall be treated as personal use by the entity. Deemed personal use by a beneficial owner under paragraph (e)(1), for example, by reason of the personal use of the unit by a sister of the beneficial owner, shall not be treated as personal use by the entity.

(B) *Exception for certain partnerships.*—If—

(1) A partnership owns an interest in a dwelling unit,

(2) A partner rents the unit from the partnership at a fair rental for use as the partner's principal residence, and

(3) The items of income, gain, loss, deduction or credit of the partnership related to the unit are allocated among the partners in accordance with their percentage ownership interest in the partnership, use of the unit by that partner as that partner's principal residence shall not be treated as personal use of the unit by the partnership for purposes of paragraph (e)(2). The partner actually making use of the unit, however, is subject to the limitations of section 280A(c)(5) with respect to items related to the unit that are allocated to that partner.

(C) *Example.*—The provisions of paragraph (e)(5)(iii)(B) of this section may be illustrated by the following example.

Example. A, B, and C form partnership P, in which each holds a one-third interest. P acquires a dwelling unit that C rents from P at fair rental for use as C's principal residence. All items of income, gain, loss, deduction, or credit of P that are related to the unit are allocated one-third to each partner. Under these circumstances, the personal use of the unit by C is not treated as personal use by P. Consequently, the use of the unit by C does not subject A and B to the limitations of section 280A(c)(5) with respect to their shares of the items related to the unit. C, however, is subject to the limitations of section 280A(c)(5) with respect to C's share of those items.

(6) *Use of the unit for repairs and maintenance.*—Notwithstanding the provisions of paragraph (e)(1) of this section, a dwelling unit shall not be deemed to have been used by the taxpayer for personal purposes on any day on which the principal purpose of the use of the unit is to perform repair or maintenance work on the unit. Whether the principal purpose of the use of the unit is to perform repair or maintenance work shall be determined in light of all the facts and circumstances including, but not limited to, the following: the amount of time devoted to repair and maintenance work, the frequency of the use for repair and maintenance purposes during a taxable year, and the presence and activities of companions. In no case, however, shall a day on which the taxpayer engages in repair and maintenance of the unit on a substantially full-time basis be considered a day of personal use by the taxpayer.

(7) *Examples.*—The provisions of this paragraph (e) may be illustrated by the following examples:

Example (1). B owns a vacation home which B rents to S, B's sister, at fair rental for 10 days. B also rents the home to C at fair rental for 11 days as a part of an arrangement whereby B is entitled to use D's home for 6 days. As a favor, B rents the home to F at a discount rate for 15 days. On the basis of the rental activity described, B is deemed to have used the home for personal purposes for 36 days.

Example (2). X Inc., an electing small business corporation in which A and B are shareholders, is the owner of a fully equipped recreational vehicle. During the month of July, the vehicle is used by three individuals. A uses the vehicle on a 7-day camping trip. D, who is B's daughter, rents the vehicle from X Inc. at fair rental for 10 days. E rents the vehicle at fair rental for 12 days under an arrangement whereby B is entitled to use an apartment owned by F, a friend of E, for 9 days. X Inc. is deemed to have used the dwelling unit for personal purposes on any day on which any of its shareholders would be deemed to have so used the unit. Therefore, X Inc. is deemed to have used the recreational vehicle for personal purposes on 29 days.

Example (3). A owns a lakeside cottage which A rents during the summer. A and B, A's spouse, arrive late Thursday evening after a long drive to prepare the cottage for the rental season. A and B prepare dinner but do no work on the unit that evening. A spends a normal work day working on the unit on Friday and Saturday; B helps for a few hours each day but spends most of the time relaxing. By Saturday evening, the necessary maintenance work is complete. Neither A nor B works on the unit on Sunday; they depart shortly before noon. The principal purpose of the use of the unit from Thursday evening through Sunday morning is to perform maintenance work on the unit. Consequently, the use during this period will not be considered personal use by A.

Example (4). C owns a mountain cabin which C rents for most of the year. C spends a week at the cabin with family members. C works on maintenance of the cabin 3 or 4 hours each day during the week. C spends the rest of the time fishing, hiking, and relaxing. C's family members, however, work substantially fulltime on the cabin on each day during the week. The principal purpose of the use of the cabin is to perform maintenance work. Therefore, the use during this period will not be considered personal use by C.

Example (5). B, an individual whose taxable year is the calendar year, uses a dwelling unit as a principal residence from January 1, 1978, to June 30, 1978. On July 1, 1978, B rents the unit at a fair rental to D, an unrelated individual, for a two-year period beginning immediately. In determining whether section 280A(c)(5) and § 1.280A-3(d) limit deductions for expenses allocable to this "qualified rental period", B is not considered to have used the unit for personal purposes from January 1, 1978, to June 30, 1978. Note, however, that section 280A(e) and § 1.280A-3(c) limit the portion of the total 1978 expenses with respect to the unit which may be attributed to the "qualified rental period." B's personal use of the unit is similarly taken into account in applying section 280A(c)(5) to any other use of the unit during the taxable year, *e.g.*, the use of a portion of the unit as a place of business.

(f) *"Day" defined*.—For purposes of section 280A, this section, and § 1.280A-3, the term "day" means generally the 24-hour period for which a day's rental would be paid. Thus, a person using a dwelling unit from Saturday afternoon through the following Saturday morning would generally be treated as having used the unit for 7 days even though the person was on the premises on 8 calendar days.

(g) *Fair rental in the case of co-owners*.—(1) *In general*.—For purposes of sections 280A, this section, and § 1.280A-3, a co-owner of a dwelling unit shall be treated as renting the unit at a fair rental if the co-owner charges an amount that is equal to the fair rental of the entire unit multiplied by that co-owner's fractional interest in the unit.

(2) *Example*.—The provisions of this paragraph may be illustrated by the following example:

Example: B and C own undivided one-half interests in a dwelling unit, fair rental for which would be $100x per month. D rents the unit from B and C for a month. B charges D $50x for the month's rental, but C charges D only $20x. B is treated as renting the unit at a fair rental for that month because B charges D $50x, which is equal to the fair rental of the entire unit ($100x), multiplied by B's one-half interest in the unit.

(h) *Coordination with section 162(a)(2)*.—Nothing in section 280A or this section shall be construed to disallow any deduction allowable under section 162(a)(2) (or any deduction which meets the tests of section 162(a)(2) but is allowable under another provision of the Internal Revenue Code) by reason of the taxpayer's being away from home in pursuit of a trade or business (other than the trade or business of renting dwelling units).

(i) *Coordination with section 183*.—If a dwelling unit is used by the taxpayer during the taxable year as a residence, section 183 (relating to activities not engaged in for profit) shall not apply with respect to the unit for the taxable year. The taxable year shall, however, be taken into account as a taxable year for purposes of determining whether the presumption described in section 183(d) applies.

Example. B owns a cottage which B rents for part of the summer in 1976, 1977, and 1978. B also uses the cottage as a residence in 1976 and 1977, but not in 1978. B's rental income for 1976 exceeds the expenses allocable to the rental activity, but in 1977 the expenses exceed the rental income. In determining whether B may claim for 1978 the benefit of the presumption described in section 183(d), the rental activity in 1976 and 1977 is taken into account even though section 183 did not apply with respect to the cottage for those years.

(j) *Effective date*.—This section and §§ 1.280A-2 and 1.280A-3 apply to taxable years beginning after December 31, 1975. [Reg. § 1.280A-1.]

§ 1.280A-2. Deductibility of expenses attributable to business use of a dwelling unit used as a residence.—(a) *Scope*.—This section describes the business uses of a dwelling unit used as a residence for which items may be deductible under an exception to the general rule of section 280A and explains the general conditions for the deductibility of items attributable to those uses. Deductions are allowable only to the extent provided in section 280A(c)(5) and in paragraph (i) of this section. See § 1.280A-1 for the general rules under section 280A.

(b) *Use as the taxpayer's principal place of business*.—(1) *In general*.—Section 280A(c)(1)(A) provides an exception to the general rule of section 280A(a) for any item to the extent that the item is allocable to a portion of the dwelling unit which is used exclusively and on a regular basis as the principal place of business for any trade or business of the taxpayer.

(2) [*Withdrawn by the IRS on 5-20-94.*]

(3) [*Withdrawn by the IRS on 5-20-94.*]

(c) *Use by patients, clients, or customers in meeting or dealing with the taxpayer in the normal course of business*.—Section 280A(c)(1)(B) provides an exception to the general rule of section 280A for any item to the extent the item is allocable to a portion of the dwelling unit which is used exclusively and on a regular basis as a place of business in which patients, clients, or customers meet or deal with the taxpayer in the normal course of the taxpayer's business. Property is so used only if the patients, clients, or customers are physically present on the premises; conversations with the taxpayer by telephone do not constitute use of the premises by patients, clients or customers. This exception applies only if the use of the dwelling unit by patients, clients, or customers is substantial and integral to the conduct of the taxpayer's business. Occasional meetings are insufficient to make this exception applicable.

(d) *Use of a separate structure not attached to the dwelling unit in connection with the taxpayer's trade or business*.—Section 280A(c)(1)(C) provides an exception to the general rule of section 280A(a) for any item to the extent that the item is allocable to a separate structure which is appurtenant to, but not attached to, the dwelling unit and is used exclusively and on a regular basis in connection with the taxpayer's trade or business. An artist's studio, a florist's greenhouse, and a carpenter's workshop are examples of structures that may be within the description of this paragraph.

(e) *Use as a storage unit for taxpayer's inventory*.—Section 280A(c)(2) provides an exception to the general rule of section 280A(a) for any item to the extent such item is allocable to space within the dwelling unit which is used on a regular basis as a storage unit for the inventory of the taxpayer held for use in the taxpayer's trade or business of selling products at retail or wholesale. The storage unit includes only the space actually used for storage; thus, if a taxpayer stores inventory in one portion of a basement, the storage unit includes only that portion even if the taxpayer makes no use of the rest of the basement. The exception provided under section 280A(c)(2) applies only if—

(1) The dwelling unit is the sole fixed location of that trade or business, and

(2) The space used is a separately identifiable space suitable for storage.

(f) *Use in providing day care services.*—(1) *In general.*—Section 280A(c)(4) provides an exception to the general rule of section 280A(a) for any item to the extent that the item is allocable to the use of any portion of the dwelling unit on a regular basis in the taxpayer's trade or business of providing day care services for children, for individuals who have attained age 65, or for individuals who are physically or mentally incapable of caring for themselves.

(2) *Day care services.*—Day care services are services which are primarily custodial in nature and which, unlike foster care, are provided for only certain hours during the day. Day care services may include educational, developmental, or enrichment activities which are incidental to the primary custodial services. If the services performed in the home are primarily educational or instructional in nature, however, they do not qualify as day care services. The determination whether particular activities are incidental to the primary custodial services generally depends upon all the facts and circumstances of the case. Educational instruction to children of nursery school age shall be considered incidental to the custodial services. Further, educational instruction to children of kindergarten age would ordinarily be considered incidental to the custodial services if the instruction is not in lieu of public instruction under a State compulsory education requirement. In addition, enrichment instruction in arts and crafts to children, handicapped individuals, or the elderly would ordinarily be considered incidental to the custodial services rendered.

(3) *State law requirements.*—This paragraph, applies to items accruing after August 31, 1977, only if the owner or operator of the day care business is, at the time the item accrues, acting in accordance with the applicable State law relating to the licensing, certification, registration, or approval of day care centers or family or group day care homes. A person satisfies the condition stated in the preceding sentence for any period for which—

(i) There is no applicable State law of the type described;

(ii) The person is exempt from the requirements of the applicable State law;

(iii) The person has whatever license, etc., is required under the applicable State law; or

(iv) The person has applied for whatever license, etc., is required under the applicable State law, provided, that the application has not been rejected, and provided that the person has corrected or removed any deficiencies that resulted in the revocation of any previous license, etc., or in the rejection of any previous application.

(g) *Exclusive use requirement.*—(1) *In general.*—Paragraph (b), (c), or (d) of this section may apply to the use of a portion of a dwelling unit for a taxable year only if there is no use of that portion of the unit at any time during the taxable year other than for business purposes. For purposes of section 280A(c)(1) and this section, the phrase "a portion of the dwelling unit" refers to a room or other separately identifiable space; it is not necessary that the portion be marked off by a permanent partition. Paragraph (b), (c), or (d) of this section may apply to a portion of a unit which is used for more than one business purpose. Necessary repair or maintenance does not constitute use for purposes of this paragraph.

(2) *Convenience of the employer.*—In the case of an employee, paragraph (b), (c), or (d) shall apply to a use of a portion of a dwelling unit only if that use is for the convenience of the employer.

(h) *Use on a regular basis.*—The determination whether a taxpayer has used a portion of a dwelling unit for a particular purpose on a regular basis must be made in light of all the facts and circumstances.

(i) *Limitation on deductions.*—(1) *In general.*—The deductions allowable under chapter 1 of the Code for a taxable year with respect to the use of a dwelling unit for one of the purposes described in paragraphs (b) through (f) of this section shall not exceed the gross income derived from such use of the unit during the taxable year, as determined under subparagraph (2) of this paragraph. Subparagraphs (3) and (4) of this paragraph provide rules for determining the expenses allocable to the business use of a unit. Subparagraph (5) of this paragraph prescribes the order in which deductions are allowable.

(2) *Gross income derived from use of unit.*—(i) *Only income from qualifying business use to be taken into account.*—For purposes of section 280A and this section, the taxpayer shall take into account, in applying the limitation on deductions, only gross income from a business use described in section 280A(c). For example, a taxpayer who teaches at school may also be engaged in a retail sales business. If the taxpayer uses a home office on a regular basis as the principal place of business for the retail sales business (a use described in section 280A(c)(1)(A)) and makes no non-business use of the office, the taxpayer shall take the gross income from the use of the office for the retail sales business into account in applying the limitation on deductions. Even if the taxpayer also corrects student papers and prepares class presentations in the home office (not a use described in section 280A(c)), no portion of the taxpayer's gross income from teaching may be taken into account in applying the limitation on deductions.

(ii) *More than one location.*—If the taxpayer engages in a business in the dwelling unit and in one or more other locations, the taxpayer shall allocate the gross income from the business to the different locations on a reasonable basis. In making this determination, the taxpayer shall take into account the amount of time that the taxpayer engages in activity related to the business at each location, the capital investment related to the business at each location, and any other facts and circumstances that may be relevant.

(iii) *Exclusion of certain amounts.*—For purposes of section 280A(c)(5)(A) and this section, gross income derived from use of a unit means gross income from the business activity in the unit reduced by expenditures required for the activity but not allocable to use of the unit itself, such as expenditures for supplies and compensation paid to other persons. For example, a physician who uses a portion of a dwelling unit for treating patients shall compute gross income derived from use of the unit by subtracting from the gross income attributable to the business activity in the unit any expenditures for nursing and secretarial services, supplies, etc.

(3) *Expenses allocable to portion of unit.*—The taxpayer may determine the expenses allocable to the portion of the unit used for business purposes by any method that is reasonable under the circumstances. If the rooms in the dwelling unit are of approximately equal size, the taxpayer may ordinarily allocate the general expenses for the unit according to the number of rooms used for the business purpose. The taxpayer may also allocate general expenses according to the percentage of the total floor space in the unit that is used for the business purpose. Expenses which are attributable only to certain portions of the unit, *e.g.*, repairs to kitchen fixtures, shall be allocated in full to those portions of the unit. Expenses which are not related to the use of the unit for business purposes, *e.g.*, expenditures for lawn care, are not taken into account for purposes of section 280A.

(4) *Time allocation for use in providing day care services.*—If the taxpayer uses a portion of a dwelling unit in providing day care services, as described in paragraph (f) of this section, and the taxpayer makes any use of that portion of the unit for nonbusiness purposes during the taxable year, the taxpayer shall make further allocation of the amounts determined under subparagraph (3) of this paragraph to be allocable to the portion of the unit used in providing day care services. The amounts allocated to the business use of the unit under this subparagraph shall bear the same proportion to the amounts determined under subparagraph (3) of this paragraph as the length of time that the portion of the unit is used for day care services bears to the length of time that the portion of the unit is available for all purposes. For example, if a portion of the unit is used for day care services for an average of 36 hours each week during the taxable year, the fraction to be used for making the allocation required under this subparagraph is 36/168 the ratio of the number of hours of day care use in a week to the total number of hours in a week.

(5) *Order of deductions.*—Business deductions with respect to the business use of a dwelling unit are allowable in the following order and only to the following extent:

(i) The allocable portions of amounts allowable as deductions for the taxable year under chapter 1 of the Code with respect to the dwelling unit without regard to any use of the unit in trade or business, *e.g.*, mortgage interest and real estate taxes, are allowable as business deductions to the extent of the gross income derived from use of the unit.

(ii) Amounts otherwise allowable as deductions for the taxable year under chapter 1 of the Code by reason of the business use of the dwelling unit (other than those which would result in an adjustment to the basis of property) are allowable to the extent the gross income derived from use of the unit exceeds the deductions allowed or allowable under subdivision (i) of this subparagraph.

(iii) Amounts otherwise allowable as deductions for the taxable year under chapter 1 of the Code by reason of the business use of the dwelling unit which would result in an adjustment to the basis of property are allowable to the extent the gross income derived from use of the unit exceeds the deductions allowed or allowable under subdivisions (i) and (ii) of this subparagraph.

(6) *Cross reference.*—For rules with respect to the deductions to be taken into account in computing adjusted gross income in the case of employees, see section 62 and the regulations prescribed thereunder.

(7) *Example.*—The provisions of this subparagraph may be illustrated by the following example:

Example. A, a self-employed individual, uses an office in the home on a regular basis as a place of business for meeting with clients of A's consulting service. A makes no other use of the office during the taxable year and uses no other premises for the consulting activity. A has a special telephone line for the office and occasionally employs secretarial assistance. A also has a gardener care for the lawn around the home during the year. A determines that 10% of the general expenses for the dwelling unit are allocable to the office. On the basis of the following figures, A determines that the sum of the allowable business deductions for the use of the office is $1,050.

	Total	Allocable to Office	
Gross income from consulting services			$1,900
Expense for secretary		$500	
Business telephone		150	
Supplies		200	
Total expenditures not allocable to use of unit			850
Gross income derived from use of unit			$1,050
Deductions allowable under subparagraph (5)(i) of this paragraph			
Mortgage interest	$5,000	$500	
Real estate taxes	2,000	200	
Amount allowable			700
Limit on further deductions			$350
Deductions allowable under subparagraph (5)(ii) of this paragraph			

	Total	Allocable to Office	
Insurance	$600	$60	
Utilities (other than residential telephone)	900	90	
Lawn care	500	0	
Amount allowable			150
Limit on further deductions			$200
Deductions allowable under subparagraph (5)(iii) of this paragraph			
	Total	Allocable to Office	
Depreciation	$3,200	$320	
Amount allowable			200

No portion of the lawn care expense is allocable to the business use of the dwelling unit. A may claim the remaining $6,300 paid for mortgage interest and real estate taxes as itemized deductions. [Reg. § 1.280A-2.]

§ 1.280A-3. Deductibility of expenses attributable to the rental of a dwelling unit used as a residence.—(a) *Scope*.—This section provides rules for determining the deductibility of expenses attributable to the rental of a dwelling unit used as a residence. Note that paragraph (c) of this section applies to any dwelling unit used by the taxpayer for personal purposes on any day during the taxable year, whether or not the taxpayer is treated as using the unit as a residence. See § 1.280A-1 for the general rules under section 280A.

(b) *Short rental period*.—If a dwelling unit used by the taxpayer as a residence during the taxable year is actually rented for less than 15 days during the taxable year,

(1) No deduction otherwise allowable because of the rental use shall be allowed, and

(2) The rental income shall not be included in gross income.

(c) *Allocation*.—(1) *In general*.—If a taxpayer uses a dwelling unit for personal purposes on any day during the taxable year, the amount deductible by reason of the rental use of the unit during the taxable year shall not exceed an amount which bears the same relationship to the total expenses paid or incurred with respect to the unit during the taxable year as the number of days on which the unit is rented at fair rental during the year bears to the total number of days that the unit is used for any purpose during the taxable year. For purposes of section 280A(e) and this section, the fact that a unit is deemed to be used for personal purposes on a particular day does not prevent that day from being counted as a day on which the unit is rented at fair rental. Use of a unit for repair and maintenance which is disregarded under § 1.280A-1(e)(6) shall be disregarded for purposes of this paragraph.

(2) *Portion of unit rented*.—If the taxpayer rents only a portion of the dwelling unit, the rule prescribed in subparagraph (1) of this paragraph shall be applied to the expenses attributable to that portion of the unit, and the days to be taken into account shall be the days on which that portion of the unit is rented at fair rental during the taxable year and the days on which that portion of the unit is used for any purpose during the taxable year. The expenses attributable to any portion of a unit shall be determined in accordance with the rules prescribed in § 1.280A-2(i)(3).

(3) *Deductions allowable without regard to rental use*.—This paragraph shall not disallow any part of those deductions with respect to a dwelling unit which are allowable without regard to the rental use of the unit.

(4) *Example*.—The provisions of this paragraph may be illustrated by the following example:

Example. A, an individual, owns a cottage which A rents to vacationers at fair rental for 120 days during the taxable year. A is deemed to have made personal use of the cottage on 15 of those 120 days. The unit is used for one or more purposes (other than repair or maintenance) on 160 days during the taxable year. The amount that A may claim as rental expenses may not exceed 120/160 of the total expenses paid or incurred with respect to the unit during the taxable year. If A itemizes deductions, A may claim the remaining 40/160 of items, such as mortgage interest and taxes, which are deductible without regard to the rental use of the unit.

(d) *Limitation on deductions if taxpayer has used dwelling unit as a residence*.—(1) *In general*.—The deductions allowable under chapter 1 of the Code for a taxable year with respect to the rental use of a dwelling unit which the taxpayer is treated as having used as a residence during such year shall not exceed the gross rental income from the unit for such year. See section 280A(d)(4) and § 1.280A-1(e)(4) for special rules affecting the determination whether the taxpayer has used a unit as a residence if any day during the taxable year is part of a "qualified rental period."

(2) *Gross rental income*.—For purposes of section 280A and this section gross rental income from a unit equals the gross receipts from rental of the unit reduced by expenditures to obtain tenants for the unit, such as realtors' fees and advertising expense. The gross rental income from a unit for a taxable year includes rental income for periods during which the unit is rented at less than a fair rental as well as rental income for periods during which the unit is rented at fair rental.

(3) *Order of deductions*.—Deductions with respect to the rental use of a dwelling unit are allowable in the following order and only to the following extent:

(i) The allocable portions of amounts otherwise allowable as deductions for the taxable year under chapter 1 of the Code with respect to the dwelling unit without regard to the rental use of the unit, *e.g.*, mortgage interest and real estate taxes, are deductible as rental expenses to the extent of the gross rental income from the unit.

(ii) The allocable portions of amounts otherwise allowable as deductions for the taxable year under chapter 1 of the Code by reason of the rental use of the dwelling unit (other than those which would result in an adjustment to the basis of property) are allowable to the extent the gross rental income exceeds the deductions allowed or allowable under subdivision (i) of this subparagraph.

(iii) The allocable portions of amounts otherwise allowable as deductions for the taxable year under chapter 1 of the Code by reason of the rental use of the dwelling unit which would result in an adjustment to the basis of property are allowable to the extent the gross rental income exceeds the deductions allowed or allowable under subdivisions (i) and (ii) of this subparagraph.

For purposes of this subparagraph, the portion of any item which is allocable to the rental use of a unit during a taxable year shall be that amount which bears the same relationship to the total amount of the item as the number of days on which the unit is rented at a fair rental during the taxable year bears to the number of days on which the unit is used for any purpose (other than repair or maintenance) during the taxable year.

(4) *Example.*—The provisions of this paragraph may be illustrated by the following example:

Example. B owns a lakeside home which B rents at a fair rental for 90 days during the taxable year. B uses the home for personal purposes on 20 other days during the taxable year and also rents it to a friend at a discount for 10 days. Thus, the home is used for some purpose (other than repair or maintenance) on 120 days during the taxable year, and the rental allocation fraction may not exceed 90/120. On the basis of the following figures, B determines that the sum of the rental expenses for the home for the taxable year that are deductible under subparagraph (3) of this paragraph is $2,200. The advertising expense and the realtor's fee are also deductible.

	Total	Allocable to rental	
Gross receipts from rental:			
90 days at $25 per day		$2,250	
10 days at $15 per day		150	
Total			$2,400
Computation of gross rental income:			
Gross receipts from rental		$2,400	
Less: Advertising and realtor's fee		200	
Gross rental income			$2,200
Deductions allowable under subparagraph (3)(i) of this paragraph:			
Mortgage interest	$1,000	$750	
Real estate taxes	800	600	
Amount allowable			1,350
Limit on further deductions			$850
Deductions allowable under subparagraph (3)(ii) of this paragraph:			
Insurance	$400	$300	
Utilities	600	450	
Amount allowable			750
Limit on further deductions			$100
Deductions allowable under subparagraph (3)(iii) of this paragraph:			
Depreciation	$1,500	$1,125	
Amount allowable			100

NOTE.—If B itemizes deductions, B may claim the other $250 in mortgage interest and the other $200 in real estate taxes as itemized deductions.

(e) *Application of the provisions of § 1.280A-1 and this section to rental pools.*—(1) *In general.*—In the case of a dwelling unit which is entered in a rental pool, as defined in subparagraph (2) of this paragraph, during the taxable year, the provisions of § 1.280A-1 and this section shall be applied in accordance with this paragraph.

(2) *Rental pool.*—For purposes of this section, the term "rental pool" means any arrangement whereby two or more dwelling units are made available for rental and those persons with interests in the units agree to share at least a substantial part of the rental income from the units without regard to the actual use of the various units. The fact that those persons with interests in a particular unit are entitled to an occupancy fee or other payment for the actual use of the unit does not prevent the arrangement from constituting a rental pool if the percentage of the rental income in which the participants in the arrangement share is substantial.

(3) *Gross rental income of participants.*—Participants in a rental pool shall include in gross rental income all amounts received or accrued by reason of participation in the rental pool (including payments such as occupancy fees) except amounts which are clearly not rental income, *e.g.*, interest earned on deposits held in escrow on behalf of the rental pool participants. Thus, a taxpayer who participates in a rental pool may have gross rental income although the unit in which the taxpayer has an interest is not actually rented during the taxable year.

(4) *Determination of use when averaging is not elected.*—(i) *Applicability.*—This paragraph (e)(4) applies with respect to a rental pool unit only for periods for which the unit is not subject to paragraph (e)(5) of this section.

(ii) *Actual use rule.*—For purposes of § 1.280A-1(d)(1) and paragraph (c) of this section, the number of days on which the unit is rented at fair rental and the number of days on which the unit is used for any purpose shall be determined by reference to the actual use of the unit. Availability for rental through the rental pool does not constitute rental at a fair rental or use of the unit for any purpose. If the taxpayer's unit is actually rented at a fair rental on any day during the taxpayer's participation in the rental pool, the taxpayer may count that day as a day on which the unit is rented at a fair rental although the taxpayer receives only a portion of the rent paid.

(iii) *Furnishing information.*—The rental agency managing the rental pool shall furnish the taxpayer within 60 days after the end of the pool season a written statement indicating the number of days the taxpayer's unit was actually rented at fair rental and the number of days the unit was used for any other purpose (other than repair and maintenance) during the pool season.

(5) *Election to average rental use.*—(i) *Applicability.*—This paragraph (e)(5) applies to a taxpayer with respect to participation in a rental pool for a pool season only if—

(A) The taxpayer signs and furnishes to the pool management a document stating that the taxpayer irrevocably consents to the application of this paragraph (e)(5) for that pool season, and

(B) The pool management sends to the taxpayer a written notice stating that there has been unanimous consent by all pool participants to the application of this paragraph (e)(5) for the pool season and providing the taxpayer with the information necessary to enable the taxpayer to comply with the rules of this paragraph (e)(5).

It is not necessary that the taxpayer furnish a separate consent for each pool season; a consent may provide that it applies to more than one pool season. If the Commissioner determines that there has not been unanimous consent to the application of this paragraph (e)(5) or that the pool management has failed to provide the required notice to pool participants, the Commissioner may require all pool participants to determine the use of their units under paragraph (e)(4) of this section.

(ii) *General rules.*—All taxpayers with interests in units participating in a rental pool during a pool season with respect to which this paragraph (e)(5) applies shall determine the number of days that the unit is rented at fair rental during its participation in the rental pool in that pool season under paragraph (e)(5)(iii) of this section. All use of the unit on days other than participation days and all use of the unit on participation days other than use at fair rental shall be determined by reference to actual use of the unit. These determinations are for purposes of applying § 1.280-1(d)(1) and paragraph (c) of this section.

(iii) *Averaging formula.*—The aggregate number of days that units in the rental pool were rented at fair rental during the pool season shall be apportioned among the units in the pool according to the following ratio:

$$\frac{\text{number of participation days of a particular unit}}{\text{aggregate number of participation days of all units.}}$$

Thus, if the aggregate number of days of rental at fair rental for all units in a pool were 300, the number of participation days of a particular unit were 80, and the aggregate number of participation days of all units in the pool were 480, the number of days of rental at fair rental to be allocated to the particular unit would be 50, computed as follows:

$$\frac{80}{480} \times 300 = 50.$$

(iv) *When pool season overlaps 2 taxable years.*—If a pool season with respect to which this paragraph (e)(5) applies overlaps 2 taxable years of a person with an interest in a unit participating in the rental pool during that pool season, that person shall apportion the number of days of fair rental allocated to that unit for that season under paragraph (e)(5)(iii) of this section between the taxable years according to the following ratio:

$$\frac{\text{number of participation days of the unit during the pool season that fall in the taxable year}}{\text{number of participation days of the unit during the pool season}}$$

(v) *"Participation day" defined.*—A "participation day" of a unit is a day for which that unit is entered in the rental pool.

(6) *Reciprocal arrangements.*—If the rental pool agreement provides that a participant whose unit is rented on a given day may make use of another unit in the pool on that day, a taxpayer who has an interest in a unit so used by another participant shall be deemed to have used the unit for personal purposes on any day on which another participant uses the unit under that provision of the agreement.

(f) *Application of the rules of § 1.280A-1 and this section to time sharing arrangement.*—(1) *In general.*—In the case of a dwelling unit which is used during the taxable year under a time sharing arrangement, as defined in subparagraph (2) of this paragraph, the provisions of § 1.280A-1 and this section shall be applied in accordance with this paragraph.

(2) *Time sharing arrangement.*—For purposes of this section, the term "time sharing arrangement" means any arrangement whereby two or more persons with interests in a dwelling unit agree to exercise control over the unit for different periods during the taxable year. For example, an arrangement under which each of twelve persons with interests in a unit is entitled to exercise control over the unit for one month during the taxable year is a time sharing arrangement. Whether all twelve persons have undivided interests in the unit for the entire year or each has the sole interest in the unit for a single month during the year is immaterial.

(3) *Use for personal purposes.*—For purposes of § 1.280A-1(d) and (e), each of the persons with an interest in the unit subject to the time sharing arrangements shall be considered to have a continuing interest in the unit regardless of the terms of the interest under local law.

(4) *Short rental period.*—The provisions of paragraph (b) of this section shall be applied on the basis of the number of days that the unit is actually rented during the entire taxable year.

(5) *Allocation rule.*—The provisions of paragraph (c) of this section shall apply if any per-

son with an interest in the unit is deemed to use the unit for personal purposes on any day during the taxable year. The provisions of paragraph (c) of this section shall be applied on the basis of the taxpayer's expenses for the unit, the number of days during the taxable year that the unit is rented at a fair rental (determined without regard to the provisions of § 1.280A-1(g)), and the number of days during the taxable year that the unit is used for any purpose.

(6) *Limitation on deductions.*—The provisions of paragraph (d) of this section shall be applied on the basis of the taxpayer's rental income and expenses with respect to the unit. [Reg. § 1.280A-3.]

Investment Tax Credit: Luxury Automobiles

Investment Tax Credit: Luxury Automobiles: Limitation on Amount of Depreciation.—Reg. §§ 1.280F-1T—1.280F-5T, relating to the limitations placed on the amount of cost recovery deductions and investment tax credit allowed for taxpayers who purchase passenger automobiles for use in a trade or business or for use in the production of income, are proposed as final and, when adopted, would become Reg. §§ 1.280F-1—1.280F-5 (published in the Federal Register on October 24, 1984).

§ 1.280F-1. Limitations on investment tax credit and recovery deductions under section 168 for passenger automobiles and certain other listed property; overview of regulations.

§ 1.280F-2. Limitations on recovery dedcutions and the invvestment tax credit for certain passenger automobiles.

§ 1.280F-3. Limitations on recovery deductions and the investment tax credit when the business use percentage of listed property is not greater than 50 percent.

§ 1.280F-4. Special rules for listed property.

§ 1.280F-5. Leased property.

Substantiation Travel, Entertainment, Gifts, Listed Property, Etc.

Business Expenses: Substantiation: Recordkeeping Requirements: Listed Property.—Amendments to Temporary Reg. §§ 1.280F-1T, 1.280F-3T and 1.280F-5T, relating to the requirement that any deduction or credit with respect to certain business-related expenses be substantiated with adequate or sufficient evidence to corroborate a taxpayer's own statement and to the limitations on cost recovery deductions and the investment tax credit for listed property, are also proposed as final (published in the Federal Register on November 6, 1985).

§ 1.280F-1. Limitations on investment tax credit and recovery deductions under section 168 for passenger automobiles and certain other listed property; overview of regulations.

§ 1.280F-3. Limitations on recovery deductions and the investment tax credit when the business use percentage of listed property is not greater than 50 percent.

§ 1.280F-5. Leased property.

Tax Year: Partnerships, S Corporations, Personal Service Corporations

Tax Year: Election: Partnerships: S Corporations: Personal Service Corporation.—Temporary Reg. §§ 1.280H-0T and 1.280H-1T, relating to the election of a taxable year by a partnership, S corporation or personal service corporation, are also proposed as final regulations (published in the Federal Register on May 27, 1988).

§ 1.280H-0. Table of contents.

§ 1.280H-1. Limitation on certain amounts paid to employee-owners by personal service corporations electing alternative taxable years.

CORPORATE DISTRIBUTIONS AND ADJUSTMENTS

Section 301 Regulations: Statutory Changes Reflected

Section 301 Regulations: Statutory Changes Reflected.—Amendments to Reg. § 1.301-1, updating existing regulations under section 301 to reflect statutory changes made by the Technical and Miscellaneous Revenue Act of 1988, which changes provide that the amount of a distribution of property made by a corporation to its shareholder is the fair market value of the distributed property, are proposed (published in the Federal Register on March 26, 2019) (corrected April 23, 2019) (REG-121694-16).

Par. 2. Section 1.301-1 is revised to read as follows:

§1.301-1. Rules applicable with respect to distributions of money and other property.— (a) *General.*—Section 301 provides the general rule for treatment of distributions made in taxable years beginning after December 31, 1986, of property by a corporation to a shareholder with respect to its stock. The term *property* is defined in section 317(a). Such distributions, except as otherwise provided in this chapter, shall be treated as provided in section 301(c). Under section 301(c), distributions may be included in gross income to the extent the amount distributed is considered a dividend under section 316, applied against and reduce the adjusted basis of the stock, treated as gain from the sale or exchange of property, or (in the case of certain distributions out of increase in value accrued before March 1, 1913) may be exempt from tax. The amount of the distributions to which section 301 applies is determined in accordance with the provisions of section 301(b). The basis of property received in a distribution to which section 301 applies is determined in accordance with the provisions of section 301(d).

(b) *Amount of distribution and determination of fair market value.*—The amount of a distribution to which section 301 applies shall be the amount of money received in the distribution, plus the fair market value of other property received in the distribution. The fair market value of any property distributed shall be determined as of the date of the distribution.

(c) *Time of inclusion in gross income and time of determination of fair market value.*—A distribution made by a corporation to its shareholders shall be included in the gross income of the distributees when the cash or other property is unqualifiedly made subject to their demands without regard to whether such date is the same as that on which the corporation made the distribution. For example, if a corporation distributes a taxable dividend in property on December 30, 2018, which is received by, or unqualifiedly made subject to the demand of, its shareholders on January 3, 2019, the amount to be included in the gross income of the shareholders will be the fair market value of such property on December 30, 2018, although such amount will not be includible in the gross income of the shareholders until January 3, 2019.

(d) *Application of section to shareholders.*—Section 301 is not applicable to an amount paid by a corporation to a shareholder unless the amount is paid to the shareholder in the shareholder's capacity as such.

(e) *Example.*—Corporation M, formed in 1998, has never been an acquiring corporation in a transaction to which section 381(a) applies. On January 1, 2019, A, an individual owned all of the stock of Corporation M, consisting of a single share, with an adjusted basis of $2,000. During 2019, A received distributions from Corporation M totaling $30,000, consisting of $10,000 in cash and listed securities having a basis in the hands of Corporation M and a fair market value on the date distributed of $20,000. Corporation M's taxable year is the calendar year. As of December 31, 2018, Corporation M had accumulated earnings and profits in the amount of $26,000, and it had no earnings and profits and no deficit for 2019. Of the $30,000 received by A, $26,000 will be treated as an ordinary dividend; the remaining $4,000 will be applied against the adjusted basis of his stock; the $2,000 in excess of the adjusted basis of his stock will be treated as gain from the sale or exchange of property under section 301(c)(3)(A). If A subsequently sells his stock in Corporation M, the basis for determining gain or loss on the sale will be zero.

(f) *Reduction for liabilities.*—(1) *General rule.*—For purposes of section 301(b)(2), no reduction in the amount of a distribution shall be made for the amount of any liability, except to the extent the liability is assumed by the shareholder within the meaning of section 357(d).

(2) *No reduction below zero.*—Any reduction pursuant to paragraph (f)(1) of this section shall not cause the amount of the distribution to be reduced below zero.

(3) *Effective dates.*—(i) *In general.*—This paragraph (f) applies to distributions occurring after January 4, 2001.

(ii) *Retroactive application.*—This paragraph (f) also applies to distributions made on or before January 4, 2001, if the distribution is made as part of a transaction described in, or substantially similar to the transaction in, Notice 99-59 (1999-2 C.B. 761), including transactions designed to reduce gain (*see* §601.601(d)(2) of this chapter). For rules for distributions on or before January 4, 2001 (other than distributions on or before that date to which this paragraph (f) applies), see rules in effect on January 4, 2001 (see §1.301-1(g) as contained in 26 CFR part 1 revised April 1, 2001).

(g) *Basis.*—The basis of property received in a distribution to which section 301 applies shall be the fair market value of such property. See paragraph (b) of this section.

(h) *Transfers for less than fair market value.*—If property is transferred by a corporation to a shareholder for an amount less than its fair market value in a sale or exchange, such shareholder shall be treated as having received a distribution to which section 301 applies. In such case, the amount of the distribution shall be the excess of the fair market value of the property over the amount paid for such property at the time of the transfer. For example, on January 3, 2019, A, a shareholder of Corporation X, purchased property from X for $20. The fair market value of such property on January 3, 2019 was $100. The amount of the distribution to A determined under section 301(b) is $80.

(i) [Reserved]

(j) *Transactions treated as distributions.*—A distribution to shareholders with respect to their stock is within the terms of section 301 although it takes place at the same time as another transaction if the distribution is in substance a separate transaction whether or not connected in a formal sense. This is most likely to occur in the case of a recapitalization, a reincorporation, or a merger of a corporation with a newly organized corporation having substantially no property. For example, if a corporation having only common stock outstanding, exchanges one share of newly issued common stock and one bond in the principal amount of $10 for each share of outstanding common stock, the distribution of the bonds will be a distribution of property (to the extent of their fair market value) to which section 301 applies, even though the exchange of common stock for common stock may be pursuant to a plan of reorganization under the terms of section 368(a)(1)(E) (recapitalization) and even though the exchange of common stock for common stock may be tax free by virtue of section 354.

(k) *Cancellation of indebtedness.*—The cancellation of indebtedness of a shareholder by a corporation shall be treated as a distribution of property.

(l) *Cross references.*—For certain rules relating to adjustments to earnings and profits and for determining the extent to which a distribution is a dividend, see sections 312 and 316 and regulations thereunder.

(m) *Split-dollar and other life insurance arrangements.*—(1) *Split-dollar life insurance arrangements.*—(i) *Distribution of economic benefits.*—The provision by a corporation to its shareholder pursuant to a split-dollar life insurance arrangement, as defined in § 1.61-22(b)(1) or (2), of economic benefits described in § 1.61-22(d) or of amounts described in § 1.61-22(e) is treated as a distribution of property, the amount of which is determined under § 1.61-22(d) and (e), respectively.

(ii) *Distribution of entire contract or undivided interest therein.*—A transfer (within the meaning of § 1.61-22(c)(3)) of the ownership of a life insurance contract (or an undivided interest therein) that is part of a split-dollar life insurance arrangement is a distribution of property, the amount of which is determined pursuant to § 1.61-22(g)(1) and (2).

(2) *Other life insurance arrangements.*—A payment by a corporation on behalf of a shareholder of premiums on a life insurance contract or an undivided interest therein that is owned by the shareholder constitutes a distribution of property, even if such payment is not part of a split-dollar life insurance arrangement under § 1.61-22(b).

(3) *When distribution is made.*—(i) *In general.*—Except as provided in paragraph (m)(3)(ii) of this section, paragraph (c) of this section shall apply to determine when a distribution described in paragraph (m)(1) or (2) of this section is taken into account by a shareholder.

(ii) *Exception.*—Notwithstanding paragraph (c) of this section, a distribution described in paragraph (m)(1)(ii) of this section shall be treated as made by a corporation to its shareholder at the time that the life insurance contract, or an undivided interest therein, is transferred (within the meaning of § 1.61-22(c)(3)) to the shareholder.

(4) *Effective date.*—(i) *General rule.*—This paragraph (m) applies to split-dollar and other life insurance arrangements entered into after September 17, 2003. For purposes of this paragraph (m)(4), a split-dollar life insurance arrangement is entered into as determined under § 1.61-22(j)(1)(ii).

(ii) *Modified arrangements treated as new arrangements.*—If a split-dollar life insurance arrangement entered into on or before September 17, 2003 is materially modified (within the meaning of § 1.61-22(j)(2)) after September 17, 2003, the arrangement is treated as a new arrangement entered into on the date of the modification.

(n) *Applicability date.*—Paragraphs (a) through (c), (e), (g), and (h) of this section apply to distributions under section 301 made after the date of publication of the Treasury decision adopting these rules as final regulations in the **Federal Register**.

Stock and Rights to Acquire Stock: Deemed Distributions

Stock and Rights to Acquire Stock: Deemed Distributions.—Amendments to Reg. §§ 1.305-1, 1.305-3 and 1.305-7, regarding deemed distributions of stock and rights to acquire stock and resolving ambiguities concerning the amount and timing of deemed distributions that are or result from adjustments to rights to acquire stock, are proposed (published in the Federal Register on April 13, 2016) (corrected July 5, 2016) (REG-133673-15).

Par. 2. Section 1.305-1 is amended by:

1. Revising paragraphs (b)(3) and (d).

2. Adding paragraph (e).

The revisions and addition read as follows:

§ 1.305-1. Stock dividends.

* * *

(b) * * *

(3) For rules determining the amount of the distribution for certain transactions, such as periodic redemptions or applicable adjustments (as defined in § 1.305-7(a)) of rights to acquire stock that are treated as distributions under section 305(b) and (c), *see* § 1.305-7 and *Examples 6, 7, 8, 9,* and *15* of § 1.305-3(e).

* * *

(d) *Definitions.*—For purposes of section 305, this section, and §§ 1.305-2 through 1.305-7:

(1) *Stock.*—The term *stock* means actual stock or a right to acquire stock.

(2) *Actual stock.*—The term *actual stock* means stock issued by a corporation, excluding rights to acquire stock as defined in paragraph (d)(3) of this section.

(3) *Right to acquire stock.*—The term *right to acquire stock* means—

(i) A right of a holder of a convertible instrument (including a debt instrument that is convertible into shares of stock and stock that is convertible into shares of another class of stock) to convert the instrument into one or more shares of stock of the corporation issuing the instrument;

(ii) A warrant, subscription right, stock right, or other option to acquire shares of stock of the corporation issuing the instrument;

(iii) A right to acquire stock of the corporation issuing such right similar to the rights described in paragraphs (d)(3)(i) and (ii) of this section; and

(iv) A right to receive an amount of cash or other property determined in whole or in part by reference to the value of a specified number of shares of stock (whether or not in lieu of such stock) of the corporation issuing the right.

(4) *Shareholder.*—The term *shareholder* means a holder of actual stock or a holder of a right to acquire stock.

(5) *Actual shareholder*.—The term *actual shareholder* means a holder of actual stock.

(6) *Deemed shareholder*.—The term *deemed shareholder* means a holder of a right to acquire stock.

(7) *Deemed distribution*.—The term *deemed distribution* means a transaction or event, other than an actual distribution of cash or property, that constitutes a distribution under section 305(b) and (c). An applicable adjustment to a right to acquire stock is not and does not result in a deemed distribution if either—

(i) The right to acquire stock is a nonqualified stock option without a readily ascertainable fair market value (*see* section 83(e) and § 1.83-7), or

(ii) Section 83(a) applies to the right to acquire stock or the stock to which the right relates or the stock is subject to a substantial risk of forfeiture, and the holder of the right has not made an election under section 83(b).

(e) *Effective/applicability date*.—Paragraphs (b)(3) and (d) of this section apply to deemed distributions under section 305(b) and (c) occurring on or after the date of publication of the Treasury decision adopting these rules as final regulations in the **Federal Register**. A taxpayer, however, may rely on these proposed regulations for deemed distributions under section 305(c) that occur prior to such date. For purposes of determining the amount of a deemed distribution to a deemed shareholder occurring prior to such date, a taxpayer may determine the amount of the deemed distribution by treating such distribution either as a distribution of a right to acquire stock or as a distribution of the actual stock to which the right relates.

Par. 3. Section 1.305-3 is amended by:

1. Revising paragraph (e) introductory text, *Example (6)*(ii), *Example (7)*(ii) and (iii).

2. Adding paragraph (f).

The revisions and addition read as follows:

§ 1.305-3. Disproportionate distributions.

* * *

(e) *Examples*.—The following examples illustrate the application of section 305(b)(2) to distributions of stock and rights to acquire stock and the application of section 305(c) to deemed distributions of stock and rights to acquire stock.

* * *

Example 6. * * *

(ii) M pays an annual cash dividend on the class A stock. At the beginning of the second year, when the conversion ratio is increased to 1.05 shares of class A stock for each share of class B stock, an applicable adjustment occurs, as defined in § 1.305-7(a), and a distribution of rights to acquire 0.05 shares of class A stock is deemed made under section 305(c) and § 1.305-7(c)(1) with respect to each share of class B stock. The proportionate interests of the class B shareholders in the assets or earnings and profits of M are increased, and the transaction has the effect described in section 305(b)(2). Accordingly, sections 305(b)(2) and 301 apply to the transaction. The amount of the deemed distribution is determined in accordance with 1.305-7(c)(4)(i) and the date and time of the deemed distribution are determined in accordance with § 1.305-7(c)(5).

Example 7. * * *

(ii) In 2017, a $1 cash dividend per share is declared and paid on the class B stock. Pursuant to the terms of the class B stock, on the date of payment, the conversion ratio of the class B stock is reduced. The reduction in conversion ratio is an applicable adjustment, as defined in § 1.305-7(a). Under section 305(c) and § 1.305-7(c)(2), the reduction is a deemed distribution of stock to the class A shareholders, since their proportionate interest in the assets or earnings and profits of the corporation is increased, and the transaction has the effect described in section 305(b)(2). Accordingly, sections 305(b)(2) and 301 apply to the transaction. The amount of the distribution is determined in accordance with § 1.305-7(c)(4)(ii), and the date and time of the deemed distribution are determined in accordance with § 1.305-7(c)(5).

(iii) In the following year a cash dividend is paid on the class A stock but not on the class B stock, and the conversion ratio of the class B stock increases. The increase in the conversion ratio of the class B shares is an applicable adjustment. Under section 305(c) and § 1.305-7(c)(1), the adjustment is a deemed distribution of rights to acquire stock to the class B shareholders since their proportionate interest in the assets or earnings and profits of the corporation is increased, and the transaction has the effect described in section 305(b)(2). Accordingly, sections 305(b)(2) and 301 apply to the transaction. The amount of the distribution is determined in accordance with § 1.305-7(c)(4)(i), and the date and time of the deemed distribution are determined in accordance with § 1.305-7(c)(5).

* * *

(f) *Effective/applicability date*.—The first sentence of paragraph (e) of this section and *Examples 6* and *7* of paragraph (e) of this section apply to deemed distributions under section 305(c) occurring on or after the date of publication of the Treasury decision adopting these rules as final regulations in the **Federal Register**. A taxpayer, however, may rely on these proposed regulations for deemed distributions under section 305(c) that occur prior to such date. For purposes of determining the amount of a deemed distribution to a deemed shareholder occurring prior to the date of publication, a taxpayer may determine the amount of the deemed distribution by treating such distribution either as a distribution of a right to acquire stock or as a distribution of the actual stock to which the right relates.

Par. 4. Section 1.305-7 is revised to read as follows:

§ 1.305-7. Certain transactions treated as distributions.—(a) *Applicable adjustment*.—For purposes of section 305, §§ 1.305-1 through 1.305-6, and this section, the term *applicable adjustment* means an adjustment to a right to acquire stock (as defined in § 1.305-1(d)(3)), including—

(1) With respect to a convertible instrument and a holder thereof, an increase in the conversion ratio or a reduction in the conversion price of such instrument;

(2) With respect to a warrant, subscription right, stock right, option, or other similar right and a holder thereof, an increase in the number of shares to be received by the holder upon exercise or a reduction in exercise price;

(3) With respect to a convertible instrument and a holder of actual stock into which such instrument may be converted, an increase in the conversion price or a reduction in the conversion ratio of such instrument;

(4) With respect to a warrant, subscription right, stock right, option, or similar right and a holder of actual stock into which such instrument is exercisable, an increase in the exercise price or a reduction in the number of shares to be received by the holder upon exercise; and

(5) An adjustment in the terms of a right to acquire stock having an effect similar to the effects of the adjustments described in paragraphs (a)(1) through (a)(4) of this section, including, for example, an extension or reduction of the term during which a right to acquire stock may be exercised.

(b) *Transactions treated as distributions.*—(1) *In general.*—Under section 305(c), an applicable adjustment, a change in redemption price, a difference between redemption price and issue price, a redemption that is treated as a distribution to which section 301 applies, or any transaction (including a recapitalization) having a similar effect on the interest of any shareholder is treated as a distribution of stock to which sections 305(b) and 301 apply if such transaction increases a shareholder's proportionate interest in the assets or earnings and profits of the corporation deemed to make such distribution, and the distribution has the result described in section 305(b)(2), (3), (4), or (5). Depending upon the facts presented, the distribution may be deemed to be made in shares of actual stock or in additional rights to acquire stock (which, in either case, may be common or preferred stock).

(c) *Applicable adjustment to right to acquire stock.*—(1) *Increase in deemed shareholder's proportionate interest.*—Under section 305(c), if an applicable adjustment has the effect of increasing a deemed shareholder's proportionate interest in the assets or earnings and profits of the corporation, and if such increase has the effect described in section 305(b)(2), (3), (4) or (5), the applicable adjustment is a deemed distribution to the deemed shareholder of a right to acquire stock, and section 301 applies to the deemed distribution. Applicable adjustments that can have this effect include, with respect to a convertible instrument, an increase in the conversion ratio or the number of shares of stock to be received upon conversion or a reduction in the conversion price.

(2) *Increase in actual shareholder's proportionate interest.*—If an applicable adjustment has the effect of reducing a deemed shareholder's proportionate interest in the assets or earnings and profits of the corporation and thereby increasing an actual shareholder's proportionate interest, and if such increase has the effect described in section 305(b)(2), (3), (4) or (5), then the applicable adjustment is a deemed distribution of stock to the actual shareholder, and section 301 applies to the deemed distribution. Applicable adjustments that can have this effect include, with respect to a convertible instrument, a reduction in the conversion ratio or in the number of shares to be received upon conversion, or an increase in the conversion price.

(3) *Exception.*—For purposes of applying section 305(c) in conjunction with section 305(b), an applicable adjustment that is made pursuant to a bona fide, reasonable adjustment formula (including but not limited to an applicable adjustment made to compensate for a distribution of stock to another shareholder) and that has the effect of preventing dilution of the proportionate interest of the holders of actual stock or rights to acquire stock does not result in a deemed distribution of stock. An applicable adjustment that is made to compensate for a cash or property distribution to another shareholder and that is taxable under section 301, 356(a)(2), 871(a)(1)(A), 881(a)(1), 852(b), or 857(b) is not made pursuant to a bona fide adjustment formula described in the preceding sentence.

(4) *Amount of deemed distribution.*—(i) *Deemed distribution to deemed shareholder.*—For a deemed distribution under section 305(b) and (c) that is made to a deemed shareholder and is an applicable adjustment, the amount of the deemed distribution is the excess of—

(A) The fair market value of the right to acquire stock held by the deemed shareholder immediately after the applicable adjustment, over

(B) The fair market value, determined immediately after the applicable adjustment, of such right to acquire stock as if no applicable adjustment had occurred.

(ii) *Deemed distribution to actual shareholder.*—For a deemed distribution under section 305(b) and (c) that is made to an actual shareholder and results from an applicable adjustment, the amount of the deemed distribution is the fair market value of the stock deemed distributed, determined in accordance with the methodology set forth in § 1.305-3(e), *Examples 8* and *9*.

(iii) *Fair market value standard.*—In determining the fair market value of a right to acquire stock for purposes of this paragraph (c)(4),

(A) Any particular facts pertaining to the deemed shareholder, including the number of rights or shares such deemed shareholder owns, will be disregarded, and

(B) Any value or reduction in value attributable to the possibility of future applicable adjustments that may result from actual or deemed distributions will not be taken into account.

(5) *Date and time of deemed distribution.*—When an applicable adjustment is a deemed distribution under paragraphs (c)(1) or (2) of this section, the deemed distribution occurs at the time such applicable adjustment occurs, in accordance with the instrument setting forth the terms of the right to acquire stock, but in no event later than the date of the distribution of cash or property that results in the deemed distribution (taking into account § 1.305-3(b)). For such applicable adjustment relating to a right to acquire publicly-traded stock, if the instrument set-

ting forth the terms of such right does not set forth the time the applicable adjustment occurs, the deemed distribution occurs immediately prior to the opening of business on the ex-dividend date for the distribution of the cash or property that results in the deemed distribution. For such an applicable adjustment relating to a right to acquire non-publicly traded stock, if the instrument setting forth the terms of such right does not set forth the time the applicable adjustment occurs, the deemed distribution occurs on the date that a holder is legally entitled to the distribution of cash or property that results in the deemed distribution.

(6) *Examples.*—The following examples and the examples in §§1.305-3(e) and 1.305-5(d) illustrate the application of section 305(c) and paragraphs (a), (b) and (c) of this section.

Example 1. (i) *Facts.* Corporation U has two classes of actual stock outstanding, class A and class B. Each class B share is convertible into class A stock. In accordance with a bona fide, reasonable antidilution provision, the conversion price is adjusted downward if the corporation transfers class A stock to anyone for consideration below the conversion price. The corporation sells class A stock to the public at the current market price, which is below the conversion price. Pursuant to the antidilution provision, the conversion price is adjusted downward.

(ii) *Analysis.* Although such a reduction in conversion price is an applicable adjustment, under paragraph (c)(3) of this section the reduction is not a distribution under section 305(c) for the purposes of section 305(b).

Example 2. (i) *Facts.* Corporation X has outstanding one class of actual common stock and convertible debt securities. The convertible securities have a bona fide, reasonable antidilution provision that provides for an increase in conversion ratio in the event stock dividends or rights to acquire stock are distributed to the common shareholders. Corporation X distributes to the common shareholders an actual stock dividend that results in an increase in the conversion ratio of the convertible securities. Pursuant to the antidilution provision, the conversion ratio is increased.

(ii) *Analysis.* Under section 305(d) and §1.305-1(d)(4), the holders of convertible securities are shareholders for purposes of section 305(b) and (c). The convertible securities are rights to acquire stock and are stock for purposes of section 305. The increase in conversion ratio caused by the distribution of the stock dividend to the common shareholders is an applicable adjustment. Because the applicable adjustment is made pursuant to a bona fide, reasonable adjustment formula within the meaning of paragraph (c)(3) of this section, the applicable adjustment is not a deemed distribution under section 305(c) of rights to acquire stock.

Example 3. (i) *Facts.* Corporation X has outstanding one class of publicly-traded common stock and convertible debt securities. The terms of the convertible securities provide for an increase in the conversion ratio in the event stock, cash, or property is distributed to the holders of the common stock. Corporation X distributes cash to the holders of the common stock, and the distribution results in an increase in the conversion ratio of the convertible securities.

(ii) *Analysis.* Under section 305(d) and §1.305-1(d)(4), the holders of the convertible securities are shareholders for purposes of section 305(b) and (c). The conversion rights in the convertible securities are rights to acquire stock (as defined in §1.305-1(d)(3)) and is stock for purposes of section 305. The increase in conversion ratio resulting from the cash distribution to the holders of common stock is an applicable adjustment. Because the applicable adjustment is not made pursuant to a bona fide, reasonable adjustment formula within the meaning of paragraph (c)(3) of this section, it is a deemed distribution to the holders of the convertible securities of rights to acquire stock under section 305(c) and paragraph (c)(1) of this section. Because the proportionate interests of these deemed shareholders in the assets or earnings and profits of Corporation X are increased by the change in conversion ratio, the distribution has the result described in section 305(b)(2) and is treated as a distribution to which section 301 applies. The amount of the deemed distribution is determined in accordance with paragraph (c)(4)(i) of this section, and the date and time of the deemed distribution are determined in accordance with paragraph (c)(5) of this section.

(d) *Recapitalizations.*—(1) *In general.*—A recapitalization (whether or not an isolated transaction) will be deemed to result in a distribution to which section 305(c) and this section apply if—

(i) It is pursuant to a plan to periodically increase a shareholder's proportionate interest in the assets or earnings and profits of the corporation, or

(ii) A shareholder owning preferred stock with dividends in arrears exchanges his stock for other stock and, as a result, increases his proportionate interest in the assets or earnings and profits of the corporation. An increase in a preferred shareholder's proportionate interest occurs in any case where the fair market value or the liquidation preference, whichever is greater, of the stock received in the exchange (determined immediately following the recapitalization), exceeds the issue price of the preferred stock surrendered.

(2) *Amount of distribution.*—In a case to which paragraph (d)(1)(ii) of this section applies, the amount of the distribution deemed under section 305(c) to result from the recapitalization is the lesser of—

(i) The amount by which the fair market value or the liquidation preference, whichever is greater, of the stock received in the exchange (determined immediately following the recapitalization) exceeds the issue price of the preferred stock surrendered, or

(ii) The amount of the dividends in arrears.

(3) *Definition.*—For purposes of applying paragraphs (d)(1) and (2) of this section with respect to stock issued before July 12, 1973, the term *issue price of the preferred stock surrendered* shall mean the greater of the issue price or the liquidation preference (not including dividends in arrears) of the stock surrendered.

(4) *Examples.*—For an illustration of the application of this paragraph (d), *see Example 12* of §1.305-3(e) and *Examples 1, 2, 3,* and *6* of §1.305-5(d).

(e) *Redemption premiums with respect to preferred stock.*—Under section 305(c), if a redemption premium exists with respect to a class of preferred stock under the circumstances described in § 1.305-5(b) and the other requirements of this section are met, the distribution will be deemed made with respect to such preferred stock, in stock of the same class. Accordingly, the preferred shareholders are considered under section 305(b)(4) and (c) to have received a deemed distribution of preferred stock to which section 301 applies.

(f) *Coordination with section 871(m).*—For coordination of sections 305 and 871(m), *see* § 1.871-15(c)(2)(ii).

(g) *Effective date.*—This section applies to deemed distributions under section 305(c) occurring on or after the date of publication of the Treasury decision adopting these rules as final regulations in the **Federal Register**. A taxpayer, however, may rely on these proposed regulations for deemed distributions under section 305(c) that occur prior to such date. For purposes of determining the amount of a deemed distribution to a deemed shareholder occurring prior to the date of publication, a taxpayer may determine the amount of the deemed distribution by treating such distribution either as a distribution of a right to acquire stock or as a distribution of the actual stock to which the right relates.

Foreign Corporations: Stock Transfer Rules: Carryover of Earnings and Taxes

Foreign Corporations: Stock Transfer Rules: Carryover of Earnings and Taxes.—Amendments to Reg. § 1.312-10, addressing (1) the carryover of certain tax attributes, such as earnings and profits and foreign income tax accounts, when two corporations combine in a section 367(b) transaction and (2) the allocation of certain tax attributes when a corporation distributes stock of another corporation in a section 367(b) transaction, are proposed (published in the Federal Register on November 15, 2000) (REG-116050-99).

☐ Par. 2. Section 1.312-10 is amended by adding paragraph (d) to read as follows:

§ 1.312-10. Allocation of earnings in certain corporate separations.

* * *

(d) For additional rules involving foreign corporations, see § 1.367(b)-8.

Qualified Property: Additional First Year Depreciation Deduction

Qualified Property: Additional First Year Depreciation Deduction.—Amendments to Reg. § 1.312-15, providing guidance regarding the additional first year depreciation deduction under section 168(k) of the Internal Revenue Code (Code), are proposed (published in the Federal Register on August 8, 2018) (REG-104397-18).

Par. 13. Section 1.312-15 is amended by adding a sentence at the end of paragraph (a)(1) and adding paragraph (e) to read as follows:

§ 1.312-15. Effect of depreciation on earnings and profits.—(a) * * *

(1) * * * Further, see § 1.168(k)-2(f)(7) with respect to the treatment of the additional first year depreciation deduction allowable under section 168(k), as amended by the Tax Cuts and Jobs Act, Public Law 115-97 (131 Stat. 2054 (December 22, 2017)), for purposes of computing the earnings and profits of a corporation.

* * *

(e) *Applicability date of qualified property.*—The last sentence of paragraph (a) of this section applies to the taxpayer's taxable years ending on or after the date of publication of a Treasury decision adopting these rules as final regulations in the **Federal Register**. However, a taxpayer may rely on the last sentence in paragraph (a) of this section in these proposed regulations for the taxpayer's taxable years ending on or after September 28, 2017, and ending before the taxpayer's taxable year that includes the date of publication of a Treasury decision adopting these rules as final regulations in the **Federal Register**.

Partnership Transactions: Equity Interests

Partnership Transactions: Equity Interests.—Amendments to Reg. § 1.337(d)-3, preventing a corporate partner from avoiding corporate-level gain through transactions with a partnership involving equity interests of the partner or certain related entities, are proposed (published in the Federal Register on March 25, 2019) REG-135671-17).

Par. 2. Section 1.337(d)-3 is amended by revising paragraphs (c)(2), (f)(2)(ii) and (i) to read as follows:

§ 1.337(d)-3. Gain recognition upon certain partnership transactions involving a partner's stock.

* * *

(c) * * *

(2) *Stock of the Corporate Partner.*—(i) *In general.*—With respect to a Corporate Partner, Stock of the Corporate Partner includes stock, warrants and other options to acquire stock, and similar interests (each an equity interest) in the Corporate Partner. Stock of the Corporate Partner also includes equity interests in a corporation that controls the Corporate Partner within the meaning of section 304(c), and which also has a direct or indirect equity interest in the Corporate Partner. Solely for purposes of determining whether a corporation that controls the Corporate Partner also has a direct or indirect equity interest in the Corporate Partner under this paragraph (c)(2), a direct or indirect ownership of an equity interest in the Corporate Partner includes ownership of Stock of the Corporate

Partner that would be attributed to a person under section 318(a)(2) (except that the 50-percent ownership limitation in section 318(a)(2)(C) does not apply) and under section 318(a)(4) (but otherwise without regard to section 318).

(ii) *Equity Interests with value attributable to Stock of the Corporate Partner.*—If an equity interest in an entity is not Stock of the Corporate Partner within the meaning of paragraph (c)(2)(i) of this section, then the equity interest will be treated as Stock of the Corporate Partner to the extent that the value of that equity interest is attributable to Stock of the Corporate Partner. The preceding sentence will apply only if either—

(A) The Corporate Partner is in control (within the meaning of section 304(c)) of that entity; or

(B) That entity owns directly or indirectly 5 percent or more, by vote or value, of the stock in the Corporate Partner.

(iii) *Determination of value attributable to Stock of the Corporate Partner.*—The value of an equity interest in an entity that is attributable to Stock of the Corporate Partner under paragraph (c)(2)(ii) of this section is equal to the product of—

(A) The fair market value of the equity interest; and

(B) The lesser of—

(1) The ratio of the fair market value of the Stock of the Corporate Partner owned (directly or indirectly (as defined in paragraph (c)(2)(i) of this section), by the entity to the fair market value of all the equity interests in the entity; or

(2) One.

* * *

(f) * * *

(2) * * *

(ii) Is not distributed to the Corporate Partner or a corporation that controls the Corporate Partner within the meaning of section 304(c) and owns directly or indirectly stock or other equity interests in the Corporate Partner. For purposes of this paragraph (f)(2), a direct or indirect ownership of an equity interest in the Corporate Partner means ownership of Stock of the Corporate Partner that would be attributed to a person under section 318(a)(2) (except that the 50-percent ownership limitation in section 318(a)(2)(C) does not apply) and under section 318(a)(4) (but otherwise without regard to section 318).

* * *

(i) *Effective/applicability date.*—The regulations in this section are effective as of the date of their publication as final regulations in the **Federal Register**.

RICs and REITs: Certain Transfers of Property

RICs and REITs: Certain Transfers of Property.—Amendments to Reg. §1.337(d)-7, imposing corporate level tax on certain transactions in which property of a C corporation becomes the property of a REIT, are proposed (published in the Federal Register on June 8, 2016) (REG-126452-15). Proposed Reg. §1.337(d)-7(b)(2)(iii) and (g)(2)(iii) adopted by T.D. 9810 on January 17, 2017. Proposed Reg. §1.337(d)-7(c)(6), (f), and (g)(2)(ii) and (iv) withdrawn by REG-113943-17 on March 26, 2019.

Par. 2. Section 1.337(d)-7 is amended by:

1. Revising paragraph (a)(1) and adding paragraphs (a)(2)(vi) and (vii).
2. Revising paragraph (b)(2)(iii).
3. Adding paragraph (b)(4).
4. Revising paragraph (c)(1).
5. Adding paragraph (c)(6).
6. Adding paragraph (f).
7. Revising paragraphs (g)(2)(ii) and (iii).
8. Adding paragraph (g)(2)(iv).

The additions and revisions read as follows:

§1.337(d)-7. Tax on property owned by a C corporation that becomes property of a RIC or REIT.—(a) *General rule.*—(1) [The text of the proposed amendment to §1.337(d)-7(a)(1) is the same as the text of §1.337(d)-7T(a)(1) as added by T.D. 9770].

(2) * * *

(vi) [The text of the proposed amendment to §1.337(d)-7(a)(2)(vi) is the same as the text of §1.337(d)-7T(a)(2)(vi) as added by T.D. 9770].

(vii) *Converted property.*—The term *converted property* means property owned by a C corporation that becomes the property of a RIC or a REIT and any other property the basis of which is determined, directly or indirectly, in whole or in part, by reference to the basis of the property owned by a C corporation that becomes the property of a RIC or a REIT.

(b) * * *

(2) * * *

(iii) [Adopted by T.D. 9810 on January 17, 2017.]

* * *

(4) [The text of the proposed amendment to §1.337(d)-7(b)(4) is the same as the text of §1.337(d)-7T(b)(4) as added by T.D. 9770].

* * *

(c) *Election of deemed sale treatment.*—(1) [The text of the proposed amendment to §1.337(d)-7(c)(1) is the same as the text of §1.337(d)-7T(c)(1) as added by T.D. 9770].

* * *

(6) [Withdrawn by REG-113943-17 on March 26, 2019.]

* * *

(f) [Withdrawn by REG-113943-17 on March 26, 2019.]

(g) * * *

(2) * * *

(ii) [Withdrawn by REG-113943-17 on March 26, 2019.]

(iii) [Adopted by T.D. 9810 on January 17, 2017.]

(iv) [Withdrawn by REG-113943-17 on March 26, 2019.]

REITs: Certain Transfers of Property

REITs: Certain Transfers of Property.—Amendments to Reg. § 1.337(d)-7, providing guidance for transactions in which property of a C corporation becomes the property of a REIT following certain corporate distributions of controlled corporation stock, are proposed (published in the Federal Register on March 26, 2019) (corrected May 3, 2019) (REG-113943-17).

Par. 2. Section 1.337(d)-7 is amended by adding paragraph (a)(2)(viii) and revising paragraphs (c)(6), (f), and (g)(2)(ii).

§ 1.337(d)-7. Tax on property owned by a C corporation that becomes property of a RIC or REIT.—(a) * * *

(2) * * *

(viii) *Distribution property.*—The term *distribution property* means—

(A) property owned immediately after a section 355 distribution by the distributing corporation, a controlled corporation (as those terms are defined in section 355(a)(1)), or a member of a separate affiliated group (as defined in section 355(b)(3)(B)) of which the distributing corporation or a controlled corporation is the common parent (but no formulation of the step transaction doctrine will be used to determine whether property acquired after the distribution is distribution property pursuant to this paragraph (a)(2)(viii)(A)), and

(B) property with a basis determined, directly or indirectly, in whole or in part, by reference to property described in paragraph (a)(2)(viii)(A) of this section.

* * *

(c) * * *

(6) *Conversion transaction following a section 355 distribution.*—(i) *In general.*—Except as provided in paragraph (c)(6)(ii) of this section, a C corporation described in paragraph (f)(1) of this section is treated as having made the election under paragraph (c)(5) of this section with respect to a conversion transaction if the conversion transaction occurs following the related section 355 distribution (as defined in paragraph (f)(1)(i) of this section) and the C corporation has not made such an election.

(ii) *Limitation.*—A C corporation treated as having made the election under paragraph (c)(5) of this section as a result of paragraph (c)(6)(i) of this section is not treated as having made the election with respect to property that the taxpayer establishes is not distribution property with respect to the related section 355 distribution. For purposes of this paragraph (c)(6)(ii), any property with an adjusted basis in excess of its fair market value as of the date of the conversion transaction will not be treated as distribution property unless the taxpayer establishes that it owned such asset immediately after the related section 355 distribution. If the limitation applies, then paragraph (b) of this section will apply to the property that is not distribution property with respect to the related section 355 distribution.

* * *

(f) *Conversion transaction preceding or following a section 355 distribution.*—(1) *In general.*—A C corporation or a REIT is described in this paragraph (f)(1) if—

(i) The C corporation or the REIT engages in a conversion transaction involving a REIT during the twenty-year period beginning on the date that is ten years before the date of a section 355 distribution (the related section 355 distribution); and

(ii) The C corporation or the REIT engaging in the related section 355 distribution is either—

(A) The distributing corporation or the controlled corporation, as those terms are defined in section 355(a)(1); or

(B) A member of the separate affiliated group (as defined in section 355(b)(3)(B)) of the distributing corporation or the controlled corporation.

(2) *Predecessors and successors.*—For purposes of this paragraph (f), any reference to a controlled corporation, a distributing corporation, or a member of the separate affiliated group of a distributing corporation or a controlled corporation includes a reference to any predecessor or successor of such corporation. Predecessors and successors include corporations which succeed to and take into account items described in section 381(c) of the distributing corporation or the controlled corporation, and corporations having such items to which the distributing corporation or the controlled corporation succeeded and took into account.

(3) *Exclusion of certain conversion transactions.*—A C corporation or a REIT is not described in paragraph (f)(1) of this section if—

(i) The distributing corporation and the controlled corporation are both REITs immediately after the related section 355 distribution (including by reason of elections under section 856(c)(1) made after the related section 355 distribution that are effective before the related section 355 distribution) and at all times during the two years thereafter;

(ii) Section 355(h)(1) does not apply to the related section 355 distribution by reason of section 355(h)(2)(B); or

(iii) The related section 355 distribution occurred before December 7, 2015 or is described in a ruling request referred to in section 311(c) of Division Q of the Consolidated Appropriations Act, 2016, Public Law 114-113, 129 Stat. 2422.

(g) * * *

(2) * * *

(ii) *Conversion transactions occurring on or after the date these regulations are published in the **Federal Register** as final regulations.*—Paragraphs (a)(1), (a)(2)(vi), (a)(2)(vii), (a)(2)(viii), (b)(4), (c)(1), (c)(6), and (f) of this section will apply to conversion transactions occurring 30 days after the date these regulations are published in the **Federal Register** as final regulations, and to conversion transactions and related section 355 distributions for which the conversion transaction occurs before, and the related section 355 distribution occurs on or after, the date that is 30 days after the date these regulations are published in the **Federal Register** as final regulations. For conversion transactions that occurred on or after June 7, 2016 and before the date that is 30 days after these regulations are published in the **Federal Register** as final regulations, see §§ 1.337(d)-7 and 1.337(d)-7T as contained in 26

CFR part 1 in effect on April 1, 2018. However, taxpayers may consistently apply paragraphs (a)(1), (a)(2)(vi), (a)(2)(vii), (a)(2)(viii), (b)(4), (c)(1), (c)(6), and (f) of this section in their entirety for all conversion transactions described in the preceding sentence. For conversion transactions that occurred on or after January 2, 2002 and before June 7, 2016, see § 1.337(d)-7 as contained in 26 CFR part 1 in effect on April 1, 2016.

* * *

Installment Obligations: Dispositions: Nonrecognition of Gain or Loss

Installment Obligations: Dispositions: Nonrecognition of Gain or Loss—Amendments to Reg. § 1.351-1, relating to the nonrecognition of gain or loss on certain dispositions of an installment obligation, are proposed (published in the Federal Register on December 23, 2014) (REG-109187-11).

☐ Par. 2. Section 1.351-1(a)(1) is amended by adding a heading and new second and third sentences to read as follows:

§ 1.351-1. Transfer to corporation controlled by transferor.—(a)(1) *In general.*—* * * See § 1.453B-1(c) for rules requiring a transferor to recognize gain or loss upon the satisfaction of an installment obligation of a corporation when the obligation is exchanged for stock in that corporation. The preceding sentence applies to satisfactions of installment obligations after the date these regulations are published as final regulations in the **Federal Register.*** * *

* * *

Active Trade or Business Requirement: Guidance

Active Trade or Business Requirement: Guidance.—Amendments to Reg. §§ 1.355-0 and 1.355-1, providing guidance regarding active trade or business requirements, is proposed (published in the Federal Register on May 8, 2007) (REG-123365-03) (corrected June 5, 2007).

☐ Par. 2. Section 1.355-0 is amended by revising the entries under § 1.355-3.

The revisions are as follows:

§ 1.355-0. Outline of sections.

* * *

§ 1.355-3 Active conduct of a trade or business.

(a) General requirements.

(b) Active conduct of a trade or business defined.

(1) In general.

(i) Directly engaged in a trade or business.

(ii) Treatment of a separate affiliated group.

(iii) Separate affiliated group defined.

(2) Active conduct of a trade or business immediately after the distribution.

(i) In general.

(ii) Trade or business.

(iii) Active conduct.

(iv) Limitations.

(v) Partner attributed the trade or business assets and activities of a partnership.

(A) In general.

(B) Significant interest.

(C) Meaningful interest.

(D) Other factors.

(3) Active conduct for the pre-distribution period.

(i) In general.

(ii) Change and expansion.

(iii) Certain transactions with partnerships that do not constitute acquisitions.

(4) Special rules for an acquisition of a trade or business.

(i) In general.

(A) Application of section 355(b)(2)(C).

(B) Application of section 355(b)(2)(D).

(C) Gain or loss recognized.

(ii) Certain transactions treated as transactions in which gain or loss is recognized.

(A) Certain tax-free acquisitions made in exchange for assets.

(B) Distributions from partnerships.

(iii) Certain transactions in which recognized gain or loss is disregarded.

(A) Transfers to controlled.

(B) Cash for fractional shares.

(C) Certain acquisitions of control of distributing.

(iv) Operating rules for acquisitions.

(A) Predecessors.

(B) Certain multi-step acquisitions of control of distributing or controlled.

(C) Certain multi-step acquisitions of a subsidiary SAG member.

(D) Certain multi-step asset acquisitions.

(E) Acquisitions involving the issuance of subsidiary stock.

(F) Acquisitions of controlled stock where controlled is or becomes a DSAG member.

(G) Treatment of stock received in certain tax-free exchanges.

(H) Situations where the separate existence of a subsidiary SAG member is respected.

(c) Definitions.

(1) Affiliate.

(2) Controlled.

(3) Distributing.

(4) Pre-distribution period.

(d) Conventions and examples.

(1) Conventions.

(2) Examples.

* * *

☐ Par. 3. Section 1.355-1 is amended by revising paragraph (a) to read as follows:

§ 1.355-1. Distribution of stock and securities of a controlled corporation.—(a) *Effective date of certain sections.*—Except as otherwise provided, §§ 1.355-1, 1.355-2, and 1.355-4 apply to transactions occurring after February 6, 1989. Section 1.355-3 applies to distributions after the date these regulations are published as final regulations in the **Federal Register.** For transactions occurring on or before that date but after February 6, 1989, see 26 CFR 1.355-3 (revised as of April 1, 2007). For all transactions occurring on or before February 6, 1989, see 26 CFR 1.355-1 through 1.355-4 (revised as of April 1, 1987). Sections 1.355-1, 1.355-2, and 1.355-4 do not reflect the amendments to section 355 made by the Revenue Act of 1987 and the Technical and Miscellaneous Revenue Act of 1988. For the effective date of §§1.355-6 and 1.355-7, see §§1.355-6(g) and 1.355-7(k), respectively.

* * *

Distribution of Stock: Device and Active Trade or Business: Guidance

Distribution of Stock: Device and Active Trade or Business: Guidance.—Amendments to Reg. §§1.355-0 and 1.355-2, clarifying the application of the device prohibition and the active business requirement of section 355 and affecting corporations that distribute the stock of controlled corporations, their shareholders, and their security holders, are proposed (published in the Federal Register on July 15, 2016) (REG-134016-15).

Par. 2. Section 1.355-0 is amended by:

1. Removing from the introductory text "1.355-7" and adding "1.355-9" in its place.
2. Revising the entry for §1.355-2(d)(2)(iv)(B).
3. Adding entries for §1.355-2(d)(2)(iv)(B)(*1*), (*2*), (*3*), (*4*), (*5*), (*6*), and (*7*).
4. Redesignating the entry for §1.355-2(d)(2)(iv)(C) as the entry for §1.355-2(d)(2)(iv)(F).
5. Adding a new entry for §1.355-2(d)(2)(iv)(C).
6. Adding entries for §1.355-2(d)(2)(iv)(C)(*1*), (*2*), and (*3*).
7. Adding an entry for §1.355-2(d)(2)(iv)(D).
8. Adding entries for §1.355-2(d)(2)(iv)(D)(*1*), (*2*), (*3*), and (*4*).
9. Adding entries for §1.355-2(d)(2)(iv)(D)(*4*)(*i*) and (*ii*).
10. Adding entries for §1.355-2(d)(2)(iv)(D)(*5*) and (*6*).
11. Adding entries for §1.355-2(d)(2)(iv)(D)(*6*)(*i*) and (*ii*).
12. Adding an entry for §1.355-2(d)(2)(iv)(D)(*7*).
13. Adding entries for §1.355-2(d)(2)(iv)(D)(*7*)(*i*) and (*ii*).
14. Adding an entry for §1.355-2(d)(2)(iv)(D)(*8*).
15. Adding an entry for §1.355-2(d)(2)(iv)(E).
16. Redesignating the entry for §1.355-2(d)(5) as the entry for §1.355-2(d)(6).
17. Adding a new entry for §1.355-2(d)(5).
18. Adding entries for §1.355-2(d)(5)(i), (ii), (iii), and (iv).
19. Adding entries for §1.355-2(i)(1), (i)(1)(i) and (ii), and (i)(2).
20. Adding an entry for §1.355-8.
21. Adding entries for §1.355-9.

The revisions and additions read as follows:

§1.355-0. Outline of sections.

* * *

§1.355-2. Limitations.

* * *

(d) * * *

(2) * * *

(iv) * * *

(B) Definitions.

(*1*) Business.

(*2*) Business Assets.

(*3*) Nonbusiness Assets.

(*4*) Total Assets.

(*5*) Nonbusiness Asset Percentage.

(*6*) Separate Affiliated Group, SAG, CSAG, and DSAG.

(*7*) 50-Percent-Owned Group, Member of a 50-Percent-Owned Group.

(C) Presence of Nonbusiness Assets as evidence of device.

(*1*) Ownership of Nonbusiness Assets.

(*2*) Difference between Nonbusiness Asset Percentages.

(*3*) Cross-reference.

(D) Operating rules.

(*1*) Multiple controlled corporations.

(*2*) Treatment of SAG as a single corporation.

(*3*) Time to identify assets and determine character of assets.

(*4*) Time to determine fair market value of assets.

(*i*) In general.

(*ii*) Consistency.

(*5*) Fair market value.

(*6*) Interest in partnership.

(*i*) In general.

(*ii*) Exception for certain interests in partnerships.

(*7*) Stock in corporation.

(*i*) In general.

(*ii*) Exception for stock in Member of a 50-Percent-Owned Group.

(*8*) Obligation between distributing corporation or controlled corporation and certain partnerships or Members of 50-Percent-Owned Groups.

(E) Anti-abuse rule.

* * *

(5) Distributions involving separation of Business Assets from Nonbusiness Assets.

(i) In general.

(ii) Definitions and operating rules.

(iii) Certain distributions involving separation of Nonbusiness Assets from Business Assets.

(iv) Anti-abuse rule.

* * *

(i) * * *

(1) Paragraph (d) of this section.

(i) In general.

(ii) Transition rule.

(2) Paragraph (g) of this section.

* * *

§1.355-8 Reserved.

§1.355-9 Minimum percentage of Five-Year-Active-Business Assets.
(a) Definitions.
(1) Distributing, Controlled.
(2) Five-Year-Active Business.
(3) Five-Year-Active-Business Assets.
(4) Non-Five-Year-Active-Business Assets.
(5) Total Assets.
(6) Five-Year-Active-Business Asset Percentage.
(7) Separate Affiliated Group, CSAG, and DSAG.
(b) Five percent minimum Five-Year-Active-Business Asset Percentage.
(c) Operating rules.
(1) Treatment of SAG and fair market value.
(2) Time to identify assets, determine character of assets, and determine fair market value of assets.
(3) Interest in partnership.
(i) In general.
(ii) Exception for certain interests in partnerships.
(d) Anti-abuse rule.
(e) Effective/applicability date.
(1) In general.
(2) Transition rule.

Par. 3. Section 1.355-2 is amended by:
1. Adding the language "federal" before the language "tax avoidance" in the second sentence of paragraph (d)(1).
2. Removing the last sentence of paragraph (d)(1) and adding two sentences at the end of the paragraph.
3. Revising paragraphs (d)(2)(iv)(A) and (B).
4. Redesignating paragraph (d)(2)(iv)(C) as (d)(2)(iv)(F).
5. Adding new paragraphs (d)(2)(iv)(C), (D), and (E).
6. Revising paragraph (d)(3)(ii).
7. Removing from paragraph (d)(3)(ii)(A) the language "the business" and adding the language "one or more Businesses (as defined in paragraph (d)(2)(iv)(B)(*1*) of this section) of the distributing corporation, the controlled corporation, or both" in its place.
8. Revising paragraph (d)(4).
9. Redesignating paragraph (d)(5) as (d)(6).
10. Adding a new paragraph (d)(5).
11. Revising newly designated paragraph (d)(6)(i).
12. Removing from newly designated paragraph (d)(6)(v) the language "subparagraph (5)" and adding the language "paragraph (d)(6)" in its place.
13. Removing from the last sentence of newly designated paragraph (d)(6)(v) *Example 1* the language "(d)(5)(i)" and adding the language "(d)(6)(i)" in its place.
14. Removing from the sixth sentence of newly designated paragraph (d)(6)(v) *Example 2* the language "(d)(5)(i)" and adding the language "(d)(6)(i)" in its place.
15. Removing from the last sentence of newly designated paragraph (d)(6)(v) *Example 2* the language "made from all the facts" and adding the language "made from either the presence of a separation of Business Assets from Nonbusiness Assets as described in paragraph (d)(5) of this section or from all the facts" in its place.
16. Adding to paragraph (h) the language "and §1.355-9 (relating to Minimum Percentage of Five-Year-Active-Business Assets)" immediately before the language "are satisfied".
17. Revising paragraph (i).
The revisions and additions read as follows:

§1.355-2. Limitations.

* * *

(d) * * *

(1) * * * However, if a transaction is specified in paragraph (d)(5)(iii) of this section, then it is considered to have been used principally as a device unless it is also specified in paragraph (d)(3)(iv) of this section or paragraph (d)(6) of this section. If a transaction is specified in paragraph (d)(6) of this section, then it is ordinarily considered not to have been used principally as a device.

(2) * * *

(iv) * * *

(A) *In general*.—The determination of whether a transaction was used principally as a device will take into account the nature, kind, amount, and use of the assets of the distributing corporation and the controlled corporation.

(B) *Definitions*.—The following definitions apply for purposes of this paragraph (d)(2)(iv):

(1) Business.—*Business* means the active conduct of a trade or business, within the meaning of section 355(b) and §1.355-3, without regard to—

(i) The requirements of section 355(b)(2)(B), (C), and (D), and §1.355-3(b)(3) and (4) (relating to active conduct throughout the five-year period preceding a distribution and acquisitions during such period);

(ii) The collection of income requirement in §1.355-3(b)(2)(ii); and

(iii) The requirement of §1.355-9 (relating to Minimum Percentage of Five-Year-Active-Business Assets (as defined in §1.355-9(a)(3))).

(2) Business Assets.—*Business Assets* of a corporation means its gross assets used in one or more Businesses. Such assets include cash and cash equivalents held as a reasonable amount of working capital for one or more Businesses. Such assets also include assets required (by binding commitment or legal requirement) to be held to provide for exigencies related to a Business or for regulatory purposes with respect to a Business. For this purpose, such assets include assets the holder is required (by binding commitment or legal requirement) to hold to

secure or otherwise provide for a financial obligation reasonably expected to arise from a Business and assets held to implement a binding commitment to expend funds to expand or improve a Business.

(3) Nonbusiness Assets.—Nonbusiness Assets of a corporation means its gross assets other than its Business Assets.

(4) Total Assets.—Total Assets of a corporation means its Business Assets and its Nonbusiness Assets.

(5) Nonbusiness Asset Percentage.—The *Nonbusiness Asset Percentage* of a corporation is the percentage determined by dividing the fair market value of its Nonbusiness Assets by the fair market value of its Total Assets.

(6) Separate Affiliated Group, SAG, CSAG, and DSAG.—Separate Affiliated Group (or *SAG*) means a separate affiliated group as defined in section 355(b)(3)(B), *CSAG* means a SAG with respect to which a controlled corporation is the common parent, and *DSAG* means a SAG with respect to which a distributing corporation is the common parent, excluding the controlled corporation and any other members of the CSAG.

(7) 50-Percent-Owned Group, Member of a 50-Percent-Owned Group.—50-Percent-Owned Group has the same meaning as SAG, except that "50-percent" is substituted for "80-percent" each place it appears in section 1504(a)(2), for purposes of section 355(b)(3)(B). A *Member of a 50-Percent-Owned Group* is a corporation that would be a member of a DSAG or a CSAG, with the substitution provided in this paragraph (d)(2)(iv)(B)(7).

(C) *Presence of Nonbusiness Assets as evidence of device.—(1) Ownership of Nonbusiness Assets.*—Ownership of Nonbusiness Assets by the distributing corporation or the controlled corporation is evidence of device. The strength of the evidence will be based on all the facts and circumstances, including the Nonbusiness Asset Percentage for each corporation. The larger the Nonbusiness Asset Percentage of either corporation, the stronger is the evidence of device. Ownership of Nonbusiness Assets ordinarily is not evidence of device if the Nonbusiness Asset Percentage of each of the distributing corporation and the controlled corporation is less than 20 percent.

(2) Difference between Nonbusiness Asset Percentages.—A difference between the Nonbusiness Asset Percentage of the distributing corporation and the Nonbusiness Asset Percentage of the controlled corporation is evidence of device, and the larger the difference, the stronger is the evidence of device. Such a difference ordinarily is not itself evidence of device (but may be considered in determining the presence or the strength of other device factors) if—

(i) The difference is less than 10 percentage points; or

(ii) The distribution is not pro rata among the shareholders of the distributing corporation, and the difference is attributable to a need to equalize the value of the controlled stock and securities (if any) distributed and the value of the distributing stock and securities (if any) exchanged therefor by the distributees.

(3) Cross-reference.—See paragraph (d)(5) of this section for a rule under which a distribution is considered to have been used principally as a device when the distributing corporation or the controlled corporation has a large Nonbusiness Asset Percentage and there is a large difference between Nonbusiness Asset Percentages of the two corporations.

(D) *Operating rules.*—The following operating rules apply for purposes of this paragraph (d)(2)(iv):

(1) Multiple controlled corporations.—If a transaction involves distributions by a distributing corporation of the stock of more than one controlled corporation, this paragraph (d)(2)(iv) applies to all such controlled corporations. If any provision in this paragraph (d)(2)(iv) requires a comparison between characteristics of the distributing corporation and the controlled corporation, the provision also requires such a comparison between the distributing corporation and each of the controlled corporations and between each controlled corporation and each other controlled corporation. If any distribution involved in the transaction is determined to have been used principally as a device by reason of this paragraph (d)(2)(iv), all distributions involved in the transaction are considered to have been used principally as a device.

(2) Treatment of SAG as a single corporation.—The members of a DSAG are treated as a single corporation, the members of a CSAG are treated as a single corporation, references to the distributing corporation include all members of the DSAG, and references to the controlled corporation include all members of the CSAG.

(3) Time to identify assets and determine character of assets.—The assets of the distributing corporation and the controlled corporation that are relevant in connection with this paragraph (d)(2)(iv), and the character of these assets as Business Assets or Nonbusiness Assets, must be determined by the distributing corporation and the controlled corporation immediately after the distribution. Accordingly, for purposes of this paragraph (d)(2)(iv), the assets of the distributing corporation do not include any asset, including stock of the controlled corporation, that is distributed in the transaction.

(4) Time to determine fair market value of assets.—(i) In general.—The distributing corporation and the controlled corporation each must determine the fair market value of its assets at the time of the distribution as of one of the following dates: immediately before the distribution; on any date within the 60-day period before the distribution; on the date of an agreement with respect to the distribution that was binding on the distributing corporation on such date and at all times thereafter; or on the date of a public announcement or filing with the Securities and Exchange Commission with respect to the distribution.

(ii) Consistency.—The distributing corporation and the controlled corporation must make the determinations described in paragraph (d)(2)(iv)(D)(4)(*i*) of this section in a manner consistent with each other and as of the same date for purposes of this paragraph (d)(2)(iv), paragraph (d)(5) of this section, and § 1.355-9. If these consistency requirements are not met, the fair market value of assets will be determined immediately before the distribution for purposes of all such provisions, unless the Commissioner

determines that the use of such date is inconsistent with the purposes of section 355 and the regulations thereunder.

(5) Fair market value.—The fair market value of an asset is determined under general federal tax principles but reduced (but not below the adjusted basis of the asset) by the amount of any liability that is described in section 357(c)(3) (relating to exclusion of certain liabilities, including liabilities the payment of which would give rise to a deduction, from the amount of liabilities assumed in certain exchanges) and relates to the asset (or to a Business with which the asset is associated). Any other liability is disregarded for purposes of determining the fair market value of an asset.

(6) Interest in partnership.—(i) In general.—Except as provided in paragraph (d)(2)(iv)(D)(6)(ii) of this section, an interest in a partnership is a Nonbusiness Asset.

(ii) Exception for certain interests in partnerships.—A distributing corporation or controlled corporation may be considered to be engaged in one or more Businesses conducted by a partnership. This determination will be made using the same criteria that would be used to determine for purposes of section 355(b) and § 1.355-3 whether the corporation is considered to be engaged in the active conduct of a trade or business conducted by the partnership (relating to the corporation's ownership interest or to its ownership interest and participation in management of the partnership). If a distributing corporation or controlled corporation is considered to be engaged in one or more Businesses conducted by a partnership, the fair market value of the corporation's interest in the partnership will be allocated between Business Assets and Nonbusiness Assets in the same proportion as the proportion of the fair market values of the Business Assets and Nonbusiness Assets of the partnership.

(7) Stock in corporation.—(i) In general.—Except as provided in paragraph (d)(2)(iv)(D)(7)(*ii*) of this section, stock in a corporation other than a member of the DSAG or the CSAG is a Nonbusiness Asset.

(ii) Exception for stock in Member of a 50-Percent-Owned Group.—If a Member of a 50-Percent-Owned Group with respect to the distributing corporation or the controlled corporation owns stock in another Member of the 50-Percent-Owned Group (other than a member of the DSAG or the CSAG, respectively), the fair market value of such stock will be allocated between Business Assets and Nonbusiness Assets in the same proportion as the proportion of the fair market values of the Business Assets and Nonbusiness Assets of the issuing corporation. This computation will be made with respect to lower-tier Members of the 50-Percent-Owned Group before the computations with respect to higher-tier members.

(8) Obligation between distributing corporation or controlled corporation and certain partnerships or Members of 50-Percent-Owned Groups.—If an obligation of the distributing corporation or the controlled corporation is held by a partnership described in paragraph (d)(2)(iv)(D)(6)(*ii*) of this section or by a Member of its 50-Percent-Owned Group, or if an obligation of a partnership described in paragraph (d)(2)(iv)(D)(6)(*ii*) of this section or of a Member of its 50-Percent-Owned Group, with respect to the distributing corporation or the controlled corporation, is held by the distributing corporation or the controlled corporation, proper adjustments will be made to prevent double inclusion of assets or inappropriate allocation between Business Assets and Nonbusiness Assets of the distributing corporation or the controlled corporation on account of such obligation. *See Examples 6* and *7* of paragraph (d)(4) of this section.

(E) *Anti-abuse rule.*—A transaction or series of transactions undertaken with a principal purpose of affecting the Nonbusiness Asset Percentage of any corporation will not be given effect for purposes of applying this paragraph (d)(2)(iv). For this purpose, a transaction or series of transactions includes a change in the form of ownership of an asset; an issuance, assumption, or repayment of indebtedness or other obligations; or an issuance or redemption of stock. However, this paragraph (d)(2)(iv)(E) generally does not apply to a non-transitory acquisition or disposition of assets, other than an acquisition from or disposition to a person the ownership of whose stock would, under section 318(a) (other than paragraph (4) thereof), be attributed to the distributing corporation or the controlled corporation, or to a non-transitory transfer of assets between the distributing corporation and the controlled corporation.

* * *

(3) * * *

(ii) *Corporate business purpose.*—A corporate business purpose for the transaction is evidence of nondevice. The stronger the evidence of device (such as the presence of the device factors specified in paragraph (d)(2) of this section), the stronger the corporate business purpose must be to prevent the determination that the transaction is being used principally as a device. Evidence of device presented by ownership of Nonbusiness Assets (as defined in paragraph (d)(2)(iv)(B)(*3*) of this section) can be outweighed by the existence of a corporate business purpose for the ownership. Evidence of device presented by a difference between the Nonbusiness Asset Percentages (as defined in paragraph (d)(2)(iv)(B)(*5*) of this section) of the distributing corporation and the controlled corporation can be outweighed by the existence of a corporate business purpose for the difference. A corporate business purpose that relates to a separation of Nonbusiness Assets from one or more Businesses or Business Assets (as defined in paragraph (d)(2)(iv)(B) of this section) is not evidence of nondevice unless the business purpose involves an exigency that requires an investment or other use of the Nonbusiness Assets in one or more Businesses of the distributing corporation, the controlled corporation, or both. The assessment of the strength of a corporate business purpose will be based on all of the facts and circumstances, including, but not limited to, the following factors:

* * *

(4) *Examples.*—The provisions of paragraphs (d)(1) through (3) of this section may be illustrated by the following examples. For purposes of these examples, A and B are individuals; P is a partnership; D and C are the distributing corporation and the controlled corporation, respectively; D and C each has no assets other than those described; there is no

other evidence of device or nondevice other than as described; D has accumulated earnings and profits; and D distributes the stock of C in a distribution which, but for the issue of whether the transaction has been used principally as a device, satisfies the requirements of section 355(a).

Example 1. Sale after distribution (device). A owns all of the stock of D, which is engaged in the warehousing business. D owns all of the stock of C, which is engaged in the transportation business. All of D's and C's assets are Business Assets. D employs B, who is extremely knowledgeable of the warehousing business in general and the operations of D in particular. B has informed A that he will seriously consider leaving D if he is not given the opportunity to purchase a significant amount of stock of D. Because of his knowledge and experience, the loss of B would seriously damage the business of D. B cannot afford to purchase any significant amount of stock of D as long as D owns C. Accordingly, D distributes the stock of C to A and A subsequently sells a portion of his D stock to B. However, instead of A selling a portion of the D stock, D could have issued additional shares to B after the distribution. In light of the fact that D could have issued additional shares to B, the sale of D stock by A is substantial evidence of device. The transaction is considered to have been used principally as a device. See paragraph (d)(1), (2)(i), (ii), and (iii)(A), (B), and (D), and (3)(i) and (ii) of this section.

Example 2. Disproportionate division of Nonbusiness Assets (device)—(i) Facts. D owns and operates a fast food restaurant in State M and owns all of the stock of C, which owns and operates a fast food restaurant in State N. The value of the Business Assets of D's and C's fast food restaurants are $100 and $105, respectively. D also has $195 cash which D holds as a Nonbusiness Asset. D and C operate their businesses under franchises granted by competing businesses F and G, respectively. G has recently changed its franchise policy and will no longer grant or renew franchises to subsidiaries or other members of the same affiliated group of corporations operating businesses under franchises granted by its competitors. Thus, C will lose its franchise if it remains a subsidiary of D. The franchise is about to expire. The lease for the State M location will expire in 24 months, and D will be forced to relocate at that time. While D has not made any plans, it is weighing its option to purchase a building for the relocation. D contributes $45 to C, which C will retain, and distributes the stock of C pro rata among D's shareholders.

(ii) *Analysis.* After the distribution, D's Nonbusiness Asset Percentage is 60 percent ($150/$250), and C's Nonbusiness Asset Percentage is 30 percent ($45/$150). D's and C's ownership of Nonbusiness Assets of at least 20 percent of their respective Total Assets is evidence of device with respect to each. The difference between D's Nonbusiness Asset Percentage and C's Nonbusiness Asset Percentage is 30 percentage points, which is also evidence of device. The corporate business purpose for the distribution does not relate to a separation of Nonbusiness Assets from one or more Businesses or Business Assets and is evidence of nondevice. However, D has no corporate business purpose for the difference of Nonbusiness Asset Percentages. While D is considering purchasing a building for use in the State M location, this purchase is not required by any exigency. The fact that the distribution is pro rata is also evidence of device. Based on all the facts and circumstances, the transaction is considered to have been used principally as a device. See paragraph (d)(1), (2)(i), (ii), (iv)(A) and (C), and (3)(i) and (ii)(A), (B), and (C) of this section.

Example 3. Proportionate division of Nonbusiness Assets (nondevice). The facts are the same as in *Example 2*, except that D contributes $95 of the cash to C instead of $45. After the distribution, D's Nonbusiness Asset Percentage is 50 percent ($100/$200) and C's Nonbusiness Asset Percentage is 47.5 percent ($95/$200), each of which is evidence of device. The difference between D's Nonbusiness Asset Percentage and C's Nonbusiness Asset Percentage (2.5 percentage points) is less than 10 percentage points and thus is not evidence of device. The corporate business purpose for the distribution is evidence of nondevice. Based on all the facts and circumstances, the transaction is considered not to have been used principally as a device. See paragraph (d)(1), (2)(i), (ii), (iv)(A) and (C), and (3)(i) and (ii)(A), (B), and (C) of this section.

Example 4. Disproportionate division of Nonbusiness Assets (nondevice). The facts are the same as in *Example 2*, except that the lease for the State M location will expire in 6 months instead of 24 months, and D will use $80 of the $150 cash it retains to purchase a nearby building for the relocation. After the distribution, D's Nonbusiness Asset Percentage is 60 percent, and C's Nonbusiness Asset Percentage is 30 percent. D's and C's ownership of Nonbusiness Assets of at least 20 percent of their respective Total Assets is evidence of device with respect to each. The difference between D's Nonbusiness Asset Percentage and C's Nonbusiness Asset Percentage is 30 percentage points, which is also evidence of device. However, D has a corporate business purpose for a significant part of the difference of Nonbusiness Asset Percentages because D's use of $80 is required by business exigencies. The fact that the distribution is pro rata is also evidence of device. The corporate business purpose for the distribution is evidence of nondevice. Based on all the facts and circumstances, the transaction is not considered to have been used principally as a device. See paragraph (d)(1), (2)(i), (ii), (iv)(A) and (C), and (3)(i) and (ii)(A), (B), and (C) of this section.

Example 5. Nonbusiness Asset Percentage (50-Percent-Owned Group)—(i) Facts. C's assets consist of 50% of the stock of S1 and other assets consisting of $10,000 of Business Assets and $5,000 of Nonbusiness Assets. S1's assets consist of 40% of the stock of S2, 60% of the stock of S3 and other assets consisting of $1,000 of Business Assets and $500 of Nonbusiness Assets. S1 has $500 of liabilities, owed to unrelated persons. S2's assets consist of $500 Business Assets and $100 Nonbusiness Assets. S2 has $200 of liabilities. S3's assets consist of $3,000 Business Assets and $1,500 Nonbusiness Assets. S3 has $3,500 of liabilities, owed to unrelated persons.

(ii) *Determination of S1's Business Assets and Nonbusiness Assets.* Because C owns at least 50% of the stock of S1, S1 is a member of C's 50-Percent-Owned Group. See paragraph (d)(2)(iv)(B)(*7*) of this section. In determining the amount of C's Business Assets and Nonbusiness Assets, whether S1's stock in S2 and S3 are Nonbusiness Assets or partially Nonbusiness Assets and partially Business Assets must first be determined. See paragraph (d)(2)(iv)(D)(*7*)(*ii*) of this section (computations are made with respect to lower-tier Members of a 50-Percent-Owned Group before the computations with respect to higher-tier members). The fair market value of S1's stock in S2 is $160 (40% of $400 ($500 + $100 - $200)). Because S1 owns less than 50% of the stock of S2, S2 is not a member of C's 50-Percent-Owned Group, and thus the S2 stock is a $160 Nonbusiness Asset in the hands of S1. See paragraph (d)(2)(iv)(B)(*7*) and (D)(*7*)(*i*) of this section. The fair market value of S1's stock in S3 is $600 (60% of $1,000 ($3,000 + $1,500 - $3,500)). Because C owns at least 50% of the stock of S1 and S1 owns at least 50% of the stock of S3, S3 is a member of C's 50-Percent-Owned Group. See paragraph (d)(2)(iv)(B)(*7*) of this section. Thus, the fair market value of the S3 stock is allocated between Business Assets and Nonbusiness Assets in the same proportion as S3's proportion of Business Assets and Nonbusiness Assets. See paragraph (d)(2)(iv)(D)(*7*)(*ii*) of this section. Because S3 has Business Assets of $3,000 and Nonbusiness Assets of $1,500, this proportion is 66 2/3% Business Assets ($3,000/$4,500) and 33 1/3% Nonbusiness Assets ($1,500/$4,500). The $600 fair market value of S1's stock in S3 is allocated $400 to Business Assets ($600 × 66 2/3%) and $200 to Nonbusiness Assets ($600 × 33 1/3%). Thus, S1's assets consist of $1,400 of Business Assets ($1,000 held directly + $400 allocated from S3) and $860 of Nonbusiness Assets ($500 held directly + $160 fair market value of its S2 stock + $200 allocated from S3).

(iii) *Determination of C's Business Assets and Nonbusiness Assets*. The fair market value of C's stock in S1 is $880 (50% of $1,760 ($160 + $600 + $1,000 + $500 - $500)). Because C owns at least 50% of the stock of S1, S1 is a member of C's 50-Percent-Owned Group. See paragraph (d)(2)(iv)(B)(*7*) of this section. Thus, the fair market value of the S1 stock is allocated between Business Assets and Nonbusiness Assets in the same proportion as the proportion of S1's Business Assets and Nonbusiness Assets. See paragraph (d)(2)(iv)(D)(*7*)(*ii*) of this section. Because S1 has Business Assets of $1,400 and Nonbusiness Assets of $860, this proportion is 61.95% Business Assets ($1,400/$2,260) and 38.05% Nonbusiness Assets ($860/$2,260). The $880 fair market value of C's S1 stock is allocated $545 to Business Assets ($880 × 61.95%) and $335 to Nonbusiness Assets ($880 × 38.05%). Thus, C's assets consist of $10,545 of Business Assets ($10,000 + $545) and $5,335 of Nonbusiness Assets ($5,000 + $335), for Total Assets of $15,880. C's Nonbusiness Asset Percentage is 33.6% ($5,335/$15,880).

Example 6. Partnership interest held by Distributing. (i) *Facts*. D has directly-held Business Assets of $1,000, directly held Nonbusiness Assets of $2,000, and a 40% partnership interest in P. P has $450 of Business Assets and $1,350 of cash, which P holds as a Nonbusiness Asset, and owes a liability of $800.

(ii) *Analysis*. Pursuant to paragraph (d)(2)(iv)(D)(*6*)(*ii*) of this section, D is allocated $100 of Business Assets from P ($400 (value of D's 40% interest in P) × 25% ($450/$1,800)) and $300 of Nonbusiness Assets from P ($400 (value of D's 40% interest in P) × 75% ($1,350/$1,800)), which are added to D's directly held Business Assets and Nonbusiness Assets, respectively. D's Nonbusiness Asset Percentage is 67.6% ($2,300 Nonbusiness Assets/$3,400 Total Assets).

Example 7. Borrowing by Distributing from partnership. (i) *Facts*. The facts are the same as in Example 6, except that D borrows $500 from P and invests the proceeds in a Nonbusiness Asset. P's directly-held Nonbusiness Assets increase by $500. The D obligation is a Nonbusiness Asset in P's hands.

(ii) *Analysis*. D's directly-held Nonbusiness Assets increase by $500, to $2,500. There is no corresponding decrease in the amount of Business Assets or Nonbusiness Assets allocated to D from P, because a Nonbusiness Asset of P ($500 cash) has been replaced by another $500 Nonbusiness Asset, the obligation from D. Effectively, because D has a 40% interest in P, D has borrowed $200 (40% of $500) from itself. Accordingly, D's Nonbusiness Assets must be decreased by $200. D's Business Assets will continue to be $1,100 ($1,000 directly held plus $100 allocated from P), and D's Nonbusiness Assets will be $2,600 ($2,500 directly held, plus $300 allocated from P less the $200 decrease to prevent double inclusion of the obligation and the obligation proceeds).

* * *

(5) *Distributions involving separation of Business Assets from Nonbusiness Assets*.—(i) *In general*.—A distribution specified in paragraph (d)(5)(iii) of this section is considered to have been used principally as a device, notwithstanding the presence of nondevice factors described in paragraph (d)(3) of this section or other facts and circumstances. However, this paragraph (d)(5)(i) does not apply to a distribution that is described in paragraph (d)(3)(iv) of this section (distributions to domestic corporations entitled to certain dividends received deductions absent application of section 355(a)) or paragraph (d)(6) of this section (transactions ordinarily not considered to be a device).

(ii) *Definitions and operating rules*.—The definitions in paragraph (d)(2)(iv)(B) of this section and the operating rules in paragraph (d)(2)(iv)(D) of this section apply for purposes of this paragraph (d)(5). For purposes of paragraph (d)(2)(iv)(D)(*1*), (*2*), and (*3*), references to paragraph (d)(2)(iv) of this section are treated as references to this paragraph (d)(5).

(iii) *Certain distributions involving separation of Nonbusiness Assets from Business Assets*.—A distribution is specified in this paragraph (d)(5)(iii) if both—

(A) The Nonbusiness Asset Percentage of the distributing corporation or the controlled corporation is 66 2/3 percent or more, and

(B) If the Nonbusiness Asset Percentage of the distributing corporation or the controlled corporation is—

(*1*) 66 2/3 percent or more but less than 80 percent, and the Nonbusiness Asset Percentage of the other corporation (the controlled corporation or the distributing corporation, as the case may be) is less than 30 percent;

(*2*) 80 percent or more but less than 90 percent, and the Nonbusiness Asset Percentage of the other corporation (the controlled corporation or the distributing corporation, as the case may be) is less than 40 percent; or

(3) 90 percent or more, and the Nonbusiness Asset Percentage of the other corporation (the controlled corporation or the distributing corporation, as the case may be) is less than 50 percent.

(iv) *Anti-abuse rule.*—The anti-abuse rule in paragraph (d)(2)(iv)(E) of this section applies for purposes of this paragraph (d)(5), with references to paragraph (d)(2)(iv) of this section treated as references to this paragraph (d)(5) and references to paragraph (d)(2)(iv)(E) of this section treated as references to this paragraph (d)(5)(iv).

(6) *Transactions ordinarily not considered as a device.*—(i) *In general.*—This paragraph (d)(6) specifies three distributions that ordinarily do not present the potential for federal tax avoidance described in paragraph (d)(1) of this section. Accordingly, such distributions are ordinarily considered not to have been used principally as a device, notwithstanding the presence of any of the device factors described in paragraph (d)(2) of this section or a separation of Business Assets from Nonbusiness Assets as described in paragraph (d)(5) of this section. A transaction described in paragraph (d)(6)(iii) or (iv) of this section is not protected by this paragraph (d)(6) from a determination that it was used principally as a device if it involves the distribution of the stock of more than one controlled corporation and facilitates the avoidance of the dividend provisions of the Code through the subsequent sale or exchange of stock of one corporation and the retention of the stock of another corporation.* * *

* * *

(i) *Effective/applicability date.*—(1) *Paragraph (d) of this section.*—(i) *In general.*—Except as provided in paragraph (i)(1)(ii) of this section, paragraph (d) of this section applies to transactions occurring on or after the date the Treasury decision adopting these regulations as final regulations is published in the **Federal Register**.

(ii) *Transition rule.*—Paragraph (d) of this section does not apply to a distribution that is—

(A) Made pursuant to an agreement, resolution, or other corporate action that is binding on or before the date the Treasury decision adopting these regulations as final regulations is published in the **Federal Register** and at all times thereafter;

(B) Described in a ruling request submitted to the Internal Revenue Service on or before July 15, 2016; or

(C) Described in a public announcement or filing with the Securities and Exchange Commission on or before the date the Treasury decision adopting these regulations as final regulations is published in the **Federal Register**.

(2) *Paragraph (g) of this section.*—Paragraph (g) of this section applies to distributions occurring after October 20, 2011. For rules regarding distributions occurring on or before October 20, 2011, *see* § 1.355-2T(i), as contained in 26 CFR part 1, revised as of April 1, 2011.

Predecessors and Successors: Limitation on Gain Recognition: Guidance

Predecessors and Successors: Limitation on Gain Recognition: Guidance.—Amendments to Reg. § 1.355-0, regarding the distribution by a distributing corporation of stock or securities of a controlled corporation without the recognition of income, gain, or loss, are proposed (published in the Federal Register on December 19, 2016) (REG-140328-15).

Par. 2. Section 1.355-0 is amended by revising the introductory text and adding an entry for § 1.355-8 to read as follows:

§ 1.355-0. Outline of sections.—In order to facilitate the use of § § 1.355-1 through 1.355-8, this section lists the major paragraphs in those sections as follows:

* * *

§ 1.355-8 Definition of predecessor and successor and limitations on gain recognition under section 355(e) and section 355(f).

(a) In general.
(1) Scope.
(2) Purpose.
(3) Overview.
(4) References.
(i) References to Distributing or Controlled.
(ii) References to a Plan or distribution.
(iii) Plan Period.
(b) Predecessor of Distributing.
(1) Definition.
(i) In general.
(ii) Pre-distribution requirements.
(A) Relevant Property.
(B) Reflection of basis.
(iii) Post-distribution requirement.
(2) Additional definitions and rules related to paragraph (b)(1) of this section.
(i) References to Distributing and Controlled.
(ii) Potential Predecessor.
(iii) Successors of Potential Predecessors.
(iv) Relevant Property; Relevant Stock.
(A) In general.
(B) Property held by Distributing.
(C) Certain reorganizations.
(v) Stock of Distributing as Relevant Property.
(A) In general.
(B) Certain reorganizations.
(vi) Substitute Asset.
(vii) Separated Property.
(viii) Underlying Property.
(ix) Scope of definition of Predecessor of Distributing.
(x) Deemed exchanges.
(c) Additional definitions.
(1) Predecessor of Controlled.
(2) Successors.
(i) In general.
(ii) Determination of Successor status.
(3) Section 381 transaction.
(d) Special acquisition rules.

(1) Deemed acquisitions of stock in section 381 transactions.

(2) Deemed acquisitions of stock after section 381 transactions.

(3) Separate counting for Distributing and each Predecessor of Distributing.

(e) Special rules for gain recognition.

(1) In general.

(2) Planned 50-percent or greater acquisitions of a Predecessor of Distributing.

(i) In general.

(ii) Operating rules.

(A) Separated Property other than Controlled stock.

(B) Controlled stock that is Separated Property.

(C) Anti-duplication rule.

(3) Planned 50-percent Acquisition of Distributing in a Section 381 transaction.

(4) Overall gain recognition.

(5) Section 336(e) election.

(f) Predecessor or Successor as a member of the affiliated group.

(g) Inapplicability of section 355(f) to certain intra-group distributions.

(1) In general.

(2) Alternative application of section 355(f).

(h) Examples.

(i) Effective/applicability date.

(1) In general.

(2) Transition rule.

(i) In general.

(ii) Definition of distribution.

(3) Exception.

Active Trade or Business Requirement: Guidance

Active Trade or Business Requirement: Guidance.—Amendments to Reg. §1.355-3, providing guidance regarding active trade or business requirements, is proposed (published in the Federal Register on May 8, 2007) (REG-123365-03) (corrected June 5, 2007).

☐ Par. 4. Section 1.355-3 is revised to read as follows:

§1.355-3. Active conduct of a trade or business.—(a) *General requirements.*—Under section 355(b)(1), a distribution of stock, or stock and securities, of controlled (as defined in paragraph (c)(2) of this section) qualifies under section 355 only if—

(1) Distributing (as defined in paragraph (c)(3) of this section) and controlled are each engaged in the active conduct of a trade or business immediately after the distribution (section 355(b)(1)(A)); or

(2) Immediately before the distribution, distributing had no assets other than stock or securities of the controlled corporations (without regard to paragraph (b)(1)(ii) of this section), and each of the controlled corporations is engaged in the active conduct of a trade or business immediately after the distribution (section 355(b)(1)(B)). A *de minimis* amount of assets held by distributing shall be disregarded for purposes of this paragraph (a)(2).

(b) *Active conduct of a trade or business defined.*—(1) *In general.*—(i) *Directly engaged in a trade or business.*—Section 355(b)(2) provides rules for determining whether a corporation is treated as engaged in the active conduct of a trade or business under section 355(b)(1). Section 355(b)(2)(A) and (b)(3)(A) provides that a corporation is treated as engaged in the active conduct of a trade or business if and only if such corporation is engaged in the active conduct of a trade or business. Accordingly, except as provided in paragraph (b)(1)(ii) of this section, a corporation is not treated as engaged in the active conduct of a trade or business under such Internal Revenue Code section solely as a result of substantially all of its assets consisting of stock, or stock and securities, of one or more corporations controlled by it (immediately after the distribution) each of which is engaged in the active conduct of a trade or business.

(ii) *Treatment of a separate affiliated group.*—Under section 355(b)(3)(B), solely for purposes of determining whether a corporation is engaged in the active conduct of a trade or business, all members of a corporation's separate affiliated group (SAG) (as defined in paragraph (b)(1)(iii) of this section) shall be treated as one corporation. This treatment applies for all purposes of determining whether a corporation is engaged in the active conduct of a trade or business. Accordingly, for this purpose, transfers of assets (or activities) that are owned (or performed) by the SAG immediately before and immediately after the transfer are disregarded and are not acquisitions under paragraph (b)(4) of this section. Further, a transaction that results in a corporation becoming a subsidiary SAG member (a SAG member that is not the common parent of such SAG) is treated as an acquisition of any assets (or activities) that are owned (or performed) by the acquired corporation at such time. Therefore, the acquisition of additional stock of a current subsidiary SAG member has no effect for purposes of applying paragraph (b)(4)(i)(A) of this section.

(iii) *Separate affiliated group defined.*—A corporation's SAG is the affiliated group which would be determined under section 1504(a) if such corporation were the common parent and section 1504(b) did not apply. Thus, the separate affiliated group of distributing (DSAG) is the affiliated group that consists of distributing as the common parent and all corporations affiliated with distributing through stock ownership described in section 1504(a)(1)(B) (regardless of whether the corporations are includible corporations under section 1504(b)). The separate affiliated group of controlled (CSAG) is determined in a similar manner (with controlled as the common parent). Accordingly, prior to a distribution, the DSAG may include CSAG members if the applicable ownership requirements are met. Further, the determination of whether a corporation is a DSAG or CSAG member shall be made separately for each distribution, and without regard to whether such corporation is a SAG member with respect to any other distribution. Any reference to DSAG or CSAG is a reference to distributing or controlled, respectively, if such corporation is not the common parent of a SAG (that is, such corporation does not own stock in any corporation that is a subsidiary member of its SAG). Further, any reference to a SAG is a reference to distributing or controlled, as the context may require, if such corporation is not the common parent of a SAG.

(2) *Active conduct of a trade or business immediately after the distribution.*—(i) *In general.*—For purposes of section 355(b), a corporation shall be treated as engaged in the active conduct of a trade or business immediately after the distribution if the assets and activities of the corporation satisfy the requirements and limitations described in paragraphs (b)(2)(ii), (b)(2)(iii), and (b)(2)(iv) of this section. See paragraph (b)(2)(v) of this section for additional special rules that apply to determine whether a corporation is attributed the trade or business assets and activities of a partnership.

(ii) *Trade or business.*—A corporation shall be treated as engaged in a trade or business immediately after the distribution if a specific group of activities is being carried on by the corporation for the purpose of earning income or profit, and the activities included in such group include every operation that forms a part of, or a step in, the process of earning income or profit. Such group of activities ordinarily must include the collection of income and the payment of expenses.

(iii) *Active conduct.*—For purposes of section 355(b), the determination of whether a trade or business is actively conducted will be made from all of the facts and circumstances. Generally, the corporation is required itself to perform active and substantial management and operational functions. Activities performed by a corporation include activities performed by employees of an affiliate (as defined in paragraph (c)(1) of this section), and in certain cases by shareholders of a closely held corporation, if such activities are performed for the corporation. For example, activities performed by a corporation include activities performed for the corporation by its sole shareholder. However, the activities of employees of affiliates (or, in certain cases, shareholders) are only taken into account during the period such corporations are affiliates (or persons are shareholders) of the corporation. A corporation will not be treated as engaged in the active conduct of a trade or business unless it (or its SAG, or a partnership from which the trade or business assets and activities are attributed) is the principal owner of the goodwill and significant assets of the trade or business for Federal income tax purposes. Activities performed by a corporation generally do not include activities performed by persons outside the corporation, including independent contractors, unless those activities are performed by employees of an affiliate (or, in certain cases, by shareholders). However, a corporation may satisfy the requirements of this paragraph (b)(2)(iii) through the activities that it performs itself, even though some of its activities are performed by persons that are not its employees, or employees of an affiliate (or, in certain cases, shareholders). Separations of real property all or substantially all of which is occupied before the distribution by the DSAG or CSAG will be carefully scrutinized in applying the requirements of section 355(b) and this section.

(iv) *Limitations.*—The active conduct of a trade or business does not include—

(A) The holding for investment purposes of stock, securities, land, or other property; or

(B) The ownership and operation (including leasing) of real or personal property used in a trade or business, unless the owner performs significant services with respect to the operation and management of the property.

(v) *Partner attributed the trade or business assets and activities of a partnership.*—(A) *In general.*—For purposes of section 355(b), a partner in a partnership will be attributed the trade or business assets and activities of that partnership during the period that such partner satisfies the requirements of paragraph (b)(2)(v)(B) or (b)(2)(v)(C) of this section. However, for purposes of this paragraph (b)(2)(v), the stock of a corporation owned by the partnership is not attributed to a partner. For purposes of determining the activities that are conducted by the partnership that may be attributed to the partner under this paragraph (b)(2)(v), the activities of independent contractors, and partners that are not affiliates (or, in certain cases, shareholders) of the partner, are not taken into account. For this purpose, the activities of partners that are affiliates (or, in certain cases, shareholders) of the partner are only taken into account during the period that such partners are affiliates (or, in certain cases, shareholders) of the partner.

(B) *Significant interest.*—The trade or business assets and activities of a partnership will be attributed to a partner if the partner (or its SAG) directly (or indirectly through one or more other partnerships) owns a significant interest in the partnership.

(C) *Meaningful interest.*—The trade or business assets and activities of a partnership will be attributed to a partner if the partner or affiliates (or, in certain cases, shareholders) of the partner performs active and substantial management functions for the partnership with respect to the trade or business assets and activities (for example, makes decisions regarding significant business issues of the partnership and regularly participates in the overall supervision, direction, and control of the employees performing the operational functions for the partnership), and the partner (or its SAG) directly (or indirectly through one or more other partnerships) owns a meaningful interest in the partnership. Whether such active and substantial management functions are performed with respect to the trade or business assets and activities of the partnership will be determined from all of the facts and circumstances. The number of partners providing management functions will not be determinative.

(D) *Other factors.*—In deciding whether the requirements of paragraph (b)(2)(v)(B) or (b)(2)(v)(C) of this section are satisfied, the formal description of the partnership interest (for example, general or limited) will not be determinative and the extent to which the partner is responsible for liabilities of the partnership will not be relevant.

(3) *Active conduct for the pre-distribution period.*—(i) *In general.*—Under section 355(b)(2), a trade or business that is relied upon to meet the requirements of section 355(b) must have been actively conducted throughout the pre-distribution period (as defined in paragraph (c)(4) of this section) by the DSAG or CSAG, or actively con-

ducted throughout the pre-distribution period and acquired during such period by the DSAG or CSAG in a transaction in which no gain or loss is recognized as provided in paragraph (b)(4) of this section. For purposes of section 355(b)(2)(B), activities that constitute a trade or business under paragraph (b)(2) of this section shall be treated as described in the preceding sentence if such activities were actively conducted throughout the pre-distribution period.

(ii) *Change and expansion.*—The fact that a trade or business underwent change during the pre-distribution period (for example, by the addition of new or the dropping of old products, changes in production capacity, and the like) shall be disregarded, provided that the changes are not of such a character as to constitute the acquisition of a new or different business. In particular, if a SAG engaged in the active conduct of one trade or business during the pre-distribution period (the original business) purchased, created, or otherwise acquired (either directly, through an interest in a partnership, or as a result of a corporation becoming a subsidiary SAG member) another trade or business (the acquired business) in the same line of business, the acquisition of the acquired business is ordinarily treated as an expansion of the original business, all of which is treated as having been actively conducted by the acquiring SAG during the pre-distribution period, unless the acquired business effects a change of such a character as to constitute the acquisition of a new or different business. For purposes of this paragraph (b)(3)(ii), in determining whether an acquired business is in the same line of business as the original business, all facts and circumstances shall be considered, including the following—

(A) Whether the product of the acquired business is similar to that of the original business;

(B) Whether the business activities associated with the operation of the acquired business are the same as the business activities associated with the operation of the original business; and

(C) Whether the operation of the acquired business involves the use of the experience and know-how that the owner of the original business developed in the operation of the original business or, alternatively, whether the operation of the acquired business draws to a significant extent on the existing experience and know-how of the owner of the original business and the success of the acquired business will depend in large measure on the goodwill associated with the original business and the name of the original business.

(iii) *Certain transactions with partnerships that do not constitute acquisitions.*—If a partner is attributed the trade or business assets and activities of a partnership under paragraph (b)(2)(v) of this section, the partner's acquisition of such trade or business assets and activities from the partnership is not, in and of itself, the acquisition of a new or different trade or business. In addition, if a partner transfers to a partnership trade or business assets and activities that the partner actively conducted immediately before the transfer and, immediately after the transfer, the partner is attributed the trade or business assets and activities of the partnership under paragraph (b)(2)(v) of this section, such transfer is not, in and of itself, the acquisition of a new or different trade or business by the transferor partner.

(4) *Special rules for an acquisition of a trade or business.*—(i) *In general.*—(A) *Application of section 355(b)(2)(C).*—Under section 355(b)(2)(C) and (b)(3), a trade or business or an interest in a partnership engaged in a trade or business relied on to meet the requirements of section 355(b) must not have been acquired by either the DSAG or CSAG during the pre-distribution period unless it was acquired in a transaction in which no gain or loss was recognized. Further, a trade or business must not have been acquired by either the DSAG or CSAG during the pre-distribution period as a result of a corporation becoming a subsidiary SAG member unless such corporation became a subsidiary SAG member as a result of one or more transactions in which no gain or loss was recognized or by reason of such transactions combined with acquisitions before the pre-distribution period. This paragraph (b)(4)(i)(A) also applies with respect to any acquisition during the pre-distribution period of a trade or business, an interest in a partnership engaged in a trade or business, or stock of a corporation engaged in a trade or business by a corporation that later becomes a subsidiary SAG member. See paragraphs (b)(4)(iv)(C) and (b)(4)(iv)(D) of this section regarding the application of this paragraph (b)(4)(i)(A) to certain multi-step acquisitions.

(B) *Application of section 355(b)(2)(D).*—Under section 355(b)(2)(D), control of distributing must not have been acquired (at the time it was conducting the trade or business to be relied on) directly or indirectly by any distributee corporation, and control of controlled must not have been acquired (at the time it was conducting the trade or business to be relied on) directly or indirectly by the DSAG, during the pre-distribution period in one or more transactions in which gain or loss was recognized. This paragraph (b)(4)(i)(B) also applies with respect to any acquisition of stock of controlled during the pre-distribution period by a corporation that later becomes a DSAG member. For purposes of this paragraph (b)(4)(i)(B), and paragraphs (b)(4)(iii)(C) and (b)(4)(iv)(B) of this section, all distributee corporations that are affiliates shall be treated as one distributee corporation. This paragraph (b)(4)(i)(B) does not apply with respect to an acquisition of stock of any corporation other than distributing or controlled. See paragraph (b)(4)(iv)(B) of this section regarding the application of this paragraph (b)(4)(i)(B) to certain multi-step acquisitions of control. Further, see paragraph (b)(4)(iv)(F) of this section regarding certain acquisitions of stock in controlled to which paragraph (b)(4)(i)(A) of this section (and not this paragraph (b)(4)(i)(B)) applies.

(C) *Gain or loss recognized.*—Any reference to gain or loss recognized includes gain or loss treated as recognized under paragraphs (b)(4)(ii) or (b)(4)(iv) of this section.

(ii) *Certain transactions treated as transactions in which gain or loss is recognized.*—The common purpose of section 355(b)(2)(C) and (D) is to prevent the direct or indirect acquisition of the trade or business to be relied on by a corporation in exchange for assets in anticipation of a distribution to which section 355 would otherwise apply. Generally, if a DSAG member or controlled acquires the trade or business solely in exchange for distributing stock, distributing acquires control of controlled solely in exchange for distributing stock, or controlled acquires the trade or business from distributing solely in exchange for stock of controlled, in a transaction in which no gain or loss was recognized, the requirements of section 355(b)(2)(C) and (D) are satisfied. On the other hand, if the trade or business is acquired in exchange for assets of distributing (other than stock of a corporation in control of distributing used in a reorganization) the requirements of section 355(b)(2)(C) and (D) are generally not satisfied. For example, acquisitions by controlled (while controlled by distributing) from an unrelated party made in exchange for controlled stock have the effect of an indirect acquisition by distributing in exchange for distributing's assets. Such acquisitions violate the purpose of section 355(b)(2)(C) even if no gain or loss is recognized. Therefore, as provided in paragraphs (b)(4)(ii)(A) and (b)(4)(ii)(B) of this section, if the DSAG or CSAG acquires a trade or business, an interest in a partnership engaged in a trade or business, or stock of a corporation engaged in a trade or business in exchange for assets of the DSAG in a transaction in which no gain or loss is recognized, for purposes of paragraph (b)(4)(i) of this section such acquisition will be treated as one in which gain or loss is recognized.

(A) *Certain tax-free acquisitions made in exchange for assets.*—An acquisition paid for in whole or in part, directly or indirectly, with assets of the DSAG will be treated as an acquisition in which gain or loss is recognized even if no gain or loss is actually recognized. Acquisitions described in this paragraph (b)(4)(ii)(A) include for example, a transaction in which the DSAG or CSAG acquires stock of a corporation engaged in the trade or business to be relied on by transferring assets not constituting the trade or business to be relied on to such corporation in exchange for stock of such corporation, the DSAG or CSAG acquires an interest in a partnership engaged in the trade or business to be relied on by contributing assets not constituting the trade or business to be relied on to the partnership, the DSAG or CSAG acquires stock of a corporation engaged in the trade or business in an exchange to which section 304(a)(1) applies, or distributing acquires a trade or business in exchange for its stock and assets in a transaction in which no loss is recognized by virtue of section 351(b). See also paragraph (b)(4)(iv)(E) of this section regarding the extent to which an acquisition involving the issuance of subsidiary stock constitutes an acquisition paid for with assets. However, the assumption by the DSAG or CSAG of liabilities of a transferor shall not, in and of itself, be treated as the payment of assets if such assumption is not treated as the payment of money or other property under any other applicable provision. In addition, an acquisition in which no gain or loss is recognized consisting of a pro rata distribution to which section 355 applies (to the extent the stock with respect to which the distribution is made was not acquired during the pre-distribution period in a transaction in which gain or loss was recognized), a distribution from a partnership that is explicitly excluded from paragraph (b)(4)(ii)(B) of this section, a reorganization described in section 368(a)(1)(E) or (F), and an exchange to which section 1036 applies, are not acquisitions described in this paragraph (b)(4)(ii)(A).

(B) *Distributions from partnerships.*—An acquisition consisting of a distribution from a partnership is generally an acquisition paid for with assets of the DSAG, and will be treated as an acquisition in which gain or loss is recognized even if no gain or loss is actually recognized. However, an acquisition consisting of a pro rata distribution from a partnership of stock or an interest in lower-tier partnership is not an acquisition described in this paragraph (b)(4)(ii)(B) (and consequently not described in paragraph (b)(4)(ii)(A) of this section) to the extent the distributee partner did not acquire the interest in the distributing partnership during the pre-distribution period in a transaction in which gain or loss was recognized and to the extent the distributing partnership did not acquire the distributed stock or partnership interest within such period. This paragraph (b)(4)(ii)(B) (and consequently paragraph (b)(4)(ii)(A) of this section) does not apply to any partnership distribution to which paragraph (b)(3)(iii) of this section (regarding distributions from partnerships that are not, in and of themselves, the acquisition of a new or different trade or business) applies.

(iii) *Certain transactions in which recognized gain or loss is disregarded.*—The common purpose of section 355(b)(2)(C) and (D) is to prevent the direct or indirect acquisition of the trade or business to be relied on by a corporation in exchange for assets in anticipation of a distribution to which section 355 would otherwise apply. An additional purpose of section 355(b)(2)(D) is to prevent a distributee corporation from acquiring control of distributing in anticipation of a distribution to which section 355 would otherwise apply, enabling the disposition of controlled stock without recognizing the appropriate amount of gain. The acquisitions described in paragraphs (b)(4)(iii)(A) through (b)(4)(iii)(C) of this section are not the types of acquisitions to which section 355(b)(2)(C) or (D) is intended to apply. Therefore, for purposes of paragraph (b)(4)(i) of this section, the recognition of gain or loss is disregarded if a trade or business, an interest in a partnership engaged in a trade or business, or stock of a corporation engaged in a trade or business is acquired in a transaction described in any of paragraphs (b)(4)(iii)(A) through (b)(4)(iii)(C) of this section.

(A) *Transfers to controlled.*—An acquisition by the CSAG from the DSAG provided the DSAG controls controlled immediately after the acquisition.

(B) *Cash for fractional shares.*—An acquisition that would satisfy the requirements of paragraph (b)(4)(i) of this section but for the payment of cash to shareholders for fractional shares in the transaction, provided that the cash paid represents a mere rounding off of the fractional shares in the exchange and is not separately bargained for consideration.

(C) *Certain acquisitions of control of distributing.*—A direct or indirect acquisition by a distributee corporation of control of distributing, in one or more transactions, where the basis of the acquired distributing stock in the hands of the distributee corporation is determined in whole by reference to the transferor's basis. This paragraph (b)(4)(iii)(C) is only applicable with respect to a distribution by the acquired distributing, and does not apply for purposes of any subsequent distribution by any distributee corporation.

(iv) *Operating rules for acquisitions.*—(A) *Predecessors.*—References to a corporation shall include references to a predecessor of such corporation. For this purpose, a predecessor of a corporation is a corporation that transfers its assets to such corporation in a transaction to which section 381 applies.

(B) *Certain multi-step acquisitions of control of distributing or controlled.*—A distributee corporation's acquisition of stock in distributing or a DSAG's acquisition of stock in controlled in one or more transactions in which gain or loss was recognized during the pre-distribution period will not prevent a distributee corporation's acquisition of distributing stock or a DSAG's acquisition of controlled stock constituting control of distributing or controlled in one or more separate transactions in which no gain or loss is recognized from satisfying the requirements of paragraph (b)(4)(i)(B) of this section, provided that, at the time control of distributing or controlled is first acquired, the acquiring distributee corporation owns an amount of distributing stock or the acquiring DSAG owns an amount of controlled stock, as the case may be, constituting control that was acquired in one or more transactions in which no gain or loss was recognized or by reason of such transactions combined with acquisitions before the pre-distribution period. The principles of this paragraph (b)(4)(iv)(B) will be applied with respect to an indirect acquisition of distributing or controlled stock.

(C) *Certain multi-step acquisitions of a subsidiary SAG member.*—An acquisition of stock in a corporation (target) by a SAG in one or more transactions in which gain or loss was recognized during the pre-distribution period will not prevent a SAG's acquisition of target stock resulting in target becoming a subsidiary SAG member in one or more separate transactions in which no gain or loss is recognized from satisfying the requirements of paragraph (b)(4)(i)(A) of this section, provided that, at the time that target first becomes a subsidiary SAG member, the SAG owns an amount of target stock meeting the requirements of section 1504(a)(2) that was acquired in one or more transactions in which no gain or loss was recognized or by reason of such transactions combined with acquisitions before the pre-distribution period. The principles of this paragraph (b)(4)(iv)(C) will be applied with respect to an indirect acquisition of target stock by the SAG.

(D) *Certain multi-step asset acquisitions.*—Notwithstanding paragraph (b)(4)(i)(A) of this section, if immediately before a SAG's direct acquisition of a trade or business (or an interest in a partnership engaged in a trade or business) held by a corporation (owner) in a transaction to which section 381 applies and in which no gain or loss is recognized, the SAG owns an amount of stock of the owner that it acquired in one or more transactions during the pre-distribution period in which gain or loss was recognized such that all of the other stock of the owner does not meet the requirements of section 1504(a)(2), such direct acquisition shall be treated as a transaction in which gain or loss was recognized. The principles of this paragraph (b)(4)(iv)(D) will be applied with respect to an indirect acquisition of the owner stock by the SAG.

(E) *Acquisitions involving the issuance of subsidiary stock.*—If a SAG directly or indirectly owns stock of a subsidiary (including a subsidiary SAG member) and the subsidiary directly or indirectly acquires a trade or business, an interest in a partnership engaged in a trade or business, or stock of a corporation engaged in a trade or business from a person other than such SAG in exchange for stock of such subsidiary in a transaction in which no gain or loss is recognized (the acquisition), solely for purposes of applying this paragraph (b)(4) with respect to the trade or business, partnership interest, or stock acquired by the subsidiary in the acquisition, the subsidiary's stock directly or indirectly owned by the SAG immediately after the acquisition is treated as acquired at the time of the acquisition in a transaction in which gain or loss is recognized.

(F) *Acquisitions of controlled stock where controlled is or becomes a DSAG member.*—With respect to an acquisition of stock in controlled, if controlled is or becomes a DSAG member, paragraph (b)(4)(i)(A) of this section applies and paragraph (b)(4)(i)(B) of this section does not apply for purposes of determining whether the requirements of section 355(b) are satisfied with respect to controlled.

(G) *Treatment of stock received in certain tax-free exchanges.*—Any stock received in a reorganization described in section 368(a)(1)(E) or (F), or in an exchange to which section 1036 applies, in which no gain or loss is recognized is treated as acquired in the same manner as the stock surrendered.

(H) *Situations where the separate existence of a subsidiary SAG member is respected.*—The separate existence of a subsidiary SAG member will be respected for purposes of determining whether a transaction qualifies for nonrecognition treatment under other provisions of the Internal Revenue Code. For example, for purposes of determining whether section 351 applies or whether the transaction qualifies as a reorganization described in section 368(a), the separate existence of the subsidiary SAG member is respected.

(c) *Definitions.*—For purposes of this section the following definitions apply:

(1) *Affiliate.*—An affiliate is any member of an affiliated group as defined in section 1504(a) (without regard to section 1504(b)).

(2) *Controlled.*—*Controlled* is the controlled corporation.

(3) *Distributing.*—*Distributing* is the distributing corporation.

(4) *Pre-distribution period.*—The *pre-distribution period* is the five-year period ending on the date of the distribution.

(d) *Conventions and examples.*—(1) *Conventions.*—The examples in paragraph (d)(2) of this section illustrate section 355(b) and this section. No inference should be drawn from any of these examples as to whether any requirements of section 355 other than those of section 355(b), as specified, are satisfied. Throughout these examples, C, D, D2, P, S, S1, S2, S3, T, X, Y, and Z are corporations, and Partnership is an entity that is treated as a partnership for Federal income tax purposes under § 301.7701-3 of this chapter. Further, assume any transfer described in *Examples 1* through *25* that is not identified as a purchase (defined in paragraph (d)(1)(iii) of this section) satisfies all the requirements of paragraph (b)(4) of this section as a transaction in which no gain or loss is recognized. Except as otherwise provided, for more than five years D has owned section 368(c) stock (as defined in paragraph (d)(1)(iv) of this section) but not section 1504(a)(2) stock (as defined in paragraph (d)(1)(v) of this section) of C. Furthermore, the following definitions apply:

(i) *ATB*.—*ATB* is any active trade or business. ATB1 and ATB2 are not in the same line of business under paragraph (b)(3)(ii) of this section.

(ii) *New subsidiary*.—A *new subsidiary* is a newly formed wholly owned corporation.

(iii) *Purchase*.—A *purchase* is an acquisition for cash.

(iv) *Section 368(c) stock*.—*Section 368(c) stock* is stock constituting control within the meaning of section 368(c).

(v) *Section 1504(a)(2) stock*.—*Section 1504(a)(2) stock* is stock meeting the requirements of section 1504(a)(2).

(2) *Examples*.—Generally, *Examples 1* and *2* illustrate the general requirements in paragraph (a) of this section, *Examples 3* through *9* illustrate the SAG rules in paragraphs (b)(1)(ii) and (b)(1)(iii) of this section, *Examples 10* through *25* illustrate the rules regarding the active trade or business and active conduct for the pre-distribution period in paragraphs (b)(2) and (b)(3) of this section, *Examples 26* through *40* illustrate the acquisition rules in paragraphs (b)(4)(i) through (b)(4)(iii) of this section, and *Examples 41* through *51* illustrate the operating rules for acquisitions in paragraph (b)(4)(iv) of this section. The examples are as follows:

Example 1. Spin-off. For more than five years, D and C have engaged in the active conduct of ATB1 and ATB2, respectively. D distributes the C stock to the D shareholders, and each corporation continues the active conduct of its respective trade or business. Because both D and C are engaged in the active conduct of a trade or business immediately after the distribution and such trades or businesses have been actively conducted by such corporations throughout the pre-distribution period, the requirements of section 355(b) have been satisfied. See paragraphs (a)(1) and (b)(3) of this section.

Example 2. Split-up. The facts are the same as *Example 1* except that D transfers all of its assets (including ATB1) other than the C stock to new subsidiary S, and then distributes the C stock and S stock to the D shareholders. Because C and S are respectively engaged in the active conduct of ATB2 and ATB1 immediately after the distribution, ATB2 has been actively conducted by C throughout the pre-distribution period, and together D (prior to the transfer to S) and S (after the transfer to S) have actively conducted ATB1 throughout the pre-distribution period, the requirements of section 355(b) have been satisfied. See paragraphs (a)(2) and (b)(3) of this section.

Example 3. Subsidiary SAG member's business. For more than five years, D has owned section 1504(a)(2) stock but not section 368(c) stock of S. Throughout this period, C and S have engaged in the active conduct of ATB1 and ATB2, respectively. In year 8, D distributes the C stock to the D shareholders. Because D owns section 1504(a)(2) stock of S, S is a DSAG member. See paragraph (b)(1)(iii) of this section. D and S are treated as one corporation for purposes of determining whether D is engaged in an active trade or business. See paragraph (b)(1)(ii) of this section. Therefore, D is engaged in the active conduct of ATB2 both throughout the pre-distribution period and immediately after the distribution. Accordingly, D and C both satisfy the requirements of section 355(b).

Example 4. Additional subsidiary SAG member shares acquired. The facts are the same as *Example 3* except that in year 6, D acquires the remaining S stock. D's acquisition of the remaining S stock in year 6 has no effect for purposes of determining whether D satisfies the requirements of section 355(b)(2)(C) because the DSAG is already engaged in the active conduct of ATB2. See paragraph (b)(1)(ii) of this section. Section 355(b)(2)(D) does not apply to D's acquisition of S stock. See paragraph (b)(4)(i)(B) of this section. Accordingly, D and C both satisfy the requirements of section 355(b).

Example 5. Segmented CSAG business. For more than five years, C has owned all the stock of S1, S2, and S3. Throughout this period, D has engaged in the active conduct of ATB1. Throughout this same period, S1, S2, and S3 have each engaged in a different essential segment of ATB2. While the three segments of ATB2 would together constitute the active conduct of a trade or business, none of S1, S2, or S3 would be considered engaged in the active conduct of an ATB individually. In year 6, D distributes the C stock to the D shareholders. C owns section 1504(a)(2) stock of S1, S2, and S3, therefore, C, S1, S2, and S3 are CSAG members. See paragraph (b)(1)(iii) of this section. C, S1, S2, and S3 are treated as one corporation for purposes of determining whether C is engaged in the active conduct of a trade or business. See paragraph (b)(1)(ii) of this section. Therefore, C is engaged in the active conduct of ATB2 both throughout the pre-distribution period and immediately after the distribution. Accordingly, D and C both satisfy the requirements of section 355(b).

Example 6. Segmented DSAG business. The facts are the same as *Example 5* except that D owns all of the C stock and all of the S3 stock, and D transfers the S3 stock to C immediately prior to the distribution. Prior to D's transfer of the S3 stock to C, D owns section 1504(a)(2) stock of S3 and C, and C owns section 1504(a)(2) stock of S1 and S2, therefore, D, C, S1, S2, and S3 are DSAG members. See paragraph (b)(1)(iii) of this section. D, C, S1, S2, and S3 are treated as one corporation for purposes of determining whether D and C are engaged in the active conduct of a trade or business, and accordingly the transfer of the S3 stock to C is disregarded. See paragraph (b)(1)(ii) of this section. After the transfer, C owns section 1504(a)(2) stock of S3, and the CSAG includes C, S1, S2, and S3. See paragraph (b)(1)(iii) of this section. C, S1, S2, and S3 are treated as one corporation for purposes of determining whether C is engaged in the active conduct of a trade or business. See paragraph (b)(1)(ii) of this section. Throughout the pre-distribution period, D, C, S1, S2, and S3 are treated as one corporation and both D and C are engaged in the active conduct of ATB1 and ATB2.

See paragraphs (b)(1) and (b)(2) of this section. Immediately after the distribution, D is engaged in the active conduct of ATB1 and C is engaged in the active conduct of ATB2. Because D and C were engaged in the active conduct of ATB1 and ATB2 throughout the pre-distribution period and, immediately after the distribution, D is engaged in the active conduct of ATB1 and C is engaged in the active conduct of ATB2, D and C both satisfy the requirements of section 355(b).

Example 7. Failed segmented business. The facts are the same as *Example 6* except that D owns section 368(c) stock but not section 1504(a)(2) stock of C. Prior to D's transfer of the S3 stock, the DSAG includes only D and S3, and the CSAG includes only C, S1, and S2. See paragraph (b)(1)(iii) of this section. Therefore, prior to the transfer of the S3 stock, ATB2 does not exist because no one SAG conducts all three of the essential segments of the trade or business. Accordingly, C does not satisfy the requirements of section 355(b) because ATB2 was not actively conducted throughout the pre-distribution period. See paragraph (b)(3)(i) of this section.

Example 8. Jointly owned partnership. For more than five years, D has owned all of the stock of C, and D and C each have owned a 17-percent interest in Partnership. Throughout this period, D and Partnership have engaged in the active conduct of ATB1 and ATB2, respectively. In year 6, D transfers its 17-percent interest in Partnership to C and distributes all of the C stock to the D shareholders. Because D owns section 1504(a)(2) stock of C, C is a DSAG member. See paragraph (b)(1)(iii) of this section. D and C are treated as one corporation for purposes of determining whether D and C are engaged in the active conduct of a trade or business. See paragraph (b)(1)(ii) of this section. Accordingly, throughout the pre-distribution period, D and C are each treated as owning a 34-percent interest in Partnership. As such, both D and C are treated as engaged in the active conduct of both ATB1 and ATB2 throughout the pre-distribution period. See paragraphs (b)(2)(v)(A) and (b)(2)(v)(B) of this section. The transfer of the Partnership interest is disregarded because it is between SAG members. See paragraph (b)(1)(ii) of this section. After the distribution, C owns 34 percent of Partnership and is therefore engaged in the active conduct of ATB2. See paragraphs (b)(2)(v)(A) and (b)(2)(v)(B) of this section. Therefore, D and C both satisfy the requirements of section 355(b).

Example 9. Sequential application of the SAG rule—(i) *Facts.* For more than five years, D2 has owned all of the stock of D, and D has owned all of the stock of C. Throughout this period, D2 has engaged in the active conduct of ATB1 and ATB2, and D has engaged in the active conduct of ATB1. C, individually, has not engaged in the active conduct of any ATB. In year 6, D distributes all of the C stock to D2 (first distribution). Immediately thereafter, D2 transfers ATB2 to C and distributes all of the C stock to the D2 shareholders (second distribution).

(ii) *Analysis - first distribution.* Because D owns section 1504(a)(2) stock of C, C is a DSAG member prior to the first distribution. See paragraph (b)(1)(iii) of this section. D and C are treated as one corporation for purposes of determining whether D and C are engaged in the active conduct of a trade or business with respect to the first distribution. See paragraphs (b)(1)(ii) and (b)(1)(iii) of this section. Accordingly, throughout the pre-distribution period, D and C are each treated as engaged in ATB1 with respect to the first distribution. However, for purposes of determining whether D's distribution of the C stock to D2 satisfies the requirements of section 355(b) immediately after the first distribution, C is the only CSAG member (D2 is not a member of any SAG with respect to the first distribution). See paragraph (b)(1)(iii) of this section. Accordingly, C does not satisfy the requirements of section 355(b) with respect to the first distribution because C is not engaged in the active conduct of an ATB immediately after the first distribution.

(iii) *Analysis - second distribution.* Because D2 owns section 1504(a)(2) stock of D and C (and D owned section 1504(a)(2) stock of C before the first distribution), D2, D, and C are D2 SAG members throughout the pre-distribution period with respect to the second distribution. See paragraph (b)(1)(iii) of this section. Further, for purposes of the second distribution D's distribution of the C stock to D2 is disregarded because it is between D2 SAG members. See paragraphs (b)(1)(ii) and (b)(1)(iii) of this section. D2, D, and C are treated as one corporation for purposes of determining whether D2 and C are engaged in the active conduct of a trade or business with respect to the second distribution. See paragraphs (b)(1)(ii) and (b)(1)(iii) of this section. Accordingly, throughout the pre-distribution period, D2 and C are each treated as engaged in the active conduct of ATB1 and ATB2 with respect to the second distribution. The transfer of ATB2 to C is disregarded because it is between D2 SAG members. See paragraph (b)(1)(ii) of this section. Immediately after the second distribution, C is engaged in the active conduct of ATB2. Therefore, D2 and C both satisfy the requirements of section 355(b) with respect to the second distribution.

Example 10. Limitations - securities and vacant land. For more than five years, D has owned investment securities and vacant land. D has conducted no activities with respect to the vacant land, but D will subsequently subdivide the vacant land, install streets and utilities, and sell the developed lots to various homebuilders. D cannot currently satisfy the requirements of section 355(b) because the holding of investment securities does not constitute the active conduct of a trade or business. See paragraph (b)(2)(iv)(A) of this section. Furthermore, no significant development activities have been conducted with respect to the vacant land. See paragraph (b)(3) of this section.

Example 11. Limitations - occupied real estate - active. For more than five years, D, a bank, has owned an eleven-story office building, the ground floor of which D has occupied while engaged in the active conduct of its banking business. The remaining ten floors are rented to various tenants. Throughout this period, the building has been managed, operated, repaired, and maintained by employees of D. D transfers the building along with the significant assets used to operate the building and the goodwill associated with the building to new subsidiary C and distributes the C stock to the D shareholders. Henceforth, C's employees will manage, operate, repair, and maintain the building. D and C both satisfy the requirements of section 355(b). See paragraph (b)(3) of this section.

Example 12. Limitations - occupied real estate - not active. For more than five years, D, a bank, has owned a two-story building, the ground floor and one half of the second floor of which D has occupied while engaged in the active conduct of its banking business. The other half of the second floor has been rented as storage space to a neighboring retail merchant. D transfers the building and the goodwill associated with the building to new subsidiary C and distributes the C stock to the D shareholders. After the distribution, D leases from C the space in the building that it formerly occupied. Under the lease, D will repair and maintain its portion of the building and pay property taxes and insurance. C does not satisfy the requirements of section 355(b) because it is not engaged in the active conduct of a trade or business immediately after the distribution. See paragraph (b)(2)(iv)(A) of this section. This example does not address the question of whether the activities of D with respect to the building prior to the separation would constitute the active conduct of a trade or business.

Example 13. No significant activities. For more than five years, D owned land on which it has engaged in the active conduct of the ranching business. Oil has been discovered in the area, and it is apparent that oil may be found under the land on which the ranching business is conducted. D has engaged in no significant activities in connection with its mineral rights. D transfers its mineral rights to new subsidiary C and distributes the C stock to the D shareholders. C will actively pursue the development of the oil producing potential of the property. C does not satisfy the requirements of section 355(b) after the distribution because D was not engaged in significant exploitation activities with respect to the mineral rights throughout the pre-distribution period. See paragraph (b)(3) of this section.

Example 14. Vertical division - state contracts. For more than five years, D has engaged in the active conduct of a single business of constructing sewage disposal plants and other facilities. D transfers one half of its assets to new subsidiary C. These assets include a contract for the construction of a sewage disposal plant in State M, construction equipment, cash, goodwill, and other tangible and significant assets. D retains a contract for the construction of a sewage disposal plant in State N, construction equipment, cash, goodwill, and other tangible and significant assets. D distributes the C stock to one of D's shareholders in exchange for all of his D stock. D and C both satisfy the requirements of section 355(b). See paragraphs (b)(2) and (b)(3)(i) of this section.

Example 15. Vertical division - location. For more than five years, D has engaged in the active conduct of owning and operating two men's retail clothing stores, one in the downtown area of the City of G and one in a suburban area of G. D transfers the store building, fixtures, inventory, and other significant assets related to the operations of the suburban store and the goodwill attributable to that store to new subsidiary C. D also transfers to C the delivery trucks and delivery personnel that formerly served both stores. Henceforth, D will contract with a local public delivery service to make its deliveries. D retains the warehouses that formerly served both stores. Henceforth, C will lease warehouse space from an unrelated public warehouse company. D then distributes the C stock to the D shareholders. D and C both satisfy the requirements of section 355(b). See paragraphs (b)(2) and (b)(3)(i) of this section.

Example 16. Horizontal division - research. For more than five years, D has engaged in the active conduct of manufacturing and sale of household products. Throughout this period, D has maintained a research department for use in connection with its manufacturing activities. The research department has 30 employees actively engaged in the development of new products. D transfers the research department (which has significant assets and goodwill) to new subsidiary C and distributes the C stock to the D shareholders. After the distribution, C continues its research operations on a contractual basis with several corporations, including D. D and C both satisfy the requirements of section 355(b). See paragraphs (b)(2) and (b)(3)(i) of this section. The result is the same if, after the distribution, C continues its research operations but furnishes its services only to D. See paragraphs (b)(2) and (b)(3)(i) of this section. However, see § 1.355-2(d)(2)(iv)(C) (related function device factor) for possible evidence of device.

Example 17. Horizontal division - sales. For more than five years, D has engaged in the active conduct of processing and selling meat products. D derives income from no other source. D separates the sales function from the processing function by transferring the significant business assets related to the sales function, the goodwill associated with the sales function, and cash for working capital to new subsidiary C. D then distributes the C stock to the D shareholders. After the distribution, C purchases for resale the meat products processed by D. D and C both satisfy the requirements of section 355(b). See paragraphs (b)(2) and (b)(3)(i) of this section. However, see § 1.355-2(d)(2)(iv)(C) (related function device factor) for possible evidence of device.

Example 18. Expansion and vertical division - location. For more than five years, D has engaged in the active conduct of owning and operating hardware stores in several states. In year 6, D purchased all of the assets of a hardware store in State M, where D had not previously conducted business. In year 8, D transfers the State M hardware store and related significant assets and goodwill to new subsidiary C and distributes the C stock to the D shareholders. After the distribution, the State M hardware store has its own manager and is operated independently of the other stores. Because—

(i) The product of the State M hardware store is similar to the product of D's hardware stores in the other states;

(ii) The business activities associated with the operation of the State M hardware store are the same as the business activities associated with the operation of D's hardware stores in the other states; and

(iii) The operation of a hardware store in State M involves the use of the experience and know-how that D developed in the operation of the hardware stores in the other states, the hardware store in State M is in the same line of business as the hardware stores in the other states. Therefore, the acquisition of the State M hardware store constitutes an expansion of D's existing business and its acquisition does not constitute the acquisition of a new or different business under paragraph (b)(3)(ii) of this section. Accordingly, D and C both satisfy the requirements of section 355(b).

Example 19. Expansion and horizontal division - Internet. For more than five years, D has engaged in the active conduct of operating a retail shoe store business, under the name D. Throughout this period, D's sales are made exclusively to customers who frequent its retail stores in shopping malls and other locations. D's business enjoys favorable name recognition, customer loyalty, and other elements of goodwill in the retail shoe market. D creates an Internet web site and begins selling shoes at retail on the web site. To a significant extent, the operation of the web site draws upon D's existing experience and know-how. The web site is named "D.com" to take advantage of the name recognition, customer loyalty, and other elements of goodwill associated with D and the D name and to enhance the web site's chances for success in its initial stages. Eight months after beginning to sell shoes on the web site, D transfers all of the web site's assets and liabilities (all of which include the significant assets and goodwill associated with the web site's business) to new subsidiary C and distributes the C stock to the D shareholders. The product of the retail shoe store business and the product of the web site are the same (shoes), and the principal business activities of the retail shoe store business are the same as those of the web site (purchasing shoes at wholesale and reselling them at retail). Although selling shoes on a web site requires some know-how not associated with operating a retail store, such as familiarity with different marketing approaches, distribution chains, and technical operations issues, the web site's operation does draw to a significant extent on D's existing experience and know-how, and the web site's success will depend in large measure on the goodwill associated with D and the D name. Therefore, the creation by D of the Internet web site does not constitute the acquisition of a new or different business under paragraph (b)(3)(ii) of this section. Accordingly, it is an expansion of D's retail shoe store business, all of which is treated as having been actively conducted throughout the pre-distribution period. Therefore, D and C both satisfy the requirements of section 355(b).

Example 20. Expansion - acquiring a SAG member. For more than five years, D has owned all of the stock of C. Throughout this period, C and unrelated T have engaged in the active conduct of ATB1. In year 6, D purchases all of the T stock. In year 8, D distributes all of the C stock to the D shareholders. Throughout the period that C is a DSAG member, D is engaged in the active conduct of ATB1. See paragraph (b)(1)(ii) of this section. Moreover, because D acquired section 1504(a)(2) stock of T, D is treated as having acquired T's assets (and activities), and that acquisition constitutes an expansion of ATB1. See paragraphs (b)(1)(ii) and (b)(3)(ii) of this section. Therefore, D and C both satisfy the requirements of section 355(b). The result would be the same if D had owned all of the T stock for more than five years, and purchased all of the C stock in year 6. See paragraphs (b)(1)(ii), (b)(3)(ii), (b)(4)(i), and (b)(4)(iv)(F) of this section.

Example 21. No expansion - acquiring only control of controlled. For more than five years, D and unrelated C have engaged in the active conduct of ATB1. In year 6, D purchases section 368(c) stock but not section 1504(a)(2) stock of C. In year 8, D distributes the C stock to the D shareholders. While D and C are in the same line of business, the acquisition does not result in an expansion of D's business under paragraph (b)(3)(ii) of this section because D is not treated as having acquired C's assets (and activities). Accordingly, D has acquired control of C in violation of section 355(b)(2)(D). See paragraph (b)(4)(i)(B) of this section. However, if D acquires additional C stock thereby causing C to become a DSAG member, D would be treated as having acquired C's assets (and activities) and the acquisition would constitute an expansion of ATB1. See paragraphs (b)(1)(ii), (b)(3)(ii), (b)(4)(i), and (b)(4)(iv)(F) of this section. In such a case, D and C both would satisfy the requirements of section 355(b).

Example 22. Partnership - meaningful but not significant. For more than five years, unrelated X and Y have owned a 20-percent and 33 1/3-percent interest, respectively, in Partnership. The remaining interests in Partnership are owned by unrelated parties. For more than five years, Partnership has manufactured power equipment. But for the performance of all its management functions by employees of X, Partnership would satisfy all the requirements of paragraph (b)(2)(i) this section. X and/or Y will be attributed the trade or business assets and activities of Partnership only if the corporation satisfies the requirements of paragraph (b)(2)(v)(B) or (b)(2)(v)(C) of this section. See paragraph (b)(2)(v)(A) of this section. While X does not satisfy the requirements of paragraph (b)(2)(v)(B) of this section because X's interest in Partnership is not significant, under paragraph (b)(2)(v)(C) of this section, X owns a meaningful interest in Partnership and performs active and substantial management functions for the trade or business assets and activities of Partnership. Therefore, X is attributed the trade or business assets and activities of Partnership. Accordingly, X is engaged in the active conduct of the business of manufacturing power equipment. See paragraph (b)(2) of this section. In determining whether Y is engaged in the business of manufacturing power equipment, the management functions performed by X for Partnership are not taken into account. See paragraph (b)(2)(v)(A) of this section. Therefore, although Y is attributed Partnership's trade or business assets and activities under paragraph (b)(2)(v)(B) of this section because Y owns a significant interest in Partnership, Y is not engaged in the business of manufacturing power equipment because neither Y nor Partnership perform any management functions for the business. See paragraph (b)(2)(iii) of this section.

Example 23. Partnership - significant but not meaningful. The facts are the same as *Example 22* except that all the management functions related to the business of Partnership are performed by employees of Partnership. Because employees of Partnership perform all of the management functions related to the trade or business assets and activities of manufacturing power equipment, Partnership itself satisfies all the requirements of paragraph (b)(2)(i) of this section. X neither owns a significant interest in Partnership nor performs active and substantial management functions with respect to the trade or business assets and activities of Partnership. Accordingly, X does not satisfy the requirements of paragraph (b)(2)(v)(B) or (b)(2)(v)(C) of this section, X is not attributed the trade or business assets and activities of Partnership's business of manufacturing power equipment, and X is not engaged in the active conduct of the business of manufacturing power equipment. On the other hand, because Y owns a significant interest in Partnership, Y satisfies the requirements of paragraph (b)(2)(v)(B) of this section. Therefore, Y is attributed the trade or business assets and activities of Partnership's business. Accordingly, Y satisfies the requirements of paragraph (b)(2)(i) of this section and is engaged in the active conduct of the business of manufacturing power equipment.

Example 24. Partnership - significant by many. The facts are the same as *Example* 23 except that X, Y, and Z each own a 33 1/3-percent interest in Partnership. Because X, Y, and Z each own a significant interest in Partnership, each of X, Y, and Z satisfies the requirements of paragraph (b)(2)(v)(B) of this section. Accordingly, each of X, Y, and Z is attributed the trade or business assets and activities of Partnership, satisfies the requirements of paragraph (b)(2)(i) of this section, and is engaged in the active conduct of the business of manufacturing power equipment.

Example 25. Non-SAG affiliates—(i) *Facts*. For more than five years, X has owned 10 percent of the stock of D2, D2 has owned all the stock of D and S, and D has owned all the stock of C. Throughout this period, D has manufactured furniture that it sells to furniture stores and has been the principal owner of the goodwill and significant assets associated with that business and C has owned and operated a laundry business and has been the principal owner of the goodwill and significant assets associated with that business. Throughout this period, however, employees of S have performed all the active and substantial management and operational functions of the furniture business for D and the laundry business for C. D distributes the C stock to D2 (first distribution) and D2 distributes the C stock to X in exchange for all of X's D2 stock (second distribution). After the distributions, employees of X perform all the active and substantial management and operational functions of the laundry business for C that the employees of S performed before the distributions and the employees of S continue to perform the same activities for D as they did before the distributions.

(ii) *Analysis - first distribution*. In determining whether the furniture manufacturing business and laundry business have been actively conducted throughout the pre-distribution period and immediately after the first distribution, the activities performed for those businesses include activities performed by employees of affiliates of D and C (even if they are not DSAG or CSAG members). Accordingly, such activities include the activities performed by the employees of S for D and C. See paragraph (b)(2)(iii) of this section. D and C own the goodwill and significant assets associated with their respective businesses both throughout the pre-distribution period and immediately after the first distribution, and are treated as performing active and substantial management and operational functions for their respective businesses both throughout the pre-distribution period and immediately after the first distribution. Therefore, D and C both satisfy the requirements of section 355(b) with respect to the first distribution.

(iii) *Analysis - second distribution*. Because D2 owns section 1504(a)(2) stock of D, C, and S (and D owned section 1504(a)(2) stock of C before the first distribution), D2, D, C, and S are D2 SAG members throughout the pre-distribution period with respect to the second distribution. See paragraph (b)(1)(iii) of this section. Accordingly, D2, D, C, and S are treated as one corporation for purposes of determining whether D2 is engaged in an active trade or business with respect to the second distribution. See paragraph (b)(1)(ii) of this section. Accordingly, for purposes of the second distribution, D2 has been engaged in the furniture manufacturing business and the laundry business throughout the pre-distribution period. Further, for purposes of the second distribution D's distribution of the C stock to D2 is disregarded because it is between D2 SAG members. See paragraph (b)(1)(ii) of this section. D and S continue to be D2 SAG members immediately after the second distribution. See paragraph (b)(1)(iii) of this section. Accordingly, D2 is engaged in the furniture manufacturing business immediately after the second distribution. In determining whether C is engaged in the active conduct of a trade or business immediately after the second distribution, the activities performed for the laundry business include activities performed by employees of affiliates of C (even if they are not CSAG members). Accordingly, immediately after the second distribution, such activities include the activities performed for C by the employees of X. See paragraph (b)(2)(iii) of this section. C owns the goodwill and significant assets associated with the laundry business both throughout the pre-distribution period and immediately after the second distribution, and is treated as performing active and substantial management and operational functions both throughout the pre-distribution period and immediately after the second distribution. Therefore, D2 and C both satisfy the requirements of section 355(b) with respect to the second distribution.

Example 26. Purchased ATB and SAG member. For more than five years, P has owned all of the stock of D and S1, and D and S1 have owned all of the stock of S2 and S3, respectively. Throughout this period, S1 and S3 have engaged in the active conduct of ATB1 and ATB2, respectively. In year 6, S2 purchases ATB1 and all of the S3 stock from S1 on the same day. In year 6, the DSAG acquired ATB1 and ATB2 (as a result of S3 becoming a DSAG member) in a transaction in which gain or loss was recognized. Accordingly, if D were to make a distribution, it could not rely on ATB1 or ATB2 to satisfy the requirements of section 355(b) unless the DSAG's year 6 acquisition of ATB1 and ATB2 is not in the pre-distribution period. See paragraph (b)(4)(i)(A) of this section. The fact that S2 acquired ATB1 and the S3 stock from an affiliate is not relevant.

Example 27. Purchased ATB prior to entering. For more than five years, T has engaged in the active conduct of ATB1. In year 6, S purchased ATB1 from T. In year 7, D acquired all of the S stock from the S shareholders solely in exchange for D stock in a transaction to which section 351 applied and in which no gain or loss was recognized. As a result, S became a DSAG member. Although S became a DSAG member in a transaction in which no gain or loss was recognized, S, a corporation that later became a DSAG member, acquired ATB1 in a transaction in which gain or loss was recognized. Accordingly, if D were to make a distribution, it could not rely on ATB1 to satisfy the requirements of section 355(b) unless S's year 6 acquisition of ATB1 is not in the pre-distribution period. See paragraph (b)(4)(i)(A) of this section.

Example 28. ATB (or new SAG member) for stock of distributing or a corporation in control of distributing in a reorganization - transfer of ATB to controlled. For more than five years, unrelated T and Z have owned all of the stock of X and Y, respectively, and X and Y have engaged in the active conduct of ATB1 and ATB2, respectively. Unrelated P owns all of the stock of D. In year 6, D acquires all of X's assets (including ATB1) from X solely in exchange for D stock in a reorganization described in section 368(a)(1)(A), and all of Y's assets (including ATB2) from Y solely in exchange for P stock in a reorganization described in section 368(a)(1)(A) by reason of section 368(a)(2)(D). No gain or loss is recognized on either acquisition. In a separate transaction, D transfers ATB2 to new subsidiary C in exchange for all of the C stock in a transaction that satisfies the requirements of section 351 and in which no gain or loss is recognized. If D were to distribute the C stock in a separate transaction, D and C can rely on ATB1 and ATB2, respectively, to satisfy the requirements of section 355(b). ATB1 and ATB2 were acquired in transactions in which no gain or loss was recognized, and were not acquired in exchange for assets of the DSAG. See paragraph (b)(4)(ii) of this section. The result would be the same if D acquired all of the assets of T (including the X stock) and Z (including the Y stock) in the reorganizations instead of acquiring the assets of X and Y, and then transferred the Y stock to C. See paragraphs (b)(1)(ii) and (b)(4)(ii) of this section.

Example 29. Taxable transfer of ATB by distributing to controlled. The facts are the same as the original facts in *Example 28* except that before and after the transfer to C, D owned section 368(c) stock but not section 1504(a)(2) stock of C, and recognized gain under section 357(c) on the transfer of ATB2 to C. D and C can rely on ATB1 and ATB2, respectively, to satisfy the requirements of section 355(b). See paragraph (b)(4)(iii)(A) of this section. The result would be the same if C purchased ATB2 from D. The result would also be the same if D acquired all of the assets of T (including the X stock) and Z (including the Y stock) in the reorganizations instead of acquiring the assets of X and Y, and then C purchased the Y stock from D. See paragraphs (b)(1)(ii) and (b)(4)(iii)(A) of this section.

Example 30. Assets for controlled stock in a section 351 transaction. For more than five years, unrelated D and C have engaged in the active conduct of ATB1 and ATB2, respectively. In year 6, D transfers trucks to C to be used in ATB2 in exchange for section 368(c) stock of C in a transaction to which section 351 applies and in which no gain or loss is recognized. If D were to distribute the C stock, C could not rely on ATB2 to satisfy the requirements of section 355(b) unless D's year 6 acquisition of the C stock is not in the pre-distribution period because D acquired section 368(c) stock of C, a corporation engaged in ATB2, in exchange for assets not constituting the trade or business. See paragraphs (b)(4)(i)(B) and (b)(4)(ii)(A) of this section. The result would be the same even if C became a DSAG member as a result of the year 6 transfer. See paragraphs (b)(4)(i)(A) and (b)(4)(ii)(A) of this section.

Example 31. ATB for controlled stock in a reorganization. For more than five years, unrelated D and T have engaged in the active conduct of ATB1 and ATB2, respectively. Throughout this period, D has owned all of the sole class of C stock. In year 6, T merges into C solely in exchange for C stock in a reorganization described in section 368(a)(1)(A) and in which no gain or loss is recognized. As a result, the T shareholders receive 20 percent of the sole class of C stock. Because C acquired ATB2 in exchange for C stock, solely for purposes of determining whether ATB2 can be relied on to satisfy the requirements of section 355(b), D is treated as having acquired its 80 percent of the C stock in year 6 in a transaction in which gain or loss was recognized. See paragraph (b)(4)(iv)(E) of this section. Accordingly, if D were to distribute the C stock, C could not rely on ATB2 to satisfy the requirements of section 355(b) unless C's year 6 acquisition of ATB2 is not in the pre-distribution period because ATB2 was in effect indirectly acquired in exchange for D's assets. See paragraphs (b)(4)(i)(A), (b)(4)(ii)(A), and (b)(4)(iv)(E) of this section.

Example 32. ATB and controlled stock for distributing stock in a section 351 transaction. For more than five years, T and unrelated C have engaged in the active conduct of ATB1 and ATB2, respectively. Unrelated P owns all of the stock of D. In year 6, P purchases ATB1 from T, and section 368(c) stock of C from the C shareholders. In year 6, P contributes the C stock and ATB1 to D solely in exchange for additional D stock in a transaction to which section 351 applies and in which no gain or loss is recognized. If D were to subsequently distribute the C stock in a separate transaction, D can rely on ATB1, and C can rely on ATB2 to satisfy the requirements of section 355(b) because neither ATB1 nor control of C was acquired in exchange for assets of the DSAG. See paragraphs (b)(4)(i)(A), (b)(4)(i)(B), and (b)(4)(ii) of this section. The fact that P, an affiliate of D, purchased ATB1 and section 368(c) stock of C in year 6 is not relevant.

Example 33. ATB for distributing stock in a section 351 transaction with section 357(c) gain. The facts are the same as *Example 32* except that D has owned section 368(c) stock of C for more than five years, P only purchases ATB1 from T, and P recognizes under section 357(c) gain on the transfer of ATB1 to D as a result of D assuming liabilities of P. D cannot rely on ATB1 to satisfy the requirements of section 355(b) until D's year 6 acquisition of ATB1 is no longer in the pre-distribution period because D acquired ATB1 in a transaction in which gain or loss was recognized. See paragraph (b)(4)(i)(A) of this section.

Example 34. Partnership distributions. For more than five years, X and Y have engaged in the active conduct of ATB1 and ATB2, respectively. Throughout this period, unrelated D has owned a 90-percent interest in Partnership. D is attributed any trade or business assets and activities of Partnership under paragraph (b)(2)(v) of this section. In year 6, Partnership purchases ATB1 from X and all of the Y stock from its owner. In year 9, Partnership distributes ATB1 and all of the Y stock to D in a non-liquidating distribution. Assume that no gain or loss is recognized by Partnership or any partner on the distribution. As a result of the distribution, Y becomes a DSAG member, and D is treated as having acquired Y's assets (and activities). See paragraphs (b)(1)(ii) and (b)(1)(iii) of this section. If D were to make a distribution, ATB1 could not be relied on to satisfy the requirements of section 355(b) unless Partnership's year 6 acquisition of ATB1 is not in the pre-distribution period. See paragraphs (b)(2)(v), (b)(3)(iii), and (b)(4)(ii)(B) of this section. If D were to make a distribution, ATB2 could not be relied on to satisfy the requirements of section 355(b) unless D's year 9 acquisition of the Y stock is not in the pre-distribution period. See paragraphs (b)(2)(v)(A) and (b)(4)(ii)(B) of this section. Alternatively, if in year 9 Partnership only makes a pro rata distribution of all the Y stock to its partners such that D receives 90 percent of the Y stock, ATB2 cannot be relied on until Partnership's year 6 acquisition of all of the Y stock is no longer in the pre-distribution period. See paragraph (b)(4)(ii)(B) of this section.

Example 35. Partnership distribution (new SAG member). For more than five years, D has owned a 50-percent interest in Partnership. The remaining interests in Partnership are owned by unrelated parties. Throughout this period, Partnership has engaged in the active conduct of ATB1, and D has been attributed the trade or business assets and activities of Partnership's ATB1 under paragraph (b)(2)(v) of this section. In year 6, pursuant to an integrated plan, Partnership contributes ATB1 to new subsidiary S, and distributes all of the S stock to D in liquidation of D's 50-percent interest in Partnership. Assume that no gain or loss is recognized by Partnership or any partner on the distribution. As a result, S becomes a DSAG member, and D is treated as having acquired S's assets (and activities). See paragraphs (b)(1)(ii) and (b)(1)(iii) of this section. Because D was attributed ATB1 immediately before the incorporation and distribution by Partnership, and S became a DSAG member as a result of the distribution, Partnership's distribution of the S stock to D is not an acquisition of ATB1. See paragraphs (b)(3)(iii) and (b)(4)(ii)(B) of this section. Accordingly, if D were to make a distribution, it could rely on ATB1 to satisfy the requirements of section 355(b).

Example 36. Transfer of partnership in a reorganization and distribution. For more than five years, T has owned a 40-percent interest in Partnership which has engaged in the active conduct of ATB1. Throughout this period, T has been attributed the trade or business assets and activities of Partnership's ATB1 under paragraph (b)(2)(v) of this section. In year 6, T merges into S, a wholly owned subsidiary of unrelated D, solely in exchange for D stock in a reorganization described in section 368(a)(1)(A) by reason of section 368(a)(2)(D). No gain or loss is recognized. If D were to make a distribution, D can rely on ATB1 because ATB1 has been actively conducted throughout the pre-distribution period, and the interest in Partnership was acquired in a transaction in which no gain or loss was recognized and was not acquired in exchange for assets of the DSAG. See paragraphs (b)(2)(v), (b)(3)(i), and (b)(4)(ii) of this section. The results would be the same if T owned only a 20-percent interest in Partnership, employees of T performed active and substantial management functions for Partnership's trade or business assets and activities prior to the merger, and employees of S (or an affiliate of S) performed active and substantial management functions for Partnership's trade or business assets and activities after the merger. See paragraphs (b)(2)(iii), (b)(2)(v), (b)(3), and (b)(4)(ii) of this section.

Example 37. Transferred ATB sold (SAG member). For more than five years, D and unrelated T have engaged in the active conduct of ATB1 and ATB2, respectively. In year 6, D contributes ATB1 to T in exchange for T stock in a transaction to which section 351 applies. No gain or loss is recognized on the contribution. Immediately after the contribution T is a DSAG member. In year 8, in response to unanticipated market changes, T sells ATB1 to an unrelated third party. Although T became a DSAG member as a result of D acquiring T stock in exchange for ATB1 in a transaction in which no gain or loss was recognized, ATB1 is not the trade or business to be relied upon. Accordingly, D cannot rely on ATB2 until the year 6 transaction is no longer in the pre-distribution period because D acquired ATB2 in exchange for D's assets not constituting the active trade or business to be relied on. See paragraphs (b)(4)(i)(A) and (b)(4)(ii)(A) of this section.

Example 38. Transferred ATB sold (partnership). The facts are the same as *Example 37* except that, in year 6, D and T contribute ATB1 and ATB2, respectively, to Partnership in a transaction to which section 721 applies. In the exchange, D and T each receive a 50-percent interest in Partnership. In year 8, in response to unanticipated market changes, Partnership sells ATB1 to an unrelated third party. If D were to make a distribution, D could not rely on ATB2 under paragraph (b)(2)(v)(B) of this section unless the year 6 transaction is not in the pre-distribution period because D acquired ATB2 in exchange for D's assets not constituting the trade or business to be relied on. See paragraphs (b)(4)(i)(A) and (b)(4)(ii)(A) of this section.

Example 39. Indirect acquisition of control of distributing's ATB. For more than five years, D and T have engaged in the active conduct of ATB1 and ATB2, respectively. All of the T stock is owned by individuals. In year 6, T purchases all the stock of D in a transaction in which gain or loss is recognized. In a separate transaction, T merges downstream into D solely in exchange for D stock in a reorganization described in section 368(a)(1)(A) and (D). No gain or loss is recognized. In year 7, D transfers ATB2 formerly conducted by T to new subsidiary C, and then distributes the C stock to the D shareholders. Although D acquired ATB2 solely in exchange for D stock in a transaction in which no gain or loss was recognized, the requirements of section 355(b) are not satisfied because ATB1, the business of D, was indirectly acquired by T, a predecessor of D, during the pre-distribution period in a transaction in which gain or loss was recognized. See paragraphs (b)(4)(i)(A) and (b)(4)(iv)(A) of this section. The result would be the same if prior to the year 6 acquisition D and wholly owned subsidiary C were engaged in the active conduct of ATB1 and ATB2, respectively, and T had no ATB.

Example 40. Exception for corporate distributee. For more than five years, T has owned all of the stock of D which in turn owned all of the stock of C. Throughout this period, D and C have engaged in the active conduct of ATB1 and ATB2, respectively. In year 6, P purchases all the stock of T. In year 7, P liquidates T in a transaction in which no gain or loss is recognized under section 332. Under section 334(b), P's basis in the D stock is determined in whole by reference to T's basis in the D stock. In year 8, D distributes the C stock to P. While the D stock was indirectly acquired in a taxable transaction, the adjusted basis that P, the distributee corporation, has in the D stock was determined in whole by reference to T's adjusted basis. Accordingly, D and C satisfy the requirements of section 355(b). See paragraph (b)(4)(iii)(C) of this section. If P were to distribute either the D stock or C stock, neither ATB1 nor ATB2 could be relied on unless the year 6 acquisition of the T stock is not in the pre-distribution period. See paragraph (b)(4)(iii)(C) of this section. The results would be the same if P acquired all of T's assets in exchange for P stock and other property in a reorganization described in section 368(a)(1)(A).

Example 41. Acquisition of section 368(c) stock of controlled, DSAG member. For more than five years, D has owned section 1504(a)(2) stock but not section 368(c) stock of C. Throughout this period, C has engaged in the active conduct of ATB1. In year 6, D purchased additional shares of C stock. As a result, D acquired section 368(c) stock of C. If D were to make a distribution of the C stock, C could rely on ATB1 to satisfy the requirement of section 355(b). C was a DSAG member, so D was engaged in ATB1 prior to the year 6 purchase of additional C stock. Accordingly, D's acquisition of additional stock of a DSAG member is disregarded in applying paragraph (b)(4)(i)(A) of this section, and paragraph (b)(4)(i)(B) of this section does not apply to this acquisition of additional C stock. See paragraphs (b)(1)(ii) and (b)(4)(iv)(F) of this section.

Example 42. Controlled becoming a DSAG member. For more than five years, D has owned section 368(c) stock but not section 1504(a)(2) stock of C. Throughout this period, D and C have engaged in the active conduct of ATB1 and ATB2, respectively. In year 6, D purchases the remaining C stock. If D distributes all the C stock, C cannot rely on ATB2 to satisfy the requirements of section 355(b) because C became a DSAG member (and thus D acquired ATB2) in a transaction in which gain or loss was recognized. See paragraphs (b)(1)(ii), (b)(4)(i)(A), and (b)(4)(iv)(F) of this section.

Example 43. Nontaxable multi-step acquisition of control. For more than five years, unrelated D and C have engaged in the active conduct of ATB1 and ATB2, respectively. C has two classes of stock outstanding. X owns all 95 shares of the class A stock of C, representing 95 percent of the voting power and 70 percent of the value, and Y owns all of the class B stock of C, representing five percent of the voting power and 30 percent of the value. In year 6, D acquires 10 shares of class A C stock from X in a transaction in which gain or loss was recognized. In year 7, in a separate transaction, D acquires an additional 80 shares of class A C stock from X solely in exchange for D voting stock in a reorganization described in section 368(a)(1)(B). No gain or loss is recognized. In year 8, in a separate transaction, D acquires the remaining five shares of class A C stock from X in a transaction in which gain or loss was recognized. Because D only acquires 70 percent of the value of C stock, C does not become a DSAG member. In year 9, D distributes the 95 shares of class A C stock to the D shareholders. At the time D first acquired control of C, D owned an amount of C stock constituting control that was acquired in a transaction in which no gain or loss was recognized. Accordingly, D and C both satisfy the requirements of section 355(b). See paragraphs (b)(4)(i)(B) and (b)(4)(iv)(B) of this section.

Example 44. Taxable multi-step acquisition of control. The facts are the same as *Example 43* except that in year 7 D acquires 70 shares of class A C stock solely in exchange for D voting stock in a reorganization described in section 368(a)(1)(B). No gain or loss is recognized. At the time D first acquired control of C, D did not own an amount of C stock constituting control that was acquired in one or more transactions in which no gain or loss was recognized or by reason of such transactions combined with acquisitions before the pre-distribution period. Accordingly, C cannot rely on ATB2 to satisfy the requirements of section 355(b) until D's year 6 acquisition of the 10 shares of class A C stock is no longer in the pre-distribution period. See paragraphs (b)(4)(i)(B) and (b)(4)(iv)(B) of this section.

Example 45. Taxable acquisition of control. For more than five years, unrelated D and C have engaged in the active conduct of ATB1 and ATB2, respectively. In year 6, D acquires section 368(c) stock but not section 1504(a)(2) stock of C from unrelated T in a reorganization described in section 368(a)(1)(A) by reason of section 368(a)(2)(E) through the use of a newly created transitory subsidiary of D. In the reorganization, T receives consideration 95 percent of which is D voting common stock and five percent of which is cash. Because D acquired control of C in a single transaction in which gain or loss was recognized, paragraph (b)(4)(iv)(B) of this section does not apply. Accordingly, C cannot rely on ATB2 to satisfy the requirements of section 355(b) until D's year 6 acquisition of control of C is no longer in the pre-distribution period. See paragraph (b)(4)(i)(B) of this section.

Example 46. Taxable multi-step indirect acquisition of control. For more than five years, C has engaged in the active conduct of ATB1. T owns exactly 80 percent of the total combined voting power of all classes of C stock entitled to vote and 80 percent of the total number of shares of all other classes of C stock, but T owns less than 80 percent of the total value of the C stock. In year 6, unrelated D acquires 10 percent of the sole outstanding class of stock of T in a transaction in which gain or loss is recognized. In year 8, in a separate transaction, T merges into D solely in exchange for D stock in a reorganization described in section 368(a)(1)(A). No gain or loss is recognized. As a result, D owns section 368(c) stock of C. Because D indirectly acquired 10 percent of the C stock owned by T in year 6, at the time D first acquired control of C, D did not own stock constituting control of C that it acquired in one or more transactions in which no gain or loss was recognized or by reason of such transactions combined with acquisitions before the pre-distribution period. Accordingly, C cannot rely on ATB1 to satisfy the requirements of section 355(b) until D's year 6 acquisition of the T stock is no longer in the pre-distribution period. See paragraphs (b)(4)(i)(B) and (b)(4)(iv)(B) of this section.

Example 47. Nontaxable multi-step acquisition of SAG member (or ATB). For more than five years, S has engaged in the active conduct of ATB1. X owns all 100 shares of the sole outstanding class of S stock. In year 6, unrelated D acquires 10 shares of S stock from X in a transaction in which gain or loss was recognized. In year 7, in a separate transaction, D acquires an additional 80 shares of S stock from X solely in exchange for D voting stock in a reorganization described in section 368(a)(1)(B). No gain or loss is recognized. As a result, S becomes a DSAG member. In year 8, in a separate transaction, D acquires another 5 shares of S stock from X in a transaction in which gain or loss was recognized. Because at the time S first became a DSAG member, D owned an amount of S stock meeting the requirements of section 1504(a)(2) that was acquired in a transaction in which no gain or loss was recognized, D can rely on ATB1 to satisfy the requirements of section 355(b) as of the year 7 transaction. See paragraphs (b)(4)(i)(A) and (b)(4)(iv)(C) of this section. The acquisition by D of other S stock in a separate transaction in which gain or loss was recognized during the pre-distribution period is disregarded. See paragraph (b)(1)(ii) of this section. The result would be the same if, in year 7, instead of acquiring S stock in a reorganization described in section 368(a)(1)(B), S merged into D in exchange for D stock in a reorganization described in section 368(a)(1)(A) in which no gain or loss was recognized. See paragraphs (b)(4)(i)(A) and (b)(4)(iv)(D) of this section.

Example 48. Taxable multi-step acquisition of SAG member (or ATB). The facts are the same as *Example 47* except that in year 6 D acquires 21 shares of S stock in a transaction in which gain or loss was recognized, and in year 7, in a separate transaction, D acquires an additional 79 shares of S stock solely in exchange for D voting stock in a reorganization described in section 368(a)(1)(B). No gain or loss is recognized, and S becomes a DSAG member. D cannot rely on ATB1 to satisfy the requirements of section 355(b) until D's year 6 acquisition of the 21 shares of S stock is no longer in the pre-distribution period because at the time S first became a DSAG member D did not own an amount of S stock meeting the requirements of section 1504(a)(2) that was acquired in one or more transactions in which no gain or loss was recognized or by reason of such transactions combined with acquisitions before the pre-distribution period. See paragraphs (b)(4)(i)(A) and (b)(4)(iv)(C) of this section. The result would be the same if, in year 7, in a separate transaction, instead of D's acquiring S stock, S merged into D in exchange for D stock in a reorganization described in section 368(a)(1)(A) in which no gain or loss was recognized. See paragraphs (b)(4)(i)(A) and (b)(4)(iv)(D) of this section. The result would also be the same if in year 6 D acquired 10 shares of S stock in a transaction in which gain or loss was recognized and, in year 7, in a separate transaction, D acquired an additional 70 shares of S stock solely in exchange for D voting stock in a reorganization described in section 368(a)(1)(B). See paragraphs (b)(4)(i)(A) and (b)(4)(iv)(C) of this section.

Example 49. Nontaxable multi-step indirect acquisition using subsidiary stock. For more than five years, X has owned all of the sole outstanding class of S stock. Throughout this period, S and unrelated T have engaged in the active conduct of ATB1 and ATB2, respectively. In year 6, T merges into S solely in exchange for S stock in a reorganization described in section 368(a)(1)(A). No gain or loss is recognized. Immediately after the merger, X and the former T shareholders own 80 percent and 20 percent of the S stock, respectively. In year 8, unrelated D acquires all of the S shares held by X solely in exchange for D voting stock in a reorganization described in section 368(a)(1)(B). No gain or loss is recognized. As a result, S becomes a DSAG member. Because D acquired ATB1 and ATB2 in a transaction in which no gain or loss was recognized, solely in exchange for D stock, D can rely on both ATB1 and ATB2 to satisfy the requirements of section 355(b). Because X is neither a predecessor of D nor a DSAG member, paragraph (b)(4)(iv)(E) of this section is not applicable.

Example 50. Taxable multi-step indirect acquisition using subsidiary stock. The facts are the same as *Example 49* except that, for more than five years, D has owned 50 percent of the sole outstanding class of X stock. In year 8, instead of D acquiring the S stock, S merges into D solely in exchange for D stock in a reorganization described in section 368(a)(1)(A). No gain or loss is recognized. Because D indirectly owned S stock and S acquired ATB2 in exchange for S stock, paragraph (b)(4)(iv)(E) of this section is applicable. Under paragraph (b)(4)(iv)(E) of this section, for purposes of applying paragraph (b)(4) of this section with respect to ATB2, D is treated as having indirectly acquired in year 6 the S stock it indirectly owns immediately after the merger of T into S in a transaction in which gain or loss was recognized. Thus, D is treated as having indirectly acquired 40 percent of the S stock in a transaction in which gain or loss is recognized at the time of the merger of T into S. Further, if the merger of T into S is in the pre-distribution period, under paragraph (b)(4)(iv)(D) of this section, D will be treated as having acquired ATB2 in a transaction in which gain or loss is recognized because, immediately before the merger of S into D, D indirectly owned 40 percent of the S stock that had been acquired in a transaction in which gain or loss was recognized. Accordingly, D cannot rely on ATB2 to satisfy the requirements of section 355(b) until the year 6 merger of T into S is no longer in the pre-distribution period. However, D can rely on ATB1 to satisfy the requirements of section 355(b). Alternatively, if X, instead of S, merged into D, S would become a DSAG member and X would be a predecessor of D. If so, for purposes of applying paragraph (b)(4) of this section with respect to ATB2, D is treated as having acquired 80 percent of the S stock in year 6 in a transaction in which gain or loss was recognized. Accordingly, D cannot rely on ATB2 to satisfy the requirements of section 355(b) until the year 6 merger of T into S is no longer in the pre-distribution period. See paragraphs (b)(1)(iii), (b)(4)(i)(A), (b)(4)(iv)(A), and (b)(4)(iv)(E) of this section. However, D can rely on ATB1 to satisfy the requirements of section 355(b).

Example 51. Taxable multi-step indirect acquisition of SAG member (or ATB). For more than five years, T has engaged in the active conduct of ATB1. Throughout this period, X owned all of the sole outstanding class of T stock, and D owned 50 percent of the sole outstanding stock of S. In year 6, S acquires 50 percent of the sole outstanding class of the X stock in a transaction in which gain or loss is recognized. In year 8, X merges into D solely in exchange for D stock. No gain or loss is recognized. As a result, T becomes a DSAG member. Because D indirectly acquired more than 20 percent of the T stock (D indirectly acquired 25 percent of T) in year 6, at the time T first became a DSAG member D did not own an amount of T stock meeting the requirements of section 1504(a)(2) that it acquired in one or more transactions in which no gain or loss was recognized or by reason of such transactions combined with acquisitions before the predistribution period. Accordingly, D cannot rely on ATB1 to satisfy the requirements of section 355(b) until D's year 6 indirect acquisition of the T stock is no longer in the pre-distribution period. See paragraphs (b)(4)(i)(A) and (b)(4)(iv)(C) of this section. The result would be the same if, instead of X, in year 8, T merged into D solely in exchange for D stock. See paragraphs (b)(4)(i) and (b)(4)(iv) of this section.

Predecessors and Successors: Limitation on Gain Recognition: Guidance

Predecessors and Successors: Limitation on Gain Recognition: Guidance.—Amendments to Reg. §1.355-8, regarding the distribution by a distributing corporation of stock or securities of a controlled corporation without the recognition of income, gain, or loss, are proposed (published in the Federal Register on December 19, 2016) (REG-140328-15).

Par. 3. Section 1.355-8 is revised to read as follows:

§1.355-8. Definition of predecessor and successor and limitations on gain recognition under section 355(e) and section 355(f).—[The text of the proposed amendments to §1.355-8(a) through (i) is the same as the text of §1.355-8T as added by T.D. 9805.]

Distribution of Stock: Device and Active Trade or Business: Guidance

Distribution of Stock: Device and Active Trade or Business: Guidance.—Reg. §§1.355-8 and 1.355-9, clarifying the application of the device prohibition and the active business requirement of section 355 and affecting corporations that distribute the stock of controlled corporations, their shareholders, and their security holders, are proposed (published in the Federal Register on July 15, 2016) (REG-134016-15).

Par. 5. Reserved §1.355-8 is added to read as follows:

§1.355-8. Definition of predecessors and successors and limitations on gain recognition.—[Reserved]

Par. 6. Section 1.355-9 is added to read as follows:

§1.355-9. Minimum percentage of Five-Year-Active-Business Assets.—(a) *Definitions.*—The following definitions apply for purposes of this section:

(1) *Distributing, Controlled.—Distributing* means the distributing corporation within the meaning of §1.355-1(b). *Controlled* means the controlled corporation within the meaning of §1.355-1(b).

(2) *Five-Year-Active Business.—Five-Year-Active Business* means the active conduct of a trade or business that satisfies the requirements and limitations of section 355(b)(2) and §1.355-3(b).

(3) *Five-Year-Active-Business Assets.—Five-Year-Active-Business Assets* of a corporation means its gross assets used in one or more Five-Year-Active Businesses. Such assets include cash and cash equivalents held as a reasonable amount of working capital for one or more Five-Year-Active Businesses. Such assets also include assets required (by binding commitment or legal requirement) to be held to provide for exigencies related to a Five-Year-Active Business or for regulatory purposes with respect to a Five-Year-Active Business. For this purpose, such assets include assets the holder is required (by binding commitment or legal requirement) to hold to secure or otherwise provide for a financial obligation reasonably expected to arise from a Five-Year-Active Business and assets held to implement a binding commitment to expend funds to expand or improve a Five-Year-Active Business.

(4) *Non-Five-Year-Active-Business Assets.—Non-Five-Year-Active-Business Assets* of a corporation means its gross assets other than its Five-Year-Active-Business Assets.

(5) *Total Assets.—Total Assets* of a corporation means its Five-Year-Active-Business Assets and its Non-Five-Year-Active-Business Assets.

(6) *Five-Year-Active-Business Asset Percentage.*—The *Five-Year-Active-Business Asset Percentage* of a corporation is the percentage determined by dividing the fair market value of its Five-Year-Active-Business Assets by the fair market value of its Total Assets.

(7) *Separate Affiliated Group, SAG, CSAG, and DSAG.—Separate Affiliated Group* (or *SAG*), *CSAG*, and *DSAG* have the same meanings as in §1.355-2(d)(2)(iv)(B)(6).

(b) *Five percent minimum Five-Year-Active-Business Asset Percentage.*—For the requirements of section 355(a)(1)(C) and section 355(b) to be satisfied with respect to a distribution, the Five-

Year-Active-Business Asset Percentage of each of Distributing and Controlled must be at least five percent.

(c) *Operating rules.*—The following operating rules apply for purposes of this section:

(1) *Treatment of SAG and fair market value.*—The operating rules in § 1.355-2(d)(2)(iv)(D)(2) (treatment of SAG as a single corporation) and (5) (fair market value) apply.

(2) *Time to identify assets, determine character of assets, and determine fair market value of assets.*—The provisions of § 1.355-2(d)(2)(iv)(D)(3) (time to identify assets and determine character of assets) apply, except that references to paragraph (d)(2)(iv) are treated as references to this section and "Business Assets or Nonbusiness Assets" is replaced with "Five-Year-Active-Business Assets or Non-Five-Year-Active-Business Assets," and the provisions of § 1.355-2(d)(2)(iv)(D)(4) (time to determine fair market value of assets) apply.

(3) *Interest in partnership.*—(i) *In general.*—Except as provided in paragraph (c)(3)(ii) of this section, an interest in a partnership is a Non-Five-Year-Active-Business Asset.

(ii) *Exception for certain interests in partnerships.*—If Distributing or Controlled is considered to be engaged in one or more Five-Year-Active-Businesses conducted by a partnership, the fair market value of the corporation's interest in the partnership will be allocated between Five-Year-Active-Business Assets and Non-Five-Year-Active-Business Assets in the same proportion as the proportion of the fair market values of the Five-Year-Active-Business Assets and Non-Five-Year-Active-Business Assets of the partnership.

(d) *Anti-abuse rule.*—A transaction or series of transactions undertaken with a principal purpose of affecting the Five-Year-Active-Business Asset Percentage of any corporation will not be given effect for purposes of applying this § 1.355-9. For this purpose, a transaction or series of transactions includes a change in the form of ownership of an asset; an issuance, assumption, or repayment of indebtedness or other obligations; or an issuance or redemption of stock. However, this paragraph (d) generally does not apply to a non-transitory acquisition or disposition of assets, other than an acquisition from or disposition to a person the ownership of whose stock would, under section 318(a) (other than paragraph (4) thereof), be attributed to Distributing or Controlled, or to a non-transitory transfer of assets between Distributing and Controlled.

(e) *Effective/applicability date.*—(1) *In general.*—Except as provided in paragraph (e)(2) of this section, this section applies to transactions occurring on or after the date the Treasury decision adopting these regulations as final regulations is published in the **Federal Register**.

(2) *Transition rule.*—This section does not apply to a distribution that is—

(i) Made pursuant to an agreement, resolution, or other corporate action that is binding on or before the date the Treasury decision adopting these regulations as final regulations is published in the **Federal Register** and at all times thereafter;

(ii) Described in a ruling request submitted to the Internal Revenue Service on or before July 15, 2016; or

(iii) Described in a public announcement or filing with the Securities and Exchange Commission on or before the date the Treasury decision adopting these regulations as final regulations is published in the **Federal Register**. [Reg. § 1.355-9.]

Section 301 Regulations: Statutory Changes Reflected

Section 301 Regulations: Statutory Changes Reflected.—Amendments to Reg. § 1.356-1, updating existing regulations under section 301 to reflect statutory changes made by the Technical and Miscellaneous Revenue Act of 1988, which changes provide that the amount of a distribution of property made by a corporation to its shareholder is the fair market value of the distributed property, are proposed (published in the Federal Register on March 26, 2019) (REG-121694-16).

Par. 3. Section 1.356-1 is amended by revising paragraph (f) to read as follows:

§ 1.356-1. Receipt of additional consideration in connection with an exchange.

* * *

(f) See § 1.301–1(j) for certain transactions which are not within the scope of section 356.

* * *

Installment Obligations: Dispositions: Nonrecognition of Gain or Loss

Installment Obligations: Dispositions: Nonrecognition of Gain or Loss—Amendments to Reg. § 1.361-1, relating to the nonrecognition of gain or loss on certain dispositions of an installment obligation, are proposed (published in the Federal Register on December 23, 2014) (REG-109187-11).

☐ Par. 3. Section 1.361-1 is amended by adding new second and third sentences to read as follows:

§ 1.361-1. Nonrecognition of gain or loss to corporations.—* * * See § 1.453B-1(c) for rules requiring a corporation transferring an installment obligation to the acquiring corporation (as that term is used in § 1.368-1) to recognize gain or loss upon the receipt of stock of the acquiring corporation or another party to the reorganization (as defined in § 1.368-2(f)) in satisfaction of that installment obligation. The preceding sentence applies to satisfactions of installment obligations after the date these regulations are published as final regulations in the **Federal Register**.* * *

Reorganizations: Foreign Corporations: Transfer of Property

Reorganizations: Foreign Corporations: Transfer of Property.—Reg. §§1.367(a)-1T and 1.367(a)-6T, relating to transfers of property to foreign corporations, are proposed (published in the Federal Register on May 16, 1986) (LR-3-86). Reg. §1.367(a)-3T was adopted as Reg. §1.367(a)-3 by T.D. 8702 on December 27, 1996. Reg. §§1.367(a)-2T and 1.367(a)-4T were adopted and §1.367(a)-5T was removed by T.D. 9803 on December 15, 2016.

§1.367(a)-1. Transfers to foreign corporations subject to section 367(a): In general.

§1.367(a)-6. Transfer of foreign branch with previously deducted losses.

Corporate Reorganizations: Foreign Corporations: Liquidating Distribution

Corporate Distributions: Foreign Corporation.—Amendments to Temporary Reg. §§1.367(a)-1T, relating to the distribution of stock and securities by a domestic corporation to a person who is not a United States person, and also relating to a liquidating distribution of property by a domestic or foreign corporation to a foreign corporation, are proposed (published in the Federal Register on January 16, 1990). Reg. §7.367(b)-1 was removed by T.D. 8862, effective February 23, 2000.

§1.367(a)-1T. Transfers to foreign corporations subject to section 367(a): In general (temporary).

Foreign Corporations: Transfers of Stock by U.S. Person

Foreign Corporations: Transfers of Stock by U.S. Person.—Reg. §1.367(a)-9, providing rules under Code Sec. 367(a) and (b) that apply to certain transfers of stock by a United States person to a foreign corporation described in Code Sec. 304(a)(1), is proposed (published in the Federal Register on February 11, 2009) (REG-147636-08).

Par. 2. Section 1.367(a)-9 is added to read as follows:

§1.367(a)-9. Treatment of deemed section 351 exchanges pursuant to section 304(a)(1).

[The text of proposed §1.367(a)-9 is the same as the text of §1.367(a)-9T as added by T.D. 9444].

Foreign Corporations: Stock Transfer Rules: Carryover of Earnings and Taxes

Foreign Corporations: Stock Transfer Rules: Carryover of Earnings and Taxes.—Reg. §1.367(b)-8 and amendments to Reg. §1.367(b)-5, addressing (1) the carryover of certain tax attributes, such as earnings and profits and foreign income tax accounts, when two corporations combine in a section 367(b) transaction and (2) the allocation of certain tax attributes when a corporation distributes stock of another corporation in a section 367(b) transaction, are proposed (published in the Federal Register on November 15, 2000) (REG-116050-99) (corrected March 12, 2001).

☐ Par. 7. Section 1.367(b)-5 is amended by: **1.** Revising paragraphs (b)(1)(ii) and (c)(2). **2.** Adding paragraph (e)(3). The revisions and addition read as follows:

§1.367(b)-5. Distributions of stock described in section 355.

* * *

(b) * * *

(1) * * *

(ii) If the distributee is an individual or a tax-exempt entity as described in §1.337(d)-4(c)(2) then, solely for purposes of determining the gain recognized by the distributing corporation, the controlled corporation shall not be considered to be a corporation, and the distributing corporation shall recognize any gain (but not loss) realized on the distribution.

* * *

(c) * * *

(2) *Adjustment to basis in stock and income inclusion.*—(i) *In general.*—If the distributee's postdistribution amount (as defined in paragraph (e)(2) of this section) with respect to the distributing or controlled corporation is less than the distributee's predistribution amount (as defined in paragraph (e)(1) of this section) with respect to such corporation, then the distributee's basis in such stock immediately after the distribution (determined under the normal principles of section 358) shall be reduced by the amount of the difference. However, the distributee's basis in such stock shall not be reduced below zero, and to the extent the foregoing reduction would have reduced basis below zero, the distributee shall instead include such amount in income as a deemed dividend from such corporation. See, e.g., paragraph (g) *Example 1* of this section.

(ii) *Exception.*—The basis reduction rule of paragraph (c)(2)(i) of this section shall apply only to the extent such reduction increases the distributee's section 1248 amount (as defined in

§1.367(b)-2(c)(1)) with respect to the distributing or controlled corporation; otherwise such basis reduction shall be replaced by the income inclusion rule of paragraph (c)(2)(i) of this section. See, e.g., §1.367(b)-8(d)(6) *Example 2*.

* * *

(e) * * *

(3) *Divisive D reorganization with a preexisting controlled corporation.*—In the case of a transaction described in §1.367(b)-8(b)(4), the predistribution amount with respect to a distributing or controlled corporation shall be computed after the allocation of the distributing corporation's earnings and profits described in §1.367(b)-8(b)(4)(i)(A) and (b)(4)(ii)(A) (without regard to the parenthetical phrase in §1.367(b)-8(b)(4)(ii)(A)), but before the reduction in the distributing corporation's earnings and profits described in §1.367(b)-8(b)(4)(i)(B). See, e.g., §1.367(b)-8(d)(6) *Example 3* and §1.367(b)-8(e)(7) *Example 3*.

* * *

□ Par. 10. Section 1.367(b)-8 is added to read as follows:

§1.367(b)-8. Allocation of earnings and profits and foreign income taxes in certain foreign corporate separations.—(a) *Scope.*—This section applies to distributions to which section 355 (or so much of section 356 as relates to section 355) applies, whether or not in connection with a section 368(a)(1)(D) reorganization (D reorganization), in which the distributing corporation or the controlled corporation (or both) is a foreign corporation (foreign divisive transaction). For purposes of this section, the terms distributing corporation and controlled corporation have the same meaning as used in section 355 and the regulations thereunder. Paragraph (b) of this section provides general rules governing the allocation and reduction of a distributing corporation's earnings and profits and foreign income taxes (pre-transaction earnings and pre-transaction taxes, respectively) in foreign divisive transactions. Paragraphs (c), (d), and (e) of this section describe special rules for the application of paragraph (b) of this section to specific situations, depending upon whether the distributing corporation or the controlled corporation (or both the distributing and the controlled corporation) is a foreign corporation.

(b) *General rules.*—(1) *Application of §1.312-10.*—(i) *In general.*—Pre-transaction earnings of a distributing corporation shall be allocated between the distributing corporation and the controlled corporation in accordance with the rules of §1.312-10(a) and shall be reduced in accordance with the rules of §1.312-10(b), except to the extent otherwise provided in this section.

(ii) *Special rules for application of §1.312-10(b).*—(A) *Distributing corporation.*—The pre-transaction earnings of a distributing corporation shall be reduced without taking into account §1.312-10(b)(2).

(B) *Controlled corporation.*—Section 1.312-10(b) shall not apply to increase or replace the earnings and profits of a controlled corporation by the amount of any decrease in the pre-transaction earnings of a distributing corporation.

(iii) *Net deficit in pre-transaction earnings.*—Nothing in this section shall permit any portion of the pre-transaction earnings of a distributing corporation that has a net deficit in pre-transaction earnings to be allocated or reduced under paragraph (b)(1)(i) of this section. See §1.312-10(c). Compare paragraph (b)(2) of this section (requiring an allocation or reduction of a pro rata portion of deficits in statutory groupings of earnings and profits when a distributing corporation has a net positive amount of pre-transaction earnings).

(iv) *Use of net bases.*—All allocations and reductions described in paragraph (b)(1)(i) of this section shall be determined in accordance with the net bases in assets. Net basis shall have the same meaning as under §1.312-10(a).

(v) *Gain recognized by distributing corporation.*—The pre-transaction earnings that are subject to allocation or reduction under paragraph (b)(1)(i) of this section shall include any increase in earnings and profits from gain recognized or income included by the distributing corporation as a result of the foreign divisive transaction. See, for example, section 367(a) and (e), section 1248(f), and §1.367(b)-5(b).

(vi) *Coordination with branch profits tax.*—An allocation or reduction in a distributing corporation's pre-transaction earnings under paragraph (b)(1)(i) of this section shall not be out of or reduce effectively connected earnings and profits or non-previously taxed accumulated effectively connected earnings and profits, as defined in section 884. See also §1.884-2T(d)(5)(iii) (providing that such earnings and profits are not subject to reduction under §1.312-10(b)).

(2) *Cross-section of earnings and profits.*—Except to the extent provided in paragraphs (b)(1)(iii), (b)(1)(vi), (d)(2)(ii), (d)(4), and (e)(4) of this section and other than any portion attributable to an inclusion under §1.367(b)-5 or paragraph (d)(2)(i) of this section, an allocation or reduction of pre-transaction earnings described in paragraph (b)(1)(i) of this section shall decrease, on a pro rata basis, the statutory groupings of earnings and profits (or deficits in statutory groupings of earnings and profits) of the distributing corporation. Thus, for example, a pro rata portion of a foreign distributing corporation's separate categories, post-1986 undistributed earnings, and annual layers of pre-1987 accumulated profits and pre-1987 section 960 earnings and profits shall be allocated or reduced.

(3) *Foreign income taxes.*—Pre-transaction taxes of a distributing corporation shall be ratably allocated or reduced only to the extent described in paragraphs (d)(3) and (e)(3) of this section. Thus, a distributing corporation's excess foreign taxes described in section 904(c) shall not be allocated or reduced under this section.

(4) *Divisive D reorganization with a preexisting controlled corporation.*—In the case of a foreign divisive transaction that includes a D reorganization with a controlled corporation that is not newly created (a preexisting controlled corporation), paragraph (b)(1)(i) of this section shall apply in the following manner:

(i) *Calculation of earnings and profits of distributing corporation.*—The pre-transaction earnings of a distributing corporation shall be reduced by the sum of—

(A) The amount of the reduction in the pre-transaction earnings of the distributing corporation as described in § 1.312-10(a) (as determined under this section); and

(B) The amount of the reduction in the pre-transaction earnings of the distributing corporation as described in § 1.312-10(b) (as determined under this section).

(ii) *Calculation of earnings and profits of controlled corporation.*—The amount of earnings and profits of the controlled corporation immediately after the foreign divisive transaction shall equal the sum of—

(A) The amount described in paragraph (b)(4)(i)(A) of this section (except to the extent such amounts are included in income as a deemed dividend pursuant to the foreign divisive transaction or are subject to the rule of § 1.367(b)-3(f)); and

(B) The amount of earnings and profits of the controlled corporation immediately before the foreign divisive transaction.

(c) *Foreign divisive transactions involving a domestic distributing corporation and a foreign controlled corporation.*—(1) *Scope.*—The rules of this paragraph (c) apply to a foreign divisive transaction involving a domestic distributing corporation and a foreign controlled corporation.

(2) *Earnings and profits allocated to a foreign controlled corporation.*—Pre-transaction earnings of a domestic distributing corporation that are allocated to a foreign controlled corporation under the rules described in paragraph (b)(1)(i) of this section shall not be included in the foreign controlled corporation's post-1986 undistributed earnings, pre-1987 accumulated profits, or pre-1987 section 960 earnings and profits. In addition, if a distribution by the domestic distributing corporation out of pre-transaction earnings immediately before the foreign divisive transaction would have been treated as a U.S. source dividend under section 861(a)(2)(A) that would not be exempt from tax under section 871(i)(2)(B) or 881(d), a distribution out of such earnings and profits by the foreign controlled corporation shall be treated as a U.S. source dividend under section 904(g) and for purposes of Chapter 3 of subtitle A of the Internal Revenue Code. See *Georday Enterprises v. Commissioner*, 126 F.2d 384 (4th Cir. 1942). See also sections 243(e) and 861(a)(2)(C) and § 1.367(b)-2(j) for other rules that may apply.

(3) *Examples.*—The following examples illustrate the application of the rules of this section to transactions described in paragraph (c)(1) of this section. The examples presume the following facts: USD is a domestic corporation engaged in manufacturing and shipping activities through Business A and Business B, respectively. FC is a foreign corporation that is wholly owned by USD. USD and FC use calendar taxable years. FC (and all of its qualified business units as defined in section 989) maintains a "u" functional currency and, except as otherwise specified, 1u = US$1 at all times. The examples are as follows:

Example 1—(i) *Facts.* The stock of USD is owned in equal parts by three shareholders, USP (a domestic corporation), USI (a United States citizen), and FP (a foreign corporation). USD owns assets with total net bases of $260 (including $100 attributable to the Business B shipping assets, which have a $160 fair market value). USD has $500 of earnings and profits (that it accumulated). The entire $500 would have been treated as a U.S. source dividend under section 861(a)(2)(A) that would not be exempt from tax under sections 871(i)(2)(B) or 881(d) if distributed by USD immediately before the foreign divisive transaction. On January 1, 2002, USD incorporates FC and transfers to FC the Business B shipping assets. USD then distributes the FC stock pro rata to USP, USI, and FP. The transaction meets the requirements of sections 368(a)(1)(D) and 355.

(ii) Result—(A) *Gain Recognition.* Under section 367(a)(5), USD recognizes gain equal to the difference between the fair market value and USD's adjusted basis in the Business B shipping assets ($160 – $100 = $60).

(B) *Calculation of USD's earnings and profits.* Under paragraph (b)(1)(v) of this section, USD's pre-transaction earnings include any gain recognized or income included as a result of the foreign divisive transaction. As described in this *Example 1* (ii)(A), USD recognizes $60 of gain as a result of the foreign divisive transaction. Accordingly, USD has $560 of pre-transaction earnings ($500 + $60). Under paragraph (b)(1)(i) of this section, USD's pre-transaction earnings are reduced by an amount equal to its pre-transaction earnings times the net bases of the assets transferred to FC divided by the net bases of the assets held by USD immediately before the foreign divisive transaction ($560 × ($160 ÷ $320) = $280). Following this reduction, USD has $280 of earnings and profits ($560 – $280).

(C) *Calculation of FC's earnings and profits.* Under paragraph (b)(1)(i) of this section, the $280 reduction in USD's pre-transaction earnings is allocated to FC. Under § 1.367(b)-2(j)(1), the $280 is translated into "u" at the spot rate on January 1, 2002, to 280u. Under paragraph (c)(2) of this section, the 280u is not included as part of FC's post-1986 undistributed earnings, pre-1987 accumulated profits, or section 960 earnings and profits.

(iii) *Post-transaction distribution.* During 2002, FC does not accumulate any earnings and profits or pay or accrue any foreign income taxes. On December 31, 2002, at a time when US$1 = 0.5u, FC distributes 180u (or $360) to its shareholders. Thus, FP, USP, and USI each receive a $120 dividend. See section 989(b)(1). Under paragraph (c)(2) of this section and § 1.367(b)-2(j)(4), $93.33 of the distribution to FP is subject to withholding under Chapter 3 of subtitle A of the Internal Revenue Code ($280 ÷ 3 = $93.33). Under section 243(e) and § 1.367(b)-2(j)(3), $93.33 of the distribution to USP is eligible for the dividends received deduction. See also section 861(a)(2)(C). Under paragraph (c)(2) of this section, the remaining $26.67 distribution to USP is treated as U.S. source under section 904(g) (and is not eligible for the dividends received deduction under section 243(e)). Under paragraph (c)(2) of this section, the $120 dividend distribution to USI is treated as U.S. source under section 904(g).

Example 2—(i) *Facts.* The stock of USD is owned by the following unrelated persons: 20 percent by USP (a domestic corporation), 20 percent by USI (a United States citizen), and 60 percent by FP (a foreign corporation). FC is a preexisting controlled corporation that was incorporated in 1995 and USD always has owned all of the FC stock. USD owns assets with total net bases of $320 (including $160 attributable to the FC stock), and USD has $500 of earnings and profits. FC has 150u of earnings and profits in the section 904(d)(1)(D) shipping separate category and has $60 of related foreign income taxes. FC's earnings and profits qualified for the high tax exception from subpart F income under section 954(b)(4), and USD elected to exclude the earnings and profits from subpart F income under section 954(b)(4) and § 1.954-1(d)(5). On January 1, 2002, USD distributes the stock of FC to its shareholders in a transaction that meets the requirements of section 355. FC is not a controlled foreign corporation after the foreign divisive transaction. On the date of the foreign divisive transaction, the FC stock has a $460 fair market value.

(ii) *Result*—(A) *Gain Recognition.* Under § 1.367(b)-5(b)(1)(ii), USD recognizes gain equal to the difference between the fair market value and USD's adjusted basis in the FC stock distributed to USI. Under § 1.367(e)-1(b)(1), USD recognizes gain equal to the difference between the fair market value and USD's adjusted basis in the FC stock distributed to FP. As a result of the transfers to USI and FP, USD recognizes gain of $240 (4/5 × ($460 − $160)), $120 of which is included in USD's income as a dividend under section 1248(a) and (f)(1) (4/5 × 150u, translated at the spot rate under section 989(b)(2)). Under section 1248(a) and (f)(1), USD includes as a dividend the difference between the fair market value and its adjusted basis in the FC stock distributed to USP to the extent of FC's earnings and profits attributable to the distributed stock. For further guidance, see also Notice 87-64 (1987-2 C.B. 375) (see also § 601.601(d)(2) of this chapter). As a result of this transfer, USD includes a $30 dividend under section 1248(a) and (f)(1) (1/5 × 150u). USD qualifies for a section 902 deemed paid foreign tax credit with respect to its $150 of section 1248 dividends.

(B) *Calculation of USD's earnings and profits.* Under paragraph (b)(1)(v) of this section, USD's pre-transaction earnings include any gain recognized or income included as a result of the foreign divisive transaction. As described in this *Example 2* (ii)(A), USD recognizes and includes a total of $270 of gain and dividend income as a result of the foreign divisive transaction. Accordingly, USD has $770 of pre-transaction earnings ($500 + $270). Under paragraphs (b)(1)(i) and (b)(1)(ii)(A) of this section, USD's pre-transaction earnings are reduced by the amount of the reduction that would have been required if USD had transferred the stock of FC to a new corporation in a D reorganization. Thus, USD's pre-transaction earnings are reduced by an amount equal to its pre-transaction earnings times its net basis in the FC stock divided by the net bases of the assets held by USD immediately before the foreign divisive transaction ($770 × ($430 ÷ $590) = $561.19). Following this reduction, USD has $208.81 of earnings and profits ($770 – $561.19).

(C) *Calculation of FC's earnings and profits.* Under paragraph (b)(1)(ii)(B) of this section, FC's earnings and profits are not increased (or replaced) as a result of the foreign divisive transaction.

Example 3—(i) *Facts.* USP, a domestic corporation, owns all of the stock of USD. FC is a preexisting controlled corporation and USD has owned all of the FC stock since FC was incorporated in 1995. USD owns assets with total net bases of $320 (including $100 attributable to the FC stock and $160 attributable to the Business B shipping assets). USD has $500 of pre-transaction earnings. FC has 150u of earnings and profits in the section 904(d)(1)(D) shipping separate category and has $60 of related foreign income taxes. FC's earnings and profits qualified for the high tax exception from subpart F income under section 954(b)(4), and USD elected to exclude the earnings and profits from subpart F income under section 954(b)(4) and § 1.954-1(d)(5). On January 1, 2002, USD transfers to FC the Business B shipping assets. USD then distributes the FC stock to USP. The transaction meets the requirements of sections 368(a)(1)(D) and 355. USD's transfer of the Business B shipping assets to FC falls within the active trade or business exception to section 367(a)(1) described in § 1.367(a)-2T. Immediately after the foreign divisive transaction, the FC stock has a $460 fair market value. USP and USD meet and comply with the requirements of section 367(a)(5) and 1248(f)(2) (and any regulations thereunder). (Sections 1.367(b)-5(b)(1)(ii) and 1.367(e)-1(b)(1) do not apply with respect to the foreign divisive transaction because the distributee, USP, is a domestic corporation.)

(ii) *Result*—(A) *Calculation of USD's earnings and profits.* Under paragraph (b)(4)(i) of this section, USD's pre-transaction earnings are reduced by the sum of the amounts described in paragraphs (b)(4)(i)(A) and (b)(4)(i)(B) of this section. Under paragraph (b)(4)(i)(A) of this section, USD's pre-transaction earnings are reduced by an amount equal to USD's pre-transaction earnings times the net bases of the assets transferred to FC divided by the total net bases of the assets held by USD immediately before the foreign divisive transaction ($500 × ($160 ÷ $320) = $250). Under paragraph (b)(4)(i)(B) of this section, USD's pre-transaction earnings are reduced by an amount equal to USD's pre-transaction earnings times USD's net basis in the stock of FC (immediately before USD's transfer of the shipping assets) divided by the total net bases of the assets held by USD immediately before the foreign divisive transaction ($500 × ($100 ÷ $320) = $156.25). The sum of the amounts described in paragraphs (b)(4)(i)(A) and (B) of this section is $406.25 ($250 + $156.25). Following the reduction described in paragraph (b)(4)(i) of this section, USD has $93.75 of earnings and profits ($500 – $406.25).

(B) *Calculation of FC's earnings and profits.* Under paragraphs (b)(4)(ii) of this section, the earnings and profits of FC immediately after the foreign divisive transaction are increased by the amount of the reduction in USD's pre-transaction earnings described in paragraph (b)(4)(i)(A) of this section ($250). Under § 1.367(b)-2(j)(1), this $250 is translated into "u" at the spot rate on January 1, 2002, to 250u. Under paragraph (c)(2) of this section, the 250u is not included as part of FC's post-1986 undistributed earnings. FC has 400u in earnings and profits (250u + 150u) immediately after the foreign divisive transaction.

(iii) *Post-transaction distribution.* FC does not accumulate any earnings and profits or pay or accrue any foreign income taxes during 2002. On December 31, 2002, FC distributes 100u as a dividend to USP, which has remained its sole shareholder. Under section 989(b)(1), the 100u distribution is translated into US$ at the spot rate on December 31, 2002, to $100. Proportionate parts of the $100 dividend are attributable to the pre-transaction earnings of FC ($37.50 = $100 × (150 ÷ 400)) and USD ($62.50 = $100 × (250 ÷ 400)). See sections 243(e) and 245. Thus, under sections 243(e) and § 1.367(b)-2(j)(3), $62.50 of the distribution is eligible for the dividends received deduction. See also section 861(a)(2)(C). The remaining $37.50 of the distribution (and $15 of related foreign income taxes) is subject to the generally applicable rules concerning dividends paid by foreign corporations.

(d) *Foreign divisive transactions involving a foreign distributing corporation and a domestic controlled corporation.*—(1) *Scope.*—The rules of this paragraph (d) apply to a foreign divisive transaction involving a foreign distributing corporation and a domestic controlled corporation.

(2) *Coordination with § 1.367(b)-3.*—(i) *In general.*—In the case of a foreign divisive transaction that includes a D reorganization, the rules of § 1.367(b)-3 are applicable with respect to the pre-transaction earnings of a foreign distributing corporation that are allocable to a domestic controlled corporation under paragraph (b)(1)(i) of this section.

(ii) *Determination of all earnings and profits amount.*—An all earnings and profits amount inclusion under paragraph (d)(2)(i) of this section shall be computed with respect to the pre-transaction earnings that are allocable to the domestic controlled corporation, without regard to the parenthetical phrase in paragraph (b)(4)(ii)(A) of this section.

(iii) *Interaction with section 358 and § 1.367(b)-2(e)(3)(ii).*—The basis increase provided in § 1.367(b)-2(e)(3)(ii) shall apply to an all earnings and profits amount inclusion under paragraph (d)(2)(i) of this section, subject to the following rules—

(A) Section 358 shall apply to determine the distributee's basis in the foreign distributing and domestic controlled corporation without regard to the all earnings and profits amount inclusion;

(B) After application of the rule in paragraph (d)(2)(iii)(A) of this section, the basis increase provided in § 1.367(b)-2(e)(3)(ii) shall be applied in a manner that attributes such basis increase solely to the exchanging shareholder's stock in the domestic controlled corporation; and

(C) the rule of paragraph (d)(2)(iii)(B) of this section shall apply prior to § 1.367(b)-5(c)(4) and (d)(4).

(iv) *Coordination with § 1.367(b)-3(c).*—In applying the rule of § 1.367(b)-3(c)(2), an exchanging shareholder described in § 1.367(b)-3(c)(1) shall recognize gain with respect to the stock of the domestic controlled corporation after the foreign divisive transaction.

(v) *Special rule for U.S. persons that own foreign distributing corporation stock after a non pro rata distribution.*—[Reserved]

(3) *Foreign income taxes.*—Pre-transaction taxes related to a foreign distributing corporation's pre-transaction earnings that are allocable or are reduced under the rules described in paragraph (b)(1)(i) of this section shall be ratably reduced. Pre-transaction taxes related to a foreign distributing corporation's pre-transaction earnings that are allocable to a domestic controlled corporation under the rules described in paragraph (b)(1)(i) of this section shall not carry over to the domestic controlled corporation. Nothing in this paragraph (d)(3) shall affect the deemed paid taxes that otherwise would accompany an inclusion under § 1.367(b)-5 or paragraph (d)(2)(i) of this section.

(4) *Previously taxed earnings and profits.*—[Reserved]

(5) *Coordination with § 1.367(b)-5.*—See also § 1.367(b)-5(c) and (d) for other rules that may apply to a foreign divisive transaction described in paragraph (d)(1) of this section.

(6) *Examples.*—The following examples illustrate the application of the rules of this section to transactions described in paragraph (d)(1) of this section. The examples presume the following facts: FD is a foreign corporation engaged in manufacturing and shipping activities through Business A and Business B, respectively. Any earnings and profits of FD described in section 904(d)(1)(D) (shipping income) qualified for the high tax exception from subpart F income under section 954(b)(4), and FD'S United States shareholders elected to exclude the earnings and profits from subpart F income under section 954(b)(4) and § 1.954-1(d)(5). USC is a domestic corporation that is wholly owned by FD. FD and USC use calendar taxable years. FD (and all of its qualified business units as defined in section 989) maintains a "u" functional currency, and 1u = US$1 at all times. The examples are as follows:

Example 1—(i) *Facts.* (A) USP, a domestic corporation, has owned all of the stock of FD since FD's incorporation in 1995. USP's adjusted basis in the FD stock is $100, and the FD stock has a fair market value of $800. FD owns assets with total net bases of 320u (including 160u attributable to the Business B shipping assets), and has the following pre-transaction earnings and pre-transaction taxes accounts:

Separate Category	*E&P*	*Foreign Taxes*
General	300u	$60
Shipping	200u	$80
	500u	$140

(B) On January 1, 2002, FD incorporates USC and transfers to USC the Business B shipping assets. FD then distributes the USC stock to USP. The transaction meets the requirements of sections 368(a)(1)(D) and 355. Immediately after the foreign divisive transaction, the FD stock and the USC stock each have a fair market value of $400.

(ii) *Results*—(A) *Calculation of FD's earnings and profits.* Under paragraph (b)(1)(i) of this section, FD's pre-transaction earnings are reduced by an amount equal to its pre-transaction earnings times the net bases of the assets transferred to USC divided by the net bases of the assets held by FD immediately before the foreign divisive transaction (500u × (160u ÷ 320u) =

250u). Following this reduction, FD has 250u of earnings and profits (500u – 250u).

(B) *All earnings and profits amount inclusion.* Under § 1.367(b)-3 and paragraph (d)(2)(i) of this section, USP includes in income as an all earnings and profits amount the pre-transaction earnings of FD that are allocable to USC under paragraph (b)(1)(i) of this section. Thus, USP's all earnings and profits amount inclusion is $250. See also section 989(b)(1) and paragraph (d)(2)(ii) of this section. Under § 1.367(b)-3(b)(3)(i) and § 1.367(b)-2(e), USP includes the all earnings and profits amount as a deemed dividend received from FD immediately before the foreign divisive transaction. Because the requirements of section 902 are met, USP qualifies for a deemed paid foreign tax credit with respect to the deemed dividend that it receives from FD. Under § 1.902-1(d)(1), the $250 deemed dividend is out of FD's separate categories and reduces foreign income taxes as follows:

Separate Category	*E&P*	*Foreign Taxes*
General	150u	$30
Shipping	100u	$40
	250u	$70

(C) *Calculation of USP's basis in USC and USC's earnings and profits.* Under paragraph (d)(2)(iii) of this section, the § 1.367(b)-2(e)(3)(ii) basis increase applies with respect to USP's all earnings and profits amount inclusion from FD and is attributed solely to USP's basis in USC (after application of section 358). Accordingly, USP has a $300 basis in the USC stock ($50 section 358 basis, determined by reference to the relative values of USP's FD and USC stock: $100 pre-transaction basis × ($400 ÷ $800) + $250 § 1.367(b)-2(e)(3)(ii) basis increase = $300). Because USP included in income as a deemed dividend under § 1.367(b)-3 and paragraph (d)(2) of this section the pre-transaction earnings of FD that are allocable to USC under paragraph (b)(1)(i) of this section, such earnings and profits are not available to increase USC's earnings and profits. As a result, USC has zero earnings and profits immediately after the foreign divisive transaction.

(D) *Application of § 1.367(b)-5(c).* The basis adjustment and income inclusion rules of § 1.367(b)-5(c)(2) apply if USP's postdistribution amount with respect to FD stock is less than its predistribution amount with respect to FD stock. Under § 1.367(b)-5(e)(1), USP's predistribution amount with respect to FD stock is USP's section 1248 amount attributable to such stock computed immediately before the distribution but after taking into account the allocation of earnings and profits as a result of the D reorganization. Thus, USP's predistribution amount with respect to FD stock is $250 (500u – 250u). See also section 989(b)(2). Under section 358, USP allocates its $100 basis in FD stock between FD stock and USC stock according to the stock blocks' relative values, yielding a $50 ($100 × ($400 ÷ $800)) basis in FD stock. See also paragraph (d)(2)(iii) of this section. Under § 1.367(b)-5(e)(2), USP's postdistribution amount with respect to FD stock is USP's section 1248 amount with respect to such stock, computed immediately after the distribution. Accordingly, USP's postdistribution amount with respect to FD stock is $250. Because USP's, postdistribution amount with respect to FD stock is not less than its predistribution amount, USP is not required to make any basis adjustment or include any income under § 1.367(b)-5(c).

(E) *FD's earnings and profits after the foreign divisive transaction.* Following the reduction described in this *Example 1* (ii)(A) and (B), FD has the following earnings and profits and foreign income taxes accounts:

Separate Category	*E&P*	*Foreign Taxes*
General	150u	$30
Shipping	100u	$40
	250u	$70

Example 2—(i) *Facts.* (A) USP, a domestic corporation, has owned all of the stock of FD since FD's incorporation in 1995. USP's adjusted basis in the FD stock is $400 and the FD stock has a fair market value of $800. USC is a preexisting controlled corporation. FD owns assets with net total bases of 320u (including 160u attributable to the USC stock), and has the following pre-transaction earnings and pre-transaction taxes accounts:

Separate Category	*E&P*	*Foreign Taxes*
General	300u	$60
Shipping	200u	$80
	500u	$140

(B) On January 1, 2002, FD distributes the USC stock to USP in a transaction that meets the requirements of section 355. Immediately after the foreign divisive transaction, the FD stock and the USC stock each have a $400 fair market value.

(ii) *Results*—(A) *Calculation of FD's earnings and profits.* Under paragraphs (b)(1)(i) and (b)(1)(ii)(A) of this section, FD's pre-transaction earnings are reduced by the amount of the reduction that would have been required if FD had transferred the stock of USC to a new corporation in a D reorganization. Thus, FD's pre-transaction earnings are reduced by an amount equal to its pre-transaction earnings times its net basis in the USC stock divided by the net bases of the assets held by FD immediately before the foreign divisive transaction (500u × (160u ÷ 320u) = 250u). Following this reduction, FD has 250u of earnings and profits (500u – 250u).

(B) *Calculation of USC's earnings and profits.* Under paragraph (b)(1)(ii)(B) of this section, USC's earnings and profits are not increased (or replaced) as a result of the foreign divisive transaction. As a result, USP is not required to include an amount in income under paragraph (d)(2)(i) of this section.

(C) *Application of §1.367(b)-5(c)*. The basis adjustment and income inclusion rules of §1.367(b)-5(c)(2) apply if USP's postdistribution amount with respect to FD stock is less than its predistribution amount with respect to FD stock. Under §1.367(b)-5(e)(1), USP's predistribution amount with respect to FD stock is USP's section 1248 amount attributable to such stock computed immediately before the distribution. Thus, USP's predistribution amount with respect to FD stock is $400 (the predistribution amount is limited to USP's built-in gain in FD stock immediately before the distribution ($800 – $400)). See also section 989(b)(2). Under section 358, USP allocates its $400 basis in FD stock between FD stock and USC stock according to the stock blocks' relative values, yielding a $200 ($400 × ($400 ÷ $800)) basis in each block. Under §1.367(b)-5(e)(2), USP's postdistribution amount with respect to FD stock is USP's section 1248 amount with respect to such stock, computed immediately after the distribution. Accordingly, USP's postdistribution amount with respect to FD stock is $200 (the postdistribution amount is limited to USP's built-in gain in FD stock immediately after the distribution ($400 – $200)). Because USP's postdistribution amount with respect to FD stock is $200 less than its predistribution amount with respect to such stock ($400 – $200), §1.367(b)-5(c)(2)(i) and (ii) require USP to reduce its basis in FD stock by the $200 difference, but only to the extent such reduction increases USP's section 1248 amount with respect to the FD stock. As a result, USP reduces its basis in the FD stock from $200 to $150 and includes $150 in income as a deemed dividend from FD. Because the requirements of section 902 are met, USP qualifies for a deemed paid foreign tax credit with respect to the deemed dividend that it receives from FD. Under §1.902-1(d)(1), the $150 deemed dividend is out of FD's separate categories and reduces foreign income taxes as follows:

Separate Category	*E&P*	*Foreign Taxes*
General	90u	$18
Shipping	60u	$24
	150u	$42

(D) *Basis adjustment*. Under §1.367(b)-5(c)(3), USP does not increase its basis in FD stock as a result of USP's $150 deemed dividend from FD. Under §1.367(b)-5(c)(4), USP increases its basis in the USC stock by the amount by which it decreased its basis in the FD stock, as well as by the amount of its deemed dividend inclusion. The §1.367(b)-5(c)(4) basis increase applies in full because USP's basis in the USC stock is not increased above the fair market value of such stock. Thus, USP increases its basis in USC stock to $400 ($200 + $50 + $150).

(E) *Reduction in FD's statutory groupings of earnings and profits*. Under paragraph (b)(2) of this section, the reduction in FD's pre-transaction earnings that is not attributable to USP's inclusion under §1.367(b)-5 decreases FD's statutory groupings of earnings and profits on a pro rata basis. Under paragraph (d)(3) of this section, FD's pre-transaction taxes also are ratably reduced. As described in this *Example 2* (ii)(A), the reduction in FD's pre-transaction earnings is 250u. As described in this *Example 2* (ii)(C), 150u of the 250u reduction is attributable to an inclusion under §1.367(b)-5. As a result, under paragraphs (b)(2) and (d)(3) of this section the remaining 100u reduction in FD's pre-transaction earnings is out of the following separate categories of earnings and profits and foreign income taxes:

Separate Category	*E&P*	*Foreign Taxes*
General	60u	$12
Shipping	40u	$16
	100u	$28

(F) *FD's earnings and profits after the foreign divisive transaction*. After the reductions described in this *Example 2* (ii)(C) and (E), FD has the following earnings and profits and foreign income taxes accounts:

Separate Category	*E&P*	*Foreign Taxes*
General	150u	$30
Shipping	100u	$40
	250u	$70

Example 3—(i) *Facts*. (A) USP, a domestic corporation, has owned all of the stock of FD since FD's incorporation in 1995. USP's adjusted basis in the FD stock is $400 and the FD stock has a fair market value of $800. USC is a preexisting controlled corporation. FD owns assets with total net bases of 320u (including 160u attributable to the USC stock and 80u attributable to the Business B shipping assets), and has the following pre-transaction earnings and pre-transaction taxes accounts:

Separate Category	*E&P*	*Foreign Taxes*
General	300u	$60
Shipping	200u	$80
	500u	$140

(B) On January 1, 2002, FD transfers to USC the Business B shipping assets. FD then distributes the USC stock to USP. The transaction meets the requirements of sections 368(a)(1)(D) and 355. Immediately after the foreign divisive transaction, the FD stock has a $200 fair market value and the USC stock has a $600 fair market value.

(ii) *Results*—(A) *Calculation of FD's earnings and profits*. Under paragraph (b)(4)(i) of this section, FD's pre-transaction earnings are reduced by the sum of the amounts described in paragraphs (b)(4)(i)(A) and (B) of this section. Under paragraph (b)(4)(i)(A) of this section, FD's pre-transaction earnings are reduced by an amount equal to FD's pre-transaction earnings times the net bases of the Business B shipping assets transferred to USC divided by the total net bases of the assets held by FD immediately before the foreign divisive transaction (500u × (80u ÷ 320u) = 125u). Under paragraph (b)(4)(i)(B) of this section, FD's pre-transaction earnings are reduced by an amount equal to FD's pre-transaction earnings times FD's net basis in the stock of USC divided by the total net bases of the assets held by FD immediately before the foreign divisive transaction (500u × (160u ÷ 320u) = 250u). The sum of the amounts described in paragraphs (b)(4)(i)(A) and (B) of this section is 375u (125u + 250u).

(B) *All earnings and profits amount inclusion.* Under §1.367(b)-3 and paragraph (d)(2)(i) of this section, USP is required to include in income as an all earnings and profits amount the pre-transaction earnings of FD that are allocable to USC under paragraph (b)(1)(i) of this section. Under paragraph (b)(4)(ii)(A) of this section, the 125u of pre-transaction earnings described in paragraph (b)(4)(i)(A) are allocable to USC. Thus, the all earnings and profits amount is $125. See also section 989(b)(1) and paragraph (d)(2)(ii) of this section. Under §§1.367(b)-3(b)(3)(i) and 1.367(b)-2(e), USP includes the all earnings and profits amount as a deemed dividend received from FD immediately before the foreign divisive transaction. Because the requirements of section 902 are met, USP qualifies for a deemed paid foreign tax credit with respect to the deemed dividend that it receives from FD. Under §1.902-1(d)(1), the $125 deemed dividend is out of FD's separate categories and reduces foreign income taxes as follows:

Separate Category	*E&P*	*Foreign Taxes*
General	75u	$15
Shipping	50u	$20
	125u	$35

(C) *Calculation of USP's basis in USC and USC's earnings and profits.* Under paragraph (d)(2)(iii) of this section, the §1.367(b)-2(e)(3)(ii) basis increase applies with respect to USP's all earnings and profits amount inclusion and is attributed solely to USP's basis in USC (after application of section 358). Accordingly, USP has a $425 basis in the USC stock ($300 section 358 basis, determined by reference to the relative values of USP's FD and USC stock: $400 pre-transaction basis × ($600 ÷ $800) + $125 §1.367(b)-2(e)(3)(ii) basis increase = $425). Because USP included in income as a deemed dividend under §1.367(b)-3 and paragraph (d)(2) of this section the pre-transaction earnings of FD that are allocable to USC under paragraph (b)(1)(i) of this section, such earnings and profits are not available to increase USC's earnings and profits. As a result, USC's earnings and profits are not increased as a result of the foreign divisive transaction.

(D) *Application of §1.367(b)-5(c).* The basis adjustment and income inclusion rules of §1.367(b)-5(c)(2) apply if USP's postdistribution amount with respect to FD stock is less than its predistribution amount with respect to FD stock. Under §1.367(b)-5(e)(1) and (3), USP's predistribution amount with respect to FD stock is USP's section 1248 amount attributable to such stock computed immediately before the distribution, after the allocation of FD's pre-transaction earnings described in paragraphs (b)(4)(i)(A) and (ii)(A) of this section, but without regard to the reduction in FD's pre-transaction earnings described in paragraph (b)(4)(i)(B) of this section. Thus, USP's predistribution amount with respect to FD stock is $375 ($500 − $125). See also section 989(b)(2). Under section 358, USP allocates its $400 basis in FD stock between FD stock and USC stock according to the stock blocks' relative values, yielding a $100 ($400 × ($200 ÷ $800)) basis in FD stock. See also paragraph (d)(2)(iii) of this section. Under §1.367(b)-5(e)(2), USP's postdistribution amount with respect to FD stock is USP's section 1248 amount with respect to such stock, computed immediately after the distribution. Accordingly, USP's postdistribution amount with respect to FD stock is $100. (While FD has earnings and profits of 125u immediately after the foreign divisive transaction, USP's postdistribution amount is limited to its built-in gain in FD stock immediately after the distribution ($200 − $100).) Because USP's postdistribution amount with respect to FD stock is $275 less than its predistribution amount with respect to such stock ($375 − $100), §1.367(b)-5(c)(2)(i) and (ii) require USP to reduce its basis in FD stock, but only to the extent such reduction increases USP's section 1248 amount with respect to the FD stock. As a result, USP reduces its basis in the FD stock from $100 to $75 and includes $250 in income as a deemed dividend from FD. Because the requirements of section 902 are met, USP qualifies for a deemed paid foreign tax credit with respect to the deemed dividend that it receives from FD. Under §1.902-1(d)(1), the $250 deemed dividend is out of FD's separate categories and reduces foreign income taxes as follows:

Separate Category	*E&P*	*Foreign Taxes*
General	150u	$30
Shipping	100u	$40
	250u	$70

(E) *Basis adjustment.* Under §1.367(b)-5(c)(3), USP does not increase its basis in FD stock as a result of USP's $250 deemed dividend from FD. Under §1.367(b)-5(c)(4), USP increases its basis in the USC stock by the amount by which it decreased its basis in the FD stock, as well as by the amount of its deemed dividend inclusion, but only up to the fair market value of USP's USC stock. As described in this *Example 3* (ii)(C), USP has already increased its basis in the USC stock to $425. Because the fair market value of FD's USC stock is $600, USP's basis increase under §1.367(b)-5(c)(4) is limited to $175. See also paragraph (d)(2)(iii)(C) of this section. Thus, USP has a $600 basis in the USC stock immediately after the foreign divisive transaction.

(F) *Reduction in FD's statutory groupings of earnings and profits.* Under paragraph (b)(2) of this section, the reduction in FD's pre-transaction earnings that is not attributable to USP's inclusion under paragraph (d)(2)(i) of this section or § 1.367(b)-5 decrease FD's statutory groupings of earnings and profits on a pro rata basis. Under paragraph (d)(3) of this section, FD's pre-transaction taxes are also ratably reduced. As described in this *Example 3* (ii)(A), the reduction in FD's pre-transaction earnings is 375u. As described in this *Example 3* (ii)(B) and (D), the entire 375u reduction was subject to inclusion as a deemed dividend by USP under paragraph (d)(2)(i) of this section or § 1.367(b)-5. Thus, none of FD's pre-transaction earnings remain to be reduced under paragraph (b)(2) of this section.

(G) *FD's earnings and profits after the foreign divisive transaction.* After the reductions described in this *Example 3* (ii)(B) and (D), FD has the following earnings and profits and foreign income taxes accounts:

Separate Category	*E&P*	*Foreign Taxes*
General	75u	$15
Shipping	50u	$20
	125u	$35

(e) *Foreign divisive transactions involving a foreign distributing corporation and a foreign controlled corporation.*—(1) *Scope.*—The rules of this paragraph (e) apply to a foreign divisive transaction involving a foreign distributing corporation and a foreign controlled corporation.

(2) *Earnings and profits of foreign controlled corporation.*—(i) *In general.*—Except to the extent specified in paragraph (e)(2)(ii) of this section, pre-transaction earnings of a foreign distributing corporation that are allocated to a foreign controlled corporation under the rules described in paragraphs (b)(1)(i) and (4) of this section shall carry over to the foreign controlled corporation in accordance with the rules described in § 1.367(b)-7.

(ii) *Special rule for pre-transaction earnings allocated to a newly created controlled corporation.*—Section 1.367(b)-9 shall apply to pre-transaction earnings that are allocated from a foreign distributing corporation to a newly created foreign controlled corporation under the rules described in paragraph (b)(1)(i) of this section.

(3) *Foreign income taxes.*—Pre-transaction taxes related to a foreign distributing corporation's pre-transaction earnings that are allocated or reduced under the rules described in paragraph (b)(1)(i) of this section shall be ratably reduced. Pre-transaction taxes related to a foreign distributing corporation's pre-transaction earnings that are allocated to a foreign controlled corporation under the rules described in paragraph (b)(1)(i) of this section shall carry over to the foreign controlled corporation in accordance with the rules of § 1.367(b)-7. Section 1.367(b)-9 shall apply to pre-transaction taxes that are allocated from a foreign distributing corporation to a newly created foreign controlled corporation under the rules described in paragraph (b)(1)(i) of this section.

(4) *Previously taxed earnings and profits.*—[Reserved]

(5) *Coordination with § 1.367(b)-5.*—See also § 1.367(b)-5(c) and (d) for other rules that may apply to a foreign divisive transaction described in paragraph (e)(1) of this section.

(6) *Examples.*—The following examples illustrate the application of the rules of this section to transactions described in paragraph (e)(1) of this section. The examples presume the following facts: FD is a foreign corporation engaged in manufacturing and shipping activities through Business A and Business B, respectively. FC is a foreign corporation that is wholly owned by FD. Any earnings and profits of FD or FC described in section 904(d)(1)(D) (shipping income) qualified for the high tax exception from subpart F income under section 954(b)(4), and FD's and FC's United States shareholders elected to exclude the earnings and profits from subpart F income under section 954(b)(4) and § 1.954-1(d)(1). FD and FC have calendar taxable years. FD and FC (and all of their respective qualified business units as defined in section 989) maintain a "u" functional currency, and 1u = US$1 at all times. The examples are as follows:

Example 1—(i) *Facts.* (A) USP, a domestic corporation, has owned all of the stock of FD since FD's incorporation in 1995. USP's adjusted basis in the FD stock is $400 and the FD stock has a fair market value of $800. FD owns assets with total net bases of 320u (including 160u attributable to the Business B shipping assets), and has the following pre-transaction earnings and pre-transaction taxes accounts:

Separate Category	*E&P*	*Foreign Taxes*
General	300u	$60
Shipping	200u	$80
	500u	$140

(B) On January 1, 2002, FD incorporates FC and transfers to FC the Business B shipping assets. FD then distributes the FC stock to USP. The transaction meets the requirements of sections 368(a)(1)(D) and 355. Immediately after the foreign divisive transaction, the FD stock and the FC stock each have a $400 fair market value.

(ii) *Result*—(A) *Calculation of FD's earnings and profits.* Under paragraph (b)(1)(i) of this section, FD's pre-transaction earnings are reduced by an amount equal to its pre-transaction earnings times the net bases of the assets transferred to FC divided by the net bases of the assets held by FD immediately before the foreign divisive transaction (500u × (160u ÷ 320u) = 250u). Following this reduction, FD has 250u of earnings and profits (500u – 250u).

(B) *Application of § 1.367(b)-5(c).* The basis adjustment and income inclusion rules of § 1.367(b)-5(c)(2) apply if USP's postdistribution amount with respect to FD or FC stock is less than its predistribution amount with respect to such stock. Under § 1.367(b)-5(e)(1), USP's predistribution amount with respect to FD or FC stock is USP's section 1248 amount attributable to such stock computed immediately before the distribution but after taking into account the allocation of earnings and profits as a result of the D reorganization. Thus, USP's predistribution amounts with respect to FD and FC stock are both $200. See also section 989(b)(2) and § 1.1248-1(d)(3). Under section 358, USP allocates its $400 basis in FD stock between FD stock and FC stock according to the stock blocks' relative values, yielding a $200 ($400 × ($400 ÷ $800)) basis in each block. Under § 1.367(b)-5(e)(2), USP's postdistribution amount with respect to FD or FC stock is USP's section 1248 amount with respect to such stock, computed immediately after the distribution. Accordingly, USP's postdistribution amounts with respect to FD and FC stock are both $200. Because USP's postdistribution amounts with respect to FD and FC stock are not less than USP's respective predistribution amounts, USP is not required to make any basis adjustment or include any income under § 1.367(b)-5(c).

(C) *Reduction in FD's statutory groupings of earnings and profits*. Under paragraph (b)(2) of this section, the 250u reduction in FD's pre-transaction earnings decreases FD's statutory groupings of earnings and profits on a pro rata basis. Under paragraph (e)(3) of this section, FD's pre-transaction taxes also are ratably reduced. Accordingly, FD's pre-transaction earnings and pre-transaction taxes are reduced by the following amounts:

Separate Category	*E&P*	*Foreign Taxes*
General	150u	$30
Shipping	100u	$40
	250u	$70

(D) *Calculation of FC's earnings and profits*. Under paragraph (e)(2) of this section, the pre-transaction earnings of FD that are allocated to FC under paragraph (b)(1)(i) of this section carry over to FC in accordance with the rules of § 1.367(b)-7, subject to the rule of § 1.367(b)-9. Under paragraph (e)(3) of this section, FD's pre-transaction taxes related to the pre-transaction earnings that are allocated to FC similarly carry over to FC in accordance with the rules of § 1.367(b)-7, subject to the rule of § 1.367(b)-9. As a result, under § 1.367(b)-7(d), FC has the following earnings and profits and foreign income taxes accounts immediately after the foreign divisive transaction:

Separate Category	*E&P*	*Foreign Taxes*
General	150u	$30
Shipping	100u	$40
	250u	$70

Example 2—(i) *Facts*. (A) USP, a domestic corporation, has owned all of the stock of FD since FD's incorporation in 1995. USP's adjusted basis in the FD stock is $300 and the FD stock has a fair market value of $1,500. FC is a preexisting controlled corporation and FD has always owned all of the FC stock. FD owns assets with total net bases of 320u (including 160u attributable to the FC stock). FD and FC have the following earnings and profits and foreign income taxes accounts:

FD:

Separate Category	*E&P*	*Foreign Taxes*
General	400u	$50
Passive	(100u)	$6
Shipping	200u	$80
	500u	$136

FC:

Separate Category	*E&P*	*Foreign Taxes*
General	600u	$100
Passive	(50u)	$6
Shipping	100u	$40
	650u	$146

(B) On January 1, 2002, FD distributes the FC stock to USP in a transaction that meets the requirements of section 355. Immediately after the foreign divisive transaction, the FD stock and the FC stock each have a $750 fair market value.

(ii) *Result*—(A) *Calculation of FD's earnings and profits*. Under paragraph (b)(1)(i) and (ii)(A) of this section, FD's pre-transaction earnings are reduced by the amount of the reduction that would have been required if FD had transferred the stock of FC to a new corporation in a D reorganization. Thus, FD's pre-transaction earnings are reduced by an amount equal to its pre-transaction earnings times its net basis in the FC stock divided by the net bases of the assets held by FD immediately before the foreign divisive transaction (500u × (160u ÷ 320u) = 250u). Following this reduction, FD has 250u of earnings and profits (500u – 250u).

(B) *Application of § 1.367(b)-5(c)*. The basis adjustment and income inclusion rules of § 1.367(b)-5(c) apply if USP's postdistribution amount with respect to FD or FC stock is less than its predistribution amount with respect to such stock. Under § 1.367(b)-5(e)(1), USP's predistribution amount with respect to FD or FC stock is USP's section 1248 amount attributable to such stock computed immediately before the distribution. Thus, USP's predistribution amounts with respect to FD and FC stock are $500 and $650, respectively. See also section 989(b)(2). Under section 358, USP allocates its $300 basis in FD stock between FD stock and FC stock according to the stock blocks' relative values, yielding a $150 ($300 × ($750 ÷ $1,500)) basis in each block. Under § 1.367(b)-5(e)(2), USP's postdistribution amount with respect to FD or FC stock is USP's section 1248 amount with respect to such stock, computed immediately after the distribution. Accordingly, USP's postdistribution amount with respect to FD stock is $250 (500u – 250u), and its postdistribution amount with respect to FC stock is $600 (while FC has 650u of earnings and profits immediately after the foreign divisive transaction, USP's postdistribution amount is limited to its built-in gain in FC stock immediately after the distribution ($750 – $150)). USP's postdistribution amount with respect to both the FD and FC stock is less than its predistribution amount with respect to such stock. This difference is $50 with respect to FC ($650 – $600), and $250 with respect to FD ($500 – $250). Under § 1.367(b)-5(c)(2)(i) and (ii), USP is required to reduce its basis in the FD and FC stock, but only to the extent such reductions increase USP's section 1248 amount with respect to the stock. Accordingly, USP reduces its basis in the FC stock by $50, and thereafter USP has a $100 basis in such stock ($150 – $100). Because a reduction in USP's basis in FD stock would not increase any of USP's section 1248 amount with respect to such stock, USP includes the entire $250 difference between its predistribution and postdistribution amounts with respect to the FD stock as a deemed dividend from FD. Because the requirements of section 902 are met, USP qualifies for a deemed paid foreign tax credit with respect to the deemed dividend that it receives from FD. Under § 1.960-1(i)(4), the 100u deficit in the section 904(d)(1)(A) passive separate category is allocated proportionately against the other separate categories for purposes of computing the deemed paid credit on the distribution. Thus, there are 333.33u (400u – (100u × (400u ÷ 600u))) of available earnings in the section 904(d)(1)(I) general separate category (along with $50 of foreign income taxes) and 166.67u (200u – (100u × (200u ÷ 600u))) of available earnings in the section 904(d)(1)(D) shipping separate category (along with $80 of foreign income taxes). Under § 1.902-1(d)(1), the $250 deemed dividend is out of FD's separate categories and reduces foreign income taxes as follows:

Separate Category	*E&P*	*Foreign Taxes*
General	166.67u	$25
Passive	0u	$0
Shipping	83.33u	$40
	250u	$65

(C) *Basis adjustments.* Under § 1.367(b)-5(c)(3), USP does not increase its basis in FD stock as a result of USP's $250 deemed dividend from FD. Under § 1.367(b)-5(c)(4), USP increases its basis in the FD and FC stock by the amount of its basis decrease or deemed dividend inclusion with respect to the other corporation, but only to the extent such basis increase does not diminish USP's postdistribution amount with respect to that other corporation and only to the extent of the other corporation's fair market value. Under these rules, USP increases its basis in the FD stock by the full amount by which it decreased its basis in FC ($150 + $50 = $200). USP does not increase its basis in the FC stock as a result of its deemed dividend from FD because any increase in the FC stock basis would diminish USP's postdistribution amount with respect to such stock.

(D) *FD's earnings and profits after the foreign divisive transaction.* Because the entire $250 reduction in FD's pre-transaction earnings was subject to inclusion under § 1.367(b)-5 (as described in this *Example 2* (ii)(B)), paragraph (b)(2) of this section does not apply. FD has the following earnings and profits and foreign income taxes accounts immediately after the foreign divisive transaction (see § 1.960-1(i)(4)):

Separate Category	*E&P*	*Foreign Taxes*
General	233.33u	$25
Passive	(100u)	$6
Shipping	116.67u	$40
	250u	$71

(E) *Calculation of FC's earnings and profits.* Under paragraph (b)(1)(ii)(B) of this section, FC's earnings and profits are not increased (or replaced) as a result of the foreign divisive transaction. FC's earnings and profits also are not reduced because USP was not required to include a deemed dividend out of FC under § 1.367(b)-5.

Example 3—(i) *Facts.* (A) USP, a domestic corporation, has owned all of the stock of FD since FD's incorporation in 1995. USP's adjusted basis in the FD stock is $100 and the FD stock has a fair market value of $2,000. FC is a preexisting controlled corporation and FD has always owned all of the FC stock. FD owns assets with total net bases of 320u (including 100u attributable to the FC stock and 160u attributable to the Business B shipping assets). FD and FC have the following earnings and profits and foreign income taxes accounts:

FD:

Separate Category	*E&P*	*Foreign Taxes*
General	300u	$50
10/50 dividends from FC1, a noncontrolled section 902 corporation	100u	$6
Shipping	200u	$80
	600u	$136

FC:

Separate Category	*E&P*	*Foreign Taxes*
General	100u	$10
Passive	(50u)	$6

Shipping	100u	$40
	150u	$56

(B) On January 1, 2002, FD transfers to FC the Business B shipping assets. FD then distributes the FC stock to USP. The transaction meets the requirements of sections 368(a)(1)(D) and 355. Immediately after the foreign divisive transaction, the FD stock and the FC stock each have a $1,000 fair market value.

(ii) *Result*—(A) *Calculation of FD's earnings and profits*. Under paragraph (b)(4)(i) of this section, FD's pre-transaction earnings are reduced by the sum of the amounts described in paragraphs (b)(4)(i)(A) and (B) of this section. Under paragraph (b)(4)(i)(A) of this section, FD's pre-transaction earnings are reduced by an amount equal to FD's pre-transaction earnings times the net bases of the Business B shipping assets transferred to FC divided by the total net bases in the assets held by FD immediately before the foreign divisive transaction (600u × (160u ÷ 320u) = 300u). Under paragraph (b)(4)(i)(B) of this section, FD's pre-transaction earnings are reduced by an amount equal to FD's pre-transaction earnings times FD's net bases in the stock of FC divided by the total net bases of the assets held by FD immediately before the foreign divisive transaction (600u × (100u ÷ 320u) = 187.50u). The sum of the amounts described in paragraphs (b)(4)(i)(A) and (B) of this section is 487.50u.

(B) *Application of §1.367(b)-5(c)*. The basis adjustment and income inclusion rules of §1.367(b)-5(c)(2) apply if USP's postdistribution amount with respect to FD or FC stock is less than its predistribution amount with respect to such stock. Under §1.367(b)-5(e)(1) and (3), USP's predistribution amount with respect to FD or FC stock is USP's section 1248 amount attributable to such stock computed immediately before the distribution, after the allocation of FD's pre-transaction earnings described in paragraphs (b)(4)(i)(A) and (ii)(A) of this section, but before the reduction in FD's pre-transaction earnings described in paragraph (b)(4)(i)(B) of this section. Thus, USP's predistribution amounts with respect to FD and FC stock are $300 (600u – 300u) and $450 (150u + 300u), respectively. See also section 989(b)(2). Under section 358, USP allocates its $100 basis in FD stock between FD stock and FC stock according to the stock blocks' relative values, yielding a $50 ($100 × ($1,000 ÷ $2,000)) basis in each block. Under §1.367(b)-5(e)(2), USP's postdistribution amount with respect to FD or FC stock is USP's section 1248 amount with respect to such stock, computed immediately after the distribution. Accordingly, USP's postdistribution amount with respect to FD stock is $112.50 (600u – 300u – 187.50u), and its postdistribution amount with respect to FC stock is $450 (150u + 300u). Because USP's postdistribution amount with respect to FC stock is not less than its predistribution amount with respect to such stock, the §1.367(b)-5(c)(2) basis adjustment and income inclusion rules do not apply with respect to the FC stock. Because USP's postdistribution amount with respect to FD stock is $187.50 less than its predistribution amount with respect to such stock ($300 – $112.50), §1.367(b)-5(c)(2)(i) and (ii) require USP to reduce its basis in FD stock, but only to the extent such reduction increases USP's section 1248 amount with respect to the FD stock. Because a reduction in USP's basis in the FD stock would not increase any of USP's section 1248 amount with respect to such stock, USP includes the entire $187.50 difference between its predistribution and postdistribution amounts with respect to the FD stock as a deemed dividend from FD. Because the requirements of section 902 are met, USP qualifies for a deemed paid foreign tax credit with respect to the deemed dividend that it receives from FD. Under §1.902-1(d)(1), the $187.50 deemed dividend is out of FD's separate categories and reduces foreign income taxes as follows:

Separate Category	*E&P*	*Foreign Taxes*
General	93.75u	$15.63
10/50 dividends from FC1	31.25u	$1.88
Shipping	62.50u	$25
	187.50u	$42.51

(C) *Basis adjustment*. Under §1.367(b)-5(c)(3), the basis increase provided in §1.367(b)-2(e)(3)(ii) does not apply with respect to USP's $187.50 deemed dividend from FD. Under §1.367(b)-5(c)(4), USP increases its basis in the FC stock by the amount of its deemed dividend inclusion from FD, but only to the extent such basis increase does not diminish USP's postdistribution amount with respect to FC stock and only up to the fair market value of the FC stock. Under these rules, USP increases its basis in the FC stock by the full amount of its deemed dividend from FD ($50 + $187.50 = $237.50).

(D) *Reduction in FD's statutory groupings of earnings and profits*. Under paragraph (b)(2) of this section, the reduction in FD's pre-transaction earnings that is not attributable to USP's inclusion under §1.367(b)-5 decreases FD's statutory groupings of earnings and profits on a pro rata basis. Under paragraph (e)(3) of this section, FD's pre-transaction taxes are also ratably reduced. As described in this *Example 3* (ii)(A), the reduction in FD's pre-transaction earnings is 487.50u. As described in this *Example 3* (ii)(B), 187.50u of the 487.50u reduction is attributable to a deemed dividend inclusion by USP under §1.367(b)-5. Thus, under paragraphs (b)(2) and (e)(3) of this section, the remaining 300u reduction in FD's pre-transaction earnings and related pre-transaction taxes is out of FD's separate categories and reduces foreign income taxes as follows:

Separate Category	*E&P*	*Foreign Taxes*
General	150u	$25
10/50 dividends from FC1	50u	$3
Shipping	100u	$40
	300u	$68

(E) *Calculation of FC's earnings and profits.* Under paragraph (b)(4)(ii) of this section, FC's earnings and profits immediately after the foreign divisive transaction equal the sum of FC's earnings and profits immediately before the foreign divisive transaction, plus the amount of the reduction in FD's earnings and profits described in paragraph (b)(4)(i)(A) of this section, except to the extent such amount was included in income as a deemed dividend pursuant to the foreign divisive transaction. The reduction in FD's earnings and profits described in paragraph (b)(4)(i)(A) of this section is 300u, none of which was included in income by USP as a deemed dividend pursuant to the foreign divisive transaction. Under paragraphs (e)(2) and (3) of this section, the 300u of pre-transaction earnings and related pre-transaction taxes carry over to FC and combine with FC's earnings and profits and foreign income taxes accounts in accordance with the rules described in §1.367(b)-7. Under §1.367(b)-7(d), FC has the following earnings and profits and foreign income taxes accounts immediately after the foreign divisive transaction:

Separate Category	*E&P*	*Hovering Deficit*	*Taxes*	*Taxes Associated w/Hovering Deficit*
General	250u		$35	
10/50 dividends from FC1	50u		$3	
Passive		(50u)		$6
Shipping	200u		$80	
	500u	(50u)	$118	$6

(F) *FD's earnings and profits after the foreign divisive transaction.* Following the reductions described in this *Example 3* (ii)(B) and (D), FD has the following earnings and profits and foreign income taxes accounts:

Separate Category	*E&P*	*Foreign Taxes*
General	56.25u	$9.37
10/50 dividends from FC1	18.75u	$1.12
Shipping	37.50u	$15
	112.50u	$25.49

(f) *Effective date.*—This section shall apply to section 367(b) exchanges that occur on or after the date 30 days after these regulations are published as final regulations in the Federal Register. [Reg. §1.367(b)-8.]

Corporate Reorganizations: Foreign Corporations

Reorganizations: Foreign Corporations: Transfer of Property.—Temporary Reg. §1.367(d)-1T, relating to transfers of property to foreign corporations, is proposed (published in the Federal Register on May 16, 1986) (LR-3-86).

§1.367(d)-1. Transfers of intangible property to foreign corporations.

Foreign Corporations: Stock Transfer Rules: Carryover of Earnings and Taxes

Foreign Corporations: Stock Transfer Rules: Carryover of Earnings and Taxes.—Amendments to Reg. §1.367(e)-1, addressing (1) the carryover of certain tax attributes, such as earnings and profits and foreign income tax accounts, when two corporations combine in a section 367(b) transaction and (2) the allocation of certain tax attributes when a corporation distributes stock of another corporation in a section 367(b) transaction, are proposed (published in the Federal Register on November 15, 2000) (REG-116050-99).

☐ Par. 12. In §1.367(e)-1, paragraph (a) is amended by adding a sentence at the end of the paragraph to read as follows:

§1.367(e)-1. Distributions described in section 367(e)(1).—(a) * * * See §1.367(b)-8(c)(3) for an example illustrating the interaction of §1.367(e)-1 with other sections of the Internal Revenue Code (such as sections 367(b) and 1248).

* * *

Section 301 Regulations: Statutory Changes Reflected

Section 301 Regulations: Statutory Changes Reflected.—Amendments to Reg. §1.368-2, updating existing regulations under section 301 to reflect statutory changes made by the Technical and Miscellaneous Revenue Act of 1988, which changes provide that the amount of a distribution of property made by a corporation to its shareholder is the fair market value of the distributed property, are proposed (published in the Federal Register on March 26, 2019) (REG-121694-16).

Par. 4. Section 1.368-2 is amended by revising the last sentence of paragraph (m)(3)(iii) to read as follows:

§1.368-2. Definition of terms.

* * *

(m) * * *

(3) * * *

(iii) * * * See §1.301-1(j).

* * *

Advance Payments for Goods and Long-Term Contracts: Existing Regulations Removed

Advance Payments for Goods and Long-Term Contracts: Existing Regulations Removed.—Amendments to Reg. §1.381(c)(4)-1, removing regulations regarding advance payments for goods and long-term contracts that are no longer necessary after the enactment of recent tax legislation, are proposed (published in the Federal Register on October 15, 2018) (REG-104872-18).

Par. 2. Section 1.381(c)(4)-1 is amended by revising the second sentence of paragraph (b)(2) to read as follows:

§1.381(c)(4)-1. Method of accounting.

* * *

(b) * * *

(2) * * * The installment method under section 453, the mark-to-market method under section 475, the amortization of bond premium under section 171, the percentage of completion method under section 460, the recurring item exception of §1.461-5, and the income deferral method under section 455 are examples of special methods of accounting.* * *

* * *

Deduction for Business Interest Expense: Limitation

Deduction for Business Interest Expense: Limitation.—Reg. §1.381(c)(20)-1, regarding the limitation on the deduction for business interest expense after the enactment of recent tax legislation, is proposed (published in the Federal Register on December 28, 2018) (REG-106089-18).

Par. 5. Section 1.381(c)(20)-1 is added to read as follows:

§1.381(c)(20)-1. Carryforward of disallowed business interest.—(a) *Carryover requirement.*—Section 381(c)(20) provides that the acquiring corporation in a transaction described in section 381(a) will succeed to and take into account the carryover of disallowed business interest described in section 163(j)(2) to taxable years ending after the date of distribution or transfer.

(b) *Carryover of disallowed business interest described in section 163(j)(2).*—For purposes of section 381(c)(20) and this section, the term *carryover of disallowed business interest described in section 163(j)(2)* means the disallowed business interest expense carryforward (within the meaning of §1.163(j)-1(b)(9)), including any disallowed disqualified interest (within the meaning of §1.163(j)-1(b)(10)), and including the distributor or transferor corporation's disallowed business interest expense from the taxable year that ends on the date of distribution or transfer. For the application of section 382 to disallowed business interest expense described in section 163(j)(2), see the regulations under section 382, including but not limited to §1.382-2.

(c) *Limitation on use of disallowed business interest expense carryforwards in the acquiring corporation's first taxable year ending after the date of distribution or transfer.*—(1) *In general.*—In determining the extent to which the acquiring corporation may use disallowed business interest expense carryforwards in its first taxable year ending after the date of distribution or transfer, the principles of §§1.381(c)(1)-1 and 1.381(c)(1)-2 apply with appropriate adjustments, including but not limited to the adjustments described in paragraphs (c)(2) and (3) of this section.

(2) *One date of distribution or transfer within the acquiring corporation's taxable year.*—If the acquiring corporation succeeds to the disallowed business interest expense carryforwards of one or more distributor or transferor corporations on a single date of distribution or transfer within one taxable year of the acquiring corporation, then, for the acquiring corporation's first taxable year ending after the date of distribution or transfer, that part of the acquiring corporation's business interest expense deduction (if any) that is attributable to the disallowed business interest expense carryforwards of the distributor or transferor corporation is limited under this paragraph (c) to an amount equal to the post-acquisition portion of the acquiring corporation's section 163(j) limitation, as defined in paragraph (c)(4) of this section.

(3) *Two or more dates of distribution or transfer in the taxable year.*—If the acquiring corporation succeeds to the disallowed business interest expense carryforwards of two or more distributor or transferor corporations on two or more dates of distribution or transfer within one taxable year of the acquiring corporation, the limitation to be applied under this paragraph (c) is determined by applying the principles of §1.381(c)(1)-2(b) to the post-acquisition portion of the acquiring corporation's section 163(j) limitation, as defined in paragraph (c)(4) of this section.

(4) *Definition.*—For purposes of this paragraph (c), the term *post-acquisition portion of the acquiring corporation's section 163(j) limitation* means the amount that bears the same ratio to the acquiring corporation's section 163(j) limitation (within the meaning of §1.163(j)-1(b)(31)) (or, if the acquiring corporation is a member of a consolidated group, the consolidated group's section 163(j) limitation) for the first taxable year ending after the date of distribution or transfer (taking into account items to which the acquiring corporation succeeds under section 381, other than disallowed business interest expense carryforwards) as the number of days in that year after the date of distribution or transfer bears to the total number of days in that year.

(5) *Examples.*—For purposes of this paragraph (c)(5), unless otherwise stated, X, Y, and Z are taxable domestic C corporations that were incorporated on January 1, 2018 and that file their tax returns on a calendar-year basis; none of X, Y, or Z is a member of a consolidated group; the small business exemption in §1.163(j)-2(d) does not apply; interest expense is deductible except to the extent of the potential application of section 163(j); and the facts set forth the only corporate activity. The principles

of this paragraph (c) are illustrated by the following examples.

(i) *Example 1: Transfer before last day of acquiring corporation's taxable year*—(A) *Facts.* On October 31, 2019, X transferred all of its assets to Y in a statutory merger to which section 361 applies. For the 2018 taxable year, X had $400x of disallowed business interest expense, and Y had $0 of disallowed business interest expense. For the taxable year ending October 31, 2019, X had an additional $350x of disallowed business interest expense (X did not deduct any of its 2018 carryforwards in its 2019 taxable year). For the taxable year ending December 31, 2019, Y had business interest expense of $100x, business interest income of $200x, and adjusted taxable income (ATI) of $1,000x. Y's section 163(j) limitation for the 2019 taxable year was $500x ($200x + (30 percent x $1,000x) = $500x).

(B) *Analysis.* Pursuant to § 1.163(j)-5(b)(2), Y deducts its $100x of current-year business interest expense (as defined in § 1.163(j)-5(a)(2)(i)) before any disallowed business interest expense carryforwards (including X's carryforwards) from a prior taxable year are deducted. The aggregate disallowed business interest expense of X carried forward under section 381(c)(20) to Y's taxable year ending December 31, 2019, is $750x. However, pursuant to paragraph (c)(2) of this section, for Y's first taxable year ending after the date of distribution or transfer, the maximum amount of X's disallowed business interest expense carryforwards that Y can deduct is equal to the post-acquisition portion of Y's section 163(j) limitation. Pursuant to paragraph (c)(4) of this section, the post-acquisition portion of Y's section 163(j) limitation means Y's section 163(j) limitation times the ratio of the number of days in the taxable year after the date of distribution or transfer to the total number of days in that year. Therefore, only $84x of the aggregate amount ($500x x (61/365) = $84x) may be deducted by Y in that year, and the remaining $666x ($750x - $84x = $666x) is carried forward to the succeeding taxable year.

(C) *Transfer on last day of acquiring corporation's taxable year.* The facts are the same as in *Example 1* in paragraph (c)(5)(i)(A) of this section, except that X's transfer of its assets to Y occurred on December 31, 2019. For the taxable year ending December 31, 2019, X had an additional $350x of disallowed business interest expense (X did not deduct any of its 2018 carryforwards in its 2019 taxable year). For the taxable year ending December 31, 2020, Y had business interest expense of $100x, business interest income of $200x, and ATI of $1,000x. Y's section 163(j) limitation for the 2020 taxable year was $500x ($200x + (30 percent x $1,000x) = $500x). The aggregate disallowed business interest expense of X carried under section 381(c)(20) to Y's taxable year ending December 31, 2020, is $750x. Paragraph (c)(2) of this section does not limit the amount of X's disallowed business interest expense carryforwards that may be deducted by Y in the 2020 taxable year. Since the amount of Y's section 163(j) limit for the 2020 taxable year was $500x, Y may deduct the full amount ($100x) of its own business interest expense for the 2020 taxable year, along with $400x of X's disallowed business interest expense carryforwards.

(ii) *Example 2: Multiple transferors on same date*—(A) *Facts.* On October 31, 2019, X and Y transferred all of their assets to Z in statutory mergers to which section 361 applies. For the 2018 taxable year, X had $300x of disallowed business interest expense, Y had $200x, and Z had $0. For the taxable year ending October 31, 2019, each of X and Y had an additional $125x of disallowed business interest expense (neither X nor Y deducted any of its 2018 carryforwards in 2019). For the taxable year ending December 31, 2019, Z had business interest expense of $100x, business interest income of $200x, and ATI of $1,000x. Z's section 163(j) limitation for the 2019 taxable year was $500x ($200x + (30 percent x $1,000x) = $500x).

(B) *Analysis.* The aggregate disallowed business interest expense of X and Y carried under section 381(c)(20) to Z's taxable year ending December 31, 2019, is $750x. However, pursuant to paragraph (c)(2) of this section, only $84x of the aggregate amount ($500x x (61/365) = $84x) may be deducted by Z in that year. Moreover, under paragraph (b)(2) of this section, this amount only may be deducted by Z in that year after Z has deducted its $100 of current-year business interest expense (as defined in § 1.163(j)-5(a)(2)(i)).

(d) *Applicability date.*—This section applies to taxable years ending after the date the Treasury decision adopting these regulations as final regulations is published in the **Federal Register**. However, taxpayers and their related parties, within the meaning of sections 267(b) and 707(b)(1), may apply the rules of this section to a taxable year beginning after December 31, 2017, so long as the taxpayers and their related parties consistently apply the rules of this section, the section 163(j) regulations (within the meaning of § 1.163(j)-1(b)(32)), and if applicable, §§ 1.263A-9, 1.381(c)(20)-1, 1.382-6, 1.383-1, 1.469-9, 1.882-5, 1.1502-13, 1.1502-21, 1.1502-36, 1.1502-79, 1.1502-91 through 1.1502-99 (to the extent they effectuate the rules of §§ 1.382-6 and 1.383-1), and 1.1504-4 to those taxable years. [Reg. § 1.381(c)(20)-1.]

Deduction for Business Interest Expense: Limitation

Deduction for Business Interest Expense: Limitation.—Amendments to Reg. §§ 1.382-1 and 1.382-2, regarding the limitation on the deduction for business interest expense after the enactment of recent tax legislation, are proposed (published in the Federal Register on December 28, 2018) (REG-106089-18).

Par. 6. Section 1.382-1 is amended by:

1. Adding entries for § 1.382-2(a)(7) and (8);
2. Revising the entry for § 1.382-2(b)(3);
3. Adding entries for § 1.382-6(b)(4), (b)(4)(i), and (b)(4)(ii);
4. Revising the entry for § 1.382-6(h); and
5. Adding entries for § 1.382-6(h)(1) and (2).

The additions and revisions read as follows:

§1.382-1. Table of contents.

* * *

§1.382-2 General rules for ownership change.

(a) * * *

(7) Section 382 disallowed business interest carryforward.

(8) Testing period.

(b) * * *

(3) Rules provided in paragraphs (a)(1)(i)(A), (a)(1)(ii), (iv), and (v), (a)(2)(iv) through (vi), (a)(3)(i), and (a)(4) through (8) of this section.

* * *

§1.382-6 Allocation of income and loss to periods before and after the change date for purposes of section 382.

* * *

(b) * * *

(4) Allocation of business interest expense.

(i) In general.

(ii) Example.

* * *

(h) Applicability date.

(1) In general.

(2) Paragraphs (b)(1) and (4) of this section.

* * *

Par. 7. Section 1.382-2 is amended by:

1. Revising paragraph (a)(1)(i)(A);
2. Removing ", or" and adding "; or" in its place at the end of paragraph (a)(1)(i)(B);
3. Revising paragraphs (a)(1)(ii) introductory text and (a)(1)(ii)(A);
4. Removing ", and" and adding "; and" in its place at the end of paragraph (a)(1)(ii)(B);
5. Removing the last sentence in paragraphs (a)(1)(iv) and (v);
6. Removing the commas and adding semicolons in their place at the end of paragraphs (a)(2)(i) and (iii);
7. Removing the period and adding a semicolon in its place at the end of paragraph (a)(2)(ii);
8. Removing ", and" and adding a semicolon in its place at the end of paragraph (a)(2)(iv);
9. Removing "1.383-1T(c)(3)." and adding §1.383-1T(c)(3); and" in its place in paragraph (a)(2)(v);
10. Adding paragraph (a)(2)(vi);
11. Removing the last sentence in paragraphs (a)(3)(i), (a)(4)(i), and (a)(5) and (6);
12. Adding paragraphs (a)(7) and (8); and
13. Revising paragraph (b)(3).

The revisions and additions read as follows:

§1.382-2. General rules for ownership change.—(a) * * *

(1) * * *

(i) * * *

(A) Is entitled to use a net operating loss carryforward, a capital loss carryover, a carryover of excess foreign taxes under section 904(c), a carryforward of a general business credit under section 39, a carryover of a minimum tax credit under section 53, or a section 382 disallowed business interest carryforward described in paragraph (a)(7) of this section;

* * *

(ii) *Distributor or transferor loss corporation in a transaction under section 381.*—Notwithstanding that a loss corporation ceases to exist under state law, if its disallowed business interest expense carryforwards, net operating loss carryforwards, excess foreign taxes, or other items described in section 381(c) are succeeded to and taken into account by an acquiring corporation in a transaction described in section 381(a), such loss corporation shall be treated as continuing in existence until—

(A) Any pre-change losses (excluding pre-change credits described in §1.383-1(c)(3)), determined as if the date of such transaction were the change date, are fully utilized or expire under section 163(j), 172, or 1212;

* * *

(2) * * *

(vi) Any section 382 disallowed business interest carryforward.

* * *

(7) *Section 382 disallowed business interest carryforward.*—The term *section 382 disallowed business interest carryforward* includes the following items:

(i) The loss corporation's disallowed business interest expense carryforwards, as defined in §1.163(j)-1(b)(9), including disallowed disqualified interest, within the meaning of §1.163(j)-1(b)(10), as of the ownership change.

(ii) The carryforward of the loss corporation's disallowed business interest expense (within the meaning of §1.163(j)-1(b)(8)) paid or accrued (without regard to section 163(j)) in the pre-change period (within the meaning of §1.382-6(g)(2)) in the year of the testing date, determined by allocating an equal portion of the disallowed business interest expense paid or accrued (without regard to section 163(j)) in the year of the testing date to each day in that year, regardless of whether the loss corporation has made a closing-of-the-books election under §1.382-6(b)(2).

(8) *Testing period.*—Notwithstanding the temporal limitations provided in §1.382-2T(d)(3)(i), the testing period for a loss corporation can begin as early as the first day of the first taxable year from which there is a section 382 disallowed business interest carryforward to the first taxable year ending after the testing date.

(b) * * *

(3) *Rules provided in paragraphs (a)(1)(i)(A), (a)(1)(ii), (iv), and (v), (a)(2)(iv) through (vi), (a)(3)(i), and (a)(4) through (8) of this section.*—The rules provided in paragraphs (a)(1)(i)(A), (a)(1)(ii), (iv), and (v), (a)(2)(iv) through (vi), (a)(3)(i), and (a)(4) through (8) of this section apply to testing dates occurring on or after the date the Treasury decision adopting these regulations as final regulations is published in the **Federal Register**. For loss corporations that have testing dates occurring before the date the Trea-

sury decision adopting these regulations as final regulations is published in the **Federal Register**, see §1.382-2 as contained in 26 CFR part 1, revised April 1, 2018. However, taxpayers and their related parties, within the meaning of sections 267(b) and 707(b)(1), may apply the rules of this section to testing dates occurring during a taxable year beginning after December 31, 2017, so long as the taxpayers and their related parties consistently apply the rules of this section, the section 163(j) regulations (within the meaning of §1.163(j)-1(b)(32)), §§1.382-5, 1.382-6, and 1.383-1, and if applicable, §§1.263A-9, 1.381(c)(20)-1, 1.469-9, 1.882-5, 1.1502-13, 1.1502-21, 1.1502-36, 1.1502-79, 1.1502-91 through 1.1502-99 (to the extent they effectuate the rules of §§1.382-2, 1.382-5, 1.382-6, and 1.383-1), and 1.1504-4 to taxable years beginning after December 31, 2017.

Carryforwards: Ownership Change: Limitations

Carryforwards: Ownership Change: Limitations.—Reg. §1.382-2T, relating to the limitation on net operating loss carryforwards and certain built-in losses following ownership changes, is proposed (published in the Federal Register on August 11, 1987) (LR-106-86). Reg. §1.382-1T was redesignated as Reg. §1.382-1 on 10/2/92 by T.D. 8440.

§1.382-2T. Definition of ownership change under section 382, as amended by the Tax Reform Act of 1986 (temporary).

Carryovers: Excess Credits: Use of Pre-change Attributes

Carryovers: Excess Credits: Use of Pre-change Attributes.—Amendments to Reg. §1.382-2T, relating to the manner and method of absorbing the Code Sec. 382 limitation with respect to certain capital losses and excess credits after there has been an ownership change of a corporation, are proposed (published in the Federal Register on September 20, 1989) (CO-69-87). Reg. §§1.383-1 and 1.383-2 were adopted by T.D. 8352 on 6/26/91.

§1.382-2T. Definition of ownership change under section 382, as amended by the Tax Reform Act of 1986 (temporary).

Deduction for Business Interest Expense: Limitation

Deduction for Business Interest Expense: Limitation.—Amendments to Reg. §§1.382-5 and 1.382-6, regarding the limitation on the deduction for business interest expense after the enactment of recent tax legislation, are proposed (published in the Federal Register on December 28, 2018) (REG-106089-18).

Par. 8. Section 1.382-5 is amended by revising the first and second sentences of paragraph (d)(1) and by adding three sentences to the end of paragraph (f) to read as follows:

§1.382-5. Section 382 limitation.

* * *

(d) * * *

(1) * * * If a loss corporation has two (or more) ownership changes, any losses or section 382 disallowed business interest carryforwards (within the meaning of §1.382-2(a)(7)) attributable to the period preceding the earlier ownership change are treated as pre-change losses with respect to both ownership changes. Thus, the later ownership change may result in a lesser (but never in a greater) section 382 limitation with respect to such pre-change losses. * * *

* * *

(f) * * * Paragraph (d)(1) of this section applies with respect to an ownership change occurring on or after the date the Treasury decision adopting these regulations as final regulations is published in the **Federal Register**. For loss corporations that have undergone an ownership change before or after the date the Treasury decision adopting these regulations as final regulations is published in the **Federal Register**, see §1.382-5 as contained in 26 CFR part 1, revised April 1, 2018. However, taxpayers and their related parties, within the meaning of sections 267(b) and 707(b)(1), may apply the rules of this section to testing dates occurring during a taxable year beginning after December 31, 2017, so long as the taxpayers and their related parties consistently apply the rules of this section, the section 163(j) regulations (within the meaning of §1.163(j)-1(b)(32)), §§1.382-2, 1.382-6, and 1.383-1, and if applicable, §§1.263A-9, 1.381(c)(20)-1, 1.469-9, 1.882-5, 1.1502-13, 1.1502-21, 1.1502-36, 1.1502-79, 1.1502-91 through 1.1502-99 (to the extent they effectuate the rules of §§1.382-2, 1.382-5, 1.382-6, and 1.383-1), and 1.1504-4 to taxable years beginning after December 31, 2017.

Par. 9. Section 1.382-6 is amended by:

1. Removing "Subject to paragraphs (b)(3)(ii) and (d)" in the first sentence of paragraph (b)(1) and adding "Subject to paragraphs (b)(3)(ii), (b)(4), and (d)" in its place;

2. Adding paragraph (b)(4); and

3. Revising paragraph (h).

The addition and revision read as follows:

§1.382-6. Allocation of income and loss to periods before and after the change date for purposes of section 382.

* * *

(b) * * *

(4) *Allocation of business interest expense.*—(i) *In general.*—Regardless of whether a loss corporation has made a closing-of-the-books election pursuant to paragraph (b) of this section, for purposes of calculating the taxable income of a loss corporation attributable to the pre-change period, the amount of the loss corporation's deduction for current-year business interest expense, within the meaning of §1.163(j)-5(a)(2)(i), is calculated based on a single tax year and is allocated between the pre-change period and the post-change period by ratably allocating an equal portion to each day in the year.

(ii) *Example.*—(A) *Facts.* X is a calendar-year C corporation that is not a member of a consolidated group. On May 26, 2019, X is acquired by Z (an unrelated third-party) in a transaction that qualifies as an ownership change under section 382(g). For calendar year 2019, X has paid or accrued $100x of current-year business interest expense (within the meaning of §1.163(j)-5(a)(2)(i)) and has an $81x section 163(j) limitation (within the meaning of §1.163(j)-1(b)(31)).

(B) *Analysis.* Pursuant to paragraph (b)(4)(i) of this section, regardless of whether X has made a closing-of-the-books election pursuant to paragraph (b) of this section, X's business interest expense deduction is ratably allocated between the pre-change and post-change periods. For calendar year 2019, X may deduct $81x of business interest expense (see §1.163(j)-2(b)), of which $32.4x ($81x x (146 days/365 days) = $32.4x) is allocable to the pre-change period. The remaining $19x of interest that was paid or accrued in calendar year 2019 is disallowed business interest expense, of which $7.6x ($19x x (146 days/365 days) = $7.6x) is allocable to the pre-change period. The $7.6x of disallowed business interest expense is treated as a section 382 disallowed business interest carryforward (see §1.382-2(a)(7)), and thus is a pre-change loss within the meaning of §1.382-2(a)(2).

* * *

(h) *Applicability date.*—(1) *In general.*—This section applies to ownership changes occurring on or after June 22, 1994.

(2) *Paragraphs (b)(1) and (4) of this section.*—Paragraphs (b)(1) and (4) of this section apply with respect to an ownership change occurring during a taxable year ending after the date the Treasury decision adopting these regulations as final regulations is published in the **Federal Register**. For ownership changes occurring during a taxable year ending before the date the Treasury decision adopting these regulations is published in the **Federal Register**, see §1.382-6 as contained in 26 CFR part 1, revised April 1, 2018. However, taxpayers and their related parties, within the meaning of sections 267(b) and 707(b)(1), may apply the rules of this section to testing dates occurring during a taxable year beginning after December 31, 2017, so long as the taxpayers and their related parties consistently apply the rules of this section, and the section 163(j) regulations (within the meaning of §1.163(j)-1(b)(32)) and §1.383-1, and if applicable, §§1.263A-9, 1.381(c)(20)-1, 1.469-9, 1.882-5, 1.1502-13, 1.1502-21, 1.1502-36, 1.1502-79, 1.1502-91 through 1.1502-99 (to the extent they effectuate the rules of §§1.382-6 and 1.383-1), and 1.1504-4 to taxable years beginning after December 31, 2017.

Advance Payments for Goods and Long-Term Contracts: Existing Regulations Removed

Advance Payments for Goods and Long-Term Contracts: Existing Regulations Removed.—Amendments to Reg. §1.382-7, removing regulations regarding advance payments for goods and long-term contracts that are no longer necessary after the enactment of recent tax legislation, are proposed (published in the Federal Register on October 15, 2018) (REG-104872-18).

Par. 3. Section 1.382-7 is amended by revising the third sentence of paragraph (a) to read as follows:

§1.382-7. Built in gains and losses.—(a) * * * Examples to which this paragraph (a) will apply include, but are not limited to, income received prior to the change date that is deferred under section 455 or Rev. Proc. 2004-34 (2004-1 CB 991 (June 1, 2004)) (or any successor revenue procedure) (see §601.601(d)(2)(ii)(*b*)).

* * *

Deduction for Business Interest Expense: Limitation

Deduction for Business Interest Expense: Limitation.—Amendments to Reg. §§1.383-0 and 1.383-1, regarding the limitation on the deduction for business interest expense after the enactment of recent tax legislation, are proposed (published in the Federal Register on December 28, 2018) (REG-106089-18).

Par. 10. Section 1.383-0 is amended by revising paragraph (a) to read as follows:

1.383-0. Effective date.—(a) The regulations under section 383 (other than the regulations described in paragraph (b) of this section) reflect the amendments made to sections 382 and 383 by the Tax Reform Act of 1986 and the amendments made to section 382 by the Tax Cuts and Jobs Act of 2017. See §1.383-1(j) for effective date rules.

* * *

Par. 11. Section 1.383-1 is amended by:

1. In paragraph (a):

a. Adding entries for paragraphs (d)(1)(i) and (ii);

b. Revising the entries for paragraphs (e)(3) and (j);

c. Adding entries for paragraphs (j)(1) and (2); and
d. Removing the entry for paragraph (k).
2. Removing "(iv)" and adding "(v)" in its place in paragraph (c)(6)(i)(B).
3. Revising paragraphs (c)(6)(ii) and (d)(1).
4. Removing the commas and adding semicolons in their place at ends of paragraphs (d)(2)(i) through (vi).
5. Revising paragraph (d)(2)(iii).
6. Redesignating paragraphs (d)(2)(iv) through (vii) as paragraphs (d)(2)(v) through (viii), respectively.
7. Adding a new paragraph (d)(2)(iv).
8. Revising newly redesignated paragraph (d)(2)(v) and paragraph (d)(3)(ii).
9. Removing "(iv)" and adding "(v)" in its place in paragraph (e)(1).
10. In paragraph (e)(2):
a. Removing "sections 11(b)(2) and (15)" and adding "section 15" in its place in the fourth sentence; and
b. Removing the last two sentences.
11. Removing and reserving paragraph (e)(3).
12. In paragraph (f):
a. Removing *Example 4;*
b. Designating *Examples 1* through 3 as paragraphs (f)(1) through (3), respectively; and
c. Revising newly designated paragraphs (f)(2) and (3).
13. In the last sentence of paragraph (g), removing "(e.g., 0.34 for taxable years beginning in 1989)".
14. In paragraph (j):
a. Revising the paragraph heading;
b. Designating the text of paragraph (j) as paragraph (j)(1) and adding a heading to newly designated paragraph (j)(1); and
c. Adding paragraph (j)(2).
15. Removing paragraph (k).
The revisions and additions read as follows:

1.383-1. Special limitations on certain capital losses and excess credits.—(a) * * *

* * *

(d) * * *

(1) * * *

(i) In general.

(ii) Ordering rule for losses or credits from same taxable year.

* * *

(e) * * *

(3) [Reserved]

* * *

(j) Applicability date.

(1) In general.

(2) Interaction with section 163(j).

* * *

(c) * * *

(6) * * *

(ii) *Example.*—L, a new loss corporation, is a calendar-year taxpayer. L has an ownership change on December 31, 2019. For 2020, L has taxable income (prior to the use of any pre-change losses) of $100,000. In addition, L has a section 382 limitation of $25,000, a pre-change net operating loss carryover of $12,000, a pre-change general business credit carryforward under section 39 of $50,000, and no items described in §1.383-1(d)(2)(i) through (iv). L's section 383 credit limitation for 2020 is the excess of its regular tax liability computed after allowing a $12,000 net operating loss deduction (taxable income of $88,000; regular tax liability of $18,480), over its regular tax liability computed after allowing an additional deduction in the amount of L's section 382 limitation remaining after the application of paragraphs (d)(2)(i) through (v) of this section, or $13,000 (taxable income of $75,000; regular tax liability of $15,750). L's section 383 credit limitation is therefore $2,730 ($18,480 minus $15,750).

(d) * * *

(1) *In general.*—(i) *In general.*—The amount of taxable income of a new loss corporation for any post-change year that may be offset by pre-change losses shall not exceed the amount of the section 382 limitation for the post-change year. The amount of the regular tax liability of a new loss corporation for any post-change year that may be offset by pre-change credits shall not exceed the amount of the section 383 credit limitation for the post-change year.

(ii) *Ordering rule for losses or credits from same taxable year.*—A loss corporation's taxable income is offset first by losses subject to a section 382 limitation, to the extent the section 382 limitation for that taxable year has not yet been absorbed, before being offset by losses of the same type from the same taxable year that are not subject to a section 382 limitation. For example, assume that Corporation X has an ownership change in Year 1 and carries over disallowed business interest expense within the meaning of §1.163(j)-1(b)(8), some of which constitutes a section 382 disallowed business interest carryforward, from Year 1 to Year 2. To the extent of its section 163(j) limitation, within the meaning of §1.163(j)-1(b)(31), and its remaining section 382 limitation, Corporation X offsets its Year 2 income with the section 382 disallowed business interest carryforward before using any of the disallowed business interest expense that is not a section 382 disallowed business interest carryforward. Similar principles apply to the use of tax credits.

(2) * * *

(iii) Pre-change losses that are described in §1.382-2(a)(2)(iii), other than losses that are pre-change capital losses, that are recognized and are subject to the section 382 limitation in such post-change year;

(iv)(A) With respect to an ownership change date occurring prior to the date the Treasury decision adopting these regulations as final regulations is published in the **Federal Register**, but during the taxable year which includes the date the Treasury decision adopting these regulations as final regulations is published in the **Federal Register**, the pre-change loss described in section 382(d)(3);

(B) With respect to an ownership change date occurring on or after the date the Treasury decision adopting these regulations as final regulations is published in the **Federal Register**, section 382 disallowed business interest carryforwards (within the meaning of § 1.382-2(a)(7));

(v) Pre-change losses not described in paragraphs (d)(2)(i) through (iv) of this section;

* * *

(3) * * *

(ii) *Example*.—L, a calendar-year taxpayer, has an ownership change on December 31, 2019. For 2020, L has taxable income of $300,000 and a regular tax liability of $63,000. L has no pre-change losses, but it has a business credit carryforward from 2018 of $25,000. L has a section 382 limitation for 2020 of $50,000. L's section 383 credit limitation is $10,500, an amount equal to the excess of L's regular tax liability ($63,000) over its regular tax liability calculated by allowing an additional deduction of $50,000 ($52,500). Pursuant to the limitation contained in section 38(c), however, L is entitled to use only $9,500 (($63,000 - $25,000) x 25 percent) of its business credit carryforward in 2020. The unabsorbed portion of L's section 382 limitation (computed pursuant to paragraph (e) of this section) is carried forward under section 382(b)(2). The unused portion of L's business credit carryforward, $1,000, is carried forward to the extent provided in section 39.

* * *

(f) * * *

(2) *Example 2*—(i) *Facts*. L, a calendar-year taxpayer, has an ownership change on December 31, 2019. For 2020, L has $750,000 of ordinary taxable income (before the application of carryovers) and a section 382 limitation of $1,500,000. L's only carryovers are from pre-2019 taxable years and consist of a $500,000 net operating loss (NOL) carryover, and a $200,000 foreign tax credit carryover (all of which may be used under the section 904 limitation). The NOL carryover is a pre-change loss, and the foreign tax credit carryover is a pre-change credit. L has no other pre-change losses or credits that can be used in 2020.

(ii) *Analysis*. The following computation illustrates the application of this section for 2020:

1. Taxable income before carryovers	$750,000
2. Pre-change NOL carryover	$500,000
3. Section 382 limitation	$1,500,000
4. Amount of pre-change NOL carryover that can be used (least of line 1, 2, or 3)	$500,000
5. Taxable income (line 1 minus line 4)	$250,000
6. Section 382 limitation remaining (line 3 minus line 4)	$1,000,000
7. Pre-change credit carryover	$200,000
8. Regular tax liability (line 5 x section 11 rates)	$52,500
9. Modified tax liability (line 5 minus line 6 (but not less than zero) x section 11 rates)	$0
10. Section 383 credit limitation (line 8 minus line 9)	$52,500
11. Amount of pre-change credits that can be used in 2020 (lesser of line 7 or line 10)	$52,500
12. Amount of pre-change credits to be carried over to 2021 under section 904(c) (line 7 minus line 11)	$147,500
13. Section 383 credit reduction amount: $52,500/0.21	$250,000
14. Section 382 limitation to be carried to 2021 under section 382(b)(2) (line 6 minus line 13)	$750,000

(3) *Example 3*—(i) *Facts*. L, a calendar-year taxpayer, has an ownership change on December 31, 2019. L has $80,000 of ordinary taxable income (before the application of carryovers) and a section 382 limitation of $25,000 for 2020, a post-change year. L's only carryover is from a pre-2019 taxable year and is a general business credit carryforward under section 39 in the amount of $10,000 (no portion of which is attributable to the investment tax credit under section 46). The general business credit carryforward is a pre-change credit. L has no other credits which can be used in 2020.

(ii) *Analysis*. The following computation illustrates the application of this section:

1. Taxable income before carryovers	$80,000
2. Section 382 limitation	$25,000
3. Pre-change credit carryover	$10,000
4. Regular tax liability (line 1 x section 11 rates)	$16,800
5. Modified tax liability ((line 1 minus line 2) x section 11 rates)	$11,550
6. Section 383 credit limitation (line 4 minus line 5)	$5,250
7. Amount of pre-change credits that can be used (lesser of line 3 or line 6)	$5,250

8. Amount of pre-change credits to be carried over to 2021 under sections 39 and 382(l)(2) (line 3 minus line 7)	$4,750
9. Regular tax payable (line 4 minus line 7)	$11,550
10. Section 383 credit reduction amount: $5,250/0.21	$25,000
11. Section 382 limitation to be carried to 2021 under section 382(b)(2) (line 2 minus line 10)	$0

* * *

(j) Applicability date.—(1) *In general.*—* * *

(2) *Interaction with section 163(j).*—Paragraphs (c)(6)(i)(B) and (c)(6)(ii), (d)(1), (d)(2)(iii) through (viii), (d)(3)(ii), (e)(1) through (3), (f), and (g) of this section apply with respect to ownership changes occurring during a taxable year ending after the Treasury decision adopting these regulations as final regulations is published in the **Federal Register**. For loss corporations that have undergone an ownership change during a taxable year ending before the date the Treasury decision adopting these regulations as final regulations is published in the **Federal Register**, see §1.383-1 as contained in 26 CFR part 1, revised April 1, 2018. However, taxpayers and their related parties, within the meaning of sections 267(b) and 707(b)(1), may apply the rules of this section to an ownership change occurring during a taxable year beginning after December 31, 2017, so long as the taxpayers and their related parties consistently apply either the rules of this section, except paragraph (d)(2)(iv)(B) of this section, the section 163(j) regulations, within the meaning of §1.163(j)-1(b)(32), and §1.382-6, and if applicable, §§1.263A-9, 1.381(c)(20)-1, 1.469-9, 1.882-5, 1.1502-13, 1.1502-21, 1.1502-36, 1.1502-79, 1.1502-91 through 1.1502-99 (to the extent they effectuate the rules of §§1.382-6 and 1.383-1), and 1.1504-4; or the rules of this section (except paragraph (d)(2)(iv)(A) of this section), the section 163(j) regulations, within the meaning of §1.163(j)-1(b)(32), and §§1.382-2, 1.382-5, 1.382-6, and 1.383-1, and if applicable, §§1.263A-9, 1.381(c)(20)-1, 1.469-9, 1.882-5, 1.1502-13, 1.1502-21, 1.1502-36, 1.1502-79, 1.1502-91 through 1.1502-99 (to the extent they effectuate the rules of §§1.382-2, 1.382-5, 1.382-6, and 1.383-1), and 1.1504-4, to those ownership changes.

Base Erosion and Anti-Abuse Tax: Guidance

Base Erosion and Anti-Abuse Tax: Guidance.—Amendments to Reg. §1.383-1, regarding the tax on base erosion payments of taxpayers with substantial gross receipts and reporting requirements thereunder, are proposed (published in the Federal Register on December 21, 2018) (REG-104259-18).

Par. 3. Section 1.383-1 is amended by adding two sentences at the end of paragraph (d)(3)(i) to read as follows:

§1.383-1. Special limitations on certain capital losses and excess credits.

* * *

(d) * * *

(3) * * *

(i) * * * The application of section 59A is not a limitation contained in subtitle A for purposes of this paragraph (d)(3)(i). Therefore, the treatment of pre-change losses and pre-change credits in the computation of the base erosion minimum tax amount will not affect whether such losses or credits result in absorption of the section 382 limitation and the section 383 credit limitation.

* * *

Indebtedness for Federal Tax Purposes: Removal of Documentation Regulations

Indebtedness for Federal Tax Purposes: Removal of Documentation Regulations.—Amendments to Reg. §§1.385-1—1.385-3, removing final regulations setting forth minimum documentation requirements that ordinarily must be satisfied in order for certain related party interests in a corporation to be treated as indebtedness for federal tax purposes (Documentation Regulations), are proposed (published in the Federal Register on September 24, 2018) (REG-130244-17).

Par. 2. Section 1.385-1 is amended by revising paragraph (a), the last sentence of paragraphs (c) introductory text and (c)(4)(iv), paragraph (d)(1)(i), the first sentence of paragraph (d)(1)(ii), and paragraphs (d)(1)(iii) and (d)(1)(iv)(A), and removing and reserving paragraph (d)(2)(i).

§1.385-1. General provisions.—(a) *Overview of section 385 regulations.*—This section and §§1.385-3 through 1.385-4T (collectively, the section 385 regulations) provide rules under section 385 to determine the treatment of an interest in a corporation as stock or indebtedness (or as in part stock and in part indebtedness) in particular factual situations. Paragraph (b) of this section provides the general rule for determining the treatment of an interest based on provisions of the Internal Revenue Code and on common law, including the factors prescribed under common law. Paragraphs (c), (d), and (e) of this section provide definitions and rules of general application for purposes of the section 385 regulations. Section 1.385-3 sets forth additional factors that, when present, control the determination of whether an interest in a corporation that is held by a member of the corporation's expanded group is treated (in whole or in part) as stock or indebtedness. * * * * *

(c) * * * For additional definitions that apply for purposes of their respective sections, see §§1.385-3(g) and 1.385-4T(e).

* * *

(4) * * *

(iv) * * * For purposes of the section 385 regulations, a corporation is a member of an expanded group if it is described in this paragraph (c)(4)(iv) of this section immediately before the relevant time for determining membership (for example, immediately before the issuance of a debt instrument (as defined in §1.385-3(g)(4)) or immediately before a distribution or acquisition that may be subject to §1.385-3(b)(2) or (3)).

* * *

(d) * * *

(1) * * *

(i) *In general.*—If a debt instrument (as defined in §1.385-3(g)(4)) is deemed to be exchanged under the section 385 regulations, in whole or in part, for stock, the holder is treated for all federal tax purposes as having realized an amount equal to the holder's adjusted basis in that portion of the debt instrument as of the date of the deemed exchange (and as having basis in the stock deemed to be received equal to that amount), and, except as provided in paragraph (d)(1)(iv)(B) of this section, the issuer is treated for all federal tax purposes as having retired that portion of the debt instrument for an amount equal to its adjusted issue price as of the date of the deemed exchange. In addition, neither party accounts for any accrued but unpaid qualified stated interest on the debt instrument or any foreign exchange gain or loss with respect to that accrued but unpaid qualified stated interest (if any) as of the deemed exchange. This paragraph (d)(1)(i) does not affect the rules that otherwise apply to the debt instrument prior to the date of the deemed exchange (for example, this paragraph (d)(1)(i) does not affect the issuer's deduction of accrued but unpaid qualified stated interest otherwise deductible prior to the date of the deemed exchange). Moreover, the stock issued in the deemed exchange is not treated as a payment of accrued but unpaid original issue discount or qualified stated interest on the debt instrument for federal tax purposes.

(ii) *Section 988.*—Notwithstanding the first sentence of paragraph (d)(1)(i) of this section, the rules of §1.988-2(b)(13) apply to require the holder and the issuer of a debt instrument that is deemed to be exchanged under the section 385 regulations, in whole or in part, for stock to recognize any exchange gain or loss, other than any exchange gain or loss with respect to accrued but unpaid qualified stated interest that is not taken into account under paragraph (d)(1)(i) of this section at the time of the deemed exchange. * * *

(iii) *Section 108(e)(8).*—For purposes of section 108(e)(8), if the issuer of a debt instrument is treated as having retired all or a portion of the debt instrument in exchange for stock under paragraph (d)(1)(i) of this section, the stock is treated as having a fair market value equal to the adjusted issue price of that portion of the debt instrument as of the date of the deemed exchange.

(iv) * * *

(A) A debt instrument that is issued by a disregarded entity is deemed to be exchanged for stock of the regarded owner under §1.385-3T(d)(4); * * *

* * *

Par. 3. Section 1.385-2 is removed.

§1.385-2. Treatment of certain interests between members of an expanded group.

Par. 4. Section 1.385-3 is amended by revising paragraph (g)(4) to read as follows:

§1.385-3. Transaction in which debt proceeds are distributed or that have a similar effect.

* * *

(g) * * *

(4) *Debt instrument.*—The term debt instrument means an interest that would, but for the application of this section, be treated as a debt instrument as defined in section 1275(a) and §1.1275-1(d).

* * *

Certain Interests in Corporations: Treated as Stock or Indebtedness

Certain Interests in Corporations: Treated as Stock or Indebtedness.—Reg. §1.385-4 and amendments to Reg. §1.385-3, addressing the treatment of instruments issued by partnerships, consolidated groups, and certain transactions involving qualified cash-management arrangements, are proposed (published in the Federal Register on October 21, 2016) (REG-130314-16).

Par. 2. Section 1.385-3 is amended by:

1. Revising paragraph (b)(3)(vii).
2. Revising paragraph (d)(4).
3. Revising paragraph (f).
4. Revising paragraphs (g)(5)-(8), (15)-(17), and (22)-(23).
5. Revising *Example 12* through *Example 19* in paragraph (h)(3).
6. Adding paragraph (k).

The revisions and additions read as follows:

§1.385-3. Transactions in which debt proceeds are distributed or that have a similar effect.

* * *

(b) * * *

(3) * * *

(vii) [The text of the proposed amendment to §1.385-3(b)(3)(vii) is the same as the text of §1.385-3T(b)(3)(vii) as added by T.D. 9790.]

* * *

(d) * * *

(4) [The text of the proposed amendment to §1.385-3(d)(4) is the same as the text of §1.385-3T(d)(4) as added by T.D. 9790.]

* * *

(f) [The text of the proposed amendment to §1.385-3(f) is the same as the text of §1.385-3T(f) as added by T.D. 9790.]

(g) * * *

(5) [The text of the proposed amendment to §1.385-3(g)(5) is the same as the text of §1.385-3T(g)(5) as added by T.D. 9790.]

(6) [The text of the proposed amendment to §1.385-3(g)(6) is the same as the text of §1.385-3T(g)(6) as added by T.D. 9790.]

(7) [The text of the proposed amendment to §1.385-3(g)(7) is the same as the text of §1.385-3T(g)(7) as added by T.D. 9790.]

(8) [The text of the proposed amendment to §1.385-3(g)(8) is the same as the text of §1.385-3T(g)(8) as added by T.D. 9790.]

* * *

(15) [The text of the proposed amendment to §1.385-3(g)(15) is the same as the text of §1.385-3T(g)(15) as added by T.D. 9790.]

(16) [The text of the proposed amendment to §1.385-3(g)(16) is the same as the text of §1.385-3T(g)(16) as added by T.D. 9790.]

(17) [The text of the proposed amendment to §1.385-3(g)(16) is the same as the text of §1.385-3T(g)(17) as added by T.D. 9790.]

* * *

(22) [The text of the proposed amendment to §1.385-3(g)(22) is the same as the text of §1.385-3T(g)(22) as added by T.D. 9790.]

(23) [The text of the proposed amendment to §1.385-3(g)(23) is the same as the text of §1.385-3T(g)(23) as added by T.D. 9790.]

* * *

(h) * * *

(3) * * *

Example 12. [The text of the proposed amendment to §1.385-3(h)(3), *Example 12* is the same as the text of §1.385-3T(h)(3), *Example 12* as added by T.D. 9790.]

Example 13. [The text of the proposed amendment to §1.385-3(h)(3), *Example 13* is the same as the text of §1.385-3T(h)(3), *Example 13* as added by T.D. 9790.]

Example 14. [The text of the proposed amendment to §1.385-3(h)(3), *Example 14* is the same as the text of §1.385-3T(h)(3), *Example 14* as added by T.D. 9790.]

Example 15. [The text of the proposed amendment to §1.385-3(h)(3), *Example 15* is the same as the text of §1.385-3T(h)(3), *Example 15* as added by T.D. 9790.]

Example 16. [The text of the proposed amendment to §1.385-3(h)(3), *Example 16* is the same as the text of §1.385-3T(h)(3), *Example 16* as added by T.D. 9790.]

Example 17. [The text of the proposed amendment to §1.385-3(h)(3), *Example 17* is the same as the text of §1.385-3T(h)(3), *Example 17* as added by T.D. 9790.]

Example 18. [The text of the proposed amendment to §1.385-3(h)(3), *Example 18* is the same as the text of §1.385-3T(h)(3), *Example 18* as added by T.D. 9790.]

Example 19. [The text of the proposed amendment to §1.385-3(h)(3), *Example 19* is the same as the text of §1.385-3T(h)(3), *Example 19* as added by T.D. 9790.]

* * *

(k) [The text of the proposed amendment to §1.385-3(k) is the same as the text of §1.385-3T(k) as added by T.D. 9790.]

Par. 3. Section 1.385-4 is added to read as follows:

§1.385-4. Treatment of consolidated groups.—[The text of proposed §1.385-4 is the same as the text of §1.385-4T as added by T.D. 9790.]

DEFERRED COMPENSATION

Pension Plans: Distributions: Phased Retirement Programs

Pension Plans: Distributions: Phased Retirement Programs.—Reg. §1.401(a)-3 and amendments to Reg. §1.401(a)-1, providing rules that permit distributions to be made from a pension plan under a phased retirement program and setting forth requirements for a bona fide phased retirement program, are proposed (published in the Federal Register on November 10, 2004) (REG-114726-04).

☐ Par. 2. In §1.401(a)-1, paragraph (b)(1)(i) is amended by adding text before the period at the end of the current sentence and a new second sentence [*proposed amendment to (b)(1)(i) adopted by T.D. 9325, 5-21-2007*], and paragraph (b)(1)(iv) to read as follows:

§1.401(a)-1. Post-ERISA qualified plans and qualified trusts; in general.

* * *

(b) * * *

(1) * * *

(i) [*Proposed amendment to (b)(1)(i) adopted by T.D. 9325, 5-21-2007.*]

* * *

(iv) Benefits may not be distributed prior to normal retirement age solely due to a reduction in hours. However, notwithstanding anything provided elsewhere in paragraph (b) of this section (including the pre-ERISA rules under §1.401-1), an employee may be treated as partially retired for purposes of paragraph (b)(1)(i) of this section to the extent provided under §1.401(a)-3 relating to a bona fide phased retirement program.

* * *

☐ Par. 3. Section 1.401(a)-3 is added to read as follows:

§1.401(a)-3. Benefits during phased retirement.—(a) *Introduction.*—(1) *General rule.*—Under section 401(a), a qualified pension plan may provide for the distribution of phased retirement benefits in accordance with the limitations of this paragraph (a) to the extent that an employee is partially retired under a bona fide phased retirement program, as defined in paragraph (c) of this section, provided the requirements set forth in paragraphs (d) and (e) of this section are satisfied.

(2) *Limitation on benefits paid during phased retirement period.*—(i) *Benefits limited to pro rata retirement benefit.*—The phased retirement benefits paid during the phased retirement period cannot exceed the phased retirement accrued benefit payable in the optional form of benefit applicable at the annuity starting date for the employee's phased retirement benefit.

(ii) *Availability of early retirement subsidies, etc.*—Except as provided in paragraph (a)(2)(iii) of this section, all early retirement benefits, retirement-type subsidies, and optional forms of benefit available upon full retirement must be available with respect to the portion of an employee's phased retirement accrued benefit that is payable as a phased retirement benefit.

(iii) *Limitation on optional forms of payment.*—Phased retirement benefits may not be paid in the form of a single sum or other form that constitutes an eligible rollover distribution under section 402(c)(4).

(3) *Limited to full-time employees who are otherwise eligible to commence benefits.*—Phased retirement benefits are only permitted to be made available to an employee who, prior to the phased retirement period, normally maintains a full-time work schedule and who would otherwise be eligible to commence retirement benefits immediately if he or she were to fully retire.

(4) *Authority of Commissioner to adopt other rules.*—The Commissioner, in revenue rulings, notices, or other guidance published in the Internal Revenue Bulletin (see §601.601(d)(2)(ii)(*b*) of this chapter), may adopt additional rules regarding the coordination of partial retirement under a phased retirement program and the qualification rules of section 401(a).

(b) *Definitions.*—(1) *In general.*—The definitions set forth in this paragraph (b) apply for purposes of this section.

(2) *Phased retirement program.*—The term *phased retirement program* means a written, employer-adopted program pursuant to which employees may reduce the number of hours they customarily work beginning on or after a date specified under the program and commence phased retirement benefits during the phased retirement period, as provided under the plan.

(3) *Phased retirement period.*—The term *phased retirement period* means the period of time that the employee and employer reasonably expect the employee to work reduced hours under the phased retirement program.

(4) *Phased retirement accrued benefit.*—The term *phased retirement accrued benefit* means the portion of the employee's accrued benefit equal to the product of the employee's total accrued benefit on the annuity starting date for the employee's phased retirement benefit, and one minus the employee's work schedule fraction.

(5) *Phased retirement benefit.*—The term *phased retirement benefit* means the benefit paid to an employee upon the employee's partial retirement under a phased retirement program, based on some or all of the employee's phased retirement accrued benefit, and payable in the optional form of benefit applicable at the annuity starting date.

(6) *Work schedule.*—With respect to an employee, the term *work schedule* means the number of hours the employee is reasonably expected to work annually during the phased retirement period (determined in accordance with paragraph (c)(4) of this section).

(7) *Full-time work schedule.*—With respect to an employee, the term *full-time work schedule* means the number of hours the employee would normally work during a year if the employee were to work on a full-time basis, determined in a reasonable and consistent manner.

(8) *Work schedule fraction.*—With respect to an employee, the term *work schedule fraction* means a fraction, the numerator of which is the employee's work schedule and the denominator of which is the employee's full-time work schedule.

(c) *Bona fide phased retirement program.*—(1) *Definition generally.*—The term *bona fide phased retirement program* means a phased retirement program that satisfies paragraphs (c)(2) through (5) of this section.

(2) *Limitation to individuals who have attained age 59 ½.*—A bona fide phased retirement program must be limited to employees who have attained age 59 ½. A plan is permitted to impose additional requirements for eligibility to participate in a bona fide phased retirement program, such as limiting eligibility to either employees who have satisfied additional age or service conditions (or combination thereof) specified in the program or employees whose benefit may not be distributed without consent under section 411(a)(11).

(3) *Participation must be voluntary.*—An employee's participation in a bona fide phased retirement program must be voluntary.

(4) *Reduction in hours requirement.*—An employee who participates in a bona fide phased retirement program must reasonably be expected (by both the employer and employee) to reduce, by 20 percent or more, the number of hours the employee customarily works. This requirement is satisfied if the employer and employee enter into an agreement, in good faith, under which they agree that the employee will reduce, by 20 percent or more, the number of hours the employee works during the phased retirement period.

(5) *Limited to employees who are not key-employee owners.*—Phased retirement benefits are not permitted to be made available to a key employee who is described in section 416(i)(1)(A)(ii) or (iii).

(d) *Conditions for commencement of phased retirement benefit.*—(1) *Imputed accruals based on full-time schedule.*—(i) *General rule.*—During the phased retirement period, in addition to being entitled to payment of the phased retirement benefit, the employee must be entitled to participate in the plan in the same manner as if the employee still maintained a full-time work schedule (including calculation of average earnings, imputation of compensation in accordance with §1.414(s)-1(f), and imputation of service in accordance with the service-crediting rules under §1.401(a)(4)-11(d)), and must be entitled to the same benefits (including early retirement benefits, retirement-type subsidies, and optional forms of benefits) upon full retirement as a similarly situated employee who has not elected phased retirement, except that the years of service credited under the plan for any plan year during the phased retirement period is determined under paragraph (d)(1)(ii) or (iii) of this section, whichever is applicable.

(ii) *Method for crediting years of service for full plan years.*—The years of service credited under the plan for any full plan year during the phased retirement period is multiplied by an adjustment ratio that is equal to the ratio of the employee's actual hours worked during that year to the number of hours that would be worked by the employee during that year under a full-time work schedule. Alternatively, on a reasonable and consistent basis, the adjustment ratio may be based on the ratio of an employee's actual compensation during the year to the compensation that would be paid to the employee during the year if he or she had maintained a full-time work schedule.

(iii) *Method for crediting years of service for partial plan years.*—In the case of a plan year only a portion of which is during a phased retirement period for an employee, the method described in paragraphs (d)(1)(i) and (ii) of this section is applied with respect to that portion of the plan year. Thus, for example, if an employee works full time until October 1 of a calendar plan year and works one-third time from October 1 through December 31 of the year, then the employee is credited with 10 months for that year (9 months plus 1/3 of 3 months).

(2) *Ancillary benefits during phased retirement period.*—(i) *Death benefits.*—If an employee dies while receiving phased retirement benefits, death benefits are allocated between the phased retirement benefit and the benefit that would be payable upon subsequent full retirement. See also § 1.401(a)-20, A-9. Thus, if an employee dies after the annuity starting date for the phased retirement benefit, death benefits are paid with respect to the phased retirement benefit in accordance with the optional form elected for that benefit, and death benefits are paid with respect to the remainder of the employee's benefit in accordance with the plan's provisions regarding death during employment.

(ii) *Other ancillary benefits.*—To the extent provided under the terms of the plan, ancillary benefits, other than death benefits described in paragraph (d)(2)(i) of this section, are permitted to be provided during the phased retirement period.

(3) *Calculation of benefit at full retirement.*—(i) *In general.*—Upon full retirement following partial retirement under a phased retirement program, the employee's total accrued benefit under the plan (including the employee's accruals during the phased retirement period, determined in accordance with paragraph (d)(1) of this section) is offset by the portion of the employee's phased retirement accrued benefit that is being distributed as a phased retirement benefit at the time of full retirement.

(ii) *Adjustment for prior payments.*—If, before full retirement, the employee's phased retirement benefit has been reduced under paragraph (d)(4) of this section, then the employee's accrued benefit under the plan is also offset upon full retirement by an amount that is actuarially equivalent to the phased retirement benefit payments that have been made during the phased retirement period that were not made with respect to the portion of the phased retirement accrued benefit that is applied as an offset under paragraph (d)(3)(i) of this section at the time of full retirement.

(iii) *Election of optional form with respect to net benefit.*—Upon full retirement, an employee is entitled to elect, in accordance with section 417, an optional form of benefit with respect to the net accrued benefit determined under paragraph (d)(3)(i) and (ii) of this section.

(iv) *New election permitted for phased retirement benefit.*—A plan is permitted to provide that, upon full retirement, an employee may elect, in accordance with section 417 and without regard to paragraph (a)(2)(iii) of this section, a new optional form of benefit with respect to the portion of the phased retirement accrued benefit that is being distributed as a phased retirement benefit. Any such new optional form of benefit is calculated at the time of full retirement as the actuarial equivalent of the future phased retirement benefits (without offset for the phased retirement benefits previously paid).

(4) *Prospective reduction in phased retirement benefit if hours are materially greater than expected.*—(i) *General rule.*—Except as otherwise provided in this paragraph (d)(4), a plan must compare annually the number of hours actually worked by an employee during the phased retirement testing period and the number of hours the employee was reasonably expected to work during the testing period for purposes of calculating the work schedule fraction. For this purpose, the phased retirement testing period is the 12 months preceding the comparison date (or such longer period permitted under paragraph(d)(4)(iv) of this section, or any shorter period that applies if there is a comparison date as a result of an agreed increase under paragraph (d)(4)(vi) of this section). In the event that the actual hours worked (determined on an annual basis) during the phased retirement testing period exceeds the work schedule, then, except as provided in paragraph (d)(4)(ii) or (v) of this section, the employee's phased retirement benefit must be reduced in accordance with the method provided in paragraph (d)(4)(iii) of this section, effective as of an adjustment date specified in the plan that is not more than 3 months later than the comparison date.

(ii) *Permitted variance in hours.*—A plan is not required to reduce the phased retirement benefit unless the hours worked during the phased retirement testing period are materially greater than the hours that would be expected to be worked under the work schedule. For this purpose, the employee's hours worked (determined on annual basis) are materially greater than the employee's work schedule if either—

(A) The employee's hours worked (determined on an annual basis) are more than 133-1/3 percent of the employee's work schedule; or

(B) The employee's hours worked (determined on an annual basis) exceed 90 percent of the full-time work schedule.

(iii) *Adjustment method.*—If a phased retirement benefit must be reduced under paragraph (d)(4) of this section, a new (i.e., reduced) phased retirement benefit must be calculated as provided in this paragraph (d)(4)(iii). First, an adjusted work schedule is determined. The adjusted work schedule is an annual schedule based on the number of hours the employee actually worked during the phased retirement testing period. The adjusted work schedule is applied to the employee's accrued benefit that was used to calculate the prior phased retirement benefit. This results in a new phased retirement accrued benefit for purposes of paragraph (b)(4) of this section. Second, a new phased retirement benefit is determined, based on the new phased retirement accrued benefit and payable in the same optional form of benefit (i.e., using the same annuity starting date and the same early retirement factor and other actuarial adjustments) as the prior phased retirement benefit. If an employee is receiving more than one phased retirement benefit (as permitted under paragraph (e)(2) of this section) and a reduction is required under paragraph (d)(4) of this section, then the reduction is applied first to the most recently commencing phased retirement benefit (and then, if necessary, to the next most recent phased retirement benefit, etc.).

(iv) *Comparison date for phased retirement testing period.*—The comparison date is any date chosen by the employer on a reasonable and consistent basis and specified in the plan, such as the last day of the plan year, December 31, or the anniversary of the annuity starting date for the employee's phased retirement benefit. As an alternative to testing the hours worked during the 12 months preceding the comparison date, the plan may, on a reasonable and consistent basis, provide that the comparison of actual hours worked to the work schedule be based on a cumulative period that exceeds 12 months beginning with either the annuity starting date for the employee's phased retirement benefit or any later date specified in the plan.

(v) *Exceptions to comparison requirement.*—(A) *In general.*—The comparison of hours described in paragraph (d)(4) of this section is not required in the situations set forth in this paragraph (d)(4)(v).

(B) *Employees recently commencing phased retirement.*—No comparison is required for an employee who commenced phased retirement benefits within the 12-month period preceding the comparison date.

(C) *Employees with short phased retirement periods.*—No comparison is required during the first 2 years of an employee's phased retirement period if—

(1) The employee has entered into an agreement with the employer under which the employee's phased retirement period will not exceed 2 years and the employee will fully retire at the end of such period; and

(2) The employee fully retires after a phased retirement period not in excess of 2 years.

(D) *Employees with proportional pay reduction.*—No comparison is required for any phased retirement testing period if the amount of compensation paid to the employee during that period does not exceed the compensation that would be paid to the employee if he or she had maintained a full-time work schedule multiplied by the work schedule fraction.

(E) *Employees at or after normal retirement age.*—No comparison is required for any phased retirement testing period ending within 3 months before the employee's normal retirement age or any time thereafter.

(vi) *Agreement to increase hours.*—(A) *General rule.*—In the event that the employer and the employee agree to increase prospectively the hours under the employee's work schedule prior to normal retirement age, then, notwithstanding the exceptions provided in paragraphs (d)(4)(v)(B) through (D) of this section, the plan must treat the effective date of the agreement to increase the employee's hours as a comparison date for purposes of paragraph (d)(4)(iv) of this section. For purposes of this paragraph (d)(4)(vi), with respect to an employee, the term *new work schedule* means the greater of the actual number of hours the employee worked (determined on an annual basis) during the prior phased retirement testing period or the annual number of hours the employee reasonably expects to work under the new agreement.

(B) *Required adjustments.*—If the employee's hours under the new work schedule are materially greater (within the meaning of paragraph (d)(4)(ii) of this section) than the hours the employee would be expected to work (based on the employee's prior work schedule), the employer is required to reduce the employee's phased retirement benefit, effective as of the date of the increase, based on the new work schedule. In this case, the employee's new work schedule is used for future comparisons under paragraph (d)(4) of this section.

(C) *Permitted adjustments.*—If the employee's hours under the new work schedule are not materially greater (within the meaning of paragraph (d)(4)(ii) of this section) than the hours the employee would be expected to work (based on the employee's prior work schedule), the employer is permitted, but not required, to reduce the employee's phased retirement benefit, effective as of the date of the increase, based on the new work schedule. If the benefit is so reduced, the employee's new work schedule is used for future comparisons under paragraph (d)(4) of this section. If the employee's phased retirement benefit is not so reduced, future comparisons are determined using the employee's prior work schedule.

(e) *Other rules.*—(1) *Highly compensated employees.*—An employee who partially retires under a phased retirement program and who was a highly compensated employee, as defined in section 414(q), immediately before the partial retirement is considered to be a highly compensated employee during the phased retirement period, without regard to the compensation actually paid to the employee during the phased retirement period.

(2) *Multiple phased retirement benefits permitted.*—(i) *In general.*—A plan is permitted to provide one or more additional phased retirement benefits prospectively to an employee who is receiving a phased retirement benefit if the conditions set forth in paragraph (e)(2)(ii) of this section are satisfied. At the later annuity starting date for the additional phased retirement benefit, the additional phased retirement benefits may not exceed the amount permitted to be paid based on the excess of—

(A) The employee's phased retirement accrued benefit at the later annuity starting date, over

(B) The portion of the employee's phased retirement accrued benefit at the earlier annuity starting date that is being distributed as a phased retirement benefit.

(ii) *Conditions.*—The additional phased retirement benefit described in paragraph (e)(2)(i) of this section may be provided only if—

(A) The prior phased retirement benefit was not based on the employee's entire phased retirement accrued benefit at the annuity starting date for the prior phased retirement benefit, or

(B) The employee's work schedule at the later annuity starting date is less than the employee's work schedule that was used to calculate the prior phased retirement benefit.

(3) *Application of section 411(d)(6).*—In accordance with § 1.411(d)-4, A-1(b)(1), the right to receive a partial distribution of an employee's accrued benefit as a phased retirement benefit is treated as an optional form of payment that is separate from the right to receive a full distribution of the accrued benefit upon full retirement.

(4) *Application of nondiscrimination rules.*—The right to receive a phased retirement benefit is a benefit, right, or feature that is subject to § 1.401(a)(4)-4.

(f) *Examples.*—The following examples illustrate the application of this section:

Example 1. (i) *Employer's Plans.* Plan X (as in effect prior to amendment to reflect the phased retirement program described below) is a defined benefit plan maintained by Employer M. Plan X provides an accrued benefit of 1.5% of the average of an employee's highest three years of pay (based on the highest 36 consecutive months of pay), times years of service (with 1,000 hours of service required for a year of service), payable as a life annuity beginning at age 65. Plan X permits employees to elect to commence actuarially reduced distributions at any time after the later of termination of employment or attainment of age 50, except that if an employee retires after age 55 and completion of 20 years of service, the applicable reduction is only 3% per year for the years between ages 65 and 62 and 6% per year for the years between ages 62 to 55. Plan X permits employees to select, with spousal consent, a single life annuity, a joint and contingent annuity with the employee having the right to select any beneficiary and a continuation percentage of 50%, 75%, or 100%, or a 10-year certain and life annuity.

(ii) *Phased Retirement Program.* Employer M adopts a voluntary phased retirement program that will only be available for employees who retire during the two-year period from February 1, 2006 to January 31, 2008. The program will not be available to employees who are not entitled to an immediate pension or who are 1 percent owners. Employer M has determined that employees typically begin to retire after attainment of age 55 with at least 15 years of service. Accordingly, to increase retention of certain employees, the program will provide that employees in certain specified work positions who have reached age $59^1/_2$ and completed 15 years of service may elect phased retirement. The program permits phased retirement to be implemented through a reduction of 25%, 50%, or 75% in the number of hours expected to be worked for up to 5 years following phased retirement (other reduced schedules may be elected with the approval of M), with the employee's compensation during the phased retirement period to be based on what a similar full-time employee would be paid, reduced by the applicable percentage reduction in hours expected to be worked. In order to participate in the program, the employee and the employer must enter into an agreement under which the employee will reduce his or her hours accordingly. The agreement also provides that the employee's compensation during phased retirement will be reduced by that same percentage. The program is announced to employees in the fall of 2005.

(iii) *Plan Provisions Regarding Phased Retirement Benefit.* (A) Plan X is amended, prior to February 1, 2006, to provide that an employee who elects phased retirement under M's phased retirement program is permitted to commence benefits with respect to a portion of his or her accrued retirement benefit (the employee's phased retirement accrued benefit), based on the applicable percentage reduction in hours expected to be worked. For example, for a 25% reduction in hours, the employee is entitled to commence benefits with respect to 25% of his or her accrued benefit. Plan X permits an employee who commences phased retirement to elect, with spousal consent, from any of the optional forms provided under the plan.

(B) During the phased retirement period, the employee will continue to accrue benefits (without regard to the plan's 1,000 hour requirement), with his or her pay for purposes of calculating benefits under Plan X increased by the ratio of 100 percent to the percentage of full-time pay that will be paid during phased retirement and with the employee's service credit to be equal to the product of the same percentage times the service credit that would apply if the employee were working full time. Upon the employee's subsequent full retirement, his or her total accrued benefit will be based on the resulting highest three years of pay and total years of service, offset by the phased retirement accrued benefit. The retirement benefit payable upon subsequent full retirement is in addition to the phased retirement benefit. Plan X does not provide for a new election with respect to the phased retirement benefit.

(C) In the case of death during the phased retirement period, the employee will be treated as a former employee to the extent of his or her phased retirement benefit and as an active employee to the extent of the retirement benefit that would be due upon full retirement.

(D) Because the terms of the phased retirement program provide that the employee's compensation during phased retirement will be reduced by that same percentage as applies to calculate phased retirement benefits, Plan X does not have provisions requiring annual testing of hours actually worked.

(iv) *Application to a Specific Employee*—(A) *Phased retirement benefit.* Employee E is age $59^1/_2$ with 20 years of credited service. Employee E's compensation is $90,000, and E's highest three years of pay is $85,000. Employee E elects phased retirement on April 1, 2006 and elects to reduce hours by 50% beginning on July 1, 2006. Thus, E's annuity starting date for the phased retirement benefit is July 1, 2006. Employee E's total accrued benefit as of July 1, 2006 as a single life annuity payable at normal retirement age is equal to $25,500 per year (1.5% times $85,000 times 20 years of service). Thus, Employee E's phased retirement accrued benefit as of July 1, 2006 as a single life annuity payable at normal retirement age is equal to $12,750 per year ($25,500 times 1 minus E's work schedule fraction of 50%). Accordingly, Employee E's phased retirement benefit payable as a straight life annuity commencing on July 1, 2006 is equal to $9,690 per year ($12,750 per year times 76% (100% minus the applicable reduction for early retirement equal to 3% for 3 years and 6% for an additional 2$^1/_2$ years)). Employee E elects a joint and 50% survivor annuity, with E's spouse as the contingent annuitant. Under Plan X, the actuarial factor for this form of benefit is 90%, so E's benefit is $8,721 per year.

(B) *Death during phased retirement.* If Employee E were to die on or after July 1, 2006 and before subsequent full retirement, E's spouse would be entitled to a 50% survivor annuity based on the joint and 50% survivor annuity being paid to E, plus a qualified preretirement survivor annuity that complies with section 417 with respect to the additional amount that would be paid to E if he or she had fully retired on the date of E's death.

(C) *Subsequent full retirement benefit.* Three years later, Employee E fully retires from Employer M. Throughout this period, E's compensation has been 50% of the compensation that would have been paid to E if he or she were working full time. Consequently, no adjustment in E's phased retirement benefit is required. E's highest consecutive 36 months of compensation would be $95,000 if E had not elected phased retirement and E has been credited with 1$^1/_2$ years of service credit for the 3 years of phased retirement (.50 times 3 years). Accordingly, prior to offset for E's phased retirement accrued benefit, E's total accrued benefit as of July 1, 2009 as a single life annuity commencing at normal retirement age is equal to $30,637.50 per year ($95,000 times 1.5% times 21.5 years of service) and, after the offset for E's phased retirement accrued benefit, E's retirement benefit as a single life annuity commencing at normal retirement age is equal to $17,887.50 ($30,637.50 minus $12,750). Thus, the amount of E's additional early retirement benefit payable as a straight life annuity at age 62$^1/_2$ is equal to $16,545.94 per year ($17,887.50 per year times 92.5% (100% minus 3% for 2$^1/_2$ years)). Employee E elects, with spousal consent, a 10-year certain and life annuity that applies to the remainder of E's accrued benefit. This annuity is in addition to the previously elected joint and 50% survivor annuity payable as E's phased retirement benefit.

Example 2. (i) *Same Plan and Phased Retirement Program, Except Annual Testing Required.* The facts with respect to the Plan X and M's phased retirement program are the same as in *Example 1*, except that the program does not provide that the employee's compensation during phased retirement will be reduced by that same percentage as is applied to calculate phased retirement benefits, but instead the compensation depends on the number of hours worked by the employee. Plan X provides for annual testing on a calendar year basis and for an employee's phased retirement benefit to be reduced proportionately if the hours worked exceed a threshold, under provisions which reflect the variance permitted paragraph (d)(4)(ii) of this section.

(ii) *Employee Has Small Increase in Hours.* The facts with respect to Employee E are the same as in *Example 1*, except that E's full time work schedule would result in 2,000 hours worked annually, E's work schedule fraction is 50%, and E works 500 hours from July 1, 2006 through December 31, 2006, 1,000 hours in 2007, 1,200 hours in 2008, and 600 hours from January 1, 2009 through E's full retirement on June 30, 2009.

(iii) *Application of Testing Rules.* No comparison of hours is required for the partial testing period that occurs in 2006. For 2007, no reduction is required in E's phased retirement benefit as a result of the hours worked by E during 2007 because the hours did not exceed E's work schedule (50% of 2,000). For 2008, although the hours worked by E exceeded E's work schedule, no reduction is required because the hours worked in 2008 were not materially greater than E's work schedule (1,200 is not more than the variance permitted under paragraph (d)(4)(ii) of this section, which is 133-$^1/_3$% of 1,000). E's total accrued benefit upon E's retirement on July 1, 2009 would be based on 21.65 years of service to reflect the actual hours worked from July 1, 2006 through June 30, 2009.

Example 3. (i) *Same Plan and Phased Retirement Program, Except Material Increase in Hours.* The facts with respect to the Plan X and M's phased retirement program are the same as in *Example 2*, except E works 1,400 hours in 2008 and 700 hours in the first half of 2009.

(ii) *Application of Testing Rules.* No comparison of hours is required for the partial testing period that occurs in 2006. For 2007, no reduction is required in E's phased retirement benefit as a result of the hours worked by E during 2007 because the hours did not exceed 50% of 2,000. However, the hours worked by E during 2008 exceed 133-$^1/_3$% of E's work schedule (50% of 2,000), so that the phased retirement benefit paid to E during 2009 must be reduced. The reduction is effective March 1, 2009. The new phased retirement benefit of $5,232.60 is based on 30% of the participant's accrued benefit as of July 1, 2006, payable as a joint and 50% survivor annuity commencing on that date (30% times $25,500 times the early retirement factor of 76% times the joint and 50% factor of 90%). This is equivalent to reducing the previously elected joint and 50% survivor annuity payable with respect to E by 40% (400 "excess" hours divided by the 1,000 hour expected reduction). When E retires fully on July 1, 2009, E's total accrued benefit as of July 1, 2009 as a single life annuity commencing at normal retirement age is $31,065 per year ($95,000 times 1.5% times 21.8 years of service). This accrued benefit is offset by (A) E's phased retirement accrued benefit (which is $7,650 (600 divided by 2,000 times $25,500)) plus (B) the actuarial equivalent of 40% of the payments that were made to E from January 1, 2008 through February 28, 2009.

Example 4. (i) *Same Plan and Phased Retirement Program, Except Employer and Employee Agree to Decrease Hours.* The facts with respect to the Plan X and M's phased retirement program are the same as in *Example 2*, except before 2008, E enters into an agreement with M to decrease E's number of hours worked from 50% of full time to 25% of full time. E works 500 hours in 2008 and 250 hours in 2009.

(ii) *Application of Multiple Benefit Rule.* Under paragraph (e)(2) of this section, Plan M may provide for an additional phased retirement benefit to be offered to E for 2008. The maximum increase would be for the phased retirement benefit paid to E during 2009 to be increased based on a phased retirement accrued benefit equal to 75% of E's accrued benefit (1,500 divided by 2,000). Thus, the amount being paid to E would be increased, effective January 1, 2008, based on the excess of 75% of E's total accrued benefit on December 31, 2007, over E's original phased retirement accrued benefit of $12,750. Employee E would have the right to elect, with spousal consent, any annuity form offered under Plan X (with the actuarial adjustment for time of commencement and form of payment to be based on the age of E and any contingent beneficiary (and E's service, if applicable) on June 1, 2008), which would be in addition to the previously elected joint and 50% survivor annuity payable as E's original phased retirement benefit. When E retires fully on July 1, 2009, Employee E's total accrued benefit as of July 1, 2009 would be offset by (A) E's original phased retirement accrued benefit plus (B) the phased retirement accrued benefit for which additional phased retirement benefits were payable beginning in 2008.

(g) *Effective date.*—The rules of this section apply to plan years beginning on or after the date of publication of the Treasury decision adopting these rules as final regulations in the Federal Register.

Governmental Pension Plans: Applicability of Normal Retirement Age Regulations

Governmental Pension Plans: Applicability of Normal Retirement Age Regulations.—Amendments to Reg. §1.401(a)-1, providing rules relating to the determination of whether the normal retirement age under a governmental plan (within the meaning of section 414(d) of the Code) that is a pension plan satisfies the requirements of section 401(a) and whether the payment of definitely determinable benefits that commence at the plan's normal retirement age satisfies these requirements, are proposed (published in the Federal Register on January 27, 2016) (REG-147310-12).

Par. 2. Section 1.401(a)-1 is amended by:

1. Revising paragraph (b)(2)(v).
2. Adding paragraph (b)(2)(vi).
3. Revising the heading and the second sentence of paragraph (b)(4).

The revisions read as follows:

§1.401(a)-1. Post-ERISA qualified plans and qualified trusts; in general.

* * *

(b) * * *

(2) * * *

(v) *Rules of application for governmental plans.*—(A) *In general.*—In the case of a governmental plan (within the meaning of section 414(d)) that provides for distributions before retirement, the general rule described in paragraph (b)(2)(i) of this section may be satisfied in accordance with paragraph (b)(2)(ii) of this section or this paragraph (b)(2)(v). In the case of a governmental plan that does not provide for distributions before retirement, the plan's normal retirement age is not required to comply with the general rule described in paragraph (b)(2)(i) of this section or this paragraph (b)(2)(v).

(B) *Age 60 and 5 years of service safe harbor.*—A normal retirement age under a governmental plan that is the later of age 60 or the age at which the participant has been credited with at least 5 years of service under the plan is deemed to be not earlier than the earliest age that is reasonably representative of the typical retirement age for the industry in which the covered workforce is employed.

(C) *Age 55 and 10 years of service safe harbor.*—A normal retirement age under a governmental plan that is the later of age 55 or the age at which the participant has been credited with at least 10 years of service under the plan is deemed to be not earlier than the earliest age that is reasonably representative of the typical retirement age for the industry in which the covered workforce is employed.

(D) *Sum of 80 safe harbor.*—A normal retirement age under a governmental plan that is the participant's age at which the sum of the participant's age plus the number of years of service that have been credited to the participant under the plan equals 80 or more is deemed to be not earlier than the earliest age that is reasonably representative of the typical retirement age for the industry in which the covered workforce is employed. For example, a normal retirement age under a governmental plan that is age 55 for a participant who has been credited with 25 years of service would satisfy the rule described in this paragraph.

(E) *Service-based combination safe harbor.*—A normal retirement age under a governmental plan that is the earlier of the participant's age at which the participant has been credited with at least 25 years of service under the plan and an age that satisfies any other safe harbor provided under paragraphs (b)(2)(v)(B) through (D) of this section is deemed to be not earlier than the earliest age that is reasonably representative of the typical retirement age for the industry in which the covered workforce is employed. For example, a normal retirement age under a governmental plan that is the earlier of the participant's age at which the participant has been credited with 25 years of service under the plan and the later of age 60 or the age at which the participant has been credited with 5 years of service under the plan would satisfy this safe harbor.

(F) *Age 50 safe harbor for qualified public safety employees.*—A normal retirement age under a governmental plan that is age 50 or later is deemed to be not earlier than the earliest age that is reasonably representative of the typical retirement age for the industry in which the covered workforce is employed if the participants to which this normal retirement age applies are qualified public safety employees (within the meaning of section 72(t)(10)(B)).

(G) *Sum of 70 safe harbor for qualified public safety employees.*—A normal retirement age under a governmental plan that is the participant's age at which the sum of the participant's age plus the number of years of service that have been credited to the participant under the plan equals 70 or more, is deemed to be not earlier than the earliest age that is reasonably representative of the typical retirement age for the industry in which the covered workforce is employed if the participants to which this normal retirement age applies are qualified public safety employees (within the meaning of section 72(t)(10)(B)).

(H) *Service-based safe harbor for qualified public safety employees.*—A normal retirement age under a governmental plan that is the age at which the participant has been credited with at least 20 years of service under the plan is deemed to be not earlier than the earliest age that is reasonably representative of the typical retirement age for the industry in which the covered workforce is employed if the participants to which this normal retirement age applies are qualified public safety employees (within the meaning of section 72(t)(10)(B)). For example, a normal retirement age that covers only qualified public safety employees and that is an employee's age when the employee has been credited with 25 years of service under a governmental plan would satisfy this safe harbor.

(I) *Reserved.*

(J) *Other normal retirement ages.*—In the case of a normal retirement age under a governmental plan that fails to satisfy any safe harbor described in paragraph (b)(2)(ii) of this section or this paragraph (b)(2)(v), whether the age is not earlier than the earliest age that is reasonably representative of the typical retirement age for the industry in which the covered workforce is employed is based on all of the relevant facts and circumstances.

(vi) *Special normal retirement age rule for certain plans.*—See section 411(f), which provides a special rule for determining a permissible normal retirement age under certain defined benefit plans.

* * *

(4) *Effective/applicability date.*—* * * In the case of a governmental plan (as defined in section 414(d)), the rules in paragraph (b)(2)(v) of this section are effective for employees hired during plan years beginning on or after the later of: January 1, 2017; or the close of the first regular legislative session of the legislative body with the authority to amend the plan that begins on or after the date that is 3 months after the final regulations are published in the **Federal Register**. However, a governmental plan sponsor may elect to apply the rules of paragraph (b)(2)(v) of this section to earlier periods. * * *

Retirement Plans: Distributions: Deferral of Receipt: Notification of Consequences

Retirement Plans: Distributions: Deferral of Receipt: Notification of Consequences.—Amendments to Reg. §§1.401(a)-13 and 1.401(a)-20, specifying that the notice required under Code Sec. 411(a)(11) to be provided to a participant of his or her right, if any, to defer receipt of an immediately distributable benefit must also describe the consequences of failing to defer receipt of the distribution, are proposed (published in the Federal Register on October 9, 2008) (REG-107318-08).

Par. 2. For each entry listed in the "Location" column, remove the language in the "Remove" column and add the language in the "Add" column in its place.

§1.401(a)-13. Assignment or alienation of benefits.

Location	Remove	Add
1.401(a)-13(g)(4)(ii), first sentence	90 days	180 days

Par. 2. For each entry listed in the "Location" column, remove the language in the "Remove" column and add the language in the "Add" column in its place.

§1.401(a)-20. Requirements of qualified joint and survivor annuity and qualified preretirement survivor annuity.

Location	Remove	Add
1.401(a)-20, A-4, third sentence	90 days	180 days
1.401(a)-20, A-10(a), fifth and sixth sentences	90 days	180 days
1.401(a)-20, A-16, sixth sentence	90 days	180 days
1.401(a)-20, A-24(a)(1), fifth sentence	90 days	180 days

Closed Defined Benefit Pensions Plans: Nondiscrimination Relief

Closed Defined Benefit Pensions Plans: Nondiscrimination Relief.—Amendments to Reg. §§1.401(a)(4)-0, 1.401(a)(4)-2—1.401(a)(4)-4, 1.401(a)(4)-8, 1.401(a)(4)-9, 1.401(a)(4)-12 and 1.401(a)(4)-13, modifying the nondiscrimination requirements applicable to certain retirement

plans that provide additional benefits to a grandfathered group of employees following certain changes in the coverage of a defined benefit plan or a defined benefit plan formula, are proposed (published in the Federal Register on January 29, 2016) (REG-125761-14).

Par. 2. Section 1.401(a)(4)-0 is amended by:

1. Adding paragraph (c)(5) to the entry for § 1.401(a)(4)-2.
2. Adding paragraph (d)(8) to the entry for § 1.401(a)(4)-4.
3. Adding paragraph (a)(4) to the entry for § 1.401(a)(4)-13.

The additions read as follows:

§ 1.401(a)(4)-0. Table of contents.

* * *

§ 1.401(a)(4)-2. Nondiscrimination in amount of employer contributions under a defined contribution plan.

* * *

(c) * * *

(5) Effective/applicability date.

* * *

§ 1.401(a)(4)-4. Nondiscriminatory availability of benefits, rights, and features.

* * *

(d) * * *

(8) Special testing rule for grandfathered group of employees.

* * *

§ 1.401(a)(4)-13. Effective dates and fresh-start rules.

(a) * * *

(4) Effective/applicability date.

* * *

Par. 3. Section 1.401(a)(4)-2 is amended by:

1. Revising paragraph (c)(3)(ii).
2. Revising *Examples 4* and *5* in paragraph (c)(4).
3. Adding *Examples 6* and *7* to paragraph (c)(4).
4. Adding paragraph (c)(5).

The revisions and additions read as follows:

§ 1.401(a)(4)-2. Nondiscrimination in amount of employer contributions under a defined contribution plan.

* * *

(c) * * *

(3) * * *

(ii) *Application of nondiscriminatory classification test.*—A rate group satisfies the nondiscriminatory classification test of § 1.410(b)-4 if and only if—

(A) The formula that is used to determine the allocation for the HCE with respect to whom the rate group is established applies to a group of employees that satisfies the reasonable classification requirement of § 1.410(b)-4(b); and

(B) The ratio percentage of the rate group is greater than or equal to the midpoint between the safe and unsafe harbor percentages applicable to the plan (or the ratio percentage of the plan, if that percentage is less).

* * *

(4) * * *

Example 4. (a) The facts are the same as in *Example 3*, except that N4 has an allocation rate of 8.0 percent. In addition, the formula that is used to determine the allocation for H2 is the same formula that is used to determine the allocation for all other employees in Plan D.

(b) There are two rate groups in Plan D. Rate group 1 consists of H1 and all those employees who have an allocation rate greater than or equal to H1's allocation rate (5.0 percent). Thus, rate group 1 consists of H1, H2 and N1 through N4. Rate group 2 consists of H2, and all those employees who have an allocation rate greater than or equal to H2's allocation rate (7.5 percent). Thus, rate group 2 consists of H2 and N4.

(c) Rate group 1 satisfies the ratio percentage test under § 1.410(b)-2(b)(2) because the ratio percentage of the rate group is 100 percent—that is, 100 percent (the percentage of all nonhighly compensated nonexcludable employees who are in the rate group) divided by 100 percent (the percentage of all highly compensated nonexcludable employees who are in the rate group).

(d) Rate group 2 does not satisfy the ratio percentage test of § 1.410(b)-2(b)(2) because the ratio percentage of the rate group is 50 percent—that is, 25 percent (the percentage of all nonhighly compensated nonexcludable employees who are in the rate group) divided by 50 percent (the percentage of all highly compensated nonexcludable employees who are in the rate group).

(e) However, under paragraph (c)(3)(ii) of this section rate group 2 satisfies the nondiscriminatory classification test of § 1.410(b)-4 because (i) the formula that is used to determine the allocation for H2 applies to a group of employees that satisfies the reasonable classification requirement of § 1.410(b)-4(b) (in this case, because it applies to all the employees) and (ii) the ratio percentage of the rate group (50 percent) is greater than the midpoint between the safe harbor and unsafe harbor percentages applicable to the plan under § 1.410(b)-4(c)(4) (40.5 percent).

(f) Under paragraph (c)(3)(iii) of this section, rate group 2 satisfies the average benefit percentage test if Plan D satisfies the average benefit percentage test. (The requirement that Plan D satisfy the average benefit percentage test applies even though Plan D satisfies the ratio percentage test and would ordinarily not need to run the average benefit percentage test.) If Plan D satisfies the average benefit percentage test, then rate group 2 satisfies section 410(b); thus, Plan D satisfies the general test in paragraph (c)(1) of this section because each rate group under the plan satisfies section 410(b).

Example 5. (a) Plan E satisfies section 410(b) by satisfying the nondiscriminatory classification test of § 1.410(b)-4 and the average benefit percentage test of § 1.410(b)-5 (without regard to § 1.410(b)-5(f)). See § 1.410(b)-2(b)(3). Plan E uses the facts-and-circumstances requirements of § 1.410(b)-4(c)(3) to satisfy the nondiscriminatory classification test of §1.410(b)-4. The safe and unsafe harbor percentages applicable to the plan under §1.410(b)-4(c)(4) are 29 and 20 percent, respectively. Plan E has a ratio percentage of 22 percent. Rate group 1 under Plan E has a ratio percentage of 23 percent. The formula that is used to determine the allocation for the HCE with respect to whom rate group 1 was formed applies to all other employees.

(b) Under paragraph (c)(3)(ii) of this section, rate group 1 satisfies the nondiscriminatory classification requirement of §1.410(b)-4, because (i) the formula that is used to determine the allocation for the HCE with respect to whom the rate group was formed applies to a group of employees that satisfies the reasonable classification requirement of §1.410(b)-4(b) (in this case, because it applies to all the employees) and (ii) the ratio percentage of the rate group (23 percent) is greater than the lesser of—

(*1*) The ratio percentage for the plan as a whole (22 percent); and

(*2*) The midpoint between the safe and unsafe harbor percentages (24.5 percent).

(c) Under paragraph (c)(3)(iii) of this section, the rate group satisfies section 410(b) because the plan satisfies the average benefit percentage test of §1.410(b)-5.

Example 6. (a) Employer Z maintains a defined contribution plan, Plan F. Employer Z has six nonexcludable employees, all of whom benefit under Plan F. There is one HCE (H1) and five NHCEs (N1 through N5). There is one rate group under Plan F. The formula that is used to determine the allocation for H1 is the greater of $20,000 or 10% of compensation for the year. The formula that applies to determine the allocation for N1 through N5 is 10% of compensation.

(b) Under paragraph (c)(3)(ii) of this section, the rate group with respect to H1 does not satisfy the nondiscriminatory classification test under §1.410(b)-4 because the formula that is used to determine the allocation for H1 (with respect to whom the rate group is established) only applies to H1. Therefore, the rate group will satisfy paragraph (c)(3) of this section only if the ratio percentage of the rate group is greater than or equal to 70 percent. This ratio percentage test applies even if H1's compensation is greater than $200,000. In such a case, the rate group will pass the ratio percentage test (and accordingly the plan will satisfy the general test of this paragraph (c)) because each employee receives an allocation of 10% of compensation and therefore the ratio percentage for the rate group is equal to 100%.

Example 7. The facts are the same as in *Example 6*, except that the classification of employees who are entitled to benefit under the formula that applies to H1 includes N1 and N2, who are identified by name. Under paragraph (c)(3)(ii) of this section, the rate group with respect to H1 does not satisfy the nondiscriminatory classification test under §1.410(b)-4 because the classification of H1, N1 and N2 by name does not satisfy the reasonable classification requirement of §1.410(b)-4(b). Therefore, the rate group with respect to H1 will satisfy paragraph (c)(3) of this section only if the ratio percentage of the rate group is greater than or equal to 70 percent.

(5) *Effective/applicability date*.—See §1.401(a)(4)-13(a)(4) for rules on the effective/applicability date of this paragraph (c).

Par. 4. In §1.401(a)(4)-3, paragraph (c)(2) is revised to read as follows:

§1.401(a)(4)-3. Nondiscrimination in amount of employer-provided benefits under a defined benefit plan.

* * *

(c) * * *

(2) *Satisfaction of section 410(b) by a rate group*.—For purposes of determining whether a rate group satisfies section 410(b), the rules of §1.401(a)(4)-2(c)(3) apply except that §1.401(a)(4)-2(c)(3)(ii)(A) is applied by substituting "benefit formula" for "formula that is used to determine the allocation." See paragraph (c)(4) of this section and §1.401(a)(4)-2(c)(4), *Example 3* through *Example 6*, for examples of this rule. See §1.401(a)(4)-13(a)(4) for rules on the effective/applicability date of this paragraph (c)(2).

* * *

Par. 5. In §1.401(a)(4)-4, paragraph (d)(8) is added to read as follows:

§1.401(a)(4)-4. Nondiscriminatory availability of benefits, rights, and features.

* * *

(d) * * *

(8) *Special testing rule for grandfathered group of employees*.—(i) *General rule*.—For a plan year that begins on or after the fifth anniversary of the closure date with respect to a closed defined benefit plan, a benefit, right, or feature under a defined benefit or defined contribution plan that is available only to a grandfathered group of employees with respect to the closed defined benefit plan is treated as satisfying paragraphs (b) and (c) of this section for the plan year, provided that—

(A) No plan amendment that affects the availability of the benefit, right, or feature (other than the closure amendment) has an applicable amendment date (within the meaning of §1.411(d)-3(g)(4)) that is within the period that begins on the closure date and ends on the last day of the plan year; and

(B) The additional requirements of paragraph (d)(8)(ii) or (iii) of this section, whichever is applicable, are satisfied.

(ii) *Additional requirements in the case of a benefit, right, or feature provided under a defined benefit plan*.—If the benefit, right, or feature is provided under a defined benefit plan, then the following additional requirements apply—

(A) The defined benefit plan under which the benefit, right, or feature is provided is the closed defined benefit plan;

(B) No plan amendment that affects the availability of the benefit, right, or feature (other than the closure amendment) has an applicable amendment date that is within the 5-year period ending on the closure date; and

(C) The closure amendment that restricted the availability of the benefit, right, or feature, making it available only to the grandfathered group of employees, must also have provided for a significant change in the type of benefit formula under the plan (such as a change from a benefit formula that is not a statutory hybrid benefit formula to a lump sum-based benefit formula).

(iii) *Additional requirements in the case of a benefit, right, or feature provided under a defined contribution plan.*—If the benefit, right, or feature is provided under a defined contribution plan, then the following additional requirements apply—

(A) The benefit, right, or feature must be a right to a rate of matching contributions provided under the defined contribution plan;

(B) The rate of matching contributions must be reasonably designed so that the matching contributions will replace some or all of the value of the benefit accruals that each employee in the grandfathered group of employees would have been provided under the closed defined benefit plan in the absence of a closure amendment (based on the terms of that plan and the section 415(b)(1)(A) dollar limit in effect immediately prior to the closure date);

(C) The closed defined benefit plan must satisfy the conditions set forth in § 1.401(a)(4)-8(b)(1)(iii)(D)*(3)*; and

(D) The rate of matching contributions must be provided in a consistent manner to all similarly situated employees.

(iv) *Certain amendments not taken into account.*—For purposes of applying the rules under this paragraph (d)(8), the following plan amendments are not taken into account (and, in the case of an amendment described in paragraph (d)(8)(iv)(C) or (D) of this section, the rules of this paragraph (d)(8) are applied as if the benefit, right, or feature provided after the amendment were the benefit, right, or feature provided before the amendment):

(A) An amendment adopted during the 5-year period ending on the closure date that extends eligibility for the benefit, right, or feature to an acquired group of employees provided that all similarly situated employees within that group are treated in a consistent manner.

(B) An amendment adopted after the closure date that expands or restricts the eligibility for the benefit, right, or feature, provided that, as of the applicable amendment date, the ratio percentage of the group of employees eligible for the benefit, right, or feature (taking into account the plan amendment) is not less than the ratio percentage of the group of employees eligible for the benefit, right, or feature provided before the amendment.

(C) An amendment adopted after the closure date that results in a replacement of the benefit, right, or feature with another benefit, right, or feature that is available to the same group of employees as the original benefit, right, or feature, provided that the original benefit, right, or feature is of inherently equal or greater value (within the meaning of paragraph (d)(4)(i)(A) of this section) than the benefit, right, or feature that replaces it.

(D) An amendment adopted after the closure date that results in a replacement of the benefit, right, or feature with another benefit, right, or feature that is available to the same group of employees as the original benefit, right, or feature, provided that there is only a *de minimis* difference between the amount payable under the original benefit, right, or feature and the amount payable under the benefit, right, or feature that replaces it.

(E) An amendment that is permitted by guidance published by the Commissioner in the Internal Revenue Bulletin.

(v) *Examples.*—The following examples illustrate the rules in this paragraph (d)(8):

Example 1—(i) *Pre-amendment defined benefit plan.* Employer A maintains Plan P, a defined benefit plan that provides for an annual benefit equal to 2% of an employee's average annual compensation multiplied by the employee's years of service. Plan P also provides for a subsidized early retirement benefit available to employees who retire between the ages of 55 and 65 with 20 years of service. Plan P was established in 2003. The plan year is a calendar year. For the 2015 plan year, Plan P satisfied the nondiscrimination requirements under sections 410(b) and 401(a)(4) without regard to the special rules under section 410(b)(6)(C) and without aggregation with any other plan.

(ii) *Plan conversion amendment.* On November 1, 2015, Employer A amends Plan P to cease future accruals under its benefit formula effective as of the close of the plan year ending December 31, 2015 and to provide future benefit accruals under a cash balance formula. The cash balance formula provides for pay credits equal to 5% of compensation and annual interest credits at an interest crediting rate of 6%. Early retirement benefits payable with respect to benefits accrued under the cash balance formula are determined as the actuarial equivalent of the hypothetical account balance, determined using reasonable actuarial assumptions that are specified in Plan P. Under the terms of the conversion amendment, an employee's benefit is equal to the employee's benefit under the prior benefit formula as of the close of the plan year ending December 31, 2015, plus the amount determined under the cash balance formula. However, any employee who had attained the age of 50 and had completed 15 years of service on or before December 31, 2015 is entitled to a plan benefit that is the greater of the benefit determined under the pre-amendment formula, or the benefit described in the prior sentence. Except for the closure amendment, there is no other plan amendment that affects the availability of Plan P's early retirement subsidy. No other significant change to Plan P's coverage or benefit formula is made with an applicable amendment date that is during the period beginning on January 1, 2011 and ending on December 31, 2015 (the 5-year period ending on the closure date).

(iii) *Applicability of special testing rule.* The plan conversion amendment is a closure amendment with a closure date of December 31, 2015. Plan P's subsidized early retirement benefit available solely to the grandfathered group of employees is a separate benefit, right, or feature that must be tested for current and effective availability under paragraphs (b) and (c) of this section. For a plan year that begins on or after January 1, 2021, Plan P's subsidized early retirement benefit is eligible for the relief provided by the special testing rule of this paragraph (d)(8) because all of the applicable requirements are satisfied. The requirement under paragraph (d)(8)(i)(A) of this section is satisfied because no other plan amendment that affects the availability of the subsidized early retirement benefit has an applicable amendment date that is on or after December 31, 2015. The additional requirements pertaining to a benefit, right, or feature provided under a defined benefit plan are also satisfied: the subsidized early retirement benefit is provided under a closed defined benefit plan as required by paragraph (d)(8)(ii)(A) of this section; no amendment that affected the availability of the subsidized early retirement benefit was made with an applicable amendment date during the 5-year period ending on the closure date as required by paragraph (d)(8)(ii)(B) of this section; and Plan P has undergone a significant change in benefit formula in connection with the closure amendment that resulted in a restriction on the availability of the subsidized early retirement benefit as required by paragraph (d)(8)(ii)(C) of this section.

Example 2—(i) *Closure of defined benefit plan.* The facts are the same as in *Example 1* of this paragraph (d)(8)(v), except that, instead of adopting a plan conversion amendment, Employer A amends Plan P to cease future accruals under the original benefit formula for all employees.

(ii) *Plan amendment to profit-sharing plan that provides enhanced rate of matching contributions.* Employer A has a profit-sharing plan that includes a qualified cash or deferred arrangement and matching contributions with respect to elective deferrals of up to 3% of compensation. On November 1, 2015, Employer A amends the plan to provide, effective January 1, 2016, for additional matching contributions of up to an additional 4% of compensation solely for employees who (1) were previously covered under the defined benefit plan, and (2) had attained the age of 50 and had 15 years of service on or before December 31, 2015. This enhanced rate of matching contributions is reasonably designed so that the matching contributions will replace some or all of the value of the benefit accruals that would have otherwise been provided to this grandfathered group of employees under Plan P. Employer A makes no other change to this enhanced rate of matching contribution after the enhanced rate is established.

(iii) *Applicability of special testing rule.* The plan amendment is a closure amendment with a closure date of December 31, 2015. The enhanced rate of matching contribution that is available solely to the grandfathered group of employees is a separate benefit, right, or feature that must be tested for current and effective availability under paragraphs (b) and (c) of this section. For a plan year that begins on or after January 1, 2021, Plan P's enhanced rate of matching contribution is eligible for the relief provided by the special testing rule of this paragraph (d)(8) because all applicable requirements are satisfied. The requirement under paragraph (d)(8)(i)(A) of this section is satisfied because no change was made to the enhanced rate of match with an applicable amendment date that is on or after December 31, 2015. The following applicable additional requirements are also satisfied: the benefit, right, or feature provided under the defined contribution plan is a rate of matching contribution as required by paragraph (d)(8)(iii)(A) of this section; the enhanced rate of matching contribution is reasonably designed so that the matching contributions will replace some of the value of the benefit accruals that each employee in the grandfathered group of employees would have otherwise been provided under Plan P immediately prior to the closure date as required by paragraph (d)(8)(iii)(B) of this section; and the rate of matching contributions is provided in a consistent manner to all similarly situated employees as required by paragraph (d)(8)(iii)(D) of this section.

(iv) *Applicability of §1.401(a)(4)-8(b)(1)(iii)(D)(3).* In addition to the requirements described in paragraph (iii) of this *Example 2*, Plan P meets the conditions for a closed defined benefit plan specified in §1.401(a)(4)-8(b)(1)(iii)(D)(3) as required by paragraph (d)(8)(iii)(C) of this section because Plan P's prior benefit formula generated equivalent normal allocation rates that increased as employees attained higher ages; Plan P satisfied the minimum coverage and nondiscrimination requirements under sections 410(b) and 401(a)(4) without regard to the special rules under section 410(b)(6)(C) and without aggregating with any other plan for the plan year preceding the closure date; and Plan P was in effect for the five-year period ending on the closure date and neither the benefit formula nor the coverage of the plan was significantly changed during this period.

(vi) *Effective/applicability dates.*—The rules of this paragraph (d)(8) apply to plan years beginning on or after the date of publication of the Treasury decision adopting these rules as final in the **Federal Register**. Taxpayers may apply the rules of this paragraph (d)(8) for plan years beginning on or after January 1, 2014.

* * *

Par. 6. Section 1.401(a)(4)-8 is amended by:

1. Revising paragraphs (b)(1)(iii)(B) through (E).
2. Removing paragraph (b)(1)(iii)(F).
3. Adding paragraph (b)(1)(iv)(E).

The revisions and additions read as follows:

§1.401(a)(4)-8. Cross-testing.

* * *

(b) * * *

(1) * * *

(iii) * * *

(B) *Defined benefit replacement allocations disregarded.*—In determining whether a plan has broadly available allocation rates for the plan year within the meaning of paragraph (b)(1)(iii)(A) of this section, the following rules in paragraphs (b)(1)(iii)(B)(*1*) and (*2*) of this section apply:

(*1*) If an employee receives a defined benefit replacement allocation (within the meaning of paragraph (b)(1)(iii)(D) of this section) for the plan year in addition to the employee's otherwise applicable allocation under the plan for the plan year, then the employee's allocation rate is determined without regard to the defined benefit replacement allocation.

(2) If an employee receives an allocation for the plan year that is the greater of the allocation for which the employee would otherwise be eligible and the defined benefit replacement allocation (within the meaning of paragraph (b)(1)(iii)(D) of this section), then the allocation for which the employee would otherwise be eligible is considered currently available to the employee, even if the employee's defined benefit replacement allocation is greater. See paragraph (b)(1)(iii)(C)(2) of this section for additional rules relating to "greater-of" plan provisions.

(C) *Plan provisions.—(1) In general.—* Plan provisions providing for defined benefit replacement allocations (within the meaning of paragraph (b)(1)(iii)(D) of this section) for the plan year must specify both the group of employees who are eligible for the defined benefit replacement allocations and the amount of the defined benefit replacement allocations.

(2) "Greater-of" plan provisions.— An allocation does not fail to be a defined benefit replacement allocation within the meaning of paragraph (b)(1)(iii)(D) of this section merely because the plan provides that each employee who is eligible for a defined benefit replacement allocation receives the greater of that allocation and the allocation for which the employee would otherwise be eligible under the plan.

*(3) Limited plan amendments.—*Except as provided in paragraph (b)(1)(iii)(D)(5) of this section, an allocation is not a defined benefit replacement allocation within the meaning of paragraph (b)(1)(iii)(D) of this section for the plan year if the plan provisions relating to the allocation are amended after the date those plan provisions are both adopted and effective.

(D) *Defined benefit replacement allocation.—(1) In general.—*A defined benefit replacement allocation is an allocation under a defined contribution plan provided only to a grandfathered group of employees with respect to a closed defined benefit plan. An allocation is treated as a defined benefit replacement allocation if—

(i) The allocation satisfies the conditions to be a replacement allocation with respect to a closed defined benefit plan in paragraph (b)(1)(iii)(D)(2) of this section;

(ii) The closed defined benefit plan satisfies the conditions in paragraph (b)(1)(iii)(D)(3) of this section; and

(iii) For each plan year that begins before the fifth anniversary of the closure date of the closed defined benefit plan, the grandfathered group of employees is a nondiscriminatory group of employees within the meaning of paragraph (b)(1)(iii)(D)(4) of this section.

*(2) Replacement allocation.—*An allocation is a replacement allocation with respect to a closed defined benefit plan under this paragraph (b)(1)(iii)(D)(2) if—

(i) The allocation is designed so that it is reasonably expected to replace some or all of the value of the benefit accruals that each employee in the grandfathered group of employees would have been provided under the closed defined benefit plan in the absence of a closure amendment (based on the terms of that plan and the section 415(b)(1)(A) dollar limit in effect immediately prior to the closure date); and

(ii) The allocation is provided in a consistent manner to all similarly situated employees.

*(3) Closed defined benefit plan.—*A closed defined benefit plan satisfies the conditions in this paragraph (b)(1)(iii)(D)(3) if—

(i) The closed defined benefit plan's benefit formula applicable to the grandfathered group of employees generated equivalent normal allocation rates that increased from year to year as employees attained higher ages or were credited with additional years of service;

(ii) The closed defined benefit plan satisfied the minimum coverage and nondiscrimination requirements under sections 410(b) and 401(a)(4) without regard to the special rules under section 410(b)(6)(C) and without aggregating with any other plan, for the plan year preceding the closure date; and

(iii) The closed defined benefit plan was in effect for the 5-year period ending on the closure date and neither the benefit formula nor the coverage of the plan was significantly changed by plan amendment with an effective date during this period.

*(4) Nondiscriminatory group of employees.—*A group of employees is a nondiscriminatory group of employees for purposes of this paragraph (b)(1)(iii)(D)(4) if the group of employees satisfies section 410(b) for the plan year (without regard to § 1.410(b)-5).

*(5) Certain amendments not taken into account.—*For purposes of determining whether the requirements of paragraphs (b)(1)(iii)(C)(3) and (b)(1)(iii)(D)(3) of this section are satisfied, the following plan amendments are not taken into account:

(i) An amendment to the closed defined benefit plan adopted during the 5-year period ending on the closure date, provided that the accrued benefit or future accruals for any employee are not increased, coverage is not expanded, and the amendment is not discriminatory within the meaning of paragraph (b)(1)(iii)(D)(6) of this section.

(ii) An amendment to the defined contribution plan under which the defined benefit replacement allocation is provided that makes *de minimis* changes in the calculation of that allocation (such as a change in the definition of compensation to include section 132(f) elective reductions).

(iii) An amendment to the defined contribution plan under which the defined benefit replacement allocation is provided that adds or removes a "greater-of" provision described under paragraph (b)(1)(iii)(C)(2) of this section.

(iv) An amendment to the defined contribution plan under which the defined benefit replacement allocation is provided that makes changes in the calculation of that allocation in a manner that is not discriminatory within the meaning of paragraph (b)(1)(iii)(D)(6) of this section.

(v) An amendment that guidance published by the Commissioner in the Internal Revenue Bulletin provides will not be taken into account.

(6) *Nondiscriminatory amendment.*—(*i*) *General rule.*—An amendment to a plan is not discriminatory if the ratio percentage of the plan is not decreased as a result of the amendment and, in the case of a plan that demonstrates compliance with the nondiscrimination in amount requirement of § 1.401(a)(4)-1(b)(2) using a method other than a safe harbor test under § 1.401(a)(4)-2(b), § 1.401(a)(4)-3(b), or paragraph (b)(3) or (c)(3) of this section, the ratio percentage for the rate group with respect to any HCE is not decreased as a result of the amendment.

(*ii*) *Timing of nondiscrimination testing.*—In determining whether the ratio percentage of the plan or the rate group is decreased as a result of an amendment, an amendment that is not in effect for an entire plan year is treated as if it were in effect for the entire plan year. In the case of an amendment that has separate portions with separate effective dates, each portion of the amendment is treated as a separate amendment that must satisfy the requirements of paragraph (b)(1)(iii)(D)(*6*)(*i*) of this section for the plan year in which it takes effect.

(*7*) *Special rules for former employers and acquired employees.*—The following special rules apply in the case of former employers and acquired employees:

(*i*) If the closed defined benefit plan was sponsored by a former employer and not by the employer, then the rules in paragraph (b)(1)(iii)(D)(*3*)(*ii*) of this section do not apply and one year is substituted for 5 years with respect to paragraph (b)(1)(iii)(D)(*3*)(*iii*) of this section;

(*ii*) An amendment adopted during the 5-year period ending on the closure date that extends the coverage or benefit formula of the closed defined benefit plan to an acquired group of employees may be applied (in addition to the amendments described in paragraph (b)(1)(iii)(D)(*5*) of this section) provided that all similarly situated employees within that group are treated in a consistent manner; and

(*iii*) If the employees of a former employer become the employees of the new employer as a result of a transaction that is a merger, acquisition, or similar event, then the transaction is treated as a closure amendment with respect to the former employer's plan as of the effective date of the acquisition.

(E) *Effective/applicability date.*—See § 1.401(a)(4)-13(a)(4) for rules on the effective/applicability date of this section.

(iv) * * *

(E) *Defined benefit replacement allocation may be disregarded.*—In determining whether a plan has a gradual age or service schedule for the plan year within the meaning of paragraph (b)(1)(iv)(A) of this section, if an employee receives a defined benefit replacement allocation (within the meaning of paragraph (b)(1)(iii)(D) of this section) for the plan year, then the plan's schedule is determined without regard to the defined benefit replacement allocation. For this purpose, the rules under paragraph (b)(1)(iii)(B) of this section apply. See § 1.401(a)(4)-13(a)(4) for rules on the effective/applicability date of this paragraph (b)(1)(iv)(E).

* * *

Par. 7. Section 1.401(a)(4)-9 is amended by:

1. Revising paragraphs (b)(2)(v)(A) and (b)(2)(v)(D)(3).
2. Adding paragraphs (b)(2)(v)(D)(4) and (5).
3. Redesignating paragraph (b)(2)(v)(F) as paragraph (b)(2)(v)(H).
4. Adding paragraphs (b)(2)(v)(F) and (b)(2)(v)(G). The revisions and additions read as follows:

§ 1.401(a)(4)-9. Plan aggregation and restructuring.

* * *

(b) * * *

(2) * * *

(v) *Eligibility for testing on a benefits basis.*—(A) *General rule.*—(*1*) *In general.*—Unless, for the plan year, a DB/DC plan is primarily defined benefit in character (within the meaning of paragraph (b)(2)(v)(B) of this section) or consists of broadly available separate plans (within the meaning of paragraph (b)(2)(v)(C) of this section), in order to be permitted to demonstrate satisfaction of the nondiscrimination in amount requirement of § 1.401(a)(4)-1(b)(2) on the basis of benefits, the DB/DC plan must satisfy the minimum aggregate allocation gateway (as described in paragraph (b)(2)(v)(D) of this section) except as provided in paragraph (b)(2)(v)(A)(*2*) of this section.

(*2*) *Additional testing options.*—A DB/DC plan that is not eligible to demonstrate satisfaction of the nondiscrimination in amount requirement of § 1.401(a)(4)-1(b)(2) on the basis of benefits under paragraph (b)(2)(v)(A)(*1*) of this section is permitted to demonstrate satisfaction of that requirement on the basis of benefits if the DB/DC plan satisfies either the closed plan rule of paragraph (b)(2)(v)(F) of this section or the lower interest rate rule of paragraph (b)(2)(v)(G) of this section.

(*3*) *Effective/applicability date.*—See § 1.401(a)(4)-13(a)(4) for rules on the effective/applicability date of this paragraph (b)(2)(v)(A).

* * *

(D) * * *

(*3*) *Averaging of rates for NHCEs.*—(*i*) *Defined benefit plan.*—For purposes of this paragraph (b)(2)(v)(D), a plan is permitted to treat each NHCE who benefits under a defined benefit plan that is part of the DB/DC plan as having an equivalent normal allocation rate equal to the average of the equivalent normal allocation rates under the defined benefit plan for all NHCEs benefitting under that plan.

(*ii*) *Defined contribution plan.*—For purposes of this paragraph (b)(2)(v)(D), a plan is permitted to treat each NHCE who benefits under a defined contribution plan that is part of the DB/DC plan as having an allocation rate equal to the average of the allocation rates under the defined contribution plan for all NHCEs benefitting under that plan.

(*iii*) *Limitations on the averaging of rates.*—For purposes of applying paragraphs (b)(2)(v)(D)(3)(*i*) and (*ii*) of this section, any equivalent normal allocation rate or allocation rate in excess of 15% of plan year compensation is treated as being 15%. The preceding sentence is applied by substituting 25% for 15% each time it appears, but only if any allocation rate or equivalent normal allocation rate higher than 15% results solely from a plan design providing allocation rates or generating equivalent normal allocation rates that are a function of age or service under which higher rates are provided to older or longer-service employees.

(4) Use of matching contributions.—For purposes of this paragraph (b)(2)(v)(D), if an NHCE is eligible for a matching contribution under a defined contribution plan that is part of the DB/DC plan, then the lesser of 3% and the average matching contribution percentage for the group of eligible NHCEs in that plan is permitted to be added to the allocation rate for that NHCE. For this purpose, the average matching contribution percentage for the group of eligible NHCEs in a plan is the actual contribution percentage (within the meaning of § 1.401(m)-5) for that group, determined without taking into account any employee contributions.

(5) Effective/applicability date.—See § 1.401(a)(4)-13(a)(4) for rules on the effective/applicability date of this paragraph (b)(2)(v)(D).

* * *

(F) *Closed plan rule.—(1) In general.*—For a plan year that begins on or after the fifth anniversary of the closure date with respect to a closed defined benefit plan, a DB/DC plan that includes a closed defined benefit plan satisfies the closed plan rule of this paragraph (b)(2)(v)(F) for the plan year if—

(i) The closed defined benefit plan was in effect for the 5-year period ending on the closure date and neither the benefit formula nor the coverage of the plan was significantly changed by plan amendment (other than the closure amendment) with an effective date during the period that begins five years before the closure date and ends on the last day of the plan year; and

(ii) For each plan year that begins on or after the closure date and before the fifth anniversary of the closure date, one of the requirements in paragraph (b)(2)(v)(F)(2) of this section is satisfied.

(2) Testing for 5 years post-closure.—A DB/DC plan meets the requirements of this paragraph (b)(2)(v)(F)(2) if—

(i) Each defined benefit plan that is part of the DB/DC plan satisfies the nondiscrimination in amount requirement of § 1.401(a)(4)-1(b)(2) on the basis of benefits without aggregation with any defined contribution plan;

(ii) The DB/DC plan satisfies the nondiscrimination in amount requirement of § 1.401(a)(4)-1(b)(2) on the basis of contributions; or

(iii) The DB/DC plan satisfies the primarily defined benefit in character requirement of paragraph (b)(2)(v)(B) of this section, or the broadly available separate plans requirement of paragraph (b)(2)(v)(C) of this section.

(3) Certain amendments not taken into account.—For purposes of this paragraph (b)(2)(v)(F), the following plan amendments are not taken into account:

(i) An amendment to the closed defined benefit plan adopted during the 5-year period ending on the closure date, provided that the accrued benefit or future accruals for any employee are not increased, coverage is not expanded, and the amendment is not discriminatory within the meaning of § 1.401(a)(4)-8(b)(1)(iii)(D)*(6)*.

(ii) An amendment adopted during the 5-year period ending on the closure date that extends the benefit formula with respect to the closed defined benefit plan to an acquired group of employees provided that all similarly situated employees within that group are treated in a consistent manner.

(iii) An amendment to the closed defined benefit plan that is adopted after the closure date that is not discriminatory within the meaning of § 1.401(a)(4)-8(b)(1)(iii)(D)*(6)*.

(iv) An amendment to the closed defined benefit plan that makes *de minimis* changes in the benefit formula.

(v) An amendment that guidance published by the Commissioner in the Internal Revenue Bulletin provides will not be taken into account.

(G) *Lower interest rate rule.*—A DB/DC plan satisfies the lower interest rate rule of this paragraph (b)(2)(v)(G) if the plan can demonstrate satisfaction of the nondiscrimination in amount requirement of § 1.401(a)(4)-1(b)(2) on the basis of benefits, provided that benefits are normalized using an interest rate of 6% rather than a standard interest rate.

* * *

Par. 8. In § 1.401(a)(4)-12, add definitions for *Closed defined benefit plan, Closure amendment, Closure date,* and *Grandfathered group of employees* in alphabetical order to read as follows:

§ 1.401(a)(4)-12. Definitions.

* * *

Closed defined benefit plan. Closed defined benefit plan means a defined benefit plan that has been amended to—

(1) Cease accruals under a benefit formula provided by the defined benefit plan for some or all employees whose benefits were previously determined under that benefit formula; or

(2) Limit participation in the defined benefit plan to a group of employees that consists of some or all of the plan participants who participated in the plan as of the closure date.

Closure amendment. A closure amendment is a plan amendment that results in a closed defined benefit plan.

Closure date. A closure date is the last day before accruals cease or participation is limited pursuant to the closure amendment.

* * *

Grandfathered group of employees. A grandfathered group of employees with respect to a closure amendment means the group of employees who, after the closure date, either continue accruals under the closed defined benefit plan's benefit formula or are entitled to an allocation formula under a defined contribution plan because those employees previously participated in the closed defined benefit plan.

* * *

Par. 9. In §1.401(a)(4)-13, paragraph (a)(4) is added to read as follows:

§1.401(a)(4)-13. Effective dates and fresh-start rules.—(a) * * *

(4) *Effective/applicability date.*—(i) *In general.*—Except as otherwise provided in this paragraph (a)(4), the rules of §1.401(a)(4)-2(c), §1.401(a)(4)-3(c)(2), §1.401(a)(4)-8(b), and §1.401(a)(4)-9(b)(2)(v)(A) and (D) apply to plan years beginning on or after the date of publication of the Treasury decision adopting these rules as final in the **Federal Register**.

(ii) *Application for earlier plan years.*—Except as provided in paragraph (a)(4)(iii) of this section, taxpayers may apply §1.401(a)(4)-2(c), §1.401(a)(4)-3(c)(2), §1.401(a)(4)-8(b), or §1.401(a)(4)-9(b)(2)(v)(A) and (D) for plan years beginning on or after January 1, 2014 and before the effective/applicability date specified under paragraph (a)(4)(i) of this section. Alternatively, for these plan years, taxpayers may apply §1.401(a)(4)-2(c), §1.401(a)(4)-3(c)(2), §1.401(a)(4)-8(b), or §1.401(a)(4)-9(b)(2)(v)(A) and (D) as contained in 26 CFR part 1 revised April 1, 2015.

(iii) *Certain rules not applicable until finalized.*—The rules of §1.401(a)(4)-9(b)(2)(v)(D)(*3*)(*ii*), (b)(2)(v)(D)(*4*), and (b)(2)(v)(G) are not permitted to be applied for plan years before the effective/applicability date specified in paragraph (a)(4)(i) of this section.

* * *

401(k) Plans: Hardship Distributions

401(k) Plans: Hardship Distributions.—Amendments to Reg. §1.401(k)-1, relating to hardship distributions from section 401(k) plans, are proposed (published in the Federal Register on November 14, 2018) (REG-107813-18).

Par. 2. Section 1.401(k)-1 is amended by:

1. Revising paragraphs (d)(1)(ii) and (iii) and adding new paragraph (d)(1)(iv).
2. Removing paragraph (d)(3)(ii) and redesignating paragraphs (d)(3)(iii), (iv) and (v) as paragraphs (d)(3)(ii), (iii) and (iv).
3. Revising newly redesignated paragraph (d)(3)(ii)(B) and adding new paragraph (d)(3)(ii)(C).
4. Revising newly redesignated paragraphs (d)(3)(iii) and (iv) and adding new paragraph (d)(3)(v).
5. In paragraph (d)(6), removing examples 3, 4, and 5 and redesignating example 6 as example 3.

The additions and revisions read as follows:

§1.401(k)-1. Certain cash or deferred arrangements.

* * *

(d) * * *

(1) * * *

(ii) In the case of a profit-sharing, stock bonus or rural cooperative plan—

(A) The employee's attainment of age $59^1/_2$; or

(B) In accordance with section 401(k)(14), the employee's hardship;

(iii) In accordance with section 401(k)(10), the termination of the plan; or

(iv) In the case of a qualified reservist distribution defined in section 72(t)(2)(G)(iii), the date the reservist was ordered or called to active duty.

* * *

(3) * * *

(ii) * * *

(B) *Deemed immediate and heavy financial need.*—A distribution is deemed to be made on account of an immediate and heavy financial need of the employee if the distribution is for—

(1) Expenses for (or necessary to obtain) medical care that would be deductible under section 213(d), determined without regard to the limitations in section 213(a) (relating to the applicable percentage of adjusted gross income and the recipients of the medical care) provided that, if the recipient of the medical care is not listed in section 213(a), the recipient is a primary beneficiary under the plan;

(2) Costs directly related to the purchase of a principal residence for the employee (excluding mortgage payments);

(3) Payment of tuition, related educational fees, and room and board expenses, for up to the next 12 months of post-secondary education for the employee, for the employee's spouse, child or dependent (as defined in section 152 without regard to section 152(b)(1), (b)(2) and (d)(1)(B)), or for a primary beneficiary under the plan;

(4) Payments necessary to prevent the eviction of the employee from the employee's principal residence or foreclosure on the mortgage on that residence;

(5) Payments for burial or funeral expenses for the employee's deceased parent, spouse, child or dependent (as defined in section 152 without regard to section 152(d)(1)(B)) or for a deceased primary beneficiary under the plan;

(6) Expenses for the repair of damage to the employee's principal residence that would qualify for the casualty deduction under section 165 (determined without regard to section 165(h)(5) and whether the loss exceeds 10% of adjusted gross income); or

(7) Expenses and losses (including loss of income) incurred by the employee on account of a disaster declared by the Federal Emergency Management Agency (FEMA) under the Robert T. Stafford Disaster Relief and Emergency Assistance Act, Pub. L. 100-707, provided that the employee's principal residence or principal place of employment at the time of the disaster was located in an area designated by FEMA for individual assistance with respect to the disaster.

(C) *Primary beneficiary under the plan.*—For purposes of paragraph (d)(3)(ii)(B) of this section, a "primary beneficiary under the plan" is an individual who is named as a beneficiary under the plan and has an unconditional right, upon the death of the employee, to all or a portion of the employee's account balance under the plan.

(iii) *Distribution necessary to satisfy financial need.*—(A) *Distribution may not exceed amount of need.*—A distribution is treated as necessary to satisfy an immediate and heavy financial need of an employee only to the extent the amount of the distribution is not in excess of the amount required to satisfy the financial need (including any amounts necessary to pay any federal, state, or local income taxes or penalties reasonably anticipated to result from the distribution).

(B) *No alternative means reasonably available.*—A distribution is not treated as necessary to satisfy an immediate and heavy financial need of an employee unless the employee has obtained all other currently available distributions (including distributions of ESOP dividends under section 404(k), but not hardship distributions) under the plan and all other plans of deferred compensation, whether qualified or nonqualified, maintained by the employer. In addition, for a distribution that is made on or after January 1, 2020, the employee must represent (in writing, by an electronic medium, or in such other form as may be prescribed by the Commissioner) that he or she has insufficient cash or other liquid assets to satisfy the need. The plan administrator may rely on the employee's representation unless the plan administrator has actual knowledge to the contrary.

(C) *Additional conditions.*—A plan generally may provide for additional conditions, such as those described in 26 CFR 1.401(k)-1(d)(3)(iv)(B) and (C) (revised as of April 1, 2018) or, for distributions made before January 1, 2020, the representation described in paragraph (d)(3)(iii)(B) of this section, to demonstrate that a distribution is necessary to satisfy an immediate and heavy financial need of an employee. For example, a plan may provide that, before a hardship distribution may be made, an employee must obtain all nontaxable loans (determined at the time a loan is made) available under the plan and all other plans maintained by the employer. However, for a distribution that is made on or after January 1, 2020, a plan may not provide for a suspension of an employee's elective contributions or employee contributions as a condition of obtaining a hardship distribution.

(iv) *Commissioner may expand standards.*—The Commissioner may prescribe additional guidance of general applicability, published in the Internal Revenue Bulletin (see § 601.601(d)(2) of this chapter), expanding the list of distributions deemed to be made on account of immediate and heavy financial needs and setting forth additional methods to demonstrate that a distribution is necessary to satisfy an immediate and heavy financial need.

(v) *Effective/applicability date.*—(A) *General rule.*—This paragraph (d)(3) applies to distributions made in plan years beginning after December 31, 2018. Except as otherwise provided in this paragraph (d)(3)(v), the rules in 26 CFR 1.401(k)-1(d)(3) (revised as of April 1, 2018) apply to distributions made in plan years beginning before January 1, 2019.

(B) *Options for earlier application.*—The last sentence of paragraph (d)(3)(iii)(C) of this section (prohibiting the suspension of contributions as a condition of obtaining a hardship distribution) may be applied as of the first day of the first plan year beginning after December 31, 2018, even if the distribution was made in the prior plan year. Thus, for example, a calendar-year plan that provides for hardship distributions under the rules in 26 CFR 1.401(k)-1(d)(3)(iv)(E) (revised as of April 1, 2018) may be amended to provide that an employee who receives a hardship distribution in the second half of the 2018 plan year will be prohibited from making contributions only until January 1, 2019 (or may continue to provide that contributions will be suspended for the originally scheduled 6 months). In addition, paragraph (d)(3)(ii)(B) of this section may be applied to distributions made on or after a date that is as early as January 1, 2018.

* * *

401(k) Plans: Hardship Distributions

401(k) Plans: Hardship Distributions.—Amendments to Reg. § 1.401(k)-3, relating to hardship distributions from section 401(k) plans, are proposed (published in the Federal Register on November 14, 2018) (REG-107813-18).

Par. 3. Section 1.401(k)-3 is amended by:

1. Revising paragraph (c)(6)(v).

2. Removing the language ", and, in the case of a hardship distribution, suspends an employee's ability to make elective contributions for 6 months in accordance with § 1.401(k)-1(d)(3)(iv)(E)" in the fifth sentence in paragraph (c)(7), *Example 1*.

3. Removing the second sentence in paragraph (j)(2)(iv).

The revision reads as follows:

§ 1.401(k)-3. Safe harbor requirements.

* * *

(c) * * *

(6) * * *

(v) *Restrictions due to limitations under the Internal Revenue Code.*—A plan may limit the amount of elective contributions made by an eligible employee under a plan—

(A) Because of the limitations of section 402(g) or 415;

(B) Due to a suspension under section 414(u)(12)(B)(ii); or

(C) Because, on account of a hardship distribution made before January 1, 2020, an employee's ability to make elective contributions has been suspended for 6 months.

* * *

401(k) Plans: Hardship Distributions

401(k) Plans: Hardship Distributions.—Amendments to Reg. § 1.401(k)-6, relating to hardship distributions from section 401(k) plans, are proposed (published in the Federal Register on November 14, 2018) (REG-107813-18).

Par. 4. Section 1.401(k)-6 is amended by:

1. Removing the fourth sentence in paragraph (2) of the definition of *Eligible employee*.

2. Removing the language ", except as provided otherwise in §1.401(k)-1(c) and (d)," in the definitions of *Qualified matching contributions (QMACs)* and *Qualified nonelective contributions (QNECs)*.

§1.401(k)-6. Definitions.

401(k) Plans: Hardship Distributions

401(k) Plans: Hardship Distributions.—Amendments to Reg. §1.401(m)-3, relating to hardship distributions from section 401(k) plans, are proposed (published in the Federal Register on November 14, 2018) (REG-107813-18).

Par. 5. Section 1.401(m)-3 is amended by revising paragraph (d)(6)(v) to read as follows:

§1.401(m)-3. Safe harbor requirements.

* * *

(d) * * *

(6) * * *

(v) *Restrictions due to limitations under the Internal Revenue Code.*—A plan may limit the amount of contributions made by an eligible employee under a plan-

(A) Because of the limitations of section 402(g) or section 415;

(B) Due to a suspension under section 414(u)(12)(B)(ii); or

(C) Because, on account of a hardship distribution made before January 1, 2020, an employee's ability to make contributions has been suspended for 6 months.

* * *

Beneficiaries

Beneficiaries: Taxability of: Sec. 401(a) Trust.—Amendments to Reg. §1.402(a)-1, relating to the taxability of beneficiaries under a trust meeting the requirements of section 401(a), are proposed (published in the Federal Register of April 30, 1975). [*Note:* Proposed Reg. §1.402(a)-1(a)(1)(iii) and (a)(2) were adopted by T.D. 9223 on August 26, 2005.]

☐ Section 1.402(a)-1 is amended by revising paragraphs (a)(1)(ii), (a)(1)(iii), (a)(2), (a)(5), (a)(6), (a)(7), (a)(9), and (b)(1) to read as follows:

§1.402(a)-1. Taxability of beneficiary under a trust which meets the requirements of section 401(a).—(a) *In general.*—(1) * * *

(ii) The provisions of section 402(a) relate only to a distribution by a trust which is described in section 401(a) and which is exempt under section 501(a) for the taxable year of the trust in which the distribution is made. With three exceptions, the distribution from such an exempt trust when received or made available is taxable to the distributee or recipient to the extent provided in section 72 (relating to annuities). First, for taxable years beginning before January 1, 1964, section 72(e)(3) (relating to the treatment of certain lump sums), as in effect before such date, shall not apply to such distributions. For taxable years beginning after December 31, 1963, such distributions may be taken into account in computations under sections 1301 through 1305 (relating to income averaging). For treatment of such total distributions, see paragraph (a)(6) of this section. Secondly, if the taxable year ends after December 31, 1969 and begins before January 1, 1974, the portion of the distribution treated as long-term capital gain is subject to the limitation under section 402(a)(5), as in effect on December 31, 1973. Thirdly, for taxable years beginning after December 31, 1973, a certain portion, described in section 402(a)(2), of a lump sum distribution, as defined in section 402(e)(4)(A) is taxable as long-term capital gain and a certain portion, described in section 402(e)(4)(E), may be taxable under section 402(e). For the treatment of such lump sum distributions, see paragraph (a)(9) of this section. Under certain circumstances, an amount representing the unrealized appreciation in the value of the securities of the employer is excludable from gross income for the year of distribution. For the rules relating to such exclusion, see paragraph (b) of this section. Furthermore, the exclusion provided by section 105(d) is applicable to a distribution from a trust described in section 401(a) and exempt under section 501(a) if such distribution constitutes wages or payments in lieu of wages for a period during which an employee is absent from work on account of a personal injury or sickness. See §1.72-15 for the rules relating to the tax treatment of accident or health benefits received under a plan to which section 72 applies.

(iii) [This proposed amendment was adopted by T.D. 9223, 8-26-2005.]

* * *

(2) [This proposed amendment was adopted by T.D. 9223, 8-26-2005.]

* * *

(5) If pension or annuity payments or other benefits are paid or made available to the beneficiary of a deceased employee or a deceased retired employee by a trust described in section 401(a) which is exempt under section 501(a), such amounts are taxable in accordance with the rules of section 402(a) and this section. In case such amounts are taxable under section 72, the "investment in the contract" shall be determined by reference to the amount contributed by the employee and by applying the applicable rules of sections 72 and 101(b)(2)(D). In case the amounts paid to, or includible in the gross income of, the beneficiaries of the deceased employee or deceased retired employee constitute a distribution to which paragraph (a)(6) or (9) (whichever applies) of this section is applicable, the extent to which the distribution is taxable is determined by reference to the contributions of the employee, by reference to any prior distributions which were excludable from gross income as a return of employee contributions, and by applying the applicable rules of sections 72 and 101(b).

(6) This subparagraph applies in the case of a total distribution made in a taxable year of the distributee or payee ending before January 1, 1970.

(i) If the total distributions payable with respect to any employee under a trust described in section 401(a) which in the year of distribution is exempt under section 501(a) are paid to, or includible in the gross income of, the distributee within one taxable year of the distributee on account of the employee's death or other separation from the service, or death after such separation from service, the amount of such distribution, to the extent it exceeds the net amount contributed by the employee, shall be considered a gain from the sale or exchange of a capital asset held for more than six months. The total distributions payable are includible in the gross income of the distributee within one taxable year if they are made available to such distributee and the distributee fails to make a timely election under section 72(h) to receive an annuity in lieu of such total distributions. The "net amount contributed by the employee" is the amount actually contributed by the employee plus any amounts considered to be contributed by the employee under the rules of section 72(f), 101(b), and paragraph (a)(3) of this section, reduced by any amounts theretofore distributed to him which were excludable from gross income as a return of employee contributions. See, however, paragraph (b) of this section for rules relating to the exclusion of amounts representing net unrealized appreciation in the value of securities of the employer corporation. In addition, all or part of the amount otherwise includible in gross income under this paragraph by a nonresident alien individual in respect of a distribution by the United States under a qualified pension plan may be excludable from gross income under section 402(a)(4). For rules relating to such exclusion, see paragraph (c) of this section. For additional rules relating to the treatment of total distributions described in this subdivision in the case of a nonresident alien individual, see sections 871 and 1441 and the regulations thereunder.

* * *

(7) The capital gains treatment provided by section 102(a)(2), as in effect for taxable years beginning before January 1, 1974, and paragraph (a)(6) of this section is not applicable to distributions paid during such years to a distributee to the extent such distributions are attributable to contributions made on behalf of an employee while he was a self-employed individual in the business with respect to which the plan was maintained. For the taxation of such amounts, see §1.72-18. For the rules for determining the amount attributable to contributions on behalf of an employee while he was self-employed, see paragraphs (b)(4) and (c)(2) of such section.

* * *

(9) For taxable years beginning after December 31, 1973, in the case of a lump sum distribution (as defined in section 402(e)(4)(A)) made to a recipient which is an individual, estate, or trust, so much of the total taxable amount (as defined in section 402(e)(4)(D) and §1.402(e)-2(d)(2)) of such lump sum distribution as is equal to the product of such total taxable amount multiplied by a fraction—

(i) The numerator of which is the number of calendar years of active participation (as determined under §1.402(e)-2(d)(3)(ii)) by the employee in such plan before January 1, 1974, and

(ii) The denominator of which is the number of calendar years of active participation (as determined under §1.402(e)-2(d)(3)(ii)) by the employee in such plan,

shall be treated as gain from the sale or exchange of a capital asset held for more than six months. For purposes of this subparagraph, in the case of an individual who at no time during his participation under the plan is an employee within the meaning of section 401(c)(1), determination of whether any distribution is a lump sum distribution shall be made without regard to the requirement that an election be made under section 402(e)(4)(B) and §1.402(e)-3.

(b) *Distributions including securities of the employer corporation.*—(1) *In general.*—(i) If a trust described in section 401(a) which is exempt under section 501(a) makes a distribution to a distributee, and such distribution includes securities of the employer corporation, the amount of any net unrealized appreciation in such securities shall be excluded from the distributee's income in the year of such distribution to the following extent:

(A) If the distribution constitutes a total distribution to which the regulations of paragraph (a)(6) of this section are applicable, or if the distribution would constitute a lump sum distribution as defined in section 402(e)(4)(A) (without regard to section 402(e)(4)(H)), the amount to be excluded is the entire net unrealized appreciation attributable to that part of the distribution which consists of securities of the employer corporation; and

(B) If the distribution is other than a total distribution to which paragraph (a)(6) of this section is applicable, or if the distribution is other than a lump sum distribution as defined in section 402(e)(4)(A) (without regard to section 402(e)(4)(H)), the amount to be excluded is that portion of the net unrealized appreciation in the securities of the employer corporation which is attributable to the amount considered to be contributed by the employee to the purchase of such securities.

The amount of net unrealized appreciation which is excludable under the regulations of (b)(1)(i)(A) and (B) of this section shall not be included in the basis of the securities in the hands of the distributee at the time of distribution for purposes of determining gain or loss on their subsequent disposition. Further, the amount of net unrealized appreciation which is not included in the basis of the securities in the hands of the distributee at the time of distribution shall be considered as a gain from the sale or exchange of a capital asset held for more than six months to the extent that such appreciation is realized in a subsequent taxable transaction. However, if the net gain realized by the distributee in a subsequent taxable transaction exceeds the amount of the net unrealized appreciation at the time of distribution, such excess shall constitute a long-term or short-term capital gain depending upon the holding period of the securities in the hands of the distributee.

(ii)(A) For purposes of section 402(a) and of this section, the term "securities" means only shares of stock and bonds or debentures issued by a corporation with interest coupons or in registered form, and the term "securities of the employer corporation" includes securities of a parent or subsidiary corporation (as defined in subsections (e) and (f) of section 425) of the employer corporation.

(B) For purposes of this paragraph, for taxable years beginning after December 31, 1973, the term "distributee" means "recipient".

* * *

Lump-Sum Distributions

Employee Plans: Lump-Sum Distributions.—Reproduced below is the text of a proposed amendment to Reg. §1.402(a)-1, relating to the election to treat no portion of a lump-sum distribution from an employee plan as long-term capital gain (published in the Federal Register on May 31, 1979).

☐ Paragraph 1. Section 1.402(a)-1(a)(9), as set forth in paragraph 10 of the appendix to the notice of proposed rulemaking of April 30, 1975, is revised by adding a new sentence at the end thereof to read as follows:

§1.402(a)-1. Taxability of beneficiary under a trust which meets the requirements of section 401(a).—(a) *In general.*—* * *

(9) * * * In the case of a lump sum distribution received by or made available to a recipient in a taxable year of the recipient beginning after December 31, 1975, the recipient may elect, in accordance with section 402(e)(4)(L) and §1.402(e)-14, to treat all calendar years of an employee's active participation in all plans in which the employee has been an active participant as years of active participation after December 31, 1973. If a recipient makes the election, no portion of any distribution received by or made available to the recipient with respect to the employee (whether in the recipient's taxable year for which the election is made, or thereafter) is taxable to the recipient as long-term capital gain under section 402(a)(2) and this subparagraph.

Employee Trusts: Effective Dates

Employee Trusts: Tax Reform Act of 1984: Effective Dates.—Temporary Reg. §1.402(a)(5)-1T is also proposed as a final regulation and, when adopted, would become Reg. §1.402(a)(5)-1 (published in the Federal Register on February 4, 1986).

§1.402(a)(5)-1. Rollovers of partial distributions from qualified trusts and annuities.

Lump-Sum Distributions: Treatment After 1973

Lump-Sum Distributions: Treatment of.—Reproduced below is the text of proposed Reg. §1.402(e)-2, relating to the treatment of lump-sum distributions (published in the Federal Register on April 30, 1975).

☐ There are added immediately after §1.402(e)-1 the following new sections:

§1.402(e)-2. Treatment of certain lump sum distributions made after 1973.—(a) *In general.*—(1) *Tax imposed; deduction allowed.*—For a taxable year, at the election of the recipient of a lump sum distribution, the ordinary income portion of such distribution is subject to the tax imposed by section 402(e)(1)(A) (hereinafter referred to as the "separate tax") and, under section 402(e)(3), an amount equal to such portion is allowable as a deduction from gross income (see section 62(11), as added by sec. 2005(c)(9) of Pub. L. No. 93-406, and the regulations thereunder) to the extent such portion is included in the gross income of the taxpayer for such year. The separate tax imposed by section 402(e)(1)(A) is an addition to the tax otherwise imposed under chapter 1 of the Code and may be elected whether or not the tax otherwise imposed by such chapter is computed under part I of subchapter Q of such chapter (relating to income averaging). This section applies with respect to distributions or payments made, or made available, to a recipient after December 31, 1973, in taxable years of the recipient beginning after that date.

(2) *Cross references.*—(i) *Computation; ordinary method.*—Paragraph (b) of this section provides rules with respect to a distribution which is not a multiple distribution, and does not include an annuity contract.

(ii) *Computation; special method (distribution including an annuity contract).*—Paragraph (c)(1) of this section provides rules with respect to a distribution which is not a multiple distribution and which includes an annuity contract.

(iii) *Computation; special method (multiple distribution).*—Paragraph (c)(2) of this section provides rules with respect to a distribution which is a multiple distribution.

(iv) *Lump sum distribution.*—For the definition of the term "lump sum distribution", see paragraph (d)(1) of this section.

(v) *Total taxable amount.*—For the definition of the term "total taxable amount", see paragraph (d)(2) of this section.

(vi) *Ordinary income portion.*—For the definition of the term "ordinary income portion", see paragraph (d)(3) of this section.

(vii) *Multiple distribution.*—For the definition of the term "multiple distribution", see paragraph (c)(2)(ii)(E) of this section.

(viii) *Election.*—For rules relating to the election of lump sum distribution treatment under this section, see §1.402(e)-3.

(b) *Ordinary method.*—(1) *In general.*—In the case of a distribution which is not included in a multiple distribution, and which does not include an annuity contract, if the recipient elects (under § 1.402(e)-3) to treat such distribution as a lump sum distribution under this section, the tax imposed by section 402(e)(1)(A) for the recipient's taxable year is an amount equal to the initial separate tax (determined under paragraph (b)(2) of this section) for such taxable year, multiplied by a fraction—

(i) The numerator of which is the ordinary income portion (determined under paragraph (d)(3) of this section) of such lump sum distribution for such taxable year, and

(ii) The denominator of which is the total taxable amount (determined under paragraph (d)(2) of this section) of such lump sum distribution for such taxable year.

(2) *Computation of initial separate tax.*—For purposes of subparagraph (1) of this paragraph, the initial separate tax is an amount equal to 10 times the tax which would be imposed by section 1(c) (relating to unmarried individuals (other than surviving spouses and heads of households)) if the recipient were an individual referred to in such section and the taxable income referred to in such section were an amount equal to one-tenth of the excess of—

(i) The total taxable amount (determined under paragraph (d)(2) of this section) of the lump sum distribution, over

(ii) The minimum distribution allowance (determined under paragraph (b)(3) of this section).

(3) *Computation of minimum distribution allowance.*—For purposes of paragraph (b)(2)(ii) of this section, the minimum distribution allowance is the lesser of—

(i) $10,000, or

(ii) One-half of the total taxable amount of the lump sum distribution for the taxable year, reduced (but not below zero) by 20 percent of the excess (if any) of such total taxable amount over $20,000.

(4) *Example.*—The application of this paragraph is illustrated by the following example:

Example. (i) On December 22, 1975, A separates from the service of the M Corporation and receives a lump sum distribution of $65,000 from the M Corporation's contributory qualified plan. A's contributions to the plan as an employee were $15,000. A has been an active participant in the plan since February 20, 1966. A and his wife, B, are each age 50. Neither received an annuity contract from a qualified plan in 1974 or 1975. Neither received a lump sum distribution in 1974. A and B file a joint return for the calendar year 1975. Their income for 1975 consists of A's salary of $15,000 from the M Corporation and of $5,000 from the N Corporation. Their deductions for 1975 (other than deductions attributable to the distribution) consist of itemized deductions of $3,000. Their average base period income (determined under section 1302(b)(1)) for the four preceding taxable years (1971 through 1974) is $14,000. Assuming there are no changes in the applicable tax law after 1974, A and B's income tax liability for 1975 is computed as follows.

(ii) A and B's gross income for 1975 is $70,000, computed by adding the total taxable amount of the lump sum distribution (determined under paragraph (d)(2) of this section) to their otherwise computed gross income [$15,000 + $5,000 + $65,000 − $15,000]. Their adjusted gross income for 1975 is $40,000 [$70,000 − ($10,000 + $20,000)]computed by reducing their gross income by the sum of the lump sum distribution deduction allowed by section 402(e)(3) with respect to the ordinary income portion of the distribution [$50,000 × 24/120]and the deduction allowed by section 1202 with respect to the capital gains portion of the distribution [($50,000 × 96/120) × 0.5]. A and B's joint taxable income is $35,500 (their itemized deductions are $3,000 and their personal exemptions total $1,500). A and B choose to apply the income averaging rules of section 1301 for 1975. Thus, A and B's income tax liability not including the separate tax on the ordinary income portion of the distribution is $8,828.

(iii) The minimum distribution allowance with respect to A's distribution is $4,000 [$10,000 − (($50,000 − $20,000) × 0.2)]. The initial separate tax on A's distribution is 10 times the tax imposed by section 1(c), computed as if the taxable income therein described were $4,600

$$\frac{[\$50,000 - \$4,000]}{10}$$

Thus, A's initial separate tax is $8,160. The separate tax on A's distribution is computed by multiplying the initial separate tax and the quotient of the ordinary income portion divided by the total taxable amount. Thus, the separate tax on A's distribution is $1,632 [$8,160 × $10,000/$50,000].

(iv) A and B's total income tax liability for 1975 is the sum of the income tax as otherwise determined and the separate tax. Thus, A and B's total income tax liability for 1975 is $10,460 [$8,828 + $1,632].

(c) *Special method.*—(1) *Computation of separate tax on distribution including annuity contract and lump sum distribution.*—(i) *Computation.*—In the case of a distribution which is not included in a multiple distribution and which includes an annuity contract, if the recipient elects (under § 1.402(e)-3) to treat the portion of such distribution not consisting of an annuity contract as a lump sum distribution under this section, the separate tax imposed by section 402(e)(1)(A) of the recipient's taxable year is the excess (if any) of the adjusted separate tax over the tax attributable to the annuity contract (determined under paragraph (c)(1)(iii) of this section).

(ii) *Definitions.*—For purposes of this section—

(A) *Adjusted separate tax.*—The adjusted separate tax is an amount equal to the adjusted initial separate tax multiplied by a fraction—

(1) The numerator of which is the ordinary income portion of the distribution, and

(2) The denominator of which is the total taxable amount (determined under paragraph (d)(2) of this section) of the lump sum distribution.

(B) *Adjusted initial separate tax.*—The adjusted initial separate tax is an amount equal to 10 times the tax which would be imposed by section 1(c) (relating to unmarried individuals (other than surviving spouses and heads of households)) if the recipient were an individual referred to in such section and the taxable income referred to in such section were an amount equal to one-tenth of the excess of—

(1) The adjusted total taxable amount of the lump sum distribution, over

(2) The adjusted minimum distribution allowance.

(C) *Adjusted total taxable amount.*—(*1*) For taxable years beginning before January 1, 1975, the adjusted total taxable amount is the sum of—

(*i*) The excess (if any) of the current actuarial value of annuity contracts distributed to the recipient, over the portion of the net amount contributed by the employee which is allocable to the contract, and

(*ii*) The total taxable amount (determined under paragraph (d)(2) of this section) of the lump sum distribution for the taxable year.

For purposes of (c)(1)(ii)(C)(*1*)(*i*) of this section, the net amount contributed by the employee which is allocable to the contract is an amount equal to the amounts considered contributed by the employee under the plan (determined by applying sections 72(f) and 101(b), and paragraph (b) of § 1.72-16) reduced by any amount theretofore distributed to the employee which were not includible in his gross income multiplied by a fraction, the numerator of which is the current actuarial value of the contract, and the denominator of which is the sum of such current actuarial value and the value of other property (including cash) distributed.

(*2*) For taxable years beginning after December 31, 1974, the adjusted total taxable amount is the sum of—

(*i*) The current actuarial value of annuity contracts distributed to the recipient, reduced by the excess, if any, of the net amount contributed by the employee (as defined in paragraph (d)(2)(ii)(A) of this section) over the cash and other property distributed, and

(*ii*) The total taxable amount (determined under paragraph (d)(2) of this section) of the lump sum distribution for the taxable year.

(D) *Adjusted ordinary income portion.*—The adjusted ordinary income portion of a lump sum distribution is the amount which would be computed under paragraph (d)(3) of this section if "adjusted total taxable amount" is substituted for "total taxable amount" in such subparagraph.

(E) *Adjusted minimum distribution allowance.*—The adjusted minimum distribution allowance is the lesser of—

(*1*) $10,000, or

(*2*) one-half of the adjusted total taxable amount of the lump sum distribution for the taxable year,

reduced (but not below zero) by 20 percent of the excess (if any) of the adjusted total taxable amount over $20,000.

(F) *Current actuarial value.*—The current actuarial value of an annuity contract is the greater of—

(*1*) The cash value of the annuity contract (determined without regard to any loans under the contract) on the date of distribution, or

(*2*) The amount determined under the appropriate tables contained in publication No. 861, entitled "Annuity Factors for Lump Sum Distributions".

(iii) *Tax attributable to an annuity contract.*—For purposes of subdivision (i) of this subparagraph, the tax attributable to an annuity contract is the product of—

(A) The quotient of the adjusted ordinary income portion (determined under paragraph (c)(1)(ii)(D) of this section) of the lump sum distribution divided by the adjusted total taxable amount (determined under paragraph (c)(1)(ii)(C) of this section), and

(B) 10 times the tax which would be imposed by section 1(c) (relating to unmarried individuals (other than surviving spouses and heads of households)) if the recipient were an individual referred to in such section and the taxable income were an amount equal to one-tenth of the excess of—

(*1*) The current actuarial value of the annuity contract, over

(*2*) The adjusted minimum distribution allowance multiplied by a fraction—

(*i*) The numerator of which is the current actuarial value of the annuity contract, and

(*ii*) The denominator of which is the adjusted total taxable amount (determined under paragraph (c)(1)(ii) of this section).

(iv) *Examples.*—The application of this subparagraph is illustrated by the following examples:

Example (1). (i) On December 29, 1975, A separates from the service of the M Corporation and receives a distribution of the balance to the credit of his account under the M Corporation's noncontributory qualified plan. The distribution consists of cash of $44,000, and an annuity contract with a current actuarial value of $6,000. A has been a participant in the plan since March 26, 1966. A and his wife, B, are each age 50. Neither received a previous distribution from a qualified plan. A and B file a joint return for 1975. Their income for 1975, other than the distribution, consists of A's salary from the M Corporation of $15,000 and of $5,000 from the N Corporation. Their deductions (other than deductions attributable to the distribution) consist of itemized deductions of $3,000. They are not otherwise permitted to use income averaging for 1975 under section 1301. Assuming there are no changes in the applicable tax law after 1974, A and B's income tax liability for 1975 is computed as follows.

(ii) A and B's gross income for 1975 is $64,000, computed by adding the total taxable amount (determined under paragraph (d)(2) of this section) of the lump sum distribution to their otherwise computed gross income [$15,000 + $5,000 + $44,000]. Their adjusted gross income for 1975 is $37,600 [$64,000—($8,800 + $17,600)], computed by reducing their gross income by the sum of the lump sum distribution deduction allowed by section 402(e)(3) with respect to the ordinary income portion of the distribution [$44,000 × 24/120] and the deduction allowed by section 1202 with respect to the capital gains portion of the distribution [($44,000 × 96/120) × 0.5]. A and B's taxable income for 1975 is $33,100 (their itemized deductions are $3,000 and their personal exemptions total $1,500). Thus, A and B's income tax liability not including the separate tax on the ordinary income portion of the distribution is $9,122.

(iii) The adjusted total taxable amount of A's distribution is the sum of the current actuarial value of the annuity contract distributed and the total taxable amount of the lump sum distribution. Thus, the adjusted total taxable amount of A's distribution is $50,000 [$6,000 + $44,000]. The adjusted minimum distribution allowance with respect to A's distribution is the lesser of $10,000 or 1/2 of the adjusted total taxable amount, reduced by 20 percent of the excess (if any) of the adjusted total taxable amount over $20,000. Thus, the adjusted minimum distribution allowance with respect to A's distribution is $4,000 [$10,000 – (($50,000 – $20,000) × 0.2)]. The adjusted initial separate tax on A's distribution is computed by multiplying 10 times the tax imposed by section 1(c) computed as if the taxable income therein described were $4,600 [($50,000 – $4,000)/10]. Thus, A's adjusted initial separate tax is $8,160. The adjusted separate tax on A's distribution is computed by multiplying the adjusted initial separate tax by the quotient of the ordinary income portion divided by the total taxable amount. Thus, the adjusted separate tax on A's distribution is $1,632 ($8,160 × $8,800/$44,000). The tax attributable to the annuity contract is 10 times the tax that would be imposed by section 1(c) computed as if the taxable income of a person described there in were $552

$$\frac{[\,\$6{,}000 - (\$4{,}000 \times (\$6{,}000/\$50{,}000))\,]}{10}$$

multiplied by the quotient described in the second preceding sentence. Thus, the tax attributable to the annuity contract is $156 [$778 × $8,800/$44,000]. The separate tax on A's distribution is computed by reducing the adjusted separate tax by the tax attributable to the annuity contract. Thus, the separate tax on A's distribution is $1,476 [$1,632 – $156].

(iv) A and B's total income tax liability for 1975 is the sum of their income tax liability, as otherwise determined, and the separate tax. Thus A and B's total income tax liability for 1975 is $10,598 [$9,122 + $1,476].

Example (2). (i) Assume the same facts as in example (1) except that the M Corporation's qualifed plan is contributory and that A's contributions under the plan as an employee were $1,760, and the current actuarial value of the annuity contract which is distributed is $5,760.

(ii) A and B's gross income for 1975 is $62,240, computed by adding the total taxable amount (determined under paragraph (d)(2) of this section) of the lump sum distribution to their otherwise computed gross income [$15,000 + $5,000 + ($44,000 – $1,760)]. Their adjusted gross income for 1975 is $36,896 [$62,240 – ($8,448 + $16,896)], computed by reducing their gross income by the sum of the lump sum distribution deduction allowed by section 402(e)(3) with respect to the ordinary income portion of the distribution [$42,240 × 24/120] and the deduction allowed by section 1202 with respect to the capital gains portion of the distribution. [($42,240 × 96/120) × 0.5]. A and B's taxable income for 1975 is $32,396 (their itemized deductions are $3,000 and their personal exemption total $1,500). Thus A and B's income tax liability not including the separate tax on the ordinary income portion of the distribution is $8,826.

(iii) The adjusted total taxable amount of A's distribution is the sum of the current actuarial value of the annuity contract distributed and the total taxable amount of the lump sum distribution. Thus, the adjusted total taxable amount of A's distribution is $48,000 [$5,760 + ($44,000 – $1,760)]. The adjusted minimum distribution allowance with respect to A's distribution is the lesser of $10,000 or 1/2 of the adjusted total taxable amount, reduced by 20 percent of the excess of the adjusted total taxable amount over $20,000. Thus, the adjusted minimum distribution allowance with respect to A's distribution is $4,400 [$10,000 – (($48,000 – $20,000) × 0.2)]. The adjusted initial separate tax on A's distribution is 10 times the tax imposed by section 1(c) computed as if the taxable income therein described were $4,360

$$\frac{[\,(\$48{,}000 - \$4{,}400)\,]}{10}$$

Thus, A's adjusted initial separate tax is $7,656. The adjusted separate tax on A's distribution is computed by multiplying the adjusted initial separate tax by the quotient of the ordinary income portion divided by the total taxable amount. Thus, the adjusted separate tax on A's distribution is $1,531 [$7,656 × $8,448/$42,240]. The tax attributable to the annuity contract is 10 times the tax that would be imposed by section 1 (c) computed as if the taxable income of a person therein described were $523

$$\frac{[\,\$5{,}760 - (\$4{,}400 \times (\$5{,}760/\$48{,}000))\,]}{10}$$

multiplied by the quotient described in the second preceding sentence. Thus, the tax attributable to the annuity contract is $147 [$735 × $8,448/$42,240]. The separate tax on A's distribution is computed by reducing the adjusted separate tax by the tax attributable to the annuity contract. Thus, the separate tax on A's distribution is $1,384 [$1,531 – $147].

(iv) A and B's total income tax liability for 1975 is the sum of their income tax liability, as otherwise determined, and the separate tax. Thus A and B's total income tax liability for 1975 is $10,210 [$1,384 + $8,826].

Example (3). (i) On December 7, 1974, C separates from the service of P Corporation and receives a distribution of the balance to the credit of his account under the P Corporation's contributory qualified plan. The distribition consists of cash of $44,000, and an annuity contract with a current actuarial value of $6,000. C has been a participant in the plan since February 20, 1965. C's contributions under the plan as an employee were $2,000. C and his wife, D, are each age 50. Neither received a previous distribution from a qualifed plan. C and D file a joint return for 1974. Their income for 1974, other than the distribution, consists of C's salary from the P Corporation of $20,000. Their deductions (other than deductions attributable to the distribution) consist of itemized deductions of $3,000. They are not otherwise permitted to use income averaging for 1974 under section 1301. C and D's income tax liability for 1974 is computed as follows.

(ii) C and D's gross income for 1974 is $62,240, computed by adding the total taxable amount (determined under paragraph (d)(2) of this section) of the lump sum distribution to their otherwise computed gross income [$20,000 + ($44,000 – $1,760)]. Their adjusted gross income for 1974 is $39,008 [$62,240 – ($4,224 + $19,008)], computed by reducing their gross income by the sum of the lump sum distribution deduction allowed by section 402(e)(3) with respect to the ordinary income portion of the distribution [$42,240 × 12/120]and the deduction allowed by section 1202 with respect to the capital gains portion of the distribution ($42,240 × 108/120) × 0.5]. C and D's taxable income for 1974 is $34,508 (their itemized deductions are $3,000 and their personal exemptions total $1,500). C and D's income tax liability for 1974 not including the separate tax on the ordinary income portion of the distribution is $9,713.

(iii) The adjusted total taxable amount of C's distribution is the sum of the current actuarial value of the annuity contract distributed and the total taxable amount of the lump sum distribution. Thus, the adjusted total taxable amount of C's distribution is $48,000 [($6,000 – $240) + ($44,000 – $1,760)]. The adjusted minimum distribution allowance with respect to C's distribution is the lesser of $10,000 or 1/2 of the adjusted total taxable amount, reduced by 20 percent of the excess of the adjusted total taxable amount over $20,000. Thus, the adjusted minimum distribution allowance with respect to C's distribution is $4,400 [$10,000 – (($48,000 – $20,000) × 0.2)]. The adjusted initial separate tax on C's distribution is 10 times the tax imposed by section 1(c) computed as if the taxable income therein described were $4,360

$$\frac{[\ (\$48{,}000 - \$4{,}400)\ ]}{10}$$

Thus, C's adjusted initial separate tax is $7,656. The adjusted separate tax on C's distribution is computed by multiplying the adjusted initial separate tax by the quotient of the ordinary income portion divided by the total taxable amount. Thus, the adjusted separate tax on C's distribution is $766 ($7,656 × $4,224/$42,240). The tax attributable to the annuity contract is 10 times the tax imposed by section 1(c) computed as if the taxable income therein described were $523

$$\frac{[\ \$5{,}760 - (\$4{,}400 \times (\$5{,}760/\$48{,}000))\ ]}{10}$$

multiplied by the quotient described in the second preceding sentence. Thus, the amount attributable to the annuity contract is $74 [$735 × ($4,224/$42,240)]. The separate tax on C's distribution is computed by reducing the adjusted separate tax by the tax attributable to the annuity contract. Thus, the separate tax on C's distribution is $692 ($766 –$74).

(iv) C and D's total income tax liability for 1974 is the sum of their income tax liability, as otherwise determined, and the separate tax. Thus, C and D's total income tax liability for 1974 is $10,405 [$9,713 + $692].

(2) *Computation of separate tax in case of multiple distribution.*—(i) *Computation.*—In the case of a payment or distribution which is included in a multiple distribution, the separate tax imposed on such multiple distribution by section 402(e)(1)(A) for the recipient's taxable year is the excess (if any) of the modified separate tax, over the sum of—

(A) The aggregate amount of the separate tax imposed by section 402(e)(1)(A) paid during the lookback period, and

(B) The modified tax attributable to the annuity contract.

(ii) *Definitions.*—For purposes of this section—

(A) *Modified separate tax.*—The term "modified separate tax" means an amount equal to the modified initial separate tax multiplied by a fraction—

(1) The numerator of which is the sum of the ordinary income portions of the lump sum distributions made within the lookback period, and

(2) The denominator of which is the sum of the total taxable amounts of the lump sum distributions made within the lookback period.

(B) *Modified initial separate tax.*—The modified initial separate tax is an amount equal to 10 times the tax which would be imposed by section 1(c) (relating to unmarried individuals (other than surviving spouses and heads of households)) if the recipient were an individual referred to in such section and the taxable income referred to in such section were an amount equal to one-tenth of the excess of

(1) The modified total taxable amount of the lump sum distribution, over

(2) The modified minimum distribution allowance.

(C) *Modified total taxable amount.*—The modified total taxable amount is the sum of the total taxable amounts (determined under paragraph (d)(2) of this section) of the distributions made during the lookback period and, in the case of a distribution made during such period to which paragraph (c)(1) of this section applied, the amount specified in paragraph (c)(1)(ii)(C)*(1)*(*i*) or (2)(*i*) of this section, whichever is applicable.

(D) *Modified minimum distribution allowance.*—The modified minimum distribution allowance is the lesser of—

(1) $10,000, or

(2) one-half of the modified total taxable amount,

reduced (but not below zero) by 20 percent of the excess of the modified total taxable amount over $20,000.

(E) *Multiple distributions.*—A distribution or payment received during a taxable year of the recipient which begins with or within a lookback period and after December 31, 1973, is included in a multiple distribution for such lookback period if—

(1) Any part of such distribution or payment (*i*) is treated as a lump sum distribution under this section or (*ii*) consists of a contract which would constitute all or a part of a lump sum distribution (determined without regard to section 402(e)(4)(B) and § 1.402(e)-3), except for the fact that it is an annuity contract, and

(2) a distribution or payment received in another such taxable year is treated as a lump sum distribution under this section.

For purposes of this subdivision (E), if the recipient of a lump sum distribution is a trust and if a beneficiary of such trust is an employee with respect to the plan under which the distribution is made, or treated as the owner of such trust for purposes of subpart E of part I of subchapter J of chapter 1 of the Code (relating to grantors and others treated as substantial owners), then such employee or owner shall be treated as the sole recipient of the lump sum distribution. For purposes of this subdivision (E), the term "an employee with respect to the plan under which the distribution is made" means an individual who, immediately before the distribution is made, is a participant in the plan under which the distribution is made.

(F) *Lookback period.*—The lookback period with respect to any recipient is a period of 6 consecutive taxable years ending on the last day of the taxable year of the recipient in which a payment or distribution which is a multiple distribution is made.

(iii) *Modified tax attributable to an annuity contract.*—For purposes of subdivision (i) of this subparagraph, the modified tax attributable to an annuity contract is equal to the product of—

(A) The quotient of the sum of the ordinary income portions (determined under paragraph (d)(3)) of the lump sum distributions received during the lookback period divided by the sum of the total taxable amounts (determined under paragraph (d)(2)) of the distributions made during the lookback period, and

(B) 10 times the tax which would be imposed by section 1(c) (relating to unmarried individuals (other than surviving spouses and heads of households)) if the recipient were an individual referred to in such section and the taxable income were an amount equal to one-tenth of the excess of—

(1) The sum of the amounts described in paragraph (c)(1)(ii)(C)(*1*)(*i*) or (2)(*i*) of this section in respect of the annuity contracts distributed during the lookback period, over

(2) The modified minimum distribution allowance multiplied by a fraction—

(i) The numerator of which is the sum of the amounts described in paragraph (c)(2)(iii)(B) in (*1*) of this section, and

(ii) The denominator of which is the modified total taxable amount (determined under paragraph (c)(2)(ii)(C) of this section).

(iv) The application of this subparagrpah is illustrated by the following examples:

Example (1). (i) On December 7, 1976, A separates from the service of N Corporation and receives a distribution of the balance to the credit of his account under the N Corporation's noncontributory qualified plan. The distribution consists of cash of $4,000 and an annuity contract with a current actuarial value of $6,000. A has been a participant in the plan since October 13, 1967. A and his wife, B, are each age 50. A and B file a joint return for 1976. Their income for 1976, other than the distribution, consists of A's salary from N Corporation of $25,000 and interest income of $3,000. Their deductions (other than deductions attributable to the distribution) consist of itemized deductions of $2,100. They are not otherwise permitted to use income averaging for 1976 under section 1301. A received a distribution in 1975 from the M Corporation and elected lump sum treatment for such distribution. The ordinary income portion of such distribution was $10,000; the total taxable amount of such distribution was $50,000; the adjusted ordinary income portion and the adjusted total taxable amount of such distribution are the same as the ordinary income portion and the total taxable amount; and they paid a separate tax on such distribution of $1,632. Assuming there are no changes in the applicable tax law after 1974, A and B's income tax liability for 1976 is computed as follows:

(ii) A and B's gross income for 1976 is $32,000, computed by adding the total taxable amount (determined under paragraph (d)(2) of this section) of the lump sum distribution to their otherwise computed gross income [$25,000 + $3,000 + $4,000]. Their adjusted gross income for 1976 is $29,400 [$32,000 – ($1,200 + $1,400)], computed by reducing their gross income by the sum of the lump sum distribution deduction allowed by section 402(e)(3) with respect to the ordinary income portion of the distribution [$4,000 × 36/120] and the deduction allowed by section 1202 with respect to the capital gains portion of the distribution [($4,000 × (84/120)) × 0.5]. A and B's taxable income for 1976 is $25,800 (their itemized deductions are $2,100 and their personal exemptions total $1,500). Thus, A and B's income tax liability for 1976, not including the separate tax on the ordinary income portion of the distribution is $6,308.

(iii) The adjusted total taxable amount of A's distribution for 1976 is the sum of the current actuarial value of the annuity contract distributed and the total taxable amount of the lump sum distribution. Thus, the adjusted total taxable amount of A's 1976 distribution is $10,000 [$6,000 + $4,000]. The modified total taxable amount is $60,000 [$50,000 + $10,000]. The modified minimum distribution allowance with respect to A's 1976 distribution is the lesser of $10,000 or 1/2 of the modified total taxable amount, reduced by 20 percent of the excess (if any) of the modified total taxable amount over $20,000. Thus, the modified minimum distribution allowance with respect to A's 1976 distribution is $2,000 [$10,000 – (($60,000 – $20,000) × 0.2)]. The modified initial separate tax on A's 1976 distribution is computed by multiplying 10 times the tax imposed by section 1(c) computed as if the taxable income therein described were $5,800

$$\frac{[(\$60{,}000 - \$2{,}000)]}{10}$$

Thus, A's modified initial separate tax is $10,680. The modified separate tax on A's 1976 distribution is computed by multiplying the modified initial separate tax by the quotient of the sum of the ordinary income portions of the lump sum distributions received during the lookback period divided by the sum of the total taxable amounts of each lump sum distribution made during such period. Thus, the modified separate tax on A's 1976 distribution is $2,215 [$10,680 × ($10,000 + $1,200)/($50,000 + $4,000)]. The modified tax attributable to the annuity contract is 10 times the tax imposed by section 1(c) computed as if the taxable income of a person described therein were $580

$$\frac{[(\$6{,}000 - ((\$6{,}000/\$60{,}000) \times \$2{,}000)]}{10}$$

multiplied by the quotient described in the second preceding sentence. Thus, the modified tax attributable to the annuity contract is $170 [$820 × ($10,000 + $1,200)/($50,000 + $4,000)]. The separate tax on A's 1976 distribution is computed by reducing the modified separate tax by the sum of the separate tax paid during the lookback period, and the modified tax attributable to the annuity contract. Thus, the separate tax on A's 1976 distribution is $413 [$2,215 – ($1,632 + $170)].

(iv) A and B's total income tax liability for 1976 is the sum of their income tax liability as otherwise determined, and the separate tax. Thus, A and B's total income tax liability for 1976 is $6,721 [$6,308 + $413].

Example (2). (i) Assume the same facts as in example (1) except that the N Corporation's qualified plan was contributory and that A's contributions under the plan as an employee were $800, and the current actuarial value of the annuity contract which is distributed is $4,800.

(ii) A and B's gross income for 1976 is $31,200, computed by adding the total taxable amount (determined under paragraph (d)(2) of this section) of the lump sum distribution to their otherwise computed gross income [$25,000 + $3,000 + ($4,000 – $800)]. Their adjusted gross income for 1976 is $29,120 [$31,200 – ($900 + $1,120)]computed by reducing their gross income by the sum of the lump sum distribution deduction allowed by section 402(e)(3) with respect to the ordinary income portion of the distribution [$3,200 × 36/120] and the deduction allowed by section 1202 with respect to the capital gains portion of the distribution [($3,200 × 84/120) × 0.5]. A and B's taxable income for 1976 is $25,520 (their itemized deductions are $2,100 and their personal exemptions total $1,500). Thus, A and B's income tax liability for 1976, not including the separate tax on the ordinary income portion of the distribution, is $6,207.

(iii) The adjusted total taxable amount of A's distribution for 1976 is the sum of the current actuarial value of the annuity contract distributed and the total taxable amount of the lump sum distribution. Thus, the adjusted total taxable amount of A's 1976 distribution is $8,000 [($4,800 + ($4,000 – $800)]. The modified total taxable amount is $58,000 [$50,000 + $8,000]. The modified minimum distribution allowance with respect to A's 1976 distribution is the lesser of $10,000 or 1/2 of the modified total taxable amount reduced by the excess, if any, of such modified total taxable amount over $20,000. Thus, the modified minimum distribution allowance with respect to A's 1976 distribution is $2,400 [$10,000 – [(($8,000 + $50,000) – $20,000 × 0.2)]]. The modified initial separate tax on A's 1976 distribution is 10 times the tax imposed by section 1(c) computed as if the taxable income therein described were $5,560

$$\frac{[(\$58{,}000 - \$2{,}400)]}{10}$$

Thus, A's modified initial separate tax to $10,176. The modified separate tax on A's 1976 distribution is computed by multiplying the modified initial separate tax by the quotient of the sum of the ordinary income portions of each lump sum distribution received during the lookback period divided by the sum of the total taxable amounts of each lump sum distribution made during such period. Thus, the modified separate tax on A's 1976 distribution is $2,096 [$10,176 × ($10,000 + $960) / ($50,000 + $3,200)]. The modified tax attributable to the annuity contract is 10 times the tax imposed by section 1(c) computed as if the taxable income therein described were $460

$$\frac{[(\$4{,}800 - (\$2{,}400 \times (\$4{,}800/\$58{,}000)))]}{10}$$

multipied by the quotient described in the second preceding sentence. Thus, the modified tax attributable to the annuity contract is $133 [$644 × ($10,000 + $960)/($50,000 + $3,200)]. The separate tax on A's 1976 distribution is computed by reducing the modified separate tax by the sum of the separate tax paid during the lookback period, and the modified tax attributable to the annuity contract. Thus, the separate tax on A's 1976 distribution is $331 [$2,096 – ($1,632 + $133)].

(iv) A and B's total income tax liability for 1976 is the sum of their income tax liability as otherwise determined, and the separate tax. Thus, A and B's total income tax liability for 1976 is $6,538 [$6,207 + $331].

Example (3). (i) Assume the same facts as in example (1) except that the distribution on December 7, 1976, from the N Corporation's noncontributory qualified plan consists only of an annuity contract with a current actuarial value of $6,000.

(ii) A and B's gross income for 1976 is $28,000, computed by adding the total taxable amount (determined under paragraph (d)(2) of this section) of the lump sum distribution to their otherwise computed gross income [$25,000 + $3,000 + 0]. Their adjusted gross income for 1976 is $28,000 [$28,000 – ($0 + $0)], computed by reducing their gross income by the sum of the lump sum distribution deduction allowed by section 402(e)(3) with respect to the ordinary income portion of the distribution [$0 × 36/120] and the deduction allowed by section 1202 with respect to the capital gains portion of the distribution [$0 × 84/120) × 0.5]. Their taxable income for 1976 is $24,000 (their itemized deductions are $2,100 and their personal exemptions total $1,500). Thus, A and B's income tax liability for 1976, not including the separate tax on the distribution is $5,804.

(iii) The adjusted total taxable amount of the A's distribution for 1976 is the sum of the current actuarial value of the annuity contract distributed and the total taxable amount of the lump sum distribution. Thus, the adjusted total taxable amount of A's 1976 distribution is $6,000 [$6,000 + $0]. The modified total taxable amount is $56,000 [$6,000 + $50,000]. The modified minimum distribution allowance with respect to A's 1976 distribution is the lesser of $10,000 or 1/2 of the modified total taxable amount, reduced by 20 percent of the excess (if any) of the modified total taxable amount over $20,000. Thus, the modified minimum distribution allowance with respect to A's 1976 distribution is $2,800 [$10,000 – (($56,000 – $20,000) × 0.2)]. The modified initial separate tax on A's 1976 distribution is computed by multiplying 10 times the tax imposed by section 1(c) computed as if the taxable income therein described were $5,320.

$$\frac{[\$56{,}000 - \$2{,}800]}{10}$$

Thus, A's modified initial separate tax is $9,672. The modified separate tax on A's 1976 distribution is computed by multiplying the modified initial separate tax by the quotient of the sum of the ordinary income portions of the lump sum distributions received during the lookback period divided by the sum of the total taxable amounts of each lump sum distribution made during such period. Thus, the modified separate tax on A's 1976 distribution is $1,934 [$9,672 × ($10,000 + $0)/($50,000 + $0)]. The modified tax attributable to the annuity contract is 10 times the tax imposed by section 1(c) computed as if the taxable income of a person described therein were $570

$$\frac{[(\$6,000 - ((\$6,000/\$56,000) \times \$2,800))]}{10}$$

multiplied by the quotient described in the second preceding sentence. Thus, the modified tax attributable to the annuity contract is $161 [$805 × ($10,000 + $0)/($50,000 + $0)]. The separate tax on A's 1976 distribution is computed by reducing the modified separate tax by the sum of the separate tax paid during the lookback period, and the modified tax attributable to the annuity contract. Thus, the separate tax on A's 1976 distribution is $141 [$1,934 – ($1,632 + $161)].

(iv) A and B's total income tax liability for 1976 is the sum of their income tax liability as otherwise determined, and the separate tax. Thus, A and B's total income tax liability for 1976 is $5,945 [$5,804 + $141].

Example (4). (i) Assume the same facts as in example (3) except that the N Corporation's qualified plan was contributory and that A's contributions under the plan as an employee were $2,000.

(ii) A and B's gross income for 1976 is $28,000, computed by adding the total taxable amount (determined under paragraph (d)(2) of this section) of the lump sum distribution to their otherwise computed gross income [$25,000 + $3,000 + 0]. Their adjusted gross income for 1976 is $28,000 [$28,000 – ($0 + $0)], computed by reducing their gross income by the sum of the lump sum distribution deduction allowed by section 402(e)(3) with respect to the ordinary income portion of the distribution [$0 × 36/120] and the deduction allowed by section 1202 with respect to the capital gains portion of the distribution [($0 × 84/120) × 0.5]. Their taxable income for 1976 is $24,400 (their itemized deductions are $2,100 and their personal exemptions total $1,500). Thus, A and B's income tax liability for 1976, not including the separate tax on the distribution is $5,804.

(iii) The adjusted total taxable amount of A's distribution for 1976 is the sum of the current actuarial value of the annuity contract distributed, reduced by the excess of the net amount contributed by the employee over the cash and other property distributed, and the total taxable amount of the lump sum distribution. Thus, the adjusted total taxable amount of A's 1976 distribution is $4,000 [($6,000 – $2,000) + $0]. The modified total taxable amount is $54,000 [$50,000 + $4,000]. The modified minimum distribution total taxable amount is $54,000. [$50,000] allowance with respect to A's 1976 distributions is the lesser of $10,000 or 1/2 of the modified total taxable amount, reduced by 20 percent of the excess (if any) of the modified total taxable amount over $20,000. Thus, the modified minimum distribution allowance with respect to A's 1976 distribution is $3,200 [$10,000 – (($54,000 – $20,000) × 0.2)]. The modified initial separate tax on A's 1976 distribution is computed by multiplying 10 times the tax imposed by section 1(c) computed as if the taxable income therein described were $5,080

$$\frac{[\$54,000 - \$3,200]}{10}$$

Thus, A's modified initial separate tax is $9,168. The modified separate tax on A's 1976 distribution is computed by multiplying the modified initial separate tax by the quotient of the sum of the ordinary income portions of the lump sum distribution received during the lookback period divided by the sum of the total taxable amounts of each lump sum distribution made during such period. Thus, the modified separate tax on A's 1976 distribution is $1,833 [$9,168 × ($10,000 + $0)/($50,000 + $0)]. The modified tax attributable to the annuity contract is 10 times the tax imposed by section 1(c) computed as if the taxable income therein described were $376

$$\frac{[\$4,000 - ((\$4,000/\$54,000) \times \$3,200)]}{10}$$

multipled by the quotient described in the second preceding sentence. Thus, the modified tax attributable to the annuity contract is $105 [$526 × ($10,000 + $0)/($50,000 + $0)]. The separate tax on A's 1976 distribution is computed by reducing the modified separate tax by the sum of the separate tax paid during the lookback period, and the modified tax attributable to the annuity contract. Thus, the separate tax on A's 1976 distribution is $96 [$1,833 – ($1,632 + $105)].

(iv) A and B's total income tax liability for 1976 is the sum of their income tax liability as otherwise determined, and the separate tax. Thus, A and B's total income tax liability for 1976 is $5,900 [$5,804 + $96].

(d) *Definitions.*—For purposes of this section and § 1.402(e)-3—

(1) *Lump sum distribution.*—(i) For taxable years of a recipient beginning after December 31, 1973, the term "lump sum distribution" means the distribution or payment within one taxable year of the recipient of the balance under the plan to the credit of an employee which becomes payable, or is made available, to the recipient—

(A) On account of the employee's death,

(B) After the employee attains age 59 1/2,

(C) In the case of an employee who at no time during his participation in the plan was an employee within the meaning of section 401(c)(1), on account of the employee's separation from the service, or

(D) In the case of an employee within the meaning of section 401(c)(1), after the employee has become disabled within the meaning of section 72(m)(7) and paragraph (f) of § 1.72-17,

from a trust forming part of a plan described in section 401(a) and which is exempt from tax under section 501(a) or from a plan described in section 403(a). Although periodic payments made under an annuity contract distributed under a plan described in the preceding sentence are taxed under section 72, solely for purposes of determining the adjusted total taxable amount or the modified total taxable amount, an annuity contract distributed from a plan described in the preceding sentence shall be treated as a lump sum distribution.

(ii)(A) A distribution or payment is not a lump sum distribution unless it constitutes the balance to the credit of the employee at the time the distribution or payment commences. For purposes of the preceding sentence, the time at which a distribution or payment commences shall be the date on which the requirements of subdivision (A), (B), (C), or (D) (whichever is applicable) of paragraph (d)(1)(i) of this section are satisfied, disregarding any previous distribution which constituted the balance to the credit of the employee.

(B) A distribution made before the death of an employee (for example, annuity payments received by the employee after retirement) will not preclude an amount paid on account of the death of the employee from being treated as a lump sum distribution by the recipient. Further, if a distribution or payment constitutes the balance to the credit of the employee, such distribution or payment shall not be treated as other than a lump sum distribution merely because an additional amount, attributable to the last or a subsequent year of service, is credited to the account of the employee and distributed.

(C) The application of this subdivision may be illustrated by the following example:

Example: A, an individual who is a calendar year taxpayer, retires from service with the M Corporation on October 31, 1975 after attaining age 59$^{1}/_{2}$. A begins to receive monthly annuity payments under the M Corporation's qualified plan on November 1, 1975. On February 3, 1976, A takes the balance to his credit under the M Corporation's plan in lieu of any future annuity payments. The balance to the credit of A under the M Corporation's plan is distributed to him on February 3, 1976, and as of such date he had not previously received any amount constituting a lump sum distribution. Such payments and distributions are not to be treated as a lump sum distribution because they are not paid within 1 taxable year of the recipient.

(iii) A payment or distribution described in paragraph (d)(1)(i) of this section which is made to more than one person (except a payment or distribution made solely to two or more trusts), shall not be treated as a lump sum distribution, unless the entire amount paid or distributed is included in the income of the employee in respect of whom the payment or distribution is made. Thus, for example, a distribution of the balance to the credit of the employee after the death of the employee made to the surviving spouse and his children cannot be treated as a lump sum distribution by the surviving spouse and children. However, a distribution to the employee's estate can be treated as a lump sum distribution even though the estate subsequently distributes the amount received to the surviving spouse and children.

(iv) The term "balance to the credit of the employee" does not include United States Retirement Plan Bonds held by a trust to the credit of an employee. Thus, a distribution or payment by a plan described in subdivision (i) of this subparagraph may constitute a lump sum distribution with respect to an employee even though the trust retains retirement plan bonds registered in the name of such employee. Similarly, the proceeds of a retirement plan bond received as a part of the balance to the credit of an employee will not be entitled to be treated as a lump sum distribution. See section 405(e) and paragraph (a)(4) of § 1.405-3.

(v) The term "balance to the credit of the employee" includes any amount to the credit of the employee under any plan which is required to be aggregated under the provisions of section 402(e)(4)(C) and paragraph (e)(1) of this section.

(vi) The term "balance to the credit of the employee" does not include any amount which has been placed in a separate account for the funding of medical benefits described in section 401(h) as defined in paragraph (a) of § 1.401-14. Thus, a distribution or payment by a plan described in subdivision (i) of this subparagraph may constitute the "balance to the credit of the employee" with respect to an employee even though the trust retains amounts attributable to the funding of medical benefits described in section 401(h).

(vii) The term "balance to the credit of the employee" includes any amount which is not forfeited under the plan as of the close of the taxable year of the recipient within which the distribution is made except that in the case of an employee who has separated from the service and incurs a break in service (within the meaning of section 411), such terms does not include an amount which is forfeited at the close of the plan year, beginning with or within such taxable year, by reason of such break in service.

(viii) The balance to the credit of the employee is includible in the gross income of the recipient if the recipient fails to make a timely election under section 72(h) to receive an annuity in lieu of such balance.

(2) *Total taxable amount.*—(i) The term "total taxable amount" means, with respect to a lump sum distribution described in the first sentence of paragraph (d)(1)(i) of this section, the amount of such lump sum distribution which exceeds the sum of—

(A) The net amount contributed by the employee, and

(B) The net unrealized appreciation attributable to that part of the distribution which consists of the securities of the employer corporation so distributed.

(ii) For purposes of paragraph (d)(2)(i)(A) of this section, the term "net amount contributed by the employee" means—

(A) For taxable years beginning after December 31, 1974, the amount actually contributed by the employee plus any amounts considered to be contributed by the employee under the rules of sections 72(f) and 101(b), and paragraph (b) of § 1.72-16, reduced by any amounts theretofore distributed to him which were excludable from gross income as a return of employee contributions.

(B) For taxable years beginning before January 1, 1975, an amount equal to the product of the amounts considered contributed by the employee under the plan (determined by applying sections 72 (f) and 101(b), and paragraph (b) of § 1.72-16) reduced by any amount theretofore distributed to the employee which were not includible in his gross income, multiplied by a fraction—

(*i*) The numerator of which is the excess, if any, of the sum of the current actuarial value of the annuity contract distributed and the value of the other property (including cash) distributed, over such current actuarial value, and

(*ii*) The denominator of which is the sum of the current actuarial value of the annuity contract distributed and the value of other property (including cash) distributed.

(iii) The provisions of this subparagraph may be illustrated by the following examples:

Example (1). A, age 60, receives a lump sum distribution from the M Corporation's noncontributory qualified plan on November 24, 1975. The distribution of $25,000 consists of cash and M Corporation securities with net unrealized appreciation of $15,000. The total taxable amount of the distribution to A is $10,000.

Example (2). B, age 60, receives a lump sum distribution from the N Corporation's contributory qualified plan on December 29, 1975. The distribution consists of $25,000 in cash. B's contributions under the plan as an employee are $5,000. The total taxable amount of the distribution to B is $20,000.

Example (3). W receives a lump sum distribution on April 1, 1975, from the M Corporation's noncontributory qualified plan as beneficiary of H on account of H's death. The distribution consists of $25,000 in cash. The total taxable amount of distribution to W is $20,000 if W is otherwise allowed a $5,000 exclusion under section 101(b).

(3) *Ordinary income portion.*—(i) The ordinary income portion of a lump sum distribution is the product of the total taxable amount of the lump sum distribution, multiplied by a fraction—

(A) the numerator of which is the number of calendar years of active participation by the employee in the plan after December 31, 1973, under which the lump sum distribution is made, and

(B) the denominator of which is the total number of calendar years of active participation by the employee in such plan.

(ii) For purposes of computing the fraction described in subdivision (i) of this subparagraph, the number of calendar years of active participation shall be the number of calendar months during the period beginning with the first month in which the employee became a participant under the plan and ending with the earliest of—

(A) The month in which the employee receives a lump sum distribution under the plan,

(B) In the case of an employee who is not an employee within the meaning of section 401(c)(1), the month in which the employee separates from the service,

(C) The month in which the employee dies, or

(D) In the case of an employee within the meaning of section 401(c)(1) who receives a lump sum distribution on account of disability, the first month in which he becomes disabled within the meaning of section 72(m)(7) and paragraph (f) of § 1.72-17.

In computing the months of active participation, in the case of active participation before January 1, 1974, a part of a calendar year in which the employee was an active participant under the plan shall be counted as 12 months, and in the case of active participation after December 31, 1973, a part of a calendar month in which an individual is an active participant under the plan shall be counted as 1 month. Thus, for example, if A, an individual, became an active participant under a plan on December 31, 1965, and continued to be an active participant under the plan until May 7, 1976, A has 108 (12 × 9) months of active participation under the plan before January 1, 1974, and A has 29 (12 + 12 + 5) months of active participation after December 31, 1973. For special rule in case of aggregation of plans, see paragraph (e)(1)(ii) of this section.

(4) *Employee; employer.*—The term "employee" includes an employee within the meaning of section 401(c)(1) and the employer of such individual is the person treated as his employer under section 401(c)(4).

(5) *Securities.*—The terms "securities" and "securities of the employer corporation" shall have the meanings provided in sections 402(a)(3)(A) and 402(a)(3)(B), respectively.

(e) *Special rules.*—(1) *Aggregation.*—(i) *Aggregation of trusts and plans.*—(A) For purposes of determining the balance to the credit of an employee, all trusts described in section 401(a) and which are exempt from tax under section 501(a) and which are part of a plan shall be treated as a single trust; all pension plans described in section 401(a) maintained by an employer shall be treated as a single plan; all profit-sharing plans described in section 401(a) maintained by an employer shall be treated as a single plan; and all stock bonus plans described in section 401(a) maintained by an employer shall be treated as a single plan. For purposes of this subdivision (i), an annuity contract shall be considered to be a trust.

(B) Trusts which are not described in section 401(a) or which are not exempt from tax under section 501(a), and annuity contracts which do not satisfy the requirements of section 404(a)(2) shall not be taken into account for purposes of subdivision (i) of this subparagraph.

(ii) *Computation of ordinary income portion.*—The ordinary income portion of a distribution from two or more plans (which are treated as a single plan under subdivision (i) of this subparagraph) shall be computed by aggregating all of the amounts which would constitute the ordinary income portion of a lump sum distribution if each plan maintained by the employer were not subject to the application of subdivision (i) of this subparagraph.

(iii) *Examples.*—The application of this subparagraph is illustrated by the following examples:

Example (1). M Corporation maintains a qualified profit-sharing plan and a qualified defnied benefit pension plan. A, who has participated in each plan for 5 years and is age 55, separates from the service on December 5, 1975. On December 5, 1975, A receives a distribution of the balance to the credit of his account under the profit-sharing plan. Payment of his pension benefits, however, will not commence until he attains age 65. A is entitled to treat his profit-sharing distribution as a lump sum distribution.

Example (2). Assume the same facts as in example (1) except that instead of a profit-sharing plan, M Corporation maintains a qualified money purchase pension plan. A is not entitled to have the amount received from the money purchase pension plan treated as a lump sum distribution.

Example (3). Assume the same facts as in example (2) except that the trust forming part of the defined benefit pension maintained by M Corporation is not a qualified trust. A is entitled to have the amount received from the money purchase plan treated as a lump sum distribution.

Example (4). N Corporation maintains profit-sharing plan X and profit-sharing plan Y which plans are qualified and are noncontributory. A is a participant in each plan. A has been a participant in the profit-sharing plan X since October 13, 1966 and a participant in profit-sharing plan Y since its inception on May 9, 1968. A, at age 55, separates from the service on December 5, 1975. He receives the balance to his credit from each plan upon separation. He receives $50,000 from profit-sharing plan X and $60,000 from profit-sharing plan Y. The ordinary income portion of his distribution from the N Corporation plans is $25,000 [($50,000 × (24/120)) + ($60,000 × (24/96))].

(2) *Community property laws.*—(i) Except as provided in paragraph (e)(2)(ii) of this section, the provisions of this section shall be applied without regard to community property laws.

(ii) In applying the provisions of section 402(e)(3), relating to the allowance of a deduction from gross income of the ordinary income portion of a lump sum distribution, community property laws shall not be disregarded. Thus, for example, if A, a married individual subject to the community property laws of a jurisdiction, receives a lump sum distribution of which the ordinary income portion is $10,000, and he and his wife, B, file separate returns for the taxable year, generally, one half of the total taxable amount of the lump sum distribution is includible in A's gross income, and he will be entitled to a deduction under section 402(e)(3) of $5,000. In this case, the other half of the total taxable amount is includible in B's gross income, and she will be entitled to a deduction of $5,000. The entire amount of the lump sum distribution, however, must be taken into account by A in computing the separate tax imposed by section 402(e)(1)(A).

(3) *Minimum period of service.*—For purposes of computing the separate tax imposed by section 402(e)(1)(A), no amount distributed or paid to an employee may be treated as a lump sum distribution under section 402(e)(4)(A) and this section unless he has been a participant in the plan for at least 5 full taxable years of such employee (preceding his taxable year in which such amount is distributed or paid). Thus, for example, if an amount, which would otherwise be a lump sum distribution, is distributed to A, an employee who has completed only 4 of his taxable years of participation in the plan before the first day of the taxable year in which the amount is distributed, A is not entitled to use the provisions of section 402(e) to compute the tax on the ordinary income portion of the amount distributed. If the amount were distributed to A's beneficiary on account of A's death, however, A's beneficiary could treat the distribution as a lump sum distribution under section 402(e) and this section.

(4) *Amounts subject to penalty.*—Section 402(e) and this section do not apply to an amount described in section 72(m)(5)(A)(ii) and § 1.72-17(e)(1)(i)(*b*) to the extent the provisions of section 72(m)(5) apply to such amount.

(5) *Distributions including securities of the employer corporation.*—For rules relating to distributions including securities of the employer corporation, see § 1.402(a)-1(b).

(6) *Liability for tax.*—(i) Except as provided in subdivision (ii) of this subparagraph the recipient shall be liable for the tax imposed by section 402(e)(1)(A).

(ii)(A) In any case in which the recipient of a lump sum distribution is a trust, if a beneficiary of such trust, is—

(1) An employee with respect to the plan under which the distribution is made, or

(2) Treated as the owner of such trust for purposes of subpart E of part I of subchapter J of chapter 1 of the Code (relating to grantors and others treated as substantial owners),

then such employee or the owner shall be treated as the sole recipient of the lump sum distribution. For purposes of *(1)* of this subdivision, the term "an employee with respect to the plan under which the distribution is made" means an individual who, immediately before the distribution is made, is a participant in the plan under which the distribution is made.

(B)*(1)* In any case in which a lump sum distribution is made within a taxable year with respect to an individual only to two or more trusts, if a beneficiary of any one of such trusts is not treated as the sole recipient of the distribution by reason of the application of (A) of this subdivision (ii), the separate tax imposed by section 402(e)(1)(A) shall be computed as if the distribution were made to a single recipient consisting of all of such trusts but the liability for such separate tax shall be allocated among the trusts according to the relative portions of the total taxable amount of the distribution received by each trust.

(2) In any case in which a lump sum distribution is made in a succeeding taxable year in a lookback period with respect to a trust described in *(1)* of this subdivision (B), the separate tax imposed by section 402(1)(A) shall be computed as if the amount described in section 402(e)(2)(A) (relating to the amount of tax imposed by section 402(e)(1)(A) paid with respect to other distributions in a lookback period) includes the separate tax determined in *(1)* of this subdivision (B) (without regard to the allocation described therein).

(7) *Change in exempt status of trust.*—For principles applicable in making appropriate adjustments if the trust was not exempt for one or more years before the year of distribution, see § 1.402(a)-1(a)(1)(iv).

(f) *Reporting.*—(1) *Information required.*—An employer who maintains a plan described in section 401(a) or 403(a), under which a distribution or payment which may be treated as a lump sum distribution is made in a taxable year of the recipient beginning after December 31, 1973, shall communicate (or cause to be communicated) in writing, to the recipient on Form 1099R the following information (where applicable):

(i) The gross amount of such distribution (including the value of any United States retirement plan bonds distributed to or held for the recipient);

(ii) The total taxable amount of such distribution;

(iii) The ordinary income portion and capital gain element of such distribution;

(iv) The net amount contributed by the employee (within the meaning of paragraph (d)(2)(ii) of this section);

(v) The portions of such distribution excludable from the gross income of the recipient under paragraph (c) of § 1.72-16 and paragraph (b) of § 1.402(a)-1;

(vi) The value of any United States retirement plan bonds distributed to or held for the recipient in excess of the net amount contributed by the employee (within the meaning of paragraph (d)(2)(ii) of this section) included in the basis of such bonds;

(vii) The current actuarial value of any annuity contract distributed as part of the balance to the credit of the employee in excess of the net amount contributed by the employee (within the meaning of paragraph (d)(2)(ii) of this section) considered to be an investment in the contract;

(viii) The net unrealized appreciation on any securities of the employer corporation.

(2) *Alternate method of communication.*—The obligation of the employer to communicate the information described in subparagraph (1) of this paragraph to the recipient shall be satisfied if the fiduciary of the trust or the payer of such distribution communicates the information to the recipient.

(3) *Taxable year of recipient.*—The report required by this paragraph may be prepared, at the option of the employer as if the taxable year of each employee were the calendar year.

(4) *Failure to satisfy requirements.*—In the event that the requirements of this paragraph are not satisfied, the information required to be furnished under this paragraph shall be furnished as part of the return required to be filed under section 6058 and the regulations thereunder.

Lump-Sum Distributions: Capital Gain Election

Employee Plans: Lump-Sum Distributions.—Reproduced below is the text of a proposed amendment of Reg. § 1.402(e)-2, relating to the election to treat no portion of a lump-sum distribution from an employee plan as long-term capital gain (published in the Federal Register on May 31, 1979).

☐ Par. 2. Section 1.402(e)-2(d)(3) as set forth in paragraph 12 of the appendix to the notice of proposed rulemaking of April 30, 1975, is revised by adding a new subdivision (iii) to read as follows:

§ 1.402(e)-2. Treatment of certain lump sum distributions made after 1973.—

* * *

(d) *Definitions.*—* * *

(3) *Ordinary income portion.*—* * *

(iii) In the case of a lump sum distribution received in a taxable year of the recipient beginning after December 31, 1975, the recipient may elect, in accordance with section 402(e)(4)(L) and § 1.402(e)-14, to treat all calendar years of an employee's active participation in all plans in which the employee has been an active participant as years of active participation after December 31, 1973. If a recipient makes the election, the ordinary income portion of any lump sum distribution received by the recipient with respect to the employee (whether in the recipient's taxable year for which the election is made, or thereafter) is equal to the total taxable amount of the distribution.

* * *

Lump-Sum Distributions: Election

Lump-Sum Distributions: Treatment of.—Reproduced below is the text of proposed Reg. § 1.402(e)-3, relating to the treatment of lump-sum distributions (published in the Federal Register on April 30, 1975).

§ 1.402(e)-3. Election to treat an amount as a lump sum distribution.—(a) *In general.*—For purposes of sections 402, 403, and this section, an amount which is described in section 402(e)(4)(A) and which is not an annuity contract may be treated as a lump sum distribution under section 402(e)(4)(A) only if the taxpayer elects for the taxable year to have all such amounts received during such year so treated. Not more than one election may be made under this section with respect to an employee after such employee has attained age 59½.

(b) *Taxpayers eligible to make the election.*—Individuals, estates, and trusts are the only taxpayers eligible to make the election provided by this section. In the case of a lump sum distribution made with respect to an employee to 2 or more trusts, the election provided by this section shall be made by the employee or by the personal representative of a deceased employee.

(c) *Procedure for making election.*—(1) *Time and scope of election.*—An election under this section shall be made for each taxable year to which such election is to apply. The election shall be made before the expiration of the period (including extensions thereof) prescribed in section 6511 for making a claim for credit or refund of the assessed tax imposed by chapter 1 of subtitle A of the Code for such taxable year.

(2) *Manner of making election.*—An election by the taxpayer with respect to a taxable year shall be made by filing Form 4972 as a part of the taxpayer's income tax return or amended return for the taxable year.

(3) *Revocation of election.*—An election made pursuant to this section may be revoked within the time prescribed in subparagraph (1) of this paragraph for making an election, only if there is filed, within such time, an amended income tax return for such taxable year, which includes a statement revoking the election and is accompanied by payment of any tax attributable to the revocation. If an election for a taxable year is revoked, another election may be made for that taxable year under paragraphs (c)(1) and (2) of this section.

(4) *Effect of election on subsequent distribution.*—An election made pursuant to this section shall be an election to treat an annuity contract distributed after December 31, 1973, in a look-back period (as defined in

§1.402(e)-2(c)(2)(iii)(F)) beginning after such date as a lump sum distribution in the taxable year of the recipient in which such contract is distributed. [Reg. §1.402(e)-3.]

Lump-Sum Distributions: Employee Plans

Employee Plans: Lump-Sum Distributions.—Reproduced below is the text of proposed Reg. §1.402(e)-14, relating to the election to treat no portion of a lump-sum distribution from an employee plan as long-term capital gain (published in the Federal Register on May 31, 1979).

☐ Par. 3. The following new section is added in the appropriate place:

§1.402(e)-14. Election to treat pre-1974 participation as post-1973 participation (the "402(e)(4)(L) election").—(a) *In general.*—Under section 402(e)(4)(L) and this section, the recipient of a lump sum distribution may elect to treat all calendar years of an employee's active participation in all plans in which the employee has been an active participant as years of active participation after December 31, 1973. This election is the "402(e)(4)(L) election." For rules relating to the treatment of distributions made on behalf of an employee with respect to whom the election is made, see §1.402(a)-1(a)(9) (relating to the capital gains portion of a lump sum distribution) and §1.402(e)-2(d)(3)(iii) (relating to the ordinary income portion of a lump sum distribution). For purposes of this section the term "lump sum distribution" means a lump sum distribution as defined in section 402(e)(4)(A), without regard to section 402(e)(4)(B).

(b) *Taxpayers not eligible to make the election.*—A taxpayer may not make the 402(e)(4)(L) election with respect to a lump sum distribution made on behalf of an employee, if—

(1) The taxpayer received a prior lump sum distribution made on behalf of the employee in a taxable year of the employee (or in a year that would have been a taxable year of the employee, but for the death of the employee) beginning after December 31, 1975, and

(2) A portion of that prior lump sum distribution was treated as long-term capital gain under section 402(a)(2) or 403(a)(2).

(c) *Time and scope of election.*—(1) *In general.*—The 402(e)(4)(L) election shall be made for the first lump sum distribution made with respect to an employee to which the election is to apply. The election does not apply to a lump sum distribution received by the recipient with respect to another employee. The 402(e)(4)(L) election is irrevocable. A revocation under §1.402(e)-3 of the election to apply the separate tax to a lump sum distribution will not revoke a 402(e)(4)(L) election.

(2) *Application of separate tax.*—Nothing in section 402(e)(4)(L) and this section changes the requirements which must be satisfied in order for a lump sum distribution to be eligible for application of the separate tax under section 402(e). Accordingly, a lump sum distribution is not taxable under section 402(e) merely because the 402(e)(4)(L) election is made with respect to, or otherwise applies to, the distribution.

(3) *Example.*—The provisions of subparagraph (2) of this paragraph may be illustrated by the following example:

Example. (i) A, a calendar year taxpayer aged 59½, separates from the service of A's employer, the M Corporation, on October 31, 1976. On December 15, 1976, A receives a distribution of the balance to A's credit under the M Corporation qualified profit sharing plan. A has been an active participant in the plan since January 1, 1971. The distribution is a lump sum distribution within the meaning of section 402(e)(4)(A) which satisfies the requirements of section 402(e)(4)(C), relating to the aggregation of certain trusts and plans, and section 402(e)(4)(H), relating to a minimum period of participation in the plan.

(ii) A makes the 402(e)(4)(L) election with respect to the distribution. Under section 402(e)(4)(L), all years of A's active participation in all plans in which A has been an active participant are treated as years of active participation after December 31, 1973. Accordingly, no portion of the distribution is taxable as long term capital gain under section 402(a)(2), and the total taxable amount of the distribution is "ordinary income" for purposes of section 402(e). A also makes the section 402(e)(4)(B) election for A's taxable year in which A receives the distribution. Accordingly, the total taxable amount of the distribution is taxable under the 10-year averaging provisions of section 402(e) (the separate tax).

(iii) On January 15, 1977, A receives a distribution of the balance of A's credit under the M Corporation qualified pension plan. A has been an active participant in the plan since January 1, 1958. The distribution is a lump sum distribution within the meaning of section 402(e)(4)(A) which satisfies the requirements of section 402(e)(4)(C), relating to the aggregation of certain trusts and plans, and section 402(e)(4)(H), relating to a minimum period of participation in the plan. No portion of the distribution is taxable as long-term capital gain under section 402(a)(2) because A made the 402(e)(4)(L) election with respect to A's 1976 distribution. In addition, no portion of the distribution is taxable under the 10-year averaging provisions of section 402(e) because A made a prior election under section 402(e)(4)(B) with respect to a distribution made on A's behalf and after A was age 59½ (the 1976 distribution).

(d) *Manner of making election.*—The 402(e)(4)(L) election shall be made in the manner indicated on the form filed pursuant to section 402(e)(4)(B) and §1.402(e)-3(c)(2) before the expiration of the period prescribed in §1.402(e)-3 for making the election to apply the separate tax to the ordinary income portion of a lump sum distribution.

(e) *Effective date.*—Taxpayers eligible under this section to make the 402(e)(4)(L) election may make the election with respect to a lump sum distribution received after December 31, 1975, and in a taxable year of the recipient beginning after that date. [Reg. §1.402(e)-14.]

Retirement Plans: Distributions: Deferral of Receipt: Notification of Consequences

Retirement Plans: Distributions: Deferral of Receipt: Notification of Consequences.—An amendment to Reg. §1.402(f)-1, specifying that the notice required under Code Sec. 411(a)(11) to be provided to a participant of his or her right, if any, to defer receipt of an immediately distributable benefit must also describe the consequences of failing to defer receipt of the distribution, is proposed (published in the Federal Register on October 9, 2008) (REG-107318-08).

Par. 2. For each entry listed in the "Location" column, remove the language in the "Remove" column and add the language in the "Add" column in its place.

§1.402(f)-1. Required explanation of eligible rollover distributions; questions and answers.

Location	Remove	Add
1.402(f)-1, A-2(a), first sentence	90 days	180 days

Lump-Sum Distributions: Taxability of Beneficiary

Lump-Sum Distributions: Treatment of.—Reproduced below is the text of proposed amendments of Reg. §1.403(a)-1, relating to the treatment of lump-sum distributions (published in the Federal Register on April 30, 1975).

☐ Section 1.403(a)-1(b) and (2) are amended to read as follows:

§1.403(a)-1. Taxability of beneficiary under a qualified annuity plan.—

* * *

(b) The amounts received by or made available to any employee referred to in paragraph (a) of this section under an annuity contract shall be included in the gross income of the employee for the taxable year in which received or made available, as provided in section 72 (relating to annuities), except that—

(1) For taxable years beginning before January 1, 1970, certain total distributions described in section 403(a)(2) (as in effect for such years) are taxable as long-term capital gains (see §1.403(a)-2 for rules applicable to such amounts), and

(2) For taxable years beginning after December 31, 1973, a portion of a lump sum distribution (as defined by section 402(e)(4)(A)) is treated as long-term capital gains (see paragraph (d) of §1.403(a)-2 for rules applicable to such portion and see §1.402(e)-2 for the computation of the separate tax on the portion of a lump sum distribution not treated as long-term capital gains).

For taxable years beginning before January 1, 1964, section 72(e)(3) (relating to treatment of certain lump sums), as in effect before such date, shall not apply to an amount described in this paragraph. For taxable years beginning after December 31, 1963, such amounts may be taken into account in computations under section 1301 through 1305 (relating to income averaging).

Lump-Sum Distributions: Certain Distributions

Lump-Sum Distributions: Treatment of.—Reproduced below are the texts of proposed amendments of Reg. §1.403(a)-2, relating to the treatment of lump-sum distributions (published in the Federal Register on April 30, 1975).

☐ Section 1.403(a)-2(a)(1) and (b) are amended; (c) is revised, (d) and (e) are added to read as follows:

§1.403(a)-2. Capital gains treatment for certain distributions.—(a) For taxable years beginning before January 1, 1970, if the total amounts payable with respect to any employee for whom an annuity contract has been purchased by an employer under a plan which—

(1) Is a plan described in section 403(a)(1) and §1.403(a)-1, and

* * *

(b) For taxable years begining before January 1, 1970—

(1) The term "total amounts" means the balance to the credit of an employee with respect to all annuities under the annuity plan which becomes payable to the payee by reason of the employee's death or other separation from the service, or by reason of his death after separation from the service. If an employee commences to receive annuity payments on retirement and then a lump sum payment is made to his widow upon his death, the capital gains treatment applies to the lump sum payment, but it does not apply to amounts received before the time the "total amounts" become payable. However, if the total amount to the credit of the employee at the time of his death or other separation from the service or death after separation from the service is paid or includible in the gross income of the payee within one taxable year of the payee, such amount is entitled to the capital gains treatment notwithstanding that in a later taxable year an additional amount is credited to the employee and paid to the payee.

* * *

(c) For taxable years beginning before January 1, 1970, the provisions of this section are not applicable to any amounts paid to a payee to the extent such amounts are attributable to contributions made on behalf of an employee while he was a self-employed individual in the business with respect to which the plan was established. For the taxation of such amounts, see §1.72-18. For such years for the rules for determining the amount attributable to contributions on behalf of an employee while he was self-employed, see paragraphs (b)(4) and (c)(2) of such section.

(d) For taxable years ending after December 31, 1969, and beginning before January 1, 1974, the portion of the total amounts described in paragraph (b)(1) of this section treated as gain from the sale or exchange of a capital asset held for more than six months is subject to the limitation of section 403(a)(2)(C), as in effect on December 31, 1973.

(e) For taxable years beginning after December 31, 1973—

(1) If a lump sum distribution (as defined in section 402(e)(4)(A) and the regulations thereunder) is received by, or made available to, the recipient under an annuity contract described in subparagraph (2)(i) of this paragraph, the ordinary income portion (as defined in section 402(e)(4)(E) and the regulations thereunder) of such distribution shall be taxable in accordance with the provisions of section 402(e) and the regulations thereunder and the portion of such distribution determined under paragraph (3) of this section shall be treated in accordance with the provisions of paragraph (2) of this section.

(2) If—

(i) An annuity contract is purchased by an employer for an employee under a plan described in section 403(a)(1) and § 1.403(a)-1,

(ii) Such plan requires that refunds of contributions with respect to annuity contracts purchased under the plan be used to reduce subsequent premiums on the contracts under the plan, and

(iii) A lump sum distribution (as defined in section 402(e)(4)(A) and the regulations thereunder) is paid to the recipient,

the amount described in paragraph (e)(3) of this section shall be treated as gain from the sale or exchange of a capital asset held for more than 6 months.

(3) For purposes of paragraph (e)(2) of this section, the portion of a lump sum distribution treated as gain from the sale or exchange of a capital asset held for more than 6 months is an amount equal to the total taxable amount of the lump sum distribution (as defined in section 402(e)(4)(D) and the regulations thereunder) multiplied by a fraction—

(i) The numerator of which is the number of calendar years of active participation (as determined under § 1.402(e)-2(d)(3)(ii)) by the employee in such plan before January 1, 1974, and

(ii) The denominator of which is the number of calendar years of active participation (as determined under § 1.402(e)-2(d)(3)(ii)) by the employee in such plan.

(4) For purposes of this paragraph—

(i) In the case of an employee who is an employee without regard to section 401(c)(1), the determination of whether or not an amount is a lump sum distribution shall be made without regard to the requirements of section 402(e)(4)(B) and § 1.402(e)-3.

(ii) No distribution to any taxpayer other than an individual, estate, or trust may be treated as a lump sum distribution under this section.

Lump-Sum Distributions: All Calendar-Year Treatment

Employee Plans: Lump-Sum Distributions.—Reproduced below is a proposed amendment of Reg. § 1.403(a)-2, relating to the election to treat no portion of a lump-sum distribution from an employee plan as long-term capital gain (published in the Federal Register on May 31, 1979).

* * *

☐ Par. 4. Section 1.403(a)-2(e)(3), as set forth in paragraph 15 of the appendix to the notice of proposed rulemaking of April 30, 1975, is revised by adding, immediately after subdivision (ii) thereof, a new sentence to read as follows:

§ 1.403(a)-2. Capital gains treatment for certain distributions.—

(e) * * *

(3) * * *

(i) * * *

(ii) * * *

In the case of a lump sum distribution received by or made available to a recipient in a taxable year of the recipient beginning after December 31, 1975, the recipient may elect, in accordance with section 402(e)(4)(L) and § 1.402(e)-14, to treat all calendar years of an employee's active participation in all plans in which the employee has been an active particpant as years of active participation after December 31, 1973. If a recipient makes the election, no portion of any distribution received by or made available to the recipient with respect to the employee (whether in the recipient's taxable year for which the election is made, or thereafter) is taxable to the recipient as long-term capital gain under section 403(a)(2) and this subparagraph.

* * *

Employee Trusts: Effective Dates

Employee Trusts: Tax Reform Act of 1984: Effective Dates.—Temporary Reg. §§ 1.404(a)-1T, 1.404(b)-1T and 1.404(d)-1T are also proposed as final regulations and, when adopted, would become Reg. §§ 1.404(a)-1, 1.404(b)-1 and 1.404(d)-1 (published in the Federal Register on February 4, 1986).

§ 1.404(a)-1. Questions and answers relating to deductibility of deferred compensation and deferred benefits for employees.

§ 1.404(b)-1. Method or arrangement of contributions, etc., deferring the receipt of compensation or providing for deferred benefits.

§ 1.404(d)-1. Questions and answers relating to deductibility of deferred compensation and deferred benefits for independent contractors.

Individual Retirement Plans: Simplified Employee Pensions

Individual Retirement Plans: Simplified Employee Pensions.—Reproduced below is the text of proposed Reg. § 1.404(h)-1, relating to individual retirement plans and simplified employee pensions (published in the Federal Register on July 14, 1981).

☐ Par. 5. There is added after § 1.404(e)-1A the following new section:

§ 1.404(h)-1. Special rules for simplified employee pensions.—(a) *In general.*—(1) Employer contributions to a simplified employee pension shall be treated as if they are made to a plan subject to the requirements of section 404. Employer contributions to a simplified employee pension are subject to the limitations of subparagraphs (2), (3), (4) and (5). For purposes of this paragraph, participants means those employees who satisfy the age, service and other requirements to participate in a simplified employee pension. For purposes of this paragraph, "compensation" means all of the compensation paid by the employer except either that for which a deduction is allowable under section 404(h) for simplified employee pensions or that for which a deduction is allowable under a plan that qualifies under section 401(a), including a plan that qualifies under section 404(a)(2) or 405.

(2) Employer contributions made for a calendar year are deductible for the taxable year of the employer with which or within which the calendar year ends.

(3) Contributions made within 3$^1/_2$ months after the close of a calendar year are treated as if they were made on the last day of such calendar year if they are made on account of such calendar year.

(4) The amount deductible for a taxable year for a simplified employee pension shall not exceed 15 percent of the compensation paid to the employees who are participants during the calendar year ending with or within the taxable year.

(5) The excess of the amount contributed over the amount deductible for a taxable year shall be deductible in the succeeding taxable years in order of time subject to the 15 percent limit of subparagraph (4).

(b) *Effect on stock bonus and profit-sharing trust.*—For any taxable year for which the employer has a deduction under section 404(h)(1), the otherwise applicable limitations in section 404(a)(3)(A) shall be reduced by the amount of the allowable deductions under section 404(h)(1) with respect to participants in the stock bonus or profit-sharing trust.

(c) *Effect on limit on deductions.*—For any taxable year for which the employer has an allowable deduction under section 404(h)(1), the otherwise applicable 25 percent limitations in section 404(a)(7) shall be reduced by the amount of the allowable deductions under section 404(h)(1) with respect to participants in the stock bonus or profit-sharing trust.

(d) *Effect on self-employed individuals or shareholder-employee.*—The limitations described in paragraphs (1), (2)(A), and (4) of section 404(e) or described in section 1379(b)(1) for any taxable year shall be reduced by the amount of the allowable deductions under section 404(h)(1) with respect to an employee within the meaning of section 401(c)(1) or a shareholder-employee (as defined in section 1379(d)).

(e) *Examples:*.—The provisions of this section may be illustrated by the following examples:

Example (1). Corporation X is a calendar-year taxpayer. On January 2, 1980, it adopts a simplified employee pension arrangement. At the end of 1980, it determines that it has paid $230,000 to all of its employees. Eight of its employees met its eligibility provisions for contributions to simplified employee pensions and their compensation totaled $140,000 before any contributions were made to their simplified employee pensions. Corporation X will be allowed to deduct its contributions to its employees' simplified employee pensions, not to exceed 15% of $140,000 or $21,000.

Example (2). Corporation Y is a calendar-year taxpayer which maintains a simplified employee pension agreement and a profit-sharing plan. The corporation has 100 employees. For the taxable year of 1980, it makes contributions to the simplified employee pensions of 75 of its employees. These contributions are 10 percent of compensation received in 1980. These same 75 employees are also participants in the corporation's profit-sharing plan. These 75 employees had total compensation paid during 1980 of $1,125,000. The corporation can deduct $112,500 under section 404(h) as its contributions to the simplified employee pension agreement. The corporation must reduce the otherwise applicable allowable deduction for contributions to the profit-sharing plan on behalf of these employees by the $112,500.

Example (3). Corporation Z is a calendar-year taxpayer which maintains a simplified employee pension arrangement and a profit-sharing plan. The corporation has 100 employees. For the taxable year of 1980, it makes contributions to the simplified employee pensions of 75 of its employees. These contributions are 10 percent of compensation received in 1980. Twenty-five of these employees are also participants in the corporation's profit-sharing plan. Each of these 75 employees had compensation for the year of $15,000, or total compensation of $1,125,000. The corporation deducts $112,500 under section 404(h) as its contribution to the simplified employee pension arrangement. The corporation must reduce the otherwise applicable allowable deduction for contributions to the profit-sharing plan on behalf of the 25 employees by $37,500, the amount contributed to the simplified employee pensions on behalf of employees covered by the profit-sharing plan.

Example (4). Corporation K is a taxpayer with a taxable year of December 1—November 30. On December 15, 1979, it adopts a simplified employee pension arrangement for its employees. It would like to make contributions to the plan on behalf of its employees for calendar year 1979. In order to make contributions to its employees' simplified employee pensions for calendar year 1979, the corporation must make the contributions by April 15, 1980. In order to receive a deduction for its taxable year ending November 30, 1980, for the contributions for calendar year 1979, the corporation must make the contributions by April 15, 1980. [Reg. §1.404(h)-1.]

ESOPs: Stock: Dividends Paid Deduction

ESOPs: Stock: Dividends Paid Deduction.—Reg. §1.404(k)-2, relating to employee stock ownership plans (ESOPs) by providing guidance concerning which corporation is entitled to the deduction for applicable dividends under Code Sec. 404(k) and by clarifying that a payment in redemption of employer securities held by an ESOP is not deductible, is proposed (published in the Federal Register on August 25, 2005) (REG-133578-05).

☐ Par. 3. Section 1.404(k)-2 is added to read as follows:

§1.404(k)-2. Dividends paid by corporation not maintaining ESOP.—

Q-1: What corporation is entitled to the deduction provided under section 404(k) for applicable dividends paid on applicable employer securities of a C corporation held by an ESOP if the ESOP benefits employees of more than one corporation or if the corporation paying the dividend is not the corporation maintaining the plan?

A-1: (a) *In general*. Under section 404(k), only the corporation paying the dividend is entitled to the deduction with respect to applicable employer securities held by an ESOP. Thus, no deduction is permitted to a corporation maintaining the ESOP if that corporation does not pay the dividend.

(b) *Example*. (i) *Facts*. S is a U.S. corporation that is wholly owned by P, an entity organized under the laws of Country A that is classified as a corporation for Federal income tax purposes. P is not engaged in a U.S. trade or business. P has a single class of common stock that is listed on a stock exchange in a foreign country. In addition, these shares are listed on the New York Stock Exchange, in the form of American Depositary Shares, and are actively traded through American Depositary Receipts (ADRs) meeting the requirements of section 409(I). S maintains an ESOP for its employees. The ESOP holds ADRs of P on Date X and receives a dividend with respect to those employer securities. The dividends received by the ESOP constitute applicable dividends as described in section 404(k)(2).

(ii) *Conclusion*. P, as the payor of the dividend, is entitled to a deduction under section 404(k) with respect to the dividends, although as a foreign corporation P does not obtain a U.S. tax benefit from the deduction. No corporation other than the corporation paying the dividend is entitled to the deduction under section 404(k). Thus, because S did not pay the dividends, S is not entitled to a deduction under section 404(k). The answer would be the same if P is a U.S. C corporation.

Q-2: What is the effective date of this section?

A-2: This section applies with respect to dividends paid on or after the date these regulations are published as final regulations in the Federal Register.

[Reg. §1.404(k)-2.]

Foreign Deferred Compensation Plans: Limitations: Deductions: Adjustments: Earnings and Profits

Foreign Deferred Compensation Plans: Limitations: Deductions: Adjustments: Earnings and Profits.—Reproduced below are the texts of proposed Reg. §§1.404A-0—1.404A-7, relating to the limitations on deductions and adjustments to earnings and profits with respect to certain foreign deferred compensation plans (published in the Federal Register on May 7, 1993).

☐ Par. 2. Sections 1.404A-0 through 1.404A-7 are added as follows:

§1.404A-0. Table of Contents.—This section 1.404A-0 lists the major headings that appear in §§1.404A-1 through 1.404A-7.

Method (2) election.
New Method Opening Amount.
Noncontrolled foreign corporation.
Nonqualified individual.
Nonqualified plan.
Old Method Closing Amount.
Open period.
Open years.
Opening reserve.
Opening year.
Pay-as-you-go method.
Period of adjustment.
Permitted plan year.
Plan year.
Primary evidence.
Prior deduction.
Protective election.
Qualified business unit.
Qualified foreign plan.
Qualified funded plan.
Qualified reserve plan.
Reasonable actuarial assumptions.
Reductions in earnings and profits.
Reserve method.
Retirement annuity.
Retroactive effective date election.
Retroactive plan-by-plan election.
Revocation of election.
Secondary evidence.
Separate funding entity.
Short taxable year.
Single plan.
Substantial risk of forfeiture.
Substantiation quality data.
Taxable year of a controlled foreign corporation.
Taxable year of a noncontrolled foreign corporation.
Taxpayer.
Termination of election.
Transition period.
Trust.
Unit credit method.
United States tax significance.
Written plan.

(f) Application of other Code requirements.
(1) Deductibility requirement.
(2) Section 461 requirements.

§1.404A-2. Rules for qualified funded plans.
(a) In general.
(b) Payment to a trust.
(1) Contribution requirements.
(2) Trust requirements.
(3) Retirement annuity.
(4) Effect of reversion of overfunded contributions.
(5) Example.
(c) Contribution deemed made before payment.
(1) Time of payment to trust.
(2) Time of designation.
(3) Irrevocable designation.
(d) Limitation for qualified funded plans.
(1) Plans with fixed or determinable benefits.
(2) Plans without fixed or determinable benefits.
(3) Limitations where more than one type of plan is maintained.
(4) Carryover contributions.
(5) Additional rules.
(e) Examples.

§1.404A-3. Rules for qualified reserve plans.
(a) Amounts taken into account with respect to qualified reserve plans.
(1) General rule.
(2) Amounts less than zero.
(3) Exclusive rules for qualified reserve plans.
(b) Reasonable addition to a reserve for liabilities.
(1) General rule.
(2) Unit credit method required.
(3) Timing of valuation.
(4) Permissible actuarial assumptions.
(c) Ten-year amortization for certain changes in reserves.
(1) Actuarial valuation.
(2) Expected value of reserve.
(3) Special rule for certain cost of living adjustments.
(4) Anti-abuse rule.
(d) Examples.

§1.404A-4. United States and foreign law limitations on amounts taken into account for qualified foreign plans.
(a) In general.
(b) Cumulative limitation.
(c) Special rule for foreign corporations in pre-pooling years.
(d) Rules relating to foreign currency.
(1) Taxable years beginning after December 31, 1986.
(2) Taxable years beginning before January 1, 1987.
(3) Special rules for the net worth method of accounting.
(e) Maintenance of more than one type of qualified foreign plan by an employer.
(f) United States and foreign law limitations not applicable.
(g) Definitions.
(1) Cumulative United States amount.
(2) Cumulative foreign amount.
(3) Appropriate foreign tax law.
(4) Aggregate amount.
(h) Examples.

§1.404A-5. Additional limitations on amounts taken into account for qualified foreign plans.
(a) Restrictions for nonqualified individuals.
(1) General rule.
(2) Determination of service attribution.
(b) Records to be provided by taxpayer.
(1) In general.
(2) Primary evidence.
(3) Additional requirements.
(4) Secondary evidence.
(5) Foreign language.
(6) Additional information required by District Director.
(7) Authorized officer to complete documents.
(8) Transitional rules.
(c) Actuarial requirements.
(1) Reasonable actuarial assumptions.
(2) Full funding limitation.

§1.404A-6. Elections under section 404A and changes in methods of accounting.
(a) Elections, changes in accounting methods, and changes in plan years.
(1) In general.

[Reg. §1.404A-0.]

§1.404A-1. General rules concerning deductions and adjustments to earnings and profits for foreign deferred compensation plans.—(a) *In general.*—Section 404A provides the exclusive means by which an employer may take a deduction or reduce earnings and profits for deferred compensation in situations other than those in which a deduction or reduction of earnings and profits is permitted under section 404. A deduction or reduction of earnings and profits is permitted under section 404A for amounts paid or accrued by an employer under a foreign deferred compensation plan, in the taxable year in which the amounts are properly taken into account under §§1.404A-1 through 1.404A-7, if each of the following requirements is satisfied:

(1) The plan is a written plan maintained by the employer that provides deferred compensation.

(2) The plan is maintained for the exclusive benefit of the employer's employees or their beneficiaries.

(3) 90 percent or more of the amounts taken into account under the plan are attributable to services performed by nonresident aliens, the compensation for which is not subject to United States federal income tax.

(4) An election under §1.404A-6 or 1.404A-7 is made to treat the plan as either a qualified funded plan or a qualified reserve plan and to select a plan year.

(b) *90-percent test.*—(1) *Reserve plans.*—Paragraph (a)(3) of this section is not satisfied by a reserve plan unless 90 percent or more of the actuarial present value of the total vested benefits (i.e., benefits not subject to substantial risk of forfeiture) accrued under the plan is attributable to services performed by nonresident aliens, the compensation for which is not subject to United States federal income tax.

(2) *Funded plans.*—(i) *Individual account plans.*—Paragraph (a)(3) of this section is not satisfied by a funded plan with individual accounts unless 90 percent or more of the amounts allocated to individual accounts (as described in section 414(i)) under the plan are allocated to the accounts of nonresident aliens and are attributable to services the compensation for which is not subject to United States federal income tax.

(ii) *Plans without individual accounts.*—Paragraph (a)(3) of this section is not satisfied by a funded plan not described in paragraph (b)(2)(i) of this section unless 90 percent or more of the actuarial present value of the total benefits accrued under the plan is attributable to services performed by nonresident aliens the compensation for which is not subject to United States federal income tax.

(c) *Calculation of 90 percent amounts.*—(1) *In general.*—In determining whether the tests described in paragraphs (b)(1) and (b)(2)(ii) of this section are satisfied, accrued benefits and the actuarial present values of accrued benefits may be calculated under any reasonable method. See § 1.404A-5(a) for rules describing the calculation of accrued benefits attributable to services for which the compensation is subject to United States federal income tax.

(2) *Safe harbor.*—The requirement of paragraph (a)(3) of this section will be deemed satisfied with respect to a plan if—

(i) The participants' benefits under the plan increase generally in proportion to their compensation taken into account under the plan; and

(ii) The sum of the following amounts does not exceed five percent of all compensation taken into account under the plan for the plan year—

(A) The compensation of United States citizens and residents taken into account under the plan; and

(B) Any other compensation subject to United States federal income tax taken into account under the plan.

(3) *Anti-abuse rule.*—Notwithstanding paragraph (c)(2) of this section, the requirement of paragraph (a)(3) of this section will not be deemed satisfied under paragraph (c)(2) of this section if the Commissioner determines that a significant purpose of the plan is to secure benefits not otherwise eligible for tax benefits under the Internal Revenue Code to participants who are United States citizens or residents.

(4) *Example.*—The principles of paragraphs (c)(2) and (c)(3) of this section are illustrated by the following example:

Example. A foreign branch of a domestic corporation maintains a deferred compensation plan under which benefits are based upon a participant's average compensation for the last five consecutive years of employment. The significant purposes of the plan do not include the provision of benefits otherwise unavailable under the Code to participants who are United States citizens or residents. The foreign branch maintains its books and records in its functional currency (FC). The taxpayer's taxable year and the plan year are coterminous with the calendar year. During the plan year in question, the compensation taken into account under the plan for all plan participants totals FC200 million. Of the FC200 million, FC6 million of the compensation taken into account under the plan is compensation for United States citizens and residents or otherwise subject to United States federal income tax. Because the FC6 million is less than five percent of all compensation taken into account under the plan for the plan year, the 90-percent requirement of paragraph (a)(3) of this section is deemed satisfied for this taxable year.

(d) *Deductions and reductions of earnings and profits.*—Deductions and reductions of earnings and profits for amounts paid by an employer to a plan that provides deferred compensation that does not meet the requirements of paragraph (a) of this section are governed exclusively by section 404, without regard to whether the plan benefits foreign employees.

(e) *Definitions.*—The following definitions apply for purposes of section 404A and §§ 1.404A-1 through 1.404A-7:

Actuarial present value. "Actuarial present value" is defined in § 1.401(a)(4)-12.

Aggregate amount. "Aggregate amount" is defined in § 1.404A-4(g)(4).

Appropriate foreign tax law. "Appropriate foreign tax law" is defined in § 1.404A-4(g)(3).

Authorized officer. "Authorized officer" is defined in § 1.404A-5(b)(7).

Carryover contributions. "Carryover contributions" are defined in § 1.404A-2(d)(4).

Change in method of accounting. "Change in method of accounting" is defined in § 1.404A-6(a).

Closing year. "Closing year" is defined in § 1.404A-6(f)(4)(ii).

Contributions accumulated to pay deferred compensation. "Contributions accumulated to pay deferred compensation" are defined in § 1.404A-2(b)(2).

Contributions to a trust. "Contributions to a trust" are defined in § 1.404A-2(b)(1).

Controlled foreign corporation. "Controlled foreign corporation" means a controlled foreign corporation as defined in sections 953(c)(1)(B) and 957.

Cumulative foreign amount. "Cumulative foreign amount" is defined in § 1.404A-4(g)(2).

Cumulative limitation. "Cumulative limitation" is defined in § 1.404A-4(b).

Cumulative United States amount. "Cumulative United States amount" is defined in § 1.404A-4(g)(1).

Deductible limit. "Deductible limit" is defined in § 1.404A-2(d)(1)(i).

Deductions. "Deductions" are defined in § 1.404A-1(f)(1).

Deferred compensation.—(i) In general.—"Deferred compensation" means any item the deductibility of which is determined by reference to section 404, without regard to whether section 404 permits a deduction and without regard to whether elections are made under § 1.404A-6 or 1.404A-7. Deferred compensation, as described in the preceding sentence, does not include deferred benefits described in section 404(b)(2)(B).

(ii) Social security.—A plan under which a foreign government (including a political subdivision, agency or instrumentality thereof) makes a contribution or a direct payment to a participant (or the participant's beneficiary) does not provide deferred compensation to the extent of such contributions or payments. Thus, for example, a foreign country's social security system generally will not be considered as providing deferred compensation. However, the fact that employers are required to maintain the plan by reason of foreign law, or the fact that the plan supplements social security benefits provided by a foreign country, or provides benefits in lieu of such social security benefits, does not prevent a plan from providing deferred compensation.

(iii) Termination indemnity plans.—The determination of whether a plan (including a termination indemnity plan) provides deferred compensation must generally be made under paragraph (i) of this definition in light of all of the facts and circumstances. Benefits paid under a plan, including a plan denominated a termina-

tion indemnity plan will generally be treated as deferred compensation if—

(A) A major purpose of the plan is to provide for the payment of retirement benefits;

(B) The plan has a benefit formula providing for payment based at least in part upon length of service;

(C) The plan provides for the payment of benefits to employees (or their beneficiaries) after the employee's retirement, death or other termination of employment; and

(D) It meets such other requirements as may be prescribed by the Commissioner in guidance of general applicability with respect to termination indemnity plans.

(iv) *Example.*—The definition of deferred compensation is illustrated by the following example:

Example. A domestic corporation maintains a branch operation in foreign country *F*. *F* requires that all employers doing business in its country provide benefits to employees under a termination indemnity plan insured by *F*'s government. The plan provides for payments to employees who terminate employment for any reason, including retirement, death, voluntary resignation and discharge for cause (other than for gross misconduct) and permits withdrawals for certain hardship conditions. Upon separation, the employee (or his or her beneficiary) receives an amount equal to the accumulation on the employer's books of one-thirteenth of his or her annual salary for each year of employment, with specified adjustments for interest and inflation. This termination indemnity plan provides deferred compensation as described in paragraph (e) of this section.

Earnings and profits. "Earnings and profits" means earnings and profits computed in accordance with sections 312 and 964(a) and, for taxable years beginning after December 31, 1986, section 986 and the regulations thereunder; and for purposes of section 902 in taxable years beginning before January 1, 1987, accumulated profits within the meaning of section 902(c) as in effect on the day before the enactment of the Tax Reform Act of 1986.

Employer. "Employer" means a person that maintains a plan for the payment of deferred compensation for services provided to it by its employees. "Employer" for purposes of the acceleration of the section 481(a) adjustment is defined in § 1.404A-6(e)(2)(iv).

Equivalent of a trust. "Equivalent of a trust" means a fund—

(i) The corpus and income of which is separately identifiable and segregated, through a separate legal entity, from the general assets of the employer;

(ii) The corpus and income of which is not subject, under the applicable foreign law, to the claims of the employer's creditors prior to the claims of employees and their beneficiaries under the plan;

(iii) The corpus and income of which, by law or by contract, cannot at any time prior to the satisfaction of all liabilities with respect to employees under the plan be used for, or diverted to, any purpose other than providing benefits under the plan; and

(iv) The corpus and income of which is held by a person who has a legally enforceable duty to operate the fund prudently.

Erroneous deduction. "Erroneous deduction" is defined in § 1.404A-7(d)(3)(ii).

Exclusive benefit. "Exclusive benefit" has the same meaning as in §§ 1.401-2 and 1.413-1(d).

Fixed or determinable benefits. "Fixed or determinable benefits" are defined in § 1.404A-2(d)(1)(i).

Full funding limitation. "Full funding limitation" is defined in § 1.404A-5(c)(2).

Functional currency. "Functional currency" (abbreviated as FC) means the functional currency of a taxpayer or a qualified business unit determined in accordance with section 985(b) and the regulations thereunder, or, for taxable years beginning before January 1, 1987, the currency in which the employer's books and records were maintained for United States tax purposes.

Funded method. "Funded method" is defined in § 1.404A-6(f)(2)(iv).

Initial aggregate amount. "Initial aggregate amount" is defined in § 1.404A-6(g)(2)(iii).

Initial Cumulative foreign amount. "Initial Cumulative foreign amount" is defined in § 1.404A-6(g)(2)(ii).

Initial Cumulative United States amount. "Initial Cumulative United States amount" is defined in § 1.404A-6(g)(2)(i).

Initial section 404A(d) amounts. "Initial section 404A(d) amounts" are defined in § 1.404A-6(g).

Liability. "Liability" is defined in § 1.404A-1(f)(2).

Majority domestic corporate shareholders. "Majority domestic corporate shareholders" are defined in § 1.404A-6(c)(2)(ii)(C).

Method of accounting. "Method of accounting" is defined in § 1.404A-6(a)(1).

Method (1) election. "Method (1) election" is defined in § 1.404A-7(g)(1).

Method (2) election. "Method (2) election" is defined in § 1.404A-7(g)(2).

New Method Opening Amount. "New Method Opening Amount" is defined in § 1.404A-6(f)(3).

Noncontrolled foreign corporation. "Noncontrolled foreign corporation" means a foreign corporation other than a controlled foreign corporation.

Nonqualified individual. "Nonqualified individual" is defined in § 1.404A-5(a)(1).

Nonqualified plan. "Nonqualified plan" is defined in § 1.404A-6(f)(3)(iii).

Old Method Closing Amount. "Old Method Closing Amount" is defined in § 1.404A-6(f)(2).

Open period. "Open period" is defined in § 1.404A-7(g)(6).

Open years. "Open years" are defined in § 1.404A-7(g)(3).

Opening reserve. "Opening reserve" is defined in § 1.404A-6(f)(3)(i).

Opening year. "Opening year" is defined in § 1.404A-6(f)(4)(i).

Pay-as-you-go method. "Pay-as-you-go method" is defined in § 1.404A-6(f)(2)(iii).

Period of adjustment. "Period of adjustment" is defined in § 1.404A-6(e)(2).

Permitted plan year. "Permitted plan year" means the plan year of a plan providing deferred compensation ending with or within the employer's taxable year.

Plan year. "Plan year" means the annual accounting period of a plan providing deferred compensation.

Primary evidence. "Primary evidence" is defined in § 1.404A-5(b)(2).

Prior deduction. "Prior deduction" is defined in § 1.404A-7(d)(3)(i).

Protective election. "Protective election" is defined in § 1.404A-7(g)(2).

Qualified business unit. "Qualified business unit" is defined in section 989(a).

Qualified foreign plan. "Qualified foreign plan" means a plan that meets the requirements of paragraph (a) of this section.

Qualified funded plan. "Qualified funded plan" means a qualified foreign plan for which an election has been made under § 1.404A-6 or 1.404A-7 by the taxpayer to treat the plan as a qualified funded plan.

Qualified reserve plan. "Qualified reserve plan" means a qualified foreign plan for which an election has been made by the taxpayer under § 1.404A-6 or 1.404A-7 to treat the plan as a qualified reserve plan.

Reasonable actuarial assumptions. "Reasonable actuarial assumptions" are defined in § 1.404A-5(c).

Reductions in earnings and profits. "Reductions in earnings and profits" are defined in § 1.404A-1(f)(1).

Reserve method. "Reserve method" is defined in § 1.404A-6(f)(2)(ii).

Retirement annuity. "Retirement annuity" is defined in § 1.404A-2(b)(3).

Retroactive effective date election. "Retroactive effective date election" is defined in § 1.404A-7(b)(1).

Retroactive period. "Retroactive period" is defined in § 1.404A-7(g)(4).

Retroactive plan-by-plan election. "Retroactive plan-by-plan election" is defined in § 1.404A-7(c)(1) and (d)(1).

Revocation of election. "Revocation of election" is defined in § 1.404A-6(d)(1).

Secondary evidence. "Secondary evidence" is defined in § 1.404A-5(b)(4).

Separate funding entity. "Separate funding entity" is defined in § 1.404A-6(f)(4)(iii).

Short taxable year. "Short taxable year" is defined in § 1.404A-7(d)(2).

Single plan. "Single plan" is defined in § 1.404A-6(a)(2).

Substantial risk of forfeiture. "Substantial risk of forfeiture" is defined in § 1.404A-3(b)(2).

Substantiation quality data. "Substantiation quality data" means less than precise data that is nevertheless the best data available for the plan year at reasonable expense.

Taxable year of a controlled foreign corporation. "Taxable year of a controlled foreign corporation" means the taxable year as defined in sections 441(b) and 7701(a)(23), subject to section 898.

Taxable year of a noncontrolled foreign corporation. "Taxable year of a noncontrolled foreign corporation" means the taxable year as defined in sections 441(b) and 7701(a)(23).

Taxpayer. "Taxpayer" is defined in section 7701(a)(14).

Termination of election. "Termination of election" is defined in § 1.404A-6(c)(1).

Transition period. "Transition period" is defined in § 1.404A-7(g)(5).

Trust. "Trust" means a trust (as defined in § 301.7701-4(a) of this chapter) or the equivalent of a trust.

Unit credit method. "Unit credit method" is defined in § 1.404A-3(b)(2).

United States tax significance. "United States tax significance" is defined in § 1.404A-6(b)(2)(ii).

Written plan. "Written plan" means a plan that is defined by plan instruments or required under the law of a foreign country, or both. An insurance contract can constitute a written plan.

(f) *Application of other Code requirements.*—(1) *Deductibility requirement.*—(i) *In general.*—In order to deduct amounts under section 404A, amounts contributed to a qualified funded plan or properly added to a reserve with respect to a qualified reserve plan must otherwise be deductible. The standards under section 404 are to be used in determining whether an amount would otherwise be deductible for this purpose. Thus, amounts may be taken into account under section 404A only to the extent that they are ordinary and necessary expenses during the taxable year in carrying on a trade or business and are compensation for personal services actually rendered before the end of the year. Similarly, in order to reduce earnings and profits under section 404A by amounts contributed to a qualified funded plan or properly added to a reserve with respect to a qualified reserve plan, earnings and profits must otherwise be able to be reduced by such amounts under the general principles of sections 312, 901, 902, 960, and 964.

(ii) *Capitalization requirements.*—In determining if an amount would otherwise be deductible (or able to be used to reduce earnings and profits) for purposes of paragraph (g)(1)(i) of this section, the fact that the amount is required to be capitalized (e.g., under section 263A) is ignored. Additionally, while section 404A and §§ 1.404A-1 through 1.404A-7 refer generally to permissible deductions or reductions of earnings and profits for deferred compensation, those references are intended to refer both to situations under which amounts may be taken into account as deductions or reductions of earnings and profits and to situations under which amounts may be taken into account through inclusion in the basis of inventory or through capitalization.

(2) *Section 461 requirements.*—In determining whether any amount of deferred compensation may be taken into account under section 404A by an accrual method taxpayer, the conditions for accrual under section 461 must be met with respect to the amount by the last day of the taxable year. For this purpose, an amount determined under §§ 1.404A-1 through 1.404A-7 establishes the fact of the liability and determines the amount of the liability with reasonable accuracy. See § 1.461-4(d)(2)(iii), which generally provides that the economic performance requirement of section 461(h) is satisfied to the extent that any amount is otherwise properly taken into account under §§ 1.404A-1 through 1.404A-7. [Reg. § 1.404A-1.]

§ 1.404A-2. Rules for qualified funded plans.—(a) *In general.*—Except as provided in this section and in §§ 1.404A-4 and 1.404A-5, the amount taken into account for a taxable year with respect to a qualified funded plan is the amount of the contributions paid by the employer to the trust in that year (regardless of whether the employer uses an accrual method of accounting). Accretions in a trust are not considered contributions to a plan.

(b) *Payment to a trust.*—(1) *Contribution requirements.*—Contributions paid under a qualified funded plan may not be taken into account unless they are—

(i) Paid to a trust which is operated in accordance with the requirements of section 401(a)(2);

(ii) Paid for a retirement annuity under which retirement benefits are provided and which is for the exclusive benefit of the employer's employees or their beneficiaries; or

(iii) Paid directly to a participant or beneficiary (rather than a trust).

(2) *Trust requirements.*—(i) *General rule.*—A contribution does not satisfy paragraph (b)(1)(i) of this section unless it is accumulated in the trust for the purpose of being distributed as deferred compensation. Whether a contribution is being accumulated in the trust for the purpose of being distributed as deferred compensation depends on the facts and circumstances. For purposes of paragraph (b)(1)(i) of this section, the fact that a trust has been (or has not been) involved in transactions that would be described in section 4975(c)(1) (and not exempted under section 4975(c)(2) or 4975(d)), e.g., contributions made in the form of a promissory note, if the plan were subject to section 4975(c)(1), is an important factor in determining whether the trust is not (or is) considered to be operated in accordance with the requirements of section 401(a)(2). In addition, a contribution to a trust does not satisfy paragraph (b)(1)(i) of this section unless it has substance.

(ii) *Effective date.*—The section 4975(c)(1) factor in determining compliance with section 401(a)(2) provided in this paragraph (b)(2) is taken into account for all transactions entered into after May 6, 1993.

(3) *Retirement annuity.*—A retirement annuity means a retirement annuity (as defined in section 404(a)(2)) except that the retirement annuity need not be part of a plan that meets the requirements of section 401(a) or 401(d). Notwithstanding the preceding sentence, the retirement annuity described therein need not be issued by an insurance company qualified to do business in a State in the United States if the taxpayer(s) and/or sponsoring employer(s) of the plan have shifted the risk of making payments under the plan to an entity that is qualified to do business in the country (or countries) where the plan is maintained.

(4) *Effect of reversion of overfunded contributions.*—If any portion of a contribution to a trust may revert to the benefit of the employer before the satisfaction of all liabilities to employees or their beneficiaries covered by the trust, no amount of the contribution may be taken into account under this section.

(5) *Example.*—The principles of paragraph (b) of this section are illustrated by the following example:

Example. A foreign subsidiary of a domestic corporation maintains a deferred compensation plan for its employees. The foreign subsidiary makes annual contributions under the plan to a trust. Each year after the contribution is made to the trust, the trustee lends the contribution back to the foreign subsidiary maintaining the plan. The foreign subsidiary executes promissory notes obligating it to repay the borrowed funds (at a reasonable rate of interest) to the trust and to pay any benefits due under the plan. Notwithstanding that the taxpayer may have designated the plan as a qualified funded plan, amounts may not be taken into account under section 404A with respect to contributions to the trust because the loans cause the trust to fail the requirements of section 401(a)(2). Even if the loans do not cause the trust to violate section 401(a)(2), the portion of any contribution that is loaned to the foreign subsidiary could not be taken into account because, to the extent of the loan (or loans), the contribution lacks substance and is not accumulated in the trust.

(c) *Contribution deemed made before payment.*—(1) *Time of payment to trust.*—Regardless of whether an employer uses the cash or an accrual method of accounting, for purposes of this section, a contribution to a trust that is paid after the close of an employer's taxable year is deemed to have been paid on the last day of that taxable year if—

(i) The payment is made on account of the taxable year and is made not later than the 15th day of the ninth month after the close of the taxable year;

(ii) The payment is treated by the plan in the same manner that the plan would treat a payment actually received on the last day of the taxable year; and

(iii) Either—

(A) The employer notifies the plan administrator or trustee in writing that the payment to the plan is designated on account of the taxable year;

(B) The taxpayer claims the payment as a deduction on its tax return for the taxable year; or

(C) The employer reduces earnings and profits with respect to the payment.

(2) *Time of designation.*—Any designation of a payment pursuant to paragraph (c)(1)(iii)(A) of this section must occur not later than the time described in paragraph (c)(1)(i) of this section.

(3) *Irrevocable designation.*—After a payment has been designated or claimed on a return in the manner provided in paragraph (c)(1)(iii)(A) of this section as being on account of a taxable year, the designation or claim may not be retracted or changed.

(d) *Limitation for qualified funded plans.*—(1) *Plans with fixed or determinable benefits.*—(i) *Limit on amount taken into account.*—Contributions made to a qualified funded plan under which the benefits are fixed or determinable are not taken into account under this section to the extent they exceed the amount that would be taken into account under section 404(a)(1)(A)(ii) and (iii) (determined without regard to the last sentence of paragraph (A) of section 404(a)(1) and without regard to whether the trust is exempt under section 501(a)). Benefits are considered fixed or determinable for this purpose if either benefits under or contributions to the plan are definitely determinable within the meaning of § 1.401-1(b)(1)(i). The limit described in the first sentence of this paragraph (d)(1)(i) is determined on the basis of the permitted plan year of the qualified foreign plan. Thus, the limit for the employer's taxable year is the limit for the plan year ending with or within the employer's taxable year.

(ii) *Actuarial valuation requirements.*—In determining the amount to be taken into account under this section, an actuarial valuation must be made not less frequently than once every three years. However, an actuarial valuation must be made for the first plan year of the plan for which an election under § 1.404A-6 is in effect. For interim years, a reasonable actuarial determination of whether the full funding limit in § 1.404A-5(c)(2) applies to the qualified funded plan must be made. The Commissioner may require a full actuarial valuation in an interim year under appropriate circumstances. See § 1.404A-6 for rules on changes in methods of accounting.

(2) *Plans without fixed or determinable benefits.*—Contributions made to a qualified funded plan under which the benefits are not fixed or determinable may not be taken into account under this section to the extent they exceed the limitations of section 404(a)(3) (determined without regard to whether the payment is made to a trust that is exempt under section 501(a)).

(3) *Limitations where more than one type of plan is maintained.*—Where payments are made for a taxable year to more than one type of qualified funded plan, the amounts that may be taken into account for the taxable year with respect to the payments are subject to the limitations of section 404(a)(7). The amount that is taken into account under this paragraph (d)(3) is determined without regard to whether the payment satisfies the minimum funding standard described in section 412.

(4) *Carryover contributions.*—In the event that the aggregate amount of contributions paid during an employer's taxable year in which an election under section 404A is in effect (reduced by an amount described in section 404A(g)(1)) exceeds the amount that may be taken into account under section 404A(a) and this section (computed without regard to section 404A(d) and § 1.404A-4), the excess contributions are treated as an amount paid in the succeeding taxable year with respect to that qualified foreign plan. A carryover contribution is also taken into account in determining whether a carryover contribution exists for a succeeding taxable year.

(5) *Additional rules.*—The Commissioner may prescribe additional rules for determining the amount that may be taken into account under this paragraph (d) in guidance of general applicability.

(e) *Examples.*—The principles of this section are illustrated by the following examples:

Example 1. A qualified funded plan under which benefits are not fixed or determinable is maintained by a foreign branch of a domestic corporation. The foreign branch computes its income in units of local currency, the FC. The taxpayer's taxable year and the plan year are coterminous with the calendar year. The plan was established in 1985, and the taxpayer made an election to apply section 404A, a qualified funded plan election as described in § 1.404A-6. For the 1985 taxable year, the employer made a FC25,000 contribution under the plan, and FC15,000 of that contribution could be taken into account under paragraph (d)(2) of this section. The cumulative foreign amount for the 1985 taxable year was FC20,000. The amount of the excess contribution carried forward was FC10,000 (FC25,000–FC15,000), because the amount of the carryover contribution is determined without regard to section 404A(d) and § 1.404A-4.

Example 2. Assume the same facts as in *Example 1,* except that the entire FC25,000 contribution made under the plan may be taken into account under paragraph (d)(2) of this section. The amount of the excess contribution carried forward was zero, even though the cumulative United States amount may have exceeded the cumulative foreign amount for the taxable year, because the amount of the excess contribution is determined without regard to section 404A(d) and § 1.404A-4.

Example 3. P, a domestic corporation, owns all of the one class of stock of foreign corporation *S.* The taxable year for *P* is the calendar year. The taxable year for *S* is the fiscal year beginning on June 1. *S* made a contribution to its qualified funded plan on February 15, 1983, and notified the plan's trustee in writing that *S* designated the contribution as a payment on account of *S'*s preceding taxable year (ending May 31, 1982). The contribution is taken into account in computing *S'*s earnings and profits for *S'*s taxable year ending May 31, 1982. [Reg. § 1.404A-2.]

§ 1.404A-3. Rules for qualified reserve plans.—(a) *Amounts taken into account with respect to qualified reserve plans.*—(1) *General rule.*—Except as provided in §§ 1.404A-4 and 1.404A-5, the amount taken into account for a taxable year with respect to a qualified reserve plan equals the sum of—

(i) The reasonable addition during the permitted plan year to a reserve for liabilities under the plan as described in paragraph (b) of this section; and

(ii) The amortization of certain increases or decreases in the plan reserve over ten years, as described in paragraph (c) of this section.

(2) *Amounts less than zero.*—If the amount to be taken into account under this section is less than zero, that amount must be treated as an increase in income and earnings and profits for the taxable year.

(3) *Exclusive rules for qualified reserve plans.*—No amounts may be taken into account with respect to a qualified reserve plan except as provided for in this section. Thus, for example, no deduction is allowed for benefit payments from the reserve. Similarly, no amount may be taken into account for any payments made by the employer that are used either to reinsure the liabilities or benefits under a qualified reserve plan or to fund separately all or a portion of the benefits under a qualified reserve plan. These amounts may, however, be taken into account as contributions to a qualified funded plan to the extent the requirements of § 1.404A-2 are satisfied.

(b) *Reasonable addition to a reserve for liabilities.*—(1) *General rule.*—Except as provided in § 1.404A-7(f)(2), the reasonable addition to a reserve for a plan year equals the increase in the reserve, determined under the unit credit method as described in paragraph (b)(2) of this section, that arises from the passage of time and from additional service and expected changes in compensation in the current plan year for employees who were included in the reserve as of the end of the prior plan year. Thus, the reasonable addition to the reserve includes an element of interest on the reserve as of the beginning of the plan year (less the interest on the benefit payments during the plan year) and the actuarial present value of the expected increase in vested benefits accrued during the current plan year for employees who were included in the reserve as of the end of the prior plan year, determined without reference to any plan amendment during the plan year.

(2) *Unit credit method required.*—The reserve for the employer's liability must be determined under the unit credit method. Thus, the reserve must be the actuarial present value of the employer's liability, taking into account service and compensation only through the valuation date. In determining the reserve under this section, benefits that are subject to a substantial risk of forfeiture may not be taken into account. The term "substantial risk of forfeiture" has the meaning stated in section 83, except that the term "property" in all events includes benefits accrued under a qualified reserve plan.

(3) *Timing of valuation.*—The determination of the reserve and the reasonable addition to the reserve must be made as of the last day of the plan year.

(4) *Permissible actuarial assumptions.*—(i) *Interest rates.*—(A) *In general.*—Notwithstanding any other provision of §§1.404A-1 through 1.404A-7, no amount may be taken into account under section 404A with respect to a qualified reserve plan unless the rate (or rates) of interest for the plan that are selected by the employer are within the permissible range. The interest rate selected by the employer for the plan under this paragraph must remain in effect for that plan until the first plan year for which that rate is no longer within the permissible range. At that time, a new rate of interest must be selected by the employer from within the permissible range applicable at that time.

(B) *Permissible range.*—For purposes of this paragraph (b)(4), the term "permissible range" means a rate of interest that is not more than 1.2 and not less than the product of 0.8 multiplied by the average rate of interest for the highest quality long-term corporate bonds denominated in the functional currency of the qualified business unit of the employer whose books reflect the plan's liabilities for the 15-year period ending on the last day before the beginning of the employer's taxable year. If there is no market in long-term corporate bonds denominated in the relevant functional currency, or if the qualified business unit computes its income or earnings and profits in dollars under §1.985-3, the employer must use a rate that can be demonstrated clearly to reflect income, based on all relevant facts and circumstances, including appropriate rates of inflation and commercial practices.

(ii) *Plan benefits.*—Except as otherwise provided by the Commissioner, changes in plan benefits or applicable foreign law that become effective (whether or not retroactively) in a future plan year may not be taken into account until the plan year the change is effective. Notwithstanding the above, the reserve calculation may take into account cost-of-living adjustments that are part of the employee's vested accrued benefit, using assumptions regarding cost-of-living adjustments that are consistent with the interest rate assumptions described in paragraph (b)(4)(i) of this section and the terms of the plan. Thus, for example, a cost-of-living adjustment that does not require any future service on the part of the employee and is not subject to employer discretion may be taken into account.

(c) *Ten-year amortization for certain changes in reserves.*—(1) *Actuarial valuation.*—Each plan year an actuarial valuation must be made as of the end of the plan year, comparing the actual reserve with the expected value of the reserve. Any difference between the actual reserve determined as of the end of the plan year and the expected value of the reserve as of that date must be amortized in level amounts of principal over ten years, beginning in the plan year of the actuarial valuation. This amortization applies regardless of whether the difference is attributable to changes in employee population, changes in plan provisions, or changes in actuarial assumptions.

(2) *Expected value of reserve.*—The expected value of the reserve as of the end of the plan year is equal to the sum of the reserve as of the end of the prior plan year plus the reasonable addition to the reserve for the plan year described in paragraph (b) of this section less the benefit payments during the plan year. Thus, the expected value of the reserve is generally determined on the basis of the plan in effect and the actuarial assumptions used as of the end of the prior plan year, but, because it includes the reasonable addition to the reserve, includes the effect of expected changes in compensation, service and vesting during the current plan year.

(3) *Special rule for certain cost of living adjustments.*—Notwithstanding the general rule that the increase in liability from a plan amendment is amortized over ten years, if under foreign law a shorter period for amortization is required, that shorter period shall be substituted for ten years in this paragraph (c) if the amendment is a cost of living adjustment that either—

(i) Relates primarily to retirees; or

(ii) Is for employees of a foreign corporation in a taxable year beginning before [*INSERT DATE THAT IS 90 DAYS AFTER THE DATE OF PUBLICATION OF FINAL REGULATIONS IN THE FEDERAL REGISTER*].

(4) *Anti-abuse rule.*—The Commissioner may reclassify any item included by a taxpayer as a reasonable addition to a reserve as instead subject to amortization over ten years if the Commissioner determines that the taxpayer's classification of that item circumvents the intent of section 404A(c)(4). Thus, for example, if the Commissioner determines that the vesting provisions of the plan cause the increase in vested benefits to be unreasonably large in a single plan year, the reasonable addition under paragraph (b) of this section must be calculated without recognizing any changes in vesting for the plan year.

(d) *Examples.*—The principles of this section are illustrated by the following examples:

Example 1. S, a foreign subsidiary of *P*, a domestic corporation, contributes funds to an irrevocable trust which is used to pay benefits provided under *S*'s reserve plan. The trust does not satisfy the requirements of section 401(a), 404(a)(4), or 404(a)(5). The funds are not used to provide benefits in addition to those provided by the reserve plan. In 1984, the year the plan was adopted, S elected to treat the plan as a qualified reserve plan. In 1984, *S* also contributed an amount to the irrevocable trust. The fact that *S* contributed an amount to the trust has no effect on the computation of the amount that *S* is entitled to take into account under this section in 1984 (or in any other year). Furthermore, no additional amount may be taken into account for the amount of the contribution to the trust beyond the amount permitted to be taken into account under this section.

Example 2. (a) Employer *Y* hired 10,000 employees in 1980, each of whom was age 40 at the beginning of the year and earned FC10,000. The employees immediately commenced participation in the plan. The plan provided that the accrued benefit at the end of X years equaled: (X multiplied by one percent) multiplied by the highest one year's compensation. The plan vesting was 20 percent per year starting after two years of service with the employer. Under the plan, once an employee was vested in a benefit, the benefit could not be forfeited for any reason other than the death of the employee. Employees who terminate employment for reasons other than death or retirement receive an immediate single sum distribution in an amount equal to the actuarial present value (calculated at eight percent interest) of the vested accrued benefit (where the actuarial present value and the vested accrued benefit are determined as of the end of the prior plan year). Reserves and expected increases in the reserve were determined using eight percent interest, five percent assumed compensation increases, the UP-84 mortality table and assuming no pre-retirement terminations other than death. However as set forth in the relevant data below, the actual experience differed from these assumptions (e.g., the actual compensation did not increase five percent each year and the mortality and termination experience were different than assumed).

Year	*End of Year Age*	*Number of Deaths*	*Number of Terminations*	*Number of Employees Remaining*
1980	41	16	5	9,979
1981	42	18	5	9,956
1982	43	20	5	9,931
1983	44	25	5	9,901
1984	45	30	25	9,846

Year	*Compensation for Each Employee*	*End of Year Accrued Benefit for Each Employee*	*End of Year Vested Accrued Benefit for Each Employee*
1980	10,000	100	0
1981	10,000	200	0
1982	10,000	300	60
1983	12,000	480	192
1984	12,000	600	360

Year	*Benefit Payments*	*End of Year Actuarial Factor*	*End of Year Reserve for Vested Benefits*
1980	0	1.049706	0
1981	0	1.136328	0
1982	0	1.230380	733,134
1983	369	1.332564	2,533,194
1984	6,396	1.443638	5,117,062

(b) *Computation of amounts taken into account for 1980.* The amount taken into account for 1980 was zero because there was no reasonable addition to the reserve (i.e., no increase in the reserve on account of the passage of time, additional service or expected changes in compensation for employees who were included in the reserve at the end of the prior year) and there were no amounts that are subject to ten-year amortization under paragraph (c) of this section.

(c) *Computation of amounts taken into account for 1981.* There was no amount taken into account for 1981 for the same reason as in 1980.

(d) *Computation of amount taken into account for 1982.* The amount taken into account in 1982 was the sum of the reasonable addition to the reserve determined under paragraph (b) of this section and the amortization of certain increases in the plan reserve over ten years determined under paragraph (c) of this section. There was no reasonable addition to the reserve (i.e., no increase in the reserve on account of the passage of time, additional service or expected changes in compensation for employees who were included in the reserve at the end of the prior year) for the 1982 year because no employee was included in the reserve as of the end of 1981. There were no benefits paid during 1981. Thus, the expected value of the reserve at the end of 1982 was zero. However, the actual value of the reserve at the end of 1982 was FC733,134 (9,931 employees x 60 x 1.230380). The difference between the expected and actual values of the reserve was taken into account over ten years beginning in 1982. Thus, the total amount taken into account for 1982 was FC73,313.

(e) *Computation of amount taken into account for 1983.* Using the employee data as of the end of 1982 and the expected rate of compensation increase for 1983, each employee's accrued benefit was expected to be 420 (10,500 × 4 years × .01) as of the end of 1983. 40 percent of this accrued benefit, or 168, was expected to be vested. Thus, the expected increase in each employee's vested accrued benefit was 108 (the difference between 168 and the vested accrued benefit as of the end of the prior year (60) for those employees who were included in the reserve as of the end of the prior year). There were 9,931 employees included in the reserve as of the end of the prior year and 9,931 × p_{43} were expected to be in the reserve as of the end of 1983. The actuarial present value factor for a deferred annuity of FC1 commencing at age 65 payable monthly is 1.332564. Thus, the actuarial present value of the expected increase in vested accrued benefits as of the end of the year was FC1,425,212 (9,931 employees × p_{43} × 108 × 1.332564). The reasonable addition to the reserve also included an element of interest on the reserve as of the end of the prior year equal to FC58,651 (8 percent × 733,134) that is offset by the interest attributable to the actual benefits paid during the year (FC15, which is interest on the benefits paid during the year (FC369) from the date of payment through the end of the year). Thus, the reasonable addition to the reserve for 1983 was FC1,483,848 (1,425,212 + 58,651 – 15) and the expected reserve at the end of the year was FC2,216,613 (733,134 + 1,483,848 – 369). The actual reserve at the end of 1983 is FC2,533,194, so there was an actuarial loss of FC316,581 (2,533,194 – 2,216,613) which was amortized over 10 years beginning in 1983. Thus, the total amount taken into account in 1983 was FC1,588,819 (1,483,848 + 73,313 + 10 percent of 316,581).

(f) *Computation of amount taken into account for 1984.* Using the employee data as of the end of 1983 and the expected rate of compensation increase for 1984, each employee's accrued benefit was expected to be 630 (12,600 × 5 years × .01) as of the end of 1984. 60 percent of this accrued benefit, or 378, was expected to be vested. Thus, the expected increase in each employee's vested accrued benefit was 186 (the difference between 378 and the vested accrued benefit as of the end of the prior year (192) for those employees who were included in the reserve as of the end of the prior year). There were 9,901 employees included in the reserve as of the end of the prior year and 9,901 × p_{44} were expected to be in the reserve as of the end of 1984. The actuarial present value factor for a deferred annuity of FC1 commencing at age 65 payable monthly is 1.443638. Thus, the actuarial present value of the expected increase in vested accrued benefits as of the end of the year was FC2,650,355 (9,901 employees × p_{44} × 186 × 1.443638). The reasonable addition to the reserve also included an element of interest on the reserve as of the end of the prior year equal to FC202,656 (8 percent × 2,533,194), offset by interest attributable to the actual benefits paid during the year (FC256, which is interest on the benefits paid during the year (FC6,396) from the date of payment through the end of the year). Thus, the reasonable addition to the reserve for 1984 was FC2,852,755 (2,650,355 + 202,656 – 256) and the expected reserve at the end of the year is FC5,379,553 (2,533,194 + 2,852,755 – 6,396). The actual reserve at the end of 1984 was FC5,117,062, so there was an actuarial gain of FC262,491 (5,379,553 – 5,117,062) which was amortized over 10 years beginning in 1984. Thus, the total amount taken into account in 1984 was FC2,931,477 (2,852,755 + 73,313 + 31,658 – 10 percent of 262,491).

(g) *Alternative computation method.* The amounts taken into account for 1982, 1983 and 1984 may also be illustrated as follows—

1982

Worksheet For Calculating Amount Taken Into Account For Qualified Reserve Plans Under §404A

(1)	Reserve at end of Prior Year	0
(2)	Interest on (1) to end of Current Year	0
(3)	Present Value of the Expected Increase in Vested Accrued Benefits for employees who were included in the reserve as of the end of the prior year.	0
(4)	Benefit Payments during current year	0
(5)	Interest on (4) from date of payment through end of Current year	0
(6)	Reasonable addition to the reserve (2) + (3) – (5)	0
(7)	Expected value of reserve (1) + (6) – (4)	0
(8)	Actual value of reserve	733,134
(9)	Amount to be amortized (8) – (7)	733,134
(10)	Remaining 10 Percent Bases from Prior Years (original amounts) (Item 12 from Prior Year)	0
(11)	10 percent Bases whose 10 years ended last year	0
(12)	(9) + (10) – (11)	733,134
(13)	10 percent of (12)	73,313
(14)	Amount Taken Into Account for Current Year [(6) + (13)]	73,313

1983

Worksheet For Calculating Amount Taken Into Account For Qualified Reserve Plans Under §404A

(1)	Reserve at end of Prior Year	733,134
(2)	Interest on (1) to end of Current Year	58,651
(3)	Present Value of the Expected Increase in Vested Accrued Benefits for employees who were included in the reserve as of the end of the prior year	1,425,212
(4)	Benefit Payments during current year	369
(5)	Interest on (4) from date of payment through end of Current year	15
(6)	Reasonable addition to the reserve (2) + (3) – (5)	1,483,848
(7)	Expected value of reserve (1) + (6) – (4)	2,216,613
(8)	Actual value of reserve	2,533,194
(9)	Amount to be amortized (8) – (7)	316,581
(10)	Remaining 10 Percent Bases from Prior Years (original amounts) (Item 12 from Prior Year)	733,134
(11)	10 percent Bases whose 10 years ended last year	0

(12)	(9) + (10) − (11)	1,049,715
(13)	10 percent of (12)	104,971
(14)	Amount Taken Into Account for Current Year [(6) + (13)]	1,588,819

1984

Worksheet For Calculating Amount Taken Into Account For Qualified Reserve Plans Under § 404A

(1)	Reserve at end of Prior Year	2,533,194
(2)	Interest on (1) to end of Current Year	202,656
(3)	Present Value of the Expected Increase in Vested Accrued Benefits for employees who were included in the reserve as of the end of the prior year.	2,650,355
(4)	Benefit Payments during current year	6,396
(5)	Interest on (4) from date of payment through end of Current year	256
(6)	Reasonable addition to the reserve (2) + (3) − (5)	2,852,755
(7)	Expected value of reserve (1) + (6) − (4)	5,379,553
(8)	Actual value of reserve	5,117,062
(9)	Amount to be amortized (8) − (7)	(262,491)
(10)	Remaining 10 Percent Bases from Prior Years (original amounts) (Item 12 from Prior Year)	1,049,715
(11)	10 percent Bases whose 10 years ended last year	0
(12)	(9) + (10) − (11)	787,224
(13)	10 percent of (12)	78,722
(14)	Amount Taken Into Account for Current Year [(6) + (13)]	2,931,477

Example 3. (a) The facts are the same as in *Example 2*, except that the interest rate used to determine the reserve as of the end of 1984 has been decreased to 7%.

(b) The amount taken into account for 1984 under the alternative calculation method is determined as follows:

1984

Worksheet For Calculating Amount Taken Into Account For Qualified Reserve Plans Under § 404A

(1)	Reserve at end of Prior Year	2,533,194
(2)	Interest on (1) to end of Current Year	202,656
(3)	Present Value of the Expected Increase in Vested Accrued Benefits for employees who were included in the reserve as of the end of the prior year.	3,402,637
(4)	Benefit Payments during current year	6,396
(5)	Interest on (4) from date of payment through end of Current year	256
(6)	Reasonable addition to the reserve (2) + (3) − (5)	3,605,037
(7)	Expected value of reserve (1) + (6) − (4)	6,131,835
(8)	Actual value of reserve	6,569,498
(9)	Amount to be amortized (8) − (7)	437,663
(10)	Remaining 10 Percent Bases from Prior Years (original amounts) (Item 12 from Prior Year)	1,049,715
(11)	10 percent Bases whose 10 years ended last year	0
(12)	(9) + (10) − (11)	1,487,378
(13)	10 percent of (12)	148,738
(14)	Amount Taken Into Account for Current Year [(6) + (13)]	3,753,775

[Reg. § 1.404A-3.]

§ 1.404A-4. United States and foreign law limitations on amounts taken into account for qualified foreign plans.—(a) *In general.*—Section 404A(d) and this section place two limits on the amount taken into account for a taxable year with respect to a qualified foreign plan under section 404A(b) and (c) and §§ 1.404A-2 and 1.404A-3. First, as set forth in paragraph (b) of this section, the cumulative amounts that are or have been taken into account under section 404A through the end of the current year may not exceed the cumulative amounts deductible under foreign law in that period. Because the foreign law deduction is cumulative, however, amounts previously disallowed under this rule are taken into account in later years as the amount deductible under foreign law increases. Second, for taxable years beginning before January 1, 1987, or such later year determined under section 902(c)(3)(A), the rule in paragraph (c) of this section further limits the amount taken into account during those taxable years. Because section 404A(d) and this section apply solely to amounts that would otherwise be taken into account under § 1.404A-2 or 1.404A-3, these limitations are applied without regard to amounts taken into account under section 481 (i.e., without regard to the portion of a section 481(a) adjustment that is taken into account during any taxable year within the section 481(a) adjustment period, as defined in § 1.404A-6(e)(2)). See § 1.404A-6, however, for rules applying the section 404A(d) limitations to the calculation of the section 481(a) adjustment.

(b) *Cumulative limitation.*—The amount taken into account with respect to a qualified foreign plan for any taxable year equals—

(1) The lesser of—

(i) The cumulative United States amount; or

(ii) The cumulative foreign amount;

(2) Reduced by the aggregate amount.

(c) *Special rule for foreign corporations in prepooling years.*—For a taxable year of a foreign corporation beginning before January 1, 1987, or such later year determined under section 902(c)(3)(A), the reduction in earnings and profits determined under paragraph (b) of this section with respect to a qualified foreign plan may not exceed the amount allowed as a deduction under the appropriate foreign tax laws for such taxable year. See *Example 3* of paragraph (h) of this section for an illustration of this rule.

(d) *Rules relating to foreign currency.*—(1) *Taxable years beginning after December 31, 1986.*—For taxable years beginning after December 31, 1986, the cumulative United States amount, the cumulative foreign amount, and the aggregate amount must be computed in the employer's functional currency. See generally section 964 and sections 985 through 989 for rules applicable to determining and translating into dollars the amount of income or loss of foreign branches and earnings and profits (or deficits in earnings and profits) of foreign corporations.

(2) *Taxable years beginning before January 1, 1987.*—For taxable years beginning before January 1, 1987, the cumulative United States amount, the cumulative foreign amount, and the aggregate amount must be computed in the currency in which the foreign branch or foreign subsidiary kept its books and records. See Rev. Rul. 75-106, 1975-1 C.B. 31 (see § 601.601(d)(2)(ii)(*b*) of this chapter), for rules for determining the amount of income or loss of foreign branches using a net worth method of accounting. See Rev. Rul. 75-107, 1975-1 C.B. 32 (see § 601.601(d)(2)(ii)(*b*) of this chapter), for rules for determining the amount of income or loss of foreign branches using a profit and loss method of accounting. See sections 312, 902, and 1248 and the regulations thereunder for rules for determining the earnings and profits of noncontrolled foreign corporations. See section 964 and the regulations thereunder for rules for determining the earnings and profits of foreign corporations for purposes of subpart F.

(3) *Special rules for the net worth method of accounting.*—For purposes of § 1.964-1(e)(4), an amount of deduction that is accrued but not paid at the end of the employer's taxable year with respect to a qualified funded plan must be treated as a short-term liability. In the case of a qualified reserve plan, for purposes of § 1.964-1(e), the amount of the reserve taken into account as a liability on the balance sheet as of the beginning of the taxable year must be limited to the aggregate amount, and the amount of the reserve taken into account as a liability on the balance sheet as of the close of the taxable year must be limited to the sum of the aggregate amount and the amount taken into account for the taxable year. For purposes of § 1.964-1(e)(4), each annual increase in the aggregate amount must be treated as a long-term liability incurred on the last day of the employer's taxable year to which the increase relates. As of the close of each taxable year, a portion of the aggregate amount equal to the amount of benefits expected to be paid during the succeeding taxable year must be reclassified as a short-term liability. The reclassified amount must be allocated to the annual increases in the aggregate amount on a first-in-first-out basis. Similar rules apply for purposes of determining the amount of reserve taken into account by a foreign branch using the net worth method of accounting for taxable years beginning before January 1, 1987, and by a qualified business unit that uses the United States dollar approximate separate transactions method of accounting under § 1.985-3 in a taxable year beginning after December 31, 1986.

(e) *Maintenance of more than one type of qualified foreign plan by an employer.*—In determining the deduction or reduction in earnings and profits when an employer maintains one plan for purposes of foreign law that is treated as two separate plans for purposes of § 1.404A-6(a)(2), the cumulative United States amount for each plan must be combined for purposes of paragraphs (a) and (b) of this section. See *Example 5* of paragraph (h) of this section for an illustration of this rule.

(f) *United States and foreign law limitations not applicable.*—The limitations set forth in this section do not apply to the adjustments required by section 481, section 446(e) and section 2(e)(3)(A) of Public Law 96-603.

(g) *Definitions.*—(1) *Cumulative United States amount.*—The term "cumulative United States amount" means (with respect to a qualified foreign plan) the amount determined under section 404A (without regard to section 404A(d)) for the taxable year of the employer and for all consecutive prior taxable years for which an election under section 404A was in effect for the plan plus the "initial section 404A amount" within the meaning of § 1.404A-6(g)(2)(i).

(2) *Cumulative foreign amount.*—The term "cumulative foreign amount" means (with respect to a qualified foreign plan) the cumulative amount allowed as a deduction under the appropriate foreign tax law for the taxable year of the employer and for all consecutive prior taxable years for which an election under section 404A was in effect for the plan plus the initial section 404A amount within the meaning of § 1.404A-6(g)(2)(ii).

(3) *Appropriate foreign tax law.*—The appropriate foreign tax law is the income tax law of the country (other than the United States) that is the principal place of business of the qualified business unit of the employer whose books reflect the plan liabilities.

(4) *Aggregate amount.*—The term "aggregate amount" means (with respect to a qualified foreign plan) amounts permitted to be taken into account under section 404A(d)(1) for all consecutive prior taxable years for which an election under section 404A was in effect for the plan

plus the initial section 404A amount required by § 1.404A-6(g)(2)(iii).

(h) *Examples.*—The principles of this section are illustrated by the following examples:

Example 1. X, a foreign subsidiary of a domestic corporation, maintains its main office in foreign country *A*, and a branch, *Y*, in foreign country *B*. The functional currency of X is the FC. *Y's* functional currency is the local currency, LC. X maintains a qualified foreign plan for the benefit of X's employees in *B*. In the year the plan was adopted, a section 404A election was made for the plan. The appropriate foreign tax law is the tax law of *B* because all the employees covered by the plan are in *B* and plan liabilities are accounted for on *Y's* books. The tax law of *B* permits X to deduct contributions to the plan. The cumulative amount allowed as a deduction under the tax law of *B* is LC80. The cumulative United States amount with respect to the plan is LC100. Therefore, the cumulative limitation is LC80. The earnings and profits of X include the profit and loss for *Y* (reflecting a reduction for contributions to the plan, computed in LC and translated into FC under the principles of section 987).

Example 2. A qualified reserve plan is maintained by a foreign branch of a domestic corporation. The foreign branch computes its income under the profit and loss method of Rev. Rul. 75-107, 1975-1 C.B. 32 (see § 601.601(d)(2)(ii)(*b*) of this chapter), in units of the local currency, the FC. The foreign branch established the qualified reserve plan in 1985 and the taxpayer made the elections described in § 1.404A-6. The taxpayer's taxable year and the plan year is the calendar year. The assumed amounts taken into account under section 404A and appropriate foreign tax law for selected years and the computations under this section which follow from the amounts, in units of FC, are shown in the following table—

		1985	*1986*	*1987*	*1988*
(1)	Amount determined with respect to the plan under section 404A for the taxable year without regard to section 404A(d)	800,000	900,000	300,000	1,000,000
(2)	Cumulative United States amount . .	800,000	1,700,000	2,000,000	3,000,000
(3)	Cumulative foreign amount	1,000,000	1,600,000	2,000,000	2,200,000
(4)	Lesser of cumulative United States or cumulative foreign amount	800,000	1,600,000	2,000,000	2,200,000
(5)	Reduced by aggregate amount (cumulative sum of (6) for prior years)	(0)	(800,000)	(1,600,000)	(2,000,000)
		800,000	800,000	400,000	200,000
(6)	Amount taken into account for the taxable year	800,000	800,000	400,000	200,000

Example 3. Assume the same facts as in *Example 2* for all taxable years, except that the qualified reserve plan is maintained by a foreign subsidiary of a domestic corporation. The foreign subsidiary computes its earnings and profits in units of the local currency, the FC. The foreign subsidiary's taxable year and the plan year are calendar years. The assumed amounts taken into account under section 404A and appropriate foreign law for selected years, and the computations under this section which follow from the amounts, in units of FC, are shown in the following table—

		1985	*1986*	*1987*	*1988*
(1)	Amount determined with respect to the plan under section 404A for the taxable year without regard to section 404A(d)	800,000	900,000	300,000	1,000,000
(2)	Amount allowed as a deduction under the appropriate foreign tax laws for the taxable year	1,000,000	600,000	400,000	200,000
(3)	Cumulative United States amount . .	800,000	1,700,000	2,000,000	3,000,000
(4)	Cumulative foreign amount	1,000,000	1,600,000	2,000,000	2,200,000
(5)	Lesser of cumulative United States or cumulative foreign amount	800,000	1,600,000	2,000,000	2,200,000
(6)	Reduced by aggregate amount (cumulative sum of (7) or (8), whichever is applicable, for prior years)	(0)	(800,000)	(1,400,000)	(2,000,000)
		800,000	800,000	600,000	200,000
(7)	Amount taken into account for taxable years before 1987 (lesser of (2) and (6))	800,000	600,000	n/a	n/a
(8)	Amount taken into account for taxable years after 1986 (same as (6))	n/a	n/a	600,000	200,000

Example 4. Z, a domestic corporation, maintains a retirement plan for employees employed in its foreign branch office. The foreign branch computes its income under the profit and loss

method Rev. Rul. 75-107, 1975-1 C.B. 32 (see §601.601(d)(2)(ii)(*b*) of this chapter), in units of local currency, the FC. The plan is a combination book reserve and funded plan, but is considered a single plan under foreign law. The total retirement benefits that a participant is eligible to receive is the sum of the benefits provided by the qualified reserve plan and the qualified funded plan. Pursuant to §1.404A-6, in the year the plan was adopted, Z made a separate qualified reserve plan and funded plan election with respect to each portion of the foreign plan. The assumed deductions under section 404A and appropriate foreign law for selected years, and the computations under this section which follow from the deductions, are shown in the following table—

	Qualified funded plan		*Qualified reserve plan*		*Combined amount—qualified foreign plans*	
	1984	*1985*	*1984*	*1985*	*1984*	*1985*
(1) Amount determined with respect to the qualified foreign plans under section 404A for the taxable year without regard to section 404A(d)	40,000	90,000	30,000	80,000		
(2) Amount allowed as a deduction under the appropriate foreign tax laws for the taxable year					60,000	185,000
(3) Cumulative United States amount	40,000	130,000	30,000	110,000		
(4) Combined cumulative United States amount (cumulative sum of (3))					70,000	240,000
(5) Cumulative foreign amount (cumulative sum of (2))					60,000	245,000
(6) Aggregate amount					0	60,000
(7) Lesser of combined cumulative United States amount or cumulative foreign amount ((4) or (5))					60,000	240,000
(9) Reduced by the aggregate amount for the qualified funded and reserve plan (cumulative sum of (10) for prior years)					(0)	(60,000)
(10) Amount taken into account for taxable year					60,000	180,000

Example 5. A qualified reserve plan is maintained by *M*, the foreign subsidiary of *N*, a domestic corporation. *M* computes its earnings and profits in units of the local currency, the FC. The taxable years of *M* and *N* and the plan year are the calendar year. *M* established the qualified reserve plan in 1984 and *N* made the elections described in §1.404A-6. In that year, the reasonable addition to the plan reserve under §1.404A-3 was FC750,000. However, the amount allowed as a deduction under the appropriate foreign tax laws for the taxable year was FC650,000. The difference between the amount taken into account under §1.404A-3 and the deduction under the appropriate foreign tax laws, FC100,000, could not be taken into account for any succeeding taxable year under §1.404A-3, but it may later reduce *M*'s earnings and profits pursuant to paragraph (a) of this section. [Reg. §1.404A-4.]

§1.404A-5. Additional limitations on amounts taken into account for qualified foreign plans.—(a) *Restrictions for nonqualified individuals.*—(1) *General rule.*—Notwithstanding any other provisions of §§1.404A-1 through 1.404A-7, no amount may be taken into account under section 404A for any contribution or amount accrued that is attributable to services performed either in the current or in a prior taxable year—

(i) By a citizen or resident of the United States who is a highly compensated [employee] (within the meaning of section 414(q)) (or, for taxable years beginning before January 1, 1989, by a citizen or resident of the United States who is an officer, shareholder, or highly compensated (within the meaning of §1.410(b)-1(d)); or

(ii) In the United States, the compensation for which is subject to tax under chapter 1 of subtitle A of the Internal Revenue Code.

(2) *Determination of service attribution.*—(i) *Not limited to actual service.*—Service performed by individuals described in paragraph (a)(1)(i) of this section includes service credited to those individuals. Service performed in the United States includes service credited in relation (directly or indirectly) to any United States service.

(ii) *Amounts attributable to service performed in the United States.*—The accrued benefit attributable to services described in this paragraph (a) is the excess, if any, of the total accrued benefit over the accrued benefit determined without credit for time spent performing services described in this paragraph (a) and without regard to the compensation levels for that time.

(b) *Records to be provided by taxpayer.*—(1) *In general.*—Notwithstanding any other provisions of §§1.404A-1 through 1.404A-7, no amount may be taken into account under section 404A for any contribution or amount accrued unless the taxpayer attaches a statement to its United States income tax return for any taxable year for which a qualified foreign plan maintained by an employer has United States tax significance. This statement must specify the name and type of qualified foreign plan; the cumulative United States amount, the cumulative foreign amount, and the aggregate amount with respect to the plan; the name and country of organization of the employer; and any other information the Commissioner may prescribe by forms and accompanying instructions or by revenue procedure.

(2) *Primary evidence.*—The statement described in paragraph (b)(1) of this section and any required forms must be completed in good faith with all of the information called for and with the calculations referenced in paragraph (b)(1) of this section. Except as provided in paragraph (b)(4) of this section, one of the following documents must be attached to the United States income tax return—

(i) A statement from the foreign tax authorities specifying the amount of the deduction allowed in computing taxable income under the appropriate foreign tax law for the relevant year or years with respect to the qualified foreign plan; or

(ii) If the return under the appropriate foreign tax law shows the deduction for plan contributions or plan reserves as a separate identifiable item, a copy of the foreign tax return for the relevant year or years with respect to the qualified foreign plan.

(3) *Additional requirements.*—The statement or return attached pursuant to paragraph (b)(2) of this section may be either the original, a duplicate original, a duly certified or authenticated copy, or a sworn copy. If only a sworn copy of a receipt or return is attached, there must be kept readily available for comparison on request the original, a duplicate original, or a duly certified or authenticated copy.

(4) *Secondary evidence.*—Where the statement or return described in paragraph (b)(2)(i) or (b)(2)(ii) of this section is not available, all of the following information must be attached to the United States income tax return—

(i) A certified statement setting forth the cumulative foreign amount for each taxable year to which section 404A applies;

(ii) The excerpts from the employer's books and records showing either the change in the reserve or contributions made with respect to the plan for the taxable year to which section 404A applies; and

(iii) The computations of the foreign deduction relating to the plan to be established by data such as excerpts from the foreign law, assessment notices, or other documentary evidence.

(5) *Foreign language.*—If the relevant returns, books, records or computations are not maintained in the English language, the taxpayer must furnish, upon request, a certified translation that is satisfactory to the District Director.

(6) *Additional information required by District Director.*—If the taxpayer upon request of the District Director fails, without justification, to furnish any additional information that is significant, the provisions of section 982 will apply.

(7) *Authorized officer to complete documents.*—The documents required by this section and by §§1.404A-6 and 1.404A-7 must be signed by an authorized officer of the taxpayer (as defined in section 6062 or 6063) who must verify under penalty of perjury that the statement and all other documents submitted are true and correct to his knowledge and belief.

(8) *Transitional rule—good faith effort.*—For taxable years ending before [*INSERT DATE THAT IS 90 DAYS AFTER THE DATE OF PUBLICATION OF FINAL REGULATIONS IN THE FEDERAL REGISTER*] a taxpayer will be treated as satisfying this paragraph (b) if it makes a good faith effort to provide reasonable documentation.

(c) *Actuarial requirements.*—(1) *Reasonable actuarial assumptions.*—Except as otherwise specifically provided in §§1.404A-2 and 1.404A-3 and this paragraph (c), in the case of a qualified reserve plan or a qualified funded plan under which benefits are fixed or determinable, no amount may be taken into account under section 404A unless costs, liabilities, rates of interest, and other factors under the plan are determined on the basis of actuarial assumptions and methods each of which is reasonable (taking into account the experience of the plan and reasonable expectations), or which, in the aggregate, result in an amount being taken into account that is equivalent to that which would be determined if each such assumption and method were reasonable, and that, in combination, offer the actuary's best estimate of anticipated experience under the plan. For plan years beginning before January 1, 1988, the preceding sentence is satisfied if costs, liabilities, rates of interest, and other factors under the plan are determined on the basis of actuarial assumptions and methods that are reasonable in the aggregate (taking into account the experience of the plan and reasonable expectations) and that, in combination, offer the actuary's best estimate of anticipated experience under the plan. Except to the extent required under that paragraph, the interest rate determined under §1.404A-3(b)(4) may not be considered in determining whether other actuarial assumptions are reasonable in the aggregate for this purpose.

(2) *Full funding limitation.*—Notwithstanding any other provisions of §§1.404A-1 through 1.404A-7, no amount may be taken into account under section 404A if the amount causes the assets in the trust (in the case of a qualified funded plan) or if taking into account the amount causes the amount of the reserve (in the case of a qualified reserve plan) to exceed the amount described in section 412(c)(7)(A)(i). [Reg. §1.404A-5.]

§1.404A-6. Elections under section 404A and changes in methods of accounting.—(a) *Elections, changes in accounting methods, and changes in plan years.*—(1) *In general.*—(i) *Methods of accounting.*—An election under section 404A with respect to a qualified foreign plan constitutes the adoption of a method of accounting if the election is made in the taxable year in which the plan is adopted. Any election under section 404A with respect to a pre-existing plan, however, constitutes a change in method of accounting requiring the Commissioner's consent under section 446 (e) and an adjustment under section 481(a). Additionally, any other change in the method used to determine the amount taken into account under section 404A(a), as well as the revocation of any election under section 404A, constitutes a change in accounting method subject to the consent and adjustment requirements of sections 446(e) and 481(a). This section provides procedures for obtaining the Commissioner's consent to make certain changes in methods of accounting under section 404A. Additionally, § 1.404A-7 provides special procedural rules applicable (along with the rules under this section) for retroactive and transition-period elections under section 404A.

(ii) *Changes not involving accounting methods.*—Any change in treatment, adjustment, or correction described in § 1.446-1(e)(2)(ii)(b) (e.g., correction of computational errors) is not a change in accounting method. While a retroactive qualified funded plan election under § 1.404A-7(c) constitutes a change in method of accounting, a mere election to apply the effective date of section 404A under § 1.404A-7(b) retroactively does not necessarily result in a change in accounting method. Additionally, a retroactive election for funded foreign branch plans under § 1.404A-7(d) will not be treated as a change in method of accounting, except to the extent that the taxpayer took erroneous deductions under its method of accounting prior to the beginning of its open period. Finally, a change of actuarial assumptions will not be treated as a change in method of accounting for purposes of this section.

(2) *Single plan.*—(i) *General rule.*—Except as otherwise provided, the rules of this section regarding elections, revocations, and re-elections, and the adoption or change of a plan year, apply separately (i.e., on a plan-by-plan basis) to each plan that qualifies as a single plan (as defined in § 1.414(l)-1(b)). For purposes of this definition, a separate reserve maintained by an employer exclusively for its liability under a plan is considered a plan asset that is available exclusively to pay benefits to employees who are covered by the plan and to their beneficiaries. Although a plan may be treated as a reserve plan under foreign law, this treatment is not binding for purposes of section 404A and this section.

(ii) *Example.*—The principles of this paragraph (a)(2) are illustrated by the following example:

Example. *S* is a wholly-owned foreign subsidiary of *P*, a domestic corporation. *S* maintains a deferred compensation plan under local law to provide benefits to its employees upon retirement based upon years of service and the highest five-year average salary. *S* decided to account for 70 percent of its deferred compensation liabilities through an unfunded book reserve (Plan One), and to account for the remaining 30 percent through a trust equivalent (Plan Two). All of the assets of Plan One and Plan Two were available for payment of liabilities under their respective plans, and were only available for payment of liabilities under their respective plans. Thus, when deferred compensation was paid to *S*'s employees, within the meaning of this paragraph (a)(2), 70 percent of the amount was paid by check drawn against the general assets of *S* and 30 percent of the amount paid was paid by check drawn on the assets of the trust equivalent. Pursuant to this section, *P* made a qualified reserve plan election for Plan One, which it defined as a plan of deferred compensation with liability for 70 percent of the amount of deferred compensation owing to each employee under *S*'s deferred compensation plan. In addition, it made a qualified funded plan election for Plan Two, which it defined as a plan of deferred compensation with liability for the remaining 30 percent. Because *S*'s reserve for its liability was treated as a plan asset with respect to 70 percent of the liability and the assets of the trust, Plan One met the requirements of a "single plan" under § 1.414(l)-1(b), and Plan Two was a separate "single plan". Thus, *S* could take into account only 70 percent of its liability to each employee under its deferred compensation plan when calculating the reasonable additions to the reserve under section 404A(c) for Plan One. Similarly, the full funding limitation and other calculations with respect to Plan Two may only be made with respect to 30 percent of *S*'s liability to each employee under the foreign deferred compensation plan.

(b) *Initial elections under section 404A.*—(1) *In general.*—The Commissioner's consent to elect initially under section 404A to treat a single plan as a qualified funded plan or as a qualified reserve plan is granted automatically if the taxpayer complies with the requirements of this paragraph (b). Except as provided in § 1.404A-7, an initial election under this section with respect to any qualified foreign plan may be made only for a taxable year beginning after December 31, 1979.

(2) *Time for making election.*—(i) *Foreign branch plans.*—Except as provided in § 1.404A-7, the initial election for a qualified foreign plan maintained by a foreign branch must be made no later than the time prescribed by law for filing the United States return (including extensions) for the first taxable year for which the election is to be effective.

(ii) *Foreign corporation plans.*—Except as provided in § 1.404A-7, the initial election for a qualified foreign plan maintained by a foreign corporation must be made no later than the time allowed for making elections under §§ 1.964-1 and 1.964-1T. Thus, the election under section 404A may be deferred until the earnings and profits of the foreign corporation have United States tax significance, as defined in §§ 1.964-1 and 1.964-1T. United States tax significance may occur in a number of ways, including, for example, a dividend distribution, an income inclusion under section 951(a), a section 1248 transaction, a step-up of basis by earnings and profits for purposes of valuing assets for interest allocation purposes under section 864(e), or an inclusion in income of the earnings of a qualified electing fund under section 1293(a)(1).

(3) *Manner in which election is to be made.*—(i) *Foreign branch plans.*—In the case of a qualified foreign plan maintained by a domestic corporation, the initial election must be made by the taxpayer by attaching a list of plans for which section 404A treatment is desired to a return filed within the time prescribed in paragraph (b)(2)(i) of this section.

(ii) *Controlled foreign corporation plans.*—If a qualified foreign plan is maintained by a controlled foreign corporation, the initial election under this section must be made in the manner prescribed by §§ 1.964-1 and 1.964-1T and must include a list of all plans for which the election is made.

(iii) *Noncontrolled foreign corporation plans.*—If a qualified foreign plan is maintained by a noncontrolled foreign corporation, the initial election under this section must be made in the manner prescribed by §§1.964-1 and 1.964-1T and must include a list of all plans for which the election is made, as if the noncontrolled foreign corporation were a controlled foreign corporation. In applying the rules of §§1.964-1 and 1.964-1T, the term "majority domestic corporate shareholders" is substituted for the term "controlling United States shareholders" wherever it appears in §§1.964-1 and 1.964-1T. The term "majority domestic corporate shareholders" has the meaning set forth in §1.985-2(c)(3)(i).

(4) *Other requirements for election.*—For each plan listed, pursuant to paragraph (b)(3) of this section, the taxpayer must designate whether it elects to treat the plan as a qualified funded plan or qualified reserve plan, and must designate a plan year. Additionally, for each plan listed, the taxpayer must disclose the amount of any section 481(a) adjustment, as well as the initial cumulative United States amount, the initial cumulative foreign amount, and the initial aggregate amount defined in paragraph (g) of this section. See §1.404A-5(b) for rules on additional information required, signing and verifying required statements, and notices and forms necessary to elect under section 404A. Additionally, see §1.404A-7(d)(1) for required agreement to assessment of tax for retroactive elections for funded foreign branch plans.

(c) *Termination of election when a plan ceases to be a qualified foreign plan.*—(1) *In general.*—An election under section 404A with respect to a foreign deferred compensation plan is terminated if at any time on or after the first day of the first taxable year for which the election is effective the plan ceases to be a qualified foreign plan by reason of a failure to satisfy the conditions of section 404A(e)(1) or (2). Thus, for example, the election is terminated (subject to the consent of the Commissioner) if more than 10 percent of the amounts taken into account under the plan are attributable to services performed by employees subject to United States federal income tax. As used in this section, the term "termination" refers only to situations under which a plan ceases to be a qualified foreign plan by reason of a failure to satisfy the conditions of section 404(e)(1) or (2). Thus, the term is distinguished from a voluntary revocation of an election (i.e., under paragraph (d)(1) of this section), which also causes a plan to cease to be a qualified foreign plan. Upon termination of an election under section 404A, a change in method of accounting is required. The conditional advance consent of the Commissioner is granted for this change in method of accounting. This conditional consent may be withdrawn, however, if the District Director determines that tax avoidance was a purpose of the termination or if the procedures in paragraph (c)(2) of this section are not satisfied.

(2) *Rules for changing method of accounting upon termination of election.*—(i) *Time for making change.*—(A) *Foreign branch plans.*—Except as provided in §1.404A-7, in the case of a plan of a foreign branch the change in method of accounting required upon termination of a section 404A election must be made no later than the time prescribed by law for filing the United States return (including extensions) for the taxable year in which the plan ceases to satisfy the requirements of section 404A(e)(1) or (2).

(B) *Foreign corporation plans.*—Except as provided in §1.404A-7, in the case of a plan of a foreign corporation the change in method of accounting required upon termination of a section 404A election shall be made no later than the first year after the termination in which the earnings and profits of the foreign corporation have United States tax significance, as defined in §§1.964-1 and 1.964-1T. See paragraph (b)(2)(ii) of this section for United States tax significance examples.

(ii) *Procedures for changing method of accounting upon termination of election.*—(A) *Foreign branch plans.*—The change in method of accounting required upon termination of a section 404A election with respect to a foreign branch plan must be made by attaching a statement to the return described in paragraph (c)(2)(i)(A) of this section disclosing the amount of any section 481(a) adjustment (required under paragraph (e) of this section and computed in accordance with paragraph (f) of this section) arising upon the change.

(B) *Controlled foreign corporation plans.*—The change in method of accounting required upon termination of a section 404A election with respect to a controlled foreign corporation plan must be made in the manner prescribed by §§1.964-1 and 1.964-1T and must include disclosure of the amount of any section 481(a) adjustment (required under paragraph (e) of this section and computed in accordance with paragraph (f) of this section) arising upon the change.

(C) *Noncontrolled foreign corporation plans.*—The change in method of accounting required upon termination of a section 404A election with respect to a noncontrolled foreign corporation plan must be made in the manner prescribed by §§1.964-1 and 1.964-1T and must include disclosure of the amount of any section 481(a) adjustment (required under paragraph (e) of this section and computed in accordance with paragraph (f) of this section) arising upon the change. In applying the rules of §§1.964-1 and 1.964-1T, the term "majority domestic corporate shareholders" is substituted for the term "controlling United States shareholders" wherever it appears in §§1.964-1 and 1.964-1T. The term "majority domestic corporate shareholders" has the meaning set forth in §1.985-2(c)(3)(i).

(d) *Other changes in methods of accounting and changes in plan year.*—(1) *Application for consent.*—Except as provided in paragraph (c) of this section or in §1.404A-7, once an initial election under section 404A is effective with respect to a plan, the taxpayer must separately apply to obtain the express consent of the Commissioner prior to changing any method of accounting with respect to a foreign deferred compensation plan. Application for the consent of the Commissioner is required whether or not the method being changed is proper or permitted under the Internal Revenue Code and regulations thereunder. Any change in method of accounting not described in this paragraph (d)(1) must be made in accordance with the requirements of section 446(e) and the regulations thereunder. The procedures prescribed in this paragraph (d), however, are the exclusive procedures for making the following changes in method of accounting—

(i) Revocation of a section 404A election;

(ii) Re-election under section 404A following termination or revocation of a section 404A election;

(iii) Changing the treatment of a plan from a qualified funded plan to a qualified reserve plan (or the converse); or

(iv) Changing the actuarial funding method used to determine costs under a qualified funded plan.

(2) *Procedures for other changes in method of accounting.*—(i) *Foreign branch plans.*—To request consent to a change in method of accounting described in paragraph (d)(1) of this section, the taxpayer must file an application on Form 3115 with the Commissioner generally within 180 days after the beginning of the taxable year in which the change is requested to be effective. In the case of a revocation of an election under section 404A, however, the 180-day period in the preceding sentence is extended to the time prescribed by law for filing the United States return for the taxable year of the change.

(ii) *Foreign corporation plans.*—For a controlled foreign corporation or a noncontrolled foreign corporation, a request for consent to revocation or to another change in method of accounting must be made in accordance with the rules of §§1.964-1 and 1.964-1T.

(3) *Plan year.*—A taxpayer must secure the consent of the Commissioner to change the plan year of a qualified foreign plan. Termination or revocation of a section 404A election will not effect a change in the plan year of the plan.

(e) *Application of section 481.*—(1) *In general.*—A change in method described in this section constitutes a change in method of accounting to which section 481 applies. Except as otherwise provided in this paragraph and in paragraph (f) of this section, this adjustment must be made in accordance with section 481 and the regulations thereunder in those circumstances. For purposes of section 481(a)(2), any change in method described in this section is considered a change in method of accounting initiated by the taxpayer.

(2) *Period of adjustment.*—(i) *In general.*—The section 481(a) adjustment period is determined under the rules of this paragraph (e)(2).

(ii) *Election or re-election.*—In the case of an election or a re-election following termination or revocation, the section 481(a) adjustment required by paragraph (e)(1) of this section must be taken into account ratably over a 15-year period, beginning with the first taxable year for which the election or re-election is effective. This section 481(a) adjustment period also applies to a change from a qualified funded plan to a qualified reserve plan.

(iii) *Termination or revocation of election and all other changes in method.*—The adjustment required by paragraph (e)(1) of this section for all changes in method (other than those described in paragraph (e)(2)(ii) of this section), including changes in election from a qualified reserve plan to a qualified funded plan, must be taken into account ratably over a six-year period, beginning with the first taxable year for which the change is effective. If an unamortized section 481(a) adjustment amount (e.g., from a previous change) remains at the end of a change in method of accounting to which this paragraph (e)(2)(iii) applies, the net amount of all of the section 481(a) adjustments must be taken into account ratably over this six-year section 481(a) adjustment period.

(iv) *Acceleration of section 481(a) adjustment.*—If the employer ceases to engage in the relevant trade or business at any time prior to the expiration of the applicable section 481(a) adjustment period provided in paragraph (e)(2)(ii) or (e)(2)(iii) of this section, the employer must take into account, in the taxable year of cessation, the balance of any section 481(a) adjustment not previously taken into account in computing taxable income (in the case of a branch) or earnings and profits (in the case of a foreign corporation). For purposes of this paragraph (e)(2)(iv), whether or not an employer ceases to engage in the trade or business is to be determined under administrative procedures issued under §1.446-1(e). In applying those procedures, "employer" is to be defined in the same manner as "taxpayer" is defined under those procedures.

(3) *Allocation and source.*—The amount of any net negative section 481(a) adjustment determined under this section and taken into account for a taxable year must be allocated and apportioned under §1.861-8 in the same manner as a deduction or reduction in earnings and profits under section 404A. Any net positive section 481(a) adjustment that is taken into account for a taxable year first must be reduced by directly allocating to such adjustment the employer's section 404A expense that is subject to apportionment (including any amount that otherwise would be capitalized); to the extent a net positive section 481(a) adjustment exceeds the amount of the employer's section 404A expense for the taxable year, such excess must be sourced or otherwise classified in the same manner as section 404A deductions or reductions in earnings and profits are allocated and apportioned.

(4) *Example.*—The principles of this paragraph (e) are illustrated by the following example:

Example. X, a domestic corporation, made an initial election under section 404A to treat an existing deferred compensation plan maintained by its foreign branch as a qualified reserve plan, effective beginning in *X*'s 1985 taxable year. *X*'s foreign branch maintains its books and records in FC, the functional currency. Previously, *X* had consistently used a permissible method of accounting with respect to the plan. The section 481(a) adjustment arising from *X*'s change in accounting method upon its section 404A election was a negative FC150,000. Beginning with its 1985 taxable year, *X* took into account a negative FC10,000 each year (FC150,000/15). Effective beginning in *X*'s 1988 taxable year, *X* received the Commissioner's express consent to change from a qualified reserve plan to a qualified funded plan. The section 481(a) adjustment attributable solely to the 1988 change was a positive FC132,000. Beginning with its 1988 taxable year, and for each of the five succeeding taxable years, *X* took into account a positive FC2,000, as computed below.

Negative 1985 section 481(a) adjustment	(FC150,000)
Less: 1985, 1986 & 1987 amounts taken into account	30,000
Subtotal	(120,000)
Positive 1988 section 481(a) adjustment	132,000
Net positive section 481(a) adjustment	12,000
Section 481(a) adjustment period	÷ 6
Net amount taken into account annually during section 481(a) adjustment period	FC2,000

(f) *Computation of section 481(a) adjustment.*—(1) *In general.*—For purposes of section 404A, except as provided in § 1.404A-7(f)(1)(ii)(C), the amount of the section 481(a) adjustment required under paragraph (e)(1) of this section equals—

(i) The Old Method Closing Amount; less

(ii) The New Method Opening Amount.

(2) *Old Method Closing Amount.*—(i) *In general.*—Except as otherwise provided in paragraph (f)(2)(ii), (iii), or (iv) of this section (or as otherwise prescribed by the Commissioner), the Old Method Closing Amount equals—

(A) The total of all past deductions taken with respect to liabilities under the plan; plus

(B) The net income earned directly or indirectly by any separate funding entity (e.g., account or trust) with respect to the plan, but only to the extent that such net income has not previously been taken into account in determining taxable income (in the case of a foreign branch) or earnings and profits (in the case of a foreign corporation); minus

(C) The total of all past payments under the plan made to plan participants and beneficiaries by the employer, the trust, or the separate funding entity.

(ii) *Taxpayer formerly using a reserve method.*—(A) *In general.*—If a taxpayer has consistently taken amounts with respect to the plan into account under a reserve method, the Old Method Closing Amount equals the closing reserve balance at the end of the closing year calculated under the taxpayer's reserve method. For purposes of the preceding sentence, a reserve method means a method of accrual based on the actuarial present value of expected future plan benefits.

(B) *Former qualified reserve plan.*—To request the Commissioner's consent in the case of a former qualified reserve plan, the closing reserve balance must be adjusted for any unamortized increases or decreases to the reserve described in § 1.404A-3(c) that have not yet been taken into account. For example, if the closing reserve balance is FC100,000, but FC10,000 of the closing reserve balance consists of an unamortized increase in the reserve that has not previously been taken into account due to the ten-year amortization requirements of § 1.404A-3(c), the Old Method Closing Amount is FC90,000.

(iii) *Taxpayer formerly using pay-as-you-go method.*—If the taxpayer has consistently taken amounts into account with respect to the plan based only on actual payments of plan benefits to participants and beneficiaries, the Old Method Closing Amount equals zero.

(iv) *Taxpayer formerly using a funded method.*—(A) *Payment to separate funding entity.*—If the taxpayer has consistently taken amounts into account with respect to the plan based only on actual payments to a separate funding entity and on payments by the employer (but not by the funding entity) to plan participants or beneficiaries, the Old Method Closing Amount equals the balance in the separate funding entity at the end of the closing year, including amounts attributable, directly or indirectly, to net investment income that has not previously been taken into account in determining taxable income (in the case of a foreign branch) or earnings and profits (in the case of a foreign corporation).

(B) *Former qualified funded plan.*—In the case of a former qualified funded plan, the Old Method Closing Amount generally equals the amount described in paragraph (f)(2)(iv)(A) of this section, adjusted, however, by—

(1) Reducing the amount properly to reflect any net limitations under section 404A(b) and (g) (e.g., the full funding limitation for a qualified funded plan) that were applied in determining amounts taken into account under the former section 404A method of accounting; and

(2) Increasing the amount properly to reflect any amounts that are not paid during the closing year but that are permitted to be taken into account in the closing year under section 404A(b)(2) (relating to payments made after the close of the taxable year).

(v) *Section 404A(d) limitation.*—In computing the Old Method Closing Amount upon the termination or revocation of an election under section 404A, the limitations of section 404A(d) and § 1.404A-4 must be taken into account. Thus, if the Old Method Closing Amount is determined under paragraph (f)(2)(ii)(B) or (f)(2)(iv)(B) of this section, the amount otherwise determined under those paragraphs shall be reduced by applying the section 404A(d) and § 1.404A-4 limitations to the extent the cumulative United States amount under § 1.404A-4 exceeds the cumulative foreign amount under § 1.404A-4.

(3) *New Method Opening Amount.*—(i) *Qualified reserve plan.*—In the case of an election to treat a plan as a qualified reserve plan, the New Method Opening Amount equals the balance of the reserve as of the end of the last day of the closing year, calculated under the rules of section 404A(c) and § 1.404A-3 based on plan information and data as of that date. The New Method Opening Amount must be reduced (or increased) for any unamortized increases (or decreases) to the reserve described in section 404A(c)(4) and § 1.404A-3(c).

(ii) *Qualified funded plan.*—In the case of an election to be treated as a qualified funded plan, the New Method Opening Amount equals the amount of funds in the trust as of the beginning of the first day of the opening year, adjusted as necessary to take into account the rules of section 404A(b) and (g). If the separate funding entity does not qualify as a trust under § 1.404A-1(e), the New Method Opening Amount in the case of a qualified funded plan is zero because there is no balance in a trust as defined in § 1.404A-1(e).

(iii) *Nonqualified plan*.—In the case of any plan that ceases to be a qualified foreign plan (either by reason of the termination or revocation of a section 404A election), the New Method Opening Amount is zero.

(iv) *Section 404A(d) limitation*.—In computing the New Method Opening Amount upon an election under section 404A, the limitation on deductions of section 404A(d) and § 1.404A-4 must be taken into account. Thus, if the New Method Opening Amount is determined under paragraph (f)(2)(i) or (f)(2)(ii) of this section, the amount otherwise determined must be reduced to the extent the cumulative United States amount computed under § 1.404A-4 exceeds the cumulative foreign amount computed under § 1.404A-4. See paragraph (g) of this section for initialization of amounts taken into account under section 404A(d).

(4) *Definitions and special rules*.—(i) *Opening year*.—For purposes of this section, the opening year is the first taxable year for which the new method of accounting is effective with respect to a plan. For example, in the case of an election to treat a foreign corporation plan as a qualified reserve plan beginning in 1989, the opening year is 1989, even though the election may not be made until 1994 pursuant to paragraph (b)(2)(ii) of this section.

(ii) *Closing year*.—For purposes of this section, the closing year is the taxable year immediately preceding the opening year.

(iii) *Separate funding entity*.—A separate funding entity described in paragraphs (f)(2)(i)(B) and (f)(2)(iv) of this section is any entity that satisfies the first requirement in the definition of the equivalent of a trust in § 1.404A-1(e) (segregation in a separate legal entity) and, in practice, also satisfies the third requirement in that definition (dedication to payment of plan benefits) with respect to benefits under the relevant plan.

(iv) *Special rules for certain foreign corporation plans*.—In the case of a foreign corporation's plan for which no method has been used for some or all prior taxable years because no calculation of earnings and profits has been necessary for those years (see, e.g., paragraph (b)(2)(ii) of this section), the employer may assume that the old method has been consistent with any method actually used consistently in immediately prior years. If no calculation of earnings and profits has been made for prior years, in determining the Old Method Closing Amount, the taxpayer may assume the method used was a method described in paragraph (f)(2)(iii) of this section. This assumed method used in the calculation of the Old Method Closing Amount must actually be used by the taxpayer for all the prior taxable years to the extent reductions of earnings and profits for those years are ever determined with respect to the plan.

(v) *Reference to rules applicable in the case of failure to consider net investment income in computing section 481(a) adjustment*.—The treatment of net investment income earned by a funding vehicle that has not previously taken into account by the taxpayer in determining taxable income (in the case of a foreign branch) or earnings and profits (in the case of a foreign corporation), and that is not properly considered (as required under paragraphs (f)(2)(i)(B) and (f)(2)(iv)(A) of this section) in determining the amount of the section 481(a) adjustment for purposes of section 404A, is determined under other applicable provisions, which may include sections 61, 671 through 679, and 1001.

(vi) *Certain section 481(a) adjustments treated as carryover contributions*.—In the case of an election for a plan to be treated as a qualified funded plan, any net positive section 481(a) adjustment is treated as a carryover contribution (within the meaning of § 1.404A-2(d)(4)) to the extent that the adjustment is attributable to limits (that would be taken into account under § 1.404A-2(d)(4)) on the amounts previously contributed to the trust under the plan that could be taken into account under section 404A.

(5) *Examples*.—The principles of paragraph (f) of this section are illustrated by the following examples:

Example 1. Nonqualified reserve plan to qualified reserve plan. A foreign subsidiary of a domestic corporation established an irrevocable balance sheet reserve for pension expenses in 1981. The subsidiary maintains its books and records in FC, the functional currency. From 1981 through 1987, the taxpayer reduced earnings and profits of the foreign subsidiary by FC150,000, the amount of the pension liability which had accrued under the plan. This method of accounting was never challenged or changed by the District Director prior to the expiration of the statute of limitations for the 1981 through 1987 taxable years. Through December 31, 1987, the last day of the closing year, actual pension payments totalled FC15,000. For the 1988 taxable year, the taxpayer made an election for the plan to be treated as a qualified reserve plan. The reserve calculated under section 404A as of the first day of the 1988 taxable year, the opening year, and based upon employee census data as of that date, was FC175,000. The Old Method Closing Amount was FC135,000 (FC150,000 less FC15,000). The New Method Opening Amount was FC175,000. The section 481(a) adjustment was a negative FC40,000 (FC135,000 less FC175,000). This adjustment is to be taken into account over the 15-year section 481(a) adjustment period prescribed in paragraph (e)(2)(ii) of this section.

Example 2. Nonqualified reserve plan to qualified reserve plan. Assume the same facts as in *Example 1*, except that the reserve calculated under section 404A as of the first day of the 1988 taxable year and based upon employee census data as of that date was FC75,000. The Old Method Closing Amount was FC135,000 (FC150,000 less FC15,000). The New Method Opening Amount was FC75,000. The section 481(a) adjustment was a positive FC60,000 (FC135,000 less FC75,000). This adjustment is to be taken into account over the 15-year section 481(a) adjustment period prescribed in paragraph (e)(2)(ii) of this section.

Example 3. Nonqualified funded plan to qualified reserve plan. *M*, a domestic corporation, wholly owns *N*, a foreign corporation. *N* maintains its books and records in FC, the local currency. From 1981 through 1988, *N* maintained a nonqualified funded plan. During this period, *N* contributed FC55,000 to the separate funding entity administering the plan and reduced earnings and profits by FC55,000. The separate funding entity realized net income of FC17,000 from investment of plan assets and paid nothing to participants. None of the FC17,000 net investment income earned in the separate funding entity was taken into account in computing *N*'s earnings and profits. As of the last day of *N*'s 1988 taxable year, the closing year, the plan's fund balance was FC72,000, comprised of FC55,000 (excess contributions) and FC17,000 (investment income). The reserve calculated under section 404A as of the first day of the 1989 taxable year, the opening year, was FC100,000. Effective for *M*'s 1989 taxable year, *M* elected under section 404A to treat *N*'s funded plan as a qualified reserve plan. The Old Method Closing Amount was FC72,000. The New Method Opening Amount was FC100,000; thus, if, in the future, *N* pays FC100,000 to plan participants or beneficiaries, that FC100,000 will not again reduce N's earnings and profits. The section 481(a) adjustment was a negative FC28,000 (FC72,000 less FC100,000). However, if the District Director later challenges and requires *N* to change its method of accounting for foreign deferred compensation used in determining its 1981 through 1988 earnings and profits in a taxable year prior to the 1989 taxable year, the section 481(a) adjustment could be changed from a negative FC28,000 to a negative FC100,000. Pursuant to the administrative procedures under section 446(e), the District Director, upon challenging the treatment of foreign deferred compensation in years prior to 1989, could require any necessary positive section 481(a) adjustment to be taken into account in one taxable year.

Example 4. Nonqualified funded plan to qualified funded plan. Y, a domestic corporation, wholly owns *X*, a foreign corporation. *X* maintains its books and records in FC, the local currency. From 1981 through 1988, *X* maintained a nonqualified funded plan. During this period, *X* reduced earnings and profits by contributions of FC55,000 to the plan. The plan paid participants FC30,000. As of the last day of *Y*'s 1988 taxable year, the plan's fund balance was FC29,000, comprised of FC25,000 (net contributions) and FC4,000 (interest income that was never previously taken into account in determining earnings and profits). Effective for *Y*'s 1989 taxable year, *Y* elected under section 404A to treat *X*'s funded plan as a qualified funded plan. The Old Method Closing Amount was FC29,000. The New Method Opening Amount was FC29,000. The section 481(a) adjustment was zero (FC29,000 less FC29,000). See *Example 3*, however, for the effects on the section 481(a) adjustment of a successful challenge to *X*'s method of accounting for foreign deferred compensation in years prior to 1989 by the District Director.

Example 5. Z, the wholly owned foreign subsidiary of *Y*, a domestic corporation, has maintained a reserve plan for its employees, beginning in 1981. *Z* maintains its books and records in FC, the local currency. Effective for 1984, *Y* elected under section 404A to treat the plan as a qualified reserve plan. The only section 481(a) adjustment required was to take into account the limitation under section 404A(d). In 1981 through 1983, prior to the section 404A election, *Z*'s earnings and profits were reduced by additions to the reserve. This method of accounting was never challenged or changed by the District Director prior to the expiration of the statute of limitations for the 1981 through 1983 taxable years. Thus, the Old Method Closing Amount equaled the balance in the reserve, which was FC300. To compute the New Method Opening Amount, the opening reserve took into account the lesser of the cumulative United States amount (FC300) or the cumulative foreign amount (FC90) as of the first day of 1984, the opening year. Thus, the New Method Opening Amount was FC90. The section 481(a) adjustment was therefore a positive FC210 (FC300—FC90); 1/15 of this amount, FC14 (FC210/15), is being taken into account as an increase in earnings and profits each year over the 15-year section 481(a) adjustment period that began in 1984.

Example 6. Nonqualified reserve plan to qualified reserve plan. Assume the same facts as in *Example 5* for all taxable years and the annual United States reduction, foreign reduction, cumulative United States amount, cumulative foreign amount and the section 481(a) adjustment shown below. The total annual reduction (or increase) in *Z*'s earnings and profits was as follows—

	1984	*1985*	*1986*	*1987*	*1988*	*1989*	*1990*
Amount determined under U.S. law with respect to the plan under section 404A for the taxable year without regard to section 404A(d)	FC(40)	FC(50)	FC(60)	FC(70)	FC(80)	FC(90)	FC(100)
Amount allowed as a deduction for the taxable year under the appropriate foreign tax laws	(70)	(260)	(50)	(40)	(30)	(20)	(10)
Cumulative U.S. amount	(340)	(390)	(450)	(520)	(600)	(690)	(790)
Cumulative foreign amount	(160)	(420)	(470)	(510)	(540)	(560)	(570)
Lesser of cumulative U.S. or foreign amount	(160)	(390)	(450)	(510)	(540)	(560)	(570)

	1984	1985	1986	1987	1988	1989	1990
Reduced by the aggregate amount	90	160	390	440	510	540	560
	(70)	(230)	(60)	(70)	(30)	(20)	(10)
Amount taken into account for the taxable year*	(70)	(230)	(50)	(70)	(30)	(20)	(10)
Positive section 481 adjustment	14	14	14	14	14	14	14
Total increase (reduction) in earnings and profits taken into account for the taxable year	FC(56)	FC(216)	FC(36)	FC(56)	FC(16)	FC(6)	FC(4)

* The limitation in § 1.404A-4(c) applies to taxable years 1984, 1985 and 1986. In 1986, the amount deductible under the appropriate foreign tax law was less than the lower of (1) the cumulative U.S. amount, or, (2) the cumulative foreign amount (then reduced by the aggregate amount).

(g) *Initial section 404A(d) amounts.*—(1) *In general.*—By making an election under section 404A, a taxpayer adopts section 404A(d) as part of its method of accounting. Section 1.404A-4 provides rules to apply the limitations of section 404A(d) in taxable years when an election under section 404A is in effect. This paragraph (g) provides rules to compute initial amounts under section 404A(d) in the opening year. These rules are based on the rules to compute the New Method Opening Amount in paragraph (f)(3) of this section.

(2) *Computation of amounts.*—As of the first day of the opening year, the initial section 404A(d) amounts are as follows:

(i) The initial cumulative United States amount equals the New Method Opening Amount without regard to any reduction under paragraph (f)(3)(iv) of this section.

(ii) The initial cumulative foreign amount equals the New Method Opening Amount computed as though the appropriate foreign tax law were the new method of accounting and without regard to paragraph (f)(3)(iv) of this section.

(iii) The initial aggregate amount equals the lesser of—

(A) The initial cumulative United States amount; and

(B) The initial cumulative foreign amount.

(3) *Example.*—The principles of paragraph (g) of this section are illustrated by the following example:

Example. A foreign subsidiary of a domestic corporation maintains its books and records in FC, the local currency. The subsidiary established a funded deferred compensation plan in 1983 but reduced earnings and profits on a pay-as-you-go basis. The plan year and the taxable year of the domestic corporation and the subsidiary are the calendar year. For the 1990 taxable year, the domestic corporation elected to treat the plan as a qualified reserve plan. The balance in the separate funding entity as of January 1, 1990, the first day of the opening year, was FC90,000. The initial United States cumulative amount (the opening reserve) was FC150,000. The initial foreign cumulative amount (the balance in the separate funding entity) was FC90,000. The initial aggregate amount was FC90,000 (the lesser of FC90,000 or FC150,000). Since the subsidiary reduced earnings and profits on the pay-as-you-go method, the Old Method Closing Amount was zero. The section 481(a) adjustment was a negative FC90,000 (zero less FC90,000 (the lesser of FC150,000 or FC90,000)). [Reg. § 1.404A-6.]

§ 1.404A-7. Effective date, retroactive elections, and transition rules.—(a) *In general.*—(1) *Effective date.*—Except as otherwise provided in this section, section 404A applies to taxable years beginning after December 31, 1979.

(2) *Overview of retroactive elections for taxable years beginning before January 1, 1980.*—(i) *Plans of foreign subsidiaries.*—Section 2(e)(2) of Public Law 96-603 permitted a taxpayer to make section 404A apply retroactively for all of its foreign subsidiaries. Paragraph (b) of this section describes and provides the time and manner to make, perfect, or revoke this retroactive effective date election. If a retroactive effective date election was made, the taxpayer was also eligible to make a qualified funded plan election or a qualified reserve plan election effective retroactively for any of its subsidiaries' plans that met the requirements of § 1.404A-1(a) (other than paragraph (4) thereof) for the relevant period. Paragraph (c) of this section describes and provides the time and manner to make, perfect, or revoke these retroactive plan-by-plan elections for foreign subsidiaries.

(ii) *Plans of foreign branches.*—Section 2(e)(3) of Public Law 96-603 permitted a taxpayer to make a qualified funded plan election retroactively for any plans maintained by a foreign branch that met the requirements of § 1.404A-1(a) (other than paragraph (4) thereof) for the relevant period. Paragraph (d) of this section describes and provides the time and manner to make this retroactive plan-by-plan qualified funded plan election for plans maintained by foreign branches.

(3) *Overview of special transition rules for election, revocation, and re-election.*—Paragraph (e) of this section provides the time and manner to make and revoke qualified funded plan and qualified reserve plan elections for a taxpayer's transition period.

(b) *Retroactive effective date elections for foreign subsidiaries.*—(1) *In general.*—Section 2(e)(2) of Public Law 96-603 permitted a taxpayer to make section 404A effective during the taxpayer's open period. If the election was made, the taxpayer accepted section 404A (including, for example, § 1.404A-1(d)) as the operative law for all foreign subsidiaries (whether or not controlled foreign corporations) during the taxpayer's entire open period. If the election was made, section 404A applies to all distributions from accumulated profits (or earnings and profits) earned after December 31, 1970 (unless the election is revoked pursuant to paragraph (b)(3) of this section, if applicable). If accumulated profits were earned prior to January 1, 1971, a change in method of accounting is required for the foreign subsidiary's taxable year that ends with or within the first taxable year in the taxpayer's open period. A section 481(a) adjustment is required for amounts taken into account prior to the beginning of the foreign subsidiary's year of change and must be computed applying the rules of § 1.404A-6(f).

(2) *Time and manner to make, perfect, or revoke election.*—The retroactive effective date election described in paragraph (b)(1) of this section is not effective unless the election was actually made no later than the time prescribed by law for filing the United States return for the first taxable year ending on or after December 31, 1980, including extensions (whether or not the time was actually extended for filing the taxpayer's return), and unless the taxpayer perfects the election by filing a statement indicating the taxpayer's agreement to perfect the election with an amended return for the first taxable year ending on or after December 31, 1980, on or before [*INSERT DATE THAT IS 365 DAYS AFTER THE DATE OF PUBLICATION OF FINAL REGULATIONS IN THE* FEDERAL REGISTER]. In order to be effective, the perfection must be made in the manner provided in § 1.404A-6(b)(3)(ii) or (iii). An election that is not perfected is considered retroactively revoked.

(3) *Requirement to amend returns.*—(i) *In general.*—In addition to the amended return required by paragraph (b)(2) of this section, the taxpayer must file any other amended United States returns that are necessary to conform the treatment of all items affected by the election or revocation to the treatment consistent with the election or revocation within the time period described in paragraph (b)(2) of this section. If no adjustments are necessary, the amended return required by paragraph (b)(2) of this section must contain a statement to that effect.

(ii) *Required statements.*—All amended returns required by this paragraph (b)(3) must be accompanied by a statement containing—

(A) The open years, open period and retroactive period of the taxpayer;

(B) The taxable year for which the election is perfected or revoked;

(C) A statement that the election (or elections) are perfected or revoked pursuant to the authority contained in § 1.404A-7; and

(D) A signature and verification as provided in § 1.404A-5(b)(7).

(c) *Retroactive plan-by-plan elections for foreign subsidiaries.*—(1) *In general.*—Any taxpayer that makes a retroactive effective date election described in paragraph (a)(2)(i) of this section under the rules of paragraph (b) of this section may, at its option, also elect to treat any foreign plan of a subsidiary that met the requirements of § 1.404A-1(a) (other than paragraph (4) thereof) for the relevant period as a qualified funded plan or as a qualified reserve plan under section 404A, beginning in any taxable year of the foreign subsidiary that ends with or within the taxpayer's open period (or for any earlier taxable year beginning after December 31, 1971, for which earnings and profits of the subsidiary had no United States tax significance). Alternatively, the taxpayer may decide to make no such plan-by-plan election with respect to any particular plan or plans of any of its foreign subsidiaries. Rules similar to those contained in § 1.404A-6 (including, where applicable, the requirement to obtain the consent of the Commissioner) are used to effect such plan-by-plan elections. If the plan existed in a taxable year beginning prior to the first year for which the election was effective, a change in method of accounting is required for the year of the election. The year of change for purposes of computing the section 481(a) adjustment is the first year that the election is effective.

(2) *Time and manner to make, perfect, or revoke election.*—A taxpayer that is eligible to make a plan-by-plan election described in paragraph (c)(1) of this section may make or perfect such an election by attaching a statement to that effect on an amended return for the year that the election is to be effective on or before [*INSERT DATE THAT IS 365 DAYS AFTER THE DATE OF PUBLICATION OF FINAL REGULATIONS IN THE* FEDERAL REGISTER]. In order to be effective, the perfection of a plan-by-plan election must be made in the manner provided in § 1.404A-6(b)(3)(ii) or (iii). An election that is not perfected is considered retroactively revoked. Any election made or perfected under this paragraph (c) will continue in effect for taxable years beginning after the taxpayer's open period, unless revoked under paragraph (c)(4) or (e) of this section or § 1.404A-6.

(3) *Requirement to amend returns.*—In addition to the amended return required by paragraph (c)(2) of this section, the taxpayer must file any other amended United States returns that are necessary to conform the treatment of all items affected by the election or revocation to the treatment consistent with the election or revocation. All amended returns must be accompanied by the statement described in paragraph (b)(3)(ii) of this section (substituting "made, perfected, or revoked" for "perfected or revoked" where applicable) and all of the information required by § 1.404A-6(b)(4) (and § 1.404A-6(c)(2)(ii), if applicable, in the case of a termination). If no adjustments are necessary, the amended return required by paragraph (c)(2) of this section must contain a statement to that effect.

(4) *Revocation after initial election and reelection permitted.*—Any taxpayer that makes an initial election for any plan under paragraph (c)(2) of this section may, under the rules of that paragraph, revoke the election for any taxable year after the sixth consecutive taxable year for which the election is effective, and may re-elect for any taxable year after the sixth consecutive taxable year for which the election is not in effect (regardless of whether the election is not in effect due to revocation or termination of the election as defined in § 1.404A-6(c)(1)). The consecutive changes in method of accounting described in the first sentence of this paragraph (c)(3) must be made under the rules in § 1.404A-6 regarding the section 481(a) adjustment period. The Commissioner may approve a letter ruling request (see

§ 601.201 of this chapter) to shorten the six-year waiting period upon a showing of extraordinary circumstances.

(5) *Examples.*—The principles of paragraphs (b) and (c) of this section are illustrated by the following examples:

Example 1. P, a domestic corporation, wholly owns two foreign subsidiaries, *S* and *T*. *S* and *T* maintain their books and records in FC, the local currency. Since 1978, *S* and *T* have maintained unfunded pension plans for their respective employees. *S* maintained two plans, Plan 1 and Plan 2, and *T* maintained one plan. The plan years and the taxable years of all three corporations are the calendar year.

(i) For 1978 and 1979, *P* reduced the earnings and profits of *S* and *T* by the amount of the pension liability that had accrued under the plans as follows—

Taxable year	*S's Plan 1*	*S's Plan 2*	*T's plan*
1978	FC30,000	FC5,000	FC70,000
1979	50,000	15,000	80,000
Total reduction in earnings and profits . . .	FC80,000	FC20,000	FC150,000
Total reduction in earnings and profits			
S	FC100,000		
T	FC150,000		

(ii) In 1981, *P* made a retroactive effective date election pursuant to section 2(e)(2) of Public Law 96-603 and paragraph (b) of this section for taxable years beginning after December 31, 1977, and ending before January 1, 1980, *P* 's open period. Thus, with respect to its open period, *P* has made section 404A the operative law for all distributions of earnings and profits (or accumulated profits) earned after December 31, 1970 for *S* and *T*. The consequences of making or not making the retroactive plan-by-plan election under section 404A for each foreign plan will be determined as though section 404A had been in effect for those years. Accordingly, earnings and profits of *S* and *T* may not be reduced with respect to amounts accrued under their respective plans unless the plans met the requirements of § 1.404A-1(a) for those years in the open period.

(iii) *P* made a retroactive plan-by-plan election to treat *S* 's Plan 1 as a qualified reserve plan for *P* 's retroactive period. The amount taken into account under § 1.404A-3 for *S* 's Plan 1 calculated under section 404A was FC25,000 for 1978 and FC35,000 for 1979. No election under section 404A was made for *S* 's Plan 2 or for *T* 's plan. Thus, no amount of the accrued but unpaid pension liability attributable to *S* 's Plan 2 or to *T* 's plan may reduce *S* 's or *T* 's respective 1978 and 1979 earnings and profits. *P* amended its tax returns for 1978 and 1979 to reflect the correct reduction of earnings and profits of FC25,000 and FC35,000 with respect to *S* 's Plan 1 and no reduction for those years with respect to *S* 's Plan 2 or *T* 's plan. Since *S* 's and *T* 's plans were established during the open period, no section 481(a) adjustment is required.

Example 2. Q, a domestic corporation, has wholly owned *R*, a foreign subsidiary, since *R* 's formation in 1968. *R* maintains its books and records in FC, the local currency. Since 1968, *R* maintained an unfunded pension plan for its employees. The plan year and the taxable year of both corporations is the calendar year. *R*, since 1968, used a method of accounting under which it reduced earnings and profits by its accrued pension liability.

(i) *R* 's earnings and profits were earned and distributed to *Q* as follows—

Taxable year	*Earnings and profits*		*Distribution of earnings and profits*
1968	FC10,000		
1969	20,000		
1970	20,000		
Subtotal		50,000	
1971	30,000		
1972	30,000		
1973	30,000		
1974	30,000		
1975	30,000		FC200,000
Subtotal		150,000	
1976	40,000		
1977	40,000		
1978	40,000		
1979	40,000		
1980	40,000		
1981	50,000		
Subtotal		250,000	
Total	FC450,000		

(ii) In 1981, *Q* made a retroactive effective date election pursuant to section 2(e)(2) of Public Law 96-603 and paragraph (b)(1) of this section for its open period. As of December 31, 1980, *Q* 's open period included the taxable years 1975 through 1979. Thus, with respect to those taxable years, *Q* has made section 404A the operative law for *R*. The consequences of making or not making the retroactive plan-by-plan election under section 404A for *R*'s foreign plan will be determined as though section 404A had been in effect for those taxable years. Thus, the earnings and profits of *R* may not be reduced with respect to amounts accrued under *R* 's plan, unless the plan met the requirements of § 1.404A-1(a) for those taxable years.

Q made a retroactive plan-by-plan election to treat *R* 's plan as a qualified reserve plan effective beginning in 1971. Of the distribution of FC200,000 to *Q* in 1975, section 404A applies to FC150,000, because these accumulated profits (or earnings and profits) were earned in taxable years beginning after December 31, 1970 and were also distributed in 1975, within *Q* 's open period. However, section 404A does not apply to the FC50,000 distribution made from accumulated profits earned before December 31, 1970. Since *R*'s plan was established before *Q* 's open period, a section 481(a) adjustment is required. This section 481(a) adjustment must be taken into account in determining earnings and profits beginning with the 1971 year of change.

(d) *Retroactive plan-by-plan qualified funded plan elections for certain plans of foreign branches.*—(1) *In general.*—Section 2(e)(3) of Public Law 96-603 permitted a taxpayer to make a qualified funded plan election retroactively for any plans maintained by a foreign branch that met the requirements of § 1.404A-1(a) (other than paragraph (4) thereof) for the relevant period. As a condition of making this election, a taxpayer is required to agree to the assessment of all deficiencies (including interest thereon) arising during those taxable years within the open period (even those taxable years that are not open years as defined in paragraph (g)(4) of this section) to the extent that the deficiencies arise from erroneous deductions claimed by the taxpayer with respect to all of the taxpayer's foreign branches that maintained a deferred compensation plan. For a taxpayer that agrees to the assessment of tax in an election under this paragraph (d), a change in method of accounting is necessary (and a section 481(a) adjustment is required in accordance with the provisions of § 1.404A-6) with respect to any erroneous deductions claimed by the taxpayer under its method of accounting in taxable years ending prior to the beginning of the open period. For such a change in method of accounting, the year of change is the first taxable year in the open period, and the method of accounting to which the taxpayer is required to change is the method permitted during the open period under this paragraph (d).

(2) *Amounts allowed as a deduction.*—If an election under section 2(e)(3) of Public Law 96-603 was made under the rules of this paragraph (d), the aggregate of the taxpayer's prior deductions is allowed as a deduction ratably over a 15-year period, beginning with the taxpayer's first taxable year beginning after December 31, 1979. A fractional part of a year which is a taxable year (as defined in sections 441(b) and 7701(a)(23)) is a taxable year for purposes of the 15-year period.

(3) *Definitions.*—(i) *Prior deduction.*—(A) *In general.*—The term "prior deduction" means a deduction with respect to a qualified funded plan (i.e., a plan that met the requirements of § 1.404A-1(a) for the relevant period, and with respect to which a qualified funded plan election was made under the rules of this paragraph (d)) maintained by a foreign branch of a taxpayer for a taxable year beginning before January 1, 1980—

(1) That the taxpayer claimed;

(2) That was not allowable under the law in effect prior to the enactment of section 404A;

(3) With respect to which, on December 1, 1980, the assessment of a deficiency was not barred by any law or rule of law; and

(4) That would have been allowable if section 404A applied to taxable years beginning before January 1, 1980.

(B) *Application of section 404A(d).*—Because the prior deductions are limited by the amounts that may be taken into account under section 404A, the computation of those prior deductions for the relevant taxable years is subject to the limitations described in section 404A(d) and § 1.404A-4. However, once the aggregate of prior deductions is calculated, the aggregate, or any portion thereof permitted to be taken into account over the 15-year period of paragraph (d)(2) of this section, is not subject to the limitations prescribed by section 404A(d) and § 1.404A-4.

(ii) *Erroneous deduction.*—The term "erroneous deduction" means an amount that is not deductible under section 404(a) (including section 404(a)(5)), that was deducted on a taxpayer's income tax return with respect to a foreign deferred compensation plan.

(4) *Time and manner to make, perfect, or revoke election.*—(i) *In general.*—A plan-by-plan election described in paragraph (d)(1) of this section is not effective unless the election was actually made no later than the time prescribed by law for filing the United States return for the first taxable year ending on or after December 31, 1980, including extensions (whether or not the time was actually extended for filing the taxpayer's return), and unless the taxpayer perfects the election by filing a statement indicating the taxpayer's agreement to perfect the election with an amended return for the first taxable year ending on or after December 31, 1980, on or before [*INSERT DATE THAT IS 365 DAYS AFTER THE DATE OF PUBLICATION OF FINAL REGULATIONS IN THE FEDERAL REGISTER*]. In order to be effective, the perfection must be made in the manner provided in § 1.404A-6(b)(3)(ii) or (iii). An election that is not perfected is considered retroactively revoked. Any election under this paragraph (d) will continue in effect for taxable years beginning after the taxpayer's open period, unless revoked under paragraph (e) of this section or § 1.404A-6.

(ii) *Requirement to amend returns.*—In addition to the amended return required by paragraph (d)(4)(i) of this section, the taxpayer must file any other amended United States returns that are necessary to conform the treatment of all items affected by the election or revocation to the treatment consistent with the election or revocation under this paragraph (d) within the time period described in paragraph (d)(4)(i) of this section. All amended returns must be accompanied by the statement described in paragraph (b)(3)(ii) of this section and all of the information required by § 1.404A-6(b)(4) (and § 1.404A-6(c)(2)(ii), if applicable, in the case of a termination). If no adjustments are necessary, the amended return required by paragraph (d)(4)(i) of this section must contain a statement to that effect.

(5) *Examples.*—The principles of this paragraph (d) are illustrated by the following examples:

Example 1. (i) During its open taxable years 1977 through 1979, *X*, a domestic corporation, maintained a nonqualified funded plan for the employees of its foreign branch. In 1981, *X* made a retroactive effective date election and a retroactive plan-by-plan election to treat this plan as a qualified funded plan. The amounts deducted on *X*'s tax returns, the amount deductible under sections 404(a) and 404A (expressed in FC, the local currency) are as follows—

	1977	*1978*	*1979*	*Total*
Amount deducted on tax return . . .	FC100	FC100	FC100	FC300
Amount deductible under section 404(a)	20	20	20	FC60
Amount deductible under section 404A	90	90	90	FC270

(ii) The assessment (including interest) for the open years 1977 through 1979 is based on adjustments to the erroneous deductions of FC240 (FC300 less FC60).

(iii) The amount of the prior deductions taken into account ratably over 15 years as provided in paragraph (d)(2) of this section, beginning in 1981, is a negative FC210 (FC60 less FC270).

(iv) No section 481(a) adjustment is required because *X* took no deductions with respect to the plan prior to the beginning of its open period.

Example 2. (i) *Z*, a domestic corporation, maintained a nonqualified funded foreign branch plan for its foreign employees, beginning in its 1965 (calendar) taxable year. In 1981, *Z* made a retroactive effective date election and a retroactive plan-by-plan election to treat this plan as a qualified funded plan. As of December 31, 1980, *Z*'s 1965 taxable year was closed, but its 1978 taxable year was open. The amounts deducted on *Z*'s tax returns, the amount deductible under sections 404(a) and 404A (expressed in FC, the local currency) are as follows—

	1965	*1978*	*Total*
Amount deducted on tax return	FC20	FC80	FC100
Amount deductible under section 404(a)	5	6	FC11
Amount deductible under section 404A	10	40	FC60

(ii) Under paragraph (d)(1) of this section, Z agreed to an assessment of deficiencies for its 1978 taxable year based on its FC74 (FC80 - FC6) of erroneous deductions as defined in paragraph (d)(3)(ii) of this section.

(iii) The FC34 (FC40—FC6) of prior deductions is permitted to be taken into account as a deduction over the 15-year period beginning with its 1980 taxable year as provided in paragraph (d)(2) of this section.

(iv) Additionally, because Z took erroneous deductions under its method of accounting prior to the beginning of its open period, it is required to change to the method of accounting permitted during the open period, and must take a section 481(a) adjustment (determined under the snapshot method of § 1.404A-6(f)) into account over the 15-year section 481(a) adjustment period of § 1.404A-6(e)(2)(ii) beginning in its 1978 year of change. See paragraph (d)(1) of this section.

Example 3. A foreign branch which computes its income under the profit and loss method of Rev. Rul. 75-107, 1975-1 C.B. 32 (see § 601.601(d)(2)(ii)(*b*) of this chapter), in units of local currency, the FC, maintains a qualified funded plan. In 1980, the taxpayer was eligible to make the elections described in this section, and did so during the 1980 taxable year. The amount determined under paragraph (d)(3)(i) of this section after taking into account the limitations prescribed [by] § 1.404A-4(a) for the open period was FC1,500,000. For the 1980 taxable year, and as provided in paragraph (d) of this section, FC100,000 of the prior deductions were deductible. The prior deductions allowed to be taken into account in the 1980 through 1994 taxable years are determined without regard to, and thus are not subject to, the limitations prescribed by § 1.404A-4(a).

(e) *Special transition rules for election, revocation and re-election.*—(1) *In general.*—This paragraph (e) provides the time and manner for making and revoking qualified funded plan and qualified reserve plan elections for a taxpayer's transition period. A taxpayer may make an election, revoke an election, and re-elect to treat any plan that met the requirements of § 1.404A-1(a) (other than paragraph (4) thereof) for the relevant period as a qualified funded plan or a qualified reserve plan under this paragraph (e) for the transition period without regard to whether a retroactive election is made under paragraph (b), (c), or (d) of this section. However, an election made under paragraph (c) or (d) of this section is deemed to continue in effect for taxable years beginning after December 31, 1979, unless revoked under paragraph (c)(4) of this section or this paragraph (e) or terminated or revoked under § 1.404A-6(f). See paragraphs (c)(2) and (d)(4)(i) of this section.

(2) *Time and manner initially to elect and revoke.*—(i) *In general.*—Taxpayers that wish to make an election under this paragraph (e) may have, but were not required to have, made a Method (1) or Method (2) election for the taxable year for which an election is made under this paragraph. Those taxpayers that wish to make (or perfect) an election under this paragraph (e) must attach a statement to that effect on an amended return for the year the election is to be effective on or before [*INSERT DATE THAT IS 365 DAYS AFTER THE DATE OF PUBLICATION OF FINAL REGULATIONS IN THE FEDERAL*

REGISTER]. An election previously made that is not perfected is considered retroactively revoked.

(ii) *Requirement to amend returns.*—In addition to the amended return required by paragraph (e)(2)(i) of this section, the taxpayer must file any other amended United States returns that are necessary to conform the treatment of all items affected by the election or revocation to the treatment consistent with the election or revocation under this paragraph (e) within the time period described in paragraph (e)(2)(i) of this section. All amended returns must be accompanied by the statement described in paragraph (b)(3)(ii) of this section (substituting "made, perfected, or revoked" for "perfected or revoked" where applicable) and all of the information required by §1.404A-6(b)(4) (and §1.404A-6(c)(2)(ii), if applicable, in the case of a termination). If no adjustments are necessary, the amended return required by paragraph (e)(2)(i) of this section must contain a statement to that effect.

(3) *Revocation after initial election and re-election permitted.*—Any taxpayer that makes an initial election for any plan under paragraph (e)(2) of this section may, under the rules of that paragraph, revoke the election for any taxable year after the sixth consecutive taxable year for which the election is effective, and may re-elect for any taxable year after the sixth consecutive taxable year for which the election is not in effect (whether the election is not in effect due to either revocation or termination of the election as defined in §1.404A-6(c)(1)). The consecutive changes in method of accounting described in the first sentence of this paragraph (e)(3) must be made under the rules in §1.404A-6 regarding the section 481(a) adjustment period. The Commissioner may approve a letter ruling request to shorten the six-year waiting period upon a showing of extraordinary circumstances.

(4) *Example.*—The principles of paragraph (e)(3) of this section are illustrated by the following example:

Example. (i) *L*, a domestic corporation, has wholly owned foreign subsidiary *M*, since *M*' s formation in 1971. *M* maintained a funded plan for its employees from 1971 through 1991. The taxable year of *L* and *M* is the calendar year. In 1981, *L* made a Method (2) election. Within 365 days after the publication of the final regulations in the Federal Register, *L* perfected its retroactive effective date election for all its foreign subsidiaries. *L*' s election terminated in 1975 due to its plan's violation of the requirements of section 404A(e)(2). Additionally, *L* perfected, revoked and re-elected on a plan-by-plan basis its election for *M*' s plan, as follows—

Plan-by-plan election effective	*Plan-by-plan election terminated or revoked*
1971—1974	1975—1981
1982—1987	1988—1993

(ii) A section 481(a) adjustment is required for the years of change 1975, 1982 and 1988.

(f) *Special data rules for retroactive elections.*—(1) *Retroactive calculation of section 481(a) adjustments.*—(i) *General rule.*—Retroactive elections may be made only if the taxpayer calculates the section 481(a) adjustment required by §1.404A-6 based on substantiation quality data. Substantiation quality data generally must be current as of the date of the change in method of accounting. Nevertheless, if contemporaneous substantiation quality data is not readily available, the taxpayer may calculate the section 481(a) adjustment based on backward projections to earlier years from the first taxable year beginning before January 1, 1980, for which sufficient contemporaneous substantiation quality data is readily available. However, such projections must satisfy the substantiation requirements in paragraph (f)(1)(ii) of this section. Furthermore, the taxpayer may not use any of the approaches provided for under this paragraph (f) if circumstances indicate that the overall result is a material distortion of the amounts allowable.

(ii) *Substantiation requirement for retroactive reserves.*—(A) *In general.*—Although reasonable actuarial estimates and projections may be used, the calculation of the opening balance of the reserve for the first year for which a qualified reserve plan election under paragraph (c)(1) of this section is effective must nonetheless be based on some actual contemporaneous evidence. Thus, the opening balance may be based on actual aggregate covered payroll, the actual number of covered employees, or a contemporaneous actuarial valuation that used reasonable actuarial methods. For example, if the taxpayer has contemporaneous records of the number of covered employees and the aggregate covered payroll, it may estimate other actuarial information, such as average age and marital status, based on reasonable actuarial methods (e.g., using substantiation quality data as of another date and adjusting for actual or expected changes for the interim years). The resulting combination of actual contemporaneous evidence and reasonably estimated data may be used to calculate the opening reserve. If a contemporaneous actuarial valuation is used as the basis of an opening reserve, the results of the valuation must be adjusted to reflect any difference between the actuarial method used in that actuarial valuation and the unit credit method, as required by section 404A(c) and §1.404A-3(b).

(B) *Interpolation.*—In cases where a taxpayer can meet the substantiation requirement of paragraph (f)(1)(ii)(A) of this section for some years, but cannot meet that requirement in intervening years (including the year of the change in method of accounting), the taxpayer may interpolate a reserve balance for the intervening years based on reasonable actuarial methods. In the absence of evidence to the contrary, it is assumed that a pro rata allocation of amounts to those intervening years is a reasonable actuarial method. This paragraph (f)(1)(ii)(B) does not authorize any interpolation for years in which other evidence indicates that it would cause a material distortion (such as a year during which the work force was on strike and no deferred compensation benefits were accrued). In addition, this paragraph (f)(1)(ii)(B) does not authorize extrapolation of reserve balances to years that are not intervening years between years that meet the substantiation requirements of paragraph (f)(1)(ii)(A) of this section.

(C) *Extrapolation.*—If the first year for which the taxpayer is able to meet the substantiation requirements of paragraph (f)(1)(ii)(A) of this section ("the substantiation year") is later than the year of the change in method of accounting, a taxpayer may use the approach described in this paragraph (f)(1)(ii)(C) to determine the section 481(a) adjustments described in § 1.404A-6(f) in years prior to the substantiation year. Under this approach, the taxpayer's closing balance under its prior method as of the date of the change in the method of accounting is compared with the opening balance in the substantiation year. If the closing balance exceeds the opening balance, the excess is the amount to be used in calculating the adjustment under section 481, as required by § 1.404A-6. However, if the closing balance of the taxpayer's reserve under its method used for years prior to the election under section 404A is less than the opening balance for the substantiation year, the opening balance as of the date of the change in method in accounting is assumed to be equal to the closing balance. Thus, if the closing balance is less than the opening balance for the substantiation year, there is no adjustment under section 481. In such a case, the difference between the opening balance as of the date of the change in method of accounting and the opening balance for the substantiation year is allocated to the years prior to the substantiation year based on reasonable actuarial methods using all available information.

(2) *Determination of reasonable addition to a reserve in interim years.*—In the case of a qualified reserve plan that is using the interpolation option of paragraph (f)(1)(ii)(B) of this section or that is described in the last sentence in paragraph (f)(1)(ii)(C) of this section, none of the increase in the reserve in the intervening year is considered a reasonable addition to the reserve under § 1.404A-3(b). Thus, the entire amount of the increase must be considered an amount to be amortized over ten years under § 1.404A-3(c).

(3) *Protective elections.*—For those taxpayers that relied on the prior position of the Internal Revenue Service by making a Method (1) election under which the section 481(a) adjustment was computed in a manner inconsistent with this section or by making a Method (2) election under which no section 481(a) adjustment was reflected in the original return, appropriate adjustments required by section 404A and its underlying regulations must be made on an amended return filed no later than [*INSERT DATE THAT IS 365 DAYS AFTER THE DATE OF PUBLICATION OF FINAL REGULATIONS IN THE FEDERAL REGISTER*] for the first year the election is effective and for all subsequent affected years for which a return has been filed. If no adjustments are necessary, an amended return should be filed for the first year stating that no adjustments are necessary.

(g) *Definitions and special rules.*—(1) *Method (1) election.*—The term "Method (1) election" means an election that was made under Method (1) (as defined in Ann. 81-114, 1981-28 I.R.B. 21) (see § 601.601(d)(2)(ii)(*b*) of this chapter) by claiming the deduction or credit allowable under section 404A on the taxpayer's income tax return for the first taxable year ending on or after December 31, 1980, including extensions (or an amended return filed no later than the end of the extended time period prescribed in section 6081, whether or not such time was actually extended for filing the taxpayer's return).

(2) *Protective or Method (2) election.*—The term "protective election" or "Method (2) election" means an election that was made under Method (2) (as defined in Ann. 81-114, 1981-28 I.R.B. 21) (see § 601.601(d)(2)(ii)(*b*) of this chapter) without claiming deductions attributable to a qualified foreign plan on the taxpayer's income tax return (or, in the case of foreign subsidiaries, without taking into account reductions of earnings and profits).

(3) *Open years of the taxpayer.*—The term "open years of the taxpayer" means open taxable years beginning after December 31, 1971, and for which, on December 31, 1980, the making of a refund, or the assessment of a deficiency, was not barred by any law or rule of law.

(4) *Retroactive period.*—The term "retroactive period" means a taxpayer's taxable years (whether or not the making of a refund, or the assessment of a deficiency, was barred by any law or rule of law for any taxable year) in the following range—

(i) Any taxable year selected by the taxpayer between taxable years beginning after December 31, 1970 and before January 1, 1980 (the beginning taxable year); and

(ii) The last taxable year beginning before January 1, 1980 (the ending taxable year).

(5) *Transition period.*—The term "transition period" means taxable years beginning after December 31, 1979, and before [*INSERT THE DATE OF PUBLICATION OF FINAL REGULATIONS IN THE FEDERAL REGISTER*].

(6) *Open period.*—For purposes of this section, the term "open period" means, with respect to any taxpayer, all taxable years beginning after December 31, 1971, and beginning before January 1, 1980, and for which, on December 31, 1980, the making of a refund, or the assessment of a deficiency, was not barred by any law or rule of law. [Reg. § 1.404A-7.]

IRAs: SEPs: Special Requirements

Individual Retirement Plans: Simplified Employee Pensions.—Reproduced below is the text of a proposed amendment of Reg. § 1.408-2, relating to individual retirement plans and simplified employee pensions (published in the Federal Register on July 14, 1981).

* * *

☐ Par. 6. Section 1.408-2 is amended by revising paragraph (c)(3) to read as follows:

§ 1.408-2. Individual retirement accounts.—

* * *

(c) * * *

(3) *Special requirement.*—There must be a separate accounting for the interest of each employee or member (or spouse of an employee or member).

* * *

IRAs: SEPs: Acceptable Contributions

Individual Retirement Plans: Simplified Employee Pensions: Qualified Voluntary Employee Contributions.—Reproduced below is the text of a proposed amendment of Reg. §1.408-2, relating to individual retirement plans, simplified employee pensions and qualified voluntary employee contributions (published in the Federal Register on January 23, 1984).

* * *

☐ Par. 2. Section 1.408-2 is amended by revising paragraph (b)(1) to read as follows:

§1.408-2. Individual retirement accounts.—

* * *

(b) * * *

(1) *Amount of acceptable contributions.*—Except in the case of a contribution to a simplified employee pension described in section 408(k) and a rollover contribution described in section 408(d)(3), 402(a)(5), 402(a)(7), 403(a)(4), 403(b)(8), 405(d)(3), or 409(b)(3)(C), the trust instrument must provide that contributions may not be accepted by the trustee for the taxable year in excess of $2,000 on behalf of any individual for whom the trust is maintained. An individual retirement account maintained as a simplified employee pension may provide for the receipt of up to the limits specified in section 408(j) for a calendar year.

IRAs: SEPs: Flexible Premiums

Individual Retirement Plans: Simplified Employee Pensions.—Reproduced below is the text of a proposed amendment of Reg. §1.408-3, relating to individual retirement plans and simplified employee pensions (published in the Federal Register on July 14, 1981).

☐ Par. 7. Section 1.408-3 is revised by adding new paragraphs (b)(6) and (f). These added provisions read as follows:

§1.408-3. Individual retirement annuities.—

* * *

(b) * * *

(6) *Flexible premium.*—(i) In the case of annuity contracts issued after November 6, 1978, the premiums under such contracts are not fixed. See paragraph (f) for the definition of an annuity contract under which "the premiums are not fixed."

(ii) In the case of a fixed premium individual retirement annuity or individual retirement endowment contract issued before November 7, 1978, the issuer of such contract may offer the holder of the contract the option of exchanging such contract for a flexible premium contract. If such an exchange is made before January 1, 1981, the exchange shall not constitute a distribution and shall be nontaxable.

* * *

(f) *Flexible premium annuity contract.*—(1) *In general.*—A flexible premium retirement annuity contract shall be considered a contract under which "the premiums are not fixed" if it provides the following:

(i) At no time after the initial premium for the contract has been paid is there a specified renewal premium required.

(ii) The contract must allow for the continuance of the contract (as a paid-up annuity) under its nonforfeiture provision if premium payments cease altogether.

(iii) The contract, if being continued on a paid-up basis (*i.e.,* if it has not been terminated by a payment in cash), will be reinstated at any date prior to its maturity date upon payment of a premium to the insurer.

(2) *Exceptions.*—(i) The insurer may require that if a premium is remitted, it will be accepted only if the amount remitted is some stated amount, not in excess of $50.

(ii) The contract may provide that if no premiums have been received under the contract for two (2) full years and the paid-up annuity benefit at maturity of the plan stipulated in the contract arising from the premium paid prior to such two-year period would be less than $20 a month, the insurer may, at its option, terminate the contract by payment in cash of the then present value of the paid-up benefit (computed on the same basis specified in the contract for determining the paid-up benefit).

(3) *Permissible provisions.*—A flexible premium contract will not be considered to have fixed premiums merely because—

(i) A maximum limit (which may be expressed as a multiple of the premium paid in the first year of the contract) is placed on the amount of the premium that the insurer will accept in any year,

(ii) An annual charge is made against the policy value,

(iii) A fee (which may be composed of a flat dollar amount plus an amount equal to the required premium tax imposed by the state government) is charged upon the acceptance of each premium by the insurer, or

(iv) The contract requires a level annual premium for a supplementary benefit, such as a waiver of premium benefit.

IRAs: SEPs: Annual Premiums

Individual Retirement Plans: Simplified Employee Pensions: Qualified Voluntary Employee Contributions.—Reproduced below is the text of a proposed amendment of Reg. §1.408-3, relating to individual retirement plans, simplified employee pensions and qualified voluntary employee contributions (published in the Federal Register on January 23, 1984).

☐ Par. 3. Section 1.408-3 is amended by revising paragraph (b)(2) to read as follows:

§1.408-3. Individual retirement annuities.—

* * *

(b) * * *

(2) *Annual premium.*—Except in the case of a contribution to a simplified employee pension described in section 408(k), the annual pre-

mium on behalf of any individual for the annuity cannot exceed $2,000. Any refund of premiums must be applied before the close of the calendar year following the year of the refund toward the payment of future premiums or the purchase of additional benefits. An individual retirement annuity maintained as a simplified employee pension may provide for an annual premium of up to the limits specified in section 408(j).

* * *

IRAs: SEPs: Rollover Contributions

Individual Retirement Plans: Simplified Employee Pensions.—Reproduced below is the text of a proposed amendment of Reg. §1.408-4, relating to individual retirement plans and simplified employee pensions (published in the Federal Register on July 14, 1981). Proposed amendments to Reg. §1.408-4(b)(4)(ii) withdrawn by REG-209459-78 on July 11, 2014.

☐ Par. 8. Section 1.408-4 is amended by: (1) adding new paragraphs (b)(3), (b)(4)(ii), and (c)(3)(ii); and (2) adding a new paragraph (h). These added provisions read as follows:

§1.408-4. Treatment of distributions from individual retirement arrangements.—

* * *

(b) *Rollover Contribution.*—* * *

(3) *To section 403(b) contract.*—Paragraph (a)(1) of this section does not apply to any amount paid or distributed from an individual retirement account or individual retirement annuity to the individual for whose benefit the account or annuity is maintained if—

(i) The entire amount received (including money and other property) represents the entire interest in the account or the entire value of the annuity,

(ii) No amount in the account and no part of the value of the annuity is attributable to any source other than a rollover contribution from an annuity contract described in section 403(b) and any earnings on such rollover,

(iii) The entire amount thereof is paid into an annuity contract described in section 403(b) (for the benefit of such individual) not later than the 60th day after the receipt of the payment or distribution, and

(iv) The distribution or transfer is made in a taxable year beginning after December 31, 1978.

(4) * * *

(ii) [Withdrawn by REG-209459-78 on July 11, 2014.]

(c) * * *

(3) *Time of inclusion.*—* * *

(ii) For taxable years beginning after December 31, 1976, the amount of net income determined under subparagraph (2) is includible in the gross income of the individual in the taxable year in which such excess contribution is made. The amount of net income thus distributed is subject to the tax imposed by section 408(f)(1) for the year includible in gross income.

* * *

(h) *Certain distributions of excess contributions after due date of return for taxable year.*—(1) *General rule.*—In the case of any individual, if the aggregate contributions (other than valid rollover contributions) paid for any taxable year to an individual retirement account or for an individual retirement annuity do not exceed $1,750, section 408(d)(1) shall not apply to the distribution of any such contribution to the extent that such contribution exceeds the amount allowable as a deduction under section 219 or 220 for the taxable year for which the contribution was paid—

(i) If such distribution is received after the date described in section 408(d)(4),

(ii) But only to the extent that no deduction has been allowed under section 219 or 220 with respect to such excess contribution.

(2) *Excess rollover contribution attributable to erroneous information.*—If the taxpayer reasonably relies on information supplied pursuant to subtitle F of the Internal Revenue Code of 1954 for determining the amount of a rollover contribution, but such information was erroneous, subparagraph (1) of this paragraph shall be applied by increasing the dollar limit set forth therein by that portion of the excess contribution which was attributable to such information.

(3) *Special rule for contributions to simplified employee pension.*—If employer contributions on behalf of the individual are paid for the taxable year to a simplified employee pension, the dollar limitation of subparagraph (1) shall be the lesser of the amount of such contributions or $7,500. See §1.219-3(a)(3)(iv) for a special rule where there is more than one employer.

(4) *Effective date.*—(1)[i] Subparagraphs (1) and (2) of this paragraph shall apply to distributions in taxable years beginning after December 31, 1975.

(ii) In the case of contributions for taxable years beginning before January 1, 1978, paragraph (5) of section 408(d) of the Internal Revenue Code of 1954 shall be applied as if such paragraph did not contain any dollar limitation.

(4)[5] *Examples.*—The provisions of this paragraph may be illustrated by the following examples:

Example (1). T, a calendar-year taxpayer, had been a participant in a government pension plan for 6 years prior to separation from service on July 31, 1976. The plan required T to make mandatory contributions and as of July 31, 1976, these mandatory contributions totaled $6,000. Upon T's separation from service, she was given the option of receiving back all of her mandatory contributions or leaving them with the plan. T elected to receive her mandatory contributions and attempted to roll over these amounts into an individual retirement account (IRA) in August of 1976. The trustee of the IRA accepted these funds and an IRA was established. In March of 1977, T discovered that the funds she received from the government plan did not qualify for rollover treatment because they were employee contributions and withdrew all of the money from her IRA. T will not have to include any of the money withdrawn from the IRA in gross income for 1977 because the transitional rule of paragraph (h)(3)(ii) permits the withdrawal of all contributions which have not been allowed as deductions under section 219 or 220 made to IRA's for taxable years beginning before January 1, 1978, regardless of the amount of the contribution.

Example (2). (i) On April 1, 1980, A, a calendar-year taxpayer, receives a lump sum distribution satisfying the requirements of section 402(e)(4)(A) and (C) under the plan of A's employer. The distribution consists of $50,000 cash. A made contributions under the plan totaling $8,000, and has received no prior distributions under the plan. However, on the form furnished to A by the employer on account of the distribution, A's contributions under the plan are listed as totaling only $4,500. A reasonably relied on this information.

(ii) A desires to establish an individual retirement account (as described in section 408(a)) with the cash received in the distribution. A desires to contribute the maximum amount permitted under the rollover rules. Under sections 402(a)(5)(B) and 402(a)(5)(D)(ii), A determines that the maximum rollover amount is $45,500, the total of the distribution ($50,000), less the amount listed as A's contributions under the plan ($4,500). The actual maximum rollover amount is $42,000, the total of the distribution ($5,000), less A's actual contribution under the plan ($8,000).

(iii) On May 23, 1980, A contributes $45,500 to an individual retirement account as a rollover contribution.

(iv) On May 1, 1981, A's employer furnishes A a corrected statement indicating that A's contributions under the plan were $8,000. On June 1, 1981, A withdraws $3,500 from the individual retirement account to correct the mistaken contribution. A will not have to include the $3,500 withdrawn from the individual retirement account in gross income for 1981 because the money was placed in the individual retirement account due to erroneous information furnished by the employer and reasonably relied upon by A and thus falls under the exception provided in section 408(d)(5)(B) to section 408(d)(1).

IRAs: SEPs: Annual Reports

Individual Retirement Accounts: Annual Information Report: Trustees and Issuers.— Reproduced below is the text of proposed Reg. §1.408-5, requiring annual reporting of information relating to individual retirement plans (published in the Federal Register on November 16, 1984).

□ Section 1.408-5 is revised to read as follows:

§1.408-5. Annual reports by trustees and issuers.—(a) *Requirement and form of report.*—The trustee of an individual retirement account or the issuer of an individual retirement annuity (including an account or annuity that is a simplified employee pension) shall make annual calendar year reports on Form 5498 concerning the status of the account or annuity. The report shall contain the following information for transactions occurring during or after the calendar year that relate to such calendar year:

(1) The name, address, and identifying number of the trustee or issuer;

(2) The name, address, and identifying number of the participant (the individual on whose behalf the account is established or in whose name the annuity is purchased (or the beneficiary of the individual or owner));

(3) The amount of contributions (exclusive of rollover contributions) made during or after the calendar year that relate to such calendar year;

(4) The amount of rollover contributions made during the calendar year;

(5) In the case of an endowment contract, the amount of the premium allocable to the cost of life insurance paid either during or after the calendar year that relates to such calendar year; and

(6) Such other information as the Commissioner may require.

(b) *Manner and time for filing.*—The report on Form 5498 shall be filed, accompanied by transmittal Form 1096, with the appropriate Internal Revenue Service Center. The report shall be filed on or before May 31 following the calendar year for which the report is required.

(c) *Statement to participants.*—(1) Each trustee or issuer required to file Form 5498 under this section shall furnish the participant a statement containing the information required to be furnished on Form 5498 plus the value of the account or annuity at the end of the calendar year. A copy of Form 5498, containing the additional information specified in the previous sentence, may be used to satisfy the statement requirement of this paragraph. If a copy of Form 5498 is not used to satisfy the statement requirement of this paragraph, the statement shall contain the following language: "This information is being furnished to the Internal Revenue Service."

(2) Each statement required by this paragraph to be furnished to participants shall be furnished to such person on or before May 31 following the calendar year for which the report on Form 5498 is required.

(d) *Penalties.*—Section 6693 prescribes penalties for failure to file an annual report required by this section.

(e) *Effective date.*—In general, this section applies to reports for calendar years beginning with 1983. For additional requirements relating to the 1985 calendar year reports, see paragraph (f) of this section. For special requirements relating to the 1983 and 1984 calendar year reports, see paragraph (g) of this section. For requirements relating to pre-1983 calendar year reports, see 26 C.F.R. §1.408-5 (1983).

(f) *Reports for calendar year 1985.*—For calendar year 1985, both Form 5498 and the statement to the participant must report, as a separate entry, the amount of contributions made during the 1985 calendar year that relate to the 1984 calendar year. This also applies, in the case of the statement to the participant, to endowment contract premiums allocable to the cost of life insurance that are paid during the 1985 calendar year but that relate to the 1984 calendar year.

(g) *Reports for calendar years 1983 and 1984.*—(1) For calendar years 1983 and 1984, neither Form 5498 nor the statement to the participant need identify the calendar year to which a contribution relates. The form and statement need only report the amount of contributions actually made during the calendar year. This also applies to endowment contract premiums allocable to the cost of life insurance and paid during the calendar year.

(2) For calendar years 1983 and 1984, Form 5498 need not report (but the statement to the participant must report), in the case of an endowment contract, the amount of the premium allocable to the cost of life insurance paid during the calendar year.

(3) For calendar year 1983, neither Form 5498 nor the statement to the participant need separately report rollover contributions made during the calendar year. Rollover contributions are to be aggregated with the amount of other contributions made during the calendar year.

(4) For calendar year 1983, the statement to the participant need not contain the language required by paragraph (c)(1) of this section.

(5) For calendar year 1983, Form 5498 shall be filed, and the statement to the participant shall be furnished, on or before June 30, 1984.

(h) *Related reports by trustees and issuers.*—See § 1.408-7 for reports relating to distributions from individual retirement plans.

IRAs: SEPs: Disclosure: Nondiscrimination

Individual Retirement Plans: Simplified Employee Pensions.—Reproduced below are the texts of proposed Reg. §§ 1.408-7 and 1.408-8 and a proposed amendment of Reg. § 1.408-6, relating to individual retirement plans and simplified employee pensions (published in the Federal Register on July 14, 1981.)

* * *

☐ Par. 9. Section 1.408-6 is amended by deleting paragraph (d)(4)(xi) and adding a new paragraph (b) to read as follows:

§ 1.408-6. Disclosure statements for individual retirement arrangements.—

* * *

(b) *Disclosure statements for spousal individual retirement arrangements.*—The trustee of an individual retirement account and the issuer of an individual retirement annuity shall furnish to the benefited individual of a spousal individual retirement arrangement a disclosure statement in accordance with paragraph (d). In the case of a spousal individual retirement arrangement that uses subaccounts, the benefited individual includes both the working and non-working spouse.

☐ Par. 10. There are added after § 1.408-6 the following new sections:

§ 1.408-7. Simplified employee pension.—(a) *In general.*—The term "simplified employee pension" means an individual retirement account or individual retirement annuity described in section 408(a), (b) or (c) with respect to which the requirements of paragraphs (b), (d), (e), (g) and (h) of this section are met and the requirements of § 1.408-8 are met with respect to any calendar year.

(b) *Establishment of simplified employee pension.*—In order to establish a simplified employee pension, the employer must execute a written instrument (hereafter referred to as the simplified employee pension arrangement) within the time prescribed for making deductible contributions. This instrument shall include: the name of the employer, the requirements for employee participation, the signature of a responsible official, and the definite allocation formula specified in section 408(k)(5) and paragraph (f) of this section.

(c) *Variation in contribution.*—(1) *Permitted variations.*—An employer's total contributions to its employees', simplified employee pensions may vary annually at the employer's discretion.

(2) *Salary reduction.*—Contributions made to a simplified employee pension under an arrangement under which the contribution will be made only if the employee receives a reduction in compensation or forgoes a compensation increase shall be treated as employer contributions to a simplified employee pension only if the arrangement precludes an individual election by the employee. If there is an individual election, then the contribution shall be treated as an employee contribution.

(d) *Participation requirements.*—(1) *Age and service requirements.*—This paragraph is satisfied with respect to a simplified employee pension arrangement for a calendar year only if for such year the employer contributes to the simplified employee pension on behalf of each individual who is an employee at any time during the calendar year who has—

(i) Attained age 25,

(ii) Performed service for the employer during at least 3 of the immediately preceding 5 calendar years, and

(iii) Received at least $200 compensation from the employer for the calendar year.

(2) *Execution of documents.*—The employer may execute any necessary documents on behalf of an employee who is entitled to a contribution to a simplified employee pension if the employee is unable or unwilling to execute such documents or the employer is unable to locate the employee.

(3) *Required employment.*—An employer may not require that an employee be employed as of a particular date in order to receive a contribution for a calendar year.

(4) *Nonresident aliens and employees covered by collective-bargaining agreements.*—An employer may exclude from participation in the simplified employee pension arrangement employees described in section 410(b)(2)(A) or 410(b)(2)(C).

(5) *Example.*—The provisions of this paragraph may be illustrated by the following example:

Example. Corporation X maintains a simplified employee pension arrangement for its employees. Individual J worked for Corporation X while in graduate school in 1976, 1977, and 1978. J never worked more than 25 days in any particular year. In October of 1979, J began to work for Corporation X on a full-time basis. J earned $5,000 from Corporation X for 1979. J became 25 on December 31, 1979. Corporation X must make a contribution to a simplified employee pension maintained on behalf of J for 1979 because as of December 31, 1979, J had met the minimum age requirement of section 408(k)(2), had performed service for Corporation X in 3 of the 5 calendar years preceding 1979, and met the minimum compensation requirements of paragraph (d)(1)(iii).

(e) *Requirement of written allocation formula.*—(1) *Requirement of definite written allocation formula.*—Employer contributions to a simplified employee pension must be made under a definite written allocation formula which specifies—

(i) The requirements which an employee must satisfy to share in an allocation, and

(ii) The manner in which the amount allocated to each employee's account is computed.

(2) *Employer may vary formula.*—An employer may vary the definite written allocation formula from year to year provided the simplified employee pension arrangement is amended by the permissible date for making contributions to indicate the new formula.

(f) *Treatment of contributions which exceed the written allocation formula.*—(1) *General rule.*—To the extent that employer contributions do not satisfy § 1.408-7(e)(1), the contributions shall be deemed to be contributions which are not made under a simplified employee pension arrangement except for purposes of section 408(a)(1), (b)(2)(B) and (d)(5). These contributions shall be deemed made to an individual retirement account or individual retirement annuity not maintained as part of a simplified employee pension arrangement.

(2) *Example.*—This paragraph is illustrated by the following example:

Example. (i) Assume that in 1979 Corporation X adopts a simplified employee pension arrangement ("SEP Arrangement"). The arrangement calls for Corporation X to contribute the same percentage of each participant's compensation exclusive of SEP contributions to a simplified employee pension (Allocation Compensation). X has three employees, A, B, and C, who satisfy the participation requirements of the SEP Arrangement. The compensation, the contributions to the individual simplified employee pension ("SEP") for A, B and C and the varying treatment of the contributions are set forth as follows:

Employee	*Gross Income*	*Net Compensation Before Contribution*	*SEP-IRA Contribution*	*Ratio of SEP-IRA Contributions to Net Compensation*
A	$11,000	$10,000	$1,000	10%
C	57,500	50,000	7,500	15%
Totals:	$80,000	$70,000	$10,000	

(ii) Under the special rule of this paragraph, because only 10 percent of compensation was allocated to A, and the allocation formula provides that the same percentage will be allocated to each participant, a certain portion of the contribution to B and C under the SEP shall be deemed made to IRA's that are not part of the SEP Arrangement.

(iii) To determine A's and B's Allocation Compensation the respective total compensation included in A's and B's gross income must be divided by 1.10 (1 plus the percentage of Allocation Compensation contributed to A under the SEP Arrangement). The excess of compensation included in gross income over Allocation Compensation is considered as a contribution under the SEP. The following table shows the result of this calculation:

Employee	*Gross Income*	*Allocation Compensation**	*SEP-IRA Contribution*	*Deemed IRA Contribution***
A	$11,000	$10,000	$1,000	$ 0
B	11,500	10,455	1,045	455
C	57,500	52,273	5,227	2,273
Totals:	$80,000	$72,728	$7,272	$2,728

* Gross Income divided by 1.10.
** Also included in Allocation Compensation.

(iv) Under section 404(h) for purposes of computing Corporation X's deduction, only the $7,272 is considered as a contribution to a SEP Arrangement described in section 408(k) under the special rule. The allowable 404(h) deduction equals $10,909 (15% of the excess of total compensation of $80,000 over the SEP contribution of $7,272 or 15% of $72,728). The other $2,728 is payment of compensation and subject to the deduction rules of section 162 or 212. Similarly, the $2,728 would not be considered as an employer SEP contribution for purposes of exemption from FICA and FUTA taxes under section 3121 and 3306.

(v) The effect of treating the $2,273 as a contribution to SEP's for purposes of section 408(a)(1), (b)(2)(B) and (d)(5) is to not disqualify the individual retirement arrangement of C for accepting non-SEP contributions in excess of $1,500 and to allow C to withdraw the excess contribution of $2,273 without including that amount in income under section 408(d)(1).

(g) *Permitted withdrawals.*—A simplified employee pension meets the requirements of this paragraph only if—

(1) Employer contributions thereto are not conditioned on the retention in such pension of any portion of the amount contributed, and

(2) There is no prohibition imposed by the employer on withdrawals from the simplified employee pension.

See section 408(d) for rules concerning the taxation of withdrawals from individual retirement accounts and annuities. See section 408(f)(1) for penalties for premature withdrawals from individual retirement accounts and annuities.

(h) *Section 401(j) plan.*—The requirements of this paragraph are met with respect to a simplified employee pension for a calendar year unless the employer maintains during any part of such year a plan—

(1) Some or all of the active participants in which are employees (within the meaning of section 401(c)(1)) or shareholder-employees (as defined in section 1379(d)), and

(2) To which section 401(j) applies. [Reg. § 1.408-7.]

§ 1.408-8. Nondiscrimination requirements for simplified employee pensions.—(a) *In general.*—The requirements of this section are met with respect to a simplified employee pension for a calendar year if for such year the contributions made by the employer to simplified employee pensions of its employees do not discriminate in favor of any employee who is—

(1) An officer,

(2) A shareholder, within the meaning of paragraph (b)(2),

(3) A self-employed individual, or

(4) Highly compensated.

(b) *Special rules.*—(1) For purposes of this section, employees described in subparagraph (A) or (C) of section 410(b)(2) shall be excluded from consideration.

(2) An individual shall be considered a shareholder if he owns (with the application of section 318) more than 10 percent of the value of the stock of the employer.

(c) *Contributions must bear a uniform relationship to total compensation.*—(1) *General rule.*—Contributions shall be considered discriminatory unless employer contributions to its employees' simplified employee pensions bear a uniform relationship to the total compensation (not in excess of the first $100,000) of each employee maintaining a simplified employee pension. A rate of contribution which decreases as compensation increases shall be considered uniform.

(2) *Definition of compensation.*—For purposes of this section, the term "compensation" has the meaning set forth in § 1.219-1, and is determined without regard to the employer contributions to the simplified employee pension arrangement.

(3) *Example.*—The provisions of this paragraph may be illustrated by the following example:

Example. Corporation X maintains a simplified employee pension arrangement which allocates employer contributions in the manner described below. First, contributions made by June 30 of each year are allocated in proportion to compensation paid from January 1 to June 30. Second, contributions made between July 1 and December 31 are allocated in proportion to compensation paid during the same period.

In 1980, the salaries paid, and contributions allocated, are shown below:

Participant	*Compensation 1/1/80—6/30/80*	*6/30/80 Allocation*	*Compensation 7/1/80—12/31/80*	*12/31/80 Allocation*
A	10,000	500	10,000	1,000
B	10,000	500	1,000	100
C	10,000	500	15,000	1,500

For 1980, A, B, and C received allocations equal to 7.5 percent, 5.45 percent, and 8 percent of compensation, respectively. These contributions are discriminatory because they do not bear a uniform relationship to total compensation.

(d) *Treatment of certain contributions and taxes.*—(1) *General rule.*—(i) Except as provided in this paragraph, employer contributions do not meet the requirements of this section unless such contributions meet the requirements of this section without taking into account contributions or benefits under Chapter 2 of the Internal Revenue Code (relating to tax on self-employment income), Chapter 21 (relating to Federal Insurance Contribution Act), Title II of the Social Security Act, or any other Federal or State law ("Social Security Taxes"). If the employer does not maintain an integrated plan at any time during the taxable year, taxes paid under section 3111(a) (relating to tax on employers) with respect to an employee may, for purposes of this section, be taken into account as a contribution by the employer to an employee's simplified employee pension. If contributions are made to the simplified employee pension of an owner-employee, the preceding sentence shall not apply unless taxes paid by all such owner-employees under section 1401(a), and the taxes which would be payable under section 1401(a) by such owner-employees but for paragraphs (4) and (5) of section 1402(c), are taken into account as contributions by the employer on behalf of such owner-employees. The amount of such taxes shall be determined in a manner consistent with § 1.401-12(h)(3).

(ii) If contributions are made to the simplified employee pension of a self-employed individual who is not an owner-employee, the arrangement may be integrated. In such a case, the portion of the earned income of such individual which does not exceed the maximum amount which may be treated as self-employment income under section 1402(b)(1) shall be treated as "wages" under section 3121(a)(1) subject to the tax imposed by section 3111(a) and such tax shall be taken into account as employer contributions.

(iii) An employer may take into account as contributions accounts not in excess of such Social Security taxes. Thus, an employer may integrate using a rate less than the maximum rate of tax under section 3111(a) or compensation less than the maximum amount specified as wages under section 3121(a).

(2) *Integrated plan defined.*—For purposes of subparagraph (1), the term "integrated plan" means a plan which meets the requirements of section 401(a), 403(a), or 405(a) but would not meet such requirements if contributions or benefits under Chapter 2 (relating to tax on self-employment income), Chapter 21 (relating to Federal Insurance Contributions Act), Title II of the Social Security Act, or any other Federal or State law were not taken into account.

(e) *Examples.*—The provisions of this section may be illustrated by the following examples:

Example (1). Corporation M adopts a simplified employee pension arrangement. The corporation would like to contribute 7.5% of an employee's first $10,000 in compensation and 5% of all compensation above $10,000. The simplified employee pension arrangement which Corporation M adopts will not be considered discriminatory within the meaning of paragraph (c) of this section because the rate of contribution decreases as compensation increases.

Example (2). Corporation L adopts a simplified employee pension plan. It wishes to contribute to the simplified employee pension of each employee who is currently performing service. The corporation would like to contribute to the simplified employee pensions 5% of the total compensation of each employee who has completed up to 5 years of service and 7% of the total compensation of each employee who has completed more than 5 years of service. The simplified employee pension plan which Corporation L adopts will be considered discriminatory within the meaning of paragraph (c) of this section because the employer contributions do not bear a uniform relationship to each employee's total compensation. [Reg. §1.408-8.]

IRAs: SEPs: Reports and Information

Individual Retirement Plans: Simplified Employee Plans.—Reproduced below is the text of proposed Reg. §1.408-9, relating to individual retirement plans and simplified employee pensions (published in the Federal Register on July 14, 1981).

§1.408-9. Reports for simplified employee pensions.—(a) *Information to be furnished upon adoption of plan.*—(1) An employer who adopts a definite written allocation formula for making contributions to an employee's simplified employee pension shall furnish the employee in writing the following information:

(i) A notice that the simplified employee pension arrangement has been adopted,

(ii) The requirements which an employee must meet in order to receive a contribution under the agreement,

(iii) The basis upon which the employer's contribution will be allocated to employees, and

(iv) Such other information that the Commissioner may require.

(2) The information in subparagraph (1) must be furnished to an employee no later than a reasonable time after the later of the time the employee becomes employed or the time of the adoption of the simplified employee pension arrangement.

(3) The Commissioner may relieve employers from furnishing any or all of the information specified in subparagraph (1).

(b) *Information to be furnished for a calendar year.*—(1) For each calendar year, the employer shall furnish to the employee a written statement indicating the amount of employer contributions made to the employee's individual retirement account or individual retirement annuity under the simplified employee pension arrangement. This requirement is satisfied if the information is on the employee's W-2 for the calendar year for which the contribution is made. Amounts described in §1.408-7(f)(1) which are not considered made under the simplified employee pension arrangement should not be included.

(2) The information required to be furnished by subparagraph (1) shall be furnished to the employee no later than the later of 30 days after the contribution or January 31 following the calendar year for which the contribution was made.

(c) The Internal Revenue Service may require reports to be filed with the Service with respect to employees who cannot be located by the employer (see §1.408-7(d)(2)). Such reports shall include such information and shall be filed in the time and manner as the Commissioner specifies.

(d) *Effective date.*—The provisions of this section are effective for calendar years beginning after December 31, 1978. [Reg. §1.408-9.]

IRAs: SEPs: Investment in Collectibles

Individual Retirement Plans: Simplified Employee Pensions: Qualified Voluntary Employee Contributions.—Reproduced below is the text of proposed Reg. §1.408-10, relating to individual retirement plans, simplified employee pensions and qualified voluntary employee contributions (published in the Federal Register on January 23, 1984).

☐ Par. 4. There is added after proposed §1.408-9, 46 Fed. Reg. 36209 (1981), the following new section:

§1.408-10. Investment in collectibles.—(a) *In general.*—The acquisition by an individual retirement account or by an individually-directed account under a plan described in section 401(a) of any collectible shall be treated (for purposes of section 402 and 408) as a distribution from such account in an amount equal to the cost to such account of such collectible.

(b) *Collectible defined.*—For purposes of this section, the term "collectible" means—

(1) Any work of art,

(2) Any rug or antique,

(3) Any metal or gem,

(4) Any stamp or coin,

(5) Any alcoholic beverage,

(6) Any musical instrument,

(7) Any historical objects (documents, clothes, etc.), or

(8) Any other tangible personal property which the Commissioner determines is a "collectible" for purposes of this section.

(c) *Individually-directed account.*—For purposes of this section, the term "individually-directed account" means an account under a plan that provides for individual accounts and that has the effect of permitting a plan participant to invest or control the manner in which the account will be invested.

(d) *Acquisition.*—For purposes of this section, the term acquisition includes purchase, exchange, contribution, or any method by which an individual retirement account or individually-directed account may directly or indirectly acquire a collectible.

(e) *Cost.*—For purposes of this section, cost means fair market value.

(f) *Premature withdrawal penalty.*—The ten percent penalty described in section 72(m)(5) and 408(f)(1) shall apply in the case of a deemed distribution from an individual retirement account described in paragraph (a) of this section.

(g) *Amounts subsequently distributed.*—When a collectible is actually distributed from an individual retirement account or an individually-directed account, any amounts included in gross income because of this section shall not be included in gross income at the time when the collectible is actually distributed.

(h) *Effective date.*—This section applies to property acquired after December 31, 1981, in taxable years ending after such date. [Reg. § 1.408-10.]

Deferred Compensation Plans: Service Providers

Deferred Compensation Plans: Service Providers.—Reg. § 1.409A-4 and amendments to Reg. § 1.409A-0, relating to the calculation of amounts includible in income under Code Sec. 409A(a) and the additional taxes imposed by such section with respect to service providers participating in certain nonqualified deferred compensation plans, are proposed (published in the Federal Register on December 8, 2008) (REG-148326-05). Proposed Reg. § 1.409A-4(a)(1)(ii)(B) withdrawn by REG-123854-12 on June 22, 2016.

Par. 2. Section 1.409A-0 is amended by adding entries for § 1.409A-4 to read as follows:

§ 1.409A-0. Table of contents.

* * *

(h) Effective/applicability date.

* * *

Par. 3. Section 1.409A-4 is added to read as follows:

§1.409A-4. Calculation of amount includible in income and additional income taxes.—(a) *Amount includible in income due to failure to meet the requirements of section 409A(a)*.—(1) *In general*.—(i) *Calculation formula*.—The amount includible in income for a service provider's taxable year due to a failure to meet the requirements of section 409A(a) with respect to a plan is the excess (if any) of—

(A) The service provider's total amount deferred under the plan for the taxable year, including the amount of any payments of amounts deferred under the plan to (or on behalf of) the service provider during such taxable year; over

(B) The portion of such amount, if any, that is either subject to a substantial risk of forfeiture (as defined in §1.409A-1(d) and applying paragraph (a)(1)(ii)(B) of this section) or has been previously included in income (as defined in §1.409A-4(a)(3)).

(ii) *Each taxable year analyzed independently*.—(A) *In general*.—An amount is includible in income under section 409A(a) for a taxable year only if a plan fails to meet the requirements of section 409A(a) during such taxable year. Whether an amount is includible in income for a taxable year due to a failure to meet the requirements of section 409A(a) during such taxable year is determined independently of whether such amounts are also includible in income due to a failure to meet the requirements of section 409A(a) in a previous or subsequent taxable year. Accordingly, an amount may be includible in income for a taxable year during which a plan fails to meet the requirements of section 409A(a), even if the same amount was includible in income in a previous taxable year, except to the extent provided in §1.409A-4(a)(3) (identification of amount previously included in income).

(B) [Reg. §1.409A-4(a)(1)(ii)(B) was withdrawn and re-proposed by REG-123854-12 on June 22, 2016.]

(iii) *Examples*.—The following examples illustrate the provisions of this paragraph (a)(1). For each of the examples, Employee A is an individual taxpayer with a calendar year taxable year. Employee A has a total amount deferred under a nonqualified deferred compensation plan of $0 in 2010, $100,000 in 2011, and $250,000 in 2012. No payments are made under the plan. The plan under which the amounts are deferred fails to meet the requirements of section 409A(a) during 2011 and 2012. The examples read as follows:

Example 1. With respect to Employee A, at no time is any deferred amount subject to a substantial risk of forfeiture. Employee A has $100,000 includible in income under section 409A(a) for 2011, because no portion of the total deferred amount for 2011 is subject to a substantial risk of forfeiture or has previously been included in income. If that $100,000 is included in income for 2011, Employee A has $150,000 includible in income under section 409A(a) for 2012 because for the taxable year 2012 the $100,000 is previously included in income (see paragraphs (a)(1)(i)(B) and (a)(3) of this section). If that $100,000 is not included in income for 2011, Employee A has $250,000 includible in income under section 409A(a) for 2012. Employee A does not avoid the requirement to include $100,000 in income under section 409A(a) for 2011 by including $250,000 in income under section 409A(a) for 2012.

Example 2. The same facts as *Example 1*, except that, with respect to Employee A, the statute of limitations on assessments has expired for 2011, but has not expired for 2012. Employee A has $250,000 includible in income under section 409A(a) for 2012, because no portion of the total deferred amount for 2012 is subject to a substantial risk of forfeiture or has previously been included in income.

(2) *Identification of the portion of the total amount deferred for a taxable year that is subject to a substantial risk of forfeiture*.—(i) *In general*.—The portion of the total amount deferred for a taxable year that is subject to a substantial risk of forfeiture (as defined in §1.409A-1(d)) is determined as of the last day of the service provider's taxable year. Accordingly, an amount may be includible in income under section 409A(a) for a taxable year even if such amount is subject to a substantial risk of forfeiture during the taxable year if the substantial risk of forfeiture lapses during such taxable year, including if the substantial risk of forfeiture lapses after the date the nonqualified deferred compensation plan under which the amount is deferred first fails to meet the requirements of section 409A(a).

(ii) *Example*.—The following example illustrates the provisions of this paragraph (a)(2): Employee B is an individual taxpayer with a calendar year taxable year. Employee B has a total amount deferred under a nonqualified deferred compensation plan of $0 for 2010, $100,000 for 2011, and $250,000 for 2012. No payments are made under the plan. Under the terms of the plan, if Employee B voluntarily separates from service before July 1, 2012, Employee B will forfeit 50 percent of the Employee B's total amount deferred under the plan. If Employee B voluntarily separates from service after June 30, 2012 but before July 1, 2013, Employee B will forfeit 20 percent of the total amount deferred under the plan. If Employee B voluntarily separates from service after June 30, 2013, Employee B will not forfeit any amount deferred under the plan. As of December 31, 2011, 50 percent of the total amount deferred under the plan ($50,000) is subject to a substantial risk of forfeiture, and the remaining amount deferred under the plan ($50,000) is not subject to a substantial risk of forfeiture. As of December 31, 2012, 20 percent of the total amount deferred under the plan ($50,000) is subject to a substantial risk of forfeiture, and the remaining amount deferred under the plan ($200,000) is not subject to a substantial risk of forfeiture. At all times the terms of the plan meet the requirements of section 409A(a) and the applicable regulations, and through May 31, 2012, the plan is operated in a manner that complies with the terms of the plan. On June 1, 2012, the plan is operated in a manner that fails to meet the requirements of section 409A(a). For purposes of determining the amount includible in income under section

409A(a), except as provided in paragraph (a)(1)(ii)(B) of this section, the portion of the total amount deferred for 2012 that is subject to a substantial risk of forfeiture is $50,000 (20 percent of $250,000).

(3) *Identification of amount previously included in income.*—(i) *In general.*—For purposes of this section, an amount is previously included in income only if the service provider has included the amount in income under an applicable provision of the Internal Revenue Code for a previous taxable year. An amount is treated as included in income for a taxable year only to the extent that the amount was properly includible in income and the service provider actually included the amount in income (including on an original or amended return or as a result of an IRS examination or a final decision of a court of competent jurisdiction). For future taxable years, the amount previously included in income is reduced to reflect any amount that was paid during the taxable year for which the amount was included in income, any amount allocated to a payment made under the plan under paragraph (f) of this section, and any amount deductible under paragraph (g) of this section.

(ii) *Examples.*—The following examples illustrate the provisions of this paragraph (a)(3). For all of the examples, Employee C is an individual taxpayer with a calendar year taxable year. Employee C has a total amount deferred under a nonqualified deferred compensation plan of $0 in 2010, $100,000 in 2011, and $250,000 in 2012. With respect to Employee C, the statute of limitations on assessments has not expired for 2011 or 2012. Except as otherwise explicitly provided in the following examples, Employee C has not included in income for 2011 on any original or amended tax return any amount deferred under the plan, none of the $250,000 total amount deferred for 2012 has previously been included in income, no payments are made under the plan, and at no time is any deferred amount subject to a substantial risk of forfeiture. The plan under which the amounts are deferred fails to meet the requirements of section 409A(a) during 2011 and 2012. The examples read as follows:

Example 1. After filing an original Federal income tax return for 2011 that did not include any amount in income under section 409A(a), on April 1, 2013, Employee C files an amended Federal income tax return for 2011 and properly includes $100,000 in income under section 409A(a) for 2011. For purposes of determining the amount includible in income under section 409A(a) for 2012, $100,000 of the $250,000 total amount deferred for 2012 has previously been included in income with respect to the plan. For 2012, Employee C includes in income $150,000 under section 409A(a) on Employee C's original Federal income tax return. As of January 1, 2013, the amount that Employee C has previously included in income under section 409A(a) with respect to the plan is $250,000.

Example 2. The facts are the same as in *Example 1,* except that Employee C receives a $10,000 payment in 2011 so that the total amount deferred for 2012 is $240,000. For purposes of determining the amount includible in income under section 409A(a) for 2012, the $100,000 amount previously included in income is reduced by the $10,000 payment so that $90,000 of the $240,000 total amount deferred for 2012 has previously been included in income. For 2012, Employee C includes in income $150,000 under section 409A(a) on Employee C's original Federal income tax return. As of January 1, 2013, the amount that Employee C has previously included in income under section 409A(a) with respect to the plan is $240,000.

Example 3. The facts are the same as in *Example 2.* Due to deemed investment losses during 2013, Employee C has an $80,000 total amount deferred under the plan for 2013. On December 31, 2013, Employee C's total amount deferred ($80,000) is paid to Employee C as a single sum payment. Pursuant to paragraph (f) of this section, $80,000 of the $240,000 amount previously included in income is allocated to the $80,000 payment so that none of the $80,000 is includible in income. In addition, pursuant to paragraph (g) of this section, Employee C is entitled to deduct $160,000 for 2013 equal to the remaining amount previously included in income the right to which is permanently lost. Because the entire $240,000 amount previously included in income has been allocated to a payment under paragraph (f) of this section or was deductible under paragraph (g) of this section, no portion of such amount is treated as previously included in income for 2014 or any subsequent taxable year. As of January 1, 2014, the amount that Employee C has previously included in income under section 409A(a) with respect to the plan is $0.

(b) *The total amount deferred under a plan for a taxable year.*—(1) *Application of general rules and specific rules for specific types of plans.*—Paragraph (b)(2) of this section provides general rules governing the determination of the total amount deferred under a plan for a taxable year, including the treatment of plans providing for alternative times and forms of payment and plans providing for certain payments the amount of which is determined by a formula that includes one or more variables dependent upon future events (formula amounts). Paragraphs (b)(3) through (b)(6) of this section provide specific rules governing the determination of the total amount deferred under certain types of plans. Except as otherwise provided, any applicable rules of paragraphs (b)(3) through (b)(6) of this section are applied in conjunction with the general rules provided in paragraph (b)(2) of this section.

(2) *General definition of total amount deferred.*—(i) *General calculation rules.*—Except as otherwise provided, the total amount deferred for a taxable year equals the present value of the future payments to which the service provider has a legally binding right under the plan as of the last day of the taxable year, plus the amount of any payments of amounts deferred under the plan to (or on behalf of) the service provider during such taxable year. For purposes of this section, present value means the value, as of a specified date, of an amount or series of amounts due thereafter, determined in accordance with the rules and assumptions of this paragraph (b)(2), as applicable, where each amount is multiplied by the probability that the condition or conditions on which payment of the amount is contingent will be satisfied, also determined in accordance with the rules and assumptions set forth in this paragraph (b)(2), as applicable, dis-

counted according to an assumed rate of interest to reflect the time value of money. For this purpose, a discount for the probability that an employee will die before commencement of benefit payments is permitted, but only to the extent that benefits will be forfeited upon death. In addition, the present value cannot be discounted for the probability that payments will not be made (or will be reduced) because of the unfunded status of the plan, the risk associated with any deemed or actual investment of amounts deferred under the plan, the risk that the service recipient, the trustee, or another party will be unwilling or unable to pay, the possibility of future plan amendments, the possibility of a future change in the law, or similar risks or contingencies. If the amount payable under a plan or the value of a benefit under a plan is expressed in a currency other than the U.S. dollar, the total amount deferred is translated from foreign currency into U.S. dollars at the spot exchange rate on the last day of the service provider's taxable year. No adjustment is made to the total amount deferred to reflect the risk that the currency in which the amount payable or the value of the benefit is expressed may in the future increase or decrease in value with respect to the U.S. dollar or any other currency.

(ii) *Actuarial assumptions and methods.*—(A) *Requirement of reasonable actuarial assumptions and methods.*—For purposes of this section, the present value must be determined as of the last day of the service provider's taxable year using actuarial assumptions and methods that are reasonable as of that date, including an interest rate for purposes of discounting for present value that is reasonable as of that date.

(B) *Use of an unreasonable actuarial assumption or method.*—If any actuarial assumption or method used to determine the total amount deferred for a taxable year under a plan is not reasonable, as determined by the Commissioner, then the total amount deferred is determined by the application of the AFR and, if applicable, the applicable mortality table under section 417(e)(3)(A)(ii)(I) (the 417(e) mortality table), both determined as of the last month of the taxable year for which the amount deferred is being determined. For purposes of this section, *AFR* means the appropriate applicable Federal rate (as defined pursuant to section 1274(d)) based on annual compounding, for the last month of the taxable year for which the amount includible in income is being determined. The period for which excess interest will be credited, beginning with the last day of the taxable year and ending with the date the excess interest will no longer be credited (determined in accordance with the payment timing assumptions set forth in paragraph (b)(2)(vi) and (vii) of this section) is used to determine the appropriate AFR (short-term, mid-term, or long-term).

(iii) *Crediting of earnings and losses.*—The earnings and losses credited under a plan as of the last day of the service provider's taxable year pursuant to the plan are given effect only to the extent the plan's terms reasonably reflect the value of the service provider's rights under the plan. For example, a plan's method of determining the amount of such earnings or losses generally will be respected for purposes of determining the total amount deferred for the taxable year, provided that the earnings and losses are credited at least once per taxable year. If earnings and losses are not credited at least annually, the total amount deferred is calculated as if the earnings or losses were credited as of the last day of the taxable year. In addition, any change in the schedule for crediting earnings during the taxable year for which the total amount deferred is calculated that would reduce the earnings credited for a taxable year in which an amount is required to be included in income under section 409A(a) is disregarded for such taxable year. For example, if a plan is amended during a taxable year that is a calendar year to change the date for crediting earnings from December 31 to July 1 of that year and the plan fails to meet the requirements of section 409A(a) during that year, the amendment is disregarded for purposes of determining the total amount deferred for the year and December 31 is treated as the date for crediting earnings and losses. If no further changes are made to the plan with respect to the crediting of earnings and losses, for subsequent taxable years, July 1 is treated as the date for crediting earnings and losses.

(iv) *Application of the general calculation rules to formula amounts.*—(A) *In general.*—With respect to a right to a payment to which this paragraph applies, the amount payable for purposes of determining the total amount deferred for the taxable year must be determined based on all of the facts and circumstances existing as of the close of the last day of the taxable year. Such determination must reflect reasonable, good faith assumptions with respect to any contingencies as to the amount of the payment, both with respect to each contingency and with respect to all contingencies in the aggregate. An assumption based on the facts and circumstances as of the close of the last day of a taxable year may be reasonable even if the facts and circumstances change in a subsequent year so that if the amount payable were determined for such subsequent year, the amount payable would be a greater (or lesser) amount. In such a case, the increase (or decrease) due to the change in the facts and circumstances is treated as earnings (or losses). This paragraph (b)(2)(iv) applies to the extent that the amount payable in a future taxable year is a formula amount to the extent that the amount payable in a future taxable year is dependent upon factors that, after applying the assumptions and other rules set out in this section, are not determinable as of the end of the taxable year for which the total amount deferred is being calculated, so that the amount payable may not readily be determined as of the end of such taxable year under the other provisions of this section. If a portion of a deferred amount is determinable under the other rules of this paragraph (b)(2), the determination of the amount deferred with respect to such portion must be determined under the rules applicable to amounts that are not formula amounts, and only the balance of the deferred amount is determined under this paragraph.

(B) *Examples.*—The following examples illustrate the provisions of this paragraph (b)(2)(iv):

Example 1. On January 1, 2020, a service provider receives a legally binding right to a payment of one percent of the service recipient's net profits for the calendar years 2020, 2021, and 2022, payable on the later of January 1, 2024 or the service provider's separation from service. The amount payable is a formula amount and this paragraph (b)(2)(iv) applies.

Example 2. On January 1, 2020, a service provider receives a legally binding right to a payment of the greater of one percent of the service recipient's net profits for the calendar years 2020, 2021, and 2022 or $10,000, payable on the later of January 1, 2024 or the service provider's separation from service. The portion of the amount payable that is a $10,000 payment, payable at the later of January 1, 2024 or the service provider's separation from service, is not a formula amount. The portion of the amount payable that is the excess, if any, of one percent of the service recipient's net profits for the calendar years 2020, 2021, and 2022 over $10,000 is a formula amount and this paragraph (b)(2)(iv) applies.

Example 3. On January 1, 2020, a service provider receives a legally binding right to payment equal to the value of 10,000 shares of service recipient stock, payable on the later of January 1, 2024 or the service provider's separation from service. Because the amount payable may increase or decrease only due to a change in value of a predetermined actual investment (10,000 shares of service recipient stock), the amount payable is not treated as a formula amount and this paragraph (b)(2)(iv) does not apply.

(v) *Treatment of payment restrictions.*—Except as specifically provided, a restriction on the payment of all or part of a deferred amount that will or may lapse under the terms of the plan, including a risk of forfeiture that is not a substantial risk of forfeiture as defined in § 1.409A-1(d) or is disregarded under § 1.409A-4(a)(1)(ii)(B), is ignored for purposes of determining the total amount deferred under the plan. Accordingly, in calculating the total amount deferred, there is no reduction to account for a risk that the amount may be forfeited if the risk of forfeiture is not a substantial risk of forfeiture. For example, if an amount deferred is subject to forfeiture under a noncompetition provision applicable for a prescribed period, the forfeiture provision is disregarded for purposes of determining the total amount deferred for the taxable year.

(vi) *Treatment of alternative times and forms of a future payment.*—(A) *In general.*—For purposes of determining the total amount deferred for a taxable year, if payment of a deferred amount may be made at alternative times or in alternative forms, each amount deferred under the plan is treated as payable at the time and under the form of payment for which the present value is highest. A time and form of payment is available to the extent a deferred amount under the plan may be payable in such time and form of payment under the plan's terms. If the service recipient has commenced payment of a deferred amount in a time and form of payment under the plan, or the service provider or service recipient has elected a time and form of payment under the plan, and under the plan's terms neither party can change such time and form of payment without the consent of the other party (and such consent requirement has substantive significance), the time and form of payment elected or the time and form of payment in which payments have commenced is treated as the sole available time and form of payment for such amount. If an alternative time and form of payment is available only at the service recipient's discretion, the time and form of payment is not available unless the service provider has a legally binding right under the principles of § 1.409A-1(b)(1) to any additional value that would be generated by the service recipient's exercise of such discretion. For purposes of determining the value of each available time and form of payment, the assumptions and methods described in this paragraph (b)(2)(vi) are applied, and then the value of each available time and form of payment is determined in accordance with the other applicable rules provided in paragraph (b) of this section.

(B) *Effect of status of service provider on available times and forms of payment.*—For purposes of determining whether a time and form of payment is available, if eligibility for a time and form of payment depends upon the service provider's status as of a future date, the service provider is assumed to continue in the service provider's status as of the last day of the taxable year. However, if the eligibility requirement is not bona fide and does not serve a bona fide business purpose, the eligibility requirement will be disregarded and the service provider will be treated as eligible for the alternative time and form of payment. For this purpose, an eligibility condition based upon the service provider's marital status (including status as a registered domestic partner or similar requirement), parental status, or status as a U.S. citizen or lawful permanent resident under section 7701(b)(6) is presumed to be bona fide and serve a bona fide business purpose. Notwithstanding the foregoing, if eligibility for a certain time or form of payment includes a bona fide requirement that the service provider provide additional services after the end of the taxable year, the time and form of payment is not treated as an available time and form of payment. The rules of this paragraph (b)(2)(vi)(B) apply regardless of whether the service provider's status changes during a subsequent taxable year.

(vii) *Treatment of payment triggers based upon events.*—(A) *In general.*—For purposes of determining the total amount deferred for a taxable year, if a payment trigger has occurred on or before the last day of the taxable year, a deferred amount payable upon such trigger is treated as payable at the time the payment is scheduled to be made under the terms of the plan. If the payment trigger has not occurred on or before the last day of the taxable year, the trigger is treated as occurring on the earliest possible date the trigger reasonably could occur based on the facts and circumstances as of the last day of the taxable year, and the deferred amount is treated as payable based upon the schedule of payments that would be triggered by such occurrence. Notwithstanding the foregoing, if the payment trigger requires a separation from service, a termination of employment, or other similar reduction or cessation of services, the service provider is treated as meeting such requirement as of the last day of the taxable year. For purposes of determining the earliest date the payment trigger reasonably could occur, whether the payment trigger actually occurs in a subsequent taxable year is disregarded. For purposes of this paragraph (b)(2)(vii), a payment trigger means an event (not including the mere passage of time) upon which an amount may become payable. Generally if an amount would be payable in a different time and form of payment depending upon some characteristic of an event, each type of event upon which an amount would become payable is treated as a separate payment trigger. For example, if an amount would be payable as a single sum payment if one subsidiary corporation of a service recipient that consists of multiple corporations is sold, but as an installment payment if another subsidiary corporation of the same service recipient is sold, then the sale of the one subsidiary corporation is treated as a separate payment trigger from the sale of the other subsidiary corporation.

(B) *Certain payment triggers disregarded.*—The possibility that the following payment triggers will occur in the future is disregarded for purposes of determining the total amount deferred (but not for purposes of determining whether the plan otherwise complies with the requirements of section 409A(a)):

(1) A payment trigger that, if the trigger were the sole trigger determining when the amount would become payable, would cause the amount to be subject to a substantial risk of forfeiture, provided that if there is more than one payment trigger applicable to an amount that otherwise would be disregarded under this paragraph (b)(2)(vii)(B)(*1*), none of such payment triggers will be disregarded unless all such payment triggers, if applied in combination as the only payment triggers, would also cause the amount to be subject to a substantial risk of forfeiture.

(2) An unforeseeable emergency (as defined in § 1.409A-3(i)(3)).

(viii) *Treatment of amounts that may qualify as short-term deferrals.*—For purposes of calculating the total amount deferred for a taxable year, the right to a payment that, under the terms of the arrangement and the facts and circumstances as of the last day of the taxable year, may be a short-term deferral as defined under § 1.409A-1(b)(4), is not included in the total amount deferred. In addition, even if such amount is not paid by the end of the applicable 2 1/2 month period so that the amount is deferred compensation, the amount is not includible in the total amount deferred until the service provider's taxable year in which the applicable 2 1/2 month period expires.

(ix) *Examples.*—The following examples illustrate the provisions of paragraphs (b)(2)(vi) through (viii) of this section. For all of the examples, the service provider is an individual taxpayer who is an employee of the service recipient, the service provider has a calendar year taxable year, and the total amount deferred is being calculated for the 68 taxable year ending December 31, 2010. In each case, the service provider is not entitled to earnings on the amount deferred. The examples read as follows:

Example 1. Employee D, who is employed by Employer Z, is entitled to commence receiving payments at age 65. The plan provides that Employee D will receive a single sum payment, except that, after Employee D attains age 62 but before Employee D attains age 64 (whether or not Employee D is then employed by Employer Z), Employee D can elect to receive payments as a single life annuity. Employee D is age 54 as of December 31, 2010. For purposes of determining the available times and forms of payment, Employee D is assumed to survive to age 62 and be eligible to elect a single life annuity. Accordingly, for purposes of determining the total amount deferred for 2010, the amount is treated as payable as either a single sum payment or a single life annuity, whichever is more valuable.

Example 2. Employee E is entitled to a single life annuity commencing on January 1, 2020 if Employee E is not married as of January 1, 2020. Employee E is entitled to either a single life annuity or a subsidized joint and survivor annuity commencing on January 1, 2020 if Employee E is married as of January 1, 2020. Employee E is not married as of December 31, 2010. For purposes of determining the total amount deferred for 2010, Employee E is assumed to remain unmarried indefinitely, so that the subsidized joint and survivor annuity is not an available form of payment. Accordingly, for purposes of determining the total amount deferred for 2010, the amount is treated as payable as a single life annuity commencing January 1, 2020.

Example 3. Employee F is entitled to a series of three payments of $1,000 due on January 1, 2020, January 1, 2021, and January 1, 2022. Under the plan's terms, Employer X has the discretion to accelerate one or more of the payments, provided that no payment may be made before January 1, 2020. Because there is no reduction in the amount payable if a payment is accelerated, an accelerated payment is more valuable than a payment made in accordance with the three-year schedule of payments. If Employee F does not have a legally binding right to a single sum payment on January 1, 2020 (or any other form of accelerated payment), then an accelerated payment is not an available time and form of payment and, for purposes of determining the total amount deferred for 2010, the amount is treated as payable as a series of three payments of $1,000 on January 1, 2020, January 1, 2021, and January 1, 2022.

Example 4. The facts are the same as in *Example 3*, except that Employer X has no discretion to accelerate one or more of the payments. Rather, Employee F has the right to accelerate one or more of the payments provided that a payment may not be paid at any date before the later of January 1, 2020 or the date 12 months after the date of such election. As of December 31, 2010, the earliest date upon which Employee F may elect to have a payment made is January 1, 2020. Because there is no reduction in the amount payable if a payment is accelerated, the earliest possible date of payment is the most valuable time and form of payment. Accordingly, for purposes of determining the total amount deferred for 2010, the amount is treated as payable as a single sum payment of $3,000 on January 1, 2020.

Example 5. Employee G is entitled to a single sum payment upon separation from service if Employee G separates from service before January 1, 2020 and a single life annuity if Employee G separates from service after December 31, 2019. As of December 31, 2010, Employee G has not separated from service. Under paragraph (b)(2)(vi)(A) of this section, the total amount deferred is determined based upon the amount that would be payable if Employee G separated from service on December 31, 2010. Accordingly, the single life annuity is not treated as an available time and form of payment, so that the amount is treated as payable as a single sum payment upon separation from service.

Example 6. Employee H is entitled to a single sum payment of deferred compensation upon the earlier of January 1, 2020 or an unforeseeable emergency. Because the payment upon an unforeseeable emergency is disregarded, for purposes of determining the total amount deferred, the deferred amount is treated as payable only on January 1, 2020.

Example 7. Employee I is entitled to a single sum payment of deferred compensation upon the earlier of January 1, 2020 or Employee I's involuntary separation from service. Under the facts and circumstances existing at the time the right to the payment was granted, if the deferred amount had been payable only upon Employee I's involuntary separation from service, the amount would have been subject to a substantial risk of forfeiture. Under paragraph (b)(2)(iv)(B) of this section, the right to a payment upon the Employee I's involuntary separation from service is disregarded, and the amount is treated as payable only on January 1, 2020.

Example 8. Employee J is entitled to a single sum payment of deferred compensation upon the earlier of January 1, 2020 or Employee J's separation from service. As of December 31, 2010, Employee J has not separated from service. Under paragraph (b)(2)(vi)(A) of this section, the total amount deferred is determined based upon the amount that would be payable if Employee J separated from service on December 31, 2010 and therefore had the right to receive the payment on December 31, 2010. The total amount deferred for 2010 is the greater of the amount that would be payable on December 31, 2010 or the present value of the amount that would be payable on January 1, 2020.

Example 9. Employee K is entitled to a single sum payment of deferred compensation upon the earlier of January 1, 2020 or the first day of the third month following Employee K's separation from service. As of December 31, 2010, Employee K has not separated from service. Under paragraph (b)(2)(vi)(A) of this section, the total amount deferred is determined based upon the amount that would be payable if Employee K separated from service on December 31, 2010, and therefore had a right to a payment on March 1, 2011. The total amount deferred for 2010 is the greater of the present value as of December 31, 2010 of the amount that would be payable on March 1, 2011 or the present value as of December 31, 2010 of the amount that would be payable on January 1, 2020.

Example 10. Employee L is entitled to a single sum payment of deferred compensation upon the earlier of January 1, 2020 or a separation from service that occurs on or before July 1, 2010. As of December 31, 2010, Employee L has not separated from service. For purposes of determining the total amount deferred, the right to be paid upon a separation from service on or before July 1, 2010 is ignored because it is no longer a possible payment trigger, and the amount is treated as payable only on January 1, 2020.

Example 11. Employee M is entitled to a single sum payment of deferred compensation upon the earliest of the date Employee M dies, Employee M attains age 65, or a child of Employee M becomes a full-time student at an accredited college or university (whether or not Employee M continues to be employed on such date). As of December 31, 2010, Employee M has a 10-year old child who is in the fifth grade. For purposes of determining the total amount deferred, the earliest time that the payment reasonably could be due upon Employee M's child entering a college or university is August 1, 2018. Thus, the total amount deferred for 2010 is the more valuable of the amount that would be payable on the Employee M's 65th birthday and the amount that would be payable on August 1, 2018. Because any additional value that would be payable upon Employee M's death is a death benefit excluded from the definition of deferred compensation under section 409A(d)(1)(B) and § 1.409A-1(a)(5), that additional value, if any, is not required to be calculated.

(3) *Account balance plans.*—(i) *In general.*—For purposes of this section, if benefits are provided under a nonqualified deferred compensation plan that is described in § 1.409A-1(c)(2)(i)(A) or (B) (an account balance plan), the present value of the amount payable equals the amount credited to the service provider's account as of the last day of the taxable year, including both the principal amount credited to the account, and any earnings or losses attributable to the principal amounts credited to the account through the last day of the taxable year. For purposes of this section, earnings or losses means any increase or decrease in the amount credited to a service provider's account that is attributable to amounts previously credited to the service provider's account, regardless of whether the plan denominates that increase or decrease as earnings or losses. For rules related to the crediting of earnings, see paragraph (b)(2)(iii) of this section. For rules relating to earnings based on an unreasonable interest rate or a rate of return based on an investment other than a single predetermined actual investment or a single reasonable interest rate, see paragraph (b)(3)(ii) of this section.

(ii) *Unreasonable rate of return.*—(A) *Application.*—This paragraph (b)(3)(ii) applies to an account balance plan under which the amount of earnings or losses credited is not based on either a predetermined actual investment, within the meaning of § 31.3121(v)(2)-1(d)(2)(i)(B) of this chapter, or a rate of interest that is not higher than a reasonable rate of interest, within the meaning of § 31.3121(v)(2)-1(d)(2)(i)(C) of this chapter, as determined by the Commissioner.

(B) *Unreasonably high interest rate.*—If the earnings or losses to be credited under a plan are based on an unreasonably high rate of interest, the amount deferred under the plan is equal to the present value as of the end of the taxable year (using a reasonable interest rate) of the amount that will be credited to the service recipient's account using the unreasonably high rate for the entire period for which the unreasonably high interest will be credited under the plan, beginning with the last day of such taxable year and ending with the date the unreasonably high interest will no longer be credited (determined in accordance with the payment timing assumptions set forth in paragraph (b)(2)(vi) and (vii) of this section). If the service recipient fails to use a reasonable interest rate to determine the amount includible in income, AFR will be used. For purposes of this section, *AFR* means the appropriate applicable Federal rate (as defined pursuant to section 1274(d)) based on annual compounding, for the last month of the taxable year for which the amount includible in income is being determined. The period described in the first sentence of this paragraph (b)(3)(ii)(B) is used to determine the appropriate AFR (short-term, mid-term, or long-term). For purposes of this paragraph (b)(3)(ii)(B), an unreasonably high interest rate includes a fixed interest rate that exceeds an interest rate that is reasonable, within the meaning of § 31.3121(v)(2)-1(d)(2)(i)(C) of this chapter.

(C) *Other rates of return*.—If the amount of earnings or losses credited is based on a rate of return that is not an unreasonably high interest rate, within the meaning of paragraph (b)(3)(ii)(B) of this section, but is also not a predetermined actual investment, within the meaning of § 31.3121(v)(2)-1(d)(2)(i)(B) of this chapter or a rate of interest that is no more than a reasonable rate of interest, within the meaning of § 31.3121(v)(2)-1(d)(2)(i)(C) of this chapter, the amount payable is a formula amount.

(4) *Reimbursement and in-kind benefit arrangements*.—For purposes of this section, if benefits for a service provider are provided under a nonqualified deferred compensation plan described in § 1.409A-1(c)(2)(i)(E) (a reimbursement arrangement), or under a nonqualified deferred compensation plan that would be described in § 1.409A-1(c)(2)(i)(E) except that the amounts, separately or in the aggregate, constitute a substantial portion of either the overall compensation earned by the service provider for performing services for the service recipient or the overall compensation received due to a separation from service, the arrangement is treated as providing for a formula amount to the extent that the expenses to be reimbursed are not explicitly identified to be a specific amount. Notwithstanding the foregoing, if the expenses eligible for reimbursement are limited, it is presumed that the limit reflects the reasonable amount of eligible expenses that the service provider will incur at the earliest possible date during the time period to which the limit applies, and for which the service provider will request reimbursement at the earliest possible date that the service provider may request reimbursement. This presumption may be rebutted only by demonstrating by clear and convincing evidence that it is unreasonable to assume that a service provider would incur such amount of expenses during the applicable time period. This presumption is not applicable to any reimbursement arrangement to which § 1.409A-3(i)(1)(iv)(B) applies (certain medical reimbursement arrangements). In addition, this paragraph (b)(4) also applies to an arrangement providing a service provider a right to in-kind benefits from the service recipient, or a payment by the service recipient directly to the person providing the goods or services to the service provider.

(5) *Split-dollar life insurance arrangements*.—For purposes of this section, if benefits for a service provider are provided under a nonqualified deferred compensation plan described in § 1.409A-1(c)(2)(i)(F) (a split-dollar life insurance arrangement), the amount of the future payment to which the service provider is entitled is treated as the amount that would be includible in income under § 1.61-22 or § 1.7872-15 (as applicable) or, if those regulations are not applicable, the amount that would be includible in income under any other applicable guidance. For this purpose, the payment timing assumptions set forth in paragraph (b)(2)(vi) and (vii) of this section generally apply. However, in the case of an arrangement subject to § 1.7872-15, to the extent the assumptions set forth in paragraph (b)(2)(vi) and (vii) of this section conflict with the provisions of § 1.7872-15, the provisions of § 1.7872-15 apply, and the conflicting assumptions set forth in paragraph (b)(2)(vi) and (vii) of this section do not apply. In either case, for purposes of determining the total amount deferred under the plan for the taxable year, the benefits under the split-dollar life insurance arrangement are included only to the extent that the right to such benefits constitutes a right to deferred compensation under § 1.409A-1(b).

(6) *Stock rights*.—If a stock right has not been exercised during the service recipient's taxable year, and remains outstanding as of the last day of the service provider's taxable year for which the total amount deferred is being calculated, the total amount deferred under the stock right for such taxable year is the excess of the fair market value of the underlying stock on the last day of the service provider's taxable year (determined in accordance with § 1.409A-1(b)(5)(iv)) over the sum of the stock right's exercise price plus any amount paid for the stock right. If a stock right has been exercised during the service provider's taxable year, the payment amount for purposes of calculating the total amount deferred for the taxable year under the stock right is the excess of the fair market value of the underlying stock (as determined in accordance with § 1.409A-1(b)(5)(iv)) on the date of exercise over the sum of the exercise price of the stock right and any amount paid for the stock right.

(7) *Anti-abuse provision*.—The Commissioner may disregard all or part of the rules of paragraphs (b)(2) through (b)(6) of this section or all or part of the plan's terms if the Commissioner determines based on all of the facts and circumstances that the plan terms have been established to eliminate or minimize the total amount deferred under the plan determined in accordance with the rules of paragraphs (b)(2) through (b)(6) of this section and if the rules of paragraphs (b)(2) through (b)(6) of this section were applied or such plan terms were given effect, the total amount deferred would not reasonably reflect the present value of the right. For example, if a plan provides that a deferred amount is payable upon a separation from service but also contains a provision that the amount will be forfeited upon a separation from service occurring on the last day of the service provider's taxable year (so that the application of paragraph (b)(2)(vii)(A) of this section treating the service provider as separating from service on the last day of the taxable year for purposes of determining the timing of the payment in calculating the total amount deferred would result in a zero amount deferred), the latter provision will be disregarded.

(c) *Additional 20 percent tax under section 409A(a)(1)(B)(i)(II)*.—With respect to an amount required to be included in income under section 409A(a) for a taxable year, the amount is subject to an additional income tax equal to 20 percent of the amount required to be included in income under section 409A(a).

(d) *Premium interest tax under section 409A(a)(1)(B)(i)(I).*—(1) *In general.*—With respect to an amount required to be included in income under section 409A(a) for a taxable year, the amount is subject to an additional income tax equal to the amount of interest at the underpayment rate plus one percentage point on the underpayments that would have occurred had the deferred compensation been includible in the service provider's gross income for the taxable year in which first deferred or, if later, the first taxable year in which such deferred compensation is not subject to a substantial risk of forfeiture. The amount required to be allocated to determine the additional tax described in this paragraph (d) is the amount required to be included in income under section 409A(a) for the taxable year, regardless of whether additional amounts were deferred under the plan in previous years.

(2) *Identification of taxable year deferred amount was first deferred or vested.*—(i) *Method of identification.*—The following method is applied for purposes of determining the taxable year or years in which an amount required to be included in income under section 409A(a) was first deferred and not subject to a substantial risk of forfeiture.

(A) For each taxable year preceding the taxable year for which the deferred amount is includible in income (the current taxable year) in which the service provider had an amount deferred under the plan that was not subject to a substantial risk of forfeiture (vested), ending with the later of the first taxable year in which the service provider had no vested amount deferred or the first taxable year beginning after December 31, 2004, calculate the vested total amount deferred for such year. For each year, include any deferred amount that was previously included in income under paragraph (a)(3) of this section but has not been paid, but exclude any amount paid to (or on behalf of) the service provider during such taxable year.

(B) Identify any payments made under the plan to (or on behalf of) the service provider for each taxable year identified in paragraph (d)(2)(i)(A) of this section.

(C) Identify any deemed net investment losses or other net decreases in the amount deferred (other than as a result of a payment) applicable to amounts that are vested for the current taxable year and each preceding taxable year identified in paragraph (d)(2)(i)(A) of this section.

(D) Starting with the first taxable year during which there was a payment identified under paragraph (d)(2)(i)(B) of this section or a loss identified under paragraph (d)(2)(i)(C) of this section (or both), subtract the total payments and loss for such taxable year from the amount determined under paragraph (d)(2)(i)(A) of this section for the earliest taxable year before such year in which there is such an amount, and from the amount determined under paragraph (d)(2)(i)(A) of this section for each subsequent taxable year ending before the taxable year in which the payment was made or the loss incurred. Do not reduce any taxable year-end balance below zero.

(E) Repeat this process for each subsequent taxable year during which there was a payment identified under paragraph (d)(2)(i)(B) of this section or a loss identified under paragraph (d)(2)(i)(C) of this section (or both).

(F) For each taxable year identified in paragraph (d)(2)(i)(A) of this section, determine the excess (if any) of the remaining amount deferred for the taxable year over the remaining amount deferred for the previous taxable year. Treat the amount deferred in taxable years beginning before January 1, 2005 as zero.

(G) Determine how much of the total amount deferred for the current taxable year was previously included in income in accordance with paragraph (a)(3) of this section.

(H) Subtract the amount determined in paragraph (d)(2)(i)(G) of this section from the excess amount determined in paragraph (d)(2)(i)(F) of this section for the earliest taxable year in which there is any such excess amount, but do not reduce the balance below zero. If the amount determined in paragraph (d)(2)(i)(G) of this section exceeds the amount determined in paragraph (d)(2)(i)(F) of this section for that earliest taxable year, subtract the excess from the amount determined in paragraph (d)(2)(i)(F) of this section for the next succeeding taxable year, but do not reduce the balance below zero. Repeat this process until the excess has been reduced to zero. The balance remaining with respect to each taxable year identified in paragraph (d)(2)(i)(A) of this section is the portion of the amount includible in income under section 409A(a) in the current taxable year that was first deferred and vested in that taxable year.

(ii) *Examples.*—The following examples illustrate the provisions of paragraph (d)(2) of this section. In all of the following examples, the service provider is an individual taxpayer with a calendar year taxable year who elects to defer a portion of the bonus that would otherwise be payable to the service provider in each of Year 1 through Year 4. All amounts deferred are deferred under the same plan, and no amount deferred under the plan is ever subject to a substantial risk of forfeiture. The plan does not fail to meet the requirements of section 409A(a) in any year prior to Year 4, and no amounts deferred under the plan are otherwise includible in income until Year 4, except for payments actually made to the service provider. The service provider had no amount deferred under the plan prior to Year 1. The plan fails to meet the requirements of section 409A(a) in Year 4. The examples read as follows:

Example 1.

	Year 1	Year 2	Year 3	Year 4
Opening Total Amount	0	110	275	495
Bonus Deferral	100	150	200	250
Net Gains (Losses)	10	15	20	25
Payments	0	0	0	0

	Year 1	Year 2	Year 3	Year 4
Closing Total Amount	110	275	495	770

(i) The amount required to be included in income under section 409A is 770. To calculate the premium interest tax, the 770 must be allocated to the year or years in which the amount was first deferred and vested.

(ii) *Step A*. Identification of vested total amount deferred excluding payments and including deferred amounts previously included in income.

Year 1	Year 2	Year 3
110	275	495

(iii) *Step B*. Identification of any payments for each year other than Year 4.

Year 1	Year 2	Year 3
0	0	0

(iv) *Step C*. Identification of any other decreases attributable to vested amounts.

Year 1	Year 2	Year 3	Year 4
0	0	0	0

(v) *Steps D and E*. Subtraction of payments and decreases from amounts deferred.

Year 1	Year 2	Year 3
110	275	495
-0	-0	-0
110	275	495

(vi) *Step F*. Subtraction of previous year total from each year's total.

Year 1	Year 2	Year 3
110	275	495
-0	-110	-275
110	165	220

(viii) Because no amount was previously included in income, Step G does not apply. Accordingly, the 770 is allocated such that 110 is treated as first deferred and vested in Year 1, 165 in Year 2, 220 in Year 3. The remainder (275) is treated as first deferred in Year 4, but is not required to be allocated for purposes of the premium interest tax because there is no hypothetical underpayment for such year.

Example 2.

	Year 1	Year 2	Year 3	Year 4
Opening Total Amount	0	110	235	365
Bonus Deferral	100	150	200	250
Net Gains (Losses)	10	(25)	(30)	25
Payments	0	0	(40)	(50)
Closing Total Amount	110	235	365	590

(i) The amount that is includible in income under section 409A(a) for Year 4 is the closing total amount (590), plus the amounts paid during Year 4 that were includible in income (50) or 640. To calculate the premium interest tax, the 640 must be allocated to the year or years in which the amount was first deferred and vested.

(ii) *Step A*. Identification of vested total amount deferred excluding payments and including deferred amounts previously included in income.

Year 1	Year 2	Year 3
110	235	365

(iii) *Step B*. Identification of any payments for each year other than Year 4.

Year 1	Year 2	Year 3
0	0	(40)

(iv) *Step C*. Identification of any other decreases attributable to vested amounts.

Year 1	Year 2	Year 3	Year 4
0	(25)	(30)	0

(v) *Steps D and E.* Subtraction of payments and decreases from amounts deferred.

Year 1	Year 2	Year 3
110	235	365
-25(Year 2)	-40(Year 3)	
-40(Year 3)	-30(Year 3)	
-30(Year 3)		
15	165	365

(vi) *Step F.* Subtraction of previous year total from each year's total.

Year 1	Year 2	Year 3
15	165	365
-0	-15	-165
15	150	200

(vii) Because no amount was previously included in income, Step G does not apply. Accordingly, the 640 is allocated such that 15 is treated as first deferred and vested in Year 1, 150 in Year 2, and 200 in Year 3. The remaining amount includible in income under section 409A for Year 4 (275) is treated as first deferred in Year 4, but is not required to be allocated for purposes of the premium interest tax because there is no hypothetical underpayment for Year 4.

Example 3. (i) The facts are the same as in *Example 2* except 125 was previously included in income under paragraph (a)(3) of this section. Accordingly, of the 590 closing total amount for Year 4 plus the 50 payment during Year 4, or 640, only 515 (640 - 125) must be included in income under section 409A(a). To calculate the premium interest tax, the 125 must be allocated to the year or years in which such amount was first deferred.

(ii) *Step G.* Allocation of amounts previously included in income.

Year 1	Year 2	Year 3
15	150	200
-15	-110	-0
0	40	200

(iii) Accordingly, for purposes of calculating the premium interest tax, the 125 previously included in income is allocated so that of the 515 includible in income under section 409A(a), 0 is treated as first deferred and vested in Year 1, 40 in Year 2, and 200 in Year 3.

(3) *Calculation of hypothetical underpayment for the taxable year during which a deferred amount was first deferred and vested.*—(i) *Calculation method.*—The hypothetical underpayment for a taxable year is determined by treating as an additional cash payment of compensation to the service provider for such taxable year, the amount determined pursuant to paragraph (d)(2) of this section to be the portion of the amount includible in income under section 409A(a) that was first deferred and vested during such taxable year. The hypothetical underpayment is calculated based on the service provider's taxable income, credits, filing status, and other tax information for the year, based on the service provider's original return filed for such year, as adjusted by any examination for such year or any amended return the service provider filed for such 82 year that was accepted by the Commissioner. The hypothetical underpayment must reflect the effect that such additional compensation would have had on the service provider's Federal income tax liability for such year, including the continued availability of any deductions taken, and the use of any carryovers such as carryover losses. For purposes of calculating a hypothetical underpayment in a subsequent year (whether or not a portion of the amount includible in income under section 409A(a) was first deferred and vested in the subsequent year), any changes to the service provider's Federal income tax liability for the subsequent year that would have occurred if the portion of the amount that was first deferred and vested during the previous taxable year had been included in the service provider's income for the previous year must be taken into account. Assumptions not based on the service provider's taxable income, credits, filing status, and other tax information for the year, based on the service provider's original return for such year, as adjusted by any examination for such year or any amended return the service provider filed for such year that was accepted by the Commissioner, may not be applied. For example, the service provider may not assume that some of the additional compensation would have been deferred under the terms of a qualified plan. If the service provider's Federal income tax liability for the taxable year in which an amount required to be included in income under section 409A(a) was first deferred and vested is adjusted (for example, by an amended return or IRS examination), and the adjustment affects the amount of the hypothetical underpayment, the service provider must recalculate the hypothetical underpayment and adjust the amount of premium interest tax due with respect to such inclusion in income under section 409A(a), as appropriate.

(ii) *Examples.*—The following examples illustrate the provisions of paragraph (d)(3)(i) of this section. In all of the following examples, Employee N is an individual taxpayer with a calendar year taxable year. For the year 2020, Employee N has a total amount deferred of $100,000 which is includible in income under section 409A(a). For purposes of determining the premium interest tax, assume that $30,000 was first deferred and vested in 2018, $35,000 was first deferred and vested in 2019, and $35,000 was first deferred and vested in 2020. The first year that Employee N had a vested deferred amount under the plan was 2018. The examples read as follows:

Example 1. For the taxable years 2018 and 2019, Employee N has no carryover losses or other items a change in which could affect the adjusted gross income for a subsequent taxable year. Employee N determines the hypothetical underpayment for 2018 by assuming an additional cash compensation payment of $30,000 for 2018, and determining the hypothetical underpayment of Federal income tax that would result. Employee N determines the hypothetical underpayment for 2019 by assuming an additional cash compensation payment of $35,000 in 2019, and determining the hypothetical underpayment of Federal income tax for 2019 that would result. There is no hypothetical underpayment with respect to hypothetical income in 2020 because the tax payment would not have been due until 2021. Therefore, Employee N is not required to determine a hypothetical underpayment for 2020.

Example 2. The facts are the same as in *Example 1*, except that in 2018, Employee N had an excess charitable contribution the deduction of which was not permitted under section 170(b), and which was carried over to subsequent taxable years under section 170(d). For purposes of determining the hypothetical underpayment for 2018, Employee N uses the charitable contribution deduction that otherwise would have been available if the $30,000 compensation payment had actually been made. Employee N must then calculate the hypothetical underpayment for all subsequent years in a manner that eliminates the portion of any carryovers of excess contributions under section 170(d) related to the charitable contribution in 2018 that would not have been available in such subsequent years as a result of having been deducted in 2018.

Example 3. The facts are the same as in *Example 2*, except that in 2021 the IRS examines Employee N's 2018 return and determines that Employee N had $20,000 in unreported income for that year. In addition to paying the tax deficiency owed for 2018, Employee N must redetermine the hypothetical underpayment for 2018 and recalculate the premium interest tax owed for 2020.

(4) *Calculation of hypothetical premium underpayment interest.*—(i) *Calculation method.*—The amount of hypothetical premium underpayment interest is determined for any taxable year by applying the applicable rate of interest under section 6621 plus one percentage point to determine the underpayment interest under section 6601 that would be due for such underpayment as of the last day of the taxable year for which the amount deferred is includible in income under section 409A(a). The amount of additional income tax under paragraph (d)(2) of this section with respect to an amount required to be included in income under section 409A(a) is the sum of all of the hypothetical premium underpayment interest for all years in which there was determined a hypothetical underpayment.

(ii) *Examples.*—The following examples illustrate the provisions of this paragraph (d)(4). In each of these examples, the service provider is an individual taxpayer with a calendar year taxable year. At all times the total amount deferred under the nonqualified deferred compensation plan is not subject to a substantial risk of forfeiture. The examples read as follows:

Example 1. Employee O has a total amount deferred under a nonqualified deferred compensation plan for 2010 of $100,000. The entire deferred amount was first deferred in 2006. For purposes of calculating the hypothetical premium underpayment interest tax, Employee O first must determine the hypothetical underpayment for taxable years 2006 through 2009 under the rules of paragraph (d)(3) of this section. Then Employee O must determine the underpayment interest under section 6601 that would have accrued, calculated using the applicable underpayment interest rate under section 6621 increased by one percentage point, applied through December 31, 2010. That amount is the premium interest tax that is due for 2010.

Example 2. Employee P has a total amount deferred under a nonqualified deferred compensation plan for 2010 of $100,000. $60,000 of that deferred amount was first deferred in 2006. $30,000 of that amount was first deferred in 2008. $10,000 of that amount was first deferred in 2010. For purposes of calculating the hypothetical premium underpayment interest tax, Employee P first must determine the hypothetical underpayment for taxable years 2006 through 2009 under the rules of paragraph (d)(3) of this section applying $60,000 of hypothetical additional compensation for 2006, and applying $30,000 of hypothetical additional compensation for 2008. The $10,000 of hypothetical additional compensation in 2010 would not result in a hypothetical underpayment because the Federal income tax applicable to that hypothetical additional compensation would not yet be due. Second, Employee P must determine the underpayment interest under section 6601 that would have accrued, calculated using the applicable underpayment interest rate under section 6621 increased by one percentage point, applied through December 31, 2010, for both the hypothetical underpayment occurring in 2006 and the hypothetical underpayment occurring in 2008. The sum of those two amounts is the premium interest tax that is due for 2010.

(e) *Amounts includible in income under section 409A(b).*—[Reserved].

(f) *Application of amounts included in income under section 409A to payments of amounts deferred.*—(1) *In general.*—Section 409A(c) provides that any amount included in gross income under section 409A is not required to be included in gross income under any other provision of this chapter or any other rule of law later than the time provided in this section. An amount included in income under section 409A that has neither been paid in the taxable year the amount was included in income under section 409A nor served as the basis for a deduction under paragraph (g) of this section is allocated to the first payment of an amount deferred under the plan in any year subsequent to the year the amount was included in income under section 409A. To the extent the amount included in income under section 409A exceeds such payment, the excess is allocated to the next payment of an amount deferred under the plan. This process is repeated until the entire amount included in income under section 409A has been paid or the service provider has become entitled to a deduction under paragraph (g) of this section.

(2) *Application of the plan aggregation rules.*—The plan aggregation rules of § 1.409A-1(c)(2) apply to the allocation of amounts previously included in income under section 409A to payments made under the plan. Accordingly, references to an amount deferred under a plan, or a payment of an amount deferred under a plan, refer to an amount deferred or a payment made under all arrangements in which a service provider participates that together are treated as a single plan under § 1.409A-1(c)(2).

(3) *Examples.*—The following examples illustrate the provisions of this section. In each of these examples, the service provider is an individual taxpayer with a calendar year taxable year. Each service provider has a total amount deferred under a nonqualified deferred compensation plan of $0 for 2010, a total amount deferred under the plan of $100,000 for 2011, a total amount deferred under the plan of $250,000 for 2012, and a total amount deferred under the plan of $400,000 for 2013. At all times the total amount deferred under the plan is not subject to a substantial risk of forfeiture. During 2011, the plan fails to comply with section 409A(a) and each service provider includes $100,000 in income under section 409A. Except as otherwise provided in the following examples, the service provider does not receive any payments of amounts deferred under the plan. The examples read as follows:

Example 1. During 2012, Employee Q receives a $10,000 payment under the plan. During 2013, Employee Q receives a $150,000 payment under the plan. For 2012, $10,000 of the $100,000 included in income under section 409A(a) is allocated under paragraph (f)(1) of this section to the $10,000 payment, so that no amount is includible in gross income as a result of such payment and Employee Q retains $90,000 of amounts previously included in income under the plan to allocate to future plan payments. For 2013, the remaining $90,000 included in income under section 409A(a) is allocated to the $150,000 payment, so that only $60,000 is includible in income as a result of such payment.

Example 2. During 2012, Employee R receives a $10,000 payment under the plan. During 2014, Employee R receives a $50,000 payment, equaling the entire amount deferred under the plan. For 2012, $10,000 of the $100,000 previously included in income is allocated pursuant to paragraph (f)(1) of this section to the $10,000 payment, so that no amount is includible in gross income as a result of such payment. For 2014, $50,000 of the $90,000 remaining amount previously included in income is allocated pursuant to paragraph (f)(1) of this section to the $50,000 payment, so that no amount is includible in gross income as a result of such payment. Provided that the requirements of paragraph (g) of this section are otherwise met, Employee R is entitled to a deduction for 2014 equal to the remaining amount ($40,000) that was previously included in income under section 409A(a) that has not been allocated to a payment under the plan.

(g) *Forfeiture or other permanent loss of right to deferred compensation.*—(1) *Availability of deduction to the service provider.*—If a service provider has included a deferred amount in income under section 409A, but has not actually received payment of such deferred amount or otherwise allocated the amount included in income under paragraph (f) of this section, the service provider is entitled to a deduction for the taxable year in which the right to that amount of deferred compensation is permanently forfeited under the plan's terms or the right to the payment of the amount is otherwise permanently lost. The deduction to which the service provider is entitled equals the deferred amount included in income under section 409A in a previous year, less any portion of such deferred amount previously included in income under section 409A that was allocated under paragraph (f) of this section to amounts paid under the plan, including any deferred amount paid in the year the right to any remaining deferred compensation is permanently forfeited or otherwise lost. For this purpose, a mere diminution in the deferred amount under the plan due to deemed investment loss, actuarial reduction, or other decrease in the amount deferred is not treated as a permanent forfeiture or loss of the right if the service provider retains the right to an amount deferred under the plan (whether or not such right is subject to a substantial risk of forfeiture as defined in § 1.409A-1(d)). In addition, a deferred amount is not treated as permanently forfeited or otherwise lost if the obligation to make the payment of such deferred amount is substituted for another deferred amount or obligation to make a payment in a future year. However, a deferred amount is treated as permanently lost if the service provider's right to receive the payment of the deferred amount becomes wholly worthless during the taxable year. Whether the right to the payment of a deferred amount has become wholly worthless is determined based on all the facts and circumstances existing as of the last day of the relevant service provider taxable year.

(2) *Application of the plan aggregation rules.*—For purposes of determining whether the right to a deferred amount is permanently forfeited or otherwise lost, the plan aggregation rules of § 1.409A-1(c) apply. Accordingly, if the right to an identified deferred amount under a plan is permanently forfeited or otherwise lost, but an additional amount remains deferred under the plan, the service provider is not entitled to a deduction.

(3) *Examples.*—The following examples illustrate the provisions of this paragraph (g). In each example, the service provider is an individual taxpayer who has a calendar year taxable year and the service recipient does not experience bankruptcy at any time or otherwise discharge any obligation to make a payment of a deferred amount, except as expressly provided in the example. The examples read as follows:

Example 1. For 2010, Employee S has a total amount deferred under an elective account balance plan of $1,000,000. The plan fails to meet the requirements of section 409A(a) during 2010 and Employee S includes $1,000,000 in income under section 409A(a) for the year 2010. In 2011, Employee S experiences investment losses but no payments before July 1, 2011, such that Employee S's account balance under the plan is $500,000. On July 1, 2011, Employee S separates from service and receives a $500,000 payment equal to the entire amount deferred under the plan, and retains no other right to deferred compensation under the plan (including all arrangements aggregated with the arrangement under which the payment was made). For 2011, Employee S is entitled to deduct $500,000 (which is the amount Employee S previously included in income under section 409A(a) ($1,000,000) less the amount actually received by Employee S ($500,000)).

Example 2. For 2010, Employee T has a total amount deferred under an elective account balance plan of $1,000,000. The plan fails to meet the requirements of section 409A(a) for 2010 and Employee T includes $1,000,000 in income under section 409A(a) for 2010. For 2011, Employee T has a total amount deferred under the plan of $500,000, due solely to the deemed investment losses attributable to Employee T's account balance (with no payments being made during 2011). Because Employee T retains the right to an amount deferred under the plan, Employee T is not entitled to a deduction for 2011 as a result of the deemed investment losses.

Example 3. For 2010, Employee U has a total amount deferred under an elective account balance plan of $1,000,000. The elective account balance plan consists of one arrangement providing for salary deferrals with an amount deferred for 2010 of $600,000, and another arrangement providing for bonus deferrals with an amount deferred for 2010 of $400,000. The plan fails to meet the requirements of section 409A(a) during 2010 and Employee U includes $1,000,000 in income under section 409A(a) for 2010. On July 1, 2011, Employee U's account balance attributable to the salary deferral arrangement is $500,000, the reduction of which is due solely to deemed investment losses in 2011 and not any payments. On July 1, 2011, Employee U is paid the $500,000 equaling the entire account balance attributable to the salary deferral arrangement. On December 31, 2011, Employee U has an account balance attributable to the bonus deferral arrangement equal to $300,000. Because Employee U retains an amount deferred under the elective account balance plan, Employee U is not entitled to a deduction for 2011 as a result of the deemed investment losses.

(h) *Effective/applicability date.*—The rules of this section apply to taxable years ending on or after the date of publication of the Treasury decision adopting these rules as final regulation in the **Federal Register**. [Reg. § 1.409A-4.]

Nonqualified Deferred Compensation Plans: Section 409A

Nonqualified Deferred Compensation Plans: Section 409A.—Amendments to Reg. §§ 1.409A-0—1.409A-4 and 1.409A-6, affecting participants, beneficiaries, sponsors, and administrators of nonqualified deferred compensation plans, are proposed (published in the Federal Register on June 22, 2016) (corrected August 4, 2016) (REG-123854-12).

Par. 2. Section 1.409A-0 is amended by:

1. Revising the entry for § 1.409A-1 by adding paragraph (b)(13).
2. Redesignating paragraph (q) as paragraph (r), and revising paragraph (q) in § 1.409A-1.
3. Revising the entry to paragraph (d) in § 1.409A-3.
4. Revising the entry to u)(4)(xiii) in § 1.409A-3.

The revisions and addition read as follows:

§ 1.409A-0. Table of contents.

* * *

§ 1.409A-1 Definitions and covered plans.

* * *

(b) * * *

(13) Recurring part-year compensation.

* * *

(q) References to a payment being made.

(r) Application of definitions and rules.

* * *

§ 1.409A-3 Permissible Payments.

* * *

(d) * * *

(1) In general.

(2) Payments due following death.

* * *

(j) * * *

(4) * * *

(xiii) Certain offsets.

(A) De minimis offset.

(B) Compliance with Federal debt collection laws.

* * *

Par. 3. Section 1.409A-1 is amended by:

1. Revising paragraph (a)(4).
2. Revising the first sentence of paragraph (b)(1).
3. Revising paragraphs (b)(3) and (b)(4)(i)(B).
4. Revising paragraph (b)(4)(ii).
5. Adding a last sentence to paragraph (b)(5)(iii)(A).
6. Revising paragraph (b)(5)(iii)(E)(*1*).
7. Revising the first sentence of paragraph (b)(5)(vi)(A).
8. Revising paragraphs (b)(5)(vi)(E) and (b)(5)(vi)(F).
9. Revising paragraph (b)(9)(iii)(A).
10. Adding a last sentence to paragraph (b)(11).
11. Adding paragraph (b)(13).
12. Revising paragraphs (h)(4) and (h)(5).
13. Redesignating paragraph (q) as paragraph (r) and revising paragraphs (q) and (r).

The revisions and additions read as follows:

§1.409A-1. Definitions and covered plans.

* * *

(a) * * *

(4) *Section 457(f) and section 457A plans.*—A deferred compensation plan under section 457(f) or a nonqualified deferred compensation plan under section 457A may be a nonqualified deferred compensation plan for purposes of this paragraph (a). The rules of section 409A apply to nonqualified deferred compensation plans separately and in addition to any requirements applicable to such plans under section 457(f) or section 457A. In addition, nonelective deferred compensation of non-employees described in section 457(e)(12) and a grandfathered plan or arrangement described in §1.457-2(k)(4) may be a nonqualified deferred compensation plan for purposes of this paragraph (a). The term *nonqualified deferred compensation plan* does not include a length of service award to a *bona fide* volunteer under section 457(e)(11)(A)(ii).

* * *

(b) * * *

(1) * * * Except as otherwise provided in paragraphs (b)(3) through (b)(13) of this section, a plan provides for the deferral of compensation if, under the terms of the plan and the relevant facts and circumstances, the service provider has a legally binding right during a taxable year to compensation that, pursuant to the terms of the plan, is or may be payable to (or on behalf of) the service provider in a later taxable year. * * *

* * *

(3) *Compensation payable pursuant to the service recipient's customary payment timing arrangement.*—A deferral of compensation does not occur solely because compensation is paid after the last day of the service provider's taxable year pursuant to the timing arrangement under which the service recipient normally compensates service providers for services performed during a payroll period described in section 3401(b), or with respect to a non-employee service provider, a period not longer than the payroll period described in section 3401(b) or if no such payroll period exists, a period not longer than the earlier of the normal timing arrangement under which the service recipient normally compensates non-employee service providers or 30 days after the end of the service provider's taxable year.

(4) * * *

(i) * * *

(B) A payment is treated as actually or constructively received for purposes of this paragraph (b)(4) if it is made in accordance with the rules in §1.409A-1(q).

* * *

(ii) *Certain delayed payments.*—A payment that otherwise qualifies as a short-term deferral under paragraph (b)(4)(i) of this section but is made after the applicable 2$^1/_2$ month period may continue to qualify as a short-term deferral if the taxpayer establishes that it was administratively impracticable for the service recipient to make the payment by the end of the applicable 2$^1/_2$ month period and, as of the date upon which the legally binding right to the compensation arose, such impracticability was unforeseeable, or the taxpayer establishes that making the payment by the end of the applicable 2$^1/_2$ month period would have jeopardized the ability of the service recipient to continue as a going concern, and provided further that the payment is made as soon as administratively practicable or as soon as the payment would no longer have such effect. For purposes of this paragraph (b)(4)(ii), an action or failure to act of the service provider or a person under the service provider's control, such as a failure to provide necessary information or documentation, is not an unforeseeable event. In addition, a payment that otherwise qualifies as a short-term deferral under paragraph (b)(4)(i) of this section but is made after the applicable 2$^1/_2$ month period may continue to qualify as a short-term deferral if the taxpayer establishes that the service recipient reasonably anticipated that the service recipient's deduction with respect to such payment otherwise would not be permitted by application of section 162(m), and, as of the date the legally binding right to the payment arose, a reasonable person would not have anticipated the application of section 162(m) at the time of the payment, and provided further that the payment is made as soon as reasonably practicable following the first date on which the service recipient anticipates or reasonably should anticipate that, if the payment were made on such date, the service recipient's deduction with respect to such payment would no longer be restricted due to the application of section 162(m). Further, a payment that otherwise qualifies as a short-term deferral under paragraph (b)(4)(i) of this section but is made after the applicable 2$^1/_2$ month period may continue to qualify as a short-term deferral if the taxpayer establishes that the service recipient reasonably anticipated that making the payment by the end of the applicable 2$^1/_2$ month period would have violated Federal securities laws or other applicable law, provided that the payment is made as soon as reasonably practicable following the first date on which the service recipient anticipates or reasonably should anticipate that making the payment would not cause such violation. The making of a payment that would cause inclusion in gross income or the application of any penalty provision or other provision of the Internal Revenue Code is not treated as a violation of applicable law. For additional rules applicable to certain transaction-based compensation, see §1.409A–3(i)(5)(iv)(A).

* * *

(5) * * *

(iii) * * *

(A) * * * The stock price will not be treated as based on a measure other than the fair market value to the extent that the amount payable upon the service provider's involuntary separation from service for cause, or the occurrence of a condition within the service provider's control such as noncompliance with a noncompetition or nondisclosure agreement (whether or not the condition is specified at the time the stock right is granted), is based on a measure that results in a payment of less than fair market value.

* * *

(E) *Eligible issuer of service recipient stock.*—*(1) In general.*—The term *eligible issuer of service recipient stock* means the corporation or other entity for which the service provider provides direct services on the date of grant of the stock right or a corporation or other entity for which it is reasonably anticipated that the service provider will begin providing direct services within 12 months after the date of grant, and any corporation or other entity (a related corporation or other entity) in a chain of corporations or other entities in which each corporation or other entity has a controlling interest in another corporation or other entity in the chain, ending with the corporation or other entity that has a controlling interest in the corporation or other entity for which the service provider provides direct services on the date of grant of the stock right or the corporation or other entity for which it is reasonably anticipated that the service provider will begin providing direct services within 12 months after the date of grant. If it is reasonably anticipated that a service provider will begin providing services for a corporation or other entity within 12 months after the date of grant, that corporation or other entity (or a related corporation or other entity) will be an eligible issuer of service recipient stock only if the services in fact commence within 12 months after the date of grant and the stock otherwise is service recipient stock at the time the services begin or, if services do not commence within that 12 month period, the right is forfeited. For this purpose, the term *controlling interest* has the same meaning as provided in § 1.414(c)-2(b)(2)(i), substituting the language "at least 50 percent" for "at least 80 percent" each place it appears in § 1.414(c)-2(b)(2)(i). In addition, if the use of such stock with respect to the grant of a stock right to a service provider is based upon legitimate business criteria, the term *controlling interest* has the same meaning as provided in § 1.414(c)-2(b)(2)(i), substituting the language "at least 20 percent" for "at least 80 percent" each place it appears in § 1.414(c)-2(b)(2)(i). For purposes of determining ownership of an interest in an organization, the rules of §§ 1.414(c)-3 and 1.414(c)-4 apply. The determination of whether a grant is based on legitimate business criteria is based on the facts and circumstances, focusing primarily on whether there is a sufficient nexus between the service provider and the issuer of the stock right so that the grant serves a legitimate non-tax business purpose other than simply providing compensation to the service provider that is excluded from the requirements of section 409A. For example, when stock of a corporation that owns an interest in a joint venture involving an operating business is granted to service providers of the joint venture who are former service providers of such corporation, that use is generally based upon legitimate business criteria, and therefore could be service recipient stock with respect to such service providers if the corporation owns at least 20 percent of the joint venture and the other requirements of this paragraph (b)(5)(iii) are met. Similarly, the legitimate business criteria requirement generally would be met if the corporate venturer issued such a right to a service provider of the joint venture who it reasonably expected would become a service provider of the corporate venturer. However, if a service provider has no real nexus with a corporate venturer, such as generally happens when the corporate venturer is a passive investor in the service recipient joint venture, a stock right issued to the service provider on the investor corporation's stock generally would not be based upon legitimate business criteria. Similarly, if a corporation holds only a minority interest in an entity that in turn holds a minority interest in the entity for which the service provider performs services, such that the corporation holds only an insubstantial indirect interest in the entity receiving the services, legitimate business criteria generally would not exist for issuing a stock right on the corporation's stock to the service provider.

* * *

(vi) * * *

(A) * * * The term *option* means the right or privilege of a person to purchase stock from a corporation by virtue of an offer of the corporation continuing for a stated period of time, whether or not irrevocable, to sell such stock at a price determined under paragraph (b)(5)(vi)(D) of this section, such person being under no obligation to purchase.

* * *

(E) *Exercise.*—The term *exercise,* when used in reference to an option, means the act of acceptance by the holder of the option of the offer to sell contained in the option. In general, the time of exercise is the time when there is a sale or a contract to sell between the corporation and the holder. A promise to pay the exercise price is not an exercise of the option unless the holder of the option is subject to personal liability on such promise. An agreement or undertaking by the service provider to make payments under a stock purchase plan is not the exercise of an option to the extent the payments made remain subject to the withdrawal by or refund to the service provider.

(F) *Transfer.*—The term *transfer,* when used in reference to the transfer to a person of a share of stock pursuant to the exercise of an option, means the transfer of ownership of such share, or the transfer of substantially all the rights of ownership. Such transfer must, within a reasonable time, be evidenced on the books of the corporation. A transfer may occur even if a share of stock is subject to a substantial risk of forfeiture or is not otherwise transferable immediately after the date of exercise. A transfer does not fail to occur merely because, under the terms of the arrangement, the person may not dispose of the share for a specified period of time, or the share is subject to a right of first refusal or a right to acquire the share at the share's fair market value at the time of the sale.

* * *

(9) * * *

(iii) * * *

(A) The separation pay (other than amounts described in paragraphs (b)(9)(iv) and (v) of this section) does not exceed two times the lesser of—

(1) The service provider's annualized compensation based upon the annual rate of pay for services provided to the service recipient for the service provider's taxable year preceding the taxable year in which the service provider has a separation from service with such service recipient (or for the taxable year in which the service provider has a separation from service if the service provider had no compensation from the service recipient in the preceding taxable year), adjusted for any increase during that year that was expected to continue indefinitely if the service provider had not separated from service; or

(2) The maximum amount that may be taken into account under a qualified

retirement plan pursuant to section 401(a)(17) for the calendar year in which the service provider has a separation from service.

* * *

(11) * * * In addition, a plan does not provide for a deferral of compensation for purposes of this paragraph (b) to the extent it provides for a payment of reasonable attorneys' fees or other reasonable expenses incurred by the service provider to enforce any *bona fide* legal claim against the service recipient with respect to the service relationship between the service provider and the service recipient.

* * *

(13) *Recurring part-year compensation.*—A plan in which a service provider participates that provides for the payment of recurring part-year compensation (as defined in § 1.409A-2(a)(14)), whether or not at the service provider's election, does not provide for a deferral of compensation for purposes of this paragraph (b) if the plan does not defer payment of any of the recurring part-year compensation to a date beyond the last day of the 13th month following the first day of the service period for which the recurring part-year compensation is paid, and the amount of the service provider's recurring part-year compensation does not exceed the annual compensation limit under section 401(a)(17) for the calendar year in which the service period commences.

* * *

(h) * * *

(4) *Asset purchase transactions.*—If as part of a sale or other disposition of assets by one service recipient (seller) to an unrelated service recipient (buyer), a service provider of the seller would otherwise experience a separation from service with the seller, the seller and the buyer may retain the discretion to specify, and may specify, whether a service provider providing services to the seller immediately before the asset purchase transaction and providing services to the buyer after and as a result of the asset purchase transaction has experienced a separation from service for purposes of this paragraph (h), provided that the asset purchase transaction results from *bona fide*, arm's length negotiations, all service providers providing services to the seller immediately before the asset purchase transaction and providing services to the buyer after and as a result of the asset purchase transaction are treated consistently (regardless of position at the seller) for purposes of applying the provisions of any nonqualified deferred compensation plan, and such treatment is specified in writing no later than the closing date of the asset purchase transaction. For purposes of this paragraph (h)(4), references to a sale or other disposition of assets, or an asset purchase transaction, refer only to a transfer of substantial assets, such as a plant or division or substantially all of the assets of a trade or business, and do not refer to a stock purchase treated as a deemed asset sale under section 338. For purposes of this paragraph (h)(4), whether a service recipient is related to another service recipient is determined under the rules provided in paragraph (f)(2)(ii) of this section.

(5) *Dual status.*—If a service provider provides services both as an employee of a service recipient and as an independent contractor of the service recipient, the service provider must separate from service both as an employee and as an independent contractor to be treated as having separated from service. Notwithstanding the foregoing, if a service provider provides services both as an employee of a service recipient and as a member of the board of directors of a corporate service recipient (or an analogous position with respect to a non-corporate service recipient), the services provided as a director are not taken into account in determining whether the service provider has a separation from service as an employee for purposes of a nonqualified deferred compensation plan in which the service provider participates as an employee that is not aggregated with any plan in which the service provider participates as a director under paragraph (c)(2)(ii) of this section. In addition, if a service provider provides services both as an employee of a service recipient and as a member of the board of directors of a corporate service recipient (or an analogous position with respect to a non-corporate service recipient), the services provided as an employee are not taken into account in determining whether the service provider has a separation from service as a director for purposes of a nonqualified deferred compensation plan in which the service provider participates as a director that is not aggregated with any plan in which the service provider participates as an employee under paragraph (c)(2)(ii) of this section.

* * *

(q) *References to a payment being made.*—A payment is made or an amount is paid or received when any taxable benefit is actually or constructively received, which includes a transfer of cash, a transfer of property includible in income under section 83, any other event that results in the inclusion in income under the economic benefit doctrine, a contribution to a trust described in section 402(b) at the time includible in income under section 402(b), a transfer or creation of a beneficial interest in a section 402(b) trust at the time includible in income under section 402(b), and the inclusion of an amount in income under 457(f)(1)(A). In addition, a payment is made or an amount is paid or received upon the transfer, cancellation, or reduction of an amount of deferred compensation in exchange for benefits under a welfare benefit plan, a fringe benefit excludible under section 119 or section 132, or any other benefit that is excludible from gross income. Notwithstanding the foregoing, the occurrence of any of the following events is not a payment:

(1) a grant of an option that does not have a readily ascertainable fair market value (as defined under § 1.83-7(b));

(2) a transfer of property (including an option that has a readily ascertainable fair market value) that is substantially nonvested (as defined under § 1.83-3(b)) with respect to which the service provider does not make a valid election under section 83(b); or

(3) a contribution to a trust described in section 402(b) or a transfer or creation of a beneficial interest in a section 402(b) trust unless and until the amount is includible in income under section 402(b).

(r) *Application of definitions and rules.*—The definitions and rules set forth in paragraphs (a) through (q) of this section apply for purposes of section 409A, this section, and §§1.409A-2 through 1.409A-6.

Par. 4. Section 1.409A-2 is amended by revising paragraph (b)(2)(i) to read as follows:

§1.409A-2. Deferral elections.

* * *

(b) * * *

(2) *Definitions of payments for purposes of subsequent changes in the time or form of payment.*—(i) *In general.*—Except as provided in paragraphs (b)(2)(ii) and (iii) of this section, the term *payment* refers to each separately identified amount to which a service provider is entitled to payment under a plan on a determinable date, and includes amounts applied for the benefit of the service provider. An amount is separately identified only if the amount may be objectively determined under a nondiscretionary formula. For example, an amount identified as 10 percent of the account balance as of a specified payment date would be a separately identified amount. The determination of whether a payment is or has been made for purposes of this paragraph (b) is made in accordance with the rules in §1.409A-1(q). For additional rules relating to the application of this paragraph (b) to amounts payable at a fixed time or pursuant to a fixed schedule, see §1.409A-3(i)(1).

* * *

Par. 5. Section 1.409A-3 is amended by:

1. Revising paragraph (b).
2. Redesignating paragraph (d) as paragraph (d)(1) and revising the heading of paragraph (d)(1).
3. Adding paragraph (d)(2).
4. Revising paragraphs (i)(5)(iii) and (i)(5)(iv)(A).
5. Revising paragraphs (j)(1) and (j)(2).
6. Revising paragraph (j)(4)(iii)(B).
7. Revising paragraphs (j)(4)(ix)(A) and (j)(4)(ix)(C).
8. Revising paragraph (j)(4)(xiii).

The revisions and additions read as follows:

§1.409A-3. Permissible payments.

* * *

(b) *Designation of payment upon a permissible payment event.*—Except as otherwise specified in this section, a plan provides for the payment upon an event described in paragraph (a)(1), (2), (3), (5), or (6) of this section if the plan provides the date of the event is the payment date, or specifies another payment date that is objectively determinable and nondiscretionary at the time the event occurs. A plan may also provide that a payment upon an event described in paragraph (a)(1), (2), (3), (5), or (6) of this section is to be made in accordance with a schedule that is objectively determinable and nondiscretionary based on the date the event occurs and that would qualify as a fixed schedule under paragraph (i)(1) of this section if the payment event were instead a fixed date, provided that the schedule must be fixed at the time the permissible payment event is designated. In addition, a plan may provide that a payment, including a payment that is part of a schedule, is to be made during a designated taxable year of the service provider that is objectively determinable and nondiscretionary at the time the payment event occurs such as, for example, a schedule of three substantially equal payments payable during the first three taxable years following the taxable year in which a separation from service occurs. A plan may also provide that a payment, including a payment that is part of a schedule, is to be made during a designated period objectively determinable and nondiscretionary at the time the payment event occurs, but only if the designated period both begins and ends within one taxable year of the service provider or the designated period is not more than 90 days and the service provider does not have a right to designate the taxable year of the payment (other than an election that complies with the subsequent deferral election rules of §1.409A-2(b)). However, in the case of a payment to be made following the death of the service provider or a beneficiary who has become entitled to payment due to the service provider's death, in addition to the permitted designated periods described in the previous sentence, the designated period may begin on the date of death and end on December 31 of the first calendar year following the calendar year during which the death occurs, and the payment recipient may have the right to designate the taxable year of payment. If a plan provides for a period of more than one day following a payment event during which a payment may be made, such as permitting payment within 90 days following the date of the event, the payment date for purposes of the subsequent deferral rules under §1.409A–2(b) is treated as the first possible date upon which a payment could be made under the terms of the plan. A plan may provide for payment upon the earliest or latest of more than one event or time, provided that each event or time is described in paragraphs (a)(1) through (6) of this section. For examples illustrating the provisions of this paragraph, see paragraph (i)(1)(vi) of this section.

* * *

(d) *When a payment is treated as made upon the designated payment date.*—(1) *In general.*—* * *

(2) *Payments due following death.*—A payment specified to be made under the plan on any date within the period beginning on the date of the death of the service provider, or of a beneficiary who has become entitled to payment due to the service provider's death, and ending on December 31 of the first calendar year following the calendar year during which the death occurs (including a payment specified to be made upon death) is treated as made on the date specified under the plan if the payment is made on any date during this period, regardless of whether the payment recipient designates the taxable year of payment. Further, any change to the time or form of a payment that is specified to be made under the plan during this period to provide that

the payment will be made on any other date during this period will not be treated as a subsequent deferral election for purposes of § 1.409A-2(b)(1) or an impermissible acceleration for purposes of § 1.409A-3(j)(1).

* * *

(i) * * *

(5) * * *

(iii) *Attribution of stock ownership.*—For purposes of paragraph (i)(5) of this section, section 318(a) applies to determine stock ownership. Stock underlying a vested option is considered owned by the person who holds the vested option (and the stock underlying a nonvested option is not considered owned by the person who holds the nonvested option). For purposes of the preceding sentence, however, if a vested option is exercisable for stock that is not substantially vested (as defined by § 1.83-3(b) and (j)), the stock underlying the option is not treated as owned by the person who holds the option.

* * *

(iv) *Special rules for certain delayed payments pursuant to a change in control event.*—(A) *Certain transaction-based compensation.*—Payments of compensation related to a change in control event described in paragraph (i)(5)(v) of this section (change in the ownership of a corporation) or paragraph (i)(5)(vii) of this section (change in the ownership of a substantial portion of a corporation's assets) that occur because a service recipient purchases its stock held by the service provider or because the service recipient or a third party purchases a stock right or a statutory stock option described in § 1.409A-1(b)(5)(ii) held by a service provider, or that are calculated by reference to the value of stock of the service recipient (collectively, transaction-based compensation), may be treated as paid on a designated date or pursuant to a payment schedule that complies with the requirements of section 409A if the transaction-based compensation is paid on the same schedule and under the same terms and conditions as apply to payments to shareholders generally with respect to stock of the service recipient pursuant to a change in control event described in paragraph (i)(5)(v) of this section (change in the ownership of a corporation) or as apply to payments to the service recipient pursuant to a change in control event described in paragraph (i)(5)(vii) of this section (change in the ownership of a substantial portion of a corporation's assets). In addition, to the extent that the transaction-based compensation is paid not later than five years after the change in control event, the payment of such compensation will not violate the initial or subsequent deferral election rules set out in § 1.409A–2(a) and (b) solely as a result of such transaction-based compensation being paid pursuant to such schedule and terms and conditions. The payment or agreement to pay transaction-based compensation payable with respect to a stock right described in § 1.409A-1(b)(5)(i)(A) or (B) or a statutory stock option described in § 1.409A-1(b)(5)(ii) also will not cause the stock right or statutory stock option to be treated as having provided for the deferral of compensation from the original grant date solely as a result of the transaction-based compensation being paid on the same schedule and under the same terms and conditions as apply to payments to shareholders generally with respect to stock of the service recipient pursuant to the change in control event described in paragraph (i)(5)(v) of this section (change in the ownership of a corporation) or as apply to payments to the service recipient pursuant to the change in control event described in paragraph (i)(5)(vii) of this section (change in the ownership of a substantial portion of a corporation's assets) and the transaction-based compensation is paid not later than five years after the change in control event. If before and in connection with a change in control event described in paragraph (i)(5)(v) or (i)(5)(vii) of this section, transaction-based compensation that would otherwise be payable as a result of such event is made subject to a condition on payment that is a substantial risk of forfeiture (as defined in § 1.409A–1(d), without regard to the provisions of that section under which additions or extensions of forfeiture conditions are disregarded) and the transaction-based compensation is payable under the same terms and conditions as apply to payments made to shareholders generally with respect to stock of the service recipient pursuant to a change in control event described in paragraph (i)(5)(v) of this section or to payments to the service recipient pursuant to a change in control event described in paragraph (i)(5)(vii) of this section, for purposes of determining whether such transaction-based compensation is a short-term deferral the requirements of § 1.409A–1(b)(4) are applied as if the legally binding right to such transaction-based compensation arose on the date that it became subject to such substantial risk of forfeiture.

* * *

(j) *Prohibition on acceleration of payments.*—(1) *In general.*—Except as provided in paragraph (j)(4) of this section, a nonqualified deferred compensation plan may not permit the acceleration of the time or schedule of any payment or amount scheduled to be paid pursuant to the terms of the plan, and no such accelerated payment may be made whether or not provided for under the terms of such plan. For purposes of determining whether a payment of deferred compensation has been made, the rules of paragraph (f) of this section (on substituted payments) apply. For purposes of this paragraph (j), an impermissible acceleration does not occur if payment is made in accordance with plan provisions or an election as to the time and form of payment in effect at the time of initial deferral (or added in accordance with the rules applicable to subsequent deferral elections under § 1.409A-2(b)) pursuant to which payment is required to be made on an accelerated schedule as a result of an intervening payment event that is an event described in paragraph (a)(1), (2), (3), (5) or (6) of this section. For such purpose, the intervening payment event may apply with respect to either the service provider or, following the service provider's death, a beneficiary who becomes entitled to payment due to the service provider's death (substituting such beneficiary for the service provider in the definitions of *disability* in paragraph (i)(4) of this section and *unforeseeable emergency* in paragraph (i)(3) of this section, as applicable). For example, a plan may provide that a participant will receive six installment payments commencing at separation from service, and also provide that if the participant dies after such payments commence but before all payments have been made, all remaining amounts will be paid in a lump sum payment. Additionally, it is not an acceleration of the time or schedule of payment of a deferral of compensation if a service recipient waives or accelerates the satisfaction of a condition constituting a substantial risk of forfeiture applicable to such deferral of compensation, provided that the requirements of section 409A (including the requirement that the payment be made upon a permissible payment event) are otherwise satisfied with respect to such deferral of compensation. For example, if a nonqualified deferred compensation plan provides for a lump sum payment of the vested benefit upon separation from service, and the benefit vests under the plan only after 10 years of service, it is not a violation of the requirements of section 409A if the service recipient reduces the vesting requirement to five years of service, even if a service provider becomes vested as a result and receives a payment in connection with a separation from service before the service provider would have completed 10 years of service. However, if the plan in this example had provided for a payment on a fixed date, rather than at separation from service, the date of payment could not be accelerated due to the accelerated vesting. For the definition of a payment for purposes of this paragraph (j), see § 1.409A–2(b)(5) (coordination of the subsequent deferral election rules with the prohibition on acceleration of payments). For other permissible payments, see § 1.409A–2(b)(2)(iii) (certain immediate payments of remaining installments) and paragraph (d) of this section (certain payments made no more than 30 days before the designated payment date).

(2) *Application to multiple payment events.*—The addition of a permissible payment event, the deletion of a permissible payment event, or the substitution of one permissible payment event for another permissible payment event, results in an acceleration of a payment if the addition, deletion, or substitution could result in the payment being made on an earlier date than such payment would have been made absent such addition, deletion, or substitution. Notwithstanding the previous sentence, the addition of death, disability (as defined in paragraph (i)(4) of this section), or an unforeseeable emergency (as defined in paragraph (i)(3) of this section), as a potentially earlier alternative or intervening payment event to an amount previously deferred will not be treated as resulting in an acceleration of a payment, even if such addition results in the payment being paid at an earlier time than such payment would have been made absent the addition of the payment event. For such purpose, the earlier alternative or intervening payment event may apply with respect to either the service provider or, following the service provider's death, a beneficiary who becomes entitled to payment due to the service provider's death (substituting such beneficiary for the service provider in the definitions of *disability* in paragraph (i)(4) of this section and *unforeseeable emergency* in paragraph (i)(3) of this section, as applicable). However, the addition of such a payment event as a potentially later alternative payment event generally is subject to the rules governing changes in the time and form of payment (see § 1.409A–2(b)).

* * *

(4) * * *

(iii) * * *

(B) *Compliance with ethics laws or conflicts of interest laws.*—A plan may provide for acceleration of the time or schedule of a payment under the plan, or a payment may be made under a plan, to the extent reasonably necessary to avoid the violation of an applicable Federal, state, local, or *bona fide* foreign ethics law or conflicts of interest law (including under circumstances in which such payment is reasonably necessary to permit the service provider to participate in activities in the normal course of his or her position in which the service provider would otherwise not be able to participate under an applicable rule). A payment is reasonably necessary to avoid the violation of a Federal, state, local, or *bona fide* foreign ethics law or conflicts of interest law if the payment is a necessary part of a course of action that results in compliance with a Federal, state, local, or *bona fide* foreign ethics law or conflicts of interest law that would be violated absent such course of action, regardless of whether other actions would also result in compliance with the Federal, state, local, or *bona fide* foreign ethics law or conflicts of interest law.

* * *

(ix) * * *

(A) The service recipient's termination and liquidation of the plan within 12 months of a corporate dissolution taxed under section 331, or with the approval of a U.S. bankruptcy court, provided that the amounts deferred under the plan are included in the participants' gross incomes in the latest of the following years (or, if earlier, the taxable year in which the amount is actually or constructively received).

(1) The calendar year in which the plan termination and liquidation occurs;

(2) The first calendar year in which the amount is no longer subject to a substantial risk of forfeiture; or

(3) The first calendar year in which the payment is administratively practicable.

* * *

(C) The service recipient's termination and liquidation of the plan, provided that—

(1) The termination and liquidation does not occur proximate to a downturn in the financial health of the service recipient;

(2) The service recipient terminates and liquidates all agreements, methods, programs, and other arrangements sponsored by the service recipient that would be aggregated with any terminated and liquidated agreements, methods, programs, and other arrangements under § 1.409A-1(c) as if there were one service provider that had deferrals of compensation under every such agreement, method, program, and other arrangement sponsored by the service recipient (for example, all elective account balance plans that the service recipient sponsors);

(3) No payments in liquidation of the plan are made within 12 months of the date the service recipient takes all necessary action to irrevocably terminate and liquidate the plan other than payments that would be payable under the terms of the plan if the action to terminate and liquidate the plan had not occurred;

(4) All payments are made within 24 months of the date the service recipient takes all necessary action to irrevocably terminate and liquidate the plan; and

(5) The service recipient does not adopt any new agreement, method, program, or other arrangement described in paragraph (C)(2) of this subsection, at any time within three years following the date the service recipient takes all necessary action to irrevocably terminate and liquidate the plan.

* * *

(xiii) *Certain offsets*.—(A) *De minimis offset*.—A plan may provide for the acceleration of the time or schedule of a payment, or a payment may be made under such plan, as satisfaction of a debt of the service provider to the service recipient, if such debt is incurred in the ordinary course of the service relationship between the service recipient and the service provider, the entire amount of reduction in any of the service recipient's taxable years does not exceed $5,000, and the reduction is made at the same time and in the same amount as the debt otherwise would have been due and collected from the service provider.

(B) *Compliance with Federal debt collection laws*.—A plan may provide for the acceleration of the time or schedule of a payment, or a payment may be made under such plan, as satisfaction of a debt of the service provider to the service recipient, to the extent reasonably necessary to comply with 31 U.S.C. sections 3711 et. seq. or similar Federal nontax law regarding debt collection relating to claims of the Federal government. A payment is reasonably necessary to comply with such a Federal debt collection law if the payment is a necessary part of a course of action that results in compliance with the Federal debt collection law that would be violated absent such course of action, regardless of whether other actions would also result in compliance with the Federal debt collection law.

* * *

Par. 6. Section 1.409A-4 (REG-148326-05), as proposed at 73 FR 74380 (December 8, 2008), is proposed to be amended by revising paragraph (a)(1)(ii)(B) to read as follows:

§1.409A-4. Calculation of amount includible in income and additional income taxes.

* * *

(a)(1)(ii)(B) *Treatment of certain deferred amounts otherwise subject to a substantial risk of forfeiture*.—For purposes of determining the amount includible in income under section 409A(a)(1) and paragraph (a)(1)(i) of this section, an amount deferred under a plan that is otherwise subject to a substantial risk of forfeiture for a taxable year is treated as not subject to a substantial risk of forfeiture for the taxable year, if during the taxable year any of the following occur:

(1) A change (including an initial deferral election) that is not authorized under §1.409A-1, §1.409A-2, or §1.409A-3 is made to a provision of the plan providing for the time or form of payment of the deferred amount, if the service recipient has not made a reasonable, good faith determination that, absent the change, the provision fails to comply with the requirements of section 409A(a).

(2) The service recipient has engaged in a pattern or practice of permitting substantially similar failures to comply with section 409A(a) under one or more nonqualified deferred compensation plans while amounts deferred under the plans are nonvested, and the facts and circumstances indicate that the deferred amount would be affected by the pattern or practice. Whether such a pattern or practice exists will depend on the facts and circumstances, including, but not limited to, whether the service recipient has taken commercially reasonable measures to identify and correct the substantially similar failures promptly upon discovery, whether the failures have affected nonvested deferred amounts with greater frequency than vested deferred amounts, whether the failures have occurred more frequently under newly adopted plans, and whether the failures appear intentional, are numerous, or repeat one or more similar past failures that were previously identified and corrected.

(3) The correction of a failure to comply with section 409A(a) affecting the deferred amount is not consistent with an applicable correction method (if one exists) set forth in applicable guidance issued by the Treasury Department and the IRS for correcting failures under section 409A(a), or the failure is not corrected in substantially the same manner as a substantially similar failure affecting a nonvested deferred amount under another plan sponsored by the service recipient. Solely with respect to the deferred amount, the requirements under applicable correction guidance with respect to eligibility, income inclusion, additional taxes, premium interest, and information reporting by the service recipient or service provider do not apply.

Par. 7. Section 1.409A-6 is amended by revising paragraph (b) to read as follows:

§1.409A-6. Application of section 409A and effective dates.

* * *

(b) *Regulatory applicability date*.—Section 1.409A-0, §1.409A-1, §1.409A-2, §1.409A-3 and this section, as amended, apply for taxable years beginning on or after publication of the Treasury decision adopting these rules as final regulations in the *Federal Register*. Section 1.409A-0, §1.409A-1, §1.409A-2, §1.409A-3 and this section as they appeared in the April 2009 edition of 26 CFR part 1 apply for taxable years beginning on or after January 1, 2009 and before publication of the Treasury decision adopting these rules as final regulations in the *Federal Register*.

Employee Plans: Vesting Standards

Qualified Employee Plans: Minimum Vesting Standards.—Temporary Reg. §1.410(a)-3T, relating to minimum vesting standards for qualified employee plans, is also proposed as a final

regulation and, when adopted, would become Reg. §1.410(a)-3 (published in the Federal Register on January 6, 1988).

§1.410(a)-3. Minimum age and service conditions.

Pension Plans: Accruals: Retirement Age

Pension Plans: Accruals: Retirement Age.—Reproduced below is the text of proposed Reg. §1.410(a)-4A, relating to the requirement for continued accruals beyond normal retirement age under employee pension plans (published in the Federal Register on April 11, 1988).

☐ Par. 2. A new §1.410(a)-4A is added immediately after §1.410(a)-4 to read as follows:

§1.410(a)-4A. Maximum age conditions after 1987.—(a) *Maximum age conditions.*—Under section 410(a)(2), a plan is not a qualified plan (and a trust forming a part of such plan is not a qualified trust) if the plan, either directly or indirectly, excludes any employee from participation on the basis of attaining a maximum age.

(b) *Effective date and transitional rule.*—If a plan contains a provision that excludes an employee from participation on the basis of attaining a maximum age, the provision may not be applied in a plan year beginning on or after January 1, 1988, to any employee (regardless of when the employee first performed an hour of service for the employer) who is credited with at least 1 hour of service on or after January 1, 1988. For purposes of determining when such an employee (who is not otherwise ineligible to participate in the plan) must become eligible to participate in the plan under section 410(a)(1)(A)(ii), section 410(a)(1)(B) and the provisions of the plan, hours of service and years of service credited to the employee before the first plan year beginning on or after January 1, 1988, are taken into account in accordance with section 410 and the regulations thereunder and in accordance with 29 CFR Part 2530. Any employee who would be eligible to participate in the plan taking such service into account and whose entry date would be prior to the first day of the first plan year beginning on or after January 1, 1988, must participate in the plan as of the first day of such plan year.

(c) *Examples.*—The provisions of this section may be illustrated by the following examples:

Example (1). Employer X maintains a defined benefit plan that uses a 12-month period beginning July 1 and ending June 30 as its plan year and that specifies a normal retirement age of 65. The plan provides that each employee of X is eligible to become a participant in the plan on the first entry date on or after the employee completes 1 year of service for X. The plan has 2 entry dates, July 1 and January 1. However, prior to the plan year beginning July 1, 1988, the plan contained a provision that excluded from participation any employee first hired within 5 years of attaining the plan's specified normal retirement age of 65. Employee A was hired by X on August 1, 1986 at age 62. A completes 1 year of service for X by August 1, 1987. If A performs at least one hour of service for X on or after January 1, 1988, the plan, in order to meet the requirements of section 410(a)(2), may not apply the maximum age provision to A on or after July 1, 1988, and A must be eligible to become a participant in the plan in accordance with the other eligibility rules contained in the plan, taking into account A's service with X performed prior to July 1, 1988 to the extent required under the terms of the plan or under section 410 and the regulations thereunder and under regulations in 29 CFR Part 2530. Accordingly, if A is still employed by X on July 1, 1988, A must become a participant in the plan on that date.

Example (2). Employer Y maintains a defined benefit plan that uses the calendar year as its plan year and that specifies a normal retirement age of 65. Employee B is first hired by Y in 1988 when B is age 66. In order for the plan to meet the requirements of section 410(a)(2), B may not be excluded from plan participation on the basis of B having attained a specified age. [Reg. §1.410(a)-4A.]

Qualified Employee Plans: Minimum Vesting Standards

Qualified Employee Plans: Minimum Vesting Standards.—Temporary Reg. §§1.410(a)-8T and 1.410(a)-9T, relating to minimum vesting standards for qualified employee plans, are also proposed as final regulations and, when adopted, would become Reg. §§1.410(a)-8 and 1.410(a)-9, respectively (published in the Federal Register on January 6, 1988).

§1.410(a)-8. Year of service; break in service.

§1.410(a)-9. Elapsed time.

Pension Plans: Continued Accruals Beyond Retirement Age

Pension Plans: Accruals: Retirement Age.—Reproduced below is the text of a proposed amendment of Reg. §1.411(a)-1, relating to the requirement for continued accruals beyond normal retirement age under employee pension plans (published in the Federal Register on April 11, 1988).

☐ Par. 3. Section 1.411(a)-1 is amended by revising paragraph (a)(3) to read as follows:

§1.411(a)-1. Minimum vesting standards; general rules.—(a) *In general.*—* * *

(3) The plan satisfies the requirements of—

(A) Section 411(a)(2) and §1.411(a)-3 (relating to vesting in accrued benefit derived from employer contributions),

(B) In the case of a defined benefit plan, section 411(b)(1) and (3) (see §§1.411(b)-1 and 1.411(b)-2, relating to accrued benefit requirements, separate accounting and accruals and allocations after a specified age), and

(C) In the case of a defined contribution plan, section 411(b)(2) and (3) (see §§1.411(b)-1(e)(2) and 1.411(b)-2, relating to accruals and allocations after a specified age and separate accounting).

* * *

Employee Plans: Vesting Standards

Qualified Employee Plans: Minimum Vesting Standards.—Temporary Reg. §§1.411(a)-3T and 1.411(a)-4T, relating to minimum vesting standards for qualified employee plans, are also proposed as final regulations and, when adopted, would become Reg. §§1.411(a)-3 and 1.411(a)-4 (published in the Federal Register on January 6, 1988).

§1.411(a)-3. Vesting in employer-derived benefits.

§1.411(a)-4. Forfeitures, suspensions, etc.

Pension Plans: Accruals: Definitions: Special Rules

Pension Plans: Accruals: Retirement Age.—Reproduced below is the text of a proposed amendment of Reg. §1.411(a)-7, relating to the requirement for continued accruals beyond normal retirement age under employee pension plans (published in the Federal Register on April 11, 1988).

☐ Par. 4. Section 1.411(a)-7 is amended by adding a new subparagraph (b)(3) to read as follows:

§1.411(a)-7. Definitions and special rules.—

* * *

(b) *Normal retirement age.*—* * *

(3) *Effect of Omnibus Budget Reconciliation Act of 1986 (OBRA).*—[RESERVED]

* * *

Employee Plans: Vesting Standards

Qualified Employee Plans: Minimum Vesting Standards.—Temporary Reg. §1.411(a)-8T, relating to minimum vesting standards for qualified employee plans, is also proposed as a final regulation and, when adopted, would become Reg. §1.411(a)-8 (published in the Federal Register on January 6, 1988).

§1.411(a)-8. Changes in vesting schedule.

Retirement Plans: Distributions: Deferral of Receipt: Notification of Consequences

Retirement Plans: Distributions: Deferral of Receipt: Notification of Consequences.—Amendments to Reg. §1.411(a)-11, specifying that the notice required under Code Sec. 411(a)(11) to be provided to a participant of his or her right, if any, to defer receipt of an immediately distributable benefit must also describe the consequences of failing to defer receipt of the distribution, are proposed (published in the Federal Register on October 9, 2008) (REG-107318-08).

Par. 2. For each entry listed in the "Location" column, remove the language in the "Remove" column and add the language in the "Add" column in its place.

Location	Remove	Add
1.411(a)-11(c)(2)(ii)	90 days	180 days
1.411(a)-11(c)(2)(iii)(A), first sentence	90 days	180 days

Par. 3. Section 1.411(a)-11 is amended as follows:
1. The second sentence of paragraph (c)(2)(i) is revised.
2. The second sentence of paragraph (c)(2)(iii)(B)(3) is revised.
3. Paragraphs (c)(2)(vi) and (h) are added.
The additions and revisions read as follows:

§1.411(a)-11. Restriction and valuation of distributions.

* * *

(c) * * *

(2) *Consent.*—(i) * * * In addition, so long as a benefit is immediately distributable, a participant must be informed of the right, if any, to defer receipt of the distribution and of the consequences of failing to defer such receipt. * * *

* * *

(iii) * * *

(B) * * *

(*3*) * * * The summary described in paragraph (c)(2)(iii)(B)(*2*) of this section must advise the participant of the right, if any, to defer receipt of the distribution and of the consequences of failing to defer such receipt, must set forth a summary of the distribution options under the plan, must refer the participant to the most recent version of the notice (and, in the case of a notice provided in any document containing information in addition to the notice, must identify that document and must provide a reasonable indication of where the notice may be found in that document, such as by index reference or by section heading), and must advise the participant that, upon request, a copy of the notice will be provided without charge.

* * *

(vi) *Consequences of failing to defer.*—(A) A notice under this paragraph (c)(2) that is required to describe the consequences of failing to defer receipt of a distribution until it is no longer immediately distributable must, to the extent applicable under the plan and in a manner designed to be easily understood, provide the participant with the information set out in paragraphs (c)(2)(vi)(A)(*1*) through (*5*) of this section and explain why it is relevant to a decision whether to defer.

(*1*) A description of the following federal tax implications of failing to defer: differences in the timing of inclusion in taxable income of an immediately commencing distribution that is not rolled over (or not eligible to be rolled over) and a distribution that is deferred until it is no longer immediately distributable (including, as applicable, differences in the taxation of distributions of designated Roth contributions within the meaning of section 402A); application of the 10% additional tax on certain distributions before age 59$^1/_2$ under section 72(t); and, in the case of a defined contribution plan, loss of the opportunity upon immediate commencement for future tax-favored treatment of earnings if the distribution is not rolled over (or not eligible to be rolled over) to an eligible retirement plan described in section 402(c)(8)(B).

(*2*) In the case of a defined benefit plan, a statement of the amount payable to the participant under the normal form of benefit both upon immediate commencement and upon commencement when the benefit is no longer immediately distributable (assuming no future benefit accruals). The statement need not vary based on the participant's marital status if the plan is permitted, pursuant to § 1.417(a)(3)-1(c)(2)(ii), to provide a QJSA explanation that does not vary based on the participant's marital status.

(*3*) In the case of a defined contribution plan, a statement that some currently available investment options in the plan may not be generally available on similar terms outside the plan and contact information for obtaining additional information on the general availability outside the plan of currently available investment options in the plan.

(*4*) In the case of a defined contribution plan, a statement that fees and expenses (including administrative or investment-related fees) outside the plan may be different from fees and expenses that apply to the participant's account and contact information for obtaining additional information on the fees and expenses that apply to the participant's account.

(*5*) An explanation of any provisions of the plan (and provisions of an accident or health plan maintained by the employer) that could reasonably be expected to materially affect a participant's decision whether to defer receipt of the distribution. Such provisions would include, for example: plan terms under which a participant who fails to defer may lose eligibility for retiree health coverage or eligibility for early retirement subsidies or social security supplements; plan terms under which the benefit of a rehired participant who failed to defer may be adversely affected by the decision not to defer; and, in the case of a defined contribution plan, plan terms under which undistributed benefits that otherwise are nonforfeitable become forfeitable upon the participant's death.

(B) *Location of information; incorporation by reference.*—In general, the information required to be provided in a notice under this paragraph (c)(2)(vi) must appear together (for example, in a list of consequences of failing to defer). However, the notice will not be treated as failing to satisfy the requirements of this paragraph (c)(2)(vi) merely because the notice includes a cross-reference to where the required information may be found in notices or other information provided or made available to the participant, as long as the notice of consequences of failing to defer includes a statement of how the referenced information may be obtained without charge and explains why the referenced information is relevant to a decision whether to defer. * * *

(h) *Consequences of Failing to Defer Effective/ Applicability Date.*—The provisions in paragraph (c) of this section that describe the requirement to notify participants of the consequences of failing to defer are effective for notices provided on or after the first day of the first plan year beginning on or after January 1, 2010.

Defined Benefit Plans: Accrual Rules

Defined Benefit Plans: Accrual Rules.—Amendments to Reg. § 1.411(b)-1, providing guidance on the application of the accrual rule for defined benefit plans under Code Sec. 411(b)(1)(B) in cases where plan benefits are determined on the basis of the greatest of two or more separate formulas, are proposed (published in the Federal Register on June 18, 2008) (REG-100464-08).

☐ Par. 2. Section 1.411(b)-1 is amended by adding new paragraph (b)(2)(ii)(G) to read as follows:

§ 1.411(b)-1. Accrued benefit requirements.

* * *

(b) * * *

(2) * * *

(ii) * * *

(G) *Special rule for multiple formulas.*—(*1*) *In general.*—Notwithstanding paragraph (a)(1) of this section, a plan that determines a participant's accrued benefit as the greatest of the benefits determined under two or more separate formulas is permitted, to the extent provided under this paragraph (b)(2)(ii)(G), to demonstrate satisfaction of section 411(b)(1)(B) and this paragraph (b) by demonstrating that each separate formula satisfies the requirements of section 411(b)(1)(B) and this paragraph (b).

(*2*) *Separate bases requirement.*—A plan is eligible for separate testing under this paragraph (b)(2)(ii)(G) if each of the separate formulas uses a different basis for determining benefits. For example, a plan is eligible for this special rule if it provides an accrued benefit equal to the greater of the benefits under two formulas, one of which determines accrued benefits on the basis of highest average compensation and the other of which determines accrued benefits on the basis of career average compensation. As another example, a defined benefit plan that bases benefits on highest average compensation and that is amended to add a statutory hybrid benefit formula (as defined in § 1.411(a)(13)-1(d)(3)) that provides for pay credits to be made based on each year's compensation is eligible for this separate testing exception if the plan provides that one or more participants are entitled to the greater of the benefit determined under the statutory hybrid benefit formula and the benefit determined under the original formula.

(3) Plans with three or more formulas.—If a plan determines a participant's benefits as the greatest of the benefits determined under three or more separate formulas, but two or more of the formulas use the same basis for determining benefits, then the plan may nonetheless apply paragraphs (b)(2)(ii)(G)(*1*) and (2) of this section by aggregating all benefit formulas that have the same basis and treating those aggregated formulas as a single formula for purposes of paragraphs (b)(2)(ii)(G)(*1*) and (*2*) of this section.

(4) Anti-abuse rule.—A plan is not eligible for separate testing under this paragraph (b)(2)(ii)(G) if the Commissioner determines that the plan's use of separate formulas with different bases is structured to evade the requirement to aggregate formulas under paragraph (a)(1) of this section (for example, if the differences between the bases of the separate formulas are minor).

(5) Effective/applicability date.—This paragraph (b)(2)(ii)(G) is applicable for plan years beginning on or after January 1, 2009.

Pension Plans: Accruals

Pension Plans: Accruals: Retirement Age.—Reproduced below are the texts of proposed Reg. § 1.411(b)-2 and a proposed amendment of Reg. § 1.411(c)-1, relating to the requirement for continued accruals beyond normal retirement age under employee pension plans (published in the Federal Register on April 11, 1988). ***Note: Taxpayers may rely on these proposed regulations pending the issuance of final regulations. The IRS will apply them in issuing rulings and in examining returns. If final regulations are less favorable, they will not be applied retroactively.***

□ Par. 5. A new section 1.411(b)-2 is added after § 1.411(b)-1 to read as follows:

§ 1.411(b)-2. Accruals and allocations after a specified age.—(a) *In general.*—Section 411(b)(1)(H) provides that a defined benefit plan does not satisfy the minimum vesting standards of section 411(a) if, under the plan, benefit accruals on behalf of a participant are discontinued or the rate of benefit accrual on behalf of a participant is reduced because of the participant's attainment of any age. Section 411(b)(2) provides that a defined contribution plan does not satisfy the minimum vesting standards of section 411(a) if, under the plan, allocations to a participant's account are reduced or discontinued or the rate of allocations to a participant's account is reduced because of the participant's attainment of any age. A defined benefit plan is not considered to discontinue benefit accruals or reduce the rate of benefit accrual on behalf of a participant because of the attainment of any age in violation of section 411(b)(1)(H) and a defined contribution plan is not considered to reduce or discontinue allocations to a participant's account or reduce the rate of allocations to a participant's account because of the attainment of any age in violation of section 411(b)(2) solely because of a positive correlation between increased age and a reduction or discontinuance in benefit accruals or account allocations under a plan. Thus, for example, if a defined benefit plan or a defined contribution plan provides for reduced or discontinued benefit accruals or account allocations on behalf of participants who have completed a specified number of years of credited service, the plan will not thereby fail to satisfy section 411(b)(1)(H) or (b)(2) solely because of a positive correlation between increased age and completion of the specified number of years of credited service. See paragraph (b)(2) of this section for rules relating to benefit and service limitations under defined benefit plans and paragraph (c)(2) of this section for rules relating to limitations on allocations under defined contribution plans. Also, if benefit accruals or the rate of benefit accrual on behalf of a participant in a defined benefit plan or allocations or the rate of allocations to the account of a participant in a defined contribution plan are reduced or discontinued under the plan and the reason for the reduction or discontinuance is neither directly nor indirectly related to the participant's attainment of a specified age, the plan does not thereby fail to satisfy the requirements of section 411(b)(1)(H) or (b)(2). Thus, for example, if a defined benefit plan is amended to cease or reduce the rate of benefit accrual for all plan participants, such cessation or reduction does not fail to satisfy the requirements of section 411(b)(1)(H).

(b) *Defined benefit plans.*—(1) *In general.*—(i) A defined benefit plan does not satisfy the minimum vesting standards of section 411(a) if, either directly or indirectly, because of the attainment of any age—

(A) A participant's accrual of benefits is discontinued or the rate of a participant's accrual of benefits is decreased, or

(B) A participant's compensation after the attainment of such age is not taken into account in determining the participant's accrual of benefits.

(ii) In determining whether a defined benefit plan satisfies paragraph (b)(1)(i) of this section, the subsidized portion of an early retirement benefit (whether provided on a temporary or permanent basis), a social security supplement (as defined in §1.411(a)-7(c)(4)(ii)) and a qualified disability benefit (as defined in §1.411(a)-7(c)(3)) are disregarded in determining the rate of a participant's accrual of benefits under the plan.

(iii) The provisions of paragraph (b)(1)(i) of this section may be illustrated by the following example. In the example, assume that the participant completes the hours of service in a plan year required under the plan to accrue a full benefit for the plan year.

Example. Employer X maintains a defined benefit plan that provides a normal retirement benefit of 1% of a participant's average annual compensation, multiplied by the participant's years of credited service under the plan. Normal retirement age under the plan is age 65. The plan contains no limitations (other than the limitations imposed by section 415) on the maximum amount of benefits the plan will pay to any participant or on the maximum number of years of credited service taken into account under the plan for purposes of determining the amount of any participant's normal retirement benefit. Participant A became a participant in the plan at age 25 and worked continuously for X until A retires at age 70. The plan will satisfy the requirements of section 411(b)(1)(H) and paragraph (b)(2) of this section if, under the plan's benefit formula, upon A's retirement, A has an accrued normal retirement benefit of at least 45% of A's average annual compensation (1% per year × 45 years).

(2) *Benefit and service limitations.*—(i) *In general.*—A defined benefit plan does not fail to satisfy section 411(b)(1)(H) and paragraph (b) of this section solely because the plan limits the amount of benefits a participant may accrue under the plan or limits the number of years of service or years of participation taken into account for purposes of determining the accrual of benefits under the plan (credited service). For this purpose, a limitation that is expressed as a percentage of compensation (whether averaged over a participant's total years of credited service for the employer or over a shorter period) and a limitation of the type described in section 401(a)(5)(D) are treated as permissible limitations on the amount of benefits a participant may accrue under the plan. However, in applying a limitation on the number of years of credited service that are taken into account under a plan, the plan may not take into account any year of service that is disregarded in determining the accrual of benefits under the plan (prior to the effective date of section 411(b)(1)(H) and this section) because of the attainment of any age.

(ii) *Limitation not based on age.*—Any limitation on the amount of benefits a participant may accrue under the plan and any limitation on the number of years of credited service taken into account under the plan may not be based, directly or indirectly, on the attainment of any age. A limitation that is determined by reference to age or that is not determinable except by reference to age is considered a limitation directly based on age. Thus, a plan provision that, for purposes of benefit accrual, disregards years of service completed after a participant becomes eligible to receive social security benefits is considered a limitation directly based on age. Similarly, a plan provision that, for purposes of benefit accrual, disregards years of service completed after the sum of a participant's age and the participant's number of years of credited service equals a specified number, is considered a limitation directly based on age. Whether a limitation is indirectly based on age is determined with reference to all the facts and circumstances.

(iii) *Examples.*—The provisions of paragraph (b)(2) of this section may be illustrated by the following examples. In each example, assume that the participant completes the hours of service in a plan year required under the plan to accrue a full benefit for the plan year.

Example (1). Assume the same facts as in the *Example* set forth in paragraph (b)(1)(ii) of this section, except that the plan provides that not more than 35 years of credited service will be taken into account in determining a participant's normal retirement benefit under the plan. Upon A's retirement at age 70, A will have a normal retirement benefit under the plan's benefit formula of 35% of A's average annual compensation (1% per year × 35 years). The plan will not fail to satisfy the requirements of section 411(b)(1)(H) and this paragraph (b) merely because the plan provides that the final 10 years of A's service under the plan is not taken into account in determining A's normal retirement benefit. The result would be the same if the plan provided that no participant could accrue a normal retirement benefit in excess of 35% of the participant's average annual compensation.

Example (2). Employer Y maintains a defined benefit plan that provides a normal retirement benefit of 50% of a participant's final average compensation. Normal retirement age under the plan is age 65. Other than the limitations imposed by section 415, the plan contains no provision that limits the accrual of the benefit payable to a participant who has less than a specified number of years of credited service for Y. Participant A is hired by Y at age 66 and commences participation in the plan at age 67. Under the plan's benefit formula, if A completes one year of credited service under the plan, A will be entitled to receive (subject to the limitations of section 415) a normal retirement benefit equal to 50% of A's final average compensation.

(3) *Different rates of benefit accrual.*—(i) *In general.*—A defined benefit plan does not fail to satisfy the requirements of section 411(b)(1)(H) and paragraph (b) of this section solely because the plan provides for the accrual of benefits at different rates with respect to participants under the plan. Accordingly, a plan under which a participant's accrued benefit is determined in accordance with the fractional rule described in section 411(b)(1)(C) and §1.411(b)-1(b)(3) will not fail to satisfy the requirements of section 411(b)(1)(H) and paragraph (b) of this section solely because the rate at which a participant's normal retirement benefit accrues differs de-

pending on the number of years of credited service a participant would have between the date of commencement of participation and the attainment of normal retirement age. In addition, a plan will not be treated as failing to satisfy section 411(b)(1)(H) and paragraph (b) of this section solely because the plan's benefit formula provides, on a uniform and consistent basis, a normal retirement benefit equal to, for example, 2% of average annual compensation multiplied by a participant's first 15 years of credited service and 1% of average annual compensation multiplied by a participant's years of credited service in excess of 15 years. The preceding sentence applies regardless of when the participant's normal retirement age occurs.

(ii) *Differences not based on age.*—Any differences in the rate of benefit accrual described in paragraph (b)(3)(i) of this section may not be based, directly or indirectly, on the attainment of any age.

(4) *Certain adjustments for delayed retirement.*—(i) *In general.*—Under section 411(b)(1)(H)(iii), a plan may provide that benefit accruals that would otherwise be required under section 411(b)(1)(H)(i) and paragraph (b) of this section for a plan year are reduced (but not below zero) as set forth in paragraph (b)(4)(ii) and (iii) of this section. This paragraph (b)(4) applies for a plan year to a participant who, as of the end of the plan year, has attained normal retirement age under the plan.

(ii) *Distribution of benefits.*—(A) A plan may provide that the benefit accrual otherwise required under section 411(b)(1)(H)(i) and paragraph (b) of this section for a plan year is reduced (but not below zero) by the actuarial equivalent of total plan benefit distributions (as determined under this paragraph (b)(4)(ii)) made to the participant by the close of the plan year.

(B) The plan benefit distributions described in this paragraph (b)(4)(ii) are limited to distributions made to the participant during plan years and periods with respect to which section 411(b)(1)(H)(i) and this section apply (including plan years and periods beginning before January 1, 1988) for which the plan could (without regard to section 401(a)(9) and the regulations thereunder) provide for the suspension of the participant's plan benefits in accordance with section 203(a)(3)(B) of the Employee Retirement Income Security Act of 1974 (ERISA) and regulations issued thereunder by the Department of Labor.

(C) For purposes of determining the total amount of plan benefit distributions that may be taken into account under this paragraph (b)(4)(ii) as of the close of a plan year, distributions shall be disregarded to the extent the total amount of distributions made to the participant by the close of the plan year exceeds the total amount of the distributions the participant would have received by the close of the plan year if the distributions had been made in accordance with the plan's normal form of benefit distribution. Accordingly, the plan is required to accrue a benefit for the plan year on behalf of a participant in accordance with the plan's benefit formula, taking into account all of the participant's years of credited service, reduced (but not below the participant's normal retirement benefit for the prior plan year) by the actuarial equivalent of total benefit distributions (taken into account under this paragraph (b)(4)(ii)) made to the participant by the close of the plan year. If, by the close of the plan year, the actuarial equivalent of total plan benefit distributions made to the participant and taken into account under this paragraph (b)(4)(ii) is greater than the total benefit accruals required under section 411(b)(1)(H)(i) and paragraph (b) of this section for the plan years during which such distributions were made, the plan is not required under section 411(b)(1)(H)(i) and paragraph (b) of this section to accrue any benefit on behalf of the participant for the plan year.

(iii) *Adjustment in benefits payable.*—(A) A plan may provide that the benefit accrual otherwise required under section 411(b)(1)(H)(i) and paragraph (b) of this section for the plan year is reduced (but not below zero) by the amount of any actuarial adjustment under the plan in the benefit payable for the plan year with respect to the participant because of a delay in the payment of plan benefits after the participant's attainment of normal retirement age.

(B) For purposes of subdivision (iii)(A), the actuarial adjustment may be taken into account for a plan year only to the extent it is made to the greater of (*1*) the participant's retirement benefit as of the close of the prior plan year, including any actuarial adjustment made under the plan for the prior plan year, and (*2*) the participant's normal retirement benefit as of the close of the prior plan year determined by including benefit accruals required by section 411(b)(1)(H)(i) and paragraph (b) of this section. If the retirement benefit, as actuarially adjusted for the plan year in accordance with this paragraph (b)(4)(iii) for delayed payment, exceeds the normal retirement benefit, as determined by including benefit accruals required for the plan year by section 411(b)(1)(H)(i) and paragraph (b) of this section, the plan shall be required to provide the retirement benefit, as actuarially adjusted in accordance with this paragraph (b)(4)(iii) under the plan. Notwithstanding the provisions of this subdivision (iii)(B), in the case of a plan that suspends benefit payments in accordance with section 203(a)(3)(B) of the Employee Retirement Income Security Act of 1974 and the regulations issued thereunder by the Department of Labor, the plan does not fail to satisfy the requirements of section 411(b)(1)(H) and paragraph (b) of this section solely because the plan provides that the retirement benefit to which a participant is entitled as of the close of a plan year ending after the participant attains normal retirement age under the plan is the greater of (*1*) the benefit payable at normal retirement age (not including benefit accruals otherwise required by section 411(b)(1)(H) and paragraph (b) of this section) actuarially adjusted under the plan to the close of the plan year for delayed payment, and (*2*) the retirement benefit determined under the plan as of the close of the plan year determined by including benefit accruals required by section 411(b)(1)(H) and paragraph (b) of this section and determined without regard to any offset that would otherwise be applicable under this paragraph (b)(4)(iii).

(iv) *Examples.*—The provisions of paragraph (b)(4) of this section may be illustrated by the following examples. In each example, assume that the participant completes the hours of service in a plan year required under the plan to accrue a full benefit for the plan year and assume that the participant is not married unless otherwise specified.

Example (1). Employer Y maintains a defined benefit plan that provides a normal retirement benefit of $20 per month multiplied by the participant's years of credited service. The plan contains no limit on the number of years of credited service taken into account for purposes of determining the normal retirement benefit provided by the plan. Participant A attains normal retirement age of 65 and continues in the full time service of Y. At age 65, A has 30 years of credited service under the plan and could receive a normal retirement benefit of $600 per month ($20 × 30 years) if A retires. The plan provides for the suspension of A's normal retirement benefit (in accordance with section 203(a)(3)(B) of the Employee Retirement Income Security Act of 1974 (ERISA) and regulations thereunder issued by the Department of Labor) during the period of A's continued employment with Y. Accordingly, the plan does not provide for an actuarial adjustment of A's normal retirement benefit because of delayed payment and the plan does not pay A's normal retirement benefit while A remains in the full time service of Y. If A retires at age 67, after completing two additional years of credited service for Y, A must receive additional accruals for the two years of credited service completed after attaining normal retirement age in order for the plan to satisfy section 411(b)(1)(H)(i). Accordingly, A is entitled to receive a normal retirement benefit of $640 per month ($20 × 32 years).

Example (2). Assume the same facts as in *Example (1),* except that the plan provides that at the time A's normal retirement benefit becomes payable, the amount of A's normal retirement benefit (determined as of A's normal retirement age and each year thereafter) will be actuarially increased for delayed retirement. The plan offsets this actuarial increase against benefit accruals in plan years ending after A's attainment of normal retirement age, as permitted by paragraph (b)(4)(iii) of this section. Accordingly, the plan does not provide for the suspension of normal retirement benefits (in accordance with section 203(a)(3)(B) of ERISA and regulations thereunder issued by the Department of Labor). Under section 411(b)(1)(H), the plan must provide A with a benefit of at least $620 per month after A completes 31 years of credited service for Y. However, under paragraph (b)(4)(iii) of this section, the plan is not required to provide A with a benefit accrual for A's additional year of credited service for Y because, under the plan, A will be entitled to receive, upon retirement at age 66 after completing 1 additional year of credited service for Y, an actuarially increased benefit of $672 per month. This monthly benefit of $672 is the greater of A's normal retirement benefit at normal retirement age ($20 × 30 years = $600) actuarially adjusted for delayed payment and A's normal retirement benefit ($20 × 31 years = $620) determined by taking into account A's year of credited service after attaining normal retirement age. Under the plan, A will be entitled to receive, upon retirement at age 67 after completing 2 additional years of credited service for Y after attaining normal retirement age, an actuarially increased benefit of $756 per month. This monthly benefit of $756 is the greater of A's actuarially adjusted normal retirement benefit at age 66 ($672) actuarially adjusted to $756 for delayed payment to age 67 and A's normal retirement benefit ($20 × 32 years = $640) determined by taking into account A's years of credited service after attaining normal retirement age.

Example (3). Assume the same facts as in *Example (1),* except that the plan neither provides for the suspension of normal retirement benefit payments (in accordance with section 203(a)(3)(B) of ERISA and regulations thereunder issued by the Department of Labor) nor provides for an actuarial increase in benefit payments because of delayed payment of benefits. Consequently, the plan provides that the normal retirement benefit will be paid to a participant, beginning at age 65 (normal retirement age) even though the participant remains in the service of Y and offsets the value of the benefit distributions against benefit accruals in plan years ending after the participant's attainment of normal retirement age, as permitted by paragraph (b)(4)(ii) of this section. Participant B (who remains in the full time service of Y) receives 12 monthly benefit payments prior to attainment of age 66. The total monthly benefit payments of $7,200 ($600 × 12 payments) have an actuarial value at age 66 of $7,559 (reflecting interest and mortality) which would produce a monthly benefit of $72 commencing at age 66. The benefit accrual for the year of credited service B completed after attaining normal retirement age is $20 per month ($20 × 1 year). Because the actuarial value (determined as a monthly benefit of $72) of the benefit payments made during the one year of credited service after B's attainment of normal retirement age exceeds the benefit accrual for the one year of credited service after B's attainment of normal retirement age, the plan is not required to accrue benefits on behalf of B for the one year of credited service after B's attainment of normal retirement age and the plan is not required to increase B's monthly benefit payment of $600 at age 66. Assume B receives 24 monthly benefit payments prior to B's retirement at age 67. The total monthly benefit payments of $14,400 ($600 × 24 payments) have an actuarial value at age 67 of $15,839 (reflecting interest and mortality) which would produce a monthly benefit payment of $156 commencing at age 67. The benefit accrual for the two years of credited service B completed after attaining normal retirement age is $40 per month ($20 × 2 years). Because the actuarial value (determined as a monthly benefit of $156) of the benefit payments made during the two years of credited service after B's normal retirement age exceeds the benefit accrual for the two years of credited service after B's normal retirement age ($20 × 2 years = $40), the plan is not required to accrue benefits on behalf of B for the second year of credited service B completed after attaining normal retirement age and the plan is not required to increase B's monthly benefit payment of $600.

Example (4). Assume that Employer Z maintains a defined benefit plan that provides a normal retirement benefit of 2% of the average of a participant's high three consecutive years of compensation multiplied by the participant's years of credited service under the plan. The plan contains no limit on the number of years of credited service taken into account for purposes of determining the normal retirement benefit provided by the plan. Participant C, who has attained normal retirement age (age 65) under the plan, continues in the full time service of Z. At normal retirement age, C has average compensation of $20,000 for C's high three consecutive years and has 10 years of credited service under the plan. Thus, at normal retirement age, C is entitled to receive an annual normal retirement benefit of $4,000 ($20,000 × .02 × 10 years). Assume further that the plan provides for the suspension of N's normal retirement benefit (in accordance with section 203(a)(3)(B) of ERISA and regulations issued thereunder by the Department of Labor) during the period of C's continued employment with Z. Accordingly, the plan does not provide for the actuarial increase of C's normal retirement benefit because of delayed payment and the plan does not pay C's normal retirement benefit while C remains in the full time service of Z. At age 70, when C retires, C has average annual compensation for C's high three consecutive years of $35,000. Under section 411(b)(1)(H), C must be credited with 15 years of credited service for Z and C's increased compensation after attaining normal retirement age must be taken into account for purposes of determining C's normal retirement benefit. At age 70, C is entitled to receive an annual normal retirement benefit of $10,500 ($35,000 × .02 × 15 years).

Example (5). Assume the same facts as in *Example (4)*, except that the payment of C's retirement benefit is not suspended (in accordance with section 203(a)(3)(B) of ERISA and regulations issued thereunder by the Department of Labor) and, accordingly, the plan provides that retirement benefits that commence after a participant's normal retirement age will be actuarially increased for late retirement. The plan offsets this actuarial increase against benefit accruals in plan years ending after C's attainment of normal retirement age, as permitted by paragraph (b)(4)(iii) of this section. Under this provision, at the close of each plan year after C's attainment of normal retirement age, C's retirement benefit is actuarially increased. Under this provision, the actuarial increase for the plan year is made to the greater of C's normal retirement benefit at the close of the prior plan year (including previous actuarial adjustments) and C's normal retirement benefit at the close of the prior plan year determined by including all benefit accruals. Accordingly, at the close of each plan year, C is entitled to receive an annual normal retirement benefit equal to the greater of C's normal retirement benefit (adjusted actuarially under the plan from the benefit to which C was entitled at the close of the prior plan year) determined at the close of the plan year and C's normal retirement benefit determined at the close of the plan year by taking into account C's years of credited service and benefit accruals after C's attainment of normal retirement age. The foregoing is illustrated in the following table with respect to certain years of credited service performed by C after attaining normal retirement age 65.

1	2	3	4	5	6
Age	*Years of credited service*	*Average compensation for high three consecutive years*	*Normal retirement benefit with additional accruals (.02 × Column 2 × Column 3)*	*Retirement benefit, as actuarially increased under the plan from the benefit at prior age (Column 6)*	*Normal retirement benefit to which C is entitled (greater of Column 4 and Column 5)*
65 . . .	10	$20,000	$4,000	N/A	$4,000
66 . . .	11	$21,000	$4,620	$4,482	$4,620
67 . . .	12	$29,000	$6,960	$5,192	$6,960
68 . . .	13	$30,000	$7,800	$7,848	$7,848
69 . . .	14	$33,000	$9,240	$8,880	$9,240
70 . . .	15	$35,000	$10,500	$10,494	$10,500

Example (6). Assume the same facts as in *Example (4)*, except that C does not retire at age 70, but continues in the full time service of Z. Upon C's attainment of age 70, the plan commences benefit payments to C. The annual benefit paid to C in the first plan year is $10,500 ($35,000 × .02 × 15 years). In determining the annual benefit payable to C in each subsequent plan year, the plan offsets the value of benefit distributions made to the participant by the close of the prior plan year against benefit accruals in plan years during which such distributions were made, as permitted by paragraph (b)(4)(ii) of this section. Accordingly, for each subsequent plan year, C is entitled under the plan to receive benefit payments based on C's benefit (at the close of the prior plan year) determined under the plan formula by taking into account all of C's years of credited service, reduced (but not below C's normal retirement benefit for the prior plan year) by the value of total benefit distributions made to C by the close of the prior plan year. The foregoing is illustrated in the following table with respect to certain years of credited service performed by C while benefits were being distributed to C.

1	2	3	4	5	6	7	8
Years of benefit distributions	*Years of credited service (as of close of the year)*	*Average compensation for high three years*	*Normal retirement benefit with additional accruals (.02 × Column 2 × Column 3)*	*Suspendible benefit distributions made during the year*	*Cumulative suspendible benefit distributions made as of close of the year*	*Annual benefit that is actuarial equivalent of cumulative suspendible benefit distributions made as of close of the year*	*Retirement benefit to which C is entitled at close of the year (Column 4 – Column 7, but not less than Column 8 for prior year)*
N/A	15	$35,000	$10,500	N/A	N/A	N/A	$10,500
1	16	$35,000	$11,200	$10,500	$10,500	$1,472	$10,500
2	17	$45,000	$15,300	$10,500	$21,000	$3,209	$12,091
3	18	$50,000	$18,000	$12,091	$33,091	$5,510	$12,490

(c) *Defined contribution plans.*—(1) *In general.*—A defined contribution plan (including a target benefit plan described in § 1.410(a)-4(a)(1)) does not satisfy the minimum vesting standards of section 411(a) if, either directly or indirectly, because of the attainment of any age—

(i) The allocation of employer contributions or forfeitures to the accounts of participants is discontinued, or

(ii) The rate at which the allocation of employer contributions or forfeitures is made to the accounts of participants is decreased.

(2) *Limitations on allocations.*—(i) A defined contribution plan (including a target benefit plan described in § 1.410(a)-4(a)(1)) does not fail to satisfy the minimum vesting standards of section 411(a) solely because the plan limits the total amount of employer contributions and forfeitures that may be allocated to a participant's account (for a particular plan year or for the participant's total years of credited service under the plan) or solely because the plan limits the total number of years of credited service for which a participant's account may receive allocations of employer contributions and forfeitures. The limitations described in the preceding sentence may not be applied with respect to the allocation of gains, losses or income of the trust to the account of a participant. Furthermore, a defined contribution plan (including a target benefit plan) does not fail to satisfy section 411(a) solely because the plan limits the number of years of credited service that may be taken into account for purposes of determining the amount of, or the rate at which, employer contributions and forfeitures are allocated to a participant's account for a particular plan year. However, in applying a credited service limitation described in this paragraph (c)(2)(i), the plan may not take into account any year of service (prior to the effective date of section 411(b)(2) and paragraph (c) of this section) that is disregarded in determining allocations to a participant's account because of the participant's attainment of any age.

(ii) Any limitation described in paragraph (c)(2)(i) of this section may not be based, directly or indirectly, on the attainment of any age. The provisions of paragraph (b)(2)(ii) of this section shall also apply for purposes of this paragraph (c).

(iii) The Commissioner shall provide such additional rules as may be necessary or appropriate with respect to the application of section 411(b)(2) and this section to target benefit plans.

(d) *Benefits and forms of benefits subject to requirements.*—(1) *General rule.*—Except as provided in paragraph (d)(2) of this section, section 411(b)(1)(H) and (b)(2) and paragraphs (b) and (c) of this section apply to all benefits (and forms of benefits) provided under a defined benefit plan and a defined contribution plan, including accrued benefits, benefits described in section 411(d)(6), ancillary benefits and other rights and features provided under the plan. Accordingly, except as provided in paragraph (d)(2) of this section, benefit accruals under a defined benefit plan and allocations under a defined contribution plan will be considered to be reduced on account of the attainment of a specified age if optional forms of benefits, ancillary benefits, or other rights or features under the plan provided with respect to benefits or allocations attributable to credited service prior to the attainment of such age are not provided (on at least as favorable a basis to participants) with respect to benefits or allocations attributable to credited service after such age. Thus, for example, a plan may not provide a lump sum payment only with respect to benefits attributable to years of credited service before the attainment of a specified age. Similarly, except as provided in paragraph (d)(2) of this section, if an optional form of benefit is available under the plan at a specified age, the availability of such form of benefit, or the method for determining the manner in which such benefit is paid, may not, directly or indirectly, be denied or provided on terms less favorable to participants because of the attainment of any higher age. Similarly, if the method for determining the amount or the rate of the subsidized portion of a joint and survivor annuity or the subsidized portion of a joint and survivor annuity or the substantial portion of a preretirement survivor annuity is less favorable with respect to participants who have attained a specified age than with respect to participants who have not attained such age, benefit accruals or account allocations under the plan will be considered to be reduced on account of the attainment of such age.

(2) *Special rule for certain benefits.*—A plan will not fail to satisfy section 411(b)(1)(H) or paragraph (b) of this section merely because the following benefits, or the manner in which such benefits are provided under the plan, vary because of the attainment of any higher age.

(i) The subsidized portion of an early retirement benefit (whether provided on a temporary or permanent basis),

(ii) A qualified disability benefit (as defined in § 1.411(a)-7(c)(3)); and

(iii) A social security supplement (as defined in § 1.411(a)-7(c)(4)(ii)).

(e) *Coordination with certain provisions.*—Notwithstanding section 411(b)(1)(H), (b)(2) and the preceding paragraphs of this section, the following rules shall apply.

(1) *Section 415 limitations.*—No allocation to the account of a participant in a defined contribution plan (including a target benefit plan described in § 1.410(a)-4(a)(1)) shall be required for a limitation year by section 411(b)(2) and no benefit accrual with respect to a participant in a defined benefit plan shall be required for a limitation year by section 411(b)(1)(H)(i) to the extent that the allocation or accrual would cause the plan to exceed the limitations of section 415(b), (c) or (e) applicable to the participant for the limitation year.

(2) *Prohibited discrimination.*—(i) No allocation to the account of a highly compensated employee in a defined contribution plan (including a target benefit plan) shall be required for a plan year by section 411(b)(2) to the extent the allocation would cause the plan to discriminate in favor of highly compensated employees within the meaning of section 401(a)(4).

(ii) No benefit accrual on behalf of a highly compensated employee in a defined benefit plan shall be required for a plan year by section 411(b)(1)(H)(i) to the extent such benefit accrual would cause the plan to discriminate in favor of highly compensated employees within the meaning of section 401(a)(4).

(iii) The Commissioner may provide additional rules relating to prohibited discrimination in favor of highly compensated employees.

(3) *Permitted disparity.*—In the case of a plan that would fail to satisfy section 401(a)(4) except for the application of section 401(l), no allocation to the account of a participant in a defined contribution plan and no benefit accrual on behalf of a participant in a defined benefit plan shall be required under section 411(b)(1)(H) or (b)(2) for a plan year to the extent such allocation or accrual would cause the plan to fail to satisfy the requirements of section 401(l) and the regulations thereunder for the plan year.

(f) *Effective dates.*—(1) *Noncollectively bargained plans.*—(i) *In general.*—Except as otherwise provided in paragraph (f)(2) of this section, section 411(b)(1)(H) and (b)(2) and paragraphs (b) and (c) of this section are effective for plan years beginning on or after January 1, 1988, with respect to a participant who is credited with at least 1 hour of service in a plan year beginning on or after January 1, 1988. Section 411(b)(1)(H) and (b)(2) and paragraphs (b) and (c) of this section are not effective with respect to a participant who is not credited with at least 1 hour of service in a plan year beginning on or after January 1, 1988.

(ii) *Defined benefit plans.*—In the case of a participant who is credited with at least 1 hour of service in a plan year beginning on or after January 1, 1988, section 411(b)(1)(H) and paragraph (b) of this section are effective with respect to all years of service completed by the participant, including years of service completed before the first plan year beginning on or after January 1, 1988. Accordingly, in the case of a participant described in the preceding sentence, a defined benefit plan does not satisfy section 411(b)(1)(H) and paragraph (b) of this section for a plan year beginning on or after January 1, 1988, if the plan disregards, because of the participant's attainment of any age, any year of service completed by the participant or any compensation earned by the participant after attaining such age. However, a defined benefit plan is not required under section 411(b)(1)(H) and paragraph (b) of this section to take into account for benefit accrual purposes any year of service completed before an employee becomes a participant in the plan. See paragraph (b)(2) of this section for rules relating to benefit and service limitations that may be imposed by a defined benefit plan.

(iii) *Defined contribution plans.*—Section 411(b)(2) and paragraph (c) of this section are not applicable with respect to allocations of employer contributions or forfeitures to the accounts of participants under a defined contribution plan for a plan year beginning before January 1, 1988. However, in the case of a defined contribution plan under which allocations to the accounts of participants for a plan year are determined on the basis of an allocation formula that takes into account service or compensation for the employer during prior plan years, section 411(b)(2) and paragraph (c) of this section are effective for plan years beginning on or after January 1, 1988, with respect to all years of service completed by the participant, including years of service completed before the first plan year beginning on or after January 1, 1988. Accordingly, in the case of a participant who has at least 1 hour of service in a plan year beginning on or after January 1, 1988, a defined contribution plan containing an allocation formula described in the preceding sentence does not satisfy section 411(b)(2) and paragraph (c) of this section with respect to allocations for a plan year beginning on or after January 1, 1988, if the plan disregards, because of the participant's attainment of any age, any year of service completed by the participant. See paragraph (c)(2) of this section for rules relating to limitations on allocations to the accounts of participants that may be imposed by a defined contribution plan.

(iv) *Employee contributions.*—In applying paragraph (f)(1)(i), (ii) and (iii) of this section to plan years beginning on or after January 1, 1988, a year of service completed before the first plan year beginning on or after January 1, 1988, will not be treated as being disregarded under a plan on account of a participant's attainment of a specified age solely because such year of service is disregarded under the plan because the participant was not eligible to make voluntary or mandatory employee contributions (as well as contributions under a cash or deferred arrangement described in section 401(k)) under the plan for such year. A plan is not required to permit a participant to make voluntary or mandatory employee contributions (as well as contributions under a cash or deferred arrangement described in section 401(k)) for a plan year beginning before January 1, 1988, in order to satisfy section 411(b)(1)(H) or (b)(2) or paragraph (b) or (c) of this section for a plan year beginning on or after January 1, 1988.

(v) *Hour of service.*—For purposes of this paragraph (f)(1), one hour of service means one hour of service recognized under the plan or required to be recognized under the plan by section 410 (relating to minimum participation standards) or section 411 (relating to minimum vesting standards). In the case of a plan that does not determine service on the basis of hours of service, one hour of service means any service recognized under the plan or required to be recognized under the plan by section 410 (relating to minimum participation standards) or section 411 (relating to minimum vesting standards).

(vi) *Examples.*—The provisions of paragraph (f)(1) of this section may be illustrated by the following examples. In each example, assume that the participant completes the hours of service in a plan year required under the plan to accrue a full benefit or receive an allocation for the plan year.

Example (1). Employer X maintains a noncontributory defined benefit plan (that is not a collectively bargained plan) that provides a normal retirement benefit equal to 1% of a participant's average annual compensation for the participant's three consecutive years of highest compensation, multiplied by the participant's years of credited service under the plan. The plan contains no limit on the number of years of credited service taken into account for purposes of determining the normal retirement benefit provided by the plan. The plan uses the calendar year as its plan year. The plan specifies a normal retirement age of 65 and provides (prior to January 1, 1988) that no compensation earned and no service performed by a participant after attainment of normal retirement age will be taken into account in determining the participant's normal retirement benefit. Participant A attains normal retirement age on December 15, 1985. A continues in the full time service of X and has at least 1 hour of service for X during the plan year beginning on January 1, 1988. As of the plan year ending December 31, 1985, A had 35 years of credited service under the plan. In accordance with the plan provisions in effect prior to January 1, 1988, A's service and compensation during the 1986 and 1987 plan years is not taken into account in determining A's normal retirement benefit for those plan years. Beginning on January 1, 1988, the plan provisions that compensation earned and years of service completed after normal retirement age are not taken into account in determining a participant's normal retirement benefit may not be applied to A. Thus, as of the plan year beginning January 1, 1988, A's normal retirement benefit under the plan must be determined without regard to those provisions. Accordingly, beginning on January 1, 1988, the plan is required to take into account A's service for X and A's compensation from X during the 1986 and 1987 plan years for purposes of determining A's normal retirement benefit in order to satisfy section 411(b)(1)(H) and paragraph (b) of this section.

Example (2). Assume the same facts as in *Example (1)*, except that the plan provides that, in determining a participant's normal retirement benefit under the plan (a) not more than 35 years of credited service will be taken into account and (b) no compensation earned after 35 years of credited service have been completed will be taken into account. Accordingly, the plan is not required to take into account A's service for X or A's compensation from X during the 1986 and 1987 plan years for purposes of determining A's normal retirement benefit in order to satisfy section 411(b)(1)(H) and paragraph (b) of this section.

Example (3). Assume the same facts as in *Example (1)*, except that A retires on December 5, 1987 and does not perform any hours of service for X after A's retirement. Accordingly, the plan is not required to take into account A's service for X and A's compensation from X during the 1986 and 1987 plan years for purposes of determining A's normal retirement benefit in order to satisfy section 411(b)(1)(H) and paragraph (b) of this section.

Example (4). Assume the same facts as in *Example (1)*, except that the plan requires, as a condition to accruing benefits attributable to employer contributions under the plan, that a participant make employee contributions under the plan. The plan provides that a participant is not eligible to make employee contributions in a plan year beginning after the plan year in which the participant attains normal retirement age under the plan. Accordingly, A does not make employee contributions during the 1986 and 1987 plan years and, therefore, does not accrue in those plan years a benefit attributable to employer contributions. The plan is not required to take into account A's service for X and A's compensation from X during the 1986 and 1987 plan years in order to satisfy section 411(b)(1)(H) and paragraph (b) of this section. In addition, the plan is not required to permit A to make employee contributions to the plan for the 1986 and 1987 plan years in order to satisfy section 411(b)(1)(H) and paragraph (b) of this section.

Example (5). Employer Y maintains a profit-sharing plan (that is not a collectively bargained plan). The plan is the only qualified plan maintained by Y and uses the calendar year as its plan year. The formula under the plan for allocating employer contributions and forfeitures to the accounts of participants contains a years of service factor. Pursuant to the allocation formula containing the years of service factor, employer contributions and forfeitures for the plan year are allocated among the accounts of participants on the basis of one unit for each full $200 of compensation of the participant for the plan year and one unit for each year of credited service for Y completed by the participant. The plan contains no limit on the number of years of credited service taken into account for purposes of determining the allocation to the account of a participant for the plan year under the plan's allocation formula. The plan specifies a normal retirement age of 65 and provides (prior to January 1, 1988) that no service performed by a participant in a plan year beginning after attainment of normal retirement age will be taken into account in determining the allocation to the participant's account for a plan year. Participant B attains normal retirement age on December 15, 1985. B continues in the full time service of Y and has at least 1 hour of service for Y during the plan year beginning January 1, 1988. As of the plan year ending December 31, 1985, B had 35 years of credited service under the plan. In accordance with the plan provisions in effect prior to January 1, 1988, B's service during the 1986 and 1987 plan years is not taken into account in determining the allocation of employer contributions and forfeitures to B's account for the 1986 and 1987 plan years. As of the plan year beginning January 1, 1988, the plan provision that years of service in plan years beginning after attainment of normal retirement age are not taken into account in determining the allocation of employer contributions and forfeitures to the accounts of participants may not be applied to B. Thus, the allocation of employer contributions and forfeitures to B's account for the 1988 plan year must be determined under the allocation formula contained in the plan without regard to that provision. Accordingly, the plan is required to take into account B's service for Y during the 1986 and 1987 plan years for purposes of determining the allocation of employer contributions and forfeitures to B's account for the 1988 plan year in order to satisfy section 411(b)(2) and paragraph (c) of this section. However, the plan is not required to provide any additional allocations to B's account under the plan for the 1986 or 1987 plan year in order to satisfy section 411 (b)(2) and paragraph (c) of this section.

Example (6). Assume the same facts as in *Example (5)*, except that the plan provides that, in determining the allocation of employer contributions and forfeitures to the account of a participant for a plan year, not more than 35 years of credited service for Y will be taken into account. Accordingly, the plan is not required to take into account B's service for Y during the 1986 or 1987 plan years for purposes of determining the allocation of employer contributions and forfeitures to B's account for the 1988 plan year under the allocation formula contained in the plan.

(2) *Collectively bargained plans.*—(i) In the case of a plan maintained pursuant to 1 or more

collective bargaining agreements between employee representatives and 1 or more employers, ratified before March 1, 1986, section 411(b)(1)(H) and (b)(2) is effective for benefits provided under, and employees covered by, any such agreement with respect to plan years beginning on or after the later of—

(A) January 1, 1988, or

(B) The date on which the last of such collective bargaining agreements terminates (determined without regard to any extension of any such agreement occurring on or after March 1, 1986).

However, notwithstanding the preceding sentence, section 411(b)(1)(H) and (b)(2) shall be effective for benefits provided under, and employees covered by, any agreement described in this paragraph (f)(2)(i) no later than with respect to the first plan year beginning on or after January 1, 1990.

(ii) The effective date provisions of paragragh (f)(1) of this section shall apply in the same manner to plans described in paragraph (f)(2)(i) of this section, except that the effective date determined under paragraph (f)(2)(i) of this section shall be substituted for the effective date determined under paragraph (f)(1) of this section.

(iii) In accordance with the provisions of paragraph (f)(2)(i) of this section, a plan described therein may be subject to different effective dates under section 411(b)(1)(H) and (b)(2) for employees who are covered by a collective bargaining agreement and employees who are not covered by a collective bargaining agreement.

(iv) For purposes of paragraph (f)(2)(i) of this section, the service crediting rules of paragraph (f)(1) of this section shall apply to a plan described in paragraph (f)(2)(i) of this section, except that in applying such rules the effective date determined under paragraph (f)(2)(i) of this section shall be substituted for the effective date determined under paragraph (f)(1) of this section. See paragraph (f)(1)(v) of this section for rules relating to the recognition of an hour of service.

(3) *Amendments to plans.*—(i) Except as provided in paragraph (f)(3)(ii) of this section, plan amendments required by section 411(b)(1)(H) and (b)(2) (the applicable sections) shall not be required to be made before the first plan year beginning on or after January 1, 1989, if the following requirements are met—

(A) The plan is operated in accordance with the requirements of the applicable section for all periods before the first plan year beginning on or after January 1, 1989, for which such section is effective with respect to the plan; and

(B) Such plan amendments are adopted no later than the last day of the first plan year beginning on or after January 1, 1989, and are made effective retroactively for all periods for which the applicable section is effective with respect to the plan.

(ii) In the case of a collectively bargained plan described in paragraph (f)(2)(i) of this section that satisfies the requirements of paragraph (f)(3)(i) of this section (as modified by this paragraph (f)(3)(ii)), paragraph (f)(3)(i) shall be applied by substituting for "the first plan year beginning on or after January 1, 1989," the first plan year beginning on or after the later of—

(A) January 1, 1989, or

(B) The date on which the last of such collective bargaining agreements terminates (determined without regard to any extension of any such agreement occurring on or after March 1, 1986).

However, notwithstanding the preceding sentence, section 411(b)(1)(H) and (b)(2) shall be applicable to plans described in this paragraph (f)(3)(ii) no later than the first plan year beginning on or after January 1, 1990. [Reg. §1.411(b)-2.]

☐ Par. 6. Section 1.411(c)-1 is amended by revising paragraph (f)(2) to read as follows:

§1.411(c)-1. Allocation of accrued benefits between employer and employee contributions.—

* * *

(f) *Suspension of benefits, etc.*—* * *

(2) *Employment after retirement.*—Except as permitted by paragraph (f)(1) of this section, a defined benefit plan must make an actuarial adjustment to an accrued benefit the payment of which is deferred past normal retirement age. See, also, section 411(b)(1)(H) (relating to continued accruals after normal retirement age) and §1.411(b)-2.

Employers-Employees: Retirement Plans: Contributions: Allocation: Accrued Benefits

Employers-Employees: Retirement Plans: Contributions: Allocation: Accrued Benefits.— An amendment to Reg. §1.411(c)-1, relating to guidance on calculation of an employee's accrued benefit derived from the employee's contributions to a qualified defined benefit pension plan, is proposed (published in the Federal Register on December 22, 1995).

☐ Par. 2. Section 1.411(c)-1 is amended by:

1. Revising paragraphs (c)(1), (c)(2), (c)(3), (c)(5) and (c)(6).
2. Revising paragraph (d).
3. Adding paragraph (g).

The additions and revisions read as follows:

§1.411(c)-1. Allocation of accrued benefits between employer and employee contributions.—

* * *

(c) *Accrued benefit derived from mandatory employee contributions to a defined benefit plan.*—(1) *General Rule.*—In the case of a defined benefit plan (as defined in section 414(j)), the accrued benefit derived from contributions made by an employee under the plan as of any applicable date in the form of an annual benefit commencing at normal retirement age and nondecreasing for the life of the participant is equal to the amount of the employee's accumulated contributions (determined under paragraph (c)(3) of this section) divided by the appropriate conversion factor with respect to that form of benefit (determined under paragraph (c)(2) of this section). Paragraph (e) of this section provides rules for actuarial adjustments where the benefit is to be determined in a form other than the form described in this paragraph (c)(1).

(2) *Appropriate conversion factor*.—For purposes of this paragraph, with respect to a form of annual benefit commencing at normal retirement age described in paragraph (c)(1), the term *appropriate conversion factor* means the present value of an annuity in the form of that annual benefit commencing at normal retirement age at a rate of $1 per year, computed using an interest rate and mortality table which would be used under the plan under section 417(e)(3) and § 1.417(e)-1T (as of the determination date).

(3) *Accumulated contributions*.—For purposes of section 411(c) and this section, the term *accumulated contributions* means the total of—

(i) All mandatory contributions made by the employee (determined under paragraph (c)(4) of this section);

(ii) Interest (if any) on such contributions, computed at the rate provided by the plan to the end of the last plan year to which section 411(a)(2) does not apply (by reason of the applicable effective dates);

(iii) Interest on the sum of the amounts determined under paragraphs (c)(3)(i) and (ii) of this section compounded annually at the rate of 5 percent per annum from the beginning of the first plan year to which section 411(a)(2) applies (by reason of the applicable effective date) to the beginning of the first plan year beginning after December 31, 1987;

(iv) Interest on the sum of the amounts determined under paragraphs (c)(3)(i) through (iii) of this section compounded annually at 120 percent of the Federal mid-term rate(s) (as in effect under section 1274(d) of the Internal Revenue Code for the first month of a plan year) for the period beginning with the first plan year beginning after December 31, 1987 and ending on the determination date; and

(v) Interest on the sum of the amounts determined under paragraphs (c)(3)(i) through (iv) of this section compounded annually, using an interest rate which would be used under the plan under section 417(e)(3) and § 1.417(e)-1T (as of the determination date), from the determination date to the date on which the employee would attain normal retirement age.

* * *

(5) *Determination date*.—(i) For purposes of section 411(c) and this section, in a case in which a participant will receive his or her entire accrued benefit derived from employee contributions in any one of the forms described in paragraph (c)(5)(ii), the term *determination date* means the date on which distribution of such benefit commences. Alternatively, in such a case, the plan may provide that the determination date is the annuity starting date with respect to that benefit, as defined in § 1.401(a)-20, Q&A-10.

(ii) Paragraph (c)(5)(i) applies to the following forms: an annuity that is substantially nonincreasing (e.g., an annuity that is nonincreasing except for automatic increases to reflect increases in the consumer price index), substantially nonincreasing installment payments for a fixed number of years, or a single sum distribution.

(iii) In a case in which a participant will receive a distribution that is not described in paragraph (c)(5)(i), the determination date will be as provided by the Commissioner.

(6) *Examples*.

(i) *Facts*. (A) In the following examples, Employer X maintains a qualified defined benefit plan that required mandatory employee contributions for 1987 and prior years, but not for years after 1987. The plan year is the calendar year. The plan provides for a normal retirement age of 65 and for 100 percent vesting in the employer-derived portion of a participant's accrued benefit after 5 years of service.

(B) The terms of the plan provide that the normal form of benefit is a level monthly amount commencing at normal retirement age and payable for the life of the participant. A plan participant who elects not to receive benefits in the form of the qualified joint and survivor annuity provided by the plan may elect to receive a single-sum distribution of the present value of his or her accrued benefit upon termination of employment.

(C) As of January 1, 1995, the plan was amended to provide that, for purposes of computing actuarially equivalent benefits, the single sum is calculated using the unisex version of the 1983 GAM mortality table (as provided in Revenue Ruling 95-6 (1995-1 C.B. 80)), and interest at the rate equal to the annual rate of interest on 30-year Treasury securities for the first calendar month preceding the first day of the plan year during which the annuity starting date occurs.

(D) Under the plan, employee contributions are accumulated at 3 percent interest for plan years beginning before 1976, 5 percent interest for plan years beginning after 1975 and before 1988, and interest at 120 percent of the Federal mid-term rate (as in effect under section 1274(d) for the first month of the plan year) for plan years beginning after 1987 until the determination date. Under the plan, the determination date is defined as the annuity starting date. For the period from the determination date until the date on which the employee attains normal retirement age, interest is credited at the interest rate which would be used under the plan under section 417(e)(3) as of the determination date.

(E) A, an unmarried participant, terminates employment with X on January 1, 1997 at age 56 with 15 years of service. As of December 31, 1987, A's total accumulated mandatory employee contributions to the plan, including interest compounded annually at 5 percent for plan years beginning after 1975 and before 1988, equaled $3,021. A receives his or her accrued benefit in the form of an annual single life annuity commencing at normal retirement age. A's annuity starting date is January 1, 2006, and therefore the determination date is January 1, 2006.

(ii) *Annuity at Normal Retirement Age—Determination of Employee-Derived and Total Plan Vested Accrued Benefit*.

Example 1.

For purposes of this example, it is assumed that A's total accrued benefit under the plan in the normal form of benefit commencing at normal retirement age is $2,949 per year. A's benefit, as of January 1, 2006, would be determined as follows:

(A) Determine A's total accrued benefit in the form of an annual single life annuity commencing at normal retirement age under the plan's formula ($2,949 per year payable at age 65).

(B) Determine A's accumulated contributions with interest to January 1, 1997. As of December 31, 1987, A's accumulated contributions with interest under the plan provisions were $3,021. A's employee contributions are accumulated from December 31, 1987 to January 1, 1997 using 120 percent of the Federal mid-term rate under section 1274(d). This rate is 10.61 percent for 1988, 11.11 percent for 1989, 9.57 percent for 1990, 9.78 percent for 1991, 8.10 percent for 1992, 7.63 percent for 1993, 6.40 percent for 1994, and 9.54 percent for 1995. It is assumed for purposes of this example that 120 percent of the Federal mid-term rate is 7.00 percent for each year between 1996 and 2006, and that the 30-year Treasury rate for December 2005 is 8.00 percent. Thus, A's contributions accumulated to January 1, 1997, equal $6,480.

(C) Determine A's accumulated contributions with interest to normal retirement age (January 1, 2006) using, for the 1996 plan year and for years until normal retirement age, 120 percent of the Federal mid-term rate under section 1274(d), which is assumed to be 7.00 percent ($11,913).

(D) Determine the accrued annual annuity benefit derived from A's contributions by dividing A's accumulated contributions determined in paragraph (C) of this *Example 1* by the plan's appropriate conversion factor. The plan's appropriate conversion factor at age 65 is 9.196, and the accrued benefit derived from A's contributions would be $11,913 ÷ 9.196 = $1,295.

(E) Determine the accrued benefit derived from employer contributions as the excess, if any, of the employee's accrued benefit under the plan over the accrued benefit derived from employee contributions ($2,949 – $1,295 = $1,654 per year).

(F) Determine the vested percentage of the accrued benefit derived from employer contributions under the plan's vesting schedule (100 percent).

(G) Determine the vested accrued benefit derived from employer contributions by multiplying the accrued benefit derived from employer contributions by the vested percentage ($1,654 × 100 percent = $1,654 per year).

(H) Determine A's vested accrued benefit in the form of an annual single life annuity commencing at normal retirement age by adding the accrued benefit derived from employee contributions and the vested accrued benefit derived from employer contributions, the sum of paragraphs (D) and (G) of this *Example 1* ($1,295 + $1,654 = $2,949 per year).

Example 2.

This example assumes the same facts as *Example 1* except that A's total accrued benefit under the plan in the normal form of benefit commencing at normal retirement age is $1,000 per year. A's benefit, as of January 1, 2006, would be determined as follows:

(A) Determine A's total accrued benefit in the form of an annual single life annuity commencing at normal retirement age under the plan's formula ($1,000 per year payable at age 65).

(B) Determine A's accumulated contributions with interest to January 1, 1997 ($6,480 from paragraph (B) of *Example 1*).

(C) Determine A's accumulated contributions with interest to normal retirement age (January 1, 2006) ($11,913 from paragraph (C) of *Example 1*).

(D) Determine the accrued annual annuity benefit derived from A's contributions by dividing A's accumulated contributions determined in paragraph (C) of this *Example 2* by the plan's appropriate conversion factor ($1,295 from paragraph (D) of *Example 1*).

(E) Determine the accrued benefit derived from employer contributions as the excess, if any, of the employee's accrued benefit under the plan over the accrued benefit derived from employee contributions. Because the accrued benefit derived from employee contributions ($1,295) is greater than the employee's accrued benefit under the plan ($1,000), the accrued benefit derived from employer contributions is zero, and A's vested accrued benefit in the form of an annual single life annuity commencing at normal retirement age is $1,295 per year.

(d) *Delegation to Commissioner.*—The Commissioner may prescribe additional guidance on calculating the accrued benefit derived from employee contributions under a defined benefit plan through publication in the Internal Revenue Bulletin of revenue rulings, notices, or other documents (see § 601.601(d)(2) of this chapter).

(e) * * *

(f) * * *

(g) *Effective date.*—Paragraphs (c)(1), (c)(2), (c)(3), (c)(5), (c)(6) and (d) of this section are effective for plan years beginning on or after January 1, 1997.

Employee Trusts: Discrimination

Employee Trusts: Vesting Schedule: Discrimination.—Reproduced below is the text of proposed Reg. §1.411(d)-1, relating to a determination if the vesting schedule of a qualified plan discriminates in favor of employees who are officers, shareholders, or highly compensated (published in the Federal Register on April 9, 1980); modifications to proposed regulations (published in the Federal Register on June 12, 1980).

§1.411(d)-1. Coordination of vesting and discrimination requirements.—(a) *General rule.*—A plan which satisfies the requirements of section 411(a)(2) shall be treated as satisfying any vesting schedule requirements resulting from the application of section 401(a)(4) unless the plan is discriminatory within the meaning of section 411(d)(1) and this section. A plan is discriminatory if there is a pattern of abuse or there is discriminatory vesting as determined under paragraphs (b) and (c) of this section, respectively. Under section 401(a)(4), a plan which discriminates in favor of employees who are officers, shareholders, or highly compensated (hereinafter referred to as "prohibited group"), is not a qualified plan under section 401(a).

(b) *Pattern of abuse.*—(1) *Definition.*—A plan is discriminatory under section 411(d)(1)(A) and shall not be considered to satisfy the requirements of section 401(a)(4) if there has been a pattern of abuse under the plan tending to discriminate in favor of the prohibited group (hereinafter referred to as "pattern of abuse").

(2) *Test for pattern of abuse.*—The determination of whether there has been a pattern of abuse shall be made on the basis of the facts and circumstances of each case. An example of a pattern of abuse is the systematic dismissal of employees before their accrued benefits vest.

(c) *Discriminatory vesting.*—(1) *Definition.*—A plan is discriminatory under section 411(d)(1)(B) and shall not be considered to satisfy the requirements of section 401(a)(4) if there have been, or there is reason to believe there will be, an accrual of benefits or forfeitures tending to discriminate in favor of the prohibited group by operation of the vesting schedule (hereinafter referred to as "discriminatory vesting").

(2) *Test for discriminatory vesting.*—The determination of whether there is, or there is reason to believe there will be, discriminatory vesting shall be made on the basis of the facts and circumstances of each case. A reasonable disparity between the vested benefits paid to or accrued by the prohibited group and the vested benefits paid to or accrued by other employees will not result in a finding that there is discriminatory vesting.

(d) [Withdrawn.]

(e) *Defined benefit plans.*—A defined benefit plan which satisfies the benefit accrual requirements of section 411(b) shall still be subject to the nondiscrimination requirements of section 401(a)(4) with regard to its benefit accrual rates. Thus, even though a plan satisfies the section 411(b) requirements, the plan may still be discriminatory under section 401(a)(4) with respect to its benefit accruals.

(f) *Effective date.*—This section shall apply to plan years beginning 30 days after the publication of this section in the FEDERAL REGISTER as a Treasury decision. [Reg. § 1.411(d)-1.]

Employees' Trusts: Minimum Funding Requirements

Employees' Trusts: Minimum Funding Requirements: Minimum Funding Excise Taxes.—Reproduced below are the texts of proposed Reg. §§ 1.412(a)-1, 1.412(b)-1 and 1.412(b)-4, 1.412(c)(2)-2, 1.412(c)(4)-1—1.412(c)(10)-1, 1.412(g)-1, proposed amendments to Reg. §§ 1.413-1 and 1.413-2, and the proposed deletions of Temporary Reg. §§ 11.412(c)-7, 11.412(c)-11 and 11.412(c)-12, relating to the minimum funding requirements for employee pension benefit plans, and to excise taxes for failure to meet the minimum funding standards (published in the Federal Register on December 1, 1982).

☐ Paragraph 1. The Income Tax Regulations, 26 CFR Part 1, are amended by adding the following new sections immediately after § 1.411(d)-3:

§ 1.412(a)-1. General scope of minimum funding standard requirements.—(a) *General rule.*—Section 412 of the Code provides minimum funding requirements for plans that include a trust qualified under section 401(a) and for plans that meet the requirements of section 403(a) or section 405(a). Generally, such plans include defined benefit pension plans, money purchase pension plans (including target benefit plans), qualified annuity plans, and qualified bond purchase plans. The minimum funding requirements continue to apply to any plan that was qualified under, or was determined to have met the requirements of, these sections for any plan year beginning on or after the effective date described in paragraph (d) of this section for the plan. Also, under section 302 of the Employee Retirement Income Security Act of 1974 ("ERISA"), the minimum funding requirements apply to employee pension benefit plans described in section 301(a) of that Act. The regulations prescribed under this section and the following sections with respect to section 412 also apply for purposes of sections 302 and 305 of ERISA. These topics are among those discussed in the following sections: maintenance of a funding standard account (including rules for combining and off-setting amounts to be amortized, rules for computing interest on amounts charged and credited to the account, rules relating to the treatment of gains and losses, and rules relating to retroactive changes in the funding standard account required by the Commissioner), § 1.412(b)-1; amortization of experience gains in connection with group deferred annuity contracts, § 1.412(b)-2; funding standard account adjustments for plan mergers and spinoffs, § 1.412(b)-3; plan terminations, § 1.412(b)-4; election of the alternative amortization method of funding, § 1.412(b)-5; determinations to be made under funding method, § 1.412(c)(1)-1; shortfall method, § 1.412(c)(1)-2; valuation of plan assets and reasonable valuation methods, § 1.412(c)(2)-1; bond valuation election, § 1.412(c)(2)-2; reasonable funding methods, § 1.412(c)(3)-1 and -2; certain changes in accrued liability, § 1.412(c)(4)-1; changes in funding method or plan year, § 1.412(c)(5)-1; full funding and the full funding limitation, § 1.412(c)(6)-1 and § 1.412(c)(7)-1; retroactive plan amendment § 1.412(c)(8)-1; frequency of actuarial valuations, § 1.412(c)(9)-1; time for making contributions to satisfy section 412, § 1.412(c)(10)-1; and maintenance of an alternative funding standard account, § 1.412(g)-1.

(b) *Exceptions.*—See section 412(h) for a list of plans not subject to the requirements of section 412. These excepted plans include profit-sharing or stock bonus plans; certain insurance contract, government, and church plans; and certain plans that do not provide for employer contributions.

(c) *Failure to meet minimum funding standards.*—A plan fails to meet the minimum funding standards for a plan year if, as of the end of that plan year, there is an accumulated funding deficiency as defined in section 412(a) and §54.4971-1(d). See regulations under section 4971 for rules relating to taxes for failure to meet the minimum funding standards.

(d) *Effective date.*—(1) *In general.*—Unless otherwise provided, this section and the following sections providing regulations under section 412 apply to any plan year to which section 412 applies. For a plan in existence on January 1, 1974, section 412 generally applies to plan years beginning in 1976. However, this time is extended by special transitional rules under section 1017(c)(2) of ERISA for such existing plans under collective bargaining agreements. For a plan not in existence on January 1, 1974, section 412 generally applies for plan years beginning after September 2, 1974.

(2) *Date when plan is in existence.*—See §1.410(a)-2(c) for rules concerning the date when a plan is considered to be in existence.

(3) *Early application of section 412.*—See §1.410(a)-2(d) for rules permitting plans in existence on January 1, 1974, to elect to have section 412, as well as other provisions added by section 1013 of ERISA, apply to a plan year beginning after September 4, 1974, and before the effective date of the provision otherwise applicable to the plan.

(4) *Transitional rule.*—The regulations issued under sections §1.412(b)-1, §1.412(b)-3, §1.412(b)-4, §1.412(c)(2)-2, §1.412(c)(4)-1, §1.412(c)(5)-1, §1.412(c)(6)-1, §1.412(c)(7)-1, §1.412(c)(8)-1, §1.412(c)(9)-1, §1.412(c) (10)-1, and §1.412(g)-1, unless otherwise indicated, are effective with respect to a particular plan when section 412 first applies to that plan. However, for plan years beginning on or before [INSERT DATE 60 DAYS AFTER PUBLICATION OF THESE REGULATIONS AS A TREASURY DECISION IN THE FEDERAL REGISTER], the plan may rely on the prior published position of the Internal Revenue Service with respect to the application of section 412. Other effective dates are included in §1.412(b)-2, §1.412(c)(1)-2, §1.412(c)(2)-1, §1.412(c)(3)-2 and §1.412(i)-1. [Reg. §1.412(a)-1.]

§1.412(b)-1. Funding standard account.—(a) *General rule.*—Generally, for each single plan subject to the minimum funding standards there must be maintained a funding standard account as prescribed by section 412(b). (See §1.414(1)-1(b)(1) for definition of "single plan".) Such an account for a money purchase pension plan reflects charges for contributions required under the plan, credits for amounts contributed, and charges and credits for amortization bases described in paragraph (b)(3) of this section.

(b) *Definitions and special rules.*—(1) *Accounting date.*—(i) *In general.*—Each charge or credit to the funding standard account is charged or credited as of an accounting date. The accounting date for an item depends on the nature of the item and must be consistent with the computation of the amount of that item.

(ii) *Specific accounting dates.*—The accounting date for each individual charge for normal cost or any charge or credit for the amortization of an amortization base is the date as of which the charge or credit is computed as due during the plan year. The last day of the plan year is the accounting date for any credit described in section 412(b)(3)(C). The first day of the plan year is the accounting date for any credit described in section 412(b)(3)(D) or for any accumulated funding deficiency or credit balance existing as of the end of the prior plan year. The accounting date for each contribution is the date the contribution is made or, if made during the period described in section 412(c)(10), the last day of the plan year. Further, any contribution made must be credited as of the accounting date.

(2) *Valuation rate.*—The term "valuation rate" means the assumed interest rate used to value plan liabilities.

(3) *Amortization base.*—For purposes of this section, the term "amortization base" means any amount established under section 412(b)(2)(B), (C), or (D) to be amortized as a charge to the funding standard account, under section 412(b)(3)(B) to be amortized as a credit to the funding standard account, any other base resulting from a combination or offset of bases or any shortfall gain or loss base under §1.412(c)(1)-2. Any base required by the Commissioner to be established pursuant to an approved change in funding method is also an amortization base. Each amortization base established under one of the provisions enumerated above with respect to a particular year is referred to as an "individual base".

(4) *Amortization period.*—The amortization period for a base is the period of years stated in section 412(b)(2) or (3) over which a particular base is to be amortized. See §1.412(c)(1)-2(g)(2) and (h)(2) for amortization periods under the shortfall method. See section 412(b)(2) and (3) for amortization periods for bases described in those sections. See paragraph (d) of this section for amortization periods of bases resulting from a combination or offset of bases. If the number of years in the amortization period is not an integer, the charge or credit in the last year will not be for the entire amortization amount but will be for the outstanding balance of the base at the time of the charge or credit.

(5) *Outstanding balance.*—The outstanding balance of a base as of the end of a plan year equals the difference between two amounts:

(i) The first amount is the outstanding balance of the base as of the beginning of the plan year (or, if later, the date as of which the base is required to be established) increased by interest at the valuation rate.

(ii) The second amount is the charge (or credit) for that year for the base increased by interest at the valuation rate.

For purposes of testing the basic funding formula in §1.412(c)(3)-1(b)(1) the outstanding balance of amortizable bases must be computed as of the valuation date (the same date as of which the present value of future benefits and the present value of normal costs over the future working lifetime of participants are determined), rather than as of the end of the plan year. In testing the basic funding formula, the outstanding balance as of a valuation date equals the difference between two amounts. The first amount is the outstanding balance as of the preceding valuation date (or, if later, the date as of which the base is required to be established) increased by interest at the valuation rate. The second amount is the charge (or credit) for the plan year preceding the plan year to which the current valuation refers increased by interest at the valuation rate.

(6) *Remaining amortization period.*—The remaining amortization period for an amortization base is the difference between the amortization period and the number of years (including whole and fractional years) for which the base has been reduced by charging or crediting the funding standard account, as the case may be, with the amortization payment for each year.

(7) *Amortization amount.*—The amortization amount is the amount of the charge or credit to the funding standard account required with respect to an amortization base for a plan year.

(8) *True and absolute values.*—See §1.404(a)-14(b)(4) for a definition of the terms "true value" and "absolute value."

(9) *Immediate gain type funding method.*—A funding method is an immediate gain type method if, under the method—

(i) The accrued liability may be determined solely from the computations with respect to the liabilities;

(ii) The accrued liability is an integral part of the funding method; and

(iii) The accrued liability is the excess of the present value, as of any valuation date, of the projected future benefit costs for all plan participants and beneficiaries over the present value of future contributions for the normal cost of all current plan participants.

Examples of the immediate gain type of funding method are the unit credit method, the entry-age normal cost method, and the individual level premium method.

(10) *Spread gain type funding method.*—A funding method is a spread gain type method if it is not an immediate gain type method. Examples of the spread gain type of funding method are the aggregate cost method, the frozen initial liability cost method and the attained age normal cost method.

(11) *Actual unfunded liability for immediate gain funding methods.*—(i) *In general.*—For a funding method of the immediate gain type, the actual unfunded liability as of any valuation date is the excess, if any, of the accrued liability over the actuarial value of assets as of that date.

(ii) *Accrued liability.*—The accrued liability is equal to the present value of future benefits less the present value of future normal costs. Generally, for purposes of computing costs for a plan year and gains and losses for a plan year, the normal cost for the plan year to which the valuation refers is considered to be a future normal cost and is not included in the accrued liability.

(iii) *Actuarial value of assets.*—The value of assets must be determined in a manner consistent with section 412(c)(2) of the Code and §1.412(c)(2)-1. Furthermore, for purposes of computing costs for a plan year and gains and losses for a plan year, the assets must be treated in a manner that is consistent with the method of calculation of the accrued liability. If, in determining the accrued liability, the normal cost for the plan year to which the valuation refers is treated as a future normal cost, then the assets used to compute the unfunded accrued liability should not include contributions that are credited to the funding standard account for the plan year to which the valuation refers or for any plan year thereafter.

(12) *Actual unfunded liability for spread gain funding methods.*—For a funding method of the spread gain type that maintains an unfunded liability, the actual unfunded liability equals the expected unfunded liability.

(13) *Expected unfunded liability.*—The expected unfunded liability as of any valuation date is determined as:

(i) The actual unfunded liability as of the prior valuation date increased with interest at the valuation rate of this later valuation date, plus

(ii) Normal costs representing accrued liabilities that were not included in determining the accrued liability as of the prior valuation date (*i.e.*, such costs were considered future normal costs as of the prior valuation date) but that are included (*i.e.*, are not considered future normal costs) in determining the accrued liability as of this later valuation date, plus interest at the valuation rate from the date as of which the normal costs were assumed payable to this valuation date, minus

(iii) The amount considered contributed by the employer to or under the plan for the plan year that was included in the calculation of the actual unfunded liability as of the prior valuation date and was included in the calculation of the actual unfunded liability as of this later valuation date, plus interest at the valuation rate from the date on which the contribution was made if made during the plan year, or under section 412(c)(10) was deemed to have been made if made after the plan year, to this later valuation date.

(14) *Plan year to which a valuation refers.*—The plan year for which the funding standard account is charged with the first normal cost determined by a valuation is the plan year to which the valuation refers. See also §1.412(c)(9)-1(b) concerning the date of a valuation.

(c) *Establishment and maintenance of amortization bases.*—(1) *Immediate gain type funding methods.*—Under a plan using an immediate gain type funding method, a new amortization base must be established to reflect each change in unfunded past service liability arising from a plan amendment, net experience gain or loss, and change in unfunded past service liability arising from a change in funding method or actuarial assumptions.

(2) *Spread gain type funding methods.*—(i) *In general.*—Under a plan using a spread gain type funding method, amortization bases may be established to reflect changes in unfunded past service liability arising from plan amendments or changes in actuarial assumptions. Alternatively, these changes in unfunded liability may be reflected in the normal cost. Whether these changes are reflected in amortization bases or in the normal cost is part of the funding method. Thus, any change from past practice constitutes a change in funding method and must be approved under section 412(c)(5). Furthermore, the method must treat increases and decreases due to any type of event consistently.

(ii) *Experience gain or loss.*—An amortization base may not be established to reflect a net experience gain or loss under a plan using a spread gain type funding method.

(3) *Special amortization bases.*—Any amortization base established to amortize a waived

funding deficiency under section 412(b)(2)(C) must continue to be maintained regardless of the type of funding method used by the plan. Also see § 1.412(b)-1(d)(1).

(d) *Combining and offsetting amounts to be amortized.*—(1) *In general.*—Under section 412(b)(4), individual bases, with the exception of bases under section 412(b)(2)(C), may be combined and offset to form a single base. This single base is computed under the provisions of paragraph (d) that follow. However, any number of amortization bases having the same remaining amortization period may be combined and offset simply by adding the outstanding balances of the individual bases, using true rather than absolute values, without regard to the computations under paragraph (d) of this section that follow. Bases under section 412(b)(2)(C) may not be combined with any bases not established under section 412(b)(2)(C).

(2) *Combined outstanding balances of bases for charges and for credits.*—Except as provided in subparagraph (1), the outstanding balances of any individual bases established for the purpose of charging the funding standard account may be combined as of any date by adding the outstanding balance of each base to be combined as of that date. Likewise, the outstanding balances of any bases for crediting the account may be combined.

(3) *Determine remaining amortization period of each combined base.*—The remaining amortization period of a combined base is determined as follows:

(i) Add the amortization amounts, based on the same mode of payment, for the individual bases being combined. Amortization amounts are of the same mode of payment if they are charged or credited on the same day of the plan year, or on the same days if charged or credited in installments during the plan year.

(ii) Divide the outstanding balance of the combined base by the combined amortization amount determined under subdivision (i).

(iii) Compute the period of years for which the amount determined under subdivision (ii) provides an annuity certain of $1 per year at the valuation rate. This number, the remaining amortization period, must be computed in terms of fractional years, if necessary. Standard present value tables may be used together with linear interpolation.

(iv) As an alternative, the amortization period may be rounded to the next lowest integer (if charge bases) or next highest integer (if credit bases) and the amortization amount must then be recomputed by dividing the outstanding balance of the combined base by the present value of an annuity certain of $1 per year at the valuation rate for the rounded amortization period.

(4) *Offset.*—Combined bases may be offset only if all charge and credit bases have been combined (except those that may not be combined pursuant to subparagraph (1)). The combined charge base and the combined credit base are offset by subtracting the lesser outstanding balance from the greater outstanding balance. The difference between these two outstanding balances is amortized over the remaining amortization period for the greater of the two outstanding balances, whether for charges or for credits. The amortization amount (charge or credit) for this offset base is the level amount payable for each plan year to reduce the outstanding balance of the base to zero over the remaining amortization period at the valuation rate. However, see paragraph (d)(3)(iv) of this section concerning an alternative method of computing the remaining amortization period.

(5) *Example.*—The principles of paragraph (d) of this section are illustrated by the following example.

Example. Assume that at the beginning of a plan year the actuary for a plan decides to combine and offset the amortization bases as reflected in the plan's funding standard account. No funding deficiency of the plan has been waived. All amortization amounts are due at the end of the plan year. The valuation rate is 5 percent. Based on pertinent information from the plan records, all amortization bases, A and B for charges and C and D for credits, are combined and offset as follows:

Base	*Outstanding balance (beginning of year)*	*Amortization amount (due end of year)*	*Remaining amortization period*
(i) *Individual bases.*			
A	$165,468	$10,000	36
B	8,863	1,000	12
C	(4,153)	(500)	11
D	(30,745)	(2,000)	30
(ii) *Combined bases.*			
AB	$174,331	$11,000	32.23
CD	(34,898)	(2,500)	24.53
(iii) *Offset base.*			
ABCD	$139,433	$8,798	32.23

(iv) The outstanding balances of the charge and credit bases were combined in step (ii) by adding outstanding balances of the like bases (165,468 + 8,863 = 174,331 and 4,153 + 30,745 = 34,898). The charge and credit base amortization amounts were similarly computed (10,000 + 1,000 = 11,000 and 500 + 2,000 = 2,500). The remaining amortization periods were derived from standard present value tables and linear interpolation as the amount having a present value at the 5 percent valuation rate for a $1 per year annuity certain equal to the ratio of the outstanding balance to the amortization amount.

(v) The combined bases were offset in step (iii) by subtracting base CD from AB to obtain the $139,433 outstanding balance, using the 32.23 remaining amortization period for base AB, and computing the $8,798 amortization amount as the level annual amount necessary to amortize the base fully over 32.23 years. (Alternatively, the amortization period may be rounded to 32 years. The amortization charge corresponding to that amortization period is $8,823.)

(e) *Interest*.—(1) *General rule*.—The funding standard account is charged or credited with interest at the valuation rate for the time between the accounting date for the item giving rise to the interest charge or credit and the end of the plan year.

(2) *Change of interest rate*.—A change of the assumed interest rate under a plan does not affect the outstanding balance or the remaining amortization period of any existing base. However, the amortization amount for each base is increased to reflect an increase in interest and decreased to reflect a decrease in interest so that the present value of future amortization amounts equals the outstanding balance of the base. This change is made in addition to creating any new base required by § 1.412(b)-1(c).

(f) *Gains and losses*.—(1) *Amortization requirements*.—(i) *Immediate gain type funding method*.—A plan that uses an immediate gain type of funding method separately amortizes experience gains and losses over the period prescribed in section 412(b)(2)(B)(iv) and (3)(B)(ii). The first year of the amortization of an experience gain or loss determined as of a particular valuation date is the plan year to which the valuation refers.

(ii) *Spread gain type funding method*.—A plan that uses a spread gain type of funding method spreads experience gains and losses over future periods as a part of the plan's normal cost. These gains and losses are reflected in the amount charged to the funding standard account under section 412(b)(2)(A) and are not separately amortized.

(2) *Amount of experience gain or loss*.—(i) *In general*.—For an immediate gain type of funding method the experience gain determined as of a valuation date is the excess of the expected unfunded liability described in § 1.412(b)-1(b)(13) over the actual unfunded liability described in § 1.412(b)-1(b)(11). The experience loss is the excess of the actual unfunded liability described in § 1.412(b)-1(b)(11) over the expected unfunded liability described in § 1.412(b)-1(b)(13).

(ii) *Special rule*.—Paragraph (f)(2)(ii) of this section applies to an immediate gain funding method if there are no other amortization charges (under section 412(b)(2)(B), (C), or (D)) or credits (under section 412(b)(3)(B)) for the first plan year in which the loss will be amortized. The experience loss as of the valuation date is the sum of—

(A) The actual unfunded liability as of the valuation date, plus

(B) Any credit balance (or minus any funding deficiency) in the funding standard account as of the first day of the first plan year in which the loss will be amortized adjusted with interest at the valuation rate to the valuation date.

(g) *Certain retroactive changes required by Commissioner*.—Under section 412(c)(3), all costs, liabilities, rates of interest, and other factors under the plan must be determined on the basis of actuarial assumptions and methods which, in the aggregate, are reasonable. Assumptions and methods are established in the first Schedule B (Form 5500) that is filed with respect to a plan year and may not be changed for that plan year. However, upon a determination by the Commissioner that the actuarial assumptions and methods used by a plan are not reasonable in the aggregate, the Commissioner may require certain retroactive adjustments to the funding standard account of the plan. The funding standard account must reflect these changes, as required by the Commissioner.

(h) *Reasonable actuarial assumptions*.—(1) *In general*.—The determination whether actuarial assumptions are reasonable in the aggregate is generally based upon the experience under the plan, unless it is established that past experience is not likely to recur and thus is not a good indication of future experience. In addition, assumptions may be considered unreasonable in the circumstances described in paragraphs (h)(2)-(4) of this section.

(2) *No counterbalancing assumptions*.—Assumptions may be considered unreasonable if an assumption used by the plan is not yet reflected in the experience of the plan, is not reasonable under the circumstances of the plan, and is not counterbalanced by another assumption. For example, if a plan with one participant who has not yet attained the normal retirement age, an assumption of an unreasonable annuity purchase rate at normal retirement age may cause assumptions to be unreasonable in the aggregate. In contrast, an unreasonable annuity purchase rate could be counterbalanced by a change in the plan interest rate.

(3) *Inconsistent with benefit structure*.—Assumptions may be unreasonable if use of an assumption is inconsistent with the benefit structure of the plan. For example, a plan which provides benefits not based on compensation may not assume a salary increase if it spreads the present value of future normal costs over the present value of future compensation.

(4) *Inconsistent assumptions*.—Assumptions may be considered unreasonable in the aggregate if one plan assumption is inconsistent with other assumptions used by the plan. For example, an assumption which projects benefits based on a salary increase of 5-percent per year may cause assumptions to be unreasonable in the aggregate in a plan which spreads normal costs over future years' compensation using an assumption of 8-percent annual compensation increases. [Reg. § 1.412(b)-1.]

☐ Par. 2. The Income Tax Regulations, 26 CFR Part 1, are amended by adding the following new sections after § 1.412(b)-2:

§ 1.412(b)-3. Funding standard account adjustments for plan mergers and spinoffs.—[RESERVED]

§ 1.412(b)-4. Plan termination and plan years of less than twelve months.—(a) *General rules*.—The minimum funding standard under section 412 applies to a plan until the end of the plan year in which the plan terminates. Therefore, the funding standard account (or the alternative funding standard account, as the case may be) must be maintained until the end of the plan year in which the plan terminates even though the plan terminates before the last day of the plan year.

(b) *Defined benefit plans.*—In the case of a defined benefit plan, the charges and credits to the funding standard account are adjusted ratably to reflect the portion of the plan year before the day of plan termination. Similarly, annual charges and credits to the funding standard account are adjusted for a short plan year. However, this ratable adjustment is not made for charges described in section 412(b)(2)(C), credits under section 412(b)(3)(A), (C), and (D), for interest charges and credits under section 412(b)(5), and for credits under section 412(c)(6).

(c) *Money purchase pension plans.*—(1) *General rule for termination.*—In the case of a money purchase pension plan, the minimum funding standard requires the funding standard account to be charged with the entire amount of any contribution due on or before the date of plan termination. However, it does not require a charge for contributions due after that date.

(2) *General rule for short plan year.*—In the case of a money purchase pension plan, the minimum funding standard requires the funding standard account to be charged with the entire amount of any contribution due as of a date within a short plan year.

(3) *Due date of contributions.*—For purposes of paragraphs (c)(1) and (2) of this section, a contribution is due as of the earlier of—

(i) The date specified in the plan, or

(ii) The date as of which the contribution is required to be allocated.

(4) *Date for allocation of contribution.*—For purposes of paragraph (c)(3)(ii) of this section, a contribution is required to be allocated as of a date if all the requirements for the allocation have been satisfied as of that date.

(d) *Date of plan termination.*—(1) *Title IV plans.*—In the case of a plan subject to Title IV of ERISA, the date of plan termination is generally the date described in section 4048 of ERISA. However, if that date precedes the tenth day after the date on which notice of intent to terminate is filed, and if any contributions made or required by Code section 412 to avoid an accumulated funding deficiency for the period ending on such tenth day would increase any participant's benefits upon termination (taking benefits guaranteed by the Pension Benefit Guaranty Corporation into account), the date of termination will be the tenth day after the date on which notice of intent to terminate is filed.

(2) *Other plans.*—In the case of a plan not subject to Title IV of ERISA, the date of plan termination occurs no earlier than the date on which the actions necessary to effect the plan termination are taken. The determination of this date is based on the facts and circumstances of each case.

(e) *Partial terminations.*—This section does not apply to a partial plan termination within the meaning of section 411(d)(3)(A).

(f) *Funding excise taxes.*—See § 54.4971-3(d) of the Pension Excise Tax Regulations (26 CFR Part 54) for the effect of plan termination on an employer's liability for taxes imposed by section 4971(a) and (b). [Reg. § 1.412(b)-4.]

☐ Par. 3. The Income Tax Regulations, 26 CFR Part 1, are amended by adding the following new section after § 1.412(c)(2)-1:

§ 1.412(c)(2)-2. Bond valuation election.—(a) *Scope of election.*—(1) *In general.*—The election described in section 412(c)(2)(B) with respect to bonds generally applies to all bonds and evidences of indebtedness including those acquired by merger. The election applies only to defined benefit plans. A defined contribution plan must value bonds and other evidences of indebtedness on the basis of fair market value.

(2) *Exception.*—The election does not apply to bonds or evidences of indebtedness at any time that they are in default as to principal or interest.

(3) *Convertible debt.*—For purposes of this section, a debt instrument which is convertible into an equity security and acquired after [THE DATE 90 DAYS AFTER THE DATE ON WHICH § 1.412(c)(2)-2 IS ADOPTED AS A TREASURY DECISION]is treated as an evidence of indebtedness until the conversion occurs.

(b) *Effect of election.*—(1) *In general.*—The effect of the election is that bonds and other evidences of indebtedness included among the plan assets are valued on an amortized basis rather than on a fair market value basis.

(2) *Amount amortized.*—(i) *In general.*—The amount amortized with respect to a bond or other evidence of indebtedness is generally the difference between its initial cost when acquired by the plan and its redemption value at the end of the amortization period. In the case of a bond or other evidence of indebtedness that was acquired by the plan in a plan year before the plan year for which the election was made, the amortized value for each year must be determined as though the election had always been in effect with respect to the bond or other evidence of indebtedness.

(ii) *Spinoffs.*—The amount amortized after a spinoff is based on the initial cost to the plan which acquired the bond or other evidence of indebtedness and not the value to the plan after the spinoff.

(iii) *Mergers.*—The amount amortized after a merger is based on the cost to the plan which first elected to value the bonds and other evidences of indebtedness on an amortized basis. In the case of a bond or other evidence of indebtedness that was acquired by any merging plan before the election was first made with respect to the bond or other evidence of indebtedness, the premium or discount shall be amortized as provided in paragraph (b)(2)(i).

(3) *Amortization period.*—The amortization period is the time from the date on which the plan acquires the bond or other evidence of indebtedness to its maturity date (or, in the case of a debt instrument that is callable prior to maturity, the earliest call date).

(c) *Effect of default.*—Once the election is made, it applies to each debt instrument held or acquired that is not in default as to principal or interest. While in default, the instrument is subject to the fair market value requirements of section 412(c)(2)(A).

(d) *Manner of making election*.—The plan administrator makes the election by preparing a statement that the election described in section 412(c)(2)(B) is being made and by filing the statement attached to the annual return required under section 6058 for the first plan year for which the election is to apply.

(e) *Revocation of election*.—(1) *Effect*.—Once consent to the revocation of the election is obtained as prescribed in paragraph (e)(2) of this section, all plan assets are valued under section 412(c)(2)(A).

(2) *Consent*.—Consent for the revocation of the election must be obtained in the manner prescribed by the Commissioner for obtaining permission to change funding methods under section 412(c)(5) and § 1.412(c)(5)-1.

(3) *Mergers*.—A plan which has acquired a bond or other evidence of indebtedness by merger must obtain the consent of the Commissioner to value bonds and other evidences of indebtedness on a basis other than amortized value if an election under section 412(c)(2)(B) with respect to the asset acquired had been made prior to the merger. [Reg. § 1.412(c)(2)-2.]

☐ Par. 4. The Income Tax Regulations, 26 CFR Part 1, are amended by adding the following new sections after § 1.412(c)(3)-2:

§ 1.412(c)(4)-1. Certain changes in accrued liability.—(a) *In general*.—In the case of immediate gain type funding methods, section 412(c)(4) treats certain increases and decreases in the accrued liability under a plan as an experience gain or loss. Plans using a spread gain type of funding method will reflect the gain or loss in determining the normal cost under the plan. Under section 412(b)(2) and (3), plans which are valued using a funding method of the immediate gain type will amortize the amount treated as an experience gain or loss in equal amounts over the period described in section 412(b). See § 1.412(b)-1(b) (9) and (10) for examples of spread gain type and immediate gain type funding methods.

(b) *Applicable changes*.—A change treated as an experience gain or loss under section 412(c)(4) includes an increase or decrease in accrued liability caused by:

(1) A change in benefits under the Social Security Act,

(2) A change in other retirement benefits created under Federal or State law,

(3) A change in the definition of "wages" under section 3121, or

(4) A change in the amount of wages under section 3121 that are taken into account for purposes of section 401(a)(5) and the regulations thereunder. [Reg. § 1.412(c)(4)-1.]

§ 1.412(c)(5)-1. Change in plan year or funding method.—Approval given under section 412(c)(5) authorizes a change in plan year or funding method. Written requests for approval are to be submitted, as directed by the Commissioner, to Commissioner of Internal Revenue, Attention: OP:E:A:P, 1111 Constitution Avenue, N.W., Washington, D.C. 20224. Such a request must be submitted before the close of the plan year for which the change is to be effective unless an extension of time for filing the request is granted. [Reg. § 1.412(c)(5)-1.]

§ 1.412(c)(6)-1. Full funding and full funding limitation.—(a) *In general*.—This section provides rules relating to full funding and the full funding limitation under section 412(c)(6) and (7). The full funding limitation for a plan year is the excess, if any, of the accrued liability under the plan plus the normal cost for the plan year over the value of the plan's assets.

(b) *Valuation*.—(1) *Timing rule*.—For purposes of this section, assets and accrued liabilities are to be valued at the usual time used by the plan for valuations.

(2) *Interest adjustments*.—If the valuation is performed before the end of the plan year, the assets and accrued liabilities (including normal cost) are projected to the end of the plan year. The projection is based on the valuation rate.

(c) *Calculation of accrued liability*.—The accrued liability of a plan is determined under the funding method used by the plan. However, if the funding method used by the plan is not an immediate gain method and, thus, does not directly calculate an accrued liability, the calculation of the accrued liability is made under the entry age normal funding method.

(d) *Calculation of normal cost*.—In general, the normal cost is the normal cost determined under the funding method used by the plan. However, if under paragraph (c) accrued liability is calculated under the entry age normal cost method, then the normal cost is also calculated under the entry age normal cost method.

(e) *Calculation of assets*.—The value of plan assets used to determine the full funding limitation is the lesser of the fair market value of the assets or the actuarial value of the assets, if different. The value of plan assets must be reduced by any credit balance existing on the first day of the plan year.

(f) *Effect of full funding on deduction limits*.—See § 1.404(a)-14(k) for provisions relating to the effect of the full funding limitation on the maximum deductible contribution limitations and 10-year amortization bases under section 404(a).

(g) *Effect of the full funding limitation on the funding standard account*.—(1) *General rule*.—If, as of the end of any plan year, the accumulated funding deficiency (calculated without regard to any credit balance for the plan year or any contributions made for that plan year) exceeds the full funding limitation of section 412(c)(7) calculated as of the valuation date and projected, if necessary, to the end of the plan year, then the following adjustments are made:

(i) The amount of such excess is credited to the funding standard account for that plan year.

(ii) As of the end of that plan year, all the amounts described in paragraphs (2)(B), (C), (D), and (3)(B) of section 412(b) which are required to be amortized shall be considered fully amortized.

(2) *Example.*—The principles of section 412(c)(6) and of paragraph (e) of this section are illustrated in the following example:

Example. Assume that a single employer plan is established on January 1, 1976, with a calendar plan year. The funding method is the accrued benefit cost method (unit credit method), the interest assumption is 5 percent, and both the normal cost and the amortization charges and credits are calculated on the basis of payment at the beginning of the year. The annual charge to the funding standard account due to the amortization (over 30 years) of the initial past service liability is $200, and the annual credit due to the amortization (over 15 years) of a 1979 experience gain is $10. A valuation is performed as of January 1, 1985, to determine costs for the 1985 plan year. There was a credit balance of $100 in the funding standard account on December 31, 1984. As of January 1, 1985, plan assets (determined in accordance with section 412(c)(7)(B) and reduced by the $100 credit balance as of January 1, 1985) were $10,400; the accrued liability under the plan was $10,000; the normal cost (for the 1985 plan year) was $1,200; and the 1985 employer contribution (made as of January 1, 1985) was $1,000. The accumulated funding deficiency (calculated ignoring the credit balance and employer contribution) as of December 31, 1985, is $1,459.50, determined as the excess of charges of $1,470 ($1,200 normal cost, plus $200 amortization charge, plus $70 interest) over the credits of $10.50 ($10 amortization credit, plus $.50 interest). The full funding limitation as of the valuation date (January 1, 1985) is $800, determined as the excess of the sum of the accrued liability ($10,000) plus normal cost ($1,200) over the adjusted plan assets ($10,400). The value of this $800 as of the end of the year (i.e., December 31, 1985) is $800 plus $40 interest, or $840.00. The excess, as of the end of the 1985 plan year, of the accumulated funding deficiency over the full funding limitation is thus $1,459.50 minus $840.00, or $619.50. The funding standard account is charged and credited as follows:

Charges		
Normal cost	$1,200.00	
Amortization charge	200.00	
Interest	70.00	
Total		$1,470.00
Credits		
Credit balance	$100.00	
Contribution	1,000.00	
Amortization credit	10.00	
Interest	55.50	
Sec. 412(c)(6) credit	619.50	
Total		$1,784.50
Credit balance December 31, 1985		$314.50

[Reg. § 1.412(c)(6)-1.]

§ 1.412(c)(7)-1. Full funding limitation.—See § 1.412(c)(6)-1 for rules relating both to full funding under section 412(c)(6) and to the full funding limitation under section 412(c)(7). [Reg. § 1.412(c)(7)-1.]

§ 1.412(c)(8)-1. Election to treat certain retroactive plan amendments as made on first day of a plan year.—The function of the Secretary of Labor described in section 412(c)(8) was transferred to the Secretary of Treasury as of December 31, 1978, by Reorganization Plan No. 4 of 1978, 1979-1 C.B. 480. Therefore, the material described in section 412(c)(8) now must be filed as directed by the Secretary of Treasury. [Reg. § 1.412(c)(8)-1.]

§ 1.412(c)(9)-1. Frequency of actuarial valuations.—(a) *Required valuation.*—Section 412(c)(9) requires an actuarial valuation not less frequently than once every three years. Paragraph (b) of this section provides general rules for performing valuations. Paragraph (d) describes certain situations in which the Commissioner may require an actuarial valuation more frequently than once every three years. These rules may be waived at the discretion of the Commissioner and do not apply to multiemployer plans within the meaning of section 414(f).

(b) *General rules for valuations.*—(1) *Date of valuation.*—Except as provided by the Commissioner, the valuation must be as of a date within the plan year to which the valuation refers or within the one month prior to that year. All assets and liabilities must be valued as of the same date. The valuation must use data as of the valuation date; it is not permissible to use adjusted data from a prior or subsequent year.

(2) *Use of prior valuations.*—A plan may not use a valuation for any subsequent plan year if that valuation was not also used for the year to which it refers. Also, a prior valuation may not be used if the plan has used any subsequent valuation for another plan year.

(c) *Funding standard account rules for years when there is no valuation.*—(1) *Amortization of bases.*—After an amortization base is established, the amortization amount of that base is charged or credited in each plan year, whether or not a valuation is performed for the year, until the outstanding balance of the base is zero. However, see § 1.412(c)(6)-1 for rules for years after a full funding limitation credit and § 1.412(b)-1 for combining and offsetting bases.

(2) *Normal cost.*—If valuations are performed less frequently than every year, then any valuation computes the normal cost for the year to which the valuation refers and for subsequent years until another valuation applies. In those subsequent years, the normal cost is—

(i) If the funding method computes normal cost as a level dollar amount, the same dollar amount as for the year to which the valuation refers;

(ii) If the funding method computes normal cost as a level percentage of pay, the same percentage of current pay as for the year to which the valuation refers, or

(iii) If the funding method computes normal cost as an amount equal to the present value of benefits accruing under the method for the year, under any reasonable method.

The rules in subdivisions (i) and (ii) apply whether the funding method computes normal cost on either an individual or an aggregate basis.

(d) *Situations when more frequent valuations are required.*—(1) *Amendments increasing actuarial costs.*—(i) *General rule.*—A valuation is required for any plan year when a plan amendment first increases the actuarial costs of a plan. For this purpose, actuarial costs consist of the plan's normal cost under section 412(b)(2)(A), amortization charges under section 412(b)(2)(B), and amortization credits under section 412(b)(3)(B).

(ii) *Exception.*—No valuation will be required under paragraph (d)(1)(i) of this section if two conditions are met: first, the plan actuary estimates that the cost increase attributable to the amendment is less than 5 percent of the actuarial cost determined without regard to the amendment; and second, the actuary files a signed statement to that effect with the annual return required under section 6058 for the year of the amendment.

(2) *Certain changes in number of participants.*—(i) *General rule.*—A valuation is required for a plan year when the actual number of plan participants that would be considered in the current valuation differs from the number of participants that were considered in the prior valuation by more than 20 percent of that number.

(ii) *Exception.*—Notwithstanding subdivision (i), no valuation will be required merely because of a change in the number of estimated participants under a plan that determines normal cost as a level percentage of payroll (on either an individual or aggregate basis) or as a level dollar amount per individual.

(iii) *Plans using shortfall method.*—No valuation will be required merely because of a change in the number of estimated participants under a plan which uses the shortfall method described in §1.412(c)(1)-2. However, a valuation is required for a plan year if the estimated units of service or production ("estimated base units" under §1.412(c)(1)-2(e)) for the prior plan year exceeds the actual number of units of service or production for that plan year by more than 20 percent.

(3) *Change in actuarial funding method or assumptions.*—A valuation is required for any plan year with respect to which a change in the funding method or actuarial assumptions of a plan is made.

(4) *Mergers and spinoffs.*—(i) *General rule.*—A valuation is required for any plan year in which a plan merger or spinoff occurs.

(ii) *Safe harbor for mergers.*—In the case of a merger, no valuation will be required under paragraph (d)(4) of this section if the *de minimis* rule in §1.414(1)-1(h) is satisfied.

(iii) *Safe harbor for spinoffs.*—In the case of a spinoff, no valuation will be required under paragraph (d)(4) of this section if the present value of all the benefits being spun off from the plan during the plan year is less than 3 percent of the plan's assets as of the beginning of the year.

(5) *Change in average age of participants.*—(i) *General rule.*—A valuation is required for any plan year with respect to which the average age of plan participants changes significantly, within the meaning of subdivisions (ii) and (iii), from the average age of plan participants at the last valuation.

(ii) *Rule for large plans.*—For a plan with 100 or more participants, an increase or decrease in average age of more than two years is a significant change.

(iii) *Rule for small plans.*—For a plan with fewer than 100 participants, an increase or decrease in average age of more than four years is a significant change.

(6) *Alternative minimum funding standard account.*—A valuation is required for each year for which the plan uses the alternative minimum funding standard account.

(7) *Deductibility considerations.*—A valuation is required when it appears that the full funding limitation has been reached for purposes of determining the maximum deductible contribution limitations of section 404(a).

(8) *Other situations.*—The Commissioner may require valuations in other situations as the facts and circumstances warrant. [Reg. §1.412(c)(9)-1.]

§1.412(c)(10)-1. Time for making contributions to satisfy section 412.—(a) *General rule.*—Under section 412(c)(10), a contribution made after the end of a plan year but no later than two and one-half months after the end of that year is deemed to have been made on the last day of that year.

(b) *Extension of general rule.*—(1) *Plan years ending before* [90 DAYS AFTER PUBLICATION DATE OF FINAL REGULATIONS].—For plan years ending before [90 DAYS AFTER PUBLICATION OF FINAL REGULATIONS], for purposes of section 412 a contribution for such a plan year that is made not later than eight and one-half months after the end of that plan year is deemed to have been made on the last day of that year.

(2) *Plan years ending on or after* [90 DAYS AFTER PUBLICATION OF FINAL REGULATIONS].—(i) *Transitional rule.*—The two and one-half month period provided in section 412(c)(10) and §1.410(c)(10)-1(a) is extended for each of the first three plan years ending after [90 DAYS AFTER PUBLICATION OF FINAL REGULATIONS]. For the first plan year ending after [90 DAYS AFTER PUBLICATION OF FINAL REGULATIONS], a contribution made not later than eight and one-half months after the end of that plan year is deemed to have been made on the last day of that year. For the second year, the two and one-half month period is extended to six and one-half months, and for the third year, the two and one-half month period is extended to four and one-half months.

(ii) *Extensions of general and transitional periods.*—The time for making contributions under the general rule described in paragraph (a) and transitional rule of paragraph (b)(2)(i) of this section may be extended to a date not beyond eight and one-half months after the end of the plan year. Extensions of the two and one-half month period and transitional years' periods are granted on an individual basis by the Commissioner. A request for extension should be submitted to the Commissioner of Internal Revenue, 1111 Constitution Avenue, N.W., Washington, D.C. 20224 (Attention OP:E:A).

(c) *Effect on section 404.*—The rules of this section, relating to the timing of contributions for purposes of section 412, operate independently from the rules under section 404(a)(6), relating to the timing of contributions for purposes of claiming a deduction under section 404. [Reg. §1.412(c)(10)-1.]

§1.412(g)-1. Alternative minimum funding standard account.—(a) *In general.*—A plan that maintains an alternative minimum funding standard account ("ASA") for any plan year under section 412(g) must satisfy the requirements of this section. To use the ASA, a plan must use a funding method that requires contributions for all years that are not less than those required under the entry age normal cost method of funding. A funding method does not affect the actual cost of plan benefits but only the incidence of contributions in different years. Thus, any funding method that requires a contribution in one year that exceeds that required by the entry age normal method (EAN) for that year must require a lesser contribution in another year. Hence, only a plan which uses the EAN cost method may use the ASA.

(b) *Special rules.*—(1) *Dual accounting.*—While maintaining an ASA, a plan must maintain the funding standard account under section 412(b) for each plan year.

(2) *Change of method.*—For any plan year, the choice of whether to use the ASA is independent of whether the ASA or funding standard account was used in the prior year. Any change from the choice made in the prior year does not require approval of the Commissioner. Further, a plan which has filed for a plan year the actuarial report described in section 6059(b) using the ASA to determine its minimum funding requirement may change to use the funding standard account to determine the funding requirement for that year. However, a plan may not switch to the ASA for a plan year after having filed the actuarial report for that year using the funding standard account.

(3) *PBGC Valuation.*—In determining charges and credits to the ASA under paragraphs (b) and (c) of this section (other than the amount in paragraph (c)(2)(i)), a plan must value its assets and liabilities on a termination basis as provided in regulations issued by the Pension Benefit Guaranty Corporation (PBGC) under sections 4041 and 4062 of the Employee Retirement Income Security Act of 1974 ("ERISA") for plans placed in trusteeship by PBGC.

(4) *Cumulative nature of account.*—When the ASA is used for a plan year after a plan year for which the ASA was not used, the credit balance and charge balance as of the first day of the year equal zero. However, during any continuous period of years for which the ASA is used, the credit or charge balance as of the end of any ASA year are carried forward as beginning balances in the next ASA year.

(c) *Charges.*—(1) *In general.*—The ASA is charged with the amounts described in paragraph (c) of this section.

(2) *Normal cost.*—The ASA is charged with the normal cost of the plan for a plan year. This amount is the normal cost for that plan year computed—

(i) Under the method of funding and actuarial assumptions used for purposes of maintaining the plan's funding standard account or, if less,

(ii) As the present value of benefits expected, on a termination basis, to accrue during the plan year.

(3) *Unfunded accrued benefits.*—The ASA is charged with the unfunded accrued benefits of the plan for a plan year. This amount is the excess of—

(i) The present value of accrued benefits under the plan, determined as of the valuation date for the plan year, over

(ii) The fair market value of plan assets, determined as of the valuation date for the plan year.

Because fair market value is used, any election to value evidences of indebtedness at amortized value does not apply in computing this value.

(4) *Credit balance from prior plan year.*—The ASA is charged as of the first day of a plan year with any ASA credit balance carried forward from the prior plan year.

(5) *Interest.*—The ASA is charged with interest on the amounts charged to the ASA under paragraph (b)(2), (b)(3) and (b)(4) of this section, as generally prescribed for the funding standard account under §1.412(b)-1(e).

(d) *Credits.*—(1) *In general.*—The ASA is credited with the amounts described in paragraph (d) of this section.

(2) *Employer contributions.*—The ASA is credited with the amount of contributions made by the employer to the plan for the plan year.

(3) *Interest.*—The ASA is credited with the interest on the amount credited under paragraph (d)(2) of this section, determined as of the end of the plan year as generally prescribed for the funding standard account under §1.412(b)-1(e). [Reg. §1.412(g)-1.]

§1.413-1. Special rules for collectively bargained plans.—

* * *

(f) *Minimum funding standard.*—The minimum funding standard for a collectively bargained plan shall be determined as if all participants in the plan were employed by a single employer.

(g) *Liability for funding tax.*—See §54.4971-3 of the Pension Excise Tax Regulations, 26 CFR Part 54, for rules under section 413(b)(6), relating to liability for excise tax on failure to meet minimum funding standards with respect to collectively bargained plans.

* * *

☐ Par. 6. The Income Tax Regulations, 26 CFR Part 1, are further amended by adding new paragraphs (e) and (f) of §1.413-2 to read as follows:

§1.413-2. Special rules for plans maintained by more than one employer.

* * *

(e) *Minimum funding standard.*—The minimum funding standard for a plan maintained by more than one employer shall be determined as if all participants in the plan were employed by a single employer.

(f) *Liability for funding tax.*—See §54.4971-3 of the Pension Excise Tax Regulations, 26 CFR Part 54, for rules under section 413(c)(5), relating to liability for excise tax on failure to meet minimum funding standards with respect to plans maintained by more than one employer.

☐ Par. 7. The Temporary Regulations under the Employee Retirement Income Security Act of 1974, 26 CFR Part 11, are amended by removing §11.412(c)-7.

§11.412(c)-7. Election to treat certain retroactive plan amendments as made on the first day of the plan year.

☐ Par. 7. The Temporary Regulations under the Employee Retirement Income Security Act of 1974, 26 CFR Part 11, are amended by removing §11.412(c)-11.

§11.412(c)-11. Election with respect to bonds.

☐ Par. 7. The Temporary Regulations under the Employee Retirement Income Security Act of 1974, 26 CFR Part 11, are amended by removing §11.412(c)-12.

§11.412(c)-12. Extension of time to make contributions to satisfy requirements of section 412.

Affiliated Service Groups: Separate Service Organizations

Employees' Trusts: Affiliated Service Groups.—Reproduced below are the texts of proposed Reg. §§1.414(m)-1—1.414(m)-4, which prescribe rules for determining whether two or more separate service organizations constitute an affiliated group and which detail how certain requirements are satisfied by a qualified retirement plan maintained by a member of an affiliated service group (published in the Federal Register on February 28, 1983).

☐ Par. 2. The following new sections are added at the appropriate place:

§1.414(m)-1. Affiliated service groups.—(a) *In general.*—Section 414(m) provides rules that require, in some circumstances, employees of separate organizations to be treated as if they were employed by a single employer for purposes of certain employee benefit requirements. For other rules requiring aggregation of employees of different organizations, see section 414(b) (relating to controlled groups of corporations) and section 414(c) (relating to trades or businesses under common control). If aggregation is required under either of the preceding provisions and also under section 414(m), the requirements with respect to all of the applicable provisions must be satisfied.

(b) *Aggregation.*—Except as provided in paragraph (c), all the employees of the members of an affiliated service group shall be treated as if they were employed by a single employer for purposes of the employee benefit requirements listed in §1.414(m)-3.

(c) *Aggregation not required.*—Pursuant to the authority contained in section 414(m)(1), a corporation, other than a professional service corporation, shall not be treated as a First Service Organization (see §1.414(m)-2) for purposes of section 414(m)(2)(A). Also, a special rule is provided in §1.414(m)-2(c)(4) for determining ownership under section 414(m)(2)(B). For purposes of this paragraph, a professional service corporation is a corporation that is organized under state law for the principal purpose of providing professional services and has at least one shareholder who is licensed or otherwise legally authorized to render the type of services for which the corporation is organized. "Professional services" means the services performed by certified or other public accountants, actuaries, architects, attorneys, chiropodists, chiropractors, medical doctors, dentists, professional engineers, optometrists, osteopaths, podiatrists, psychologists, and veterinarians. The Commissioner may expand the list of services in the preceding sentence. However, no such expansion will be effective with respect to any organization until the first day of the first plan year beginning at least 180 days after the publication of such change. [Reg. §1.414(m)-1.]

§1.414(m)-2. Definitions.—(a) *Affiliated service group.*—"Affiliated service group" means a group consisting of a service organization (First Service Organization) and

(1) One or more A Organizations described in paragraph (b), or

(2) One or more B Organizations described in paragraph (c), or

(3) One or more A Organizations described in paragraph (b) and one or more B Organizations described in paragraph (c).

(b) *A Organizations.*—(1) *General rule.*—A service organization is an A Organization if it:

(i) Is a partner or shareholder in the First Service Organization (regardless of the percentage interest it owns in the First Service Organization but determined with regard to the constructive ownership rules of paragraph (d)); and

(ii) Regularly performs services for the First Service Organization, or is regularly associated with the First Service Organization in performing services for third persons.

It is not necessary that any of the employees of the organization directly perform services for the First Service Organization; it is sufficient that the organization is regularly associated with the First Service Organization in performing services for third persons.

(2) *Regularly performs services for.*—The determination of whether a service organization regularly performs services for the First Service Organization or is regularly associated with the First Service Organization in performing services for third persons shall be made on the basis of the facts and circumstances. One factor that is relevant in making this determination is the amount of the earned income that the organization derives from performing services for the First Service Organization, or from performing services for third persons in association with the First Service Organization.

(3) *Examples.*—The provisions of this paragraph may be illustrated by the following examples.

Example (1). A Organization. (i) Attorney N is incorporated, and the corporation is a partner in a law firm. Attorney N and his corporation are regularly associated with the law firm in performing services for third persons.

(ii) Considering the law firm as a First Service Organization, the corporation is an A Organization because it is a partner in the law firm and it is regularly associated with the law firm in performing services for third persons. Accordingly, the corporation and the law firm constitute an affiliated service group.

Example (2). Corporation. (i) Corporation F is a service organization that is a shareholder in Corporation G, another service organization. F regularly provides services for G. Neither corporation is a professional service corporation within the meaning of subsection (1)(c).

(ii) Neither corporation may be considered a First Service Organization for purposes of this paragraph and, thus, aggregation will not be required by operation of the A Organization test. However, G or F may be treated as a First Service Organization and the other organization may be a B Organization under the rules of subsection (2)(c).

Example (3). Regularly associated with. (i) R, S & T is a law partnership with offices in numerous cities. The office in the city of D is incorporated, and the corporation is a partner in the law firm. All of the employees of the corporation work directly for the corporation, and none of them work directly for any of the other offices of the law firm.

(ii) Considering the law firm as a First Service Organization, the corporation is an A Organization because it is a partner in the First Service Organization and is regularly associated with the law firm in performing services for third persons. Accordingly, the corporation and the law firm constitute an affiliated service group.

(c) *B Organizations.*—(1) *General rule.*—An organization is a B Organization if:

(i) A significant portion of the business of the organization is the performance of services for the First Service Organization, for one or more A Organizations determined with respect to the First Service Organization, or for both,

(ii) Those services are of a type historically performed by employees in the service field of the First Service Organization or the A Organizations, and

(iii) Ten percent or more of the interests in the organization is held, in the aggregate, by persons who are designated group members (as defined in subparagraph (4)) of the First Service Organization or of the A Organizations, determined using the constructive ownership rules of paragraph (d).

(2) *Significant portion.*—(i) *General rule.*—Except as provided in subdivisions (ii) and (iii), the determination of whether providing services for the First Service Organization, for one or more A Organizations, or for both, is a significant portion of the business of an organization will be based on the facts and circumstances. Wherever it appears in this paragraph (2), "one or more A Organizations" means one or more A Organizations determined with respect to the First Service Organization.

(ii) *Service Receipts safe harbor.*—The performance of services for the First Service Organizations, for one or more A Organizations, or for both, will not be considered a significant portion of the business of an organization if the Service Receipts Percentage is less than five percent.

(iii) *Total Receipts threshold test.*—The performance of services for the First Service Organization, for one or more A Organizations, or for both, will be considered a significant portion of the business of an organization if the Total Receipts Percentage is ten percent or more.

(iv) *Service Receipts Percentage.*—The Service Receipts Percentage is the ratio of the gross receipts of the organization derived from performing services for the First Service Organization, for one or more A Organizations, or for both, to the total gross receipts of the organization derived from performing services. This ratio is the greater of the ratio for the year for which the determination is being made or for the three year period including that year and the two preceding years (or the period of the organization's existence, if less).

(v) *Total Receipts Percentage.*—The Total Receipts Percentage is calculated in the same manner as the Service Receipts Percentage, except that gross receipts in the denominator are determined without regard to whether they were derived from performing services.

(3) *Historically performed.*—Services will be considered of a type historically performed by employees in a particular service field if it was not unusual for the services to be performed by employees of organizations in that service field (in the United States) on December 13, 1980.

(4) *Designated group.*—(i) *Definition.*—"Designated group" members are the officers, the highly compensated employees, and the common owners of an organization (as defined in subdivision (ii)). However, even though a person is not a common owner, the interests the person holds in the potential B Organization will be taken into account if the person is an officer or a highly compensated employee of the First Service Organization or of an A Organization.

(ii) *Common owner.*—A person who is an owner of a First Service Organization or of an A Organization is a common owner if at least three percent of the interests in the organization is, in the aggregate, held by persons who are owners of the potential B Organization (determined using the constructive ownership rules of paragraph (d)).

(5) *Owner.*—The term "owner" includes organizations that have an ownership interest described in paragraph (e).

(6) *Aggregation of ownership interests.*—It is not necessary that a single designated group member of the First Service Organization or of an A Organization own ten percent or more of the interests, determined using the constructive ownership rules of paragraph (d), in the organization for the organization to be a B Organization. It is sufficient that the sum of the interests, determined using the constructive ownership rules of paragraph (d), held by all of the designated group members of the First Service Organization, and the designated group members of the A Organizations, is ten percent or more of the interests in the organization.

(7) *Non-service organization.*—An organization may be a B Organization even though it does not qualify as a service organization under paragraph (f).

(8) *Examples.*—The provisions of this paragraph may be illustrated by the following examples.

Example (1). B Organization. (i) R is a service organization that has 11 partners. Each partner of R owns one percent of the stock in Corporation D. The corporation provides services to the partnership of a type historically performed by employees in the service field of the partnership. A significant portion of the business of the corporation consists of providing services to the partnership.

(ii) Considering the partnership as a First Service Organization, the corporation is a B Organization because a significant portion of the business of the corporation is the performance of services for the partnership of a type historically performed by employees in the service field of the partnership, and more than ten percent of the interests in the corporation is held, in the aggregate, by the designated group members (consisting of the 11 common owners of the partnership). Accordingly, the corporation and the partnership constitute an affiliated service group.

(iii) A similar result would be obtained if no more than 8 percent of the 11 percent ownership in Corporation D were held by highly compensated employees of R who were not owners of R (even though no one group of the three preceding groups held 10 percent or more of the stock of Corporation D).

Example (2). Other aggregation rules. (i) C, an individual, is a 60 percent partner in D, a service organization, and regularly performs services for D. C is also an 80 percent partner in F. A significant portion of the gross receipts of F are derived from providing services to D of a type historically performed by employees in the service field of D.

(ii) Viewing D as a First Service Organization, F is a B Organization because a significant portion of gross receipts of F are derived from performing services for D of a type historically performed by employees in that service field, and more than ten percent of the interests in F is held by the designated group member C (who is a common owner of D). Accordingly, D and F constitute an affiliated service group. Additionally, the employees of D and F are aggregated under the rules of section 414(c). Thus, any plan maintained by a member of the affiliated service group must satisfy the aggregation rules of sections 414(c) and 414(m).

Example (3). Common owner. (i) Corporation T is a service organization. The sole function of Corporation W is to provide services to Corporation T of a type historically performed by employees in the service field of Corporation T. Individual C owns all of the stock of Corporation W and two percent of the stock of Corporation T. C is not an officer or a highly compensated employee of Corporation T.

(ii) Considering Corporation T as a First Service Organization, Corporation W is not a B Organization because it is not 10 percent owned by designated group members. Because C owns less than 3 percent of Corporation T, C is not a common owner of T.

Example (4). B Organization. (i) Individual M owns one-third of an employee benefit consulting firm. M also owns one-third of an insurance agency. A significant portion of the business of the consulting firm consists of assisting the insurance agency in developing employee benefit packages for sale to third persons and providing services to the insurance company in connection with employee benefit programs sold to other clients of the insurance agency. Additionally, the consulting firm frequently provides services to clients who have purchased insurance arrangements from the insurance company for the employee benefit plans they maintain. The insurance company frequently refers clients to the consulting firm to assist them in the design of their employee benefit plans. The percentage of the total gross receipts of the consulting firm that represent gross receipts from the performance of these services for the insurance agency is 20 percent.

(ii) Considering the insurance agency as a First Service Organization, the consulting firm is a B Organization because a significant portion of the business of the consulting firm (as determined under the Total Receipts Percentage Test) is the performance of services for the insurance agency of a type historically performed by employees in the service field of insurance, and more than 10 percent of the interests in the consulting firm is held by owners of the insurance agency. Thus, the insurance agency and the consulting firm constitute an affiliated service group.

Example (5). B Organization. (i) Attorney T is incorporated, and the corporation is a 6% shareholder in a law firm (which is also incorporated). All of the work of Corporation T is performed for the law firm.

(ii) Under the principles of section 267(c), T is deemed to own the shares of the law firm owned by T Corporation. Thus, T is a common owner of the law firm. Considering the law firm as a First Service Organization, Corporation T is a B Organization because a significant portion of the business of Corporation T consists of performing services for the law firm of a type historically performed by employees, and 100 percent of Corporation T is owned by a common owner of the law firm.

Example (6). Significant portion. (i) The income of Corporation X is derived from both performing services and other business activities. The amount of its receipts derived from performing services for, and its total receipts derived from, Corporation Z and the total for all other customers is set forth below:

	Origin of income	*Corporation Z*	*All customers*
Year 1	Services	$4	$100
	Total		$120
Year 2	Services	$9	$150
	Total		$180
Year 3	Services	$42	$200
	Total		$240

(ii) In year 1 (the first year of existence of Corporation X), the Services Receipts Percentage for Corporation X (for its business with Corporation Z) is less than five percent ($4/$100, or 4%).

Thus performing services for Corporation Z will not be considered a significant portion of the business of Corporation X.

(iii) In year 2, the Services Receipts Percentage is the greater of the ratio for that year ($9/$150, or 6%) or for years 1 and 2 combined ($13/$250, or 5.2%), which is six percent. The Total Receipts Percentage is the greater of the ratio for that year ($9/$180, or 5%) or for years 1 and 2 combined ($13/$300, or 4.3%), which is five percent. Because the Services Receipts Percentage is greater than five percent and the Total Receipts Percentage is less than ten percent, whether performing services for Corporation Z constitutes a significant portion of the business of Corporation X is determined by the facts and circumstances.

(iv) In year 3, the Services Receipts Percentage is the greater of the ratio for that year ($42/$200, or 21%) or for years, 1, 2, and 3 combined ($55/$450, or 12.2%), which is 21 percent. The Total Receipts Percentage is the greater of the ratio for that year ($42/$240, or 17.5%) or for years 1, 2, and 3 combined ($55/$540, or 10.1%), which is 17.5 percent. Because the Total Receipts Percentage is greater than ten percent and the Services Receipts Percentage is not less than five percent, a significant portion of the business of Corporation X is considered to be the performances of services for Corporation Z.

(d) *Ownership.*—(1) *Constructive ownership.*—Except as otherwise provided in the regulations under section 414(m), the principles of section 267(c) (relating to constructive ownership of stock) shall apply in determining ownership for purposes of section 414(m). Accordingly, the rules of section 267(c) shall apply to partnership interests as well as to stock.

(2) *Qualified plans.*—In determining ownership for purposes of section 414(m), an individual's interest under a plan that qualifies under section 401(a) will be taken into account.

(3) *Special rules.*—For purposes of section 414(m):

(i) Stock or partnership interests owned, directly or indirectly, by or for a corporation, partnership, estate, or trust shall be considered as being owned proportionately by or for its shareholders, partners, or beneficiaries;

(ii) An individual shall be considered as owning the stock or partnership interests owned, directly or indirectly, by or for his family;

(iii) An individual owning (otherwise than by the application of subdivision (ii)) any stock in a corporation or interest in a partnership shall be considered as owning the stock or partnership interests owned, directly or indirectly, by or for his partner;

(iv) The family of an individual shall include only his brothers and sisters (whether by the whole or half blood), spouse, ancestors, and lineal descendants; and

(v) Stock or partnership interests constructively owned by a person by reason of the application of subdivision (i) shall, for the purpose of applying subdivision (i), (ii), or (iii), be treated as actually owned by such person, but stock or partnership interests constructively owned by an individual by reason of the application of subdivision (ii) or (iii) shall not be treated as owned by him for the purpose of again applying either of such subdivisions in order to make another the constructive owner of such stock or partnership interests.

(4) *Examples.*—The provisions of this paragraph may be illustrated by the following examples.

Example (1). Constructive ownership. (i) Individual K is incorporated as K Corporation, and K Corporation is a partner in a management consulting firm K & F. K regularly performs services for the management consulting firm K & F. The secretarial services for the consulting firm are performed by Corporation M. A significant portion of the business of the secretarial corporation, M, consists of providing services to the consulting firm. All of the stock of the secretarial corporation, M, is owned by individual K.

(ii) Considering the consulting firm as a First Service Organization, Corporation K is an A Organization because it is a partner in the consulting firm and regularly performs services for the firm or is regularly associated with the firm in performing services for third persons.

(iii) Under the principles of section 267(c), individual K is deemed to own the partnership interest in the consulting firm that is held by K Corporation. Thus, K is considered to be an owner of the consulting firm.

(iv) Considering the consulting firm as a First Service Organization, the secretarial corporation is a B Organization because a significant portion of its business consists of performing services for the consulting firm or for Corporation K of a type historically performed by employees in the service field of management consulting, and at least ten percent of the interests in the secretarial corporation, M, is held by individual K, an owner of the consulting firm.

Example (2). Constructive ownership. (i) J is the office manager and a highly compensated employee of an accounting partnership H & H. The secretarial services for the partnership are provided by Corporation W. J owns fifty percent of the stock of the secretarial corporation. A significant portion of the business of the secretarial corporation consists of providing services to the partnership.

(ii) Considering the partnership as a First Service Organization, the secretarial corporation is a B Organization because a significant portion of the business of the secretarial corporation is the performance of services for the partnership of a type historically performed by employees of accounting firms, and more than ten percent of the interest in the corporation is held by a highly compensated employee of the partnership.

(iii) Under the principles of section 267(c), the result would be the same, for example, if the stock were held (instead of by J) by the spouse of J, the children of J, the parents or grandparents of J, a trust for the benefit of J's children, or by a combination of such relatives.

Example (3). Qualified plan. (i) T is the chief executive officer of W Corporation, which is a consulting firm. T is also a participant in the W Corporation Profit-Sharing Plan, which qualifies under section 401(a). T's account balance in the plan is $150,000, and it consists of 25 percent of the stock of X Corporation. The sole function of X Corporation is to provide secretarial services to W Corporation.

(ii) Considering W Corporation as a First Service Organization, X Corporation is a B Organization because a significant portion of the business of X Corporation consists of providing secretarial services to W Corporation, secretarial services are of a type historically performed by employees in the field of consulting, and 25 percent of the stock of X Corporation is considered to be owned by T, a highly compensated employee of W Corporation, using the principles of section 267(c). Accordingly, W Corporation and X Corporation constitute an affiliated service group.

(e) *Organization.*—(1) *General rule.*—The term "organization" includes a sole proprietorship, partnership, corporation, or any other type of entity regardless of its ownership format.

(2) *Special rule.*—[Reserved.]

(f) *Service organization.*—(1) *Non-capital intensive organizations.*—The principal business of an organization will be considered the performance of services if capital is not a material income-producing factor for the organization, even though the organization is not engaged in a field listed in subparagraph (2). Whether capital is a material income-producing factor must be determined by reference to all the facts and circumstances of each case. In general, capital is a material income-producing factor if a substantial portion of the gross income of the business is attributable to the employment of capital in the business, as reflected, for example, by a substantial investment in inventories, plant, machinery, or other equipment. Additionally, capital is a material income-producing factor for banks and similar institutions. However, capital is not a material income-producing factor if the gross income of the business consists principally of fees, commissions, or other compensation for personal services performed by an individual.

(2) *Specific fields.*—Regardless of whether subparagraph (1) applies, an organization engaged in any one or more of the following fields is a service organization:

(i) Health;

(ii) Law;

(iii) Engineering;

(iv) Architecture;

(v) Accounting;

(vi) Actuarial science;

(vii) Performing arts;

(viii) Consulting; and

(ix) Insurance.

Notwithstanding the preceding sentence, an organization will not be considered to be performing services merely because it is engaged in the manufacture or sale of equipment or supplies used in the above fields, or merely because it is engaged in performing research or publishing in the above fields. An organization will not be considered to be a service organization under this subparagraph (2) merely because an employee provides one of the enumerated services to the organization or to other employees of the organization unless the organization is also engaged in the performance of the same services for third parties.

(3) *Other organizations.*—Organizations engaged in performing services and that are not described in subparagraph (1) or (2) shall not be considered to be service organizations. The Commissioner may expand the list of fields contained in subparagraph (2). However, no such expansion will be effective until the first day of the first plan year beginning at least 180 days after the publication of such change.

(4) *Exempted organizations.*—The Commissioner may determine that certain organizations, or types of organizations, should not be considered as subject to the requirements of section 414(m), even though the organizations are described in subparagraph (1) or (2).

(g) *Multiple affiliated service groups.*—(1) *Multiple First Service Organizations.*—Two or more affiliated service groups will not be aggregated simply because an organization is an A Organization or a B Organization with respect to each affiliated service group.

(2) *Multiple A or B Organizations.*—If an organization is a First Service Organization with respect to two or more A Organizations or two or more B Organizations, or both, all of the organizations shall be considered to constitute a single affiliated service group.

(3) The provisions of this paragraph may be illustrated by the following examples.

Example (1). Multiple First Service Organizations. (i) Corporation P provides secretarial service to numerous dentists in a medical building, each of whom maintains his own separate unincorporated practice. Dentist T owns 20 percent of the secretarial corporation and accounts for 20 percent of its gross receipts. Dentist W owns 25 percent of the corporation and accounts for 25 percent of its gross receipts.

(ii) Considering Dentist T as a First Service Organization, the secretarial corporation, P, is a B Organization because 20 percent of the gross receipts of the corporation are derived from performing services for Dentist T of a type historically performed by employees of dentists, and 20 percent of the interests in the corporation is owned by Dentist T. Accordingly, Dentist T and the corporation constitute an affiliated service group.

(iii) Considering Dentist W as a First Service Organization, the secretarial corporation, P, is a B Organization because 25 percent of the gross receipts of the corporation are derived from performing services for Dentist W of a type historically performed by employees of dentists, and 25 percent of the interests in the corporation is owned by Dentist W. Accordingly, Dentist W and the corporation constitute an affiliated service group. However, this affiliated service group does not include Dentist T even though the secretarial corporation, P, is a B Organization with respect to both dentists. Thus, there are two affiliated service groups.

Example (2). Multiple B Organizations. (i) Doctor N is incorporated as Corporation N. Secretarial services are provided to Corporation N by Corporation Q. Corporation N owns 20 percent of the interests in the secretarial corporation and provides 20 percent of its gross receipts. Nursing services are provided to Corporation N by Corporation R. Corporation N owns 25 percent of the interests in the nursing corporation and provides 25 percent of its gross receipts.

(ii) Considering Corporation N as a First Service Organization, the secretarial corporation, Q, is a B Organization because 20 percent of the gross receipts of the secretarial corporation, Q, are derived from performing services for Corporation N of a type historically performed by employees of doctors, and 20 percent of the secretarial corporation is owned by the owner of

Corporation N. Accordingly, Corporation N and the secretarial corporation, Q, constitute an affiliated service group.

(iii) Considering Corporation N as a First Service Organization, the nursing corporation, R, is a B Organization because 25 percent of the gross receipts of the nursing corporation, R, are derived from performing services for Corporation N of a type historically performed by employees of doctors, and 25 percent of the nursing corporation is owned by the owner of Corporation N. Accordingly, Corporation N and the nursing corporation constitute an affiliated service group.

(iv) For purposes of section 414(m), there will be considered to be one affiliated service group consisting of Corporation N, the secretarial corporation, Q, and the nursing corporation, R. [Reg. § 1.414(m)-2.]

§ 1.414(m)-3. Employee benefit requirements.—(a) *Employee benefit requirements affected.*—All of the employees of the members of an affiliated service group shall be treated as employed by a single employer for purposes of the following employee benefit requirements:

(1) Sections 401(a)(3) and 410 (relating to minimum participation requirements);

(2) Section 401(a)(4) (requiring that contributions or benefits do not discriminate in favor of employees who are officers, shareholders, or highly compensated);

(3) Sections 401(a)(7) and 411 (relating to minimum vesting standards);

(4) Sections 401(a)(16) and 415 (relating to limitations on contributions and benefits);

(5) Section 408(k) (relating to simplified employee pensions);

(6) Section 105(h) (relating to self-insured medical reimbursement plans);

(7) Section 125 (relating to cafeteria plans); and

(8) Pursuant to the authority granted in section 414(m)(6), section (a)(10) (relating to plans providing contributions or benefits to owner-employees).

(b) *Special requirements.*—If a plan maintained by a member of an affiliated service group covers an employee described in section 401(c)(1) (self-employed individual), an owner-employee within the meaning of section 401(c)(3), or a shareholder-employee within the meaning of section 1379(d), the plan must also satisfy the following requirements to the extent they apply:

(1) Section 401(a)(9) (relating to special distribution requirements for plans benefiting self-employed individuals);

(2) Section 401(a)(17) (relating to a limitation on the compensation base of plans benefiting self-employed individuals or shareholder-employees); and

(3) Section 401(a)(18) (relating to special requirements for defined benefit plans benefiting self-employed individuals or shareholder-employees). Pursuant to the authority granted in section 414(m)(6), a plan that covers a self-employed individual, an owner-employee, or a shareholder-employee will be subject to the preceding requirements, even though that individual is not employed by the member of the affiliated service group maintaining the plan. These requirements apply only if the earned income of the self-employed individual or owner-employee or the compensation received as a shareholder-employee is taken into account in computing contributions or benefits under the plan.

(c) *Multiple employer plans.*—(1) *General rule.*—If a plan maintained by a member of an affiliated service group covers an individual who is not an employee of the member, but who is an employee of another member of that affiliated service group, the plan will be considered to be maintained by the member that does employ that individual. Thus, the plan will be considered to be maintained by more than one employer for purposes of section 413(c)(2) (relating to the exclusive benefit rule), (4) (relating to funding), (5) (relating to liability for funding tax), and (6) (relating to deductions). Therefore, a member of an affiliated service group may deduct contributions on behalf of individuals who are not employees of that member, if the individuals are employed by another member of that affiliated service group.

(2) *Special rule.*—The multiple employer plan rule contained in subparagraph (1) shall not apply in the case of a controlled group of corporations (as described in section 414(b)) or a group of trades or businesses under common control (as described in section 414(c)).

(d) *Discrimination.*—In testing for discrimination under section 401(a)(4) (requiring that contributions or benefits do not discriminate in favor of employees who are officers, shareholders, or highly compensated), all of the compensation paid to an employee must be considered in determining the contributions or benefits under a plan maintained by a member of an affiliated service group, without regard to the percentage of the organization employing the individual owned by the member maintaining the plan.

(e) *Example.*—The provisions of this section may be illustrated by the following example:

(1) T is incorporated and Corporation T is a partner in a service organization. Corporation T employs only its sole shareholder and maintains a retirement plan. W and Z, the other partners in the service organization, are not incorporated. Each partner has a one-third interest, in the service organization. The partnership has eight common law employees.

(2) Considering the partnership as a First Service Organization, Corporation T is an A Organization because it is a partner in the First Service Organization and regularly performs services for the partnership or is regularly associated with the partnership in performing services for third persons. Accordingly, the partnership and Corporation T constitute an affiliated service group.

(3) If the retirement plan maintained by Corporation T covers any of the common law employees of the partnership, it will be benefiting individuals who are not employees of the member of the affiliated service group maintaining the plan (Corporation T). As such, the plan will be considered to be maintained by more than one employer, and will be subject to the rules of section 413(c)(2), (4), (5), and (6) and the regulations thereunder. Thus, contributions by Corporation T on behalf of these individuals will not fail to be deductible under section 404 merely because they are not employees of Corporation T. In testing for discrimination under section 401(a)(4), all of the compensation paid to the

employees of the partnership must be taken into account in determining their contributions or benefits under the plan, without regard to the percentage of the partnership owned by Corporation T.

(4) If the plan maintained by Corporation T covers partners W and Z, the plan must also satisfy the requirements listed in paragraph (b), to the extent they are applicable. [Reg. §1.414(m)-3.]

§1.414(m)-4. Effective dates.—(a) *Effective dates.*—(1) *New plans.*—In the case of a plan that was not in existence on November 30, 1980, section 414(m) and the regulations thereunder apply to plan years ending after November 30, 1980.

(2) *Existing plans.*—In the case of a plan in existence on November 30, 1980, section 414(m) and the regulations thereunder shall apply to plan years beginning after November 30, 1980.

(b) *Frozen plan.*—(1) *Defined contribution plans.*—In the case of a defined contribution plan in existence on November 30, 1980, that fails to satisfy the requirements of section 401(a) solely because of the application of section 414(m), the trust shall be treated as continuing to satisfy the requirements of section 401(a) after the effective date of section 414(m) if the plan is terminated and all amounts are distributed to the participants within 180 days after the latest of:

(i) [insert the date of publication of this requlation in the Federal Register as a Treasury decision],

(ii) The date on which notice of the final determination with respect to a request for a determination letter is issued by the Internal Revenue Service, such request is withdrawn, or such request is finally disposed of by the Internal Revenue Service, provided the request for a determination letter was pending on [insert the date of the publication of this regulation in the Federal Register as a Treasury decision] or, in the case of a request for a determination letter on the plan termination, was made within 60 days after [insert the date of the publication of this regulation in the Federal Register as a Treasury decision].

(iii) If a petition is timely filed with the United States Tax Court for a declaratory judgment under section 7476 with respect to the final determination (or the failure of the Internal Revenue Service to make a final determination) in response to such request, the date on which the decision of the United States Tax Court in such proceeding becomes final.

(2) *Defined benefit plans.*—In the case of a defined benefit plan in existence on November 30, 1980, that fails to satisfy the requirements of section 401(a) solely because of the application of section 414(m), the trust shall be treated as continuing to satisfy the requirements of section 414(m) if the plan is terminated within 180 days after the latest of the dates determined in a manner consistent with paragraph (b)(1). However, deductions for contributions to the plan for plan years after the effective date of section 414(m) are limited to those necessary to satisfy the minimum funding standards of section 412. [Reg. §1.414(m)-4.]

Affiliated Service Groups: Employee Leasing, Etc.

Employee Trusts: Affiliated Service Groups, Employee Leasing and Other Arrangements.—Reproduced below is the text of proposed Reg. §1.414(o)-1, relating to affiliated service groups, employee leasing and other arrangements (published in the Federal Register on August 27, 1987).

□ Par. 2. The following new section is added immediately following §1.414(m)-4 and reads as follows:

§1.414(o)-1. Avoidance of employee benefit requirements through the use of separate organizations, employee leasing, or other arrangements.—(a) *In general.*—(1) Pursuant to section 414(o), this section provides rules, in addition to the rules contained in sections 414(m) and 414(n) and the regulations thereunder, to prevent the avoidance of any employee benefit requirement listed in either §1.414(m)-3 or §1.414(n)-3, through the use of separate organizations, employee leasing, or other arrangements.

(2) For the definition of the terms "person" and "leased employee", see §1.414(n)-1(b). For the definition of the term "organization", see §1.414(m)-5(a)(2). For the definition of the terms "management functions" and "management activities or services", see §1.414(m)-5(c).

(3) For purposes of this section, the term "plan" means a stock bonus, pension, or profit-sharing plan qualified under section 401(a) or a simplified employee pension under section 408(k).

(4) For purposes of this section, the term "employee" includes a "self-employed individual" as defined in section 401(c)(1).

(5) For purposes of this section, the term "maintained", when used in the context of a plan maintained by any person, means "maintained at any time".

(6) For purposes of this section, services performed for a person other than as an employee of such person means services performed directly or indirectly for such person.

(b) *Services performed by leased owners.*—(1) *In general.*—(i) If an individual is a leased owner with respect to a recipient, then for purposes of determining whether any qualified plan actually maintained by the recipient and whether any qualified plan maintained by a leasing organization in which the leased owner is a participant (or in which the leased owner has or had an accrued benefit) satisfies the employee benefit requirements of section 1.414(n)-3(a) (except for paragraph (a)(6) of that section) for a plan year, the leased owner's interest in the leasing organization's qualified plan attributable to services performed by the leased owner for the recipient is to be treated as provided under a separate qualified plan maintained by the recipient covering only the leased owner and the leased owner is to be treated as an employee of the recipient. If a separate qualified plan is treated as maintained by the recipient with respect to a leased owner and such leased owner also participates in a qualified plan actually maintained by the recipient, the leased owner's interest in the leasing organization's qualified plan attributable to the leased owner's performance of services for the recipient that is treated as provided to the leased owner under a separate qualified plan of the recipient is to be treated as provided to the leased owner under the qualified plan actually maintained by the recipient for purposes of determining whether such qualified plan satisfies the applicable employee benefit requirements. If either the separate qualified plan for the leased owner that is treated as maintained by the recipient or any qualified plan that is actually maintained by the recipient fails to satisfy any of the applicable employee benefit requirements, then except as provided in paragraphs (b)(1)(ii) and (b)(1)(iii) of this section, the following qualified plans shall be treated as not satisfying such requirements: any qualified plan actually maintained by the recipient in which the leased owner is a participant (or has or had an accrued benefit) and any qualified plan that is actually maintained by a leasing organization in which the leased owner has an interest that is attributable to the leased owner's performance of services for the recipient.

(ii) The Commissioner will not apply paragraph (b)(1)(i) of this section so as to disqualify a plan actually maintained by a recipient unless the Commissioner determines that, taking into account all the facts and circumstances, the disqualification of a leasing organization's plan would be ineffective as a means of securing compliance with the applicable employee benefit requirements. For example, it may be appropriate to disqualify the recipient's plan where a leasing organization's plan was terminated or substantial assets were removed therefrom in a year for which the statute of limitations has run with respect to the employer, employee, or trust.

(iii) If pursuant to paragraph (b)(1)(i) of this section, more than one leasing organization plan is subject to disqualification and at least one of the plans would not be disqualified if another plan or plans were disqualified first, all affected plan sponsors may, by agreement, elect the plan or plans subject to disqualification, provided that such election is not inconsistent with the purposes of this paragraph (b), such as where the plan or plans elected were terminated or substantial assets were removed therefrom in a year for which the statute of limitations has run with respect to the employer, employee, or trust. In the absence of such an election, the Commissioner, taking into account all the facts and circumstances, shall have the discretion to determine which plan or plans shall be disqualified.

(2) *Leased owner.*—(i) For purposes of this paragraph (b), an individual is a "leased owner" with respect to a recipient if during the plan year of a plan maintained by a leasing organization the individual (A) performs any services for a recipient other than as an employee of the recipient and (B) is, at the time such services are performed, a five-percent owner of the recipient. The fact that an individual may also perform services as an employee of the recipient does not affect his status as a leased owner. If an individual becomes a leased owner with respect to a recipient, such individual is from that point on always to be considered a leased owner with respect to the recipient, notwithstanding anything in this paragraph (b) to the contrary, even if subsequently all services performed by the individual for the recipient are performed as an employee of the recipient.

(ii) Except as provided in paragraph (b)(2)(iii) of this section, and notwithstanding the first sentence of paragraph (b)(2)(i) of this section to the contrary, an individual is not a leased owner with respect to a recipient for purposes of a plan year of a plan maintained by a leasing organization if, during each calendar year containing at least one day of such plan year, less than 25 percent of his total hours actually worked for substantial compensation are for all recipients with respect to which he is a leased owner (but for the application of this paragraph (b)(2)(ii)) and less than 25 percent of his total compensation is derived from performing services for all such recipients. For purposes of this paragraph (b)(2)(ii), performing services for the recipient includes services performed as an employee of the recipient and in any other capacity. For purposes of this paragraph (b)(2)(ii), the term "compensation" means (A) with respect to services performed as a common-law employee, compensation reportable on Form W-2, and (B) with respect to services performed other than as a common-law employee, earned income as defined in section 401(c)(2). See section 414(s) for the definition of "compensation" for years beginning after December 31, 1986.

(iii) Paragraph (b)(2)(ii) of this section does not apply to an individual who (A) is a leased owner with respect to a recipient pursuant to the application of the first sentence of paragraph (b)(2)(i) of this section, and (B) performs professional services (as defined in § 1.414(m)-1(c)) for the recipient, whether or not as an employee of the recipient, during the plan year of the plan maintained by the leasing organization, of the same type as the professional services performed by the recipient for third parties.

(3) *Recipient.*—For purposes of this paragraph (b), the term "recipient" has the same meaning as in paragraphs (b)(2) and (b)(6) of § 1.414(n)-1, except that "leased owner" is substituted for "leased employee".

(4) *Leasing organization.*—For purposes of this paragraph (b), the term "leasing organization" has the same meaning as in § 1.414(n)-1(b)(1), except that "leased owner" is substituted for "leased employee" and that "or provided" is added after "provides".

(5) *Five-percent owner.*—For purposes of this paragraph (b), an individual is a five-percent owner of a recipient if such individual is a 5-percent owner (as defined in section 416(i)) of any person included in the recipient.

(6) *Contributions, benefit, etc., provided to a leased owner.*—For purposes of this paragraph (b), a leased owner's interest in a leasing organization (as defined in § 1.414(n)-2(b)(1)(i)) and in a leasing organization's qualified plan (as defined in § 1.414(n)-2(b)(1)(i)), to the extent attributable to services for the recipient by the leased owner, is, for purposes of the applicable employee benefit requirements, treated as provided by the recipient or under a plan of the recipient. For rules relating to the application of this requirement, see paragraph (b)(2) of § 1.414(n)-2.

(7) *Effect on employee rules.*—To the extent that a leased owner performs services for a recipient other than in the capacity of an employee, a leased owner is not an employee of the recipient

and may not be actually covered by a plan of the recipient. Such leased owner may, however, qualify as a leased employee under section 414(n) and the regulations thereunder.

(c) [(c) through (j) withdrawn: 4/27/93]

(k) *Effective dates.*—(1) [(k)(1) withdrawn: 4/27/93]

(2) The provisions of paragraph (b) of this section are effective for tax years of recipients beginning after December 31, 1983. Therefore, the provisions of paragraph (b) apply to plan years beginning during and after the first tax year of a recipient beginning after December 31, 1983. For purposes of applying paragraph (b) to plan years beginning during and after the first tax year of a recipient beginning after December 31, 1983, contributions, forfeitures and benefits provided during any plan year beginning prior to the first tax year of a recipient beginning after December 31, 1983, shall be taken into account if they would have been taken into account had paragraph (b) been effective for such prior plan year.

(3) [(k)(3) withdrawn: 4/27/93]

(4) [(k)(4) withdrawn: 4/27/93]

[Reg. §1.414(o)-1.]

Employee Trusts: Highly Compensated Employees

Employee Benefit Plans: Highly Compensated Employees: Compensation: Definition.— Temporary Reg. §1.414(q)-1T, relating to the scope and meaning of the terms "highly compensated employee" and "compensation", is also proposed as a final regulation and, when adopted, would become Reg. §1.414(q)-1 (published in the Federal Register on February 19, 1988).

§1.414(q)-1. Highly compensated employee.

Qualified Plans: Automatic Contribution Arrangements

Qualified Plans: Automatic Contribution Arrangements.—Reg. §1.414(w)-1, relating to automatic contribution arrangements allowed by certain qualified plans, was adopted by T.D. 9447 on February 23, 2009 (published in the Federal Register on November 8, 2007) (REG-133300-07).

⋙→ Caution: Proposed Reg. §1.414(w)-1, below, was adopted by T.D. 9447 on February 23, 2009. Final Reg. §1.414(w)-1 applies for plan years beginning on or after January 1, 2010. For plan years beginning prior to January 1, 2010, a plan that operates in accordance with this proposed Reg. §1.414(w)-1 or final Reg. §1.414(w)-1 will be treated as operating in accordance with a good faith interpretation of Code Sec. 414(w).

☐ Par. 13. Section 1.414(w)-1 is added to read as follows:

§1.414(w)-1. Permissible withdrawals from eligible automatic contribution arrangements.—(a) *Overview.*—Section 414(w) provides rules under which certain employees are permitted to elect to make a withdrawal from an eligible automatic contribution arrangement. This section sets forth the rules applicable to permissible withdrawals from an eligible automatic contribution arrangement within the meaning of section 414(w). Paragraph (b) of this section defines an eligible automatic contribution arrangement. Paragraph (c) of this section describes a permissible withdrawal and addresses which employees are eligible to elect a withdrawal, the timing of the withdrawal election, and the amount of the withdrawal. Paragraph (d) of this section describes the tax and other consequences of the withdrawal. Paragraph (e) of this section includes the definitions applicable to this section.

(b) *Eligible automatic contribution arrangement.*—(1) *In general.*—An eligible automatic contribution arrangement is an automatic contribution arrangement under an applicable employer plan that, for the plan year, satisfies the uniformity requirement under paragraph (b)(2) of this section, the notice requirement under paragraph (b)(3) of this section, and the default investment requirement under (b)(4) of this section.

(2) *Uniformity requirement.*—An eligible automatic contribution arrangement must provide that the default elective contribution is a uniform percentage of compensation. An arrangement does not violate the uniformity requirement of this paragraph (b)(2) merely because the percentage varies in a manner that is permitted under §1.401(k)-3(j)(2)(iii), except that the rules of §§1.401(k)-3(j)(2)(iii)(A) and 1.401(k)-3(j)(2)(iii)(B) are applied without regard to whether the arrangement is intended to be a qualified automatic contribution arrangement.

(3) *Notice requirement.*—(i) *General rule.*—The notice requirement of this paragraph (b)(3) is satisfied for a plan year if each eligible employee is given notice of the employee's rights and obligations under the arrangement. The notice must be sufficiently accurate and comprehensive to apprise the employee of such rights and obligations, and be written in a manner calculated to be understood by the average employee to whom the arrangement applies. The notice must be in writing, however, see §1.401(a)-21 for rules permitting the use of electronic media to provide applicable notices.

(ii) *Content requirement.*—The notice must include the provisions found in §1.401(k)-3(d)(2)(ii) to the extent those provisions apply to the arrangement. A notice is not considered sufficiently accurate and comprehensive unless the notice accurately describes—

(A) The level of elective contributions which will be made on the employee's behalf if the employee does not make an affirmative election;

(B) The employee's rights to elect not to have default elective contributions made to the plan on his or her behalf or to have a different percentage of compensation or amount of elective contributions made to the plan on his or her behalf;

(C) How contributions made under the arrangement will be invested in the absence of any investment election by the employee; and

(D) The employee's rights to make a permissible withdrawal, if applicable, and the procedures to elect such a withdrawal.

(iii) *Timing.*—(A) *General rule.*—The timing requirement of this paragraph (b)(3)(iii) is satisfied if the notice is provided within a reasonable period before the beginning of each plan year (or, in the year an employee becomes an eligible employee, within a reasonable period before the employee becomes an eligible employee). In addition, a notice satisfies the timing requirements of paragraph (b)(3) of this section only if it is provided sufficiently early so that the employee has a reasonable period of time after receipt of the notice and before the first elective contribution is made under the arrangement to make the election described under paragraph (b)(ii)(A) of this section.

(B) *Deemed satisfaction of timing requirement.*—The timing requirement of this paragraph (b)(3)(iii) is satisfied if at least 30 days (and no more than 90 days) before the beginning of each plan year, the notice is given to each eligible employee for the plan year. In the case of an employee who does not receive the notice within the period described in the previous sentence because the employee becomes an eligible employee after the 90th day before the beginning of the plan year, the timing requirement is deemed to be satisfied if the notice is provided no more than 90 days before the employee becomes an eligible employee (and no later than the date the employee becomes an eligible employee).

(4) *Default investment requirement.*—To the extent the plan is subject to Title I of ERISA, default elective contributions under an eligible automatic contribution arrangement must be invested in accordance with regulations prescribed by the Secretary of Labor under section 404(c)(5) of ERISA.

(c) *Permissible withdrawal.*—(1) *In general.*—If the plan provides, any employee who has default elective contributions made under the eligible automatic contribution arrangement may elect to make a withdrawal of such contributions (and earnings attributable thereto) in accordance with the requirements of this paragraph (c). An applicable employer plan that includes an eligible automatic contribution arrangement will not fail to satisfy the prohibition on in-service withdrawals under sections 401(k)(2)(B), 403(b)(7), 403(b)(11), or 457(d)(1) merely because it permits withdrawals that satisfy the timing requirement of paragraph (c)(2) of this section and the amount requirement of paragraph (c)(3) of this section.

(2) *Timing.*—The election to withdraw default elective contributions must be made no later than 90 days after the date of the first default elective contribution under the eligible automatic contribution arrangement. The date of the first default elective contribution is the date that the compensation that is subject to the cash or deferred election would otherwise have been included in gross income. The effective date of an election described in this paragraph (c)(2) cannot be later than the last day of the payroll period that begins after the date the election is made.

(3) *Amount of distributions.*—(i) *In general.*—A distribution satisfies the requirement of this paragraph (c)(3) if the distribution is equal to the amount of default elective contributions made under the eligible automatic contribution arrangement through the effective date of the election described in paragraph (c)(2) of this section (adjusted for allocable gains and losses to the date of distribution). If default elective contributions are separately accounted for in the participant's account, the amount of the distribution will be the total amount in that account. However, if default elective contributions are not separately accounted for under the plan, the amount of the allocable gains and losses will be determined under rules similar to those provided under § 1.401(k)-2(b)(2)(iv) for the distribution of excess contributions.

(ii) *Fees.*—The distribution amount as determined under this paragraph (c)(3) may be reduced by any generally applicable fees. However, the plan may not charge a different fee for a distribution under section 414(w) than applies to other distributions.

(d) *Consequences of the withdrawal.*—(1) *Income tax consequences.*—(i) *Year of inclusion.*—The amount of the withdrawal is includible in the eligible employee's gross income for the taxable year in which the distribution is made. However, the portion of the distribution consisting of designated Roth contributions is not included in an employee's gross income a second time. The portion of the withdrawal that is treated as an investment in the contract is determined without regard to any plan contributions other than those distributed as withdrawal default elective contributions.

(ii) *No additional tax on early distributions from qualified retirement plans.*—The withdrawal is not subject to the additional tax under section 72(t).

(iii) *Reporting.*—The amount of the withdrawal is reported on Form 1099-R, Distributions From Pensions, Annuities, Retirement or Profit-Sharing Plans, IRAs, Insurance Contracts, etc., as described in the applicable instructions.

(2) *Forfeiture of matching contributions.*—In the case of any withdrawal made under paragraph (c) of this section, employer matching contributions with respect to the amount withdrawn must be forfeited.

(3) *Consent rules.*—A withdrawal made under paragraph (c) of this section may be made without regard to any notice or consent otherwise required under section 401(a)(11) or 417.

(e) *Definitions.*—Unless indicated otherwise, the following definitions apply for purposes of section 414(w) and this section.

(1) *Applicable employer plan.*—An applicable employer plan means a plan that—

(i) Is qualified under section 401(a);

(ii) Satisfies the requirements of section 403(b); or

(iii) Is a section 457(b) eligible governmental plan described in § 1.457-2(f).

(2) *Automatic contribution arrangement.*—An automatic contribution arrangement means an arrangement that provides for a cash or deferred election that provides that in the absence of an eligible employee's affirmative election, a default election applies under which the employee is treated as having elected to have default elective contributions made on his or her behalf under the plan. This default election ceases to apply with respect to an employee if

the employee makes an affirmative election (that remains in effect) to—

(i) Not have any default elective contributions made on his or her behalf; or

(ii) Have default elective contributions made in a different amount or percentage of compensation.

(3) *Default elective contributions.*—Default elective contributions means contributions made at a specified level or amount under an automatic contribution arrangement that are—

(i) Contributions described in section 402(g)(3)(A) or 402(g)(3)(C); or

(ii) Contributions made pursuant to a cash or deferred election within the meaning of section 457(b)(4) where the contributions are under a section 457(b) eligible governmental plan.

(4) *Eligible employee.*—An eligible employee means an employee who is eligible to make a cash or deferred election under the plan.

(f) *Effective date.*—Section 414(w) and this section apply to plan years beginning on or after January 1, 2008. [Reg. § 1.414(w)-1.]

Qualified Plans: Compensation: Treatment of Income from Indian Fishing Rights-Related Activity

Qualified Plans: Compensation: Treatment of Income from Indian Fishing Rights-Related Activity.—Amendments to Reg. § 1.415(c)-2, clarifying that amounts paid to an Indian tribe member as remuneration for services performed in a fishing rights-related activity may be treated as compensation for purposes of applying the limits on qualified plan benefits and contributions, are proposed (published in the Federal Register on November 15, 2013) (REG-120927-13).

☐ Par. 2. Section 1.415(c)-2 is amended by adding paragraphs (g)(9) and (h) to read as follows:

§ 1.415(c)-2. Compensation.

* * *

(g) * * *

(9) *Income derived by Indians from exercise of fishing rights.*—Amounts paid to a member of an Indian tribe directly or through a qualified Indian entity (within the meaning of section 7873(b)(3)) as compensation for services performed in a fishing rights-related activity (as defined in section 7873(b)(1)) of the tribe do not fail to constitute compensation under paragraphs (b)(1) and (b)(2) of this section and are not excluded from the definition of compensation pursuant to paragraph (c)(4) of this section merely because those amounts are not subject to income or employment taxes as a result of section 7873(a)(1) and (2). Thus, the determination of whether an amount constitutes wages, salaries, or earned income for purposes of paragraph (b)(1) or (a)(2) of this section is made without regard to the exemption from taxation under section 7873(a)(1) and (2).

(h) *Effective/applicability date.*—Section 1.415(c)-2(g)(9) shall apply for plan years ending on or after the date of publication of the Treasury decision adopting these rules as final regulations in the **Federal Register**.

Retirement Plans: Distributions: Deferral of Receipt: Notification of Consequences

Retirement Plans: Distributions: Deferral of Receipt: Notification of Consequences.—Amendments to Reg. § 1.417(e)-1, specifying that the notice required under Code Sec. 411(a)(11) to be provided to a participant of his or her right, if any, to defer receipt of an immediately distributable benefit must also describe the consequences of failing to defer receipt of the distribution, are proposed (published in the Federal Register on October 9, 2008) (REG-107318-08).

Par. 2. For each entry listed in the "Location" column, remove the language in the "Remove" column and add the language in the "Add" column in its place.

§ 1.417(e)-1. Restrictions and valuations of distributions from plans subject to sections 401(a)(11) and 417.

Location	Remove	Add
1.417(e)-1(b)(3)(i)	90 days	180 days
1.417(e)-1(b)(3)(ii), first sentence	90 days	180 days
1.417(e)-1 (b)(3)(iii)	90 days	180 days
1.417(e)-1 (b)(3)(vi), second sentence	90 days	180 days
1.417(e)-1(b)(3)(vii)	90 days	180 days
1.417(e)-1(b)(3)(vii)	90-day	180-day

Minimum Present Value Requirements: Benefit Plan Distributions: Update

Minimum Present Value Requirements: Benefit Plan Distributions: Update.—Amendments to Reg. § 1.417(e)-1, relating to the minimum present value requirements applicable to certain defined benefit pension plans, are proposed (published in the Federal Register on November 25, 2016) (REG-107424-12).

Par. 2. Section 1.417(e)-1 is amended by:
1. Revising paragraphs (d)(1)(i), (d)(2), (d)(3), (d)(4), and (d)(6).
2. Adding paragraph (d)(8)(vi).
3. Revising paragraph (d)(9).
4. Removing paragraph (d)(10).
The addition and revisions read as follows:

§1.417(e)-1. Restrictions and valuations of distributions from plans subject to sections 401(a)(11) and 417.

* * *

(d) *Present value requirement.*—(1) *General rule.*—(i) *Defined benefit plans.*—(A) *In general.*—A defined benefit plan must provide that the present value of any accrued benefit and the amount (subject to sections 411(c)(3) and 415) of any distribution, including a single sum, must not be less than the amount calculated using the applicable mortality table described in paragraph (d)(2) of this section and the applicable interest rate described in paragraph (d)(3) of this section, as determined for the month described in paragraph (d)(4) of this section. The present value of any optional form of benefit, determined in accordance with the preceding sentence, cannot be less than the present value of the accrued benefit payable at normal retirement age, except to the extent that, for an optional form of benefit payable after normal retirement age, the requirements for suspension of benefits under section 411(a)(3)(B) are satisfied. The same rules used for the plan under this paragraph (d) must also be used to compute the present value of the benefit for purposes of determining whether consent for a distribution is required under paragraph (b) of this section.

(B) *Payment of a portion of a participant's benefit.*—The rules of this paragraph (d)(1) apply with respect to a payment of only a portion of the accrued benefit in the same manner as these rules would apply to a distribution of the entire accrued benefit. See paragraph (d)(7) of this section.

(C) *Special rules for applicable defined benefit plans.*—See section 411(a)(13) and the regulations thereunder for an exception from the rules of section 417(e)(3) and this paragraph (d) that applies to certain distributions from certain applicable defined benefit plans.

* * *

(2) *Applicable mortality table.*—(i) *In general.*—The applicable mortality table for a calendar year is the mortality table that is prescribed by the Commissioner in guidance published in the Internal Revenue Bulletin. See §601.601(d)(2) of this chapter. This mortality table is to be based on the table specified under section 430(h)(3)(A), but without regard to section 430(h)(3)(C) or (D).

(ii) *Mortality discounts.*—(A) *In general.*—Except as provided under paragraph (d)(2)(ii)(B) of this section, the probability of death under the applicable mortality table is taken into account for purposes of determining the present value under this paragraph (d) without regard to the death benefits provided under the plan (other than a death benefit that is part of the normal form of benefit or part of another optional form of benefit, as described in §1.411(d)-3(g)(6)(ii)(B), for which present value is determined).

(B) *Special rule for employee-provided benefit.*—For purposes of determining the present value under this paragraph (d) with respect to the accrued benefit derived from employee contributions (that is determined in accordance with the requirements of section 411(c)(3)), the probability of death during the assumed deferral period, if any, is not taken into account. For purposes of the preceding sentence, the assumed deferral period is the period between the date of the present value determination and the assumed commencement date for the annuity attributable to contributions made by an employee.

(3) *Applicable interest rate.*—(i) *In general.*—The applicable interest rate for a month is determined using the first, second, and third segment rates for that month under section 430(h)(2)(C), as modified pursuant to section 417(e)(3)(D) (and without regard to the segment rate stabilization rules of section 430(h)(2)(C)(iv)). The applicable interest rate is specified by the Commissioner in revenue rulings, notices, or other guidance published in the Internal Revenue Bulletin, and is applied under rules similar to the rules under §1.430(h)(2)-1(b). Thus, for example, in determining the present value of a straight life annuity, the first segment is applied with respect to payments expected to be made during the 5-year period beginning on the annuity starting date, the second segment rate is applied with respect to payments expected to be made during the 15-year period following the end of that 5-year period, and the third segment rate is applied with respect to payments expected to be made after the end of that 15-year period. The interest rates that are published by the Commissioner are to be used for this purpose without further adjustment.

(ii) *Examples.*—The following examples illustrate the rules of paragraphs (d)(2) and (3) of this section.

Example 1. (i) Plan A is a non-contributory single-employer defined benefit plan with a calendar-year plan year, a one-year stability period coinciding with the calendar year, and a two-month lookback used for determining the applicable interest rate. The normal retirement age is 65, and all participant elections are made with proper spousal consent. Plan A provides for optional single sum payments equal to the present value of the participant's accrued benefit. Plan A provides that the applicable interest rates are the segment rates as specified by the Commissioner for the second full calendar month preceding the calendar year that contains the annuity starting date. The applicable mortality table is the table specified by the Commissioner for the calendar year that contains the annuity starting date.

(ii) Participant P retires in May 2017 at age 60 and elects (with spousal consent) to receive a single-sum payment. P has an accrued benefit of $2,000 per month payable as a life annuity beginning at the plan's normal retirement age of 65. The applicable mortality rates for 2017 apply. The applicable interest rates published by the Commissioner for November 2016 are 1.57%, 3.45%, and 4.39% for the first, second, and third segment rates, respectively. The deferred annuity factor calculated based on these interest rates and the applicable mortality table for 2017 is 10.931 for a participant age 60. To satisfy the requirements of section 417(e)(3) and this paragraph (d), the single-sum payment received by P cannot be less than $262,344 (that is, $2,000 x 12 x 10.931).

Example 2. (i) The facts are the same as for *Example 1* of this paragraph (d)(3)(ii), except that Plan A provides for mandatory employee contributions. Participant Q retires in May 2017 at age 60 and elects (with spousal consent) to receive a single-sum payment of Q's entire accrued benefit. Q has an accrued benefit of $2,000 per month payable as a life annuity beginning at Plan A's normal retirement age of 65, consisting of an accrued benefit derived from employee contributions determined in accordance with section 411(c)(2) (Q's employee-provided accrued benefit) of $500 per month and an accrued benefit derived from employer contributions (Q's employer-provided accrued benefit) of $1,500 per month.

(ii) Pursuant to paragraph (d)(2)(ii)(B) of this section, the single-sum payment used to settle Q's employee-provided accrued benefit cannot be less than the present value of that portion of Q's accrued benefit determined using the applicable interest and mortality rates described in paragraphs (d)(3)(i) and (d)(2)(ii) of this section, determined without taking the probability of death during the assumed deferral period into account. The deferred annuity factor calculated based on the interest and mortality rates specified in *Example 1* of this paragraph (d)(3)(ii) (taking the probability of death only after age 65 into account) is 11.266 for a participant age 60. To satisfy the requirement of section 417(e)(3) and this paragraph (d), the single-sum payment received by Q with respect to the employee-provided portion of the accrued benefit cannot be less than the minimum present value of $67,596 (that is, $500 x 12 x 11.266).

(iii) The single-sum payment used to settle Q's employer-provided accrued benefit cannot be less than the present value of that portion of Q's accrued benefit determined using the applicable interest and mortality rates. However, for this purpose, Plan A is permitted to take the probability of death during the assumed deferral period into account. The single-sum payment received by Q with respect to the employer-provided portion of the accrued benefit cannot be less than $196,758 (that is, $1,500 x 12 x 10.931).

(iv) The total single-sum payment received by Q cannot be less than the sum of the minimum present value of Q's employee- and employer-provided accrued benefits, or $264,354 ($67,596 + $196,758).

(4) *Time for determining interest rate and mortality table.*—(i) *Interest rate general rule.*—Except as provided in paragraph (d)(4)(v) or (vi) of this section, the applicable interest rate to be used for a distribution is the applicable interest rate determined under paragraph (d)(3) of this section for the applicable lookback month. The applicable lookback month for a distribution is the lookback month (as described in paragraph (d)(4)(iv) of this section) for the stability period (as described in paragraph (d)(4)(iii) of this section) that contains the annuity starting date for the distribution. The time and method for determining the applicable interest rate for each participant's distribution must be determined in a consistent manner that is applied uniformly to all participants in the plan.

(ii) *Mortality table general rule.*—The applicable mortality table to be used for a distribution is the mortality table that is published for the calendar year during which the stability period containing the annuity starting date begins.

(iii) *Stability period.*—A plan must specify the period for which the applicable interest rate remains constant (the stability period). This stability period may be one calendar month, one plan quarter, one calendar quarter, one plan year, or one calendar year. This same stability period also applies to the applicable mortality table.

(iv) *Lookback month.*—A plan must specify the lookback month that is used to determine the applicable interest rate with respect to a stability period. The lookback month may be the first, second, third, fourth, or fifth full calendar month preceding the first day of the stability period.

(v) *Permitted average interest rate.*—A plan may apply the rules of paragraph (d)(4)(i) of this section by substituting a permitted average applicable interest rate with respect to the plan's stability period for the applicable interest rate determined under paragraph (d)(3) of this section for the applicable lookback month for the stability period. For this purpose, a permitted average applicable interest rate with respect to a stability period is the applicable interest rate that is computed by averaging the applicable interest rates determined under paragraph (d)(3) of this section for two or more consecutive months from among the first, second, third, fourth, and fifth calendar months preceding the first day of the stability period. For this paragraph (d)(4)(v) to apply, a plan must specify the manner in which the permitted average interest rate is computed.

(vi) *Additional determination dates.*—The Commissioner may prescribe, in guidance published in the Internal Revenue Bulletin, other times that a plan may provide for determining the applicable interest rate.

(vii) *Example.*—The following example illustrates the rules of this paragraph (d)(4):

Example. (i) The facts are the same as *Example 1* of paragraph (d)(3)(ii) of this section, except that Plan A provides that the applicable interest rates are the rates for the third full calendar month preceding the beginning of the plan quarter that contains the annuity starting date. Plan A also provides that the applicable mortality table is the table specified by the Commissioner for the calendar year that contains the beginning of the stability period.

(ii) The segment interest rates that apply for annuity starting dates during the period beginning April 1, 2017 and ending June 30, 2017 are the segment rates for January 2017. This plan design permits the applicable interest rate to be fixed for each plan quarter and for the applicable interest rate for all distributions made during each plan quarter to be determined before the beginning of the plan quarter.

* * *

(6) *Exceptions.*—(i) *In general.*—This paragraph (d) (other than the provisions relating to section 411(d)(6) requirements in paragraph (d)(9) of this section) does not apply to the amount of a distribution paid in the form of an annual benefit that—

(A) Does not decrease during the life of the participant, or, in the case of a QPSA, the life of the participant's spouse; or

(B) Decreases during the life of the participant merely because of—

(1) The death of the survivor annuitant (but only if the reduction is to a level not below 50 percent of the annual benefit payable before the death of the survivor annuitant): or

(2) The cessation or reduction of a social security supplement or qualified disability benefit (as defined in section 411(a)(9)).

(ii) *Example.*—The following example illustrates the rules of this paragraph (d)(6).

Example. (i) The facts are the same as *Example 1* of paragraph (d)(3)(ii) of this section. Plan A also provides an optional distribution in the form of a Social Security level income option. Under this provision, the participant's benefit is adjusted so that a larger amount is payable until age 65, at which time it is reduced to provide a level income in combination with the participant's estimated social security benefit beginning at age 65. Participant R's reduced early retirement benefit payable as a straight life annuity benefit commencing at age 60 is $1,300 per month (which is less than the actuarially equivalent benefit that would have been determined using the applicable interest and mortality rates under section 417(e)(3)) and R's estimated social security benefit is $1,000 per month beginning at age 65.

(ii) Because the benefit payable under the social security level income option decreases at age 65 and the decrease is not on account of the death of the participant or a beneficiary or the cessation or reduction of social security supplements or qualified disability benefits, the benefits payable under the social security level income option are subject to the minimum present value requirements of section 417(e)(3). As illustrated in *Example 1* of paragraph (d)(3)(ii) of this section, the minimum present value of Participant R's benefits under section 417(e)(3) is $262,344, which is based on the present value of R's accrued benefit, not R's benefit that would be payable as a straight life annuity at the annuity starting date.

(iii) The deferred annuity factor for a participant age 60 with lifetime benefits commencing at age 65, based on the November 2016 segment rates and the applicable mortality table for 2017, is 10.931. The corresponding temporary annuity factor to age 65 is 4.752. The minimum benefits payable to Participant R in the form of a social security level income option (with a decrease of $1,000 – equal to the participant's estimated social security benefit – occurring at age 65) are $2,090.99 per month until age 65 and $1,090.99 per month thereafter. Any amounts less than this would have a present value smaller than the required amount of $262,344, and thus would fail to satisfy the minimum present value requirement of section 417(e)(3).

* * *

(8) * * *

(vi) *Applicability date for provisions reflecting PPA '06 updates and other rules.*—Paragraphs (d)(1) through (4) of this section apply to distributions with annuity starting dates in plan years beginning on or after the date regulations that finalize these proposed regulations are published in the **Federal Register**. Prior to this applicability date, taxpayers must continue to apply the provisions of §1.417(e)-1(d) as contained in 26 CFR part 1 as in effect immediately before publication of those final regulations, except to the extent superseded by statutory changes and guidance of general applicability relating to those statutory changes.

(9) *Relationship with section 411(d)(6).*—(i) *In general.*—A plan amendment that changes the interest rate or the mortality assumptions used for the purposes described in paragraph (d)(1) of this section (including a plan amendment that changes the time for determining those assumptions) is generally subject to section 411(d)(6). However, for certain exceptions to the rule in the preceding sentence, see paragraph (d)(7)(iv) of this section, §1.411(d)-4, Q&A-2(b)(2)(v) (with respect to plan amendments relating to involuntary distributions), and section 1107(a)(2) of the Pension Protection Act of 2006, Public Law 109-280, 120 Stat. 780 (2006) (PPA '06) (with respect to certain plan amendments that were made pursuant to a change to the Internal Revenue Code by PPA '06 or regulations issued thereunder).

(ii) *Section 411(d)(6) relief for change in time for determining interest rate and mortality table.*—Notwithstanding the general rule of paragraph (d)(9)(i) of this section, if a plan amendment changes the time for determining the applicable interest rate (and, if the amendment changes the stability period described in paragraph (d)(4)(iii) of this section, the time for determining the applicable mortality table), including an indirect change as a result of a change in plan year, the amendment will not be treated as reducing accrued benefits in violation of section 411(d)(6) merely on account of this change if the conditions of this paragraph (d)(9)(ii) are satisfied. If the plan amendment is effective on or after the date the amendment is adopted, any distribution for which the annuity starting date occurs in the one-year period commencing at the time the amendment is effective must be determined using the interest rate and mortality table provided under the plan determined at either the date for determining the interest rate and mortality table before the amendment or the date for determining the interest rate and mortality table after the amendment, whichever results in the larger distribution. If the plan amendment is adopted retroactively (that is, the amendment is effective prior to the adoption date), the plan must use the interest rate and mortality table determination dates resulting in the larger distribution for distributions with annuity starting dates occurring during the period beginning with the effective date and ending one year after the adoption date.

* * *

Employee Trusts: Effective Dates

Employee Trusts: Tax Reform Act of 1984: Effective Dates.—Temporary Reg. §§1.419-1T and 1.419A-1T are also proposed as final regulations and, when adopted, would become Reg. §§1.419-1 and 1.419A-1, respectively (published in the Federal Register on February 4, 1986).

§1.419-1. Treatment of welfare benefit funds.

§1.419A-1. Qualified asset account limitation of additions to account.

Welfare Benefit Funds: Collective Bargaining

Welfare Benefit Fund: Collective Bargaining: Limits on Contributions and Reserves.— Temporary Reg. §1.419A-2T, relating to welfare benefit funds maintained pursuant to collective bargaining agreements, is also proposed as a final regulation and, when adopted, would become Reg. §1.419A-2 (published in the Federal Register on July 3, 1985).

§1.419A-2. Qualified asset account limitation for collectively bargained funds.

Defined Benefit Plans: Multiemployer Plan Funding Guidance

Defined Benefit Plans: Multiemployer Plan Funding Guidance.—Reg. §§1.432(a)-1 and 1.432(b)-1, providing additional rules for certain multiemployer defined benefit plans that are in effect on July 16, 2006 and affecting multiemployer plans that are either endangered or critical status, are proposed (published in the Federal Register on March 18, 2008) (REG-151135-07).

☐ Par. 2. Section 1.432(a)-1 is added to read as follows:

§1.432(a)-1. General rules relating to section 432.—(a) *In general.*—(1) *Overview.*—This section provides rules relating to multiemployer plans (within the meaning of section 414(f)) that are in endangered status or critical status under section 432. Section 432 and this section only apply to multiemployer plans that are in effect on July 16, 2006. Paragraph (b) of this section sets forth definitions of terms that apply for purposes of section 432. Paragraph (c) of this section sets forth special rules for plans described in section 404(c) and for the treatment of nonbargained participation.

(2) *Plans in endangered status.*—(i) *Plan sponsor must adopt funding improvement plan.*—If a plan is in endangered status, the plan sponsor must adopt and implement a funding improvement plan that satisfies the requirements of section 432(c).

(ii) *Restrictions applicable to plans in endangered status.*—If a plan is in endangered status, the plan and plan sponsor must satisfy the requirements of section 432(d)(1) during the funding plan adoption period specified in section 432(c)(8).

(iii) *Restrictions applicable after the adoption of funding improvement plan.*—In the case of a plan that is in endangered status after adoption of the funding improvement plan, the plan and the plan sponsor must satisfy the requirements of section 432(d)(2) until the end of the funding improvement period.

(3) *Plans in critical status.*—(i) *Plan sponsor must adopt rehabilitation plan.*—If a plan is in critical status, the plan sponsor must adopt and implement a rehabilitation plan that satisfies the requirements of section 432(e).

(ii) *Restrictions applicable to plans in critical status.*—If a plan is in critical status, the plan and the plan sponsor must satisfy the requirements of section 432(f)(4) during the rehabilitation plan adoption period as defined in section 432(e)(5). The plan must also apply the restrictions on single sum and other accelerated benefits set forth in paragraph (a)(3)(iii) of this section.

(iii) *Restrictions on single sums and other accelerated benefits.*—(A) *In general.*—A plan in critical status is required to provide that, effective on the date the notice of certification of the plan's critical status for the initial critical year under §1.432(b)-1(e) is sent, no payment in excess of the monthly amount payable under a single life annuity (plus any social security supplements described in the last sentence of section 411(a)(9)), and no payment for the purchase of an irrevocable commitment from an insurer to pay benefits, may be made except as provided in section 432(f)(2). A plan amendment that provides for these restrictions does not violate section 411(d)(6).

(B) *Exceptions.*—Pursuant to section 432(f)(2)(B), the restrictions under this paragraph (a)(3)(iii) do not apply to a benefit which under section 411 (a)(11) may be immediately distributed without the consent of the participant or to any makeup payment in the case of a retroactive annuity starting date or any similar payment of benefits owed with respect to a prior period.

(C) [Reserved.]

(D) *Correction of erroneous restrictions.*—If the notice described in §1.432(b)-1(e) has been sent and the restrictions provided under this paragraph (a)(3)(iii) have been applied, and it is later determined that the restrictions should not have been applied, then the plan must correct any benefit payments that were restricted in error. Thus, for example, if pursuant to section 212(e)(2) of the Pension Protection Act of 2006, Public Law 109-280, 120 Stat. 780 the enrolled actuary for the plan certified that it was reasonably expected that the plan would be in critical status with respect to the first plan year beginning after 2007, and the notice described in §1.432(b)-1(e)(3)(i) was sent, but the plan is not later certified to be in critical status for that plan year, then the plan must correct any benefit payments that were restricted after the notice was sent. Similarly, if the enrolled actuary for the plan certified that it was reasonably expected that the plan would be in critical status with respect to the first plan year beginning after 2007, and the notice described in § 1.432(b)-1(e)(3)(i) was sent before the first day of that plan year, the restriction on benefits under section 432(f)(2) first applies beginning on the first day of the first plan year beginning after 2007. If the plan restricts benefits before that date, then the plan must correct any improperly restricted benefits.

(iv) *Restrictions applicable after the adoption of rehabilitation plan.*—In the case of a plan that is in critical status after the adoption of the rehabilitation plan, the plan and the plan sponsor must satisfy the requirements of section 432(f)(1) until the end of the rehabilitation period.

(b) *Definitions.*—The following definitions apply for purposes of section 432 and the regulations:

(1) *Accumulated funding deficiency.*—The term accumulated funding deficiency has the same meaning as the term accumulated funding deficiency under section 431(a).

(2) *Active participant.*—The term active participant means a participant who is in covered service under the plan.

(3) *Bargaining party.*—Except as provided in paragraph (c)(1) of this section, the term bargaining party means an employer who has an obligation to contribute under the plan and an employee organization which, for purposes of collective bargaining, represents plan participants employed by an employer which has an obligation to contribute under the plan.

(4) *Benefit commencement date.*—The term benefit commencement date means the annuity starting date (or in the case of a retroactive annuity starting date, the date on which benefit payments begin).

(5) *Critical status.*—A multiemployer plan is in critical status if the plan meets one of the tests set forth in § 1.432(b)-1(c).

(6) *Endangered status.*—A plan is in endangered status if the plan meets one of the tests set forth in § 1.432(b)-1(b).

(7) *Funded percentage.*—The term funded percentage means a fraction (expressed as a percentage) the numerator of which is the actuarial value of the plan's assets as determined under section 431(c)(2) and the denominator of which is the accrued liability of the plan, determined using the actuarial assumptions described in section 431(c)(3) and the unit credit funding method.

(8) *Funding improvement period for endangered or seriously endangered plans.*—The term funding improvement period means the period that begins on the first day of the first plan year beginning after the earlier of the second anniversary of the date of the adoption of the funding improvement plan, or the expiration of the collective bargaining agreements that are in effect on the due date for the actuarial certification of endangered status for the initial endangered year and which cover, as of such due date, at least 75 percent of the active participants in the plan. The funding improvement period ends on the last day of the 10th year (15 years for seriously endangered plans, except as provided in section 432(c)(5)) after it begins or, if earlier, the date of the change in status described in section 432(c)(4)(C).

(9) *Funding plan adoption period.*—The term funding plan adoption period means the period that begins on the date of the actuarial certification for the initial endangered year and ends on the day before the first day of the funding improvement period.

(10) *Inactive participant.*—The term inactive participant means —

(i) A participant who is not an active participant,

(ii) A beneficiary under the plan, or

(iii) An alternate payee under the plan.

(11) *Initial critical year.*—The term initial critical year means the first year for which the enrolled actuary for the plan has certified that the plan is or will be in critical status. If a plan is in critical status in one year, emerges from critical status in a subsequent year and then returns to critical status, the year of reentry into critical status is treated as the initial critical year with respect to subsequent years.

(12) *Initial endangered year.*—The term initial endangered year means the first year for which the enrolled actuary for the plan has certified that the plan is in endangered status. If a plan is in endangered status in one year, changes from endangered status in a subsequent year and then returns to endangered status, the year of reentry into endangered status is treated as the initial endangered year with respect to subsequent years.

(13) *Nonbargained participant.*—The term nonbargained participant means a participant in the plan whose participation is other than pursuant to a collective bargaining agreement within the meaning of section 7701(a)(46). A participant will not be treated as a nonbargained participant merely because the participant is no longer covered by the collective bargaining agreement solely as a result of retirement or severance from employment.

(14) *Obligation to contribute.*—The term obligation to contribute means an obligation to contribute arising under one or more collective bargaining (or related) agreements or as a result of a duty under applicable labor-management relations law.

(15) *Plan sponsor.*—Except as provided in paragraph (c)(1) of this section, the term plan sponsor means the association, committee, joint board of trustees, or other similar group of representatives of the parties who establish or maintain the plan.

(16) *Rehabilitation period.*—The term rehabilitation period means the period that begins on the first day of the first plan year beginning after the earlier of the second anniversary of the date of the adoption of the rehabilitation plan, or the expiration of the collective bargaining agreements that are in effect on the due date for the actuarial certification of critical status for the initial critical year and which cover, as of such due date, at least 75 percent of the active participants in the plan. The rehabilitation period ends on the last day of the 10th year after it begins or, if earlier, the plan year preceding the plan year in which the plan has emerged from critical status as described in section 432(e)(4)(B).

(17) *Rehabilitation plan adoption period.*—The term rehabilitation plan adoption period

means the period that begins on the date of the actuarial certification for the initial critical year and ends on the day before the first day of the rehabilitation period.

(18) *Seriously endangered status.*—A plan is in seriously endangered status if the plan is in endangered status and is described in both §1.432(b)-1(b)(2) and (3).

(c) *Special rules.*—(1) *Plan described in section 404(c).*—In the case of a plan described in section 404(c), or a continuation of such a plan, the association of employers that is the employer settlor of the plan is treated as a bargaining party and is treated as the plan sponsor for purposes of section 432.

(2) *Plans covering both bargained and nonbargained participants.*—In the case of an employer that contributes to a plan with respect to both employees who are covered by one or more collective bargaining agreements and employees who are nonbargained participants, if the plan is in endangered status or critical status, benefits of and contributions for the nonbargained participants (including surcharges on those contributions) are determined as if those nonbargained participants were covered under the employer's collective bargaining agreement in effect when the plan entered endangered or critical status that is the first to expire.

(3) *Plans covering nonbargained participants only.*—In the case of an employer that contributes to a multiemployer plan only with respect to employees who are not covered by a collective bargaining agreement, section 432 and the regulations thereunder are applied as if the employer were the bargaining party, and its participation agreement with the plan were a collective bargaining agreement with a term ending on the first day of the plan year beginning after the employer is provided the schedules described in sections 432(c) and (e).

(d) *Effective/applicability date.*—These regulations apply to plan years ending after March 18, 2008, but only with respect to plan years that begin on or after January 1, 2008. [Reg. §1.432(a)-1.]

☐ Par. 3. Section 1.432(b)-1 is added to read as follows:

§1.432(b)-1. Determination of status and adoption of a plan.—(a) *In general.*—This section provides rules relating to multiemployer plans (within the meaning of section 414(f)) that are in endangered status or critical status under section 432. Section 432 and this section only apply to multiemployer plans that are in effect on July 16, 2006. Paragraph (b) of this section sets forth the factors for determining whether a plan is in endangered status. Paragraph (c) of this section sets forth the factors for determining whether a plan is in critical status. Paragraph (d) sets forth the requirements for the annual certification by the plan's enrolled actuary. Paragraph (e) of this section describes the notice to employees that is required for plans that are in endangered or critical status.

(b) *Determination of endangered status.*—(1) *In general.*—A plan is in endangered status for a plan year if, as determined by the enrolled actuary for the plan, the plan is not in critical status for the plan year and if, as of the beginning of the plan year, the plan is described either in paragraph (b)(2) of this section or paragraph (b)(3) of this section. The enrolled actuary's determination of whether a plan is in endangered status is made under the rules of paragraph (d)(5) of this section.

(2) *Endangered status based on funding percentage.*—A plan is described in this paragraph (b)(2) for a plan year if the plan's funded percentage for such plan year is less than 80 percent.

(3) *Endangered status based on projection of funding deficiency.*—A plan is described in this paragraph (b)(3) for a plan year if the plan has an accumulated funding deficiency for such plan year (or is projected to have such an accumulated funding deficiency for any of the 6 succeeding plan years), taking into account any extension of amortization periods under section 431(d).

(c) *Critical Status.*—(1) *In general.*—A multiemployer plan is in critical status for a plan year if, as determined by the enrolled actuary for the plan, the plan is described in one or more of paragraphs (c)(2) through (c)(6) of this section as of the beginning of the plan year. The enrolled actuary's determination of critical status must be made in accordance with the rules of paragraph (d)(5) of this section. Notwithstanding paragraph (d)(5)(iii) of this section, for purposes of applying the critical status tests described in paragraphs (c)(2) and (c)(5) of this section, the actuary must assume that the terms of all collective bargaining agreements pursuant to which the plan is maintained for the current plan year continue in effect for succeeding plan years.

(2) *Critical status based on 6-year projection of benefit payments.*—A plan is described in this paragraph (c)(2) if the funded percentage of the plan is less than 65 percent, and the present value of all nonforfeitable benefits projected to be payable under the plan during the current plan year and each of the 6 succeeding plan years (plus administrative expenses for such plan years) is greater than the sum of—

(i) The fair market value of plan assets, plus

(ii) The present value of the reasonably anticipated employer contributions for the current plan year and the 6 succeeding plan years.

(3) *Critical status based on short term funding deficiency.*—A plan is described in this paragraph (c)(3) if—

(i) The plan has an accumulated funding deficiency for the current plan year, not taking into account any extension of amortization periods under section 431(d), or

(ii) The plan is projected to have an accumulated funding deficiency for any of the 3 succeeding plan years (4 succeeding plan years if the funded percentage of the plan is 65 percent or less), not taking into account any extension of amortization periods under section 431(d).

(4) *Critical status based on contributions less than normal cost plus interest.*—A plan is described in this paragraph (c)(4) if—

(i) The present value of the reasonably anticipated employer and employee contributions for the current plan year is less than the sum of—

(A) The plan's normal cost (determined under the unit credit funding method), and

(B) Interest (determined at the rate used for determining costs under the plan) on the excess if any of—

(1) The accrued liability of the plan (determined using the actuarial assumptions described in section 431(c)(3) and the unit credit funding method) over

(2) The actuarial value of assets determined under section 431(c)(2),

(ii) The present value, as of the beginning of the current plan year, of nonforfeitable benefits of inactive participants is greater than the present value of nonforfeitable benefits of active participants, and

(iii) The plan has an accumulated funding deficiency for the current plan year (or is projected to have such a deficiency for any of the 4 succeeding plan years), not taking into account any extension of amortization periods under section 431(d).

(5) *Critical status based on 4-year projection of benefit payments.*—A plan is described in this paragraph (c)(5) if the present value of all benefits projected to be payable under the plan during the current plan year or any of the 4 succeeding plan years (plus administrative expenses for such plan years) is greater than the sum of—

(i) The fair market value of plan assets, plus

(ii) The present value of the reasonably anticipated employer contributions for the current plan year and each of the 4 succeeding plan years.

(6) *Critical status based on failure to meet emergence criteria.*—A plan is described in this paragraph (c)(6) if—

(i) The plan was in critical status for the immediately preceding plan year, and

(ii) The enrolled actuary for the plan has certified that the plan is projected to have an accumulated funding deficiency for the plan year or any of the 9 succeeding plan years, without regard to the use of the shortfall funding method but taking into account any extensions of the amortization periods under section 431(d).

(d) *Annual certification by the plan's enrolled actuary.*—(1) *In general.*—Not later than the 90th day of each plan year of a multiemployer plan, the enrolled actuary for the plan must certify to the Secretary of the Treasury and to the plan sponsor—

(i) Whether or not the plan is in endangered status for such plan year;

(ii) Whether or not the plan is or will be in critical status for such plan year, and

(iii) In the case of a plan which is in a funding improvement or rehabilitation period, whether or not the plan is making the scheduled progress in meeting the requirements of its funding improvement or rehabilitation plan.

(2) *Transmittal of certification.*—(i) *Transmittal to the plan sponsor.*—The certification of plan status described in paragraph (d)(1) must be submitted to the plan sponsor at the address stated by the plan sponsor on their Annual Report (Form 5500) or such other address as the plan sponsor may designate in writing for receipt of this certification.

(ii) *Transmittal to the Secretary of the Treasury.*—Except as provided in guidance of general applicability to be published in the Internal Revenue Bulletin, the annual certification of plan status described in paragraph (d)(1) must be transmitted to the Secretary of the Treasury by mailing the certification to:

Internal Revenue Service
Employee Plans Compliance Unit
Group 7602 (SE:TEGE:EP)
Room 1700 - 17th Floor
230 S. Dearborn Street
Chicago, IL 60604

(3) *Content of annual certification.*—(i) *In general.*—The annual certification must contain the information described in this paragraph (d)(3). The Secretary may add to or otherwise modify the requirements in this paragraph (d)(3) in guidance of general applicability to be published in the Internal Revenue Bulletin.

(ii) *Plan identification.*—The annual certification must include the name of the plan; the plan number; the name, address, and telephone number of the plan sponsor; and the plan year for which the certification is being made.

(iii) *Enrolled actuary identification.*—The annual certification must include the name, address and telephone number of the enrolled actuary signing the certification; the actuary's enrollment identification number; the actuary's signature, and the date of the signature.

(iv) *Information on plan status.*—The annual certification must state whether the plan is in endangered status (which includes seriously endangered status); critical status, or neither endangered nor critical status.

(v) *Information on scheduled progress.*—If the annual certification is made with respect to a plan year that is within the plan's funding improvement period or rehabilitation period arising from a prior certification of endangered or critical status, the actuary must also certify whether or not the plan is making scheduled progress in meeting the requirements of its funding improvement or rehabilitation plan.

(4) *Penalty for failure to secure timely actuarial certification.*—A failure of a plan's actuary to certify the plan's status under this paragraph (d) by the date specified in paragraph (d)(1) of this section is treated as a failure or refusal by the plan administrator to file the annual report required to be filed with the Secretary of Labor under section 101(b)(4) of the Employee Retirement Income Security Act of 1974.

(5) *Actuarial projections of assets and liabilities.*—(i) *In general.*—In making the determinations and projections under section 432(b) and this section, the enrolled actuary for the plan must make projections required for the current and succeeding plan years of the current value of the assets of the plan and the present value of all liabilities to participants and beneficiaries under the plan for the current plan year as of the beginning of such year. These projections must be based on reasonable actuarial estimates, assumptions, and methods in accordance with section 431(c)(3) and that offer the actuary's best estimate of anticipated experience under the plan. Notwithstanding the previous sentence, the actuary is permitted to rely on the plan sponsor's projection of activity in the industry provided

under paragraph (d)(5)(iii) of this section. The projected present value of liabilities as of the beginning of such year must be determined based on the most recent information reported on the most recent of either—

(A) The actuarial statement required under section 103(d) of the Employee Retirement Income Security Act of 1974 that has been filed with respect to the most recent year, or

(B) The actuarial valuation for the preceding plan year.

(ii) *Determinations of future contributions.*—Any actuarial projection of plan assets shall assume either—

(A) Reasonably anticipated employer contributions for the current and succeeding plan years, assuming that the terms of the one or more collective bargaining agreements pursuant to which the plan is maintained for the current plan year continue in effect for succeeding plan years, or

(B) That employer contributions for the most recent plan year will continue indefinitely, but only if the enrolled actuary for the plan determines there have been no significant demographic changes that would make such assumption unreasonable.

(iii) *Projected industry activity.*—The plan sponsor shall provide any necessary projection of activity in the industry, including future covered employment, to the plan actuary. For this purpose, the plan sponsor must act reasonably and in good faith.

(6) *Treatment of amortization extensions under section 412(e).*—For purposes of section 432, if the plan received an extension of any amortization period under section 412(e), the extension is treated the same as an extension under section 431(d). Thus, such an extension is not taken into account in determining whether a plan has or will have an accumulated funding deficiency under paragraph (c)(3) and (c)(4) of this section, but it is taken into account in determining whether a plan has or will have an accumulated funding deficiency under paragraph (b)(3) of this section.

(e) *Notice of endangered or critical status.*—(1) *In general.*—In any case in which the enrolled actuary for the plan certifies that a multiemployer plan is or will be in endangered or critical status for a plan year, the plan sponsor must, not later than 30 days after the date of the certification, provide notification of the endangered or critical status to the participants and beneficiaries, the bargaining parties, the Pension Benefit Guaranty Corporation, and the Secretary of Labor.

(2) *Plans in critical status.*—If it is certified that a multiemployer plan is or will be in critical status for a plan year, the plan sponsor must include in the notice an explanation of the possibility that adjustable benefits (as defined in section 432(e)(8)) may be reduced, and such reductions may apply to participants and beneficiaries whose benefit commencement date is on or after the date such notice is provided for the first plan year in which the plan is in critical status. If the plan provides benefits that are restricted under section 432(f)(2), the notice must also include an explanation that the plan cannot pay single sums and similar benefits described in section 432(f)(2) that are greater than the monthly amount due under a single life annuity. A plan sponsor that sends the model notice issued by the Secretary of Labor pursuant to section 432(b)(3)(D)(iii) satisfies this requirement.

(3) *Transition rules.*—(i) *Early notice permitted.*—If, after August 17, 2006, the enrolled actuary for the plan certifies that a plan is reasonably expected to be in critical status with respect to the first plan year beginning after 2007, then the notice described in this paragraph (e) may be provided before the date the actuary certifies the plan is in critical status for that plan year. The ability to provide early notice does not extend the otherwise applicable deadline for providing the notice under paragraph (e)(1) of this section.

(ii) *Reformation of prior notice.*—If notice has been provided prior to the date required under paragraph (e)(1) of this section, but the notice did not include all of the information described in paragraph (e)(2) of this section, then that notice will not satisfy the requirements for notice under section 432(b)(3)(D). Accordingly, the restrictions under section 432(f)(2) will not apply as a result of the issuance of such a notice. However, if prior to the date notice is required to be provided under paragraph (e)(1) of this section additional notice is provided that includes all of the information required under paragraph (e)(2) of this section, then the notice requirements of section 432(b)(3)(D) are satisfied as of the date of that additional notice and the restrictions of section 432(f)(2) will apply beginning on that date. In such a case, the date of the earlier notice will still apply for purposes of section 432(e)(8)(A)(ii) provided that the earlier notice included all of the information required under section 432(b)(3)(D)(ii).

(f) *Effective/applicability date.*—These regulations apply to plan years ending after March 18, 2008, but only with respect to plan years that begin on or after January 1, 2008. [Reg. § 1.432(b)-1.]

ACCOUNTING PERIODS AND METHODS OF ACCOUNTING

Foreign Corporations: Tax Years

Foreign Corporations: Tax Years.—Amendments to Reg. § 1.442-1, relating to the required taxable year of those foreign corporations beginning after July 10, 1989, are proposed (published in the Federal Register on January 5, 1993).

☐ Par. 3. Section 1.442-1 is amended by adding a sentence to the end of paragraphs (a)(1), (b)(3) and (c)(5), to read as follows:

§ 1.442-1. Change of annual accounting period.—(a) * * *

(1) * * * For special rules relating to controlled foreign corporations and foreign personal holding companies that are specified foreign corporations, within the meaning of section 898 and § 1.898-2, see section 898 and the regulations under that section.

* * *

(b) * * *

(3) * * * For special rules relating to controlled foreign corporations and foreign personal holding companies that are specified foreign corporations, within the meaning of section 898 and § 1.898-2, see section 898 and the regulations under that section.

* * *

(c) * * *

(5) * * * For special rules relating to controlled foreign corporations and foreign personal holding companies that are specified foreign corporations, within the meaning of section 898 and § 1.898-2, see section 898 and the regulations under that section.

* * *

Taxable Year: Partnerships, S Corporations, Personal Service Corporations

Taxable Year: Election: Partnership: S Corporation: Personal Service Corporation.— Temporary Reg. §§ 1.444-0T—1.444-3T, relating to the election of a taxable year by a partnership, S corporation or personal service corporation, are also proposed as final regulations and, when adopted, would become Reg. §§ 1.444-0—1.444-3 (published in the Federal Register on May 27, 1988).

§ 1.444-0. Table of contents.

§ 1.444-1. Election to use a taxable year other than the required taxable year.

§ 1.444-2. Tiered structure.

§ 1.444-3. Manner and time of making section 444 election.

Commodities: Securities: Mark-to-Market Accounting

Commodities: Securities: Mark-to-Market Accounting.—Amendments to Reg. § 1.446-1, regarding the election to use the mark-to-market method of accounting for dealers in commodities and traders in securities or commodities, are proposed (published in the Federal Register on January 28, 1999) (REG-104924-98).

□ Par. 2. In § 1.446-1, paragraph (c)(2)(iii) is added to read as follows:

§ 1.446-1. General rule for methods of accounting.

* * *

(c) * * *

(2) * * *

(iii) Section 475 is the exclusive authority on which a taxpayer may rely to use the mark-to-market method of accounting for nonfinancial customer paper, as defined in section 475(c)(4)(B). Thus, except to the extent provided in § 1.475(c)-2(d), the mark-to-market method of accounting is not a permissible method of accounting for nonfinancial customer paper. In addition, the lower-of-cost-or-market method of accounting is not a permissible method of accounting for these assets. See § 1.471-12. This paragraph (c)(2)(iii) applies to all tax years ending on or after January 28, 1999.

* * *

Debt Instruments: Allocation of Interest: Certain Small Transactions

Debt Instruments: Allocation of Interest: Certain Small Transactions.—An amendment to Reg. § 1.446-2, relating to the tax treatment of debt instruments with original issue discount and the imputation of interest on deferred payments under certain contracts for the sale or exchange of property, is proposed (published in the Federal Register on December 22, 1992) (FI-189-84). (Reg. § 1.446-2 was adopted by T.D. 8517 on January 27, 1994. T.D. 8517, however, states that Reg. § 1.446-2(e)(3) of the proposed regulations issued on December 22, 1992, remains in proposed form.)

§ 1.446-2. Method of accounting for interest.

* * *

(e) *Allocation of interest to payments.*—* * *

(3) *Allocation respected in certain small transactions.*—(i) *In general.*—If the aggregate amount of interest and principal payable under a contract does not exceed $250,000 and section 483 does not apply to the loan, an express allocation of the payments between interest and principal by the parties is respected. Similarly, if section 483 applies to a contract under which the aggregate amount payable does not exceed $250,000, but does not apply to a party to the contract (as, for example, in the case of an obligor under a debt instrument given in consideration for the sale or exchange of personal use property), an express allocation of the payments between interest and principal by the parties is respected for purposes of determining the tax liability of the party not subject to section 483.

(ii) *Prepaid interest.*—The amount of interest allocated to any payment under this paragraph (e)(3) is treated as prepaid interest to the extent the amount exceeds—

(A) The aggregate amount of accrued interest as of the date the payment becomes due; reduced (but not below zero) by

(B) The aggregate amount of interest allocated to prior payments under this paragraph (e)(3).

(iii) *Accounting for prepaid interest.*—Prepaid interest must be included in income by a lender when received, regardless of the lender's method of accounting. Except as otherwise provided in section 461(g)(2), prepaid interest is not deductible before such interest accrues (as determined under paragraph (c) of this section).

* * *

Notional Principal Contracts: Timing of Income and Deductions

Notional Principal Contracts: Timing of Income and Deductions.—An amendment to Reg. §1.446-3, relating to notional principal contracts, is proposed (published in the Federal Register on July 10, 1991). (Reg. §1.446-3 was adopted by T.D. 8491 on October 8, 1993. T.D. 8491, however, states that the special rules found in Reg. §1.446-3(e)(4)(iv) of the proposed regulations issued on July 10, 1991, remain in proposed form.)

§1.446-3. Notional principal contracts.

* * *

(e) *Taxable year of inclusion and deduction.—*

* * *

(4) *Special rules.*—(i) *Compound and disguised notional principal contracts.—** * *

(iv) *Caps and floors that are significantly in-the-money.*—If, on the date that a cap or floor is entered into, the current value of the specified index in a cap agreement exceeds the cap rate by a significant amount, or the floor rate exceeds the current value of the specified index in a floor agreement by a significant amount, then the cap or floor is treated as including one or more loans. The time value component of a cap or floor that is significantly in-the-money is recognized as interest for all purposes of the Code. For any taxable year during the term of the agreement, this time value component is deemed to be the lesser of:

(A) the ratable daily portion of the cap or floor premium that is recognized for the taxable year under paragraph (a)(3)(ii) (C) of this section, multiplied by the discount rate used by the parties to determine the amount paid for the cap or floor compounded from the date the premium is paid to the earlier of the date such option contracts expire or the end of the taxable year; or

(B) the net income or deduction from the cap or floor for the taxable year under paragraph (e)(1) of this section, computed without regard to this paragraph (e)(4)(iv).

In the case of an interest rate cap or an interest rate floor, a significant amount for purposes of this paragraph (e)(4)(iv) is more than 25 basis points. Interest recognized under this paragraph (e)(4)(iv) is not included in the net income or deduction from the cap or floor under paragraph (e)(1) of this section.

* * *

Notional Principal Contracts: Contingent Nonperiodic Payments

Notional Principal Contracts: Contingent Nonperiodic Payments.—Amendments to Reg. §1.446-3, relating to the inclusion into income or deduction of a contingent nonperiodic payment provided for under a notional principal contract, are proposed (published in the Federal Register on February 26, 2004) (corrected March 23, 2004) (REG-166012-02).

☐ Par. 4. Section 1.446-3 is amended by:

1. Revising the introductory text of paragraph (a) and the table of contents in paragraph (a).
2. Adding paragraph (c)(5).
3. Revising paragraphs (d), (f)(2)(i), (f)(2)(iii)(A), and (g)(4).
4. Redesignating the text of paragraph (g)(6) as paragraph (g)(7).
5. Adding new paragraph (g)(6).
6. Amending the newly designated text of paragraph (g)(7) by:
   (a) Revising the heading for *Example 3*.
   (b) Adding *Example 5* through *Example 9*.
7. Revising paragraphs (i) and (j).

The revisions and additions read as follows:

§1.446-3. Notional principal contracts.— (a) *Table of contents.*—This paragraph (a) lists captioned paragraphs contained in this section.

§1.446-3 Notional principal contracts

(iii) Alternative methods for swaps.

(A) Prepaid swaps.

(B) Other nonperiodic swap payments.

(iv) General rule for caps and floors.

(v) Alternative methods for caps and floors that hedge debt instruments.

(A) Prepaid caps and floors.

(B) Other caps and floors.

(C) Special method for collars.

(vi) Additional methods.

(3) Term of extendible or terminable contracts.

(4) Examples.

(g) Special rules.

(1) Disguised notional principal contracts.

(2) Hedged notional principal contracts.

(3) Options and forwards to enter into notional principal contracts.

(4) Swaps with significant nonperiodic payments.

(5) Caps and floors that are significantly in-the-money. [Reserved]

(6) Notional principal contracts with contingent nonperiodic payments.

(i) Definitions.

(A) Noncontingent nonperiodic payments.

(B) Contingent nonperiodic payments.

(ii) Noncontingent swap method.

(iii) Determining projected amount of contingent payment.

(A) Payment based on actively traded futures or forward contracts.

(B) Payment based on extrapolation from current market prices.

(C) Payment based on reasonable estimate.

(iv) Redeterminations of projected payments and level payment amounts.

(A) General rule.

(B) Special rule for fixed but deferred contingent nonperiodic payments.

(v) Adjustments following redeterminations.

(vi) Adjustments for differences between projected and actual payments.

(vii) Recordkeeping requirements.

(7) Examples.

(h) Termination payments.

(1) Definition.

(2) Taxable year of inclusion and deduction by original parties.

(3) Taxable year of inclusion and deduction by assignees.

(4) Special rules.

(i) Assignment of one leg of a contract.

(ii) Substance over form.

(5) Examples.

(i) Election to mark to market.

(1) General rule.

(2) Scope of election.

(3) Determination of fair market value.

(i) Determination based on readily ascertainable value.

(ii) Determination based on value used for financial statements.

(iii) Determination based on counterparty's mark-to-market value.

(iv) Determination based on value used in determining net asset value.

(4) Requirements for use of financial statement values. [Reserved]

(5) Notional principal contracts accruing interest on significant nonperiodic payments.

(i) General rule.

(ii) Special rules for significant contingent nonperiodic payments.

(iii) Nonapplicability to regulated investment companies.

(6) Election.

(j) Effective dates.

(1) General rule.

(2) Exception.

* * *

(c) * * *

(5) *Risk-free interest rate and determination date.*—(i) *Risk-free interest rate.*—The risk-free interest rate is the applicable Federal rate determined in accordance with section 1274(d)(1) for a determination date and the period remaining in the term of the contract on the determination date.

(ii) *Determination date.*—A determination date is the commencement date of the swap, each redetermination date as defined in paragraph (g)(6)(ii) of this section, and each special redetermination date as defined in paragraph (g)(6)(iv)(B) of this section.

(d) *Taxable year of inclusion and deduction; adjustment of gain or loss.*—(1) *Inclusion and deduction.*—For all purposes of the Internal Revenue Code, the net income or net deduction from a notional principal contract for a taxable year is taken into account for that taxable year. The net income or net deduction from a notional principal contract for a taxable year equals the total of all of the periodic payments that are recognized from that contract for the taxable year under paragraph (e) of this section, all of the nonperiodic payments that are recognized from that contract for the taxable year under paragraph (f) of this section, and the mark-to-market income inclusions and deductions recognized from that contract under paragraph (i) of this section.

(2) *Adjustment of gain or loss.*—Proper adjustment shall be made in the amount of any gain or loss realized on a sale, exchange, or termination of a notional principal contract for inclusions or deductions pursuant to paragraphs (d)(1) and (g)(4) of this section and for payments or receipts with respect to the notional principal contract.

* * *

(f) * * *

(2) *Recognition rules.*—(i) *In general.*—All taxpayers, regardless of their method of accounting, must recognize the ratable daily portion of a nonperiodic payment for the taxable year to which that portion relates. Generally, a nonperiodic payment must be recognized over the term of a notional principal contract in a manner that reflects the economic substance of the contract. See paragraph (g)(6) of this section for additional rules for contingent nonperiodic payments.

* * *

(iii) * * *

(A) *Prepaid swaps.*—An upfront payment on a swap may be amortized by assuming that the nonperiodic payment represents the present value of a series of equal payments made throughout the term of the swap contract (the level payment method), adjusted as appropriate to take account of increases or decreases in the notional principal amount. The discount rate used in this calculation must be the rate (or rates) used by the parties to determine the amount of the nonperiodic payment. If that rate is not readily ascertainable, the discount rate used must be a rate that is reasonable under the circumstances. Under this method, an upfront payment is allocated by dividing each equal payment into its principal recovery and time value components. The principal recovery components of the equal payments are treated as periodic payments that are deemed to be made on each of the dates that the swap contract provides for periodic payments by the payor of the nonperiodic payment or, if none, on each of the dates that the swap contract provides for periodic payments by the recipient of the nonperiodic payment. The sum of the principal recovery components equals the amount of the upfront payment. The time value component is used to compute the amortization of the nonperiodic payment but is otherwise disregarded. See paragraph (f)(4) *Example 5* of this section.

* * *

(g) * * *

(4) *Swaps with significant nonperiodic payments.*—The parties to a swap with one or more significant nonperiodic payments must treat the contract as two or more separate transactions consisting of an on-market swap and one or more loans. The parties must account for the loans separately from the swap. The payments associated with the on-market swap are included in the net income or net deduction from the swap under paragraph (d) of this section. The time value components associated with the loans are not included in the net income or net deduction from the swap under paragraph (d) of this section but are recognized as interest for all purposes of the Internal Revenue Code. The on-market swap must result in recognition of the payments associated with the swap in a manner that complies with the principles set forth in paragraph (f)(2)(i) of this section. See paragraph (g)(7) *Example 3* of this section for a situation in which the on-market swap payments for a party making a significant nonperiodic upfront payment will be level payments that may be constructed through a combination of the actual payments on the swap and level payments computed under the level payment method provided by paragraph (f)(2)(iii)(A) of this section. In certain cases, a swap with significant nonperiodic payments other than an upfront payment may be treated as if the swap provided for a series of level payment loan advances having a present value equal to the present value of the nonperiodic payments, with the amount of each loan advance being immediately returned as a level payment on the swap. See paragraph (g)(7) *Example 5* of this section. For purposes of section 956, the Commissioner may treat any nonperiodic swap payment, whether or not it is significant, as one or more loans.

* * *

(6) *Notional principal contracts with contingent nonperiodic payments.*—(i) *Definitions.*—(A) *Noncontingent nonperiodic payments.*—A noncontingent nonperiodic payment is a nonperiodic payment that either is fixed on or before the end of the taxable year in which a contract commences or is equal to the sum of amounts that would be periodic payments if they are paid when they become fixed (including amounts determined as interest accruals).

(B) *Contingent nonperiodic payments.*—A contingent nonperiodic payment is any nonperiodic payment other than a noncontingent nonperiodic payment.

(ii) *Noncontingent swap method.*—Under the noncontingent swap method, a taxpayer, regardless of its method of accounting, recognizes each contingent nonperiodic payment with respect to a notional principal contract by determining the projected amount of the payment and by applying to that projected amount the level payment method described in paragraphs (f)(2)(iii)(A) and (B) of this section. The projected amount of a contingent nonperiodic payment is the reasonably expected amount of the payment, which is determined by using one of the methods described in paragraph (g)(6)(iii) of this section and by using the risk-free interest rate in applying the level payment method. On each successive anniversary date for the notional principal contract (a redetermination date) and each special redetermination date (as defined in paragraph (g)(6)(iv)(B) of this section), the taxpayer must redetermine the projected amount of each contingent nonperiodic payment, reapply the level payment method as provided in paragraph (g)(6)(iv) of this section, and make the adjustments specified in paragraph (g)(6)(v) of this section. If paragraph (g)(4) of this section applies to the notional principal contract, redeterminations and adjustments must also be made to account for the time value components of the transaction as interest in accordance with that paragraph. Except for contingent nonperiodic payments governed by paragraph (g)(6)(iv)(B) of this section, in the taxable year in which a contingent payment is made or received, the parties must make appropriate adjustments to the amount of income or deductions attributable to the notional principal contract for any differences between projected and actual contingent nonperiodic payments as provided in paragraph (g)(6)(vi) of this section.

(iii) *Determining projected amount of contingent payment.*—(A) *Payment based on actively traded futures or forward contracts.*—If a contingent nonperiodic payment is determined under the contract by reference to the value of a specified index on a designated future date, the projected amount of the payment may be determined on the basis of the future value for the specified index in actively traded futures or forward contracts, if any, providing for delivery or settlement on the designated future date. If no actively traded contract exists for the designated future date, a determination from the future values for the specified index in actively traded futures or forward contracts, if any, providing for delivery or settlement on dates within three months of the designated future date may be used.

(B) *Payment based on extrapolation from current market prices.*—If a contingent nonperiodic payment is determined under the contract by reference to the value of a specified index on a designated future date, the projected amount of the payment may be determined on the basis of the current value of the specified index as established by objective financial information adjusted to convert the current value to a future value for the specified index on the designated future date. The current value is converted to a future value by adding to the current value an amount equal to the accrual of interest on the current value under a constant yield method at the risk-free interest rate with appropriate compounding and by making appropriate adjustments for expected cash payments on the property underlying the specified index.

(C) *Payment based on reasonable estimate.*—If the methods provided in paragraphs (g)(6)(iii)(A) and (B) of this section do not result in a reasonable estimate of the amount of the contingent payment, the taxpayer must use another method that does result in a reasonable estimate of the amount of the contingent payment and that is based on objective financial information.

(iv) *Redeterminations of projected payments and level payment amounts.*—(A) *General rule.*—On each redetermination date, the taxpayer must redetermine the projected amount using current values on the redetermination date and the same method that was used on the commencement date of the notional principal contract, and must reapply the level payment method as of the commencement date of the notional principal contract on the basis of the new projected payment amount and the risk-free interest rate in effect on the redetermination date.

(B) *Special rule for fixed but deferred contingent nonperiodic payments.*—If a contingent nonperiodic payment is fixed more than six months before it is due, and if the date the payment is fixed is in a different taxable year from the date the payment is due, the date on which the payment is fixed is a special redetermination date. As of that date, the taxpayer must treat the fixed amount as the projected amount for that contingent nonperiodic payment and apply paragraphs (g)(6)(iv) and (v) of this section as if the special redetermination date were a redetermination date.

(v) *Adjustments following redeterminations.*—Following each redetermination of projected payments and level payment amounts, the taxpayer must apply the new schedule of level payments for purposes of determining amounts to be recognized in the current and subsequent taxable years with respect to the contingent nonperiodic payments. Any difference between the amounts recognized in prior taxable years and the amounts that would have been recognized in those years had the new level payment schedule been in effect for those years is taken into account as additional payments or receipts with respect to the contract ratably over the one-year period beginning with the redetermination date and, to the extent attributable to a difference in the interest amounts calculated under paragraph (g)(4) of this section, is recognized as interest for all purposes of the Internal Revenue Code.

(vi) *Adjustments for differences between projected and actual payments.*—Any difference between the amounts taken into account under paragraph (f) and this paragraph (g)(6) on the one hand and the amount of the actual payment under the contract on the other hand is taken into account as an adjustment to the net income or net deduction from the notional principal contract for the taxable year during which the payment occurs, and not as an adjustment to interest income or expense.

(vii) *Recordkeeping requirements.*—The books and records maintained by a taxpayer must contain a description of the method used to determine the projected amount of a contingent payment, projected payment schedules, any adjustments following redeterminations, and any adjustments for differences between projected and actual contingent payments.

(7) * * *

Example 3. Upfront significant nonperiodic payment. * * *

* * *

Example 5. Backloaded significant nonperiodic payment. (i) On January 1, 2003, unrelated parties *P* and *Q* enter into an interest rate swap contract. Under the terms of the contract, *P* agrees to make five annual payments to *Q* equal to LIBOR times a notional principal amount of $100,000,000. In return, *Q* agrees to pay *P* 6% of $100,000,000 annually, plus $24,420,400 on December 31, 2007. At the time *P* and *Q* enter into this swap agreement the rate for similar on-market swaps is LIBOR to 10%. Assume that on January 1, 2003, the risk-free rate is 10%.

(ii) The $24,420,400 payment from *Q* to *P* is significant when compared to the present value of the total payments due from *Q* under the contract. Accordingly, pursuant to paragraph (g)(4) of this section, the transaction is recharacterized as two separate transactions. First, *P* is treated as paying to *Q* a series of $4,000,000 level payment loan advances. The present value of the level payment loan advances equals the present value of $24,420,400, the significant nonperiodic payment. Stated differently, the sum of the level payment loan advances and accrued interest on those advances equals the significant nonperiodic payment.

(iii) Next, *Q* is treated as using each loan advance to fund five annual level swap payments of $4,000,000. The level payment loan advances and accrued interest on the advances computed with annual compounding at 10% are as follows:

	Level Payment	*Accrued Interest*
2003	$ 4,000,000	$ 0
2004	4,000,000	400,000
2005	4,000,000	840,000
2006	4,000,000	1,324,000
2007	4,000,000	1,856,400
	$20,000,000	$4,420,400

(iv) *P* recognizes interest income, and *Q* accrues interest expense, each taxable year equal to the interest accruals on the deemed level payment loan advances. These interest amounts are not included in the parties' net income or net deduction from the swap contract under paragraph (d) of this section.

(v) The level payment amounts of $4,000,000 are taken into account in determining the parties' net income and deductions on the swap pursuant to paragraph (d) of this section.

Example 6. Contingent nonperiodic payment on an equity swap. (i) On January 1, 2005, unrelated parties *V* and *W* enter into an equity swap contract. Under the terms of the contract, *V* agrees to make three annual payments to *W* equal to 1-year LIBOR times a notional principal amount of $50,000,000. In return, *W* agrees to make a single payment on December 31, 2007, equal to the appreciation, if any, of a $50,000,000 investment in a basket of equity securities over the term of the swap. *V* is obligated to make a single payment on December 31, 2007, equal to the depreciation, if any, in the same $50,000,000 investment in the basket of equity securities. Assume that on January 1, 2005, 1-year LIBOR is 9.5%, and the risk-free rate is 10.0%.

(ii) This contract is a notional principal contract as defined in paragraph (c)(1) of this section. The annual LIBOR-based payments from *V* to *W* are periodic payments and the single payment on December 31, 2007, is a contingent nonperiodic payment.

(iii) Pursuant to the method described in (g)(6)(iii)(B) of this section, the parties determine that the projected amount of the contingent nonperiodic payment that *W* will pay *V* on December 31, 2007, is $16,550,000. The present value of this projected fixed payment is significant when compared to the present value of the total payments due from *W* under the contract. Accordingly, pursuant to paragraph (g)(4) of this section, the transaction is recharacterized as two separate transactions.

(iv) As a preliminary step, using the risk-free rate of 10.0% as the discount rate, the parties determine the level payment amounts that have a present value equal to the present value of $16,550,000, the projected significant nonperiodic payment. Stated differently, the sum of the level payment amounts and accrued interest at 10.0% on those amounts must equal the projected significant nonperiodic payment. The level payment amounts thus determined are $5,000,000.

(v) Next, *V* is treated as paying to *W* a series of $5,000,000 loan advances.

(vi) Then, *W* is treated as using each loan advance to fund one of the three annual level swap payments of $5,000,000. The level payment loan advances and accrued interest on the advances computed with annual compounding at 10.0% are as follows:

	Level Payment	*Accrued Interest*
2005	$ 5,000,000	$ 0
2006	5,000,000	500,000
2007	5,000,000	1,050,000
	$15,000,000	$1,550,000

(vii) No interest amount is taken into account for the contract year 2005.

(viii) The level payment amount of $5,000,000 is taken into account for the contract year 2005 in determining the parties' net income and deductions on the swap pursuant to paragraph (d) of this section.

(ix) For the contract year 2005, *V* makes a swap payment to *W* equal to 1-year LIBOR at 9.5% times $50,000,000, or $4,750,000, and *W* is deemed to make a swap payment to *V* equal to the annual level payment of $5,000,000. The net of the ratable daily portions of these payments determines the annual net income or deduction from the contract for both *V* and *W*.

Example 7. Initial Adjustment. (i) The terms of the equity swap agreement are the same as in *Example 6*. In addition, assume that on January 1, 2006, the first redetermination date, 1-year LIBOR is 10.0%, and the risk-free rate is 10.5%. On that date, the parties redetermine the projected amount of the contingent nonperiodic payment using current values in effect on that date. Under the method described in (g)(6)(iii)(B) of this section, the parties determine that the reprojected amount of the contingent nonperiodic payment that *W* will pay *V* on December 31, 2007, is $23,261,500. The present value as of January 1, 2005, of this projected fixed payment is significant when compared to the present value of the total payments due from *W* under the contract. Accordingly, pursuant to paragraph (g)(4) of this section, the transaction is recharacterized as two separate transactions.

(ii) The parties use the redetermined projected amount of $23,261,500, to reapply the method provided by paragraph (g)(4) of this section effective as of the commencement date of the swap. As a preliminary step, using the risk-free rate of 10.5% as the discount rate, the parties determine the level payment amounts that have a present value equal to the present value of $23,261,500, the reprojected significant nonperiodic payment. Stated differently, the sum of the level payment amounts and accrued interest at 10.5% on those amounts must equal the reprojected significant nonperiodic payment. The level payment amounts thus determined are $6,993,784.

(iii) Next, *V* is treated as paying to *W* a series of $6,993,784 loan advances.

(iv) Then, *W* is treated as using each loan advance to fund one of the three annual level swap payments of $6,993,784. The level payment loan advances and accrued interest on the advances computed with annual compounding at 10.5%, are as follows:

	Level Payment	*Accrued Interest*
2005	$ 6,993,784	$ 0
2006	6,993,784	734,347
2007	6,993,784	1,545,801
	$20,981,352	$2,280,148

(v) For the contract year 2006, *V* recognizes interest income, and *W* accrues interest expense equal to the accrued interest of $734,347 on the deemed level payment loan advance. These interest amounts are not included in the parties' net income or net deduction from the swap contract under paragraph (d) of this section.

(vi) The level payment amount of $6,993,784 is taken into account for the contract year 2006 in determining the parties' net income and deductions on the swap pursuant to paragraph (d) of this section.

(vii) The parties also take into account for the contract year 2006 the difference between the amount recognized for 2005 and the amount that would have been recognized in 2005 had the new level payment schedule in this *Example 7* been in effect in 2005. Thus, for purposes of paragraph (d) of this section, *W* is treated as making a swap payment, and *V* is treated as receiving a swap payment of $1,993,784 ($6,993,784 – $5,000,000) for purposes of paragraph (d) of this section.

(viii) For the contract year 2006, *V* makes a swap payment to *W* equal to 1-year LIBOR at 10.0% times $50,000,000, or $5,000,000, and *W* is deemed to make a swap payment to *V* equal to the annual level payment of $6,993,784 and the adjustment amount of $1,993,784. The net of the ratable daily portions of these payments determines the annual net income or deduction from the contract for both *V* and *W*.

Example 8. Subsequent Adjustment. (i) The terms of the equity swap agreement are the same as in *Example 7.* In addition, assume that on January 1, 2007, the second redetermination date, 1-year LIBOR is 11.0%, and the risk-free rate is also 11.0%. On that date, the parties redetermine the projected amount of the contingent nonperiodic payment using current values in effect on that date. The parties determine that the reprojected amount of the contingent nonperiodic payment that *W* will pay *V* on December 31, 2007, is $11,050,000. The present value as of January 1, 2005, of this projected fixed payment is significant when compared to the present value of the total payments due from *W* under the contract. Accordingly, pursuant to paragraph (g)(4) of this section, the transaction is recharacterized as two separate transactions.

(ii) The parties use the redetermined projected amount of $11,050,000, to reapply the method provided by paragraph (g)(4) effective as of the commencement date of the swap. As a preliminary step, using the risk-free rate of 11.0% as the discount rate, the parties determine the level payment amounts that have a present value equal to the present value of $11,050,000, the reprojected significant nonperiodic payment. Stated differently, the sum of the level payment amounts and accrued interest at 11.0% on those amounts must equal the reprojected significant nonperiodic payment. The level payment amounts thus determined are $3,306,304.

(iii) Next, *V* is treated as paying to *W* a series of $3,306,304 loan advances.

(iv) Then, *W* is treated as using each loan advance to fund one of the three annual level swap payments of $3,306,304. The level payment loan advances and accrued interest on the loan advances computed with annual compounding at 11.0% are as follows:

	Level Payment	*Accrued Interest*
2005	$3,306,304	$0
2006	3,306,304	363,693
2007	3,306,304	767,393
	$9,918,912	$1,131,086

(v) For 2007, *V* recognizes interest income, and *W* accrues interest expense equal to the $767,393 accrued interest amount for 2007 on the deemed loan advances. In addition, *V* has a net interest expense item and *W* has a net interest income item equal to $370,654 ($734,347 – $363,693), the difference between the interest accrual taken into account for 2006 and the amount that would have been taken into account for 2006 had the new level payment schedule in this *Example 8* been in effect for 2006. As a result, *V* has net interest income and *W* has net interest expense in the amount of $396,739 for 2007. These interest amounts are not included in the parties' net income or net deduction from the swap contract under paragraph (d) of this section.

(vi) The level payment amount of $3,306,304 is taken into account for the contract year 2007 in determining the parties' net income and deductions on the swap pursuant to paragraph (d) of this section.

(vii) For 2007, the parties also take into account for 2007 the difference between the amounts previously recognized for 2005 and 2006 and the amounts that would have been recognized for those years had the new level payment schedule in this *Example 8* been in effect in 2005 and 2006. The amounts previously recognized were: a total of $6,993,784 for 2005, which is the sum of $5,000,000 (in 2005) and $1,993,784 (in 2006), and a total of $6,993,784 for 2006 (in 2006). The adjustment amount, therefore, equals two times $3,687,480 ($6,993,784 – $3,306,304), or $7,374,960. This amount is taken into account as a payment for purposes of paragraph (d) of this section.

(viii) For the contract year 2007, *V* makes a swap payment to *W* equal to 1-year LIBOR at 11.0% times $50,000,000, or $5,500,000. *W* is deemed to make a swap payment to *V* equal to the annual level payment for 2007 of $3,306,304, and *V* is deemed to make a swap payment to *W* equal to the adjustment amount of $7,374,960. The net of the ratable daily portions of these payments determines the annual net income or deduction from the contract for both *V* and *W*.

Example 9. Adjustment for actual payment. (i) The terms of the equity swap agreement are the same as in *Example 8.* In addition, on December 31, 2007, *W* makes a payment to *V* of $25,000,000, an amount equal to the appreciation of a $50,000,000 investment in the basket of equity securities.

(ii) For 2007, $13,950,000, the difference between $25,000,000 and $11,050,000, the projected amount of the contingent payment as of January 1, 2007, is taken into account as an adjustment to the parties' net income or deductions for each party's taxable year that contains December 31, 2007, pursuant to paragraph (d) of this section.

* * *

(i) *Election to mark to market.*—A taxpayer may elect to mark to market notional principal contracts providing for nonperiodic payments. The rules of paragraphs (f) (other than (f)(2)(i)), (g)(6)(ii) through (vii), and (h) of this section do not apply to contracts to which this paragraph (i) applies. See paragraph (i)(5) of this section for rules respecting interest accruals under paragraph (g)(4) of this section for contracts providing for significant nonperiodic payments to which this paragraph (i) applies.

(1) *General rule.*—In the case of any contract held at the close of the taxable year to which this paragraph (i) applies, the taxpayer shall determine income inclusions and deductions by reference to the gain or loss that would be realized if the contract were sold for its fair market value on the last business day of the taxable year. Proper adjustment shall be made in the amount of any gain or loss subsequently realized (or calculated) for the income inclusions and deductions taken into account by reason of this paragraph (i)(1) as provided in paragraph (d)(2) of this section.

(2) *Scope of election.*—The election provided by this paragraph is available for notional principal contracts that are—

(i) Of a type that is actively traded within the meaning of § 1.1092(d)-1(c) (determined without regard to the limitation in § 1.1092(d)-1(c)(2));

(ii) Marked to market by the taxpayer for purposes of determining the taxpayer's financial income provided the taxpayer satisfies the requirements in paragraph (i)(4) of this section;

(iii) Subject to an agreement by a party to the contract that is subject to section 475 to supply to the taxpayer the value that it uses in applying section 475(a)(2); or

(iv) Marked to market by a regulated investment company described in section 1296(e)(2).

(3) *Determination of fair market value.*—For purposes of paragraph (i)(1) of this section, fair market value is determined by applying the rules set forth in paragraphs (i)(3)(i) through (iv) of this section.

(i) *Determination based on readily ascertainable value.*—For a contract described in paragraph (i)(2)(i) of this section, fair market value is determined based on the mean between the bid and asked prices quoted for the contract on an established financial market as defined in § 1.1092(d)-1(b)(1), or, if bid and asked prices are not available, comparable prices determined on the basis of recent price quotations described in § 1.1092(d)-1(b)(2).

(ii) *Determination based on value used for financial statements.*—For a contract described in paragraph (i)(2)(ii) of this section that is not described in paragraph (i)(2)(i) of this section, fair market value is the value used by the taxpayer for purposes of preparing its financial statements under paragraph (i)(4) of this section.

(iii) *Determination based on counterparty's mark-to-market value.*—For a contract described in paragraph (i)(2)(iii) of this section that is not described in paragraph (i)(2)(i) of this section, fair market value is the mark-to-market value provided by a counterparty as being the value the counterparty used for purposes of section 475(a)(2).

(iv) *Determination based on value used in determining net asset value.*—Notwithstanding paragraphs (i)(3)(i) through (iii) of this section, for a contract described in paragraph (i)(2)(iv) of this section, fair market value is the value used by the taxpayer in determining its net asset value.

(4) *Requirements for use of financial statement values.*—[Reserved].

(5) *Notional principal contracts accruing interest on significant nonperiodic payments.*—(i) *General rule.*—If a notional principal contract that is marked to market under this paragraph (i) provides for one or more significant nonperiodic payments, paragraph (g)(4) of this section applies to the contract (computed with regard to the rule in paragraph (i)(5)(ii) of this section). Proper adjustment shall be made in the amount of any income inclusions or deductions recognized under paragraph (i)(1) of this section to take into account amounts recognized as interest under paragraph (g)(4) of this section and the payment or receipt of the nonperiodic payment or payments.

(ii) *Special rules for significant contingent nonperiodic payments.*—In the case of a contract providing for a significant contingent nonperiodic payment, the projected amount of the payment is determined by applying one of the methods described in paragraph (g)(6)(iii) of this section or by applying the deemed equivalent value method described in this paragraph (i)(5)(ii). The amount of the payment is not redetermined except as provided in paragraph (g)(6)(iv)(B) of this section. The deemed equivalent value method may be applied if the contract fixes the timing and amount of all of the payments under the contract, except for a sole significant contingent nonperiodic payment. Under the deemed equivalent value method, the amount of the significant contingent nonperiodic payment is the amount that, as of the date the terms of the contract are fixed, causes the present value of all of the payments by the taxpayer to equal the present value of all of the payments of the counterparty to the contract. The present value of each payment of the contract is determined by applying the risk-free interest rate.

(iii) *Nonapplicability to regulated investment companies.*—Paragraphs (i)(5)(i) and (ii) of this section do not apply to a regulated investment company described in paragraph (i)(2)(iv) of this section that makes an election under paragraph (i) of this section.

(6) *Election.*—An election to apply this paragraph (i) must be made with respect to all notional principal contracts described in paragraph (i)(2) of this section to which the taxpayer is a party. The election must be made in the time and manner prescribed by the Commissioner and is effective for the taxable year for which made and all subsequent taxable years, unless revoked with the consent of the Commissioner.

(j) *Effective dates.*—(1) *General rule.*—Except as provided in paragraph (j)(2) of this section, this section is applicable for notional principal contracts entered into on or after December 13, 1993.

(2) *Exception.*—Paragraphs (g)(6) (other than (g)(6)(i)) and (i) of this section are applicable for notional principal contracts entered into on or after 30 days after the date a Treasury decision based on these proposed regulations is published in the Federal Register.

Section 1256 Contracts: Swap Exclusions

Section 1256 Contracts: Swap Exclusions.—Amendment to Reg. § 1.446-3, providing guidance on the category of swaps and similar agreements that are within the scope of Code Sec. 1256(b)(2)(B), are proposed (published in the Federal Register on September 16, 2011) (REG-111283-11).

☐ Par. 2. Section 1.446-3 is amended by:

1. Revising the entries for the table of contents in § 1.446-3(a) for paragraphs (c) and (j).
2. Revising paragraphs (c)(1), (c)(2), and (c)(3).
3. Adding and reserving paragraph (c)(5).
4. Adding paragraph (c)(6).
5. Adding two sentences to the end of paragraph (j).

The revisions and additions read as follows:

§1.446-3. Notional principal contracts.

* * *

(c) Definitions and scope.

(1) Notional principal contract.

(i) In general.

(ii) Payment defined.

(iii) Included contracts.

(A) Special rule for credit default swaps.

(B) Special rule for nonfunctional currency notional principal contracts.

(iv) Excluded contracts.

(v) Transactions within section 475.

(vi) Transactions within section 988.

(2) Specified index.

(i) Specified financial index.

(ii) Specified non-financial index.

(3) Notional principal amount.

(4) Special definitions.

(i) Related person and party to the contract.

(ii) Objective financial information.

(iii) Dealer in notional principal contracts.

(5) [Reserved]

(6) Examples.

* * *

(j) Effective/applicability date.

* * *

(c) *Definitions and scope.*—(1) *Notional principal contract.*—(i) *In general.*—A notional principal contract is a financial instrument that requires one party to make two or more payments to the counterparty at specified intervals calculated by reference to a specified index upon a notional principal amount in exchange for specified consideration or a promise to pay similar amounts. An agreement between a taxpayer and a qualified business unit (as defined in section 989(a)) of the taxpayer, or among qualified business units of the same taxpayer, is not a notional principal contract because a taxpayer cannot enter into a contract with itself.

(ii) *Payment defined.*—For purposes of paragraph (c)(1)(i) of this section, a payment includes an amount that is fixed on one date and paid or otherwise taken into account on a later date. Thus, for example, a contract that provides for a settlement payment referenced to the appreciation or depreciation on a specified number of shares of common stock, adjusted for actual dividends paid during the term of the contract, is treated as a contract with more than one payment with respect to that leg of the contract. See *Example 2* of this paragraph (c).

(iii) *Included contracts.*—Notional principal contracts governed by this section include contracts commonly referred to as interest rate swaps, currency swaps, basis swaps, interest rate caps, interest rate floors, commodity swaps, equity swaps, equity index swaps, credit default swaps, weather-related swaps, and similar agreements that satisfy the requirements of paragraph (c)(1)(i). A collar is not itself a notional principal contract, but a cap and a floor that comprise a collar may be treated as a single notional principal contract under paragraph (f)(2)(v)(C) of this section. A contract may be a notional principal contract governed by this section even though the term of the contract is subject to termination or extension. Each confirmation under a master agreement to enter into an agreement covered by this section is treated as a separate notional principal contract (or as more than one notional principal contract if the confirmation creates more than one notional principal contract). Notwithstanding the rule under paragraph (c)(3) of this section—

(A) *Special rule for credit default swaps.*—A credit default swap contract that permits or requires the delivery of specified debt instruments in satisfaction of one leg of the contract is a notional principal contract if it otherwise satisfies the requirements of paragraph (c)(1)(i) of this section.

(B) *Special rule for nonfunctional currency notional principal contracts.*—A notional principal contract that permits or requires the delivery of specified currency in satisfaction of one or both legs of the contract but that otherwise qualifies as a nonfunctional currency notional principal contract under §1.988-1(a)(2)(iii)(B) is a notional principal contract.

(iv) *Excluded contracts.*—A forward contract, an option, and a guarantee are not notional principal contracts. An instrument or contract that constitutes indebtedness under general Federal income tax law is not a notional principal contract. An option or forward contract that entitles or obligates a person to enter into a notional principal contract is not a notional principal contract, but payments made under such an option or forward contract may be governed by paragraph (g)(3) of this section.

(v) *Transactions within section 475.*—To the extent that the rules provided in paragraphs (e) and (f) of this section are inconsistent with the rules that apply to any notional principal contract that is governed by section 475 and the regulations thereunder, the rules of section 475 and the regulations thereunder govern.

(vi) *Transactions within section 988.*—To the extent that the rules provided in this section are inconsistent with the rules that apply to any notional principal contract that is also a section 988 transaction or that is integrated with other property or debt pursuant to section 988(d), the rules of section 988 and the regulations thereunder govern. The rules of §1.446-3(g)(4) are not considered to be inconsistent with the rules of section 988. See §1.988-2(e)(3)(iv).

(2) *Specified index.*—A specified index may be either a specified financial index or a specified non-financial index.

(i) *Specified financial index.*—A specified financial index is—

(A) A fixed rate, price, or amount;

(B) A fixed rate, price, or amount applicable in one or more specified periods followed by one or more different fixed rates, prices, or amounts applicable in other periods;

(C) An index that is based on objective financial information (as defined in paragraph (c)(4)(ii) of this section); and

(D) An interest rate index that is regularly used in normal lending transactions between a party to the contract and unrelated persons.

(ii) *Specified non-financial index.*—A specified non-financial index is any objectively determinable information that—

(A) Is not within the control of any of the parties to the contract and is not unique to one of the parties' circumstances;

(B) Is not financial information; and

(C) Cannot be reasonably expected to front-load or back-load payments accruing under the contract.

(3) *Notional principal amount.*—For purposes of this section, a notional principal amount is any specified amount of money or property that, when multiplied by either a specified financial index or a specified non-financial index, measures a party's rights and obligations under the contract, but is not borrowed, loaned, or sold between the parties as part of the contract. The notional principal amount may vary over the term of the contract, provided that it is set in advance or varies based on objective financial information (as defined in paragraph (c)(4)(ii) of this section). If a notional principal contract references a notional principal amount that varies, or that references a different notional principal amount for each party, and a principal purpose for entering into the contract is to avoid the application of the rules in this section, the Commissioner may recharacterize the contract according to its substance, including by separating the contract into a series of notional principal contracts for purposes of applying the rules of this section or by treating the contract, in whole or in part, as a loan.

* * *

(5) [Reserved]

(6) *Examples.*—The following examples illustrate the application of paragraph (c) of this section.

Example 1. Forward rate agreement. (i) On January 1, 2012, A enters into a contract with unrelated counterparty B under which on December 31, 2013, A will pay or receive from B, as the case may be, an amount determined by subtracting 6% multiplied by a notional amount of $10 million from 3 month LIBOR on December 31, 2013 multiplied by the same notional amount ((3 month LIBOR × $10,000,000) - (6% × $10,000,000)). The contract provides for no other payments.

(ii) Because this contract provides for a single net payment between A and B determined by interest rates in effect on the settlement date of the contract, the contract is not a notional principal contract defined in § 1.446-3(c)(1)(i).

Example 2. Equity total return contract with dividend adjustments. (i) On January 1, 2012, A enters into a contract with unrelated counterparty B under which on December 31, 2013, A will receive from B an amount equal to the appreciation (if any) on a notional amount of 1 million shares of XYZ common stock, plus any dividends or other distributions that are paid on 1 million shares of XYZ common stock during the term of the contract. In return, on December 31, 2013 A will pay B an amount equal to any depreciation on 1 million shares of XYZ common stock, and an amount equal to 3 month LIBOR multiplied by the notional value of 1 million shares of XYZ stock on January 1, 2012 compounded over the term of the contract. All payments are netted such that A and B are only liable for the net payment due under the contract on December 31, 2013.

(ii) Because both legs of this contract provide for payments that become fixed during the term of the contract (the dividend payments and the LIBOR-based payments), each leg of the contract is treated as providing for more than one payment. In addition, since the indices referenced in the contract are specified indices described in paragraph (c)(2)(i) of this section, and the 1 million shares of XYZ common stock are a notional principal amount described in paragraph (c)(3) of this section, the contract is a notional principal contract defined in § 1.446-3(c)(1)(i).

* * *

(j) *Effective/applicability date.*—* * * The rules of paragraph (c) of this section apply to notional principal contracts entered into on or after the date of publication of a Treasury decision adopting these rules as final regulations in the **Federal Register**. Section 1.446-3(c) as contained in 26 CFR part 1 revised April 1, 2011, continues to apply to notional principal contracts entered into before the date of publication of a Treasury decision adopting these rules as final regulations in the **Federal Register**.

Notional Principal Contracts: Nonperiodic Payments: Swaps

Notional Principal Contracts: Nonperiodic Payments: Swaps.—Amendments to Reg. § 1.446-3, providing that, subject to certain exceptions, a notional principal contract with a nonperiodic payment, regardless of whether it is significant, must be treated as two separate transactions consisting of one or more loans and an on-market, level payment swap, are proposed (published in the Federal Register on May 8, 2015) (REG-102656-15; REG-107548-11).

Par. 2. Section 1.446-3 is amended by:

1. Revising paragraph (g)(4).
2. Revising paragraph (g)(6), *Examples* 2, 3 and 4.
3. Revising paragraph (j)(2).

The revisions read as follows:

§ 1.446-3. Notional principal contracts.

* * *

(g) * * *

(4) [The text of the proposed amendment to § 1.446-3(g)(4) is the same as the text of § 1.446-3T(g)(4) as added by T.D. 9719].

* * *

(6) * * *

Example 2. [The text of proposed amendment to § 1.446-3(g)(6) *Example* 2 is the same as the text of § 1.446-3T(g)(6) *Example* 2 as added by T.D. 9719].

Example 3. [The text of proposed amendment to § 1.446-3(g)(6) *Example* 3 is the same as the text of § 1.446-3T(g)(6) *Example* 3 as added by T.D. 9719].

Example 4. [The text of proposed amendment to § 1.446-3(g)(6) *Example 4* is the same as the text of § 1.446-3T(g)(6) *Example 4* as added by T.D. 9719].

* * *

(j) * * *

(2) [The text of the proposed amendment to § 1.446-3(j)(2) is the same as the text of § 1.446-3T(j)(2) as added by T.D. 9719].

Deduction for Business Interest Expense: Limitation

Deduction for Business Interest Expense: Limitation.—Amendments to Reg. § 1.446-3, regarding the limitation on the deduction for business interest expense after the enactment of recent tax legislation, are proposed (published in the Federal Register on December 28, 2018) (REG-106089-18).

Par. 12. Section 1.446-3 is amended by revising paragraphs (g)(4) and (j)(2) to read as follows:

§ 1.446-3. Notional principal contracts.

* * *

(g) * * *

(4) *Swaps with significant nonperiodic payments.*—For swaps with significant nonperiodic payments, see § 1.163(j)-1(b)(20)(ii).

* * *

(j) * * *

(2) The rules provided in paragraph (g)(4) of this section apply to notional principal contracts entered into on or after the date of publication of a Treasury decision adopting these rules as final regulations in the **Federal Register**. Taxpayers may apply the rules provided in paragraph (g)(4) of this section to notional principal contracts entered into before the date of publication of a Treasury decision adopting these rules as final regulations in the **Federal Register**.

Foreign Personal Holding Company Income: Foreign Currency Gain or Loss: Exclusion

Foreign Personal Holding Company Income: Foreign Currency Gain or Loss: Exclusion—Amendments to Reg. § 1.446-4, providing guidance on the treatment of foreign currency gain or loss of a controlled foreign corporation under the business needs exclusion from foreign personal holding company income, are proposed (published in the Federal Register on December 19, 2017) (REG-119514-15).

Par. 2. Section 1.446-4 is amended by:

1. Revising the first sentence of paragraph (a).
2. Revising the heading of paragraph (g) and adding a sentence at the end of paragraph (g).
3. Removing paragraph (h).

The revisions and addition read as follows:

§ 1.446-4. Hedging transactions.—(a) *In general.*—Except as provided in this paragraph (a), a hedging transaction as defined in § 1.1221-2(b) (whether or not the character of gain or loss from the transaction is determined under § 1.1221-2) and a bona fide hedging transaction as defined in § 1.954-2(a)(4)(ii) must be accounted for under the rules of this section. * * *

* * *

(g) *Applicability date.*—* * * This section applies to a bona fide hedging transaction (as defined in § 1.954-2(a)(4)(ii)) entered into on or after the date that these regulations are published as final regulations in the *Federal Register*.

Limitation on Cash Method of Accounting

Accounting Methods: Cash Method: Limitations.—Temporary Reg. § 1.448-1T, relating to the limitation on the use of the cash method of accounting, is proposed and, when adopted, would become Reg. § 1.448-1 (published in the Federal Register on June 16, 1987).

§ 1.448-1. Limitation on the use of the cash receipts and disbursements method of accounting.

Imputed Interest: Original Issue Discount

Imputed Interest: Original Issue Discount: Safe Haven Interest Rates.—Reproduced below is the text of a proposed amendment to Reg. § 1.451-1, relating to (1) the tax treatment of debt instruments issued after July 1, 1982, that contain original issue discount, (2) the imputation of and the accounting for interest with respect to sales and exchanges of property occurring after December 31, 1984, and (3) safe haven interest rates for loans or advances between commonly controlled taxpayers and safe haven leases between such taxpayers (published in the Federal Register on April 8, 1986).

□ Par. 9. In paragraph (d) of § 1.451-1 the heading and text are revised to read as follows:

§ 1.451-1. General rule for taxable year of inclusion.—

* * *

(d) *Special rule for inclusion of original issue discount.*—For inclusion of original issue discount in respect of certain debt instruments issued after May 27, 1969, see section 1272.

* * *

Imputed Interest: Original Issue Discount

Imputed Interest: Original Issue Discount: Safe Haven Interest Rates.—Reproduced below is the text of a proposed amendment to Reg. §1.451-2, relating to (1) the tax treatment of debt instruments issued after July 1, 1982, that contain original issue discount, (2) the imputation of and the accounting for interest with respect to sales and exchanges of property occurring after December 31, 1984, and (3) safe haven interest rates for loans or advances between commonly controlled taxpayers and safe haven leases between such taxpayers (published in the Federal Register on April 8, 1986).

□ Par. 10. Paragraph (b) of §1.451-2 is amended by removing the eighth and ninth sentences and adding in their place new sentences to read as follows:

§1.451-2. Constructive receipt of income.—

* * *

(b) *Examples of constructive receipt.*—* * * However, in the case of certain deposits made after December 31, 1970, in banks, domestic building and loan associations, and similar financial institutions, the inclusion rules of section 1272 apply. See §§1.1232-3A and 1.1272-1. * * *

* * *

Advance Payments for Goods and Long-Term Contracts: Existing Regulations Removed

Advance Payments for Goods and Long-Term Contracts: Existing Regulations Removed.—Amendments to Reg. §1.451-5, removing regulations regarding advance payments for goods and long-term contracts that are no longer necessary after the enactment of recent tax legislation, are proposed (published in the Federal Register on October 15, 2018) (REG-104872-18).

Par. 4. Section 1.451-5 is removed.

§1.451-5. Advance payments for goods and long-term contracts.

Installment Sales Reporting

Installment Sales Reporting: Sales Occurring After October 19, 1980: General Rules.— Temporary Reg. §§15A.453-0 and 15A.453-1, relating to installment sales or reporting of gain for sales occurring after October 19, 1980, have also been proposed as final regulations and, when adopted, would become Reg. §§1.453-0 and 1.453-1 (published in the Federal Register on February 4, 1981).

§15A.453-0. Taxable years affected.

§15A.453-1. Installment method reporting for sales of real proerty and casual sales of personal property.

Installment Obligations

Installment Obligations: Nonrecognition Transactions.—Reproduced below is the text of a proposed amendment of Reg. §1.453-1, relating to installment obligations received in certain nonrecognition transactions (published in the Federal Register on May 3, 1984).

□ Paragraph. Section 1.453-1 is amended by revising paragraph (f) to read as follows:

§1.453-1. Installment method reporting for sales of real property and casual sales of personal property.

* * *

(f) *Installment obligations received in certain nonrecognition exchanges.*—(1) *Exchanges described in section 1031(b).*—(i) *In general.*—The provisions of paragraph (f)(1) of this section apply to exchanges described in section 1031(b) ("section 1031(b) exchanges") in which the taxpayer receives as boot (property which is "other property" under section 1031(b)) an installment obligation issued by the other party to the exchange, as well as property with respect to which no gain or loss is recognized ("permitted property" for purposes of paragraph (f)(1) of this section). However, an exchange otherwise described in section 1036 in which the receipt of an installment obligation is treated as a dividend (or would be treated as a dividend if the issuing corporation had adequate earnings and profits) is not a section 1031(b) exchange for purposes of this section.

(ii) *Exclusion from payment.*—Receipt of permitted property will not be considered payment for purposes of paragraph (c) of this section.

(iii) *Installment method determinations.*—In a section 1031(b) exchange, the taxpayer's basis in the property transferred by the taxpayer, including nondeductible expenses of the exchange, will first be allocated to the permitted property received by the taxpayer up to, but not in excess of, the fair market value of such property. If the taxpayer's basis exceeds the fair market value of the permitted property, that excess amount of basis is "excess basis." In making all required installment method determinations, the exchange is treated as if the taxpayer had made an installment sale of appreciated property (with a basis equal to the amount of excess basis) in which the consideration received was the installment obligation and any other boot. In a section 1031(b) exchange, only net qualifying indebtedness is taken into account in determining the amount of qualifying indebtedness (as defined in

§ 1.453-1A(b)(2)(iv)). For this purpose, net qualifying indebtedness is the excess of—

(A) Liabilities of the taxpayer (or liabilities encumbering the property) assumed or taken subject to by the other party to the exchange as part of the consideration to the taxpayer, over

(B) The sum of any net cash paid (cash paid less any cash received) by the taxpayer in the exchange and any liability assumed or taken subject to by the taxpayer in the exchange.

Therefore, for purposes of installment method determinations, the selling price is the sum of the face value of the installment obligation (reduced by any portion of the obligation characterized as interest by section 483 or 1232), any net qualifying indebtedness, any cash received (in excess of any cash paid) by the taxpayer, and the fair market value of any other boot. The basis is the excess basis. The total contract price is the selling price less any net qualifying indebtedness that does not exceed the excess basis. Finally, payment in the year of exchange includes any net qualifying indebtedness that exceeds the excess basis.

(iv) *Examples.*—The provisions of paragraph (f)(1) of this section are illustrated by the following examples:

Example (1). In 1981, A makes a section 1031(b) exchange of real property held for investment (basis $400,000) for permitted property worth $200,000, and an $800,000 installment obligation issued by the other party to the exchange bearing adequate stated interest. Neither the property transferred by A nor the property received in the exchange is mortgaged property. A's basis of $400,000 is allocated first to the permitted property received, up to the fair market value of $200,000. A's excess basis is $200,000 ($400,000 – $200,000). Since the installment obligation is the only boot received by A in the exchange, A's entire excess basis of $200,000 is allocable to it. Under the installment method, the selling price is $800,000 (the face amount of the installment obligation), and the contract price is also $800,000 (selling price less qualifying indebtedness, $800,000 – 0). The gross profit is $600,000 (selling price less excess basis allocated to the installment obligation, $800,000 – $200,000), and the gross profit ratio is 75% ($600,000/$800,000). A recognizes no gain until payments are received on the installment obligation. As A receives payments (exclusive of interest) on the installment obligation, 75% of each payment will be gain attributable to the exchange and 25% of each payment will be recovery of basis. A will hold the permitted property received in the exchange with a basis of $200,000.

Example (2). The facts are the same as in example (1), except that in the exchange A receives permitted property worth $200,000, a $600,000 installment obligation, and $200,000 in cash. A is treated as having sold appreciated property (basis equal to the $200,000 excess basis) for $200,000 cash and a $600,000 installment obligation. As in example (1), the contract price and the selling price are $800,000, the gross profit is $600,000, and the gross profit ratio is 75%. Accordingly, A will recognize gain of $150,000 on receipt of the cash (75% of the $200,000 payment). A holds the permitted property with a basis of $200,000.

Example (3). The facts are the same as in example (2), except that A does not receive $200,000 in cash. Instead, the property transferred by A in the exchange was subject to a mortgage (meeting the definition of qualifying indebtedness) of $200,000 to which the other party to the exchange took subject. The permitted property received by A in the exchange was not subject to a mortgage. A is treated as having sold appreciated property (basis equal to $200,000 excess basis) for $600,000 cash and $200,000 net relief of mortgage liability. The mortgage liability of which A is deemed relieved ($200,000), reduced by any cash paid by A and any mortgage liability encumbering the like-kind property received by A in the simultaneous exchange ($0), is treated as qualifying indebtedness. Since the qualifying indebtedness ($200,000) does not exceed A's excess basis ($200,000), B's taking subject to such indebtedness does not constitute payment to A in the year of exchange. Under the installment method, the selling price is $800,000 and the total contract price is $600,000 (selling price of $800,000 less $200,000 of qualifying indebtedness that does not exceed A's excess basis). Gross profit is also $600,000 (800,000 selling price less $200,000 excess basis), and the gross profit ratio is 1 ($600,000/600,000). A recognizes no gain until payments are received on the installment obligation. As A receives payment (exclusive of interest) in the $600,000 installment obligation, the full amount received will be gain attributable to the exchange. A holds the permitted property with a basis of $200,000.

Example (4). The facts are the same as in example (2), except that A's basis in the property transferred by A was only $160,000. Since A's basis first must be allocated to permitted property received in the exchange up to the fair market value ($200,000) of that permitted property, there is no excess basis. Accordingly, A will recognize gain equal to the full amount of cash received ($200,000), and will hold the installment obligation at a basis of zero. A will hold the permitted property at a basis of $160,000.

(2) *Certain exchanges described in section 356(a).*—(i) *In general.*—The provisions of paragraph (f)(2) of this section apply to exchanges described in section 356(a)(1) ("section 356(a)(1) exchanges") in which the taxpayer receives as boot (property which is "other property" under section 356(a)(1)(B)) an installment obligation issued by a qualifying corporation which is not treated as a dividend to the taxpayer. For purposes of section 453(f)(6) and paragraph (f)(2) of this section, any such section 356(a)(1) exchange shall be treated as a disposition of property by the taxpayer to the qualifying corporation and an acquisition of such property by the qualifying corporation from the taxpayer. If section 354 would apply to the exchange but for the receipt of boot, the term "qualifying corporation" means a corpoation the stock of which could be received by the taxpayer in the exchange without recognition of gain or loss. If section 355 would apply to the exchange but for the receipt of boot, the term "qualifying corporation" means the distributing corporation (referred to in section 355(a)(1)(A)). Receipt of an installment obligation is treated as a dividend if section 356(a)(2) applies (determined without regard to the presence or absence of accumulated earnings and

profits), or if section 356(e) (relating to certain exchanges for section 306 stock) applies to the taxpayer's receipt of the installment obligation.

(ii) *Exclusion from payment.*—Receipt of permitted property shall not be considered payment for purposes of paragraph (c) of this section. For purposes of paragraph (f)(1) of this section, "permitted property" means property, the receipt of which does not result in recognition of gain under section 356(a)(1) (i.e., stock of a qualifying corporation).

(iii) *Installment method determinations.*—Installment method determinations with respect to an installment obligation received in an exchange to which paragraph (f)(2) of this section applies shall be made in accordance with the rules prescribed in paragraph (f)(1)(iii) of this section. In applying such rules, a section 356(a)(1) exchange shall be treated as a section 1031(b) exchange and permitted property shall mean permitted property described in paragraph (f)(2) of this section.

(iv) *Examples.*—The provisions of paragraph (f)(2) of this section are illustrated by the following examples:

Example (1). T corporation and P corporation are unrelated closely held corporations. A owns 10% of the stock of T. A is not related to any other T stockholder or to any P stockholder. S corporation is a wholly-owned subsidiary of P. Pursuant to a plan of reorganization, T merges with and into S. In the merger, the T shares held by A are exchanged for shares of P worth $100,000 and a $300,000 installment obligation (bearing adequate interest) issued by P. In the merger the other stockholders of T exchange their T shares solely for P shares worth, in the aggregate, $3,600,000. The merger is a reorganization described in sections 368(a)(1)(A) and (a)(2)(D), and T, S, and P each is a party to the reorganization under section 368(b). P is a qualifying corporation and A is party to a section 356(a)(1) exchange in which receipt by A of the installment obligation will not be treated as a dividend to A. Because, for purposes of section 453(f)(6), this transaction is treated as a direct exchange between P and A, no gain or loss is recognized by S with respect to the P obligation. Assume A's basis in the T shares exchanged by A was $150,000. A's basis is allocated first to the permitted property (P shares) received, up to the fair market value of $100,000. A's excess basis is $50,000 ($150,000 − $100,000). Since the installment obligation is the only boot received by A in the exchange, the entire excess basis of $50,000 is allocable to it. Under the installment method, the contract price is $300,000 (face amount of the installment obligation), the gross profit is $250,000 (contract price less $50,000 excess basis allocated to the installment obligation), and the gross profit ratio is 5/6 ($250,000/$300,000). A recognizes no gain until payments are received on the installment obligation. As A receives payments (exclusive of interest) on the installment obligation, 5/6ths of each payment will be gain attributable to the exchange and 1/6th of each payment will be recovery of basis. A will hold the permitted property (P stock) received in the exchange at a basis of $100,000.

Example (2). The facts are the same as in exmaple (1). B, who also owns 10% of the stock of T directly and owns no other stock by T by attribution within the meaning of 318(a), exchanges the T shares in the merger for $400,000 installment obligation issued by P (bearing adequate interest). Although section 356(a)(1) will not apply to this exchange becasue B receives no P stock in the transaction and the character of the gain is determined under section 302(a), for purposes of section 453 and paragraph (a) of this section, B is treated as having sold the T shares to P in exchange for P's installment obligation. B will report the installment sale on the installment method unless B elects under paragraph (e) of this section not to report the transaction on the installment method. If, by reason of constructive ownership of T shares under section 381(a) and failure to meet the requirements of section 302(c)(2), the character of the transaction as to B were determined under section 302(d), section 453 would not apply to the exchange by B.

Example (3). The facts are the same as in examples (1) and (2), except that the P stock is voting stock and S merges into T in a reorganization described in section 368(a)(2)(E). The results are the same as in examples (1) and (2).

Example (4) (i). T Corporation and larger P Corporation are unrelated public corporations the stock of each of which is widely held. A is a stockholder of T. S Corporation is a wholly owned subsidiary of P. On December 31, 1981, pursuant to a plan of reorganization which provides for a "note option" election, T merges with and into S. In the merger, A exercises the note option and the T shares held by A are exchanged for a $30,000 installment obligation (bearing adequate interest) issued by P, 1,000 P shares (worth $10 per share on the date of merger), and a non-negotiable certificate evidencing a right to receive (within 5 years from the date of merger) up to 1,000 additional P shares (plus adequate interest) if certain earnings conditions are satisfied. Neither the installment obligation nor the certificate evidencing the right to receive additional P shares is readily tradable within the meaning of § 1.453-1A(c)(4)(iv)(C). There is a valid business reason for not issuing all of the P shares immediately. Certain of the other T shareholders exercise the note option and exchange their T shares for a similar package. Other T shareholders do not exercise the note option and receive in the merger P shares plus a non-negotiable right to receive up to an equal number of additional P shares (plus adequate interest) within 5 years. In the aggregate, the total outstanding T shares are exchanged for 20% P installment obligations, 40% P shares, and rights to receive an equal number of additional P shares within 5 years. The merger of T into S qualifies as a reorganization under section 368(a)(1)(A) and (a)(2)(D). P is a qualifying corporation, the P shares received and which may subsequently be received by A are permitted property, and the exchange to which A is a party is a section 356(a)(1) exchange.

(ii) Assume A's basis in the T shares exchanged by A was $25,000. A's basis is allocated first to permitted property (P shares) up to fair market value. In the exchange A has received 1,000 P shares (worth $10,000) and may receive up to an additional 1,000 P shares in the future. In allocating A's basis, it is assumed that all contingencies contemplated by the merger agreement will be met or otherwise resolved in a manner that will maximize the consideration A will receive. It is further assumed that each P share, when received, will have a fair market value equal to the fair market value ($10) of a P share at the date of merger. Accordingly, since A may receive a maximum of 2,000 P shares, $20,000 (2,000 × $10) of A's basis will be allocated to the 1,000 P shares A has received ($10 per share) and to A's right to receive up to an additional 1,000 P shares (at $10 per share). A's excess basis of $5,000 ($25,000 – $20,000) is allocated to the $30,000 P installment obligation.

(iii) In 1983 the earnings condition is fully satisfied and A receives an additional 1,000 P shares (plus adequate interest). Each P share held by A has a basis of $10.

(iv) Assume instead that the earnings condition is only partly satisfied and, by the close of 1986, A has received only an additional 600 P shares and is not entitled to receive any further P shares. Initially, each P share received by A was assigned a basis of $10. Of A's $25,000 basis in the T shares exchanged, $4,000 ($20,000 initially allocated to P shares received and to be received less $16,000 (1,600 P shares × $10)) now must be accounted for. The $4,000 of remaining basis will be assigned to the P shares than held by A. Thus, if A continues to hold all 1,600 P shares, A's basis in each P share will be increased by $2.50 ($4,000 divided by 1,600 P shares), If A previously sold 800 P shares and retains only 800 P shares, A's basis in each retained P share will be increased by $5 ($4,000 divided by 800 P shares). If A retains no P shares, and if all of the additional 600 P shares were issued to A and sold by A before the final year of the five year earn-out term (*i.e.*, by the end of 1985), A's remaining basis of $4,000 will be added to the basis at which A holds the unpaid portion of the P installment obligation (up to but not in excess of the maximum amount remaining payable under that obligation less A's remaining basis in the installment obligation determined immediately before the addition to basis). If A has previously disposed of the P installment obligation, so that A holds neither P shares nor the P installment obligation to which the remaining $4,000 of A's basis can be allocated, A will be allowed a $4,000 loss in 1986. Similarly, if A continues to hold the P installment obligation but the facts are such that the maximum amount thereafter payable under the obligation is only $3,000 in excess of A's basis in the obligation determined immediately before assignment of A's remaining $4,000 basis, $3,000 of that remaining basis would be assigned to the installment obligation and P would be allowed a $1,000 loss in 1986.

Example (5). Pursuant to a plan to acquire all the stock of T corporation, P purchases 90% of the T stock for cash. To acquire the remaining 10% of T stock P creates S corporation and transfers P stock and P's newly issued installment notes to S in exchange for all of S's stock. The P notes are not readily tradable. Thereafter S merges into T, and P stock and P's installment notes are distributed to the T minority shareholders, and the S stock held by P is automatically converted into T stock. Assume that for federal tax purposes the existence of S is disregarded and the transaction is treated as a sale of T stock to P in exchange for P stock and P's installment notes. The minority shareholders will report the gain realized on the receipt of the P installment notes on the installment method unless they elect otherwise. The receipt of P stock will be treated as a payment in the year of sale.

Example (6). The facts are the same as example (5) except P transferred only P's installment notes to S and only these notes were distributed to T minority shareholders. As in example (5) the transaction is treated as a sale of T stock to P in exchange for P's installment notes. Each minority shareholder realizing gain on the receipt of the installment notes will report the gain on the installment method unless electing otherwise.

(3) *Other partial recognition exchanges.*—(i) *In general.*—The provisions of paragraph (f)(3) of this section apply to exchanges not described in paragraph (f)(1) or (2) of this section in which a taxpayer, in exchange for appreciated property, receives both permitted property (*i.e.*, property with respect to which no gain or loss would be recognized but which, in the hands of the taxpayer, would have as basis for determining gain or loss the same basis in whole or in part as the property exchanged) and boot that includes an installment obligation issued by the other party to the exchange. Ordinarily, the installment method rules set forth in paragraph (f)(1)(ii) and (iii) of this section will apply to an exchange described in paragraph (f)(3) of this section subject to such variations, if any, as may be required under the applicable provisions of the Code.

(ii) *Exchanges to which section 351 applies.*—If a taxpayer receives, in an exchange to which section 351(b) applies (a "section 351(b) exchange"), an installment obligation that is not a security within the meaning of section 351(a), the installment obligation is boot and the stock and securities (within the meaning of section 351(a)) are permitted property (within the meaning of paragraph (f)(1)(ii) of this section). The taxpayer will report the installment obligation on the installment method and any other boot received will be treated as a payment made in the year of the exchange. In applying the rules of paragraph (f)(1)(iii) of this section to a section 351(b) exchange the excess basis is the amount, if any, by which the taxpayer's basis in the property transferred (plus any cash transferred) by the taxpayer exceeds the sum of the transferred liabilities which are not treated as money received under section 357 plus the fair market value of permitted property received by the taxpayer. In determining selling price and total contract price, transferred liabilities which are not treated as money received under section 357 shall be disregarded. For purposes of paragraph (f)(3)(ii) of this section, transferred liabilities are liabilities described in section 357(a)(2). Solely for the purpose of applying section 358(a)(1), the taxpayer shall be treated as if the taxpayer elected not to report receipt of the installment obligation on the installment method. Under section 362(a)(1) the corporation's basis in the property received from the taxpayer is the taxpayer's basis in the property increased by the gain recognized by the taxpayer at the time of the exchange. As the taxpayer recognizes gain on the installment method, the corporation will increase its basis in the property by an amount equal to the amount of gain recognized by the taxpayer.

(iii) *Examples.*—The provisions of paragraph (f)(3) of this section are illustrated by the following examples. In each example, assume that adequate stated interest means both a reasonable rate of interest within the meaning of any applicable regulation promulgated under section 385 and a rate of interest not less than the test rate prescribed in the regulations under section 483, and that the debt to equity ratio of the issuing corporation is a permissible ratio under any applicable regulation promulgated under section 385.

Example (1). A owns Blackacre, unimproved real property, with a basis of $300,000. The fair market value of Blackacre is $700,000. Blackacre is encumbered by a longstanding mortgage of $200,000. A transfers Blackacre, subject to the mortgage, to a newly organized X corporation. A receives in exchange all of the stock of X, worth $400,000, and a $100,000 installment obligation (bearing adequate stated interest) issued by X. A realizes $400,000 of gain on the exchange. The installment obligation calls for a single payment of the full $100,000 face amount three years following the date of issue. The installment obligation is not a "security" within the meaning of section 351(a), and thus the exchange by A is a transaction described in section 351(b). The installment obligation is boot received by A in the exchange and the X stock is permitted property received by A in exchange. In applying the provisions of paragraph (f)(1)(ii) and (iii) of this section to a section 351(b) exchange, reference is required to section 357(a) under which the $200,000 mortgage liability is not treated as money or other property received by A in the exchange, and to section 358(a)(1) under which the basis of the X stock in the hands of A will be determined. These rules apply as follows: Neither receipt of the X stock nor relief of the mortgage encumbrance is treated as payment to A and thus A will recognize no gain in the year of the exchange. A's basis of $300,000 in Blackacre is reduced by the $200,000 mortgage from which A is deemed relieved in the exchange. The remaining basis of $100,000 is allocated to the X stock (but not in excess of the fair market value of the X stock); since the fair market value of the X stock is $400,000, the basis of the X stock in the hands of A is $100,000. Accordingly, in A's hands the installment obligation has a basis of zero. In the hands of X, the initial basis of Blackacre, determined under section 362(a), is $300,000 (the basis of the property in the hands of A), increased by the amount of gain recognized by A at the time of the transfer ($0)). As A receives payments on the installment obligation and recognizes gain, X's basis in Blackacre will be increased, at that time, in an amount equal to the gain recognized by A. Thus, if the $100,000 installment obligation is paid in full on the third anniversary date, A will recognize gain of $100,000 (because A's basis in the installment obligation is zero) and X at that time will increase the basis at which it holds Blackacre by $100,000. If in the third year X had sold the property for cash before making payment on the installment obligation, X would recognize a loss of $100,000 when X paid the obligation in that amount to A on the third anniversary date.

Example (2). B owns Whiteacre, unencumbered, unimproved real property, with a basis of $250,000. The fair market value of Whiteacre is $300,000. A transfers Whiteacre to newly organized Y corporation in exchange for all of the stock of Y corporation (worth $200,000) and a $100,000 installment obligation (bearing adequate interest). The installment obligation is payable in full on the second anniversary of the date of issue. The installment obligation is not a "security" within the meaning of section 351(a), and thus the transaction is a section 351(b) exchange. Applying the rules summarized in example (1) to the facts of this case, receipt of the installment obligation is not treated as payment to A, $200,000 of A's basis of $250,000 in Whiteacre is allocated to the Y stock (equal to the fair market value of the Y stock), and the excess basis of $50,000 is allocated to the installment obligation. In the hands of Y, the basis of Whiteacre initially is $250,000, and will be increased by $50,000 when the installment obligation is paid and A recognizes gain of $50,000.

Example (3). D owns a machine which is unencumbered 5-year recovery property with an adjusted basis of $500,000. The recomputed basis (as defined in section 1245(a)(2)) of the machine in the hands of D is $1 million. The fair market value of the machine also is $1 million. D transfers the machine to newly organized X corporation, and E, an unrelated individual, simultaneously transfers property worth $1 million to X corporation. D receives in exchange 400 shares of X common stock worth $400,000, a $400,000 15-year debenture issued by X (worth its face amount), and a $200,000 installment obligation (bearing adequate interest) issed by X. The installment obligation calls for a single payment of the full $200,000 face amount two years following the date of issue. E receives in the exchange 1,000 shares of X common stock worth $1 million. D and E are in control (as defined in section 368(c)) of X immediately after the exchange. The debenture received by D is a "security" within the meaning of section 351(a), but the installment obligation received by D is not a "security" within the meaning of that section and thus the exchange by D is a transaction described in section 351(b). The installment obligation is boot received by D in the exchange and the X stock and X debenture are permitted property received by D in the exchange. Since the aggregate fair market value ($800,000) of X stock ($400,000) and the X debenture ($400,000) received by D exceeds D's $500,000 adjusted basis in the machine, all of that basis is allocated proportionately among the items of permitted property. Thus, D will hold the X stock with a basis of $250,000 and the X debenture with a basis of $250,000. Since there is no excess basis, in the hands of D the installment obligation has a basis of zero. In the hands of X, the adjusted basis of the machine remains $500,000. When D receives payment from X on the $200,000 installment obligation, D will recognize gain of $200,000, all of which gain will be treated as ordinary income. See sections 1245(a)(1) and 453B(a). At that time, X's adjusted basis in the machine will be increased in an amount equal to the $200,000 gain recognized by D.

Example (4). In 1976 H and W purchased Blackacre as their principal residence for $50,000. In 1981 H and W, both of whom are less than 55 years of age, sold Blackacre to A for $90,000: $15,000 cash, A's assumption of the $40,000 mortgage, and A's promise to pay H and W $7,000 (with adequate stated interest) in each of the next 5 years. Within 2 years of the sale of Blackacre, H and W acquire Whiteacre, an unencumbered property, which will be their principal residence, for $80,000. Of the $40,000 gain that H and W realized upon the sale of Whiteacre, $30,000 will not be recognized pursuant to the provisions of section 1034. Unless H and W elect not to report the transaction on the installment method, they will treat the $10,000 gain to be recognized as the gross profit for purposes of calculating the gross profit ratio. Accordingly the gross profit ratio is 1/5 ($10,000 gross profit/ $50,000 contract price) and H and W will report as gain $3,000 (1/5 × $15,000) in the year of the sale and $1,400 (1/5 × $7,000) in each of the next five years.

(4) *Installment obligations received as distributions in redemptions of stock pursuant to section 302(a)*.—If a corporation redeems its stock and the redemption is treated as a distribution in part or full payment in exchange for the stock under section 302(a), then an installment obligation which meets the requirements of section 453 and is distributed in the redemption shall be reported on the installment method unless the taxpayer elects otherwise.

Example. A owns 10% of the stock of X corporation and is not considered as owning (under section 318(a)) any other shares of X corporation. X redeems all of A's X shares and distributes its installment obligation to A in full payment. The reduction is treated as a sale of the X shares by A under section 302(b)(3). A will report any gain realized in the redemption on the installment method unless A elects otherwise.

* * *

Installment Obligations: Dispositions: Nonrecognition of Gain or Loss

Installment Obligations: Dispositions: Nonrecognition of Gain or Loss—Reg. §1.453B-1, relating to the nonrecognition of gain or loss on certain dispositions of an installment obligation, is proposed (published in the Federal Register on December 23, 2014) (REG-109187-11).

□ Par. 4. Section 1.453B-1 is added to read as follows:

§1.453B-1. Gain or loss on disposition of installment obligations.—(a) *General rule.*—[Reserved].

(b) *Basis of obligation.*—[Reserved].

(c) *Dispositions on which no gain or loss is recognized.*—(1) *Certain nonrecognition transactions.*—(i) *In general.*—If the Internal Revenue Code provides an exception to the recognition of gain or loss for certain dispositions, no gain or loss shall be recognized under section 453B on the disposition of an installment obligation within that exception. These exceptions include—

(A) Certain transfers to corporations under sections 351 and 361;

(B) Contributions to a partnership under section 721; and

(C) Distributions by a partnership to a partner under section 731 (except as provided by sections 704(c)(1)(B), 736, 737, and 751(b)).

(ii) *Transactions resulting in a satisfaction of installment obligations.*—Paragraph (c)(1)(i) of this section does not apply to a disposition that results in a satisfaction of an installment obligation, regardless of whether the disposition occurs as part of a transaction for which the Internal Revenue Code provides an exception to the recognition of gain or loss. These dispositions include, but are not limited to—

(A) The receipt of stock of a corporation from the corporation in satisfaction of an installment obligation of the corporation; and

(B) The receipt of an interest in a partnership from the partnership in satisfaction of an installment obligation of the partnership.

(2) *Effective/applicability date.*—This paragraph (c) applies to satisfactions, distributions, transmissions, sales, or other dispositions of installment obligations after the date these regulations are published as final regulations in the **Federal Register**. [Reg. §1.453B-1.]

Imputed Interest: Original Issue Discount: Safe Haven Rates

Imputed Interest: Original Issue Discount: Safe Haven Interest Rates.—Reproduced below is the text of a proposed amendment of Reg. §1.454-1, relating to (1) the tax treatment of debt instruments issued after July 1, 1982, that contain original issue discount, (2) the imputation of and the accounting for interest with respect to sales and exchanges of property occurring after December 31, 1984, and (3) safe haven interest rates for loans or advances between commonly controlled taxpayers and safe haven leases between such taxpayers (published in the Federal Register on April 8, 1986).

□ Par. 11. Paragraph (a)(1)(i) of §1.454-1 is revised to read as follows:

§1.454-1. Obligations issued at discount.—

(a) *Certain non-interest bearing obligations issued at discount.*—(1) *Election to include increase in income currently.*—If a taxpayer owns—

(i) A non-interest bearing obligation issued at a discount and redeemable for fixed amounts increasing at stated intervals (other than a debt instrument issued after May 27, 1969, as to which inclusion of original issue discount is required under section 1272), or

* * *

Deferred Compensation Plans: State and Local Governments: Tax-Exempt Entities

Deferred Compensation Plans: State and Local Governments: Tax-Exempt Entities.—Reg. §1.457-11 and amendments to Reg. §§1.457-1, 1.457-2, 1.457-4, 1.457-6, 1.457-7, 1.457-9 and 1.457-10—1.457-13, prescribing rules under section 457 of the Internal Revenue Code for the taxation of compensation deferred under plans established and maintained by State or local

governments or other tax exempt organizations, are proposed (published in the Federal Register on June 22, 2016) (REG-147196-07).

Par. 2. Section 1.457-1 is revised to read as follows:

§ 1.457-1. General overview of section 457.—Section 457 provides rules for nonqualified deferred compensation plans established by eligible employers as defined under § 1.457-2(d). Eligible employers may establish either deferred compensation plans that are eligible plans that meet the requirements of section 457(b) and §§ 1.457-3 through 1.457-10, or deferred compensation plans that do not meet the requirements of section 457(b) and §§ 1.457-3 through 1.457-10 (and therefore are ineligible plans which are generally subject to federal income tax treatment under section 457(f) and § 1.457-12(a)). Plans described in § 1.457-11 are not subject to section 457 or are treated as not providing for a deferral of compensation for purposes of section 457 (and, accordingly, the rules under §§ 1.457-3 through 1.457-10 and § 1.457-12(a) do not apply to these plans).

Par. 3. Section 1.457-2 is amended by:

1. Revising the introductory text.
2. Revising the second sentence of paragraph (f).
3. Revising the last sentence of paragraph (i).
4. Revising paragraph (k).

The revisions read as follows:

§ 1.457-2. Definitions.—This section sets forth the definitions that are used under §§ 1.457-1 through 1.457-12.

* * *

(f) * * * An eligible governmental plan is an eligible plan that is established and maintained by a State as defined in paragraph (l) of this section and that meets the requirements of section 401(a)(37). * * *

* * *

(i) * * * Solely for purposes of section 457 and §§ 1.457-2 through 1.457-12, the term *nonelective employer contribution* includes employer contributions that would be described in section 401(m) if they were contributions to a qualified plan.

* * *

(k) *Plan.*—*Plan* includes any agreement, method, program, or other arrangement (including an individual employment agreement) under which the payment of compensation for services rendered to an eligible employer is deferred (whether by salary reduction, nonelective employer contribution, or otherwise). However, the plans described in § 1.457-11 are either not subject to section 457 or are treated as not providing for a deferral of compensation for purposes of section 457, even if the payment of compensation is deferred under the plan.

* * *

Par. 4. Section 1.457-4 is amended by:

1. Revising paragraphs (a), (b), and the last sentence of (e)(1).
2. Removing the language "§ 1.457-11" wherever it appears in paragraphs (e)(1), (e)(2), (e)(3), and (e)(5) *Example 1* and adding the language "§ 1.457-12" in its place.

The revisions read as follows:

§ 1.457-4. Annual deferrals, deferral limitations, and deferral agreements under eligible plans.—(a) *Taxation of annual deferrals.*—With the exception of designated Roth contributions (which are not excludable from gross income), annual deferrals that satisfy the requirements of paragraphs (b) and (c) of this section are excluded from the gross income of a participant in the year deferred or contributed and are not includible in gross income until paid to the participant in the case of an eligible governmental plan, or until paid or otherwise made available to the participant in the case of an eligible plan of a tax-exempt entity. See § 1.457-7.

(b) *Agreement for deferral.*—(1) *In general.*—To be an eligible plan, the plan must provide that compensation for any calendar month may be deferred by salary reduction only if an agreement providing for the deferral has been entered into before the first day of the month in which the compensation to be deferred under the agreement would otherwise be paid or made available, and any modification or revocation of such an agreement may not become effective before the first day of the month following the month in which the modification or revocation occurs. However, a new employee may defer compensation in the first calendar month of employment if an agreement providing for the deferral is entered into on or before the first day the participant performs services for the eligible employer. An eligible plan may provide that if a participant enters into an agreement providing for deferral by salary reduction under the plan, the agreement will remain in effect until the participant revokes or alters the terms of the agreement. Nonelective employer contributions to an eligible plan are not subject to the timing rules for salary reduction agreements described in this paragraph (b)(1).

(2) *Designated Roth contributions in plans maintained by eligible governmental employers.*—(i) *Elections.*—An election by a participant to make a designated Roth contribution (as defined in section 402A(c)(1)) to an eligible governmental plan in lieu of all or a portion of the amount that the participant could elect to contribute to the plan on a pre-tax basis must be irrevocably designated as an elective deferral that is not excludable from gross income in accordance with the timing rules under paragraph (b)(1) of this section. Designated Roth contributions are treated the same as pre-tax contributions for purposes of §§ 1.457-1 through 1.457-10, except as otherwise specifically provided in those sections.

(ii) *Separate accounting*.—Contributions and withdrawals of a participant's designated Roth contributions must be credited and debited to a designated Roth account maintained for the participant, and the plan must maintain a record of the participant's investment in the contract (that is, designated Roth contributions that have not been distributed) with respect to the participant's designated Roth account. In addition, gains, losses, and other credits or charges must be separately allocated on a reasonable and consistent basis to the designated Roth account and other accounts under the plan. However, forfeitures may not be allocated to the designated Roth account, and no contributions other than designated Roth contributions and rollover contributions described in section 402A(c)(3)(B) may be allocated to such account. The separate accounting requirement described in this paragraph applies to a plan at the time a designated Roth contribution is contributed to the plan and continues to apply until all designated Roth contributions (and the earnings attributable thereto) are distributed from the plan. See A-13 of § 1.402A-1 for additional requirements for separate accounting.

* * *

(e) * * *

(1) * * * Thus, an excess deferral is includible in gross income when deferred or, if later, when the excess deferral first ceases to be subject to a substantial risk of forfeiture, under the rules described in § 1.457-12(e).

* * *

Par. 5. Section 1.457-6 is amended by revising the first sentence of paragraph (b)(1) to read as follows:

§ 1.457-6. Timing of distributions under eligible plans.

* * *

(b) * * *

(1) * * * An employee has a severance from employment with the eligible employer if the employee dies, retires, or otherwise has a severance from employment (including as described in section 414(u)(12)(B)) with the eligible employer.* * *

* * *

Par. 6. Section 1.457-7 is amended by revising the section heading and paragraph (b)(1), redesignating paragraph (b)(4) as (b)(5), and adding a new paragraph (b)(4) to read as follows:

§ 1.457-7. Taxation of distributions under eligible plans.

* * *

(b) * * *

(1) *Amounts included in gross income in year paid under an eligible governmental plan*.—Except as provided in paragraphs (b)(2), (3), and (4) of this section (or in § 1.457-10(c) relating to payments to a spouse or former spouse pursuant to a qualified domestic relations order), amounts deferred under an eligible governmental plan are includible in the gross income of a participant or beneficiary for the taxable year in which paid to the participant or beneficiary under the plan. Distributions from designated Roth accounts are excludable from gross income to the extent provided in section 402A and §§ 1.402A-1 and 1.402A-2.

* * *

(4) *Certain amounts from an eligible governmental plan not in excess of the amount paid for qualified health insurance premiums*.—Amounts paid to a participant who is an eligible retired public safety officer from an eligible governmental plan are excludible from gross income to the extent provided in section 402(l).

* * *

Par. 7. Section 1.457-9 is amended by revising the third sentence of paragraph (a) and the last sentence of paragraph (b) to read as follows:

§ 1.457-9. Effect on eligible plans when not administered in accordance with eligibility requirements.—(a) * * * If a plan ceases to be an eligible governmental plan, amounts subsequently deferred by participants are includible in gross income when deferred, or, if later, when the amounts deferred first cease to be subject to a substantial risk of forfeiture, under the rules described in § 1.457-12(e). * * *

(b) * * * See § 1.457-12 for rules regarding the treatment of an ineligible plan.

Par. 8. Section 1.457-10 is amended by removing the language "§ 1.457-11" wherever it appears in paragraphs (a)(2)(i), (a)(3) *Example 2* (ii), (c)(2) *Example 1* (ii) and *Example 2* (ii) and adding the language "§ 1.457-12" in its place.

§ 1.457-10. Miscellaneous provisions.

Par. 10. Add a new § 1.457-11 to read as follows:

§ 1.457-11. Exclusions and exceptions for certain plans.—(a) *In general*.—The plans described in paragraphs (b) and (c) of this section either are not subject to section 457 or are treated as not providing for a deferral of compensation for purposes of section 457, and, accordingly, the provisions of §§ 1.457-3 through 1.457-10 and 1.457-12(a) do not apply to these plans.

(b) *Plans not subject to section 457*.—The following plans are not subject to section 457:

(1) Any plan satisfying the conditions in section 1107(c)(4) of the Tax Reform Act of 1986, Public Law 99-514 (100 Stat. 2494) (TRA '86) (relating to certain plans for State judges);

(2) Any of the following plans (to which specific transitional statutory exclusions apply):

(i) A plan of a tax-exempt entity in existence prior to January 1, 1987, if the conditions of section 1107(c)(3)(B) of the TRA '86, as amended by section 1011(e)(6) of the Technical and Miscellaneous Revenue Act of 1988, Public Law 100-647 (102 Stat. 3342) (TAMRA), are satisfied (see § 1.457-2(b)(4) for a different rule that may apply to the annual deferrals permitted under this type of plan);

(ii) A collectively bargained nonelective deferred compensation plan in effect on December 31, 1987, if the conditions of section 6064(d)(2) of TAMRA are satisfied;

(iii) Amounts deferred under plans described in section 6064(d)(3) of TAMRA (relating to amounts deferred under certain nonelective deferred compensation plans in effect before 1989); and

(iv) Any plan satisfying the conditions in section 1107(c)(4) and (5) of TRA '86 (relating to certain plans for certain individuals with respect to which the IRS issued guidance before 1977); and

(3) Any plan described in section 457(e)(12) that provides only nonelective deferred compensation attributable to services not performed as an employee (for example, a plan providing nonelective deferred compensation attributable to services performed by independent contractors). For this purpose, deferred compensation is nonelective only if all individuals, other than those who have not satisfied any applicable initial service requirement, with the same relationship to the payor are covered under the same plan with no individual variations or options under the plan.

(c) *Plans treated as not providing for a deferral of compensation.*—The following plans are treated as not providing for a deferral of compensation for purposes of section 457, §§ 1.457-1 through 1.457-10, and § 1.457-12:

(1) A bona fide vacation leave, sick leave, compensatory time, severance pay, disability pay, or death benefit plan, as described in section 457(e)(11)(A)(i) (see paragraph (d) of this section for the definition of a bona fide severance pay plan, paragraph (e) of this section for the definitions of a bona fide death benefit plan and a bona fide disability pay plan, and paragraph (f) of this section for the requirements for a bona fide sick or vacation leave plan); and

(2) A plan described in section 457(e)(11)(A)(ii) paying solely length of service awards that are based on service accrued after December 31,1996, to bona fide volunteers (and their beneficiaries) on account of qualified services performed by those volunteers.

(d) *Definition of bona fide severance pay plan.*—(1) *In general.*—A bona fide severance pay plan is an arrangement that meets the following requirements:

(i) Except as provided in paragraph (d)(3) of this section, benefits are payable only upon involuntary severance from employment, as defined in paragraph (d)(2) of this section (see § 1.457-6(b) for the meaning of severance from employment);

(ii) The amount payable does not exceed two times the participant's annualized compensation based upon the annual rate of pay for services provided to the eligible employer for the calendar year preceding the calendar year in which the participant has a severance from employment with the eligible employer (or the current calendar year if the participant had no compensation for services provided to the eligible employer in the preceding calendar year), adjusted for any increase during the year used to measure the rate of pay that was expected to continue indefinitely if the participant had not had a severance from employment; and

(iii) The entire severance benefit must be paid to the participant no later than the last day of the second calendar year following the calendar year in which the severance from employment occurs, pursuant to a requirement contained in a written plan document.

(2) *Involuntary severance from employment.*—(i) *In general.*—For purposes of paragraph (d)(1)(i) of this section, an *involuntary severance from employment* means a severance from employment due to the independent exercise of the eligible employer's unilateral authority to terminate the participant's services, other than due to the participant's implicit or explicit request, if the participant was willing and able to continue performing services. An involuntary severance from employment may include an eligible employer's failure to renew a contract at the time the contract expires, provided that the employee was willing and able to execute a new contract providing terms and conditions substantially similar to those in the expiring contract and to continue providing such services. The determination of whether a severance from employment is involuntary is based on all the facts and circumstances without regard to any characterization of the reason for the payment by the employer or participant.

(ii) *Severance from employment for good reason.*—(A) *In general.*—Notwithstanding paragraph (d)(2)(i) of this section, a participant's voluntary severance from employment will be treated as an involuntary severance from employment, for purposes of paragraph (d)(1)(i) of this section, if the severance occurs under certain bona fide conditions that are pre-specified in writing (referred to herein as a severance from employment for good reason), provided that the avoidance of the requirements of section 457 is not the primary purpose of the inclusion of the conditions or of the actions by the employer in connection with the satisfaction of the conditions, and a voluntary severance from employment under such conditions effectively constitutes an involuntary severance from employment. Notwithstanding the previous sentence, once the bona fide conditions have been established, the elimination of one or more of the conditions may result in the extension of a substantial risk of forfeiture, the recognition of which would be subject to the rules discussed in § 1.457-12(e)(2).

(B) *Material negative change required.*—A severance from employment for good reason will be treated as an involuntary severance from employment only if the relevant facts and circumstances demonstrate that it was the result of unilateral employer action that caused a material negative change to the participant's relationship with the eligible employer. Some factors that may provide evidence of such a material negative change include a material reduction in the duties to be performed, a material negative change in the conditions under which the duties are to be performed, or a material reduction in the compensation to be received for performing such services. Other factors to be considered in determining whether a severance from employment due to good reason will be treated as an involuntary severance from employment include the extent to which the payments upon a severance from employment for good reason are in the same amount and made at the same time and in the same form as payments that would be made upon an actual involuntary severance from employment, and whether the employee is required to give the employer notice of the existence of the condition that would result in the treatment of a severance from employment as being for good reason and a reasonable opportunity to remedy the condition.

(C) *Safe harbor*.—The requirements of paragraph (d)(2)(ii)(B) of this section are deemed to be satisfied if a severance from employment occurs under the conditions described in paragraph (d)(2)(ii)(C)(*1*) of this section, those conditions are specified in writing by the time the legally binding right to the payment arises, and the plan also satisfies the requirements in paragraphs (d)(2)(ii)(C)(*2*) and (*3*) of this section.

(*1*) The severance from employment occurs during a limited period of time not to exceed two years following the initial existence of one or more of the following conditions arising without the consent of the participant:

(*i*) A material diminution in the participant's base compensation;

(*ii*) A material diminution in the participant's authority, duties, or responsibilities;

(*iii*) A material diminution in the authority, duties, or responsibilities of the supervisor to whom the participant is required to report, including a requirement that a participant report to a corporate officer or employee instead of reporting directly to the board of directors (or similar governing body) of an organization;

(*iv*) A material diminution in the budget over which the participant retains authority;

(*v*) A material change in the geographic location at which the participant must perform services; or

(*vi*) Any other action or inaction that constitutes a material breach by the eligible employer of the agreement under which the participant provides services.

(*2*) The amount, time, and form of payment upon the severance from employment is substantially the same as the amount, time, and form of payment that would have been made upon an actual involuntary severance from employment, to the extent such right to payment exists.

(*3*) The participant is required to provide notice to the eligible employer of the existence of the applicable condition(s) described in paragraph (d)(2)(ii)(C)(*1*) of this section within a period not to exceed 90 days after the initial existence of the condition(s), upon the notice of which, the employer must be provided a period of at least 30 days during which it may remedy the condition(s) and not be required to pay the amount.

(3) *Window programs*.—The requirement in paragraph (d)(1)(i) of this section that benefits be payable only upon involuntary severance from employment does not apply to a bona fide severance pay plan that provides benefits upon a severance from employment pursuant to a window program. For this purpose, a *window program* means a program established by an employer to provide separation pay in connection with an impending severance from employment, if the program is made available by the employer for a limited period of time (typically no longer than 12 months) to participants who have a severance from employment during that period or to participants who have a severance from employment during that period under specified circumstances. A program is not considered a window program for purposes of this paragraph if it is part of a pattern of multiple similar programs that, if offered as a single program, would not be a window program under this paragraph. Whether multiple programs constitute a pattern of similar programs is determined based on the relevant facts and circumstances. Although no one factor is determinative, relevant factors include whether the benefits are on account of a specific reduction in workforce (or some other entity-related operational condition), the degree to which the separation pay relates to an event or condition, and whether the event or condition is temporary or discrete or is a permanent aspect of the employer's practices.

(4) *Voluntary early retirement incentive plans*.—(i) *In general*.—Notwithstanding paragraph (d)(1) of this section, an applicable voluntary early retirement incentive plan (as defined in section 457(e)(11)(D)(ii)) is treated as a bona fide severance pay plan for purposes of this section with respect to payments or supplements made as an early retirement benefit, a retirement-type subsidy, or an early retirement benefit described in the last sentence of section 411(a)(9), if the payments or supplements are made in coordination with a defined benefit pension plan that is qualified under section 401(a) maintained by an eligible employer described in section 457(e)(1)(A) or by an education association described in section 457(e)(11)(D)(ii)(II). See section 1104(d)(4) of the Pension Protection Act of 2006, Public Law 109-280 (120 Stat. 780), regarding the application of the Internal Revenue Code and certain other laws to any plan, arrangement, or conduct to which section 457(e)(11)(D) does not apply.

(ii) *Definitions*.—The definitions in § 1.411(d)-3(g)(6)(i) and (iv) apply for purposes of determining whether payments or supplements are an early retirement benefit or a retirement-type subsidy, and the definition in § 1.411(a)-7(c)(4) applies for purposes of determining whether payments or supplements are an early retirement benefit described in the last sentence of section 411(a)(9).

(e) *Bona fide death benefit or disability pay plans*.—(1) *Bona fide death benefit plan*.—For purposes of section 457(e)(11)(A)(i) and this section, a *bona fide death benefit plan* is a plan providing death benefits as defined in § 31.3121(v)(2)-1(b)(4)(iv)(C) of this chapter, provided that, for purposes of this paragraph (e)(1), the death benefits may be provided through insurance and the lifetime benefits payable under the plan are not treated as including the value of any term life insurance coverage provided under the plan that is includible in gross income.

(2) *Bona fide disability pay plan.*—For purposes of section 457(e)(11)(A)(i) and this section, a *bona fide disability pay plan* is a plan that pays benefits (whether or not insured) only in the event that a participant is disabled, provided that, for purposes of this paragraph (e)(2), the value of any disability insurance coverage provided under the plan that is included in gross income is disregarded. For this purpose, a participant is considered disabled only if the participant meets one of the following conditions:

(i) The participant is unable to engage in any substantial gainful activity by reason of any medically determinable physical or mental impairment that can be expected to result in death or last for a continuous period of not less than 12 months;

(ii) The participant is, by reason of any medically determinable physical or mental impairment that can be expected to result in death or last for a continuous period of not less than 12 months, receiving income replacement benefits for a period of not less than three months under an accident and health plan covering employees of the eligible employer; or

(iii) The participant is determined to be totally disabled by the Social Security Administration or Railroad Retirement Board.

(f) *Bona fide sick and vacation leave plans.*—(1) *In general.*—For purposes of section 457(e)(11)(A)(i) and this section, the determination of whether a sick or vacation leave plan is a bona fide sick or vacation leave plan is made based on the relevant facts and circumstances. In general, a plan is treated as a bona fide sick or vacation leave plan, and not an arrangement to defer compensation, if the facts and circumstances demonstrate that the primary purpose of the plan is to provide participants with paid time off from work because of sickness, vacation, or other personal reasons. Factors used in determining whether a plan is a bona fide sick or vacation leave plan include whether the amount of leave provided could reasonably be expected to be used in the normal course by an employee (before the employee ceases to provide services to the eligible employer) absent unusual circumstances, the ability to exchange unused accumulated leave for cash or other benefits (including nontaxable benefits and the use of leave to postpone the date of termination of employment), the applicable restraints (if any) on the ability to accumulate unused leave and carry it forward to subsequent years in circumstances in which the accumulated leave may be exchanged for cash or other benefits, the amount and frequency of any in-service distributions of cash or other benefits offered in exchange for accumulated and unused leave, whether any payment of unused leave is made promptly upon severance from employment (or instead is paid over a period after severance from employment), and whether the program (or a particular feature of the program) is available only to a limited number of employees.

(2) *Delegation of authority to Commissioner.*—The Commissioner may provide additional rules regarding the requirements of a bona fide sick or vacation leave plan under section 457, in revenue rulings, notices, or other guidance published in the Internal Revenue Bulletin (see § 601.601(d)(2)(ii)(*b*) of this chapter), as the Commissioner determines to be necessary or appropriate.

Pars. 9 and 11. Redesignate § 1.457-11 as § 1.457-12 and revise newly-redesignated § 1.457-12 to read as follows:

§ 1.457-12. Tax treatment of participants if plan is not an eligible plan.—(a) *Tax treatment of an ineligible plan under section 457(f).*—(1) *In general.*—Pursuant to section 457(f)(1), if an eligible employer provides for a deferral of compensation under an ineligible plan, amounts will be included in income in accordance with paragraphs (a)(2) through (4) of this section, except as otherwise provided in this paragraph (a) or paragraph (b) of this section. See § 1.457-11 for plans that are not subject to section 457 or are not treated as providing for a deferral of compensation for purposes of section 457.

(2) *Income inclusion.*—The present value of compensation deferred under an ineligible plan is includible in the gross income of a participant or beneficiary under section 457(f) on the applicable date. For this purpose, the applicable date is the later of the first date on which there is a legally binding right to the compensation or, if the compensation is subject to a substantial risk of forfeiture, the first date on which the substantial risk of forfeiture (within the meaning of section 457(f)(3)(B) and paragraph (e) of this section) lapses. Paragraph (c) of this section provides rules for determining the present value of the compensation deferred under the plan, including a requirement that the amount of compensation deferred under an ineligible plan as of an applicable date includes any earnings on the compensation as of that date.

(3) *Treatment of earnings after income inclusion.*—Earnings credited on compensation deferred under an ineligible plan after the date on which the compensation is includible in gross income under section 457(f)(1) pursuant to paragraph (a)(2) of this section are includible in the gross income of a participant or beneficiary when paid or made available to the participant or beneficiary.

(4) *Income inclusion when compensation is paid or made available.*—Amounts paid or made available to a participant or beneficiary under an ineligible plan are includible in the gross income of the participant or beneficiary under section 72, relating to annuities. For this purpose, an amount is paid or made available if there is actual or constructive receipt (within the meaning of § 1.451-2) of any taxable or nontaxable benefit, including a transfer of cash, a transfer of property includible in income under section 83, any other event that results in the inclusion in income under the economic benefit doctrine, a contribution to (or transfer or creation of a beneficial interest in) a trust described in section 402(b) at a time when contributions to the trust are includible in income under section 402(b), or inclusion of an amount in income under section 457A. An amount is also paid or made available for this purpose if there is a transfer, cancellation, or reduction of an amount of deferred compensation in exchange for benefits under a welfare benefit plan, a fringe benefit excludible

under section 119 or section 132, or any other benefit that is excludible from gross income.

(5) *Investment in the contract.*—For purposes of applying section 72 to amounts that are paid or made available as described in paragraph (a)(4) of this section, a participant is treated as having an investment in the contract to the extent that compensation has been included in gross income by the participant in accordance with paragraph (a)(2) of this section. An amount is treated as included in income for a taxable year only to the extent that the amount was properly includible in income and the participant actually included the amount in income (including on an original or amended federal income tax return or as a result of an IRS examination or a final decision of a court of competent jurisdiction).

(b) *Exceptions.*—(1) *In general.*—Section 457(f)(1) and paragraph (a) of this section do not apply to a plan or a portion of a plan described in this paragraph (b). The determination of whether a plan or a portion of a plan is described in this paragraph (b) is made as of the date on which the legally binding right to an amount arises. However, a plan or portion of a plan will cease to be a plan that is described in this paragraph (b) on the first date that it no longer meets the requirements described in this paragraph (b).

(2) *Certain retirement plans.*—Annuity plans and contracts described in section 403 and plans described in section 401(a) are not subject to the provisions of section 457(f)(1) and paragraph (a) of this section.

(3) *Section 402(b) trusts.*—(i) *Section 402(b).*—The portion of a plan that consists of a trust to which section 402(b) applies is not subject to the provisions of section 457(f)(1) and paragraph (a) of this section.

(ii) *Example.*—The provisions of this paragraph (b)(3) are illustrated in the following example:

Example. (i) *Facts.* On October 1, 2017, an eligible employer establishes an ineligible plan covering only one participant (a highly compensated employee under section 414(q)) under which the participant obtains an unconditional right to be paid $150,000 (plus interest at a specified reasonable rate) on October 1, 2021. As part of the plan, the employer simultaneously establishes a trust described in section 402(b) in the United States for the sole benefit of the participant. Under the terms of the plan and trust, the assets of the trust are also payable to the participant on October 1, 2021, and the amount that the employer is otherwise obligated to pay under the plan will be reduced (offset) by the amount paid to the participant from the trust. Section 402(b)(4) applies to the trust, and the trust has assets of $98,000 on October 1, 2017 and $100,000 on December 31, 2017.

(ii) *Conclusion.* Section 457(f) and this section apply only to the portion of the plan that is not funded through the section 402(b) trust. Thus, the participant has income under section 457(f) equal to the present value of the portion of the compensation deferred under the plan that is not funded through the section 402(b) trust on the date on which there is a legally binding right to the compensation (October 1, 2017). This present value is equal to $52,000 ($150,000 - $98,000), which is included in the participant's gross income on October 1, 2017. The participant must also include $100,000 in gross income on December 31, 2017 pursuant to section 402(b)(4)(A).

(4) *Qualified governmental excess benefit arrangements under section 415(m).*—A qualified governmental excess benefit arrangement described in section 415(m) is not subject to the provisions of section 457(f)(1) and paragraph (a) of this section.

(5) *Nonqualified annuities under section 403(c).*—(i) *Section 403(c) annuities.*—The portion of a plan in which premiums are paid by an employer for an annuity contract to which section 403(c) applies is not subject to the provisions of section 457(f)(1) and paragraph (a) of this section.

(ii) *Examples.*—The provisions of this paragraph (b)(5) are illustrated by the following examples:

Example 1. (i) *Facts.* A tax-exempt entity pays a premium for an annuity contract (described in section 403(c)) for the benefit of a participant. The annuity contract has a value of $135,000, and the participant is substantially vested (as defined in § 1.83-3(b)) at the time the premium is paid. The participant includes the full value ($135,000) in income under section 403(c) in the year the employer pays the premium.

(ii) *Conclusion.* Although the participant has a legally binding right to payments under the annuity contract that will be made in a subsequent taxable year, the participant's interest in the annuity contract is not subject to section 457(f)(1) and paragraph (a) of this section.

Example 2. (i) *Facts.* The facts are the same as in *Example 1 of this paragraph (b)(5)*, except the participant's rights in the annuity contract are not substantially vested (as defined in § 1.83-3(b)) at the time the premium is paid and do not become substantially vested until a future taxable year. The participant does not include the full value of the contract in income under section 403(c) in the year the employer pays the premium.

(ii) *Conclusion.* Neither the payment of the premium nor the participant's interest in the annuity contract is subject to section 457(f)(1) or paragraph (a) of this section.

(6) *Transfer of property under section 83.*—(i) *Section 83.*—The portion of a plan that consists of a transfer of property to which section 83 applies is not subject to the provisions of section 457(f)(1) and paragraph (a) of this section. Specifically, section 457(f)(1) and paragraph (a) of this section do not apply if, on or before the first date on which compensation deferred under a plan is not subject to a substantial risk of forfeiture (within the meaning of section 457(f)(3)(B) and paragraph (e) of this section), the amount is paid through a transfer of property described in section 83. However, section 457(f)(1) and paragraph (a) of this section do apply if the first date on which compensation deferred under a plan is not subject to a substantial risk of forfeiture (as defined in section 457(f)(3)(B) and paragraph (e) of this section) precedes the date on which the amount is paid through a transfer of property described in section 83. If deferred compensation payable in property is includible in gross income under section 457(f)(1)(A), then, as provided in section 72, the amount includible in gross income when that property is later transferred or

made available to the participant or beneficiary is the excess of the value of the property at that time over the amount previously included in gross income under section 457(f)(1)(A).

(ii) *Examples*.—The provisions of this paragraph (b)(6) are illustrated by the following examples:

Example 1. (i) *Facts*. On December 1, 2017, an eligible employer agrees to transfer property that is substantially vested (within the meaning of § 1.83-3(b)) and has a fair market value equal to a specified dollar amount, to a participant on January 15, 2020. The participant's rights under the agreement are not subject to a substantial risk of forfeiture (within the meaning of section 457(f)(3)(B) and paragraph (e) of this section).

(ii) *Conclusion*. Because there is no substantial risk of forfeiture (within the meaning of section 457(f)(3)(B) and paragraph (e) of this section) with respect to the agreement to transfer property in 2020, the present value of the amount on the applicable date (December 1, 2017) is includible in the participant's gross income under section 457(f)(1)(A). Under paragraph (a)(4) of this section, when the substantially vested property is transferred to the participant on January 15, 2020, the amount includible in the participant's gross income is equal to the excess of the fair market value of the property on that date over the amount that was included in gross income for 2017.

Example 2. (i) *Facts*. Under a bonus plan, an eligible employer agrees in 2021 to transfer property that is substantially nonvested (within the meaning of § 1.83-3(b)) to Participants A and B in 2023 if they are continuously employed by the eligible employer through the date of the transfer (which condition constitutes a substantial risk of forfeiture within the meaning of section 457(f)(3)(B) and paragraph (e) of this section). In 2023, the eligible employer transfers the property to Participants A and B, subject to a substantial risk of forfeiture (within the meaning of § 1.83-3(c)), that lapses in 2025. Participant A makes a timely election to include the fair market value of the property in gross income under section 83(b). Participant B does not make this election.

(ii) *Conclusion*. The compensation deferred for both Participants A and B is not subject to section 457(f)(1) or paragraph (a) of this section because section 83 applies to the transfer of property on or before the date on which the property is not subject to a substantial risk of forfeiture (within the meaning of section 457(f)(3)(B) and paragraph (e) of this section). Because of the section 83(b) election, Participant A includes the fair market value of the property (disregarding lapse restrictions) in gross income for 2023 under section 83(b)(1). Participant B includes the value of the property in gross income when the substantial risk of forfeiture lapses in 2025 under section 83(a).

(7) *Applicable employment retention plan*.—The portion of a plan that is an applicable employment retention plan as described in section 457(f)(4) with respect to any participant is not subject to the provisions of section 457(f)(1) and paragraph (a) of this section. See also section 1104(d)(4) of the Pension Protection Act of 2006, Public Law 109-280 (120 Stat. 780), regarding the application of the Internal Revenue Code and certain other laws to any plan, arrangement, or conduct to which section 457(f)(2)(F) does not apply.

(c) *Amount included in income*.—(1) *Calculation of present value*.—(i) *In general*.—Except as otherwise provided in this paragraph (c), the present value of compensation deferred under an ineligible plan as of an applicable date equals the present value of the future payments to which the participant has a legally binding right (as described in paragraph (d) of this section). For this purpose, present value is determined in accordance with the provisions of this paragraph (c)(1)(i) by multiplying the amount of a payment (or the amount of each payment in a series of payments) by the probability that any condition or conditions on which the payment is contingent will be satisfied and discounting the amount using an assumed rate of interest to reflect the time value of money.

(ii) *Actuarial assumptions*.—(A) *In general*.—*(1) Reasonable actuarial assumptions*.—For purposes of paragraph (c)(1)(i) of this section, present value is determined using actuarial assumptions and methods that, based on all of the facts and circumstances, are reasonable as of the applicable date, including an interest rate that is reasonable as of that date and other assumptions necessary to determine the present value (without regard to whether the present value of the compensation deferred under the plan is reasonably ascertainable as described in § 31.3121(v)(2)-1(e)(4)(i)(B) of this chapter).

(2) Probability of death before the payment of benefits.—For purposes of paragraph (c)(1)(i) of this section, the probability that a participant will die before a payment is made is permitted to be taken into account only to the extent that the payment is forfeitable upon death.

(3) Probability that the payment will not be made.—For purposes of paragraph (c)(1)(i) of this section, the probability that payments will not be made (or will be reduced) because of the unfunded status of a plan, the risk associated with any deemed or actual investment of compensation deferred under the plan, the risk that the eligible employer or another party will be unwilling or unable to pay, the possibility of future plan amendments, the possibility of a future change in the law, or similar risks or contingencies are not taken into account.

(B) *Payments made in foreign currency*.—The rules in § 1.409A-4(b)(2)(i) apply for purposes of determining the treatment of payments in foreign currency.

(C) *Treatment of payment triggers based upon events*.—*(1) In general*.—Except as provided in paragraph (c)(1)(ii)(C)(2) of this section, the rules in § 1.409A-4(b)(2)(vii) apply for purposes of determining the treatment of payment triggers based upon events.

(2) Treatment of severance from employment.—If the date on which a payment will be made depends on the date the participant has a severance from employment (as described in § 1.457-6(b)) and the participant has not had a severance from employment by the applicable date, then for purposes of paragraph (c)(1)(ii)(A)(*1*) of this section, the severance from employment may be treated as occurring on any date that is not later than the fifth anniversary of the applicable date, unless this assumption

would be unreasonable under the facts and circumstances.

(iii) *Unreasonable assumptions.*—If any actuarial assumption or method used to determine the present value of compensation deferred under the plan is not reasonable, as determined by the Commissioner, then the Commissioner will determine the present value using actuarial assumptions and methods that the Commissioner determines to be reasonable, including the AFR and the applicable mortality table under section 417(e)(3)(B) as of the applicable date. For purposes of this section, *AFR* means the mid-term applicable federal rate (as defined pursuant to section 1274(d)) for January 1 of the relevant calendar year, compounded annually.

(iv) *Account balance plans.*—(A) *In general.*—To the extent benefits are provided under an account balance plan, as defined in § 31.3121(v)(2)-1(c)(1)(ii) and (iii) of this chapter, to which earnings (or losses, if applicable) are credited at least annually, the present value of compensation deferred under the plan as of an applicable date is the amount credited to the participant's account, including both the principal amount credited to the account and any earnings or losses attributable to the principal amount that have been credited to the account, as of that date.

(B) *Unreasonable rates of return.*—This paragraph (c)(1)(iv)(B) applies to an account balance plan under which the income credited is based on neither a predetermined actual investment, within the meaning of § 31.3121(v)(2)-1(d)(2)(i)(B) of this chapter, nor a rate of interest that is reasonable, within the meaning of § 31.3121(v)(2)-1(d)(2)(i)(C) of this chapter, as determined by the Commissioner. The present value of compensation deferred under that type of plan as of an applicable date is equal to the amount credited to the participant's account as of that date, plus the present value of the excess (if any) of the earnings to be credited under the plan over the earnings that would be credited through the projected payment date using a reasonable rate of interest. If the present value of compensation deferred under the plan is not determined and is not taken into account by the taxpayer in this manner, the present value of the compensation deferred under the plan will be treated as equal to the amount credited to the participant's account as of the applicable date, plus the present value of the excess (if any) of the earnings to be credited under the plan through the projected payment date over the earnings that would be credited using the AFR.

(C) *Combinations of predetermined actual investments or interest rates.*—If the amount of earnings or losses credited under an account balance plan is based on the greater of two or more rates of return (each of which would be a predetermined actual investment or a reasonable interest rate if the earnings or losses credited were based on only one of those rates of return), then the amount included in income on the applicable date is the sum of the amount credited to the participant's account as of the applicable date and the present value (determined under paragraph (c)(1)(i) of this section) of the right to future earnings.

(D) *Examples.*—The following examples illustrate the provisions of paragraphs (c)(1)(i) through (iv) of this section. For purposes of these examples, assume that the arrangements are either not subject to section 409A or 457A or otherwise comply with the requirements of those provisions, and that the parties are not under examination for any of the tax years in question.

Example 1. (i) *Facts.* On October 1, 2017, an eligible employer agrees to pay $100,000 to a participant on January 1, 2024, if the participant is alive on that date. The employer determines that the October 1, 2017 present value of that payment is $75,000 based on the second segment rate used for purposes of section 417(e)(3)(C) on October 1, 2017, and using the mortality table applicable under section 417(e)(3)(B) on October 1, 2017.

(ii) *Conclusion.* The present value has been determined in accordance with paragraph (c)(1)(i) of this section.

Example 2. (i) *Facts.* On October 1, 2018, an eligible employer agrees to pay $100,000 to a participant at severance from employment. The assumptions that the employer uses to determine the present value are that the participant will have a severance from employment on October 1, 2023 (the fifth anniversary of the date the participant obtains the right to the payment in accordance with paragraph (c)(1)(ii)(C)(2) of this section) and that the present value will be determined using a rate of 4.5% compounded monthly.

(ii) *Conclusion.* Assuming, solely for purposes of this example, that the employer's severance from employment date and interest rate assumptions are reasonable, the value included in income on the applicable date (October 1, 2018) is $79,885.

Example 3. (i) *Facts.* On October 1, 2017, an eligible employer agrees to pay $100,000 to a participant at severance from employment, but no payment will be made if the severance from employment occurs on or after October 1, 2021.

(ii) *Conclusion.* Although paragraph (c)(1)(ii)(C)(2) of this section provides that for purposes of determining when a payment will be made, severance may be treated as if it occurred on the fifth anniversary of the applicable date, that assumption would be unreasonable under these facts and circumstances and would not be permitted under paragraph (c)(1)(ii)(C)(2) of this section. Accordingly, for purposes of determining the present value, an assumption that severance from employment would occur after September 30, 2021 would be unreasonable.

Example 4. (i) *Facts.* An eligible employer maintains a supplemental executive retirement plan that provides a subsidized early retirement benefit payable to participants between age 60 and 65. A 60 year old participant becomes vested in the right to the subsidized early retirement benefit on December 31, 2017.

(ii) *Conclusion.* The assumption under paragraph (c)(1)(ii)(C)(2) of this section would not be permitted for purposes of determining the amount to be included in income because the nature of the subsidized early retirement benefit causes it to decline in value until it becomes worthless upon attainment of age 65. In other words, the value of the subsidized early retirement benefit using the assumption permitted in paragraph (c)(1)(ii)(C)(2) of this section would result in a value of $0 and would be unreasonable under the facts and circumstances.

Example 5. (i) *Facts.* On October 1, 2017, an eligible employer agrees to provide compensation to an employee for prior services in an amount equal to $100,000, plus interest at a reasonable rate, with payment to be made at the time of the employee's severance from employment. The participant's right to the compensation is not subject to a substantial risk of forfeiture at any time.

(ii) *Conclusion.* Because the agreement provides for a reasonable rate of interest, the amount included in income on the applicable date (October 1, 2017) is $100,000.

Example 6. (i) *Facts.* The facts are the same as in *Example 5* of this paragraph (c)(1)(iv)(D), except that the right is subject to a requirement that the participant continue to provide substantial services for three additional years (which constitutes a substantial risk of forfeiture as described in paragraph (e) of this section). On October 1, 2020, when the substantial risk of forfeiture lapses, the account balance is $116,147.

(ii) *Conclusion.* The amount included in income on the applicable date (October 1, 2020) is $116,147.

Example 7. (i) *Facts.* The facts are the same as in *Example 5* of this paragraph (c)(1)(iv)(D), except that the rate of interest credited on the account is 5% above a reasonable rate of interest. On October 1, 2017, the sum of the $100,000 account balance, plus the present value of the right to receive the difference between a reasonable rate of return and the rate of return being credited on the account (from October 1, 2017 until October 1, 2022) is $128,336. The participant has a severance from employment on October 16, 2020, and is paid $135,379 on that date.

(ii) *Conclusion.* The amount included in income on the applicable date (October 1, 2017) is $128,336. Pursuant to paragraph (a)(5) of this section, the $128,336 is treated as investment in the contract for purposes of section 72 and, pursuant to paragraph (a)(4) of this section, the participant recognizes an additional $7,043 ($135,379, minus the $128,336 that was previously included in gross income for 2017) in income attributable to the payment on October 16, 2020.

Example 8. (i) *Facts.* The facts are the same as in *Example 5* of this paragraph (c)(1)(iv)(D), except that the employer also agrees to pay the participant an amount that is estimated to be equal to the federal, state, and local income taxes due (based on a fixed percentage that is pre-specified in the agreement) attributable to the amount included in income on the applicable date (October 1, 2017). In exchange for that tax payment, the amount payable upon severance from employment is to be reduced by an amount equal to the federal, state, and local income taxes for the taxable year of payment that the employer estimates would otherwise have been due but for the income inclusion in 2017. In satisfaction of this obligation to make the tax payment, the employer pays the participant $66,667 on April 15, 2018.

(ii) *Conclusion.* The present value on the applicable date (October 1, 2017) is $100,000, plus the present value of the $66,667 payment to be made on April 15, 2018, minus the present value of the reduction that will be applied at the time of payment (which, if reasonable, may be assumed to be October 1, 2022 in accordance with paragraph (c)(1)(ii)(C)(*2*) of this section).

Example 9. (i) *Facts.* An eligible employer credits $100,000 on December 31, 2017, to the account of a participant under an ineligible plan, subject to the condition that the amount will be forfeited if the participant voluntarily terminates employment before December 31, 2019. The account balance will be credited with notional annual earnings based on the greater of the return of a designated S&P 500 index fund or a specified rate of interest and will be paid on December 31, 2025.

(ii) *Conclusion.* Under paragraph (c)(1)(iv)(C) of this section, the sum of the amount credited to the participant's account as of the applicable date (December 31, 2019) and the present value (determined under paragraph (c)(1)(i) of this section) of the right to future earnings based on the greater of the return of the designated S&P 500 index fund or the specified rate of interest must be included in the participant's gross income on the applicable date.

(v) *Application of the general calculation rules to formula amounts.*—With respect to a right to receive a formula amount, the amount or amounts of future payments under the plan, for purposes of determining the present value as of an applicable date, is determined based on all of the facts and circumstances existing as of that date. This determination must reflect reasonable, good faith assumptions with respect to any contingencies as to the amount of the payment, both with respect to each contingency and with respect to all contingencies in the aggregate. An assumption based on the facts and circumstances as of the applicable date may be reasonable even if the facts and circumstances change in the future so that when the amount payable is determined in a subsequent year, the amount payable is a greater (or lesser) amount. In such a case, the increase (or decrease) due to the change in the facts and circumstances is treated as earnings (or losses). For purposes of this paragraph (c)(1)(v), an amount payable is a formula amount to the extent that the amount payable in a future taxable year is dependent upon factors that, after applying the assumptions and other rules set forth in this section, are not determinable as of the applicable date, such that the amount payable may not be readily determined as of that date under the other provisions of this section. If some portion of an amount payable is not a formula amount, the amount payable with respect to such portion is determined under the rules applicable to amounts that are not formula amounts, and only the balance of the amount payable is determined under the rules applicable to formula amounts.

(vi) *Treatment of payment restrictions.*—The rules in § 1.409A-4(b)(2)(v) apply for purposes of determining the treatment of payment restrictions.

(vii) *Treatment of alternative times and forms of a future payment.*—The rules in § 1.409A-4(b)(2)(vi) apply for purposes of determining the treatment of alternative times and forms of a future payment.

(viii) *Reimbursement and in-kind benefit arrangements.*—The rules in § 1.409A-4(b)(4) apply for purposes of determining the present value of reimbursement and in-kind benefit arrangements.

(ix) *Split-dollar life insurance arrangements.*—The rules in § 1.409A-4(b)(5) apply for purposes of determining the present value of benefits provided under a split-dollar life insurance arrangement.

(2) *Forfeiture or other permanent loss of right to compensation previously included in income.*—(i) *In general.*—If a participant has included compensation under a plan in income pursuant to paragraph (a)(2) or (4) of this section, but all or a portion of that compensation is never paid under the plan, the participant is entitled to a deduction for the taxable year in which the entire remaining right to the payment of the compensation is permanently forfeited under the plan's terms or otherwise permanently lost. The deduction to which the participant is entitled equals the excess of the amounts included in income under paragraphs (a)(2) and (4) of this section with respect to the compensation over the total amount of the compensation actually received that constitutes investment in the contract under paragraph (a)(5) of this section.

(ii) *Forfeiture or permanent loss of right.*—For purposes of this paragraph (c)(2), a mere diminution in the amount payable under the plan due to a deemed investment loss, an actuarial reduction, or any other decrease in the amount deferred under the plan is not treated as a forfeiture or permanent loss of the right if the participant retains the right to any payment under the plan (whether or not such right is subject to a substantial risk of forfeiture as described in paragraph (e) of this section). In addition, an amount payable under a plan is not treated as forfeited or otherwise permanently lost if another amount or an obligation to make a payment in a future year is substituted for the original amount. However, an amount payable under a plan is treated as permanently lost if the participant's right to receive payment of the amount becomes wholly worthless during the taxable year. Whether the right to receive payment has become wholly worthless is determined based on the relevant facts and circumstances existing as of the last day of the relevant taxable year.

(iii) *Examples.*—The provisions of this paragraph (c)(2) are illustrated in the following examples:

Example 1. (i) *Facts.* On October 1, 2017, an eligible employer establishes an ineligible plan for a participant under which the employer agrees to pay the amount credited to the participant's account when the participant has a severance from employment. The obligation to make the payment is not subject to a substantial risk of forfeiture. The account balance on October 1, 2017 is $125,000, and the participant includes $125,000 in income in 2017. The plan subsequently experiences notional investment losses, and the participant receives $75,000 from the plan in a lump-sum distribution in 2024, when the participant has a severance from employment. The $75,000 lump-sum distribution represents all amounts due to the participant under the plan.

(ii) *Conclusion.* For 2024, the participant is entitled to deduct $50,000 (the excess of the amount included in income under paragraph (a)(2) of this section ($125,000) over the amount actually received that constitutes investment in the contract under paragraph (a)(5) of this section ($75,000)).

Example 2. (i) *Facts.* The facts are the same facts as in *Example 1* of this paragraph (c)(2)(iii), except that the plan provides that the participant will receive the deferred compensation in three installments (1/3 of the account balance in 2024, 1/2 of the then remaining account balance in 2025, and the remaining balance in 2026), and that the sum of all three installments is $75,000.

(ii) *Conclusion.* The participant is entitled to deduct $50,000 in the taxable year of the last installment payment (2026) ($125,000, reduced by the sum of the amounts received in 2024, 2025, and 2026 ($75,000)).

(d) *Definition of deferral of compensation.*—(1) *In general.*—(i) *Legally binding right.*—A plan provides for the deferral of compensation with respect to a participant for purposes of section 457(f) and this section if, under the terms of the plan and the relevant facts and circumstances, the participant has a legally binding right during a calendar year to compensation that, pursuant to the terms of the plan, is or may be payable to (or on behalf of) the participant in a later calendar year. Whether a plan provides for the deferral of compensation for purposes of section 457(f) and this section is determined based on the relevant facts and circumstances at the time that the participant obtains a legally binding right to the compensation, or, if later, when a plan is amended to convert a right that does not provide for a deferral of compensation into a right that does provide for a deferral of compensation. For example, if a plan providing for retiree health care does not initially provide for a deferral of compensation but is later amended to provide the ability to receive future cash payments instead of health benefits, it may become a plan that provides for the deferral of compensation at the time of the amendment. An amount of compensation deferred under a plan that provides for the deferral of compensation within the meaning of section 457(f) and this section does not cease to be an amount subject to section 457(f) and this section by reason of any change to the plan that would otherwise recharacterize the right to the amount as a right that does not provide for the deferral of compensation with respect to such amount. In addition, any change under the plan that results in an exchange of an amount deferred under the plan for some other right or benefit that would otherwise be excluded from the participant's gross income does not affect the characterization of the plan as one that provides for a deferral of compensation.

(ii) *Discretion to reduce or eliminate compensation.*—A participant does not have a legally binding right to compensation to the extent that the compensation may be reduced or eliminated unilaterally by the employer or another person after the services creating the right to the compensation have been performed. However, if the facts and circumstances indicate that the discretion to reduce or eliminate the compensation is available or exercisable only upon a condition, or the discretion to reduce or eliminate the compensation lacks substantive significance, a participant is considered to have a legally binding right to the compensation. Whether the discretion to reduce or eliminate compensation lacks substantive significance depends on all the relevant facts and circumstances. However, if the participant to whom the compensation may be paid has effective control of the person retaining the discretion to reduce or eliminate the compensation, or has effective control over any portion of the compensation of the person retaining the discretion to reduce or eliminate the compensation, or is a member of the family (as defined in section 267(c)(4) but also including the spouse of any member of the family) of the person retaining the discretion to reduce or eliminate the compensation, the discretion to reduce or eliminate the compensation is not treated as having substantive significance. Compensation is not considered subject to unilateral reduction or elimination merely because it may be reduced or eliminated by operation of the objective terms of the plan, such as the application of a nondiscretionary, objective provision creating a substantial risk of forfeiture or the application of a formula that provides for benefits to be offset by benefits provided under another plan (such as a plan that is qualified under section 401(a)).

(2) *Short-term deferrals.*—For purposes of section 457(f) and this section, a deferral of compensation does not occur under a plan with respect to any payment for which a deferral of compensation does not occur under section 409A pursuant to § 1.409A-1(b)(4) (short-term deferrals), except that, for purposes of this paragraph, in applying the rules provided in § 1.409A-1(b)(4) the meaning of *substantial risk of forfeiture* under § 1.457-12(e) applies in each place that term is used (and not the meaning of *substantial risk of forfeiture* provided under § 1.409A-1(d)).

(3) *Recurring part-year compensation.*—For purposes of section 457(f) and this section and notwithstanding paragraph (d)(2) of this section, a deferral of compensation does not occur under a plan with respect to an amount that is recurring part-year compensation (as defined in § 1.409A-2(a)(14)), if the plan does not defer payment of any of the recurring part-year compensation to a date beyond the last day of the 13th month following the first day of the service period for which the recurring part-year compensation is paid, and the amount of the recurring part-year compensation does not exceed the annual compensation limit under section 401(a)(17) for the calendar year in which the service period commences.

(4) *Certain other exceptions.*—For purposes of section 457(f) and this section, a deferral of compensation does not occur to the extent that a plan provides for:

(i) The payment of expense reimbursements, medical benefits, or in-kind benefits, as described in § 1.409A-1(b)(9)(v)(A), (B), or (C);

(ii) Certain indemnification rights, liability insurance, or legal settlements, as described in § 1.409A-1(b)(10), or (11); or

(iii) Taxable educational benefits for an employee (which, for this purpose, means solely benefits consisting of educational assistance, as defined in section 127(c)(1) and the regulations thereunder, attributable to the education of an employee, and does not include any benefits provided for the education of any other person, including any spouse, child, or other family member of the employee).

(5) *Interaction with section 409A.*—(i) *In general.*—The rules of section 457(f) apply to an ineligible plan separately and in addition to any requirements applicable to the plan under section 409A.

(ii) *Acceleration of the time or schedule of a payment.*—Although section 457(f) and this section do not preclude the acceleration of payments, see § 1.409A-3(a) for the general rules and exceptions relating to the acceleration of payments that are subject to section 409A.

(iii) *Example.*—The provisions of this paragraph (d)(5) are illustrated in the following example:

Example. (i) *Facts.* On December 1, 2017, an eligible employer establishes an account balance plan for an employee that is subject to section 457(f), under which an initial amount is credited to the account and is increased periodically by earnings based on a reasonable specified rate of interest. The entire account balance is subject to a substantial risk of forfeiture until December 1, 2021. Under the terms of the plan, the account balance will be paid in three annual installments on each January 15, beginning in 2024 (one third of the balance for the first installment, one half of the then remaining balance for the second installment, and the remaining balance for the third installment). However, in 2022, the plan is amended to provide for payments to begin in 2023, such that the plan fails to comply with the requirements of section 409A during 2022. The account balance is: $100,000 on December 1, 2021; $118,000 on December 31, 2022; $120,000 on January 15, 2023 (so that the payment made that day is $40,000 ($120,000/3)); $88,000 on January 15, 2024 (so that the payment made that day is $44,000 ($88,000/2)); and $50,000 on January 15, 2025 (so that the payment made that day is $50,000).

(ii) *Conclusion: Federal income tax treatment in 2021.* The plan provides for a deferral of compensation to which section 457(f) applies. Under section 457(f) and paragraph (a)(2) of this section, the $100,000 amount of the account balance on December 1, 2021, when the benefits cease to be subject to a substantial risk of forfeiture, is included in the employee's gross income on that date.

(iii) *Conclusion: Federal income tax treatment after 2021—(1) Treatment in 2022 under section 409A.* Because the arrangement fails to meet the requirements of section 409A in 2022, the employee has gross income under section 409A equal to the account balance on December 31, 2022, reduced by the amount previously included in income. Accordingly, the amount included in gross income under section 409A is equal to $18,000 (the $118,000 account balance on December 31, 2022, reduced by the $100,000 previously included in income under section 457(f) for 2021). The amount included in gross income under section 409A is subject to an additional 20 percent tax under section 409A(a)(1)(B)(i)(II) and a premium interest tax under section 409A(a)(1)(B)(i)(I).

(2) *Federal income tax treatment of first installment payment in 2023—(i) Earnings previously included under section 409A.* The first $18,000 of the $40,000 payment in 2023 is excluded from gross income under section 409A as a result of the earlier inclusion of that amount in income in

2022 due to the section 409A violation. See §1.409A-4(f).

(*ii*) *Deferral of compensation under section 457(f)*. The amount of the investment in the contract (described in paragraph (a)(5) of this section) allocated to the remaining $22,000 of the installment paid in 2023 is $33,333 ($100,000/3), so no amount is included in gross income for 2023.

(*3*) *Federal income tax treatment of second installment payment in 2024*. The employee has unused investment in the contract from 2023 in the amount of $11,333 ($33,333 - $22,000). Assuming that the employee elects to redetermine the amount recognized for the current and subsequent years in 2024 pursuant to §1.72-4(d)(3)(ii), the amount included in gross income for 2024 is $5,000 (the payment of $44,000, reduced by the portion of the remaining investment in the contract that is allocable to the installment, which is $39,000 (($100,000 – $22,000)/2)).

(*4*) *Federal income tax treatment of third installment payment in 2025*. The amount included in gross income for 2025 is $11,000 (the payment of $50,000, reduced by the remaining investment in the contract of $39,000).

(e) *Rules relating to substantial risk of forfeiture*.—(1) *Substantial risk of forfeiture*.—(i) *In general*.—An amount of compensation is subject to a substantial risk of forfeiture only if entitlement to the amount is conditioned on the future performance of substantial services, or upon the occurrence of a condition that is related to a purpose of the compensation if the possibility of forfeiture is substantial. An amount is not subject to a substantial risk of forfeiture if the facts and circumstances demonstrate that the forfeiture condition is unlikely to be enforced (see paragraph (e)(1)(v) of this section). If a plan provides that entitlement to an amount is conditioned on involuntary severance from employment without cause (which includes, for this purpose, a voluntary severance from employment that is treated as involuntary under §1.457-11(d)(2)(ii)), the right is subject to a substantial risk of forfeiture if the possibility of forfeiture is substantial.

(ii) *Substantial future services*.—For purposes of paragraph (e)(1)(i) of this section, the determination of whether an amount of compensation is conditioned on the future performance of substantial services is based on the relevant facts and circumstances, such as whether the hours required to be performed during the relevant period are substantial in relation to the amount of compensation.

(iii) *Condition related to a purpose of the compensation*.—For purposes of paragraph (e)(1)(i) of this section, a condition related to a purpose of the compensation must relate to the participant's performance of services for the employer or to the employer's governmental or tax-exempt activities (as applicable) or organizational goals.

(iv) *Noncompetition conditions*.—For purposes of paragraph (e)(1)(i) of this section, an amount of compensation will not be treated as subject to a substantial risk of forfeiture merely because the right to payment of the amount is conditioned, directly or indirectly, upon the employee refraining from the future performance of certain services, unless each of the of the following conditions is satisfied:

(A) The right to payment of the amount is expressly conditioned upon the employee refraining from the future performance of services pursuant to an enforceable written agreement.

(B) The employer makes reasonable ongoing efforts to verify compliance with noncompetition agreements (including the noncompetition agreement applicable to the employee).

(C) At the time that the enforceable written agreement becomes binding, the facts and circumstances demonstrate that the employer has a substantial and bona fide interest in preventing the employee from performing the prohibited services and that the employee has bona fide interest in, and ability to, engage in the prohibited competition. Factors taken into account for this purpose include the employer's ability to show significant adverse economic consequences that would likely result from the prohibited services; the marketability of the employee based on specialized skills, reputation, or other factors; and the employee's interest, financial need, and ability to engage in the prohibited services.

(v) *Enforcement of forfeiture condition*.—To constitute a substantial risk of forfeiture, the possibility of actual forfeiture in the event that the forfeiture condition occurs must be substantial based on the relevant facts and circumstances. Factors to be considered for this purpose include, but are not limited to, the extent to which the employer has enforced forfeiture conditions in the past, the level of control or influence of the employee with respect to the organization and the individual(s) who would be responsible for enforcing the forfeiture condition, and the likelihood that such provisions would be enforceable under applicable law.

(2) *Addition or extension of risk of forfeiture*.—(i) *General rule*.—The initial addition or extension of any risk of forfeiture after a legally binding right to compensation arises, including the application of a risk of forfeiture to a plan providing for deferrals of current compensation (an additional or extended risk of forfeiture), will be disregarded unless the plan meets the requirements of paragraphs (e)(2)(ii) through (v) of this section.

(ii) *Benefit must be materially greater*.—A deferred amount will not be subject to a substantial risk of forfeiture for purposes of section 457 and this section after the date on which an employee could have received the amount, unless the present value of the amount made subject to the additional or extended substantial risk of forfeiture (disregarding the risk of forfeiture in determining the present value of the amount) is materially greater than the present value of the amount the employee otherwise would have received absent the initial or extended risk of forfeiture. For purposes of this paragraph (e)(2)(ii), present value is determined in accordance with the rules described in paragraph (c) of this section as of the applicable date for the amount the employee otherwise would have received absent the initial or extended risk of forfeiture. In addition, an amount is materially greater for purposes of this paragraph (e)(2)(ii) only if the present value of the amount subject to the additional or extended substantial risk of forfeiture is more than 125 percent of the present value of the amount that the employee would have received absent the additional or extended risk of forfeiture. For this purpose, compensation that the participant would receive for continuing to perform services, regardless of whether the deferred amount is subjected to an additional or extended substantial risk of forfeiture, is not taken into account.

(iii) *Minimum two years of substantial future services*.—The employee must be required to perform substantial services in the future, or refrain from competing pursuant to an agreement that meets the requirements of paragraph (e)(1)(iv) of this section, for a minimum of two years after the date that the employee could have received the compensation in the absence of the additional or extended substantial risk of forfeiture. For example, if an employee elects to defer a fixed percentage from each semi-monthly payroll, the two year minimum applies to each semi-monthly payroll amount that would otherwise have been paid. Notwithstanding the two year minimum, a plan may provide that that the substantial future service condition will lapse upon death, disability, or involuntary severance from employment without cause.

(iv) *Timing*.—The parties must agree in writing to any addition or extension of a substantial risk of forfeiture under this paragraph (e)(2). In the case of an initial addition of a substantial risk of forfeiture if none previously existed (for example, in the case of a deferral of current compensation), this written agreement must be entered into before the beginning of the calendar year in which any services that give rise to the compensation are performed, and, in the case of an extension of a substantial risk of forfeiture, the written agreement must be entered into at least 90 days before an existing substantial risk of forfeiture would have lapsed. If an employee with respect to whom compensation is made subject to an initial or extended substantial risk of forfeiture was not providing services to the employer at least 90 days before the addition or extension, the addition or extension may be agreed to in writing within 30 days after commencement of employment but only with respect to amounts attributable to services rendered after the addition or extension is agreed to in writing.

(v) *Substitutions*.—For purposes of paragraph (e)(2) of this section, if an amount is forfeited or relinquished and replaced, in whole or part, with a right to another amount (or benefit) that is a substitute for the amount that was forfeited or relinquished and that is subject to a risk of forfeiture, the risk of forfeiture will be disregarded unless the requirements of paragraphs (e)(2)(ii) through (iv) of this section are satisfied.

(3) *Examples*.—The provisions of this paragraph (e) are illustrated in the following examples:

Example 1. (i) *Facts*. On January 15, 2017, an employee has a severance from employment with an eligible employer and enters into an agreement with the eligible employer under which the eligible employer agrees to pay the employee $250,000 on January 15, 2018, if the employee provides consulting services to the employer until that date. The consulting services required are insubstantial in relation to the payment. The employee provides the required consulting services for the employer through January 15, 2018.

(ii) *Conclusion*. The consulting services provided by the former employee do not constitute substantial services because they are insubstantial in relation to the payment. Accordingly, the present value of $250,000 payable on January 15, 2018 is includible in the employee's gross income on January 15, 2017.

Example 2. (i) *Facts*. On January 27, 2020, an eligible employer agrees to pay an employee an amount equal to $120,000 on January 1, 2023, provided that the employee continues to provide substantial services to the employer through that date. In 2021, the parties enter into a written agreement to extend the date through which substantial services must be performed to January 1, 2025, in which event, the employer will pay an amount that has a present value of $145,000 on January 1, 2023.

(ii) *Conclusion*. As of the date the initial risk of forfeiture would have lapsed, the present value of the compensation subject to the extended substantial risk of forfeiture is not materially greater than the present value of the amount previously deferred under the plan ($145,000 is not more than 125% of $120,000) and, therefore, the intended extension of the substantial risk of forfeiture is disregarded under the provisions of paragraph (e)(2) of this section. Accordingly, the employee will recognize income, on the applicable date (January 1, 2023) in an amount equal to $120,000 (the amount that is not subject to a substantial risk of forfeiture on that date, disregarding the intended extension). With respect to the amount that is ultimately paid under the plan on January 1, 2025, the employee is treated as having investment in the contract of $120,000 (pursuant to paragraph (a)(5) of this section).

Example 3. (i) *Facts*. On December 31, 2017, a participant enters into an agreement to defer $15,000 of the participant's current compensation that would otherwise be paid during 2018, with payment of the deferred amounts to be made on December 31, 2024, but only if the participant continues to provide substantial services until December 31, 2024. Under the terms of the agreement, the participant's periodic payments of current compensation are reduced, and a corresponding amount is credited (with a 30% employer match) to an account earning a reasonable rate of interest. The present value of the amount payable on December 31, 2024 is 130% of the present value of the amount deferred.

(ii) *Conclusion*. The amounts deferred are subject to a substantial risk of forfeiture because the plan satisfies the requirements of paragraphs (e)(2)(ii) through (v) of this section.

Example 4. (i) *Facts*. Employee A is a well-known college sports coach with a long history of success in a sports program at University X. University X reasonably expects that the loss of Employee A would be substantially detrimental to its sports program and would result in significant financial losses. Employee A has bona fide interest in continuing to work as a college sports coach and is highly marketable. On June 1, 2020, Employee A and University X enter into a written agreement under which Employee A agrees to provide substantial services to University X until June 1, 2023. The parties further agree that University X will pay $500,000 to Employee A on June 1, 2025 if Employee A has not performed services as a sports coach before that date for any other college or university with a sports program similar to that of University X. The agreement is enforceable under applicable law and University X would be reasonably expected to enforce it.

(ii) *Conclusion*. The $500,000 payable under the agreement is subject to a substantial risk of forfeiture until June 1, 2025, and includible in Employee A's gross income on that date

Pars. 9 and 12. Redesignate §1.457-12 as §1.457-13 and revise newly-redesignated §1.457-13 to read as follows:

§1.457-13. Applicability dates.—(a) *General applicability date.*—Except as otherwise provided in paragraph (b) of this section, §§1.457-1 through 1.457-12 apply to compensation deferred under a plan for calendar years beginning after the date of publication of the Treasury decision adopting these rules as final regulations in the **Federal Register,** including deferred amounts to which the legally binding right arose during prior calendar years that were not previously included in income during one or more prior calendar years.

(b) *Special applicability dates.*—(1) *Plans maintained pursuant to collective bargaining agreements.*—In the case of a plan maintained pursuant to one or more collective bargaining agreements that have been ratified and are in effect on the date of publication of the Treasury decision adopting these rules as final regulations in the **Federal Register**, these regulations will not apply with respect to compensation deferred under the plan before the earlier of:

(i) The date on which the last of the collective bargaining agreements terminates (determined without regard to any extension thereof after the date of publication of the Treasury decision adopting these rules as final regulations in the **Federal Register**); or

(ii) The first day of the third calendar year beginning after the date of publication of the Treasury decision adopting these rules as final regulations in the **Federal Register**.

(2) *Governmental plans.*—If legislation is required to amend a governmental plan, these regulations will not apply to compensation deferred under that plan in taxable years ending before the day following the end of the second legislative session of the legislative body with the authority to amend the plan that begins after the date of publication of the Treasury decision adopting these rules as final regulations in the **Federal Register**.

Long-Term Contracts: Home Construction Contracts: Rules

Long-Term Contracts: Home Construction Contracts: Rules.—Amendments to Reg. §§1.460-3, 1.460-4, 1.460-5 and 1.460-6, regarding accounting for certain long-term construction contracts that qualify as home construction contracts, are proposed (published in the Federal Register on August 4, 2008) (REG-120844-07).

Par. 2. Section 1.460-3 is amended by:

1. Revising paragraph (b)(1)(ii).

2. Redesignating paragraphs (b)(2)(ii), (b)(2)(iii) and (b)(2)(iv) as paragraphs (b)(2)(iii), (b)(2)(iv) and (b)(2)(v), respectively, and revising them.

3. Adding a new paragraph (b)(2)(ii).

The revisions and addition read as follows:

§1.460-3. Long-term construction contracts.

* * *

(b) * * *

(1) * * *

(ii) Construction contract, other than a home construction contract, that a taxpayer estimates (when entering into the contract) will be completed within 2 years of the contract commencement date, provided the taxpayer satisfies the $10,000,000 gross receipts test described in paragraph (b)(3) of this section.

(2) * * *

(ii) *Land improvements.*—For purposes of paragraph (b)(2)(i)(B) of this section, improvements to real property directly related to, and located on the site of, the dwelling units consist of improvements to land on which dwelling units (as described in paragraph (b)(2)(i)(A) of this section) are constructed, and common improvements as defined in paragraph (b)(2)(iv) of this section. A long-term construction contract is a home construction contract if a taxpayer (including a subcontractor working for a general contractor) meets the 80% test in paragraph (b)(2)(i) of this section as applied to either paragraph (b)(2)(i)(A) of this section or paragraph (b)(2)(i)(B) of this section, or both paragraphs (b)(2)(i)(A) and (b)(2)(i)(B) of this section, collectively.

(iii) *Townhouses and rowhouses.*—For purposes of determining whether a long-term construction contract is a home construction contract under paragraph (b)(2) of this section, each townhouse or rowhouse is a separate building. For this purpose, the term townhouse and rowhouse includes an individual condominium unit.

(iv) *Common improvements.*—(A) *In general.*—A taxpayer includes in the cost of a dwelling unit or land its allocable share of the cost that the taxpayer incurs for any common improvements that benefit the dwelling unit or land.

(B) *Definition.*—For purposes of this section, a *common improvement* is an improvement that the taxpayer is contractually obligated, or required by law, to construct within the tract or tracts of land containing the dwelling units (or the land on which dwelling units are to be constructed) and that benefits the dwelling units (or the land on which dwelling units are to be constructed). In general, a common improvement does not solely benefit any particular dwelling unit or any particular lot on which a dwelling unit is constructed. However, land clearing and grading are common improvements, even when performed on a particular lot. Other examples of common improvements are sidewalks, sewers, roads and clubhouses.

(v) *Mixed use costs.*—If a contract involves the construction of both commercial units and dwelling units, a taxpayer must allocate the costs among the commercial units and dwelling units using a reasonable method or combination of reasonable methods. In general, the reasonableness of an allocation method will be based on facts and circumstances. Examples of methods that may be reasonable are specific identification, square footage, or fair market value.

* * *

Par. 3. Section 1.460-4 is amended by:

1. Revising the third sentence in paragraph (c)(1).

2. Redesignating paragraph (g) as paragraph (g)(1) and revising newly redesignated paragraph (g)(1).

3. Adding a paragraph (g)(2).

4. Revising *Example 5.* of paragraph (h).

The revisions and additions read as follows:

§1.460-4. Methods of accounting for long-term contracts.

* * *

(c) * * *

(1) * * * Permissible exempt contract methods are the PCM, the EPCM described in paragraph (c)(2) of this section, the CCM described in paragraph (d) of this section, the accrual method, and any other permissible method. * * *

* * *

(g) *Method of accounting.*—(1) *In general.*—A taxpayer must apply its method(s) of accounting for long-term contracts consistently for all similarly classified long-term contracts until the taxpayer obtains the Commissioner's consent under section 446(e) to change to another method of accounting.

(2) *Taxpayer-initiated change in method of accounting.*—(i) *Change to PCM for long-term contracts for which PCM is required.*—A taxpayer-initiated change in method of accounting for long-term contracts (or portion thereof) for which income must be determined using the PCM described in paragraph (b) of this section and the costs allocation rules described in §1.460-5(b) or (c) (required PCM contracts) from a method of accounting that does not comply with paragraph (b) of this section and §1.460-5(b) or (c) to a method that complies with paragraph (b) of this section and §1.460-5(b) or (c) must be applied to all required PCM contracts entered into before the year of change and not reported as completed as of the beginning of the year of change. Accordingly, a section 481(a) adjustment will be required.

(ii) *Change from a permissible PCM method to another permissible PCM method for long-term contracts for which PCM is required.*—A taxpayer initiated change in method of accounting for required PCM contracts, as defined in paragraph (g)(2)(i) of this section (or a portion thereof), from a method of accounting that complies with paragraph (b) of this section and §1.460-5(b) or (c) to another method of accounting that complies with paragraph (b) of this section and §1.460-5(b) or (c) must be made on a cut-off basis and applied only to contracts entered into during and after the year of change. Accordingly, a section 481(a) adjustment will be neither permitted nor required.

(iii) *Change to an exempt contract method for home construction contracts.*—A taxpayer-initiated change in method of accounting for home construction contracts, as defined in §1.460-3(b)(2), to a permissible exempt contract method, as described in paragraph (c)(1) of this section, must be applied to all home construction contracts entered into before the year of change and not reported as completed as of the beginning of the year of change. Accordingly, a section 481(a) adjustment will be required.

(iv) *Change to an exempt contract method for exempt contracts other than home construction contracts.*—A taxpayer-initiated change in method of accounting for long-term contracts (or portion thereof) not described in paragraphs (g)(2)(i), (ii) and (iii) of this section to a permissible exempt contract method as described in paragraph (c)(1) of this section must be applied to all contracts that are eligible to use the exempt contract method entered into before the year of change and not reported as completed as of the beginning of the year of change. Accordingly, a section 481(a) adjustment will be required.

(h) * * *

* * *

Example 5. PCM—contract terminated. C, whose taxable year ends December 31, determines the income from long-term contracts using the PCM. During 2001, C buys land and begins constructing a building that will contain 50 apartment units on that land. C enters into a contract to sell the building to B for $2,400,000. B gives C a $50,000 deposit toward the purchase price. By the end of 2001, C has incurred $500,000 of allocable contract costs on the building and estimates that the total allocable contract costs on the building will be $1,500,000. Thus, for 2001, C reports gross receipts of $800,000 ($500,000 / $1,500,000 × $2,400,000), current-year costs of $500,000, and gross income of $300,000 ($800,000 − $500,000). In 2002, after C has incurred an additional $250,000 of allocable contract costs on the building, B files for bankruptcy protection and defaults on the contract with C, who is permitted to keep B's $50,000 deposit as liquidated damages. In 2002, C reverses the transaction with B under paragraph (b)(7) of this section and reports a loss of $300,000 ($500,000 − $800,000). In addition, C obtains an adjusted basis in the building sold to B of $700,000 ($500,000 (current-year costs deducted in 2001) − $50,000 (B's forfeited deposit) + $250,000 (current-year costs incurred in 2002). C may not apply the look-back method to this contract in 2002.

* * *

Par. 4. Section 1.460-5 is amended by:

1. Adding a new sentence to the end of paragraph (c)(2).
2. Revising paragraph (g).

The revision and addition read as follows:

§1.460-5. Cost allocation rules.

* * *

(c) * * *

(2) * * * Further, this election is not available if a taxpayer is changing from a cost allocation method other than as prescribed in paragraph (b) of this section, in which case the taxpayer must follow the procedures under §1.446-1(e) for obtaining the Commissioner's consent for the change in method of accounting.

* * *

(g) *Method of accounting*.—A taxpayer that adopts, elects, or otherwise changes to a cost allocation method of accounting (or changes to another cost allocation method of accounting with the Commissioner's consent) must apply that method consistently for all similarly classified contracts, until the taxpayer obtains the Commissioner's consent under section 446 to change to another cost allocation method. A taxpayer-initiated change in cost allocation method from a method that does not comply with the cost allocation rules of this section to a method that complies with the cost allocation rules of this section must be applied to all long-term contracts to which the rules of this section apply, including contracts entered into before the year of change and not reported as completed as of the beginning of the year of change. Accordingly, a section 481(a) adjustment is required. Any other taxpayer-initiated change in cost allocation method to a method permitted under the rules of this section must be made on a cut-off basis and applied only to contracts entered into during and after the year of change, in which case a section 481(a) adjustment will be neither permitted nor required.

Par. 5. Section 1.460-6 is amended by:

1. Adding paragraph (c)(3)(vii).
2. Redesignating paragraph (d)(2)(iv) as paragraph (d)(2)(v).
3. Adding a new paragraph (d)(2)(iv).

The additions and revision read as follows:

§1.460-6. Look-back method.

* * *

(c) * * *

(3) * * *

(vii) *Section 481(a) adjustments*.—For purposes of determining the hypothetical underpayment or overpayment of tax for any year, amounts reported as section 481(a) adjustments shall be taken into account in the tax year or years they are reported. However, any portion of a section 481(a) adjustment not yet reported as of the tax year in which the contract is completed shall be taken into account in the tax year the contract is completed for purposes of determining the hypothetical underpayment or overpayment of tax.

* * *

(d) * * *

(2) * * *

(iv) *Section 481(a) adjustments*.—For purposes of determining the hypothetical underpayment or overpayment of tax for any year under the simplified marginal impact method, amounts reported as section 481(a) adjustments shall be taken into account in the tax year or years they are reported. However, any portion of a section 481(a) adjustment not yet reported as of the tax year in which the contract is completed shall be taken into account in the tax year the contract is completed for purposes of determining the hypothetical underpayment or overpayment of tax.

* * *

Deduction Limited to Amount at Risk

Deduction Limited to Amount at Risk.—Reproduced below are the texts of proposed Reg. §§1.465-1—1.465-7, 1.465-9—1.465-13 and 1.465-22—1.465-26, relating to the determination of amounts at risk with respect to certain activities (published in the Federal Register on June 5, 1979). Proposed Reg. §§1.465-8 and 1.465-20 were adopted by T.D. 9124 on April 30, 2004.

§1.465-1. General rules; limitation of deductions to amount at risk.—(a) *In general*.—For taxable years beginning after December 31, 1975, section 465 generally limits the amount of any loss described in section 465(d) that is otherwise deductible in connection with an activity described in section 465(c)(1). Under section 465 the amount of the loss is allowed as a deduction only to the extent that the taxpayer is at risk with respect to the activity at the close of the taxable year. The determination of the amount the taxpayer is at risk in cases where the activity is engaged in by an entity separate from the taxpayer is made as of the close of the taxable year of the entity engaging in the activity (for example, a partnership). For the purposes of these regulations, in cases where the activity is engaged in by an entity separate from the taxpayer references to a taxable year shall apply to the taxable year of the entity unless otherwise stated. For rules determining the amount at risk and for more specific rules regarding the effective dates, see §§1.465-20 through 1.465-25 and 1.465-95.

(b) *Substance over form*.—In applying section 465 and these regulations, substance will prevail over form. Regardless of the form a transaction may take, the taxpayer's amount at risk will not be increased if the transaction is inconsistent with normal commercial practices or is, in essence, a device to avoid section 465. See §1.465-4 for rules regarding attempts to avoid the at risk provisions.

(c) *Activities*.—See sections 465(c)(1)(A) through (D) and §§1.465-42 through 1.465-45 for the activities to which section 465 applies for taxable years beginning generally after December 31, 1975. These activities are holding, producing, or distributing movies and video tapes, farming, leasing of personal property, and exploring for or exploiting oil and gas resources. See section 465(c)(3) and section 465(c)(1)(E) for additional activities to which section 465 applies for taxable years beginning generally after December 31, 1978.

(d) *Taxpayers affected by at risk provisions.*—(1) For taxable years beginning generally after December 31, 1975, section 465 applies to all noncorporate taxpayers, to electing small business corporations (as defined in section 1371(b)), and to personal holding companies (as defined in section 542). For special rules relating to electing small business corporations, see § 1.465-10.

(2) See section 465(a)(1)(C) for additional taxpayers to whom section 465 applies for taxable years beginning generally after December 31, 1978.

(e) *Basis.*—The provisions of section 465 and the regulations thereunder are only intended to limit the extent to which certain losses in connection with covered activities may be deducted in a given year by a taxpayer. Section 465 does not apply for other purposes, such as determining adjusted basis. Thus, for example, the adjusted basis of a partner in a partnership interest is not affected by section 465. [Reg. § 1.465-1.]

§ 1.465-2. General rules; allowance of deductions.—(a) *In general.*—In any taxable year, there are two ways in which deductions allocable to an activity to which section 465 applies will be allowable under section 465. First, deductions allocable to an activity and otherwise allowable will be allowable in a taxable year to the extent of income received or accrued from the activity in that taxable year. See the example at § 1.465-11(c)(2). Thus, to the extent there is income from the activity in a taxable year, deductions allocable to that activity will be allowable without regard to the amount at risk. Second, losses from the activity (that is, the excess of deductions allocable to the activity over the income received or accrued from the activity) will be allowable to the extent the taxpayer is at risk with respect to that activity at the close of the taxable year. See the example at § 1.465-11(a)(2). Also see §§ 1.465-11 through 1.465-13 for the definition of loss.

(b) *Carryover of loss.*—A loss which is disallowed by reason of section 465(a) shall be treated as a deduction for the succeeding taxable year with respect to the same activity to which it is allocable. In the succeeding taxable year there will again be two ways for the deduction to be allowable. There is no limit to the number of years to which a taxpayer may carry over a loss disallowed solely by reason of section 465(a). [Reg. § 1.465-2.]

§ 1.465-3. General rules; amount at risk below zero.—(a) *Loss deductions.*—The amount of loss which is allowed for a taxable year cannot reduce a taxpayer's amount at risk below zero. Otherwise allowable losses for a taxable year which exceed a taxpayer's amount at risk shall be treated in accordance with § 1.465-2.

(b) *Negative at risk.*—A taxpayer's amount at risk may be reduced below zero. For example, if a taxpayer's amount at risk in an activity is $100 and if $120 is distributed to the taxpayer from the activity, (or if a $120 recourse loan is converted to nonrecourse), the taxpayer's amount at risk is reduced to negative $20. In that event for the taxpayer to restore the amount the taxpayer is at risk in the activity to zero, the amount at risk must be increased by $20. Thus, in such a case if in the succeeding taxable year the taxpayer incurs a loss described in section 465(d) of $40, the amount at risk must be increased by $60 ($40 + $20) in order for the full $40 to be allowed under section 465.

(c) *Recapture of certain loss deductions.*—For taxable years beginning after December 31, 1978 see section 465(e) for rules relating to the recapture of certain loss deductions. [Reg. § 1.465-3.]

§ 1.465-4. General rules; rules regarding attempts to avoid the at risk provisions.—(a) *General rule.*—If a taxpayer engages in a pattern of conduct which is not within normal commercial practice or has the effect of avoiding the provisions of section 465, the taxpayer's amount at risk may be adjusted to reflect more accurately the amount which is actually at risk. For example, increases in the amount at risk occurring toward the close of a taxable year which have the effect of increasing the amount of losses which will be allowed to the taxpayer under section 465 for the taxable year will be examined closely. If, considering all the facts and circumstances, it appears that the event which increases the amount at risk at the close of the taxable year will be accompanied by an event which decreases the amount at risk after the close of the taxable year, these amounts will be disregarded in determining the amount at risk unless the taxpayer can establish—

(1) The existence of a valid business purpose for increasing and then decreasing the amount at risk; and

(2) That the increases and decreases are not a device for avoiding section 465.

(b) *Facts and circumstances.*—The facts and circumstances to be considered include—

(1) The length of time between the increase and decrease in the amount at risk;

(2) The nature of the activity and deviations from normal business practice in the conduct of that activity;

(3) The use of those amounts which increased the amount at risk toward the close of the taxable year;

(4) Contractual arrangements between parties to the activity; and

(5) The occurrence of unanticipated events which make the decrease in the amount at risk necessary. [Reg. § 1.465-4.]

§ 1.465-5. General rules; recourse liabilities which become nonrecourse upon the occurrence of an event.—In the case of liabilities which are recourse for a period of time and then after the occurrence of an event or lapse of a period of time become nonrecourse, a taxpayer shall be considered at risk during the period of recourse liability if—

(a) On the basis of all the facts and circumstances, the reasons for entering into such a borrowing arrangement are primarily business motivated and not primarily related to Federal income tax consequences; and

(b) Such a borrowing arrangement is consistent with the normal commercial practice of financing the activity for which the money is being borrowed. [Reg. § 1.465-5.]

§ 1.465-6. General rules; amounts protected against loss.—(a) *In general.*—Notwithstanding any other provision in any regulation under section 465, assets of a taxpayer (including money) contributed to an activity shall not be treated as increasing the taxpayer's amount at risk to the extent the taxpayer is protected against loss of such assets. In addition, amounts borrowed by a taxpayer shall not be considered at risk to the extent the taxpayer is protected against loss of the borrowed amount. Similarly, such amounts shall not be considered at risk if the taxpayer is protected against loss of the property pledged as security and the taxpayer is not personally liable for repayment.

(b) *Contributions from other partners.*—A partner shall not be at risk with respect to any partnership liability to the extent the partner would be entitled to contributions from other partners if the partner were called upon to pay the partnership's creditor, because to that extent the partner is protected against loss. See § 1.465-24(a)(2)(ii) for an example relating to the treatment of contributions by partners.

(c) *Contingent liabilities.*—If a taxpayer is liable for repayment of an amount borrowed only upon the occurrence of a contingency, the taxpayer shall not be considered at risk with respect to such amount if the likelihood of the contingency occurring is such that the taxpayer is effectively protected against loss. Conversely, the taxpayer will be considered at risk if the likelihood of the contingency occurring is such that the taxpayer is not effectively protected against loss, or if the protection against loss does not cover all likely possibilities. For example, a taxpayer who obtains casualty insurance or insurance protection against tort liability will not ordinarily be considered "not at risk" solely because of such hazard insurance protection.

(d) *Guarantors.*—If a taxpayer guarantees repayment of an amount borrowed by another person (primary obligor) for use in an activity, the guarantee shall not increase the taxpayer's amount at risk. If the taxpayer repays to the creditor the amount borrowed by the primary obligor, the taxpayer's amount at risk shall be increased at such time as the taxpayer has no remaining legal rights against the primary obligor.

(e) *Examples.*—The provisions of this section may be illustrated by the following examples:

Example (1). A, an individual, borrows $6,000 from a bank for use in an activity described in section 465(c)(1). A is not personally liable for repayment of the loan but instead pledges as security assets not used in the activity with a net fair market value of $6,000. However B, a third party, guarantees A that A's entire loss from the activity will be repaid to A by B. Since A is protected against loss on the loan, A's amount at risk is not increased as a result of the entire transaction.

Example (2). Assume the same facts as in example (1) except that B, instead of guaranteeing A's entire loss from the activity, guarantees A against loss of A's security in excess of $2,000. Accordingly, A is considered as having pledged as security assets with a net fair market value of $2,000. Under § 1.465-25(a)(1), A's amount at risk is increased by $2,000.

Example (3). C, an individual, is engaged in the activity of farming. C borrows $10,000 for use on the farm from an unrelated third party. As security C pledges future crops. Under the general terms of the loan agreement, C is not personally liable for repayment of the $10,000. There is, however, one exception to this general provision. C will be personally liable if the crops are destroyed as the result of flooding. While drought is a constant concern for farmers in the area, flooding is not. Accordingly, although C is personally liable in the event of flooding, C's amount at risk will not be increased unless flooding actually occurs and destroys the crops, because the likelihood of flooding is such that C is effectively protected against loss. If the contingency does occur, C's amount at risk is increased at the end of the year in which it occurs.

Example (4). D, an individual calendar year taxpayer, is engaged in the activity or producing motion picture films. In 1979 D borrows $100,000 for use in the activity from E, the promoter. D is personally liable for repayment of the loan. E has neither a capital interest in the activity nor an interest in the net profits of the activity. Therefore, E is not considered a person with an interest in the activity other than that of a creditor. See § 1.465-8(b). However, E agrees to protect D against loss of up to the first $40,000 of losses from the activity. Thus, under the agreement D will not bear the economic burden of any loss until the total losses exceed $40,000. All of the losses in excess of $40,000 will be borne by D. As a result of this protection-against-loss agreement, the $100,000 borrowed for use in the activity will increase D's amount at risk by $60,000. At the close of 1979, D's losses from the activity amount to $70,000. However, because D's amount at risk is only $60,000, D will only be permitted to deduct $60,000. The remaining $10,000 of deductions shall be treated in accordance with § 1.465-2(b). [Reg. § 1.465-6.]

§ 1.465-7. General rules; amounts loaned to the activity by the taxpayer.—(a) *Partners.*—The amount at risk in an activity of a partner who lends the partnership money for use in the activity shall be increased by the amount by which that partner's basis in the partnership is increased under § 1.752-1(e) due to the incurrence by the partnership of that liability. The amount at risk of any other partners shall not be increased as a result of the loan.

(b) *Shareholders of electing small business corporations.*—For rules relating to amounts loaned by a shareholder to an electing small business corporation, see § 1.465-10(c).

(c) *Special rules.*—For special rules relating to amounts borrowed from persons with an interest in the activity other than that of creditor and amounts borrowed from persons with a special relationship to the taxpayer, see section 465(b)(3) and §§ 1.465-8 and 1.465-20. [Reg. § 1.465-7.]

§ 1.465-9. General rules; rules of construction.—(a) *Amounts protected against loss.*—Section 465(b)(4) and § 1.465-6 provide special rules relating to amounts protected against loss which override the other rules contained in section 465. Where the regulations under section 465 refer to cash or property contributed to an activity and amounts borrowed for use in an activity, it may be assumed that such cash, property, or amounts are not protected against loss under section 465(b)(4) unless expressly provided otherwise.

(b) *Amounts borrowed for use in an activity.*—Section 465(b)(3) and § 1.465-20 contain special rules relating to treatment of amounts borrowed from certain persons. Where the regulations under section 465 refer to amounts borrowed for use in an activity, it may be assumed that such amounts are borrowed neither from a person with an interest (other than an interest as a creditor) in the activity nor from a person who has a special relationship to the taxpayer specified within any one of the paragraphs of section 267(b), unless expressly provided otherwise.

(c) *Use of the term "activity".*—For the purposes of the regulations under section 465, unless expressly provided otherwise, use of the term "activity" shall refer to an activity which is described in section 465(c)(1).

(d) *Single activity.*—For the purposes of the regulations under section 465, unless otherwise stated, it is assumed that an entity conducting an activity is engaged only in that one activity.

(e) *Double counting of additions and reductions to amount at risk.*—An amount, or portion of an amount (which is contributed, borrowed, etc.), can only increase or decrease a taxpayer's amount at risk one time. Thus, if a portion of an amount increases a taxpayer's amount at risk under more than one section of the regulations, that portion can increase the taxpayer's amount at risk in the activity only once.

(f) *Personal funds or personal assets.*—For the purposes of the regulations under section 465, unless otherwise stated, the terms "personal funds" and "personal assets" of a taxpayer refer to funds and assets which—

(1) Are owned by the taxpayer;

(2) Are not acquired through borrowing; and

(3) Have a basis equal to their fair market value.

(g) *Foreclosure.*—If a foreclosure occurs within an activity, it will be treated as a disposition of the asset which is the subject of the foreclosure. For rules relating to dispositions, see § 1.465-66. [Reg. § 1.465-9.]

§ 1.465-10. General rules; rules relating to subchapter S corporations and their shareholders.—(a) *In general.*—In the case of electing small business corporations (as defined in section 1371(b)) the at risk rules of section 465 apply at both the corporate level and the shareholder level. Therefore, losses from an activity can be deducted by the corporation only to the extent that the corporation is at risk in the activity. In addition, each shareholder will be allowed a loss in the activity only to the extent that the shareholder is at risk in the activity.

(b) *Determination of corporation's amount at risk.*—(1) *General rule.*—Except as provided in paragraph (b)(2) of this section, an electing small business corporation's amount at risk in an activity is determined in the same manner as that of any other taxpayer.

(2) *Special rule for certain borrowed amounts.*—Amounts borrowed by an electing small business corporation from one or more of its shareholders may increase the corporation's amount at risk, notwithstanding the fact that the shareholders have an interest in the activity other than that of a creditor.

(c) *Determination of shareholder's amount at risk.*—The amount at risk of a shareholder of an electing small business corporation (as described in section 1371(b)) shall be adjusted to reflect any increase or decrease in the adjusted basis of any indebtedness of the corporation to the shareholder described in section 1374(c)(2)(B).

(d) *Example.*—The provisions of this section may be illustrated by the following example:

Example. A is the single shareholder in X, an electing small business corporation engaged in an activity described in section 465(c)(1). A contributed $50,000 to X in exchange for its stock under section 351. In addition, A borrowed $40,000 for which A assumed personal liability A then loaned the entire amount to X for use in the activity. During its taxable year, X had a net operating loss of $75,000. At the close of the taxable year (without reduction for any losses of X) A's amount at risk is $90,000 ($50,000 + $40,000). However, it is also necessary to determine X's amount at risk in the activity. X is also at risk for the $40,000 borrowed from A and expended in the activity. Therefore, X's amount at risk in the activity is $90,000 ($50,000 + $40,000). Because X's amount at risk in the activity ($90,000) exceeds the net operating loss ($75,000), the entire loss is allowed to the corporation and allocated to A. Since A's amount at risk ($90,000) also exceeds the loss ($75,000) A will be allowed the entire loss deduction. [Reg. § 1.465-10.]

§ 1.465-11. Definition of loss; in general.—(a) *In general.*—(1) *Loss.*—A taxpayer has a loss described in section 465(d) in a taxable year in an amount equal to the excess of allowable deductions allocable to an activity over the income received or accrued from the activity by the taxpayer for the taxable year. Such loss is referred to as a section 465(d) loss in the regulations under section 465. See § 1.465-13 for the definition of allowable deductions allocable to an activity and § 1.465-12 for a definition of income from the activity.

(2) *Example.*—The application of this paragraph may be illustrated by the following example:

Example. In 1977 B, a calendar year individual, contributes $15,000 to an activity described in section 465(c)(1). During 1977 B has income of $20,000 from the activity and has allowable deductions of $45,000 from the activity. From this $45,000 of allowable deductions, B must first take a deduction of $20,000 to reflect the income received by B from the activity in 1977. The remaining $25,000 ($45,000 – $20,000) is B's section 465(d) loss. Assuming B's amount at risk in the activity is $15,000 at the close of 1977, B is also allowed to deduct $15,000 of the $25,000 section 465(d) loss for 1977. The remaining $10,000 ($25,000 – $15,000) of the section 465(d) loss which is not allowed as a deduction for 1977 will be treated as a deduction allocable to the activity for 1978.

(b) *Carryover loss.*—For the carryover of losses disallowed by section 465, see § 1.465-2(b).

(c) *Loss with no amount at risk.*—(1) *In general.*—A section 465(d) loss is determined without regard to the amount at risk. Thus, even if the taxpayer has no amount at risk in the activity, deductions are allowable under section 465 for a taxable year to the extent there is income from the activity in that taxable year.

(2) *Example.*—The provisions of this paragraph may be illustrated by the following example:

Example. Before taking into account any gain or loss during 1978, the amount that C, a calendar year taxpayer, is at risk in an activity described in section 465(c)(1) is equal to minus $20,000. During 1978 C has deductions of $10,000 allocable to the activity and income of $15,000 from the activity. Because the income from the activity exceeds the amount of allocable deductions from the activity, there is no section 465(d) loss in 1978 to be disallowed under section 465(a). Thus, although C has a negative amount at risk, C is permitted to take deductions in the amount of $10,000 for 1978. [Reg. § 1.465-11.]

§ 1.465-12. Definition of loss; income from the activity.—(a) *In general.*—Income received or accrued from an activity includes gain recognized upon the disposition of the activity or an interest in the activity in accordance with § 1.465-66. For the purposes of this section and the determinations made under section 465(d), the character of any gain is irrelevant. Thus, all short-term capital gains and long-term capital gains attributable to the activity shall be included as income from the activity. For more rules relating to income from an activity see §§ 1.465-42 through 1.465-45.

(b) *Example.*—The provisions of this section may be illustrated by the following example:

Example. On February 1, 1977, A, an individual on a calendar year, purchases a piece of equipment to be used in an activity described in section 465(c)(1)(C). A bought the equipment for $50,000, paying $5,000 from personal assets and borrowing $45,000 from a bank on a nonrecourse basis secured only by the newly purchased equipment. On February 1, 1977, A has a basis in the activity of $50,000 and an initial amount at risk of $5,000. At the close of 1977 after the application of section 465, A's basis has been reduced to $35,000, A's amount at risk has been reduced to zero, and A has a loss of $10,000 disallowed by reason of section 465(a). In 1978, the bank forecloses on the equipment when it is still encumbered by the $45,000 loan. Assuming there were no other transactions relating to this activity, A recognizes a $10,000 gain ($45,000 – $35,000) on this disposition. For purposes of section 465(d), this $10,000 of gain is income from the activity, and the $10,000 of disallowed loss in 1977 is treated as a deduction for 1978. Since the income from the activity for 1978 ($10,000) is equal to the deductions attributable to the activity for 1978 ($10,000), there is no section 465(d) loss for 1978. Therefore, the $10,000 of gain is included in the gross income in 1978 and the $10,000 of disallowed loss is allowed as a deduction for 1978. [Reg. § 1.465-12.]

§ 1.465-13. Definition of loss; deductions from the activity.—(a) *General rule.*—For the purposes of section 465 allowable deductions allocable to an activity are those otherwise allowable deductions incurred in a trade or business or for the production of income from the activity. For the purposes of this section capital losses shall be treated as deductions without regard to section 1211. See § 1.465-38 for rules relating to the order in which deductions are to be allowed and § 1.465-2(b) for the treatment of loss deductions which are disallowed by section 465.

(b) *Capital gain.*—(1) *In general.*—For the purposes of section 465 the deduction for capital gains provided for in section 1202 shall not be treated as a deduction allocable to an activity. Therefore, the capital gain deduction described in section 1202 will not be subject to the limitations of section 465(a) and has no effect on the amount at risk.

(2) *Example.*—The provision of paragraph (b)(1) of this section may be illustrated by the following example:

Example. At the close of 1976 A, an individual and a calendar year taxpayer, has $1,000 of section 465(d) losses disallowed under section 465(a) for an activity described in section 465(c)(1). Before A has any other deductions allocable to the activity, A sells the entire activity, realizing $1,900 of long term capital gain. For 1977 A is allowed a deduction of $950 under section 1202. Other than the disallowed loss of $1,000 and the section 1202 deduction, A has no other deductions. In accordance with § 1.465-66 A has received $1,900 income from the activity. Since the $950 deduction under section 1202 is not allocable to the activity, the only deduction allocable to the activity for 1977 is the $1,000 disallowed in 1976. Therefore, for 1977 $1,900 will be included in gross income, $950 is allowed as a deduction, and in addition the full disallowed loss of $1,000 is allowed as a deduction since it is not in excess of the income from the activity ($1,900).

(c) *Dual use of assets or personnel.*—Proper allocation rules are necessary if assets or personnel are used either in two or more separate activities referred to in section 465(c)(2), or in one or more activities referred to in section 465(c)(2) and an activity to which section 465 does not apply. In such a case the deductions attributable to the use of these assets or personnel must be allocated between the activities on a reasonable basis. [Reg. § 1.465-13].

§ 1.465-22. Effect on amount at risk of money transactions.—(a) *Money contributed to activity.*—A taxpayer's amount at risk in an activity shall be increased by the amount of personal funds the taxpayer contributes to the activity. For this purpose a contribution by a partner to a partnership conducting only one activity is a contribution to the activity. However, a partner's amount at risk shall not be increased by the amount which the partner is required under the partnership agreement to contribute until such time as the contribution is actually made. Neither shall a partner's amount at risk be increased in the case of a note payable to the partnership for which a partner is personally liable until such time as the proceeds of the note are actually devoted to the activity. See § 1.465-10 for rules relating to amounts loaned by a shareholder to an electing small business corporation. See § 1.465-7(a) for the treatment of a loan by a partner to the partnership.

(b) *Withdrawal of money from the activity.*—A taxpayer's amount at risk in an activity shall be decreased by the amount of money withdrawn from the activity by or on behalf of the taxpayer. Amounts withdrawn from an activity include distributions from a partnership or an electing small business corporation (as defined in section 1371(b)). In the case of a taxpayer who is a shareholder of an electing small business corporation (as defined in section 1371(b)), withdrawals shall include repayments of any indebtedness of the corporation to the shareholder described in section 1374(c)(2)(B) to the extent of any decrease in the shareholder's adjusted basis of such indebtedness. For the treatment of amounts already used in an activity which are used to repay a loan, see §§1.465-24(b)(2)(i) and 1.465-25(b)(2).

(c) *Effect of income and loss from activity on amount of risk.*—(1) *Income.*—A taxpayer's amount at risk in an activity shall be increased by an amount equal to the excess of the taxpayer's share of all items of income received or accrued from the activity during the taxable year over the taxpayer's share of allowable deductions which are allocable to the activity for the taxable year. A taxpayer's amount at risk in an activity shall also be increased by the taxpayer's share of tax-exempt receipts of the activity.

(2) *Loss.*—A taxpayer's amount at risk in an activity shall be decreased by the amount of loss from the activity allowed as a deduction to the taxpayer under section 465(a). A loss shall reduce a taxpayer's amount at risk in the activity at the close of the taxable year after the taxable year for which the loss is allowable. A taxpayer's amount at risk in an activity shall be decreased by the taxpayer's share of expenses relating to the production of tax-exempt receipts of the activity which are not deductible in determining taxable income from the activity.

(3) *Cross references.*—For the definition of income from the activity, see §1.465-12. For definition of loss from the activity, see section 465(d) and §1.465-11. For the timing of increases and decreases to the amount at risk, see §1.465-39.

(d) *Payment to seller.*—Payment by a purchaser to the seller for an interest in an activity shall be treated by the purchaser as if the payment to the seller were a contribution to the activity. For rules relating to the contribution of borrowed amounts see §§1.465-20, 1.465-24, and 1.465-25. [Reg. §1.465-22.]

§1.465-23. Effect on amount at risk of property transactions.—(a) *Contributions of property.*—(1) *Contribution of unencumbered property.*—When a taxpayer contributes unencumbered property to an activity, the taxpayer's amount at risk in the activity shall be increased by the adjusted basis of the contributed property. However, see §§1.465-20, 1.465-24, and 1.465-25 for rules relating to the contribution to the activity of property that has been purchased with borrowed funds.

(2) *Contribution of encumbered property.*—(i) Except as may otherwise result due to the application of §1.465-20, when a taxpayer contributes to an activity property that is subject only to liabilities for which the taxpayer is personally liable for repayment, the taxpayer's amount at risk in the activity shall be increased by the adjusted basis of the contributed property.

(ii) Except as may otherwise result due to the application of §1.465-20, when a taxpayer contributes to an activity property that is subject to a liability for which the taxpayer is not personally liable for repayment, the taxpayer's amount at risk is increased by the adjusted basis in the property and is decreased by the amount of encumbrances to which the property is subject which would not have increased the taxpayer's amount at risk if incurred for use in the activity. If after contribution of the property to the activity such an encumbrance is reduced, it shall be treated as the repayment of a loan used in the activity for which the taxpayer is not personally liable and for which there is no property used outside the activity pledged as security. See §1.465-25(b)(2)(i).
If the basis of such property is decreased (for example, due to depreciation) prior to contribution to the activity, the portion of the basis consisting of amounts which would have increased the taxpayer's amount at risk if contributed directly to the activity will be decreased first.

(iii) The provisions of this paragraph may be illustrated by the following examples.

Example (1). In 1976 A, a calendar year individual taxpayer, purchases an asset for $5,000 financed in part by a $3,000 nonrecourse loan secured only by the asset and in part by $2,000 of cash from personal funds. Thereafter, in 1976 A contributes the asset to an activity before any of the nonrecourse debt has been repaid. Under §1.465-23(a)(2)(ii), A's amount at risk in the activity will be increased to the extent the taxpayer's adjusted basis in the asset consists of amounts which would have increased the taxpayer's amount at risk if contributed directly to the activity. In this instance the $3,000 nonrecourse loan is secured by an asset used in the activity. Because these loan proceeds would not increase the amount at risk if contributed directly to the activity, they will not increase the amount at risk in this case. However, the $2,000 of personal funds used for part payment of the asset would have increased A's amount at risk in the activity by $2,000 if contributed directly to the activity. Consequently, A's amount at risk in the activity is increased by $2,000 as a result of the contribution of the asset to the activity.

Example (2). In 1976 B, a calendar year individual taxpayer, purchases an asset for $5,000 financed in part by a $3,000 nonrecourse loan secured only by the asset and in part by $2,000 of cash from personal funds. B uses the asset in an activity to which section 465 does not apply and takes $1,000 of depreciation. Thereafter, B contributes the asset to an activity described in section 465(c)(1). None of the nonrecourse debt had been repaid at the time of the contribution. Under §1.465-23(a)(2)(ii) the $1,000 of depreciation will be deducted first from the portion of the basis that consists of amounts which would have increased the taxpayer's amount at risk in the activity if contributed directly to the activity. This means that at the time of contribution to the activity the asset has an adjusted basis of $4,000, consisting in part of a $3,000 nonrecourse loan and in part of $1,000 of personal funds which would have increased B's amount at risk in the activity if contributed directly to the activity. Consequently, B's amount at risk in the activity is increased by $1,000 as a result of the contribution of the asset to the activity.

(b) *Adjusted basis.*—(1) For the purpose of this section the adjusted basis is that adjusted basis which would have been used in determining the amount of loss if the property were sold immediately after being contributed to the activity.

(2) The provisions of this paragraph may be illustrated by the following examples:

Example (1). In 1972 A, an individual calendar year taxpayer, purchases a car for $5,000 using personal assets to pay the seller. From 1972 through 1975 the car is used solely for A's personal nonbusiness needs. On January 1, 1976, A converts the use of the car and begins using the car solely for business purposes. On January 1, 1976, the fair market value of the car is $2,400. For 1976 A is allowed a deduction of $600 for depreciation of the car. On January 1, 1977, A contributes the car to an activity described in section 465(c)(1). If on January 1, 1977, the car had been sold the allowable loss would have been the excess (if any) of $1,800 ($2,400 – $600) over the amount realized on the sale (see § 1.165-7(a)(5)). As a result of contributing the car, A's amount at risk in the activity is increased by $1,800.

Example (2). Assume the same facts as in example (1) except that A contributes the car to the activity described in section 465(c)(1) on January 1, 1976. On that date the car is converted from personal use to use in a trade or business or for the production of income. If the car were to be sold thereafter, the loss would be determined with reference to an adjusted basis of $2,400. Accordingly, A's amount at risk is increased by $2,400.

(c) *Distribution of property.*—A taxpayer's amount at risk in an activity shall be decreased by—

(1) The adjusted basis in the hands of the taxpayer of property (other than money) which is withdrawn by or on behalf of the taxpayer from the activity; less

(2) The amount of liabilities to which the property is subject to for which the taxpayer is not personally liable.

If a taxpayer is distributed property described in this paragraph, repayment of the liability by the taxpayer after the distribution shall not increase the taxpayer's amount at risk.

(d) *Use of property as security for a nonrecourse loan.*—For rules relating to the treatment of a taxpayer's amount at risk when the taxpayer pledges property as security for a nonrecourse loan, see § 1.465-25.

(e) *Contribution of property previously serving as security for a nonrecourse loan.*—For rules relating to the treatment of a taxpayer's amount at risk when the taxpayer contributes to an activity property that had served as security for a nonrecourse loan used in the activity, see § 1.465-25(a)(3). [Reg. § 1.465-23.]

§ 1.465-24. Effect on amount at risk of loans for which borrower is personally liable for repayment.—(a) *Creation of loan.*—(1) *General rule.*—A taxpayer's amount at risk in an activity is increased by the amount of any liability incurred in the conduct of an activity for use in the activity to the extent the taxpayer is personally liable for repayment of the liability.

(2) *Partnerships.*—(i) When a partnership incurs a liability in the conduct of an activity and under state law members of the partnership may be held personally liable for repayment of the liability, each partner's amount at risk is increased to the extent the partner is not protected against loss. To the extent the partner is protected against loss (such as through a right of contribution), the liability shall be treated in the same manner as amounts borrowed for which the taxpayer has no personal liability and for which no security is pledged. See § 1.465-25.

(ii) The application of this paragraph may be illustrated by the following example:

Example. A and B are equal general partners in partnership AB, which is engaged solely in an activity described in section 465(c)(1). AB borrows $25,000 from a bank to purchase equipment to be used in the activity. In addition to giving the bank a security interest in the newly purchased equipment, A and B each assumes personal liability for the loan. Although either A or B could be called upon by the bank to repay the entire $25,000, in such instance the partner who paid would be entitled to $12,500 from the other partner. Thus, although each is personally liable for $25,000, each is protected against loss in excess of $12,500. Accordingly, the loan increases the amount each is at risk with respect to the activity by $12,500.

(3) *Small business corporations.*—The amount at risk of a shareholder of an electing small business corporation (as defined in section 1371(b)) shall not be increased by indebtedness incurred by the corporation from persons other than that shareholder. For treatment of indebtedness described in section 1374(c)(2)(B) (relating to loans by shareholders to electing small business corporations), see § 1.465-10(c).

(b) *Repayment of loan.*—(1) *General rule.*—(i) Except as otherwise provided in this paragraph, the repayment by the taxpayer of a liability for which the taxpayer is personally liable does not affect the taxpayer's amount at risk. For this purpose, whether a taxpayer is considered personally liable for repayment of a liability is determined at the time of repayment.

(ii) The provisions of paragraph (b)(1) of this section, may be illustrated by the following examples:

Example (1). In 1977 A, an individual calendar year taxpayer, borrows $10,000 from a bank, assuming personal liability for repayment, for use in partnership AB, which is engaged solely in an activity. At the close of 1977 A's amount at risk is $10,000. In December of 1978 A takes $3,000 of personal funds and uses these funds to repay the bank. If no other factors occur during the year to affect A's amount at risk in the activity, A's amount at risk will be $10,000 at the close of 1978 because the repayment with personal assets of a liability for which A was personally liable does not affect A's amount at risk in the activity.

Example (2). In 1977 B, a calendar year taxpayer borrows $5,000 for use in an activity. B is personally liable for the repayment of the loan. At the end of 1977 B's amount at risk in the activity is $5,000. In 1978 when the amount of the loan is still $5,000, the loan obligation is purchased by C, a person who has an interest (other than interest as a creditor) in the activity. As a result of C's interest in the activity the loan is not treated in the same manner as a loan for which B is personally liable for repayment as long as C is the holder of the note. See § 1.465-20. Accordingly, B's amount at risk in the activity is decreased by $5,000, and repayments on the note made by B to C are not governed by this section. See § 1.465-5 for the effect on the amount at risk of loans which convert from recourse to nonrecourse. See § 1.465-25 for the effect on the amount at risk of repayments of a loan for which the borrower is not personally liable for repayment.

(2) *Repayments using amounts which would not increase the taxpayer's amount at risk if contributed to the activity.*—(i) If a taxpayer repays a loan for which the taxpayer is personally liable with assets already in the activity, the taxpayer's

amount at risk in the activity will be decreased by the adjusted basis (as defined in §1.465-23(b)(1)) of such assets. If the taxpayer repays a loan for which the taxpayer is personally liable with funds which, if contributed to the activity, would not increase the taxpayer's amount at risk, the taxpayer's amount at risk shall be decreased to the extent of the repayment. Thus, for example, if a taxpayer repays a loan for which the taxpayer is personally liable with funds received from a nonrecourse loan secured by property used in the activity, the taxpayer's amount at risk shall be decreased to the extent of the repayment. The payment by a partnership of a liability which, pursuant to paragraph (a)(2) of this section, is deemed to be incurred by a partner in the conduct of the activity shall decrease the partner's amount at risk in the activity to the extent such partner's basis in the partnership is decreased due to the payment of the liability by the partnership.

(ii) The provisions of paragraph (b)(2) of this section may be illustrated by the following example:

Example. In 1977 A, an individual calendar year taxpayer, borrows $10,000 from a bank, assuming personal liability for repayment, for use in partnership AB, which is engaged solely in an activity described in section 465(c)(1). At the close of 1977 A's amount at risk in the activity is $10,000. In December of 1978 A borrows $3,000 for which A is not personally liable and which is secured by property used in the activity, and uses the funds to pay the bank. If no other factors occur during the year to affect A's amount at risk in the activity, A's amount at risk will be decreased by the amount of the repayment, because A used funds for the repayment which would not have increased A's amount at risk had they been contributed to the activity. Therefore, at the close of 1978 A's amount at risk is $7,000. The result would be the same if the $3,000 used for the repayment of the loan were withdrawn from AB. See §1.465-22.

(3) *Repayment of a loan for which others are personally liable.*—Where more than one person is personally liable for repayment of a loan, repayment of that portion of the loan for which the taxpayer is personally liable and not protected against loss shall be treated in accordance with §1.465-24(b). Repayment of that portion of the loan for which the taxpayer is protected against loss (such as through a right of contribution) shall be treated as a repayment of a loan for which the taxpayer has no personal liability and for which no security is pledged. See §1.465-25. Also, see the example at paragraph (a)(2) of this section. [Reg. §1.465-24.]

§1.465-25. Effect on amount at risk of loan for which borrower is not personally liable for repayment.—(a) *Nonrecourse loan for which taxpayer pledges property not used in the activity.*—(1) *In general.*—A taxpayer's amount at risk in an activity is increased by amounts borrowed for use in the activity when the taxpayer is not personally liable for repayment of the loan if the taxpayer pledges as security property not used in the activity. However, the amount of the increase shall not exceed the net fair market value (as defined in paragraph (a)(4) of this section) of the pledged property. If the net fair market value of the security changes (in accordance with paragraph (a)(4) of this section) after the loan is made, a redetermination shall be made of the taxpayer's amount at risk in the activity using the new net fair market value.

(2) *Repayment of loan.*—To the extent a taxpayer's amount at risk is increased by a portion of a liability described in paragraph (a)(1) of this section, the taxpayer's repayment of that portion of the liability will be treated in the same manner as the repayment of a loan for which the taxpayer is personally liable in accordance with §1.465-24(b). However, to the extent the amount of the liability exceeds the net fair market value of property not used in the activity which secures the loan, repayment of that portion of the liability is considered as the repayment of a loan for which the taxpayer is not personally liable and has not pledged property used outside the activity in accordance with paragraph (b)(2)(i) of this section. Repayments of the loan are considered to be made first in respect of that portion of the loan which exceeds the net fair market value of property not used in the activity which secures the loan. If a portion of an amount borrowed is used in the activity and a portion is used outside the activity, repayment will be considered made first in respect of the portion used outside the activity.

(3) *Contribution of security to activity.*—If property which is pledged as security for an amount borrowed for use in an activity is subsequently contributed to the activity, the amount at risk shall be redetermined in accordance with this section as though the net fair market value of the security had been reduced to zero. This will reduce the amount at risk in accordance with §1.465-25(a)(1). Furthermore, the contribution of the property to the activity will be treated as a contribution of unencumbered property and will increase the amount at risk in accordance with §1.465-23(a)(1).

(4) *Net fair market value; changes in net fair market value.*—The net fair market value of property is the amount by which the property's fair market value at the date it is pledged as security exceeds the total amount of superior liens to which it is subject. Subsequent changes in the fair market value of the property are not taken into account for purposes of determining net fair market value. However, to the extent the amount of superior liens changes during a taxable year the net fair market value shall be adjusted at the close of the taxable year. Thus, the net fair market value of property will be reduced to the extent of increases in superior liens to which the property is subject and will be increased to the extent of decreases in superior liens of which the property is relieved. For purposes of determining the effect of superior liens on the calculations described in this paragraph, it is not relevant that other property is also subject to any such superior lien. If a portion of an amount borrowed which is secured by property described in this section is not contributed to an activity, that portion shall be treated as a superior lien on such property, thus reducing its net fair market value in accordance with §1.465-25(a)(4).

(b) *Nonrecourse loan for which a taxpayer pledges assets used in the activity.*—(1) *In general.*—(i) *Borrowed funds used in the activity.*—A taxpayer's amount at risk is unaffected by amounts borrowed for use in an activity where the taxpayer is not personally liable for repayment of the loan and has not pledged as security property used outside the activity. Thus, a taxpayer's amount at risk in a partnership activity is unaffected to the extent the taxpayer borrows for use in the partnership money secured only by the partnership interest. Where a partnership borrows amounts for use in the activity pledging only property used in the activity for repayment of the loan, and neither the partnership nor any partner is personally liable for repayment of the loan, the loan shall be treated by each partner as a loan which is described in this paragraph.

(ii) *Borrowed funds used outside the activity.*—A taxpayer's amount at risk is affected by amounts borrowed for use outside the activity where the taxpayer is not personally liable for repayment of the loan and has pledged as security only property used in the activity. In such a case, the taxpayer's amount at risk in the activity is decreased by an amount equal to the amount borrowed for use outside the activity. This result is unchanged if the only security for the loan is the taxpayer's interest in the activity. If the taxpayer has pledged as security property, some of which is used in the activity (including for this purpose the taxpayer's interest in the activity) and some of which is not, the taxpayer's amount at risk in the activity shall be reduced by the excess, if any, of amounts borrowed for use outside the activity over the net fair market value of the security not used in the activity.

(2) *Repayment of loan.*—(i) *Borrowed funds used in the activity.*—Where a taxpayer's amount at risk was not increased as a result of the rule contained in paragraph (b)(1)(i) of this section, a subsequent repayment of the loan by the taxpayer will increase the taxpayer's amount at risk to the extent of the repayment. However, if the amount used to repay the loan would not have increased the taxpayer's amount at risk in the activity if the amount had been contributed to the activity, the repayment will not increase the taxpayer's amount at risk. Thus, for example, if a nonrecourse loan (the proceeds of which were used in the activity) which did not increase the taxpayer's amount at risk is repaid with money borrowed by the taxpayer with a second nonrecourse loan secured only by property used in the activity, the taxpayer's amount at risk will not be increased by the repayment. When a liability described in paragraph (b)(1)(i) of this section is repaid with assets already used in the activity, the taxpayer's amount at risk will not be affected as a result of the repayment. Therefore, when a partnership incurs such a liability and thereafter repays it with assets used in the activity, no partner's amount at risk is affected upon the incurrence of the liability or upon repayment.

(ii) *Borrowed funds not used in the activity.*—A taxpayer's amount at risk is affected by the repayment by the taxpayer of amounts borrowed for use outside the activity where the taxpayer is not personally liable for repayment of the loan and has pledged as security only property used in the activity (including for this purpose the taxpayer's interest in the activity). In such a case the taxpayer's amount at risk in the activity is increased by the amount of the repayment. If the taxpayer has pledged as security property, some of which is used in the activity and some of which is not, upon repayment the taxpayer's amount at risk in the activity will be increased by the lesser of the amount of the repayment made by the taxpayer or the amount (if any) by which the outstanding liability (immediately before repayment) exceeds the net fair market value of the property not used in the activity which is pledged as security. However, if the amount used to repay the loan would not have increased the taxpayer's amount at risk in the activity if the amount had been contributed to the activity, the repayment will not increase the amount at risk. Thus, if the repayment is made using assets already in the activity, the repayment will not increase the taxpayer's amount at risk.

(3) *Examples.*—The provisions of this section may be illustrated by the following examples:

Example (1). (i) In 1977 A, a calendar year individual, pledges A's house (which is not used in the activity) as well as an asset used in the activity as security to borrow $8,000 on a nonrecourse basis to be used in an activity. On the day the house is pledged as security, its fair market value is $60,000, and it is subject to a superior lien of $54,000. If the amount of the superior lien is not reduced during the balance of the year, at the close of 1977 the net fair market value of the house is $6,000 ($60,000 – $54,000), since the net fair market value of the security ($6,000) is less than the amount borrowed ($8,000), the increase in A's amount at risk is limited to $6,000.

(ii) In 1978 A reduces the amount of the superior lien on the house to $53,000. Accordingly, the house's net fair market value at the close of 1978 is $7,000 ($60,000 – $53,000). In accordance with paragraph (a)(4) of this section, a redetermination of the amount at risk is made using the new net fair market value. Using the new value, the amount borrowed ($8,000) is still more than the net fair market value ($7,000). Therefore, the new net fair market value would be used to measure the increase in A's amount at risk in the activity. The new amount determined under paragraph (a)(4) of this section ($7,000) exceeds the earlier amount determined under this section ($6,000) by $1,000. Thus, A's amount at risk is increased by $1,000.

(iii) In 1979 the fair market value of A's house increases to $75,000. On December 31, 1979, A obtains a $10,000 second mortgage on the house. The second mortgage is made superior to the lien for the $8,000 loan made in 1977. At the close of 1979 the original lien on the house has been reduced to $52,000 and the second mortgage is $10,000. Since changes in the fair market value of security are ignored for purposes of determining net fair market value, the net fair market value of the house at the end of 1979 is determined by comparing its fair market value at the time the $8,000 was borrowed in 1977, $60,000, with the amount of superior liens outstanding at the end of 1979, $62,000 ($52,000 + $10,000). Since the fair market value of the house as so determined is less than the total of the superior liens to which the house is subject at the end of 1979, the net fair market value of the house at that time is 0. In accordance with paragraph (a)(4) of this section a redetermination of the amount at risk is made using the new net fair market value. Using the new value the amount borrowed ($8,000) is still more than the net fair market value (0). Therefore, the new net fair market value would be used to measure the increase in A's amount at risk in the activity. The new amount determined under paragraph (a)(4) of this section (0) is less than the earlier amount determined under this section ($7,000) by $7,000. Thus, A's amount at risk is decreased by $7,000.

Example (2). (i) In 1977 B, a calendar year individual, pledges shares of stock that are not used in the activity as security to borrow $20,000 on a nonrecourse basis to be used in an activity. On the day the shares are pledged, they are worth $40,000 and are not subject to any superior liens. At the close of 1977 the fair market value of the shares is $30,000. Nevertheless, at the close of 1977 the net fair market value of the shares is $40,000, because changes in the fair market value of security are ignored for purposes of determining net fair market value. Since the net fair market value of the shares ($40,000) is greater than the amount borrowed ($20,000), B's amount at risk in the activity is increased by $20,000.

(ii) In 1978, B, using personal assets, repays $4,000 of the loan secured by the shares of stock. In accordance with paragraph (a)(2) of this section, repayments of such a loan are treated like repayments of a loan for which the taxpayer is personally liable. Thus, B's amount at risk is not affected by the repayment.

(iii) In 1979 the shares of stock are made subject to a $30,000 lien superior to the previous lien. At the close of 1979 the net fair market value of the shares of stock is $10,000 ($40,000 fair market value minus $30,000 superior lien). Accordingly, a redetermination must be made of B's amount at risk. Since the new net fair market value of the shares of stock ($10,000) is less than the amount of the loan outstanding ($16,000), the net fair market value is used to measure any change in A's amount at risk. The new amount determined under this section ($10,000) is less than the earlier amount determined under this section ($16,000) by $6,000. Thus, in accordance with paragraph (a) of this section B's amount at risk is decreased under this section by $6,000.

(iv) In 1980 B repays $7,000 of the loan secured by the shares of stock. In accordance with paragraph (a)(2) of this section, the repayment is first deemed to be made in respect of that portion of the loan, $6,000, which exceeds the net fair market value of property not used in the activity which secures the loan. Pursuant to paragraph (b)(2)(i) of this section the repayment will result in a corresponding increase of $6,000 in the amount at risk. The remaining $1,000 repayment is treated under paragraph (a)(2) of this section in the same manner as the repayment of a loan for which the taxpayer is personally liable. Repayment of such a loan results in no change in the amount at risk. Accordingly, as a result of the $7,000 repayment, B's amount at risk is increased by $6,000.

Example (3). (i) In 1977 C, a calendar year individual, purchases an asset for $10,000 for use in an activity. C pays for the asset with $2,000 of personal funds and a purchase money mortgage of $8,000 on which C is not personally liable. At the end of 1977 C still owes $8,000 on the purchase money mortgage. As a result of this transaction C's amount at risk in the activity is increased by $2,000.

(ii) In 1978 C repays $3,000 of the purchase money mortgage, $2,000 with personal funds from outside the activity and $1,000 with funds from within the activity. Since the $2,000 of funds from outside the activity can increase C's amount at risk if contributed to the activity, their use to repay the loan will increase C's amount at risk by $2,000. The additional $1,000 of repayment is from funds already within the activity. Accordingly, the use of those funds to repay the loan does not increase C's amount at risk in the activity.

Example (4). (i) In 1977 D, a calendar year individual, borrows $5,000 for use in a farming activity described in section 465(c)(1)(B). D is personally liable on the loan. At the end of 1977 the $5,000 loan remains outstanding. Accordingly, D's amount at risk in the activity is increased by $5,000.

(ii) In 1979 D requests the lender to convert the $5,000 loan into a nonrecourse loan secured by assets in the farming activity. The lender agrees to the request. Assuming that § 1.465-5 applies and the recourse loan increases D's amount at risk prior to conversion, the conversion of the loan from recourse to nonrecourse reduces D's amount at risk by $5,000 at the close of 1979.

(iii) In 1980 D repays $1,000 of the $5,000 loan with personal funds from outside the activity and $2,000 with money from the activity. The repayment of $3,000 of the loan increases D's amount at risk to the extent a contribution of amounts used to repay the loan would have increased the taxpayer's amount at risk in the activity. Since $2,000 from the activity was used to repay the loan, D's amount at risk in the activity is not increased to the extent of that $2,000. However, the $1,000 from outside the activity would have increased the amount at risk if it were contributed to the activity. Therefore, at the end of 1980 D's amount at risk will be increased by $1,000.

Example (5). E and F form partnership EF to engage in an activity described in section 465(c)(1). Partnership EF borrows $20,000 secured by a purchase money mortgage for which neither of the partners is personally liable and uses the funds to purchase an asset for use in the activity. This transaction does not increase the amount E and F are at risk in the activity. Thereafter, EF repays $5,000 of the purchase money mortgage with funds from the activity. Pursuant to paragraph (c) of this section the repayment by EF has no effect on the amount E and F are at risk in the activity.

Example (6). A, an individual calendar year taxpayer, is engaged in a farming activity described in section 465(c)(1)(B). On January 6, 1978, A borrows $8,000 using machinery from the activity as security. A is not personally liable for repayment of the loan. A uses the $8,000 (along with $2,000 from personal funds) to purchase an automobile for use outside the activity. Subsequently, A pledges the automobile as security to borrow $8,000. A uses this $8,000 to purchase a truck which is contributed to the farming activity in August of 1978. Section 465(b)(2) provides that no property shall be taken into account as security if it is directly or indirectly financed by indebtedness which is secured by property used in the activity. Accordingly, if no other events affecting A's amount at risk occur in 1978, A's amount at risk in the farming activity at the close of 1978 will be the same as it was at the close of 1977.

(c) *Repayment of nonrecourse liability by a partnership.*—The repayment by a partnership of a liability for which a taxpayer is not personally liable and for which that taxpayer has not pledged as security assets used outside the activity shall not affect the taxpayer's amount at risk. [Reg. § 1.465-25.]

§ 1.465-26. Effect of transfers by gift or at death on amount at risk; cross reference.—For rules relating to the effect on the amount at risk of transfers by gift or at death, see §§ 1.465-57 through 1.465-59. [Reg. § 1.465-26.]

Deduction Limited to Amount at Risk

Deduction Limited to Amount at Risk.—Reproduced below are the texts of proposed Reg. §§ 1.465-38, 1.465-39, 1.465-41—1.465-45, 1.465-66—1.465-69, 1.465-75—1.465-79 and 1.465-95, relating to the determination of amounts at risk with respect to certain activities (published in the Federal Register on June 5, 1979).

§ 1.465-38. Ordering rules.—(a) *In general.*—In determining which items of deductions otherwise allowable are to be allowed under section 465(a), the following ordering system shall be used:

(1) First, all capital losses shall be allowed.

(2) Second, all items of deduction entering into the computation under section 1231 shall be allowed.

(3) Third, all items of deduction to the extent they do not constitute items of tax preference under section 57 and are not described in paragraph (a)(1) or (2) of this section shall be allowed.

(4) Fourth, all items of tax preference under section 57 not described in paragraph (a)(1) or (2) of this section shall be allowed.

(b) *Retention of identity.*—When treated as deductions in succeeding taxable years, deductions which are disallowed under section 465(a) shall retain their identity according to the classifications enumerated in paragraph (a) of this section.

(c) *Special rule.*—Deductions described in paragraph (a)(4) of this section (relating to tax preference items) which are disallowed by section 465(a) shall be further subdivided according to the taxable year in which they were originally paid or accrued. When such deductions are allowed, those deductions paid or accrued in the earliest taxable years shall be allowed first.

(d) *Examples.*—The provisions of this section may be illustrated by the following examples:

Example (1). A, an individual calendar year taxpayer, is engaged in an activity described in section 465(c)(1). At the close of 1977 A is at risk $1000 in the activity. During 1978 A had $3000 of income from the activity and $7500 of deductions allocated to the activity. Of the $7500 of deductions $2500 are of the type described in § 1.465-38(a)(3) and $5000 are of the type described in § 1.465-38(a)(4). Assuming nothing else has occurred during 1978 to affect A's amount at risk, A will be allowed $4000 of deductions and $3500 of deductions will be disallowed. Since A has no deductions described in § 1.465-38(a)(1) or § 1.465-38(a)(2), the $4000 of allowed deductions will consist of the entire $2500 described in § 1.465-38(a)(3) and $1500 of the $5000 deductions described in § 1.465-38(a)(4). The $3500 deductions disallowed will consist of deductions in § 1.465-38(a)(4).

Example (2). Assume the same facts as in example (1), and in addition during 1979 A has income from the activity of $10,000. During 1979 A incurred $14,000 of deductions of which $4,000 are described in § 1.465-38(a)(3) and $10,000 are described in § 1.465-38(a)(4). When A's current deductions are added to the deductions which were not allowed and therefore carried over from 1978, A's total deductions from the activity for 1979 are $17,500 ($14,000 + $3,500), of which $4,000 are described in § 1.465-38(a)(3) and $13,500 are described in § 1.465-38(a)(4) ($10,000 + $3,500). Of the $13,500 of deductions described in § 1.465-38(a)(4), $3,500 are from 1978 and $10,000 are from 1979. Assuming nothing occurs during 1979 to affect A's amount at risk, A will be allowed deductions from the activity in the amount of $10,000 (see § 1.465-2(a)). Since A has no deductions described in § 1.465-38(a)(1) or § 1.465-38(a)(2), the entire $10,000 of deductions will come from those deductions described in § 1.465-38(a)(3) and § 1.465-38(a)(4). Of A's $17,500 of deductions from the activity the entire $4,000 described in § 1.465-38(a)(3) will be allowed. Of the $13,500 deductions described in § 1.465-38(a)(4), $6,000 will be allowed. Pursuant to § 1.465-38(c) deductions described in § 1.465-38(a)(4) and occurring in the earliest years shall be allowed first. Accordingly, the $6,000 deductions described in § 1.465-38(a)(4) which are to be allowed shall consist of the entire $3,500 attributable to 1978 and $2,500 of the $10,000 deductions described in § 1.465-38(a)(4) attributable to 1979. The remaining $7,500 of deductions described in § 1.465-38(a)(4) and attributable to 1979 will be carried over and treated as deductions from the activity for 1980. [Reg. § 1.465-38.]

§ 1.465-39. Timing of increases and decreases to the amount at risk.—(a) *General rule.*—Except as provided in paragraph (b) of this section, factors which increase or decrease the amount a taxpayer is at risk in a taxable year shall so increase or decrease the amount at risk before determining the amount of section 465(d) loss which is allowed for the year.

(b) *Exception.*—Section 465(d) losses which are allowed as deductions for a taxable year under section 465 reduce the amount a taxpayer is at risk with respect to that activity at the close of the immediately succeeding taxable year of the taxpayer.

(c) *Procedure.*—The amount a taxpayer is at risk in an activity at the close of a taxable year of the taxpayer is determined by—

(1) Reducing the amount at risk in the activity at the close of the preceding taxable year by the amount of the section 465(d) loss which was allowed as a deduction in the preceding taxable year;

(2) Increasing the amount at risk in the activity (determined after the application of paragraph (c)(1) of this section) by all factors occurring during the taxable year which increase the amount at risk; and

(3) Decreasing the amount at risk in the activity (determined after the application of paragraph (c)(2) of this section) by all factors occurring during the taxable year which decrease the amount at risk.

See § 1.465-41 for illustrations of the operation of this section. [Reg. § 1.465-39.]

§ 1.465-41. Examples.—The provisions of §§ 1.465-1 through 1.465-40 may be illustrated by the following examples:

Example (1). On January 1, 1976, A and B as equal partners form partnership AB. Both A and B, as well as partnership AB, are calendar year taxpayers. On January 1, 1976, A and B each contributes $5,000 from personal assets to AB. On August 1, 1976, AB borrows $6,000 from a bank with A and B each assuming personal liability. On December 31, 1976, AB reduces the amount outstanding on the loan to $4,500. AB has neither loss nor income for 1976. As of December 31, 1976, A's amount at risk in the activity engaged in by AB is determined as follows:

Amount at risk in activity as of 1/1/76	$0
Plus:	
Contributions	5,000
Allocable share of loan for which personal liability was assumed ($6,000) ÷ 2)	3,000
	$8,000
Less:	
Allocable share of net reduction in personal liability (See § 1.465-24(b)(2)(i)) $\left(\frac{\$6{,}000 - \$4{,}500}{2}\right)$	750
Amount at risk in activity as of 12/31/76	$7,250

Example (2). Assume the same facts as in example (1) and in addition on February 1, 1977, AB borrows $20,000 under a nonrecourse financing arrangement with the lender taking as security equipment purchased with the newly acquired funds. On May 1, 1977 AB reduces the amount outstanding on the loan on which A and B have assumed personal liability to $4,000 ($4,500 – $500). On August 1, 1977 AB reduces the principal amount due on the nonrecourse loan to $19,000. On October 1, 1977 AB distributes $2,000 each to both A and B. On December 1, 1977 AB reduces the amount outstanding on the loan on which A and B have assumed personal liability to $2,500 ($4,000 – $1,500). A and B are each allocated $3,000 as their distributive share of partnership income for its taxable year ending December 31, 1977. As of December 31, 1977, A's amount at risk in the activity engaged in by AB is determined as follows:

Amount at risk in activity as of 1/1/77		$7,250
Plus:		
Income from the activity		3,000
		$10,250
Less:		
Allocable share of net reduction in personal liability—5/1/77 ($500 ÷ 2)	$250	
Allocable share of net reduction in personal liability—12/1/77 ($1,500 ÷ 2)	750	
Distribution	2,000	3,000
Amount at risk in activity as of 12/31/77		$7,250

The $20,000 nonrecourse loan does not affect the amount at risk of either A or B because neither of them assumed personal liability and neither of them pledged property not used in the activity as security. Under § 1.465-25(b)(2) the reduction in the nonrecourse liability did not reduce either partner's amount at risk, because the loan was repaid with amounts already in the activity. Under § 1.465-24(b)(2) the reduction in personal liability did reduce the amount at risk, because the repayment was made with amounts already in the activity.

Example (3). Assume the same facts as in example (2) and in addition on March 1, 1978, A and B each contributes $1,000 to AB. On September 1, 1978 A and B each contributes $1,500 to AB and on the same date AB reduces the outstanding amount due on the loan for which A and B are personally liable to zero, and also repays $500 on the loan for which A and B had not assumed personal liability. For AB's taxable year ending December 1978 A and B each has $10,500 of section 465(d) losses. As of December 31, 1978, A's amount at risk for the activity engaged in by AB is determined as follows:

Amount at risk in activity as of 1/1/78	$7,250
Plus:	
Contribution—3/1/78	1,000
Contribution—9/1/78	1,500
	$9,750
Less:	
Allocable share of net reduction in personal liability ($2,500 ÷ 2)	1,250
Amount at risk in activity as of 12/31/78	$8,500

A was allocated $10,500 in partnership losses. Since A's amount at risk as of December 31, 1978 is only $8,500, A's loss deduction for the activity will also be so limited. Thus, A may take a loss deduction of $8,500 for 1978. This deduction will decrease A's amount at risk at the close of 1979. The $2,000 not allowed as a loss deduction for 1978 will be treated as a deduction in 1979. Under § 1.465-25(b)(2)(i) the reduction in nonrecourse liability did not reduce either partner's amount at risk, because the loan was repaid with amounts already in the activity.

Example (4). Assume the facts as in example (3) and in addition on March 1, 1979, A and B each contributes $1,000 to AB. For AB's taxable year ending December 31, 1979, A and B are each allocated $500 as their share of partnership income (which is calculated without regard to the $2,000 loss deduction disallowed in 1978). As of December 31, 1979, A's amount at risk in the activity engaged in by AB is determined as follows:

Amount at risk in activity as of 1/1/79	$8,500
Less:	
Loss allowed in 1978	8,500
	$0
Plus: Contribution	1,000
Amount at risk in activity as of 12/31/79	$1,000

A had a $2,000 loss deduction which was not allowed in 1978 and is treated as a deduction for 1979. Since $500 is A's distributive share of partnership income (which is calculated without regard to such deduction), A's section 465(d) loss for 1979 is $1,500 ($2,000 – $500). Since A is at risk $1,000 as of December 31, 1979, only $1,000 is allowable as loss deduction for 1979. The remaining $500 is treated as a deduction for 1980. Therefore, of the $2,000 disallowed loss deduction for 1978 treated as a deduction for 1979, $500 is deductible by reason of A's share of partnership income, $1,000 is deductible because A was at risk $1,000, and the remaining $500 is not deductible for 1979 but is treated as a deduction allocable to the activity for 1980.

Example (5). On July 1, 1976, C, along with many other persons, forms partnership W. C is a calendar year taxpayer and partnership W is on a taxable year ending June 30. On July 1, 1976, C contributes $3,000 to W. On August 1, 1976, W borrows a sum of money for which C's allocable share of personal liability is $7,500. On October 1, 1976, W borrows a sum of money under a nonrecourse financing arrangement with respect to which C's allocable share is $10,000. On March 1, 1977, W repays a portion of the loan for which C is personally liable, thereby reducing C's personal liability to $6,000. C's allocable share of W's losses for the taxable year ending June 30, 1977, is $13,000. On September 1, 1977, C contributes unencumbered personal assets with an adjusted basis of $6,000 to W. On November 1, 1977, W repays another portion of the loan for which C is personally liable, reducing C's personal liability to $5,000. On December 1, 1977, W repays part of the nonrecourse loan thereby reducing C's allocable portion of the amount outstanding to $8,000. The amount of loss deduction which C is allowed for 1977 is determined as follows:

Amount at risk in activity as of 7/1/76 (prior to contribution)	$0
Plus:	
Contribution—7/1/76	3,000
Allocable share of loan for which personal liability was assumed	7,500
	$10,500
Less:	
Allocable share of net reduction in personal liability	$1,500
Amount at risk in activity as of 6/30/77	$9,000

Although C's allocable share of W's losses for the taxable year ending June 30, 1977, is $13,000, C's allowable loss deduction is limited to the amount at risk as of the close of the partnership's taxable year. Thus, C's loss deduction for the taxable year ending December 31, 1977, is $9,000. The $4,000 not allowed as a loss deduction in 1977 will be treated as a deduction in 1978. The fact that prior to December 31, 1977, but after the close of W's taxable year on June 30, 1977, C made a contribution to W does not increase the amount of loss which C may deduct for 1977. That amount is limited to the amount C was at risk in the activity as of the close of W's taxable year.

Example (6). Assume the same facts as in example (5), and in addition for the taxable year ending June 30, 1978, C's allocable share of W's losses is $250 (which is calculated without regard to the $4,000 loss deduction carryover from 1977). On October 1, 1978, W distributes $2,000 to C. The amount of loss deduction which C is allowed for 1978 is determined as follows:

Amount at risk in activity as of 7/1/77	$9,000
Less:	
Loss allowed in 1977	9,000
	$0
Plus:	
Contribution—9/1/77	6,000
Less:	
Net reduction in personal liability 11/1/77	1,000
Amount at risk in activity as of 6/30/78	$5,000

C has $4,000 of deductions which were not allowed in 1977 as well as $250 of current loss for W's taxable year ending June 30, 1978. Since $4,250, the entire amount of section 465(d) loss ($4,000 + $250), is less than the amount at risk as of the close of W's taxable year, the entire amount is allowable as a deduction for C's taxable year ending December 31, 1978. The fact that prior to December 31, 1978, but after the close of W's taxable year on June 30, 1978, W made a distribution to C does not decrease the amount of allowable loss which C may deduct in 1978 unless § 1.465-4 is found to apply.

Example (7). Assume the facts as in example (6), and in addition for W's taxable year ending June 30, 1979, C's allocable share of income is $1,000. No other events occur which affect C's amount at risk. C's amount at risk as of June 30, 1979, is determined as follows:

Amount at risk in activity as of 7/1/78	$5,000
Less:	
Loss allowed in 1978	4,250
	$750
Plus:	
Income from the activity	1,000
	$1,750
Less:	
Distribution—10/1/78	2,000
Amount at risk in activity as of 6/30/79	$(250)

For the recapture of certain losses where the amount at risk is less than zero, see section 465(e). [Reg. § 1.465-41.]

§ 1.465-42. Activities to which section 465 applies; holding, producing, or distributing motion picture films or video tapes.—(a) *In general.*—Section 465 applies to any taxpayer described in § 1.465-1(d) who is engaged in the activity of holding, producing, or distributing motion picture films or video tapes either as a trade or business or for the production of income.

(b) *Loss.*—All receipts related to holding, producing, or distributing motion picture films or video tapes and all items of deduction incurred with respect to such receipts are to be taken into account in determining whether there is a section 465(d) loss.

(c) *Separate activities.*—(1) *General rule.*—Except in the case of a partner's interest in a partnership or a shareholder's interest in an electing small business corporation, a taxpayer's interest in each different film or video tape shall be considered a separate activity. Thus, if an individual has an interest in four different films, each film represents a separate activity to that individual and that individual has a separate section 465(d) loss and a separate amount at risk with respect to each film.

(2) *Partners and shareholders.*—In the case of a partner's interest in a partnership or a shareholder's interest in an electing small business corporation, all films and video tapes in which the partnership or corporation has an interest shall be treated as one activity of the partner or shareholder. Thus, if a partnership has an interest in three different films and two different video tapes, the five films and video tapes will constitute one activity for each partner. This means that all items of income allocated to a partner from the films and video tapes shall be aggregated with all items of deductions allocated to that partner from the films and video tapes so as to result in one amount at risk and one section 465(d) loss (if any) for each partner.

(d) *Different film or video tape.*—(1) *General rule.*—For the purposes of paragraph (c) of this section, a different film or video tape is one—

(i) In which the finished product is viewed as a single work; and

(ii) Which is of a length such that individuals could normally be expected to view it in one sitting.

For the purposes of paragraph (c) of this section, a movie or video tape can consist of more than one reel.

(2) *Special rule.*—In cases where more than one film or video tape exists as a result of applying paragraph (d)(1)(ii) of this section, each portion of the film or video tape which is intended to be viewed in a separate sitting shall be a different film or video tape. [Reg. § 1.465-42.]

§ 1.465-43. Activities to which section 465 applies; farming.—(a) *In general.*—Section 465 applies to any taxpayer described in § 1.465-1(d) who is engaged in farming (as defined in section 464(e)) as a trade or business or for the production of income.

(b) *Loss.*—All receipts related to the farming activity and all items of deduction incurred with respect to such receipts are to be taken into account in determining whether there is a section 465(d) loss.

(c) *Separate activities.*—For each farm rules similar to those found in § 1.465-42(c) shall apply for purposes of determining what constitutes a separate activity.

(d) *Farm.*—As used in this section, the term "farm" includes all property where the cultivation of land or the raising or harvesting of any agricultural or horticultural commodity occurs, including the raising, shearing, feeding, caring for, training, and management of animals. For purposes of the preceding sentence, trees (other than trees bearing fruit or nuts) shall not be treated as an agricultural or horticultural commodity.

(e) *Farm activity.*—When a procedure for the processing of products grown or animals raised on a farm is carried on within the physical boundaries of a farm, it is necessary to determine whether such activity constitutes a farm activity. In such event, the facts and circumstances of each case must be evaluated. Generally, the most significant facts and circumstances in making this determination include—

(1) The similarity of the product as processed to the product as it is being grown or raised;

(2) The consistency with normal commercial practice of conducting the procedure within the physical boundaries of a farm; and

(3) The necessity of the procedure to obtain a marketable product.

If it is determined that the processing procedure is a nonfarm activity, receipts and expenditures from the farm activity and the nonfarm activity cannot be aggregated, and section 465 shall apply only to the receipts and expenditures from the farm activity.

(f) *Examples.*—The provisions of paragraph (e) of this section may be illustrated by the following examples:

Example (1). A operates a farm where A plants and harvests potatoes. On one portion of the farm A also operates a plant in which the potatoes are processed into potato chips. These potato chips are then shipped to various distributors who bag and sell the potato chips to retailers. The processing of potato chips by A shall not be considered a farm activity. The processing neither results in a final product (potato chip) similar to the product as grown (potato) nor is it necessary to obtain a marketable product.

Example (2). B is engaged in the farm activity of growing tobacco. Among the steps B takes to produce a product that is marketable is to maintain a warehouse within the physical boundaries of the farm for the purpose of curing and packing the tobacco that B has grown on the farm. There is no market for the tobacco in the form it takes when harvested. The curing and packing aspect of B's operations is a farm activity, because the final product as processed is similar to the product as grown, and the procedure is necessary to obtain a marketable product.

Example (3). C is engaged in growing wine grapes. In addition, C operates a winery within the boundaries of the farm. The capacity of C's winery is such that C purchases grapes from neighboring farms for use in making the wine in addition to using grapes grown in C's own vineyard. Most of the grape growers in the region of C's vineyard do not operate their own wineries but, instead, sell their grapes to a winery. Therefore the operation of the winery on the farm is not consistent with normal commercial practice. Thus, the operation of the winery is not a farm activity. The end product of the winery (wine) is not similar to the product as grown (grapes). In addition, harvested grapes are a marketable commodity without further processing. The result is the same even if the size of C's winery is such that it can only accommodate the grapes grown by C.

Example (4). D operates a farm on which D raises Black Angus steers. In addition, D maintains facilities on the farm to slaughter the steers. D has a contract with several grocery stores and restaurants in the area to provide them with this meat. Under these circumstances the slaughtering facilities will not be considered a farm activity. [Reg. § 1.465-43.]

§ 1.465-44. Activities to which section 465 applies; leasing section 1245 property.—(a) *In general.*—Section 465 applies to any taxpayer described in § 1.465-1(d)(1) who is engaged in the leasing of any section 1245 property (as defined in section 1245(a)(3)) as a trade or business or for the production of income. However, see section 465(c)(3)(D)(ii) for special exceptions relating to certain corporations engaged in equipment leasing.

(b) *Loss.*—All receipts related to the leasing of section 1245 property and all items of deduction incurred with respect to such receipts are to be taken into account in determining whether there is a section 465(d) loss.

(c) *Separate activities.*—(1) *General rule.*—For each section 1245 property which is leased or held for leasing, rules similar to those found in § 1.465-42(c) shall apply for purposes of determining what constitutes a separate activity.

(2) *Section 1245 property.*—For the purposes of section 465 where several section 1245 properties, such as parts of a computer system, comprise one unit under the same lease agreement and are neither separately financed nor subject to different lease terms, the properties will be considered one section 1245 property.

(d) *Lease.*—For the purposes of section 465, a lease is any arrangement or agreement, formal or informal, written or oral, whereby the owner of property receives consideration in any form for the use of the property by another party. Whether a specific transaction constitutes a lease or sale shall be determined on the basis of the particular facts and circumstances.

(e) *Ancillary leasing of section 1245 property.*—Section 465 shall not apply to amounts received or accrued where the leasing of section 1245 property is incidental to making real property available as living accommodations (such as where an unfurnished rental apartment is equipped with a stove or refrigerator). Section 465 shall also not apply to amounts received or accrued where the leasing of section 1245 property is incidental to the furnishing of services. [Reg. § 1.465-44.]

§ 1.465-45. Activities to which section 465 applies; exploring for, or exploiting, oil and gas resources.—(a) *In general.*—Section 465 applies to any taxpayer described in § 1.465-1(d) who is engaged in exploring for, or exploiting, oil and gas resources as a trade or business or for the production of income.

(b) *Loss.*—All receipts related to exploring for, or exploiting, oil and gas resources and which constitute gross income from the property within the meaning of section 613, and all items of deduction incurred with respect to such receipts, are to be taken into account in determining whether there is a section 465(d) loss.

(c) *Separate activities.*—For each separate oil and gas property (as defined under section 614) rules similar to those found in § 1.465-42(c) shall apply for purposes of determining what constitutes a separate activity.

(d) *Depletion.*—In the case of exploring for, or exploiting, oil and gas resources a taxpayer's allowable deduction under section 611 (relating to an allowance for depletion) shall be considered a deduction incurred in the production of income from the activity. Therefore, it must be taken into account in determining the taxpayer's section 465(d) loss. A taxpayer's amount at risk in an activity shall be increased by the excess of the deductions for depletion over the basis of the property (used within the activity) subject to depletion. [Reg. § 1.465-45.]

§ 1.465-66. Transfers and dispositions; general rule.—(a) *General rule.*—In the case of a transfer or other disposition of all or part of either an activity or an interest in an activity during a taxable year, any gain recognized on the transfer or disposition shall be treated as income from the activity in accordance with § 1.465-12. In the case of a liquidation by a partnership of a partner's interest in that partnership, or complete redemption by an electing small business corporation of a shareholder's stock in that corporation, the provisions of this section shall apply. In general, this section will cause amounts disallowed by section 465 in previous taxable years to be allowed for the taxable year of transfer or disposition. In addition, any gain recognized as the result of a transfer or disposition of an asset which was at one time used in an activity shall be treated as income from the activity, notwithstanding the fact that the taxpayer's participation in the activity ended prior to the transfer or disposition.

(b) *Examples.*—The provisions of this section may be illustrated by the following examples:

Example (1). On January 1, 1976, A and B as equal partners form partnership AB. A and B, as well as AB, are calendar year taxpayers. After the close of taxable year 1978 A's basis in AB is $3,000, A's amount at risk is zero, and A has $7,000 of losses from the activity which would have been allowed but for section 465(a). AB's assets are subject to a nonrecourse loan of $20,000, of which A's share is $10,000. On January 1, 1979, C purchases A's interest in AB for $11,000. C pays A $1,000 in cash and takes a 50 percent interest in the partnership, which is renamed BC. BC's assets are still encumbered to the extent of $20,000. A's amount realized is $11,000, which includes $1,000 cash as well as the amount of the encumbrance on A's share of AB's assets ($10,000). Therefore, A's gain is $8,000 ($11,000 – $3,000). This $8,000 is income from the activity. Assuming A is entitled to no deductions allocable to the activity for 1979 other than those disallowed in 1978 under section 465(a), income allocable to the activity for 1979 ($8,000) will exceed the deductions ($7,000). Consequently, A will not have a section 465(d) loss from the activity in 1979 because $7,000 is less than the amount of income from the activity for 1979 ($8,000). The $7,000 of deductions will be allowed for 1979.

Example (2). On January 1, 1978, D, an individual, purchases a piece of equipment to be used in an activity described in section 465(c)(1)(C). D purchases the equipment for $10,000, paying $1,000 from personal assets and borrowing $9,000 from a bank. The loan from the bank is a nonrecourse loan secured by the equipment. After the close of 1980 D's basis in the equipment is $2,000 and the amount at risk in the activity is zero. As of the beginning of 1981 D has $7,000 of losses which would be allowed but for section 465(a). The equipment is still encumbered by the $9,000 loan. On January 1, 1981, D gives the piece of equipment to a relative, E. The fair market value of the equipment at the time of the transfer is $9,500. E pays no cash to D but takes the equipment still subject to the nonrecourse loan. D's amount realized on the transfer is $9,000, attributable to the liabilities to which the equipment is subject. D must recognize $7,000 ($9,000 – $2,000) of income on the disposition. This $7,000 is income from the activity. Assuming D is entitled to no deductions allocable to the activity for 1981 other than those disallowed in 1980 under section 465(a) the income allocable from the activity for 1981 ($7,000) will equal the deductions allocable to the activity for 1981 ($7,000). Consequently, D will not have a section 465(d) loss from the activity in 1981 and the $7,000 of deductions will be allowed for 1981, because there is an equal amount of income from the activity in that year.

Example (3). E, an individual calendar year taxpayer, is a partner in partnership EFGH, which is also a calendar year taxpayer. At the close of 1978 E's amount at risk is zero, E's adjusted basis is $350, and E has deductions disallowed by section 465 in the amount of $50. E's share of nonrecourse liabilities of the partnership is $400. At the close of 1979 none of the figures has changed and EFGH distributes property (which is not described in section 751) to E in complete liquidation of E's interest in EFGH. Under section 752(b) E is treated as receiving $400. Under section 732(b), E's basis of $350 is reduced to zero. E must recognize $50 of gain ($400 – $350). Under this section, E has income from the activity in the amount of the gain recognized ($50). This will allow E to deduct the $50 deductions previously suspended. In 1979 E will not have a section 465(d) loss from the activity [Reg. § 1.465-66.]

§ 1.465-67. Transfers and dispositions; pass through of losses suspended under section 465(a).—(a) *Applicability.*—This section shall apply to any transfer or disposition in which—

(1) The taxpayer transfers or disposes of such taxpayer's entire interest in the activity or the entity conducting the activity,

(2) The basis of the transferee is determined in whole or in part by reference to the basis of the transferor; and

(3) The transferor has suspended losses under section 465(a) at the time of the transfer or disposition.

For the treatment of any gain recognized by the transferor, see § 1.465-66.

(b) *Pass through of suspended losses.*—If at the close of the taxable year in which the transfer or disposition occurs, the amount of the transferor's section 465(d) loss from the activity is in excess of the transferor's amount at risk in the activity, such excess shall be added to the transferor's basis in the activity. The preceding sentence is to be applied after the determination of any gain to the transferor and is to be used solely for the purpose of determining the basis of the property in the hands of the transferee. [Reg. § 1.465-67.]

§ 1.465-68. Transfers and dispositions; amounts at risk in excess of losses disallowed.—(a) *Applicability.*—This section shall apply to any transfer or disposition (except a transfer at death) in which—

(1) The taxpayer transfers or disposes of such taxpayer's entire interest in the activity or the entity conducting the activity;

(2) The basis of the transferee is determined in whole or in part by reference to the basis of the transferor; and

(3) The transferor has an amount at risk which is in excess of losses from the activity.

(b) *General rule.*—At the close of the transferor's taxable year in which the transfer or disposition occurs, the transferor's amount at risk in the activity (after being reduced by the transferor's losses from that activity for that taxable year) shall be added to the transferee's amount at risk. In addition, the transferee's amount at risk shall be increased by the amount that the transferee's basis is increased under section 1015(d) (relating to gift tax paid by the transferor).

(c) *Limitation.*—The amount by which the transferee's amount at risk is increased under paragraph (b) of this section shall be limited to the amount of the transferee's basis which exceeds the amount considered paid by the transferee at the time of the transfer. For the purposes of this section the amount considered paid by the transferee includes the amount of liabilities to which the transferred property is subject.

(d) *Examples.*—The provisions of this section may be illustrated by the following examples:

Example (1). On December 31, 1978, F, an individual, makes a gift to G of F's entire interest in an activity described in section 465(c)(1). F had engaged in the activity as an individual. As of the close of 1978 F's amount at risk in the activity is $500, F's adjusted basis in the activity is $9,500, the fair market value of the activity is $20,000, and the activity is subject to a nonrecourse liability of $9,000. G does not pay any cash to F but takes the gift subject to the $9,000 liability. Since F's amount at risk in the activity is $500 at the close of the year, this amount shall be added to G's amount at risk. This amount is not limited by paragraph (c) of this section, because the amount of G's adjusted basis which exceeds the amount G is considered to have paid at the time of the transfer is also $500 ($9,500 – $9,000). Therefore, G is at risk in the amount of $500.

Example (2). Assume the same facts as in example (1), except that in addition to G taking the gift subject to the $9,000 liability, G also pays F $1,500 in cash. Regardless of how much F is at risk, G's amount at risk will not be increased as the result of this section. This is because the amount of increase is limited to the excess of G's basis ($10,500, consisting of the $9,000 liability, plus the $1,500 cash paid to F) over the amount G is considered to have paid F ($9,000 + $1,500 = $10,500). Since the excess is zero ($10,500 – $10,500), the amount of increase under § 1.465-68(b) is also zero. G's amount at risk will be increased, however, under § 1.465-22(d) by the $1,500 cash paid to F, and therefore, G's amount at risk is $1,500. [Reg. § 1.465-68.]

§ 1.465-69. Transfers and dispositions; amounts at risk in excess of losses disallowed with respect to transfers at death.—(a) *Applicability.*—If after the close of the taxable year in which a decedent dies, the decedent's amount at risk in the activity (after being reduced by losses previously suspended under section 465(a)) is greater than zero, such amount shall be added to the successor's amount at risk. However, this amount must be adjusted to reflect changes, if any, in the amount at risk occurring as the result of the decedent's death. The successor's amount at risk shall also be increased by the amount which the successor's basis in the activity is increased under section 1014 or 1023(h), (c), (d), and (e).

(b) *Example.*—The provisions of this section may be illustrated by the following example:

Example. H, an individual, is engaged in an activity described in section 465(c)(1) for a taxable year in which section 1023 applies. On December 31 of such year, H dies. On that date H's basis in the activity is $6,000, H's amount at risk in the activity is $2,500, and the fair market value of the activity is $12,500. Under H's will, J is the sole beneficiary of H's interest in the activity. During the period between H's death and the time J succeeded to the activity nothing occurred which affected the amount at risk. Under sections 1023(h), (c), (d), and (e), the basis of the activity in the hands of J is increased by $5,000, which when added to H's basis of $6,000, gives J a basis in the activity of $11,000. To determine J's amount at risk in the activity, H's amount at risk in the activity ($2,500) is added to the amount by which J's basis in the activity is increased under sections 1023(h), (c), (d), and (e) ($5,000). Therefore, J's amount at risk in the activity is $7,500 ($2,500 + $5,000). [Reg. § 1.465-69.]

§ 1.465-75. Amounts at risk with respect to activities begun prior to effective date; in general.—Section 465 generally applies to losses attributable to amounts paid or incurred in taxable years beginning after December 31, 1975. For the purposes of applying the at risk limitation to activities begun before the effective date of the provision (and which were not excepted from application of the provision), it is necessary to determine the amount at risk as of the first day of the first taxable year beginning after December 31, 1975. The amount at risk in an activity as of the first day of the first taxable year of the taxpayer beginning after December 31, 1975 (for the purposes of §§ 1.465-75 through 1.465-79, such first day shall be referred to as the effective date) shall be determined according to the rules provided in §§ 1.465-76 through 1.465-79. [Reg. § 1.465-75.]

§ 1.465-76. Amounts at risk with respect to activities begun prior to effective date; determination of amount at risk.—(a) *Initial amount.*—The amount a taxpayer is at risk on the effective date with respect to an activity to which section 465 applies shall be determined in accordance with this section. The initial amount the taxpayer is at risk in the activity shall be the taxpayer's initial basis in the activity as modified by disregarding amounts described in section 465(b)(3) or (4) (relating generally to amounts protected against loss or borrowed from related persons).

(b) *Succeeding adjustments.*—For each taxable year ending before the effective date, the initial amount at risk shall be increased and decreased by the items which increased and decreased the taxpayer's basis in the activity in that year as modified by disregarding the amounts described in section 465(b)(3) or (4).

(c) *Application of losses and withdrawals.*—(1) Losses described in section 465(d) which are incurred in taxable years beginning prior to January 1, 1976 and deducted in such taxable years will be treated as reducing first that portion of the taxpayer's basis which is attributable to amounts not at risk. On the other hand, withdrawals made in taxable years beginning before January 1, 1976 will be treated as reducing the amount which the taxpayer is at risk.

(2) Therefore, if in a taxable year beginning prior to January 1, 1976 there is a loss described in section 465(d), it shall reduce the amount at risk only to the extent it exceeds the amount of the taxpayer's basis which is not at risk. For the purposes of this paragraph the taxpayer's basis which is not at risk is that portion of the taxpayer's basis in the activity (as of the close of the taxable year and prior to reduction for the loss) which is attributable to amounts described in section 465(b)(3) or (4).

(d) *Amount at risk shall not be less than zero.*—If, after determining the amount described in paragraph (a), (b), and (c) of this section, the amount at risk (but for this paragraph) would be less than zero, the amount at risk on the effective date shall be zero. [Reg. § 1.465-76.]

§ 1.465-77. Amounts at risk with respect to activities begun prior to effective date; allocation of loss for different taxable years.—If the taxable year of the entity conducting the activity differs from that of the taxpayer, the loss attributable to the activity for the first taxable year of the entity ending after the beginning of the first taxable year of the taxpayer beginning after December 31, 1975, shall be allocated in the following manner: That portion of the loss from the activity for such taxable year of the entity which is attributable to taxable years of the taxpayer beginning before January 1, 1976, is that portion which bears the same ratio to the total loss as the number of days in such taxable year before January 1, 1976, bears to the total number of days in the entire taxable year. Consequently, that portion shall be treated in accordance with § 1.465-76. [Reg. § 1.465-77.]

§ 1.465-78. Amounts at risk with respect to activities begun prior to effective date; insufficient records.—If sufficient records do not exist to accurately determine under § 1.465-76 the amount which a taxpayer is at risk on the effective date, the amount at risk shall be the taxpayer's basis in the activity reduced (but not below zero) by the taxpayer's share of amounts described in section 465(b)(3) or (4) with respect to the activity on the day before the effective date [Reg. § 1.465-78.]

§ 1.465-79. Amounts at risk with respect to activities begun prior to effective date; examples.—The provisions of § 1.465-75 and § 1.465-76 may be illustrated by the following examples:

Example (1). J and K, as equal partners, form partnership JK on January 1, 1975 to engage in an activity described in section 465(c)(1). Both J and K, as well as JK, are calendar year taxpayers. On January 1, 1975, each partner contributes $10,000 in cash from personal assets to JK. On July 1, 1975, JK borrows $40,000 (of which J's share is $20,000) from a bank under a nonrecourse financing arrangement secured only by the new equipment purchased with the $40,000 for use in the activity. On Septebmer 1, 1975, JK reduces the amount due on the loan to $36,000 (of which J's share is $18,000). On October 1, 1975, JK distributes $3,000 to each partner. For taxable year 1975, JK has no income or loss. Although J's basis in the activity is $25,000 ($10,000 + $18,000 – $3,000), J's amount at risk on the effective date is $7,000, determined as follows:

Initial amount at risk	$10,000
Plus:	
Items which increased basis other than amounts described in section 465 (b)(3) or (4)	$0
	$10,000
Less:	
Distribution	3,000
J's amount at risk on effective date	$7,000

Example (2). Assume the same facts as in example (1) except that JK has a section 465(d) loss for 1975, of which J's share is $12,000. Although J's basis in the activity is $13,000 ($10,000 + $18,000 – ($3,000 + $12,000)), J's amount at risk on the effective date is $7,000, determined as follows:

Initial amount at risk	$10,000
Plus:	
Items which increased basis other than amounts described in section 465 (b)(3) or (4)	0
	$10,000
Less:	
Distribution plus	
Portion of loss ($12,000) in excess of portion of basis not at risk ($18,000) ($3,000 + 0)	3,000
J's amount at risk on effective date	$7,000

Example (3). Assume the same facts as in example (1) except that JK has a section 465(d) loss for 1975, and J's share is $23,000. J's basis in the activity is $2,000 ($10,000 + $18,000 – ($3,000 + $23,000)). The amount at risk on the effective date is determined as follows:

Initial amount at risk		$10,000
Plus:		
Items which increased basis other than amounts described in section 465(b)(3) or (4)		0
		$10,000
Less:		
Distribution	$3,000	
Portion of loss ($23,000) in excess of portion of basis not at risk ($18,000)	5,000	8,000
J's amount at risk on the effective date		$2,000

[Reg. § 1.465-79.]

§ 1.465-95. Effective date.—(a) *In general.*—Except as otherwise provided, the regulations under section 465 shall apply to losses attributable to amounts paid or incurred in taxable years beginning after December 31, 1975. For purposes of this paragraph, any amount allowed or allowable for depreciation, amortization, or depletion for any period shall be treated as an amount paid or incurred in such period.

(b) *Special rules.*—For special rules relating to the effective date of section 465 with respect to certain leasing activities and certain movie and video tape activities, see section 204(c)(2) and (3) of the Tax Reform Act of 1976 (90 Stat. 1532). [Reg. § 1.465-95.]

Deduction Limited to Amount at Risk

Deduction Limited to Amount at Risk.—Amendments to Reg. §§7.465-1—7.465-5, relating to the determination of amounts at risk with respect to certain activities, are proposed (published in the Federal Register on June 5, 1979).

□ Par. 2. Sections 7.465-1 through 7.465-5 of this chapter (26 CFR Part 7), promulgated by Treasury Decision 7504, are hereby revoked.

§7.465-1. Amounts at risk with respect to activities begun prior to effective date; in general (Temporary).

§7.465-2. Determination of amount at risk (Temporary).

§7.465-3. Allocation of loss for different taxable years (Temporary).

§7.465-4. Insufficient records (Temporary).

§7.465-5. Examples (Temporary).

Nuclear Decommissioning Funds: Contributions to Trusts: Deductions

Nuclear Decommissioning Funds: Contributions to Trusts: Deductions.—Amendments to Reg. §1.468A-1, relating to deductions for contributions to trusts maintained for decommissioning nuclear power plants and the use of the amounts in those trusts to decommission nuclear plants, are proposed (published in the Federal Register on December 29, 2016) (REG-112800-16).

Par. 2. Section §1.468A-1 is amended by revising paragraph (b)(6) to read as follows:

§1.468A-1. Nuclear decommissioning costs; general rules.

* * *

(b) * * *

(6)(i) The term *nuclear decommissioning costs* or *decommissioning costs* includes all otherwise deductible expenses to be incurred in connection with the entombment, decontamination, dismantlement, removal and disposal of the structures, systems and components of a nuclear power plant, whether that nuclear power plant will continue to produce electric energy or has permanently ceased to produce electric energy. Such term includes all otherwise deductible expenses to be incurred in connection with the preparation for decommissioning, such as engineering and other planning expenses, and all otherwise deductible expenses to be incurred with respect to the plant after the actual decommissioning occurs, such as physical security and radiation monitoring expenses. An expense is otherwise deductible for purposes of this paragraph (b)(6) if it would be deductible or recoverable through depreciation or amortization under chapter 1 of the Internal Revenue Code without regard to section 280B.

(ii) The term nuclear decommissioning costs or decommissioning costs also includes costs incurred in connection with the construction, operation, and ultimate decommissioning of a facility used solely to store, pending delivery to a permanent repository or disposal, spent nuclear fuel generated by the nuclear power plant or plants located on the same site as the storage facility (for example, an Independent Spent Fuel Storage Installation). Such term does not include otherwise deductible expenses to be incurred in connection with the disposal of spent nuclear fuel under the Nuclear Waste Policy Act of 1982 (Public Law 97-425).

* * *

Nuclear Decommissioning Funds: Contributions to Trusts: Deductions

Nuclear Decommissioning Funds: Contributions to Trusts: Deductions.—Amendments to Reg. §1.468A-5, relating to deductions for contributions to trusts maintained for decommissioning nuclear power plants and the use of the amounts in those trusts to decommission nuclear plants, are proposed (published in the Federal Register on December 29, 2016) (REG-112800-16).

Par. 3. Paragraph §1.468A-5 is amended by revising the heading and paragraphs (b)(2)(i) and (d)(3)(i) to read as follows:

§1.468A-5. Nuclear decommissioning fund—miscellaneous provisions.

* * *

(b) * * *

(2) * * *

(i) A payment by a nuclear decommissioning fund for the purpose of satisfying, in whole or in part, the liability of the electing taxpayer for decommissioning costs of the nuclear power plant to which the nuclear decommissioning fund relates, whether such payment is made to an unrelated party in satisfaction of the decommissioning liability or to the plant operator or other otherwise disqualified person as reimbursement solely for actual expenses paid by such person in satisfaction of the decommissioning liability;

* * *

(d) * * *

(3) * * *

(i) The substantial completion of the decommissioning of a nuclear power plant occurs on the date on which all Federal, state, local, and contractual decommissioning requirements are fully satisfied (the substantial completion date). Except as otherwise provided in paragraph (d)(3)(ii) of this section, the substantial completion date is also the termination date.

* * *

Escrow Funds: Reporting of Income: Qualified Settlement Funds

Escrow Funds: Reporting of Income: Qualified Settlement Funds: Qualified Trusts: Escrow Accounts—Reg. §§1.468B-8, relating to the designation of the person required to report the income earned on qualified settlement funds and certain other funds, trusts, and escrow accounts, and other related rules, is proposed (published in the Federal Register on February 1, 1999) (REG-209619-93). Proposed Reg. §§1.468B-7 and 1.468B-9 and proposed amendments to Reg. §§1.468B-0, 1.468B-1 and 1.468B-5 were adopted by T.D. 9249 on February 3, 2006. Proposed Reg. §1.468B-6 was withdrawn on February 7, 2006.

☐ Par. 5. [Section 1.468B-8 is] added to read as follows:

§1.468B-8. Contingent at-closing escrows.—(a) *Scope*.—This section provides rules under section 468B(g) for the taxation of income earned on a contingent at-closing escrow, which is defined in paragraph (b) of this section. No inference should be drawn from this section concerning the tax treatment of a contingent at-closing escrow, or of parties to the escrow, under sections of the Internal Revenue Code other than section 468B. See also paragraph (d) of this section.

(b) *Definitions*.—For purposes of this section, the following definitions apply—

Administrator means an escrow agent, escrow holder, trustee, or other person responsible for administering an escrow account, trust, or fund (the purchaser or the seller may be the administrator);

Contingent at-closing escrow means an escrow account, trust, or fund that satisfies the following requirements—

(1) The escrow is established in connection with the sale or exchange (other than an exchange to which section 354, 355, or 356 applies) of real or personal property used in a trade or business or held for investment (including stock in a corporation or an interest in a partnership);

(2) Depending on whether events specified in the agreement between the purchaser and the seller that are subject to bona fide contingencies (not including events that are certain, or reasonably certain, to occur, such as the passage of time, or that are certain, or reasonably certain, not to occur) either occur or fail to occur, the escrow's assets (except for assets set aside for taxes or expenses) will be distributable—

(i) Entirely to the purchaser;

(ii) Entirely to the seller; or

(iii) In part, to the purchaser with the remainder to the seller; and

(3) The escrow is not a qualified escrow account or qualified trust established in connection with a deferred exchange under section 1031(a)(3);

Determination date means the date on which (or by which) the last of the events subject to a bona fide contingency specified in the agreement between the purchaser and the seller (referred to in the definition of *contingent at-closing escrow*) has either occurred or failed to occur;

Purchaser means, in the case of an exchange of property, the transferee of the property; and

Seller means, in the case of an exchange of property, the transferor of the property.

(c) *Tax liability of purchaser and seller for the period prior to the determination date*.—For the period prior to the determination date, the purchaser is treated as owning the assets of the contingent at-closing escrow for federal income tax purposes. Thus, in computing the purchaser's income tax liability, the purchaser must take into account all items of income, deduction, and credit (including capital gains and losses) of the escrow until the determination date.

(d) *Transfer of interest in the assets of the escrow on the determination date*.—No inference should be drawn from this section whether, for purposes of Internal Revenue Code sections other than 468B, there is a transfer of ownership of the assets of a contingent at-closing escrow on the determination date from the purchaser to the seller or from the seller to the purchaser, or the tax consequences of such a transfer. Thus, for example, if there is a transfer of ownership of the assets of the escrow from the purchaser to the seller on the determination date for purposes of other Code sections, no inference should be drawn from this section whether any portion of the amount transferred is unstated interest. See §1.483-4.

(e) *Tax liability of purchaser and seller for the period beginning on the determination date*.—For the period beginning on the determination date, the purchaser and the seller must each take into account in determining their income tax liabilities the income, deductions, and credits (including capital gains and losses) corresponding to their ownership interests in the assets of the escrow.

(f) *Statement required to be provided to administrator within 30 days after the determination date*.—Within 30 days after the determination date, the purchaser and the seller must provide the administrator with a written statement that—

(1) Is signed by the purchaser and the seller;

(2) Specifies the determination date; and

(3) Specifies the purchaser's and seller's ownership interests in each asset of the escrow.

(g) *Reporting obligations of the administrator*.—(1) *In general*.—The administrator of a contingent at-closing escrow must, for each calendar year (or portion thereof) that the escrow is in existence, report the income of the escrow on Forms 1099 in accordance with the information reporting requirements of subpart B, Part III, subchapter A, chapter 61, Subtitle F of the Internal Revenue Code. The Forms 1099 must show as payor the administrator of the escrow and as payee the person (or persons) treated as the payee (or payees) under paragraph (g)(2) of this section.

(2) *Person treated as payee*.—In satisfying the reporting obligations of paragraph (g)(1) of this section, the following rules apply to the administrator—

(i) For the period prior to the determination date, the administrator must treat the purchaser as the payee of the income of the escrow;

(ii) For the period beginning on the determination date, if the written statement described in paragraph (f) of this section is timely provided to the administrator, the administrator must treat as the payee (or payees) of the income of the escrow the purchaser or seller (or both) in accordance with their respective ownership interests as shown on the statement; and

(iii) If the written statement described in paragraph (f) of this section is not provided to the administrator, the administrator must continue to treat the purchaser as the payee of the income of the escrow.

(3) *Relief from penalties for filing incorrect information return or payee statement.*—For purposes of sections 6721 and 6722, the administrator will not be treated as failing to file or furnish a correct information return or payee statement solely because, in preparing a Form 1099, the administrator relies on a statement described in paragraph (f) of this section and therefore treats the purchaser or seller (or both) as the payee (or payees) of the income of the escrow in accordance with their respective ownership interests in the assets of the escrow as shown on the statement. If a statement described in paragraph (f) of this section is not provided to the administrator, the administrator will not be treated as failing to file or furnish a correct information return or payee statement solely because, in preparing a Form 1099, the administrator relies on the absence of the statement and therefore treats the purchaser as the payee.

(h) *Effective date.*—(1) *In general.*—The provisions of this section apply to contingent at-closing escrows that are established after the date of publication of final regulations in the Federal Register.

(2) *Transition rule.*—With respect to a contingent at-closing escrow established after August 16, 1986, but on or before the date of publication of final regulations in the Federal Register, the Internal Revenue Service will not challenge a reasonable, consistently applied method of taxation for income earned by the escrow. The Internal Revenue Service will also not challenge a reasonable, consistently applied method for reporting such income.

(i) [Reserved]

(j) *Example.*—The provisions of this section may be illustrated by the following example:

Example. (i) P and S are corporations. In 1999, P enters into a contract with S for the purchase of rental real estate. On October 1, 1999, the date of sale, S transfers the real estate to P, and P pays S a portion of the purchase price, $9,000,000. P deposits the remaining portion of the purchase price, $850,000, into an escrow account as required by the contract. H is the escrow holder.

(ii) The contract provides that the escrow balance as of November 1, 2000, is payable entirely to P, entirely to S, or partially to P and partially to S depending on the amount, if any, by which the average rental income from the real estate during a specified testing period ending on September 30, 2000, exceeds one or more specified earnings targets.

(iii) According to the terms of the contract, the income earned on the escrow must be accumulated and is not currently distributable to P or S during the period prior to November 1, 2000.

(iv) During the testing period specified in the contract between P and S, the average rental income earned on the property exceeds one (but not all) of the specified earnings targets. As a result, on September 30, 2000, the end of the testing period, P became entitled to 40% of the escrow assets and S became entitled to 60% of the escrow assets.

(v) On October 30, 2000, P and S provide H with the written statement described in paragraph (f) of this section. The written statement is thus provided within 30 days of September 30, 2000. The statement indicates that P's ownership interest in each asset of the escrow is 40 percent and S's ownership interest in each asset is 60 percent.

(vi) The escrow is a contingent at-closing escrow. September 30, 2000, is the determination date because this is the date on which the testing period ends. As of this date, all contingencies specified in the contract are resolved.

(vii) P must take into account all of the income, deductions, and credits (including capital gains and losses) of the escrow in computing P's income tax liability for the period prior to September 30, 2000. See paragraph (c) of this section.

(viii) For the period beginning on September 30, 2000, P must take into account in computing P's income tax liability 40 percent of each item of income, deduction, and credit of the escrow (including capital gains and losses), and S must take into account in computing S's income tax liability 60 percent of these items. See paragraph (e) of this section.

(ix) H is subject to the information reporting requirements of paragraph (g)(1) of this section. H must file Forms 1099 and furnish payee statements to reflect the fact that prior to September 30, 2000, P is the payee of all the income of the escrow, and for the period beginning on September 30, 2000, P is the payee of 40 percent of the income, and S is the payee of 60 percent of the income.

[Reg. § 1.468B-8.]

Passive Activity Losses and Credits: Limitations

Passive Activity Losses and Credits: Limitations.—Reg. §§1.469-1T, 1.469-2T, 1.469-3T and 1.469-5T, relating to the limitations on passive activity losses and credits, are proposed (published in the Federal Register on February 24, 1988) (LR-14-88). Reg. §1.469-11T was adopted by T.D. 8417 on May 11, 1992.

§1.469-1T. General rules (temporary).

§1.469-2T. Passive activity loss (temporary).

§1.469-3T. Passive activity credit (temporary).

§1.469-5T. Material participation (temporary).

Passive Activity Losses and Credits: Limitations

Passive Activity Losses and Credits: Limitations.—Amendments to Reg. §§1.469-0, 1.469-5, 1.469-5T and 1.469-9, regarding the definition of an "interest in a limited partnership as a limited partner" for purposes of determining whether a taxpayer materially participates in an activity under section 469 of the Internal Revenue Code, are proposed (published in the Federal Register on November 28, 2011) (REG-109369-10).

☐ Par. 2. Section 1.469–0 is amended by:

1. Revising the entries for §1.469–5(a), (b), (c), (d), and (e).
2. Removing the entries for §1.469–5T(e)(1), (e)(2), and (e)(3).

The revisions read as follows:

§1.469-0. Table of contents.

* * *

* * *

☐ Par. 3. In §1.469–5, paragraphs (a), (b), (c), (d), and (e) are revised to read as follows:

§1.469-5. Material participation.—(a) through (d) [Reserved].

(e) *Treatment of an interest in a limited partnership as a limited partner.*—(1) *In general.*—Except as otherwise provided in this paragraph (e), an individual shall not be treated as materially participating in any activity in which the individual owns an interest in a limited partnership as a limited partner (as defined in paragraph (e)(3)(i) of this section) for purposes of applying section 469 and the regulations thereunder to—

(i) The individual's share of any income, gain, loss, deduction, or credit from such activity that is attributable to an interest in a limited partnership as a limited partner; and

(ii) Any gain or loss from such activity recognized upon a sale or exchange of such an interest.

(2) *Exceptions.*—Paragraph (e)(1) of this section shall not apply to an individual's share of income, gain, loss, deduction, and credit for a taxable year from any activity in which the individual would be treated as materially participating for the taxable year under paragraphs (a)(1), (a)(5), or (a)(6) of § 1.469-5T if the individual did not own an interest in a limited partnership as a limited partner (as defined in paragraph (e)(3)(i) of this section) for such taxable year.

(3) *Interest in a limited partnership as a limited partner.*—(i) *In general.*—Except as provided in paragraph (e)(3)(ii) of this section, for purposes of section 469(h)(2) and this paragraph (e), an interest in an entity shall be treated as an interest in a limited partnership as a limited partner if—

(A) The entity in which such interest is held is classified as a partnership for Federal income tax purposes under § 301.7701-3; and

(B) The holder of such interest does not have rights to manage the entity at all times during the entity's taxable year under the law of the jurisdiction in which the entity is organized and under the governing agreement.

(ii) *Individual holding an interest other than an interest in a limited partnership as a limited partner.*—An individual shall not be treated as holding an interest in a limited partnership as a limited partner for the individual's taxable year if such individual also holds an interest in the partnership that is not an interest in a limited partnership as a limited partner (as defined in paragraph (e)(3)(i) of this section), such as a state-law general partnership interest, at all times during the entity's taxable year ending with or within the individual's taxable year (or the portion of the entity's taxable year during which the individual (directly or indirectly) owns such interest in a limited partnership as a limited partner).

(4) *Effective/applicability date.*—This section applies to taxable years beginning on or after the date of publication of the Treasury decision adopting these rules as a final regulation in the **Federal Register.**

* * *

☐ Par. 4. Section 1.469–5T paragraph (e) is revised to read as follows:

§1.469-5T. Material participation (Temporary).

* * *

(e) *Treatment of Limited Partners.*—[Reserved]. See § 1.469-5(e) for rules relating to this paragraph (e).

* * *

☐ Par. 5. Section 1.469–9 paragraph (f)(1) is revised to read as follows:

§1.469-9. Rules for certain rental real estate activities.

* * *

(f) *Limited partnership interests in rental real estate activities.*—(1) *In general.*—If a taxpayer elects under paragraph (g) of this section to treat all interests in rental real estate as a single rental real estate activity, and at least one interest in rental real estate is held by the taxpayer as an interest in a limited partnership as a limited partner (within the meaning of § 1.469-5(e)(3)), the combined rental real estate activity of the taxpayer will be treated as an interest in a limited partnership as a limited partner for purposes of determining material participation. Accordingly, the taxpayer will not be treated under this section as materially participating in the combined rental real estate activity unless the taxpayer materially participates in the activity under the tests listed in § 1.469-5(e)(2) (dealing with the tests for determining the material participation of a limited partner).

* * *

Deduction for Business Interest Expense: Limitation

Deduction for Business Interest Expense: Limitation.—Amendments to Reg. §1.469-9, regarding the limitation on the deduction for business interest expense after the enactment of recent tax legislation, are proposed (published in the Federal Register on December 28, 2018) (REG-106089-18).

Par. 13. Section 1.469-9 is amended by revising paragraph (b)(2) to read as follows:

§1.469-9. Rules for certain rental real estate activities.

* * *

(b) * * *

(2) *Real property trade or business.*—The following terms have the following meanings in determining whether a trade or business is a real property trade or business for purposes of section 469(c)(7)(C) and this section.

(i) *Real property.*—(A) *In general.*—The term *real property* includes land, buildings, and other inherently permanent structures that are permanently affixed to land. Any interest in real property, including fee ownership, co-ownership, a leasehold, an option, or a similar interest is real property under this section. Tenant improvements to land, buildings, or other structures that are inherently permanent or otherwise classified as real property within the meaning of this section are real property for purposes of section 469(c)(7)(C). However, property produced for sale that is not real property in the hands of the producing taxpayer or a related person, but that may be incorporated into real property by an unrelated person, is not treated as real property of the producing taxpayer for purposes of section 469(c)(7)(C) and this section (for example, bricks, nails, paint, and windowpanes).

(B) *Land.*—The term *land* includes water and air space superjacent to land and natural products and deposits that are unsevered from the land. Natural products and deposits, such as plants, crops, trees, water, ores, and minerals, cease to be real property when they are harvested, severed, extracted, or removed from the land. Accordingly, any trade or business that involves the cultivation and harvesting of plants, crops, or trees, or severing, extracting, or removing natural products or deposits from land is not a real property trade or business for purposes of section 469(c)(7)(C) and this section. The storage or maintenance of severed or extracted natural products or deposits, such as plants, crops, trees, water, ores, and minerals, in or upon real property does not cause the stored property to be recharacterized as real property, and any trade or business relating to or involving such storage or maintenance of severed or extracted natural products or deposits is not a real property trade or business, even though such storage or maintenance otherwise may occur upon or within real property.

(C) *Inherently permanent structure.*—The term *inherently permanent structure* means any permanently affixed building or other permanently affixed structure. If the affixation is reasonably expected to last indefinitely, based on all the facts and circumstances, the affixation is considered permanent. However, an asset that serves an active function, such as an item of machinery or equipment (for example, HVAC system, elevator or escalator), is not a building or other inherently permanent structure, and therefore is not real property for purposes of section 469(c)(7)(C) and this section, even if such item of machinery or equipment is permanently affixed to or becomes incorporated within a building or other inherently permanent structure. Accordingly, a trade or business that involves the manufacture, installation, operation, maintenance, or repair of any asset that serves an active function will not be a real property trade or business, or a unit or component of another real property trade or business, for purposes of section 469(c)(7)(C) and this section.

(D) *Building.*—*(1) In general.*—A *building* encloses a space within its walls and is generally covered by a roof or other external upper covering that protects the walls and inner space from the elements.

(2) Types of buildings.—Buildings include the following assets if permanently affixed to land: houses; townhouses; apartments; condominiums; hotels; motels; stadiums; arenas; shopping malls; factory and office buildings; warehouses; barns; enclosed garages; enclosed transportation stations and terminals; and stores.

(E) *Other inherently permanent structures.*—*(1) In general.*—Other inherently permanent structures include the following assets if permanently affixed to land: parking facilities; bridges; tunnels; roadbeds; railroad tracks; pipelines; storage structures such as silos and oil and gas storage tanks; and stationary wharves and docks.

(2) Facts and circumstances determination.—The determination of whether an asset is an inherently permanent structure is based on all the facts and circumstances. In particular, the following factors must be taken into account:

(i) The manner in which the asset is affixed to land and whether such manner of affixation allows the asset to be easily removed from the land;

(ii) Whether the asset is designed to be removed or to remain in place indefinitely on the land;

(iii) The damage that removal of the asset would cause to the asset itself or to the land to which it is affixed;

(iv) Any circumstances that suggest the expected period of affixation is not indefinite (for example, a lease that requires or permits removal of the asset from the land upon the expiration of the lease); and

(v) The time and expense required to move the asset from the land.

(ii) *Other definitions.*—(A) through (G) [Reserved]

(H) *Real property operation.*—The term *real property operation* means handling, by a direct or indirect owner of the real property, the day-to-day operations of a trade or business, within the meaning of paragraph (b)(1) of this section, relating to the maintenance and occupancy of the real property that affect the availability and functionality of that real property used, or held out for use, by customers where payments received from customers are principally for the customers' use of the real property. The principal purpose of such business operations must be the provision of the use of the real property, or physical space accorded by or within the real property, to one or more customers, and not the provision of other significant or extraordinary personal services, within the meaning of §1.469-1T(e)(3)(iv) and (v), to customers in conjunction with the customers' incidental use of the real property or physical space. If the real property or physical space is provided to a customer to be used to carry on the customer's trade or business, the principal purpose of the business operations must be to provide the customer with exclusive use of the real property or physical space in furtherance of the customer's trade or business, and not to provide other significant or extraordinary personal services to the customer in addition to or in conjunction with the use of the real property or physical space, regardless of whether the customer pays for the services separately. However, other incidental personal services may be provided to the customer in conjunction with the use of real property or physical space, as long as such services are insubstantial in relation to the customer's use of the real property or physical space and the receipt of such services is not a significant factor in the customer's decision to use the real property or physical space.

(I) *Real property management.*—The term *real property management* means handling, by a professional manager, the day-to-day operations of a trade or business, within the meaning of paragraph (b)(1) of this section, relating to the maintenance and occupancy of real property that affect the availability and functionality of that property used, or held out for use, by customers where payments received from customers are principally for the customers' use of the real property. The principal purpose of such business operations must be the provision of the use of the real property, or physical space accorded by or within the real property, to one or more customers, and not the provision of other significant or extraordinary personal services, within the meaning of §1.469-1T(e)(3)(iv) and (v), to customers in conjunction with the customers' incidental use of the real property or physical space. If the real property or physical space is provided to a customer to be used to carry on the customer's trade or business, the principal purpose of the business operations must be to provide the customer with exclusive use of the real property or physical space in furtherance of the customer's trade or business, and not to provide other significant or extraordinary personal services to the customer in addition to or in conjunction with the use of the real property or physical space, regardless of whether the customer pays for the services separately. However, other incidental personal services may be provided to the customer in conjunction with the use of real property or physical space, as long as such services are insubstantial in relation to the customer's use of the real property or physical space and the receipt of such services is not a significant factor in the customer's decision to use the real property or physical space. A professional manager is a person responsible, on a full-time basis, for the overall management and oversight of the real property or properties and who is not a direct or indirect owner of the real property or properties.

(J) and (K) [Reserved]

(iii) *Examples.*—The following examples illustrate the operation of this paragraph (b)(2):

(A) *Example 1.* A owns farmland and uses the land in A's farming business to grow and harvest crops of various kinds. As part of this farming business, A utilizes a greenhouse that is an inherently permanent structure to grow certain crops during the winter months. Under the rules of this section, any trade or business that involves the cultivation and harvesting of plants, crops, or trees is not a real property trade or business for purposes of section 469(c)(7)(C) and this section, even though the cultivation and harvesting of crops occurs upon or within real property. Accordingly, under these facts, A is not engaged in a real property trade or business for purposes of section 469(c)(7)(C) and this section.

(B) *Example 2.* B is a retired farmer and owns farmland that B rents exclusively to C to operate a farm. The arrangement between B and C is a trade or business (within the meaning of paragraph (b)(1) of this section) where payments by C are principally for C's use of B's real property. B also provides certain farm equipment for C's use. However, C is solely responsible for the maintenance and repair of the farm equipment along with any costs associated with operating the equipment. B also occasionally provides oral advice to C regarding various aspects of the farm operation, based on B's prior experience as a farmer. Other than the provision of this occasional advice, B does not provide any significant or extraordinary personal services to C in connection with the rental of the farmland to C. Under these facts, B is engaged in a real property trade or business (which does not include the use or deemed rental of any farm equipment) for purposes of section 469(c)(7)(C) and this section, and B's oral advice is an incidental personal service that B provides in conjunction with C's use of the real property. Nevertheless, under these facts, C is not engaged in a real property trade or business for purposes of section 469(c)(7)(C) and this section because C is engaged in the business of farming.

(C) *Example 3.* D owns a building in which D operates a restaurant and bar. Even though D provides customers with use of the physical space inside the building, D is not engaged in a trade or business where payments by customers are principally for the use of real property or physical space. Instead, the payments by D's customers are principally for the receipt of significant or extraordinary personal services (within the meaning of §1.469-1T(e)(3)(iv) and (v)), mainly food and beverage preparation and presentation services, and the use of the physical space by customers is incidental to the receipt of these personal services. Under the rules of this section, any trade or business that involves the provision of significant or extraordinary personal services to customers in conjunction with the customers' incidental use of real property or physical space is not a real property trade or business, even though the business operations occur upon or within real property. Accordingly, under these facts, D is not engaged in a real property trade or business for purposes of section 469(c)(7)(C) and this section.

(D) *Example 4.* E owns a majority interest in an S corporation, X, that is engaged in the trade or business of manufacturing industrial cooling systems for installation in commercial buildings and for other uses. E also owns a majority interest in an S corporation, Y, that purchases the industrial cooling systems from X and that installs, maintains, and repairs those systems in both existing commercial buildings and commercial buildings under construction. Under the rules of this section, any trade or business that involves the manufacture, installation, operation, maintenance, or repair of any machinery or equipment that serves an active function will not be a real property trade or business (or a unit or component of another real property trade or business) for purposes of section 469(c)(7)(C) and this section, even though the machinery or equipment will be permanently affixed to real property once it is installed. In this case, the industrial cooling systems are machinery or equipment that serves an active function. Accordingly, under these facts, E, X and Y will not be treated as engaged in one or more real property trades or businesses for purposes of section 469(c)(7)(C) and this section.

(E) *Example 5.* (*1*) F owns an interest in P, a limited partnership. P owns and operates a luxury hotel. In addition to providing rooms and suites for use by customers, the hotel offers many additional amenities such as in-room food and beverage service, maid and linen service, parking valet service, concierge service, front desk and bellhop service, dry cleaning and laundry service, and in-room barber and hairdresser service. P contracted with M to provide maid and janitorial services to P's hotel. M is an S corporation principally engaged in the trade or business of providing maid and janitorial services to various types of businesses, including hotels. G is a professional manager employed by M who handles the day-to-day business operations relating to M's provision of maid and janitorial services to M's various customers, including P.

(*2*) Even though the personal services that P provides to the customers of its hotel are significant personal services within the meaning of §1.469-1T(e)(3)(iv), the principal purpose of P's hotel business operations is the provision of use of the hotel's rooms and suites to customers, and not the provision of the significant personal services to P's customers in conjunction with the customers' incidental use of those rooms or suites. The provision of these significant personal services by P to P's customers is incidental to the customers' use of the hotel's real property. Accordingly, under these facts, F and P are treated as engaged in a real property trade or business for purposes of section 469(c)(7)(C) and this section.

(*3*) With respect to the maid and janitorial services provided by M, M's operations affect the availability and functionality of real property used, or held out for use, by customers in a trade or business where payments by customers are principally for the use of real property (in this case, P's hotel). However, M does not operate or manage real property. Instead, M is engaged in a trade or business of providing maid and janitorial services to customers, such as P, that are engaged in real property trades or businesses. Thus, M's business operations are merely ancillary to real property trades or businesses. Therefore, M is not engaged in real property operations or management as defined in this section. Accordingly, under these facts, M is not engaged in a real property trade or business within the meaning of section 469(c)(7)(C) and this section.

(*4*) With respect to the day-to-day business operations that G handles as a professional manager of M, the business operations that G manages is not the provision of use of P's hotel rooms and suites to customers. G does not operate or manage real property. Instead, G manages the provision of maid and janitorial services to customers, including P's hotel. Therefore, G is not engaged in real property management as defined in this section. Accordingly, under these facts, G is not engaged in a real property trade or business within the meaning of section 469(c)(7)(C) and this section.

* * *

Deduction for Business Interest Expense: Limitation

Deduction for Business Interest Expense: Limitation.—Amendments to Reg. §1.469-11, regarding the limitation on the deduction for business interest expense after the enactment of recent tax legislation, are proposed (published in the Federal Register on December 28, 2018) (REG-106089-18).

Par. 14. Section 1.469-11 is amended by:

1. Removing the period at the end of paragraph (a)(1) and adding a semicolon in its place;
2. Revising paragraph (a)(3);
3. Redesignating paragraphs (a)(4) and (5) as paragraphs (a)(5) and (6), respectively; and
4. Adding a new paragraph (a)(4).

The revision and addition read as follows:

§1.469-11. Effective date and transition rules.—(a) * * *

(3) The rules contained in §1.469-9, other than paragraph (a)(4) of this section, apply for taxable years beginning on or after January 1, 1995, and to elections made under §1.469-9(g) with returns filed on or after January 1, 1995, and the rules contained in §1.469-11(a)(4) apply for taxable years beginning on or after the date of the Treasury decision adopting these regulations

as final regulations is published in the **Federal Register**;

(4) The rules contained in § 1.469-9(b)(2) apply to taxable years beginning after December 31, 2018. Paragraph (b) of this section applies to loss corporations that have undergone an ownership change during a taxable year ending after the date of the Treasury decision adopting these regulations as final regulations is published in the **Federal Register**. However, taxpayers and their related parties, within the meaning of sections 267(b) and 707(b)(1), may rely on the rules of this section if applied consistently by the taxpayers and their related parties, until the date the Treasury decision adopting these regulations as final regulations is published in the **Federal Register**;

* * *

Commodities: Securities: Mark-to-Market Accounting

Commodities: Securities: Mark-to-Market Accounting.—Reg. § 1.471-12, regarding the election to use the mark-to-market method of accounting for dealers in commodities and traders in securities or commodities, is proposed (published in the Federal Register on January 28, 1999) (REG-104924-98).

☐ Par. 3. Section 1.471-12 is added as follows:

§ 1.471-12. Nonfinancial customer paper.—Nonfinancial customer paper, as defined in section 475(c)(4)(B), may not be treated as inventory except as provided in § 1.475(c)-2(d). This section applies to taxable years ending on or after January 28, 1999. [Reg. § 1.471-12.]

Last-In, First-Out Rule: Increase in Value of Inventories

Inventories: Last-In, First-Out Rule: Increase in Value: Three-Year Averaging Method.—Reproduced below is the text of a proposed amendment to Reg. § 1.472-2, relating to 3-year averaging for increases in inventory value (published in the Federal Register on February 10, 1983).

☐ Paragraph. Section 1.472-2 is amended as follows:

1. Paragraph (c) is revised to read as set forth below.
2. Paragraph (f) is deleted.

§ 1.472-2. Requirements incident to the adoption and use of LIFO inventory method.—

* * *

(c)(1) Goods of the specified type included in the opening inventory of the taxable year for which the method is first used shall be considered as having been acquired at the same time and at a unit cost equal to the actual cost of the aggregate divided by the number of units on hand. The actual cost of the aggregate shall be determined pursuant to the inventory method employed by the taxpayer under the regulations applicable to the prior taxable year with the exception that restoration to the opening inventory of the taxable year for which the LIFO method is first used shall be made with respect to any writedown to market values resulting from the pricing of former inventories.

(2) In the case of a taxpayer first using the LIFO method before January 1, 1982, goods of the specified type on hand as of the close of the taxable year preceding the taxable year for which this inventory method is first used shall be included in the taxpayer's closing inventory for such preceding taxable year at a cost determined in the manner prescribed in paragraph (c)(1) of this section.

(3) In the case of a taxpayer first using the LIFO method after December 31, 1981—

(i) The amount arising from the restoration referred to in paragraph (c)(1) of this section shall be included in the taxpayer's gross income ratably in each of the three taxable years beginning with the taxable year for which the LIFO method is first used.

(ii) Neither an adjustment to the closing inventory nor an amended return shall be required for the taxable year preceding the taxable year for which the LIFO method is first used.

(iii) The provisions of paragraph (c)(3) of this section may be illustrated by the following example:

Example. X, a calendar year taxpayer, first adopts the LIFO method for 1982 and the closing inventory for 1981 included a writedown to market values of $9,000. Such writedown amount shall be restored to the 1982 opening inventory and $3,000 shall be included in X's gross income in each of the taxable years 1982, 1983, and 1984.

LIFO Inventories: Inventory Price Index Computation Method Pools

LIFO Inventories: Inventory Price Index Computation Method Pools.—Amendments to Reg. § 1.472-8, relating to the establishment of dollar-value last-in, first-out (LIFO) inventory pools by certain taxpayers that use the inventory price index computation (IPIC) pooling method, are proposed (published in the Federal Register on November 28, 2016) (REG-125946-10).

Par. 2. Section 1.472-8 is amended as follows:

1. Paragraph (b)(4) is revised.
2. Paragraph (c)(2) is revised.
3. Paragraph (e)(3)(ii) is revised.
4. Paragraph (e)(3)(iii)(B)(*2*) is amended by removing "Table 6 (Producer price indexes and percent changes for commodity groupings and individual items, not seasonally adjusted)" and adding in its place "Table 9 (formerly Table 6) (Producer price indexes and percent changes for commodity and service groupings and individual items, not seasonally adjusted)" in the first sentence; and removing "Table 6" and adding in its place "Table 9" in the second sentence.

5. Paragraphs (e)(3)(iii)(C)(*1*) and (*2*) are amended by removing "Table 6" and adding in its place "Table 9".

6. Paragraph (e)(3)(v) is revised.

The revisions read as follows:

§1.472-8. Dollar-value method of pricing LIFO inventories.

* * *

(b) * * *

(4) *IPIC method pools.*—(i) *In general.*—A manufacturer or processor that elects to use the inventory price index computation method described in paragraph (e)(3) of this section (IPIC method) for a trade or business may elect to establish dollar-value pools for those manufactured or processed items accounted for using the IPIC method as provided in this paragraph (b)(4)(i) based on the 2-digit commodity codes (that is, major commodity groups) in Table 9 (formerly Table 6) (Producer price indexes and percent changes for commodity and service groupings and individual items, not seasonally adjusted) of the "PPI Detailed Report" published monthly by the United States Bureau of Labor Statistics (available at http://www.bls.gov). A taxpayer electing to establish dollar-value pools under this paragraph (b)(4)(i) may combine IPIC pools of manufactured or processed goods that comprise less than 5 percent of the total current-year cost of all dollar-value pools for that trade or business to form a single miscellaneous manufactured or processed IPIC pool. A taxpayer electing to establish dollar-value pools under this paragraph (b)(4)(i) may combine a miscellaneous manufactured or processed IPIC pool that comprises less than 5 percent of the total current-year cost of all dollar-value pools with the largest manufactured or processed IPIC pool. Each of these 5-percent rules is a method of accounting. A taxpayer may not change to, or cease using, either 5-percent rule without obtaining the Commissioner's prior consent. Whether a specific manufactured or processed IPIC pool or the miscellaneous manufactured or processed IPIC pool satisfies the applicable 5-percent rule must be determined in the year of adoption or year of change, whichever is applicable, and redetermined every third taxable year. Any change in pooling required or permitted as a result of a 5-percent rule is a change in method of accounting. A taxpayer must secure the consent of the Commissioner pursuant to §1.446-1(e) before combining or separating manufactured or processed IPIC pools and must combine or separate its manufactured or processed IPIC pools in accordance with paragraph (g)(2) of this section.

(ii) *Pooling of goods a manufacturer or processor purchased for resale.*—A manufacturer or processor electing to establish dollar-value pools under paragraph (b)(4)(i) of this section and that is also engaged, within the same trade or business, in wholesaling or retailing goods purchased from others (resale), must establish pools for its resale goods in accordance with paragraph (c)(2)(i) of this section. A manufacturer or processor that must establish dollar-value pools for resale goods under this paragraph (b)(4)(ii) may combine IPIC pools of resale goods that comprise less than 5 percent of the total current-year cost of all dollar-value pools for that trade or business to form a single miscellaneous resale IPIC pool. The single miscellaneous resale IPIC pool established pursuant to this paragraph (b)(4)(ii) may not be combined with any other IPIC pool. This 5-percent rule is a method of accounting. A taxpayer may not change to, or cease using, this 5-percent rule without obtaining the Commissioner's prior consent. Whether a specific resale IPIC pool satisfies the 5-percent rule must be determined in the year of adoption or year of change, whichever is applicable, and redetermined every third taxable year. Any change in pooling required or permitted as a result of this 5-percent rule is a change in method of accounting. A taxpayer must secure the consent of the Commissioner pursuant to §1.446-1(e) before combining or separating resale IPIC pools and must combine or separate its resale IPIC pools in accordance with paragraph (g)(2) of this section.

(iii) *No commingling of manufactured goods and resale goods within a pool.*—Notwithstanding any other rule provided in paragraph (b) or (c) of this section, a manufacturer or processor electing to establish dollar-value pools under paragraph (b)(4)(i) of this section and that is also engaged in retailing or wholesaling may not include manufactured or processed goods in the same IPIC pool as goods purchased for resale. Further, in applying the 5-percent rules described in paragraphs (b)(4)(i) and (ii) of this section, a taxpayer may not combine an IPIC pool of manufactured or processed goods that comprises less than 5 percent of the total current-year cost of all dollar-value pools for that trade or business with a resale IPIC pool that comprises less than 5 percent of the total current-year cost of all dollar-value pools for the purpose of forming a single miscellaneous IPIC pool.

(iv) *Examples.*—The rules of paragraph (b)(4) of this section may be illustrated by the following examples:

Example 1. (i) Taxpayer is engaged in the trade or business of manufacturing products A, B, and C. In order to cover temporary shortages, Taxpayer also purchases a small quantity of identical products for resale to customers. Taxpayer treats its manufacturing and resale activities as a single trade or business. Taxpayer uses the IPIC method described in paragraph (e)(3) of this section. Pursuant to its election, Taxpayer establishes dollar-value pools for the manufactured items under paragraph (b)(4)(i) of this section, based on the 2-digit commodity codes in Table 9 of the PPI Detailed Report. Taxpayer also establishes dollar-value pools for the items purchased for resale under paragraph (b)(4)(ii) of this section, based on the 2-digit commodity codes in Table 9 of the PPI Detailed Report. Taxpayer does not choose to use the 5-percent rules under paragraphs (b)(4)(i) and (ii) of this section.

(ii) Even though Taxpayer has manufactured items and resale items that share the same 2-digit commodity codes, under paragraph (b)(4)(iii) of this section, Taxpayer's manufactured goods may not be included in the same IPIC pool as its goods purchased for resale.

Example 2. (i) The facts are the same as in *Example 1*, except Taxpayer establishes three IPIC pools for its manufacturing activities and three IPIC pools for its resale activities. Further, Taxpayer chooses to use the 5-percent rules of paragraphs (b)(4)(i) and (ii) of this section. The percentage of total current-year cost of each IPIC pool to the current-year cost of all dollar-value pools for the trade or business is as follows:

	Percentage of total current-year cost of IPIC pool to current-year cost of all dollar-value pools
Manufacturing Pools:	
Pool A	90%
Pool B	1%
Pool C	1%
Resale Pools:	
Pool D	6%
Pool E	1%
Pool F	1%
	100%

(ii) For purposes of applying the 5-percent rules to Taxpayer's manufacturing operations under paragraph (b)(4)(i) of this section, because Pools B and C each comprise less than 5 percent of the total current-year cost of all dollar-value pools, Pools B and C may be combined to form a single miscellaneous pool of manufactured or processed goods (new Pool G).

(iii) For purposes of applying the 5-percent rules to Taxpayer's resale operations under paragraph (b)(4)(ii) of this section, because Pools E and F each comprise less than 5 percent of the total current-year cost of all dollar-value pools, Pools E and F may be combined to form a single miscellaneous pool of resale goods (new Pool H).

(iv) Because Pool G comprises less than 5 percent of the total current-year cost of all dollar-value pools, under paragraph (b)(4)(i) of this section, Pool G may be combined with Pool A, the largest IPIC pool of manufactured goods.

(v) Although Pool H also comprises less than 5 percent of the total current-year cost of all dollar-value pools, under paragraph (b)(4)(ii) of this section, Pool H may not be combined with Pool A, the largest pool of manufactured goods, or Pool D, the largest pool of resale goods.

* * *

(c) * * *

(2) *IPIC method pools.*—(i) *In general.*—A retailer that elects to use the inventory price index computation method described in paragraph (e)(3) of this section (IPIC method) for a trade or business may elect to establish dollar-value pools for those purchased items accounted for using the IPIC method as provided in this paragraph (c)(2)(i) based on either the general expenditure categories (that is, major groups) in Table 3 (Consumer Price Index for all Urban Consumers (CPI-U): U.S. city average, detailed expenditure categories) of the "CPI Detailed Report" or the 2-digit commodity codes (that is, major commodity groups) in Table 9 (formerly Table 6) (Producer price indexes and percent changes for commodity and service groupings and individual items, not seasonally adjusted) of the "PPI Detailed Report." A wholesaler, jobber, or distributor that elects to use the IPIC method for a trade or business may elect to establish dollar-value pools for any group of resale goods accounted for using the IPIC method based on the 2-digit commodity codes (that is, major commodity groups) in Table 9 (Producer price indexes and percent changes for commodity and service groupings and individual items, not seasonally adjusted) of the "PPI Detailed Report." The "CPI Detailed Report" and the "PPI Detailed Report" are published monthly by the United States Bureau of Labor Statistics (BLS) (available at http://www.bls.gov). A taxpayer electing to establish dollar-value pools under this paragraph (c)(2)(i) may combine IPIC pools of resale goods that comprise less than 5 percent of the total current-year cost of all dollar-value pools for that trade or business to form a single miscellaneous resale IPIC pool. A taxpayer electing to establish pools under this paragraph (c)(2)(i) may combine a miscellaneous resale IPIC pool that comprises less than 5 percent of the total current-year cost of all dollar-value pools with the largest resale IPIC pool. Each of these 5-percent rules is a method of accounting. A taxpayer may not change to, or cease using, either 5-percent rule without obtaining the Commissioner's prior consent. Whether a specific resale IPIC pool or the miscellaneous resale IPIC pool satisfies the applicable 5-percent rule must be determined in the year of adoption or year of change, whichever is applicable, and redetermined every third taxable year. Any change in pooling required or permitted under a 5-percent rule is a change in method of accounting. A taxpayer must secure the consent of the Commissioner pursuant to § 1.446-1(e) before combining or separating resale IPIC pools and must combine or separate its resale IPIC pools in accordance with paragraph (g)(2) of this section.

(ii) *Pooling of manufactured or processed goods of a wholesaler, retailer, jobber, or distributor.*—A wholesaler, retailer, jobber, or distributor electing to establish dollar-value pools under paragraph (c)(2)(i) of this section and that is also engaged, within the same trade or business, in manufacturing or processing, must establish pools for its manufactured or processed goods in accordance with paragraph (b)(4)(i) of this section. A wholesaler, retailer, jobber, or distributor that must establish dollar-value pools for manufactured or processed goods under this paragraph (c)(2)(ii) may combine IPIC pools of manufactured or processed goods that comprise less than 5 percent of the total current-year cost of all dollar-value pools for that trade or business to form a single miscellaneous manufactured or processed IPIC pool. The single miscellaneous manufactured or processed IPIC pool established pursuant to this paragraph (c)(2)(ii) may not be combined with any other IPIC pool. This 5-percent rule is a method of accounting. A taxpayer may not change to, or cease using, this 5-percent rule without obtaining the Commissioner's prior consent. Whether a specific manufactured or processed IPIC pool satisfies the 5-percent rule must be determined in the year of adoption or year of change, whichever is applicable, and redetermined every third taxable year. Any change in pooling required or permitted as a result of a 5-percent rule is a change in method of accounting. A taxpayer must secure the consent of the Commissioner pursuant to § 1.446-1(e) before combining or separating manufactured or processed IPIC pools and must combine or separate its manufactured or processed IPIC pools in accordance with paragraph (g)(2) of this section.

(iii) *No commingling of manufactured goods and purchased goods within a pool.*—Notwithstanding any other rule provided in paragraph (b) or (c) of this section, a wholesaler, retailer, jobber, or distributor electing to establish dollar-value pools under paragraph (c)(2)(i) of this section and that is also engaged in manufacturing or processing may not include manufactured or processed goods in the same IPIC pool as goods purchased for resale. Further, in applying the 5-percent rules described in paragraphs (c)(2)(i) and (ii) of this section, a taxpayer may not combine an IPIC pool of manufactured or processed goods that comprises less than 5 percent of the total current-year cost of all dollar-value pools with a resale IPIC pool that comprises less than 5 percent of the total current-year cost of all dollar-value pools for purposes of forming a single miscellaneous IPIC pool.

(iv) *Examples.*—The rules of paragraph (c)(2) of this section may be illustrated by the following examples:

Example 1. (i) Taxpayer is engaged in the trade or business of wholesaling products A, B, and C. Taxpayer also manufactures a small quantity of identical products for sale to customers. Taxpayer treats its wholesaling and manufacturing activities as a single trade or business. Taxpayer uses the IPIC method described in paragraph (e)(3) of this section. Pursuant to its election, Taxpayer establishes dollar-value pools for the wholesale items purchased for resale under paragraph (c)(2)(i) of this section, based on the 2-digit commodity codes in Table 9 of the PPI Detailed Report. Taxpayer also establishes dollar-value pools for the manufactured items under paragraph (c)(2)(ii) of this section, based on the 2-digit commodity codes in Table 9 of the PPI Detailed Report. Taxpayer does not choose to use the 5-percent rules under paragraphs (c)(2)(i) and (ii) of this section.

(ii) Even though Taxpayer has resale and manufactured items that share the same 2-digit commodity codes, under paragraph (c)(2)(iii) of this section, Taxpayer's resale goods may not be included in the same IPIC pool as its manufactured goods.

Example 2. (i) The facts are the same as in *Example 1,* except Taxpayer establishes three IPIC pools for its wholesale activities and three IPIC pools for its manufacturing activities. Further, Taxpayer chooses to use the 5-percent rules of paragraphs (c)(2)(i) and (ii) of this section. The percentage of total current-year cost of each IPIC pool to the current-year cost of all dollar-value pools for the trade or business is as follows:

	Percentage of total current-year cost of IPIC pool to current-year cost of all dollar-value pools
Wholesaling Pools:	
Pool J	90%
Pool K	1%
Pool L	1%
Manufacturing Pools:	
Pool M	6%
Pool N	1%
Pool O	1%
	100%

(ii) For purposes of applying the 5-percent rules to Taxpayer's wholesaling operations under paragraph (c)(2)(i) of this section, because Pools K and Pool L each comprise less than 5 percent of the total current-year cost of all dollar-value pools, Pools K and L may be combined to form a single miscellaneous pool of wholesale goods (new Pool P).

(iii) For purposes of applying the 5-percent rules to Taxpayer's manufacturing operations under paragraph (c)(2)(ii) of this section, because Pools N and O each comprise less than 5 percent of the total current-year cost of all dollar-value pools, Pools N and O may be combined to form a single miscellaneous pool of manufactured goods (new Pool Q).

(iv) Because Pool P comprises less than 5 percent of the total current-year cost of all dollar-value pools, under paragraph (c)(2)(i) of this section, Pool P may be combined with Pool J, the largest IPIC pool of resale goods.

(v) Although Pool Q also comprises less than 5 percent of the total current-year cost of all dollar-value pools, under paragraph (c)(2)(ii) of this section, Pool Q may not be combined with Pool J, the largest pool of resale goods, or Pool M, the largest pool of manufactured goods.

* * *

(e) * * *

(3) * * *

(ii) *Eligibility*.—Any taxpayer electing to use the dollar-value LIFO method may elect to use the IPIC method. Except as provided in other published guidance, a taxpayer that elects to use the IPIC method for a specific trade or business must use that method to account for all items of dollar-value LIFO inventory.

* * *

(v) *Effective/applicability date*.—The rules of this paragraph (e)(3) and paragraphs (b)(4) and (c)(2) of this section are applicable for taxable years ending on or after the date the Treasury decision adopting these rules as final regulations is published in the **Federal Register**.

* * *

Methods of Accounting: Mark-to-Market Method: Dealers in Securities

Methods of Accounting: Mark-to-Market Method: Dealers in Securities.—Reproduced below are the texts of proposed Reg. §§1.475(a)-1, 1.475(a)-2 and 1.475(b)-3, relating to the mark-to-market method of accounting for securities that is required to be used by a dealer in securities (published in the Federal Register on January 4, 1995) (FI-42-94). Reg. §§1.475-0, 1.475(a)-3 and 1.475(b)-4 and amendments to Reg. §§1.475(c)-1, 1.475(c)-2 and 1.475(e)-1 were adopted by T.D. 8700 on December 23, 1996.

□ Par. 3. Section 1.475(a)-1 is added as follows:

§1.475(a)-1. Mark to market of debt instruments.—(a) *Overview*.—This section provides rules for taking into account interest accruals and gain and loss on a debt instrument to which section 475(a) applies. Paragraph (b) of this section clarifies that the mark-to-market computation affects neither the amount treated as interest earned from a debt instrument nor the taxable year in which that interest is taken into account. Paragraph (c) of this section prescribes general rules. Paragraph (d) of this section prescribes additional rules for instruments acquired with market discount. Paragraph (e) of this section provides rules for taking into account market discount that accrued on a bond before the bond became subject to the mark-to-market requirements. Paragraph (f) of this section prescribes rules for computing the mark-to-market gain or loss on partially or wholly worthless debts, and paragraph (g) provides rules for dealers accounting for bad debts using a reserve method of accounting.

(b) *No effect on amount of market discount, acquisition premium, or bond premium*.—Marking a debt instrument to market does not create, increase, or reduce market discount, acquisition premium, or bond premium, nor does it affect the adjusted issue price of, or accruals of original issue discount (OID) on, a bond issued with OID.

(c) *Accrual of interest, discount, and premium*.—In general, the amount of gain or loss from marking a debt instrument to market is computed after adjustments to basis for accruals of stated interest, discount, and premium.

(1) *Qualified stated interest*.—Immediately before a debt instrument is marked to market under section 475(a), the holder of the instrument must take any unpaid accrued qualified stated interest into account and must correspondingly increase the basis of the instrument. The holder must later decrease the basis of the instrument when accrued qualified stated interest is actually received. (See §1.1273-1(c) for the definition of qualified stated interest and §1.446-2(b) for the rule governing its accrual.)

(2) *General rule regarding accrual of discount*.—If a bond that was acquired with OID or market discount is marked to market under section 475(a), then, immediately before the bond is marked to market, the discount accrued through that date (determined under section 1272, 1275(d), or 1276, as applicable) is included in gross income, to the extent not previously included, and the bond's basis is correspondingly increased for amounts so included. (Because accrued OID is determined under all of the rules of section 1272 and the regulations thereunder, it is computed taking into account the reduction for acquisition premium that is required by section 1272(a)(7).) See paragraph (d) of this section, which requires the current inclusion in income of market discount on bonds marked to market. See paragraph (e) of this section for exceptions, and additional rules, for market discount bonds that become subject to section 475(a) after acquisition.

(3) *Bond premium*.—If a debt instrument that is subject to the basis adjustment required by section 1016(a)(5) or (6) is marked to market under section 475(a), then, immediately before the debt instrument is marked to market, the required basis adjustment must be made. Accordingly, the mark-to-market adjustment is computed after the basis of the debt instrument has been adjusted under section 1016(a)(5) or (6) for disallowed amortizable bond premium (in the case of tax-exempt bonds) or deductible bond premium (in the case of taxable bonds). If an election under section 171(c) is made after the first taxable year in which section 475(a) applies to the bond, the amount of bond premium is determined under section 171(b)(1) without regard to any basis adjustments that may have been required as a result of the bond being marked to market in prior taxable years. See paragraph (b) of this section for the rule that marking a debt instrument to market does not affect bond premium.

(d) *Mandatory current inclusion of market discount*.—(1) *General rule*.—If section 475(a) applies to a bond during any portion of a taxable year, gross income for that taxable year includes the market discount attributable to the portion of the year to which section 475(a) applies (as determined under section 1276(b)). Section 1276 does not apply to the bond except with respect to market discount, if any, that accrued before the bond became subject to section 475(a). Similarly, section 1277 does not apply to the bond except with respect to any net direct interest expense (as defined in section 1277(c)) that accrued before the bond became subject to section 475(a). See paragraph (e) of this section for additional rules governing this situation. For purposes of the Code other than the purposes described in the last sentence of section 1278(b)(1), any amount included in gross income under this paragraph (d)(1) is treated as interest. The bond's basis is correspondingly increased for any amount so included in gross income.

(2) *Interaction with section 1278(b).*—Paragraph (d)(1) of this section applies to a dealer, even if the dealer has not elected under section 1278(b) to include market discount currently. If the dealer has not made that election, however, this paragraph (d) does not require current inclusion of market discount on any bond to which section 475(a) does not apply.

(e) *Recognition of market discount that accrued before section 475(a) applies to a market discount bond.*—(1) *General rule.*—In the case of a debt instrument that is acquired with market discount, that is not subject to an election under section 1278(b), and that first becomes subject to section 475(a) in the taxpayer's hands on a date after its acquisition, this paragraph (e) governs the recognition of market discount that is attributable (as determined under section 1276(b)) to any period before section 475(a) applies to the debt instrument. To the extent that the market discount described in the preceding sentence is greater than the excess, if any, of the fair market value of the debt instrument at the time it became subject to section 475(a) over its adjusted basis at that time, section 1276(a)(1) applies to any gain recognized under section 475(a). To the extent of any remaining market discount that had accrued before section 475(a) became applicable, section 1276(a) applies no later than it would have applied if section 475(a) did not apply to the bond. For example, section 1276(a) applies to the previously accrued market discount as partial principal payments are made. Except as provided in the preceding sentences, gain recognized under section 475(a) is not recharacterized as interest by section 1276(a).

(2) *Examples.*—The rules of paragraphs (d) and (e) of this section are illustrated by the following examples:

Example 1.

(i) *Facts.* Bond *X* was issued on January 1, 1996, for $1,000. Bond *X* matures on December 31, 2005, provides for a principal payment of $1,000 on the maturity date, and provides for interest payments at a rate of 8%, compounded annually, on December 31 of each year. *D* is a dealer in securities within the meaning of section 475(c)(1). On January 1, 1997, *D* purchased bond *X* for $955. *D* had not elected under section 1278(b) to include market discount in gross income currently. Under section 475(b), section 475(a) did not apply to bond *X* until January 1, 1999, at which time bond *X* had a fair market value of $961. On December 31, 1999, bond *X* had a fair market value of $980.

(ii) *Holdings.* In the absence of an election under section 1276(b)(2), market discount on bond *X* accrues under section 1276(b)(1) at the rate of $5 per year. On January 1, 1999, when bond *X* became subject to section 475(a), $10 of market discount had accrued, but the excess of the bond's fair market value on January 1, 1999, over its adjusted basis on that date (the built-in gain) was only $6 ($961 – $955). During 1999, *D* is required to include as interest income the $5 of market discount that accrues during that year, and *D* increases by that amount its basis in the bond and the amount to be used in computing mark-to-market gain or loss. On December 31, 1999, *B* must mark bond *X* to market and recognize a gain of $14 ($980 – [$961 + $5]). Under section 1276(a)(1) and (4) and paragraph (e)(1) of this section, $4 of that $14 gain is treated as interest income. The $4 is the amount by which the market discount of $10 that had accrued on January 1, 1999, exceeded the $6 built-in gain on that date.

Example 2.

(i) *Facts.* The facts are the same as in *Example 1*, except that, in addition, *D* sells bond *X* for its fair market value of $1,000 on June 30, 2000.

(ii) *Holdings.* Immediately before the sale, *D* is required to include as interest income the $2.50 of market discount that accrued during the portion of the year through June 30, and *D* increases by that amount its basis in the bond and the amount to be used in computing mark-to-market gain or loss. Also, under § 1.475(a)-2, immediately before the sale, *D* recognizes $17.50 of mark-to-market gain (the increase in value since the preceding mark to market less the basis increase of $2.50 from the market discount accrual. See § 1.475(a)-2). On the sale, *D* also recognizes the $6 of built-in gain, all of which is recharacterized as ordinary interest income under section 1276(a)(4).

Example 3.

(i) *Facts.* The facts are the same as in *Example 1*, except that, during 2001, the issuer of bond *X* made a partial principal payment in the amount of $20.

(ii) *Holdings.* Under paragraph (e)(1) of this section and section 1276(a)(4), $6 of the partial principal payment is included in *D*'s 2001 income as interest income. The $6 is the portion of the $10 of market discount that had accrued at the time bond *X* became subject to section 475(a) and that had not previously caused gain or a partial principal payment to be treated as interest income.

(f) *Worthless debts.*—(1) *Computation of mark-to-market gain or loss.*—This paragraph (f) applies to any dealer that, under section 475(a)(2), marks to market either a debt that was charged off during the year because it became partially worthless or a debt that became wholly worthless during the taxable year (without regard to whether the debt was charged off). Any gain or loss attributable to marking a debt to market is determined by deeming the debt's adjusted basis to be the debt's adjusted basis under § 1.1011-1, less the amount charged off during the taxable year or during any prior taxable year, to the extent that amount has not previously reduced tax basis. A debt that becomes wholly worthless is deemed to have an adjusted basis of zero. The deemed adjusted basis, however, is used solely for this paragraph (f). Thus, any portion of a loss attributable to a bad debt continues to be accounted for under the bad debt provisions of the Code, and the basis of the debt continues to be adjusted as otherwise required under the Code.

(2) *Treatment of mark-to-market gain or loss.*—To the extent that a debt has been previ-

ously charged off, mark-to-market gain is treated as a recovery. Thus, for example, a dealer using the section 585 reserve method of accounting for bad debts must credit to the reserve any portion of mark-to-market gain that is treated as a recovery of a bad debt previously charged to the reserve account, and the dealer must include any excess in gross income as required by § 1.585-3(a). Similarly, if a dealer is a large bank that changed to the specific charge-off method of accounting for bad debts using the elective cut-off procedures described in § 1.585-7, the dealer must charge to the reserve for pre-disqualification loans all losses recognized as a result of marking to market a debt that is a pre-disqualification loan within the meaning of § 1.585-7(b)(2). Marking a pre-disqualification loan to market, however, is not a disposition of that loan under § 1.585-7(d).

(g) *Additional rules applicable to reserve-method taxpayers.*—If a dealer accounts for bad debts using the reserve method of accounting under section 585 or 593, the following additional rules apply in computing a reasonable addition to a reserve—

(1) To determine the amount of total loans outstanding, the outstanding balance on a debt that is marked to market is increased or decreased by the amount of any mark-to-market gain or loss recognized, except that the outstanding balance of the debt may never exceed the actual balance currently due; and

(2) If the reasonable addition to the reserve is computed based on a percentage of taxable income, any gain or loss attributable to marking a debt to market must be taken into account in computing taxable income.

(h) *Example.*—This example illustrates paragraphs (f) and (g) of this section.

Example.

(i) *B*, a calendar year taxpayer, is a dealer that marks some of its debts to market under section 475(a)(2). Additionally, *B* is a bank that accounts for bad debts using the section 585 reserve method of accounting. *B* has not made an election to use the conformity method of accounting described in § 1.166-2(d)(3).

(ii) On December 31, 1995, *B* has total loans outstanding of $1,000,000 and a bad debt reserve balance of $1000. Among the loans that *B* marks to market is loan *X*. On January 1, 1995, loan *X* had a book and tax basis of $100. During the taxable year, loan *X* became partially worthless, and *B* charged off the loan by $5. Thus, loan *X* had a book basis of $95 and a tax basis of $100. The fair market value of loan *X* was $94 on December 31, 1995.

(iii) *B* computes the amount of gain or loss to be taken into account under section 475(a)(2) with respect to loan *X* using the rules of paragraph (f) of this section. Under paragraph (f)(1) of this section, *B* treats the adjusted tax basis of loan *X* as having been reduced by the $5 charge-off. Thus, *B* determines that it is required to take into account a $1 mark-to-market loss based on the difference between *B*'s adjusted basis in loan *X* of $95, as determined under paragraph (f)(1) of this section, and loan *X*'s fair market value of $94.

(iv) Further, *B* decides to claim a bad debt deduction with respect to loan *X* in 1995, rather than waiting until loan *X* becomes totally worthless. Thus, *B* charges the $5 of partial worthlessness to its reserve for bad debts. In computing a reasonable addition to the reserve under section 585(b), *B* reduces the amount of its total loans outstanding by $6 ($5 charged to the reserve for bad debts, plus $1 mark-to-market loss).

(v) On December 31, 1997, loan *X* has a fair market value of $93 and an adjusted basis (and outstanding principal balance) of $90. No additional worthlessness occurred with respect to loan *X* in 1996 or 1997. *X* determines that it is required to recognize a $3 mark-to-market gain with respect to loan *X*. Because *B* previously charged $5 to the bad debt reserve with respect to loan *X*, the entire $3 is a recovery item and must be credited to the bad debt reserve. See paragraph (f)(2) of this section. In computing a reasonable addition to the reserve for 1997, *B* does not increase the balance of its total loans outstanding by the $3 mark-to-market gain, because that adjustment would increase the balance to an amount in excess of the actual outstanding principal balance of $90. See paragraph (g)(1) of this section.

[Reg. § 1.475(a)-1.]

□ Par. 4. Section 1.475(a)-2 is added as follows:

§ 1.475(a)-2. Mark to market upon disposition of security by a dealer.—

(a) *General rule.*—If a dealer in securities ceases to be the owner of a security for federal income tax purposes and if the security would have been marked to market under section 475(a) if the dealer's taxable year had ended immediately before the dealer ceases to own it, then (whether or not the security is inventory in the hands of the dealer) the dealer must recognize gain or loss on the security as if it were sold for its fair market value immediately before the dealer ceases to own it, and gain or loss is taken into account at that time. The amount of any gain or loss subsequently realized must be properly adjusted, in the form of a basis adjustment or otherwise, for gain or loss taken into account under this paragraph (a). See § 1.475(b)-4(b) for the rule governing when a security with substituted basis must be identified if it is to be exempted from the application of section 475(a).

(b) *Example.*—The rule of paragraph (a) of this section is illustrated by the following example.

Example.

(i) *Facts.* *D* is a dealer in securities within the meaning of section 475(c)(1) and is a member of a consolidated group that uses the calendar year as its taxable year. On February 1, 1995, *D* acquired for $100 a debt instrument issued by an unrelated party. On June 1, 1995, *D* sold the debt instrument to another member of the group, *M1*, for $110, which was the fair market value of the security on that date. *D* would have been required to mark the debt instrument to market under section 475(a) if its taxable year had ended immediately before it sold the debt instrument to *M1*.

(ii) *Holding*. Under paragraph (a) of this section, *D* marks the debt instrument to market immediately before the sale to *M1* and takes into account $10 of gain. The gain is not deferred intercompany gain. As a result, *D*'s basis in the debt instrument increases to $110 immediately before the sale. Accordingly, there is no gain or loss on the sale, and *M1*'s basis in the debt instrument is $110.

[Reg. § 1.475(a)-2.]

☐ Par. 6. Section 1.475(b)-3 is added as follows:

§ 1.475(b)-3. Exemption of securities in certain securitization transactions.—

(a) *Exemption of contributed assets.*—If a taxpayer expects to contribute securities (for example, mortgages) to a trust or other entity, including a REMIC, in exchange for interests therein (including ownership interests or debt issued by the trust or other entity), the contributed securities qualify as held for investment (within the meaning of section 475(b)(1)(A)) or not held for sale (within the meaning of section 475(b)(1)(B)) only if the taxpayer expects each of the interests received (whether or not a security within the meaning of section 475(c)(2)) to be either held for investment or not held for sale to customers in the ordinary course of the taxpayer's trade or business.

(b) *Exemption of resulting interests.*—(1) *General rule.*—If a taxpayer contributes securities to a trust or other entity in exchange for interests therein (including ownership interests or debt issued by the trust or other entity) and if, for federal income tax purposes, the ownership of the interests received is not treated as ownership of the securities contributed, the interests received may be identified as being described in section 475(b)(1), even if some or all of the contributed securities were not so described and could not have been so identified. For purposes of determining the timeliness of an identification of an interest received, the interest is treated as acquired on the day of its receipt.

(2) *Examples.*—The following examples illustrate the principles of paragraph (b)(1) of this section.

Example 1. Identification of REMIC regular interests. If a taxpayer holds mortgages that are marked to market under section 475 and the taxpayer contributes the mortgages to a REMIC in exchange for REMIC regular interests that are described in section 475(b)(1), the taxpayer may identify the regular interests as exempt from mark-to-market treatment. This is permissible because REMIC regular interests are debt securities issued by the REMIC and do not represent continued ownership of the contributed mortgages.

Example 2. Identification of interests in a grantor trust. If a taxpayer contributes securities to a grantor trust and receives beneficial interests therein and if the taxpayer marked the contributed securities to market under section 475, the taxpayer cannot identify the beneficial interests in the grantor trust as exempt from mark-to-market treatment. Because ownership of a beneficial interest in a grantor trust represents continued ownership of an undivided interest in the contributed assets, no new security has been acquired.

[Reg. § 1.475(b)-3.]

Commodities: Securities: Mark-to-Market Accounting

Commodities: Securities: Mark-to-Market Accounting.—Reg. §§ 1.475(e)-1, 1.475(f)-1 and 1.475(f)-2 and amendments to Reg. §§ 1.475(c)-1, 1.475(c)-2 and redesignated 1.475(g)-1, regarding the election to use the mark-to-market method of accounting for dealers in commodities and traders in securities or commodities, are proposed (published in the Federal Register on January 28, 1999) (REG-104924-98).

☐ Par. 4. In § 1.475(c)-1, paragraphs (b)(3)(i) and (b)(4)(ii) are revised to read as follows:

§ 1.475(c)-1. Definitions—dealer in securities.

* * *

(b) * * *

(3) * * *

(i) For purposes of section 471, the taxpayer accounts for any security (as defined in section 475(c)) as inventory;

* * *

(4) * * *

(ii) *Continued applicability of an election.*—(A) *In general.*—Except as provided in paragraph (b)(4)(ii)(B) of this section, an election under this paragraph (b)(4) continues in effect for subsequent taxable years until revoked. The election may be revoked only with the consent of the Commissioner.

(B) *Taxable years ending after July 22, 1998.*—An election under this paragraph (b)(4) is ineffective for taxable years ending after July 22, 1998.

* * *

☐ Par. 5. In § 1.475(c)-2, paragraph (d) is added to read as follows:

§ 1.475(c)-2. Definitions—security.

* * *

(d) *Inventory.*—(1) *Nonfinancial customer paper is generally not marked to market under section 475.*—Except as provided in paragraph (d)(3) of this section, nonfinancial customer paper (as defined in section 475(c)(4)(B)) is not a security even if it is inventory.

(2) *Treatment of nonfinancial customer paper under other sections of the Internal Revenue Code.*—For nonfinancial customer paper that is not a security, the mark-to-market method of accounting and the lower-of-cost-or-market method of accounting are not permissible methods of accounting. See §§ 1.446-1(c)(2)(iii) and 1.471-12.

(3) *Nonfinancial customer paper treated as inventory.*—[Reserved].

☐ Par. 7. New § 1.475(e)-1 and §§ 1.475(f)-1 and 1.475(f)-2 are added to read as follows:

§1.475(e)-1. Election of mark-to-market accounting for dealers in commodities.—(a) *Time and manner of making election.*—An election under section 475(e)(1) must be made in the time and manner prescribed by the Commissioner.

(b) *Application of securities dealer rules to electing commodities dealers.*—Except as otherwise provided in this section or in other guidance prescribed by the Commissioner, the rules and administrative interpretations under section 475 for dealers in securities apply to dealers in commodities that make an election under section 475(e)(1).

(c) *Commodity derivatives deemed not held for investment.*—(1) *In general.*—Except as otherwise determined by the Commissioner in a revenue ruling, revenue procedure, or letter ruling, if a dealer in commodities that made an election under section 475(e)(1) holds a commodity described in section 475(e)(2)(B) or (C) (describing certain notional principal contracts and commodity derivatives), section 475(b)(1)(A) (exempting from mark-to-market accounting certain positions that are held for investment) does not apply to that commodity.

(2) *Character of commodity derivatives required to be marked to market.*—If a commodity is required to be marked to market because of the application of paragraph (c)(1) of this section, the gain or loss with respect to that commodity is ordinary.

(d) *Same day identification.*—An identification of a commodity as exempt from mark-to-market accounting under section 475(b)(2) is not effective unless it is made before the close of the day on which the commodity was acquired, originated, or entered into. [Reg. §1.475(e)-1.]

§1.475(f)-1. Procedures for electing mark-to-market accounting for traders.—(a) *Time and manner of making election.*—An election under section 475(f)(1) or (2) must be made in the time and manner prescribed by the Commissioner.

(b) *Coordination with section 475(a).*—If a dealer in securities also has a securities or commodities trading business or a commodities dealing business, the dealer may make an election under section 475(e)(1), (f)(1), or (f)(2) for that business. [Reg. §1.475(f)-1.]

§1.475(f)-2. Election of mark-to-market accounting for traders in securities or commodities.—(a) *Securities not held in connection with trading activities.*—(1) *Taxpayer identification of investment securities.*—If a trader in securities makes an election under section 475(f)(1)(A) (electing trader) and holds a security other than in connection with that trading business, the electing trader must identify that security in accordance with section 475(f)(1)(B)(ii). If the electing trader is also a dealer in securities, however, the preceding sentence applies only to securities described in section 475(b)(1) (without regard to section 475(b)(2)).

(2) *Satisfaction of Commissioner.*—In no event is the requirement of section 475(f)(1)(B)(i) satisfied unless the electing trader demonstrates by clear and convincing evidence that a security has no connection to its trading activities.

(3) *Substantially similar securities held for trading and investment.*—An electing trader that holds a security other than in connection with its trading business and also trades the same or substantially similar securities in no event satisfies the requirement of section 475(f)(1)(B)(i) unless the security is held in a separate, nontrading account maintained with a third party.

(4) *Consequences of failure to identify investment securities.*—If an electing trader holds a security that is not held in connection with its trading business and fails to identify the security in a manner that satisfies the requirements of section 475(f)(1)(B)(ii)—

(i) The consequences described in section 475(d)(2) apply to the security; and

(ii) The character of the gain or loss with respect to the security is ordinary.

(5) *Commissioner identification of investment securities.*—Notwithstanding paragraph (a)(4) of this section, the Commissioner may treat a security described in that paragraph as meeting the requirements of section 475(f)(1)(B)(i) and (ii).

(b) *Character of securities marked to market.*—The gain or loss with respect to a security that is marked to market under section 475(f)(1)(A) is ordinary.

(c) *Application of securities dealer rules to electing traders.*—Except as otherwise provided in this section or in other guidance prescribed by the Commissioner, the principles of the rules and administrative interpretations under section 475 for dealers in securities apply to traders in securities that make an election under section 475(f)(1).

(d) *Same day identification.*—An identification of a security as exempt from mark-to-market accounting under section 475(f)(1)(B) is not effective unless it is made before the close of the day on which the security was acquired, originated, or entered into.

(e) *Application to traders in commodities.*—(1) *General rule.*—If a trader in commodities makes an election under section 475(f)(2), paragraphs (a), (b), (c), and (d) of this section apply to the trader in the same manner that they apply to a trader in securities who makes an election under section 475(f)(1).

(2) *Coordination with section 1256.*—If a trader in commodities makes an election under section 475(f)(2) and trades section 1256 contracts that are commodities as defined in section 475(e)(2), then the rules of section 475(f) and paragraph (e)(1) of this section apply to those contracts, and not the capital character rules of section 1256. [Reg. §1.475(f)-2.]

☐ Par. 6. Section 1.475(e)-1 is redesignated as §1.475(g)-1. [*NOTE: Reg. §1.475(e)-1 was redesignated as Reg. §1.475(g)-1 by T.D. 9328 on June 11, 2007.*]

☐ Par. 8. Newly designated §1.475(g)-1 is amended by revising paragraphs (h)(2) and (i) and adding paragraphs (k), (l), and (m) to read as follows:

§1.475(g)-1. Effective dates.

* * *

(h) * * *

(2) Section 1.475(c)-1(b) (concerning sellers of nonfinancial goods and services) applies as follows:

(i) Except as otherwise provided in this paragraph (h)(2), § 1.475(c)-1(b) applies to taxable years ending on or after December 31, 1993.

(ii) Section 1.475(c)-1(b)(4)(ii)(B) applies to taxable years ending after July 22, 1998.

* * *

(i) Section 1.475(c)-2 (concerning the definition of security) applies as follows:

(1) Section 1.475(c)-2(a), (b), and (c) (concerning the definition of security) applies to taxable years ending on or after December 31, 1993. By its terms, however, § 1.475(c)-2(a)(3) applies only to residual interests or to interests or arrangements acquired on or after January 4, 1995; and the integrated transactions that are referred to in § 1.475(c)-2(a)(2) and (b) exist only after August 13, 1996 (the effective date of § 1.1275-6).

(2) Section 1.475(c)-2(d) applies as follows:

(i) Section 1.475(c)-2(d)(1) applies to taxable years ending after July 22, 1998.

(ii) Section 1.475(c)-2(d)(2) applies to taxable years ending on or after January 28, 1999.

* * *

(k) Section 1.475(e)-1(a) (concerning the time and manner for making the mark-to-market election for dealers in commodities) applies to taxable years ending on or after January 28, 1999. Section 1.475(e)-1(b), (c) and (d) applies to commodities acquired on or after March 1, 1999.

(l) Section 1.475(f)-1 (procedures for electing mark-to-market accounting for traders in securities or commodities) applies to taxable years ending on or after January 28, 1999.

(m) Section 1.475(f)-2 (concerning the mark-to-market rules for traders in securities or commodities) applies to securities or commodities acquired on or after March 1, 1999.

Global Dealing Operations: Allocation and Sourcing of Income and Deductions

Global Dealing Operations: Allocation and Sourcing of Income and Deductions.—Reg. § 1.475(g)-2 and amendments to Reg. §§ 1.482-0 and 1.482-1, relating to the allocation and sourcing of income, deductions, gains and losses from a global dealing operation, are proposed (published in the Federal Register on March 6, 1998) (REG-208299-90).

☐ Par. 2. Section 1.475(g)-2 is added as follows:

§ 1.475(g)-2. Risk transfer agreements in a global dealing operation.—(a) *In general.*—This section provides computational rules to coordinate the application of section 475 and § 1.446-4 with rules for allocation and sourcing under the global dealing regulations. If the requirements in paragraph (c) of this section are met, a risk transfer agreement (RTA) (as defined in paragraph (b) of this section) is accounted for under the rules of paragraph (d) of this section.

(b) *Definition of risk transfer agreement.*—For purposes of this section, a risk transfer agreement (RTA) is a transfer of risk between two qualified business units (QBUs) (as defined in § 1.989(a)-1(b)) of the same taxpayer such that—

(1) The transfer is consistent with the business practices and risk management policies of each QBU;

(2) The transfer is evidenced in each QBU's books and records;

(3) Each QBU records the RTA on its books and records at a time no later than the time the RTA is effective; and

(4) Except to the extent required by paragraph (b)(3) of this section, the entry in the books and records of each QBU is consistent with that QBU's normal accounting practices.

(c) *Requirements for application of operational rule.*—(1) The position in the RTA of one QBU (the hedging QBU) would qualify as a hedging transaction (within the meaning of § 1.1221-2(b)) with respect to that QBU if—

(i) The RTA were a transaction entered into with an unrelated party; and

(ii) For purposes of determining whether the hedging QBU's position satisfies the risk reduction requirement in § 1.1221-2(b), the only risks taken into account are the risks of the hedging QBU (that is, the risks that would be taken into account if the hedging QBU were a separate corporation that had made a separate-entity election under § 1.1221-2(d)(2));

(2) The other QBU (the marking QBU) is a regular dealer in securities (within the meaning of § 1.482-8(a)(2)(iii));

(3) The marking QBU would mark to market its position in the RTA under section 475 if the RTA were a transaction entered into with an unrelated party; and

(4) Income of the marking QBU is subject to allocation under § 1.482-8 to two or more jurisdictions or is sourced under § 1.863-3(h) to two or more jurisdictions.

(d) *Operational rule.*—If the requirements in paragraph (c) of this section are met, each QBU that is a party to a RTA (as defined in paragraph (b) of this section) takes its position in the RTA into account as if that QBU had entered into the RTA with an unrelated party. Thus, the marking QBU marks its position to market, and the hedging QBU accounts for its position under § 1.446-4. Because this section only effects coordination with the allocation and sourcing rules, it does not affect factors such as the determination of the amount of interest expense that is incurred by either QBU and that is subject to allocation and apportionment under section 864(e) or 882(c). [Reg. § 1.475(g)-2.]

☐ Par. 3. Section 1.482-0 is amended as follows: 1. The introductory text is revised. 2. The section heading and entries for § 1.482-8 are redesignated as the section heading and entries for § 1.482-9. 3. A new section heading and entries for § 1.482-8 are added. The addition and revision read as follows:

§ 1.482-0. Outline of regulations under section 482.—This section contains major captions for §§ 1.482-1 through 1.482-9.

* * *

§ 1.482-8. Allocation of income earned in a global dealing operation.

(a) General requirements and definitions.

(1) In general.

(2) Definitions.
(i) Global dealing operation.
(ii) Participant.
(iii) Regular dealer in securities.
(iv) Security.
(3) Factors for determining comparability for a global dealing operation.
(i) Functional analysis.
(ii) Contractual terms.
(iii) Risk.
(iv) Economic conditions.
(4) Arm's length range.
(i) General rule.
(ii) Reliability.
(iii) Authority to make adjustments.
(5) Examples.
(b) Comparable uncontrolled financial transaction method.
(1) General rule.
(2) Comparability and reliability.
(i) In general.
(ii) Adjustments for differences between controlled and uncontrolled transactions.
(iii) Data and assumptions.
(3) Indirect evidence of the price of a comparable uncontrolled financial transaction.
(i) In general.
(ii) Public exchanges or quotation media.
(iii) Limitation on use of public exchanges or quotation media.
(4) Arm's length range.
(5) Examples.
(c) Gross margin method.
(1) General rule.
(2) Determination of an arm's length price.
(i) In general.
(ii) Applicable resale price.
(iii) Appropriate gross profit.
(3) Comparability.
(i) In general.
(ii) Adjustments for differences between controlled and uncontrolled transactions.
(iii) Reliability.
(iv) Data and assumptions.
(A) In general.
(B) Consistency in accounting.
(4) Arm's length range.
(5) Example.
(d) Gross markup method.
(1) General rule.
(2) Determination of an arm's length price.
(i) In general.
(ii) Appropriate gross profit.
(3) Comparability and reliability.
(i) In general.
(ii) Adjustments for differences between controlled and uncontrolled transactions.
(iii) Reliability.
(iv) Data and assumptions.
(A) In general.
(B) Consistency in accounting.
(4) Arm's length range.
(e) Profit split method.
(1) General rule.
(2) Appropriate share of profit and loss.
(i) In general.
(ii) Adjustment of factors to measure contribution clearly.
(3) Definitions.
(4) Application.
(5) Total profit split.
(i) In general.
(ii) Comparability.
(iii) Reliability.
(iv) Data and assumptions.
(A) In general.
(B) Consistency in accounting.
(6) Residual profit split.
(i) In general.
(ii) Allocate income to routine contributions.
(iii) Allocate residual profit.
(iv) Comparability.
(v) Reliability.
(vi) Data and assumptions.
(A) General rule.
(B) Consistency in accounting.
(7) Arm's length range.
(8) Examples.
(f) Unspecified methods.
(g) Source rule for qualified business units.

☐ Par. 4. Section 1.482-1 is amended as follows: 1. In paragraph (a)(1), remove the last sentence and add two new sentences in its place. 2. Revise paragraph (b)(2)(i). 3. In paragraph (c)(1), revise the last sentence. 4. In paragraph (d)(3)(v), revise the last sentence. 5. In paragraph (i), revise the introductory text. The additions and revisions read as follows:

§1.482-1. Allocation of income and deductions among taxpayers.—(a) *In general.*—(1) *Purpose and scope.*—* * * Section 1.482-8 elaborates on the rules that apply to controlled entities engaged in a global securities dealing operation. Finally, §1.482-9 provides examples illustrating the application of the best method rule.

* * *

(b) * * *

(2) * * *

(i) *Methods.*—Sections 1.482-2 through 1.482-6 and §1.482-8 provide specific methods to be used to evaluate whether transactions between or among members of the controlled group satisfy the arm's length standard, and if they do not, to determine the arm's length result.

(c) *Best method rule.*—(1) *In general.*—* * * See §1.482-9 for examples of the application of the best method rule.

* * *

(d) * * *

(3) * * *

(v) *Property or services.*—* * * For guidance concerning the specific comparability considerations applicable to transfers of tangible and intangible property, see §§1.482-3 through 1.482-6 and §1.482-8; see also §1.482-3(f), dealing with the coordination of the intangible and tangible property rules.

* * *

(i) *Definitions.*—The definitions set forth in paragraphs (i)(1) through (10) of this section apply to §§1.482-1 through 1.482-9.

* * *

Foreign Corporations: Certain Transfers of Property

Foreign Corporations: Certain Transfers of Property.—Amendments to Reg. § 1.482-1, relating to certain transfers of property by United States persons to foreign corporations and affecting United States persons that transfer certain property, including foreign goodwill and going concern value, to foreign corporations in nonrecognition transactions described in section 367 of the Internal Revenue Code, are proposed (published in the Federal Register on September 16, 2015) (REG-139483-13).

Par. 14. Section 1.482-1 is amended by revising paragraphs (f)(2)(i) and (f)(2)(ii)(B) and adding paragraph (j)(7) to read as follows:

§ 1.482-1. Allocation of income and deductions among taxpayers.—[The text of the proposed amendments to § 1.482-1 is the same as the text of § 1.482-1T(f)(2)(i), (f)(2)(ii)(B), and (j)(7) as added by T.D. 9738].

Global Dealing Operations: Allocation and Sourcing of Income and Deductions

Global Dealing Operations: Allocation and Sourcing of Income and Deductions.—Amendments to Reg. § 1.482-2, relating to the allocation and sourcing of income, deductions, gains and losses from a global dealing operation, are proposed (published in the Federal Register on March 6, 1998) (REG-208299-90).

☐ Par. 5. Section 1.482-2 is amended as follows:

1. In paragraph (a)(3)(iv), revise the first sentence.
2. Revise paragraph (d).

The revisions read as follows:

§ 1.482-2. Determination of taxable income in specific situations.—(a) * * *

(3) * * *

(iv) Fourth, section 482 and paragraphs (b) through (d) of this section and §§ 1.482-3 through 1.482-8, if applicable, may be applied by the district director to make any appropriate allocations, other than an interest rate adjustment, to reflect an arm's length transaction based upon the principal amount of the loan or advance and the interest rate as adjusted under paragraph (a)(3)(i), (ii), or (iii) of this section. * * *

* * *

(d) *Transfer of property.*—For rules governing allocations under section 482 to reflect an arm's length consideration for controlled transactions involving the transfer of property, see §§ 1.482-3 through 1.482-6 and § 1.482-8.

Global Dealing Operations: Allocation and Sourcing of Income and Deductions

Global Dealing Operations: Allocation and Sourcing of Income and Deductions.—Reg. § 1.482-8 and an amendment to Reg. § 1.482-8, relating to the allocation and sourcing of income, deductions, gains and losses from a global dealing operation, are proposed (published in the Federal Register on March 6, 1998) (REG-208299-90).

☐ Par. 6. Section 1.482-8 is redesignated as § 1.482-9 and a new § 1.482-8 is added to read as follows:

§ 1.482-8. Allocation of income earned in a global securities dealing operation.—(a) *General requirements and definitions.*—(1) *In general.*—Where two or more controlled taxpayers are participants in a global dealing operation, the allocation of income, gains, losses, deductions, credits and allowances (referred to herein as income and deductions) from the global dealing operation is determined under this section. The arm's length allocation of income and deductions related to a global dealing operation must be determined under one of the methods listed in paragraphs (b) through (f) of this section. Each of the methods must be applied in accordance with all of the provisions of § 1.482-1, including the best method rule of § 1.482-1(c), the comparability analysis of § 1.482-1(d), and the arm's length range of § 1.482-1(e), as those sections are supplemented or modified in paragraphs (a)(3) and (a)(4) of this section. The available methods are—

(i) The comparable uncontrolled financial transaction method, described in paragraph (b) of this section;

(ii) The gross margin method, described in paragraph (c) of this section;

(iii) The gross markup method, described in paragraph (d) of this section;

(iv) The profit split method, described in paragraph (e) of this section; and

(v) Unspecified methods, described in paragraph (f) of this section.

(2) *Definitions.*—(i) *Global dealing operation.*—A global dealing operation consists of the execution of customer transactions, including marketing, sales, pricing and risk management activities, in a particular financial product or line of financial products, in multiple tax jurisdictions and/or through multiple participants, as defined in paragraph (a)(2)(ii) of this section. The taking of proprietary positions is not included within the definition of a global dealing operation unless the proprietary positions are entered into by a regular dealer in securities in its capacity as such a dealer under paragraph (a)(2)(iii) of this section. Lending activities are not included within the definition of a global dealing operation. Therefore, income earned from such lending activities or from securities held for investment is not income from a global dealing operation and is not governed by this section. A

global dealing operation may consist of several different business activities engaged in by participants. Whether a separate business activity is a global dealing operation shall be determined with respect to each type of financial product entered on the taxpayer's books and records.

(ii) *Participant*.—(A) A participant is a controlled taxpayer, as defined in § 1.482-1(i)(5), that is—

(1) A regular dealer in securities as defined in paragraph (a)(2)(iii) of this section; or

(2) A member of a group of controlled taxpayers which includes a regular dealer in securities, but only if that member conducts one or more activities related to the activities of such dealer.

(B) For purposes of paragraph (a)(2)(ii)(A)*(2)* of this section, such related activities are marketing, sales, pricing, risk management or brokering activities. Such related activities do not include credit analysis, accounting services, back office services, general supervision and control over the policies of the controlled taxpayer, or the provision of a guarantee of one or more transactions entered into by a regular dealer in securities or other participant.

(iii) *Regular dealer in securities*.—For purposes of this section, a regular dealer in securities is a taxpayer that—

(A) Regularly and actively offers to, and in fact does, purchase securities from and sell securities to customers who are not controlled taxpayers in the ordinary course of a trade or business; or

(B) Regularly and actively offers to, and in fact does, enter into, assume, offset, assign or otherwise terminate positions in securities with customers who are not controlled entities in the ordinary course of a trade or business.

(iv) *Security*.—For purposes of this section, a security is a security as defined in section 475(c)(2) or foreign currency.

(3) *Factors for determining comparability for a global dealing operation*.—The comparability factors set out in this paragraph (a)(3) must be applied in place of the comparability factors described in § 1.482-1(d)(3) for purposes of evaluating a global dealing operation.

(i) *Functional analysis*.—In lieu of the list set forth in § 1.482-1(d)(3)(i)(A) through (H), functions that may need to be accounted for in determining the comparability of two transactions are—

(A) Product research and development;

(B) Marketing;

(C) Pricing;

(D) Brokering; and

(E) Risk management.

(ii) *Contractual terms*.—In addition to the terms set forth in § 1.482-1(d)(3)(ii)(A), and subject to § 1.482-1(d)(3)(ii)(B), significant contractual terms for financial products transactions include—

(A) Sales or purchase volume;

(B) Rights to modify or transfer the contract;

(C) Contingencies to which the contract is subject or that are embedded in the contract;

(D) Length of the contract;

(E) Settlement date;

(F) Place of settlement (or delivery);

(G) Notional principal amount;

(H) Specified indices;

(I) The currency or currencies in which the contract is denominated;

(J) Choice of law and jurisdiction governing the contract to the extent chosen by the parties; and

(K) Dispute resolution, including binding arbitration.

(iii) *Risk*.—In lieu of the list set forth in § 1.482-1(d)(3), significant risks that could affect the prices or profitability include—

(A) Market risks, including the volatility of the price of the underlying property;

(B) Liquidity risks, including the fact that the property (or the hedges of the property) trades in a thinly traded market;

(C) Hedging risks;

(D) Creditworthiness of the counterparty; and

(E) Country and transfer risk.

(iv) *Economic conditions*.—In lieu of the list set forth in § 1.482-1(d)(3)(iv)(A) through (H), significant economic conditions that could affect the prices or profitability include—

(A) The similarity of geographic markets;

(B) The relative size and sophistication of the markets;

(C) The alternatives reasonably available to the buyer and seller;

(D) The volatility of the market; and

(E) The time the particular transaction is entered into.

(4) *Arm's length range*.—(i) *General rule*.—Except as modified in this paragraph (a)(4), § 1.482-1(e) will apply to determine the arm's length range of transactions entered into by a global dealing operation as defined in paragraph (a)(2)(i) of this section. In determining the arm's length range, whether the participant is a buyer or seller is a relevant factor.

(ii) *Reliability*.—In determining the reliability of an arm's length range, it is necessary to consider the fact that the market for financial products is highly volatile and participants in a global dealing operation frequently earn only thin profit margins. The reliability of using a statistical range in establishing a comparable price of a financial product in a global dealing operation is based on facts and circumstances. In a global dealing operation, close proximity in time between a controlled transaction and an uncontrolled transaction may be a relevant factor in determining the reliability of the uncontrolled transaction as a measure of the arm's length price. The relevant time period will depend on the price volatility of the particular product.

(iii) *Authority to make adjustments*.—The district director may, notwithstanding § 1.482-1(e)(1), adjust a taxpayer's results under a method applied on a transaction by transaction basis if a valid statistical analysis demonstrates that the taxpayer's controlled prices, when analyzed on an aggregate basis, provide results that are not arm's length. See § 1.482-1(f)(2)(iv). This may occur, for example, when there is a pattern of prices in controlled transactions that are higher or lower than the prices of comparable uncontrolled transactions.

(5) *Examples.*—The following examples illustrate the principles of this paragraph (a).

Example 1. Identification of participants. (i) B is a foreign bank that acts as a market maker in foreign currency in country X, the country of which it is a resident. C, a country Y resident corporation, D, a country Z resident corporation, and USFX, a U.S. resident corporation are all members of a controlled group of taxpayers with B, and each acts as a market maker in foreign currency. In addition to market-making activities conducted in their respective countries, C, D, and USFX each employ marketers and traders, who also perform risk management with respect to their foreign currency operations. In a typical business day, B, C, D, and USFX each enter into several hundred spot and forward contracts to purchase and sell Deutsche marks (DM) with unrelated third parties on the interbank market. In the ordinary course of business, B, C, D, and USFX also enter into contracts to purchase and sell DM with each other.

(ii) Under § 1.482-8(a)(2)(iii), B, C, D, and USFX are each regular dealers in securities because they each regularly and actively offer to, and in fact do, purchase and sell currencies to customers who are not controlled taxpayers, in the ordinary course of their trade or business. Consequently, each controlled taxpayer is also a participant. Together, B, C, D, and USFX conduct a global dealing operation within the meaning of § 1.482-8(a)(2)(i) because they execute customer transactions in multiple tax jurisdictions. Accordingly, the controlled transactions between B, C, D, and USFX are evaluated under the rules of § 1.482-8.

Example 2. Identification of participants. (i) The facts are the same as in Example 1, except that USFX is the only member of the group of controlled taxpayers that buys from and sells foreign currency to customers. C performs marketing and pricing activities with respect to the controlled group's foreign currency operation. D performs accounting and back office services for B, C, and USFX, but does not perform any marketing, sales, pricing, risk management or brokering activities with respect to the controlled group's foreign currency operation. B provides guarantees for all transactions entered into by USFX.

(ii) Under § 1.482-8(a)(2)(iii), USFX is a regular dealer in securities and therefore is a participant. C also is a participant because it performs activities related to USFX's foreign currency dealing activities. USFX's and C's controlled transactions relating to their DM activities are evaluated under § 1.482-8. D is not a participant in a global dealing operation because its accounting and back office services are not related activities within the meaning of § 1.482-8(a)(2)(ii)(B). B also is not a participant in a global dealing operation because its guarantee function is not a related activity within the meaning of § 1.482-8(a)(2)(ii)(B). Accordingly, the determination of whether transactions between B and D and other members of the controlled group are at arm's length is not determined under § 1.482-8.

Example 3. Scope of a global dealing operation. (i) C, a U.S. resident commercial bank, conducts a banking business in the United States and in countries X and Y through foreign branches. C regularly and actively offers to, and in fact does, purchase from and sell foreign currency to customers who are not controlled taxpayers in the ordinary course of its trade or business in the United States and countries X and Y. In all the same jurisdictions, C also regularly and actively offers to, and in fact does, enter into, assume, offset, assign, or otherwise terminate positions in interest rate and cross-currency swaps with customers who are not controlled taxpayers. In addition, C regularly makes loans to customers through its U.S. and foreign branches. C regularly sells these loans to a financial institution that repackages the loans into securities.

(ii) C is a regular dealer in securities within the meaning of § 1.482-8(a)(2)(ii) because it purchases and sells foreign currency and enters into interest rate and cross-currency swaps with customers. Because C conducts these activities through U.S. and foreign branches, these activities constitute a global dealing operation within the meaning of § 1.482-8(a)(2)(i). The income, expense, gain or loss from C's global dealing operation is sourced under §§ 1.863-3(h) and 1.988-4(h). Under § 1.482-8(a)(2)(i), C's lending activities are not, however, part of a global dealing operation.

Example 4. Dissimilar products. The facts are the same as in Example 1, but B, C, D, and USFX also act as a market maker in Malaysian ringgit-U.S. dollar cross-currency options in the United States and countries X, Y, and Z. The ringgit is not widely traded throughout the world and is considered a thinly traded currency. The functional analysis required by § 1.482-8(a)(3)(i) shows that the development, marketing, pricing, and risk management of ringgit-U.S. dollar cross-currency option contracts are different than that of other foreign currency contracts, including option contracts. Moreover, the contractual terms, risks, and economic conditions of ringgit-U.S. dollar cross-currency option contracts differ considerably from that of other foreign currency contracts, including option contracts. See § 1.482-8(a)(3)(ii) through (iv). Accordingly, the ringgit-U.S. dollar cross-currency option contracts are not comparable to contracts in other foreign currencies.

Example 5. Relevant time period. (i) USFX is a U.S. resident corporation that is a regular dealer in securities acting as a market maker in foreign currency by buying from and selling currencies to customers. C performs marketing and pricing activities with respect to USFX's foreign currency operation. Trading in Deutsche marks (DM) is conducted between 10:00 a.m. and 10:30 a.m. and between 10:45 a.m. and 11:00 a.m. under the following circumstances.

10:00 a.m.	1.827DM: $1	Uncontrolled Transaction
10:04 a.m.	1.827DM: $1	Controlled Transaction
10:06 a.m.	1.826DM: $1	Uncontrolled Transaction
10:08 a.m.	1.825DM: $1	Uncontrolled Transaction
10:10 a.m.	1.827DM: $1	Controlled Transaction
10:12 a.m.	1.824DM: $1	Uncontrolled Transaction
10:15 a.m.	1.825DM: $1	Uncontrolled Transaction

10:18 a.m.	1.826DM: $1	Controlled Transaction
10:20 a.m.	1.824DM: $1	Uncontrolled Transaction
10:23 a.m.	1.825DM: $1	Uncontrolled Transaction
10:25 a.m.	1.825DM: $1	Uncontrolled Transaction
10:27 a.m.	1.827DM: $1	Controlled Transaction
10:30 a.m.	1.824DM: $1	Uncontrolled Transaction
10:45 a.m.	1.822DM: $1	Uncontrolled Transaction
10:50 a.m.	1.821DM: $1	Uncontrolled Transaction
10:55 a.m.	1.822DM: $1	Uncontrolled Transaction
11:00 a.m.	1.819DM: $1	Uncontrolled Transaction

(ii) USFX and C are participants in a global dealing operation under § 1.482-8(a)(2)(i). Therefore, USFX determines its arm's length price for its controlled DM contracts under § 1.482-8(a)(4). Under § 1.482-8(a)(4), the relevant arm's length range for setting the prices of USFX's controlled DM transactions occurs between 10:00 a.m. and 10:30 a.m. Because USFX has no controlled transactions between 10:45 a.m. and 11:00 a.m., and the price movement during this later time period continued to decrease, the 10:45 a.m. to 11:00 a.m. time period is not part of the relevant arm's length range for pricing USFX's controlled transactions.

(b) *Comparable uncontrolled financial transaction method.*—(1) *General rule.*—The comparable uncontrolled financial transaction (CUFT) method evaluates whether the amount charged in a controlled financial transaction is arm's length by reference to the amount charged in a comparable uncontrolled financial transaction.

(2) *Comparability and reliability.*—(i) *In general.*—The provisions of § 1.482-1(d), as modified by paragraph (a)(3) of this section, apply in determining whether a controlled financial transaction is comparable to a particular uncontrolled financial transaction. All of the relevant factors in paragraph (a)(3) of this section must be considered in determining the comparability of the two financial transactions. Comparability under this method depends on close similarity with respect to these factors, or adjustments to account for any differences. Accordingly, unless the controlled taxpayer can demonstrate that the relevant aspects of the controlled and uncontrolled financial transactions are comparable, the reliability of the results as a measure of an arm's length price is substantially reduced.

(ii) Adjustments for differences between controlled and *uncontrolled transactions.* If there are differences between controlled and uncontrolled transactions that would affect price, adjustments should be made to the price of the uncontrolled transaction according to the comparability provisions of § 1.482-1(d)(2) and paragraph (a)(3) of this section.

(iii) *Data and assumptions.*—The reliability of the results derived from the CUFT method is affected by the completeness and accuracy of the data used and the reliability of the assumptions made to apply the method. See § 1.482-1(c)(2)(ii). In the case of a global dealing operation in which the CUFT is set through the use of indirect evidence, participants generally must establish data from a public exchange or quotation media contemporaneously to the time of the transaction, retain records of such data, and upon request furnish to the district director any pricing model used to establish indirect evidence of a CUFT, in order for this method to be a reliable means of evaluating the arm's length nature of the controlled transactions.

(3) *Indirect evidence of the price of a comparable uncontrolled financial transaction.*—(i) *In general.*—The price of a CUFT may be derived from data from public exchanges or quotation media if the following requirements are met—

(A) The data is widely and routinely used in the ordinary course of business in the industry to negotiate prices for uncontrolled sales;

(B) The data derived from public exchanges or quotation media is used to set prices in the controlled transaction in the same way it is used for uncontrolled transactions of the taxpayer, or the same way it is used by uncontrolled taxpayers; and

(C) The amount charged in the controlled transaction is adjusted to reflect differences in quantity, contractual terms, counterparties, and other factors that affect the price to which uncontrolled taxpayers would agree.

(ii) *Public exchanges or quotation media.*—For purposes of paragraph (b)(3)(i) of this section, an established financial market, as defined in § 1.1092(d)-1(b), qualifies as a public exchange or a quotation media.

(iii) *Limitation on use of data from public exchanges or quotation media.*—Use of data from public exchanges or quotation media is not appropriate under extraordinary market conditions. For example, under circumstances where the trading or transfer of a particular country's currency has been suspended or blocked by another country, causing significant instability in the prices of foreign currency contracts in the suspended or blocked currency, the prices listed on a quotation medium may not reflect a reliable measure of an arm's length result.

(4) *Arm's length range.*—See § 1.482-1(e)(2) and paragraph (a)(4) of this section for the determination of an arm's length range.

(5) *Examples.*—The following examples illustrate the principles of this paragraph (b).

Example 1. Comparable uncontrolled financial transactions. (i) B is a foreign bank resident in country X that acts as a market maker in foreign currency in country X. C, a country Y resident corporation, D, a country Z resident corporation, and USFX, a U.S. resident corporation are all members of a controlled group of taxpayers with B, and each acts as a market maker in foreign currency. In addition to market marking activities conducted in their respective countries, C, D, and USFX each employ marketers and traders, who also perform risk management with respect to their foreign currency operations. In a typical business day, B, C, D, and USFX each enter into several hundred spot and forward contracts to purchase and sell Deutsche marks (DM) with unrelated third parties on the interbank market. In the ordinary course of business, B, C, D, and USFX also each enter into contracts to purchase and sell DM with each other. On a typical day, no more than 10% of USFX's DM trades are with controlled taxpayers. USFX's DM-denominated spot and forward contracts do not vary in their terms, except as to the volume of DM purchased or sold. The differences in volume of DM purchased and sold by USFX do not affect the pricing of the DM. USFX maintains contemporaneous records of its trades, accounted for by type of trade and counterparty. The daily volume of USFX's DM-denominated spot and forward contracts consistently provides USFX with third party transactions that are contemporaneous with the transactions between controlled taxpayers.

(ii) Under § 1.482-8(a)(2)(iii), B, C, D, and USFX each are regular dealers in securities because they each regularly and actively offer to, and in fact do, purchase and sell currencies to customers who are not controlled taxpayers, in the ordinary course of their trade or business. Consequently, each controlled taxpayer is also a participant. Together, B, C, D, and USFX conduct a global dealing operation within the meaning of § 1.482-8(a)(2)(i) because they execute customer transactions in multiple tax jurisdictions. To determine the comparability of USFX's controlled and uncontrolled DM-denominated spot and forward transactions, the factors in § 1.482-8(a)(3) must be considered. USFX performs the same functions with respect to controlled and uncontrolled DM-denominated spot and forward transactions. See § 1.482-8(a)(3)(i). In evaluating the contractual terms under § 1.482-8(a)(3)(ii), it is determined that the volume of DM transactions varies, but these variances do not affect the pricing of USFX's uncontrolled DM transactions. Taking into account the risk factors of § 1.482-8(a)(3)(iii), USFX's risk associated with both the controlled and uncontrolled DM transactions does not vary in any material respect. In applying the significant factors for evaluating the economic conditions under § 1.482-8(a)(3)(iv), USFX has sufficient third party DM transactions to establish comparable economic conditions for evaluating an arm's length price. Accordingly, USFX's uncontrolled transactions are comparable to its controlled transactions in DM spot and forward contracts.

Example 2. Lack of comparable uncontrolled financial transactions. The facts are the same as in Example 1, except that USFX trades Italian lira (lira) instead of DM. USFX enters into few uncontrolled and controlled lira-denominated forward contracts each day. The daily volume of USFX's lira forward purchases and sales does not provide USFX with sufficient third party transactions to establish that uncontrolled transactions are sufficiently contemporaneous with controlled transactions to be comparable within the meaning of § 1.482-8(a)(3). In applying the comparability factors of § 1.482-8(a)(3), and of paragraph (a)(3)(iv) of this section in particular, USFX's controlled and uncontrolled lira forward purchases and sales are not entered into under comparable economic conditions. Accordingly, USFX's uncontrolled transactions in lira forward contracts are not comparable to its controlled lira forward transactions.

Example 3. Indirect evidence of the price of a comparable uncontrolled financial transaction. (i) The facts are the same as in Example 2, except that USFX uses a computer quotation system (CQS) that is an interdealer market, as described in § 1.1092(d)-1(b)(2), to set its price on lira forward contracts with controlled and uncontrolled taxpayers. Other financial institutions also use CQS to set their prices on lira forward contracts. CQS is an established financial market within the meaning of § 1.1092(d)-1(b).

(ii) Because CQS is an established financial market, it is a public exchange or quotation media within the meaning of § 1.482-8(b)(3)(i). Because other financial institutions use prices from CQS in the same manner as USFX, prices derived from CQS are deemed to be widely and routinely used in the ordinary course of business in the industry to negotiate prices for uncontrolled sales. See § 1.482-8(b)(3)(i)(A) and (B). If USFX adjusts the price quoted by CQS under the criteria specified in § 1.482-8(b)(2)(ii)(A)(3), the controlled price derived by USFX from CQS qualifies as indirect evidence of the price of a comparable uncontrolled financial transaction.

Example 4. Indirect evidence of the price of a comparable uncontrolled financial transaction—internal pricing models. (i) T is a U.S. resident corporation that acts as a market maker in U.S. dollar-denominated notional principal contracts. T's marketers and traders work together to sell notional principal contracts (NPCs), primarily to T's North and South American customers. T typically earns 4 basis points at the inception of each standard 3 year U.S. dollar-denominated interest rate swap that is entered into with an unrelated, financially sophisticated, creditworthy counterparty. TS, T's wholly owned U.K. subsidiary, also acts as a market maker in U.S. dollar-denominated NPCs, employing several traders and marketers who initiate contracts primarily with European customers. On occasion, for various business reasons, TS enters into a U.S. dollar-denominated NPC with T. The U.S. dollar-denominated NPCs that T enters into with unrelated parties are comparable in all material respects to the transactions that T enters into with TS. TS prices all transactions with T using the same pricing models that TS uses to price transactions with third parties. The pricing models analyze relevant data, such as interest rates and volatilities, derived from public exchanges. TS records the data that were used to determine the price of each transaction at the time the transaction was entered into. Because the price produced by the pricing models is a mid-market price, TS adjusts the price so that it receives the same 4 basis point spread on its transaction with T that it would earn on comparable transactions with comparable counterparties during the same relevant time period.

(ii) Under § 1.482-8(a)(2), T and TS are participants in a global dealing operation that deals in U.S. dollar-denominated NPCs. Because the prices produced by TS's pricing model are derived from information on public exchanges and TS uses the same pricing model to set prices for controlled and uncontrolled transactions, the requirements of § 1.482-8(b)(3)(i)(A) and (B) are met. Because the U.S. dollar-denominated NPCs that T enters into with customers (uncontrolled transactions) are comparable to the transactions between T and TS within the meaning of § 1.482-8(a)(3) and TS earns 4 basis points at inception of its uncontrolled transactions that are comparable to its controlled transactions, TS has also satisfied the requirements of

§1.482-8(b)(3)(i)(C). Accordingly, the price produced by TS's pricing model constitutes indirect evidence of the price of a comparable uncontrolled financial transaction.

(c) *Gross margin method.*—(1) *General rule.*—The gross margin method evaluates whether the amount allocated to a participant in a global dealing operation is arm's length by reference to the gross profit margin realized on the sale of financial products in comparable uncontrolled transactions. The gross margin method may be used to establish an arm's length price for a transaction where a participant resells a financial product to an unrelated party that the participant purchased from a related party. The gross margin method may apply to transactions involving the purchase and resale of debt and equity instruments. The method may also be used to evaluate whether a participant has received an arm's length commission for its activities in a global dealing operation when the participant has not taken title to a security or has not become a party to a derivative financial product. To meet the arm's length standard, the gross profit margin on controlled transactions should be similar to that of comparable uncontrolled transactions.

(2) *Determination of an arm's length price.*—(i) *In general.*—The gross margin method measures an arm's length price by subtracting the appropriate gross profit from the applicable resale price for the financial product involved in the controlled transaction under review.

(ii) *Applicable resale price.*—The applicable resale price is equal to either the price at which the financial product involved is sold in an uncontrolled sale or the price at which contemporaneous resales of the same product are made. If the product purchased in the controlled sale is resold to one or more related parties in a series of controlled sales before being resold in an uncontrolled sale, the applicable resale price is the price at which the product is resold to an uncontrolled party, or the price at which contemporaneous resales of the same product are made. In such case, the determination of the appropriate gross profit will take into account the functions of all members of the controlled group participating in the series of controlled sales and final uncontrolled resales, as well as any other relevant factors described in paragraph (a)(3) of this section.

(iii) *Appropriate gross profit.*—The appropriate gross profit is computed by multiplying the applicable resale price by the gross profit margin, expressed as a percentage of total revenue derived from sales, earned in comparable uncontrolled transactions.

(3) *Comparability and reliability.*—(i) *In general.*—The provisions of §1.482-1(d), as modified by paragraph (a)(3) of this section, apply in determining whether a controlled transaction is comparable to a particular uncontrolled transaction. All of the factors described in paragraph (a)(3) of this section must be considered in determining the comparability of two financial products transactions, including the functions performed. The gross margin method considers whether a participant has earned a sufficient gross profit margin on the resale of a financial product (or line of products) given the functions performed by the participant. A reseller's gross profit margin provides compensation for performing resale functions related to the product or products under review, including an operating profit in return for the reseller's investment of capital and the assumption of risks. Accordingly, where a participant does not take title, or does not become a party to a financial product, the reseller's return to capital and assumption of risk are additional factors that must be considered in determining an appropriate gross profit margin. An appropriate gross profit margin primarily should be derived from comparable uncontrolled purchases and resales of the reseller involved in the controlled sale. This is because similar characteristics are more likely to be found among different resales of a financial product or products made by the same reseller than among sales made by other resellers. In the absence of comparable uncontrolled transactions involving the same reseller, an appropriate gross profit margin may be derived from comparable uncontrolled transactions of other resellers.

(ii) *Adjustments for differences between controlled and uncontrolled transactions.*—If there are material differences between controlled and uncontrolled transactions that would affect the gross profit margin, adjustments should be made to the gross profit margin earned in the uncontrolled transaction according to the comparability provisions of §1.482-1(d)(2) and paragraph (a)(3) of this section. For this purpose, consideration of operating expenses associated with functions performed and risks assumed may be necessary because differences in functions performed are often reflected in operating expenses. The effect of a difference in functions performed on gross profit, however, is not necessarily equal to the difference in the amount of related operating expenses.

(iii) *Reliability.*—In order for the gross margin method to be considered a reliable measure of an arm's length price, the gross profit should ordinarily represent an amount that would allow the participant who resells the product to recover its expenses (whether directly related to selling the product or more generally related to maintaining its operations) and to earn a profit commensurate with the functions it performed. The gross margin method may be a reliable means of establishing an arm's length price where there is a purchase and resale of a financial product and the participant who resells the property does not substantially participate in developing a product or in tailoring the product to the unique requirements of a customer prior to the resale.

(iv) *Data and assumptions.*—(A) *In general.*—The reliability of the results derived from the gross margin method is affected by the completeness and accuracy of the data used and the reliability of the assumptions made to apply the method. See §1.482-1(c)(2)(ii). A participant may establish the gross margin by comparing the bid and offer prices on a public exchange or quotation media. In such case, the prices must be contemporaneous to the controlled transaction, and the participant must retain records of such data.

(B) *Consistency in accounting.*—The degree of consistency in accounting practices between the controlled transaction and the uncontrolled transactions may affect the reliability of the gross margin method. For example, differences as between controlled and uncontrolled transactions in the method used to value similar financial products (including methods of accounting, methods of estimation, and the timing for changes of such methods) could affect the gross profit. The ability to make reliable adjustments for such differences could affect the reliability of the results.

(4) *Arm's length range.*—See § 1.482-1(e)(2) and paragraph (a)(4) of this section for the determination of an arm's length range.

(5) *Example.*—The following example illustrates the principles of this paragraph (c).

Example 1. Gross margin method. (i) T is a U.S. resident financial institution that acts as a market maker in debt and equity instruments issued by U.S. corporations. Most of T's sales are to U.S.-based customers. TS, T's U.K. subsidiary, acts as a market maker in debt and equity instruments issued by European corporations and conducts most of its business with European-based customers. On occasion, however, a customer of TS wishes to purchase a security that is either held by or more readily accessible to T. To facilitate this transaction, T sells the security it owns or acquires to TS, who then promptly sells it to the customer. T and TS generally derive the majority of their profit on the difference between the price at which they purchase and the price at which they sell securities (the bid/offer spread). On average, TS's gross profit margin on its purchases and sales of securities from unrelated persons is 2%. Applying the comparability factors specified in § 1.482-8(a)(3), T's purchases and sales with unrelated persons are comparable to the purchases and sales between T and TS.

(ii) Under § 1.482-8(a)(2), T and TS are participants in a global dealing operation that deals in debt and equity securities. Since T's related purchases and sales are comparable to its unrelated purchases and sales, if TS's gross profit margin on purchases and sales of comparable securities from unrelated persons is 2%, TS should also typically earn a 2% gross profit on the securities it purchases from T. Thus, when TS resells for $100 a security that it purchased from T, the arm's length price at which TS would have purchased the security from T would normally be $98 ($100 sales price minus (2% gross profit margin × $100)).

(d) *Gross markup method.*—(1) *General rule.*—The gross markup method evaluates whether the amount allocated to a participant in a global dealing operation is arm's length by reference to the gross profit markup realized in comparable uncontrolled transactions. The gross markup method may be used to establish an arm's length price for a transaction where a participant purchases a financial product from an unrelated party that the participant sells to a related party. This method may apply to transactions involving the purchase and resale of debt and equity instruments. The method may also be used to evaluate whether a participant has received an arm's length commission for its role in a global dealing operation when the participant has not taken title to a security or has not become a party to a derivative financial product. To meet the arm's length standard, the gross profit markup on controlled transactions should be similar to that of comparable uncontrolled transactions.

(2) *Determination of an arm's length price.*—(i) *In general.*—The gross markup method measures an arm's length price by adding the appropriate gross profit to the participant's cost or anticipated cost, of purchasing, holding, or structuring the financial product involved in the controlled transaction under review (or in the case of a derivative financial product, the initial net present value, measured by the anticipated cost of purchasing, holding, or structuring the product).

(ii) *Appropriate gross profit.*—The appropriate gross profit is computed by multiplying the participant's cost or anticipated cost of purchasing, holding, or structuring a transaction by the gross profit markup, expressed as a percentage of cost, earned in comparable uncontrolled transactions.

(3) *Comparability and reliability.*—(i) *In general.*—The provisions of § 1.482-1(d), as modified by paragraph (a)(3) of this section, apply in determining whether a controlled transaction is comparable to a particular uncontrolled transaction. All of the factors described in paragraph (a)(3) of this section must be considered in determining the comparability of two financial products transactions, including the functions performed. The gross markup method considers whether a participant has earned a sufficient gross markup on the sale of a financial product, or line of products, given the functions it has performed. A participant's gross profit markup provides compensation for purchasing, hedging, and transactional structuring functions related to the transaction under review, including an operating profit in return for the investment of capital and the assumption of risks. Accordingly, where a participant does not take title, or does not become a party to a financial product, the reseller's return to capital and assumption of risk are additional factors that must be considered in determining the gross profit markup. An appropriate gross profit markup primarily should be derived from comparable uncontrolled purchases and sales of the participant involved in the controlled sale. This is because similar characteristics are more likely to be found among different sales of property made by the same participant than among sales made by other resellers. In the absence of comparable uncontrolled transactions involving the same participant, an appropriate gross profit markup may be derived from comparable uncontrolled transactions of other parties whether or not such parties are members of the same controlled group.

(ii) *Adjustments for differences between controlled and uncontrolled transactions.*—If there are material differences between controlled and uncontrolled transactions that would affect the gross profit markup, adjustments should be made to the gross profit markup earned in the uncontrolled transaction according to the comparability provisions of § 1.482-1(d)(2) and paragraph (a)(3) of this section. For this purpose, consideration of operating expenses associated with the functions performed and risks assumed may be necessary, because differences in functions performed are often reflected in operating expenses. The effect of a difference in functions on gross profit, however, is not necessarily equal to the difference in the amount of related operating expenses.

(iii) *Reliability.*—In order for the gross markup method to be considered a reliable measure of an arm's length price, the gross profit should ordinarily represent an amount that would allow the participant who purchases the product to recover its expenses (whether directly related to selling the product or more generally related to maintaining its operations) and to earn a profit commensurate with the functions it performed. As with the gross margin method, the gross markup method may be a reliable means of establishing an arm's length price where there is a purchase and resale of a financial product and the participant who resells the property does not substantially participate in developing a product or in tailoring the product to the unique requirements of a customer prior to the resale.

(iv) *Data and assumptions.*—(A) *In general.*—The reliability of the results derived from the gross markup method is affected by the completeness and accuracy of the data used and the reliability of the assumptions made to apply the method. See § 1.482-1(c)(2)(ii). A participant may establish the gross markup by comparing the bid and offer prices on a public exchange or quotation media. In such case, the prices must be contemporaneous with the controlled transaction, and the participant must retain records of such data.

(B) *Consistency in accounting.*—The degree of consistency in accounting practices between the controlled transaction and the uncontrolled transactions may affect the reliability of the gross markup method. For example, differences as between controlled and uncontrolled transactions in the method used to value similar financial products (including methods in accounting, methods of estimation, and the timing for changes of such methods) could affect the gross profit. The ability to make reliable adjustments for such differences could affect the reliability of the results.

(4) *Arm's length range.*—See § 1.482-1(e)(2) and paragraph (a)(4) of this section for the determination of an arm's length range.

(e) *Profit split method.*—(1) *General rule.*—The profit split method evaluates whether the allocation of the combined operating profit or loss of a global dealing operation to one or more participants is at arm's length by reference to the relative value of each participant's contribution to that combined operating profit or loss. The combined operating profit or loss must be derived from the most narrowly identifiable business activity of the participants for which data is available that includes the controlled transactions (relevant business activity).

(2) *Appropriate share of profit and loss.*—(i) *In general.*—The relative value of each participant's contribution to the global dealing activity must be determined in a manner that reflects the functions performed, risks assumed, and resources employed by each participant in the activity, consistent with the comparability provisions of § 1.482-1(d), as modified by paragraph (a)(3) of this section. Such an allocation is intended to correspond to the division of profit or loss that would result from an arrangement between uncontrolled taxpayers, each performing functions similar to those of the various controlled taxpayers engaged in the relevant business activity. The relative value of the contributions of each participant in the global dealing operation should be measured in a manner that most reliably reflects each contribution made to the global dealing operation and each participant's role in that contribution. In appropriate cases, the participants may find that a multi-factor formula most reliably measures the relative value of the contributions to the profitability of the global dealing operation. The profit allocated to any particular participant using a profit split method is not necessarily limited to the total operating profit from the global dealing operation. For example, in a given year, one participant may earn a profit while another participant incurs a loss, so long as the arrangement is comparable to an arrangement to which two uncontrolled parties would agree. In addition, it may not be assumed that the combined operating profit or loss from the relevant business activity should be shared equally or in any other arbitrary proportion. The specific method must be determined under paragraph (e)(4) of this section.

(ii) *Adjustment of factors to measure contribution clearly.*—In order to reliably measure the value of a participant's contribution, the factors, for example, those used in a multi-factor formula, must be expressed in units of measure that reliably quantify the relative contribution of the participant. If the data or information is influenced by factors other than the value of the contribution, adjustments must be made for such differences so that the factors used in the formula only measure the relative value of each participant's contribution. For example, if trader compensation is used as a factor to measure the value added by the participants' trading expertise, adjustments must be made for variances in compensation paid to traders due solely to differences in the cost of living.

(3) *Definitions.*—The definitions in this paragraph (e)(3) apply for purposes of applying the profit split methods in this paragraph (e).

Gross profit is gross income earned by the global dealing operation.

Operating expenses includes all expenses not included in the computation of gross profit, except for interest, foreign income taxes as defined in § 1.901-2(a), domestic income taxes, and any expenses not related to the global dealing activity that is evaluated under the profit split method. With respect to interest expense, see section 864(e) and the regulations thereunder and § 1.882-5.

Operating profit or loss is gross profit less operating expenses, and includes all income, expense, gain, loss, credits or allowances attributable to each global dealing activity that is evaluated under the profit split method. It does not include income, expense, gain, loss, credits or allowances from activities that are not evaluated under the profit split method, nor does it include extraordinary gains or losses that do not relate to the continuing global dealing activities of the participant.

(4) *Application.*—Profit or loss shall be allocated under the profit split method using either the total profit split, described in paragraph (e)(5) of this section, or the residual profit split, described in paragraph (e)(6) of this section.

(5) *Total profit split.*—(i) *In general.*—The total profit split derives the percentage of the combined operating profit of the participants in a global dealing operation allocable to a participant in the global dealing operation by evaluating whether uncontrolled taxpayers who perform similar functions, assume similar risks,

and employ similar resources would allocate their combined operating profits in the same manner.

(ii) *Comparability.*—The total profit split evaluates the manner by which comparable uncontrolled taxpayers divide the combined operating profit of a particular global dealing activity. The degree of comparability between the controlled and uncontrolled taxpayers is determined by applying the comparability standards of § 1.482-1(d), as modified by paragraph (a)(3) of this section. In particular, the functional analysis required by § 1.482-1(d)(3)(i) and paragraph (a)(3)(i) of this section is essential to determine whether two situations are comparable. Nevertheless, in certain cases, no comparable ventures between uncontrolled taxpayers may exist. In this situation, it is necessary to analyze the remaining factors set forth in paragraph (a)(3) of this section that could affect the division of operating profits between parties. If there are differences between the controlled and uncontrolled taxpayers that would materially affect the division of operating profit, adjustments must be made according to the provisions of § 1.482-1(d)(2) and paragraph (a)(3) of this section.

(iii) *Reliability.*—As indicated in § 1.482-1(c)(2)(i), as the degree of comparability between the controlled and uncontrolled transactions increases, the reliability of a total profit split also increases. In a global dealing operation, however, the absence of external market benchmarks (for example, joint ventures between uncontrolled taxpayers) on which to base the allocation of operating profits does not preclude use of this method if the allocation of the operating profit takes into account the relative contribution of each participant. The reliability of this method is increased to the extent that the allocation has economic significance for purposes other than tax (for example, satisfying regulatory standards and reporting, or determining bonuses paid to management or traders). The reliability of the analysis under this method may also be enhanced by the fact that all parties to the controlled transaction are evaluated under this method. The reliability of the results, however, of an analysis based on information from all parties to a transaction is affected by the reliability of the data and assumptions pertaining to each party to the controlled transaction. Thus, if the data and assumptions are significantly more reliable with respect to one of the parties than with respect to the others, a different method, focusing solely on the results of that party, may yield more reliable results.

(iv) *Data and assumptions.*—(A) *In general.*—The reliability of the results derived from the total profit split method is affected by the quality of the data used and the assumptions used to apply the method. See § 1.482-1(c)(2)(ii). The reliability of the allocation of income, expense, or other attributes between the participants' relevant business activities and the participants' other activities will affect the reliability of the determination of the combined operating profit and its allocation among the participants. If it is not possible to allocate income, expense, or other attributes directly based on factual relationships, a reasonable allocation formula may be used. To the extent direct allocations are not made, the reliability of the results derived from application of this method is reduced relative to the results of a method that requires fewer allocations of income, expense, and other attributes. Similarly, the reliability of the results derived from application of this method is affected by the extent to which it is possible to apply the method to the participants' financial data that is related solely to the controlled transactions. For example, if the relevant business activity is entering into interest rate swaps with both controlled and uncontrolled taxpayers, it may not be possible to apply the method solely to financial data related to the controlled transactions. In such case, the reliability of the results derived from application of this method will be reduced.

(B) *Consistency in accounting.*—The degree of consistency between the controlled and uncontrolled taxpayers in accounting practices that materially affect the items that determine the amount and allocation of operating profit affects the reliability of the result. Thus, for example, if differences in financial product valuation or in cost allocation practices would materially affect operating profit, the ability to make reliable adjustments for such differences would affect the reliability of the results.

(6) *Residual profit split.*—(i) *In general.*—The residual profit split allocates the combined operating profit or loss between participants following the two-step process set forth in paragraphs (e)(6)(ii) and (iii) of this section.

(ii) *Allocate income to routine contributions.*—The first step allocates operating income to each participant to provide an arm's length return for its routine contributions to the global dealing operation. Routine contributions are contributions of the same or similar kind as those made by uncontrolled taxpayers involved in similar business activities for which it is possible to identify market returns. Routine contributions ordinarily include contributions of tangible property, services, and intangibles that are generally owned or performed by uncontrolled taxpayers engaged in similar activities. For example, transactions processing and credit analysis are typically routine contributions. In addition, a participant that guarantees obligations of or otherwise provides credit support to another controlled taxpayer in a global dealing operation is regarded as making a routine contribution. A functional analysis is required to identify the routine contributions according to the functions performed, risks assumed, and resources employed by each of the participants. Market returns for the routine contributions should be determined by reference to the returns achieved by uncontrolled taxpayers engaged in similar activities, consistent with the methods described in §§ 1.482-2 through 1.482-4 and this § 1.482-8.

(iii) *Allocate residual profit.*—The allocation of income to the participant's routine contributions will not reflect profits attributable to each participant's valuable nonroutine contributions to the global dealing operation. Thus, in cases where valuable nonroutine contributions are present, there normally will be an unallocated residual profit after the allocation of income described in paragraph (e)(6)(ii) of this section. Under this second step, the residual profit generally should be divided among the participants based upon the relative value of each of their nonroutine contributions. Nonroutine contributions are contributions so integral to the global dealing operation that it is impossible to segregate them from the operation and find a separate market return for the contribution. Pricing and risk managing financial products almost invariably involve nonroutine contributions. Similarly, product development and information technology are generally nonroutine contributions. Marketing may be a nonroutine contribution if the marketer substantially participates in developing a product or in tailoring the product to the unique requirements of a customer. The relative value of the nonroutine contributions of each participant in the global dealing operation should be measured in a manner that most reliably reflects each nonroutine contribution made to the global dealing operation and each participant's role in the nonroutine contributions.

(iv) *Comparability*.—The first step of the residual profit split relies on external market benchmarks of profitability. Thus, the comparability considerations that are relevant for the first step of the residual profit split are those that are relevant for the methods that are used to determine market returns for routine contributions. In the second step of the residual profit split, however, it may not be possible to rely as heavily on external market benchmarks. Nevertheless, in order to divide the residual profits of a global dealing operation in accordance with each participant's nonroutine contributions, it is necessary to apply the comparability standards of § 1.482-1(d), as modified by paragraph (a)(3) of this section. In particular, the functional analysis required by § 1.482-1(d)(3)(i) and paragraph (a)(3)(i) of this section is essential to determine whether two situations are comparable. Nevertheless, in certain cases, no comparable ventures between uncontrolled taxpayers may exist. In this situation, it is necessary to analyze the remaining factors set forth in paragraph (a)(3) of this section that could affect the division of operating profits between parties. If there are differences between the controlled and uncontrolled taxpayers that would materially affect the division of operating profit, adjustments must be made according to the provisions of § 1.482-1(d)(2) and paragraph (a)(3) of this section.

(v) *Reliability*.—As indicated in § 1.482-1(c)(2)(i), as the degree of comparability between the controlled and uncontrolled transactions increases, the reliability of a residual profit split also increases. In a global dealing operation, however, the absence of external market benchmarks (for example, joint ventures between uncontrolled taxpayers) on which to base the allocation of operating profits does not preclude use of this method if the allocation of the residual profit takes into account the relative contribution of each participant. The reliability of this method is increased to the extent that the allocation has economic significance for purposes other than tax (for example, satisfying regulatory standards and reporting, or determining bonuses paid to management or traders). The reliability of the analysis under this method may also be enhanced by the fact that all parties to the controlled transaction are evaluated under this method. The reliability of the results, however, of an analysis based on information from all parties to a transaction is affected by the reliability of the data and assumptions pertaining to each party to the controlled transaction. Thus, if the data and assumptions are significantly more reliable with respect to one of the parties than with respect to the others, a different method, focusing solely on the results of that party, may yield more reliable results.

(vi) *Data and assumptions*.—(A) *General rule*.—The reliability of the results derived from the residual profit split is measured under the standards set forth in paragraph (e)(5)(iv)(A) of this section.

(B) *Consistency in accounting*.—The degree of accounting consistency between controlled and uncontrolled taxpayers is measured under the standards set forth in paragraph (e)(5)(iv)(B) of this section.

(7) *Arm's length range*.—See § 1.482-1(e)(2) and paragraph (a)(4) of this section for the determination of an arm's length range.

(8) *Examples*.—The following examples illustrate the principles of this paragraph (e).

Example 1. Total profit split. (i) P, a U.S. corporation, establishes a separate U.S. subsidiary (USsub) to conduct a global dealing operation in over-the-counter derivatives. USsub in turn establishes subsidiaries incorporated and doing business in the U.K. (UKsub) and Japan (Jsub). USsub, UKsub, and Jsub each employ marketers and traders who work closely together to design and sell derivative products to meet the particular needs of customers. Each also employs personnel who process and confirm trades, reconcile trade tickets and provide ongoing administrative support (back office services) for the global dealing operation. The global dealing operation maintains a single common book for each type of risk, and the book is maintained where the head trader for that type of risk is located. Thus, notional principal contracts denominated in North and South American currencies are booked in USsub, notional principal contracts denominated in European currencies are booked in UKsub, and notional principal contracts denominated in Japanese yen are booked in Jsub. However, each of the affiliates has authorized a trader located in each of the other affiliates to risk manage its books during periods when the booking location is closed. This grant of authority is necessary because marketers, regardless of their location, are expected to sell all of the group's products, and need to receive pricing information with respect to products during their clients' business hours, even if the booking location is closed. Moreover, P is known for making a substantial amount of its profits from trading activities, and frequently does not hedge the positions arising from its customer transactions in an attempt to profit from market changes. As a result, the traders in "off-hours" locations must have a substantial amount of trading authority in order to react to market changes.

(ii) Under § 1.482-8(a)(2), USsub, UKsub and Jsub are participants in a global dealing operation in over-the-counter derivatives. P determines that the total profit split method is the best method to allocate an arm's length amount of income to each participant. P allocates the operating profit from the global dealing operation between USsub, UKsub and Jsub on the basis of the relative compensation paid to marketers and traders in each location. In making the allocation, P adjusts the compensation amounts to account for factors unrelated to job performance, such as the higher cost of living in certain jurisdictions. Because the traders receive significantly greater compensation than marketers in order to account for their greater contribution to the profits of the global dealing operation, P need not make additional adjustments or weight the compensation of the traders more heavily in allocating the operating profit between the affiliates. For rules concerning the source of income allocated to USsub, UKsub and Jsub (and any U.S. trade or business of the participants), see § 1.863-3(h).

Example 2. Total profit split. The facts are the same as in Example 1, except that the labor market in Japan is such that traders paid by Jsub are paid the same as marketers paid by Jsub at the same seniority level, even though the traders contribute substantially more to the profitability of the global dealing operation. As a result, the allocation method used by P is unlikely to compensate the functions provided by each affiliate so as to be a reliable measure of an arm's length result under §§ 1.482-8(e)(2) and 1.482-1(c)(1), unless P weights the compensation of traders more heavily than the compensation of marketers or develops another method of measuring the contribution of traders to the profitability of the global dealing operation.

Example 3. Total profit split. The facts are the same as in Example 2, except that, in P's annual report to shareholders, P divides its operating profit from customer business into "dealing profit" and "trading profit." Because both marketers and traders are involved in the dealing function, P divides the "dealing profit" between the affiliates on the basis of the relative compensation of marketers and traders. However, because only the traders contribute to the trading profit, P divides the trading profit between the affiliates on the basis of the relative compensation only of the traders. In making that allocation, P must adjust the compensation of traders in Jsub in order to account for factors not related to job performance.

Example 4. Total profit split. The facts are the same as in Example 1, except that P is required by its regulators to hedge its customer positions as much as possible and therefore does not earn any "trading profit." As a result, the marketing intangibles, such as customer relationships, are relatively more important than the intangibles used by traders. Accordingly, P must weight the compensation of marketers more heavily than the compensation of traders in order to take into account accurately the contribution each function makes to the profitability of the business.

Example 5. Residual profit split. (i) P is a U.S. corporation that engages in a global dealing operation in foreign currency options directly and through controlled taxpayers that are incorporated and operate in the United Kingdom (UKsub) and Japan (Jsub). Each controlled taxpayer is a participant in a global dealing operation. Each participant employs marketers and traders who work closely together to design and sell foreign currency options that meet the particular needs of customers. Each participant also employs salespeople who sell foreign currency options with standardized terms and conditions, as well as other financial products offered by the controlled group. The traders in each location risk manage a common book of transactions during the relevant business hours of each location. P has a AAA credit rating and is the legal counterparty to all third party transactions. The traders in each location have discretion to execute contracts in the name of P. UKsub employs personnel who process and confirm trades, reconcile trade tickets, and provide ongoing administrative support (back office services) for all the participants in the global dealing operation. The global dealing operation has generated $192 of operating profit for the period.

(ii) After analyzing the foreign currency options business, P has determined that the residual profit split method is the best method to allocate the operating profit of the global dealing operation and to determine an arm's length amount of compensation allocable to each participant in the global dealing operation.

(iii) The first step of the residual profit split method (§ 1.482-8(e)(6)(ii)) requires P to identify the routine contributions performed by each participant. P determines that the functions performed by the salespeople are routine. P determines that the arm's length compensation for salespeople is $3, $4, and $5 in the United States, the United Kingdom, and Japan, respectively. Thus, P allocates $3, $4, and $5 to P, UKsub, and Jsub, respectively.

(iv) Although the back office function would not give rise to participant status, in the context of a residual profit split allocation, the back office function is relevant for purposes of receiving remuneration for routine contributions to a global dealing operation. P determines that an arm's length compersation for the back office is $20. Since the back office services constitute routine contributions, $20 of income is allocated to UKsub under step 1 of the residual profit split method. In addition, P determines that the comparable arm's length compensation for the risk to which P is subject as counterparty is $40. Accordingly, $40 is allocated to P as compensation for acting as counterparty to the transactions entered into in P's name by Jsub and UKsub.

(v) The second step of the residual profit split method (§ 1.482-8(e)(6)(iii)) requires that the residual profit be allocated to participants according to the relative value of their nonroutine contributions. Under P's transfer pricing method, P allocates the residual profit of $120 ($192 gross income minus $12 salesperson commissions minus $20 payment for back office services minus $40 compensation for the routine contribution of acting as counterparty) using a multi-factor formula that reflects the relative value of the nonroutine contributions. Applying the comparability factors set out in § 1.482-8(a)(3), P allocates 40% of the residual profit to UKsub, 35% of the residual profit to P, and the remaining 25% of residual profit to Jsub. Accordingly, under step 2, $48 is allocated to UKsub, $42 is allocated to P, and $30 is allocated to Jsub. See § 1.863-3(h) for the source of income allocated to P with respect to its counterparty function.

(f) *Unspecified methods.*—Methods not specified in paragraphs (b), (c), (d), or (e) of this section may be used to evaluate whether the amount charged in a controlled transaction is at arm's length. Any method used under this paragraph (f) must be applied in accordance with the provisions of § 1.482-1 as modified by paragraph (a)(3) of this section.

(g) *Source rule for qualified business units.*—See § 1.863-3(h) for application of the rules of this section for purposes of determining the source of income, gain or loss from a global dealing operation among qualified business units (as defined in section 989(c) and § § 1.863-3(h)(3)(iv) and 1.989(a)-1). [Reg. § 1.482-8.]

EXEMPT ORGANIZATIONS

Exemption from Tax: Social Welfare Organizations: Guidance on Candidate-Related Political Activities

Exemption from Tax: Social Welfare Organizations: Guidance on Candidate-Related Political Activities.—Amendments to Reg. § 1.501(c)(4)-1, providing guidance to tax-exempt social welfare organizations on political activities related to candidates that will not be considered to promote social welfare, are proposed (published in the Federal Register on November 29, 2013) (REG-134417-13).

☐ Par. 2. Section 1.501(c)(4)-1 is proposed to be amended by revising the first sentence of paragraph (a)(2)(ii) and adding paragraphs (a)(2)(iii) and (c) to read as follows:

§ 1.501(c)(4)-1. Civic organizations and local associations of employees.—(a) * * *

(2) * * *

(ii) * * * The promotion of social welfare does not include direct or indirect candidate-related political activity, as defined in paragraph (a)(2)(iii) of this section. * * *

(iii) *Definition of candidate-related political activity.*—(A) *In general.*—For purposes of this section, candidate-related political activity means:

(1) Any communication (as defined in paragraph (a)(2)(iii)(B)*(3)* of this section) expressing a view on, whether for or against, the selection, nomination, election, or appointment of one or more clearly identified candidates or of candidates of a political party that—

(i) Contains words that expressly advocate, such as "vote," "oppose," "support," "elect," "defeat," or "reject;" or

(ii) Is susceptible of no reasonable interpretation other than a call for or against the selection, nomination, election, or appointment of one or more candidates or of candidates of a political party;

(2) Any public communication (defined in paragraph (a)(2)(iii)(B)*(5)* of this section) within 30 days of a primary election or 60 days of a general election that refers to one or more clearly identified candidates in that election or, in the case of a general election, refers to one or more political parties represented in that election;

(3) Any communication the expenditures for which are reported to the Federal Election Commission, including independent expenditures and electioneering communications;

(4) A contribution (including a gift, grant, subscription, loan, advance, or deposit) of money or anything of value to or the solicitation of contributions on behalf of—

(i) Any person, if the transfer is recognized under applicable federal, state, or local campaign finance law as a reportable contribution to a candidate for elective office;

(ii) Any section 527 organization; or

(iii) Any organization described in section 501(c) that engages in candidate-related political activity within the meaning of this paragraph (a)(2)(iii) (see special rule in paragraph (a)(2)(iii)(D) of this section);

(5) Conduct of a voter registration drive or "get-out-the-vote" drive;

(6) Distribution of any material prepared by or on behalf of a candidate or by a section 527 organization including, without limitation, written materials, and audio and video recordings;

(7) Preparation or distribution of a voter guide that refers to one or more clearly identified candidates or, in the case of a general election, to one or more political parties (including material accompanying the voter guide); or

(8) Hosting or conducting an event within 30 days of a primary election or 60 days of a general election at which one or more candidates in such election appear as part of the program.

(B) *Related definitions.*—The following terms are defined for purposes of this paragraph (a)(2)(iii) only:

(1) "*Candidate*" means an individual who publicly offers himself, or is proposed by another, for selection, nomination, election, or appointment to any federal, state, or local public office or office in a political organization, or to be a Presidential or Vice-Presidential elector, whether or not such individual is ultimately selected, nominated, elected, or appointed. Any officeholder who is the subject of a recall election shall be treated as a candidate in the recall election.

(2) "*Clearly identified*" means the name of the candidate involved appears, a photograph or drawing of the candidate appears, or the identity of the candidate is apparent by reference, such as by use of the candidate's recorded voice or of terms such as "the Mayor," "your Congressman," "the incumbent," "the Democratic nominee," or "the Republican candidate for County Supervisor." In addition, a candidate may be "clearly identified" by reference to an issue or characteristic used to distinguish the candidate from other candidates.

(3) "*Communication*" means any communication by whatever means, including written, printed, electronic (including Internet), video, or oral communications.

(4) "*Election*" means a general, special, primary, or runoff election for federal, state, or local office; a convention or caucus of a political party that has authority to nominate a candidate for federal, state or local office; a primary election held for the selection of delegates to a national nominating convention of a political party; or a primary election held for the expression of a preference for the nomination of indi-

viduals for election to the office of President. A special election or a runoff election is treated as a primary election if held to nominate a candidate. A convention or caucus of a political party that has authority to nominate a candidate is also treated as a primary election. A special election or a runoff election is treated as a general election if held to elect a candidate. Any election or ballot measure to recall an individual who holds state or local elective public office is also treated as a general election.

(5) *"Public communication"* means any communication (as defined in paragraph (a)(2)(iii)(B)(3) of this section)—

(*i*) By broadcast, cable, or satellite;

(*ii*) On an Internet Web site;

(*iii*) In a newspaper, magazine, or other periodical;

(*iv*) In the form of paid advertising; or

(*v*) That otherwise reaches, or is intended to reach, more than 500 persons.

(6) *"Section 527 organization"* means an organization described in section 527(e)(1) (including a separate segregated fund described in section 527(f)(3)), whether or not the organization has filed notice under section 527(i).

(C) *Attribution*.—For purposes of this section, activities conducted by an organization include activities paid for by the organization or conducted by an officer, director, or employee acting in that capacity or by volunteers acting under the organization's direction or supervision. Communications made by an organization include communications the creation or distribution of which is paid for by the organization or that are made in an official publication of the organization (including statements or material posted by the organization on its Web site), as part of the program at an official function of the organization, by an officer or director acting in that capacity, or by an employee, volunteer, or other representative authorized to communicate on behalf of the organization and acting in that capacity.

(D) *Special rule regarding contributions to section 501(c) organizations*.—For purposes of paragraph (a)(2)(iii)(A)(4) of this section, a contribution to an organization described in section 501(c) will not be treated as a contribution to an organization engaged in candidate-related political activity if—

(*1*) The contributor organization obtains a written representation from an authorized officer of the recipient organization stating that the recipient organization does not engage in such activity (and the contributor organization does not know or have reason to know that the representation is inaccurate or unreliable); and

(*2*) The contribution is subject to a written restriction that it not be used for candidate-related political activity within the meaning of this paragraph (a)(2)(iii).

(c) *Effective/applicability date*.—Paragraphs (a)(2)(ii) and (iii) of this section apply on and after the date of publication of the Treasury decision adopting these rules as final regulations in the **Federal Register**.

Exemption from Tax: VEBA: Geographic Locale Restriction

Exemption from Tax: VEBA: Geographic Locale Restriction.—Reproduced below is the text of a proposed amendment to Reg. §1.501(c)(9)-2, relating to the qualification of voluntary employees' beneficiary associations under Code Sec. 501(c)(9) (published in the Federal Register on August 7, 1992).

☐ Par. 2. In §1.501(c)(9)-2, paragraph (a)(1) is amended by adding a sentence between the fourth and fifth sentences, and a new paragraph (d) is added, to read as follows:

§1.501(c)(9)-2. Membership in a voluntary employees' beneficiary association; employees; voluntary association of employees.—(a) * * *

(1) *In general*.—* * * (See paragraph (d) of this section for the meaning of geographic locale.) * * *

* * *

(d) *Meaning of geographic locale*.—(1) *Three-state safe harbor*.—An area is a single geographic locale for purposes of paragraph (a)(1) of this section if it does not exceed the boundaries of three contiguous states, *i.e.*, three states each of which shares a land or river border with at least one of the others. For this purposes, Alaska and Hawaii are deemed to be contiguous with each other and with each of the following states: Washington, Oregon, and California.

(2) *Discretionary authority to recognize larger areas as geographic locales*.—In determining whether an organization covering employees of employers engaged in the same line of business is a voluntary employees' beneficiary association (VEBA) described in section 501(c)(9), the Commissioner may recognize an area that does not satisfy the three-state safe harbor in paragraph (d)(1) of this section as a single geographic locale if—

(i) It would not be economically feasible to cover employees of employers engaged in that line of business in that area under two or more separate VEBAs each extending over fewer states; and

(ii) Employment characteristics in that line of business, population characteristics, or other regional factors support the particular states included. This paragraph (d)(2)(ii) is deemed satisfied if the states included are contiguous.

(3) *Examples*.—The following examples illustrate this paragraph (d).

Example 1. The membership of the W Association is made up of employers whose business consists of the distribution of produce in Virginia, North Carolina, and South Carolina. Because Virginia and South Carolina each share a land border with North Carolina, the three states are contiguous states and form a single geographic locale.

Example 2. The membership of the X Association is made up of employers whose business consists of the retail sale of computer software in Montana, Wyoming, North Dakota, South Dakota, and Nebraska, which are contiguous states. X establishes the X Trust to provide life, sick, accident, or other benefits for the employees of its members. The X Trust applies for recognition of exemption as a VEBA, stating that it intends to permit employees of any employer that is a member of X to join the proposed VEBA. In its application, the X Trust provides summaries of employer data and economic analyses showing that no division of the region into smaller groups of states would enable X to establish two or more separate VEBAs each with enough members to make the formation of those separate VEBAs economically feasible. Furthermore, although some possible divisions of the region into three-state or four-state areas could form an economically feasible VEBA, any such division of the five-state region covered by X would leave employees of X's employer-members located in at least one state without a VEBA. The Commissioner may, as a matter of administrative discretion, recognize the X Trust as a VEBA described in section 501(c)(9) based on its showing that the limited number of employees in each state would make any division of the region into two or more VEBAs economically infeasible.

Example 3. The membership of the Y Association is made up of employers whose business consists of shipping freight by barge on the Mississippi and Ohio Rivers. Some of the members of Y conduct their business out of ports in Louisiana, while other operate out of ports in Arkansas, Missouri, and Ohio. Y establishes the Y Trust to provide life, sick, accident, or other benefits to the employees of its members. The Y Trust applies for recognition of exemption as a VEBA, stating that it intends to permit the employees of any employer that is a member of Y to join the proposed VEBA. In its application, the Y Trust sets forth facts tending to show that there are so few members of Y in each of the four states that any division of those states into two or more separate regions would result in creating VEBAs that would be too small to be economically feasible, that all of the members of Y are engaged in river shipping between inland and Gulf ports that are united by the existence of a natural waterway, and that the labor force engaged in providing transportation by river barge is distinct from that engaged in providing other means of transportation. Even though Ohio, Louisiana, Arkansas, and Missouri are not contiguous, because Ohio does not share a land or river border with any of the other three states, the Commissioner may, as a matter of administrative discretion, recognize the Y Trust as a VEBA described in section 501(c)(9) based on its showing that the establishment of separate characteristics of the river shipping business justify permitting a VEBA to cover the scattered concentrations of employees in that business located in Louisiana, Arkansas, Missouri, and Ohio.

Example 4. The membership of the Z Association is made up of employers whose business consists of the retail sale of agricultural implements in the states west of the Mississippi River except California, Alaska, and Hawaii. There are 21 states in the region covered by Z. Z established the Z1 Trust, the Z2 Trust, and the Z3 Trust to provide life, sick, accident or other benefits to the employees of its members. The trusts cover different subregions which were formed by dividing the Z region into three areas each consisting of seven contiguous states. Each trust applies for recognition of exemption as a VEBA, stating that it intends to permit the employees of any employer that is member of Z located within its subregion to join its proposed VEBA. Each trust sets forth facts in its application tending to show that four states within its particular subregion would be needed to create a VEBA large enough to be economically feasible, so that any further division of its seven-state subregion would leave employees of at least some of Z's employer-members located in the subregion in an area too small to support an economically feasible VEBA. The applications contain no justification for the choice of three seven-state subregions. Since the applicants have not shown that it would not be economically feasible to divide the Z region into smaller subregions (*e.g.*, four containing four states and one containing five states), the applicants have not satisifed paragraph (d)(2)(i) of this section, and the Commissioner does not have the discretion to recognize the Z1, Z2, and Z3 Trusts as VEBAs described in section 501(c)(9).

Qualified Group Legal Services Plans

Qualified Group Legal Services Plans.—Reproduced below is the text of proposed Reg. §1.501(c)(20)-1, relating to qualified group legal services plans (published in the Federal Register on April 29, 1980).

☐ Par. 3. There is added in the appropriate place the following new section:

§1.501(c)(20)-1. Qualified group legal services plan trust.—(a) *Qualified group legal services plan.*—For purposes of this section, a "qualified group legal services plan" is a plan that satisfies the requirements of section 120(b) and §1.120-2.

(b) *General requirements for exemption.*—Under section 501(c)(20), an organization or trust created or organized in the United States is exempt as provided in section 501(a) if the exclusive function of the organization or trust is to form part of a qualified group legal services plan or plans.

(c) *Exception for trust associated with section 501(c) organization.*—As described in section 120(c)(5)(C), employer contributions under a qualified group legal services plan may be paid to an organization described in section 501(c) if that organization is permitted by section 501(c) to receive payments from an employer for support of a qualified group legal services plan. However, that organization must, in turn, pay or credit the contributions to an organization or trust described in section 501(c)(20). In such a case, the organization or trust to which the contributions are finally paid or credited is considered to satisfy the requirement that the *exclusive* function of the organization or trust be to form part of a qualified group legal services plan or plans, notwithstanding that the organization or trust provides legal services or indemnification against the cost of legal services unassociated with such a qualified plan. This exception applies, however, only if any such legal service or indemnification is provided under a program established and maintained by the organization described in section 501(c) to which the employer contributions under a qualified group legal services plan are first paid under section 120(c)(5)(C). Whether providing legal services or indemnification against the cost of legal services unassociated with a qualified group legal services plan is a permissible activity of an organization described in section 501(c) is determined under the rules under that paragraph of section 501(c) in which the organization is described. [Reg. § 1.501(c)(20)-1.]

Charitable Hospitals: Additional Requirements

Charitable Hospitals: Additional Requirements.—Reg. §§ 1.501(r)-0—1.501(r)-7, providing guidance regarding the requirements for charitable hospital organizations relating to financial assistance and emergency medical care policies, charges for certain care provided to individuals eligible for financial assistance, and billing and collections, are proposed (published in the Federal Register on June 26, 2012) (REG-130266-11) (corrected August 10, 2012).

Proposed Reg. §§1.501(r)-0—1.501(r)-7 were adopted by T.D. 9708 on December 29, 2014. However, for tax years beginning on or before December 29, 2015, a hospital may rely on the final regulations or the 2012 and/or 2013 proposed regulations (REG-130266-11 and/or REG-106499-12).

☐ Par. 2. Section 1.501(r)-0 is added to read as follows:

§ 1.501(r)-0. Outline of regulations.—This section lists the table of contents for §§ 1.501(r)-1 through 1.501(r)-7.

§ 1.501(r)-1. Definitions.

(a) Application.

(b) Definitions.

(1) Amounts generally billed (AGB).

(2) AGB percentage.

(3) Application period.

(4) Billing and collections policy.

(5) Completion deadline.

(6) Disregarded entity.

(7) Emergency medical care.

(8) Emergency medical conditions.

(9) Extraordinary collection action (ECA).

(10) Financial assistance policy (FAP).

(11) FAP application.

(12) FAP application form.

(13) FAP-eligible individual.

(14) Gross charges.

(15) Hospital facility.

(16) Hospital organization.

(17) Medicare fee-for-service.

(18) Notification period.

(19) Plain language summary.

(20) Primary payer.

(21) Private health insurer.

(22) Referring.

§ 1.501(r)-2. Failures to satisfy section 501(r) requirements. [Reserved]

§ 1.501(r)-3. Community health needs assessments. [Reserved]

§ 1.501(r)-4. Financial assistance policy and emergency medical care policy.

(a) In general.

(b) Financial assistance policy.

(1) In general.

(2) Eligibility criteria and basis for calculating amounts charged to patients.

(3) Method for applying for financial assistance.

(4) Actions that may be taken in the event of nonpayment.

(5) Widely publicizing the FAP.

(6) Readily obtainable information.

(c) Emergency medical care policy.

(1) In general.

(2) Interference with provision of emergency medical care.

(3) Relation to federal law governing emergency care.

(4) Examples.

(d) Establishing the FAP and other policies.

(1) In general.

(2) Authorized body.

(3) Implementing a policy.

(4) Establishing a policy for more than one hospital facility.

§ 1.501(r)-5. Limitation on charges.

(a) In general.

(b) Amounts generally billed.

(1) Look-back method.

(2) Prospective Medicare method.

(3) Examples.

(c) Gross charges.

(d) Safe harbor for certain charges in excess of AGB.

§ 1.501(r)-6. Billing and collection.

(a) In general.

(b) Extraordinary collection actions.

(c) Reasonable efforts.

(1) In general.

(2) Notification.

(3) Incomplete FAP applications.

(4) Complete FAP applications.

(5) Suspending ECAs while a FAP application is pending.

(6) Waiver does not constitute reasonable efforts.

(7) Agreements with other parties.

(8) Clear and conspicuous placement.

§ 1.501(r)-7. Effective/applicability dates.

(a) Statutory effective/applicability date.

(1) In general.

(2) Community health needs assessment.

(b) Effective/applicability date of regulations.

[Reg. § 1.501(r)-0.]

☐ Par. 3. Section 1.501(r)-1 is added to read as follows:

§ 1.501(r)-1. Definitions.—(a) *Application.*—The definitions set forth in this section apply to §§ 1.501(r)-2 through 1.501(r)-7.

(b) *Definitions.*—(1) *Amounts generally billed (AGB)* means the amounts generally billed for emergency or other medically necessary care to individuals who have insurance covering such care, determined in accordance with § 1.501(r)-5(b).

(2) *AGB percentage* means a percentage of gross charges that a hospital facility uses under § 1.501(r)-5(b)(1) to determine the AGB for any emergency or other medically necessary care it provides to a FAP-eligible individual.

(3) *Application period* means the period during which a hospital facility must accept and process an application for assistance under its financial assistance policy (FAP) submitted by an individual in order to have made reasonable efforts to determine whether the individual is FAP-eligible. With respect to any care provided by a hospital facility to an individual, the application period begins on the date the care is provided to the individual and ends on the 240th day after the hospital facility provides the individual with the first billing statement for the care.

(4) *Billing and collections policy* means a written policy that includes all of the elements described in § 1.501(r)-4(b)(4).

(5) *Completion deadline* means the date after which a hospital facility may initiate or resume extraordinary collection actions against an individual who has submitted an incomplete FAP application if that individual has not provided the hospital facility with the missing information and/or documentation necessary to complete the application. The completion deadline must be specified in a written notice (as described in § 1.501(r)-6(c)(3)(i)(C)) and must be no earlier than the later of—

(i) 30 days after the hospital facility provides the individual with this written notice; or

(ii) The last day of the application period described in paragraph (b)(3) of this section.

(6) *Disregarded entity* means an entity that is generally disregarded as separate from its owner for federal tax purposes under § 301.7701-3 of this chapter. One example of a disregarded entity is a domestic single member limited liability company that does not elect to be classified as an association taxable as a corporation for federal tax purposes.

(7) *Emergency medical care* means care provided by a hospital facility for emergency medical conditions.

(8) *Emergency medical conditions* means emergency medical conditions as defined in section 1867 of the Social Security Act (42 U.S.C. 1395dd).

(9) *Extraordinary collection action (ECA)* means an action described in § 1.501(r)-6(b).

(10) *Financial assistance policy (FAP)* means a written policy that meets the requirements described in § 1.501(r)-4(b).

(11) *FAP application* means the information and accompanying documentation that a hospital facility requires an individual to submit to apply for financial assistance under the facility's FAP. A FAP application is considered complete if it contains information and documentation sufficient for the hospital facility to determine whether the applicant is FAP-eligible and incomplete if it does not contain such information and documentation.

(12) *FAP application form* means the application form (and any accompanying instructions) that a hospital facility requires an individual to submit as part of his or her FAP application.

(13) *FAP-eligible individual* means an individual eligible for financial assistance under a hospital facility's FAP, without regard to whether the individual has applied for assistance under the FAP.

(14) *Gross charges*, or the *chargemaster rate*, means a hospital facility's full, established price for medical care that the hospital facility consistently and uniformly charges all patients before applying any contractual allowances, discounts, or deductions.

(15) *Hospital facility* means a facility that is required by a state to be licensed, registered, or similarly recognized as a hospital. Except as otherwise provided in published guidance, a hospital organization may treat multiple buildings operated under a single state license as a single hospital facility. For purposes of this paragraph (b)(15), the term "state" includes only the 50 states and the District of Columbia and not any U.S. territory or foreign country. References to a hospital facility taking actions include instances in which the hospital organization operating the hospital facility takes action through or on behalf of the hospital facility.

(16) *Hospital organization* means an organization recognized (or seeking to be recognized) as described in section 501(c)(3) that operates one or more hospital facilities, including a hospital facility operated through a disregarded entity.

(17) *Medicare fee-for-service* means health insurance available under Medicare Part A and Part B of Title XVIII of the Social Security Act.

(18) *Notification period* means the period during which a hospital facility must notify an individual about its FAP in accordance with § 1.501(r)-6(c)(2) in order to have made reasonable efforts to determine whether the individual is FAP-eligible. With respect to any care provided by a hospital facility to an individual, the notification period begins on the first date care is provided to the individual and ends on the 120th day after the hospital facility provides the individual with the first billing statement for the care.

(19) *Plain language summary* means a written statement that notifies an individual that the hospital facility offers financial assistance under a FAP and provides the following additional information in language that is clear, concise, and easy to understand—

(i) A brief description of the eligibility requirements and assistance offered under the FAP;

(ii) The direct website address (or URL) and physical location(s) (including a room number, if applicable) where the individual can obtain copies of the FAP and FAP application form;

(iii) Instructions on how the individual can obtain a free copy of the FAP and FAP application form by mail;

(iv) The contact information, including the telephone number(s) and physical location (including a room number, if applicable), of hospital facility staff who can provide an individual with information about the FAP and the FAP application process, as well as of the nonprofit organizations or government agencies, if any, that the hospital facility has identified as available sources of assistance with FAP applications;

(v) A statement of the availability of translations of the FAP, FAP application form, and plain language summary in other languages, if applicable; and

(vi) A statement that no FAP-eligible individual will be charged more for emergency or other medically necessary care than AGB.

(20) *Primary payer* means a health insurer (whether a private health insurer or a public payer such as Medicare) that pays first on a claim for medical care (usually after a deductible has been paid by the insured) up to the limits of the policy or program, regardless of other insurance coverage the insured may have. Primary payers are distinguished from secondary payers that pay second on a claim for medical care to the extent payment has not been made by the primary payer.

(21) *Private health insurer* means any organization that offers insurance for medical care that is not a governmental unit described in section 170(c)(1). For purposes of § 1.501(r)-5(b), claims paid under Medicare Advantage (Part C of Title XVIII of the Social Security Act) are treated as claims paid by a private health insurer.

(22) *Referring* an individual's debt to a debt collection agency or other party includes contracting with, delegating, or otherwise using the debt collection agency or other party to collect amounts owed by the individual to the hospital facility while still maintaining ownership of the debt. [Reg. § 1.501(r)-1.]

☐ Par. 4. Sections 1.501(r)-2 and 1.501(r)-3 are added and reserved to read as follows:

§ 1.501(r)-2. Failures to satisfy section 501(r) requirements.—[Reserved].

§ 1.501(r)-3. Community health needs assessments.—[Reserved].

☐ Par. 5. Sections 1.501(r)-4, 1.501(r)-5, 1.501(r)-6, and 1.501(r)-7 are added to read as follows:

§ 1.501(r)-4. Financial assistance policy and emergency medical care policy.—(a) *In general.*—A hospital organization meets the requirements of section 501(r)(4) with respect to a hospital facility it operates if the hospital organization establishes for that hospital facility—

(1) A written financial assistance policy (FAP) that meets the requirements described in paragraph (b) of this section; and

(2) A written emergency medical care policy that meets the requirements described in paragraph (c) of this section.

(b) *Financial assistance policy.*—(1) *In general.*—To satisfy paragraph (a)(1) of this section, a hospital facility's FAP must apply to all emergency and other medically necessary care provided by the hospital facility and include—

(i) Eligibility criteria for financial assistance and whether such assistance includes free or discounted care;

(ii) The basis for calculating amounts charged to patients;

(iii) The method for applying for financial assistance;

(iv) In the case of a hospital facility that does not have a separate billing and collections policy, the actions that may be taken in the event of nonpayment; and

(v) Measures to widely publicize the FAP within the community served by the hospital facility.

(2) *Eligibility criteria and basis for calculating amounts charged to patients.*—(i) *In general.*—To satisfy paragraphs (b)(1)(i) and (b)(1)(ii) of this section, the FAP must—

(A) Specify all financial assistance available under the FAP, including all discount(s) and free care and, if applicable, the amount(s) (for example, gross charges) to which any discount percentages will be applied;

(B) Specify all of the eligibility criteria that an individual must satisfy to receive each such discount, free care, or other level of assistance;

(C) State that following a determination of FAP-eligibility, a FAP-eligible individual will not be charged more for emergency or other medically necessary care than the amounts generally billed to individuals who have insurance covering such care (AGB);

(D) Describe which method under § 1.501(r)-5(b) the hospital facility uses to determine AGB; and

(E) If the hospital facility uses the look-back method described in § 1.501(r)-5(b)(1) to determine AGB, either state the hospital facility's AGB percentage(s) and describe how the hospital facility calculated such percentage(s) or explain how members of the public may readily obtain this information in writing and free of charge.

(ii) *Examples.*—The following examples illustrate this paragraph (b)(2):

Example 1. Q is a hospital facility that establishes a FAP that provides assistance to all uninsured and underinsured individuals whose family income is less than or equal to x% of the Federal Poverty Level (FPL), with the level of discount for which an individual is eligible under Q's FAP determined based upon the individual's family income as a percentage of FPL. Q's FAP defines the meaning of "uninsured," "underinsured," "family income," and "Federal Poverty Level" and specifies that all emergency and other medically necessary care provided by Q is covered under the FAP. Q's FAP also states that Q determines AGB by multiplying the gross charges for any emergency or other medically necessary care it provides to a FAP-eligible individual by 50 percent. The FAP states, further, that Q calculated the AGB percentage of 50 percent based on all claims paid in full to Q by Medicare and private health insurers and the individuals they insured over a specified 12-month period, divided by the associated gross charges for those claims. Q's FAP contains the following chart, specifying each discount available under the FAP, the amounts (gross charges) to which these discounts will be applied, and the specific eligibility criteria for each such discount:

Family income as % of FPL	Discount off of gross charges
>y% - x%	50%
>z% - y%	75%
≤z%	Free

Q's FAP also contains a statement that no FAP-eligible individual will be charged more for emergency or other medically necessary care than AGB because Q's AGB percentage is 50 percent of gross charges and the most a FAP-eligible individual will be charged is 50 percent of gross charges. Q's FAP satisfies the requirements of this paragraph (b)(2).

Example 2. R is a hospital facility that establishes a FAP that provides assistance based on household income. R's FAP defines the meaning of "household income" and specifies that all emergency and other medically necessary care provided by R is covered under the FAP. R's FAP contains the following chart, specifying the assistance available under the FAP and the specific eligibility criteria for each level of assistance offered, which R updates occasionally to account for inflation:

Household income	Maximum amount individual will be responsible for paying
>$b - $a	40% of gross charges, up to the lesser of AGB or x% of annual household income
>$c - $b	20% of gross charges, up to the lesser of AGB or y% of annual household income
≤$c	$0 (free)

R's FAP contains a statement that no FAP-eligible individual will be charged more for emergency or other medically necessary care than AGB. R's FAP also states that R determines AGB by multiplying the gross charges for any emergency or other medically necessary care it provides by AGB percentages, which are based on claims paid under Medicare. In addition, the FAP provides a web address individuals can visit, and a telephone number they can call, if they would like to obtain an information sheet stating R's AGB percentages and explaining how these AGB percentages were calculated. This information sheet, which R makes available on its website and provides to any individual who requests it, states that R's AGB percentages are 35 percent of gross charges for inpatient care and 60 percent of gross charges for outpatient care. It also states that these percentages were based on all claims paid to R for emergency or other medically necessary inpatient and outpatient care by Medicare and Medicare beneficiaries over a specified 12-month period, divided by the associated gross charges for those claims. R's FAP satisfies the requirements of this paragraph (b)(2).

(3) *Method for applying for financial assistance.*—(i) *In general.*—To satisfy paragraph (b)(1)(iii) of this section, a hospital facility's FAP must describe how an individual applies for financial assistance under the FAP. In addition, either the hospital facility's FAP or FAP application form (including accompanying instructions) must describe the information and documentation the hospital facility may require an individual to submit as part of his or her FAP application and provide the contact information described in §1.501(r)-1(b)(19)(iv). The hospital facility may not deny financial assistance under the FAP based on an applicant's failure to provide information or documentation that the hospital facility's FAP or FAP application form does not require an individual to submit as part of a FAP application.

(ii) *Example.*—The following example illustrates this paragraph (b)(3):

Example. S is a hospital facility with a FAP that bases eligibility solely on an individual's household income. S's FAP provides that an individual may apply for financial assistance by completing and submitting S's FAP application form. S's FAP also describes how individuals can obtain copies of the FAP application form. S's FAP application form contains lines on which the applicant lists all items of household income received by the applicant's household over the last three months and the names of the applicant's household members. The instructions to S's FAP application form tell applicants where to submit the application and provide that an applicant must attach to his or her FAP application form proof of household income in the form of the applicant's most recent federal tax return, payroll check stubs from the last three months, documentation of the applicant's qualification for certain specified state meanstested programs, or other reliable evidence of the applicant's earned and unearned household income. S does not require FAP applicants to submit any information or documentation not mentioned in the FAP application form instructions. S's FAP application form instructions also provide the contact information of hospital facility staff who can provide an applicant with information about the FAP and FAP application process. S's FAP satisfies the requirements of this paragraph (b)(3).

(4) *Actions that may be taken in the event of nonpayment.*—(i) *In general.*—To satisfy paragraph (b)(1)(iv) of this section, either a hospital facility's FAP or a separate written billing and collections policy established by the hospital facility must describe—

(A) Any actions that the hospital facility (or other authorized party) may take relating to obtaining payment of a bill for medical care, including, but not limited to, any extraordinary collection actions described in §1.501(r)-6(b);

(B) The process and time frames the hospital facility (or other authorized party) uses in taking the actions described in paragraph (b)(4)(i)(A) of this section, including, but not limited to, the reasonable efforts it will make to determine whether an individual is FAP-eligible before engaging in any extraordinary collection actions, as described in § 1.501(r)-6(c); and

(C) The office, department, committee, or other body with the final authority or responsibility for determining that the hospital facility has made reasonable efforts to determine whether an individual is FAP-eligible and may therefore engage in extraordinary collection actions against the individual.

(ii) *Separate billing and collections policy.*—In the case of a hospital facility that satisfies paragraph (b)(1)(iv) of this section by establishing a separate written billing and collections policy, the hospital facility's FAP must state that the actions the hospital facility may take in the event of nonpayment are described in a separate billing and collections policy and explain how members of the public may readily obtain a free copy of this separate policy.

(5) *Widely publicizing the FAP.*—(i) *In general.*—To satisfy paragraph (b)(1)(v) of this section, a FAP must include, or explain how members of the public may readily obtain a free written description of, measures taken by the hospital facility to—

(A) Make the FAP, FAP application form, and a plain language summary of the FAP (as defined in § 1.501(r)-1(b)(19)) widely available on a website, as described in paragraph (b)(5)(iv) of this section;

(B) Make paper copies of the FAP, FAP application form, and plain language summary of the FAP available upon request and without charge, both in public locations in the hospital facility and by mail, in English and in the primary language of any populations with limited proficiency in English that constitute more than 10 percent of the residents of the community served by the hospital facility;

(C) Inform and notify visitors to the hospital facility about the FAP through conspicuous public displays or other measures reasonably calculated to attract visitors' attention; and

(D) Inform and notify residents of the community served by the hospital facility about the FAP in a manner reasonably calculated to reach those members of the community who are most likely to require financial assistance.

(ii) *Meaning of inform and notify.*—For purposes of paragraphs (b)(5)(i)(C) and (b)(5)(i)(D) of this section, a measure will inform and notify visitors to a hospital facility or residents of a community about the hospital facility's FAP if the measure, at a minimum, notifies the reader or listener that the hospital facility offers financial assistance under a FAP and informs him or her about how or where to obtain more information about the FAP.

(iii) *Meaning of reasonably calculated.*—Whether one or more measures to widely publicize a hospital facility's FAP are reasonably calculated to inform and notify visitors to a hospital facility or residents of a community about the hospital facility's FAP in the manner described in paragraphs (b)(5)(i)(C) and (b)(5)(i)(D) of this section will depend on all of the facts and circumstances, including the primary language(s) spoken by the residents of the community served by the hospital facility and other attributes of the community and the hospital facility.

(iv) *Widely available on a website.*—For purposes of paragraph (b)(5)(i)(A) of this section, a hospital facility makes its FAP, FAP application form, and plain language summary of the FAP widely available on a website only if—

(A) The hospital facility conspicuously posts complete and current versions of these documents in English and in the primary language of any populations with limited proficiency in English that constitute more than 10 percent of the residents of the community served by the hospital facility on—

(1) The hospital facility's website;

(2) If the hospital facility does not have its own website separate from the hospital organization that operates it, the hospital organization's website; or

(3) A website established and maintained by another entity, but only if the website of the hospital facility or hospital organization (if the facility or organization has a website) provides a conspicuously-displayed link to the web page on which the document is posted, along with clear instructions for accessing the document on that website;

(B) Any individual with access to the Internet can access, download, view, and print a hard copy of these documents without requiring special computer hardware or software (other than software that is readily available to members of the public without payment of any fee) and without payment of a fee to the hospital facility, hospital organization, or other entity maintaining the website; and

(C) The hospital facility provides any individual who asks how to access a copy of the FAP, FAP application form, or plain language summary of the FAP online with the direct website address, or URL, of the web page on which these documents are posted.

(v) *Limited English proficient populations.*—For purposes of paragraphs (b)(5)(i)(B) and (b)(5)(iv)(A) of this section, a hospital facility may determine whether any language minority with limited proficiency in English constitutes more than 10 percent of the residents of the community served by the hospital facility based on the latest data available from the U.S. Census Bureau or other similarly reliable data.

(vi) *Examples.*—The following examples illustrate this paragraph (b)(5):

Example 1. (i) Z is a hospital facility whose FAP states that Z will make its FAP, FAP application form, and a plain language summary of its FAP widely available through its website. In accordance with its FAP, the home page and main billing page of Z's website conspicuously display the following message: "Need help paying your bill? You may be eligible for financial assistance. Click *here* for more information." When readers click on the link, they are taken to a web page that explains the various discounts available under Z's FAP and the specific eligibility criteria for each such discount. This web page also provides a telephone number and room number of Z that individuals can call or visit for more information about the FAP, as well as the name and contact information of a few nonprofit organizations and government agencies that Z has identified as capable and available sources of assistance with FAP applications. In addition, the web page contains prominently-displayed links that allow readers to download PDF files of the FAP and the FAP application form, free of charge. Z provides any individual who asks how to access a copy of the FAP, FAP application form, or plain language summary of the FAP online with the URL of this web page. Z's FAP includes measures to make the FAP widely available on a website within the meaning of paragraph (b)(5)(i)(A) of this section.

(ii) Z's FAP also states that Z will make paper copies of the FAP, FAP application form, and plain language summary of the FAP available upon request and without charge, both by mail and in its billing office, admissions and registrations areas, and emergency room, and will inform and notify visitors to the hospital facility about the FAP in these same locations using signs and brochures. In accordance with its FAP, Z conspicuously displays a sign in large font regarding the FAP in its billing office, admissions and registrations areas, and emergency room. The sign says: "Uninsured? Having trouble paying your hospital bill? You may be eligible for financial assistance." The sign also provides the URL of the web page where Z's FAP and FAP application form can be accessed. In addition, the sign provides a telephone number and room number of Z that individuals can call or visit with questions about the FAP or the FAP application process. Underneath each sign, Z conspicuously displays copies of a brochure that contains all of the information required to be included in a plain language summary of the FAP (as defined in § 1.501(r)-1(b)(19)). Z makes these brochures available in quantities sufficient to meet visitor demand. Z also makes paper copies of its FAP and FAP application form available upon request and without charge in these same locations and by mail. Z's FAP includes measures to widely publicize the FAP within the meaning of paragraphs (b)(5)(i)(B) and (b)(5)(i)(C) of this section.

(iii) In addition, Z's FAP states that Z will inform and notify members of the community served by the hospital facility about the FAP through its quarterly newsletter and by distributing copies of its FAP brochures to physicians and local nonprofit organizations and public agencies that address the health needs of lowincome people. In accordance with its FAP, Z distributes copies of the brochure and its FAP application form to all of its referring staff physicians and to the community health centers serving its community. Z also distributes copies of these documents to the local health department and to numerous public agencies and nonprofit organizations in its community that address the health issues and other needs of low-income populations, in quantities sufficient to meet demand. In addition, every issue of the quarterly newsletter that Z mails to the individuals in its customer database contains a prominently-displayed advertisement informing readers that Z offers financial assistance and that people having trouble paying their hospital bills may be eligible for financial assistance. The advertisement also provides readers with the URL of the web page where Z's FAP and FAP application form can be accessed and a telephone number and room number of Z that individuals can call or visit with questions about the FAP or the FAP application process. Z's FAP includes measures to widely publicize its FAP within the meaning of paragraph (b)(5)(i)(D) of this section.

(iv) Because Z's FAP includes measures to widely publicize the FAP described in paragraphs (b)(5)(i)(A), (b)(5)(i)(B), (b)(5)(i)(C), and (b)(5)(i)(D) of this section, Z's FAP meets the requirements of this paragraph (b)(5).

Example 2. Assume the same facts as *Example 1*, except that Z serves a community in which 11 percent of the residents speak Spanish and have limited proficiency in English. Z's FAP states that Z will provide all of the information described in *Example 1*, including the FAP itself, in both Spanish and English. In accordance with its FAP, Z translates its FAP, FAP application form, and FAP brochure (which constitutes a plain language summary of the FAP) into Spanish, and displays and distributes Spanish versions of these documents in its hospital facility and in the Spanish-speaking portions of the community it serves, using all of the measures described in *Example 1*. Moreover, the home page and main billing page of Z's website conspicuously display an "¿Habla Español?" link that takes readers to a web page that summarizes the FAP in Spanish and contains links that allow readers to download PDF files of the Spanish versions of the FAP and FAP application form, free of charge. Z's FAP meets the requirements of this paragraph (b)(5) by including measures to widely publicize the FAP within the community served by Z.

Example 3. Assume the same facts as *Example 1*, except that instead of including generalized summaries of the measures Z will take to widely publicize its FAP in the FAP itself, Z's FAP states that a task force established by Z with control over a set budget will meet at least annually to develop and adopt a plan to widely publicize Z's FAP. The FAP further states that the task force will summarize this plan in a one-page information sheet that will be made available upon request in Z's billing office and posted on the web page through which Z makes its FAP and FAP application form widely available. In year 1, the task force considers the needs of Z's patients and the surrounding community and adopts and implements a plan to take all of the measures described in *Example 1*. The task force prepares a one-page information sheet summarizing this plan that is made available as described in the FAP. Z's FAP meets the requirements of this paragraph (b)(5) in year 1 by including measures to widely publicize the FAP within the community served by Z.

(6) *Readily obtainable information.*—For purposes of this paragraph (b), members of the public may readily obtain information if a hospital facility makes the information available free of charge both on a website and in writing upon request in a manner similar to that described in paragraphs (b)(5)(i)(A) and (b)(5)(i)(B) of this section.

(c) *Emergency medical care policy.*—(1) *In general.*—To satisfy paragraph (a)(2) of this section, a hospital facility must establish a written policy that requires the hospital facility to provide, without discrimination, care for emergency medical conditions to individuals regardless of whether they are FAP-eligible.

(2) *Interference with provision of emergency medical care.*—A hospital facility's emergency medical care policy will not be described in paragraph (c)(1) of this section unless it prohibits the hospital facility from engaging in actions that

discourage individuals from seeking emergency medical care, such as by demanding that emergency department patients pay before receiving treatment for emergency medical conditions or by permitting debt collection activities in the emergency department or in other areas of the hospital facility where such activities could interfere with the provision, without discrimination, of emergency medical care.

(3) *Relation to federal law governing emergency medical care.*—Subject to paragraph (c)(2) of this section, a hospital facility's emergency medical care policy will be described in paragraph (c)(1) of this section if it requires the hospital facility to provide the care for emergency medical conditions that the hospital facility is required to provide under Subchapter G of Chapter IV of Title 42 of the Code of Federal Regulations (or any successor regulations).

(4) *Examples.*—The following examples illustrate this paragraph (c):

Example 1. F is a hospital facility with a dedicated emergency department that is subject to the Emergency Medical Treatment and Labor Act (EMTALA) and is not a critical access hospital. F establishes a written emergency medical care policy requiring F to comply with EMTALA by providing medical screening examinations and stabilizing treatment and referring or transferring an individual to another facility, when appropriate, and to provide emergency services in accordance with 42 CFR §482.55 (or any successor regulation). F's emergency medical care policy also states that F prohibits any actions that would discourage individuals from seeking emergency medical care, such as by demanding that emergency department patients pay before receiving treatment for emergency medical conditions or permitting debt collection activities in the emergency department or in other areas of the hospital facility where such activities could interfere with the provision, without discrimination, of emergency medical care. F's emergency medical care policy is described in paragraph (c)(1) of this section.

Example 2. G is a rehabilitation hospital facility. G does not have a dedicated emergency department, nor does it have specialized capabilities that would make it appropriate to accept transfers of individuals who need stabilizing treatment for an emergency medical condition. G establishes a written emergency medical care policy that addresses how it appraises emergencies, provides initial treatment, and refers or transfers an individual to another facility, when appropriate, in a manner that complies with 42 CFR §482.12(f)(2) (or any successor regulation). G's emergency medical care policy also states that G prohibits any actions that would discourage individuals from seeking emergency medical care, such as by permitting debt collection activities in any areas of the hospital facility where such activities could interfere with the provision, without discrimination, of emergency medical care. G's emergency medical care policy is described in paragraph (c)(1) of this section.

(d) *Establishing the FAP and other policies.*—(1) *In general.*—A hospital organization has established a FAP, a billing and collections policy, or an emergency medical care policy for a hospital facility only if an authorized body of the hospital organization has adopted the policy for the hospital facility and the hospital facility has implemented the policy.

(2) *Authorized body.*—For purposes of this paragraph (d), an authorized body of a hospital organization means—

(i) The governing body (that is, the board of directors, board of trustees, or equivalent controlling body) of the hospital organization;

(ii) A committee of the governing body, which may be composed of any individuals permitted under state law to serve on such a committee, to the extent that the committee is permitted by state law to act on behalf of the governing body;

(iii) To the extent permitted under state law, other parties authorized by the governing body of the hospital organization to act on its behalf; or

(iv) In the case of a hospital facility (operated by the hospital organization) that has its own governing body and is recognized as an entity under state law but is a disregarded entity for federal tax purposes, the governing body of that disregarded entity (or a committee of or other parties authorized by that governing body as described in paragraphs (d)(2)(ii) or (d)(2)(iii) of this section).

(3) *Implementing a policy.*—For purposes of this paragraph (d), a hospital facility has implemented a policy if the hospital facility has consistently carried out the policy.

(4) *Establishing a policy for more than one hospital facility.*—Although a hospital organization operating more than one hospital facility must separately establish a FAP and emergency medical care policy for each hospital facility it operates, such policies may contain the same operative terms. However, different AGB percentages and methods of determining AGB and the unique attributes of the communities that different hospital facilities serve may require the hospital facilities to include in their FAPs (or otherwise make available) different information regarding AGB and different measures to widely publicize the FAP in order to meet the requirements of paragraphs (b)(2) and/or (b)(5) of this section. [Reg. §1.501(r)-4.]

§1.501(r)-5. Limitation on charges.—(a) *In general.*—A hospital organization meets the requirements of section 501(r)(5) with respect to a hospital facility it operates if the hospital facility limits the amount charged for care it provides to any individual who is eligible for assistance under its financial assistance policy (FAP) to—

(1) In the case of emergency or other medically necessary care, not more than the amounts generally billed to individuals who have insurance covering such care (AGB), as determined under paragraph (b) of this section; and

(2) In the case of all other medical care, less than the gross charges for such care, as described in paragraph (c) of this section.

(b) *Amounts generally billed.*—In order to meet the requirements of paragraph (b)(1) of this section, a hospital facility must determine AGB for emergency or other medically necessary care using a method described in either paragraph (b)(1) or (b)(2) of this section. A hospital facility may use only one of these methods to determine AGB. After choosing a particular method, a hospital facility must continue to use that method.

(1) *Look-back method.*—(i) *In general.*—A hospital facility may determine AGB for any emergency or other medically necessary care it provides to a FAP-eligible individual by multiplying the hospital facility's gross charges for the care provided to the individual by one or more percentages of gross charges (AGB percentages). The hospital facility must calculate its AGB percentage(s) at least annually by dividing the sum of all claims for emergency and other medically necessary care described in either paragraph (b)(1)(i)(A) or (b)(1)(i)(B) of this section that have been paid in full to the hospital facility during a prior 12-month period by the sum of the associated gross charges for those claims:

(A) Claims paid by Medicare fee-for-service as the primary payer, including any associated portions of the claims paid by Medicare beneficiaries in the form of co-insurance or deductibles; or

(B) Claims paid by both Medicare fee-for-service and all private health insurers as primary payers, together with any associated portions of these claims paid by Medicare beneficiaries or insured individuals in the form of co-payments, co-insurance, or deductibles.

(ii) *One or multiple AGB percentages.*—A hospital facility's AGB percentage that is calculated using the method described in this paragraph (b)(1) may be one average percentage of gross charges for all emergency and other medically necessary care provided by the hospital facility. Alternatively, a hospital facility may calculate multiple AGB percentages for separate categories of care (such as inpatient and outpatient care or care provided by different departments) or for separate items or services, as long as the hospital facility calculates AGB percentages for all emergency and other medically necessary care provided by the hospital facility.

(iii) *Start date for applying AGB percentages.*—For purposes of determining AGB under this paragraph (b)(1), with respect to any AGB percentage that a hospital facility has calculated, the hospital facility must begin applying the AGB percentage by the 45th day after the end of the 12-month period the hospital facility used in calculating the AGB percentage.

(2) *Prospective Medicare method.*—As an alternative to the method described in paragraph (b)(1) of this section, a hospital facility may determine AGB for any emergency or other medically necessary care provided to a FAP-eligible individual by using the billing and coding process the hospital facility would use if the FAP-eligible individual were a Medicare fee-for-service beneficiary and setting AGB for the care at the amount the hospital facility determines would be the amount Medicare and the Medicare beneficiary together would be expected to pay for the care.

(3) *Examples.*—The following examples illustrate this paragraph (b):

Example 1. On January 15 of year 1, Y, a hospital facility, generates data on all claims paid to it in full for emergency or other medically necessary care by all private health insurers and Medicare fee-for-service as primary payers over the immediately preceding calendar year. Y determines that it received a total of $360 million on these claims from the private health insurers and Medicare and another $40 million from their insured patients and Medicare beneficiaries in the form of deductibles, co-insurance, and co-payments. Y's gross charges for these claims totaled $800 million. Y calculates that its AGB percentage is 50 percent of gross charges ($400 million/$800 million × 100). Y determines AGB for any emergency or other medically necessary care it provides to a FAP-eligible individual between February 1 of year 1 (less than 45 days after the end of the 12-month claim period) and January 31 of year 2 by multiplying the gross charges for the care provided to the individual by 50%. Y has determined AGB in accordance with this paragraph (b).

Example 2. On September 20 of year 1, X, a hospital facility, generates data on all claims paid to it in full for emergency or other medically necessary care by Medicare fee-for-service as the primary payer over the 12 months ending on August 31 of year 1. X determines that, of these claims for inpatient services, it received a total of $80 million from Medicare and another $20 million from Medicare beneficiaries in the form of co-insurance or deductibles. X's gross charges for these inpatient claims totaled $250 million. Of the claims for outpatient services, X received a total of $100 million from Medicare and another $25 million from Medicare beneficiaries. X's gross charges for these outpatient claims totaled $200 million. X calculates that its AGB percentage for inpatient services is 40 percent of gross charges ($100 million/$250 million × 100) and its AGB percentage for outpatient services is 62.5 percent of gross charges ($125 million/$200 million × 100). Between October 15 of year 1 (45 days after the end of the 12-month claim period) and October 14 of year 2, X determines AGB for any emergency or other medically necessary inpatient care it provides to a FAP-eligible individual by multiplying the gross charges for the inpatient care it provides to the individual by 40% and AGB for any emergency or other medically necessary outpatient care it provides to a FAP-eligible individual by multiplying the gross charges for the outpatient care it provides to the individual by 62.5%. X has determined AGB in accordance with this paragraph (b).

Example 3. Z is a hospital facility. Whenever Z provides emergency or other medically necessary care to a FAP-eligible individual, Z determines the AGB for the care by using the billing and coding process it would use if the individual were a Medicare fee-for-service beneficiary and setting AGB for the care at the amount it determines Medicare and the Medicare beneficiary together would be expected to pay for the care. Z determines AGB in accordance with this paragraph (b).

(c) *Gross charges.*—A hospital facility must charge a FAP-eligible individual less than the gross charges for any medical care provided to that individual. However, a billing statement issued to a FAP-eligible individual for medical care provided by a hospital facility may state the gross charges for such care as the starting point to which various contractual allowances, discounts, or deductions are applied, as long as the actual amount the individual is expected to pay is less than the gross charges for such care.

(d) *Safe harbor for certain charges in excess of AGB.*—A hospital facility will be deemed to meet the requirements of paragraph (a) of this section, even if it charges more than AGB for emergency or other medically necessary care (or gross charges for any medical care) provided to a FAP-eligible individual if—

(1) The FAP-eligible individual has not submitted a complete FAP application to the hospital facility as of the time of the charge; and

(2) The hospital facility has made and continues to make reasonable efforts to determine whether the individual is FAP-eligible, as described in § 1.501(r)-6(c), during the applicable time periods described in that section (including by correcting the amount charged if the individual is subsequently found to be FAP-eligible). [Reg. § 1.501(r)-5.]

§ 1.501(r)-6. Billing and collection.—(a) *In general.*—A hospital organization meets the requirements of section 501(r)(6) with respect to a hospital facility it operates if the hospital facility does not engage in extraordinary collection actions (ECAs), as defined in paragraph (b) of this section, against an individual before the hospital facility has, consistent with paragraph (c) of this section, made reasonable efforts to determine whether the individual is eligible for assistance under its financial assistance policy (FAP). For purposes of this section, with respect to any debt owed by an individual for care provided by a hospital facility—

(1) ECAs against the individual include ECAs against any other individual who has accepted or is required to accept responsibility for the individual's hospital bills; and

(2) The hospital facility will be deemed to have engaged in an ECA against the individual if any purchaser of the individual's debt or any debt collection agency or other party to which the hospital facility has referred the individual's debt has engaged in an ECA against the individual.

(b) *Extraordinary collection actions.*—ECAs are actions taken by a hospital facility against an individual related to obtaining payment of a bill for care covered under the hospital facility's FAP that require a legal or judicial process or involve selling an individuals' debt to another party or reporting adverse information about the individual to consumer credit reporting agencies or credit bureaus. For purposes of this paragraph (b), actions that require a legal or judicial process include, but are not limited to, actions to—

(1) Place a lien on an individual's property;

(2) Foreclose on an individual's real property;

(3) Attach or seize an individual's bank account or any other personal property;

(4) Commence a civil action against an individual;

(5) Cause an individual's arrest;

(6) Cause an individual to be subject to a writ of body attachment; and

(7) Garnish an individual's wages.

(c) *Reasonable efforts.*—(1) *In general.*—With respect to any care provided by a hospital facility to an individual, the hospital facility will have made reasonable efforts to determine whether the individual is FAP-eligible only if the hospital facility—

(i) Notifies the individual about its FAP during the notification period (as defined in § 1.501(r)-1(b)(18)), as described in paragraph (c)(2) of this section;

(ii) In the case of an individual who submits an incomplete FAP application during the application period (as defined in § 1.501(r)-1(b)(3)), meets the requirements described in paragraph (c)(3) of this section; and

(iii) In the case of an individual who submits a complete FAP application during the application period, meets the requirements described in paragraph (c)(4) of this section.

(2) *Notification.*—(i) *In general.*—Except as provided in paragraph (c)(2)(ii) of this section, with respect to any care provided by a hospital facility to an individual, a hospital facility will have notified the individual about its FAP for purposes of paragraph (c)(1)(i) of this section only if the hospital facility—

(A) Distributes a plain language summary of the FAP (as defined in § 1.501(r)-1(b)(19)) and offers a FAP application form to the individual before discharge from the hospital facility;

(B) Includes a plain language summary of the FAP with all (and at least three) billing statements for the care and all other written communications regarding the bill provided to the individual during the notification period;

(C) Informs the individual about the FAP in all oral communications with the individual regarding the amount due for the care that occur during the notification period; and

(D) Provides the individual with at least one written notice that—

(1) Informs the individual about the ECAs the hospital facility or other authorized party may take if the individual does not submit a FAP application or pay the amount due by a deadline (specified in the notice) that is no earlier than the last day of the notification period; and

(2) Is provided to the individual at least 30 days before the deadline specified in the written notice.

(ii) *Notification when FAP application is submitted.*—If an individual submits a complete or incomplete FAP application to a hospital facility during the application period, the hospital facility will be deemed to have notified the individual about its FAP for purposes of paragraph (c)(1)(i) of this section as of the day the application is submitted. However, to have made reasonable efforts to determine whether such an individual is FAP-eligible, the hospital facility must meet the requirements of paragraphs (c)(3) and (c)(4) of this section, as applicable.

(iii) *When no FAP application is submitted.*—If an individual fails to submit a FAP application during the notification period (or, if later, by the deadline specified in the written notice described in paragraph (c)(2)(i)(D) of this section) and the hospital facility has notified (and documented that it has notified) the individual as described in paragraph (c)(2)(i) of this section, the hospital facility will have satisfied paragraph (c)(1)(i) of this section. Until and unless the individual subsequently submits a FAP application during the remainder of the application period, paragraphs (c)(1)(ii) and (c)(1)(iii) do not apply. As a result, the hospital facility will have made reasonable efforts to determine whether the individual is FAP-eligible and may engage in one or more ECAs against the individual.

(iv) *Example.*—The following example illustrates this paragraph (c)(2):

Example. Individual A receives care from hospital facility T on February 1 and February 2. When A is discharged from T on February 2, T gives A its FAP application form and a plain language summary of its FAP. On March 1, April 15, and May 30, T sends A billing statements that include a one-page insert that provides a plain language summary of the FAP. With the May 30 billing statement, T also includes a letter that informs A that if she does not pay the amount owed or submit a FAP application form by June 29 (120 days after the first billing statement was provided on March 1), T may report A's delinquency to credit reporting agencies, seek to obtain a judgment against A, and, if such a judgment is obtained, seek to attach and seize A's bank account or other personal property, which are the only ECAs that T (or any party to which T refers A's debt) may take in accordance with T's billing and collections policy. T does not have any other written or oral communications with A about her bill before June 29. T keeps electronic records showing that it provided a plain language summary and FAP application to A on discharge and included the letter regarding ECAs and the plain language summaries with the billing statements sent to A. A does not submit a FAP application form by June 29. T has made reasonable efforts to determine whether A is FAP-eligible, and thus may engage in ECAs against A, as of June 30.

(3) *Incomplete FAP applications.*—(i) *In general.*—With respect to any care provided by a hospital facility to an individual, if the individual submits an incomplete FAP application during the application period, the hospital facility will have made reasonable efforts to determine whether the individual is FAP-eligible only if the hospital facility—

(A) Suspends any ECAs against the individual as described in paragraph (c)(5) of this section;

(B) Provides the individual with a written notice that describes the additional information and/or documentation required under the FAP or FAP application form that the individual must submit to the hospital facility to complete his or her FAP application and includes a plain language summary of the FAP with this notice; and

(C) Provides the individual with at least one written notice that—

(1) Informs the individual about the ECAs the hospital facility or other authorized party may initiate or resume if the individual does not complete the FAP application or pay the amount due by a completion deadline (specified in the notice) that is no earlier than the later of the last day of the application period or 30 days after the hospital facility provides the individual with the written notice; and

(2) Is provided to the individual at least 30 days before the completion deadline.

(ii) *FAP application completed by the completion deadline.*—If an individual who has submitted an incomplete FAP application during the application period completes the FAP application by the completion deadline, the individual will be considered to have submitted a complete FAP application during the application period, and the hospital facility will therefore only have made reasonable efforts to determine whether the individual is FAP-eligible if it meets the requirements for complete FAP applications described in paragraph (c)(4) of this section.

(iii) *FAP application not completed by the completion deadline.*—If an individual who submits an incomplete FAP application to a hospital facility during the application period fails to complete the FAP application by the completion deadline and the hospital facility has met the requirements described in paragraph (c)(3)(i) of this section, the hospital facility will have made reasonable efforts to determine whether the individual is FAP-eligible and may initiate or resume ECAs against the individual after the completion deadline.

(iv) *Examples.*—The following examples illustrate this paragraph (c)(3):

Example 1. (i) Assume the same facts as the example in paragraph (c)(2)(iv) of this section and the following additional facts: A submits an incomplete FAP application to T on October 13, two weeks before the last day of the application period on October 27 (240 days after the first billing statement was provided on March 1). Eligibility for assistance under T's FAP is based solely on an individual's family income and the instructions to T's FAP application form require applicants to attach certain documentation verifying family income to their application forms. The FAP application form that A submits to T on October 13 includes all of the required income information, but A fails to attach the required documentation verifying her family income. After receiving A's incomplete FAP application on October 13, T does not initiate any new ECAs against A and does not take any further action on the ECAs T previously initiated against A. On October 15, a member of T's staff calls A to inform her that she failed to attach any of the required documentation of her family income and explain what kind of documentation A needs to submit and how she can submit it. On October 16, T sends a letter to A explaining the kind of documentation of family income that A must provide to T to complete her application and informing A about the ECAs that T (or any other authorized party) may initiate or resume against A if A does not submit the missing documentation or pay the amount due by November 15 (30 days after October 16). T includes a plain language summary of the FAP with the letter. T has met the requirements of this paragraph (c)(3).

(ii) On November 15, A provides T with the missing documentation. Because A provides the missing documentation by the completion deadline, she has submitted a complete FAP application during the application period. As a result, to have made reasonable efforts to determine whether A is FAP-eligible, T must assess the documentation to determine whether A is FAP-eligible and otherwise meet the requirements for complete FAP applications described in paragraph (c)(4) of this section.

Example 2. Individual B receives care from hospital facility U on January 10. U has established a FAP that provides assistance to all individuals whose household income is less than $y, and the instructions to U's FAP application form specify the documentation that applicants must provide to verify their household income. Upon discharge, U's staff gives B a plain language summary of the FAP and a copy of its FAP application form. On January 20, B submits a

FAP application form to U indicating that he has household income of less than $y. The FAP application form includes all of the required income information, but B fails to attach the required documentation verifying household income. On February 1, U sends B the first billing statement for the care and includes with the statement another plain language summary of the FAP. U also includes with the billing statement a letter informing B that the income information he provided on his FAP application form indicates that he may be eligible to pay only x% of the amount stated on the billing statement if he can provide documentation that verifies his household income. In addition, this letter describes the type of documentation (also described in the instructions to U's FAP application form) that B needs to provide to complete his FAP application. By August 30, B has not provided the missing documentation. U sends B a written notice on August 30 informing him about the ECAs U (or any other authorized party) may initiate against B if B does not submit the missing documentation or pay the amount due by September 29 (240 days after the first billing statement was provided on February 1 and the last day of the application period). B fails to provide the missing documentation by September 29. U has made reasonable efforts to determine whether B is FAP-eligible, and thus may engage in ECA's against B, as of September 30.

(4) *Complete FAP applications.*—(i) *In general.*—With respect to any care provided by a hospital facility to an individual, if the individual submits a complete FAP application during the application period, the hospital facility will have made reasonable efforts to determine whether the individual is FAP-eligible only if the hospital facility does the following in a timely manner—

(A) Suspends any ECAs against the individual as described in paragraph (c)(5) of this section;

(B) Makes and documents a determination as to whether the individual is FAP-eligible;

(C) Notifies the individual in writing of the eligibility determination (including, if applicable, the assistance for which the individual is eligible) and the basis for this determination;

(D) If the hospital facility determines the individual is FAP-eligible, does the following—

(1) Provides the individual with a billing statement that indicates the amount the individual owes as a FAP-eligible individual and shows, or describes how the individual can get information regarding, the AGB for the care and how the hospital facility determined the amount the individual owes as a FAP-eligible individual;

(2) If the individual has made payments to the hospital facility (or any other party) for the care in excess of the amount he or she is determined to owe as a FAP-eligible individual, refunds those excess payments; and

(3) Takes all reasonably available measures to reverse any ECA (with the exception of a sale of debt) taken against the individual to collect the debt at issue; such reasonably available measures generally include, but are not limited to, measures to vacate any judgment against the individual, lift any lien or levy on the individual's property, and remove from the individual's credit report any adverse information that was reported to a consumer reporting agency or credit bureau.

(ii) *Determination based on complete FAP applications.*—If a hospital facility has met the requirements described in paragraph (c)(4)(i) of this section and not violated the anti-abuse rule described in paragraph (c)(4)(iii) of this section, the hospital facility has made reasonable efforts to determine whether the individual is FAP-eligible and may initiate or resume ECAs against the individual. To have made reasonable efforts to determine the FAP-eligibility of an individual who has submitted a complete FAP application during the application period, the hospital facility must meet the requirements described in this paragraph (c)(4) regardless of whether the hospital facility has previously made such reasonable efforts under paragraphs (c)(2)(iii) or (c)(3)(iii) of this section.

(iii) *Anti-abuse rule for complete FAP applications.*—A hospital facility will not have made reasonable efforts to determine whether an individual is FAP-eligible if the hospital facility bases its determination that the individual is not FAP-eligible on information that the hospital facility has reason to believe is unreliable or incorrect or on information obtained from the individual under duress or through the use of coercive practices. For purposes of this paragraph (c)(4)(iii), a coercive practice includes delaying or denying emergency medical care to an individual until the individual has provided the requested information.

(iv) *Presumptive eligibility permitted.*—A hospital facility will have made reasonable efforts to determine whether an individual is FAP-eligible if the hospital facility determines that the individual is eligible for the most generous assistance (including free care) available under the FAP based on information other than that provided by the individual as part of a complete FAP application and the hospital facility meets the requirements described in paragraph (c)(4)(i) of this section.

(v) *Examples.*—The following examples illustrate this paragraph (c)(4):

Example 1. V is a hospital facility with a FAP under which the specific assistance for which an individual is eligible depends exclusively upon that individual's household income. The most generous assistance offered for care under V's FAP is 90 percent off of gross charges up to a maximum amount due of $1,000. On March 3, D, an individual, receives care from V, the gross charges for which are $500. Although D does not submit a FAP application to V, V learns that D is eligible for certain benefits under a state program that bases eligibility on household income. Based on this knowledge, V determines that D is eligible under V's FAP to receive the most generous assistance under the FAP, resulting in D owing $50 (90 percent off of the $500 in gross charges) for the March 3 care. V documents this determination, and, on March 21, sends D a billing statement that informs him that V determined he was eligible for the 90% discount based on his eligibility for the benefits under the state program and the fact that his bill, after the discount, was not more than $1,000. This billing statement indicates an amount owed of $50, shows that V arrived at $50 by applying a 90 percent discount to the gross charges for the care, and provides a telephone number D can call to obtain the AGB for the care he received. V has made reasonable efforts to determine whether D is FAP-eligible as of March 21.

Example 2. Individual C receives care from hospital facility W on September 1. W has established a FAP that provides assistance only to individuals whose family income is less than or equal to x% of the Federal Poverty Level (FPL), which, in the case of C's family size, is $y. Upon discharge, W's staff gives C a plain language summary of the FAP and a FAP application form and informs C that if she needs assistance in filling out the form, W has a social worker on staff who can assist her. C expresses interest in getting assistance with a FAP application while she is still on site and is directed to K, one of W's social workers. K explains the eligibility criteria in W's FAP to C, and C realizes that to determine her family income as a percentage of FPL she needs to look at her prior year's tax returns. On September 20, after returning home and obtaining the necessary information, C submits a FAP application to W that contains all of the information and documentation required in the FAP application form instructions. W's staff promptly examines C's FAP application and, based on the information and documentation therein, determines that C's family income is well in excess of $y. On October 1, W sends C her first billing statement for the care she received on September 1. With the billing statement, W includes a letter informing C that she is not eligible for financial assistance because her FAP application indicates that she has family income in excess of x% of FPL ($y for a family the size of C's family) and W only provides financial assistance to individuals with family income that is less than x% of FPL. W has made reasonable efforts to determine whether C is FAP-eligible as of October 1.

Example 3. E, an individual, receives care from P, a hospital facility, in February. P provides E with the first billing statement for the care on March 1. P notifies E about its FAP as described in paragraph (c)(2)(i) of this section, but E fails to submit a FAP application by P's specified deadline of June 30 (120 days after the initial March 1 billing statement and the last day of the notification period). In September, P seeks and obtains a judgment against E, in which the court determines that E owes P $1,200 for the care P provided and states that E has 30 days to pay this amount. E does not pay any of the $1,200 in 30 days. By October 20, P has seized E's bank account and obtained a total of $450 in funds from the account. E submits a complete FAP application to P on October 20, before the last day of the application period on October 27 (240 days after the initial March 1 billing statement). Upon receiving this application, P does not seize any additional funds from E's bank account and also does not initiate any additional ECAs against E. P promptly examines the application and determines that E is eligible under P's FAP to receive a discount that results in E only owing $150 for the care she received. P also determines that the AGB for the care is $500. P documents this determination, seeks to vacate the judgment against E, lifts the levy on E's bank account, and sends E a letter that informs her about the FAP discount for which she is eligible and explains the basis for this eligibility determination. P includes with this letter a check for $300 (the $450 that P seized from E's bank account minus the $150 that E owes as a FAP-eligible individual) and a billing statement that indicates a $300 refund, shows how P applied the FAP discount for which E is eligible to arrive at an amount owed of $150, and states that the AGB for the care is $500. P has made reasonable efforts to determine whether E is FAP-eligible.

Example 4. R, a hospital facility, has established a FAP that provides financial assistance only to individuals whose family income is less than or equal to x% of the Federal Poverty Level (FPL), as based on their prior year's federal tax return. Individual L receives care from R. While L is being discharged from R, she is approached by M, an employee of a debt collection company that has a contract with R to handle all of R's patient billing. M asks L for her family income information, telling L that this information is needed to determine whether L is eligible for financial assistance. L tells M that she does not know what her family income is and would need to consult her tax returns to determine it. M tells L that she can just provide a "rough estimate" of her family income. L states that her family income may be around $y, an amount slightly above the amount that would allow her to qualify for financial assistance. M enters $y on the income line of a FAP application form with L's name on it and marks L as not FAP-eligible. Based on M's information collection, R determines that L is not FAP-eligible and notifies L of this determination with her first billing statement. Because M had reason to believe that the income estimate provided by L was unreliable, R has violated the anti-abuse rule described in paragraph (c)(4)(iii) of this section. Thus, R has not made reasonable efforts to determine whether L is FAP-eligible.

(5) *Suspending ECAs while a FAP application is pending.*—If an individual submits a complete or incomplete FAP application during the application period, the hospital facility will have made reasonable efforts to determine whether the individual is FAP-eligible only if the hospital facility does not initiate any ECAs, or take further action on any previously-initiated ECAs, against the individual after receiving the application and until either—

(i) The hospital facility has met the requirements described in paragraph (c)(4) of this section; or

(ii) In the case of an incomplete FAP application, the completion deadline has passed without the individual having completed the FAP application.

(6) *Waiver does not constitute reasonable efforts.*—For purposes of this paragraph (c), obtaining a signed waiver from an individual, such as a signed statement that the individual does not wish to apply for assistance under the FAP or receive the information described in paragraphs (c)(2) or (c)(3) of this section, will not constitute a determination of FAP-eligibility and will not satisfy the requirement to make reasonable efforts to determine whether the individual is FAP-eligible before engaging in ECAs against the individual.

(7) *Agreements with other parties.*—If a hospital facility refers or sells an individual's debt to another party during the application period, the hospital facility will have made reasonable ef-

forts to determine whether the individual is FAP-eligible only if it first obtains (and, to the extent applicable, enforces) a legally binding written agreement from the party that—

(i) In the case of any debt referred to the party during the notification period, the party will refrain from engaging in ECAs against the individual until the hospital facility has met (and documented that it has met) the requirements necessary to have made reasonable efforts under paragraph (c)(2)(iii), (c)(3)(iii), or (c)(4)(ii) of this section;

(ii) If the individual submits a FAP application during the application period, the party will suspend any ECAs against the individual as described in paragraph (c)(5) of this section;

(iii) If the individual submits a FAP application during the application period and the hospital facility determines the individual to be FAP-eligible, the party will do the following in a timely manner—

(A) Adhere to procedures specified in the agreement that ensure that the individual does not pay, and has no obligation to pay, the party and the hospital facility together more than he or she is required to pay as a FAP-eligible individual; and

(B) If applicable and if the party (rather than the hospital facility) has the authority to do so, takes all reasonably available measures to reverse any ECA (other than the sale of a debt) taken against the individual as described in paragraph (c)(4)(i)(D)(3) of this section; and

(iv) If the party refers or sells the debt to yet another party during the application period, the party will obtain a written agreement from that other party including all of the elements described in this paragraph (c)(7).

(8) *Clear and conspicuous placement.*—A hospital facility may print any written notice or communication described in this paragraph (c), including any plain language summary of the FAP, on a billing statement or along with other descriptive or explanatory matter, as long as the required information is conspicuously placed and of sufficient size to be clearly readable. [Reg. § 1.501(r)-6.]

§ 1.501(r)-7. Effective/applicability dates.—(a) *Statutory effective/applicability date.*—(1) *In general.*—Except as provided in paragraph (a)(2) of this section, section 501(r) applies to taxable years beginning after March 23, 2010.

(2) *Community health needs assessment.*—The requirements of section 501(r)(3) apply to taxable years beginning after March 23, 2012.

(b) *Effective/applicability date of regulations.*—The rules of § 1.501(r)-1 and §§ 1.501(r)-4 through 1.501(r)-6 apply to taxable years beginning on or after the date these regulations are published as final regulations in the **Federal Register**. [Reg. § 1.501(r)-7.]

Charitable Hospitals: Community Health Needs Assessments

Charitable Hospitals: Community Health Needs Assessments.—Reg. §§ 1.501(r)-2 and 1.501(r)-3, and amendments to Reg. §§ 1.501(r)-0, 1.501(r)-1 and 1.501(r)-7, providing guidance to charitable hospital organizations on the community health needs assessment (CHNA) requirements, and related excise tax and reporting obligations, enacted as part of the Patient Protection and Affordable Care Act of 2010, are proposed (published in the Federal Register on April 5, 2013) (REG-106499-12) (corrected May 21, 2013).

Proposed Reg. §§ 1.501(r)-2 and 1.501(r)-3 and proposed amendments to Reg. §§ 1.501(r)-0, 1.501(r)-1 and 1.501(r)-7 were adopted by T.D. 9708 on December 29, 2014. However, for tax years beginning on or before December 29, 2015, a hospital may rely on the final regulations or the 2012 and/or 2013 proposed regulations (REG-130266-11 and/or REG-106499-12).

□ Par. 2. Section 1.501(r)-0 as proposed to be amended at 77 FR 38160 (June 26, 2012) is proposed to be further amended as follows:

1. Adding a new entry to § 1.501(r)-1, paragraph (c).
2. Adding new entries to § 1.501(r)-2 and § 1.501(r)-3.
3. Revising the entry to § 1.501(r)-7.

The revision and additions to read as follows:

§ 1.501(r)-0. Outline of regulations.

* * *

§ 1.501(r)-1 Definitions.

* * *

(c) Additional definitions.
(1) Authorized body of a hospital facility.
(2) Operating a hospital facility.
(3) Partnership agreement.
(4) Widely available on a Web site.

§ 1.501(r)-2 Failures to satisfy section 501(r).

(a) Revocation of section 501(c)(3) status.
(b) Minor and inadvertent omissions and errors.
(c) Excusing certain failures if hospital facility corrects and discloses.
(d) Taxation of noncompliant hospital facilities.
(1) In general.
(2) Noncompliant facility income.
(3) No aggregation.
(4) Interaction with other Code provisions.

§ 1.501(r)-3 Community health needs assessments.

(a) In general.
(b) Conducting a CHNA.
(1) In general.
(2) Date a CHNA is conducted.
(3) Community served by the hospital facility.
(4) Assessing community health needs.
(5) Persons representing the broad interests of the community.
(6) Medically underserved populations.
(7) Documentation of a CHNA.
(8) Making the CHNA report widely available to the public.
(c) Implementation strategy.
(1) In general.
(2) Description of how the hospital facility plans to address a significant health need.
(3) Description of why a hospital facility is not addressing a significant health need.
(4) Joint implementation strategies.

(5) When the implementation strategy must be adopted.

(d) New hospital facilities.

(e) Transition rules.

(1) CHNA conducted in taxable year beginning before March 23, 2012.

(2) CHNA conducted in first taxable year beginning after March 23, 2012.

* * *

§ 1.501(r)-7 Effective/applicability dates.

(a) Effective/applicability date.

(b) Reliance and transition period.

☐ Par. 3. Section 1.501(r)-1 as proposed to be amended at 77 FR 38160 (June 26, 2012) is proposed to be further amended by revising paragraphs (b)(15) and (b)(16) and adding new paragraph (c) to read as follows:

§ 1.501(r)-1. Definitions.

* * *

(b) * * *

(15) *Hospital facility* means a facility that is required by a state to be licensed, registered, or similarly recognized as a hospital. Multiple buildings operated under a single state license are considered to be a single hospital facility. For purposes of this paragraph (b)(15), the term "state" includes only the 50 states and the District of Columbia and not any U.S. territory or foreign country. References to a hospital facility taking actions include instances in which the hospital organization operating the hospital facility takes actions through or on behalf of the hospital facility.

(16) *Hospital organization* means an organization recognized (or seeking to be recognized) as described in section 501(c)(3) that operates one or more hospital facilities. If the section 501(c)(3) status of such an organization is revoked, the organization will, for purposes of section 4959, continue to be treated as a hospital organization during the taxable year in which such revocation becomes effective.

* * *

(c) *Additional definitions.*—(1) *Authorized body of a hospital facility* means

(i) The governing body (that is, the board of directors, board of trustees, or equivalent controlling body) of the hospital organization that operates the hospital facility, or a committee of, or other party authorized by, that governing body to the extent such committee or other party is permitted under state law to act on behalf of the governing body; or

(ii) If the hospital facility has its own governing body and is recognized as an entity under state law but is a disregarded entity for federal tax purposes, the governing body of that hospital facility, or a committee of, or other party authorized by, that governing body to the extent such committee or other party is permitted under state law to act on behalf of the governing body.

(2) *Operating a hospital facility* includes operating the facility through the organization's own employees or contracting out to another organization to operate the facility. For example, if an organization hires a management company to operate the facility, the hiring organization is considered to operate the facility. An organization also operates a hospital facility if it is the sole member or owner of a disregarded entity that operates the hospital facility. In addition, an organization operates a hospital facility if it owns a capital or profits interest in, or is a member of, a joint venture, limited liability company, or other entity treated as a partnership for federal income tax purposes that operates the hospital facility unless either—

(i) The organization does not have control over the operation of the hospital facility sufficient to ensure that the operation of the hospital facility furthers an exempt purpose described in section 501(c)(3) and thus treats the operation of the hospital facility, including the facility's provision of medical care, as an unrelated trade or business described in section 513(a) with respect to the hospital organization; or

(ii) At all times since March 23, 2010, the organization has been organized and operated primarily for educational or scientific purposes and has not engaged primarily in the operation of one or more hospital facilities and, pursuant to a partnership agreement entered into prior to March 23, 2010,—

(A) Does not own more than 35 percent of the capital or profits interest in the partnership (determined in accordance with section 707(b)(3));

(B) Does not own a general partner interest, managing-member interest, or similar interest in the partnership; and

(C) Does not have control over the operation of the hospital facility sufficient to ensure that the hospital facility complies with the requirements of section 501(r).

(3) *Partnership agreement*, for purposes of paragraph (c)(2)(ii) of this section, includes all written agreements among the partners, or between one or more partners and the partnership, concerning affairs of the partnership and responsibilities of the partners, whether or not embodied in a document referred to by the partners as the partnership agreement, entered into before March 23, 2010. A partnership agreement also includes any modifications to the agreement agreed to by all partners, or adopted in any other manner provided by the partnership agreement, but no such modifications adopted on or after March 23, 2010, that affect whether or not the agreement is described in paragraph (c)(2)(ii) of this section. In addition, a partnership agreement includes provisions of federal, state, or local law, as in effect before March 23, 2010, that govern the affairs of the partnership or are considered under such law to be part of the agreement.

(4) *Widely available on a Web site* means—

(i) The hospital facility conspicuously posts a complete and current version of the document on—

(A) The hospital facility's Web site;

(B) If the hospital facility does not have its own Web site separate from the hospital organization that operates it, the hospital organization's Web site; or

(C) A Web site established and maintained by another entity, but only if the Web site of the hospital facility or hospital organization (if the facility or organization has a Web site) provides a conspicuously-displayed link to the web page on which the document is posted, along with clear instructions for accessing the document on that Web site;

(ii) Individuals with access to the Internet can access, download, view, and print a hard copy of the document without requiring special computer hardware or software (other than software that is readily available to members of the public without payment of any fee); without payment of a fee to the hospital facility, hospital organization, or other entity maintaining the Web site; and without creating an account or being otherwise required to provide personally identifiable information; and

(iii) The hospital facility provides individuals who ask how to access a copy of the document online with the direct Web site address, or URL, of the web page on which the document is posted.

☐ Par. 4. Sections 1.501(r)-2 and 1.501(r)-3 are added to read as follows:

§1.501(r)-2. Failures to satisfy section 501(r).—(a) *Revocation of section 501(c)(3) status.*—Except as otherwise provided in paragraphs (b) and (c) of this section, a hospital organization failing to meet one or more of the requirements of section 501(r) separately with respect to one or more hospital facilities it operates may have its section 501(c)(3) status revoked as of the first day of the taxable year in which the failure occurs. In determining whether to continue to recognize the section 501(c)(3) status of a hospital organization that fails to meet one or more of the requirements of section 501(r) with respect to one or more hospital facilities, the Commissioner will consider all relevant facts and circumstances including, but not limited to, the following—

(1) Whether the organization has previously failed to meet the requirements of section 501(r), and, if so, whether the same type of failure previously occurred;

(2) The size, scope, nature, and significance of the organization's failure(s);

(3) In the case of an organization that operates more than one hospital facility, the number, size, and significance of the facilities that have failed to meet the section 501(r) requirements relative to those that have complied with these requirements;

(4) The reason for the failure(s);

(5) Whether the organization had, prior to the failure(s), established practices and procedures (formal or informal) reasonably designed to promote and facilitate overall compliance with the section 501(r) requirements;

(6) Whether the practices and procedures had been routinely followed and the failure(s) occurred through an oversight or mistake in applying them;

(7) Whether the organization has implemented safeguards that are reasonably calculated to prevent similar failures from occurring in the future;

(8) Whether the organization corrected the failure(s) as promptly after discovery as is reasonable given the nature of the failure(s); and

(9) Whether the organization took the measures described in paragraphs (a)(7) and (a)(8) of this section before the Commissioner discovered the failure(s).

(b) *Minor and inadvertent omissions and errors.*—A hospital facility's omission of required information from a policy or report described in §1.501(r)-3 or §1.501(r)-4, or error with respect to the implementation or operational requirements described in §1.501(r)-3 through §1.501(r)-6, will not be considered a failure to meet a requirement of section 501(r) if—

(1) Such omission or error was minor, inadvertent, and due to reasonable cause; and

(2) The hospital facility corrects such omission or error as promptly after discovery as is reasonable given the nature of the omission or error.

(c) *Excusing certain failures if hospital facility corrects and discloses.*—Pursuant to guidance set forth by revenue procedure, notice, or other guidance published in the Internal Revenue Bulletin, a hospital facility's failure to meet one or more of the requirements described in §1.501(r)-3 through §1.501(r)-6 that is neither willful nor egregious shall be excused for purposes of this section if the hospital facility corrects and makes disclosure in accordance with the rules set forth in the guidance. If a hospital facility's failure was willful or egregious, the failure will not be excused, even if the hospital facility corrects and makes disclosure in accordance with the guidance, and no presumption will be created by a hospital facility's correction and disclosure that the failure was neither willful nor egregious. For purposes of this paragraph (c), willful is to be interpreted consistent with the meaning of that term in the context of civil penalties, which would include a failure due to gross negligence, reckless disregard, or willful neglect. Furthermore, notwithstanding a hospital facility's compliance with such future guidance, a hospital facility may, in the discretion of the IRS, be subject to an excise tax under section 4959 for failures to meet the requirements of section 501(r)(3).

(d) *Taxation of noncompliant hospital facilities.*—(1) *In general.*—Except as otherwise provided in paragraphs (b) and (c) of this section, if a hospital organization that operates more than one hospital facility fails to meet one or more of the requirements of section 501(r) separately with respect to a hospital facility during a taxable year, the income derived from the noncompliant hospital facility ("noncompliant facility income") during that taxable year will be subject to tax computed as provided in section 11 (or as provided in section 1(e) if the hospital organization is a trust described in section 511(b)(2)), but substituting "noncompliant facility income" for "taxable income," if—

(i) The hospital organization continues to be recognized as described in section 501(c)(3) during the taxable year, but

(ii) The hospital organization would not continue to be recognized as described in section 501(c)(3) during the taxable year based on the facts and circumstances described in paragraph (a) of this section (but disregarding paragraph (a)(3)) if the noncompliant hospital facility were the only hospital facility operated by the organization.

(2) *Noncompliant facility income.*—(i) *In general.*—For purposes of this paragraph (d), the

noncompliant facility income derived from a hospital facility during a taxable year will be the gross income derived from that hospital facility during the taxable year, less the deductions allowed by chapter 1 of the Internal Revenue Code (Code) that are directly connected to the operation of that hospital facility during the taxable year, excluding any gross income and deductions taken into account in computing any unrelated business taxable income described in section 512 that is derived from the facility during the taxable year.

(ii) *Directly connected deductions.*—For purposes of this paragraph (d), to be directly connected with the operation of a hospital facility that has failed to meet the requirements of section 501(r), an item of deduction must have proximate and primary relationship to the operation of the hospital facility. Expenses, depreciation, and similar items attributable solely to the operation of a hospital facility are proximately and primarily related to such operation, and therefore qualify for deduction to the extent that they meet the requirements of section 162, section 167, or other relevant provisions of the Code. Where expenses, depreciation, and similar items are attributable to a noncompliant hospital facility and other hospital facilities operated by the hospital organization (and/or to other activities of the hospital organization unrelated to the operation of hospital facilities), such items shall be allocated between the hospital facilities (and/or other activities) on a reasonable basis. The portion of any such item so allocated to a noncompliant hospital facility is proximately and primarily related to the operation of that facility and shall be allowable as a deduction in computing the facility's noncompliant facility income in the manner and to the extent it would meet the requirements of section 162, section 167, or other relevant provisions of the Code.

(3) *No aggregation.*—In computing the noncompliant facility income of a hospital facility, the gross income from (and the deductions allowed with respect to) the hospital facility may not be aggregated with the gross income from (and the deductions allowed with respect to) the hospital organization's other noncompliant hospital facilities subject to tax under this paragraph (d) or its unrelated trade or business activities described in section 513.

(4) *Interaction with other Code provisions.*—(i) *Hospital organization operating a noncompliant hospital facility continues to be treated as tax-exempt.*—A hospital organization operating a noncompliant hospital facility subject to tax under this paragraph (d) shall continue to be treated as an organization that is exempt from tax under section 501(a) because it is described in section 501(c)(3) for all purposes of the Code. Thus, for example, the application of this paragraph (d) shall not, by itself, affect the tax-exempt status of bonds issued to finance the noncompliant hospital facility.

(ii) *Noncompliant hospital facility operated by a tax-exempt hospital organization is subject to tax.*—A noncompliant hospital facility described in paragraph (d)(1) of this section is subject to tax under this paragraph (d), notwithstanding the fact that the hospital organization operating the hospital facility is otherwise exempt from tax under section 501(a) and subject to tax under section 511(a) and that § 1.11-1(a) of this chapter states such organizations are not liable to the tax imposed under section 11.

(iii) *Noncompliant hospital facility not a business entity.*—A noncompliant hospital facility subject to tax under this paragraph (d) is not considered a business entity for purposes of § 301.7701-2(b)(7) of this chapter. [Reg. § 1.501(r)-2.]

§ 1.501(r)-3. Community health needs assessments.—(a) *In general.*—With respect to any taxable year, a hospital organization meets the requirements of section 501(r)(3) with respect to a hospital facility it operates only if—

(1) The hospital facility has conducted a community health needs assessment (CHNA) that meets the requirements of paragraph (b) of this section in such taxable year or in either of the two taxable years immediately preceding such taxable year; and

(2) An authorized body of the hospital facility (as defined in § 1.501(r)-1(c)(1)) has adopted an implementation strategy to meet the community health needs identified through the CHNA, as described in paragraph (c) of this section, by the end of the taxable year in which the hospital facility conducts the CHNA.

(b) *Conducting a CHNA.*—(1) *In general.*—To conduct a CHNA for purposes of paragraph (a) of this section, a hospital facility must complete all of the following steps—

(i) Define the community it serves;

(ii) Assess the health needs of that community;

(iii) In assessing the health needs of the community, take into account input from persons who represent the broad interests of that community, including those with special knowledge of or expertise in public health;

(iv) Document the CHNA in a written report ("CHNA report") that is adopted for the hospital facility by an authorized body of the hospital facility; and

(v) Make the CHNA report widely available to the public.

(2) *Date a CHNA is conducted.*—For purposes of this section, a hospital facility will be considered to have conducted a CHNA on the date it has completed all of the steps described in paragraph (b)(1) of this section. Solely for purposes of determining the date on which a CHNA has been conducted, a hospital facility will be considered to have made the CHNA report widely available to the public on the date it first makes the CHNA report widely available to the public as described in paragraph (b)(8)(i) of this section.

(3) *Community served by the hospital facility.*—In defining the community it serves for purposes of paragraph (b)(1)(i) of this section, a hospital facility may take into account all of the relevant facts and circumstances, including the geographic area served by the hospital facility, target populations served (for example, children, women, or the aged), and principal functions (for example, focus on a particular specialty area or targeted disease). A hospital facility may define its community to include populations in addition to its patient populations and geographic areas outside of those in which its patient populations reside. However, a hospital facility may not define its community to exclude medically underserved, low-income, or minority populations who are part of its patient popula-

tions, live in geographic areas in which its patient populations reside (unless they are not part of the hospital facility's target populations or affected by its principal functions), or otherwise should be included based on the method the hospital facility uses to define its community. In addition, if a hospital facility's method of defining its community takes into account patient populations, the hospital facility must treat as patients all individuals who receive care from the hospital facility, without regard to whether (or how much) they or their insurers pay for the care received or whether they are eligible for assistance under the hospital facility's financial assistance policy.

(4) *Assessing community health needs.*—To assess the health needs of the community it serves for purposes of paragraph (b)(1)(ii) of this section, a hospital facility must identify significant health needs of the community, prioritize those health needs, and identify potential measures and resources (such as programs, organizations, and facilities in the community) available to address the health needs. For these purposes, the health needs of a community include requisites for the improvement or maintenance of health status in both the community at large and in particular parts of the community (such as particular neighborhoods or populations experiencing health disparities). A hospital facility may determine whether a health need is significant based on all of the facts and circumstances present in the community it serves. In addition, a hospital facility may use any criteria to prioritize the significant health needs it identifies, including, but not limited to, the burden, scope, severity, or urgency of the health need; the estimated feasibility and effectiveness of possible interventions; the health disparities associated with the need; or the importance the community places on addressing the need.

(5) *Persons representing the broad interests of the community.*—To take into account input from persons who represent the broad interests of the community it serves (including those with special knowledge of or expertise in public health) for purposes of paragraph (b)(1)(iii) of this section, a hospital facility must take into account input from the sources listed in paragraphs (b)(5)(i), (b)(5)(ii), and (b)(5)(iii) of this section in assessing the health needs of its community. Input from these persons includes, but is not limited to, input on any financial and other barriers to access to care in the community. In addition, a hospital facility may take into account input from a broad range of persons located in or serving its community, including, but not limited to, health care consumers and consumer advocates, nonprofit and community-based organizations, academic experts, local government officials, local school districts, health care providers and community health centers, health insurance and managed care organizations, private businesses, and labor and workforce representatives. A hospital facility must take into account input from the following sources in assessing the health needs of its community—

(i) At least one state, local, tribal, or regional governmental public health department (or equivalent department or agency) with knowledge, information, or expertise relevant to the health needs of that community;

(ii) Members of medically underserved, low-income, and minority populations in the community served by the hospital facility, or individuals or organizations serving or representing the interests of such populations; and

(iii) Written comments received on the hospital facility's most recently conducted CHNA and most recently adopted implementation strategy.

(6) *Medically underserved populations.*—For purposes of this paragraph (b), medically underserved populations include populations experiencing health disparities or at risk of not receiving adequate medical care as a result of being uninsured or underinsured or due to geographic, language, financial, or other barriers.

(7) *Documentation of a CHNA.*—(i) *In general.*—For purposes of paragraph (b)(1)(iv) of this section, the CHNA report adopted for the hospital facility by an authorized body of the hospital facility must include—

(A) A definition of the community served by the hospital facility and a description of how the community was determined;

(B) A description of the process and methods used to conduct the CHNA;

(C) A description of how the hospital facility took into account input from persons who represent the broad interests of the community it serves;

(D) A prioritized description of the significant health needs of the community identified through the CHNA, along with a description of the process and criteria used in identifying certain health needs as significant and prioritizing such significant health needs; and

(E) A description of the potential measures and resources identified through the CHNA to address the significant health needs.

(ii) *Process and methods used to conduct the CHNA.*—A hospital facility's CHNA report will be considered to describe the process and methods used to conduct the CHNA for purposes of paragraph (b)(7)(i)(B) of this section if the CHNA report describes the data and other information used in the assessment, as well as the methods of collecting and analyzing this data and information, and identifies any parties with whom the hospital facility collaborated, or with whom it contracted for assistance, in conducting the CHNA.

(iii) *Input from persons who represent the broad interests of the community served by the hospital facility.*—A hospital facility's CHNA report will be considered to describe how the hospital facility took into account input from persons who represent the broad interests of the community it serves for purposes of paragraph (b)(7)(i)(C) of this section if the CHNA report summarizes, in general terms, the input provided by such persons and how and over what time period such input was provided (for example, whether through meetings, focus groups, interviews, surveys, or written comments and between what dates); provides the names of organizations providing input and summarizes the nature and extent of the organization's input; and describes the medically underserved, low-income, or minority populations being represented by organizations or individuals that provided input. A CHNA report does not need to name or otherwise individually identify any individuals participating in community forums, focus groups, survey samples, or similar groups.

(iv) *Separate CHNA reports*.—While a hospital facility may conduct its CHNA in collaboration with other organizations and facilities (including, but not limited to, related and unrelated hospital organizations and facilities, for-profit and government hospitals, governmental departments, and nonprofit organizations), every hospital facility must document the information described in this paragraph (b)(7) in a separate CHNA report to satisfy paragraph (b)(1)(iv) of this section unless it is eligible to adopt a joint CHNA report as described in paragraph (b)(7)(v) of this section. However, if a hospital facility is collaborating with other facilities and organizations in conducting its CHNA or if another organization has conducted a CHNA for all or part of the hospital facility's community, portions of the hospital facility's CHNA report may be substantively identical to portions of a CHNA report of a collaborating hospital facility or the other organization conducting a CHNA, if appropriate under the facts and circumstances. For example, if a hospital facility conducts a survey of the health needs of residents of homeless shelters located in the community in collaboration with other hospital facilities, the description of that survey in the hospital facility's CHNA report may be identical to the description contained in the CHNA reports for the other collaborating hospital facilities. Similarly, if the state or local public health department with jurisdiction over the community served by the hospital facility conducts an inventory of community health improvement resources available in that community, the hospital facility may include that inventory in its CHNA report.

(v) *Joint CHNA reports*.—(A) *In general*.—A hospital facility that collaborates with other hospital facilities in conducting its CHNA will satisfy paragraph (b)(1)(iv) of this section if an authorized body of the hospital facility adopts for the hospital facility a joint CHNA report produced for all of the collaborating hospital facilities, as long as all of the collaborating hospital facilities define their community to be the same and conduct a joint CHNA process, and the joint CHNA report is clearly identified as applying to the hospital facility.

(B) *Example*.—The following example illustrates this paragraph (b)(7)(v):

Example. P is one of ten hospital facilities located in and serving the populations of a particular Metropolitan Statistical Area (MSA). P and the other nine facilities in the MSA, some of which are unrelated to P, decide to collaborate in conducting a CHNA for the MSA and to each define their community as constituting the entire MSA. The ten hospital facilities work together with the state and local health departments of jurisdictions in the MSA to assess the health needs of the MSA and collaborate in conducting surveys and holding public forums to receive input from the MSA's residents, including its medically underserved, low-income, and minority populations. The hospital facilities then work together to prepare a joint CHNA report documenting this joint CHNA process that contains all of the elements described in paragraph (b)(7)(i) of this section. The joint CHNA report identifies all of the collaborating hospital facilities, including P, by name, both within the report itself and on the cover page. The board of directors of the hospital organization operating P adopts the joint CHNA report for P. P has complied with the requirements of this paragraph (b)(7)(v) and, accordingly, has satisfied paragraph (b)(1)(iv) of this section.

(8) *Making the CHNA report widely available to the public*.—(i) *In general*.—For purposes of paragraph (b)(1)(v) of this section, a hospital facility's CHNA report is made widely available to the public only if the hospital facility—

(A) Makes the CHNA report widely available on a Web site, as defined in § 1.501(r)-1(c)(4), at least until the date the hospital facility has made widely available on a Web site its two subsequent CHNA reports; and

(B) Makes a paper copy of the CHNA report available for public inspection without charge at the hospital facility at least until the date the hospital facility has made available for public inspection without charge a paper copy of its two subsequent CHNA reports.

(ii) *Making draft CHNA reports widely available*.—Notwithstanding paragraph (b)(8)(i) of this section, if a hospital facility makes widely available on a Web site (and/or for public inspection) a version of the CHNA report that is expressly marked as a draft on which the public may comment, the hospital facility will not be considered to have made the CHNA report widely available to the public for purposes of determining the date on which the hospital facility has conducted a CHNA under paragraph (a) of this section.

(c) *Implementation strategy*.—(1) *In general*.—For purposes of paragraph (a)(2) of this section, a hospital facility's implementation strategy to meet the community health needs identified through the hospital facility's CHNA is a written plan that, with respect to each significant health need identified through the CHNA, either—

(i) Describes how the hospital facility plans to address the health need; or

(ii) Identifies the health need as one the hospital facility does not intend to address and explains why the hospital facility does not intend to address the health need.

(2) *Description of how the hospital facility plans to address a significant health need*.—In describing how a hospital facility plans to address a significant health need identified through a CHNA for purposes of paragraph (c)(1)(i) of this section, the implementation strategy must describe the actions the hospital facility intends to take to address the health need, the anticipated impact of these actions, and a plan to evaluate such impact. The implementation strategy must also identify the programs and resources the hospital facility plans to commit to address the health need. Finally, the implementation strategy must describe any planned collaboration between the hospital facility and other facilities or organizations in addressing the health need.

(3) *Description of why a hospital facility is not addressing a significant health need*.—In explaining why it does not intend to address a significant health need for purposes of paragraph (c)(1)(ii) of this section, a hospital facility may provide a brief explanation of its reason for not addressing the health need, including, but

not limited to, resource constraints, other facilities or organizations in the community addressing the need, relative lack of expertise or competencies to effectively address the need, a relatively low priority assigned to the need, and/or a lack of identified effective interventions to address the need.

(4) *Joint implementation strategies.*—A hospital facility may develop an implementation strategy in collaboration with other facilities and organizations, including, but not limited to, related and unrelated hospital organizations and facilities, for-profit and government hospitals, governmental departments, and nonprofit organizations. In general, a hospital facility that collaborates with other facilities and organizations in developing its implementation strategy must still document its implementation strategy in a separate written plan that is tailored to the particular hospital facility, taking into account its specific programs and resources. However, a hospital facility that adopts a joint CHNA report described in paragraph (b)(7)(v) of this section may also adopt a joint implementation strategy that, with respect to each significant health need identified through the joint CHNA, either describes how the collaborating hospital facilities plan to address the health need or identifies the health need as one the hospital facilities do not intend to address and explains why the hospital facilities do not intend to address the health need, as long as the joint implementation strategy—

(i) Is clearly identified as applying to the hospital facility;

(ii) Clearly identifies the hospital facility's particular role and responsibilities in taking the actions described in the implementation strategy and the programs and resources the hospital facility plans to commit to such actions; and

(iii) Includes a summary or other tool that helps the reader easily locate those portions of the joint implementation strategy that relate to the hospital facility.

(5) *When the implementation strategy must be adopted.*—(i) *In general.*—For purposes of paragraph (a)(2) of this section, in order to have adopted an implementation strategy to meet the health needs identified through a hospital facility's CHNA by the end of the same taxable year in which the hospital facility conducts that CHNA, an authorized body of the hospital facility must adopt the implementation strategy during the taxable year in which the hospital facility completes the final step for the CHNA described in paragraph (b)(1) of this section, regardless of whether the hospital facility began working on the CHNA in a prior taxable year.

(ii) *Example.*—The following example illustrates this paragraph (c)(5):

Example. M is a hospital facility that last conducted a CHNA and adopted an implementation strategy in Year 1. In Year 3, M defines the community it serves, assesses the health needs of that community, and takes into account input from persons who represent the broad interests of that community. In Year 4, M documents its CHNA in a CHNA report that is adopted by an authorized body of M, makes the CHNA report widely available on a Web site, and makes paper copies available for public inspection. To meet the requirements of paragraph (a)(2) of this section, an authorized body of M must adopt an implementation strategy to meet the health needs identified through that CHNA by the last day of Year 4.

(d) *New hospital facilities.*—A hospital facility that is newly acquired or placed into service, or that becomes newly subject to the requirements of section 501(r) because the hospital organization that operates it is newly recognized as described in section 501(c)(3), must meet the requirements of section 501(r)(3) by the last day of the second taxable year beginning after the date, respectively, the hospital facility is acquired; licensed, registered, or similarly recognized by its state as a hospital; or newly subject to the requirements of section 501(r) as a result of the hospital organization operating it being recognized as described in section 501(c)(3).

(e) *Transition rules.*—(1) *CHNA conducted in taxable year beginning before March 23, 2012.*—A hospital facility that conducted a CHNA described in section 501(r)(3) in either its first taxable year beginning after March 23, 2010, or its first taxable year beginning after March 23, 2011, does not need to meet the requirements of section 501(r)(3) again until the third taxable year following the taxable year in which the hospital facility conducted that CHNA, provided that the hospital facility has adopted an implementation strategy to meet the community health needs identified through that CHNA on or before the 15th day of the fifth calendar month following the close of its first taxable year beginning after March 23, 2012.

(2) *CHNA conducted in first taxable year beginning after March 23, 2012.*—A hospital facility that conducts a CHNA described in section 501(r)(3) in its first taxable year beginning after March 23, 2012, will be deemed to satisfy paragraph (a)(2) of this section during that taxable year if an authorized body of the hospital facility adopts an implementation strategy to meet the community health needs identified through that CHNA on or before the 15th day of the fifth calendar month following the close of its first taxable year beginning after March 23, 2012. [Reg. § 1.501(r)-3.]

☐ Par. 5. Section 1.501(r)-7 as proposed to be amended at 77 FR 38169 (June 26, 2012) is proposed to be further amended by revising the section to read as follows:

§ 1.501(r)-7. Effective/applicability dates.—(a) *Effective/applicability date.*—The rules of § 1.501(r)-1 through § 1.501(r)-6 are effective on the date of publication of the Treasury decision adopting these rules as final or temporary regulations.

(b) *Reliance and transition period.*—A hospital facility may rely on § 1.501(r)-3 of the proposed regulations published in the **Federal Register** on April 5, 2013, for any CHNA conducted or implementation strategy adopted on or before the date that is six months after these regulations are published as final or temporary regulations in the **Federal Register**. [Reg. § 1.501(r)-7.]

Employee Trusts: Effective Dates

Employee Trusts: Tax Reform Act of 1984: Effective Dates.—Temporary Reg. §1.505(c)-1T is proposed as a final regulation and, when adopted, would become Reg. §1.505(c)-1 (published in the Federal Register on February 4, 1986).

§1.505(c)-1. Questions and answers relating to the notification requirement for recognition of exemption under paragraphs (9), (17) and (20) of section 501(c).

Section 501(c)(4) Organization: Notification of Intent to Operate

Section 501(c)(4) Organization: Notification of Intent to Operate.—Reg. §1.506-1, relating to the requirement, added by the Protecting Americans from Tax Hikes Act of 2015, that organizations must notify the IRS of their intent to operate under section 501(c)(4) of the Internal Revenue Code (Code), is proposed (published in the Federal Register on July 12, 2016) (REG-101689-16).

Par. 2. Section 1.506-1 is added to read as follows:

§1.506-1. Organizations required to notify Commissioner of intent to operate under section 501(c)(4).—[The text of proposed §1.506-1 is the same as the text for §1.506-1T as added by T.D. 9775].

Type I and Type III Supporting Organizations: Requirements

Type I and Type III Supporting Organizations: Requirements.—Amendments to Reg. §1.509(a)-4, regarding the prohibition on certain contributions to Type I and Type III supporting organizations and the requirements for Type III supporting organizations, are proposed (published in the Federal Register on February 19, 2016) (REG-118867-10).

Par. 2. Section 1.509(a)-4 is amended by:

1. Revising paragraphs (f)(5)(ii), (i)(2)(i) introductory text, (i)(2)(i)(A), (i)(2)(iii), and (i)(3)(i);
2. Adding *Example 3* to paragraph (i)(3)(iv);
3. Revising paragraphs (i)(4)(ii)(A)(1), (i)(4)(ii)(B), (i)(4)(iii) and (iv), (i)(5)(ii)(A) and (B), (i)(5)(iii)(A), *Example 4* of paragraph (i)(5)(iii)(D), the third sentence of paragraph (i)(6) introductory text, and paragraphs (i)(6)(iii) and (v) introductory text and (l).

The revisions and additions read as follows:

§1.509(a)-4. Supporting organizations.

* * *

(f) * * *

(5) * * *

(ii) *Meaning of control.*—For purposes of paragraph (f)(5)(i) of this section, the governing body of a supported organization will be considered *controlled* by a person described in paragraph (f)(5)(i)(A) of this section if that person, alone or by aggregating the person's votes or positions of authority with persons described in paragraph (f)(5)(i)(B) or (C) of this section, may require the governing body of the supported organization to perform any act that significantly affects its operations or may prevent the governing body of the supported organization from performing any such act. The governing body of a supported organization will generally be considered to be controlled directly or indirectly by one or more persons described in paragraph (f)(5)(i)(A), (B), or (C) of this section if the voting power of such persons is 50 percent or more of the total voting power of such governing body or if one or more of such persons have the right to exercise veto power over the actions of the governing body of the supported organization. However, all pertinent facts and circumstances will be taken into consideration in determining whether one or more persons do in fact directly or indirectly control the governing body of a supported organization.

* * *

(i) * * *

(2) * * *

(i) *Annual notification.*—For each taxable year (the Reporting Year), a Type III supporting organization must provide the following documents to each of its supported organizations:

(A) A written notice addressed to a principal officer of the supported organization describing the type and amount of all of the support (including all of the distributions described in paragraph (i)(6) of this section if applicable) the supporting organization provided to the supported organization during the supporting organization's taxable year immediately preceding the Reporting Year (and during any other taxable year of the supporting organization ending after December 28, 2012, for which such support information has not previously been provided);

* * *

(iii) *Due date.*—The notification documents required by this paragraph (i)(2) shall be delivered or electronically transmitted by the last day of the fifth calendar month of the Reporting Year.

* * *

(3) * * *

(i) *General rule.*—A supporting organization meets the responsiveness test only if it is responsive to the needs or demands of each of its supported organizations. Except as provided in paragraph (i)(3)(v) of this section, in order to meet this test, a supporting organization must satisfy the requirements of paragraphs (i)(3)(ii) and (iii) of this section with respect to each of its supported organizations.

* * *

(iv) * * *

Example 3. Z is described in section 501(c)(3). Z's organizational documents provide that it supports ten different organizations, each of which is described in section 509(a)(1). One of the directors of S (one of the supported organizations) is a voting member of Z's board of directors and participates in Z's regular board meetings. Officers of Z hold regular face-to-face or telephonic meetings during the year to which officers of all the supported organizations are invited. Z's meetings with the supported organizations may be held jointly or separately. Prior to the meetings, Z makes available to the supported organizations (including by email) up-to-date information about its activities including its assets and liabilities, receipts and distributions, and investment policies and returns. In the meetings, officers of each of the supported organizations have an opportunity to ask questions and discuss with officers of Z the projected needs of their organizations, as well as Z's investment and grant making policies and practices. In addition to holding these meetings with the supported organizations, Z provides the contact information of one of its officers to each of the supported organizations and encourages them to contact that officer if they have questions, or if they wish to schedule additional meetings to discuss the projected needs of their organization and how Z should distribute its income and invest its assets. Z provides the information required under paragraph (i)(2) of this section and a copy of its annual audited financial statements to the principal officers of the supported organizations. Z meets the relationship test of paragraph (i)(3)(ii)(B) or (C) of this section with respect to each of its supported organizations. Based on these facts, Z also satisfies the significant voice requirement of paragraph (i)(3)(iii) of this section, and therefore meets the responsiveness test of this paragraph (i)(3) with respect to each of its ten supported organizations.

* * *

(4) * * *

(ii) * * *

(A) * * *

(1) Directly further the exempt purposes of one or more supported organizations by performing the functions of, or carrying out the purposes of, such supported organization(s); and

* * *

(B) *Meaning of substantially all.*—For purposes of paragraph (i)(4)(ii)(A) of this section, in determining whether substantially all of a supporting organization's activities directly further the exempt purposes of one or more supported organization(s), all pertinent facts and circumstances will be taken into consideration.

* * *

(iii) *Parent of supported organization(s).*—For purposes of paragraph (i)(4)(i)(B) of this section, in order for a supporting organization to qualify as the parent of each of its supported organizations, the supporting organization and its supported organizations must be part of an integrated system (such as a hospital system), the supporting organization must engage in activities typical of the parent of an integrated system, and a majority of the officers, directors, or trustees of each supported organization must be appointed or elected, directly or indirectly, by the governing body, members of the governing body, or officers (acting in their official capacities) of the supporting organization. For purposes of this paragraph (i)(4)(iii), examples of activities typical of the parent of an integrated system of supported organizations include (but are not limited to) coordinating the activities of the supported organizations and engaging in overall planning, policy development, budgeting, and resource allocation for the supported organizations.

(iv) *Supporting a governmental supported organization.*—(A) *In general.*—A supporting organization satisfies the requirements of this paragraph (i)(4)(iv) if—

(1) The supporting organization supports only governmental supported organizations, and, if the supporting organization supports more than one governmental supported organization, all of the governmental supported organizations either—

(i) Operate within the same geographic region; or

(ii) Work in close coordination or collaboration with one another to conduct a service, program, or activity that the supporting organization supports; and

(2) A substantial part of the supporting organization's total activities are activities that directly further, as defined by paragraph (i)(4)(ii)(C) of this section, the exempt purposes of its governmental supported organization(s).

(B) *Governmental supported organization defined.*—For purposes of paragraph (i)(4)(iv)(A) of this section, the term *governmental supported organization* means a supported organization that is—

(1) A governmental unit described in section 170(c)(1); or

(2) An organization described in section 170(c)(2) and (b)(1)(A) (other than in clauses (vii) and (viii)) that is an instrumentality of one or more governmental units described in section 170(c)(1).

(C) *Geographic region defined.*—For purposes of paragraph (i)(4)(iv)(A)(1) of this section, the term *geographic region* means a city, county, or metropolitan area.

(D) *Close cooperation or coordination.*—To satisfy the close cooperation or coordination requirement of paragraph (i)(4)(iv)(A)*(1)* of this section, the supporting organization shall maintain on file a letter from each of the governmental supported organizations (or a joint letter from all of them) describing their collaborative or cooperative efforts with respect to the particular service, program, or activity.

(E) *Exception for organizations supporting a governmental supported organization on or before February 19, 2016.*—A Type III supporting organization in existence on or before February 19, 2016 will be treated as meeting the requirements of this paragraph (i)(4)(iv) if it met and continues to meet the following requirements—

(1) It supports one or more governmental supported organizations described in paragraph (i)(4)(iv)(B) of this section and does not support more than one supported organization that is not a governmental supported organization;

(2) Each of the supported organizations is designated by the supporting organization as provided in paragraph (d)(4) of this section on or before February 19, 2016; and

(3) A substantial part of the supporting organization's total activities are activities that directly further, as defined by paragraph (i)(4)(ii)(C) of this section, the exempt purposes of its governmental supported organization(s).

(F) *Transition rule for supporting organizations in existence on or before February 19, 2016.*—Until the earlier of the first day of the organization's first taxable year beginning after the date final regulations are published in the **Federal Register** under this paragraph (i)(4)(iv) or the first day of the organization's second taxable year beginning after February 19, 2016, a Type III supporting organization in existence on or before February 19, 2016 will be treated as meeting the requirements of this paragraph (i)(4)(iv) if it met and continues to meet the following requirements—

(1) It supports at least one supported organization that is a governmental entity to which the supporting organization is responsive within the meaning of paragraph (i)(3) of this section; and

(2) It engages in activities for or on behalf of the governmental supported organization described in paragraph (i)(4)(iv)(F)*(1)* of this section that perform the functions of, or carry out the purposes of, that governmental supported organization and that, but for the involvement of the supporting organization, would normally be engaged in by the governmental supported organization itself.

* * *

(5) * * *

(ii) * * *

(A) *Annual distribution.*—With respect to each taxable year, a supporting organization must make distributions described in paragraph (i)(6) of this section in a total amount equaling or exceeding the supporting organization's distributable amount for the taxable year, as defined in paragraph (i)(5)(ii)(B) of this section, on or before the last day of the taxable year.

(B) *Distributable amount.*—Except as provided in paragraphs (i)(5)(ii)(D) and (E) of this section, the distributable amount for a taxable year is an amount equal to the greater of 85 percent of the supporting organization's adjusted net income (as determined by applying the principles of section 4942(f) and §53.4942(a)-2(d) of this chapter) for the taxable year immediately preceding the taxable year of the required distribution (immediately preceding taxable year) or its minimum asset amount (as defined in paragraph (i)(5)(ii)(C) of this section) for the immediately preceding taxable year.

* * *

(iii) * * *

(A) *General rule.*—With respect to each taxable year, a non-functionally integrated Type III supporting organization must distribute one-third or more of its distributable amount to one or more supported organizations that are attentive to the operations of the supporting organization (within the meaning of paragraph (i)(5)(iii)(B) of this section).

* * *

(D) * * *

Example 4. O is an organization described in section 501(c)(3). O is organized to support five private universities, V, W, X, Y, and Z, each of which is described in section 509(a)(1). O meets the responsiveness test described in paragraph (i)(3) of this section with respect to each of its supported organizations. Each year, O distributes an aggregate amount that equals its distributable amount described in paragraph (i)(5)(ii)(B) of this section and distributes an equal amount to each of the five universities. O distributes annually to each of V and W an amount that equals more than 10 percent of each university's total annual support received in its most recently completed taxable year. Based on these facts, O meets the requirements of paragraph (i)(5)(iii) of this section because it distributes two-fifths (more than the required one-third) of its distributable amount to supported organizations that are attentive to O.

(6) *Distributions that count toward distribution requirement.*—* * * Distributions by the supporting organization that count toward the distribution requirement imposed in paragraph (i)(5)(ii) of this section are limited to thefollowing—

* * *

(iii) Any reasonable and necessary—

(A) Administrative expenses paid to accomplish the exempt purposes of the supported organization, which do not include expenses incurred in the production of investment income or the conduct of fundraising activities, except as provided in paragraph (i)(6)(iii)(B) of this section; and

(B) Expenses incurred to solicit contributions that are received directly by a supported organization, but only to the extent the amount of such expenses does not exceed the amount of contributions actually received by the supported organization as a result of the solicitation, as substantiated in writing by the supported organization;

* * *

(v) Any amount set aside for a specific project that accomplishes the exempt purposes of a supported organization, with such set-aside counting toward the distribution requirement for the taxable year in which the amount is set aside but not in the year in which it is actually paid, if at the time of the set-aside, the supporting organization—

* * *

(l) *Effective/applicability dates.*—(1) Paragraphs (a)(6), (f)(5), and (i) of this section are effective on December 28, 2012, except—

(i) Paragraphs (i)(4)(ii)(C), (i)(5)(ii)(C) and (D), (i)(6)(iv), (i)(7)(ii), and (i)(8) of this section are applicable on December 21, 2015; and

(ii) Paragraphs (f)(5)(ii), (i)(2)(i) and (iii), (i)(3)(i), (i)(4)(ii)(A)(1), (i)(4)(ii)(B), (i)(4)(iii) and (iv), (i)(5)(ii)(A) and (B), (i)(5)(iii)(A), (i)(6)(i), (iii) and (v) of this section, *Example 3* of paragraph (i)(3)(iv) of this section, and *Example 4* of paragraph (i)(5)(iii)(D) of this section are effective on the date the Treasury decision adopting these rules as final or temporary regulations is published in the **Federal Register**.

(2) See paragraphs (i)(5)(ii)(B) and (C) and (i)(8) of §1.509(a)–4T contained in 26 CFR part 1, revised as of April 1, 2015, for certain rules regarding non-functionally integrated Type III supporting organizations effective before December 21, 2015. See paragraphs (i)(5)(ii)(A) and (B) and (i)(5)(iii)(D) of §1.509(a)-4 (as effective December 21, 2015), for certain rules regarding non-functionally integrated Type III supporting organizations effective before the date the Treasury decision adopting these rules as final or temporary regulations is published in the Federal Register.

Guidance under Section 529A: Qualified ABLE Programs

Guidance under Section 529A: Qualified ABLE Programs.—Amendments to Reg. §1.511-2, regarding programs under The Stephen Beck, Jr., Achieving a Better Life Experience Act of 2014 and rules under which States or State agencies or instrumentalities may establish and maintain a new type of tax-favored savings program through which contributions may be made to the account of an eligible disabled individual to meet qualified disability expenses, are proposed (published in the Federal Register on June 22, 2015) (REG-102837-15).

Par. 2. Section 1.511-2 is amended by adding paragraph (e) to read as follows:

§1.511-2. Organizations subject to tax.

* * *

(e) *ABLE programs.*—(1) *Unrelated business taxable income.*—A qualified ABLE program described in section 529A generally is exempt from income taxation, but is subject to taxes imposed by section 511 relating to the imposition of tax on unrelated business income. A qualified ABLE program is required to file Form 990-T, "Exempt Organization Business Income Tax Return," if such filing would be required under the rules of §§1.6012-2(e) and 1.6012-3(a)(5) if the ABLE program were an organization described in those sections.

(2) *Effective/applicability dates.*—This paragraph (e) applies to taxable years beginning after December 31, 2014.

Exempt Organizations: Calculation of Unrelated Business Taxable Income (UBTI)

Exempt Organizations: Calculation of Unrelated Business Taxable Income (UBTI).—Reg. §1.512(a)-5, providing guidance on how certain organizations that provide employee benefits must calculate unrelated business taxable income (UBTI), are proposed (published in the Federal Register on February 6, 2014) (REG-143874-10).

☐ Par. 2. Section 1.512(a)-5 is added to read as follows:

§1.512(a)-5. Questions and answers relating to the unrelated business taxable income of organizations described in paragraphs (9) or (17) of section 501(c).—

Q-1. What does section 512(a)(3) provide with respect to organizations described in paragraphs (9) or (17) of section 501(c)?

A-1. (a) In general, section 512(a)(3) provides rules for determining the unrelated business income tax of voluntary employees' beneficiary associations (VEBAs) and supplemental unemployment benefit trusts (SUBs). Under section 512(a)(3)(A), a Covered Entity's "unrelated business taxable income" means all income except exempt function income. Under section 512(a)(3)(B), exempt function income includes income that is set aside for exempt purposes, as described in Q&A-2 of this section, subject to certain limits, as described in Q&A-3 of this section.

(b) For purposes of this section, a "Covered Entity" means a VEBA or a SUB.

Q-2. What is exempt function income?

A-2. (a) Under section 512(a)(3)(B), the exempt function income of a Covered Entity for a taxable year means the sum of—

(1) amounts referred to in the first sentence of section 512(a)(3)(B) that are paid by members of the Covered Entity and employer contributions to the Covered Entity (collectively "member contributions"); and

(2) other income of the Covered Entity (including earnings on member contributions) that is set aside for—

(i) a purpose specified in section 170(c)(4) and reasonable costs of administration directly connected with such purpose, or

(ii) subject to the limitation of section 512(a)(3)(E) (as described in Q&A-3 of this section), the payment of life, sick, accident, or other benefits and reasonable costs of administration directly connected with such purpose.

(b) The other income described in paragraph (a)(2) of this Q&A-2 does not include the gross income derived from any unrelated trade or business (as defined in section 513) regularly carried on by the Covered Entity, computed as if the organization were subject to section 512(a)(1).

Q-3. What are the limits on the amount that may be set aside?

A-3. (a) Pursuant to section 512(a)(3)(E)(i), and except as provided in paragraph (b) of this Q&A-3, the amount of investment income (as defined in paragraph (c)(1) of this Q&A-3) set aside by a Covered Entity as of the close of a taxable year of such Covered Entity to provide for the payment of life, sick, accident, or other benefits (and administrative costs associated with the provision of such benefits) is not taken into account for purposes of determining the amount of that income that constitutes "exempt function income" to the extent that the total amount of the assets of the Covered Entity at the end of the taxable year to provide for the payment of life, sick, accident, or other benefits (and related administrative costs) exceeds the applicable account limit for such taxable year of the Covered Entity (as described in paragraph (d) of this section). Accordingly, any investment income a Covered Entity earns during the taxable year is subject to unrelated business income tax to the extent the Covered Entity's year-end assets exceed the applicable account limit. This rule applies regardless of whether the Covered Entity spends or retains (or is deemed to spend or deemed to retain) that investment income during the course of the year. Thus, in addition to the unrelated business taxable income derived by a Covered Entity from any unrelated trade or business (as defined in section 513) regularly carried on by it, computed as if the organization were subject to section 512(a)(1), the unrelated business taxable income of a Covered Entity for a taxable year of such an organization includes the lesser of—

(1) the investment income of the Covered Entity for the taxable year, or

(2) the excess of the total amount of the assets of the Covered Entity (excluding amounts set aside for a purpose described in section 170(c)(4)) as of the close of the taxable year over the applicable account limit for the taxable year.

(b) In accordance with section 512(a)(3)(E)(iii), a Covered Entity is not subject to the limits described in this Q&A-3 if substantially all of the contributions to the Covered Entity are made by employers who were tax exempt throughout the five year taxable period ending with the taxable year in which the contributions are made.

(c) For purposes of this section, a Covered Entity's "investment income"—

(1) means all income except -

(i) member contributions described in paragraph (a)(1) of Q&A-2 of this section;

(ii) income set aside as described in paragraph (a)(2)(i) of Q&A-2 of this section; or

(iii) income from any unrelated trade or business described in paragraph (b) of Q&A-2 of this section; and

(2) includes gain realized by the Covered Entity on the sale or disposition of any asset during such year (other than gain on the sale or disposition of assets of an unrelated trade or business described in paragraph (b) of Q&A-2 of this section). The gain realized by a Covered Entity on the sale or disposition of an asset is equal to the amount realized by the organization over the basis of such asset in the hands of the organization reduced by any qualified direct costs attributable to such asset (under paragraphs (b), (c), and (d) of Q&A-6 of § 1.419A-1T).

(d) In calculating the total amount of the assets of a Covered Entity as of the close of the taxable year, certain assets with useful lives extending substantially beyond the end of the taxable year (for example, buildings, and licenses) are not to be taken into account to the extent they are used in the provision of life, sick, accident, or other benefits. By contrast, cash and securities (and other similar investments) held by a Covered Entity are taken into account in calculating the total amount of the assets of a Covered Entity as of the close of the taxable year because they are used to pay welfare benefits, rather than merely used in the provision of such benefits.

(e) The determination of the applicable account limit for purposes of this Q&A-3 is made under the rules of sections 419A(c) and 419A(f)(7), except that a reserve for post-retirement medical benefits under section 419A(c)(2)(A) is not to be taken into account. See § 1.419A-2T for special rules relating to collectively bargained welfare benefit funds.

(f) The limits of this Q&A-3 apply to a Covered Entity that is part of a 10 or more employer plan, as defined in section 419A(f)(6). For this purpose, the account limit is determined as if the plan is not subject to the exception under section 419A(f)(6).

(g) *Examples.* The following examples illustrate the calculation of a VEBA's UBTI:

Example 1 (a) Employer *X* establishes a VEBA as of January 1, 2013, through which it provides health benefits to active employees. The plan year is the calendar year. The VEBA has no employee contributions or member dues, receives no income from an unrelated trade or business regularly carried on by the VEBA, and has no income set aside for a purpose specified in section 170(c)(4). The VEBA's investment income in 2013 is $1,000. As of December 31, 2013, the applicable account limit under section 512(a)(3)(E)(i) is $5,000 and the total amount of assets is $7,000.

(b) The UBTI for 2013 is $1,000. This is because the UBTI is the lesser of (1) the investment income for the year ($1,000) and (2) the excess of the VEBA assets over the account limit at the end of the year ($7,000 over $5,000, or $2,000).

Example 2 (a) The facts are the same as in *Example 1,* except that the VEBA's applicable account limit under section 512(a)(3)(E)(i) as of December 31, 2013, is $6,500.

(b) The UBTI for 2013 is $500. This is because the UBTI for 2013 is the lesser of (1) the investment income for the year ($1,000) and (2) the excess of the VEBA assets over the account limit at the end of the year ($7,000 over $6,500, or $500).

Example 3 (a) Employer Y contributes to a VEBA through which *Y* provides health benefits to active and retired employees. The plan year is the calendar year. At the end of 2012, there was no carryover of excess contributions within the meaning of section 419(d), the balance in the VEBA was $25,000, the Incurred but Unpaid (IBU) claims reserve was $6,000, the reserve for post-retirement medical benefits (PRMB) (computed in accordance with section 419A(c)(2)) was $19,000, and there were no existing reserves within the meaning of section 512(a)(3)(E)(ii). During 2013, the VEBA received $70,000 in employer contributions and $5,000 in investment income, paid $72,000 in benefit payments and $7,000 in administrative expenses, and received no income from an unrelated trade or business regularly carried on by the VEBA. All the 2013 benefit payments are with respect to active employees and the IBU claims reserve (that is, the account limit under section 419A(c)(1)) at the end of 2013 was $7,200. The reserve for PRMB at the end of 2013 was $20,000. All amounts designated as "administrative expenses" are expenses incurred in connection with the administration of the employee health benefits. "Investment income" is net of administrative costs incurred in the production of the investment income (for example, investment management and/or brokerage fees). Only employers contributed to the VEBA (that is, there were no employee contributions or member dues/fees). The VEBA did not set aside any income for the a purpose specified in section 170(c)(4).

(b) The total amount of assets of the VEBA at the end of 2013 is $21,000 (that is, $25,000 beginning of year balance + $70,000 contributions + $5,000 investment income - ($72,000 in benefit payments + $7,000 in administrative expenses))

(c) The applicable account limit under section 512(a)(3)(E)(i) (that is, the account limit under section 419A(c), excluding the reserve for post retirement medical benefits) is the IBU claims reserve ($7,200).

(d) The total amount of assets of the VEBA as of the close of the year ($21,000) exceeds the applicable account limit ($7,200) by $13,800.

(e) The unrelated business taxable income is $5,000 (that is, the lesser of investment income ($5,000) and the excess of the amount of assets of the VEBA as of the close of the taxable year over the applicable account limit ($13,800)).

Example 4 (a) The facts are the same as in *Example 3* except that the 2012 year-end balance was $15,000.

(b) The total amount of assets in the VEBA at the end of 2013 is $11,000 (that is, $15,000 beginning of year balance + $70,000 contributions + $5,000 investment income - ($72,000 in benefit payments + $7,000 in administrative expenses))

(c) The applicable account limit under section 512(a)(3)(E)(i) remains $7,200.

(d) The total amount of assets of the VEBA as of the close of the year ($11,000) exceeds the applicable account limit ($7,200) by $3,800.

(e) The unrelated business taxable income is $3,800 (that is, the lesser of investment income ($5,000) and the excess of the total amount of assets of the VEBA at the close of the taxable year over the applicable account limit ($3,800)).

Q-4. What is the effective date of the amendments to section 512(a)(3) and what transition rules apply to "existing reserves for post-retirement medical or life insurance benefits"?

A-4. (a) The amendments to section 512(a)(3), made by the Tax Reform Act of 1984, apply to income earned by a Covered Entity after December 31, 1985, in the taxable years of such an organization ending after such date.

(b) Section 512(a)(3)(E)(ii)(I) provides that income that is attributable to "existing reserves for post-retirement medical or life insurance benefits" will not be treated as unrelated business taxable income. This includes income that is either directly or indirectly attributable to existing reserves. An "existing reserve for post-retirement medical or life insurance benefits" (as defined in section 512(a)(3)(E)(ii)(II)) is the total amount of assets actually set aside by a Covered Entity on July 18, 1984 (calculated in the manner set forth in Q&A-3 of this section, and adjusted under paragraph (c) of Q&A-11 of § 1.419-1T), reduced by employer contributions to the fund on or before such date to the extent such contributions are not deductible for the taxable year of the employer containing July 18, 1984, and for any prior taxable year of the employer, for purposes of providing such post-retirement benefits. For purposes of the preceding sentence only, an amount that was not actually set aside on July 18, 1984, will be treated as having been actually set aside on such date if—

(1) such amount was incurred by the employer (without regard to section 461(h)) as of the close of the last taxable year of the Covered Entity ending before July 18, 1984, and

(2) such amount was actually contributed to the Covered Entity within 8 1/2 months following the close of such taxable year.

(c) In addition, section 512(a)(3)(E)(ii)(I) applies to existing reserves for such post-retirement benefits only to the extent that such "existing reserves" do not exceed the amount that could be accumulated under the principles set forth in Revenue Rulings 69-382, 1969-2 CB 28; 69-478, 1969-2 CB 29; and 73-599, 1973-2 CB 40. Thus, amounts attributable to any such excess "existing reserves" are not within this transition rule even though they were actually set aside on July 18, 1984. See § 601.601(d)(2)(ii)(b).

(d) All post-retirement medical or life insurance benefits (or other benefits to the extent paid with amounts set aside to provide post-retirement medical or life insurance benefits) provided after July 18, 1984 (whether or not the employer has maintained a reserve or fund for such benefits) are to be charged, first, against the "existing reserves" within this transition rule (including amounts attributable to "existing reserves" within this transition rule) for post-retirement medical benefits or for post-retirement life insurance benefits (as the case may be) and, second, against all other amounts. For this purpose, the qualified direct cost of an asset with a useful life extending substantially beyond the end of the taxable year (as determined under Q&A-6 of § 1.419-1T) will be treated as a benefit provided and thus charged against the "existing reserve" based on the extent to which such asset is used in the provision of post-retirement medical benefits or post-retirement life insurance benefits (as the case may be). All plans of an employer providing post-retirement medical benefits are to be treated as one plan for purposes of section 512(a)(3)(E)(ii)(III), and all plans of an employer providing post-retirement life insurance benefits are to be treated as one plan for purposes of section 512(a)(3)(E)(ii)(III).

(e) In calculating the unrelated business taxable income of a Covered Entity for a taxable year of such organization, the total income of the Covered Entity for the taxable year is reduced by the income attributable to "existing reserves" within the transition rule before such income is compared to the excess of the total amount of the assets of the Covered Entity as of the close of the taxable year over the applicable account limit for the taxable year.

(f) The following example illustrates the calculation of a VEBA's UBTI:

Example. Assume that the total income of a VEBA for a taxable year is $1,000, and that the excess of the total amount of the assets of the VEBA as of the close of the taxable year over the applicable account limit is $600. Assume also that of the $1,000 of total income, $540 is attributable to "existing reserves" within the transition rule of section 512(a)(3)(E)(ii)(I). The unrelated business taxable income of this VEBA for the taxable year is equal to the lesser of the following two amounts: (1) the total income of the VEBA for the taxable year, reduced by the extent to which such income is attributable to "existing reserves" within the meaning of the transition rule ($1,000 - $540 = $460); or (2) the excess of the total amount of the assets of the VEBA as of the close of the taxable year over the applicable account limit ($600). Thus, the unrelated business income of this VEBA for the taxable year is $460.

Q-5. What is the effective/applicability date of this section?

A-5. Except as otherwise provided in this paragraph, this section is applicable to taxable years ending on or after the date of publication of the final regulation. For rules that apply to earlier periods, see 26 CFR 1.512(a)-5T (revised as of April 1, 2013). [Reg. § 1.512(a)-5.]

Section 1256 Contracts: Swap Exclusions

Section 1256 Contracts: Swap Exclusions.—Amendment to Reg. § 1.512(b)-1, providing guidance on the category of swaps and similar agreements that are within the scope of Code Sec.

1256(b)(2)(B), are proposed (published in the Federal Register on September 16, 2011) (REG-111283-11).

Par. 3. Section 1.512(b)-(1) is amended by:

1. Revising paragraph (a)(1).
2. Adding two sentences to the end of paragraph (a)(3).

The revision and addition read as follows:

§1.512(b)-1. Modifications.

* * *

(a) *Certain Investment Income.*—(1) *In general.*—Dividends, interest, payments with respect to securities loans (as defined in section 512(a)(5)), annuities, income from notional principal contracts (as defined in §1.446-3(c)), other substantially similar income from ordinary and routine investments to the extent determined by the Commissioner, and all deductions directly connected with any of the foregoing items of income shall be excluded in computing unrelated business taxable income.

* * *

(3) * * * The rules of paragraph (a)(1) of this section apply to notional principal contracts as defined in §1.446-3(c) that are entered into on or after the date of publication of a Treasury decision adopting these rules as final regulations in the **Federal Register**. Section 1.512(b)-1(a)(1) as contained in 26 CFR part 1 revised April 1, 2011, continues to apply to notional principal contracts entered into before the date of publication of a Treasury decision adopting these rules as final regulations in the **Federal Register**.

* * *

Guidance under Section 529A: Qualified ABLE Programs

Guidance under Section 529A: Qualified ABLE Programs.—Amendments to Reg. §1.513-1, regarding programs under The Stephen Beck, Jr., Achieving a Better Life Experience Act of 2014 and rules under which States or State agencies or instrumentalities may establish and maintain a new type of tax-favored savings program through which contributions may be made to the account of an eligible disabled individual to meet qualified disability expenses, are proposed (published in the Federal Register on June 22, 2015) (REG-102837-15).

Par. 3. Section 1.513-1 is amended by adding *Example 4* to paragraph (d)(4)(i) to read as follows:

§1.513-1. Definition of unrelated trade or business.

* * *

(d) * * *

(4) * * *

(i) * * *

Example 4. P is a qualified ABLE program described in section 529A. P receives amounts in order to open or maintain ABLE accounts, as administrative or maintenance fees and other similar fees including service charges. Because the payment of these amounts are essential to the operation of a qualified ABLE program, the income generated from the activity does not constitute gross income from an unrelated trade or business.

* * *

Partnerships: Tax-Exempt Organization Partners: Fractions Rule

Partnerships: Tax-Exempt Organization Partners: Fractions Rule.—Amendments to Reg. §1.514(c)-2, relating to the application of section 514(c)(9)(E) of the Internal Revenue Code (Code) to partnerships that hold debt-financed real property and have one or more (but not all) qualified tax-exempt organization partners within the meaning of section 514(c)(9)(C), are proposed (published in the Federal Register on November 23, 2016) (REG-136978-12).

Par. 2. Section 1.514(c)-2 is amended by:

1. In paragraph (a), adding entries for (d)(2)(i) through (iii), adding entries for (d)(3)(i) and (ii), revising the entry for (d)(6), removing entries for (d)(6)(i) and (ii), and (d)(7), adding entries for (k)(1)(i) through (iv), revising the entries for (k)(2)(i) and (ii), adding an entry for (k)(2)(iii), and revising the entry for (n).
2. Revising paragraphs (d)(2) and (3).
3. Removing paragraph (d)(6).
4. Redesignating paragraph (d)(7) as paragraph (d)(6).
5. Revising newly redesignated paragraph (d)(6) *Example 1* paragraph (i) and adding paragraph (iv).
6. Removing the language "(i.e., reverse)" in paragraph (e)(1)(i) and adding the language "(that is, reverse)" in its place.
7. Removing the language "other partners; and" at the end of paragraph (e)(1)(iii) and adding the language "other partners;" in its place.
8. Removing the language "of §1.704-1(b)(2)(ii)(*d*)." at the end of paragraph (e)(1)(iv) and adding the language "of §1.704-1(b)(2)(ii)(*d*);" in its place.
9. Removing the language "the regulations thereunder." at the end of paragraph (e)(1)(v) and adding the language "the regulations thereunder;" in its place.
10. Adding new paragraphs (e)(1)(vi) and (vii).
11. Adding *Example 5* to paragraph (e)(5).
12. Removing the word "and" at the end of paragraph (f)(3).
13. Redesignating paragraph (f)(4) as paragraph (f)(5) and adding new paragraph (f)(4).
14. Revising paragraph (k)(1).
15. Revising the subject heading for paragraph (k)(2)(i).
16. Revising paragraph (k)(2)(i)(A).

17. Redesignating paragraph (k)(2)(ii) as paragraph (k)(2)(iii) and adding new paragraph (k)(2)(ii).
18. Revising paragraph (k)(3)(ii)(B).
19. Removing the second sentence in paragraph (m)(1)(ii).
20. Revising *Example 3*(ii) of paragraph (m)(2).
21. Revising the subject heading for paragraph (n).
22. Adding a sentence to the end of paragraph (n)(2).
The revisions and additions read as follows:

§1.514(c)-2. Permitted allocations under section 514(c)(9)(E).—(a) *Table of contents.*—* * *

(d) * * *

(2) * * *

(i) In general.

(ii) Limitation.

(iii) Distributions disregarded.

(3) * * *

(i) In general.

(ii) Reasonable guaranteed payments may be deducted only when paid in cash.

* * *

(6) Examples.

* * *

(k) * * *

(1) * * *

(i) In general.

(ii) Acquisition of partnership interests after initial formation of partnership.

(iii) Capital commitment defaults or reductions.

(iv) Examples.

(2) * * *

(i) Qualified organizations.

(ii) Non-qualified organizations.

(iii) Example.

* * *

(n) Effective/applicability dates.

* * *

(d) * * *

(2) *Preferred returns.*—(i) *In general.*—Items of income (including gross income) and gain that may be allocated to a partner with respect to a current or cumulative reasonable preferred return for capital (including allocations of minimum gain attributable to nonrecourse liability (or partner nonrecourse debt) proceeds distributed to the partner as a reasonable preferred return) are disregarded in computing overall partnership income or loss for purposes of the fractions rule. Similarly, if a partnership agreement effects a reasonable preferred return with an allocation of what would otherwise be overall partnership income, those items comprising that allocation are disregarded in computing overall partnership income for purposes of the fractions rule.

(ii) *Limitation.*—Except as otherwise provided in paragraph (d)(2)(iii) of this section, items of income and gain (or part of what would otherwise be overall partnership income) that may be allocated to a partner in a taxable year with respect to a reasonable preferred return for capital are disregarded under paragraph (d)(2)(i) of this section for purposes of the fractions rule only if the partnership agreement requires the partnership to make distributions first to pay any accrued, cumulative, and compounding unpaid preferred return to the extent such accrued but unpaid preferred return has not otherwise been reversed by an allocation of loss prior to such distribution.

(iii) *Distributions disregarded.*—A distribution is disregarded for purposes of paragraph (d)(2)(ii) of this section if the distribution—

(A) Is made pursuant to a provision in the partnership agreement intended to facilitate the partners' payment of taxes imposed on their allocable shares of partnership income or gain;

(B) Is treated as an advance against distributions to which the distributee partner would otherwise be entitled under the partnership agreement; and

(C) Does not exceed the distributee partner's allocable share of net partnership income and gain multiplied by the sum of the highest statutory federal, state, and local tax rates applicable to such partner.

(3) *Guaranteed payments.*—(i) *In general.*—A current or cumulative reasonable guaranteed payment to a qualified organization for capital or services is treated as an item of deduction in computing overall partnership income or loss, and the income that the qualified organization may receive or accrue from the current or cumulative reasonable guaranteed payment is not treated as an allocable share of overall partnership income or loss. The treatment of a guaranteed payment as reasonable for purposes of section 514(c)(9)(E) does not affect its possible characterization as unrelated business taxable income under other provisions of the Internal Revenue Code.

(ii) *Reasonable guaranteed payments may be deducted only when paid in cash.*—If a partnership that avails itself of paragraph (d)(3)(i) of this section would otherwise be required (by virtue of its method of accounting) to deduct a reasonable guaranteed payment to a qualified organization earlier than the taxable year in which it is paid in cash, the partnership must delay the deduction of the guaranteed payment until the taxable year it is paid in cash. For purposes of this paragraph (d)(3)(ii), a guaranteed payment that is paid in cash on or before the due date (not including extensions) for filing the partnership's return for a taxable year may be treated as paid in that prior taxable year.

* * *

(6) * * *

Example 1. * * *

(i) The partnership agreement provides QO a 10 percent preferred return on its unreturned capital. The partnership agreement provides that the preferred return may be compounded (at 10 percent) and may be paid in future years and requires that when distributions are made, they must be made first to pay any accrued, cumulative, and compounding unpaid preferred return not previously reversed by a loss allocation. The partnership agreement also allows distributions to be made to facilitate a partner's payment of federal, state, and local taxes. Under the partnership agreement, any such distribution is treated as an advance against distributions to which the distributee partner would otherwise be entitled and must not exceed the partner's allocable share of net partnership income or gain for that taxable year multiplied by the sum of the highest statutory federal, state, and local tax rates applicable to the partner. The partnership agreement first allocates gross income and gain 100 percent to QO, to the extent of the preferred return. All remaining income or loss is allocated 50 percent to QO and 50 percent to TP.

* * *

(iv) The facts are the same as in paragraph (i) of this *Example 1*, except the partnership makes a distribution to TP of an amount computed by a formula in the partnership agreement equal to TP's allocable share of net income and gain multiplied by the sum of the highest statutory federal, state, and local tax rates applicable to TP. The partnership satisfies the fractions rule. The distribution to TP is disregarded for purposes of paragraph (d)(2)(ii) of this section because the distribution is made pursuant to a provision in the partnership agreement that provides that the distribution is treated as an advance against distributions to which TP would otherwise be entitled and the distribution did not exceed TP's allocable share of net partnership income or gain for that taxable year multiplied by the sum of the highest statutory federal, state, and local tax rates applicable to TP. The income and gain that is specially allocated to QO with respect to its preferred return is disregarded in computing overall partnership income or loss for purposes of the fractions rule because the requirements of paragraph (d) of this section are satisfied. After disregarding those allocations, QO's fractions rule percentage is 50 percent (see paragraph (c)(2) of this section), and, under the partnership agreement, QO may not be allocated more than 50 percent of overall partnership income in any taxable year.

(e) * * *

(1) * * *

(vi) Allocations of what would otherwise be overall partnership income that may be made to chargeback (that is, reverse) prior allocations of partner-specific expenditures that were disregarded in computing overall partnership income or loss for purposes of the fractions rule under paragraph (f) of this section; and

(vii) Allocations of what would otherwise be overall partnership income that may be made to chargeback (that is, reverse) prior allocations of unlikely losses and deductions that were disregarded in computing overall partnership income or loss for purposes of the fractions rule under paragraph (g) of this section.

* * *

(5) * * *

Example 5. Chargeback of prior allocations of unlikely losses and deductions. (i) Qualified organization (QO) and taxable corporation (TP) are equal partners in a partnership that holds encumbered real property. The partnership agreement generally provides that QO and TP share partnership income and deductions equally. QO contributes land to the partnership, and the partnership agreement provides that QO bears the burden of any environmental remediation required for that land, and, as such, the partnership will allocate 100 percent of the expense attributable to the environmental remediation to QO. In the unlikely event of the discovery of environmental conditions that require remediation, the partnership agreement provides that, to the extent its cumulative net income (without regard to the remediation expense) for the taxable year the partnership incurs the remediation expense and for subsequent taxable years exceeds $500x, after allocation of the $500x of cumulative net income, net income will first be allocated to QO to offset any prior allocation of the environmental remediation expense deduction. On January 1 of Year 3, the partnership incurs a $100x expense for the environmental remediation of the land. In that year, the partnership had gross income of $60x and other expenses of $30x for total net income of $30x without regard to the expense associated with the environmental remediation. The partnership allocated $15x of income to each of QO and TP and $100x of remediation expense to QO.

(ii) The partnership satisfies the fractions rule. The allocation of the expense attributable to the remediation of the land is disregarded under paragraph (g) of this section. QO's share of overall partnership income is 50 percent, which equals QO's share of overall partnership loss.

(iii) In Year 8, when the partnership's cumulative net income (without regard to the remediation expense) for the taxable year the partnership incurred the remediation expense and subsequent taxable years is $480x (the $30x from Year 3, plus $450x of cumulative net income for Years 4-7), the partnership has gross income of $170x and expenses of $50x, for total net income of $120x. The partnership's cumulative net income for all years from Year 3 to Year 8 is $600x ($480x for Years 3-7 and $120x for Year 8). Pursuant to the partnership agreement, the first $20x of net income for Year 8 is allocated equally between QO and TP because the partnership must first earn cumulative net income in excess of $500x before making the offset allocation to QO. The remaining $100x of net income for Year 8 is allocated to QO to offset the environmental remediation expense allocated to QO in Year 3.

(iv) Pursuant to paragraph (e)(1)(vii) of this section, the partnership's allocation of $100x of net income to QO in Year 8 to offset the prior environmental remediation expense is disregarded in computing overall partnership income or loss for purposes of the fractions rule. The allocation does not cause the partnership to violate the fractions rule.

(f) * * *

(4) Expenditures for management and similar fees, if such fees in the aggregate for the taxable year are not more than 2 percent of the partner's capital commitments; and * * *

* * *

(k) *Special rules.*—(1) *Changes in partnership allocations arising from a change in the partners' interests.*—(i) *In general.*—A qualified organization that acquires a partnership interest from another qualified organization is treated as a continuation of the prior qualified organization partner (to the extent of that acquired interest) for purposes of applying the fractions rule. Changes in partnership allocations that result from other transfers or shifts of partnership interests will be closely scrutinized (to determine whether the transfer or shift stems from a prior agreement, understanding, or plan or could otherwise be expected given the structure of the transaction), but generally will be taken into account only in determining whether the partnership satisfies the fractions rule in the taxable year of the change and subsequent taxable years.

(ii) *Acquisition of partnership interests after initial formation of partnership.*—Changes in partnership allocations due to an acquisition of a partnership interest by a partner (new partner) after the initial formation of a partnership will not be closely scrutinized under paragraph (k)(1)(i) of this section, but will be taken into account only in determining whether the partnership satisfies the fractions rule in the taxable year of the change and subsequent taxable years, and disproportionate allocations of income, loss, or deduction to the partners to adjust the partners' capital accounts as a result of, and to reflect, the new partner acquiring the partnership interest and the resulting changes to the other partners' interests will be disregarded in computing overall partnership income or loss for purposes of the fractions rule if such changes and disproportionate allocations are not inconsistent with the purpose of the fractions rule under paragraph (k)(4) of this section and—

(A) The new partner acquires the partnership interest no later than 18 months following the formation of the partnership (applicable period);

(B) The partnership agreement and other relevant documents anticipate the new partners acquiring the partnership interest during the applicable period, set forth the time frame in which the new partners will acquire the partnership interests, and provide for the amount of capital the partnership intends to raise;

(C) The partnership agreement and other relevant documents specifically set forth the method for determining any applicable interest factor and for allocating income, loss, or deduction to the partners to account for the economics of the arrangement in the partners' capital accounts after the new partner acquires the partnership interest; and

(D) The interest rate for any applicable interest factor is not greater than 150 percent of the highest applicable Federal rate, at the appropriate compounding period or periods, at the time the partnership was formed.

(iii) *Capital commitment defaults or reductions.*—Changes in partnership allocations that result from an unanticipated partner default on a capital contribution commitment or an unanticipated reduction in a partner's capital contribution commitment, that are effected pursuant to provisions prescribing the treatment of such events in the partnership agreement, and that are not inconsistent with the purpose of the fractions rule under paragraph (k)(4) of this section, will not be closely scrutinized under paragraph (k)(1)(i) of this section, but will be taken into account only in determining whether the partnership satisfies the fractions rule in the taxable year of the change and subsequent taxable years. In addition, partnership allocations of income, loss, or deduction to partners made pursuant to the partnership agreement to adjust partners' capital accounts as a result of unanticipated capital contribution defaults or reductions will be disregarded in computing overall partnership income or loss for purposes of the fractions rule. The adjustments may include allocations to adjust partners' capital accounts to be consistent with the partners' adjusted capital commitments.

(iv) *Examples.*—The following examples illustrate the provisions of paragraph (k)(1) of this section.

Example 1. Staged closing. (i) On July 1 of Year 1, two taxable partners (TP1 and TP2) form a partnership that will invest in debt-financed real property. The partnership agreement provides that, within an 18-month period, partners will be added so that an additional $1000x of capital can be raised. The partnership agreement sets forth the method for determining the applicable interest factor that complies with paragraph (k)(1)(ii)(D) of this section and for allocating income, loss, or deduction to the partners to account for the economics of the arrangement in the partners' capital accounts. During the partnership's Year 1 taxable year, partnership had $150x of net income. TP1 and TP2, each, is allocated $75x of net income.

(ii) On January 1 of Year 2, qualified organization (QO) joins the partnership. The partnership agreement provides that TP1, TP2, and QO will be treated as if they had been equal partners from July 1 of Year 1. Assume that the interest factor is treated as a reasonable guaranteed payment to TP1 and TP2, the expense from which is taken into account in the partnership's net income of $150x for Year 2. To balance capital accounts, the partnership allocates $100x of the income to QO ($50x, or the amount of one-third of Year 1 income that QO was not allocated during the partnership's first taxable year, plus $50x, or one-third of the partnership's income for Year 2) and the remaining income equally to TP1 and TP2. Thus, the partnership allocates $100x to QO and $25x to TP1 and TP2, each.

(iii) The partnership's allocation to QO would violate the fractions rule because QO's overall percentage of partnership income for Year 2 of 66.7 percent is greater than QO's fractions rule percentage of 33.3 percent. However, the special allocation of $100x to QO for Year 2 is disregarded in determining QO's percentage of overall partnership income for purposes of the fractions rule because the requirements in paragraph (k)(1)(ii) of this section are satisfied.

Example 2. Capital call default. (i) On January 1 of Year 1, two taxable partners, (TP1 and TP2) and a qualified organization (QO) form a partnership that will hold encumbered real property and agree to share partnership profits and losses, 60 percent, 10 percent, and 30 percent, respectively. TP1 agreed to a capital commitment of $120x, TP2 agreed to a capital commitment of $20x, and QO agreed to a capital commitment of $60x. The partners met half of their commitments upon formation of the partnership. The partnership agreement requires a partner's interest to be reduced if the partner defaults on a capital call. The agreement also allows the nondefaulting partners to make the contribution and to increase their own interests in the partnership. Following a capital call default, the partnership agreement requires allocations to adjust capital accounts to reflect the change in partnership interests as though the funded commitments represented the partner's interests from the partnership's inception.

(ii) In Year 1, partnership had income of $100x, which was allocated to the partners $60x to TP1, $10x to TP2, and $30x to QO.

(iii) In Year 2, partnership required each partner to contribute the remainder of its capital commitment, $60x from TP1, $10x from TP2, and $30x from QO. TP1 could not make its required capital contribution, and QO contributed $90x, its own capital commitment, in addition to TP1's. TP1's default was not anticipated. As a result and pursuant to the partnership agreement, TP1's interest was reduced to 30 percent and QO's interest was increased to 60 percent. Partnership had income of $60x and losses of $120x in Year 2, for a net loss of $60x. Partnership allocated to TP1 $48x of loss (special allocation of $30x of gross items of loss to adjust capital accounts and $18x of net loss (30 percent of $60x net loss)), TP2 $6x of net loss (10 percent of $60x net loss), and QO $6x of loss (special allocation of $30x of gross items of income to adjust capital accounts - $36x of net loss (60 percent of $60x net loss)). At the end of Year 2, TP1's capital account equals $72x (capital contribution of $60x + $60x income from Year 1 - $48x loss from Year 2); TP2's capital account equals $24x (capital contributions of $20x + $10x income from Year 1 - $6x loss from Year 2); and QO's capital account equals $144x (capital contributions of $120x ($30x + $90x) + $30x income from Year 1 - $6x loss from Year 2).

(iv) The changes in partnership allocations to TP1 and QO due to TP1's unanticipated default on its capital contribution commitment were effected pursuant to provisions prescribing the treatment of such events in the partnership agreement. Therefore these changes in allocations will not be closely scrutinized under paragraph (k)(1)(i) of this section, but will be taken into account only in determining whether the partnership satisfies the fractions rule in the taxable year of the change and subsequent taxable years. In addition, pursuant to paragraph (k)(1)(iii) of this section, the special allocations of $30x additional loss to TP1 and $30x additional income to QO to adjust their capital accounts to reflect their new interests in the partnership are disregarded when calculating QO's percentage of overall partnership income and loss for purposes of the fractions rule.

(2) * * *

(i) *Qualified organizations.*—* * *

(A) Qualified organizations do not hold (directly or indirectly through a partnership), in the aggregate, interests of greater than five percent in the capital or profits of the partnership; and

* * *

(ii) *Non-qualified organizations.*—Section 514(c)(9)(B)(vi) does not apply to a partnership otherwise subject to that section if—

(A) All partners other than qualified organizations do not hold (directly or indirectly through a partnership), in the aggregate, interests of greater than five percent in the capital or profits of the partnership; and

(B) Allocations have substantial economic effect without application of the special rules in §1.704-1(b)(2)(iii)(*c*) (regarding the presumption that there is a reasonable possibility that allocations will affect substantially the dollar amounts to be received by the partners from the partnership if there is a strong likelihood that offsetting allocations will not be made in five years, and the presumption that the adjusted tax basis (or book value) of partnership property is equal to the fair market value of such property).

* * *

(3) * * *

(ii) * * *

(B) $1,000,000.

* * *

(m) * * *

(2) * * *

Example 3. * * *

(ii) P2 satisfies the fractions rule with respect to the P2/P1A chain. See §1.702-1(a)(8)(ii) (for rules regarding separately stating partnership items). P2 does not satisfy the fractions rule with respect to the P2/P1B chain.

(n) *Effective/applicability dates.*—* * *

(2) * * * However, paragraphs (d)(2)(ii) and (iii), (d)(6) *Example 1*(i) and (iv), (e)(1)(vi) and (vii), (e)(5) *Example 5*, (f)(4), (k)(1)(ii) through (iv), (k)(2)(i)(A), (k)(2)(ii), (k)(3)(ii)(B), (m)(1)(ii), and (m)(2) *Example 3*(ii) of this section apply to taxable years ending on or after the date these regulations are published as final regulations in the **Federal Register**.

* * *

Exempt Organizations

Exempt Organizations: Unrelated Trade or Business: Bingo Games.—Reproduced below is the text of a proposed amendment of Reg. §1.527-3, relating to the treatment of proceeds from bingo games (published in the Federal Register on August 28, 1979).

☐ Par. 2. Section 1.527-3(b)[(a)](1) is revised to read as follows:

§1.527-3. Political organization taxable income.—

* * *

(b)[a] *Exempt function income defined.*—(1) *In general.*—For purposes of section 527 and these regulations the term "exempt function income" means any amount received as—

(i) A contribution of money or other property;

(ii) Membership dues, fees, or assessments from a member of a political organization;

(iii) Proceeds from a political fund raising or entertainment event, or proceeds from the sale of political campaign materials, which are not received in the ordinary course of any trade or business; and

(iv) Proceeds from the conduct of any bingo game (as defined in section 513(f)(2)) unless the proceeds were held on October 21, 1978, by the political organization that conducted the bingo games and thereafter were used by that organization to make a contribution or expenditure (as defined in section 301(e) and (f) of the Federal Election Campaign Act of 1971; 2 U.S.C. 431(e), (f)) in connection with an election held before January 1, 1979,

to the extent such amount is segregated for use only for the exempt function of the political organization. (See also §1.527-4 regarding the treatment of expenditures for a judicially determined illegal activity.)

* * *

Qualified State Tuition Programs: Distributions: Reporting Requirements

Qualified State Tuition Programs: Distributions: Reporting Requirements.—Reg. §§1.529-0—1.529-6, relating to qualified state tuition programs (QSTPs) and affecting QSTPs established and maintained by a state, or an agency or instrumentality of a state, and individuals receiving distributions from QSTPs, are proposed (published in the Federal Register on August 24, 1998) (REG-106177-97).

☐ Par. 2. An undesignated center heading [Qualified State Tuition Programs] and §§1.529-0 through 1.529-6 are added to read as follows:

§1.529-0. Table of contents.—This section lists the following captions contained in §§1.529-1 through 1.529-6:

[Reg. §1.529-0.]

§1.529-1. Qualified State tuition program, unrelated business income tax and defini-

tions.—(a) *In general.*—A qualified State tuition program (QSTP) described in section 529 is exempt from income tax, except for the tax imposed under section 511 on the QSTP's unrelated business taxable income. A QSTP is not required to file Form 990, Return of Organization Exempt From Income Tax, Form 1041, U.S. Income Tax Return for Estates and Trusts, or Form 1120, U.S. Corporation Income Tax Return. A QSTP may be required to file Form 990-T, Exempt Organization Business Income Tax Return. See §§1.6012-2(e) and 1.6012-3(a)(5) for requirements for filing Form 990-T.

(b) *Unrelated business income tax rules.*—For purposes of section 529, this section and §§1.529-2 through 1.529-6:

(1) *Application of section 514.*—An interest in a QSTP shall not be treated as debt for purposes of section 514. Consequently, a QSTP's investment income will not constitute debt-financed income subject to the unrelated business income tax merely because the program accepts contributions and is obligated to pay out or refund such contributions and certain earnings attributable thereto to designated beneficiaries or to account owners. However, investment income of a QSTP shall be subject to the unrelated business income tax as debt-financed income to the extent the program incurs indebtedness when acquiring or improving income-producing property.

(2) *Penalties and forfeitures.*—Earnings forfeited on prepaid educational arrangements or contracts and educational savings accounts and retained by a QSTP, or amounts collected by a QSTP as penalties on refunds or excess contributions are not unrelated business income to the QSTP.

(3) *Administrative and other fees.*—Amounts paid, in order to open or maintain prepaid educational arrangements or contracts and educational savings accounts, as administrative or maintenance fees, and other similar fees including late fees, service charges, and finance charges, are not unrelated business income to the QSTP.

(c) *Definitions.*—For purposes of section 529, this section and §§1.529-2 through 1.529-6:

Account means the formal record of transactions relating to a particular designated beneficiary when it is used alone without further modification in these regulations. The term includes prepaid educational arrangements or contracts described in section 529(b)(1)(A)(i) and educational savings accounts described in section 529(b)(1)(A)(ii).

Account owner means the person who, under the terms of the QSTP or any contract setting forth the terms under which contributions may be made to an account for the benefit of a designated beneficiary, is entitled to select or change the designated beneficiary of an account, to designate any person other than the designated beneficiary to whom funds may be paid from the account, or to receive distributions from the account if no such other person is designated.

Contribution means any payment directly allocated to an account for the benefit of a designated beneficiary or used to pay late fees or administrative fees associated with the account. In the case of a tax-free *rollover*, within the meaning of this paragraph (c), into a QSTP account, only the portion of the rollover amount that constituted *investment in the account*, within the meaning of this paragraph (c), is treated as a contribution to the account as required by §1.529-3(a)(2).

Designated beneficiary means—

(1) The individual designated as the beneficiary of the account at the time an account is established with the QSTP;

(2) The individual who is designated as the new beneficiary when beneficiaries are changed; and

(3) The individual receiving the benefits accumulated in the account as a scholarship in the case of a QSTP account established by a State or local government or an organization described in section 501(c)(3) and exempt from taxation under section 501(a) as part of a scholarship program operated by such government or organization.

Distributee means the designated beneficiary or the account owner who receives or is treated as receiving a distribution from a QSTP. For example, if a QSTP makes a distribution directly to an eligible educational institution to pay tuition and fees for a designated beneficiary or a QSTP makes a distribution in the form of a check payable to both a designated beneficiary and an eligible educational institution, the distribution shall be treated as having been made in full to the designated beneficiary.

Distribution means any disbursement, whether in cash or in-kind, from a QSTP. Distributions include, but are not limited to, tuition credits or certificates, payment vouchers, tuition waivers or other similar items. Distributions also include, but are not limited to, a refund to the account owner, the designated beneficiary or the designated beneficiary's estate.

Earnings attributable to an account are the total account balance on a particular date minus the investment in the account as of that date.

Earnings ratio means the amount of earnings allocable to the account on the last day of the calendar year divided by the total account balance on the last day of that calendar year. The earnings ratio is applied to any distribution made during the calendar year. For purposes of computing the earnings ratio, the earnings allocable to the account on the last day of the calendar year and the total account balance on the last day of the calendar year include all distributions made during the calendar year and any amounts that have been forfeited from the account during the calendar year.

Eligible educational institution means an institution which is described in section 481 of the Higher Education Act of 1965 (20 U.S.C 1088) as in effect on August 5, 1997, and which is eligible to participate in a program under title IV of such Act. Such institutions generally are accredited post-secondary educational institutions offering credit toward a bachelor's degree, an associate's degree, a graduate level or professional degree, or another recognized post-secondary credential. Certain proprietary institutions and post-secondary vocational institutions also are eligible institutions. The institution must be eligible to participate in Department of Education student aid programs.

Final distribution means the distribution from a QSTP account that reduces the total account balance to zero.

Forfeit means that earnings and contributions allocable to a QSTP account are withdrawn by the QSTP from the account or deducted by the QSTP from a distribution to pay a penalty as required by § 1.529-2(e).

Investment in the account means the sum of all contributions made to the account on or before a particular date less the aggregate amount of contributions included in distributions, if any, made from the account on or before that date.

Member of the family means an individual who is related to the designated beneficiary as described in paragraphs (1) through (9) of this definition. For purposes of determining who is a member of the family, a legally adopted child of an individual shall be treated as the child of such individual by blood. The terms brother and sister include a brother or sister by the halfblood. Member of the family means—

(1) A son or daughter, or a descendant of either;

(2) A stepson or stepdaughter;

(3) A brother, sister, stepbrother, or stepsister;

(4) The father or mother, or an ancestor of either;

(5) A stepfather or stepmother;

(6) A son or daughter of a brother or sister;

(7) A brother or sister of the father or mother;

(8) A son-in-law, daughter-in-law, father-in-law, mother-in-law, brother-in-law, or sister-in-law; or

(9) The spouse of the designated beneficiary or the spouse of any individual described in paragraphs (1) through (8) of this definition.

Person has the same meaning as under section 7701(a)(1).

Qualified higher education expenses means—

(1) Tuition, fees, and the costs of books, supplies, and equipment required for the enrollment or attendance of a designated beneficiary at an eligible educational institution; and

(2) The costs of room and board (as limited by paragraph (2)(i) of this definition) of a designated beneficiary (who meets requirements of paragraph (2)(ii) of this definition) incurred while attending an eligible educational institution:

(i) The amount of room and board treated as qualified higher education expenses shall not exceed the minimum room and board allowance determined in calculating costs of attendance for Federal financial aid programs under section 472 of the Higher Education Act of 1965 (20 U.S.C. 1087ll) as in effect on August 5, 1997. For purposes of these regulations, room and board costs shall not exceed $1,500 per academic year for a designated beneficiary residing at home with parents or guardians. For a designated beneficiary residing in institutionally owned or operated housing, room and board costs shall not exceed the amount normally assessed most residents for room and board at the institution. For all other designated beneficiaries the amount shall not exceed $2,500 per academic year. For this purpose the term academic year has the same meaning as that term is given in 20 U.S.C. 1088(d) as in effect on August 5, 1997.

(ii) Room and board shall be treated as qualified higher education expenses for a designated beneficiary if they are incurred during any academic period during which the designated beneficiary is enrolled or accepted for enrollment in a degree, certificate, or other program (including a program of study abroad approved for credit by the eligible educational institution) that leads to a recognized educational credential awarded by an eligible educational institution. In addition, the designated beneficiary must be enrolled at least half-time. A student will be considered to be enrolled at least half-time if the student is enrolled for at least half the full-time academic workload for the course of study the student is pursuing as determined under the standards of the institution where the student is enrolled. The institution's standard for a full-time workload must equal or exceed the standard established by the Department of Education under the Higher Education Act and set forth in 34 CFR 674.2(b).

Rollover distribution means a distribution or transfer from an account of a designated beneficiary that is transferred to or deposited within 60 days of the distribution into an account of another individual who is a member of the family of the designated beneficiary. A distribution is not a rollover distribution unless there is a change in beneficiary. The new designated beneficiary's account may be in a QSTP in either the same State or a QSTP in another State.

Total account balance means the total amount or the total fair market value of tuition credits or certificates or similar benefits allocable to the account on a particular date. For purposes of computing the *earnings ratio*, the total account balance is adjusted as described in this paragraph (c).

[Reg. § 1.529-1.]

§ 1.529-2. Qualified State tuition program described.—(a) *In general.*—To be a QSTP, a program must satisfy the requirements described in paragraphs (a) through (i) of this section. A QSTP is a program established and maintained by a State or an agency or instrumentality of a State under which a person—

(1) May purchase tuition credits or certificates on behalf of a designated beneficiary that entitle the beneficiary to the waiver or payment of qualified higher education expenses of the beneficiary; or

(2) May make contributions to an account that is established for the purpose of meeting the qualified higher education expenses of the designated beneficiary of the account.

(b) *Established and maintained by a State or agency or instrumentality of a State.*—(1) *Established.*—A program is established by a State or an agency or instrumentality of a State if the program is initiated by State statute or regulation, or by an act of a State official or agency with the authority to act on behalf of the State.

(2) *Maintained.*—A program is maintained by a State or an agency or instrumentality of a State if—

(i) The State or agency or instrumentality sets all of the terms and conditions of the program, including but not limited to who may contribute to the program, who may be a designated beneficiary of the program, what benefits the program may provide, when penalties will apply to refunds and what those penalties will be; and

(ii) The State or agency or instrumentality is actively involved on an ongoing basis in the administration of the program, including supervising all decisions relating to the investment of assets contributed to the program.

(3) *Actively involved.*—Factors that are relevant in determining whether a State, agency or instrumentality is actively involved include, but are not limited to: whether the State provides services or benefits (such as tax, student aid or other financial benefits) to account owners or designated beneficiaries that are not provided to persons who are not account owners or designated beneficiaries; whether the State or agency or instrumentality establishes detailed operating rules for administering the program; whether officials of the State or agency or instrumentality play a substantial role in the operation of the program, including selecting, supervising, monitoring, auditing, and terminating any private contractors that provide services under the program; whether the State or agency or instrumentality holds the private contractors that provide services under the program to the same standards and requirements that apply when private contractors handle funds that belong to the State or provide services to the State; whether the State provides funding for the program; and, whether the State or agency or instrumentality acts as trustee or holds program assets directly or for the benefit of the account owners or designated beneficiaries. If the State or an agency or instrumentality thereof exercises the same authority over the funds invested in the program as it does over the investments in or pool of funds of a State employees' defined benefit pension plan, then the State or agency or instrumentality will be considered actively involved on an ongoing basis in the administration of the program.

(c) *Permissible uses of contributions.*—Contributions to a QSTP can be placed into either a prepaid educational arrangement or contract described in section 529(b)(1)(A)(i) or an educational savings account described in section 529(b)(1)(A)(ii), or both, but cannot be placed into any other type of account.

(1) A prepaid educational services arrangement or contract is an account through which tuition credits or certificates or other rights are acquired that entitle the designated beneficiary of the account to the waiver or payment of qualified higher education expenses.

(2) An educational savings account is an account that is established exclusively for the purpose of meeting the qualified higher education expenses of a designated beneficiary.

(d) *Cash contributions.*—A program shall not be treated as a QSTP unless it provides that contributions may be made only in cash and not in property. A QSTP may accept payment, however, in cash, or by check, money order, credit card, or similar methods.

(e) *Penalties on refunds.*—(1) *General rule.*—A program shall not be treated as a QSTP unless it imposes a more than de minimis penalty on the earnings portion of any distribution from the program that is not—

(i) Used exclusively for qualified higher education expenses of the designated beneficiary;

(ii) Made on account of the death or disability of the designated beneficiary;

(iii) Made on account of the receipt of a scholarship (or allowance or payment described in section 135(d)(1)(B) or (C)) by the designated beneficiary to the extent the amount of the distribution does not exceed the amount of the scholarship, allowance, or payment; or

(iv) A rollover distribution.

(2) *More than de minimis penalty.*—(i) *In general.*—A penalty is more than de minimis if it is consistent with a program intended to assist individuals in saving exclusively for qualified higher education expenses. Except as provided in paragraph (e)(2)(ii) of this section, whether any particular penalty is more than de minimis depends on the facts and circumstances of the particular program, including the extent to which the penalty offsets the federal income tax benefit from having deferred income tax liability on the earnings portion of any distribution.

(ii) *Safe harbor.*—A penalty imposed on the earnings portion of a distribution is more than de minimis if it is equal to or greater than 10 percent of the earnings.

(3) *Separate distributions.*—For purposes of applying the penalty, any single distribution described in paragraph (e)(1) of this section will be treated as a separate distribution and not part of a single aggregated annual distribution by the program, notwithstanding the rules under §1.529-3 and §1.529-4.

(4) *Procedures for verifying use of distributions and imposing and collecting penalties.*—(i) *In general.*—To be treated as imposing a more than de minimis penalty as required in paragraph (e)(1) of this section, a program must implement practices and procedures to identify whether a distribution is subject to a penalty and collect any penalty that is due.

(ii) *Safe harbor.*—A program that falls within the safe harbor described in paragraphs (e)(4)(ii)(A) through (E) of this section will be treated as implementing practices and procedures to identify whether a more than de minimis penalty must be imposed as required in paragraph (e)(1) of this section.

(A) *Distributions treated as payments of qualified higher education expenses.*—The program treats distributions as being used to pay for qualified higher education expenses only if—

(1) The distribution is made directly to an eligible educational institution;

(2) The distribution is made in the form of a check payable to both the designated beneficiary and the eligible educational institution;

(3) The distribution is made after the designated beneficiary submits substantiation to show that the distribution is a reimbursement for qualified higher education expenses that the designated beneficiary has already paid and the program has a process for reviewing the validity of the substantiation prior to the distribution; or

(4) The designated beneficiary certifies prior to the distribution that the distribution will be expended for his or her qualified higher education expenses within a reasonable time after the distribution; the program requires the designated beneficiary to provide substantiation of payment of qualified higher education expenses within 30 days after making the distribution and has a process for reviewing the substantiation; and the program retains an account balance that is large enough to collect any penalty owed on the distribution if valid substantiation is not produced.

(B) *Treatment of all other distributions.*—The program collects a penalty on all distributions not treated as made to pay qualified higher education expenses except where—

(1) Prior to the distribution the program receives written third party confirmation that the designated beneficiary has died or become disabled or has received a scholarship (or allowance or payment described in section 135(d)(1)(B) or (C)) in an amount equal to the distribution; or

(2) Prior to the distribution the program receives a certification from the account owner that the distribution is being made because the designated beneficiary has died or become disabled or has received a scholarship (or allowance or payment described in section 135(d)(1)(B) or (C)) received by the designated beneficiary (and the distribution is equal to the amount of the scholarship, allowance, or payment) and the program withholds and reserves a portion of the distribution as a penalty. Any penalty withheld by the program may be refunded after the program receives third party confirmation that the designated beneficiary has died or become disabled or has received a scholarship or allowance (or payment described in section 135(d)(1)(B) or (C)).

(C) *Refunds of penalties.*—The program will refund a penalty collected on a distribution only after the designated beneficiary substantiates that he or she had qualified higher education expenses greater than or equal to the distribution, and the program has reviewed the substantiation.

(D) *Documentation of amounts refunded and not used for qualified higher education expenses.*—The program requires the distributee, defined in §1.529-1(c), to provide a signed statement identifying the amount of any refunds received from eligible educational institutions at the end of each year in which distributions for qualified higher education expenses were made and of the next year.

(E) *Procedures to collect penalty.*—The program collects required penalties by retaining a sufficient balance in the account to pay the amount of penalty, withholding an amount equal to the penalty from a distribution, or collecting the penalty on a State income tax return.

(f) *Separate accounting.*—A program shall not be treated as a QSTP unless it provides separate accounting for each designated beneficiary. Separate accounting requires that contributions for the benefit of a designated beneficiary and any earnings attributable thereto must be allocated to the appropriate account. If a program does not ordinarily provide each account owner an annual account statement showing the total account balance, the investment in the account, earnings, and distributions from the account, the program must give this information to the account owner or designated beneficiary upon request. In the case of a prepaid educational arrangement or contract described in section 529(b)(1)(A)(i) the total account balance may be shown as credits or units of benefits instead of fair market value.

(g) *No investment direction.*—A program shall not be treated as a QSTP unless it provides that any account owner in, or contributor to, or designated beneficiary under, such program may not directly or indirectly direct the investment of any contribution to the program or directly or indirectly direct the investment of any earnings attributable to contributions. A program does not violate this requirement if a person who establishes an account with the program is permitted to select among different investment strategies designed exclusively by the program, only at the time the initial contribution is made establishing the account. A program will not violate the requirement of this paragraph (g) if it permits a person who establishes an account to select between a prepaid educational services account and an educational savings account. A program also will not violate the requirement of this paragraph (g) merely because it permits its board members, its employees, or the board members or employees of a contractor it hires to perform administrative services to purchase tuition credits or certificates or make contributions as described in paragraph (c) of this section.

(h) *No pledging of interest as security.*—A program shall not be treated as a QSTP unless the terms of the program or a state statute or regulation that governs the program prohibit any interest in the program or any portion thereof from being used as security for a loan. This restriction includes, but is not limited to, a prohibition on the use of any interest in the program as security for a loan used to purchase such interest in the program.

(i) *Prohibition on excess contributions.*—(1) *In general.*—A program shall not be treated as a QSTP unless it provides adequate safeguards to prevent contributions for the benefit of a designated beneficiary in excess of those necessary to provide for the qualified higher education expenses of the designated beneficiary.

(2) *Safe harbor.*—A program satisfies this requirement if it will bar any additional contributions to an account as soon as the account reaches a specified account balance limit applicable to all accounts of designated beneficiaries with the same expected year of enrollment. The total contributions may not exceed the amount determined by actuarial estimates that is necessary to pay tuition, required fees, and room and board expenses of the designated beneficiary for five years of undergraduate enrollment at the highest cost institution allowed by the program. [Reg. §1.529-2.]

§1.529-3. Income tax treatment of distributees.—(a) *Taxation of distributions.*—(1) *In general.*—Any distribution, other than a rollover distribution, from a QSTP account must be included in the gross income of the distributee to the extent of the earnings portion of the distribution and to the extent not excluded from gross income under any other provision of chapter 1 of the Internal Revenue Code. If any amount of a distribution is forfeited under a QSTP as required by §1.529-2(e), this amount is neither included in the gross income of the distributee nor deductible by the distributee.

(2) *Rollover distributions.*—No part of a rollover distribution is included in the income of the distributee. Following the rollover distribution, that portion of the rollover amount that constituted investment in the account, defined in §1.529-1(c), of the account from which the distribution was made is added to the investment in the account of the account that received the distribution. That portion of the rollover amount

that constituted earnings of the account that made the distribution is added to the earnings of the account that received the distribution.

(b) *Computing taxable earnings.*—(1) *Amount of taxable earnings in a distribution.*—(i) *Educational savings account.*—In the case of an educational savings account, the earnings portion of a distribution is equal to the product of the amount of the distribution and the earnings ratio, defined in § 1.529-1(c). The return of investment portion of the distribution is equal to the amount of the distribution minus the earnings portion of the distribution.

(ii) *Prepaid educational services account.*—In the case of a prepaid educational services account, the earnings portion of a distribution is equal to the value of the credits, hours, or other units of education distributed at the time of distribution minus the return of investment portion of the distribution. The value of the credits, hours, or other units of education may be based on the tuition waived or the cash distributed. The return of investment portion of the distribution is determined by dividing the investment in the account at the end of the year in which the distribution is made by the number of credits, hours, or other units of education in the account at the end of the calendar year (including all credits, hours, or other units of education distributed during the calendar year), and multiplying that amount by the number of credits, hours, or other units of education distributed during the current calendar year.

(2) *Adjustment for programs that treated distributions and earnings in a different manner for years beginning before January 1, 1999.*—For calendar years beginning after December 31, 1998, a QSTP must treat taxpayers as recovering investment in the account and earnings ratably with each distribution. Prior to January 1, 1999, a program may have treated distributions in a different manner and reported them to taxpayers accordingly. In order to adjust to the method described in this section, if distributions were treated as coming first from the investment in the account, the QSTP must adjust the investment in the account by subtracting the amount of the investment in the account previously treated as distributed. If distributions were treated as coming first from earnings, the QSTP must adjust the earnings portion of the account by subtracting the amount of earnings previously treated as distributed. After the adjustment is made, the investment in the account is recovered ratably in accordance with this section. If no previous distribution was made but earnings were treated as taxable to the taxpayer in the year they were allocated to the account, the earnings treated as already taxable are treated as additional contributions and added to the investment in the account.

(3) *Examples.*—The application of this paragraph (b) is illustrated by the following examples. The rounding convention used (rounding to three decimal places) in these examples is for purposes of illustration only. A QSTP may use another rounding convention as long as it consistently applies the convention. The examples are as follows:

Example 1. (i) In 1998, an individual, A, opens a prepaid educational services account with a QSTP on behalf of a designated beneficiary. Through the account A purchases units of education equivalent to eight semesters of tuition for full-time attendance at a public four-year university covered by the QSTP. A contributes $16,000 that includes payment of processing fees to the QSTP. In 2011 the designated beneficiary enrolls at a public four-year university. The QSTP makes distributions on behalf of the designated beneficiary to the university in August for the fall semester and in December for the spring semester. Tuition for full-time attendance at the university is $7,500 per academic year in 2011 and 2012, $7,875 for the academic year in 2013, and $8,200 for the academic year in 2014. The only expense covered by the QSTP distribution is tuition for four academic years. The calculations are as follows:

2011		
Investment in the account as of 12/31/2011	=	$16,000
Units in account	=	8
Per unit investment	=	$2,000
Units distributed in 2011	=	2
Investment portion of distribution in 2011 ($2,000 per unit × 2 units)	=	$4,000
Current value of two units distributed in 2011	=	$7,500
Earnings portion of distribution in 2011 ($7,500 - $4,000)	=	$3,500
2012		
Investment in the account as of 12/31/2012 ($16,000-$4,000)	=	$12,000
Units in account	=	6
Per unit investment	=	$2,000
Units distributed in 2012	=	2
Investment portion of distribution in 2012 ($2,000 per unit × 2 units)	=	$4,000
Current value of two units distributed in 2012	=	$7,500
Earnings portion of distribution in 2012 ($7,500 - $4,000)	=	$3,500
2013		
Investment in the account as of		

12/31/2013 ($12,000-$4000)	=	$8,000
Units in account	=	4
Per unit investment	=	$2,000
Units distributed in 2013	=	2
Investment portion of distribution in 2013 ($2,000 per unit × 2 units)	=	$4,000
Current value of two units distributed in 2013	=	$7,875
Earnings portion of distribution in 2013 ($7,875 - $4,000)	=	$3,875
2014		
Investment in the account as of 12/31/2014 ($8,000-$4000)	=	$4,000
Units in account	=	2
Per unit investment	=	$2,000
Units distributed in 2014	=	2
Investment portion of distribution in 2014 ($4,000 per unit × 2 units)	=	$4,000
Current value of two units distributed in 2014	=	$8,200
Earnings portion of distribution in 2014 ($8,200 - $4,000)	=	$4,200
12/31/2014 (after distributions) Investment in the account as of 12/31/2014 ($4,000-$4000)	=	0

(ii) In each year the designated beneficiary includes in his or her gross income the earnings portion of the distribution for tuition.

Example 2. (i) In 1998, an individual, B, opens a college savings account with a QSTP on behalf of a designated beneficiary. B contributes $18,000 to the account that includes payment of processing fees to the QSTP. On December 31, 2011, the total balance in the account for the benefit of the designated beneficiary is $30,000 (including distributions made during the year 2011). In 2011 the designated beneficiary enrolls at a four-year university. The QSTP makes distributions on behalf of the designated beneficiary to the university in August for the fall semester and in December for the spring semester. Tuition for full-time attendance at the university is $7,500 per academic year in 2011 and 2012, $7,875 for the academic year in 2013, and $8,200 for the academic year in 2014. The only expense covered by the QSTP distributions is tuition for four academic years. On the last day of the calendar year the account is allocated earnings of 5% on the total account balance on that day. Under the terms of the QSTP, a penalty of 15% is applied to the earnings not used to pay tuition. The calculations are as follows:

2011		
Investment in the account	=	$18,000
Total account balance as of 12/31/2011	=	$30,000
Earnings as of 12/31/2011	=	$12,000
Distributions in 2011	=	$7,500
Earnings ratio for 2011 ($12,000 ÷ $30,000)	=	40%
Earnings portion of distributions in 2011 ($7,500 × .4)	=	$3,000
Return of investment portion of distributions in 2011 ($7,500 - $3,000)	=	$4,500
2012		
Investment in the account as of 12/31/2012 ($18,000 - $4,500)	=	$13,500
Total account balance as of 12/31/12 [($30,000-$7,500) × 105%]	=	$23,625
Earnings as of 12/31/2012	=	$10,125
Distributions in 2012	=	$7,500
Earnings ratio for 2012 ($10,125 ÷ $23,625)	=	42.9%
Earnings portion of distributions in 2012 ($7,500 × .429)	=	$3,217.50
Return of investment portion of distributions in 2012 ($7,500 - $3,217.50)	=	$4,282.50
2013		
Investment in the account as of		

12/31/2013 ($13,500 - $4,282.50)	=	$9,217.50
Total account balance as of 12/31/13 [($23,625-$7,500) × 105%]	=	$16,931.25
Earnings as of 12/31/2013	=	$7,713.75
Distributions in 2013	=	$7,875
Earnings ratio for 2013 ($7,713.75 ÷ $16,931.25)	=	45.6%
Earnings portion of distributions in 2013 ($7,875 × .456)	=	$3,591
Return of investment portion of distributions in 2013 ($7,875 - $3,591)	=	$4,284
2014		
Investment in the account as of 12/31/2014 ($9,217.50 - $4,284)	=	$4,933.50
Total account balance as of 12/31/14 [($16,931.25 - $7,875) × 105%]	=	$9,509.06
Earnings as of 12/31/2014	=	$4,575.56
Distributions in 2014 for qualified higher education expenses (QHEE)	=	$8,200
Distributions in 2014 not for qualified higher education expenses (Non-QHEE)	=	$1,309.06
Total distributions	=	$9,509.06
Earnings portion of QHEE distribution in 2014 [($8,200 ÷ $9,509.06) × $4,575.56]	=	$3,945.68
Return of investment portion of QHEE distribution in 2014	=	$4,254.32
Earnings portion of Non-QHEE distribution subject to penalty [($1,309.06 ÷ $9,509.06) × $4,575.56)]	=	$629.89
Return of investment portion of non-QHEE distribution in 2014	=	$679.17

(ii) In years 2011 through 2013 the designated beneficiary includes in gross income the earnings portion of the distributions for tuition. In year 2014 the designated beneficiary includes in gross income the earnings portion of the distribution for tuition, $3,945.68, plus the earnings portion of the distribution that was not used for tuition after reduction for the penalty, i.e. $535.41 ($629.89 minus a 15% penalty of $94.48).

(c) *Change in designated beneficiaries.*—(1) *General rule.*—A change in the designated beneficiary of a QSTP account is not treated as a distribution if the new designated beneficiary is a member of the family of the transferor designated beneficiary. However, any change of designated beneficiary not described in the preceding sentence is treated as a distribution to the account owner, provided the account owner has the authority to change the designated beneficiary. For rules related to a change in the designated beneficiary pursuant to a rollover distribution see §§1.529-1(c) and 1.529-3(a)(2).

(2) *Scholarship program.*—Notwithstanding paragraph (c)(1) of this section, the requirement that the new beneficiary be a member of the family of the transferor beneficiary shall not apply to a change in designated beneficiary of an interest in a QSTP account purchased by a State or local government or an organization described in section 501(c)(3) as part of a scholarship program.

(d) *Aggregation of accounts.*—If an individual is a designated beneficiary of more than one account under a QSTP, the QSTP shall treat all contributions and earnings as allocable to a single account for purposes of calculating the earnings portion of any distribution from that QSTP. For purposes of determining the effect of the distribution on each account, the earnings portion and return of investment in the account portion of the distribution shall be allocated pro rata among the accounts based on total account value as of the close of the current calendar year. [Reg. §1.529-3.]

§1.529-4. Time, form, and manner of reporting distributions from QSTPs and backup withholding.—(a) *Taxable distributions.*—The portion of any distribution made during the calendar year by a QSTP that represents earnings shall be reported by the payor as described in this section.

(b) *Requirement to file return.*—(1) *Form of return.*—A payor must file a return required by this section on Form 1099-G. A payor may use forms containing provisions similar to Form 1099-G if it complies with applicable revenue procedures relating to substitute Forms 1099. A payor must file a separate return for each distributee who receives a taxable distribution.

(2) *Payor.*—For purposes of this section, the term "payor" means the officer or employee having control of the program, or their designee.

(3) *Information included on return.*—A payor must include on Form 1099-G—

(i) The name, address, and taxpayer identifying number (TIN) (as defined in section 7701(a)(41)) of the payor;

(ii) The name, address, and TIN of the distributee;

(iii) The amount of earnings distributed to the distributee in the calendar year; and

(iv) Any other information required by Form 1099-G or its instructions.

(4) *Time and place for filing return.*—A payor must file any return required by this paragraph (b) on or before February 28 of the year following the calendar year in which the distribution is made. A payor must file the return with the IRS office designated in the instructions for Form 1099-G.

(5) *Returns required on magnetic media.*—If a payor is required to file at least 250 returns during the calendar year, the returns must be filed on magnetic media. If a payor is required to file fewer than 250 returns, the prescribed paper form may be used.

(6) *Extension of time to file return.*—For good cause, the Commissioner may grant an extension of time in which to file Form 1099-G for reporting taxable earnings under section 529. The application for extension of time must be submitted in the manner prescribed by the Commissioner.

(c) *Requirement to furnish statement to the distributee.*—(1) *In general.*—A payor that must file a return under paragraph (b) of this section must furnish a statement to the distributee. The requirement to furnish a statement to the distributee will be satisfied if the payor provides the distributee with a copy of the Form 1099-G (or a substitute statement that complies with applicable revenue procedures) containing all the information filed with the Internal Revenue Service and all the legends required by paragraph (c)(2) of this section by the time required by paragraph (c)(3) of this section.

(2) *Information included on statement.*—A payor must include on the statement that it must furnish to the distributee—

(i) The information required under paragraph (b)(3) of this section;

(ii) The telephone number of a person to contact about questions pertaining to the statement; and

(iii) A legend as required on the official Internal Revenue Service Form 1099-G.

(3) *Time for furnishing statement.*—A payor must furnish the statement required by paragraph (c)(1) of this section to the distributee on or before January 31 of the year following the calendar year in which the distribution was made. The statement will be considered furnished to the distributee if it is mailed to the distributee's last known address.

(4) *Extension of time to furnish statement.*—For good cause, the Commissioner may grant an extension of time to furnish statements to distributees of taxable earnings under section 529. The application for extension of time must be submitted in the manner prescribed by the Commissioner.

(d) *Backup withholding.*—Distributions from a QSTP are not subject to backup withholding.

(e) *Effective date.*—The reporting requirements set forth in this section apply to distributions made after December 31, 1998. [Reg. §1.529-4.]

§1.529-5. Estate, gift, and generation-skipping transfer tax rules relating to qualified State tuition programs.—(a) *Gift and generation-skipping transfer tax treatment of contributions after August 20, 1996, and before August 6, 1997.*—A contribution on behalf of a designated beneficiary to a QSTP (or to a program that meets the transitional rule requirements under §1.529-6(b)) after August 20, 1996, and before August 6, 1997, is not treated as a taxable gift. The subsequent waiver of qualified higher education expenses of a designated beneficiary by an educational institution (or the subsequent payment of higher education expenses of a designated beneficiary to an educational institution) under a QSTP is treated as a qualified transfer under section 2503(e) and is not treated as a transfer of property by gift for purposes of section 2501. As such, the contribution is not subject to the generation-skipping transfer tax imposed by section 2601.

(b) *Gift and generation-skipping transfer tax treatment of contributions after August 5, 1997.*—(1) *In general.*—A contribution on behalf of a designated beneficiary to a QSTP (or to a program that meets the transitional rule requirements under §1.529-6(b)) after August 5, 1997, is a completed gift of a present interest in property under section 2503(b) from the person making the contribution to the designated beneficiary. As such, the contribution is eligible for the annual gift tax exclusion provided under section 2503(b). The portion of a contribution excludible from taxable gifts under section 2503(b) also satisfies the requirements of section 2642(c)(2) and, therefore, is also excludible for purposes of the generation-skipping transfer tax imposed under section 2601. A contribution to a QSTP after August 5, 1997, is not treated as a qualified transfer within the meaning of section 2503(e).

(2) *Contributions that exceed the annual exclusion amount.*—(i) Under section 529(c)(2)(B) a donor may elect to take certain contributions to a QSTP into account ratably over a five year period in determining the amount of gifts made during the calendar year. The provision is applicable only with respect to contributions not in excess of five times the section 2503(b) exclusion amount available in the calendar year of the contribution. Any excess may not be taken into account ratably and is treated as a taxable gift in the calendar year of the contribution.

(ii) The election under section 529(c)(2)(B) may be made by a donor and his or her spouse with respect to a gift considered to be made one-half by each spouse under section 2513.

(iii) The election is made on Form 709, Federal Gift Tax Return, for the calendar year in which the contribution is made.

(iv) If in any year after the first year of the five year period described in section 529(c)(2)(B), the amount excludible under section 2503(b) is increased as provided in section 2503(b)(2), the donor may make an additional contribution in any one or more of the four remaining years up to the difference between the exclusion amount as increased and the original exclusion amount for the year or years in which the original contribution was made.

(v) *Example.*—The application of this paragraph (b)(2) is illustrated by the following example:

Example. In Year 1, when the annual exclusion under section 2503(b) is $10,000, P makes a contribution of $60,000 to a QSTP for the benefit of P's child, C. P elects under section 529(c)(2)(B) to account for the gift ratably over a five year period beginning with the calendar year of contribution. P is treated as making an excludible gift of $10,000 in each of Years 1 through 5 and a taxable gift of $10,000 in Year 1. In Year 3, when the annual exclusion is increased to $12,000, P makes an additional contribution for the benefit of C in the amount of $8,000. P is treated as making an excludible gift of $2,000 under section 2503(b); the remaining $6,000 is a taxable gift in Year 3.

(3) *Change of designated beneficiary or rollover.*—(i) A transfer which occurs by reason of a change in the designated beneficiary, or a rollover of credits or account balances from the account of one beneficiary to the account of another beneficiary, is not a taxable gift and is not subject to the generation-skipping transfer tax if the new beneficiary is a member of the family of the old beneficiary, as defined in § 1.529-1(c), and is assigned to the same generation as the old beneficiary, as defined in section 2651.

(ii) A transfer which occurs by reason of a change in the designated beneficiary, or a rollover of credits or account balances from the account of one beneficiary to the account of another beneficiary, will be treated as a taxable gift by the old beneficiary to the new beneficiary if the new beneficiary is assigned to a lower generation than the old beneficiary, as defined in section 2651, regardless of whether the new beneficiary is a member of the family of the old beneficiary. The transfer will be subject to the generation-skipping transfer tax if the new beneficiary is assigned to a generation which is two or more levels lower than the generation assignment of the old beneficiary. The five year averaging rule described in paragraph (b)(2) of this section may be applied to the transfer.

(iii) *Example.*—The application of this paragraph (b)(3) is illustrated by the following example:

Example. In Year 1, P makes a contribution to a QSTP on behalf of P's child, C. In Year 4, P directs that a distribution from the account for the benefit of C be made to an account for the benefit of P's grandchild, G. The rollover distribution is treated as a taxable gift by C to G, because, under section 2651, G is assigned to a generation below the generation assignment of C.

(c) *Estate tax treatment for estates of decedents dying after August 20, 1996, and before June 9, 1997.*—The gross estate of a decedent dying after August 20, 1996, and before June 9, 1997, includes the value of any interest in any QSTP which is attributable to contributions made by the decedent to such program on behalf of a designated beneficiary.

(d) *Estate tax treatment for estates of decedents dying after June 8, 1997.*—(1) *In general.*—Except as provided in paragraph (d)(2) of this section, the gross estate of a decedent dying after June 8, 1997, does not include the value of any interest in a QSTP which is attributable to contributions made by the decedent to such program on behalf of any designated beneficiary.

(2) *Excess contributions.*—In the case of a decedent who made the election under section 529(c)(2)(B) and paragraph (b)(3)(i) of this section who dies before the close of the five year period, that portion of the contribution allocable to calendar years beginning after the date of death of the decedent is includible in the decedent's gross estate.

(3) *Designated beneficiary decedents.*—The gross estate of a designated beneficiary of a QSTP includes the value of any interest in the QSTP. [Reg. § 1.529-5.]

§ 1.529-6. Transition rules.—(a) *Effective date.*—Section 529 is effective for taxable years ending after August 20, 1996, and applies to all contracts entered into or accounts opened on August 20, 1996, or later.

(b) *Programs maintained on August 20, 1996.*—Transition relief is available to a program maintained by a State under which persons could purchase tuition credits, certification or similar rights on behalf of, or make contributions for educational expenses of, a designated beneficiary if the program was in existence on August 20, 1996. Such program must meet the requirements of a QSTP before the later of August 20, 1997, or the first day of the first calendar quarter after the close of the first regular session of the State legislature that begins after August 20, 1996. If a State has a two-year legislative session, each year of such session shall be deemed to be a separate regular session of the State legislature. The program, as in effect on August 20, 1996, shall be treated as a QSTP with respect to contributions (and earnings allocable thereto) pursuant to contracts entered into under the program. This relief is available for contributions (and earnings allocable thereto) made before, and the contracts entered into before, the first date on which the program becomes a QSTP. The provisions of the program, as in effect on August 20, 1996, shall apply in lieu of section 529(b) with respect to such contributions and earnings. A program shall be treated as meeting the transition rule if it conforms to the requirements of section 529, §§ 1.529-1 through 1.529-5 and this section by the date this document is published as final regulations in the Federal Register.

(c) *Retroactive effect.*—No income tax liability will be asserted against a QSTP for any period before the program meets the requirements of section 529, §§ 1.529-1 through 1.529-5 and this section if the program qualifies for the transition relief described in paragraph (b) of this section.

(d) *Contracts entered into and accounts opened before August 20, 1996.*—(1) *In general.*—A QSTP may continue to maintain agreements in connection with contracts entered into and accounts opened before August 20, 1996, without jeopardizing its tax exempt status even if maintaining the agreements is contrary to section 529(b) provided that the QSTP operates in accordance with the restrictions contained in this paragraph (d). However, distributions made by the QSTP, regardless of the terms of any agreement executed before August 20, 1996, are subject to tax according to the rules of § 1.529-3 and subject to the reporting requirements of § 1.529-4.

(2) *Interest in program pledged as security for a loan.*—An interest in the program, or a portion of an interest in the program, may be used as security for a loan if the contract giving rise to the interest was entered into or account was opened prior to August 20, 1996 and the agreement permitted such a pledge.

(3) *Member of the family.*—In the case of an account opened or a contract entered into before August 20, 1996, the rules regarding a change in beneficiary, including the rollover rule in § 1.529-3(a) and the gift tax rule in § 1.529-5(b)(3),

shall be applied by treating any transferee beneficiary permitted under the terms of the account or contract as a member of the family of the transferor beneficiary.

(4) *Eligible educational institution.*—In the case of an account opened or contract entered into before August 20, 1996, an eligible educational institution is an educational institution in which the beneficiary may enroll under the terms of the account or contract. [Reg. § 1.529-6.]

Guidance under Section 529A: Qualified ABLE Programs

Guidance under Section 529A: Qualified ABLE Programs.—Reg. §§ 1.529A-0—1.529A-7, regarding programs under The Stephen Beck, Jr., Achieving a Better Life Experience Act of 2014 and rules under which States or State agencies or instrumentalities may establish and maintain a new type of tax-favored savings program through which contributions may be made to the account of an eligible disabled individual to meet qualified disability expenses, are proposed (published in the Federal Register on June 22, 2015) (corrected August 7, 2015) (REG-102837-15).

Par. 4. An undesignated center heading [Qualified ABLE Programs] is added immediately following § 1.528-10 and §§ 1.529A-0 through 1.529A-7 are added to read as follows:

§ 1.529A-0. Table of contents.—This section lists the following captions contained in §§ 1.529A-1 through 1.529A-7.

(1) In general.

(2) Time and manner of furnishing statement.

(3) Copy of Form 5498-QA.

(e) Request for TIN of designated beneficiary.

(f) Penalties.

(1) Failure to file return.

(2) Failure to furnish TIN.

(g) Effective/applicability date.

§1.529A-6 Reporting of distributions from and termination of an ABLE account.

(a) In general.

(b) Requirement to file return.

(1) Form of return.

(2) Information included on return.

(3) Time and manner of filing return.

(c) Requirement to furnish statement.

(1) In general.

(2) Time and manner of furnishing statement.

(3) Copy of Form 1099-QA.

(d) Request for TIN of contributor(s).

(e) Penalties.

(1) Failure to file return.

(2) Failure to furnish TIN.

(f) Effective/applicability date.

§1.529A-7 Electronic furnishing of statements to designated beneficiaries and contributors.

(a) Electronic furnishing of statements.

(1) In general.

(2) Consent.

(3) Required disclosures.

(4) Format.

(5) Notice.

(6) Access period.

(b) Effective/applicability date.

[Reg. §1.529A-0.]

§1.529A-1. Exempt status of qualified ABLE program and definitions.—(a) *In general.*—A qualified ABLE program described in section 529A is exempt from income tax, except for the tax imposed under section 511 on the unrelated business taxable income of that program.

(b) *Definitions.*—For purposes of section 529A, this section and §§1.529A-2 through 1.529A-7—

(1) *ABLE account* means an account established under a qualified ABLE program and owned by the designated beneficiary of that account.

(2) *Contracting State* means a State without a qualified ABLE program of its own, which, in order to make ABLE accounts available to its residents who are eligible individuals, contracts with another State having such a program.

(3) *Contribution* means any payment directly allocated to an ABLE account for the benefit of a designated beneficiary.

(4) *Designated beneficiary* means the individual who is the owner of the ABLE account and who either established the account at a time when he or she was an eligible individual or who has succeeded the former designated beneficiary in that capacity (successor designated beneficiary). If the designated beneficiary is not able to exercise signature authority over his or her ABLE account or chooses to establish an ABLE account but not exercise signature authority, references to the designated beneficiary with respect to his or her actions include actions by the designated beneficiary's agent under a power of attorney or, if none, a parent or legal guardian of the designated beneficiary.

(5) *Disability certification* means a certification deemed sufficient by the Secretary to establish a certain level of physical or mental impairment that meets the requirements described in §1.529A-2(e).

(6) *Distribution* means any payment from an ABLE account. A *program-to-program transfer* is not a distribution.

(7) *Earnings* attributable to an account are the excess of the total account balance on a particular date over the *investment in the account* as of that date.

(8) *Earnings ratio* means the amount of earnings attributable to the account as of the last day of the calendar year in which the designated beneficiary's taxable year begins, divided by the total account balance on that same date, after taking into account all distributions made during that calendar year and all contributions received during that same year other than those (if any) returned in accordance with §1.529A-2(g)(4).

(9) *Eligible individual* for a taxable year means an individual who either:

(i) Is entitled during that taxable year to benefits based on blindness or disability under title II or XVI of the Social Security Act, provided that such blindness or disability occurred before the date on which the individual attained age 26 (and, for this purpose, an individual is deemed to attain age 26 on his or her 26th birthday); or

(ii) Is the subject of a disability certification filed with the Secretary for that taxable year.

(10) *Excess contribution* means the amount by which the amount contributed during the taxable year of the designated beneficiary to an ABLE account exceeds the limit in effect under section 2503(b) for the calendar year in which the taxable year of the designated beneficiary begins.

(11) *Excess aggregate contribution* means the amount contributed during the taxable year of the designated beneficiary that causes the total of amounts contributed since the establishment of the ABLE account (or of an ABLE account for the same designated beneficiary that was rolled into the current ABLE account) to exceed the limit in effect under section 529(b)(6). In the context of the safe harbor in §1.529A-2(g)(3), however, excess aggregate contribution means a contribution that causes the account balance to exceed the limit in effect under section 529(b)(6).

(12) *Investment in the account* means the sum of all contributions made to the account, reduced by the aggregate amount of contributions included in distributions, if any, made from the account. In the case of a rollover into an ABLE account the amount included as investment in the recipient account is not the full amount of the rollover contribution, but instead is equal to the amount of the rollover contribution that constituted the investment in the account from which the rollover was made.

(13) *Member of the family* means a sibling, whether by blood or by adoption. Such term includes a brother, sister, stepbrother, stepsister, half-brother, and half-sister.

(14) *Program-to-program transfer* means the direct transfer of the entire balance of an ABLE account into an ABLE account of the same designated beneficiary in which the transferor ABLE account is closed upon completion of the transfer, or of part or all of the balance to an ABLE account of another eligible individual who is a member of the family of the former designated beneficiary, without any intervening distribution or deemed distribution to the designated beneficiary.

(15) *Qualified ABLE program* means a program established and maintained by a State, or agency or instrumentality of a State, under which an ABLE account may be established by and for the benefit of the account's designated beneficiary who is an eligible individual, and that meets the requirements described in § 1.529A-2.

(16) *Qualified disability expenses* means any expenses incurred at a time when the designated beneficiary is an eligible individual that relate to the blindness or disability of the designated beneficiary of an ABLE account, including expenses that are for the benefit of the designated beneficiary in maintaining or improving his or her health, independence, or quality of life. *See* § 1.529A-2(h). Any expenses incurred at a time when a designated beneficiary is neither disabled nor blind within the meaning of § 1.529A-1(b)(9)(i) or § 1.529A-2(e)(1)(i) are not qualified disability expenses.

(17) *Rollover* means a contribution to an ABLE account of a designated beneficiary (or of an eligible individual who is a member of the family of the designated beneficiary) of all or a portion of an amount withdrawn from the designated beneficiary's ABLE account, provided the contribution is made within 60 days of the date of the withdrawal and, in the case of a rollover to the designated beneficiary's ABLE account, no rollover has been made to an ABLE account of the designated beneficiary within the prior 12 months.

(c) *Effective/applicability date.*—This section applies to taxable years beginning after December 31, 2014. [Reg. § 1.529A-1.]

§ 1.529A-2. Qualified ABLE program.—(a) *In general.*—A qualified ABLE program is a program established and maintained by a State, or an agency or instrumentality of a State, that satisfies all of the requirements of this section and under which—

(1) An ABLE account may be established for the purpose of meeting the qualified disability expenses of the designated beneficiary of the account;

(2) The designated beneficiary must be a resident of such State or a resident of a Contracting State (as residence is determined under the law of the State of the designated beneficiary's residence);

(3) A designated beneficiary is limited to only one ABLE account at a time except as otherwise provided with respect to program-to-program transfers and rollovers;

(4) Any person may make contributions to such an ABLE account, subject to the limitations described in paragraph (g) of this section; and

(5) Distributions (other than rollovers and returns of contributions as described in paragraph (g)(4) of this section) may be made only to or for the benefit of the designated beneficiary of the ABLE account.

(b) *Established and maintained by a State or agency or instrumentality of a State.*—(1) *Established.*—A program is established by a State or its agency or instrumentality if the program is initiated by State statute or regulation or by an act of a State official or agency with the authority to act on behalf of the State.

(2) *Maintained.*—A program is maintained by a State or an agency or instrumentality of a State if—

(i) The State or its agency or instrumentality sets all of the terms and conditions of the program, including but not limited to who may contribute to the program, who may be a designated beneficiary of the program, and what benefits the program may provide; and

(ii) The State or its agency or instrumentality is actively involved on an ongoing basis in the administration of the program, including supervising the implementation of decisions relating to the investment of assets contributed under the program. Factors that are relevant in determining whether a State or its agency or instrumentality is actively involved in the administration of the program include, but are not limited to: whether the State or its agency or instrumentality provides services to designated beneficiaries that are not provided to persons who are not designated beneficiaries; whether the State or its agency or instrumentality establishes detailed operating rules for administering the program; whether officials of the State or its agency or instrumentality play a substantial role in the operation of the program, including selecting, supervising, monitoring, auditing, and terminating the relationship with any private contractors that provide services under the program; whether the State or its agency or instrumentality holds the private contractors that provide services under the program to the same standards and requirements that apply when private contractors handle funds that belong to the State or its agency or instrumentality or provide services to the State or its agency or instrumentality; whether the State or its agency or instrumentality provides funding for the program; and whether the State or its agency or instrumentality acts as trustee or holds program assets directly or for the benefit of the designated beneficiaries. For example, if the State or its agency or instrumentality thereof exercises the same authority over the funds invested in the program as it does over the investments in or pool of funds of a State employees' defined benefit pension plan, then the State or its agency or instrumentality will be considered actively involved on an ongoing basis in the administration of the program.

(3) *Community Development Financial Institutions (CDFIs).*—Some or all of the services described in paragraphs (b)(2)(i) and (ii) of this section may be performed by one or more Community Development Financial Institutions (CDFIs) with whom the State (or its agency or instrumentality) contracts for that purpose.

(c) *Establishment of an ABLE account.*—(1) *In general.*—Except as otherwise provided in this paragraph (c), a qualified ABLE program must provide that an ABLE account may be established only for an eligible individual under a qualified ABLE program of the State in which the eligible individual is a resident. The qualified ABLE program also may allow the establishment of an ABLE account for an eligible individual who is a resident of a *Contracting State* as defined in §1.529A-1(b)(2). If an eligible individual is unable to establish an ABLE account on his or her own behalf, the ABLE account may be established on behalf of the eligible individual by the eligible individual's agent under a power of attorney or, if none, by a parent or legal guardian of the eligible individual.

(2) *Only one ABLE account.*—(i) *In general.*—Except in the case of rollovers or program-to-program transfers, a designated beneficiary is limited to one ABLE account at a time, regardless of where located. To ensure that this requirement is met, a qualified ABLE program must obtain a verification, signed under penalties of perjury, that the eligible individual has no other existing ABLE account (other than an ABLE account that will terminate with the rollover or program-to-program transfer into the new ABLE account) before that program can permit the establishment of an ABLE account for that eligible individual. In the case of a rollover, the ABLE account from which amounts were rolled must be closed as of the 60th day after the amount was distributed from the ABLE account in order for the account that received the rollover to be treated as an ABLE account.

(ii) *Treatment of additional accounts.*—Except in the case of rollovers or program-to-program transfers, if an ABLE account is established for a designated beneficiary who already has an ABLE account in existence, an additional account will not be treated as an ABLE account. However, if all contributions made to that account are returned in accordance with the rules that apply to excess contributions and excess aggregate contributions under paragraph (g)(4) of this section, the additional account will be treated as never having been established.

(3) *Beneficial interest.*—The eligible individual for whose benefit an ABLE account is established is the designated beneficiary of the account. A person other than the designated beneficiary with signature authority over the account of the designated beneficiary may neither have nor acquire any beneficial interest in the account during the lifetime of the designated beneficiary and must administer the account for the benefit of the designated beneficiary of the account.

(d) *Eligible individual.*—(1) *In general.*—Whether an individual is an eligible individual (as defined in §1.529A-1(b)(9)) is determined for each taxable year, and that determination applies for the entire year. A qualified ABLE program must specify the documentation that an individual must provide, both at the time an ABLE account is established for that individual and thereafter, in order to ensure that the designated beneficiary of the ABLE account is, and continues to be, an eligible individual. For purposes of determining whether an individual is an eligible individual, a disability certification will be deemed to be filed with the Secretary once the qualified ABLE program has received the disability certification (as described in paragraph (e) of this section) or a disability certification has been deemed to have been received under the rules of the qualified ABLE program, which information the qualified ABLE program will file in accordance with the filing requirements under §1.529A-5(c)(2)(iv).

(2) *Frequency of recertification.*—(i) *In general.*—A qualified ABLE program may choose different methods of ensuring a designated beneficiary's status as an eligible individual and may impose different periodic recertification requirements for different types of impairments.

(ii) *Considerations.*—In developing its rules on recertification, a qualified ABLE program may take into consideration whether an impairment is incurable and, if so, the likelihood that a cure may be found in the future. For example, a qualified ABLE program may provide that the initial certification will be deemed to be valid for a stated number of years, which may vary with the type of impairment. If the qualified ABLE program imposes an enforceable obligation on the designated beneficiary or other person with signature authority over the ABLE account to promptly report changes in the designated beneficiary's condition that would result in the designated beneficiary's failing to satisfy the definition of eligible individual, the program also may provide that a certification is valid until the end of the taxable year in which the change in the designated beneficiary's condition occurred.

(3) *Loss of qualification as an eligible individual.*—If the designated beneficiary of an ABLE account ceases to be an eligible individual, then for each taxable year in which the designated beneficiary is not an eligible individual, the account will continue to be an ABLE account, the designated beneficiary will continue to be the designated beneficiary of the ABLE account (and will be referred to as such), and the ABLE account will not be deemed to have been distributed. However, beginning on the first day of the designated beneficiary's first taxable year for which the designated beneficiary does not satisfy the definition of an eligible individual, additional contributions to the designated beneficiary's ABLE account must not be accepted by the qualified ABLE program. Additionally, no amounts incurred during that year and each subsequent year in which the designated beneficiary does not satisfy the definition of an eligible individual will be qualified disability expenses. If the designated beneficiary subsequently again becomes an eligible individual, contributions to the designated beneficiary's ABLE account again may be accepted subject to the contribution limits under section 529A, and expenses incurred that meet the definition of a qualified disability expense will be qualified disability expenses

(e) *Disability certification.*—(1) *In general.*—Except as provided in paragraph (e)(3) of this section or additional guidance described in paragraph (e)(4) of this section, a disability certification with respect to an individual is a certification signed under penalties of perjury by the individual, or by the other individual establishing (or with signature authority over) the ABLE account for the individual, that—

(i) The individual—

(A) Has a medically determinable physical or mental impairment that results in marked and severe functional limitations (as defined in paragraph (e)(2) of this section), and that—

(1) Can be expected to result in death; or

(2) Has lasted or can be expected to last for a continuous period of not less than 12 months; or

(B) Is blind (within the meaning of section 1614(a)(2) of the Social Security Act);

(ii) Such blindness or disability occurred before the date on which the individual attained age 26 (and, for this purpose, an individual is deemed to attain age 26 on his or her 26th birthday); and

(iii) Includes a copy of the individual's diagnosis relating to the individual's relevant impairment or impairments, signed by a physician meeting the criteria of section 1861(r)(1) of the Social Security Act (42 U.S.C. 1395x(r)).

(2) *Marked and severe functional limitations.*—For purposes of paragraph (e)(1) of this section, the phrase "marked and severe functional limitations" means the standard of disability in the Social Security Act for children claiming Supplemental Security Income for the Aged, Blind, and Disabled (SSI) benefits based on disability (*see* 20 CFR 416.906). Specifically, this is a level of severity that meets, medically equals, or functionally equals the severity of any listing in appendix 1 of subpart P of 20 CFR part 404, but without regard to age. (*See* 20 CFR 416.906, 416.924 and 416.926a.) Such phrase also includes any impairment or standard of disability identified in future guidance published in the Internal Revenue Bulletin (*see* § 601.601(d)(2) of this chapter). Consistent with the regulations of the Social Security Administration, the level of severity is determined by taking into account the effect of the individual's prescribed treatment. (*See* 20 CFR 416.930.)

(3) *Compassionate allowance list.*—Conditions listed in the "List of Compassionate Allowances Conditions" maintained by the Social Security Administration (at *www.socialsecurity.gov/compassionateallowances/conditions.htm*) are deemed to meet the requirements of section 529A(e)(1)(B) regarding the filing of a disability certification, if the condition was present before the date on which the individual attained age 26. To establish that an individual with such a condition meets the definition of an eligible individual, the individual must identify the condition and certify to the qualified ABLE program both the presence of the condition and its onset prior to age 26, in a manner specified by the qualified ABLE program.

(4) *Additional guidance.*—Additional guidance on conditions deemed to meet the requirements of section 529A(e)(1)(B) may be identified in future guidance published in the Internal Revenue Bulletin. *See* § 601.601(d)(2) of this chapter.

(5) *Restriction on use of certification.*—No inference may be drawn from a disability certification described in this paragraph (e) for purposes of establishing eligibility for benefits under title II, XVI, or XIX of the Social Security Act.

(f) *Change of designated beneficiary.*—A qualified ABLE program must permit a change in the designated beneficiary of an ABLE account, but only during the life of the designated beneficiary. At the time of the change, the successor designated beneficiary must be an eligible individual.

(g) *Contributions.*—(1) *Permissible property.*—Except in the case of program-to-program transfers, contributions to an ABLE account may only be made in cash. A qualified ABLE program may allow cash contributions to be made in the form of a check, money order, credit card, electronic transfer, or similar method.

(2) *Annual contributions limit.*—A qualified ABLE program must provide that no contribution to an ABLE account will be accepted to the extent such contribution, when added to all other contributions (whether from the designated beneficiary or one or more other persons) to that ABLE account made during the designated beneficiary's taxable year causes the total of such contributions to exceed the amount in effect under section 2503(b) for the calendar year in which the designated beneficiary's taxable year begins. For this purpose, contributions do not include rollovers or program-to-program transfers.

(3) *Cumulative limit.*—(i) *In general.*—A qualified ABLE program maintained by a State or its agency or instrumentality must provide adequate safeguards to prevent aggregate contributions on behalf of a designated beneficiary in excess of the limit established by that State under section 529(b)(6). For purposes of the preceding sentence, aggregate contributions include contributions to any prior ABLE account maintained by any State or its agency or instrumentality for the same designated beneficiary or any prior designated beneficiary.

(ii) *Safe harbor.*—A qualified ABLE program maintained by a State or its agency or instrumentality satisfies the requirement in paragraph (g)(3)(i) of this section if it refuses to accept any additional contribution to an ABLE account once the balance in that account reaches the limit established by that State under section 529(b)(6). Once the account balance falls below such limit, additional contributions again may be accepted, subject to the limits under this paragraph (g)(3)(i) of this section.

(4) *Return of excess contributions and excess aggregate contributions.*—If an excess contribution as defined in § 1.529A-1(b)(10) or an excess aggregate contribution as defined in § 1.529A-1(b)(11) is allocated to or deposited into the ABLE account of a designated beneficiary, a qualified ABLE program must return that excess contribution or excess aggregate contribution, including all net income attributable to that excess contribution or excess aggregate contribution, as determined under the rules set forth in § 1.408-11 (treating an IRA as an ABLE account and returned contributions under section 408(d)(4) as excess contributions or excess aggregate contributions), to the person or persons who made that contribution. An excess contribution or excess aggregate contribution must be returned to its contributor(s) on a last-in-first-out basis until the entire excess contribution or excess aggregate contribution, along with all net income attributable to such contribution, has been returned. Returned contributions must be received by the contributor(s) on or before the due date (including extensions) for the Federal income tax return of the designated beneficiary for the taxable year in which the excess contribution or excess aggregate contribution was made. *See* § 1.529A-3(e) for income tax considerations for the contributor(s). If an excess contribution or excess aggregate contribution and the net income attributable to the excess contribution or excess aggregate contribu-

tion are returned to a contributor other than the designated beneficiary, the qualified ABLE program must notify the designated beneficiary of such return at the time of the return.

(h) *Qualified disability expenses.*—(1) *In general.*—Qualified disability expenses, as defined in § 1.529A-1(b)(16), are expenses incurred that relate to the blindness or disability of the designated beneficiary of the ABLE account and are for the benefit of that designated beneficiary in maintaining or improving his or her health, independence, or quality of life. Such expenses include, but are not limited to, expenses related to the designated beneficiary's education, housing, transportation, employment training and support, assistive technology and related services, personal support services, health, prevention and wellness, financial management and administrative services, legal fees, expenses for oversight and monitoring, and funeral and burial expenses, as well as other expenses that may be identified from time to time in future guidance published in the Internal Revenue Bulletin. *See* § 601.601(d)(2) of this chapter. Qualified disability expenses include basic living expenses and are not limited to items for which there is a medical necessity or which solely benefit a disabled individual. A qualified ABLE program must establish safeguards to distinguish between distributions used for the payment of qualified disability expenses and other distributions, and to permit the identification of the amounts distributed for housing expenses as that term is defined for purposes of the Supplemental Security Income program of the Social Security Administration.

(2) *Example.*—The following example illustrates this paragraph (h):

Example. B, an individual, has a medically determined mental impairment that causes marked and severe limitations on her ability to navigate and communicate. A smart phone would enable B to navigate and communicate more safely and effectively, thereby helping her to maintain her independence and to improve her quality of life. Therefore, the expense of buying, using, and maintaining a smart phone that is used by B would be considered a qualified disability expense.

(i) *Separate accounting.*—A program will not be treated as a qualified ABLE program unless it provides separate accounting for each ABLE account. Separate accounting requires that contributions for the benefit of a designated beneficiary and any earnings attributable thereto must be allocated to that designated beneficiary's account. Whether or not a program provides each designated beneficiary an annual account statement showing the total account balance, the investment in the account, the accrued earnings, and the distributions from the account, the program must give this information to the designated beneficiary upon request.

(j) *Program-to-program transfers.*—A qualified ABLE program may permit a change of qualified ABLE program or a change of designated beneficiary by means of a program-to-program transfer as defined in § 1.529A-1(b)(14). In that event, subject to any contrary provisions or limitations adopted by the qualified ABLE program, rules similar to the rules of § 1.401(a)(31)-1, Q&A-3 and 4 (which apply for purposes of a direct rollover from a qualified plan to an eligible retirement plan) apply for purposes of determining whether an amount is paid in the form of a program-to-program transfer.

(k) *Carryover of attributes.*—Upon a rollover or program-to-program transfer, all of the attributes of the former ABLE account relevant for purposes of calculating the investment in the account and applying the annual and cumulative limits on contributions are applicable to the recipient ABLE account. The portion of the rollover or transfer amount that constituted investment in the account from which the distribution or transfer was made is added to investment in the recipient ABLE account. Similarly, the portion of the rollover or transfer amount that constituted earnings of the account from which the distribution or transfer was made is added to the earnings of the recipient ABLE account.

(l) *Investment direction.*—A program will not be treated as a qualified ABLE program unless it provides that the designated beneficiary of an ABLE account established under such program may direct, whether directly or indirectly, the investment of any contributions to the program (or any earnings thereon) no more than two times in any calendar year.

(m) *No pledging of interest as security.*—A program will not be treated as a qualified ABLE program unless the terms of the program, or a state statute or regulation that governs the program, prohibit any interest in the program or any portion thereof from being used as security for a loan. This restriction includes, but is not limited to, a prohibition on the use of any interest in the ABLE program as security for a loan used to purchase such interest in the program.

(n) *No sale or exchange.*—A qualified ABLE program must ensure that no interest in an ABLE account may be sold or exchanged.

(o) *Change of residence.*—A qualified ABLE program may continue to maintain the ABLE account of a designated beneficiary after that designated beneficiary changes his or her residence to another State.

(p) *Post-death payments.*—A qualified ABLE program must provide that a portion or all of the balance remaining in the ABLE account of a deceased designated beneficiary must be distributed to a State that files a claim against the designated beneficiary or the ABLE account itself with respect to benefits provided to the designated beneficiary under that State's Medicaid plan established under title XIX of the Social Security Act. The payment of such claim (if any) will be made only after providing for the payment from the designated beneficiary's ABLE account of all outstanding payments due for his or her qualified disability expenses, and will be limited to the amount of the total medical assistance paid for the designated beneficiary after the establishment of the ABLE account (the date on which the ABLE account, or any ABLE account from which amounts were rolled or transferred to the ABLE account of the same designated beneficiary, was opened) over the amount of any premiums paid, whether from the ABLE account or otherwise by or on behalf of the designated beneficiary, to a Medicaid Buy-In program under any such State Medicaid plan.

(q) *Reporting requirements.*—A qualified ABLE program must comply with all applicable reporting requirements, including without limitation those described in §§1.529A-5 through 1.529A-7.

(r) *Effective/applicability dates.*—This section applies to taxable years beginning after December 31, 2014. [Reg. §1.529A-2.]

§1.529A-3. Tax treatment.—(a) *Taxation of distributions.*—Each distribution from an ABLE account consists of earnings (computed in accordance with paragraph (c) of this section) and investment in the account. If the total amount distributed from an ABLE account to or for the benefit of the designated beneficiary of that ABLE account during his or her taxable year does not exceed the qualified disability expenses of the designated beneficiary for that year, no amount distributed is includible in the gross income of the designated beneficiary for that year. If the total amount distributed from an ABLE account to or for the benefit of the designated beneficiary of that ABLE account during his or her taxable year exceeds the qualified disability expenses of the designated beneficiary for that year, the distributions from the ABLE account, except to the extent excluded from gross income under this section or any other provision of chapter 1 of the Internal Revenue Code, must be included in the gross income of the designated beneficiary in the manner provided under this section and section 72. In such a case, the earnings portion of the distribution includible in gross income is equal to the earnings portion of the distribution reduced by an amount that bears the same ratio to the earnings portion as the amount of qualified disability expenses during the year bears to the total distributions during the year. For this purpose, all amounts relevant under section 72 are determined as of December 31 of the year in which the designated beneficiary's taxable year begins, and all amounts distributed from an ABLE account to or for the benefit of the designated beneficiary during his or her taxable year are treated as one distribution. If an excess contribution or excess aggregate contribution is returned within the time period required in §1.529A-2(g)(4), any net income distributed is includible in the gross income of the contributor(s) in the taxable year in which the excess contribution or excess aggregate contribution was made.

(b) *Additional exclusions from gross income.*—(1) *Rollover.*—A rollover as defined in §1.529A-1(b)(17) is not includible in gross income under paragraph (a) of this section.

(2) *Program-to-program transfers.*—A program-to-program transfer as defined in §1.529A-1(b)(14) is not a distribution and is not includible in gross income under paragraph (a) of this section.

(3) *Change of designated beneficiary.*—(i) *In general.*—A change of designated beneficiary of an ABLE account is not treated as a distribution for purposes of section 529A, and is not includible in gross income under paragraph (a) of this section, if the successor designated beneficiary is—

(A) An eligible individual for such calendar year; and

(B) A member of the family of the former designated beneficiary. 58

(ii) *Other designated beneficiary changes.*—In the case of any change of designated beneficiary not described in paragraph (b)(3)(i) of this section, the former designated beneficiary of that ABLE account will be treated as having received a distribution of the fair market value of the assets in that ABLE account on the date on which the change is made to the new designated beneficiary.

(4) *Payments to creditors post-death.*—Distributions made after the death of the designated beneficiary in payment of outstanding obligations due for qualified disability expenses of the designated beneficiary are not includible in the gross income of the designated beneficiary or his or her estate. Included among these obligations is the post-death payment of any part of a claim filed against the designated beneficiary or the ABLE account by a State under a State Medicaid plan.

(c) *Computation of earnings.*—The earnings portion of a distribution is equal to the product of the amount of the distribution and the earnings ratio, as defined in §1.529A-1(b)(8). The balance of the distribution (the amount of the distribution minus the earnings portion of that distribution) is the portion of that distribution that constitutes the return of investment in the account.

(d) *Additional tax on amounts includible in gross income.*—(1) *In general.*—If any amount of a distribution from an ABLE account is includible in the gross income of a person for any taxable year under paragraph (a) of this section (the "includible amount"), the tax imposed on that person by Chapter 1 of the Internal Revenue Code shall be increased by an amount equal to 10 percent of the includible amount.

(2) *Exceptions.*—(i) *Distributions on or after the death of the designated beneficiary.*—Paragraph (d)(1) of this section does not apply to any distribution made from the ABLE account on or after the death of the designated beneficiary to the estate of the designated beneficiary, to an heir or legatee of the designated beneficiary, or to a creditor described in paragraph (b)(4) of this section.

(ii) *Returned excess contributions and additional accounts.*—Paragraph (d)(1) of this section does not apply to any return made in accordance with §1.529A-2(g)(4) of an excess contribution, excess aggregate contribution, or additional account.

(e) *Tax on excess contributions.*—Under section 4973(h), a contribution to an ABLE account in excess of the annual contributions limit described in §1.529A-2(g)(2) is subject to an excise tax in an amount equal to 6 percent of the excess contribution. However, if the excess contribution is returned in accordance with the provisions of §1.529A-2(g)(4), it is treated as an amount not contributed.

(f) *Filing requirements.*—A qualified ABLE program is not required to file Form 990, "Return of Organization Exempt From Income Tax," Form 1041, "U.S. Income Tax Return for Estates and Trusts," or Form 1120, "U.S. Corporation Income Tax Return." However, a qualified ABLE program is required to file Form 990-T, "Exempt Organization Business Income Tax Return," if such filing would be required under the rules of §§1.6012-2(e) and 1.6012-3(a)(5) if the ABLE program were an organization described in those sections.

(g) *Effective/applicability dates.*—This section applies to taxable years beginning after December 31, 2014. [Reg. § 1.529A-3.]

§ 1.529A-4. Gift, estate, and generation-skipping transfer taxes.—(a) *Contributions.*—(1) *In general.*—Each contribution by a person to an ABLE account other than by the designated beneficiary of that account is treated as a completed gift to the designated beneficiary of the account for gift tax purposes. Under the applicable gift tax rules, a contribution from a corporation, partnership, trust, estate, or other entity is treated as a gift by the shareholders, partners, or other beneficial owners in proportion to their respective ownership interests in the entity. *See* § 25.2511-1(c) and (h). A gift into an ABLE account is not treated as either a gift of a future interest in property, or a qualified transfer under section 2503(e). To the extent a contributor's gifts to the designated beneficiary, including gifts paid into the designated beneficiary's ABLE account, do not exceed the annual limit in section 2503(b), the contribution is not subject to gift tax. This provision, however, does not change any other provision applicable to the transfer. For example, a contribution by the employer of the designated beneficiary's parent continues to constitute earned income to the parent and then a gift by the parent to the designated beneficiary.

(2) *Generation-skipping transfer (GST) tax.*—To the extent the contribution into an ABLE account is a nontaxable gift for gift tax purposes, the inclusion ratio for purposes of the GST tax will be zero pursuant to section 2642(c)(1).

(3) *Designated beneficiary as contributor.*—A designated beneficiary may make a contribution to fund his or her own ABLE account. That contribution is not a gift. However, in the event of any change of designated beneficiary, the portion of the then fair market value of the ABLE account attributable to that contribution and any earnings attributable to that contribution will constitute a gift by the designated beneficiary to the successor designated beneficiary, and the usual gift and GST tax rules will apply.

(b) *Distributions.*—No distribution from an ABLE account to or for the benefit of the designated beneficiary is treated as a taxable gift to that designated beneficiary.

(c) *Change of designated beneficiary.*—Neither gift tax nor generation-skipping transfer tax applies to a change of designated beneficiary if the successor designated beneficiary is both an eligible individual and a member of the family (as described in § 1.529A-1(b)(13)) of the designated beneficiary. The previous sentence does not apply to any other change of designated beneficiary.

(d) *Transfer tax on death of designated beneficiary.*—Upon the death of the designated beneficiary, the designated beneficiary's ABLE account is includible in his or her gross estate for estate tax purposes under section 2031. The payment of outstanding qualified disability expenses and the payment of certain claims made by a State under its Medicaid plan may be deductible for estate tax purposes if the requirements of section 2053 are satisfied.

(e) *Effective/applicability date.*—This section applies to taxable years beginning after December 31, 2014. [Reg. § 1.529A-4.]

§ 1.529A-5. Reporting of the establishment of and contributions to an ABLE account.—(a) *In general.*—A filer defined in paragraph (b)(1) of this section must, with respect to each ABLE account—

(1) File an annual information return, as described in paragraph (c) of this section, with the Internal Revenue Service; and

(2) Furnish an annual statement, as described in paragraph (d) of this section, to the designated beneficiary of the ABLE account.

(b) *Additional definitions.*—In addition to the definitions in § 1.529A-1(b), the following definitions also apply for purposes of this section—

(1) *Filer* means the State or its agency or instrumentality that establishes and maintains the qualified ABLE program under which an ABLE account is established. The filing may be done by either an officer or employee of the State or its agency or instrumentality having control of the qualified ABLE program, or the officer's or employee's designee.

(2) *TIN* means taxpayer identification number as defined in section 7701(a)(41).

(c) *Requirement to file return.*—(1) *Form of return.*—For purposes of reporting the information described in paragraph (c)(2) of this section, the filer must file Form 5498-QA, "ABLE Account Contribution Information," or any successor form, together with Form 1096, "Annual Summary and Transmittal of U.S. Information Returns."

(2) *Information included on return.*—With respect to each ABLE account, the filer must include on the return—

(i) The name, address, and TIN of the designated beneficiary of the ABLE account;

(ii) The name, address, and TIN of the filer;

(iii) Information regarding the establishment of the ABLE account, as required by the form and its instructions;

(iv) Information regarding the disability certification or other basis for eligibility of the designated beneficiary, as required by the form and its instructions. For further information regarding eligibility and disability certification, *see* § 1.529A-2(d) and (e), respectively;

(v) The total amount of any contributions made with respect to the ABLE account during the calendar year;

(vi) The fair market value of the ABLE account as of the last day of the calendar year; and

(vii) Any other information required by the form, its instructions, or published guidance. *See* §§ 601.601(d) and 601.602 of this chapter.

(3) *Time and manner of filing return.*—(i) *In general.*—Except as provided in paragraph (c)(3)(ii) of this section, the information returns required under this paragraph must be filed on or before May 31 of the year following the calendar year with respect to which the return is being filed, in accordance with the forms and their instructions.

(ii) *Extensions of time.*—*See* §§ 1.6081-1 and 1.6081-8 of this chapter for rules relating to extensions of time to file information returns required in this section.

(iii) *Electronic filing.*—*See* § 301.6011-2 of this chapter for rules relating to electronic filing.

(iv) *Substitute forms.*—The filer may file the returns required under this paragraph (c) on a substitute form. A substitute form must comply with applicable revenue procedures (*see* § 601.601(d)(2) of this chapter) or other guidance published by the IRS, including Publication 1179, "General Rules and Specifications for Substitute Forms 1096, 1098, 1099, 5498, and Certain Other Information Returns."

(d) *Requirement to furnish statement.*—(1) *In general.*—The filer must furnish a statement to the designated beneficiary of the ABLE account for which it is required to file a Form 5498-QA (or any successor form). The statement must include—

(i) The information required under paragraph (c)(2) of this section;

(ii) A legend that identifies the statement as important tax information that is being furnished to the Internal Revenue Service; and

(iii) The name and address of the office or department of the filer that is the information contact for questions regarding the ABLE account to which the Form 5498-QA relates.

(2) *Time and manner of furnishing statement.*—(i) *In general.*—Except as provided in paragraph (d)(2)(ii) of this section, the filer must furnish the statement described in paragraph (d)(1) of this section to the designated beneficiary on or before March 15 of the year following the calendar year with respect to which the statement is being furnished. If mailed, the statement must be sent to the designated beneficiary's last known address. The statement may be furnished electronically, as provided in § 1.529A-7.

(ii) *Extensions of time.*—The Internal Revenue Service may grant an extension of time to furnish statements required in this section upon a showing of good cause. *See* the instructions to Form 5498-QA.

(3) *Copy of Form 5498-QA.*—The filer may satisfy the requirement of this paragraph (d) by furnishing either a copy of Form 5498-QA (or successor form) or another document that contains the information required by paragraph (d)(1) of this section, if the document complies with applicable revenue procedures (*see* § 601.601(d)(2) of this chapter) or other guidance published by the IRS relating to substitute statements, including Publication 1179, "General Rules and Specifications for Substitute Forms 1096, 1098, 1099, 5498, and Certain Other Information Returns."

(e) *Request for TIN of designated beneficiary.*—The filer must request the TIN of the designated beneficiary at the time the ABLE account is opened if the filer does not already have a record of the designated beneficiary's correct TIN. The filer must clearly notify the designated beneficiary that the law requires the designated beneficiary to furnish a TIN so that it may be included on an information return to be filed by the filer. The designated beneficiary may provide his or her TIN in any manner including orally, in writing, or electronically. If the TIN is furnished in writing, no particular form is required. Form W-9, "Request for Taxpayer Identification Number and Certification," may be used, or the request may be incorporated into the forms related to the establishment of the ABLE account.

(f) *Penalties.*—(1) *Failure to file return.*—The section 6693 penalty may apply to the filer that fails to file information returns at the time and in the manner required by this section, unless it is shown that such failure is due to reasonable cause. *See* section 6693 and the regulations thereunder.

(2) *Failure to furnish TIN.*—The section 6723 penalty may apply to any designated beneficiary who fails to furnish his or her TIN to the filer. *See* section 6723, and the regulations thereunder, for rules relating to the penalty for failure to furnish a TIN.

(g) *Effective/applicability date.*—The rules of this section apply to information returns required to be filed, and payee statements required to be furnished, after December 31, 2015. [Reg. § 1.529A-5.]

§ 1.529A-6. Reporting of distributions from and termination of an ABLE account.—(a) *In general.*—The filer as defined in § 1.529A-5(b)(1) must, with respect to each ABLE account from which any distribution is made or which is terminated during the calendar year—

(1) File an annual information return, as described paragraph (b) of this section, with the Internal Revenue Service; and

(2) Furnish an annual statement, as described in paragraph (c) of this section, to the designated beneficiary of the ABLE account and to each contributor who received a returned contribution in accordance with § 1.529A-2(g)(4) attributable to the calendar year.

(b) *Requirement to file return.*—(1) *Form of return.*—For purposes of reporting the information in paragraph (b)(2) of this section, the filer must file Form 1099-QA, "Distributions from ABLE Accounts," or any successor form, together with Form 1096, "Annual Summary and Transmittal of U.S. Information Returns."

(2) *Information included on return.*—The filer must include on the return—

(i) The name, address, and TIN of the designated beneficiary of the ABLE account or of any contributor who received a returned contribution in accordance with § 1.529A-2(g)(4) attributable to the calendar year, as applicable;

(ii) The name, address, and TIN of the filer;

(iii) The aggregate amount of distributions from the ABLE account during the calendar year;

(iv) Information as to basis and earnings with respect to such distributions or returns of contributions;

(v) Information regarding termination (if any) of the ABLE account;

(vi) Information regarding each rollover and any program-to-program transfer to or from the ABLE account during the designated beneficiary's taxable year;

(vii) Whether the return is being furnished to the designated beneficiary or to a contributor; and

(viii) Any other information required by the form, its instructions, or published guidance. *See* § § 601.601(d) and 601.602 of this chapter.

(3) *Time and manner of filing return.*—(i) *In general.*—Except as provided in paragraph (b)(3)(ii) of this section, the Forms 1099-QA and 1096 must be filed on or before February 28 (March 31 if filing electronically) of the year following the calendar year with respect to

which the return is being filed, in accordance with the forms and their instructions.

(ii) *Extensions of time.—See* §§1.6081-1 and 1.6081-8 of this chapter for rules relating to extensions of time to file information returns required in this section.

(iii) *Electronic filing.—See* §301.6011-2 of this chapter for rules relating to electronic filing.

(iv) *Substitute forms.*—The filer may file the return required under this paragraph (b) on a substitute form. A substitute form must comply with applicable revenue procedures (*see* §601.601(d)(2) of this chapter) or other guidance published by the IRS, including Publication 1179, "General Rules and Specifications for Substitute Forms 1096, 1098, 1099, 5498, and Certain Other Information Returns."

(c) *Requirement to furnish statement.*—(1) *In general.*—The filer must furnish a statement to the designated beneficiary and each contributor (if any) of the ABLE account for which it is required to file a Form 1099-QA (or any successor form). The statement must include—

(i) The information required under paragraph (b)(2) of this section.

(ii) A legend that identifies the statement as important tax information that is being furnished to the Internal Revenue Service;

(iii) The name and address of the office or department of the filer that is the information contact for questions regarding the ABLE account to which the Form 1099-QA relates.

(2) *Time and manner of furnishing statement.*—(i) *In general.*—Except as provided in paragraph (c)(2)(ii) of this section, a filer must furnish the statement described in paragraph (c)(1) of this section to the designated beneficiary on or before January 31 of the year following the calendar year with respect to which the statement is being furnished. If mailed, the statement must be sent to the recipient's last known address. The statement may be furnished electronically, as provided in §1.529A-7.

(ii) *Extensions of time.*—The Internal Revenue Service may grant an extension of time to furnish statements required in this section upon a showing of good cause. *See* the instructions to Form 1099-QA.

(3) *Copy of Form 1099-QA.*—A filer may satisfy the requirement of this paragraph (c) by furnishing either a copy of Form 1099-QA (or successor form) or another document that contains the information required by paragraph (c)(1) of this section and that complies with applicable revenue procedures (*see* §601.601(d)(2) of this chapter) or other guidance published by the IRS relating to substitute statements, including Publication 1179, "General Rules and Specifications for Substitute Forms 1096, 1098, 1099, 5498, and Certain Other Information Returns."

(d) *Request for TIN of contributor(s).*—A filer must request the TIN for each contributor to the ABLE account at the time a contribution is made, if the filer does not already have a record of that person's correct TIN. The filer must clearly notify each contributor to the account that the law requires that person to furnish a TIN so that it may be included on an information return to be filed by the filer. The contributor may provide his or her TIN in any manner including orally, in writing, or electronically. If the TIN is furnished in writing, no particular form is required. Form W-9, "Request for Taxpayer Identification Number and Certification," may be used, or the request may be incorporated into the forms related to the establishment of the ABLE account.

(e) *Penalties.*—(1) *Failure to file return.*—The section 6693 penalty may apply to a filer that fails to file information returns at the time and in the manner required by this section, unless it is shown that such failure is due to reasonable cause. *See* section 6693 and the regulations thereunder.

(2) *Failure to furnish TIN.*—The section 6723 penalty may apply to any contributor who fails to furnish his or her TIN to the filer. *See* section 6723, and the regulations thereunder, for rules relating to the penalty for failure to furnish a TIN.

(f) *Effective/applicability date.*—The rules of this section apply to information returns required to be filed, and payee statements required to be furnished, after December 31, 2015. [Reg. §1.529A-6.]

§1.529A-7. Electronic furnishing of statements to designated beneficiaries and contributors.—(a) *Electronic furnishing of statements.*—(1) *In general.*—A filer required under §1.529A-5 or §1.529A-6 of this chapter to furnish a written statement to a designated beneficiary of or contributor to an ABLE account may furnish the statement in an electronic format in lieu of a paper format. A filer who meets the requirements of paragraphs (a)(2) through (6) of this section is treated as furnishing the required statement.

(2) *Consent.*—(i) *In general.*—The recipient of the statement must have affirmatively consented to receive the statement in an electronic format. The consent may be made electronically in any manner that reasonably demonstrates that the recipient can access the statement in the electronic format in which it will be furnished to the recipient. Alternatively, the consent may be made in a paper document if it is confirmed electronically.

(ii) *Withdrawal of consent.*—The consent requirement of this paragraph (a)(2) is not satisfied if the recipient withdraws the consent and the withdrawal takes effect before the statement is furnished. The filer may provide that a withdrawal of consent takes effect either on the date it is received by the filer or on another date no more than 60 days later. The filer also may provide that a request for a paper statement will be treated as a withdrawal of consent.

(iii) *Change in hardware or software requirements.*—If a change in the hardware or software required to access the statement creates a material risk that the recipient will not be able to access the statement, the filer must, prior to changing the hardware or software, provide the recipient with a notice. The notice must describe the revised hardware and software required to access the statement and inform the recipient that a new consent to receive the statement in the revised electronic format must be provided to the filer if the recipient does not want to withdraw the consent. After implementing the revised hardware and software, the filer must obtain from the recipient, in the manner described in paragraph (a)(2)(i) of this section, a new consent or confirmation of consent to receive the statement electronically.

(iv) *Examples.*—For purposes of the following examples that illustrate the rules of this paragraph (a)(2), assume that the requirements of § 1.529A-7(a)(3) have been met:

Example 1. Filer F sends Recipient R a letter stating that R may consent to receive statements required under § 1.529A-5 or § 1.529A-6 electronically on a Web site instead of in a paper format. The letter contains instructions explaining how to consent to receive the statements electronically by accessing the Web site, downloading the consent document, completing the consent document, and e-mailing the completed consent back to F. The consent document posted on the Web site uses the same electronic format that F will use for the electronically furnished statements. R reads the instructions and submits the consent in the manner provided in the instructions. R has consented to receive the statements electronically in the manner described in paragraph (a)(2)(i) of this section.

Example 2. Filer F sends Recipient R an e-mail stating that R may consent to receive statements required under § 1.529A-5 or § 1.529A-6 electronically instead of in a paper format. The e-mail contains an attachment instructing R how to consent to receive the statements electronically. The e-mail attachment uses the same electronic format that F will use for the electronically furnished statements. R opens the attachment, reads the instructions, and submits the consent in the manner provided in the instructions. R has consented to receive the statements electronically in the manner described in paragraph (a)(2)(i) of this section.

Example 3. Filer F posts a notice on its Web site stating that Recipient R may receive statements required under § 1.529A-5 or § 1.529A-6 electronically instead of in a paper format. The Web site contains instructions on how R may access a secure Web page and consent to receive the statements electronically. By accessing the secure Web page and giving consent, R has consented to receive the statements electronically in the manner described in paragraph (a)(2)(i) of this section.

(3) *Required disclosures.*—(i) *In general.*—Prior to, or at the time of, a recipient's consent, the filer must provide to the recipient a clear and conspicuous disclosure statement containing each of the disclosures described in paragraphs (a)(3)(ii) through (viii) of this section.

(ii) *Paper statement.*—The recipient must be informed that the statement will be furnished on paper if the recipient does not consent to receive it electronically.

(iii) *Scope and duration of consent.*—The recipient must be informed of the scope and duration of the consent. For example, the recipient must be informed whether the consent applies to statements furnished every year after the consent is given until it is withdrawn in the manner described in paragraph (a)(3)(v)(A) of this section, or only to the statement required to be furnished on or before the due date immediately following the date on which the consent is given.

(iv) *Post-consent request for a paper statement.*—The recipient must be informed of any procedure for obtaining a paper copy of the recipient's statement after giving the consent and whether a request for a paper statement will be treated as a withdrawal of consent.

(v) *Withdrawal of consent.*—The recipient must be informed that—

(A) The recipient may withdraw a consent by writing (electronically or on paper) to the person or department whose name, mailing address, and e-mail address is provided in the disclosure statement;

(B) The filer will confirm, in writing (either electronically or on paper), the withdrawal and the date on which it takes effect; and

(C) A withdrawal of consent does not apply to a statement that was furnished electronically in the manner described in this paragraph (a) before the date on which the withdrawal of consent takes effect.

(vi) *Notice of termination.*—The recipient must be informed of the conditions under which a filer will cease furnishing statements electronically to the recipient.

(vii) *Updating information.*—The recipient must be informed of the procedures for updating the information needed by the filer to contact the recipient. The filer must inform the recipient of any change in the filer's contact information.

(viii) *Hardware and software requirements.*—The recipient must be provided with a description of the hardware and software required to access, print, and retain the statement, and the date when the statement will no longer be available on the Web site.

(4) *Format.*—The electronic version of the statement must contain all required information and comply with applicable revenue procedures or other guidance published by the IRS relating to substitute statements to recipients, including Publication 1179, "General Rules and Specifications for Substitute Forms 1096, 1098, 1099, 5498, and Certain Other Information Returns."

(5) *Notice.*—(i) *In general.*—If the statement is furnished on a Web site, the filer must notify the recipient that the statement is posted on a Web site. The notice may be delivered by mail, electronic mail, or in person. The notice must provide instructions on how to access and print the statement. The notice must include the following statement in capital letters, "IMPORTANT TAX RETURN DOCUMENT AVAILABLE." If the notice is provided by electronic mail, the foregoing statement must be on the subject line of the electronic mail.

(ii) *Undeliverable electronic address.*—If an electronic notice described in paragraph (a)(5)(i) of this section is returned as undeliverable, and the correct electronic address cannot be obtained from the filer's records or from the recipient, then the filer must furnish the notice by mail or in person within 30 days after the electronic notice is returned.

(iii) *Corrected statements.*—If the filer has corrected a recipient's statement that was furnished electronically, the filer must furnish the corrected statement to the recipient electronically. If the recipient's statement was furnished through a Web site posting and the filer has corrected the statement, the filer must notify the recipient that it has posted the corrected statement on the Web site within 30 days of such posting in the manner described in paragraph (a)(5)(i) of this section. The corrected statement or the notice must be furnished by mail or in person if—

(A) An electronic notice of the Web site posting of an original statement or the corrected statement was returned as undeliverable; and

(B) The recipient has not provided a new e-mail address.

(6) *Access period.*—Statements furnished on a Web site must be retained on the Web site through October 15 of the year following the calendar year to which the statements relate (or the first business day after such October 15 if October 15 falls on a Saturday, Sunday, or legal holiday). The filer must maintain access to corrected statements that are posted on the Web site through October 15 of the year following the calendar year to which the statements relate (or the first business day after such October 15 if October 15 falls on a Saturday, Sunday, or legal holiday) or the date 90 days after the corrected statements are posted, whichever is later. The rules in this paragraph (a)(6) do not replace the filer's obligation to keep records under section 6001 and § 1.6001-1(a) of this chapter.

(b) *Effective/applicability date.*—This section applies to statements required to be furnished after December 31, 2015. [Reg. § 1.529A-7.]

CORPORATIONS USED TO AVOID INCOME TAX ON SHAREHOLDERS

Foreign Corporations: Tax Years

Foreign Corporations: Tax Years.—Reproduced below are the texts of proposed Reg. § 1.563-3 and a proposed amendment to Reg. § 1.563-3, relating to the required taxable year of those foreign corporations beginning after July 10, 1989 (published in the Federal Register on January 5, 1993).

□ Par. 5. Section 1.563-3 is redesignated as Reg. § 1.563-4 and a new Reg. § 1.563-3 is added as follows:

§ 1.563-3. Foreign personal holding company tax; procedure for designation of a dividend as being taken into account under section 563(c).—In determining the deduction for dividends paid under section 561, a foreign personal holding company may designate a dividend paid after the close of any taxable year beginning after July 10, 1989, and on or before the 15th day of the third month following the close of that taxable year, as being taken into account under section 563(c) and this section by making the designation on an attachment to Schedule N of Form 5471. The designation must set forth the date of the distribution and a statement indicating the extent to which the distribution is being taken into account under section 563(c), and any other information required by Form 5471 and the instructions to that form. The designation must be signed and dated by a duly authorized corporate officer of the foreign personal holding company. If a foreign personal holding company took a dividend paid into account under section 563(c) for any taxable year beginning after July 10, 1989, and ending prior to [INSERT DATE THAT IS 120 DAYS AFTER DATE OF PUBLICATION OF FINAL REGULATIONS IN THE FEDERAL REGISTER] but did not follow the procedures set forth in this paragraph, then a designation on an attachment to Schedule N of Form 5471 setting forth the information required above should be signed in a manner set forth above and attached to the first Form 5471 and, if applicable, Form 1120F, to be filed after [INSERT DATE THAT IS 120 DAYS AFTER DATE OF PUBLICATION OF FINAL REGULATIONS IN THE FEDERAL REGISTER.][Reg. § 1.563-3.]

BANKING INSTITUTIONS

Minimum Addition to Reserves for Losses: Mutual Savings Banks

Minimum Addition to Reserves for Losses: Mutual Savings Banks.—Reproduced below is the text of a proposed amendment of Reg. § 1.581-2, relating to the minimum addition to reserves for losses on loans of mutual savings banks and other organizations (published in the Federal Register on December 19, 1983).

§ 1.581-2. Mutual savings banks, building and loan associations, and cooperative banks.

□ Par. 2. Section 1.581-2(b) is amended by removing the phrase "See section 593 and § 1.593-1" and inserting in its place "See section 593 and § § 1.593-1 through 1.593-8".

Imputed Interest: Original Issue Discount: Safe Haven Rates

Imputed Interest: Original Issue Discount: Safe Haven Interest Rates.—Reproduced below is the text of a proposed amendment of Reg. § 1.582-1, relating to (1) the tax treatment of debt instruments issued after July 1, 1982, that contain original issue discount, (2) the imputation of and the accounting for interest with respect to sales and exchanges of property occurring after December 31, 1984, and (3) safe haven interest rates for loans or advances between commonly controlled taxpayers and safe haven leases between such taxpayers (published in the Federal Register on April 8, 1986).

§ 1.582-1. Bad debts, losses, and gains with respect to securities held by financial institutions.

□ Par. 14. In § 1.582-1, paragraphs (d) and (e)(3)(i) are amended by removing the phrase "section 1232" from each place that it appears and adding in its place the phrase "sections 1271 through 1275".

Minimum Addition to Reserves for Losses: Mutual Savings Banks

Minimum Addition to Reserves for Losses: Mutual Savings Banks.—Reproduced below are the texts of proposed amendments to Reg. §§1.591-1, relating to the minimum addition to reserves for losses on loans of mutual savings banks and other organizations (published in the Federal Register on December 19, 1983).

☐ Par. 3. Section 1.591-1 is amended as follows:

1. Paragraph (a)(2) is amended by inserting "or a mutual savings bank described in section 591(b)" after "domestic building and loan association".

2. Paragraph (c)(2) is removed and paragraph (c)(1) is redesignated as paragraph (c)(2).

3. Paragraph (c)(2) as so redesignated is amended by inserting "and before the first day of the taxpayer's first taxable year ending after August 13, 1981," after "October 16, 1962," and by removing "; and" and inserting a period in lieu thereof.

4. A new paragraph (c)(1) is added which reads as follows:

§1.591-1. Deduction for dividends paid on deposits.

* * *

(c) *Effective date.*—* * *

(1) Dividends or interest paid or credited during a taxable year ending after August 13, 1981, by any taxpayer which (at the time of such payment or credit) qualifies as (i) a mutual savings bank (including a mutual savings bank which has capital stock represented by shares and which is subject to, and operates under, Federal or State laws relating to mutual savings banks), (ii) a domestic building and loan association (as defined in section 7701(a)(19)), (iii) a cooperative bank (as defined in section 7701(a)(32)), or (iv) any other savings institution chartered and supervised as a savings and loan or similar association under Federal or State law; and

* * *

NATURAL RESOURCES

Depletion: Lease of Mineral Property: Uniform Capitalization Rules: Treatment of Delay Rental

Depletion: Lease of Mineral Property: Uniform Capitalization Rules: Treatment of Delay Rental.—Amendments to Reg. §1.612-3, conforming regulations relating to delay rental to the requirements of Code Sec. 263A relating to capitalization and inclusion in inventory of costs of certain expenses, are proposed (published in the Federal Register on February 8, 2000) (REG-103882-99).

☐ Par. 2. In §1.612-3, the second sentence of paragraph (c)(2) is removed and two sentences are added in its place to read as follows:

§1.612-3. Depletion; treatment of bonus and advanced royalty.

* * *

(c) * * *

(2) * * * To the extent the delay rental is not required to be capitalized under section 263A and the regulations thereunder, the payor may at his election deduct such amount or under section 266 and the regulations thereunder, charge it to depletable capital account. The second sentence of this paragraph (c)(2) applies to delay rentals paid with respect to leasing transactions entered into on or after the date these regulations are published as final regulations in the Federal Register.

* * *

Partners and Partnerships: Sales or Exchanges: Certain Distributions

Partners and Partnerships: Sales or Exchanges: Certain Distributions.—Amendments to Reg. §1.617-4, prescribing how a partner should measure its interest in a partnership's unrealized receivables and inventory items, and that provide guidance regarding the tax consequences of a distribution that causes a reduction in that interest, are proposed (published in the Federal Register on November 3, 2014) (REG-151416-06).

☐ Par. 2. Section 1.617-4 is amended by adding a new sentence at the end of paragraph (c)(3)(ii)(*g*) to read as follows:

§1.617-4. Treatment of gain from disposition of certain mining property.

* * *

(c) * * *

(3) * * *

(ii) * * *

(*g*) * * * *See also* §§1.732-1(c)(2)(iii) and 1.755-1(c)(2)(iii) for rules governing the application of section 617 to partnership property in certain situations.

* * *

Imputed Interest: Original Issue Discount: Safe Haven Rates

Imputed Interest: Original Issue Discount: Safe Haven Interest Rates.—Reproduced below is the text of a proposed amendment of Reg. §1.636-1, relating to (1) the tax treatment of debt instruments issued after July 1, 1982, that contain original issue discount, (2) the imputation of and the accounting for interest with respect to sales and exchanges of property occurring after December 31, 1984, and (3) safe haven interest rates for loans or advances between commonly controlled taxpayers and safe haven leases between such taxpayers (published in the Federal Register on April 8, 1986).

☐ Par. 15. In §1.636-1, paragraph (a)(1)(ii) is amended by removing the phrase "section 1232" and adding in its place the phrase "section 1271".

§1.636-1. Treatment of production payments as loans.

* * *

ESTATES, TRUSTS, BENEFICIARIES, AND DECEDENTS

Electing Small Business Trusts: Potential Current Beneficiaries: Nonresident Aliens

Electing Small Business Trusts: Potential Current Beneficiaries: Nonresident Aliens.—Amendments to Reg. §1.641(c)-1, regarding the recent statutory expansion of the class of permissible potential current beneficiaries of an electing small business trust to include nonresident aliens, are proposed (published in the Federal Register on April 19, 2019) (REG-117062-18).

Par. 2. Section 1.641(c)-1 is amended by:

1. Revising paragraphs (b)(1) and (2).
2. Adding a sentence to the end of paragraph (k).
3. In paragraph (l), designating *Examples 1* through *5* as paragraphs (l)(1) through (5).
4. In newly designated paragraph (l)(3)(i), removing the language "*Example 2*" and adding "*Example 2* in paragraph (l)(2) of this section" in its place.
5. Adding paragraph (l)(6).

The revisions and additions read as follows:

§1.641(c)-1. Electing small business trust.

* * *

(b) * * *

(1) *Grantor portion.*—(i) *In general.*—Subject to paragraph (b)(1)(ii) of this section, the grantor portion of an ESBT is the portion of the trust that is treated as owned by the grantor or another person under subpart E of the Code.

(ii) *Nonresident alien deemed owner.*—If, pursuant to section 672(f)(2)(A)(ii), the deemed owner of a grantor portion of the ESBT is a nonresident alien, as defined in section 7701(b)(1)(B) (NRA), the items of income, deduction, and credit from that grantor portion must be reallocated from the grantor portion to the S portion, as defined in paragraph (b)(2) of this section, of the ESBT.

(2) *S portion.*—(i) *In general.*—Subject to paragraph (b)(2)(ii) of this section, the S portion of an ESBT is the portion of the trust that consists of S corporation stock and that is not treated as owned by the grantor or another person under subpart E of the Code.

(ii) *NRA deemed owner of grantor portion.*—The S portion of an ESBT also includes the grantor portion of the items of income, deduction, and credit reallocated under paragraph (b)(1)(ii) of this section from the grantor portion of the ESBT to the S portion of the ESBT.

* * *

(k) * * * Paragraphs (b)(1) and (2) of this section, and *Example 6* in paragraph (l)(6) of this section, apply to all ESBTs after December 31, 2017.

(l) * * *

(6) *Example 6: NRA as potential current beneficiary.*—Domestic Trust (DT) has a valid ESBT election in effect. DT owns S corporation stock. The S corporation owns U.S. and foreign assets. The foreign assets produce foreign source income. B, an NRA, is the grantor and the only trust beneficiary and potential current beneficiary of DT. B is not a resident of a country with which the United States has an income tax treaty. Under section 677(a), B is treated as the owner of DT because, under the trust documents, income and corpus may be distributed only to B during B's lifetime. Paragraph (b)(2)(ii) of this section requires that the S corporation income of the ESBT that otherwise would have been allocated to B under the grantor trust rules must be reallocated from B's grantor portion to the S portion of DT. In this example, the S portion of DT is treated as including the grantor portion of the ESBT, and thus all of DT's income from the S corporation is taxable to DT.

Charitable Contributions: Substantiation

Charitable Contributions: Substantiation Requirements.—Amendments to Reg. §1.642(c)-1, relating to deductions in excess of $5,000 claimed for charitable contributions of property, are proposed (published in the Federal Register on May 5, 1988).

* * *

☐ Par. 2. Paragraph (a)(1) of §1.642(c)-1 is amended by revising the first sentence to read as set forth below.

§1.642(c)-1. Unlimited deduction for amounts paid for charitable purpose.—(a) *In general.*—(1) Any part of the gross income of an estate or trust which, pursuant to the terms of the governing instrument, is paid (or treated under paragraph (b) of this section as paid) during the taxable year for a purpose specified in section 170(c) shall be allowed as a deduction to such estate or trust in lieu of the limited charitable contributions deduction authorized by section 170(a) (provided that the recordkeeping and return requirements for charitable contribution deductions contained in §1.170A-13 are satisfied). * * *

Charitable Contributions: Substantiation

Charitable Contributions: Substantiation Requirements.—Amendments to Reg. § 1.642(c)-2, relating to deductions in excess of $5,000 claimed for charitable contributions of property, are proposed (published in the Federal Register on May 5, 1988).

☐ Par. 3. Section 1.642(c)-2 is amended by adding a new paragraph (e) immediately after paragraph (d) to read as set forth below.

§ 1.642(c)-2. Unlimited deduction for amounts permanently set aside for a charitable purpose.—

* * *

(e) *Substantiation requirements.*—No deduction shall be allowed under paragraphs (a), (b)(2), or (c) of this section unless the recordkeeping and return requirements for charitable contribution deductions contained in § 1.170A-13 are satisfied.

Charitable Contribution Deductions: State or Local Tax Credits

Charitable Contribution Deductions: State or Local Tax Credits.—Amendments to Reg. § 1.642(c)-3, providing rules governing the availability of charitable contribution deductions under section 170 when a taxpayer receives or expects to receive a corresponding state or local tax credit, are proposed (published in the Federal Register on August 27, 2018) (REG-112176-18).

Par. 4. Section 1.642(c)-3 is amended by adding paragraph (g) to read as follows:

§ 1.642(c)-3. Adjustments and other special rules for determining unlimited charitable contributions deduction.

* * *

(g) *Payments resulting in state or local tax benefits.*—(1) *In general.*—If the trust or decedent's estate makes a payment of gross income for a purpose specified in section 170(c), and the trust or decedent's estate receives or expects to receive a state or local tax benefit in consideration for such payment, § 1.170A-1(h)(3) applies in determining the charitable contribution deduction under section 642(c).

(2) *Effective/applicability date.*—Paragraph (g)(1) of this section applies to payments of gross income after August 27, 2018.

Gross Income of Beneficiary

Gross Income of Beneficiary: Character of Amounts.—Reproduced below is the text of the proposed amendment of Reg. § 1.652(b)-1, relating to the character of amounts included in the gross income of a beneficiary (published in the Federal Register on April 30, 1975).

☐ Section 1.652(b)-1 is amended by deleting "72(n)" and inserting in lieu thereof "402(a)(2)". As amended § 1.652(b)-1 reads as follows:

§ 1.652(b)-1. Character of amounts.—In determining the gross income of a beneficiary, the amounts includible under § 1.652(a)-1 have the same character in the hands of the beneficiary as in the hands of the trust. For example, to the extent that the amounts specified in § 1.652(a)-1 consist of income exempt from tax under section 103, such amounts are not included in the beneficiary's gross income. Similarly, dividends distributed to a beneficiary retain their original character in the beneficiary's hands for purposes of determining the availability to the beneficiary of the dividends received credit under section 34 (for dividends received on or before December 31, 1964) and the dividend exclusion under section 116. Also, to the extent that the amounts specified in § 1.652(a)-1 consist of "earned income" in the hands of the trust under the provisions of section 1348 such amount shall be treated under section 1348 as "earned income" in the hands of the beneficiary. Similarly, to the extent the amounts specified in § 1.652(a)-1 consist of an amount received as a part of a lump sum distribution from a qualified plan and to which the provisions of section 402(a)(2) would apply in the hands of the trust, such amount shall be treated as subject to such section in the hands of the beneficiary except where such amount is deemed under section 666(a) to have been distributed in a preceding taxable year of the trust and the partial tax described in section 668(a)(2) is determined under section 668(b)(1)(B). The tax treatment of amounts determined under § 1.652(a)-1 depends upon the beneficiary's status with respect to them, not upon the status of the trust. Thus, if a beneficiary is deemed to have received foreign income of a foreign trust, the includibility of such income in his gross income depends upon his taxable status with respect to that income.

Estates and Trusts: Charitable Remainder Trusts

Estates and Trusts: Charitable Remainder Trusts.—Reproduced below is the text of a proposed amendment of Reg. § 1.664-1, relating to transfers for public, charitable and religious uses (published in the Federal Register on December 19, 1975).

☐ Paragraph (f) of § 1.664-1 is amended by revising the heading of subparagraph (3) and by adding a new subparagraph (4) at the end thereof. These revised and added provisions read as follows:

§ 1.664-1. Charitable remainder trusts.

* * *

(f) *Effective date.*—* * *

(3) *Amendment of certain trusts created after July 31, 1969.*—* * *

(4) *Certain wills and trusts in existence on September 21, 1974.*—(i) In the case of a will exe-

cuted before September 21, 1974, or a trust created (within the meaning of applicable local law) after July 31, 1969, and before September 21, 1974, which is amended pursuant to section 2055(e)(3) and §20.2055-2(g), a charitable remainder trust resulting from such amendment will be treated as a charitable remainder trust from the date it would be deemed created under §1.664-1(a)(4) and (5), whether or not such date is after September 20, 1974.

(ii) Property transferred to a trust created (within the meaning of applicable local law) before August 1, 1969, whose governing instrument provides that an organization described in section 170(c) receives an irrevocable remainder interest in such trust shall be deemed transferred to a trust created on the date of such transfer, provided that the transfer occurs after July 31, 1969, and prior to October 18, 1971, and pursuant to an amendment provided in §20.2055-2(g), the transferred property and any undistributed income therefrom is severed and placed in a separate trust as of the date of the amendment.

* * *

Application of the Grantor Trust Rules to Nonexempt Employees' Trusts

Application of the Grantor Trust Rules to Nonexempt Employees' Trusts.—Amendments to Reg. §§1.671-1 and 1.671-2, relating to the application of the grantor trust rules to nonexempt employees' trusts, are proposed (published in the Federal Register on September 27, 1996) (REG-209826-96).

□ Par. 2. Section 1.671-1 is amended by adding paragraphs (g) and (h) to read as follows:

§1.671-1. Grantors and others treated as substantial owners; scope.

* * *

(g) *Domestic nonexempt employees' trust.*—(1) *General rule.*—An employer is not treated as an owner of any portion of a nonexempt employees' trust described in section 402(b) that is part of a deferred compensation plan, and that is not a foreign trust within the meaning of section 7701(a)(31), regardless of whether the employer has a power or interest described in sections 673 through 677 over any portion of the trust. See section 402(b)(3) and §1.402(b)-1(b)(6) for rules relating to treatment of a beneficiary of a nonexempt employees' trust as the owner of a portion of the trust.

(2) *Example.*—The following example illustrates the rules of paragraph (g)(1) of this section:

Example. Employer X provides nonqualified deferred compensation through Plan A to certain of its management employees. Employer X has created Trust T to fund the benefits under Plan A. Assets of Trust T may not be used for any purpose other than to satisfy benefits provided under Plan A until all plan liabilities have been satisfied. Trust T is classified as a trust under §301.7701-4 of this chapter, and is not a foreign trust within the meaning of section 7701(a)(31). Under §1.83-3(e), contributions to Trust T are considered transfers of property to participants within the meaning of section 83. On these facts, Trust T is a nonexempt employees' trust described in section 402(b). Because Trust T is a nonexempt employees' trust described in section 402(b) that is part of a deferred compensation plan, and that is not a foreign trust within the meaning of section 7701(a)(31), Employer X is not treated as an owner of any portion of Trust T.

(h) *Foreign employees' trust.*—(1) *General rules.*—Except as provided under section 679 or as provided under this paragraph (h)(1), an employer is not treated as an owner of any portion of a foreign employees' trust (as defined in paragraph (h)(2) of this section), regardless of whether the employer has a power or interest described in sections 673 through 677 over any portion of the trust.

(i) *Plan of CFC employer.*—If a controlled foreign corporation (as defined in section 957) maintains a deferred compensation plan funded through a foreign employees' trust, then, with respect to the controlled foreign corporation, the provisions of subpart E apply to the portion of the trust that is the fractional interest described in paragraph (h)(3) of this section.

(ii) *Plan of U.S. employer.*—If a United States person (as defined in section 7701(a)(30)) maintains a deferred compensation plan that is funded through a foreign employees' trust, then, with respect to the U.S. person, the provisions of subpart E apply to the portion of the trust that is the fractional interest described in paragraph (h)(3) of this section.

(iii) *Plan of U.S.-related foreign partnership employer.*—(A) *General rule.*—If a U.S.-related foreign partnership (as defined in paragraph (h)(1)(iii)(B) of this section) maintains a deferred compensation plan funded through a foreign employees' trust, then, with respect to the U.S.-related foreign partnership, the provisions of subpart E apply to the portion of the trust that is the fractional interest described in paragraph (h)(3) of this section.

(B) *U.S.-related foreign partnership.*—For purposes of this paragraph (h), a U.S.-related foreign partnership is a foreign partnership in which a U.S. person or a controlled foreign corporation owns a partnership interest either directly or indirectly through one or more partnerships.

(iv) *Application of §1.1297-4 to plan of foreign non-CFC employer.*—A foreign employer that is not a controlled foreign corporation may be treated as an owner of a portion of a foreign employees' trust as provided in §1.1297-4.

(v) *Application to employer entity.*—The rules of paragraphs (h)(1)(i) through (h)(1)(iv) of this section apply to the employer whose employees benefit under the deferred compensation plan funded through a foreign employees' trust, or, in the case of a deferred compensation plan covering independent contractors, the recipient of services performed by those independent contractors, regardless of whether the plan is maintained through another entity. Thus, for example, where a deferred compensation plan benefitting employees of a controlled foreign corporation is funded through a foreign employees' trust, the controlled foreign corporation is considered to be the grantor of the foreign employees' trust for purposes of applying paragraph (h)(1)(i) of this section.

(2) *Foreign employees' trust.*—A foreign employees' trust is a nonexempt employees' trust described in section 402(b) that is part of a deferred compensation plan, and that is a foreign trust within the meaning of section 7701(a)(31).

(3) *Fractional interest for paragraph (h)(1).*—(i) *In general.*—The fractional interest for a foreign employees' trust used for purposes of paragraph (h)(1) of this section for a taxable year of the employer is an undivided fractional interest in the trust for which the fraction is equal to the relevant amount for the employer's taxable year divided by the fair market value of trust assets for the employer's taxable year.

(ii) *Relevant amount.*—(A) *In general.*—For purposes of applying paragraph (h)(3)(i) of this section, and except as provided in paragraph (h)(3)(iii) of this section, the relevant amount for the employer's taxable year is the amount, if any, by which the fair market value of trust assets, plus the fair market value of any assets available to pay plan liabilities that are held in the equivalent of a trust within the meaning of section 404A(b)(5)(A), exceed the plan's accrued liability. The following rules apply for this purpose:

(1) The plan's accrued liability is determined using a projected unit credit funding method that satisfies the requirements of §1.412(c)(3)-1, taking into account only liabilities relating to services performed through the measurement date for the employer or a predecessor employer.

(2) The plan's accrued liability is reduced (but not below zero) by any liabilities that are provided for under annuity contracts held to satisfy plan liabilities.

(3) Any amount held under an annuity contract that exceeds the amount that is needed to satisfy the liabilities provided for under the contract (e.g., the value of a participation right under a participating annuity contract) is added to the fair market value of any assets available to pay plan liabilities that are held in the equivalent of a trust.

(4) If the relevant amount as determined under this paragraph (h)(3)(ii), without regard to this paragraph (h)(3)(ii)(A)(4), is greater than the fair market value of trust assets, then the relevant amount is equal to the fair market value of trust assets.

(B) *Permissible actuarial assumptions for accrued liability.*—For purposes of paragraph (h)(3)(ii)(A) of this section, a plan's accrued liability must be calculated using an interest rate and other actuarial assumptions that the Commissioner determines to be reasonable. It is appropriate in determining this interest rate to look to available information about rates implicit in current prices of annuity contracts, and to look to rates of return on high-quality fixed-income investments currently available and expected to be available during the period prior to maturity of the plan benefits. If the qualified business unit computes its income or earnings and profits in dollars pursuant to the dollar approximate separate transactions method under §1.985-3, the employer must use an exchange rate that can be demonstrated to clearly reflect income, based on all relevant facts and circumstances, including appropriate rates of inflation and commercial practices.

(iii) *Exception for reasonable funding.*—The relevant amount does not include an amount that the taxpayer demonstrates to the Commissioner is attributable to amounts that were properly contributed to the trust pursuant to a reasonable funding method, applied using actuarial assumptions that the Commissioner determines to be reasonable, or any amount that the taxpayer demonstrates to the Commissioner is attributable to experience that is favorable relative to any actuarial assumptions used that the Commissioner determines to be reasonable. For this paragraph (h)(3)(iii) to apply to a controlled foreign corporation employer described in paragraph (h)(1)(i) of this section, the taxpayer must indicate on a statement attached to a timely filed Form 5471 that the taxpayer is relying on this rule. For purposes of this paragraph (h)(3)(iii), an amount is considered contributed pursuant to a reasonable funding method if the amount is contributed pursuant to a funding method permitted to be used under section 412 (e.g., the entry age normal funding method) that is consistently used to determine plan contributions. In addition, for purposes of this paragraph (h)(3)(iii), if there has been a change to that method from another funding method, an amount is considered contributed pursuant to a reasonable funding method only if the prior funding method is also a funding method described in the preceding sentence that was consistently used to determine plan contributions. For purposes of this paragraph (h)(3)(iii), a funding method is considered reasonable only if the method provides for any initial unfunded liability to be amortized over a period of at least 6 years, and for any net change in accrued liability resulting from a change in funding method to be amortized over a period of at least 6 years.

(iv) *Reduction for transition amount.*—The relevant amount is reduced (but not below zero) by any transition amount described in paragraphs (h)(5), (h)(6), or (h)(7) of this section.

(v) *Fair market value of assets.*—For purposes of paragraphs (h)(3)(i) and (ii) of this section, for a taxable year of the employer, the fair market value of trust assets, and the fair market value of other assets held in the equivalent of a trust within the meaning of section 404A(b)(5)(A), equals the fair market value of those assets, as of the measurement date for the employer's taxable year, adjusted to include contributions made after the measurement date and by the end of the employer's taxable year.

(vi) *Annual valuation.*—For purposes of determining the relevant amount for a taxable year of the employer, the fair market value of plan assets, and the plan's accrued liability as described in paragraphs (h)(3)(ii) and (iii) of this section, and the normal cost as described in paragraph (h)(4) of this section, must be determined as of a consistently used annual measurement date within the employer's taxable year.

(vii) *Special rule for plan funded through multiple trusts.*—In cases in which a plan is funded through more than one foreign employees' trust, the fractional interest determined under paragraph (h)(3)(i) of this section in each trust is determined by treating all of the trusts as if their assets were held in a single trust for which the fraction is determined in accordance with the rules of this paragraph (h)(3).

(4) *De minimis exception.*—If the relevant amount is not greater than the plan's normal cost for the plan year ending with or within the employer's taxable year, computed using a funding method and actuarial assumptions as described in paragraph (h)(3)(ii) of this section or as described in paragraph (h)(3)(iii) of this section if the requirements of that paragraph are met, that are used to determine plan contributions, then the relevant amount is considered to be zero for purposes of applying paragraph (h)(3)(i) of this section.

(5) *General rule for transition amount.*—(i) *General rule.*—If paragraphs (h)(6) and (h)(7) of this section do not apply to the employer, the transition amount for purposes of paragraph (h)(3)(iv) of this section is equal to the preexisting amount multiplied by the applicable percentage for the year in which the employer's taxable year begins.

(ii) *Preexisting amount.*—The preexisting amount is equal to the relevant amount of the trust, determined without regard to paragraphs (h)(3)(iv) and (h)(4) of this section, computed as of the measurement date that immediately precedes September 27, 1996 disregarding contributions to the trust made after the measurement date.

(iii) *Applicable percentage.*—The applicable percentage is equal to 100 percent for the employer's first taxable year ending after this document is published as a final regulation in the Federal Register and prior taxable years of the employer, and is reduced (but not below zero) by 10 percentage points for each subsequent taxable year of the employer.

(6) *Transition amount for new CFCs.*—(i) *General rule.*—In the case of a new controlled foreign corporation employer, the transition amount for purposes of paragraph (h)(3)(iv) is equal to the pre-change amount multiplied by the applicable percentage for the year in which the new controlled foreign corporation employer's taxable year begins.

(ii) *Pre-change amount.*—The pre-change amount for purposes of paragraph (h)(6)(i) is equal to the relevant amount of the trust, determined without regard to paragraphs (h)(3)(iv) and (h)(4) of this section and disregarding contributions to the trust made after the measurement date, for the new controlled foreign corporation employer's last taxable year ending before the corporation becomes a new controlled foreign corporation employer.

(iii) *Applicable percentage.*—(A) *General rule.*—Except as provided in paragraph (h)(6)(iii)(B) of this section, the applicable percentage is equal to 100 percent for a new controlled foreign corporation employer's first taxable year ending after the corporation becomes a controlled foreign corporation. The applicable percentage is reduced (but not below zero) by 10 percentage points for each subsequent taxable year of the new controlled foreign corporation.

(B) *Interim rule.*—For any taxable year of a new controlled foreign corporation employer that ends on or before the date this document is published as a final regulation in the Federal Register, the applicable percentage is equal to 100 percent. The applicable percentage is reduced by 10 percentage points for each subsequent taxable year of the new controlled foreign corporation employer that ends after the date this document is published as a final regulation in the Federal Register.

(iv) *New CFC employer.*—For purposes of paragraph (h)(6) of this section, a new controlled foreign corporation employer is a corporation that first becomes a controlled foreign corporation within the meaning of section 957 after September 27, 1996. A new controlled foreign corporation employer includes a corporation that was a controlled foreign corporation prior to, but not on, September 27, 1996 and that first becomes a controlled foreign corporation again after September 27, 1996.

(v) *Anti-stuffing rule.*—Notwithstanding paragraph (h)(6)(iii) of this section, if, prior to becoming a controlled foreign corporation, a corporation contributes amounts to a foreign employees' trust with a principal purpose of obtaining tax benefits by increasing the pre-change amount, the applicable percentage with respect to those amounts is 0 percent for all taxable years of the new controlled foreign corporation employer.

(7) *Transition amount for new U.S.-related foreign partnerships.*—(i) *General rule.*—In the case of a new U.S.-related foreign partnership employer, the transition amount for purposes of paragraph (h)(3)(iv) of this section is equal to the pre-change amount multiplied by the applicable percentage for the year in which the new U.S.-related foreign partnership employer's taxable year begins.

(ii) *Pre-change amount.*—The pre-change amount for purposes of paragraph (h)(7)(i) of this section is equal to the relevant amount of the trust, determined without regard to paragraphs (h)(3)(iv) and (h)(4) of this section and disregarding contributions to the trust made after the measurement date, for the entity's last taxable year ending before the entity becomes a new U.S.-related foreign partnership employer.

(iii) *Applicable percentage.*—(A) *General rule.*—Except as provided in paragraph (h)(7)(iii)(B) of this section, the applicable percentage is equal to 100 percent for a new U.S.-related foreign partnership employer's first taxable year ending after the entity becomes a new U.S.-related foreign partnership employer. The applicable percentage is reduced (but not below zero) by 10 percentage points for each subsequent taxable year of the new U.S.-related foreign partnership employer.

(B) *Interim rule.*—For any taxable year of a new U.S.-related foreign partnership employer that ends on or before the date this document is published as a final regulation in the Federal Register, the applicable percentage is equal to 100 percent. The applicable percentage is reduced by 10 percentage points for each subsequent taxable year of the new U.S.-related foreign partnership employer that ends after the date this document is published as a final regulation in the Federal Register.

(iv) *New U.S.-related foreign partnership employer.*—For purposes of paragraph (h)(7) of this section, a new U.S.-related foreign partnership employer is an entity that was a foreign corporation other than a controlled foreign corporation, or that was a foreign partnership other than a U.S.-related foreign partnership, and that changes from this status to a U.S.-related foreign partnership after September 27, 1996. A new U.S.-related foreign partnership employer includes a corporation that was a U.S.-related foreign partnership prior to, but not on, September 27, 1996 and that first becomes a U.S.-related foreign partnership again after September 27, 1996.

(v) *Anti-stuffing rule.*—Notwithstanding paragraph (h)(7)(iii) of this section, if, prior to becoming a new U.S.-related foreign partnership employer, an entity contributes amounts to a foreign employees' trust with a principal purpose of obtaining tax benefits by increasing the pre-change amount, the applicable percentage with respect to those amounts is 0 percent for all taxable years of the new U.S.-related foreign partnership employer.

(8) *Examples.*—The following examples illustrate the rules of paragraph (h) of this section. In each example, the employer has a power or interest described in sections 673 through 677 over the foreign employees' trust, and the monetary unit is the applicable functional currency (FC) determined in accordance with section 985(b) and the regulations thereunder.

Example 1. (i) Employer X is a controlled foreign corporation (as defined in section 957). Employer X maintains a defined benefit retirement plan for its employees. Employer X's taxable year is the calendar year. Trust T, a foreign employees' trust, is the sole funding vehicle for the plan. Both the plan year of the plan and the taxable year of Trust T are the calendar year.

(ii) As of December 31, 1997, Trust T's measurement date, the fair market value (as described in paragraph (h)(3)(iv) of this section) of Trust T's assets is FC 1,000,000, and the amount of the plan's accrued liability is FC 800,000, which includes a normal cost for 1997 of FC 50,000. The preexisting amount for Trust T is FC 40,000. Thus, the relevant amount for 1997 is FC 160,000 (which is greater than the plan's normal cost for the year). Employer X's shareholder does not indicate on a statement attached to a timely filed Form 5471 that any of the relevant amount qualifies for the exception described in paragraph (h)(3)(iii) of this section. Therefore, the fractional interest for Employer X's taxable year ending on December 31, 1997, is 16 percent. Employer X is treated as the owner for federal income tax purposes of an undivided 16 percent interest in each of Trust T's assets for the period from January 1, 1997 through December 31, 1997. Employer X must take into account a 16 percent pro rata share of each item of income, deduction or credit of Trust T during this period in computing its federal income tax liability.

Example 2. Assume the same facts as in *Example 1*, except that Employer X's shareholder indicates on a statement attached to a timely filed Form 5471 and can demonstrate to the satisfaction of the Commissioner that, in reliance on paragraph (h)(3)(iii) of this section, FC 100,000 of the fair market value of Trust T's assets is attributable to favorable experience relative to reasonable actuarial assumptions used. Accordingly, the relevant amount for 1997 is FC 60,000. Because the plan's normal cost for 1997 is less than FC 60,000, the de minimis exception of paragraph (h)(4) of this section does not apply. Therefore, the fractional interest for Employer X's taxable year ending on December 31, 1997, is 6 percent. Employer X is treated as the owner for federal income tax purposes of an undivided 6 percent interest in each of Trust T's assets for the period from January 1, 1997, through December 31, 1997. Employer X must take into account a 6 percent pro rata share of each item of income, deduction or credit of Trust T during this period in computing its federal income tax liability.

(9) *Effective date.*—Paragraphs (g) and (h) of this section apply to taxable years of an employer ending after September 27, 1996.

☐ Par. 3. Section 1.671-2 is amended by adding paragraph (f) to read as follows:

§1.671-2. Applicable principles.

* * *

(f) For purposes of subtitle A of the Internal Revenue Code, a person that is treated as the owner of any portion of a trust under subpart E is considered to own the trust assets attributable to that portion of the trust.

PARTNERS AND PARTNERSHIPS

Personal Service Corporation: Taxable Years

Personal Service Corporations: Partnerships: S Corporations: Taxable Years.—Temporary Reg. §1.702-3T is also proposed as a final regulation and, when adopted, would become Reg. §1.702-3 (published in the Federal Register on December 23, 1987).

§1.702-3. 4-year spread.

Partnerships: Equity for Services

Partnerships: Equity for Services.—Amendments to Reg. §1.704-1, providing that the transfer of a partnership interest in connection with the performance of services is subject to Code Sec. 83 and providing rules for coordinating Code Sec. 83 with partnership taxation principles, are proposed (published in the Federal Register on May 24, 2005) (REG-105346-03).

☐ Par. 4. Section 1.704-1 is amended as follows:

1. In paragraph (b)(0), an entry is added to the table for §1.704-1(b)(4)(xii).
2. In paragraph (b)(1)(ii)(*a*), a sentence is added at the end of the paragraph.
3. Paragraph (b)(2)(iv)(*b*)(*1*) is revised.
4. Paragraph (b)(2)(iv)(*f*)(*5*)(*iii*) is revised.
5. Paragraph (b)(4)(xii) is added.
6. Paragraph (b)(5) *Example 29* is added.

The additions and revisions read as follows:

§1.704-1. Partner's distributive share.

* * *

(b) * * * (0) * * *

* * *

Substantialy nonvested interests . . . . 1.704-1(b)(4)(xii)

* * *

(1) * * *

(ii) * * * *(a)* * * * In addition, paragraph (b)(4)(xii) and paragraph (b)(5) *Example 29* of this section apply to compensatory partnership interests (as defined in §1.721-1(b)(3)) that are transferred on or after the date final regulations are published in the Federal Register.

* * *

(2) * * *

(iv) * * *

(b) * * *

(1) the amount of money contributed by that partner to the partnership and, in the case of a compensatory partnership interest (as defined in §1.721-1(b)(3)) that is transferred on or after the date final regulations are published in the Federal Register, the amount included on or after that date in the partner's compensation income under section 83(a), (b), or (d)(2).

* * *

(f) * * *

(5) * * *

(iii) In connection with the transfer or vesting of a compensatory partnership interest (as defined in §1.721-1(b)(3)) that is transferred on or after the date final regulations are published in the Federal Register, but only if the transfer or vesting results in the service provider recognizing income under section 83 (or would result in such recognition if the interest had a fair market value other than zero).

* * *

(4) * * *

(xii) *Substantially nonvested interests.*—*(a) In general.*—If a section 83(b) election has been made with respect to a substantially nonvested interest, the holder of the nonvested interest may be allocated partnership income, gain, loss, deduction, or credit (or items thereof) that will later be forfeited. For this reason, allocations of partnership items while the interest is substantially nonvested cannot have economic effect.

(b) Deemed Compliance with Partners' Interests in the Partnership.—If a section 83(b) election has been made with respect to a substantially nonvested interest, allocations of partnership items while the interest is substantially nonvested will be deemed to be in accordance with the partners' interests in the partnership if—

(1) The partnership agreement requires that the partnership make forfeiture allocations if the interest for which the section 83(b) election is made is later forfeited; and

(2) All material allocations and capital account adjustments under the partnership agreement not pertaining to substantially nonvested partnership interests for which a section 83(b) election has been made are recognized under section 704(b).

(c) Forfeiture allocations.—Forfeiture allocations are allocations to the service provider (consisting of a pro rata portion of each item) of gross income and gain or gross deduction and loss (to the extent such items are available) for the taxable year of the forfeiture in a positive or negative amount equal to—

(1) The excess (not less than zero) of the—

(i) Amount of distributions (including deemed distributions under section 752(b) and the adjusted tax basis of any property so distributed) to the partner with respect to the forfeited partnership interest (to the extent such distributions are not taxable under section 731); over

(ii) Amounts paid for the interest and the adjusted tax basis of property contributed by the partner (including deemed contributions under section 752(a)) to the partnership with respect to the forfeited partnership interest; minus

(2) The cumulative net income (or loss) allocated to the partner with respect to the forfeited partnership interest.

(d) Positive and negative amounts.—For purposes of paragraph (b)(4)(xii)*(c)* of this section, items of income and gain are reflected as positive amounts, and items of deduction and loss are reflected as negative amounts.

(e) Exception.—Paragraph (b)(4)(xii)*(b)* of this section shall not apply to allocations of partnership items made with respect to a substantially nonvested interest for which the holder has made a section 83(b) election if, at the time of the section 83(b) election, there is a plan that the interest will be forfeited. In such a case, the partners' distributive shares of partnership items shall be determined in accordance with the partners' interests in the partnership under paragraph (b)(3) of this section. In determining whether there is a plan that the interest will be forfeited, the Commissioner will consider all of the facts and circumstances (including the tax status of the holder of the forfeitable compensatory partnership interest).

(f) Cross references.—Forfeiture allocations may be made out of the partnership's items for the entire taxable year of the forfeiture. See §1.706-3(b) and paragraph (b)(5) *Example 29* of this section.

* * *

(5) * * *

Example 29. (i) In Year 1, A and B each contribute cash to LLC, a newly formed limited liability company classified as a partnership for Federal tax purposes, in exchange for equal units in LLC. Under LLC's operating agreement, each unit is entitled to participate equally in the profits and losses of LLC. The operating agreement also provides that the partners' capital accounts will be determined and maintained in accordance with paragraph (b)(2)(iv) of this section, that liquidation proceeds will be distributed in accordance with the partners' positive capital account balances, and that any partner with a deficit balance in that partner's capital account following the liquidation of the partner's interest must restore that deficit to the partnership. At the beginning of Year 3, SP agrees to perform services for LLC. In connection with the performance of SP's services and a payment of $10 by SP to LLC, LLC transfers a 10% interest in LLC to SP. SP's interest in LLC is substantially nonvested (within the meaning of § 1.83-3(b)). At the time of the transfer of the LLC interest to SP, LLC's operating agreement is amended to provide that, if SP's interest is forfeited, then SP is entitled to a return of SP's $10 initial contribution, and SP's distributive share of all partnership items (other than forfeiture allocations under § 1.704-1(b)(4)(xii)) will be zero with respect to that interest for the taxable year of the partnership in which the interest was forfeited. The operating agreement is also amended to require that LLC make forfeiture allocations if SP's interest is forfeited. Additionally, the operating agreement is amended to provide that no part of LLC's compensation deduction is allocated to the service provider to whom the interest is transferred. SP makes an election under section 83(b) with respect to SP's interest in LLC. Upon receipt, the fair market value of SP's interest in LLC is $100. In each of Years 3, 4, 5, and 6, LLC has operating income of $100 (consisting of $200 of gross receipts and $100 of deductible expenses), and makes no distributions. SP forfeits SP's interest in LLC at the beginning of Year 6. At the time of the transfer of the interest to SP, there is no plan that SP will forfeit the interest in LLC.

(ii) Because a section 83(b) election is made, SP recognizes compensation income in the year of the transfer of the LLC interest. Therefore, SP recognizes $90 of compensation income in the year of the transfer of the LLC interest (the excess of the fair market value of SP's interest in LLC, $100, over the amount SP paid for the interest, $10). Under paragraph (b)(2)(iv)(*b*)(*1*) of this section, in Year 3, SP's capital account is initially credited with $100, the amount paid for the interest ($10) plus the amount included in SP's compensation income upon the transfer under section 83(b) ($90). Under § § 1.83-6(b) and 1.721-1(b)(2), LLC does not recognize gain on the transfer of the interest to SP. LLC is entitled to a compensation deduction of $90 under section 83(h). Under the terms of the operating agreement, the deduction is allocated equally to A and B.

(iii) As a result of SP's election under section 83(b), SP is treated as a partner starting from the date of the transfer of the LLC interest to SP in Year 3. Section 1.761-1(b). In each of years 3, 4 and 5, SP's distributive share of partnership income is $10 (10% of $100), A's distributive share of partnership income is $45 (45% of $100), and B's distributive share of partnership income is $45 (45% of $100). In accordance with the operating agreement, SP's capital account is increased (to $130) by the end of Year 5 by the amounts allocated to SP, and A's and B's capital accounts are increased by the amounts allocated to A and B. Because LLC satisfies the requirements of paragraph (b)(4)(xii) of this section, LLC's allocations in years 3, 4 and 5 are deemed to be in accordance with the partners' interests in the partnership.

(iv) As a result of the forfeiture of the LLC interest by SP in year 6, LLC is required to recognize income ($90) equal to the amount of the allowable deduction on the transfer of the LLC interest to SP under § 1.83-6(c). LLC repays SP's $10 capital contribution to SP, reducing SP's capital account to $120. Under the terms of the operating agreement, because SP forfeited SP's interest, SP's distributive share of all partnership items (other than forfeiture allocations) is zero for Year 6. To reverse SP's prior allocations of LLC income, LLC makes forfeiture allocations of $30 of deductions ($0 (the difference between the $10 distributed to SP and the $10 contributed to LLC by SP) minus $30 (the cumulative net LLC income allocated to SP) to SP in Year 6. Notwithstanding section 706(c) and (d), these allocations may be made out of LLC's partnership items for the entire taxable year of the forfeiture. Thus, in Year 6, $30 of deductions are allocated to SP, and the remaining $220 of net operating income ($200 of gross receipts and $90 of income under § 1.83-6(c) less $70 of remaining deductions) are allocated to A and B equally for tax purposes. In accordance with section 83(b)(1) (last sentence), SP does not receive a deduction or capital loss for the amount ($90) that was included in SP's compensation income. Because LLC satisfies the requirements of paragraph (b)(4)(xii) of this section, LLC's allocations in year 6 are deemed to be in accordance with the partners' interests in the partnership.

* * *

Partners and Partnerships: Sales or Exchanges: Certain Distributions

Partners and Partnerships: Sales or Exchanges: Certain Distributions.—Amendments to Reg. § § 1.704-1 and 1.704-3, prescribing how a partner should measure its interest in a partnership's unrealized receivables and inventory items, and that provide guidance regarding the tax consequences of a distribution that causes a reduction in that interest, are proposed (published in the Federal Register on November 3, 2014) (REG-151416-06).

☐ Par. 3. Section 1.704-1 is amended by:

a. Revising paragraph (b)(2)(iv)(*f*) introductory text.

b. Redesignating paragraph (b)(2)(iv)(*f*)(*5*)(*v*) as paragraph (b)(2)(iv)(*f*)(*5*)(*vi*).

c. Adding new paragraph (b)(2)(iv)(*f*)(*5*)(*v*).

d. Designating the undesignated text after paragraph (b)(2)(iv)(*f*)(*5*)(*vi*) as paragraph (b)(2)(iv)(*f*)(*5*)(*vii*).

The revisions and additions read as follows:

§ 1.704-1. Partner's distributive share.

* * *

(b) * * *

(2) * * *

(iv) * * *

(*f*) *Revaluations of property.*—A partnership agreement may, upon the occurrence of certain events, and must in the circumstances described in § 1.751-1(b)(2)(iv), increase or decrease the capital accounts of the partners to reflect a revaluation of partnership property (including intangible assets such as goodwill) on the partnership's books. If a partnership that revalues its property pursuant to this paragraph owns an interest in another partnership, that partnership in which it owns an interest may also revalue its property in accordance with this section. Similarly, if an interest in a partnership that revalues its property pursuant to this paragraph is owned by another partnership, the partnership owning that interest may also revalue its property in accordance with this section. Capital accounts so adjusted will not be considered to be determined and maintained in accordance with the rules of this paragraph (b)(2)(iv) unless—

* * *

(5) * * *

(v) In connection with an agreement to change (other than a de minimis change) the manner in which the partners share any item or class of items of income, gain, loss, deduction or credit of the partnership under the partnership agreement, or

* * *

☐ Par. 4. Section 1.704-3 is amended in paragraph (a)(9) by adding a sentence immediately following the first sentence to read as follows:

§1.704-3. Contributed property.—(a) * * *

(9) * * * If a partnership (the upper-tier partnership) owns an interest in another partnership (the lower-tier partnership), and both the upper-tier partnership and the lower-tier partnership simultaneously revalue partnership property pursuant to §1.704-1(b)(2)(iv)(f), the principles of this paragraph (a)(9) shall apply to any reverse section 704(c) allocations created upon the revaluation. * * *

* * *

☐ Par. 18. For each section listed in the table, remove the language in the "Remove" column and add in its place the language in the "Add" column as set forth below:

Section	Remove	Add
§1.704-3, paragraph (a)(6)(ii)	§1.743-1(b) or 1.751-1(a)(2)	§1.743-1(b), 1.751-1(a)(2), or 1.751-1(b)

Partnerships: Creditable Foreign Taxes: Allocation

Partnerships: Creditable Foreign Taxes: Allocation.—Amendments to Reg. §1.704-1, providing guidance relating to the allocation by a partnership of foreign income taxes, are proposed (published in the Federal Register on February 4, 2016) (REG-100861-15).

Par. 2. Section 1.704-1 is amended as follows:

1. In paragraph (b)(0):

i. Add an entry for §1.704-1 (b)(1)(ii)(*b*)(*1*).

ii. Revise the entries for (b)(4)(viii)(*c*)(*1*) through (*4*) and (b)(4)(viii)(*d*)(*1*).

2. Revise paragraphs (b)(1)(ii)(*b*)(*1*), (b)(1)(ii)(*b*)(*3*)(*B*), (b)(4)(viii)(*a*)(*1*), (b)(4)(viii)(*c*)(*1*), (b)(4)(viii)(c)(2)(*ii*) and (*iii*), (b)(4)(viii)(*c*)(*3*) and (*4*), (b)(4)(viii)(*d*)(*1*), and *Example* 25 of paragraph (b)(5).

3. Add *Examples 36* and *37* to paragraph (b)(5).

The revisions read as follows:

§1.704-1. Partner's distributive share.

* * *

(b) * * *

(0) [The text of the proposed amendments to §1.704-1(b)(0) is the same as the text of §1.704-1T(b)(0) as added by T.D. 9748.]

(1) * * *

(ii) * * *

(*b*) *Rules relating to foreign tax expenditures.*—(*1*) [The text of the proposed amendments to §1.704-1(b)(1)(ii)(*b*)(*1*) is the same as the text of §1.704-1T(b)(1)(ii)(*b*)(*1*) as added by T.D. 9748.]

* * *

(*3*) * * *

(*B*) [The text of the proposed amendments to §1.704-1(b)(1)(ii)(*b*)(*3*)(*B*) is the same as the text of §1.704-1T(b)(1)(ii)(*b*)(*3*)(*B*) as added by T.D. 9748.]

* * *

(4) * * *

(viii) * * *

(*a*) * * *

(*1*) [The text of the proposed amendments to §1.704-1(b)(4)(viii)(*a*)(*1*) is the same as the text of §1.704-1T(b)(4)(viii)(*a*)(*1*) as added by T.D. 9748.]

* * *

(*c*) *Income to which CFTEs relate.*—(*1*) [The text of the proposed amendments to §1.704-1(b)(4)(viii)(*c*)(*1*) is the same as the text of §1.704-1T(b)(4)(viii)(*c*)(*1*) as added by T.D. 9748.]

(*2*) * * *

(*ii*) [The text of the proposed amendments to §1.704-1(b)(4)(viii)(*c*)(*2*)(*ii*) is the same as the text of §1.704-1T(b)(4)(viii)(*c*)(2)(*ii*) as added by T.D. 9748.]

(*iii*) [The text of the proposed amendments to §1.704-1(b)(4)(viii)(*c*)(*2*)(*iii*) is the same as the text of §1.704-1T(b)(4)(viii)(*c*)(2)(*iii*) as added by T.D. 9748.]

(*3*) [The text of the proposed amendments to §1.704-1(b)(4)(viii)(*c*)(*3*) is the same as the text of §1.704-1T(b)(4)(viii)(*c*)(*3*) as added by T.D. 9748.]

(*4*) [The text of the proposed amendments to §1.704-1(b)(4)(viii)(*c*)(*4*) is the same as the text of §1.704-1T(b)(4)(viii)(*c*)(*4*) as added by T.D. 9748.]

* * *

(*d*) *Allocation and apportionment of CFTEs to CFTE categories.*—(*1*) [The text of the proposed amendments to §1.704-1(b)(4)(viii)(*d*)(*1*) is the same as the text of §1.704-1T(b)(4)(viii)(*d*)(*1*) as added by T.D. 9748.]

* * *

(5) * * *

Example 25. [The text of the proposed amendments to § 1.704-1(b)(5) *Example 24* is the same as the text of § 1.704-1T(b)(5) *Example 25* as added by T.D. 9748.]

* * *

Example 36. [The text of the proposed amendments to § 1.704-1(b)(5) *Example 36* is the same as the text of § 1.704-1T(b)(5) *Example 36* as added by T.D. 9748.]

Example 37. [The text of the proposed amendments to § 1.704-1(b)(5) *Example 37* is the same as the text of § 1.704-1T(b)(5) *Example 37* as added by T.D. 9748.]

* * *

Foreign Tax Credit: Covered Asset Acquisitions

Foreign Tax Credit: Covered Asset Acquisitions.—Amendments to Reg. § 1.704-1, relating to transactions that generally are treated as asset acquisitions for U.S. income tax purposes and either are treated as stock acquisitions or are disregarded for foreign income tax purposes, are proposed (published in the Federal Register on December 7, 2016) (REG-129128-14).

Par. 2. Section 1.704-1, as proposed to be amended at 81 FR 5967, February 4, 2016, is further amended by adding two sentences at the end of paragraph (b)(1)(ii)(b)(*1*) and by adding paragraphs (b)(4)(viii)(*c*)(*4*)(*v*) through (b)(4)(viii)(*c*)(*4*)(*vii*) to read as follows:

§ 1.704-1. Partner's distributive share.

* * *

(b) * * *

(1) * * *

(ii) * * *

(b) * * *

(1) * * * Paragraphs (b)(4)(viii)(*c*)(*4*)(*v*) through (*vii*) of this section apply to covered asset acquisitions (CAAs) (as defined in § 1.901(m)-1(a)(8)) occurring on or after the date of publication of a Treasury decision adopting these rules as final regulations in the **Federal Register.** Taxpayers may, however, rely on paragraphs (b)(4)(viii)(*c*)(*4*)(*v*) through (*vii*) of this section prior to the date paragraphs (b)(4)(viii)(*c*)(*4*)(*v*) through (*vii*) of this section are applicable provided that they consistently apply paragraphs (b)(4)(viii)(*c*)(*4*)(*v*) through (*vii*) of this section, § 1.901(m)-1, and §§ 1.901(m)-3 through 1.901(m)-8 (excluding § 1.901(m)-4(e)) to all CAAs occurring on or after January 1, 2011, and consistently apply § 1.901(m)-2 (excluding § 1.901(m)-2(d)) to all CAAs occurring on or after December 7, 2016.

* * *

(4) * * *

(viii) * * *

(c) * * *

(4) * * *

(v) Adjustments related to section 901(m).—If one or more assets owned by a partnership are relevant foreign assets (or RFAs) with respect to a foreign income tax, then, solely for purposes of applying the safe harbor provisions of paragraph (b)(4)(viii)(*a*)(*1*) of this section to allocations of CFTEs with respect to that foreign income tax, the net income in a CFTE category that includes partnership items of income, deduction, gain, or loss attributable to the RFA shall be increased by the amount described in paragraph (b)(4)(viii)(*c*)(*4*)(*vi*) of this section and reduced by the amount described in paragraph (b)(4)(viii)(*c*)(*4*)(*vii*) of this section. Similarly, a partner's CFTE category share of income shall be increased by the portion of the amount described in paragraph (b)(4)(viii)(*c*)(*4*)(*vi*) of this section that is allocated to the partner under § 1.901(m)-5(d) and reduced by the portion of the amount described in paragraph (b)(4)(viii)(*c*)(*4*)(*vii*) of this section that is allocated to the partner under § 1.901(m)-5(d). The principles of this paragraph (b)(4)(viii)(*c*)(*4*)(*v*) apply similarly when a partnership owns an RFA indirectly through one or more other partnerships. For purposes of paragraphs (b)(4)(viii)(*c*)(*4*)(*v*), (b)(4)(viii)(*c*)(*4*)(*vi*), and (b)(4)(viii)(*c*)(*4*)(*vii*) of this section, basis difference is defined in § 1.901(m)-4, cost recovery amount is defined in § 1.901(m)-5(b)(2), disposition amount is defined in § 1.901(m)-5(c)(2), foreign income tax is defined in § 1.901(m)-1(a)(21), RFA is defined in § 1.901(m)-2(c), U.S. disposition gain is defined in § 1.901(m)-1(a)(43), and U.S. disposition loss is defined in § 1.901(m)-1(a)(44).

(vi) Adjustment amounts for RFAs with a positive basis difference.—With respect to RFAs with a positive basis difference, the amount referenced in (b)(4)(viii)(*c*)(*4*)(*v*) is the sum of any cost recovery amounts and disposition amounts attributable to U.S. disposition loss that correspond to partnership items that are included in the net income in the CFTE category and that are taken into account for the U.S. taxable year of the partnership under § 1.901(m)-5(d).

(vii) Adjustment amounts for RFAs with a negative basis difference.—With respect to RFAs with a negative basis difference, the amount referenced in (b)(4)(viii)(*c*)(*4*)(*v*) is the sum of any cost recovery amounts and disposition amounts attributable to U.S. disposition gain that correspond to partnership items that are included in the net income in the CFTE category and that are taken into account for the U.S. taxable year of the partnership under § 1.901(m)-5(d).

* * *

Liabilities: Recourse Partnership Liabilities

Liabilities: Recourse Partnership Liabilities.—Amendments to Reg. § 1.704-1, addressing when certain obligations to restore a deficit balance in a partner's capital account are disregarded under section 704 of the Internal Revenue Code (Code) and when partnership liabilities are treated as recourse liabilities under section 752, are proposed (published in the Federal Register on October 5, 2016) (REG-122855-15).

Par. 2. Section 1.704-1 is amended by:

1. Adding two sentences to the end of paragraph (b)(1)(ii)(*a*).

2. Adding a sentence to the end of paragraph (b)(2)(ii)(*b*)(3) introductory text.
3. Removing the undesignated paragraph following paragraph (b)(2)(ii)(*b*)(3).
4. Adding paragraphs (b)(2)(ii)(*b*)(4) through (7).
5. Revising paragraph (b)(2)(ii)(*c*).
The additions and revisions read as follows:

§1.704-1. Partner's distributive share.

* * *

(b) * * *

(1) * * *

(ii) * * *

(a) * * * Furthermore, the last sentence of paragraph (b)(2)(ii)(*b*)(3) of this section and paragraphs (b)(2)(ii)(*b*)(4) through (7) and (b)(2)(ii)(*c*) of this section apply on or after the date these regulations are published as final regulations in the **Federal Register**. However, taxpayers may rely on the last sentence of paragraph (b)(2)(ii)(*b*)(3) of this section and paragraphs (b)(2)(ii)(*b*)(4) through (7) and (b)(2)(ii)(*c*) of this section on or after October 5, 2016 and before the date these regulations are published as final regulations in the **Federal Register**.

* * *

(2) * * *

(ii) * * *

(b) * * *

(3) * * * Notwithstanding the partnership agreement, an obligation to restore a deficit balance in a partner's capital account, including an obligation described in paragraph (b)(2)(ii)(*c*)(*1*) of this section, will not be respected for purposes of this section to the extent the obligation is disregarded under paragraph (b)(2)(ii)(*c*)(*4*) of this section.

(4) For purposes of paragraphs (b)(2)(ii)(*b*)(*1*) through (3) of this section, a partnership taxable year shall be determined without regard to section 706(c)(2)(A).

(5) The requirements in paragraphs (b)(2)(ii)(*b*)(2) and (3) of this section are not violated if all or part of the partnership interest of one or more partners is purchased (other than in connection with the liquidation of the partnership) by the partnership or by one or more partners (or one or more persons related, within the meaning of section 267(b) (without modification by section 267(e)(1)) or section 707(b)(1), to a partner) pursuant to an agreement negotiated at arm's length by persons who at the time such agreement is entered into have materially adverse interests and if a principal purpose of such purchase and sale is not to avoid the principles of the second sentence of paragraph (b)(2)(ii)(*a*) of this section.

(6) The requirement in paragraph (b)(2)(ii)(*b*)(2) of this section is not violated if, upon the liquidation of the partnership, the capital accounts of the partners are increased or decreased pursuant to paragraph (b)(2)(iv)(*f*) of this section as of the date of such liquidation and the partnership makes liquidating distributions within the time set out in the requirement in paragraph (b)(2)(ii)(*b*)(2) of this section in the ratios of the partners' positive capital accounts, except that it does not distribute reserves reasonably required to provide for liabilities (contingent or otherwise) of the partnership and installment obligations owed to the partnership, so long as such withheld amounts are distributed as soon as practicable and in the ratios of the partners' positive capital account balances.

(7) See examples (1)(i) and (ii), (4)(i), (8)(i), and (16)(i) of paragraph (b)(5) of this section for issues concerning paragraph (b)(2)(ii)(*b*) of this section.

(c) Obligation to restore deficit.—(1) Other arrangements treated as obligations to restore deficits.—If a partner is not expressly obligated to restore the deficit balance in such partner's capital account, such partner nevertheless will be treated as obligated to restore the deficit balance in his capital account (in accordance with the requirement in paragraph (b)(2)(ii)(*b*)(*3*) of this section and subject to paragraph (b)(2)(ii)(*c*)(2) of this section) to the extent of—

(A) The outstanding principal balance of any promissory note (of which such partner is the maker) contributed to the partnership by such partner (other than a promissory note that is readily tradable on an established securities market), and

(B) The amount of any unconditional obligation of such partner (whether imposed by the partnership agreement or by state or local law) to make subsequent contributions to the partnership (other than pursuant to a promissory note of which such partner is the maker).

(2) Satisfaction requirement.—For purposes of paragraph (b)(2)(ii)(*c*)(*1*) of this section, a promissory note or unconditional obligation is taken into account only if it is required to be satisfied at a time no later than the end of the partnership taxable year in which such partner's interest is liquidated (or, if later, within 90 days after the date of such liquidation). If a promissory note referred to in paragraph (b)(2)(ii)(*c*)(*1*) of this section is negotiable, a partner will be considered required to satisfy such note within the time period specified in this paragraph (b)(2)(ii)(*c*)(2) if the partnership agreement provides that, in lieu of actual satisfaction, the partnership will retain such note and such partner will contribute to the partnership the excess, if any, of the outstanding principal balance of such note over its fair market value at the time of liquidation. See paragraph (b)(2)(iv)(*d*)(2) of this section. See examples (1)(ix) and (x) of paragraph (b)(5) of this section.

(3) Related party notes.—For purposes of paragraph (b)(2) of this section, if a partner contributes a promissory note to the partnership during a partnership taxable year beginning after December 29, 1988, and the maker of such note is a person related to such partner (within the meaning of §1.752-4(b)(1)), then such promissory note shall be treated as a promissory note of which such partner is the maker.

(4) Obligations disregarded.—(A) General rule.—A partner in no event will be considered obligated to restore the deficit balance in his capital account to the partnership (in accordance with the requirement in paragraph (b)(2)(ii)(*b*)(3) of this section) to the extent such partner's obligation is a bottom dollar payment obligation that is not recognized under

§ 1.752-2(b)(3) or is not legally enforceable, or the facts and circumstances otherwise indicate a plan to circumvent or avoid such obligation. See paragraphs (b)(2)(ii)(*f*), (b)(2)(ii)(*h*), and (b)(4)(vi) of this section for other rules regarding such obligation. To the extent a partner is not considered obligated to restore the deficit balance in the partner's capital account to the partnership (in accordance with the requirement in paragraph (b)(2)(ii)(*b*)(*3*) of this section), the obligation is disregarded and paragraph (b)(2) of this section and § 1.752-2 are applied as if the obligation did not exist.

(B) Factors indicating plan to circumvent or avoid obligation.—In the case of an obligation to restore a deficit balance in a partner's capital account upon liquidation of a partnership, paragraphs (b)(2)(ii)(*c*)(*4*)(*B*)(*i*) through (*iv*) of this section provide a nonexclusive list of factors that may indicate a plan to circumvent or avoid the obligation. For purposes of making determinations under this paragraph (b)(2)(ii)(*c*)(*4*), the weight to be given to any particular factor depends on the particular case and the presence or absence of any particular factor is not, in itself, necessarily indicative of whether or not the obligation is respected. The following factors are taken into consideration for purposes of this paragraph (b)(2):

(i) The partner is not subject to commercially reasonable provisions for enforcement and collection of the obligation.

(ii) The partner is not required to provide (either at the time the obligation is made or periodically) commercially reasonable documentation regarding the partner's financial condition to the partnership.

(iii) The obligation ends or could, by its terms, be terminated before the liquidation of the partner's interest in the partnership or when the partner's capital account as provided in § 1.704-1(b)(2)(iv) is negative.

(iv) The terms of the obligation are not provided to all the partners in the partnership in a timely manner.

* * *

U.S. Persons: Partnerships with Foreign Partners: Transfers of Appreciated Property

U.S. Persons: Partnerships with Foreign Partners: Transfers of Appreciated Property.—Amendments to Reg. § 1.704-1, addressing transfers of appreciated property by U.S. persons to partnerships with foreign partners related to the transferor, are proposed (published in the Federal Register on January 19, 2017) (REG-127203-15).

Par. 3. Section 1.704-1 is amended by adding paragraph (b)(2)(iv)(f)(6) following the undesignated paragraph at the end of paragraph (b)(2)(iv)(f)(5) and adding paragraph (f) to read as follows:

§ 1.704-1. Partner's distributive share.

* * *

(b) * * *

(2) * * *

(iv) * * *

(*f*) * * *

(*6*) [The text of proposed § 1.704-1(b)(2)(iv)*f*)(*6*) is the same as the text of § 1.704-1T(b)(2)(iv)*f*)(*6*) as added by T.D. 9814].

* * *

(f) [The text of proposed § 1.704-1(f) is the same as the text of § 1.704-1T(f) as added by T.D. 9814].

* * *

Partnerships: Centralized Partnership Audit Regime

Partnerships: Centralized Partnership Audit Regime.—Amendments to Reg. § 1.704-1, implementing the centralized partnership audit regime that have not been finalized to reflect the changes made by the Technical Corrections Act of 2018, contained in Title II of the Consolidated Appropriations Act of 2018 (TTCA), are proposed (published in the Federal Register on August 17, 2018) (REG-136118-15; REG-119337-17; REG-118067-17; REG-120232-17 and REG-120233-17).

Par. 2. Section 1.704-1 is amended by:

1. Adding paragraph (b)(1)(viii).
2. Adding a sentence to the end of paragraph (b)(2)(iii)(*a*).
3. Adding paragraphs (b)(2)(iii)(*f*), (b)(2)(iv)(*i*)(*4*), and (b)(4)(xi) through (xv).

The additions read as follows:

§ 1.704-1. Partner's distributive share.

* * *

(b) * * *

(1) * * *

(viii) *Items relating to a final determination under the centralized partnership audit regime.—(a) In general.*—Certain items of income, gain, loss, deduction or credit may result from a final determination under subchapter C of chapter 63 of the Internal Revenue Code (subchapter C of chapter 63) (relating to the centralized partnership audit regime). Special rules under section 704(b) and § 1.704-1(b) apply to these items that take into account that the item relates to the reviewed year (as defined in § 301.6241-1(a)(8) of this chapter) but occurs in the adjustment year (as defined in § 301.6241-1(a)(1) of this chapter). See paragraphs (b)(2)(iii)(*a*) and (*f*), (b)(2)(iv)(*i*)(*4*), and (b)(4)(xi) through (xv) of this section.

(b) Successors.—(1) In general.—In the case of a transfer or liquidation of a partnership interest subsequent to a reviewed year, a successor has the meaning provided in paragraph (b)(1)(viii)(*b*) of this section. In the case of a subsequent transfer by a successor of a partnership interest, the principles of paragraph (b)(1)(viii)(*b*) of this section will also apply to the new successor.

(2) Identifiable transferee partner.—Except as otherwise provided in paragraph (b)(1)(viii)(*b*)(*3*) of this section, in the case of a transfer of all or part of a partnership interest during or subsequent to the reviewed year, a

successor is the partner to which the reviewed year transferor partner's capital account carried over (or would carry over if the partnership maintained capital accounts) under paragraph (b)(2)(iv)(*l*) of this section (an identifiable transferee partner).

(3) Unidentifiable transferee partner.—If, after exercising reasonable diligence, the partnership cannot determine an identifiable transferee partner under paragraph (b)(1)(viii)(*b*)(*2*) of this section, each partner in the adjustment year that is not an identifiable transferee partner and was not a partner in the reviewed year, (an unidentifiable transferee partner) is a successor to the extent of the proportion of its interest in the partnership to the total interests of unidentifiable transferee partners in the partnership (considering all facts and circumstances).

(4) Liquidation of partnership interest.—In the case of a liquidation of a partner's entire interest in the partnership during or subsequent to the reviewed year, the successors to the liquidated partner are certain adjustment year partners (as defined in § 301.6241-1(a)(2) of this chapter) as provided in this paragraph (b)(1)(viii)(*b*)(*4*). The determination of the extent to which the adjustment year partners are treated as successors under this section must be made in a manner that reflects the extent to which the adjustment year partners' interests in the partnership increased as a result of the liquidating distribution (considering all facts and circumstances).

(2) * * *

(iii) * * *

(a) * * *Notwithstanding any other sentence of this paragraph (b)(2)(iii)(*a*), an allocation of any of the following will be substantial only if the allocation is described in paragraph (b)(2)(iii)(*f*) of this section: an expenditure for any payment required to be made by a partnership under subchapter C of chapter 63 (relating to the centralized partnership audit regime), adjustments reflected on a statement furnished to a pass-through partner (as defined in § 301.6241-1(a)(5) of this chapter) under § 301.6226-3(e)(4) of this chapter, or interest, penalties, additions to tax, or additional amounts described in section 6233.

* * *

(f) Certain expenditures under the centralized partnership audit regime.—(1) In general.—The economic effect of an allocation of an expenditure for any payment required to be made by a partnership under subchapter C of chapter 63 (as described in § 301.6241-4(a) of this chapter) is substantial only if the expenditure is allocated in the manner described in this paragraph (b)(2)(iii)(*f*). For partnerships with allocations that do not satisfy paragraph (b)(2)(ii) of this section, see paragraph (b)(4)(xi) of this section.

(2) Expenditures for imputed underpayments or similar amounts.—Except as otherwise provided, an expenditure for an imputed underpayment, as defined in § 301.6241-1(a)(3) of this chapter, is allocated to the reviewed year partner (or its successor, as defined in paragraph (b)(1)(viii)(*b*) of this section) in proportion to the allocation of the notional item (as described in § 301.6225-4(b) of this chapter) to which the expenditure relates, taking into account modifications under § 301.6225-2 of this chapter attributable to that partner.

(3) Interest, penalties, additions to tax, or additional amounts described in section 6233.—An expenditure for interest, penalties, additions to tax, or additional amounts as determined under section 6233 (or penalties and interest described in § 301.6226-3(e)(4)(iv) of this chapter) is allocated to the reviewed year partner (or its successor, as defined in paragraph (b)(1)(viii)(*b*) of this section) in proportion to the allocation of the portion of the imputed underpayment with respect to which the penalty applies or related notional item to which it relates (whichever is appropriate), taking into account modifications under § 301.6225-2 of this chapter attributable to that partner.

(4) Imputed underpayments unrelated to notional items.—In the case of an imputed underpayment that results from a partnership adjustment for which no notional items are created under § 301.6225-4(b)(2) of this chapter, the expenditure must be allocated to the reviewed year partner (or its successor, as defined in paragraph (b)(1)(viii)(*b*) of this section) that would have borne the economic benefit or burden of the partnership adjustment if the partnership and its partners had originally reported in a manner consistent with the partnership adjustment that resulted in the imputed underpayment with respect to the reviewed year.

(iv) * * *

(i) * * *

(4) Certain expenditures under the centralized partnership audit regime.—Notwithstanding paragraph (b)(2)(iv)(*i*)(*1*) of this section, the economic effect of an allocation of an expenditure for any payment required to be made by a partnership under subchapter C of chapter 63 (as described in § 301.6241-4(a) of this chapter) is substantial only if the expenditure is allocated in the manner described in paragraph (b)(2)(iii)(*f*) of this section. For partnerships with allocations that do not satisfy paragraph (b)(2)(ii) of this section, see paragraph (b)(4)(xii) of this section.

* * *

(4) * * *

(xi) *Notional items under the centralized partnership audit regime.*—An allocation of a notional item (as described in § 301.6225-4(b)(3) of this chapter) does not have substantial economic effect within the meaning of paragraph (b)(2) of this section. However, the allocation of a notional item of income or gain described in § 301.6225-4(b)(3)(ii) and (iv) of this chapter, or expense or loss described in § 301.6225-4(b)(3)(iii) and (v) of this chapter, will be deemed to be in accordance with the partners' interests in the partnership if the notional item is allocated in the manner in which the corresponding actual item would have been allocated in the reviewed year under the rules of this section, treating successors (as defined in paragraph (b)(1)(viii)(*b*) of this section) as reviewed year partners. Additionally, the allocation of a notional item of expense or loss described in § 301.6225-4(b)(3)(iv) of this chapter, or a notional item of income or gain described in § 301.6225-4(b)(3)(v) of this chapter, will be deemed to be in accordance with the partners' interests in the partnership if the notional item is allocated to the reviewed year partners (or their successors as defined in paragraph (b)(1)(viii)(*b*) of this section) in the manner in which the excess item was allocated in the reviewed year.

(xii) *Certain section 705(a)(2)(B) expenditures under the centralized partnership audit regime.*—An allocation of an expenditure for any payment required to be made by a partnership under subchapter C of chapter 63 (relating to the centralized partnership audit regime and as described in §301.6241-4(a) of this chapter) will be deemed to be in accordance with the partners' interests in the partnership, as provided in paragraph (b)(3) of this section, only if the expenditure is allocated in the manner described in paragraph (b)(2)(iii)(*f*) of this section and if the partners' distribution rights are reduced by the partners' shares of the imputed underpayment.

(xiii) *Partnership adjustments that do not result in an imputed underpayment under the centralized partnership audit regime.*—An allocation of an item arising from a partnership adjustment that does not result in an imputed underpayment (as defined in §301.6225-1(f) of this chapter) does not have substantial economic effect within the meaning of paragraph (b)(2) of this section. However, the allocation of such an item will be deemed to be in accordance with the partners' interests in the partnership if allocated in the manner in which the item would have been allocated in the reviewed year under the rules of this section, treating successors as defined in paragraph (b)(1)(viii)(*b*) of this section as reviewed year partners.

(xiv) *Partnership adjustments subject to an election under section 6226.*—An allocation of an item arising from a partnership adjustment that results in an imputed underpayment for which an election is made under §301.6226-1 of this chapter does not have substantial economic effect within the meaning of paragraph (b)(2) of this section. However, the allocation of such an item will be deemed to be in accordance with the partners' interests in the partnership if allocated in the adjustment year (as defined in §301.6241-1(a)(1) of this chapter) in the manner in which the item would have been allocated under the rules of this section (or otherwise taken into account under subtitle A of the Code) in the reviewed year (as defined in §301.6241-1(a)(8) of this chapter), followed by any intervening years (as defined in §301.6226-3(b)(3) of this chapter), concluding with the reporting year (as defined in §301.6226-3(a) of this chapter).

(xv) *Substantial economic effect under sections 168(h) and 514(c)(9)(E)(i)(II).*—An allocation described in paragraphs (b)(4)(xi) through (xiv) of this section will be deemed to have substantial economic effect for purposes of sections 168(h) and 514(c)(9)(E)(i)(II) if the allocation is deemed to be in accordance with the partners' interests in the partnership under the applicable rules set forth in paragraphs (b)(4)(xi) through (xiv) of this section.

* * *

Qualified Property: Additional First Year Depreciation Deduction

Qualified Property: Additional First Year Depreciation Deduction.—Amendments to Reg. §§1.704-1 and 1.704-3, providing guidance regarding the additional first year depreciation deduction under section 168(k) of the Internal Revenue Code (Code), are proposed (published in the Federal Register on August 8, 2018) (REG-104397-18).

Par. 14. Section 1.704-1 is amended by adding two sentences at the end of paragraph (b)(1)(ii)(*a*) and adding a sentence at the end of paragraph (b)(2)(iv)(*g*)(*3*) to read as follows:

§1.704-1. Partner's distributive share.

* * *

(b) * * *

(1) * * *

(ii) * * *

(*a*) * * * The last sentence of paragraph (b)(2)(iv)(*g*)(*3*) of this section is applicable for partnership taxable years ending on or after the date of publication of a Treasury decision adopting these rules as final regulations in the **Federal Register**. However, a partnership may rely on the last sentence in paragraph (b)(2)(iv)(*g*)(*3*) of this section in these proposed regulations for the partnership's taxable years ending on or after September 28, 2017, and ending before the partnership's taxable year that includes the date of publication of a Treasury decision adopting these rules as final regulations in the **Federal Register**.

* * *

(2) * * *

(iv) * * *

(*g*) * * *

(*3*) * * * For purposes of the preceding sentence, additional first year depreciation deduction under section 168(k) is not a reasonable method.

* * *

Par. 15. Section 1.704-3 is amended by:

1. Adding a sentence at the end of paragraph (d)(2);
2. Revising the first sentence in paragraph (f); and
3. Adding two sentences at the end of paragraph (f).

The additions and revision read as follows:

§1.704-3. Election of limitation of tax for individuals.

* * *

(d) * * *

(2) * * * However, the additional first year depreciation deduction under section 168(k) is not a permissible method for purposes of the preceding sentence and, if a partnership has acquired property in a taxable year for which the additional first year depreciation deduction under section 168(k) has been used of the same type as the contributed property, the portion of the contributed property's book basis that exceeds its adjusted tax basis must be recovered under a reasonable method. See §1.168(k)-2(b)(3)(iv)(B).

* * *

(f) * * * With the exception of paragraphs (a)(1), (a)(8)(ii) and (iii), and (a)(10) and (11) of this section, and of the last sentence in paragraph (d)(2) of this section, this section applies to properties contributed to a partnership and to restatements pursuant to § 1.704-1(b)(2)(iv)(*f*) on or after December 21, 1993. * * * The last sentence of paragraph (d)(2) of this section applies to property contributed to a partnership on or after the date of publication of a Treasury decision adopting these rules as final regulations in the **Federal Register**. However, a taxpayer may rely on the last sentence in paragraph (d)(2) of this section in these proposed regulations for property contributed to a partnership on or after September 28, 2017, and ending before the date of publication of a Treasury decision adopting these rules as final regulations in the **Federal Register**.

* * *

U.S. Persons: Partnerships with Foreign Partners: Transfers of Appreciated Property

U.S. Persons: Partnerships with Foreign Partners: Transfers of Appreciated Property.—Amendments to Reg. § 1.704-3, addressing transfers of appreciated property by U.S. persons to partnerships with foreign partners related to the transferor, are proposed (published in the Federal Register on January 19, 2017) (REG-127203-15).

Par. 4. Section 1.704-3 is amended by adding paragraphs (a)(13), (d)(5)(iii), and (g) to read as follows:

§ 1.704-3. Contributed property.—(a) * * *

(13) [The text of proposed § 1.704-3(a)(13) is the same as the text of § 1.704-3T(a)(13) as added by T.D. 9814].

* * *

(d) * * *

(5) * * *

(iii) [The text of proposed § 1.704-3(d)(5)(iii) is the same as the text of § 1.704-3T(d)(5)(iii) as added by T.D. 9814].

* * *

(g) [The text of proposed § 1.704-3(g) is the same as the text of § 1.704-3T(g) as added by T.D. 9814].

Partnerships: Distribution of Property: Assets-Over Merger

Partnerships: Distribution of Property: Assets-Over Merger.—Amendments to Reg. §§ 1.704-3 and 1.704-4, providing rules concerning the application of Code Secs. 704(c)(1)(B) and 737 to distributions of property after two partnerships engage in an assets-over merger, are proposed (published in the Federal Register on August 22, 2007) (REG-143397-05) (corrected November 6, 2007).

☐ Par. 2. Section 1.704-3 is amended as follows:

1. Paragraphs (a)(9) through (a)(12) are redesignated as paragraphs (a)(10) through (a)(13), respectively.

2. New paragraph (a)(9) is added.

3. Paragraph (f) is amended by revising the paragraph heading and adding one additional sentence at the end of the paragraph.

The revisions and additions read as follows:

§ 1.704-3. Contributed Property.

(a) * * *

(9) *Section 704(c) property transferred in an assets-over merger*.—Assets transferred to a transferee partnership from the transferor partnership in an assets-over merger as defined in § 1.708-1(c)(3)(i) (the transferor partnership being the partnership considered to have been terminated under § 1.708-1(c)(1) and the transferee partnership being the partnership considered to be the resulting partnership under § 1.708-(1)(c)(1)) may have both original section 704(c) gain or loss (see § 1.704-4(c)(4)(ii)(A) for the definition of original section 704(c) gain or loss) and new section 704(c) gain or loss. The transferee partnership may continue to use the section 704(c) allocation method adopted by the transferor partnership with respect to section 704(c) property originally contributed to the transferor partnership or it may adopt another reasonable section 704(c) method. Also, the transferee partnership may continue to use the section 704(c) allocation method adopted by the transferor partnership with respect to new section 704(c) gain or loss to account for differences between book value and adjusted tax basis as a result of a prior revaluation. In addition, the transferee partnership may adopt any reasonable section 704(c) method with respect to new section 704(c) gain or loss in excess of the amount of new section 704(c) gain or loss described in the prior sentence. With respect to both original and new section 704(c) gain or loss, the transferee partnership must use a reasonable method that is consistent with the purpose of sections 704(b) and 704(c).

* * *

(f) *Effective/applicability date.*—* * * Paragraph (a)(9) is effective for any distribution of property after January 19, 2005, if such property was contributed in a merger using the assets-over form after May 3, 2004.

☐ Par. 3. Section 1.704-4 is amended as follows:

1. Paragraph (a)(1) is amended by removing the phrase "five years" and adding in its place the phrase "seven years."

2. Paragraph (a)(4)(i) is amended by removing the phrase "five-year" and adding in its place the phrase "seven-year."

3. Paragraph (a)(4)(ii) is amended by removing the phrase "five-year" and adding in its place the phrase "seven-year."

4. Paragraphs (c)(4)(i) and (c)(4)(ii) are added.

5. Paragraph (c)(7) is redesignated as paragraph (c)(8).
6. A new paragraph (c)(7) is added.
7. Paragraphs (f)(2), *Examples (1) and (2)* are amended by removing the language "five-year" and replacing it with the language "seven-year" wherever it appears throughout both examples.
8. Paragraph (g) is amended by revising the paragraph heading and adding two sentences at the end of the paragraph.

The revisions and additions read as follows:

§ 1.704-4. Distribution of contributed property.

* * *

(c) * * *

(4) *Complete transfer to another partnership (Assets-Over Merger).*—(i) *In general.*—Section 704(c)(1)(B) and this section do not apply to the transfer in an assets-over merger as defined in § 1.708-1(c)(3)(i) by a partnership (the transferor partnership, which is considered to be the terminated partnership as a result of the merger) of all of its assets and liabilities to another partnership (the transferee partnership, which is considered to be the resulting partnership after the merger), followed by a distribution of the interest in the transferee partnership in liquidation of the transferor partnership as part of the same plan or arrangement.

(ii) *Subsequent distributions.*—Except as provided in paragraph (c)(4)(E) below, section 704(c)(1)(B) and this section apply to the subsequent distribution by the transferee partnership of section 704(c) property contributed by the transferor partnership to the transferee partnership in an assets-over merger, as provided in paragraphs (c)(4)(ii)(A) through (D) of this section.

(A) *Original section 704(c) gain or loss.*—The seven-year period in section 704(c)(1)(B) does not restart with respect to original section 704(c) gain or loss as a result of the transfer of the section 704(c) property to the transferee partnership. For purposes of this paragraph (c)(4)(ii)(A), the amount of original section 704(c) gain or loss is the difference between the property's fair market value and the contributing partner's adjusted tax basis, at the time of contribution, to the extent such difference has not been eliminated by section 704(c) allocations, prior revaluations, or in connection with the merger. See §§ 1.704-4(a) and (b) for post-merger distributions of property contributed to the transferee partnership prior to the merger. A subsequent distribution by the transferee partnership of property with original section 704(c) gain or loss to a partner other than the partner that contributed such property to the transferor partnership is subject to section 704(c)(1)(B) if the distribution occurs within seven years of the contribution of the property to the transferor partnership. See § 1.704-4(c)(4)(ii)(B) for rules relating to the distribution of property with new section 704(c) gain or loss. See § 1.737-2(b)(1)(ii)(A) for a similar rule in the context of section 737.

(B) *New section 704(c) gain or loss.*—A subsequent distribution of property with new section 704(c) gain or loss by the transferee partnership to a partner other than the contributing partner is subject to section 704(c)(1)(B) if the distribution occurs within seven years of the contribution of the property to the transferee partnership by the transferor partnership. For these purposes, a partner of the transferor partnership is deemed to have contributed to the transferee partnership an undivided interest in the property of the transferor partnership. The determination of the partners' undivided interest for this purpose shall be determined by the transferor partnership using any reasonable method. New section 704(c) gain or loss shall be allocated among the partners of the transferor partnership in a manner consistent with the principles of §§ 1.704-3(a)(7) and 1.704-3(a)(10). See § 1.737-2(b)(1)(ii)(B) for a similar rule in the context of section 737.

(C) *Ordering Rule.*—(1) *Post-merger revaluation.*—Revaluations after a merger that reflect a reduction in the amount of built-in gain or loss inherent in property will reduce new section 704(c) gain or loss prior to reducing original section 704(c) gain or loss.

(2) *Post-merger partial recognition.*—For purposes of this section, if less than all of a section 704(c) property is distributed, then a proportionate amount of original and new section 704(c) gain or loss must be recognized.

(D) *Subsequent Mergers.*—If the transferee partnership (first transferee partnership) is subsequently merged into another partnership (new transferee partnership) the new section 704(c) gain or loss that resulted from the merger of the transferor partnership into the first transferee partnership shall be subject to section 704(c)(1)(B) for seven years from the time of the contribution by the transferor partnership to the first transferee partnership (original merger) and new section 704(c) gain or loss that resulted from the merger of the first transferee into the new transferee (subsequent merger) shall be subject to section 704(c)(1)(B) for seven years from the time of the subsequent merger. See § 1.737-2(b)(1)(ii)(D) for a similar rule in the context of section 737.

(E) *Identical Ownership or De Minimis Change in Ownership Exception.*—Section 704(c)(1)(B) and this section do not apply to new section 704(c) gain or loss in property transferred by the transferor partnership to the transferee partnership if both the transferor partnership and the transferee partnership are owned by the same owners in the same proportions or the difference in ownership is de minimis. The transferor partnership and the transferee partnership are owned by the same owners in the same proportions if each partner owns identical interests in book capital and in each item of income, gain, loss, deduction, and credit, and identical shares of distributions and liabilities in each of the transferor and transferee partnerships. A difference in ownership is de minimis if ninety seven percent of the interests in book capital and in each item of income, gain, loss, deduction and credit and shares of distributions, and liabilities of the transferor partnership and transferee partnership are owned by the same owners in the same proportions. See § 1.737-2(b)(1)(ii)(E) for a similar rule in the context of section 737.

(F) *Examples.*—The following examples illustrate the rules of paragraph (c)(4)(ii) of this section.

Example (1). New section 704(c) gain. (i) *Facts* . On January 1, 2005, A contributes Asset 1, with a basis of $200x and a fair market value of $300x, to partnership PRS1 in exchange for a 50 percent interest. On the same date, B contributes $300x of cash to PRS1 in exchange for a 50 percent interest. Also on January 1, 2005, C contributes Asset 2, with a basis of $100x and a fair market value of $200x, to partnership PRS2 in exchange for a 50 percent interest. D contributes $200x of cash to PRS2 in exchange for a 50 percent interest. On January 1, 2008, PRS1 and PRS2 undertake an assets-over partnership merger in which PRS1 is the continuing partnership and PRS2 is the terminating partnership for both state law and federal tax purposes. At the time of the merger, PRS1's only assets are Asset 1, with a fair market value of $900x, and $300x in cash. PRS2's only assets are Asset 2, with a fair market value of $600x, and $200x in cash. After the merger, the partners have book capital and profits interests in PRS1 as follows: A, 30 percent; B, 30 percent; C, 20 percent; and D, 20 percent. PRS1 and PRS2 both have provisions in their respective partnership agreements requiring the revaluation of partnership property upon entry of a new partner. PRS1 would not be treated as an investment company (within the meaning of section 351) if it were incorporated. Neither partnership holds any unrealized receivables or inventory for purposes of section 751. In addition, neither partnership has a section 754 election in place. Asset 1 and Asset 2 are nondepreciable capital assets. On January 1, 2013, PRS1 has the same assets that it had after the merger. Each asset has the same value that it had at the time of the merger. On this date, PRS1 distributes Asset 2 to A in liquidation of A's interest.

(ii) *Analysis*. On the date of the merger of PRS2 into PRS1, the fair market value of Asset 2 ($600x) exceeded its adjusted tax basis ($100x). Thus, pursuant to § 1.704-4(c)(4)(ii)(A), when Asset 2 was contributed to PRS1 in the merger, it was section 704(c) gain property. The total amount of the section 704(c) gain was $500x ($600x (fair market value) — $100x (adjusted basis)). The amount of original section 704(c) gain attributable to Asset 2 equals $100x, the difference between its fair market value ($200x) and adjusted tax basis ($100x) upon contribution to PRS2 by C. The amount of new section 704(c) gain attributable to Asset 2 equals $400x, the total amount of section 704(c) gain ($500x) less the amount of the original section 704(c) gain ($100x). The distribution of Asset 2 to A occurs more than seven years after the contribution by C of Asset 2 to PRS2. Therefore, pursuant to § 1.704-4(c)(4)(ii)(A), section 704(c)(1)(B) does not apply to the $100x of original section 704(c) gain. The distribution of Asset 2 to A, however, occurs within seven years of the contribution in the merger of Asset 2 to PRS1 by PRS2. Pursuant to § 1.704-4(c)(4)(ii)(B), section 704(c)(1)(B) applies to the new section 704(c) gain. As the transferees of PRS2's partnership interest in PRS1, C and D succeed to one-half of the $400x of the new section 704(c) gain created by the merger. Thus, as a result of the distribution of Asset 2 to A within seven years of the merger, C and D are required to recognize $200x of gain each. See § 1.737-2(b)(1)(ii)(F), *Example (1)* for analysis of a similar example under section 737.

Example (2). Revaluation gain and merger gain. (i) *Facts* . The facts are the same as *Example (1)*, except that during 2005, PRS2 admitted E as a new partner in PRS2 at a time when the fair market value of Asset 2 was $300x and PRS2's only other asset was cash of $200X. In exchange for a contribution of cash of $250x, E was admitted as a one-third partner in PRS2. In accordance with the terms of PRS2's partnership agreement, the partnership revalued its assets pursuant to § 1.704-1(b)(2)(iv)(f) upon admission of E so that the unrealized gain of $100X attributable to Asset 2 was allocated equally between C and D, or $50X each. On January 1, 2008, PRS2 merges into PRS1. At the time of the merger, PRS1's only assets are Asset 1, with a fair market value of $550x, and $300x in cash. PRS2's only assets are Asset 2, with a fair market value of $400x, and $400x in cash. After the merger, the partners have book capital and profits and loss interests in PRS1 as follows: A, 25.76 percent; B, 25.76 percent; C, 16.16 percent; D, 16.16 percent; and E, 16.16 percent. On January 1, 2011, Asset 2 is distributed to A when its value is still $400x.

(ii) Analysis. On the date of the merger of PRS2 into PRS1, the fair market value of Asset 2 ($400x) exceeded its adjusted tax basis ($100x). Thus, when Asset 2 was contributed to PRS1 in the merger, it was section 704(c) gain property. The total amount of the section 704(c) gain was $300x ($400x (fair market value) - $100x (adjusted basis)). The amount of the original section 704(c) gain attributable to Asset 2 equals $100x, the difference between its fair market value of $200x and adjusted tax basis $100x upon contribution to PRS2 by C. The amount of the new section 704(c) gain attributable to Asset 2 equals $200x, the total section 704(c) gain ($300x) less the amount of the original section 704(c) gain ($100x). The distribution of Asset 2 to A occurs within seven years after the contribution by C to PRS2. Therefore, pursuant to § 1.704-4(c)(4)(ii)(A), section 704(c)(1)(B) applies to the original section 704(c) gain. The distribution of Asset 2 to A also occurs within seven years of the contribution of Asset 2 to PRS1 by PRS2. Pursuant to § 1.704-4(c)(4)(ii)(B), section 704(c)(1)(B) applies to the new section 704(c) gain. As the transferees of PRS2's partnership interest in PRS1, C and D each succeed to $50x of new section 704(c) gain as a result of the revaluation of Asset 2 upon admission of E as a partner. Moreover, C, D and E each succeed to $33.33x of new section 704(c) gain as a result of the merger. C also has $100x of original section 704(c) gain as a result of the original contribution of Asset 2 to PRS2. Thus, as a result of the distribution of Asset 2 to A within seven years of the merger, C, D and E are each required to recognize gain. C will recognize a total of $183.33x of gain ($100x of original section 704(c) gain and $83.33x of new section 704(c) gain). D will recognize a total of $83.33x of gain (all new section 704(c) gain) and E will recognize $33.33x of gain (all new section 704(c) gain). See § 1.737-2(b)(1)(ii)(F), *Example (2)* for a similar example under section 737.

Example (3). Revaluation loss and merger gain. (i) *Facts*. The facts are the same as *Example (1)* except that during 2005, PRS2 admitted E as a new partner in PRS2 at a time when the fair market value of Asset 2 was $150x and PRS2's only other asset was cash of $200x. In exchange for a contribution of cash of $175x, E was admitted as a one-third partner in PRS2. In accordance with the terms of PRS2's partnership agreement, the partnership revalued its assets upon admission of E so that the unrealized loss of $50x attributable to Asset 2 was allocated equally between C and D, or $25x each. On January 1, 2008, PRS 2 merges into PRS1. At the time of the merger, PRS1's only assets are Asset 1, with a fair market value of $900x, and $300x in cash. PRS2's only assets are Asset 2, with a fair market value of $600x, and $375x in cash. After the merger, the partners have book capital and profits and loss interests in PRS1 as follows: A, 27.5 percent; B, 27.5 percent; C, 15 percent; D, 15 percent; and E, 15 percent. On January 1, 2013, Asset 2 is distributed to A when its value is still $600x.

(ii) *Analysis*. On the date of the merger of PRS2 into PRS1, the fair market value of Asset 2 ($600x) exceeded its adjusted tax basis ($100x). Thus, when Asset 2 was contributed to PRS1 in the merger, it was section 704(c) gain property. The total amount of the section 704(c) gain was $500x ($600x (fair market value) – $100x (adjusted basis)). The amount of the original section 704(c) gain attributable to Asset 2 equals $50x, the difference between its fair market value ($200x) and adjusted tax basis ($100x) upon contribution to PRS2 by C, less the unrealized loss ($50X) attributable to the revaluation of PRS2 on the admission of E as a partner in PRS2. The amount of the new section 704(c) gain attributable to Asset 2 equals $450x, the total section 704(c) gain ($500x) less the amount of the original section 704(c) gain ($50x). The distribution of Asset 2 to A occurs more than seven years after the contribution by C to PRS2. Therefore, pursuant to § 1.704-4(c)(4)(ii)(A), section 704(c)(1)(B) does not apply to the original section 704(c) gain. The distribution of Asset 2 to A, however, occurs within seven years of the contribution of Asset 2 to PRS1 and PRS2. Pursuant to § 1.704-4(c)(4)(ii)(B), section 704(c)(1)(B) applies to the new section 704(c) gain. As the transferees of PRS2's partnership interest in PRS1, C, D and E each succeed to $150x of new section 704(c) gain. Thus, as a result of the distribution of Asset 2 to A within seven years of the merger, C, D and E are each required to recognize $150x of gain.

Example (4). Reverse section 704(c) gain. (i) *Facts*. The facts are the same as *Example (1)*, except that on January 1, 2013, PRS1 distributes Asset 1 to C in liquidation of C's interest in PRS1.

(ii) *Analysis*. The distribution of Asset 1 to C occurs more than seven years after the contribution of Asset 1 to PRS1. Thus, pursuant to § 1.704-4(c)(4)(ii)(A), section 704(c)(1)(B) does not apply to the original section 704(c) gain. Pursuant to § 1.704-4(c)(7), section 704(c)(1)(B) does not apply to reverse section 704(c) gain in Asset 1 resulting from a revaluation of PRS1's partnership property at the time of the merger. Accordingly, neither A nor B will recognize gain under section 704(c)(1)(B) as a result of the distribution of Asset 1 to C. See § 1.737-2(b)(1)(ii)(F), *Example (4)* for a similar example under section 737.

Example (5). Identical ownership exception. (i) *Facts*. In 1990, A, an individual, and B, a subchapter C corporation, formed PRS1, a partnership. A owned 75 percent of the interests in the book capital (as determined for purposes of § 1.704-1(b)(2)(iv)), profits, losses, distributions, and liabilities (under section 752) of PRS1. B owned the remaining 25 percent interest in the book capital, profits, losses, distributions, and liabilities of PRS1. In the same year, A and B also formed another partnership, PRS2, with A owning 75 percent of the interests in the book capital, profits, losses, distributions, and liabilities of PRS2 and B owning the remaining 25 percent of the book capital, profits, losses, distributions, and liabilities. Upon formation of the partnerships, A contributed Asset X to PRS1 and Asset Y to PRS2 and B contributed cash. Both Assets X and Y had section 704(c) built-in gain at the time of contribution to the partnerships.

(ii) In January 2005, PRS1 is merged into PRS2 in an assets-over merger in which PRS1 is the terminating partnership and PRS2 as the continuing partnership for both state law and federal income tax purposes. At the time of the merger, both Asset X and Y had increased in value from the time they were contributed to PRS1 and PRS2, respectively. As a result, a new layer of section 704(c) gain was created with respect to Asset X in PRS1, and reverse section 704(c) gain was created with respect to Asset Y in PRS2. After the merger, A had a 75 percent interest in PRS2's capital, profits, losses, distributions, liabilities, and all other items. B held the remaining 25 percent interest in PRS2's capital, profits, losses, distributions, liabilities, and all other items. In 2006, PRS2 distributes Asset X to A.

(iii) *Analysis*. The 2006 distribution of Asset X occurs more than seven years after the formation of the partnerships and the original contribution of both Assets X and Y to the partnerships. Therefore, the original layer of built-in gain created on the original contribution of Asset X to PRS1 is not taken into account in applying section 704(c)(1)(B) to the proposed distribution. In addition, paragraph (c)(4)(ii)(E) of this section provides that section 704(c)(1)(B) and paragraph (c)(4)(ii)(B) of this section do not apply to new section 704(c) gain or loss in property transferred by the transferor partnership to the transferee partnership if both the transferor partnership and the transferee partnership are owned by the same owners in the same proportions. The transferor partnership and the transferee partnership are owned by the same owners in the same proportions if each partner's percentage interest in the transferor partnership's book capital, profits, losses, distributions, and liabilities, is the same as the partner's percentage interest in those items of the transferee partnership. In this case, A owned 75 percent and B owned 25 percent of the interests in the book capital, and in each item of income, gain, loss and credit, and share of distributions and liabilities of PRS1 and PRS2 prior to the merger and 75 percent and 25 percent, respectively, of PRS2 after the merger. As a result, the requirements of the identical ownership exception of paragraph (c)(4)(ii)(E) of this section are satisfied. Thus, the new built-in gain created upon contribution of Asset X in connection with the partnership merger will not be taken into account in applying section 704(c)(1)(B) to the proposed distribution. See § 1.737-2(b)(1)(ii)(F), *Example (5)* for a similar example under section 737.

* * *

(7) *Reverse section 704(c) gain or loss.*—Section 704(c)(1)(B) and this section do not apply to reverse section 704(c) gain or loss as described in § 1.704-3(a)(6)(i).

* * *

(g) *Effective/applicability date.*—* * * Paragraphs (a)(1), (a)(4)(i), (a)(4)(ii), and (f)(2), *Examples (1) and (2),* are effective August 22, 2007. Paragraphs (c)(4) and (c)(7) are effective for any distributions of property after January 19, 2005, if such property was contributed in a merger using the assets-over form after May 3, 2004.

Partners and Partnerships: American Jobs Creation Act of 2004 and Taxpayer Relief Act of 1997: Guidance

Partners and Partnerships: American Jobs Creation Act of 2004 and Taxpayer Relief Act of 1997: Guidance.—Amendments to Reg. §§1.704-3 and 1.704-4, providing guidance on certain provisions of the American Jobs Creation Act of 2004, conforming the regulations to statutory changes in the Taxpayer Relief Act of 1997, modifying the basis allocation rules to prevent certain unintended consequences of the current basis allocation rules for substituted basis transactions and providing additional guidance on allocations resulting from revaluations of partnership property, are proposed (published in the Federal Register on January 16, 2014) (REG-144468-05) (corrected April 15, 2014).

☐ Par. 2. Section 1.704-3 is amended by:

1. Revising paragraph (a)(3)(ii).
2. Adding paragraph (a)(3)(iii).
3. Revising paragraph (a)(6)(i).
4. Adding paragraph (a)(6)(iii).
5. Adding paragraph (a)(6)(iv).
6. Revising paragraph (a)(7).
7. Revising the first sentence in paragraph (a)(10) by removing the word "allocation" before the word "method".
8. Redesignating paragraph (f) as paragraph (g).
9. Adding a new paragraph (f).
10. Adding a sentence at the end of newly redesignated paragraph (g).

The revisions and additions read as follows.

§1.704-3. Contributed property.—(a) * * *

(3) * * *

(ii) *Built-in gain and built-in loss.*—The built-in gain on section 704(c) property is the excess of the property's book value over the contributing partner's adjusted tax basis upon contribution. The built-in gain is thereafter reduced by decreases in the difference between the property's book value and adjusted tax basis (other than decreases to the property's book value pursuant to § 1.704-1(b)(2)(iv)(*f*) or § 1.704-1(b)(2)(iv)(*s*)). The built-in loss on section 704(c) property is the excess of the contributing partner's adjusted tax basis over the property's book value upon contribution. The built-in loss is thereafter reduced by decreases in the difference between the property's adjusted tax basis and book value (other than increases to the property's book value pursuant to § 1.704-1(b)(2)(iv)(*f*) or § 1.704-1(b)(2)(iv)(*s*)). For purposes of paragraph (a)(6)(iii) and (iv) of this section, a built-in gain or built-in loss referred to in this paragraph shall be referred to as a forward section 704(c) allocation. *See* § 1.460-4(k)(3)(v)(A) for a rule relating to the amount of built-in income or built-in loss attributable to a contract accounted for under a long-term contract method of accounting.

(iii) *Effective/applicability date.*—The provisions of paragraph (a)(3)(ii) of this section apply to partnership contributions and transactions occurring on or after the date of publication of the Treasury decision adopting these rules as final regulations in the **Federal Register**. * * *

* * *

(6)(i) *Revaluations under section 704(b).*—The principles of this section apply with respect to property for which differences between book value and adjusted tax basis are created when a partnership revalues partnership property pursuant to § 1.704-1(b)(2)(iv)(*f*) or § 1.704-1(b)(2)(iv)(*s*) (reverse section 704(c) allocations). Each such revaluation creates a separate amount of built-in gain or built-in loss, as the case may be (a section 704(c) layer), that must be tracked separately from built-in gain or built-in loss arising from contribution (a forward section 704(c) layer) and any other revaluation (a reverse section 704(c) layer). For instance, one section 704(c) layer with respect to a particular property may be of built-in gain, and another section 704(c) layer with respect to the same property may be of built-in loss.

* * *

(iii) *Allocation method.*—A partnership may use any reasonable method to allocate the items of income, gain, loss, and deduction associated with an item of property among the property's forward and reverse section 704(c) layers.

(iv) *Effective/applicability date.*—The provisions of paragraph (a)(6)(iii) of this section apply to partnership contributions and transactions occurring on or after the date of publication of the Treasury decision adopting these rules as final regulations in the **Federal Register.**

* * *

(7) *Transfers of a partnership interest..*—If a contributing partner transfers a partnership interest, built-in gain must be allocated to the transferee partner as it would have been allocated to the transferor partner. If the contributing partner transfers a portion of the partnership interest, the share of built-in gain proportionate to the interest transferred must be allocated to the transferee partner. Rules for the allocation of builtin loss are provided in paragraph (f) of this section.

* * *

(f) *Special rules for built-in loss property.*—(1) *General principles.*—(i) *Contributing partner.*—If a partner contributes section 704(c)(1)(C) property (as defined in paragraph (f)(2)(i) of this section) to a partnership, the excess of the adjusted basis of the section 704(c)(1)(C) property (determined without regard to paragraph (f)(1)(ii) of this section) over its fair market value immediately before the contribution will be taken into account only in determining the amount of items allocated to the section 704(c)(1)(C) partner (as defined in paragraph (f)(2)(ii) of this section) that contributed such section 704(c)(1)(C) property.

(ii) *Non-contributing partners.*—In determining the amount of items allocated to partners other than the section 704(c)(1)(C) partner, the initial basis of section 704(c)(1)(C) property in the hands of the partnership is equal to the property's fair market value at the time of contribution.

(2) *Definitions.*—For purposes of this section—

(i) *Section 704(c)(1)(C) property.*—The term *section 704(c)(1)(C) property* means section 704(c) property (as defined in paragraph (a)(3)(i) of this section) with a built-in loss at the time of contribution. Section 704(c)(1)(C) property does not include a § 1.752-7 liability (within the meaning of § 1.752-7(b)(3)) or property for which differences between book value and adjusted tax basis are created when a partnership revalues property pursuant to § 1.704-1(b)(2)(iv)(*f*) or § 1.704-1(b)(2)(iv)(*s*).

(ii) *Section 704(c)(1)(C) partner.*—The term *section 704(c)(1)(C) partner* means a partner that contributes section 704(c)(1)(C) property to a partnership.

(iii) *Section 704(c)(1)(C) basis adjustment.*—A property's section 704(c)(1)(C) basis adjustment is initially equal to the excess of the adjusted basis of section 704(c)(1)(C) property (determined without regard to paragraph (f)(1)(ii) of this section) over its fair market value immediately before the contribution, and is subsequently adjusted for the recovery of the section 704(c)(1)(C) basis adjustment under paragraph (f)(3)(ii)(D) of this section.

(3) *Operational rules.*—(i) *In general.*—Except as provided in this section, section 704(c)(1)(C) property is subject to the rules and regulations applicable to section 704(c) property. *See*, for example, § 1.704-3(a)(9).

(ii) *Effect of section 704(c)(1)(C) basis adjustment.*—(A) *In general.*—The section 704(c)(1)(C) basis adjustment is an adjustment to the basis of partnership property with respect to the section 704(c)(1)(C) partner only. A section 704(c)(1)(C) basis adjustment amount is excluded from the partnership's basis of section 704(c)(1)(C) property. Thus, for purposes of calculating income, deduction, gain, and loss, the section 704(c)(1)(C) partner will have a special basis for section 704(c)(1)(C) property in which the partner has a section 704(c)(1)(C) basis adjustment. The section 704(c)(1)(C) basis adjustment has no effect on the partnership's computation of any item under section 703.

(B) *Computation of section 704(c)(1)(C) partner's distributive share of partnership items.*—The partnership first computes its items of income, deduction, gain, or loss at the partnership level under section 703. The partnership then allocates the partnership items among the partners, including the section 704(c)(1)(C) partner, in accordance with section 704, and adjusts the partners' capital accounts accordingly. The partnership then adjusts the section 704(c)(1)(C) partner's distributive share of the items of partnership income, deduction, gain, or loss in accordance with paragraphs (f)(3)(ii)(C) and (D) of this section, to reflect the effects of the section 704(c)(1)(C) partner's section 704(c)(1)(C) basis adjustment. These adjustments to the section 704(c)(1)(C) partner's distributive share must be reflected on Schedules K and K-1 of the partnership's return (Form 1065). The adjustments to the section 704(c)(1)(C) partner's distributive shares do not affect the section 704(c)(1)(C) partner's capital account.

(C) *Effect of section 704(c)(1)(C) basis adjustment in determining items of income, gain, or loss.*—The amount of a section 704(c)(1)(C) partner's income, gain, or loss from the sale or exchange of partnership property in which the section 704(c)(1)(C) partner has a section 704(c)(1)(C) basis adjustment is equal to the section 704(c)(1)(C) partner's share of the partnership's gain or loss from the sale of the property (including any remedial allocations under § 1.704-3(d)), minus the section 704(c)(1)(C) partner's section 704(c)(1)(C) basis adjustment for the partnership property.

(D) *Effect of section 704(c)(1)(C) basis adjustment in determining items of deduction.*—*(1) In general.*—If section 704(c)(1)(C) property is subject to amortization under section 197, depreciation under section 168, or other cost recovery in the hands of the section 704(c)(1)(C) partner, the section 704(c)(1)(C) basis adjustment associated with the property is recovered in accordance with section 197(f)(2), section 168(i)(7), or another applicable Internal Revenue Code section. The amount of any section 704(c)(1)(C) basis adjustment that is recovered by the section 704(c)(1)(C) partner in any year is added to the section 704(c)(1)(C) partner's distributive share of the partnership's depreciation or amortization deductions for the year. The basis adjustment is adjusted under section 1016(a)(2) to reflect the recovery of the section 704(c)(1)(C) basis adjustment.

(2) Example.—A contributes Property, with an adjusted basis of $12,000 and a fair market value of $5,000 on January 1 of the year of contribution, and B contributes $5,000 to PRS, a partnership. Prior to the contribution, A depreciates Property under section 168 over 10 years using the straight-line method and the half-year convention. On the contribution date, Property has 7.5 years remaining in its recovery period. Property is section 704(c)(1)(C) property, and A's section 704(c)(1)(C) basis adjustment is $7,000. PRS's basis in Property is $5,000 (fair market value) and, in accordance with section 168(i)(7), the depreciation is $667 per year ($5,000 divided by 7.5 years), which is shared equally between A and B. A's $7,000 section 704(c)(1)(C) basis adjustment is subject to depreciation of $933 per year in accordance with section 168(i)(7) ($7,000 divided by 7.5 years), which is taken into account by A.

(iii) *Transfer of section 704(c)(1)(C) partner's partnership interest.*—(A) *General rule.*—Except as provided in paragraph (f)(3)(iii)(B) of this section, if a section 704(c)(1)(C) partner transfers its partnership interest, the portion of the section 704(c)(1)(C) basis adjustment attributable to the interest transferred is eliminated and the transferee is not treated as the section 704(c)(1)(C) partner with respect to the interest transferred. The transferor remains the section 704(c)(1)(C) partner with respect to any remaining section 704(c)(1)(C) basis adjustment.

(B) *Special rules.—(1) General rule for transfer of partnership interest in nonrecognition transaction.*—Except as provided in paragraph (f)(3)(iii)(B)(2) of this section, paragraph (f)(3)(iii)(A) of this section does not apply to the extent a section 704(c)(1)(C) partner transfers its partnership interest in a nonrecognition transaction. Instead, the transferee of all or a portion of a section 704(c)(1)(C) partner's partnership interest succeeds to the transferor's section 704(c)(1)(C) basis adjustments in an amount attributable to the interest transferred and the transferee will be treated as the section 704(c)(1)(C) partner with respect to the transferred interest. Regardless of whether a section 754 election is in effect or a substantial built in loss exists with respect to the transfer, the amount of any section 704(c)(1)(C) basis adjustment with respect to section 704(c)(1)(C) property to which the transferee succeeds shall be decreased by the amount of any negative section 743(b) adjustment that would be allocated to the section 704(c)(1)(C) property pursuant to the provisions of § 1.755-1 if the partnership had a section 754 election in effect upon the transfer. If the nonrecognition transaction is described in section 168(i)(7)(B), then the rules in section 168(i)(7)(A) apply with respect to transferor's cost recovery deductions under section 168. If gain or loss is recognized on the transaction, appropriate adjustments must be made to the section 704(c)(1)(C) basis adjustment.

(2) Exception for gifts.—Paragraph (f)(3)(iii)(B)(*1*) of this section does not apply to the transfer of all or a portion of a section 704(c)(1)(C) partner's partnership interest by gift.

(C) *Examples.*—The following examples illustrate the principles of this paragraph (f)(3)(iii)—

Example 1. Sale of entire partnership interest. In Year 1, A contributes nondepreciable Property, with an adjusted basis of $11,000 and a fair market value of $5,000, and B and C each contribute $5,000 cash to PRS, a partnership. PRS's basis in Property is $5,000, and A's section 704(c)(1)(C) basis adjustment in Property is $6,000. In Year 3, Property's fair market value is unchanged and A's section 704(c)(1)(C) basis adjustment remains $6,000. D purchases A's interest in PRS for its fair market value of $5,000. PRS does not have a section 754 election in effect in Year 3. A recognizes a loss of $6,000 on the sale, which equals the excess of its basis in PRS ($11,000) over the amount realized on the sale ($5,000). Pursuant to paragraph (f)(3)(iii)(A) of this section, D does not succeed to A's section 704(c)(1)(C) basis adjustment, which is eliminated upon the sale.

Example 2. Sale of portion of partnership interest. Assume the same facts as *Example 1* except that D purchases 50 percent of A's interest in PRS for its fair market value of $2,500. A recognizes a loss of $3,000 on the sale, which equals the excess of its basis in the 50 percent interest in PRS ($5,500) over the amount realized on the sale ($2,500). Pursuant to paragraph (f)(3)(iii)(A) of this section, D does not succeed to A's section 704(c)(1)(C) basis adjustment, and A's section 704(c)(1)(C) basis adjustment is reduced to $3,000 upon the sale.

Example 3. Section 721 transaction—(i) Assume the same facts as *Example 1* except that instead of selling its interest in PRS to D in Year 3, A contributes its interest in PRS to UTP, a partnership, in exchange for a 50 percent interest in UTP. Following the contribution, UTP's basis in PRS is $5,000 plus a $6,000 section 704(c)(1)(C) basis adjustment solely allocable to A. Under the facts of this example, UTP's share of basis in PRS property is the same.

(ii) Under paragraph (f)(3)(iii)(B)(*1*) of this section, UTP succeeds to A's $6,000 section 704(c)(1)(C) basis adjustment in Property. PRS does not have a section 754 election in effect and does not have a substantial built-in loss (within the meaning of § 1.743-1(a)(2)(i)) with respect to the transfer. Paragraph (f)(3)(iii)(B)(*1*) of this section requires PRS to reduce the amount of the section 704(c)(1)(C) basis adjustment by the amount of the negative section 743(b) adjustment that would be allocated to Property if PRS had an election under section 754 in effect. Because UTP's basis in PRS equals UTP's share of basis in PRS property, no negative section 743(b) adjustment would result from the transfer. Accordingly, UTP's section 704(c)(1)(C) basis adjustment in Property is $6,000. Pursuant to paragraph (a)(9) of this section, UTP must allocate its distributive share of PRS's items with respect to the section 704(c)(1)(C) basis adjustment solely to A.

(iii) In Year 3, PRS sells Property for its fair market value of $5,000. PRS realizes no gain or loss on the sale. Pursuant to paragraph (f)(3)(ii)(C) of this section, PRS reduces UTP's allocable gain from the sale of Property ($0) by the amount of UTP's section 704(c)(1)(C) basis adjustment for Property ($6,000). Thus, UTP is allocated a $6,000 loss. Pursuant to paragraph (a)(9) of this section, UTP must allocate the $6,000 loss with respect to the section 704(c)(1)(C) basis adjustment to A. A's basis in UTP decreases from $11,000 to $5,000 and its section 704(c)(1)(C) basis adjustment in UTP is eliminated.

Example 4. Interaction with section 362(e)(2)(A)—(i) Assume the same facts as *Example 1* except that instead of selling its interest in PRS to D in Year 3, A contributes its interest in PRS to Y Corp, a corporation, in a transfer described in section 351. PRS has a section 754 election in effect. A's basis in its Y Corp stock is $11,000 under section 358.

(ii) A and Y Corp do not elect to apply the provisions of section 362(e)(2)(C). Therefore, section 362(e)(2)(A) will apply because Y Corp's basis in PRS ($11,000) would exceed the fair market value of PRS ($5,000) immediately after the transaction. Thus, pursuant to section 362(e)(2)(B), Y Corp's basis in PRS will be $5,000. Y Corp succeeds to A's $6,000 section 704(c)(1)(C) basis adjustment in Property pursuant to paragraph (f)(3)(iii)(B)(*1*) of this section. Pursuant to § 1.743-1, Y Corp's section 743(b) adjustment is ($6,000), or the difference between Y Corp's basis in PRS of $5,000 and Y Corp's share of the adjusted basis of PRS's property of $11,000 (which is Y Corp's cash on liquidation of $5,000, increased by the $6,000 tax loss that would be allocated to Y Corp upon a hypothetical transaction). The ($6,000) section 743(b) adjustment will be allocated to PRS's property in accordance with section 755 and the regulations thereunder.

Example 5. Gift of partnership interest. Assume the same facts as *Example 1* except that instead of selling its PRS interest to D in Year 3, A makes a gift of its PRS interest to D. Pursuant to paragraph (f)(3)(iii)(B)(2) of this section, D does not succeed to any of A's section 704(c)(1)(C) basis adjustment in Property. The $6,000 section 704(c)(1)(C) basis adjustment is eliminated upon the gift.

(iv) *Transfer of section 704(c)(1)(C) property by partnership.*—(A) *Like-kind exchange.*—*(1) General rule.*—If a partnership disposes of section 704(c)(1)(C) property in a like-kind exchange described in section 1031 and the regulations thereunder, the substituted basis property (as defined in section 7701(a)(42)) received by the partnership is treated, solely with respect to the section 704(c)(1)(C) partner, as section 704(c)(1)(C) property with the same section 704(c)(1)(C) basis adjustment as the section 704(c)(1)(C) property disposed of by the partnership (with appropriate adjustments for any portion of the section 704(c)(1)(C) basis adjustment taken into account in determining the section 704(c)(1)(C) partner's gain or loss recognized on the transfer).

(2) Example.—A contributes Property 1 with an adjusted basis of $12,000 and a fair market value of $10,000 and B contributes $10,000 cash to PRS, a partnership. A has a $2,000 section 704(c)(1)(C) basis adjustment in Property 1, and PRS has an adjusted basis in Property 1 of $10,000, or its fair market value. PRS subsequently engages in a like-kind exchange under section 1031 of Property 1 when the fair market value of Property 1 is $13,000 and receives Property 2 with a fair market value of $12,000 and $1,000 cash in exchange. PRS's gain on the transaction is $3,000 ($13,000 minus PRS's $10,000 adjusted basis) but is recognized only to the extent of the cash received of $1,000, of which $500 is allocable to A. As provided in paragraph (f)(3)(iv)(A)(*1*) of this section, Property 2 is treated as section 704(c)(1)(C) property with respect to A and has the same section 704(c)(1)(C) basis adjustment as Property 1. Because PRS recognized gain on the transaction, A must use $500 of its section 704(c)(1)(C) basis adjustment to reduce A's gain to $0. Therefore, A's $2,000 section 704(c)(1)(C) basis adjustment is reduced to $1,500.

(B) *Contribution of 704(c)(1)(C) property in section 721 transaction.*—*(1) In general.*—The rules set forth in this paragraph (f)(3)(iv)(B) apply if a section 704(c)(1)(C) partner contributes section 704(c)(1)(C) property to an upper-tier partnership, and that upper-tier partnership subsequently contributes the section 704(c)(1)(C) property to a lower-tier partnership in a transaction described in section 721(a) (whether as part of a single transaction or as separate transactions). The interest in the lower-tier partnership received by the upper-tier partnership is treated as the section 704(c)(1)(C) property with the same section 704(c)(1)(C) basis adjustment as the contributed property. The lower-tier partnership determines its basis in the contributed property by excluding the existing section 704(c)(1)(C) basis adjustment under the principles of paragraph (f)(3)(ii)(A) of this section. However, the lower-tier partnership also succeeds to the upper-tier partnership's section 704(c)(1)(C) basis adjustment. The portion of the upper-tier partnership's basis in its interest in the lower-tier partnership attributable to the section 704(c)(1)(C) basis adjustment must be segregated and allocated solely to the section 704(c)(1)(C) partner for whom the initial section 704(c)(1)(C) basis adjustment was made. Similarly, the section 704(c)(1)(C) basis adjustment to which the lower-tier partnership succeeds must be segregated and allocated solely to the uppertier partnership, and the section 704(c)(1)(C) partner for whom the initial section 704(c)(1)(C) basis adjustment was made. If gain or loss is recognized on the transaction, appropriate adjustments must be made to the section 704(c)(1)(C) basis adjustment.

(2) Special rules.—*(a)* To the extent that any section 704(c)(1)(C) basis adjustment in a tiered partnership is recovered under paragraphs (f)(3)(ii)(C) or (D) of this section, or is otherwise reduced, upper- or lower-tier partnerships in the tiered structure must make conforming reductions to related section 704(c)(1)(C) basis adjustments to prevent duplication of loss.

(b) Section 704(c)(1)(C) property that is contributed by an upper-tier partnership to a lower-tier partnership will have an additional section 704(c)(1)(C) basis adjustment if the value of the section 704(c)(1)(C) property is less than its tax basis (as adjusted under paragraph (f)(3)(ii) of this section) at the time of the transfer to the lower-tier partnership. Any additional section 704(c)(1)(C) basis adjustment determined under this paragraph will be allocated among the partners of the upper-tier partnership in a manner that reflects their relative shares of that loss.

(3) Example 1.—(i) In Year 1, A contributes Property with an adjusted basis of $11,000 and a fair market value of $5,000, and B contributes $5,000 cash to UTP, a partnership. Later in Year 1, when Property's basis has not changed, and Property is worth at least $5,000, UTP contributes Property to LTP in a section 721 transaction for a 50-percent interest in LTP. In Year 2, LTP sells Property for its fair market value of $29,000.

(ii) A has a $6,000 section 704(c)(1)(C) basis adjustment in Property. After the section 721 transaction, A's section 704(c)(1)(C) basis adjustment in Property becomes A's section 704(c)(1)(C) adjustment in UTP's interest in LTP. UTP has a section 704(c)(1)(C) adjustment in Property in the amount of A's section 704(c)(1)(C) adjustment in Property. This section 704(c)(1)(C) adjustment must be segregated and allocated solely to A. UTP's basis in its interest in LTP is determined without reference to the section 704(c)(1)(C) adjustment. Thus, UTP's basis in LTP is $5,000. LTP's basis in Property is determined without reference to the section 704(c)(1)(C) basis adjustment; therefore, LTP's basis in Property is $5,000.

(iii) Upon the sale of Property, LTP realizes a gain of $24,000 ($29,000 fair market value minus $5,000 adjusted basis). UTP's allocable share of the $24,000 gain from the sale of Property by LTP is $12,000, reduced by UTP's $6,000 section 704(c)(1)(C) basis adjustment in

Property. Because UTP's section 704(c)(1)(C) basis adjustment must be segregated and allocated solely to A, UTP allocates the $12,000 of gain equally between A and B, but allocates the recovery of the $6,000 section 704(c)(1)(C) basis adjustment to A. Therefore, pursuant to paragraph (f)(3)(ii)(C) of this section, A recognizes no gain or loss on the sale (A's $6,000 share of UTP's gain minus the $6,000 section 704(c)(1)(C) basis adjustment). Because UTP's section 704(c)(1)(C) adjustment in Property is used, A's section 704(c)(1)(C) basis adjustment in UTP's interest in LTP is reduced to $0 to prevent duplication of loss pursuant to paragraph (f)(3)(iv)(B)(*2*)(*a*) of this section.

Example 2— Assume the same facts as *Example 1*, except that in Year 2, UTP sells its entire interest in LTP to D for its fair market value of $17,000. UTP recognizes a $12,000 gain on the sale, which equals the excess of UTP's amount realized on the sale ($17,000) over UTP's basis in LTP ($5,000). UTP allocates the $12,000 gain equally to A and B. However, A's $6,000 section 704(c)(1)(C) adjustment in UTP's interest in LTP offsets A's share of the gain. Therefore, A recognizes no gain or loss on the sale. D does not receive any of UTP's section 704(c)(1)(C) basis adjustment in Property, which is eliminated upon the sale.

Example 3—(i) Assume the same facts as *Example 1*, except that at the time UTP contributes Property to LTP, the fair market value of Property has fallen to $2,000. In Year 2, LTP sells Property for its fair market value of $2,000.

(ii) A has a $6,000 section 704(c)(1)(C) basis adjustment in Property. After the section 721 transaction, pursuant to paragraph (f)(3)(iv)(B)(*1*) of this section, A's section 704(c)(1)(C) basis adjustment in Property becomes A's section 704(c)(1)(C) adjustment in UTP's interest in LTP. Pursuant to paragraph (f)(3)(iv)(B)(*1*) of this section, UTP has a section 704(c)(1)(C) adjustment in Property in the amount of A's section 704(c)(1)(C) adjustment in Property. This section 704(c)(1)(C) adjustment must be segregated and allocated solely to A. Because UTP's basis in Property ($5,000) exceeds the fair market value of Property ($2,000) by $3,000 at the time of UTP's contribution to LTP, UTP has an additional section 704(c)(1)(C) adjustment of $3,000 in Property pursuant to paragraph (f)(3)(iv)(B)(2)(*b*) of this section. Partners A and B share equally in this $3,000 section 704(c)(1)(C) adjustment. UTP's basis in its interest in LTP is determined without reference to A's section 704(c)(1)(C) adjustment. Thus, UTP's basis in LTP is $5,000. Pursuant to paragraph (f)(3)(iv)(B)(*1*) of this section, LTP's basis in Property is determined without reference to either section 704(c)(1)(C) basis adjustment; therefore, LTP's basis in Property is $2,000.

(iii) Upon the sale of Property, LTP recognizes no gain or loss ($2,000 sales price minus $2,000 adjusted basis). However, the sale of Property triggers UTP's two separate section 704(c)(1)(C) basis adjustments. First, UTP applies the $3,000 section 704(c)(1)(C) adjustment attributable to the built-in loss in Property arising after A contributed Property to UTP. This results in an allocation of ($1,500) of loss to each of A and B. Next, UTP applies the $6,000 section 704(c)(1)(C) basis adjustment attributable to A's initial contribution of Property to UTP, resulting in an additional ($6,000) of loss allocated to A. Thus, the sale of Property by LTP results in A recognizing ($7,500) of loss, and B recognizing ($1,500) of loss. Pursuant to paragraph (f)(3)(iv)(B)(*2*)(*a*) of this section, because UTP's section 704(c)(1)(C) adjustment in Property is used, A's section 704(c)(1)(C) basis adjustment in UTP's interest in LTP is reduced to $0 to prevent duplication of loss

(C) *Section 351 transactions.*—(*1*) *Basis in transferred property.*—A corporation's adjusted basis in property transferred to the corporation by a partnership in a transaction described in section 351 is determined under section 362 (including for purposes of applying *section 362(e)*) by taking into account any section 704(c)(1)(C) basis adjustment for the property (other than any portion of a section 704(c)(1)(C) basis adjustment that reduces a partner's gain under paragraph (f)(3)(iv)(C)(*2*) of this section).

(*2*) *Partnership gain.*—The amount of gain, if any, recognized by the partnership on the transfer of property by the partnership to a corporation in a transfer described in section 351 is determined without regard to any section 704(c)(1)(C) basis adjustment for the transferred property. The amount of gain, if any, recognized by the partnership on the transfer that is allocated to the section 704(c)(1)(C) partner is adjusted to reflect the partner's section 704(c)(1)(C) basis adjustment in the transferred property.

(*3*) *Basis in stock.*—The partnership's adjusted basis in stock received from a corporation in a transfer described in section 351 is determined without regard to the section 704(c)(1)(C) basis adjustment in property transferred to the corporation in the section 351 exchange. A partner with a section 704(c)(1)(C) basis adjustment in property transferred to the corporation, however, has a basis adjustment in the stock received by the partnership in the section 351 exchange in an amount equal to the partner's section 704(c)(1)(C) basis adjustment in the transferred property, reduced by any portion of the section 704(c)(1)(C) basis adjustment that reduced the partner's gain under paragraph (f)(3)(iv)(C)(2) of this section.

(*4*) *Example.*—The following example illustrates the provisions of this paragraph (f)(3)(iv)(C).

Example. Section 351 transaction—(i) In Year 1, A contributes $10,000 cash and B contributes Property with an adjusted basis of $18,000 and a fair market value of $10,000 to PRS, a partnership. PRS takes Property with a basis of $10,000. B's section 704(c)(1)(C) basis adjustment for Property is $8,000. PRS contributes Property to Y Corp in a section 351 transaction. Under section 362(e)(2)(A), Y Corp takes a $10,000 basis in Property. PRS's basis in its Y Corp stock is $10,000 under section 358. Pursuant to paragraph (f)(3)(iv)(C)(*3*) of this section, B has a section 704(c)(1)(C) basis adjustment of $8,000 in the Y Corp stock received by PRS in the section 351 exchange.

(ii) In Year 2, Y Corp sells Property for its fair market value of $10,000. Y Corp recognizes no gain or loss on the sale of Property. Pursuant to paragraph (f)(3)(iv)(C)(*1*) of this section, B does not take into account its section 704(c)(1)(C) basis adjustment upon the sale by Y Corp of Property. Instead, B will take the section

704(c)(1)(C) basis adjustment into account when PRS disposes of the Y Corp stock.

(D) *Section 708(b)(1)(B) transactions.*—(1) *In general.*—A partner with a section 704(c)(1)(C) basis adjustment in section 704(c)(1)(C) property held by a partnership that terminates under section 708(b)(1)(B) will continue to have the same section 704(c)(1)(C) basis adjustment for section 704(c)(1)(C) property deemed contributed by the terminated partnership to the new partnership under § 1.708-1(b)(4). In addition, the deemed contribution of property by a terminated partnership to a new partnership is not subject to this section and does not create a section 704(c)(1)(C) basis adjustment.

(2) *Example.*—A contributes Property with an adjusted basis of $11,000 and a fair market value of $5,000 and B contributes $5,000 cash to PRS, a partnership. B sells its entire interest in PRS to C for its fair market value of $5,000, which terminates PRS under section 708(b)(1)(B). Under § 1.708-1(b)(4), PRS is deemed to contribute all of its assets and liabilities to a new partnership (New PRS) in exchange for an interest in New PRS. Immediately thereafter, PRS is deemed to distribute its interest in New PRS equally to A and C in complete liquidation of PRS. New PRS takes Property with a basis of $5,000 and A retains its $6,000 section 704(c)(1)(C) basis adjustment related to Property inside New PRS.

(E) *Disposition in an installment sale.*—If a partnership disposes of section 704(c)(1)(C) property in an installment sale (as defined in section 453(b)), the installment obligation received by the partnership is treated as the section 704(c)(1)(C) property with the same section 704(c)(1)(C) basis adjustment as the section 704(c)(1)(C) property disposed of by the partnership (with appropriate adjustments for any gain recognized on the installment sale).

(F) *Contributed contracts.*—If a partner contributes to a partnership a contract that is section 704(c)(1)(C) property, and the partnership subsequently acquires property pursuant to the contract in a transaction in which less than all of the loss is recognized, then the acquired property is treated as section 704(c)(1)(C) property with the same section 704(c)(1)(C) basis adjustment as the contract (with appropriate adjustments for any gain or loss recognized on the acquisition). For this purpose, the term *contract* includes, but is not limited to, options, forward contracts, and futures contracts.

(v) *Distributions.*—(A) *Current distribution of section 704(c)(1)(C) property to section 704(c)(1)(C) partner.*—If a partnership distributes property to a partner and the partner has a section 704(c)(1)(C) basis adjustment for the property, the section 704(c)(1)(C) basis adjustment is taken into account under section 732. *See* § 1.732-2(a). For certain adjustments to the basis of remaining partnership property after the distribution of section 704(c)(1)(C) property to the section 704(c)(1)(C) partner, see § 1.734-2(c).

(B) *Distribution of section 704(c)(1)(C) property to another partner.*—If a partner receives a distribution of property in which another partner has a section 704(c)(1)(C) basis adjustment, the distributee does not take the section 704(c)(1)(C) basis adjustment into account under section 732. If section 704(c)(1)(B) applies to treat the section 704(c)(1)(C) partner as recognizing loss on the sale of the distributed property, the section 704(c)(1)(C) basis adjustment is taken into account in determining the amount of the loss. A section 704(c)(1)(C) partner with a section 704(c)(1)(C) basis adjustment in the distributed property that is not taken into account as described in the prior sentence reallocates the section 704(c)(1)(C) basis adjustment among the remaining items of partnership property under § 1.755-1(c).

(C) *Distributions in complete liquidation of a section 704(c)(1)(C) partner's interest.*—If a section 704(c)(1)(C) partner receives a distribution of property (whether or not the partner has a section 704(c)(1)(C) basis adjustment in the property) in liquidation of its interest in the partnership, the adjusted basis to the partnership of the distributed property immediately before the distribution includes the section 704(c)(1)(C) partner's section 704(c)(1)(C) basis adjustment for the property in which the section 704(c)(1)(C) partner relinquished an interest. For purposes of determining the section 704(c)(1)(C) partner's basis in distributed property under section 732, the partnership reallocates any section 704(c)(1)(C) basis adjustment from section 704(c)(1)(C) property retained by the partnership to distributed properties of like character under the principles of § 1.755-1(c)(i), after applying sections 704(c)(1)(B) and 737. If section 704(c)(1)(C) property is retained by the partnership, and no property of like character is distributed, then that property's section 704(c)(1)(C) basis adjustment is not reallocated to the distributed property for purposes of applying section 732. *See* § 1.734-2(c)(2) for rules regarding the treatment of any section 704(c)(1)(C) adjustment that is not fully utilized by the section 704(c)(1)(C) partner.

(D) *Examples.*—The following examples illustrate the principles of this paragraph (f)(3)(v).

Example 1. Current distribution of section 704(c)(1)(C) property to section 704(c)(1)(C) partner—(i) A contributes Property 1 with an adjusted basis of $15,000 and a fair market value of $10,000 and Property 2 with an adjusted basis of $5,000 and a fair market value of $20,000 and B contributes $30,000 cash to PRS, a partnership. Property 1 and Property 2 are both capital assets. When Property 1 has a fair market value of $12,000, and neither A nor B's basis in PRS has changed, PRS distributes Property 1 to A in a current distribution.

(ii) Property 1 has an adjusted basis to PRS of $10,000, and A has a section 704(c)(1)(C) basis adjustment of $5,000 in Property 1. Pursuant to § 1.732-2(c) and paragraph (f)(3)(v)(A) of this section, for purposes of section 732(a)(1), the adjusted basis of Property 1 to PRS immediately before the distribution is $15,000 (PRS's $10,000 adjusted basis increased by A's $5,000 section 704(c)(1)(C) basis adjustment for Property 1) and, therefore. A takes a $15,000 adjusted basis in Property 1 upon the distribution. Accordingly, no adjustment is required to PRS's property under section 734.

Example 2. Current distribution of section 704(c)(1)(C) property to another partner. Assume the same facts as *Example 1* except PRS distributes Property 1 to B in a distribution to which section 704(c)(1)(B) does not apply. B does not take any portion of A's section 704(c)(1)(C) basis adjustment into account. Accordingly, pursuant to § 1.732-1(a) and paragraph (f)(3)(v)(B) of this section, for purposes of section 732(a)(1), the adjusted basis of Property 1 to PRS immediately before the distribution is $10,000 and, therefore, B takes a $10,000 adjusted basis in Property 1 upon the distribution. Accordingly, no adjustment is required to PRS's property under section 734. A's section 704(c)(1)(C) basis adjustment in Property 1 is reallocated to Property 2 in accordance with § 1.755-1(c).

Example 3. (i) *Liquidating distribution to section 704(c)(1)(C) partner.* In Year 1, A contributes Property 1 with an adjusted basis of $15,000 and a fair market value of $10,000 and Property 2 with an adjusted basis of $5,000 and a fair market value of $20,000 and B and C each contribute $30,000 cash to PRS, a partnership. Property 1 and Property 2 are both capital assets. In a later year, when the fair market value of Property 2 is still $20,000, and no partner's basis in PRS has changed, PRS distributes Property 2 and $10,000 to A in complete liquidation of A's partnership interest in a distribution to which section 737 does not apply. PRS has a section 754 election in effect for the year of the distribution.

(ii) Property 2 has an adjusted basis to PRS of $5,000, and A has a section 704(c)(1)(C) basis adjustment of $5,000 in Property 1. Pursuant to § 1.732-2(c) and paragraph (f)(3)(v)(C) of this section, for purposes of section 732(b), the adjusted basis of Property 2 to PRS immediately before the distribution is $10,000 (PRS's $5,000 adjusted basis in Property 2 increased by A's $5,000 section 704(c)(1)(C) basis adjustment for Property 1), and A's adjusted basis in Property 2 upon the distribution is $10,000 (A's $20,000 basis in PRS minus the $10,000 cash distributed). Therefore, no adjustment is required to PRS's property under section 734.

(vi) *Returns.*—A partnership that owns property with a section 704(c)(1)(C) basis adjustment must attach a statement to the partnership return for the year of the contribution setting forth the name and taxpayer identification number of the section 704(c)(1)(C) partner as well as the section 704(c)(1)(C) basis adjustment and the section 704(c)(1)(C) property to which the adjustment relates.

(g) * * *. The provisions of paragraph (f) of this section apply to partnership contributions occurring on or after the date of publication of the Treasury decision adopting these rules as final regulations in the **Federal Register.**

☐ Par. 3. Section 1.704-4 is amended as follows:

1. In paragraph (a)(1), by removing "five years" and adding in its place "seven years".

2. In paragraph (a)(4) by removing "five-year" and adding in its place "seven-year" each time it appears.

3. By revising paragraph (a)(4)(i).

4. In paragraph (f)(2), *Examples 1* and 2, by removing the phrase "five-year" and adding in its place "seven-year" each time it appears and removing "2000" and adding in its place "2002" each time it appears.

5. By adding a sentence to the end of paragraph (g).

The revision and addition read as follows:

§ 1.704-4. Distribution of contributed property.—(a) * * *

(4) *Determination of seven-year period.*—(i) *General rule.*—The seven-year period specified in paragraph (a)(1) of this section begins on, and includes, the date of contribution and ends on, and includes, the last date that is within seven years of the contribution. For example, if a partner contributes section 704(c) property to a partnership on May 15, 2016, the seven-year period with respect to the section 704(c) property ends on, and includes, May 14, 2023.

* * *

(g) * * * The provisions of this section relating to the seven-year period for determining the applicability of section 704(c)(1)(B) are applicable for partnership contributions occurring on or after the date of publication of the Treasury decision adopting these rules as final regulations in the **Federal Register.**

Partnerships: Centralized Partnership Audit Regime

Partnerships: Centralized Partnership Audit Regime.—Amendments to Reg. § 1.705-1, implementing the centralized partnership audit regime that have not been finalized to reflect the changes made by the Technical Corrections Act of 2018, contained in Title II of the Consolidated Appropriations Act of 2018 (TTCA), are proposed (published in the Federal Register on August 17, 2018) (REG-136118-15; REG-119337-17; REG-118067-17; REG-120232-17 and REG-120233-17).

Par. 3. Section 1.705-1 is amended by adding paragraph (a)(10) to read as follows:

§ 1.705-1. Determination of basis of partner's interest.—(a) * * *

(10) For rules relating to determining the adjusted basis of a partner's interest in a partnership following a final determination under subchapter C of chapter 63 of the Internal Revenue Code (relating to the centralized partnership audit regime), see §§ 301.6225-4 and 301.6226-4 of this chapter.

* * *

Partnerships: Allocable Cash Basis: Tiered Partnership Items

Partnerships: Allocable Cash Basis: Tiered Partnership Items.—Amendments to Reg. § 1.706-0, regarding the determination of a partner's distributive share of certain allocable cash basis items and items attributable to an interest in a lower-tier partnership during a partnership taxable year in which a partner's interest changes, are proposed (published in the Federal Register on August 3, 2015) (corrected October 29, 2015) (REG-109370-10).

Par. 2. Section 1.706-0 is amended by removing the entry for § 1.706-2T and adding entries for § § 1.706-2, 1.706-3, and 1.706-6 to read as follows:

§ 1.706-0. Table of contents.

* * *

Partnerships: Taxable Year: Related Parties

Deductions: Losses: Interest: Transactions Between Related Taxpayers.—Temporary Reg. § 1.706-2T, relating to deductions, timing of deductions and losses in transactions between certain related taxpayers, is also proposed as a final regulation and, when adopted, would become Reg. § 1.706-2 (published in the Federal Register on November 30, 1984).

§ 1.706-2. Temporary regulations; questions and answers under the Tax Reform Act of 1984.

Partnerships: Allocable Cash Basis: Tiered Partnership Items

Partnerships: Allocable Cash Basis: Tiered Partnership Items.—Reg. § 1.706-2 and amendments to Temporary Reg. § 1.706-2T, regarding the determination of a partner's distributive share of certain allocable cash basis items and items attributable to an interest in a lower-tier partnership during a partnership taxable year in which a partner's interest changes, are proposed (published in the Federal Register on August 3, 2015) (corrected October 29, 2015) (REG-109370-10).

Par. 3. Section 1.706-2 is added to read as follows:

§ 1.706-2. Certain allocable cash basis items.—(a) *Allocable cash basis items prorated over period to which attributable.*—(1) *In general.*—If during any taxable year of the partnership there is a change in any partner's interest in the partnership, then each partner's distributive share of any allocable cash basis item shall be determined—

(i) By assigning the appropriate portion of such item to each day in the period to which it is attributable; and

(ii) By allocating the portion assigned to any such day among the partners in proportion to their interests in the partnership at the close of such day.

(2) *Allocable cash basis item.*—For purposes of this section, the term *allocable cash basis item* means any of the following items of deduction, loss, income, or gain with respect to which the partnership uses the cash receipts and disbursements method of accounting:

(i) Interest;

(ii) Taxes;

(iii) Payments for the use of property or for services (other than deductions for the transfer of an interest in the partnership in connection with the performance of services; such deductions generally must be allocated under the rules for extraordinary items in § 1.706-4(e));

(iv) Any allowable deduction that had been previously deferred under section 267(a)(2);

(v) Any deduction, loss, income, or gain item that accrues over time and that would, if not allocated as an allocable cash basis item, result in the significant misstatement of a partner's income.

(3) *Items attributable to periods not within taxable year.*—If any portion of any allocable cash basis item is attributable to—

(i) Any period before the beginning of the taxable year, such portion shall be assigned under paragraph (a)(1)(i) of this section to the first day of the taxable year, or

(ii) Any period after the close of the taxable year, such portion shall be assigned under paragraph (a)(1)(i) of this section to the last day of the taxable year.

(4) *Treatment of deductible items attributable to prior periods.*—If any portion of a deductible cash basis item is assigned under paragraph (a)(3)(i) of this section to the first day of any taxable year—

(i) Such portion shall be allocated among persons who are partners in the partnership during the period to which such portion is attributable in accordance with their varying interests in the partnership during such period; and

(ii) Any amount allocated under paragraph (a)(4)(i) of this section to a person who is not a partner in the partnership on such first day shall be capitalized by the partnership and allocated among partnership assets under the principles of section 755 (applying the principles of § 1.755-1(b) for partners who sold or exchanged their interest, and the principles of § 1.755-1(c) for partners who received a distribution from the partnership in exchange for their interest).

(b) *Example 1.* On January 1, 2015, A, B, and C are equal one-third partners in PRS, a calendar year partnership that uses the cash receipts and disbursements method of accounting. On July 1, 2015, A sells her entire interest in PRS to D. On

December 1, 2015, PRS pays a $12,000 interest expense that is attributable to every day in PRS's taxable year. Assume the de minimis exception of paragraph (c) of this section does not apply, and that the $12,000 interest expense must be allocated under the rules of paragraph (a) of this section. A was a partner in PRS for 181 days, and D was a partner in PRS for 184 days, including on July 1 pursuant to paragraph (a)(1)(ii) of this section. Under paragraph (a) of this section, A is entitled to 181/365 of her otherwise allocable share of deductions for the $12,000 interest expense, and D is entitled to 184/365 of his otherwise allocable share of deductions for the $12,000 interest expense. Thus, PRS allocates the interest expense deductions $1,983.56 to A, $2,016.44 to D, and $4,000 to each B and C.

Example 2. In 2015, E, F, and G are equal one-third partners in PRS, a calendar year partnership that uses the cash receipts and disbursements method of accounting. On December 31, 2015, E sells her entire interest in PRS to H. In November 2016, PRS makes a $6,000 payment for the use of property that is attributable to the period from January 1, 2015 to December 31, 2016. Assume the de minimis exception of paragraph (c) of this section does not apply, and that the $6,000 payment for the use of property must be allocated under the rules of paragraph (a) of this section. Under paragraph (a)(3)(i) of this section, half of the $6,000 expense is attributable to 2015 and must be assigned to January 1, 2016. Of this $3,000 assigned to January 1, 2016, one-third is allocable to each E, F, and G under paragraph (a)(4)(i) of this section. However, because E is not a partner in 2016, PRS must capitalize E's $1,000 share of the expense under paragraph (a)(4)(ii) of this section. Because E sold her interest to H, PRS must treat the capitalized $1,000 similar to a section 743(b) adjustment for H allocated among PRS's property under the principles of § 1.755-1(b).

Example 3. Assume the same facts as Example 2, except that on December 31, 2015, PRS distributed property to E in complete redemption of E's interest, and H never becomes a partner in PRS. PRS must capitalize E's $1,000 share of the expense under paragraph (a)(4)(ii) of this section. However, because E was redeemed, PRS must instead treat the capitalized $1,000 similar to a section 734(b) common basis adjustment allocated among PRS's property under the principles of § 1.755-1(c).

(c) *De minimis exception.*—An item described in paragraph (a)(2) of this section will not be subject to the rules of this section if, for the partnership's taxable year the total amount of the particular class of allocable cash basis items described in paragraph (a)(2)(i) through (v) of this section (but in no event counting an item more than once) is less than five percent of the partnership's gross income, including tax-exempt income described in section 705(a)(1)(B), in the case of income or gain items, or gross expenses and losses, including section 705(a)(2)(B) expenditures, in the case of losses and expense items; and the total amount of allocable cash basis items from all classes of allocable cash basis items amounting to less than five percent of the partnership's gross income, including tax-exempt income described in section 705(a)(1)(B), in the case of income or gain items, or gross expenses and losses, including section 705(a)(2)(B) expenditures, in the case of losses and expense items, does not exceed $10 million in the taxable year, determined by treating all such allocable cash basis items as positive amounts.

(d) *Effective/applicability date.*—This section applies to taxable years beginning on or after the date of publication of the Treasury decision adopting these rules as a final regulation in the **Federal Register**. [Reg. § 1.706-2.]

Par. 4. Section 1.706-2T is removed.

§ 1.706-2T. Temporary regulations; question and answer under the Tax Reform Act of 1984 (Temporary).

Partnerships: Equity for Services

Partnerships: Equity for Services.—Reg. § 1.706-3, providing that the transfer of a partnership interest in connection with the performance of services is subject to Code Sec. 83 and providing rules for coordinating Code Sec. 83 with partnership taxation principles, is proposed (published in the Federal Register on May 24, 2005) (REG-105346-03). Proposed Reg. § 1.706-3(a) withdrawn by REG-109370-10 on August 3, 2015; REG-109370-10 also proposed to redesignate Reg. § 1.706-3(b) and (c) as Reg. § 1.706-6(a) and (b).

☐ Par. 5. Section 1.706-3 is added to read as follows.

§ 1.706-3. Property transferred in connection with the performance of services.—(a) [Withdrawn by REG-109370-10 on August 3, 2015.]

(b) *Forfeiture allocations.*—If an election under section 83(b) is made with respect to a partnership interest that is substantially nonvested (within the meaning of § 1.83-3(b)), and that interest is later forfeited, the partnership must make forfeiture allocations to reverse prior allocations made with respect to the forfeited interest. See § 1.704-1(b)(4)(xii). Although the person forfeiting the interest may not have been a partner for the entire taxable year, forfeiture allocations may be made out of the partnership's items for the entire taxable year.

(c) *Effective date.*—This section applies to transfers of property on or after the date final regulations are published in the Federal Register. [Reg. § 1.706-3.]

Partnerships: Allocable Cash Basis: Tiered Partnership Items

Partnerships: Allocable Cash Basis: Tiered Partnership Items.—Reg. § 1.706-3 and amendments to Reg. §§ 1.706-3 and 1.706-4, regarding the determination of a partner's distributive share

of certain allocable cash basis items and items attributable to an interest in a lower-tier partnership during a partnership taxable year in which a partner's interest changes, are proposed (published in the Federal Register on August 3, 2015) (corrected October 29, 2015) (REG-109370-10).

Par. 5. Section 1.706-3 is added to read as follows:

§1.706-3. Items attributable to interest in lower-tier partnership..—(a) *General rule.*—Except as provided in paragraphs (b) and (c) of this section, if during any taxable year of the partnership—

(1) There is a change in any partner's interest in the partnership (the upper-tier partnership); and

(2) Such partnership is a partner in another partnership (the lower-tier partnership), then each partner's distributive share of any item of the upper-tier partnership attributable to the lower-tier partnership shall be determined by assigning the appropriate portion (determined by applying principles similar to the principles of §1.706-2(a)(3) and (4)) of each such item to the appropriate days during which the upper-tier partnership is a partner in the lower-tier partnership and by allocating the portion assigned to any such day among the partners in proportion to their interests in the upper-tier partnership at the close of such day. An upper-tier partnership's distributive share of any items of income, gain, loss, deduction, or credit from a lower-tier partnership is considered to be realized or sustained by the upper-tier partnership at the same time and in the same manner as such items were realized or sustained by the lower-tier partnership. For an additional example of the application of the principles of this paragraph (a), see Revenue Ruling 77-311, 1977-2 CB 218. *See* section 601.601(d)(2)(ii)(b).

(b) *De minimis upper-tier partnership exception.*—A de minimis upper-tier partnership is not required to, but may, apply paragraph (a) of this section. For purposes of this paragraph, a de minimis upper-tier partnership is a partnership that directly owns an interest in less than 10 percent of the profits and capital of the lower-tier partnership. This paragraph (b) only applies if all de minimis upper-tier partnerships own an interest in, in the aggregate, less than 30 percent of the profits and capital of the lower-tier partnership, and if no partnership is created with a purpose of avoiding the application of this section.

(c) *Example 1.* On January 1, 2015, A, B, and C are equal one-third partners in UTP, a calendar year partnership that uses the proration method and calendar day convention to account for variations during its taxable year. UTP is itself a partner in a lower-tier partnership, LTP, which is also a calendar year partnership. UTP owns a 15 percent interest in the profits and capital of LTP throughout 2015. On August 1, 2015, A sells her entire interest in UTP to D. During 2015, LTP incurred $100,000 of ordinary deductions, which were attributable to the period from January 1, 2015, to July 1, 2015. None of LTP's deductions were extraordinary items within the meaning of §1.706-4(e). UTP's distributive share of LTP's deductions is $15,000. Under paragraph (a) of this section, UTP must assign the $15,000 equally among all days from January 1, 2015 to July 1, 2015, and allocate the assigned daily portions among its partners in accordance with their interests in UTP on those days. Accordingly, A, B, and C are each allocated $5,000 of the deduction, and D is not allocated any portion of the deduction.

Example 2. Assume the same facts as Example 1, except that UTP owned a 9 percent interest in the profits and capital of LTP throughout 2015, and that LTP had only one other partner, which owned the remaining 91 percent of LTP. UTP's distributive share of LTP's $100,000 ordinary deductions is $9,000. UTP qualifies as a de minimis upper-tier partnership under paragraph (b) of this section, and therefore UTP is not required to apply the rules of paragraph (a) of this section. Instead, UTP may apply the rules of §1.706-4 to the $9,000 ordinary deduction. If UTP decides to apply the rules of §1.706-4, UTP prorates the $9,000 deduction equally over its entire taxable year, and allocates it according to its partners' interests on each day. Because A was a partner in UTP for 213 days, and D was a partner in UTP for 152 days, UTP allocates the $9,000 deduction $3,000 to each of B and C, $1,750.68 to A, and $1,249.32 to D.

Example 3. Assume the same facts as Example 2, except that UTP uses the interim closing method rather than the proration method. UTP qualifies as a de minimis upper-tier partnership under paragraph (b) of this section, and therefore UTP is not required to apply the rules of paragraph (a) of this section. Instead, UTP may apply the rules of §1.706-4 to the $9,000 ordinary deduction. UTP's distributive share of LTP items is considered to have been realized or sustained by UTP at the same time and in the same manner as such items were realized or sustained by LTP. Accordingly, even if UTP decides to apply the rules of §1.706-4, UTP's application of the interim closing method of §1.706-4 to the $9,000 deduction results in UTP allocating to each of A, B, and C $3,000 of the deduction, and not allocating any portion of the deduction to D. UTP would reach the same result if it had instead chosen to apply the rules of paragraph (a) of this section.

(d) *Effective/applicability date.*—This section applies to partnership taxable years beginning on or after the date of publication of the Treasury decision adopting these rules as a final regulation in the **Federal Register**. [Reg. §1.706-3.]

Par. 6. As proposed to be added May 24, 2005 (70 FR 29675), redesignate §1.706-3(b) and (c) as §1.706-6(a) and (b).

§1.706-3. Items attributable to interest in lower-tier partnership.

Par. 7. Section 1.706-4 is amended by:

a. Adding a new sentence to the end of paragraph (b)(2);

b. Revising paragraph (e)(1);

c. Redesignating paragraphs (e)(2)(ix), (x), and (xi) as paragraphs (e)(2)(xi), (xii), and (xiii) respectively;

d. Adding new paragraphs (e)(2)(ix) and (e)(2)(x);

e. Adding a new sentence to the end of paragraph (e)(3);

f. Revising paragraph (e)(4) Example 3; and

g. Revising the first sentence of paragraph (f).

The additions and revisions read as follows:

§1.706-4. Determination of distributive share when a partner's interest varies

***

(b) ***

(2) * * * However, this paragraph (b)(2) does not apply to any deduction for the transfer of an interest in the partnership in connection with the performance of services. Instead, such deduction must be allocated under the extraordinary item rules of paragraphs (e)(1) and (2) of this section.

***

(e) ***

(1) *General principles.*—Extraordinary items may not be prorated. The partnership must allocate extraordinary items among the partners in proportion to their interests in the partnership item at the time of day on which the extraordinary item occurred, regardless of the method (interim closing or proration method) and convention (daily, semi-monthly, or monthly) otherwise used by the partnership. These rules require the allocation of extraordinary items as an exception to the proration method, which would otherwise ratably allocate the extraordinary items across the segment, and the conventions, which could otherwise inappropriately shift extraordinary items between a transferor and transferee. However, publicly traded partnerships (as defined in section 7704(b)) that are treated as partnerships may, but are not required to, apply their selected convention in determining who held publicly traded units (as described in §1.7704-1(b) or §1.7704-1(c)(1)) at the time of the occurrence of any extraordinary item except extraordinary items described in paragraph (e)(2)(ix) of this section. Publicly traded partnerships that choose to treat items described in paragraph (e)(2)(ix) of this section as extraordinary items must allocate those items among the partners in proportion to their interests in those items at the time of day on which the items are deemed to have occurred according to the special timing rules for those items in paragraph (e)(2)(ix) of this section, regardless of the method and convention otherwise used by the partnership. Extraordinary items continue to be subject to any special limitation or requirement relating to the timing or amount of income, gain, loss, deduction, or credit applicable to the entire partnership taxable year (for example, the limitation for section 179 expenses).

(2) ***

(ix) For publicly traded partnerships (as defined in section 7704(b)), any item of income that is an amount subject to withholding as defined in §1.1441-2(a) (excluding amounts effectively connected with the conduct of a trade or business within the United States) or a withholdable payment under §1.1473-1(a) occurring during a taxable year if the partners agree (within the meaning of paragraph (e) of this section) to consistently treat all such items as extraordinary items for that taxable year. If the partners so agree, then for purposes of section 706 such items shall be treated as occurring at the next time as of which the recipients of a distribution by the partnership are determined, or, to the extent such income items arise between the final time during the taxable year as of which the recipients of a distribution by the partnership are determined and the end of the taxable year, such items shall be treated as occurring at the final time during the taxable year as of which the recipients of a distribution by the partnership are determined. This paragraph (e)(2)(ix) does not apply unless the partnership has a regular practice of making at least four distributions (other than de minimis distributions) to its partners during each taxable year.

(x) Any deduction for the transfer of an interest in the partnership in connection with the performance of services. Such an extraordinary item is treated as occurring immediately before the transfer or vesting of the partnership interest that results in compensation income for the person who performs the services, but in no case shall the item be treated as occurring prior to the beginning of the partnership's taxable year.

***

(3) * * * However, this paragraph (e)(3) does not apply to any deduction for the transfer of an interest in the partnership in connection with the performance of services. Instead, such deduction must be allocated under the extraordinary item rules of paragraphs (e)(1) and (2) of this section.

(4) ***

Example 3. (i) Assume the same facts as in *Example 2*, except that PRS is a publicly traded partnership (within the meaning of section 7704(b)), A held a publicly traded unit (as described in §1.7704-1(b) or §1.7704-1(c)(1)) in PRS, and the extraordinary item recognized at 3:15 p.m. on December 7, 2016 is not described in paragraph (e)(2)(ix) of this section. Under PRS's monthly convention, the December 12 variation is deemed to have occurred for purposes of this section at the end of the day on November 30, 2016. Pursuant to paragraph (e)(1) of this section, a publicly traded partnership (as defined in section 7704(b)) may choose to respect its conventions in determining who held its publicly traded units (as described in §1.7704-1(b) or §1.7704-1(c)(1)) at the time of the occurrence of an extraordinary item, except for extraordinary items described in paragraph (e)(2)(ix) of this section. Therefore, PRS may choose to treat A as not having been a partner in PRS for purposes of this paragraph (e) at the time the extraordinary item arose, and thus PRS may choose not to allocate A any share of the extraordinary item.

(ii) Assume the same facts as in paragraph (i) of this *Example 3*, except that on November 5, 2016, PRS recognizes an item of income that is an amount subject to withholding as defined in §1.1441-2(a) (and that is not effectively connected with the conduct of a trade or business within the United States). PRS has a regular practice of making quarterly distributions to its partners each taxable year. PRS determines that the recipients of its fourth-quarter distribution will be interest holders of record at the close of business on December 15, 2016. The partners of PRS agree (within the meaning of paragraph (f) of this section) to consistently treat all such items during the taxable year as extraordinary items. Pursuant to paragraph (e)(2)(ix) of this section, the item of income that arose on November 5 is treated as an extraordinary item occurring at the next time as of which the recipients of a distribution by the partnership are determined (unless that time occurs in a different taxable year). Because December 15 occurs before the end of PRS's taxable year, the item of income is treated as occurring at the close of business on December 15, and must be allocated according to PRS's partners' interests at that time, determined without regard to PRS's applicable convention. Therefore, A will not be allocated any share of the item because A disposed of its entire interest in PRS before the close of business on December 15.

(iii) Assume the same facts as in paragraph (ii) of this *Example 3*, except that PRS determines that the recipients of its fourth-quarter distribution will be interest holders of record at the close of business on January 15, 2017, and PRS determines that the recipients of its third-quarter distribution will be interest holders of record at the close of business on October 21, 2016. Therefore, the last time during 2016 as of which the recipients of a distribution by PRS are determined is at the close of business on October 21, 2016. Pursuant to paragraph (e)(2)(ix) of this section, because the item of income subject to withholding as defined in §1.1441-2(a) which arises on November 5 arises between the final time during the taxable year as of which the recipients of a distribution are determined and the end of the taxable year, such item shall be treated as occurring at the final time during the taxable year as of which the recipients of a distribution by the partnership are determined. Therefore, the item of income subject to withholding as defined in §1.1441-2(a) which arises on November 5, 2016 is treated as occurring at the close of business on October 21, 2016, and must be allocated according to PRS's partners' interests at that time.

(f) *Agreement of the partners.*—For purposes of paragraphs (a)(3)(iii) (relating to selection of the proration method), (c)(3) (relating to selection of the semi-monthly or monthly convention), (d)(1) (relating to performance of regular semi-monthly or monthly interim closings), (e)(2)(ix) (relating to a publicly traded partnership's treatment of all amounts subject to withholding as defined in §1.1441-2(a) that are not effectively connected with the conduct of a trade or business within the United States or withholdable payments under §1.1473-1(a) as extraordinary items), and (e)(2)(xi) (relating to selection of additional extraordinary items) of this section, the term agreement of the partners means either an agreement of all the partners to select the method, convention, or extraordinary item in a dated, written statement maintained with the partnership's books and records, including, for example, a selection that is included in the partnership agreement, or a selection of the method, convention, or extraordinary item made by a person authorized to make that selection, including under a grant of general authority provided for by either state law or in the partnership agreement, if that person's selection is in a dated, written statement maintained with the partnership's books and records.

* * *

Partnerships: Centralized Partnership Audit Regime

Partnerships: Centralized Partnership Audit Regime.—Amendments to Reg. §1.706-4, implementing the centralized partnership audit regime that have not been finalized to reflect the changes made by the Technical Corrections Act of 2018, contained in Title II of the Consolidated Appropriations Act of 2018 (TTCA), are proposed (published in the Federal Register on August 17, 2018) (REG-136118-15; REG-119337-17; REG-118067-17; REG-120232-17 and REG-120233-17).

Par. 4. Section 1.706-4 is amended by redesignating paragraphs (e)(2)(viii) through (xi) as paragraphs (e)(2)(ix) through (xii), respectively, and adding a new paragraph (e)(2)(viii) to read as follows:

§1.706-4. Determination of distributive share when a partner's interest varies.

* * *

(e) * * *

(2) * * *

(viii) Any item arising from a final determination under subchapter C of chapter 63 of the Internal Revenue Code (relating to the centralized partnership audit regime) with respect to a partnership adjustment resulting in an imputed underpayment for which no election is made under §301.6226-1 of this chapter or for which a pass-through partner (as defined in §301.6241-1(a)(5)) pays an imputed underpayment under §301.6226-3(e)(4).

Partnerships: Equity for Services

Partnerships: Equity for Services.—Amendments to Reg. §1.707-1, providing that the transfer of a partnership interest in connection with the performance of services is subject to Code Sec. 83 and providing rules for coordinating Code Sec. 83 with partnership taxation principles, are proposed (published in the Federal Register on May 24, 2005) (REG-105346-03).

☐ Par. 6. In §1.707-1, paragraph (c) is amended by revising the second sentence to read as follows:

§1.707-1. Transactions between partner and partnership.

* * *

(c) *Guaranteed Payments.*—* * * However, except as otherwise provided in section 83 and the regulations thereunder, a partner must include such payments as ordinary income for that partner's taxable year within or with which ends the partnership taxable year in which the partnership deducted such payments as paid or accrued under its method of accounting. * * *

* * *

Disguised Payments: Services

Disguised Payments: Services.—Amendments to Reg. §§1.707-0 and 1.707-1, relating to disguised payments for services under section 707(a)(2)(A) of the Internal Revenue Code and providing guidance to partnerships and their partners regarding when an arrangement will be treated as a disguised payment for services, are proposed (published in the Federal Register on July 23, 2015) (REG-115452-14).

Par. 2. Section 1.707-0 is amended by revising § 1.707-2 to read as follows:

§1.707-0. Table of contents.

* * *

* * *

Par. 3. Section 1.707-1 is amended by adding a sentence at the end of paragraph (a) and revising paragraph (c) Example 2 to read as follows.

§1.707-1. Transactions between partner and partnership.—(a) * * * For arrangements pursuant to which a purported partner performs services for a partnership and the partner receives a related direct or indirect allocation and distribution from the partnership, see § 1.707-2 to determine whether the arrangement should be treated as a disguised payment for services.

(c) * * *

Example 2. Partner C in the CD partnership is to receive 30 percent of partnership income, but not less than $10,000. The income of the partnership is $60,000, and C is entitled to $18,000 (30 percent of $60,000). Of this amount, $10,000 is a guaranteed payment to C. The $10,000 guaranteed payment reduces the partnership's net income to $50,000 of which C receives $8,000 as C's distributive share.

* * *

Disguised Payments: Services

Disguised Payments: Services.—Reg. §1.707-2, relating to disguised payments for services under section 707(a)(2)(A) of the Internal Revenue Code and providing guidance to partnerships and their partners regarding when an arrangement will be treated as a disguised payment for services, is proposed (published in the Federal Register on July 23, 2015) (corrected August 19, 2015) (REG-115452-14).

Par. 4. Section 1.707-2 is added to read as follows:

§1.707-2. Disguised payments for services.—(a) *In general.*—This section prescribes rules for characterizing arrangements as disguised payments for services. Paragraph (b) of this section outlines the elements necessary to characterize an arrangement as a payment for services, and it provides operational rules regarding application and timing of this section. Paragraph (c) of this section identifies the factors that weigh in the determination of whether an arrangement includes the elements described in paragraph (b) of this section that make it appropriate to characterize the arrangement as a payment for services. Paragraph (d) of this section provides examples applying these rules to determine whether an arrangement is a payment for services.

(b) *Elements necessary to characterize arrangements as disguised payments for services.*—(1) *In general.*—An arrangement will be treated as a disguised payment for services if—

(i) A person (service provider), either in a partner capacity or in anticipation of becoming a partner, performs services (directly or through its delegate) to or for the benefit of a partnership;

(ii) There is a related direct or indirect allocation and distribution to such service provider; and

(iii) The performance of such services and the allocation and distribution, when viewed together, are properly characterized as a transaction occurring between the partnership and a person acting other than in that person's capacity as a partner.

(2) *Application and timing.*—(i) *Timing and effect of the determination.*—Whether an arrangement is properly characterized as a payment for services is determined at the time the arrangement is entered into or modified and without regard to whether the terms of the arrangement require the allocation and distribution to occur in the same taxable year. An arrangement that is treated as a payment for services under this paragraph (b) is treated as a payment for services for all purposes of the Internal Revenue Code, including for example, sections 61, 409A, and 457A (as applicable). The amount paid to a person in consideration for services under this section is treated as a payment for services provided to the partnership, and, when appropriate, the partnership must capitalize these amounts (or otherwise treat such amounts in a manner consistent with their recharacterization). The partnership must also treat the arrangement as a payment to a non-partner in determining

the remaining partners' shares of taxable income or loss.

(ii) *Timing of inclusion.*—The inclusion of income by the service provider and deduction (if applicable) by the partnership of amounts paid pursuant to an arrangement that is characterized as a payment for services under paragraph (b)(1) of this section is taken into account in the taxable year as required under applicable law by applying all relevant sections of the Internal Revenue Code, including for example, sections 409A and 457A (as applicable), to the allocation and distribution when they occur (or are deemed to occur under all other provisions of the Internal Revenue Code).

(3) *Application of disguised payment rules.*—If a person purports to provide services to a partnership in a capacity as a partner or in anticipation of becoming a partner, the rules of this section apply for purposes of determining whether the services were provided in exchange for a disguised payment, even if it is determined after applying the rules of this section that the service provider is not a partner. If after applying the rules of this section, no partnership exists as a result of the service provider failing to become a partner under the arrangement, then the service provider is treated as having provided services directly to the other purported partner.

(c) *Factors considered.*—Whether an arrangement constitutes a payment for services (in whole or in part) depends on all of the facts and circumstances. Paragraphs (c)(1) through (6) of this section provide a non-exclusive list of factors that may indicate that an arrangement constitutes (in whole or in part) a payment for services. The presence or absence of a factor is based on all of the facts and circumstances at the time the parties enter into the arrangement (or if the parties modify the arrangement, at the time of the modification). The most important factor is significant entrepreneurial risk as set forth in paragraph (c)(1) of this section. An arrangement that lacks significant entrepreneurial risk constitutes a payment for services. An arrangement that has significant entrepreneurial risk will generally not constitute a payment for services unless other factors establish otherwise. For purposes of making determinations under this paragraph (c), the weight to be given to any particular factor, other than entrepreneurial risk, depends on the particular case and the absence of a factor is not necessarily indicative of whether or not an arrangement is treated as a payment for services.

(1) The arrangement lacks significant entrepreneurial risk. Whether an arrangement lacks significant entrepreneurial risk is based on the service provider's entrepreneurial risk relative to the overall entrepreneurial risk of the partnership. Paragraphs (c)(1)(i) through (v) of this section provide facts and circumstances that create a presumption that an arrangement lacks significant entrepreneurial risk and will be treated as a disguised payment for services unless other facts and circumstances establish the presence of significant entrepreneurial risk by clear and convincing evidence:

(i) Capped allocations of partnership income if the cap is reasonably expected to apply in most years;

(ii) An allocation for one or more years under which the service provider's share of income is reasonably certain;

(iii) An allocation of gross income;

(iv) An allocation (under a formula or otherwise) that is predominantly fixed in amount, is reasonably determinable under all the facts and circumstances, or is designed to assure that sufficient net profits are highly likely to be available to make the allocation to the service provider (e.g. if the partnership agreement provides for an allocation of net profits from specific transactions or accounting periods and this allocation does not depend on the long-term future success of the enterprise); or

(v) An arrangement in which a service provider waives its right to receive payment for the future performance of services in a manner that is non-binding or fails to timely notify the partnership and its partners of the waiver and its terms.

(2) The service provider holds, or is expected to hold, a transitory partnership interest or a partnership interest for only a short duration.

(3) The service provider receives an allocation and distribution in a time frame comparable to the time frame that a non-partner service provider would typically receive payment.

(4) The service provider became a partner primarily to obtain tax benefits that would not have been available if the services were rendered to the partnership in a third party capacity.

(5) The value of the service provider's interest in general and continuing partnership profits is small in relation to the allocation and distribution.

(6) The arrangement provides for different allocations or distributions with respect to different services received, the services are provided either by one person or by persons that are related under sections 707(b) or 267(b), and the terms of the differing allocations or distributions are subject to levels of entrepreneurial risk that vary significantly.

(d) *Examples.*—The following examples illustrate the application of this section:

Example 1. Partnership ABC constructed a building that is projected to generate $100,000 of gross income annually. A, an architect, performs services for partnership ABC for which A's normal fee would be $40,000 and contributes cash in an amount equal to the value of a 25 percent interest in the partnership. In exchange, A will receive a 25 percent distributive share for the life of the partnership and a special allocation of $20,000 of partnership gross income for the first two years of the partnership's operations. The ABC partnership agreement satisfies the requirements for economic effect contained in §1.704-1(b)(2)(ii), including requiring that liquidating distributions are made in accordance with the partners' positive capital account balances. Under paragraph (c) of this section, whether the arrangement is treated as a payment for services depends on the facts and circumstances. The special allocation to A is a capped amount and the cap is reasonably expected to apply. The special allocation is also made out of gross income. Under paragraphs (c)(1)(i) and (iii) of this section, the capped allocations of income and gross income allocations described are presumed to lack significant entrepreneurial risk. No additional facts and circumstances establish otherwise by clear and convincing evidence. Thus, the allocation lacks significant entrepreneurial risk. Accordingly, the arrangement provides for a disguised payment for services as of the date that A and ABC enter into the arrangement and, pursuant to paragraph (b)(2)(ii) of this section, should be included in income by A in the time and manner required under applicable law as determined by applying all relevant sections of the Internal Revenue Code to the arrangement.

Example 2. A, a stock broker, agrees to effect trades for Partnership ABC without the normal brokerage commission. A contributes 51 percent of partnership capital and in exchange, receives a 51 percent interest in residual partnership profits and losses. In addition, A receives a special allocation of gross income that is computed in a manner which approximates its foregone commissions. The special allocation to A is computed by means of a formula similar to a normal brokerage fee and varies with the value and amount of services rendered rather than with the income of the partnership. It is reasonably expected that Partnership ABC will have sufficient gross income to make this allocation. The ABC partnership agreement satisfies the requirements for economic effect contained in § 1.704-1(b)(2)(ii), including requiring that liquidating distributions are made in accordance with the partners' positive capital account balances. Under paragraph (c) of this section, whether the arrangement is treated as a payment for services depends on the facts and circumstances. Under paragraphs (c)(1)(iii) and (iv) of this section, because the allocation is an allocation of gross income and is reasonably determinable under the facts and circumstances, it is presumed to lack significant entrepreneurial risk. No additional facts and circumstances establish otherwise by clear and convincing evidence. Thus, the allocation lacks significant entrepreneurial risk. Accordingly, the arrangement provides for a disguised payment for services as of the date that A and ABC enter into the arrangement and, pursuant to paragraph (b)(2)(ii) of this section, should be included in income by A in the time and manner required under applicable law as determined by applying all relevant sections of the Internal Revenue Code to the arrangement.

Example 3. (i) M performs services for which a fee would normally be charged to new partnership ABC, an investment partnership that will acquire a portfolio of investment assets that are not readily tradable on an established securities market. M will also contribute $500,000 in exchange for a one percent interest in ABC's capital and profits. In addition to M's one percent interest, M is entitled to receive a priority allocation and distribution of net gain from the sale of any one or more assets during any 12-month accounting period in which the partnership has overall net gain in an amount intended to approximate the fee that would normally be charged for the services M performs. A, a company that controls M, is the general partner of ABC and directs all operations of the partnership consistent with the partnership agreement, including causing ABC to purchase or sell an asset during any accounting period. A also controls the timing of distributions to M including distributions arising from M's priority allocation. Given the nature of the assets in which ABC will invest and A's ability to control the timing of asset dispositions, the amount of partnership net income or gains that will be allocable to M under the ABC partnership agreement is highly likely to be available and reasonably determinable based on all facts and circumstances available upon formation of the partnership. A will be allocated 10 percent of any net profits or net losses of ABC earned over the life of the partnership. A undertakes an enforceable obligation to repay any amounts allocated and distributed pursuant to this interest (reduced by reasonable allowances for tax payments made on A's allocable shares of partnership income and gain) that exceed 10 percent of the overall net amount of partnership profits computed over the life of the partnership (a "clawback obligation"). It is reasonable to anticipate that A could and would comply fully with any repayment responsibilities that arise pursuant to this obligation. The ABC partnership agreement satisfies the requirements for economic effect contained in § 1.704-1(b)(2)(ii), including requiring that liquidating distributions are made in accordance with the partners' positive capital account balances.

(ii) Under paragraph (c) of this section, whether A's arrangement is treated as a payment for services in directing ABC's operations depends on the facts and circumstances. The most important factor in this facts and circumstances determination is the presence or absence of significant entrepreneurial risk. The arrangement with respect to A creates significant entrepreneurial risk under paragraph (c)(1) of this section because the allocation to A is of net profits earned over the life of the partnership, the allocation is subject to a clawback obligation and it is reasonable to anticipate that A could and would comply with this obligation, and the allocation is neither reasonably determinable nor highly likely to be available. Additionally, other relevant factors do not establish that the arrangement should be treated as a payment for services. Thus, the arrangement with respect to A does not constitute a payment for services for purposes of paragraph (b)(1) of this section.

(iii) Under paragraph (c) of this section, whether M's arrangement is treated as a payment for services depends on the facts and circumstances. The most important factor in this facts and circumstances determination is the presence or absence of entrepreneurial risk. The priority allocation to M is an allocation of net profit from any 12-month accounting period in which the partnership has net gain, and thus it does not depend on the overall success of the enterprise. Moreover, the sale of the assets by ABC, and hence the timing of recognition of gains and losses, is controlled by A, a company related to M. Taken in combination, the facts indicate that the allocation is reasonably determinable under all the facts and circumstances and that sufficient net profits are highly likely to be available to make the priority allocation to the service provider. As a result, the allocation presumptively lacks significant entrepreneurial risk. No additional facts and circumstances establish otherwise by clear and convincing evidence. Accordingly, the arrangement provides for a disguised payment for services as of the date M and ABC enter into the arrangement and, pursuant to paragraph (b)(2)(ii) of this section, should be included in income by M in the time and manner required under applicable law as determined by applying all relevant sections of the Internal Revenue Code to the arrangement.

(iv) Assume the facts are the same as paragraph (i) of this example, except that the partnership can also fund M's priority allocation and distribution of net gain from the revaluation of any partnership assets pursuant to §1.704-1(b)(2)(iv)(f). As the general partner of ABC, A controls the timing of events that permit revaluation of partnership assets and assigns values to those assets for purposes of the revaluation. Under paragraph (c) of this section, whether M's arrangement is treated as a payment for services depends on the facts and circumstances. The most important factor in this facts and circumstances determination is the presence or absence of significant entrepreneurial risk. Under this arrangement, the valuation of the assets is controlled by A, a company related to M, and the assets of the company are difficult to value. This fact, taken in combination with the partnership's determination of M's profits by reference to a specified accounting period, causes the allocation to be reasonably determinable under all the facts and circumstances or to ensure that net profits are highly likely to be available to make the priority allocation to the service provider. No additional facts and circumstances establish otherwise by clear and convincing evidence. Accordingly, the arrangement provides for a disguised payment for services as of the date M and ABC enter into the arrangement and, pursuant to paragraph (b)(2)(ii) of this section, should be included in income by M in time and manner required under applicable law as determined by applying all relevant sections of the Internal Revenue Code to the arrangement.

Example 4. (i) The facts are the same as in *Example 3*, except that ABC's investment assets are securities that are readily tradable on an established securities market, and ABC is in the trade or business of trading in securities and has validly elected to mark-to-market under section 475(f)(1). In addition, M is entitled to receive a special allocation and distribution of partnership net gain attributable to a specified future 12-month taxable year. Although it is expected that one or more of the partnership's assets will be sold for a gain, it cannot reasonably be predicted whether the partnership will have net profits with respect to its entire portfolio in that 12-month taxable year.

(ii) Under paragraph (c) of this section, whether the arrangement is treated as a payment for services depends on the facts and circumstances. The most important factor in this facts and circumstances determination is the presence or absence of significant entrepreneurial risk. The special allocation to M is allocable out of net profits, the partnership assets have a readily ascertainable market value that is determined at the close of each taxable year, and it cannot reasonably be predicted whether the partnership will have net profits with respect to its entire portfolio for the year to which the special allocation would relate. Accordingly, the special allocation is neither reasonably determinable nor highly likely to be available because the partnership assets have a readily ascertainable fair market value that is determined at the beginning of the year and at the end of the year. Thus, the arrangement does not lack significant entrepreneurial risk under paragraph (c)(1) of this section. Additionally, the facts and circumstances do not establish the presence of other factors that would suggest that the arrangement is properly characterized as a payment for services. Accordingly, the arrangement does not constitute a payment for services under paragraph (b)(1) of this section.

Example 5. (i) A is a general partner in newly-formed partnership ABC, an investment fund. A is responsible for providing management services to ABC, but has delegated that management function to M, a company controlled by A. Funds that are comparable to ABC commonly require the general partner to contribute capital in an amount equal to one percent of the capital contributed by the limited partners, provide the general partner with an interest in 20 percent of future partnership net income and gains as measured over the life of the fund, and pay the fund manager annually an amount equal to two percent of capital committed by the partners.

(ii) Upon formation of ABC, the partners of ABC execute a partnership agreement with terms that differ from those commonly agreed upon by other comparable funds. The ABC partnership agreement provides that A will contribute nominal capital to ABC, that ABC will annually pay M an amount equal to one percent of capital committed by the partners, and that A will receive an interest in 20 percent of future partnership net income and gains as measured over the life of the fund. A will also receive an additional interest in future partnership net income and gains determined by a formula (the "Additional Interest"). The parties intend that the estimated present value of the Additional Interest approximately equals the present value of one percent of capital committed by the partners determined annually over the life of the fund. However, the amount of net profits that will be allocable to A under the Additional Interest is neither highly likely to be available nor reasonably determinable based on all facts and circumstances available upon formation of the partnership. A undertakes a clawback obligation, and it is reasonable to anticipate that A could and would comply fully with any repayment responsibilities that arise pursuant to this obligation. The ABC partnership agreement satisfies the requirements for economic effect contained in §1.704-1(b)(2)(ii), including requiring that liquidating distributions are made in accordance with the partners' positive capital account balances.

(iii) Under paragraph (c) of this section, whether the arrangement relating to the Additional Interest is treated as a payment for services depends on the facts and circumstances. The most important factor in this facts and circumstances determination is the presence or absence of significant entrepreneurial risk. The arrangement with respect to A creates significant entrepreneurial risk under paragraph (c)(1) of this section because the allocation to A is of net profits, the allocation is subject to a clawback obligation over the life of the fund and it is reasonable to anticipate that A could and would comply with this obligation, and the allocation is neither reasonably determinable nor highly likely to be available. Additionally, the facts and circumstances do not establish the presence of other factors that would suggest that the arrangement is properly characterized as a payment for services. Accordingly, the arrangement does not constitute a payment for services under paragraph (b)(1) of this section.

Example 6. (i) A is a general partner in limited partnership ABC, an investment fund. A is responsible for providing management services to ABC, but has delegated that management function to M, a company controlled by A. The ABC partnership agreement provides that A must contribute capital in an amount equal to one percent of the capital contributed by the limited partners, that A is entitled to an interest in 20 percent of future partnership net income and gains as measured over the life of the fund, and that M is entitled to receive an annual fee in an amount equal to two percent of capital committed by the partners. The amount of partnership net income or gains that will be allocable to A under the ABC partnership agreement is neither highly likely to be available nor reasonably determinable based on all facts and circumstances available upon formation of the partnership. A also undertakes a clawback obligation, and it is reasonable to anticipate that A could and would comply fully with any repayment responsibilities that arise pursuant to this obligation.

(ii) ABC's partnership agreement also permits M (as A's appointed delegate) to waive all or a portion of its fee for any year if it provides written notice to the limited partners of ABC at least 60 days prior to the commencement of the partnership taxable year for which the fee is payable. If M elects to waive irrevocably its fee pursuant to this provision, the partnership will, immediately following the commencement of the partnership taxable year for which the fee would have been payable, issue to M an interest determined by a formula in subsequent partnership net income and gains (the "Additional Interest"). The parties intend that the estimated present value of the Additional Interest approximately equals the estimated present value of the fee that was waived. However, the amount of net income or gains that will be allocable to M is neither highly likely to be available nor reasonably determinable based on all facts and circumstances available at the time of the waiver of the fee. The ABC partnership agreement satisfies the requirements for economic effect contained in § 1.704-1(b)(2)(ii), including requiring that liquidating distributions are made in accordance with the partners' positive capital account balances. The partnership agreement also requires ABC to maintain capital accounts pursuant to § 1.704-1(b)(2)(iv) and to revalue partner capital accounts under § 1.704-1(b)(2)(iv)(f) immediately prior to the issuance of the partnership interest to M. M undertakes a clawback obligation, and it is reasonable to anticipate that M could and would comply fully with any repayment responsibilities that arise pursuant to this obligation.

(iii) Under paragraph (c) of this section, whether the arrangements relating to A's 20 percent interest in future partnership net income and gains and M's Additional Interest are treated as payment for services depends on the facts and circumstances. The most important factor in this facts and circumstances determination is the presence or absence of significant entrepreneurial risk. The allocations to A and M do not presumptively lack significant entrepreneurial risk under paragraph (c)(1) of this section because the allocations are based on net profits, the allocations are subject to a clawback obligation over the life of the fund and it is reasonable to anticipate that A and M could and would comply with this obligation, and the allocations are neither reasonably determinable nor highly likely to be available. Additionally, the facts and circumstances do not establish the presence of other factors that would suggest that the arrangement is properly characterized as a payment for services. Accordingly, the arrangements do not constitute payment for services under paragraph (b)(1) of this section. [Reg. § 1.707-2.]

Disguised Payments: Services

Disguised Payments: Services.—Amendments to Reg. § 1.707-9, relating to disguised payments for services under section 707(a)(2)(A) of the Internal Revenue Code and providing guidance to partnerships and their partners regarding when an arrangement will be treated as a disguised payment for services, are proposed (published in the Federal Register on July 23, 2015) (REG-115452-14).

Par. 5. Section 1.707-9 is amended by:

a. Redesignating paragraph (b) as paragraph (c);

b. Redesignating paragraph (a) as paragraph (b); and

c. Adding new paragraph (a).

The addition reads as follows:

§ 1.707-9. Effective dates and transitional rules.—(a) *Section 1.707-2.*—(1) *In general.*—Section 1.707-2 applies to all arrangements entered into or modified after the date of publication of the Treasury decision adopting that section as final regulations in the **Federal Register**. To the extent that an arrangement permits a service provider to waive all or a portion of its fee for any period subsequent to the date the arrangement is created, then the arrangement is modified for purposes of this paragraph on the date or dates that the fee is waived.

(2) *Arrangements entered into or modified before final regulations are published in the* **Federal** *Register.*—In the case of any arrangement entered into or modified that occurs on or before final regulations are published in the **Federal Register**, the determination of whether the arrangement is a disguised fee for services under section 707(a)(2)(A) is to be made on the basis of the statute and the guidance provided regarding that provision in the legislative history of section 73 of the Tax Reform Act of 1984 (Pub. L. 98-369, 98 Stat. 494). See H.R. Rep. No. 861, 98th Cong., 2d Sess. 859-2 (1984); S. Prt. No. 169 (Vol. I), 98th Cong., 2d Sess. 223-32 (1984); H.R. Rep. No. 432 (Pt. 2), 98th Cong., 2d Sess. 1216-21 (1984).

* * *

Liabilities: Recourse Partnership Liabilities

Liabilities: Recourse Partnership Liabilities.—Amendments to Reg. §§1.707-0, 1.707-5 and 1.707-9, addressing when certain obligations to restore a deficit balance in a partner's capital account are disregarded under section 704 of the Internal Revenue Code (Code) and when partnership liabilities are treated as recourse liabilities under section 752, are proposed (published in the Federal Register on October 5, 2016) (REG-122855-15).

Par. 3. Section 1.707-0 is amended by revising the entries for §1.707-5(a)(2)(i) and (ii) to read as follows:

§1.707-0. Table of contents.

* * *

§1.707-5 Disguised sales of property to partnership; special rules relating to liabilities.

(a) * * *

(2) * * *

(i) In general.

(ii) Partner's share of §1.752-7 liability.

* * *

Par. 4. Section 1.707-5 is amended by revising paragraph (a)(2) and *Examples 2, 3, 7, and 8* of paragraph (f) to read as follows:

§1.707-5. Disguised sales of property to partnership; special rules relating to liabilities.— (a) * * *

(2) [The text of proposed §1.707-5(a)(2) is the same as the text of §1.707-5T(a)(2) as added by T.D. 9788].

* * *

(f) * * *

Example 2. [The text of proposed §1.707-5(f) *Example 2* is the same as the text of §1.707-5T(f) *Example 2* as added by T.D. 9788].

Example 3. [The text of proposed §1.707-5(f) *Example 3* is the same as the text of §1.707-5T(f) *Example 3* as added by T.D. 9788].

* * *

Example 7. [The text of proposed §1.707-5(f) *Example 7* is the same as the text of §1.707-5T(f) *Example 7* as added by T.D. 9788].

Example 8. [The text of proposed §1.707-5(f) *Example 8* is the same as the text of §1.707-5T(f) *Example 8* as added by T.D. 9788].

* * *

Par. 5. Section 1.707-9 is amended by adding paragraph (a)(5) to read as follows:

§1.707-9. Effective dates and transitional rules.—(a) * * *

(5) [The text of proposed §1.707-9(a)(5) is the same as the text of §1.707-9T(a)(5) as added by T.D. 9788].

* * *

Partnership Liabilities: Disguised Sale Purposes

Partnership Liabilities: Disguised Sale Purposes.—Amendments to Reg. §§1.707-5 and 1.707-5T, concerning how partnership liabilities are allocated for disguised sale purposes, are proposed (published in the Federal Register on June 19, 2018) (REG-131186-17).

Par. 2. Section 1.707-5 is amended by revising paragraph (a)(2) and *Examples 2, 3, 7,* and *8* in paragraph (f) to read as follows:

§1.707-5. Disguised sales of property to partnership; special rules relating to liabilities.— (a) * * *

(2) *Partner's share of liability.*—A partner's share of any liability of the partnership is determined under the following rules:

(i) *Recourse liability.*—A partner's share of a recourse liability of the partnership equals the partner's share of the liability under the rules of section 752 and the regulations thereunder. A partnership liability is a recourse liability to the extent that the obligation is a recourse liability under §1.752-1(a)(1) or would be treated as a recourse liability under that section if it were treated as a partnership liability for purposes of that section.

(ii) *Nonrecourse liability.*—A partner's share of a nonrecourse liability of the partnership is determined by applying the same percentage used to determine the partner's share of the excess nonrecourse liability under §1.752-3(a)(3). A partnership liability is a nonrecourse liability of the partnership to the extent that the obligation is a nonrecourse liability under §1.752-1(a)(2) or would be a nonrecourse liability of the partnership under §1.752-1(a)(2) if it were treated as a partnership liability for purposes of that section.

* * *

(f) * * *

Example 2. Partnership's assumption of recourse liability encumbering transferred property. (i) C transfers property Y to a partnership. At the time of its transfer to the partnership, property Y has a fair market value of $10,000,000 and is subject to an $8,000,000 liability that C incurred, immediately before transferring property Y to the partnership, in order to finance other expenditures. Upon the transfer of property Y to the partnership, the partnership assumed the liability encumbering that property. The partnership assumed this liability solely to acquire property Y. Under section 752 and the regulations thereunder, immediately after the partnership's assumption of the liability encumbering property Y, the liability is a recourse liability of the partnership and C's share of that liability is $7,000,000.

(ii) Under the facts of this example, the liability encumbering property Y is not a qualified liability. Accordingly, the partnership's assumption of the liability results in a transfer of consideration to C in connection with C's transfer of property Y to the partnership in the amount of $1,000,000 (the excess of the liability assumed by the partnership ($8,000,000) over C's share of the liability immediately after the assumption ($7,000,000)). See paragraphs (a)(1) and (2) of this section.

Example 3. Subsequent reduction of transferring partner's share of liability. (i) The facts are the same as in *Example 2*. In addition, property Y is a fully leased office building, the rental income from property Y is sufficient to meet debt service, and the remaining term of the liability is ten years. It is anticipated that, three years after the partnership's assumption of the liability, C's share of the liability under section 752 will be reduced to zero because of a shift in the allocation of partnership losses pursuant to the terms of the partnership agreement. Under the partnership agreement, this shift in the allocation of partnership losses is dependent solely on the passage of time.

(ii) Under paragraph (a)(3) of this section, if the reduction in C's share of the liability was anticipated at the time of C's transfer, was not subject to the entrepreneurial risks of partnership operations, and was part of a plan that has as one of its principal purposes minimizing the extent of sale treatment under § 1.707-3 (that is, a principal purpose of allocating a large percentage of losses to C in the first three years when losses were not likely to be realized was to minimize the extent to which C's transfer would be treated as part of a sale), C's share of the liability immediately after the assumption is treated as equal to C's reduced share.

* * *

Example 7. Partnership's assumptions of liabilities encumbering properties transferred pursuant to a plan. (i) Pursuant to a plan, G and H transfer property 1 and property 2, respectively, to an existing partnership in exchange for interests in the partnership. At the time the properties are transferred to the partnership, property 1 has a fair market value of $10,000 and an adjusted tax basis of $6,000, and property 2 has a fair market value of $10,000 and an adjusted tax basis of $4,000. At the time properties 1 and 2 are transferred to the partnership, a $6,000 nonrecourse liability (liability 1) is secured by property 1 and a $7,000 recourse liability of F (liability 2) is secured by property 2. Properties 1 and 2 are transferred to the partnership, and the partnership takes subject to liability 1 and assumes liability 2. G and H incurred liabilities 1 and 2 immediately prior to transferring properties 1 and 2 to the partnership and used the proceeds for personal expenditures. The liabilities are not qualified liabilities. Assume that G and H are each allocated $2,000 of liability 1 in accordance with § 1.707-5(a)(2)(ii) (which determines a partner's share of a nonrecourse liability). Assume further that G's share of liability 2 is $3,500 and H's share is $0 in accordance with § 1.707-5(a)(2)(i) (which determines a partner's share of a recourse liability).

(ii) G and H transferred properties 1 and 2 to the partnership pursuant to a plan. Accordingly, the partnership's taking subject to liability 1 is treated as a transfer of only $500 of consideration to G (the amount by which liability 1 ($6,000) exceeds G's share of liabilities 1 and 2 ($5,500)), and the partnership's assumption of liability 2 is treated as a transfer of only $5,000 of consideration to H (the amount by which liability 2 ($7,000) exceeds H's share of liabilities 1 and 2 ($2,000)). G is treated under the rule in § 1.707-3 as having sold $500 of the fair market value of property 1 in exchange for the partnership's taking subject to liability 1 and H is treated as having sold $5,000 of the fair market value of property 2 in exchange for the assumption of liability 2.

Example 8. Partnership's assumption of liability pursuant to a plan to avoid sale treatment of partnership assumption of another liability. (i) The facts are the same as in *Example 7*, except that—

(A) H transferred the proceeds of liability 2 to the partnership; and

(B) H incurred liability 2 in an attempt to reduce the extent to which the partnership's taking subject to liability 1 would be treated as a transfer of consideration to G (and thereby reduce the portion of G's transfer of property 1 to the partnership that would be treated as part of a sale).

(ii) Because the partnership assumed liability 2 with a principal purpose of reducing the extent to which the partnership's taking subject to liability 1 would be treated as a transfer of consideration to G, liability 2 is ignored in applying paragraph (a)(3) of this section. Accordingly, the partnership's taking subject to liability 1 is treated as a transfer of $4,000 of consideration to G (the amount by which liability 1 ($6,000) exceeds G's share of liability 1 ($2,000)). On the other hand, the partnership's assumption of liability 2 is not treated as a transfer of any consideration to H because H's share of that liability equals $7,000 as a result of H's transfer of $7,000 in money to the partnership.

* * *

Par. 3. Section 1.707-5T is removed.

§ 1.707-5T. Disguised sales of property to partnership; special rules relating to liabilities (temporary).

Partnership Liabilities: Disguised Sale Purposes

Partnership Liabilities: Disguised Sale Purposes.—Amendments to Reg. §§ 1.707-9 and 1.707-9T, concerning how partnership liabilities are allocated for disguised sale purposes, are proposed (published in the Federal Register on June 19, 2018) (REG-131186-17).

Par. 4. Section 1.707-9 is amended by revising paragraph (a)(4) and removing paragraph (a)(5). The revisions read as follows:

§ 1.707-9. Effective dates and transitional rules.—(a) * * *

(4) *Section 1.707-5(a)(2) and (f) Examples 2, 3, 7, and 8*.—(i) Section 1.707-5(a)(2) and (f) *Ex-*

amples 2, 3, 7, and *8,* as contained in 26 CFR part 1 revised as of April 1, 2016, apply to any transaction with respect to which any transfers occur before January 3, 2017.

(ii) For any transaction with respect to which all transfers occur on or after January 3, 2017, and any of such transfers occurs before the date that is thirty days after the date these regulations are published as final in the *Federal Register,* see §1.707-9T(a)(5) as contained in 26 CFR part 1 revised as of April 1, 2017.

(iii) Section 1.707-5(a)(2) and (f) *Examples 2, 3, 7,* and *8* apply to any transaction with respect to which all transfers occur on or after the date that is thirty days after the date these regulations are published as final in the *Federal Register.*

* * *

Par. 5. Section 1.707-9T is removed.

§1.707-9T. Effective dates and transitional rules (temporary).

Partnerships: Equity for Services

Partnerships: Equity for Services.—Amendments to Reg. §1.721-1, providing that the transfer of a partnership interest in connection with the performance of services is subject to Code Sec. 83 and providing rules for coordinating Code Sec. 83 with partnership taxation principles, are proposed (published in the Federal Register on May 24, 2005) (REG-105346-03).

☐ Par. 7. In §1.721-1, paragraph (b) is revised to read as follows.

§1.721-1. Nonrecognition of gain or loss on contribution.

* * *

(b)(1) Except as otherwise provided in this section or §1.721-2, section 721 does not apply to the transfer of a partnership interest in connection with the performance of services or in satisfaction of an obligation. The transfer of a partnership interest to a person in connection with the performance of services constitutes a transfer of property to which section 83 and the regulations thereunder apply. To the extent that a partnership interest transferred in connection with the performance of services rendered by a decedent prior to the decedent's death is transferred after the decedent's death to the decedent's successor in interest, the fair market value of such interest is an item of income in respect of a decedent under section 691.

(2) Except as provided in section 83(h) and 1.83-6(c), no gain or loss shall be recognized by a partnership upon—

(i) The transfer or substantial vesting of a compensatory partnership interest; or

(ii) The forfeiture of a compensatory partnership interest. See §1.704-1(b)(4)(xii) for rules regarding forfeiture allocations of partnership items that may be required in the taxable year of a forfeiture.

(3) For purposes of this section, a compensatory partnership interest is an interest in the transferring partnership that is transferred in connection with the performance of services for that partnership (either before or after the formation of the partnership), including an interest that is transferred on the exercise of a compensatory partnership option. A compensatory partnership option is an option to acquire an interest in the issuing partnership that is granted in connection with the performance of services for that partnership (either before or after the formation of the partnership).

(4) To the extent that a partnership interest is—

(i) Transferred to a partner in connection with the performance of services rendered to the partnership, it is a guaranteed payment for services under section 707(c);

(ii) Transferred in connection with the performance of services rendered to a partner, it is not deductible by the partnership, but is deductible only by such partner to the extent allowable under Chapter 1 of the Code.

(5) This paragraph (b) applies to interests that are transferred on or after the date final regulations are published in the Federal Register.

* * *

Installment Obligations: Dispositions: Nonrecognition of Gain or Loss

Installment Obligations: Dispositions: Nonrecognition of Gain or Loss—Amendments to Reg. §1.721-1, relating to the nonrecognition of gain or loss on certain dispositions of an installment obligation, are proposed (published in the Federal Register on December 23, 2014) (REG-109187-11).

☐ Par. 5. Section 1.721-1(a) is amended by adding new ninth and tenth sentences to read as follows:

§1.721-1. Nonrecognition of gain or loss on contribution.—(a) * * * For rules in determining a partner's gain or loss when an installment obligation of a partnership is contributed to the partnership, see section 453B and §1.453B-1(c). The preceding sentence applies to satisfactions of installment obligations after the date these regulations are published as final regulations in the **Federal Register**.

* * *

U.S. Persons: Partnerships with Foreign Partners: Transfers of Appreciated Property

U.S. Persons: Partnerships with Foreign Partners: Transfers of Appreciated Property.—Reg. §§1.721(c)-1—1.721(c)-7, addressing transfers of appreciated property by U.S. persons to partner-

ships with foreign partners related to the transferor, are proposed (published in the Federal Register on January 19, 2017) (REG-127203-15).

Par. 5. Section 1.721(c)-1 is added to read as follows:

§1.721(c)-1. Overview, definitions, and rules of general application.—[The text of proposed §1.721(c)-1 is the same as the text of §1.721(c)-1T as added by T.D. 9814]. [Reg. §1.721(c)-1.]

Par. 6. Section 1.721(c)-2 is added to read as follows:

§1.721(c)-2. Recognition of gain on certain contributions of property to partnerships with related foreign partners.—[The text of proposed §1.721(c)-2 is the same as the text of §1.721(c)-2T as added by T.D. 9814]. [Reg. §1.721(c)-2.]

Par. 7. Section 1.721(c)-3 is added to read as follows:

§1.721(c)-3. Gain deferral method.—[The text of proposed §1.721(c)-3 is the same as the text of §1.721(c)-3T as added by T.D. 9814]. [Reg. §1.721(c)-3.]

Par. 8. Section 1.721(c)-4 is added to read as follows:

§1.721(c)-4. Acceleration events.—[The text of proposed §1.721(c)-4 is the same as the text of §1.721(c)-4T as added by T.D. 9814]. [Reg. §1.721(c)-4.]

Par. 9. Section 1.721(c)-5 is added to read as follows:

§1.721(c)-5. Acceleration event exceptions.—[The text of proposed §1.721(c)-5 is the same as the text of §1.721(c)-5T as added by T.D. 9814]. [Reg. §1.721(c)-5.]

Par. 10. Section 1.721(c)-6 is added to read as follows:

§1.721(c)-6. Procedural and reporting requirements.—[The text of proposed §1.721(c)-6 is the same as the text of §1.721(c)-6T as added by T.D. 9814]. [Reg. §1.721(c)-6.]

Par. 11. Section 1.721(c)-7 is added to read as follows:

§1.721(c)-7. Examples.—[The text of proposed §1.721(c)-7 is the same as the text of §1.721(c)-7T as added by T.D. 9814]. [Reg. §1.721(c)-7.]

Partners and Partnerships: Sales or Exchanges: Certain Distributions

Partners and Partnerships: Sales or Exchanges: Certain Distributions.—Amendments to Reg. §1.732-1, prescribing how a partner should measure its interest in a partnership's unrealized receivables and inventory items, and that provide guidance regarding the tax consequences of a distribution that causes a reduction in that interest, are proposed (published in the Federal Register on November 3, 2014) (REG-151416-06).

☐ Par. 5. Section 1.732-1 is amended by adding paragraphs (c)(2)(iii), (iv), (v), (vi), and (vii), and revising paragraph (c)(5) to read as follows:

§1.732-1. Basis of distributed property other than money.

***

(c) ***

(2) ***

(iii) *Property subject to section 1245.*—Any increase in basis allocated to capital gain property pursuant to the second sentence in paragraph (c)(2)(ii) of this section is not taken into account in determining the recomputed or adjusted basis in the property for purposes of section 1245(a)(1). Notwithstanding the prior sentence, any depreciation or amortization of the increase in basis that is allowed or allowable is taken into account in computing the property's recomputed basis. In the case of property that is subject to section 617(d)(1), section 1250(a)(1), section 1252(a)(1), or section 1254(a)(1), rules similar to the rule in this paragraph (c)(2)(iii) shall apply. *See Examples* 2 and 3 in §1.755-1(c)(6).

(iv) *Section 1231 property.*—Any increase in basis allocated to capital gain property pursuant to the second sentence in paragraph (c)(2)(ii) of this section is not taken into account in determining section 1231 gain and loss, as defined in section 1231(a)(3). *See Examples* 2 and 3 in §1.755-1(c)(6).

(v) *Property subject to section 1248.*—Any increase in basis allocated to stock in a foreign corporation pursuant to the second sentence in paragraph (c)(2)(ii) of this section or any decrease in basis allocated to stock in a foreign corporation pursuant to the second sentence in paragraph (c)(2)(i) of this section is not taken into account in determining the amount of gain recognized on the sale or exchange of such stock for purposes of section 1248(a). In the case of property that is subject to section 995(c), rules similar to the rule set forth in this paragraph (c)(2)(v) shall apply. *See Examples* 8 and 9 in §1.751-1(g).

(vi) *Special rule.*—Any basis adjustment to an asset that is not taken into account under paragraph (c)(2)(iii), (iv), or (v) of this section shall, upon a taxable disposition, be treated as gain or loss, as the case may be, from the sale or exchange of a capital asset with the same holding period as the underlying asset. *See Examples 2* and *3* in § 1.755-1(c)(6).

(vii) *Election not to apply the provisions of paragraphs (c)(2)(iii), (iv), and (v).—See* § 1.755-1(c)(2)(vi) for rules regarding an election to have the provisions of paragraphs (c)(2)(iii), (iv), and (v) of this section, and § 1.755-1(c)(2)(iii), (iv), and (v) not apply. *See Examples 2* and *3* in § 1.755-1(c)(6).

* * *

(5) *Effective/applicability date.*—This paragraph (c) applies to distributions of property from a partnership that occur on or after December 15, 1999, except that paragraphs (c)(2)(iii), (iv), (v), (vi), and (vii) of this section apply to distributions of property from a partnership that occur on or after the date of publication of a Treasury decision adopting these rules as final regulations in the **Federal Register**.

* * *

Partners and Partnerships: American Jobs Creation Act of 2004 and Taxpayer Relief Act of 1997: Guidance

Partners and Partnerships: American Jobs Creation Act of 2004 and Taxpayer Relief Act of 1997: Guidance.—Amendments to Reg. § 1.732-2, providing guidance on certain provisions of the American Jobs Creation Act of 2004, conforming the regulations to statutory changes in the Taxpayer Relief Act of 1997, modifying the basis allocation rules to prevent certain unintended consequences of the current basis allocation rules for substituted basis transactions and providing additional guidance on allocations resulting from revaluations of partnership property, are proposed (published in the Federal Register on January 16, 2014) (REG-144468-05).

☐ Par. 4. Section 1.732-2 is amended by:

1. Redesignating paragraph (b) introductory text as (b)(1) introductory text and revising it.
2. Adding paragraph (b)(2.
3. Redesignating paragraph (c) as paragraph (d).
4. Adding a new paragraph (c).

The revisions and addition reads as follows:

§ 1.732-2. Special partnership basis of distributed property.

* * *

(b) *Adjustments under section 743(b).*—(1) *In general.*—In the case of a distribution of property to a partner who acquired any part of its interest in a transfer, if there was an election under section 754 in effect with respect to the transfer, or if the partnership had a substantial built-in loss (as defined in § 1.743-1(a)(2)(i)) immediately after the transfer, then, for purposes of section 732 (other than subsection (d) thereof), the adjusted partnership basis of the distributed property shall take into account, in addition to any adjustments under section 734(b), the transferee's special basis adjustment for the distributed property under section 743(b). The application of this paragraph may be illustrated by the following example:

* * *

(2) *Effective/applicability date.*—Paragraph (b)(1) of this section relating to substantial built-in losses is applicable for partnership distributions occurring on or after the date of publication of the Treasury decision adopting these rules as final regulations in the **Federal Register**.

(c) *Adjustments under section 704(c)(1)(C).*—(1) *In general.*—In the case of a distribution of property to a section 704(c)(1)(C) partner (as defined in § 1.704-3(f)(2)(ii)), for purposes of section 732 (other than subsection (d) thereof), the adjusted partnership basis of the distributed property shall take into account, in addition to any adjustments under section 734(b), the distributee's section 704(c)(1)(C) basis adjustment (if any) for the distributed property.

(2) *Effective/applicability date.*—Paragraph (c)(1) of this section is applicable for partnership distributions occurring on or after the date of publication of the Treasury decision adopting these rules as final regulations in the **Federal Register**.

* * *

Partners and Partnerships: American Jobs Creation Act of 2004 and Taxpayer Relief Act of 1997: Guidance

Partners and Partnerships: American Jobs Creation Act of 2004 and Taxpayer Relief Act of 1997: Guidance.—Amendments to Reg. §§ 1.734-1 and 1.734-2, providing guidance on certain provisions of the American Jobs Creation Act of 2004, conforming the regulations to statutory changes in the Taxpayer Relief Act of 1997, modifying the basis allocation rules to prevent certain unintended consequences of the current basis allocation rules for substituted basis transactions and providing additional guidance on allocations resulting from revaluations of partnership property, are proposed (published in the Federal Register on January 16, 2014) (REG-144468-05) (corrected April 15, 2014).

☐ Par. 5. Section 1.734-1 is amended by:

1. Revising the section heading.
2. Revising paragraph (a).
3. Revising paragraph (b)(2)(i).
4. Adding *Example 3 following paragraph (b)(2)(ii).*
5. Adding a sentence at the end of paragraph (d).
6. Adding paragraphs (f), (g), and (h).

The revisions and additions read as follows:

§1.734-1. Adjustment to basis of undistributed partnership property where partnership has a section 754 election or there is a substantial basis reduction with respect to a distribution.—(a) *General rule.*—(1) *Adjustments to basis.*—A partnership shall not adjust the basis of partnership property as the result of a distribution of property to a partner unless the election provided in section 754 (relating to optional adjustment to basis of partnership property) is in effect or there is a substantial basis reduction (within the meaning of paragraph (a)(2)(i) of this section) with respect to the distribution.

(2) *Substantial basis reduction.*—(i) *In general.*—For purposes of this section, there is a substantial basis reduction with respect to a distribution of property or properties to a partner if the sum of the amounts described in section 734(b)(2)(A) and (b)(2)(B) exceeds $250,000. If there is a substantial basis reduction under this section, the partnership is treated as having an election under section 754 in effect solely for the distribution to which the substantial basis reduction relates.

(ii) *Special rules for tiered partnerships.*—See paragraph (f) of this section for special rules regarding tiered partnerships.

(iii) *Special rules for securitization partnerships.*—See paragraph (g) of this section for special rules regarding securitization partnerships.

(b) ***

(2) *Decrease in basis.*—(i) When a partnership with a section 754 election in effect makes a distribution in liquidation of a partner's entire interest in the partnership, or when there is a substantial basis reduction (within the meaning of paragraph (a)(2)(i) of this section), the partnership shall decrease the adjusted basis of the remaining partnership property by—

(ii) ***

Example 3—(i) A, B, and C each contribute $2 million to PRS, a partnership. PRS purchases Property 1 and Property 2, both of which are capital assets, for $1 million and $5 million respectively. In Year 2, the fair market value of Property 1 increases to $3 million and the fair market value of Property 2 increases to $6 million. Also in Year 2, PRS distributes Property 1 to C in liquidation of C's interest in PRS at a time when C's basis in its PRS interest is still $2 million. PRS does not have an election under section 754 in effect.

(ii) Under section 732, the basis of Property 1 in the hands of C is $2 million. Because the excess of C's adjusted basis in Property 1 ($2 million) over PRS's adjusted basis in Property 1 ($1 million) is $1 million, the amount described in section 734(b)(2)(B) ($1 million) exceeds $250,000, and therefore, there is a substantial basis reduction with respect to the distribution. Accordingly, pursuant to paragraph (a)(2)(i) of this section, PRS is treated as having a section 754 election in effect in Year 2 and must reduce its basis in Property 2 in accordance with paragraph (b)(2)(i) of this section.

***

(d) *** A partnership required to adjust the basis of partnership property following the distribution of property because there is a substantial basis reduction (within the meaning of paragraph (a)(2)(i) of this section) with respect to the distribution is subject to, and required to comply with, the provisions of this paragraph (d) solely with respect to the distribution to which the substantial basis reduction relates.

***

(f) *Adjustments with respect to tiered partnerships.*—(1) *In general.*—If an upper-tier partnership makes an adjustment under paragraph (b) of this section to the basis of an interest it holds in a lower-tier partnership that has an election under section 754 in effect, the lower-tier partnership must make adjustments under paragraph (b) of this section to the upper-tier partnership's share of the lower-tier partnership's assets. The amount of the lower-tier partnership's adjustment is equal to the adjustment made by the upper-tier partnership to the basis of its interest in the lower-tier partnership. The lower-tier partnership's adjustment to the upper-tier partnership's share of its assets is for the upper-tier partnership only and does not affect the basis in the lower-tier partnership's property for the other partners of the lower-tier partnership. Additionally, if there is a substantial basis reduction (within the meaning of paragraph (a)(2)(i) of this section) with respect to a distribution by an upper-tier partnership that (either directly or indirectly through one or more partnerships) holds an interest in a lower-tier partnership, each lower-tier partnership is treated, solely with respect to the distribution, as if it had made an election under section 754 for the taxable year in which the distribution occurs. For additional examples of the application of the principles of this paragraph (f)(1), see Revenue Ruling 92-15, 1992-1 CB 215. *See* §601.601(d)(2)(ii)(b)

(2) *Example.*—(i) *Facts.*—A, B, and C are equal partners in UTP, a partnership. Each partner's interest in UTP has an adjusted basis and fair market value of $3 million. UTP owns two capital assets with the following adjusted bases and fair market values:

	Adjusted basis	Fair market value
Property 1	$2.2 million	$3 million
Property 2	$2.8 million	$3 million

UTP also owns a 50 percent interest in LTP, a partnership. UTP's interest in LTP has an adjusted basis of $4 million and a fair market value of $3 million. LTP owns one asset, Property 3, a capital asset, which has an adjusted basis of $8 million and a fair market value of $6 million. Neither UTP nor LTP has an election under section 754 in effect.

(ii) *Liquidating distribution to A of Property 1.*—UTP distributes Property 1 to A in complete liquidation of A's interest in UTP. Under section 732(b), the adjusted basis of Property 1 to A is $3 million. Therefore, there is a substantial basis reduction with respect to the distribution to A because the sum of the amounts described in section 734(b)(2)(A) ($0) and section 734(b)(2)(B) (the excess of $3 million over $2.2 million, or $800,000) exceeds $250,000. Therefore, pursuant to paragraph (b)(2) of this section, UTP must decrease the basis of its property by $800,000.

Under § 1.755-1(c), UTP must decrease the adjusted basis of its 50 percent interest in LTP by $800,000. Likewise, pursuant to paragraph (f)(1) of this section, LTP must decrease its basis in UTP's share of Property 3 by $800,000 in accordance with § 1.755-1(c).

(g) *Securitization partnerships.*—A securitization partnership (as defined in § 1.743-1(o)(2)) shall not be treated as having a substantial basis reduction with respect to any distribution of property to a partner.

(h) *Effective/applicability date.*—The rules relating to substantial basis reductions in paragraphs (a) and (b) of this section and paragraphs (f) and (g) of this section apply to partnership distributions occurring on or after the date of publication of the Treasury decision adopting these rules as final regulations in the **Federal Register**.

☐ Par. 6. Section 1.734-2 is amended by revising the section heading and adding paragraph (c) to read as follows:

§ 1.734-2. Adjustment after distribution to transferee partner or section 704(c)(1)(C) partner.

* * *

(c)(1) Section 704(c)(1)(C) basis adjustments will be taken into account in determining the basis adjustment under section 734(b). However, section 704(c)(1)(C) basis adjustments, other than a section 704(c)(1)(C) basis adjustment applied as an adjustment to the basis of partnership property pursuant to paragraph (c)(2) of this section, will not be taken into account in making allocations under § 1.755-1(c).

(2) *Liquidating distributions.*—If a section 704(c)(1)(C) partner receives a distribution of property (including money) in liquidation of its entire partnership interest, the section 704(c)(1)(C) partner's section 704(c)(1)(C) basis adjustments that are treated as basis in the distributed property pursuant to section 732 will be taken into account in determining the basis adjustment under section 734(b), regardless of whether the distributed property is section 704(c)(1)(C) property. If any section 704(c)(1)(C) basis adjustment cannot be reallocated to distributed property in connection with the distribution, then that remaining section 704(c)(1)(C) basis adjustment shall be treated as a positive section 734(b) adjustment. If the distribution also gives rise to a negative section 734(b) adjustment without regard to the section 704(c)(1)(C) basis adjustment reallocation, then the negative section 734(b) adjustment and the section 704(c)(1)(C) basis adjustment reallocation are netted together, and the net amount is allocated under § 1.755-1(c). If the partnership does not have a section 754 election in effect at the time of the liquidating distribution, the partnership shall be treated as having made a section 754 election solely for purposes of computing any negative section 734(b) adjustment that would arise from the distribution.

(3) The following examples illustrate the provisions of this paragraph (c).

Example 1—(i) In Year 1, A contributes $5,000 cash and Property A, a capital asset, with an adjusted basis of $7,000 and a fair market value of $5,000; B contributes $8,000 cash and Property B, a capital asset, with an adjusted basis and fair market value of $2,000; and C contributes $7,000 cash and Property C, a capital asset, with an adjusted basis and fair market value of $3,000 to PRS, a partnership. In Year 3, Property B has appreciated in value to $8,000. PRS distributes Property B and $4,000 to C in complete liquidation of C's interest in PRS at a time when no partner's basis in PRS has changed. PRS revalues its property under § 1.704-1(b)(2)(iv)(f) in connection with the distribution, and makes an election under section 754. C recognizes no gain or loss on the distribution.

(ii) C receives Property B with a basis of $6,000 (C's adjusted basis in PRS of $10,000 minus the $4,000 cash distributed). Because PRS has an election under section 754 in effect, PRS must reduce its basis in remaining partnership property under § 1.734-1(b)(2)(ii) by $4,000 (C's $6,000 basis in Property B minus PRS's $2,000 adjusted basis in Property B prior to the distribution. Under § 1.755-1(c)(2)(ii), that basis reduction must be allocated within a class first to properties with unrealized depreciation in proportion to their respective amounts of unrealized depreciation. Any remaining decrease must be allocated in proportion to the properties' adjusted bases. Because there is no unrealized depreciation in either Property A (disregarding A's section 704(c)(1)(C) basis adjustment) or Property C, the decrease must be allocated between the two properties in proportion to their adjusted bases, $2,500 ($4,000 multiplied by $5,000 divided by $8,000) to Property A and $1,500 ($4,000 multiplied by $3,000 divided by $8,000) to Property C.

(iii) In a subsequent year, PRS sells Property A for its fair market value of $7,500 and recognizes $5,000 of gain ($7,500 amount realized minus adjusted basis of $2,500). Pursuant to § 1.704-3(f)(3)(ii)(B), A's $2,500 distributive share of the $5,000 gain from the sale of Property A is reduced by A's $2,000 section 704(c)(1)(C) basis adjustment. Therefore, A recognizes a gain of $500 on the sale.

Example 2—(i) A contributes Property 1 with an adjusted basis of $15,000 and a fair market value of $10,000 and Property 2 with an adjusted basis of $15,000 and a fair market value of $20,000, and B and C each contribute $30,000 cash to PRS, a partnership. A has a section 704(c)(1)(C) basis adjustment of $5,000 with respect to Property 1. PRS's adjusted bases in Property 1 and Property 2 are $10,000 and $15,000, respectively. When the fair market value of A's interest in PRS is still $30,000, and no partner's basis in its PRS interest has changed, PRS makes a liquidating distribution to A of $30,000 cash, which results in A realizing no gain or loss. PRS has an election under section 754 in effect.

(ii) A is unable to take into account A's section 704(c)(1)(C) basis adjustment in Property 1 upon the distribution of the cash as described in paragraph (c)(2) of this section because A cannot increase the basis of cash under § 1.704-3(f)(3)(v)(C). Thus, A's $5,000 section 704(c)(1)(C) basis adjustment is treated as a positive section 734(b) adjustment to the partnership's assets retained. PRS's $5,000 section 734(b) adjustment will be allocated to Property 2, increasing its basis from $15,000 to $20,000 under §1.755-1(c).

Example 3—(i) A contributes Property 1 with an adjusted basis of $35,000 and a fair market value of $30,000, B contributes Property 2 with an adjusted basis and fair market value of $30,000, and C contributes $30,000 cash to PRS, a partnership. Property 1 is a capital asset, and Property 2 is inventory (as defined in section 751(d)). PRS's adjusted basis in Property 1 is $30,000 under section 704(c)(1)(C)(ii), and A has a section 704(c)(1)(C) basis adjustment of $5,000 with respect to Property 1. Later, at a time when the value and bases of the properties have not changed, PRS distributes $30,000 cash to A in complete liquidation of A's interest. A recognizes a ($5,000) loss under section 731(a)(2) on the distribution. PRS has an election under section 754 in effect.

(ii) The distribution results in a negative section 734(b) adjustment to capital gain property of ($5,000) (the amount of loss A recognizes under section 731(a)(2)). Additionally, because A is unable to take into account A's section 704(c)(1)(C) basis adjustment in Property 1 upon the distribution of the cash, A's $5,000 section 704(c)(1)(C) basis adjustment is treated as a positive section 734(b) adjustment. Pursuant to paragraph (c)(2) of this section, these two adjustments are netted together, resulting in no adjustment under section 734(b). Therefore, the partnership's basis in Property 1 and Property 2 remains $30,000.

Example 4—(i) Assume the same facts as in *Example 3* except that PRS distributes Property 2 to A in complete liquidation of A's interest in a transaction to which section 704(c)(1)(B) and section 737 do not apply.

(ii) Pursuant to §1.704-3(f)(v)(C), A cannot include A's section 704(c)(1)(C) basis adjustment in the basis of the distributed property, because the section 704(c)(1)(C) property and the distributed property are not of like character. Accordingly, the basis to A of Property 2 is $30,000. A also recognizes a $5,000 capital loss under section 731(a)(2), resulting in a ($5,000) basis adjustment under section 734(b). Because the section 704(c)(1)(C) basis adjustment to Property 1 was not reallocated in connection with the distribution, that remaining $5,000 section 704(c)(1)(C) basis adjustment is treated as a positive section 734(b) adjustment. Pursuant to paragraph (c)(2) of this section, these two adjustments are netted together, resulting in no adjustment under section 734(b). Therefore, the basis of Property 1 remains $30,000.

(4) *Effective/applicability date.*—This paragraph (c) applies to partnership distributions occurring on or after the date of publication of the Treasury decision adopting these rules as final regulations in the **Federal Register**.

Partners and Partnerships: Sales or Exchanges: Certain Distributions

Partners and Partnerships: Sales or Exchanges: Certain Distributions.—Amendments to Reg. §1.736-1, prescribing how a partner should measure its interest in a partnership's unrealized receivables and inventory items, and that provide guidance regarding the tax consequences of a distribution that causes a reduction in that interest, are proposed (published in the Federal Register on November 3, 2014) (REG-151416-06).

□ Par. 6. Section 1.736-1 is amended in paragraph (b)(4) by removing the language "paragraph (b)(3)(iii)" from the last sentence and adding the language "paragraph (b)(3)" in its place.

§1.736-1. Payments to a retiring partner or a deceased partner's successor in interest.

Disguised Payments: Services

Disguised Payments: Services.—Amendments to Reg. §1.736-1, relating to disguised payments for services under section 707(a)(2)(A) of the Internal Revenue Code and providing guidance to partnerships and their partners regarding when an arrangement will be treated as a disguised payment for services, are proposed (published in the Federal Register on July 23, 2015) (REG-115452-14).

Par. 6. Section 1.736-1 is amended by adding a sentence at the end of paragraph (a)(1)(i) to read as follows:

§1.736-1. Payments to a retiring partner or a deceased partner's successor in interest.—(a) * * *

(1)(i) * * * Section 736 does not apply to arrangements treated as disguised payments for services under §1.707-2.

* * *

Partnerships: Distribution of Property: Assets-Over Merger

Partnerships: Distribution of Property: Assets-Over Merger.—Amendments to Reg. §§1.737-1, 1.737-2 and 1.737-5, providing rules concerning the application of Code Secs. 704(c)(1)(B) and 737 to distributions of property after two partnerships engage in an assets-over merger, are proposed (published in the Federal Register on August 22, 2007) (REG-143397-05) (corrected November 6, 2007).

□ Par. 4. Section 1.737-1(c)(1) is amended by removing the phrase "five years" and adding in its place the phrase "seven years."

§1.737-1. Recognition of precontribution gain.

□ Par. 5. Section 1.737-2 is amended as follows:

1. Paragraph (b) is revised.
2. Paragraph (e) is redesignated as paragraph (f).
3. New paragraph (e) is added.

The additions and revisions read as follows:

§1.737-2. Exceptions and special rules.

* * *

(b) *Transfers to another partnership.*—(1) *Complete transfer to another partnership (Assets-over merger).*—(i) *In General.*—Section 737 and this section do not apply to a transfer in an assets-over merger as defined in §1.708-1(c)(3) by a partnership (the transferor partnership, which is considered to be the terminated partnership as a result of the merger) of all of its assets and liabilities to another partnership (the transferee partnership, which is considered to be the resulting partnership after the merger) followed by a distribution of the interest in the transferee partnership in liquidation of the transferor partnership as part of the same plan or arrangement.

(ii) *Subsequent distributions.*—(A) *Original section 704(c) gain.*—If, immediately before the assets-over merger, the transferor partnership holds property that has original built-in gain (as defined in §1.704-4(c)(4)(ii)(A)), the seven year period in section 737(b) does not restart with respect to such gain as a result of the transfer of such section 704(c) property to the transferee partnership. A subsequent distribution of other property by the transferee partnership to the partner who contributed the original section 704(c) gain property to the transferor partnership is only subject to section 737 with respect to the original section 704(c) gain if the distribution occurs within seven years of the time such property was contributed to the transferor partnership. See §1.704-4(c)(4)(ii)(A) for a similar provision in the context of section 704. See §1.737-1 for post-merger distribution of property contributed to the transferee partnership prior to the merger.

(B) *New section 704(c) gain.*—Except as provided in paragraph (b)(1)(ii)(E) of this section, if new built-in gain is created upon the contribution of assets by the transferor partnership to the transferee partnership, a subsequent distribution by the transferee partnership of property to a partner of the transferee partnership (other than property deemed contributed by such partner) is subject to section 737, if such distribution occurs within seven years of the contribution by the transferor partnership to the transferee partnership. For these purposes, a partner of the transferor partnership is deemed to have contributed to the transferee partnership an undivided interest in the property of the transferor partnership. The determination of the partner's undivided interest for this purpose shall be determined by the transferor partnership using any reasonable method. See §1.704-4(c)(4)(ii)(B) for a similar provision in the context of section 704.

(C) *Ordering Rule.*—For purposes of this section, if a partner is required to recognize gain under this section, the partner shall recognize a proportionate amount of original and new section 704(c) gain.

(D) *Subsequent Mergers.*—If the transferee partnership (first transferee partnership) is subsequently merged into another partnership (new transferee partnership) the section 704(c) gain that resulted from the merger of the transferor partnership into the first transferee partnership shall be subject to section 737 for seven years from the time of the contribution by the transferor partnership to the first transferee partnership (original merger) and section 704(c) gain that resulted from the merger of the first transferee partnership into the new transferee partnership shall be subject to section 737 for seven years from the time of the contribution by the first transferee partnership to the new transferee partnership (subsequent merger). See §1.704-4(c)(4)(ii)(D) for a similar rule in the context of section 704.

(E) *Identical Ownership or De Minimis Change In Ownership.*—For purposes of section 737(b) and this section, net precontribution gain does not include new section 704(c) gain in property transferred by the transferor partnership to the transferee partnership if both the transferor partnership and the transferee partnership are owned by the same owners in the same proportions or if the difference in ownership is de minimis. The transferor partnership and the transferee partnership are owned by the same owners in the same proportions if each partner owns identical interests in book capital and each item of income, gain, loss, deduction, and credit, and identical shares of distributions and liabilities in each of the transferor and transferee partnerships. A difference in ownership is de minimis if ninety seven percent of interests in book capital and each item of income, gain, loss, deduction and credit and shares in distributions and liabilities of the transferor partnership and transferee partnership are owned by the same owners in the same proportions. See §1.704-4(c)(4)(ii)(E) for a similar provision in the context of section 704.

(F) *Examples.*—The following examples illustrate the rules of paragraph (b)(3) of this section.

Example (1). No net precontribution gain. (i) *Facts* . On January 1, 2005, A contributes Asset 1, with a basis of $200x and a fair market value of $300x, to partnership PRS1 in exchange for a 50 percent interest. On the same date, B contributes $300x of cash to PRS1 in exchange for a 50 percent interest. Also on January 1, 2005, C contributes Asset 2, with a basis of $100x and a fair market value of $200x, to partnership PRS2 in exchange for a 50 percent interest. D contributes $200x of cash to PRS2 in exchange for a 50 percent interest. On January 1, 2008, PRS1 and PRS2 undertake an assets-over partnership merger in which PRS1 is the continuing partnership and PRS2 is the terminating partnership for both state law and federal tax purposes. At the time of the merger, PRS1's only assets are Asset 1, with a fair market value of $900x, and $300x in cash. PRS2's only assets are Asset 2, with a fair market value of $600x and $200x in cash. After the merger, the partners have capital and profits interests in PRS1 as follows: A, 30 percent; B, 30 percent; C, 20 percent; and D, 20 percent. PRS1 and PRS2 both have provisions in their respective partnership agreements requiring the revaluation of partnership property upon entry of a new partner. PRS1 would not be treated as an investment company (within the meaning of section 351) if it were incorporated. Neither partnership holds any unrealized receivables or inventory for purposes of section 751. In addition, neither partnership has a section 754 election in place. Asset 1 and Asset 2 are nondepreciable capital assets. On January 1, 2013, PRS1 has the same assets that it had after the merger. Each asset has the same value that it had at the time of the merger. On this date, PRS1 distributes Asset 2 to A in liquidation of A's interest.

(ii) *Analysis*. Section 737(a) requires A to recognize gain when it receives a distribution of property in an amount equal to the lesser of the excess distribution or the partner's net precontribution gain. The distribution of Asset 2 to A results in an excess distribution of $400x ($600x fair market value of Asset 2 - $200x adjusted basis in A's partnership interest). However, the distribution of Asset 2 to A occurs more than seven years after the contribution by A of Asset 1 to PRS1 and A made no subsequent contributions to PRS1. Therefore, A's net precontribution gain for purposes of section 737(b) at the time of the distribution is zero. The $600x of reverse section 704(c) gain in Asset 1, resulting from a revaluation of PRS1's partnership property at the time of the merger, is not net precontribution gain (See § 1.737-2(e)). Accordingly, A will not recognize gain under section 737 as a result of the distribution of Asset 2. See § 1.704-4(c)(4)(ii)(F), *Example (1)* for a similar example under section 704.

Example (2). Revaluation gain and merger gain. (i) *Facts* . The facts are the same as *Example (1)*, except that on January 1, 2007, E joins PRS2 as a one-third partner for $250x in cash. At the time E joins the partnership, Asset 2 has a fair market value of $300x. On January 1, 2008, PRS2 merges into PRS1. At the time of the merger, Asset 1 and Asset 2 both have a fair market value of $400x. On January 1, 2011, Asset 1 is distributed to C when its value is $275x.

(ii) *Analysis*. Section 737(a) requires A to recognize gain when it receives a distribution of property in an amount equal to the lesser of the excess distribution or the partner's net precontribution gain. The distribution of Asset 1 to C results in an excess distribution of $175x ($275x fair market value of Asset 1 - $100x adjusted basis in C's partnership interest). The distribution of Asset 1 to C occurs within seven years of the original contribution of Asset 2 by C to PRS2. Therefore, C's net precontribution gain at the time of the distribution is $183.33x, which includes C's original section 704(c) gain from the contribution of Asset 2 to PRS2 of $100x plus C's share of new section 704(c) gain of $83.33x ($50x of reverse section 704(c) gain upon the admission of E, plus $33.33x of additional section 704(c) gain upon merger). C's excess distribution is less than C's net precontribution gain. Thus, C will recognize $175x of gain upon receipt of Asset 1 in accordance with section 737(a). See § 1.704-4(c)(4)(ii)(F), *Example (2)* for a similar example under section 704.

Example (3). Fluctuations in the value of an asset. (i) *Facts*. The facts are the same as *Example (1)*, except that on January 1, 2011, Asset 1 is distributed to C when its fair market value is $300x. Immediately prior to the distribution, PRS1 revalues its property in accordance with § 1.704-1(b)(2)(iv)(f).

(ii) *Analysis*. The distribution of Asset 1 to C occurs within seven years of the original contribution of Asset 2 by C to PRS2 and within seven years of the date of the merger. Therefore, C's net precontribution gain at the time of the distribution equals $300x ($100x of original section 704(c) gain from the contribution of Asset 2 to PRS2 and $200x of new section 704(c) gain). The distribution of Asset 1 to C results in an excess distribution of $200x ($300x fair market value of Asset 1 - $100x adjusted basis in C's partnership interest). Accordingly, in accordance with section 737(a), C will recognize gain of $200x upon receipt of Asset 1.

Example (4). Reverse section 704(c) gain. (i) Facts. The facts are the same as *Example (1)*, except that on January 1, 2011, PRS1 distributes Asset 2 to A in liquidation of A's interest in PRS1. At the time of the distribution, Asset 2 has a value of $600x.

(ii) *Analysis*. Section 737(a) requires A to recognize gain when it receives a distribution of property in an amount equal to the lesser of the excess distribution or the partner's net precontribution gain. The distribution of Asset 2 to A results in an excess distribution of $400x ($600x fair market value -200x adjusted basis in A's partnership interest). The distribution of Asset 2 to A occurs within seven years after the contribution of Asset 1 to PRS1 by A. Thus, A's net precontribution gain for purposes of section 737(b) at the time of the distribution is $100x (A's original section 704(c) gain from the contribution of Asset 1 to PRS1). Under § 1.737-2(e), A's net precontribution gain does not include A's reverse section 704(c) gain upon the revaluation of the Assets of PRS1 prior to the merger. Accordingly, A will recognize $100x of gain (the lesser of the excess distribution or net precontribution gain) under section 737 as a result of the distribution of Asset 2. See § 1.704-4(c)(4)(ii)(F), *Example (4)* for a similar example under section 704.

Example (5). Identical ownership exception. (i) *Facts*. In 1990, A, an individual, and B, a subchapter C corporation, formed PRS1, a partnership. A owned 75 percent of the interests in the book capital, profits, losses, distributions, and liabilities of PRS1. B owned the remaining 25 percent interest in the book capital, profits, losses, distributions, and liabilities of PRS1. In the same year, A and B also formed another partnership, PRS2, with A owning 75 percent of the interests in PRS2 and B owning the remaining 25 percent. Upon formation of the partnerships, A contributed Asset X to PRS1 and Asset Y to PRS2 and B contributed cash. Both Assets X and Y had section 704(c) built-in gain at the time of contribution to the partnerships.

(ii) In January 2005, PRS1 is merged into PRS2 in an assets-over merger in which PRS1 is the terminating partnership and PRS2 as the continuing partnership for both state law and federal income tax purposes. At the time of the merger, both Assets X and Y had increased in value from the time they were contributed to PRS1 and PRS2, respectively. As a result, a new layer of section 704(c) gain was created with respect to Asset X in PRS1. After the merger, A had a 75 percent interest in PRS2's book capital, profits, losses, distributions, and liabilities. B held the remaining 25 percent interest in PRS2's book capital, profits, losses, distributions, and liabilities. In 2006, PRS2 distributes Asset X to A.

(iii) *Analysis*. The 2006 distribution by PRS2 occurs more than seven years after the formation of the partnerships and the original contribution of Asset X to the partnerships. Therefore, the original layer of built-in gain created on the original contribution of Asset X to the partnerships should not be taken into account in applying section 737 to the proposed liquidation. In addition, paragraph (b)(1)(ii)(E) of this section provides that section 737(a) does not apply to newly created section 704(c) gain in property transferred by the transferor partnership to the transferee partnership if both the transferor partnership and the transferee partnership are owned by the same owners in the same proportions. The transferor partnership and the transferee partnership are owned by the same owners in the same proportions if each partner's percentage interest in the transferor partnership's book capital, profits, losses, distributions, and liabilities is the same as the partner's percentage interest in those items of the transferee partnership. In this case, A owned 75 percent and B owned 25 percent of the interests in the book capital, profits, losses, distributions, and liabilities of PRS1 and PRS2 prior to the merger and 75 percent and 25 percent, respectively, of PRS2 after the merger. As a result, the requirements of the identical ownership exception of paragraph (b)(1)(ii)(E) of this section are satisfied. Thus, the new built-in gain created upon contribution of Asset X in connection with the partnership merger will not be taken into account in applying section 737 to the proposed distribution. See § 1.704-4(c)(4)(ii)(F), *Example (5)* for a similar example under section 704.

(2) *Certain divisive transactions*.—(i) *In general*.—Section 737 and this section do not apply to a transfer by a partnership (transferor partnership) of all of the section 704(c) property contributed by a partner to a second partnership (transferee partnership) in an exchange described in section 721, followed by a distribution as part of the same plan or arrangement of an interest in the transferee partnership (and no other property) in complete liquidation of the interest of the partner that originally contributed the section 704(c) property to the transferor partnership (divisive transactions).

(ii) *Subsequent distributions*.—After a divisive transaction referred to in paragraph (b)(2)(i) of this section, a subsequent distribution of property by the transferee partnership to a partner of the transferee partnership that was formerly a partner of the transferor partnership is subject to section 737 to the same extent that a distribution from the transferor partnership would have been subject to section 737.

* * *

(e) *Reverse section 704(c) gain*.—For purposes of section 737(b), net precontribution gain does not include reverse section 704(c) gain as described in § 1.704-3(a)(6)(i).

☐ Par. 6. Section 1.737-5 is amended by revising the section heading and adding two additional sentences at the end of the paragraph to read as follows:

§ 1.737-5. Effective/applicability date.

* * * Section 1.737-1(c) is effective as of August 22, 2007. Section 1.737-2(b)(1) is effective for any distribution of property after January 19, 2005, if such property was contributed in a merger using the assets-over form after May 3, 2004.

Partners and Partnerships: American Jobs Creation Act of 2004 and Taxpayer Relief Act of 1997: Guidance

Partners and Partnerships: American Jobs Creation Act of 2004 and Taxpayer Relief Act of 1997: Guidance.—Amendments to Reg. § 1.737-1, providing guidance on certain provisions of the American Jobs Creation Act of 2004, conforming the regulations to statutory changes in the Taxpayer Relief Act of 1997, modifying the basis allocation rules to prevent certain unintended consequences of the current basis allocation rules for substituted basis transactions and providing additional guidance on allocations resulting from revaluations of partnership property, are proposed (published in the Federal Register on January 16, 2014) (REG-144468-05).

☐ Par. 7. Section 1.737-1 is amended by revising paragraph (c)(1) and adding paragraphs (c)(3) and (4) to read as follows:

§ 1.737-1. Recognition of precontribution gain.

* * *

(c) *Net precontribution gain*.—(1) *General rule*.—The distributee partner's net precontribution gain is the net gain (if any) that would have been recognized by the distributee partner under section 704(c)(1)(B) and § 1.704-4 if all property that had been contributed to the partnership by the distributee partner within seven years of the distribution and is held by the partnership immediately before the distribution had been distributed by the partnership to another partner other than the partner who owns, directly or indirectly, more than 50 percent of the capital or profits interest in the partnership.

* * *

(3) *Determination of seven-year period*.—(i) *General rule*.—The seven-year period specified in paragraph (c)(1) of this section begins on, and includes, the date of contribution and ends on, and includes, the last date that is within seven years of the contribution. For example, if a partner contributes 704(c) property to a partnership on May 15, 2016, the seven-year period with respect to the section 704(c) property ends on, and includes, May 14, 2023.

(ii) *Section 708(b)(1)(B) terminations*.—A termination of the partnership under section 708(b)(1)(B) does not begin a new seven-year period for each partner with respect to built-in gain and built-in loss property that the terminated partnership is deemed to contribute to the new partnership under § 1.708-1(b)(4). *See* § 1.704-3(a)(3)(ii) for the definitions of built-in gain and built-in loss on section 704(c) property.

(4) *Effective/applicability date*.—The provisions of paragraph (c)(1) and (3) of this section

relating to the seven-year period for determining the applicability of section 737(b) apply for partnership contributions occurring on or after the date of publication of the Treasury decision adopting these rules as final regulations in the **Federal Register**.

* * *

Partners and Partnerships: American Jobs Creation Act of 2004 and Taxpayer Relief Act of 1997: Guidance

Partners and Partnerships: American Jobs Creation Act of 2004 and Taxpayer Relief Act of 1997: Guidance.—Amendments to Reg. §1.743-1, providing guidance on certain provisions of the American Jobs Creation Act of 2004, conforming the regulations to statutory changes in the Taxpayer Relief Act of 1997, modifying the basis allocation rules to prevent certain unintended consequences of the current basis allocation rules for substituted basis transactions and providing additional guidance on allocations resulting from revaluations of partnership property, are proposed (published in the Federal Register on January 16, 2014) (REG-144468-05).

☐ Par. 8. Section 1.743-1 is amended by:

1. Revising the section heading.
2. Revising paragraph (a).
3. Revising paragraph (b).
4. Redesignating paragraph (f) introductory text as paragraph (f)(1) introductory text and revising it.
5. Adding paragraph (f)(2).
6. In paragraph (h)(1), removing "§1.708-1(b)(1)(iv)" and adding in its place "§1.708-1(b)(4)".
7. Revising paragraph (j)(3)(ii) *Example 1*.
8. Revising paragraph (j)(3)(ii) *Example 3*.
9. Revising paragraph (k)(1)(iii).
10. Adding paragraph (k)(2)(iv).
11. Redesignating paragraph (l) as paragraph (p).
12. Adding a new paragraph (l).
13. Adding paragraphs (m), (n), and (o).
14. Revising newly redesignated paragraph (p).

The revisions and additions read as follows:

§1.743-1. Special rules where partnership has a section 754 election in effect or has a substantial built-in loss immediately after transfer of partnership interest.— (a) *Generally*.—(1) *Adjustment to basis*.—The basis of partnership property is adjusted as a result of the transfer of an interest in a partnership by sale or exchange or on the death of a partner if the election provided by section 754 (relating to optional adjustments to the basis of partnership property) is in effect with respect to the partnership, or if the partnership has a substantial built-in loss (within the meaning of paragraph (a)(2)(i) of this section) immediately after the transfer.

(2) *Substantial built-in loss*.—(i) *In general*.—A partnership has a substantial built-in loss with respect to a transfer of an interest in a partnership if the partnership's adjusted basis in partnership property exceeds the fair market value of the property (as determined in paragraph (a)(2)(iii) of this section) by more than $250,000 immediately after the transfer.

(ii) *Impact of section 743 basis adjustments and section 704(c)(1)(C) basis adjustments*.—For purposes of paragraph (a)(2)(i) of this section, any section 743 or section 704(c)(1)(C) basis adjustments (as defined in §1.704-3(f)(2)(iii)) (other than the transferee's section 743(b) basis adjustments or section 704(c)(1)(C) basis adjustments) to partnership property are disregarded.

(iii) *Determination of fair market value in tiered situation*.—For purposes of paragraph (a)(2)(i) of this section, an upper-tier partnership's fair market value in a lower-tier partnership is equal to the sum of—

(A) The amount of cash that the upper-tier partnership would receive if the lowertier partnership sold all of its property for cash to an unrelated person for an amount equal to the fair market value of such property, satisfied all of its liabilities (other than §1.752-7 liabilities), paid an unrelated person to assume all of its §1.752-7 liabilities in a fully taxable, arm's-length transaction, and liquidated; and

(B) The upper-tier partnership's share of the lower-tier partnership's liabilities as determined under section 752 and the regulations.

(iv) *Example*.—A and B are equal partners in PRS, a partnership. PRS owns Property 1, with an adjusted basis of $3 million and a fair market value of $2 million, and Property 2, with an adjusted basis of $1 million and a fair market value of $1 million. In Year 2, A sells 50 percent of its interest in PRS to C for its fair market value of $750,000. PRS does not have section 754 election in effect. Under paragraph (a)(2)(i) of this section, PRS has a substantial built-in loss because, immediately after the transfer, the adjusted basis of PRS's property ($4 million) exceeds the fair market value of the property ($3 million) by more than $250,000. Thus, pursuant to paragraph (a)(1) of this section, PRS must adjust the bases of its properties as if PRS had made a section 754 election for Year 2.

(b) *Determination of adjustment*.—In the case of the transfer of an interest in a partnership, either by sale or exchange or as a result of the death of a partner, a partnership that has an election under section 754 in effect or that has a substantial built-in loss (within the meaning of paragraph (a)(2)(i) of this section) —

* * *

(f) *Subsequent transfers*.—(1) *In general*.— Where there has been more than one transfer of a partnership interest, a transferee's basis adjustment is determined without regard to any prior transferee's basis adjustment. In the case of a gift of an interest in a partnership, the donor is treated as transferring, and the donee as receiving, that portion of the basis adjustment attributable to the gifted partnership interest. The following example illustrates the provisions of this paragraph (f)(1):

* * *

(2) *Special rules for substituted basis transactions.*—Where a partner had a basis adjustment under section 743(b) allocated pursuant to § 1.755-1(b)(2) through (b)(4) that is attributable to an interest that is subsequently transferred in a substituted basis transaction (within the meaning of § 1.755-1(b)(5)), the provisions of paragraph (f)(1) of this section do not apply. Instead, the transferee succeeds to that portion of the transferor's basis adjustment attributable to the transferred partnership interest. The basis adjustment to which the transferee succeeds is taken into account for purposes of determining the transferee's share of the adjusted basis to the partnership of the partnership's property for purposes of paragraph (b) of this section and § 1.755-1(b)(5). To the extent a transferee would be required to decrease the adjusted basis of an item of partnership property pursuant to §§ 1.743-1(b)(2) and 1.755-1(b)(5), the decrease first reduces the positive section 743(b) adjustment, if any, that the transferee succeeds to. The following example illustrates the provisions of this paragraph (f)(2):

Example—(i) A and B are partners in LTP, a partnership. A owns a 60 percent interest, and B owns a 40 percent interest, in LTP. B owns the LTP interest with an adjusted basis of $50 and a fair market value of $70. LTP owns two assets: Capital Asset 1 with an adjusted basis of $25 and a fair market value of $100, and Capital Asset 2 with an adjusted basis of $100 and a fair market value of $75. B sells its interest in LTP to UTP. Both LTP and UTP have a section 754 election in effect. Pursuant to § 1.755-1(b)(3), UTP's $20 section 743(b) adjustment is allocated $30 to Capital Asset 1 and ($10) to Capital Asset 2.

(ii) UTP distributes its LTP interest to C, a partner in UTP, when the adjusted bases and fair market values of the LTP interest and LTP's assets have not changed. C's adjusted basis in its UTP interest at the time of the distribution is $40. Pursuant to paragraph (f)(2) of this section, C succeeds to UTP's section 743(b) adjustment. Also pursuant to paragraph (f)(2) of this section, the section 743(b) adjustment is taken into account in determining C's share of the adjusted basis of LTP property. Thus, C also has a $30 negative section 743(b) adjustment that must be allocated pursuant to § 1.755-1(b)(5). That is, C's interest in the partnership's previously taxed capital is $70 (C would be entitled to $70 cash on liquidation and there is no increase or decrease for tax gain or tax loss from the hypothetical transaction, taking into account UTP's section 743(b) adjustment to which C succeeds). Pursuant to § 1.755-1(b)(5)(iii)(B), the $30 negative section 743(b) adjustment must be allocated within the capital class first to properties with unrealized depreciation in proportion to C's share of the respective amounts of unrealized depreciation before the decrease. Taking into account UTP's section 743(b) adjustment to which C succeeds, C has no share of LTP's unrealized depreciation. Pursuant to § 1.755-1(b)(5)(iii)(B), any remaining decrease must be allocated among Capital Asset 1 and Capital Asset 2 in proportion to C's share of their adjusted bases. Taking into account UTP's section 743(b) adjustment to which C succeeds, C's share of the adjusted basis in Capital Asset 1 is $40 ($10 share of LTP's basis and $30 of UTP's section 743(b) adjustment to which C succeeded) and in Capital Asset 2 is $30 ($40 share of LTP's basis and ($10) of UTP's section 743(b) adjustment). Thus, 40/70 of the $30 adjustment, $17.14, is allocated to Capital Asset 1 and 30/70 of the $30 adjustment, $12.86, is allocated to Capital Asset 2. The decrease allocated to Capital Asset 1 first reduces UTP's section 743(b) adjustment to which C succeeds. Thus, C has a net section 743(b) adjustment in Capital Asset 1 of $12.86 ($30 minus $17.14) and in Capital Asset 2 of ($22.86) (($10) plus ($12.86)). If Capital Asset 1 is subject to the allowance for depreciation or amortization, C's net $12.86 positive basis adjustment is recovered pursuant to paragraph (j)(4)(i)(B).

(iii) If C later transfers its LTP interest to D in a transaction that is not a substituted basis transaction within the meaning of § 1.755-1(b)(5), under paragraph (f)(1) of this section, D does not succeed to any of C's section 743(b) adjustment.

* * *

(j) * * *

(3) * * *

(ii) * * *

Example 1. A and B form equal partnership PRS. A and B each contribute $100 cash, and PRS purchases nondepreciable property for $200. Later, at a time when the property value has decreased to $100, C contributes $50 cash for a 1/3 interest in PRS. Under § 1.704-1(b)(2)(iv)(f)(5), PRS revalues its property in connection with the admission of C, allocating the $100 unrealized loss in the property equally between A and B under the partnership agreement, which provides for the use of the traditional method under § 1.704-3(b). A subsequently sells its interest in PRS to T for $50. PRS has an election in effect under section 754. T receives a negative $50 basis adjustment under section 743(b) that, under section 755, is allocated to the nondepreciable property. PRS later sells the property for $120. PRS recognizes a book gain of $20 (allocated equally between T, B, and C), and a tax loss of $80. T will receive an allocation of $40 of tax loss under the principles of section 704(c). However, because T has a negative $50 basis adjustment in the nondepreciable property, T recognizes a $10 gain from the partnership's sale of the property.

* * *

Example 3. A and B form equal partnership PRS. A and B each contribute $75 cash. PRS purchases nondepreciable property for $150. Later, at a time when the property value has decreased to $100, C contributes $50 cash for a 1/3 interest in PRS. Under § 1.704-1(b)(2)(iv)(*f*)(5), PRS revalues its property in connection with the admission of C. The $50 unrealized loss in the property is allocated equally to A and B under the partnership agreement, which provides for the use of the remedial allocation method described in § 1.704-3(d). A subsequently sells its interest in PRS to T for $50. PRS has an election in effect under section 754. T receives a negative $25 basis adjustment under section 743(b) that, under section 755, is allocated to the nondepreciable property. PRS later sells the property for $112. PRS recognizes a book gain of $12 (allocated equally between T, B, and C), and a tax loss of $38 (allocated equally between T and B). To match its share of book gain, C will be allocated $4 of remedial gain, and T and B will each be allocated an offsetting $2 remedial loss. T was allocated a total of $21 of tax loss with respect to the property. However, because T has a negative $25 basis adjustment in the nondepreciable property, T recognizes a $4 gain from the partnership's sale of the property.

* * *

(k) * * *

(1) * * *

(iii) *Rules for substantial built-in loss transactions.*—A partnership required to adjust the basis of partnership property following the transfer of an interest in a partnership by sale or exchange or on the death of a partner as the result of the partnership having a substantial built-in loss (as defined in paragraph (a)(2)(i) of this section) immediately after such transfer is subject to, and required to comply with, this paragraph (k)(1), and may rely on, and must comply with, paragraphs (k)(3), (k)(4), and (k)(5) of this section solely with respect to the transfer to which the substantial built-in loss relates as if an election under section 754 were in effect at the time of the transfer. *See* paragraph (k)(2) of this section for additional rules for transferees and paragraph (n) of this section for special reporting rules relating to electing investment partnerships.

(2) * * *

(iv) *Special rules for transferees subject to the substantial built-in loss provisions.*—The transferee of an interest in a partnership that is required to reduce the bases of partnership property in accordance with the rules in paragraph (a)(2) of this section must comply with this paragraph (k)(2) as if an election under section 754 were in effect at the time of the transfer.

(l) *Basis adjustments with respect to tiered partnerships.*—(1) *General rule.*—If an interest in an upper-tier partnership that holds an interest in a lower-tier partnership is transferred by sale or exchange or upon the death of a partner, and the upper-tier partnership and the lower-tier partnership both have elections in effect under section 754, then for purposes of section 743(b) and section 754, an interest in the lower-tier partnership will be deemed similarly transferred in an amount equal to the portion of the upper-tier partnership's interest in the lower-tier partnership that is attributable to the interest in the upper-tier partnership being transferred. Additionally, if an interest in an upper-tier partnership that holds (directly or indirectly through one or more partnerships) an interest in a lower-tier partnership is transferred by sale or exchange or on the death of a partner, and the upper-tier partnership has a substantial built-in loss (within the meaning of paragraph (a)(2)(i) of this section) with respect to the transfer, each lower-tier partnership is treated, solely with respect to the transfer, as if it had made a section 754 election for the taxable year of the transfer. For additional examples of the application of the principles of this paragraph (l), see Revenue Ruling 87-115, 1987-2 CB 163. *See* § 601.601(d)(2)(ii)(b).

(2) *Example.*—The following example illustrates the principles of this paragraph (l).

Example. A and B are equal partners in UTP, a partnership. UTP has no liabilities and owns a 25 percent interest in LTP, a partnership. UTP's interest in LTP has a fair market value of $100,000 and an adjusted basis of $500,000. LTP has no liabilities and owns Land, which has a fair market value of $400,000 and an adjusted basis of $2 million. In Year 3, when UTP and LTP do not have section 754 elections in effect, B sells 50 percent of its interest in UTP to C for its fair market value of $25,000. Because the adjusted basis of UTP's interest in LTP ($500,000) exceeds the fair market value of UTP's interest in LTP ($100,000) by more than $250,000 immediately after the transfer, UTP has a substantial built-in loss with respect to the transfer. Thus, pursuant to paragraph (l) of this section, UTP must adjust the basis of its interest in LTP, and LTP must adjust the basis of Land, as if it had made a section 754 election for Year 3.

(m) *Anti-abuse rule for substantial built-in loss transactions.*—Provisions relating to substantial built-in loss transactions in paragraph (a) and paragraphs (k), (l), (n), and (o) of this section must be applied in a manner consistent with the purposes of these paragraphs and the substance of the transaction. Accordingly, if a principal purpose of a transaction is to achieve a tax result that is inconsistent with the purpose of one or more of these paragraphs, the Commissioner may recast the transaction for Federal income tax purposes, as appropriate, to achieve tax results that are consistent with the purpose of these paragraphs. Whether a tax result is inconsistent with the purposes of the provisions is determined based on all the facts and circumstances. For example, under the provisions of this paragraph (m)—

(1) Property held by related partnerships may be aggregated if the properties were transferred to the related partnerships with a principal purpose of avoiding the application of the substantial built-in loss provisions in section 743 and the regulations; and

(2) A contribution of property to a partnership may be disregarded if the transfer of the property was made with a principal purpose of avoiding the application of the substantial built-in loss provisions in section 743 and the regulations thereunder.

(n) *Electing investment partnerships.*—(1) *No adjustment of partnership basis.*—For purposes of this section, an electing investment partnership (as defined in paragraph (n)(6) of this section) shall not be treated as having a substantial built-in loss (within the meaning of paragraph (a)(2)(i) of this section) with respect to any transfer occurring while the election in paragraph (n)(6)(i) of this section is in effect.

(2) *Loss deferral for transferee partner.*—In the case of a transfer of an interest in an electing investment partnership, the transferee partner's distributive share of losses (without regard to gains) from the sale or exchange of partnership property shall not be allowed except to the extent that it is established that such losses exceed the loss (if any) recognized by the transferor partner (or by any prior transferor to the extent not fully offset by a prior disallowance under this paragraph (n)(2)) on the transfer of the partnership interest. If an electing investment partnership allocates losses with a different character from the sale or exchange of property to the

transferee (such as ordinary or section 1231 losses and capital losses) and the losses allocated to that partner are limited by this paragraph (n)(2), then a proportionate amount of the losses disallowed under this paragraph (n)(2) shall consist of each loss of a separate character that is allocated to the transferee partner.

(3) *No reduction in partnership basis.*—Losses disallowed under paragraph (n)(2) of this section shall not decrease the transferee partner's basis in the partnership interest.

(4) *Effect of termination of partnership.*—This paragraph (n) shall be applied without regard to any termination of a partnership under section 708(b)(1)(B).

(5) *Certain basis reductions treated as losses.*—In the case of a transferee partner whose basis in property distributed by the partnership is reduced under section 732(a)(2), the amount of the loss recognized by the transferor on the transfer of the partnership interest that is taken into account under paragraph (n)(2) of this section shall be reduced by the amount of such basis reduction.

(6) *Electing investment partnership.*—For purposes of this section, the term *electing investment partnership* means any partnership if—

(i) The partnership makes an election under paragraph (n)(10) of this section to have this paragraph (n) apply;

(ii) The partnership would be an investment company under section 3(a)(1)(A) of the Investment Company Act of 1940 but for an exemption under paragraph (1) or (7) of section 3(c) of such Act;

(iii) The partnership has never been engaged in a trade or business (see paragraph (n)(7) of this section for additional rules regarding this paragraph (n)(6)(iii));

(iv) Substantially all of the assets of the partnership are held for investment;

(v) At least 95 percent of the assets contributed to the partnership consist of money;

(vi) No assets contributed to the partnership had an adjusted basis in excess of fair market value at the time of contribution;

(vii) All partnership interests of the partnership are issued by the partnership pursuant to a private offering before the date that is 24 months after the date of the first capital contribution to the partnership; (viii) The partnership agreement of the partnership has substantive restrictions on each partner's ability to cause a redemption of the partner's interest (see paragraphs (n)(8) and (n)(9) of this section for additional rules regarding this paragraph (n)(6)(viii)); and

(ix) The partnership agreement of the partnership provides for a term that is not in excess of 15 years (see paragraph (n)(9) of this section for additional rules regarding this paragraph (n)(6)(ix)).

(7) *Trade or business.*—For purposes of paragraph (n)(6)(iii) of this section, whether a partnership is engaged in a trade or business is based on the all the facts and circumstances. Notwithstanding the prior sentence—

(i) A partnership will not be treated as engaged in a trade or business if, based on all the facts and circumstances, the partnership is not engaged in a trade or business under the rules in § 1.731-2(e)(3).

(ii) In the case of a tiered partnership arrangement, a partnership (upper-tier partnership) will not be treated as engaged in a trade or business of a partnership in which it owns an interest (lower-tier partnership) if the upper-tier partnership can establish that, at all times during the period in which the upper-tier partnership owns an interest in the lower-tier partnership, the adjusted basis of its interest in the lower-tier partnership is less than 25 percent of the total capital that is required to be contributed to the upper-tier partnership by its partners during the entire term of the upper-tier partnership. Otherwise, the upper-tier partnership will be treated as engaged in the trade or business of the lower-tier partnership.

(8) *Substantive restrictions.*—For purposes of paragraph (n)(6)(viii) of this section, substantive restrictions include cases in which a redemption is permitted under a partnership agreement only if the redemption is necessary to avoid a violation of state, federal, or local laws (such as ERISA or the Bank Holding Company Act) or the imposition of a federal excise tax on, or a change in the federal tax-exempt status of, a tax-exempt partner.

(9) *Special rules for partnerships in existence on June 4, 2004.*—In the case of a partnership in existence on June 4, 2004, paragraph (n)(6)(viii) of this section will not apply to the partnership and paragraph (n)(6)(ix) of this section is applied by substituting "20 years" for "15 years."

(10) *Election.*—(i) *Eligibility.*—A partnership is eligible to make the election described in paragraph (n)(6)(i) of this section if the partnership meets the definition of an electing investment partnership in paragraph (n)(6) of this section and does not have an election under section 754 in effect.

(ii) *Manner of making election.*—A partnership must make the election by attaching a written statement to an original return for the taxable year for which the election is effective. The original return must be filed not later than the time prescribed by § 1.6031(a)-1(e) of the Procedure and Administration Regulations (including extensions) for filing the return for the taxable year for which the election is effective. If the partnership is not otherwise required to file a partnership return, the election shall be made in accordance with the rules in § 1.6031(a)-1(b)(5) of the Procedure and Administration Regulations. The statement must—

(A) Set forth the name, address, and tax identification number of the partnership making the election;

(B) Contain a representation that the partnership is eligible to make the election; and

(C) Contain a declaration that the partnership elects to be treated as an electing investment partnership.

(iii) *Effect and duration of election.*—Once the election is made, the election is effective for all transfers during the partnership's taxable year for which the election is effective and all succeeding taxable years, except as provided in paragraphs (n)(10)(iv) and (n)(10)(v) of this section.

(iv) *Termination of election.*—(A) *In general.*—The election terminates if the partnership fails to meet the definition of an electing investment partnership. The electing investment partnership's election also terminates if the partnership files an election under section 754.

(B) *Effect of termination.*—If the election terminates, the partnership will be subject to the substantial built-in loss provisions in this section with respect to the first transfer of a partnership interest that occurs after the partnership ceases to meet the definition of an electing investment partnership (or the first transfer that occurs after the effective date of the section 754 election) and to each subsequent transfer. In addition, any losses that are subsequently allocated to a partner to whom a partnership interest was transferred while the election was in effect shall remain subject to the rules in paragraph (n)(2) of this section.

(v) *Revocation of election.*—(A) *In general.*—The election, once made, shall be irrevocable except with the consent of the Commissioner. The application for consent to revoke the election must be submitted to the Internal Revenue Service in the form of a letter ruling request.

(B) *Effect of revocation.*—If the election is properly revoked, the partnership will be subject to the substantial built-in loss provisions in this section with respect to the first transfer of a partnership interest that occurs after the effective date of the revocation and to each subsequent transfer. In addition, any losses that are subsequently allocated to a partner to whom a partnership interest was transferred while the election was in effect shall remain subject to the rules in paragraph (n)(2) of this section.

(11) *Transferor partner required to provide information to transferee partner and partnership.*—(i) *In general.*—Except as provided in paragraph (n)(11)(ii) of this section, if an electing investment partnership interest is transferred in a sale or exchange or upon the death of a partner, the transferor (or, in the case of a partner who dies, the partner's executor, personal representative, or other successor in interest) must notify the transferee and the partnership in writing. If the transferor is a nominee (within the meaning of §1.6031(c)-1T), then the nominee, and not the beneficial owner of the transferred interest, must supply the information to the transferee and the partnership. The notice must be provided within 30 days after the date on which the transferor partner (or the executor, personal representative, or other successor in interest) receives a Schedule K-1 from the partnership for the partnership's taxable year in which the transfer occurred. The notice must be signed under penalties of perjury, must be retained by the transferee and the partnership as long as the contents thereof may be material in the administration of any internal revenue law, and must include—

(A) The name, address, and tax identification number of the transferor;

(B) The name, address, and tax identification number of the transferee (if ascertainable);

(C) The name of the electing investment partnership;

(D) The date of the transfer (and, in the case of the death of a partner, the date of the death of the partner);

(E) The amount of loss, if any, recognized by the transferor on the transfer of the interest, together with the computation of the loss;

(F) The amount of losses, if any, recognized by any prior transferors to the extent the losses were subject to disallowance under paragraph (n)(2) of this section in the hands of a prior transferee and have not been offset by prior loss disallowances under paragraph (n)(2) of this section; and

(G) Any other information necessary for the transferee to compute the amount of loss disallowed under paragraph (n)(2) of this section.

(ii) *Exception.*—The rules of paragraph (n)(11)(i) of this section do not apply if the transferor recognizes a gain on the transfer and no prior transferor recognized a loss on any transfer.

(iii) *Effect of failure to notify transferee partner.*—If the transferor partner, its legal representative in the case of a transfer by death, or the nominee (if the transferor is a nominee) fails to provide the transferee partner with the statement, the transferee partner must treat all losses allocated from the electing investment partnership as disallowed under paragraph (n)(2) of this section unless the transferee partner obtains, from the partnership or otherwise, the information necessary to determine the proper amount of losses disallowed under paragraph (n)(2) of this section. If the transferee does not have the information necessary to determine the proper amount of losses disallowed under paragraph (n)(2) of this section, but does have information sufficient to determine the maximum amount of losses that could be disallowed, then the transferee may treat the amount of losses disallowed under paragraph (n)(2) of this section as being equal to that maximum amount. For example, if the transferee is able to ascertain the adjusted basis that a prior transferor had in its partnership interest, but is not able to ascertain the amount realized by that transferor, the transferee may assume, for purposes of calculating the amount of losses disallowed under paragraph (n)(2) of this section, that the sales price when the prior transferor sold its interest was zero. If, following the filing of a return pursuant to the previous sentence, the transferor partner or the partnership provides the required information to the transferee partner, the transferee partner should make appropriate adjustments in an amended return for the year of the loss allocation from the partnership in accordance with section 6511 or other applicable rules.

(iv) *Additional rules..*—See paragraph (n)(12)(i) of this section for additional reporting requirements when the electing investment partnership is not required to file a partnership return.

(12) *Electing investment partnership required to provide information to partners.*—(i) *Distributive shares of partnership items.*—An electing investment partnership is required to separately state on Schedule K and K-1 of the partnership's return (Form 1065) all allocations of losses to all of its partners under §1.702-1(a)(8)(ii), including losses that, in the absence of section 743(e), could be netted against gains at the partnership level. If a partnership's election to be treated as an electing investment partnership is terminated or revoked under paragraphs (n)(10)(iv) or (n)(10)(v) of this section, the partnership must continue to state such gains and losses separately in future returns relating to any period

during which the partnership has one or more transferee partners that are subject to section paragraph (n)(2) of this section. If an electing investment partnership is not required to file a partnership return, the transferee of a partnership interest may be required to provide the Commissioner similar information regarding the partner's distributive share of gross gains and losses of the partnership under §1.6031(a)-1(b)(4).

(ii) *Annual statement.*—An electing investment partnership must provide an annual statement to all of its partners. The statement must be attached to every statement provided to a partner or nominee under section 6031(b) that is issued with respect to any taxable year for which an election to be treated as an electing investment partnership is in effect (whether or not the election is in effect for the entire taxable year). The statement must include the following—

(A) A statement that the partnership has elected to be treated as an electing investment partnership;

(B) A statement that, unless the transferor partner recognizes a gain on the transfer and no prior transferor recognized a loss on any transfer, if a partner transfers an interest in the partnership to another person, the transferor partner must, within 30 days after receiving a Schedule K-1 from the partnership for the taxable year that includes the date of the transfer, provide the transferee with certain information, including the amount, if any, of loss that the transferor recognized on the transfer of the partnership interest, and the amount of losses, if any, recognized by prior transferors with respect to the same interest; and

(C) A statement that if an interest in the partnership is transferred to a transferee partner, the transferee is required to reduce its distributive share of losses from the partnership, determined without regard to gains from the partnership, to the extent of any losses recognized by the transferor partner when that partner transferred the partnership interest to the transferee (and to the extent of other losses recognized on prior transfers of the same partnership interest that have not been offset by prior loss disallowances). The statement must also notify the transferee that it is required to reduce its share of losses as reported to the transferee by the partnership each year by the amount of any loss recognized by the transferor partner (or any prior transferor to the extent not already offset by prior loss disallowances) until the transferee has reduced its share of partnership losses by the total amount of losses required to be disallowed. Finally, the statement must state that if the transferor partner (or its nominee), or its legal representative in the case of a transfer by death, fails to provide the transferee with the required statement, the transferee must treat all losses allocated from the partnership as disallowed unless the transferee obtains, from the partnership or otherwise, the information necessary to determine the proper amount of losses disallowed.

(o) *Securitization partnerships.*—(1) *General rule.*—A securitization partnership (as defined in paragraph (o)(2) of this section) shall not be treated as having a substantial built-in loss with respect to any transfer.

(2) *Definition of securitization partnership.*—A *securitization partnership* means any partnership the sole business activity of which is to issue securities that provide for a fixed principal (or similar) amount and that are primarily serviced by the cash flows of a discrete pool (either fixed or revolving) of receivables or other financial assets that by their terms convert into cash in a finite period, but only if the sponsor of the pool reasonably believes that the receivables and other financial assets comprising the pool are not acquired for the purpose of being disposed of.

(p) *Effective/applicability date.*—* * * Paragraph (f)(2) of this section and the provisions relating to substantial built-in losses in paragraph (a) and paragraphs (k), (l), (m), (n), and (o) of this section are effective for transfers of partnership interests occurring on or after the date of publication of the Treasury decision adopting these rules as final regulations in the **Federal Register**.

Qualified Property: Additional First Year Depreciation Deduction

Qualified Property: Additional First Year Depreciation Deduction.—Amendments to Reg. §1.743-1, providing guidance regarding the additional first year depreciation deduction under section 168(k) of the Internal Revenue Code (Code), are proposed (published in the Federal Register on August 8, 2018) (REG-104397-18).

Par. 16. Section 1.743-1 is amended by:

1. Adding three sentences to the end of paragraph (j)(4)(i)(B)(*1*) and adding two sentences at the end of paragraph (l) to read as follows:

§1.743-1. Optional adjustment to basis of partnership property.

* * *

(j) * * *

(4) * * *

(i) * * *

(B) * * *

(*1*) * * * Notwithstanding the above, the partnership is allowed to deduct the additional first year depreciation under section 168(k) and §1.168(k)-2 for an increase in the basis of qualified property, as defined in section 168(k) and §1.168(k)-2, under section 743(b) in a class of property, as defined in §1.168(k)-2(e)(1)(ii)(A) through (F), even if the partnership made the election under section 168(k)(7) and §1.168(k)-2(e)(1) not to deduct the additional first year depreciation for all other qualified property of the partnership in the same class of property, as defined in §1.168(k)-2(e)(1)(ii)(A) through (F), and placed in service in the same taxable year, provided the section 743(b) basis adjustment meets all requirements of section 168(k) and §1.168(k)-2. Further, the partnership may make an election under section 168(k)(7) and §1.168(k)-2(e)(1) not to deduct the additional first year depreciation for an increase in the basis of qualified property, as defined in section 168(k) and §1.168(k)-2, under section 743(b) in a class of property, as defined in

§ 1.168(k)-2(e)(1)(ii)(A) through (F), and placed in service in the same taxable year, even if the partnership does not make that election for all other qualified property of the partnership in the same class of property, as defined in § 1.168(k)-2(e)(1)(ii)(A) through (F), and placed in service in the same taxable year. In this case, the section 743(b) basis adjustment must be recovered under a reasonable method.

* * *

(l) * * * The last three sentences of paragraph (j)(4)(i)(B)(*1*) of this section apply to transfers of partnership interests that occur on or after the date of publication of a Treasury decision adopting these rules as final regulations in the **Federal Register**. However, a partnership may rely on the last three sentences in paragraph (j)(4)(i)(B)(*1*) of this section in these proposed regulations for transfers of partnership interests that occur on or after September 28, 2017, and ending before the date of publication of a Treasury decision adopting these rules as final regulations in the **Federal Register**.

Partners and Partnerships: Sales or Exchanges: Certain Distributions

Partners and Partnerships: Sales or Exchanges: Certain Distributions.—Amendments to Reg. § 1.751-1, prescribing how a partner should measure its interest in a partnership's unrealized receivables and inventory items, and that provide guidance regarding the tax consequences of a distribution that causes a reduction in that interest, are proposed (published in the Federal Register on November 3, 2014) (corrected January 26, 2015) (REG-151416-06).

□ Par. 7. Section 1.751-1 is amended by:

a. Revising paragraphs (a)(1) and (2).

b. Revising the first sentence of paragraph (b)(1)(i) and adding a new sentence at the end of paragraph (b)(1)(i).

c. Removing the last four sentences of paragraph (b)(1)(ii).

d. Revising paragraphs (b)(1)(iii) and (b)(2) and (3).

e. Redesignating paragraphs (b)(4) and (5) as paragraphs (b)(5) and (6).

f. Adding a new paragraph (b)(4).

g. Revising the paragraph heading of newly designated paragraph (b)(5).

h. Further redesignating newly redesignated paragraph (b)(5)(ii) as paragraph (b)(5)(vi) and adding paragraphs (b)(5)(ii), (iii), (iv), and (v).

i. Revising newly designated paragraph (b)(6).

j. Revising paragraph (c)(4)(vi).

k. Adding paragraph (c)(4)(x).

l. Removing paragraphs (c)(5) and (6).

m. Revising the first and second sentences of paragraph (d)(1).

n. Revising paragraphs (e), (f), and (g).

The additions and revisions read as follows:

§ 1.751-1. Unrealized receivables and inventory items.—(a) * * *

(1) *Character of amount realized.*—To the extent that money or property received by a partner in exchange for all or part of his partnership interest is attributable to his share of the value of partnership unrealized receivables or inventory items, the money or fair market value of the property received shall be considered as an amount realized from the sale or exchange of property other than a capital asset. The remainder of the total amount realized on the sale or exchange of the partnership interest is realized from the sale or exchange of a capital asset under section 741. For definition of "unrealized receivables" and "inventory items," see section 751(c) and (d). *See* paragraph (e) of this section for the definition of section 751 property.

(2) *Determination of gain or loss.*—The income or loss realized by a partner upon the sale or exchange of its interest in section 751 property is the amount of income or loss from section 751 property (taking into account allocations of tax items applying the principles of section 704(c), including any remedial allocations under § 1.704-3(d), and any section 743 basis adjustment pursuant to § 1.743-1(j)(3)) that would have been allocated to the partner (to the extent attributable to the partnership interest sold or exchanged) if the partnership had sold all of its property in a fully taxable transaction for cash in an amount equal to the fair market value of such property (taking into account section 7701(g)) immediately prior to the partner's transfer of the interest in the partnership. Any gain or loss recognized that is attributable to section 751 property will be ordinary gain or loss. The difference between the amount of capital gain or loss that the partner would realize in the absence of section 751 and the amount of ordinary income or loss determined under this paragraph (a)(2) is the transferor's capital gain or loss on the sale of its partnership interest. For purposes of section 751(a) and paragraph (a) of this section, the amount of money or the fair market value of property received by the partner in exchange for all or part of his partnership interest must take into account the partner's share of income or gain from section 751 property. *See Example 1* in paragraph (g) of this section. *See* § 1.460-4(k)(2)(iv)(E) for rules relating to the amount of ordinary income or loss attributable to a contract accounted for under a long-term contract method of accounting.

* * *

(b) *Certain distributions treated as sales or exchanges.*—(1) *In general.*—(i) Certain distributions to which section 751(b) applies are treated in whole or in part as sales or exchanges of property, and not as distributions to which sections 731 through 736 apply. * * * For purposes of section 751 and this section, a partner's interest in the partnership's section 751 property includes allocations of tax items applying the principles of section 704(c).

* * *

(iii) If a distribution is a section 751(b) distribution, as described in paragraph (b)(2)(i) of this section, the tax consequences of the section 751(b) distribution, as determined under paragraph (b)(3) of this section, shall first apply, and then the rules of sections 731 through 736 shall apply. *See* paragraph (b)(5)(vi) of this section for treatment of payments under section 736(a).

(2) *Distributions to which section 751(b) applies.*—(i) *Section 751(b) amount.*—A distribution is a section 751(b) distribution if it gives rise to a "section 751(b) amount" for any partner. A partner's section 751(b) amount (if any) associated with a distribution of partnership property (including money) equals the greatest of—

(A) The amount by which the partner's net section 751 unrealized gain immediately before the distribution exceeds the partner's net section 751 unrealized gain immediately after the distribution;

(B) The amount by which the partner's net section 751 unrealized loss immediately after the distribution exceeds the partner's net section 751 unrealized loss immediately before the distribution; and

(C) The amount of the partner's net section 751 unrealized gain immediately before the distribution, increased by the total amount of the partner's net section 751 unrealized loss immediately after the distribution (where neither of those numbers equals zero).

(ii) *Net section 751 unrealized gain or loss before a distribution.*—A partner's net section 751 unrealized gain or loss immediately before a distribution equals the amount of net income or loss, as the case may be, from section 751 property that would be allocated to the partner if the partnership disposed of all of the partnership's assets for cash in an amount equal to the fair market value of such property (taking into account section 7701(g)). For this purpose, a partner's net section 751 unrealized gain or loss includes any remedial allocations under § 1.704-3(d), and takes into account any section 743(b) basis adjustment pursuant to § 1.743-1(j)(3) and any carryover basis adjustment described in §§ 1.743-1(g)(2)(ii), 1.755-1(b)(5)(iii)(D), or 1.755-1(c)(4) as though the carryover basis adjustment was applied to the basis of new partnership section 751 property with fair market value of zero.

(iii) *Net section 751 unrealized gain or loss after a distribution.*—A partner's net section 751 unrealized gain or loss immediately after a distribution equals the sum of (to the extent applicable)—

(A) With respect to a partner remaining in the partnership immediately after the distribution (including a distributee partner remaining in the partnership), the amount of net income or loss, as the case may be (including any remedial allocations under § 1.704-3(d) and taking into account any section 743(b) basis adjustment pursuant to § 1.743-1(j)(3) and any carryover basis adjustment described in §§ 1.743-1(g)(2)(ii), 1.755-1(b)(5)(iii)(D), or 1.755-1(c)(4) as though the carryover basis adjustment was applied to the basis of new partnership section 751 property with fair market value of zero), from section 751 property that would be allocated to the partner if the partnership disposed of all of the partnership's assets for cash in an amount equal to the fair market value of such property (taking into account section 7701(g)); and

(B) With respect to a partner receiving a distribution, the amount of net income or loss, as the case may be, from section 751 property that would be recognized by the distributee if, immediately after the distribution, the distributee disposed of the distributed assets for cash in an amount equal to the fair market value of such property (taking into account section 7701(g)).

(iv) *Revaluation of assets.*—For a partnership that distributes money or property (other than a de minimis amount) to a partner as consideration for an interest in the partnership, and that owns section 751 property immediately after the distribution, if the partnership maintains capital accounts in accordance with § 1.704-1(b)(2)(iv), the partnership must revalue its assets immediately prior to the distribution in accordance with § 1.704-1(b)(2)(iv)(*f*). If a partnership does not maintain capital accounts in accordance with § 1.704-1(b)(2)(iv), the partnership must comply with this section by computing its partners' shares of partnership gain or loss immediately before the distribution as if the partnership assets were sold for cash in a fully taxable transaction (taking into account section 7701(g)), and by taking those computed shares of gain or loss into account under the principles of section 704(c) (making subsequent adjustments for cost recovery and other events that affect the basis of the property). In addition, if the partnership (upper-tier partnership) owns another partnership directly or indirectly through one or more partnerships (lower-tier partnership), and the same persons own, directly or indirectly (through one or more entities), more than 50 percent of the capital and profits interests in both the upper-tier partnership and the lower-tier partnership, the lower-tier partnership must also revalue its assets immediately prior to the distribution in accordance with § 1.704-1(b)(2)(iv)(f) if the lower-tier partnership owns section 751 property. If the same persons do not own, directly or indirectly, more than 50 percent of the capital and profits interests in both the upper-tier partnership and the lower-tier partnership, the upper-tier partnership must allocate its distributive share of the lower-tier partnership's items among its partners in a manner that reflects the allocations that would have been made had the lower-tier partnership revalued its property.

(3) *Tax consequences of a section 751(b) distribution.*—(i) *Reasonable approach.*—In the case of a section 751(b) distribution described in paragraph (b)(2) of this section, the partnership must choose a reasonable approach that is consistent with the purpose of section 751(b) under which each partner with a section 751(b) amount recognizes ordinary income (or takes it into account by eliminating a basis adjustment) equal to that section 751(b) amount immediately prior to the section 751(b) distribution. In certain circumstances described in paragraph (b)(3)(ii) of this section, a distributee partner may also be permitted or required to recognize capital gain. To be reasonable, an approach must conform to the general principles and anti-abuse rules described in paragraph (b)(4) of this section. An approach is not necessarily unreasonable merely because another approach would result in a higher aggregate tax liability. Once the partnership has

adopted a reasonable approach, it must apply that approach consistently for all section 751(b) distributions, including for any distributions the partnership makes after a termination of the partnership under section 708(b)(1)(B). If the application of the adopted approach to a later section 751(b) distribution produces results inconsistent with the purpose of section 751, the partnership must adopt another reasonable approach that achieves the purposes of section 751 for that distribution only. *See Example 3* through *Example 8* in paragraph (g) of this section.

(ii) *Gain Recognition.*—(A) *Mandatory recognition.*—A partner's net section 751 unrealized gain or net section 751 unrealized loss for purposes of paragraph (b)(3)(i) of this section is determined before taking into account any basis adjustments required by paragraph (b)(3)(iii) of this section. In certain instances, the application of paragraph (b)(3)(iii) of this section may cause a partner to receive distributed property with a basis that differs from the basis of the property in the hands of the distributing partnership. If an adjustment to the basis of the distributed section 751 property results in a section 734(b) basis adjustment, and that basis adjustment would have altered the amount of net section 751 unrealized gain or loss computed under paragraph (b)(2) of this section if the section 734(b) adjustment had been included immediately prior to the distribution, then the distributee partner must recognize capital gain immediately prior to the distribution in an amount sufficient to eliminate that section 734(b) basis adjustment. *See Examples 5* and *6* in paragraph (g) of this section. If, however, the partnership makes an election under § 1.755-1(c)(2)(vi), then the partner must characterize all or a portion of the gain recognized under this paragraph as ordinary income or a dividend, as appropriate, to preserve the character of the gain in the adjusted asset. *See Example 9* in paragraph (g) of this section.

(B) *Elective recognition.*—A distributee partner may elect to recognize capital gain (in addition to amounts required to be recognized under this section) to eliminate section 732(a)(2) or (b) basis adjustments to the asset or assets received in distribution if, and to the extent that, the basis adjustments required by paragraph (b)(3)(iii) of this section would otherwise cause the distributee partner's net section 751 unrealized gain to be greater immediately after the distribution than it was immediately before the distribution or would cause the distributee partner's net section 751 unrealized loss to be less immediately after the distribution than it was immediately before the distribution. A distributee partner elects under this paragraph (b)(3)(ii)(B) by providing the partnership with written notification of its intent to make the election and reporting the capital gain on its return. An extension of time to make an election under this paragraph (b)(3)(ii)(B) will not be granted under § 301.9100-3 of this chapter. The requirement in paragraph (b)(1)(i) of this section that a partnership apply a chosen reasonable method consistently across all partnership distributions does not apply for purposes of this paragraph. *See Example 7* in paragraph (g) of this section.

(iii) *Adjustments to Basis.*—The partnership and its partners must make appropriate adjustments to the adjusted basis of the partners' interests in the partnership, and of section 751 property and other property held by the partnership or partners, in a manner consistent with the adopted approach to reflect any ordinary income or capital gain recognized upon application of paragraph (b)(3) of this section, and section 704(c) amounts must be adjusted accordingly.

(4) *General principles and anti-abuse rules.*—(i) The purpose of section 751 is to prevent a partner from converting its rights to ordinary income into capital gain, including by relying on the rules of section 704(c) to defer ordinary income while monetizing most of the value of the partnership interest. The partnership and all partners of the partnership must apply the rules of section 751 and § 1.751-1 in a manner consistent with the purpose of section 751. Accordingly, if a principal purpose of a transaction is to achieve a tax result that is inconsistent with the purpose of section 751, the Commissioner may recast the transaction for federal tax purposes as appropriate to achieve tax results that are consistent with the purpose of section 751. The Commissioner will determine whether a tax result is inconsistent with the purpose of section 751 based on all the facts and circumstances. The existence of one or more of the situations set forth below is presumed to establish that a transaction is inconsistent with the purpose of section 751 and disclosure to the Internal Revenue Service in accordance with § 1.751-1(b)(4)(ii) is required.

(A) Circumstances in which a partner received a distribution that would otherwise be subject to section 751(b), but for the application of the principles of section 704(c), and one or more of the following conditions exist (whether at the time of the distribution or, in the case of paragraph (b)(4)(i)(A)*(2), (3), (4)*, or *(5)* of this section, a later date):

(1) The partner's interest in net section 751 unrealized gain is at least four times greater than the partner's capital account immediately after the distribution, pursuant to § 1.704-1(b)(2)(iv) (or comparable amount for partnerships not maintaining capital accounts under § 1.704-1(b)(2)(iv));

(2) The partner is substantially protected from losses from the partnership's activities and has little or no participation in the profits from the partnership's activities other than a preferred return that is in the nature of a payment for the use of capital;

(3) The partner engages in a transaction that, at the time of the transaction, causes the net value of the partner (or its successor) to be less than the tax liability that the partner (or its successor) would incur with respect to its interest in the partnership's section 751 property upon a sale of its partnership interest for its fair market value at the time of the transaction. For this purpose, the net value of the partner (or its successor) equals—

(i) The fair market value of all assets owned by the partner (or its successor) that may be subject to creditor's claims under local law (including the partner's enforceable right to contributions from its owner or owners), less

(ii) All obligations of the partner (or its successor) other than the partner's obligation with respect to the tax liability for which the net value is being determined;

(4) The partner transfers a portion of its partnership interest within five years after the distribution in a manner that does not trigger ordinary income recognition, and ordinary income or gain with respect to the partnership interest is subject to Federal income tax in the hands of the transferor partner immediately before the transfer, but any ordinary income or gain with respect to the partnership interest is exempt from, or otherwise not subject to, Federal income tax in the hands of the transferee partner immediately after the transfer;

(5) The partnership transfers to a corporation in a nonrecognition transaction section 751 property other than pursuant to a transfer of all property used in a trade or business (excluding assets that are not material to a continuation of the trade or business); or

(B) The partners agree to change (other than a de minimis change) the manner in which the partners share any item or class of items of income, gain, loss, deduction or credit of the partnership under the partnership agreement and that change reduces the partner's net section 751 unrealized gain.

(ii) If a partner participates in a transaction described in paragraph (b)(4)(i)(A) or (B) of this section and does not recognize and report its share of ordinary income from section 751 property on its tax return for the taxable year of the transaction, the partner must file Form 8275-R, Regulation Disclosure Statement, or any appropriate successor form, disclosing its participation in the transaction for the taxable year in which the transaction occurred.

(5) *Special rules.*—* * *

* * *

(ii) The transferee in a nonrecognition transaction of all or a portion of the partnership interest of a contributing partner is treated as the contributing partner for purposes of section 751(b)(2) in an amount attributable to the interest transferred.

(iii) For purposes of section 751(b)(2), if a partnership disposes of contributed section 751 property in a nonrecognition transaction, the substituted basis property (within the meaning of section 7701(a)(42)) received in exchange for such substituted basis property is treated as the contributed section 751 property with regard to the contributing partner. If a partnership transfers contributed section 751 property together with other property in a nonrecognition transaction, the substituted basis property (within the meaning of section 7701(a)(42)) is treated as the contributed section 751 property with regard to the contributing partner in the same proportion as the fair market value of the contributed section 751 property, at the time of the transfer, bears to the fair market value of the other property transferred at the time of the transfer. If a transfer described in this paragraph (b)(5)(iii) was in exchange for an interest in an entity, the interest in the entity will not be treated as the contributed section 751 property with regard to the contributing partner to the extent the value of the interest is attributable to other property the partnership contributed to the entity.

(iv) For purposes of section 751(b)(2), an interest in an entity previously contributed to the partnership is not treated as previously contributed property to the extent the value of the interest is attributable to property the partnership contributed to the entity after the interest was contributed to the partnership. The preceding sentence does not apply to the extent that the property contributed to the entity was contributed to the partnership by the partner that also contributed the interest in the entity to the partnership.

(v) For purposes of section 751(b)(2), the distribution of an undivided interest in property is treated as the distribution of previously contributed property to the extent that the undivided interest does not exceed the undivided interest, if any, contributed by the distributee partner in the same property.

* * *

(6) *Statements required.*—(i) *Partnership.*—A partnership that makes a section 751(b) distribution must submit with its return for the year of the distribution a statement for each section 751(b) distribution made during the year that includes the following:

(A) A caption identifying the statement as the disclosure of a section 751(b) distribution and the date of the distribution; and

(B) A brief description of the reasonable approach adopted by the partnership pursuant to paragraph (b)(3)(i) of this section for recognizing the ordinary income; if applicable, the capital gain required to be recognized; and if relevant, whether the approach varies from an approach previously adopted within any of the three tax years preceding the current tax year.

(ii) *Partner.*—A partnership that makes a section 751(b) distribution during the partnership's tax year must submit with its return for the year of the distribution a statement for each partner that has a section 751(b) amount greater than $0 in connection with that distribution. The statement must be attached to the statement for that partner required by section 6031(b) and § 1.6031(b)-1T(a), and must include the following:

(A) The date of the section 751(b) distribution;

(B) The amount of ordinary income the partner recognized pursuant to paragraph (b)(3)(i) of this section; and

(C) The amount of capital gain the partner recognized, if any, pursuant to paragraph (b)(3)(ii)(A) or (B) of this section.

(c) * * *

(4) * * *

(vi) With respect to any taxable year of a partnership beginning after July 18, 1984, amounts treated as ordinary income under section 467 are treated as ordinary income under this section in the same manner as amounts treated as ordinary income under section 1245 (*see* paragraph (c)(4)(iii) of this section) or section 1250 (*see* paragraph (c)(4)(v) of this section).

* * *

(x) With respect to any taxable year of a partnership beginning after July 18, 1984, the term *unrealized receivables,* for purposes of this section and sections 731, 732, and 741 (but not for purposes of section 736), includes any market discount bond (as defined in section 1278) and any short-term obligation (as defined in section 1283) but only to the extent of the amount that would be treated as ordinary income if (at the time of the transaction described in this section or section 731, 732, or 741, as the case may be) such property had been sold by the partnership.

* * *

(d) *Inventory items which have substantially appreciated in value.*—(1) *Substantial appreciation.*—Partnership inventory items shall be considered to have appreciated substantially in value if, at the time of the distribution, the total fair market value of all the inventory items of the partnership exceeds 120 percent of the aggregate adjusted basis for such property in the hands of the partnership (without regard to any special basis adjustment to the partner). The terms "inventory items which have appreciated substantially in value" or "substantially appreciated inventory items" refer to the aggregate of all partnership inventory items but do not include any unrealized receivables. * * *

* * *

(e) *Section 751 property and other property.*—For purposes of paragraph (a) of this section, *section 751 property* means unrealized receivables or inventory items. For purposes of paragraph (b) of this section, *section 751 property* means unrealized receivables or substantially appreciated inventory items. For purposes of all paragraphs of this section, *other property* means all property (including money) that is not section 751 property.

(f) *Applicability date.*—The rules contained in paragraph (a)(2) of this section apply to transfers of partnership interests that occur on or after November 3, 2014. The rules contained in paragraph (a)(3) of this section apply to transfers of partnership interests that occur on or after December 15, 1999. The rules contained in paragraphs (b)(2) and (3) of this section apply to distributions of partnership property that occur on or after the date of publication of a Treasury decision adopting these rules as final regulations in the **Federal Register**. However, a partnership and its partners may apply the rules contained in paragraph (b)(2) of this section for purposes of determining a partner's interest in the partnership's section 751 property on or after November 3, 2014, provided the partnership and its partners apply paragraphs (a)(2), (b)(2), and (b)(4) of this section, and proposed § 1.704-1(b)(2)(iv)(f), consistently for all partnership sales, exchanges, and distributions occurring on or after November 3, 2014, including for any distributions the partnership makes after a termination of the partnership under section 708(b)(1)(B).

(g) *Examples.*—Application of the provisions of section 751 may be illustrated by the following examples. In each of *Examples 2* through 9 of this paragraph (g), none of the section 751 property qualifies as property that the distributee previously contributed as described in section 751(b)(2)(A), and no distribution to a retiring partner is a payment described in section 736(a):

Example 1. (i)(A) A and B are equal partners in personal service partnership PRS. A contributed nondepreciable capital assets (the "Capital Assets") to PRS with a basis and fair market value of $14,000. B contributed unrealized receivables described in paragraph (c) of this section (the "Unrealized Receivables") to PRS with a basis of zero and fair market value of $14,000. Later, when the fair market value of the Capital Assets had declined to $2,000, B transferred its interest in PRS to T for $9,000 when PRS's balance sheet (reflecting a cash receipts and disbursements method of accounting) was as follows:

Assets

	Adjusted Basis	Fair Market Value
Cash	$ 4,000	$ 4,000
Capital Assets	14,000	2,000
Unrealized Receivables	0	14,000
Total	18,000	20,000

Liabilities and Capital

	Adjusted Basis	Fair Market Value
Liabilities	$2,000	$2,000
Capital:		
A	15,000	9,000
B	1,000	9,000
Total	18,000	20,000

(B) The total amount realized by B is $10,000, consisting of the cash received, $9,000, plus $1,000, B's share of the partnership liabilities assumed by T. *See* section 752. B's interest in the partnership property includes an interest in the partnership's Unrealized Receivables. B's basis in its partnership interest is $2,000 ($1,000, plus $1,000, B's share of partnership liabilities). If section 751(a) did not apply to the sale, B would recognize $8,000 of capital gain from the sale of the interest in PRS. However, section 751(a) does apply to the sale.

(ii) For purposes of section 751(a), the amount of money or the fair market value of property received by the partner in exchange for all or part of his partnership interest must take into account the partner's share of income or gain from section 751 property. If PRS sold all of its section 751 property in a fully taxable transaction immediately prior to the transfer of B's partnership interest to T, B would have been allocated $14,000 of ordinary income from the sale of PRS's Unrealized Receivables under section 704(c). Therefore, B will recognize $14,000 of ordinary income with respect to the Unrealized Receivables. The difference between the amount of capital gain or loss that the partner would realize in the absence of section 751 ($8,000) and the amount of ordinary income or loss determined under paragraph (a)(2) of this section ($14,000) is the transferor's capital gain or loss on the sale of its partnership interest. In this case, B will recognize a $6,000 capital loss.

Example 2. (i) A, B, and C each contribute $120 to partnership ABC in exchange for a 1/3 interest. A, B, and C each share in the profits and losses of ABC in accordance with their 1/3 interest. ABC purchases land for $100 in Year 1. At the end of Year 3, when ABC holds $260 in cash and land with a value of $100 and has generated

$90 in zero-basis unrealized receivables, ABC distributes $50 cash to C in a current distribution, reducing C's interest in ABC from 1/3 to 1/4. ABC has a section 754 election in effect. To determine if the distribution is a distribution to which section 751(b) applies, ABC must apply the test set forth in paragraph (b)(2) of this section.

(ii)(A) Pursuant to paragraph (b)(2)(iv) of this section, ABC revalues its assets and its partners' capital accounts are increased under § 1.704-1(b)(2)(iv)(f) to reflect each partner's share of the unrealized gain in the partnership's assets. Before the distribution, ABC's balance sheet is as follows:

	Tax	Book	Capital	Tax	Book
Cash	$260	$260	A	$120	$150
Unrealized Receivable	0	90	B	120	150
Real Property	100	100	C	120	150
Totals	360	450		360	450

(B) If ABC disposed of all of its assets for cash in an amount equal to the fair market value of such property immediately before the distribution, A, B, and C would each be allocated $30 of net income from ABC's section 751 property. Accordingly, A, B, and C's net section 751 unrealized gain immediately before the distribution is $30 each under paragraph (b)(2)(ii) of this section.

(iii)(A) After the distribution (but before taking into account any consequences under this section), ABC's balance sheet would be as follows:

	Tax	Book	Capital	Tax	Book
Cash	$210	$210	A	$120	$150
Unrealized Receivable	0	90	B	120	150
Real Property	100	100	C	70	100
Totals	310	400		310	400

(B) If ABC disposed of all of its assets in exchange for cash in amounts equal to the fair market values of those assets immediately after the distribution, A, B, and C would each still be allocated $30 of net income from ABC's section 751 property pursuant to § 1.704-3(a)(6). C did not receive any section 751 property in the distribution. Accordingly, A, B, and C's net section 751 unrealized gain immediately after the distribution is $30 each under paragraph (b)(2)(iii) of this section.

(iv) Because no partner's net section 751 unrealized gain is greater immediately before the distribution than immediately after the distribution, and because no partner's net section 751 unrealized loss is greater immediately after the distribution than immediately before the distribution, the distribution is not a section 751(b) distribution under paragraph (b)(2)(i) of this section. Accordingly, section 751(b) does not apply to the distribution.

Example 3. (i) Assume the same facts as in *Example 2* of this paragraph (g), but assume ABC distributes $150 cash to C in complete liquidation of C's interest. To determine if the distribution is a distribution to which section 751(b) applies, ABC must apply the test set forth in paragraph (b)(2) of this section.

(ii)(A) Pursuant to paragraph (b)(2)(iv) of this section, ABC revalues its assets and its partners' capital accounts are increased under § 1.704-1(b)(2)(iv)(f) to reflect each partner's share of the unrealized gain in the partnership's assets. Before the distribution, ABC's balance sheet is as follows:

	Tax	Book	Capital	Tax	Book
Cash	$260	$260	A	$120	$150
Unrealized Receivable	0	90	B	120	150
Real Property	100	100	C	120	150
Totals	360	450		360	450

(B) If ABC disposed of all of its assets in exchange for cash in amounts equal to the fair market values of these assets immediately before the distribution, A, B, and C would each be allocated $30 of net income from ABC's section 751 property. Accordingly, A, B, and C's net section 751 unrealized gain immediately before the distribution is $30 each under paragraph (b)(2)(ii) of this section.

(iii)(A) Because ABC has elected under section 754, and because A recognizes $30 gain on the distribution of cash, the basis of the real property is increased to $130 under section 734(b). After the distribution (but before taking into account any consequences under this section), ABC's balance sheet would be as follows:

	Tax	Book	Capital	Tax	Book
Cash	$110	$110	A	$120	$150
Unrealized Receivable	0	90	B	120	150
Real Property	130	100	C	0	0
Totals	240	300		240	300

(B) Because C is no longer a partner in ABC, C would not be allocated any net income from ABC's section 751 property immediately after the distribution. Also, C did not receive any section 751 property in the distribution. Accordingly, C's net section 751 unrealized gain immediately after the distribution is $0 under paragraph (b)(2)(iii) of this section.

(iv) Because C's net section 751 unrealized gain is greater immediately before the distribution than immediately after the distribution, section 751(b) applies to the distribution. Under paragraph (b)(2)(i) of this section, C has a section 751(b) amount equal to $30, the amount by which C's share of pre-distribution net section 751 unrealized gain ($30) exceeds C's share of post-distribution net section 751 unrealized gain ($0). Accordingly, paragraph (b)(3)(i) of this section requires C to recognize $30 of ordinary income using a reasonable approach consistent with the purpose of this section. ABC considers two approaches, the first of which is described in paragraphs (v) and (vi) of this example, and the second of which is described in paragraphs (vii) and (viii) of this example.

(v) Assume ABC adopts an approach under which, immediately before the section 751(b) distribution, C is deemed to recognize $30 of ordinary income. To reflect C's recognition of $30 of ordinary income, C increases its basis in its ABC partnership interest by $30, and the partnership increases its basis in the unrealized receivable by the $30 of income recognized by C, immediately before the distribution. Provided the partnership applies the approach consistently for all section 751(b) distributions, ABC's adopted approach is reasonable. After taking into account the tax consequences of the section 751(b) distribution immediately prior to the cash distribution, ABC's modified balance sheet is as follows:

	Tax	Book	Capital	Tax	Book
Cash	$260	$260	A	$120	$150
Unrealized Receivable	30	90	B	120	150
Real Property	100	100	C	150	150
Totals	390	450		390	450

(vi) After determining the tax consequences of the section 751(b) distribution, the rules of sections 731 through 736 apply. Accordingly, C recognizes no gain or loss under section 731(a) upon the distribution. Because C recognizes no gain on the distribution, the basis of the partnership real property is not adjusted. After the distribution, ABC's balance sheet is as follows:

	Tax	Book	Capital	Tax	Book
Cash	$110	$110	A	$120	$150
Unrealized Receivable	30	90	B	120	150
Real Property	100	100	C	0	0
Totals	240	300		240	300

(vii) Assume alternatively that ABC adopts an approach under which, immediately before the section 751(b) distribution, C is deemed to—

(A) Receive a distribution of ABC's unrealized receivables with a fair market value of $30 and a tax basis of $0;

(B) Sell the unrealized receivable to ABC in exchange for $30, recognizing $30 of ordinary income; and

(C) Contribute the $30 to ABC. Provided the partnership applies the approach consistently for all section 751(b) distributions, ABC's adopted approach is reasonable. After taking into account the tax consequences of the section 751(b) distribution immediately prior to the cash distribution, ABC's modified balance sheet is the same as the balance sheet shown in paragraph (v) of this example.

(viii) After determining the tax consequences of the section 751(b) distribution, the rules of sections 731 through 736 apply. The tax consequences under the rules of sections 731 through 736 are the same tax consequences described in paragraph (vi) of this example.

Example 4. (i) A and B are equal partners in a partnership, AB, that owns Unrealized Receivable with a fair market value of $50 and nondepreciable real property with a basis of $50 and a fair market value of $100. A has an adjusted basis in its partnership interest of $25, and B has an adjusted basis in its partnership interest of $50. The partnership has a section 754 election in effect, and B has a basis adjustment under section 743(b) of $25 that is allocated to Unrealized Receivable. AB distributes Unrealized Receivable to A in a current distribution. To determine if the distribution is a distribution to which section 751(b) applies, AB must apply the test set forth in paragraph (b)(2) of this section.

(ii)(A) AB makes a non-mandatory revaluation of its assets and its partners' capital accounts are increased under § 1.704-1(b)(2)(iv)(f) to reflect each partner's share of the unrealized gain in the partnership's assets. Before the distribution, AB's balance sheet is as follows:

	Tax	Basis Adj.	Book	Capital	Tax	Special Basis	Book
Unrealized Receivable	0	25	50	A	25		75
Real Property	50		100	B	25	25	75
Totals	50	25	150		50	25	150

(B) If AB disposed of all of its assets in exchange for cash in amounts equal to the fair market values of these assets immediately before the distribution, A and B would each be allocated $25 of net income from AB's section 751 property. However, B's net income from Unrealized Receivable would be offset by its $25 section 743 adjustment. § 1.743-1(j)(3). Accordingly, A and B's net section 751 unrealized gain immediately before the distribution is $25 and $0, respectively, under paragraph (b)(2)(ii) of this section.

(iii)(A) After the distribution (but before taking into account any consequences under this section), AB's balance sheet would be as follows:

	Tax	Basis Adj.	Book	Capital	Tax	Carryover Adjustment	Book
Carryover Adjustment		25	0	A	25		25
Real Property	50		100	B	25	25	75
Totals	50	25	100		50	25	100

(B) If AB disposed of all of its assets in exchange for cash in amounts equal to the fair market values of those assets immediately after the distribution, no partner would be allocated net income or loss from section 751 property. However, B has a carryover basis adjustment to ordinary income property of $25 under §§1.743-1(g)(2)(ii) and 1.755-1(c)(4), which B must treat as applied to section 751 property with fair market value of $0 pursuant to paragraph (b)(2)(ii) of this section. Accordingly, B's net section 751 unrealized loss immediately after the distribution is $25 under paragraph (b)(2)(iii)(A) of this section. If, immediately after the distribution, A disposed of Unrealized Receivable in exchange for $50 cash, A would recognize $50 of net income from section 751 property. Accordingly, A's net section 751 unrealized gain immediately after the distribution is $50 under paragraph (b)(2)(iii)(B) of this section.

(iv) Because B's net section 751 unrealized loss immediately after the distribution ($25) exceeds B's net section 751 unrealized loss immediately before the distribution ($0), the distribution is a section 751(b) distribution. Under paragraph (b)(2)(i) of this section, B has a section 751(b) amount equal to $25, the difference of B's share of pre-distribution net section 751 unrealized gain ($0) and B's share of post-distribution net section 751 unrealized loss ($25). Accordingly, paragraph (b)(3)(i) of this section requires B to account for $25 of ordinary income using a reasonable approach consistent with the purpose of this section.

(v) Assume AB adopts an approach under which, immediately before the section 751(b) distribution, B is deemed to—

(A) Receive a distribution of Unrealized Receivable with a fair market value of $25 and a tax basis of $25 (which consists of B's section 743(b) basis adjustment and is determined solely for purposes of applying a reasonable method consistent with the purposes of section 751(b));

(B) Sell Unrealized Receivable to AB in exchange for $25, so that B recognizes $0 of ordinary income, and AB receives Unrealized Receivable with a basis of $25; and

(C) Contribute the $25 to AB. Provided the partnership applies the approach consistently for all section 751(b) distributions, AB's adopted approach is reasonable. After taking into account the tax consequences of the section 751(b) distribution, AB's modified balance sheet is as follows:

	Tax	Book	Capital	Tax	Book
			A	0	25
Real Property	50	100	B	50	75
Totals	50	100		50	100

(vi) After determining the tax consequences of the section 751(b) distribution, the rules of sections 731 through 736 apply. Accordingly, A recognizes no gain on the distribution of Unrealized Receivable, which A takes with a basis of $25.

Example 5. Capital Gain Recognition Required. (i) A, B, and C are each 1/3 partners in a partnership, ABC, that holds Unrealized Receivable 1 with a fair market value of $90, Unrealized Receivable 2 with a fair market value of $30, and nondepreciable real property with a fair market value of $180. The partnership has a section 754 election in effect. Each of the partners has an adjusted basis in its partnership interest of $0 with a fair market value of $100. None of the partners has a capital loss carryforward. ABC distributes to A Unrealized Receivable 1 in a current distribution. To determine if the distribution is a distribution to which section 751(b) applies, ABC must apply the test set forth in paragraph (b)(2) of this section.

(ii)(A) Pursuant to paragraph (b)(2)(iv) of this section, ABC revalues its assets and its partners' capital accounts are increased under §1.704-1(b)(2)(iv)(f) to reflect each partner's share of the unrealized gain in the partnership's assets. Before the distribution, ABC's balance sheet is as follows:

	Tax	Book	Capital	Tax	Book
Unrealized Receivable 1	$0	$90	A	$0	$100
Unrealized Receivable 2	0	30	B	0	100
Real Property	0	180	C	0	100
Totals	0	300		0	300

(B) If ABC disposed of all of its assets for cash in an amount equal to the fair market value of such property immediately before the distribution, A, B, and C would each be allocated $40 of net income from ABC's section 751 property ($30 each from Unrealized Receivable 1 and $10 each from Unrealized Receivable 2). Accordingly, A, B, and C's net section 751 unrealized gain immediately before the distribution is $40 each under paragraph (b)(2)(ii) of this section.

(iii)(A) After the distribution (but before taking into account any consequences under this section), ABC's balance sheet would be as follows:

	Tax	Book	Capital	Tax	Book
Unrealized Receivable 2	$0	$30	A	$0	$10
			B	0	100
Real Property	0	180	C	0	100
Totals	0	210		0	210

(B) If ABC disposed of all of its assets in exchange for cash in amounts equal to the fair market values of those assets immediately after the distribution, A, B, and C would each be allocated $10 of net income from ABC's section 751 property ($10 each from Unrealized Receivable 2). If immediately after the distribution, A disposed of Unrealized Receivable 1 in exchange for $90 cash, A would recognize $90 of net income from section 751 property. Accordingly, B and C's net section 751 unrealized gain immediately after the distribution is $10 each under paragraph (b)(2)(iii)(A) of this section, and A's is $100 under paragraphs (b)(2)(iii)(A) and (B) of this section.

(iv) Because B and C's net section 751 unrealized gain is greater immediately before the distribution than immediately after the distribution, the distribution is a section 751(b) distribution. Under paragraph (b)(2)(i) of this section, each of B and C has a section 751(b) amount equal to $30, the amount by which each partner's share of pre-distribution net section 751 unrealized gain ($40) exceeds its share of post-distribution net section 751 unrealized gain ($10). Accordingly, paragraph (b)(3)(i) of this section requires each of B and C to recognize $30 of ordinary income using a reasonable approach consistent with the purpose of this section. ABC considers three approaches, the first of which is described in paragraphs (v) and (vi) of this example, the second of which is described in paragraphs (vii) and (viii) of this example, and the third of which is described in paragraph (ix) of this example.

(v) Assume ABC adopts an approach under which, immediately before the section 751(b) distribution, B and C are each deemed to recognize $30 of ordinary income. To reflect B and C's recognition of $30 of ordinary income, B and C increase their bases in their ABC partnership interests by $30 each, and the partnership increases its basis in Unrealized Receivable 1 by $60 immediately before the distribution to A. Following the distribution to A, A's basis in Unrealized Receivable 1 is $0 under section 732(a)(2). Because ABC has elected under section 754, the distribution of Unrealized Receivable 1 to A would result in a $60 section 734(b) adjustment to Unrealized Receivable 2. *See* §1.755-1(c)(1). Because that basis adjustment would have altered the amount of net section 751 unrealized gain or loss computed under paragraph (b)(2) of this section, A must recognize $60 of capital gain prior to the distribution of Unrealized Receivable 1 pursuant to paragraph (b)(3)(ii)(A) of this section. This gain recognition increases A's basis in its ABC partnership interest by $60 immediately before the distribution to A, eliminating the section 734(b) adjustment. *See* section 732(a)(2). In addition, the partnership increases its basis in Real Property by $60 pursuant to paragraph (b)(3)(iii) of this section, and treats A's gain recognized as reducing A's $60 reverse section 704(c) amount in the Real Property. Provided the partnership applies the approach consistently for all section 751(b) distributions, ABC's adopted approach is reasonable. After taking into account the tax consequences of the deemed gain approach described in this example, ABC's modified balance sheet immediately prior to the distribution is as follows:

	Tax	Book	Capital	Tax	Book
Unrealized Receivable 1	$60	$90	A	$60	$100
Unrealized Receivable 2	0	30	B	30	100
Real Property	60	180	C	30	100
Totals	120	300		120	300

(vi) After determining the tax consequences of the section 751(b) distribution, the rules of sections 731 through 736 apply. Thus, Unrealized Receivable 1 would take a $60 basis in A's hands under section 732(a), and no section 734(b) adjustment would be made to Unrealized Receivable 2. After the distribution, ABC's balance sheet is as follows:

	Tax	Book	Capital	Tax	Book
Unrealized Receivable 2	$0	$30	A	$0	$10
			B	30	100
Real Property	60	180	C	30	100
Totals	60	210		60	210

(vii) Assume alternatively that ABC adopts an approach under which, immediately before the section 751(b) distribution, B and C are each deemed to:

(A) Receive a distribution of Unrealized Receivable 1 with a fair market value of $30 and tax basis of $0;

(B) Sell the unrealized receivable to ABC for $30, recognizing $30 of ordinary income; and

(C) Contribute the $30 to ABC. For the same reasons stated in paragraph (v) of this example, A recognizes capital gain of $60. To accomplish this, A, immediately before the section 751(b) distribution, is deemed to:

(*1*) Receive a distribution of Real Property with a fair market value of $60 and tax basis of $0;

(*2*) Sell the Real Property to ABC for $60, recognizing $60 of capital gain; and

(*3*) Contribute the $60 to ABC.

(viii) The partnership treats the $60 of gain recognized by A as reducing A's $60 reverse section 704(c) amount in the Real Property. Provided the partnership applies the approach consistently for all section 751(b) distributions, ABC's adopted approach is reasonable. Before taking into account the tax consequences of the section 751(b) distribution, ABC's balance sheet is the same as the balance sheet shown in paragraph (v) of this example. After determining the tax consequences of the section 751(b) distribution, the rules of sections 731 through 736 apply. The tax consequences under the rules of sections 731 through 736 are the same tax consequences described in paragraph (vi) of this example.

(ix) Assume alternatively that A does not recognize capital gain of $60. As a result, upon the distribution of Unrealized Receivable 1 to A, ABC makes a $60 section 734(b) adjustment to Unrealized Receivable 2. The adopted approach is not reasonable because it is contrary to paragraph (b)(3)(ii)(A) of this section.

Example 6. Capital Gain Recognition Required. (i)(A) Assume the same facts as *Example 5* of this paragraph (g), except that Unrealized Receivable 1 has a $9 tax basis, and each of the partners has an adjusted basis in its partnership interest of $3. Before the distribution, ABC's balance sheet is as follows:

	Tax	Book	Capital	Tax	Book
Unrealized Receivable 1	$9	$90	A	$3	$100
Unrealized Receivable 2	0	30	B	3	100
Real Property	0	180	C	3	100
Totals	9	300		9	300

(B) If ABC disposed of all of its assets for cash in an amount equal to the fair market value of such property immediately before the distribution, A, B, and C would each be allocated $37 of net income from ABC's section 751 property ($27 each from Unrealized Receivable 1 and $10 each from Unrealized Receivable 2). Accordingly, A, B, and C's net section 751 unrealized gain immediately before the distribution is $37 each under paragraph (b)(2)(ii) of this section.

(ii)(A) After the distribution (but before taking into account any consequences under this section), ABC's balance sheet would be as follows:

	Tax	Book	Capital	Tax	Book
Unrealized Receivable 2	$6	$30	A	$0	$10
			B	3	100
Real Property	0	180	C	3	100
Totals	6	210		6	210

(B) If ABC disposed of all of its assets for cash in an amount equal to the fair market value of such property immediately after the distribution, taking into account the $6 section 734(b) adjustment allocated to Unrealized Receivable 2, A, B, and C would each be allocated $8 of net income from ABC's section 751 property ($8 each from Unrealized Receivable 2). If, immediately after the distribution, A disposed of Unrealized Receivable 1 for cash in an amount equal to its fair market value, A would recognize $87 of net income from section 751 property. Accordingly, B and C's net section 751 unrealized gain immediately after the distribution is $8 each under paragraph (b)(2)(iii)(A) of this section, and A's is $95 under paragraphs (b)(2)(iii)(A) and (B) of this section.

(iii) Because B and C's net section 751 unrealized gain is greater immediately before the distribution than immediately after the distribution, the distribution is a section 751(b) distribution. Under paragraph (b)(2)(i) of this section, each of B and C has a section 751(b) amount equal to $29, the amount by which each partner's share of pre-distribution net section 751 unrealized gain ($37) exceeds its share of post-distribution net section 751 unrealized gain ($8). Accordingly, paragraph (b)(3)(i) of this section requires each of B and C to recognize $29 of ordinary income using a reasonable approach consistent with the purpose of this section. ABC considers two approaches, the first of which is described in paragraphs (iv) and (v) of this example, and the second of which is described in paragraphs (vi) and (vii) of this example.

(iv) Assume ABC adopts an approach under which, immediately before the section 751(b) distribution, B and C are each deemed to recognize $29 of ordinary income. To reflect B and C's recognition of $29 of ordinary income, B and C increase their bases in their ABC partnership interests by $29 each, and the partnership increases its basis in Unrealized Receivable 1 by $58 to $67 immediately before the distribution to A. Following the distribution to A, A's basis in Unrealized Receivable 1 is $3 under section 732(a)(2). Because ABC has elected under section 754, the distribution of Unrealized Receivable 1 to A would result in a $64 section 734(b) adjustment to Unrealized Receivable 2 (rather than the $6 section 734(b) adjustment computed prior to the application of this section). *See* § 1.755-1(c)(1). Because that additional basis adjustment would have altered the amount of net section 751 unrealized gain or loss computed under paragraph (b)(2) of this section, A must recognize $58 of capital gain prior to the distribution of Unrealized Receivable 1 pursuant to paragraph (b)(3)(ii)(A) of this section. This gain recognition increases A's basis in its ABC partnership interest by $58 to $61 immediately before the distribution to A. In addition, the partnership increases its basis in Real Property by $58 pursuant to paragraph (b)(3)(iii) of this section, and treats A's gain recognized as reducing A's $60 reverse section 704(c) amount in the Real Property. Provided the partnership applies the approach consistently for all section 751(b) distributions, ABC's adopted approach is reasonable. After taking into account the tax consequences of the deemed gain approach described in this example, ABC's modified balance sheet immediately prior to the distribution is as follows:

	Tax	Book	Capital	Tax	Book
Unrealized Receivable 1	$67	$90	A	$61	$100
Unrealized Receivable 2	0	30	B	32	100
Real Property	58	180	C	32	100
Totals	125	300		125	300

(v) After determining the tax consequences of the section 751(b) distribution, the rules of sections 731 through 736 apply. Thus, A would take a $61 tax basis in Unrealized Receivable 1 under section 732(a), and a $6 section 734(b) adjustment would be made to Unrealized Receivable 2. After the distribution, ABC's balance sheet is as follows:

	Tax	Book	Capital	Tax	Book
Unrealized Receivable 2	$6	$30	A	$0	$10
			B	32	100
Real Property	58	180	C	32	100
Totals	64	210		64	210

(vi) Assume alternatively that ABC adopts an approach under which, immediately before the section 751(b) distribution, B and C are each deemed to:

(A) Receive a distribution of Unrealized Receivable 1 with a fair market value of $29 and tax basis of $0;

(B) Sell the unrealized receivable to ABC for $29, recognizing $29 of ordinary income; and

(C) Contribute the $29 to ABC. For the same reasons stated in paragraph (iv) of this example, A recognizes capital gain of $58. To accomplish this, A, immediately before the section 751(b) distribution, is deemed to:

(*1*) Receive a distribution of Real Property with a fair market value of $58 and tax basis of $0;

(*2*) Sell the Real Property to ABC for $58, recognizing $58 of capital gain; and

(*3*) Contribute the $58 to ABC.

(vii) The partnership treats the $58 of gain recognized by A as reducing A's $60 reverse section 704(c) amount in the Real Property. Provided the partnership applies the approach consistently for all section 751(b) distributions, ABC's adopted approach is reasonable. After taking into account the tax consequences of the section 751(b) distribution, ABC's balance sheet is the same as the balance sheet shown in paragraph (iv) of this example. After determining the tax consequences of the section 751(b) distribution, the rules of sections 731 through 736 apply. The tax consequences under the rules of sections 731 through 736 are the same tax consequences described in paragraph (v) of this example.

Example 7. Capital Gain Recognition Elective. (i)(A) Assume the same facts as described in Example 6 of this paragraph (g), including that ABC adopts the deemed gain approach described in paragraph (iv), except that ABC does not have a section 754 election in effect. As in *Example 6*, each of A, B, and C has net section 751 unrealized gain of $37 immediately before the distribution. After the distribution (but before taking into account any consequences under this section), ABC's balance sheet would be as follows:

	Tax	Book	Capital	Tax	Book
Unrealized Receivable 2	$0	$30	A	0	10
			B	3	100
Real Property	0	180	C	3	100
Totals	0	210		6	210

(B) If ABC disposed of all of its assets for cash in an amount equal to the fair market value of such property immediately after the distribution, because there is no section 734(b) adjustment allocated to Unrealized Receivable 2, A, B, and C would each be allocated $10 of net income from ABC's section 751 property ($10 each from Unrealized Receivable 2). If, immediately after the distribution, A disposed of Unrealized Receivable 1 for cash in an amount equal to its fair market value, A would recognize $87 of net income from section 751 property. Accordingly, B and C's net section 751 unrealized gain immediately after the distribution is $10 each under paragraph (b)(2)(iii)(A) of this section, and A's is $97 under paragraphs (b)(2)(iii)(A) and (B) of this section.

(ii) Because B and C's net section 751 unrealized gain is greater immediately before the distribution than immediately after the distribution, the distribution is a section 751(b) distribution. Under paragraph (b)(2)(i) of this section B and C each have a section 751(b) amount equal to $27, the amount by which those partners' shares of pre-distribution net section 751 unrealized gain ($37), exceeds their shares of post-distribution net section 751 unrealized gain ($10). Accordingly, paragraph (b)(3)(i) of this section requires each of B and C to recognize $27 of ordinary income using a reasonable approach consistent with the purpose of this section.

(iii) Assume ABC adopts an approach under which, immediately before the section 751(b) distribution, B and C are each deemed to recognize

$27 of ordinary income. To reflect B and C's recognition of $27 of ordinary income, B and C increase their bases in their ABC partnership interests by $27, and the partnership increases its basis in Unrealized Receivable 1 by $54 to $63 immediately before the distribution to A. The distribution to A results in an adjustment to the basis of the distributed Unrealized Receivable 1 under section 732(a)(2), reducing the basis of Unrealized Receivable 1 in the hands of A to $3. Because ABC has not elected under section 754 and does not have a substantial basis reduction under section 734(d), this $60 decrease to the basis of Unrealized Receivable 1 will not affect the basis of other assets held by ABC. Thus, the distribution does not alter the amount of net section 751 unrealized gain or loss computed under paragraph (b)(2) of this section. Accordingly, A is not obligated under paragraph (b)(3)(ii)(A) of this section to recognize gain or income upon the distribution of Unrealized Receivable 1. However, A may elect to recognize $60 of capital gain under paragraph (b)(3)(ii)(B) of this section to eliminate the section 732 basis adjustment to the distributed Unrealized Receivable 1 which would otherwise cause A's net section 751 unrealized gain to be greater immediately after the distribution than it was immediately before the distribution. This gain recognition increases A's basis in its ABC partnership interest by $60 immediately before the distribution to A. In addition, the partnership increases its basis in Real Property by $60 pursuant to paragraph (b)(3)(iii) of this section, and treats A's gain recognized as reducing A's $60 reverse section 704(c) amount in the Real Property. A receives the distributed Unrealized Receivable 1 with a basis of $63, so that the distribution does not increase A's net section 751 unrealized gain. After the distribution, ABC's balance sheet is as follows:

	Tax	Book	Capital	Tax	Book
Unrealized Receivable 2	$0	$30	A	0	10
			B	30	100
Real Property	60	180	C	30	100
Totals	60	210		60	210

Example 8. (i) A, B, and C, each domestic corporations, are 1/3 partners in a domestic partnership ABC. ABC purchased 100% of the stock in two foreign corporations, X and Y. X and Y each have one share of stock outstanding. ABC has a basis of $15 in its X share with a fair market value of $150, and a basis of $3 in its Y share with a fair market value of $30. The earnings and profits of X that are attributable to ABC's X stock under section 1248 are $135; the earnings and profits of Y that are attributable to ABC's Y stock are $27. ABC has a section 754 election in effect. Each of A, B, and C has a partnership interest with an adjusted basis of $6 and a fair market value of $60. On January 1, 2013, ABC distributes the Y share to A in a current distribution. To determine if the distribution is a distribution to which section 751(b) applies, ABC must apply the test set forth in paragraph (b)(2) of this section.

(ii)(A) Pursuant to paragraph (b)(2)(iv) of this section, ABC revalues its assets. Its partners' capital accounts are increased under § 1.704-1(b)(2)(iv)(f) to reflect each partner's share of the unrealized gain in the partnership's assets. Before the distribution, ABC's balance sheet is as follows (with the shares of X and Y each reflected as having both an unrealized receivable component and a capital gain component):

	Tax	Book	Capital	Tax	Book
X stock (total)	$15	$150	A	$6	$60
Unrealized receivable	0	135	B	6	60
Capital gain asset	15	15	C	6	60
Y stock (total)	3	30			
Unrealized receivable	0	27			
Capital gain asset	3	3			
Totals	18	180		18	180

(B) If ABC disposed of all of its assets for cash in an amount equal to the assets' fair market value immediately before the distribution, A, B, and C would each be allocated $54 of net income from ABC's section 751 property ($45 each from X stock and $9 each from Y stock). Accordingly, A, B, and C's net section 751 unrealized gain immediately before the distribution is $54 each under paragraph (b)(2)(ii) of this section.

(iii)(A) After the distribution (but before taking into account any consequences under this section), ABC's balance sheet is as follows:

	Tax	Book	Capital	Tax	Book
X stock (total)	$15	$150	A	$3	$30
Unrealized receivable	0	135	B	6	60
Capital gain asset	15	15	C	6	60
Totals	15	150		15	150

(B) If ABC disposed of its asset for cash in an amount equal to the fair market value of that asset immediately after the distribution, A, B, and C would each be allocated $45 of net income from ABC's section 751 property pursuant to § 1.704-3(a)(6). A, however, received Y stock, which continues to be section 751 property in A's hands under section 735(a), with a holding period that includes the partnership's holding period under section 735(b). If A disposed of its Y stock for cash in an amount equal to its fair market value, A would recognize $27 of gain under section 751(b) on the Y stock (a foreign corporation described in section 1248) that is included in A's income under section 1248 as a dividend to the extent of the attributable earnings. Accordingly, B and C's net section 751 unrealized gain immediately after the distribution is $45 each under paragraph (b)(2)(iii)(A) of this section, and A's is $72 under paragraphs (b)(2)(iii)(A) and (B) of this section.

(iv) Because B and C's net section 751 unrealized gain is greater immediately before the distribution than immediately after the distribution, the distribution is a section 751(b) distribution. Under paragraph (b)(2)(i) of this section, B and C each have a section 751(b) amount equal to $9, the amount by which those partners shares of pre-distribution net section 751 unrealized gain ($54) exceeds their shares of post-distribution net section 751 unrealized gain ($45). Accordingly, paragraph (b)(3)(i) of this section requires each of B and C to recognize $9 as a dividend under section 1248 using a reasonable approach consistent with the purpose of this section. ABC considers two approaches, the first of which is described in paragraphs (v) and (vi) of this example, and the second of which is described in paragraph (vii) of this example.

(v) Assume ABC adopts an approach under which, immediately before the section 751(b) distribution, B and C are each deemed to recognize $9 of gain includible as a dividend with respect to the distribution of the Y stock, which is treated as a sale or exchange for purposes of section 1248. To reflect B and C's recognition of $9 of dividend income, B and C increase the bases in their ABC partnership interests by $9 each, and the partnership increases its basis in the Y share unrealized receivable component by $18 immediately before the distribution. The portion of the unrealized receivable component of the Y share that is deemed to be sold or exchanged under section 1248 has a new holding period beginning on the day after the section 751(b) distribution ("the new holding period portion"). The earnings and profits of $18 attributable to the new holding period portion of the Y share are 2/3 of the total earnings and profits attributable to the Y share immediately before the distribution (B and C's $18 aggregate gain recognized under section 751(b) divided by $27, the aggregate of all the partners' net section 751 unrealized gain immediately before the distribution). The remaining earnings and profits are allocated to the remainder of the Y share. Provided the partnership applies the approach consistently for all section 751(b) distributions, ABC's adopted approach is reasonable. After taking into account the tax consequences of the deemed gain approach described in this example, ABC's modified balance sheet immediately before the distribution is as follows:

	Tax	Book	Capital	Tax	Book
X stock	$15	$150	A	$6	$60
Unrealized receivable	0	135	B	15	60
Capital gain asset	15	15	C	15	60
Y stock	21	30			
New holding period portion	18	18			
Unrealized receivable	0	9			
Capital gain asset	3	3			
Totals	36	180		36	180

(vi) After determining the tax consequences of the section 751(b) distribution, the rules of sections 731 through 736 apply. Accordingly, the basis of the distributed Y stock in A's hands is limited under section 732(a)(2) to A's $6 basis in its partnership interest. Pursuant to section 732(c)(3)(B), the $15 decrease in basis from $21 to $6 must be allocated to the distributed components of the Y stock in proportion to their respective adjusted bases. A must allocate the $15 decrease in basis in the Y stock between the new holding period portion (which has a basis of $18) and the remainder of the Y share (which has a basis of $3). Accordingly, A receives the new holding period portion of the Y share with an adjusted basis of $5.14 ($6 multiplied by ($18 divided by $21)), and the remainder of the Y share with an adjusted basis of $0.86 ($6 multiplied by ($3 divided by $21)). Because the basis of the distributed Y stock in A's hands was reduced from $21 (the basis of the Y stock in the hands of ABC) to $6 (the basis in A's hands), ABC must increase the basis of its remaining asset under section 734(b)(1)(B) by $15. ABC must allocate the $15 under §1.755-1(c)(1)(i) to the capital gain portion of the X stock. After the distribution, ABC's balance sheet is as follows:

	Tax	Book	Capital	Tax	Book
X stock	$30	$150	A	$0	$30
Unrealized receivable	0	135	B	15	60
Capital gain asset	30	15	C	15	60
Totals	30	150		30	150

(vii) Assume alternatively that ABC adopts an approach under which, immediately before the section 751(b) distribution, B and C are each deemed to:

(A) Receive a distribution of the portion of the partnership's Y stock with a fair market value of $9 and a tax basis of $0;

(B) Sell the Y stock back to ABC for $9, recognizing $9 of gain includible as a dividend; and

(C) Contribute the $9 to ABC. ABC will be deemed to have purchased for $18 a portion of the Y stock unrealized receivable component, which will have a new holding period. The deemed sale of Y stock by B and C to ABC will be treated as a sale or exchange for purposes of section 1248. Provided that the partnership applies the approach consistently for all section 751(b) distributions, Partnership ABC's adopted approach is reasonable. After taking into account the tax consequences of the deemed transaction, ABC's balance sheet is the same as the balance sheet shown in paragraph (v) of this example. After taking into account the tax consequences of the section 751(b) distribution, ABC's balance sheet is the same as the balance sheet shown in paragraph (vi) of this example.

(viii) Assume that in a later unrelated transaction, A sells its Y stock at a time when its fair market value, earnings and profits, and adjusted basis have not changed. The sale of Y stock by A is a sale or exchange subject to section 1248. Pursuant to § 1.732-1(c)(2)(v), in determining the dividend portion of its gain on the Y stock under section 1248, A does not take into account the $15 decrease in basis under section 732. Accordingly, upon the sale of the Y stock, A recognizes $9 of gain, the lesser of $9 ($0 gain on the new holding period portion ($18 fair market value minus $18 basis) plus $9 gain on the remainder ($12 fair market value minus $3 basis)) or $9 (earnings and profits attributable to the remainder of the Y share) as dividend income under section 1248. A recognizes $15 of capital gain in addition to the $9 of dividend income ($30 amount realized minus $15 ($6 aggregate basis in Y share plus $9 section 1248 dividend income)).

(ix) Assume that ABC also sells its X stock in a later unrelated transaction at a time when its fair market value has declined to $120 but earnings and profits have remained the same. ABC has not made an election under § 1.755-1(c)(2)(vi). In determining the dividend portion of its gain on the X stock under section 1248, ABC does not take into account the $15 increase in basis under section 734(b). Upon the sale of the stock, ABC recognizes $105, the lesser of $105 ($120 - $15) or $135 (earnings and profits attributable to the X stock for the partnership's holding period) as dividend income. In addition to the $105 of gain includible as a dividend, ABC recognizes $15 of capital loss ($120 amount realized minus $135 ($30 aggregate basis in X stock plus $105 section 1248 dividend income)).

Example 9. (i) Assume the same facts as in *Example 8* of this paragraph (g), except assume that Partnership ABC makes an election under § 1.755-1(c)(2)(vi). As in *Example 8*, paragraph (b)(3)(i) of this section requires each of B and C to recognize $9 as a dividend under section 1248 using a reasonable approach consistent with the purpose of this section for the reasons described in paragraphs (ii) through (iv) of *Example 8*. Further assume that ABC adopts the deemed gain approach described in paragraph (v) of *Example 8*. As in *Example 8*, B and C are each deemed to recognize $9 of dividend income with respect to the distribution of the Y stock, which is treated as a sale or exchange for purposes of section 1248. To reflect B and C's recognition of $9 of dividend income, B and C increase the bases in their ABC partnership interests by $9 each. The partnership increases its basis in the Y share unrealized receivable component by $18 immediately before the distribution. The portion of the unrealized receivable component of the Y share that is deemed to be sold or exchanged under section 1248 has a new holding period beginning on the day after the section 751(b) distribution ("the new holding period portion").

(ii) Because ABC makes an election under § 1.755-1(c)(2)(vi), the distribution of the Y share to A results in a $15 section 734(b) adjustment to the unrealized receivable component of the X share. Because that basis adjustment would have altered the amount of net section 751 unrealized gain or loss computed under paragraph (b)(2) of this section, A must recognize $15 of gain with respect to the X share pursuant to paragraph (b)(3)(ii)(A) of this section. Also pursuant to paragraph (b)(3)(ii)(A) of this section, A's recognition of income with respect to the X stock is a sale or exchange for purposes of section 1248 and begins a new holding period for this portion of ABC's X stock, including for purposes of attributing earnings and profits. This income recognition increases A's basis in its ABC partnership interest by $15 immediately before the distribution to A. In addition, the partnership increases its basis in the X share by $15, immediately before the distribution to A. The partnership treats the $15 of dividend income recognized by A as reducing A's $15 reverse section 704(c) amount in the X stock. Provided the partnership applies the approach consistently for all section 751(b) distributions, ABC's adopted approach is reasonable. After taking into account the tax consequences of the deemed gain approach described above, ABC's balance sheet is as follows:

	Tax	Book	Capital	Tax	Book
X stock	$30	$150	A	$21	$60
Unrealized receivable	0	120	B	15	60
Capital gain asset	30	30	C	15	60
Y stock	21	30			
Unrealized receivable	0	9			
Capital gain asset	21	21			
Totals	51	180		51	180

(iii)(A) After determining the tax consequences of the section 751(b) distribution, the rules of sections 731 through 736 apply. Accordingly, the Y stock would take a $21 basis in A's hands under section 732(a), and no section 734(b) adjustment would be made to the X stock. After the distribution, ABC's balance sheet is as follows:

	Tax	Book	Capital	Tax	Book
X stock	$30	$150	A	$0	$30
Unrealized receivable	0	120	B	15	60
Capital gain asset	30	30	C	15	60
Totals	30	150		30	150

(B) If the partnership sells the X stock, the gain recognized is $120 ($150 - $30), all of which is recharacterized as a dividend under section 1248. Because A's recognition of $15 of dividend income reduced A's reverse section 704(c) amount in the X stock, this gain is allocated $45 to B, $45 to C, and $30 to A.

☐ Par. 18. For each section listed in the table, remove the language in the "Remove" column and add in its place the language in the "Add" column as set forth below:

Section	Remove	Add
§ 1.751-1, paragraph (c)(4)(i) first and last sentences	sections 731, 736, 741, and 751	sections 731, 732, and 741 (but not for purposes of section 736)
§ 1.751-1, paragraph (c)(4)(ii), first and last sentences	sections 731, 736, 741, and 751	sections 731, 732, and 741 (but not for purposes of section 736)
§ 1.751-1, paragraph (c)(4)(iii) first and last sentences	sections 731, 736, 741, and 751	sections 731, 732, and 741 (but not for purposes of section 736)
§ 1.751-1, paragraph (c)(4)(iv) first and last sentences	sections 731, 736, 741, and 751	sections 731, 732, and 741 (but not for purposes of section 736)
§ 1.751-1, paragraph (c)(4)(v) first and last sentences	sections 731, 736, 741, and 751	sections 731, 732, and 741 (but not for purposes of section 736)
§ 1.751-1, paragraph (c)(4)(vii) first and last sentences	sections 731, 736, 741, and 751	sections 731, 732, and 741 (but not for purposes of section 736)
§ 1.751-1, paragraph (c)(4)(viii) First and last sentences	sections 731, 736, 741, and 751	sections 731, 732, and 741 (but not for purposes of section 736)
§ 1.751-1, paragraph (c)(4)(ix) first and last sentences	sections 731, 736, 741, and 751	sections 731, 732, and 741 (but not for purposes of section 736)
§ 1.751-1, paragraph (d)(2)(i) last sentence	section 1221(1)	section 1221(a)(1)
§ 1.751-1, paragraph (d)(2)(ii) second sentence	section 1221(4)	section 1221(a)(4)

Section 752: Related Party Rules: Recourse Liabilities of a Partnership

Section 752: Related Party Rules: Recourse Liabilities of a Partnership.—Amendments to Reg. §§1.752-0 and 1.752-2, relating to recourse liabilities of a partnership and the special rules for related persons, are proposed (published in the Federal Register on December 16, 2013) (REG-136984-12).

☐ Par. 2. Section 1.752-0 is amended by:

1. Revising the entry for § 1.752-2(a) and adding new entries for § 1.752-2(a)(1) and (a)(2).

2. Revising the entry for § 1.752-4(b)(2); removing the entries for § 1.752-4(b)(2)(i), (b)(2)(ii), and (b)(2)(iii); redesignating the entries for § 1.752-4(b)(2)(iv), (b)(2)(iv)(A) and (b)(2)(iv)(B) as § 1.752-4(b)(4), (b)(4)(i), and (b)(4)(ii), respectively; and removing the entry for § 1.752-4(b)(2)(iv)(C).

3. Adding new entries for § 1.752-4(b)(3) and (b)(5).

The revisions and additions read as follows:

§ 1.752-0. Table of contents.

§ 1.752-2. Partner's share of recourse liabilities.

(a) *Special rules.*—Partner's share of recourse liabilities.

(1) In general.

(2) Overlapping economic risk of loss.

* * *

§ 1.752-4. Special rules.

* * *

(b) * * *

(2) Related partner exception.

(3) Person related to more than one partner.

(4) Special rule where entity structured to avoid related person status.

(i) In general.

(ii) Ownership interest.

(5) Examples.

☐ Par. 3. Section 1.752-2 is amended by:

1. Redesignating paragraph (a) as paragraph (a)(1) and adding a heading to paragraph (a).

2. Adding paragraph (a)(2).

3. Adding *Example 9 to* paragraph (f).

4. Revising paragraphs (i)(1) and (2).

5. Adding a sentence to the end of paragraph (l).

The additions and revisions read as follows:

§1.752-2. Partner's share of recourse liabilities.—(a) *Partner's share of recourse liabilities.*—* * *

(2) *Overlapping economic risk of loss.*—For purposes of determining a partner's share of a recourse partnership liability, the amount of the partnership liability is taken into account only once. If the aggregate amount of the economic risk of loss that all partners are determined to bear with respect to a partnership liability (or portion thereof) under paragraph (a)(1) of this section (without regard to this paragraph (a)(2)) exceeds the amount of such liability (or portion thereof), then the economic risk of loss borne by each partner with respect to such liability shall equal the amount determined by multiplying:

(i) The amount of such liability (or portion thereof) by

(ii) The fraction obtained by dividing the amount of the economic risk of loss that such partner is determined to bear with respect to that liability (or portion thereof) under paragraph (a)(1) of this section, by the sum of such amounts for all partners.

* * *

(f) * * *

Example 9. Overlapping economic risk of loss. (i) A and B are unrelated equal members of limited liability company, AB. AB is treated as a partnership for federal tax purposes. AB borrows $1,000 from Bank. A guarantees payment for the entire amount of AB's $1,000 liability and B guarantees payment for $500 of the liability. Both A and B waive their rights of contribution against each other.

(ii) Because the aggregate amount of A's and B's economic risk of loss under paragraph (a)(1) of this section ($1,500) exceeds the amount of AB's liability ($1,000), the economic risk of loss borne by A and B each is determined under paragraph (a)(2) of this section. Under paragraph (a)(2) of this section, A's economic risk of loss equals $1,000 multiplied by $1,000/$1,500 or $667, and B's economic risk of loss equals $1,000 multiplied by $500/$1,500 or $333.

* * *

(i) * * *

(1) The amount of liabilities with respect to which the upper-tier partnership has the payment obligation or is the lender as provided in paragraph (c) of this section; and

(2) The amount of any other liabilities with respect to which partners of the upper-tier partnership bear the economic risk of loss, provided the partner is not a partner in the lower-tier partnership.

* * *

(l) * * * Paragraphs (a)(2), (f) *Example 9*, and (i) of this section apply to liabilities incurred or assumed by a partnership on or after the date these proposed regulations are published as final regulations in the **Federal Register**, other than liabilities incurred or assumed by a partnership pursuant to a written binding contract in effect prior to that date.

Liabilities: Recourse Partnership Liabilities

Liabilities: Recourse Partnership Liabilities.—Amendments to Reg. §§1.752-0 and 1.752-2, addressing when certain obligations to restore a deficit balance in a partner's capital account are disregarded under section 704 of the Internal Revenue Code (Code) and when partnership liabilities are treated as recourse liabilities under section 752, are proposed (published in the Federal Register on October 5, 2016) (REG-122855-15).

Par. 6. Section 1.752-0 is amended by:

1. Adding entries for §1.752-2(b)(3)(i) and (ii), (b)(3)(ii)(A) and (B), (b)(3)(ii)(C), (b)(3)(ii)(C)(*1*) through (3), (b)(3)(ii)(D), and (b)(3)(iii).
2. Adding entries for §1.752-2(j)(2)(i) and (ii).
3. Adding entries for §1.752-2(j)(3)(i) through (iii).
4. Revising the entries for §1.752-2(j)(3) and (4).
5. Adding an entry for §1.752-2(k).

The revisions and additions read as follows:

§1.752-0. Table of contents.

* * *

§1.752-2 Partner's share of recourse liabilities.

* * *

(b) * * *

(3) * * *

(i) In general.

(ii) Special rules for bottom dollar payment obligations.

(A) In general.

(B) Exception.

(C) Definition of bottom dollar payment obligation.

(*1*) In general.

(*2*) Exceptions.

(*3*) Benefited party defined.

(D) Disclosure of bottom dollar payment obligations.

(iii) Special rule for indemnities and reimbursement agreements.

* * *

(j) * * *

(2) * * *

(i) In general.

(ii) Economic risk of loss.

(3) Plan to circumvent or avoid an obligation.

(i) General rule.

(ii) Factors indicating plan to circumvent or avoid an obligation.

(iii) Deemed plan to circumvent or avoid an obligation.

(4) Examples.

(k) Effective/applicability dates.

* * *

Par. 7. Section 1.752-2 is amended by:

1. Revising the last sentence of paragraph (a).
2. Revising paragraph (b)(3) and the last sentence of paragraph (b)(6).

3. Adding a sentence to the end of paragraph (f) introductory text and adding *Examples 10* and *11* to paragraph (f).
4. Revising paragraphs (j)(2) and (3).
5. Adding paragraph (j)(4).
6. Removing paragraph (k).
7. Redesignating paragraph (l) as paragraph (k) and revising it.
The revisions and additions read as follows:

§1.752-2. Partner's share of recourse liabilities.—(a) * * * The determination of the extent to which a partner bears the economic risk of loss for a partnership liability is made under the rules in paragraphs (b) through (j) of this section.

(b) * * *

(3) [The text of proposed §1.752-2(b)(3) is the same as the text of §1.752-2T(b)(3) as added by T.D. 9788].

* * *

(6) * * * See paragraph (j) of this section.

* * *

(f) *Examples.*—* * * Unless otherwise provided, for purposes of the following examples, assume that any obligation of a partner or related person to make a payment is recognized under paragraph (b)(3) of this section.

* * *

Example 10. [The text of proposed §1.752-2(f) *Example 10* is the same as the text of §1.752-2T(f) *Example 10* as added by T.D. 9788].

Example 11. [The text of proposed §1.752-2(f) *Example 11* is the same as the text of §1.752-2T(f) *Example 11* as added by T.D. 9788].

* * *

(j) * * *

(2) [The text of proposed §1.752-2(j)(2) is the same as the text of §1.752-2T(j)(2) as added by T.D. 9788].

(3) *Plan to circumvent or avoid an obligation.*—(i) *General rule.*—An obligation of a partner or related person to make a payment is not recognized under paragraph (b) of this section if the facts and circumstances evidence a plan to circumvent or avoid the obligation.

(ii) *Factors indicating plan to circumvent or avoid an obligation.*—In the case of a payment obligation, other than an obligation to restore a deficit capital account upon liquidation of a partnership, paragraphs (j)(3)(ii)(A) through (G) of this section provide a non-exclusive list of factors that may indicate a plan to circumvent or avoid the payment obligation. The presence or absence of a factor is based on all of the facts and circumstances at the time the partner or related person makes the payment obligation or if the obligation is modified, at the time of the modification. For purposes of making determinations under this paragraph (j)(3), the weight to be given to any particular factor depends on the particular case and the presence or absence of a factor is not necessarily indicative of whether a payment obligation is or is not recognized under paragraph (b) of this section.

(A) The partner or related person is not subject to commercially reasonable contractual restrictions that protect the likelihood of payment, including, for example, restrictions on transfers for inadequate consideration or distributions by the partner or related person to equity owners in the partner or related person.

(B) The partner or related person is not required to provide (either at the time the payment obligation is made or periodically) commercially reasonable documentation regarding the partner's or related person's financial condition to the benefited party.

(C) The term of the payment obligation ends prior to the term of the partnership liability, or the partner or related person has a right to terminate its payment obligation, if the purpose of limiting the duration of the payment obligation is to terminate such payment obligation prior to the occurrence of an event or events that increase the risk of economic loss to the guarantor or benefited party (for example, termination prior to the due date of a balloon payment or a right to terminate that can be exercised because the value of loan collateral decreases). This factor typically will not be present if the termination of the obligation occurs by reason of an event or events that decrease the risk of economic loss to the guarantor or benefited party (for example, the payment obligation terminates upon the completion of a building construction project, upon the leasing of a building, or when certain income and asset coverage ratios are satisfied for a specified number of quarters).

(D) There exists a plan or arrangement in which the primary obligor or any other obligor (or a person related to the obligor) with respect to the partnership liability directly or indirectly holds money or other liquid assets in an amount that exceeds the reasonable foreseeable needs of such obligor.

(E) The payment obligation does not permit the creditor to promptly pursue payment following a payment default on the partnership liability, or other arrangements with respect to the partnership liability or payment obligation otherwise indicate a plan to delay collection.

(F) In the case of a guarantee or similar arrangement, the terms of the partnership liability would be substantially the same had the partner or related person not agreed to provide the guarantee.

(G) The creditor or other party benefiting from the obligation did not receive executed documents with respect to the payment obligation from the partner or related person before, or within a commercially reasonable period of time after, the creation of the obligation.

(iii) *Deemed plan to circumvent or avoid an obligation.*—Evidence of a plan to circumvent or avoid an obligation is deemed to exist if the facts and circumstances indicate that there is not a reasonable expectation that the payment obligor will have the ability to make the required payments if the payment obligation becomes due and payable. For purposes of this section, a payment obligor includes an entity disregarded as an entity separate from its owner under section 856(i), section 1361(b)(3), or §§301.7701-1 through 301.7701-3 of this chapter (a disregarded entity), and a trust to which subpart E of part I of subchapter J of chapter 1 of the Code applies.

(4) *Examples.*—The following examples illustrate the principles of paragraph (j) of this section.

Example 1. Gratuitous guarantee. (i) In 2016, A, B, and C form a domestic limited liability company (LLC) that is classified as a partnership for federal tax purposes. Also in 2016, LLC receives a loan from a bank. A, B, and C do not bear the economic risk of loss with respect to that partnership liability, and, as a result, the liability is treated as nonrecourse under §1.752-1(a)(2) in 2016. In 2018, A guarantees the entire amount of the liability. The bank did not request the guarantee and the terms of the loan did not change as a result of the guarantee. A did not provide any executed documents with respect to A's guarantee to the bank. The bank also did not require any restrictions on asset transfers by A and no such restrictions exist.

(ii) Under paragraph (j)(3) of this section, A's 2018 guarantee (payment obligation) is not recognized under paragraph (b)(3) of this section if the facts and circumstances evidence a plan to circumvent or avoid the payment obligation. In this case, the following factors indicate a plan to circumvent or avoid A's payment obligation: (1) the partner is not subject to commercially reasonable contractual restrictions that protect the likelihood of payment, such as restrictions on transfers for inadequate consideration or equity distributions; (2) the partner is not required to provide (either at the time the payment obligation is made or periodically) commercially reasonable documentation regarding the partner's or related person's financial condition to the benefited party; (3) in the case of a guarantee or similar arrangement, the terms of the liability are the same as they would have been without the guarantee; and (4) the creditor did not receive executed documents with respect to the payment obligation from the partner or related person at the time the obligation was created. Absent the existence of other facts or circumstances that would weigh in favor of respecting A's guarantee, evidence of a plan to circumvent or avoid the obligation exists and, pursuant to paragraph (j)(3)(i) of this section, A's guarantee is not recognized under paragraph (b) of this section. As a result, LLC's liability continues to be treated as nonrecourse.

Example 2. Underfunded disregarded entity payment obligor. (i) In 2016, A forms a wholly owned domestic limited liability company, LLC, with a contribution of $100,000. A has no liability for LLC's debts, and LLC has no enforceable right to a contribution from A. Under §301.7701-3(b)(1)(ii) of this chapter, LLC is a treated for federal tax purposes as a disregarded entity. Also in 2016, LLC contributes $100,000 to LP, a limited partnership with a calendar year taxable year, in exchange for a general partnership interest in LP, and B and C each contributes $100,000 to LP in exchange for a limited partnership interest in LP. The partnership agreement provides that only LLC is required to restore any deficit in its capital account. On January 1, 2017, LP borrows $300,000 from a bank and uses $600,000 to purchase nondepreciable property. The $300,000 is secured by the property and is also a general obligation of LP. LP makes payments of only interest on its $300,000 debt during 2017. LP has a net taxable loss in 2017, and, under §§1.705-1(a) and 1.752-4(d), LP determines its partners' shares of the $300,000 debt at the end of its taxable year, December 31, 2017. As of that date, LLC holds no assets other than its interest in LP.

(ii) Because LLC is a disregarded entity, A is treated as the partner in LP for federal income tax purposes. Only LLC has an obligation to make a payment on account of the $300,000 debt if LP were to constructively liquidate as described in paragraph (b)(1) of this section. Therefore, paragraph (j)(3)(iii) of this section is applied to the LLC and not to A. LLC has no assets with which to pay if the payment obligation becomes due and payable. As such, evidence of a plan to circumvent or avoid the obligation is deemed to exist and, pursuant to paragraph (j)(3)(i) of this section, LLC's obligation to restore its deficit capital account is not recognized under paragraph (b) of this section. As a result, LP's $300,000 debt is characterized as nonrecourse under §1.752-1(a)(2) and is allocated among A, B, and C under §1.752-3.

(k) *Effective/applicability dates.*—(1) Paragraph (h)(3) of this section applies to liabilities incurred or assumed by a partnership on or after October 11, 2006, other than liabilities incurred or assumed by a partnership pursuant to a written binding contract in effect prior to that date. The rules applicable to liabilities incurred or assumed (or pursuant to a written binding contract in effect) prior to October 11, 2006, are contained in §1.752-2 in effect prior to October 11, 2006, (see 26 CFR part 1 revised as of April 1, 2006). The last sentence of paragraphs (a), (b)(6), and (f) of this section and paragraphs (j)(3) and (4) of this section apply to liabilities incurred or assumed by a partnership and to payment obligations imposed or undertaken with respect to a partnership liability on or after the date these regulations are published as final regulations in the **Federal Register**, other than liabilities incurred or assumed by a partnership and payment obligations imposed or undertaken pursuant to a written binding contract in effect prior to that date. Taxpayers may rely on these regulations for the period between October 5, 2016 and the date these regulations are published as final regulations in the **Federal Register**.

(2) [The text of proposed §1.752-2(k)(2) is the same as the text of §1.752-2T(l)(2) as added by T.D. 9788.]

(3) [The text of proposed §1.752-2(k)(3) is the same as the text of §1.752-2T(l)(3) as added by T.D. 9788.]

Certain Interests in Partnerships: Treated as Stock or Indebtedness

Certain Interests in Partnerships: Treated as Stock or Indebtedness.—Amendments to Reg. §1.752-2, addressing the treatment of instruments issued by partnerships, consolidated groups, and certain transactions involving qualified cash-management arrangements, are proposed (published in the Federal Register on October 21, 2016) (REG-130314-16).

Par. 4. Section 1.752-2 is amended by:

1. Revising paragraph (c)(3).
2. Revising paragraph (l)(4).

The addition and revision read as follows

§1.752-2. Partner's share of recourse liabilities.

* * *

(c) * * *

(3) [The text of the proposed amendment to §1.752-2(c)(3) is the same as the text of §1.752-2T(c)(3) as added by T.D. 9790.]

* * *

(l) * * *

(4) [The text of the proposed amendment to §1.752-2(l)(4) is the same as the text of §1.752-2T(l)(4) as added by T.D. 9790.]

Section 752: Related Party Rules: Recourse Liabilities of a Partnership

Section 752: Related Party Rules: Recourse Liabilities of a Partnership.—Amendments to Reg. §§1.752-4 and 1.752-5, relating to recourse liabilities of a partnership and the special rules for related persons, are proposed (published in the Federal Register on December 16, 2013) (REG-136984-12).

☐ Par. 4. Section 1.752-4 is amended by:

1. Removing the word "and" at the end of paragraph (b)(1)(ii).
2. Removing "267(f)(1)(A)." at the end of (b)(1)(iii) and adding in its place "267(f)(1)(A); and".
3. Adding paragraph (b)(1)(iv).
4. Revising paragraph (b)(2).
5. Adding paragraphs (b)(3), (4), and (5).

The additions and revisions read as follows:

§1.752-4. Special rules.

* * *

(b) * * *

(1) * * *

(iv) Disregard section 267(c)(1) in determining whether stock of a corporation owned, directly or indirectly, by or for a partnership is considered as being owned proportionately by or for its partners if the corporation is a lender as provided in §1.752-2(c) or has a payment obligation with respect to a liability of the partnership.

(2) *Related partner exception.*—Notwithstanding paragraph (b)(1) of this section (which defines related person), if a person who owns (directly or indirectly through one or more partnerships) an interest in a partnership is a lender as provided in §1.752-2(c) or has a payment obligation with respect to a partnership liability, or portion thereof, then other persons owning interests directly or indirectly (through one or more partnerships) in that partnership are not treated as related to that person for purposes of determining the economic risk of loss borne by each of them for such partnership liability, or portion thereof. This paragraph (b)(2) does not apply when determining a partner's interest under the de minimis rules in §1.752-2(d) and (e).

(3) *Person related to more than one partner.*—If a person that is a lender as provided in §1.752-2(c) or that has a payment obligation with respect to a partnership liability, or portion thereof, is related to more than one partner under paragraph (b)(1) of this section, the partnership liability, or a portion thereof, is shared equally among such partners.

(4) *Special rule where entity structured to avoid related person status.*—(i) *In general.*—If—

(A) A partnership liability is owed to or guaranteed by another entity that is a partnership, an S corporation, a C corporation, or a trust;

(B) A partner or related person owns (directly or indirectly) a 20 percent or more ownership interest in the other entity; and

(C) A principal purpose of having the other entity act as a lender or guarantor of the liability was to avoid the determination that the partner that owns the interest bears the economic risk of loss for federal income tax purposes for all or part of the liability; then the partner is treated as holding the other entity's interest as a creditor or guarantor to the extent of the partner's or related person's ownership interest in the entity.

(ii) *Ownership interest.*—For purposes of paragraph (b)(4)(i) of this section, a person's ownership interest in:

(A) A partnership equals the partner's highest percentage interest in any item of partnership loss or deduction for any taxable year;

(B) An S corporation equals the percentage of the outstanding stock in the S corporation owned by the shareholder;

(C) A C corporation equals the percentage of the fair market value of the issued and outstanding stock owned by the shareholder; and

(D) A trust equals the percentage of the actuarial interests owned by the beneficial owner of the trust.

(5) *Examples.*—The following examples illustrate the principles of paragraph (b) of this section.

Example 1. Person related to more than one partner. A owns 100 percent of X, a corporation. X owns 100 percent of Y, a corporation. A and X are equal members of P, a limited liability company treated as a partnership for federal tax purposes. Y guarantees payment of a liability of P of $1,000. A and X are not lenders as provided in §1.752-2(c) and do not otherwise have a payment obligation with respect to the liability. Therefore, paragraph (b)(2) of this section does not apply for purposes of determining the economic risk of loss borne by A and X. Under paragraph (b)(1) of this section, Y is related to A and X. Therefore, under paragraph (b)(3) of this section, A and X each have a $500 share of the $1,000 liability.

Example 2. Related partner exception. A owns 100 percent of two corporations, X and Y. A and Y are members of P, a limited liability company treated as a partnership for federal tax purposes. P borrows $1,000 from Bank. A and X each guarantee payment of the $1,000 debt owed to Bank. A and Y are not treated as related to each other pursuant to paragraph (b)(2) of this section because A has the payment obligation with respect to the $1,000 debt pursuant to § 1.752-2(b). Y is therefore not treated as related to X. Because A is the only partner that bears the economic risk of loss for P's $1,000 liability, A's share of the liability is $1,000 under § 1.752-2(a)(1).

Example 3. Related partner exception. A owns 100 percent of two corporations, X and Y. X owns 79 percent of a corporation, Z, and Y owns the remaining 21 percent of Z. X and Y are members of P, a limited liability company treated as a partnership for federal tax purposes. P borrows $2,000 from Bank. Both X and Z guarantee payment of the $2,000 debt owed to Bank. X has a payment obligation with respect to P's $2,000 liability; therefore, paragraph (b)(2) of this section applies and X and Y are not treated as related for purposes of determining the economic risk of loss borne by each of them for P's $2,000 liability. Because X and Y are not treated as related, and neither owns an 80 percent or more interest in Z, neither X nor Y is treated as related to Z under paragraph (b)(1) of this section. Because X bears the economic risk of loss for P's $2,000 liability, X's share of the liability is $2,000 under § 1.752-2(a)(1).

Example 4. Related partner exception and person related to more than one partner. Same facts as in *Example 3*, but X guarantees payment of only $1,200 of the debt owed to Bank and Z guarantees payment of $2,000. Pursuant to paragraph (b)(2) of this section, X and Y are not treated as related to the extent of X's $1,200 guarantee. Because X bears the economic risk of loss for $1,200 of P's $2,000 liability, X's share of the liability is $1,200 under § 1.752-2(a)(1). In addition, because paragraph (b)(2) of this section does not apply with respect to the remaining portion of the liability that X did not guarantee, X and Y are treated as related for purposes of the remaining $800 of the liability pursuant to paragraph (b)(1) of this section. Therefore, Z is treated as related to X and Y under paragraph (b)(1) of this section. Pursuant to paragraph (b)(3) of this section, X and Y share the $800 equally. In sum, X's share of P's $2,000 liability is $1,600 ($1,200 under § 1.752-2(a)(1) and $400 under paragraph (b)(3) of this section) and Y's share of P's $2,000 liability is $400 under paragraph (b)(3) of this section.

Example 5. Entity structured to avoid related person status. A, B, and C form a general partnership, ABC. A, B, and C are equal partners, each contributing $1,000 to the partnership. A and B want to loan money to ABC and have the loan treated as nonrecourse for purposes of section 752. A and B form partnership AB to which each contributes $50,000. A and B share losses equally in partnership AB. Partnership AB loans partnership ABC $100,000 on a nonrecourse basis secured by the property ABC buys with the loan. Under these facts and circumstances, A and B bear the economic risk of loss with respect to the partnership liability equally based on their percentage interest in losses of partnership AB.

* * *

☐ Par. 5. Section 1.752-5 is amended by adding a second sentence in paragraph (a) and removing the word "However" at the beginning of the third sentence and adding in its place "In addition".

The addition reads as follows:

§ 1.752-5. Effective dates and transition rules.—(a) * * * However, § 1.752-4(b)(1)(iv), (b)(2), (b)(3), and (b)(5) *Examples 1, 2, 3,* and *4* apply to any liability incurred or assumed by a partnership on or after the date that these regulations are published as final regulations in the **Federal Register**, other than a liability incurred or assumed by a partnership pursuant to a written binding contract in effect prior to that date. * * *

* * *

Section 754 Election Statement: Steamlining

Section 754 Election Statement: Steamlining.—Amendments to Reg. § 1.754-1, relating to the requirements for making a valid election under section 754 of the Internal Revenue Code of 1986, are proposed (published in the Federal Register on October 12, 2017) (REG-116256-17).

Par 2. Section 1.754-1 is amended by revising the fourth sentence of paragraph (b)(1) and adding new paragraph (d) to read as follows:

§ 1.754-1. Time and manner of making election to adjust basis of partnership property.

* * *

(b) * * *

(1) * * * The statement required by this paragraph (b)(1) must set forth the name and address of the partnership making the election, and contain a declaration that the partnership elects under section 754 to apply the provisions of section 734(b) and section 743(b). * * *

* * *

(d) Applicability date.—The fourth sentence of paragraph (b)(1) of this section applies to taxable years ending on or after the date these regulations are published as final regulations in the Federal Register. Taxpayers may, however, rely on the fourth sentence of paragraph (b)(1) of this section for periods prior to the date these regulations are published as final regulations in the Federal Register.

Partners and Partnerships: American Jobs Creation Act of 2004 and Taxpayer Relief Act of 1997: Guidance

Partners and Partnerships: American Jobs Creation Act of 2004 and Taxpayer Relief Act of 1997: Guidance.—Amendments to Reg. § 1.755-1, providing guidance on certain provisions of the American Jobs Creation Act of 2004, conforming the regulations to statutory changes in the Taxpayer Relief Act of 1997, modifying the basis allocation rules to prevent certain unintended consequences of the current basis allocation rules for substituted basis transactions and providing

additional guidance on allocations resulting from revaluations of partnership property, are proposed (published in the Federal Register on January 16, 2014) (REG-144468-05) (corrected April 15, 2014).

☐ Par. 9. Section 1.755-1 is amended by:

1. Revising paragraph (b)(5).
2. Redesignating paragraph (e) as paragraph (f).
3. Adding a new paragraph (e).
4. Revising newly redesignated paragraph (f).

The revisions and addition read as follows:

§1.755-1. Rules for allocation of basis.

* * *

(b) * * *

* * *

(5) *Substituted basis transactions.*—(i) *In general.*—This paragraph (b)(5) applies to basis adjustments under section 743(b) that result from exchanges in which the transferee's basis in the partnership interest is determined in whole or in part by reference to the transferor's basis in that interest and from exchanges in which the transferee's basis in the partnership interest is determined by reference to other property held at any time by the transferee. For example, this paragraph (b)(5) applies if a partnership interest is contributed to a corporation in a transaction to which section 351 applies, if a partnership interest is contributed to a partnership in a transaction to which section 721(a) applies, or if a partnership interest is distributed by a partnership in a transaction to which section 731(a) applies.

(ii) *Allocations between classes of property.*—(A) *No adjustment.*—If the total amount of the basis adjustment under section 743(b) is zero, then no adjustment to the basis of partnership property will be made under this paragraph (b)(5).

(B) *Increases.*—If there is an increase in basis to be allocated to partnership assets, the increase must be allocated between capital gain property and ordinary income property in proportion to, and to the extent of, the gross gain or gross income (including any remedial allocations under §1.704-3(d)) that would be allocated to the transferee (to the extent attributable to the acquired partnership interest) from the hypothetical sale of all property in each class. Any remaining increase must be allocated between the classes in proportion to the fair market value of all property in each class.

(C) *Decreases.*—If there is a decrease in basis to be allocated to partnership assets, the decrease must be allocated between capital gain property and ordinary income property in proportion to, and to the extent of, the gross loss (including any remedial allocations under §1.704-3(d)) that would be allocated to the transferee (to the extent attributable to the acquired partnership interest) from the hypothetical sale of all property in each class. Any remaining decrease must be allocated between the classes in proportion to the transferee's shares of the adjusted bases of all property in each class (as adjusted under the preceding sentence).

(iii) *Allocations within the classes.*—(A) *Increases.*—If, under paragraph (b)(5)(ii) of this section, there is an increase in basis to be allocated within a class, the increase must be allocated first to properties with unrealized appreciation in proportion to the transferee's share of the respective amounts of unrealized appreciation (to the extent attributable to the acquired partnership interest) before the increase (but only to the extent of the transferee's share of each property's unrealized appreciation). Any remaining increase must be allocated among the properties within the class in proportion to their fair market values.

(B) *Decreases.*—If, under paragraph (b)(5)(ii) of this section, there is a decrease in basis to be allocated within a class, the decrease must be allocated first to properties with unrealized depreciation in proportion to the transferee's shares of the respective amounts of unrealized depreciation (to the extent attributable to the acquired partnership interest) before the decrease (but only to the extent of the transferee's share of each property's unrealized depreciation). Any remaining decrease must be allocated among the properties within the class in proportion to the transferee's shares of their adjusted bases (as adjusted under the preceding sentence).

(C) *Limitation in decrease of basis.*—Where, as a result of a transaction to which this paragraph (b)(5) applies, a decrease in basis must be allocated to capital gain assets, ordinary income assets, or both, and the amount of the decrease otherwise allocable to a particular class exceeds the transferee's share of the adjusted basis to the partnership of all assets in that class, the basis of the property is reduced to zero (but not below zero).

(D) *Carryover adjustment.*—Where a transferee's negative basis adjustment under section 743(b) cannot be allocated to any asset, the adjustment is made when the partnership subsequently acquires property of a like character to which an adjustment can be made.

(iv) *Examples.*—The provisions of this paragraph (b)(5) are illustrated by the following examples—

Example 1. * * *

Example 2. * * *

Example 3—(i) A is a one-third partner in UTP, a partnership, which has a valid election in effect under section 754. The three partners in UTP have equal interests in the capital and profits of UTP. UTP has three assets with the following adjusted bases and fair market values:

Assets	Adjusted basis	Fair market value
Intangible 1	$30	$200
Land	$200	$200
50% interest in LTP	$190	$200

LTP, a partnership, has a section 754 election in effect for the year of the distribution. LTP owns three assets with the following adjusted bases and fair market values:

Assets	Adjusted basis	Fair market value
Intangible 2	$340	$100
Intangible 3	$20	$280
Inventory	$20	$20

UTP distributes its interest in LTP in redemption of A's interest in UTP. At the time of the distribution, A's adjusted basis in its UTP interest is $140. A recognizes no gain or loss on the distribution. Under section 732(b), A's basis in the distributed LTP interest is $140. Under sections 734(b) and 755, UTP increases its adjusted basis in Intangible 1 by $50, the amount of the basis adjustment to the LTP interest in the hands of A.

(ii) The amount of the basis adjustment with respect to LTP under section 743(b) is the difference between A's basis in LTP of $140 and A's share of the adjusted basis to LTP of partnership property. A's share of the adjusted basis to LTP of partnership property is equal to the sum of A's share of LTP's liabilities of $0 plus A's interest in the previously taxed capital of LTP of $190 ($200, A's cash on liquidation, increased by $120, the amount of tax loss allocated to A from the sale of Intangible 2 in the hypothetical transaction, decreased by $130, the amount of tax gain allocated to A from the sale of Intangible 3 in the hypothetical transaction). Therefore, the amount of the negative basis adjustment under section 743(b) to partnership property is $50.

(iii) Under this paragraph (b)(5), LTP must allocate $50 of A's negative basis adjustment between capital gain property and ordinary income property in proportion to, and to the extent of, the gross loss (including any remedial allocations under § 1.704-3(d)) that would be allocated to A from the hypothetical sale of all property in each class. If LTP disposed of its assets in a hypothetical sale, A would be allocated $120 of gross loss from Intangible 2 only. Accordingly, the $50 negative adjustment must be allocated to capital assets. Under paragraph (b)(5)(iii)(B) of this section, the $50 negative adjustment must be allocated to the assets in the capital class first to properties with unrealized depreciation in proportion to the transferee's shares of the respective amounts of unrealized depreciation. Thus, the $50 negative adjustment must be allocated entirely to Intangible 2.

Example 4—(i) A is a one-third partner in LTP. The three partners in LTP have equal interests in the capital and profits of LTP. LTP has two assets: accounts receivable with an adjusted basis of $300 and a fair market value of $240 and a nondepreciable capital asset with an adjusted basis of $60 and a fair market value of $240. A contributes its interest in LTP to UTP in a transaction described in section 721. At the time of the transfer, A's basis in its LTP interest is $90. Under section 723, UTP's basis in its interest in LTP is $90. LTP makes an election under section 754 in connection with the transfer.

(ii) The amount of the basis adjustment under section 743(b) is the difference between UTP's $90 basis in its LTP interest and UTP's share of the adjusted basis to LTP of LTP's property. UTP's share of the adjusted basis to LTP of LTP's property is equal to the sum of UTP's share of LTP's liabilities of $0 plus UTP's interest in the previously taxed capital of LTP of $120 ($160, the amount of cash on liquidation, increased by $20, the amount of tax loss allocated to UTP from the hypothetical transaction, and decreased by $60, the amount of tax gain allocated to UTP from the hypothetical transaction). Therefore, the amount of the negative basis adjustment under section 743(b) to partnership property is $30.

(iii) The total amount of gross loss that would be allocated to UTP from the hypothetical sale of LTP's ordinary income property is $20 (one third of the excess of the basis of the accounts receivable ($300) over their fair market value ($240)). The hypothetical sale of LTP's capital gain property would result in a net gain. Therefore, under this paragraph (b)(5), $20 of the $30 basis adjustment must be allocated to ordinary income property. Because LTP holds only one ordinary income property, the $20 decrease must be allocated entirely to the accounts receivable. Pursuant to paragraph (b)(5)(ii)(C) of this section, the remaining $10 basis adjustment must be allocated between ordinary income property and capital gain property according to UTP's share of the adjusted bases of such properties. Therefore, $8 ($10 multiplied by $80 divided by $100) would be allocated to the accounts receivable and $2 ($10 multiplied by $20 divided by $100) would be allocated to the nondepreciable capital asset. * * *

* * *

(e) *No allocation of basis decrease to stock of corporate partner.*—(1) *In general.*—In making an allocation under section 755(a) of any decrease in the adjusted basis of partnership property under section 734(b)—

(i) No allocation may be made to stock in a corporation (or any person related (within the meaning of sections 267(b) or 707(b)(1)) to such corporation) that is a partner in the partnership; and

(ii) Any amount not allocable to stock by reason of paragraph (c)(1) of this section shall be allocated under section 755(a) to other partnership property.

(2) *Recognition of gain.*—Gain shall be recognized to the partnership to the extent that the amount required to be allocated under paragraph (e)(1)(ii) of this section to other partnership property exceeds the aggregate adjusted basis of such other property immediately before the allocation required by paragraph (e)(1)(ii) of this section.

(3) *Example.*—A, B, and C are equal partners in PRS, a partnership. C is a corporation. The adjusted basis and fair market value for A's interests in PRS is $100. PRS owns Capital Asset 1 with an adjusted basis of $0 and a fair market value of $100, Capital Asset 2 with an adjusted basis of $150 and a fair market value of $50, and stock in Corp, a corporation that is related to C under section 267(b), with an adjusted basis of $250 and fair market value of $150. PRS has a section 754 election in effect. PRS distributes Capital Asset 1 to A in liquidation of A's interest

in PRS. PRS will reduce the basis of its remaining assets under section 734(b) by $100, to be allocated under section 755. Pursuant to the general rule of paragraph (c) of this section, PRS would reduce the basis of Capital Asset 2 by $50 and the stock of Corp by $50. However, pursuant to paragraph (e)(1)(i) of this section, the basis of the Corp stock is not adjusted. Thus, the basis of Capital Asset 2 is reduced by $100 from $150 to $50.

(f) *Effective date.*—(1) *Generally.*—Except as provided in paragraph (f)(2) of this section, this section applies to transfers of partnership interests and distributions of property from a partnership that occur on or after December 15, 1999.

(2) *Special rules.*—Paragraphs (a) and (b)(3)(iii) of this section apply to transfers of partnership interests and distributions of property from a partnership that occur on or after June 9, 2003. Paragraph (b)(5) of this section applies to transfers of partnership interests occurring on or after January 16, 2014. Paragraph (e) of this section applies to transfers of partnership interests occurring on or after the date of publication of the Treasury decision adopting these rules as final regulations in the **Federal Register**.

* * *

Partners and Partnerships: Sales or Exchanges: Certain Distributions

Partners and Partnerships: Sales or Exchanges: Certain Distributions.—Amendments to Reg. §1.755-1, prescribing how a partner should measure its interest in a partnership's unrealized receivables and inventory items, and that provide guidance regarding the tax consequences of a distribution that causes a reduction in that interest, are proposed (published in the Federal Register on November 3, 2014) (corrected January 26, 2015) (REG-151416-06).

☐ Par. 8. Section 1.755-1 is amended by:

a. Adding paragraphs (c)(2)(iii), (iv), (v), and (vi).

b. Revising the paragraph heading and the introductory text of paragraph (c)(6).

c. Removing the paragraph heading "*Example.*" in paragraph (c)(6) and adding "*Example 1.*" in its place.

d. Adding *Examples 2* and *3* to paragraph (c)(6).

e. Revising paragraph (e)(2).

The additions and revisions read as follows:

§1.755-1. Rules for allocation of basis.

* * *

(c) * * *

(2) * * *

(iii) *Coordination with section 1245 and similar provisions.*—Any increase in basis allocated to capital gain property pursuant to the second sentence in paragraph (c)(2)(i) of this section is not taken into account in determining the recomputed or adjusted basis in the property for purposes of section 1245(a)(1). Notwithstanding the prior sentence, any depreciation or amortization of the increase in basis that is allowed or allowable is taken into account in computing the property's recomputed basis. In the case of property that is subject to section 617(d)(1), 1250(a)(1), 1252(a)(1), or 1254(a)(1), rules similar to the rule in this paragraph (c)(2)(iii) shall apply.

(iv) *Coordination with section 1231.*—Any increase in basis allocated to capital gain property pursuant to the second sentence in paragraph (c)(2)(i) of this section is not taken into account in determining section 1231 gain and loss, as defined in section 1231(a)(3). Any basis adjustment to an asset not taken into account pursuant to this paragraph (c)(2)(iv) shall be treated as gain from the sale or exchange of a capital asset with the same holding period as the underlying asset.

(v) *Coordination with sections 1248 and 995.*—Any increase in basis allocated to stock in a foreign corporation pursuant to the second sentence in paragraph (c)(2)(i) of this section, or any decrease in basis allocated to stock in a foreign corporation pursuant to the second sentence in paragraph (c)(2)(ii) of this section, is not taken into account in determining the amount of gain recognized on the sale or exchange of such stock for purposes of section 1248(a). In the case of property that is subject to section 995(c), rules similar to the rule set forth in this paragraph (c)(2)(v) shall apply.

(vi) *Election not to apply the provisions of paragraphs (c)(2)(iii), (iv), and (v).*—A partnership may elect not to apply paragraphs (c)(2)(iii), (iv), and (v) of this section, and §1.732-1(c)(2)(iii), (iv), and (v). An election made under this paragraph (c)(2)(vi) shall apply to all property distributions taking place in the partnership taxable year for which the election is made and in all subsequent partnership taxable years (including after a termination of the partnership under section 708(b)(1)(B)). An election under this paragraph (c)(2)(vi) must be made in a written statement filed with the partnership return for the first taxable year in which any of paragraph (c)(2)(iii), (iv), or (v) of this section, or §1.732-1(c)(2)(iii), (iv), or (v), would have applied if no election was made. An election under this paragraph (c)(2)(vi) is valid only if the required statement is included with a partnership return that is filed not later than the time prescribed by paragraph (e) of this section or §1.6031(a)-1 (including extensions thereof) for filing the return for such taxable year. This election is a method of accounting under section 446, and once the election is made, it can be revoked only with the consent of the Commissioner. The revocation of the election, or the making of a late election, under this paragraph (c)(2)(vi) is a change in method of accounting to which the provisions of section 446(e) and the regulations under section 446(e) apply. *See* paragraph (c)(6), *Example 3*, of this section for the treatment of a section 734(b) adjustment if an election under this paragraph (c)(2)(vi) is made, and certain consequences of the election under section 751(b). The statement required by this paragraph (c)(2)(vi) shall—

(A) Set forth the name and address of the partnership making the election;

(B) Be signed by any officer, manager, or member of the partnership who is authorized (under local law or the partnership's organizational documents) to make the election and who represents to having such authorization under penalties of perjury; and

(C) Contain a declaration that the partnership elects not to apply paragraphs (c)(2)(iii), (iv), and (v) of this section and § 1.732-1(c)(2)(iii), (iv), and (v).

* * *

(6) *Examples.*—The following examples illustrate this paragraph (c):

* * *

Example 2. (i) A, B, and C are equal partners in ABC. Each partner has an outside basis in its partnership interest of $20. ABC owns depreciable equipment X with an adjusted basis of $30 and a fair market value of $150 and depreciable equipment Y with an adjusted basis of $30 and a fair market value of $30. ABC has made an election under section 754.

(ii) The depreciable equipment X has $120 of adjustments reflected in its adjusted basis within the meaning of § 1.1245-2(a)(2). Accordingly, the entire $120 of the gain with respect to depreciable equipment X would be treated as gain to which section 1245(a)(1) would apply if the partnership sold the depreciable equipment X for its fair market value. ABC, therefore, has a $120 unrealized receivable within the meaning of § 1.751-1(c)(4)(iii). Assume ABC makes a current distribution of the depreciable equipment Y to A. Because A's basis in his partnership interest is only $20, A's basis in the depreciable equipment Y will be limited to $20 under section 732(a). Under section 734(b), ABC will increase the basis in its capital gain property by $10 and will not adjust the basis of ordinary income property. Assume ABC has not made an election under § 1.755-1(c)(2)(vi).

(iii) *Allocation between classes.* Pursuant to § 1.755-1(a)(1), ABC's $120 unrealized receivable associated with the depreciable equipment X is treated as a separate asset that is ordinary income property. Thus, ABC is treated as having two assets (each actually a component of the single asset, equipment X) after the distribution, one that is capital gain property with a basis of $30 and a fair market value of $30, and one that is ordinary income property with a basis of $0 and a fair market value of $120.

(iv) *Allocation within class.* ABC must allocate the $10 basis increase entirely to the capital gain portion of the depreciable equipment X, as it holds no other capital gain property after it distributes the depreciable equipment Y to A. Therefore, ABC increases the basis of the capital gain property to $40.

(v) *Treatment of section 734(b) adjustment.* Pursuant to paragraph (c)(2)(iii) of this section, if ABC sold its depreciable equipment X for $150 immediately after the distribution to A, ABC would not take into account the $10 section 734(b) adjustment in determining ABC's recomputed or adjusted basis in the depreciable equipment X for purposes of section 1245(a)(1) and, accordingly, would recognize $120 of ordinary income. Also pursuant to paragraph (c)(2)(iv) of this section, the $10 section 734(b) adjustment is not taken into account for purposes of determining section 1231 gain or loss. Thus, pursuant to paragraph (c)(2)(vi) of this section, ABC would recognize a $10 capital loss.

(vi) *Treatment of additional depreciation and appreciation.* (A) Assume, instead, that ABC continues to own the equipment and takes additional depreciation deductions of $16 ($15 with respect to the original remaining $30 basis and $1 with respect to the additional $10 basis resulting from the section 734(b) adjustment). At a time when the equipment has appreciated in value to $170, ABC sells the depreciable equipment X for $170 in a taxable transaction. In that same taxable year, ABC does not sell any other property used in its trade or business.

(B) Pursuant to section 1245(a)(1), ABC must recognize ordinary income in an amount by which the lesser of the following two amounts exceeds ABC's adjusted basis in the depreciable equipment X—

(*1*) ABC's recomputed basis in the depreciable equipment, or

(*2*) ABC's amount realized;

(C) Pursuant to section 1245(a)(2)(A), ABC's recomputed basis is an amount equal to the sum of—

(*1*) ABC's adjusted basis of the property, plus

(*2*) The amount of adjustments reflected in the adjusted basis on account of deductions allowed or allowable.

(D) Pursuant to (c)(2)(iii) of this section, the $9 remaining section 734(b) adjustment is not taken into account in determining ABC's recomputed or adjusted basis in the property for purposes of section 1245(a)(1). Thus, ABC's adjusted basis in the property is $15 (the remaining original basis). Also pursuant to (c)(2)(iii) of this section, however, any depreciation, or amortization of the section 734(b) adjustment that is allowed or allowable is taken into account in computing the property's recomputed basis. Thus, ABC's amount of adjustments reflected in the adjusted basis is $136 (the original $120 adjustment for depreciation deductions plus the additional $15 adjustment for depreciation deductions plus the additional $1 adjustment for depreciation deductions taken with respect to the section 734(b) adjustment). Accordingly, ABC's recomputed basis is $151 ($15 adjusted basis plus $136 of adjustments), which is lower than ABC's amount realized of $170. ABC, therefore, must recognize ordinary income in an amount by which ABC's recomputed basis of $151 exceeds ABC's adjusted basis in the depreciable equipment X. Pursuant to (c)(2)(iii) of this section, the $9 remaining section 734(b) adjustment is not taken into account in determining the adjusted basis in the property for purposes of section 1245(a)(1). Accordingly, ABC must recognize $136 of ordinary income (the excess of ABC's $151 recomputed basis in the depreciable equipment X over ABC's $15 adjusted basis in the depreciable equipment X).

(E) Pursuant to paragraph (c)(2)(iv) of this section, the section 734(b) adjustment is not taken into account in determining ABC's section 1231 gain or loss. Accordingly, pursuant to section 1231(a)(1), ABC recognizes $19 of capital gain (ABC's $170 amount realized on the disposition of the depreciable equipment X over ABC's adjusted basis of $15 in the depreciable equipment X, reduced by the $136 of ordinary income ABC recognized under section

1245(a)(1)). Pursuant to paragraph (c)(2)(vi) of this section, ABC also recognizes a capital loss equal to the remaining $9 section 734(b) adjustment.

Example 3. (i) Assume the same facts as *Example 2* of this paragraph (c), except ABC has made an election under paragraph (c)(2)(vi) of this section.

(ii) *Treatment of section 734(b) adjustment.* Because ABC has made an election under paragraph (c)(2)(vi) of this section, paragraph (c)(2)(iii) of this section does not apply. Thus, if ABC sold its depreciable equipment X immediately after the distribution to A, ABC would take into account the $10 section 734(b) adjustment in determining ABC's recomputed or adjusted basis in the depreciable equipment X for purposes of section 1245(a)(1) and, accordingly, would recognize $110 of ordinary income (including for purposes of applying section 751).

* * *

(e) * * *

(2) *Special rules.*—Paragraphs (a) and (b)(3)(iii) of this section apply to transfers of partnership interests and distributions of property from a partnership that occur on or after June 9, 2003, and paragraphs (c)(2)(iii), (iv), (v), (vi), and (c)(6) of this section and *Examples 2* and *3* of paragraph (c) of this section apply to distributions of property from a partnership that occur on or after the date of publication of a Treasury decision adopting these rules as final regulations in the **Federal Register**.

Partnerships: Equity for Services

Partnerships: Equity for Services.—Amendments to Reg. §1.761-1, providing that the transfer of a partnership interest in connection with the performance of services is subject to Code Sec. 83 and providing rules for coordinating Code Sec. 83 with partnership taxation principles, are proposed (published in the Federal Register on May 24, 2005) (REG-105346-03).

☐ Par. 8. Section 1.761-1(b) is amended by adding two sentences to the end of the paragraph to read as follows:

§1.761-1. Terms defined.

* * *

(b) * * * If a partnership interest is transferred in connection with the performance of services, and that partnership interest is substantially nonvested (within the meaning of §1.83-3(b)), then the holder of the partnership interest is not treated as a partner solely by reason of holding the interest, unless the holder makes an election with respect to the interest under section 83(b). The previous sentence applies to partnership interests that are transferred on or after the date final regulations are published in the Federal Register.

* * *

Partnership Interest: Treatment of Grantor of an Option

Partnership Interest: Treatment of Grantor of an Option.—Amendments to Reg. §1.761-3, relating to the tax treatment of noncompensatory options and convertible instruments issued by a partnership, are proposed (published in the Federal Register on February 5, 2013) (REG-106918-08).

☐ Par 2. Section 1.761-3 is amended by adding paragraph (c)(1)(iv) to read as follows:

§1.761-3. Certain option holders treated as partners.

* * *

(c) * * *

(1) * * *

(iv) An event described in paragraphs (c)(1)(iv)(A), (B), or (C) of this section, provided the event is pursuant to a plan in existence at the time of the issuance or modification of the noncompensatory option that has as a principal purpose the substantial reduction of the present value of the aggregate Federal tax liabilities of the partners and the noncompensatory option holder (under paragraph (a)(1)(ii) of this section):

(A) Issuance, transfer, or modification of an interest in, or liquidation of, the issuing partnership;

(B) Issuance, transfer, or modification of an interest in any look-through entity (as defined in paragraph (b)(1) of this section) that directly, or indirectly through one or more look-through entities, owns the noncompensatory option;

(C) Issuance, transfer, or modification of an interest in any look-through entity that directly, or indirectly through one or more look-through entities, owns an interest in the issuing partnership.

* * *

INSURANCE COMPANIES

Life Insurance Companies: Property and Casualty Insurance Companies: Life Insurance Reserves

Life Insurance Companies: Property and Casualty Insurance Companies: Life Insurance Reserves.—Amendments to Reg. §1.801-4, permitting the recomputation of certain life insurance reserves if such reserves were initially computed or estimated on other than an actuarial basis, are proposed (published in the Federal Register on January 2, 1997) (REG-246018-96).

Par. 2. Section 1.801-4 is amended by adding a new paragraph (g) to read as follows:

§1.801-4. Life insurance reserves.

* * *

(g) *Recomputation of life insurance reserves.*—(1) *General.*—If an insurance company does not compute or estimate its reserves for contracts involving, at the time with respect to which the reserves are computed, life, accident or health contingencies, on the basis of mortality or morbidity tables and assumed rates of interest, then the taxpayer or the Commissioner may recompute reserves for those contracts on the basis of mortality or morbidity tables and assumed rates of interest.

(2) *Effect of recomputation.*—If reserves are recomputed pursuant to paragraph (g)(1) of this section, the recomputed reserves satisfy the requirements of section 816(b)(1)(A).

(3) *Mean reserve.*—For purposes of section 816(b)(4) and § 1.801-3(i), if reserves are recomputed pursuant to paragraph (g)(1) of this section for a taxable year, the reserves must be recomputed for both the beginning and the end of the taxable year.

(4) *Subsequently acquired information.*—No information acquired after the date as of which a reserve was initially computed or estimated may be taken into account in recomputing that reserve under paragraph (g)(1) of this section.

(5) *Effective date.*—This section is applicable with respect to returns filed for taxable years beginning after the date final regulations are filed with the Office of the Federal Register.

Imputed Interest: Original Issue Discount: Safe Haven Rates

Imputed Interest: Original Issue Discount: Safe Haven Interest Rates.—Reproduced below is the text of a proposed amendment of Reg. § 1.818-3, relating to (1) the tax treatment of debt instruments issued after July 1, 1982, that contain original issue discount, (2) the imputation of and the accounting for interest with respect to sales and exchanges of property occurring after December 31, 1984, and (3) safe haven interest rates for loans or advances between commonly controlled taxpayers and safe haven leases between such taxpayers (published in the Federal Register on April 8, 1986).

☐ Par. 16. In § 1.818-3, paragraph (f) is amended by removing the phrase "section 1232(a) (relating to the taxation of bonds and other evidences of indebtedness)" and adding in its place the phrase "section 1271 (relating to the treatment of amounts received on retirement or sale or exchange of debt instruments)", and by removing the phrase "section 1232(a)(2)(C)" and adding in its place the phrase "section 1271(d)".

§ 1.818-3. Amortization of premium and accrual of discount.

Insurance Companies: Modification of Discounting Rules

Insurance Companies: Modification of Discounting Rules.—Amendments to Reg. §§ 1.846-0—1.846-4 and Temporary Reg. §§ 1.846-2T and 1.846-4T, providing guidance on new discounting rules for unpaid losses and estimated salvage recoverable of insurance companies for Federal income tax purposes, are proposed (published in the Federal Register on November 7, 2018) (REG-103163-18).

Par. 2. Section 1.846-0 is removed.

§ 1.846-0. Outline of provisions.

Par. 3. Section 1.846-1 is amended by:

1. Removing "section 846(f)(3)" from the first sentence of paragraph (a)(1) and adding "section 846(e)(3)" in its place.
2. Removing "and § 1.846-3(b) contains guidance relating to discount factors applicable to accident years prior to the 1987 accident year" from the third sentence of paragraph (a)(1).
3. Removing the last sentence of paragraph (a)(1).
4. Removing paragraph (a)(2) and redesignating paragraphs (a)(3) and (4) as paragraphs (a)(2) and (3), respectively.
5. In the first sentence of paragraph (b)(1), removing "section 846(f)(6)" and adding "section 846(e)(6)" in its place; and removing ", in § 1.846-2 (relating to a taxpayer's election to use its own historical loss payment pattern)".
6. Removing "for accident years after 1987" from the heading for paragraph (b)(3)(i).
7. Removing the designation "(A)" and the accompanying heading "Accident years after 1991" after the heading of paragraph (b)(3)(ii).
8. Removing paragraphs (b)(3)(ii)(B), and (b)(3)(iii) and (iv).
9. Removing paragraph (b)(4) and redesignating paragraph (b)(5) as paragraph (b)(4).
10. Adding paragraphs (c), (d), and (e).

The additions read as follows:

§ 1.846-1. Application of discount factors.

* * *

(c) *Determination of annual rate.*—The applicable interest rate is the annual rate determined by the Secretary for any calendar year on the basis of the corporate bond yield curve (as defined in section 430(h)(2)(D)(i), determined by substituting "60-month period" for "24-month period" therein). The annual rate for any calendar year is determined on the basis of a yield curve that reflects the average, for the most recent 60-month period ending before the beginning of the calendar year, of monthly yields on corporate bonds described in section 430(h)(2)(D)(i). The annual rate is the average of that yield curve's monthly spot rates with times to maturity of not more than seventeen and one-half years.

(d) *Determination of loss payment pattern.*—(1) *In general.*—Under section 846(d)(1), the loss payment pattern determined by the Secretary for each line of business is determined by reference to the historical loss payment pattern applicable to such line of business determined in accordance with the method of determination set forth in section 846(d)(2) and the computational rules prescribed in section 846(d)(3) on the basis of the annual statement data from annual statements described in section 846(d)(2)(A) and (B). However, the Secretary may adjust the loss payment pattern for any line of business as provided in paragraph (d)(2) of this section.

(2) *Smoothing adjustments*.—The Secretary may adjust the loss payment pattern for any line of business using a methodology described by the Secretary in other published guidance if necessary to avoid negative payment amounts and otherwise produce a stable pattern of positive discount factors less than one.

(e) *Applicability date*.—(1) Except as provided in paragraph (e)(2) of this section, this section applies to taxable years beginning after December 31, 1986.

(2) Paragraphs (c) and (d) of this section apply to taxable years beginning after December 31, 2017.

Par. 4. Section 1.846-2 is removed.

§1.846-2. Election by taxpayer to use its own historical loss payment pattern.

Par. 5. Section 1.846-2T is removed.

§1.846-2T. Election by taxpayer to use its own historical loss payment pattern (temporary).

Par. 6. Section 1.846-3 is removed.

§1.846-3. Fresh start and reserve strengthening.

Par. 7. Section 1.846-4 is removed.

§1.846-4. Effective/applicability date.

Par. 8. Section 1.846-4T is removed.

§1.846-4T. Effective dates (temporary).

REGULATED INVESTMENT COMPANIES AND REAL ESTATE INVESTMENT TRUSTS

Deduction for Business Interest Expense: Limitation

Deduction for Business Interest Expense: Limitation.—Amendments to Reg. §1.860C-2, regarding the limitation on the deduction for business interest expense after the enactment of recent tax legislation, are proposed (published in the Federal Register on December 28, 2018) (REG-106089-18).

Par. 15. Section 1.860C-2 is amended by revising paragraph (b)(2) to read as follows:

§1.860C-2. Determination of REMIC taxable income or net loss.

* * *

(b) * * *

(2) *Deduction allowable under section 163*.—(i) A REMIC is allowed a deduction, determined without regard to section 163(d), for any interest expense accrued during the taxable year.

(ii) For taxable years beginning after December 31, 2017, a REMIC is allowed a deduction, determined without regard to section 163(j), for any interest expense accrued during the taxable year.

* * *

Definition of Registered Form: Guidance

Definition of Registered Form: Guidance.—Amendments to Reg. §1.860D-1, providing guidance on the definitions of registration-required obligation and registered form, including guidance on the issuance of pass-through certificates and participation interests in registered form, are proposed (published in the Federal Register on September 19, 2017) (REG-125374-16).

Par. 6. Section 1.860D-1(b)(5)(i)(A) is amended by removing the language "§5f.103-1(c)" and adding in its place the language "§1.163-5(b)."

§1.860D-1. Definition of a REMIC.

REMICs: Reporting Information: Extension of Time

REMICs: Reporting Information: Extension of Time.—An amendment to Reg. §1.860F-4, relating to real estate mortgage investment conduits, is proposed (published in the Federal Register on September 30, 1991).

☐ Par. 3. Section 1.860F-4 is amended by revising paragraph (e)(2)(i) to read as follows:

§1.860F-4. REMIC reporting requirements and other administrative rules.

* * *

(e) * * *

(2) * * *

(i) In general, Schedule Q must be mailed (or otherwise delivered) to each holder of a residual interest during a calendar quarter no later than the 41st day following the close of the calendar quarter.

* * *

Stock and Rights to Acquire Stock: Deemed Distributions

Stock and Rights to Acquire Stock: Deemed Distributions.—Amendments to Reg. §1.860G-3, regarding deemed distributions of stock and rights to acquire stock and resolving ambiguities concerning the amount and timing of deemed distributions that are or result from adjustments to rights to acquire stock, are proposed (published in the Federal Register on April 13, 2016) (REG-133673-15).

Par. 5. Section 1.860G-3(b)(1) is amended by removing the language "1.1441-2(d)(4)" in the last sentence, and adding the language "1.1441-2(d)(1)(ii)(C)" in its place, and by removing the language "1.1441-5(b)(2)(i)(A), and" and adding the language "1.1441-5(b)(2)(i)(A), 1.1471-2(a)(4)(i)(B)(4), and" in its place.

§1.860G-3. Treatment of foreign persons.

SOURCES WITHIN OR WITHOUT THE U.S.

Imputed Interest: Original Issue Discount: Safe Haven Rates

Imputed Interest: Original Issue Discount: Safe Haven Interest Rates.—Reproduced below is the text of a proposed amendment of Reg. §1.861-2, relating to (1) the tax treatment of debt instruments issued after July 1, 1982, that contain original issue discount, (2) the imputation of and the accounting for interest with respect to sales and exchanges of property occurring after December 31, 1984, and (3) safe haven interest rates for loans or advances between commonly controlled taxpayers and safe haven leases between such taxpayers (published in the Federal Register on April 8, 1986).

§1.861-2. Interest.

☐ Par. 17. In §1.861-2, paragraph (a)(4) is amended by removing the phrase "section 1232(b)(1)" and adding in its place the phrase "section 1273(a)(1)".

Stock and Rights to Acquire Stock: Deemed Distributions

Stock and Rights to Acquire Stock: Deemed Distributions.—Amendments to Reg. §1.861-3, regarding deemed distributions of stock and rights to acquire stock and resolving ambiguities concerning the amount and timing of deemed distributions that are or result from adjustments to rights to acquire stock, are proposed (published in the Federal Register on April 13, 2016) (REG-133673-15).

Par. 6. Section 1.861-3 is amended by:

1. In paragraph (a)(6), removing "A substitute dividend payment is a payment" in the first sentence and adding "A substitute dividend payment is a payment or a deemed payment" in its place, and adding a new second sentence.

2. In paragraph (d), replacing the third sentence with a new sentence.

The additions read as follows:

§1.861-3. Dividends.—(a) * * *

(6) *Substitute dividend payments.*—* * * A deemed payment is a payment deemed to have been made in the amount (as determined under §1.305-7(c)(4)) of a deemed distribution (as defined in §1.305-1(d)(7)) that the owner of the transferred security is entitled to during the term of the transaction. * * *

* * *

(d) *Effective/applicability date.*—* * * Paragraph (a)(6) of this section applies to payments made on or after the date of publication of the Treasury decision adopting these rules as final regulations in the **Federal Register**; however, a taxpayer may rely on the rule in the second sentence of paragraph (a)(6) of this section for all deemed distributions (as defined in §1.305-1(d)(7)) occurring on or after January 1, 2016, until the date of publication of a Treasury decision adopting these rules as final regulations in the **Federal Register**. * * *

Compensation for Labor or Personal Services: Artists: Athletes

Compensation for Labor or Personal Services: Artists: Athletes.—Amendments to Reg. §1.861-4, clarifying the determination of source of compensation of a person, including an artist or athlete, who is compensated for labor or personal services performed at specific events, are proposed (filed in the Federal Register on October 17, 2007) (REG-114125-07).

☐ Par. 2. Section 1.861-4 is amended by:

1. Removing the heading for paragraph (b)(1)(i).

2. Redesignating paragraph (b)(1)(i) as paragraph (b)(1).

3. In the last sentence of newly designated paragraph (b)(1), adding the language "or on the event basis as defined in paragraph (b)(2)(ii)(G) of this section," after the language "paragraph (b)(2)(ii)(E) of this section,".

4. In the last sentence of paragraph (b)(2)(i), adding the language "or on the event basis as defined in paragraph (b)(2)(ii)(G) of this section," after the language "paragraph (b)(2)(ii)(E) of this section,".

5. In the first sentence of paragraph (b)(2)(ii)(C)(1)(i), adding the language ", including an event basis as defined in paragraph (b)(2)(ii)(G) of this section," after the language "alternative basis" wherever the language "alternative basis" appears in the sentence.

6. In the first sentence of paragraph (b)(2)(ii)(C)(1)(ii), adding the language "event basis as defined in paragraph (b)(2)(ii)(G) of this section or other" after the language "partly without the United States under an".

7. Removing paragraph (b)(2)(ii)(C)(3).

8. In the first sentence of paragraph (b)(2)(ii)(E), removing the language "individual's" and adding the language "person's" in its place, removing the language "individual" and adding the language "person" in its place, and removing the language "his or hers" and adding the language "such person's" in its place.

9. In the second sentence of paragraph (b)(2)(ii)(F), removing the language "an individual" and adding the language "a person" in its place.

10. Redesignating paragraphs (c) and (d) as new paragraphs (d) and (e), respectively.

11. Redesignating paragraph (b)(2)(ii)(G) as new paragraph (c).

12. Adding a new paragraph (b)(2)(ii)(G).

13. In the introductory language of newly-designated paragraph (c), removing the language "paragraph (b)(2)(ii)" and adding the language "section" in its place.

14. Adding new *Examples 7*, *8*, *9*, and *10* to newly-designated paragraph (c).

15. Redesignating paragraph (b)(1)(ii) *Example*, as new *Example 11* in newly-designated paragraph (c), revising the paragraph heading and removing paragraph (b)(1)(ii).

16. Adding a new sentence at the end of newly-designated paragraph (e) and revising the paragraph heading.

The additions read as follows:

§1.861-4. Compensation for labor or personal services.

* * *

(b) * * *

(2) * * *

(ii) * * *

(G) *Event basis.*—The amount of compensation for labor or personal services determined on an event basis is the amount of the person's compensation which, based on the facts and circumstances, is attributable to the labor or personal services performed at the location of a specific event. The source of compensation for labor or personal services determined on an event basis is the location of the specific event. A basis that purports to determine the source of compensation from the performance of labor or personal services at a specific event, whether on a time basis or otherwise, by taking into account the location of labor or personal services performed in preparation for the performance of labor or personal services at the specific event will generally not be the basis that most correctly determines the source of the compensation.

(c) *Examples.*—* * *

Example 7. P, a citizen and resident of Country A, is paid by Company Z to make a presentation in the United States in 2009. In 2010, Company Z pays P to make 10 presentations, four of which are in the United States and six of which are outside the United States. P is compensated separately by Company Z for each presentation. For some presentations P receives a flat fee from Company Z. For the remaining presentations P receives compensation that is based on a formula. Under the facts and circumstances of the particular case, the source of the compensation for each presentation is most correctly reflected on an event basis, as defined in paragraph (b)(2)(ii)(G) of this section. Because P is compensated separately for each presentation, the source of P's compensation from Company Z for the 2009 presentation within the United States and the four 2010 presentations in the United States will be from sources in the United States. The amounts will be determined based on the flat fee or the formula as contractually determined.

Example 8. (i) *Facts.* Group B, a Country N corporation, is a musical group. All of the members of Group B are citizens and residents of Country N. Group B has an employment arrangement with Corp Y, a Country N corporation, to perform as directed by Corp Y. Corp Y and a tour promoter enter into a contract to provide the services of Group B to perform in musical concerts in the United States and Country M during a 45-day period. Under the contract, Group B performs concerts in 15 cities, 10 of which are in the United States. Prior to entering the United States, Group B spends 60 days rehearsing and preparing in Country N. Under the contract with Corp Y, Group B receives a flat fee of $10,000,000 for performing in all 15 cities. The fee is based on expected revenues from the musical concerts. Each concert is expected to require a similar amount and type of labor or personal services by Group B. At the end of the tour, an analysis of the revenues from all of the concerts shows that 80% of the total revenues from the tour were from the performances within the United States.

(ii) *Analysis.* Under the facts and circumstances basis of paragraph (b)(1) of this section, the source of the compensation received under the contract is most correctly reflected on an event basis, as defined in paragraph (b)(2)(ii)(G) of this section, with amounts determined based on the relative gross receipts attributable to the performances within and without the United States. Thus, of the $10,000,000 of compensation included in Group B's gross income, $8,000,000 ($10,000,000 × .80) is attributable to labor or personal services performed by Group B within the

United States and $2,000,000 ($10,000,000 × .20) is attributable to the labor or personal services performed by Group B without the United States.

Example 9. (i) *Facts.* A, a citizen and resident of Country M, is an employee of Corp X, a Country M corporation. During 2008, Corp X is contractually obligated to provide A's services to perform in a specific athletic event in the United States. Under A's employment contract with Corp X, A is required to perform at a professional level that requires training and other preparation prior to the event. A undertakes all of this preparation in Country M. Solely as a result of A's performance at the athletic event in the United States, A receives $2,000,000 from Corp. X.

(ii) *Analysis.* The entire $2,000,000 received by A for performing labor or personal services at the athletic event in the United States is income from sources within the United States on an event basis as defined in paragraph (b)(2)(ii)(G) of this section. A's compensation is attributable entirely to labor or personal services performed within the United States at the athletic event. It is inappropriate to conclude that the source of A's compensation for labor or personal services is performed partly within and partly without the United States simply because A's preparation for the athletic event involved activities in Country M.

Example 10. (i) *Facts.* X, a citizen and resident of Country M, is employed under a standard player's contract by a professional sports team (Team) that plays its games both within and without the United States during its season. The term of the contract is for twelve months beginning on October 1. Under the contract, X's salary could be paid in semi-monthly installments beginning with the first game of the regular season and ending with the final game played by the Team. Alternatively, because the regular playing season was shorter than the one-year period covered by the contract, X had the option to receive his salary over a twelve-month period. X elected this option. In addition, during the period of this employment contract, X, as an employee of Team, was required to practice at the direction of the Team as well as to participate in games. During 2008, X participated in all practices and games of Team and received a salary. Team qualified for postseason games in 2008. X also received in 2008 additional amounts for playing in preseason and postseason games for the Team.

(ii) *Analysis.* The salary paid to X by the Team is considered to be personal services compensation of X that X received as an employee of the Team. The source of this compensation within the United States is determined under the time basis method described in paragraph (b)(2)(ii)(A) of this section and accordingly is determined based upon the number of days X performed services for the Team within the United States during 2008 over the total number of days that X performed services for the Team during 2008. The source of the additional amounts X received for playing in preseason and postseason games is determined under the event basis method described in paragraph (b)(2)(ii)(G) of this section and accordingly is determined based on the location where each such preseason or postseason game was played.

Example 11. * * *

* * *

(e) *Effective/applicability date.*—* * * The revisions in paragraphs (b)(1), (b)(2)(i), and (b)(2)(ii)(C)(1)(i) and (ii) of this section which refer to the event basis; the revisions of paragraphs (b)(2)(ii)(C)(e), (b)(2)(ii)(E), (b)(2)(ii)(F), (b)(2)(ii)(G), and (c) of this section; and *Examples 7* through *11* of paragraph (c) of this section apply to taxable years beginning after the date final regulations are published in the Federal Register.

Determination of the Foreign Tax Credit: Guidance

Determination of the Foreign Tax Credit: Guidance.—Amendments to Reg. §§1.861-8—1.861-12, relating to the determination of the foreign tax credit under the Internal Revenue Code, including changes made by the Tax Cuts and Jobs Act, are proposed (published in the Federal Register on December 7, 2018) (REG-105600-18).

Par. 3. Section 1.861-8 is amended by:

1. Removing the last sentence of paragraph (a)(1).
2. Removing the third sentence through fifth sentences of paragraph (a)(4).
3. Removing paragraph (a)(5).
4. Revising paragraphs (c)(2) and (d)(2).
5. Adding two sentences after the sixth sentence in paragraph (e)(1).
6. Removing the first sentence of paragraph (e)(6)(i).
7. Adding a new first sentence and a new second sentence to paragraph (e)(6)(i).
8. Removing paragraphs (e)(6)(iii) and (e)(12)(iv).
9. Adding paragraphs (e)(13) through (e)(15).
10. Revising paragraph (f)(1)(i).
11. Adding paragraph (h).

The revisions and additions read as follows:

§1.861-8. Computation of taxable income from sources within the United States and from other sources and activities.

* * *

(c) * * *

(2) *Apportionment based on assets.*—Certain taxpayers are required by paragraph (e)(2) of this section and §1.861-9T to apportion interest expense on the basis of assets. A taxpayer may apportion other deductions based on the comparative value of assets that generate income within each grouping, provided that this method reflects the factual relationship between the deduction and the groupings of income and is applied in accordance with the rules of §1.861-9T(g). In general, such apportionments must be made either on the basis of the tax book value of those assets or, except in the case of interest expense, on the basis of their fair market value. *See* §1.861-9(h). Taxpayers using the fair

market value method for their last taxable year beginning before January 1, 2018, must change to the tax book value method (or the alternative tax book value method) for purposes of apportioning interest expense for their first taxable year beginning after December 31, 2017. The Commissioner's approval is not required for this change. In the case of any corporate taxpayer that—

(i) Uses tax book value or alternative tax book value, and

(ii) Owns directly or indirectly (within the meaning of § 1.861-12T(c)(2)(ii)(B)) 10 percent or more of the total combined voting power of all classes of stock entitled to vote in any other corporation (domestic or foreign) that is not a member of the affiliated group (as defined in section 864(e)(5)), the taxpayer must adjust its basis in that stock in the manner described in § 1.861-12(c)(2).

* * *

(d) * * *

(2) *Allocation and apportionment to exempt, excluded, or eliminated income.*—(i) *In general.*—[Reserved]. For further guidance, see § 1.861-8T(d)(2)(i).

(ii) *Exempt income and exempt asset defined.*—(A) *In general.*—For purposes of this section, the term *exempt income* means any gross income to the extent that it is exempt, excluded, or eliminated for Federal income tax purposes. The term *exempt asset* means any asset to the extent income from the asset is (or is treated as under paragraph (d)(2)(ii)(B) or (C) of this section) exempt, excluded, or eliminated for Federal income tax purposes.

(B) [Reserved]. For further guidance, see § 1.861-8T(d)(2)(ii)(B).

(C) *Foreign-derived intangible income and inclusions under section 951A(a).*—*(1) Exempt income.*—The term "exempt income" includes an amount of a domestic corporation's gross income included in foreign-derived intangible income (as defined in section 250(b)(1)), and also includes an amount of a domestic corporation's gross income from an inclusion under section 951A(a) and the gross up under section 78 attributable to such an inclusion, in each case equal to the amount of the deduction allowed under section 250(a) for such gross income (taking into account the reduction under section 250(a)(2)(B), if any). Therefore, for purposes of apportioning deductions using a gross income method, gross income does not include gross income included in foreign-derived intangible income, an inclusion under section 951A(a), or the gross up under section 78 attributable to an inclusion under section 951A(a), in an amount equal to the amount of the deduction allowed under section 250(a)(1)(A), (B)(i), or (B)(ii), respectively (taking into account the reduction under section 250(a)(2)(B), if any).

(2) Exempt assets.—*(i) Assets that produce foreign-derived intangible income.*—The term "exempt asset" includes the portion of a domestic corporation's assets that produce gross income included in foreign-derived intangible income equal to the amount of such assets multiplied by the fraction that equals the amount of the domestic corporation's deduction allowed under section 250(a)(1)(A) (taking into account the reduction under section 250(a)(2)(B)(i), if any) divided by its foreign-derived intangible income. No portion of the value of stock in a foreign corporation is treated as an exempt asset by reason of this paragraph (d)(2)(ii)(C)(*2*)(*i*), including by reason of a transfer of intangible property to a foreign corporation subject to section 367(d) that gives rise to income eligible for a deduction under section 250(a)(1)(A).

(ii) Controlled foreign corporation stock that gives rise to inclusions under section 951A(a).—The term "exempt asset" includes a portion of the value of a United States shareholder's stock in a controlled foreign corporation if the United States shareholder is a domestic corporation that is eligible for a deduction under section 250(a) with respect to income described in section 250(a)(1)(B)(i) and all or a portion of the domestic corporation's stock in the controlled foreign corporation is characterized as GILTI inclusion stock. The portion of foreign corporation stock that is treated as an exempt asset for a taxable year equals the portion of the value of such foreign corporation stock (determined in accordance with §§ 1.861-9(g), 1.861-12, and 1.861-13) that is characterized as GILTI inclusion stock multiplied by a fraction that equals the amount of the domestic corporation's deduction allowed under section 250(a)(1)(B)(i) (taking into account the reduction under section 250(a)(2)(B)(ii), if any) divided by its GILTI inclusion amount (as defined in § 1.951A-1(c)(1) or, in the case of a member of a consolidated group, § 1.1502-51(b)) for such taxable year. The portion of controlled foreign corporation stock treated as an exempt asset under this paragraph (d)(2)(ii)(C)(*2*)(*ii*) is treated as attributable to the relevant categories of GILTI inclusion stock described in each of paragraphs (d)(2)(ii)(C)(*3*)(*i*) through (*v*) of this section based on the relative value of the portion of the stock in each such category.

(3) GILTI inclusion stock.—For purposes of paragraph (d)(2)(ii)(C)(*2*)(*ii*) of this section, the term *GILTI inclusion stock* means the aggregate of the portions of the value of controlled foreign corporation stock that are—

(i) Assigned to the section 951A category under § 1.861-13(a)(2);

(ii) Assigned to a particular treaty category under § 1.861-13(a)(3)(i) (relating to resourced gross tested income stock);

(iii) Assigned under § 1.861-13(a)(1) to the gross tested income statutory grouping within the foreign source passive category less the amount described in § 1.861-13(a)(5)(iii)(A);

(iv) Assigned under § 1.861-13(a)(1) to the gross tested income statutory grouping within the U.S. source general category less the amount described in § 1.861-13(a)(5)(iv)(A); and

(v) Assigned under § 1.861-13(a)(1) to the gross tested income statutory grouping within the U.S. source passive category less the amount described in § 1.861-13(a)(5)(iv)(B).

(4) Non-applicability to section 250(b)(3).—This paragraph (d)(2)(ii)(C) does not apply when apportioning deductions for purposes of determining deduction eligible income under the operative section of section 250(b)(3).

(5) Example.—The following example illustrates the application of this paragraph (d)(2)(ii)(C).

(*i*) *Facts.* USP, a domestic corporation, directly owns all of the stock of CFC1 and CFC2, both of which are controlled foreign corporations. The tax book value of CFC1 and CFC2's stock is $10,000 and $9,000, respectively. Pursuant to § 1.861-13(a), $6,100 of the stock of CFC1 is assigned to the section 951A category under § 1.861-13(a)(2) ("section 951A category stock") and the remaining $3,900 of the stock of CFC1 is assigned to the general category ("general category stock"). Additionally, $4,880 of the stock of CFC2 is section 951A category stock and the remaining $4,120 of the stock of CFC2 is general category stock. Under section 951A and the section 951A regulations (as defined in § 1.951A-1(a)(1)), USP's GILTI inclusion amount is $610. The portion of USP's deduction under section 250 described in section 250(a)(1)(B)(i) is $305. No portion of USP's deduction is reduced by reason of section 250(a)(2)(B)(ii).

(*ii*) *Analysis.* Under paragraph (d)(2)(ii)(C)(*1*) of this section, $305 of USP's gross income attributable to its GILTI inclusion amount is exempt income for purposes of apportioning deductions for purposes of section 904. Under paragraph (d)(2)(ii)(C)(*3*) of this section, the GILTI inclusion stock of CFC1 is the $6,100 of stock that is section 951A category stock and the GILTI inclusion stock of CFC2 is the $4,880 of stock that is section 951A category stock. Under paragraph (d)(2)(ii)(C)(*2*) of this section, the portion of the value of the stock of CFC1 and CFC2 that is treated as an exempt asset equals the portion of the value of the stock of CFC1 and CFC2 that is GILTI inclusion stock multiplied by 50% ($305/$610). Accordingly, the exempt portion of the stock of CFC1 is $3,050 (50% x $6,100) and the exempt portion of CFC2's stock is $2,440 (50% x $4,880). Therefore, the stock of CFC1 taken into account for purposes of apportioning deductions is $3,050 of non-exempt section 951A category stock and $3,900 of general category stock. The stock of CFC2 taken into account for purposes of apportioning deductions is $2,440 of non-exempt section 951A category stock and $4,120 of general category stock.

(d)(2)(iii) through (d)(2)(iii)(B) [Reserved]. For further guidance, see § 1.861-8T(d)(2)(iii) through § 1.861-8T(d)(2)(iii)(B).

(C) Dividends for which a deduction is allowed under section 245A;

(D) Foreign earned income as defined in section 911 and the regulations thereunder (however, the rules of § 1.911-6 do not require the allocation and apportionment of certain deductions, including home mortgage interest, to foreign earned income for purposes of determining the deductions disallowed under section 911(d)(6)); and

(E) Inclusions for which a deduction is allowed under section 965(c). *See* § 1.965-6(d).

(iv) *Value of stock attributable to previously taxed earnings and profits.*—No portion of the value of stock in a controlled foreign corporation is treated as an exempt asset by reason of the adjustment under § 1.861-12(c)(2) in respect of previously taxed earnings and profits described in section 959(c)(1) or (c)(2) (including earnings and profits described in section 959(c)(2) by reason of section 951A(f)(1) and § 1.951A-6(b)(1)). *See also* § 1.965-6(d).

(e) * * *

(1) * * * Paragraphs (e)(13) and (14) of this section contain rules with respect to the allocation and apportionment of the deduction allowed under section 250(a). Paragraph (e)(15) of this section contains rules with respect to the allocation and apportionment of a taxpayer's distributive share of a partnership's deductions. * * *

* * *

(6) * * *

(i) *In general.*—The deduction for foreign income, war profits and excess profits taxes (*foreign income taxes*) allowed by section 164 is allocated and apportioned among the applicable statutory and residual groupings under the principles of § 1.904-6(a)(1)(i), (ii), and (iv). The deduction for state and local taxes (*state income taxes*) allowed by section 164 is considered definitely related and allocable to the gross income with respect to which such state income taxes are imposed. * * *

* * *

(13) *Foreign-derived intangible income.*—The portion of the deduction that is allowed for foreign-derived intangible income under section 250(a)(1)(A) (taking into account the reduction under section 250(a)(2)(B)(i), if any) is considered definitely related and allocable to the class of gross income included in the taxpayer's foreign-derived deduction eligible income (as defined in section 250(b)(4)). If necessary, the portion of the deduction is apportioned within the class ratably between the statutory grouping (or among the statutory groupings) of gross income and the residual grouping of gross income based on the relative amounts of foreign-derived deduction eligible income in each grouping.

(14) *Global intangible low-taxed income and related section 78 gross up.*—The portion of the deduction that is allowed for the global intangible low-taxed income amount described in section 250(a)(1)(B)(i) (taking into account the reduction under section 250(a)(2)(B)(ii), if any) is considered definitely related and allocable to the class of gross income included under section 951A(a). If necessary (for example, because a portion of the inclusion under section 951A(a) is passive category income or U.S. source income), the portion of the deduction is apportioned within the class ratably between the statutory grouping (or among the statutory groupings) of gross income and the residual grouping of gross income based on the relative amounts of gross income in each grouping. Similar rules apply to allocate and apportion the portion of the deduction that is allowed for the section 78 gross up under section 250(a)(1)(B)(ii).

(15) *Distributive share of partnership deductions.*—In general, if deductions are incurred by a partnership in which the taxpayer is a partner, the taxpayer's deductions that are allocated and apportioned include the taxpayer's distributive share of the partnership's deductions. See §§ 1.861-9(e), 1.861-17(f), and 1.904-4(n)(1)(ii) for special rules for apportioning a partner's distributive share of deductions of a partnership.

(f) * * *

(1) * * *

(i) *Separate foreign tax credit limitations.*—Section 904(d)(1) and other sections described in § 1.904-4(m) require that a separate foreign tax credit limitation be determined with respect to each separate category of income specified in those sections. Accordingly, the foreign source income within each separate category described in § 1.904-5(a)(4)(v) constitutes a separate statutory grouping of income. U.S. source income is treated as income in the residual category for purposes of determining the limitation on the foreign tax credit.

* * *

(h) *Applicability date.*—This section applies to taxable years that both begin after December 31, 2017, and end on or after December 4, 2018.

Par. 4. Section 1.861-9 is amended by:

1. Revising the section heading.
2. Revising paragraphs (a) through (e)(1).
3. Removing the last sentences in paragraph (e)(2) and (e)(3).
4. Revising paragraphs (e)(4) through (f)(3)(i).
5. Revising the heading of paragraph (f)(4).
6. Removing the language "noncontrolled section 902 corporations" wherever it appears in paragraphs (f)(4)(i) and (f)(4)(ii) and adding the language "noncontrolled 10-percent owned foreign corporations" in its place.
7. Removing the last sentence of paragraph (f)(4)(ii).
8. Revising paragraph (f)(4)(iii).
9. Revising paragraphs (f)(5) through (h)(3), and (h)(5).
10. Revising the first and second sentences of paragraph (i)(2)(i).
11. Removing the language "paragraph (i)(2)" from the third and fourth sentences of paragraph (i)(2) and adding the language "paragraph (i)(2)(i)" in its place.
12. Revising paragraphs (j) and (k).

The revisions and additions read as follows:

§ 1.861-9. Allocation and apportionment of interest expense and rules for asset-based apportionment.—(a) through (c)(4) [Reserved]. For further guidance, see § 1.861-9T(a) through (c)(4).

(5) *Section 163(j).*—If a taxpayer is subject to section 163(j), the taxpayer's deduction for business interest expense is limited to the sum of the taxpayer's business interest income, 30 percent of the taxpayer's adjusted taxable income for the taxable year, and the taxpayer's floor plan financing interest expense. In the taxable year that any deduction is permitted for business interest expense with respect to a disallowed business interest carryforward, that business interest expense is apportioned for purposes of this section under rules set forth in paragraphs (d), (e), or (f) of this section (as applicable) as though it were incurred in the taxable year in which the expense is deducted.

(d) through (e)(1) [Reserved]. For further guidance, see § 1.861-9T(d) through (e)(1).

* * *

(4) *Entity rule for less than 10 percent limited partners and less than 10 percent corporate general partners.*—(i) *Partnership interest expense.*—A limited partner (whether individual or corporate) or corporate general partner whose ownership, together with ownership by persons that bear a relationship to the partner described in section 267(b) or section 707, of the capital and profits interests of the partnership is less than 10 percent directly allocates its distributive share of partnership interest expense to its distributive share of partnership gross income. Under § 1.904-4(n)(1)(ii), such a partner's distributive share of foreign source income of the partnership is treated as passive income (subject to the high-taxed income exception of section 904(d)(2)(B)(iii)(II)), except in the case of income from a partnership interest held in the ordinary course of the partner's active trade or business, as defined in § 1.904-4(n)(1)(ii)(B). A partner's distributive share of partnership interest expense (other than partnership interest expense that is directly allocated to identified property under § 1.861-10T) is apportioned in accordance with the partner's relative distributive share of gross foreign source income in each separate category and of gross domestic source income from the partnership. To the extent that partnership interest expense is directly allocated under § 1.861-10T, a comparable portion of the income to which such interest expense is allocated is disregarded in determining the partner's relative distributive share of gross foreign source income in each separate category and domestic source income. The partner's distributive share of the interest expense of the partnership that is directly allocable under § 1.861-10T is allocated according to the treatment, after application of § 1.904-4(n)(1), of the partner's distributive share of the income to which the expense is allocated.

(e)(4)(ii) through (e)(7) [Reserved]. For further guidance, see § 1.861-9T(e)(4)(ii) through (e)(7).

(8) *Special rule for specified partnership loans.*—(i) *In general.*—For purposes of apportioning interest expense that is not directly allocable under paragraph (e)(4) of this section or § 1.861-10T, the disregarded portion of a specified partnership loan is not considered an asset of a SPL lender. The disregarded portion of a specified partnership loan is the portion of the value of the loan (as determined under paragraph (h)(4)(i) of this section) that bears the same proportion to the total value of the loan as the matching income amount that is included by the SPL lender for a taxable year with respect to the loan bears to the total amount of SPL interest income that is included directly or indirectly in gross income by the SPL lender with respect to the loan during that taxable year.

(ii) *Treatment of interest expense and interest income attributable to a specified partnership loan.*—If a SPL lender (or any other person in the same affiliated group as the SPL lender) takes into account a distributive share of SPL interest expense, the SPL lender includes the matching income amount for the taxable year that is attributable to the same loan in gross income in the same statutory and residual groupings as the statutory and residual groupings of gross income from which the SPL interest expense is deducted by the SPL lender (or any other person in the same affiliated group as the SPL lender).

(iii) *Anti-avoidance rule for third party back-to-back loans.*—If, with a principal purpose of avoiding the rules in this paragraph (e)(8), a person makes a loan to a person that is not related (within the meaning of section 267(b) or 707) to the lender, the unrelated person makes a loan to a partnership, and the first loan would constitute a specified partnership loan if made directly to the partnership, then the rules of this paragraph (e)(8) apply as if the first loan was made directly to the partnership. Such a series of loans will be subject to this recharacterization rule without regard to whether there was a principal purpose of avoiding the rules in this paragraph (e)(8) if the loan to the unrelated person would not have been made or maintained on substantially the same terms irrespective of the loan of funds by the unrelated person to the partnership. The principles of this paragraph (e)(8)(iii) also apply to similar transactions that involve more than two loans and regardless of the order in which the loans are made.

(iv) *Anti-avoidance rule for loans held by CFCs.*—A loan receivable held by a controlled foreign corporation with respect to a loan to a partnership in which a United States shareholder (as defined in § 1.904-5(a)(4)(vi)) of the controlled foreign corporation owns an interest, directly or indirectly through one or more other partnerships or other pass-through entities (as defined in § 1.904-5(a)(4)(iv)), is recharacterized as a loan receivable held directly by the United States shareholder with respect to the loan to such partnership for purposes of this paragraph (e)(8) if the loan was made or transferred with a principal purpose of avoiding the rules in this paragraph (e)(8).

(v) *Interest equivalents.*—The principles of this paragraph (e)(8) apply in the case of a partner, or any person in the same affiliated group as the partner, that takes into account a distributive share of an expense or loss (to the extent deductible) that is allocated and apportioned in the same manner as interest expense under § 1.861-9T(b) and has a matching income amount with respect to the transaction that gives rise to that expense or loss.

(vi) *Definitions.*—For purposes of this paragraph (e)(8), the following definitions apply.

(A) *Affiliated group.*—The term *affiliated group* has the meaning provided in § 1.861-11(d)(1).

(B) *Matching income amount.*—The term *matching income amount* means the lesser of the total amount of the SPL interest income included directly or indirectly in gross income by the SPL lender for the taxable year with respect to a specified partnership loan or the total amount of the distributive shares of the SPL interest expense of the SPL lender (or any other person in the same affiliated group as the SPL lender) with respect to the loan.

(C) *Specified partnership loan.*—The term *specified partnership loan* means a loan to a partnership for which the loan receivable is held, directly or indirectly through one or more other partnerships, either by a person that owns an interest, directly or indirectly through one or more other partnerships, in the partnership, or by any person in the same affiliated group as that person.

(D) *SPL interest expense.*—The term *SPL interest expense* means an item of interest expense paid or accrued with respect to a specified partnership loan, without regard to whether the expense was currently deductible (for example, by reason of section 163(j)).

(E) *SPL interest income.*—The term *SPL interest income* means an item of gross interest income received or accrued with respect to a specified partnership loan.

(F) *SPL lender.*—The term *SPL lender* means the person that holds the receivable with respect to a specified partnership loan. If a partnership holds the receivable, then any partner in the partnership (other than a partner described in paragraph (e)(4)(i) of this section) is also considered a SPL lender.

(9) *Characterizing certain partnership assets as foreign branch category assets.*—For purposes of applying this paragraph (e) to section 904 as the operative section, a partner that is a United States person that has a distributive share of partnership income that is treated as foreign branch category income under § 1.904-4(f)(1)(i)(B) characterizes its pro rata share of the partnership assets that give rise to such income as assets in the foreign branch category.

(f) through (f)(1) [Reserved]. For further guidance, see § 1.861-9T(f) through (f)(1).

(2) *Section 987 QBUs of domestic corporations.*—(i) *In general.*—In the application of the asset method described in paragraph (g) of this section, a domestic corporation—

(A) Takes into account the assets of any section 987 QBU (as defined in § 1.987-1(b)(2)), translated according to the rules set forth in paragraph (g) of this section, and

(B) Combines with its own interest expense any deductible interest expense incurred by a section 987 QBU, translated according to the rules of section 987 and the regulations under that section.

(ii) *Coordination with section 987(3).*—For purposes of computing foreign currency gain or loss under section 987(3) (including section 987 gain or loss recognized under § 1.987-5), the rules of this paragraph (f)(2) do not apply. *See* § 1.987-4.

(iii) *Example.*—The following example illustrates the application of this paragraph (f)(2).

(A) *Facts.* X is a domestic corporation that operates B, a branch doing business in a foreign country. B is a section 987 QBU (as defined in § 1.987-1(b)(2)) as well as a foreign branch (as defined in § 1.904-4(f)(3)(iii)). In 2020, without regard to B, X has gross domestic source income of $1,000 and gross foreign source general category income of $500 and incurs $200 of interest expense. Using the tax book value method of apportionment, X, without regard to B, determines the value of its assets that generate domestic source income to be $6,000 and the value of its assets that generate foreign source general category income to be $1,000. Applying the translation rules of section 987, X (through B) earned $500 of gross foreign source foreign branch category income and incurred $100 of interest expense. B incurred no other expenses. For 2020, the average functional currency book value of B's assets that generate foreign source foreign branch category income translated at the year-end rate for 2020 is $3,000.

(B) *Analysis.* The combined assets of X and B for 2020 (averaged under § 1.861-9T(g)(3)) consist 60% ($6,000/$10,000) of assets generating domestic source income, 30% ($3,000/$10,000) of assets generating foreign source foreign branch category income, and 10% ($1,000/$10,000) of assets generating foreign source general category income. The combined interest expense of X and B is $300. Thus, $180 ($300 x 60%) of the combined interest expense is apportioned to domestic source income, $90 ($300 x 30%) is apportioned to foreign source foreign branch category income, and $30 ($300 x 10%) is apportioned to foreign source general category income, yielding net U.S. source income of $820 ($1,000 – $180), net foreign source foreign branch category income of $410 ($500 – $90), and net foreign source general category income of $470 ($500 – $30).

(3) *Controlled foreign corporations.*—(i) *In general.*—For purposes of computing subpart F income and tested income and computing earnings and profits for all Federal income tax purposes, the interest expense of a controlled foreign corporation may be apportioned using either the asset method described in paragraph (g) of this section or the modified gross income method described in paragraph (j) of this section, subject to the rules of paragraph (f)(3)(ii) and (iii) of this section.

* * *

(4) *Noncontrolled 10-percent owned foreign corporations.*—* * *

(iii) *Stock characterization.*—The stock of a noncontrolled 10-percent owned foreign corporation is characterized under the rules in § 1.861-12(c)(4).

(5) [Reserved]. For further guidance, see § 1.861-9T(f)(5).

(g) through (g)(1)(i) [Reserved]. For further guidance, see § 1.861-9T(g) through (g)(1)(i).

(ii) A taxpayer may elect to determine the value of its assets on the basis of either the tax book value or the fair market value of its assets. However, for taxable years beginning after December 31, 2017, the fair market value method is not allowed with respect to allocations and apportionments of interest expense. *See* section 864(e)(2). For rules concerning the application of an alternative method of valuing assets for purposes of the tax book value method, see paragraph (i) of this section. For rules concerning the application of the fair market value method, see paragraph (h) of this section.

(iii) [Reserved]

(iv) For rules relating to earnings and profits adjustments by taxpayers using the tax book value method for the stock in certain 10 percent owned corporations, see § 1.861-12(c)(2).

(v) [Reserved]

(2) *Asset values.*—(i) *General rule.*—(A) *Average of values.*—For purposes of determining the value of assets under this section, an average of values (book or market) within each statutory grouping and the residual grouping is computed for the year on the basis of values of assets at the beginning and end of the year. For the first taxable year beginning after December 31, 2017 (*post-2017 year*), a taxpayer that determined the value of its assets on the basis of the fair market value method for purposes of apportioning interest expense in its prior taxable year may choose to determine asset values under the tax book value method (or the alternative tax book value method) by treating the value of its assets as of the beginning of the post-2017 year as equal to the value of its assets at the end of the first quarter of the post-2017 year, provided that each member of the affiliated group (as defined in § 1.861-11T(d)) determines its asset values on the same basis. Where a substantial distortion of asset values would result from averaging beginning-of-year and end-of-year values, as might be the case in the event of a major corporate acquisition or disposition, the taxpayer must use a different method of asset valuation that more clearly reflects the average value of assets weighted to reflect the time such assets are held by the taxpayer during the taxable year.

(B) *Tax book value method.*—Under the tax book value method, the value of an asset is determined based on the adjusted basis of the asset. For purposes of determining the value of stock in a 10 percent owned corporation at the beginning and end of the year under the tax book value method, the tax book value is determined without regard to any adjustments under section 961(a) or 1293(d), see § 1.861-12(c)(2)(i)(B)(*1*), and before the adjustment required by § 1.861-12(c)(2)(i)(A) to the basis of stock in the 10 percent owned corporation. The average of the tax book value of the stock at the beginning and end of the year is then adjusted with respect to earnings and profits as described in § 1.861-12(c)(2)(i).

(g)(2)(ii) through (g)(2)(ii)(A)(*1*) [Reserved]. For further guidance, see § 1.861-9T(g)(2)(ii) through (g)(2)(ii)(A)(*1*).

(*2*) *United States dollar approximate separate transactions method.*—In the case of a branch to which the United States dollar approximate separate transactions method of accounting described in § 1.985-3 applies, the beginning-of-year dollar amount of the assets is determined by reference to the end-of-year balance sheet of the branch for the immediately preceding taxable year, adjusted for United States generally accepted accounting principles and United States tax accounting principles, and translated into U.S. dollars as provided in § 1.985-3(c). The end-of-year dollar amount of the assets of the branch is determined in the same manner by reference to the end-of-year balance sheet for the current taxable year. The beginning-of-year and end-of-year dollar tax book value of assets, as so determined, within each grouping is then averaged as provided in paragraph (g)(2)(i) of this section.

(g)(2)(ii)(B) through (g)(3) [Reserved]. For further guidance, see § 1.861-9T(g)(2)(ii)(B) through (g)(3).

(h) *Fair market value method.*—An affiliated group (as defined in section 1.861-11T(d)) or other taxpayer (the *taxpayer*) that elects to use the fair market value method of apportionment values its assets according to the methodology described in this paragraph (h). Effective for taxable years beginning after December 31, 2017, the fair market value method is not allowed for purposes of apportioning interest expense. *See* section 864(e)(2). However, a taxpayer may continue to apportion deductions other than interest expense that are properly apportioned based on fair market value according to the methodology described in this paragraph (h). *See* §1.861-8(c)(2).

(h)(1) through (h)(3) [Reserved]. For further guidance, see §1.861-9T(h)(1) through (h)(3).

* * *

(5) *Characterizing stock in related persons.*—Stock in a related person held by the taxpayer or by another related person shall be characterized on the basis of the fair market value of the taxpayer's pro rata share of assets held by the related person attributed to each statutory grouping and the residual grouping under the stock characterization rules of §1.861-12T(c)(3)(ii), except that the portion of the value of intangible assets of the taxpayer and related persons that is apportioned to the related person under §1.861-9T(h)(2) shall be characterized on the basis of the net income before interest expense of the related person within each statutory grouping or residual grouping (excluding income that is passive under §1.904-4(b)).

* * *

(i) * * *

(2) * * *

(i) Except as provided in this paragraph (i)(2)(i), a taxpayer may elect to use the alternative tax book value method. For the taxpayer's first taxable year beginning after December 31, 2017, the Commissioner's approval is not required to switch from the fair market value method to the alternative tax book value method for purposes of apportioning interest expense. * * *

* * *

(j) through (j)(2)(i) [Reserved]. For further guidance, see §1.861-9T(j) through (j)(2)(i).

(ii) *Step 2.*—Moving to the next higher-tier controlled foreign corporation, combine the gross income of such corporation within each grouping with its pro rata share (as determined under principles similar to section 951(a)(2)) of the gross income net of interest expense of all lower-tier controlled foreign corporations held by such higher-tier corporation within the same grouping adjusted as follows:

(A) Exclude from the gross income of the higher-tier corporation any dividends or other payments received from the lower-tier corporation other than interest income received from the lower-tier corporation;

(B) Exclude from the gross income net of interest expense of any lower-tier corporation any gross subpart F income, net of interest expense apportioned to such income;

(C) Exclude from the gross income net of interest expense of any lower-tier corporation any gross tested income as defined in §1.951A-2(c)(1), net of interest expense apportioned to such income;

(D) Then apportion the interest expense of the higher-tier controlled foreign corporation based on the adjusted combined gross income amounts; and

(E) Repeat paragraphs (j)(2)(ii)(A) through (D) of this section for each next higher-tier controlled foreign corporation in the chain.

(k) *Applicability date.*—This section applies to taxable years that both begin after December 31, 2017, and end on or after December 4, 2018.

Par. 5. Section 1.861-10 is amended by:

1. Revising paragraph (e)(8)(vi).

2. Removing and reserving paragraph (e)(10).

3. Adding paragraph (f).

The revisions and additions read as follows:

§1.861-10. Special allocations of interest expense.

* * *

(e) * * *

(8) * * *

(vi) *Classification of hybrid stock.*—In determining the amount of its related group indebtedness for any taxable year, a U.S. shareholder must not treat stock in a related controlled foreign corporation as related group indebtedness, regardless of whether the related controlled foreign corporation claims a deduction for interest under foreign law for distributions on such stock. For purposes of determining the foreign base period ratio under paragraph (e)(2)(iv) of this section for a taxable year that ends on or after December 4, 2018, the rules of this paragraph (e)(8)(vi) apply to determine the related group debt-to-asset ratio in each taxable year included in the foreign base period, including in taxable years that end before December 4, 2018.

* * *

(10) [Reserved]

* * *

(f) *Applicability date.*—This section applies to taxable years that end on or after December 4, 2018.

Par. 6. Section 1.861-11 is amended by:

1. Revising paragraphs (a) through (c).

2. Removing the language ", except that section 936 corporations are also included within the affiliated group to the extent provided in paragraph (d)(2) of this section" from the first sentence of paragraph (d)(1).

3. Removing and reserving paragraph (d)(2).

4. Adding paragraph (h).

The revisions and addition read as follows:

§1.861-11. Special rules for allocating and apportioning interest expense of an affiliated group of corporations.—(a) [Reserved]. For further guidance, see §1.861-11T(a).

(b) *Scope of application.*—(1) *Application of section 864(e)(1) and (5) (concerning the definition and treatment of affiliated groups).*—Section 864(e)(1) and (5) and the portions of this section implementing section 864(e)(1) and (5) apply to the computation of foreign source taxable income for purposes of section 904 (relating to various limitations on the foreign tax credit).

Section 864(e)(1) and (5) and the portions of this section implementing section 864(e)(1) and (5) also apply in connection with section 907 to determine reductions in the amount allowed as a foreign tax credit under section 901. Section 864(e)(1) and (5) and the portions of this section implementing section 864(e)(1) and (5) also apply to the computation of the combined taxable income of the related supplier and a foreign sales corporation (FSC) (under sections 921 through 927) as well as the combined taxable income of the related supplier and a domestic international sales corporation (DISC) (under sections 991 through 997).

(b)(2) through (c) [Reserved]. For further guidance, see § 1.861-11T(b)(2) through (c).

(d) * * *

(2) [Reserved]

* * *

(h) *Applicability dates.*—This section applies to taxable years that both begin after December 31, 2017, and end on or after December 4, 2018.

Par. 7. Section 1.861-12 is amended by:

1. Revising paragraphs (a) through (c)(1).
2. Revising the heading of paragraph (c)(2).
3. Removing the language ", for taxable years beginning after April 25, 2006," from paragraph (c)(2)(i)(A).
4. Revising paragraphs (c)(2)(i)(B) through (c)(3).
5. Revising paragraph (c)(4).
6. Removing paragraph (c)(5).
7. Revising paragraphs (d) through (j).
8. Adding paragraph (k).

The revisions and additions read as follows:

§ 1.861-12. Characterization rules and adjustments for certain assets.—(a) *In general.*—The rules in this section are applicable to taxpayers in apportioning expenses under an asset method to income in the various separate categories described in § 1.904-5(a)(4)(v), and supplement other rules provided in §§ 1.861-9 through 1.861-11T. The principles of the rules in this section are also applicable in apportioning expenses among statutory and residual groupings for any other operative section. See also § 1.861-8(f)(2)(i) for a rule requiring conformity of allocation methods and apportionment principles for all operative sections. Paragraph (b) of this section describes the treatment of inventories. Paragraph (c)(1) of this section concerns the treatment of various stock assets. Paragraph (c)(2) of this section describes a basis adjustment for stock in 10 percent owned corporations. Paragraph (c)(3) of this section sets forth rules for characterizing the stock in controlled foreign corporations. Paragraph (c)(4) of this section describes the treatment of stock of noncontrolled 10-percent owned foreign corporations. Paragraph (d)(1) of this section concerns the treatment of notes. Paragraph (d)(2) of this section concerns the treatment of notes of controlled foreign corporations. Paragraph (e) of this section describes the treatment of certain portfolio securities that constitute inventory or generate income primarily in the form of gains. Paragraph (f) of this section describes the treatment of assets that are subject to the capitalization rules of section 263A. Paragraph (g) of this section concerns the treatment of FSC stock and of assets of the related supplier generating foreign trade income. Paragraph (h) of this section concerns the treatment of DISC stock and of assets of the related supplier generating qualified export receipts. Paragraph (i) of this section is reserved. Paragraph (j) of this section sets forth an example illustrating the rules of this section, as well as the rules of § 1.861-9(g).

(b) through (c)(1) [Reserved]. For further guidance, see § 1.861-12T(b) through (c)(1).

(2) *Basis adjustment for stock in 10 percent owned corporations.*—(i) * * *

(B) *Computational rules.—(1) Adjustments to basis.—(i) Application of section 961 or 1293(d).*—For purposes of this section, a taxpayer's adjusted basis in the stock of a foreign corporation does not include any amount included in basis under section 961 or 1293(d) of the Code.

(ii) Application of section 965(b).—If a taxpayer owned the stock of a specified foreign corporation (as defined in § 1.965-1(f)(45)) as of the close of the last taxable year of the specified foreign corporation that began before January 1, 2018, the taxpayer's adjusted basis in the stock of the specified foreign corporation for that taxable year and any subsequent taxable year is determined as if the taxpayer made the election described in § 1.965-2(f)(2)(i) (regardless of whether the election was actually made) but does not include the amount included (or that would be included if the election were made) in basis under § 1.965-2(f)(2)(ii)(A) (without regard to whether any portion of the amount is netted against the amounts of any other basis adjustments under § 1.965-2(h)(2)).

(2) Amount of earnings and profits.—For purposes of this paragraph (c)(2), earnings and profits (or deficits) are computed under the rules of section 312 and, in the case of a foreign corporation, sections 964(a) and 986 for taxable years of the 10 percent owned corporation ending on or before the close of the taxable year of the taxpayer. Accordingly, the earnings and profits of a controlled foreign corporation includes all earnings and profits described in section 959(c). The amount of the earnings and profits with respect to stock of a foreign corporation held by the taxpayer is determined according to the attribution principles of section 1248 and the regulations under section 1248. The attribution principles of section 1248 apply without regard to the requirements of section 1248 that are not relevant to the determination of a shareholder's pro rata portion of earnings and profits, such as whether earnings and profits (or deficits) were derived (or incurred) during taxable years beginning before or after December 31, 1962.

(3) Annual noncumulative adjustment.—The adjustment required by paragraph (c)(2)(i)(A) of this section is made annually and is noncumulative. Thus, the adjusted basis of the

stock (determined without regard to prior years' adjustments under paragraph (c)(2)(i)(A) of this section) is adjusted annually by the amount of accumulated earnings and profits (or deficits) attributable to the stock as of the end of each year.

(4) *Translation of non-dollar functional currency earnings and profits.*—Earnings and profits (or deficits) of a qualified business unit that has a functional currency other than the dollar must be computed under this paragraph (c)(2) in functional currency and translated into dollars using the exchange rate at the end of the taxpayer's current taxable year (and not the exchange rates for the years in which the earnings and profits or deficits were derived or incurred).

(C) *Examples.*—The following examples illustrate the application of paragraph (c)(2)(i)(B) of this section.

(1) *Example 1: No election described in §1.965-2(f)(2)(i)*—(i) *Facts.* USP, a domestic corporation, owns all of the stock of CFC1 and CFC2, both controlled foreign corporations. USP, CFC1, and CFC2 all use the calendar year as their U.S. taxable year. USP owned CFC1 and CFC2 as of December 31, 2017, and CFC1 and CFC2 were specified foreign corporations with respect to USP. USP did not make the election described in §1.965-2(f)(2)(i), but if USP had made the election, USP's basis in the stock of CFC1 would have been increased by $75 under §1.965-2(f)(2)(ii)(A) and USP's basis in the stock of CFC2 would have been decreased by $75 under §1.965-2(f)(2)(ii)(B). For purposes of determining the value of the stock of CFC1 and CFC2 at the beginning of the 2019 taxable year, without regard to amounts included in basis under section 961 or 1293(d), USP's adjusted basis in the stock of CFC1 is $100 and its adjusted basis in the stock of CFC2 is $350 (before the application of this paragraph (c)(2)(i)(B)).

(*ii*) *Analysis.* Under paragraph (c)(2)(i)(B)(*1*) of this section, USP's adjusted basis in CFC1 and CFC2 is determined as if USP had made the election described in §1.965-2(f)(2)(i), and therefore USP's adjusted basis in CFC2 includes the $75 reduction USP would have made to its basis in that stock under §1.965-2(f)(2)(ii)(B). However, USP's adjusted basis in the stock of CFC1 does not include the $75 that USP would have included in its basis in that stock under §1.965-2(f)(2)(ii)(A). Accordingly, for purposes of determining the value of stock of CFC1 and CFC2 at the beginning of the 2019 taxable year, USP's adjusted basis in the stock of CFC1 is $100 and USP's adjusted basis in the stock of CFC2 is $275 ($350 – $75).

(2) *Example 2: Election described in §1.965-2(f)(2)(i)*—(i) *Facts.* USP, a domestic corporation, owns all of the stock of CFC1, which owns all of the stock of CFC2, both foreign corporations. USP, CFC1, and CFC2 all use the calendar year as their U.S. taxable year. USP owned CFC1, and CFC1 owned CFC2 as of December 31, 2017, and CFC1 and CFC2 were specified foreign corporations with respect to USP. USP made the election described in §1.965-2(f)(2)(i). As a result of the election, USP was required to increase its basis in CFC1 by $90 under §1.965-2(f)(2)(ii)(A), and to decrease its basis in CFC1 by $90 under §1.965-2(f)(2)(ii)(B). Pursuant to §1.965-2(h)(2), USP netted the increase of $90 against the decrease of $90 and made no net adjustment to the basis of the stock of CFC1. For purposes of determining the value of the stock of CFC1 at the beginning of the 2019 taxable year, without regard to amounts included in basis under section 961 or 1293(d), USP's adjusted basis in the stock of CFC1 is $600 (before the application of this paragraph (c)(2)(i)(B)).

(*ii*) *Analysis.* Under paragraph (c)(2)(i)(B)(*1*) of this section, USP's adjusted basis in CFC1 is determined as if USP had made the election described in §1.965-2(f)(2)(i), and therefore USP's adjusted basis in CFC1 includes the $90 reduction USP would have made to its basis in that stock, without regard to the netting rule described in §1.965-2(h)(2). However, USP's adjusted basis in the stock of CFC1 does not include the amount that would have been included in basis under §1.965-2(f)(2)(ii)(A) without regard to the netting rule described in §1.965-2(h)(2). Accordingly, for purposes of determining the value of stock of CFC1 at the beginning of the 2019 taxable year, USP's adjusted basis in the stock of CFC1 is $510 ($600 – $90).

(c)(2)(ii) through (c)(2)(vi) [Reserved]. For further guidance, see §1.861-12T(c)(2)(ii) through (c)(2)(vi).

(3) *Characterization of stock of controlled foreign corporations.*—(i) *Operative sections.*—(A) *Operative sections other than section 904.*—For purposes of applying this section to an operative section other than section 904, stock in a controlled foreign corporation (as defined in section 957) is characterized as an asset in the relevant groupings on the basis of the asset method described in paragraph (c)(3)(ii) of this section, or the modified gross income method described in paragraph (c)(3)(iii) of this section. Stock in a controlled foreign corporation whose interest expense is apportioned on the basis of assets is characterized in the hands of its United States shareholders under the asset method described in paragraph (c)(3)(ii) of this section. Stock in a controlled foreign corporation whose interest expense is apportioned on the basis of modified gross income is characterized in the hands of its United States shareholders under the modified gross income method described in paragraph (c)(3)(iii) of this section.

(B) *Section 904 as operative section.*—For purposes of applying this section to section 904 as the operative section, §1.861-13 applies to characterize the stock of a controlled foreign corporation as an asset producing foreign source income in the separate categories described in §1.904-5(a)(4)(v), or as an asset producing U.S. source income in the residual grouping, in the hands of the United States shareholder, and to determine the portion of the stock that gives rise to an inclusion under section 951A(a) that is treated as an exempt asset under §1.861-8(d)(2)(ii)(C). Section 1.861-13 also provides rules for subdividing the stock in the various separate categories and the residual grouping into a section 245A subgroup and a non-section 245A subgroup in order to determine the amount of the adjustments required by section 904(b)(4) and §1.904(b)-3(c) with respect to the section 245A subgroup, and provides rules for determining the portion of the stock that gives rise to a dividend eligible for a deduction under section 245(a)(5) that is treated as an exempt asset under §1.861-8(d)(2)(ii)(B).

(ii) [Reserved]. For further guidance, see § 1.861-12T(c)(3)(ii).

(iii) *Modified gross income method.*—Under the modified gross income method, the taxpayer characterizes the tax book value of the stock of the first-tier controlled foreign corporation based on the gross income, net of interest expense, of the controlled foreign corporation (as computed under § 1.861-9T(j) to include certain gross income, net of interest expense, of lower-tier controlled foreign corporations) within each relevant category for the taxable year of the controlled foreign corporation ending with or within the taxable year of the taxpayer. For this purpose, however, the gross income, net of interest expense, of the first-tier controlled foreign corporation includes the total amount of gross subpart F income, net of interest expense, of any lower-tier controlled foreign corporation that was excluded under the rules of § 1.861-9(j)(2)(ii)(B). The gross income, net of interest expense, of the first-tier controlled foreign corporation also includes the total amount of gross tested income, net of interest expense, of any lower-tier controlled foreign corporation that was excluded under the rules of § 1.861-9(j)(2)(ii)(C).

(4) *Characterization of stock of noncontrolled 10-percent owned foreign corporations.*—(i) *In general.*—Except in the case of a nonqualifying shareholder described in paragraph (c)(4)(ii) of this section, the principles of § 1.861-12(c)(3), including the relevant rules of § 1.861-13 when section 904 is the operative section, apply to characterize stock in a noncontrolled 10-percent owned foreign corporation (as defined in section 904(d)(2)(E)). Accordingly, stock in a noncontrolled 10-percent owned foreign corporation is characterized as an asset in the various separate categories on the basis of either the asset method described in § 1.861-12T(c)(3)(ii) or the modified gross income method described in § 1.861-12(c)(3)(iii). Stock in a noncontrolled 10-percent owned foreign corporation the interest expense of which is apportioned on the basis of assets is characterized in the hands of its shareholders under the asset method described in § 1.861-12T(c)(3)(ii). Stock in a noncontrolled 10-percent owned foreign corporation the interest expense of which is apportioned on the basis of gross income is characterized in the hands of its shareholders under the modified gross income method described in § 1.861-12(c)(3)(iii).

(ii) *Nonqualifying shareholders.*—Stock in a noncontrolled 10-percent owned foreign corporation is characterized as a passive category asset in the hands of a shareholder that either is not a domestic corporation or is not a United States shareholder with respect to the noncontrolled 10-percent owned foreign corporation for the taxable year. Stock in a noncontrolled 10-percent owned foreign corporation is characterized as in the separate category described in section 904(d)(4)(C)(ii) in the hands of any shareholder with respect to whom look-through treatment is not substantiated. *See also* § 1.904-5(c)(4)(iii)(B). In the case of a noncontrolled 10-percent owned foreign corporation that is a passive foreign investment company with respect to a shareholder, stock in the noncontrolled 10-percent owned foreign corporation is characterized as a passive category asset in the hands of the shareholder if such shareholder does not meet the ownership requirements described in section 904(d)(2)(E)(i)(II).

(d) *Treatment of notes.*—(1) *General rule.*—[Reserved]. For further guidance, see § 1.861-12T(d)(1).

(2) *Characterization of related controlled foreign corporation notes.*—The debt of a controlled foreign corporation is characterized in the same manner as the interest income derived from that debt obligation. See §§ 1.904-4 and 1.904-5(c)(2) for rules treating interest income as income in a separate category.

(e) through (j) [Reserved]. For further guidance, see § 1.861-12T(e) through (j).

(k) *Applicability date.*—This section applies to taxable years that both begin after December 31, 2017, and end on or after December 4, 2018. Section 1.861-12(c)(2)(i)(*B*)(*1*)(*ii*) also applies to the last taxable year of a foreign corporation that begins before January 1, 2018, and with respect to a United States person, the taxable year in which or with which such taxable year of the foreign corporation ends.

Income from U.S. Sources: Allocation and Apportionment

Income from U.S. Sources: Allocation and Apportionment of Expenses.—Temporary Reg. §§ 1.861-8T—1.861-12T, relating to the allocation and apportionment of interest expense and certain other expenses for purposes of the foreign tax credit rules and certain other international tax provisions, are also proposed as final regulations and, when adopted, would become §§ 1.861-8—1.861-12 (published in the Federal Register on September 14, 1988).

§ 1.861-8. Computation of taxable income from sources within the United States and from other sources and activities.

§ 1.861-9. Allocation and apportionment of income expense.

§ 1.861-10. Special allocations of interest expense.

§ 1.861-11. Special rules for allocating and apportioning interest expense of an affiliated group of corporations.

§ 1.861-12. Characterization rules and adjustments for certain assets.

Income from U.S. Sources: Transition Rules

Income from Source: Interest Expense Allocation.—Amendments of Temporary Reg. §1.861-9T, relating to transition rules for the allocation and apportionment of interest expense for the purposes of the foreign tax credit rules and certain other international tax provisions, are also proposed as final (published in the Federal Register on August 2, 1989).

§1.861-9. Allocation and apportionment of interest expense.

Determination of the Foreign Tax Credit: Guidance

Determination of the Foreign Tax Credit: Guidance.—Reg. §1.861-13, relating to the determination of the foreign tax credit under the Internal Revenue Code, including changes made by the Tax Cuts and Jobs Act, is proposed (published in the Federal Register on December 7, 2018) (REG-105600-18).

Par. 8. §1.861-13 is added to read as follows:

§1.861-13. Payment and returns of tax withheld by the acquiring agency.—(a) *Methodology.*—For purposes of allocating and apportioning deductions for purposes of section 904 as the operative section, stock in a controlled foreign corporation owned directly or indirectly through a partnership or other pass-through entity by a United States shareholder is characterized by the United States shareholder under the rules described in this section. In general, paragraphs (a)(1) through (5) of this section characterize the stock of the controlled foreign corporation as an asset in the various statutory groupings and residual grouping based on the type of income that the stock of the controlled foreign corporation generates, has generated, or may reasonably be expected to generate when the income is included by the United States shareholder.

(1) *Step 1: Characterize stock as generating income in statutory groupings under the asset or modified gross income method.*—(i) *Asset method.*—United States shareholders using the asset method to characterize stock of a controlled foreign corporation must apply the asset method described in §1.861-12T(c)(3)(ii) to assign the assets of the controlled foreign corporation to the statutory groupings described in paragraphs (a)(1)(i)(A)(*1*) through (*10*) and (a)(1)(i)(B) of this section. If the controlled foreign corporation owns stock in a lower-tier noncontrolled 10-percent owned foreign corporation, the assets of the lower-tier noncontrolled 10-percent owned foreign corporation are assigned to a gross subpart F income grouping to the extent such assets generate income that, if distributed to the controlled foreign corporation, would be gross subpart F income of the controlled foreign corporation. *See also* §1.861-12(c)(4).

(A) *General and passive categories.*—Within each of the controlled foreign corporation's general category and passive category, each of the following subgroups within each category is a separate statutory grouping—

(*1*) Foreign source gross tested income;

(*2*) For each applicable treaty, U.S. source gross tested income that, when taken into account by a United States shareholder under section 951A, is resourced in the hands of the United States shareholder (*resourced gross tested income*);

(*3*) U.S. source gross tested income not described in paragraph (a)(1)(i)(A)(2) of this section;

(*4*) Foreign source gross subpart F income;

(*5*) For each applicable treaty, U.S. source gross subpart F income that, when included by a United States shareholder under section 951(a)(1), is resourced in the hands of the United States shareholder (*resourced gross subpart F income*);

(*6*) U.S. source gross subpart F income not described in paragraph (a)(1)(i)(A)(*5*) of this section;

(*7*) Foreign source gross section 245(a)(5) income;

(*8*) U.S. source gross section 245(a)(5) income;

(*9*) Any other foreign source gross income (*specified foreign source general category income* or *specified foreign source passive category income*, as the case may be); and

(*10*) Any other U.S. source gross income (*specified U.S. source general category gross income* or *specified U.S. source passive category gross income*, as the case may be).

(B) *Section 901(j) income.*—For each country described in section 901(j), all gross income from sources in that country.

(ii) *Modified gross income method.*—United States shareholders using the modified gross income method to characterize stock in a controlled foreign corporation must apply the modified gross income method under §1.861-12(c)(3)(iii) to assign the modified gross income of the controlled foreign corporation to the statutory groupings described in paragraphs (a)(1)(i)(A)(*1*) through (*10*) and (a)(1)(i)(B) of this section. For this purpose, the rules described in §§1.861-12(c)(3)(iii) and 1.861-9T(j)(2) apply to combine gross income in a statutory grouping that is earned by the controlled foreign corporation with gross income of lower-tier controlled foreign corporations that is in the same statutory grouping. For example, foreign source general category gross tested income (net of interest expense) earned by the controlled foreign corporation is combined with its pro rata share of the foreign source general category gross tested income (net of interest expense) of lower-tier controlled foreign corporations. If the controlled foreign corporation owns stock in a lower-tier noncontrolled 10-percent owned foreign corporation, gross income of the lower-tier noncontrolled 10-percent owned foreign corporation is assigned to a gross subpart F income grouping to the extent that the income, if distributed to the upper-tier controlled foreign corporation, would be gross subpart F income of the upper-tier controlled foreign corporation. *See also* § 1.861-12(c)(4).

(2) *Step 2: Assign stock to the section 951A category.*—A controlled foreign corporation is not treated as earning section 951A category income. The portion of the value of the stock of the controlled foreign corporation that is assigned to the section 951A category equals the value of the portion of the stock of the controlled foreign corporation that is assigned to the foreign source gross tested income statutory groupings within the general category (*general category gross tested income stock*) multiplied by the United States shareholder's inclusion percentage. Under § 1.861-8(d)(2)(ii)(C)(*2*)(*ii*), a portion of the value of stock assigned to the section 951A category may be treated as an exempt asset. The portion of the general category gross tested income stock that is not characterized as a section 951A category asset remains a general category asset and may result in expenses being disregarded under section 904(b)(4). See paragraph (a)(5)(ii) of this section and § 1.904(b)-3. No portion of the passive category gross tested income stock or U.S. source gross tested income stock is assigned to the section 951A category.

(3) *Step 3: Assign stock to a treaty category.*—(i) *Inclusions under section 951A(a).*—The portion of the value of the stock of the controlled foreign corporation that is assigned to a particular treaty category due to an inclusion of U.S. source income under section 951A(a) that was resourced under a particular treaty equals the value of the portion of the stock of the controlled foreign corporation that is assigned to the resourced gross tested income statutory grouping within each of the controlled foreign corporation's general or passive categories (*resourced gross tested income stock*) multiplied by the United States shareholder's inclusion percentage. Under § 1.861-8(d)(2)(ii)(C)(*2*)(*ii*), a portion of the value of stock assigned to a particular treaty category by reason of this paragraph (a)(3)(i) may be treated as an exempt asset. The portion of the resourced gross tested income stock that is not characterized as a treaty category asset remains a U.S. source general or passive category asset, as the case may be, that is in the residual grouping and may result in expenses being disregarded under section 904(b)(4) for purposes of determining entire taxable income under section 904(a). *See* paragraph (a)(5)(iv) of this section and § 1.904(b)-3.

(ii) *Inclusions under section 951(a)(1).*—The portion of the value of the stock of the controlled foreign corporation that is assigned to a particular treaty category due to an inclusion of U.S. source income under section 951(a)(1) that was resourced under a treaty equals the value of the portion of the stock of the controlled foreign corporation that is assigned to the resourced gross subpart F income statutory grouping within each of the controlled foreign corporation's general category or passive category.

(4) *Step 4: Aggregate stock within each separate category and assign stock to the residual grouping.*—The portions of the value of stock of the controlled foreign corporation assigned to foreign source statutory groupings that were not specifically assigned to the section 951A category under paragraph (a)(2) of this section (Step 2) are aggregated within the general category and the passive category to characterize the stock as general category stock and passive category stock, respectively. The portions of the value of stock of the controlled foreign corporation assigned to U.S. source statutory groupings that were not specifically assigned to a particular treaty category under paragraph (a)(3) of this section (Step 3) are aggregated to characterize the stock as U.S. source category stock, which is in the residual grouping. Stock assigned to the separate category for income described in section 901(j)(1) remains in that category.

(5) *Step 5: Determine section 245A and non-section 245A subgroups for each separate category and U.S. source category.*—(i) *In general.*—In the case of stock of a controlled foreign corporation that is held directly or indirectly through a partnership or other pass-through entity by a United States shareholder that is a domestic corporation, stock of the controlled foreign corporation that is general category stock, passive category stock, and U.S. source category stock is subdivided between a section 245A subgroup and a non-section 245A subgroup under paragraphs (a)(5)(ii) through (v) of this section for purposes of applying section 904(b)(4) and § 1.904(b)-3(c). Each subgroup is treated as a statutory grouping under § 1.861-8(a)(4) for purposes of allocating and apportioning deductions under §§ 1.861-8 through 1.861-14T and 1.861-17 in applying section 904 as the operative section. Deductions apportioned to each section 245A subgroup are disregarded under section 904(b)(4). *See* § 1.904(b)-3. Deductions apportioned to the statutory groupings for gross section 245(a)(5) income are not disregarded under section 904(b)(4); however, a portion of the stock assigned to those groupings is treated as exempt under § 1.861-8T(d)(2)(ii)(B).

(ii) *Section 245A subgroup of general category stock.*—The portion of the general category stock of the controlled foreign corporation that is assigned to the section 245A subgroup of the general category equals the value of the general category gross tested income stock of the controlled foreign corporation that is not assigned to the section 951A category under paragraph (a)(2) of this section (Step 2), plus the value of the portion of the stock of the controlled foreign corporation that is assigned to the specified foreign source general category income statutory grouping.

(iii) *Section 245A subgroup of passive category stock.*—The portion of passive category stock of the controlled foreign corporation that is assigned to the section 245A subcategory of the passive category equals the sum of—

(A) The value of the portion of the stock of the controlled foreign corporation that is assigned to the gross tested income statutory grouping within foreign source passive category income multiplied by a percentage equal to 100 percent minus the United States shareholder's inclusion percentage for passive category gross tested income; and

(B) The value of the portion of the stock of the controlled foreign corporation that was assigned to the specified foreign source passive category income statutory grouping.

(iv) *Section 245A subgroup of U.S. source category stock.*—The portion of U.S. source category stock of the controlled foreign corporation that is assigned to the section 245A subgroup of the U.S. source category equals the sum of—

(A) The value of the portion of the stock of the controlled foreign corporation that is assigned to the U.S. source general category gross tested income statutory grouping multiplied by a percentage equal to 100 percent minus the United States shareholder's inclusion percentage for the general category;

(B) The value of the portion of the stock of the controlled foreign corporation that is assigned to the U.S. source passive category gross tested income statutory grouping multiplied by a percentage equal to 100 percent minus the United States shareholder's inclusion percentage for the passive category;

(C) The value of the resourced gross tested income stock of the controlled foreign corporation that is not assigned to a particular treaty category under paragraph (a)(3)(i) of this section (Step 3);

(D) The value of the portion of the stock of the controlled foreign corporation that is assigned to the specified U.S. source general category gross income statutory grouping; and

(E) The value of the portion of the stock of the controlled foreign corporation that is assigned to the specified U.S. source passive category gross income statutory grouping.

(v) *Non-section 245A subgroup*.—The value of stock of a controlled foreign corporation that is not assigned to the section 245A subgroup within the general or passive category or the residual grouping is assigned to the non-section 245A subgroup within such category or grouping. The value of stock of a controlled foreign corporation that is assigned to the section 951A category, the separate category for income described in section 901(j)(1), or a particular treaty category is always assigned to a non-section 245A subgroup.

(b) *Definitions*.—This paragraph (b) provides definitions that apply for purposes of this section.

(1) *Gross section 245(a)(5) income*.—The term *gross section 245(a)(5) income* means all items of gross income described in section 245(a)(5)(A) and (B).

(2) *Gross subpart F income*.—The term *gross subpart F income* means all items of gross income that are taken into account by a controlled foreign corporation in determining its subpart F income under section 952, except for items of gross income described in section 952(a)(5).

(3) *Gross tested income*.—The term *gross tested income* has the meaning provided in §1.951A-1(c)(1).

(4) *Inclusion percentage*.—The term *inclusion percentage* has the meaning provided in §1.960-2(c)(2).

(5) *Separate category*.—The term *separate category* has the meaning provided in §1.904-5(a)(4)(v).

(6) *Treaty category*.—The term *treaty category* means a category of income earned by a controlled foreign corporation for which section 904(a), (b), and (c) are applied separately as a result of income being resourced under a treaty. See, for example, section 245(a)(10), 865(h), or 904(h)(10). A United States shareholder may have multiple treaty categories for amounts of income resourced by the United States shareholder under a treaty. *See* §1.904-5(m)(7).

(7) *U.S. source category*.—The term *U.S. source category* means the aggregate of U.S. source income in each separate category listed in section 904(d)(1).

(c) *Examples*.—The following examples illustrate the application of the rules in this section.

(1) *Example 1: Asset method*—(i) *Facts*—(A) USP, a domestic corporation, directly owns all of the stock of a controlled foreign corporation, CFC1. The tax book value of CFC1's stock is $20,000. USP uses the asset method described in §1.861-12T(c)(3)(ii) to characterize the stock of CFC1. USP's inclusion percentage is 70%.

(B) CFC1 owns the following assets with the following values as determined under §§1.861-9(g)(2) and 1.861-9T(g)(3): assets that generate income described in the foreign source gross tested income statutory grouping within the general category ($4,000), assets that generate income described in the foreign source gross subpart F income statutory grouping within the general category ($1,000), assets that generate specified foreign source general category income ($3,000), and assets that generate income described in the foreign source gross subpart F income statutory grouping within the passive category ($2,000).

(C) CFC1 also owns all of the stock of CFC2, a controlled foreign corporation. The tax book value of CFC1's stock in CFC2 is $5,000. CFC2 owns the following assets with the following values as determined under §§1.861-9(g)(2) and 1.861-9T(g)(3): assets that generate income described in the foreign source gross subpart F income statutory grouping within the general category ($2,250) and assets that generate specified foreign source general category income ($750).

(ii) *Analysis*—(A) *Step 1*—(*1*) *Characterization of CFC2 stock*. CFC2 has total assets of $3,000, $2,250 of which are in the foreign source gross subpart F income statutory grouping within the general category and $750 of which are in the specified foreign source general category income statutory grouping. Accordingly, CFC2's stock is characterized as $3,750 ($2,250/$3,000 x $5,000) in the foreign source gross subpart F income statutory grouping within the general category and $1,250 ($750/$3,000 x $5,000) in the specified foreign source general category income statutory grouping.

(*2*) *Characterization of CFC1 stock*. CFC1 has total assets of $15,000, $4,000 of which are in the foreign source gross tested income statutory grouping within the general category, $4,750 of which are in the foreign source gross subpart F income statutory grouping within the general category (including the portion of CFC2 stock assigned to that statutory grouping), $4,250 of which are in the specified foreign source general category income statutory grouping (including the portion of CFC2 stock assigned to that statutory grouping), and $2,000 of which are in the foreign source gross subpart F income statutory grouping within the passive category. Accordingly, CFC1's stock is characterized as $5,333 ($4,000/$15,000 x $20,000) in the foreign source gross tested income statutory grouping within the general category, $6,333 ($4,750/$15,000 x $20,000) in the foreign source gross subpart F income statutory grouping within the general category, $5,667 ($4,250/$15,000 x $20,000) in the specified foreign source general category income statutory grouping, and $2,667 ($2,000/$15,000 x $20,000) in the foreign source gross subpart F income statutory grouping within the passive category.

(B) *Step 2*. The portion of the value of the stock of CFC1 that is general category gross tested income stock is $5,333. USP's inclusion percentage is 70%. Accordingly, under paragraph (a)(2) of this section, $3,733 of the stock of CFC1 is assigned to the section 951A category and a portion thereof may be treated as an exempt asset under § 1.861-8(d)(2)(ii)(C)(*2*)(*ii*). The remainder, $1,600, remains a general category asset.

(C) *Step 3*. No portion of the stock of CFC1 is resourced gross tested income stock or assigned to the resourced gross subpart F income statutory grouping in any treaty category. Accordingly, no portion of the stock of CFC1 is assigned to a treaty category under paragraph (a)(3) of this section.

(D) *Step 4—(1) General category stock*. The total portion of the value of the stock of CFC1 that is general category stock is $13,600, which is equal to $1,600 (the portion of the value of the general category stock of CFC1 that was not assigned to the section 951A category in Step 2) plus $5,667 (the value of the portion of the stock of CFC1 assigned to the specified foreign source income statutory grouping within the general category) plus $6,333 (the value of the portion of the stock of CFC1 assigned to the foreign source gross subpart F income statutory grouping within the general category).

(2) *Passive category stock*. The total portion of the value of the stock of CFC1 that is passive category stock is $2,667.

(3) *U.S source category stock*. No portion of the value of the stock of CFC1 is U.S. source category stock.

(E) *Step 5—(1) General category stock*. Under paragraph (a)(5)(ii) of this section, the value of the stock of CFC1 assigned to the section 245A subgroup of general category stock is $7,267, which is equal to $1,600 (the portion of the value of the general category stock of CFC1 that was not assigned to the section 951A category in Step 2) plus $5,667 (the value of the portion of the stock of CFC1 assigned to the specified foreign source general category income statutory grouping). Under paragraph (a)(5)(v) of this section, the remainder of the general category stock of CFC1, $6,333, is assigned to the non-section 245A subgroup of general category stock.

(2) *Passive category stock*. No portion of the passive category stock of CFC1 is in the foreign source gross tested income statutory grouping or the specified foreign source passive category income statutory grouping. Accordingly, under paragraph (a)(5)(iii) of this section, no portion of the value of the stock of CFC1 is assigned to the section 245A subgroup of passive category stock. Under paragraph (a)(5)(v) of this section, the passive category stock of CFC1, $2,667 is assigned to the non-section 245A subgroup of passive category stock.

(3) *Section 951A category stock*. Under paragraph (a)(5)(v) of this section, all of the section 951A category stock, $3,733, is assigned to the non-section 245A subgroup of section 951A category stock.

(F) *Summary*. For purpose of the allocation and apportionment of expenses, $13,600 of the stock of CFC1 is characterized as general category stock, $7,267 of which is in the section 245A subgroup and $6,333 of which is in the non-section 245A subgroup; $2,667 of the stock of CFC1 is characterized as passive category stock, all of which is in the non-section 245A subgroup; and $3,733 of the stock of CFC1 is characterized as section 951A category stock, all of which is in the non-section 245A subgroup.

(2) *Example 2: Asset method with noncontrolled 10-percent owned foreign corporation*—(i) *Facts*. The facts are the same as in paragraph (c)(1)(i) of this section, except that CFC1 does not own CFC2 and instead owns 20% of the stock of FC2, a foreign corporation that is a noncontrolled 10-percent owned foreign corporation. The tax book value of CFC1's stock in FC2 is $5,000. FC2 owns assets with the following values as determined under §§ 1.861-9(g)(2) and 1.861-9T(g)(3): assets that generate specified foreign source general category income ($3,000). All of the assets of FC2 generate income that, if distributed to CFC1 as a dividend, would be foreign source gross subpart F income in the general category to CFC1.

(ii) *Analysis*—(A) *Step 1—(1) Characterization of FC2 stock*. All of the assets of FC2 generate income that, if distributed to CFC1, would be foreign source gross subpart F income in the general category to CFC1. Accordingly, under paragraph (a)(1)(i) of this section, all of CFC1's stock in FC2 ($5,000) is characterized as in the foreign source gross subpart F income statutory grouping within the general category.

(2) *Characterization of CFC1 stock*. CFC1 has total assets of $15,000, $4,000 of which are in the foreign source gross tested income statutory grouping within the general category, $6,000 of which are in the foreign source gross subpart F income statutory grouping within the general category (including the FC2 stock assigned to that statutory grouping), $3,000 of which are in the specified foreign source general category income statutory grouping, and $2,000 of which are in the foreign source gross subpart F income statutory grouping within the passive category. Accordingly, CFC1's stock is characterized as $5,333 ($4,000/$15,000 x $20,000) in the foreign source gross tested income statutory grouping within the general category, $8,000 ($6,000/$15,000 x $20,000) in the foreign source gross subpart F income statutory grouping within the general category, $4,000 ($3,000/$15,000 x $20,000) in the specified foreign source general category income statutory grouping, and $2,667 ($2,000/$15,000 x $20,000) in the foreign source gross subpart F income statutory grouping within the passive category.

(B) *Step 2*. The analysis is the same as in paragraph (c)(1)(ii)(B) of this section.

(C) *Step 3*. The analysis is the same as in paragraph (c)(1)(ii)(C) of this section.

(D) *Step 4—(1) General category stock*. The total portion of the value of the stock of CFC1 that is general category stock is $13,600, which is equal to $1,600 (the portion of the value of the general category stock of CFC1 that was not assigned to the section 951A category in Step 2) plus $4,000 (the value of the portion of the stock of CFC1 assigned to the specified foreign source income statutory grouping within the general category general category) plus $8,000 (the value of the portion of the stock of CFC1 assigned to the foreign source gross subpart F income statutory grouping within the general category).

(2) *Passive category stock.* The analysis is the same as in paragraph (c)(1)(ii)(D)(2) of this section.

(E) *Step 5—(1) General category stock.* Under paragraph (a)(5)(ii) of this section, the value of the stock of CFC1 assigned to the section 245A subgroup of general category stock is $5,600, which is equal to $1,600 (the portion of the value of the general category stock of CFC1 that was not assigned to the section 951A category in Step 2) plus $4,000 (the value of the portion of the stock of CFC1 assigned to the specified foreign source general category income statutory grouping). Under paragraph (a)(5)(v) of this section, the remainder of the general category stock of CFC1, $8,000, is assigned to the non-section 245A subgroup of general category stock.

(2) *Passive category stock.* The analysis is the same as in paragraph (c)(1)(ii)(E)(2) of this section.

(3) *Section 951A category stock.* The analysis is the same as in paragraph (c)(1)(ii)(E)(3) of this section.

(F) *Summary.* For purpose of the allocation and apportionment of expenses, $13,600 of the stock of CFC1 is characterized as general category stock, $5,600 of which is in the section 245A subgroup and $8,000 of which is in the non-section 245A subgroup; $2,667 of the stock of CFC1 is characterized as passive category stock, all of which is in the non-section 245A subgroup; and $3,733 of the stock of CFC1 is characterized as section 951A category stock, all of which is in the non-section 245A subgroup.

(3) *Example 3: Modified gross income method*—(i) *Facts*—(A) USP, a domestic corporation, directly owns all of the stock of a controlled foreign corporation, CFC1. The tax book value of CFC1's stock is $100,000. CFC1 owns all of the stock of CFC2, a controlled foreign corporation. USP uses the modified gross income method described in § 1.861-12(c)(3)(iii) to characterize the stock in CFC1. USP's inclusion percentage is 100%.

(B) CFC1 earns $1,500 of foreign source gross tested income within the general category and $500 of foreign source gross subpart F income within the passive category. CFC1 incurs $200 of interest expense.

(C) CFC2 earns $3,000 of foreign source gross tested income within the general category, $2,000 of foreign source gross subpart F income within the general category, and $1,000 of specified foreign source general category income. CFC2 incurs $3,000 of interest expense.

(ii) *Analysis*—(A) *Step 1—(1) Determination of CFC2 gross income (net of interest expense).* CFC2 has total gross income of $6,000. CFC2's $3,000 of interest expense is apportioned among the statutory groupings of gross income based on the gross income of CFC2 to determine the gross income (net of interest expense) of CFC2 in each statutory grouping. As a result, $1,500 ($3,000/$6,000 x $3,000) of interest expense is apportioned to foreign source gross tested income within the general category, $1,000 ($2,000/$6,000 x $3,000) of interest expense is apportioned to foreign source gross subpart F income within the general category, and $500 ($1,000/$6,000 x $3,000) of interest expense is apportioned to specified foreign source general category income. Accordingly, CFC2 has the following amounts of gross income (net of interest expense): $1,500 ($3,000 – $1,500) of foreign source gross tested income within the general category, $1,000 ($2,000 – $1,000) of foreign source gross subpart F income within the general category, and $500 ($1,000 – $500) of specified foreign source general category income.

(2) *Determination of CFC1 gross income (net of interest expense).* Before including the gross income consisting of subpart F income and tested income (net of interest expense) of CFC2, CFC1 has total gross income of $2,500, including $500 of CFC2's specified foreign source general category income which is combined with CFC1's items of gross income under § 1.861-9(j)(2)(ii). CFC1's $200 of interest expense is apportioned among the statutory groupings of gross income of CFC1 to determine the gross income (net of interest expense) of CFC1 in each statutory grouping. As a result, $120 ($1,500/$2,500 x $200) of interest expense is apportioned to foreign source gross tested income within the general category, $40 ($500/$2,500 x $200) to foreign source gross subpart F income within the passive category, and $40 ($500/$2,500 x $200) to specified foreign source general category income. Accordingly, CFC1 has the following amounts of gross income (net of interest expense) before including the gross income (net of interest expense) of CFC2: $1,380 ($1,500 – $120) of foreign source gross tested income within the general category, $460 ($500 – $40) of foreign source gross subpart F income within the passive category, and $460 ($500 – $40) of specified foreign source general category income. After including the gross income consisting of subpart F income and tested income (net of interest expense) of CFC2, CFC1 has the following amounts of gross income (net of interest expense): $2,880 ($1,380 + $1,500) of foreign source gross tested income within the general category, $1,000 of foreign source gross subpart F income within the general category, $460 of specified foreign source general category income, and $460 of foreign source gross subpart F income within the passive category.

(3) *Characterization of CFC1 stock.* CFC1 is considered to have a total of $4,800 of gross income (net of interest expense) for purposes of characterizing the stock of CFC1. Accordingly, CFC1's stock is characterized as $60,000 ($2,880/$4,800 x $100,000) in the foreign source gross tested income statutory grouping within the general category, $20,834 ($1,000/$4,800 x $100,000) in the foreign source gross subpart F income statutory grouping within the general category, $9,583 ($460/$4,800 x $100,000) in the specified foreign source general category income statutory grouping, and $9,583 ($460/$4,800 x $100,000) in the foreign source gross subpart F income statutory grouping within the passive category.

(B) *Step 2.* The portion of the value of the stock of CFC1 that is general category gross tested income stock is $60,000. USP's inclusion percentage is 100%. Accordingly, under paragraph (a)(2) of this section, all of the $60,000 of the stock of CFC1 is assigned to the section 951A category.

(C) *Step 3.* No portion of the stock of CFC1 is resourced gross tested income or assigned to the resourced gross subpart F income statutory group in any treaty category. Accordingly, no portion of the stock of CFC1 is assigned to a treaty category under paragraph (a)(3) of this section.

(D) *Step 4—(1) General category stock.* The total portion of the value of the stock of CFC1 that is general category stock is $30,417, which is equal to $20,834 (the value of the portion of the stock of CFC1 assigned to the subpart F income statutory grouping within the general category income statutory grouping) plus $9,583 (the value of the portion of the stock of CFC1 assigned to the specified foreign source general category income statutory grouping).

(2) Passive category stock. The total portion of the value of the stock of CFC1 that is passive category stock is $9,583.

(3) U.S. source category stock. No portion of the value of the stock of CFC1 is U.S. source category stock.

(E) *Step 5—(1) General category stock.* All of the value of the general category gross tested income stock of CFC1 was assigned to the section 951A category in Step 2. Accordingly, under paragraph (a)(5)(ii) of this section, the value of the stock of CFC1 assigned to the section 245A subgroup of general category stock is $9,583, which is equal to the value of the portion assigned to the specified foreign source general category income statutory grouping. Under paragraph (a)(5)(v) of this section, the remainder of the general category stock of CFC1, $20,834, is assigned to the non-section 245A subgroup of general category stock.

(2) Passive category stock. No portion of the passive category stock of CFC1 is in the foreign source gross tested income statutory grouping or the specified foreign source passive category income statutory grouping. Accordingly, under paragraph (a)(5)(iii) of this section, no portion of the value of the stock of CFC1 is assigned to the section 245A subgroup. Under paragraph (a)(5)(v) of this section, the passive category stock of CFC1, $9,534, is assigned to the non-section 245A subgroup of passive category stock.

(3) Section 951A category stock. Under paragraph (a)(5)(v) of this section, all of the section 951A category stock, $60,000, is assigned to the non-section 245A subgroup of section 951A category stock.

(F) *Summary.* For purposes of the allocation and apportionment of expenses, $60,000 of the stock of CFC1 is characterized as section 951A category stock, all of which is in the non-section 245A subgroup; $30,417 of the stock of CFC1 is characterized as general category stock, $9,583 of which is in the section 245A subgroup and $20,834 of which is in the non-section 245A subgroup; and $9,583 of the stock of CFC1 is characterized as passive category stock, all of which is in the non-section 245A subgroup.

(d) *Applicability dates.*—This section applies for taxable years that both begin after December 31, 2017, and end on or after December 4, 2018. [Reg. § 1.861-13.]

Income from U.S. Sources: Transition Rules

Income from Source: Interest Expense Allocation.—Temporary Reg. § 1.861-13T, relating to transition rules for the allocation and apportionment of interest expense for the purposes of the foreign tax credit rules and certain other international tax provisions, is also proposed as final (published in the Federal Register on August 2, 1989).

§ 1.861-13. Transition rules for interest expenses.

Determination of the Foreign Tax Credit: Guidance

Determination of the Foreign Tax Credit: Guidance.—Amendments to Reg. § 1.861-14, relating to the determination of the foreign tax credit under the Internal Revenue Code, including changes made by the Tax Cuts and Jobs Act, are proposed (published in the Federal Register on December 7, 2018) (REG-105600-18).

Par. 9. Section 1.861-14 is amended by:

1. Removing the language ", except that section 936 corporations (as defined in § 1.861-11(d)(2)(ii)) are also included within the affiliated group to the extent provided in paragraph (d)(2) of this section" from the first sentence of paragraph (d)(1).

2. Removing and reserving paragraph (d)(2).

§ 1.861-14. Special rules for allocating and apportioning certain expenses (other than interest expense) of an affiliated group of corporations.

Income from U.S. Sources: Allocation and Apportionment

Income from U.S. Sources: Allocation and Apportionment of Expenses.—Temporary Reg. § 1.861-14T, relating to the allocation and apportionment of interest expense and certain other expenses for purposes of the foreign tax credit rules and certain other international tax provisions, is also proposed as final regulations and, when adopted, would become § 1.861-14 (published in the Federal Register on September 14, 1988).

§ 1.861-14. Special rules for allocating and apportioning certain expenses (other than interest expense) of an affiliated group of corporations.

Determination of the Foreign Tax Credit: Guidance

Determination of the Foreign Tax Credit: Guidance.—Amendments to Reg. §1.861-17, relating to the determination of the foreign tax credit under the Internal Revenue Code, including changes made by the Tax Cuts and Jobs Act, are proposed (published in the Federal Register on December 7, 2018) (REG-105600-18).

Par. 10. Section 1.861-17 is amended by:

1. Adding paragraph (e)(3).
2. Removing and reserving paragraph (g).
3. Adding paragraph (i).

The additions and revisions read as follows:

§1.861-17. Allocation and apportionment of research and experimental expenditures.

* * *

(e) * * *

(3) *Change of method for first taxable year beginning after December 31, 2017.*—A taxpayer otherwise subject to the binding election described in paragraph (e)(1) of this section may change its method once for its first taxable year beginning after December 31, 2017, without the prior consent of the Commissioner. The taxpayer's use of a new method constitutes a binding election to use the new method for its return filed for the first year for which the taxpayer uses the new method and for four taxable years thereafter.

* * *

(g) [Reserved]

* * *

(i) *Applicability date.*—This section applies to taxable years that both begin after December 31, 2017, and end on or after December 4, 2018.

Advance Payments for Goods and Long-Term Contracts: Existing Regulations Removed

Advance Payments for Goods and Long-Term Contracts: Existing Regulations Removed.—Amendments to Reg. §1.861-18, removing regulations regarding advance payments for goods and long-term contracts that are no longer necessary after the enactment of recent tax legislation, are proposed (published in the Federal Register on October 15, 2018) (REG-104872-18).

Par. 5. Section 1.861-18 is amended in paragraph (i)(4) by:

1. Removing *Example 2;*
2. Designating *Examples 1* and 3 as paragraphs (i)(4)(i) and (ii), respectively; and
3. In the heading for newly designated paragraph (i)(4)(ii), removing "3" and adding "2" in its place.

§1.861-18. Classification of transactions involving computer programs.

Global Dealing Operations: Allocation and Sourcing of Income and Deductions

Global Dealing Operations: Allocation and Sourcing of Income and Deductions.—Amendments to Reg. §1.863-3, relating to the allocation and sourcing of income, deductions, gains and losses from a global dealing operation, are proposed (published in the Federal Register on March 6, 1998) (REG-208299-90).

Par. 7. Section 1.863-3 is amended as follows:

1. Paragraph (h) is redesignated as paragraph (i).
2. A new paragraph (h) is added.

The addition reads as follows:

§1.863-3. Allocation and apportionment of income from certain sales of inventory.

* * *

(h) *Income from a global dealing operation.*—(1) *Purpose and scope.*—This paragraph (h) provides rules for sourcing income, gain and loss from a global dealing operation that, under the rules of §1.482-8, is earned by or allocated to a controlled taxpayer qualifying as a participant in a global dealing operation under §1.482-8(a)(2)(ii). This paragraph (h) does not apply to income earned by or allocated to a controlled taxpayer qualifying as a participant in a global dealing operation that is specifically sourced under sections 861, 862 or 865, or to substitute payments earned by a participant in a global dealing operation that are sourced under §1.861-2(a)(7) or §1.861-3(a)(6).

(2) *In general.*—The source of any income, gain or loss to which this section applies shall be determined by reference to the residence of the participant. For purposes of this paragraph (h), the residence of a participant shall be determined under section 988(a)(3)(B).

(3) *Qualified business units as participants in global dealing operations.*—(i) *In general.*—Except as otherwise provided in this paragraph (h), where a single controlled taxpayer conducts a global dealing operation through one or more qualified business units (QBUs), as defined in section 989(a) and §1.989(a)-1, the source of income, gain or loss generated by the global dealing operation and earned by or allocated to the controlled taxpayer shall be determined by applying the rules of §1.482-8 as if each QBU that performs activities of a regular dealer in securities as defined in §1.482-8(a)(2)(ii)(A) or the related activities described in §1.482-8(a)(2)(ii)(B) were a separate controlled taxpayer qualifying as a participant in the global dealing operation

within the meaning of § 1.482-8(a)(2)(ii). Accordingly, the amount of income sourced in the United States and outside of the United States shall be determined by treating the QBU as a participant in the global dealing operation, allocating income to each participant under § 1.482-8, as modified by paragraph (h)(3)(ii) of this section, and sourcing the income to the United States or outside of the United States under § 1.863-3(h)(2).

(ii) *Economic effects of a single legal entity.*—In applying the principles of § 1.482-8, the taxpayer shall take into account the economic effects of conducting a global dealing operation through a single entity instead of multiple legal entities. For example, since the entire capital of a corporation supports all of the entity's transactions, regardless of where those transactions may be booked, the payment of a guarantee fee within the entity is inappropriate and will be disregarded.

(iii) *Treatment of interbranch and interdesk amounts.*—An agreement among QBUs of the same taxpayer to allocate income, gain or loss from transactions with third parties is not a transaction because a taxpayer cannot enter into a contract with itself. For purposes of this paragraph (h)(3), however, such an agreement, including a risk transfer agreement (as defined in § 1.475(g)-2(b)) may be used to determine the source of global dealing income from transactions with third parties in the same manner and to the same extent that transactions between controlled taxpayers in a global dealing operation may be used to allocate income, gain or loss from the global dealing operation under the rules of § 1.482-8.

(iv) *Deemed QBU.*—For purposes of this paragraph (h)(3), a QBU shall include a U.S. trade or business that is deemed to exist because of the activities of a dependent agent in the United States, without regard to the books and records requirement of § 1.989(a)-1(b).

(v) *Examples.*—The following examples illustrate this paragraph (h)(3).

Example 1. Use of comparable uncontrolled financial transactions method to source global dealing income between branches. (i) F is a foreign bank that acts as a market maker in foreign currency through branch offices in London, New York, and Tokyo. In a typical business day, the foreign exchange desk in F's U.S. branch (USFX) enters into several hundred spot and forward contracts on the interbank market to purchase and sell Deutsche marks (DM) with unrelated third parties. Each of F's branches, including USFX, employs both marketers and traders for their foreign currency dealing. In addition, USFX occasionally transfers risk with respect to its third party DM contracts to F's London and Tokyo branches. These interbranch transfers are entered into in the same manner as trades with unrelated third parties. On a typical day, risk management responsibility for no more than 10% of USFX's DM trades are transferred interbranch. F records these transfers by making notations on the books of each branch that is a party to the transfers. The accounting procedures are nearly identical to those followed when a branch enters into an offsetting hedge with a third party. USFX maintains contemporaneous records of its interbranch transfers and third party transactions, separated according to type of trade and counterparty. Moreover, the volume of USFX's DM spot purchases and sales each day consistently provides USFX with third party transactions that are contemporaneous with the transfers between the branches.

(ii) As provided in paragraph (h)(3)(i) of this section, USFX and F's other branches that trade DM are participants in a global dealing operation. Accordingly, the principles of § 1.482-8 apply in determining the source of income earned by F's qualified business units that are participants in a global dealing operation. Applying the comparability factors in § 1.482-8(a)(3) shows that USFX's interbranch transfers and uncontrolled DM-denominated spot and forward contracts have no material differences. Because USFX sells DM in uncontrolled transactions and transfers risk management responsibility for DM-denominated contracts, and the uncontrolled transactions and interbranch transfers are consistently entered into contemporaneously, the interbranch transfers provide a reliable measure of an arm's length allocation of third party income from F's global dealing operation in DM-denominated contracts. This allocation of third party income is treated as U.S. source in accordance with §§ 1.863-3(h) and 1.988-4(h) and accordingly will be treated as income effectively connected with F's U.S. trade or business under § 1.864-4.

Example 2. Residual profit split between branches. (i) F is a bank organized in country X that has a AAA credit rating and engages in a global dealing operation in foreign currency options through branch offices in London, New York, and Tokyo. F has dedicated marketers and traders in each branch who work closely together to design and sell foreign currency options that meet the particular needs of customers. Each branch also employs general salespeople who sell standardized foreign currency options, as well as other financial products and foreign currency offered by F. F's traders work from a common book of transactions that is risk managed at each branch during local business hours. Accordingly, all three branches share the responsibility for risk managing the book of products. Personnel in the home office of F process and confirm trades, reconcile trade tickets, and provide ongoing administrative support (back office services) for the other branches. The global dealing operation has generated $223 of operating profit for the period.

(ii) Under § 1.863-3(h), F applies § 1.482-8 to allocate global dealing income among its branches, because F's London, New York, and Tokyo branches are treated as participants in a global dealing operation that deals in foreign currency options under § 1.482-8(a)(2). After analyzing the foreign currency options business, F has determined that the residual profit split method is the best method to determine an arm's length amount of compensation allocable to each participant in the global dealing operation.

(iii) Under the first step of the residual profit split method (§ 1.482-8(e)(6)(ii)), F identifies and compensates the routine contributions performed by each participant. F determines that an arm's length compensation for general salespeople is $3, $4, and $5 in New York, London, and Tokyo, respectively, and that the home office incurred $11 of expenses in providing the back office services. Since F's capital legally supports all of the obligations of the branches, no amount is allocated to the home office of F for the provision of capital.

(iv) The second step of the residual profit split method (§1.482-8(e)(6)(iii)) requires that the residual profit be allocated to participants according to their nonroutine contributions. F determines that a multi-factor formula best reflects these contributions. After a detailed functional analysis, and applying the comparability factors in §1.482-8(a)(3), 40% of the residual profit is allocated to the London branch, 35% to the New York branch, and the remaining 25% to the Tokyo branch. Thus, the residual profit of $200 ($223 operating profit minus $12 general salesperson commissions minus $11 back office allocation) is allocated $80 to London (40% allocation × $200), $70 to New York (35% × $200) and $50 to Tokyo (25% × $200).

Example 3. Residual profit split—deemed branches. (i) P, a U.K. corporation, conducts a global dealing operation in notional principal contracts, directly and through a U.S. subsidiary (USsub) and a Japanese subsidiary (Jsub). P is the counterparty to all transactions entered into with third parties. P, USsub, and Jsub each employ marketers and traders who work closely together to design and sell derivative products to meet the particular needs of customers. USsub also employs personnel who process and confirm trades, reconcile trade tickets and provide ongoing administrative support (back office services) for the global dealing operation. The global dealing operation maintains a single common book for each type of risk, and the book is maintained where the head trader for that type of risk is located. However, P, USsub, and Jsub have authorized a trader located in each of the other affiliates to risk manage its books during periods when the primary trading location is closed. This grant of authority is necessary because marketers, regardless of their location, are expected to sell all of the group's products, and need to receive pricing information with respect to products during their clients' business hours, even if the booking location is closed. The global dealing operation has generated $180 of operating profit for the period.

(ii) Because employees of USsub have authority to enter into contracts in the name of P, P is treated as being engaged in a trade or business in the United States through a deemed QBU. §1.863-3(h)(3)(iv). Similarly, under U.S. principles, P would be treated as being engaged in business in Japan through a QBU. Under §1.482-8(a)(2), P, USsub, and Jsub are participants in the global dealing operation relating to notional principal contracts. Additionally, under §1.863-3(h)(3), the U.S. and Japanese QBUs are treated as participants in a global dealing operation for purposes of sourcing the income from that operation. Under §1.863-3(h), P applies the methods in §1.482-8 to determine the source of income allocated to the U.S. and non-U.S. QBUs of P.

(iii) After analyzing the notional principal contract business, P has concluded that the residual profit split method is the best method to allocate income under §1.482-8 and to source income under §1.863-3(h).

(iv) Under the first step of the residual profit split method (§1.482-8(e)(6)(ii)), P identifies and compensates the routine contributions performed by each participant. Although the back office function does not give rise to participant status, in the context of a residual profit split allocation, the back office function is relevant for purposes of receiving remuneration for a routine contribution to a global dealing operation. P determines that an arm's length compensation for the back office is $20. Since the back office services constitute a routine contribution, $20 of income is allocated to USsub under step 1 of the residual profit split method. Similarly, as the arm's length compensation for the risk to which P is subject as counterparty is $40, $40 is allocated to P as compensation for acting as counterparty.

(v) The second step of the residual profit split method (§1.482-8(e)(6)(iii)) requires that the residual profit be allocated to participants according to the relative value of their nonroutine contributions. Under P's transfer pricing method, P allocates the residual profit of $120 ($180 gross income minus $20 for back office services minus $40 compensation for the routine contribution of acting as counterparty) using a multi-factor formula that reflects the relative value of the nonroutine contributions. Applying the comparability factors set out in §1.482-8(a)(3), P allocates 40% of the residual profit to P, 35% of the residual profit to USsub, and the remaining 25% of residual profit to Jsub. Accordingly, under step 2, $48 is allocated to P, $42 is allocated to USsub, and $30 is allocated to Jsub. Under §1.863-3(h), the amounts allocated under the residual profit split is sourced according to the residence of each participant to which it is allocated.

(vi) Because the $40 allocated to P consists of compensation for the use of capital, the allocation is sourced according to where the capital is employed. Accordingly, the $40 is sourced 35% to P's deemed QBU in the United States under §1.863-3(h)(3)(iv) and 65% to non-U.S. sources.

* * *

Income from U.S. Sources: Allocation and Apportionment

Income from U.S. Sources: Allocation and Apportionment of Expenses.—Temporary Reg. §1.863-3T (redesignated as Temporary Reg. §1.863-3AT by T.D. 8687), relating to the allocation and apportionment of interest expense and certain other expenses for purposes of the foreign tax credit rules and certain other international tax provisions, is also proposed as a final regulation and, when adopted, would become §1.863-3A (published in the Federal Register on September 14, 1988).

§1.863-3A. Income from the sale of personal property derived partly from within and partly from without the United States.

Global Dealing Operations: Allocation and Sourcing of Income and Deductions

Global Dealing Operations: Allocation and Sourcing of Income and Deductions.—Amendments to Reg. §1.863-7, relating to the allocation and sourcing of income, deductions, gains and losses from a global dealing operation, are proposed (published in the Federal Register on March 6, 1998) (REG-208299-90).

☐ Par. 8. Section 1.863-7(a)(1) is amended by revising the second sentence to read as follows:

§1.863-7. Allocation of income attributable to certain notional principal contracts under section 863(a).—(a) *Scope.*—(1) *Introduction.*—* * * This section does not apply to income from a section 988 transaction (as defined in section 988(c) and §1.988-1(a)), or to income from a global dealing operation (as defined in §1.482-8(a)(2)(i)) that is sourced under the rules of §1.863-3(h). * * *

* * *

Section 1256 Contracts: Swap Exclusions

Section 1256 Contracts: Swap Exclusions.—Amendment to Reg. §1.863-7, providing guidance on the category of swaps and similar agreements that are within the scope of Code Sec. 1256(b)(2)(B), are proposed (published in the Federal Register on September 16, 2011) (REG-111283-11).

☐ Par. 4. Section 1.863-7 is amended by:

1. Revising the third sentence and removing the fourth sentence of paragraph (a)(1).
2. Adding two sentences to the end of paragraph (a)(2).

The revision and addition read as follows:

§1.863-7. Allocation of income attributable to certain notional principal contracts under section 863(a).—(a) *Scope.*—(1) *Introduction.*—* * * Notional principal contract income is income attributable to a notional principal contract as defined in §1.446-3(c). * * *

(2) * * * The rules of this section apply to notional principal contracts as defined in §1.446-3(c) that are entered into on or after the date of publication of a Treasury decision adopting these rules as final regulations in the **Federal Register**. Section 1.863-7 as contained in 26 CFR part 1 revised April 1, 2011, continues to apply to notional principal contracts entered into before the date of publication of a Treasury decision adopting these rules as final regulations in the **Federal Register**.

* * *

Global Dealing Operations: Allocation and Sourcing of Income and Deductions

Global Dealing Operations: Allocation and Sourcing of Income and Deductions.—Amendments to Reg. §§1.864-4 and 1.864-6, relating to the allocation and sourcing of income, deductions, gains and losses from a global dealing operation, are proposed (published in the Federal Register on March 6, 1998) (REG-208299-90).

☐ Par. 9. Section 1.864-4 is amended as follows:

1. Paragraphs (c)(2)(iv), (c)(2)(v), (c)(3)(ii), and (c)(5)(vi)(*a*) and (*b*) are redesignated as (c)(2)(v), (c)(2)(vi), (c)(3)(iii), and (c)(5)(vi)(*b*) and (*c*), respectively.
2. New paragraphs (c)(2)(iv), (c)(3)(ii), and (c)(5)(vi)(*a*) are added.

The additions read as follows:

§1.864-4. U.S. source income effectively connected with U.S. business.

* * *

(c) * * *

(2) * * *

(iv) *Special rule relating to a global dealing operation.*—An asset used in a global dealing operation, as defined in §1.482-8(a)(2)(i), will be treated as an asset used in a U.S. trade or business only if and to the extent that the U.S. trade or business is a participant in the global dealing operation under §1.863-3(h)(3), and income, gain or loss produced by the asset is U.S. source under §1.863-3(h) or would be treated as U.S. source if §1.863-3(h) were to apply to such amounts.

* * *

(3) * * *

(ii) *Special rule relating to a global dealing operation.*—A U.S. trade or business shall be treated as a material factor in the realization of income, gain or loss derived in a global dealing operation, as defined in §1.482-8(a)(2)(i), only if and to the extent that the U.S. trade or business is a participant in the global dealing operation under §1.863-3(h)(3), and income, gain or loss realized by the U.S. trade or business is U.S. source under §1.863-3(h) or would be treated as U.S. source if §1.863-3(h) were to apply to such amounts.

* * *

(5) * * *

(vi) * * *

(*a*) *Certain income earned by a global dealing operation.*—Notwithstanding paragraph (c)(5)(ii) of this section, U.S. source interest, including substitute interest as defined in §1.861-2(a)(7), and dividend income, including substitute dividends as defined in §1.861-3(a)(6), derived by a participant in a global dealing operation, as defined in §1.482-8(a)(2)(i), shall be treated as attributable to the foreign corporation's U.S. trade or business, only if and to the extent that the income would be treated as U.S. source if §1.863-3(h) were to apply to such amounts.

☐ Par. 10. Section 1.864-6 is amended as follows: 1. Paragraph (b)(2)(ii)(*d*)(*3*) and (b)(3)(ii)(*c*) are added. 2. Paragraph (b)(3)(i) is revised by adding a new sentence after the last sentence. The additions and revision read as follows:

§1.864-6. Income, gain or loss attributable to an office or other fixed place of business in the United States.

* * *

(b) * * *

(2) * * *

(ii) * * *

(*d*) * * *

(*3*) *Certain income earned by a global dealing operation.*—Notwithstanding paragraphs (b)(2)(ii)(*a*) or (*b*) of this section, foreign source interest, including substitute interest as defined in §1.861-2(a)(7), or dividend income, including substitute dividends as defined in §1.861-3(a)(6), derived by a participant in a global dealing operation, as defined in §1.482-8(a)(2)(i) shall be treated as attributable to the foreign corporation's U.S. trade or business only if and to the extent that the income would be treated as U.S. source if §1.863-3(h) were to apply to such amounts. * * *

(3) * * *

(i) * * * Notwithstanding paragraphs (b)(3)(i)(*1*) and (*2*) of this section, an office or other fixed place of business of a nonresident alien individual or a foreign corporation which is located in the United States and which is a participant in a global dealing operation, as defined in §1.482-8(a)(2)(i), shall be considered to be a material factor in the realization of foreign source income, gain or loss, only if and to the extent that such income, gain or loss would be treated as U.S. source if §1.863-3(h) were to apply to such amounts.

(ii) * * *

(*c*) *Property sales in a global dealing operation.*—Notwithstanding paragraphs (b)(3)(ii)(*a*) or (*b*) of this section, personal property described in section 1221(1) and sold in the active conduct of a taxpayer's global dealing operation, as defined in §1.482-8(a)(2)(i), shall be presumed to have been sold for use, consumption, or disposition outside of the United States only if and to the extent that the income, gain or loss to which the sale gives rise would be sourced outside of the United States if §1.863-3(h) were to apply to such amounts.

Income from U.S. Sources: Related Person

Controlled Foreign Corporations: Investment of Earnings in U.S. Property: Related Person Factoring Income.—Temporary Reg. §1.864-8T, relating to the treatment of related person factoring income, is also proposed as a final regulation and, when adopted, would become Reg. §1.864-8 (published in the Federal Register on June 14, 1988).

§1.864-8. Treatment of related persons.

Foreign Taxpayers: Derivative Financial Instruments: Safe Harbors

Foreign Taxpayers: Derivative Financial Instruments: Safe Harbors.—Reg. §1.864(b)-1, providing that foreign taxpayers who effect transactions in derivative financial instruments for their own accounts are not thereby engaged in a trade or business in the United States if they are not dealers in stocks, securities, commodities or derivatives, is proposed (published in the Federal Register on June 12, 1998) (REG-106031-98) (corrected 7/15/98).

☐ Par. 2. Section 1.864(b)-1 is added to read as follows:

§1.864(b)-1. Trading in derivatives.—(a) *Trading for taxpayer's own account.*—As used in part I (section 861 and following) and part II (section 871 and following), subchapter N, chapter 1 of the Internal Revenue Code (Code), and chapter 3 (section 1441 and following) of the Code, and the regulations thereunder, if a taxpayer is an eligible nondealer, the term *engaged in trade or business within the United States* does not include effecting transactions in derivatives for the taxpayer's own account, including hedging transactions within the meaning of §1.1221-2.

(b) *Definitions.*—(1) *Eligible nondealer.*—For purposes of this section, an *eligible nondealer* is a foreign corporation or a person that is not a resident of the United States, and either of which is not, at any place (domestic or foreign), nor at any time during that person's taxable year, any of the following—

(i) A dealer in stocks or securities as defined in §1.864-2(c)(2)(iv)(*a*);

(ii) A dealer in commodities as that term is used in §1.864-2(d); or

(iii) A person that regularly offers to enter into, assume, offset, assign or otherwise terminate positions in derivatives with customers in the ordinary course of a trade or business, including regularly holding oneself out, in the ordinary course of one's trade or business, as being willing and able to enter into either side of a derivative transaction.

(2) *Derivative.*—For purposes of this section, the term *derivative* includes—

(i) An interest rate, currency (as defined in paragraph (b)(3) of this section), equity, or commodity (as the term is used in section 864(b)(2)(B) and §1.864-2(d)) notional principal contract (as the term is used in section 475(c)(2)); or

(ii) An evidence of an interest, or a derivative financial instrument (including any option, forward contract, short position and any similar financial instrument), in any—

(A) Commodity (as the term is used in section 864(b)(2)(B) and §1.864-2(d));

(B) Currency (as defined in paragraph (b)(3) of this section);

(C) Share of stock (as the term is used in §1.864-2(c)(2));

(D) Partnership or beneficial ownership interest in a widely held or publicly traded partnership or trust;

(E) Note, bond, debenture, or other evidence of indebtedness; or

(F) Notional principal contract described in paragraph (b)(2)(i) of this section.

(3) *Limitation.*—For purposes of this section, the term *currency* is limited to currencies of a kind customarily dealt in on an organized commodity exchange. [Reg. § 1.864(b)-1.]

Gain or Loss of Foreign Person: Sale or Exchange: Partnership Interest

Gain or Loss of Foreign Person: Sale or Exchange: Partnership Interest.—Reg. § 1.864(c)(8)-1, affecting certain foreign persons that recognize gain or loss from the sale or exchange of an interest in a partnership that is engaged in a trade or business within the United States, is proposed (published in the Federal Register on December 27, 2018) (REG-113604-18).

Par. 2. Section 1.864(c)(8)-1 is added to read as follows:

§ 1.864(c)(8)-1. Gain or loss by foreign persons on the disposition of certain partnership interests.—(a) *Overview.*—This section provides rules and definitions under section 864(c)(8). Paragraph (b) of this section provides the general rule treating gain or loss recognized by a nonresident alien individual or foreign corporation from the sale or exchange of a partnership interest as effectively connected gain or effectively connected loss. Paragraph (c) of this section provides rules for determining the limitation on the amount of effectively connected gain or effectively connected loss under section 864(c)(8) and paragraph (b) of this section. Paragraph (d) of this section provides rules regarding coordination with section 897. Paragraph (e) of this section provides rules regarding certain tiered partnerships. Paragraph (f) of this section provides rules regarding U.S. income tax treaties. Paragraph (g) of this section provides definitions. Paragraph (h) of this section provides a rule regarding certain contributions of property to a partnership. Paragraph (i) of this section contains examples illustrating the rules set forth in this section. Paragraph (j) of this section provides the applicability date.

(b) *Gain or loss treated as effectively connected gain or loss.*—(1) *In general.*—Notwithstanding any other provision of subtitle A of the Internal Revenue Code, if a foreign transferor owns, directly or indirectly, an interest in a partnership that is engaged in the conduct of a trade or business within the United States, outside capital gain, outside capital loss, outside ordinary gain, or outside ordinary loss (each as defined in paragraph (b)(2) of this section) recognized by the foreign transferor on the transfer of all (or any portion) of the interest is treated as effectively connected gain or effectively connected loss, subject to the limit described in paragraph (b)(3) of this section. Except as provided in paragraph (d) of this section, this section does not apply to prevent any portion of the gain or loss that is otherwise treated as effectively connected gain or effectively connected loss under provisions of the Internal Revenue Code other than section 864(c)(8) from being so treated.

(2) *Determination of outside gain and loss.*—(i) *In general.*—The amount of gain or loss recognized by the foreign transferor in connection with the transfer of its partnership interest is determined under all relevant provisions of the Internal Revenue Code and the regulations thereunder. See, e.g., §§ 1.741-1(a) and 1.751-1(a)(2). For purposes of this section, the amount of gain or loss that is treated as capital gain or capital loss under sections 741 and 751 is referred to as *outside capital gain* or *outside capital loss*, respectively. The amount of gain or loss that is treated as ordinary gain or ordinary loss under sections 741 and 751 is referred to as *outside ordinary gain* or *outside ordinary loss*, respectively.

(ii) *Nonrecognition provisions.*—A foreign transferor's gain or loss recognized in connection with the transfer of its partnership interest does not include gain or loss to the extent that the gain or loss is not recognized by reason of one or more nonrecognition provisions of the Internal Revenue Code.

(3) *Limitations.*—This paragraph (b)(3) limits the amount of gain or loss recognized by a foreign transferor that may be treated as effectively connected gain or effectively connected loss.

(i) *Capital gain limitation.*—Outside capital gain recognized by a foreign transferor is treated as effectively connected gain to the extent it does not exceed aggregate deemed sale EC capital gain determined under paragraph (c)(3)(ii)(B) of this section.

(ii) *Capital loss limitation.*—Outside capital loss recognized by a foreign transferor is treated as effectively connected loss to the extent it does not exceed aggregate deemed sale EC capital loss determined under paragraph (c)(3)(ii)(B) of this section.

(iii) *Ordinary gain limitation.*—Outside ordinary gain recognized by a foreign transferor is treated as effectively connected gain to the extent it does not exceed aggregate deemed sale EC ordinary gain determined under paragraph (c)(3)(ii)(A) of this section.

(iv) *Ordinary loss limitation.*—Outside ordinary loss recognized by a foreign transferor is treated as effectively connected loss to the extent it does not exceed aggregate deemed sale EC ordinary loss determined under paragraph (c)(3)(ii)(A) of this section.

(c) *Amount treated as effectively connected with the conduct of a trade or business within the United States.*—This paragraph (c) describes the steps to be followed in computing the limitations described in paragraph (b)(3) of this section.

(1) *Step 1: Determine deemed sale gain and loss.*—Determine the amount of gain or loss that the partnership would recognize with respect to each of its assets (other than interests in partnerships described in paragraph (e) of this section) upon a deemed sale of all of the partnership's assets on the date of the transfer of the partnership interest described in paragraph (b)(1) of this section (deemed sale). For this purpose, a deemed sale is a hypothetical sale by the part-

nership to an unrelated person of each of its assets (tangible and intangible) in a fully taxable transaction for cash in an amount equal to the fair market value of each asset (taking into account section 7701(g)) immediately before the partner's transfer of the interest in the partnership. For rules concerning the deemed sale of certain partnership interests, see paragraph (e) of this section.

(2) *Step 2: Determine deemed sale EC gain and loss.*—(i) *In general.*—With respect to each asset deemed sold in paragraph (c)(1) of this section, determine the amount of gain or loss from the deemed sale that would be treated as effectively connected gain or effectively connected loss (including by reason of section 897, taking into account any exceptions thereto, such as section 897(k) or section 897(l)). Gain described in this paragraph (c)(2) is referred to as *deemed sale EC gain*, and loss described in this paragraph (c)(2) is referred to as *deemed sale EC loss*. Section 864 and the regulations thereunder apply for purposes of determining whether gain or loss that would arise in a deemed asset sale would be treated as effectively connected gain or loss. For purposes of this paragraph (c)(2)(i), gain or loss from the deemed sale of an asset is treated as attributable to an office or other fixed place of business maintained by the partnership in the United States, and is not treated as sold for use, disposition, or consumption outside the United States in a sale in which an office or other fixed place of business maintained by the partnership in a foreign country materially participated in the sale.

(ii) *Exception.*—Gain or loss from the deemed sale of an asset described in paragraph (c)(2)(i) of this section (other than a United States real property interest) is not treated as deemed sale EC gain or deemed sale EC loss if—

(A) No income or gain produced by the asset was taxable as income that was effectively connected with the conduct of a trade or business within the United States by the partnership (or a predecessor of the partnership) during the ten-year period ending on the date of the transfer; and

(B) The asset has not been used, or held for use, in the conduct of a trade or business within the United States by the partnership (or a predecessor of the partnership) during the ten-year period ending on the date of the transfer.

(3) *Step 3: Determine the foreign transferor's distributive share of deemed sale EC gain or deemed sale EC loss.*—(i) *In general.*—Determine the foreign transferor's distributive share of deemed sale EC gain and deemed sale EC loss. A foreign transferor's distributive share of deemed sale EC gain or deemed sale EC loss with respect to each asset is the amount of the deemed sale EC gain and deemed sale EC loss determined under paragraph (c)(2) of this section that would have been allocated to the foreign transferor by the partnership under all applicable Code sections (including section 704) upon the deemed sale described in paragraph (c)(1) of this section, taking into account allocations of tax items applying the principles of section 704(c), including any remedial allocations under § 1.704-3(d), and any section 743 basis adjustment pursuant to § 1.743-1(j)(3)).

(ii) *Aggregate deemed sale EC items.*—(A) *Ordinary gain or loss.*—A foreign transferor's *aggregate deemed sale EC ordinary gain* (if the aggregate results in a gain) or *aggregate deemed sale EC ordinary loss* (if the aggregate results in a loss) is the sum of—

(1) The portion of the foreign transferor's distributive share of deemed sale EC gain and deemed sale EC loss that is attributable to the deemed sale of the partnership's assets that are section 751(a) property; and

(2) Deemed sale EC gain and deemed sale EC loss from the sale of assets that are section 751(a) property that would be allocated to the foreign transferor with respect to interests in partnerships that are engaged in the conduct of a trade or business within the United States under paragraph (e)(1)(ii) of this section upon the deemed asset sales described in paragraph (e)(1)(i) of this section.

(B) *Capital gain or loss.*—A foreign transferor's *aggregate deemed sale EC capital gain* (if the aggregate of the foreign transferor's distributive share of the deemed sale EC capital gain and loss results in a gain) or *aggregate deemed sale EC capital loss* (if the aggregate of the foreign transferor's distributive share of the deemed sale EC capital gain and loss results in a loss) is the sum of—

(1) The portion of the foreign transferor's distributive share of deemed sale EC gain and deemed sale EC loss that is attributable to the deemed sale of assets that are not section 751(a) property; and

(2) Deemed sale EC gain and deemed sale EC loss from the sale of assets that are not section 751(a) property and that would be allocated to the foreign transferor with respect to all interests in partnerships that are engaged in the conduct of a trade or business within the United States under paragraph (e)(1)(ii) of this section upon the deemed asset sales described in paragraph (e)(1)(i) of this section.

(iii) *Partial transfers.*—If a foreign transferor transfers less than all of its interest in a partnership, then for purposes of paragraph (c)(3)(i) of this section, the foreign transferor's distributive share of deemed sale EC gain and deemed sale EC loss is determined by reference to the amount of deemed sale EC gain or deemed sale EC loss determined under paragraph (c)(3)(i) of this section that is attributable to the portion of the foreign transferor's partnership interest that was transferred.

(d) *Coordination with section 897.*—If a foreign transferor transfers an interest in a partnership in a transfer that is subject to section 864(c)(8), and the partnership owns one or more United States real property interests (as defined in section 897(c)), then the foreign transferor determines its effectively connected gain and effectively connected loss under this section, and not pursuant to section 897(g). Accordingly, with respect to a transfer described in the preceding sentence, section 864(c)(8)(C) does not reduce the amount of gain or loss treated as effectively connected gain or loss under this section. For rules regarding a transfer not subject to section 864(c)(8) of an interest in a partnership that owns one or more United States real property interests, see section 897(g) and the regulations thereunder.

(e) *Tiered partnerships.*—(1) *Transfers of upper-tier partnerships.*—Assets sold in a deemed sale described in paragraph (c)(1) of this section do not include interests in partnerships that are engaged in the conduct of a trade or business within the United States or interests in partnerships that hold, directly or indirectly, partnerships that are engaged in the conduct of a trade or business within the United States. Rather, if a foreign transferor transfers an interest in a partnership (upper-tier partnership) that owns, directly or indirectly, an interest in one or more partnerships that are engaged in the conduct of a trade or business within the United States, then—

(i) Beginning with the lowest-tier partnership that is engaged in the conduct of a trade or business within the United States in a chain of partnerships and going up the chain, each partnership that is engaged in the conduct of a trade or business within the United States is treated as selling its assets in a deemed sale in accordance with the principles of paragraph (c)(1) of this section; and

(ii) Each partnership must determine its deemed sale EC gain and deemed sale EC loss in accordance with the principles of paragraph (c)(2) of this section, and determine the distributive share of deemed sale EC gain and deemed sale EC loss for each partner that is either a partnership (in which the foreign transferor is a direct or indirect partner) or a foreign transferor, in accordance with the principles of paragraph (c)(3)(i) of this section.

(2) *Transfers by upper-tier partnerships.*—If a foreign transferor is a direct or indirect partner in an upper-tier partnership and the upper-tier partnership transfers an interest in a partnership that is engaged in the conduct of a trade or business within the United States (including a partnership held indirectly through one or more partnerships), then the principles of this section (including paragraph (e)(1) of this section) apply with respect to the gain or loss on the transfer that is allocated to the foreign transferor by the upper-tier partnership.

(3) *Coordination with section 897.*—For purposes of this paragraph (e), a lower-tier partnership that holds one or more United States real property interests is treated as engaged in the conduct of a trade or business within the United States.

(f) *Income tax treaties.*—(1) *In general.*—This paragraph (f) describes how the provisions of a U.S. income tax treaty apply to the transfer by a foreign transferor that is eligible for benefits under the treaty of an interest in a partnership that is engaged in the conduct of a trade or business within the United States.

(2) *Application of gains article.*—Treaty provisions applicable to gains from the alienation of property forming part of a permanent establishment, including gains from the alienation of a permanent establishment in the United States, apply to the transfer by a foreign transferor of an interest in a partnership with a permanent establishment in the United States.

(3) *Coordination rule.*—For purposes of applying paragraph (c) of this section to gains described in paragraph (f)(2) of this section, a foreign transferor's distributive share of deemed sale EC gain and deemed sale EC loss are determined with respect to the assets of the partnership that form part of the partnership's permanent establishment in the United States and that are not otherwise exempt from U.S. taxation under the treaty.

(g) *Definitions.*—The following definitions apply for purposes of this section.

(1) *Effectively connected gain.*—The term *effectively connected gain* means gain that is treated as effectively connected with the conduct of a trade or business within the United States.

(2) *Effectively connected loss.*—The term *effectively connected loss* means loss treated as effectively connected with the conduct of a trade or business within the United States.

(3) *Foreign transferor.*—The term *foreign transferor* means a nonresident alien individual or foreign corporation.

(4) *Section 751(a) property.*—The term *section 751(a) property* means unrealized receivables described in section 751(c) and inventory items described in section 751(d).

(5) *Transfer.*—The term *transfer* means a sale, exchange, or other disposition, and includes a distribution from a partnership to a partner to the extent that gain or loss is recognized on the distribution, as well as a transfer treated as a sale or exchange under section 707(a)(2)(B).

(h) *Anti-stuffing rule.*—If a foreign transferor (or a person that is related to a foreign transferor within the meaning of section 267(b) or 707(b)) transfers property (including another partnership interest) to a partnership in a transaction with a principal purpose of reducing the amount of gain treated as effectively connected gain, or increasing the amount of loss treated as effectively connected loss, under section 864(c)(8) or section 897, the transfer is disregarded for purposes of section 864(c)(8) or section 897, as appropriate, or otherwise recharacterized in accordance with its substance.

(i) *Examples.*—This paragraph provides examples that illustrate the rules of this section. For purposes of this paragraph, unless otherwise provided, the following facts are presumed. FP is a foreign corporation. USP is a domestic corporation. PRS is a partnership that was formed on January 1, 2018, when FP and USP each contributed $100x in cash. PRS has made no distributions and received no contributions other than those described in paragraph (i)(1)(iii) of this section. FP's adjusted basis in its interest in PRS is $100x. X is a foreign corporation that is unrelated to FP, USP, or PRS. Upon the formation of PRS, FP and USP entered into an agreement providing that all income, gain, loss, and deduction of PRS will be allocated equally between FP and USP. PRS is engaged in the conduct of a trade or business within the United States (the U.S. Business) and an unrelated business in Country A (the Country A Business). In a deemed sale described in paragraph (c)(1) of this section, gain or loss on assets of the U.S. Business would be treated as effectively connected gain or effectively connected loss, and gain or loss on assets of the Country A Business would not be so treated (including by reason of paragraph (c)(2)(ii) of this section). PRS has no liabilities. FP does not qualify for the benefits of an income tax treaty between the United States and another country.

(1) *Example 1. Deemed sale limitation*—(i) *Facts.* On January 1, 2019, FP sells its entire interest in PRS to X for $105x. Immediately before the sale, PRS's balance sheet appears as follows:

	Adjusted Basis	Fair Market Value
U.S. Business capital asset	$100x	$104x
Country A Business capital asset	100x	106x
Total	$200x	$210x

(ii) *Analysis*—(A) *Outside gain or loss.* FP is a foreign transferor (within the meaning of paragraph (g)(3) of this section) and transfers (within the meaning of paragraph (g)(5) of this section) its interest in PRS to X. FP recognizes a $5x capital gain under section 741, which is an outside capital gain within the meaning of paragraph (b)(2)(i) of this section. Under paragraph (b)(1) of this section, FP's $5x capital gain is treated as effectively connected gain to the extent that it does not exceed the limitation described in paragraph (b)(3)(i) of this section, which is FP's aggregate deemed sale EC capital gain.

(B) *Deemed sale.* FP's aggregate deemed sale EC capital gain is determined according to the three-step process set forth in paragraph (c) of this section. First, the amount of gain or loss that PRS would recognize with respect to each of its assets upon a deemed sale described in paragraph (c)(1) of this section is a $4x gain with respect to the U.S. Business capital asset and a $6x gain with respect to the Country A Business capital asset. Second, under paragraph (c)(2) of this section, PRS's deemed sale EC gain is $4x. PRS recognizes no deemed sale EC gain or loss with respect to the Country A Business capital asset under section 864 and paragraph (c)(2)(ii) of this section. Third, under paragraph (c)(3)(ii)(B) of this section, FP's aggregate deemed sale EC capital gain is $2x (that is, the aggregate of its distributive share of deemed sale EC gain attributable to the deemed sale of assets that are not section 751(a) property, which is 50% of $4x).

(C) *Limitation.* Under paragraph (b)(3)(i) of this section, the $5x outside capital gain recognized by FP is treated as effectively connected gain to the extent that it does not exceed FP's $2x aggregate deemed sale EC capital gain. Accordingly, FP recognizes $2x of capital gain that is treated as effectively connected gain.

(2) *Example 2. Outside gain limitation*—(i) *Facts.* On January 1, 2019, FP sells its entire interest in PRS to X for $110x. Immediately before the sale, PRS's balance sheet appears as follows:

	Adjusted Basis	Fair Market Value
U.S. Business capital asset	$100x	$150x
Country A Business capital asset	100x	70x
Total	$200x	$220x

(ii) *Analysis*—(A) *Outside gain or loss.* FP is a foreign transferor (within the meaning of paragraph (g)(3) of this section) and transfers (within the meaning of paragraph (g)(5) of this section) its interest in PRS to X. FP recognizes a $10x capital gain under section 741, which is an outside capital gain within the meaning of paragraph (b)(2)(i) of this section. Under paragraph (b)(1) of this section, FP's $10x capital gain is treated as effectively connected gain to the extent that it does not exceed the limitation described in paragraph (b)(3)(i) of this section, which is FP's aggregate deemed sale EC capital gain.

(B) *Deemed sale.* FP's aggregate deemed sale EC capital gain is determined according to the three-step process set forth in paragraph (c) of this section. First, the amount of gain or loss that PRS would recognize with respect to each of its assets upon a deemed sale described in paragraph (c)(1) of this section is a $50x gain with respect to the U.S. Business capital asset and a $30x loss with respect to the Country A Business capital asset. Second, under paragraph (c)(2) of this section, PRS's deemed sale EC gain is $50x. PRS recognizes no deemed sale EC gain or loss with respect to the Country A Business capital asset under section 864 and paragraph (c)(2)(ii) of this section. Third, under paragraph (c)(3) of this section, FP's aggregate deemed sale EC capital gain is $25x (that is, the aggregate of its distributive share of deemed sale EC gain attributable to the deemed sale of assets that are not section 751(a) property, which is 50% of $50x).

(C) *Limitation.* Under paragraph (b)(3)(i) of this section, the $10x outside capital gain recognized by FP is treated as effectively connected gain to the extent that it does not exceed FP's $25x aggregate deemed sale EC capital gain. Accordingly, FP recognizes $10x of capital gain that is treated as effectively connected gain.

(3) *Example 3. Interaction with section 751(a)*—(i) *Facts.* On January 1, 2019, FP sells its entire interest in PRS to X for $95x. Through both its U.S. Business and its Country A Business, PRS holds inventory items that are section 751 property (as defined in § 1.751-1(a)). Immediately before the sale, PRS's balance sheet appears as follows:

	Adjusted Basis	Fair Market Value
U.S. Business capital asset	$20x	$50x
U.S. Business inventory	30x	50x
Country A Business capital asset	100x	80x
Country A Business inventory	50x	10x
Total	$200x	$190x

(ii) *Analysis*—(A) *Outside gain or loss.* FP is a foreign transferor (within the meaning of paragraph (g)(3) of this section) and transfers (within the meaning of paragraph (g)(5) of this section) its interest in PRS to X. Under sections 741 and 751, FP recognizes a $10x ordinary loss and a $5x capital gain. See § 1.751-1(a). Under paragraph (b)(2)(i) of this section, FP has outside ordinary loss equal to $10x and outside capital gain equal to $5x. Under paragraph (b)(1) of this section,

FP's outside ordinary loss and outside capital gain are treated as effectively connected loss and effectively connected gain to the extent that each does not exceed the applicable limitation described in paragraph (b)(3) of this section. In the case of FP's outside ordinary loss, the applicable limitation is FP's aggregate deemed sale EC ordinary loss. In the case of FP's outside capital gain, the applicable limitation is FP's aggregate deemed sale EC capital gain.

(B) *Deemed sale.* FP's aggregate deemed sale EC ordinary loss and aggregate deemed sale EC capital gain are determined according to the three-step process set forth in paragraph (c) of this section.

(1) *Step 1.* The amount of gain or loss that PRS would recognize with respect to each of its assets upon a deemed sale described in paragraph (c)(1) of this section is as follows:

Asset	Gain/(Loss)
U.S. Business capital asset	$30x
U.S. Business inventory	20x
Country A Business capital asset	(20x)
Country A Business inventory	(40x)

(2) *Step 2.* Under paragraph (c)(2) of this section, PRS's deemed sale EC gain and deemed sale EC loss must be determined with respect to each asset. The amounts determined under paragraph (c)(2) of this section are as follows:

Asset	Deemed Sale EC Gain/(Loss)
U.S. Business capital asset	$30x
U.S. Business inventory	20x
Country A Business capital asset	0
Country A Business inventory	0

(3) *Step 3.* Under paragraph (c)(3) of this section, FP's aggregate deemed sale EC capital gain is $15x (that is, the aggregate of its distributive share of deemed sale EC gain that is attributable to the deemed sale of assets that are not section 751(a) property, which is 50% of $30x) and FP's aggregate deemed sale EC ordinary loss is $0 (that is, the aggregate of its distributive share of deemed sale EC loss that is attributable to the deemed sale of assets that are section 751(a) property).

(C) *Limitation*—(i) *Capital gain.* Under paragraph (b)(3)(i) of this section, the $5x outside capital gain recognized by FP is treated as effectively connected gain to the extent that it does not exceed FP's $15x aggregate deemed sale EC capital gain. Accordingly, the amount of FP's capital gain that is treated as effectively connected gain is $5x.

(ii) *Ordinary loss.* Under paragraph (b)(3)(iv) of this section, the $10x outside ordinary loss recognized by FP is treated as effectively connected loss to the extent that it does not exceed FP's $0 aggregate deemed sale EC ordinary loss. Accordingly, the amount of FP's ordinary loss that is treated as effectively connected loss is $0.

(j) *Applicability date.*—This section applies to transfers occurring on or after November 27, 2017. [Reg. § 1.864(c)(8)-1.]

Definition of Registered Form: Guidance

Definition of Registered Form: Guidance.—Amendments to Reg. § 1.871-14, providing guidance on the definitions of registration-required obligation and registered form, including guidance on the issuance of pass-through certificates and participation interests in registered form, are proposed (published in the Federal Register on September 19, 2017) (REG-125374-16).

Par. 7. Section 1.871-14 is amended by:

1. Revising the heading for paragraph (c).
2. Revising paragraph (c)(1)(i).
3. Revising the heading for paragraph (d).
4. Revising paragraphs (d)(1) and (2).
5. Adding paragraphs (j)(4) and (5).

The revisions and additions read as follows:

§ 1.871-14. Rules relating to repeal of tax on interest of nonresident alien individuals and foreign corporations received from certain portfolio debt investments.

* * *

(c) *Obligations in registered form.*—(1) *In general.*—(i) *Registered form.*—For purposes of this section, the rules of § 1.163-5(b) apply to determine when an obligation is in registered form.

* * *

(d) *Application of repeal of 30-percent withholding to pass-through certificates or participation interests.*—(1) *In general.*—(i) *Pass-through certificates.*—Interest received on a pass-through certificate (as defined in § 1.163-5(a)(3)(i)(B)) qualifies as portfolio interest under section 871(h)(2) or 881(c)(2) if the interest satisfies the conditions described in paragraph (c)(1)(ii) of this section or the conditions described in paragraph (e) of this section, without regard to whether any obligation held by the grantor trust, or similar fund, to which the pass-through certificate relates is described in paragraph (c)(1)(ii) or (e) of this section. For purposes of this paragraph (d)(1)(i), a similar fund includes an entity that, under §§ 301.7701-1 through 301.7701-3 of this chapter, is disregarded as an entity separate from its owner or classified as a partnership for federal tax purposes, without regard to the fund has the power to vary the assets in the fund or the sequence of payments made to holders. In addition, for purposes of this paragraph (d)(1)(i), a similar fund does not include a business entity that is classified as a corporation under §301.7701-2 of this chapter.

(ii) *Participation interests.*—Interest received on a participation interest described in §1.163-5(a)(3)(ii) qualifies as portfolio interest under section 871(h)(2) or 881(c)(2) if the interest satisfies the conditions described in paragraph (c)(1)(ii) of this section or the conditions described in paragraph (e) of this section, without regard to whether the obligation to which the participation interest relates is described in paragraph (c)(1)(ii) or (e) of this section.

(2) *Interest in REMICs.*—Interest received on a regular or residual interest in a REMIC, as defined in sections 860D and 860G and the regulations thereunder, qualifies as portfolio interest under section 871(h)(2) or 881(c)(2) if the interest satisfies the conditions described in paragraph (c)(1)(ii) of this section or the conditions described in paragraph (e) of this section. For purposes of paragraphs (c)(1)(ii) and (e) of this section, interest on a regular interest in a REMIC is not considered interest on any mortgage obligations held by the REMIC. The rule in the preceding sentence, however, applies only to payments made to the holder of the regular interest in the REMIC from the REMIC and does not apply to payments made to the REMIC. For purposes of paragraphs (c)(1)(ii) and (e) of this section, interest on a residual interest in a REMIC is considered to be interest on or with respect to the obligations held by the REMIC, and not on or with respect to the residual interest.

* * *

(j) * * *

(4) *Registered form.*—Paragraph (c)(1)(i) of this section applies to obligations issued after March 18, 2012. For the rules that apply to obligations issued on or before March 18, 2012, see §1.871-14 as contained in 26 CFR part 1, revised as of the date of the most recent annual revision.

(5) *Pass-through certificates, participation interests, and interests in REMICs.*—Paragraph (d) of this section applies to pass-through certificates, participation interests, or interests in REMICs issued after the date of publication of a Treasury decision adopting these rules as final regulations in the **Federal Register**.

Sources within the United States: Dividend Equivalents

Sources within the United States: Dividend Equivalents.—Amendments to Reg. §1.871-15, relating to certain financial products providing for payments that are contingent upon or determined by reference to U.S. source dividend payments, are proposed (published in the Federal Register on January 24, 2017) (REG-135122-16).

Par. 2. Section 1.871-15 is amended by revising paragraph (a)(1), paragraph (g)(4)(ii)(B), paragraphs (p)(1)(ii) through (p)(1)(iv), and paragraph (p)(5) to read as follows:

§1.871-15. Treatment of dividend equivalents.—(a) * * *

(1) [The text of the proposed amendments to §1.871-15(a)(1) is the same as the text of §1.871-15T(a)(1) as added by T.D. 9815.]

* * *

(g) * * *

(4) * * *

(ii) * * *

(B) [The text of the proposed amendments to §1.871-15(g)(4)(ii)(B) is the same as the text of §1.871-15T(g)(4)(ii)(B) as added by T.D. 9815.]

* * *

(p) * * *

(1) * * *

(ii) [The text of the proposed amendments to §1.871-15(p)(1)(ii) is the same as the text of §1.871-15T(p)(1)(ii) as added by T.D. 9815.]

(iii) [The text of the proposed amendments to §1.871-15(p)(1)(iii) is the same as the text of §1.871-15T(p)(1)(iii) as added by T.D. 9815.]

(iv) [The text of the proposed amendments to §1.871-15(p)(1)(iv) is the same as the text of §1.871-15T(p)(1)(iv) as added by T.D. 9815.]

* * *

(5) [The text of the proposed amendments to §1.871-15(p)(5) is the same as the text of §1.871-15T(p)(5) as added by T.D. 9815.]

* * *

Definition of Registered Form: Guidance

Definition of Registered Form: Guidance.—Amendments to Reg. §1.881-3, providing guidance on the definitions of registration-required obligation and registered form, including guidance on the issuance of pass-through certificates and participation interests in registered form, are proposed (published in the Federal Register on September 19, 2017) (REG-125374-16).

Par. 8. Section 1.881-3(e) is amended by:

1. Removing *Examples 10* and *19*.

2. Redesignating *Examples 11* through *18* as *Examples 10* through *17* and *Examples 20* through *26* as *Examples 18* through *24*.

§1.881-3. Conduit financing arrangements.

Foreign Corporations: Determination of Interest Expense Deduction: Branch Profits Tax

Foreign Corporations: Determination of Interest Expense Deduction: Branch Profits Tax.—Amendments to Reg. §1.882-5, relating to the determination of the interest expense deduction of foreign corporations and the branch profits tax, are proposed (published in the Federal Register on March 8, 1996).

☐ Par. 2. Section 1.882-5 is amended as follows:

1. The text of paragraph (b)(2)(iv) is added.
2. The text of paragraph (c)(2)(v) is added.
3. In paragraph (c)(5), *Example 4*, *Example 6*, and *Example 7* are added.
4. The text of paragraph (d)(2)(vi) is added.
5. In paragraph (d)(6), *Example 4* is added.
6. The text of paragraph (e)(3) is added.
7. In paragraph (e)(5), *Example 2* is added.
8. The text of paragraph (f)(2) is added.

The added provisions read as follows:

§1.882-5. Determination of interest deduction

* * *

(b) * * *

(2) * * *

(iv) *Adjustment to basis of financial instruments.*—The basis of a security or contract that is marked to market pursuant to section 475 or section 1256 will be determined as if each determination date were the last business day of the taxpayer's taxable year. A financial instrument with a fair market value of less than zero is a liability, not an asset, for purposes of this section. [*NOTE:* Proposed Reg. §1.882-5(b)(2)(iv) was adopted as Temporary Reg. §1.882-5T(b)(3)(ii) by T.D. 9281 on August 15, 2006.]

* * *

(c) * * *

(2) * * *

(v) *Hedging transactions.*—A transaction (or transactions) that hedges an asset or liability, or a pool of assets or a pool of liabilities, will be taken into account in determining the value, amount and currency denomination of the asset or liability that it hedges. A transaction will be considered to hedge an asset or liability only if the transaction meets the requirements of §1.1221-2.

* * *

(5) * * *

Example 4. Partnership liabilities. X and Y are each foreign corporations engaged in the active conduct of a trade or business within the United States through a partnership, *P*. Under the partnership agreement, X and *Y* each have a 50% interest in the capital and profits of *P*, and *X* is also entitled to a return of 6% per annum on its capital account that is a guaranteed payment under section 707(c). In addition, *P* has incurred a liability of $100x to an unrelated bank, *B*. Under paragraph (c)(2)(vi) of this section, *X* and *Y* each share equally in *P's* liability to *B*. In accordance with U.S. tax principles, *P's* obligation to make guaranteed payments to *X* does not constitute a liability of *P*, and therefore neither *X* nor *Y* take into account that obligation of the partnership in computing their actual ratio.

* * *

Example 6. Securities in ratio as assets. FC is a foreign corporation engaged in a trade or business in the United States through a U.S. branch. FC is a dealer in securities within the meaning of section 475(c)(1)(B) because it regularly offers to enter into positions in currency spot and forward contracts with customers in the ordinary course of its trade or business. FC has not elected to use the fixed ratio. On December 31, 1996, the end of FC's taxable year, the mark-to-market value of the spot and forward contracts entered into by FC worldwide is 1000x, which includes a mark-to-market gain of 500x with respect to the spot and forward contracts that are shown on the books of its U.S. branch and that produce effectively connected income. On its December 31, 1996, determination date, FC includes 500x in its U.S. assets, and 1000x in its worldwide assets.

Example 7. Securities in ratio as assets and liabilities. The facts are the same as in *Example 4*, except that on December 31, 1996, the mark-to-market value of the spot and forward contracts entered into by FC worldwide is 1000x, and FC has a mark-to-market loss of 500x with respect to the spot and forward contracts that are shown on the books of its U.S. branch and that would produce effectively connected income. On its December 31, 1996, determination date, FC includes the 1000x in its worldwide assets for purposes of determining its ratio of worldwide liabilities to worldwide assets. For purposes of Step 3, however, FC has U.S-booked liabilities in the United States equal to the 500x U.S. loss position.

(d) * * *

(2) * * *

(vi) *Hedging transactions.*—A transaction (or transactions) that hedges a U.S. booked liability, or a pool of U.S. booked liabilities, will be taken into account in determining the currency denomination, amount of, and interest rate associated with, that liability. A transaction will be considered to hedge a U.S. booked liability only if the transaction meets the requirements of §1.1221-2(a), (b), and (c), and is identified in accordance with the requirements of §1.1221-2(e).

* * *

(6) * * *

Example 4. Liability hedge—(i) *Facts.* FC is a foreign corporation that meets the definition of a bank, as defined in section 585(a)(2)(B) (without regard to the second sentence thereof), and that is engaged in a banking business in the United States through its branch, *B*. *FC*'s corporate policy is to match the currency denomination of its assets and liabilities, thereby minimizing potential gains and losses from currency fluctuations. Thus, at the close of each business day, *FC* enters into one or more hedging transactions as needed to maintain a balanced currency position, and instructs each branch to do the same. At the close of business on December 31, 1998, *B* has 100x of U.S. dollar assets, and U.S. booked liabilities of 90x U.S. dollars and 1000x Japanese yen (exchange rate: $1 = 100). To eliminate the currency mismatch in this situation, *B* enters into a forward contract with an unrelated third party that requires *FC* to pay 10x dollars in return for 1000x yen. Through this hedging transaction, *FC* has effectively converted its 1000x Japanese yen liability into a U.S. dollar liability. *FC* uses its actual ratio of 90% in 1998 for Step 2, the adjusted U.S. booked liabilities method for purposes of Step 3, and is a calendar year taxpayer.

(ii) *Analysis.* Under paragraph 1.882-5(d)(2)(vi), *FC* is required to take into account hedges of U.S. booked liabilities in determining the currency denomination, amount, and interest rate associated with those liabilities. Accordingly, *FC* must treat the Japanese yen liabilities booked in the United States on December 31, 1998, as U.S. dollar liabilities to determine both the amount of the liabilities and the interest paid or accrued on U.S. booked liabilities for purposes of this section. Moreover, in applying the scaling ratio prescribed in paragraph (d)(4)(i) of this section, *FC* must scale back both the U.S. booked liabilities and the hedge(s) of those liabilities. Assuming that *FC*'s average U.S. booked liabilities for the year ending December 31, 1998, exceed its U.S.-connected liabilities determined under paragraphs (a)(1) through (c)(5) of this section by 10%, *FC* must scale back by 10% both its interest expense associated with U.S. booked liabilities, and any income or loss from the forward contract to purchase Japanese yen that hedges its U.S. booked liabilities.

(e) * * *

(3) *Hedging transactions.*—A transaction (or transactions) that hedges a liability, or a pool of liabilities, will be taken into account in determining the amount of, or interest rate associated with, that liability. A transaction will be considered to hedge a liability only if the transaction meets the requirements of §1.1221-2(a),(b), and (c).

* * *

(5) * * *

Example 2. Asset hedge—(i) *Facts. FC* is a foreign corporation that meets the definition of a bank, as defined in section 585(a)(2)(B) (without regard to the second sentence thereof), and that is engaged in the banking business in the United States through its branch, *B*. *FC*'s corporate policy is to match the currency denomination of its assets and liabilities, thereby minimizing potential gains and losses from currency fluctuations. Thus, at the close of each business day, *FC* enters into one or more hedging transactions as needed to maintain a balanced currency position, and instructs each branch to do the same. At the close of business on December 31, 1998, *B* has two U.S. assets, a loan of 90x U.S. dollars and a loan of 1000x Japanese yen (exchange rate: $1 = ¥100). *B* has U.S. booked liabilities, however, of 100x U.S. dollars. To eliminate the currency mismatch, *B* enters into a forward contract with an unrelated third party that requires *FC* to pay 1000x yen in return for 10x dollars. Through this hedging transaction, *FC* has effectively converted its 1000x Japanese yen asset into a U.S. dollar asset. *FC* uses its actual ratio of 90% in 1998 for Step 2, has elected the separate currency pools method in paragraph (e) of this section, and is a calendar year taxpayer.

(ii) *Analysis.* Under paragraph (e)(1)(i) of this section, *FC* must take into account any transaction that hedges a U.S. asset in determining the currency denomination and value of that asset. *FC*'s Japanese yen asset will therefore be treated as a U.S. dollar asset in determining its U.S. assets in each currency. Accordingly, *FC* will be treated as having only U.S. dollar assets in making its separate currency pools computation.

(f) * * *

(2) *Special rules for financial products.*—Paragraphs (b)(2)(iv), (c)(2)(v), (d)(2)(vi), and (e)(3) of this section will be effective for taxable years beginning on or after the date these regulations are published as final regulations in the Federal Register.

Deduction for Business Interest Expense: Limitation

Deduction for Business Interest Expense: Limitation.—Amendments to Reg. §1.882-5, regarding the limitation on the deduction for business interest expense after the enactment of recent tax legislation, are proposed (published in the Federal Register on December 28, 2018) (REG-106089-18).

Par. 16. Section 1.882-5 is amended by adding a sentence to the end of paragraph (a)(5) to read as follows:

§1.882-5. Determination of interest deduction.—(a) * * *

(5) * * * For rules regarding the coordination of this section and section 163(j), see §1.163(j)-8(e).

* * *

Foreign Corporations: Determination of Interest Expense Deduction: Branch Profits Tax

Foreign Corporations: Determination of Interest Expense Deduction: Branch Profits Tax.—Amendments to Reg. §1.884-1, relating to the determination of the interest expense deduction of foreign corporations and the branch profits tax, are proposed (published in the Federal Register on March 8, 1996).

☐ Par. 3. Section 1.884-1 is amended as follows:

1. Paragraph (c)(2)(iii) is added.
2. Paragraph (d)(2) is amended as follows:
   a. Paragraph (d)(2)(vii) is revised.
   b. In paragraph (d)(2)(xi), *Example 6* through *Example 8* are added.
3. The text of paragraph (d)(6)(v) is added.
4. In paragraph (i)(4), a sentence is added at the end of the existing text.

The revised and added provisions read as follows:

§1.884-1. Branch profits tax.

* * *

(c) * * *

(2) * * *

(iii) *Hedging transactions.*—A transaction that hedges a U.S. asset, or a pool of U.S. assets, will be taken into account in determining the amount of that asset (or pool of assets) to the extent that income or loss from the hedging transaction produces ECI or reduces ECI. A transaction that hedges a U.S. asset, or pool of U.S. assets, is also taken into account in determining the currency denomination of the U.S. asset (or pool of U.S. assets). A transaction will be considered to hedge a U.S. asset only if the transaction meets the requirements of §1.1221-2(a), (b), and (c), and is identified in accordance with the requirements of §1.1221-2(e).

(d) * * *

(2) * * *

(vii) *Financial instruments.*—A financial instrument, including a security as defined in section 475 and a section 1256 contract, shall be treated as a U.S. asset of a foreign corporation in the same proportion that the income, gain, or loss from such security is ECI for the taxable year.

* * *

(xi) * * *

Example 6. Hedging transactions—(i) *Facts.* FC is a foreign corporation engaged in a trade or business in the United States through a U.S. branch. The functional currency of FC's U.S. branch is the U.S. dollar. On January 1, 1997, in the ordinary course of its business, the U.S. branch of FC enters into a forward contract with an unrelated party to purchase 100 German marks (DM) on March 31, 1997, for $50. To hedge the risk of currency fluctuation on this transaction, the U.S. branch also enters into a forward contract with another unrelated party to sell 100 DM on March 31, 1997, for $52, identifying this contract as a hedging transaction in accordance with the requirements of §1.1221-2(e). FC marks its foreign currency transactions to market for U.S. tax purposes.

(ii) *Net assets.* At the end of FC's taxable year, the value of the forward contract to purchase 100 DM is marked to market, resulting in gain of $10 being realized and recognized as U.S. source effectively connected income by FC. Similarly, FC marks to market the contract to sell 100 DM, resulting in $8 of realized and recognized loss by FC. Pursuant to paragraph (c)(2)(iii) of this section, FC must increase or decrease the amount of its U.S. assets to take into account any transaction that hedges the contract to purchase 100 DM. Consequently, FC has a U.S. asset of $2 ($10 (the adjusted basis of the contract to purchase 100 DM) - $8 (the loss on the contract to sell 100 DM)).

Example 7. Split hedge. The facts are the same as in *Example 5*, except that the contract to sell 100 DM is entered into with an unrelated third party by the home office of FC. FC includes the contract to sell 100 DM in a pool of assets treated as producing income effectively connected with the U.S. trade or business of FC. Therefore, under paragraph (c)(2)(iii) of this section, at its next determination date FC will report a U.S. asset of $2, computed as in *Example 5*.

Example 8. Securities. FC is a foreign corporation engaged in a U.S. trade or business through a branch in the United States. During the taxable year 1997, FC derives $100 of income from securities, of which $60 is treated as U.S. source effectively connected income under the terms of an Advance Pricing Agreement that uses a profit split methodology. Accordingly, pursuant to paragraph (d)(2)(vii) of this section, FC has a U.S. asset equal to 60% ($60 of ECI divided by $100 of gross income from securities) of the amount of the securities.

* * *

(6) * * *

(v) *Computation of E&P basis of financial instruments.*—For purposes of this section, the E&P basis of a security that is marked to market under section 475 and a section 1256 contract shall be adjusted to take into account gains and losses recognized by reason of section 475 or section 1256. The E&P basis must be further adjusted to take into account a transaction that hedges a U.S. asset, as provided in paragraph (c)(2)(ii) of this section.

* * *

(i) * * *

(4) * * * Paragraphs (c)(2)(iii), (d)(2)(vii), and (d)(6)(v) of this section will be effective for taxable years beginning on or after the date these regulations are published as final regulations in the Federal Register.

* * *

Foreign Corporations: Branch Profits Tax

Foreign Corporations: Branch Profits Tax.—Reg. §§1.884-2T and 1.884-3T, relating to the branch profits tax, are proposed (published in the Federal Register on September 2, 1988) (INTL-934-86). Reg. §§1.884-0, 1.884-1, 1.884-4 and 1.884-5 were adopted 9/10/92 by T.D. 8432.

§1.884-2. Special rules for termination or incorporation of a U.S. trade or business or liquidation or reorganization of a foreign corporation or its domestic subsidiary.

§1.884-3. Coordination of branch profits tax with second-tier withholding.

Foreign Governments and International Organizations

Income of Foreign Governments and International Organizations.—Temporary Reg. §§1.892-1T—1.892-7T, relating to current taxation of income of foreign governments from investment sources within the United States, are also proposed as final regulations and, when adopted, would become Reg. §§1.892-1—1.892-7 (published in the Federal Register on June 27, 1988).

§1.892-1. Purpose and scope of regulations.

Foreign Governments and International Organizations: Income from Sources within the United States

Foreign Governments and International Organizations: Income from Sources within the United States.—Reg. §1.892-4 and amendments to Reg. §1.892-5, relating to the taxation of the income of foreign governments from investments in the United States under section 892 of the Internal Revenue Code, are proposed (published in the Federal Register on November 3, 2011) (REG-146537-06) (corrected November 23, 2011).

☐ Par. 2. Section 1.892-4 is added to read as follows:

§1.892-4. Commercial activities.—(a) through (c) [Reserved]. For further guidance, see §1.892-4T(a) through (c).

(d) *In general.*—Except as provided in paragraph (e) of this section, all activities (whether conducted within or outside the United States) which are ordinarily conducted for the current or future production of income or gain are commercial activities. Only the nature of the activity, not the purpose or motivation for conducting the activity, is determinative of whether the activity is commercial in character. An activity may be considered a commercial activity even if such activity does not constitute a trade or business for purposes of section 162 or does not constitute (or would not constitute if undertaken in the United States) the conduct of a trade or business in the United States for purposes of section 864(b).

(e) *Activities that are not commercial.*—(1) *Investments.*—(i) *In general.*—Subject to the provisions of paragraphs (e)(1)(ii) and (iii) of this section, the following are not commercial activities: investments in stocks, bonds, and other securities (as defined in §1.892-3T(a)(3)); loans; investments in financial instruments (as defined in §1.892-3T(a)(4)); the holding of net leases on real property; the holding of real property which is not producing income (other than on its sale or from an investment in net leases on real property); and the holding of bank deposits in banks. Transferring securities under a loan agreement which meets the requirements of section 1058 is an investment for purposes of this paragraph (e)(1)(i). An activity will not cease to be an investment solely because of the volume of transactions of that activity or because of other unrelated activities.

(ii) *Trading.*—Effecting transactions in stocks, bonds, other securities (as defined in §1.892-3T(a)(3)), commodities, or financial instruments (as defined in §1.892-3T(a)(4)) for a foreign government's own account does not constitute a commercial activity regardless of whether such activity constitutes a trade or business for purposes of section 162 or constitutes (or would constitute if undertaken within the United States) the conduct of a trade or business in the United States for purposes of section 864(b). Such transactions are not commercial activities regardless of whether they are effected by the foreign government through its employees or through a broker, commission agent, custodian, or other independent agent and regardless of whether or not any such employee or agent has discretionary authority to make decisions in effecting the transactions. Such transactions undertaken as a dealer (as determined under the principles of §1.864-2(c)(2)(iv)(a)), however, constitute commercial activity. For purposes of this paragraph (e)(1)(ii), the term *commodities* means commodities of a kind customarily dealt in on an organized commodity exchange but only if the transaction is of a kind customarily consummated at such place.

(iii) *Banking, financing, etc.*—Investments (including loans) made by a banking, financing, or similar business constitute commercial activities, even if the income derived from such investments is not considered to be income effectively connected with the active conduct of a banking, financing, or similar business in the U.S. by reason of the application of §1.864-4(c)(5).

(iv) *Disposition of a U.S. real property interest.*—A disposition (including a deemed disposition under section 897(h)(1)) of a U.S. real property interest (as defined in section 897(c)), by itself, does not constitute the conduct of a commercial activity. As described in §1.892-3T(a), however, gain derived from a disposition of a U.S. real property interest defined in section 897(c)(1)(A)(i) will not qualify for exemption from tax under section 892.

(2) through (5) [Reserved]. For further guidance, see §1.892-4T(c)(2) through (c)(5).

(f) *Effective/applicability date.*—This section applies on the date the regulations are published as final regulations in the **FEDERAL REGISTER**. See §1.892-4T for the rules that apply before the date the regulations are published as final regulations in the **FEDERAL REGISTER**. [Reg. §1.892-4.]

☐ Par. 3. Section 1.892-5 is revised to read as follows:

§1.892-5. Controlled commercial entity.—(a) *In general.*—(1) *General rule and definition of the term "controlled commercial entity".*—Under section 892(a)(2)(A)(ii) and (a)(2)(A)(iii), the exemption generally applicable to a foreign government (as defined in §1.892-2T) for income described in §1.892-3T does not apply to income received by a controlled commercial entity or received (directly or indirectly) from a controlled commercial entity, or to income derived from the disposition of any interest in a controlled commercial entity. For purposes of section 892 and the regulations thereunder, the term *entity* means and includes a corporation, a partnership, a trust (including a pension trust described in §1.892-2T(c)), and an estate, and the term *controlled commercial entity* means any entity (including a controlled entity as defined in §1.892-2T(a)(3)) engaged in commercial activities (as defined in §§1.892-4 and 1.892-4T) (whether conducted within or outside the United States) if the government—

(i) Holds (directly or indirectly) any interest in such entity which (by value or voting power) is 50 percent or more of the total of such interests in such entity, or

(ii) Holds (directly or indirectly) any other interest in such entity which provides the foreign government with effective practical control of such entity.

(2) *Inadvertent commercial activity.*—(i) *General rule.*—For purposes of determining whether an entity is a controlled commercial entity for purposes of section 892(a)(2)(B) and paragraph (a)(1) of this section, an entity that conducts only inadvertent commercial activity will not be considered to be engaged in commercial activities. However, any income derived from such inadvertent commercial activity will not qualify for exemption from tax under section 892. Commercial activity of an entity will be treated as inadvertent commercial activity only if:

(A) Failure to avoid conducting the commercial activity is reasonable as described in paragraph (a)(2)(ii) of this section;

(B) The commercial activity is promptly cured as described in paragraph (a)(2)(iii) of this section; and

(C) The record maintenance requirements described in paragraph (a)(2)(iv) of this section are met.

(ii) *Reasonable failure to avoid commercial activity.*—(A) *In general.*—Subject to paragraphs (a)(2)(ii)(B) and (C) of this section, whether an entity's failure to prevent its worldwide activities from resulting in commercial activity is reasonable will be determined in light of all the facts and circumstances. Due regard will be given to the number of commercial activities conducted during the taxable year and in prior taxable years, as well as the amount of income earned from, and assets used in, the conduct of the commercial activities in relationship to the entity's total income and assets, respectively. For purposes of this paragraph (a)(2)(ii)(A) and paragraph (a)(2)(ii)(C) of this section, where a commercial activity conducted by a partnership is attributed under paragraph (d)(5)(i) of this section to an entity owning an interest in the partnership—

(1) Assets used in the conduct of the commercial activity by the partnership are treated as assets used in the conduct of commercial activity by the entity in proportion to the entity's interest in the partnership; and

(2) The entity's distributive share of the partnership's income from the conduct of the commercial activity shall be treated as income earned by the entity from the conduct of commercial activities.

(B) *Continuing due diligence requirement.*—A failure to avoid commercial activity will not be considered reasonable unless there is continuing due diligence to prevent the entity from engaging in commercial activities within or outside the United States as evidenced by having adequate written policies and operational procedures in place to monitor the entity's worldwide activities. A failure to avoid commercial activity will not be considered reasonable if the management-level employees of the entity have not undertaken reasonable efforts to establish, follow, and enforce such written policies and operational procedures.

(C) *Safe Harbor.*—Provided that adequate written policies and operational procedures are in place to monitor the entity's worldwide activities as required in paragraph (a)(2)(ii)(B) of this section, the entity's failure to avoid commercial activity during the taxable year will be considered reasonable if:

(1) The value of the assets used in, or held for use in, all commercial activity does not exceed five percent of the total value of the assets reflected on the entity's balance sheet for the taxable year as prepared for financial accounting purposes, and

(2) The income earned by the entity from commercial activity does not exceed five percent of the entity's gross income as reflected on its income statement for the taxable year as prepared for financial accounting purposes.

(iii) *Cure requirement.*—A timely cure shall be considered to have been made if the entity discontinues the conduct of the commercial activity within 120 days of discovering the commercial activity. For example, if an entity that holds an interest as a general partner in a partnership discovers that the partnership is conducting commercial activity, the entity will satisfy the cure requirement if, within 120 days of discovering the commercial activity, the entity discontinues the conduct of the activity by divesting itself of its interest in the partnership (including by transferring its interest in the partnership to a related entity), or the partnership discontinues its conduct of commercial activity.

(iv) *Record maintenance.*—Adequate records of each discovered commercial activity and the remedial action taken to cure that activity must be maintained. The records shall be retained so long as the contents thereof may become material in the administration of section 892.

(3) *Annual determination of controlled commercial entity status.*—If an entity described in paragraph (a)(1)(i) or (ii) of this section engages in commercial activities at any time during a taxable year, the entity will be considered a controlled commercial entity for the entire taxable

year. An entity not otherwise engaged in commercial activities during a taxable year will not be considered a controlled commercial entity for a taxable year even if the entity engaged in commercial activities in a prior taxable year.

(b) through (d)(4) [Reserved]. For further guidance, see § 1.892-5T(b) through (d)(4).

(5) *Partnerships*.—(i) *General rule*.—Except as provided in paragraph (d)(5)(ii) or paragraph (d)(5)(iii) of this section, the commercial activities of an entity classified as a partnership for federal tax purposes will be attributable to its partners for purposes of section 892. For example, if an entity described in paragraph (a)(1)(i) or (ii) of this section holds an interest as a general partner in a partnership that is engaged in commercial activities, the partnership's commercial activities will be attributed to that entity for purposes of determining if the entity is a controlled commercial entity within the meaning of section 892(a)(2)(B) and paragraph (a) of this section.

(ii) *Trading activity exception*.—An entity not otherwise engaged in commercial activities will not be considered to be engaged in commercial activities solely because the entity is a member of a partnership (whether domestic or foreign) that effects transactions in stocks, bonds, other securities (as defined in § 1.892-3T(a)(3)), commodities (as defined in § 1.892-4(e)(1)(ii)), or financial instruments (as defined in § 1.892-3T(a)(4)) for the partnership's own account or solely because an employee of such partnership, or a broker, commission agent, custodian, or other agent, pursuant to discretionary authority granted by such partnership, effects such transactions for the account of the partnership. This exception shall not apply to any member in the case of a partnership that is a dealer in stocks, bonds, other securities, commodities, or financial instruments, as determined under the principles of § 1.864-2(c)(2)(iv)(a).

(iii) *Limited partner exception*.—(A) *General rule*.—An entity that is not otherwise engaged in commercial activities (including, for example, performing services for a partnership as described in section 707(a) or section 707(c)) will not be deemed to be engaged in commercial activities solely because it holds an interest as a limited partner in a limited partnership. Nevertheless, pursuant to sections 875, 882, and 892(a)(2)(A)(i), a foreign government member's distributive share of partnership income will not be exempt from taxation under section 892 to the extent that the partnership derived such income from the conduct of a commercial activity. For example, where a controlled entity described in § 1.892-2T(a)(3) that is not otherwise engaged in commercial activities holds an interest as a limited partner in a limited partnership that is a dealer in stocks, bonds, other securities, commodities, or financial instruments in the United States, although the controlled entity partner will not be deemed to be engaged in commercial activities solely because of its interest in the limited partnership, its distributive share of partnership income derived from the partnership's activity as a dealer will not be exempt from tax under section 892 because it was derived from the conduct of a commercial activity.

(B) *Interest as a limited partner in a limited partnership*.—Solely for purposes of paragraph (d)(5)(iii) of this section, an interest in an entity classified as a partnership for federal tax purposes shall be treated as an interest as a limited partner in a limited partnership if the holder of such interest does not have rights to participate in the management and conduct of the partnership's business at any time during the partnership's taxable year under the law of the jurisdiction in which the partnership is organized or under the governing agreement. Rights to participate in the management and conduct of a partnership's business do not include consent rights in the case of extraordinary events such as admission or expulsion of a general or limited partner, amendment of the partnership agreement, dissolution of the partnership, disposition of all or substantially all of the partnership's property outside of the ordinary course of the partnership's activities, merger, or conversion.

(iv) *Illustration*.—The following example illustrates the application of this paragraph (d)(5):

Example 1. K, a controlled entity of a foreign sovereign, has investments in various stocks and bonds of United States corporations and in a 20% interest in Opco, a limited liability company that is classified as a partnership for federal tax purposes. Under the governing agreement of Opco, K has the authority to participate in the management and conduct of Opco's business. Opco has investments in various stocks and bonds of United States corporations and also owns and manages an office building in New York. Because K has authority to participate in the management and conduct of Opco's business, its interest in Opco is not a limited partner interest. Therefore, K will be deemed to be engaged in commercial activities because of attribution of Opco's commercial activity, even if K does not actually make management decisions with regard to Opco's commercial activity, the operation of the office building. Accordingly, K is a controlled commercial entity, and all of its income, including its distributive share of partnership income from its interest in Opco and its income from the stocks and bonds it owns directly, will not be exempt from tax under section 892.

Example 2. The facts are the same as in *Example 1*, except that Opco has hired a real estate management firm to lease offices and manage the office building. Notwithstanding the fact that an independent contractor is performing the activities, Opco will still be deemed to be engaged in commercial activities. Accordingly, K is a controlled commercial entity, and all of its income, including its distributive share of partnership income from its interest in Opco and its income from the stocks and bonds it owns directly, will not be exempt from tax under section 892.

Example 3. The facts are the same as in *Example 1*, except that K is a member that has no right to participate in the management and conduct of Opco's business. Assume further that K is not otherwise engaged in commercial activities. Under paragraph (d)(5)(iii) of this section, Opco's commercial activities will not be attributed to K. Accordingly, K will not be a controlled commercial entity, and its income derived from the stocks and bonds it owns directly and the portion of its distributive share of partnership income from its interest in Opco that is derived from stocks and bonds will be exempt from tax under section 892. The portion of K's distributive share of partnership income from its interest in Opco that is derived from the operation of the office building will not be exempt from tax under section 892 and § 1.892-3T(a)(1).

(e) *Effective/applicability date.*—This section applies on the date these regulations are published as final regulations in the **FEDERAL REGISTER**. See § 1.892-5(a) as issued under TD 9012 (August 1, 2002) for rules that apply on or after January 14, 2002, and before the date these regulations are published as final regulations in the **FEDERAL REGISTER**. See § 1.892-5T(a) for rules that apply before January 14, 2002, and § 1.892-5T(b) through (d) for rules that apply before the date these regulations are published as final regulations in the **FEDERAL REGISTER**. [Reg. § 1.892-5.]

Global Dealing Operations: Allocation and Sourcing of Income and Deductions

Global Dealing Operations: Allocation and Sourcing of Income and Deductions.—Amendments to Reg. § 1.894-1, relating to the allocation and sourcing of income, deductions, gains and losses from a global dealing operation, are proposed (published in the Federal Register on March 6, 1998) (REG-208299-90).

☐ Par. 11. Section 1.894-1 is amended as follows:

1. Paragraph (d) is redesignated as paragraph (e).
2. New paragraph (d) is added.

The addition reads as follows:

§ 1.894-1. Income affected by treaty.

* * *

(d) *Income from a global dealing operation.*—If a taxpayer that is engaged in a global dealing operation, as defined in § 1.482-8(a)(2)(i), has a permanent establishment in the United States under the principles of an applicable U.S. income tax treaty, the principles of § 1.863-3(h), § 1.864-4(c)(2)(iv), § 1.864-4(c)(3)(ii), § 1.864-4(c)(5)(vi)(a) or § 1.864-6(b)(2)(ii)(*d*)(*3*) shall apply for purposes of determining the income attributable to that U.S. permanent establishment.

* * *

Dispositions of Investment in U.S. Real Property

Nonresident Aliens and Foreign Corporations: Disposition of Investment in U.S. Real Property.—Temporary Reg. §§ 1.897-4AT and 1.897-5T—1.897-9T, relating to dispositions of U.S. real property interests by nonresident aliens and foreign corporations, are also proposed as final regulations and, when adopted, would become Reg. §§ 1.897-4A and 1.897-5—1.897-9 (published in the Federal Register on May 5, 1988).

§ 1.897-4A. Table of contents.

§ 1.897-5. Corporate distributions.

§ 1.897-6. Nonrecognition exchanges applicable to corporations, their shareholders, and other taxpayers, and certain transfers of property in corporate reorganizations.

§ 1.897-7. Treatment of certain partnership interests as entirely U.S. real property interests under sections 897(g) and 1445(e).

§ 1.897-8. Status of a U.S. real property holding corporation as a condition for electing section 897(i) pursuant to § 1.897-3.

§ 1.897-9. Treatment of certain interest in publicly traded corporations, definition of foreign person, and foreign governments and international organizations.

Gain or Loss of Foreign Person: Sale or Exchange: Partnership Interest

Gain or Loss of Foreign Person: Sale or Exchange: Partnership Interest.—Reg. § 1.897-7, affecting certain foreign persons that recognize gain or loss from the sale or exchange of an interest in a partnership that is engaged in a trade or business within the United States, is proposed (published in the Federal Register on December 27, 2018) (REG-113604-18).

Par. 3. Section 1.897-7 is added to read as follows:

§ 1.897-7. Treatment of certain partnership interests, trusts and estates under section 897(g).—(a) through (b) [Reserved]. For further guidance, see § 1.897-7T(a) through (b).

(c) *Coordination with section 864(c)(8).*—Except as provided in § 1.864(c)(8)-1, the amount of any money, and the fair market value of any property, received by a nonresident alien individual or foreign corporation in exchange for all or part of its interest in a partnership, trust, or estate shall, to the extent attributable to United States real property interests, be considered as an amount received from the sale or exchange in the United States of such property. See also § 1.864(c)(8)-1(h) for an anti-stuffing rule that may apply to transactions subject to section 897. This paragraph applies to transfers occurring on or after November 27, 2017. [Reg. § 1.897-7.]

Gain or Loss of Foreign Person: Sale or Exchange: Partnership Interest

Gain or Loss of Foreign Person: Sale or Exchange: Partnership Interest.—Amendments to Temporary Reg. §1.897-7T, affecting certain foreign persons that recognize gain or loss from the sale or exchange of an interest in a partnership that is engaged in a trade or business within the United States, are proposed (published in the Federal Register on December 27, 2018) (REG-113604-18).

Par. 4. Section 1.897-7T is amended by adding paragraph (c) to read as follows:

§1.897-7T. Treatment of certain partnership interests as entirely U.S. real property interests under sections 897(g) and 1445(e) (temporary).

* * *

(c) *Coordination with section 864(c)(8).* [Reserved]. For further guidance, see §1.897-7(c). [Reg. §1.897-7T.]

Foreign Corporations: Tax Years

Foreign Corporations: Tax Years.—Reproduced below are the texts of proposed Reg. §§1.898-0—1.898-4, relating to the required taxable year of those foreign corporations beginning after July 10, 1989 (published in the Federal Register on January 5, 1993). See below for a proposed amendment to proposed Reg. §1.898-4.

☐ Par. 6. Sections 1.898-0—1.898-4 are added as follows:

§1.898-0. Outline of regulations for section 898.—This section lists the major paragraphs contained in §§1.898-1 through 1.898-4.

§1.898-1. Taxable year of certain foreign corporations.

(a) In general.

(b) Effective dates.

(c) Exceptions to section 898.

(1) Specified foreign corporations with no section 951(a) or foreign personal holding company income.

(2) Elections to be treated as domestic corporations.

§1.898-2. Definition of specified foreign corporation.

(a) In general.

(b) Ownership requirements.

(1) In general.

(2) Ownership by attribution.

(3) Definition of United States shareholder.

(i) In general.

(ii) Certain captive insurance companies.

(iii) Foreign personal holding companies.

(4) Illustrations.

(c) Special rule for foreign personal holding companies that are not controlled foreign corporations.

(1) In general.

(2) Illustrations.

§1.898-3. Determining the required year.

(a) Controlled foreign corporations.

(1) In general.

(2) One-month deferral election.

(3) Majority U.S. shareholder year.

(i) In general.

(ii) Passthrough entities.

(4) Inconsistent majority U.S. shareholder years.

(i) In general.

(ii) Formula for determining least aggregate deferral.

(iii) Illustrations.

(iv) Procedural requirements and effective date.

(5) Testing days.

(i) In general.

(ii) Illustration.

(iii) Additional testing days.

(iv) Illustration.

(v) Anti-abuse rule.

(b) Foreign personal holding companies.

(1) In general.

(2) One-month deferral election not available.

(3) Testing days.

§1.898-4. Special rules.

(a) Changes in the required year of a specified foreign corporation for its first taxable year beginning after July 10, 1989.

(1) In general.

(2) Procedure for a specified foreign corporation to conform to the required year for the first taxable year beginning after July 10, 1989.

(i) No section 898(c)(1)(B) election.

(ii) With section 898(c)(1)(B) election.

(iii) Filing requirement.

(b) Changes in the required year of a specified foreign corporation during a taxable year of a specified foreign corporation subsequent to its first taxable year beginning after July 10, 1989.

(1) In general.

(2) Procedure for the change to a new required year of a specified foreign corporation for taxable years subsequent to its first taxable year beginning after July 10, 1989.

(i) Different majority shareholder year.

(ii) Election under section 898(c)(1)(B).

(iii) Procedure for prior years.

(iv) Making a second election under section 898(c)(1) (B).

(v) Procedure for obtaining the consent of the Commissioner to change the required year of specified foreign corporations.

(3) Short period.

(i) In general.

(ii) Illustrations.

(4) Conforming changes in the majority U.S. shareholder year.

(c) Nonconforming foreign and United States taxable years of a specified foreign corporation.

(1) In general.

(2) Computation of income and earnings and profits of a specified foreign corporation.

(i) Separate books of account.

(ii) Income and earnings and profits computation in lieu of separate books.

(iii) Illustration.

(3) 52-53-week taxable year.

(i) In general.

(ii) Majority United States shareholder with a 52-53 week taxable year.

(iii) Specified foreign corporation with a 52-53 week taxable year.

(iv) Illustrations.

(4) Certain captive insurance companies that elect to treat their related person insurance income as income effectively connected with the conduct of a United States trade or business.

(d) Four-year income spread.

[Reg. §1.898-0.]

§1.898-1. Taxable year of certain foreign corporations.—(a) *In general.*—Pursuant to section 898(a), the taxable year of a specified foreign corporation is the required year. The required year is generally the majority U.S. shareholder year. These regulations define specified foreign corporation and United States shareholder, for purposes of these rules, at §1.898-2(a) and (b)(3), respectively. The ownership requirements of a specified foreign corporation, which are a part of the definition of specified foreign corporation, are set forth at §1.898-2 (b)(1) and (2). A special rule for determining whether a foreign corporation that meets the ownership requirements of a foreign personal holding company is a specified foreign corporation is located at §1.898-2(c). Section 1.898-3 sets forth the rules for the determination of the required year, including rules by which a specified foreign corporation that is a controlled foreign corporation may elect a taxable year beginning one month earlier than the majority U.S. shareholder year. Section 1.898-4 sets forth special rules including rules at paragraphs (a) and (b) of that section on changes in the required year, rules at paragraph (c) of that section covering situations where the required year under section 898 is different from the specified foreign corporation's foreign taxable year (the taxable year for purposes of computing income tax liabilities due a foreign country), and rules at paragraph (d) of that section regarding the four-year spread of certain income.

(b) *Effective dates.*—Sections 1.898-1 through 1.898-4 are effective for taxable years of specified foreign corporations beginning after July 10, 1989. However, §§1.898-3 (a)(4)(regarding situations in which inconsistent majority U.S. shareholder years exist) and 1.898-3 (a)(5)(iii)(regarding situations in which additional testing days are required) are effective for taxable years beginning after [INSERT DATE 120 DAYS AFTER DATE OF PUBLICATION OF FINAL REGULATIONS IN THE FEDERAL REGISTER], and section 1.898-4 (b) is effective for changes in the required year of a specified foreign corporation subsequent to its first taxable year beginning after July 10, 1989.

(c) *Exceptions to section 898.*—(1) *Specified foreign corporations with no section 951(a) or foreign personal holding company income.*—A specified foreign corporation is not required to conform its taxable year to the required year so long as its United States shareholders do not have any amount includible in gross income pursuant to section 951(a) and do not receive any actual or deemed distributions attributable to amounts described in section 553 with respect to that corporation. Once any United States shareholder of that specified foreign corporation has any amount includible in gross income pursuant to section 951(a) or receives any actual or deemed distributions attributable to amounts described in section 553 with respect to that corporation, then the specified foreign corporation must comply with section 898 and §§1.898-3 and 1.898-4 beginning with its first taxable year subsequent to the taxable year to which that shareholder's income is attributable. Once the specified foreign corporation is required to conform its taxable year to the required year, the fact that the shareholders of the corporation cease to have any such amount includible in gross income pursuant to section 951(a) or section 553 is not relevant. Section 898 continues to apply.

(2) *Elections to be treated as domestic corporations.*—A foreign corporation that is a foreign insurance company and that elects to be treated as a domestic corporation pursuant to section 953(d) is treated as a domestic corporation for all purposes of the Code and, thus, is not subject to section 898. Likewise, a foreign corporation organized under the laws of a contiguous foreign country and described in section 1504(d) is not subject to section 898 if the foreign corporation is treated as a domestic corporation in accordance with section 1504(d). [Reg. §1.898-1.]

§1.898-2. Definition of specified foreign corporation.—(a) *In general.*—For purposes of section 898 and §§1.898-1 through 1.898-4, a specified foreign corporation means any foreign corporation with respect to which the ownership requirements of section 898(b)(2) and paragraph (b) of this section are met and which either is treated as a controlled foreign corporation for any purpose under sections 951 through 964 of the Code (including sections 957(a), 957(b) and 953(c)), or is a foreign personal holding company, as defined in section 552.

(b) *Ownership requirements.*—(1) *In general.*—The ownership requirements of section 898(b)(2) and this paragraph (b)(1) are met with respect to any foreign corporation if a United States shareholder owns, or is considered to own by applying the attribution rules set forth in paragraph (b)(2) of this section, on each testing day, more than 50 percent of the total voting power of all classes of stock of the foreign corporation entitled to vote, or more than 50 percent of the total value of all classes of stock of the foreign corporation.

(2) *Ownership by attribution.*—For purposes of section 898(b)(2)(A) and paragraph (b)(1) of this section, the rules contained in the following sections of the Internal Revenue Code apply in determining ownership—

(i) Section 958(a) and (b) for determining direct, indirect, and constructive stock ownership of a controlled foreign corporation;

(ii) Section 551(f) pertaining to the stock of a foreign personal holding company held through a foreign entity; and,

(iii) Section 554 for determining stock ownership of a foreign personal holding company.

(3) *Definition of United States shareholder.*—(i) *In general.*—For purposes of §§1.898-1 through 1.898-4, United States shareholder has the meaning given to it by section 951(b), except that, in the case of a foreign corporation having related person insurance income, as defined in section 953(c)(2), a person will be treated as a United States shareholder for purposes of section 898 if that person is treated as a United States shareholder under section 953(c)(1). *See* section 898(b)(3)(A).

(ii) *Certain captive insurance companies.*—The determination of whether certain shareholders are United States shareholders under section 953(c)(1) and, consequently, whether the foreign corporation is a controlled foreign corporation for a particular taxable year, depends on the proportion of related person insurance income to total insurance income earned by the foreign corporation during the taxable year. If the related person insurance income of the foreign corporation is less than 20 percent of its total insurance income for the year, then the special rules of section 953(c) for captive insurance companies will not apply. The determination of whether the related person insurance income of a foreign corporation is less than 20 percent of its total insurance income for a particular taxable year cannot be made until the end of that year. Consequently, a foreign corporation that derives related person insurance income generally will not be required to consider non-10 percent United States shareholders (*i.e.*, persons who are United States shareholders only because of the special captive insurance rules) in determining whether it is a controlled foreign corporation on the first day of the foreign corporation's taxable year to determine further whether it is a specified foreign corporation and, therefore, subject to section 898, unless the foreign corporation was treated as a controlled foreign corporation because of the special captive insurance rules for the immediately preceding taxable year. When a foreign corporation is both a captive insurance company and a specified foreign corporation, it must consider all persons who are United States shareholders under both sections 951(b) and 953(c) in determining its required year.

(iii) *Foreign personal holding companies.*—In the case of any foreign personal holding company as defined in section 552, which is not also a specified foreign corporation by reason of being a controlled foreign corporation under section 898(b)(1)(A)(i), United States shareholder means any person who is treated as a United States shareholder under section 551(a).

(4) *Illustrations.*—The application of this paragraph (b) may be illustrated by the following examples:

Example 1. Z is a publicly traded United States corporation that owns all of the outstanding stock of FY, a foreign corporation. FY is not a foreign personal holding company. FY owns 51 percent (of both voting power and value) of all of the outstanding stock of FX, which is also a foreign corporation. The remainder of the stock is owned by an unrelated foreign corporation. FY is a controlled foreign corporation and a specified foreign corporation. In addition, pursuant to section 958(a)(2), Z is considered to own its proportionate share (*i.e.*, 51 percent) of the stock of FX which is owned by FY. Thus, FX is also both a controlled foreign corporation and [a] specified foreign corporation, as defined in section 898(b) and this section.

Example 2. Z is a United States citizen who owns 51 percent of the value, but none of the voting stock, of FY, a foreign corporation. The remaining 49 percent of the value of FY, as well as all of FY's voting stock, is owned by a nonresident alien individual who is not related to Z. FY owns 51 percent (of both voting power and value) of all of the outstanding stock of FX, which is also a foreign corporation. FY is not a controlled foreign corporation because it does not have a United States shareholder within the meaning of section 951(b)(although if FY had related person insurance income it may be a controlled foreign corporation under the rules of section 953(c)). FY was a foreign personal holding company for its prior year. FY is a foreign personal holding company and a specified foreign corporation for the current year for purposes of section 898 because Z is a United States shareholder within the meaning of section 551(a) who owns 51 percent of the total value of the stock of FY. *See* section 552(a)(2)(B). Under section 551(f), however, the stock of FX owned by FY is not treated as being owned proportionately by Z. Accordingly, FX is not subject to section 898.

Example 3. FX has 20 equal shareholders, all of whom are related United States persons. Thus, FX does not qualify as a controlled foreign corporation under the general subpart F rules applicable to insurance companies because none of the United States persons are United States shareholders. However, if FX earns related person insurance income in a particular taxable year, then it will be considered a controlled foreign corporation for that year, unless the amount of the related person insurance income was less than 20 percent of its total insurance income for that year. If, in its taxable year ending December 31, 1990, FX earns related person insurance income in an amount that is less than 20 percent of its total insurance income and, thus, is not considered a controlled foreign corporation, then FX would not be required to determine its required year on January 1, 1991. Alternatively, if FX earns related person insurance income in its taxable year ending December 31, 1990, in excess of the 20 percent *de minimis* amount and, thus, is considered a controlled foreign corporation, FX would be required to determine whether it is a specified foreign corporation on January 1, 1991, and in making that determination, would be required to treat all United States persons owning its stock as United States shareholders.

(c) *Special rule for foreign personal holding companies that are not controlled foreign corporations.*—(1) *In general.*—A foreign corporation that is not a controlled foreign corporation for 30 days or more during the current taxable year will be required to determine whether it is a specified foreign corporation on any testing day during the current year only if the foreign corporation—

(i) meets the ownership requirements of section 552(a)(2)(ownership requirements for a foreign personal holding company) for the current taxable year, and

(ii) was a foreign personal holding company for its taxable year immediately preceding the current taxable year.

(2) *Illustrations.*—The application of this paragraph (c) may be illustrated by the following examples:

Example 1. (i) FX is a foreign corporation that uses the calendar year as its taxable year. For calendar year 1989, its last taxable year beginning before the effective date of section 898, FX met the stock ownership requirements of section 552(a)(2) for a foreign personal holding company. More than 50 percent of the total value of all classes of stock of FX is owned by Y, a United States shareholder with a taxable year ending June 30. The remaining value of FX stock, and all of FX's voting stock, is owned by Z, a nonresident alien individual who is unrelated to Y. FX is not a controlled foreign corporation.

(ii) On January 1, 1990 (FX's first testing day after the effective date of section 898), FX examined its gross income for the taxable year ending December 31, 1989. FX met the gross income requirement of section 552(a)(1) for a foreign personal holding company for that year. Therefore, under the rules of this paragraph (c), FX was deemed to be a foreign personal holding company, for purposes of section 898, for the current taxable year beginning January 1, 1990. Accordingly, FX was required to determine whether it was a specified foreign corporation on January 1, 1990. FX was a specified foreign corporation on that date and, therefore, was required to change its taxable year to the required year ending on June 30.

Example 2. The facts are the same as in *Example 1,* with the additional fact that FX did not meet the gross income requirement for a foreign personal holding company for the short taxable year beginning January 1, 1990, and ending June 30, 1990. Nevertheless, FX will be required to maintain a taxable year beginning July 1, 1990, as its required year under section 898(c). [Reg. §1.898-2.]

§1.898-3. Determining the required year.—(a) *Controlled foreign corporations.*—(1) *In general.*—The required year is the majority U.S. shareholder year prescribed in section 898(c)(1)(C) and paragraph (a)(3) of this section. If, however, there are inconsistent majority U.S. shareholder years, then the required year is the taxable year prescribed in section 898(c)(1)(A)(ii) and paragraph (a)(4) of this section.

(2) *One-month deferral election.*—A specified foreign corporation that is a controlled foreign corporation may elect under section 898(c)(1)(B) and §1.898-4(a)(2)(ii) and (b)(2)(ii) of this section a taxable year beginning one month earlier than the majority U.S. shareholder year. The specified foreign corporation may revoke this election; see §1.898-4(b). If the specified foreign corporation revokes the election, it may re-elect the one-month deferral only if it follows the procedures set forth in §1.898-4(b)(2)(iv) and (v). A specified foreign corporation that is a foreign personal holding company, but is not a controlled foreign corporation, may not make this election. Also, this election may not be made by a specified foreign corporation that is a controlled foreign corporation, but whose required year is the taxable year prescribed by section 898(c)(1)(A)(ii) and paragraph (a)(4) of this section because there are inconsistent majority U.S. shareholder years.

(3) *Majority U.S. shareholder year.*—(i) *In general.*—For the purpose of determining the required year of a specified foreign corporation, the majority U.S. shareholder year under section 898(c)(1)(C)(i) means the taxable year (if any) which, on each testing day as defined in paragraph (a)(5) of this section, constitutes the taxable year of a United States shareholder described in either paragraph (a)(3)(i)(A) or (B) of this section.

(A) Each United States shareholder, as defined in section 898(b)(3)(A) and §1.898-2(b)(3), that owns more than 50 percent of the voting power of all classes of stock of the specified foreign corporation entitled to vote, or more than 50 percent of the total value of all classes of stock of the specified foreign corporation, after application of the attribution rules of section 898(b)(2)(B). This shareholder is described in section 898(b)(2)(A) and is referred to in this section as a "more than 50 percent United States shareholder."

(B) Each United States shareholder, as defined in section 898(b)(3)(A) and §1.898-2(b)(3), that is not a more than 50 percent United States shareholder and whose stock was treated as owned under section 898(b)(2)(B) (the attribution rules) by a more than 50 percent United States shareholder.

(ii) *Passthrough entities.*—For the purpose of determining the required year of a specified foreign corporation, if each United States shareholder described in paragraph (a)(3)(i)(A) or (B) of this section is a passthrough entity, such as an S corporation, partnership, trust, or estate, then the majority U.S. shareholder year is the taxable year which, on a testing day, constitutes the taxable year of the passthrough entity and not the taxable year or years of the passthrough entity's shareholders, partners, or beneficiaries.

(4) *Inconsistent majority U.S. shareholder years.*—(i) *In general.*—There may exist more than one majority U.S. shareholder year under section 898(c)(1)(C)(i) and paragraph (a)(3) of this section because the taxable years of shareholders described in paragraph (a)(3)(i)(A) or (B) of this section may be different taxable years. If the majority U.S. shareholder years are inconsistent, then the specified foreign corporation must adopt the taxable year that results in the least aggregate deferral of income to all United States shareholders of the specified foreign corporation, even if that taxable year is not a majority U.S. shareholder year. See paragraph (a)(4)(iii), *Example 2,* of this section. If the required year is the taxable year prescribed by this paragraph (a)(4) because there are inconsistent majority U.S. shareholder years, then the one-month deferral election under section 898(c)(1)(B) and paragraph (a)(2) of this section is not available.

(ii) *Formula for determining least aggregate deferral.*—The aggregate deferral of income for a particular year is equal to the sum of the products determined by multiplying, on each testing day as defined in paragraph (a)(5) of this section, the number of month(s) of deferral for each United States shareholder, that are shareholders on the testing day, that would be generated by that year end by that United States shareholder's percentage interest in deemed distributions from the specified foreign corporation.

The United States shareholder's taxable year that produces the lowest sum when compared to the other United States shareholders' taxable years is the taxable year that results in the least aggregate deferral of income to the United States shareholders. For purposes of this section, the number of months of deferral for a United States shareholder of a specified foreign corporation is measured by the number of months from the end of the taxable year of the specified foreign corporation to the end of the taxable year of the United States shareholder. Part of a month is treated as a month. If the calculation results in more than one taxable year qualifying as the taxable year with the least aggregate deferral, the specified foreign corporation may select any one of such taxable years as its required year. However, if one of such qualifying taxable years is also the specified foreign corporation's existing taxable year, the specified foreign corporation must maintain its existing taxable year.

(iii) *Illustrations.*—The application of this paragraph (a)(4) may be illustrated by the following examples:

Example 1. (i) FX is a foreign corporation with two classes of stock, only one of which is voting stock. Each class of stock shares equally in distributions. FX has a June 30 taxable year. FX's shareholders, A, B and C are U.S. citizens. A owns 45 percent of each class of stock, B owns 35 percent of each class of stock, and C owns the remaining 20 percent of each class of stock. A is B's grandfather and C is unrelated to A and B. A and C are calendar year taxpayers. B's taxable year ends on June 30. Under sections 958(b)(1) and 318(a)(1)(A), A is considered to own the stock owned by B. Under section 898(c)(1)(C)(i)(I), A is a more than 50 percent United States shareholder and under section 898(c)(1)(C)(i)(II), B is a United States shareholder whose stock is considered to be owned by a more than 50 percent United States shareholder. Accordingly, FX has two majority U.S. shareholder years, the calendar year and the fiscal year ending June 30. These majority U.S. shareholder years are inconsistent.

(ii) Beginning July 1, 1990, the first day of FX's first taxable year beginning after July 10, 1989, FX must conform its taxable year to the required year by adopting the taxable year that results in the least aggregate deferral of income, taking into consideration the taxable year of each United States shareholder, including C. The taxable year ending December 31 produces .35 × 6 (B's percentage share of distributions from FX multiplied by the number of months of deferral if December 31 is the required year), or a product of 2.1. The taxable year ending June 30 produces [.45 × 6] plus [.20 × 6] (A and C's percentage shares of distributions from FX multiplied by the number of months of deferral if June 30 is the required year), or a product of 3.9. Accordingly, the taxable year ending December 31 is the required year. However, if C's year end were also June 30, or if only the nonvoting stock shared in distributions and B owned all of the nonvoting stock, then the taxable year ending June 30 would produce the least aggregate deferral of income, and would be the required year.

Example 2. (i) LX is a calendar year foreign corporation with one class of stock. LX's shareholders, A, B and C are U.S. citizens. A is B's grandfather and C is unrelated to A and B. A owns 10 percent of LX's stock and has a taxable year ending June 30. B owns 45 percent of LX's stock and has a taxable year ending March 31. C owns the remaining 45 percent of LX and has a September 30 taxable year. Under sections 958(b)(1) and 318(a)(1) (A), A is considered to own the stock owned by B. Under section 898(c)(1)(C)(i)(I), A is a more than 50 percent United States shareholder and under section 898(c)(1)(C) (i)(II), B is a United States shareholder whose stock is considered to be owned by a more than 50 percent United States shareholder. Accordingly, LX has two inconsistent majority U.S. shareholder years, the fiscal year ending June 30 and the fiscal year ending March 31.

(ii) Beginning January 1, 1990, the first day of LX's first taxable year beginning after July 10, 1989, LX must conform its taxable year to the required year by adopting the taxable year that results in the least aggregate deferral of income, taking into consideration the taxable year of each United States shareholder. The taxable year ending June 30 produces [.45 × 3] plus [.45 × 9] (B and C's, respective percentage shares of distributions multiplied by the number of months of deferral), or a product of 5.4. The taxable year ending March 31 produces [.1 × 9] plus [.45 × 6] (A and C's percentage shares of distributions multiplied by the number of months of deferral), or a product of 3.6. The taxable year ending September 30 produces [.1 × 3] plus [.45 × 6] (A and B's percentage shares of distributions multiplied by the number of months of deferral), or a product of 3.0. Accordingly, September 30 is the required year.

(iv) *Procedural requirements and effective date.*—This paragraph (a)(4) is effective for taxable years beginning after [INSERT DATE 120 DAYS AFTER DATE OF PUBLICATION OF FINAL REGULATIONS IN THE FEDERAL REGISTER]. In order to show that the requirements of this paragraph (a)(4) are satisfied, a statement setting forth the computations required to establish the taxable year that results in the least aggregate deferral of income to the United States shareholders of the specified foreign corporation must be attached to Form 5471 and, if applicable, to Form 1120F, and must indicate the following at the top of page one of the statement: "FILED UNDER § 1.898-3(a)(4)."

(5) *Testing days.*—(i) *In general.*—A specified foreign corporation must identify its majority U.S. shareholder year(s), if any, for the purpose of determining its required year. The specified foreign corporation must determine its majority U.S. shareholder year on each testing day. In general, the testing day is the first day of the specified foreign corporation's taxable year for U.S. tax purposes, determined without regard to section 898. *See* section 898(c)(1)(C)(ii).

(ii) *Illustration.*—The application of paragraph (a)(5)(i) of this section may be illustrated by the following example:

Example. FX is a foreign corporation that, prior to the effective date of section 898, used the calendar year as its taxable year. Thus, on January 1, 1990, the first day of FX's first taxable year beginning after July 10, 1989, FX determined whether it was a specified foreign corporation and, thus, required to change its taxable year to the required year under section 898(c). Based on this test, FX changed to a taxable year ending on June 30 (because FX was a specified foreign corporation and its majority U.S. shareholder year ends on June 30). Accordingly, FX had a short period taxable year for the period beginning January 1, 1990, and ending June 30, 1990. On July 1, 1990, the first day of its new taxable year, FX again tested to determine whether it was using the required year.

(iii) *Additional testing days.*—For taxable years of specified foreign corporations beginning after [INSERT DATE THAT IS 120 DAYS AFTER FINAL REGULATIONS ARE PUBLISHED IN THE FEDERAL REGISTER], a specified foreign corporation must determine its majority U.S. shareholder year on each day, since the most recent testing day described in paragraph (a) (5)(i) of this section, on which a substantial change occurs in the United States ownership of the stock of the specified foreign corporation. A substantial change in the United States ownership of the stock of a specified foreign corporation is a change that results in a new more than 50 percent United States shareholder of the foreign corporation.

(iv) *Illustration.*—The application of paragraph (a) (5)(iii) of this section may be illustrated by the following example:

Example. FX is a controlled foreign corporation with one class of stock and a taxable year ending on June 30. Y, the majority United States shareholder of FX, owns 51 percent of the stock of FX. Y also has a taxable year ending June 30. Thus, FX is a specified foreign corporation subject to section 898. On May 1, 1994, Y sold 10 percent of the stock in FX to Z, an unrelated United States corporation that owned 41 percent of the stock of FX before the sale. Z obtained, therefore, a sufficient amount of FX stock to qualify as a "more than 50 percent United States shareholder" of FX. Z has a taxable year ending on April 30. Consequently, on May 1, 1994, FX determined that its new required year was a taxable year ending April 30. FX has a taxable year ending June 30, 1994, and a short taxable year beginning July 1, 1994, and ending April 30, 1995. *See* § 1.898-4(b)(3).

(v) *Anti-abuse rule.*—The district director may require the use of a testing day other than that identified in paragraph (a)(5)(i) or (iii) of this section that will reflect more accurately the ownership of the specified foreign corporation and thereby the aggregate deferral of income to the United States shareholders of the specified foreign corporation where the United States shareholders engage in a transaction (or transactions) that has as its principal purpose the avoidance of the principles of this section. Thus, the anti-abuse rule of the preceding sentence would apply, for example, when there is a transfer of an interest in a specified foreign corporation that results in a temporary transfer of that interest principally for the purpose of qualifying for a specific taxable year under the principles of this section.

(b) *Foreign personal holding companies.*—(1) *In general.*—The required year is the majority U.S. shareholder year prescribed by section 898(c)(1)(A) and paragraph (a) (3) of this section. If, however, there are inconsistent majority U.S. shareholder years, then the required year is the taxable year determined under the provisions of paragraph (a)(4) of this section.

(2) *One-month deferral election not available.*—A specified foreign corporation that is a foreign personal holding company, but is not a controlled foreign corporation, may not make the one-month deferral election of paragraph (a)(2) of this section.

(3) *Testing days. See.*—paragraph (a)(5) of this section. [Reg. § 1.898-3.]

§ 1.898-4. Special rules.—(a) *Changes in the required year of a specified foreign corporation for its first taxable year beginning after July 10, 1989.*—(1) *In general.*—A specified foreign corporation must conform its taxable year to the required year as defined in section 898(c) for taxable years beginning after July 10, 1989. In addition, section 898(c) (1)(B) permits a specified foreign corporation that is a controlled foreign corporation to elect a taxable year beginning one month earlier than the majority U.S. shareholder year.

(2) *Procedure for a specified foreign corporation to conform to the required year for the first taxable year beginning after July 10, 1989.*—(i) *No section 898(c)(1)(B) election.*—If no election under section 898(c)(1)(B) can be made because the specified foreign corporation is a foreign personal holding company, or no election is being made for a specified foreign corporation that is a controlled foreign corporation, but the specified foreign corporation is changing its first taxable year beginning after July 10, 1989, to conform to the required year, then unless the instructions to the forms provide otherwise, the words "Change in Taxable Year" must be placed in the upper left hand corner of the first page of Form 5471 and, if applicable, on Form 1120F, with respect to the specified foreign corporation for the taxable year for which the change is made. If a specified foreign corporation is not required to change its taxable year, then no notation concerning this fact need appear on Form 5471 and, if applicable, on Form 1120F.

(ii) *With section 898(c)(1)(B) election.*—The election under section 898(c)(1)(B) may be made for a specified foreign corporation that is a controlled foreign corporation for its first taxable year beginning after July 10, 1989, by indicating on Form 5471 and, if applicable, on Form 1120F, that the taxable year shown on the form with respect to the controlled foreign corporation was determined in accordance with section 898(c)(1)(B). The following words must be used unless the instructions to the forms provide otherwise:

(A) If the election involves a change in the taxable year of the controlled foreign corporation, the words "Section 898(c)(1)(B) Election – Change in Taxable Year" must be placed in the upper left hand corner of the first page of Form 5471 and, if applicable, on Form 1120F; and

(B) If the election does not involve a change in the taxable year of the controlled foreign corporation, the words, "Section 898(c)(1)(B) Election" must be placed in the upper left hand corner of the first page of Form 5471 and, if applicable, on Form 1120.

(iii) *Filing requirement.*—If a specified foreign corporation changed its required year for its first taxable year beginning after July 10, 1989, to conform to the requirements of section 898 and § 1.898-3 but did not follow the procedures set forth in Rev. Proc. 90-26 and this paragraph (a)(2), a statement must be attached to the first

Form 5471 and, if applicable, Form 1120F, to be filed after [INSERT DATE THAT IS 120 DAYS AFTER DATE OF PUBLICATION OF FINAL REGULATIONS IN THE FEDERAL REGISTER]indicating that the corporation's taxable year was changed to conform to the requirements of section 898. If a specified foreign corporation has not conformed its first taxable year beginning after July 10, 1989, to the taxable year required by section 898 and § 1.898-3, an amended return with an amended Form 5471 (or Form 1120F) must be filed to satisfy the requirements of section 898, § 1.898-3 and this paragraph (a)(2).

(b) *Changes in the required year of a specified foreign corporation during a taxable year of a specified foreign corporation subsequent to its first taxable year beginning after July 10, 1989.*—(1) *In general.*—A specified foreign corporation must conform its taxable year to a different required year should circumstances arise in which the required year changes under the rules of § 1.898-3, such as when a substantial change in ownership of a specified foreign corporation results in a new more than 50 percent United States shareholder with a different majority U.S. shareholder year. The change in taxable year of a specified foreign corporation made to conform to a different required year shall be treated as initiated by the taxpayer and as having been made with the consent of the Commissioner. The requirements set forth in this paragraph (b) are effective for taxable years subsequent to a specified foreign corporation's first taxable year beginning after July 10, 1989.

(2) *Procedure for the change to a new required year of a specified foreign corporation for taxable years subsequent to its first taxable year beginning after July 10, 1989.*—(i) *Different majority U.S. shareholder year.*—If the specified foreign corporation is changing its taxable year to conform to a different required year under paragraph (b)(1) of this section, unless the instructions to the forms provide otherwise, the words "Change in Taxable Year" must be placed in the upper left hand corner of the first page of Form 5471 and, if applicable, on Form 1120F, with respect to the specified foreign corporation for the taxable year for which the change is made. This paragraph covers terminations of prior elections under section 898(c)(1)(B) made in conjunction with that change.

(ii) *Election under section 898(c)(1)(B).*—If the specified foreign corporation that is a controlled foreign corporation is changing its taxable year to conform to a different required year under paragraph (b) of this section and an election under section 898(c)(1)(B) is made, the change in taxable year and the election under section 898 (c)(1)(B) are to be noted on Form 5471 and, if applicable, on Form 1120F, with respect to that corporation for the taxable year for which the change and election are made. Unless the instructions to the forms provide otherwise, the words "Section 898(c)(1)(B) Election – Change in Taxable Year" must be placed in the upper left hand corner of the first page of each form. This paragraph covers terminations of prior elections under section 898(c)(1)(B) made in conjunction with that election.

(iii) *Procedure for prior years.*—If a specified foreign corporation conformed its taxable year to that required by section 898 and § 1.898-3 prior to [INSERT DATE THAT IS 120 DAYS AFTER DATE OF PUBLICATION OF FINAL REGULATIONS IN THE FEDERAL REGISTER] but did not follow the procedures set forth in this paragraph (b)(2), a statement must be attached to the first Form 5471 and, if applicable, Form 1120F, to be filed after [INSERT DATE THAT IS 120 DAYS AFTER DATE OF PUBLICATION OF FINAL REGULATIONS IN THE FEDERAL REGISTER] indicating that the corporation's taxable year was changed to conform to the requirements of section 898 and § 1.898-3. If a specified foreign corporation has not conformed a taxable year subsequent to its first taxable year beginning after July 10, 1989, to the taxable year required by section 898 and § 1.898-3, an amended return, with an amended Form 5471 (or Form 1120F) must be filed to satisfy the requirements of section 898, § 1.898-3 and this paragraph (b)(2).

(iv) *Making a second election under section 898(c)(1)(B).*—Except for an election under section 898(c)(1)(B) that is made in conjunction with a change in its taxable year to conform to a different required year under paragraph (b)(2)(ii) of this section, a specified foreign corporation that has elected the one-month deferral under section 898(c)(1)(B) and subsequently revoked that election shall not be eligible to make an election under section 898(c)(1)(B) for any taxable year before its fifth taxable year which begins after the first taxable year for which the revocation is effective, unless the consent of the Commissioner pursuant to the procedures set forth in paragraph (b)(2)(v) of this section is obtained.

(v) *Procedure for obtaining the consent of the Commissioner to change the required year of specified foreign corporations.*—In the circumstance described in paragraph (b)(2)(iv) of this section, a specified foreign corporation must request the approval of the Commissioner for a change in taxable year by completing and filing Form 1128 (Application for Change in Accounting Period) (or successor form) with the Commissioner. The application may be filed either by the majority United States shareholder on behalf of the specified foreign corporation or by the specified foreign corporation. The application must be filed on or before the 15th day of the second calendar month following the close of the short period for which a return is required to effect the change in taxable year. Reference to this regulation must be made part of the application by placing the following statement at the top of page one of the application: "FILED UNDER § 1.898-4." Approval of a change in taxable year described in paragraph (b)(2)(iv) of this section will not be granted unless the taxpayer agrees to the terms, conditions, and adjustments, as set forth by the Commissioner, under which the change will be effected. Unless the instructions to the forms indicate otherwise, re-election of section 898(c)(1)(B) must be noted on Form 5471 and, if applicable, on Form 1120F, for the taxable year for which the re-election is made. Unless the instructions to the forms indicate otherwise, the words "Re-elected Section 898(c)(1)(B) Election – Change in Taxable Year" must be placed in the upper left hand corner of the first page of each form.

(3) *Short period.*—(i) *In general.*—Any short period required for a specified foreign corporation to effect the change in taxable year de-

scribed in paragraph (b)(1) of this section will begin on the first day of the specified foreign corporation's current taxable year and will end on the last day of the new required year within which the change in ownership of the specified foreign corporation (or other event that necessitates a change in taxable year) occurs. If, however, the last day of the specified foreign corporation's current taxable year occurs prior to the last day of the new required year within which the change in ownership of the specified foreign corporation (or other event resulting in a new required year) occurs, then the short period will begin the day following the last day of the specified foreign corporation's current taxable year and end on the last day of the new required year subsequent to the required year within which the change in ownership of the specified foreign corporation (or other event resulting in a new required year) occurred. In no case shall the taxable year of the specified foreign corporation be in excess of one year.

(ii) *Illustrations.*—The application of this paragraph (b)(3) may be illustrated by the following examples:

Example 1. FX is a foreign corporation that is a specified foreign corporation within the meaning of section 898(b). FX had been a calendar year taxpayer. On July 1, 1991, FX was purchased by a United States shareholder with a September 30 fiscal year. Accordingly, the short period required to change the taxable year of FX to the required year began on January 1, 1991, the first day of FX's current taxable year, and ended on September 30, 1991, the last day of the new required year within which the change in ownership of FX occurred.

Example 2. The facts are the same as in *Example 1* except that on July 1, 1991, FX was purchased by a United States shareholder with a June 30 fiscal year. Accordingly, the short period required to change the taxable year of FX to the required year did not begin until January 1, 1992, the day following the last day of FX's current taxable year because the last day of FX's current taxable year occurs prior to the last day of the new required year within which the change in ownership occurred. The short period will begin January 1, 1992, and will end June 30, 1992.

(4) *Conforming changes in the majority U.S. shareholder year.*—The requirements of section 898 and §§1.898-3 and 1.898-4 may be satisfied by a majority United States shareholder of a specified foreign corporation changing its taxable year to conform to the taxable year of the specified foreign corporation. However, any change to the United States shareholder's taxable year requires the approval of the Commissioner, and must be made in accordance with section 442 and the regulations under that section, relating to changes of annual accounting period.

(c) *Nonconforming foreign and United States taxable years of a specified foreign corporation.*—(1) *In general.*—If a specified foreign corporation's foreign taxable year (for purposes of computing income tax liabilities due a foreign country) does not conform to the required year pursuant to section 898(c) and §1.898-3, then the United States shareholders must compute any income inclusion relating to the specified foreign corporation including, but not limited to, subpart F income, increase in earnings invested in United States property, foreign personal holding company income, and section 864(d) income in accordance with the rules set forth in paragraphs (c)(2) and (3) of this section. However, see section 338 and the regulations under that section for rules applicable to certain domestic and foreign corporations, and the shareholders of those corporations where an election under that section is made.

(2) *Computation of income and earnings and profits of a specified foreign corporation.*—(i) *Separate books of account.*—A specified foreign corporation that has a foreign taxable year different from its required year, as determined under section 898(c) and §1.898-3, will have portions of two foreign annual accounting periods in each required year. In this case, either separate books of account for the specified foreign corporation based upon the required year may be maintained, or income (and earnings and profits) shall be computed as set forth in paragraph (c)(2)(ii) of this section. Books of account must be maintained on a consistent basis for each foreign annual accounting period.

(ii) *Income and earnings and profits computation in lieu of separate books.*—In lieu of maintaining separate books of account, income and earnings and profits shall be computed in two steps. First, for the foreign annual accounting period of the specified foreign corporation which ends within its required year, the income (and earnings and profits) of the specified foreign corporation is the entire income (or earnings and profits) of the foreign annual accounting period, less the income (or earnings and profits), if any, of that foreign annual accounting period properly allocable to the preceding taxable year, determined under a consistent application of the principles of section 964 and the regulations under that section. Second, for the foreign annual accounting period of the specified foreign corporation which ends after its required year, the income (and earnings and profits) of the specified foreign corporation is the income (and earnings and profits) of each month (or quarter) which has ended within the required year determined on the basis of interim actual book closings and computed by a consistent application of the principles of section 964 and the regulations under that section. If the amount of income properly includable in the gross income of United States shareholders in the preceding taxable year is different from the amount of income actually included by United States shareholders in the preceding taxable year, then an adjustment must be made by each United States person affected by means of an amended return for that preceding taxable year.

(iii) *Illustration.*—The application of this paragraph (c)(2) may be illustrated by the following example:

Example. (i) FX is a specified foreign corporation organized in foreign country, FC. FX's annual accounting period and taxable year, for FC purposes, end March 31. FX's required year is the calendar year. FX did not conform its FC taxable year to the required year. Separate books for United States tax purposes are not maintained. Accordingly, FX's required year, Calendar Year 1, will include portions of two FC annual accounting periods and FC taxable years.

(ii) For the FC period ending March 31, during Calendar Year 1, FX's income (in U.S. dollars) was $1,000, all of which was foreign personal holding company income. This amount was determined on the basis of FX's annual March 31, FC financial reports, adjusted in accordance with section 964 and the regulations under that section. Of the $1,000, it was determined from the annual financial reports that $350 was earned during the months ending in Calendar Year 1. For the period April 1, during Calendar Year 1, to the end of Calendar Year 1, FX's income was $1,200, determined on the basis of FX's monthly interim FC books of account. Accordingly, the income of FX subject to inclusion in the gross income of United States shareholders for Calendar Year 1, is $1,550. However, based on FX's annual March 31, Year 2, financial reports (adjusted in accordance with section 964 and the regulations under that section), FX's income for the period April 1, during Calendar Year 1, to the end of Calendar Year 1 was $1,300, not $1,200. Accordingly, each United States shareholder of FX must file an amended return for Calendar Year 1 showing its portion of the additional $100 of income.

(3) *52-53-week taxable year.*—(i) *Majority United States shareholder with a 52-53-week taxable year.*—If a majority United States shareholder elects to follow a 52-53-week taxable year (determined under section 441(f) and the regulations under that section), and the specified foreign corporation does not intend to follow a 52-53-week taxable year, then the required year of the specified foreign corporation, as determined under section 898(c) and § 1.898-3, shall be a 12-month taxable year, which must end on the last day of the same month used in determining the 52-53-week taxable year of its majority United States shareholder. If the election of the one-month deferral under section 898(c)(1)(B) and § 1.898-3(a)(2) is made, the election will be valid, and the specified foreign corporation may retain a 12-month taxable year, subject to the condition that the 12-month taxable year must end on the last day of the month which immediately precedes the month used in determining the 52-53-week taxable year of its majority United States shareholder.

(ii) *Specified foreign corporation with a 52-53-week taxable year.*—If a specified foreign corporation elects to follow a 52-53-week taxable year, and the majority United States shareholder does not intend to follow a 52-53-week taxable year, then the required year, as determined under section 898(c) and § 1.898-3, of the specified foreign corporation shall be a 52-53-week taxable year, which must end within a seven-day period from the last day of the 12-month taxable year of its majority United States shareholder. If the election of the one-month deferral under section 898(c)(1)(B) and § 1.898-3(a)(2) is made, the election will be valid and the specified foreign corporation may retain a 52-53-week taxable year, subject to the condition that the 52-53-week taxable year must end within a seven-day period from the last day of the month which immediately precedes the 12-month taxable year of its majority United States shareholder.

(iii) *Illustrations.*—The application of this paragraph (c)(3) may be illustrated by the following examples:

Example 1. X is a United States corporation created on January 1, 1990, that elected to follow a 52-53-week taxable year which ends on the Friday nearest the end of December. Thus, X's first United States taxable year began on Monday, January 1, 1990, and ended on Friday, December 28, 1990; its next taxable year began on Saturday, December 29, 1990, and ended on Friday, January 3, 1992. X owns 100 percent of FY, a specified foreign corporation that is a controlled foreign corporation which follows a 12-month taxable year ending on November 30. In these circumstances, X's taxable year may end either earlier or later than one month after the end of FY's taxable year. Nonetheless, an election under section 898(c)(1)(B), which would permit FY to retain its current taxable year, will be effective because FY's taxable year ends on the last day of the month which immediately precedes the same month used in determining the 52-53-week taxable year of X, its majority United States shareholder.

Example 2. Y is a United States person with a taxable year ending September 30. Y also is the majority United States shareholder of FX, a specified foreign corporation which is a controlled foreign corporation that wishes to make the one-month deferral election under section 898(c)(1)(B). FX follows a 52-53-week taxable year that ends on the Monday closest to the last day of August. In 1990, the last day of August fell on a Friday. Thus, FX's taxable year ended on Monday, September 3, 1990, a date within a seven-day period from the last day of the month which immediately precedes the 12-month taxable year of its majority United States shareholder, Y. In 1994, FX's taxable year will end on Monday, August 29, and its next taxable year will begin on August 30, 1994. Thus, in 1994, FX's taxable year will begin more than one month before the beginning of Y's United States taxable year. Nevertheless, the election made under section 898(c)(1)(B) will be effective because FX's taxable year will end within a seven-day period from the last day of the month which immediately precedes the 12-month taxable year of its majority United States shareholder.

(4) *Certain captive insurance companies that elect to treat their related person insurance income as income effectively connected with the conduct of a United States trade or business.*—Section 953(c)(3)(C) permits a foreign corporation to elect to treat its related person insurance income as income effectively connected with the conduct of a trade or business in the United States. Under § 1.953-7(c)(3) of proposed regulations, such a foreign corporation must utilize the calendar year as its annual accounting period for United States tax purposes, as required by section 843. Further, if an election is made for the first taxable year beginning after December 31, 1987, or any subsequent taxable year, the election is effective from the first day of the taxable year for which the election is made (and all subsequent taxable years). Therefore, a foreign corporation that has a fiscal taxable year prior to making the election must file a short-year return for the period from the first day the election becomes effective to the last day of the calendar year in which the election is made. The rules under section 953(c)(3)(C) and § 1.953-7 will prevail over the rules under section 898 and this section. Thus, if a captive insurance company that is a specified foreign corporation makes an election pursuant to section 953(c)(3)(C) and § 1.953-7(c), it must use the calendar year as its annual accounting period for United States tax purposes,

regardless of the taxable year of its majority United States shareholder. However, if a captive insurance company that is a specified foreign corporation does not make the election pursuant to section 953(c)(3)(C) and the regulations thereunder, it must conform its United States taxable year to that of its majority United States shareholder.

(d) *Four-year income spread.*—For its first taxable year beginning after July 10, 1989, if, because of the change necessitated by section 898 in the taxable year of the specified foreign corporation, any United States person was required to include in gross income for one taxable year amounts attributable to two taxable years of the specified foreign corporation, the amount that the United States person would otherwise have included in gross income for the one taxable year by reason of the short taxable year of the specified foreign corporation resulting from the change shall be included in that person's gross income ratably over a four-taxable-year period beginning with that one taxable year. A United States person who is required by reason of section 898 to include in gross income amounts attributable to two taxable years of a specified foreign corporation may not waive the four-year ratable inclusion of such gross income. [Reg. §1.898-4.]

Accounting Periods: Adoptions: Changes: Retentions

Accounting Periods: Adoptions: Changes: Retentions.—Amendments to proposed Reg. §1.898-4 (see above), relating to certain adoptions, changes, and retentions of annual accounting periods, are proposed (published in the Federal Register on June 13, 2001) (REG-106917-99).

☐ Par. 9. Section 1.898-4, as proposed to be added at 58 FR 297, January 5, 1993, is amended by adding paragraph (c)(3)(iv) to read as follows:

§1.898-4. Special rules.

* * *

(c) * * *

(3) * * *

(iv) *Recognition of income and deductions.*—See §1.441-2(e) for rules regarding the recognition of income and deductions (e.g., amounts includible in gross income pursuant to sections 951(a) or 553) if either the majority United States shareholder, or the specified foreign corporation, or both, elect to use a 52-53-week taxable year under this paragraph (c)(3).

* * *

Foreign Tax Credit: Determining the Amount of Taxes Paid

Foreign Tax Credit: Determining the Amount of Taxes Paid.—Amendments to Reg. §1.901-2, providing guidance relating to the determination of the amount of taxes paid, are proposed (published in the Federal Register on March 30, 2007) (REG-156779-06). The amendments to Reg. §1.901-2(e)(5)(iv) were adopted as Temporary Reg. §1.901-2T(e)(5)(iv) by T.D. 9416 on July 15, 2008.

☐ Par. 2. Section 1.901-2 is amended by adding paragraphs (e)(5)(iii) and (iv) [see sentence, above, regarding (e)(5)(iv)], and revising paragraph (h) to read as follows:

Caution: Proposed Reg. §1.901-2(e)(5)(iii) will be effective for tax years beginning after the final regulations are published in the Federal Register. Taxpayers can rely on Proposed Reg. §1.901-2(e)(5)(iii) for tax years ending on or after March 29, 2007, and beginning on or before the date the final regulations are published. See Notice 2007-95.

§1.901-2. Income, war profits, or excess profits tax paid or accrued.

* * *

(e)(5) * * *

(iii) *U.S.-owned foreign entities.*—(A) *In general.*—If a U.S. person described in section 901(b) directly or indirectly owns stock possessing 80 percent or more of the total voting power and total value of one or more foreign corporations (or, in the case of a non-corporate foreign entity, directly or indirectly owns an interest in 80 percent or more of the income of one or more such foreign entities), the group comprising such foreign corporations and entities (the "U.S.-owned group") shall be treated as a single taxpayer for purposes of paragraph (e)(5) of this section. Therefore, if one member of such a U.S.-owned group transfers or surrenders a net loss for the taxable year to a second member of the U.S.-owned group and the loss reduces the foreign tax due from the second member pursuant to a foreign law group relief or similar regime, foreign tax paid by the first member in a different year does not fail to be a compulsory payment solely because such tax would not have been due had the member that transferred or surrendered the net loss instead carried over the loss to reduce its own income and foreign tax liability in that year. Similarly, if one or more members of the U.S.-owned group enter into a combined settlement under foreign law of two or more issues involving different members of the group, such settlement will be evaluated on an overall basis, not on an issue-by-issue or entity-by-entity basis, in determining whether an amount is a compulsory amount. The provisions of this paragraph (e)(5)(iii) apply solely for purposes of determining whether amounts paid are compulsory payments of foreign tax and do not, for example, modify the provisions of section 902 requiring separate pools of post-1986 undistributed earnings and post-1986 foreign income taxes for each member of a qualified group.

(B) *Special rules.*—All domestic corporations that are members of a consolidated group (as that term is defined in §1.1502-1(h)) shall be treated as one domestic corporation for purposes of this paragraph (e)(5)(iii). For purposes of this paragraph (e)(5)(iii), indirect ownership of stock or another equity interest (such as an interest in a partnership) shall be determined in accordance with the principles of section 958(a)(2), whether the interest is owned by a U.S. or foreign person.

(C) *Examples.*—The following examples illustrate the rules of this paragraph (e)(5)(iii):

»»→ *Caution: Proposed Reg. §1.901-2(e)(5)(iii) will be effective for tax years beginning after the final regulations are published in the Federal Register. Taxpayers can rely on Proposed Reg. §1.901-2(e)(5)(iii) for tax years ending on or after March 29, 2007, and beginning on or before the date the final regulations are published. See Notice 2007-95.*

Example 1. (i) *Facts.* A, a domestic corporation, wholly owns B, a country X corporation. B, in turn, wholly owns several country X corporations, including C and D. B, C, and D participate in group relief in country X. Under the country X group relief rules, a member with a net loss may choose to surrender the loss to another member of the group. In year 1, C has a net loss of (1,000x) and D has net income of 5,000x for country X tax purposes. Pursuant to the group relief rules in country X, C agrees to surrender its year 1 net loss to D and D agrees to claim the net loss. D uses the net loss to reduce its year 1 net income to 4,000x for country X tax purposes, which reduces the amount of country X tax D owes in year 1 by 300x. In year 2, C earns 3,000x with respect to which it pays 900x of country X tax. Country X permits a taxpayer to carry forward net losses for up to ten years.

(ii) *Result.* Paragraph (e)(5)(i) of this section provides, in part, that an amount paid to a foreign country does not exceed the amount of liability under foreign law for tax if the taxpayer determines such amount in a manner that is consistent with a reasonable interpretation and application of the substantive and procedural provisions of foreign law (including applicable tax treaties) in such a way as to reduce, over time, the taxpayer's reasonably expected liability under foreign law for tax. Under paragraph (e)(5)(iii)(A) of this section, B, C, and D are treated as a single taxpayer for purposes of testing whether the reasonably expected foreign tax liability has been minimized over time, because A directly and indirectly owns 100 percent of each of B, C, and D. Accordingly, none of the 900x paid by C in year 2 fails to be a compulsory payment solely because C could have reduced its year 2 country X tax liability by 300x by choosing to carry forward its year 1 net loss to year 2 instead of surrendering it to D to reduce D's country X liability in year 1.

Example 2. (i) *Facts.* L, M, and N are country Y corporations. L owns 100 percent of the common stock of M, which owns 100 percent of the stock of N. O, a domestic corporation, owns a security issued by M that is treated as debt for country Y tax purposes and as stock for U.S. tax purposes. As a result, L owns 100 percent of the stock of M for country Y purposes while O owns 99 percent of the stock of M for U.S. tax purposes. L, M, and N participate in group relief in country Y. Pursuant to the group relief rules in country Y, M may surrender its loss to any member of the group. In year 1, M has a net loss of $10 million, N has net income of $25 million, and L has net income of $15 million. M chooses to surrender its year 1 net loss to L. Country Y imposes tax of 30 percent on the net income of country Y corporations. Accordingly, in year 1, the loss surrender has the effect of reducing L's country Y tax by $3 million. In year 1, N makes a payment of $7.5 million to country Y with respect to its net income of $25 million. If M had surrendered its net loss to N instead of L, N would have had net income of $15 million, with respect to which it would have owed only $4.5 million of country Y tax.

(ii) *Result.* M and N, but not L, are treated as a single taxpayer for purposes of paragraph (e)(5) of this section because O directly and indirectly owns 99 percent of each of M and N, but owns no direct or indirect interest in L. Accordingly, in testing whether M and N's reasonably expected foreign tax liability has been minimized over time, L is not considered the same taxpayer as M and N, collectively, and the $3 million reduction in L's year 1 country Y tax liability through the surrender to L of M's $10 million country Y net loss in year 1 is not considered to reduce M and N's collective country Y tax liability.

* * *

(h) *Effective date.*—Paragraphs (a) through (e)(5)(ii) and paragraph (g) of this section, § 1.901-2A, and § 1.903-1 apply to taxable years beginning after November 14, 1983. Paragraphs (e)(5)(iii) and (iv) of this section are effective for foreign taxes paid or accrued during taxable years of the taxpayer ending on or after the date on which these regulations are published as final regulations in the Federal Register.

Determination of the Foreign Tax Credit: Guidance

Determination of the Foreign Tax Credit: Guidance.—Reg. § 1.901(j)-1, relating to the determination of the foreign tax credit under the Internal Revenue Code, including changes made by the Tax Cuts and Jobs Act, is proposed (published in the Federal Register on December 7, 2018) (REG-105600-18).

Par. 11. Section 1.901(j)-1 is added to read as follows:

§ 1.901(j)-1. Payment and returns of tax withheld by the acquiring agency.—(a) *Sourcing rule for related party payments and inclusions.*—Any income paid or accrued through one or more entities is treated as income from sources within a country described in section 901(j)(2) if the income was, without regard to such entities, from sources within that country.

(b) *Applicability date.*—This section applies to taxable years that end on or after December 4, 2018. [Reg. § 1.901(j)-1.]

Foreign Tax Credit: Covered Asset Acquisitions

Foreign Tax Credit: Covered Asset Acquisitions.—Reg. §§ 1.901(m)-1—1.901(m)-8, relating to transactions that generally are treated as asset acquisitions for U.S. income tax purposes and either are treated as stock acquisitions or are disregarded for foreign income tax purposes, are proposed (published in the Federal Register on December 7, 2016) (REG-129128-14).

Par. 3. Section 1.901(m)-1 is added to read as follows:

§1.901(m)-1. Definitions.—(a) *Definitions.*—[The text of proposed §1.901(m)-1(a) is the same as the text of §1.901(m)-1T(a) as added by T.D. 9800.]

(1) The term *aggregate basis difference* means, with respect to a foreign income tax and a foreign payor, the sum of the allocated basis differences for a U.S. taxable year of a section 901(m) payor, plus any aggregate basis difference carryover from the immediately preceding U.S. taxable year of the section 901(m) payor with respect to the foreign income tax and foreign payor, as adjusted under §1.901(m)-6(c). For purposes of this definition, if foreign law imposes tax on the combined income (within the meaning of §1.901-2(f)(3)(ii)) of two or more foreign payors, all foreign payors whose items of income, deduction, gain, or loss are included in the U.S. taxable income or earnings and profits of the section 901(m) payor are treated as a single foreign payor. Aggregate basis difference is determined with respect to each separate category described in §1.904-4(m).

(2) The term *aggregate basis difference carryover* has the meaning provided in §1.901(m)-3(c).

(3) The term *aggregated CAA transaction* means a series of related CAAs occurring as part of a plan.

(4) The term *allocable foreign income* means the portion of foreign income of a foreign payor that relates to the foreign income tax amount of the foreign payor that is paid or accrued by, or considered paid or accrued by, a section 901(m) payor.

(5) The term *allocated basis difference* means, with respect to an RFA and a foreign income tax, the sum of the cost recovery amounts and disposition amounts assigned to a U.S. taxable year of the section 901(m) payor under §1.901(m)-5.

(6) through (8) [The text of proposed §§1.901(m)-1(a)(6) through (8) is the same as the text of §§1.901(m)-1T(a)(6) through (8) as added by T.D. 9800.]

(9) The term *cumulative basis difference exemption* has the meaning provided in §1.901(m)-7(b)(2).

(10) through (11) [The text of proposed §§1.901(m)-1(a)(10) through (11) is the same as the text of §§1.901(m)-1T(a)(10) through (11) as added by T.D. 9800.]

(12) The term *disqualified tax amount* has the meaning provided in §1.901(m)-3(b).

(13) through (14) [The text of proposed §§1.901(m)-1(a)(13) through (14) is the same as the text of §§1.901(m)-1T(a)(13) through (14) as added by T.D. 9800.]

(15) The term *foreign basis* means the adjusted basis of an asset determined for purposes of a foreign income tax.

(16) The term *foreign basis election* has the meaning provided in §1.901(m)-4(c).

(17) The term *foreign country creditable tax* (or *FCCT*) means, with respect to a foreign income tax amount, the amount of income, war profits, or excess profits tax paid or accrued to a foreign country or possession of the United States and claimed as a foreign tax credit for purposes of determining the foreign income tax amount. To qualify as a FCCT, the tax imposed by the foreign country or possession must be a foreign income tax or a withholding tax determined on a gross basis as described in section 901(k)(1)(B).

(18) through (21) [The text of proposed §§1.901(m)-1(a)(18) through (21) is the same as the text of §§1.901(m)-1T(a)(18) through (21) as added by T.D. 9800.]

(22) The term *foreign income tax amount* means, with respect to a foreign income tax, the amount of tax (including an amount of tax that is zero) reflected on a foreign tax return (as properly amended or adjusted). If foreign law imposes tax on the combined income (within the meaning of §1.901-2(f)(3)(ii)) of two or more foreign payors, however, a foreign income tax amount means the amount of tax imposed on the combined income, regardless of whether the tax is reflected on a single foreign tax return.

(23) The term *foreign payor* means an individual or entity (including a disregarded entity) subject to a foreign income tax. If a foreign income tax imposes tax on the combined income (within the meaning of §1.901-2(f)(3)(ii)) of two or more individuals or entities, each such individual or entity is a foreign payor. An individual or entity may be a foreign payor with respect to more than one foreign income tax for purposes of applying section 901(m).

(24) The term *foreign taxable year* means a taxable year for purposes of a foreign income tax.

(25) The term *mid-year transaction* means a transaction in which a foreign payor that is a corporation or a disregarded entity has a change in ownership or makes an election pursuant to §301.7701-3 to change its entity classification, or a transaction in which a foreign payor that is a partnership terminates under section 708(b)(1), provided in each case that the foreign payor's foreign taxable year does not close as a result of the transaction, and, if the foreign payor is a corporation or a partnership, the foreign payor's U.S. taxable year closes.

(26) through (28) [The text of proposed §§1.901(m)-1(a)(26) through (28) is the same as the text of §§1.901(m)-1T(a)(26) through (28) as added by T.D. 9800.]

(29) The term *reverse hybrid* has the meaning provided in §1.909-2(b)(1)(iv).

(30) The term *RFA class exemption* has the meaning provided in §1.901(m)-7 (b)(3).

(31) The term *RFA owner (U.S.)* means a person that owns an RFA for U.S. income tax purposes.

(32) The term *RFA owner (foreign)* means an individual or entity (including a disregarded entity) that owns an RFA for purposes of a foreign income tax.

(33) through (34) [The text of proposed §§1.901(m)-1(a)(33) through (34) is the same as the text of §§1.901(m)-1T(a)(33) through (34) as added by T.D. 9800.]

(35) The term *section 901(m) payor* means a person eligible to claim the foreign tax credit allowed under section 901(a), regardless of whether the person chooses to claim the foreign tax credit, as well as a section 902 corporation (as defined in section 909(d)(5)). If members of a U.S. affiliated group of corporations (as defined in section 1504) file a consolidated return, each member is a separate section 901(m) payor. If individuals file a joint return, those individuals are treated as a single section 901(m) payor.

(36) through (38) [The text of proposed §§1.901(m)-1(a)(36) through (38) is the same as the text of §§1.901(m)-1T(a)(36) through (38) as added by T.D. 9800.]

(39) The term *tentative disqualified tax amount* has the meaning provided in §1.901(m)-3(b)(2).

(40) through (41) [The text of proposed §§1.901(m)-1(a)(40) through (41) is the same as the text of §§1.901(m)-1T(a)(40) through (41) as added by T.D. 9800.]

(42) The term *U.S. basis deduction* has the meaning provided in §1.901(m)-5(b)(3).

(43) through (45) [The text of proposed §§1.901(m)-1(a)(43) through (45) is the same as the text of §§1.901(m)-1T(a)(43) through (45) as added by T.D. 9800.]

(b) *Effective/applicability date.*—(1) Paragraphs (a)(1), (2), (3), (4), (5), (9), (12), (15), (16), (17), (22), (23), (24), (25), (29), (30), (31), (32), (35), (39), and (42) of this section apply to CAAs occurring on or after the date of publication of the Treasury decision adopting these rules as final regulations in the **Federal Register**.

(2) [The text of proposed §1.901(m)-1(b)(2) is the same as the text of §1.901(m)-1T(b)(2) as added by T.D. 9800.]

(3) Taxpayers may, however, rely on this section prior to the date this section is applicable provided that they both consistently apply this section, §1.704-1(b)(4)(viii)(*c*)(*4*)(*v*) through (*vii*), and §§1.901(m)-3 through 1.901(m)-8 (excluding §1.901(m)-4(e)) to all CAAs occurring on or after January 1, 2011, and consistently apply §1.901(m)-2 (excluding §1.901(m)-2(d)) to all CAAs occurring on or after December 7, 2016. For this purpose, persons that are related (within the meaning of section 267(b) or 707(b)) will be treated as a single taxpayer. [Reg. §1.901(m)-1.]

Par. 4. Section 1.901(m)-2 is added to read as follows:

§1.901(m)-2. Covered asset acquisitions and relevant foreign assets.—(a) through (b)(3) [The text of proposed §§1.901(m)-2(a) through (b)(3) is the same as the text of §§1.901(m)-2T(a) through (b)(3) as added by T.D. 9800.]

(4) Any transaction (or series of transactions occurring pursuant to a plan) to the extent it is treated as an acquisition of assets for purposes of U.S. income tax and as the acquisition of an interest in a fiscally transparent entity for purposes of a foreign income tax;

(5) Any transaction (or series of transactions occurring pursuant to a plan) to the extent it is treated as a partnership distribution of one or more assets the U.S. basis of which is determined by section 732(b) or 732(d) or which causes the U.S. basis of the partnership's remaining assets to be adjusted under section 734(b), provided the transaction results in an increase in the U.S. basis of one or more of the assets distributed by the partnership or retained by the partnership without a corresponding increase in the foreign basis of such assets; and

(6) Any transaction (or series of transactions occurring pursuant to a plan) to the extent it is treated as an acquisition of assets for purposes of both U.S. income tax and a foreign income tax, provided the transaction results in an increase in the U.S. basis without a corresponding increase in the foreign basis of one or more assets.

(c) *Relevant foreign asset.*—(1) [The text of proposed §1.901(m)-2(c)(1) is the same as the text of §1.901(m)-2T(c)(1) as added by T.D. 9800.]

(2) *RFA status with respect to a foreign income tax.*—An asset is relevant in determining foreign income if income, deduction, gain, or loss attributable to the asset is taken into account in determining foreign income immediately after the CAA, or would be taken into account in determining foreign income immediately after the CAA if the asset were to give rise to income, deduction, gain, or loss at such time.

(3) *Subsequent RFA status with respect to another foreign income tax.*—After a CAA, an asset will become an RFA with respect to another foreign income tax if, pursuant to a plan or series of related transactions that have a principal purpose of avoiding the application of section 901(m), an asset that was not relevant in determining foreign income for purposes of that foreign income tax immediately after the CAA becomes relevant in determining such foreign income. A principal purpose of avoiding section 901(m) will be deemed to exist if income, deduction, gain, or loss attributable to the asset is taken into account in determining such foreign income within the one-year period following the CAA, or would be taken into account in determining such foreign income during such time if the asset were to give rise to income, deduction, gain, or loss within the one-year period.

(d) [The text of proposed §1.901(m)-2(d) is the same as the text of §1.901(m)-2T(d) as added by T.D. 9800.]

(e) *Examples.*—The following examples illustrate the rules of this section:

Example 1. CAA involving an acquisition of a partnership interest for foreign income tax purposes—(i) *Facts.* (A) FPS is an entity organized in Country F that is treated as a partnership for both U.S. and Country F income tax purposes. FPS is owned 50/50 by FC1 and FC2, each of which is a corporation organized in Country F and treated as a corporation for both U.S. and Country F income tax purposes. FPS has a single asset, Asset A. USP, a domestic corporation, owns all the interests in DE, a disregarded entity.

(B) Pursuant to the same transaction, USP acquires FC1's interest in FPS, and DE acquires FC2's interest in FPS. For U.S. income tax purposes, with respect to USP, the acquisition of the interests in FPS is treated as the acquisition of Asset A by USP. *See* Rev. Rul. 99-6, 1999-1 C.B. 432. For Country F tax purposes, the acquisitions of the interests of FPS by USP and DE are treated as acquisitions of partnership interests.

(ii) *Result.* The transaction is a CAA under paragraph (b)(4) of this section because it is treated as the acquisition of Asset A for U.S. income tax purposes and the acquisition of interests in a partnership for Country F tax purposes.

Example 2. CAA involving an asset acquisition for purposes of both U.S. income tax and a foreign income tax —(i) *Facts.* (A) USP, a domestic corporation, wholly owns CFC1, a foreign corporation, and CFC1 wholly owns CFC2, also a foreign corporation. CFC1 and CFC2 are organized in Country F. CFC1 owns Asset A.

(B) In an exchange described in section 351, CFC1 transfers Asset A to CFC2 in exchange for CFC2 common stock and cash. CFC1 recognizes gain on the exchange under section 351(b). Under section 362(a), CFC2's U.S. basis in Asset A is increased by the gain recognized by CFC1. For Country F tax purposes, gain or loss is not recognized on the transfer of Asset A to CFC2, and therefore there is no increase in the foreign basis in Asset A.

(ii) *Result*. The transaction is a CAA under paragraph (b)(6) of this section because it is treated as an acquisition of Asset A by CFC2 for both U.S. and Country F income tax purposes, and it results in an increase in the U.S. Basis of Asset A without a corresponding increase in the foreign basis of Asset A.

Example 3. RFA status determined immediately after CAA; application of principal purpose rule—(i) *Facts*. (A) USP1 and USP2 are unrelated domestic corporations. USP1 wholly owns USSub, also a domestic corporation. On January 1 of Year 1, USP2 acquires all of the stock of USSub from USP1 in a qualified stock purchase (as defined in section 338(d)(3)) to which section 338(a) applies. Immediately after the acquisition, none of the income, deduction, gain, or loss attributable to any of the assets of USSub is taken into account in determining foreign income for purposes of a foreign income tax nor would such items be taken into account in determining foreign income for purposes of a foreign income tax immediately after the acquisition if such assets were to give rise to income, deduction, gain, or loss immediately after the acquisition.

(B) On December 1 of Year 1, USSub contributes all its assets to FSub, its wholly owned subsidiary, which is a corporation for both U.S. and Country X income tax purposes, in a transfer described in section 351 (subsequent transfer). USSub recognizes no gain or loss for U.S. or Country X income tax purposes as a result of the subsequent transfer. As a result of the subsequent transfer, income, deduction, gain, or loss attributable to the assets of USSub that were transferred to FSub is taken into account in determining foreign income of FSub for Country X tax purposes.

(ii) *Result*. (A) Under paragraph (b)(1) of this section, the acquisition by USP2 of the stock of USSub is a section 338 CAA. Under paragraph (c)(1) of this section, none of the assets of USSub are RFAs immediately after the CAA, because none of the income, deduction, gain, or loss attributable to such assets is taken into account for purposes of determining foreign income with respect to any foreign income tax immediately after the CAA (nor would such items be taken into account for purposes of determining foreign income immediately after the CAA if such assets were to give rise to income, deduction, gain, or loss at such time).

(B) Although the subsequent transfer is not a CAA under paragraph (b) of this section, the subsequent transfer causes the assets of USSub to become relevant in the hands of FSub in determining foreign income for Country X tax purposes. Because the subsequent transfer occurred within the one-year period following the CAA, it is presumed to have a principal purpose of avoiding section 901(m). Accordingly, under paragraph (c)(2) of this section, the assets of USSub with respect to the CAA occurring on January 1 of Year 1 become RFAs with respect to Country X tax as a result of the subsequent transfer. Thus, a basis difference with respect to Country X tax must be computed for the RFAs and taken into account under section 901(m).

(f) *Effective/applicability date*.—(1) [The text of proposed § 1.901(m)-2(f)(1) is the same as the text of § 1.901(m)-2T(f)(1) as added by T.D. 9800.]

(2) Paragraphs (b)(4) through (b)(6), (c)(2), (c)(3), and (e) of this section apply to CAAs occurring on or after the date of publication of the Treasury decision adopting these rules as final regulations in the **Federal Register**.

(3) Taxpayers may, however, rely on this section prior to the date this section is applicable provided that they both consistently apply this section (excluding paragraph (d) of this section) to all CAAs occurring on or after December 7, 2016 and consistently apply § 1.704-1(b)(4)(viii)(*c*)(*4*)(*v*) through (*vii*), § 1.901(m)-1, and § § 1.901(m)-3 through 1.901(m)-8 (excluding § 1.901(m)-4(e)) to all CAAs occurring on or after January 1, 2011. For this purpose, persons that are related (within the meaning of section 267(b) or 707(b)) will be treated as a single taxpayer. [Reg. § 1.901(m)-2.]

Par. 5. Section 1.901(m)-3 is added to read as follows:

§ 1.901(m)-3. Disqualified tax amount and aggregate basis difference carryover.—(a) *In general*.—If a section 901(m) payor has an aggregate basis difference, with respect to a foreign income tax and a foreign payor, for a U.S. taxable year, the section 901(m) payor must determine the portion of a foreign income tax amount that is disqualified under section 901(m) (disqualified tax amount). Paragraph (b) of this section provides rules for determining the disqualified tax amount. Paragraph (c) of this section provides rules for determining what portion, if any, of aggregate basis difference will be carried forward to the next U.S. taxable year (aggregated basis difference carryover). Paragraph (d) of this section provides the effective/applicability date.

(b) *Disqualified tax amount*.—(1) *In general*.—A section 901(m) payor's disqualified tax amount is not taken into account in determining the credit allowed under section 901(a). If the section 901(m) payor is a section 902 corporation, the disqualified tax amount is not taken into account for purposes of section 902 or 960. Sections 78 and 275 do not apply to the disqualified tax amount. The disqualified tax amount is allowed as a deduction to the extent otherwise deductible (see sections 164, 212, and 964 and the regulations under those sections).

(2) *Determination of disqualified tax amount*.—(i) *In general*.—Except as provided in paragraph (b)(2)(iv) of this section, the disqualified tax amount is equal to the lesser of the foreign income tax amount that is paid or accrued by, or considered paid or accrued by, the section 901(m) payor for the U.S. taxable year or the tentative disqualified tax amount. All calculations are determined with respect to each separate category described in § 1.904-4(m).

(ii) *Tentative disqualified tax amount.*—The tentative disqualified tax amount is equal to the amount determined under paragraph (b)(2)(ii)(A) of this section reduced (but not below zero) by the amount described in paragraph (b)(2)(ii)(B) of this section.

(A) The product of—

(1) The sum of the foreign income tax amount and the FCCTs that are paid or accrued by, or considered paid or accrued by, the section 901(m) payor, and

(2) A fraction, the numerator of which is the aggregate basis difference, but not in excess of the allocable foreign income, and the denominator of which is the allocable foreign income.

(B) The amount of the FCCT that is a disqualified tax amount of the section 901(m) payor with respect to another foreign income tax.

(iii) *Allocable foreign income.*—(A) *No allocation required.*—Except as provided in paragraph (b)(2)(iii)(D) of this section, if the entire foreign income tax amount is paid or accrued by, or considered paid or accrued by, a single section 901(m) payor, then the allocable foreign income is equal to the entire foreign income, determined with respect to each separate category described in § 1.904-4(m).

(B) *Allocation required.*—Except as provided in paragraph (b)(2)(iii)(D) of this section, if the foreign income tax amount is allocated to, and considered paid or accrued by, more than one person, a section 901(m) payor's allocable foreign income is equal to the portion of the foreign income that relates to the foreign income tax amount allocated to that section 901(m) payor, determined with respect to each separate category described in § 1.904-4(m).

(C) *Rules for allocations.*—This paragraph (b)(2)(iii)(C) provides allocation rules that apply to determine allocable foreign income in certain cases.

(1) If the foreign payor is involved in a mid-year transaction and the foreign income tax amount is allocated under § 1.336-2(g)(3)(ii), 1.338-9(d), or 1.901-2(f)(4), then, to the extent any portion of the foreign income tax amount is allocated to, and considered paid or accrued by, a section 901(m) payor, the allocable foreign income of the section 901(m) payor is determined in accordance with the principles of § 1.1502-76(b). To the extent the foreign income tax amount is allocated to an entity that is a partnership for U.S. income tax purposes, a portion of the foreign income is first allocated to the partnership in accordance with the principles of § 1.1502-76(b), which is then allocated under the rules of paragraph (b)(2)(iii)(C)(2) of this section to determine the allocable foreign income of a section 901(m) payor that owns an interest in the partnership directly or indirectly through one or more other partnerships for U.S. income tax purposes.

(2) If the foreign income tax amount is considered paid or accrued by a section 901(m) payor for a U.S. taxable year under § 1.702-1(a)(6), the determination of the allocable foreign income must be consistent with the allocation of the foreign income tax amount that relates to the foreign income. *See* § 1.704-1(b)(4)(viii).

(3) If the foreign income tax amount that is allocated to, and considered paid or accrued by, a section 901(m) payor for a U.S. taxable year is determined under § 1.901-2(f)(3)(i), the allocable foreign income is determined in accordance with § 1.901-2(f)(3)(iii).

(D) *Failure to substantiate allocable foreign income.*—If, pursuant to section 901(m)(3)(A), a section 901(m) payor fails to substantiate its allocable foreign income to the satisfaction of the Secretary, then allocable foreign income will equal the amount determined by dividing the sum of the foreign income tax amount and the FCCTs that are paid or accrued by, or considered paid or accrued by, the section 901(m) payor, by the highest marginal tax rate applicable to income of the foreign payor under foreign tax law.

(iv) *Special rule.*—A section 901(m) payor's disqualified tax amount is zero for a U.S. taxable year if:

(A) The section 901(m) payor's aggregate basis difference for the U.S. taxable year is a negative amount;

(B) Foreign income is less than or equal to zero for the foreign taxable year of the foreign payor; or

(C) The foreign income tax amount that is paid or accrued by, or considered paid or accrued by, the section 901(m) payor for the U.S. taxable year is zero.

(3) *Examples.*—The following examples illustrate the rules of paragraph (b)(2) of this section. For purposes of all the examples, unless otherwise specified: USP is a domestic corporation. CFC1, CFC2, DE1, and DE2 are organized in Country F and are treated as corporations for Country F tax purposes. CFC1 and CFC2 are section 902 corporations (as defined in section 909(d)(5)). DE1 and DE2 are disregarded entities. USP, CFC1, and CFC2 have a calendar year for both U.S. and Country F income tax purposes, and DE1 and DE2 have a calendar year for Country F tax purposes. Country F and Country G each impose a single tax that is a foreign income tax. CFC1, CFC2, DE1, and DE2 each have a functional currency of the u with respect to all activities. At all relevant times, 1u equals $1. All amounts are stated in millions. The examples assume that the applicable cost recovery method for property results in basis being recovered ratably over the life of the property beginning on the first day of the U.S. taxable year in which the property is acquired or placed into service; there is a single § 1.904-4(m) separate category with respect to a foreign income and foreign income tax amount; and a section 901(m) payor properly substantiates its allocable foreign income to the satisfaction of the Secretary.

Example 1. Determining aggregate basis difference; multiple foreign payors—(i) *Facts.* CFC1 wholly owns CFC2 and DE1. DE1 wholly owns DE2. Assume that the tax laws of Country F do not allow combined income reporting or the filing of consolidated income tax returns. Accordingly, CFC1, CFC2, DE1, and DE2 file separate tax returns for Country F tax purposes. USP acquires all of the stock of CFC1 in a qualified stock purchase (as defined in section 338(d)(3)) to which section 338(a) applies for both CFC1 and CFC2.

(ii) *Result.* (A) The acquisition of CFC1 gives rise to four separate CAAs under

§1.901(m)-2(b). The acquisition of the stock of CFC1 and the deemed acquisition of the stock of CFC2 under section 338(h)(3)(B) is each a Section 338 CAA under §1.901(m)-2(b)(1). Furthermore, because the deemed acquisition of the assets of DE1 and DE2 for U.S. income tax purposes is disregarded for Country F tax purposes, each acquisition is a CAA under §1.901(m)-2(b)(2). Because these four CAAs occur pursuant to a plan, under §1.901(m)-1(a)(3) they are part of an aggregated CAA transaction. Under §1.901(m)-1(a)(31), CFC1 is the RFA owner (U.S.) with respect to its assets and those of DE1 and DE2. CFC2 is the RFA owner (U.S.) with respect to its assets. Under §1.901(m)-1(a)(23), CFC1, CFC2, DE1, and DE2 are each a foreign payor for Country F tax purposes. Under §1.901(m)-1(a)(35), CFC1 is the section 901(m) payor with respect to foreign income tax amounts for which CFC1, DE1, and DE2 are the foreign payors (see §§1.901-2(f)(1) and 1.901-2(f)(4)(ii)). CFC2 is the section 901(m) payor with respect to foreign income tax amounts for which CFC2 is the foreign payor (see §1.901-2(f)(1)).

(B) In determining aggregate basis difference under §1.901(m)-1(a)(1) for a U.S. taxable year of CFC1, CFC1 has three computations with respect to Country F tax, because there are three foreign payors for Country F tax purposes whose foreign income tax amount, if any, is considered paid or accrued by CFC1 as the section 901(m) payor. Furthermore, for each U.S. taxable year, CFC1 will compute a separate disqualified tax amount and aggregate basis difference Carryover (if any) under paragraph (b)(2) of this section, with respect to each foreign payor.

(C) In determining aggregate basis difference for a U.S. taxable year of CFC2 under §1.901(m)-1(a)(1), CFC2 has a single computation with respect to Country F tax, because there is a single foreign payor (CFC2) for Country F tax purposes whose foreign income tax amount, if any, is considered paid or accrued by CFC2 as the section 901(m) payor. Furthermore, for each U.S. taxable year, CFC2 will compute a disqualified tax amount and aggregate basis difference Carryover (if any) under paragraph (b)(2) of this section.

(iii) *Alternative facts*. Assume the same facts as in paragraph (i) of this *Example 1*, except that foreign income for Country F tax purposes is based on combined income (within the meaning of §1.901-2(f)(3)(ii)) of CFC1, CFC2, DE1, and DE2. For purposes of determining an aggregate basis difference for a U.S. taxable year of CFC1 under §1.901(m)-1(a)(1), CFC1, DE1, and DE2 are treated as a single foreign payor because all of the items of income, deduction, gain, or loss with respect to CFC1, DE1, and DE2 are included in the earnings and profits of CFC1 for U.S. income tax purposes. For each U.S. taxable year, CFC1 will therefore compute a single aggregate basis difference, disqualified tax amount, and aggregate basis difference carryover. The result for CFC2 under the alternative facts is the same as in paragraph (ii)(C) of this *Example 1*.

Example 2. Computation of disqualified tax amount—(i) *Facts*. On December 31 of Year 0, USP acquires all of the stock of CFC1 in a qualified stock purchase (as defined in section 338(d)(3)) to which section 338(a) applies (Acquisition). CFC1 owns four assets (Asset A, Asset B, Asset C, and Asset D, and collectively, Assets) and conducts activities in Country F and in a Country G branch. The activities conducted by CFC1 in Country G are not subject to tax in Country F. The tax rate is 25% in Country F and 30% in Country G. For Country F tax purposes, CFC1's foreign income and foreign income tax amount for each foreign taxable year 1 through 15 is 100u and $25 (25u translated at the exchange rate of $1 = 1u), respectively. For Country G tax purposes, CFC1's foreign income and foreign income tax amount for each foreign taxable year 1 through 5 is 400u and $120 (120u translated at the exchange rate of $1 = 1u), respectively. No dispositions occur for any of the Assets during the applicable cost recovery period. Additional facts relevant to each of the Assets are summarized below.

Assets	Relevant foreign income tax	Basis Difference	Applicable Cost Recovery Period	Cost Recovery Amount
Asset A	Country F tax	150u	15 years	10u (150u / 15)
Asset B	Country F tax	50u	5 years	10u (50u / 5)
Asset C	Country G tax	300u	5 years	60u (300u / 5)
Asset D	Country G tax	(100u)	5 years	negative 20u (negative 100 / 5)

(ii) *Result*. (A) Under §1.901(m)-2(b)(1), the Acquisition of the stock of CFC1 is a Section 338 CAA. Under §1.901(m)-2(c)(1), Assets A and B are RFAs with respect to Country F tax, because they are relevant in determining foreign income of CFC1 for Country F tax purposes and were owned by CFC1 when the Acquisition occurred. Assets C and D are RFAs with respect to Country G tax, because they are relevant in determining foreign income of CFC1 for Country G tax purposes and were owned by CFC1 when the Acquisition occurred. Under §1.901(m)-1(a)(31), CFC1 is the RFA owner (U.S.) with respect to all of the RFAs. Under §1.901(m)-1(a)(35) and (a)(23), CFC1 is the section 901(m) payor and the foreign payor for Country F and Country G tax purposes.

(B) In determining aggregate basis difference for a U.S. taxable year of CFC1, CFC1 has two computations, one with respect to Country F tax and one with respect to Country G tax. Under §1.901(m)-1(a)(1), the aggregate basis difference for a U.S. taxable year with respect to Country F tax is equal to the sum of the allocated basis differences with respect to Assets A and B for the U.S. taxable year. Under §1.901(m)-1(a)(5), allocated basis differences are comprised of cost recovery amounts and disposition amounts. Because there are no dispositions, the only allocated basis differences taken into account in determining an aggregate basis difference are cost recovery amounts. Under §1.901(m)-5(b), any cost recovery amounts are attributed to CFC1, because CFC1 is the section 901(m) payor and RFA owner (U.S.) with respect to all of the Assets. For each U.S. taxable year, CFC1 will compute a separate disqualified tax amount and aggregate basis difference carryover (if any) with respect to Country F tax and Country G tax under paragraph (b)(2) of this section. For purposes of both disqualified tax amount computations, because CFC1 is the section 901(m) payor and foreign payor, the foreign income tax amount paid or accrued by CFC1 with respect to Country F tax and Country G tax, respectively, will be the entire foreign income tax amount and CFC1's allocable foreign income will be the entire foreign income.

(C) With respect to Country F tax, in U.S. taxable years 1 through 5, CFC1 has an aggregate basis difference of 20u each year (10u cost recovery amount with respect to Asset A plus 10u cost recovery amount with respect to Asset B). For U.S. taxable years 1 through 5, under paragraph (b)(2) of this section, the disqualified tax amount each year is $5, the lesser of two amounts: the tentative disqualified tax amount, in this case, $5 ($25 foreign income tax amount x (20u aggregate basis difference / 100u allocable foreign income)), or the foreign income tax amount paid or accrued by CFC1, in this case, $25. After U.S. taxable year 5, Asset B has no unallocated basis difference with respect to Country F tax. Accordingly, in U.S. taxable years 6 through 15, CFC1 has an aggregate basis difference of 10u each year. Accordingly, for U.S. taxable years 6 through 15, the disqualified tax amount each year is $2.50, the lesser of two amounts: the tentative disqualified tax amount, in this case, $2.50 ($25 foreign income tax amount x (10u aggregate basis difference / 100u allocable foreign income)), or the foreign income tax amount paid or accrued by CFC1, in this case, $25. After U.S. taxable year 15, Asset A has no unallocated basis difference with respect to Country F tax and, therefore, CFC1 has no disqualified tax amount with respect to Country F Tax.

(D) With respect to Country G tax, in U.S. taxable years 1 through 5, CFC1 has an aggregate basis difference of 40u each year (60u cost recovery amount with respect to Asset C + (20u) cost recovery amount with respect to Asset D). For U.S. taxable years 1 through 5, under paragraph (b)(2) of this section, the disqualified tax amount each year is $12, the lesser of two amounts: the tentative disqualified tax amount, in this case, $12 ($120 foreign income tax amount x (40u aggregate basis difference / 400u allocable foreign income)), or the foreign income tax amount paid or accrued by CFC1, in this case, $120. After U.S. taxable year 5, Asset C and Asset D have no unallocated basis difference with respect to Country G tax. Accordingly, in U.S. taxable years 6 through 15, CFC1 has no disqualified tax amount with respect to Country G Tax.

Example 3. FCCT—(i) *Facts*. In U.S. taxable year 1, USP acquires all of the interests in DE1 in a transaction (Transaction) that is treated as a stock acquisition for Country F tax purposes. Immediately after the Transaction, DE1 owns assets (Pre-Transaction Assets), all of which are used in a Country G branch and give rise to income that is taken into account for Country F tax and Country G tax purposes. After the Transaction, DE1 acquires additional assets (Post-Transaction Assets), which are not used by the Country G branch. Both Country F and Country G have a tax rate of 30%. Country F imposes worldwide tax on its residents and provides a foreign tax credit for taxes paid to other jurisdictions. In foreign taxable year 3, 100u of income is attributable to DE1's Post-Transaction Assets and 100u of income is attributable to DE1's Pre-Transaction Assets. For Country G tax purposes, the foreign income is 100u and foreign income tax amount is 30u (30% x 100u). For Country F tax purposes, the foreign income is 200u and the pre-foreign tax credit tax is 60u (30% x 200u). The 60u of Country F pre-foreign tax credit tax is reduced by the 30u foreign income tax amount imposed for Country G tax purposes. Thus, the foreign income tax amount for Country F tax purposes is $30 (30u translated into dollars at the exchange rate of $1 = 1u). Assume that for U.S. taxable year 3 USP has 100u aggregate basis difference with respect to Country F tax and 100u aggregate basis difference with respect to Country G tax. USP does not dispose of DE1 or any assets of DE1 in U.S. taxable year 3.

(ii) *Result*. (A) Under § 1.901(m)-2(b)(2), the Transaction is a CAA. Under § 1.901(m)-2(c)(1), the Pre-Transaction Assets are RFAs with respect to both Country F tax and Country G tax, because they are relevant in determining the foreign income of DE1 for Country F tax and Country G tax purposes and were owned by DE1 when the Transaction occurred. Under § 1.901(m)-1(a)(31), USP is the RFA owner (U.S.) with respect to the RFAs. Under § 1.901(m)-1(a)(23), DE1 is a foreign payor for Country F tax and Country G tax purposes. Under § 1.901(m)-1(a)(35), USP is the section 901(m) payor with respect to foreign income tax amounts for which DE1 is the foreign payor (see § 1.901-2(f)(4)(ii)). Because the Country G foreign income tax amount is claimed as a credit for purposes of determining the Country F foreign income tax amount, the Country G foreign income tax amount is an FCCT under § 1.901(m)-1(a)(17).

(B) Under § 1.901(m)-1(a)(1), for each U.S. taxable year, USP will separately compute the aggregate basis difference with respect to Country F tax and with respect to Country G tax, and will use those amounts to separately compute a disqualified tax amount and aggregate basis difference carryover (if any) with respect to each foreign income tax. Because DE1 is a disregarded entity owned by USP during the entire U.S. taxable year 3, the foreign income tax amount paid or accrued by DE1 is not subject to allocation. Accordingly, for purposes of each of the disqualified tax amount computations, the foreign income tax amount paid or accrued by USP with respect to Country F tax and Country G tax, respectively, is the entire foreign income tax amount paid or accrued by DE1, and, under paragraph (b)(2)(iii)(A) of this section, USP's allocable foreign income will be equal to DE1's entire foreign income.

(C) As stated in paragraph (i) of this *Example 3*, for U.S. taxable year 3 USP has 100u aggregate basis difference with respect to Country F tax and 100u aggregate basis difference with respect to Country G tax. With respect to Country G tax, in U.S. taxable year 3, under paragraph (b)(2) of this section, the disqualified tax amount is $30, the lesser of the two amounts: the tentative disqualified tax amount, in this case, $30 ($30 foreign income tax amount x (100u aggregate basis difference / 100u allocable foreign income)), or the foreign income tax amount considered paid or accrued by USP, in this case, $30.

(D) With respect to Country F tax, in U.S. taxable year 3, under paragraph (b)(2) of this section, the disqualified tax amount is $0, the lesser of two amounts: the tentative disqualified tax amount, in this case $0 (($30 foreign income tax amount + $30 Country G FCCT) x (100u aggregate basis difference / 200u foreign income) = $30 reduced by $30 Country G FCCT that is a disqualified tax amount of USP), or the foreign income tax amount considered paid or accrued by USP, in this case, $30.

(c) *Aggregate basis difference carryover.*—(1) *In general.*—If a section 901(m) payor has an aggregate basis difference carryover for a U.S. taxable year, as determined under this paragraph (c), the aggregate basis difference carryover is taken into account in computing the section 901(m) payor's aggregate basis difference for the next U.S. taxable year. For successor rules that apply to an aggregate basis difference carryover, see § 1.901(m)-6(c).

(2) *Amount of aggregate basis difference carryover.*—(i) If a section 901(m) payor's disqualified tax amount is zero, all of the section 901(m) payor's aggregate basis difference (positive or negative) for the U.S. taxable year gives rise to an aggregate basis difference carryover to the next U.S. taxable year.

(ii) If a section 901(m) payor's disqualified tax amount is not zero, then aggregate basis difference carryover can arise in either or both of the following two situations:

(A) If a section 901(m) payor's aggregate basis difference for the U.S. taxable year exceeds its allocable foreign income, the excess gives rise to an aggregate basis difference carryover.

(B) If the tentative disqualified tax amount exceeds the disqualified tax amount, the excess tentative disqualified tax amount is converted into aggregate basis difference carryover by multiplying such excess by a fraction, the numerator of which is the allocable foreign income, and the denominator of which is the sum of the foreign income tax amount and the FCCTs that are paid or accrued by, or considered paid or accrued by, the section 901(m) payor.

(3) *Example.*—The following example illustrates the rule of paragraph (c) of this section.

Example. Aggregate basis difference carryover; section 901(m) payor's U.S. taxable year differs from the foreign taxable year of foreign payor—(i) *Facts.* (A) On July 1 of Year 1, CFC1 acquires all of the interests of DE1 in a transaction (Transaction) that is treated as a stock acquisition for Country F tax purposes. CFC1 and DE1 are organized in Country F and are treated as corporations for Country F tax purposes. CFC1 is a section 902 corporation (as defined in section 909(d)(5)), and DE1 is a disregarded entity. CFC1 has a calendar year for U.S. income tax purposes, and DE1 has a June 30 year-end for Country F tax purposes. Country F imposes a single tax that is a foreign income tax. CFC1 and DE1 each have a functional currency of the u with respect to all activities. Immediately after the Transaction, DE1 owns one asset, Asset A, that gives rise to income that is taken into account for Country F tax purposes. For the first U.S. taxable year (U.S. taxable year 1) there is a cost recovery amount with respect to Asset A of 9u, and for each subsequent U.S. taxable year until the U.S. basis is fully recovered, there is a cost recovery amount with respect to Asset A of 18u. There is no disposition of Asset A.

(ii) *Result.* (A) Under § 1.901(m)-2(b)(2), the Transaction is a CAA. Under § 1.901(m)-2(c)(1), Asset A is an RFA with respect to Country F tax because it is relevant in determining the foreign income of DE1 for Country F tax purposes and was owned by DE1 when the Transaction occurred. Under § 1.901(m)-1(a)(31), CFC1 is the RFA owner (U.S.) with respect to Asset A. Under § 1.901(m)-1(a)(23), DE1 is a foreign payor for Country F tax purposes. Under § 1.901(m)-1(a)(35), CFC1 is the section 901(m) payor with respect to foreign income tax amounts for which DE1 is the foreign payor (see § 1.901-2(f)(4)(ii)).

(B) Under § 1.901(m)-1(a)(1), in determining the aggregate basis difference for U.S. taxable year 1, CFC1 has one computation with respect to Country F tax. Under § 1.901(m)-1(a)(1), aggregate basis difference with respect to Country F tax is equal to the sum of allocated basis differences with respect to all RFAs, which, in this case, is only Asset A. Under § 1.901(m)-1(a)(5), allocated basis differences are comprised of cost recovery amounts and disposition amounts. Because there is no disposition of Asset A, the only allocated basis difference taken into account in determining an aggregate basis difference are cost recovery amounts with respect to Asset A. Under § 1.901(m)-5(b), any cost recovery amounts are assigned to a U.S taxable year of CFC1, because CFC1 is the section 901(m) payor and RFA owner (U.S.) with respect to Asset A. Under paragraph (b)(2) of this section, for each U.S. taxable year, CFC1 will compute a disqualified tax amount and aggregate basis difference carryover with respect to the aggregate basis difference. Because DE1 is a disregarded entity owned by CFC1, the foreign income tax amount paid or accrued by DE1 is not subject to allocation. Accordingly, for purposes of the disqualified tax amount computation, the foreign income tax amount paid or accrued by CFC1 with respect to Country F tax is the entire foreign income tax amount paid or accrued by DE1, and under paragraph (b)(2)(iii)(A) of this section, CFC1's allocable foreign income will be equal to DE1's entire foreign income.

(C) In U.S. taxable year 1, CFC1 has an aggregate basis difference of 9u (the 9u cost recovery amount with respect to Asset A for U.S. taxable year 1). However, because the foreign taxable year of DE1, the foreign payor, will not end between July 1 and December 31, there will not be a foreign income tax amount for U.S. taxable year 1. Because the foreign income tax amount considered paid or accrued by CFC1 for U.S. taxable year 1 is zero, under paragraph (b)(2)(iv) of this section, the disqualified tax amount for U.S. taxable year 1 of CFC1 is also zero. Furthermore, because the disqualified tax amount is zero, under paragraph (c)(2)(i) of this section, CFC1 has an aggregate basis difference carryover equal to 9u, the entire amount of the aggregate basis difference for U.S. taxable year 1. Under paragraph (c)(1) of this section, the 9u aggregate basis difference carryover is taken into account in computing CFC1's aggregate basis difference for U.S. taxable year 2. Accordingly, in U.S. taxable year 2, CFC1 has an aggregate basis difference of 27u (18u cost recovery amount for

U.S. taxable year 2, plus 9u aggregate basis difference carryover from U.S. taxable year 1).

(d) *Effective/applicability date.*—This section applies to CAAs occurring on or after the date of publication of the Treasury decision adopting these rules as final regulations in the **Federal Register**. Taxpayers may, however, rely on this section prior to the date this section is applicable provided that they both consistently apply this section, § 1.704-1(b)(4)(viii)(*c*)(*4*)(*v*) through (*vii*), § 1.901(m)-1, and §§ 1.901(m)-4 through 1.901(m)-8 (excluding § 1.901(m)-4(e)) to all CAAs occurring on or after January 1, 2011, and consistently apply § 1.901(m)-2 (excluding § 1.901(m)-2(d)) to all CAAs occurring on or after December 7, 2016. For this purpose, persons that are related (within the meaning of section 267(b) or 707(b)) will be treated as a single taxpayer. [Reg. § 1.901(m)-3.]

Par. 6. Section 1.901(m)-4 is added to read as follows:

§ 1.901(m)-4. Determination of basis difference.—(a) through (b) [The text of proposed §§ 1.901(m)-4(a) through (b) is the same as the text of §§ 1.901(m)-4T(a) through (b) as added by T.D. 9800.]

(c) *Foreign basis election.*—(1) An election (foreign basis election) may be made to apply section 901(m)(3)(C)(i)(II) by reference to the foreign basis immediately after the CAA instead of the U.S. basis immediately before the CAA. Accordingly, if a foreign basis election is made, basis difference is the U.S. basis in the RFA immediately after the CAA, less the foreign basis in the RFA immediately after the CAA. For this purpose, the foreign basis immediately after the CAA takes into account any adjustment to that foreign basis resulting from the CAA for purposes of the foreign income tax.

(2) Except as otherwise provided in this paragraph (c), a foreign basis election is made by the RFA owner (U.S.). If, however, the RFA owner (U.S.) is a partnership, each partner in the partnership (and not the partnership) may independently make a foreign basis election. In the case of one or more tiered partnerships, the foreign basis election is made at the level at which a partner is not also a partnership.

(3) The election may be made separately for each CAA, and with respect to each foreign income tax and each foreign payor. For purposes of making the foreign basis election, all CAAs that are part of an aggregated CAA transaction are treated as a single CAA. Furthermore, for purposes of making the foreign basis election, if foreign law imposes tax on the combined income (within the meaning of § 1.901-2(f)(3)(ii)) of two or more foreign payors, all foreign payors whose items of income, deduction, gain, or loss for U.S. income tax purposes are included in the U.S. taxable income or earnings and profits of a single section 901(m) payor are treated as a single foreign payor.

(4) A foreign basis election is made by using foreign basis to determine basis difference for purposes of computing a disqualified tax amount and an aggregate basis difference carryover for the U.S. taxable year, as provided under § 1.901(m)-3. A separate statement or form evidencing the foreign basis election need not be filed. Except as provided in paragraph (c)(5) and (6) of this section, in order for a foreign basis election to be effective, the election must be reflected on a timely filed original federal income tax return (including extensions) for the first U.S. taxable year that the foreign basis election is relevant to the computation of any amounts reported on such return, including on any required schedules.

(5) If the RFA owner (U.S.) is a partnership, a foreign basis election reflected on a partner's timely filed amended federal income tax return is also effective if all of the following conditions are satisfied:

(i) The partner's timely filed original federal income tax return (including extensions) for the first U.S. taxable year of the partner in which a foreign basis election is relevant to the computation of any amounts reported on such return, including on any required schedules, does not reflect the application of section 901(m);

(ii) The information provided by the partnership to the partner for purposes of applying section 901(m) and any information required to be reported by the partnership is based solely on computations that use foreign basis to determine basis difference; and

(iii) Prior to the due date of the original federal income tax return (including extensions) described in paragraph (c)(5)(i) of this section, the partner delegated the authority to the partnership to choose whether to provide the partner with information to apply section 901(m) using foreign basis, either pursuant to a written partnership agreement (within the meaning of § 1.704-1(b)(2)(ii)(*h*)) or written notice provided by the partner to the partnership.

(6) If, pursuant to paragraph (g)(3) of this section, a taxpayer chooses to have this section apply to CAAs occurring on or after January 1, 2011, a foreign basis election will be effective if the election is reflected on a timely filed amended federal income tax return (or tax returns, as applicable) filed no later than one year following the date of publication of the Treasury decision adopting these rules as final regulations in the **Federal Register**.

(7) The foreign basis election is irrevocable. Relief under § 301.9100-1 is not available for the foreign basis election.

(d) *Determination of basis difference in a section 743(b) CAA.*—(1) [The text of proposed § 1.901(m)-4(d)(1) is the same as the text of § 1.901(m)-4T(d)(1) as added by T.D. 9800.]

(2) *Foreign basis election.*—If a foreign basis election is made with respect to a section 743(b) CAA, then, for purposes of paragraph (d)(1) of this section, the section 743(b) adjustment is determined by reference to the foreign basis of the RFA, determined immediately after the CAA.

(e) [The text of proposed § 1.901(m)-4(e) is the same as the text of § 1.901(m)-4T(e) as added by T.D. 9800.]

(f) *Examples.*—The following examples illustrate the rules of this section:

Example 1. Scope of basis choice; identifying separate CAAs, RFA owners (U.S.), and foreign payors in an aggregated CAA transaction —(i) *Facts.* CFC1 wholly owns CFC2, both of which are section 902 corporations (as defined in section

909(d)(5)), organized in Country F, and treated as corporations for Country F tax purposes. CFC1 also wholly owns DE1, and DE1 wholly owns DE2. DE1 and DE2 are entities organized in Country F treated as corporations for Country F tax purposes and as disregarded entities for U.S. income tax purposes. Country F imposes a single tax that is a foreign income tax. All of the stock of CFC1 is acquired in a qualified stock purchase (within the meaning of section 338(d)(3)) to which section 338(a) applies for both CFC1 and CFC2. For Country F tax purposes, the transaction is treated as an acquisition of the stock of CFC1.

(ii) *Result.* (A) The acquisition of CFC1 gives rise to four separate CAAs described in §1.901(m)-2. Under §1.901(m)-2(b)(1), the acquisition of the stock of CFC1 and the deemed acquisition of the stock of CFC2 under section 338(h)(3)(B) are each a section 338 CAA. Furthermore, because the deemed acquisition of the assets of each of DE1 and DE2 for U.S. income tax purposes is disregarded for Country F tax purposes, the deemed acquisitions are CAAs under §1.901(m)-2(b)(2). Because the four CAAs occurred pursuant to a plan, under §1.901(m)-1(a)(3), all of the CAAs are part of an aggregated CAA transaction. Under §1.901(m)-1(a)(31), CFC1 is the RFA owner (U.S.) with respect to its assets and the assets of DE1 and DE2 that are RFAs. CFC2 is the RFA owner (U.S.) with respect to its assets that are RFAs. Under §1.901(m)-1(a)(23), CFC1, CFC2, DE1, and DE2 are each a foreign payor for Country F tax purposes.

(B) Under paragraph (c) of this section, a foreign basis election may be made by the RFA owner (U.S.). The election is made separately with respect to each CAA (for this purpose, treating all CAAs that are part of an aggregated CAA transaction as a single CAA) and with respect to each foreign income tax and foreign payor. Thus, in this case, CFC1 can make a separate foreign basis election for one or more of the following three groups of RFAs: RFAs that are relevant in determining foreign income of CFC1; RFAs that are relevant in determining foreign income of DE1; and RFAs that are relevant in determining foreign income of DE2. Furthermore, CFC2 can make a foreign basis election for all of its RFAs that are relevant in determining its foreign income.

Example 2. Scope of basis choice; RFA owner (U.S.) is a partnership—(i) *Facts.* USPS is a domestic partnership for which a section 754 election is in effect. USPS owns two assets, the stock of DE1 and DE2. DE1 is an entity organized in Country X and treated as a corporation for Country X tax purposes. DE2 is an entity organized in Country Y and treated as a corporation for Country Y tax purposes. DE1 and DE2 are disregarded entities. Country X and Country Y each impose a single tax that is a foreign income tax. US1 and US2, unrelated domestic corporations, and FP, a foreign person unrelated to US1 and US2, acquire partnership interests in USPS from existing partners of USPS pursuant to the same plan.

(ii) *Result.* Under §1.901(m)-2(b)(3), the acquisitions of the partnership interests in USPS by US1, US2, and FP each give rise to separate section 743(b) CAAs, but under §1.901(m)-1(a)(3), they are treated as an aggregated CAA transaction because they occur as part of a plan. Under §1.901(m)-1(a)(31), USPS is the RFA owner (U.S.) with respect to the assets of DE1 and DE2 that are RFAs. Under §1.901(m)-1(a)(23), DE1 is a foreign payor for Country X tax purposes and DE2 is a foreign payor for Country Y tax purposes. Because the RFA owner (U.S.) is a partnership, paragraph (c)(2) of this section provides that US1, US2, and FP (the relevant partners in USPS) separately choose whether to make a foreign basis election for purposes of determining basis difference. Furthermore, under paragraph (c)(3) of this section, the choice to make the election is made separately by each partner with respect to each foreign payor. Thus, in this case, each partner may make separate elections for the RFAs that are relevant in determining foreign income of DE1 for Country X tax purposes and the RFAs that are relevant in determining foreign income of DE2 for Country Y tax purposes.

(g) *Effective/applicability date.*—(1) [The text of proposed §1.901(m)-4(g)(1) is the same as the text of §1.901(m)-4T(g)(1) as added by T.D. 9800.]

(2) Except for paragraphs (a), (b), (d)(1), and (e) of this section, this section applies to CAAs occurring on or after the date of publication of the Treasury decision adopting these rules as final regulations in the **Federal Register**.

(3) Taxpayers may, however, rely on this section prior to the date this section is applicable provided that they both consistently apply this section (excluding paragraph (e) of this section), §1.704-1(b)(4)(viii)(*c*)(*4*)(*v*) through (*vii*), §1.901(m)-1, §1.901(m)-3, and §§1.901(m)-5 through 1.901(m)-8 to all CAAs occurring on or after January 1, 2011, and consistently apply §1.901(m)-2 (excluding §1.901(m)-2(d)) to all CAAs occurring on or after December 7, 2016. For this purpose, persons that are related (within the meaning of section 267(b) or 707(b)) will be treated as a single taxpayer. [Reg. §1.901(m)-4.]

Par. 7. Section 1.901(m)-5 is added to read as follows:

§1.901(m)-5. Basis difference taken into account.—(a) *In general.*—This section provides rules for determining the amount of basis difference with respect to an RFA that is taken into account in a U.S. taxable year for purposes of determining the disqualified portion of a foreign income tax amount. Paragraph (b) of this section provides rules for determining a cost recovery amount and assigning that amount to a U.S. taxable year of a single section 901(m) payor when the RFA owner (U.S.) is the section 901(m) payor. Paragraph (c) of this section provides rules for determining a disposition amount and assigning that amount to a U.S. taxable year of a single section 901(m) payor when the RFA owner (U.S.) is the section 901(m) payor. Paragraph (d) of this section provides rules for allocating cost recovery amounts and disposition amounts when the RFA owner (U.S.) is a fiscally transparent entity for U.S. income tax purposes. Paragraph (e) of this section provides special rules for allocating cost recovery amounts and disposition amounts with respect to certain section 743(b) CAAs. Paragraph (f) of this section provides special rules for allocating certain disposition amounts when a foreign payor is transferred in a mid-year transaction. Paragraph (g) of this section provides special rules for allocating both cost recovery amounts and disposition amounts in certain cases in which the RFA owner (U.S.) either is a reverse hybrid or a fiscally transparent entity for both U.S. and foreign income tax purposes that is directly or indirectly owned by a reverse hybrid. Paragraph (h) of this section provides examples illustrating the application of this section. Paragraph (i) of this section provides the effective/applicability date.

(b) *Basis difference taken into account under applicable cost recovery method.*—(1) *In general.*—When the RFA owner (U.S.) is a section 901(m) payor, all of a cost recovery amount is attributed to the section 901(m) payor and assigned to the U.S. taxable year of the section 901(m) payor in which the corresponding U.S. basis deduction is taken into account under the applicable cost recovery method. This is the case regardless of whether the deduction is deferred or disallowed for U.S. income tax purposes. If instead the RFA owner (U.S.) is a fiscally transparent entity for U.S. income tax purposes, a cost recovery amount is allocated to one or more section 901(m) payors under paragraph (d) of this section, except as provided in paragraphs (e) and (g) of this section. If a cost recovery amount arises from an RFA with respect to a section 743(b) CAA, in certain cases the cost recovery amount is allocated to a section 901(m) payor under paragraph (e) of this section. In certain cases in which the RFA owner (U.S.) either is a reverse hybrid or a fiscally transparent entity for both U.S. and foreign income tax purposes that is directly or indirectly owned by a reverse hybrid, a cost recovery amount is allocated to one or more section 901(m) payors under paragraph (g) of this section.

(2) *Determining a cost recovery amount.*—(i) [The text of proposed § 1.901(m)-5(b)(2)(i) is the same as the text of § 1.901(m)-5T(b)(2)(i) as added by T.D. 9800.]

(ii) *U.S. basis subject to multiple cost recovery methods.*—If the entire U.S. basis is not subject to the same cost recovery method, the applicable cost recovery method for determining the cost recovery amount is the cost recovery method that applies to the portion of the U.S. basis that corresponds to the basis difference.

(3) *Applicable cost recovery method.*—For purposes of section 901(m), an applicable cost recovery method includes any method for recovering the cost of property over time for U.S. income tax purposes (each application of a method giving rise to a "U.S. basis deduction"). Such methods include depreciation, amortization, or depletion, as well as a method that allows the cost (or a portion of the cost) of property to be expensed in the year of acquisition or in the placed-in-service year, such as under section 179. Applicable cost recovery methods do not include any provision allowing the U.S. basis to be recovered upon a disposition of an RFA.

(c) *Basis difference taken into account as a result of a disposition.*—(1) *In general.*—Except as provided in paragraph (f) of this section, when the RFA owner (U.S.) is a section 901(m) payor, all of a disposition amount is attributed to the section 901(m) payor and assigned to the U.S. taxable year of the section 901(m) payor in which the disposition occurs. If instead the RFA owner (U.S.) is a fiscally transparent entity for U.S. income tax purposes, except as provided in paragraphs (e), (f), and (g) of this section, a disposition amount is allocated to one or more section 901(m) payors under paragraph (d) of this section. If a disposition amount arises from an RFA with respect to a section 743(b) CAA, in certain cases the disposition amount is allocated to a section 901(m) payor under paragraph (e) of this section. If there is a disposition of an RFA in a foreign taxable year of a foreign payor during which there is a mid-year transaction, in certain cases a disposition amount is allocated under paragraph (f) of this section. In certain cases in which the RFA owner (U.S.) either is a reverse hybrid or a fiscally transparent entity for both U.S. and foreign income tax purposes that is directly or indirectly owned by a reverse hybrid, a disposition amount is allocated to one or more section 901(m) payors under paragraph (g) of this section.

(2) [The text of proposed § 1.901(m)-5(c)(2) is the same as the text of § 1.901(m)-5T(c)(2) as added by T.D. 9800.]

(d) *General rules for allocating and assigning a cost recovery amount or a disposition amount when the RFA owner (U.S.) is a fiscally transparent entity.*—(1) *In general.*—Except as provided in paragraphs (e), (f), and (g) of this section, this paragraph (d) provides rules for allocating a cost recovery amount or a disposition amount when the RFA owner (U.S.) is a fiscally transparent entity for U.S. income tax purposes in which a section 901(m) payor directly or indirectly owns an interest, as well as for assigning the allocated amount to a U.S. taxable year of the section 901(m) payor. For purposes of this paragraph (d), unless otherwise indicated, a reference to direct or indirect ownership in an entity means for U.S. income tax purposes. For purposes of this paragraph (d), a person indirectly owns an interest in an entity for U.S. income tax purposes if the person owns the interest through one or more fiscally transparent entities for U.S. income tax purposes, and at least one of the fiscally transparent entities is not a disregarded entity. For purposes of this paragraph (d), a person indirectly owns an interest in an entity for foreign income tax purposes if the person owns the interest through one or more fiscally transparent entities for foreign income tax purposes. If the RFA owner (U.S.) is a lower-tier fiscally transparent entity for U.S. income tax purposes in which the section 901(m) payor indirectly owns an interest, the rules of this section apply in a manner consistent with the application of these rules when the section 901(m) payor directly owns an interest in the RFA owner (U.S.).

(2) *Allocation of a cost recovery amount.*—A cost recovery amount is allocated to a section 901(m) payor that directly or indirectly owns an interest in the RFA owner (U.S.) to the extent the U.S. basis deduction that corresponds to the cost recovery amount is (or will be) included in the section 901(m) payor's distributive share of the income of the RFA owner (U.S.) for U.S. income tax purposes.

(3) *Allocation of a disposition amount attributable to foreign disposition gain or foreign disposition loss.*—(i) *In general.*—Except as provided in paragraph (f) of this section, a disposition

amount attributable to foreign disposition gain or foreign disposition loss (as determined under paragraph (d)(5) of this section) is allocated under paragraph (d)(3)(ii) or (d)(3)(iii) of this section to a section 901(m) payor that directly or indirectly owns an interest in the RFA owner (U.S.).

(ii) *First allocation rule.*—This paragraph (d)(3)(ii) applies when a section 901(m) payor, or a disregarded entity directly owned by a section 901(m) payor, is the foreign payor whose foreign income includes a distributive share of the foreign income of the RFA owner (foreign) and, therefore, all of the foreign income tax amount of the foreign payor is paid or accrued by, or considered paid by, the section 901(m) payor. Thus, this paragraph (d)(3)(ii) applies when the RFA owner (U.S.) is a fiscally transparent entity for both U.S. and foreign income tax purposes and a section 901(m) payor either directly owns an interest in the RFA owner (U.S.) or directly owns an interest in another fiscally transparent entity for U.S. and foreign income tax purposes, which, in turn, directly or indirectly owns an interest in the RFA owner (U.S.) for both U.S. and foreign income tax purposes. In these cases, the section 901(m) payor is allocated the portion of a disposition amount that is equal to the product of the disposition amount attributable to foreign disposition gain or foreign disposition loss, as applicable, and a fraction, the numerator of which is the portion of the foreign disposition gain or foreign disposition loss recognized by the RFA owner (foreign) for foreign income tax purposes that is (or will be) included in the foreign payor's distributive share of the foreign income of the RFA owner (foreign), and the denominator of which is the foreign disposition gain or foreign disposition loss.

(iii) *Second allocation rule.*—This paragraph (d)(3)(iii) applies when neither a section 901(m) payor nor a disregarded entity directly owned by a section 901(m) payor is the foreign payor with respect to the foreign income of the RFA owner (foreign). Instead, a section 901(m) payor directly or indirectly owns an interest in the foreign payor, which is a fiscally transparent entity for U.S. income tax purposes (other than a disregarded entity directly owned by the section 901(m) payor), and, therefore, the section 901(m) payor is considered to pay or accrue only its allocated portion of the foreign income tax amount of the foreign payor. This will be the case when the foreign payor is either the RFA owner (U.S.), another fiscally transparent entity for U.S. income tax purposes (other than a disregarded entity directly owned by a section 901(m) payor) that directly or indirectly owns an interest in the RFA owner (U.S.) for both U.S. and foreign income tax purposes, or a disregarded entity directly owned by the RFA owner (U.S.). In these cases, the section 901(m) payor is allocated the portion of a disposition amount that is equal to the product of the disposition amount attributable to foreign disposition gain or foreign disposition loss, as applicable, and a fraction, the numerator of which is the portion of the foreign disposition gain or foreign disposition loss that is included in the allocable foreign income of the section 901(m) payor, and the denominator of which is the foreign disposition gain or foreign disposition loss. If allocable foreign income is not otherwise required to be determined because there is no foreign income tax amount, the numerator is the portion of the foreign disposition gain or foreign disposition loss that would be included in the allocable foreign income of the section 901(m) payor if there were a foreign income tax amount.

(4) *Allocation of a disposition amount attributable to U.S. disposition gain or U.S. disposition loss.*—A section 901(m) payor that directly or indirectly owns an interest in the RFA owner (U.S.) is allocated the portion of a disposition amount that is equal to the product of the disposition amount attributable to U.S. disposition gain or U.S. disposition loss (as determined under paragraph (d)(5) of this section), as applicable, and a fraction, the numerator of which is the portion of the U.S. disposition gain or U.S. disposition loss that is (or will be) included in the section 901(m) payor's distributive share of income of the RFA owner (U.S.) for U.S. income tax purposes, and the denominator of which is the U.S. disposition gain or U.S. disposition loss.

(5) *Determining the extent to which a disposition amount is attributable to foreign or U.S. disposition gain or loss.*—(i) *RFA with a positive basis difference.*—When there is a disposition of an RFA with a positive basis difference and the disposition results in either a foreign disposition gain or a U.S. disposition loss, but not both, the entire disposition amount is attributable to foreign disposition gain or U.S. disposition loss, as applicable, even if the disposition amount exceeds the foreign disposition gain or the absolute value of the U.S. disposition loss. If the disposition results in both a foreign disposition gain and a U.S. disposition loss, the disposition amount is attributable first to foreign disposition gain to the extent thereof, and the excess disposition amount, if any, is attributable to the U.S. disposition loss, even if the excess disposition amount exceeds the absolute value of the U.S. disposition loss.

(ii) *RFA with a negative basis difference.*—When there is a disposition of an RFA with a negative basis difference and the disposition results in either a foreign disposition loss or a U.S. disposition gain, but not both, the entire disposition amount is attributable to foreign disposition loss or U.S. disposition gain, as applicable, even if the absolute value of the disposition amount exceeds the absolute value of the foreign disposition loss or the U.S. disposition gain. If the disposition results in both a foreign disposition loss and a U.S. disposition gain, the disposition amount is attributable first to foreign disposition loss to the extent thereof, and the excess disposition amount, if any, is attributable to the U.S. disposition gain, even if the absolute value of the excess disposition amount exceeds the U.S. disposition gain.

(6) *U.S. taxable year of a section 901(m) payor to which an allocated cost recovery amount or disposition amount is assigned.*—A cost recovery amount or a disposition amount allocated to a section 901(m) payor under paragraph (d) of this section is assigned to the U.S. taxable year of the section 901(m) payor that includes the last day of the U.S. taxable year of the RFA owner (U.S.) in which, in the case of a cost recovery amount, the RFA owner (U.S.) takes into account the corresponding U.S. basis deduction (without regard to whether the deduction is deferred or disallowed for U.S. income tax purposes), or in the

case of a disposition amount, the disposition occurs.

(e) *Special rules for certain section 743(b) CAAs*.—If a section 901(m) payor acquires a partnership interest in a section 743(b) CAA, including a section 743(b) CAA with respect to a lower-tier partnership that results from a direct acquisition by the section 901(m) payor of an interest in an upper-tier partnership, and subsequently there is a cost recovery amount or a disposition amount that arises from an RFA with respect to that section 743(b) CAA, all of the cost recovery amount or the disposition amount is allocated to that section 901(m) payor. The U.S. taxable year of the section 901(m) payor to which the cost recovery amount or the disposition amount is assigned is the U.S. taxable year in which, in the case of a cost recovery amount, the section 901(m) payor takes into account the corresponding U.S. basis deduction (without regard to whether the deduction is deferred or disallowed for U.S. income tax purposes), or in the case of a disposition amount, the disposition occurs.

(f) *Mid-year transactions*.—(1) *In general*.—When a disposition of an RFA occurs in the same foreign taxable year that a foreign payor is involved in a mid-year transaction, the portion of the disposition amount that is attributable to foreign disposition gain or foreign disposition loss (as determined under paragraph (d)(5) of this section) is allocated to a section 901(m) payor and assigned to a U.S. taxable year of the section 901(m) payor under this paragraph (f). To the extent the disposition amount is attributable to U.S. disposition gain or U.S. disposition loss (as determined under paragraph (d)(5) of this section), see paragraph (c)(1) or (d) of this section, as applicable.

(2) *Allocation rule*.—To the extent a disposition amount is attributable to foreign disposition gain or foreign disposition loss, a section 901(m) payor is allocated the portion of the disposition amount equal to the product of the disposition amount attributable to foreign disposition gain or foreign disposition loss, as applicable, and a fraction, the numerator of which is the portion of the foreign disposition gain or foreign disposition loss that is included in the allocable foreign income of the section 901(m) payor, and the denominator of which is the foreign disposition gain or foreign disposition loss. If allocable foreign income is not otherwise required to be determined because there is no foreign income tax amount, the numerator is the portion of the foreign disposition gain or foreign disposition loss that would be included in the allocable foreign income of the section 901(m) payor if there were a foreign income tax amount.

(3) *Assignment to a U.S. taxable year of a section 901(m) Payor*.—A disposition amount allocated to a section 901(m) payor under paragraph (f)(2) of this section is assigned to the U.S. taxable year of the section 901(m) payor in which the foreign disposition gain or foreign disposition loss (or portion thereof) is included in allocable foreign income of the section 901(m) payor or, if allocable foreign income is not otherwise required to be determined because there is no foreign income tax amount, the U.S. taxable year in which the foreign disposition gain or foreign disposition loss would be included in allocable foreign income if there were a foreign income tax amount.

(g) *Reverse hybrids*.—(1) *In general*.—This paragraph (g) provides rules for allocating a cost recovery amount or a disposition amount when the RFA owner (U.S.) is either a reverse hybrid or a fiscally transparent entity for U.S. and foreign income tax purposes that is directly or indirectly owned by a reverse hybrid for U.S. and foreign income tax purposes, and in each case, the foreign payor whose foreign income includes a distributive share of the foreign income of the RFA owner (foreign) directly or indirectly owns an interest in the reverse hybrid for foreign income tax purposes. Application of the allocation rules under paragraphs (g)(2) and (g)(3) of this section depend upon whether a section 901(m) payor or a disregarded entity directly owned by a section 901(m) payor is the foreign payor, or, instead, a section 901(m) payor directly or indirectly owns an interest in the foreign payor. For purposes of this paragraph (g), unless otherwise indicated, a reference to direct or indirect ownership in an entity means for U.S. income tax purposes. For purposes of this paragraph (g), a person indirectly owns an interest in an entity for U.S. income tax purposes if the person owns the interest through one or more fiscally transparent entities for U.S. income tax purposes, and at least one of the fiscally transparent entities is not a disregarded entity. For purposes of this paragraph (g), a person indirectly owns an interest in an entity for foreign income tax purposes if the person owns the interest through one or more fiscally transparent entities for foreign income tax purposes. If the RFA owner (U.S.) is a lower-tier fiscally transparent entity for U.S. income tax purposes in which the reverse hybrid indirectly owns an interest, the rules of this section apply in a manner consistent with the application of these rules when the reverse hybrid directly owns an interest in the RFA owner (U.S.).

(2) *First allocation rule*.—(i) *Allocation to a section 901(m) payor*.—This paragraph (g)(2)(i) applies when a section 901(m) payor, or a disregarded entity directly owned by a section 901(m) payor, is the foreign payor whose foreign income includes a distributive share of the foreign income of the RFA owner (foreign), and, therefore, all of the foreign income tax amount of the foreign payor is paid or accrued by, or considered paid or accrued by, the section 901(m) payor. Thus, this paragraph (g)(2)(i) applies when a section 901(m) payor either directly owns an interest in the reverse hybrid or directly owns an interest in a fiscally transparent entity for U.S. and foreign income tax purposes, which, in turn, directly or indirectly owns an interest in the reverse hybrid for both U.S. and foreign income tax purposes. In these cases, the section 901(m) payor is allocated the portions of cost recovery amounts or disposition amounts (or both) with respect to RFAs that are equal to the product of the sum of the cost recovery amounts and the disposition amounts and a fraction, the numerator of which is the portion of the foreign income of the RFA owner (foreign) that is included in the foreign income of the foreign payor, and the denominator of which is the foreign income of the RFA owner (foreign).

(ii) *Assignment to a U.S. taxable year of a section 901(m) Payor*.—This paragraph (g)(2)(ii) applies when a cost recovery amount or a disposition amount, or portion thereof, is allocated to a section 901(m) payor under paragraph (g)(2)(i) of this section. If the reverse hybrid is the RFA owner (U.S.), a cost recovery amount or disposition amount, or portion thereof, is assigned to the U.S. taxable year of the section 901(m) payor that includes the last day of the U.S. taxable year of the reverse hybrid in which, in the case of a cost recovery amount, the reverse hybrid takes into account the corresponding U.S. basis deduction (without regard to whether the deduction is deferred or disallowed for U.S. income tax purposes), or, in the case of a disposition amount, the disposition occurs. If the reverse hybrid is not the RFA owner (U.S.) but instead the reverse hybrid directly or indirectly owns an interest in the RFA owner (U.S.) for both U.S. and foreign income tax purposes, a cost recovery amount or disposition amount, or portion thereof, is assigned to the U.S. taxable year of the section 901(m) payor that includes the last day of the U.S. taxable year of the reverse hybrid, which, in turn, includes the last day of the U.S. taxable year of the RFA owner (U.S.) in which, in the case of a cost recovery amount, the RFA owner (U.S.) takes into account the corresponding U.S. basis deduction (without regard to whether the deduction is deferred or disallowed for U.S. income tax purposes), or, in the case of a disposition amount, the disposition occurs.

(3) *Second allocation rule.*—(i) *Allocation to a section 901(m) payor.*—This paragraph (g)(3)(i) applies when neither a section 901(m) payor nor a disregarded entity directly owned by a section 901(m) payor is the foreign payor with respect to the foreign income of the RFA owner (foreign). Instead, a section 901(m) payor directly or indirectly owns an interest in the foreign payor, which is a fiscally transparent entity for U.S. income tax purposes (other than a disregarded entity directly owned by the section 901(m) payor), and, therefore, the section 901(m) payor is considered to pay or accrue only its allocated portion of the foreign income tax amount of the foreign payor. In these cases, the section 901(m) payor is allocated the portions of cost recovery amounts or disposition amounts (or both) with respect to RFAs that are equal to the product of the sum of the cost recovery amounts and the disposition amounts and a fraction, the numerator of which is the portion of the foreign income of the RFA owner (foreign) that is included in the foreign income of the foreign payor and included in the allocable foreign income of the section 901(m) payor, and the denominator of which is the foreign income of the RFA owner (foreign). If allocable foreign income is not otherwise required to be determined for a section 901(m) payor because there is no foreign income tax amount, the numerator is the foreign income of the RFA owner (foreign) that is included in the foreign income of the foreign payor and that would be included in allocable foreign income of the section 901(m) payor if there were a foreign income tax amount.

(ii) *Assignment to a U.S. taxable year of a section 901(m) payor.*—A cost recovery amount or a disposition amount, or portion thereof, that is allocated to a section 901(m) payor under paragraph (g)(3)(i) of this section is assigned to the U.S. taxable year of the section 901(m) payor in which the foreign income of the RFA owner (foreign) described in paragraph (g)(3)(i) of this section is included in the allocable foreign income of the section 901(m) payor, or, if there is no foreign income tax amount, the U.S. taxable year of the section 901(m) payor in which the foreign income of the RFA owner (foreign) described in paragraph (g)(3)(i) of this section would be included in allocable foreign income if there were a foreign income tax amount.

(h) *Examples.*—The following examples illustrate the rules of this section. In addition to any facts described in a particular example, the following facts apply to all the examples unless otherwise specified: CFC1, CFC2, and DE are organized in Country F and treated as corporations for Country F tax purposes. CFC1 and CFC2 are each a section 902 corporation (as defined in section 909(d)(5)) that is wholly owned by the same U.S. corporation, and DE is a disregarded entity. CFC1 and CFC2 have a U.S. taxable year that is a calendar year, and CFC1, CFC2, and DE have a foreign taxable year that is a calendar year. Country F imposes a single tax that is a foreign income tax. CFC1, CFC2, and DE each have a functional currency of the u with respect to all activities. At all relevant times, 1u equals $1. All amounts are stated in millions. The examples assume that the applicable cost recovery method for property results in basis being recovered ratably over the life of the property beginning on the first day of the U.S. taxable year in which the property is acquired or placed into service.

Example 1. CAA followed by disposition: fully taxable for both U.S. income tax and foreign income tax purposes—(i) *Facts.* (A) On January 1, Year 1, USP acquires all of the stock of CFC1 in a qualified stock purchase (as defined in section 338(d)(3)) to which section 338(a) applies (Section 338 Acquisition). At the time of the Section 338 Acquisition, CFC1 owns a single asset (Asset A) that is located in Country F. Asset A gives rise to income that is taken into account for Country F tax purposes. Asset A is tangible personal property that, under the applicable cost recovery method in the hands of CFC1, is depreciable over 5 years. There are no cost recovery deductions available for Country F tax purposes with respect to Asset A. Immediately before the Section 338 Acquisition, Asset A has a U.S. basis of 10u and a foreign basis of 40u. Immediately after the Section 338 Acquisition, Asset A has a U.S. basis of 100u and foreign basis of 40u.

(B) On July 1, Year 2, Asset A is transferred to an unrelated third party in exchange for 120u in a transaction in which all realized gain is recognized for both U.S. income tax and Country F tax purposes (subsequent transaction). For U.S. income tax purposes, CFC1 recognizes U.S. disposition gain of 50u (amount realized of 120u, less U.S. basis of 70u (100u cost basis, less 30u of accumulated depreciation)) with respect to Asset A. The 30u of accumulated depreciation is the sum of 20u of depreciation in Year 1 (100u cost basis/5 years) and 10u of depreciation in Year 2 ((100u cost basis/5 years) x 6/12). For Country F tax purposes, CFC1 recognizes foreign disposition gain of 80u (amount realized of 120u, less foreign basis of 40u) with respect to Asset A. Immediately after the subsequent transaction, Asset A has a U.S. basis and a foreign basis of 120u.

(ii) *Result.* (A) Under § 1.901(m)-2(b)(1), USP's acquisition of the stock of CFC1 in the Section 338 Acquisition is a section 338 CAA. Under § 1.901(m)-2(c)(i), Asset A is an RFA with respect to Country F tax because it is relevant in determining the foreign income of CFC1 for Country F tax purposes. Under § 1.901(m)-4(b), the basis difference with respect to Asset A is 90u (100u – 10u). Under Section 901(m)-1(a)(31), CFC1 is the RFA owner (U.S.) with respect to Asset A. Under § 1.901(m)-1(a)(23), CFC1 is a foreign payor for Country F tax purposes. Under § 1.901(m)-1(a)(35), CFC1 is the section 901(m) payor with respect to a foreign income tax amount for which CFC1 is the foreign payor (see § 1.901-2(f)(1)).

(B) Under § 1.901(m)-1(a)(5), allocated basis differences are comprised of cost recovery amounts and disposition amounts. In Year 1, Asset A has an allocated basis difference that includes only a cost recovery amount. Under paragraph (b)(2) of this section, the cost recovery amount for Year 1 is determined by applying the applicable cost recovery method of Asset A in the hands of CFC1 to the basis difference with respect to Asset A. Accordingly the cost recovery amount is 18u (90u basis difference/5 years). Under paragraph (b)(1) of this section, all of the 18u cost recovery amount is attributed to CFC1 and assigned to Year 1, because CFC1 is a section 901(m) payor and RFA owner (U.S.) with respect to Asset A and Year 1 is the U.S. taxable year of CFC1 in which it takes into account the corresponding 20u of depreciation. Immediately after Year 1, under § 1.901(m)-1(a)(40), unallocated basis difference is 72u with respect to Asset A (90u – 18u).

(C) In Year 2, Asset A has an allocated basis difference that includes both a cost recovery amount and a disposition amount. Under paragraph (b)(2) of this section, the cost recovery amount for Year 2, as of the date of the subsequent transaction, is 9u ((90u basis difference/5 years) x 6/12). Under § 1.901(m)-1(a)(10), the subsequent transaction is a disposition of Asset A, because the subsequent transaction is an event that results in an amount of gain being recognized for U.S. income tax and Country F tax purposes. Because all realized gain in Asset A is recognized for U.S. income tax and Country F tax purposes, the rule in paragraph (c)(2)(i) of this section applies to determine the disposition amount. Under that rule, the disposition amount for Year 2 is the unallocated basis difference of 63u (90u basis difference, less total 27u taken into account as cost recovery amounts in Year 1 and Year 2). Accordingly, the allocated basis difference for Year 2 is 72u (9u of cost recovery amount, plus 63u of disposition amount). Under paragraphs (b)(1) and (c)(1) of this section, all of the 72u of allocated basis difference is attributed to CFC1 and assigned to Year 2, because CFC1 is a section 901(m) payor and the RFA owner (U.S.) with respect to Asset A and Year 2 is the U.S. taxable year of CFC1 in which it takes into account the corresponding 10u of depreciation and in which the disposition occurred.

(D) Unallocated basis difference with respect to Asset A, as determined immediately after the subsequent transaction, is 0u (90u basis difference less 90u basis difference taken into account as 27u total cost recovery amount in Year 1 and Year 2 and as a 63u disposition amount in Year 2). Accordingly, because there is no unallocated basis difference with respect to Asset A attributable to the Section 338 Acquisition, the subsequent transaction is not a successor transaction as defined in § 1.901(m)-6(b)(2). Furthermore, the subsequent transaction is not a CAA under § 1.901(m)-2(b). For these reasons, section 901(m) no longer applies to Asset A.

Example 2. CAA followed by Disposition: nontaxable for U.S. income tax purposes and taxable for foreign income tax purposes—(i) *Facts.* The facts are the same as in paragraph (i)(A) of *Example 1* but the facts in paragraph (i)(B) of *Example 1* are instead that on July 1, Year 2, Asset A is transferred to CFC2, in exchange for 100u of stock of CFC2 (subsequent transaction). For U.S. income tax purposes, CFC1 does not recognize any U.S. disposition gain or U.S. disposition loss with respect to Asset A. For Country F tax purposes, CFC1 recognizes foreign disposition gain of 60u (amount realized of 100u, less foreign basis of 40u) with respect to Asset A. Immediately after the subsequent transaction, Asset A has a U.S. basis of 70u (100u cost basis less 30u accumulated depreciation) and a foreign basis of 100u. The 30u of accumulated depreciation is the sum of 20u of depreciation in Year 1 (100u cost basis/5 years) and 10u in Year 2 ((100u cost basis/5 years) x 6/12).

(ii) *Result.* (A) The results described in paragraph (ii)(A) of *Example 1* also apply to this *Example 2.*

(B) The result for Year 1 is the same as in paragraph (ii)(B) of *Example 1.*

(C) In Year 2, Asset A has an allocated basis difference that includes both a cost recovery amount and a disposition amount. Under paragraph (b)(2) of this section, the cost recovery amount for Year 2, as of the date of the subsequent transaction, is 9u ((90u basis difference/5 years) x 6/12). Under § 1.901(m)-1(a)(10), the Transaction is a disposition of Asset A, because the subsequent transaction is an event that results in an amount of gain being recognized for Country F tax purposes. Because the disposition is not also fully taxable for U.S. income tax purposes, the rule in paragraph (c)(2)(ii) of this section applies to determine the disposition amount. Under that rule, the disposition amount is 60u, the lesser of (i) 60u (60u foreign disposition gain plus absolute value of 0u U.S. disposition loss), and (ii) 63u unallocated basis difference (90 basis difference less total 27u taken into account as cost recovery amounts, 18u in Year 1 and 9u in Year 2). Accordingly, the allocated basis difference for the first half of Year 2 is 69u (9u of cost recovery amount, plus 60u of disposition amount). Under paragraphs (b)(1) and (c)(1) of this section, all of the 69u of allocated basis difference is attributed to CFC1 and assigned to Year 2, because CFC1 is a section 901(m) payor and the RFA owner (U.S.) with respect to Asset A and Year 2 is the U.S. taxable year of CFC1 in which it takes into account the corresponding 10u of depreciation and in which the disposition occurred.

(D) Unallocated basis difference with respect to Asset A immediately after the subsequent transaction is 3u (90u basis difference less 87u basis difference taken into account as a 27u total cost recovery amount in Year 1 and Year 2 and as a 60u disposition amount in Year 2). Accordingly, because there is unallocated basis difference of 3u with respect to Asset A attributable to the Section 338 Acquisition, as determined immediately after the subsequent transaction, the subsequent transaction is a successor transaction as defined in §1.901(m)-6(b)(2). Following the subsequent transaction, the unallocated basis difference of 3u must be taken into account as cost recovery amounts or disposition amounts (or both) by CFC2, the new section 901(m) payor and RFA owner (U.S.) of Asset A. See §1.901(m)-6(b)(3)(ii). Because the subsequent transaction is not a CAA under §1.901(m)-2(b), there is no additional basis difference with respect to Asset A as a result of the subsequent transaction.

Example 3. CAA followed by disposition: nontaxable for both U.S. income tax and foreign income tax purposes—(i) *Facts*. The facts are the same as in paragraph (i)(A) of *Example 1* but the facts in paragraph (i)(B) of *Example 1* are instead that on July 1, Year 2, CFC1 transfers Asset A to CFC2, in exchange for 110u of stock of CFC2 (subsequent transaction). For U.S. income tax purposes, CFC1 does not recognize any U.S. disposition gain or U.S. disposition loss with respect to Asset A as a result of the subsequent transaction. Furthermore, for Country F tax purposes, CFC1 recognizes no foreign disposition gain or foreign disposition loss with respect to Asset A as a result of the subsequent transaction. Immediately after the subsequent transaction, Asset A has a U.S. basis of 70u (100u cost basis less 30u accumulated depreciation) and a foreign basis of 40u. The 30u of accumulated depreciation is the sum of 20u of depreciation in Year 1 (100u cost basis/5 years) and 10u in Year 2 ((100u cost basis/5 years) x 6/12).

(ii) *Result*. (A) The result for Year 1 is the same as in paragraph (ii)(A) of *Example 1*.

(B) The result for Year 1 is the same as in paragraph (ii)(B) of *Example 1*.

(C) In Year 2, Asset A has an allocated basis difference that includes only a cost recovery amount. Under paragraph (b)(2) of this section, the cost recovery amount for Year 2, as of the date of the subsequent transaction, is 9u ((90u basis difference/5 years) x 6/12). Under §1.901(m)-1(a)(10), the subsequent transaction does not constitute a disposition of Asset A, because the subsequent transaction is not an event that results in an amount of gain or loss being recognized for U.S. income tax or for Country F tax purposes. Therefore, no disposition amount is taken into account for Asset A in Year 2. Under paragraph (b)(1) of this section, all of the 9u of allocated basis difference is attributed to CFC1 and assigned to Year 2, because CFC1 is a section 901(m) payor and RFA owner (U.S.) with respect to Asset A and Year 2 is the U.S. taxable year of CFC1 in which it takes into account the corresponding 10u of depreciation.

(D) Unallocated basis difference with respect to Asset A immediately after the subsequent transaction is 63u (90u basis difference, less 27u total cost recovery amounts, 18u in Year 1 and 9u in Year 2). Accordingly, because there is unallocated basis difference of 63u with respect to Asset A attributable to the CAA, as determined immediately after the subsequent transaction, the subsequent transaction is a successor transaction as defined in §1.901(m)-6(b)(2). Following the subsequent transaction, the unallocated basis difference of 63u must be taken into account as cost recovery amounts or disposition amounts (or both) by CFC2, the new section 901(m) payor and RFA owner (U.S.) of Asset A. See §1.901(m)-6(b)(3)(ii). Because the subsequent transaction is not a CAA under §1.901(m)-2(b), there is no additional basis difference with respect to Asset A as a result of the subsequent transaction.

(i) *Effective/applicability date*.—(1) Except for paragraphs (b)(2)(i) and (c)(2) of this section, this section applies to CAAs occurring on or after the date of publication of the Treasury decision adopting these rules as final regulations in the **Federal Register**.

(2) [The text of proposed §1.901(m)-5(i)(2) is the same as the text of §1.901(m)-5T(i)(2) as added by T.D. 9800.]

(3) Taxpayers may, however, rely on this section prior to the date this section is applicable provided that they both consistently apply this section, §1.704-1(b)(4)(viii)(*c*)(*4*)(*v*) through (*vii*), §1.901(m)-1, §1.901(m)-3, §1.901(m)-4 (excluding §1.901(m)-4(e)), §1.901(m)-6, §1.901(m)-7, and §1.901(m)-8 to all CAAs occurring on or after January 1, 2011, and consistently apply §1.901(m)-2 (excluding §1.901(m)-2(d)) to all CAAs occurring on or after December 7, 2016. For this purpose, persons that are related (within the meaning of section 267(b) or 707(b)) will be treated as a single taxpayer. [Reg. §1.901(m)-5.]

Par. 8. Section 1.901(m)-6 is added to read as follows:

§1.901(m)-6. Successor rules.—(a) through (b)(2) [The text of proposed §§1.901(m)-6(a) through (b)(2) is the same as the text of §§1.901(m)-6T(a) through (b)(2) as added by T.D. 9800.]

(3) *Special considerations*.—(i) If an asset is an RFA with respect to more than one foreign income tax, this paragraph (a) applies separately with respect to each foreign income tax.

(ii) Any subsequent cost recovery amount for an RFA transferred in a successor transaction is determined based on the post-transaction applicable cost recovery method, as described in §1.901(m)-5(b)(3), that applies to the U.S. basis (or portion thereof) that corresponds to the unallocated basis difference.

(4)(i) [The text of proposed §1.901(m)-6(b)(4)(i) is the same as the text of §1.901(m)-6T(b)(4)(i) as added by T.D. 9800.]

(ii) *Foreign basis election*.—If a foreign basis election is made under §1.901(m)-4(c) with respect to a foreign income tax in a subsequent CAA, any unallocated basis difference with respect to one or more prior CAAs will not be taken into account under section 901(m). The only basis difference that will be taken into account after the subsequent CAA with respect to that foreign income tax is the basis difference with respect to the subsequent CAA.

(b)(4)(iii) [The text of proposed §1.901(m)-6(b)(4)(iii) is the same as the text of §1.901(m)-6T(b)(4)(iii) as added by T.D. 9800.]

(5) [The text of proposed §1.901(m)-6(b)(5) is the same as the text of §1.901(m)-6T(b)(5) as added by T.D. 9800.]

(c) *Successor rules for aggregate basis difference carryover.*—(1) *Transfers of a section 901(m) payor's aggregate basis difference carryover to another person.*—If a corporation acquires the assets of a section 901(m) payor in a transaction to which section 381 applies, that corporation succeeds to any aggregate basis difference carryovers of the section 901(m) payor.

(2) *Transfers of a section 901(m) payor's aggregate basis difference carryover with respect to a foreign payor to another foreign payor.*—If a section 901(m) payor has an aggregate basis difference carryover, with respect to a foreign income tax and a foreign payor, and substantially all of the assets of the foreign payor are transferred to another foreign payor in which the section 901(m) payor owns an interest, the section 901(m) payor's aggregate basis difference carryover with respect to the first foreign payor is transferred to the section 901(m) payor's aggregate basis difference carryover with respect to the other foreign payor. In such a case, the section 901(m) payor's aggregate basis difference carryover with respect to the first foreign payor is reduced to zero.

(3) *Anti-abuse rule.*—If a section 901(m) payor has an aggregate basis difference carryover with respect to a foreign income tax and a foreign payor and, with a principal purpose of avoiding the application of section 901(m), assets of the foreign payor are transferred to another foreign payor in a transaction not described in paragraph (c)(1) or (2) of this section, then a portion of the aggregate basis difference carryover of the section 901(m) payor is transferred either to the aggregate basis difference carryover of the section 901(m) payor with respect to the other foreign payor or to another section 901(m) payor, as appropriate. The portion of the aggregate basis difference carryover transferred is determined based on the ratio of fair market value of the assets transferred to the fair market value of all of the assets of the foreign payor that transferred the assets. Similar principles apply when, with a principle purpose of avoiding the application of section 901(m), there is a change in the allocation of foreign income for foreign income tax purposes or the allocation of foreign income tax amounts for U.S. income tax purposes that would otherwise separate foreign income tax amounts from the related aggregate basis difference carryover.

(4) *Ownership.*—For purposes of this paragraph (c), a section 901(m) payor owns an interest in a foreign payor if the section 901(m) payor owns the interest directly or indirectly through one or more fiscally transparent entities for U.S. income tax purposes.

(d) *Effective/applicability date.*—(1) [The text of proposed §1.901(m)-6(d)(1) is the same as the text of §1.901(m)-6T(d)(1) as added by T.D. 9800.]

(2) Paragraphs (b)(3), (b)(4)(ii), and (c) of this section apply to CAAs occurring on or after the date of publication of the Treasury decision adopting these rules as final regulations in the **Federal Register**.

(3) Taxpayers may, however, rely on this section prior to the date this section is applicable provided that they both consistently apply this section, §1.704-1(b)(4)(viii)(*c*)(*4*)(*v*) through (*vii*), §1.901(m)-1, §§1.901(m)-3 through 1.901(m)-5 (excluding §1.901(m)-4(e)), §1.901(m)-7, and §1.901(m)-8 to all CAAs occurring on or after January 1, 2011, and consistently apply §1.901(m)-2 (excluding §1.901(m)-2(d)) to all CAAs occurring on or after December 7, 2016. For this purpose, persons that are related (within the meaning of section 267(b) or 707(b)) will be treated as a single taxpayer. [Reg. §1.901(m)-6.]

Par. 9. Section 1.901(m)-7 is added to read as follows:

§1.901(m)-7. De minimis rules.—(a) *In general.*—This section provides rules describing basis difference that is not taken into account under section 901(m) because a CAA results in a de minimis amount of basis difference. Paragraph (b) of this section sets forth the general rule for determining whether the de minimis threshold is met. Paragraph (c) of this section provides modifications to the general rule in the case of CAAs involving related persons and CAAs that are part of an aggregated CAA transaction. Paragraph (d) of this section provides rules for applying this section, and paragraph (e) of this section provides an anti-abuse rule applicable to related persons. Paragraph (f) of this section provides examples that illustrate the application of this section. Paragraph (g) of this section provides the effective/applicability date.

(b) *General rule.*—(1) *In general.*—A basis difference with respect to an RFA and a foreign income tax is not taken into account under section 901(m) if the requirements under either the cumulative basis difference exemption or the RFA class exemption are satisfied.

(2) *Cumulative basis difference exemption.*—Except as provided in paragraph (c) of this section, a basis difference, with respect to an RFA and a foreign income tax, is not taken into account under section 901(m) (cumulative basis difference exemption) if the sum of that basis difference and all other basis differences (including negative basis differences), with respect to a single CAA and a single RFA owner (U.S.), is less than the greater of:

(i) $10 million, or

(ii) 10 percent of the total U.S. basis of all the RFAs immediately after the CAA.

(3) *RFA class exemption.*—(i) Except as provided in paragraph (c) of this section, a basis difference, with respect to an RFA and a foreign income tax, is not taken into account under section 901(m) (RFA class exemption) if the RFA is part of a class of RFAs and the absolute value of the sum of the basis differences (including negative basis differences), with respect to a single CAA and a single RFA owner, for all the RFAs in that class is less than the greater of:

(A) $2 million, or

(B) 10 percent of the total U.S. basis of all the RFAs in that class of RFAs immediately after the CAA.

(ii) For purposes of this paragraph (b)(3), the classes of RFAs are the seven asset classes defined in §1.338-6(b), regardless of whether the CAA is a section 338 CAA.

(c) *Special rules*.—(1) *Modification of de minimis rules for related persons*.—If the transferor and transferee in the CAA are related persons (as described in section 267(b) or 707(b)), the cumulative basis difference exemption and the RFA class exemption, as described in paragraph (b) of this section, are applied by replacing the terms "$10 million," "10 percent", and "$2 million" wherever they occur in that paragraph with the terms "$5 million," "5 percent," and "$1 million," respectively.

(2) *CAA part of an aggregated CAA transaction*.—If a CAA is part of an aggregated CAA transaction and a single RFA owner (U.S.) does not own all the RFAs attributable to the CAAs that are part of the aggregated CAA transaction, the cumulative basis difference exemption and the RFA class exemption apply to such CAA only if, in addition to satisfying the requirements of paragraph (b)(2) or (b)(3) of this section, respectively, determined without regard to this paragraph (c)(2), the cumulative basis difference exemption or the RFA class exemption, as modified by this paragraph (c)(2), is satisfied. Solely for purposes of this paragraph (c)(2), the cumulative basis difference exemption and the RFA class exemption are applied taking into account all the basis differences with respect to all the RFAs owned by all the RFA owners (U.S.) that are attributable to the CAAs that are part of the aggregated CAA transaction.

(d) *Rules of application*.—The following rules apply for purposes of this section.

(1) Whether a basis difference qualifies for the cumulative basis difference exemption or the RFA class exemption is determined when an asset first becomes an RFA with respect to a CAA. In the case of a subsequent CAA described in § 1.901(m)-6(b)(4), the application of the cumulative basis difference exemption and the RFA class exemption is based on basis difference, if any, that results from the subsequent CAA.

(2) If there is an aggregated CAA transaction, the cumulative basis difference exemption and each RFA class exemption are applied by treating all CAAs that are part of the aggregated CAA transaction as a single CAA.

(3) Basis difference is computed in accordance with § 1.901(m)-4 except that a foreign basis election need not be evidenced if either the cumulative basis difference exemption or an RFA class exemption apply to all RFAs with respect to the CAA.

(4) Basis difference is translated into U.S. dollars (if necessary) using the spot rate determined under the principles of § 1.988-1(d) on the date of the CAA.

(e) *Anti-abuse rule*.—The cumulative basis difference exemption and an RFA class exemption are not available if the transferor and transferee in the CAA are related persons (as described in section 267(b) or 707(b)) and the CAA was entered into, or structured, with a principal purpose of avoiding the application of section 901(m). See also § 1.901(m)-8(c), which provides that certain built-in loss assets are not taken into account for purposes of applying this section.

(f) *Examples*.—The following examples illustrate the rules of this section:

Example 1. De minimis; cumulative basis difference exemption —(i) *Facts*. USP, a domestic corporation, as part of a plan, purchases all of the stock of CFC1 and CFC2 from a single seller. CFC1 and CFC2 are section 902 corporations (as defined in section 909(d)(5)), organized in Country F, and treated as corporations for Country F tax purposes. Country F imposes a single tax that is a foreign income tax. Each acquisition is a qualified stock purchase (as defined in section 338(d)(3)) to which section 338(a) applies. A foreign basis election is not made under § 1.901(m)-4(c). Immediately after the acquisition of the stock of CFC1 and CFC2, the assets of CFC1 and CFC2 give rise to income that is taken into account for Country F tax purposes, and those assets are in a single class, as defined in § 1.338-6(b). At all relevant times, 1u equals $1. All amounts are stated in millions. The additional facts are summarized below.

Relevant Foreign Assets	Total U.S. Basis Immediately Before	Total U.S. Basis Immediately After	Total Basis Difference
Assets of CFC1	48u	60u	12u
Assets of CFC2	100u	96u	(4)u
Total	148u	156u	8u

(ii) *Result*. (A) Under § 1.901(m)-2(b)(1), USP's acquisitions of the stock of CFC1 and CFC2 are each a section 338 CAA. Under 1.901(m)-1(a)(3), the two section 338 CAAs constitute an aggregated CAA transaction because the acquisitions occur as part of a plan. Under § 1.901(m)-2(c)(1), the assets of CFC1 and CFC2 are RFAs for Country F tax purposes because they are relevant in determining foreign income of CFC1 and CFC 2, respectively, for Country F tax purposes. Under § 1.901(m)-1(a)(31), CFC1 is the RFA owner (U.S.) with respect to its assets, and CFC2 is the RFA owner (U.S.) with respect to its assets.

(B) Under paragraph (b)(2) of this section, the application of the cumulative basis difference exemption is based on a single CAA and a single RFA owner (U.S.), subject to the requirements under paragraph (c)(2) of this section that apply when there is an aggregated CAA transaction. In the case of the section 338 CAA with respect to CFC1, without regard to paragraph (c)(2) of this section, the requirements of the cumulative basis difference exemption are satisfied if the sum of the basis differences is less than the threshold of $10 million, the greater of $10 million or $6 million (10% of the total U.S. basis of $60 million (60 million u translated into dollars at the exchange rate of $1 = 1u)). In this case, the sum of the basis differences is $12 million (12 million u translated into dollars at the exchange rate of $1 = 1 u). Because the sum of the basis differences of $12 million is not less than the threshold of $10 million, the requirements of the cumulative basis difference exemption are not satisfied. Because the requirements of the cumulative basis difference exemption are not satisfied, without regard to paragraph (c)(2) of this section, paragraph (c)(2) of this section is not applicable. Finally, the RFA class exemption is not relevant because all of the RFAs of CFC1 are in a single class. Accordingly, the basis differences with respect to all of the RFAs of CFC1 must be taken into account under section 901(m).

(C) In the case of the section 338 CAA with respect to CFC2, without regard to paragraph (c)(2) of this section, the requirements of the cumulative basis difference exemption are satisfied if the sum of the basis differences is less than the threshold of $10 million, the greater of $10 million or $ 9.6 million (10% of the total U.S. basis of $96 million (96 million u translated into dollars at the exchange rate of $1 = 1u)) In this case, the sum of the basis differences is ($4) million ((4) million u translated into dollars at the exchange rate of $1 = 1 u). Because the sum of the basis differences of ($4) million is less than the threshold of $10 million, the requirements of the cumulative basis difference exemption are satisfied. However, because the section 338 CAA with respect to CFC2 is part of an aggregate CAA transaction that includes the section 338 CAA with respect to CFC1, paragraph (c)(2) of this section is applicable. Under paragraph (c)(2) of this section, the requirements of the cumulative basis difference exemption must also be satisfied taking into account all of the RFAs of both CFC2 and CFC1. In this case, the requirements of the cumulative basis difference exemption for purposes of paragraph (c)(2) of this section are satisfied if the sum of the basis differences with respect to all of the RFAs of CFC2 and CFC1 is less than the threshold of $15.6 million, the greater of $10 million or $15.6 million (10% of the total U.S. basis of $156 million (156 million u translated into dollars at the exchange rate of $1 = 1u)) In this case, the sum of the basis differences is $8 million (8 million u translated into dollars at the exchange rate of $1 = 1 u). Because the sum of the basis differences of $8 million is less than the threshold of $15.6 million, the requirements of the cumulative basis difference exemption are satisfied in the case of the section 338 CAA with respect to CFC2. Accordingly, none of the basis differences with respect to the RFAs of CFC2 are taken into account under section 901(m).

Example 2. De minimis; RFA Class Exemption—(i) *Facts.* USP, a domestic corporation, acquires all the stock of CFC, a section 902 corporation (as defined in section 909(d)(5)) organized in Country F and treated as a corporation for Country F tax purposes, in a qualified stock purchase (as defined in section 338(d)(3)) to which section 338(a) applies. Country F imposes a single tax that is a foreign income tax. A foreign basis election is not made under § 1.901(m)-4(c). Immediately after the acquisition of CFC, the assets of CFC give rise to income that is taken into account for Country F tax purposes. At all relevant times, 1u equals $1. All amounts are stated in millions. The additional facts are summarized below.

Relevant Foreign Assets	Total U.S. Basis Immediately Before	Total U.S. Basis Immediately After	Total Basis Difference
Cash (Class I)	10u	10u	0u
Inventory (Class IV)	14u	15u	1u
Buildings (Class V)	19u	30u	11u
Total	43u	55u	12u

(ii) *Result.* (A) Under § 1.901(m)-2(b)(1), USP's acquisition of the stock of CFC is a section 338 CAA. Under § 1.901(m)-2(c)(1), the assets of CFC are RFAs for Country F tax purposes because they are relevant in determining foreign income of CFC for Country F tax purposes.

(B) Under paragraph (b)(2) of this section, the requirements of the cumulative basis difference exemption are satisfied if the sum of the basis differences is less than the threshold of $10 million, the greater of $10 million or $5.5 million (10% of the total U.S. basis of $55 million (55 million u translated into dollars at the exchange rate of $1 = 1u)). In this case, the sum of the basis differences is $12 million (12 million u translated into dollars at the exchange rate of $1 = 1 u). Because the sum of the basis differences of $12 million is not less than the threshold of $10 million, the requirements of the cumulative basis difference exemption are not satisfied.

(C) Under paragraph (b)(3) of this section, each of CFC's assets is allocated to its class under § 1.338-6(b) for purposes of the RFA class exemption. The requirements of the RFA class exemption with respect to the Class IV RFAs (in this case, inventory) are satisfied if the absolute value of the sum of the basis differences with respect to the Class IV RFAs is less than the threshold of $2 million, the greater of $2 million or $1.5 million (10% of the total U.S. basis of Class IV RFAs of $15 million (15 million u translated into dollars at the exchange rate of $1 = 1u)) In this case, the absolute value of the sum of the basis differences is $1 million (1 million u translated into dollars at the exchange rate of $1 = 1 u). Because the sum of the basis differences of $1 million is less than the threshold of $2 million, the requirements of the RFA class exemption are satisfied. Accordingly, the basis differences with respect to the Class IV RFAs are not taken into account under section 901(m).

(D) The requirements of the RFA class exemption with respect to the Class V RFAs (in this case, buildings) is satisfied if the absolute value of the sum of the basis differences with respect to the Class V RFAs is less than the threshold of $3 million, the greater of $2 million or $3 million (10% of the total U.S. basis of Class V RFAs of $30 million (30 million u translated into dollars at the exchange rate of $1 = 1u)). In this case, the absolute value of the sum of the basis differences is $11 million (11 million u translated into dollars at the exchange rate of $1 = 1 u). Because the sum of the basis differences of $11 million is not less than the threshold of $3 million, the requirements of the RFA class exemption are not satisfied. Accordingly, the basis differences with respect to the Class V RFAs are taken into account under section 901(m).

(E) The Class I RFAs (in this case, cash) are irrelevant because there is no basis differences with respect to those RFAs.

(g) *Effective/applicability date.*—This section applies to CAAs occurring on or after the date of publication of the Treasury decision adopting these rules as final regulations in the **Federal Register**. Taxpayers may, however, rely on this section prior to the date this section is applicable provided that they both consistently apply this section, §1.704-1(b)(4)(viii)(*c*)(*4*)(*v*) through (*vii*), §1.901(m)-1, §§1.901(m)-3 through 1.901(m)-6 (excluding §1.901(m)-4(e)), and §1.901(m)-8 to all CAAs occurring on or after January 1, 2011, and consistently apply §1.901(m)-2 (excluding §1.901(m)-2(d)) to all CAAs occurring on or after December 7, 2016. For this purpose, persons that are related (within the meaning of section 267(b) or 707(b)) will be treated as a single taxpayer. [Reg. §1.901(m)-7.]

Par. 10. Section 1.901(m)-8 is added to read as follows:

§1.901(m)-8. Miscellaneous.—(a) *In general.*—This section provides guidance on other matters under section 901(m). Paragraph (b) of this section provides guidance on the application of section 901(m) to pre-1987 foreign income taxes. Paragraph (c) of this section provides anti-abuse rules relating to built-in loss assets. Paragraph (d) of this section provides the effective/applicability date.

(b) *Application of section 901(m) to pre-1987 foreign income taxes.*—Section 901(m) and §§1.901(m)-1 through -8 apply to pre-1987 foreign income taxes (as defined in §1.902-1(a)(10)(iii)) of a section 902 corporation.

(c) *Anti-abuse rule for built-in loss RFAs.*—A basis difference with respect to an RFA described in section 901(m)(3)(C)(ii) (built-in loss RFA) will not be taken into account for purposes of computing an allocated basis difference for a U.S. taxable year of a section 901(m) payor if any RFA, including an RFA other than built-in loss RFAs, is acquired with a principal purpose of using one or more built-in loss RFAs to avoid the application of section 901(m). Furthermore, a basis difference with respect to a built-in loss RFA will not be taken into account for purposes of the cumulative basis difference exemption or the RFA class exemption under §1.901(m)-7 if any RFAs, including RFAs other than built-in loss RFAs, are acquired with a principal purpose of avoiding the application of section 901(m).

(d) *Effective/applicability date.*—This section applies to CAAs occurring on or after the date of publication of the Treasury decision adopting these rules as final regulations in the **Federal Register**. Taxpayers may, however, rely on this section prior to the date this section is applicable provided that they both consistently apply this section, §1.704-1(b)(4)(viii)(*c*)(*4*)(*v*) through (*vii*), §1.901(m)-1, and §§1.901(m)-3 through 1.901(m)-7 (excluding §1.901(m)-4(e)) to all CAAs occurring on or after January 1, 2011, and consistently apply §1.901(m)-2 (excluding §1.901(m)-2(d)) to all CAAs occurring on or after December 7, 2016. For this purpose, persons that are related (within the meaning of section 267(b) or 707(b)) will be treated as a single taxpayer. [Reg. §1.901(m)-8.]

Section 301 Regulations: Statutory Changes Reflected

Section 301 Regulations: Statutory Changes Reflected.—Amendments to Reg. §1.902-1, updating existing regulations under section 301 to reflect statutory changes made by the Technical and Miscellaneous Revenue Act of 1988, which changes provide that the amount of a distribution of property made by a corporation to its shareholder is the fair market value of the distributed property, are proposed (published in the Federal Register on March 26, 2019) (REG-121694-16).

Par. 5. In §1.902-1(a)(12), remove the reference "§1.301-1(b)" and add in its place "§1.301-1(c)".

§1.902-1. Credit for domestic corporate shareholder of a foreign corporation for foreign income taxes paid by the foreign corporation.

Section 301 Regulations: Statutory Changes Reflected

Section 301 Regulations: Statutory Changes Reflected.—Amendments to Reg. §1.902-3, updating existing regulations under section 301 to reflect statutory changes made by the Technical and Miscellaneous Revenue Act of 1988, which changes provide that the amount of a distribution of property made by a corporation to its shareholder is the fair market value of the distributed property, are proposed (published in the Federal Register on March 26, 2019) (REG-121694-16).

Par. 6. In §1.902-3(a)(7), remove the reference "§1.301-1(b)" and add in its place "§1.301-1(c)".

§1.902-3. Credit for domestic corporate shareholder of a foreign corporation for foreign income taxes paid with respect to accumulated profits of taxable years of the foreign corporation beginning before January 1, 1987.

Determination of the Foreign Tax Credit: Guidance

Determination of the Foreign Tax Credit: Guidance.—Amendments to Reg. §§1.904-1—1.904-6, relating to the determination of the foreign tax credit under the Internal Revenue Code, including changes made by the Tax Cuts and Jobs Act, are proposed (published in the Federal Register on December 7, 2018) (REG-105600-18).

Par. 12. §1.904-1 is revised to read as follows:

§1.904-1. Limitation on credit for foreign taxes.—(a) *In general.*—For each separate category described in §1.904-5(a)(4)(v), the total credit for taxes paid or accrued (including those deemed to have been paid or accrued other than by reason of section 904(c)) shall not exceed that proportion of the tax against which such credit is taken which the taxpayer's taxable income from foreign sources (but not in excess of the taxpayer's entire taxable income) in such separate category bears to his entire taxable income for the same taxable year.

(b) *Special computation of taxable income.*—For purposes of computing the limitation under paragraph (a) of this section, the taxable income in the case of an individual, estate, or trust is computed without any deduction for personal exemptions under section 151 or 642(b).

(c) *Joint return.*—In the case of spouses making a joint return, the applicable limitation prescribed by section 904(a) on the credit for taxes paid or accrued to foreign countries and possessions of the United States is applied with respect to the aggregate taxable income in each separate category from sources without the United States, and the aggregate taxable income from all sources, of the spouses.

(d) *Consolidated group.*—For rules relating to the computation of the foreign tax credit limitation for a consolidated group, see § 1.1502-4.

(e) *Applicability dates.*—This section applies to taxable years that both begin after December 31, 2017, and end on or after December 4, 2018.

Par. 13. Section 1.904-2 is amended by:

1. Revising paragraphs (a) through (d).

2. Removing the language "904(d)" and adding the language "904(c)" in its place in paragraph (e).

3. Removing and reserving paragraph (g).

4. Revising paragraphs (h) and (i).

5. Adding paragraphs (j) and (k).

The revisions and additions read as follows:

§ 1.904-2. Carryback and carryover of unused foreign tax.—(a) *Credit for foreign tax carryback or carryover.*—A taxpayer who chooses to claim a credit under section 901 for a taxable year is allowed a credit under that section not only for taxes otherwise allowable as a credit but also for taxes deemed paid or accrued in that year as a result of a carryback or carryover of an unused foreign tax under section 904(c). However, the taxes so deemed paid or accrued are not allowed as a deduction under section 164(a). Foreign tax paid or accrued with respect to section 951A category income, including section 951A category income that is reassigned to a separate category for income resourced under a treaty, may not be carried back or carried forward or deemed paid or accrued under section 904(c). For special rules regarding these computations in case of taxes paid, accrued, or deemed paid with respect to foreign oil and gas extraction income or foreign oil related income, see section 907(f) and the regulations under that section.

(b) *Years to which foreign taxes are carried.*—If the taxpayer chooses the benefits of section 901 for a taxable year, any unused foreign tax paid or accrued in that year is carried first to the immediately preceding taxable year and then, as applicable, to each of the ten succeeding taxable years, in chronological order, but only to the extent not absorbed as taxes deemed paid or accrued under paragraph (d) of this section in a prior taxable year.

(c) *Definitions.*—This paragraph (c) provides definitions that apply for purposes of this section.

(1) *Unused foreign tax.*—The term *unused foreign tax* means, with respect to each separate category for any taxable year, the excess of the amount of creditable foreign tax paid or accrued, or deemed paid under section 902 (as in effect on December 21, 2017) or section 960, in such year, over the applicable foreign tax credit limitation under section 904 for the separate category in such year. Unused foreign tax does not include any amount for which a credit is disallowed, including foreign income taxes for which a credit is disallowed or reduced when the tax is paid, accrued, or deemed paid.

(2) *Separate category.*—The term *separate category* has the same meaning as provided in § 1.904-5(a)(4)(v).

(3) *Excess limitation.*—(i) *In general.*—The term *excess limitation* means, with respect to a separate category for any taxable year (the *excess limitation year*) and an unused foreign tax carried from another taxable year (the *excess credit year*), the amount (if any) by which the limitation for that separate category with respect to that excess limitation year exceeds the sum of—

(A) The creditable foreign tax actually paid or accrued or deemed paid under section 902 (as in effect on December 21, 2017) or section 960 with respect to the separate category in the excess limitation year, and

(B) The portion of any unused foreign tax for a taxable year preceding the excess credit year that is absorbed as taxes deemed paid or accrued in the excess limitation year under paragraph (a) of this section.

(ii) *Deduction years.*—Excess limitation for a taxable year absorbs unused foreign tax, regardless of whether the taxpayer chooses to claim a credit under section 901 for the year. In such case, the amount of the excess limitation, if any, for the year is determined in the same manner as though the taxpayer had chosen to claim a credit under section 901 for that year. For purposes of this determination, if the taxpayer has an overall foreign loss account, the excess limitation in a deduction year is determined based on the amount of the overall foreign loss the taxpayer would have recaptured if the taxpayer had chosen to claim a credit under section 901 for that year and had not made an election under § 1.904(f)-2(c)(2) to recapture more of the overall foreign loss account than is required under § 1.904(f)-2(c)(1).

(d) *Taxes deemed paid or accrued.*—(1) *Amount deemed paid or accrued.*—The amount of unused foreign tax with respect to a separate category that is deemed paid or accrued in any taxable year to which such unused foreign tax may be carried under paragraph (b) of this section is equal to the smaller of—

(i) The portion of the unused foreign tax that may be carried to the taxable year under paragraph (b) of this section, or

(ii) The amount, if any, of the excess limitation for such taxable year with respect to such unused foreign tax.

(2) *Carryback or carryover tax deemed paid or accrued in the same separate category.*—Any unused foreign tax, which is deemed to be paid or accrued under section 904(c) in the year to which it is carried, is deemed to be paid or accrued with respect to the same separate category as the category to which it was assigned in the year in which it was actually paid or accrued. However, see paragraphs (h) through (j) of this section for transition rules in the case of certain carrybacks and carryovers.

(3) *No duplicate disallowance of creditable foreign tax.*—Foreign income taxes for which a credit is partially disallowed, including when the tax is paid, accrued, or deemed paid, are not reduced again by reason of the unused foreign tax being deemed to be paid or accrued in the year to which it is carried under section 904(c).

* * *

(g) [Reserved]

(h) *Transition rules for carryovers of pre-2003 unused foreign tax and carrybacks of post-2002 unused foreign tax paid or accrued with respect to dividends from noncontrolled section 902 corporations.*—For transition rules for carryovers of pre-2003 unused foreign tax, and carrybacks of post-2002 unused foreign tax, paid or accrued with respect to dividends from noncontrolled section 902 corporations, see 26 CFR § 1.904-2(h) (revised as of April 1, 2018).

(i) *Transition rules for carryovers of pre-2007 unused foreign tax and carrybacks of post-2006 unused foreign tax.*—For transition rules for carryovers of pre-2007 unused foreign tax, and carrybacks of post-2006 unused foreign tax, see 26 CFR § 1.904-2(i) (revised as of April 1, 2018).

(j) *Transition rules for carryovers and carrybacks of pre-2018 and post-2017 unused foreign tax.*—(1) *Carryover of unused foreign tax.*—(i) *In general.*—For purposes of this paragraph (j), the terms *post-2017 separate category*, *pre-2018 separate category*, and *specified separate category* have the meanings set forth in § 1.904(f)-12(j)(1). The rules of this paragraph (j)(1) apply to reallocate to the taxpayer's post-2017 separate categories for foreign branch category income, general category income, passive category income, and specified separate categories of income, any unused foreign taxes (as defined in paragraph (c)(1) of this section) that were paid or accrued or deemed paid under sections 902 and 960 with respect to income in a pre-2018 separate category.

(ii) *Allocation to the same separate category.*—Except as provided in paragraph (j)(1)(iii) of this section, to the extent any unused foreign taxes paid or accrued or deemed paid with respect to a separate category of income are carried forward to a taxable year beginning after December 31, 2017, such taxes are allocated to the same post-2017 separate category as the pre-2018 separate category from which the unused foreign taxes are carried.

(iii) *Exception for certain general category unused foreign taxes.*—(A) *In general.*—To the extent any unused foreign taxes paid or accrued (but not taxes deemed paid) with respect to general category income are carried forward to a taxable year beginning after December 31, 2017, a taxpayer may choose to allocate those taxes to the taxpayer's post-2017 separate category for foreign branch category income to the extent those taxes would have been allocated to the taxpayer's post-2017 separate category for foreign branch category income if the taxes were paid or accrued in a taxable year beginning after December 31, 2017. Any remaining unused foreign taxes paid or accrued or deemed paid with respect to general category income carried forward to a taxable year beginning after December 31, 2017, are allocated to the taxpayer's post-2017 separate category for general category income.

(B) *Rules regarding the exception.*—A taxpayer applying the exception described in paragraph (j)(1)(iii)(A) of this section (the *branch carryover exception*) must apply the exception to all of its unused foreign taxes paid or accrued with respect to general category income that are carried forward to all taxable years beginning after December 31, 2017. A taxpayer may choose to apply the branch carryover exception on a timely filed original return (including extensions) or an amended return. A taxpayer that applies the exception on an amended return must make appropriate adjustments to eliminate any double benefit arising from application of the exception to years that are not open for assessment.

(2) *Carryback of unused foreign tax.*—(i) *In general.*—The rules of this paragraph (j)(2) apply to any unused foreign taxes that were paid or accrued, or deemed paid under section 960, with respect to income in a post-2017 separate category.

(ii) *Passive category income and specified separate categories of income described in § 1.904-4(m).*—Any unused foreign taxes paid or accrued or deemed paid with respect to passive category income or a specified separate category of income in a taxable year beginning after December 31, 2017, that are carried back to a taxable year beginning before January 1, 2018, are allocated to the same pre-2018 separate category as the post-2017 separate category from which the unused foreign taxes are carried.

(iii) *General category income and foreign branch category income.*—Any unused foreign taxes paid or accrued or deemed paid with respect to general category income or foreign branch category income in a taxable year beginning after December 31, 2017, that are carried back to a taxable year beginning before January 1, 2018, are allocated to the taxpayer's pre-2018 separate category for general category income.

(k) *Applicability date.*—Paragraphs (a) through (i) of this section apply to taxable years that both begin after December 31, 2017, and end on or after December 4, 2018. Paragraph (j) of this section applies to taxable years beginning after December 31, 2017. Paragraph (j)(2) of this section also applies to the last taxable year beginning before January 1, 2018.

Par. 14. Section 1.904-3 is amended by:

1. Revising the section heading.

2. Removing the language "a husband and wife" and adding the language "spouses" in its place in paragraphs (a), (b), (c), and (d).

3. Adding a sentence to the end of paragraph (a).
4. Removing the second and third sentences in paragraph (d).
5. Revising paragraph (e).
6. Revising paragraphs (f)(1) through (f)(3).
7. Removing the language "904(d)" and adding the language "904(c)" in its place in paragraphs (f)(5)(i) and (ii).
8. Removing paragraph (f)(6).
9. Removing and reserving paragraph (g).
10. Adding paragraph (h).

The additions and revisions read as follows:

§1.904-3. Carryback and carryover of unused foreign tax by spouses making a joint return.—(a) * * * The rules in this section apply separately with respect to each separate category as defined in §1.904-5(a)(4)(v).

* * *

(e) *Amounts carried from or through a joint return year to or through a separate return year.*—(1) *In general.*—It is necessary to allocate to each spouse the spouse's share of an unused foreign tax or excess limitation for any taxable year for which the spouses filed a joint return if—

(i) The spouses file separate returns for the current taxable year and an unused foreign tax is carried thereto from a taxable year for which they filed a joint return;

(ii) The spouses file separate returns for the current taxable year and an unused foreign tax is carried to such taxable year from a year for which they filed separate returns but is first carried through a year for which they filed a joint return; or

(iii) The spouses file a joint return for the current taxable year and an unused foreign tax is carried from a taxable year for which they filed joint returns but is first carried through a year for which they filed separate returns.

(2) *Computation and adjustments.*—In the cases described in paragraph (e)(1) of this section, the separate carryback or carryover of each spouse to the current taxable year shall be computed in the manner described in §1.904-2 but with the modifications set forth in paragraph (f) of this section. Where applicable, appropriate adjustments are made to take into account the fact that, for any taxable year involved in the computation of the carryback or the carryover, either spouse has combined foreign oil and gas income described in section 907(b) with respect to which the limitation in section 907(a) applies.

(f) * * *

(1) *Separate category limitation.*—The limitation in a separate category of a particular spouse for a taxable year for which a joint return is made shall be the portion of the limitation on the joint return which bears the same ratio to such limitation as such spouse's foreign source taxable income (with gross income and deductions taken into account to the same extent as taken into account on the joint return) in such separate category (but not in excess of the joint foreign source taxable income) bears to the joint foreign source taxable income in such separate category.

(2) *Unused foreign tax.*—For purposes of this section, the term *unused foreign tax* means, with respect to a particular spouse and separate category for a taxable year for which a joint return is made, the excess of the foreign tax paid or accrued by that spouse with respect to that separate category over that spouse's separate category limitation.

(3) *Excess limitation.*—For purposes of this section, the term *excess limitation* means, with respect to a particular spouse and separate category for a taxable year for which a joint return is made, the excess of that spouse's separate category limitation over the foreign taxes paid or accrued by such spouse with respect to such separate category for such taxable year.

* * *

(g) [Reserved]

(h) *Applicability date.*—This section is applicable for taxable years that both begin after December 31, 2017, and end on or after December 4, 2018.

Par. 15. §1.904-4 is amended by:
1. Revising paragraph (a).
2. Removing the language "1248; or" from paragraph (b)(2)(i)(A) and adding the language "1248;" in its place.
3. Removing the language "1293." from paragraph (b)(2)(i)(B) and adding the language "1293;" in its place.
4. Adding paragraphs (b)(2)(i)(C) and (D).
5. Revising the first and second sentences of paragraph (b)(2)(ii).
6. Removing the language "shall not be" from the first sentence of paragraph (c)(1) and adding the language "is not" in its place.
7. Revising the second, third, and fourth sentences of paragraph (c)(1).
8. Removing the last sentence of paragraph (c)(1).
9. Revising the second, third, and fourth sentences, and adding a new sentence after the fourth sentence, of paragraph (c)(3).
10. Revising paragraph (c)(4).
11. Revising paragraph (c)(5)(ii).
12. Removing the second and third sentences of paragraphs (c)(5)(iii)(A) and (B).
13. Revising the first sentence of paragraph (c)(6)(i).
14. Removing the language "deemed paid or accrued" and adding the language "deemed paid" in its place in the second sentence in paragraph (c)(6)(i).
15. Removing the word "taxable" from the last sentence of paragraph (c)(6)(i).
16. Revising the first, fourth, fifth, and sixth sentences of paragraph (c)(6)(iii).

17. Removing the word "taxable" in the second sentence of paragraph (c)(6)(iii).
18. Removing the language "deemed paid or accrued" and adding the language "deemed paid" in its place in the third sentence of paragraph (c)(6)(iii).
19. Revising paragraph (c)(6)(iv).
20. Revising the second sentence and the sixth sentence of paragraph (c)(7)(i).
21. Removing the language "general category income" and adding the language "income in another separate category" in its place in the third sentence of paragraph (c)(7)(iii).
22. Adding paragraph (d) and revising paragraph (e)(1).
23. Removing and reserving paragraph (e)(2)(i)(W).
24. Removing the last sentence of paragraph (e)(3)(ii).
25. Removing paragraph (e)(5).
26. Adding paragraphs (f) and (g).
27. Revising paragraphs (h)(2), (h)(5)(i), (h)(5)(ii), and paragraphs (k) through (n).
28. Adding paragraphs (o),(p), and (q).
The revisions and additions read as follows:

§1.904-4. Separate application of section 904 with respect to certain categories of income.—(a) *In general.*—A taxpayer is required to compute a separate foreign tax credit limitation for income received or accrued in a taxable year that is described in section 904(d)(1)(A) (section 951A category income), 904(d)(1)(B) (foreign branch category income), 904(d)(1)(C) (passive category income), 904(d)(1)(D) (general category income), or paragraph (m) of this section (specified separate categories). For purposes of this section, the definitions in §1.904-5(a)(4) apply.

(b) * * *

(2) * * *

(i) * * *

(C) Distributive shares of partnership income treated as passive category income under paragraph (n)(1) of this section, and income from the sale of a partnership interest treated as passive category income under paragraph (n)(2) of this section; or

(D) Income treated as passive category income under the look-through rules in §1.904-5.

(ii) *Exceptions.*—Passive income does not include any export financing interest (as defined in paragraph (h) of this section), any high-taxed income (as defined in paragraph (c) of this section), financial services income (as defined in paragraph (e)(1)(ii) of this section), or any active rents and royalties (as defined in paragraph (b)(2)(iii) of this section). In addition, passive income does not include any income that would otherwise be passive but is excluded from passive category income under §1.904-5(b)(1).* * *

* * *

(c) * * *

(1) * * * Income is considered to be high-taxed income if, after allocating expenses, losses, and other deductions of the United States person to that income under paragraph (c)(2) of this section, the sum of the foreign income taxes paid or accrued, and deemed paid under section 960, by the United States person with respect to such income (reduced by any portion of such taxes for which a credit is not allowed) exceeds the highest rate of tax specified in section 1 or 11, whichever applies (and with reference to section 15 if applicable), multiplied by the amount of such income (including the amount treated as a dividend under section 78). If, after application of this paragraph (c), income that would otherwise be passive income is determined to be high-taxed income, the income is treated as general category income, foreign branch category income, section 951A category income, or income in a specified separate category, as determined under the rules of this section, and any taxes imposed on that income are considered related to the same separate category of income under §1.904-6. If, after application of this paragraph (c), passive income is zero or less than zero, any taxes imposed on the passive income are considered related to the same separate category of income to which the passive income (if not reduced to zero or less than zero) would have been assigned had the income been treated as high-taxed income (general category, foreign branch category, section 951A category, or a specified separate category). * * *

* * *

(3) * * * Paragraph (c)(4) of this section provides additional rules for inclusions under section 951(a)(1) or 951A(a) that are passive income, dividends from a controlled foreign corporation or noncontrolled 10-percent owned foreign corporation that are passive income, and income that is received or accrued by a United States person through a foreign QBU that is passive income. For purposes of this paragraph (c), a foreign QBU is a qualified business unit (as defined in section 989(a)), other than a controlled foreign corporation or noncontrolled 10-percent owned foreign corporation, that has its principal place of business outside the United States. These rules apply whether the income is received from a controlled foreign corporation of which the United States person is a United States shareholder, from a noncontrolled 10-percent owned foreign corporation of which the United States person is a United States shareholder that is a domestic corporation, or from any other person. In applying these rules, passive income is not treated as subject to a withholding tax or other foreign tax for which a credit is disallowed in full, for example, under section 901(k). * * *

(4) *Dividends and inclusions from controlled foreign corporations, dividends from noncontrolled 10-percent owned foreign corporations, and income attributable to foreign QBUs.*—Except as provided in paragraph (c)(5) of this section, the rules of this paragraph (c)(4) apply to all dividends and all amounts included in gross income of a United States shareholder under section 951(a)(1) or 951A(a) with respect to the foreign corporation that (after application of the look-through rules of section 904(d)(3) and §1.904-5) are attributable to passive income received or accrued by a controlled foreign corporation, all dividends from a noncontrolled 10-percent owned foreign corporation that are received or accrued by a United States shareholder that (after application of the look-through rules of section 904(d)(4) and §1.904-5) are treated as passive income, and all

amounts of passive income received or accrued by a United States person through a foreign QBU. The grouping rules of paragraph (c)(3)(i) through (iv) of this section apply separately to dividends, to inclusions under section 951(a)(1) and to inclusions under section 951A(a) with respect to each controlled foreign corporation of which the taxpayer is a United States shareholder, and to dividends with respect to each noncontrolled 10-percent owned foreign corporation of which the taxpayer is a United States shareholder that is a domestic corporation. The grouping rules of paragraph (c)(3)(i) through (iv) of this section also apply separately to income attributable to each foreign QBU of a controlled foreign corporation, noncontrolled 10-percent owned foreign corporation, any other look-through entity as defined in § 1.904-5(i), or any United States person.

(5) * * *

(ii) *Treatment of partnership income.*—A partner's distributive share of income from a foreign or United States partnership that is treated as passive income under paragraph (n)(1)(ii) of this section (generally providing that a less than 10 percent partner's distributive share of partnership income is passive income) is treated as a single item of income and is not grouped with other amounts. A distributive share of income from a partnership that is treated as passive income under paragraph (n)(1)(i) of this section is grouped according to the rules in paragraph (c)(3) of this section, except that the portion, if any, of the distributive share of income attributable to income earned by a United States partnership through a foreign QBU is separately grouped under the rules of paragraph (c)(4) of this section.

* * *

(6) * * *

(i) * * * The determination of whether an amount included in gross income under section 951(a)(1) or 951A(a) is high-taxed income is made in the taxable year the income is included in the gross income of the United States shareholder under section 951(a) or 951A(a) (for purposes of this paragraph (c), the *year of inclusion*). * * *

* * *

(iii) * * * If an item of income is considered high-taxed income in the year of inclusion and paragraph (c)(6)(i) of this section applies, then any increase in foreign income taxes imposed with respect to that item are considered to be related to the same separate category to which the income was assigned in the taxable year of inclusion. * * * The taxpayer shall treat any taxes paid or accrued, or deemed paid, on the distribution in excess of this amount as taxes related to the same category of income to which such inclusion would have been assigned had the income been treated as high-taxed income in the year of inclusion (general category income, section 951A category income, or income in a specified separate category). If these additional taxes are not creditable in the year of distribution, the carryover rules of section 904(c) apply (see section 904(c) and § 1.904-2(a) for rules disallowing carryovers in the section 951A category). For purposes of this paragraph (c)(6), the foreign tax on an inclusion under section 951(a)(1) or 951A(a) is considered increased on distribution of the earnings and profits associated with that inclusion if the total of taxes paid and deemed paid on the inclusion and the distribution (taking into account any reductions in tax and any withholding taxes) exceeds the total taxes deemed paid in the year of inclusion. * * *

(iv) *Increase in taxes paid by successors.*—If passive earnings and profits previously included in income of a United States shareholder are distributed to a person that was not a United States shareholder of the distributing corporation in the year the earnings were included, any increase in foreign taxes paid or accrued, or deemed paid, on that distribution is treated as tax related to general category income (or income in a specified separate category, if applicable) in the case of earnings and profits previously included under section 951(a)(1), and is treated as tax related to section 951A category income (or income in a specified separate category, if applicable) in the case of earnings and profits previously included under section 951A(a), regardless of whether the previously-taxed income was considered high-taxed income under section 904(d)(2)(F) in the year of inclusion.

(7) * * *

(i) * * * If the inclusion is considered to be high-taxed income, then the taxpayer shall treat the inclusion as general category income, section 951A category income or income in a specified separate category as provided in paragraph (c)(1) of this section. * * * For this purpose, the foreign tax on an inclusion under section 951(a)(1) or 951A(a) shall be considered reduced on distribution of the earnings and profits associated with the inclusion if the total taxes paid and deemed paid on the inclusion and the distribution (taking into account any reductions in tax and any withholding taxes) is less than the total taxes deemed paid in the year of inclusion. * * *

* * *

(d) *General category income.*—The term *general category income* means all income other than passive category income, foreign branch category income, section 951A category income, and income in a specified separate category. Any item that is excluded from the passive category under section 904(d)(2)(B)(iii) or § 1.904-5(b)(1) is included in general category income only to the extent that such item does not meet the definition of another separate category. General category income also includes income treated as general category income under the look-through rules referenced in § 1.904-5(a)(2).

(e) * * *

(1) *In general.*—(i) *Treatment of financial services income.*—Financial services income that meets the definition of foreign branch category income is treated as income in that category. Financial services income of a controlled foreign corporation that is included in gross income of a United States shareholder under section 951A(a) is treated as section 951A category income in the hands of the United States shareholder. Financial services income that is neither treated as foreign branch category income nor treated as section 951A category income is treated as general category income.

(ii) *Definition of financial services income.*—The term *financial services income* means income derived by a financial services entity, as defined in paragraph (e)(3) of this section, that is:

(A) Income derived in the active conduct of a banking, insurance, financing, or similar business (active financing income as defined in paragraph (e)(2) of this section);

(B) Passive income as defined in section 904(d)(2)(B) and paragraph (b) of this section as determined before the application of the exception for high-taxed income but after the application of the exception for export financing interest; or

(C) Incidental income as defined in paragraph (e)(4) of this section.

(2) * * *

(i) * * *

(W) [Reserved]

* * *

(f) *Foreign branch category income.*—(1) *Foreign branch category income.*—(i) *In general.*—Except as provided in paragraph (f)(1)(ii) of this section, the term *foreign branch category income* means income of a United States person, other than a pass-through entity, that is—

(A) Income attributable to foreign branches of the United States person held directly or indirectly through disregarded entities;

(B) A distributive share of partnership income that is attributable to foreign branches held by the partnership directly or indirectly through disregarded entities, or held indirectly by the partnership through another partnership or other pass-through entity that holds the foreign branch directly or indirectly through disregarded entities; and

(C) Income from other pass-through entities determined under principles similar to those described in paragraph (f)(1)(i)(B) of this section.

(ii) *Passive category income excluded from foreign branch category income.*—Income assigned to the passive category under paragraph (b) of this section is not foreign branch category income, regardless of whether the income is described in paragraph (f)(1)(i) of this section. Income that is treated as passive category income under the look-through rules in § 1.904-5 is also excluded from foreign branch category income, regardless of whether the income is attributable to a foreign branch. However, income that would be passive category income but for the application of section 904(d)(2)(B)(iii) (export financing interest and high-taxed income) or 904(d)(2)(C) (financial services income) and the regulations under those sections and also meets the definition of foreign branch category income is foreign branch category income.

(2) *Gross income attributable to a foreign branch.*—(i) *In general.*—Except as provided in this paragraph (f)(2), gross income is attributable to a foreign branch to the extent the gross income (as adjusted to conform to Federal income tax principles) is reflected on the separate set of books and records (as defined in § 1.989(a)-1(d)(1) and (2)) of the foreign branch. Gross income that is not attributable to the foreign branch and is therefore attributable to the foreign branch owner is treated as income in a separate category (other than the foreign branch category) under the other rules of this section.

(ii) *Income attributable to U.S. activities.*—Gross income attributable to a foreign branch does not include items arising from activities carried out in the United States, regardless of whether the items are reflected on the foreign branch's separate books and records.

(iii) *Income arising from stock.*—(A) *In general.*—Except as provided in paragraph (f)(2)(iii)(B) of this section, gross income attributable to a foreign branch does not include items of income arising from stock of a corporation (whether foreign or domestic), including gain from the disposition of such stock or any inclusion under sections 951(a), 951A(a), or 1293(a).

(B) *Exception for dealer property.*—Paragraph (f)(2)(iii)(A) of this section does not apply to gain recognized from dispositions of stock in a corporation, if the stock would be dealer property (as defined in § 1.954-2(a)(4)(v)) if the foreign branch were a controlled foreign corporation.

(iv) *Disposition of interests in certain entities.*—(A) *In general.*—Except as provided in paragraph (f)(2)(iv)(B) of this section, gross income attributable to a foreign branch does not include gain from the disposition of an interest in a partnership or other pass-through entity or an interest in a disregarded entity. See also paragraph (n)(2) of this section for general rules relating to the sale of a partnership interest.

(B) *Exception for sales by a foreign branch in the ordinary course of business.*—The rule in paragraph (f)(2)(iv)(A) of this section does not apply to gain from the sale or exchange of an interest in a partnership or other pass-through entity or an interest in a disregarded entity if the gain is reflected on the books and records of a foreign branch and the interest is held by the foreign branch in the ordinary course of its active trade or business. An interest is considered to be held in the ordinary course of the foreign branch's active trade or business if the foreign branch engages in the same or a related trade or business as the partnership or other pass-through entity (other than through a less than 10 percent interest) or disregarded entity.

(v) *Adjustments to items of gross income reflected on the books and records.*—If a principal purpose of recording or failing to record an item of gross income on the books and records of a foreign branch, or of making a disregarded payment described in paragraph (f)(2)(vi) of this section, is the avoidance of Federal income tax, the purposes of section 904, or the purposes of section 250 (in connection with section 250(b)(3)(A)(i)(VI)), the item must be attributed to one or more foreign branches or the foreign branch owner in a manner that reflects the substance of the transaction. For purposes of this paragraph (f)(2)(v), interest received by a foreign branch from a related person is presumed to be attributable to the foreign branch owner (and not to the foreign branch) unless the interest income meets the definition of financial services income under paragraph (e)(1)(ii) of this section. For purposes of this paragraph (f)(2)(v), a related person is any person that bears a relationship to the foreign branch owner described in section 267(b) or 707.

(vi) *Attribution of gross income to which disregarded payments are allocable.*—(A) *In general.*—If a foreign branch makes a disregarded payment to its foreign branch owner and the disregarded payment is allocable to non-passive category gross income of the foreign branch reflected on the foreign branch's separate set of books and records under paragraph (f)(2)(i) of this section, the gross income attributable to the foreign branch is adjusted downward to reflect the allocable amount of the disregarded payment, and the general category gross income attributable to the foreign branch owner is adjusted upward by the same amount, translated (if necessary) from the foreign branch's functional currency to U.S. dollars at the spot rate, as defined in § 1.988-1(d), on the date of the disregarded payment. Similarly, if a foreign branch owner makes a disregarded payment to its foreign branch and the disregarded payment is allocable to general category gross income of the foreign branch owner that was not reflected on the separate set of books and records of any foreign branch of the foreign branch owner, the gross income attributable to the foreign branch owner is adjusted downward to reflect the allocable amount of the disregarded payment, and the gross income attributable to the foreign branch is adjusted upward by the same amount, translated (if necessary) from U.S. dollars to the foreign branch's functional currency at the spot rate, as defined in § 1.988-1(d), on the date of the disregarded payment. An adjustment to the attribution of gross income under this paragraph (f)(2)(vi) does not change the total amount, character, or source of the United States person's gross income. Similar rules apply in the case of disregarded payments between a foreign branch and another foreign branch with the same foreign branch owner.

(B) *Allocation of disregarded payments.—(1) In general.*—Whether a disregarded payment is allocable to gross income of a foreign branch or its foreign branch owner, and the source and separate category of the gross income to which the disregarded payment is allocable, is determined under the following rules:

(i) Disregarded payments from a foreign branch owner to its foreign branch are allocable to gross income attributable to the foreign branch owner to the extent a deduction for that payment, if regarded, would be allocated and apportioned to general category gross income of the foreign branch owner under the principles of §§ 1.861-8 through 1.861-14T and 1.861-17 by treating foreign source general category gross income and U.S. source general category gross income each as a statutory grouping; and

(ii) Disregarded payments from a foreign branch to its foreign branch owner are allocable to gross income attributable to the foreign branch to the extent a deduction for that payment, if regarded, would be allocated and apportioned to gross income of the foreign branch under the principles of §§ 1.861-8 through 1.861-14T and 1.861-17 by treating foreign source gross income in the foreign branch category and U.S. source gross income in the foreign branch category each as a statutory grouping.

(2) Disregarded sales of property.—The principles of paragraph (f)(2)(vi)(B)(*1*)(*i*) and (*ii*) of this section apply in the case of disregarded payments in consideration for the transfer of property between a foreign branch and its foreign branch owner to the extent the disregarded payment, if regarded, would, for purposes of determining gross income, be subtracted from gross receipts that are regarded for Federal income tax purposes.

(3) Conditions and timing of reallocation.—The gross income attributable to the foreign branch is adjusted only in the taxable year, and only to the extent, that a disregarded payment, if regarded, would be allowed as a deduction or otherwise would be taken into account (for example, as an increase to cost of goods sold).

(C) *Exclusion of certain disregarded payments.*—Paragraph (f)(2)(vi)(A) of this section does not apply to the following payments, accruals, or other transfers between a foreign branch and its foreign branch owner that are disregarded for Federal income tax purposes:

(1) Interest and interest equivalents that, if regarded, would be described in § 1.861-9T(b);

(2) Remittances from the foreign branch to its foreign branch owner, except as provided in paragraph (f)(2)(vi)(D) of this section; or

(3) Contributions of money, securities, and other property from the foreign branch owner to its foreign branch, except as set forth in paragraph (f)(2)(vi)(D) of this section.

(D) *Certain transfers of intangible property.*—For purposes of applying this paragraph (f)(2)(vi), the amount of gross income attributable to a foreign branch (and the amount of gross income attributable to its foreign branch owner) that is not passive category income must be adjusted under the principles of paragraph (f)(2)(vi)(B) of this section to reflect all transactions that are disregarded for Federal income tax purposes in which property described in section 367(d)(4) is transferred to or from a foreign branch, whether or not a disregarded payment is made in connection with the transfer. In determining the amount of gross income that is attributable to a foreign branch that must be adjusted by reason of this paragraph (f)(2)(vi)(D), the principles of sections 367(d) and 482 apply. For example, if a foreign branch owner transfers property described in section 367(d)(4), the principles of section 367(d) are applied by treating the foreign branch as a separate corporation to which the property is transferred in exchange for stock of the corporation in a transaction described in section 351.

(E) *Amount of disregarded payments.*—The amount of each disregarded payment used to make an adjustment under this paragraph (f)(2)(vi) (or the absence of any adjustment) must be determined in a manner that results in the attribution of the proper amount of gross income to each of a foreign branch and its foreign branch owner under the principles of section 482, applied as if the foreign branch were a corporation.

(F) *Ordering rules.*—For purposes of applying this paragraph (f)(2)(vi), adjustments related to disregarded payments from a foreign branch to its foreign branch owner are computed first, followed by adjustments related to disregarded payments from a foreign branch owner to its foreign branch.

(3) *Definitions.*—The following definitions apply for purposes of this paragraph (f).

(i) *Disregarded entity.*—The term *disregarded entity* means an entity described in § 301.7701-2(c)(2) of this chapter that is disregarded as an entity separate from its owner for Federal income tax purposes.

(ii) *Disregarded payment*.—The term *disregarded payment* means any amount described in paragraph (f)(3)(ii)(A) or (B) of this section.

(A) *Payments to or from a disregarded entity*.—An amount described in this paragraph (f)(3)(ii)(A) is an amount that is paid to or by a disregarded entity in connection with a transaction that is disregarded for Federal income tax purposes and that is reflected on the separate set of books and records of a foreign branch.

(B) *Other disregarded amounts*.—An amount described in this paragraph (f)(3)(ii)(B) is any amount reflected on the separate set of books and records of a foreign branch that would constitute an item of income, gain, deduction, or loss (other than an amount described in paragraph (f)(3)(ii)(A) of this section) if the transaction to which the amount is attributable were regarded for Federal income tax purposes.

(iii) *Foreign branch*.—(A) *In general*.—The term *foreign branch* means a qualified business unit (QBU), as defined in § 1.989(a)-1(b)(2)(ii) and (b)(3), that conducts a trade or business outside the United States. For an illustration of the principles of this paragraph (f)(3)(iii), see paragraph (f)(4)(i) *Example 1* of this section.

(B) *Trade or business outside the United States*.—Activities carried out in the United States, whether or not such activities are described in § 1.989(a)-1(b)(3), do not constitute the conduct of a trade or business outside the United States. Activities carried out outside the United States that constitute a permanent establishment under the terms of an income tax treaty between the United States and the country in which the activities are carried out are presumed to constitute a trade or business conducted outside the United States for purposes of this paragraph (f)(3)(iii)(B). In determining whether activities constitute a trade or business under § 1.989(a)-1(c), disregarded payments are taken into account and may give rise to a trade or business, provided that the activities (together with any other activities of the QBU) would otherwise satisfy the rule in § 1.989(a)-1(c).

(C) *Activities of a partnership, estate, or trust*.—*(1) Treatment as a foreign branch*.—For purposes of this paragraph (f)(3)(iii), the activities of a partnership, estate, or trust that conducts a trade or business that satisfies the requirements of § 1.989(a)-1(b)(2)(ii)(A) (as modified by paragraph (f)(3)(iii)(B) of this section) are—

(i) Deemed to satisfy the requirements of § 1.989(a)-1(b)(2)(ii)(B); and

(ii) Comprise a foreign branch.

(2) Separate set of books and records.—A foreign branch described in this paragraph (f)(3)(iii)(C) is treated as maintaining a separate set of books and records with respect to the activities described in paragraph (f)(3)(iii)(C)*(1)* of this section, and must determine, as the context requires, the items of gross income, disregarded payments, and any other items that would be reflected on those books and records in applying this paragraph (f) with respect to the foreign branch.

(iv) *Foreign branch owner*.—The term *foreign branch owner* means, with respect to a foreign branch, the person (including a foreign or domestic partnership or other pass-through entity) that owns the foreign branch, either directly or indirectly through one or more disregarded entities. For this purpose, the foreign branch owner does not include the foreign branch or another foreign branch of the person that owns the foreign branch.

(v) *Remittance*.—The term *remittance* means a transfer of property (within the meaning of section 317(a)) by a foreign branch that would be treated as a distribution if the foreign branch were treated as a separate corporation.

(4) *Examples*.—The following examples illustrate the application of this paragraph (f).

(i) *Example 1: Determination of foreign branches and foreign branch owner*—(A) *Facts*—*(1)* P, a domestic corporation, is a partner in PRS, a domestic partnership. All other partners in PRS are unrelated to P. PRS conducts activities solely in Country A (the Country A Business), and those activities constitute a trade or business outside the United States within the meaning of paragraph (f)(3)(iii)(B) of this section. PRS reflects items of income, gain, loss, and expense of the Country A Business on the books and records of PRS's home office. PRS's functional currency is the U.S. dollar. PRS is in the business of manufacturing bicycles.

(2) PRS owns FDE1, a disregarded entity organized in Country B. FDE1 conducts activities in Country B (the Country B Business), and those activities constitute a trade or business outside the United States within the meaning of paragraph (f)(3)(iii)(B) of this section. FDE1 maintains a set of books and records that are separate from those of PRS, and the separate set of books and records reflects items of income, gain, loss, and expense with respect to the Country B Business. Country B Business's functional currency is the U.S. dollar. FDE1 is in the business of selling bicycles manufactured by PRS.

(3) FDE1 owns FDE2, a disregarded entity organized in Country C. FDE2 conducts activities in Country C (the Country C Business), and those activities constitute a trade or business outside the United States within the meaning of paragraph (f)(3)(iii)(B) of this section. FDE2 maintains a set of books and records that are separate from those of PRS and FDE1, and the separate set of books and records reflects items of income, gain, loss, and expense with respect to the Country C Business. Country C Business's functional currency is the U.S. dollar. FDE2 sells paper. FDE2's paper business is not related to FDE1's bicycle sales business, and FDE1 does not hold its interest in FDE2 in the ordinary course of its trade or business.

(B) *Analysis*—*(1)* Country A Business's activities comprise a trade or business conducted outside the United States within the meaning of § 1.989(a)-1(b)(2)(ii)(A) and (b)(3) (in each case, as modified by paragraph (f)(3)(iii) of this section). PRS does not maintain a separate set of books and records with respect to the Country A Business. However, under paragraph (f)(3)(iii)(C) of this section, the Country A Business's activities are deemed to satisfy the requirement of § 1.989(a)-1(b)(2)(ii)(B) that a QBU maintain a separate set of books and records with respect to the relevant activities. Thus, for purposes of this paragraph (f), the activities of the Country A Business constitute a QBU as defined in § 1.989-1(b)(2)(ii) and (b)(3), as modified by paragraph (f)(3)(iii) of this section, that conducts a trade or business outside the United States. Accordingly, the activities of the Country A Business constitute a foreign branch within the meaning of paragraph (f)(3)(iii) of this section. PRS, the person that owns the Country A Business, is the foreign branch owner, within the meaning of paragraph (f)(3)(iv) of this section, with respect to the Country A Business.

(2) Country B Business's activities comprise a trade or business outside the United States within the meaning of § 1.989(a)-1(b)(2)(ii)(A) and (b)(3) (in each case, as modified by paragraph (f)(3)(iii) of this section). PRS maintains a separate set of books and records with respect to the Country B Business, as described in § 1.989(a)-1(b)(2)(ii)(B). Thus, for purposes of this section, the activities of the Country B Business constitute a QBU as defined in § 1.989-1(b)(2)(ii) and (b)(3), as modified by paragraph (f)(3)(iii) of this section, that conducts a trade or business outside the United States. Accordingly, the activities of the Country B Business constitute a foreign branch within the meaning of paragraph (f)(3)(iii) of this section. Under paragraph (f)(3)(iv) of this section, PRS, the person that owns the Country B Business indirectly through FDE1 (a disregarded entity), but not including the activities of PRS that constitute the Country A business, is the foreign branch owner with respect to the Country B Business.

(3) The same analysis that applies to the Country B Business applies to the Country C Business. Accordingly, the activities of the Country C Business constitute a foreign branch within the meaning of paragraph (f)(3)(iii) of this section. PRS, the person that owns the Country C Business indirectly through FDE1 and FDE2 (disregarded entities), but not including the activities of PRS that constitute the Country A Business, is the foreign branch owner with respect to the Country C Business.

(ii) *Example 2: Sale of foreign branch*—(A) *Facts*. The facts are the same as in paragraph (f)(4)(i)(A) of this section, except that in 2019, FDE1 sold FDE2 to an unrelated person, recording gain from the sale on its books and records. In 2020, PRS sells FDE1 to another unrelated person, recording gain from the sale on its books and records. In each year, PRS allocates a portion of the gain to P.

(B) *Analysis*—(1) *Sale of FDE2*. Under paragraph (f)(1)(i)(B) of this section, P's distributive share of gain recognized by PRS in connection with the sales of FDE1 and FDE2 constitutes foreign branch category income if it is attributable to a foreign branch held by PRS directly or indirectly through one or more disregarded entities. PRS's gross income from the 2019 sale of FDE2 is reflected on the separate set of books and records maintained with respect to the Country B Business (a foreign branch) operated by FDE1. Therefore, absent an exception, under paragraph (f)(2)(i) of this section PRS's gross income from the sale of FDE2 would be attributable to the Country B Business, and would constitute foreign branch category income. However, under paragraph (f)(2)(iv) of this section, gross income attributable to the Country B Business does not include gain from the sale or exchange of an interest in FDE2, a disregarded entity, unless the interest in FDE2 is held by the Country B Business in the ordinary course of its active trade or business (within the meaning of paragraph (f)(2)(iv)(B) of this section). In this case, the Country B Business does not hold FDE2 in the ordinary course of its active trade or business within the meaning of paragraph (f)(2)(iv)(B) of this section. As a result, P's distributive share of gain from the sale of FDE2 is not attributable to a foreign branch, and is not foreign branch category income.

(2) *Sale of FDE1*. The analysis of PRS's sale of FDE1 in 2020 is the same as the analysis for the sale of FDE2, except that PRS, through its Country A Business, holds FDE1 in the ordinary course of its active trade or business within the meaning of paragraph (f)(2)(iv)(B) of this section because the Country A Business engages in a trade or business that is related to the trade or business of FDE1. Therefore, P's distributive share of gain from the sale of FDE1 is attributable to a foreign branch, and is foreign branch category income.

(iii) *Example 3: Disregarded payment for services*—(A) *Facts*. P, a domestic corporation, owns FDE, a disregarded entity that is a foreign branch within the meaning of paragraph (f)(3)(iii) of this section. FDE's functional currency is the U.S. dollar. In 2019, P accrued and recorded on its books and records (and not FDE's books and records) $1,000 of gross income from the performance of services to unrelated parties that was not passive category income, $400 of which was foreign source income in respect of services performed outside the United States by employees of FDE and $600 of which was United States source income in respect of services performed in the United States. Absent the application of paragraph (f)(2)(vi) of this section, the $1,000 of gross income earned by P would be general category income that would not be attributable to FDE. FDE provided services in support of P's gross income from services. P compensated FDE for its services with an arm's length payment of $400, which was disregarded for Federal income tax purposes. The deduction for the payment of $400 from P to FDE would be allocated and apportioned to the $400 of P's foreign source services income if the payment were regarded for Federal income tax purposes.

(B) *Analysis*. The disregarded payment from P, a United States person, to FDE, its foreign branch, is not recorded on FDE's separate books and records (as adjusted to conform to Federal income tax principles) within the meaning of paragraph (f)(2)(i) of this section because it is disregarded for United States tax purposes. However, the disregarded payment is allocable to gross income attributable to P because a deduction for the payment, if it were regarded, would be allocated to P's $1,000 of gross services income and apportioned between U.S. and foreign source income under § 1.861-8. Under paragraph (f)(2)(vi)(A) of this section, the amount of gross income attributable to the FDE foreign branch (and the gross income attributable to P) is adjusted to take the disregarded payment into account. As such, all of P's $400 of foreign source gross income from the performance of services is attributable to the FDE foreign branch for purposes of this section. Therefore, $400 of the foreign source gross income that P earned with respect to its services in 2019 constitutes gross income that is assigned to the foreign branch category.

(g) *Section 951A category income.*—(1) *In general.*—Except as provided in paragraph (g)(2) of this section, the term *section 951A category income* means amounts included (directly or indirectly through a pass-through entity) in gross income of a United States person under section 951A(a).

(2) *Exceptions for passive category income.*—Section 951A category income does not include any amounts included under section 951A(a) that are allocable to passive category income under §1.904-5(c)(6). Section 951A category income also does not include any amounts treated as passive category income under paragraph (n)(2) of this section.

(h) * * *

(2) *Treatment of export financing interest.*—Except as provided in paragraph (h)(3) of this section, if a taxpayer (including a financial services entity) receives or accrues export financing interest from an unrelated person, then that interest is not treated as passive category income. Instead, the interest income is treated as foreign branch category income, section 951A category income, general category income, or income in a specified separate category under the rules of this section.

* * *

(5) * * *

(i) *Income other than interest.*—If any foreign person receives or accrues income that is described in section 864(d)(7) (income on a trade or service receivable acquired from a related person in the same foreign country as the recipient) and such income would also meet the definition of export financing interest if section 864(d)(1) applied to such income (income on a trade or service receivable acquired from a related person treated as interest), then the income is considered to be export financing interest and is not treated as passive category income. The income is treated as foreign branch category income, section 951A category income, general category income, or income in a specified separate category under the rules of this section.

(ii) *Interest income.*—If export financing interest is received or accrued by any foreign person and that income would otherwise be treated as related person factoring income of a controlled foreign corporation under section 864(d)(6) if section 864(d)(7) did not apply, section 904(d)(2)(B)(iii)(I) applies and the interest is not treated as passive category income. The income is treated as general category income in the hands of the controlled foreign corporation.

* * *

(k) *Separate category under section 904(d)(6) for items resourced under treaties.*—(1) *In general.*—Except as provided in paragraph (k)(4)(i) of this section, sections 904(a), (b), (c), (d), (f), and (g), and sections 907 and 960 are applied separately to any item of income that, without regard to a treaty obligation of the United States, would be treated as derived from sources within the United States, but under a treaty obligation of the United States such item of income would be treated as arising from sources outside the United States, and the taxpayer chooses the benefits of such treaty obligation.

(2) *Aggregation of items of income in each other separate category.*—For purposes of applying the general rule of paragraph (k)(1) of this section, items of income in each other separate category of income that are resourced under each applicable treaty are aggregated in a single separate category for income in that separate category that is resourced under that treaty. For example, all items of general category income that would otherwise be treated as derived from sources within the United States but which the taxpayer chooses to treat as arising from sources outside the United States pursuant to a provision of a bilateral U.S. income tax treaty are treated as income in a separate category for general category income resourced under the particular treaty. Resourced items are not combined with other income that is foreign source income under the Code, even if the other income arises from sources within the treaty country and is included in the same separate category to which the resourced income would be assigned without regard to section 904(d)(6).

(3) *Related taxes.*—Foreign taxes are allocated to each separate category described in paragraph (k)(2) of this section in accordance with §1.904-6.

(4) *Coordination with certain income tax treaty provisions*—.—(i) *Exception for special relief from double taxation for individual residents of treaty countries.*—Section 904(d)(6)(A) and paragraph (k)(1) of this section do not apply to any item of income deemed to be from foreign sources by reason of the relief from double taxation rules in any U.S. income tax treaty that is solely applicable to United States citizens who are residents of the other Contracting State.

(ii) *U.S. competent authority assistance.*—For purposes of applying paragraph (k)(1) of this section, if, under the mutual agreement procedure provisions of an applicable income tax treaty, the U.S. competent authority agrees to allow a taxpayer to treat an item of income as foreign source income, where such item of income would otherwise be treated as derived from sources within the United States, then the taxpayer is considered to have chosen the benefits of such treaty obligation to treat the item as foreign source income.

(5) *Coordination with other Code provisions.*—Section 904(d)(6)(A) and paragraph (k)(1) of this section do not apply to any item of income to which any of sections 245(a)(10), 865(h), or 904(h)(10) applies. *See* paragraph (l) of this section.

(l) *Priority rule.*—Income that meets the definitions of a specified separate category and another category of income described in section 904(d)(1) is subject to the separate limitation described in paragraph (m) of this section and is not treated as general category income, foreign branch category income, passive category income, or section 951A category income.

(m) *Income treated as allocable to a specified separate category.*—If section 904(a), (b), and (c) are applied separately to any category of income under the Internal Revenue Code and regulations (for example, under section 245(a)(10), 865(h), 901(j), 904(d)(6), or 904(h)(10), and the regulations under those sections), that category of income is treated for all purposes of the Internal Revenue Code and regulations as if it were a separate category listed in section 904(d)(1). For purposes of this section, a separate category that is treated as if it were listed in section 904(d)(1) by reason of the first sentence in this paragraph (m) is referred to as a *specified separate category.*

(n) *Income from partnerships and other pass-through entities.*—(1) *Distributive shares of partnership income.*—(i) *In general.*—Except as provided in paragraph (n)(1)(ii) of this section, a partner's distributive share of partnership income is characterized as passive category income to the extent that the distributive share is a share of income earned or accrued by the partnership in the passive category. A partner's distributive share of partnership income that is not described in the first sentence of this paragraph is treated as foreign branch category income, section 951A category income, general category income, or income in a specified separate category under the rules of this section. Similar principles apply for a person's share of income from any other pass-through entity.

(ii) *Less than 10 percent partners partnership interests.*—(A) *In general.*—Except as provided in paragraph (n)(1)(ii)(B) of this section, if any limited partner or corporate general partner owns less than 10 percent of the value in a partnership, the partner's distributive share of partnership income from the partnership is passive income to the partner (subject to the high-taxed income exception of section 904(d)(2)(B)(iii)(II)), and the partner's distributive share of partnership deductions from the partnership is allocated and apportioned under the principles of section 1.861-8 only to the partner's passive income from that partnership. See also § 1.861-9(e)(4) for rules for apportioning partnership interest expense.

(B) *Exception for partnership interest held in the ordinary course of business.*—If a partnership interest described in paragraph (n)(1)(ii)(A) of this section is held in the ordinary course of a partner's active trade or business, the rules of paragraph (n)(1)(i) of this section apply for purposes of characterizing the partner's distributive share of the partnership income. A partnership interest is considered to be held in the ordinary course of a partner's active trade or business if the partner (or a member of the partner's affiliated group of corporations (within the meaning of section 1504(a) and without regard to section 1504(b)(3))) engages (other than through a less than 10 percent interest in a partnership) in the same or a related trade or business as the partnership.

(2) *Income from the sale of a partnership interest.*—(i) *In general.*—To the extent a partner recognizes gain on the sale of a partnership interest, that income shall be treated as passive category income to the partner, unless the income is considered to be high-taxed under section 904(d)(2)(B)(iii)(II) and paragraph (c) of this section.

(ii) *Exception for sale by 25-percent owner.*—Except as provided in paragraph (f)(2)(iv) of this section, in the case of a sale of an interest in a partnership by a partner that is a 25-percent owner of the partnership, determined by applying section 954(c)(4)(B) and substituting "partner" for "controlled foreign corporation" every place it appears, for purposes of determining the separate category to which the income recognized on the sale of the partnership interest is assigned such partner is treated as selling the proportionate share of the assets of the partnership attributable to such interest.

(3) *Value of a partnership interest.*—For purposes of paragraphs (n)(1) and (2) of this section, a partner will be considered as owning 10 percent of the value of a partnership for a particular year if the partner, together with any person that bears a relationship to the partner described in section 267(b) or 707, owns 10 percent of the capital and profits interest of the partnership. For this purpose, value will be determined at the end of the partnership's taxable year.

(o) *Separate category of section 78 gross up.*—The amount included in income under section 78 by reason of taxes deemed paid under section 960 is assigned to the separate category to which the taxes are allocated under § 1.904-6(b).

(p) *Separate category of foreign currency gain or loss.*—Foreign currency gain or loss recognized under section 986(c) with respect to a distribution of previously taxed earnings and profits (as described in section 959 or 1293(c)) is assigned to the separate category or categories of the previously taxed earnings and profits from which the distribution is made. See § 1.987-6(b) for rules on assigning section 987 gain or loss on a remittance from a section 987 QBU to a separate category or categories.

(q) *Applicability dates.*—This section applies for taxable years that both begin after December 31, 2017, and end on or after December 4, 2018.

Par. 16. § 1.904-5 is amended by:

1. Revising paragraphs (a), (b), and (c)(1).

2. Revising the third and fourth sentences of paragraph (c)(2)(i).

3. Removing the language "noncontrolled section 902 corporation" and adding the language "noncontrolled 10-percent owned foreign corporation" in its place in the heading and text of paragraph (c)(2)(iii).

4. Revising paragraph (c)(3).

5. Revising the first sentence, and removing the language "paragraph" and adding the language "paragraph (c)(4)" in its place in the second sentence, of paragraph (c)(4)(i).

6. Revising paragraph (c)(4)(iii).

7. Adding paragraphs (c)(5) and (6).

8. Revising paragraphs (d)(1) and (2).

9. Removing and reserving paragraph (f)(1).

10. Removing paragraph (f)(3).

11. Removing the language "section 904(d)(3) and this section" and adding the language "paragraph (c) of this section" in its place in the first sentence of paragraph (g).

12. Removing the last sentence of paragraph (g).

13. Revising paragraph (h).

14. Removing the language "paragraphs (i)(2), (3), and (4)" and adding the language "paragraphs (i)(2) and (3)" in its place in the first sentence of paragraph (i)(1).

15. Removing the language "noncontrolled section 902 corporation" and adding the language "noncontrolled 10-percent owned foreign corporation" in its place in the second sentence of paragraph (i)(1).

16. Removing the language "paragraph (i)(4)" and adding the language "paragraph (i)(3)" in its place in the second sentence of paragraph (i)(1).

17. Revising the sixth and seventh sentences of paragraph (i)(1).

18. Revising paragraph (i)(2) and (3).

19. Removing and reserving paragraph (i)(4).

20. Removing the last sentence of paragraph (j).

21. Adding the language "under §1.904-4" after the language "characterized" in the first sentence of paragraph (k)(1).

22. Revising paragraph (k)(2)(iii).

23. Removing the language "noncontrolled section 902 corporation" and adding the language "noncontrolled 10-percent owned foreign corporation" in its place in paragraph (m)(1).

24. Removing the language "or amount treated as a dividend, including" and adding the language "which, for purposes of this paragraph (m), includes" in its place in the third sentence of paragraph (m)(1).

25. Removing the language "951(a)(1)(A)," and adding the language "951(a)(1)(A), 951A(a)," in its place in the fourth sentence of paragraph (m)(1).

26. Revising paragraphs (m)(2)(ii), (m)(4)(i), and the first sentence of paragraph (m)(5)(i).

27. Removing the language "section 902(a) and section 960(a)(1)" and adding the language "section 960" in its place in paragraph (m)(6).

28. Removing the language "904(g)(6)" from the first sentence of paragraph (m)(7)(i) and adding the language "904(h)(6)" in its place.

29. Removing the language "904(g)" from the first sentence of paragraph (m)(7)(i) and adding the language "904(h)" in its place.

30. Removing the language "(d) and (f)" from the second sentence of paragraph (m)(7)(i) and adding the language "(d), (f), and (g)" in its place.

31. Removing the language "902," from the second sentence of paragraph (m)(7)(i).

32. Removing the language "noncontrolled section 902 corporation" and adding the language "noncontrolled 10-percent owned foreign corporation" in its place, and by removing the language "section 904(d)(1)" and adding "§1.904-4" in its place in the first sentence of paragraph (n).

33. Revising the last sentence of paragraph (n).

34. Revising paragraph (o).

The additions and revisions read as follows:

§1.904-5. Look-through rules as applied to controlled foreign corporations and other entities.—(a) *Scope and definitions.*—(1) *Look-through rules under section 904(d)(3) to passive category income.*—Paragraph (c) of this section provides rules for determining the extent to which dividends, interest, rents, and royalties received or accrued by certain eligible persons, and inclusions under sections 951(a)(1) and 951A(a), are treated as passive category income. Paragraph (g) of this section provides rules applying the principles of paragraph (c) of this section to foreign source interest, rents, and royalties paid by a United States corporation to a related corporation. Paragraph (h) of this section provides rules for assigning a partnership payment to a partner described in section 707 to the passive category. Paragraph (i) of this section provides rules applying the principles of this section to assign distributions and payments from certain related entities to the passive category or to treat the distributions and payments as not in the passive category.

(2) *Other look-through rules under section 904(d).*—Under section 904(d)(4) and paragraph (c)(4)(iii) of this section, certain dividends from noncontrolled 10-percent owned foreign corporations are treated as income in a separate category. Under section 904(d)(3)(H) and paragraph (j) of this section, certain inclusions under section 1293 are treated as income in a separate category. Paragraph (i) of this section provides rules applying the principles of this section to assign distributions from certain related entities to separate categories.

(3) *Other rules provided in this section.*—Paragraph (b) of this section provides operative rules for this section. Paragraph (d) of this section provides rules addressing exceptions to passive category income for certain purposes in the case of controlled foreign corporations that meet the requirements of section 954(b)(3)(A) (de minimis rule) or section 954(b)(4) (high-tax exception). Paragraph (e) of this section provides rules for characterizing a controlled foreign corporation's foreign base company income and gross insurance income when section 954(b)(3)(B) (full inclusion rule) applies. Paragraph (f) of this section modifies the look-through rules for certain types of income. Paragraph (k) of this section provides ordering rules for applying the look-through rules. Paragraph (l) of this section provides examples illustrating the application of certain rules in this section. Paragraphs (m) and (n) of this section provide rules related to the resourcing rules described in section 904(h).

(4) *Definitions.*—For purposes of this section, the following definitions apply:

(i) The term *controlled foreign corporation* has the meaning given such term by section 957 (taking into account the special rule for certain captive insurance companies contained in section 953(c)).

(ii) The term *look-through rules* means the rules described in this section that assign income to a separate category based on the separate category of the income to which it is allocable.

(iii) The term *noncontrolled 10-percent owned foreign corporation* has the meaning provided in section 904(d)(2)(E)(i).

(iv) The term *pass-through entity* means a partnership, S corporation, or any other person (whether domestic or foreign) other than a corporation to the extent that the income or deductions of the person are included in the income of one or more direct or indirect owners or beneficiaries of the person. For example, if a domestic trust is subject to Federal income tax on a portion of its income and its owners are subject to tax on the remaining portion, the domestic trust is treated as a domestic pass-through entity with respect to such remaining portion.

(v) The term *separate category* means, as the context requires, any category of income described in 904(d)(1)(A), (B), (C), or (D), any specified separate category of income as defined in §1.904-4(m), or any category of earnings and profits to which income described in such provisions is attributable.

(vi) The term *United States shareholder* has the meaning given such term by section 951(b) (taking into account the special rule for certain captive insurance companies contained in section 953(c)), except that for purposes of this section, a United States shareholder includes any member of the controlled group of the United States shareholder. For this purpose the controlled group is any member of the affiliated group within the meaning of section 1504(a)(1) except that "more than 50 percent" is substituted for "at least 80 percent" wherever it appears in section 1504(a)(2). When used in reference to a noncontrolled 10-percent owned foreign corporation described in section 904(d)(2)(E)(i)(II), the term *United States shareholder* also means a taxpayer that meets the stock ownership requirements described in section 904(d)(2)(E)(i)(II).

(b) *Operative rules.*—(1) *Assignment of income not assigned under the look-through rules.*—Except as provided by the look-through rules, dividends, interest, rents, and royalties received or accrued by a taxpayer from a controlled foreign corporation in which the taxpayer is a United States shareholder are excluded from passive category income. Income excluded from the passive category under this paragraph (b)(1) is assigned to another separate category (other than the passive category) under the rules in §1.904-4.

(2) *Priority and ordering of look-through rules.*—Except as provided in §1.904-4(l), to the extent the look-through rules assign income to a separate category, the income is assigned to that separate category rather than the separate category to which the income would have been assigned under §1.904-4 (not taking into account §1.904-4(l)). See paragraph (k) of this section for ordering rules for applying the look-through rules.

(c) * * *

(1) *Scope.*—Subject to the exceptions in paragraph (f) of this section, paragraphs (c)(2) through (c)(6) (other than paragraph (c)(4)(iii)) of this section provide look-through rules with respect to interest, rents, royalties, dividends, and inclusions under section 951(a)(1) and 951A(a) that are received or accrued from a controlled foreign corporation in which the taxpayer is a United States shareholder. Paragraph (c)(4)(iii) of this section provides a look-through rule for dividends received from a noncontrolled 10-percent owned foreign corporation by a domestic corporation that is a United States shareholder in the foreign corporation.

(2) * * *

(i) * * * Related person interest is treated as passive category income to the extent it is allocable to passive category income of the controlled foreign corporation. If related person interest is received or accrued from a controlled foreign corporation by two or more persons, the amount of interest received or accrued by each person that is allocable to passive category income is determined by multiplying the amount of related person interest allocable to passive category income by a fraction. * * *

* * *

(3) *Rents and royalties.*—Any rents or royalties received or accrued from a controlled foreign corporation in which the taxpayer is a United States shareholder are treated as passive category income to the extent they are allocable to passive category income of the controlled foreign corporation under the principles of §§1.861-8 through 1.861-14T.

(4) * * *

(i) * * * Except as provided in paragraph (d)(2) of this section, any dividend paid or accrued out of the earnings and profits of any controlled foreign corporation is treated as passive category income in proportion to the ratio of the portion of earnings and profits attributable to passive category income to the total amount of earnings and profits of the controlled foreign corporation. * * *

* * *

(iii) *Look-through rule for dividends from noncontrolled 10-percent owned foreign corporations.*—(A) *In general.*—Except as provided in paragraph (c)(4)(iii)(B) of this section, any dividend that is distributed by a noncontrolled 10-percent owned foreign corporation and received or accrued by a domestic corporation that is a United States shareholder of such foreign corporation is treated as income in a separate category in proportion to the ratio of the portion of earnings and profits attributable to income in such category to the total amount of earnings and profits of the noncontrolled 10-percent owned foreign corporation.

(B) *Inadequate substantiation.*—A dividend distributed by a noncontrolled 10-percent owned foreign corporation is treated as income in the separate category described in section 904(d)(4)(C)(ii) if the Commissioner determines that the look-through characterization of the dividend cannot reasonably be determined based on the available information.

* * *

(5) *Inclusions under section 951(a)(1)(A).*—(i) Any amount included in gross income under section 951(a)(1)(A) is treated as passive category income to the extent the amount included is attributable to income received or accrued by the controlled foreign corporation that is passive category income. All other amounts included in gross income under section 951(a)(1)(A) are treated as general category income or income in a specified separate category under the rules in §1.904-4. For rules concerning a distributive share of partnership income, see §1.904-4(n). For rules concerning the gross up under section 78, see §1.904-4(o). For rules concerning inclusions under section 951(a)(1)(B), see paragraph (c)(4)(i) of this section.

(ii) [Reserved]

(6) *Inclusions under section 951A(a).*—Any amount included in gross income under section

951A(a) is treated as passive category income to the extent the amount included is attributable to income received or accrued by the controlled foreign corporation that is passive category income. All other amounts included in gross income under section 951A(a) are treated as section 951A category income or income in a specified separate category under the rules in § 1.904-4. For rules concerning a distributive share of partnership income, see § 1.904-4(n). For rules concerning the gross up under section 78, see § 1.904-4(o).

(d) * * *

(1) *De minimis amount of subpart F income.*—If the sum of a controlled foreign corporation's gross foreign base company income (determined under section 954(a) without regard to section 954(b)(5)) and gross insurance income (determined under section 953(a)) for the taxable year is less than the lesser of 5 percent of gross income or $1,000,000, then none of that income is treated as passive category income. In addition, if the test in the first sentence of this paragraph is satisfied, for purposes of paragraphs (c)(2)(ii)(D) and (E) of this section (apportionment of interest expense to passive income using the asset method), any passive category assets are not treated as passive category assets but are treated as assets in the general category or a specified separate category. The determination in the first sentence is made before the application of the exception for certain income subject to a high rate of foreign tax described in paragraph (d)(2) of this section.

(2) *Exception for certain income subject to high foreign tax.*—Except as provided in § 1.904-4(c)(7)(iii) (relating to reductions in tax upon distribution), for purposes of the dividend look-through rule of paragraph (c)(4)(i) of this section, an item of net income that would otherwise be passive income (after application of the priority rules of § 1.904-4(l)) and that is received or accrued by a controlled foreign corporation is not treated as passive category income, and the earnings and profits attributable to such income is not treated as passive category earnings and profits, if the taxpayer establishes to the satisfaction of the Secretary under section 954(b)(4) that the income was subject to an effective rate of income tax imposed by a foreign country greater than 90 percent of the maximum rate of tax specified in section 11 (with reference to section 15, if applicable). Such income is treated as general category income or income in a specified separate category under the rules in § 1.904-4. The first sentence of this paragraph has no effect on amounts (other than dividends) paid or accrued by a controlled foreign corporation to a United States shareholder of such controlled foreign corporation to the extent those amounts are allocable to passive category income of the controlled foreign corporation.

* * *

(f) * * *

(1) [Reserved]

* * *

(h) *Application of look-through rules to payments from a partnership or other pass-through entity.*—Payments to a partner described in section 707 (e.g., payments to a partner not acting in capacity as a partner) are characterized as passive category income to the extent that the payment is attributable under the principles of § 1.861-8 and this section to passive category income of the partnership, if the payments are interest, rents, or royalties that would be characterized under the controlled foreign corporation look-through rules of paragraph (c) of this section if the partnership were a foreign corporation, and the partner who receives the payment owns 10 percent or more of the value of the partnership (as determined under § 1.904-4(n)(3)). A payment by a partnership to a member of the controlled group (as defined in paragraph (a)(4)(vi) of this section) of the partner is characterized under the look-through rules of this paragraph (h) if the payment would be a section 707 payment entitled to look-through treatment if it were made to the partner. Similar principles apply for a payment from any other pass-through entity. The rules in this paragraph (h) do not apply with respect to interest to the extent the interest income is assigned to a separate category under the specified partnership loan rules described in § 1.861-9(e)(8).

(i) * * *

(1) * * * For purposes of this paragraph (i)(1), indirect ownership of stock is determined under section 318 and the regulations under that section. In the case of a partnership or other pass-through entity, indirect ownership and value is determined under the rules in paragraph (i)(2) of this section.

(2) *Indirect ownership and value of a partnership interest.*—A person is considered as owning, directly or indirectly, more than 50 percent of the value of a partnership if the person, together with any other person that bears a relationship to the first person that is described in section 267(b) or 707, owns more than 50 percent of the capital and profits interests of the partnership. For this purpose, value will be determined at the end of the partnership's taxable year. Similar principles apply for a person that owns a pass-through entity other than a partnership.

(3) *Special rule for dividends between certain foreign corporations.*—Solely for purposes of dividend payments between controlled foreign corporations, noncontrolled 10-percent owned foreign corporations, or a controlled foreign corporation and a noncontrolled 10-percent owned foreign corporation, the two foreign corporations are considered related look-through entities if the same person is a United States shareholder of both foreign corporations.

(4) [Reserved]

* * *

(k) * * *

(2) * * *

(iii) Inclusions under sections 951(a)(1)(A) and 951A(a) and distributive shares of partnership income;

* * *

(m) * * *

(2) * * *

(ii) *Interest payments from noncontrolled 10-percent owned foreign corporations.*—If interest is received or accrued by a shareholder from a noncontrolled 10-percent owned foreign corporation (where the shareholder is a domestic corporation that is a United States shareholder of such noncontrolled 10-percent owned foreign corporation), the rules of paragraph (m)(2)(i) of this section apply in determining the portion of the interest payment that is from sources within the United States, except that the related party interest rules of paragraph (c)(2)(ii)(C) of this section do not apply.

* * *

(4) * * *

(i) *Rule.*—Any dividend or distribution treated as a dividend under this paragraph (m) (including an amount included in gross income under section 951(a)(1)(B)) that is received or accrued by a United States shareholder from a controlled foreign corporation, or any dividend that is received or accrued by a domestic corporation from a noncontrolled 10-percent owned foreign corporation with respect to which the shareholder is a United States shareholder, are treated as income in a separate category derived from sources within the United States in proportion to the ratio of the portion of the earnings and profits of the controlled foreign corporation or noncontrolled 10-percent owned foreign corporation in the corresponding separate category from United States sources to the total amount of earnings and profits of the controlled foreign corporation or noncontrolled 10-percent owned foreign corporation in that separate category.

* * *

(5) * * *

(i) * * * Any amount included in the gross income of a United States shareholder of a controlled foreign corporation under section 951(a)(1)(A), 951A, or in the gross income of a domestic corporation that is a United States shareholder of a noncontrolled 10-percent owned foreign corporation described in section 904(d)(2)(E)(i)(II) that is a qualified electing fund under section 1293 is treated as income subject to a separate category that is derived from sources within the United States to the extent the amount is attributable to income of the controlled foreign corporation or qualified electing fund, respectively, in the corresponding category of income from sources within the United States. * * *

* * *

(n) * * * Section 904(d)(3), (d)(4), and (h), and this section are then applied for purposes of characterizing and sourcing income received, accrued, or included by a United States shareholder of the foreign corporation that is attributable or allocable to income or earnings and profits of the foreign corporation.

(o) *Applicability dates.*—This section is applicable for taxable years that both begin after December 31, 2017, and end on or after December 4, 2018.

Par. 17. § 1.904-6 is amended by:

1. Revising the first sentence, and adding two sentences after the fourth sentence, of paragraph (a)(1)(i).

2. Removing the language "(unless it is a withholding tax that is not the final tax payable on the income as described in § 1.904-4(d))" and adding the language "(as defined in section 901(k)(1)(B))" in its place in the new seventh sentence of paragraph (a)(1)(i).

3. Revising paragraph (a)(1)(iv).

4. Adding paragraphs (a)(2) and (3).

5. Revising paragraph (b).

6. Adding paragraph (d).

The revisions and additions read as follows:

§ 1.904-6. Allocation and apportionment of taxes.—(a) * * *

(1) * * *

(i) * * * The amount of foreign taxes paid or accrued with respect to a separate category (as defined in § 1.904-5(a)(4)(v)) of income (including United States source income within the separate category) includes only those taxes that are related to income in that separate category. * * * Income included in the foreign tax base is calculated under foreign law, but characterized as income in a separate category under United States tax principles. For example, a foreign tax imposed on an amount realized on the disposition of controlled foreign corporation stock that is characterized as a capital gain under foreign law but as a dividend under section 1248 is generally assigned to the general category, not the passive category. * * *

* * *

(iv) *Base and timing differences.*—If, under the law of a foreign country or possession of the United States, a tax is imposed on a type of item that does not constitute income under Federal income tax principles (a *base difference*), such as gifts or life insurance proceeds, that tax is treated as imposed with respect to income in the separate category described in section 904(d)(2)(H)(i). If, under the law of a foreign country or possession of the United States, a tax is imposed on an item of income that constitutes income under Federal income tax principles but is not recognized for Federal income tax purposes in the current year (a *timing difference*), that tax is allocated and apportioned to the appropriate separate category or categories to which the tax would be allocated and apportioned if the income were recognized under Federal income tax principles in the year in which the tax was imposed. If the amount of an item of income as computed for foreign tax purposes is positive but is greater than the amount of income that is currently recognized for Federal income tax purposes, for example, due to a difference in depreciation conventions or the timing of recognition of gross income, or because of a permanent difference between U.S. and foreign tax law in the amount of deductions that are allowed to reduce gross income, the tax is allocated or apportioned to the separate category to which the income is assigned, and no portion of the tax is attributable to a base difference. In addition, a tax imposed on a distribution that is excluded from gross income under section 959(a) or section 959(b) is treated as attributable to a timing difference (and not a base difference) and is treated as tax imposed on the earnings and profits from which the distribution was paid.

(2) *Special rules for foreign branches.*—(i) *In general.*—Except as provided in this paragraph (a)(2), any foreign tax reflected on the books and records of a foreign branch under the principles of § 1.987-2(b) is allocated and apportioned under the rules of paragraph (a)(1) of this section.

(ii) *Disregarded reallocation transactions.*—(A) *Foreign branch to foreign branch owner.*—In the case of a disregarded payment from a foreign branch to a foreign branch owner that is treated as a disregarded reallocation transaction that results in foreign branch category income being reallocated to the general category, any foreign tax imposed solely by reason of that payment, such as a withholding tax imposed on the disregarded payment, is allocated and apportioned to the general category.

(B) *Foreign branch owner to foreign branch.*—In the case of a disregarded payment from a foreign branch owner to a foreign branch that is treated as a disregarded reallocation transaction that results in general category income being reallocated to the foreign branch category, any foreign tax imposed solely by reason of that transaction is allocated and apportioned to the foreign branch category.

(iii) *Other disregarded payments.*—(A) *Foreign branch to foreign branch owner.*—In the case of a disregarded payment from a foreign branch to a foreign branch owner that is not a disregarded reallocation transaction, foreign tax imposed solely by reason of that disregarded payment is allocated and apportioned to a separate category under the principles of paragraph (a)(1) of this section based on the nature of the item (determined under Federal income tax principles) that is included in the foreign tax base. For example, if a remittance of an appreciated asset results in gain recognition under foreign law, the tax imposed on that gain is treated as attributable to a timing difference with respect to recognition of the gain, and is allocated and apportioned to the separate category to which gain on a sale of that asset would have been assigned if it were recognized for Federal income tax purposes. However, a gross basis withholding tax on a remittance is attributable to a timing difference in taxation of the income out of which the remittance is made, and is allocated and apportioned to the separate category or categories to which a section 987 gain or loss would be assigned under § 1.987-6(b).

(B) *Foreign branch owner to foreign branch.*—In the case of a disregarded payment from a foreign branch owner to a foreign branch that is not a disregarded reallocation transaction, any foreign tax imposed solely by reason of that disregarded payment is allocated and apportioned to the foreign branch category.

(iv) *Definitions.*—The following definitions apply for purposes of this paragraph (a)(2):

(A) *Disregarded reallocation transaction.*—The term *disregarded reallocation transaction* means a disregarded payment or a transfer described in § 1.904-4(f)(2)(vi)(D) that results in an adjustment to the gross income attributable to the foreign branch under § 1.904-4(f)(2)(vi)(A).

(B) The terms *disregarded payment, foreign branch, foreign branch owner,* and *remittance* have the same meaning given to those terms in § 1.904-4(f)(3).

(3) *Taxes imposed on high-taxed income.*—For rules on the treatment of taxes imposed on high-taxed income, see § 1.904-4(c).

(b) *Allocation and apportionment of deemed paid taxes and certain creditable foreign tax expenditures.*—(1) *Taxes deemed paid under section 960(a) or (d).*—If a domestic corporation that is a United States shareholder includes any amount in gross income under sections 951(a)(1)(A) or 951A(a), any foreign tax deemed paid with respect to such amount under section 960(a) or (d) is allocated to the separate category to which the inclusion is assigned.

(2) *Taxes deemed paid under section 960(b)(1).*—If a domestic corporation that is a United States shareholder receives a distribution of previously taxed earnings and profits from a first-tier corporation that is excluded from the domestic corporation's income under section 959(a) and § 1.959-1, any foreign tax deemed paid under section 960(b)(1) with respect to such distribution is allocated to the same separate category as the annual PTEP account and PTEP group (as defined in § 1.960-3(c)) from which the distribution is made.

(3) *Taxes deemed paid under section 960(b)(2).*—If a controlled foreign corporation receives a distribution of previously taxed earnings and profits from an immediately lower-tier corporation that is excluded from such controlled foreign corporation's gross income under section 959(b) and § 1.959-2, any foreign tax deemed paid under section 960(b)(2) with respect to such distribution is allocated to the same separate category as the annual PTEP account and PTEP group (as defined in § 1.960-3(c)) from which the distribution is made. *See also* § 1.960-3(c)(2).

(4) *Creditable foreign tax expenditures.*—(i) *In general.*—Except as provided in paragraph (b)(4)(ii) of this section, creditable foreign tax expenditures (CFTEs) allocated to a partner under § 1.704-1(b)(4)(viii)(*a*) are allocated for purposes of this section to the same separate category as the separate category to which the taxes were allocated in the hands of the partnership under the rules of paragraph (a) of this section.

(ii) *Foreign branch category.*—CFTEs allocated to a partner in a partnership under § 1.704-1(b)(4)(viii)(*a*) are allocated and apportioned to the foreign branch category of the partner to the extent that:

(A) The CFTEs are allocated and apportioned by the partnership under the rules of paragraph (a) of this section to the general category;

(B) In the hands of the partnership, the CFTEs are related to general category income attributable to a foreign branch (as described in § 1.904-4(f)(2)) under the principles of paragraph (a) of this section; and

(C) The partner's distributive share of the income described in paragraph (b)(4)(ii)(B) of this section is foreign branch category income of the partner under § 1.904-4(f)(1)(i)(B).

* * *

(d) *Applicability dates.*—This section is applicable for taxable years that both begin after December 31, 2017, and end on or after December 4, 2018.

Foreign Tax Credit: Foreign Loss Recapture: Property Disposition

Foreign Tax Credit: Foreign Loss Recapture: Property Disposition.—Amendments to Reg. § 1.904-4, providing guidance regarding the coordination of the rules for determining high-taxed income with capital gains adjustments and the allocation and recapture of overall foreign losses

and overall domestic losses, as well as the coordination of the recapture of overall foreign losses on certain dispositions of property and other rules concerning overall foreign losses and overall domestic losses, are proposed (published in the Federal Register on June 25, 2012) (REG-134935-11).

☐ Par. 2. Section 1.904-4 is amended by adding paragraph (c)(2)(iii) and by adding a sentence at the end of paragraph (n) to read as follows:

§1.904-4. Separate application of section 904 with respect to certain categories of income.

* * *

(c) * * *

(2) * * *

(iii) *Coordination with section 904(b), (f) and (g).*—The determination of whether foreign-source passive income is high-taxed is made before taking into account any adjustments under section 904(b) or any allocation or recapture of a separate limitation loss, overall foreign loss or overall domestic loss under section 904(f) and (g).

* * *

(n) * * * Paragraph (c)(2)(iii) of this section applies to taxable years ending on or after the date of publication of a Treasury decision adopting these rules as final regulations in the **Federal Register.**

Controlled Foreign Corporations: Hybrid Branches: Subpart F Income

Controlled Foreign Corporations: Hybrid Branches: Subpart F Income.—Amendments to Reg. §1.904-5, relating to the treatment under subpart F of certain transactions involving hybrid branches, are proposed (published in the Federal Register on July 13, 1999) (REG-113909-98).

☐ Par. 2. In §1.904-5, paragraph (k)(1) is revised to read as follows:

§1.904-5. Look-through rules as applied to controlled foreign corporations and other entities.

* * *

(k) *Ordering rules.*—(1) *In general.*—Income received or accrued by a related person to which the look-through rules apply is characterized before amounts included from, or paid or distributed by, that person and received or accrued by a related person. For purposes of determining the character of income received or accrued by a person from a related person if the payor or another related person also receives or accrues income from the recipient and the look-through rules apply to the income in all cases, the rules of paragraph (k)(2) of this section apply. Notwithstanding any other provision of this section, the principles of §1.954-1(c)(1)(i) will apply to any expense subject to §1.954-1(c)(1)(i).

* * *

Determination of the Foreign Tax Credit: Guidance

Determination of the Foreign Tax Credit: Guidance.—Reg. §1.904(b)-3, relating to the determination of the foreign tax credit under the Internal Revenue Code, including changes made by the Tax Cuts and Jobs Act, is proposed (published in the Federal Register on December 7, 2018) (REG-105600-18).

Par. 18. Section 1.904(b)-3 is added to read as follows:

§1.904(b)-3. Disregard of certain dividends and deductions under section 904(b)(4).—(a) *Disregard of certain dividends and deductions.*—(1) *In general.*—For purposes of section 904(a), in the case of a domestic corporation which is a United States shareholder with respect to a specified 10-percent owned foreign corporation (as defined in section 245A(b)), the domestic corporation's foreign source taxable income in a separate category and entire taxable income is determined without regard to the following items:

(i) Any dividend for which a deduction is allowed under section 245A;

(ii) Deductions properly allocable or apportioned to gross income in the section 245A subgroup as determined under paragraphs (b) and (c)(1) of this section; and

(iii) Deductions properly allocable or apportioned to stock of specified 10-percent owned foreign corporations in the section 245A subgroup as determined under paragraphs (b) and (c) of this section.

(2) *Deductions properly allocable or apportioned to the residual grouping.*—Deductions that are properly allocable or apportioned to gross income or stock in the section 245A subgroup of the residual grouping (consisting of U.S. source income) are disregarded solely for purposes of determining entire taxable income under section 904(a).

(b) *Determining properly allocable or apportioned deductions.*—The amount of deductions properly allocable or apportioned to gross income or stock described in paragraphs (a)(1)(ii) and (iii) of this section is determined by subdividing the United States shareholder's gross income and assets in each separate category described in §1.904-5(a)(4)(v) into a section 245A subgroup and a non-section 245A subgroup. Gross income and assets in the residual grouping for U.S. source income are also subdivided into a section 245A subgroup and a non-section 245A subgroup. Each section 245A subgroup is treated as a statutory grouping under §1.861-8(a)(4). Deductions properly allocable or apportioned to dividends or stock described in paragraphs (a)(1)(ii) and (iii) of this section only include those deductions that are allocated and apportioned under §§1.861-8 through 1.861-14T and 1.861-17 to the section 245A subgroups. The deduction allowed under section 245A(a) for dividends is allocated and apportioned solely among the section 245A subgroups on the basis of the relative amounts of gross income from such dividends in each section 245A subgroup.

(c) *Income and assets in the 245A subgroups.*—(1) *In general.*—For purposes of applying the allocation and apportionment rules under §§1.861-8 through 1.861-14T and 1.861-17 to the deductions of a United States shareholder, the only gross income included in a section 245A subgroup is dividend income for which a deduction is allowed under section 245A. The only asset included in a section 245A subgroup is the portion of the value of stock of each specified 10-percent owned foreign corporation that is assigned to the section 245A subgroup determined under paragraph (c)(2) of this section.

(2) *Assigning stock to a subgroup.*—The value of stock of a specified 10-percent owned foreign corporation is characterized as an asset in a separate category described in §1.904-5(a)(4)(v) or the residual grouping for U.S. source income under the rules of §1.861-12(c). If the specified 10-percent owned foreign corporation is not a controlled foreign corporation, all of the value of its stock (other than the portion of stock assigned to the statutory groupings for gross section 245(a)(5) income under §§1.861-12(c)(4) and 1.861-13) in each separate category and in the residual grouping for U.S. source income is assigned to the section 245A subgroup in such separate category or residual grouping. If the specified 10-percent owned foreign corporation is a controlled foreign corporation, a portion of the value of stock in each separate category and in the residual grouping for U.S. source income is subdivided between a section 245A and non-section 245A subgroup under §1.861-13(a)(5).

(d) *Coordination with OFL and ODL rules.*—Section 904(b)(4) and this section apply before the operation of the overall foreign loss rules in section 904(f) and the overall domestic loss rules in section 904(g).

(e) *Example.*—The following example illustrates the application of this section.

(1) *Facts*—(i) *Income and assets of USP*. USP is a domestic corporation. USP owns a factory in the United States with a tax book value of $21,000. USP also directly owns all of the stock of each of the following three controlled foreign corporations: CFC1, CFC2, and CFC3. USP's tax book value in each of CFC1, CFC2, and CFC3 is $10,000. USP incurs $1,500 of interest expense and earns $1,600 of U.S. source gross income. Under section 951A and the section 951A regulations (as defined in §1.951A-1(a)(1)), USP's GILTI inclusion amount is $2,200. USP's deduction under section 250 is $1,100 ("section 250 deduction"), all of which is by reason of section 250(a)(1)(B)(i). No portion of USP's section 250 deduction is reduced by reason of section 250(a)(2)(B). None of the CFCs makes any distributions.

(ii) *Characterization of CFC stock*. After application of §1.861-13(a), USP determined that $7,300 of the stock of each of CFC1, CFC2, and CFC3 is assigned to the section 951A category ("section 951A category stock") in the non-section 245A subgroup and the remaining $2,700 of the stock of each of CFC1, CFC2, and CFC3 is assigned to the general category ("general category stock") in the section 245A subgroup. Additionally, under §1.861-8(d)(2)(ii)(C)(2), $3,650 of the stock of each of CFC1, CFC2, and CFC3 that is section 951A category stock is an exempt asset. Accordingly, with respect to the stock of its controlled foreign corporations in the aggregate, USP has $10,950 of section 951A category stock in a non-section 245A subgroup; $8,100 of general category stock in a section 245A subgroup; and $10,950 of stock that is an exempt asset.

(iii) *Apportioning of expenses*. Taking into account USP's factory and its stock in CFC1, CFC2, and CFC3, the tax book value of USP's assets for purposes of apportioning expenses is $40,050 (excluding the $10,950 of exempt assets). Under §1.861-9T(g), USP's $1,500 of interest expense is apportioned as follows: $410 ($1,500 x $10,950/$40,050) to section 951A category income, $303 ($1,500 x $8,100/$40,050) to general category income, and the remaining $787 ($1,500 x $21,000/$40,050) to the residual U.S. source grouping. Under §1.861-8(e)(14), all of USP's section 250 deduction is allocated and apportioned to section 951A category income.

(2) *Analysis*—(i) *USP's pre-credit U.S. tax*. USP's worldwide taxable income is $1,200, which equals its GILTI inclusion amount of $2,200 plus its U.S. source gross income of $1,600, less its deduction under section 250 of $1,100 and its interest expense of $1,500. For purposes of applying section 904(a), before taking into account any foreign tax credit under section 901, USP's federal income tax liability is 21% of $1,200, or $252.

(ii) *Application of section 904(b)(4)*. Under section 904(d)(1), USP applies section 904(a) separately to each separate category of income.

(A) *General category income*. Before application of section 904(b)(4) and the rules in this section, USP's foreign source taxable income in the general category is a loss of $303, which equals $0 (USP's foreign source general category income) less $303 (interest expense apportioned to general category income), and USP's worldwide taxable income is $1,200. Under paragraph (d) of this section, the rules in section 904(f) and (g) apply after section 904(b)(4) and the rules in this section. Under paragraphs (b) and (c)(1) of this section, USP has no deductions properly allocable or apportioned to gross income in the section 245A subgroup because USP has no dividend income in the general category for which a deduction is allowed under section 245A. Under paragraphs (b) and (c) of this section, USP has $303 of deductions for interest expense that are properly allocable or apportioned to stock of specified 10-percent owned foreign corporations in the section 245A subgroup because USP's only general category assets are the general category stock of CFC1, CFC2, and CFC3, all of which are in the section 245A subgroup. Therefore, under paragraph (a) of this section, USP's foreign source taxable income in the general category and its worldwide taxable income are determined without regard to the $303 of deductions for interest expense. Accordingly, USP's foreign source taxable income in the general category is $0 and its worldwide taxable income is $1,503, and therefore, there is no separate limitation loss for purposes of section 904(f). Under section 904(a) and (d)(1) USP's foreign tax credit limitation for the general category is $0.

(B) *Section 951A category income*. Before application of section 904(b)(4) and the rules in this section, USP's foreign source taxable income in the section 951A category is $690, which equals

$2,200 (USP's GILTI inclusion amount) less $1,100 (USP's section 250 deduction) less $410 (interest apportioned to section 951A category income). Under paragraphs (b) and (c)(1) of this section, USP has no deductions properly allocable and apportioned to gross income in a section 245A subgroup of the section 951A category. Under paragraphs (b) and (c) of this section, USP has no deductions properly allocable and apportioned to stock of specified 10-percent owned foreign corporations in a section 245A subgroup of section 951A category stock because no portion of section 951A category stock is assigned to a section 245A subgroup. *See* § 1.861-13(a)(5)(v). Therefore, under paragraph (a) of this section no adjustment is made to USP's foreign source taxable income in the section 951A category. However, the adjustments to USP's worldwide taxable income described in paragraph (e)(2)(ii)(A) of this section apply for purposes of calculating USP's foreign tax credit limitation for the section 951A category. Accordingly, USP's foreign source taxable income in the section 951A category is $690 and its worldwide taxable income is $1,503. Under section 904(a) and (d)(1), USP's foreign tax credit limitation for the section 951A category is $116 ($252 x $690/$1,503).

(f) *Applicability date.*—Except as provided in this paragraph (f), this section applies to taxable years beginning after December 31, 2017. For a taxable year that both begins before January 1, 2018, and ends after December 31, 2017, this section applies without regard to the rules relating to inclusions arising under section 951A. [Reg. § 1.904(b)-3.]

Determination of the Foreign Tax Credit: Guidance

Determination of the Foreign Tax Credit: Guidance.—Amendments to Reg. § 1.904(f)-12, relating to the determination of the foreign tax credit under the Internal Revenue Code, including changes made by the Tax Cuts and Jobs Act, are proposed (published in the Federal Register on December 7, 2018) (corrected March 6, 2019) (REG-105600-18).

Par. 19. § 1.904(f)-12 is amended by adding and reserving paragraph (i) and adding paragraph (j) to read as follows:

§ 1.904(f)-12. Payment and returns of tax withheld by the acquiring agency.

* * *

(i) [Reserved]

(j) *Recapture in years beginning after December 31, 2017, of separate limitation losses, overall foreign losses, and overall domestic losses incurred in years beginning before January 1, 2018.*—(1) *Definitions.*—(i) The term *pre-2018 separate categories* means the separate categories of income described in section 904(d) and any specified separate categories of income, as applicable to taxable years beginning before January 1, 2018.

(ii) The term *post-2017 separate categories* means the separate categories of income described in section 904(d) and any specified separate categories of income, as applicable to taxable years beginning after December 31, 2017.

(iii) The term *specified separate category* has the meaning set forth in § 1.904-4(m)).

(2) *Losses related to pre-2018 passive category income or a specified separate category of income.*—(i) *Allocation of separate limitation loss or overall foreign loss account incurred in a pre-2018 separate category for passive category income or a specified separate category of income.*—To the extent that a taxpayer has a balance in any separate limitation loss or overall foreign loss account in a pre-2018 separate category for passive category income or a specified separate category of income at the end of the taxpayer's last taxable year beginning before January 1, 2018, the amount of such balance is allocated on the first day of the taxpayer's next taxable year to the same post-2017 separate category as the pre-2018 separate category of the separate limitation loss or overall foreign loss account.

(ii) *Recapture of separate limitation loss or overall domestic loss that reduced pre-2018 passive category income or a specified separate category of income.*—To the extent that at the end of the taxpayer's last taxable year beginning before January 1, 2018, a taxpayer has a balance in any separate limitation loss or overall domestic loss account which offset pre-2018 separate category income that was passive category income or income in a specified separate category, such loss is recaptured in subsequent taxable years as income in the same post-2017 separate category as the pre-2018 separate category of income that was offset by the loss.

(3) *Losses related to pre-2018 general category income.*—(i) *Allocation of separate limitation loss or overall foreign loss account incurred in a pre-2018 separate category for general category income.*—To the extent that a taxpayer has a balance in any separate limitation loss or overall foreign loss account in a pre-2018 separate category for general category income at the end of the taxpayer's last taxable year beginning before January 1, 2018, the amount of such balance is allocated on the first day of the taxpayer's next taxable year to the taxpayer's post-2017 separate category for general category income, or, if the taxpayer applies the exception described in § 1.904-2(j)(1)(iii), on a pro rata basis to the taxpayer's post-2017 separate categories for general category and foreign branch category income, based on the proportion in which any unused foreign taxes in the same pre-2018 separate category for general category income are allocated under § 1.904-2(j)(1)(iii)(A). If the taxpayer has no unused foreign taxes in the pre-2018 separate category for general category income, then any loss account balance in that category is allocated to the post-2017 separate category for general category income.

(ii) *Recapture of separate limitation loss or overall domestic loss that reduced pre-2018 general category income.*—To the extent that a taxpayer's separate limitation loss or overall domestic loss offset pre-2018 separate category income that was general category income, the balance in the loss account at the end of the taxpayer's last taxable year beginning before January 1, 2018, is recaptured in subsequent taxable years as income in the post-2017 separate category for general category income, or, if the taxpayer applies the exception described in § 1.904-2(j)(1)(iii), on a pro rata basis as income in the post-2017 separate categories for general category and foreign branch category income, based on the proportion in which any unused foreign taxes in the pre-2018 separate category for general category income are allocated under §1.904-2(j)(1)(iii)(A). If the taxpayer has no unused foreign taxes in the pre-2018 separate category for general category income, then the loss account balance shall be recaptured in subsequent taxable years solely as income in the post-2017 separate category for general category income.

(4) *Treatment of foreign losses that are part of net operating losses incurred in pre-2018 taxable years which are carried forward to post-2017 taxable years.*—A foreign loss that is part of a net operating loss incurred in a taxable year beginning before January 1, 2018, which is carried forward, pursuant to section 172, to a taxable year beginning after December 31, 2017, will be carried forward under the rules of §1.904(g)-3(b)(2). For purposes of applying those rules, the portion of a net operating loss carryforward that is attributable to a foreign loss from the pre-2018 separate category for passive category income or a specified separate category of income will be treated as a loss in the same post-2017 separate category as the pre-2018 separate category. The portion of a net operating loss carryforward that is attributable to a foreign loss from the pre-2018 separate category for general category income must be treated as a loss in the post-2017 separate category for general or branch category income under the allocation principles of paragraph (j)(3)(i) of this section.

(5) *Applicability date.*—This paragraph (j) applies to taxable years beginning after December 31, 2017.

Foreign Tax Credit: Foreign Loss Recapture: Property Disposition

Foreign Tax Credit: Foreign Loss Recapture: Property Disposition.—Amendments to Reg. §1.904(g)-3, providing guidance regarding the coordination of the rules for determining high-taxed income with capital gains adjustments and the allocation and recapture of overall foreign losses and overall domestic losses, as well as the coordination of the recapture of overall foreign losses on certain dispositions of property and other rules concerning overall foreign losses and overall domestic losses, are proposed (published in the Federal Register on June 25, 2012) (REG-134935-11).

☐ Par. 3. Section 1.904(g)-3 is amended by revising paragraph (f), adding paragraph (i) and adding a sentence at the end of paragraph (k) to read as follows:

§1.904(g)-3. Ordering rules for the allocation of net operating losses, net capital losses, U.S. source losses, and separate limitation losses, and for the recapture of separate limitation losses, overall foreign losses, and overall domestic losses.

* * *

(f) *Step Five: Recapture of overall foreign loss accounts.*—If the taxpayer's separate limitation income for the taxable year (reduced by any losses carried over under paragraph (b) of this section) exceeds the sum of the taxpayer's U.S. source loss and separate limitation losses for the year, so that the taxpayer has separate limitation income remaining after the application of paragraphs (d)(1) and (e) of this section, then the taxpayer shall recapture prior year overall foreign losses, if any, in accordance with §1.904(f)-2, and reduce overall foreign loss accounts in accordance with §1.904(f)-2. Such recapture shall include amounts determined under §1.904(f)-2(c) and (d)(3) but not §1.904(f)-2(d)(4).

* * *

(i) *Step Eight: Dispositions under section 904(f)(3) in which gain would not otherwise be recognized.*—The taxpayer shall determine the amount of gain that would otherwise not be recognized but that must be recognized in accordance with §1.904(f)-2(d)(4) (not exceeding the taxpayer's applicable overall foreign loss account) and then apply §1.904(f)-2(a) and (b) to recapture overall foreign loss accounts in an amount equal to the gain recognized. To the extent this recognition of gain in a taxable year increases the amount of a net operating loss carryover to that taxable year, paragraphs (b) through (e) of this section shall be applied to determine the allocation of the additional net operating loss, but only after the applicable overall foreign loss account has been recaptured as provided in this paragraph (i).

(k) * * * Paragraphs (f) and (i) of this section apply to taxable years ending on or after the date of publication of a Treasury decision adopting these rules as final regulations in the **Federal Register**.

Foreign Tax Credit

Foreign Tax Credits: Foreign Tax Redeterminations: Notification.—Temporary Reg. §§1.905-3T—1.905-5T, relating to a taxpayer's obligation to file notification of a foreign tax redetermination, to make adjustments to a taxpayer's pools of foreign taxes and earnings and profits, and the imposition of the civil penalty for failure to file such notice or report such adjustments, are also proposed as final regulations and, when adopted, would become Reg. §§1.905-3—1.905-5 (published in the Federal Register on June 23, 1988).

§1.905-3. Adjustments to the pools of foreign taxes and earnings and profits when the allowable foreign tax credit changes.

§1.905-4. Notification and redetermination of United States tax liability.

§1.905-5. Foreign tax redeterminations and currency translation rules for foreign tax redeterminations occurring in taxable years beginning prior to January 1, 1987.

Foreign Tax Credit: Foreign Tax Redeterminations

Foreign Tax Credit: Foreign Tax Redeterminations.—Reg. §§1.905-3, 1.905-4 and 1.905-5, relating to a taxpayer's obligation under Code Sec. 905(c) to notify the IRS of a foreign tax redetermination, are proposed (published in the Federal Register on November 7, 2007) (REG-209020-86).

☐ Par. 2. Section 1.905-3 is added to read as follows:

§1.905-3. Adjustments to United States tax liability and to the pools of post-1986 undistributed earnings and post-1986 foreign income taxes as a result of a foreign tax redetermination.

[The text of this section is the same as the text of §1.905-3T(a) through (e) as added by T.D. 9362].

☐ Par. 3. Section 1.905-4 is added to read as follows:

§1.905-4. Notification of foreign tax redetermination.

[The text of this section is the same as the text of §1.905-4T(a) through (f)(2) as added by T.D. 9362].

☐ Par. 3. Section 1.905-5 is added to read as follows:

§1.905-5. Foreign tax redeterminations and currency translation rules for foreign tax redeterminations occurring in taxable years beginning prior to January 1, 1987.

[The text of this section is the same as the text of §1.905-5T(a) through (f) as added by T.D. 9362].

Domestic International Sales Corporations

Domestic International Sales Corporations: Taxation of Income.—Reproduced below is the text of a proposed amendment of Temporary Reg. §1.921-1T, relating to the taxation to income allocable to a DISC for taxable years beginning after 1984 (published in the Federal Register on February 3, 1987).

☐ Par. 3. Paragraph (b)(6) of §1.921-1T is removed.

§1.921-1T. Temporary regulations providing transition rules for DISCs and FSCs.

FSCs: Export Property

Foreign Sales Corporations.—Temporary Reg. §§1.927(a)-1T and 1.927(d)-2T, relating to foreign sales corporations, are also proposed as final regulations and, when adopted, would become Reg. §§1.927(a)-1 and 1.927(d)-2, respectively (published in the Federal Register on March 3, 1987).

§1.927(a)-1. Definition of export property.

§1.927(d)-2. Definitions and special rules relating to foreign sales corporation.

Possessions Credit

Possessions Corporations Credit: Qualified Possession Source Investment Income.—Reproduced below are the texts of proposed Reg. §§1.936-2, 1.936-3 and 1.936-3A, defining the term "qualified possession source investment income" (published in the Federal Register on January 21, 1986).

* * *

☐ Par. 2. New §§1.936-2, 1.936-3 and 1.936-3A are added after §1.936-1 to read as follows:

§1.936-2. Source of income.—(a) *In general.*—Except as provided in §1.936-2(b) (relating to certain interest), for purposes of section 936(d)(2), the determination as to whether gross income is from sources within a particular possession shall be made in accordance with §1.863-6.

(b) *Certain interest.*—(1) Interest paid by a possessions corporation that meets the condition of section 936(a)(2)(A) with respect to a particular possession is from sources within that possession.

(2) Interest paid or credited on deposit accounts with a possession branch of a corporation or partnership is from sources within the possession if, at the time of payment or crediting, the branch is engaged within the possession in the commercial banking business or the business of a savings and loan or similar association. [Reg. §1.936-2.]

§1.936-3. Investment in a possession (for use therein).—For purposes of section 936(d)(2), interest and certain dividends derived after April 17, 1984 (less deductions allocable and apportionable thereto) by a domestic corporation engaged in the active conduct of a trade or business in Puerto Rico shall be treated as attributable to investment in Puerto Rico (for use therein) if the interest or certain dividends qualify for exemption from Puerto Rican Income Tax under regulations issued by the Secretary of the Treasury of Puerto Rico, as in effect on April 17, 1984 under the authority of the Acts No. 6 of December 15, 1953, 57 of June 13, 1963, and 25 of June 2, 1978, as amended, to determine the institutions which are eligible to receive funds from exempted businesses under those Acts.

In the case of any investment of funds made by the possessions corporation after [Date that is 30 days after the date of publication in the Federal Register of this regulation as a Treasury decision], the preceding sentence shall not apply unless the possessions corporation receives, at the time the funds are delivered for investment, the written agreement of the institution receiving the funds that the funds will be invested by the institution so as to qualify for exemption under the foregoing regulations of Puerto Rico. Interest derived after September 30, 1976 and before April 18, 1984 shall be treated as attributable to investment in Puerto Rico (for use therein) if the interest qualifies for exemption from Puerto Rican Income Tax under regulations issued by the Secretary of the Treasury of Puerto Rico as in effect on September 28, 1976 under the authority of section 2(j) of the Puerto Rico Industrial Incentive Act of 1963, as amended. [Reg. § 1.936-3.]

§ 1.936-3A. Funds derived from a possession.—(a) *In general.*—Funds treated as derived from the active conduct of a trade or business in a possession or from investment of such funds in a possession ("qualified funds") include—

(1) Taxable income from sources without the United States derived from the active conduct of a trade or business in the possession, and

(2) Qualified possession source investment income,

reduced by any distributions paid with respect to such income and by any losses (not otherwise taken into account under subparagraph (1) or (2)) from such activity or investment. The amount of any capital contributions to a possessions corporation is not treated as qualified funds.

(b) *Limitation on investment.*—Notwithstanding paragraph (a), the amount of qualified funds which may be invested in a possession and give rise to income which is treated as qualified possession source investment income is limited to the total qualified funds for the taxable year and for all prior taxable years which are not already invested in a possession. For this purpose, qualified possession source investment income is not included in total qualified funds for the current taxable year, but is included with respect to prior taxable years.

(c) *Illustration:*.—The principles of paragraphs (a) and (b) of this section are illustrated by the following example:

Example: X has operated in Puerto Rico as a section 936 corporation since January 1, 1980. In 1980 X earned $30,000 from the active conduct of a business in Puerto Rico and paid a dividend of $20,000. On January 1, 1981 X invested $20,000 in a Puerto Rican financial institution. For the year 1981 X had a loss of $10,000 from the conduct of its business and received $1500 in interest. For the years 1982 and 1983 X earned $40,000 and $60,000 respectively from its business and $2000 each year from its investments which qualify under § 1.936-3 and paid dividends of $20,000 and $30,000 respectively. On January 1, 1984 X deposited $80,000 in the same Puerto Rican financial institution for a total deposit of $100,000. For 1984 X had a $5000 loss from its business, but received $15,000 of interest from its investments.

For 1981, the interest received from the investment in the Puerto Rican financial institution was not qualified possession source investment income since there were no qualified funds for 1981. The $30,000 of income received by X from the active conduct of its business in 1980 was reduced to zero by a $20,000 dividend in 1980 and a $10,000 loss in 1981.

For 1982 and 1983 the $20,000 originally deposited in 1981 and not withdrawn are treated as qualified funds and all of the income derived therefrom as qualified possession source investment income assuming the requirements of §§ 1.936-2 and 1.936-3 are met. (The zero qualified funds at the end of 1981 were increased to $20,000 in 1982, representing $40,000 of active business income less $20,000 of dividends; in 1983, the qualified funds available for investment were further increased to $52,000, representing $60,000 of active business income in 1983 less dividend payment of $30,000 (or $30,000) plus $2000 of qualified possession source investment income accrued in 1982). The $1500 of interest earned in 1981 was not derived from qualified funds and, therefore, was not qualified possession source investment income. In addition, this amount and any amount of interest derived therefrom can never be qualified funds since the $1500 was neither derived initially from the active conduct of a trade or business in Puerto Rico nor was it qualified possession source investment income.

For 1984, $7350 of the $15,000 of interest received on the $100,000 investment constitutes qualified possession source investment income since only $49,000 of the $100,000 deposited was from qualified funds ($52,000 of qualified funds at the end of 1983 reduced by the $5000 of loss incurred in 1984 and increased by the $2000 of qualified possession source investment income accrued in 1983). [Reg. § 1.936-3A.]

* * *

☐ Par. 4. Section 7.936-1 is removed.

§ 7.936-1. Qualified possession source investment income (temporary).

Qualified Caribbean Basin Countries: Investments: Requirements

Qualified Caribbean Basin Countries: Investments: Requirements.—Reproduced below is the text of a proposed amendment to Reg. § 1.936-10, relating to the use of Code Sec. 936 funds to finance an investment that qualifies as a privatization (published in the Federal Register on May 13, 1991).

☐ Par. 2. Section 1.936-10 is amended as follows:

1. Paragraph (c)(5)(i)(A) is amended by adding a new sentence at the end of the paragraph to read as set forth below.

2. Paragraph (c)(5)(i)(B)(*1*) is amended by removing the word "or" at the end of the paragraph.

3. Paragraph (c)(5)(i)(B)(*2*) is amended by adding the word "or" at the end of the paragraph, and paragraph (c)(5)(i)(B)(*3*) is added to read as set forth below.

4. Paragraph (c)(5)(v) is added to read as set forth below.

5. Paragraphs (c)(9)(i) and (ii) are revised to read as set forth below.

§1.936-10. Qualified investments.

* * *

(c) * * *

(5) * * *

(i) * * *

(A) * * * Solely for purposes of a qualified privatization described in paragraph (c)(5)(v) of this section, the amounts disbursed under the loan or bond issue may also be applied to an investment in a corporation, partnership, or trust.

(B) * * *

(*3*) A qualified privatization described in paragraph (c)(5)(v) of this section;

* * *

(v) *Qualified privatization*.—This paragraph (c)(5)(v) is effective for investments made by a possessions corporation in a financial institution for investments in accordance with a specific authorization granted by the Commissioner of Financial Institutions of Puerto Rico (or his delegate) on or after [INSERT DATE THAT IS 30 DAYS AFTER PUBLICATION OF THE FINAL REGULATIONS IN THE FEDERAL REGISTER]. For purposes of this section, a qualified privatization is a financing transaction that satisfies all of the requirements of this paragraph (c)(5)(v).

(A) The loan must be made to finance the acquisition, directly or through an investment in a corporation, partnership or trust, of any assets that are currently used in a trade or business or were used in a trade or business but are no longer so used at the time of acquisition and a plan exists to continue or resume using those assets in the conduct of an active trade or business. The loan can also be used to finance other costs associated with acquiring the trade or business or placing assets back in service, within the limits set forth in paragraph (c)(4)(iii) of this section.

(B) After the acquisition, the assets must be used in a trade or business conducted as a qualified business activity.

(C) The United States Agency for International Development (USAID) or the Overseas Private Investment Corporation (OPIC) must certify, prior to the acquisition, that, as a result of the transfer of the activity from the public to the private sector, the acquisition is expected to have a significant positive developmental impact in the qualified Caribbean Basin country where the trade or business is conducted. The determination of whether an acquisition has significant positive developmental impact depends upon an analysis measuring the extent to which incremental developmental benefits exceed incremental negative effects. Generally, developmental effects will be measured in relation to the impact of the acquisition on those economic factors generally used to measure the effect of an activity on the economy of a qualified Caribbean Basin country. Those factors include (but are not limited to) increased economic efficiency and innovation conducive to self-sustaining growth, decreased government expenditures or increased direct revenues to the government, an improved balance of payments of the qualified Caribbean Basin country (through expanded exports of goods or services), increased employment over time, reduced cost of capital, increased expenditures for maintenance and operations, increased capital expenditures, increased net output and improved market competitiveness. Negative factors include (but are not limited to) increased capital outflows (*e.g.*, expenditures abroad and repatriation to any foreign shareholders).

(D) During the 3-year period preceding the acquisition, the government of the qualified Caribbean Basin country must have owned an interest, directly or indirectly, in the acquired assets that, by value or voting interest, represented 50 percent or more of the total of such interests in the acquired assets, and such government must have exercised effective control over such assets.

(E) After the acquisition and during all the time that the loan is outstanding, no government or government-controlled entity may own, directly or indirectly, any interest in the acquired assets.

(F) No government or government-controlled entity may exercise any effective control, or managerial or operational responsibility or authority, over the acquired assets at any time during the time that the loan is outstanding. This restriction is not intended to restrict the normal exercise of regulatory authority by a government, provided such power is not exercised in a way that would defeat the intent of the provisions in this paragraph (c)(5)(v)(F).

* * *

(9) * * *

(i) In the case of an investment described in paragraph (c)(4) of this section (relating to investments in active business assets) or in paragraph (c)(5)(v) of this section (relating to qualified privatization), a qualified recipient is a person that carries on a qualified business activity in a qualified Caribbean Basin country, and complies with the agreement and certification requirements described in paragraph (c)(11)(i) of this section at all times during the period in which the investment remains outstanding.

(ii) In the case of an investment described in paragraph (c)(5) of this section (relating to investments in development projects), other than an investment described in paragraph (c)(5)(v) of this section, a qualified recipient is the borrower (including a person empowered by the borrower to authorize expenditures for the investment in the development project) that has authority to comply, and complies, with the agreement and certification requirements described in paragraph (c)(11)(i) of this section at all times during the period in which the investment remains outstanding.

U.S. Possessions: Residence Rules

U.S. Possessions: Residence Rules.—Amendments to Reg. §1.937-1, determining whether an individual is a bona fide resident of a U.S. territory.and affecting individuals establishing bona fide residency in a U.S. territory by allowing additional days of constructive presence in a U.S. territory, are proposed (published in the Federal Register on August 27, 2015) (REG-109813-11).

Par. 2. Section 1.937-1 is amended as follows:

1. Revising paragraph (c)(3)(i)(B) and paragraph (c)(3)(i)(C)(2).
2. Adding paragraph (c)(3)(i)(D).
3. Revising *Example 1* of paragraph (g).
4. Redesignating *Examples 2* through *10* of paragraph (g) as *Examples 5* through *13* respectively.
5. Adding new *Examples 2, 3,* and *4* to paragraph (g).
6. Revising newly re-designated *Example 5* of paragraph (g).
7. Adding a new sentence to the end of paragraph (i).

The revisions and additions read as follows:

§1.937-1. Bona fide residency in a possession.

* * *

(c) * * *

(3) * * *

(i) * * *

(B) Any day that an individual is outside of the relevant possession to receive, or to accompany on a full-time basis a parent, spouse, or child (as defined in section 152(f)(1)) who is receiving, qualifying medical treatment as defined in paragraph (c)(4) of this section;

(C) * * *

(1) * * *

(2) Period for which a mandatory evacuation order is in effect for the geographic area in the relevant possession in which the individual's place of abode is located; and

(D) Any day not described in paragraph (c)(3)(i)(B) or (C) of this section that an individual is outside of the United States and the relevant possession, except that an individual will not be considered present in the relevant possession under this paragraph (c)(3)(i)(D) for more than 30 days during the taxable year, and this paragraph (c)(3)(i)(D) does not apply for purposes of calculating the required minimum 60 days of presence in the relevant possession under paragraph (c)(1)(ii) of this section. Furthermore, this paragraph (c)(3)(i)(D) applies only if the number of days that the individual is considered to be present in the relevant possession during the taxable year, determined without regard to this paragraph (c)(3)(i)(D), exceeds the number of days that the individual is considered to be present in the United States during the taxable year.

* * *

(g) * * *

Example 1. Presence test. H, a U.S. citizen, is engaged in a profession that requires frequent travel. In each of the years 2016 and 2017, H spends 195 days in Possession N and the balance of the year in the United States. In 2018, H spends 160 days in Possession N and the balance of the year in the United States. Thus, H spends a total of 550 days in Possession N for the three-year period consisting of years 2016, 2017, and 2018. Under paragraph (c)(1)(ii) of this section, H satisfies the presence test of paragraph (c) of this section with respect to Possession N for taxable year 2018 because H is present in Possession N for more than the required 549 days during the three-year period of 2016 through 2018 and is present in Possession N for at least 60 days during each of those taxable years. Assuming that in 2018 H does not have a tax home outside of Possession N and does not have a closer connection to the United States or a foreign country under paragraphs (d) and (e) of this section respectively, then regardless of whether H was a bona fide resident of Possession N in 2016 and 2017, H is a bona fide resident of Possession N for taxable year 2018.

Example 2. Presence test. Same facts as *Example 1,* except that in 2018, H spends 130 days in Possession N, 110 days in foreign countries, and 125 days in the United States. Because H satisfies the requirements of paragraph (c)(3)(i)(D) of this section, 30 of the days spent in foreign countries during 2018 are treated as days of presence in Possession N. Thus, H will be treated as being present for 160 days in Possession N for 2018. Under paragraph (c)(1)(ii) of this section, H meets the presence test of paragraph (c) of this section with respect to Possession N for taxable year 2018 because H is present in Possession N for 550 days (more than the required 549 days) during the three-year period of 2016 through 2018 and is present in Possession N for at least 60 days in each of those taxable years. As in *Example 1,* assuming that in 2018 H does not have a tax home outside of Possession N and does not have a closer connection to the United States or a foreign country under paragraphs (d) and (e) of this section respectively, then regardless of whether H was a bona fide resident of Possession N in 2016 and 2017, H is a bona fide resident of Possession N in 2018.

Example 3. Presence test. Same facts as *Example 1,* except that in 2018, H spends 130 days in Possession N, 100 days in foreign countries, and 135 days in the United States. Under these facts, H does not satisfy paragraph (c)(1)(ii) of this section for taxable year 2018 because H is present in Possession N for only 520 days (less than the required 549 days) during the three-year period of 2016 through 2018. The rule of paragraph (c)(3)(i)(D) of this section (treating up to 30 days spent in foreign countries as days of presence in Possession N) is not available because H fails to satisfy the condition that H be present more days in Possession N than in the United States during 2018, determined without regard to the application of paragraph (c)(3)(i)(D) of this section.

Example 4. Presence test. Same facts as *Example 1,* except that in 2016, H spends 360 days in Possession N and six days in the United States; in 2017, H spends 45 days in Possession N, 290 days in foreign countries, and 30 days in the United States; and in 2018, H spends 180 days in Possession N and 185 days in the United States. Under these facts, H does not satisfy paragraph (c)(1)(ii) of this section for taxable year 2018.

During the three-year period from 2016 through 2018, H is present in Possession N for 615 days, including 30 of the days spent in foreign countries in 2017, which are treated under paragraph (c)(3)(i)(D) of this section as days of presence in Possession N. Although H is present in Possession N for more than the required 549 days during the three-year period, H is only present for 45 days in Possession N during one of the taxable years (2017) of the period, less than the 60 days of minimum presence required under paragraph (c)(1)(ii) of this section. The rule of paragraph (c)(3)(i)(D) of this section does not apply for purposes of determining whether H is present in Possession N for the 60-day minimum required under paragraph (c)(1)(ii) of this section.

Example 5. Presence test. W, a U.S. citizen, owns a condominium in Possession P where she spends part of the taxable year. W also owns a house in State N near her grown children and grandchildren. W is retired and her income consists solely of pension payments, dividends, interest, and Social Security benefits. For 2016, W spends 145 days in Possession P, 101 days in Europe and Asia on vacation, and 120 days in State N. For taxable year 2016, W is not present in Possession P for at least 183 days, is present in the United States for more than 90 days, and has a significant connection to the United States by reason of her permanent home. However, under paragraph (c)(1)(iv) of this section, W still satisfies the presence test of paragraph (c) of this section with respect to Possession P for taxable year 2016 because she has no earned income in the United States and is present for more days in Possession P than in the United States.

* * *

(i) * * * Notwithstanding the foregoing, paragraph (c)(3)(i)(D) and *Examples 1, 2, 3, 4,* and *5* of paragraph (g) of this section apply for taxable years beginning after the date these regulations are published as final regulations in the **Federal Register**.

Global Intangible Low-Taxed Income: Guidance

Global Intangible Low-Taxed Income: Guidance.—Amendments to Reg. §1.951-1, implementing section 951A of the Internal Revenue Code, which was enacted on December 22, 2017, are proposed (published in the Federal Register on October 10, 2018) (REG-104390-18).

Par. 2. Section 1.951-1 is amended by:

1. Revising the introductory language in paragraph (a).
2. Revising paragraphs (e) and (g)(1).
3. Adding paragraphs (h) and (i).

The revisions and additions read as follows:

§1.951-1. Amounts included in gross income of United States shareholders.—(a) *In general.*—If a foreign corporation is a controlled foreign corporation (within the meaning of section 957) at any time during any taxable year of such corporation, every person—

* * *

(e) *Pro rata share of subpart F income defined.*—(1) *In general.*—(i) *Hypothetical distribution.*—For purposes of paragraph (b) of this section, a United States shareholder's pro rata share of a controlled foreign corporation's subpart F income for a taxable year is the amount that bears the same ratio to the corporation's subpart F income for the taxable year as the amount of the corporation's current earnings and profits that would be distributed with respect to the stock of the corporation which the United States shareholder owns (within the meaning of section 958(a)) for the taxable year bears to the total amount of the corporation's current earnings and profits that would be distributed with respect to the stock owned by all the shareholders of the corporation if all the current earnings and profits of the corporation for the taxable year (not reduced by actual distributions during the year) were distributed (*hypothetical distribution*) on the last day of the corporation's taxable year on which such corporation is a controlled foreign corporation (*hypothetical distribution date*).

(ii) *Determination of current earnings and profits.*—For purposes of this paragraph (e), the amount of current earnings and profits of a controlled foreign corporation for a taxable year is treated as the greater of the following two amounts:

(A) The earnings and profits of the corporation for the taxable year determined under section 964; or

(B) The sum of the subpart F income (as determined under section 952 and increased as provided under section 951A(c)(2)(B)(ii) and §1.951A-6(d)) of the corporation for the taxable year and the tested income (as defined in section 951A(c)(2)(A) and §1.951A-2(b)(1)) of the corporation for the taxable year.

(2) *One class of stock.*—If a controlled foreign corporation for a taxable year has only one class of stock outstanding, the amount of the corporation's current earnings and profits distributed in the hypothetical distribution with respect to each share in the class of stock is determined as if the hypothetical distribution were made pro rata with respect to each share in the class of stock.

(3) *More than one class of stock.*—If a controlled foreign corporation for a taxable year has more than one class of stock outstanding, the amount of the corporation's current earnings and profits distributed in the hypothetical distribution with respect to each class of stock is determined under this paragraph (e)(3) based on the distribution rights of each class of stock on the hypothetical distribution date, and then further distributed pro rata with respect to each share in the class of stock. Subject to paragraphs (e)(4) through (6) of this section, the distribution rights of a class of stock are determined taking into account all facts and circumstances related to the economic rights and interest in the current earnings and profits of the corporation of each class, including the terms of the class of stock, any agreement among the shareholders and, where appropriate, the relative fair market value of shares of stock.

(4) *Special rules.*—(i) *Redemptions, liquidations, and returns of capital.*—Notwithstanding the terms of any class of stock of the controlled foreign corporation or any agreement or arrangement with respect thereto, no amount of current earnings and profits is distributed in the hypothetical distribution with respect to a particular class of stock to the extent that a distribution of such amount would constitute a distribution in redemption of stock (even if such redemption would be treated as a distribution of property to which section 301 applies pursuant to section 302(d)), a distribution in liquidation, or a return of capital.

(ii) *Certain cumulative preferred stock.*—If a controlled foreign corporation has outstanding a class of redeemable preferred stock with cumulative dividend rights and dividend arrearages that do not compound at least annually at a rate that equals or exceeds the applicable Federal rate (as defined in section 1274(d)(1)) (*AFR*), the amount of the corporation's current earnings and profits distributed in the hypothetical distribution with respect to the class of stock may not exceed the amount of dividends actually paid during the taxable year with respect to the class of stock plus the present value of the unpaid current dividends with respect to the class determined using the AFR that applies on the date the stock is issued for the term from such issue date to the mandatory redemption date and assuming the dividends will be paid at the mandatory redemption date. For purposes of this paragraph (e)(4)(ii), if the class of preferred stock does not have a mandatory redemption date, the mandatory redemption date is the date that the class of preferred stock is expected to be redeemed based on all facts and circumstances.

(iii) *Dividend arrearages.*—If there is an arrearage in dividends for prior taxable years with respect to a class of preferred stock of a controlled foreign corporation, an amount of the corporation's current earnings and profits is distributed in the hypothetical distribution to the class of preferred stock by reason of the arrearage only to the extent the arrearage exceeds the accumulated earnings and profits of the controlled foreign corporation remaining from prior taxable years beginning after December 31, 1962, as of the beginning of the taxable year, or the date on which such stock was issued, whichever is later. If there is an arrearage in dividends for prior taxable years with respect to more than one class of preferred stock, the previous sentence is applied to each class in order of priority, except that the accumulated earnings and profits remaining after the applicable date are reduced by the earnings and profits necessary to satisfy arrearages with respect to classes of stock with a higher priority. For purposes of this paragraph (e)(4)(iii), the amount of any arrearage is determined by taking into account the time value of money principles in paragraph (e)(4)(ii) of this section.

(5) *Restrictions or other limitations on distributions.*—(i) *In general.*—A restriction or other limitation on distributions of an amount of earnings and profits by a controlled foreign corporation is not taken into account in determining the amount of the corporation's current earnings and profits distributed in a hypothetical distribution to a class of stock of the controlled foreign corporation.

(ii) *Definition.*—For purposes of paragraph (e)(5)(i) of this section, a restriction or other limitation on distributions includes any limitation that has the effect of limiting the distribution of an amount of earnings and profits by a controlled foreign corporation with respect to a class of stock of the corporation, other than currency or other restrictions or limitations imposed under the laws of any foreign country as provided in section 964(b).

(iii) *Exception for certain preferred distributions.*—For purposes of paragraph (e)(5)(i) of this section, the right to receive periodically a fixed amount (whether determined by a percentage of par value, a reference to a floating coupon rate, a stated return expressed in terms of a certain amount of U.S. dollars or foreign currency, or otherwise) with respect to a class of stock the distribution of which is a condition precedent to a further distribution of earnings and profits that year with respect to any class of stock (not including a distribution in partial or complete liquidation) is not a restriction or other limitation on the distribution of earnings and profits by a controlled foreign corporation.

(iv) *Illustrative list of restrictions and limitations.*—Except as provided in paragraph (e)(5)(iii) of this section, restrictions or other limitations on distributions include, but are not limited to—

(A) An arrangement that restricts the ability of a controlled foreign corporation to pay dividends on a class of stock of the corporation until a condition or conditions are satisfied (for example, until another class of stock is redeemed);

(B) A loan agreement entered into by a controlled foreign corporation that restricts or otherwise affects the ability to make distributions on its stock until certain requirements are satisfied; or

(C) An arrangement that conditions the ability of a controlled foreign corporation to pay dividends to its shareholders on the financial condition of the corporation.

(6) *Transactions and arrangements with a principal purpose of reducing pro rata shares.*—For purposes of this paragraph (e), any transaction or arrangement that is part of a plan a principal purpose of which is the avoidance of Federal income taxation, including, but not limited to, a transaction or arrangement to reduce a United States shareholder's pro rata share of the subpart F income of a controlled foreign corporation, which transaction or arrangement would avoid Federal income taxation without regard to this paragraph (e)(6), is disregarded in determining such United States shareholder's pro rata share of the subpart F income of the corporation. This paragraph (e)(6) also applies for purposes of the pro rata share rules described in § 1.951A-1(d) that reference this paragraph (e), including the rules in § 1.951A-1(d)(3) that determine the pro rata share of qualified business asset investment based on the pro rata share of tested income.

(7) *Examples.*—The application of this section is illustrated by the examples in this paragraph (e)(7).

(i) Common facts for examples in paragraph (e)(7). Except as otherwise stated, the following facts are assumed for purposes of the examples.

(A) FC1 is a controlled foreign corporation.

(B) USP1, USP2, and USP3 are domestic corporations and United States shareholders of FC1.

(C) Individual A is a foreign individual, and FC2 is a foreign corporation.

(D) All persons use the calendar year as their taxable year.

(E) Any ownership of FC1 by any shareholder is for all of Year 1.

(F) The common shareholders of FC1 are entitled to dividends when declared by FC1's board of directors.

(G) There are no accrued but unpaid dividends with respect to preferred shares, and common shares have positive liquidation value.

(H) FC1 makes no distributions during Year 1.

(I) There are no other facts and circumstances related to the economic rights and interest of any class of stock in the current earnings and profits of a foreign corporation, and no transaction or arrangement was entered into as part of a plan a principal purpose of which is the avoidance of Federal income taxation.

(J) FC1 does not have tested income within the meaning of section 951A(c)(2)(A) and § 1.951A-2(b)(1) or tested loss within the meaning of section 951A(c)(2)(B) and § 1.951A-2(b)(2).

(ii) *Example 1: single class of stock*—(A) *Facts*. FC1 has outstanding 100 shares of one class of stock. USP1 owns 60 shares of FC1. USP2 owns 40 shares of FC1. For Year 1, FC1 has $1,000x of earnings and profits and $100x of subpart F income within the meaning of section 952.

(B) *Analysis*. FC1 has one class of stock. Therefore, under paragraph (e)(2) of this section, FC1's current earnings and profits of $1,000x are distributed in the hypothetical distribution pro rata to each share of stock. Accordingly, under paragraph (e)(1) of this section, for Year 1, USP1's pro rata share of FC1's subpart F income is $60x ($100x x $600x/$1,000x) and USP2's pro rata share of FC1's subpart F income is $40x ($100x x $400x/$1,000x).

(iii) *Example 2: common and preferred stock*—(A) *Facts*. FC1 has outstanding 70 shares of common stock and 30 shares of 4% nonparticipating, voting preferred stock with a par value of $10x per share. USP1 owns all of the common shares. Individual A owns all of the preferred shares. For Year 1, FC1 has $100x of earnings and profits and $50x of subpart F income within the meaning of section 952. In Year 1, FC1 distributes as a dividend $12x to Individual A with respect to Individual A's preferred shares.

(B) *Analysis*. The distribution rights of the preferred shares are not a restriction or other limitation within the meaning of paragraph (e)(5) of this section. Under paragraph (e)(3) of this section, the amount of FC1's current earnings and profits distributed in the hypothetical distribution with respect to Individual A's preferred shares is $12x and with respect to USP1's common shares is $88x. Accordingly, under paragraph (e)(1) of this section, USP1's pro rata share of FC1's subpart F income is $44x ($50x x $88x/$100x) for Year 1.

(iv) *Example 3: restriction based on cumulative income*—(A) *Facts*. FC1 has outstanding 10 shares of common stock and 400 shares of 2% nonparticipating, voting preferred stock with a par value of $1x per share. USP1 owns all of the common shares. FC2 owns all of the preferred shares. USP1 and FC2 cause the governing documents of FC1 to provide that no dividends may be paid to the common shareholders until FC1 cumulatively earns $100,000x of income. For Year 1, FC1 has $50x of earnings and profits and $50x of subpart F income within the meaning of section 952. In Year 1, FC1 distributes as a dividend $8x to FC2 with respect to FC2's preferred shares.

(B) *Analysis*. The agreement restricting FC1's ability to pay dividends to common shareholders until FC1 cumulatively earns $100,000x of income is a restriction or other limitation within the meaning of paragraph (e)(5) of this section. Therefore, the restriction is disregarded for purposes of determining the amount of FC1's current earnings and profits distributed in the hypothetical distribution to a class of stock. The distribution rights of the preferred shares are not a restriction or other limitation within the meaning of paragraph (e)(5) of this section. Under paragraph (e)(3) of this section, the amount of FC1's current earnings and profits distributed in the hypothetical distribution with respect to FC2's preferred shares is $8x and with respect to USP1's common shares is $42x. Accordingly, under paragraph (e)(1) of this section, USP1's pro rata share of FC1's subpart F income is $42x for Year 1.

(v) *Example 4: redemption rights*—(A) *Facts*. FC1 has outstanding 40 shares of common stock and 10 shares of 4% nonparticipating, voting preferred stock with a par value of $50x per share. Pursuant to the terms of the preferred stock, FC1 has the right to redeem at any time, in whole or in part, the preferred stock. FC2 owns all of the preferred shares. USP1, wholly owned by FC2, owns all of the common shares. For Year 1, FC1 has $100x of earnings and profits and $100x of subpart F income within the meaning of section 952. In Year 1, FC1 distributes as a dividend $20x to FC2 with respect to FC2's preferred shares.

(B) *Analysis*. If FC1 were treated as having redeemed any preferred shares, the redemption would be treated as a distribution to which section 301 applies under section 302(d) due to FC2's constructive ownership of the common shares. However, under paragraph (e)(4)(i) of this section, no amount of earnings and profits is distributed in the hypothetical distribution to the preferred shareholders on the hypothetical distribution date as a result of FC1's right to redeem, in whole or in part, the preferred shares. FC1's redemption rights with respect to the preferred shares cannot affect the distribution of current earnings and profits in the hypothetical distribution to FC1's shareholders. As a result, the amount of FC1's current earnings and profits distributed in the hypothetical distribution with respect to FC2's preferred shares is $20x and with respect to USP1's common shares is $80x. Accordingly, under paragraph (e)(1) of this section, USP1's pro rata share of FC1's subpart F income is $80x for Year 1.

(vi) *Example 5: shareholder owns common and preferred stock*—(A) *Facts*. FC1 has outstanding 40 shares of common stock and 60 shares of 6% nonparticipating, nonvoting preferred stock with a par value of $100x per share. USP1 owns

30 shares of the common stock and 15 shares of the preferred stock during Year 1. The remaining 10 shares of common stock and 45 shares of preferred stock of FC1 are owned by Individual A. For Year 1, FC1 has $1,000x of earnings and profits and $500x of subpart F income within the meaning of section 952.

(B) *Analysis*. Under paragraph (e)(5)(iii) of this section, the right of the holder of the preferred stock to receive 6% of par value is not a restriction or other limitation within the meaning of paragraph (e)(5) of this section. The amount of FC1's current earnings and profits distributed in the hypothetical distribution with respect to FC1's preferred shares is $360x (0.06 x $100x x 60) and with respect to its common shares is $640x ($1,000x - $360x). As a result, the amount of FC1's current earnings and profits distributed in the hypothetical distribution to USP1 is $570x, the sum of $90x ($360x x 15/60) with respect to its preferred shares and $480x ($640x x 30/40) with respect to its common shares. Accordingly, under paragraph (e)(1) of this section, USP1's pro rata share of the subpart F income of FC1 is $285x ($500x x $570x/$1,000x).

(vii) *Example 6: subpart F income and tested income*—(A) *Facts*. FC1 has outstanding 700 shares of common stock and 300 shares of 4% nonparticipating, voting preferred stock with a par value of $100x per share. USP1 owns all of the common shares. USP2 owns all of the preferred shares. For Year 1, FC1 has $10,000x of earnings and profits, $2,000x of subpart F income within the meaning of section 952, and $9,000x of tested income within the meaning of section 951A(c)(2)(A) and § 1.951A-2(b)(1).

(B) *Analysis*—(1) *Pro rata share of subpart F income*. The current earnings and profits of FC1 determined under paragraph (e)(1)(ii) of this section are $11,000x, the greater of FC1's earnings and profits as determined under section 964 ($10,000x) or the sum of FC1's subpart F income and tested income ($2,000x + $9,000x). The amount of FC1's current earnings and profits distributed in the hypothetical distribution with respect to USP2's preferred shares is $1,200x (.04 x $100x x 300) and with respect to USP1's common shares is $9,800x ($11,000x - $1,200x). Accordingly, under paragraph (e)(1) of this section, USP1's pro rata share of FC1's subpart F income is $1,782x ($2,000x x $9,800x/$11,000x), and USP2's pro rata share of FC1's subpart F income is $218x ($2,000x x $1,200x/$11,000x).

(2) *Pro rata share of tested income*. The same analysis applies for the hypothetical distribution with respect to the tested income as under paragraph (ii)(A) of this *Example 6* with respect to the subpart F income. Accordingly, under § 1.951A-1(d)(2), USP1's pro rata share of FC1's tested income is $8,018x ($9,000x x $9,800x/$11,000x), and USP2's pro rata share of FC1's tested income is $982x ($9,000x x $1,200x/$11,000x) for Year 1.

(viii) *Example 7: subpart F income and tested loss*—(A) *Facts*. The facts are the same as in paragraph (A) of *Example 6*, except that for Year 1, FC1 has $8,000x of earnings and profits, $10,000x of subpart F income within the meaning of section 952 (but without regard to the limitation in section 952(c)), and $2,000x of tested loss within the meaning of section 951A(c)(2)(B) and § 1.951A-2(b)(2). Under section 951A(c)(2)(B)(ii) and § 1.951A-6(d), the earnings and profits of FC1 are increased for purposes of section 952 by the amount of FC1's tested loss. Accordingly, taking into account section 951A(c)(2)(B)(ii) and § 1.951A-6(d), the subpart F income of FC1 is $10,000x.

(B) *Analysis*—(1) *Pro rata share of subpart F income*. The current earnings and profits determined under paragraph (e)(1)(ii) of this section are $10,000x, the greater of the earnings and profits of FC1 determined under section 964 ($8,000x) or the sum of FC1's subpart F income and tested income ($10,000x + $0). The amount of FC1's current earnings and profits distributed in the hypothetical distribution with respect to USP2's preferred shares is $1,200x (.04 x $100x x 300) and with respect to Corp A's common shares is $8,800x ($10,000x - $1,200x). Accordingly, under paragraph (e)(1) of this section, for Year 1, USP1's pro rata share of FC1's subpart F income is $8,800x and USP2's pro rata share of FC1's subpart F income is $1,200x.

(2) *Pro rata share of tested loss*. The current earnings and profits determined under § 1.951A-1(d)(4)(i)(B) are $2,000x, the amount of FC1's tested loss. Under § 1.951A-1(d)(4)(i)(C), the entire $2,000x tested loss is distributed in the hypothetical distribution with respect to USP1's common shares. Accordingly, USP1's pro rata share of the tested loss is $2,000x.

* * *

(g) * * *

(1) *In general*.—For purposes of sections 951 through 964, the term "United States shareholder" means, with respect to a foreign corporation, a United States person (as defined in section 957(c)) who owns within the meaning of section 958(a), or is considered as owning by applying the rules of ownership of section 958(b), 10 percent or more of the total combined voting power of all classes of stock entitled to vote of such foreign corporation, or 10 percent or more of the total value of shares of all classes of stock of such foreign corporation.

* * *

(h) *Special rule for partnership blocker structures*.—(1) *In general*.—For purposes of sections 951 through 964, a controlled domestic partnership is treated as a foreign partnership in determining the stock of a controlled foreign corporation owned (within the meaning of section 958(a)) by a United States person if the following conditions are satisfied—

(i) Without regard to this paragraph (h), the controlled domestic partnership owns (within the meaning of section 958(a)) stock of a controlled foreign corporation; and

(ii) If the controlled domestic partnership (and all other controlled domestic partnerships in the chain of ownership of the controlled foreign corporation) were treated as foreign—

(A) The controlled foreign corporation would continue to be a controlled foreign corporation; and

(B) At least one United States shareholder of the controlled foreign corporation would be treated as owning (within the meaning of section 958(a)) stock of the controlled foreign corporation through another foreign corporation that is a direct or indirect partner in the controlled domestic partnership.

(2) *Definition of a controlled domestic partnership*.—For purposes of paragraph (h)(1) of this section, the term *controlled domestic partnership*

means, with respect to a United States shareholder described in paragraph (h)(1)(ii)(B) of this section, a domestic partnership that is controlled by the United States shareholder and persons related to the United States shareholder. For purposes of this paragraph (h)(2), control generally is determined based on all the facts and circumstances, except that a partnership will be deemed to be controlled by a United States shareholder and related persons in any case in which those persons, in the aggregate, own (directly or indirectly through one or more partnerships) more than 50 percent of the interests in the partnership capital or profits. For purposes of this paragraph (h)(2), a related person is, with respect to a United States shareholder, a person that is related to the United States shareholder within the meaning of section 267(b) or 707(b)(1).

(3) *Example.*—(i) *Facts.*—USP, a domestic corporation, owns all of the stock of CFC1 and CFC2. CFC1 and CFC2 own 60% and 40%, respectively, of the interests in the capital and profits of DPS, a domestic partnership. DPS owns all of the stock of CFC3. Each of CFC1, CFC2, and CFC3 is a controlled foreign corporation. USP, DPS, CFC1, CFC2, and CFC3 all use the calendar year as their taxable year. For Year 1, CFC3 has $100x of subpart F income (as defined under section 952) and $100x of earnings and profits.

(ii) *Analysis.*—DPS is a controlled domestic partnership with respect to USP within the meaning of paragraph (h)(2) of this section because more than 50% of the interests in its capital or profits are owned by persons related to USP within the meaning of section 267(b) (that is, CFC1 and CFC2), and thus DPS is controlled by USP and related persons. Without regard to paragraph (h) of this section, DPS is a United States shareholder that owns (within the meaning of section 958(a)) stock of CFC3, a controlled foreign corporation. If DPS were treated as foreign, CFC3 would continue to be a controlled foreign corporation, and USP would be treated as owning (within the meaning of section 958(a)) stock in CFC3 through CFC1 and CFC2, which are both partners in DPS. Thus, under paragraph (h)(1) of this section, DPS is treated as a foreign partnership for purposes of determining the stock of CFC3 owned (within the meaning of section 958(a)) by USP. Accordingly, USP's pro rata share of CFC3's subpart F income for Year 1 is $100x, and USP includes in its gross income $100x under section 951(a)(1)(A). DPS is not a United States shareholder of CFC3 for purposes of sections 951 through 964.

(i) *Applicability dates.*—Paragraphs (a), (e)(1)(ii)(B), and (g)(1) of this section apply to taxable years of foreign corporations beginning after December 31, 2017, and to taxable years of United States shareholders with or within which such taxable years of foreign corporations end. Except for paragraph (e)(1)(ii)(B), paragraph (e) of this section applies to taxable years of United States shareholders ending on or after October 3, 2018. Paragraph (h) of this section applies to taxable years of domestic partnerships ending on or after May 14, 2010.

* * *

Global Intangible Low-Taxed Income: Guidance

Global Intangible Low-Taxed Income: Guidance.—Reg. §§1.951A-0—1.951A-7, implementing section 951A of the Internal Revenue Code, which was enacted on December 22, 2017, are proposed (published in the Federal Register on October 10, 2018) (REG-104390-18).

Par. 3. Section 1.951A-0 is added to read as follows:

§1.951A-0. Outline of section 951A regulations.—This section lists the headings for §§1.951A-1 through 1.951A-7.

§1.951A-1 General provisions.

(a) Overview.

(1) In general.

(2) Scope.

(b) Inclusion of global intangible low-taxed income.

(c) Determination of GILTI inclusion amount.

(1) In general.

(2) Definition of net CFC tested income.

(3) Definition of net deemed tangible income return.

(i) In general.

(ii) Definition of deemed tangible income return.

(iii) Definition of specified interest expense.

(4) Determination of GILTI inclusion amount for consolidated groups.

(d) Determination of pro rata share.

(1) In general.

(2) Tested income.

(i) In general.

(ii) Special rule for prior allocation of tested loss.

(3) Qualified business asset investment.

(i) In general.

(ii) Special rule for preferred stock in case of excess QBAI.

(iii) Examples.

(4) Tested loss.

(i) In general.

(ii) Special rule in case of accrued but unpaid dividends.

(iii) Special rule for stock with no liquidation value.

(iv) Examples.

(5) Tested interest expense.

(6) Tested interest income.

(e) Definitions.

(1) CFC inclusion date.

(2) CFC inclusion year.

(3) Section 958(a) stock.

(4) U.S. shareholder inclusion year.

§1.951A-2 Tested income and tested loss.

(a) Scope.

(b) Definitions related to tested income and tested loss.

(1) Tested income and tested income CFC.

(2) Tested loss and tested loss CFC.

(c) Rules relating to the determination of tested income and tested loss.

(1) Definition of gross tested income.

(2) Determination of gross tested income and allowable deductions.

(3) Allocation of deductions to gross tested income.
(4) Nonapplication of section 952(c).
(i) In general.
(ii) Example.
(5) Disregard of basis in property related to certain transfers during the disqualified period.
(i) In general.
(ii) Definition of specified property.
(iii) Definition of disqualified basis.
(iv) Example.

§1.951A-3 Qualified business asset investment.
(a) Scope.
(b) Definition of qualified business asset investment.
(c) Specified tangible property.
(1) In general.
(2) Tangible property.
(d) Dual use property.
(1) In general.
(2) Dual use ratio.
(3) Example.
(e) Determination of adjusted basis of specified tangible property.
(1) In general.
(2) Effect of change in law.
(3) Specified tangible property placed in service before enactment of section 951A.
(f) Special rules for short taxable years.
(1) In general.
(2) Determination of quarter closes.
(3) Reduction of qualified business asset investment.
(4) Example.
(g) Partnership property.
(1) In general.
(2) Definitions related to partnership QBAI.
(i) In general.
(ii) Partnership QBAI ratio.
(iii) Partnership specified tangible property.
(3) Determination of adjusted basis.
(4) Examples.
(h) Anti-abuse rules for certain transfers of property.
(1) Disregard of basis in specified tangible property held temporarily.
(2) Disregard of basis in specified tangible property related to transfers during the disqualified period.
(i) In general.
(ii) Determination of disqualified basis.
(A) In general.
(B) Definition of qualified gain amount.
(C) Definition of disqualified transfer.
(D) Definition of disqualified period.
(E) Related person.
(iii) Examples.

§1.951A-4 Tested interest expense and tested interest income.
(a) Scope.
(b) Definitions related to specified interest expense.
(1) Tested interest expense.
(i) In general.
(ii) Interest expense.
(iii) Qualified interest expense.
(iv) Qualified CFC.
(2) Tested interest income.
(i) In general.
(ii) Interest income.
(iii) Qualified interest income.
(c) Examples.

§1.951A-5 Domestic partnerships and their partners.
(a) Scope.
(b) In general.
(1) Determination of GILTI inclusion amount of a U.S. shareholder partnership.
(2) Determination of distributive share of U.S. shareholder partnership's GILTI inclusion amount of partner other than a U.S. shareholder partner.
(c) Determination of GILTI inclusion amount of a U.S. shareholder partner.
(d) Tiered U.S. shareholder partnerships.
(e) Definitions.
(1) CFC tested item.
(2) Partnership CFC.
(3) U.S. shareholder partner.
(4) U.S. shareholder partnership.
(f) Reporting requirement.
(g) Examples.

§1.951A-6 Treatment of GILTI inclusion amount and adjustments to earnings and profits and basis related to tested loss CFCs.
(a) Scope.
(b) Treatment as subpart F income for certain purposes.
(1) In general.
(2) Allocation of GILTI inclusion amount to tested income CFCs.
(i) In general.
(ii) Example.
(iii) Translation of portion of GILTI inclusion amount allocated to tested income CFC.
(c) Treatment as an amount includible in the gross income of a United States person.
(1) In general.
(2) Special rule for a United States shareholder that is a domestic partnership.
(d) Increase of earnings and profits of tested loss CFC for purposes of section 952(c)(1)(A).
(e) Adjustments to basis related to net used tested loss.
(1) In general.
(i) Disposition of stock of a controlled foreign corporation.
(ii) Disposition of stock of an upper-tier controlled foreign corporation.
(iii) Disposition of an interest in a foreign entity other than a controlled foreign corporation.
(iv) Order of application of basis reductions.
(v) No duplicative adjustments.
(2) Net used tested loss amount.
(i) In general.
(ii) Used tested loss amount.
(3) Net offset tested income amount.
(i) In general.
(ii) Offset tested income amount.
(4) Attribution to stock.
(i) In general.
(ii) Nonrecognition transactions.
(5) Section 381 transactions.
(6) Other definitions.
(i) Domestic corporation.
(ii) Disposition.

(7) Special rule for disposition by controlled foreign corporation less than 100 percent owned by a single domestic corporation.

(8) Special rules for members of a consolidated group.

(9) Examples.

§1.951A-7 Applicability dates.

[Reg. §1.951A-0.]

Par. 4. Section 1.951A-1 is added to read as follows:

§1.951A-1. General provisions.—(a) *Overview.*—(1) *In general.*—This section and §§1.951A-2 through 1.951A-7 (collectively, the *section 951A regulations*) provide rules to determine a United States shareholder's income inclusion under section 951A and certain definitions for purposes of section 951A and the section 951A regulations. This section provides general rules for determining a United States shareholder's inclusion of global intangible low-taxed income. Section 1.951A-2 provides rules for determining a controlled foreign corporation's tested income or tested loss. Section 1.951A-3 provides rules for determining a controlled foreign corporation's qualified business asset investment. Section 1.951A-4 provides rules for determining a controlled foreign corporation's tested interest expense and tested interest income. Section 1.951A-5 provides rules relating to the application of section 951A and the section 951A regulations to domestic partnerships and their partners. Section 1.951A-6 provides rules relating to the treatment of the inclusion of global intangible low-taxed income for certain purposes and adjustments to earnings and profits and basis of a controlled foreign corporation related to a tested loss. Section 1.951A-7 provides dates of applicability.

(2) *Scope.*—Paragraph (b) of this section provides the general rule requiring a United States shareholder to include in gross income its global intangible low-taxed income for a U.S. shareholder inclusion year. Paragraph (c) of this section provides rules for determining the amount of a United States shareholder's global intangible low-taxed income for the U.S. shareholder inclusion year, including a rule for the application of section 951A and the section 951A regulations to consolidated groups. Paragraph (d) of this section provides rules for determining a United States shareholder's pro rata share of certain items for purposes of determining the United States shareholder's global intangible low-taxed income. Paragraph (e) of this section provides additional general definitions for purposes of this section and the section 951A regulations.

(b) *Inclusion of global intangible low-taxed income.*—Each person who is a United States shareholder (as defined in section 951(b)) of any controlled foreign corporation (as defined in section 957) and owns section 958(a) stock (as defined in paragraph (e)(3) of this section) in any such controlled foreign corporation includes in gross income in the U.S. shareholder inclusion year (as defined in paragraph (e)(4) of this section) the shareholder's GILTI inclusion amount (as defined in paragraph (c) of this section), if any, for the U.S. shareholder inclusion year.

(c) *Determination of GILTI inclusion amount.*—(1) *In general.*—Except as provided in paragraph (c)(4) of this section, the term *GILTI inclusion amount* means, with respect to a United States shareholder and a U.S. shareholder inclusion year, the excess (if any) of—

(i) The shareholder's net CFC tested income (as defined in paragraph (c)(2) of this section) for the year, over

(ii) The shareholder's net deemed tangible income return (as defined in paragraph (c)(3) of this section) for the year.

(2) *Definition of net CFC tested income.*—The term *net CFC tested income* means, with respect to a United States shareholder and a U.S. shareholder inclusion year, the excess (if any) of—

(i) The aggregate of the shareholder's pro rata share of the tested income of each tested income CFC (as defined in §1.951A-2(b)(1)) for the year, over

(ii) The aggregate of the shareholder's pro rata share of the tested loss of each tested loss CFC (as defined in §1.951A-2(b)(2)) for the year.

(3) *Definition of net deemed tangible income return.*—(i) *In general.*—The term *net deemed tangible income return* means, with respect to a United States shareholder and a U.S. shareholder inclusion year, the excess (if any) of—

(A) The shareholder's deemed tangible income return (as defined in paragraph (c)(3)(ii) of this section) for the year, over

(B) The shareholder's specified interest expense (as defined in paragraph (c)(3)(iii) of this section) for the year.

(ii) *Definition of deemed tangible income return.*—The term *deemed tangible income return* means, with respect to a United States shareholder and a U.S. shareholder inclusion year, 10 percent of the aggregate of the shareholder's pro rata share of the qualified business asset investment (as defined in §1.951A-3(b)) of each tested income CFC for the year.

(iii) *Definition of specified interest expense.*—The term *specified interest expense* means, with respect to a United States shareholder and a U.S. shareholder inclusion year, the excess (if any) of—

(A) The aggregate of the shareholder's pro rata share of the tested interest expense (as defined in §1.951A-4(b)(1)) of each controlled foreign corporation for the year, over

(B) The aggregate of the shareholder's pro rata share of the tested interest income (as defined in §1.951A-4(b)(2)) of each controlled foreign corporation for the year.

(4) *Determination of GILTI inclusion amount for consolidated groups.*—For purposes of section 951A and the section 951A regulations, a member of a consolidated group (as defined in §1.1502-1(h)) determines its GILTI inclusion amount under the rules provided in §1.1502-51.

(d) *Determination of pro rata share.*—(1) *In general.*—For purposes of paragraph (c) of this section, each United States shareholder that owns section 958(a) stock in a controlled foreign corporation as of a CFC inclusion date (as defined in paragraph (e)(1) of this section) determines for a U.S. shareholder inclusion year that includes such CFC inclusion date its pro rata share (if any) of the controlled foreign corporation's tested income, tested loss, qualified business asset investment, tested interest expense, and tested interest income (each a *CFC tested item*), as applicable, for the CFC inclusion year (as defined in paragraph (e)(2) of this section). Except as otherwise provided in this paragraph (d), a United States shareholder's pro rata share of each CFC tested item is determined independently of its pro rata share of any other CFC tested item. Except as modified in this paragraph (d), a United States shareholder's pro rata share of any CFC tested item is determined under the rules of section 951(a)(2) and § 1.951-1(b) and (e) in the same manner as those provisions apply to subpart F income. Under section 951(a)(2) and § 1.951-1(b) and (e), as modified by this paragraph (d), a United States shareholder's pro rata share of any CFC tested item for a U.S. shareholder inclusion year is determined with respect to the section 958(a) stock of the controlled foreign corporation owned by the United States shareholder on the CFC inclusion date. A United States shareholder's pro rata share of any CFC tested item is translated into United States dollars using the average exchange rate for the CFC inclusion year of the controlled foreign corporation. Paragraphs (d)(2) through (5) of this section provide rules for determining a United States shareholder's pro rata share of each CFC tested item of a controlled foreign corporation.

(2) *Tested income.*—(i) *In general.*—Except as provided in paragraph (d)(2)(ii) of this section, a United States shareholder's pro rata share of the tested income of each tested income CFC for a U.S. shareholder inclusion year is determined under section 951(a)(2) and § 1.951-1(b) and (e), substituting "tested income" for "subpart F income" each place it appears, other than in § 1.951-1(e)(1)(ii)(B).

(ii) *Special rule for prior allocation of tested loss.*—In any case in which tested loss has been allocated to any class of stock in a prior CFC inclusion year under paragraph (d)(4)(iii) of this section, tested income is first allocated to each such class of stock in the order of its liquidation priority to the extent of the excess (if any) of the sum of the tested loss allocated to each such class of stock for each prior CFC inclusion year under paragraph (d)(4)(iii) of this section, over the sum of the tested income allocated to each such class of stock for each prior CFC inclusion year under this paragraph (d)(2)(ii). Paragraph (d)(2)(i) of this section applies for purposes of determining a United States shareholder's pro rata share of the remainder of the tested income, except that, for purposes of the hypothetical distribution of section 951(a)(2)(A) and § 1.951-1(b) and (e), the amount of current earnings and profits of the tested income CFC is reduced by the amount of tested income allocated under the first sentence of this paragraph (d)(2)(ii). For an example of the application of this paragraph (d)(2), see *Example 2* of paragraph (d)(4)(iv) of this section.

(3) *Qualified business asset investment.*—(i) *In general.*—Except as provided in paragraph (d)(3)(ii) of this section, a United States shareholder's pro rata share of the qualified business asset investment of a tested income CFC for a U.S. shareholder inclusion year bears the same ratio to the total qualified business asset investment of the tested income CFC for the CFC inclusion year as the United States shareholder's pro rata share of the tested income of the tested income CFC for the U.S. shareholder inclusion year bears to the total tested income of the tested income CFC for the CFC inclusion year.

(ii) *Special rule for preferred stock in case of excess QBAI.*—If a tested income CFC's qualified business asset investment for a CFC inclusion year exceeds 10 times its tested income for the CFC inclusion year (such excess, *excess QBAI*), a United States shareholder's pro rata share of the tested income CFC's qualified business asset investment is the sum of its pro rata share determined under paragraph (d)(3)(i) of this section without regard to the excess QBAI, plus its pro rata share determined under paragraph (d)(3)(i) of this section solely with respect to the excess QBAI and without regard to tested income allocated to any share of preferred stock of the tested income CFC under paragraph (d)(2) of this section.

(iii) *Examples.*—The following examples illustrate the application of paragraphs (d)(2) and (3) of this section. See also § 1.951-1(e)(7), *Example 6* (illustrating a United States shareholder's pro rata share of tested income).

(A) *Example 1*—(1) *Facts*. FS, a controlled foreign corporation, has outstanding 70 shares of common stock and 30 shares of 4% nonparticipating, cumulative preferred stock with a par value of $10x per share. P Corp, a domestic corporation and a United States shareholder of FS, owns all of the common shares. Individual A, a United States shareholder, owns all of the preferred shares. Both FS and P Corp use the calendar year as their taxable year. Individual A and P Corp are shareholders of FS for all of Year 4. At the beginning of Year 4, FS had no dividend arrearages with respect to its preferred stock. For Year 4, FS has $100x of earnings and profits, $120x of tested income, and no subpart F income within the meaning of section 952. FS also has $750x of qualified business asset investment for Year 4.

(2) *Analysis*—(i) *Determination of pro rata share of tested income.* For purposes of determining P Corp's pro rata share of FS's tested income under paragraph (d)(2) of this section, the amount of FS's current earnings and profits for purposes of the hypothetical distribution described in § 1.951-1(e)(1)(i) is $120x, the greater of its earnings and profits as determined under section 964 ($100x) or the sum of its subpart F income and tested income ($0 + $120x). Under paragraph (d)(2) of this section and § 1.951-1(e)(3), the amount of FS's current earnings and profits distributed in the hypothetical distribution is $12x (.04 x $10x x 30) with respect to Individual A's preferred shares and $108x ($120x - $12x) with respect to P Corp's common shares. Accordingly, under paragraph (d)(2) of this section and § 1.951-1(e)(1), Individual A's pro rata share of FS's tested income is $12x, and P Corp's pro rata share of FS's tested income is $108x for Year 4.

(ii) *Determination of pro rata share of qualified business asset investment.* The special rule of paragraph (d)(3)(ii) of this section does not apply because FS's qualified business asset investment of $750x does not exceed $1,200x, which is 10 times FS's tested income of $120x. Accordingly, under the general rule of paragraph (d)(3)(i) of this section, Individual A's and P Corp's pro rata share of FS's qualified business asset investment bears the same ratio to FS's total qualified business asset investment as Individual A's and P Corp's pro rata share, respectively, of FS's tested income bears to FS's total tested income. Thus, Individual A's pro rata share of FS's qualified business asset investment is $75x ($750x x $12x/$120x), and P Corp's pro rata share of FS's qualified business asset investment is $675x ($750x x $108x/$120x).

(B) *Example 2*—(1) *Facts*. The facts are the same as in paragraph (i) of *Example 1*, except that FS has $1,500x of qualified business asset investment for Year 4.

(2) *Analysis*. (i) *Determination of pro rata share of tested income*. The analysis and the result are the same as in paragraph (ii)(A) of *Example 1*.

(ii) *Determination of pro rata share of qualified business asset investment*. The special rule of paragraph (d)(3)(ii) of this section applies because FS's qualified business asset investment of $1,500x exceeds $1,200x, which is 10 times FS's tested income of $120x. Under paragraph (d)(3)(ii) of this section, Individual A's and P Corp's pro rata share of FS's qualified business asset investment is the sum of their pro rata share determined under paragraph (d)(3)(i) of this section without regard to the excess QBAI plus their pro rata share with respect to the excess QBAI but without regard to tested income allocated to preferred stock under paragraph (d)(2) of this section. Without regard to the excess QBAI of $300x, Individual A's pro rata share of FS's qualified business asset investment is $120x ($1,200x x $12x/$120x), and P Corp's pro rata share of FS's qualified business asset investment is $1,080x ($1,200x x $108x/$120x). Solely with respect to the excess QBAI and without regard to tested income allocated to the preferred stock under paragraph (d)(2) of this section, Individual A's pro rata share of FS's qualified business asset investment is $0 ($300x x $0/$108x), and P Corp's pro rata share of FS's qualified business asset investment is $300x ($300x x $108x/$108x). Thus, Individual A's pro rata share of FS's qualified business asset investment is $120x ($120x + $0), and P Corp's pro rata share of FS's qualified business asset investment is $1,380x ($1,080x + $300x).

(4) *Tested loss*.—(i) *In general*.—A United States shareholder's pro rata share of the tested loss of each tested loss CFC for a U.S. shareholder inclusion year is determined under section 951(a)(2) and § 1.951-1(b) and (e) with the following modifications—

(A) "Tested loss" is substituted for "subpart F income" each place it appears;

(B) For purposes of the hypothetical distribution described in section 951(a)(2)(A) and § 1.951-1(e)(1)(i), the amount of current earnings and profits of a controlled foreign corporation for a CFC inclusion year is treated as being equal to the tested loss of the tested loss CFC for the CFC inclusion year;

(C) Except as provided in paragraphs (d)(4)(ii) and (iii) of this section, the hypothetical distribution described in section 951(a)(2)(A) and § 1.951-1(e)(1)(i) is treated as made solely with respect to the common stock of the tested loss CFC; and

(D) The amount of the dividend received by any other person for purposes of section 951(a)(2)(B) and § 1.951-1(b)(1)(ii) is treated as being equal to the amount of the tested loss of the tested loss CFC for the CFC inclusion year (regardless of whether, or the extent to which, the other person actually receives a dividend).

(ii) *Special rule in case of accrued but unpaid dividends*.—If a tested loss CFC's earnings and profits that have accumulated since the issuance of preferred shares are reduced below the amount necessary to satisfy any accrued but unpaid dividends with respect to such preferred shares, then the amount by which the tested loss reduces the earnings below the amount necessary to satisfy the accrued but unpaid dividends is distributed in the hypothetical distribution described in section 951(a)(2)(A) and § 1.951-1(e)(1)(i) with respect to the preferred stock of the tested loss CFC and the remainder of the tested loss is distributed with respect to the common stock of the tested loss CFC.

(iii) *Special rule for stock with no liquidation value*.—If a tested loss CFC's common stock has a liquidation value of zero and there is at least one other class of equity with a liquidation preference relative to the common stock, then the tested loss is distributed in the hypothetical distribution described in section 951(a)(2)(A) and § 1.951-1(e)(1)(i) with respect to the most junior class of equity with a positive liquidation value to the extent of such liquidation value. Thereafter, tested loss is distributed with respect to the next most junior class of equity to the extent of its liquidation value and so on. All determinations of liquidation value are to be made as of the beginning of the CFC inclusion year of the tested loss CFC.

(iv) *Examples*.—The following examples illustrate the application of this paragraph (d)(4). See also § 1.951-1(e)(7), *Example 7* (illustrating a United States shareholder's pro rata share of subpart F income and tested loss).

(A) *Example 1*—(1) *Facts*. FS, a controlled foreign corporation, has outstanding 70 shares of common stock and 30 shares of 4% nonparticipating, cumulative preferred stock with a par value of $10x per share. P Corp, a domestic corporation and a United States shareholder of FS, owns all of the common shares. Individual A, a United States citizen and a United States shareholder, owns all of the preferred shares. FS, Individual A, and P Corp all use the calendar year as their taxable year. Individual A and P Corp are shareholders of FS for all of Year 5. At the beginning of Year 5, FS had earnings and profits of $120x, which accumulated after the issuance of the preferred stock. At the end of Year 5, the accrued but unpaid dividends with respect to the preferred stock are $36x. For Year 5, FS has a $100x tested loss, and no other items of income, gain, deduction or loss. At the end of Year 5, FS has earnings and profits of $20x.

(2) *Analysis*. FS is a tested loss CFC for Year 5. Before taking into account the tested loss in Year 5, FS had sufficient earnings and profits to satisfy the accrued but unpaid dividends of $36x. The amount of the reduction in earnings below the amount necessary to satisfy the accrued but unpaid dividends attributable to the tested loss is $16x ($36x - ($120x - $100x)). Accordingly, under paragraph (d)(4)(ii) of this sec-

tion, Individual A's pro rata share of the Year 5 tested loss is $16x, and P Corp's pro rata share of the tested loss is $84x ($100x - $16x).

(B) *Example* 2—(1) *Facts*. FS, a controlled foreign corporation, has outstanding 100 shares of common stock and 50 shares of 4% nonparticipating, cumulative preferred stock with a par value of $100x per share. P Corp, a domestic corporation and a United States shareholder of FS, owns all of the common shares. Individual A, a United States citizen and a United States shareholder, owns all of the preferred shares. FS, Individual A, and P Corp all use the calendar year as their taxable year. Individual A and P Corp are shareholders of FS for all of Year 1 and Year 2. At the beginning of Year 1, the common stock had no liquidation value and the preferred stock had a liquidation value of $5,000x and no accrued but unpaid dividends. In Year 1, FS has a tested loss of $1,000x and no other items of income, gain, deduction, or loss. In Year 2, FS has tested income of $3,000x and no other items of income, gain, deduction, or loss and paid no dividends. FS has earnings and profits of $3,000x for Year 2. At the end of Year 2, FS has accrued but unpaid dividends of $400x with respect to the preferred stock ($5000x x 0.04 for Year 1 and $5000x x 0.04 for Year 2).

(2) *Analysis*—(i) *Year 1*. FS is a tested loss CFC in Year 1. The common stock of FS has liquidation value of zero and the preferred stock has a liquidation preference relative to the common stock. The tested loss ($1,000x) does not exceed the liquidation value of the preferred stock ($5,000x). Accordingly, under paragraph (d)(4)(iii) of this section, the tested loss is distributed with respect to the preferred stock in the hypothetical distribution described in section 951(a)(2)(A) and § 1.951-1(e). Individual A's pro rata share of the tested loss is $1,000x, and P Corp's pro rata share of the tested loss is $0.

(ii) *Year 2*. FS is a tested income CFC in Year 2. Because $1,000x of tested loss was allocated to the preferred stock in Year 1 under paragraph (d)(4)(iii) of this section, the first $1,000x of tested income in Year 2 is allocated to the preferred stock under paragraph (d)(2)(ii) of this section. P Corp's and Individual A's pro rata shares of the remaining $2,000x of tested income are determined under the general rule of paragraph (d)(2)(i) of this section, except that for purposes of the hypothetical distribution the amount of FS's current earnings and profits is reduced by the tested income allocated under paragraph (d)(2)(ii) of this section to $2,000x ($3,000x - $1,000x). Accordingly, under paragraph (d)(2)(i) of this section, the amount of FS's current earnings and profits distributed in the hypothetical distribution with respect to Individual A's preferred stock is $400x ($400x of accrued but unpaid dividends) and with respect to P Corp's common stock is $1,600x ($2,000x - $400x). Individual A's pro rata share of the tested income is $1,400x ($1,000x + $400x), and P Corp's pro rata share of the tested income is $1,600x.

(5) *Tested interest expense*.—A United States shareholder's pro rata share of tested interest expense of a controlled foreign corporation for a U.S. shareholder inclusion year is equal to the amount by which the tested interest expense reduces the shareholder's pro rata share of tested income of the controlled foreign corporation for the U.S. shareholder inclusion year, increases the shareholder's pro rata share of tested loss of the controlled foreign corporation for the U.S. shareholder inclusion year, or both.

(6) *Tested interest income*.—A United States shareholder's pro rata share of tested interest income of a controlled foreign corporation for a U.S. shareholder inclusion year is equal to the amount by which the tested interest income increases the shareholder's pro rata share of tested income of the controlled foreign corporation for the U.S. shareholder inclusion year, reduces the shareholder's pro rata share of tested loss of the controlled foreign corporation for the U.S. shareholder inclusion year, or both.

(e) *Definitions*.—This paragraph (e) provides additional definitions that apply for purposes of the section 951A regulations. Other definitions relevant to the section 951A regulations are included in §§ 1.951A-2 through 1.951A-6.

(1) *CFC inclusion date*.—The term *CFC inclusion date* means the last day of a CFC inclusion year on which a foreign corporation is a controlled foreign corporation.

(2) *CFC inclusion year*.—The term *CFC inclusion year* means any taxable year of a foreign corporation beginning after December 31, 2017, at any time during which the corporation is a controlled foreign corporation.

(3) *Section 958(a) stock*.—The term *section 958(a) stock* means stock of a controlled foreign corporation owned (directly or indirectly) by a United States shareholder within the meaning of section 958(a).

(4) *U.S. shareholder inclusion year*.—The term *U.S. shareholder inclusion year* means a taxable year of a United States shareholder that includes a CFC inclusion date of a controlled foreign corporation of the United States shareholder. [Reg. § 1.951A-1.]

Par. 5. Section 1.951A-2 is added to read as follows:

§ 1.951A-2. Tested income and tested loss.—(a) *Scope*.—This section provides general rules for determining the tested income or tested loss of a controlled foreign corporation for purposes of determining a United States shareholder's net CFC tested income under § 1.951A-1(c)(2). Paragraph (b) of this section provides definitions related to tested income and tested loss. Paragraph (c) of this section provides rules for determining the gross tested income of a controlled foreign corporation and the deductions that are properly allocable to gross tested income.

(b) *Definitions related to tested income and tested loss*.—(1) *Tested income and tested income CFC*.—The term *tested income* means the excess (if any) of a controlled foreign corporation's gross tested income for a CFC inclusion year, over the allowable deductions (including taxes) properly allocable to the gross tested income for the CFC inclusion year (a controlled foreign corporation with tested income for a CFC inclusion year, a *tested income CFC*).

(2) *Tested loss and tested loss CFC*.—The term *tested loss* means the excess (if any) of a

controlled foreign corporation's allowable deductions (including taxes) properly allocable to gross tested income (or that would be allocable to gross tested income if there were gross tested income) for a CFC inclusion year, over the gross tested income of the controlled foreign corporation for the CFC inclusion year (a controlled foreign corporation without tested income for a CFC inclusion year, a *tested loss CFC*).

(c) *Rules relating to the determination of tested income and tested loss.*—(1) *Definition of gross tested income.*—The term *gross tested income* means the gross income of a controlled foreign corporation for a CFC inclusion year determined without regard to—

(i) Items of income described in section 952(b),

(ii) Gross income taken into account in determining the subpart F income of the corporation,

(iii) Gross income excluded from the foreign base company income (as defined in section 954) or the insurance income (as defined in section 953) of the corporation solely by reason of an election made under section 954(b)(4) and § 1.954-1(d)(5),

(iv) Dividends received by the corporation from related persons (as defined in section 954(d)(3)), and

(v) Foreign oil and gas extraction income (as defined in section 907(c)(1)) of the corporation.

(2) *Determination of gross income and allowable deductions.*—For purposes of determining tested income and tested loss, the gross income and allowable deductions of a controlled foreign corporation for a CFC inclusion year are determined under the rules of § 1.952-2 for determining the subpart F income of a controlled foreign corporation.

(3) *Allocation of deductions to gross tested income.*—Any deductions of a controlled foreign corporation allowable under paragraph (c)(2) of this section are allocated and apportioned to gross tested income under the principles of section 954(b)(5) and § 1.954-1(c), by treating gross tested income that falls within a single separate category (as defined in § 1.904-5(a)(1)) as a single item of gross income, in addition to the items set forth in § 1.954-1(c)(1)(iii).

(4) *Nonapplication of section 952(c).*—(i) *In general.*—The gross tested income and allowable deductions properly allocable to gross tested income of a controlled foreign corporation for a CFC inclusion year are determined without regard to the application of section 952(c).

(ii) *Example.*—The following example illustrates the application of this paragraph (c)(4).

(A) *Example*—(1) *Facts.* A Corp, a domestic corporation, owns 100% of the single class of stock of FS, a controlled foreign corporation. Both A Corp and FS use the calendar year as their taxable year. In Year 1, FS has foreign base company income of $100x, a loss in foreign oil and gas extraction income of $100x, and earnings and profits of $0. FS has no other income. In Year 2, FS has gross income of $100x and earnings and profits of $100x. Without regard to section 952(c)(2), in Year 2 FS has no income described in any of the categories of income excluded from gross tested income in paragraphs (c)(1)(i) through (v) of this section. FS has no allowable deductions properly allocable to gross tested income for Year 2.

(2) *Analysis.* As a result of the earnings and profits limitation of section 952(c)(1), FS has no subpart F income in Year 1, and A Corp has no inclusion with respect to FS under section 951(a)(1)(A). Under paragraph (c)(4)(i) of this section, the gross tested income of FS is determined without regard to section 952(c)(1). Therefore, in determining the gross tested income of FS in Year 1, the $100x foreign base company income of FS in Year 1 is excluded under paragraph (c)(1)(ii) of this section, and FS has no gross tested income in Year 1. In Year 2, under section 952(c)(2), FS's earnings and profits ($100x) in excess of its subpart F income ($0) are treated as subpart F income. Therefore, FS has subpart F income of $100x in Year 2, and A Corp has an inclusion of $100x with respect to FS under section 951(a)(1)(A). Under paragraph (c)(4)(i) of this section, the gross tested income of FS is determined without regard to section 952(c)(2). Accordingly, FS's income in Year 2 is not subpart F income described in paragraph (c)(1)(ii) of this section, and FS has $100x of gross tested income in Year 2.

(5) *Disregard of basis in property related to certain transfers during the disqualified period.*—(i) *In general.*—Any deduction or loss attributable to disqualified basis of any specified property allocated and apportioned to gross tested income under paragraph (c)(3) of this section is disregarded for purposes of determining tested income or tested loss of a controlled foreign corporation. For purposes of this paragraph (c)(5), in the case that a deduction or loss arises with respect to specified property with disqualified basis and adjusted basis other than disqualified basis, the deduction or loss is treated as attributable to the disqualified basis in the same proportion that the disqualified basis bears to the total adjusted basis of the property.

(ii) *Definition of specified property.*—The term *specified property* means property that is of a type with respect to which a deduction is allowable under section 167 or 197.

(iii) *Definition of disqualified basis.*—Solely for purposes of paragraph (c)(5)(i) of this section, the term *disqualified basis* has the meaning set forth in § 1.951A-3(h)(2)(ii) (including with respect to property owned by a partnership by reason of § 1.951A-3(g)(3)), except that, in applying the provisions of § 1.951A-3(h)(2) to determine the disqualified basis, the term "specified property" is substituted for "specified tangible property" and the term "controlled foreign corporation" is substituted for "tested income CFC" each place they appear.

(iv) *Example.*—(A) *Facts.* USP, a domestic corporation, owns all of the stock of CFC1 and CFC2, each a controlled foreign corporation. Both USP and CFC1 use the calendar year as their taxable year. CFC2 uses a taxable year ending November 30. On November 1, 2018, before the start of its first CFC inclusion year, CFC2 sells intangible property to CFC1 that is amortizable under section 197 in exchange for $100x of cash. The intangible property has a basis of $20x in the hands of CFC2, and CFC2 recognizes $80x of gain as a result of the sale ($100x - $20x). CFC2's gain is not subject to U.S. tax or taken into account in determining USP's inclusion under section 951(a)(1)(A).

(B) *Analysis*. The sale by CFC1 is a disqualified transfer (within the meaning of § 1.951A-3(h)(2)(ii)(C), as modified by paragraph (c)(5)(iii) of this section) because it is a transfer of specified property, CFC2 and CFC1 are related persons, and the transfer occurs during the disqualified period (within the meaning of § 1.951A-3(h)(2)(ii)(D)). The disqualified basis is $80x, the excess of CFC1's adjusted basis in the property immediately after the disqualified transfer ($100x), over the sum of CFC2's basis in the property immediately before the transfer ($20x) and the qualified gain amount (as defined in § 1.951A-3(h)(2)(ii)(B)) ($0). Accordingly, under paragraph (c)(5)(i) of this section, any deduction or loss attributable to the disqualified basis is disregarded for purposes of determining the tested income or tested loss of any CFC for any CFC inclusion year. [Reg. § 1.951A-2.]

Par. 6. Section 1.951A-3 is added to read as follows:

§ 1.951A-3. Qualified business asset investment.—(a) *Scope*.—This section provides general rules for determining the qualified business asset investment of a controlled foreign corporation for purposes of determining a United States shareholder's deemed tangible income return under § 1.951A-1(c)(3)(ii). Paragraph (b) of this section defines qualified business asset investment. Paragraph (c) of this section defines tangible property and specified tangible property. Paragraph (d) of this section provides rules and examples for determining the portion of property that is specified tangible property when the property is used in the production of both gross tested income and gross income that is not gross tested income. Paragraph (e) of this section provides rules for determining the adjusted basis of specified tangible property. Paragraph (f) of this section provides rules for determining qualified business asset investment of a tested income CFC with a short taxable year. Paragraph (g) of this section provides rules and examples for increasing the qualified business asset investment of a tested income CFC by reason of property owned through a partnership. Paragraph (h) of this section provides anti-abuse rules that disregard the basis of specified tangible property transferred in certain transactions when determining the qualified business asset investment of a tested income CFC.

(b) *Definition of qualified business asset investment*.—The term *qualified business asset investment* means the average of a tested income CFC's aggregate adjusted bases as of the close of each quarter of a CFC inclusion year in specified tangible property that is used in a trade or business of the tested income CFC and is of a type with respect to which a deduction is allowable under section 167. A tested loss CFC has no qualified business asset investment. See paragraph (f) of this section for rules relating to the qualified business asset investment of a tested income CFC with a short taxable year.

(c) *Specified tangible property*.—(1) *In general*.—The term *specified tangible property* means, subject to paragraph (d) of this section, tangible property used in the production of gross tested income. None of the tangible property of a tested loss CFC is specified tangible property.

(2) *Tangible property*.—The term *tangible property* means property for which the depreciation deduction provided by section 167(a) is eligible to be determined under section 168 without regard to section 168(f)(1), (2), or (5) and the date placed in service.

(d) *Dual use property*.—(1) *In general*.—In the case of tangible property of a tested income CFC that is used in both the production of gross tested income and the production of gross income that is not gross tested income in a CFC inclusion year, the portion of the adjusted basis in the property treated as adjusted basis in specified tangible property for the CFC inclusion year is determined by multiplying the average of the tested income CFC's adjusted basis in the property by the dual use ratio with respect to the property for the CFC inclusion year.

(2) *Dual use ratio*.—The term *dual use ratio* means, with respect to specified tangible property:

(i) In the case of specified tangible property that produces directly identifiable income for a CFC inclusion year, the ratio of the gross tested income produced by the property for the CFC inclusion year to the total amount of gross income produced by the property for the CFC inclusion year.

(ii) In the case of specified tangible property that does not produce directly identifiable income for a CFC inclusion year, the ratio of the gross tested income of the tested income CFC for the CFC inclusion year to the total amount of gross income of the tested income CFC for the CFC inclusion year.

(3) *Example*.—The following example illustrates the application of this paragraph (d).

(i) *Example*—(A) *Facts*. FS is a tested income CFC. FS owns a machine that only packages Product A. In Year 1, FS sells Product A to related and unrelated resellers and earns $1,000x of gross income. For Year 1, sales of Product A produce gross tested income of $750x and foreign base company sales income (as defined in section 954(d)) of $250x. The average adjusted basis of the machine for Year 1 in the hands of FS is $4,000x. FS also owns an office building for its administrative functions with an average adjusted basis for Year 1 of $10,000x. The office building does not produce directly identifiable income. FS has no other specified tangible property. For year 1, FS also earns $1,250x of gross tested income and $2,750x of foreign base company sales income from sales of Product B. Neither the machine nor the office building is used in the production of income related to Product B. For Year 1, FS's gross tested income is $2,000x and its total gross income is $5,000x.

(B) *Analysis*. The machine and office building are both property for which the depreciation deduction provided by section 167(a) is eligible to be determined under section 168. Therefore, under paragraph (c)(2) of this section, the machine and office building are tangible property. Under paragraph (d)(1) of this section, the portion of the basis in the machine treated as basis in specified tangible property is equal to FS's average basis in the machine for the year ($4,000x), multiplied by the dual use ratio under paragraph (d)(2)(i) of this section (75%), which is the proportion that the gross tested income produced by the property ($750x) bears to the total gross income produced by the property ($1,000x). Accordingly, $3,000x ($4,000x x 75%) of FS's adjusted basis in the machine is taken into account in determining the average of FS's aggregate adjusted bases described in paragraph (b) of this section. Under paragraph (d)(1) of this section, the portion of the basis in the office building treated as basis in specified tangible property is equal to FS's average basis in the office building for the year ($10,000x), multiplied by the dual use ratio under paragraph (d)(2)(ii) of this section (40%), which is the ratio of FS's gross tested income for Year 1 ($2,000x) to FS's total gross income for Year 1 ($5,000x). Accordingly, $4,000x ($10,000x x 40%) of FS's adjusted basis in the office building is taken into account in determining the average of FS's aggregate adjusted bases described in paragraph (b) of this section.

(e) *Determination of adjusted basis of specified tangible property.*—(1) *In general.*—The adjusted basis in specified tangible property is determined by using the alternative depreciation system under section 168(g), and by allocating the depreciation deduction with respect to such property for the CFC inclusion year ratably to each day during the period in the taxable year to which such depreciation relates.

(2) *Effect of change in law.*—The determination of adjusted basis for purposes of paragraph (b) of this section is made without regard to any provision of law enacted after December 22, 2017, unless such later enacted law specifically and directly amends the definition of qualified business asset investment under section 951A.

(3) *Specified tangible property placed in service before enactment of section 951A.*—The adjusted basis in property placed in service before December 22, 2017, is determined using the alternative depreciation system under section 168(g), as if this system had applied from the date that the property was placed in service.

(f) *Special rules for short taxable years.*—(1) *In general.*—In the case of a tested income CFC that has a CFC inclusion year that is less than twelve months (a *short taxable year*), the rules for determining the qualified business asset investment of the tested income CFC under this section are modified as provided in paragraphs (f)(2) and (3) of this section with respect to the CFC inclusion year.

(2) *Determination of quarter closes.*—For purposes of determining quarter closes, in determining the qualified business asset investment of a tested income CFC for a short taxable year, the quarters of the tested income CFC for purposes of this section are the full quarters beginning and ending within the short taxable year (if any), determining quarter length as if the tested income CFC did not have a short taxable year, plus one or more short quarters (if any).

(3) *Reduction of qualified business asset investment.*—The qualified business asset investment of a tested income CFC for a short taxable year is the sum of—

(i) The sum of the tested income CFC's aggregate adjusted bases in specified tangible property as of the close of each full quarter (if any) in the CFC inclusion year divided by four, plus

(ii) The tested income CFC's aggregate adjusted bases in specified tangible property as of the close of each short quarter (if any) in the CFC inclusion year multiplied by the sum of the number of days in each short quarter divided by 365.

(4) *Example.*—The following example illustrates the application of this paragraph (f).

(i) *Example*—(A) *Facts.* USP1, a domestic corporation, owns all of the stock of FS, a controlled foreign corporation. USP1 owns FS from the beginning of Year 1. On July 15, Year 1, USP1 sells FS to USP2, an unrelated person. USP2 makes a section 338(g) election with respect to the purchase of FS, as a result of which FS's taxable year is treated as ending on July 15. USP1, USP2, and FS all use the calendar year as their taxable year. FS's aggregate adjusted bases in specified tangible property are $250x as of March 31, $300x as of June 30, $275x as of July 15, $500x as of September 30, and $450x as of December 31.

(B) *Analysis*—(1) *Determination of short taxable years and quarters.* FS has two short taxable years in Year 1. The first short taxable year is from January 1 to July 15, with two full quarters (January 1-March 31 and April 1-June 30) and one short quarter (July 1-July 15). The second taxable year is from July 16 to December 31, with one short quarter (July 16-September 30) and one full quarter (October 1-December 31).

(2) *Calculation of qualified business asset investment for the first short taxable year.* Under paragraph (f)(2) of this section, for the first short taxable year in Year 1, FS has three quarter closes (March 31, June 30, and July 15). Under paragraph (f)(3) of this section, the qualified business asset investment of FS for the first short taxable year is $148.80x, the sum of $137.50x (($250x + $300x)/4) attributable to the two full quarters and $11.30x ($275x x 15/365) attributable to the short quarter.

(3) *Calculation of qualified business asset investment for the second short taxable year.* Under paragraph (f)(2) of this section, for the second short taxable year in Year 1, FS has two quarter closes (September 30 and December 31). Under paragraph (f)(3) of this section, the qualified business asset investment of FS for the second short taxable year is $217.98x, the sum of $112.50x ($450x/4) attributable to the one full quarter and $105.48x ($500x x 77/365) attributable to the short quarter.

(g) *Partnership property.*—(1) *In general.*—For purposes of paragraph (b) of this section, if a tested income CFC holds an interest in one or more partnerships as of the close of the CFC inclusion year, the qualified business asset investment of the tested income CFC for the CFC inclusion year is increased by the sum of the tested income CFC's partnership QBAI with respect to each partnership for the CFC inclusion year. A tested loss CFC has no partnership QBAI for a CFC inclusion year.

(2) *Definitions related to partnership QBAI.*—(i) *In general.*—The term *partnership QBAI* means the sum of the tested income CFC's share of the partnership's adjusted basis in partnership specified tangible property as of the close of a partnership taxable year that ends with or within a CFC inclusion year. A tested income CFC's share of the partnership's adjusted basis in partnership specified tangible property is de-

termined separately with respect to each partnership specified tangible property of the partnership by multiplying the partnership's adjusted basis in the property by the partnership QBAI ratio with respect to the property. If the partnership's taxable year is less than twelve months, the principles of paragraph (f) of this section apply in determining a tested income CFC's partnership QBAI with respect to the partnership.

(ii) *Partnership QBAI ratio.*—The term *partnership QBAI ratio* means, with respect to partnership specified tangible property:

(A) In the case of partnership specified tangible property that produces directly identifiable income for a partnership taxable year, the ratio of the tested income CFC's distributive share of the gross income produced by the property for the partnership taxable year that is included in the gross tested income of the tested income CFC for the CFC inclusion year to the total gross income produced by the property for the partnership taxable year.

(B) In the case of partnership specified tangible property that does not produce directly identifiable income for a partnership taxable year, the ratio of the tested income CFC's distributive share of the gross income of the partnership for the partnership taxable year that is included in the gross tested income of the tested income CFC for the CFC inclusion year to the total amount of gross income of the partnership for the partnership taxable year.

(iii) *Partnership specified tangible property.*—The term *partnership specified tangible property* means tangible property (as defined in paragraph (c)(2) of this section) of a partnership that is—

(A) Used in the trade or business of the partnership,

(B) Of a type with respect to which a deduction is allowable under section 167, and

(C) Used in the production of tested income.

(3) *Determination of adjusted basis.*—For purposes of this paragraph (g), a partnership's adjusted basis in partnership specified tangible property is determined based on the average of the partnership's adjusted basis in the property as of the close of each quarter in the partnership taxable year. The principles of paragraphs (e) and (h) of this section apply for purposes of determining a partnership's adjusted basis in partnership specified tangible property and the portion of such adjusted basis taken into account in determining a tested income CFC's partnership QBAI.

(4) *Examples.*—The following examples illustrate the rules of this paragraph (g).

(i) *Example 1*—(A) *Facts.* FC, a tested income CFC, is a partner in PRS. Both FC and PRS use the calendar year as their taxable year. PRS owns two assets, Asset A and Asset B, both of which are tangible property used in PRS's trade or business that it depreciates under section 168. The average of PRS's adjusted basis as of the close of each quarter of PRS's taxable year in Asset A is $100x and the average of PRS's adjusted basis as of the end of each quarter of PRS's taxable year in Asset B is $50x. Asset A produces $10x of directly identifiable gross income in Year 1, and Asset B produces $50x of directly identifiable gross income in Year 1. FC's distributive share of the gross income from Asset A is $8x and its distributive share of the gross income from Asset B is $10x. FC's entire distributive share of income from Asset A and Asset B is included in FC's gross tested income for Year 1. PRS partners' distributive shares satisfy the requirements of section 704.

(B) *Analysis.* Each of Asset A and Asset B is partnership specified tangible property because each is tangible property, of a type with respect to which a deduction is allowable under section 167, used in PRS's trade or business, and used in the production of tested income. FC's partnership QBAI ratio for Asset A is 80%, the ratio of FC's distributive share of the gross income from Asset A for Year 1 that is included in FC's gross tested income ($8x) to the total gross income produced by Asset A for Year 1 ($10x). FC's partnership QBAI ratio for Asset B is 20%, the ratio of FC's distributive share of the gross income from Asset B for Year 1 that is included in FC's gross tested income ($10x) to the total gross income produced by Asset B for Year 1 ($50x). FC's share of the average of PRS's adjusted basis of Asset A is $80x, PRS's adjusted basis in Asset A of $100x multiplied by FC's partnership QBAI ratio for Asset A of 80%. FC's share of the average of PRS's adjusted basis of Asset B is $10x, PRS's adjusted basis in Asset B of $50x multiplied by FC's partnership QBAI ratio for Asset B of 20%. Therefore, FC's partnership QBAI with respect to PRS is $90x ($80x + $10x). Accordingly, under paragraph (g)(1) of this section, FC increases its qualified business asset investment for Year 1 by $90x.

(ii) *Example 2*—(A) *Facts.* FC, a tested income CFC, owns a 50% interest in PRS. PRS owns Asset A, which is specified tangible property. The average of PRS's adjusted basis as of the close of each quarter of PRS's taxable year in Asset A is $100x. FC has the same taxable year as PRS. Asset A produces $20x of directly identifiable gross income in Year 1, and PRS has $22x of expenses in Year 1 that are properly allocable to such income. Therefore, FC's allocation of net income or loss from PRS is $1x loss, which is comprised of FC's distributive share of the gross income from Asset A of $10x, all of which is included in FC's gross tested income for Year 1, and FC's distributive share of the expenses related to Asset A of $11x, all of which is taken into account in determining its tested income under § 1.951-2(c). PRS has no other income or loss in Year 1. FC also has $8x of gross tested income from other sources in Year 1, and no deductions properly allocable to such income. PRS partners' distributive shares satisfy the requirements of section 704.

(B) *Analysis.* FC's partnership QBAI ratio for Asset A is 50%, the ratio of FC's distributive share of the gross income from Asset A for Year 1 that is included in FC's gross tested income ($10x) to the total gross income produced by Asset A for Year 1 ($20x). FC's share of the average of PRS's adjusted basis in Asset A is $50x, PRS's adjusted basis in Asset A of $100x multiplied by FC's partnership QBAI ratio for Asset A of 50%. FC increases its qualified business asset investment by $50x, notwithstanding that FC would not be a tested income CFC but for its $8x of gross tested income from other sources.

(h) *Anti-abuse rules for certain transfers of property.*—(1) *Disregard of basis in specified tangible property held temporarily.*—If a tested income CFC (*acquiring CFC*) acquires specified tangible property (as defined in paragraph (c)(1) of this section) with a principal purpose of reducing the GILTI inclusion amount of a United States shareholder for any U.S. shareholder inclusion year, and the tested income CFC holds the property temporarily but over at least the close of one quarter, the specified tangible property is disregarded in determining the acquiring CFC's average adjusted basis in specified tangible property for purposes of determining the acquiring CFC's qualified business asset investment for any CFC inclusion year during which the tested income CFC held the property. For purposes of this paragraph (h)(1), specified tangible property held by the tested income CFC for less than a twelve month period that includes at least the close of one quarter during the taxable year of a tested income CFC is treated as temporarily held and acquired with a principal purpose of reducing the GILTI inclusion amount of a United States shareholder for a U.S. shareholder inclusion year if such acquisition would, but for this paragraph (h)(1), reduce the GILTI inclusion amount of a United States shareholder for a U.S. shareholder inclusion year.

(2) *Disregard of basis in specified tangible property related to transfers during the disqualified period.*—(i) *In general.*—For purposes of determining the qualified business asset investment of a tested income CFC for a CFC inclusion year, in applying the alternative depreciation system under section 168(g) to determine the tested income CFC's adjusted basis in specified tangible property, any disqualified basis with respect to the specified tangible property is not taken into account.

(ii) *Determination of disqualified basis.*—(A) *In general.*—The term *disqualified basis* means, with respect to specified tangible property, the excess (if any) of the property's adjusted basis immediately after a disqualified transfer, over the sum of the property's adjusted basis immediately before the disqualified transfer and the qualified gain amount with respect to the disqualified transfer. Disqualified basis may be reduced or eliminated through depreciation, amortization, sales or exchanges, section 362(e), and other methods. In such circumstances, in the case of specified tangible property with disqualified basis and adjusted basis other than disqualified basis, the disqualified basis is reduced or eliminated in the same proportion that the disqualified basis bears to the total adjusted basis of the property.

(B) *Definition of qualified gain amount.*—The term *qualified gain amount* means, with respect to a disqualified transfer, the sum of the following amounts:

(1) The amount of gain recognized by a controlled foreign corporation (*transferor CFC*) on the disqualified transfer of the specified tangible property that is subject to U.S. federal income tax under section 882 (except to the extent the gain is subject to a reduced rate of tax, or is exempt from tax, pursuant to an applicable treaty obligation of the United States); and

(2) Any United States shareholder's pro rata share of the gain recognized by the transferor CFC on the disqualified transfer of the specified tangible property (determined without regard to properly allocable deductions) taken into account in determining the United States shareholder's inclusion under section 951(a)(1)(A), excluding any amount that is described in paragraph (h)(2)(ii)(B)(*1*) of this section.

(C) *Definition of disqualified transfer.*—The term *disqualified transfer* means a transfer of specified tangible property during a transferor CFC's disqualified period by the transferor CFC to a related person in which gain was recognized, in whole or in part, by the transferor CFC, regardless of whether the property was specified tangible property in the hands of the transferor CFC. For purposes of the preceding sentence, a transfer includes any disposition, sale or exchange, contribution, or distribution of the specified tangible property, and includes an indirect transfer (for example, a transfer of an interest in a partnership is treated as a transfer of the assets of the partnership and transfer by or to a partnership is treated as a transfer by or to its partners).

(D) *Definition of disqualified period.*—The term *disqualified period* means, with respect to a transferor CFC, the period beginning on January 1, 2018, and ending as of the close of the transferor CFC's last taxable year that is not a CFC inclusion year. A transferor CFC that has a CFC inclusion year beginning January 1, 2018, has no disqualified period.

(E) *Related person.*—For purposes of this paragraph (h)(2), a person is related to a controlled foreign corporation if the person bears a relationship to the controlled foreign corporation described in section 267(b) or 707(b) immediately before or immediately after the transfer.

(iii) *Examples.*—The following examples illustrate the application of this paragraph (h)(2).

(A) *Example 1*—(1) *Facts.* USP, a domestic corporation, owns all of the stock of CFC1 and CFC2, each a controlled foreign corporation. Both USP and CFC1 use the calendar year as their taxable year. CFC2 uses a taxable year ending November 30. On November 1, 2018, before the start of its first CFC inclusion year, CFC2 sells specified tangible property that has a basis of $10x in the hands of CFC2 to CFC1 in exchange for $100x of cash. CFC2 recognizes $90x of gain as a result of the sale ($100x - $10x), $30x of which is foreign base company income (within the meaning of section 954). USP includes in gross income under section 951(a)(1)(A) its pro rata share of the subpart F income of $30x. CFC2's gain is not otherwise subject to U.S. tax or taken into account in determining USP's inclusion under section 951(a)(1)(A).

(2) *Analysis.* The transfer is a disqualified transfer because it is a transfer of specified tangible property; CFC1 and CFC2 are related persons; and the transfer occurs during the disqualified period, the period that begins on January 1, 2018, and ends the last day before the first CFC inclusion year of CFC2 (November 30, 2018). The disqualified basis is $60x, the excess of CFC1's adjusted basis in the property immediately after the disqualified transfer ($100x), over the sum of CFC2's basis in the property immediately before the transfer ($10x) and USP's pro rata share of the gain recognized by CFC1 on the

transfer of the property taken into account by USP under section 951(a)(1)(A) ($30x). Accordingly, under paragraph (h)(2)(i) of this section, for purposes of determining the qualified business asset investment of any tested income CFC for any CFC inclusion year, in applying section 168(g) to determine the CFC's basis in the specified tangible property, the $60x disqualified basis of the property is not taken into account.

(B) *Example 2*—(1) *Facts*. The facts are the same as in paragraph (i) of *Example 1*, except that CFC2 uses the calendar year as its taxable year.

(2) *Analysis*. Because CFC2 has a taxable year beginning January 1, 2018, CFC2 has no disqualified period. Accordingly, the property was not transferred during a disqualified period of CFC2, and there is no disqualified basis with respect to the property. [Reg. § 1.951A-3.]

Par. 7. Section 1.951A-4 is added to read as follows:

§ 1.951A-4. Tested interest expense and tested interest income.—(a) *Scope*.—This section provides general rules for determining the tested interest expense and tested interest income of a controlled foreign corporation for purposes of determining a United States shareholder's specified interest expense under § 1.951A-1(c)(3)(iii). Paragraph (b) of this section provides the definitions related to tested interest expense and tested interest income. Paragraph (c) of this section provides examples illustrating these definitions and the application of § 1.951A-1(c)(3)(iii). The amount of specified interest expense determined under § 1.951A-1(c)(3)(iii) and this section is the amount of interest expense described in section 951A(b)(2)(B).

(b) *Definitions related to specified interest expense*.—(1) *Tested interest expense*.—(i) *In general*.—The term *tested interest expense* means interest expense paid or accrued by a controlled foreign corporation taken into account in determining the tested income or tested loss of the controlled foreign corporation for the CFC inclusion year under § 1.951A-2(c), reduced by the qualified interest expense of the controlled foreign corporation.

(ii) *Interest expense*.—The term *interest expense* means any expense or loss that is treated as interest expense by reason of the Internal Revenue Code or the regulations thereunder, and any other expense or loss incurred in a transaction or series of integrated or related transactions in which the use of funds is secured for a period of time if such expense or loss is predominately incurred in consideration of the time value of money.

(iii) *Qualified interest expense*.—The term *qualified interest expense* means, with respect to a qualified CFC, the interest expense paid or accrued by the qualified CFC taken into account in determining the tested income or tested loss of the qualified CFC for the CFC inclusion year, multiplied by the fraction (not to exceed one) described in paragraph (b)(1)(iii)(A) of this section, and then reduced (but not to less than zero) by the amount described in paragraph (b)(1)(iii)(B) of this section.

(A) The numerator of the fraction described in this paragraph (b)(1)(iii)(A) is the average of the aggregate adjusted bases as of the close of each quarter of obligations or financial instruments held by the qualified CFC that give rise to income excluded from foreign personal holding company income (as defined in section 954(c)(1)) by reason of section 954(h) or (i), and the denominator is the average of the aggregate adjusted bases as of the close of each quarter of all assets held by the qualified CFC. For purposes of this paragraph (b)(1)(iii)(A), the basis of the stock of another qualified CFC held by a qualified CFC is treated as basis of an obligation or financial instrument giving rise to income excluded from foreign personal holding company income by reason of section 954(h) or (i) in an amount equal to the basis of the stock multiplied by the fraction described in this paragraph (b)(1)(iii)(A) determined with respect to the assets of such other qualified CFC.

(B) The amount described in this paragraph (b)(1)(iii)(B) is the amount of interest income of the qualified CFC for the CFC inclusion year that is excluded from foreign personal holding company income (as defined in section 954(c)(1)) by reason of section 954(c)(3) or (6).

(iv) *Qualified CFC*.—The term *qualified CFC* means an eligible controlled foreign corporation (within the meaning of section 954(h)(2)) or a qualifying insurance company (within the meaning of section 953(e)(3)).

(2) *Tested interest income*.—(i) *In general*.—The term *tested interest income* means interest income included in the gross tested income of a controlled foreign corporation for the CFC inclusion year, reduced by qualified interest income of the controlled foreign corporation.

(ii) *Interest income*.—The term *interest income* means any income or gain that is treated as interest income by reason of the Internal Revenue Code or the regulations thereunder, and any other income or gain recognized in a transaction or series of integrated or related transactions in which the forbearance of funds is secured for a period of time if such income or gain is predominately derived from consideration of the time value of money.

(iii) *Qualified interest income*.—The term *qualified interest income* means, with respect to a qualified CFC, interest income of the qualified CFC included in the gross tested income of the qualified CFC for the CFC inclusion year that is excluded from foreign personal holding company income (as defined in section 954(c)(1)) by reason of section 954(h) or (i).

(c) *Examples*.—The following examples illustrate the application of this section.

(1) *Example 1: wholly-owned CFCs*—(i) *Facts*. A Corp, a domestic corporation, owns 100% of the single class of stock of each of FS1 and FS2, each a controlled foreign corporation. A Corp, FS1, and FS2 all use the calendar year as their taxable year. In Year 1, FS1 pays $100x of interest to FS2. Also, in Year 1, FS2 pays $100x of interest to a bank that is not related to A Corp, FS1, or FS2. The interest paid by each of FS1 and FS2 is taken into account in determining the tested income and tested loss of FS1 and FS2 under § 1.951A-2(c), and the interest received by FS2 is not foreign personal holding company income (as defined in section 954(c)(1)) by reason of section 954(c)(6) and thus is included in gross

tested income. For Year 1, taking into account interest income and expense, FS1 has $500x of tested income and FS2 has $400x of tested loss. Neither FS1 nor FS2 is a qualified CFC.

(ii) *Analysis*—(A) *CFC-level determination; tested interest expense and tested interest income.* FS1 has $100x of tested interest expense for Year 1. FS2 has $100x of tested interest expense and $100x of tested interest income for Year 1.

(B) *United States shareholder-level determination; pro rata share and specified interest expense.* Under § 1.951A-1(d)(5) and (6), A Corp's pro rata share of FS1's tested interest expense is $100x, its pro rata share of FS2's tested interest expense is $100x, and its pro rata share of FS2's tested interest income is $100x. For Year 1, A Corp's aggregate pro rata share of tested interest expense is $200x and its aggregate pro rata share of tested interest income is $100x. Accordingly, under § 1.951A-1(c)(3)(iii), A Corp's specified interest expense is $100x ($200x - $100x) for Year 1.

(2) *Example 2: less than wholly-owned CFCs*—(i) *Facts.* The facts are the same as in paragraph (i) of *Example 1,* except that A Corp owns 50% of the single class of stock of FS1 and 80% of the single class of stock of FS2.

(ii) *Analysis.* (A) *CFC-level determination; tested interest expense and tested interest income.* The analysis is the same as in paragraph (ii)(A) of *Example 1.*

(B) *United States shareholder-level determination; pro rata share and specified interest expense.* Under § 1.951A-1(d)(5) and (6), A Corp's pro rata share of FS1's tested interest expense is $50x ($100x x 0.50), its pro rata share of FS2's tested interest expense is $80x ($100x x 0.80), and its pro rata share of FS2's tested interest income is $80x ($100x x 0.80). For Year 1, A Corp's aggregate pro rata share of the tested interest expense is $130x and its aggregate pro rata share of the tested interest income is $80x. Accordingly, under § 1.951A-1(c)(3)(iii), A Corp's specified interest expense is $50x ($130x - $80x) for Year 1.

(3) *Example 3: qualified CFC*—(i) *Facts.* B Corp, a domestic corporation, owns 100% of the single class of stock of each of FS1 and FS2, each a controlled foreign corporation. B Corp, FS1, and FS2 all use the calendar year as their taxable year. FS2 is an eligible controlled foreign corporation within the meaning of section 954(h)(2). In Year 1, FS1 pays $100x of interest to FS2, which interest income is excluded from the foreign personal holding company income (as defined in section 954(c)(1)) of FS2 by reason of section 954(c)(6). Also, in Year 1, FS2 pays $250x of interest to a bank, and receives an additional $300x of interest from customers that are not related to FS2, which interest income is excluded from foreign personal holding company income by reason of section 954(h). The interest paid by each of FS1 and FS2 is taken into account in determining the tested income and tested loss of FS1 and FS2, and the interest received by FS2 is included in gross tested income. FS1 is not a qualified CFC. FS2 does not own stock in any qualified CFC. FS2's average adjusted bases in obligations or financial instruments that give rise to income excluded from foreign personal holding company income by reason of section 954(h) is $8,000x, and FS2's average adjusted bases in all its assets is $10,000x.

(ii) *Analysis*—(A) *CFC-level determination; tested interest expense and tested interest income.* FS1 has $100x of tested interest expense for Year 1. FS2 is a qualified CFC because it is an eligible controlled foreign corporation within the meaning of section 954(h)(2). As a result, in determining the tested interest income and tested interest expense of FS2, the qualified interest income and qualified interest expense of FS2 are excluded. FS2 has qualified interest income of $300x, the amount of FS2's interest income that is excluded from foreign personal holding company income by reason of section 954(h). In addition, FS2 has qualified interest expense of $100x, the amount of FS2's interest expense taken into account in determining FS2's tested income or tested loss under § 1.951A-2(c) ($250x), multiplied by a fraction, the numerator of which is FS2's average adjusted bases in obligations or financial instruments that give rise to income excluded from foreign personal holding company income by reason of section 954(h) ($8,000x), and the denominator of which is F2's average adjusted bases in all its assets ($10,000x), and then reduced by the amount of the interest income received from FS1 excluded from foreign personal holding company income by reason of section 954(c)(6) ($100x). Therefore, for Year 1, FS2 has tested interest income of $100x ($400x - $300x) and tested interest expense of $150x ($250x - $100x).

(B) *United States shareholder-level determination; pro rata share and specified interest expense.* Under § 1.951A-1(d)(5) and (6), B Corp's pro rata share of FS1's tested interest expense is $100x, its pro rata share of FS2's tested interest expense is $150x, and its pro rata share of FS2's tested interest income is $100x. For Year 1, B Corp's aggregate pro rata share of tested interest expense is $250x ($100x + $150x) and its aggregate pro rata share of tested interest income is $100x ($0 + $100x). Accordingly, under § 1.951A-1(c)(3)(iii), B Corp's specified interest expense is $150x ($250x - $100x) for Year 1. [Reg. § 1.951A-4.]

Par. 8. Section 1.951A-5 is added to read as follows:

§ 1.951A-5. Domestic partnerships and their partners.—(a) *Scope.*—This section provides rules regarding the application of section 951A and the section 951A regulations to domestic partnerships that own (within the meaning of section 958(a)) stock in one or more controlled foreign corporations and to partners of such domestic partnerships, including United States persons (within the meaning of section 957(c)). Paragraph (b) of this section provides rules for the determination of the GILTI inclusion amount of a domestic partnership and the distributive share of such amount of a partner that is not a United States shareholder with respect to one or more controlled foreign corporations owned by the domestic partnership. Paragraph (c) of this section provides rules for the determination of the GILTI inclusion amount of a partner that is a United States shareholder with respect to one or more controlled foreign corporations owned by a domestic partnership. Paragraph (d) of this section provides rules for tiered domestic partnerships. Paragraph (e) of this section provides the definitions of CFC tested item, partnership CFC,

U.S. shareholder partner, and U.S. shareholder partnership. Paragraph (f) of this section requires a domestic partnership to provide certain information to each partner necessary for the partner to determine its GILTI inclusion amount or its distributive share of the partnership's GILTI inclusion amount. Paragraph (g) of this section provides examples illustrating the rules of this section. For rules regarding the treatment of certain controlled domestic partnerships owned through one or more foreign corporations as foreign partnerships for purposes of sections 951 through 964, including section 951A and the section 951A regulations, see § 1.951-1(h).

(b) *In general.*—(1) *Determination of GILTI inclusion amount of a U.S. shareholder partnership.*—A U.S. shareholder partnership determines its GILTI inclusion amount for its U.S. shareholder inclusion year under the general rules applicable to United States shareholders in section 951A and the section 951A regulations.

(2) *Determination of distributive share of U.S. shareholder partnership's GILTI inclusion amount of a partner other than a U.S. shareholder partner.*—Each partner of a U.S. shareholder partnership that is not a U.S. shareholder partner takes into account its distributive share of the U.S. shareholder partnership's GILTI inclusion amount (if any) for the U.S. shareholder inclusion year in accordance with section 702 and § 1.702-1(a)(8)(ii).

(c) *Determination of GILTI inclusion amount of a U.S. shareholder partner.*—For purposes of section 951A and the section 951A regulations, section 958(a) stock of a partnership CFC owned by a U.S. shareholder partnership is treated as section 958(a) stock owned proportionately by each U.S. shareholder partner that is a United States shareholder of the partnership CFC in the same manner as if the U.S. shareholder partnership were a foreign partnership under section 958(a)(2) and § 1.958-1(b). Accordingly, for purposes of determining a U.S. shareholder partner's GILTI inclusion amount, the U.S. shareholder partner determines its pro rata share of any CFC tested item of a partnership CFC based on the section 958(a) stock owned by the U.S. shareholder partner by reason of this paragraph (c). In addition, a U.S. shareholder partner's distributive share of the GILTI inclusion amount of a U.S. shareholder partnership is determined without regard to the partnership's pro rata share of any CFC tested item of a partnership CFC with respect to which the U.S. shareholder partner is a United States shareholder.

(d) *Tiered U.S. shareholder partnerships.*—In the case of tiered U.S. shareholder partnerships, section 958(a) stock of a partnership CFC treated as owned under paragraph (c) of this section by a U.S. shareholder partner that is also a U.S. shareholder partnership is treated as section 958(a) stock owned by the U.S. shareholder partnership for purposes of applying paragraph (c) of this section to a U.S. shareholder partner of such U.S. shareholder partnership.

(e) *Definitions.*—The following definitions apply for purposes of this section:

(1) *CFC tested item.*—The term *CFC tested item* has the meaning set forth in § 1.951A-1(d)(1).

(2) *Partnership CFC.*—The term *partnership CFC* means, with respect to a U.S. shareholder partnership, a controlled foreign corporation stock of which is owned (within the meaning of section 958(a)) by the U.S. shareholder partnership.

(3) *U.S. shareholder partner.*—The term *U.S. shareholder partner* means, with respect to a U.S. shareholder partnership and a partnership CFC of the U.S. shareholder partnership, a United States person that is a partner in the U.S. shareholder partnership and that is also a United States shareholder (as defined in section 951(b)) of the partnership CFC.

(4) *U.S. shareholder partnership.*—The term *U.S. shareholder partnership* means a domestic partnership (within the meaning of section 7701(a)(4)) that is a United States shareholder of one or more controlled foreign corporations.

(f) *Reporting requirement.*—A U.S. shareholder partnership must furnish to each partner on or with such partner's Schedule K-1 (Form 1065 or successor form) for each U.S. shareholder inclusion year of the partnership the partner's distributive share of the partnership's GILTI inclusion amount (if any) and, with respect to a U.S. shareholder partner, the partner's proportionate share of the partnership's pro rata share (if any) of each CFC tested item of each partnership CFC of the partnership and any other information required in the form or instructions. See section 6031(b).

(g) *Examples.*—The following examples illustrate the rules of this section. None of the persons in the following examples own an interest in any controlled foreign corporation other than as described.

(1) *Example 1: domestic partnership with partners that are not United States shareholders.* (i) *Facts.* Eleven U.S. citizens ("individuals") each own a 9% interest of PRS, a domestic partnership. The remaining 1% interest of PRS is owned by X Corp, a domestic corporation. None of the individuals or X Corp are related. PRS owns 100% of the single class of stock of FC, a controlled foreign corporation. The individuals, X Corp, PRS, and FC all use the calendar year as their taxable year. In Year 1, FC has $130x of tested income and $50x of qualified business asset investment.

(ii) *Analysis*—(A) *Partnership-level calculation.* PRS is a U.S. shareholder partnership with respect to FC. Under paragraph (b)(1) of this section, PRS determines its GILTI inclusion amount for Year 1. PRS's pro rata share of FC's tested income is $130x. PRS's pro rata share of FC's qualified business asset investment is $50x. PRS's net CFC tested income is $130x. PRS's net deemed tangible income return is $5x ($50x x 0.10). PRS's GILTI inclusion amount for Year 1 is $125x ($130x - $5x).

(B) *Partner-level calculation.* Neither X Corp nor the individuals are U.S. shareholder partners with respect to FC. Accordingly, under paragraph (b)(2) of this section, each of the individuals and X Corp includes its distributive share of PRS's GILTI inclusion amount ($11.25x each for the individuals and $1.25x for X Corp) in gross income for Year 1.

(2) *Example 2: domestic partnership with partners that are United States shareholders; multiple partnership CFCs.* (i) *Facts.* X Corp and Y Corp are domestic corporations that own 40% and 60%, respectively, of PRS, a domestic partnership. PRS owns 100% of the single class of stock of FC1 and of FC2, each a controlled foreign corporation. X Corp, Y Corp, PRS, FC1, and FC2 all use the

calendar year as their taxable year. In Year 1, FC1 has $130x of tested income and $50x of qualified business asset investment, and FC2 has $30x of tested loss.

(ii) *Analysis*—(A) *Partnership-level calculation.* PRS is a U.S. shareholder partnership with respect to each of FC1 and FC2. Under paragraph (b)(1) of this section, PRS determines its GILTI inclusion amount for Year 1. PRS's pro rata share of FC1's tested income is $130x and of FC2's tested loss is $30x. PRS's pro rata share of FC1's qualified business asset investment is $50x. PRS's net CFC tested income is $100x ($130x – $30x). PRS's net deemed tangible income return is $5x ($50x x 0.10). PRS's GILTI inclusion amount for Year 1 is $95x ($100x - $5x).

(B) *Partner-level calculation.* X Corp and Y Corp are U.S. shareholder partners with respect to FC1 and FC2. Accordingly, under paragraph (c) of this section, X Corp and Y Corp are treated as owning section 958(a) stock of FC1 and FC2 proportionately as if PRS were a foreign partnership. Thus, X Corp's pro rata share of FC1's tested income is $52x ($130x x 0.40), and its pro rata share of FC2's tested loss is $12x ($30x x 0.40). X Corp's pro rata share of FC1's qualified business asset investment is $20x ($50x x 0.40). Accordingly, X Corp's net CFC tested income is $40x ($52x - $12x), and its net deemed tangible income return is $2x ($20x x 0.10). X Corp's GILTI inclusion amount for Year 1 is $38x ($40x - $2x). Y Corp's pro rata share of FC1's tested income is $78x ($130x x 0.60), and its pro rata share of FC2's tested loss is $18x ($30x x 0.60). Y Corp's pro rata share of FC1's qualified business asset investment is $30x ($50x x 0.60). Accordingly, Y Corp's net CFC tested income is $60x ($78x - $18x), and its net deemed tangible income return is $3x ($30x x 0.10). Y Corp's GILTI inclusion amount for Year 1 is $57x ($60x - $3x). Because X Corp and Y Corp are both U.S. shareholder partners with respect to FC1 and FC2, the only partnership CFCs of PRS, X Corp and Y Corp each includes its proportionate share of PRS's share of each CFC tested item of FC1 and FC2 under paragraph (c) of this section rather than including a distributive share of the GILTI inclusion amount of PRS.

(3) *Example 3: domestic partnership with partners that are United States shareholders with respect to some, but not all, of the controlled foreign corporations owned by the domestic partnership.* (i) *Facts.* X Corp and Y Corp are domestic corporations that own 40% and 60%, respectively, of PRS, a domestic partnership. PRS owns 20% of the single class of stock of FC1 and 10% of the single class of stock of FC2. In addition, Y Corp owns 100% of the single class of stock of FC3. FC1, FC2, and FC3 are controlled foreign corporations. X Corp, Y Corp, PRS, FC1, FC2, and FC3 all use the calendar year as their taxable year. In Year 1, FC1 has $100x of tested income, FC2 has $80x of tested income, and FC3 has $10x of tested loss.

(ii) *Analysis.* (A) *Partnership-level calculation.* PRS is a U.S. shareholder partnership with respect to each of FC1 and FC2. Under paragraph (b)(1) of this section, PRS determines its GILTI inclusion amount for Year 1. PRS's pro rata share of FC1's tested income is $20x ($100x x 0.20) and of FC2's tested income is $8x ($80x x 0.10). PRS's net CFC tested income is $28x ($20x + $8x). PRS has no net deemed tangible income return. PRS's GILTI inclusion amount for Year 1 is $28x.

(B) *Partner-level calculation*—(1) *X Corp.* X Corp is not a U.S. shareholder partner with respect to either FC1 or FC2 because X Corp owns (within the meaning of section 958) less than 10% of each of FC1 (40% x 20% = 8%) and FC2 (40% x 10% = 4%). Accordingly, under paragraph (b)(2) of this section, X Corp includes in income its distributive share, or $11.20x ($28x x 0.40), of PRS's GILTI inclusion amount in Year 1.

(2) *Y Corp.* Y Corp is a United States shareholder of FC3. Y Corp is also a U.S. shareholder partner with respect to FC1, because it owns (within the meaning of section 958) at least 10% (60% x 20% = 12%) of the stock of FC1, but not with respect to FC2, because Y Corp owns (within the meaning of section 958) less than 10% of the stock of FC2 (60% x 10% = 6%). Accordingly, under paragraph (c) of this section, Y Corp is treated as owning section 958(a) stock of FC1 proportionately as if PRS were a foreign partnership. Thus, Y Corp's pro rata share of FC1's tested income is $12x ($20x x 0.60). Y Corp's pro rata share of FC3's tested loss is $10x ($10x x 1). Accordingly, Y Corp's net CFC tested income is $2x ($12x - $10x) and Y Corp has no net deemed tangible income return. Y Corp's GILTI inclusion amount for Year 1 is $2x. In addition, under paragraph (c) of this section, for purposes of determining Y Corp's distributive share of PRS's GILTI inclusion amount, Y Corp's distributive share of PRS's GILTI inclusion amount is determined without regard to PRS's pro rata share of any item of FC1. PRS's GILTI inclusion amount computed solely with respect to FC2 is $8x ($80x x 0.10). Y Corp's distributive share of PRS's GILTI inclusion amount is $4.80x ($8x x 0.60) in Year 1.

(4) *Example 4: tiered domestic partnerships*—(i) *Facts.* X Corp and Y Corp are domestic corporations that own, respectively, a 20% interest and an 80% interest in PRS1, an upper-tier domestic partnership. PRS1 owns a 40% interest in PRS2, a lower-tier domestic partnership. The remaining 60% of PRS2 is owned by Z Corp, a controlled foreign corporation. PRS2 is not a controlled domestic partnership within the meaning of §1.951-1(h)(2) (because no United States shareholder of Z Corp (or related persons) controls PRS2). PRS2 owns 80% of the single class of stock of FC, a controlled foreign corporation. X Corp, Y Corp, Z Corp, PRS1, PRS2, and FC all use the calendar year as their taxable year. In Year 1, FC has $100x of tested income and $50x of qualified business asset investment.

(ii) *Analysis.* (A) *Lower-tier partnership-level calculation.* PRS2 is a U.S. shareholder partnership with respect to FC, because PRS2 directly owns 80% of the single class of stock of FC. Under paragraph (b)(1) of this section, PRS2 determines its GILTI inclusion amount for its taxable year. PRS2's pro rata share of FC's tested income is $80x ($100x x 0.80). PRS2's pro rata share of FC's qualified business asset investment is $40x ($50x x 0.80). PRS2's net CFC tested income is $80x, and its net deemed tangible income return is $4x ($40x x 0.10). PRS2's GILTI inclusion amount for Year 1 is $76x ($80x - $4x).

(B) *Non-U.S. shareholder partner calculation.* Z Corp is not a U.S. shareholder partner of FC. Therefore, under paragraph (b)(2) of this section, in Year 1, Z Corp includes in income Z Corp's distributive share of PRS2's GILTI inclusion amount, or $45.60x ($76x x 0.60). Z Corp's gross tested income in Year 1 includes this amount.

(C) *Upper-tier partnership-level calculation*. PRS1 is a U.S. shareholder partner with respect to FC because it owns (within the meaning of section 958) more than 10% of the stock of FC (40% x 100% (by reason of the application of section 958(b)(2)) = 40%). Accordingly, under paragraph (c) of this section, PRS1 is treated as owning section 958(a) stock of FC proportionately as if PRS2 were a foreign partnership. Thus, PRS1's pro rata share of FC's tested income is $32x ($100x x 0.80 x 0.40), and its pro rata share of FC's qualified business asset investment is $16x ($50x x 0.80 x 0.40). PRS1's net CFC tested income is $32x, and its net deemed tangible income return is $1.60x ($16x x 0.10). PRS1's GILTI inclusion amount for Year 1 is $30.40x ($32x - $1.60x).

(D) *Upper-tier partnership partner-level calculation*—(*1*) *Treatment of upper-tier partnership*. For purposes of applying paragraph (c) of this section to determine X Corp and Y Corp's GILTI inclusion amount, PRS1 is treated as owning section 958(a) stock of FC.

(*2*) *X Corp*. X Corp is not a U.S. shareholder partner with respect to FC because it owns (within the meaning of section 958) less than 10% (20% x 40% x 100% (by reason of the application of section 958(b)(2)) = 8%) of the stock of FC. Accordingly, under paragraph (b)(2) of this section, X Corp includes its distributive share of PRS1's GILTI inclusion amount in Year 1, which is $6.08x ($30.40x x 0.20).

(*3*) *Y Corp*. Y Corp is a U.S. shareholder partner with respect to FC because it owns (within the meaning of section 958) more than 10% (80% x 40% x 100% (by reason of the application of section 958(b)(2)) = 32%) of the stock of FC. Accordingly, under paragraphs (c) and (d) of this section, Y Corp is treated as owning section 958(a) stock of FC proportionately as if PRS1 and PRS2 were foreign partnerships. Thus, Y Corp's pro rata share of FC's tested income is $25.60x ($100x x 0.80 x 0.40 x 0.80), and its pro rata share of FC's qualified business asset investment is $12.80x ($50x x 0.80 x 0.40 x 0.80). Y Corp's net CFC tested income is $25.60x, its net deemed tangible income return is $1.28x ($12.80x x 0.10), and its GILTI inclusion amount is $24.32x ($25.60x - $1.28x). Because Y Corp is a U.S. shareholder partner with respect to FC, the only partnership CFC of PRS1, Y Corp has no distributive share of the GILTI inclusion amount of PRS1 under paragraph (c) of this section.

(5) *Example 5: S corporation and its shareholders*—(i) *Facts*. Individual A, a U.S. citizen, and Grantor Trust, a trust all of which is treated under sections 671 through 679 as owned by Individual B, a U.S. citizen, respectively own 5% and 95% of the single class of stock of Corporation X, an S corporation. Corporation X owns 100% of the single class of stock of FC, a controlled foreign corporation. Individual A, Grantor Trust, Individual B, Corporation X, and FC all use the calendar year as their taxable year. In Year 1, FC has $200x of tested income and $100x of qualified business asset investment.

(ii) *Analysis*—(A) *S corporation-level calculation*. An S corporation is treated as a partnership for purposes of sections 951 through 965 under section 1373. Corporation X is a U.S. shareholder partnership with respect to FC, a partnership CFC. Accordingly, under paragraph (b)(1) of this section, Corporation X determines its GILTI inclusion amount for Year 1. Corporation X's pro rata share of FC's tested income is $200x, and its pro rata share of FC's qualified business asset investment is $100x. Corporation X's net CFC tested income is $200x, and its net deemed tangible income return is $10x ($100x x 0.10). Corporation X's GILTI inclusion amount for Year 1 is $190x ($200x - $10x).

(B) *S corporation shareholder-level calculation*-(*1*) *Individual A*. Individual A is not a U.S. shareholder partner with respect to FC because it owns (within the meaning of section 958) less than 10% (5% x 100% = 5%) of the FC stock. Accordingly, under paragraph (b)(2) of this section, Individual A includes in gross income its proportionate share of Corporation X's GILTI inclusion amount, which is $9.50x ($190x x 0.05).

(*2*) *Grantor Trust*. Because Individual B is treated as owning all of Grantor Trust under sections 671 through 679, Individual B is treated as if it directly owns the shares of stock in Corporation X owned by Grantor Trust. As a result, Individual B is treated as a U.S. shareholder partner with respect to FC because it owns (within the meaning of section 958) more than 10% (95% x 100% = 95%) of the FC stock. Accordingly, under paragraph (c) of this section, Individual B is treated as owning section 958(a) stock of FC proportionately as if Corporation X were a foreign partnership. Thus, Individual B's pro rata share of FC's tested income is $190x ($200x x 0.95) and its pro rata share of FC's qualified business asset investment is $95x ($100x x 0.95). Individual B's net CFC tested income is $190x, and its net deemed tangible income return is $9.50x ($95x x 0.10). Individual B's GILTI inclusion amount for Year 1 is $180.5x ($190x - $9.50x). Because Individual B is a U.S. shareholder partner with respect to FC, the only partnership CFC of Corporation X, Individual B has no distributive share of the GILTI inclusion amount of Corporation X under paragraph (c) of this section.

(6) *Example 6: domestic partnership with no GILTI inclusion amount*—(i) *Facts*. X Corp is a domestic corporation that owns a 90% interest in PRS, a domestic partnership. The remaining 10% of PRS is owned by Y, a foreign individual. PRS owns 100% of the single class of stock of FC1, a controlled foreign corporation, and 100% of the single class of stock of FC2, a controlled foreign corporation. X Corp owns 100% of the single class of stock of FC3, a controlled foreign corporation. X Corp, PRS, FC1, FC2, and FC3 all use the calendar year as their taxable year. In Year 1, FC1 has $100x of tested loss and $80x of tested interest expense, FC2 has $50x of tested income, and FC3 has $150x of tested income and $500x of qualified business asset investment in Year 1.

(ii) *Analysis*—(A) *Partnership-level calculation*. PRS is a U.S. shareholder partnership with respect to FC1 and FC2. Under paragraph (b)(1) of this section, PRS determines its GILTI inclusion amount for Year 1. PRS's pro rata share of FC1's tested loss is $100x, and PRS's pro rata share of FC2's tested income is $50x. PRS's net CFC tested income is $0 ($50x - 100x), and therefore PRS has no GILTI inclusion amount for Year 1.

(B) *Partner-level calculation*. X Corp is a U.S. shareholder partner with respect to FC1 and FC2 because X Corp owns (within the meaning of section 958) at least 10% of each (90% x 100% = 90%). Accordingly, under paragraph (c) of this section, X Corp is treated as owning section 958(a) stock of FC1 and FC2 proportionately as if PRS were a foreign partnership. X Corp's pro rata share of FC1's tested loss is $90x ($100x x 0.90), and X Corp's pro rata share of FC1's tested interest expense is $72x ($80 x 0.90). X Corp's pro rata share of FC2's tested income is $45x ($50x x 0.90). X Corp's pro rata share of FC3's tested income is $150x, and its pro rata share of FC3's qualified business asset investment is $500x. X Corp's net CFC tested income is $105x ($45x + $150x - $90x). X Corp's deemed tangible income return is $50x ($500x x 0.10), but its net deemed tangible income return is $0 ($50x - $72x). X Corp has a GILTI inclusion amount of $105x ($105x - $0) for Year 1. [Reg. §1.951A-5.]

Par. 9. Section 1.951A-6 is added to read as follows:

§1.951A-6. Treatment of GILTI inclusion amount and adjustments to earnings and profits and basis related to tested loss CFCs.—(a) *Scope.*—This section provides rules relating to the treatment of GILTI inclusion amounts and adjustments to earnings and profits and basis to account for tested losses. Paragraph (b) of this section provides that a GILTI inclusion amount is treated in the same manner as an amount included under section 951(a)(1)(A) for purposes of applying certain sections of the Code. Paragraph (c) of this section provides rules for the treatment of amounts taken into account in determining the net CFC tested income when applying sections 163(e)(3)(B)(i) and 267(a)(3)(B). Paragraph (d) of this section provides rules that increase the earnings and profits of a tested loss CFC for purposes of section 952(c)(1)(A). Paragraph (e) of this section provides rules for certain basis adjustments to the stock of a controlled foreign corporation by reason of tested losses used to reduce a domestic corporation's net CFC tested income upon the disposition of the stock of the controlled foreign corporation.

(b) *Treatment as subpart F income for certain purposes.*—(1) *In general.*—A GILTI inclusion amount is treated in the same manner as an amount included under section 951(a)(1)(A) for purposes of applying sections 168(h)(2)(B), 535(b)(10), 851(b), 904(h)(1), 959, 961, 962, 993(a)(1)(E), 996(f)(1), 1248(b)(1), 1248(d)(1), 1411, 6501(e)(1)(C), 6654(d)(2)(D), and 6655(e)(4), and with respect to other sections of the Internal Revenue Code as provided in other guidance published in the Internal Revenue Bulletin.

(2) *Allocation of GILTI inclusion amount to tested income CFCs.*—(i) *In general.*—For purposes of the sections referred to in paragraph (b)(1) of this section, the portion of the GILTI inclusion amount of a United States shareholder treated as being with respect to each controlled foreign corporation of the United States shareholder for the U.S. shareholder inclusion year is—

(A) In the case of a tested loss CFC, zero, and

(B) In the case of a tested income CFC, the portion of the GILTI inclusion amount of the United States shareholder which bears the same ratio to such inclusion amount as the United States shareholder's pro rata share of the tested income of the tested income CFC for the U.S. shareholder inclusion year bears to the aggregate amount of the United States shareholder's pro rata share of the tested income of each tested income CFC for the U.S. shareholder inclusion year.

(ii) *Example.*—(A) *Facts.* USP, a domestic corporation, owns all of the stock of three controlled foreign corporations, CFC1, CFC2, and CFC3. USP, CFC1, CFC2, and CFC3 all use the calendar year as their taxable year. In Year 1, CFC1 has tested income of $100x, CFC2 has tested income of $300x, and CFC3 has tested loss of $50x. Neither CFC1 nor CFC2 has qualified business asset investment.

(B) *Analysis.* In Year 1, USP has a GILTI inclusion amount of $350x ($100x + $300x - $50x). The aggregate amount of USP's pro rata share of tested income from CFC1 and CFC2 is $400x ($100x + $300x). The portion of USP's GILTI inclusion amount treated as being with respect to CFC1 is $87.50x ($350x x $100x/$400x). The portion of USP's GILTI inclusion amount treated as being with respect to CFC2 is $262.50x ($350x x $300x/$400x). The portion of USP's GILTI inclusion amount treated as being with respect to CFC3 is $0 because CFC3 is a tested loss CFC.

(iii) *Translation of portion of GILTI inclusion amount allocated to tested income CFC.*—The portion of the GILTI inclusion amount of a United States shareholder allocated to a tested income CFC under section 951A(f)(2) and paragraph (b)(2)(i) of this section is translated into the functional currency of the tested income CFC using the average exchange rate for the CFC inclusion year of the tested income CFC.

(c) *Treatment as an amount includible in the gross income of a United States person.*—(1) *In general.*—For purposes of sections 163(e)(3)(B)(i) and 267(a)(3)(B), an item (including original issue discount) is treated as includible in the gross income of a United States person to the extent that such item increases a United States shareholder's pro rata share of tested income of a controlled foreign corporation for a U.S. shareholder inclusion year, reduces the shareholder's pro rata share of tested loss of a controlled foreign corporation for the U.S. shareholder inclusion year, or both.

(2) *Special rule for a United States shareholder that is a domestic partnership.*—In the case of a United States shareholder that is a domestic partnership (within the meaning of section 7701(a)(4)), an item is described in paragraph (c)(1) of this section only to the extent one or more United States persons (other than domestic partnerships) that are direct or indirect partners of the domestic partnership include in gross income their distributive share of the GILTI inclusion amount (if any) of the domestic partnership for the U.S. shareholder inclusion year of the domestic partnership in which such item accrues or such item is taken into account under paragraph (c)(1) of this section by a U.S. shareholder partner (within the meaning of §1.951A-5(e)(3)) of the domestic partnership by reason of §1.951A-5(c).

(d) *Increase of earnings and profits of tested loss CFC for purposes of section 952(c)(1)(A).*—For purposes of section 952(c)(1)(A) with respect to a

CFC inclusion year, the earnings and profits of a tested loss CFC are increased by an amount equal to the tested loss of the tested loss CFC for the CFC inclusion year.

(e) *Adjustments to basis related to net used tested loss*.—(1) *In general*.—(i) *Disposition of stock of a controlled foreign corporation*.—In the case of a disposition of section 958(a) stock of a controlled foreign corporation owned (directly or indirectly) by a domestic corporation (*specified stock*), the adjusted basis of the specified stock is reduced immediately before the disposition by the domestic corporation's net used tested loss amount with respect to the controlled foreign corporation (if any) attributable to the specified stock. If the reduction described in the preceding sentence exceeds the adjusted basis in the specified stock immediately before the disposition, such excess is treated as gain from the sale or exchange of the stock for the taxable year in which the disposition occurs.

(ii) *Disposition of stock of an upper-tier controlled foreign corporation*.—In the case of a disposition of specified stock of a controlled foreign corporation (*upper-tier CFC*) by reason of which a domestic corporation owns, or has owned, section 958(a) stock of any other controlled foreign corporation (*lower-tier CFC*), for purposes of determining the reduction under paragraph (e)(1)(i) of this section, the domestic corporation's net used tested loss amount (if any) with respect to the upper-tier CFC attributable to the specified stock is—

(A) Increased by the sum of the domestic corporation's net used tested loss amounts with respect to each lower-tier CFC attributable to the specified stock; and

(B) Reduced (but not below zero) by the sum of the domestic corporation's net offset tested income amounts with respect to the upper-tier CFC and each lower-tier CFC attributable to the specified stock.

(iii) *Disposition of an interest in a foreign entity other than a controlled foreign corporation*.—In the case of a disposition of an interest in a foreign entity other than a controlled foreign corporation through which entity a domestic corporation owns section 958(a) stock of a controlled foreign corporation, for purposes of paragraph (e)(1)(i) and (ii) of this section, the controlled foreign corporation is treated as a lower-tier CFC, the interest in the entity is treated as specified stock of a controlled foreign corporation, and the entity is treated as an upper-tier CFC with respect to which the domestic corporation has neither a net used tested loss amount nor a net offset tested income amount.

(iv) *Order of application of basis reductions*.—In the event of an indirect disposition described in paragraph (e)(6)(ii)(B) of this section, the basis reduction described in paragraph (e)(1)(i) of this section is deemed to occur at the lowest-tier CFC first and, thereafter, up the chain of ownership until adjustments are made to the specified stock directly owned by the person making the disposition described in paragraph (e)(6)(ii)(A) of this section.

(v) *No duplicative adjustments*.—No item is taken into account under this paragraph (e)(1) to adjust the basis of specified stock of a controlled foreign corporation to the extent that such amount has previously been taken into account with respect to a prior basis adjustment with respect to such stock under this paragraph (e)(1). Moreover, the basis of specified stock is not reduced to the extent a taxpayer can demonstrate to the satisfaction of the Secretary that such adjustments would duplicate prior reductions to the basis of such stock under section 362(e)(2).

(2) *Net used tested loss amount*.—(i) *In general*.—The term *net used tested loss amount* means, with respect to a domestic corporation and a controlled foreign corporation, the excess (if any) of—

(A) The aggregate of the domestic corporation's used tested loss amount with respect to the controlled foreign corporation for each U.S. shareholder inclusion year, over

(B) The aggregate of the domestic corporation's offset tested income amount with respect to the controlled foreign corporation for each U.S. shareholder inclusion year.

(ii) *Used tested loss amount*.—The term *used tested loss amount* means, with respect to a domestic corporation and a tested loss CFC for a U.S. shareholder inclusion year—

(A) In the case of a domestic corporation that has net CFC tested income for the U.S. shareholder inclusion year, the domestic corporation's pro rata share of the tested loss of the tested loss CFC for the U.S. shareholder inclusion year, or

(B) In the case of a domestic corporation without net CFC tested income for the U.S. shareholder inclusion year, the amount that bears the same ratio to the domestic corporation's pro rata share of the tested loss of the tested loss CFC for the U.S. shareholder inclusion year as the aggregate of the domestic corporation's pro rata share of the tested income of each tested income CFC for the U.S. shareholder inclusion year bears to the aggregate of the domestic corporation's pro rata share of the tested loss of each tested loss CFC for the U.S. shareholder inclusion year.

(3) *Net offset tested income amount*.—(i) *In general*.—The term *net offset tested income amount* means, with respect to a domestic corporation and a controlled foreign corporation, the excess (if any) of the amount described in paragraph (e)(2)(i)(B) of this section over the amount described in paragraph (e)(2)(i)(A) of this section.

(ii) *Offset tested income amount*.—The term *offset tested income amount* means, with respect to a domestic corporation and a tested income CFC for a U.S. shareholder inclusion year—

(A) In the case of a domestic corporation that has net CFC tested income for the U.S. shareholder inclusion year, the amount that bears the same ratio to the domestic corporation's pro rata share of the tested income of the tested income CFC for the U.S. shareholder inclusion year as the aggregate of the domestic corporation's pro rata share of the tested loss of each tested loss CFC for the U.S. shareholder inclusion year bears to the aggregate of the domestic corporation's pro rata share of the tested income of each tested income CFC for the U.S. shareholder inclusion year, or

(B) In the case of a domestic corporation without net CFC tested income for the U.S. shareholder inclusion year, the domestic corporation's pro rata share of the tested income of the tested income CFC for the U.S. shareholder inclusion year.

(4) *Attribution to stock.*—(i) *In general.*—The portion of a domestic corporation's net used tested loss amount or net offset tested income amount with respect to a controlled foreign corporation (including a lower-tier CFC) attributable to specified stock for purposes of paragraph (e)(1) of this section is determined based on the domestic corporation's pro rata share of the tested loss and tested income, as applicable, of the controlled foreign corporation for each U.S. shareholder inclusion year with respect to such specified stock. See § 1.951A-1(d)(1), (2), and (4) for rules regarding the determination of pro rata share amounts of tested income and tested loss.

(ii) *Nonrecognition transactions.*—In the case of specified stock acquired by a domestic corporation in a nonrecognition transaction (as defined in section 7701(a)(45)), the principles of § 1.1248-8 apply to determine the domestic corporation's net used tested loss amount or net offset tested income amount with respect to a controlled foreign corporation attributable to specified stock. For purposes of applying the principles of § 1.1248-8, tested income is treated as earnings and profits and tested loss is treated as a deficit in earnings and profits.

(5) *Section 381 transactions.*—If a controlled foreign corporation with respect to which a United States shareholder has a net used tested loss amount or net offset tested income amount is a distributor or transferor corporation in a transaction described in section 381(a) (*acquired CFC*) in which a controlled foreign corporation is the acquiring corporation (*acquiring CFC*), the domestic corporation's net used tested loss amount or net offset tested income amount with respect to the acquiring CFC is increased by the amount of the net used tested loss amount or net offset tested income amount of the acquired CFC. This paragraph (e)(5) does not apply to the extent that the acquiring CFC is an upper-tier CFC and such amounts would be taken into account under paragraph (e)(1)(ii) of this paragraph if the stock of the acquiring CFC were disposed of.

(6) *Other definitions.*—The following additional definitions apply for purposes of this paragraph (e):

(i) *Domestic corporation.*—The term *domestic corporation* means a domestic corporation other than a real estate investment trust (as defined in section 856) or a regulated investment company (as defined in section 851).

(ii) *Disposition.*—The term *disposition* means—

(A) Any transfer of specified stock that is taxable, in whole or in part, including a sale or exchange, contribution, or distribution of the stock, including a deemed sale or exchange by reason of the specified stock becoming worthless within the meaning of section 165(g), or

(B) Any indirect disposition of specified stock of a lower-tier CFC as a result of a disposition described in paragraph (e)(6)(ii)(A) of this section of specified stock of an upper-tier CFC.

(7) *Special rule for disposition by controlled foreign corporation less than 100 percent owned by a single domestic corporation.*—In the case of a disposition by a controlled foreign corporation that is not 100 percent owned, within the meaning of section 958(a), by a single domestic corporation, if a reduction to basis described in paragraph (e)(1) of this section by reason of a domestic corporation's net used tested loss amount results in an increase to the controlled foreign corporation's foreign personal holding company income (as defined in section 954(c)(1)), the domestic corporation's pro rata share of the subpart F income of the controlled foreign corporation, as otherwise determined under section 951(a)(2) and § 1.951-1(b) and (e), is increased by the amount of such increase, and no other shareholder takes such subpart F income into account under section 951(a)(1)(A).

(8) *Special rules for members of a consolidated group.*—For purposes of the section 951A regulations, a member determines its net used tested loss amount and the adjustments made as a result of the amount under the rules provided in § 1.1502-51(c).

(9) *Examples.*—The following examples illustrate the application of the rules in this paragraph (e).

(i) *Example 1*—(A) *Facts.* USP, a domestic corporation, owns 100% of the single class of stock of CFC1 and CFC2. USP1, CFC1, and CFC2 all use the calendar year as their taxable year. In Year 1, CFC2 has $90x of tested loss and CFC1 has $100x of tested income. At the beginning of Year 2, USP sells all of the stock of CFC2 to an unrelated buyer for cash. USP has no used tested loss amount or offset tested income amount with respect to CFC2 in any year prior to Year 1. USP has not owned stock in any other CFC by reason of owning stock of CFC1 and CFC2.

(B) *Analysis.* At the time of the disposition, USP has a net used tested loss amount of $90x with respect to CFC2 attributable to the CFC2 stock, which is the specified stock. Because USP does not own (and has not owned), within the meaning of section 958(a)(2), stock in any lower-tier CFCs by reason of the CFC2 stock, there is no adjustment to the net used tested loss amount of $90x pursuant to paragraph (e)(1)(ii) of this section. Accordingly, immediately before the disposition of the CFC2 stock, the basis of the CFC2 stock is reduced by $90x under paragraph (e)(1)(i) of this section.

(ii) *Example 2*—(A) *Facts.* The facts are the same as in paragraph (A) of *Example 1*, except that USP sells only 90% of the shares of CFC2.

(B) *Analysis.* The analysis is the same as in paragraph (B) of *Example 1*, except that USP's net used tested loss amount attributable to the CFC2 stock that was disposed of is only $81x (90% x $90x) under paragraph (e)(4)(i) of this section. Accordingly, immediately before the disposition of such stock, the basis in the CFC2 stock disposed of is reduced by $81x under paragraph (e)(1)(i) of this section.

(iii) *Example 3*—(A) *Facts.* The facts are the same as in paragraph (A) of *Example 1*, except that USP sells the CFC2 stock at the beginning of Year 3 and during Year 2 CFC1 has $10x of tested loss that offsets Year 2 tested income of CFC2.

(B) *Analysis.* USP has a net used tested loss amount of $80x with respect to CFC2 attributable to the CFC2 stock, the amount of USP's used tested loss amount with respect to CFC2 attributable to the CFC2 stock in Year 1 of $90x reduced by USP's offset tested income amount with respect to CFC2 attributable to the CFC2 stock in Year 2 of $10x. Accordingly, immediately before the disposition of the CFC2 stock, the basis of the CFC2 stock is reduced by $80x under paragraph (e)(1)(i) of this section.

(iv) *Example 4*—(A) *Facts*. USP, a domestic corporation, owns 100% of the single class of stock of CFC1, and CFC1 owns 100% of the single class of stock of CFC2. USP1, CFC1, and CFC2 all use the calendar year as their taxable year. In Year 1, CFC1 has $100x of tested loss that offsets CFC2's $100x of tested income. USP sells the stock of CFC1 at the beginning of Year 2. USP has no used tested loss amount or offset tested income amount with respect to CFC1 of CFC2 in any year prior to Year 1. USP has not owned stock in any other CFC by reason of owning stock of CFC1 and CFC2.

(B) *Analysis*. (1) *Direct disposition*. At the time of the disposition, USP has a net used tested loss amount of $100x with respect to CFC1 attributable to the CFC1 stock. However, because USP owns, within the meaning of section 958(a)(2), CFC2 stock by reason of the CFC1 stock, USP's $100x net used tested loss amount with respect to CFC1 attributable to the CFC1 stock is reduced by USP's $100x net offset tested income amount with respect to CFC2 attributable to the CFC1 stock. Accordingly, there is no adjustment to the basis of the CFC1 stock under paragraph (e)(1)(i) of this section.

(2) *Indirect disposition*. Under paragraph (e)(6)(ii)(B) of this section, USP's disposition of the CFC1 stock also constitutes an indirect disposition of the CFC2 stock because CFC1 is an upper-tier CFC and CFC2 is a lower-tier CFC within the meaning of paragraph (e)(1)(ii) of this section. However, USP has no net used tested loss amount with respect to CFC2 attributable to the CFC2 stock. Accordingly, there is no adjustment to the basis of the CFC2 stock under paragraph (e)(1) of this section.

(v) *Example 5*—(A) *Facts*. The facts are the same as in paragraph (A) of *Example 4*, except that in Year 1 CFC2 has $100x of tested loss that offsets CFC1's $100x of tested income. CFC1 sells the stock of CFC2 at the beginning of Year 2.

(B) *Analysis*. USP, a domestic corporation, owns within the meaning of section 958(a) stock of CFC2. Accordingly, immediately before the disposition, CFC1's basis in the CFC2 stock is reduced by USP's net used tested loss amount with respect to CFC2 attributable to the CFC2 stock of $100x under paragraph (e)(1)(i) of this section.

(vi) *Example 6*—(A) *Facts*. The facts are the same as in paragraph (A) of *Example 5*, except that instead of CFC1 selling the stock of CFC2, USP sells the stock of CFC1.

(B) *Analysis*—(1) *Direct disposition*. USP has no net used tested loss amount with respect to CFC1 attributable to the stock of CFC1. However, because USP owns, within the meaning of section 958(a)(2), stock of CFC2 by reason of owning stock of CFC1, under paragraph (e)(1)(ii) of this section, USP's net used tested loss amount attributable to the stock of CFC1 ($0) is increased by USP's net used tested loss amount with respect to CFC2 attributable to the CFC1 stock ($100x), and reduced by USP's net offset tested income amount with respect to CFC1 attributable to the CFC1 stock ($100x). Accordingly, there is no adjustment to the basis of the CFC1 stock under paragraph (e)(1) of this section.

(2) *Indirect disposition*. Under paragraph (e)(6)(ii)(B) of this section, USP's disposition of CFC1 stock also constitutes an indirect disposition of the CFC2 stock because CFC1 is an upper-tier CFC and CFC2 is a lower-tier CFC within the meaning of paragraph (e)(1)(ii) of this section. Accordingly, immediately before the disposition, CFC1's basis in the CFC2 stock is reduced by USP's net used tested loss amount with respect to CFC2 attributable to the CFC2 stock of $100x under paragraph (e)(1)(i) of this section. Under paragraph (e)(1)(iv) of this section, the basis reduction to CFC2's shares is deemed to occur immediately before any reductions occur with respect to the stock of CFC1, of which there are none.

(vii) *Example 7*—(A) *Facts*. USP1, a domestic corporation, owns 90% of the single class of stock of CFC1, and CFC1 owns 100% of the single class of stock of CFC2. USP1 also owns 100% of the single class of stock of CFC3. The remaining 10% of the stock of CFC1 is owned by USP2, a person unrelated to USP1. USP2 owns no other CFCs. USP1, USP2, CFC1, CFC2, and CFC3 all use the calendar year as their taxable year. In Year 1, CFC1 has no tested income or tested loss, CFC2 has tested loss of $100x, and CFC3 has tested income of $100x. CFC1 has no other earnings or income in Year 1. At the beginning of Year 2, CFC1 sells CFC2. Without regard to this paragraph (e), CFC1 would recognize no gain or loss with respect to the CFC2 stock. USP1 has not owned stock in any other controlled foreign corporation by reason of owning stock of CFC1, CFC2, and CFC3.

(B) *Analysis*. At the time of the disposition, USP2 has no net used tested loss amount with respect to CFC2. At the time of the disposition, USP1 has a net used tested loss amount of $90x with respect to CFC2 attributable to the CFC2 stock, which is the specified stock. Because USP1 does not own (and has not owned), within the meaning of section 958(a)(2), stock in any lower-tier CFCs by reason of the CFC2 stock, there is no adjustment to the net used tested loss amount of $90x pursuant to paragraph (e)(1)(ii) of this section. Accordingly, immediately before the disposition of the CFC2 stock, the basis of the CFC2 stock is reduced by $90x under paragraph (e)(1)(i) of this section. As a result, CFC1 recognizes gain of $90x on the disposition of the CFC2 stock, which results in $90x of foreign personal holding company income and $90x of earnings and profits. Under paragraph (e)(7) of this section, USP1's pro rata share of the subpart F income of CFC1 is increased by $90x, and USP2 does not take such subpart F income into account under section 951(a)(1)(A).

(viii) *Example 8*—(A) *Facts*. USP, a domestic corporation, owns 100% of the single class of stock of CFC1 and CFC2, and CFC1 owns 100% of the single class of stock of CFC3 and CFC4. USP, CFC1, CFC2, CFC3, and CFC4 all use the calendar year as their taxable year. In Year 1, CFC1 has no tested income or tested loss, CFC2 has $200x of tested income, and CFC3 and CFC4 each have tested loss of $100x. During Year 2, CFC3 liquidates into CFC1 in a nontaxable transaction described under section 332, and CFC1 sells the stock of CFC4 to an unrelated third party for cash. During Year 2, none of CFC1, CFC2, CFC3, or CFC4 earn tested income or tested loss. At the beginning of Year 3, USP sells the stock of CFC1 to an unrelated third party for cash. USP has not owned stock in any other CFC by reason of owning stock in CFC1, CFC2, CFC3, or CFC4.

(B) *Analysis*. (1) CFC3's liquidation into CFC1 is not a disposition within the meaning of paragraph (e)(6)(ii)(A) of this section because CFC1 does not recognize gain or loss in whole or in part with respect to the stock of CFC3 under section 332. Furthermore, CFC1 does not inherit CFC3's net used tested loss amount under paragraph (e)(5) of this section because CFC1 is an upper-tier CFC with respect to CFC3 and would take such amounts into account under paragraph (e)(1)(ii) of this section at the time of a future disposition. That is, the CFC3 stock is section 958(a) stock that USP has owned by reason of its ownership of CFC1 within the meaning of paragraph (e)(1)(ii) of this section.

(2) At the time of CFC1's sale of the stock of CFC4, USP has a $100x net used tested loss amount with respect to CFC4 attributable to the CFC4 stock, which is the specified stock. Because USP has not owned, within the meaning of section 958(a)(2), stock in any lower-tier CFCs by reason of the CFC4 stock, there is no adjustment to the net used tested loss amount of $100x pursuant to paragraph (e)(1)(ii) of this section. Accordingly, immediately before the disposition of the CFC4 stock, the basis of the CFC4 stock is reduced by $100x under paragraph (e)(1)(i) of this section.

(3) At the time of USP's sale of CFC1, USP has no net used tested loss amount with respect to CFC1 attributable to the CFC1 stock. However, USP has owned, within the meaning of section 958(a)(2), stock of lower-tier CFCs (CFC3 and CFC4) by reason of its ownership of CFC1. Thus, USP's net used tested loss amount attributable to the stock of CFC1 ($0) is increased by USP's net used tested loss amounts with respect to CFC3 and CFC4 attributable to the CFC1 stock ($200x). Accordingly, immediately before the disposition of the CFC1 stock, the basis of the CFC1 stock is reduced by $200x under paragraph (e)(1)(i) of this section. The rule prohibiting duplicative adjustments under paragraph (e)(1)(v) of this section does not prevent this basis reduction because the net used tested loss amounts with respect to the CFC3 and CFC4 stock were not previously taken into account to reduce the basis of CFC1 stock. [Reg. § 1.951A-6.]

Par. 10. Section 1.951A-7 is added to read as follows:

§ 1.951A-7. Applicability dates.—Sections 1.951A-1 through 1.951A-6 apply to taxable years of foreign corporations beginning after December 31, 2017, and to taxable years of United States shareholders in which or with which such taxable years of foreign corporations end. [Reg. § 1.951A-7.]

Determination of the Foreign Tax Credit: Guidance

Determination of the Foreign Tax Credit: Guidance.—Amendments to Reg. § 1.952-1, relating to the determination of the foreign tax credit under the Internal Revenue Code, including changes made by the Tax Cuts and Jobs Act, are proposed (published in the Federal Register on December 7, 2018) (REG-105600-18).

Par. 20. Section 1.952-1 is amended by removing the language "§ 1.904-5(a)(1)" and adding in its place the language "§ 1.904-5(a)(4)(v)" in the first sentence of paragraph (e)(5).

§ 1.952-1. Subpart F income defined.

CFCs: Insurance Income: After 1986

Controlled Foreign Corporations: Insurance Income: Tax Years After 1986.—Reproduced below are the texts of proposed Reg. §§ 1.953-0—1.953-7 and proposed amendments to Reg. §§ 1.953-1—1.953-6, relating to the election to expense certain depreciable business assets (published in the Federal Register on April 17, 1991).

☐ Par. 2. Sections 1.953-1—1.953-6 are redesignated as §§ 1.953-1A—1.953-6A, and a new center heading is added preceding newly designated § 1.953-1A to read as follows:

REGULATIONS APPLICABLE TO TAXABLE YEARS BEGINNING BEFORE JANUARY 1, 1987

☐ Par. 5. A new center heading is added to follow newly designated § 1.953-6A and to precede § 1.960-1:

REGULATIONS APPLICABLE TO TAXABLE YEARS BEGINNING AFTER DECEMBER 31, 1986

☐ Par. 3. A new center heading and new §§ 1.953-0 through 1.953-7 are added to read as follows:

REGULATIONS APPLICABLE TO TAXABLE YEARS BEGINNING AFTER DECEMBER 31, 1986

§ 1.953-0. Introduction.—(a) This paragraph lists the topics covered in §§ 1.953-0 through 1.953-7.

(ii) Changes in the amount of the letter of credit.

(10) Underpayment of tax due.

(11) Termination or revocation of election.

(i) Termination.

(ii) Revocation with consent.

(iii) Unilateral revocation by Commissioner.

(b) *Effective dates.*—(1) The provisions of §§1.953-1 through 1.953-7 apply to taxable years of a controlled foreign corporation beginning after December 31, 1986. However, the amendments to section 953(c)(2) and (c)(3) by section 1012(i)(3)(A) and (B)(i) and (ii) of the Technical and Miscellaneous Revenue Act of 1988 shall apply to taxable years beginning after December 31, 1987 to the extent such amendments add the phrase "(directly or indirectly)." Further, the risk location rules of §1.953-2 shall apply only to periods of coverage that begin on or after June 17, 1991. Prior to the effective date of §1.953-2, taxpayers may determine the location of risks by using the principles of §1.953-2A of the regulations, but those principles shall be applied to determine whether risks are located in or outside the controlled foreign corporation's country of incorporation rather than in or outside the United States. Finally, the apportionment of reserves, losses, policyholder dividends, and policy acquisition expenses between premium and investment income within the SCI, and, in certain circumstances, within the RPII category as provided in §1.953-5(c)(3) shall apply to taxable years beginning on or after April 17, 1991. For taxable years beginning prior to April 17, 1991, taxpayers may use a reasonable apportionment formula.

(2) The provisions of §§1.953-1A through 1.953-6A apply to taxable years of a controlled foreign corporation beginning before January 1, 1987. All references therein to sections of the Code are to the Internal Revenue Code of 1954 prior to the amendments made by the Tax Reform Act of 1986. [Reg. §1.953-0.]

§1.953-1. Taxation of foreign insurance operations.—(a) *In general.*—The income from the insurance operations of a controlled foreign corporation may be subject to inclusion in the gross income of a United States shareholder under subpart F of the Code either as insurance income under section 953 or as foreign personal holding company income under sections 954(a)(1) and (c). Section 953 insurance income is income (including premium and investment income) attributable to the issuing or reinsuring of any insurance or annuity contract in connection with risks located in a country other than the country (the "home country") under the laws of which the controlled foreign corporation is created or organized and which would be taxed under subchapter L of the Code if the income were the income of a domestic insurance company. The term "home country" includes any area within the jurisdiction (as recognized by the United States) of the country of incorporation of a controlled foreign corporation or within the jurisdiction of a possession of such country. A risk is located in a country other than the home country if it is located on the high seas outside the home country. Insurance income exists only with respect to bona fide contracts of insurance (or reinsurance) or annuity contracts. There are two categories of section 953 insurance income: income that constitutes related person insurance income under §1.953-3(b)(1) (the "RPII category") and income that is subject to section 953 but is not related person insurance income (the "nonRPII category"). Income, whether premium or investment income, derived from issuing or reinsuring insurance or annuity contracts in connection with risks located in the country in which the controlled foreign corporation is created or organized is referred to as same country insurance ("SCI") income. Investment income attributable to premiums that constitute SCI income may be includable in the gross income of the United States shareholders of a controlled foreign corporation as foreign personal holding company income under sections 954(a)(1) and (c). However, the premiums attributable to issuing or reinsuring insurance or annuity contracts in connection with risks located in the controlled foreign corporation's home country are not generally treated as subpart F income.

(b) *Determining subpart F inclusions of income from insurance operations.*—(1) *Procedure.*—The following procedures are used to determine the amount of a controlled foreign corporation's section 953 insurance income and its foreign personal holding company income derived from insurance operations:

(i) Determine whether premiums from insurance, reinsurance, and annuity contracts issued by the controlled foreign corporation constitute section 953 insurance income or SCI income by determining the location of the risks under the contracts (*see* §1.953-2);

(ii) Determine whether the premiums that constitute section 953 insurance income are attributable to the RPII or nonRPII categories (*see* §1.953-3);

(iii) Allocate and apportion investment income to the RPII, nonRPII, and SCI categories (*see* §1.953-4); and

(iv) Allocate and apportion deductions to the RPII, nonRPII, and SCI categories; within the SCI category and, under certain circumstances, within the RPII category, further allocate and apportion deductions between SCI premium income and SCI investment income (*see* §1.953-5).

(2) *Cross reference to additional provisions.*—Section 1.953-6 contains rules relating to the application of subchapter L of the Code (insurance companies), subpart F of part III of subchapter N (controlled foreign corporations), and certain additional Code provisions to income derived from the conduct of insurance operations. Section 1.953-7 contains rules regarding certain exceptions to the inclusion of related person insurance income in the gross income of certain United States shareholders.

(c) *Effective date.*—For regulations under section 953 that apply to the taxable years of a controlled foreign corporation beginning before January 1, 1987, *see* §§1.953-1A through 1.953-6A. The provisions of §1.953-1 and §§1.953-3 through 1.953-7 apply to the taxable years of a controlled foreign corporation beginning after December 31, 1986. However, the amendments to section 953(c)(2) and (c)(3) by section 1012(i)(3)(A) and (B)(i) and (ii) of the Technical and Miscellaneous Revenue Act of 1988 shall apply to taxable years beginning after December 31, 1987 to the extent such amendments add the phrase "(directly or indirectly)." Also, the regulations under § 1.953-2 regarding the location of risks will apply only to periods of coverage, regardless of when the contract was issued, that begin on or after June 17, 1991. Prior to the effective date of § 1.953-2, taxpayers may determine the location of risks by using the principles of § 1.953-2A of the regulations, but those principles shall be applied to determine whether risks are located in or outside the controlled foreign corporation's country of incorporation rather than in or outside the United States. Finally, the apportionment of reserves, losses, policyholder dividends, and policy acquisition expenses between premium and investment income within the SCI, and, in certain circumstances, within the RPII category as provided in § 1.953-5(c)(3) shall apply to taxable years beginning on or after April 17, 1991. For taxable years beginning prior to April 17, 1991, taxpayers may use a reasonable apportionment formula. [Reg. § 1.953-1.]

§ 1.953-2. Premiums attributable to the section 953 insurance income category and the SCI income category.—(a) *In general.*—Premiums on any insurance, reinsurance, or any annuity contract (including an annuity certain, which is an annuity that guarantees payments for a fixed period without reference to life contingencies) must be classified as either section 953 insurance income or SCI income. To determine whether premiums paid for an annuity certain are section 953 insurance income or SCI income, the annuity certain shall be treated as a contract covering risks in connection with life or health. Premiums written (less return premiums and premiums paid for reinsurance) before the first taxable year of the controlled foreign corporation beginning after December 31, 1986 that become earned under section 832(b)(4) in such taxable year or succeeding taxable years must be classified as either section 953 insurance income or SCI income. (*See* § 1.953-3, below, for rules allocating premiums that constitute section 953 insurance income to the RPII or nonRPII categories.)

(1) *Section 953 insurance income premiums.*—Premiums constitute section 953 insurance income if they relate to risks that are—

(i) In connection with property located in a country other than the home country, as described in paragraph (e) of this section;

(ii) In connection with a liability arising out of an activity conducted in a country other than the home country, as described in paragraph (f) of this section;

(iii) In connection with the life or health of a resident of a country other than the home country, as described in paragraph (g) of this section; or

(iv) In connection with risks not described in paragraph (a)(1)(i) through (iii) of this section as a result of any arrangement whereby another person receives a substantially equal amount of premiums or other consideration in respect of issuing (or reinsuring) a contract described in paragraph (a)(1)(i) through (iii) of this section. (*See* paragraph (h) of this section).

(2) *SCI income premiums.*—Premiums constitute SCI income if they relate to risks that are—

(i) In connection with property located in the home country, as described in paragraph (e) of this section;

(ii) In connection with a liability arising out of an activity conducted in the home country, as described in paragraph (f) of this section; or

(iii) In connection with the life or health of a resident of the home country, as described in paragraph (g) of this section.

(b) *Method of attributing premiums to the section 953 insurance income or SCI income categories.*—(1) *In general.*—Whether the premiums from an insurance, reinsurance, or annuity contract constitute section 953 insurance income or SCI income is determined by the location of the risks during the period or periods of coverage under the contract to which the premiums relate. A period of coverage is a period no longer than one year during which insurance coverage is provided or an annuity contract is in force and which begins or ends with or within the taxable year of the controlled foreign corporation. A period of coverage begins when coverage under the contract commences or on the anniversary of that date. A period of coverage ends on the last day preceding a new period of coverage, on the day the contract terminates or is canceled, or on the day the risk under the contract has been transferred in a reinsurance transaction in which the reinsurer assumes all rights and obligations under the reinsured policies. The determination of where a risk is located must be made separately for each period of coverage applicable to the taxable year.

(2) *Examples.*—The following examples illustrate the principles of paragraph (b)(1) of this section.

Example 1. Controlled foreign corporation X, incorporated in country M, issues to corporation Z an insurance contract which provides coverage for a 2 1/2 year period beginning on July 1, 1987. Under the insurance contract, premiums are paid monthly. Corporation X uses the calendar year as the taxable year. For premiums included in gross income for the 1987 taxable year, the period of coverage under the contract is July 1, 1987 to June 30, 1988. For premiums included in gross income for the 1988 taxable year, there are two applicable periods of coverage: July 1, 1987 to June 30, 1988 and July 1, 1988 to June 30, 1989. Whether the premiums attributable to each such period of coverage constitute section 953 insurance income or SCI insurance income must be made by considering only the facts pertinent to each period of coverage separately. For the 1989 taxable year, the periods of coverage are July 1, 1988 to June 30, 1989 and July 1, 1989 to December 31, 1989. Again, whether the premiums attributable to each such period of coverage constitute section 953 insurance income or SCI insurance income must be made by considering only the facts pertinent to each period of coverage separately.

Example 2. The facts are the same as in *Example 1* except that Z cancels the contract on August 31, 1987. For the 1987 taxable year, the period of coverage is July 1, 1987 to August 31, 1987.

Example 3. The facts are the same as in *Example 1* except that on January 15, 1989, X cedes risks under the insurance contract in a reinsurance transaction (other than a reinsurance transaction in which the reinsurer assumes all rights and obligations under the reinsured contracts) to controlled foreign corporation W, which also uses the calendar year as the taxable year. For the 1988 taxable year, the periods of coverage for X are July 1, 1987 to June 30, 1988 and July 1, 1988 to June 30, 1989. For 1989, the periods of coverage for both X and W are July 1, 1988 to June 30, 1989 and July 1, 1989 to December 31, 1989.

Example 4. The facts are the same as in *Example 1* except that corporation X issues to corporation Z an insurance contract which covers the marine risks of shipping a machine to and from countries other than country M. The contract does not specify the dates during which the machine is covered, but provides coverage from the time the machine is delivered alongside a named vessel at the port of embarkation until the time the machine is delivered alongside the vessel at the port of debarkation. The deliveries are commenced and completed during the period beginning February 1, 1987 and ending February 28, 1987. For the 1987 taxable year, the period of coverage is February 1 to February 28, 1987.

(c) *Definition of premiums.*—For a controlled foreign corporation that would be taxed as a life insurance company under part I of subchapter L (relating to life insurance companies) of the Code if it were a domestic insurance company, the term "premiums," for purposes of this section and § 1.953-3, means the items taken into account for the taxable year under section 803(a)(1). For a controlled foreign corporation that would be taxed under part II of subchapter L (relating to insurance companies other than life insurance companies), the term "premiums," for purposes of this section and § 1.953-3, means premiums written, as defined in section 832(b)(4)(A). If a policy of insurance, such as a reporting form policy or other policy, does not require premiums to be paid until the policy term expires, then the deposits required during the term of the policy must be included in premiums. In the case of a mutual fire or flood insurance company described in section 832(b)(1)(D), the term "premiums," for purposes of this section and § 1.953-3, means the entire amount of premiums deposited. In addition, for taxable years beginning after December 31, 1986 and before January 1, 1993, if the foreign corporation was a controlled foreign corporation (as defined in section 957 of the Code prior to its amendment by the Tax Reform Act of 1986) in the most recent taxable year beginning before January 1, 1987, the term "premiums" also includes an amount equal to 3 1/3 percent of the unearned premiums at the end of the most recent taxable year beginning before January 1, 1987 that are sourced within the United States under section 861(a)(7). *See* section 832(b)(4)(C). Premiums included in gross income by virtue of the preceding sentence are attributable to risks located outside the controlled foreign corporation's home country.

(d) *Allocation and apportionment of premiums.*—*(1) Risks both in and outside the home country.*—If the risks covered by a contract of insurance or reinsurance or annuity contract are located both in and outside the home country during any period of coverage, the premium for insuring the risks must be allocated to or apportioned between risks incurred in the home country and risks incurred outside the home country. Allocation of a premium means that there is a direct correlation between the premium charged and the location of the insured risks in or outside the home country. Apportionment means that there is a reasonable basis for dividing the premium between risks incurred in the home country and risks incurred outside the home country, but there is no direct correlation between the premium charged and the location of the risks. If a premium is apportioned between home country risks and risks incurred outside the home country, each premium payment shall be considered to be partly related to home country risks and partly related to risks incurred outside the home country. The allocation or apportionment of premiums to or between risks located in the home country and risks located outside the home country must be reasonable in relation to the location of the insured risks during the period of coverage. In considering whether a method of allocation or apportionment is reasonable, consideration shall be given to the types of risks covered and the terms of the insurance, reinsurance, or annuity contract including, but not limited to, provisions which separately describe each risk covered, the period of coverage of each risk, the special warranties for each risk, the premium for each risk, and the conditions for paying the premium for each risk. The allocation and apportionment of premiums must be consistent with the rules prescribed in paragraphs (e), (f), and (g) of this section. In addition, once a particular method has been adopted for allocating and apportioning premiums under a contract, that method must be used as long as the contract is in force.

(2) *Examples.*—The following examples illustrate the rules of paragraph (d)(1) of this section.

Example 1. X is a country F controlled foreign corporation with a calendar taxable year. X insures from July 1, 1987 through June 30, 1988 a particular piece of machinery that is located in country F. The machine is moved outside country F on January 1, 1988. The contract provides for $500 in premiums to be paid on June 30, 1987 and $1,000 on January 1, 1988. The larger premium payment on January 1, 1988 reflects the increased risks associated with locating the machine outside country F. For the 1987 and 1988 taxable years, the period of coverage is July 1, 1987 to June 30, 1988. Because there is a direct correlation between the premium payments and the location of the risks, the premiums must be allocated. The $500 premium payment included in X's gross income for the 1987 taxable year relates to risks incurred while the property is located in country F; therefore, all $500 in premiums constitute SCI income. The $1,000 included in X's gross income in the 1988 taxable year relates to coverage while the property is outside country F; therefore, all $1,000 constitutes section 953 insurance income.

Example 2. Z is a country F controlled foreign corporation with a calendar taxable year. Z issues a policy of insurance covering risks of damage to railroad rolling stock that only travels a particular route between country F and country M. The railroad rolling stock travels an equal number of miles in both countries. A $1,000 premium is required by Z to insure the railroad rolling stock from July 1, 1987 through June 30, 1988. The premium is paid in two installments: $500 on June 30, 1987 and $500 on January 1, 1988. Based on the types of risks covered by the contract of insurance and the terms of the contract, Z, in conformance with paragraph (e)(2)(i) of this section, chooses an apportionment method based on mileage. Because the premium is apportioned, $250 of the $500 premium included in the gross income of Z in the 1987 taxable year is attributable to home country risks and $250 is attributable to risks outside the home country. The result for the 1988 taxable year is the same.

(3) *80 percent rule.*—(i) *In general.*—If 80 percent or more of the premiums for a period of coverage of a particular contract are apportioned to risks located in the home country or to risks located outside the home country, then all of the premiums for the period of coverage are apportioned to risks incurred in or outside the home country, as the case may be.

(ii) *Example.*—The following example illustrates the operation of the 80 percent rule of paragraph (d)(3)(i) of this section.

Example. Controlled foreign corporation X, which is incorporated in country F and uses the calendar year as its taxable year, issues an insurance contract insuring a machine owned by Y against damage for a one year period commencing on May 1, 1987. When the contract was issued, the machine was located in country F; however, on April 1, 1988, Y moved the machine to a branch located outside country F. Y is required to pay premiums of $100 per month under the terms of the insurance contract. For the taxable years ending December 31, 1987 and December 31, 1988, the period of coverage is May 1, 1987 to April 30, 1988. For that period of coverage 1/12 ($100/$1200) of the premiums are related to risks located outside country F. Because approximately 92% of the premiums are related to home country risks, all the premiums under the contract are attributable to home country risks. Therefore, the $800 of premiums received by X from Y in the taxable year ending December 31, 1987 and the $400 of premiums received in the taxable year ending December 31, 1988 are attributable entirely to home country risks and constitute SCI income.

(e) *Location of risks in connection with property.*—(1) *In general.*—Risks in connection with property covered by a contract of insurance or reinsurance are located where the property is located during the period or periods of coverage applicable to the taxable year. A risk is in connection with property if it is related to an interest of an insured in tangible (whether real or personal) or intangible property. An interest in real property includes, but is not limited to, the interest of an owner, landlord, tenant, licensee, licensor, mortgagor, mortgagee, trustee, beneficiary, or partner. Where property is located depends on all the facts and circumstances. (*See* paragraph (e)(2) of this section for specific rules locating certain types of property.) The determination of where property is located must be made separately under each contract of insurance or reinsurance and for each item of property covered by the contract for each period of coverage applicable to the taxable year. (However, *see* paragraph (e)(3)(i) of this section which permits property to be aggregated in certain circumstances for purposes of determining location of risks.)

(2) *Specific rules for locating certain types of property.*—(i) *Commercial transportation property.*—Premiums related to insuring or reinsuring risks in connection with any motor vehicle, ship or boat, aircraft, railroad rolling stock, or any container transported thereby ("commercial transportation property") that is used predominantly in the commercial transportation of persons or property are attributable to risks located in the home country if the property is located in the home country for the entire period of coverage, or outside the home country if the property is located outside the home country for the entire period of coverage. If the commercial transportation property is located both in and outside the home country, then the premiums shall be allocated or apportioned between risks located in the home country and risks located outside the home country on any reasonable basis (such as time or mileage) that gives due regard to the risk being insured and that complies with the requirements of paragraphs (d)(1) and (d)(3) of this section. *See* paragraph (e)(3)(iii) of this section for rules relating to the location of moveable property, which includes commercial transportation property, if the location of such property cannot be determined by the end of the taxable year.

(ii) *Examples.*—The following examples illustrate the operation of paragraph (e)(2)(i) of this section.

Example 1. Controlled foreign corporation Y, which is incorporated in country F, issues a property and liability insurance contract covering a helicopter that is used in rescue operations in country F as well as other countries. More than 60 percent of the miles traversed by the helicopter are outside country F. However, the helicopter is located in a hangar in country F for more than 90 percent of the period of coverage. Y apportions the premiums based on the time the helicopter is located in and outside the country of incorporation. An apportionment based on the amount of time that the helicopter is located in and outside country F is not reasonable in light of the types of risks insured and the activities in which the helicopter is engaged. Therefore, Y's apportionment of the premium will not be respected.

Example 2. Corporation Y, a country F controlled foreign corporation, insures an airplane that is used exclusively for the commercial transportation of persons or property. Of the total miles travelled by the airplane, 60 percent are traversed outside country F, and 40 percent are traversed in country F. The airplane is grounded only for repairs, and the repairs are made at the location of the airplane at the time the repairs are needed. The premiums must be apportioned on a reasonable basis between risks incurred while the plane is in country F and risks incurred while it is outside country F. On the facts presented in this example, an apportionment based on total miles traversed in and outside country F would be reasonable. Thus, 60 percent of the premiums would constitute section 953 insurance income and 40 percent of the premiums would constitute SCI income.

Example 3. The facts are the same as in *Example 2* except that of the total miles travelled by the airplane, 85 percent are traversed outside the home country and 15 percent are traversed in the home country. Under the 80 percent rule of paragraph (d)(3) of this section, all of the premiums are apportioned to risks located outside country F.

(iii) *Noncommercial transportation property.*—Premiums related to risks incurred in connection with any motor vehicle, ship or boat, aircraft, or railroad rolling stock not used predominantly in the commercial transportation of persons or property are attributable to risks located outside the home country if the noncommercial transportation property is registered during the period of coverage with a country other than the home country (including any political subdivision or agency of such country) or if the owner of the property is a citizen of, resident of, or entity organized under the laws of a country other than the home country. In all other cases, noncommercial transportation property shall be deemed to be located in the home country.

(iv) *Property exported by ship or aircraft.*—Premiums related to risks in connection with property exported from the home country by ship or aircraft are attributable to risks incurred while the exported property is located in the home country if the insured risks terminate when the exported property is placed aboard the ship or aircraft for export. Premiums are attributable to risks incurred while the exported property is located outside the home country if the insured risks commence when the exported property is placed aboard the ship or aircraft for export. If the insured risks commence before the exported property is placed aboard the ship or aircraft for export and terminate after the departure of the ship or aircraft from the home country, the premiums must be allocated or apportioned between risks incurred while the exported property is located in the home country and risks incurred while the property is located outside the home country on any reasonable basis (such as time or mileage) that gives due regard to the risk being insured and that complies with the requirements of paragraphs (d)(1) and (d)(3) of this section.

(v) *Property imported by ship or aircraft.*—Premiums related to risks in connection with property imported into the home country by ship or aircraft are attributable to risks incurred outside the home country if the insured risks terminate when the imported property is unloaded at the home country port of entry. If the insured risks commence after the imported property is unloaded from the ship or aircraft at the home country port of entry, the premiums are attributable to risks incurred while the imported property is in the home country. If the insured risks commence before and terminate after the imported property is unloaded from the ship or aircraft at the home country port of entry, the premiums must be allocated or apportioned to or between risks incurred while the imported property is located in the home country and risks incurred while the imported property is located outside the home country on any reasonable basis (such as time or mileage) that gives due regard to the risk being insured and that complies with the requirements of paragraphs (d)(1) and (d)(3) of this section.

(vi) *Shipments originating and terminating in the home country.*—Premiums related to risks incurred in connection with property transported from one place in the home country to another place in the home country on or over another country, or on or over the high seas outside the territorial waters of the home country are attributable to risks in the home country unless the premiums are allocated, in a reasonable manner, under the terms of the insurance contract to risks incurred while the property is located in the home country and risks incurred while the property is located outside the home country.

(vii) *Shipments originating and terminating in a country other than the home country.*—Premiums related to risks in connection with property transported on or over the home country to and from points outside the home country are attributable to risks located outside the home country unless the premiums are allocated, in a reasonable manner, under the terms of the insurance contract to risks incurred while the property is located in the home country and risks incurred while the property is located outside the home country.

(3) *Related assets and certain moveable property.*—(i) *Related assets.*—If a contract of insurance or reinsurance covers a group of related assets, such as inventory, which are located in and outside the home country, premiums under the contract may be allocated or apportioned, on any reasonable basis, between risks located in the home country and risks located outside the home country by reference to such property taken in the aggregate.

(ii) *Example.*—The following example illustrates the related assets rule of paragraph (e)(3)(i) of this section.

Example. X is a controlled foreign corporation incorporated in country F. X issues a contract of insurance to M covering M's inventory. M maintains its inventory in warehouses in country F and other countries. The risks to which the inventory is exposed are similar in each country in which the inventory is stored. For the applicable period of coverage, 40 percent of M's inventory is located in country F and 60 percent is located outside country F. The location of the property is determined on the basis of the average value of inventory warehoused in and outside of country F during the period of coverage. X may apportion 40 percent of the premiums under the contract with M to the SCI income category and 60 percent to the section 953 insurance income category.

(iii) *Moveable property.*—In any case in which a contract of insurance or reinsurance covers moveable property (other than noncommercial transportation property) and the determination of the location of the property in or outside the home country during a period of coverage cannot practicably be made by the close of the controlled foreign corporation's taxable year, the controlled foreign corporation may apportion the premiums in conformance with a reasonable expectation of where the property will be located during the period of coverage, provided that the apportionments made on all contracts to which this paragraph (e)(3)(iii) applies do not result in a material distortion. A material distortion results if the amount of premiums apportioned to the SCI or section 953 insurance income category determined by reference to the actual facts pertinent to the period of coverage, as ascertained within 90 days after the end of the period of coverage, would result in at least a 10 percentage point difference when compared to the amount of premiums apportioned to those categories under a reasonable expectation of where the property will be located during the period of coverage. In order to avail itself of this method, the controlled foreign corporation must maintain records that demonstrate the reasonableness of its apportionment, disclose the actual location of the property as ascertained within 90 days after the end of the period of coverage, and demonstrate that the apportionment did not result in a material distortion. If such records are not maintained, the apportionment method of this paragraph may not be used and the property shall be located under the rule of this paragraph (e) that would apply in absence of the method prescribed by this paragraph (e)(2)(iii). In the event of a material distortion, the United States shareholders or, if an election is made under §1.953-7(c), the controlled foreign corporation, must file amended income tax returns and apportion premiums based on the actual location of the property and the rules of paragraphs (d) and (e) of this section.

(iv) *Example.*—The following example illustrates the moveable property rule of paragraph (e)(3)(iii) of this section.

Example. X is a controlled foreign corporation incorporated in country F. It uses the calendar year as its taxable year. X issues a contract of insurance covering a ship from July 1, 1988 to June 30, 1989. The contract is the only one issued by X that covers moveable property. The owner of the ship leases the ship to third persons on a per voyage basis. Based on information provided by the shipowner, 30 percent of the total miles traversed during the 12 month period immediately preceding the issuance of the contract were in home country waters and 70 percent outside the home country. X may apportion 30 percent of the premiums received to the SCI income category and 70 percent to the section 953 insurance income category. Within 90 days after the end of the policy period, X obtains information demonstrating that the ship was used in the territorial waters of the home country 25 percent of the time and outside the territorial waters 75 percent of the time. The apportionment method used by X is reasonable and does not result in a material distortion because an apportionment based on the facts pertinent to the period of coverage would not have resulted in at least a 10 percentage point difference in the amount of premiums apportioned to the SCI or section 953 insurance income categories. Thus, X may use the apportionment method described in paragraph (e)(3)(iii) of this section provided it maintains the records required by that paragraph.

(f) *Location of risks in connection with liability arising out of activity.*—(1) *Definition of risks in connection with liability.*—A risk covered by a contract of insurance or reinsurance is in connection with liability arising out of an activity if the insured is covered against a liability resulting from the actions of a person or a juridical entity, including actions that result in a tort, violation of contract, violation of property rights, or any other cause of action pursuant to the operation of law. The term not only includes a direct liability, which, for example, may be incurred by a tortfeasor to the person harmed, but also an indirect liability, such as the liability of one person to another resulting from the actions of an independent contractor. Moreover, a risk in connection with liability includes any loss of an insured (except a loss in connection with property described in paragraph (e) of this section) which could arise from the occurrence of an event insured against. For example, in the case of a promoter of outdoor sporting events, a risk in connection with liability arising out of an activity includes the loss that could arise from the cancellation of a sporting event because of inclement weather.

(2) *Location of risk.*—(i) *In general.*—A risk in connection with an activity is located where the activity that could give rise to a liability or loss is performed. For purposes of allocating and apportioning premiums between risks located in and outside the home country, where an activity is performed depends on the facts and circumstances of each case. Among the factors to be considered in making the determination are the location of the assets associated with the activity, the place where services comprising the activity are performed, the place where activities intended to result in a sale occur, and the place where sales actually occur.

(ii) *Examples.*—The following examples illustrate the location of risk rules of paragraph (f)(2)(i) of this section.

Example 1. X is a controlled foreign corporation that issues liability insurance and is incorporated in country M. It uses a calendar year as its taxable year. X issues a contract of insurance to Z, which owns and operates department stores in country M and other countries. The contract covers all of Z's stores. It provides coverage against "liability for bodily injury or property damage arising out of the ownership, maintenance, or use of the insured premises and all operations necessary or incidental thereto." Assuming X cannot allocate the premiums between home country and other country risks, it must apportion the premiums between those risks on a reasonable basis taking into account where the stores are located and the level of covered activities in each of those stores.

Example 2. Y is a controlled foreign corporation incorporated in country F. Y writes worker's compensation coverage. Y issues a contract to Z, which has employees in country F and other countries, covering all of Z's employees. The premiums paid by Z are not allocable to risks located in the home country and risks located outside the home country. Z must apportion the premiums on a reasonable basis taking into account where Z's employees perform services.

(3) *Specific rules locating certain activities.*—(i) *Liability with respect to property manufactured, produced, constructed, or assembled.*—Premiums under a policy of insurance or reinsurance that insures a person that manufactures, produces, constructs, or assembles property against claims arising from the consumption or use of such property are attributable to risks from an activity performed where the consumption or use of the property takes place, or if the place of consumption or use cannot be known, where the property is manufactured, produced, constructed, or assembled. If the consumption or use of the property could arise in or outside the home country, the premiums must be allocated to or apportioned between risks located in the home country and risks located outside the home country on any reasonable basis that gives due regard to the risk being insured and that complies with the

requirements of paragraphs (d)(1) and (d)(3) of this section.

(ii) *Examples.*—The following examples illustrate the rule of paragraph (f)(3)(i) of this section.

Example 1. X is a contractor that constructs apartment buildings. X uses a system of pre-fabricated construction that entails constructing parts of the apartment buildings in country F and assembling them outside of country F. The only completed apartment buildings constructed by X are outside of country F. X is insured by Z, a country F controlled foreign corporation, against liability for the improper construction of, or the failure to construct, an apartment building. Z is insuring risks in connection with an activity that arises outside of country F because that is where the use of the property takes place.

Example 2. M manufactures automobiles in facilities located in country W. M is covered by a single policy of insurance issued by F, a controlled foreign corporation organized in country W. M sells its automobiles through independent dealers all over the world, including country W. F charges a single premium to insure M against any liability for harm to persons or damage to property arising from a manufacturing defect. F must apportion the premium between risks located in W and risks located outside W on a reasonable basis because the use of the automobiles occurs in and outside of country W. However, if it cannot be known where the automobiles are used, then F is deemed to be insuring risks in connection with an activity that arises in country W because that is where the automobiles are manufactured.

(iii) *Location of activities in connection with transportation property.*—Premiums under a contract of insurance or reinsurance covering risks in connection with the operation of a motor vehicle, ship or boat, aircraft, or railroad rolling stock are attributable to risks in connection with an activity performed where the transportation property is located under the principles of paragraph (e)(2)(i) and (iii) of this section relating to the location of transportation property.

(iv) *Example.*—The following example illustrates the rule of paragraph (f)(3)(iii) of this section.

Example. X is a controlled foreign corporation created under the laws of country F and uses the calendar year as its taxable year. X insures B, a pilot for a commercial airline, against any damage to persons or property arising from B's professional activities. X charges a $10,000 premium, payable $5,000 at the inception of the policy and $5,000 on January 1, 1988, for a one year policy providing coverage from July 1, 1987 to June 30, 1988. B always pilots the same round trip flight from country F to country R and back. For both the 1987 and 1988 taxable years, the period of coverage is July 1, 1987 to June 30, 1988. On each trip from F to R the aircraft traverses half of the total mileage in country F and half in country R. Because the aircraft B flies is located in the home country one-half of the time, a reasonable basis exists for apportioning one-half of the premiums paid by B to risks arising from his activities outside the home country and one-half to activities arising in the home country. Thus, for the 1987 taxable year, the $5,000 of premiums are apportioned so that $2,500 of the premiums are attributable to home country risks and $2,500 of the premiums are attributable to risks located outside the home country. For the 1988 taxable year, the results are the same.

(v) *Selling activity.*—The liability of a person arises from selling activity only if, and to the extent that, the liability does not relate to liability in connection with property manufactured, produced, constructed, or assembled, as described in paragraph (f)(3)(i) of this section, or liability for activities in connection with transportation property, as described in paragraph (f)(3)(iii) of this section. A person is engaged in selling activity if the person engages in any activity which is intended to result in the sale of property. Premiums received on a contract of insurance or reinsurance covering risks in connection with selling activity are attributable to risks incurred where the selling activity takes place regardless of whether the property passes through, or is delivered in, the country in which the selling activity is carried on. Selling activity takes place where the activities preparatory to the sale, such as advertising, negotiating, and distributing, take place.

(vi) *Example.*—The following example illustrates the rule of paragraph (f)(3)(v) of this section.

Example. Corporation M, a country W corporation, insures a wholesale distributor against liability arising out of a breach of warranty. The wholesale distributor negotiates and processes orders in country W, but sells its inventory exclusively in countries other than country W by advertising in trade publications and distributing sales catalogues in those countries. The premiums on the policy issued to M are attributable to risks arising from activities performed both in and outside country W and M must allocate and apportion, on a reasonable basis, the premiums received for insuring the wholesale distributor between risks located in country W and risks located outside country W.

(g) *Location of risks in connection with life or health.*—(1) *In general.*—Risks in connection with life or health include risks under contracts of insurance, reinsurance, annuity contracts, or noncancellable health and accident contracts defined in section 816(a) (relating to the definition of a life insurance company). Risks under cancelable health and accident contracts are also risks in connection with life or health. An annuity certain, under which annuity payments are not determined by reference to life contingencies, is treated, for purposes of section 953 as a contract covering risks in connection with life or health. The risk under any insurance, reinsurance, or annuity contract covered by this paragraph (g)(1) is located in the country where the person with respect to whom the risk is located (the "determining life") is resident. The determining life with respect to any life, accident, or health insurance or reinsurance contract is the person whose life or health is covered by the contract. The determining life with respect to a life annuity contract is the person by whose life the annuity payments are measured. The determining life with respect to an annuity certain is the life of the person who purchases the annuity contract and the life of the person for whose benefit the annuity was purchased. Thus, risks in connection with an annuity certain are deemed to be located in their entirety outside a controlled foreign corporation's home country if either the purchaser of the contract or the recipient of the annuity payments resides outside the home country, as determined in accordance with the rules of this paragraph. The person with the determining life is presumed to be resident at the last address given to the controlled foreign corporation as such person's residence, unless the controlled foreign corporation knows or has reason to know that such person is resident at a different address. Premiums received under a contract of group life or health insurance must be apportioned between risks located in the home country and risks outside the home country on the basis of the last known addresses of the residences of the persons insured under the contract or, in the case where the contract is issued to an employer, where the persons covered by the contract are employed.

(2) *Example*.—The following example illustrates the rules of paragraph (g)(1) of this section.

Example. Controlled foreign corporation X, a country F corporation and a calendar year taxpayer, is engaged in the life insurance business. On July 1, 1987, X issues a three year term life insurance contract on the life of B. Premiums under the contract are payable on July 1 and December 31 of each year the contract is in force. B gives to X an address in country F as the address of his primary residence. On November 1, 1987, B changes his primary residence from country F to country Z. B notifies X of the change of address on February 1, 1988. For X's 1987 taxable year the premiums received on July 1, 1987 and December 31, 1987 are allocable to the SCI income category. Because X did not have knowledge, and had no reason to know, of B's change of address until February 1, 1988, it may rely, for all premium payments received before February 1, 1988, on the address B initially provided at the time the contract was approved. However, all premiums received after February 1, 1988 constitute section 953 insurance income because X had knowledge at the time those premiums were received that B had his or her primary residence outside of country F.

(h) *Risks deemed to be located in a country other than the home country*.—(1) *Artificial arrangements*.—The section 953 insurance income of a controlled foreign corporation includes any insurance income from issuing or reinsuring insurance policies or annuity contracts covering risks located in the home country if the insurance, reinsurance, or annuity contracts are attributable to any direct or indirect cross-insurance arrangement whereby the controlled foreign corporation provides insurance, reinsurance, or annuity contracts relating to home country risks and, in exchange, another person provides insurance, reinsurance, or annuity contracts relating to risks located outside the home country. Arrangements to which this rule applies include those entered into by the controlled foreign corporation, persons related (within the meaning of section 954(d)(3)) to the controlled foreign corporation, the United States shareholders of the controlled foreign corporation, and persons related to such shareholders.

(2) *Evidence of arrangements*.—The determination of whether an arrangement referred to in paragraph (h)(1) of this section exists depends on all the facts and circumstances. Facts to be considered in determining the existence of such an arrangement include the premiums charged in relation to the risks insured, the profit margin expected from the contracts, and the loss experience of the risks which the other person insures or reinsures compared with the loss experience of the risks which the controlled foreign corporation insures or reinsures. Further, consideration will be given to the existence of common directors or owners between the parties executing the reciprocal insurance arrangement. The period in which the controlled foreign corporation receives premiums and the period of coverage for which the premiums are received need not be the same as, or identical in length with, that of the other person or limited to a single taxable year of the controlled foreign corporation.

(3) *Examples*.—The following examples illustrate the principles of paragraph (h) of this section.

Example 1. Controlled foreign corporation X is incorporated in country F and is a wholly owned subsidiary of corporation M, a United States corporation. Foreign corporation Y is a wholly owned subsidiary of foreign corporation R. R is not a controlled foreign corporation. Corporations M and R, which are not related, agree that from July 1, 1987 through December 31, 1987, Y corporation will reinsure certain policies issued by M covering risks that are located outside country F, and that from January 1, 1988 through June 30, 1988, X will reinsure certain policies issued by R covering risks that are located in country F. The premiums received by X corporation from reinsuring the risks of R are attributable to risks located outside country F and constitute section 953 insurance income.

Example 2. The facts are the same as in *Example 1* except that one-third of the risks of M to be reinsured are reinsured with Y and two-thirds of the risks are reinsured with Z, another wholly owned foreign subsidiary of R. The premiums received by X from reinsuring the policies of R are attributable to risks located outside country F and constitute section 953 insurance income.

Example 3. The facts are the same as in *Example 1* except that X and V, another wholly owned foreign subsidiary of M, reinsure the risks of R. The premiums received by X and V from reinsuring the policies of R are attributable to risks located outside country F and constitute section 953 insurance income. [Reg. § 1.953-2.]

§ 1.953-3. Allocation of premiums to the RPII or nonRPII categories of section 953 insurance income.—(a) *In general*.—All premiums that constitute section 953 insurance income are included within one of two categories: premiums that constitute related person insurance income ("RPII premiums") under paragraph (b) of this section and premiums that do not constitute RPII premiums ("nonRPII premiums"). RPII premiums are not recharacterized as nonRPII premiums even though the exceptions of § 1.953-7 are applicable. However, if the exceptions of § 1.953-7(a) or (b) apply, persons that are United States shareholders solely by virtue of section 953(c)(1)(A) and paragraph (b)(2) of this section of a controlled foreign corporation, as defined in section 953(c)(1)(B) and paragraph (b)(2) of this section, do not include RPII income in their gross income. Persons that are United States shareholders within the meaning of section 951(b) of a controlled foreign corporation as defined in section 957 must always include RPII income in their gross income, regardless of whether the exceptions of § 1.953-7(a) or (b) apply. However, the special pro rata share rules of section 953(c)(5) and § 1.953-6(h)(1) shall not apply if the conditions of section 953(c)(3)(A) and (B) and § 1.953-7(a) and (b) are met.

(b) *Related person insurance income.*—(1) *In general.*—Related person insurance income is included within the meaning of the term "insurance income" as that term is used in section 953. Related person insurance income is premium and investment income attributable to a policy of insurance or reinsurance that provides insurance coverage to a related insured on risks located outside the controlled foreign corporation's country of incorporation, or premium and investment income attributable to an annuity contract that is purchased by or for the benefit of a related insured if the determining life is located outside the controlled foreign corporation's country of incorporation. For this purpose, a related insured is any insured, purchaser of an annuity contract, or recipient of annuity payments that is a United States shareholder of the controlled foreign corporation or a related person (within the meaning of section 954(d)(3)) to a United States shareholder.

(2) *Definitions.*—(i) *United States shareholder, related person, and controlled foreign corporation.*—For purposes of determining whether insurance income is related person insurance income, the terms "United States shareholder," "related person to a United States shareholder," and "controlled foreign corporation" are specifically defined. The term "controlled foreign corporation" means any foreign corporation if 25 percent or more of the total combined voting power of all classes of stock of the foreign corporation entitled to vote or 25 percent or more of the total value of the stock of the foreign corporation is owned (within the meaning of section 958(a)), or is considered as owned by applying the rules of ownership of section 958(b), by United States shareholders on any day during the taxable year of the foreign corporation. For purposes of applying this section to a foreign mutual insurance company, the term stock includes any certificate entitling the holder to voting power in the mutual company. *See* section 958(a)(3). A "United States shareholder" for these purposes is any United States person (as defined in section 957(c)) who owns (within the meaning of section 958(a)) any stock of the foreign corporation at any time during the foreign corporation's taxable year. A person is a related person to a United States shareholder if the person is related within the meaning of section 954(d)(3) of the Code to the United States shareholder. Thus, a person is related to a United States shareholder if the person controls (within the meaning of section 954(d)(3)), or is controlled by, the United States shareholder, or the person is controlled by the same person (or persons) that controls the United States shareholder. In addition, in the case of any policy of insurance covering liability arising from services performed as a director, officer, or employee of a corporation, or as a partner or employee of a partnership, the person performing such services and the entity for which such services are performed shall be treated as related persons.

(ii) *Examples.*—The following examples illustrate the definitions of paragraph (b)(2)(i) of this section.

Example 1. X is a country F corporation that provides insurance coverage to its 100 shareholders. X has voting common stock and nonvoting preferred stock issued and outstanding. All of the voting common stock is owned by 75 foreign persons. None of the foreign shareholders are related persons within the meaning of section 954(d)(3). All of the nonvoting preferred stock is owned by 25 United States persons. The nonvoting preferred stock accounts for 25 percent of the total value of both classes of stock outstanding. Therefore, each United States person is a United States shareholder and X is a controlled foreign corporation under section 953(c)(2)(B). The premiums from policies of insurance issued to the twenty-five United States shareholders constitute RPII premiums to the extent those premiums relate to risks located outside country F. The premiums from the 75 foreign shareholders constitute nonRPII premiums to the extent those premiums relate to risks located outside country F.

Example 2. The facts are the same as in *Example 1* except that all of the nonvoting preferred stock is owned by a foreign corporation, all of the stock of which is owned by the 25 United States persons. Under section 958(a)(2), the United States persons are considered as owning the stock owned by the foreign corporation. Therefore, X is a controlled foreign corporation and the 25 United States persons are United States shareholders.

Example 3. The facts are the same as in *Example 1* except that 5 of the nonvoting preferred stock shareholders are insured by X and 20 are not. X is a controlled foreign corporation and all 25 United States persons are United States shareholders. A United States person need not be insured by the controlled foreign corporation to be a United States shareholder of that corporation.

Example 4. Y is a foreign corporation that issues polices of insurance and reinsurance. The one class of Y stock outstanding is owned equally by 25 shareholders who are United States persons. None of the shareholders of Y are insured by Y; however, five of the policies issued by Y are issued to wholly-owned foreign subsidiaries of five of Y's shareholders. The premiums attributable to the policies of insurance issued with respect to the foreign subsidiaries constitute RPII premiums. The insured foreign subsidiaries are related persons to United States shareholders because those subsidiaries are controlled, within the meaning of section 954(d)(3), by United States shareholders.

(iii) *United States shareholder: exception for indirect ownership; publicly traded stock.*—A United States person who is not insured or reinsured (directly or indirectly) by a foreign corporation (the "insuring foreign corporation") and is not related to a person insured (directly or indirectly) by the insuring foreign corporation shall not be treated as a United States shareholder of the insuring foreign corporation by virtue of section 958(a)(2) because of such person's ownership of stock in another foreign corporation which owns stock (directly or indirectly) in the insuring foreign corporation if:

(A) The stock of the other foreign corporation is publicly traded;

(B) The United States person owns less than five percent of the combined voting power of all classes of stock entitled to vote and less than five percent of the total value of the stock of the other foreign corporation; and

(C) The stock of the insuring foreign corporation constitutes less than five percent of the gross value of all the assets of the other foreign corporation.

(iv) *Example.*—The following example illustrates the indirect ownership exception of paragraph (b)(2)(iii) of this section.

Example. X is a foreign corporation which writes policies of insurance for its shareholders and unrelated persons. X has one class of stock outstanding. Five shareholders of X, who are United States persons, each own 4 percent of X's stock. These shareholders are also insured by X. The remaining 80 percent of the X stock is owned by corporation Y, a foreign corporation the stock of which is publicly traded. X insures certain risks of Y. All of the stock of Y is owned by United States persons, but no shareholder of Y owns more than 5 percent of the stock of Y by vote or value or is insured by X. None of the United States persons are related to Y or to each other. The X stock owned by Y constitutes less than five percent of the total value of all of Y's assets. The United States persons who own the stock of Y are not considered United States shareholders of X under section 958(a)(2) because the requirements of paragraph (b)(2)(iii) of this section are met. Therefore, only 20 percent of the X stock is owned by United States persons and X is not a controlled foreign corporation.

(v) *Controlled foreign corporation: shipowner's protection and indemnity association.*—A controlled foreign corporation meeting the definition of paragraph (b)(2)(i) of this section and also qualifying as a shipowner's protection and indemnity association under section 526 of the Code is a controlled foreign corporation subject to the provisions of §§1.953-1 through 1.953-7. Thus, a United States shareholder of such an association must include its pro rata share of the receipts of such an association that constitute section 953 insurance income, including premiums, dues, and assessments, less appropriately allocated and apportioned expenses, losses and other deductions, in such shareholder's gross income as required by §1.953-6(h) notwithstanding section 526. *See* §1.952-2(c)(1) which states that subchapter F does not apply in determining the gross income of a controlled foreign corporation.

(3) *Reinsurance.*—(i) *In general.*—Related person insurance income includes income attributable to contracts of reinsurance, including reinsurance arrangements in which the reinsurer accepts all the rights and obligations under the reinsured contracts, pursuant to which the controlled foreign corporation reinsures contracts issued by its United States shareholders, or related persons to such shareholders.

(ii) *Examples.*—The following examples illustrate the rule of paragraph (b)(3)(i) of this section.

Example 1. Twenty-five domestic corporations, which are engaged in the business of issuing property insurance policies to unrelated commercial entities, formed Z under the laws of country W to reinsure a portion of the risks insured by the domestic corporations. Each of the twenty-five domestic corporations owns an equal amount of the one class of stock of Z outstanding. Z has no business other than reinsuring the policies issued by its shareholders. The premiums received by Z constitute RPII premiums.

Example 2. The facts are the same as in *Example 1.* However, X, one of the shareholders of Z, enters a portfolio (assumption) reinsurance agreement with Z under which Z assumes all of the rights and obligations under certain policies issued by X. Z notifies the policyholders that it is assuming all the rights and obligations under the policies issued by X. The premiums from the reinsured policies constitute related person insurance income even though X no longer has any rights or obligations under the policies.

(4) *Indirectly insuring a related insured: fronting.*—(i) *In general.*—For taxable years beginning after December 31, 1987, premiums received on insurance contracts, or contracts reinsuring insurance contracts, that indirectly insure United States shareholders of a controlled foreign corporation or persons related to such shareholders are included within the definition of related person insurance income. A contract indirectly insures a United States shareholder or person related to such shareholder if the contract is issued by an unrelated person and the contract is ultimately reinsured with the controlled foreign corporation in which the United States shareholder owns stock. For taxable years beginning after December 31, 1987, premiums received on annuity contracts, or contracts reinsuring annuity contracts, that are indirectly purchased by, or indirectly provide annuity benefits to, a United States shareholder or persons related to such shareholders are included within the definition of related person insurance income.

(ii) *Example.*—The following example illustrates the rule of paragraph (b)(4)(i) of this section.

Example. Z is a domestic corporation that has issued a policy of insurance to Y. Y is a domestic corporation which owns stock in X, a controlled foreign corporation within the meaning of section §1.953-3(b)(2)(i). Z does not own any of the stock of X. Z reinsures with X part of the risk it insures under the policy issued to Y. The premiums received by X for reinsuring the policy issued to Y are RPII premiums because one of its United States shareholders, Y, is indirectly an insured of X.

(5) *Cross-insurance arrangements.*—(i) *In general.*—Related person insurance income includes insurance income attributable to a direct or indirect cross-insurance arrangement whereby the controlled foreign corporation issues an insurance, reinsurance, or annuity contract to a person other than a related insured (as defined in paragraph (b)(1) of this section) in return for another person issuing an insurance, reinsurance, or annuity contract to a person that would be a related insured if the controlled foreign corporation were to issue an insurance, reinsurance, or annuity contract to such person. *See* §1.953-2(h).

(ii) *Example.*—The following example illustrates the rule of paragraph (b)(5)(i) of this section.

Example. Controlled foreign corporation X is owned by 30 United States shareholders engaged in a similar line of business. Controlled foreign corporation Y is owned by 32 United States shareholders engaged in the same line of business as the 30 shareholders of X. Both X and Y provide insurance to businesses engaged in the line of business in which their shareholders are engaged as well as other types of business. X agrees to provide insurance protection to Y's shareholders and Y agrees to provide insurance to X's shareholders. The premiums of both X and Y that relate to insuring the shareholders of the other corporation constitute related person insurance income.

(6) *Specific premium rules.*—(i) *Premiums received prior to January 1, 1987.*—Related person insurance income includes premiums written (less return premiums and premiums paid for reinsurance) before the first taxable year of the controlled foreign corporation beginning after December 31, 1986 that become earned under section 832(b)(4) in a taxable year beginning after December 31, 1986, or succeeding taxable years, provided that the premiums otherwise qualify as related person insurance income.

(ii) *Apportionment of premiums if stock owned for less than entire taxable year.*—If, during a taxable year of a controlled foreign corporation, an insurance, reinsurance, or annuity contract that relates to a United States shareholder remains in force beyond the period during which the United States shareholder owns stock in the controlled foreign corporation, the amount of the premiums, as defined in § 1.953-2(c), attributable to the contract must be apportioned between the RPII category and the nonRPII category. The amount apportioned to the RPII category is equal to the amount of premiums on the contract included in the gross income of the controlled foreign corporation in the taxable year multiplied by a fraction, the numerator of which is the number of days in the period of coverage which fall within the taxable year during which the United States shareholder owned stock in the controlled foreign corporation, and the denominator of which is the total number of days in the period of coverage that fall within the taxable year. The remainder of the premiums on the contract are apportioned to the nonRPII category.

(iii) *Examples.*—The following examples illustrate the rule of paragraph (b)(6)(ii) of this section.

Example 1. Y is a country F controlled foreign corporation with a calendar taxable year. Y issues a policy of insurance to M, one of its United States shareholders, covering risks of property damage to a plant owned by M. The plant is located outside country F. The policy covers risks incurred from July 1, 1987 to June 30, 1988. M pays premiums of $1,000 on July 1, 1987 and $1,000 on January 1, 1988. On September 30, 1987, M sells all of its stock in Y. In Y's 1987 taxable year, there are 183 days during which M is insured. M is a stockholder in Y for 92 days during the 1987 taxable year. Therefore, of the $1,000 of premiums from M included in Y's gross income in its 1987 taxable year, $503 ($1,000 × 92/183) is allocated to the RPII premium category and $497 is allocated to the nonRPII premium category. For the 1988 taxable year, all $1,000 of premiums from M are allocated to the nonRPII premium category because M owns no stock in Y on any day of the period of coverage falling within the 1988 taxable year.

Example 2. The facts are the same as in *Example 1* except that M sells only a part of its Y stock on September 30, 1987. Because M remains a shareholder in Y, all the premiums received from M in the 1987 and 1988 taxable years are allocated to the RPII premium category.

(iv) *Anti-abuse rule.*—If the facts and circumstances indicate that the premiums charged on an insurance, reinsurance, or annuity contract that gives rise to related person insurance income are below the premium rate charged on comparable contracts issued to unrelated persons, then the district director can recast capital contributions or other amounts paid or deposited by the United States shareholder as premiums on an insurance, reinsurance, or annuity contract. *See also* section 482 (allocation of income and deductions among taxpayers) and section 845 (certain reinsurance agreements).

(v) *Example.*—The following example illustrates the anti-abuse rule of paragraph (b)(6)(iv) of this section.

Example. X is a controlled foreign corporation incorporated in country F that insures the risks of its shareholders, all of whom are United States persons, as well as the risks of unrelated persons. In 1987, X issued fire insurance policies to some of its shareholders and to unrelated persons covering property located outside country F. The premium rates charged to the shareholders under the policies were less than those charged to similarly situated unrelated persons. The shareholders who are insured under the fire insurance policies also purchased preferred stock on which X has call rights which become effective on the same dates that the policies expire. The facts indicate that the amounts paid for the preferred stock are actually part of the cost of the insurance provided to the shareholders. All or part of the amounts paid for the preferred stock may be recharacterized as premiums paid on insurance policies. [Reg. § 1.953-3.]

§ 1.953-4. Allocation and apportionment of items of investment income.—(a) *In general.*—(1) *Investment income.*—This section prescribes the rules for determining the amount of investment income within the RPII, nonRPII, and SCI categories. Except as provided in paragraph (a)(2) of this section, investment income for this purpose is any type of income of a controlled foreign corporation for the taxable year other than premiums as defined in § 1.953-2(c). Thus, investment income includes, but is not limited to, gain from the sale or disposition of property under section 832(b)(1)(B), interest, dividends, and rents. Investment income also includes, to the extent prescribed in paragraph (a)(2) of this section, income resulting from the decrease in section 807(c) items under section 807(a), income resulting from the decrease in section 807(c)(1) items included in unearned premiums of a property and casualty insurance company under section 832(b)(4), and income resulting from a reduction of discounted unpaid losses under section 832(b)(5). An item of investment income is allocated to a particular category, whether the RPII, nonRPII, or SCI category, only if the income results from a decrease in reserves attributable under the principles of § 1.953-5(a) to a particular category or if the requirements of paragraph (b) of this section are met. If an item of investment income cannot be allocated to the RPII, nonRPII, or SCI categories, it is apportioned to the different categories in accordance with paragraph (c) of this section. If the investment income within each of the RPII, nonRPII, and SCI categories is determined under the apportionment method of paragraph (c) of this section, then the investment income within each category shall be deemed to consist of each type of investment income (*e.g.*, dividends, interest, tax-exempt interest, and capital gains) in the same proportion that the aggregate amount of a particular type of investment income earned during the taxable year bears to the total amount of all types of investment income earned during the taxable year.

(2) *Decreases in reserves*.—(i) *In general*.—In the case of each of the RPII, nonRPII, and SCI categories of income, if a decrease in section 807(c) items or a decrease in section 846 discounted unpaid losses occurs as the result of the payment of claims and benefits accrued and losses incurred, as described in section 805(a)(1), or as the result of losses paid, as described in section 832(b)(5)(A)(i), then the income resulting from the decrease in reserves shall be deemed to consist of premium and investment income in the same proportion that the claims, benefits, or losses that result in the decrease in the reserve are apportioned between premium and investment income under § 1.953-5(c)(3)(iii)(A). Section 807(c) items include section 807(c)(1) reserves included in the unearned premiums of a property and casualty insurance company under section 832(b)(4). If a decrease in section 807(c) items and section 846 unpaid losses attributable under the principles of § 1.953-5(a) to the SCI category and to the RPII category (if the elections under section 953(c)(3)(C) and section 831(b) are made) occurs as the result of any actuarial redetermination, the amount of income included in gross income in accordance with section 807(f), in the case of a foreign life insurance company, or in accordance with section 481, in the case of a foreign property and casualty insurance company, shall be considered investment income equal to the amount obtained by multiplying the decrease in section 807(c) items or section 846 discounted unpaid losses by a fraction. The numerator of the fraction shall be the amount of the increase in section 807(c) items or section 846 discounted unpaid losses that have been apportioned against investment income under § 1.953-5(c)(3)(iii)(B) and (C) during the five taxable years (or the period during which the controlled foreign corporation has been in existence, if less than five taxable years) preceding the current taxable year. The denominator of the fraction shall be the total amount of deductions attributable to the increases in section 807(c) items and section 846 discounted unpaid losses during the five taxable years (or shorter period, if applicable) preceding the current taxable year. The remainder of the decrease in section 807(c) items and section 846 discounted unpaid losses attributable to the SCI category and, if appropriate, the RPII category shall be treated as giving rise to premium income. In the case of section 807(c) items and section 846 discounted unpaid losses attributable to the nonRPII category and the RPII category, if the section 953(c)(3)(C) and section 831(b) elections have not been made, the entire decrease in section 807(c) items and section 846 discounted unpaid losses shall be treated as investment income.

(ii) *Examples*.—The following examples illustrate the principles of paragraph (a)(2)(i) of this section.

Example 1. Y is a life insurance company and is a controlled foreign corporation. In 1988 Y's section 807(c)(1) life insurance reserves decrease from $10,000 to $8,000, resulting in $2,000 of income under sections 803(a)(2) and 807(a). The decrease resulted from the payment of a death benefit that, under § 1.953-5(c)(3)(iii)(A), is apportioned against investment income and premium income in the amount of $1,500 and $500, respectively. The $2,000 decrease results in $1,500 of investment income ($2,000 × $1,500/$2,000) and $500 of premium income ($2,000 × $500/$2,000).

Example 2. X is a property and casualty insurance company and is a controlled foreign corporation. Under section 832(b)(5), X had, for its 1987 taxable year, discounted unpaid losses of $100,000 attributable to contracts the premiums from which were allocable to the SCI category of income. For 1988, X had losses paid of $50,000 and discounted unpaid losses of $25,000 allocable to contracts giving rise to SCI premiums. Section 832(b)(5) requires X to reduce its 1988 losses paid by the excess of discounted unpaid losses for 1987 over the current year discounted unpaid losses. Thus, X has $25,000 of income resulting from the decrease in discounted unpaid losses computed as follows: 1988 losses paid of $50,000 minus the difference between 1987 discounted unpaid losses of $100,000 and 1988 discounted unpaid losses of $25,000 ($50,000 − [$100,000 − $25,000]) = $25,000. Assuming that section 481 applies, X will take the premium and investment income into account in accordance with that section. If over the past five years, the increase in discounted unpaid losses is $50,000, of which $10,000 was allocated to investment income and $40,000 to premium income under § 1.953-5(c)(3)(iii)(B) and (C), then 1/5th ($10,000/$50,000) of the amounts taken into income in each taxable year in accordance with section 481 will be treated as investment income and 4/5ths ($40,000/$50,000) will be treated as premium income.

(b) *Allocation of investment income*.—(1) *In general*.—An item of investment income is allocated to a particular category of income if the item directly relates to a contract (or that part of a contract) which gives rise to premiums allocable to the same category of income. An item of investment income is considered to be directly related to a contract (or that part of a contract) which gives rise to premiums allocable to a particular category if the income is derived from an asset which is identified on the controlled foreign corporation's books and records as an asset relating to RPII, nonRPII, or SCI contracts and the controlled foreign corporation separately accounts for the various income, exclusion, deduction, reserve, and other liability items properly attributable to such contracts.

(2) *Examples*.—The following examples illustrate the rules of paragraph (b)(1) of this section.

Example 1. The facts are the same as in *Example 2* of paragraph (a)(2)(ii) of this section. The amount of investment income included in gross income in each taxable year in accordance with section 481 is allocable to the SCI category.

Example 2. Z is a country F controlled foreign corporation which issues life insurance contracts. Among the contracts issued by Z are variable life insurance contracts issued to residents of country F. The life insurance contracts qualify as variable contracts under section 817(d) of the Code. The amounts received under the contracts are allocated pursuant to country F law to an account which is segregated from the general asset accounts of Z, and the amount of the death benefits under the contracts are adjusted on the basis of the investment return and the market value of the segregated asset account. Z's books of account identify the assets relating to the variable life insurance contracts issued to residents of country F, and Z separately accounts for the various income, exclusion, deduction, reserve, and other liability items properly attributable to such contracts. Therefore, all of the investment income attributable to the variable contracts is allocable to the SCI income category.

(c) *Apportionment of investment income.*—(1) *Life insurance companies.*—(i) *In general.*—A foreign corporation that would determine its insurance income under part I of subchapter L (relating to life insurance companies) if it were a domestic company shall apportion its investment income to each of the RPII, nonRPII, and SCI categories, in the same proportion that—

(A) The sum of the means of each of the items described in section 807(c) attributable to contracts which give rise to premiums within the particular income category bears to

(B) The sum of the means of the items described in section 807(c) for the taxable year attributable to all contracts.

(ii) *Section 807(c) items attributable to RPII, nonRPII, and SCI contracts.*—The amount of an item described in section 807(c) that is attributable to a particular income category is that amount which would result if the section 807(c) item were computed, using the assumptions required under section 807, as modified by § 1.953-6(e), only with respect to the contracts the premiums from which are apportioned to that particular income category.

(2) *Property and casualty companies.*—(i) *In general.*—A foreign corporation that would determine its insurance income under part II of subchapter L (relating to insurance companies other than life insurance companies) if it were a domestic company shall apportion its investment income to each of the RPII, nonRPII, and SCI categories, in the same proportion that—

(A) The sum of the premiums written, as defined in section 832(b)(4)(A), for the current taxable year, plus the amount of unearned premiums as of the close of the previous taxable year, plus the amount of the section 846 discounted unpaid losses as of the close of the previous taxable year attributable to the particular income category, bears to

(B) The sum of the premiums written, as defined in section 832(b)(4)(A), for the current taxable year, plus the amount of unearned premiums as of the close of the previous taxable year, plus the amount of the section 846 discounted unpaid losses as of the close of the previous taxable year attributable to all categories of income.

(ii) *Unpaid losses attributable to a particular category.*—The amount of the section 846 discounted unpaid losses that are attributable to a particular income category is that amount which would result if the unpaid losses were computed, using the assumptions required by section 846, as modified by § 1.953-6(e), only with respect to the contracts the premiums from which are apportioned to that particular income category.

(3) *Examples.*—The following examples illustrate the principles of paragraph (c) of this section.

Example 1. X is a property and casualty insurance company and a controlled foreign corporation that is not engaged in a trade or business in the United States. X is a calendar year taxpayer. In 1987, X had $600 of premiums written from contracts issued to related insureds and $300 of premiums written from contracts issued to unrelated persons. At the end of 1986, X had $400 in unearned premiums from contracts issued to related insureds and $200 of unearned premiums from contracts issued to unrelated persons. X also had unpaid losses at the end of 1986 of $500 with respect to its related insured contracts and $250 with respect to its contracts issued to unrelated persons. In 1987, X had $1,000 of taxable interest income and $2,000 of tax exempt income. The total of X's premiums written for the current year, plus previous year unearned premiums, plus previous year unpaid loss reserves on RPII business is $1,500 ($600 + $400 + $500) and on nonRPII business is $750 ($300 + $200 + $250). Therefore, $2,000 of investment income ($1,500/$2,250 × $3,000) is apportioned to the RPII category and $1,000 ($750/$2,250 × $3,000) is apportioned to the nonRPII category. Pursuant to paragraph (a)(1) of this section, of the $2,000 apportioned to the RPII category, $666.67 ($2,000 × $1,000/$3,000) is taxable interest income and $1,333.33 ($2,000 × $2,000/$3,000) is tax-exempt interest. Of the $1,000 apportioned to the nonRPII category, $333.33 ($1,000 × $1,000/$3,000) is taxable interest income and $666.67 ($1,000 × $2,000/$3,000) is tax-exempt interest income.

Example 2. Y is a controlled foreign corporation that issues life insurance policies and would, if it were a domestic corporation, be taxable under part I of subchapter L of the Code. Y is not engaged in a trade or business within the United States. In 1987, its first year in business, Y only issues insurance policies to its United States shareholders or persons related to its United States shareholders. Y received $3,000 in premiums for the year and at the end of the year had a reserve under section 807(c)(1) of $2,000. In 1988, Y only issues life insurance policies to persons other than its United States shareholders or persons related to those shareholders. Y receives $5,000 in premiums in 1988. In 1988, Y's year-end section 807(c)(1) reserves with respect to contracts issued to related persons is $1,000 and with respect to unrelated persons is $4,000. Investment income in 1988 is $1,000, all of which is taxable interest income. The mean of the 807(c) items for 1988 are computed in Table 1 below.

Table 1

Mean section 807(c) items attributable to RPII contracts in force in 1988:		
Mean of life insurance reserves attributable to RPII policies:		
1987 closing reserve	$2,000	
1988 closing reserve	$1,000	
Mean = ($2,000 + $1,000)/2		$1,500
Mean of life insurance reserves attributable to nonRPII policies:		
1987 closing reserve	$0	
1988 closing reserve	$4,000	
Mean = $4,000/2		$2,000

Based on the computations in Table 1, the investment income apportioned to the RPII category equals $1,000 × ($1,500/3,500) or $428.57, and investment income apportioned to the nonRPII category equals $1,000 × ($2,000/$3,500) or $571.42. [Reg. § 1.953-4.]

§ 1.953-5. Allocation and apportionment of expenses.—(a) *Allocation of deductions to RPII, nonRPII, and SCI categories.*—To compute the amount of section 953 insurance income or foreign personal holding company income that a controlled foreign corporation has derived from insurance operations, items of expenses, losses, and other deductions (collectively referred to as "deductions") must be allocated to and apportioned among the RPII, nonRPII, and SCI categories of income. Allocation of expenses shall be made in accordance with § § 1.861-8, 1.861-8T, 1.861-9T, 1.861-10T, and 1.861-12T, and this section. The deduction under section 832(b)(4)(B) for unearned premiums is allocable to the categories to which the unearned premiums relate as determined by § § 1.953-2 and 1.953-3. The deductions for death benefits, increases in reserves, policyholder dividends, consideration in respect of the assumption by another person of liabilities, and reimbursable dividends under section 805(a)(1), (2), (3), (6), and (7) are allocable to the particular category of income to which those deductions relate. The deductions for losses paid and discounted unpaid losses, under section 832(b)(5), and dividends and similar distributions paid or declared to policyholders in their capacity as such, under section 832(c)(11), are also allocable to the particular category of income to which those deductions relate. The amount of the deductions specified in the preceding two sentences of this paragraph shall be considered to relate to the RPII, nonRPII, and SCI categories to the extent the deduction is attributable to contracts that give rise to premiums allocated to a particular category. Deductions not specifically addressed in this paragraph (a) may be allocated to the RPII, nonRPII, or SCI category of income if the controlled foreign corporation identifies on its books and records the assets which relate to RPII, nonRPII, or SCI contracts, and the controlled foreign corporation separately accounts for the various income, exclusion, deduction, reserve, and other liability items properly attributable to such contracts.

(b) *Apportionment of expenses to RPII, nonRPII, and SCI categories.*—(1) *In general.*—Those expenses which cannot be allocated must be apportioned among the RPII, nonRPII, and SCI categories.

(2) *Life insurance companies.*—(i) *Investment deductions.*—A controlled foreign corporation that would be taxable under part I of subchapter L (relating to life insurance companies) if it were a domestic insurance company shall apportion to the RPII, nonRPII, and SCI categories its deductions that are allocable or apportionable to investment income under § § 1.861-8, 1.861-8T, 1.861-9T, 1.861-10T, and 1.861-12T in the same proportion that investment income for the current taxable year is apportioned to those categories under § 1.953-4(c).

(ii) *Other deductions.*—A controlled foreign corporation that would be taxable under part I of subchapter L (relating to life insurance companies) if it were a domestic insurance company shall apportion to the RPII, nonRPII, and SCI categories a deduction that is not allocable or apportionable to investment income under § § 1.861-8, 1.861-8T, 1.861-9T, 1.861-10T, and 1.861-12T in the same proportion as the numerator in paragraph (b)(2)(ii)(A) of this section bears to the denominator in paragraph (b)(2)(ii)(B) of this section.

(A) *Numerator.*—For purposes of this paragraph (b)(2)(ii) the numerator equals:

(1) The amount of premiums determined under section 803(a)(1) allocable to the income category, plus

(2) The decrease in section 807(c) items allocable to the income category as determined under section 807(a), minus

(3) The increase in section 807(c) items allocable to the income category as determined under section 807(b).

(B) *Denominator.*—For purposes of this paragraph (b)(2)(ii) the denominator equals:

(1) The amount of premiums determined under section 803(a)(1) for all categories of income, plus

(2) The decrease in section 807(c) items for all categories of income as determined under section 807(a), minus

(3) The increase in section 807(c) items for all categories of income as determined under section 807(b).

(3) *Property and casualty companies.*—(i) *Investment deductions.*—A controlled foreign corporation that would be taxable under part II of subchapter L (relating to insurance companies other than life companies) if it were a domestic insurance company shall apportion to the RPII, nonRPII, and SCI categories its deductions that are allocable or apportionable to investment income under § § 1.861-8, 1.861-8T, 1.861-9T, 1.861-10T, and 1.861-12T in the same proportion that investment income for the current taxable year is apportioned to those categories under § 1.953-4(c).

(ii) *Other deductions.*—A controlled foreign corporation that would be taxable under part II of subchapter L (relating to insurance companies other than life insurance companies) if it were a domestic insurance company shall apportion to the RPII, nonRPII, and SCI categories a deduction that is not allocable or apportionable to investment income under §§1.861-8, 1.861-8T, 1.861-9T, 1.861-10T, and 1.861-12T in the same proportion that the premiums earned, as defined in section 832(b)(4), allocated to a particular income category bears to the total of the premiums earned in all of the income categories.

(c) *Allocation and apportionment of deductions between premium and investment income after the deductions have been allocated or apportioned to the SCI or RPII categories.*—(1) *In general.*—Deductions within the SCI category must be allocated to or apportioned between premium income and investment income. Deductions within the RPII category must be allocated to or apportioned between premium and investment income if an election is made under section 953(c)(3)(C) (relating to the treatment of RPII income as effectively connected with the conduct of a United States trade or business) and under section 831(b) (alternative tax for certain small companies). Allocation and apportionment of deductions to or between premium and investment income within the SCI category and, if applicable, the RPII category is made in accordance with §§1.861-8, 1.861-8T, 1.861-9T, 1.861-10T, and 1.861-12T and paragraph (c)(3) of this section.

(2) *Examples.*—The following examples illustrate the rule of paragraph (c)(1) of this section.

Example 1. X is a life insurance company that issues policies insuring the lives of persons residing in X's country of incorporation. X requires its insureds to undergo medical examinations by physicians approved and paid by X. Under the principles of §§1.861-8, 1.861-8T, 1.861-9T, 1.861-10T, and 1.861-12T and this section, the medical expenses paid by X are allocable to the class of gross income consisting of X's SCI premiums.

Example 2. Z is a life insurance company that issues policies only in its country of incorporation. Z has an investment department that is in charge of investing Z's funds. The amount expended by Z in compensating the employees of its investment department is allocable under the principles of §1.861-8 and this section to the class of gross income consisting of Z's SCI investment income.

(3) *Apportionment of reserves, losses, policyholder dividends, and policy acquisition expenses and certain other deductions between investment and premium income.*—(i) *In general.*—For taxable years beginning on or after April 17, 1991, the amount of the deduction for reserves, the deduction for losses, the deduction for policyholder dividends, the deduction for policy acquisition expenses, and certain other deductions apportioned against investment income within the SCI category and, if applicable, within the RPII category, shall be—

(A) The amount of investment income required to be added to reserves and required to fund losses within the SCI and, if applicable, the RPII category as computed in paragraph (c)(3)(iii) of this section;

(B) Investment income's proportionate share of policyholder dividends within the SCI and, if applicable, the RPII category as determined under paragraph (c)(3)(iv) of this section; and

(C) The amount of policy acquisition expenses and certain other deductions determined under paragraph (c)(3)(v) of this section. The remainder of the deductions for reserves, losses, policyholder dividends, policy acquisition expenses, and certain other deductions within the SCI and, if applicable, the RPII category shall be apportioned against and reduce premium income. For taxable years beginning prior to April 17 1991, taxpayers may use a reasonable apportionment formula.

(ii) *Deduction for reserves and losses defined.*—For purposes of paragraph (c)(3)(i) of this section, the phrase "deduction for losses" means current year deductions for claims, benefits, and losses under section 805(a)(1)(other than discounted unpaid losses under section 846), losses paid under section 832(b)(5)(A)(i), and unpaid losses on life insurance contracts. The phrase "deduction for reserves" means, for purposes of paragraph (c)(3)(i) of this section: the increase in section 807(c) reserves, as adjusted by section 807(b), of a foreign life insurance company; the increase in section 807(c)(1) reserves, as adjusted under section 807(b), included in unearned premiums of a foreign property and casualty company; and the increase in section 846 discounted unpaid losses as computed under section 832(b)(5)(ii).

(iii) *Investment income required to be added to reserves and required to fund losses.*—The total amount of investment income required to be added to reserves and to fund current year losses within the SCI and, if applicable, the RPII category is computed as the sum of the following:

(A) The investment income portion of current year losses within the SCI and, if applicable, the RPII category: This amount is the excess of—

(1) The amount of current year losses within the appropriate category, less

(2) The amount of current year losses within the appropriate category divided by one plus one-half of the annual interest rate specified in §1.953-6(e)(4) for computing reserves.

(B) The investment income portion attributable to current-year premiums that have been added to reserves within the SCI and, if applicable, the RPII category: This amount shall be computed as—

(1) The amount of current-year premiums added to reserves within the appropriate category multiplied by one-half of the annual interest rate specified in §1.953-6(e)(4) for computing reserves, or

(2) If the amount of current-year premiums added to the reserves is not known, the excess of—

(i) The year-end reserves within the appropriate category attributable to current-year premiums within the appropriate category, less

(ii) The year-end reserves within the appropriate category divided by one plus one-half of the annual interest rate specified in §1.953-6(e)(4) for computing reserves.

(C) The investment income portion attributable to reserves within the SCI and, if applicable, the RPII category existing as of the end of the preceding taxable year and still in existence as of the end of the current taxable year: This amount shall be computed as the excess of—

(1) The amount of the reserves within the appropriate category at the end of the taxable year, less the sum of the amount of reserves within the appropriate category attributable to current-year premiums plus the investment income portion attributable to current-year premiums as computed under paragraph (c)(3)(iii)(B) of this section, over

(2) The amount obtained by dividing the amount computed under paragraph (c)(3)(iii)(C)*(1)* of this section by one plus the annual interest rate specified in § 1.953-6(e)(4) for computing reserves.

(D) If the amount of a reserve within the SCI and, if applicable, the RPII category is increased because of any actuarial redetermination, the investment income portion of the increase shall be treated as the amount of the adjustment multiplied by a fraction, the numerator of which is the amount of reserves within the appropriate category that have been deducted against gross investment income under paragraph (c)(3)(iii)(B) and (D) of this section during the five taxable years preceding the current taxable year (or for the life of the corporation preceding the current taxable year if the foreign corporation has been in existence for less than five taxable years), and the denominator of which is the total amount of deductions attributable to reserves within the appropriate category during the five taxable years preceding the current taxable year (or for the life of the corporation preceding the current taxable year, as may be applicable).

(iv) *Investment income's proportionate share of policyholder dividends.*—For purposes of this paragraph (c)(3), investment income's proportionate share of policyholder dividends, as defined in section 808(a) and (b) and section 832(c)(11), is an amount equal to the deduction for policyholder's dividends determined under sections 808, 809, and 832(c)(11) for the taxable year multiplied by a fraction, the numerator of which is gross investment income within the SCI and, if applicable, the RPII category, for the taxable year, reduced by the amounts determined under paragraph (c)(3)(i)(A) of this section, and the denominator of which is total gross income within the appropriate category reduced by the excess, if any, of the closing balance of items described in section 807(c) or discounted unpaid losses under section 846 within the appropriate category, over the opening balance of such items and losses within the appropriate category. For purposes of paragraph (c)(3)(iv) of this section, the denominator of the fraction shall be determined by including tax-exempt interest and by applying section 807(a)(2)(B) as if it did not contain section 807(a)(2)(B)(i) thereof.

(v) *Apportionment of policy acquisition expenses and certain other deductions.*—For purposes of this paragraph (c)(3), specified policy acquisition expenses, as defined in section 848(c)(1), and general deductions, as defined in section 848(c)(2), shall be apportioned to investment income within the SCI category and, if applicable, the RPII category, in the same proportion as the numerator in paragraph (c)(3)(v)(A) of this section bears to the denominator in paragraph (c)(3)(v)(B) of this section.

(A) *Numerator.*—For purposes of this paragraph (c)(3)(v), the numerator equals the amount of investment income allocated or apportioned to the SCI category and, if applicable, the RPII category, minus the amount of the deduction for reserves apportioned to investment income under this paragraph (c)(3), to the extent that such reserves qualify as life insurance reserves within the meaning of section 816(b).

(B) *Denominator.*—For purposes of this paragraph (c)(3)(v), the denominator equals the amount of premium income allocated or apportioned to the SCI category and, if applicable, the RPII category, plus the amount determined under paragraph (c)(3)(v)(A) of this section. For purposes of paragraph (c)(3)(v)(B) of this section, premium income is the amount of premiums within the meaning of section 803(a)(1) and (b), in the case of a controlled foreign corporation that would be taxable under part I of subchapter L (relating to life insurance companies) if it were a domestic insurance company. In the case of a controlled foreign corporation that would be taxable under part II of subchapter L (relating to insurance companies other than life companies) if it were a domestic insurance company, premium income is the amount of premiums within the meaning of section 832(b)(4). All computations entering into the determination of premium income for purposes of paragraph (c)(3)(v)(B) of this section shall be made in the manner required under section 811(a) for life insurance companies. The fraction set forth in this paragraph (c)(3)(v), determined for each taxable year, applies to the amount of specified policy acquisition expenses computed under section 848(c)(1) for that taxable year, which are capitalized and allowed as a deduction in such taxable year and in subsequent taxable years in accordance with section 848(a). The fraction set forth in this paragraph (c)(3)(v), determined for each taxable year, also applies to the amount, if any, by which general deductions (as defined in section 848(c)(2)) deductible in such taxable year exceed specified policy acquisition expenses for such year (as computed and capitalized under section 848). Such general deductions are subject to the apportionment formula set forth in this paragraph (c)(3)(v), even if the capitalization requirements of section 848 do not apply to the company or to certain contracts issued by it. For purposes of this paragraph (c)(3)(v), the terms "net premiums" and "general deductions," as defined in sections 848(d) and 848(c)(2), respectively, shall be computed by taking into account only amounts that have been allocated or apportioned to the SCI category and, if applicable, the RPII category.

(vi) *Example.*—The following example demonstrates the calculation of the amount of investment income required to be added to reserves and fund losses under paragraph (c)(3)(i) of this section.

Example. X is a country F controlled foreign corporation that has income from issuing life insurance contracts to persons who reside in country F. At the end of its 1988 taxable year, X has a reserve under section 807(c)(1) of $12,292 of which $7,000 is from the addition of current-year premiums plus $350 of investment income attributable to those premiums. At the end of the 1987 taxable year X's reserves were $7,350. Thus, X's reserves have increased a total of $4,942. X paid

$3,000 in death benefits in 1988. The appropriate interest rate for computing X's life insurance reserves on all of X's policies is 10% per annum. The amount of reserves and losses apportioned to premium and investment income is computed as follows:

The investment income portion of X's current year losses paid:

Losses – [Losses/(1 + .5(10%)] $3,000 – ($3,000/1.05) = $142.86.

The investment income portion of X's current year premiums that have been added to reserves:

There are two methods for computing this amount:

(a) Current year premiums added to reserves × .5(annual interest rate for determining reserves).

$7,000 × .05 = $350

(b) Year-end reserves attributable to current-year premiums less [such year-end reserves divided by 1 + .5(annual interest rate)].

$7,350 – [$7,350/(1 + .5(10%)]=

$7,350 – $7,000 = $350.

The investment income portion attributable to section 807(c) reserves existing at the end of the preceding taxable year that were in existence at the end of the current taxable year.

[Year-end reserves less the sum of reserves attributable to current-year premiums plus the investment income portion attributable to current-year premiums minus the amount obtained in the previous term divided by (1 + 10%)]

[$12,292 – ($7,000 + $350)] – [($12,292 – ($7,000 + $350))/1.10] =

$4,942 – $4,492.72 = $449.28

Thus, of $3,000 in losses, $142.86 is apportioned to gross investment income and $2,857.14 is allocated to premium income. Of the $4,942 increase in reserves, $350 is the amount of investment income required to be added to current-year premiums and $449.28 is the amount of investment income required to be added to reserves that were in existence throughout the year. Thus, $799.28 of the $4,942.28 increase in reserves is apportioned to investment income and $4,142.72 ($4,942 – $799.28) of the increase in reserves is apportioned to premium income.

(4) *Alternative method for life insurance companies.*—(i) *In general.*—As an alternative to the computations required by paragraph (c)(3)(i) of this section, a controlled foreign corporation that would be subject to part I of subchapter L if it were a domestic insurance company may apportion against investment income within the SCI and, if applicable, the RPII category, the deductions for reserves, losses, and policyholder dividends in an amount equal to the policy interest plus gross investment income's proportionate share of policyholder dividends as computed under section 812(b). The remaining amount, if any, of the deductions for reserves, losses, and policyholder dividends shall be apportioned to gross premium income.

(ii) *Example.*—The following example demonstrates the principles of paragraph (c)(4)(i) of this section.

Example. X is a controlled foreign corporation that would be taxable as a life insurance company under part I of subchapter L if it were a domestic insurance company. In 1988, X has a reserve of $1,000. In 1989, X has a reserve of $1,500. Under section 812(b)(2)(A), and using the interest rate prescribed in § 1.953-6(e)(4) for computing reserves, X has policy interest equal to $200. Rather than using the method set forth in paragraph (c)(3)(i) of this section, the increase in reserves may be apportioned between premium and investment income by apportioning the policy interest to investment income and by apportioning the increase in the reserves less the policy interest against premium income. Thus, $200 is apportioned to investment income and $300 ($500 – $200) is apportioned to premium income.

(5) *Losses in excess of premium or investment income.*—If the total amount of deductions allocated and apportioned to premium income within the RPII and nonRPII categories exceeds the amount of premium income within those categories, then the excess shall be allocated to investment income within the same category. If the total amount of deductions allocated and apportioned to premium income within the SCI category exceeds the amount of premium income within that category, then the excess shall not be allocated to investment income within the SCI category and shall not be allocated to any other category of subpart F income. However, if an election is made under section 952(c)(1)(B)(vii), the deductions allocated and apportioned to premium income within the SCI category shall be allocated to investment income within the SCI category. If the total amount of deductions allocated or apportioned to investment income within each of the RPII and nonRPII categories exceeds the amount of investment income within those categories, then the excess deductions shall be allocated to premium income within the same category. If the total amount of deductions allocated or apportioned to investment income within the SCI category exceeds the amount of investment income within that category, then the excess deductions shall be allocated to the RPII or nonRPII categories in accordance with paragraph (c)(6) of this section. However, if an election is made under section 952(c)(1)(B)(vii), deductions allocated or apportioned to investment income with the SCI category that exceed the income within that category shall first reduce premium income within the same category.

(6) *Losses within the RPII, nonRPII, and SCI categories.*—If, after allocating and apportioning deductions, there is a loss within the RPII or nonRPII categories, within the investment income portion of the SCI category, or, if an election is made under section 952(c)(1)(B)(vii), within the entire SCI category, then a loss in one category will be treated as reducing income in another category only for purposes of calculating the pro rata share of RPII, nonRPII, or SCI income to be included by United States shareholders as defined in section 951(b). Thus, persons that are United States shareholders solely by virtue of section 953(c)(1)(A) may not use a loss within the nonRPII or SCI categories to reduce income within the RPII category. [Reg. § 1.953-5.]

§ 1.953-6. Application of subchapter L and certain sections of subchapter N of the Code.—(a) *Applicability of subchapter L.*—(1) *In general.*—A controlled foreign corporation which has insurance income under section 953 or foreign personal holding company income that is SCI investment income shall compute its insurance income or SCI investment income either under part I of subchapter L of the Code (relating to life insurance companies) or under part II of subchapter L of the Code (relating to other insurance companies) as modified by this section and § 1.952-2. If a controlled foreign corporation does not file an annual statement with an insurance regulatory authority of any State, such corporation must complete those portions of the annual statement prescribed by the National Association of Insurance Commissioners which are necessary to make the determinations and computations required under subchapter L of the Code. If a controlled foreign corporation uses the reserves described in paragraph (d)(1)(ii) of this section (relating to reserves on United States business for which no NAIC statement is required) to qualify as a life insurance company subject to part I under subchapter L, then the foreign corporation shall compute its reserves, for purposes of the NAIC annual statement, by following the laws and regulations of New York or the laws of the State of the United States where the insured risks are located, whichever is applicable under paragraph (d)(1)(ii) of this section. In all other circumstances, the controlled foreign corporation shall complete the necessary portion of the NAIC annual statement by following the rules prescribed in § § 1.953-1 through 1.953-7 and, to the extent not inconsistent with those sections, the rules prescribed by the National Association of Insurance Commissioners.

(2) *Applicability of section 7702.*—[Reserved]

(3) *Applicability of section 817.*—[Reserved]

(b) *Special rules regarding use of subchapter L to compute RPII, nonRPII, and SCI income.*—(1) *Certain provisions not to apply.*—The following provisions of subchapter L do not apply in computing section 953 insurance income or foreign personal holding company income that is SCI investment income:

(i) Section 806, relating to the small life insurance company deduction;

(ii) Section 805(a)(5), relating to the operations loss deduction; and

(iii) Section 832(c)(5), relating to certain capital losses.

(2) *Allocation and apportionment of certain items.*—The items referred to in section 803(a)(1)(relating to gross amount of premiums and other considerations), section 803(a)(2)(relating to net decrease in reserves), section 805(a)(2)(relating to net increase in reserves), and section 832(b)(4)(relating to premiums earned on insurance contracts) shall be taken into account in computing income within a particular category, whether the RPII, nonRPII, and SCI, categories, only to the extent they relate to a contract issued or reinsured by the controlled foreign corporation that gives rise to premiums within that particular category. For rules relating to the allocation of premiums, *see* § § 1.953-2 and 1.953-3. For rules relating to increases or decreases in reserves, *see* § § 1.953-4 and 1.953-5.

(c) *Alternative tax for certain small companies.*—Any controlled foreign corporation that computes its taxable income under part II of subchapter L (relating to insurance companies other than life insurance companies) and makes the election under § 1.953-7(c) to have its related person insurance income treated as effectively connected with the conduct of a trade or business in the United States may elect to have its related person insurance income, as well as its income effectively connected with the conduct of a United States trade or business that is excluded from subpart F income under section 952(b), taxed under section 831(b)(alternative tax for certain small companies) if the requirements of that section are met. To determine whether a corporation meets the net written premium requirement of section 831(b), the premiums on all policies (including SCI policies) of insurance or reinsurance or annuity contracts issued by the corporation must be taken into account.

(d) *Computation of reserves to determine applicability of part I of subchapter L.*—(1) *Reserves required by law.*—The reserves set forth in this paragraph (d)(1) are the only reserves to be taken into account as reserves required by law under section 816(b)(2) to determine for any taxable year whether a controlled foreign corporation is subject to part I of subchapter L (relating to life insurance companies):

(i) *Reserves with respect to United States business.*—The reserves which are required by the law of the state or states of the United States, including the District of Columbia, to which the business of the controlled foreign corporation is subject, but only with respect to its United States business, if any, which is taxable under section 842(a).

(ii) *Reserves deemed to be required.*—To the extent the controlled foreign corporation is not subject to section 842(a) but issues a policy of insurance or an annuity contract to a resident of the United States—

(A) Except as provided in paragraph (d)(1)(ii)(B) of this section, the reserves that would be required by applying the minimum standards of the law of New York as if the controlled foreign corporation were an insurance company transacting all of its insurance business (other than its insurance business carried on within the United States that is subject to section 842(a)) for the taxable year in New York, and

(B) With respect to all United States risks covered by insurance ceded to the controlled foreign corporation by an insurance company subject to subchapter L of the Code, determined without regard to section 501, and in respect of which an election is made by or on behalf of the controlled foreign corporation to determine its reserves in accordance with paragraph (d)(1)(ii)(B) of this section, the amount of reserves against such risks which would result if the reserves were determined by applying the law of the state of the United States where the risks are located as if the controlled foreign corporation were an insurance company in that state engaged in reinsuring the risks.

(iii) *Reserves with respect to foreign business.*—In the case of a reserve on a contract that is not described in paragraph (d)(1)(i) and (ii) of this section, the reserve determined under the laws, regulations, or administrative guidance of the insurance regulatory authority of the home country, or the reserve determined under the laws of the country of residence of the insured, if the controlled foreign corporation is subject to the insurance regulatory authority of the insured's country of residence. If the reserves of a controlled foreign corporation are subject to the laws of more than one foreign jurisdiction, the amount of reserves taken into account shall be the largest reserve required by any such foreign jurisdiction. If neither the home country nor the country of residence of the insured require reserves to be established, then the reserve shall be computed using the mortality tables prescribed by section 807(d) but using the interest rate prescribed in paragraph (e)(4) of this section applicable to qualified contracts.

(2) *SCI reserves to be taken into account.*—The total reserves of a controlled foreign corporation are taken into account to determine whether the corporation is to compute its taxable income under part I of subchapter L. Thus, reserves which relate to the lives or health of residents of the home country are taken into account.

(e) *Computation of reserves for purposes of computing taxable income.*—(1) *Actual reserves required.*—For all purposes of §§1.953-1 through 1.953-7, a controlled foreign corporation will be considered to have a reserve only to the extent the reserve has been actually held during the taxable year for which the reserve is claimed.

(2) *Life insurance reserves.*—For purposes of computing the taxable income from insurance operations, the section 807(c)(1) items of a controlled foreign corporation that would be taxable under part I or part II of subchapter L of the Code if it were a domestic insurance company that are related to a nonqualified contract, as defined in this paragraph, shall be determined under the rules of section 807(d). The amount of life insurance reserves under section 807(c)(1) relating to qualified foreign contracts shall be determined under the rules of section 807(e)(4) and paragraph (e)(4) of this section. For purposes of this paragraph, a qualified foreign contract means a contract insuring life or health issued by a controlled foreign corporation if the person with the determining life, as defined in §1.953-2(g)(1), is a resident of the country in which the controlled foreign corporation is incorporated and such country is not contiguous to the United States. A nonqualified foreign contract is any contract that is not a qualified foreign contract.

(3) *Discounted unpaid losses of a property and casualty company.*—If a controlled foreign corporation would be taxable under part II of subchapter L of the Code if it were a domestic insurance company or if it would be subject to part I but has discounted unpaid losses as defined in section 846, the amount of its discounted unpaid losses shall be determined under the rules of section 846 except to the extent modified by paragraph (e)(4) of this section.

(4) *Interest rates used for determining reserves.*—(i) *Qualified foreign contracts and property and liability contracts.*—For purposes of applying section 807(d)(2)(B) and section 812(b)(2)(A) to qualified foreign contracts as defined in paragraph (e)(2) of this section, the term "prevailing State assumed interest rate" shall mean the highest assumed interest rate permitted to be used in computing life insurance reserves for insurance contracts or annuity contracts under the laws of each country in which the controlled foreign corporation conducts an insurance business. For purposes of applying sections 807 and 812 to qualified foreign contracts, as defined in paragraph (e)(2) of this section, and for purposes of applying section 846 to contracts covering risks located outside the United States, the applicable federal interest rate shall be a foreign currency rate of interest analogous to the applicable federal mid-term rates as defined in section 1274(d), but based on annual compounding. An analogous foreign currency rate of interest is a rate of interest based on yields (with an appropriate compounding period) of the highest grade of outstanding marketable obligations denominated in the currency of the country pursuant to the laws of which the controlled foreign corporation computes its reserves (excluding any obligations that benefit from special tax exemptions or preferential tax rates not available to debt instruments generally) with due consideration given to the maturities of the obligations. If a controlled foreign corporation that would be subject to part II of subchapter L if it were a domestic insurance company uses the loss payment patterns prescribed by the Secretary under section 846(d) for discounting unpaid losses (rather than the company's historical payment pattern as permitted under section 846(e)), the company must compute the year-end discounted fraction of unpaid losses and the reserve discount factors by using the applicable federal interest rate required by this paragraph and may not use the year-end discounted fraction of unpaid losses and the reserve discount factors prescribed by the Secretary for any accident year.

(ii) *Nonqualified foreign contracts.*—For purposes of applying sections 807 and 812 to nonqualified foreign contracts, as defined in paragraph (e)(2) of this section, the prevailing state assumed interest rate shall be the rate defined in section 807(d)(4)(B) and the applicable federal interest rate shall be the rate defined in section 807(d)(4)(A).

(f) *Corporations not qualifying as insurance companies.*—(1) *In general.*—The United States shareholders of a controlled foreign corporation must include their pro rata share of that corporation's section 953 insurance income even if the foreign corporation would not be taxed under subchapter L of the Code if it were a domestic corporation. Such a corporation shall compute its section 953 insurance income and its foreign personal holding company income that is SCI investment income under the rules of part I or part II of subchapter L as modified by section 953(b) and §§1.953-1 through 1.953-7, to the extent not inconsistent with the rules of this paragraph, as if it were a domestic insurance company. A controlled foreign corporation will compute its insurance income as if it were a domestic insurance company subject to part I of subchapter L (relating to life insurance companies) only if it can meet the requirements of section 816(a) of the Code taking into account only that portion of its business which involves the issuing or reinsuring of insurance or annuity contracts. If the requirements of section 816(a) cannot be met, then the controlled foreign corporation must compute its insurance income under part II of subchapter L.

(2) *Items of gross income attributable to insurance operations of a non-insurance company.*—(i) *Corporations computing taxable income under part I of subchapter L.*—The taxable income of a controlled foreign corporation described under paragraph (f)(1) of this section that computes its insurance income under part I of subchapter L, shall include in its insurance income, together with the items of gross income that directly relate to its life insurance business, the items of income described in section 803(a)(3) which are

not directly related to its insurance business, and which are not directly related to any other trade or business, in the proportion that the numerator determined under paragraph (f)(2)(i)(A) of this section bears to the denominator determined under paragraph (f)(2)(i)(B) of this section.

(A) *Numerator*.—The numerator used for the apportionment under paragraph (f)(2)(i) of this section is the sum of the means of the items described in section 807(c) at the beginning and end of the taxable year.

(B) *Denominator*.—The denominator used for the apportionment under paragraph (f)(2)(ii) of this section is the mean of the value of the total assets held by the controlled foreign corporation at the beginning and the end of the taxable year, determined by taking bills, accounts, notes receivable, and open accounts at face value and all other assets at their adjusted basis under section 1011 of the Code, unless there is affirmative evidence that more accurately reflects the value of the assets.

(ii) *Example*.—The following example illustrates the principles of paragraph (f)(2)(i) of this section.

Example. X is a controlled foreign corporation incorporated in country M engaged in the business of selling product V. It uses the calendar year as its taxable year. All of X's sales are to persons who reside outside of country M. A division of X issues contracts of credit life insurance to ensure payment of the purchase price of X's products. X does not, however, do enough business as an insurer to qualify as an insurance company under subchapter L of the Code. In 1988, X receives $500 in premiums and $3,000 in sales from product V. X also has interest, dividends, and gains from the sale of investment properties in the amount of $10,000. The investment income is not specifically allocable to the insurance or non-insurance businesses. The mean of X's reserves under section 807(c) determined as of the beginning and end of 1988 is $1,000. The mean of the value of X's total assets held at the beginning and the end of the taxable year is $5,000. The $3,000 received as part of the sales price of product V are directly related to V's non-insurance business and do not constitute insurance income. The $500 in premiums are directly related to V's insurance business and do constitute insurance income under section 953. Of X's $10,000 in investment income $2,000 ($10,000 × $1,000/$5,000) is insurance income under section 953.

(iii) *Corporations computing taxable income under part II of subchapter L*.—The taxable income of a controlled foreign corporation described in paragraph (f)(1) of this section that computes its insurance income as if it were a domestic insurance company subject to part II of subchapter L shall include in its insurance income, together with the items of gross income that directly relate to its insurance business, the items of income described in section 832(b)(1) which are not directly related to its insurance business, and which are not directly related to any other trade or business, in the proportion that the numerator determined under paragraph (f)(2)(iii)(A) of this section bears to the denominator determined under paragraph (f)(2)(iii)(B) of this section.

(A) *Numerator*.—The numerator used for the apportionment under paragraph (f)(2)(iii) of this section is the sum of—

(1) The mean of the controlled foreign corporation's unearned premiums at the beginning and end of the taxable year, determined under section 832(b)(4)(B);

(2) The mean of the controlled foreign corporation's discounted unpaid losses at the beginning and end of the taxable year, determined under section 846; plus

(3) The mean of the items described in section 807(c)(4) at the beginning and end of the taxable year, to the extent allowable under section 832(c)(11).

(B) *Denominator*.—The denominator used for the apportionment under paragraph (f)(2)(iii) of this section is the mean of the value of the total assets held by the controlled foreign corporation at the beginning and the end of the taxable year, determined by taking bills, accounts, notes receivable, and open accounts at face value and all other assets at their adjusted basis under section 1011 of the Code, unless there is affirmative evidence that more accurately reflects the value of the assets.

(g) *Relationship between sections 953 and 954*.—(1) *Priority of application*.—(i) *In general*.—For purposes of determining the subpart F income of a controlled foreign corporation, the provisions of section 953 and §§1.953-1 through 1.953-7 must be applied before the provisions of section 954 (relating to foreign base company income). Further, the provisions of section 954 apply only to income that is not insurance income under section 953. For example, the provisions of section 954 are applied to the investment income attributable to premiums received with respect to insured risks located in the controlled foreign corporation's country of incorporation only after §§1.953-1 through 1.953-7 have been applied to determine the amount of section 953 insurance income and SCI income and the deductions allocated and apportioned to those categories of income. Notwithstanding the foregoing, foreign base company oil related income as defined in section 954(a)(5) and (g) shall not be treated as insurance income subject to section 953 and shall not be subject to §§1.953-1 through 1.953-7.

(ii) *Examples*.—The following examples illustrate the principles of paragraph (g)(1)(i) of this section.

Example 1. X is a controlled foreign corporation incorporated in country F. X's only trade or business is the insurance business. All of X's premiums are received under contracts insuring risks located outside country F. X earns interest, dividends, and rents from the investment of the premiums it receives. The interest, dividends, and rents are insurance income under section 953 and not foreign personal holding company income under section 954.

Example 2. Y is a controlled foreign corporation incorporated in country W. Y owns all of the outstanding stock of Z, also a country W corporation. Y writes contracts that give rise to premiums allocable to the nonRPII and SCI categories. In its taxable year ending in 1988, Y receives a dividend from Z. Y must allocate or apportion that dividend income to the nonRPII and SCI categories under §1.953-4 before applying the exception of section 954(c)(3)(relating to dividends from same-country related corporations) to the SCI investment income.

(2) *Decrease or increase in income not material.*—(i) *In general.*—For purposes of computing the subpart F income of a controlled foreign corporation deriving income from insurance, reinsurance, or annuity contracts, deductions are allowed if they are allowed under subchapter L of the Code as modified by section 953 regardless of whether they are allocated or apportioned to section 953 insurance income or SCI investment income which constitutes section 954(c) foreign personal holding company income. Further, the amount of section 953 insurance income and the amount of foreign personal holding company income attributable to SCI investment income shall be determined in accordance with subchapter L of the Code, as modified by section 953, even though those rules result in a greater amount of subpart F income compared to the amount determined under section 954. Thus, in applying section 953 to income of a controlled foreign corporation that would, but for section 953, be subject to the provisions of section 954, the exceptions under section 954(c) which would not require a United States shareholder to include in gross income dividends, interest, rents, royalties, gains from the sale or exchange of property described in section 954(c)(1)(B), net gains from commodities transactions described in section 954(c)(1)(C), and net gains from foreign currency transactions described in section 954(c)(1)(D), are irrelevant.

(ii) *Examples.*—The principles of this paragraph (g)(2) are illustrated in the following examples.

Example 1. Z is a controlled foreign corporation that only issues and reinsures property and casualty insurance policies covering home country risks. Z may allocate a part of its discounted unpaid losses under section 846 to its SCI investment income which is foreign personal holding company income under section 954(c).

Example 2. X, a controlled foreign corporation, receives dividends and interest from a subsidiary which is incorporated in the same country as X and has a substantial part of its trade or business assets located in that country. All of X's income is attributable to the RPII or nonRPII categories. The dividends, after the appropriate allocation and apportionment, are included in the gross income of X's United States shareholders without regard to section 954(c)(3)(relating to dividends and interest from same-country related corporations).

(h) *Inclusion of pro rata share of subpart F income derived from insurance operations.*—(1) *Inclusion of pro rata share of related person insurance income.*—Each section 953(c) shareholder, as defined in this paragraph (h)(1), must include in its gross income (subject to the section 952(c) earnings and profits limitation) the lesser of—

(i) The "pro rata amount," which is the amount that would be determined under section 951(a)(2) if only related person insurance income were taken into account; if the number of shares of stock owned (within the meaning of section 958(a)) by section 953(c) shareholders in the aggregate on the last day of the taxable year were the total number of shares in the foreign corporation; and if only distributions received by section 953(c) shareholders were taken into account under section 951(a)(2)(B); or

(ii) The "limitation amount," which is the amount that would be determined under section 951(a)(2) if all of the taxable income of the foreign corporation for the taxable year were subpart F income.

A section 953(c) shareholder is a United States shareholder as defined in section 953(c)(1)(A) and § 1.953-3(b)(2) and includes a United States shareholder as defined in section 951(b).

(2) *Inclusion of subpart F income other than related person insurance income.*—Each United States shareholder as defined in section 951(b)(a "section 951(b) shareholder") must include, in addition to its pro rata share of income within the RPII category computed under paragraph (h)(1) of this section, its pro rata share of subpart F income other than related person insurance income, as computed under section 951(a)(2) and paragraph (h)(3) of this section. A section 951(b) shareholder must include its pro rata share of income within the RPII category as computed under this paragraph (h)(2) regardless of whether the exceptions of section 953(c)(3)(A) and (B) and § 1.953-7(a) and (b) apply.

(3) *Earnings and profits limitation.*—Pursuant to section 952(c)(1)(A), the subpart F income of any controlled foreign corporation for any taxable year shall not exceed the earnings and profits of such corporation for such taxable year. Thus, a United States shareholder's inclusion of subpart F income shall not exceed such shareholder's pro rata share, computed under the principles of section 951(a)(2), of the earnings and profits of the controlled foreign corporation. If the sum of a United States shareholder's pro rata share of related person insurance income and subpart F income other than related person insurance income exceeds such shareholder's pro rata share of the controlled foreign corporation's earnings and profits, then the section 952(c)(1)(A) earnings and profits limitation shall be applied by first including the United States shareholder's pro rata share of related person insurance income.

(4) *Examples.*—The following examples illustrate the principles of paragraph (h) of this section.

Example 1. X is a country M corporation and is a controlled foreign corporation under section 957, section 953(c)(1)(B), and § 1.953-3(b)(2). It has 100 shares of one class of stock outstanding. A owns 5 shares, B owns 5 shares, C owns 70 shares, and F owns 20 shares. A, B, and C are unrelated United States persons; F is a foreign person. A, B and C are considered section 953(c) shareholders. Only C, however, is a section 951(b) shareholder. During the current taxable year, X has $1,000 of related person insurance income and $1,000 of earnings and profits. A and B will each include $50 and C will include $700 of related person insurance income in gross income, computed as set forth below.

Computation of pro rata share of related person insurance income.

Lesser of:

Pro rata amount:

A:	5/80 × $1,000	=	$62.50

B:	5/80 × $1,000	=	$62.50
C:	70/80 × $1,000	=	$875.00

or

Limitation amount:

A:	5/100 × $1,000	=	$50.00
B:	5/100 × $1,000	=	$50.00
C:	70/100 × $1,000	=	$700.00

Example 2. The facts are the same as in *Example 1* except that there is $2,000 of related person insurance income and $1,500 of earnings and profits. The amount of related person insurance income included in gross income of A, B, and C is $75, $75, and $1,050, respectively, as computed below.

Computation of pro rata share of related person insurance income.

Lesser of:

Pro rata amount:

A:	5/80 × $2,000	=	$125
B:	5/80 × $2,000	=	$125
C:	70/80 × $2,000	=	$1,750

or

Limitation amount:

A:	5/100 × $2,000	=	$100
B:	5/100 × $2,000	=	$100
C:	70/100 × $2,000	=	$1,400

Computation of section 952(c)(1)(A) earnings and profits limitation.

A:	5/100 × $1,500	=	$75
B:	5/100 × $1,500	=	$75
C:	70/100 × $1,500	=	$1,050

The amount of related person insurance income included in the gross income of each shareholder is limited by their pro rata share of earnings and profits as computed under section 952(c) because that amount is less than both the pro rata amount and the limitation amount.

Example 3. The facts are the same as in *Example 1* except that X has $1,000 in related person insurance income, $1,000 in subpart F income other than related person insurance income, and $1,500 in earnings and profits.

Computation of pro rata share of related person insurance income.

Lesser of:

Pro rata amount:

A:	5/80 × $1,000	=	$62.50
B:	5/80 × $1,000	=	$62.50
C:	70/80 × $1,000	=	$875.00

or

Limitation amount:

A:	5/100 × $2,000	=	$100
B:	5/100 × $2,000	=	$100
C:	70/100 × $2,000	=	$1,400

Computation of the pro rata share of subpart F income other than related person insurance income.

C is the only section 951(b) shareholder.

C:	70/100 × $1,000	=	$700

Computation of pro rata share of earnings and profits.

A:	5/100 × $1,500	=	$75
B:	5/100 × $1,500	=	$75
C:	70/100 × $1,500	=	$1,050

With respect to A and B, the pro rata amount of related person insurance income is less than their pro rata share of X's earnings and profits. Thus, A and B will each include $62.50 in gross income as related person insurance income.

The sum of C's pro rata share of related person insurance income (the pro rata amount of $875) and subpart F income other than related person insurance income ($700) equals $1,575. That sum exceeds C's pro rata share of X's earnings and profits ($1,050). Thus, C must include $875 of related person insurance income and $175 ($1,050 – $875) of subpart F income other than related person insurance income.

(5) *Controlled foreign corporation for less than entire year.*—(i) *In general.*—If a foreign corporation with related person insurance income is a controlled foreign corporation for less than the entire taxable year, for purposes of computing the limitation amount, only the taxable income of the foreign corporation for that portion of the taxable year during which the foreign corporation was a controlled foreign corporation, computed as if such income were earned ratably throughout the taxable year, shall be treated as subpart F income.

(ii) *Example.*—The rule of this paragraph (h)(5) is illustrated in the following example.

Example. X, a foreign corporation, was incorporated on January 1, 1987 by A, B and F. As of that date, A and B, who are United States persons, each own 5 shares and F, who is not a United States person, owns 90 shares of the 100 shares of the single class of stock issued and outstanding. On July 1, 1987, F sells 70 of his shares to C, a United States person. At the end of the calendar year, which is also X's taxable year, X has $1,000 of income from providing insurance to its United States shareholders and persons related to those shareholders. X also has $1,000 of earnings and profits for the year. A and B must each include $25.00 in gross income and C must include $349.00. The computations necessary to determine related person insurance income are set forth below.

Computation of pro rata share of related person insurance income.

Lesser of:				
	Pro rata amount:			
	A:	5/80 × (182/365 × $1,000)	=	$31.00
	B:	5/80 × (182/365 × $1,000)	=	$31.00
	C:	70/80 × (182/365 × $1,000)	=	$436.00
or				
	Limitation amount:			
	A:	5/100 × (182/365 × $1,000)	=	$25.00
	B:	5/100 × (182/365 × $1,000)	=	$25.00
	C:	70/100 × (182/365 × $1,000)	=	$349.00

Thus, the amount of related person insurance income to be included by A, B, and C is the limitation amount.

(6) *Distributions.*—(i) *In general.*—Only distributions to United States shareholders, as defined in section 951(b) or section 953(c)(1)(A), are to be taken into account for purposes of computing the pro rata amount, as defined in paragraph (h)(1)(i) of this section. However, for purposes of computing the limitation amount under paragraphs (h)(1)(ii) of this section, distributions to shareholders other than United States shareholders shall be taken into account.

(ii) *Example.*—The following example illustrates the rule of paragraph (h)(6)(i) of this section.

Example. X is a controlled foreign corporation within the meaning of section 953(c)(1) and § 1.953-3(b)(2) and has 100 shares of one class of stock outstanding. F, who is not a United States person, owned all 100 shares of X's outstanding stock until July 1, 1987, when A, a United States person, acquired 60 shares of the stock from F. On June 30, 1987, before A had acquired X's stock from F, X made a distribution of $2 per share for a total of $200 to F. At the end of the calendar year, which is also X's taxable year, X had $2,000 of taxable income, of which $1,000 is related person insurance income. X also had earnings and profits for the taxable year of $2,000. The computation for determining A's pro rata share of related person insurance income is set forth below.

Computation of pro rata share of related person insurance income.

(i)	*Pro rata amount:*		
	A: 60/60 × 182/365 × $1,000	=	$499.00
(ii)	*Limitation amount:*		
	A: 60/100 × 182/365 × $2,000	=	$598.00
	minus lesser of:		
	$120 dividend on shares purchased		
	or		
	60% × 182/365 × $2,000 ($598.00)	=	($120.00)
			$478.00

Thus, A must include $478 of related person insurance income in gross income.

(7) *Mutual insurance companies.*—For purposes of sections 951(a)(2) and 953(c)(5) and paragraph (h) of this section, a United States shareholder that is a policyholder in a mutual insurance company shall compute its pro rata share by reference to the amount that would be distributed with respect to the United States shareholder's policy or policies owned on the last day of the controlled foreign corporation's taxable year if all the related person insurance income and all the subpart F income other than related person insurance income were distributed to the policyholders. In making the determination of a mutual policyholder's pro rata share of subpart F income the rules set forth in paragraph (h)(7)(i) through (iii) of this section are applied in the order given and the first rule to result in the determination of a specific amount to be included in the policyholder's gross income is the rule that shall be applied. The mutual policyholder's pro rata share of subpart F income shall be determined as:

(i) The amount that would be distributed annually under the terms of the policy or the by-laws of the corporation;

(ii) The amount that would be distributed if the mutual company were liquidated; or

(iii) The amount that would be distributed to a policyholder if earnings and profits were distributed in the same proportion that premiums paid by the policyholder over a five-year period ending on the last day of the controlled foreign corporation's taxable year bears to the total amount of premiums paid by all policyholders who hold ownership interests on the last day of the taxable year and have held their interest over the five-year period.

(i) *Application of sections 959, 961, and 1248.*—If a foreign corporation that is a controlled foreign corporation under section 953(c) makes a distribution with respect to its stock, section 959(a)(1) shall apply to any United States shareholder as defined in section 953(c)(1)(A) and § 1.953-3(b)(2). Earnings and profits attributable to related person insurance income included in the gross income of a United States shareholder with less than 10 percent of the combined voting power of the stock of the controlled foreign corporation shall be treated as earnings and profits which have been included in the gross income of a United States shareholder for purposes of sections 956 and 959(a)(2). In addition, the adjustments made to the basis of stock in a controlled foreign corporation required by section 961 shall apply to any United States shareholder as defined in section 953(c)(1)(A) and §1.953-3(b)(2). Any United States person who is a United States shareholder, as defined in section 953(c)(1)(A) and §1.953-3(b)(2), of a controlled foreign corporation, as defined in section 953(c)(1)(B) and §1.953-3(b)(2), shall be treated as meeting the stock ownership requirements of section 1248(a)(2). In addition, any controlled foreign corporation, within the meaning of section 953(c)(1)(B) and §1.953-3(b)(2), shall be treated as a controlled foreign corporation for purposes of section 1248.

(j) *Application of section 367(b)*.—[Reserved]

(k) *Interaction with section 954(b)(3)*.—Income that would not be considered subpart F income but for the operation of section 954(b)(3)(B) shall not be considered related person insurance income. Thus, if foreign base company income and insurance income exceed 70 percent of gross income, United States persons who are United States shareholders solely by operation of section 953(c)(1)(A) and §1.953-3(b)(2) must include in their gross income only their pro rata share of related person insurance income. Any person who is a United States shareholder as defined in section 951(b) shall, however, include his pro rata share, as determined under this section, of the entire amount of subpart F income of the controlled foreign corporation. [Reg. §1.953-6.]

§1.953-7. Exceptions to inclusion of related person insurance income for certain shareholders.—(a) *Corporation not held by insureds*.—(1) *In general*.—A person that is a United States shareholder solely by virtue of section 953(c)(1) shall not include in gross income such person's pro rata share of income that qualifies as related person insurance income if, at all times during the taxable year of the foreign corporation, less than 20 percent of the total combined voting power of all classes of stock of the corporation entitled to vote and less than 20 percent of the total value (both stock and policies) of the corporation is owned (directly or indirectly under the principles of section 883(c)(4)) by persons who are the insured under any insurance or reinsurance contract, who are the purchasers or beneficiaries of any annuity contract issued or reinsured by the foreign corporation, or who are related persons (within the meaning of section 954(d)(3)) to any such insured. For purposes of this paragraph, the term "insured" means only United States persons, as defined in section 957(c), or persons related to United States persons (within the meaning of section 954(d)(3)) who are insured or reinsured by the foreign corporation, persons who have purchased or are beneficiaries under any annuity contract issued or reinsured by the foreign corporation, or persons insured by the foreign corporation in a cross-insurance arrangement described in §1.953-3(b)(5).

(2) *Examples*.—The principles of this paragraph (a) are illustrated in the following examples.

Example 1. X is a country Y corporation which issues property and liability insurance policies for risks located outside country Y. X has one class of voting stock outstanding. Z, a domestic corporation, owns 60 percent of X's stock. Z has 100 shareholders each of which owns one percent of Z. Of the remaining shareholders of X, four are foreign corporations, each of which owns five percent of the X stock, and four are domestic corporations which also own five percent each. X has issued policies of insurance to 25 of Z's shareholders, the four foreign corporations which own stock in X, and to W, one of the domestic corporate shareholders of X. None of the other shareholders of X are insured by X. The 25 insureds who own stock in Z own, indirectly under the principles of section 883(c)(4), 15 percent of the stock of X (25% × 60%). The insurance income attributable to the policy of insurance issued to W is related person insurance income that is includable in the gross income of the four domestic corporate shareholders of X because 20 percent of the stock of X is owned directly or indirectly by insureds who are United States persons: 15 percent by 25 of the shareholders of Z plus 5 percent owned by W. In addition, because Z is a United States shareholder as defined in section 951(b), as well as in section 953(c)(1), it must include its pro rata share of the related person insurance of income of X, plus the section 953(a) insurance income that is not related person insurance income, regardless of whether 20 percent or more of the corporation is owned, directly or indirectly, by insureds who are United States persons.

Example 2. Y is a controlled foreign corporation. Its one class of stock outstanding is owned equally by 20 domestic corporations, none of which are insured by Y. Nine of the shareholder corporations are the parent corporations of nine unrelated, wholly owned foreign subsidiaries which are insured by Y. Because the insureds are related persons, within the meaning of section 954(d)(3), to United States shareholders (the domestic corporate shareholders), the income from insuring the foreign subsidiaries is related person insurance income. Moreover, because nine domestic corporate shareholders of Y control the subsidiaries, within the meaning of section 954(d)(3), they are related persons. Therefore, 45 percent (9 × 5%) of the stock of Y is owned by United States shareholders that are related to the insureds and the exception to inclusion in gross income of paragraph (a)(1) of this section is inapplicable. The 20 domestic shareholders must include Y's related person insurance income in their gross income.

(b) *De minimis insurance exception*.—(1) *In general*.—A person that is a United States shareholder solely by virtue of section 953(c)(1) shall not include in gross income such person's pro rata share of income that qualifies as related person insurance income if the related person insurance income, determined on a gross basis, of the foreign corporation is less than 20 percent of the foreign corporation's total insurance income for the taxable year, determined on a gross basis, without regard to those provisions of section 953(a)(1) and §1.953-2(a)(1) which limit section 953 insurance income to income from countries other than the country in which the corporation was created or organized. Related person insurance income determined on a gross basis means life insurance gross income within the meaning of section 803 or gross income within the meaning of section 832(b)(1), whichever is applicable, except that the phrase "premiums earned (within the meaning of section 832(b)(4)" shall be substituted for the term "underwriting income," where that term appears in section 832(b)(1)(A).

(2) *Examples.*—The following examples illustrate the principles of paragraph (b)(1) of this section.

Example 1. X is a country Y corporation engaged in the business of issuing liability insurance. All of the stock of X is owned by United States shareholders. Each of the United States shareholders owns less than 10 percent of X's one class of stock outstanding. For its 1987 taxable year, X has $100,000 of gross income of which $10,000 constitutes section 953 insurance income within the RPII category and $50,000 constitutes section 953 insurance income within the nonRPII category. Of the remaining $40,000 of income, $10,000 would have been premium and investment income within the RPII category of section 953 insurance income and $30,000 would have been premium and investment income within the nonRPII category of insurance income except that those amounts relate to contracts insuring risks located in the home country. Thus, without regard to the same country exception, $20,000 of income ($10,000 from the RPII category and $10,000 from the SCI category) would have been within the RPII category of section 953 insurance income. X does not meet the de minimis insurance exception of paragraph (b)(1) of this section because 20 percent ($20,000/$100,000) of its insurance income, determined without regard to those provisions of section 953(a)(1) and §1.953-2(a)(3) which limit insurance income to income from insuring risks located outside the home country, is related person insurance income.

Example 2. The facts are the same as in *Example 1* except that $3,000 of premiums that constitute income within the RPII category is paid to another insurer pursuant to a reinsurance contract. X does meet the de minimis insurance exception because under section 832(b)(4)(A) premiums paid for reinsurance are deducted from premiums written in arriving at premiums earned. Thus, approximately 17.5 percent ($17,000/$97,000) of X's insurance income is related person insurance income.

(3) *Anti-abuse rule.*—(i) *In general.*—In determining insurance income on a gross basis, the District Director may exclude income attributable to an insurance or reinsurance contract covering the life, health, property, or liability of a person other than a United States shareholder, or person related to such shareholder, or attributable to an annuity contract, or a contract reinsuring annuity contracts, that are purchased by, or provide annuity payments to, a person other than a United States shareholder or person related to such shareholder, if the primary purpose for entering into the contract is to qualify for the de minimis insurance exception. *See also* section 845. In making this determination, the District Director will consider all the facts and circumstances. Among the factors to be considered are whether there is a true transfer of risk, whether the predominant purpose for the transaction is a bona fide business purpose, and whether the terms of the insurance or reinsurance contract reflect the terms that unrelated parties would agree to in a similar transaction.

(ii) *Examples.*—The following examples illustrate the principles of paragraph (b)(3) of this section.

Example 1. The facts are the same as in *Example 1* in paragraph (b)(2) of this section, except that near the end of its taxable year, X cedes to another insurance company, Z, under a contract of reinsurance some of the insurance policies that were issued by X to persons other than related insureds. X receives a ceding commission from Z of $30,000 and thereby increases its gross income other than RPII income by $30,000. Thus, approximately 15 percent ($20,000/$130,000) of X's income is RPII income without regard to the same country exception. At the beginning of the following taxable year, Z reinsures with S, a subsidiary controlled by X, a block of insurance which is similar to the policies X reinsured with Z. W pays Z a ceding commission of $30,000. Based on the facts and circumstances, X will be regarded as having engaged in the reinsurance transaction with Z in order to qualify for the de minimis exception. Therefore, the $30,000 of income from the reinsurance transaction will be ignored in determining whether X qualifies for the de minimis exception.

Example 2. The facts are the same as in *Example 1* in paragraph (b)(2) of this section except, that near the end of the taxable year, X enters a reinsurance agreement with M under which X receives $30,000 in nonRPII premiums. At the beginning of the following taxable year, X cedes to F all of the risks of M that X reinsured at the end of 1988, transferring the $30,000 in premiums to F. The $30,000 in nonRPII premiums received by X under the reinsurance agreement will be ignored for purposes of determining whether X qualifies for the de minimis related person insurance income exception.

(c) *Election to treat income as effectively connected.*—(1) *In general.*—A controlled foreign corporation, other than a disqualified corporation, may elect in accordance with the procedures set forth in this paragraph to treat its related person insurance income that is not actually effectively connected income under section 864(c) as if it were income effectively connected with the conduct of a trade or business in the United States. To make the election, the foreign corporation must waive all benefits (other than with respect to section 884) with respect to related person insurance income granted by the United States under any treaty, including any friendship, commerce and navigation treaty, between the United States and any foreign country.

(2) *Corporations which may make the election.*—(i) *In general.*—The election may be made by any corporation that is not a disqualified corporation. A corporation is a disqualified corporation if, for any taxable year beginning after December 31, 1986, it is a controlled foreign corporation as defined in section 957(a) or (b) (without regard to section 953(c)(1)(B) and §1.953-3(b)(2)) for an uninterrupted period of 30 days or more during the taxable year and a United States shareholder, as defined in section 951(b), owns, directly or indirectly, within the

meaning of section 958(a) (without regard to the constructive ownership rules of section 958(b)), stock in the corporation at some time during the taxable year.

(ii) *Successor corporation.*—A corporation that is a successor to another corporation that, during any taxable year beginning after December 31, 1986, was a disqualified corporation may not make the election. The term "successor corporation" means any foreign corporation that acquires assets of another foreign corporation having a fair market value of 50 percent or more of the fair market value of all the assets held by the acquired foreign corporation immediately before the acquisition, if 50 percent or more of the combined voting power of all classes of stock entitled to vote or 50 percent or more of the value of all classes of stock in the acquiring corporation is owned, directly or indirectly, at the time of the acquisition by one or more persons who at any time during which the acquired foreign corporation was a disqualified corporation owned, directly or indirectly, 50 percent or more of the combined voting power of all classes of stock entitled to vote or 50 percent or more of the value of all classes of stock in the acquired foreign corporation.

(iii) *Examples.*—The following examples illustrate the principles of paragraph (c)(2) of this section.

Example 1. Subsequent to December 31, 1986, 50 domestic corporations, all engaged in business within the same industry, form M, a foreign corporation to insure the risks of the 50 corporations and their subsidiaries. Each of the corporations owns two percent of the one class of voting stock of M outstanding. M may make the election under section 953(c)(3)(C) to have its related person insurance income treated as if it were effectively connected with the conduct of a trade or business within the United States because it has never been a controlled foreign corporation within the meaning of section 957(a) or (b).

Example 2. The facts are the same as in *Example 1,* except that four of the 50 domestic corporate shareholders, W, X, Y, and Z, each own 7 percent of the stock of M and are wholly-owned subsidiaries of V, a domestic corporation. None of the other shareholders of M are 10 percent or greater shareholders. M is a controlled foreign corporation under section 957(b) because more than 25 percent of its stock is owned by United States shareholders as defined in section 951(b). Under the attribution rules of section 958(b), W, X, Y, and Z are each considered as owning 28 percent of the stock of M and therefore are United States shareholders under section 951(b) because each is considered as owning the stock of the others by attribution through V. Because each of W, X, Y, and Z own stock in M directly under section 958(a), M is a disqualified corporation.

Example 3. On January 1, 1987, X, a domestic corporation, formed Z under the laws of country F as a reinsurance company constituting a mutual insurance company under the laws of country F. X capitalized Z by contributing interest bearing reserve fund certificates which entitle X to 30 percent of the voting power in Z. Z reinsures policies issued by X, none of which relate to risks located in country F. Under the laws of country F, the policyholders under the policies issued by X and reinsured by Z are members of Z and have voting rights. None of these policyholders hold 10 percent or more of the voting power of Z. However, only those policyholders may receive policyholder dividends from Z. X is not entitled to any nonliquidating distributions from Z. Z is a controlled foreign corporation within the meaning of section 957(b). Even though neither X nor the United States policyholders have had inclusions of insurance income in their gross income by virtue of subpart F of the Code, because Z is a controlled foreign corporation under section 957(b) it cannot make the election under section 953(c)(3)(C) to have its related person insurance income treated as if it were effectively connected with the conduct of a trade or business within the United States.

(3) *Taxable year of corporation making election.*—A corporation making the election to treat related person insurance income as income effectively connected with the conduct of a trade or business in the United States must utilize the calendar year as its annual accounting period for United States tax purposes, as required by section 843.

(4) *Period during which election is in effect.*—(i) *Elections that become effective in taxable years beginning after December 31, 1987.*—If an election under paragraph (c)(3) of this section is made for the first taxable year beginning after December 31, 1987 or any subsequent taxable year, the election is effective from the first day of the taxable year for which the election is made (and all subsequent taxable years). Therefore, a foreign corporation that has a fiscal taxable year prior to making the election must file a short-year return for the period from the first day the election becomes effective to the last day of the calendar year in which the election is made.

(ii) *Examples.*—The following examples illustrate the rule of paragraph (c)(4)(i) of this section.

Example 1. X is a controlled foreign corporation that keeps its books and records on a calendar year basis. X makes an election under paragraph (c)(3) of this section for the 1988 taxable year. X's election is effective as of January 1, 1988.

Example 2. Y is a controlled foreign corporation that keeps its books and records on a July 1 to June 30 fiscal year basis. Y makes an election under paragraph (c)(3) of this section for the 1988 taxable year. Y's election is effective as of July 1, 1988. Y must file a short-year return covering the period from July 1, 1988 to December 31, 1988.

(iii) *Elections that become effective in first taxable year beginning after December 31, 1986.*—For any foreign corporation that makes an election under paragraph (c) of this section for the first taxable year beginning after December 31, 1986, the election is effective as of the date indicated by the corporation on its election statement and for all subsequent taxable years. A foreign corporation that had a fiscal taxable year prior to making the election must file a short-year return covering the period from the beginning of its 1987 fiscal year to the last day of its 1987 fiscal year. The foreign corporation must include in its gross income for the taxable year in which the election becomes effective the amount of related person insurance income that is attributable to the period from the date the election becomes effective through the last day of the calendar year. The amount of the related person insurance income attributable to such period is that amount determined by allocating to each day in the taxable year its ratable portion of related person insurance income. However, if the corporation keeps adequate books and records that, in the district director's discretion, accurately reflect the actual amount of the income earned in such period, the corporation may include such amount in gross income rather than the daily pro rata amount.

(iv) *Examples.*—The following examples illustrate the principles of paragraph (c)(4)(iii) of this section.

Example 1. X is a controlled foreign corporation that keeps its books and records on a calendar year basis. X makes an election under paragraph (c) of this section for the 1987 taxable year. In its election statement, X chose September 15, 1987 as the effective date of its election. X must include in gross income the related person insurance income attributable to the period from September 15, 1987 to December 31, 1987 in its calendar year 1987 tax return.

Example 2. Y is a controlled foreign corporation that keeps its books and records on a July 1 to June 30 fiscal year basis. Y makes an election under this paragraph (c) of this section for the 1987 taxable year and chooses to make the election effective as of September 1, 1987. Y must file a short-year return covering the period from July 1, 1987 to August 31, 1987. The related person insurance income of Y that, under Y's method of accounting, is attributable to the period from July 1, 1987 to August 31, 1987 must be included in the gross income of Y's United States shareholders. In addition, X must also file another short-year return covering the period from September 1, 1987 to December 31, 1987 and must include in its gross income for that period the related person insurance income attributable to that period.

(5) *Effect of election: taxation under section 882; alternative minimum tax; dividends received deduction; pre-1987 deficits in earnings and profits, and net operating losses.*—If a foreign corporation makes an election under paragraph (c) of this section, all income that is actually effectively connected with the conduct of a trade or business in the United States (as determined under sections 864(c) and 842) and all related person insurance income that is not effectively connected with the conduct of a trade or business within the United States but is treated as if it were effectively connected by virtue of the election under this paragraph (c) of this section will be taxable under section 882. The branch profits tax imposed by section 884 and the tax imposed on interest described in section 884(f) will apply to an electing corporation to the same extent and in the same manner that those taxes would have applied if the corporation had not made the election. Thus, the exclusion from the branch profits tax contained in section 884(d)(2)(D) (relating to income treated as effectively connected under section 953(c)(3)(C)) does not apply to income which is actually effectively connected with the conduct of a trade or business within the United States under sections 864(c) and 842. Further, a controlled foreign corporation that makes the election under section 953(c)(3)(C) shall continue to be treated as a controlled foreign corporation for purposes of section 864(c)(4)(D)(ii). Thus, related person insurance income that is treated as income effectively connected with the conduct of a United States trade or business shall not be subject to the branch profits tax under section 884 solely by virtue of making the election under section 953(c)(3)(C). *But see* section 842(b) with respect to the minimum effectively connected net investment income of a foreign corporation conducting an insurance business within the United States. Related person insurance income that is treated as if it were effectively connected with the conduct of a United States trade or business is subject to the alternative minimum tax provisions of sections 55 and 56 of the Code. For purposes of section 245 (dividends from certain foreign corporations), related person insurance income that is treated as if it were effectively connected by virtue of an election under paragraph (c)(3) of this section shall be treated as effectively connected for purposes of determining post-1986 undistributed U.S. earnings under section 245(a)(5). Net operating loss deductions and deficits in earnings and profits of a corporation making the election under paragraph (c)(3) of this section that would be carried over from, or incurred in, taxable years beginning before January 1, 1986 cannot be carried over to, or used in, taxable years beginning after December 31, 1986.

(6) *Exemption from tax imposed by section 4371.*—The tax imposed by section 4371 (relating to policies issued or reinsured by foreign insurers) shall not apply to premiums that are subject to the election under paragraph (c) of this section to treat related person insurance income which is not otherwise effectively connected income under section 864(c) as if it were effectively connected with the conduct of a trade or business within the United States. The exemption from the tax imposed by section 4371 begins after the later of the date of acceptance of the election or the first day of the first taxable year for which the election is made. An election is accepted on the date when the closing agreement has been executed by the taxpayer and the Commissioner. A copy of the election statement that has been stamped as accepted by the Commissioner will serve to place others on notice of the exemption. If an election has an effective date prior to the date on which the election is accepted, any excise taxes that have been paid on any related person insurance income received prior to the acceptance of the election may be refunded to the person who remitted the taxes. *See also* section 4373, which exempts from the excise tax under section 4371 income which is effectively connected with the conduct of a trade or business within the United States.

(7) *Procedure for making election under section 953(c)(3)(C).*—(i) *In general.*—In order to make a valid election to treat related person insurance income as income effectively connected with the conduct of a trade or business in the United States, a foreign corporation must provide the Internal Revenue Service with a signed election statement, a signed closing agreement, and a letter of credit.

(ii) *When election must be made.*—In order for the election to be effective for a taxable year, an election statement must be filed on or before the due date of the electing corporation's tax return reporting the related person insurance income earned during the taxable year.

(iii) *Election.*—An election is made by mailing an original and one copy of an election statement to the Internal Revenue Service, Assistant Commissioner (International), IN:C:C:51, 950 L'Enfant Plaza South, S.W., Washington, D.C. 20024. The statement must be signed under penalty of perjury by a responsible corporate officer, within the meaning of section 6062, stating that the statement and accompanying documents are true and complete to the best of the officer's knowledge and belief. A copy of the accepted election statement must be attached to the first tax return of the electing corporation that includes related person insurance income to which the election under paragraph (c) of this section applies. The election statement must be made in the following (or substantially similar) form:

FOREIGN CAPTIVE INSURANCE COMPANY ELECTION UNDER SECTION 953(c)(3)(C)

(1) ______________________________

(Name, address, tax identification number [a number will automatically be assigned to those corporations not already having a number], and place of incorporation of the corporation) hereby elects under section 953(c)(3)(C) to treat its related person insurance income, as defined in section 953(c)(2), that is not actually effectively connected with the conduct of a trade or business in the United States under sections 864 or 842, as income effectively connected with the conduct of a trade or business within the United States.

(2) *(Name of corporation).*—waives all benefits (other than with respect to section 884) with respect to related person insurance income under any treaty, including any friendship, commerce and navigation treaty, between the United States and any foreign country.

(3) *(Name of corporation).*—agrees to timely file a United States income tax return and timely remit the income tax due on its related person insurance income, determined as if all such income were effectively connected with the conduct of a United States trade or business.

(4) Attached to this election statement is a complete list of all United States shareholders, as defined in section 953(c)(1)(A) and § 1.953-3(b)(2), which own stock in *(Name of corporation)* as of a date no more than 90 days prior to the date this election statement is mailed. The list includes the name, address, tax identification number, and ownership percentage for each such United States shareholder. *(Name of corporation)* agrees to file an updated list containing the information prescribed in this paragraph determined as of the last day of each taxable year. This updated list will be filed with the United States tax return reporting the related person insurance income earned by the corporation for each taxable year the election is in effect. [Attach listing].

(5) *(Name of corporation).*—agrees to file a complete list of all United States persons (whether or not listed as United States persons who own stock in *(Name of corporation))* whose risks are insured or reinsured by *(Name of corporation)*, or who have purchased annuities or will receive annuity payments from *(Name of corporation)* as of the last day of each taxable year. The list will include the name, address, and tax identification number of each United States person so insured or reinsured. The list will be filed with the United States tax return reporting related person insurance income earned by *(Name of corporation)* for each taxable year the election is in effect.

(6) *(Name of corporation).*—agrees to provide security for the payment of tax due on its related person insurance income. The security will be in an amount and upon the terms as stated in a closing agreement to be executed between the Internal Revenue Service and *(Name of corporation)*.

(7) Attached is the power of attorney, Form 2848, of the person authorized to negotiate a closing agreement on behalf of *(Name of corporation)*.

The undersigned declares under penalty of perjury that the statements contained in this election and accompanying documents are true and complete to the best of his/her knowledge and belief.

__________ ______________________________

Date (Title)

(Name of Corporation)

(8) *Closing agreement.*—After the receipt of the election statement, the controlled foreign corporation's designated representative will be provided with a model closing agreement and further instructions on completing the election process.

(9) *Letter of credit.*—(i) *In general.*—A foreign corporation that makes the election under paragraph (c)(3) of this section must provide a letter of credit issued in favor of the Internal Revenue Service. The letter of credit must generally be in an amount equal to 10 percent of the gross premium income from insuring or reinsuring the risks of United States shareholders and persons related to such shareholders in the 12 month period preceding the filing of the election. In the case of a corporation that did not receive gross premiums from United States shareholders or related persons in the previous 12 month period, the amount of the letter of credit required will be based on an estimate of the projected gross premiums of the corporation for the first year of the election. For purposes of paragraph (c)(9)(i) and (ii) of this section, the term "gross premiums" means the amount of gross premiums written on insurance contracts during the taxable year without adjustment for return premiums, premiums for reinsurance, premiums and other consideration arising out of indemnity reinsurance, or increases in unearned premiums. In all cases, a minimum amount of $75,000 will be required and the maximum amount required will not exceed $10,000,000. The foreign corporation must provide, under

penalty of perjury, evidence to support the computation of the amount of the letter of credit it proposes as security under paragraph (c) of this section.

(ii) *Changes in the amount of the letter of credit.*—Once the amount of the letter of credit has been determined for a taxable year, no change in the amount of the letter of credit is required unless in a subsequent taxable year there is an increase in gross premiums to more than 120 percent of the amount of the gross premiums used to compute the letter of credit (the "base year gross premiums"). If for any taxable year, the foreign corporation has gross premium income constituting more than 120 percent of the base year gross premiums, the amount of the letter of credit must be increased within 30 days of the filing of the tax return for that year. If a letter of credit in a greater amount must be provided, it must be in the amount of 10 percent of the gross premiums for the taxable year. No change in the letter of credit is required if gross premiums for a taxable year decline from the base year premium level; however, the taxpayer may submit a new letter of credit equal to 10 percent of the gross premiums for the taxable year in replacement of the outstanding letter of credit.

(10) *Underpayment of tax due.*—If it is determined that there is a deficiency or underpayment of any tax due pursuant to the election, the Commissioner will issue a notice of deficiency or notice and demand in the amount of the deficiency or underpayment determined, plus any applicable interest and penalties. Assessment and collection of any deficiency or underpayment of tax will be as provided by the Internal Revenue Code and payment of all additional amounts due will be in accordance with the terms specified in any statement of notice and demand sent to the foreign corporation. If the tax is not paid in accordance with the terms of the statement of notice and demand, collection of the deficiency will be made by resorting to the letter of credit before any levy or proceeding in court for collection is instituted against the controlled foreign corporation or its shareholders. However, nothing in paragraph (c)(3)(10) of this section shall be construed to preclude the Secretary's ability to use the jeopardy assessment procedures of sections 6861 through 6864 of the Code. If the letter of credit is drawn upon, it must be reinstated to the level as provided for under the closing agreement within 60 days after the date drawn upon.

(11) *Termination or revocation of election.*—(i) *Termination.*—If a controlled foreign corporation that made the election to treat its related person insurance income as effectively connected income for any taxable year becomes a disqualified corporation, as defined in paragraph (c)(2) of this section, in any subsequent taxable year, the election will not apply to any taxable year beginning after the taxable year in which the corporation becomes a disqualified corporation. If a foreign corporation's election is terminated by virtue of the corporation's becoming a disqualified corporation, the corporation will be barred from making another election under section 953(c)(3)(C).

(ii) *Revocation with consent.*—The election to treat related person insurance income as effectively connected with the conduct of a trade or business within the United States can be revoked only with the consent of the Commissioner. In order to obtain a revocation, the taxpayer must request a ruling from the Associate Chief Counsel (International). To determine whether a request for revocation should be granted, consideration will be given to all the facts and circumstances. Among the circumstances that will be considered as favorable to a determination to allow revocation of an election will be whether the foreign corporation would qualify for the de minimis ownership exception of paragraph (a)(1) of this section or the de minimis related person insurance exception of paragraph (b)(2) of this section. If after having made an election under paragraph (c) of this section the foreign corporation makes an election under section 953(d) (relating to the election of a foreign insurance company to be treated as a domestic corporation), the election under this paragraph shall be treated as revoked with the Commissioner's consent beginning with the period that the election under section 953(d) is in effect. The revocation of an election is effective for the taxable year indicated by the Commissioner in the consent. Any foreign corporation that receives the consent of the Commissioner to revoke an election may not make a subsequent election for a period of four years from the end of the first taxable year in which the election is not in effect.

(iii) *Unilateral revocation by Commissioner.*—If an electing corporation fails to timely file a return, fails to pay the tax due with respect to related person insurance income that it elects to have taxed as effectively connected income, fails to make the estimated tax payments required by section 6655, or fails to maintain or provide a letter of credit in the appropriate amount, the election may be revoked by the Commissioner for the taxable year in which the electing corporation fails to file a return, pay the tax due, pay the estimated tax, or fails to maintain or provide the appropriate letter of credit or in any subsequent taxable year. If the revocation is made in a taxable year subsequent to the taxable year in which the failure occurs, the Commissioner can make the revocation effective retroactively to the taxable year in which the failure occurred or any subsequent taxable year. Revocation of the election may cause the United States shareholders of the foreign corporation to be liable for subpart F inclusions and make the foreign corporation liable for the unpaid excise tax on premiums under section 4371 for insurance or reinsurance issued by the foreign corporation. Funds obtained under the letter of credit will be applied to the taxes due from the foreign corporation, its shareholders, or both, with respect to related person insurance income. Any foreign corporation (or successor corporation, as defined in paragraph (c)(2)(ii) of this section) the election of which is unilaterally revoked by the Commissioner shall be barred from making another election under section 953(c)(3)(C). [Reg. §1.953-7.]

CFCs: Insurance Income: After 1986: Election to Expense

Controlled Foreign Corporations: Insurance Income: Tax Years After 1986.—Reproduced below is a proposed amendment to Temporary Reg. § 1.954-1T (Reg. § 1.954-1T was redesignated as Reg. § 4.954-1 by T.D. 8618 on 9/6/95), relating to the election to expense certain depreciable business assets (published in the Federal Register on April 17, 1991).

□ Par. 4. Section 1.954-1T is amended by revising paragraph (c) to read as follows:

§ 1.954-1T. Foreign base company income; taxable years beginning after December 31, 1986 (Temporary).

* * *

(c) *Computation of net foreign base company income.*—(1) *General rule.*—The net foreign base company income of a controlled foreign corporation is computed by reducing (but not below zero) the amount of gross income in each of the categories of adjusted gross foreign base company income described in paragraph (b)(2) of this section, so as to take into account deductions allocable and apportionable to such income. For purposes of section 954 and this section, expenses must be allocated and apportioned consistent with the allocation and apportionment of expenses for purposes of section 904(d). For purposes of this § 1.954-1T, an item of net foreign base company income must be categorized according to the category of adjusted gross foreign base company income from which it is derived. Thus, an item of net foreign base company income must be categorized as a net item of—

(i) Foreign personal holding company income,

(ii) Foreign base company sales income,

(iii) Foreign base company services income,

(iv) Foreign base company shipping income,

(v) Foreign base company oil related income, or

(vi) Full inclusion foreign base company income.

(2) *Computation of net foreign base company income derived from same country insurance income.*—Deductions relating to foreign base company income derived from insurance, reinsurance, or annuity contracts covering risks located in the country in which the controlled foreign corporation is created or organized shall be allocated and apportioned in accordance with the rules set forth in § 1.953-5.

Controlled Foreign Corporations: Hybrid Branches: Subpart F Income

Controlled Foreign Corporations: Hybrid Branches: Subpart F Income.—Amendments to Reg. §§ 1.954-0 and 1.954-1, relating to the treatment under subpart F of certain transactions involving hybrid branches, are proposed (published in the Federal Register on July 13, 1999) (REG-113909-98).

□ Par. 3. Section 1.954-0(b) is amended as follows:

1. The entry for § 1.954-1(c)(1)(i) is revised.
2. Entries for § 1.954-1(c)(1)(i)(A) through (c)(1)(i)(E) are added.
3. An entry for § 1.954-2(a)(5) is added.
4. An entry for § 1.954-2(a)(6) is added.

The revision and additions read as follows:

§ 1.954-0. Introduction.

* * *

(b) * * *

§ 1.954-1 Foreign base company income

* * *

(c) * * *

(1) * * *

(i) Deductions.

(A) Deductions against gross foreign base company income.

(B) Special rule for deductible payments to certain non-fiscally transparent entities.

(C) Limitations.

(D) Example.

(E) Effective date.

* * *

§ 1.954-2 Foreign personal holding company income.

(a) * * *

(5) Special rules applicable to distributive share of partnership income.

(i) Application of related person exceptions where payment reduces foreign tax of payor.

(ii) Certain other exceptions applicable to foreign personal holding company income. [Reserved]

(iii) Effective date.

(6) Special rules applicable to exceptions from foreign personal holding company income treatment in circumstances involving hybrid branches.

(i) In general.

(ii) Exception where no tax reduction or tax disparity.

(iii) Effective date.

* * *

□ Par. 4. Section 1.954-1 is amended as follows: **1.** Paragraphs (c)(1)(i) heading and introductory text and (c)(1)(i)(A) through (c)(1)(i)(D) are redesignated as paragraphs (c)(1)(i)(A) heading and introductory text and (c)(1)(i)(A)(*1*) through (c)(1)(i)(A)(*4*), respectively. **2.** A heading for paragraph (c)(1)(i) is added. **3.** Paragraphs (c)(1)(i)(B) through (c)(1))(i)(E) are added. The additions read as follows:

§1.954-1. Foreign base company income

* * *

(c) * * *

(1) * * *

(i) *Deductions.*—(A) *Deductions against gross foreign base company income.*—* * *

(B) *Special rule for deductible payments to certain non-fiscally transparent entities.*—Notwithstanding any other provision of this section, except as provided in paragraph (c)(1)(i)(C) of this section, an expense (including a distributive share of any expense) that would otherwise be allocable under section 954(b)(5) against the subpart F income of a controlled foreign corporation shall not be allocated against subpart F income of the controlled foreign corporation resulting from the payment giving rise to the expense if—

(1) Such expense arises from a payment between the controlled foreign corporation and a partnership in which the controlled foreign corporation is a partner and the partnership is not regarded as fiscally transparent, as defined in §1.954-9(a)(7), by any country in which the controlled foreign corporation does business or has substantial assets; and

(2) The payment from which the expense arises would have reduced foreign tax, under §1.954-9(a)(3), and would have fallen within the tax disparity rule of §1.954-9(a)(5)(iv), if those provisions had been applicable to the payment.

(C) *Limitations.*—Paragraph (c)(1)(i)(B) of this section shall not apply to the extent that the controlled foreign corporation partner has no income against which to allocate the expense, other than its distributive share of a payment described in paragraph (c)(1)(i)(B) of this section. Similarly, to the extent an expense described in paragraph (c)(1)(i)(B) of this section exceeds the controlled foreign corporation partner's distributive share of the payment from which the expense arises, such excess amount of the expense may reduce subpart F income (other than such payment) to which it is properly allocable or apportionable under section 954(b)(5).

(D) *Example.*—The following example illustrates the application of paragraphs (c)(1)(i)(B) and (C) of this section:

Example. CFC, a controlled foreign corporation in Country A, is a 70 percent partner in partnership P, located in Country B. Country A's tax laws do not classify P as a fiscally transparent entity. The rate of tax in country B is 15 percent of the tax rate in country A. P loans $100 to CFC at a market rate of interest. In year 1, CFC pays P $10 of interest on the loan. The interest payment would have caused the recharacterization rules of §1.954-9 to apply if the payment were made between the entities described in §1.954-9(a)(2). CFC's distributive share of P's interest income is $7, which is foreign personal holding company income to CFC under section 954(c). Under paragraph (c)(1)(i)(B) of this section, $7 of the $10 interest expense may not be allocated against any of CFC's subpart F income. However, to the extent the remaining $3 of interest expense is properly allocable to subpart F income of CFC other than its distributive share of P's interest income, this expense may offset such other subpart F income.

(E) *Effective date.*—Paragraph (c)(1)(i)(B), (C) and (D) of this section shall be applicable for all payments made or accrued in taxable years commencing after [date that is 5 years after publication of the final regulations in the federal register], under hybrid arrangements, unless such payments are made pursuant to an arrangement that would qualify for permanent relief under §1.954-9(c)(2) if made between a controlled foreign corporation and its hybrid branch, in which case the relief afforded under that section shall also be afforded under this section.

* * *

Foreign Personal Holding Company Income: Foreign Currency Gain or Loss: Exclusion

Foreign Personal Holding Company Income: Foreign Currency Gain or Loss: Exclusion.—Amendments to Reg. §1.954-0, providing guidance on the treatment of foreign currency gain or loss of a controlled foreign corporation under the business needs exclusion from foreign personal holding company income, are proposed (published in the Federal Register on December 19, 2017) (REG-119514-15).

Par. 3. Section 1.954-0(b) is amended by:

1. Redesignating the entry for §1.954-2(g)(2)(ii)(D) as the entry for §1.954-2(g)(2)(ii)(E).

2. Redesignating the entries for §1.954-2(g)(2)(ii)(C), (g)(2)(ii)(C)(*1*), (g)(2)(ii)(C)(2), (g)(2)(ii)(C)(2)(*i*), (g)(2)(ii)(C)(2)(*ii*), and (g)(2)(ii)(C)(2)t(*iii*) as the entries for §1.954-2(g)(2)(ii)(D), (g)(2)(ii)(D)(*1*), (g)(2)(ii)(D)(2), (g)(2)(ii)(D)(2)(*i*), (g)(2)(ii)(D)(2)(*ii*), and (g)(2)(ii)(D)(2)(*iii*), respectively.

3. Adding new entries for §1.954-2(g)(2)(ii)(C), (g)(2)(ii)(C)(*1*), and (g)(2)(ii)(C)(2).

4. Revising the entry for §1.954-2(g)(2)(iii).

The additions and revision read as follows:

§1.954-0. Introduction

* * *

(b) * * *

§1.954-2 Foreign personal holding company income.

* * *

(g) * * *

(2) * * *

(ii) * * *

(C) Foreign currency gains and losses arising from a transaction or property that gives rise to both non-subpart F income and subpart F income or from a bona fide hedging transaction with respect to such a transaction or property.

(1) In general.

(2) Financial statement hedging transaction with respect to the net investment in a qualified business unit.

* * *

(iii) Special rule for foreign currency gain or loss from an interest-bearing liability and bona fide hedges of an interest-bearing liability.

* * *

Determination of the Foreign Tax Credit: Guidance

Determination of the Foreign Tax Credit: Guidance.—Amendments to Reg. §1.954-1, relating to the determination of the foreign tax credit under the Internal Revenue Code, including changes made by the Tax Cuts and Jobs Act, are proposed (published in the Federal Register on December 7, 2018) (REG-105600-18).

Par. 21. Section 1.954-1 is amended by:

1. Removing the language "§1.904-5(a)(1)" and adding in its place the language "§1.904-5(a)(4)(v)" in the introductory text of paragraph (c)(1)(iii)(A).
2. Removing the language "section 960" and adding in its place the language "section 960(a) and §1.960-2(b)(1)" in the first sentence of paragraph (d)(3)(i).
3. Removing the language "section 960" and adding in its place the language "section 960(a)" in the second sentence of paragraph (d)(3)(i).
4. Revising the last sentence of paragraph (d)(3)(i).
5. Adding a sentence at the end of paragraph (d)(3)(i).
6. Removing the language "section 960" and adding in its place the language "section 960(a) and §1.960-2(b)(1)" in paragraph (d)(3)(ii).
7. Adding a sentence at the end of paragraph (d)(3)(ii).
8. Removing paragraph (g)(4).
9. Adding paragraph (h).

The revision and additions read as follows:

§1.954-1. Foreign base company income.

* * *

(d) * * *

(3) * * *

(i) * * * Except as provided in the next sentence, the amount of foreign income taxes paid or accrued with respect to a net item of income, determined in the manner provided in this paragraph (d), is not affected by a subsequent reduction in foreign income taxes attributable to a distribution to shareholders of all or part of such income. To the extent the foreign income taxes paid or accrued by the controlled foreign corporation are reasonably certain to be returned by the foreign jurisdiction imposing such taxes to a shareholder, directly or indirectly, through any means (including, but not limited to, a refund, credit, payment, discharge of an obligation, or any other method) on a subsequent distribution to such shareholder, the foreign income taxes are not treated as paid or accrued for purposes of this paragraph (d)(3)(i).

(ii) * * * However, notwithstanding the rules in §1.904-4(c)(7), to the extent the foreign income taxes paid or accrued by the controlled foreign corporation are reasonably certain to be returned by the foreign jurisdiction imposing such taxes to a shareholder, directly or indirectly, through any means (including, but not limited to, a refund, credit, payment, discharge of an obligation, or any other method) on a subsequent distribution to such shareholder, the foreign income taxes are not treated as paid or accrued for purposes of this paragraph (d)(3)(ii).

* * *

(h) *Applicability dates.*—(1) *Paragraphs (d)(3)(i) and (ii).*—Paragraphs (d)(3)(i) and (ii) of this section apply to taxable years of a controlled foreign corporation ending on or after December 4, 2018.

(2) *Paragraph (g).*—Paragraph (g) of this section applies to taxable years of a controlled foreign corporation beginning on or after July 23, 2002.

Controlled Foreign Corporations: Hybrid Branches: Subpart F Income

Controlled Foreign Corporations: Hybrid Branches: Subpart F Income.—Amendments to Reg. §1.954-2, relating to the treatment under subpart F of certain transactions involving hybrid branches, are proposed (published in the Federal Register on July 13, 1999) (REG-113909-98).

☐ Par. 5. In §1-954-2, paragraphs (a)(5) and (a)(6) are added to read as follows:

§1.954-2. Foreign personal holding company income.—(a) * * *

(5) *Special rules applicable to distributive share of partnership income.*—(i) *Application of related person exceptions where payment reduces foreign tax of payor.*—If a partnership receives an item of income that reduced the foreign income tax of the payor (determined under the principles of §1.954-9(a)(3)), to determine the extent to which a controlled foreign corporation's distributive share of such item of income is foreign personal holding company income, the exceptions contained in section 954(c)(3) shall apply only if—

(A)*(1)* Any such exception would have applied to exclude the income from foreign personal holding company income if the controlled foreign corporation had earned the income directly (determined by testing, with reference to such controlled foreign corporation, whether an entity is a related person, within the meaning of section 954(d)(3), or is organized under the laws of, or uses property in, the foreign country in which the controlled foreign corporation is created or organized); and

(2) The distributive share of such income is not in respect of a payment made by the controlled foreign corporation to the partnership; and

(B)*(1)* The partnership is created or organized, and uses a substantial part of its assets in a trade or business in the country under the laws of which the controlled foreign corporation is created or organized (determined under the principles of paragraph (b)(4) of this section);

(2) The partnership is regarded as fiscally transparent, as defined in §1.954-9(a)(7), by all countries under the laws of which the controlled foreign corporation is created or organized or has substantial assets; or

(3) The income is taxed in the year when earned at an effective rate of tax (determined under the principles of § 1.954-1(d)(2)) that is not less than 90 percent of, and not more than five percentage points less than, the effective rate of tax that would have applied to such income under the laws of the country in which the controlled foreign corporation is created or organized if such income were earned directly by the controlled foreign corporation partner from local sources.

(ii) *Certain other exceptions applicable to foreign personal holding company income.*—[Reserved].

(iii) *Effective date.*—Paragraph (a)(5)(i) of this section shall apply to all amounts paid or accrued in taxable years commencing after [date that is 5 years after publication of the final regulations in the federal register], under hybrid arrangements, unless such payments are made pursuant to an arrangement which would qualify for permanent relief under § 1.954-9(c)(2) if made between a controlled foreign corporation and its hybrid branch, in which case the relief afforded under that section shall also be afforded under this section.

(6) *Special rules applicable to exceptions from foreign personal holding company income treatment in circumstances involving hybrid branches.*—(i) *In general.*—In the case of a payment between a controlled foreign corporation (or its hybrid branch, as defined in § 1.954-9(a)(6)) and the hybrid branch of a related controlled foreign corporation, the exceptions contained in section 954(c)(3) shall apply only if the payment would have qualified for the exception if the payor were a separate controlled foreign corporation created or organized in the jurisdiction where foreign tax is reduced and the payee were a separate controlled foreign corporation created or organized under the laws of the jurisdiction in which the payment is subject to tax (other than a withholding tax).

(ii) *Exception where no tax reduction or tax disparity.*—Paragraph (a)(6)(i) of this section shall not apply unless the payment would have reduced foreign tax, under § 1.954-9(a)(3), and fallen within the tax disparity rule of § 1.954-9(a)(5)(iv) if those provisions had been applicable to the payment.

(iii) *Effective date.*—The rules of this section shall apply to all amounts paid or accrued in taxable years commencing after [date that is 5 years after publication of the final regulations in the federal register], under hybrid arrangements, unless such payments are made pursuant to an arrangement which would qualify for permanent relief under § 1.954-9(c)(2) if made between a controlled foreign corporation and its hybrid branch, in which case the relief afforded under that section shall also be afforded under this section.

Section 1256 Contracts: Swap Exclusions

Section 1256 Contracts: Swap Exclusions.—Amendment to Reg. § 1.954-2, providing guidance on the category of swaps and similar agreements that are within the scope of Code Sec. 1256(b)(2)(B), are proposed (published in the Federal Register on September 16, 2011) (REG-111283-11).

☐ Par. 5. Section 1.954-2 is amended by:

1. Revising paragraph (h)(3)(i).
2. Adding paragraph (h)(3)(iii).

The revision and addition read as follows:

§ 1.954-2. Foreign personal holding company income.

* * *

(3) *Notional principal contracts.*—(i) In general.—Income equivalent to interest includes income from notional principal contracts (as defined in § 1.446-3(c)) denominated in the functional currency of the taxpayer (or a qualified business unit of the taxpayer, as defined in section 989(a)), the value of which is determined solely by reference to interest rates or interest rate indices, to the extent that the income from such transactions accrues on or after August 14, 1989.

* * *

(iii) *Effective/applicability date.*—The rules of paragraph (h)(3) of this section apply to notional principal contracts as defined in § 1.446-3(c) that are entered into on or after the date of publication of a Treasury decision adopting these rules as final regulations in the **Federal Register**. Section 1.954-2(h)(3) as contained in 26 CFR part 1 revised April 1, 2011, continues to apply to notional principal contracts entered into before the date of publication of a Treasury decision adopting these rules as final regulations in the **Federal Register**.

* * *

Foreign Personal Holding Company Income: Foreign Currency Gain or Loss: Exclusion

Foreign Personal Holding Company Income: Foreign Currency Gain or Loss: Exclusion.—Amendments to Reg. § 1.954-2, providing guidance on the treatment of foreign currency gain or loss of a controlled foreign corporation under the business needs exclusion from foreign personal holding company income, are proposed (published in the Federal Register on December 19, 2017) (REG-119514-15).

Par. 4. Section 1.954-2 is amended by:

1. Adding a sentence after the first sentence in paragraph (a)(4)(ii)(A).
2. Redesignating paragraph (g)(2)(ii)(D) as paragraph (g)(2)(ii)(E).
3. Redesignating paragraph (g)(2)(ii)(C) as paragraph (g)(2)(ii)(D).
4. In newly redesignated paragraph (g)(2)(ii)(D)(2)(*i*), removing "paragraph (g)(2)(ii)(C)" and adding "paragraph (g)(2)(ii)(D)" in its place and removing "paragraph (g)(2)(ii)(C)(*1*)" and adding "paragraph (g)(2)(ii)(D)(*1*)" in its place.

5. In newly redesignated paragraph (g)(2)(ii)(D)(2)(*ii*), removing "paragraph (g)(2)(ii)(C)(2)(*i*)" and adding "paragraph (g)(2)(ii)(D)(2)(*i*)" each place it appears.

6. In newly redesignated paragraph (g)(2)(ii)(D)(2)(*iii*), removing "paragraph (g)(2)(ii)(C)(2)" and adding "paragraph (g)(2)(ii)(D)(2)" in its place.

7. Adding new paragraph (g)(2)(ii)(C).

8. Revising paragraph (g)(2)(iii).

9. Revising paragraph (g)(3)(iii).

10. Revising paragraph (g)(4)(iii).

11. Adding two sentences after the third sentence in paragraph (i)(2).

The additions and revisions read as follows:

§1.954-2. Foreign personal holding company income.

(a) * * *

(4) * * *

(ii) * * *

(A) * * * Additionally, the acquisition of a debt instrument by a controlled foreign corporation may be treated as a bona fide hedging transaction with respect to an interest-bearing liability of the controlled foreign corporation, provided that the acquisition of the debt instrument has the effect of managing the controlled foreign corporation's exchange rate risk with respect to the liability within the meaning of §1.1221-2(c)(4) and (d), determined without regard to §1.1221-2(d)(5), and otherwise meets the requirements of paragraph (a)(4)(ii) of this section. * * *

* * *

(g) * * *

(2) * * *

(ii) * * *

(C) *Foreign currency gains and losses arising from a transaction or property that gives rise to both non-subpart F income and subpart F income or from a bona fide hedging transaction with respect to such a transaction or property.—(1) In general.—* If a foreign currency gain or loss would be directly related to the business needs of the controlled foreign corporation pursuant to paragraph (g)(2)(ii)(B)(*1*) or (*2*) of this section except that it arises from a transaction or property that gives rise, or is reasonably expected to give rise, to both non-subpart F income and subpart F income (other than foreign currency gain or loss), or from a bona fide hedging transaction with respect to such a transaction or property, the amount of foreign currency gain or loss that is allocable to non-subpart F income under this paragraph (g)(2)(ii)(C)(*1*) is directly related to the business needs of the controlled foreign corporation. The amount of foreign currency gain or loss arising from a transaction or property described in this paragraph (g)(2)(ii)(C)(*1*), or from a bona fide hedging transaction with respect to such a transaction or property, that is allocable to non-subpart F income equals the product of the total amount of foreign currency gain or loss arising from the transaction or property and the ratio of non-subpart F income (other than foreign currency gain or loss) that the transaction or property gives rise to, or is reasonably expected to give rise to, to the total income that the transaction or property gives rise to, or is reasonably expected to give rise to. However, none of the foreign currency gain or loss arising from property that does not give rise to income (as defined in paragraph (e)(3) of this section), or from a bona fide hedging transaction with respect to such property, is allocable to non-subpart F income.

(*2*) *Financial statement hedging transaction with respect to a qualified business unit.*—If foreign currency gain or loss arises from a financial statement hedging transaction (as defined in this paragraph (g)(2)(ii)(C)(*2*)) with respect to a qualified business unit (as defined in §1.989(a)-1) (QBU) of a controlled foreign corporation that is not treated as an entity separate from the controlled foreign corporation for federal income tax purposes, either because it is a branch or division of the controlled foreign corporation or because it is a business entity that is disregarded as separate from its owner under §301.7701-3 of this chapter, the amount of the qualifying portion (as determined under this paragraph (g)(2)(ii)(C)(*2*)) of foreign currency gain or loss that is allocable to non-subpart F income under this paragraph (g)(2)(ii)(C)(*2*) is directly related to the business needs of the controlled foreign corporation. Generally, the controlled foreign corporation must allocate the qualifying portion of foreign currency gain or loss arising from the financial statement hedging transaction between subpart F income and non-subpart F income in the same proportion as it would characterize gain or loss determined under section 987 as subpart F income and non-subpart F income under the principles of §1.987-6(b). A *financial statement hedging transaction* is a transaction that is entered into by a CFC for the purpose of managing exchange rate risk with respect to part or all of that CFC's net investment in a QBU that is included in the consolidated financial statements of a United States shareholder of the CFC (or a corporation that directly or indirectly owns such United States shareholder). The qualifying portion of foreign currency gain or loss is the amount of foreign currency gain or loss arising from a financial statement hedging transaction that is properly accounted for under U.S. generally accepted accounting principles as a cumulative foreign currency translation adjustment to shareholders' equity.

* * *

(iii) *Special rule for foreign currency gain or loss from an interest-bearing liability and bona fide hedges of an interest-bearing liability.*—Except as provided in paragraph (g)(2)(ii)(D)(*2*) or (g)(5)(iv) of this section, foreign currency gain or loss arising from an interest-bearing liability is characterized as subpart F income and non-subpart F income in the same manner that interest expense associated with the liability would be allocated and apportioned between subpart F income and non-subpart F income under §§1.861-9T and 1.861-12T. Likewise, foreign currency gain or loss arising from a bona fide hedging transaction entered into by the controlled foreign corporation that has the effect of managing exchange rate risk with respect to an interest-bearing liability that is not subject to paragraph (g)(2)(ii)(D)(*2*) (certain interest-bearing liabilities treated as dealer property) or (g)(5)(iv) (gain or loss allocated under § 1.861-9) of this section is characterized as subpart F income and non-subpart F income in the same manner that interest expense associated with the interest-bearing liability would be allocated and apportioned between subpart F income and non-subpart F income under §§ 1.861-9T and 1.861-12T. Paragraph (g)(2)(ii) of this section does not apply to any foreign currency gain or loss described in this paragraph (g)(2)(iii).

(3) * * *

(iii) *Revocation of election.*—This election is effective for the taxable year of the controlled foreign corporation for which it is made and all subsequent taxable years of such corporation unless revoked by the Commissioner or the controlling United States shareholders (as defined in § 1.964-1(c)(5)) of the controlled foreign corporation. The controlling United States shareholders of a controlled foreign corporation may revoke such corporation's election at any time. If an election has been revoked under this paragraph (g)(3)(iii), a new election under paragraph (g)(3) of this section cannot be made until the sixth taxable year following the year in which the previous election was revoked, and such subsequent election cannot be revoked until the sixth taxable year following the year in which the subsequent election was made. The controlling United States shareholders revoke an election on behalf of a controlled foreign corporation by filing a statement that clearly indicates such election has been revoked with their original or amended income tax returns for the taxable year of such United States shareholders ending with or within the taxable year of the controlled foreign corporation for which the election is revoked.

* * *

(4) * * *

(iii) *Revocation of election.*—This election is effective for the taxable year of the controlled foreign corporation for which it is made and all subsequent taxable years of such corporation unless revoked by the Commissioner or the controlling United States shareholders (as defined in § 1.964-1(c)(5)) of the controlled foreign corporation. The controlling United States shareholders of a controlled foreign corporation may revoke such corporation's election at any time. If an election has been revoked under this paragraph (g)(4)(iii), a new election under paragraph (g)(4) of this section cannot be made until the sixth taxable year following the year in which the previous election was revoked, and such subsequent election cannot be revoked until the sixth taxable year following the year in which the subsequent election was made. The controlling United States shareholders revoke an election on behalf of a controlled foreign corporation by filing a statement that clearly indicates such election has been revoked with their original or amended income tax returns for the taxable year of such United States shareholders ending with or within the taxable year of the controlled foreign corporation for which the election is revoked.

* * *

(i) * * *

(2) *Other paragraphs.*—* * * The second sentence of paragraph (a)(4)(ii)(A), paragraph (g)(2)(ii)(C)(*1*), and the second sentence of paragraph (g)(2)(iii) apply to a bona fide hedging transaction entered into on or after the date the proposed regulations are published as final regulations in the *Federal Register*. Paragraphs (g)(2)(ii)(C) (other paragraph (g)(2)(ii)(C)(*1*), insofar as it applies to a bona fide hedging transaction), (g)(3)(iii), and (g)(4)(iii) of this section apply to taxable years of controlled foreign corporations ending on or after the date that these regulations are published as final regulations in the *Federal Register*.

Controlled Foreign Corporations: Hybrid Branches: Subpart F Income

Controlled Foreign Corporations: Hybrid Branches: Subpart F Income.—Reg. §1.954-9, relating to the treatment under subpart F of certain transactions involving hybrid branches, is proposed (published in the Federal Register on July 13, 1999) (REG-113909-98).

☐ Par. 6. Section 1.954-9 is added to read as follows:

§1.954-9. Hybrid branches.—(a) *Subpart F income arising from certain payments involving hybrid branches.*—(1) *Payment causing foreign tax reduction gives rise to additional subpart F income.*—The non-subpart F income of a controlled foreign corporation will be recharacterized as subpart F income, to the extent provided in paragraph (a)(5) of this section, if—

(i) A hybrid branch payment, as defined in paragraph (a)(6) of this section, is made between the entities described in paragraph (a)(2) of this section;

(ii) The hybrid branch payment reduces foreign tax, as determined under paragraph (a)(3) of this section; and

(iii) The hybrid branch payment is treated as falling within a category of foreign personal holding company income under the rules of paragraph (a)(4) of this section.

(2) *Hybrid branch payment between certain entities.*—(i) *In general.*—Paragraph (a)(1) of this section shall apply to hybrid branch payments between—

(A) A controlled foreign corporation and its hybrid branch;

(B) Hybrid branches of a controlled foreign corporation;

(C) A partnership in which a controlled foreign corporation is a partner (either directly or through one or more branches or other partnerships) and a hybrid branch of the partnership; or

(D) Hybrid branches of a partnership in which a controlled foreign corporation is a partner (either directly or through one or more branches or other partnerships).

(ii) *Hybrid branch payment involving partnership.*—(A) *Fiscally transparent partnership.*—To the extent of the controlled foreign corporation's proportionate share of a hybrid branch payment, the rules of paragraphs (a)(3), (4) and (5) of this section shall be applied by treating the hybrid branch payment between the partnership and the hybrid branch as if it were made directly between the controlled foreign corporation and the hybrid branch, or as if the hybrid branches of the partnership were hybrid branches of the controlled foreign corporation, if the hybrid branch payment is made between—

(1) A fiscally transparent partnership in which a controlled foreign corporation is a partner (either directly or through one or more branches or other fiscally transparent partnerships) and the partnership's hybrid branch; or

(2) Hybrid branches of a fiscally transparent partnership in which a controlled foreign corporation is a partner (either directly or through one or more branches or other fiscally transparent partnerships).

(B) *Non-fiscally transparent partnership.*—To the extent of the controlled foreign corporation's proportionate share of a hybrid branch payment, the rules of paragraphs (a)(3) and (4) and (a)(5)(iv) of this section shall be applied to the non-fiscally transparent partnership as if it were the controlled foreign corporation, if the hybrid branch payment is made between—

(1) A non-fiscally transparent partnership in which a controlled foreign corporation is a partner (either directly or through one or more branches or other partnerships) and the partnership's hybrid branch; or

(2) Hybrid branches of a non-fiscally transparent partnership in which a controlled foreign corporation is a partner (either directly or through one or more branches or other partnerships).

(C) *Examples.*—The following examples illustrate the application of this paragraph (a)(2)(ii):

Example 1. CFC, a controlled foreign corporation in Country A, is a 90 percent partner in partnership P, which is treated as fiscally transparent under the laws of Country A. P has a hybrid branch, BR, in Country B. P makes an interest payment of $100 to BR. Under Country A law, CFC's 90 percent share of the payment reduces CFC's Country A income tax. Under paragraph (a)(2)(ii)(A) of this section, the recharacterization rules of this section are applied by treating the payment as if made by CFC to BR. Ninety dollars of CFC's non-subpart F income, to the extent available, and subject to the earnings and profits and tax rate limitations of paragraph (a)(5) of this section, is recharacterized as subpart F income.

Example 2. CFC, a controlled foreign corporation in country A, is a 90 percent partner in partnership P, which is treated as fiscally transparent under the laws of Country A. P has two branches in Country B, BR1 and BR2. BR1 is treated as fiscally transparent under the laws of Country A. BR2 is a hybrid branch. BR1 makes an interest payment of $100 to BR2. Under paragraph (a)(2)(ii)(A) of this section, the payment by BR1, the fiscally transparent branch, is treated as a payment by P, and the deemed payment by P, a fiscally transparent partnership, is treated as made by CFC. Under Country A law, CFC's 90 percent share of BR1's payment reduces CFC's Country A income tax. Ninety dollars of CFC's non-subpart F income, to the extent available, and subject to the earnings and profits and tax rate limitations of paragraph (a)(5) of this section, is recharacterized as subpart F income.

(3) *Application when payment reduces foreign tax.*—For purposes of paragraph (a)(1) of this section, a hybrid branch payment reduces foreign tax when the foreign tax imposed on the income of the payor, or any person that is a related person with respect to the payor (as determined under the principles of section 954(d)(3)), is less than the foreign tax that would have been imposed on such income had the hybrid branch payment not been made, or the hybrid branch payment creates or increases a loss or deficit or other tax attribute which may be carried back or forward to reduce the foreign income tax of the payor or any owner in another year (determined by taking into account any refund of such tax made to the payor, payee or any other person).

(4) *Hybrid branch payment that is included within a category of foreign personal holding company income.*—(i) *In general.*—For purposes of paragraph (a)(1) of this section, whether the hybrid branch payment is treated as income included within a category of foreign personal holding company income is determined by treating a hybrid branch that is either the payor or recipient of the hybrid branch payment as a separate wholly-owned subsidiary corporation of the controlled foreign corporation that is incorporated in the jurisdiction under the laws of which such hybrid branch is created, organized for foreign law purposes, or has substantial assets. Thus, the hybrid branch payment will be treated as included within a category of foreign personal holding company income if, taking into account any specific exceptions for that category, the payment would be included within a category of foreign personal holding company income if the branch or branches were treated as separately incorporated for U.S. tax purposes.

(ii) *Extent to which controlled foreign corporation and hybrid branches treated as separate entities.*—For purposes of this section, other than the determination under paragraph (a)(4)(i) of this section, a controlled foreign corporation and its hybrid branch, a partnership and its hybrid branch, or hybrid branches shall not be treated as separate entities. Thus, for example, if a controlled foreign corporation, including all of its hybrid branches, has an overall deficit in earnings and profits to which section 952(c) applies, the limitation of such section on the amount includible in the subpart F income of such corporation will apply. Similarly, for purposes of applying the de minimis and full inclusion rules of section 954(b)(3), a controlled foreign corporation and its hybrid branch, or hybrid branches shall not be treated as separate corporations. Further, a hybrid branch payment that would reduce foreign personal holding company income under section 954(b)(5) if made between two separate entities will not create an expense if made between a controlled foreign corporation and its hybrid branch, a partnership and its hybrid branch, or hybrid branches.

(5) *Recharacterization of income attributable to current earnings and profits as subpart F income.*—(i) *General rule.*—Non-subpart F income of a controlled foreign corporation in an amount equal to the excess of earnings and profits of the controlled foreign corporation for the taxable year over subpart F income, as defined in section

952(a), will be recharacterized as subpart F income under paragraph (a)(1) of this section only to the extent provided under paragraphs (a)(5)(ii) through (vi) of this section.

(ii) *Subpart F income.*—For purposes of determining the excess of current earnings and profits over subpart F income under paragraph (a)(1) of this section, the amount of subpart F income is determined before the application of the rules of this section but after the application of the rules of sections 952(c) and 954(b). Further, such amount is determined by treating the controlled foreign corporation and all of its hybrid branches as a single corporation.

(iii) *Recharacterization limited to gross amount of hybrid branch payment.*—(A) *In general.*—The amount recharacterized as subpart F income under paragraph (a)(1) of this section is limited to the amount of the hybrid branch payment.

(B) *Exception for duplicative payments.*—[Reserved].

(iv) *Tax disparity rule.*—(A) *In general.*—Paragraph (a)(1) of this section will apply only if the hybrid branch payment falls within the tax disparity rule. The hybrid branch payment falls within the tax disparity rule if it is taxed in the year when earned at an effective rate of tax that is less than 90 percent of, and at least 5 percentage points less than, the hypothetical effective rate of tax imposed on the hybrid branch payment, as determined under paragraph (a)(5)(iv)(B) of this section.

(B) *Hypothetical effective rate of tax.*—*(1) In general.*—The hypothetical effective rate of tax imposed on the hybrid branch payment is—

(i) For the taxable year of the payor in which the hybrid branch payment is made, the amount of income taxes that would have been paid or accrued by the payor if the hybrid branch payment had not been made, less the amount of income taxes paid or accrued by the payor; divided by

(ii) The amount of the hybrid branch payment.

(2) Hypothetical effective rate of tax when hybrid branch payment causes or increases loss or deficit.—If the hybrid branch payment causes or increases a loss or deficit of the payor for foreign tax purposes, and such loss or deficit can be carried forward or back, the hypothetical effective rate of tax imposed on the hybrid branch payment is the effective rate of tax that would be imposed on the taxable income of the payor for the year in which the payment is made if the payor's taxable income were equal to the amount of the hybrid branch payment.

(C) *Examples.*—The application of this paragraph (a)(5)(iv) is illustrated by the following examples:

Example 1. In 2006, CFC organized in Country A had net income of $60 from manufacturing for Country A tax purposes. It also had a branch (BR) in Country B. BR is a hybrid entity under paragraph (a)(1) of this section. CFC made a payment of $40 to BR, which was a hybrid branch payment under paragraph (a)(6) of this section, and was treated by CFC as a deductible payment for Country A tax purposes. CFC paid $30 of Country A taxes in 2006. It would have paid $50 of Country A taxes without the deductible payment. Country A did not impose any withholding tax on the $40 payment to BR. Country B also did not impose a tax on the $40 received by BR. Therefore, the effective rate of tax on that payment is 0%. Furthermore, the hypothetical effective rate of tax on the $40 hybrid branch payment is 50% ($50 – $30/$40). The effective rate of tax (0%) is less than 90% of, and more than 5 percentage points less than, this hypothetical rate of tax of 50%. As a result, the $40 hybrid branch payment falls within the tax disparity rule of this paragraph (a)(5)(iv).

Example 2. Assume the same facts as in *Example 1*, except that CFC has a loss of $100 for the year for Country A tax purposes. Under Country A law, CFC can carry the loss forward for use in subsequent years. CFC paid no Country A taxes in 2006. The rate of tax in Country A is graduated from 20% to 50%. If the $40 hybrid branch payment were the only item of taxable income of CFC, Country A would have imposed tax at an effective rate of 30%. The effective rate of tax (0%) is less than 90% of, and more than 5 percentage points less than, the hypothetical effective rate of tax (30%) imposed on the hybrid branch payment. As a result, the $40 hybrid branch payment falls within the tax disparity rule of this paragraph (a)(5)(iv).

Example 3. Assume the same facts as in *Example 1*, except that Country B imposes tax on the $40 hybrid payment to BR at an effective rate of 50%. The effective rate of 50% is equal to the hypothetical effective rate of tax. As a result, the hybrid branch payment does not fall within the tax disparity rule of this paragraph (a)(5)(iv) and, thus, the recharacterization rules of paragraph (a)(1) of this section do not apply. See also the special high tax exception of paragraph (a)(5)(v) of this section.

(v) *Special high tax exception.*—(A) *In general.*—Paragraph (a)(1) of this section shall not apply if the non-subpart F income that would be recharacterized as subpart F income under this section was subject to foreign income taxes imposed by a foreign country or countries at an effective rate that is greater than 90 percent of the maximum rate of tax specified in section 11 for the taxable year of the controlled foreign corporation.

(B) *Effective rate of tax.*—The effective rate of tax imposed on the non-subpart F income that would be recharacterized as subpart F income under this section is determined under the principles of § 1.954-1(d)(2) and (3). See paragraph (b) of this section for the application of section 960 to amounts recharacterized as subpart F income under this section.

(vi) *No carryback or carryforward of amounts in excess of current year earnings and profits limitation.*—To the extent that some or all of the amount required to be recharacterized under this section is not recharacterized as subpart F income because the hybrid branch payment exceeds the amount that can be recharacterized, as determined under paragraph (a)(5)(i) of this section, this excess shall not be carried back or forward to another year.

(6) *Definitions for this section.*—For purposes of this section:

(i) *Arrangement.*—shall mean any agreement to pay interest, rents, royalties or similar amounts. It shall also include the declaration and payment of a dividend (but not an agreement or undertaking to pay future, unspecified dividends). An arrangement shall not, however, include the mere formation or acquisition (or similar event) of a hybrid branch that is intended to become a party to an arrangement.

(ii) *Entity*.—means any person that is treated by the United States or any jurisdiction as other than an individual.

(iii) *Hybrid branch*.—means an entity that—

(A) Is disregarded as an entity separate from its owner for federal tax purposes and is owned (including ownership through branches) by either a controlled foreign corporation or a partnership in which a controlled foreign corporation is a partner (either directly or indirectly through one or more branches or partnerships);

(B) Is treated as fiscally transparent by the United States; and

(C) Is treated as non-fiscally transparent by the country in which the payor entity, any owner of a fiscally-transparent payor entity, the controlled foreign corporation, or any intermediary partnership is created, organized or has substantial assets.

(iv) *Hybrid branch payment*.—means the gross amount of any payment (including any accrual) which, under the tax laws of any foreign jurisdiction to which the payor is subject, is regarded as a payment between two separate entities but which, under U.S. income tax principles, is not income to the recipient because it is between two parts of a single entity.

(7) *Fiscally transparent and non-fiscally transparent*.—For purposes of this section an entity shall be treated as fiscally transparent with respect to an interest holder of the entity, if such interest holder is required, under the laws of any jurisdiction to which it is subject, to take into account separately, on a current basis, such interest holder's share of all items which, if separately taken into account by such interest holder, would result in an income tax liability for the interest holder in such jurisdiction different from that which would result if the interest holder did not take the share of such items into account separately. A non-fiscally transparent entity is an entity that is not fiscally transparent under this paragraph (a)(7).

(b) *Application of section 960*.—For purposes of determining the amount of taxes deemed paid under section 960, the amount of non-subpart F income recharacterized as subpart F income under this section shall be treated as attributable to income in separate categories, as defined in §1.904-5(a)(1), in proportion to the ratio of non-subpart F income in each such category to the total amount of non-subpart F income of the controlled foreign corporation for the taxable year.

(c) *Effective dates*.—(1) *In general*.—This section shall be applicable for all amounts paid or accrued in taxable years commencing after [date that is 5 years after publication of the final regulations in the federal register], under hybrid arrangements, except as otherwise provided.

(2) *Permanent relief*.—(i) *In general*.—This section shall not apply to any payments made under hybrid arrangements entered into before June 19, 1998. This exception shall be permanent so long as the arrangement is not substantially modified, within the meaning of paragraph (c)(2)(ii) of this section, on or after June 19, 1998.

(ii) *Substantial modification*.—(A) *In general*.—Substantial modification of a hybrid arrangement includes—

(1) The expansion of the hybrid arrangement (other than de minimis expansion);

(2) A more than 50% change in the U.S. ownership (direct or indirect) of any entity that is a party to the hybrid arrangement, other than—

(i) A transfer of ownership of such party within a controlled group determined under section 1563(a), without regard to section 1563(a)(4); or

(ii) A change in ownership of the entire controlled group (determined under section 1563(a), without regard to section 1563(a)(4)) of which such party is a member;

(3) Any measure taken by a party to the arrangement (or any related party) that materially increases the tax benefit of the hybrid arrangement, regardless of whether such measure alters the legal relationship between the parties to the arrangement. For example, in the case of a hybrid branch payment determined with reference to a percentage of sales, a growth in the amount of the hybrid branch payment (and, thus, the tax benefit) caused by a growth of sales will not, in general, be a substantial modification. However, in the case of a significant sales growth resulting from a transfer of assets by a related party, that transfer would be a measure which materially increased the benefit of the arrangement, and that arrangement would be deemed to have been substantially modified.

(B) *Transactions not treated as substantial modification*.—Substantial modification of a hybrid arrangement does not include—

(1) The daily reissuance of a demand loan by operation of law;

(2) The renewal of a loan, license or rental agreement on the same terms and conditions if—

(i) The renewal occurs pursuant to the terms of the agreement and without more than a de minimis amount of action of any party thereto;

(ii) As contemplated by the original agreement, the same parties agree to renew the agreement without modification; or

(iii) The renewal occurs solely by reason of a subsequent drawdown under a grandfathered master credit facility agreement;

(3) The renewal of a loan, license, or rental agreement by the same parties on terms which do not increase the tax benefit of the arrangement (other than a de minimis increase);

(4) The making of payments under a license agreement in respect of copyrights or patents (or know-how associated with such copyrights or patents), not in existence at the time the agreement was entered into, but only where the development of such property was anticipated by the agreement, and such property is substantially derived from (or otherwise incorporates substantial features of) copyrights and patents (or know-how associated with such copyrights or patents) in existence at the time of, and covered under, the original agreement;

(5) A final transfer pricing adjustment made by the taxation authorities of the jurisdiction in which the tax reduction occurs, so

long as such adjustment would not have been a substantial valuation misstatement (as defined in section 6662(e)(1)(B)) if the adjustment had been made by the Internal Revenue Service; or

(6) A de minimis periodic adjustment by the parties to the arrangement made annually (or more frequently) to conform the payments to the requirements of section 482. [Reg. § 1.954-9.]

Corporate Shareholders: Amount Determined Under Section 956

Corporate Shareholders: Amount Determined Under Section 956.—Amendments to Reg. § 1.956-1, reducing the amount determined under section 956 of the Internal Revenue Code with respect to certain domestic corporations, are proposed (published in the Federal Register on November 5, 2018) (REG-114540-18).

Par. 2. Section 1.956-1 is amended by:

1. Revising paragraph (a).

2. In the first sentence of paragraph (g)(1), removing the language "Paragraph (a)" and adding in its place "Paragraph (a)(1)".

3. Adding paragraphs (g)(4) and (5).

The revisions and additions read as follows:

§ 1.956-1. Shareholder's pro rata share of the average of the amounts of United States property held by a controlled foreign corporation.—(a) *Overview and scope.*—(1) *In general.*—Subject to the provisions of section 951(a) and the regulations thereunder, a United States shareholder of a controlled foreign corporation is required to include in gross income the amount determined under section 956 with respect to the shareholder for the taxable year but only to the extent not excluded from gross income under section 959(a)(2) and the regulations thereunder.

(2) *Reduction for certain United States shareholders.*—(i) *In general.*—For a taxable year of a controlled foreign corporation, the amount determined under section 956 with respect to each share of stock of the controlled foreign corporation owned (within the meaning of section 958(a)) by a United States shareholder is the amount that would be determined under section 956 with respect to such share for the taxable year, absent the application of this paragraph (a)(2) for the taxable year (such amount, the *tentative section 956 amount*, and in the aggregate with respect to all shares owned (within the meaning of section 958(a)) by the United States shareholder, the *aggregate tentative section 956 amount*), reduced by the amount of the deduction under section 245A that the shareholder would be allowed if the shareholder received as a distribution from the controlled foreign corporation an amount equal to the tentative section 956 amount with respect to such share on the last day during the taxable year on which the foreign corporation is a controlled foreign corporation (*hypothetical distribution*).

(ii) *Determination of the amount of the deduction that would be allowed under section 245A with respect to a hypothetical distribution.*—For purposes of determining the amount of the deduction under section 245A that a United States shareholder would be allowed with respect to a share of stock of a controlled foreign corporation by reason of a hypothetical distribution, the following rules apply—

(A) If a United States shareholder owns a share of stock of a controlled foreign corporation indirectly (within the meaning of section 958(a)(2)), then—

(1) Sections 245A(a) through (d), 246(a), and 959 apply to the hypothetical distribution as if the United States shareholder directly owned (within the meaning of section 958(a)(1)(A)) the share;

(2) Section 245A(e) applies to the hypothetical distribution as if the distribution were made to the United States shareholder through each entity by reason of which the United States shareholder indirectly owns such share and pro rata with respect to the equity that gives rise to such indirect ownership;

(3) To the extent that a distribution treated as made to a controlled foreign corporation pursuant to the hypothetical distribution by reason of paragraph (a)(2)(ii)(A)(2) of this section would be subject to section 245A(e)(2), the United States shareholder is treated as not being allowed a deduction under section 245A by reason of the hypothetical distribution; and

(4) Section 246(c) applies to the hypothetical distribution by substituting the phrase "owned (within the meaning of section 958(a))" for the term "held" each place it appears in section 246(c); and

(B) Section 246(c) applies to the hypothetical distribution by substituting "the last day during the taxable year on which the foreign corporation is a controlled foreign corporation" for the phrase "the date on which such share becomes ex-dividend with respect to such dividend" in section 246(c)(1)(A).

(3) *Examples.*—The following examples illustrate the application of paragraph (a)(2) of this section.

(i) *Example 1.* (A) *Facts. (1)* USP, a domestic corporation, owns all of the single class of stock of CFC1, which is treated as equity for U.S. income tax purposes and under the laws of the jurisdiction in which CFC1 is organized and liable to tax as a resident. The stock of CFC1 consists of 100 shares, and USP satisfies the holding period requirement of section 246(c) (as modified by paragraph (a)(2)(ii)(B) of this section) with respect to each share of CFC1 stock. CFC1 owns all of the stock of USS, a domestic corporation. CFC1's adjusted basis in the stock of USS is $0x.

(2) The functional currency of CFC1 is the U.S. dollar. CFC1 has $100x of undistributed earnings as defined in section 245A(c)(2), $90x of which constitute undistributed foreign earnings as defined in section 245A(c)(3), and $10x of which are described in section 245(a)(5)(B) (that is, earnings attributable to a dividend that CFC1 received from USS). CFC1 would not receive a deduction or other tax benefit with respect to any income, war profits, or excess profits taxes on a distribution. None of the earnings and profits of CFC1 are described in section 959(c)(1) or

(2) or are earnings and profits attributable to income excluded from subpart F income under section 952(b). CFC1's applicable earnings (as defined in section 956(b)(1)) are $100x. CFC1 also has held an obligation of USP with an adjusted basis of $120x on every day during the taxable year that was acquired while all of its stock was owned by USP.

(B) *Analysis*. Because USP directly owns all of the stock of CFC1 at the end of CFC1's taxable year, USP's aggregate tentative section 956 amount with respect to CFC1 is $100x, the lesser of USP's pro rata share of the average amounts of United States property held by CFC1 ($120x) and its pro rata share of CFC1's applicable earnings ($100x). Under paragraph (a)(2)(i) of this section, USP's section 956 amount with respect to CFC1 is its aggregate tentative section 956 amount with respect to CFC1 reduced by the deduction under section 245A that USP would be allowed if USP received an amount equal to its aggregate tentative section 956 amount as a distribution with respect to the CFC1 stock. With respect to the tentative distribution from CFC1 to USP, USP would be allowed a $90x deduction under section 245A with respect to the foreign-source portion of the $100x hypothetical distribution (that is, an amount of the dividend that bears the same ratio to the dividend as the $90x of undistributed foreign earnings bears to the $100x of undistributed earnings). Accordingly, USP's section 956 amount with respect to CFC1 is $10x, its aggregate tentative section 956 amount ($100x) with respect to CFC1 reduced by the amount of the deduction that USP would have been allowed under section 245A with respect to the hypothetical distribution ($90x).

(ii) *Example 2. (A) Facts*. The facts are the same as in paragraph (A) of *Example 1* in this paragraph (a)(3)(i) of this section, except that all $100x of CFC1's undistributed earnings are described in section 959(c)(2).

(B) *Analysis*. As in paragraph (B) of *Example 1* in this paragraph (a)(3)(i) of this section, USP's aggregate tentative section 956 amount with respect to CFC1 is $100x, the lesser of USP's pro rata share of the average amounts of United States property held by CFC1 ($120x) and its pro rata share of CFC1's applicable earnings ($100x). However, paragraph (a)(2) of this section does not reduce USP's section 956 amount, because USP would not be allowed any deduction under section 245A with respect to the $100x hypothetical distribution by reason of section 959(a) and (d). Accordingly, USP's section 956 amount is $100x. However, under sections 959(a)(2) and 959(f)(1), USP's inclusion under section 951(a)(1)(B) with respect to CFC1 is $0, because USP's section 956 amount with respect to CFC1 does not exceed the earnings and profits of CFC1 described in section 959(c)(2) with respect to USP. The $100x of earnings and profits of CFC1 described in section 959(c)(2) are reclassified as earnings and profits described in section 959(c)(1).

(iii) *Example 3*. (A) *Facts*. *(1)* USP, a domestic corporation, owns all of the single class of stock of CFC1, and has held such stock for five years. CFC1 has held 70% of the single class of stock of CFC2 for three years. The other 30% of the CFC2 stock has been held by a foreign individual unrelated to USP or CFC1 since CFC2's formation. All of the stock of each of CFC1 and CFC2 is treated as equity for U.S. income tax purposes and under the laws of the jurisdiction in which each respective corporation is organized and liable to tax as a resident. CFC2 has a calendar taxable year. On December 1, Year 1, CFC1 acquires the remaining 30% of the stock of CFC2 for cash. On June 30, Year 2, CFC1 sells to a third party the 30% of CFC2 stock acquired in Year 1 at no gain. CFC2 made no distributions during Year 1.

(2) The functional currency of CFC1 and CFC2 is the U.S. dollar. CFC2 has $120x of undistributed earnings as defined in section 245A(c)(2), all of which constitute undistributed foreign earnings. Neither CFC1 nor CFC2 would receive a deduction or other tax benefit with respect to any income, war profits, or excess profits taxes on a distribution. None of the earnings and profits of CFC2 are described in section 959(c)(1) or (2) or are earnings and profits attributable to income excluded from subpart F income under section 952(b). CFC2's applicable earnings (as defined in section 956(b)(1)) are $120x. CFC2 has held an obligation of USP with an adjusted basis of $100x on every day of Year 1 that was acquired while USP owned all of the stock of CFC1 and CFC1 held 70% of the single class of stock of CFC2.

(B) *Analysis*. Because USP indirectly owns (within the meaning of section 958(a)) all of the stock of CFC2 at the end of Year 1, USP's aggregate tentative section 956 amount with respect to CFC2 for Year 1 is $100x, the lesser of USP's pro rata share of the average amounts of United States property held by CFC2 ($100x) and its pro rata share of CFC2's applicable earnings ($120x). Under paragraph (a)(2)(i) of this section, USP's section 956 amount with respect to CFC2 for Year 1 is its aggregate tentative section 956 amount with respect to CFC2 reduced by the deduction under section 245A that USP would be allowed if USP received an amount equal to its aggregate tentative section 956 amount as a distribution with respect to the CFC2 stock that USP owns indirectly within the meaning of section 958(a)(2). For purposes of determining the consequences of this hypothetical distribution, under paragraph (a)(2)(ii)(A)(*1*) of this section, USP is treated as owning the CFC2 stock directly. In addition, under paragraph (a)(2)(ii)(A)(*4*) of this section, the holding period requirement of section 246(c) is applied by reference to the period during which USP owned (within the meaning of section 958(a)) the stock of CFC2. Therefore, with respect to the hypothetical distribution from CFC2 to USP, USP would satisfy the holding period requirement under section 246(c) with respect to the 70% of the CFC2 stock that USP indirectly owned for three years through CFC1, but not with respect to the 30% of the CFC2 stock that USP indirectly owned through CFC1 for a period of less than 365 days. Accordingly, USP's section 956 amount with respect to CFC2 for Year 1 is $30x, its aggregate tentative section 956 amount ($100x) reduced by the amount of the deduction that USP would have been allowed under section 245A with respect to the hypothetical distribution ($70x).

* * *

(g) * * *

(4) Paragraphs (a)(2) and (3) of this section apply to taxable years of controlled foreign

corporations beginning on or after the date of publication of the Treasury decision adopting paragraphs (a)(2) and (3) of this section as final regulations in the **Federal Register**, and to taxable years of a United States shareholder in which or with which such taxable years of the controlled foreign corporation end.

(5) Paragraph (e)(6) of this section applies to property acquired in exchanges occurring on or after June 24, 2011.

CFCs: Earnings and Profits: Shareholder's Share

Controlled Foreign Corporations: Investment of Earnings in U.S. Property: Related Person Factoring Income.—Amendments to Temporary Reg. §§1.956-1T and 1.956-2T, relating to the treatment of related person factoring income, are proposed (published in the Federal Register on June 14, 1988). Amendments to Reg. §§1.956-1(b)(4), 1.956-2(d)(2) and 1.956-3(b)(2)(ii) withdrawn by REG-122387-16 on November 3, 2016; Temporary Reg. §1.956-3T adopted by T.D. 9792 on November 2, 2016.

§1.956-1. Shareholder's pro rata share of a controlled foreign corporation's increase in earnings invested in United States property.

§1.956-2. Definition of United States property.

Notional Principal Contracts: Nonperiodic Payments: Swaps

Notional Principal Contracts: Nonperiodic Payments: Swaps.—Amendments to Reg. §1.956-2, providing that, subject to certain exceptions, a notional principal contract with a nonperiodic payment, regardless of whether it is significant, must be treated as two separate transactions consisting of one or more loans and an on-market, level payment swap, are proposed (published in the Federal Register on May 8, 2015) (REG-102656-15; REG-107548-11).

Par. 3. Section 1.956-2 is amended by revising paragraphs (b)(1)(xi) and (f) to read as follows:

§1.956-2. Definition of United States property.

* * *

(b)(1)(xi) [The text of this proposed amendment is the same as the text of §1.956-2T(b)(1)(xi) as added by T.D. 9719].

* * *

(f) [The text of this proposed amendment is the same as the text of §1.956-2T(f) as added by T.D. 9719].

United States Property: Controlled Foreign Corporations: Partnerships with Special Allocations

United States Property: Controlled Foreign Corporations: Partnerships with Special Allocations.—Amendments to Reg. §1.956-4, regarding the determination of the amount of United States property treated as held by a controlled foreign corporation (CFC) through a partnership, are proposed (published in the Federal Register on November 3, 2016) (corrected December 28, 2016) (REG-114734-16).

Par. 2. Section 1.956-4 is amended by:

1. Revising paragraph (b)(2)(ii).
2. Adding paragraph (b)(2)(iii).
3. Adding a sentence at the end of paragraph (i) of *Example 2* of paragraph (b)(3).
4. Revising paragraph (ii) of *Example 2* of paragraph (b)(3).
5. Revising *Example 3* of paragraph (b)(3).
6. Adding *Example 4* to paragraph (b)(3).
7. Revising paragraph (f)(1).

The revisions and additions read as follows:

§1.956-4. Certain rules applicable to partnerships.

* * *

(b) * * *

(2) * * *

(ii) *Special allocations.*—Except as otherwise provided in paragraph (b)(2)(iii) of this section, for purposes of paragraph (b)(1) of this section, if a partnership agreement provides for the allocation of book income (or, where appropriate, book gain) from a subset of the property of the partnership to a partner other than in accordance with the partner's liquidation value percentage in a particular taxable year (a *special allocation*), then the partner's attributable share of that property is determined solely by reference to the partner's special allocation with respect to the property, provided the special allocation will be respected for Federal income tax purposes under section 704(b) and the regulations thereunder and does not have a principal purpose of avoiding the purposes of section 956.

(iii) *Limitation on special allocations in the case of a controlled partnership.*—Paragraph (b)(2)(ii) of this section does not apply to determine a partner's attributable share of partnership property in the case of a partnership controlled by the partner. For purposes of this paragraph (b)(2)(iii), a partner controls a partnership when the partner and the partnership are related within the meaning of section 267(b) or section 707(b), determined by substituting "at least 80 percent" for "more than 50 percent" wherever it appears.

(3) * * *

Example 2. (i) *Facts.* * * * FS does not control FPRS within the meaning of paragraph (b)(2)(iii) of this section.

(ii) *Result.* Under paragraph (b)(1) of this section, for purposes of section 956, FS is treated as holding its attributable share of the property held by FPRS with an adjusted basis equal to its attributable share of FPRS's adjusted basis in such property. In general, FS's attributable share of property held by FPRS is determined in accordance with FS's liquidation value percentage. However, because FS does not control FPRS within the meaning of paragraph (b)(2)(iii) of this section and because the special allocation does not have a principal purpose of avoiding the purposes of section 956, under paragraph (b)(2)(ii) of this section, FS's attributable share of the FPRS property is determined by reference to its special allocation. FS's special allocation percentage for the FPRS property is 80%, and thus FS's attributable share of the FPRS property is 80% and its attributable share of FPRS's basis in the FPRS property is $80x. Accordingly, for purposes of determining the amount of United States property held by FS as of the close of quarter 1 of year 1, FS is treated as holding United States property with an adjusted basis of $80x.

Example 3. (i) *Facts.* USP, a domestic corporation, wholly owns FS, a controlled foreign corporation, which, in turn, owns a 25% capital and profits interest in FPRS, a foreign partnership. The remaining 75% capital and profits interest in FPRS is owned by an unrelated foreign person. Thus, FS does not control FPRS within the meaning of paragraph (b)(2)(iii) of this section. FPRS holds property (the "FPRS property") that would be United States property if held by FS directly. The FPRS property has an adjusted basis of $100x and is anticipated to appreciate in value but generate relatively little income. The FPRS partnership agreement, which satisfies the requirements of section 704(b), specially allocates 80% of the income with respect to the FPRS property to the unrelated foreign person and 80% of the gain with respect to the disposition of FPRS property to FS. The special allocation does not have a principal purpose of avoiding the purposes of section 956.

(ii) *Result.* Because FPRS is not controlled by FS within the meaning of paragraph (b)(2)(iii) of this section, and the special allocation does not have a principal purpose of avoiding the purposes of section 956, under paragraph (b)(2)(ii) of this section, FS's attributable share of the FPRS property is determined by reference to a special allocation with respect to the FPRS property. Given the income and gain anticipated with respect to the FPRS property, it is appropriate to determine FS's attributable share of the property in accordance with the special allocation of gain. Accordingly, for purposes of determining the amount of United States property held by FS in each year that FPRS holds the FPRS property, FS's attributable share of the FPRS property is 80% and its attributable share of FPRS's basis in the FPRS property is $80x. Thus, FS is treated as holding United States property with an adjusted basis of $80x.

Example 4. (i) *Facts.* The facts are the same as in *Example 3* of this paragraph (b)(3), except that USP owns the 75% capital and profits interest in FPRS rather than an unrelated foreign person. Thus, FS controls FPRS within the meaning of paragraph (b)(2)(iii) of this section. At the close of quarter 1 of year 1, the liquidation value percentage, as determined under paragraph (b)(2) of this section, for FS with respect to FPRS is 25%.

(ii) *Result.* Because FPRS is controlled by FS within the meaning of paragraph (b)(2)(iii) of this section, under paragraph (b)(2)(iii) of this section, FS's attributable share of the FPRS property is not determined by reference to the special allocation of gain with respect to the FPRS property. Accordingly, for purposes of determining the amount of United States property held by FS in each year that FPRS holds the FPRS property, FS's attributable share of the FPRS property is determined under paragraph (b)(2)(i) in accordance with FS's liquidation value percentage, which is 25%, and its attributable share of FPRS's basis in the FPRS property is $25x. Thus, FS is treated as holding United States property with an adjusted basis of $25x.

* * *

(f) * * *

(1) Except as otherwise provided in this paragraph (f)(1), paragraph (b) of this section applies to taxable years of controlled foreign corporations ending on or after November 3, 2016, and taxable years of United States shareholders in which or with which such taxable years end, with respect to property acquired on or after November 3, 2016. Paragraphs (b)(2)(ii) and (iii) of this section, as well as *Example 2*, *Example 3*, and *Example 4* of paragraph (b)(3) of this section, apply to taxable years of controlled foreign corporations ending on or after the date of publication in the **Federal Register** of the Treasury decision adopting this rule as a final regulation, and taxable years of United States shareholders in which or with which such taxable years end, with respect to property acquired on or after the date of publication in the **Federal Register** of the Treasury decision adopting this rule as a final regulation. For purposes of this paragraph (f)(1), a deemed exchange of property pursuant to section 1001 on or after November 3, 2016 constitutes an acquisition of the property on or after that date, and a deemed exchange of property pursuant to section 1001 on or after the date of publication in the **Federal Register** of the Treasury decision adopting this rule as a final regulation constitutes an acquisition of the property on or after that date.

See § 1.956-2(a)(3), as contained in 26 CFR part 1 revised as of April 1, 2016, for the rules applicable to taxable years of a controlled foreign corporation beginning on or after July 23, 2002, and ending before November 3, 2016, and with respect to property acquired before November 3, 2016, to taxable years of a controlled foreign corporation beginning on or after July 23, 2002.

CFCs: Previously Taxed Earnings and Profits: Exclusion from Gross Income: Basis Adjustments

CFCs: Previously Taxed Earnings and Profits: Exclusion from Gross Income: Basis Adjustments.—Amendments to Reg. §§1.959-1—1.959-4, providing guidance relating to the exclusion from gross income of previously taxed earnings and profits under Code Sec. 959 and related basis adjustments under Code Sec. 961, are proposed (published in the Federal Register on August 29, 2006) (REG-121509-00) (corrected December 8, 2006).

☐ Par. 2. Section 1.959-1 is revised to read as follows:

§1.959-1. Exclusion from gross income of United States persons of previously taxed earnings and profits.—(a) *In general.*—Section 959(a) provides an exclusion whereby the earnings and profits of a foreign corporation attributable to amounts which are, or have been, included in a United States shareholder's gross income under section 951(a) are not taxed again when distributed (directly or indirectly through a chain of ownership described in section 958(a)) from such foreign corporation to such shareholder (or any other United States person who acquires from any person any portion of the interest of such United States shareholder in such foreign corporation, but only to the extent of such portion, and subject to such proof of the identity of such interest as the Secretary may by regulations prescribe). Section 959(a) also excludes from gross income of a United States shareholder earnings and profits attributable to amounts which are, or have been, included in the gross income of such shareholder under section 951(a) which would, but for section 959(a)(2), be again included in the gross income of such shareholder (or any other United States person who acquires from any person any portion of the interest of such United States shareholder in such foreign corporation, but only to the extent of such portion, and subject to such proof of the identity of such interest as the Secretary may by regulations prescribe) under section 951(a)(1)(B). Section 959(b) provides that for purposes of section 951(a), the earnings and profits of a CFC attributable to amounts that are, or have been, included in the gross income of a United States shareholder under section 951(a) shall not, when distributed through a chain of ownership described in section 958(a), be included in the gross income of a CFC in such chain for purposes of the application of section 951(a) to such CFC with respect to such United States shareholder (or any other United States person who acquires from any person any portion of the interest of such United States shareholder in such foreign corporation, but only to the extent of such portion, and subject to such proof of the identity of such interest as the Secretary may by regulations prescribe). Section 959(c) provides rules for the allocation of distributions to the various categories of previously taxed earnings and profits of a foreign corporation and the foreign corporation's non-previously taxed earnings and profits. Section 959(d) provides that, except as provided in section 960(a)(3), any distribution excluded from gross income under section 959(a) shall be treated as a distribution which is not a dividend; except that such distribution shall immediately reduce earnings and profits. Section 959(e) provides that, for purposes of sections 959 and 960(b), any amount included in the gross income of any person as a dividend by reason of subsection (a) or (f) of section 1248 shall be treated as an amount included in the gross income of such person (or, in any case to which section 1248(e) applies, of the domestic corporation referred to in section 1248(e)(2)) under section 951(a)(1)(A). Section 959(f)(1) provides rules for the allocation of amounts which would, but for section 959(a)(2), be included in gross income under section 951(a)(1)(B) to certain previously taxed earnings and profits of a foreign corporation and non-previously taxed earnings and profits. Section 959(f)(2) provides an ordering rule pursuant to which the rules of section 959 are applied first to actual distributions and then to amounts which would, but for section 959, be included in gross income under section 951(a)(1)(B). Paragraph (b) of this section provides a list of definitions. Paragraph (c) of this section provides rules for the exclusion from gross income under section 959(a)(1) of distributions of earnings and profits by a foreign corporation and the exclusion from gross income under section 959(a)(2) of amounts which would, but for section 959, be included in gross income under section 951(a)(1)(B). Paragraph (d) of this section provides for the establishment and acquisition of previously taxed earnings and profits accounts by shareholders of foreign corporations. Section 1.959-2 provides rules for the exclusion from gross income of a CFC of distributions of previously taxed earnings and profits from another CFC in a chain of ownership described in section 958(a). Section 1.959-3 provides rules for the allocation of distributions and section 956 amounts to the earnings and profits of a CFC and for the maintenance and adjustment of previously taxed earnings and profits accounts by shareholders of foreign corporations. Section 1.959-4 provides for the treatment of actual distributions that are excluded from gross income under section 959(a).

(b) *Definitions.*—For purposes of this section through §1.959-4 and §1.961-1 through §1.961-4, the terms listed in this paragraph are defined as follows:

(1) *Previously taxed earnings and profits* means the earnings and profits of a foreign corporation, computed in accordance with sections 964 and 986(b) and the regulations thereunder, attributable to section 951(a) inclusions.

(2) *Previously taxed earnings and profits account* means an account reflecting the previously taxed earnings and profits of a foreign corporation (if any).

(3) *Dollar basis* means the United States dollar amounts included in a United States shareholder's income with respect to the previously taxed earnings and profits included in a shareholder's previously taxed earnings and profits account.

(4) *Covered shareholder* means a person who is one of the following—

(i) A United States person who owns stock (within the meaning of section 958(a)) in a foreign corporation and who has had a section

951(a) inclusion with respect to its stock in such corporation;

(ii) A successor in interest, as defined in paragraph (b)(5) of this section; or

(iii) A corporation that is not described in paragraphs (b)(4)(i) or (ii) of this section and that owns stock (within the meaning of section 958(a)) in a foreign corporation in which another corporation is a covered shareholder described in paragraph (b)(4)(i) or (ii) of this section, if both the first mentioned corporation and the covered shareholder are members of the same consolidated group.

(5) *Successor in interest* means a United States person who acquires, from any person, ownership (within the meaning of section 958(a)) of stock in a foreign corporation, for which there is a previously taxed earnings and profits account and who establishes to the satisfaction of the Director of Field Operations the right to the exclusion from gross income provided by section 959(a) and this section. To establish the right to the exclusion, the shareholder must attach to its return for the taxable year a statement that provides that it is excluding amounts from gross income because it is a successor in interest succeeding to one or more previously taxed earnings and profits accounts with respect to shares it owns in a foreign corporation. Included in the statement shall be the name of the foreign corporation. In addition, that shareholder must be prepared to provide the following information within 30 days upon request by the Director of Field Operations—

(i) The name, address, and taxable year of the foreign corporation and of all the other corporations, partnerships, trusts, or estates in any applicable chain of ownership described in section 958(a);

(ii) The name, address, and taxpayer identification number, if any, of the person from whom the stock interest was acquired;

(iii) A description of the stock interest acquired and its relation, if any, to a chain of ownership described in section 958(a);

(iv) The amount for which an exclusion under section 959(a) and paragraph (c) of this section is claimed; and

(v) Evidence showing that the earnings and profits for which an exclusion is claimed are previously taxed earnings and profits, that such amounts were not previously excluded from the gross income of a United States person, and the identity of the United States shareholder who originally included such amounts in gross income under section 951(a). The acquiring person shall also furnish to the Director of Field Operations such other information as may be required by the Director of Field Operations in support of the exclusion.

(6) *Block of stock* shall have the meaning provided in §1.1248-2(b) with the additional requirement that the previously taxed earnings and profits attributable to each share of stock in such block must be the same.

(7) *Consolidated group* shall have the meaning provided in §1.1502-1(h).

(8) *Member* shall have the meaning provided in §1.1502-1(b).

(9) *Section 951(a) inclusion* means a section 951(a)(1)(A) inclusion or an amount included in the gross income of a United States shareholder under section 951(a)(1)(B).

(10) *Section 951(a)(1)(A) inclusion* means—

(i) An amount included in a United States shareholder's gross income under section 951(a)(1)(A);

(ii) An amount included in the gross income of any person as a dividend by reason of subsection (a) or (f) of section 1248 (or, in any case to which section 1248(e) applies, an amount included in the gross income of the domestic corporation referred to in section 1248(e)(2)); or

(iii) An amount described in section 1293(c).

(11) *Section 956 amount* means an amount determined under section 956 for a United States shareholder with respect to a single share or, if a shareholder maintains a previously taxed earnings and profits account with respect to a block of stock, a block of such shareholder's stock in the CFC.

(12) *Section 959(c)(1) earnings and profits* means the previously taxed earnings and profits of a foreign corporation attributable to amounts that have been included in the gross income of a United States shareholder under section 951(a)(1)(B) (or which would have been included except for section 959(a)(2) and §1.959-2) and amounts that have been included in gross income under section 951(a)(1)(C) as it existed prior to its repeal (or which would have been included except for section 959(a)(3) as it existed prior to its repeal).

(13) *Section 959(c)(2) earnings and profits* means the previously taxed earnings and profits of a foreign corporation attributable to section 951(a)(1)(A) inclusions.

(14) *Non-previously taxed earnings and profits* means the earnings and profits of a foreign corporation other than the corporation's previously taxed earnings and profits.

(15) *CFC* means a controlled foreign corporation within the meaning of either section 953(c)(1)(B) or section 957.

(16) *United States shareholder* means a United States person who qualifies as a United States shareholder under either section 951(b) or section 953(c)(1)(A).

(c) *Amount excluded from gross income.*—(1) *Distributions.*—In the case of a distribution of earnings and profits to a covered shareholder with respect to stock in a foreign corporation, an amount shall be excluded from such shareholder's gross income equal to the total amount by which such shareholder's previously taxed earnings and profits account with respect to such stock is decreased under §1.959-3 because of the distribution.

(2) *Section 956 amounts.*—In a case where a covered shareholder has a section 956 amount for a CFC's taxable year, an amount shall be excluded from such shareholder's gross income equal to the amount of section 959(c)(2) earnings and profits in any shareholder's previously taxed earnings and profits account that are reclassified as section 959(c)(1) earnings and profits under §1.959-3 because of that section 956 amount.

(d) *Shareholder accounts.*—(1) *In general.*—Any person who is subject to §1.959-3 shall maintain a previously taxed earnings and profits account with respect to each share of stock it owns (within the meaning of section 958(a)) in a foreign corporation. Although the account is share specific, the account may be maintained with respect to each block of the stock in the foreign corporation. Such account shall be maintained in accordance with § 1.959-3.

(2) *Acquisition of account.*—(i) *In general.*—If any person acquires, from any other person, ownership of shares of stock in a foreign corporation (within the meaning of section 958(a)) the prior shareholder's previously taxed earnings and profits account with respect to such stock becomes the previously taxed earnings and profits account of the acquirer.

(ii) *Acquisition of account by a person other than a successor in interest.*—If such acquirer is not a successor in interest (a foreign person for example), the previously taxed earnings and profits account with respect to the stock acquired shall remain unchanged for the period that the stock is owned by such acquirer. See also § 1.959-3(e), providing account adjustment rules that apply only for acquired PTI accounts if the acquirer is a successors in interest.

(3) *Examples.*—The application of this paragraph (d) is illustrated by the following examples:

Example 1. Shareholder's previously taxed earnings and profits account. (i) *Facts.* DP, a United States shareholder owns all of the 100 shares of the only class of stock in FC, a CFC. The 100 shares are a block of stock. DP and FC use the calendar year as their taxable year and FC uses the U.S. dollar as its functional currency. In year 1, FC earns $100x of subpart F income and $100x of non-subpart F income. DP includes $100x in gross income under section 951(a).

(ii) *Analysis.* As a result of DP's inclusion of $100x of gross income under section 951(a), DP has a previously taxed earnings and profits account with respect to each of its 100 shares equal to $1x or should DP choose to maintain its previously taxed earnings and profits account on a block basis, an account of $100x with respect to its entire interest in FC.

Example 2. Acquisition of previously taxed earnings and profits account. (i) *Facts.* Assume the same facts as *Example 1*, but that in year 2, a nonresident alien, FP, contributes property to FC to acquire 1000 newly issued shares of FC of the same class held by DP. In year 10, DP sells all of its FC shares to FP. In year 15, FP sells all of its shares in FC to USP, a United States person. Any income earned by FC after year 1 is non-subpart F income. The only distributions by FC during this period are a $100x pre-sale distribution to FP in year 15 and another $100x distribution in year 16 to USP.

(ii) *Analysis.* In year 2, DP retains its previously taxed earnings and profits account of $100x as result of its section 951(a) inclusion in year 1 regardless of the fact that FC is no longer a CFC and DP no longer holds a sufficient interest in FC to be a United States shareholder with respect to FC. In year 10, pursuant to paragraph (d)(2)(i) of this section, FP acquires a $100x previously taxed earnings and profits account with respect to DP's block of stock in FC that FP acquired. In year 15, FP receives a distribution of $100x of earnings and profits from FC, but FP may not exclude any of this distribution from gross income because FP is a nonresident alien. Consequently, pursuant to paragraph (d)(2)(ii) of this section, even though it acquired a previously taxed earnings and profits account from DP of $100x the account remains unchanged during FP's ownership of the FC stock. However, if USP can make the showing required in paragraph (b)(5) of this section, USP may exclude the $100x distribution in year 16 under section 959(a)(1) and paragraph (c) of this section to the extent that the distribution results in a decrease of the $100x previously taxed earnings and profits account that USP acquired from FP pursuant to the account adjustment rules of § 1.959-3. [Reg. § 1.959-1.]

☐ Par. 3. Section 1.959-2 is revised to read as follows:

§ 1.959-2. Exclusion from gross income of CFCs of previously taxed earnings and profits.—(a) *Exclusion from gross income.*—(1) *In general.*—The earnings and profits of a CFC (lower-tier CFC) attributable to amounts which are, or have been, included in the gross income of a United States shareholder under section 951(a) shall not, when distributed through a chain of ownership described in section 958(a), be also included in the gross income of the CFC receiving the distribution (upper-tier CFC) in such chain for purposes of the application of section 951(a) to such upper-tier CFC with respect to such United States shareholder. The amount of the exclusion provided under this paragraph is the entire amount distributed by the lower-tier CFC to the upper-tier CFC that gave rise (in whole or in part) to an adjustment of the United States shareholder's previously taxed earnings and profits accounts with respect to the stock it owns (within the meaning of section 958(a)) in the lower-and upper-tier CFC under § 1.959-3(e)(3). This amount shall not exceed the earnings and profits of the lower-tier CFC attributable to amounts described in section 951(a)(1) (without regard to pro rata share). The exclusion from the income of such upper-tier CFC also applies with respect to any other United States shareholder who is a successor in interest.

(2) *Examples.*—The application of this paragraph (a) is illustrated by the following examples:

Example 1. Distribution attributable to subpart F income of lower-tier CFC. (i) *Facts.* FC, a CFC, is 70% owned by DP, a United States person, and 30% owned by FP, a nonresident alien. FC owns all the stock in FS, a CFC. DP, FP, FC and FS all use the calendar year as their taxable year and FC and FS use the U.S. dollar as their functional currency. In year 1, FS earns $100x of passive income described in section 954(c) and $50x of non-subpart F income. On the last day of year 1, FS distributes $100x to FC that would qualify as subpart F income of FC. On the last day of year 1, FC distributes $70x to DP and $30x to FP.

(ii) *Analysis.* DP is required to include $70x in its gross income under section 951(a) as a result of FS's earning $100x of subpart F income for the year. Consequently, the section 959(c)(2) earnings and profits in DP's previously taxed earnings and profits account with respect to its indirect ownership of stock in FS is increased to $70x. Under § 1.959-3(e)(3), as a result of the $100x distribution paid by FS to FC, DP's previously taxed earnings and profits account is reduced by its pro rata share of the distribution ($70x). In addition, FS's non-previously taxed earnings and profits are reduced by the remaining $30x. Under paragraph (a) of this section, the amount of the exclusion under paragraph (a) is equal to the amount distributed, not to exceed the amount of earnings and profits that gave rise to the previously taxed income that is being distributed. Consequently, the entire $100x distribution (as opposed to only $70x) is excluded from FC's gross income for purposes of determining whether DP has an inclusion under section 951(a) as a result of FC's receiving the distribution from FS. The receipt of the distribution from FS increases FC's earnings and profits by $100x ($70x of which is previously taxed earnings and profits and $30x of which is non-previously taxed earnings and profits).

Example 2. Transferee shareholder. (i) *Facts*. The facts are the same as in *Example 1* except that neither FS nor FC makes any distributions in year 1. In year 2, FP sells its stock in FC to DT, a United States person. On the last day of year 2, FS distributes $100x to FC that would qualify as subpart F income of FC. FS has no earnings and profits for year 2, and FC has no earnings and profits for year 2 other than the distribution from FS.

(ii) *Analysis*. With respect to DP, the analysis is the same as that in *Example 1*. However, for purposes of DT's determination of the amount includible in its gross income under section 951(a) with respect to FC for year 2, none of the $100x distribution is excluded from FC's gross income for purposes of applying section 951(a) with respect to DT's interest in FC because none of earnings and profits distributed by FS to FC are attributable to amounts which are, or have been, included in the gross income of DT or the person to whom DT is a successor in interest (FP). Consequently, DT must include $30x in gross income under section 951(a) for year 2 as its pro rata share of FC's subpart F income of $100x ($100x × 30%). Thereafter, DT has a previously taxed earnings and profits account consisting of $30x with respect to its stock in FC and FC has $100x of previously taxed earnings and profits.

Example 3. Mixed distribution. (i) *Facts*. The facts are the same as in *Example 1*, except that on the last day of year 1, FS distributes $150x to FC that would qualify as subpart F income of FC, which in turn distributes $105x to DP and $45x to FP.

(ii) *Analysis*. Under the analysis in *Example 1* and pursuant to paragraph (a) of this section, $100x of the distribution from FS to FC is excluded from FC's gross income for purposes of determining DP's inclusion under section 951(a) with respect to FC's receipt of the distribution from FS. However, DP's pro rata share of the remaining $50x, or $35x ($50x × 70%), is included in DP's gross income under section 951(a). Consequently, the previously taxed earnings and profits in DP's previously taxed earnings and profits account with respect to its stock in FC is increased from $70x to $105x pursuant to § 1.959-3(e)(2)(i). That account is then reduced to $0, as a result of the distribution of $105x to DP pursuant to § 1.959-3(e)(2)(ii) and DP excludes the distribution of $105x from FC from its gross income for year 1 under section 959(a)(1) and § 1.959-1(c).

(b) *Section 304(a)(1) transactions.*—(1) *Deemed redemption treated as a distribution.*—In the case of a stock acquisition under section 304(a)(1) treated as a distribution to which section 301 applies, the selling CFC shall be deemed for purposes of section 959(b) and paragraph (a) of this section to receive such distributions through a chain of ownership described under section 958(a).

(2) *Example.*—The application of this paragraph (c) is illustrated by the following example:

Example. Cross-chain acquisition of CFC stock by a CFC from another CFC. (i) *Facts*. DP, a domestic corporation, owns all of the stock in two foreign corporations, FX and FY. FX owns all of the stock in foreign corporation FZ. DP, FX, FY, and FZ all use the calendar year as their taxable year and the U.S. dollar as their functional currency. During year 1, FY purchases all of the stock in FZ from FX for $80x in a transaction described in section 304(a)(1). At the end of year 1, before taking into account the purchase of FZ's stock, FY has section 959(c)(2) earnings and profits of $20x and non-previously taxed earnings and profits of $10x, and FZ has section 959(c)(2) earnings and profits of $50x and non-previously taxed earnings and profits of $0.

(ii) *Analysis*. Under section 304(a)(1), FX is deemed to have transferred the FZ stock to FY in exchange for FY stock in a transaction to which section 351 applies, and FY is treated as having redeemed, for $80x, the FY stock deemed issued to FX. The payment of $80x is treated as a distribution to which section 301 applies. Under section 304(b)(2), the determination of the amount which is a dividend (and the source) is made as if the distribution were made, first, by FY to the extent of its earnings and profits, $30x, and then by FX to the extent of its earnings and profits, $50x. Under paragraph (c)(1) of this section, FX is deemed to receive the distributions from FY and FZ through a chain of ownership described in section 958(a). Under paragraph (a) of this section, the amount of FY's previously taxed earnings and profits, $20x, and the amount of FZ's previously taxed earnings and profits, $50x, distributed to FX are excluded from the gross income of FX. Accordingly, only $10x is included in FX's gross income. [Reg. § 1.959-2.]

☐ Par. 4. Section 1.959-3 is revised to read as follows:

§ 1.959-3. Maintenance and adjustment of previously taxed earnings and profits accounts.—(a) *In general.*—This section provides rules for the maintenance and adjustment of previously taxed earnings and profits accounts by shareholders and with respect to foreign corporations. Paragraph (b) of this section provides general rules governing the accounting of previously taxed earnings and profits at the shareholder level and corporate level. Paragraph (c) of this section provides rules regarding the treatment of foreign taxes when previously taxed earnings and profits are distributed by a foreign corporation through a chain of ownership described in section 958(a). Paragraph (d) of this section provides rules regarding the allocation of other expenses to previously taxed earnings and profits. Paragraph (e)(1) of this section addresses the adjustment of shareholder-level previously taxed earnings and profits accounts as a result of certain transactions. Paragraph (e)(2) of this section provides rules establishing the order in which adjustments are to be made to a covered shareholder's previously taxed earnings and profits account. Paragraph (e)(3) of this section provides rules regarding distributions of previously taxed earnings and profits in a chain of ownership described in section 958(a). Paragraph (e)(4) of this section provides for the maintenance and adjustment of aggregate categories of previously taxed and non-previously taxed earnings and profits at the corporate level with adjustments to individual shareholder-level accounts. Paragraph (e)(5) of this section provides rules for the effect of a foreign corporation's deficit in earnings and profits on previously taxed earnings and profits. Paragraph (f) of this section provides rules regarding the treatment of previously taxed earnings and profits when a shareholder has multiple previously taxed earnings and profits accounts. Paragraph (g) of this section provides rules regarding the treatment of previously taxed earnings and profits when more than one shareholder in a foreign corporation is a member of the same consolidated group. Paragraph (h) of this section provides rules governing the adjustment of previously taxed earnings and profits accounts in the case of a redemption.

(b) *Corporate-level and shareholder-level accounting of previously taxed earnings and profits.*—(1) *Shareholder-level accounting.*—A shareholder's previously taxed earnings and profits account with respect to its stock in a foreign corporation shall identify the amount of section 959(c)(1) earnings and profits and the amount of section 959(c)(2) earnings and profits attributable to such stock for each taxable year of the foreign corporation and shall be maintained in the functional currency of such foreign corporation. A shareholder account must also reflect the annual dollar basis of each category of previously taxed earnings and profits in the account. See §1.959-3(e) of this section for rules regarding the adjustment of shareholder previously taxed earnings and profits accounts.

(2) *Corporate-level accounting.*—Separate aggregate categories of section 959(c)(1), section 959(c)(2) and non-previously taxed earnings and profits (earnings and profits described in section 959(c)(3)) shall be maintained with respect to a foreign corporation. These categories of earnings and profits of the foreign corporation shall be maintained in the functional currency of the foreign corporation. For purposes of this section, distributions are allocated to a foreign corporation's earnings and profits under section 316(a) by applying first section 316(a)(2) and then section 316(a)(1) to each of these three categories of earnings and profits. Section 956 amounts shall be treated as attributable first to section 959(c)(2) earnings and profits and then to non-previously taxed earnings and profits. These allocations are made in conjunction with the rules for making corporate-level adjustments to previously taxed earnings and profits under §1.959-3(e)(4).

(3) *Classification of earnings and profits.*—(i) *In general.*—For purposes of this section, earnings and profits are classified as to year and category of earnings and profits in the taxable year of the foreign corporation in which such amounts are included in gross income of a United States shareholder under section 951(a) and are reclassified as to category of earnings and profits in the taxable year of the foreign corporation in which such amounts would be so included in the gross income of a United States shareholder under section 951(a) but for the provisions of section 959(a)(2) and §1.959-1(c)(2). Such classifications do not change by reason of a subsequent distribution of such amounts to an upper-tier corporation in a chain of ownership described in section 958(a). This paragraph shall apply to distributions by one foreign corporation to another foreign corporation and by a foreign corporation to a United States person.

(ii) *Dollar basis pooling election.*—For purposes of computing foreign currency gain or loss under section 986(c) and adjustments to stock basis under section 961(b) and (c) with respect to distributions of previously taxed earnings and profits of any foreign corporation, in lieu of maintaining annual dollar basis accounts with respect to previously taxed earnings and profits described in paragraph (b)(1) of this section, a taxpayer may maintain an aggregate dollar basis pool that reflects the dollar basis of all of the corporation's previously taxed earnings and profits described in sections 959(c)(1) and 959(c)(2) and treat a pro rata portion of the dollar basis pool as attributable to distributions of such previously taxed earnings and profits. A taxpayer makes this election by using a dollar basis pool to compute foreign currency gain or loss under section 986(c) with respect to distributions of previously taxed earnings and profits of the foreign corporation, or to compute gain or loss with respect to its stock in the foreign corporation, whichever occurs first. Any subsequent change in the taxpayer's method of assigning dollar basis may be made only with the consent of the Commissioner.

(4) *Examples.*—The application of this paragraph (b) is illustrated by the following examples:

Example 1. Distribution. (i) *Facts.* DP, a United States shareholder, owns 100% of the only class of stock in FC, a CFC, which, in turn, owns 100% of the only class of stock in FS, a CFC. DP, FC and FS all use the calendar year as their taxable year. FC and FS both use the u as their functional currency. During year 1, FC earns 100u of non-subpart F income and invests 100u in United States property. DP must include 100u in its gross income for year 1 under section 951(a)(1)(B) with respect to FC. For year 2, FS has no subpart F income or investment of earnings in United States property but FS has 100u of non-previously taxed earnings and profits which it distributes to FC. The distribution of 100u to FC is subpart F income of FC and DP must include the 100u in its gross income for year 2 under section 951(a)(1)(A). Also in year 2, FC has non-subpart F income of 100u. The exchange rates at all times in year 1 and year 2, respectively, are 1u = $1 and 1u = $1.20.

(ii) *Analysis.* With respect to FC, the earnings and profits are classified as follows: 100u of section 959(c)(1) earnings and profits from year 1, 100u of section 959(c)(2) earnings and profits from year 2, and 100u of non-previously taxed earnings and profits from year 2. The dollar basis with respect to the section 959(c)(1) earnings and profits is $100 and the dollar basis with respect to the section 959(c)(2) earnings and profits is $120.

Example 2. Subsequent distribution in a later year. (i) *Facts.* Assume the same facts as in *Example 1,* except that during year 3 neither FC nor FS has any earnings and profits or deficit in earnings and profits or section 956 amount, but FC distributes 100u to DP on December 31, year 3, at which time the spot exchange rate is 1u = $1.30.

(ii) *Analysis.* For purposes of section 959 and 961, the 100u distribution of FC shall be considered attributable to FC's section 959(c)(1) earnings and profits for year 1. The section 959(c)(1) earnings and profits are reduced by 100u and the dollar basis of the account is reduced by $100. Since the spot rate at the time of the 100u distribution to DP is 1u = $1.30, DP recognizes foreign currency gain of $30 ((100 × 1.3) – (100 × 1)).

Example 3. Dollar basis pooling election. (i) *Facts.* Assume the same facts as in *Example 2,* except that DP elected to maintain the dollar basis of its previously taxed earnings and profits account on a pooled basis for purposes of section 986(c) and section 961 as provided in paragraph (b)(3)(ii) of this section.

(ii) *Analysis.* The section 959(c)(1) earnings and profits are reduced by 100u, but the dollar basis of the account is reduced by $110 ((100u/200u) × $220). In addition, DP recognizes foreign currency gain under section 986(c) of $20 ($130 – ((100u/200u) × $220)).

(c) *Treatment of certain foreign taxes.*—(1) For purposes of this section, when previously taxed earnings and profits are distributed by a foreign corporation to another foreign corporation through a chain of ownership described in section 958(a) such earnings and profits shall be reduced by the functional currency amount of any income, war profits, or excess profits taxes imposed by any foreign country or a possession of the United States on or with respect to such earnings and profits. Any such taxes shall not be included in the distributee foreign corporation's pools of post-1986 foreign income taxes maintained for purposes of sections 902 and 960(a)(1). Such taxes shall be maintained in a separate account and allowed as a credit as provided under section 960(a)(3) when the associated previously taxed earnings and profits are distributed. The taxpayer's dollar basis in the previously taxed earnings and profits account shall be reduced by the dollar amount of such taxes, translated in accordance with section 986(a).

(2) *Example.*—The application of this paragraph (c) is illustrated by the following example:

Example. Imposition of foreign taxes on a CFC. (i) *Facts.* DP, a United States shareholder, owns 100% of the only class of stock in foreign corporation FC, a CFC, which, in turn, owns 100% of the only class of stock in FS, a CFC. DP, FC, and FS all use the calendar year as their taxable year. FC and FS both use the u as their functional currency. During year 1, FS earns 90u of subpart F income, after incurring 10u of foreign income tax allocable to such income under § 1.954-1(c), has earnings and profits in excess of 90u, and makes no distributions. DP must include 90u, translated at the average exchange rate for the year of 1u=$1 as provided in section 989(b)(3), in its gross income for year 1 under section 951(a)(1)(A)(i). As of the end of year 1, FS has section 959(c)(2) earnings and profits of 90u. During year 2, FS has neither earnings and profits nor a deficit in earnings and profits but distributes 90u to FC, and, by reason of section 959(b) and § 1.959-2, such amount is not includible in the gross income of DP for year 2 under section 951(a) with respect to FC. FC incurs a withholding tax of 9u on the 90u distribution from FS (10% of 90u) and an additional foreign income tax of 11u by reason of the inclusion of the distribution in its taxable income for foreign tax purposes in year 2. The average exchange rate for year 2 is 1u = $2.

(ii) *Analysis.* At the end of year 2, FS has section 959(c)(2) earnings and profits of 0 (90u - 90u); and FC has section 959(c)(2) earnings and profits of 70u (90u - 9u - 11u). DP's dollar basis in the 70u section 959(c)(2) earnings and profits account with respect to FC is $50 ($90 inclusion – $18 withholding tax – $22 income tax). The $40 of foreign taxes imposed on FC with respect to the previously taxed earnings and profits are not included in FC's post-1986 foreign income taxes pool. A foreign tax credit with respect to the $40 of foreign tax attributable to the 70u of previously taxed earnings and profits will be allowed under section 960(a)(3) upon distribution of such previously taxed earnings and profits.

(d) *Treatment of other expenses.*—Except as provided in paragraph (c) of this section, no expense paid or accrued by a foreign corporation shall be allocated or apportioned to the previously taxed earnings and profits of such corporation.

(e) *Adjustments to previously taxed earnings and profits account.*—(1) *In general.*—A covered shareholder's previously taxed earnings and profits account (including the dollar basis in such account) is adjusted in the manner provided in paragraphs (e)(2), (f) and (g) of this section, except as otherwise provided in paragraph (e)(3) of this section. For adjustments to a previously taxed earnings and profits account in the case of redemptions, see paragraph (h) of this section.

(2) *Order and amount of adjustments.*—As of the close of a foreign corporation's taxable year, and for the taxable year of the covered shareholder in which or with which such taxable year of the foreign corporation ends, the covered shareholder shall make any of the following adjustments that are applicable for that year to the previously taxed earnings and profits account for the stock owned for any portion of such year (within the meaning of section 958(a)) in the foreign corporation in the following order—

(i) *Step 1. Section 951(a)(1)(A) inclusion.*—Increase the amount of section 959(c)(2) earnings and profits and the associated dollar basis in the account by the amount of the section 951(a)(1)(A) inclusion with respect to such stock;

(ii) *Step 2. Distributions on such stock.*—(A) Decrease the amount of the section 959(c)(1) earnings and profits in the account (but not below zero), and then the amount of section 959(c)(2) earnings and profits in the account (but not below zero) by the amount of earnings and profits distributed to the covered shareholder during the year with respect to such stock, decrease the dollar basis in the account by the dollar amount attributable to the distributed earnings and profits; and

(B) Increase the amount of the earnings and profits and associated dollar basis, in the account first to the extent provided under paragraph (f)(1) of this section and then to the extent provided under paragraph (g)(1) of this section and then reduce the account to zero;

(iii) *Step 3. Reallocation from other accounts with respect to redemptions.*—Increase the amount of the earnings and profits and associated dollar basis in the account to the extent provided under paragraph (h)(3)(ii) of this section.

(iv) *Step 4. Section 956 amount.*—Reclassify the section 959(c)(2) earnings and profits and associated dollar basis in such shareholder's previously taxed earnings and profits account with respect to such stock as section 959(c)(1) earnings and profits in an amount equal to the lesser of—

(A) The covered shareholder's section 956 amount for the taxable year with respect to such stock; or

(B) The amount of the section 959(c)(2) earnings and profits attributable to such stock.

(v) *Step 5. Reallocation to other accounts with respect to distributions.*—Decrease the amount of section 959(c)(1) earnings and profits and associated dollar basis in the account, and thereafter the amount of section 959(c)(2) earnings and profits and associated dollar basis in the account to the extent provided under paragraph (f)(1) of this section and then under paragraph (g)(1) of this section;

(vi) *Step 6. Reclassification with respect to section 956 amounts.*—Reclassify the section 959(c)(2) earnings and profits and the associated dollar basis attributable to such stock as section 959(c)(1) earnings and profits to the extent provided under paragraph (f)(2) of this section and then to the extent provided in paragraph (g)(2) of this section.

(vii) *Step 7. Further adjustment for section 956 amounts.*—Increase the amount of section 959(c)(1) earnings and profits and the associated dollar basis in the account by any amount included in the covered shareholder's gross income for the year under section 951(a)(1)(B) with respect to such stock.

(3) *Intercorporate distributions.*—If a foreign corporation receives a distribution of earnings and profits from another foreign corporation that is in a chain of ownership described in section 958(a), a covered shareholder's previously taxed earnings and profits accounts with respect to the stock in each foreign corporation in such chain shall be adjusted at the end of the respective corporation's taxable year, and for the taxable year of the covered shareholder in which or with which such taxable year of the foreign corporation ends, as follows:

(i) The covered shareholder's previously taxed earnings and profits account with respect to stock in the distributor shall be decreased (but not below zero), at the same time that the covered shareholder would make adjustments under paragraph (e)(2)(ii) of this section, by the amount of the distribution and the associated dollar basis. Such decrease to the covered shareholder's previously taxed earnings and profits account shall be made first to the section 959(c)(1) earnings and profits and thereafter to the section 959(c)(2) earnings and profits in such account.

(ii) Except as provided in paragraph (c) of this section, the section 959(c)(1) earnings and profits and section 959(c)(2) earnings and profits in the covered shareholder's previously taxed earnings and profits account with respect to the stock in the distributee shall be increased, at the same time that the covered shareholder would make adjustments under paragraph (e)(2)(i) of this section, by an amount equal to the decrease under paragraph (e)(3)(i) of this section and to the extent the distribution is out of non-previously taxed earnings and profits of the distributor, to the extent provided under paragraph (e)(2) of this section. If the receiving corporation uses a non-dollar functional currency that differs from the functional currency used by the distributing corporation, then—

(A) The amount of increase shall be the spot value of the distribution in the receiving corporation's functional currency at the time of the distribution; and

(B) The dollar basis of the amount distributed shall be carried over from the distributing corporation to the receiving corporation.

(4) *Effect on foreign corporation's earnings and profits.*—Adjustments to a shareholder's previously taxed earnings and profits account in accordance with this section shall result in corresponding adjustments to the appropriate aggregate category or categories of earnings and profits of the foreign corporation. If an adjustment to a foreign corporation's earnings and profits is required (other than as a result of the previous sentence) the adjustment shall be made only to the non-previously taxed earnings and profits of the corporation except to the extent provided in paragraph (h)(2)(i) of this section. Moreover, if a distribution to a taxpayer exceeds such taxpayer's previously taxed earnings and profits account with respect to stock it owns (within the meaning of section 958(a)) in the foreign corporation making the distribution, the distribution may only be treated as a dividend under section 316 by applying section 316(a)(1) and (2) to the non-previously taxed earnings and profits of the foreign corporation.

(5) *Deficits in earnings and profits.*—If a foreign corporation has a deficit in earnings and profits, as determined under section 964(a) and §1.964-1, for any taxable year, a covered shareholder's previously taxed earnings and profits account with respect to its stock in such foreign corporation shall not be adjusted to take into account the deficit and the deficit shall be applied only to the non-previously taxed earnings and profits of the foreign corporation.

(6) *Examples.*—The application of this paragraph (e) is illustrated by the following examples:

Example 1. Distribution to a United States shareholder. (i) *Facts.* DP, a United States shareholder, owns 100% of the only class of stock in FC, a CFC. Both DP and FC use the calendar year as their taxable year. FC uses the "u" as its functional currency. During year 1, FC derives 100u of subpart F income, and such amount is included in DP's gross income under section 951(a)(1)(A). The average exchange rate for year 1 is 1u = $1. At the end of year 1, FC's current and accumulated earnings and profits (before taking into account distributions made during year 1) are 500u. Also, on December 31, year 1, when the spot exchange rate is 1u = $1.10, FC distributes 50u of earnings and profits to DP.

(ii) *Analysis.* At the end of year 1, the section 959(c)(2) earnings and profits in DP's previously taxed earnings and profits account are first increased from 0 to 100u, pursuant to paragraph (e)(2)(i) of this section as a result of the subpart F inclusion of 100u and then reduced from 100u to 50u, pursuant to paragraph (e)(2)(ii) of this section as a result of the distribution. DP's dollar basis in the 100u of previously taxed earnings and profits is $100 (the dollar amount of the income inclusion under section 951(a)(1)(A)). See section 989(b)(3). The 50u distribution is excluded from DP's gross income pursuant to §1.959-1(c)(1). Pursuant to paragraph (e)(4) of this section, at the end of year 1, FC has section 959(c)(2) earnings and profits of 50u and non-previously taxed earnings and profits of 400u. DP's dollar basis in the previously taxed earnings and profits account is reduced by a pro rata share of the dollar amount included in income under section 951(a)(1)(A), or by $50 (50u distribution/100u previously taxed earnings and profits × $100 dollar basis). DP recognizes foreign currency gain under section 986(c) of $5 ($55 spot value of 50u distribution – $50 basis).

Example 2. Net deficit in earnings and profits. (i) *Facts.* Assume the same facts as in *Example 1,* except that FC has a net deficit in earnings and profits of 500u for year 2. At the end of Year 1, FC has 50u of section 959(c)(2) earnings and profits and 400u of non-previously taxed earnings and profits.

(ii) *Analysis.* At the end of year 2, DP's section 959(c)(2) earnings and profits for year 1 remains at 50u, pursuant to paragraph (e)(5) of this paragraph, because a shareholder's previously taxed earnings and profits account is not adjusted to take into account the CFC's deficit in earnings and profits. Pursuant to paragraph (e)(4) of this section, at the end of year 2, FC's non-previously taxed earnings and profits are reduced to (100u), and no adjustment is made to FC's previously taxed earnings and profits, which remains at 50u.

Example 3. Distribution and section 956 inclusion in same year. Assume the same facts as in *Example 1,* except that DP also has a section 956 amount for year 1 with respect to its stock in FC of 200u.

(ii) *Analysis.* At the end of year 1, adjustments are made to DP's previously taxed earnings and profits account in its FC stock in the following order: First, the section 959(c)(2) earnings and profits in DP's previously taxed earnings and profits account are increased from 0 to 100u pursuant to paragraph (e)(2)(i) of this section as a result of the subpart F inclusion. Then, the section 959(c)(2) earnings and profits in DP's previously taxed earnings and profits account are reduced from 100u to 50u pursuant to paragraph (e)(2)(ii) of this section as a result of the distribution and the 50u distribution is excluded from DP's gross income pursuant to §1.959-1(c)(1). Then, the remaining 50u of section 959(c)(2) earnings and profits in DP's previously taxed earnings and profits account are reclassified as section 959(c)(1) earnings and profits pursuant to paragraph (e)(2)(iv) of this section as a result of FC's investment in United States property and 50u of the 200u section 956 amount is excluded from DP's gross income pursuant to §1.959-1(c)(2). Finally, the remaining 150u section 956 amount equal to $165 (150u × 1.1) is included in DP's gross income pursuant to section 951(a)(1)(B) and the section 959(c)(1) earnings and profits in DP's previously taxed earnings and profits account are increased from 50u to 200u pursuant to paragraph (e)(2)(vii) of this section. Pursuant to paragraph (e)(4) of this section, at the end of year 1, FC has section 959(c)(1) earnings and profits of 200u and non-previously taxed earnings and profits of 250u. DP's dollar basis in the previously taxed earnings and profits account at the end of year 1 is $215 (the $50 attributable to the reclassified 50u of earnings and $165 attributable to the 150u of section 956 inclusion). See section 989(b)(4).

Example 4. Section 956 amount in following year. (i) *Facts.* Assume the same facts as in *Example 3,* except that in year 2, DP has an additional section 956 amount of 200u with respect to its stock in FC and the spot exchange rate on December 31, year 2 is 1u = $1.20.

(ii) *Analysis.* As in *Example 3,* at the end of year 1, DP has a section 959(c)(1) earnings and profits account with respect to its stock in FC of 200u. Although DP has 200u of section 959(c)(1) earnings and profits in its previously taxed earnings and profits account with respect to its stock in FC, section 959(c)(1) earnings and profits are generated by the inclusion of a section 956 amount in a United States shareholder's gross income or the reclassification of section 959(c)(2) earnings and profits to exclude a section 956 amount from a United States shareholder's gross income and cannot be used to exclude any additional section 956 amounts from a United States shareholder's gross income. Consequently, at the end of year 2, the section 959(c)(1) earnings and profits in DP's previously taxed earnings and profits account are increased from 200u to 400u pursuant to paragraph (e)(2)(vii) of this section and the 200u section 956 amount is included in DP's gross income pursuant to section 959(a)(1)(B). Pursuant to paragraph (e)(4) of this section, at the end of year 2, FC has section 959(c)(1) earnings and profits of 400u and non-previously taxed earnings and profits of 50u. DP's dollar basis in its 200u of year 2 section 959(c)(1) earnings and profits is $240.

Example 5. Section 951(a)(1)(A) inclusion and distribution in following year. (i) *Facts.* Assume the same facts as in *Example 4,* except that in year 3, FC derives 250u of subpart F income, which is included in DP's income under section 951(a)(1)(A), makes a 250u distribution to DP, and has 700u of current and accumulated earnings and profits (before taking into account distributions made during year 3). The average exchange rate for year 3 is 1u = $1.10, so DP includes $275 in income (250u × $1.10/1u).

(ii) *Analysis.* As in *Example 4,* at the end of year 2, DP has a previously taxed earnings and profits account with respect to its stock in FC of 400u of section 959(c)(1) earnings and profits. At the end of year 3, adjustments are made in the following order. First, DP's section 959(c)(2) earnings and profits are increased from 0 to 250u pursuant to paragraph (e)(2)(i) of this section as a result of the subpart F inclusion. Then the section 959(c)(1) earnings and profits in DP's previously taxed earnings and profits account are reduced from 400u to 150u and the 250u distribution to DP is excluded from DP's gross income pursuant to § 1.959-1(c)(1). Pursuant to paragraph (e)(4) of this section, at the end of year 3, FC has 150u of section 959(c)(1) earnings and profits, 250u of section 959(c)(2) earnings and profits, and 50u of non-previously taxed earnings and profits. If DP has not made the dollar basis pooling election described in paragraph (b)(3)(ii) of this section, then the 250u distribution out of section 959(c)(1) earnings is assigned a dollar basis of $293.75 ($240 basis in 200u of year 2 earnings and $53.75 basis in 50u of year 1 earnings (50u/200u × $215)). DP's remaining dollar basis in the year 1 section 959(c)(1) earnings is $161.25 ($215 – $53.75). If DP elected to maintain the dollar basis of its previously taxed earnings and profits account on a pooled basis as provided in paragraph (b)(3)(ii) of this section, then the 250u distribution out of section 959(c)(1) earnings is assigned a dollar basis of $280.77 (250u/650u × ($215 + $240 + $275)), and DP's dollar basis in its remaining 400u previously taxed earnings accounts is $449.23 ($730 – $280.77).

Example 6. Distribution to a United States shareholder and a foreign shareholder. (i) *Facts.* DP, a United States shareholder, owns 70% and FP, a nonresident alien, owns 30% of the only class of stock in FC, a CFC that uses the U.S. dollar as its functional currency. Both DP and FC use the calendar year as their taxable year. During year 1, FC derives $100x of subpart F income, $70x of which is included in DP's gross income under section 951(a)(1)(A). FC's current and accumulated earnings and profits (before taking into account distributions made during year 1) are $500x. Also, during year 1, FC distributes $50x of earnings and profits, $35x distribution to DP and $15x distribution to FP.

(ii) *Analysis.* At the end of year 1, the section 959(c)(2) earnings and profits in DP's previously taxed earnings and profits account are increased from $0 to $70x, pursuant to paragraph (e)(2)(i) of this section as a result of the subpart F inclusion. The section 959(c)(2) earnings and profits in DP's previously taxed earnings and profits account are then reduced from $70x to $35x, pursuant to paragraph (e)(2)(ii) of this section as a result of the distribution. Pursuant to paragraph (e)(4) of this section, at the end of year 1, FC has section 959(c)(2) earnings and profits of $35x and non-previously taxed earnings and profits of $415x.

Example 7. Intercorporate Distribution. (i) *Facts.* DP, a United States shareholder, owns 70% and FP, a nonresident alien, owns 30% of the only class of stock in FC, a CFC. FC owns 100% of the only class of stock in FS, a CFC. FC uses the "u" as its functional currency and FS uses the "y" as its functional currency. DP, FC, and FS all use the calendar year as their taxable year. During year 1, FS derives 100y of subpart F income. The average y:$ exchange rate for year 1 is 1y = $1. On December 31, year 2, FS distributes 100y to FC. The y:u exchange rate on December 31, year 2, is 1y = 0.5u.

(ii) *Analysis.* (A) *Year 1.* At the end of year 1, DP's pro rata share of 70y of subpart F income is included in DP's gross income pursuant to section 951(a)(1)(A)(i) and the section 959(c)(2) earnings and profits in DP's previously taxed earnings and profits account with respect to the stock it indirectly owns in FS are correspondingly increased from 0 to 70y pursuant to paragraph (e)(2)(i) of this section as a result of the subpart F income. The dollar basis of the previously taxed earnings and profits in DP's account with respect to its stock in FS is $70. At the end of year 2, FS has section 959(c)(2) earnings and profits of 70y and non-previously taxed earnings and profits of 30y.

(B) *Year 2.* Upon the distribution of 100y=50u from FS to FC on December 31, year 2, the section 959(c)(2) earnings and profits in DP's previously taxed earnings and profits account with respect to the stock it indirectly owns in FS are reduced from 70y to 0 and the section 959(c)(2) earnings and profits in DP's earnings and profits account with respect to its stock in FC are correspondingly increased from 0 to 35u pursuant to paragraph (e)(3) of this section. The entire 100y=50u distribution is excluded from FC's income for purposes of determining FC's subpart F income under section 951(a) for year 2 with respect to DP pursuant to § 1.959-2(a)(1). Pursuant to paragraph (e)(4) of this section, at the end of year 2, FS has 0 earnings and profits and FC has section 959(c)(2) earnings and profits of 35u and non-previously taxed earnings and profits of 15u. DP's dollar basis in its 35u of section 959(c)(2) earnings and profits in its earnings and profits account with respect to its stock in FC is $70, carried over from DP's original dollar basis in its 70y of section 959(c)(2) earnings and profits in its previously taxed earnings and profits account with respect to its stock in FS.

Example 8. Sale of CFC stock. (i) *Facts.* DP1, a United States shareholder, owns 100% of the only class of stock in FC, a CFC. At the beginning of year 1, DP1 has a zero basis in its stock in FC. Both DP1 and FC use the calendar year as their taxable year. FC uses the U.S. dollar as its functional currency. During year 1, FC derives $100x of subpart F income and $100x of other income. On December 31 of year 1, DP1 sells all of its stock in FC to DP2, a U.S. person for $200x. Year 1 is a year beginning on or after December 31, 1962.

(ii) *Analysis.* First, DP1 includes the $100x of subpart F income in gross income under section 951(a)(1)(A). The section 959(c)(2) earnings and profits in DP1's previously taxed earnings and profits account with respect to its stock in FC are increased from $0 to $100x pursuant to paragraph (e)(2)(i) of this section and DP1's basis in its FC stock is increased from $0 to $100x pursuant to § 1.961-1(b). FC's section 959(c)(2) earnings and profits are increased from $0 to $100x and its non-previously taxed earnings and profits are correspondingly increased from $0 to $100x pursuant to paragraph (e)(4) of this section. Then pursuant to section 1248(a), because FC has $100x of non-previously taxed earnings and profits attributable to DP1's stock that are attributable to a taxable year beginning on or after December 31, 1962 during which FC was a CFC and DP1 owned its stock in FC, the $100x of gain recognized by DP1 on the sale of its stock ($200x proceeds – $100x basis) is included in DP1's gross income as a dividend. Consequently, the section 959(c)(2) earnings and profits in DP1's previously taxed earnings and profits account with respect to its stock in FC are increased from $100x to $200x pursuant to paragraph (e)(2)(i) of this section. Upon the sale, DP2 acquires from DP1 a previously taxed earnings and profits account with respect to the FC stock of $200x of section 959(c)(2) earnings and profits and takes a cost basis of $200x in the FC stock pursuant to section 1012.

(f) *Special rule for shareholders with more than one previously taxed earnings and profits account.*—(1) *Adjustments for distributions.*—If a covered shareholder owns (within the meaning of section 958(a)) more than one share of stock in a foreign corporation as of the last day of the foreign corporation's taxable year, to the extent that the total amount of any distributions of earnings and profits made with respect to any particular share for the foreign corporation's taxable year would exceed the previously taxed earnings and profits account with respect to such share (an excess distribution amount), the following adjustments shall be made:

(i) *Adjustment of other accounts.*—The covered shareholder's previously taxed earnings and profits accounts with respect to the shareholder's other shares of stock in the foreign corporation that are owned by the covered shareholder as of the last day of the CFC's taxable year shall be decreased, in the aggregate, by an amount equal to such excess distribution amount, but not below zero. Such decrease shall be made on a pro rata basis by reference to the amount of the previously taxed earnings and profits in those other accounts and shall be allocated to the section 959(c)(1) and (c)(2) earnings and profits in those accounts in the same manner as a distribution is allocated to such earnings and profits pursuant to the rules of section 959(c) and paragraph (e)(2)(ii)(A) of this section.

(ii) *Adjustment of deficient account.*—The covered shareholder's previously taxed earnings and profits account for the first-mentioned share of stock shall correspondingly be increased by the same amount, and then shall be adjusted to zero as provided under paragraph (e)(2)(ii)(B) of this section.

(2) *Adjustments for section 956 amounts.*—If a United States shareholder, who owns more than one share of stock in a CFC as of the last day of the CFC's taxable year, has a section 956 amount with respect to its stock in the CFC for a taxable year, to the extent that the section 956 amount with respect to any particular share of stock exceeds the section 959(c)(2) earnings and profits in such shareholder's previously taxed earnings and profits account with respect to such share (an excess section 956 amount), the covered shareholder's section 959(c)(2) earnings and profits in its previously taxed earnings and profits accounts with respect to its other shares of stock that are owned by the United States shareholder on the last day of the CFC's taxable year shall be reclassified as section 959(c)(1) earnings and profits, in the aggregate, by an amount equal to such excess section 956 amount. Such reclassification shall be made on a pro rata basis by reference to the amount of the section 959(c)(2) earnings and profits in each of the United States shareholder's other previously taxed earnings and profits accounts with respect to its stock in the CFC prior to reclassification under this paragraph (f)(2).

(3) *Examples.*—The application of this paragraph (f) is illustrated by the following examples:

Example 1. Two blocks of stock. (i) *Facts.* DP, a United States shareholder, owns two blocks, block 1 and block 2, of shares of class A stock in FC, a CFC that uses the U.S. dollar as its functional currency. Both DP and FC use the calendar year as their taxable year. Entering year 1, DP has a previously taxed earnings and profits account with respect to its block 1 shares consisting of $25x of section 959(c)(2) earnings and profits and a previously taxed earnings and profits account with respect to its block 2 shares consisting of $65x of section 959(c)(2) earnings and profits. Entering year 1, FC has section 959(c)(2) earnings and profits of $90x and non-previously taxed earnings and profits of $200x. During year 1, FC makes a distribution of earnings and profits on its Class A stock of $50x on each of block 1 and block 2.

(ii) *Analysis.* First, as a result of the distribution, the section 959(c)(2) earnings and profits in DP's previously taxed earnings and profits account with respect to block 1 are decreased from $25x to $0 and the section 959(c)(2) earnings and profits in DP's previously taxed earnings and profits account with respect to block 2 are decreased from $65x to $15x pursuant to paragraph (e)(2)(ii) of this section. Because there are insufficient previously taxed earnings and profits with respect to block 1, DP may access its excess previously taxed earnings and profits with respect to its block 2 stock, after taking into account any distributions or section 956 amounts with respect to block 2. Accordingly, the section 959(c)(2) earnings and profits in DP's previously taxed earnings and profits account with respect to block 2 are decreased from $15x to $0 pursuant to paragraphs (e)(2)(v) and (f)(1)(i) of this section and the section 959(c)(2) earnings and profits in DP's previously taxed earnings and profits account with respect to block 2 are increased from $0 to $15x and then decreased from $15x to $0 pursuant to paragraphs (e)(2)(ii)(B) and (f)(1)(ii) of this section. The $40x ($25x + $15x) of the distribution with respect to block 1 and $50x of the distribution with respect to block 2 are excluded from DP's gross income pursuant to § 1.959-1(c)(1). The remaining $10x of the distribution of earnings and profits with respect to block 1 is included in DP's gross income as a dividend. Pursuant to paragraph (e)(4) of this section, at the end of year 1, FC has section 959(c)(2) earnings and profits of $0 and non-previously taxed earnings and profits of $190x.

Example 2. Multiple classes of stock. (i) *Facts.* Assume the same facts as in *Example 1,* except that DP also owns a block, block 3, of class B stock in FC. Entering year 1, DP has a previously taxed earnings and profits account with respect to block 3 consisting of $60x of section 959(c)(2) earnings and profits. Entering year 1, FC has $150x of section 959(c)(2) earnings and profits and $200x of non-previously taxed earnings and profits.

(ii) *Analysis.* First, as in *Example 1,* the section 959(c)(2) earnings and profits in DP's previously taxed earnings and profits account with respect to block 1 are decreased from $25x to $0 and the section 959(c)(2) earnings and profits in DP's previously taxed earnings and profits account with respect to block 2 are decreased from $65x to $15x pursuant to paragraph (e)(2)(ii) of this section. Because there are insufficient previously taxed earnings and profits with respect to block 1, DP may access its excess previously taxed earnings and profits with respect to block 2 and block 3, after taking into account any distributions or section 956 amounts with respect to those blocks. In addition, the previously taxed earnings and profits from blocks 2 and 3 are decreased pro rata based on the relative previously taxed earnings and profits in the previously taxed earnings and profits accounts with respect to both blocks after taking into account any distributions or section 956 amounts with respect to those blocks. Thus, the section 959(c)(2) earnings and profits in DP's previously taxed earnings and profits account with respect to block 2 are decreased from $15x to $10x ($15x/$75x × $25x) and the section 959(c)(2) earnings and profits in DP's previously taxed earnings and profits account with respect to block 3 are decreased from $60x to $40x ($60x/$75x × $25x) pursuant to paragraphs (e)(2)(v) and (f)(1)(i) of this section. The section 959(c)(2) earnings and profits in DP's previously taxed earnings and profits account with respect to block 1 are increased from $0 to $25x and then decreased from $25x to $0 pursuant to paragraphs (e)(2)(ii)(B) and (f)(1)(ii) of this section. The entire $50x distribution with respect to block 1 and $50x distribution with respect to block 2 are excluded from DP's gross income pursuant to § 1.959-1(c)(1). Pursuant to paragraph (e)(4) of this section, at the end of year 1, FC has section 959(c)(2) earnings and profits of $50x and non-previously taxed earnings and profits of $200x.

Example 3. Distribution in excess of aggregate previously taxed earnings and profits. (i) *Facts.* Assume the same facts as in *Example* 2, except that instead of a total distribution of $100x on Class A shares in year 1, FC makes a total distribution of $200x on its Class A shares in year 1, consisting of a $100x distribution to block 1 and a $100 distribution to block 2.

(ii) *Analysis.* First, as a result of the distribution, the section 959(c)(2) earnings and profits in DP's previously taxed earnings and profits account with respect to block 1 are decreased from $25x to $0 and the section 959(c)(2) earnings and profits in DP's previously taxed earnings and profits account with respect to block 2 are decreased from $65x to $0 pursuant to paragraph (e)(2)(ii) of this section. Because there are insufficient previously taxed earnings and profits in DP's previously taxed earning and profits accounts with respect to blocks 1 and 2, DP may access its excess previously taxed earnings and profits in its previously taxed earnings and profits account with respect to block3 after taking into account any distributions or section 956 amounts with respect to block 3. Consequently, the section 959(c)(2) earnings and profits in DP's previously taxed earnings and profits account with respect to block 3 are decreased from $60x to $0 pursuant to paragraphs (e)(2)(v) and (f)(1)(i) of this section. Of the total $200x distribution from FC to DP, $150x is excluded from DP's gross income pursuant to § 1.959-1(c)(1). The remaining $50x of the distribution is included in DP's gross income pursuant to section 951(a)(1)(A). Pursuant to paragraph (e)(4) of this section, at the end of year 1, FC has section 959(c)(2) earnings and profits of $0 and non-previously taxed earnings and profits of $150x.

Example 4. Sale. (i) *Facts.* Assume the same facts as in *Example 2*, except that DP sells block 3 before the end of year 1.

(ii) *Analysis.* First, as in *Example* 2, the distribution results in a decrease of the section 959(c)(2) earnings and profits in DP's previously taxed earnings and profits account with respect to block 1 from $25x to $0 and the section 959(c)(2) earnings and profits in DP's previously taxed earnings and profits account with respect to block 2 from $65x to $15x pursuant to paragraph (e)(2)(ii) of this section. Because DP does not own block 3 on the last day of year 1, DP cannot use the previously taxed earnings and profits account with respect to block 3 to exclude a distribution in that year to block 1 or 2 from gross income. Therefore, the section 959(c)(2) earnings and profits in DP's previously taxed earnings and profits account with respect to block 2 are decreased from $15x to $0 pursuant to paragraphs (e)(2)(v) and (f)(1)(i) of this section and the section 959(c)(2) earnings and profits in DP's previously taxed earnings and profits account with respect to block 1 are increased from $0 to $15x and then decreased from $15x to $0 pursuant to paragraphs (e)(2)(ii)(B) and (f)(1)(ii) of this section. The $40x ($25x + $15x) of the distribution with respect to block 1 and $50x of the distribution with respect to block 2 are excluded from DP's gross income pursuant to § 1.959-1(c)(1). The remaining $10x of the distribution with respect to block 1 is included in DP's gross income as a dividend. Pursuant to paragraph (e)(4) of this section, at the end of year 1, FC has section 959(c)(2) earnings and profits of $60x and non-previously taxed earnings and profits of $190x.

Example 5. Section 956 amount. (i) *Facts.* Assume the same facts as in *Example* 2, except that, in addition, during year 1, FC has a section 956 amount of $30x, $5x of which is allocable to each of blocks 1 and 2, and $20x of which is allocable to block 3.

(ii) *Analysis.* Pursuant to paragraph (f)(2) of this section, account adjustments are made for the distribution from FC before any account adjustments are made for the section 956 amount. After account adjustments are made for the distribution from FC as illustrated in *Example* 2, DP has a previously taxed earnings and profits account with respect each block as follows: block 1: $0, block 2: $10x of section 959(c)(2) earnings and profits, block 3: $40x of section 959(c)(2) earnings and profits. As a result of the section 956 amount with respect to block 2, pursuant to paragraph (e)(2)(vi) of this section, $5x of DP's section 959(c)(2) earnings and profits in its previously taxed earnings and profits account with respect to block 2 is reclassified as section 959(c)(1) earnings and profits. Consequently, block 2 is left with a previously taxed earnings and profits account consisting of $5x of section 959(c)(1) earnings and profits and $5x of section 959(c)(2) earnings and profits. In addition, pursuant to paragraph (e)(2)(vi) of this section, $20x of DP's section 959(c)(2) earnings and profits in its previously taxed earnings and profits account with respect to block 3 are reclassified as section 959(c)(1) earnings and profits. Consequently, block 3 is left with a previously taxed earnings and profits account consisting of $20x of section 959(c)(1) earnings and profits and $20x of section 959(c)(2) earnings and profits. The total $25x section 956 amount with respect to blocks 2 and 3 is excluded from DP's gross income pursuant to § 1.959-1(c)(2). Because there are insufficient previously taxed earnings and profits in the previously taxed earnings and profits account with respect to block 1, DP may access its excess previously taxed earnings and profits in the previously taxed earnings and profits accounts with respect to blocks 2 and 3 after taking into account any distributions or section 956 amounts with respect to those blocks. In addition, the previously taxed earnings and profits in the previously taxed earnings and profits accounts with respect to blocks 2 and 3 are reclassified pro rata based on the relative previously taxed earnings and profits in those accounts after taking into account any distributions or section 956 amounts with respect to those blocks. Accordingly, pursuant to paragraphs (e)(2)(vi) and (f)(2) of this section, an additional $1x ($5x/$25x × $5x) of the section 959(c)(2) earnings and profits in DP's previously taxed earnings and profits account with respect to block 2 are reclassified as section 959(c)(1) earnings and profits and an additional $4x($20x/$25x × $5x) of the section 959(c)(2) earnings and profits in DP's previously taxed earnings and profits account with respect to block 3 are reclassified as section 959(c)(1) earnings and profits. The $5x section 956 amount with respect to block 1 is also excluded from DP's gross income pursuant to § 1.959-1(c)(2). At the end of year 1, DP's previously taxed earnings and profits accounts with respect to its various blocks of stock are as follows: block 1 has no previously taxed earnings and profits, block 2 has $6x ($5x + $1x) of section 959(c)(1) earnings and profits and $4x ($5x – $1x) of section 959(c)(2) earnings and profits and block 3 has $24x ($20x + $4x) of section 959(c)(1) earnings and profits and $16x ($20x – $4x) of section 959(c)(2) earnings and profits. Pursuant to paragraph (e)(4) of this section, at the end of year 1, FC has $30x of section 959(c)(1) earnings and profits, $20x of section 959(c)(2) earnings and profits, and $200x of non-previously taxed earnings and profits.

(g) *Special rule for shareholder included in a consolidated group.*—(1) *Adjustments for distributions.*—(i) *In general.*—In the case of a covered shareholder who is a member of a consolidated group, to the extent that the total amount of any distributions of earnings and profits with respect to such covered shareholder's stock in a foreign corporation during such foreign corporation's taxable year would exceed the covered shareholder's previously taxed earnings and profits account with respect to all of the covered shareholder's stock of the foreign corporation (an excess distribution amount) the previously taxed earnings and profits accounts of the covered shareholder and of the other members of the covered shareholder's consolidated group that own stock in the same foreign corporation and are members of the covered shareholder's consolidated group on the last day of the foreign corporation's taxable year shall be adjusted as follows.

(A) *Adjustment of other members' accounts.*—The previously taxed earnings and profits accounts of the other members of the consolidated group that own (within the meaning of section 958(a)) stock in the same foreign corporation and are members of the covered shareholder's consolidated group on the last day of the foreign corporation's taxable year shall be decreased, in the aggregate, by the amount of such excess distribution amount, but not below zero. Such decrease shall be made on a pro rata basis by reference to the amount of such other members' previously taxed earnings and profits accounts and shall be allocated to the section 959(c)(1) and (c)(2) earnings and profits in such accounts in the same manner as a distribution is allocated to such earnings and profits pursuant to section 959(c) and paragraph (e)(2)(ii)(A) of this section.

(B) *Adjustment of the deficient account.*—The deficient previously taxed earnings and profits account of such covered shareholder shall correspondingly be increased by the same amount, and then adjusted to zero under paragraph (e)(2)(ii)(B) of this section.

(ii) *Insufficient previously taxed earnings and profits.*—If more than one member of the consolidated group is a covered shareholder that has an excess distribution amount with respect to all of its stock in the foreign corporation and there is insufficient previously taxed earnings and profits available in the previously taxed earnings and profits accounts of other consolidated group members to exclude the combined excess distribution amounts of the covered shareholders, the other consolidated group members' previously taxed earnings and profits shall be allocated between the covered shareholders' deficient previously taxed earnings and profits accounts in proportion to each covered shareholder's excess distribution amount.

(2) *Adjustments for section 956 amounts.*—(i) *In general.*—If a United States shareholder, who is a member of a consolidated group, has a section 956 amount with respect to its stock in a CFC for a taxable year, to the extent that the section 956 amount exceeds the section 959(c)(2) earnings and profits in such United States shareholder's previously taxed earnings and profits accounts with respect to all of its stock in the CFC (an excess section 956 amount), the section 959(c)(2) earnings and profits in the previously taxed earnings and profits accounts of consolidated group members, who are members of the United States shareholder's consolidated group on the last day of the CFC's taxable year, with respect to their stock in the CFC shall be reclassified as section 959(c)(1) earnings and profits, in the aggregate, by an amount equal to such excess section 956 amount. The amount that is reclassified with respect to each such account of such other members shall be proportionate to the amount of section 959(c)(2) earnings and profits in those accounts prior to reclassification under this paragraph (g).

(ii) *Insufficient section 959(c)(2) earnings and profits.*—If more than one member of the consolidated group is a United States shareholder that has an excess section 956 amount with respect to its stock in the CFC for the taxable year and there is insufficient aggregate section 959(c)(2) earnings and profits in other consolidated group members' previously taxed earnings and profits accounts to exclude the combined excess section 956 amounts of the Untied States shareholders, the amount of any consolidated group members' section 959(c)(2) earnings and profits that are reclassified on behalf of each United States shareholder shall be proportionate to the excess section 956 amount for each such United States shareholder.

(3) *Stock basis adjustments of members.*—See § 1.1502-32 for rules addressing investment adjustments resulting from the application of this paragraph.

(4) *Examples.*—The application of this paragraph (g) is illustrated by the following examples:

Example 1. Two consolidated group members. (i) *Facts.* DP1, a United States shareholder, owns one block, block 1, of shares of Class A stock in FC, a CFC that uses the U.S. dollar as its functional currency. DP2, a United States shareholder and a member of DP1's consolidated group, owns one block, block 2, of shares of Class A stock in FC. DP1, DP2 and FC all use the calendar year as their taxable year and FC uses the U.S. dollar as its functional currency. Entering year 1, DP1 has a previously taxed earnings and profits account with respect to block 1 consisting of $50x of section 959(c)(2) earnings and profits and DP2 has a previously taxed earnings and profits account with respect to block 2 consisting of $200x of section 959(c)(2) earnings and profits. Entering year 1, FC has section 959(c)(2) earnings and profits of $250x and non-previously taxed earnings and profits of $100x. In year 1, FC generates no earnings and profits and makes a distribution of earnings and profits on its Class A stock, a $100x distribution of earnings and profits to block 1 and a $100x distribution of earnings and profits to block 2.

(ii) *Analysis.* First, pursuant to paragraph (e)(2)(ii) of this section, the section 959(c)(2) earnings and profits in DP1's previously taxed earnings and profits account with respect to block 1 are decreased from $50x to $0 and the section 959(c)(2) earnings and profits in DP2's previously taxed earnings and profits account with respect to block 2 are decreased from $200x to $100x. Then, pursuant to paragraphs (e)(2)(v) and (g)(1)(i)(A) of this section, the section 959(c)(2) earnings and profits in DP2's previously taxed earnings and profits account with respect to block 2 are decreased from $100x to $50x and, pursuant to paragraphs (e)(2)(ii)(B) and (g)(1)(i)(B) of this section, the section 959(c)(2) earnings and profits in DP1's previously taxed earnings and profits account with respect to block 1 are increased from $0 to $50x and then decreased from $50x to $0. Pursuant to section 959(a) and § 1.959-1(c), the entire $100x distribution to block 1 and $100x distribution to block 2 are excluded from DP1's and DP2's gross incomes respectively. Pursuant to paragraph (e)(4) of this section, at the end of year 1, FC has section 959(c)(2) earnings and profits of $50x and non-previously taxed earnings and profits of $100x.

Example 2. Two consolidated group members; multiple classes of stock. (i) *Facts.* Assume the same facts as in *Example 1*, except that DP1 also owns one block, block 3, of shares of class B stock in FC. DP1 has a previously taxed earnings and profits account with respect to block 3 consisting of $40x of section 959(c)(2) earnings and profits. Entering year 1, FC has section 959(c)(2) earnings and profits of $290x and non-previously taxed earnings and profits of $100x.

(ii) *Analysis.* First, pursuant to paragraph (e)(2)(ii) of this section, the section 959(c)(2) earnings and profits in DP1's previously taxed earnings and profits account with respect to block 1 are decreased from $50x to $0 and the section 959(c)(2) earnings and profits in DP2's previously taxed earnings and profits account with respect to block 2 are decreased from $200x to $100x. Then, pursuant to paragraphs (e)(2)(v) and (f)(1)(i) of this section, the section 959(c)(2) earnings and profits in DP1's previously taxed earnings and profits account with respect to block 3 are decreased from $40x to $0 and, pursuant to paragraphs (e)(2)(ii)(B) and (f)(1)(ii) of this section, the section 959(c)(2) earnings and profits in DP1's previously taxed earnings and profits account with respect to block 1 are increased from $0 to $40x and then decreased from $40x to $0. Finally, pursuant to paragraphs (e)(2)(v) and (g)(1)(i)(A) of this section, the section 959(c)(2) earnings and profits in DP2's previously taxed earnings and profits account with respect to block 2 are decreased from $100x to $90x and, pursuant to paragraphs (e)(2)(ii)(B) and (g)(1)(i)(B) of this section, the section 959(c)(2) earnings and profits in DP1's previously taxed earnings and profits account with respect to block 1 are increased from $0 to $10x and then decreased from $10x to $0. Pursuant to section 959(a) and § 1.959-1(c), the entire $100x distribution to block 1 and $100x distribution to block 2 are excluded from DP1's and DP2's gross incomes respectively. Pursuant to paragraph (e)(4) of this section, at the end of year 1, FC has section 959(c)(2) earnings and profits of $90x and non-previously taxed earnings and profits of $100x.

Example 3. Three consolidated group members; multiple classes of stock. (i) *Facts.* Assume the same facts as in *Example 2*, except that DP3, a United States shareholder and a member of DP1's consolidated group, owns one block, block 4, of shares of class B stock in FC. DP3 has a previously taxed earnings and profits account with respect to block 4 consisting of $25x of section 959(c)(2) earnings and profits. Entering year 1, FC has section 959(c)(2) earnings and profits of $315x and non-previously taxed earnings and profits of $100x.

(ii) *Analysis.* First, pursuant to paragraph (e)(2)(ii) of this section, the section 959(c)(2) earnings and profits in DP1's previously taxed earnings and profits account with respect to block 1 are decreased from $50x to $0 and the section 959(c)(2) earnings and profits in DP2's previously taxed earnings and profits account with respect to block 2 are decreased from $200x to $100x. Then, pursuant to paragraphs (e)(2)(v) and (f)(1)(i) of this section, the section 959(c)(2) earnings and profits in DP1's previously taxed earnings and profits account with respect to block 3 are decreased from $40x to $0 and, pursuant to paragraphs (e)(2)(ii)(B) and (f)(1)(ii) of this section, the section 959(c)(2) earnings and profits in DP1's previously taxed earnings and profits account with respect to block 1 are increased from $0 to $40x and then decreased from $40x to $0. Finally, pursuant to paragraphs (e)(2)(v) and (g)(1)(i)(A) of this section, the section 959(c)(2) earnings and profits in DP2's and DP3's previously taxed earnings and profits accounts with respect to blocks 2 and 4 are decreased pro rata from $100x to $92x and from $25x to $23x respectively, and, pursuant to paragraphs (e)(2)(ii)(B) and (g)(1)(i)(B) of this section, the section 959(c)(2) earnings and profits in DP1's previously taxed earnings and profits account with respect to block 1 are increased from $0 to $10x and then decreased from $10x to $0. Pursuant to section 959(a) and § 1.959-1(c), the entire amounts of the $100x distribution to block 1 and the $100x distribution to block 2 are excluded from DP1's and DP2's gross incomes respectively. Pursuant to paragraph (e)(4) of this section, at the end of year 1, FC has section 959(c)(2) earnings and profits of $115x and non-previously taxed earnings and profits of $100x.

Example 4. Section 956 Amount. (i) *Facts*. Assume the same facts as in *Example 3*, except that instead of a distribution of 200x on its class A stock, FC has a section 956 amount for year 1 of $180x, 45x of which is allocable to each of blocks 1 through 4.

(ii) *Analysis*. First, pursuant to paragraph (e)(2)(iv) of this section, the section 959(c)(2) earnings and profits in each shareholder's previously taxed earnings profits account are reclassified as section 959(c)(1) earnings and profits leaving each block of stock with the following account: block 1: $45x of section 959(c)(1) earnings and profits, $5x of section 959(c)(2) earnings and profits; block 2: $45x of section 959(c)(1) earnings and profits and $155x of section 959(c)(2) earnings and profits; block 3: $40x of section 959(c)(1) earnings and profits and $0 of section 959(c)(2) earnings and profits; block 4: $25x of section 959(c)(1) earnings and profits and $0 of section 959(c)(2) earnings and profits. After the above reclassifications, DP1 has an excess section 956 amount of $5x with respect to block 3. Therefore, pursuant to paragraphs (e)(2)(vi) and (f)(2) of this section, the remaining $5x of section 959(c)(2) earnings and profits in DP1's previously taxed earnings and profits account with respect to block 1 are reclassified as section 959(c)(1) earnings and profits, leaving DP1 with $50x of section 959(c)(1) earnings and profits and $0 of section 959(c)(2) earnings and profits in its previously taxed earnings and profits account with respect to block 1. The entire $45x section 956 amount with respect to blocks 1 and 3 are excluded from DP1's gross income pursuant to paragraph (c)(2) of this section. After the above reclassifications, DP3 has an excess section 956 amount of $20x with respect to block 4. Therefore, pursuant to paragraphs (e)(2)(vi) and (g)(2)(i) of this section, $20x of the section 959(c)(2) earnings and profits in DP2's previously taxed earnings and profits account with respect to block 2 are reclassified as section 959(c)(1) earnings and profits, leaving DP2 with $65x of section 959(c)(1) earnings and profits and $135x of section 959(c)(2) earnings and profits. The entire $45x section 956 amount with respect to blocks 2 and 4 are excluded from DP2's and DP3's gross incomes, respectively, pursuant to § 1.959-1(c)(2). Pursuant to paragraph (e)(4) of this section, at the end of year 1, FC has section 959(c)(1) earnings and profits of $180x, section 959(c)(2) earnings and profits of $135x, and non-previously taxed earnings and profits of $100x.

Example 5. Ex-member. (i) *Facts*. DP1, a United States shareholder, owns one block, block 1, of shares of Class A stock in FC, a CFC that uses the U.S. dollar as its functional currency. DP2 and DP3, both United States shareholders and members of DP1's consolidated group, own one block each, blocks 2 and 3 respectively, of shares of Class A stock in FC. DP1, DP2, DP3 and FC all use the calendar year as their taxable year. Entering year 1, DP1 has a previously taxed earnings and profits account with respect to block 1 consisting of $50x of section 959(c)(2) earnings and profits, DP2 has a previously taxed earnings and profits account with respect to block 2 consisting of $100x of section 959(c)(2) earnings and profits, and DP3 has a previously taxed earnings and profits account with respect to block 3 consisting of $200x of section 959(c)(2) earnings and profits. Entering year 1, FC has section 959(c)(2) earnings and profits of $350x and non-previously taxed earnings and profits of $100x. On March 15 of year 1, FC makes a distribution of earnings and profits on its Class A stock consisting of a $100x distribution of earnings and profits to each of blocks 1, 2 and 3. On July 4 of year 1, DP3 is sold to DP4, a United States person who is not a member of the consolidated group, and DP3 ceases to be a member of the consolidated group.

(ii) *Analysis*. First, pursuant to paragraph (e)(2)(ii) of this section, the section 959(c)(2) earnings and profits in DP1's previously taxed earnings and profits account with respect to block 1 are decreased from $50x to $0, the section 959(c)(2) earnings and profits in DP2's previously taxed earnings and profits account with respect to block 2 are decreased from $100x to $0, and the section 959(c)(2) earnings and profits in DP3's previously taxed earnings and profits account with respect to block 3 are decreased from $200x to $100x. Because DP3 was not a member of DP1's consolidated group on the last day of year 1, the remaining $100x of section 959(c)(2) earnings and profits in DP3's previously taxed earnings and profits account with respect to its stock in FC cannot be used to exclude the remaining $50x distribution to DP1 from DP1's gross income. Consequently, pursuant to § 1.959-1(c)(1), $50x of the distribution to block 1, the entire $100x of the distribution to block 2, and the entire $100x of the distribution to block 3 are excluded from DP1's, DP2's, and DP3's gross incomes respectively. The remaining $50x distribution to DP1 is included in DP1's gross income pursuant to section 951(a)(1)(a). Pursuant to paragraph (e)(4) of this section, at the end of year 1, FC has section 959(c)(2) earnings and profits of $150x and non-previously taxed earnings and profits of $50x.

Example 6. Insufficient excess previously taxed earnings and profits. (i) *Facts*. DP1, a United States shareholder, owns one block, block 1, of shares of Class A stock in FC, a CFC that uses the U.S. dollar as its functional currency. DP2 and DP3, both United States shareholders and members of DP1's consolidated group, own one block each, blocks 2 and 3 respectively, of shares of Class A stock in FC. DP1, DP2, DP3 and FC all use the calendar year as their taxable year. Entering year 1, DP1 has a previously taxed earnings and profits account with respect to block 1 consisting of $40x of section 959(c)(2) earnings and profits, DP2 has a previously taxed earnings and profits account with respect to block 2 consisting of $60x of section 959(c)(2) earnings and profits, and DP3 has a previously taxed earnings and profits account with respect to block 3 consisting of $150x of section 959(c)(2) earnings and profits. Entering year 1, FC has section 959(c)(2) earnings and profits of $250x and non-previously taxed earnings and profits of $100x. On March 15 of year 1, FC makes a distribution of earnings and profits on its Class A stock consisting of a $100x distribution of earnings and profits to each of blocks 1, 2 and 3.

(ii) *Analysis*. First, pursuant to paragraph (e)(2)(ii) of this section, the section 959(c)(2) earnings and profits in DP1's previously taxed earnings and profits account with respect to block 1 are decreased from $40x to $0, the section 959(c)(2) earnings and profits in DP2's previously taxed earnings and profits account with respect to block 2 are decreased from $60x to $0, and the section 959(c)(2) earnings and profits in DP3's previously taxed earnings and profits account with respect to block 3 are decreased from $150x to $50x. Then, pursuant to paragraph (g)(1)(i)(A) of this section, the section 959(c)(2) earnings and profits in DP3's previously taxed earnings and profits account with respect to its stock in FC are reduced from $50x to $0 and, pursuant to paragraphs (g)(1)(i)(B) and (g)(1)(ii) of this section, the section 959(c)(2) earnings and profits in DP1's and DP2's previously taxed earnings and profits accounts with respect to their stock in FC are increased from $0 to $30x ($60x /$100x × $50x) and $0 to $20x ($40x/$100x x $50x) respectively and then immediately reduce to $0. Pursuant to § 1.959-1(c), $70x ($40x + $30x) of the distribution to DP1, $80x ($60x + $20x) of the distribution to DP2, and $100x of the distribution to DP3 are excluded from gross income. The remaining $30x distributed to DP1 and $20x distributed to DP2 are included in gross income pursuant to section 951(a)(1)(A). Pursuant to paragraph (e)(4) of this section, at the end of year 1, FC has non-previously taxed earnings and profits of $50x.

(h) *Adjustments in the case of redemptions.*—(1) *In general.*—In the case of a foreign corporation's redemption of stock (a redemption distribution), the effect on the covered shareholder's previously taxed earnings and profits account and on the earnings and profits of the redeeming corporation depends on whether the distribution is treated as a payment in exchange for stock or as a distribution of property to which section 301 applies. For the treatment of deemed redemption distributions in transactions described in section 304(a)(1), see paragraph (h)(4) of this section.

(2) *Exchange treatment.*—(i) *Effect on foreign corporation's earnings and profits.*—In the case of a redemption distribution that is treated as a payment in exchange for stock under section 302(a) or section 303, the amount of the distribution properly chargeable to the earnings and profits of the redeeming foreign corporation is the amount determined under section 312(a), subject to the limitation in section 312(n)(7) and this paragraph (h)(2)(i). For purposes of section 312(n)(7), the amount properly chargeable to the earnings and profits of the redeeming foreign corporation shall not exceed the sum of—

(A) The amount of the previously taxed earnings and profits account with respect to the redeemed shares of stock (without adjustment for any income inclusion under section 1248 resulting from the redemption); and

(B) A ratable portion of the redeeming corporation's non-previously taxed earnings and profits. Such chargeable amount of earnings and profits shall be allocated to earnings and profits in accordance with section 959(c) and this section.

(ii) *Cessation of previously taxed earnings and profits account.*—In the case of a redemption distribution that is treated as a payment in exchange for stock, the redeemed covered shareholder's previously taxed earnings and profits account with respect to the redeemed shares ceases to exist and is not transferred to any other previously taxed earnings and profits account. In such a case, any previously taxed earnings and profits in the redeemed covered shareholder's previously taxed earnings and profits account, after being reduced under paragraph (h)(2)(i) of this section, become non-previously taxed earnings and profits of the foreign corporation.

(iii) *Examples.*—The application of this paragraph (h)(2) is illustrated by the following examples:

Example 1. Complete redemption treated as exchange; previously taxed earnings and profits account is depleted. (i) *Facts*. DP, a United States shareholder, owns 70% and FP, a nonresident alien who is unrelated to DP under section 318, owns 30% of the only class of stock in FC, a CFC that uses the U.S. dollar as its functional currency. Both DP and FC use the calendar year as their taxable year and both DP and FC are wholly owned by the same domestic corporation, USP. DP has a previously taxed earnings and profits account consisting of $50x of section 959(c)(2) earnings and profits with respect to its stock in FC and DP has a $50 basis in its FC stock pursuant to section 961(a). FC has $50x of section 959(c)(2) earnings and profits and $50x of non-previously taxed earnings and profits attributable to taxable years of FC beginning on or after December 31, 1962 during which FC was a CFC and during which DP held its shares of stock in FC. FC redeems all of DP's stock for $100x in a redemption that is treated as a payment in exchange for the stock under section 302(a).

(ii) *Analysis*. DP includes $35x ($50x × 70%) in gross income as a dividend pursuant to section 1248(a) as a result of the deemed exchange. FC adjusts its earnings and profits as a result of the exchange under paragraph (h)(2)(i) of this section in the following manner: first, FC's section 959(c)(2) earnings and profits are reduced from $50x to $0; then, FC's non-previously taxed earnings and profits are decreased from $50x to $15x to reflect DP's $35x ratable share of FC's non-previously taxed earnings and profits. DP's previously taxed earnings and profits account ceases to exist and is not transferred to any other previously taxed earnings and profits account.

Example 2. Complete redemption treated as exchange; previously taxed earnings and profits account is not depleted. (i) *Facts*. Assume the same facts as *Example 1*, except that the amount of the redemption distribution by FC to DP is $25x.

(ii) *Analysis*. DP recognizes a $25x loss as a result of the deemed exchange. FC's section 959(c)(2) earnings and profits are decreased from $50x to $25x, pursuant to paragraph (h)(2)(i) of this section. DP's previously taxed earnings and profits account ceases to exist, and the remaining $25x of section 959(c)(2) earnings and profits in such account is not transferred to any other previously taxed earnings and profits account. However, pursuant to paragraph (h)(2)(ii) of this section, the $25x of previously taxed earnings and profits is converted to non-previously taxed earnings and profits of DC.

(3) *Distribution treatment.*—(i) *Adjustment of shareholder previously taxed earnings and profits*

accounts and foreign corporation's earnings and profits.—In the case of a redemption distribution by a foreign corporation that is treated as a distribution of property to which section 301 applies, § 1.959-1 and this section shall apply in the same manner as they would apply to any distribution of property to which section 301 applies.

(ii) *Transfer to remaining shares.*—To the extent that the previously taxed earnings and profits account with respect to stock redeemed in a transaction described in paragraph (h)(3)(i) of this section exceeds the amount chargeable to the earnings and profits of the corporation under the rules of that paragraph, the excess previously taxed earnings and profits shall be reallocated to the previously taxed earnings and profits accounts with respect to the remaining stock in the foreign corporation in a manner consistent with, and in proportion to, the proper adjustments of the basis in the remaining shares pursuant to § 1.302-2(c).

(iii) *Examples.*—The application of this paragraph (h)(3) is illustrated by the following examples:

Example 1. Redemption in exchange for cash that is treated as a distribution. (i) *Facts.* DP, a United States shareholder, owns 100% of the stock in FC, a CFC that uses the U.S. dollar as its functional currency. Both DP and FC use the calendar year as their taxable year. DP owns two blocks of stock in FC, block 1 and block 2. At the beginning of year 1, DP has a previously taxed earnings and profits account with respect to block 1 consisting of $50x of section 959(c)(2) earnings and profits and FC has section 959(c)(2) earnings and profits of $50x and non-previously taxed earnings and profits of $100x. In year 1, FC redeems block 1 for $100x in a redemption that is treated as a distribution of property to which section 301 applies under section 302(d).

(ii) *Analysis.* The section 959(c)(2) earnings and profits in DP's previously taxed earnings and profits account with respect to block 1 are reduced from $50x to $0 and FC's section 959(c)(2) earnings and profits are correspondingly reduced from $50x to $0. The remaining $50x is included in DP's gross income as a dividend under section 301(c)(1) and FC's non-previously taxed earnings and profits are reduced from $100x to $50x.

Example 2. Redemption in exchange for cash that is treated as a distribution. (i) *Facts.* Assume the same facts as *Example 1*, except that DP is redeemed for $25x.

(ii) *Analysis.* The section 959(c)(2) earnings and profits in DP's previously taxed earnings and profits account with respect to block 1 are reduced from $50x to $25x and FC's section 959(c)(2) earnings and profits are correspondingly reduced from $50x to $25x. FC's non-previously taxed earnings and profits remain at $100x. Pursuant to paragraph (h)(3)(ii) of this section the remaining $25x of section 959(c)(2) earnings and profits in DP's previously taxed earnings and profits account with respect to block 1 are reallocated with respect to the remaining stock in FC in a manner consistent with, and in proportion to, the proper adjustments of the basis of the remaining FC shares pursuant to § 1.302-2(c).

(4) *Section 304 transactions.*—(i) *Deemed redemption treated as a distribution.*—In the case of a stock acquisition described in section 304(a)(1), that is treated as a distribution of property to which section 301 applies, a covered shareholder receiving an amount treated as a distribution of earnings and profits shall have a previously taxed earnings and profits account with respect to stock in each foreign corporation treated as distributing its earnings and profits under section 304(b)(2), even if such person did not otherwise have a previously taxed earnings and profits account with respect to stock in such corporation or corporations. In such a case, § 1.959-1 and this section shall apply in the same manner as these regulations would apply to any distribution to which section 301 applies.

(ii) *Example.*—The application of this paragraph (h)(4) is illustrated by the following example:

Example. Cross-chain acquisition of first-tier CFC. (i) *Facts.* DP, a domestic corporation, owns all of the stock in DS, a domestic corporation, and F1, a CFC. DP and DS are members of the same consolidated group. DS owns all of the stock in F2, a CFC. DP, DS, F1 and F2 all use the calendar year as their taxable year and F1 and F2 each use the U.S. dollar as its functional currency. During year 1, F1 purchases all the stock in F2 from DS for $80x in a transaction described in section 304(a)(1). At the end of year 1, before taking into account the purchase of F2's stock, DP has a previously taxed earnings and profits account consisting of $20x of section 959(c)(2) earnings and profits with respect to its stock in F1, and F1 has previously taxed earnings and profits consisting of $20x of section 959(c)(2) earnings and profits and non-previously taxed earnings and profits of $10x. At the end of year1, before taking into account the purchase of F2's stock, DS has a previously taxed earnings and profits account consisting of $50x of section 959(c)(2) earnings and profits with respect to its stock in F2, and F2 has section 959(c)(2) earnings and profits of $50x and non-previously taxed earnings and profits of $0.

(ii) *Analysis.* Under section 304(a)(1), DS is deemed to have transferred the F2 stock to F1 in exchange for F1 stock in a transaction to which section 351(a) applies, and F1 is treated as having redeemed, for $80x, the F1 stock deemed issued to DS. The payment of $80x is treated as a distribution of property to which section 301 applies. Under section 304(b)(2), the determination of the amount which is a dividend is made as if the distribution were made, first, by F1 to the extent of its earnings and profits ($30x), and then by F2 to the extent of its earnings and profits ($50x). Before taking into account the deemed distributions, DS had a previously taxed earnings and profits account consisting of $50x of section 959(c)(2) earnings and profits with respect to its stock in F2, and DP had a previously taxed earnings and profits account consisting of $20x of section 959(c)(2) earnings and profits with respect to its stock in F1. Under paragraph (h)(4)(i) of this section, DS has a previously taxed earnings and profits account with respect to the stock in F1. Under paragraph (g)(1)(i) of this section, the section 959(c)(2) earnings and profits in DP's previously taxed earnings and profits account with respect to the F1 stock are reduced from $20x to $0 and the section 959(c)(2) earnings and profits in DS's previously taxed earnings and profits account with respect to the F1 stock are increased from $0 to $20x. The distribution by F1 causes the section 959(c)(2) earnings and profits in DS's previously taxed earnings and profits account with respect to F1 stock to be reduced from $20x to $0, and causes F1's section 959(c)(2) earnings and profits to be reduced from $20x to $0 and its non-previously taxed earnings and profits to be reduced from $10x to $0. The deemed distribution by F2 causes the section 959(c)(2) earnings and profits in DS's previously taxed earnings and profits account with respect to F2 stock to be reduced from $50x to $0, and causes F2's section 959(c)(2) earnings and profits to be reduced from $50x to $0. Of the distribution of $80x, $70x is excluded from DS's gross income pursuant to § 1.959-1(c)(1), and $10x is included in DS's gross income as a dividend.

[Reg. § 1.959-3.]

☐ Par. 5. Section 1.959-4 is revised to read as follows:

§ 1.959-4. Distributions of amounts excluded under section 959(a).—Except as provided in section 960(a)(3) and § 1.960-1, any distribution excluded from gross income of a covered shareholder under section 959(a)(1) and § 1.959-1(c)(1) shall be treated, for purposes of chapter 1 (relating to normal taxes and surtaxes) of subtitle A (relating to income taxes) of the Internal Revenue Code as a distribution which is not a dividend, except such a distribution shall immediately reduce earnings and profits.

Determination of the Foreign Tax Credit: Guidance

Determination of the Foreign Tax Credit: Guidance.—Amendments to Reg. §§ 1.960-1—1.960-7, relating to the determination of the foreign tax credit under the Internal Revenue Code, including changes made by the Tax Cuts and Jobs Act, are proposed (published in the Federal Register on December 7, 2018) (REG-105600-18).

Par. 22. Section 1.960-1 is revised to read as follows:

§ 1.960-1. Overview, definitions, and computational rules for determining foreign income taxes deemed paid under section 960(a), (b), and (d).—(a) *Overview.*—(1) *Scope of §§ 1.960-1 through 1.960-3.*—This section and §§ 1.960-2 and 1.960-3 provide rules to associate foreign income taxes of a controlled foreign corporation with the income that a domestic corporation that is a United States shareholder of the controlled foreign corporation takes into account in determining a subpart F inclusion or GILTI inclusion amount of the domestic corporation, as well as to associate foreign income taxes of a controlled foreign corporation with distributions of previously taxed earnings and profits. These regulations provide the exclusive rules for determining the foreign income taxes deemed paid by a domestic corporation. Therefore, only foreign income taxes of a controlled foreign corporation that are associated under these rules with a subpart F inclusion or GILTI inclusion amount of a domestic corporation that is a United States shareholder of the controlled foreign corporation, or with previously taxed earnings and profits, are eligible to be deemed paid. This section provides definitions and computational rules for determining foreign income taxes deemed paid under section 960(a), (b), and (d). Section 1.960-2 provides rules for computing the amount of foreign income taxes deemed paid by a domestic corporation that is a United States shareholder of a controlled foreign corporation under section 960(a) and (d). Section 1.960-3 provides rules for computing the amount of foreign income taxes deemed paid by a domestic corporation that is a United States shareholder of a controlled foreign corporation, or by a controlled foreign corporation, under section 960(b).

(2) *Scope of this section.*—Paragraph (b) of this section provides definitions for purposes of this section and §§ 1.960-2 and 1.960-3. Paragraph (c) of this section provides computational rules to coordinate the various calculations under this section and §§ 1.960-2 and 1.960-3. Paragraph (d) of this section provides rules for computing the income in an income group within a section 904 category, and for associating foreign income taxes with an income group. Paragraph (e) of this section provides a rule for the creditability of taxes associated with the residual income group. Paragraph (f) of this section provides an example illustrating the application of this section.

(b) *Definitions.*—The following definitions apply for purposes of this section and §§ 1.960-2 and 1.960-3.

(1) *Annual PTEP account.*—The term *annual PTEP account* has the meaning set forth in § 1.960-3(c)(1).

(2) *Controlled foreign corporation.*—The term *controlled foreign corporation* means a foreign corporation described in section 957(a).

(3) *Current taxable year.*—The term *current taxable year* means the U.S. taxable year of a controlled foreign corporation that is an inclusion year, or during which the controlled foreign corporation receives a section 959(b) distribution or makes a section 959(a) distribution or a section 959(b) distribution.

(4) *Current year taxes.*—The term *current year taxes* means foreign income taxes paid or accrued by a controlled foreign corporation in a current taxable year. Foreign income taxes accrue when all the events have occurred that establish the fact of the liability and the amount of the liability can be determined with reasonable accuracy. *See* §§ 1.446-1(c)(1)(ii)(A) and 1.461-4(g)(6)(iii)(B) (economic performance exception for certain foreign taxes). Withholding taxes described in section 901(k)(1)(B) that are withheld from a payment accrue when the payment is made. Foreign income taxes calculated on the basis of net income recognized in a foreign taxable year accrue on the last day of the foreign taxable year. Accordingly, current year taxes include foreign withholding taxes that are withheld from payments made to the controlled foreign corporation during the current taxable year, and foreign income taxes that accrue in the controlled foreign corporation's current taxable year in which or with which its foreign taxable year ends. Additional payments of foreign in-

come taxes resulting from a redetermination of foreign tax liability, including contested taxes that accrue when the contest is resolved, "relate back" and are considered to accrue as of the end of the foreign taxable year to which the taxes relate.

(5) *Foreign income taxes*.—The term *foreign income taxes* means income, war profits, and excess profits taxes as defined in § 1.901-2(a), and taxes included in the term income, war profits, and excess profits taxes by reason of section 903 and § 1.903-1(a), that are imposed by a foreign country or a possession of the United States, including any such taxes that are deemed paid by a controlled foreign corporation under section 960(b). Income, war profits, and excess profits taxes do not include amounts excluded from the definition of those taxes pursuant to section 901 and the regulations under that section. See, for example, section 901(f), (g), and (i). Foreign income taxes also do not include taxes paid by a controlled foreign corporation for which a credit is disallowed at the level of the controlled foreign corporation. See, for example, sections 245A(e)(3), 901(k)(1), (l), and (m), 909, and 6038(c)(1)(B). Foreign income taxes, however, include taxes that may be deemed paid but for which a credit is reduced or disallowed at the level of the United States shareholder. See, for example, sections 901(e), 901(j), 901(k)(2), 908, 965(g) and 6038(c)(1)(A).

(6) *Foreign taxable year*.—The term *foreign taxable year* has the meaning set forth in section 7701(a)(23), applied by substituting "under foreign law" for the phrase "under subtitle A."

(7) *GILTI inclusion amount*.—The term *GILTI inclusion amount* has the meaning set forth in § 1.951A-1(c)(1) (or, in the case of a member of a consolidated group, § 1.1502-51(b)).

(8) *Gross tested income*.—The term *gross tested income* has the meaning set forth in § 1.951A-2(c)(1).

(9) *Inclusion percentage*.—The term *inclusion percentage* has the meaning set forth in § 1.960-2(c)(2).

(10) *Inclusion year*.—The term *inclusion year* means the U.S. taxable year of a controlled foreign corporation which ends during or with the taxable year of a United States shareholder of the controlled foreign corporation in which the United States shareholder includes an amount in income under section 951(a)(1) or 951A(a) with respect to the controlled foreign corporation.

(11) *Income group*.—The term *income group* means a group of income described in paragraph (d)(2)(ii) of this section.

(12) *Partnership CFC*.—The term *partnership CFC* has the meaning set forth in § 1.951A-5(e)(2).

(13) *Passive category*.—The term *passive category* means the separate category of income described in section 904(d)(1)(C) and § 1.904-4(b).

(14) *Previously taxed earnings and profits*.—The term *previously taxed earnings and profits* means earnings and profits described in section 959(c)(1) or (2), including earnings and profits described in section 959(c)(2) by reason of section 951A(f)(1) and § 1.951A-6(b)(1).

(15) *PTEP group*.—The term *PTEP group* has the meaning set forth in § 1.960-3(c)(2).

(16) *PTEP group taxes*.—The term *PTEP group taxes* has the meaning set forth in § 1.960-3(d)(1).

(17) *Recipient controlled foreign corporation*.—The term *recipient controlled foreign corporation* has the meaning set forth in § 1.960-3(b)(2).

(18) *Reclassified previously taxed earnings and profits*.—The term *reclassified previously taxed earnings and profits* has the meaning set forth in § 1.960-3(c)(4).

(19) *Reclassified PTEP group*.—The term *reclassified PTEP group* has the meaning set forth in § 1.960-3(c)(4).

(20) *Residual income group*.—The term *residual income group* has the meaning set forth in paragraph (d)(2)(ii)(D) of this section.

(21) *Section 904 category*.—The term *section 904 category* means a separate category of income described in § 1.904-5(a)(4)(v).

(22) *Section 951A category*.—The term *section 951A category* means the separate category of income described in section 904(d)(1)(A) and § 1.904-4(g).

(23) *Section 959 distribution*.—The term *section 959 distribution* means a section 959(a) distribution or a section 959(b) distribution.

(24) *Section 959(a) distribution*.—The term *section 959(a) distribution* means a distribution excluded from the gross income of a United States shareholder under section 959(a).

(25) *Section 959(b) distribution*.—The term *section 959(b) distribution* means a distribution excluded from the gross income of a controlled foreign corporation for purposes of section 951(a) under section 959(b).

(26) *Section 959(c)(2) PTEP group*.—The term *section 959(c)(2) PTEP group* has the meaning set forth in § 1.960-3(c)(4).

(27) *Subpart F inclusion*.—The term *subpart F inclusion* has the meaning set forth in § 1.960-2(b)(1).

(28) *Subpart F income*.—The term *subpart F income* has the meaning set forth in section 952 and § 1.952-1(a).

(29) *Subpart F income group*.—The term *subpart F income group* has the meaning set forth in paragraph (d)(2)(ii)(B)(*1*) of this section.

(30) *Tested foreign income taxes*.—The term *tested foreign income taxes* has the meaning set forth in § 1.960-2(c)(3).

(31) *Tested income*.—The term *tested income* means the amount with respect to a controlled foreign corporation that is described in section 951A(c)(2)(A) and § 1.951A-2(b)(1).

(32) *Tested income group*.—The term *tested income group* has the meaning set forth in paragraph (d)(2)(ii)(C) of this section.

(33) *United States shareholder*.—The term *United States shareholder* has the meaning set forth in section 951(b).

(34) *U.S. shareholder partner*.—The term *U.S. shareholder partner* has the meaning set forth in § 1.951A-5(e)(3).

(35) *U.S. shareholder partnership*.—The term *U.S. shareholder partnership* has the meaning set forth in § 1.951A-5(e)(4).

(36) *U.S. taxable year*.—The term *U.S. taxable year* has the same meaning as that of the term *taxable year* set forth in section 7701(a)(23).

(c) *Computational rules*.—(1) *In general*.—For purposes of computing foreign income taxes deemed paid by either a domestic corporation that is a United States shareholder with respect to a controlled foreign corporation under §1.960-2 or 1.960-3 or by a controlled foreign corporation under §1.960-3 for the current taxable year, the following rules apply in the following order, beginning with the lowest-tier controlled foreign corporation in a chain with respect to which the domestic corporation is a United States shareholder:

(i) First, items of gross income of the controlled foreign corporation for the current taxable year other than a section 959(b) distribution are assigned to section 904 categories and included in income groups within those section 904 categories under the rules in paragraph (d)(2) of this section. The receipt of a section 959(b) distribution by the controlled foreign corporation is accounted for under §1.960-3(c)(3).

(ii) Second, deductions (other than for current year taxes) of the controlled foreign corporation for the current taxable year are allocated and apportioned to reduce gross income in the section 904 categories and the income groups within a section 904 category. See paragraph (d)(3)(i) of this section. Additionally, the functional currency amounts of current year taxes of the controlled foreign corporation for the current taxable year are allocated and apportioned to reduce gross income in the section 904 categories and the income groups within a section 904 category, and to reduce earnings and profits in any PTEP groups that were increased as provided in paragraph (c)(1)(i) of this section. See paragraph (d)(3)(ii) of this section. For purposes of computing foreign taxes deemed paid, current year taxes allocated and apportioned to income groups and PTEP groups in the section 904 categories are translated into U.S. dollars in accordance with section 986(a). See paragraph (c)(3) of this section.

(iii) Third, current year taxes deemed paid under section 960(a) and (d) by the domestic corporation with respect to income of the controlled foreign corporation are computed under the rules of §1.960-2. In addition, foreign income taxes deemed paid under section 960(b)(2) with respect to the receipt of a section 959(b) distribution by the controlled foreign corporation are computed under the rules of §1.960-3(b).

(iv) Fourth, any previously taxed earnings and profits of the controlled foreign corporation resulting from subpart F inclusions and GILTI inclusion amounts with respect to the controlled foreign corporation's current taxable year are separated from other earnings and profits of the controlled foreign corporation and added to an annual PTEP account, and a PTEP group within the PTEP account, under the rules of §1.960-3(c).

(v) Fifth, paragraphs (c)(1)(i) through (iv) of this section are repeated for each next higher-tier controlled foreign corporation in the chain.

(vi) Sixth, with respect to the highest-tier controlled foreign corporation in a chain that is owned directly (or indirectly through a partnership) by the domestic corporation, foreign income taxes that are deemed paid under section 960(b)(1) in connection with the receipt of a section 959(a) distribution by the domestic corporation are computed under the rules of §1.960-3(b).

(2) *Inclusion of current year items.*—For a current taxable year, the items of income and deductions (including for taxes), and the U.S. dollar amounts of current year taxes, that are included in the computations described in this section and assigned to income groups and PTEP groups for the taxable year are the items that the controlled foreign corporation accrues and takes into account during the current taxable year.

(3) *Functional currency and translation.*—The computations described in this paragraph (c) that relate to income and earnings and profits are made in the functional currency of the controlled foreign corporation (as determined under section 985), and references to taxes deemed paid are to U.S. dollar amounts (translated in accordance with section 986(a)).

(d) *Computing income in a section 904 category and an income group within a section 904 category.*—(1) *Scope.*—This paragraph (d) provides rules for assigning gross income (including gains) of a controlled foreign corporation for the current taxable year to a section 904 category and income group within a section 904 category, and for allocating and apportioning deductions (including losses and current year taxes) and the U.S. dollar amount of current year taxes of the controlled foreign corporation for the current taxable year among the section 904 categories, income groups within a section 904 category, and PTEP groups. For rules regarding maintenance of previously taxed earnings and profits in an annual PTEP account, and assignment of those previously taxed earnings and profits to PTEP groups, see §1.960-3.

(2) *Assignment of gross income to section 904 categories and income groups within a category.*—(i) *Assigning items of gross income to section 904 categories.*—Items of gross income of the controlled foreign corporation for the current taxable year are first assigned to a section 904 category of the controlled foreign corporation under §§1.904-4 and 1.904-5, and under §1.960-3(c)(1) in the case of gross income relating to a section 959(b) distribution received by the controlled foreign corporation. Income of a controlled foreign corporation, other than gross income relating to a section 959(b) distribution, cannot be assigned to the section 951A category or the foreign branch category. *See* §1.904-4(f) and (g).

(ii) *Grouping gross income within a section 904 category.*—(A) *In general.*—Gross income within a section 904 category is assigned to an income group under the rules of this paragraph (d)(2)(ii), or to a PTEP group under the rules of §1.960-3(c)(3). Gross income other than a section 959(b) distribution is assigned to a subpart F income group, tested income group, or residual income group.

(B) *Subpart F income groups.*—*(1) In general.*—The term *subpart F income group* means an income group within a section 904 category that consists of income that is described in paragraph (d)(2)(ii)(B)(2) of this section. Gross income that is treated as a single item of income under §1.954-1(c)(1)(iii) is in a separate subpart F income group under paragraph (d)(2)(ii)(B)(2)(*i*) of this section. Items of gross income that give rise to income described in paragraph (d)(2)(ii)(B)(2)(*ii*) of this section are aggregated and treated as gross income in a separate subpart F income group. Similarly, items of gross income that give rise to income described in each one of paragraphs (d)(2)(ii)(B)(2)(*iii*) through (*v*) of this section are aggregated and treated as gross income in a separate subpart F income group.

(2) *Income in subpart F income groups*.—The income included in subpart F income groups is:

(*i*) Items of foreign base company income treated as a single item of income under § 1.954-1(c)(1)(iii);

(*ii*) Insurance income described in section 952(a)(1);

(*iii*) Income subject to the international boycott factor described in section 952(a)(3);

(*iv*) Income from certain bribes, kickbacks and other payments described in section 952(a)(4); and

(*v*) Income subject to section 901(j) described in section 952(a)(5).

(C) *Tested income groups*.—The term *tested income group* means an income group that consists of tested income within a section 904 category. Items of gross tested income in each section 904 category are aggregated and treated as gross income in a separate tested income group.

(D) *Residual income group*.—The term *residual income group* means the income group within a section 904 category that consists of income not described in paragraph (d)(2)(ii)(B) or (C) of this section.

(E) *Examples*.—The following examples illustrate the application of this paragraph (d)(2)(ii).

(1) *Example 1: Subpart F income groups*—(*i*) *Facts*. CFC, a controlled foreign corporation, is incorporated in Country X. CFC uses the "u" as its functional currency. At all relevant times, 1u=$1. CFC earns from sources outside of Country X portfolio dividend income of 100,000u, portfolio interest income of 1,500,000u, and 70,000u of royalty income that is not derived from the active conduct of a trade or business. CFC also earns 50,000u from the sale of personal property to a related person for use outside of Country X that gives rise to foreign base company sales income under section 954(d). Finally, CFC earns 45,000u for performing consulting services outside of Country X for related persons that gives rise to foreign base company services income under section 954(e). None of the income is taxed by Country X. The dividend income is subject to a 15 percent third-country withholding tax after application of the applicable income tax treaty. The interest income and the royalty income are subject to no third-country withholding tax. CFC incurs no expenses.

(*ii*) *Analysis*. Under paragraph (d)(2)(i) of this section and § 1.904-4, the interest income, dividend income, and royalty income are passive category income and the sales and consulting income are general category income. Under paragraph (d)(2)(ii)(B) of this section, CFC has a separate subpart F income group within the passive category with respect to the 100,000u of dividend income, which is foreign personal holding company income described in § 1.954-1(c)(1)(iii)(A)(*1*)(*i*) (dividends, interest, rents, royalties and annuities) that falls within a single group of income under § 1.904-4(c)(3)(i) for passive income that is subject to withholding tax of fifteen percent or greater. CFC also has a separate subpart F income group within the passive category with respect to the 1,500,000u of interest income and the 70,000u of royalty income (in total 1,570,000u) which together are foreign personal holding company income described in § 1.954-1(c)(1)(iii)(A)(*1*)(*i*) (dividends, interest, rents, royalties and annuities) that falls within a single group of income under § 1.904-4(c)(3)(iii) for passive income that is subject to no withholding tax or other foreign tax. With respect to its 50,000u of sales income, CFC has a separate subpart F income group with respect to foreign base company sales income described in § 1.954-1(c)(1)(iii)(A)(*2*)(*i*) within the general category. With respect to its 45,000u of services income, CFC has a separate subpart F income group with respect to foreign base company services income described in § 1.954-1(c)(1)(iii)(A)(*2*)(*ii*) within the general category.

(2) *Example 2: Tested income groups*—(*i*) *Facts*. CFC, a controlled foreign corporation, is incorporated in Country X. CFC uses the "u" as its functional currency. At all relevant times, 1u=$1. CFC earns 500u from the sale of goods to unrelated parties. CFC also earns 75u for performing consulting services for unrelated parties. All of its income is gross tested income. CFC incurs no deductions.

(*ii*) *Analysis*. Under paragraph (d)(2)(i) of this section and section 904 and § 1.904-4, the sales income and services income are both general category income. Under paragraph (d)(2)(ii)(C) of this section, with respect to the 500u of sales income and 75u services income (in total 575u), CFC has one tested income group within the general category.

(3) *Allocation and apportionment of deductions among section 904 categories, income groups within a section 904 category, and certain PTEP groups*.—(i) *In general*.—Gross income of the controlled foreign corporation in each income group within each section 904 category is reduced by deductions (including losses) of the controlled foreign corporation for the current taxable year under the following rules.

(A) First, the rules of sections 861 through 865 and 904(d) and the regulations under those sections (taking into account the rules of section 954(b)(5) and § 1.954-1(c), and section 951A(c)(2)(A)(ii) and § 1.951A-2(c)(3), as appropriate) apply to allocate and apportion to reduce gross income (or create a loss) in each section 904 category and income group within a section 904 category any deductions of the controlled foreign corporation that are definitely related to less than all of the controlled foreign corporation's gross income as a class. See paragraph (d)(3)(ii) of this section for special rules for allocating and apportioning current year taxes to section 904 categories, income groups, and PTEP groups.

(B) Second, related person interest expense is allocated to and apportioned among the subpart F income groups within the passive category under the principles of § 1.904-5(c)(2) and § 1.954-1(c)(1)(i).

(C) Third, any remaining deductions are allocated and apportioned to reduce gross income (or create a loss) in the section 904 categories and income groups within each section 904 category under the rules referenced in paragraph (d)(3)(i)(A) of this section. No deductions of the controlled foreign corporation for the current taxable year other than a deduction for current year taxes imposed solely by reason of the receipt of a section 959(b) distribution are allocated or apportioned to reduce earnings and profits in a PTEP group.

(ii) *Allocation and apportionment of current year taxes.*—(A) *In general.*—Current year taxes are allocated and apportioned among the section 904 categories under the rules of § 1.904-6(a)(1)(i) and (ii) on the basis of the amount of taxable income computed under foreign law in each section 904 category that is included in the foreign tax base. Current year taxes in a section 904 category are then allocated and apportioned among the income groups within a section 904 category under the principles of § 1.904-6(a)(1)(i) and (ii). If the amount of previously taxed earnings and profits in a PTEP group is increased in the current taxable year of the controlled foreign corporation under § 1.960-3(c)(3) by reason of the receipt of a section 959(b) distribution, then for purposes of allocating and apportioning current year taxes that are imposed solely by reason of the receipt of the section 959(b) distribution under this paragraph (d)(3)(ii)(A), the PTEP group is treated as an income group within the section 904 category. In applying § 1.904-6(a)(1)(i) and (ii) for purposes of this paragraph (d)(3)(ii)(A), the gross items of income and deduction calculated under foreign law that are included in a section 904 category, income group, or PTEP group that is treated as an income group are the items that are included in taxable income under foreign law for the foreign taxable year of the controlled foreign corporation that ends with or within the controlled foreign corporation's current taxable year. For purposes of determining foreign income taxes deemed paid under the rules in §§ 1.960-2 and 1.960-3, the U.S. dollar amounts of current year taxes are assigned to the section 904 categories, income groups, and PTEP groups, if any, to which the current year taxes are allocated and apportioned.

(B) *Base and timing differences.*—*(1) In general.*—Current year taxes that are attributable to a base difference described in § 1.904-6(a)(1)(iv) are not allocated and apportioned to any subpart F income group, tested income group or PTEP group, but are treated as related to income in the residual income group. Except as provided in paragraph (d)(3)(ii)(B)(*2*) of this section, current year taxes that are attributable to a timing difference described in § 1.904-6(a)(1)(iv) are treated as related to the appropriate section 904 category and income group within a section 904 category to which the particular tax would be assigned if the income on which the tax is imposed were recognized under Federal income tax principles in the year in which the tax was imposed.

(2) Tax on previously taxed earnings and profits.—Current year taxes imposed solely by reason of the controlled foreign corporation's receipt of a section 959(b) distribution are not allocated and apportioned under the general rule for timing differences but are allocated or apportioned to a PTEP group. Current year taxes imposed with respect to previously taxed earnings and profits by reason of any other timing difference are allocated or apportioned, under the general rule described in paragraph (d)(3)(ii)(B)(*1*) of this section, to the income group to which the income that gave rise to the previously taxed earnings and profits was assigned in the inclusion year. For example, a net basis tax imposed on a controlled foreign corporation's receipt of a section 959(b) distribution by the corporation's country of residence is allocated or apportioned to a PTEP group. Similarly, a withholding tax imposed with respect to a controlled foreign corporation's receipt of a section 959(b) distribution is allocated and apportioned to a PTEP group. In contrast, a withholding tax imposed on a disregarded payment from a disregarded entity to its controlled foreign corporation owner is treated as a timing difference and is never treated as related to a PTEP group, even if all of the controlled foreign corporation's earnings are previously taxed earnings and profits, because the tax is not imposed solely by reason of a section 959(b) distribution. Such a withholding tax, however, may be treated as related to a subpart F income group or tested income group under the general rule for timing differences.

(e) *No deemed paid credit for current year taxes related to residual income group.*—Current year taxes paid or accrued by a controlled foreign corporation that are allocated and apportioned under paragraph (d)(3)(ii) of this section to a residual income group cannot be deemed paid under section 960 for any taxable year.

(f) *Example.*—The following example illustrates the application of this section and § 1.960-3.

(1) *Facts*—(i) *Income of CFC1 and CFC2.* CFC1, a controlled foreign corporation, conducts business in Country X. CFC1 uses the "u" as its functional currency. At all relevant times, 1u=$1. CFC1 owns all of the stock of CFC2, a controlled foreign corporation. CFC1 and CFC2 both use the calendar year as their U.S. and foreign taxable years. In 2019, CFC1 earns 2,000,000u of gross income that is foreign oil and gas extraction income, within the meaning of section 907(c)(1), and 2,000,000u of interest income from unrelated persons, for both U.S. and Country X tax law purposes. Country X exempts interest income from tax. In 2019, CFC1 also receives a section 959(b) distribution from CFC2 of 4,000,000u of previously taxed earnings and profits attributable to an inclusion under section 965(a) for CFC2's 2017 U.S. taxable year. The inclusion under section 965(a) was income in the general category. There are no PTEP group taxes associated with the previously taxed earnings and profits distributed by CFC2 at the level of CFC2. The section 959(b) distribution is treated as a dividend taxable to CFC1 under Country X law. In 2019, CFC2 earns no gross income and receives no distributions.

(ii) *Pre-tax deductions of CFC1 and CFC2.* For both U.S. and Country X tax purposes, in 2019, CFC1 incurs 1,500,000u of deductible expenses other than current year taxes that are allocable to all gross income. For U.S. tax purposes, under §§ 1.861-8 through 1.861-14T, 750,000u of such deductions are apportioned to each of CFC1's foreign oil and gas extraction income and interest income. Under Country X law, 1,000,000u of deductions are allocated and apportioned to the 4,000,000u treated as a dividend, and 500,000u of deductions are allocated and apportioned to the 2,000,000u of foreign oil and gas extraction income. Under Country X law, no deductions are allocable to the interest income. Country X imposes tax of 900,000u on a base of 4,500,000u (6,000,000u gross income − 1,500,000u deductions) consisting of 3,000,000u (4,000,000u − 1,000,000u) attributable to CFC1's section 959(b) distribution and 1,500,000u (2,000,000u − 500,000u) attributable to CFC1's foreign oil and gas extraction income. In 2019, CFC2 has no expenses (including current year taxes).

(iii) *United States shareholders of CFC1.* All of the stock of CFC1 is owned (within the meaning of section 958(a)) by corporate United States shareholders that use the calendar year as their U.S. taxable year. In 2019, the United States shareholders of CFC1 include in gross income subpart F inclusions in the passive category totaling $1,250,000 with respect to 1,250,000u of subpart F income of CFC1.

(2) *Analysis*—(i) *CFC2.* Under paragraph (c)(1) of this section, the computational rules of paragraph (c)(1) of this section are applied beginning with CFC2. However, CFC2 has no gross income or expenses in 2019 (the "current taxable year"). Accordingly, the computational rules described in paragraph (c)(1)(i) through (iv) of this section are not relevant with respect to CFC2. Under paragraph (c)(1)(v) of this section, the rules in paragraph (c)(1)(i) through (iv) of this section are then applied to CFC1.

(ii) *CFC1.* (A) *Step 1.* Under paragraph (c)(1)(i) of this section, CFC1's items of gross income for the current taxable year are assigned to section 904 categories and included in income groups within those section 904 categories. In addition, CFC1's receipt of a section 959(b) distribution is assigned to a PTEP group. Under paragraph (d)(2)(i) of this section and § 1.904-4, the interest income is passive category income and the foreign oil and gas extraction income is general category income. Under paragraph (d)(2)(ii) of this section, the 2,000,000u of interest income is assigned to a subpart F income group (the "subpart F income group") within the passive category because it is foreign personal holding company income described in § 1.954-1(c)(1)(iii)(A)(*1*)(*i*) that falls within a single group of income under § 1.904-4(c)(3)(iii) for passive income that is subject to no withholding tax or other foreign tax. The 2,000,000u of foreign oil and gas extraction income is assigned to the residual income group within the general category. Under § 1.960-3(c), the 4,000,000u section 959(b) distribution is assigned to the PTEP group described in § 1.960-3(c)(2)(vii) within the 2017 annual PTEP account (the "PTEP group") within the general category.

(B) *Step 2—(1) Allocation and apportionment of deductions for expenses other than taxes.* Under paragraph (c)(1)(ii) of this section, CFC1's deductions for the current taxable year are allocated and apportioned among the section 904 categories, income groups within a section 904 category, and any PTEP groups that were increased as provided in paragraph (c)(1)(i) of this section. Under paragraph (d)(3)(i) of this section and § 1.861-8 through 1.861-14T, 750,000u of deductions are allocated and apportioned to the residual income group within the general category, and 750,000u of deductions are allocated and apportioned to the subpart F income group within the passive category. Therefore, CFC1 has 1,250,000u (2,000,000u − 750,000u) of pre-tax income attributable to the residual income group within the general category and 1,250,000u (2,000,000u − 750,000u) of pre-tax income attributable to the subpart F income group within the passive category. For U.S. tax purposes, no deductions other than current year taxes are allocated and apportioned to the 4,000,000u in CFC1's PTEP group.

(2) *Allocation and apportionment of current year taxes.* Under paragraph (c)(1)(ii) of this section, CFC1's current year taxes are allocated and apportioned among the section 904 categories, income groups within a section 904 category, and any PTEP groups that were increased as provided in paragraph (c)(1)(i) of this section. Under paragraphs (d)(3)(i) and (ii) of this section, for purposes of allocating and apportioning taxes to reduce the income in a section 904 category, an income group, or PTEP group, § 1.904-6(a)(1) and (ii) are applied to determine the amount of taxable income computed under Country X law in each section 904 category, income group, and PTEP group that is included in the Country X tax base. For Country X purposes, 1,000,000u of deductions are apportioned to CFC1's PTEP group within the general category, 500,000u of deductions are apportioned to the residual income group within the general category, and no deductions are apportioned to the subpart F income group in the passive category. Therefore, for Country X purposes, CFC1 has 3,000,000u of income attributable to the PTEP group within the general category, 1,500,000u of income attributable to the residual income group within the general category, and no income attributable to the subpart F income group within the passive category. Under paragraph (d)(3)(ii) of this section, 600,000u (3,000,000u/4,500,000u x 900,000u) of the 900,000u current year taxes paid by CFC1 are related to the PTEP group within the general category, and 300,000u (1,500,000u/4,500,000u x 900,000u) are related to the residual income group within the general category. No current year taxes are allocated or apportioned to the subpart F income group within the passive category because the interest expense is exempt from Country X tax. Thus, for U.S. tax purposes, CFC1 has 3,400,000u of previously taxed earnings and profits (4,000,000u − 600,000u) in the PTEP group within the general category, 1,250,000u of income in the subpart F income group within the passive category, and 950,000u of income (1,250,000u − 300,000u) in the residual income group within the general category. For purposes of determining foreign taxes deemed paid under section 960, CFC1 has $600,000 of foreign income taxes in the PTEP group within the general category and $300,000 of current year taxes in the residual income group within the general category. Under paragraph (e) of this section, the United States shareholders of CFC1 cannot claim a credit with respect to the $300,000 of taxes on CFC1's income in the residual income group.

(C) *Step 3.* Under paragraph (c)(1)(iii) of this section, the United States shareholders of CFC1 compute current year taxes deemed paid under section 960(a) and (d) and the rules of § 1.960-2. None of the Country X tax is allocated to CFC1's subpart F income group. Therefore, there are no current year taxes deemed paid by CFC1's United States shareholders with respect to their passive category subpart F inclusions. See § 1.960-2(b)(5) and (c)(7) for examples of the application of section 960(a) and (d) and the rules in §1.960-2. Additionally, under paragraph (c)(1)(iii) of this section, foreign income taxes deemed paid under section 960(b)(2) by CFC1 are determined with respect to the section 959(b) distribution from CFC2 under the rules of §1.960-3. There are no PTEP group taxes associated with the previously taxed earnings and profits distributed by CFC2 in the hands of CFC2. Therefore, there are no foreign income taxes deemed paid by CFC1 under section 960(b)(2) with respect to the section 959(b) distribution from CFC2. See §1.960-3(e) for examples of the application of section 960(b) and the rules in §1.960-3.

(D) *Step 4*. Under paragraph (c)(1)(iv) of this section, previously taxed earnings and profits resulting from subpart F inclusions and GILTI inclusion amounts with respect to CFC1's current taxable year are separated from CFC1's other earnings and profits and added to an annual PTEP account and PTEP group within the PTEP account, under the rules of §1.960-3(c). The United States shareholders of CFC1 include in gross income subpart F inclusions totaling $1,250,000 with respect to 1,250,000u of subpart F income of CFC1, and the subpart F inclusions are passive category income. Therefore, under §1.960-3(c)(2), 1,250,000u of previously taxed earnings and profits resulting from the subpart F inclusions is added to CFC1's PTEP group described in §1.960-3(c)(2)(x) within the 2019 annual PTEP account within the passive category.

(E) *Step 5*. Paragraph (c)(1)(v) of this section does not apply because CFC1 is the highest-tier controlled foreign corporation in the chain.

(F) *Step 6*. Paragraph (c)(1)(vi) of this section does not apply because CFC1 did not make a section 959(a) distribution.

Par. 23. Section 1.960-2 is revised to read as follows:

§1.960-2. Foreign income taxes deemed paid under sections 960(a) and (d).—(a) *Scope*.—Paragraph (b) of this section provides rules for computing the amount of foreign income taxes deemed paid by a domestic corporation that is a United States shareholder of a controlled foreign corporation under section 960(a). Paragraph (c) of this section provides rules for computing the amount of foreign income taxes deemed paid by a domestic corporation that is a United States shareholder of a controlled foreign corporation under section 960(d).

(b) *Foreign income taxes deemed paid under section 960(a)*.—(1) *In general*.—If a domestic corporation that is a United States shareholder of a controlled foreign corporation includes in gross income under section 951(a)(1)(A) its pro rata share of the subpart F income of the controlled foreign corporation (a *subpart F inclusion*), the domestic corporation is deemed to have paid the amount of the controlled foreign corporation's foreign income taxes that are properly attributable to the items of income in a subpart F income group of the controlled foreign corporation that give rise to the subpart F inclusion of the domestic corporation that is attributable to the subpart F income group. For each section 904 category, the domestic corporation is deemed to have paid foreign income taxes equal to the sum of the controlled foreign corporation's foreign income taxes that are properly attributable to the items of income in the subpart F income groups to which the subpart F inclusion is attributable. See §1.904-6(b)(1) for rules on assigning the foreign income tax to a section 904 category. No foreign income taxes are deemed paid under section 960(a) with respect to an inclusion under section 951(a)(1)(B).

(2) *Properly attributable*.—The amount of the controlled foreign corporation's foreign income taxes that are properly attributable to the items of income in the subpart F income group of the controlled foreign corporation to which a subpart F inclusion is attributable equals the domestic corporation's proportionate share of the current year taxes of the controlled foreign corporation that are allocated and apportioned under §1.960-1(d)(3)(ii) to the subpart F income group. No other foreign income taxes are considered properly attributable to an item of income of the controlled foreign corporation.

(3) *Proportionate share*.—(i) *In general*.—A domestic corporation's proportionate share of the current year taxes of a controlled foreign corporation that are allocated and apportioned under §1.960-1(d)(3)(ii) to a subpart F income group within a section 904 category of the controlled foreign corporation is equal to the total U.S. dollar amount of current year taxes that are allocated and apportioned under §1.960-1(d)(3)(ii) to the subpart F income group multiplied by a fraction (not to exceed one), the numerator of which is the portion of the domestic corporation's subpart F inclusion that is attributable to the subpart F income group and the denominator of which is the total net income in the subpart F income group, both determined in the functional currency of the controlled foreign corporation. If the numerator or denominator of the fraction is zero or less than zero, then the proportionate share of the current year taxes that are allocated and apportioned under §1.960-1(d)(3)(ii) to the subpart F income group is zero.

(ii) *Effect of qualified deficits*.—Neither an accumulated deficit nor any prior year deficit in the earnings and profits of a controlled foreign corporation reduces its net income in a subpart F income group. Accordingly, any such deficit does not affect the denominator of the fraction described in paragraph (b)(3)(i) of this section. However, the first sentence of this paragraph (b)(3)(ii) does not affect the application of section 952(c)(1)(B) for purposes of determining the domestic corporation's subpart F inclusion. Any reduction to the domestic corporation's subpart F inclusion under section 952(c)(1)(B) is reflected in the numerator of the fraction described in paragraph (b)(3)(i) of this section.

(iii) *Effect of current year E&P limitation or chain deficit*.—To the extent that an amount of income in a subpart F income group is excluded from the subpart F income of the controlled foreign corporation under section 952(c)(1)(A) or (C), the net income in the subpart F income group that is the denominator of the fraction described in paragraph (b)(3)(i) of this section is reduced (but not below zero) by the amount excluded. The domestic corporation's subpart F inclusion that is the numerator of the fraction described in paragraph (b)(3)(i) of this section is based on the controlled foreign corporation's subpart F income computed with the application of section 952(c)(1)(A) and (C).

(4) *Domestic partnerships.*—For purposes of applying this paragraph (b), in the case of a domestic partnership that is a U.S. shareholder partnership with respect to a partnership CFC, the distributive share of a U.S. shareholder partner of the U.S. shareholder partnership's subpart F inclusion with respect to the partnership CFC is treated as a subpart F inclusion of the U.S. shareholder partner with respect to the partnership CFC.

(5) *Example.*—The following example illustrates the application of this paragraph (b).

(i) *Facts.* USP, a domestic corporation, owns 80% of the stock of CFC, a controlled foreign corporation. The remaining portion of the stock of CFC is owned by an unrelated person. USP and CFC both use the calendar year as their U.S. taxable year, and CFC also uses the calendar year as its foreign taxable year. CFC uses the "u" as its functional currency. At all relevant times, 1u=$1. For its U.S. taxable year ending December 31, 2018, after the application of the rules in § 1.960-1(d) the income of CFC after foreign taxes is assigned to the following income groups: 1,000,000u of dividend income in a subpart F income group within the passive category ("subpart F income group 1"); 2,400,000u of gain from commodities transactions in a subpart F income group within the passive category ("subpart F income group 2"); and 1,800,000u of foreign base company services income in a subpart F income group within the general category ("subpart F income group 3"). CFC has current year taxes, translated into U.S. dollars, of $740,000 that are allocated and apportioned as follows: $50,000 to subpart F income group 1; $240,000 to subpart F income group 2; and $450,000 to subpart F income group 3. USP has a subpart F inclusion with respect to CFC of 4,160,000u = $4,160,000, of which 800,000u is attributable to subpart F income group 1, 1,920,000u to subpart F income group 2, and 1,440,000u to subpart F income group 3.

(ii) *Analysis*—(A) *Passive category.* Under paragraphs (b)(2) and (3) of this section, the amount of CFC's current year taxes that are properly attributable to items of income in subpart F income group 1 to which a subpart F inclusion is attributable equals USP's proportionate share of the current year taxes that are allocated and apportioned under § 1.960-1(d)(3)(ii) to subpart F income group 1, which is $40,000 ($50,000 x 800,000u/1,000,000u). Under paragraphs (b)(2) and (3) of this section, the amount of CFC's current year taxes that are properly attributable to items of income in subpart F income group 2 to which a subpart F inclusion is attributable equals USP's proportionate share of the current year taxes that are allocated and apportioned under § 1.960-1(d)(3)(ii) to subpart F income group 2, which is $192,000 ($240,000 x 1,920,000u/2,400,000u). Accordingly, under paragraph (b)(1), USP is deemed to have paid $232,000 ($40,000 + $192,000) of passive category foreign income taxes of CFC with respect to its $2,720,000 subpart F inclusion in the passive category.

(B) *General category.* Under paragraphs (b)(2) and (3) of this section, the amount of CFC's current year taxes that are properly attributable items of income in subpart F income group 3 to which a subpart F inclusion is attributable equals USP's proportionate share of the foreign income taxes that are allocated and apportioned under § 1.960-1(d)(3)(ii) to subpart F income group 3, which is $360,000 ($450,000 x 1,440,000u/1,800,000u). CFC has no other subpart F income groups within the general category. Accordingly, under paragraph (b)(1) of this section, USP is deemed to have paid $360,000 of general category foreign income taxes of CFC with respect to its $1,440,000 subpart F inclusion in the general category.

(c) *Foreign income taxes deemed paid under section 960(d).*—(1) *In general.*—If a domestic corporation that is a United States shareholder of one or more controlled foreign corporations includes an amount in gross income under section 951A(a) and § 1.951A-1(b), the domestic corporation is deemed to have paid an amount of foreign income taxes equal to 80 percent of the product of its inclusion percentage multiplied by the sum of all tested foreign income taxes in the tested income group within each section 904 category of the controlled foreign corporation or corporations.

(2) *Inclusion percentage.*—The term *inclusion percentage* means, with respect to a domestic corporation that is a United States shareholder of one or more controlled foreign corporations, the domestic corporation's GILTI inclusion amount divided by the aggregate amount described in section 951A(c)(1)(A) and § 1.951A-1(c)(2)(i) with respect to the United States shareholder.

(3) *Tested foreign income taxes.*—The term *tested foreign income taxes* means, with respect to a domestic corporation that is a United States shareholder of a controlled foreign corporation, the amount of the controlled foreign corporation's foreign income taxes that are properly attributable to tested income taken into account by the domestic corporation under section 951A and § 1.951A-1.

(4) *Properly attributable.*—The amount of the controlled foreign corporation's foreign income taxes that are properly attributable to tested income taken into account by the domestic corporation under section 951A(a) and § 1.951A-1(b) equals the domestic corporation's proportionate share of the current year taxes of the controlled foreign corporation that are allocated and apportioned under § 1.960-1(d)(3)(ii) to the tested income group within each section 904 category of the controlled foreign corporation. No other foreign income taxes are considered properly attributable to tested income.

(5) *Proportionate share.*—A domestic corporation's proportionate share of current year taxes of a controlled foreign corporation that are allocated and apportioned under § 1.960-1(d)(3)(ii) to a tested income group within a section 904 category of the controlled foreign corporation is the U.S. dollar amount of current year taxes that are allocated and apportioned under § 1.960-1(d)(3)(ii) to a tested income group within a section 904 category of the controlled foreign corporation multiplied by a fraction (not to exceed one), the numerator of which is the portion of the tested income of the controlled foreign corporation in the tested income

group within the section 904 category that is included in computing the domestic corporation's aggregate amount described in section 951A(c)(1)(A) and § 1.951A-1(c)(2)(i), and the denominator of which is the income in the tested income group within the section 904 category, both determined in the functional currency of the controlled foreign corporation. If the numerator or denominator of the fraction is zero or less than zero, the domestic corporation's proportionate share of the current year taxes allocated and apportioned under § 1.960-1(d)(3)(ii) to the tested income group is zero.

(6) *Domestic partnerships.*—See § 1.951A-5 for rules regarding the determination of the GILTI inclusion amount of a U.S. shareholder partner.

(7) *Examples.*—The following examples illustrate the application of this paragraph (c).

(i) *Example 1: Directly owned controlled foreign corporation*—(A) *Facts.* USP, a domestic corporation, owns 100% of the stock of a number of controlled foreign corporations, including CFC1. USP and CFC1 each use the calendar year as their U.S. taxable year. CFC1 uses the "u" as its functional currency. At all relevant times, 1u=$1. For its U.S. taxable year ending December 31, 2018, after application of the rules in § 1.960-1(d), the income of CFC1 is assigned to a single income group: 2,000u of income from the sale of goods in a tested income group within the general category ("tested income group"). CFC1 has current year taxes, translated into U.S. dollars, of $400 that are all allocated and apportioned to the tested income group. For its U.S. taxable year ending December 31, 2018, USP has a GILTI inclusion amount determined by reference to all of its controlled foreign corporations, including CFC1, of $6,000, and an aggregate amount described in section 951A(c)(1)(A) and § 1.951A-1(c)(2)(i) of $10,000. All of the income in CFC1's tested income group is included in computing USP's aggregate amount described in section 951A(c)(1)(A) and § 1.951A-1(c)(2)(i).

(B) *Analysis.* Under paragraph (c)(5) of this section, USP's proportionate share of the current year taxes that are allocated and apportioned under § 1.960-1(d)(3)(ii) to CFC1's tested income group is $400 ($400 x 2,000u/2,000u). Therefore, under paragraph (c)(4) of this section, the amount of current year taxes properly attributable to tested income taken into account by USP under section 951A(a) and § 1.951A-1(b) is $400. Under paragraph (c)(3) of this section, USP's tested foreign income taxes with respect to CFC1 are $400. Under paragraph (c)(2) of this section, USP's inclusion percentage is 60% ($6,000/$10,000). Accordingly, under paragraph (c)(1) of this section, USP is deemed to have paid $192 of the foreign income taxes of CFC1 (80% x 60% x $400).

(ii) *Example 2: Controlled foreign corporation owned through domestic partnership*—(A) *Facts*—(*1*) US1, a domestic corporation, owns 95% of PRS, a domestic partnership. The remaining 5% of PRS is owned by US2, a domestic corporation that is unrelated to US1. PRS owns all of the stock of CFC1, a controlled foreign corporation. In addition, US1 owns all of the stock of CFC2, a controlled foreign corporation. US1, US2, PRS, CFC1, and CFC2 all use the calendar year as their taxable year. CFC1 and CFC2 both use the "u" as their functional currency. At all relevant times, 1u=$1. For its U.S. taxable year ending December 31, 2018, after application of the rules in § 1.960-1(d), the income of CFC1 is assigned to a single income group: 300u of income from the sale of goods in a tested income group within the general category ("CFC1's tested income group"). CFC1 has current year taxes, translated into U.S. dollars, of $100 that are all allocated and apportioned to CFC1's tested income group. The income of CFC2 is also assigned to a single income group: 200u of income from the sale of goods in a tested income group within the general category ("CFC2's tested income group"). CFC2 has current year taxes, translated into U.S. dollars, of $20 that are allocated and apportioned to CFC2's tested income group.

(*2*) In the same year, US1 is a U.S. shareholder partner with respect to CFC1, a partnership CFC, and accordingly, determines its GILTI inclusion amount under § 1.951A-5(c), as if US1 owned (within the meaning of section 958(a)) 95% of the stock of CFC1. Taking into account both CFC1 and CFC2, US1 has a GILTI inclusion amount in the general category of $485, and an aggregate amount described in section 951A(c)(1)(A) and § 1.951A-1(c)(2)(i) within the general category of $485. 285u (95% x 300u) of the income in CFC1's tested income group and 200u of the income in CFC2's tested income group is included in computing US1's aggregate amount described in section 951A(c)(1)(A) and § 1.951A-1(c)(2)(i) within the general category. Because US2 is not a U.S. shareholder partner with respect to CFC1, US2 does not take into account CFC1's tested income in determining its GILTI inclusion amount. However, under § 1.951A-5(b)(2), US2 includes in income $15, its distributive share of PRS's GILTI inclusion amount.

(B) *Analysis*—(*1*) *US1*—(*i*) *CFC1.* Under paragraph (c)(5) and (6) of this section, US1's proportionate share of the current year taxes that are allocated and apportioned under § 1.960-1(d)(3)(ii) to CFC1's tested income group is $95 ($100 x 285u/300u). Therefore, under paragraph (c)(4) of this section, the amount of the current year taxes properly attributable to tested income taken into account by US1 under section 951A(a) and § 1.951A-1(b) is $95. Under paragraph (c)(3) of this section, US1's tested foreign income taxes with respect to CFC1 are $95. Under paragraph (c)(2) of this section, US1's inclusion percentage is 100% ($485/$485). Accordingly, under paragraph (c)(1) of this section, US1 is deemed to have paid $76 of the foreign income taxes of CFC1 (80% x 100% x $95).

(*ii*) *CFC2.* Under paragraph (c)(5) of this section, US1's proportionate share of the foreign income taxes that are allocated and apportioned under § 1.960-1(d)(3)(ii) to CFC2's tested income group is $20 ($20 x 200u/200u). Therefore, under paragraph (c)(4) of this section, the amount of foreign income taxes properly attributable to tested income taken into account by US1 under section 951A(a) and § 1.951A-1(b) is $20. Under paragraph (c)(3) of this section, US1's tested foreign income taxes with respect to CFC2 are $20. Under paragraph (c)(2) of this section, US1's inclusion percentage is 100% ($485/$485). Accordingly, under paragraph (c)(1) of this section, US1 is deemed to have paid $16 of the foreign income taxes of CFC2 (80% x 100% x $20).

(2) *US2.* US2 is not a United States shareholder of CFC1 or CFC2. Accordingly, under paragraph (c)(1) of this section, US2 is not deemed to have paid any of the foreign income taxes of CFC1 or CFC2.

Par. 24. Section 1.960-3 is revised to read as follows:

§1.960-3. Foreign income taxes deemed paid under section 960(b).—(a) *Scope.*—Paragraph (b) of this section provides rules for computing the amount of foreign income taxes deemed paid by a domestic corporation that is a United States shareholder of a controlled foreign corporation, or by a controlled foreign corporation, under section 960(b). Paragraph (c) of this section provides rules for the establishment and maintenance of PTEP groups within an annual PTEP account. Paragraph (d) of this section defines the term PTEP group taxes. Paragraph (e) of this section provides examples illustrating the application of this section.

(b) *Foreign income taxes deemed paid under section 960(b).*—(1) *Foreign income taxes deemed paid by a domestic corporation with respect to a section 959(a) distribution.*—If a controlled foreign corporation makes a distribution to a domestic corporation that is a United States shareholder with respect to the controlled foreign corporation and that distribution is, in whole or in part, a section 959(a) distribution with respect to a PTEP group within a section 904 category, the domestic corporation is deemed to have paid the amount of the foreign corporation's foreign income taxes that are properly attributable to the section 959(a) distribution with respect to the PTEP group and that have not been deemed to have been paid by a domestic corporation under section 960 for the current taxable year or any prior taxable year. See §1.965-5(c)(1)(iii) for rules disallowing credits in relation to a distribution of certain previously taxed earnings and profits resulting from the application of section 965. For each section 904 category, the domestic corporation is deemed to have paid foreign income taxes equal to the sum of the controlled foreign corporation's foreign income taxes that are properly attributable to section 959(a) distributions with respect to all PTEP groups within the section 904 category. See §1.904-6(b)(2) for rules on assigning the foreign income tax to a section 904 category.

(2) *Foreign income taxes deemed paid by a controlled foreign corporation with respect to a section 959(b) distribution.*—If a controlled foreign corporation (*distributing controlled foreign corporation*) makes a distribution to another controlled foreign corporation (*recipient controlled foreign corporation*) and the distribution is, in whole or in part, a section 959(b) distribution from a PTEP group within a section 904 category, the recipient controlled foreign corporation is deemed to have paid the amount of the distributing controlled foreign corporation's foreign income taxes that are properly attributable to the section 959(b) distribution from the PTEP group and that have not been deemed to have been paid by a domestic corporation under section 960 for the current taxable year or any prior taxable year. See §1.904-6(b)(3) for rules on assigning the foreign income tax to a section 904 category.

(3) *Properly attributable.*—The amount of foreign income taxes that are properly attributable to a section 959 distribution from a PTEP group within a section 904 category equals the domestic corporation's or recipient controlled foreign corporation's proportionate share of the PTEP group taxes with respect to the PTEP group within the section 904 category. No other foreign income taxes are considered properly attributable to a section 959 distribution.

(4) *Proportionate share.*—A domestic corporation's or recipient controlled foreign corporation's proportionate share of the PTEP group taxes with respect to a PTEP group within a section 904 category is equal to the total amount of the PTEP group taxes with respect to the PTEP group multiplied by a fraction (not to exceed one), the numerator of which is the amount of the section 959 distribution from the PTEP group, and the denominator of which is the total amount of previously taxed earnings and profits in the PTEP group, both determined in the functional currency of the controlled foreign corporation. If the numerator or denominator of the fraction is zero or less than zero, then the proportionate share of the PTEP group taxes with respect to the PTEP group is zero.

(5) *Domestic partnerships.*—For purposes of applying this paragraph (b), in the case of a domestic partnership that is a U.S. shareholder partnership with respect to a partnership CFC, the distributive share of a U.S. shareholder partner of a U.S. shareholder partnership's section 959(a) distribution from the partnership CFC is treated as a section 959(a) distribution received by the U.S. shareholder partner from the partnership CFC.

(c) *Accounting for previously taxed earnings and profits.*—(1) *Establishment of annual PTEP account.*—A separate, annual account (*annual PTEP account*) must be established for the previously taxed earnings and profits of the controlled foreign corporation to which inclusions under section 951(a) and GILTI inclusion amounts of United States shareholders of the CFC are attributable. Each account must correspond to the inclusion year of the previously taxed earnings and profits and to the section 904 category to which the inclusions under section 951(a) or GILTI inclusion amounts were assigned at the level of the United States shareholders. Accordingly, a controlled foreign corporation may have an annual PTEP account in the section 951A category or a treaty category (as defined in §1.861-13(b)(6)), even though income of the controlled foreign corporation that gave rise to the previously taxed earnings and profits cannot initially be assigned to the section 951A category or a treaty category.

(2) *PTEP groups within an annual PTEP account.*—The amount in an annual PTEP account is further assigned to one or more of the following groups of previously taxed earnings and profits (each, a *PTEP group*) within the account:

(i) Earnings and profits described in section 959(c)(1)(A) by reason of section 951(a)(1)(B) and not by reason of the application of section 959(a)(2);

(ii) Earnings and profits described in section 959(c)(1)(A) that were initially described in section 959(c)(2) by reason of section 965(a);

(iii) Earnings and profits described in section 959(c)(1)(A) that were initially described in section 959(c)(2) by reason of section 965(b)(4)(A);

(iv) Earnings and profits described in section 959(c)(1)(A) that were initially described in section 959(c)(2) by reason of section 951A;

(v) Earnings and profits described in section 959(c)(1)(A) that were initially described in section 959(c)(2) by reason of section 951(a)(1)(A) (other than as a result of the application of section 965);

(vi) Earnings and profits described in section 959(c)(1)(B);

(vii) Earnings and profits described in section 959(c)(2) by reason of section 965(a);

(viii) Earnings and profits described in section 959(c)(2) by reason of section 965(b)(4)(A);

(ix) Earnings and profits described in section 959(c)(2) by reason of section 951A;

(x) Earnings and profits described in section 959(c)(2) by reason of section 951(a)(1)(A) (other than as a result of the application of section 965).

(3) *Accounting for distributions of previously taxed earnings and profits.*—With respect to a recipient controlled foreign corporation that receives a section 959(b) distribution, such distribution amount is added to the annual PTEP account, and PTEP group within the annual PTEP account, that corresponds to the inclusion year and section 904 category of the annual PTEP account, and PTEP group within the annual PTEP account, from which the distributing controlled foreign corporation is treated as making the distribution under section 959 and the regulations under that section. Similarly, with respect to a controlled foreign corporation that makes a section 959 distribution, such distribution amount reduces the annual PTEP account, and PTEP group within the annual PTEP account, that corresponds to the inclusion year and section 904 category of the annual PTEP account, and PTEP group within the annual PTEP account, from which the controlled foreign corporation is treated as making the distribution under section 959 and the regulations under that section. Earnings and profits in a PTEP group are reduced by the amount of current year taxes that are allocated and apportioned to the PTEP group under § 1.960-1(d)(3)(ii), and the U.S. dollar amount of the taxes are added to an account of PTEP group taxes under the rules in paragraph (d)(1) of this section.

(4) *Accounting for reclassifications of earnings and profits described in section 959(c)(2) to earnings and profits described in section 959(c)(1).*—If an amount of previously taxed earnings and profits that is in a PTEP group described in paragraphs (c)(2)(vii) through (x) of this section (each, a *section 959(c)(2) PTEP group*) is reclassified as previously taxed earnings and profits described in section 959(c)(1) (*reclassified previously taxed earnings and profits*), the section 959(c)(2) PTEP group is reduced by the functional currency amount of the reclassified previously taxed earnings and profits. This amount is added to the corresponding PTEP group described in paragraphs (c)(2)(ii) through (v) of this section (each, a *reclassified PTEP group*) in the same section 904 category and same annual PTEP account as the reduced section 959(c)(2) PTEP group.

(d) *PTEP group taxes.*—(1) *In general.*—The term *PTEP group taxes* means the U.S. dollar amount of foreign income taxes (translated in accordance with section 986(a)) that are paid, accrued, or deemed paid with respect to an amount in each PTEP group within an annual PTEP account. The foreign income taxes that are paid, accrued, or deemed paid with respect to a PTEP group within an annual PTEP account of a controlled foreign corporation are—

(i) The sum of—

(A) The current year taxes paid or accrued by the controlled foreign corporation that are allocated and apportioned to the PTEP group under § 1.960-1(d)(3)(ii);

(B) Foreign income taxes that are deemed paid under section 960(b)(2) and paragraph (b)(2) of this section by the controlled foreign corporation with respect to a section 959(b) distribution received by the controlled foreign corporation, the amount of which is added to the PTEP group under paragraph (c)(3) of this section; and

(C) In the case of a reclassified PTEP group of the controlled foreign corporation, reclassified PTEP group taxes that are attributable to the section 959(c)(2) PTEP group that corresponds to the reclassified PTEP group;

(ii) Reduced by—

(A) Foreign income taxes that were deemed paid under section 960(b)(2) and paragraph (b)(2) of this section by another controlled foreign corporation that received a section 959(b) distribution from the controlled foreign corporation, the amount of which is subtracted from the controlled foreign corporation's PTEP group under paragraph (c)(3) of this section;

(B) Foreign income taxes that were deemed paid under section 960(b)(1) and paragraph (b)(1) of this section by a domestic corporation that is a United States shareholder of the controlled foreign corporation that received a section 959(a) distribution from the controlled foreign corporation, the amount of which is subtracted from the controlled foreign corporation's PTEP group under paragraph (c)(3) of this section; and

(C) In the case of a section 959(c)(2) PTEP group of the controlled foreign corporation, reclassified PTEP group taxes.

(2) *Reclassified PTEP group taxes.*—Reclassified PTEP group taxes are foreign income taxes that are initially included in PTEP group taxes with respect to a section 959(c)(2) PTEP group under paragraph (d)(1)(i)(A) or (B) of this section multiplied by a fraction, the numerator of which is the portion of the previously taxed earnings and profits in the section 959(c)(2) PTEP group that become reclassified previously taxed earnings and profits, and the denominator of which is the total previously taxed earnings and profits in the section 959(c)(2) PTEP group.

(3) *Foreign income taxes deemed paid with respect to PTEP groups established for pre-2018 inclusion years.*—Foreign income taxes paid or accrued with respect to an annual PTEP account, and a PTEP group within such account, that was established for an inclusion year that begins before January 1, 2018, are treated as PTEP group

taxes of a controlled foreign corporation for purposes of this section only if those foreign income taxes were—

(i) Paid or accrued in a taxable year of the controlled foreign corporation that began before January 1, 2018;

(ii) Not included in a controlled foreign corporation's post-1986 foreign income taxes (as defined in section 902(c)(2) as in effect on December 21, 2017) used to compute foreign taxes deemed paid under section 902 (as in effect on December 21, 2017) in any taxable year that began before January 1, 2018; and

(iii) Not treated as deemed paid under section 960(a)(3) (as in effect on December 21, 2017) by a domestic corporation that was a United States shareholder of the controlled foreign corporation.

(e) *Examples*.—The following examples illustrate the application of this section.

(1) *Example 1: Establishment of PTEP groups and PTEP accounts*—(i) *Facts*. USP, a domestic corporation, owns all of the stock of CFC1, a controlled foreign corporation. CFC1 owns all of the stock of CFC2, a controlled foreign corporation. USP, CFC1, and CFC2 each use the calendar year as their U.S. taxable year. CFC1 and CFC2 use the "u" as their functional currency. At all relevant times, 1u = $1. With respect to CFC2, USP includes in gross income a subpart F inclusion of 1,000,000u = $1,000,000 for the taxable year ending December 31, 2018. The inclusion is with respect to passive category income. In its U.S. taxable year ending December 31, 2019, CFC2 distributes 1,000,000u to CFC1. CFC2 has no earnings and profits except for the 1,000,000u of previously taxed earnings and profits resulting from USP's 2018 taxable year subpart F inclusion. CFC2's country of organization, Country X, imposes a withholding tax on CFC1 of 300,000u on CFC2's distribution to CFC1. Under § 1.960-1(d)(3)(ii), CFC1's 300,000u of current year taxes are allocated and apportioned to the PTEP group within the annual PTEP account within the section 904 category to which the 1,000,000u of previously taxed earnings and profits are assigned.

(ii) *Analysis*—(A) Under paragraph (c)(1) of this section, a separate annual PTEP account in the passive category for the 2018 taxable year is established for CFC2 as a result of USP's subpart F inclusion. Under paragraph (c)(2) of this section, this account contains one PTEP group, which is described in paragraph (c)(2)(x) of this section.

(B) Under paragraph (c)(3) of this section, in the 2019 taxable year, the 1,000,000u related to the section 959(b) distribution from CFC2 is added to CFC1's annual PTEP account for the 2018 taxable year in the passive category and to the PTEP group within such account described in paragraph (c)(2)(x) of this section. Similarly, CFC2's 2018 taxable year annual PTEP account within the passive category, and the PTEP group within such account described in paragraph (c)(2)(x) of this section, is reduced by the amount of the 1,000,000u section 959(b) distribution to CFC1. Additionally, CFC1's annual PTEP account for the 2018 taxable year in the passive category, and the PTEP group within such account described in paragraph (c)(2)(x) of this section, is reduced by the 300,000u of withholding taxes imposed on CFC1 by Country X. Therefore, CFC1's annual PTEP account for the 2018 taxable year within the passive category and the PTEP group within such account described in paragraph (c)(2)(x) of this section is 700,000u.

(C) Under paragraph (d)(1) of this section, the 300,000u of withholding tax is translated into U.S. dollars and $300,000 is added to the PTEP group taxes with respect to CFC1's PTEP group described in paragraph (c)(2)(x) of this section within the annual PTEP account for the 2018 taxable year within the passive category.

(2) *Example 2: Foreign income taxes deemed paid under section 960(b)*—(i) *Facts*. USP, a domestic corporation, owns 100% of the stock of CFC1, which in turn owns 60% of the stock of CFC2, which in turn owns 100% of the stock of CFC3. USP, CFC1, CFC2, and CFC3 all use the calendar year as their U.S. taxable year. CFC1, CFC2, and CFC3 all use the "u" as their functional currency. At all relevant times, 1u=$1. On July 1, 2020, CFC2 distributes 600u to CFC1 and the entire distribution is a section 959(b) distribution ("distribution 1"). On October 1, 2020, CFC1 distributes 800u to USP and the entire distribution is a section 959(a) distribution ("distribution 2"). CFC1 and CFC2 make no other distributions in the year ending December 31, 2020, earn no other income, and incur no taxes on distribution 1 or distribution 2. Before taking into account distribution 1, CFC2 has 1,000u in a PTEP group described in paragraph (c)(2)(x) of this section within an annual PTEP account for the 2016 taxable year within the general category. The previously taxed earnings and profits in CFC2's PTEP group relate to subpart F income of CFC3 that was included by USP in 2016. CFC3 distributed the earnings and profits to CFC2 before the 2020 taxable year and, solely as a result of the distribution of the previously taxed earnings and profits, CFC2 incurred withholding and net basis tax, resulting in $150 of PTEP group taxes with respect to the PTEP group. Before taking into account distribution 1 and distribution 2, CFC1 has 200u in a PTEP group described in paragraph (c)(2)(ix) of this section within an annual PTEP account for the 2018 taxable year within the section 951A category. The previously taxed earnings and profits in CFC1's PTEP group relate to the portion of a GILTI inclusion amount that was included by USP in 2018 and allocated to CFC2 under section 951A(f)(2) and § 1.951A-6(b)(2). CFC2 distributed the earnings and profits to CFC1 before the 2020 taxable year and, solely as a result of the distribution of the previously taxed earnings and profits, CFC1 incurred withholding and net basis tax, resulting in $25 of PTEP group taxes with respect to the PTEP group.

(ii) *Analysis*—(A) *Foreign income taxes deemed paid by CFC1*. With respect to distribution 1 from CFC2 to CFC1, under paragraph (b)(4) of this section CFC1's proportionate share of PTEP group taxes with respect to CFC2's PTEP group described in paragraph (c)(2)(x) of this section within an annual PTEP account for the 2016 taxable year within the general category is $90 ($150 x 600u/1,000u). Under paragraph (b)(3) of this section, the amount of foreign income taxes that are properly attributable to distribution 1 is $90. Accordingly, under paragraph (b)(2) of this section, CFC1 is deemed to have paid $90 of general category foreign income taxes of CFC2 with respect to its 600u section 959(b) distribution in the general category.

(B) *Adjustments to PTEP accounts of CFC1 and CFC2.* Under paragraph (c)(3) of this section, the 600u related to distribution 1 is added to CFC1's PTEP group described in paragraph (c)(2)(x) of this section within an annual PTEP account for the 2016 taxable year within the general category. Similarly, CFC2's PTEP group described in paragraph (c)(2)(x) of this section within an annual PTEP account for the 2016 taxable year within the general category is reduced by 600u, the amount of the section 959(b) distribution to CFC1. Additionally, under paragraph (d) of this section, CFC1's PTEP group taxes with respect to its PTEP group described in paragraph (c)(2)(x) of this section within an annual PTEP account for the 2016 taxable year within the general category are increased by $90 and CFC2's PTEP group described in paragraph (c)(2)(x) of this section within an annual PTEP account for the 2016 taxable year within the general category are reduced by $90.

(C) *Foreign income taxes deemed paid by USP.* With respect to distribution 2 from CFC1 to USP, because CFC1 has PTEP groups in more than one section 904 category, this section is applied separately to each section 904 category (that is, distribution 2 of 800u is applied separately to the 200u of CFC1's PTEP group described in paragraph (c)(2)(ix) of this section and 600u of CFC1's PTEP group described in paragraph (c)(2)(x) of this section).

(*1*) *Section 951A category.* Under paragraph (b)(4) of this section, USP's proportionate share of PTEP group taxes with respect to CFC1's PTEP group described in paragraph (c)(2)(ix) of this section within an annual PTEP account for the 2018 taxable year within the section 951A category is $25 ($25 x 200u/200u). Under paragraph (b)(3) of this section, the amount of foreign income taxes within the section 951A category that are properly attributable to distribution 2 is $25. Accordingly, under paragraph (b)(1) of this section USP is deemed to have paid $25 of section 951A category foreign income taxes of CFC1 with respect to its 200u section 959(a) distribution in the section 951A category.

(*2*) *General category.* Under paragraph (b)(4) of this section, USP's proportionate share of PTEP group taxes with respect to CFC1's PTEP group described in paragraph (c)(2)(x) of this section within an annual PTEP account for the 2016 taxable year within the general category is $90 ($90 x 600u/600u). Under paragraph (b)(3) of this section, the amount of foreign income taxes that are properly attributable to distribution 2 is $90. Accordingly, under paragraph (b)(1), USP is deemed to have paid $90 of general category foreign income taxes of CFC1 with respect to its 600u section 959(a) distribution in the general category.

Par. 25. Section 1.960-4 is amended by:

1. Removing the language "960(b)(1)" and adding the language "960(c)(1)" in its place wherever it appears.

2. Adding two sentences at the end of paragraph (a)(1).

3. Revising the last sentence of paragraph (d).

The addition and revision read as follows:

§1.960-4. Additional foreign tax credit in year of receipt of previously taxed earnings and profits.—(a) * * *

(1) * * * For purposes of this section, an amount included in gross income under section 951A(a) is treated as an amount included in gross income under section 951(a). The amount of the increase in the foreign tax credit limitation allowed by this section is determined with regard to each separate category of income described in § 1.904-5(a)(4)(v).

* * *

(d) * * * For purposes of this paragraph (d), the term "foreign income taxes" includes foreign income taxes paid or accrued, foreign income taxes deemed paid or accrued under section 904(c), and foreign income taxes deemed paid under section 960, for the taxable year of inclusion.

* * *

Par. 26. Section 1.960-5 is amended by removing the language "951(a)" and adding the language "951(a) or 951A(a)" in its place in paragraph (a)(1).

§1.960-5. Credit for taxable year of inclusion binding for taxable year of exclusion.

Par. 27. Section 1.960-6 is amended by removing the language "960(b)(1)" and adding the language "960(c)(1)" in its place in paragraph (a).

§1.960-6. Overpayments resulting from increase in limitation for taxable year of exclusion.

Par. 28. Section 1.960-7 is revised to read as follows:

§1.960-7. Applicability dates.—*Applicability dates.* Sections 1.960-1 through 1.960-6 apply to a taxable year of a foreign corporation beginning after December 31, 2017, and a taxable year of a domestic corporation that is a United States shareholder of the foreign corporation in which or with which such taxable year of such foreign corporation ends.

CFCs: Previously Taxed Earnings and Profits: Exclusion from Gross Income: Basis Adjustments

CFCs: Previously Taxed Earnings and Profits: Exclusion from Gross Income: Basis Adjustments.—Reg. §§1.961-3 and 1.961-4 and amendments to Reg. §§1.961-1 and 1.961-2, providing guidance relating to the exclusion from gross income of previously taxed earnings and profits under Code Sec. 959 and related basis adjustments under Code Sec. 961, are proposed (published in the Federal Register on August 29, 2006) (REG-121509-00) (corrected December 8, 2006).

☐ Par. 6. Section 1.961-1 is revised to read as follows:

§1.961-1. Increase in basis of stock in CFCs and of other property.—(a) *Definitions.*—See §1.959-1(b) for a list of defined terms applicable to §1.961-1 through §1.961-4.

(b) *Increase in basis.*—(1) *In general.*—Except as provided in paragraphs (b)(2) and (b)(3) of this section, the adjusted basis of a United States shareholder's stock in a CFC or property (as defined in paragraph (c)(1) of this section) by reason of the ownership of which such United States shareholder is considered under section 958(a) as owning stock in a CFC shall be increased under section 961(a) each time, and to the extent that, such United States shareholder's previously taxed earnings and profits account with respect to the stock in that CFC is increased pursuant to the steps outlined in §1.959-3(e)(2).

(2) *Limitation on amount of increase in case of election under section 962.*—[Reserved].

(3) *Deemed inclusions under sections 1293(c) and 959(e).*—Paragraph (b)(1) of this section shall not apply in the case of a deemed section 951(a) inclusion pursuant to section 1293(c) or 959(e).

(c) *Rules of application.*—(1) *Property defined.*—The property of a United States shareholder referred to in paragraph (b)(1) of this section shall consist of—

(i) Stock in a foreign corporation;

(ii) An interest in a foreign partnership; or

(iii) A beneficial or ownership interest in a foreign estate or trust (as defined in section 7701(a)(31)).

(2) *Increase with respect to each share or ownership unit.*—Any increase under paragraph (b) of this section in the basis of a United States shareholder's stock in a foreign corporation or property (as defined in paragraph (c)(1) of this section) by reason of the ownership of which such United States shareholder is considered under section 958(a) as owning stock in a foreign corporation shall be made on a pro rata basis with respect to each share of such stock or each ownership unit of such property.

(3) *Translation rules.*—For purposes of determining an increase in basis under this section, in cases in which the previously taxed earnings and profits account is maintained in a non-United States dollar functional currency, section 951(a) inclusions shall be translated into United States dollars at the appropriate exchange rate as described in section 989(b). Any other increase in basis pursuant to paragraph (b) of this section (for example, a basis increase resulting from the application of §1.959-3(f) or (g)) shall be in the amount of the transferor's dollar basis attributable to the previously taxed earnings and profits transferred.

(c) [(d)] *Examples.*—The application of this section is illustrated by the following examples:

Example 1. Basis adjustment for income inclusion. (i) *Facts.* DP, a United States shareholder, owns 800 of the 1,000 shares of the one class of stock in FC and has a basis of $50 in each of its shares. DP and FC use the calendar year as a taxable year and FC is a CFC. FC uses the u as its functional currency. The average exchange rate for year 1 is 1u = $1. In year 1, its first year of operation, FC has 100,000u of subpart F income after the payment of 11,250u of foreign income taxes. DP is required to include in gross income 80,000u (800/1,000 × 100,000u) equal to $80,000 under section 951(a), and 9,000u (80,000u/100,000u × 11,250u) equal to $9,000 under section 78.

(ii) *Analysis.* On December 31, of year 1, DP increases the section 959(c)(2) earnings and profits in its previously taxed earnings and profits account with respect to its stock in FC by 80,000u pursuant to §1.959-3(e)(2)(i) to reflect the inclusion of 80,000u, or $80,000, in DP's gross income pursuant to section 959(a), and correspondingly increases the basis of each share of its stock in FC by $100 ($80,000/800) from $50 to $150 pursuant to paragraphs (b)(1) and (c)(2) of this section.

Example 2. Sale of CFC stock. (i) *Facts.* Assume the same facts as in *Example 1*, except that in year 2, DP sells all of its stock in FC to DP2, a United States person that is DP's successor in interest (as defined in §1.959-1(b)(5)), for $200 per share. At the time of sale, the exchange rate is 1u = $1 and DP has a basis of $150 per share in its FC stock and a previously taxed earnings and profits account with respect to its FC stock consisting of 80,000u of section 959(c)(2) earnings and profits with a dollar basis of $80,000. Also, at the time of sale, FC has 50,000u of non-previously taxed earnings and profits, attributable to taxable years of FC beginning on or after December 31,1962 during which FC was a CFC and DP held its shares of stock in FC.

(ii) *Analysis.* Pursuant to section 1248(a), because FC has 40,000u of non-previously taxed earnings and profits attributable to DP's stock (50,000u × 800/1,000), the $40,000 of gain, equal to 40,000u, recognized by DP on the sale of it stock (($200 - $150) × 800) is included in DP's gross income as a dividend. Consequently, the section 959(c)(2) earnings and profits in DP's previously taxed earnings and profits account with respect to its stock in FC are increased from 80,000u to 120,000u pursuant to §1.959-3(e)(2)(i). DP's basis in each share of its stock in FC is not adjusted, pursuant to paragraph (b)(3) of this section, because the adjustment to DP's previously taxed earnings and profits account results from a deemed section 951(a) inclusion pursuant to section 959(e). Upon the sale, DP2 acquires a previously taxed earnings and profits account with respect to the FC stock of 120,000u pursuant to §1.959-1(d)(2)(i) and can utilize the account if it qualifies as a successor in interest under §1.959-1(b)(5). DP2 takes a cost basis of $200 per share in the FC stock pursuant to section 1012.

[Reg. §1.961-1.]

☐ Par. 7. Section 1.961-2 is revised to read as follows:

§1.961-2. Reduction in basis of stock in foreign corporations and of other property.—(a) *Reduction in basis.*—(1) *In general.*—Except as provided in paragraph (a)(2) of this section, the adjusted basis of a covered shareholder's stock in a foreign corporation or property (as defined in §1.961-1(c)) by reason of the ownership of which such covered shareholder is considered under section 958(a) as owning stock in a foreign corporation shall be reduced under section 961(b) each time, and to the extent, that such covered shareholder's dollar basis in a previously taxed earnings and profits account with respect to the stock in such foreign corporation is decreased pursuant to the steps outlined in §1.959-3(e)(2) and shall also be reduced by the dollar amount of any foreign income taxes allowed as a credit under section 960(a)(3) with respect to the earnings and profits accounted for by that decrease.

(2) *Limitation on amount of reduction in case of election under section 962.*—[Reserved].

(b) *Rules of application.*—(1) *Reduction with respect to each ownership unit.*—Any reduction under paragraph (a) of this section in the adjusted basis of a covered shareholder's stock in a foreign corporation or property (as defined in paragraph (b)(1) of this section) by reason of the ownership of which it is considered under section 958(a) as owning stock in a foreign corporation shall be made on a pro rata basis with respect to each share of such stock or each ownership unit of such property.

(2) *Translation rules.*—For purposes of determining a decrease in basis under this section, in cases in which the previously taxed earnings and profits account is maintained in a non-United States dollar functional currency, distributions of previously taxed earnings and profits shall be translated using the dollar basis of the earnings distributed. See §1.959-3(b)(1) and (b)(3)(ii) for rules regarding the dollar basis of previously taxed earnings and profits. If the covered shareholder elects to maintain dollar basis accounts of previously taxed earnings and profits as described in § 1.959-3(b)(3)(ii), the dollar basis of the earnings distributed shall be determined according to the following formula: (functional currency distributed/total functional currency previously taxed earnings and profits) × total dollar basis of previously taxed earnings and profits. See section 989(b)(1) for the appropriate exchange rate applicable to distributions for purposes of section 986(c).

(c) *Amount in excess of basis.*—To the extent that the amount of the reduction in the adjusted basis of property provided by paragraph (a) of this section exceeds such adjusted basis, the amount shall be treated as gain from the sale or exchange of property.

(d) *Examples.*—The application of this section is illustrated by the following examples:

Example 1. Successor in interest. (i) *Facts.* DP, a United States shareholder, owns all of the 1,000 shares of the one class of stock in FC, which owns all of the 500 shares of the one class of stock in FS. Each share of DP's stock in FC has a basis of $200. DP, FC, and FS use the calendar year as a taxable year and FC and FS are CFCs throughout the period here involved. FC and FS both use the u as their functional currency. In year 1, FS has 100,000u of subpart F income after the payment of 50,000u of foreign income taxes. The average exchange rate for year 1 and year 2 is 1u = $1. For year 1, DP includes 100,000u in gross income under section 951(a) with respect to FS. In accordance with the provisions of §1.961-1, DP increases the basis of each of its 1,000 shares of stock in FC to $300 ($200+$100,000/1,000) as of December 31, of year 1. On July 31 of year 2, DP sells 250 of its shares of stock in FC to domestic corporation DT at a price of $350 per share. DT satisfies the requirements of paragraph (d) of §1.959-1 so as to qualify as DP's successor in interest. On September 30 of year 2, the earnings and profits attributable to the 100,000u included in DP's gross income under section 951(a) for year 1 are distributed to FC which incurs a withholding tax of 10,000u on such distribution (10% of 100,000u) and an additional foreign income tax of 33 1/3% or 30,000u by reason of the inclusion of the net distribution of 90,000u (100,000u minus 10,000u) in its taxable income for year 2. On June 30 of year 3, FC distributes the remaining 60,000u of such earnings and profits to DP and DT: DP receives 45,000u (750/1,000×60,000u) and excludes such amount from gross income under section 959(a) and §1.959-1(c); DT receives 15,000u (250/1,000× 60,000u) and, as DP's successor in interest, excludes such amount from gross income under section 959(a) and §1.959-1(c).

(ii) *Analysis.* As of June 30 of year 3, DP must reduce the adjusted basis of each of its 750 shares of stock in FC to $200 ($300 minus ($45,000/750+$10,000/1,000+ $30,000/1,000)); and DT must reduce the basis of each of its 250 shares of stock in FC to $250 ($350 minus ($15,000/250+ $10,000/1,000+$30,000/1,000)).

Example 2. Sale of lower-tier CFC. (i) *Facts.* Assume the same facts as in *Example 1,* except that in addition, on July 31 of year 2, FC sells its 500 shares of stock in FS to domestic corporation DT2 at a price of $600 per share. DT2 satisfies the requirements of §1.959-1(b)(5) so as to qualify as DP's successor in interest. On September 30 of year 2, FS distributes 100,000u of earnings and profits to DT2, which earnings and profits are attributable to the 100,000u included in DP's gross income under section 951(a) for year 1. As DP's successor in interest, DT2 excludes the 100,000u it receives from gross income under section 959(a) and §1.959-1(c).

(ii) *Analysis.* As of September 30 of year 2, DT2 must reduce the basis of each of its 500 shares of stock in FS to $400 ($600 minus ($100,000/500)).

Example 3. Section 956 amount. (i) *Facts.* DP, a United States shareholder, owns all of the 1,000 shares of the one class of stock in FC, which owns all of the 500 shares of the one class of stock in FS. Each share of DP's stock in FC has a basis of $200. DP, FC, and FS use the calendar year as a taxable year and FC and FS are CFCs throughout the period here involved. FC and FS both use the u as their functional currency. In year 1, FS has 100,000u of subpart F income after the payment of 50,000u of foreign income taxes. The average exchange rate for year 1 and year 2 is 1u = $1. For year 1, DP includes 100,000u in gross income under section 951(a) with respect to FS. In accordance with the provisions of §1.959-3(e)(2)(i) and §1.961-1, DP increases the section 959(c)(2) earnings and profits in its earnings and profits account with respect to its FC stock by 100,000u and correspondingly adjusts the basis of each of its 1,000 shares of stock in FC to $300 ($200+$100,000/1,000) as of December 31 of year 1. In year 2, DP has a section 956 amount with respect to its stock in FC of 100,000u.

(ii) *Analysis.* On December 31 of year 2, DP reclassifies 100,000u of section 959(c)(2) earnings and profits as section 959(c)(1) earnings and profits pursuant to § 1.959-3(e)(2)(iv). DP's basis in each of its 1,000 shares of stock in FC remains unchanged at $300 per share.

[Reg. § 1.961-2.]

☐ Par. 8. Section 1.961-3 is added to read as follows:

§ 1.961-3. Basis adjustments in stock held by foreign corporation.—(a) *Where the upper-tier entity is 100% owned by a single United States shareholder.*—(1) *In general.*—If a United States shareholder is treated under section 958(a) as owning stock in a CFC (lower-tier CFC) by reason of owning, either directly or pursuant to the application of section 958(a), stock in one or more other CFCs (each an "upper-tier CFC"), any increase to such United States shareholder's basis in stock or other property under § 1.961-1 of this section resulting from an adjustment to such United States shareholder's previously taxed earnings and profits account with respect to its stock in the lower-tier CFC shall also be made to each upper-tier CFC's basis in either the stock in the lower-tier CFC or the property by reason of which it is considered to own stock in the lower-tier CFC under section 958(a), but only for purposes of determining the amount included under section 951 in the gross income of such United States shareholder or its successor in interest. In addition, any downward adjustment to such United States shareholder's (or its successor in interest's) previously taxed earnings and profits account with respect to its stock in a distributor under § 1.959-3(e)(3) shall result in a corresponding reduction of the basis of the distributee's stock in the distributor for purposes of determining the amount included in such United States shareholder's gross income under section 951(a).

(2) *Examples.*—The application of this paragraph (a) is illustrated by the following examples:

Example 1. Intercorporate dividend from lower-tier CFC to upper-tier CFC. (i) *Facts.* DP, a United States shareholder, owns all of the stock in FC, a CFC, and FC owns all of the stock in FS, a CFC. DP, FC and FS all use the calendar year as their taxable year and FC and FS both use the U.S. dollar as their functional currency. In year 1, FS has $100x of subpart F income that is included in DP's gross income under section 951(a)(1). In year 2, FS pays a dividend of $100x to FC.

(ii) *Analysis.* On December 31 of year 1, the section 959(c)(2) earnings and profits in DP's previously taxed earnings and profits account with respect to its stock in FS are increased by $100x pursuant to § 1.959-3(e)(2)(i) to reflect the inclusion of $100x in DP's gross income under section 951(a)(1)(A). DP's basis in its stock in FC is correspondingly increased by $100x pursuant to § 1.961-1(b). FC's basis in its stock in FS is also increased by $100x pursuant to paragraph (a) of this section, but only for purposes of determining the amount included in DP's gross income under section 951. At the end of year 2, the section 959(c)(2) earnings and profits in DP's previously taxed earnings and profits account with respect to its stock in FS are decreased by $100x and its previously taxed earnings and profits account with respect to its stock in FC are increased by $100x pursuant to § 1.959-3(e)(3) to reflect the transfer of the previously taxed earnings and profits from FS to FC. The $100x distribution is excluded from FC's income for purposes of determining the amount included in DP's gross income pursuant to § 1.959-2(a). FC's basis in its stock in FS, for purposes of determining the amount included in DP's gross income under section 951, is decreased by $100x pursuant to paragraph (a) of this section.

Example 2. Sale of upper-tier CFC stock. (i) *Facts.* DP, a United States shareholder, owns all of the stock in FC, a CFC. FC owns all of the stock in FS1, a CFC, and FS1 owns all of the stock in FS2, a CFC. DP, FC, FS1, and FS2 all use the calendar year as their taxable year and FC, FS1 and FS2 all use the U.S. dollar as their functional currency. In year 1, FS2 has $100x of subpart F income which is included in DP's gross income under section 951(a)(1)(A). In year 2, FC sells FS1 to FT, a nonresident alien, and recognizes $100x of gain on the sale.

(ii) *Analysis.* On December 31 of year 1, the section 959(c)(2) earnings and profits in DP's previously taxed earnings and profits account with respect to its stock in FS2 are increased by $100x pursuant to § 1.959-3(e)(2)(i) to reflect the inclusion of $100x in DP's gross income under section 951(a)(1). DP's basis in its stock in FC is correspondingly increased by $100x under § 1.961-1(b). FC's basis in its stock in FS1 and FS1's basis in its stock in FS2 are also each increased by $100x under paragraph (a) of this section, but only for purposes of determining the amount included in the gross income of DP under section 951. In year 2, the $100x of gain on FC's sale of FS1 stock would be subpart F income that would be includible in DP gross income under section 951(a)(1)(A). However, since FC has an additional $100x of basis in its stock in FS1 for purposes of determining the amount included in DP's gross income under section 951, the sale of FS1 by FC does not generate any subpart F income to DP.

(b) *Exception where the upper-tier entity is less than 100 percent owned by a single United States shareholder.*—(1) *In general.*—If United States shareholders are treated, under section 958(a), as owning stock in a CFC (lower-tier CFC) by reason of owning, either directly or pursuant to the application of section 958(a), stock in one or more other CFCs (each an "upper-tier CFC"), and if, in the aggregate, the lower-tier CFC is less than wholly indirectly owned by a single United States shareholder, any increase to any United States shareholder's basis in stock or other property under § 1.961-1(b) of this section resulting from an increase to such United States shareholder's previously taxed earnings and profits account with respect to its stock in such lower-tier CFC shall result in an increase to each upper-tier CFC's basis in either the stock in the lower-tier CFC or the property by reason of which such upper-tier CFC is considered to own stock in the lower-tier CFC under section 958(a), but only for purposes of determining the amount included under section 951 in the gross income of such United States shareholder or its successor in interest. The amount of the increase to each upper-tier CFC's basis in either the stock in the lower-tier CFC or the property by reason of which such upper-tier CFC is considered to own stock in the lower-tier CFC under section 958(a) shall be equal to the amount that would be excluded from the gross income of such upper-tier CFC pursuant to section 959(b) and § 1.959-2(a) if the amount that gave rise to the adjustment to the United States shareholder's previously taxed earnings and profits account with respect to its stock in the lower-tier CFC were actually distributed through a chain of ownership to such upper-tier CFC. In addition, any decrease to such United States shareholder's (or successor in interest's) previously taxed earnings and profits account with respect to its stock in a distributor under § 1.959-3(e)(3) shall result in a corresponding reduction of the basis of the distributee's stock in the distributor. The reduction of the basis of the distributee's stock in the distributor shall be equal to the amount that would be excluded from the gross income of the distributee pursuant to section 959(b) and § 1.959-2(a).

(2) *Example*.—The application of this paragraph (b) is illustrated by the following example:

Example. Less than wholly owned CFC. (i) *Facts*. DP, a United States shareholder, owns 70%, and FP, a nonresident alien, owns 30% of the stock in FC, a CFC. FC in turn owns 100% of the stock in FS, a CFC. Each of DP, FC, FN and FS use the calendar year as their taxable year and both FC and FS use the U.S. dollar as their functional currency. Entering year 1, DP has a basis of $50x in FC and FC has a basis of $50x in FS. In year 1, FS earns $100x of subpart F income. In year 2, FC sells FS for $150x.

(ii) *Analysis*. On December 31 of year 1, DP includes $70x of the $100x of subpart F income earned by FS in gross income under section 951(a)(1)(A). DP increases its section 959(c)(2) earnings and profits in its earnings and profits account with respect to its stock in FS by $70x pursuant to § 1.959-3(e)(2)(i). DP increases its basis in FC from $50x to $120x pursuant to § 1.961-1(b). FC increases its basis in FS from $50x to $150x pursuant to paragraph (b)(1) of this section (but only for purposes of determining FC's subpart F income with respect to DP) because if the $100x amount of subpart F income of FS that caused the $70x increase to DP's previously taxed earnings and profits account with respect to its stock in FS had been distributed to FC, the entire $100x would be excluded from FC's gross income pursuant to section 959(b) and § 1.959-2(a) for purposes of determining DP's inclusion under section 951(a)(1)(A). In year 2, when FC sells FS, for purposes of determining DP's subpart F inclusion, FC is treated as recognizing $0 on the sale ($150x sale proceeds - $150x basis). Therefore, DP includes $0 in income under section 951(a)(1)(A) as a result of the sale. Although the sale does not generate gain for purposes of determining DP's subpart F inclusion, it does cause FC's non-previously taxed earnings and profits to be increased by $100x ($150x sale proceeds - $50x basis).

(c) *Translation rules*.—Rules similar to those provided in § 1.961-1(c)(3) and § 1.961-2(b)(3) shall apply for purposes of determining the exchange rates used to reflect any change to the basis of stock or other property under this section. [Reg. § 1.961-3.]

☐ Par. 9. Section 1.961-4 is added to read as follows:

§ 1.961-4. Section 304 transactions.—(a) *Deemed redemption treated as a distribution*.—(1) *In general*.—In the case of a stock acquisition described in section 304(a)(1) that is treated as a distribution of earnings and profits of a foreign acquiring corporation or a foreign issuing corporation or both, basis adjustments shall be made in accordance with the rules of §§ 1.961-1, 1.961-2, and 1.961-3.

(2) *Examples*.—The application of this section is illustrated by the following examples:

Example 1. Cross-chain acquisition of first-tier CFC. (i) *Facts*. DP, a domestic corporation, owns all of the stock in DS, a domestic corporation, and F1, a CFC. DS owns all of the stock in F2, a CFC. DP, DS, F1 and F2 all use the calendar year as their taxable year and F1 and F2 use the U.S. dollar as their functional currency. During year 1, F1 purchases all of the stock in F2 from DS for $80x in a transaction described in section 304(a)(1). At the end of year 1, before taking into account the purchase of F2's stock, DP has a previously taxed earnings and profits account consisting of $20x of section 959(c)(2) earnings and profits with respect to its stock in F1, and F1 has section 959(c)(2) earnings and profits of $20x and non-previously taxed earnings and profits of $10x. At the end of year 1, before taking into account the purchase of F2's stock, DS has a previously taxed earnings and profits account consisting of $50x of section 959(c)(2) earnings and profits with respect to its stock in F2 and F2 has section 959(c)(2) earnings and profits of $50x and non-previously taxed earnings and profits of $0. Before taking into account the purchase of F2's stock, DP's basis in F1's stock is $30x and DS's basis in F2's stock is $60x.

(ii) *Analysis*. Under section 304(a)(1), DS is deemed to have transferred the F2 stock to F1 in exchange for F1 stock in a transaction to which section 351(a) applies, and F1 is treated as having redeemed, for $80x, the F1 stock hypothetically issued to DS. The payment of $80x is treated as a distribution to which section 301 applies. Under section 304(b)(2), the determination of the amount which is a dividend is made as if the distribution were made, first, by F1 to the extent of its earnings and profits ($30x), and then by F2 to the extent of its earnings and profits ($50x). Before taking into account the deemed distributions, DS had a previously taxed earnings and profits account of $50x with respect to its stock in F2, and DP had a previously taxed earnings and profits account of $20x with respect to its stock in F1. Under § 1.959-3(h)(4)(i), DS is deemed to have a previously taxed earnings and profits account with respect to stock in F1. Under § 1.959-3(g)(1), the section 959(c)(2) earnings and profits in DP's previously taxed earnings and profits account with respect to F1 stock are reduced from $20x to $0. As a result, DP's basis in F1's stock is reduced from $30x to $10x under § 1.961-2(a). The deemed distribution of earnings and profits by F2 causes the section 959(c)(2) earnings and profits in DS's previously taxed earnings and profits account with respect to F2 stock to be reduced from $50x to $0. Under § 1.961-2(a) and § 1.961-3(a), F1's basis in its newly acquired F2's stock is reduced from $60x to $10x. F1 has a transferred basis of $10x in F2's stock.

Example 2. Cross-chain acquisition of lower-tier CFC. (i) *Facts.* DP, a domestic corporation, owns all of the stock in two CFCs, FX and FY. FX owns all of the stock in FZ, a CFC. FX, FY and FZ use the U.S. dollar as their functional currency. During year 1, FY purchases all of the stock in FZ from FX for $80x in a transaction described in section 304(a)(1). On December 31 of year 1, before taking into account the purchase of FZ's stock, FY has section 959(c)(2) earnings and profits of $20x and non-previously taxed earnings and profits of $10x, and FZ has section 959(c)(2) earnings and profits of $50x and non-previously taxed earnings and profits of $0. Before taking into account FX's purchase of FZ's stock, DP's basis in FX's stock is $60x; DP's basis in FY's stock is $30x; and FX's basis in FZ's stock, for purposes of determining the amount includible in DP's gross income under section 951(a), is $60x.

(ii) *Analysis.* Under section 304(a)(1), FX is deemed to have transferred the FZ stock to FY in exchange for FY stock in a transaction to which section 351(a) applies, and FY is treated as having redeemed, for $80x, the FY stock hypothetically issued to FX. The payment of $80x is treated as a distribution of property to which section 301 applies. Under section 304(b)(2), the determination of the amount which is a dividend is made as if the distribution were made, first, by FY to the extent of its earnings and profits, $30x, and then by FX to the extent of its earnings and profits, $50x. Under § 1.959-2(b), FX is deemed to receive the distributions from FY and FZ through a chain of ownership described in section 958(a), and $70x is excluded from FX's gross income under section 959(b) and § 1.959-2(a). Under § 1.959-3(e)(3), the section 959(c)(2) earnings and profits in DP's previously taxed earnings and profits account for the stock in FY are reduced from $20x to $0; the section 959(c)(2) earnings and profits in DP's previously taxed earnings and profits account for the stock in FZ are reduced from $50x to $0; and the section 959(c)(2) earnings and profits in DP's previously taxed earnings and profits account for the stock in FX are increased from $0 to $70x (and such account is further increased to $80x due to the inclusion of $10x of subpart F income in DP's gross income under section 951(a)). Under § 1.961-2(a), DP's basis in the stock in FY is reduced from $30x to $10x. DP's basis in the stock in FX is first reduced by $50x under § 1.961-2(a), and then increased by $80x under § 1.961-1(b), for a net increase of $30x, to $90x. Under § 1.961-3(a), FY's basis in the stock in FZ, for purposes of determining the amount includible in DP's gross income under section 951(a), is reduced by $50x to $10x.

[Reg. § 1.961-4.]

Foreign-Derived Intangible Income: Global Intangible Low-Taxed Income: Deduction

Foreign-Derived Intangible Income: Global Intangible Low-Taxed Income: Deduction.—Amendments to Reg. § 1.962-1, providing guidance to determine the amount of the deduction for foreign-derived intangible income and global intangible low-taxed income, are proposed (published in the Federal Register on March 6, 2019) (REG-104464-18).

Par. 3. Section 1.962-1 is amended by adding paragraphs (b)(1)(i)(A)(2), (b)(1)(i)(B)(*3*), and revising paragraph (d) to read as follows:

§ 1.962-1. Limitation of tax for individuals on amounts included in gross income under section 951(a).

* * *

(b) * * *

(1) * * *

(i) * * *

(A) * * *

(2) His GILTI inclusion amount (as defined in § 1.951A-1(c)(1)) for the taxable year; plus

* * *

(B) * * *

(3) The portion of the deduction under section 250 and § 1.250(a)-1 that would be allowed to a domestic corporation equal to the percentage applicable to global intangible low-taxed income for the taxable year under section 250(a)(1)(B) (including as modified by section 250(a)(3)(B)) multiplied by the sum of the amount described in paragraph (b)(1)(i)(A)(2) of this section and the amount described in paragraph (b)(1)(i)(A)(*3*) of this section that is attributable to the amount described in paragraph (b)(1)(i)(A)(2) of this section.

* * *

(d) *Applicability dates.*—Except as otherwise provided in this paragraph (d), paragraph (b)(1)(i) of this section applies beginning the last taxable year of a foreign corporation that begins before January 1, 2018, and with respect to a United States person, for the taxable year in which or with which such taxable year of the foreign corporation ends. Paragraph (b)(1)(i)(B)(3) applies to taxable years of a foreign corporation ending on or after March 4, 2019, and with respect to a United States person, for the taxable year in which or with which such taxable year of the foreign corporation ends.

CFCs: Insurance Income: After 1986: Tax Adjustments

Controlled Foreign Corporations: Insurance Income: Tax Years After 1986.—Reproduced below is a proposed amendment to Reg. § 1.964-1, relating to the election to expense certain depreciable business assets (published in the Federal Register on April 17, 1991).

☐ Par. 6. Section 1.964-1 is amended by adding the following language to the end of paragraph (c)(5):

§1.964-1. Determination of the earnings and profits of a foreign corporation

* * *

(c) *Tax adjustments.*—* * *

(5) *Controlling United States shareholders.*— * * * In the event that a foreign corporation is a controlled foreign corporation solely by virtue of section 953(c)(1)(B), the controlling United States shareholders of the foreign corporation shall be those United States shareholders (as defined in section 953(c)(1)(A)) who, in the aggregate, own (within the meaning of section 958(a)) more than 25 percent of the total combined voting power of all classes of the stock of such corporation entitled to vote. In the event that the foreign corporation is a controlled foreign corporation solely by virtue of section 953(c)(1)(B) but the United States shareholders (as defined in section 953(c)(1)(A)) do not, in the aggregate, own (within the meaning of section 958(a)) more than 25 percent of the total combined voting power of all classes of the stock of such corporation entitled to vote, the controlling shareholders of the foreign corporation shall be all those United States shareholders (within the meaning of section 953(c)(1)(A)) who own (within the meaning of section 958(a)) stock of such corporation.

Foreign Corporations: Tax Accounting Elections

Foreign Corporations: Tax Accounting Elections.—Amendments to Reg. §1.964-1, clarifying the rules for controlling domestic shareholders to adopt or change a method of accounting or taxable year on behalf of a foreign corporation, are proposed (published in the Federal Register on November 4, 2011) (REG-114749-09). Amendments to Reg. §§1.952-2 and 1.964-1, proposed on July 1, 1992, are withdrawn.

☐ Par. 2. Section 1.964-1 is amended as follows:

1. Adding a new paragraph (a)(4).

2. In paragraph (b)(3), revising the introductory text, redesignating *Example (1)* as *Example*, and removing *Example (2)*.

3. Revising the first sentence of paragraph (c)(1).

4. Revising paragraph (c)(1)(iii) and removing paragraphs (c)(1)(iii)(*a*), (c)(1)(iii)(*b*), and (c)(1)(iii)(*c*).

5. Revising paragraph (c)(1)(v).

6. Inserting a sentence after the fourth sentence of paragraph (c)(2), revising the fifth sentence of paragraph (c)(2), and adding a sentence at the end of paragraph (c)(2).

7. Revising paragraph (c)(8).

8. Adding a new paragraph (c)(9).

9. Revising paragraph (d).

The additions and revisions read as follows:

§1.964-1. Determination of the earnings and profits of a foreign corporation

* * *

(a)(4) *Example.*—The rules of this paragraph (a) are illustrated by the following example.

Example. (i) *Facts.* P, a domestic corporation, owns all of the outstanding stock of FX, a controlled foreign corporation. In preparing its books for purposes of accounting to its shareholders, FX uses an accounting method (Local Books Method) to determine the amount of its depreciation expense that does not conform to accounting principles generally accepted in the United States (U.S. GAAP) or to U.S. income tax accounting standards as described in paragraph (c). The amount of the adjustment necessary to conform the depreciation expense determined under the Local Books Method with the amount that would be determined under U.S. GAAP for purposes of paragraph (a)(1)(ii) of this section if FX were a domestic corporation is not material. However, the adjustment necessary to conform the amount of the depreciation expense under the Local Books Method to U.S. income tax accounting standards for purposes of paragraph (a)(1)(iii) of this section is material.

(ii) *Result.* Although FX is not required to make the adjustment necessary to conform the amount of its tax expense reserve deduction determined under the Local Books Method to the amount that would be determined under U.S. GAAP, FX is required to make the adjustment necessary to conform the amount of the depreciation expense determined under the Local Books Method to the amount of depreciation expense for the current year that would be allowed under U.S. income tax accounting standards as described in paragraph (c).

(b) * * *

(3) *Example.*—The rules of this paragraph (b) are illustrated by the following example.

* * *

(c) * * *

(1) *In general.*—Except as otherwise provided in the Code and regulations (for example, section 952(c)(3) (earnings and profits determined without regard to section 312(n)(4)-(6) for purposes of section 952(c)), the tax accounting standards to be applied in making the adjustments required by paragraph (a)(1)(iii) of this section shall be those applied to domestic corporations, including but not limited to the following:

* * *

(iii) *Depreciation and amortization.*—Depreciation and amortization shall be computed in accordance with the provisions of section 312(k) and the regulations under that section. In the case of a foreign corporation described in section 312(k)(4) (one with less than 20 percent U.S.-source gross income), depreciation and amortization of items that are not described in section 312(k)(2) or (k)(3) shall be determined under the rules for determining taxable income. For example, amortization for amortizable section 197 intangibles (as defined in section 197(c)) is calculated in accordance with section 197, and depreciation for real property is calculated in accordance with section 168(g)(2)(C)(iii). For any taxable year beginning before July 1, 1972, depreciation shall be computed in accordance with section 167 and the regulations under that section.

* * *

(v) *Taxable years.*—The period for computation of taxable income and earnings and profits known as the taxable year shall reflect the provisions of sections 441 and 898 and the regulations under those sections.

* * *

(2) *Adoption or change of method or taxable year.*—* * * Once adopted, a method of accounting or taxable year may be changed by or on behalf of the foreign corporation only in accordance with the applicable provisions of the Code and regulations. Adjustments to the appropriate separate category (as defined in § 1.904-5(a)(1)) of earnings and profits and income of the foreign corporation (including a category of subpart F income described in section 952(a) or, in the case of foreign base company income, described in § 1.954-1(c)(1)(iii)) shall be required under section 481 to prevent any duplication or omission of amounts attributable to previous years that would otherwise result from any change in a method of accounting. * * * See paragraph (c)(9) of this section for rules if the change in method of accounting is required in connection with an audit of the foreign corporation's controlling domestic shareholders (as defined in paragraph (c)(5) of this section).

* * *

(8) *Examples.*—The following examples illustrate the application of paragraph (c) of this section:

Example 1. P, a domestic corporation, owns all of the outstanding stock of FX, a controlled foreign corporation organized in 2012. In maintaining its books for the purpose of accounting to its shareholders, FX deducts additions to a reserve for bad debts. Assume that if FX were a domestic corporation, it would be required to use the specific charge-off method under section 166 with respect to allowable bad debt losses. In accordance with paragraph (c)(1)(i) of this section, FX's reserve deductions must be adjusted (if the adjustments are material) in order to compute its earnings and profits in accordance with U.S. income tax accounting standards as described in paragraph (c). Accordingly, P must compute FX's earnings and profits using the specific charge-off method of accounting for bad debts in accordance with section 166.

Example 2. FX, a controlled foreign corporation, maintains its books for the purpose of accounting to its shareholders by capitalizing research and experimental expenses. A, B, and C, the United States shareholders (as defined in section 951(b)) of FX, own 45 percent, 30 percent, and 25 percent, respectively, of its only class of outstanding stock. For the first taxable year of FX, pursuant to paragraph (c)(3) of this section, B and C adopt on its behalf the section 174 method of currently deducting research and experimental expenses. Regardless of whether A objects to this action or receives the notice required by paragraph (c)(3)(iii) of this section, adjustments must be made to reflect the use of the section 174 method in computing the earnings and profits of FX with respect to A as well as with respect to B and C.

Example 3. (i) P, a calendar year domestic corporation that uses the fair market value method of apportioning interest expense, owns all of the outstanding stock of FX, a controlled foreign corporation organized in 2002 that uses the calendar year as its taxable year for foreign tax purposes. On June 1, 2012, FX makes a distribution to P. Prior to that distribution, none of the significant events specified in paragraph (c)(6) of this section had occurred. In addition, neither P nor FX had ever made or adopted, or been required to make or adopt, an election or method of accounting or taxable year for United States tax purposes with respect to FX. FX does not act to make any election or adopt any method of accounting or a taxable year for United States tax purposes.

(ii) P must compute FX's earnings and profits for FX's 2002 through 2012 taxable years in order to determine if any portion of the 2012 distribution is taxable as a dividend and to determine P's deemed paid foreign tax credit on such portion under section 902. Under paragraph (c)(2) of this section, P may make an election or adopt a method or methods of accounting and a taxable year on behalf of FX by satisfying the requirements of paragraph (c)(3) of this section by the due date (with extensions) of P's Federal income tax return for 2012, its taxable year with which ends FX's 2012 taxable year. Under paragraph (c)(4) of this section, any such election or adoption will govern the computation of FX's earnings and profits for its taxable years beginning in 2002 and subsequent taxable years for purposes of determining the Federal income tax liability of P and any subsequent shareholders of FX in 2012 and subsequent taxable years, unless the Commissioner consents to a change.

(iii) If P fails to satisfy the requirements under paragraph (c)(3) of this section and such failure is not shown to the satisfaction of the Commissioner to be due to reasonable cause, the earnings and profits of FX will be computed on the basis of a calendar taxable year as if no elections were made and any permissible methods of accounting not requiring an election and reflected in FX's books were adopted. Any subsequent attempt by FX or P to change an accounting method or taxable year of FX shall be effective only if the Commissioner consents to the change.

Example 4. (i) The facts are the same as in *Example 3*, except that P owns 80 percent, rather than all, of the outstanding stock of FX. M, a calendar year domestic corporation, owns the remaining 20 percent of the stock of FX beginning in 2002. M uses the tax book value method to allocate its interest expense under section 864(e)(4).

(ii) M, but not P, must compute FX's earnings and profits beginning in 2002 in order to determine the adjustment under § 1.861-12(c) and § 1.861-12T(c) to M's basis in the stock of FX for M's 2002 through 2011 taxable years. Because P, the controlling domestic shareholder of FX, has not made or adopted, or been required to make or adopt, an election or a method of accounting or taxable year with respect to FX, the earnings and profits of FX for 2002 through 2011 will be computed on the basis of a calendar taxable year as if no elections were made and any permissible methods of accounting not requiring an election and reflected in FX's books were adopted. However, a properly filed, timely election or adoption of a method of accounting or taxable year by, or on behalf of, FX with respect to FX's taxable year ending in 2012, when FX's earnings and profits are first significant for United States tax purposes for P, FX's controlling domestic shareholder, shall not be treated as a change in accounting method or a change in taxable year for any pre-2012 taxable year of FX. M will not be required to recompute its basis adjustments for 2002 through 2011 by reason of P's adoption of a method or methods of accounting or taxable year with respect to FX for 2012. See paragraph (c)(4)(iii) of this section. However, any method of accounting or taxable year adopted on behalf of FX by P pursuant to this paragraph (c) with respect to FX is binding on P, FX, and M for purposes of computing FX's earnings and profits in 2002 and subsequent taxable years for purposes of determining the Federal income tax liability of P, M, and any subsequent shareholders of FX in 2012 and subsequent taxable years, unless the Commissioner consents to a change.

Example 5. (i) In 1987, P, a calendar year domestic corporation that uses the tax book value method to allocate its interest expense under section 864(e)(4), acquired 50 percent of the outstanding stock of 10/50 Corp, a noncontrolled section 902 corporation organized in 1980. For taxable years beginning on or before April 25, 2006, the provisions of this paragraph (c) did not provide a mechanism for shareholders of noncontrolled section 902 corporations to make elections or adopt methods of accounting or a taxable year on behalf of noncontrolled section 902 corporations. However, P had to compute 10/50 Corp's earnings and profits in order to determine the adjustment under §1.861-12(c) and §1.861-12T(c) to P's basis in the stock of 10/50 Corp beginning with P's 1987 taxable year.

(ii) For taxable years beginning on or before April 25, 2006, P was required to compute 10/50 Corp's earnings and profits as if any permissible method of accounting not requiring an election and reflected in 10/50 Corp's books had been adopted. See paragraph (c)(4)(ii) of this section. In taxable years beginning after April 25, 2006, in accordance with paragraph (c)(3) of this section P may request the consent of the Commissioner to change any method of accounting or the taxable year on behalf of 10/50 Corp.

(9) *Change of method on audit.*—If, in connection with an audit (or audits) of one or more shareholders of the foreign corporation who collectively would constitute the foreign corporation's controlling domestic shareholder(s) if they undertook to act on the corporation's behalf, the Commissioner determines that a method of accounting of the foreign corporation does not clearly reflect income, the computation of earnings and profits shall be made in a manner which, in the opinion of the Commissioner, does clearly reflect income. See section 446 and the related regulations. The Commissioner shall provide written notice of the change in method of accounting to each such shareholder and to all other persons known by the Commissioner to be domestic shareholders who own (within the meaning of section 958(a)) stock of the foreign corporation. However, the failure of the Commissioner to provide such notice to any such other person shall not invalidate the change of method, which shall bind both the foreign corporation and all of its domestic shareholders as to the computation of the foreign corporation's earnings and profits for the taxable year of the foreign corporation for which the method of accounting is changed and in subsequent taxable years unless the Commissioner consents to a change.

(d) *Effective/applicability date.*—This section applies in computing earnings and profits of foreign corporations in taxable years of foreign corporations beginning on or after the date of publication of these regulations as final regulations in the **Federal Register**, and taxable years of shareholders with or within which such taxable years of the foreign corporations end. See 26 CFR §1.964-1 (revised as of April 1, 2011) for rules applicable to taxable years beginning before such date.

Determination of the Foreign Tax Credit: Guidance

Determination of the Foreign Tax Credit: Guidance.—Amendments to Reg. §1.965-5, relating to the determination of the foreign tax credit under the Internal Revenue Code, including changes made by the Tax Cuts and Jobs Act, are proposed (published in the Federal Register on December 7, 2018) (REG-105600-18).

Par. 29. Section 1.965-5, as proposed to be added at 83 FR 39562 (August 9, 2018), is amended by adding paragraph (c)(1)(iii) to read as follows:

§1.965-5. Allowance of a credit or deduction for foreign income taxes.

* * *

(c) * * *

(1) * * *

(iii) *Foreign income taxes deemed paid under section 960(b) (as applicable to taxable years of controlled foreign corporations beginning after December 31, 2017, and to taxable years of United States persons in which or with which such taxable years of foreign corporations end).*—No credit is allowed for the applicable percentage of foreign income taxes deemed paid under section 960(b) (as in effect for a taxable year of a controlled foreign corporation beginning after December 31, 2017, and a taxable year of a United States person in which or with which such controlled foreign corporation's taxable year ends) and §1.960-3(b)(1) with respect to distributions to the domestic corporation of section 965(a) previously taxed earnings and profits or section 965(b) previously taxed earnings and profits. The foreign income taxes deemed paid under §1.960-3(b)(1) with respect to a distribution to the domestic corporation of section 965(a) previously taxed earnings and profits or section 965(b) previously taxed earnings and profits is equal to the foreign income taxes properly attributable to a distribution from the distributing controlled foreign corporation's individual PTEP groups described in §1.960-3(c)(2)(ii), (iii), (vii), or (viii).

For purposes of this paragraph (c)(1)(iii), the terms "properly attributable" and "PTEP group" have the meanings set forth in §1.960-3(b)(3) and (c)(2) respectively. In addition, foreign income taxes that would have been deemed paid under section 960(a)(1) (as in effect on December 21, 2017) with respect to the portion of a section 965(a) earnings amount that was reduced under §1.965-1(b)(2) or §1.965-8(b) are not eligible to be deemed paid under section 960(b) and §1.960-3(b)(1) or any other section of the Code.

* * *

Determination of the Foreign Tax Credit: Guidance

Determination of the Foreign Tax Credit: Guidance.—Amendments to Reg. §1.965-7, relating to the determination of the foreign tax credit under the Internal Revenue Code, including changes made by the Tax Cuts and Jobs Act, are proposed (published in the Federal Register on December 7, 2018) (corrected March 6, 2019) (REG-105600-18).

Par. 30. Section 1.965-7, as proposed to be added at 83 FR 39,564 (August 9, 2018), is amended by adding three sentences at the end of paragraph (e)(1)(i) and adding paragraph (e)(1)(iv) to read as follows:

§1.965-7. Elections, payment, and other special rules.

* * *

(e) * * *

(1) * * *

(i) * * * If the section 965(n) election creates or increases a net operating loss under section 172 for the taxable year, then the taxable income of the person for the taxable year cannot be less than the amount described in paragraph (e)(1)(ii) of this section. The amount of deductions equal to the amount by which a net operating loss is created or increased for the taxable year by reason of the section 965(n) election (the "deferred amount") is not taken into account in computing taxable income or the separate foreign tax credit limitations under section 904 for that year. The source and separate category (as defined in §1.904-5(a)(4)(v)) components of the deferred amount are determined in accordance with paragraph (e)(1)(iv) of this section.

* * *

(iv) *Effect of section 965(n) election.*—(A) *In general.*—The section 965(n) election for a taxable year applies solely for purposes of determining the amount of net operating loss under section 172 for the taxable year and determining the amount of taxable income for the taxable year (computed without regard to the deduction allowable under section 172) that may be reduced by net operating loss carryovers or carrybacks to such taxable year under section 172. Paragraph (e)(1)(iv)(B) of this section provides a rule for coordinating the section 965(n) election's effect on section 172 with the computation of the separate foreign tax credit limitations under section 904.

(B) *Ordering rule for allocation and apportionment of deductions for purposes of the section 904 limitation.*—The effect of a section 965(n) election with respect to a taxable year on the computation of the separate foreign tax credit limitations under section 904 is computed as follows and in the following order.

(1) Deductions that would have been allowed for the taxable year but for the section 965(n) election, other than the amount of any net operating loss carryover or carryback to that year that is not allowed by reason of the section 965(n) election, are allocated and apportioned under §§1.861-8 through 1.861-17 to the relevant statutory and residual groupings, taking into account the amount described in paragraph (e)(1)(ii) of this section. The source and separate category of the net operating loss carryover or carryback to the taxable year, if any, is determined under the rules of §1.904(g)-3(b), taking into account the amount described in paragraph (e)(1)(ii) of this section. Therefore, if the amount of the net operating loss carryover or carryback to the taxable year (as reduced by reason of the section 965(n) election) exceeds the U.S. source loss component of the net operating loss that is carried over under §1.904(g)-3(b)(3)(i), but such excess is less than the potential carryovers (or carrybacks) of the separate limitation losses that are part of the net operating loss, the potential carryovers (or carrybacks) are proportionately reduced as provided in §1.904(g)-3(b)(3)(ii) or (iii), as applicable.

(2) If a net operating loss is created or increased for the taxable year by reason of the section 965(n) election, the deferred amount (as defined in paragraph (e)(1)(i) of this section) is not allowed as a deduction for the taxable year. See paragraph (e)(1)(i) of this section. The deferred amount (which is the corresponding addition to the net operating loss for the taxable year) comprises a ratable portion of the deductions (other than the deduction allowed under section 965(c)) allocated and apportioned to each statutory and residual grouping under paragraph (e)(1)(iv)(B)(*1*) of this section. Such ratable portion equals the deferred amount multiplied by a fraction, the numerator of which is the deductions allocated and apportioned to the statutory or residual grouping under paragraph (e)(1)(iv)(B)(*1*) of this section (other than the section 965(c) deduction) and the denominator of which is the total deductions (other than the section 965(c) deduction) described in paragraph (e)(1)(iv)(B)(*1*) of this section. Accordingly, the fraction described in the previous sentence takes into account the deferred amount.

(3) Taxable income and the separate foreign tax credit limitations under section 904 for the taxable year are computed without taking into account any deferred amount. Deductions allocated and apportioned to the statutory and residual groupings under paragraph (e)(1)(iv)(B)(*1*)) of this section, to the extent deducted in the taxable year rather than deferred to create or increase a net operating loss, are combined with income in the statutory and residual groupings to which those deductions are assigned in order to compute the amount of separate limitation income or loss in each separate category and U.S. source income or loss for the taxable year. Section 904(b), (f), and (g) are then applied to determine the applicable foreign tax credit limitations for the taxable year.

* * *

Foreign Currency Gain or Loss: Recognition and Deferral

Foreign Currency Gain or Loss: Recognition and Deferral.—Amendments to Reg. §§1.987-1—1.987-4, 1.987-6—1.987-8 and 1.987-12, relating to the recognition and deferral of foreign currency gain or loss under section 987 with respect to a qualified business unit (QBU) in connection with certain QBU terminations and certain other transactions involving partnerships, are proposed (published in the Federal Register on December 8, 2016) (REG-128276-12).

Par. 2. Section 1.987-1 is amended by adding paragraphs (b)(1)(iii), (b)(6), (c)(1)(ii)(B), (c)(3)(i)(E), (d)(3), (f), (g)(2)(i)(B) and (C), and (g)(3)(i)(E) through (H) to read as follows:

§1.987-1. Scope, definitions, and special rules.

* * *

(b) * * *

(1) * * *

(iii) [The text of the proposed amendment to §1.987-1(b)(1)(iii) is the same as the text of §1.987-1T(b)(1)(iii) as added by T.D. 9795].

* * *

(6) [The text of the proposed amendment to §1.987-1(b)(6) is the same as the text of §1.987-1T(b)(6) as added by T.D. 9795].

* * *

(c) * * *

(1) * * *

(ii) * * *

(B) [The text of the proposed amendment to §1.987-1(c)(1)(ii)(B) is the same as the text of §1.987-1T(c)(1)(ii)(B) as added by T.D. 9795]

* * *

(3) * * *

(i) * * *

(E) [The text of the proposed amendment to §1.987-1(c)(3)(i)(E) is the same as the text of §1.987-1T(c)(3)(i)(E) as added by T.D. 9795].

* * *

(d) * * *

(3) [The text of the proposed amendment to §1.987-1(d)(3) is the same as the text of §1.987-1T(d)(3) as added by T.D. 9795].

* * *

(f) [The text of the proposed amendment to §1.987-1(f) is the same as the text of §1.987-1T(f) as added by T.D. 9795].

* * *

(g) * * *

(2) * * *

(i) * * *

(B) [The text of the proposed amendment to §1.987-1(g)(2)(i)(B) is the same as the text of §1.987-1T(g)(2)(i)(B) as added by T.D. 9795].

(C) [The text of the proposed amendment to §1.987-1(g)(2)(i)(C) is the same as the text of §1.987-1T(g)(2)(i)(C) as added by T.D. 9795].

* * *

(3) * * *

(i) * * *

(E) [The text of the proposed amendment to §1.987-1(g)(3)(i)(E) is the same as the text of §1.987-1T(g)(3)(i)(E) as added by T.D. 9795].

(F) [The text of the proposed amendment to §1.987-1(g)(3)(i)(F) is the same as the text of §1.987-1T(g)(3)(i)(F) as added by T.D. 9795].

(G) [The text of the proposed amendment to §1.987-1(g)(3)(i)(G) is the same as the text of §1.987-1T(g)(3)(i)(G) as added by T.D. 9795].

(H) [The text of the proposed amendment to §1.987-1(g)(3)(i)(H) is the same as the text of §1.987-1T(g)(3)(i)(H) as added by T.D. 9795].

* * *

Par. 3. Section 1.987-2 is amended by adding paragraph (c)(9) to read as follows:

§1.987-2. Attribution of items to eligible QBUs; definition of a transfer and related rules.

* * *

(c) * * *

(9) [The text of the proposed amendment to §1.987-2(c)(9) is the same as the text of §1.987-2T(c)(9) as added by T.D. 9795].

* * *

Par. 4. Section 1.987-3 is amended by adding paragraphs (b)(2)(ii), (b)(4), (c)(2)(ii) and (v), (d), and *Example 9* through *Example 14* of paragraph (e) to read as follows:

§1.987-3. Determination of section 987 taxable income or loss of an owner of a section 987 QBU.

* * *

(b) * * *

(2) * * *

(ii) [The text of the proposed amendment to §1.987-3(b)(2)(ii) is the same as the text of §1.987-3T(b)(2)(ii) as added by T.D. 9795].

* * *

(4) [The text of the proposed amendment to §1.987-3(b)(4) is the same as the text of §1.987-3T(b)(4) as added by T.D. 9795].

* * *

(c) * * *

(2) * * *

(ii) [The text of the proposed amendment to §1.987-3(c)(2)(ii) is the same as the text of §1.987-3T(c)(2)(ii) as added by T.D. 9795].

* * *

(v) [The text of the proposed amendment to §1.987-3(c)(2)(v) is the same as the text of §1.987-3T(c)(2)(v) as added by T.D. 9795].

(d) [The text of the proposed amendment to §1.987-3(d) is the same as the text of §1.987-3T(d) as added by T.D. 9795].

(e) *Examples.*—* * *

Example 9 [The text of the proposed amendment to §1.987-3(e) *Example 9* is the same as the text of §1.987-3T(e) *Example 9* as added by T.D. 9795].

Example 10 [The text of the proposed amendment to §1.987-3(e) *Example 10* is the same as the text of § 1.987-3T(e) *Example 10* as added by T.D. 9795].

Example 11 [The text of the proposed amendment to § 1.987-3(e) *Example 11* is the same as the text of § 1.987-3T(e) *Example 11* as added by T.D. 9795].

Example 12 [The text of the proposed amendment to § 1.987-3(e) *Example 12* is the same as the text of § 1.987-3T(e) *Example 12* as added by T.D. 9795].

Example 13 [The text of the proposed amendment to § 1.987-3(e) *Example 13* is the same as the text of § 1.987-3T(e) *Example 13* as added by T.D. 9795].

Example 14 [The text of the proposed amendment to § 1.987-3(e) *Example 14* is the same as the text of § 1.987-3T(e) *Example 14* as added by T.D. 9795].

* * *

Par. 5. Section 1.987-4 is amended by adding paragraphs (c)(2) and (f) to read as follows:

§ 1.987-4. Determination of net unrecognized section 987 gain or loss of a section 987 QBU.

* * *

(c) * * *

(2) [The text of the proposed amendment to § 1.987-4(c)(2) is the same as the text of § 1.987-4T(c)(2) as added by T.D. 9795].

* * *

(f) [The text of the proposed amendment to § 1.987-4(f) is the same as the text of § 1.987-4T(f) as added by T.D. 9795].

* * *

Par. 6. Section 1.987-6 is amended by adding paragraph (b)(4) to read as follows:

§ 1.987-6. Character and source of section 987 gain or loss.

* * *

(b) * * *

(4) [The text of the proposed amendment to § 1.987-6(b)(4) is the same as the text of § 1.987-6T(b)(4) as added by T.D. 9795].

* * *

Par. 7. Section 1.987-7 is amended by adding paragraph (b) to read as follows:

§ 1.987-7. Section 987 aggregate partnerships.

* * *

(b) [The text of the proposed amendment to § 1.987-7(b) is the same as the text of § 1.987-7T(b) as added by T.D. 9795].

* * *

Par. 8. Section 1.987-8 is amended by adding paragraph (d) to read as follows:

§ 1.987-8. Termination of a section 987 QBU.

* * *

(d) [The text of the proposed amendment to § 1.987-8(d) is the same as the text of § 1.987-8T(d) as added by T.D. 9795].

* * *

Par. 9. Section 1.987-12 is revised to read as follows:

§ 1.987-12. Deferral of section 987 gain or loss.—[The text of the proposed amendment to § 1.987-12 is the same as the text of § 1.987-12T as added by T.D. 9795].

Gain or Loss: Nonfunctional Currency Transactions

Gain or Loss: Nonfunctional Currency Transactions.—Amendments to Reg. §§ 1.988-1 and 1.988-2, relating to the taxation of gain or loss from certain foreign currency transactions, are proposed (published in the Federal Register on March 17, 1992) (REG-208202-91) [originally issued as INTL-15-91]. Amendments to Reg. § 1.988-2(b)(15), (d)(5), (e)(3)(iv) and (e)(7) were adopted 1/12/2000 by T.D. 8860. Amendments to Reg. § 1.988-1(a)(3), (4) and (5) were withdrawn on 8/29/2003 by REG-106486-98; INTL-0015-91.

☐ Par. 2. Section 1.988-1 is amended by adding paragraphs (a)(3), (4), and (5), and adding *Example 12* to paragraph (a)(6) to read as follows [amendments to Reg. § 1.988-1(a)(3), (4) and (5) were withdrawn on 8/29/2003 by REG-106486-98, leaving only the amendment to Reg. § 1.988-1(a)(6), below]:

§ 1.988-1. Certain definitions and special rules.

(a) * * *

(6) * * *

Example 12. (i) On January 1, 1993, X issues a 3 year bond with the following terms. The bond is priced at par with a principal amount of $100. X agrees to make three payments on December 31 of each year of $5.28 and, upon maturity, will repay 200 Swiss francs (Sf) in satisfaction of the principal due. The spot rate on January 1, 1993 is Sf1 = $.50.

(ii) The debt instrument is a dual currency debt instrument within the meaning of paragraph (a)(4) of this section. The dual currency debt instrument is separated into two component hypothetical debt instruments. The first is a hypothetical Swiss franc denominated zero coupon bond with a stated redemption price at maturity of Sf200 discounted at a rate consistent with the rules of § 1.1273-2(d)(2)(iv) (assume 5% compounded annually) to determine an issue price of Sf172.77. The second is a 3 year hypothetical dollar self-amortizing installment obligation with annual payments of $5.28, a principal amount of $13.62 [$100 – (Sf172.77 × $.50)] and a yield to maturity of 8% compounded annually. Issuing a hypothetical dollar denominated installment obligation is not a section 988 transaction. Issuing the hypothetical Swiss franc zero coupon bond is a section 988 transaction subject to the computational rules of § 1.988-2(b).

☐ Par. 3. Section 1.988-2 is amended by adding paragraphs (b)(14) and (15), (d)(5), (e)(3)(iv) and (e)(7) as follows [amendments to Reg. § 1.988-2(b)(15), (d)(5), (e)(3)(iv) and (e)(7) were adopted 1/12/2000 by T.D. 8860, leaving only the amendments to Reg. § 1.988-2(b)(14), below]:

§ 1.988-2. Recognition and computation of exchange gain or loss.

* * *

(b) * * *

(14) *Nonfunctional currency debt replaced by other related person debt denominated in a different currency.*—(i) *In general.*—If a debt instrument denominated in a nonfunctional currency (or the payments of which are determined with reference to a nonfunctional currency) is entered into between related persons as defined in sections 267(b) and 707(b), and the instrument is disposed of or otherwise terminated prior to maturity in a transaction in which exchange gain or loss would be recognized, the District Director or the Assistant Commissioner (International) may defer such gain or loss if he determines that the debt has in effect been replaced with other debt denominated in a different currency (replacement debt) entered into with the same or another related person (regardless of whether the replacement debt is denominated in, or determined by reference to, the taxpayer's functional currency). Such deferral, however, shall not exceed the earlier of the date the replacement debt is terminated in a transaction in which gain or loss is recognized or the maturity date of the replacement debt (so long as such debt is not replaced with debt of a related person in a different currency).

(ii) *Debt for debt exchanges in the same nonfunctional currency.*—[RESERVED]

(iii) *Example.*—The following example illustrates the application of this paragraph (b)(14).

Example. X is a calendar year corporation with the dollar as its functional currency. On January 1, 1995, X issues a par bond with a principal amount of 3,500,000 British pounds (£) to Y, a related person under section 267(b). The bond pays interest at the rate of 10% compounded semi-annually and matures on December 31, 2009. The £3,500,000 have a spot value of $5,000,000 on January 1, 1995. On January 1, 1997, X and Y agree to convert X's pound obligation to a dollar obligation in the principal amount of $5,300,000, the spot value of the pound principal amount on that date. Assume that but for paragraph (b)(14) of this section, X would realize and recognize a $300,000 exchange loss on January 1, 1997. However, the District Director may defer X's $300,000 exchange loss until the $5,300,000 obligation matures or is otherwise terminated in a transaction in which gain or loss is recognized.

(iv) *Effective date.*—Paragraph (b)(14)(i) of this section shall be effective for transactions entered into after March 17, 1992.

* * *

Section 1256 Contracts: Swap Exclusions

Section 1256 Contracts: Swap Exclusions.—Amendment to Reg. § 1.988-1, providing guidance on the category of swaps and similar agreements that are within the scope of Code Sec. 1256(b)(2)(B), are proposed (published in the Federal Register on September 16, 2011) (REG-111283-11).

☐ Par. 6. Section 1.988-1 is amended by:

1. Revising paragraph (a)(2)(iii)(B)(*2*).

2. Adding two sentences to the end of paragraph (a)(2)(iii)(C) The revision and addition read as follows:

§ 1.988-1. Certain definitions and special rules.—(a) * * *

(2) * * *

(iii) * * *

(B) * * *

(*2*) Definition of notional principal contract. Generally, the term "notional principal contract" means a contract defined in § 1.446-3(c). However, a "notional principal contract" shall only be considered as described in paragraph (a)(2)(iii)(B)(*1*) of this section if the underlying property to which the instrument ultimately relates is money (for example, functional currency), nonfunctional currency, or property the value of which is determined by reference to an interest rate. Thus, the term "notional principal contract" includes a currency swap as defined in § 1.988-2(e)(2)(ii), but does not include a swap referenced to a commodity or equity index.

(C) * * * The rules of this paragraph (a)(2)(iii) apply to notional principal contracts as defined in § 1.446-3(c) that are entered into on or after the date of publication of a Treasury decision adopting these rules as final regulations in the **Federal Register**. Section 1.988-1(a)(2)(iii) as contained in 26 CFR part 1 revised April 1, 2011, continues to apply to notional principal contracts entered into before the date of publication of a Treasury decision adopting these rules as final regulations in the **Federal Register**.

* * *

Foreign Currency Gain or Loss: Recognition and Deferral

Foreign Currency Gain or Loss: Recognition and Deferral.—Amendments to Reg. §§ 1.988-1 and 1.988-2, relating to the recognition and deferral of foreign currency gain or loss under section 987 with respect to a qualified business unit (QBU) in connection with certain QBU terminations

and certain other transactions involving partnerships, are proposed (published in the Federal Register on December 8, 2016) (REG-128276-12).

Par. 10. Section 1.988-1 is amended by adding paragraph (a)(3) to read as follows:

§1.988-1. Certain definitions and special rules.

* * *

(a) * * *

(3) [The text of the proposed amendment to §1.988-1(a)(3) is the same as the text of §1.988-1T(a)(3) as added by T.D. 9795].

* * *

Par. 11. Section 1.988-2 is amended by revising paragraph (b)(16) and adding paragraph (i) to read as follows:

§1.988-2. Recognition and computation of exchange gain or loss.

* * *

(b) * * *

(16) [The text of the proposed amendment to §1.988-2(b)(16) is the same as the text of §1.988-2T(b)(16) as added by T.D. 9795].

* * *

(i) [The text of the proposed amendment to §1.988-2(i) is the same as the text of §1.988-2T(i) as added by T.D. 9795].

Global Dealing Operations: Allocation and Sourcing of Income and Deductions

Global Dealing Operations: Allocation and Sourcing of Income and Deductions.—Amendments to Reg. §1.988-4, relating to the allocation and sourcing of income, deductions, gains and losses from a global dealing operation, are proposed (published in the Federal Register on March 6, 1998) (REG-208299-90).

☐ Par. 12. Section 1.988-4 is amended as follows:

1. Paragraph (h) is redesignated as paragraph (i).
2. A new paragraph (h) is added.

The addition and revision read as follows:

§1.988-4. Source of gain or loss realized on a section 988 transfer.

* * *

(h) *Exchange gain or loss from a global dealing operation.*—Notwithstanding the provisions of this section, exchange gain or loss derived by a participant in a global dealing operation, as defined in §1.482-8(a)(2)(i), shall be sourced under the rules set forth in §1.863-3(h).

* * *

Gain or Loss: Nonfunctional Currency Transactions

Gain or Loss: Nonfunctional Currency Transactions.—Amendments to Reg. §1.988-5, relating to the taxation of gain or loss from certain foreign currency transactions, are proposed (published in the Federal Register on March 17, 1992) (REG-208202-91) [originally issued as INTL-15-91].

☐ Par. 4. Section 1.988-5 is amended by adding paragraphs (d) and (f) to read as follows:

§1.988-5. Section 988(d) hedging transactions.

* * *

(d) *Hedges of certain nonfunctional currency payments.*—(1) *In general.*—If a qualified payment, as defined in paragraph (d)(2)(ii) of this section, and a hedge, as defined [in] paragraph (d)(2)(iii) of this section, satisfy the requirements of paragraph (d)(2)(i) of this section, the qualified payment and the hedge shall be integrated as provided in paragraph (d)(3) of this section. A transaction integrated in accordance with the provisions of this section shall be referred to as a "hedged qualified payment." For purposes of this paragraph (d), the rules of paragraph (b)(3)(ii) of this section shall apply.

(2) *Requirements and definitions.*—(i) *Requirements of hedged qualified payment.*—A qualified payment as defined in paragraph (d)(2)(ii) of this section and a hedge as defined in paragraph (d)(2)(iii) of this section must satisfy the following requirements in order to be treated as a hedged qualified payment under paragraph (d)(1) of this section.

(A) The qualified payment and the hedge are identified as an integrated transaction under the rules of paragraph (b)(3) of this section.

(B) The hedge is entered into (or in the case of nonfunctional currency deposited in a separate account with a bank or other financial institution, such currency is acquired and deposited) on or after the date the qualified payment becomes fixed (or declared in the case of a dividend), and before the accrual date as defined in paragraph (d)(2)(iv) of this section.

(C) The qualified payment is hedged in whole or in part throughout the period beginning with the date the hedge is identified in accordance with paragraph (b)(3) of this section and ending on or after the accrual date (but not later than the payment date).

(D) None of the parties to the hedge are related. For this purpose, parties are related if they satisfy any of the relationships defined in sections 267(b) and 707(b).

(E) In the case of a qualified business unit with a residence, as defined in section 988(a)(3)(B), outside of the United States, both the qualified payment and the hedge are properly reflected on the books of that qualified business unit.

(F) Subject to the limitations of paragraph (d)(2)(i)(E) of this section, both the qualified payment and the hedge are entered into by the same individual, partnership, trust, estate, or corporation. With respect to a corporation, the same corporation must enter into both the qualified payment and the hedge whether or not such corporation is a member of an affiliated group of corporations that files a consolidated return.

(G) With respect to a foreign person engaged in a U.S. trade or business that enters into a qualified payment or hedge through such trade or business, all items of income and expense associated with the qualified payment and the hedge would have been effectively connected with such U.S. trade or business throughout the term of the hedged qualified payment had this paragraph (d) not applied.

(ii) *Qualified payment.*—A qualified payment is—

(A) A declared but unpaid dividend denominated in or determined by reference to a nonfunctional currency with respect to the recipient; or

(B) An unaccrued rent or royalty payment denominated in or determined by reference to a nonfunctional currency of the taxpayer (whether the taxpayer is the payor or recipient), the amount of which is fixed on the date the hedge is entered into.

(iii) *Hedge.*—(A) *In general.*—For purposes of this paragraph (d), the term hedge means a deposit of nonfunctional currency in a hedging account (as defined [in] paragraph (d)(3)(iii)(D) of this section), a contract described in §1.988-1(a)(1)(ii) and (2)(iii), or combination thereof, that reduces the risk of exchange rate fluctuations by reference to the taxpayer's functional currency with respect to nonfunctional currency payments made or received under a qualified payment (as defined in paragraph (d)(2)(ii) of this section). The term hedge includes an option contract described in §1.988-1(a)(1)(ii) and (2)(iii) only if the option contract expires on or before the accrual date and is exercised on or before such date. The premium paid for an option that lapses shall be integrated with the qualified payment.

(B) *Special rule for series of hedges.*—A series of hedges as defined in paragraph (d)(3)(iii)(A) of this section shall be considered a hedge if the qualified payment is hedged in whole or in part throughout the period beginning with the date the hedge is identified in accordance with paragraph (d)(2)(i)(A) of this section and ending on or after the accrual date. A taxpayer that enters into a series of hedges will be deemed to have satisfied the preceding sentence if the hedge that succeeds a hedge that has been terminated is entered into on the business day following such termination.

(C) *Special rules for historical rate rollovers.*—The principles of paragraph (b)(2)(iii)(C) of this section shall apply for purposes of this paragraph (d).

(D) *Special rules regarding deposits of nonfunctional currency in a hedging account.*—The principles of paragraph (b)(2)(iii)(D) of this section shall apply for purposes of this paragraph (d).

(E) *Interest income on deposit of nonfunctional currency in a hedging account.*—The principles of paragraph (b)(2)(iii)(E) of this section shall apply for purposes of this paragraph (d).

(iv) *Accrual date.*—The accrual date is the date when a dividend, rent or royalty that is a qualified payment is required to be accrued (or otherwise taken into account) under the taxpayer's method of accounting. A taxpayer may use any reasonable convention consistently applied to translate an accrued payment or receipt into the taxpayer's functional currency.

(v) *Payment date.*—The payment date is the date when payment is made or received with respect to a qualified payment or the subsequent account payable or receivable arising from such qualified payment.

(3) *Effect of hedged qualified payment.*—(i) *In general.*—A taxpayer that has entered into a transaction that is treated as a hedged qualified payment shall treat amounts paid or received under the hedge as paid or received under the qualified payment, or any subsequent account payable or receivable, or that portion to which the hedge relates. Thus, for example, any gain or loss on the hedge shall have the same source and character as the source and character of the qualified payment. The taxpayer shall recognize no exchange gain or loss on the hedge. The taxpayer shall recognize no exchange gain or loss with respect to an account payable or receivable that arises from a qualified payment during the period that the account payable or receivable is covered by the hedge.

(ii) *Partially hedged qualified payments.*—The effect of integrating a qualified payment and a hedge that partially hedges such qualified payment is to treat the amounts paid or received under the hedge as paid or received under the portion of the qualified payment being hedged, or any subsequent account payable or receivable. The income or expense resulting from qualified payment that is attributable to that portion of the qualified payment that is not hedged shall be translated into functional currency on the accrual date. The taxpayer shall realize exchange gain or loss shall with respect to any unhedged payable or receivable arising from the qualified payment.

(iii) *Disposition of a hedge or termination of the qualified payment prior to the accrual date.*—(A) *In general.*—If a taxpayer identifies a qualified payment as part of a hedged qualified payment as defined in paragraph (d)(2) of this section, and the qualified payment is disposed of or otherwise terminated prior to the accrual date (by transfer, cancellation, or otherwise), the taxpayer shall treat the hedge as sold for its fair market value on the date the qualified payment is terminated and shall realize and recognize any gain or loss with respect to that hedge on such date. Such gain or loss shall be an adjustment to the amount received or expended with respect to the disposition or termination, if any. The spot rate on the date the hedge is treated as sold shall be used to determine subsequent exchange gain or loss on the hedge. If a taxpayer identifies a hedge as part of a hedged qualified payment as defined in paragraph (d)(2) of this section, and disposes of the hedge prior to the accrual date, any gain or loss realized by the taxpayer on such disposition shall not be recognized and shall be an adjustment to the income or expense from the qualified payment.

(B) *Certain events in a series of hedges treated as a termination of the hedged qualified payment.*—If the rules of paragraph (d)(2)(iii)(B) of this section are not satisfied, the hedged qualified payment shall be terminated and the provisions of paragraph (d)(3)(iii)(A) of this section shall apply to any gain or loss actually realized with respect to such hedge. Any subsequent transactions entered into to reduce the risk of exchange rate movements with respect to such qualified payment shall not be considered a hedge as defined in paragraph (d)(2)(iii) of this section.

(C) *Qualified payments between related persons.—(1) In general.*—Notwithstanding any other provision of this paragraph (d), if the parties to a qualified payment are related within the meaning of sections 267(b) and 707(b), and the hedge or qualified payment is disposed of or otherwise terminated prior to the accrual date, the District Director or the Assistant Commissioner (International) may redetermine the timing, source, and character of gain or loss from the hedge or the qualified payment if he determines that a significant purpose for disposing of the hedge or terminating the qualified payment prior to the accrual date was to affect the timing, source, or character of income, gain, expense, or loss for Federal income tax purposes.

(2) Special source rule for certain hedges of dividends between related persons.—If a hedged qualified payment is entered into by a U.S. person and consists of a declared but unpaid dividend between related persons (as defined in section 267(b)) and a hedge, and the dividend is not paid, then any loss realized with respect to the hedge shall reduce foreign source income described in section 904 (d)(1)(I) and any gain shall be treated as from U.S. sources.

(iv) *Disposition of a hedge on or after the accrual date.*—If a taxpayer identifies a hedge as part of a hedged qualified payment as defined in paragraph (d)(2) of this section, and disposes of the hedge on or after the accrual date, the taxpayer shall recognize no gain or loss on the hedge and the booking date, as defined in § 1.988-2(c)(2), of the payable or receivable for purposes of computing exchange gain or loss shall be the date such hedge is disposed of.

(v) *Special rule for foreign persons that enter into hedged qualified payments giving rise to U.S. source income not effectively connected with a U.S. trade or business.*—If a foreign person enters into a hedged qualified payment that gives rise to U.S. source income not effectively connected with a U.S. trade or business of such foreign person, for purposes of sections 871(a), 881, 1441, 1442 and 6049, the provisions of this paragraph (d) shall not apply and such sections of the Internal Revenue Code shall be applied separately to the qualified payment and the hedge. To the extent relevant to any foreign person, if the requirements of this paragraph (d) are otherwise met, the provisions of this paragraph (d) shall apply for all other purposes of the Internal Revenue Code (*e.g.*, for purposes of calculating the earnings and profits of a controlled foreign corporation that enters into a hedged qualified payment through a qualified business unit resident outside the United States, income or expense with respect to such hedged qualified payment shall be calculated under the provisions of this paragraph (d)).

(vi) *Sections 263(g), 1092, and 1256 do not apply.*—Sections 263(g), 1092, and 1256 do not apply with respect to a qualified payment or hedge which comprises a hedged qualified payment as defined in paragraph (d)(2) of this section. However, sections 263(g), 1092 and 1256 may apply to the hedged qualified payment if such transaction is part of a straddle.

(vii) *Examples.*—The principles set forth in paragraph (d) of this section are illustrated in the following examples. The examples assume that K is an accrual method, calendar year U.S. corporation with the dollar as its functional currency.

Example 1. (i) K is a U.S. corporation that has a qualified business unit, Q. Q's principal place of business is in Canada, and it has the U.S. dollar (US$) as its functional currency. On January 1, 1993, Q enters into a 3 year lease to rent an office in Canada for annual payments of 50,000 Canadian dollars (C$). On February 1, 1993, 1994, and 1995, Q enters into a forward contract to buy C$50,00O for US$24,500, US$24,000, and US$23,500 respectively. Assume Q satisfies the identification requirements of paragraph (d)(2)(i)(A) of this section.

(ii) The obligation to pay rent denominated in nonfunctional currency as set forth above is a qualified payment as defined in paragraph (d)(2)(ii) of this section. Further, the forward contracts constitute a hedge as defined in paragraph (d)(2)(iii) of this section. Assuming the requirements of paragraph (d)(2)(i) of this section are satisfied, Q may integrate the forward contracts with the rental payments. Accordingly, Q is treated as having paid US$24,500 in rent in 1993, US$24,000 in rent in 1994, and US$23,500 in 1995.

Example 2. (i) B is a wholly owned Danish subsidiary of K, a U.S. corporation. B was organized on January 1, 1995, and its functional currency is the Danish Kroner. On September 1, 1995, the board of directors of B declares a dividend payable on December 31, 1995 in the amount of Krl00,000, which equals $10,000 at the spot rate on September 1, 1995. On the same day, K enters into a forward contract to sell Kr100,000 for $9,750 on September 1, 1995. Assume K satisfies the identification requirements of paragraph (d)(2)(i)(A) of this section. B pays a dividend of Kr100,000 on December 31, 1995. At the end of 1995, B's pool of post-1986 undistributed earnings is Kr300,000 of non-subpart F foreign source earnings and profits, and B's pool of post-1986 foreign income taxes is $3,000.

(ii) The declared dividend denominated in Kroner as set forth above is a qualified payment as defined in paragraph (d)(2)(ii) of this section. Further, the forward contract constitutes a hedge as defined in paragraph (d)(2)(iii) of this section. Assuming the requirements of paragraph (d)(2)(i) of this section are satisfied, K may integrate the forward contract with the dividend. Accordingly, K is treated as having received a $9,750 dividend in 1995.

(iii) The amount of foreign taxes deemed paid with respect to the dividend is $1,000 (Kr100,000/Kr300,000 × $3,000). If B had not hedged the dividend, the amount of the foreign taxes deemed paid would still be $1,000, computed in the same manner.

(iv) Assume that B does not pay the Kr100,000 dividend and K realizes a $250 loss on December 31, 1995, when the forward contract is terminated. Under paragraph (d)(3)(iii)(C)(2) of this section, the $250 loss shall reduce foreign source income described in section 904(d)(1)(I).

(4) *Effective date.*—This paragraph (d) shall be effective for transactions entered into on or after [DATE FINAL REGULATIONS ARE PUBLISHED IN THE FEDERAL REGISTER].

* * *

(f) *Mark to market method of accounting for taxpayers that are not acting in the capacity of a dealer.*—(1) *Scope.*—This paragraph (f) shall apply to any taxpayer that makes an election as provided in paragraph (f)(2) of this section. However, this election is not available to a qualified business unit that uses the United States dollar approximate separate transactions method of accounting described in § 1.985-3.

(2) *Operative rules.*—(i) *In general.*—A taxpayer described in paragraph (f)(1) of this section may elect to realize for the taxable year exchange gain or loss on section 988 transactions that results from changes in exchange rates between the date a financial accounting period begins and the date a financial accounting period closes (but no less frequently than quarterly), provided such treatment is consistent with the taxpayer's method of accounting for financial reporting purposes (and that method conforms to U.S. generally accepted accounting principles). Realizing the gain or loss resulting from changes in exchange rates between the date a financial accounting period begins and the date a financial accounting period closes shall hereafter be referred to as marking to market.

(ii) *Treatment of gain or loss.*—Proper adjustment for gain or loss realized under the preceding paragraph shall be made in the amount of any gain or loss subsequently realized. The character and source of gain or loss realized under the preceding paragraph shall be determined under § 1.988-3 and § 1.988-4.

(iii) *Exception.*—The method of accounting described in this paragraph (f) shall not apply to transactions entered into by a taxpayer in its capacity as a dealer or trader (as defined in § 1.446-4(b)) in nonfunctional currency or nonfunctional currency denominated instruments.

(3) *Treatment of hedging transactions.*—(i) *Hedging election by the taxpayer.*—Except as provided in this paragraph (f)(3), all section 988 transactions must be accounted for as if they were not hedging any transaction (*i.e.*, without regard to the taxpayer's treatment of hedging transaction for financial accounting purposes). A taxpayer that makes an election under this paragraph (f) shall account for section 988 hedging transactions as provided in paragraphs (a) through (e) of this section. Thus, if a taxpayer that has made an election under this paragraph (f) fully hedges all payments under a nonfunctional currency borrowing so as to create a synthetic functional currency borrowing that satisfies the requirements of paragraph (a) of this section, such nonfunctional currency borrowing and the related hedges shall not be marked to market under paragraph (f)(2) of this section. In contrast, if the taxpayer elects hedge accounting treatment for financial accounting purposes with respect to the transaction described in the preceding sentence, but does not comply with paragraph (a) of this section (*e.g.*, fails to satisfy the identification requirements of paragraph (a)(8) of this section), the nonfunctional currency borrowing and related hedges must be marked to market under paragraph (f)(2) of this section.

(ii) *Authority of the District Director.*—Nothing in this paragraph (f) shall prevent the District Director (or Assistant Commissioner (International)) from applying the rules of paragraphs (a) through (d) of this section.

(4) *Consistency rules.*—If a taxpayer elects the mark to market method of accounting of this paragraph (f) each person who is related to the taxpayer within the meaning of section 267(b) or 707(b) (whether or not such person is uses U.S. generally accepted accounting principles) shall be deemed to make the election described in paragraph (f)(2) of this section. The deemed election shall not apply to persons who otherwise would not be eligible to make the election described in paragraph (f)(2) of this section.

(5) *Time and manner of making election.*—(i) *Time for making the election.*—A taxpayer's election under this paragraph (f) is effective for any taxable year (and subsequent taxable years) only if it is made by the due date (including extensions) of the taxpayer's federal income tax return for the year.

(ii) *Manner of making the election.*—A taxpayer shall make the election provided in this paragraph (f) by attaching a statement entitled "Election of mark to market method of accounting with respect to section 988 transactions" to the taxpayer's return for the first taxable year for which the election is to be effective. The statement must contain the following information:

(A) A brief description of the taxpayer's method of accounting for financial purposes; and

(B) A statement that this method of accounting applies consistently to all related persons (except for the dealing or trading activities of such person) within the meaning of sections 267(b) and 707(b) except qualified business units that use the United States dollar approximate separate transactions method of accounting described in § 1.985-3.

(iii) *Election by a partnership, trust or controlled foreign corporation.*—In the case of a partnership, the election shall be made on behalf of all partners by the general partners; in the case of a trust (other than a grantor trust) the election shall be made by the trustees. In the case of a controlled foreign corporation, the election shall be made on behalf of all shareholders by its controlling United States shareholders under § 1.964-1(c)(3).

(iv) *Revocation.*—The election under this paragraph (f) cannot be revoked without the consent of the Commissioner.

(6) *Interaction with § 1.988-2(b)(14).*—Section 1.988-2(b)(14) (relating to nonfunctional currency related person debt replaced by other related person debt in a different currency) shall not apply to exchange gain or loss realized with respect to a debt instrument which is subject to the mark to market method of accounting elected under this paragraph (f).

(7) *Examples.*—The following examples illustrate the rules of this paragraph (f):

Example 1. (i) X is a calendar year U.S. corporation with the dollar as its functional currency. X is on the accrual method of accounting, and has properly elected the mark to market method of accounting of § 1.988-5(f) under which X's section 988 transactions are marked to market monthly. X also uses a spot rate convention to determine the spot rate as provided in §1.988-1(d)(3). Pursuant to X's spot rate convention, the spot rate at which a transaction within a month is booked is determined by the spot rate at the end of the prior month. Under X's method of accounting, nonfunctional currency denominated transactions (other than inventory and property accounts) on the books at the end of the month are revalued at the spot rate on the last day of the month. Inventory and property accounts (which are not section 988 transactions and therefore are not eligible for mark to market treatment) on the balance sheet are recorded exclusively at historical cost translated on the day of purchase. On January 1, 1995, X's only financial asset is a £ 2,000 bank account, which pursuant to X's spot rate convention is equal to $4,000 (the December 31, 1994 spot rate is £1 = $2, multiplied by £ 2,000). X also has inventory of $500 (translated at the historical rate). Assume that all of X's inventory was purchased on the same day. X has no liabilities.

(ii) On January 15, 1995, X receives £100 from the issuance of a note payable on January 15, 2000, and deposits the £100 into the bank account. The December 31, 1994 spot rate of £1 = $2 is used to book the cash and the note, not the spot rate on January 15, 1995. X has no other transactions during the month of January. The spot rate at the end of January is £1 = $2.50. Accordingly, X will realize $1,050 of exchange gain [(£2,100 × $2.50 = $5,250) – (£2,100 × $2.00 = $4,200)] with respect to X's pound cash account. Additionally, X will realize $50 of exchange loss [(£100 × $2.00 = $200) – (£100 × $2.50 = $250)] with respect to X's liability. Thus, X's total exchange gain for the [month of] January is $1,000. Because the acquisition of the inventory is not a section 988 transaction (and accordingly is recorded at historical cost and not revalued), no gain or loss is realized with respect to the inventory.

(iii) On February 21, 1995, X sells half of its inventory for £195, in exchange for an account receivable. The January 31, 1995 spot rate of £1 = $2.50 is used to book the receivable and to determine the amount realized on the inventory sale, not the spot rate on February 21, 1995. X has no other transactions during the month of February. The spot rate at the end of February is £ 1 = $2.75. X will realize $548.50 of exchange gain computed as follows:

(A) X will realize $573.50 of exchange gain on its assets subject to section 988 computed as follows. With respect to X's pound cash account, X will realize $525 of exchange gain [(£2,100 × $2.75 = $5,775) – (£2,100 × $2.50 = $5,250)]. With respect to the account receivable, X will realize $48.50 of exchange gain [(£195 × $2.75 = $536.25) – (£195 × $2.50 = $487.75)].

(B) X will realize $25 of exchange loss [(£100 × $2.50 = $250) – (£100 × $2.75 = $275)] with respect to X's £100 liability.

X will compute gain on the sale of its inventory by translating the £195 realized at the January 31, 1995 rate of £1 = $2.50 to equal $487.50 and subtracting the assumed basis of $250. Thus, X's gain on the sale of inventory is $237.50, none of which is exchange gain or loss under section 988.

(iv) On March 22, 1995, X is paid £195 in satisfaction of the account receivable, and deposits that amount in its bank account. The February 28, 1995 spot rate of £1 = $2.75 is used to book payment of the receivable and the amount deposited. X has no other transactions during the month of March. The spot rate at the end of March is £1 = $3.00. X will realize $550.75 of exchange gain computed as follows:

(A) X will realize $575.75 of exchange gain on its assets computed as follows. With respect to X's pound cash account, X will realize $575.75 of exchange gain [(£2,295 × $3.00 = $6,887) – (£2,295 × $2.75 = $6,311.25)]. With respect to the account receivable, X will not realize exchange gain or loss because it is terminated within the month of March.

(B) X will realize $25 of exchange loss [(£100 × $2.75 = $275) – (£100 × $3.00 = $300)] with respect to X's £100 liability.

(v) On April 15, 1995, (when the spot rate is £ 1 = $3.25) X withdraws £1000 from its bank account that it uses to purchase a machine. The basis of the machine is $3000 (the spot rate on March 31, 1995 of £1 = $3.00 times £1000).

Example 2. H is a calendar year U.S. corporation with the dollar as its functional currency that has properly elected the mark to market method of accounting of paragraph (f)(2) of this section. Under this method, H revalues its nonfunctional currency positions at the close of each month. H owns 100 percent of L, a foreign corporation. L has the local currency as its functional currency. On August 4, 1995, H enters into a forward contract which it designates for financial accounting purposes as a hedge of its net investment in L. Under H's method of financial accounting, gain or loss on the forward contract is not included in profit and loss but is treated as an adjustment to the equity account of H. Under paragraph (f)(2) of this section, the forward contract is not treated as hedging any transaction and therefore must be revalued on August 31, 1995 and gain or loss realized.

(8) *Effective date*.—This paragraph (f) shall be effective for taxable years ending on or after [DATE FINAL REGULATIONS ARE PUBLISHED IN THE FEDERAL REGISTER].

Foreign Personal Holding Company Income: Foreign Currency Gain or Loss: Exclusion

Foreign Personal Holding Company Income: Foreign Currency Gain or Loss: Exclusion.—Reg. §1.988-7, providing guidance on the treatment of foreign currency gain or loss of a controlled foreign corporation under the business needs exclusion from foreign personal holding company income, is proposed (published in the Federal Register on December 19, 2017) (REG-119514-15).

Par. 5. Section 1.988-7 is added to read as follows:

§1.988-7. Election to mark-to-market foreign currency gain or loss on section 988 transactions.—(a) *In general*.—Except as provided in paragraph (b) of this section, a taxpayer may elect under this section to apply the foreign currency mark-to-market method of accounting described in this section with respect to all section 988 transactions (including the acquisition and holding of nonfunctional currency described in section 988(c)(1)(C)(ii)). Under the foreign currency mark-to-market method of accounting, the timing of section 988 gain or loss on section 988 transactions is determined under the principles of section 1256. Only section 988 gain or loss is taken into account under the foreign currency mark-to-market method of accounting. Consistent with section 1256(a)(2), appropriate adjustments must be made to prevent the section 988 gain or loss from being taken into account again under section 988 or another provision of the Code or regulations. A section 988 transaction subject to this election is not subject to the "netting rule" of section 988(b) and § 1.988-2(b)(8), under which exchange gain or loss is limited to overall gain or loss realized in a transaction, in taxable years prior to the taxable year in which section 988 gain or loss would be recognized with respect to such section 988 transaction but for this election.

(b) *Exceptions.*—The election described in paragraph (a) of this section does not apply to:

(1) Any security, commodity, or section 1256 contract that is marked to market under any other provision, including section 475 or section 1256;

(2) Any security, commodity, or section 1256 contract that, pursuant to an election or an identification made by the taxpayer, is excepted from mark-to-market treatment under another provision, including section 475 or section 1256;

(3) Any transaction of a qualified business unit (as defined in section 1.989(a)-1(b)) that is subject to section 987; or

(4) Any section 988 transaction denominated in, or determined by reference to, a hyperinflationary currency. See § 1.988-2(b)(15), (d)(5), and (e)(7) for rules relating to such transactions.

(c) *Time and manner of election.*—A taxpayer makes the election under paragraph (a) of this section by filing a statement that clearly indicates that such election has been made with the taxpayer's timely-filed original federal income tax return for the taxable year for which the election is made. In the case of a controlled foreign corporation, the controlling United States shareholders (as defined in § 1.964-1(c)(5)) make the election under paragraph (a) of this section on behalf of the controlled foreign corporation by filing a statement that clearly indicates that such election has been made with their timely-filed, original federal income tax returns for the taxable year of such United States shareholders ending with or within the taxable year of the controlled foreign corporation for which the election is made.

(d) *Revocation and subsequent election.*—A taxpayer may revoke its election under paragraph (a) of this section at any time. If an election has been revoked under this paragraph (d), a new election under paragraph (a) of this section cannot be made until the sixth taxable year following the year in which the previous election was revoked, and such subsequent election cannot be revoked until the sixth taxable year following the year in which the subsequent election was made. A taxpayer revokes the election by filing a statement that clearly indicates that such election has been revoked with its original or amended federal income tax return for the taxable year for which the election is revoked. In the case of a controlled foreign corporation, the controlling United States shareholders revoke the election on behalf of the controlled foreign corporation by filing a statement that clearly indicates that such election has been revoked with their original or amended federal income tax returns for the taxable year of such United States shareholders ending with or within the taxable year of the controlled foreign corporation for which the election is revoked.

(e) *Applicability dates.*—This section applies to taxable years of taxpayers (including controlled foreign corporations) ending on or after the date these regulations are published as final regulations in the *Federal Register*. [Reg. § 1.988-7.]

DISCs: Taxation of Income

Domestic International Sales Corporations: Taxation of Income.—Reproduced below are the texts of proposed amendments of Reg. § 1.991-1, relating to the taxation of income allocable to a DISC for taxable years beginning after 1984 (published in the Federal Register on February 3, 1987).

* * *

☐ Par. 4. Section 1.991-1 is amended as follows:

1. In the third sentence of paragraph (a), the phrase "and the interest equalization tax" is removed, and three new sentences are added at the end of paragraph (a).
2. a. In paragraph (b)(1) the third sentence is revised;
   b. In paragraph (b)(2) a new sentence is added immediately after the fourth sentence;
   c. Paragraph (b)(3) is revised; and
   d. Paragraphs (b)(4) and (5) are removed.
3. New paragraphs (e) and (f) are added immediately after paragraph (d).

§ 1.991-1. Taxation of a domestic international sales corporation (DISC).—(a) *In general.*—* * * For taxable years of a DISC beginning after 1984, the shareholders of the DISC are required to pay an annual interest charge on the shareholder's DISC-related deferred tax liability. The interest charge is imposed on the DISC shareholder, not the DISC. See section 995(f) and § 1.995(f)-1.

* * *

(b) *Determination of taxable income.*—(1) *In general.*—* * * For example, a DISC may choose its accounting methods and inventory method, or elect, under section 168(b)(3), different recovery percentages for its recovery property than those prescribed under section 168(b)(1), as if the DISC were a domestic corporation which had not elected to be treated as a DISC. * * *

(2) *Choice of accounting methods.*—* * * See also, section 267 for rules that may apply to transactions between a DISC and a related taxpayer requiring the matching of certain items of income and deduction and the deferral of certain losses. * * *

(3) *Annual accounting period.*—For taxable years beginning after March 21, 1984, a DISC cannot choose or change its taxable year without regard to the taxable year of its principal shareholder. In general, a DISC and its principal shareholder must use the same taxable year. See section 441(h) and § 1.441-1.

* * *

(e) *Close of taxable year and termination of DISC election for all DISCs on December 31, 1984; Reelection required; Exemption of pre-1985 accumulated DISC income from tax.*—Under section 805(b)(1)(A) of the Tax Reform Act of 1984, Pub. L. 98-369, the last taxable year of a DISC beginning before 1985 ended on December 31, 1984. The corporation's DISC election is also deemed revoked as of the close of business on December 31, 1984. A new DISC election must be made on Form 4876A in order for the corporation to be treated as a DISC for any taxable year beginning after December 31, 1984. See § 1.921-1T(b). See section 805(b)(2) of the Act and § 1.921-1T(a) for the tax treatment after 1984 of the accumulated DISC income derived before 1985 by certain DISCs.

(f) *Interest charge imposed on DISC shareholders after 1984.*—Section 995(f) requires that for each taxable year beginning after 1984, each shareholder of a DISC shall pay an interest charge on the shareholder's DISC-related deferred tax liability. The shareholder's DISC-related deferred tax liability is computed only with reference to the DISC's accumulated DISC income (earned in periods after 1984) and deferred by the DISC for more than one taxable year. Thus, in general, a DISC shareholder will not have a DISC-related deferred tax liability (and thus, no interest charge) until the close of the shareholder's taxable year following the taxable year with which or within which the first taxable year of the DISC (ending after 1984) ends. See § 1.995(f)-1.

DISCs: Taxation of Income: Elections

Domestic International Sales Corporations: Taxation of Income.—Reproduced below are the texts of proposed amendments of Reg. §§ 1.992-1 and 1.992-2, relating to the taxation of income allocable to a DISC for taxable years beginning after 1984 (published in the Federal Register on February 3, 1987).

□ Par. 5. Section 1.992-1 is amended as follows:

1. At the end of paragraph (a)(7), "and" is removed; at the end of paragraph (a)(8), the period is removed and ", and" is added in its place; immediately following paragraph (a)(8) the following new paragraph is added: "(9) Is not a member of any controlled group (as defined in section 993(a)(3) and § 1.993-1(k)) of which a FSC or a small FSC (as defined in section 992) is a member. See paragraph (j) of this section."; and in the sentence immediately following paragraph (a)(9), the language "subparagraphs (1) through (8) of this paragraph" is removed and the language "paragraphs (a)(1), through (a)(9) of this section" is added in its place.

2. The text of paragraph (e) is redesignated as paragraph (e)(1) and new paragraph (e)(2) is added to read as set forth below.

3. A new paragraph (j) is added to read as set forth below.

§ 1.992-1. Requirements of a DISC.—

* * *

(e) *Election in effect.*—(1) * * *

(2) Section 805(b)(1)(A) of the Tax Reform Act of 1984 provides that the last taxable year of any DISC beginning in 1984, shall end on December 31, 1984, and under § 1.921-1T(a)(1) the corporation's DISC election is also deemed revoked as of the close of business on that date. A new DISC election must be filed on Form 4876A in order for the corporation to be treated as a DISC for any taxable year beginning after December 31, 1984. See § 1.992-2(a) and (b).

* * *

(j) *Effect on a DISC of a FSC election.*—(1) *General rule.*—(i) Under section 992(a)(1)(E) and paragraph (a)(9) of this section, a corporation shall not be treated as a DISC for a taxable year if at any time during such taxable year such corporation is a member of a controlled group (as defined in section 993(a)(3) and § 1.993-1(k)) of which a FSC or a small FSC (as defined in section 922) is a member. For purposes of this paragraph (j), a FSC also includes a small FSC. A FSC election within a group will prevail over any DISC election within such group. Thus, no corporation can make an election to be treated as a DISC for any taxable year if on any day of such taxable year such corporation is a member of a controlled group of which a FSC is a member. Further, the election of a corporation to be treated as a DISC is terminated on the first day for which the election of another corporation to be treated as a FSC becomes effective, if at any time during the DISC's taxable year such corporations are members of the same controlled group. Except as provided in paragraph (j)(2) of this section (relating to certain corporate acquisitions and reorganizations), the termination of the DISC election on such date means that such corporation shall not be treated as a DISC for its entire taxable year which includes such date, and the corporation shall be subject to tax on its taxable income for such entire taxable year. A revocation of the corporation's DISC election under section 992(b)(3) is not required.

(ii) The following example illustrates the provisions of this paragraph (j)(1):

Example. D, a calendar year corporation, has made a proper DISC election for 1985 and succeeding years. F, a corporation having a fiscal year beginning on July 1, is a member of the same controlled group of which D is a member. On May 1, 1986, F files an election to be treated as a FSC effective for F's taxable year beginning July 1, 1986. D's DISC election is treated as terminated on July 1, 1986, and D is not a DISC for its taxable year which begins January 1, 1986, and ends on December 31, 1986. F's election to be treated as a FSC for its taxable year beginning July 1, 1986, is not affected by the termination of D's DISC election.

(2) *Exception for certain acquisitions and reorganizations.*—(i) In the case of a DISC and a FSC described in paragraph (j)(2)(ii) of this section for a taxable year, paragraph (j)(1) of this

section shall not apply, and the domestic corporation may be treated as a DISC or the foreign corporation may be treated as a FSC for a short taxable year ending on the day preceding the day the DISC and the FSC became members of the same controlled group. If the DISC election is terminated, the DISC is required to satisfy all requirements to be treated as a DISC (including the 95 percent qualified export receipts and assets requirement of section 992(a)(1)) for the short taxable year, and may satisfy those requirements by making the distributions to meet such requirements provided in section 992(c). The $10 million limitation on qualified export receipts under section 995(b)(1)(E) for the short taxable year must be pro rated on a daily basis as provided in § 1.995-8(a). If the FSC election is terminated, the FSC is required to satisfy all requirements to be treated as a FSC for the short taxable year, and if the FSC is a small FSC, the $5 million foreign trading gross receipts limitation under section 924(b)(2) for the short taxable year must be pro rated on a daily basis. The controlled group of corporations shall make its choice to terminate the election of either the DISC or the FSC by filing the short period return required for the corporation whose election as a DISC or FSC (as the case may be) is to be terminated within the due date (including extensions) prescribed by section 6072(b). If the group fails to terminate the election of either the DISC or the FSC within such period, the DISC election of the domestic corporation shall be terminated as provided by paragraph (j)(1) of this section.

(ii) A DISC and a FSC are described in this paragraph (j)(2)(ii) for a taxable year if—

(A) Both the DISC and the FSC had an immediately preceding taxable year and each was treated as a DISC and as a FSC, respectively, for such immediately preceding taxable year,

(B) The DISC and the FSC were not members of the same controlled group on the first day of the taxable year, and

(C) The DISC and the FSC became members of the same controlled group of corporations during the taxable year by reason of the acquisition, directly or indirectly, of a member of the controlled group which includes such DISC (or FSC, as the case may be) by either—

(1) A member of the controlled group which includes such FSC (or DISC, as the case may be) (thereby making the DISC and the FSC members of the same parent-subsidiary controlled group), or

(2) The 5 or fewer persons who are individuals, estates or trusts who control the corporation which controls such FSC (or DISC, as the case may be) (thereby making the DISC and the FSC members of the same brother-sister controlled group).

(iii) The provisions of this paragraph (j)(2) may be illustrated by the following example:

Example—(i) *Facts.* Z corporation owns all the stock of D, a corporation which has elected to be treated as a DISC. X corporation owns all the stock of F, a corporation which has elected to be treated as a small FSC. Z, X, D and F use the calendar year as the taxable year. D was treated as a DISC, and F was treated as a small FSC, for their taxable years ending December 31, 1986. On January 1, 1987, Z and X are not members of the same controlled group. On August 1, 1987, Z purchases all of the stock of X, thereby making D and F members of the same controlled group.

(ii) *Result.* (A) If the group chose to retain the small FSC and terminate the DISC, under paragraph (j)(2)(i) of this section, D is permitted to end its taxable year on July 31, 1987, and may be treated as a DISC for such short year if it satisfies the requirements of section 992(a)(1) with respect to such short taxable year. The $10 million amount under section 995(b)(1)(E) for the short taxable year is limited to $5,808,219 ($10 million × 212/365). D's DISC election is terminated on August 1, 1987. F's small FSC election and $5 million amount under section 924(b)(2) are not affected by the acquisition.

(B) Alternatively, the group could choose to retain the DISC and terminate the small FSC with the same short taxable year ending July 31, 1987. F's $5 million amount for such short year would be limited to $2,904,110 ($5 million × 212/365), and D's DISC election and $10 million amount under section 995(b)(1)(E) would not be affected by the acquisition.

□ Par. 6. Section 1.992-2 is amended by removing "Form 4876" each place it appears and adding in their place the words "Form 4876A", and by revising paragraphs (a) and (b)(2) to read as follows:

§ 1.992-2. Election to be treated as a DISC.—(a) *Manner and Time of election.*—(1) *Manner.*—The election to be treated as a DISC is made by the corporation by filing Form 4876A (Form 4876 for taxable years beginning before January 1, 1985) with the service center with which it would file its income tax return if the corporation were subject for such taxable year to all the taxes imposed by subtitle A of the Internal Revenue Code. The Form 4876A shall be signed by any person authorized to sign the corporation's return under section 6062, and shall contain the information required by such Form. Except as provided in paragraphs (b)(3) and (c) of this section, such election to be treated as a DISC shall be valid only if the statement of consent of every person who is a shareholder of the corporation as of the beginning of the first taxable year for which such election is to be effective is made on or is attached to such Form 4876A when filed with the service center.

(2) *Time for making election.*—In the case of a corporation making an election to be treated as a DISC for the corporation's first taxable year, the election shall be made within 90 days after the beginning of such taxable year. In the case of a corporation making an election to be treated as a DISC for a taxable year which is not the corporation's first taxable year, the election shall be made during the 90 day period immediately preceding the first day of such taxable year.

(3) *Special rule for re-electing DISC status in 1985.*—Under section 805(b) of the Tax Reform Act of 1985, the last taxable year of any DISC beginning in 1984 ended on December 31, 1984, and under § 1.921-1T(a)(1), the corporation's election to be treated as a DISC is deemed revoked after the close of business on such date. A corporation which was a DISC on December 31,

1984, and which wishes to be treated as a DISC for its first taxable year beginning after December 31, 1984, must make a new DISC election by filing Form 4876A in accordance with the instructions thereon and in accordance with paragraph (a)(1) of this section on or before June 3, 1987. The Form 4876A is to be filed within such period with the service center with which the corporation files its DISC return.

(b) *Consent by shareholders.*—* * *

(2) *Transitional rule for certain corporations re-electing DISC status in 1985.*—Notwithstanding paragraph (b)(1) of this section, if the corporation was a DISC on December 31, 1984, and the corporation files its election to be treated as a DISC for the corporation's first taxable year beginning after December 31, 1984, within the time prescribed in paragraph (a)(3) of this section, the election shall be valid if the consent of each person who was a shareholder of the corporation on January 1, 1985, is filed with the service center with which the election was filed on or before December 31, 1987. The form of such consent shall be the same as that prescribed in paragraph (b)(1) of this section. A copy of the corporation's statement of election, Form 4876A, shall be attached to the consent.

* * *

Imputed Interest: OID: Safe Haven Interest Rates

Imputed Interest: Original Issue Discount: Safe Haven Interest Rates.—Reproduced below is the text of a proposed amendment of Reg. §1.993-1, relating to (1) the tax treatment of debt instruments issued after July 1, 1982, that contain original issue discount, (2) the imputation of and the accounting for interest with respect to sales and exchanges of property occurring after December 31, 1984, and (3) safe haven interest rates for loans or advances between commonly controlled taxpayers and safe haven leases between such taxpayers (published in the Federal Register on April 8, 1986).

* * *

☐ Par. 18. In §1.993-1, paragraph (g) is amended by removing the phrase "section 1232" and adding in its place the phrase "section 1272".

* * *

DISCs: Deemed Distributions

Domestic International Sales Corporations: Taxation of Income.—Reproduced below are the texts of proposed Reg. §1.995-2A and proposed amendments to Reg. §1.995-2, relating to the taxation of income allocable to a DISC for taxable years beginning after 1984 (published in the Federal Register on February 3, 1987).

* * *

☐ Par. 7. Section 1.995-2 is amended by revising the title of the section and by adding two new sentences immediately before the first sentence in paragraph (a) to read as follows:

§1.995-2. Deemed distributions in qualified years ending before 1985.—(a) *General rule.*—This section applies to taxable years of a DISC ending before January 1, 1985. See §1.995-2A for taxable years of a DISC beginning after December 31, 1984. * * *

☐ Par. 8. New section 1.995-2A is added immediately after §1.995-2 to read as follows:

§1.995-2A. Deemed distributions in qualified years beginning after 1984.—(a) *General rule.*—This section applies to taxable years of a DISC beginning after December 31, 1984. See §1.995-2 for taxable years beginning before January 1, 1985. Under section 995(b)(1), each shareholder of a DISC shall be treated as having received a distribution taxable as a dividend with respect to the shareholder's stock on the last day of each taxable year of the DISC beginning after December 31, 1984, in an amount equal to the shareholder's pro rata share of the sum (as limited by paragraph (b) of this section) of the following items:

(1) The gross interest derived by the DISC during such year from producer's loans (as defined in §1.993-4).

(2) The lower of—

(i) Any gain recognized by the DISC during such year on the sale or exchange of property (other than property which in the hands of the DISC is a qualified export asset) which was previously transferred to it in a transaction in which the transferor realized gain which was not recognized in whole or in part, or

(ii) The amount of the transferor's gain which was not recognized on the previous transfer of the property to the DISC.

For purposes of this paragraph (a)(2), each item of property shall be considered separately. See paragraph (d) of this section for special rules with respect to certain tax-free acquisitions of property by the DISC.

(3) The lower of—

(i) Any gain recognized by the DISC during such year on the sale or exchange of property which in the hands of the DISC is a qualified export asset (other than stock in trade or property described in section 1221(1)) and which was previously transferred to the DISC in a transaction in which the transferor realized gain which was not recognized in whole or in part, or

(ii) The amount of the transferor's gain which was not recognized on the previous transfer of the property to the DISC and which would have been includible in the transferor's gross income as ordinary income if its entire realized gain had been recognized upon the transfer.

For purposes of this paragraph (a)(3), each item of property shall be considered separately. See paragraph (d) of this section for special rules with respect to certain tax-free acquisitions of property by the DISC.

(4) Fifty (50) percent of the taxable income of the DISC for the taxable year attributable to military property (as defined in §1.995-6).

(5) The taxable income of the DISC for the taxable year attributable to qualified export receipts of the DISC for such year which exceed $10,000,000 (as determined under § 1.995-8).

(6) The sum of—

(i) In the case of a shareholder which is a C corporation, an amount equal to one-seventeenth ($^1/_{17}$) of the excess, if any, of the taxable income of the DISC for the taxable year, before reduction for any distributions during such year, over the sum of the amounts deemed distributed for the taxable year in accordance with paragraphs (a)(1) through (5) of this section,

(ii)(A) In the case of a shareholder which is a C corporation—

(1) An amount equal to $^{16}/_{17}$ of the excess described in paragraph (a)(6)(i), multiplied by the international boycott factor as determined under section 999(c)(1), or

(2) In lieu of the amount determined under subparagraph (ii)(A)(*1*), $^{16}/_{17}$ of such excess as is described in section 999(c)(2), or

(B) In the case of a shareholder which is not a C corporation—

(1) An amount equal to all of the excess described in paragraph (a)(6)(i), multiplied by the international boycott factor as determined under section 999(c)(1), or

(2) In lieu of the amount determined under subparagraph (ii)(B)(*1*), the amount of such excess as is described in section 999(c)(2), and

(iii) An amount equal to the sum of any illegal bribes, kickbacks, or other payments paid by or on behalf of the DISC directly or indirectly to an official, employee, or agent in fact of a government. An amount is paid by a DISC where it *is* paid directly or indirectly by any officer, director, employee, shareholder, or agent of the DISC for the benefit of such DISC. For purposes of this section, the principles of section 162(c) and the regulations thereunder shall apply. The amount of an illegal payment made in the form of property or services shall be considered to be equal to the fair market value of such property or services at the time such property is transferred or such services are performed.

(7) The amount of foreign investment attributable to producer's loans of the DISC, as of the close of the "group taxable year" ending with such taxable year of the DISC, determined in accordance with § 1.995-5. The amount of such foreign investment attributable to producer's loans so determined for any taxable year of a former DISC shall be deemed distributed as a dividend to the shareholders of such former DISC on the last day of such taxable year. See § 1.995-3(e) for the effect that such deemed distribution has on scheduled installments of deemed distributions or accumulated DISC income under § 1.995-3(a) upon disqualification.

(b) *Limitation on amount of deemed distributions under section 995(b)(1).*—(1) *General rule.*—The sum of the amounts described in paragraphs (a)(1) through (a)(6) of this section which is deemed distributed pro rata to the DISC's shareholders as a dividend for any taxable year of the DISC shall not exceed the DISC's earnings and profits for such year.

(2) *Foreign investment attributable to producer's loans.*—The amount of foreign investment attributable to producer's loans of the DISC (as described in paragraph (a)(7) of this section) which is deemed to be distributed pro rata to the DISC's shareholders as a dividend for any taxable year of the DISC shall not exceed the lesser of the DISC's accumulated DISC income at the beginning of such year or the corporation's accumulated earnings and profits at the beginning of such year (but not less than zero)—

(i) Increased by any DISC income of the corporation for such year as defined in § 1.996-3(b)(2) (that is, any excess of the DISC's earnings and profits for such year over the sum of the amounts described in paragraphs (a)(1) through (a)(6) of this section), or

(ii) Decreased by any deficit in the DISC's earnings and profits for such year.

For example, if a DISC has a deficit in accumulated earnings and profits at the beginning of a taxable year of $10,000, current earnings and profits of $12,000, no amounts described in paragraphs (a)(1) through (a)(6) of this section for the year, and foreign investment attributable to producer's loans for the taxable year of $5,000, the DISC would have a deemed distribution described in paragraph (a)(7) of this section of $5,000 for the taxable year. As a further example, assume that the DISC had accumulated earnings and profits of $13,000 at the beginning of the taxable year, accumulated DISC income of $10,000 at the beginning of the taxable year, a deficit in earnings and profits for the taxable year of $12,000, no amounts described in paragraphs (a)(1) through (a)(6) of this section for the taxable year, and foreign investment attributable to producer's loans for the taxable year of $5,000. Under these facts the DISC would have no deemed distribution described in paragraph (a)(7) of this section for the taxable year because the DISC had no DISC income for the taxable year and the current year's deficit in earnings and profits subtracted from the DISC's accumulated DISC income at the beginning of the year produces a negative amount. For rules relating to the carryover to a subsequent year of the $5,000 of foreign investment attributable to producer's loans, see § 1.995-5(a)(6).

(3) *Ordering rule when limitation applies.*—If, by reason of the limitation described in paragraph (b)(1) of this section, less than the sum of the amounts described in paragraphs (a)(1) through (a)(6) of this section is deemed distributed, then the portion of such sum which is deemed distributed shall be attributed first to the amount described in paragraph (a)(1), to the extent thereof; second to the amount described in paragraph (a)(2), to the extent thereof; third to the amount described in paragraph (a)(3), to the extent thereof; and so forth, and finally to the amount described in paragraph (a)(6).

(c) *Examples.*—Paragraphs (a) and (b) of this section may be illustrated by the following examples:

Example (1). Y is a corporation which uses the calendar year as its taxable year and elects to be treated as a DISC beginning with its taxable year beginning January 1, 1985. X, a corporation, is Y's sole shareholder. In 1985, X transfers certain property to Y in exchange for Y's stock in a transaction in which X does not recognize gain or loss by reason of the application of section 351(a). Included in the property transferred to Y is depreciable property described in paragraph (a)(3) of this section on which X realizes, and does not recognize by reason of the application of section 1245(b)(3), a gain of $20,000. If X had sold such property for cash, the $20,000 gain would have been recognized as ordinary income under section 1245. Also included in the transfer to Y are 100 shares of stock in a third corporation (which is not a related foreign export corporation) on which X realizes, but does not recognize, a gain of $5,000. In 1986, Y sells such property and recognizes a gain of $25,000 on the depreciable property and $8,000 on the 100 shares of stock. Y has accumulated earnings and profits at the beginning of 1986 of $5,000, earnings and profits for 1986 of $72,000, and taxable income for 1986 of $100,000. At the beginning of 1986, Y has $6,000 of accumulated DISC income, no previously taxed income, and a deficit of $1,000 of other earnings and profits. The total qualified export receipts of Y for 1986 are less than $10 million and there were no transactions in military property. Under these facts and the additional facts assumed in the table below, X is treated as having received a deemed distribution taxable as a dividend of $46,000 on December 31, 1986, determined as follows:

(1)	Gross interest derived by Y in 1986 from producer's loans		$7,000
(2)	Amount of gain on depreciable property (lesser of Y's recognized gain ($25,000) or X's gain not recognized on section 1245 property ($20,000))		20,000
(3)	Amount of gain on stock (lesser of Y's recognized gain ($8,000) or X's gain not recognized ($5,000))		5,000
(4)	One-seventeenth of the excess of the DISC's taxable income for 1986 over the sum of lines (1), (2) and (3) (1/17 of $100,000 minus $32,000))		$4,000
(5)	Limitation on lines (1) through (4):		
	(a)	Sum of lines (1) through (4)	$36,000
	(b)	Earnings and profits for 1986	72,000
	(c)	Lesser of lines (5)(a) or (b)	$36,000
(6)	Amount determined under paragraph (a)(7) of this section:		
	(a)	Foreign investment attributable to producer's loans under § 1.995-5	$10,000
	(b)	Sum of the lesser of accumulated earnings and profits at beginning of 1986 ($5,000) or accumulated DISC income at beginning of 1986 ($6,000), plus excess of earnings and profits for 1986 over line (5)(c) ($72,000 minus $36,000)	$41,000
	(c)	Lesser of lines (6)(a) or (b)	$10,000
(7)	Total deemed distribution for 1986 (sum of lines (5)(c) and (6)(c))		$46,000

Example (2). Assume the facts are the same as in example (1), except that the earnings and profits for 1986 are only $30,000. Under these facts, X is treated as receiving a deemed distribution taxable as a dividend of $35,000 on December 31, 1986, determined as follows:

(5)	Limitation on lines (1) through (4) of example (1):		
	(a)	Line (5)(a) of example (1)	$36,000
	(b)	Earnings and profits for 1986	$30,000
	(c)	Lesser of lines (5)(a) or (b)	$30,000
(6)	Amount determined under paragraph (a)(7) of this section:		
	(a)	Line (6)(a) of example (1)	$10,000
	(b)	Sum of the lesser of accumulated earnings and profits at beginning of 1986 ($5,000) or accumulated DISC income at beginning of 1986 ($6,000), plus excess of earnings and profits for 1986 over line (5)(c) ($30,000 minus $30,000)	$5,000
	(c)	Lesser of lines (6)(a) or (b)	$5,000
(7)	Total deemed distribution for 1986 (sum of lines (5)(c) and (6)(c)		$35,000

Example (3). Assume the facts are the same as in example (1), except that Y has a deficit in accumulated earnings and profits at the beginning 1986 of $4,000. This deficit is comprised of accumulated DISC income of $1,000, no previously taxed income and a deficit in other earnings and profits of $5,000. Assume also that Y has earnings and profits for 1986 of $45,000. Under these facts, X is treated as receiving a deemed distribution taxable as a dividend in the amount of $45,000 on December 31, 1986, determined as follows:

(5)	Limitation on lines (1) through (4) of example (1):		
	(a)	Line (5)(a) of example (1)	$36,000
	(b)	Earnings and profits for 1986	$45,000
	(c)	Lesser of lines (5)(a) or (b)	$36,000
(6)	Amount determined under paragraph (a)(7) of this section:		
	(a)	Line (6)(a) of example (1)	$10,000

	(b)	Sum of the lesser of accumulated earnings and profits at beginning of 1986 ($4,000 deficit—but not less than zero) or accumulated DISC income at beginning of 1986 ($1,000), plus excess of earnings and profits for 1986 over amount on line (5)(c) ($45,000 minus $36,000)	$9,000
	(c)	Lesser of lines (6)(a) or (b)	$9,000
(7)		Total deemed distribution for 1986 (sum of lines (5)(c) and (6)(c))	$45,000

(d) *Special rules for certain tax-free acquisitions of property by the DISC.*—(1) *Exchanges by DISC.*—For purposes of paragraph (a)(2)(i) and (3)(i) of this section, if—

(i) A DISC acquires property in a first transaction and in a second transaction it disposes of such property in exchange for other property, and

(ii) By reason of the application of section 1031 (relating to like-kind exchanges) or section 1033 (relating to involuntary conversions), the basis in the DISC's hands of the other property acquired in such second transaction is determined in whole or in part with reference to the basis of the property acquired in the first transaction,

then upon a disposition of such other property in a third transaction by the DISC such other property shall be treated as though it had been transferred to the DISC in the first transaction. Thus, if the first transaction is a purchase of the property for cash, then paragraph (a)(2) and (3) of this section will not apply to a sale by the DISC of the other property acquired in the second transaction.

(2) *Transfer to another DISC.*—For purposes of paragraph (a)(2)(i) and (3)(i) of this section, if a DISC acquires property in a first transaction and it transfers such property to a transferee DISC in a second transaction in which the transferor DISC's gain is not recognized in whole or in part, then such property shall be treated as though it had been transferred to the transferee DISC in the same manner in which it was acquired in the first transaction by the transferor DISC. For example, if X and Y are both DISCs, and if X transfers property to Y in a second transaction in which gain or loss is not recognized, paragraph (a)(2) or (3) of this section does not apply to a sale of such property by Y in a third transaction if X had acquired the property in a first transaction by a cash purchase. If, however, X acquired the property from a transferor other than a DISC in the first transaction in which the transferor's realized gain was not recognized, then paragraph (a)(2) or (3) of this section may apply to a sale by Y if the other conditions of paragraph (a)(2) or (3) are met.

(3) *Limitation on amount recognized by DISC.*—If a DISC acquires property in a second transaction described in paragraph (d)(1) or (2) of this section in which it (or, in the case of a second transaction described in paragraph (d)(2), the transferor DISC) recognizes a portion (but not all) of the realized gain, then the amount described in paragraph (a)(2)(ii) or (a)(3)(ii) of this section with respect to a disposition by the DISC of such acquired property in a third transaction shall not exceed the amount of the transferor's gain which was not recognized on the first transaction minus the amount of gain recognized by the DISC (or transferor DISC) on the second transaction.

(4) *Examples.*—The provisions of this paragraph (d) are illustrated by the following examples:

Example (1). X and Y are corporations each of which qualifies as a DISC and uses the calendar year as its taxable year. In 1985, X acquires section 1245 property in a first transaction in which the transferor's entire realized gain of $17 is not recognized. In 1986, X transfers such property to Y in a second transaction in which X realizes a gain of $20 of which only $4 is recognized. (On December 31, 1986, X's shareholders are treated as having received a distribution taxable as a dividend which includes such $4 under paragraph (a)(3) of this section, provided the limitation in paragraph (b) of this section is met.) Assume further that in a third transaction in 1987, Y sells such property and recognizes a gain of $25. Under section 995(b)(1)(C) and paragraph (a)(3)(ii) of this section, Y's shareholders are treated as having received a distribution taxable as a dividend on December 31, 1987, of $13, which is the amount of the gain not recognized on the first transaction ($17) reduced by the amount recognized by X on the second transaction ($4).

Example (2). Z is a DISC which uses the calendar year as its taxable year. In a first transaction in 1985, Z acquires section 1245 property in exchange for its stock from A, an individual who is Z's sole shareholder, in a transaction in which A's realized gain of $30 is not recognized by reason of section 351(a). In a second transaction in 1986, Z exchanges such property for other property in a like-kind exchange to which section 1031(b) applies and recognizes $10 of a realized gain of $35. (On December 31, 1986, A is treated as having received a distribution taxable as a dividend which includes such $10 under paragraph (a)(3) of this section, provided the limitation in paragraph (b) of this section is met.) In a third transaction in 1987, Z sells the property acquired in the like-kind exchange and recognizes a gain of $25. Under section 995(b)(1)(C) and paragraph (a)(3)(ii) of this section, A is treated as having received a distribution taxable as a dividend on December 31, 1987, of $20, which is the amount of gain not recognized by A on the first transaction ($30) reduced by the amount of gain recognized by Z on the second transaction ($10).

(e) *Carryback of net operating loss and capital loss to prior DISC taxable year.*—For purposes of sections 991, 995 and 996, the amount of the deduction for the taxable year under section 172 for a net operating loss carryback or carryover or under section 1212 for a capital loss carryback or carryover shall be determined in the same manner as if the DISC were a domestic corporation which had not elected to be treated as a DISC. Thus, the amount of the deduction will be the same whether or not the corporation was a DISC in the year the loss is incurred or in the year to which the loss is carried. For provisions setting forth adjustments to the DISCs, or former DISCs, deemed distributions, adjustments to its divisions of earnings and profits, and other tax consequences arising from such carrybacks, see §1.996-8. See §1.996-9 for the reduction of the amount of any net operating loss or capital loss carryforward of a DISC to the extent of the DISC's accumulated DISC income as of December 31, 1984. [Reg. §1.995-2A.]

* * *

Partners and Partnerships: Sales or Exchanges: Certain Distributions

Partners and Partnerships: Sales or Exchanges: Certain Distributions.—Amendments to Reg. §1.995-4, prescribing how a partner should measure its interest in a partnership's unrealized receivables and inventory items, and that provide guidance regarding the tax consequences of a distribution that causes a reduction in that interest, are proposed (published in the Federal Register on November 3, 2014) (REG-151416-06).

☐ Par. 9. Section 1.995-4 is amended by revising the section heading and adding a new sentence at the end of paragraph (a)(1) to read as follows:

§1.995-4. Gain on certain dispositions of stock in a DISC.—(a) * * *

(1) * * * *But see* §§1.732-1(c)(2)(v) and 1.755-1(c)(2)(v) for rules governing the application of section 995(c) to partnership property in situations in which the basis of the property is increased or decreased under section 732 or 734(b).

* * *

DISCs: Deemed Distributions

Domestic International Sales Corporations: Taxation of Income.—Reproduced below are the texts of proposed Reg. §§1.995-8 and 1.995-(f)-1, relating to the taxation of income allocable to a DISC for taxable years beginning after 1984 (published in the Federal Register on February 3, 1987).

* * *

☐ Par. 10. A new section 1.995-8 is added immediately after §1.995-7, to read as follows:

§1.995-8. Taxable income attributable to qualified export receipts which exceed $10 million for a taxable year ending after 1984.—(a) *In general.*—This section provides rules for the computation of the taxable income of the DISC attributable to qualified export receipts (as defined in section 993(a) and the regulations thereunder) of the DISC which exceed $10 million for a taxable year beginning after December 31, 1984. Section 995(b)(1)(E) treats the amount of such taxable income as a deemed distribution pro rata to the shareholders of the DISC for taxable years of the DISC beginning after December 31, 1984. If the DISC's qualified export receipts for the taxable year exceed the $10 million amount, the corporation does not lose its status as a DISC, but there will be a deemed distribution of all of the DISC's taxable income attributable to the qualified export receipts for the taxable year which exceed the $10 million amount. Under section 995(b)(4) and paragraph (f) of this section, only one $10 million amount is allowed among all DISCs which are members of the same controlled group (as defined in section 993(a)(3)). If the DISC's taxable year is a short period as defined in section 443, and for such year the DISC is not a member of a controlled group which includes any other DISC, the $10 million amount for such year shall be reduced to the amount which bears the same ratio to $10 million as the number of days in such short period bears to 365, and for purposes of this section, all references to the $10 million amount shall refer to such reduced amount. If the qualified export receipts of the DISC for the taxable year do not exceed the $10 million amount, section 995(b)(1)(E) and this section do not apply. The $10 million amount is an annual amount; thus, if $10 million exceeds the DISC's qualified export receipts for the taxable year, such excess may not be carried or applied to any other taxable year. For purposes of this section, the term "excess receipts" means the qualified export receipts of the DISC for the taxable year which exceed the $10 million amount. See paragraph (d) of this section for coordination of the deemed distribution under section 995(b)(1)(E) and the other deemed distributions under section 995(b)(1).

(b) *Determination of qualified export receipts which exceed $10 million.*—(1) *General rule.*—If the qualified export receipts of the DISC for the taxable year exceed the $10 million amount, the DISC shall segregate the qualified export receipts for the taxable year into two amounts, those which shall be considered not to exceed the $10 million amount, and those which shall be considered to exceed the $10 million amount. Except as provided in paragraphs (b)(2) and (3) of this section, the selection of the excess receipts may be made by the DISC in any manner. In general, the selection of the excess receipts permits the DISC to allocate the $10 million amount to the qualified export receipts of those transactions during the taxable year which permit the greatest amount of taxable income to be allocated to the DISC under the inter-company pricing rules of section 994. Except as provided in paragraphs (b)(2) and (3) of this section, the allocation may be made on a transaction-by-transaction basis among all the transactions occurring during the taxable year, or on the basis of groupings consistent with the groupings used by the DISC for purposes of applying the inter-company pricing rules under §1.994-1(c)(7). Specifically, the $10 million amount is not required to be allocated to transactions in the order in which they occur during the taxable year, nor is the amount required to be allocated ratably to all transactions occurring during the taxable year. The allocation of the $10 million amount shall be made by the DISC on or before the due date of the DISC's return for the taxable year. The allocation of the $10 million amount may thereafter be amended only if (i) the DISC and all of the DISC's shareholders file amended returns consistent with any change in the allocation of the $10 million amount, and (ii) at the time such amended returns are filed, at least 12 full months remain in the statutory period (including extensions) for the assessment of a deficiency against any shareholder of the DISC. If less than 12 full months of such period remain with respect to any such shareholder, the director of the service center with which such shareholder files its income tax return will, upon request, enter into an agreement extending such statutory period for the limited purpose of assessing any deficiency against such shareholder attributable to the change in the allocation of the $10 million amount.

(2) *Exception for related and subsidiary services.*—Notwithstanding paragraph (b)(1) of this section, if qualified export receipts for the taxable year arise from a transaction in which services are or are to be provided which are related and subsidiary to any qualified sale, exchange, lease, rental, or other disposition of export property (within meaning of section 993(a)(1)(C) and § 1.993-1(d)), the total amount of the qualified export receipts derived from such transaction must either be allocated in total, or not allocated at all to the $10 million amount. For example, if the qualified export receipts derived from a transaction are $50, of which $4 are attributable to related and subsidiary services and $46 are attributable to the sale of export property, the DISC must allocate either $50 or $0 of the qualified export receipts from such transaction to the $10 million amount; the DISC may not chose to allocate to the $10 million amount only the $4 attributable to the services or only the $46 attributable to the export property.

(3) *Ratable allocation where last transaction selected exceeds $10 million amount.*—If, in selecting among the qualified export receipts of the taxable year, the qualified export receipts of the last transaction so selected by the DISC (when added to the receipts selected from other transactions) result in the DISC exceeding the $10 million amount for such year, the amount of qualified export receipts and taxable income attributable to such transaction which, for purposes of section 995(b)(1)(E) and this section shall be considered not to exceed the $10 million amount, shall be apportioned in proportion to (i) the amount of the qualified export receipts of the transaction that do not (when added to the receipts selected from other transactions) cause the DISC to exceed the $10 million amount, to (ii) the total amount of qualified export receipts from such transaction. The remainder shall be considered attributable to excess receipts for the taxable year. The deductions and the taxable income attributable to such transaction shall also be apportioned in the same manner. For example, assume that for the taxable year the DISC has selected nine transactions having total qualified export receipts of $9,975,000 as transactions to which the $10 million amount is to be applied, and that the tenth transaction the DISC would select has qualified export receipts of $40,000. In this instance, $25,000 ($10,000,000 – $9,975,000) of the qualified export receipts from such tenth transaction shall be considered not to exceed the $10 million amount, and $15,000 ($40,000 – $25,000) of such receipts shall be considered to be excess receipts. Accordingly, 37.5 percent (15/40) of the taxable income attributable to such transaction shall be deemed to be attributable to excess receipts.

(c) *Deductions taken into account.*—After identifying the transactions of the taxable year which are considered to exceed the $10 million amount, the DISC shall reduce such excess receipts by, where applicable, the cost of goods sold attributable to such excess receipts, and the deductions of the DISC properly allocated and apportioned to such excess receipts in accordance with § 1.861-8. Such deductions include all applicable deductions from gross income for the taxable year provided under part VI of subchapter B of chapter 1 of the Code. The difference between the amount of the excess receipts and the deductions attributable to such excess receipts is the taxable income of the DISC attributable to qualified export receipts of the DISC for the taxable year which exceed the $10 million amount. Except as provided in paragraph (d) of this section, this amount of taxable income is treated as the deemed distribution under section 995(b)(1)(E) for the taxable year.

(d) *Coordination with other deemed distributions under section 995(b)(1).*—If (but for this paragraph (d)) an amount of taxable income would be treated as distributed for the taxable year under section 995(b)(1)(E) and also under subparagraph (A), (B), (C) or (D) of section 995(b)(1), such amount of taxable income shall be treated as distributed for such taxable year under that other subparagraph and not under section 995(b)(1)(E) and shall be subtracted from the amount determined under paragraph (c) of this section. In the case of military property, as defined in section 995(b)(3)(B) and § 1.995-6(c), 50 percent of the taxable income of the DISC for the taxable year attributable to such property is deemed distributed under section 995(b)(1)(D) and § 1.995-6. The remainder of the taxable income attributable to military property is deemed distributed under section 995(b)(1)(E) unless all of the gross receipts attributable to such property is allocated to the $10 million amount.

(e) *Illustration.*—The principles of this section may be illustrated by the following example:

Example—(i) *Facts.* P is a C corporation that uses the fiscal year ending September 30 as the taxable year. P owns all of the stock in Corporation D. D elects to be treated as a DISC for its taxable year beginning January 1, 1985. Under section 441(h), D must use the same taxable year as P. Accordingly, D's taxable year beginning January 1, 1985, will end on September 30, 1985. Assume that in D's taxable year ending September 30, 1985, D sold four aircraft in separate transactions (S1, S2, M1, M2). Two of the sales (M1 and M2) were of military property. D also derived $12,000 of interest from producer's loans during the taxable year. D's qualified export receipts for the taxable year are $9,762,000, and assume that the deductions properly allocated and apportioned thereto are $8,550,000, as follows:

	Receipts	*Deductions*	*Taxable income*
Producer's loan interest	$12,000	–0–	$12,000
Sales: S1	3,750,000	3,330,000	420,000
S2	3,000,000	2,670,000	330,000

	Receipts	Deductions	Taxable income
M1	1,500,000	1,200,000	300,000
M2	1,500,000	1,350,000	150,000
	$9,762,000	$8,550,000	$1,212,000

(ii) *Limitation on $10 million amount.* D's taxable year ending September 30, 1985, is a short period consisting of 273 days. Accordingly, the $10 million amount specified in section 995(b)(1)(E) is limited to $7,479,452 (273/365 × $10 million) for the taxable year.

(iii) *Amount distributed under section 995(b)(1)(E).* D allocates all of the qualified export receipts from S1 and S2, and $729,452 of the receipts from M1 against the $7,479,452 amount ($3,750,000 + $3,000,000 + $729,452 = $7,479,452), leaving the following amounts, reduced by the deductions properly apportioned and allocated thereto, as the amount distributed for the taxable year under section 995(b)(1)(E):

	Excess Receipts	Deductions	Taxable income
M1	$1,500,000	$1,200,000	$300,000
Less: Amount of M1 not in excess of limitation	(729,452)	(583,562)[1]	(145,890)
M1 Excess receipts	$770,548	$616,438	$154,110
M2	1,500,000	1,350,000	150,000
Producer's loan interest	12,000	–0 –	12,000
Taxable income attributable to excess receipts, see § 1.995-8(c)			$316,110
Less: Amounts otherwise distributed under section 995(b)(1), see § 1.995-8(d):			
Section 995(b)(1)(A)—Producer's loan interest			$(12,000)
Section 995(b)(1)(D)—50% of taxable income attributable to sales of military property:			
M1 $154,110 × 50%			(77,055)
M2 $150,000 × 50%			(75,000)
Deemed distribution under section 995(b)(1)(E) for taxable year			$152,055

[1] $729,452/$1,500,000 × $1,200,000 = $583,562. See paragraph (b)(3) of this section.

(iv) *Deemed distribution for 1985.* The amount of D's deemed distribution under section 995(b)(1) for D's taxable year ending September 30, 1985, is $437,464 determined as follows:

Section 995(b)(1):		Amount
(A)	Producer's loan interest	$12,000
(D)	One-half of taxable income attributable to military property (50% of $450,000)	225,000
(E)	Taxable income attributable to excess receipts	152,055
(F)	One-seventeenth of the excess of taxable income less amounts in (A), (D) and (E) $^{1}/_{17}$ × ($1,212,000 – $12,000 – $225,000 – $152,055)	48,409
		$437,464

(f) *Members of a controlled group limited to one $10 million amount.*—(1) *General rule.*—For purposes of section 995(b)(1)(E) and this section, in the case of a controlled group of corporations (as defined in section 993(a)(3) and § 1.993-1(k)), all DISCs which are members of such controlled group on a December 31, shall, for their taxable years which include such December 31, be limited to one $10 million amount. The $10 million amount shall be allocated equally among the member DISCs of such controlled group for their taxable years including such December 31, unless all of the member DISCs consent to an apportionment plan providing for an unequal allocation of the $10 million amount. Such a plan shall provide for the apportionment of a fixed dollar amount to one or more of the corporations, and the sum of the amounts so apportioned shall not exceed the $10 million amount. If the taxable year including such December 31 of any member DISC is a short period (as defined in section 443), the portion of the $10 million amount allocated to such member DISC for such short period under the preceding sentence shall be reduced to the amount which bears the same ratio to the amount so allocated as the number of days in such short period bears to 365. The consent of each member DISC to the apportionment plan for the taxable year shall be signified by a statement which satisfies the requirements of and is filed in the manner specified in § 1.1561-3(b). An apportionment plan may be amended in the manner prescribed in § 1.1561-3(c), except that an original or an amended plan may not be adopted with respect to a particular December 31 if at the time such original or amended plan is sought to be adopted, less than 12 full months remain in the statutory period (including extensions) for the assessment of a deficiency against any shareholder of a member DISC the tax liability of which would change by the adoption of such original or amended plan. If less than 12 full months of such period remain with respect to any such shareholder, the director of the service center with which such shareholder files its income tax return will, upon request, enter into an agreement extending such statutory period for the limited purpose of assessing any deficiency against such shareholder attributable to the adoption of such original or amended apportionment plan.

(2) *Membership determined under section 1563(b).*—For purposes of paragraph (f) of this section, the determination of whether a DISC is a member of a controlled group of corporations with respect to any taxable year shall be made in

the manner prescribed in section 1563(b) and the regulations thereunder.

(3) *Certain short taxable years.*—(i) *General rule.*—If a DISC has a short period (as defined in section 443) which does not include a December 31, and such DISC is a member of a controlled group of corporations which includes one or more other DISCs with respect to such short period, then the amount described in section 995(b)(1)(E) with respect to the short period of such DISC shall be determined by (A) dividing $10 million by the number of DISCs which are members of such group on the last day of such short period, and (B) multiplying the result by a fraction, the numerator of which is the number of days in such short period and the denominator of which is 365. For purposes of the preceding sentence, section 1563(b) shall be applied as if the last day of such short period were substituted for December 31. Except as provided in paragraph (f)(3)(ii) of this section, a DISC having a short period not including a December 31 may not enter into an apportionment plan with respect to such short period.

(ii) *Exception.*—If the short period not including a December 31 of two or more DISCs begins on the same date and ends on the same date and such DISCs are members of the same controlled group, such DISCs may enter into an apportionment plan for such short period in the manner provided in paragraph (f)(1) of this section with respect to the combined amount allowed to each of such DISCs under paragraph (f)(3)(i).

(4) *Effect on DISC shareholders.*—The computation of the deemed distribution under section 995(b)(1)(E) and this section for a taxable year, as affected by the controlled group rules of this paragraph (f), applies to a shareholder of a DISC whether or not such shareholder is a member of the controlled group which includes such DISC. [Reg. § 1.995-8.]

□ Par. 11. New § 1.995(f)-1 is added immediately after § 1.995-8 to read as follows:

§ 1.995(f)-1. Interest charge on DISC-related deferred tax liability for periods after 1984.—(a) *Interest charge.*—(1) *In general.*—Effective for taxable years ending after December 31, 1984, section 995(f) requires that each shareholder of a DISC shall pay for each taxable year interest on the shareholder's DISC-related deferred tax liability (as defined in paragraph (d) of this section) for such year at a rate of interest equal to the base period T-bill rate (as defined in paragraph (b)(2) of this section). See paragraph (b) of this section for the computation of the amount of the interest charge. The interest charge is computed on Form 8404. For purposes of this section, the term "DISC" includes a former DISC as defined in section 992(a)(3). Accordingly, a shareholder of a former DISC is required to pay the annual interest charge on such shareholder's DISC-related deferred tax liability.

(2) *Related rules.*—(i) The interest charge is an annual charge and is imposed on the shareholder of the DISC. The interest charge is not imposed on the DISC. Under section 995(f)(6), the amount of a shareholder's interest charge for any taxable year is treated for all purposes of the Code as interest paid or accrued on an underpayment of tax. Accordingly, subject to all otherwise applicable limitations on the deduction for interest, the amount of the annual interest charge imposed on the shareholder is deductible by the shareholder for the taxable year in which the amount of the interest charge is paid, in the case of a shareholder which uses the cash receipts and disbursements method of accounting, or accrued, in the case of a shareholder which uses the accrual method of accounting. See paragraph (j)(2) of this section. Because the interest charge imposed on the shareholder is treated as interest, the payment or accrual of the interest charge does not increase or decrease the shareholder's basis in the stock of the DISC, and does not increase or decrease the taxable income or earnings and profits of the DISC.

(ii) Under section 995(f)(2), the shareholder's DISC-related deferred tax liability for a taxable year, that is, the amount considered to be the "principal" amount of the "loan" on which the interest charge is computed, is determined only with reference to the accumulated DISC income (A) derived by the DISC in periods after 1984, and (B) derived by the DISC in taxable years of the DISC that ended before the taxable year of the shareholder for which the interest charge is being determined.

(iii) No payments of estimated tax under section 6654 (in the case of individuals) or 6154 (in the case of corporations) are required with respect to the interest charge imposed by section 995(f)(1).

(iv) Paragraph (g) of this section contains rules for determining the interest charge for a taxable year in which shares in the DISC are transferred or redeemed. Paragraph (h) of this section proivdes rules for the computation and allocation of the interest charge where the DISC's shares are held by S corporations, trusts, estates or partnerships.

(b) *Computation of the interest charge.*—(1) *General rule.*—Under section 995(f)(1), the amount of the interest charge imposed on a DISC shareholder for a taxable year is equal to the product of—

(i) The shareholder's DISC-related deferred tax liability for such year, multiplied by,

(ii) A factor which is equal to the base period T-bill rate compounded daily for the number of days in the shareholder's taxable year for which the interest charge is being computed. See section 6622 for the requirement that all interest required to be paid under the Code be compounded daily. See paragraph (c) of this section for obtaining the table of base period T-bill rate factors reflecting daily compounding of the base period T-bill rate. See paragraph (g) of this section for special rules for computing the amount of the interest charge for a taxable year in which the shareholder transfers or acquires stock in the DISC.

(2) *Base period T-bill rate.*—Under section 995(f)(4), the "base period T-bill rate" is the annual rate of interest determined by the Secretary to be equivalent to the average investment yield of United States Treasury bills with maturities of 52 weeks which were auctioned during the one-year period ending on September 30 of the calendar year ending with (or, if the shareholder's taxable year is not the calendar year, of the most

recent calendar year ending before) the close of the taxable year of the DISC shareholder for which the shareholder's interest charge is being determined. For example, if a DISC shareholder's taxable year is a fiscal year ending on June 30, the base period T-bill rate applicable to the shareholder's taxable year ending June 30, 1987, would be the rate determined for the one-year period ending September 30, 1986. If the shareholder's taxable year is the calendar year, the base period T-bill rate applicable to the shareholder's taxable year ending December 31, 1987, would be the rate determined for the one-year period ending September 30, 1987.

(c) *Publication of base period T-bill rate and use of the table of factors for daily compounding.*—The base period T-bill rate for each one-year period ending on September 30, as determined by the Secretary, shall be certified to the Commissioner and shall be published in a revenue ruling in the Internal Revenue Bulletin. Such revenue ruling shall also contain a table of factors reflecting daily compounding of the base period T-bill rate. To compute the amount of the interest charge for the taxable year under paragraph (b) of this section the shareholder shall use the base period T-bill rate factor corresponding to the number of days in the shareholder's taxable year for which the interest charge is being computed. Generally, the factor to be used will be the factor for 365 days. The factor to be used will be other than the factor for 365 days if the shareholder's taxable year for which the interest charge is being determined is a short taxable year, if the shareholder uses the 52-53 week taxable year, or if the shareholder's taxable year is a leap year. For example, if a DISC shareholder which had been using the calendar year as the taxable year changes its taxable year to the fiscal year ending January 31, then in computing the interest charge for the short taxable year January 1 to January 31 required to effect such change, the shareholder will use the factor for a taxable year of 31 days.

(d) *DISC-related deferred tax liability.*—(1) *Purpose.*—For taxable years of a DISC shareholder ending after December 31, 1984, the shareholder's DISC-related deferred tax liability represents, in general terms, the cumulative amount of income tax that is considered to have been deferred from taxation in prior taxable years (ending after 1984) of the shareholder by use of the DISC. A separate interest charge is imposed on the shareholder for each taxable year of the shareholder until the deferred DISC income is distributed or deemed distributed by the DISC. The amount of the shareholder's DISC-related deferred tax liability is determined for each taxable year by taking the difference between the shareholder's income tax liability for the taxable year computed first with, and then without, the accumulated DISC income that has been deferred from taxation in prior taxable years of the shareholder. See paragraph (f) of this section for the definition of "deferred DISC income." This paragraph (d) provides certain special rules to be used solely for the purpose of determining the amount of the shareholder's DISC-related deferred tax liability. For any taxable year, these rules may result in the amount of the shareholder's DISC-related deferred tax liability being different than the amount of additional income tax that the shareholder would owe for such year if the deferred DISC income were received by the shareholder in an actual distribution to which section 996(a) applies.

(2) *In general.*—(i) Under section 995(f)(2), the "shareholder's DISC-related deferred tax liability", with respect to any taxable year of a DISC shareholder ending after 1984, is the excess of—

(A) The amount which would be the tax liability (as defined in paragraph (e) of this section) of the shareholder for the taxable year if the amount of the deferred DISC income (as described in paragraph (f) of this section) of such shareholder for such taxable year were included in the shareholder's gross income as ordinary income, over

(B) The actual amount of the shareholder's tax liability for such taxable year.

(ii) If in the taxable year the shareholder owns stock in more than one DISC, the deferred DISC income of such shareholder for the taxable year is the sum of the amounts of deferred DISC income of such shareholder with respect to each of such DISCs.

(iii) Where the DISC shareholder is a member of an affiliated group of corporations that files a consolidated return, the affiliated group's DISC-related deferred tax liability for the taxable year is the excess of (A) the amount which would be the group's tax liability (as defined in paragraph (e) of this section) including in gross income the deferred DISC income for the taxable year of each DISC shareholder which is a member of the group, over (B) the amount of the group's actual tax liability for such taxable year.

(iv) Except as provided in paragraphs (d) and (e) of this section, the computations necessary to determine the shareholder's DISC-related deferred tax liability shall be made under the law and the rates of tax applicable to the shareholder's taxable year for which the computations are made.

(v) The shareholder's DISC-related deferred tax liability for a taxable year is computed on Form 8404. See paragraph (j) of this section for the manner and time for filing or amending Form 8404 and paying the interest charge.

(3) *Carrybacks not taken into account.*—Under section 995(f)(2)(A), the shareholder's DISC-related deferred tax liability for any taxable year is determined without regard to any net operating loss or capital loss carryback or any credit carryback to such taxable year from any succeeding taxable year. For example, if for 1987 a calendar year shareholder of a DISC has a DISC-related deferred tax liability for the taxable year and thereby incurs an interest charge for such taxable year, and if the shareholder thereafter has a net operating loss (as defined in section 172(c)) for calendar year 1988, all or a portion of which is a net operating loss carryback to the 1987 taxable year, the shareholder's DISC-related deferred tax liability and interest charge for the 1987 taxable year are not affected by such net operating loss carryback, even if the shareholder recovers the total amount of the tax it paid for taxable year 1987, and has a net operating loss carryover to future taxable years.

(4) *Carryovers not taken into account.*—(i) *General rule.*—Under section 995(f)(2)(A)(i), the determination of the shareholder's tax liability for the taxable year including the deferred DISC income shall be made by not taking into

account any loss, deduction or credit to the extent that such loss, deduction or credit may be carried by the shareholder to any other taxable year. If, however, the taxable year is the last taxable year to which the amount of a carryforward (of either a deduction or a credit) may be carried, the shareholder's tax liability including the deferred DISC income shall be computed with regard to the full amount of such carryforward, because the amount of the carryforward cannot be carried to another taxable year of the shareholder.

(ii) *Examples*.—The provisions of this paragraph (d)(4) may be illustrated by the following examples:

Example (1). Assume that in 1986, a calendar year DISC shareholder recognizes only ordinary business income of $10,000, and has deferred DISC income for the taxable year of $5000. If the shareholder also had a net operating loss carryforward to 1986 of $12,000, the shareholder would be allowed a $10,000 net operating loss deduction for 1986 and would have a net operating loss carryforward to 1987 of $2000. For purposes of determining the shareholder's DISC-related deferred tax liability for 1986, the shareholder's computation of its tax liability including the deferred DISC income under section 995(f)(2)(A)(i) may take into account a net operating loss deduction of only $10,000, because $2000 of the total loss carryforward may be carried to the shareholder's following taxable year. Accordingly, the shareholder's taxable income for 1986 including the deferred DISC income is $5000 ($10,000 of ordinary income, plus $5000 of deferred DISC income, less the net operating loss deduction of $10,000). However, if 1986 were the last taxable year to which the $12,000 net operating loss carryforward could be carried, then the shareholder's tax liability including the deferred DISC income under section 995(f)(2)(A)(i) may be computed by taking the full amount of the loss carryforward into account.

Example (2). Assume that in 1986, a calendar year DISC shareholder places in service an amount of property such that the amount of the investment credit determined for the taxable year under section 46 is $25,000, and that the shareholder has no credit carryforwards to the taxable year from any earlier taxable year. Assume that for the shareholder's 1986 taxable year the amount of the credit allowed is limited to $20,000, because of the limitation on the amount of the credit allowed under section 38(c), and that the remaining $5000 of the credit determined for the taxable year may be carried back 3 years or forward 15 years. In determining the shareholder's DISC-related deferred tax liability for the 1986 taxable year, the amount of the credit that may be allowed to reduce the shareholder's tax liability including the deferred DISC income under section 995(f)(2)(A)(i) is limited to $20,000, because the remaining $5000 of the credit may be carried to another taxable year.

Example (3). The facts are the same as in example (2). Assume that $2000 of the $5000 excess credit for 1986 was applied to reduce 1985 taxes, and that none of the remaining $3000 could be carried back to any other taxable year. If in 1987, all of the $3000 credit carried over from 1986 is applied to reduce the shareholder's 1987 actual tax liability, that $3000 credit is also to be used to reduce the shareholder's 1987 tax liability including the deferred DISC income under section 995(f)(2)(A)(i).

(5) *Adjustments not involving carryovers or carrybacks*.—In computing the amount of the DISC shareholder's taxable income and tax liability including the deferred DISC income under section 995(f)(2)(A)(i), there shall be taken into account adjustments in amounts allowable as deductions and in amounts excluded from or included in gross income to the extent that such adjustments do not result in amounts which may be carried back or forward by the shareholder to any other taxable year. For example, in the case of a DISC shareholder who is an individual, the amount of medical expenses allowable as a deduction under section 213 must be redetermined when computing the individual's taxable income and tax liability including the deferred DISC income under section 995(f)(2)(A)(i). The amount of medical expenses allowable as a deduction decreases because the taxpayer's adjusted gross income, increased by the amount of the deferred DISC income, would increase the limitation on the deductible amount of medical expenses, and the medical expenses not allowed may not be carried to any other taxable year. As a further example, in the case of an individual or a corporation which is a DISC shareholder, the amount allowable as a charitable deduction under section 170 is not redetermined when computing the taxpayer's taxable income and tax liability including the deferred DISC income under section 995(f)(2)(A)(i), because the amount of charitable contributions made for the taxable year which are not allowable as a deduction for such year by reason of the percentage of income limitations under section 170(b) may be carried over to subsequent taxable years under section 170(d).

(6) *Deferred tax liability determined without regard to any consequential deduction or credit*.—Except as provided in paragraph (d)(8) of this section, in computing the amount of the DISC shareholder's tax liability including the deferred DISC income under section 995(f)(2)(A)(i), there shall not be taken into account any additional deduction or credit that would be allowable for any item that would be paid or accrued if the deferred DISC income were actually distributed to the shareholder. For example, when computing the shareholder's tax liability including the deferred DISC income, no deduction shall be taken into account for the additional state or local income or franchise taxes that would be due if such deferred DISC income were actually distributed to the shareholder. In addition, to simplify the calculations, in the case of a DISC shareholder who uses the accrual method of accounting, no deduction for the current year's interest charge shall be taken into account in computing the shareholder's DISC-related deferred tax liability for the current taxable year. However, after the amount of the interest charge for the current taxable year has been determined, such amount may be taken into account as a deduction for the current taxable year in determining the amount of the shareholder's income tax liability under chapter 1 of the Code for the taxable year in the circumstances described in paragraph (j)(2)(ii) of this section.

(7) *Source of deferred DISC income*.—The source of the deferred DISC income which is considered included in the shareholder's gross income for purposes of section 995(f)(2)(A)(i)

shall be determined under section 861(a)(2)(D) and § 1.861-3(a)(5) in the same manner as if such amount were actually distributed to the DISC shareholder as a dividend.

(8) *Deemed paid foreign tax credit; separate limitation.*—In the case of a DISC shareholder that is a corporation, if the shareholder elects the foreign tax credit for the taxable year, such shareholder shall, in computing its tax liability including the deferred DISC income, take into account any increase in the amount of the deemed paid foreign tax credit under section 902(a) for foreign income taxes paid by the DISC to the extent that the deferred DISC income is treated as income from sources without the United States. In such case, in accordance with section 78, the shareholder shall also include the amount of such foreign income tax in computing its gross income including the deferred DISC income. Any increase in the amount of the foreign tax credit that would be allowable against the tax liability determined under section 995(f)(2)(A)(i) with respect to the amount of the deferred DISC income shall be subject to the separate limitation required by section 904(d)(1)(F) in the same manner as if such amount were actually distributed to the DISC shareholder as a dividend.

(e) *Tax liability.*—(1) *General rule.*—Except as provided in paragraphs (e)(2) and (e)(3) of this section, for purposes of the two tax computations ("with and without" the deferred DISC income) required by section 995(f)(2) and paragraph (d) of this section, the term "tax liability" means the amount of the tax imposed on the DISC shareholder for the taxable year by chapter 1 of the Code, reduced by the credits (but not the credit carrybacks or carryovers described in paragraphs (d)(3) and (d)(4) of this section) allowable against such tax.

(2) *Certain taxes not to be taken into account.*—For purposes of section 995 (f)(2) and paragraph (e)(1) of this section, any tax imposed by any of the following provisions shall not be treated as tax imposed by chapter 1 of the Code:

(i) Section 55 (relating to the alternative minimum tax) and

(ii) Any other provisions described in section 26(b)(2) (relating to certain other taxes treated as not imposed by chapter 1 of the Code).

(3) *Certain credits not taken into account.*—For purposes of section 995(f)(2) and paragraph (e)(1) of this section, the credits allowed for the taxable year by the following sections shall not be taken into account in determining the DISC shareholder's tax liability:

(i) Section 31 (relating to taxes withheld on wages),

(ii) Section 32 (relating to the earned income credit), and

(iii) Section 34 (relating to the fuels credit).

(f) *Deferred DISC income.*—(1) *In general.*—Under section 995(f)(3)(A), for any taxable year of a DISC shareholder, the term "deferred DISC income" means the excess of—

(i) The shareholder's pro rata share of the DISC's accumulated DISC income (earned by the DISC in taxable years ending after December 31, 1984) as of the close of the computation year (as defined in paragraph (f)(2) of this section), over

(ii) The amount (if any) of distributions-in-excess-of-income (as defined in paragraph (f)(3) of this section) made by the DISC during the taxable year of the DISC immediately following the computation year.

Thus, in the simple case where the DISC has only one shareholder and the DISC and the shareholder have the same taxable year, the shareholder's deferred DISC income for the taxable year is the excess of the DISC's accumulated DISC income (derived from periods after 1984) at the beginning of the taxable year over the amount (if any) by which actual distributions for the taxable year which are considered to be made out of accumulated DISC income exceed the amount of DISC income for such year. Where shareholders of the DISC have a taxable year different from that of the DISC, the deferred DISC income is measured from the computation year, as described in paragraph (f)(2) of this section.

(2) *Computation year.*—(i) *General rule.*—Under section 995(f)(3)(B), with respect to any taxable year of a DISC shareholder, the "computation year" is the taxable year of the DISC ending with (or within, if the DISC and the shareholder do not have the same taxable year) the taxable year of the shareholder which precedes the taxable year of the shareholder for which the amount of deferred DISC income is being determined.

(ii) *Example.*—The following example illustrates the relationship between the shareholder's taxable year and the DISC's computation year:

Example. Assume that a DISC, D, has two shareholders, A, the principal shareholder, and B, a minority shareholder. Shareholder A uses the calendar year as the taxable year, and shareholder B's taxable year is the fiscal year ending June 30. Under section 441(h), D must use the calendar year as the taxable year. In determining the amount of shareholder A's deferred DISC income for A's taxable year ending December 31, 1987, the computation year is D's taxable year ending December 31, 1986, that is, D's taxable year ending with shareholder A's taxable year preceding the taxable year of A for which A's deferred DISC income is being determined. In determining the amount of shareholder B's deferred DISC income for B's taxable year ending June 30, 1987, the computation year is D's taxable year ending December 31, 1985, that is, D's taxable year ending within B's taxable year preceding the taxable year of B for which B's deferred DISC income is being determined.

(3) *Distributions-in-excess-of-income.*—Under section 995(f)(3)(C), with respect to any taxable year of a DISC, the term "distributions-in-excess-of-income", means the excess (if any) of—

(i) The amount of actual distributions made to the shareholder during such taxable year out of accumulated DISC income (as determined under section 996), over

(ii) The shareholder's pro rata share of the DISC income (as defined in section 996(f)) for such taxable year.

(4) *Illustrations.*—The provisions of paragraph (f) of this section may be illustrated by the following example:

Example—(i) Facts. P corporation, which uses the calendar year as the taxable year, owns all of the stock of D, a domestic corporation which elects to be treated as a DISC for its taxable year beginning January 1, 1985. Under section 441(h), D must adopt the same taxable year as P; accordingly, D's taxable year beginning January 1, 1985, will end on December 31, 1985.

Assume that D has the following amounts for its three taxable years ending December 31, 1985, 1986 and 1987:

	1985	*1986*	*1987*
Taxable income and earnings and profits for the year	$45,000	$60,000	$40,000
Deemed distribution under section 995(b)(1)	5,000	10,000	15,000
DISC income for year	$40,000	$50,000	$25,000
Actual distributions during year	$-0-	$20,000	$60,000
Accumulated DISC income—end of year	$40,000	$85,000	$65,000
Previously taxed income—end of year	5,000	-0-	-0-
Accumulated earnings and profits—end of year	$45,000	$85,000	$65,000

(ii) *Result—1985.* Under section 995(f)(3), P will have no deferred DISC income for P's taxable year ending December 31, 1985, because D does not have accumulated DISC income derived from periods after 1984 as of the close of the computation year. With respect to P's taxable year ending December 31, 1985, the computation year under section 995(f)(3)(B) would be D's taxable year ending with or within P's taxable year ending December 31, 1984, which is prior to D's current election to be treated as a DISC. Accordingly, because P has no deferred DISC income for its taxable year ending December 31, 1985, P will have no DISC-related deferred tax liability and therefore no interest charge for the taxable year.

(iii) *Result—1986.* Under section 995(f)(3), P will have deferred DISC income for P's taxable year ending December 31, 1986, of $40,000 determined as follows. With respect to P's taxable year ending December 31, 1986, the computation year is D's taxable year ending December 31, 1985. D's accumulated DISC income as of the close of the computation year is $40,000, and D made no distributions-in-excess-of-income in D's taxable year following the computation year (that is, in D's taxable year ending December 31, 1986, of the actual distributions of $20,000, only $5000 of this amount is treated as made out of accumulated DISC income, and because the DISC income for the year is $50,000, none of the actual distributions for the year reduce the accumulated DISC income as of the beginning of the taxable year.)

Accordingly, because P's deferred DISC income for the taxable year ending December 31, 1986, is $40,000, P must compute its tax liability for the year with and then without the $40,000 amount under section 995(f)(2) to determine its DISC-related deferred tax liability. P's interest charge for the taxable year ending December 31, 1986, under section 995(f)(1) will be the amount of the DISC-related deferred tax liability (the tax on $40,000) multiplied by the base period T-bill rate factor for the 365 day taxable year. See paragraph (b) of this section.

(iv) *Result-1987.* Under section 995 (f)(3), P will have deferred DISC income for P's taxable year ending December 31, 1987, of $65,000 computed as follows:

	D's accumulated DISC income derived from periods after 1984 as of the close of the computation year (D's taxable year ending December 31, 1986)	$85,000
Less:	Amount of D's distributions-in-excess-of-income made in D's taxable year ending December 31, 1987	20,000
	P's deferred DISC income for taxable year ending December 31, 1987	$65,000

The $20,000 amount of distributions-in-excess-of-income for D's taxable year ending December 31, 1987, may be determined as follows:

	Amount of D's actual distributions for D's taxable year ending December 31, 1987		$60,000
Less:	D's previously taxed income at close of previous taxable year	$-0-	
	Deemed distribution for current year	15,000	
	Total amount of previously taxed income available for distributions during D's taxable year ending December 31, 1987	$15,000	15,000
	Difference-Amount of actual distributions for current year out of accumulated DISC income		$45,000
Less:	DISC income for current year		25,000
	Distributions-in-excess-of-income for D's taxable year ending December 31, 1987		$20,000

Accordingly, because P's deferred DISC income for its taxable year ending December 31, 1987 is $65,000, P must compute its tax liability for the taxable year with and then without the $65,000 amount to determine its DISC-related deferred tax liability under section 995(f)(2). P's interest charge for the taxable year ending December 31, 1987, under section 995(f)(1) will be the amount of the DISC-related deferred tax liability (the tax on the $65,000) multiplied by the base period T-bill rate factor for the 365 day taxable year.

(g) *Special rules for computation of the interest charge where DISC stock is transferred during taxable year.*—(1) *General rule.*—If the same number of shares of stock in the DISC are not held by the shareholder for the shareholder's entire taxable year, the amount of the interest charge for the taxable year with respect to the shares transferred or acquired by the shareholder shall be equal to the amount of the DISC-related deferred tax liability with respect to such transferred or acquired shares computed as if the shareholder held such shares for the shareholder's entire taxable year, multiplied by the base period T-bill rate factor corresponding to the number of days in the shareholder's taxable year that the shareholder held such transferred or acquired shares. In determining the number of days in the shareholder's taxable year that the shareholder held such transferred or acquired shares, the transferor shareholder shall include the day of the transfer and the transferee shareholder shall exclude the day of the transfer.

(2) *Adjustment for gain recognized on disposition.*—(i) *Transferor.*—For purposes of determining the deferred DISC income for the taxable year of a shareholder who disposes of stock in the DISC during the taxable year, the amount of gain recognized with respect to such stock which is treated under section 995(c) and § 1.995-4 as a dividend shall be treated as an actual distribution made by the DISC to such shareholder out of accumulated DISC income for the taxable year of the DISC which includes the date of such disposition. Accordingly, the amount of such gain which exceeds the shareholder's pro rata share of the DISC income for such taxable year shall be treated under section 995(f)(3)(C) and paragraph (f) of this section as a distribution-in-excess-of-income which reduces the amount of such shareholder's deferred DISC income for the taxable year of the shareholder in which the disposition of the shares occurs.

(ii) *Transferee.*—For purposes of determining the amount of any transferee shareholder's deferred DISC income for a taxable year, if under section 996(d)(1) and § 1.996-4(a) such shareholder would be permitted to treat an amount of an actual distribution by the DISC made out of accumulated DISC income as made out of previously taxed income, such transferee shareholder's deferred DISC income for such taxable year shall be reduced by such amount.

(3) *Examples.*—The provisions of this paragraph (g) may be illustrated by the following examples:

Example (1). X, an individual, uses the calendar year as the taxable year and owns all of the stock of D, a calendar year corporation which elects to be treated as a DISC for 1985. On May 1, 1987, X makes a gift to Y, a calendar year individual, of all the stock in D. On December 31, 1986, D had accumulated DISC income of $1000, and during its taxable year ending December 31, 1987, D made no distributions-in-excess-of-income. X recognizes no gain on the transfer of stock to Y. Accordingly, for the taxable year ending December 31, 1987, X and Y each have deferred DISC income of $1000, and each must compute a DISC-related deferred tax liability for 1987 with respect to this $1000 of deferred DISC income as if each of them owned the stock for the entire year. X will multiply X's DISC-related deferred tax liability by the base period T-bill rate factor for 121 days, and Y will multiply Y's DISC-related deferred tax liability by the base period T-bill rate factor for 244 days, to reflect the number of days during their taxable year that each held the stock in the DISC. If during the taxable year Y received a distribution-in-excess-of-income of $200, Y's deferred DISC income for the taxable year would be $800, and X's deferred DISC income for the year would also be $800, even though the actual distribution was received by Y.

Example (2). (i) Corporations A and D use the calendar year as the taxable year. A owns all of the stock of D, which elects to be treated as a DISC for 1985. On December 31, 1987, A sells all of its stock in D to B corporation, and recognizes a gain on the sale of $400. B corporation uses the fiscal year ending June 30 as the taxable year. Assume that D had accumulated DISC income at the close of 1986 of $600, and that D realized $250 of DISC income for 1987. Assume also that D made no actual distributions out of accumulated DISC income during 1987. Accordingly, D has accumulated DISC income at December 31, 1987, of $850 ($600 plus $250), all of which was accumulated during the period A held the stock in the DISC. Under section 995(c) and § 1.995-4, all of A's recognized gain of $400 on the disposition of the stock in the DISC is treated as a dividend, because A's recognized gain ($400) does not exceed the accumulated DISC income of D attributable to the stock disposed of by A ($850).

(ii) Under paragraph (g)(2) of this section, for purposes of section 995(f)(3), the $400 amount that A must treat as a dividend is treated as an actual distribution to A for 1987 out of accumulated DISC income. Accordingly, A's deferred DISC income for its taxable year ending December 31, 1987, is $450, determined as follows:

Accumulated DISC income of D at close of computation year (1986)		$600
Amount of gain realized by A in 1987 treated as an actual distribution out of accumulated DISC income	$400	
Less: DISC income for 1978	250	
Difference: Amount treated as a distribution-in-excess-of- income . . .	$150	150
Deferred DISC income		$450

A will use this $450 amount of deferred DISC income to compute its DISC-related deferred tax liability and interest charge for A's 365 day taxable year ending December 31, 1987.

(iii) Because B purchased the stock in D on December 31, 1987, B will have a part-year interest charge for B's taxable year ending June 30, 1988. D's computation year with respect to B's taxable year ending June 30, 1988, is D's taxable year ending December 31, 1986. B's deferred DISC income for its taxable year ending June 30, 1988, is $450, the same amount that A had with respect to A's taxable year ended December 31, 1987, because B is permitted, under section 996(d), to take into account as a reduction in accumulated DISC income, the amount of gain A recognized on the disposition which was treated as an actual distribution to A out of accumulated DISC income. Accordingly, B must compute its DISC-related deferred tax liability and interest charge for the taxable year ending June 30, 1988, with respect to the $450 of deferred DISC income. The interest charge for B's taxable year ending June 30, 1988, is determined by multiplying B's DISC-related deferred tax liability (the tax on the $450 of deferred DISC income) by the base period T-bill rate factor for 182 days (January 1 to June 30, 1988), because B held the stock for only 182 days in B's taxable year ended June 30, 1988.

(iv) Note that under section 441(h), D must change its taxable year from the calendar year to the fiscal year ending June 30, because there has been a change in the taxable year of D's "principal shareholder" by reason of B's acquisition of D. See §1.441-1(h)(3).

(h) *Special rules for computation of the interest charge where DISC stock is held by certain pass-through entities.*—(1) *Partnerships.*—For purposes of section 995(f) and this section, if stock in a DISC is held by a partnership, the deferred DISC income of such partnership for the taxable year shall be attributed to each partner in proportion to the partner's interest in partnership income for the taxable year. Thus, each partner shall take into account its share of the partnership's deferred DISC income for the partnership taxable year ending with or within the taxable year of the partner, and each partner shall determine its DISC-related deferred tax liability and the interest charge thereon for the partner's taxable year as if the partner directly owned stock in the DISC.

(2) *S corporations.*—For purposes of section 995(f) and this section, if stock in a DISC is held by an S corporation, the deferred DISC income of such S corporation for the taxable year shall be attributed to each shareholder in proportion to the shareholder's pro rata share of the S corporation's nonseparately computed income or loss (determined under section 1366(a)(1)(B)) for the taxable year. Thus, each shareholder shall take into account its share of the S corporation's deferred DISC income for the taxable year of the S corporation ending with or within the taxable year of the shareholder, and shall determine its DISC-related deferred tax liability and the interest charge thereon for the taxable year as if the shareholder directly owned stock in the DISC.

(3) *Estates or trusts.*—For purposes of section 995(f) and this section, if stock in a DISC is held by an estate or trust, the deferred DISC income allocable to the stock in the DISC held by the estate or trust shall not be attributed to the beneficiaries of such estate or trust. The interest charge is imposed on the estate or trust. The estate or trust is required to determine its DISC-related deferred tax liability and interest charge for the taxable year in the same manner as other taxpayers. For this purpose, the tax rates applicable to estates and trusts for the taxable year under section 1(e) shall apply. In computing the taxable income of the estate or trust for the taxable year including the deferred DISC income under section 995(f)(2)(A)(i), the estate or trust shall not take into account a deduction under section 651 or 661 (relating to deductions for distributions) greater than the deduction for distributions allowed in computing the estate or trust's actual tax liability for such year under section 995(f)(2)(A)(ii).

(i) [There is no paragraph (i).]

(j) *Character, payment, assessment and collection of the interest charge.*—(1) *Character.*—Under section 995(f)(6), the interest charge imposed on a DISC shareholder for any taxable year is treated for all purposes of the Code in the same manner as interest on an underpayment of tax under section 6601. Thus, the interest charge may be deducted from the shareholder's gross income only to the extent the shareholder may deduct interest on an underpayment of tax, and subject to all applicable limitations on the deduction for interest.

(2) *Taxable year for which interest charge is deductible.*—(i) *Cash method shareholder.*—If the DISC shareholder uses the cash receipts and disbursements method of accounting, to the extent that the interest charge for a taxable year is deductible, it is deductible in the taxable year in which the shareholder pays the interest charge. For example, assume that on March 15, 1987, a cash method, calendar year DISC shareholder that is a C corporation pays $100, representing the full amount of the shareholder's interest charge for its taxable year ending December 31, 1986. The $100 amount is a proper interest deduction for the shareholder's taxable year ending December 31, 1987, the taxable year in which the cash method shareholder paid the interest charge.

(ii) *Accrual method shareholder.*—If the DISC shareholder uses the accrual method of accounting, under the all events test the fact of the shareholder's liability for the interest charge for a taxable year is not fixed, and the amount of the interest charge cannot be determined, until the close of the period in which the shareholder can receive a distribution-in-excess-of-income with respect to such year. Prior to that time, all or any amount of the interest charge for the taxable year may be eliminated by such a distribution. Generally, however, if the DISC shareholder uses the accrual method and if the DISC and the shareholder have the same taxable year, then to the extent that the interest charge for a taxable year is deductible, the amount of the shareholder's interest charge is a proper deduction for such taxable year, because the period in which the DISC can make a distribution-in-excess-of-income to the shareholder with respect to such taxable year ends on the last day of such shareholder's taxable year. For example, assume that on March 10, 1987, an accrual method, calendar year DISC shareholder that is a C corporation pays $150, representing the full amount of the shareholder's interest charge for its taxable year ending December 31, 1986. Assume also that the DISC uses the calendar year as the taxable year. When the DISC's 1986 taxable year closed, the shareholder could no longer receive a distribution-in-excess-of-income under section 995(f)(3)(A)(ii) with respect to the shareholder's 1986 taxable year. Accordingly, the $150 interest charge is a proper interest deduction for the shareholder's taxable year ending December 31, 1986, the taxable year in which the interest charge accrued under section 461.

(3) *Payment, assessment and collection of the interest charge.*—(i) Under section 995(f)(6), the interest charge imposed on the DISC shareholder for any taxable year is required to be paid on the same date the shareholder's income tax return for such taxable year is required to be filed, without regard to extensions.

If the interest charge is not paid by that date, interest, compounded daily, at the rate specified under section 6621 shall be imposed on the amount of the unpaid interest charge from that date until the date the interest charge is paid. The interest charge for the taxable year shall be computed on a current Form 8404, which must be completed in accordance with the instructions thereon, and filed by the DISC shareholder together with a separate payment of the interest charge. The payment of the interest charge shall be made, and the Form 8404 shall be filed with the service center with which the shareholder's income tax return for the taxable year is required to be filed. In order to assure proper handling of the Form 8404 and crediting of payment of the interest charge to the shareholder's account, the Form 8404 and the payment of the interest charge should not be attached to or mailed together with the shareholder's income tax return for the taxable year. Payment of the interest charge may not be made by designating any portion of an overpayment of tax as an amount to be applied in payment of the interest charge.

(ii) Payments of estimated tax under section 6654 (in the case of an individual), or 6154 (in the case of a corporation) are not required with respect to the interest charge.

(iii) The interest charge is to be assessed, and may be collected in the same manner as interest on an underpayment of tax under section 6601.

(4) *Subsequent change in interest charge amount; amended Form 8404.*—If the shareholder's actual tax liability for a taxable year changes, either by reason of an audit adjustment or by the filing of an amended return, the shareholder is required to file an amended Form 8404 only if the amount of the shareholder's DISC-related deferred tax liability (as defined in § 1.995(f)-1(d)) for such taxable year also changes. If so required, the shareholder shall file the amended Form 8404 by (i) clearly labeling across the top of a Form 8404 "Amended Form 8404 for Shareholder's Taxable Year Ending 19XX", (ii) by attaching to the amended Form 8404 a computation and an explanation of the change in the shareholder's DISC-related deferred tax liability and interest charge for such taxable year, and (iii) by enclosing payment for the amount of any additional interest charge or a statement of the amount of the interest charge required to be refunded to the shareholder. The amended Form 8404 should be attached to the copy of the shareholder's amended income tax return for the taxable year involved, or mailed separately to the service center with which the shareholder would file an amended income tax return for the taxable year involved. [Reg. § 1.995(f)-1.]

DISCs: Deemed Distributions

Domestic International Sales Corporations: Taxation of Income.—Reproduced below are the texts of proposed Reg. §1.996-9 and proposed amendments to Reg. §1.996-1, relating to the taxation of income allocable to a DISC for taxable years beginning after 1984 (published in the Federal Register on February 3, 1987).

* * *

☐ Par. 12. Paragraph (b)(2) of § 1.996-1 is revised to read as follows:

§ 1.996-1. Rules for actual distributions and certain deemed distributions.—* * *

(b) *Rules for qualifying distributions and deemed distributions under section 995(b)(1)(G).*— * * *

(2) *Special rules.*—(i) *1976-1984.*—For taxable years beginning after December 31, 1975, and before January 1, 1985, paragraph (b)(1) of this section shall apply to one-half of the amount of an actual distribution made pursuant to § 1.992-3 to satisfy the condition of § 1.992-1(b) (the gross receipts test) and paragraph (a) of this section shall apply to the remaining one-half of such amount.

(ii) *After 1984.*—For taxable years beginning after December 31, 1984, in the case of a DISC shareholder which is a C corporation, paragraph (b)(1) of this section shall apply to $^{16}/_{17}$ of the amount of an actual distribution made pursuant to § 1.992-3 to satisfy the condition of § 1.992-1(b) (the gross receipts test) and paragraph (a) of this section shall apply to one-seventeenth ($^{1}/_{17}$) of such amount.

* * *

☐ Par. 12. A new section 1.996-9 is added immediately after § 1.996-8 to read as follows:

§ 1.996-9. Adjustments attributable to the Tax Reform Act of 1984.—(a) *Exemption of pre-1985 accumulated DISC income from tax.*—(1) *In general.*—Under section 805(b)(2) of the Tax Reform Act of 1984, Pub. L. 98-369, 98 Stat. 494, 1001, in the case of actual distributions made after December 31, 1984, by a DISC or former DISC which was a DISC on such date, any accumulated DISC income of such DISC or former DISC which was derived before January 1, 1985, shall be treated as previously taxed income with respect to which there had previously been a deemed distribution to which section 996(e)(1) applied. For purposes of this section such accumulated DISC income shall be referred to as "exempt accumulated DISC income". For purposes of this section, a distribution includes any distribution in liquidation of a corporation.

(2) *Exception for previously disqualified DISCs.*—Paragraph (a)(1) of this section does not apply to the amount of any actual or deemed distribution of any accumulated DISC income of a DISC or former DISC derived before January 1, 1985, which is scheduled to be received as a deemed distribution under section 995(b)(2) and § 1.995-3 by reason of the disqualification, termination or revocation of the DISC election of such corporation (a "disqualified DISC"). Thus, in the case of a corporation which was a disqualified DISC with respect to one or more prior taxable years ending before 1985, but which has reelected to be treated as a DISC for one or more succeeding taxable years including the taxable year ending December 31, 1984, this paragraph (a)(2) applies to any accumulated DISC income scheduled to be received as a deemed distribution under section 995(b)(2), and paragraph (a)(1) of this section applies to any accumulated DISC income derived before 1985 which is not

required to be distributed under section 995(b)(2).

(3) *Exception for amounts distributed to meet qualification requirements.*—Paragraph (a)(1) of this section does not apply to the amount of any accumulated DISC income derived before January 1, 1985, which is distributed (or is required to be distributed) under section 992(c) after December 31, 1984, in order to satisfy the requirements of section 992(a)(1)(A) (relating to the 95 percent qualified export receipts test) or section 992(a)(1)(B) (relating to the 95 percent qualified export assets test), with respect to any taxable year ending before January 1, 1985.

(b) *Effect of distributions by DISC to shareholders.*—(1) *Scope.*—This paragraph (b) applies only to distributions made after December 31, 1984, by a DISC (including a corporation which has elected to be treated as an interest charge DISC for any period after 1984) or a former DISC which has any amount of exempt accumulated DISC income (as defined in paragraph (a)(1) of this section), and it shall not apply after such corporation has distributed, under the ordering rules of this paragraph (b), all of its exempt accumulated DISC income. This paragraph (b) shall apply notwithstanding section 996(a)(1).

(2) *Ordering rule for distributions made before July 1, 1985.*—Any actual distribution to a shareholder after December 31, 1984, and before July 1, 1985, by a DISC or former DISC described in paragraph (b)(1) of this section, which is made out of earnings and profits shall be treated as made—

(i) First, out of previously taxed income, to the extent thereof,

(ii) Second, out of accumulated DISC income derived after 1984, to the extent thereof, and

(iii) Third, out of other earnings and profits (including current earnings and profits in the case of a former DISC).

Any distribution which is treated as made out of previously taxed income under paragraph (b)(2)(i) shall be treated as made first out of exempt accumulated DISC income, to the extent thereof, and second, out of other previously taxed income.

(3) *Ordering rule for distributions made after June 30, 1985.*—Any actual distribution to a shareholder after June 30, 1985, by a DISC or former DISC described in paragraph (b)(1) of this section, which is made out of earnings and profits shall be treated as made—

(i) First, out of other earnings and profits (including current earnings and profits in the case of a former DISC), to the extent thereof,

(ii) Second, out of previously taxed income, to the extent thereof, and

(iii) Third, out of accumulated DISC income derived after 1984.

Any distribution which is treated as made out of previously taxed income under paragraph (b)(3)(ii) shall be treated as made first out exempt accumulated DISC income, to the extent thereof, and second, out of other previously taxed income.

(4) *Exception for qualifying distributions and foreign investments attributable to producer's loans.*—This paragraph (b) shall not apply to any actual distribution made pursuant to section 992(c) (relating to distributions to meet qualification requirements), or to any deemed distribution pursuant to section 995(b)(1)(G) (relating to foreign investment attributable to producer's loans). Such distributions shall be treated as described in section 996(a)(2).

(c) *Earnings and profits attributable to exempt income.*—The earnings and profits of a corporation which receives a distribution directly or indirectly from a DISC or former DISC shall be increased by the amount of money and the adjusted basis of any property received in a distribution which is treated as made out of previously taxed income attributable to exempt accumulated DISC income.

(d) *No adjustment to basis in stock of DISC for exempt income.*—Notwithstanding section 996(e), a shareholder's basis in the stock of a DISC or former DISC shall not be increased by the amount of exempt accumulated DISC income which is treated as previously taxed income, and such basis shall not be reduced by the receipt of such amount as previously taxed income in a distribution to which paragraph (b) of this section applies.

(e) *Carryover basis in property received in a distribution of exempt income.*—If property other than money is received in a distribution of exempt accumulated DISC income as previously taxed income, and if such property was a qualified export asset (as defined in section 993(b)) on December 31, 1984, then for purposes of section 311, no gain or loss shall be recognized on the distribution of such property, and the shareholder who receives such property shall have a basis in such property equal to the basis of such property in the hands of the DISC or former DISC.

(f) *Reduction of net operating loss and capital loss carryovers.*—In the case of a DISC (including a corporation which has elected to be treated as an interest charge DISC for any period after 1984) or a former DISC which was a DISC on December 31, 1984, the amount of any net operating loss or capital loss of such corporation that was incurred in a taxable year in which such corporation was a DISC and which is a net operating loss or capital loss carryover to any taxable year ending after December 31, 1984, shall be reduced by the amount of exempt accumulated DISC income (as defined in paragraph (a)(1) of this section) of such corporation as of December 31, 1984. If the sum of such carryovers exceeds the amount of such exempt accumulated DISC income, the exempt accumulated DISC income shall first be applied to reduce the amount of such net operating loss carryover, and the amount of such exempt accumulated DISC income (if any) which exceeds such net operating loss carryover shall be applied to reduce the amount of such capital loss carryover to the extent of such excess.

(g) *No credit allowed for foreign taxes attributable to exempt accumulated DISC income.*—Notwithstanding sections 901(d) and 902, no credit shall be allowed for the amount of any income, war profits, or excess profits taxes paid or deemed paid to any foreign country or possession of the United States to the extent that such taxes are attributable to any exempt accumulated DISC income of a DISC or former DISC. [Reg. § 1.996-9.]

* * *

International Boycotts

International Boycotts: Loss of Tax Benefits: Computation of International Boycott Factor.—Reproduced below is the text of proposed Reg. §1.999-1, relating to the computation of the international boycott factor (published in the Federal Register on February 24, 1977).

§1.999-1. Computation of the International Boycott Factor.—(a) *In general.*—Sections 908(a), 952(a)(3), and 995(b)(1)(F) provide that certain benefits of the foreign tax credit, deferral of earnings of foreign corporations, and DISC are denied if a person or a member of a controlled group (within the meaning of section 993(a)(3)) that includes that person participates in or cooperates with an international boycott (within the meaning of section 999(b)(3)). The loss of tax benefits may be determined by multiplying the otherwise allowable tax benefits by the "international boycott factor." Section 999(c)(1) provides that the international boycott factor is to be determined under regulations prescribed by the Secretary. The method of computing the international boycott factor is set forth in paragraph (c) of this section. A special rule for computing the international boycott factor of a person that is a member of two or more controlled groups is set forth in paragraph (d). Transitional rules for making adjustments to the international boycott factor for years affected by the effective dates are set forth in paragraph (e). The definitions of the terms used in this section are set forth in paragraph (b).

(b) *Definitions.*—For purposes of this section:

(1) *Boycotting country.*—In respect of a particular international boycott, the term "boycotting country" means any country described in section 999(a)(1)(A) or (B) that requires participation in or cooperation with that particular international boycott.

(2) *Participation in or cooperation with an international boycott.*—For the definition of the term "participation in or cooperation with an international boycott", see section 999(b)(3) and Parts H through M of the Treasury Department's International Boycott Guidelines.

(3) *Operations in or related to a boycotting country.*—For the definitions of the terms "operations", "operations in a boycotting country", "operations related to a boycotting country", and "operations with the government, a company, or a national of a boycotting country", see Part B of the Treasury Department's International Boycott Guidelines.

(4) *Clearly demonstrating clearly separate and identifiable operations.*—For the rules for "clearly demonstrating clearly separate and identifiable operations", see Part D of the Treasury Department's International Boycott Guidelines.

(5) *Purchase made from a country.*—The terms "purchase made from a boycotting country" and "purchases made from any country other than the United States" mean, in respect of any particular country, the gross amount paid in connection with the purchase of, the use of, or the right to use:

(i) Tangible personal property (including money) from a stock of goods located in that country,

(ii) Intangible property (other than securities) in that country,

(iii) Securities by a dealer to a beneficial owner that is a resident of that country (but only if the dealer knows or has reason to know the country of residence of the beneficial owner),

(iv) Real property located in that country, or

(v) Services performed in, and the end product of services performed in, that country (other than payroll paid to a person that is an officer or employee of the payor).

(6) *Sales made to a country.*—The terms "sales made to a boycotting country" and "sales made to any country other than the United States" mean, in respect of any particular country, the gross receipts from the sale, exchange, other disposition, or use of:

(i) Tangible personal property (including money) for direct use, consumption, or disposition in that country,

(ii) Services performed in that country,

(iii) The end product of services (wherever performed) for direct use, consumption, or disposition in that country,

(iv) Intangible property (other than securities) in that country,

(v) Securities by a dealer to a beneficial owner that is a resident of that country (but only if the dealer knows or has reason to know the country of residence of the beneficial owner), or

(vii) Real property located in that country.

To determine the country of direct use, consumption, or disposition of tangible personal property and the end product of services, see paragraph (b)(10) of this section.

(7) *Sales made from a country.*—The terms "sales made from a boycotting country" and "sales made from any country other than the United States" mean, in respect of a particular country, the gross receipts from the sale, exchange, other disposition, or use of:

(i) Tangible personal property (including money) from a stock of goods located in that country,

(ii) Intangible property (other than securities) in that country, or

(iii) Services performed in, and the end product of services performed in, that country.

However, gross receipts from any such sale, exchange, other disposition, or use by a person that are included in the numerator of that person's international boycott factor by reason of paragraph (b)(6) of this section shall not again be included in the numerator by reason of this subparagraph.

(8) *Payroll paid or accrued for services performed in a country.*—The terms "payroll paid or accrued for services performed in a boycotting country" and "payroll paid or accrued for services performed in any country other than the United States" mean, in respect of a particular country, the total amount paid or accrued as compensation to officers and employees, including wages, salaries, commissions, and bonuses, for services performed in that country.

(9) *Services performed partly within and partly without a country.*—(i) *In general.*—Except

as provided in paragraph (b)(9)(ii) of this section, for purposes of allocating to a particular country—

(A) The gross amount paid in connection with the purchase or use of,

(B) The gross receipts from the sale, exchange, other disposition or use of, and

(C) the payroll paid or accrued for services performed, or the end product of services performed, partly within and partly without that country, the amount paid, received, or accrued to be allocated to that country, unless the facts and circumstances of a particular case warrant a different amount, will be that amount that bears the same relation to the total amount paid, received, or accrued as the number of days of performance of the services within that country bears to the total number of days of performance of services for which the total amount is paid, received, or accrued.

(ii) *Transportation, telegraph, and cable services.*—Transportation, telegraph, and cable services performed partly within one country and partly within another country are allocated between the two countries as follows:

(A) In the case of a purchase of such services performed from Country A to Country B, fifty percent of the gross amount paid is deemed to be a purchase made from Country A and the remaining fifty percent is deemed to be a purchase made from Country B.

(B) In the case of a sale of such services performed from Country A to Country B, fifty percent of the gross receipts is deemed to be a sale made from Country A and the remaining fifty percent is deemed to be a sale made to Country B.

(10) *Country of use, consumption, or disposition.*—As a general rule, the country of use, consumption, or disposition of a tangible personal property (including money) and the end product of services (wherever performed) is deemed to be the country of destination of the tangible personal property or the end product of the services. (Thus, if legal services are performed in one country and an opinion is given for use by a client in a second country, the end product of the legal services is used, consumed, or disposed of in the second country.) The occurrence in a country of a temporary interruption in the shipment of the tangible personal property or the delivery of the end product of services shall not constitute such country the country of destination. However, if at the time of the transaction the person providing the tangible personal property or the end product of services knew, or should have known from the facts and circumstances surrounding the transaction, that the tangible personal property or the end product of services probably would not be used, consumed, or disposed of in the country of destination, that person must determine the country of ultimate use, consumption or disposition of the tangible personal property or the end product of services. Notwithstanding the preceding provisions of this subparagraph, a person that sells, exchanges, otherwise disposes of, or makes available for use, tangible personal property to any person all of whose business except for an insubstantial part consists of selling from inventory to retail customers at retail outlets all within one country may assume at the time of such sale to such person that the tangible personal property will be used, consumed, or disposed of within such country.

(11) *Controlled group taxable year.*—The term "controlled group taxable year" means the taxable year of the controlled group's common parent corporation. In the event that no common parent corporation exists, the members of the group shall elect the taxable year of one of the members of the controlled group to serve as the controlled group taxable year. The taxable year election is a binding election to be changed only with the approval of the Secretary or his delegate. The election is to be made in accordance with the procedures set forth in the instructions to Form 5713, the International Boycott Report.

(c) *Computation of international boycott factor.*—(1) *In general.*—The method of computing the international boycott factor of a person that is not a member of a controlled group is set forth in paragraph (c)(2) of this section. The method of computing the international boycott factor of a person that is a member of a controlled group is set forth in paragraph (c)(3) of this section. For purposes of paragraphs (c)(2) and (3), purchases and sales made by, and payroll paid or accrued by, a partnership are deemed to be made or paid or accrued by a partner in that production that the partner's distributive share bears to the purchases and sales made by, and the payroll paid or accrued by, the partnership. Also for purposes of paragraphs (c)(2) and (3), purchases and sales made by, and payroll paid or accrued by, a trust referred to in section 671 are deemed to be made both by the trust (for purposes of determining the trust's international boycott factor), and by a person treated under section 671 as the owner of the trust (but only in that proportion that the portion of the trust that such person is considered as owning under section 671 through 679 bears to the purchases and sales made by, and the payroll paid and accrued by, the trust).

(2) *International boycott factor of a person that is not a member of a controlled group.*—The international boycott factor to be applied by a person that is not a member of a controlled group (within the meaning of section 993(a)(3)) is a fraction.

(i) The numerator of the fraction is the sum of the—

(A) Purchases made from all boycotting countries associated in carrying out a particular international boycott,

(B) Sales made to or from all boycotting countries associated in carrying out a particular international boycott, and

(C) Payroll paid or accrued for services performed in all boycotting countries associated in carrying out a particular international boycott

by that person during that person's taxable year, minus the amount of such purchases, sales, and payroll that is clearly demonstrated to be attributable to clearly separate and identifiable operations in connection with which there was no participation in or cooperation with that international boycott.

(ii) The denominator of the fraction is the sum of the—

(A) Purchases made from any country other than the United States,

(B) Sales made to or from any country other than the United States, and

(C) Payroll paid or accrued for services performed in any country other than the United States

by that person during that person's taxable year.

(3) *International boycott factor of a person that is a member of a controlled group.*—The international boycott factor to be applied by a person that is a member of a controlled group (within the meaning of section 993(a)(3)) shall be computed in the manner described in paragraph (c)(2) of this section, except that there shall be taken into account the purchases and sales made by, and the payroll paid or accrued by, each member of the controlled group during each member's own taxable year that ends with or within the controlled group taxable year that ends with or within that person's taxable year.

(d) *Computation of the international boycott factor of a person that is a member of two or more controlled groups.*—The international boycott factor to be applied under sections 908(a), 952(a)(3), and 995(b)(1)(F) by a person that is a member of two or more controlled groups shall be determined in the manner described in paragraph (c)(3), except that the purchases, sales, and payroll included in the numerator and denominator shall include the purchases, sales, and payroll of that person and of all other members of the two or more controlled groups of which that person is a member.

(e) *Transitional rules.*—(1) *Pre-November 3, 1976 boycotting operations.*—The international boycott factor to be applied under sections 908(a), 952(a)(3), and 995(b)(1)(F) by a person that is not a member of a controlled group, for that person's taxable year that includes November 3, 1976, or a person that is a member of a controlled group, for the controlled group taxable year that includes November 3, 1976, shall be computed in the manner described in paragraphs (c)(2) and (c)(3), respectively, of this section. However, the following adjustments shall be made—

(i) There shall be excluded from the numerators described in paragraphs (c)(2)(i) and (c)(3)(i) of this section purchases, sales, and payroll clearly demonstrated to be attributable to clearly separate and identifiable operations—

(A) that were completed on or before November 3, 1976, or

(B) in respect of which it is demonstrated that the agreements constituting participation in or cooperation with the international boycott were renounced, the renunciations were communicated on or before November 3, 1976, to the governments or persons with which the agreements were made, and the agreements have not been reaffirmed after November 3, 1976, and

(ii) The international boycott factor resulting after the numerator has been modified in accordance with paragraph (e)(1)(i) of this section shall be further modified by multiplying it by a fraction. The numerator of that fraction shall be the number of days in that person's taxable year (or, if applicable, in that person's controlled group taxable year) remaining after November 3, 1976, and the denominator shall be 366.

The principles of this subparagraph are illustrated in the following example:

Example. Corporation A, a calendar year taxpayer, is not a member of a controlled group. During the 1976 calendar year, Corporation A had three operations in a boycotting country under three separate contracts, each of which contained agreements constituting participation in or cooperation with an international boycott. Each contract was entered into on or after September 2, 1976. Operation (1) was completed on November 1, 1976. The sales made to a boycotting country in connection with Operation (1) amounted to $10. Operation (2) was not completed during the taxable year, but on November 1, 1976, Corporation A communicated a renunciation of the boycott agreement covering that operation to the government of the boycott country. The sales made to a boycotting country in connection with Operation (2) amounted to $40. Operation (3) was not completed during the taxable year, nor was any renunciation of the boycott agreement made. The sales made to a boycotting country in connection with Operation (3) amounted to $25. Corporation A had no purchases made from, sales made from, or payroll paid or accrued for services performed in, a boycotting country. Corporation A had $500 of purchases made from, sales made from, sales made to, and payroll paid or accrued for services performed in, countries other than the United States. Company A's boycott factor for 1976, computed under paragraph (c)(2) of this section (before the application of this subparagraph) would be:

$$\frac{\$10 + \$40 + \$25}{\$500} = \frac{\$75}{\$500}$$

However, the $10 is eliminated from the numerator by reason of paragraph (e)(1)(i)(A) of this section, and the $40 is eliminated from the numerator by reason of paragraph (e)(1)(i)(B) of this section. Thus, before the application of paragraph (e)(1)(ii) of this section, Corporation A's international boycott factor is $25/$500. After the application of paragraph (e)(1)(ii), Corporation A's international boycott factor is:

$$\frac{\$25}{\$500} \times \frac{58}{366}$$

(2) *Pre-December 31, 1977 boycotting operations.*—The international boycott factor to be applied under sections 908(a), 952(a)(3), and 995(b)(1)(F) by a person that is not a member of a controlled group, for that person's taxable year that includes December 31, 1977, or by a person that is a member of a controlled group, for the controlled group taxable year that includes December 31, 1977, shall be computed in the manner described in paragraphs (c)(2) and (c)(3), respectively, of this section. However, the following adjustments shall be made—

(i) There shall be excluded from the numerators described in paragraphs (c)(2)(i) and (c)(3)(i) of this section purchases, sales, and payroll clearly demonstrated to be attributable to clearly separate and identifiable operations that were carried out in accordance with the terms of binding contracts entered into before September 2, 1976, and—

(A) That were completed on or before December 31, 1977, or

(B) In respect of which it is demonstrated that the agreements constituting participation in or cooperation with the international boycott were renounced, the renunciations were communicated on or before December 31, 1977, to the governments or persons with which the agreements were made, and the agreements were not reaffirmed after December 31, 1977, and

(ii) In the case of clearly separate and identifiable operations that are carried out in accordance with the terms of binding contracts entered into before September 2, 1976, but that do not meet the requirements of paragraph (e)(2)(i) of this section, the numerators described in paragraphs (c)(2)(i) and (c)(3)(i) of this section shall be adjusted by multiplying the purchases, sales, and payroll clearly demonstrated to be attributable to those operations by a fraction, the numerator of which is the number of days in such person's taxable year (or, if applicable, in such person's controlled group taxable year) remaining after December 31, 1977, and the denominator of which is 365.

The principles of this subparagraph are illustrated in the following example:

Example. Corporation A is not a member of a controlled group and reports on the basis of a July 1—June 30 fiscal year. During the 1977-1978 fiscal year, Corporation A had 2 operations carried out pursuant to the terms of separate contracts, each of which had a clause that constituted participation in or cooperation with an international boycott. Neither operation was completed during the fiscal year, nor were either of the boycotting clauses renounced. Operation (1) was carried out in accordance with the terms of a contract entered into on November 15, 1976. Operation (2) was carried out in accordance with the terms of a binding contract entered into before September 2, 1976. Corporation A had sales made to a boycotting country in connection with Operation (1) in the amount of $50, and in connection with Operation (2) in the amount of $100. Corporation A had sales made to countries other than the United States in the amount of $500. Corporation A had no purchases made from, sales made from, or payroll paid or accrued for services performed in, any country other than the United States. In the absence of this subparagraph, Corporation A's international boycott factor would be

$$\frac{\$50 + \$100}{\$500}$$

However, by reason of the application of this subparagraph, Corporation A's international boycott factor is reduced to

$$\frac{\$50 + \$100 \left(\frac{181}{365}\right)}{\$500}$$

(3) *Incomplete controlled group taxable year.*—If, at the end of the taxable year of a person that is a member of a controlled group, the controlled group taxable year that includes November 3, 1976 has not ended, or the taxable year of one or more members of the controlled group that includes November 3, 1976 has not ended, then the international boycott factor to be applied under sections 908(a), 952(a)(3) and 995(b)(1)(F) by such person for the taxable year shall be computed in the manner described in paragraph (c)(3) of this section. However, the numerator and the denominator in that paragraph shall include only the purchases, sales, and payroll of those members of the controlled group whose taxable years ending after November 3, 1976 have ended as the end of the taxable year of such person.

(f) *Effective date.*—This section applies to participation in or cooperation with an international boycott after November 3, 1976. In the case of operations which constitute participation in or cooperation with an international boycott and which are carried out in accordance with the terms of a binding contract entered into before September 2, 1976, this section applies to such participation or cooperation after December 31, 1977. [Reg. § 1.999-1].

GAIN OR LOSS ON DISPOSITION OF PROPERTY

Annuity Contracts: Exchanges of Property

Annuity Contracts: Exchanges of Property.—Amendments to Reg. § 1.1001-1, providing guidance on the taxation of the exchange of property for an annuity contract, are proposed (published in the Federal Register on October 18, 2006) (REG-141901-05).

☐ Par. 3. In § 1.1001-1, paragraphs (h), (i) and (j) are added to read as follows:

§ 1.1001-1. Computation of gain or loss.

* * *

(h) [Reserved.]

(i) [Reserved.]

(j) *Certain annuity contracts received in exchange for property.*—(1) *In general.*—If an annuity contract (other than an annuity contract that either is a debt instrument subject to sections 1271 through 1275, or is received from a charitable organization in a bargain sale governed by § 1.1011-2) is received in exchange for property, receipt of the contract shall be treated as a receipt of property in an amount equal to the fair market value of the contract, whether or not the contract is the equivalent of cash. The amount realized attributable to the annuity contract is the fair market value of the annuity contract at the time of the exchange, determined under section 7520. For the timing of the recognition of gain or loss, if any, see § 1.451-1(a). In the case of a transfer in part a sale and in part a gift, see paragraph (e) of this section. In the case of an annuity contract that is a debt instrument subject to sections 1271 through 1275, see paragraph (g) of this section. In the case of a bargain sale to a charitable organization, see § 1.1011-2.

(2) *Effective date.*—(i) *In general.*—Except as provided in paragraph (j)(2)(ii), this paragraph (j) is effective for exchanges of property for an annuity contract (other than an annuity contract that either is a debt instrument subject to sections 1271 through 1275, or is received from a charitable organization in a bargain sale governed by § 1.1011-2) after October 18, 2006.

(ii) This paragraph (j) is effective for exchanges of property for an annuity contract (other than an annuity contract that either is a debt instrument subject to sections 1271 through 1275, or is received from a charitable organization in a bargain sale governed by § 1.1011-2) after April 18, 2007, if the following conditions are met —

(A) The issuer of the annuity contract is an individual;

(B) The obligations under the annuity contract are not secured, either directly or indirectly; and

(C) The property transferred in exchange for the annuity contract is not subsequently sold or otherwise disposed of by the transferee during the two-year period beginning on the date of the exchange. For purposes of this provision, a disposition includes without limitation a transfer to a trust (whether a grantor trust, a revocable trust, or any other trust) or to any other entity even if solely owned by the transferor.

State and Local Governments: Tax-Exempt Bonds

State and Local Governments: Tax-Exempt Bonds.—Amendments to Reg. §1.1001-3, addressing when tax-exempt bonds are treated as retired for purposes of section 103 and sections 141 through 150 of the Internal Revenue Code, are proposed (published in the Federal Register on December 31, 2018) (REG-141739-08).

Par. 3. Section 1.1001-3 is amended by:

1. Revising paragraph (a)(2).
2. Revising the paragraph (h) subject heading.
3. Revising the first sentence of paragraph (h)(1).
4. Revising the paragraph (h)(2) subject heading.
5. Adding paragraph (h)(3).

The revisions and addition read as follows:

§1.1001-3. Modifications of debt instruments.—(a) * * *

(2) *Qualified tender bonds.*—For special rules governing whether tax-exempt bonds that are qualified tender bonds are retired for purposes of sections 103 and 141 through 150, see §1.150-3.

* * *

(h) *Applicability date.*—* * *

(1) * * * Except as otherwise provided in paragraphs (h)(2) and (3) of this section, this section applies to alterations of the terms of a debt instrument on or after September 24, 1996. * * *

(2) *Alteration or modification results in an instrument or property right that is not debt.* * * *

(3) *Qualified tender bonds.*—Paragraph (a)(2) of this section applies to events and actions taken with respect to qualified tender bonds that occur on or after the date that is 90 days after the date of publication of the Treasury decision adopting these rules as final regulations in the **Federal Register.**

Imputed Interest: OID: Safe Haven Rates: Related Party Sales

Imputed Interest: Original Issue Discount: Safe Haven Interest Rates.—Reproduced below is the text of a proposed amendment to Reg. §1.1012-2, relating to (1) the tax treatment of debt instruments issued after July 1, 1982, that contain original issue discount, (2) the imputation of and the accounting for interest with respect to sales and exchanges of property occurring after December 31, 1984, and (3) safe haven interest rates for loans or advances between commonly controlled taxpayers and safe haven leases between such taxpayers (published in the Federal Register on April 8, 1986).

□ Par. 21. Section 1.1012-2 is revised to read as follows:

§1.1012-2. Certain sales or exchanges between related parties.—(a) *In general.*—In the case of a sale or exchange of property in which the relationship between the seller and the buyer is such that the sale or exchange is not necessarily an arm's-length transaction, the transaction shall be examined to determine whether the value of the consideration provided by the buyer is greater than or less than the value of the property. If the value of the consideration exceeds the value of the property, this excess shall not be treated as relating to the sale or exchange and will be recharacterized according to the relationship between the parties. If the value of the property exceeds the value of the consideration, this excess generally shall be treated as transferred from the seller to the buyer based on the relationship between the parties and not as transferred in exchange for the debt instrument. The preceding sentence shall not apply to any transaction that would be characterized as in part a gift and in part a sale under §1.170A-4(c)(2) and §1.1011-2(b) or under §1.1015-4.

(b) *Value.*—In applying this section to any sale or exchange where all or a part of the consideration furnished by the buyer consists of one or more debt instruments issued by the buyer to the seller, then, for purposes of this section—

(1) The value of any such debt instrument to which section 1274 applies or which has adequate stated interest within the meaning of section 1274(c)(2) or §1.483-2 shall be its issue price;

(2) The value of any such debt instrument issued under a contract to which section 483 applies shall be the amount described in §1.483-3(a)(2)(i); and

(3) In determining whether the value of the consideration furnished by the buyer exceeds the value of the property, the value of the property shall be determined by reference to the price that an unrelated buyer (having the same creditworthiness as the actual buyer) would be willing to pay for the property in an arm's-length transaction if seller financing (taken into account at its issue price) were offered on the same terms as those offered to the actual buyer.

(c) *Examples.*—The provisions of this section may be illustrated by the following examples:

Example (1). (i) On January 1, 1986, Corporation X sells nonpublicly traded property to A, the sole shareholder of X. In consideration for the sale, A makes a down payment of $200,000 and issues a debt instrument calling for a single payment of $1,000,000 due in five years. No interest is provided for in the debt instrument. Because A is the sole shareholder of X, the transaction must be examined to determine whether the value of the property exceeds the value of the consideration furnished by A. For this purpose, the value of the property is its fair market value (determined without regard to any seller financing).

(ii) Assume that the fair market value of the property is $900,000 and that the issue price of the debt instrument under § 1.1274-4 is $643,928. Thus, the value of the consideration furnished by A is $843,928 (the sum of $200,000 (the portion of the consideration attributable to the down payment) and $643,928 (the portion of the consideration attributable to the debt instrument)). Since the value of the property ($900,000) exceeds the value of the consideration ($843,928), X Corporation is treated as having made a distribution to shareholder A to which section 301 applies. The amount of the distribution is $56,072 (the difference between $900,000 and $843,928). The basis of the property in the hands of A is $900,000 ($843,928 (consideration actually furnished by A) increased by $56,072 (the amount of the section 301 distribution)).

Example (2). The facts are the same as in Example (1) except that the fair market value of the property is $800,000. X is not treated as having made a section 301 distribution to A and A's basis in the property is $800,000. The transaction need not be examined for excessive consideration since a sale from a corporation to a shareholder ordinarily would not be used to disguise a contribution to capital from the shareholder to the corporation.

Example (3). (i) C sells nonpublicly traded property to his employer D for $300,000 in cash and D's debt instrument having a face amount of $1,000,000, payable in 5 years with interest payable semiannually at a rate of 9 percent. Because D is C's employer, the transaction must be examined to determine if a portion of the amount designated as consideration for the property is in fact disguised compensation.

(ii) Assume that the fair market value of the property (assuming no seller financing), is $1,000,000 and that the issue price of D's debt instrument is $1,000,000. Assume further that a buyer unrelated to D and having the same creditworthiness as C would be willing to pay $1,200,000 for the property if allowed to pay $300,000 in cash and $900,000 in the form of a 5-year debt instrument calling for semiannual payments of interest at a rate of 9 percent. The value of the consideration furnished by D is $1,300,000 (cash of $300,000 plus a debt instrument having an issue price of $1,000,000). Since this amount exceeds the value of the property by $100,000, only $200,000 of the $300,000 transferred from D to C is treated as consideration furnished for the property. The remaining $100,000 is treated as compensation. D's basis in the property is $1,200,000 (cash consideration of $200,000 plus a debt instrument with an issue price of $1,000,000).

Example (4). The facts are the same as in Example (3) except that the property could be sold to the unrelated buyer for $1,400,000 (assuming a down payment of $300,000 and 5-year seller financing at 9 percent for the balance of the purchase price). Because the value of the consideration furnished by D ($1,300,000) does not exceed the value of the property ($1,400,000), D is not treated as having paid compensation to C. D's basis in the property is $1,300,000. The transaction need not be examined for insufficient consideration since employees ordinarily do not make bargain sales to their employers. [Reg. § 1.1012-2.]

Estate and Person Acquiring Property from Decedent: Consistent Basis Reporting

Estate and Person Acquiring Property from Decedent: Consistent Basis Reporting.—Reg. §1.1014-10, providing guidance regarding the requirement that a recipient's basis in certain property acquired from a decedent be consistent with the value of the. property as finally determined for Federal estate tax purposes, is proposed (published in the Federal Register on March 4, 2016) (REG-127923-15).

Par. 2. Section 1.1014-10 is added to read as follows:

§1.1014-10. Basis of property acquired from a decedent must be consistent with Federal estate tax return.—(a) *Consistent basis requirement.*—(1) *In general.*—The taxpayer's initial basis in property described in paragraph (b) of this section may not exceed the property's final value within the meaning of paragraph (c) of this section. This requirement applies whenever the taxpayer reports a taxable event with respect to the property to the Internal Revenue Service (IRS) (for example depreciation or amortization) and continues to apply until the property is sold, exchanged, or otherwise disposed of in one or more transactions that result in the recognition of gain or loss for Federal income tax purposes, regardless of whether the owner on the date of the sale, exchange, or disposition is the same taxpayer who acquired the property from the decedent or as a result of the decedent's death.

(2) *Subsequent basis adjustments.*—The final value within the meaning of paragraph (c) of this section is the taxpayer's initial basis in the property. In computing at any time after the decedent's date of death the taxpayer's basis in property acquired from the decedent or as a result of the decedent's death, the taxpayer's initial basis in that property may be adjusted due to the operation of other provisions of the Internal Revenue Code (Code) governing basis without violating paragraph (a)(1) of this section. Such adjustments may include, for example, gain recognized by the decedent's estate or trust upon distribution of the property, post-death capital improvements and depreciation, and post-death adjustments to the basis of an interest in a partnership or S corporation. The existence of recourse or non-recourse debt secured by property at the time of the decedent's death does not affect the property's basis, whether the gross value of the property and the outstanding debt are reported separately on the estate tax return or the net value of the property is reported. Therefore, post-death payments on such debt do

not result in an adjustment to the property's basis.

(b) *Property subject to consistency requirement.*—(1) *In general.*—Property subject to the consistency requirement in paragraph (a)(1) of this section is any property that is includable in the decedent's gross estate under section 2031,any property subject to tax under section 2106, and any other property the basis of which is determined in whole or in part by reference to the basis of such property (for example as the result of a like-kind exchange or involuntary conversion) that generates a tax liability under chapter 11 of subtitle B of the Code (chapter 11) on the decedent's estate in excess of allowable credits, except the credit for prepayment of tax under chapter 11.

(2) *Exclusions.*—For purposes of paragraph (b)(1) of this section, property that qualifies for an estate tax charitable or marital deduction under section 2055, 2056, or 2056A, respectively, does not generate a tax liability under chapter 11 and therefore is excluded from the property subject to the consistency requirement in paragraph (a)(1) of this section. For purposes of paragraph (b)(1) of this section, tangible personal property for which an appraisal is not required under § 20.2031-6(b) is deemed not to generate a tax liability under chapter 11 and therefore also is excluded from the property subject to the consistency requirement in paragraph (a)(1) of this section.

(3) *Application.*—For purposes of paragraph (b)(1) of this section, if a liability under chapter 11 is payable after the application of all available credits (other than a credit for a prepayment of estate tax), the consistency requirement in paragraph (a)(1) of this section applies to the entire gross estate (other than property excluded under paragraph (b)(2) of this section) because all such property contributes to the liability under chapter 11 and therefore is treated as generating a tax liability under chapter 11. If, however, after the application of all such available credits, no tax under chapter 11 is payable, the entire gross estate is excluded from the application of the consistency requirement.

(c) *Final value.*—(1) *Finality of estate tax value.*—The *final value* of property reported on a return filed pursuant to section 6018 is its value as finally determined for purposes of the tax imposed by chapter 11. That value is—

(i) The value reported on a return filed with the Internal Revenue Service (IRS) pursuant to section 6018 once the period of limitations for assessment of the tax under chapter 11 has expired without that value having been timely adjusted or contested by the IRS,

(ii) If paragraph (c)(1)(i) of this section does not apply, the value determined or specified by the IRS once the periods of limitations for assessment and for claim for refund or credit of the tax under chapter 11 have expired without that value having been timely contested;

(iii) If paragraphs (c)(1)(i) and (ii) of this section do not apply, the value determined in an agreement, once that agreement is final and binding on all parties; or

(iv) If paragraphs (c)(1)(i), (ii), and (iii) of this section do not apply, the value determined by a court, once the court's determination is final.

(2) *No finality of estate tax value.*—Prior to the determination, in accordance with paragraph (c)(1) of this section, of the final value of property described in paragraph (b) of this section, the recipient of that property may not claim an initial basis in that property in excess of the value reported on the statement required to be furnished under section 6035(a). If the final value of the property subsequently is determined under paragraph (c)(1) of this section and that value differs from the value reported on the statement required to be furnished under section 6035(a), then the taxpayer may not rely on the statement initially furnished under section 6035(a) for the value of the property and the taxpayer may have a deficiency and underpayment resulting from this difference.

(3) *After-discovered or omitted property.*—(i) *Return under section 6018 filed.*—In the event property described in paragraph (b)(1) of this section is discovered after the estate tax return under section 6018 has been filed or otherwise is omitted from that return (after-discovered or omitted property), the final value of that property is determined under section (c)(3)(i)(A) or (B) of this section.

(A) *Reporting prior to expiration of period of limitation on assessment.*—The final value of the after-discovered or omitted property is determined in accordance with paragraph (c)(1) or (2) of this section if the executor, prior to the expiration of the period of limitation on assessment of the tax imposed on the estate by chapter 11, files with the IRS an initial or supplemental estate tax return under section 6018 reporting the property.

(B) *No reporting prior to expiration of period of limitation on assessment.*—If the executor does not report the after-discovered or omitted property on an initial or supplemental Federal estate tax return filed prior to the expiration of the period of limitation on assessment of the tax imposed on the estate by chapter 11, the final value of that unreported property is zero. See *Example 3* of paragraph (e) of this section.

(ii) *No return under section 6018 filed.*—If no return described in section 6018 has been filed, and if the inclusion in the decedent's gross estate of the after-discovered or omitted property would have generated or increased the estate's tax liability under chapter 11, the final value, for purposes of section 1014(f), of all property described in paragraph (b) of this section is zero until the final value is determined under paragraph (c)(1) or (2) of this section. Specifically, if the executor files a return pursuant to section 6018(a) or (b) that includes this property or the IRS determines a value for the property, the final value of all property described in paragraph (b) of this section includible in the gross estate then is determined under paragraph (c)(1) or (2) of this section.

(d) *Executor.*—For purposes of this section, *executor* has the same meaning as in section 2203 and includes any other person required under section 6018(b) to file a return.

(e) *Examples.*—The following examples illustrate the application of this section.

Example 1. (i) At D's death, D owned 50% of Partnership P, which owned a rental building with a fair market value of $10 million subject to nonrecourse debt of $2 million. D's sole beneficiary is C, D's child. P is valued at $8 million. D's interest in P is reported on the return required by section 6018(a) at $4 million. The IRS accepts the return as filed and the time for assessing the tax under chapter 11 expires. C sells the interest for $6 million in cash shortly thereafter.

(ii) Under these facts, the final value of D's interest is $4 million under paragraph (c)(1)(i) of this section. Under section 742 and § 1.742-1, C's basis in the interest in P at the time of its sale is $5 million (the final value of D's interest ($4 million) plus 50% of the $2 million nonrecourse debt). Following the sale of the interest, C reports taxable gain of $1 million. C has complied with the consistency requirement of paragraph (a)(1) of this section.

(iii) Assume instead that the IRS adjusts the value of the interest in P to $4.5 million, and that value is not contested before the expiration of the time for assessing the tax under chapter 11. The final value of D's interest in P is $4.5 million under paragraph (c)(1)(ii) of this section. Under section 742 and § 1.742-1, C claims a basis of $5.5 million at the time of sale and reports gain on the sale of $500,000. C has complied with the consistency requirement of paragraph (a)(1) of this section.

Example 2. (i) At D's death, D owned (among other assets) a private residence that was not encumbered. D's sole beneficiary is C. D's executor reports the value of the residence on the return required by section 6018(a) as $600,000 and pays the tax liability under chapter 11. The IRS timely contests the reported value and determines that the value of the residence is $725,000. The parties enter into a settlement agreement that provides that the value of the residence for purposes of the tax imposed by chapter 11 is $650,000. Pursuant to paragraph (c)(1)(iii) of this section, the final value of the residence is $650,000.

(ii) Several years later, C adds a master suite to the residence at a cost of $45,000. Pursuant to section 1016(a), C's basis in the residence is increased by $45,000 to $695,000. Subsequently, C sells the residence to an unrelated third party for $900,000. C claims a basis in the residence of $695,000 and reports a gain of $205,000 ($900,000 – $695,000). C has complied with the consistency requirement of paragraph (a)(1) of this section.

Example 3. (i) The facts are the same as in *Example 2* but, after the expiration of the period for assessing the tax imposed by chapter 11, the executor discovers property that had not been reported on the return required by section 6018(a) but which, if reported, would have generated additional chapter 11 tax on the entire value of the newly discovered property. Pursuant to paragraph (c)(3)(i)(B) of this section, C's basis in the residence of $695,000 does not change, but the final value of the additional unreported property is zero.

(ii) Alternatively, assume that no return was required to be filed under section 6018 before discovering the additional property (and none in fact was filed) but, after the application of the applicable credit amount, D's taxable estate including the unreported property would have been $200,000. Pursuant to paragraph (c)(3)(ii) of this section, the final value of all property included in D's gross estate that is described in paragraph (b) of this section is zero until the executor files an estate tax return with the IRS pursuant to section 6018 or the IRS determines a value for the property. In either of those events, the final value of property described in paragraph (b) of this section reported on the return is determined in accordance with paragraph (c)(1) or (c)(2) of this section.

Example 4. (i) At D's death, D's gross estate includes a residence valued at $300,000 encumbered by nonrecourse debt in the amount of $100,000. Title to the residence is held jointly by D and C (D's daughter) with rights of survivorship. D provided all the consideration for the residence and the entire value of the residence was included in D's gross estate. The executor reports the value of the residence as $200,000 on the return required by section 6018 filed with the IRS for D's estate and claims no other deduction for the debt. The statement required by section 6035 reports the value of the residence as $300,000. C sells the residence before the final value is determined under paragraph (c)(1) of this section for $375,000 and claims a gain of $75,000 on C's Federal income tax return.

(ii) A court subsequently determines that the value of the residence was $290,000 and the time for contesting this value in any court expires before the expiration of the period for assessing C's income tax for the year of C's sale of the property. The final value of the residence is $290,000 pursuant to paragraphs (c)(1)(iv) and (c)(2) of this section. Because C claimed a basis in the residence that exceeds the final value, C may have a deficiency and underpayment.

(f) *Effective/applicability date.*—Upon the publication of the Treasury Decision adopting these rules as final in the **Federal Register**, this section will apply to property acquired from a decedent or by reason of the death of a decedent whose return required by section 6018 is filed after July 31, 2015. Persons may rely upon these rules before the date of publication of the Treasury Decision adopting these rules as final in the **Federal Register**. [Reg. § 1.1014-10.]

Accelerated Cost Recovery System

Accelerated Cost Recovery System.—Reproduced below are the texts of proposed amendments of Reg. §§1.1016-3 and 1.1016-4, relating to the Accelerated Cost Recovery System for recovering capital costs of eligible property (published in the Federal Register on February 16, 1984).

☐ Par. 4. Paragraph (a)(3) of § 1.1016-3 is redesignated as (a)(4), and a new paragraph (a)(3) is added to read as follows:

§ 1.1016-3. Exhaustion, wear and tear, obsolescence, amortization, and depletion for periods since February 28, 1913.—(a) *In general.*—

* * *

(3) *Adjustment for amount allowable where no cost recovery deduction claimed under section 168.*—(i) Except as provided in subdivision (iii) of this subparagraph (3), if the taxpayer has not taken a deduction under section 168 (hereinafter

referred to as ACRS deduction) either in the taxable year or for any prior taxable year, the adjustments to basis of the property for the ACRS deduction allowable shall be determined by using the recovery method described in section 168(b)(1) or (2) or, where applicable, section 168(f)(2)(A) or (B).

(ii) If the taxpayer with respect to any recovery property has properly taken an ACRS deduction under one of the methods provided in section 168 for one or more years but has omitted the deduction in other years, the adjustment to basis for the ACRS deduction allowable in such a case will be the deduction under the method which was used by the taxpayer with respect to that property. Thus, for example, A acquired property in 1981 for which he properly elected to compute his ACRS deduction by use of one of the optional straight line percentages described in section 168(b)(3) for the first recovery year but did not take a deduction in the second and third years of the asset's recovery period. The adjustment to basis for the ACRS deduction allowable for the second and third recovery years will be computed using the optional straight line percentages which were elected.

(iii) If the taxpayer has made an election under §1.168-5(e)(5) (relating to special election rules for foreign taxpayers) to use an optional straight line percentage with respect to recovery property, the adjustments to basis of the property for the ACRS deduction allowable shall be determined pursuant to that election.

(iv) The provisions of subdivision (iii) of this subparagraph (3) may be illustrated by the following example:

Example. In 1981, Corporation F (a calendar year taxpayer) purchases for $100,000 and places in service in a foreign country 5-year recovery property which has a present class life of 7.5 years. F is not subject to United States income tax, other than under section 881, and is not required to compute earnings and profits under section 964. On January 1, 1983, F begins engaging in a trade or business in the United States (making it subject to tax under section 882), and uses the property in the United States in connection with that trade or business. Under §1.168-5(e)(5)(ii), F may elect to use the optional recovery percentages with respect to the property placed in service in 1981 by submitting the requisite information on its income tax return for the taxable year beginning in 1983. That election will apply with respect to such property from the taxable year in which it is placed in service. Thus, if F elects the optional recovery percentages based on a 12-year recovery period under §1.168-2(g)(3), the allowable ACRS deductions for 1981 and 1982 would be $4,000 (*i.e.*, .04 × $100,000) and $9,000 (*i.e.*, .09 × $100,000), respectively, and F's adjusted basis in the property on January 1, 1983, would be $87,000 (*i.e.*, $100,000 – $13,000). For the deduction allowable to F with respect to the property in 1983, see §1.168-2(j)(4)(i) and (j)(6) (relating to change in status).

* * *

☐ Par. 5. Section 1.1016-4 is amended by adding a new sentence at the end of paragraph (b) thereof, to read as follows:

§1.1016-4. Exhaustion, wear and tear, obsolescence, amortization, and depletion; periods during which income was not subject to tax.—

* * *

(b) * * *

For purposes of this section, the amount that would have been allowable as a deduction shall be determined without reference to section 168.

Imputed Interest: OID: Safe Haven Rates: Basis Adjustments

Imputed Interest: Original Issue Discount: Safe Haven Interest Rates.—Reproduced below is the text of a proposed amendment of Reg. §1.1016-5, relating to (1) the tax treatment of debt instruments issued after July 1, 1982, that contain original issue discount, (2) the imputation of and the accounting for interest with respect to sales and exchanges of property occurring after December 31, 1984, and (3) safe haven interest rates for loans or advances between commonly controlled taxpayers and safe haven leases between such taxpayers (published in the Federal Register on April 8, 1986).

☐ Par. 22. In §1.1016-5, paragraph(s) is revised to read as follows:

§1.1016-5. Miscellaneous adjustments to basis.

* * *

(s) *Original issue discount.*—In the case of certain debt instruments issued at a discount after May 27, 1969, the basis shall be increased under section 1272(b)(2) by the amount of original issue discount included in the holder's gross income pursuant to section 1272.

Allocation Rules: Code Sec. 1060 Coordination

Gains and Losses: Asset Acquisitions: Allocation Rules.—Temporary Reg. §1.1031(d)-1T, relating to allocation rules for certain asset acquisitions under Code Sec. 1060, is also proposed as a final regulation and, when adopted, would become Reg. §1.1031(d)-1 (published in the Federal Register on July 18, 1988).

§1.1031(d)-1. Coordination of section 1060 with section 1031 (temporary).

Imputed Interest: OID: Safe Haven Rates: Certain Exchanges

Imputed Interest: Original Issue Discount: Safe Haven Interest Rates.—Reproduced below is the text of a proposed amendment of Reg. §1.1037-1, relating to (1) the tax treatment of debt instruments issued after July 1, 1982, that contain original issue discount, (2) the imputation of and the accounting for interest with respect to sales and exchanges of property occurring after December 31, 1984, and (3) safe haven interest rates for loans or advances between commonly controlled taxpayers and safe haven leases between such taxpayers (published in the Federal Register on April 8, 1986).

☐ Par. 23. Section 1.1037-1 is amended as follows:

1. In paragraph (a) by removing the phrase "the first sentence of section 1232(a)(2)(B)," and adding in its place "section 1271(c)(2)(A)", by removing the phrase "section 1232(b)(2)" each place that is appears in *Example (6)* and *Example (7)* and adding in its place the phrase "section 1273(b)(1)", by removing the phrase "section 1232(a)(2)(B)" each place it appears in *Example (7)* and adding in its place the phrase "section 1271(c)(2)(A)", and by removing the phrase "section 1232(a)(2)(B)(ii)" each place it appears in *Example (6)* and *Example (7)* and adding in its place the phrase "section 1271(c)(2)(A)(ii)".

2. In paragraph (b) by removing the phrase "section 1232" from the heading and adding in its place the phrase "section 1271", by removing the phrase "section 1232(a)(2)(B)" each place that it appears and adding in its place the phrase "section 1271(c)(2)(A)", and by removing the phrase "section 1232" from the heading of paragraph (b)(6) and adding in its place the phrase "section 1271".

§1.1037-1. Certain exchanges of United States obligations.

Transfers Between Spouses

Transfers: Alimony, Separate Maintenance, and Dependency Exemption.—Temporary Reg. §1.1041-1T, relating to the treatment of transfers of property between spouses and former spouses, the tax treatments of alimony and separate maintenance payments, and the dependency exemption in the case of a child of divorced parents, is also proposed as a final regulation and, when adopted, would become Reg. §1.1041-1 (published in the Federal Register on August 31, 1984).

§1.1041-1. Treatment of transfers of property between spouses or incident to divorce.

Employee Trusts: Effective Dates

Employee Trusts: Tax Reform Act of 1984: Effective Dates.—Temporary Reg. §1.1042-1T is also proposed as a final regulation and, when adopted, would become Reg. §1.1042-1 (published in the Federal Register on February 4, 1986).

§1.1042-1. Questions and answers relating to the sales of stock to employee stock ownership plans or certain cooperatives.

Employee Stock Ownership Plans: Sale of Stock: Notarized Statements of Purchase

Employee Stock Ownership Plans: Sale of Stock: Notarized Statements of Purchase.—Amendments to Temporary Reg. §1.1042-1T, relating to notarized statements of purchase under Code Sec. 1042 and affecting taxpayers making an election to defer the recognition of gain under Code Sec. 1042 on the sale of stock to an employee stock ownership plan, are proposed (published in the Federal Register on July 10, 2003) (REG-121122-03).

☐ Par. 2. In §1.1042-1T, A-3, in the undesignated paragraph following paragraph (b)(6), the penultimate sentence is removed and three sentences added in its place to read as follows:

§1.1042-1T. Questions and answers relating to the sales of stock to employee stock ownership plans or certain cooperatives (temporary).

* * *

Q-3. * * *

A-3. * * *

(b) * * *

(6) * * *

* * * Such statement of purchase must be notarized not later than the time the taxpayer files the income tax return for the taxable year in which the sale of qualified securities occurred in any case in which any qualified replacement property was purchased by such time and during the qualified replacement period. If qualified replacement property is purchased after such filing date but during the qualified replacement period, the statement of purchase must be notarized not later than the time the taxpayer's income tax return is filed for the taxable year following the year for which the election under section 1042(a) was made. The previous two sentences apply to taxable years of sellers ending on or after the date final regulations are published in the Federal Register. * * *

* * *

Transfers of Securities Under Agreements

Transfers of Securities Under Agreements.—Reproduced below are the texts of proposed Reg. §§1.1058-1 and 1.1058-2, relating to transfers of securities under certain agreements (published in the Federal Register on July 26, 1983).

☐ Paragraph 1. The following sections are inserted in the appropriate place.

§1.1058-1. Transfers of securities under certain agreements.—(a) *In general.*—Section 1058 provides rules for the nonrecognition of gain or loss with respect to certain transfers of securities occurring after December 31, 1976. In order to qualify for treatment under this section, the transfer must be pursuant to an agreement which contains the provisions required by paragraph (b) of this section and those provisions must be complied with. If this section does apply, the lender will not recognize gain or loss on the exchange of the securities for the obligation of the borrower under the agreement nor will the lender recognize gain or loss on the exchange of the rights under such agreement in return for securities identical to the securities transferred by the lender.

(b) *Agreement requirements.*—The agreement between the borrower and lender described in paragraph (a) of this section must be in writing and must—

(1) Require the borrower to return to the lender securities identical to those which were lent to the borrower. For the purposes of this section securities are defined in section 1236(c). Identical securities are securities of the same class and issue as the securities lent to the borrower. If, however, the agreement permits the borrower to return equivalent securities in the event of reorganization, recapitalization or merger of the issuer of the securities during the term of the loan, this requirement will be deemed to be satisfied.

(2) Require the borrower to make payments to the lender of amounts equivalent to all interest, dividends, and other distributions which the owner of the securities is entitled to for the period during which the securities are borrowed.

(3) Not reduce the lender's risk of loss or opportunity for gain. Accordingly, the agreement must provide that the lender may terminate the loan upon notice of not more than 5 business days.

See section 512(a)(5) and the regulations thereunder for additional requirements with respect to loans of securities made by exempt organizations.

(c) *Basis.*—(1) *Lender's basis in securities.*—If this section applies, the lender's basis in the identical securities returned by the borrower shall be the same as the lender's basis in the securities lent to the borrower.

(2) *Lender's basis in contractual obligation.*—If this section applies, the lender's basis in the contractual obligation received from the borrower in exchange for the lender's securities is equal to the lender's basis in the securities exchanged.

(d) *Treatment of payments to lender.*—Except as otherwise provided in section 512(a)(5), a payment of amounts required to be paid by the borrower that are equivalent to all interest, dividends, and other distributions as provided in paragraph (b)(2) of this section, shall be treated by the lender as a fee for the temporary use of property. Thus, for example, an amount received by the lender that is equivalent to a dividend paid during the term of the loan shall not constitute a dividend to the lender for purposes of the Internal Revenue Code, but shall be taken into account as ordinary income.

(e) *Noncompliance with section 1058.*—(1) If a transfer of securities is intended to comply with section 1058 and fails to do so because the contractual obligation does not meet the requirements of section 1058(b) and §1.1058-1(b), gain or loss is recognized in accordance with section 1001 and §1.1001-1(a) upon the initial transfer of the securities. However, see section 1091 of the Code for disallowance of loss from wash sales of stock or securities.

(2) If securities are transferred pursuant to an agreement which meets the requirements of section 1058(b) and §1.1058-1(b) and the borrower fails to return to the lender securities identical to the securities transferred as required by the agreement, or otherwise defaults under the agreement, gain or loss is recognized on the day the borrower fails to return identical securities as required by the agreement, or otherwise defaults under the agreement. However, see section 1091 of the Code for disallowance of loss from wash sales of stock or securities.

(f) *Special rule.*—For purposes of determining the tax consequences to the lender of securities when a merger, recapitalization or reorganization (including, but not limited to, a reorganization described in section 368(a)(1) of the Internal Revenue Code) of the issuer occurs during the term of a loan to which section 1058 applies, the section 1058 loan transaction is deemed terminated immediately prior to the merger, recapitalization or reorganization and a second section 1058 transaction is deemed entered into immediately following the merger, recapitalization or reorganization. Therefore, the borrower of the securities is deemed to have returned the securities to the lender immediately prior to the merger, recapitalization or reorganization and immediately following the merger, recapitalization or reorganization the lender and borrower are deemed to have entered into a second section 1058 loan transaction, on terms identical to the original section 1058 loan transaction. The special rule in this paragraph (f) shall not apply in the case where the lender ultimately is repaid with securities identical to the securities originally transferred.

(g) *Cross reference.*—For rules relating to the lender's holding period, see §1.1223-2. [Reg. §1.1058-1.]

§1.1058-2. Examples.—The provisions of §1.1058-1 may be illustrated by the following examples:

Example (1). A owns 1,000 shares of XYZ common stock. A instructs A's broker, B, to sell the XYZ stock. B sells to C. After the sale, B learns that A will not be able to deliver to B certificates representing the 1,000 shares in time for B to deliver them to C on the settlement date. B decides to effect the delivery by borrowing stock from a third party. To this end, B enters into a written agreement with D, a non-exempt corporation having a large stock portfolio of XYZ common stock. The agreement includes the following terms:

(1) D will transfer to B certificates representing 1,000 shares of XYZ common stock.

(2) B will pay D an amount equivalent to any dividends or other distributions paid on the XYZ stock during the period of the loan.

(3) Regardless of any increases or decreases in the market value of XYZ common stock, B will transfer to D 1,000 shares of the XYZ common stock of the same issue as that of the XYZ common stock transferred from D to B.

(4) B agrees that upon notice of 5 business days, B will return identical securities to D.

The agreement between B and D satisfies the requirements of paragraph (b) of § 1.1058-1. The agreement is in writing. It requires the borrower, B, to return to the lender, D, identical securities and to pay to the lender, D, amounts equivalent to any dividends or other distributions paid on the stock during the period of the loan. It does not reduce D's risk of loss or opportunity for gain because, regardless of fluctuations in the market value of XYZ common stock, B is obligated to return 1,000 shares of XYZ common stock.

Example (2). Assume the same facts as in Example (1) except that the agreement between B and D includes the following additional terms:

(1) Upon D's transfer to B of the certificates representing the 1,000 shares of XYZ common stock, B will transfer to D, cash equal to the market value of the XYZ common stock on the business day preceding the transfer, as collateral for the stock. The collateral will be increased or decreased daily to reflect increases or decreases in the market value of the XYZ stock during the period of the loan.

(2) B agrees that upon notice of 5 business days, B will return to D 1,000 shares of XYZ common stock, or the equivalent thereof in the event of reorganization, recapitalization, or merger of XYZ during the term of the loan. Upon delivery of the stock to D, D will return the cash collateral to B.

The agreement between B and D satisfies the requirements of paragraph (b) of this section. If XYZ is merged into another corporation and B returns to D an equivalent amount of stock in the resulting corporation, paragraph (f) of this section provides that the section 1058 transaction is deemed terminated immediately before the merger. Thus, D is deemed to be the owner of the XYZ common stock at the time of the merger. Furthermore, paragraph (a) of this section provides that D does not recognize gain or loss upon the transfer of the XYZ common stock to B or upon the return of the stock of the resulting corporation to D. Nonetheless, gain or loss may be recognized with respect to the merger. If the merger is described in section 368(a)(1), gain will be recognized to the extent section 354(a)(2) or 356 applies to the merger. If the merger is not described in section 368(a)(1), D generally will recognize the entire gain or loss with respect to such stock as a result of the merger.

Example (3). Assume the same facts as in example (2) and in addition that on March 1, D transfers certificates representing 1,000 shares of XYZ common stock to B. D's basis in the stock is $60,000. On the business day preceding the transfer, the stock has a market value of $75 a share. Consequently, B transfers to D $75,000 as collateral for the stock. B then uses the certificates to complete a timely delivery to C. On March 20, when the market value of XYZ common stock is $69 a share, D gives B notice of termination. On March 24, B delivers to D 1,000 shares of XYZ common stock of the same issue as that of the XYZ common stock transferred to B on March 1. D returns the $69,000 cash collateral to B. (Because the market value of the stock had declined during the period of the loan, the collateral was adjusted to reflect the new market value and the $6,000 had previously been returned to B.) Because the agreement between B and D contains the provisions required by paragraph (b) of § 1.1058-1 and such provisions were complied with, D does not recognize gain on the transfer of the XYZ common stock to B. Nor does D recognize gain upon the return of XYZ common stock. D's basis in the XYZ common stock returned to it by B is $60,000. As to the holding period of the XYZ common stock returned to D, see § 1.1223-2(a).

Example (4). Assume the same facts as in example (3) and in addition that on March 3, XYZ pays a dividend on its common stock. B pays to D an amount equivalent to the dividend. The amount paid by B does not constitute a dividend to D, but rather constitutes a fee for the temporary use of property as provided in § 1.1058-1(d).

Example (5). (i) Assume the same facts as in example (3) except that on March 24 B notifies D that delivery of the 1,000 shares of XYZ common stock, of the same issue as that of the XYZ common stock transferred to B on March 1, cannot be completed on March 24. Assume further that B informs D that delivery would be completed on March 27.

(ii) If B and D agree to extend the time period in which B is to return the identical securities to D till March 27, then the section 1058 agreement will not be treated as breached when B delivers the securities on March 27, pursuant to the modified section 1058 agreement. As a result, D does not recognize gain on the transfer of XYZ common stock to B. Nor does D recognize gain upon the return of XYZ common stock.

(iii) If B and D do not agree to extend the time period, in which B is to return the identical securities to D, then as of March 25 B's failure to transfer the identical securities as required by the agreement will be treated as a breach of the agreement. As a result D will be treated as selling the XYZ common stock on March 25. D must then recognize gain or (subject to section 1091) loss, whichever is appropriate, on the sale of the securities. [Reg. § 1.1058-2.]

Tax Straddles: Loss Deferral: Wash Sales

Tax Straddles: Loss Deferral: Wash Sales.—Temporary Reg. §§ 1.1092(b)-1T, 1.1092(b)-2T and 1.1092(b)-5T, relating to the application of the loss deferral and wash sale rules and treatment of holding periods and losses with respect to straddle positions, are also proposed as final regula-

tions and, when adopted, would become Reg. §§1.1092(b)-1, 1.1092(b)-2 and 1.1092(b)-5, respectively (published in the Federal Register on January 24, 1985).

§1.1092(b)-1. Coordination of loss deferral rules and wash sale rules.

§1.1092(b)-2. Treatment of holding periods and losses with respect to straddle positions.

§1.1092(b)-5. Definitions.

Tax Straddles: Mixed Straddles

Tax Straddles: Mixed Straddles: Identification.—Temporary Reg. §§1.1092(b)-3T and 1.1092(b)-4T, relating to mixed straddles, are also proposed as final regulations and, when adopted, would become Reg. §§1.1092(b)-3 and 1.1092(b)-4 (published in the Federal Register on January 24, 1985).

§1.1092(b)-3. Mixed straddles; straddle-by-straddle identification under section 1092(b)(2)(A)(i)(I).

§1.1092(b)-4. Mixed straddles; mixed straddle account.

Straddles: Personal Property Defined

Straddles: Personal Property Defined.—An amendment to Reg. §1.1092(d)-2, relating to the definition of personal property for purposes of the straddle rules, is proposed (published in the Federal Register on May 2, 1995).

☐ Par. 2. Section 1.1092(d)-2 is revised to read as follows:

§1.1092(d)-2. Personal property.—(a) *Special rules for stock.*—As defined by section 1092(d)(l), *personal property* includes—

(1) Any stock if the stock is of a type that is actively traded and the stock is part of a straddle at least one of the offsetting positions of which is—

(i) An option with respect to that stock or substantially identical stock or securities; or

(ii) Under paragraphs (b) and (c) of this section, a position with respect to substantially similar or related property (other than stock); and

(2) Any stock, whether or not of a type that is actively traded, of a corporation formed or availed of to take positions in personal property as defined by section 1092(d)(1) that offset positions taken, directly or indirectly, by any shareholder.

(b) *Substantially similar or related property.*—For purposes of section 1092(d)(3)(B)(i)(II) and this section, the term *substantially similar or related property* is defined in §1.246-5 (other than §1.246-5(b)(3)). The rule in §1.246-5(c)(6) does not narrow the related party rule in section 1092(d)(4).

(c) *Position with respect to substantially similar or related property (other than stock).*—For purposes of section 1092(d)(3)(B)(i)(II) and this section, a *position with respect to substantially similar or related property (other than stock)* does not include direct ownership of stock or a short sale of stock but includes any other position with respect to substantially similar or related property.

(d) *Example.*—The following example illustrates the application of this section.

(1) *Facts*—(i) *The stock. A* acquired 10,000 shares of actively traded *X* stock during 1990. On September 29, 1995, those shares had a fair market value of $1,000,000.

(ii) *The swap.* On September 29, 1995, *A* entered into an *equity swap* contract with unrelated counterparty *C*, for a term of three years. Under the terms of that contract, on the last business day of each calendar quarter, *A* must pay to C an amount equal to the appreciation, if any, during the quarter on 10,000 shares of *X* stock. *A* also must pay to C an amount equal to the dividends, if any, that were paid during the quarter on 10,000 shares of *X* stock. On the last business day of each calendar quarter, *A* is to receive from C an amount equal to the depreciation, if any, during the quarter on 10,000 shares of *X* stock. *A* also is to receive from C an amount equal to the 3-month London Interbank Offered Rate (LIBOR), as determined at the close of the prior quarter, multiplied by the value of the *X* stock on that date.

(2) *Holdings*—(i) *The two legs as offsetting positions.* Because holding the equity swap substantially diminishes *A*'s risk of loss from holding the *X* stock, the *X* stock and the equity swap are offsetting positions within the meaning of section 1092(c). The remaining question is whether these are positions with respect to personal property.

(ii) *The swap leg as a position with respect to personal property.* The equity swap contract is a position with respect to personal property as defined by section 1092(d)(1). Although section 1092(d)(3)(A) generally excludes stock from the definition of personal property, this exclusion does not apply to interests in stock. Therefore, stock can be personal property when testing whether an interest in the stock, other than a direct interest in, or a short sale of, the stock, is a position with respect to personal property. Because the equity swap contract is an interest in actively traded stock, the equity swap contract is a position with respect to personal property.

(iii) *The stock leg as personal property.* As described below, ownership of the *X* stock is also a position with respect to personal property.

(A) *The rule of section 1092(d)(3)(B)(i)(II).* Under section 1092(d)(3)(B)(i)(II) and paragraph (a)(1)(ii) of this section, stock is not excluded from the definition of personal property if it is part of a straddle at least one of the offsetting positions of which is a position with respect to substantially similar or related property (other than stock).

(B) *The swap as a position with respect to substantially similar or related property (other than stock) for purposes of section 1092(d)(3)(B)(i)(II).* Under paragraph (b) of this section, the equity swap contract is a position with respect to property that is substantially similar or related to the *X* stock because *A* is entitled to payments under the equity swap contract that are attributable to the decline in the value of the *X* stock. See § 1.246-5(c)(7). Under section 1092(d)(3)(B)(i)(II) and paragraph (c) of this section, the equity swap contract is a position with respect to substantially similar or related property (other than stock) because it is not direct ownership of stock or a short sale of stock.

(C) *The stock as part of a straddle for purposes of the test of section 1092(d)(3)(B)(i)(II).* In determining whether the X stock is part of a straddle for purposes of the test of section 1092(d)(3)(B)(i) and paragraph (a)(1) of this section, section 1092(d)(3)(C) treats the *X* stock as personal property. Because the stock is treated as personal property for this purpose, because the equity swap contract is a position with respect to personal property (see paragraph (d)(2)(ii) of this section), and because the *X* stock and the equity swap contract are offsetting positions (see paragraph (d)(2)(i) of this section), the straddle test in section 1092(d)(3)(B)(i) and paragraph (a)(1) of this section is satisfied. Accordingly, under section 1092(d)(3)(B), the stock is personal property for all purposes of section 1092.

(iv) *The two legs as a straddle.* Because ownership of the *X* stock and the equity swap contract are offsetting positions with respect to personal property, the *X* stock and the equity swap contract are a straddle to *A* within the meaning of section 1092(c)(1).

(e) *Effective dates.*—(1) *In general.*—Except as provided in paragraph (e)(2) of this section, this section applies to positions established on or after May 1, 1995.

(2) *Special rules for substantially similar or related property.*—(i) *In general.*—Paragraph (b) of this section applies to positions established on or after March 17, 1995.

(ii) *Special rule for certain straddles.*—Paragraph (b) of this section applies to positions established after March 1, 1984, if the taxpayer substantially diminished its risk of loss by holding substantially similar or related property involving the following types of transactions—

(A) Holding offsetting positions consisting of stock and a convertible debenture of the same corporation where the price movements of the two positions are related; or

(B) Holding a short position in a stock index regulated futures contract (or alternatively an option on such a regulated futures contract or an option on the stock index) and stock in an investment company whose principal holdings mimic the performance of the stocks included in the stock index (or alternatively a portfolio of stocks whose performance mimics the performance of the stocks included in the stock index).

CAPITAL GAINS AND LOSSES

Transfers of Securities Under Agreements

Transfers of Securities Under Agreements.—Reproduced below is the text of proposed Reg. § 1.1223-2, relating to transfers of securities under certain agreements (published in the Federal Register on July 26, 1983).

□ Par. 2. The following is inserted immediately after § 1.1223-1.

§ 1.1223-2. Rules relating to securities lending transactions.—(a) *General rule.*—In the case of a transfer of securities pursuant to an agreement which meets the requirements of section 1058 (relating to transfers of securities under certain agreements), the holding period in the hands of the lender of the securities received by the lender from the borrower shall include—

(1) The period for which the lender held the securities which were transferred to the borrower; and

(2) The period between the transfer of the securities from the lender to the borrower and the return of the securities to the lender.

(b) *Failure to comply with section 1058.*—(1) If a transfer of securities is intended to comply with section 1058 and fails to do so because the contractual obligation does not meet the requirements of section 1058(b) and § 1.1058-1(b), the holding period in the hands of the lender of the securities transferred to the borrower shall terminate on the day the securities are transferred to the borrower, and the holding period in the hands of the borrower of the property transferred to it shall begin on the date that the securities are delivered pursuant to the transfer loan agreement.

(2) If securities are transferred pursuant to an agreement which meets the requirements of section 1058(b) and § 1.1058-1(b) and the borrower fails to return identical securities as required by the agreement or otherwise defaults under the agreement, the holding period in the hands of the lender of the securities transferred to the borrower shall terminate on the day the borrower fails to return identical securities as required by the agreement or otherwise defaults under the agreement, and the holding period in the hands of the borrower of the securities transferred to it shall begin on the day the borrower fails to return identical securities as required by the agreement or otherwise defaults under the agreement. [Reg. § 1.1223-2.]

Partners and Partnerships: Sales or Exchanges: Certain Distributions

Partners and Partnerships: Sales or Exchanges: Certain Distributions.—Amendments to Reg. §1.1231-1, prescribing how a partner should measure its interest in a partnership's unrealized receivables and inventory items, and that provide guidance regarding the tax consequences of a distribution that causes a reduction in that interest, are proposed (published in the Federal Register on November 3, 2014) (REG-151416-06).

☐ Par. 10. Section 1.1231-1 is amended by adding a new sentence after the third sentence in the introductory text of paragraph (d) to read as follows:

§1.1231-1. Gains and losses from the sale or exchange of certain property used in the trade or business.

* * *

(d) * * * *See also* §§1.732-1(c)(2)(iv) and 1.755-1(c)(2)(iv) for rules governing the application of section 1231 to partnership property in situations in which the basis of the property is increased under section 732 or 734(b). * * *

* * *

Imputed Interest: OID: Safe Haven Rates

Imputed Interest: Original Issue Discount: Safe Haven Interest Rates.—Reproduced below are the texts of proposed amendments of Reg. §§1.1232-1—1.1232-3 and 1.1232-3A, relating to (1) the tax treatment of debt instruments issued after July 1, 1982, that contain original issue discount, (2) the imputation of and the accounting for interest with respect to sales and exchanges of property occurring after December 31, 1984, and (3) safe haven interest rates for loans or advances between commonly controlled taxpayers and safe haven leases between such taxpayers (published in the Federal Register on April 8, 1986).

☐ Par. 24. Section 1.1232-1 is amended as follows:

1. In paragraph (a) by revising the heading to read "Bonds and other evidences of indebtedness issued before July 2, 1982; scope of section"; by removing the first sentence and adding the following new sentence as the first sentence of the paragraph, and by removing the phrase "after May 27, 1969," from the fourth sentence and adding in its place the phrase "after May 27, 1969, and before July 2, 1982,". The added sentence reads as follows: "Section 1232 as in effect before its repeal by section 42(a) of the Tax Reform Act of 1984 applies to any bond, debenture, note, or certificate of indebtedness (referred to in this section and §§1.1232-2 through 1.1232-4 as an obligation) (1) which is a capital asset in the hand of the taxpayer, and (2) which is issued by any corporation, or by any government or political subdivision thereof."

2. In paragraph (c)(3) by removing the phrase "December 31, 1975," from the heading and adding in its place the phrase "December 31, 1975, and before July 2, 1982"; and by adding the phrase "and before July 2, 1982" immediately after the first parenthetical in the first sentence thereof.

§1.1232-1. Bonds and other evidences of indebtedness; scope of section.

☐ Par. 25. The heading of §1.1232-2 is revised to read "Retirement of an obligation issued before July 2, 1982."

§1.1232-2. Retirement.

☐ Par. 26. Section 1.1232-3 is amended as follows: **1.** The heading is amended by adding the phrase "and before July 2, 1982," immediately following the phrase "December 31, 1954." **2.** Paragraph (a) is amended by removing the phrase "after May 27, 1969" from the heading and from each place that it appears and adding in its place the phrase "after May 27, 1969, and before July 2, 1982". **3.** Paragraph (f), the first sentence, is amended by removing the phrase "after December 31, 1954," and inserting the phrase "after December 31, 1954, and before August 17, 1984," in its place.

§1.1232-3. Gain upon sale or exchange of obligations issued at a discount.

☐ Par. 27. Section 1.1232-3A is amended as follows: **1.** The heading and paragraph (a) are amended by removing the phrase "after May 27, 1969," and adding in its place the phrase "after May 27, 1969, and before July 2, 1982." **2.** Paragraph (f) is amended by removing the phrase "after December 31, 1975" and by adding in its place the phrase "after December 31, 1975, and before July 2, 1982."

§1.1232-3A. Inclusion as interest of original issue discount on certain obligations issued after May 27, 1969.

Partnership Interest: Treatment of Grantor of an Option

Partnership Interest: Treatment of Grantor of an Option.—Amendments to Reg. §1.1234-3, relating to the tax treatment of noncompensatory options and convertible instruments issued by a partnership, are proposed (published in the Federal Register on February 5, 2013) (REG-106918-08).

☐ Par 3. Section 1.1234-3 is amended by adding a sentence at the end of paragraph (b)(2) to read as follows:

§ 1.1234-3. Special rules for the treatment of grantors of certain options granted after September 1, 1976.

* * *

(b) * * *

(2) * * * For purposes of the preceding sentence, for options granted on or after February 5, 2013, the term *securities* includes partnership interests.

* * *

Notional Principal Contracts: Contingent Nonperiodic Payments

Notional Principal Contracts: Contingent Nonperiodic Payments.—Reg. § 1.1234A-1, relating to the inclusion into income or deduction of a contingent nonperiodic payment provided for under a notional principal contract, is proposed (published in the Federal Register on February 26, 2004) (REG-166012-02).

☐ Par. 5. Section 1.1234A-1 is added to read as follows:

§ 1.1234A-1. Notional principal contracts, bullet swaps, and forward contracts.—(a) *General rule.*—If a taxpayer has a position in a notional principal contract governed by the rules of § 1.446-3, any gain or loss arising from a termination payment as defined in § 1.446-3(h)(1) is treated as gain or loss from a termination of the notional principal contract.

(b) *Nonapplicability to payments other than termination payments.*—For purposes of section 1234A, none of the following payments terminate or cancel a right or obligation: a periodic payment described in § 1.446-3(e), a nonperiodic payment described in § 1.446-3(f), a contingent nonperiodic payment described in § 1.446-3(g)(6) to which § 1.446-3(g)(6)(ii) applies, or mark-to-market income inclusions and deductions described in § 1.446-3(i)(1). Accordingly, section 1234A does not apply to any of these items, including any final scheduled payment. If a payment made or received pursuant to a notional principal contract is not a termination payment as defined in § 1.446-3(h)(1), the payment constitutes ordinary income or expense. See sections 162 and 212 and the regulations thereunder.

(c) *Bullets swaps and forward contracts.*—(1) Any gain or loss arising from the settlement of obligations under a bullet swap or forward contract (including a payment pursuant to the terms of the obligations) is treated as gain or loss from a termination of the bullet swap or forward contract.

(2) *Definition of bullet swap.*—A bullet swap is a financial instrument that is not an excluded contract as defined in § 1.446-3(c)(1)(ii), that provides for the computation of an amount or amounts due from one party to another by reference to a specified index upon a notional principal amount, and that provides for settlement of all the parties' obligations at or close to maturity of the contract.

(d) *Effective date.*—Paragraphs (b)(1) and (c) of this section are applicable to notional principal contracts, bullet swaps, and forward contracts entered into on or after 30 days after the date a Treasury decision based on these proposed regulations is published in the Federal Register. [Reg. § 1.1234A-1.]

Partners and Partnerships: Sales or Exchanges: Certain Distributions

Partners and Partnerships: Sales or Exchanges: Certain Distributions.—Amendments to Reg. § 1.1245-1, prescribing how a partner should measure its interest in a partnership's unrealized receivables and inventory items, and that provide guidance regarding the tax consequences of a distribution that causes a reduction in that interest, are proposed (published in the Federal Register on November 3, 2014) (REG-151416-06).

☐ Par. 18. For each section listed in the table, remove the language in the "Remove" column and add in its place the language in the "Add" column as set forth below:

§ 1.1245-1. General rule for treatment of gain from dispositions of certain depreciable property.

Section	Remove	Add
§ 1.1245-1, paragraph (a) last sentence	see section 1245(b) and § 1.1245-4.	*see* section 1245(b), and §§ 1.732-1(c)(2)(iii), 1.755-1(c)(2)(iii), and 1.1245-4.

Partners and Partnerships: Sales or Exchanges: Certain Distributions

Partners and Partnerships: Sales or Exchanges: Certain Distributions.—Amendments to Reg. §§ 1.1245-2 and 1.1245-4, prescribing how a partner should measure its interest in a partnership's unrealized receivables and inventory items, and that provide guidance regarding the tax consequences of a distribution that causes a reduction in that interest, are proposed (published in the Federal Register on November 3, 2014) (REG-151416-06).

☐ Par. 11. Section 1.1245-2 is amended by removing paragraph (c)(6)(ii) and redesignating paragraph (c)(6)(iii) as paragraph (c)(6)(ii).

☐ Par. 18. For each section listed in the table, remove the language in the "Remove" column and add in its place the language in the "Add" column as set forth below:

§1.1245-2. Definition of recomputed basis.

Section	Remove	Add
§1.1245-2, paragraph (c)(6)(i)	1245(b)(6)(B)	1245(b)(5)(B)

☐ Par. 12. Section 1.1245-4 is amended by revising paragraphs (f)(2)(ii) and (f)(3) and *Example 2* to read as follows:

§1.1245-4. Exceptions and limitations.

* * *

(f) * * *

(2) * * *

(ii) The portion of such potential section 1245 income which is recognized as ordinary income under paragraphs (b)(3)(i) and (b)(4)(i) of §1.751-1.

(3) * * *

Example 2. Assume the same facts as in *Example 1* of this paragraph (f) except that the machine had been purchased by the partnership. Assume further that upon the distribution, $4,000 of gain is recognized as ordinary income under section 751(b). Under section 1245(b)(3), gain to be taken into account under section 1245(a)(1) by the partnership is limited to $4,000. Immediately after the distribution, the amount of adjustments reflected in the adjusted basis of the property is $2,000 (that is, potential section 1245 income of the partnership, $6,000, minus gain recognized under section 751(b), $4,000). Thus, if the adjusted basis of the machine in the hands of C were $10,000, the recomputed basis of the machine would be $12,000 ($10,000 plus $2,000).

* * *

Controlled Foreign Corporations: Insurance Income: Tax Years After 1986

Controlled Foreign Corporations: Insurance Income: Tax Years After 1986.—Reproduced below is a proposed amendment to Reg. §1.1248-1, relating to the election to expense certain depreciable business assets (published in the Federal Register on April 17, 1991).

☐ Par. 7. Section 1.1248-1 is amended by revising paragraph (a)(2) to read as follows:

§1.1248-1. Treatment of gain from certain sales or exchanges of stock in certain foreign corporations.—(a) *In general.*—* * *

(2) In respect of a United States person who sells or exchanges stock in a foreign corporation, the conditions referred to in paragraph (a)(1) of this section are satisfied only if—

(i) Such person owned, within the meaning of section 958(a), or was considered as owning by applying the rules of ownership of section 958(b), 10 percent or more of the total combined voting power of all classes of stock entitled to vote of the foreign corporation at any time during the 5-year period ending on the date of the sale or exchange and during that time the foreign corporation was a controlled foreign corporation as defined in section 957, or

(ii) Such person owned, within the meaning of section 958(a), any stock in the foreign corporation at any time during the 5-year period ending on the date of the sale or exchange and during that time the foreign corporation was a controlled foreign corporation as defined in section 953(c)(1)(B).

Partners and Partnerships: Sales or Exchanges: Certain Distributions

Partners and Partnerships: Sales or Exchanges: Certain Distributions.—Amendments to Reg. §1.1248-1, prescribing how a partner should measure its interest in a partnership's unrealized receivables and inventory items, and that provide guidance regarding the tax consequences of a distribution that causes a reduction in that interest, are proposed (published in the Federal Register on November 3, 2014) (REG-151416-06).

☐ Par. 13. Section 1.1248-1 is amended by adding a new sentence at the end of paragraph (a)(1) to read as follows:

§1.1248-1. Treatment of gain from certain sales or exchanges of stock in certain foreign corporations.—(a) * * *

(1) * * * *See also* §§1.732-1(c)(2)(v) and 1.755-1(c)(2)(v) for rules governing the application of section 1248 to partnership property in situations in which the basis of the property is increased or decreased under section 732 or 734(b).

* * *

Partners and Partnerships: Sales or Exchanges: Certain Distributions

Partners and Partnerships: Sales or Exchanges: Certain Distributions.—Amendments to Reg. §1.1250-1, prescribing how a partner should measure its interest in a partnership's unrealized receivables and inventory items, and that provide guidance regarding the tax consequences of a distribution that causes a reduction in that interest, are proposed (published in the Federal Register on November 3, 2014) (REG-151416-06).

☐ Par. 14. Section 1.1250-1 is amended by revising the section heading and adding a new sentence at the end of paragraph (f) to read as follows:

§1.1250-1. Gain from disposition of certain depreciable property.

* * *

(f) * * * *See also* §§1.732-1(c)(2)(iii) and 1.755-1(c)(2)(iii) for rules governing the application of section 1250 to partnership property in situations in which the basis of the property is increased under section 732 or 734(b).

* * *

Partners and Partnerships: Sales or Exchanges: Certain Distributions

Partners and Partnerships: Sales or Exchanges: Certain Distributions.—Amendments to Reg. §1.1252-2, prescribing how a partner should measure its interest in a partnership's unrealized receivables and inventory items, and that provide guidance regarding the tax consequences of a distribution that causes a reduction in that interest, are proposed (published in the Federal Register on November 3, 2014) (REG-151416-06).

☐ Par. 15. Section 1.1252-2 is amended by adding a new sentence at the end of paragraph (c)(2)(vii) to read as follows:

§1.1252-2. Special rules.

* * *

(c) * * *

(2) * * *

(vii) * * * *See also* §§1.732-1(c)(2)(iii) and 1.755-1(c)(2)(iii) for rules governing the application of section 1252 to partnership property in situations in which the basis of the property is increased under section 732 or 734(b).

* * *

Partners and Partnerships: Sales or Exchanges: Certain Distributions

Partners and Partnerships: Sales or Exchanges: Certain Distributions.—Amendments to Reg. §1.1254-5, prescribing how a partner should measure its interest in a partnership's unrealized receivables and inventory items, and that provide guidance regarding the tax consequences of a distribution that causes a reduction in that interest, are proposed (published in the Federal Register on November 3, 2014) (REG-151416-06).

☐ Par. 16. Section 1.1254-5 is amended by revising the introductory text of paragraph (b)(1) to read as follows:

§1.1254-5. Special rules for partnerships and their partners.

* * *

(b) *Determination of gain treated as ordinary income under section 1254 upon the disposition of natural resource recapture property by a partnership.*—(1) *General rule.*—Upon a disposition of natural resource recapture property by a partnership, the amount treated as ordinary income under section 1254 is determined at the partner level. *See also* §§1.732-1(c)(2)(iii) and 1.755-1(c)(2)(iii) for rules governing the application of section 1254 to partnership property in certain situations. Each partner must recognize as ordinary income under section 1254 the lesser of—

* * *

Cost-Sharing Payments: Conservation Payments

Cost-Sharing Payments: Conservation Payments: Exclusions: Recapture.—Temporary Reg. §§16A.1255-1 and 16A.1255-2, relating to cost-sharing payments, are also proposed as final regulations (published in the Federal Register on May 21, 1981).

§16A.1255-1. General rule for treatment of gain from disposition of section 126 property.

§16A.1255-2. Special rules.

Section 1256 Contracts: Swap Exclusions

Section 1256 Contracts: Swap Exclusions.—Reg. §§1.1256(b)-1 and 1.1256(g)-1, providing guidance on the category of swaps and similar agreements that are within the scope of Code Sec. 1256(b)(2)(B), are proposed (published in the Federal Register on September 16, 2011) (REG-111283-11).

☐ Par. 7. Section 1.1256(b)-1 is added to read as follows:

§1.1256(b)-1. Section 1256 contract defined.—(a) *General rule.*—A section 1256 contract does not include any contract, or option on such contract, that is a notional principal contract as defined in §1.446-3(c). A contract that is defined as both a notional principal contract in §1.446-3(c) and as a section 1256 contract in section 1256(b)(1) is treated as a notional principal contract and not as a section 1256 contract.

(b) *Regulated futures contract.*—A regulated futures contract is a section 1256 contract only if the contract is a futures contract—

(1) With respect to which the amount required to be deposited and the amount which may be withdrawn depends on a system of marking to market;

(2) That is traded on or subject to the rules of a qualified board or exchange; and

(3) That is not required to be reported as a swap under the Commodity Exchange Act.

(c) *Effective/applicability date.*—The rules of this section apply to contracts entered into on or after the date the final regulations are published in the **Federal Register**. [Reg. §1.1256(b)-1.]

☐ Par. 8. Section 1.1256(g)-1 is added to read as follows:

§1.1256(g)-1. Qualified board or exchange defined.—(a) *General rule.*—A qualified board or exchange means a national securities exchange registered with the Securities Exchange Commission, a domestic board of trade designated as a contract market by the Commodity Futures Trading Commission, or any other exchange, board of trade, or other market for which the Secretary determines in published guidance in the **Federal Register** or in the Internal Revenue Bulletin (see §601.601(d)(2)(ii) of this chapter) that such market has rules adequate to carry out the purposes of section 1256.

(b) *Effective/applicability date.*—The rule of this section applies to taxable years ending on or after the date the final regulations are published in the **Federal Register**. [Reg. §1.1256(g)-1.]

REMICs: Regular Interests: Accrual of OID

REMICs: Regular Interests: Accrual of OID.—Amendments to Reg. §§1.1271-0 and 1.1275-2, relating to the accrual of original issue discount (OID) on certain real estate mortgage investment conduit (REMIC) regular interests and providing guidance to REMICs, REMIC regular interest holders and information reporters regarding the accrual of OID, are proposed (published in the Federal Register on August 25, 2004) (REG-108637-03).

☐ Par. 2. Section 1.1271-0 is amended by adding entries for §1.1275-2(l) and (m) to read as follows:

§1.1271-0. Original issue discount; effective date; table of contents.

* * *

§1.1275-2 Special rules relating to debt instruments.

* * *

(l) [Reserved]

(m) Special rule for certain REMIC regular interests.

(1) Scope.

(2) General rules.

(3) Special rule for calculation of OID in final accrual period.

(4) Definition of record date.

(5) Accrual of qualified stated interest.

(6) Example.

(7) Treatment of REMIC regular interests if the record dates and the payment dates are separated by more than thirty-one days.

(8) Effective date.

* * *

☐ Par. 3. Section 1.1275-2 is amended by adding new paragraphs (l) and (m) to read as follows:

§1.1275-2. Special rules relating to debt instruments.

* * *

(l) [Reserved].

(m) *Special rules for certain REMIC regular interests.*—(1) *Scope.*—If the terms of a REMIC regular interest (as defined in section 860G(a)(1)) provide for a delay between its record dates and the associated payment dates, the initial accrual period and final accrual period for that regular interest are determined under this paragraph (m). Except as provided in paragraph (m)(7) of this section, this paragraph (m) does not apply to a REMIC regular interest if the record dates and the payment dates are separated by more than thirty-one days.

(2) *General rules.*—(i) *Initial accrual period.*—The initial accrual period for a REMIC regular interest subject to this paragraph (m) begins on issuance of the REMIC regular interest.

(ii) *Final accrual period.*—The final accrual period for a REMIC regular interest subject to this paragraph (m) ends on the final record date of the REMIC regular interest.

(3) *Special rule for calculation of OID in final accrual period.*—In applying section 1272(a)(6)(A) to calculate OID in the final accrual period for a REMIC regular interest subject to this paragraph (m), payments after the end of the final accrual period of amounts included in the stated redemption price at maturity are treated as payments during the final accrual period.

(4) *Definition of record date.*—For purposes of this paragraph (m), a *record date* of a REMIC regular interest is a date, provided by the terms of the REMIC regular interest, on which the holder becomes entitled to a payment (of interest or principal) that is to be made on a subsequent payment date.

(5) *Accrual of qualified stated interest.*—See §1.446-2 for the accrual of qualified stated interest.

(6) *Example.*—The following example illustrates the application of this paragraph (m).

Example. REMIC X issues regular interests on January 1, 2009. The terms of the regular interests provide for payments of interest and principal to the persons who hold the regular interests on the last day of the calendar month (the record date). Each such payment is to be made on the fifteenth day of the succeeding calendar month (the payment date). The last payment with respect to the regular interests issued by REMIC X is to be made on January 15, 2014, to persons who hold the regular interests on December 31, 2013. Under this paragraph (m), the initial accrual period begins on the date of issuance, January 1, 2009, and the last accrual period ends on the last record date, December 31, 2013.

(7) *Treatment of REMIC regular interests if the record dates and the payment dates are separated by more than thirty-one days.*—[Reserved]

(8) *Effective date.*—(i) *In general.*—This paragraph (m) applies to REMIC regular interests issued after the date the final regulations are published in the Federal Register.

(ii) *Automatic consent to change method of accounting.*—Taxpayers are hereby granted the Commissioner's consent under section 446(e) to change their method of accounting for REMIC regular interests to which this paragraph (m) applies if—

(A) The change involves changing accrual periods to accrual periods allowed by this paragraph (m);

(B) The change is made for the first taxable year of the taxpayer during which the taxpayer holds a REMIC regular interest to which the rules of this paragraph (m) apply; and

(C) The change in method of accounting is effected on a cut-off basis.

Indebtedness for Federal Tax Purposes: Removal of Documentation Regulations

Indebtedness for Federal Tax Purposes: Removal of Documentation Regulations.—Amendments to Reg. §1.1275-1, removing final regulations setting forth minimum documentation requirements that ordinarily must be satisfied in order for certain related party interests in a corporation to be treated as indebtedness for federal tax purposes (Documentation Regulations), are proposed (published in the Federal Register on September 24, 2018) (REG-130244-17).

Par. 5. Section 1.1275-1 is amended by revising the last sentence of paragraph (d) to read as follows:

§1.1275-1. Definitions.

* * *

(d) * * * See §1.385-3 for rules that treat certain instruments that otherwise would be treated as indebtedness as stock for federal tax purposes.

* * *

Definition of Registered Form: Guidance

Definition of Registered Form: Guidance.—Amendments to Reg. §1.1287-1, providing guidance on the definitions of registration-required obligation and registered form, including guidance on the issuance of pass-through certificates and participation interests in registered form, are proposed (published in the Federal Register on September 19, 2017) (REG-125374-16).

Par. 9. Section 1.1287-1 is amended by:

1. Revising paragraph (a).
2. Redesignating paragraphs (b)(1) and (2) as (b)(2) and (3), respectively.
3. Adding a new paragraph (b)(1).
4. Revising the paragraph heading and first sentence of newly redesignated paragraph (b)(2).
5. Redesignating paragraph (d) as paragraph (d)(1).
6. Revising the paragraph heading and the first sentence of newly redesignated paragraph (d)(1).
7. Adding a new paragraph heading for paragraph (d).
8. Adding paragraph (d)(2).

The revisions and additions read as follows:

§1.1287-1. Denial of capital gains treatment for gains on registration-required obligations not in registered form.—(a) *In general.*—Except as provided in paragraph (c) of this section, any gain on the sale or other disposition of a registration-required obligation held after December 31, 1982, that is not in registered form shall be treated as ordinary income unless the issuance of the obligation was subject to tax under section 4701. The term *registration-required obligation* has the meaning given to that term in section 163(f)(2) and §1.163-5(a)(2)(i). The term *holder* means the person that would be denied a loss deduction under section 165(j)(1) or denied capital gain treatment under section 1287(a).

(b) *Registered form.*—(1) *Obligations issued after March 18, 2012.*—With respect to obligations issued after March 18, 2012, the term *registered form* has the meaning given that term in §1.163-5(b).

(2) *Obligations issued after September 21, 1984 and on or before March 18, 2012.*—With respect to any obligation originally issued after September 21, 1984, and on or before March 18, 2012, the term *registered form* has the meaning given that term in §5f.103-1 of this chapter. * * *

* * *

(d) *Applicability date.*—(1) *In general.*—Except as provided in paragraph (d)(2) of this section, these regulations apply generally to obligations issued after January 20, 1987. * * *

(2) *Obligations issued after March 18, 2012.*—Paragraph (a) of this section applies to obligations issued after March 18, 2012.

Passive Foreign Investment Companies: Passive Income Characterization: Certain Foreign Banks and Securities Dealers: Exceptions To

Passive Foreign Investment Companies: Passive Income Characterization: Certain Foreign Banks and Securities Dealers: Exception To.—Amendments to Reg. §1.1291-0, relating to the application of the exceptions to passive income contained in section 1296(b) for foreign banks, securities dealers and brokers, are proposed (published in the Federal Register on April 28, 1995).

☐ Par. 2. Section 1.1291-0T is redesignated as §1.1291-0.

☐ Par. 3. Newly designated §1.1291-0 is amended as follows:

1. The section heading for newly designated §1.1291-0 is revised.
2. The introductory language for newly designated §1.1291-0 is revised.
3. Entries for §§1.1296-4 and 1.1296-6 are added in numerical order.

The revisions and additions read as follows:

§1.1291-0. Passive foreign investment companies—table of contents..—This section lists headings under sections 1291, 1294, 1296 and 1297 of the Internal Revenue Code.

* * *

* * *

Passive Foreign Investment Companies: Qualified Electing Funds: Shareholders

Passive Foreign Investment Companies: Qualified Electing Funds: Shareholders.—Reproduced below is the text of proposed Reg. §1.1291-1, relating to the taxation of shareholders of certain passive foreign investment companies (PFICs) upon payment of distributions by such companies or upon the disposition of stock of such companies (published in the Federal Register on April 1, 1992) (INTL-941-86; INTL-656-87; INTL-704-87). Proposed Reg. §1.1291-1(b)(2)(ii), (b)(2)(v), (b)(7), (b)(8) and (i) withdrawn by REG-113350-13 on December 31, 2013.

☐ Par. 5. Section 1.1291-1 is added to read as follows:

§1.1291-1. Taxation of U.S. persons that are shareholders of section 1291 funds.—(a) *In general.*—A U.S. person that is a shareholder (within the meaning of paragraph (b)(7) of this section) of a section 1291 fund (as defined in paragraph (b)(2)(v) of this section) is subject to the special rules under section 1291 and these regulations with respect to gain recognized on direct and indirect dispositions of stock of the section 1291 fund and upon certain direct and indirect distributions by the section 1291 fund. This section provides definitions and rules applicable to all PFICs and their shareholders. For rules governing the taxation of distributions and dispositions, *see* §§1.1291-2 and 1.1291-3, respectively. For rules governing the determination of the deferred tax amount, *see* §1.1291-4. For rules governing the determination of the foreign tax credit that a shareholder of a section 1291 fund may claim on distributions and certain dispositions, *see* §1.1291-5. For rules governing the recognition of gain on a direct or indirect disposition of stock of a section 1291 fund notwithstanding an otherwise applicable nonrecognition provision, *see* §1.1291-6. For guidance for regulated investment companies making a mark-to-market election, *see* §1.1291-8. For the time and manner of making the deemed sale and dividend elections under section 1291(d)(2), *see* §§1.1291-9 and 1.1291-10, respectively.

(b) *Definitions.*—(1) *PFIC.*—(i) *In general.*—A passive foreign investment company (PFIC) is a foreign corporation that satisfies either the income test of section 1296(a)(1) or the asset test of section 1296(a)(2). A corporation will not be treated as a PFIC with respect to a shareholder for those days included in the shareholder's holding period before the shareholder became a United States person within the meaning of section 7701(a)(30).

(ii) *PFIC characterization continued.*—A corporation will be treated as a PFIC with respect to a shareholder even if the corporation satisfies neither the income test nor the asset test of section 1296(a), if the corporation (or its predecessor in a reorganization described in section 368(a)(1)(F)) was a section 1291 fund with respect to the shareholder at any time during the shareholder's holding period of the corporation's stock.

(2) *Types of PFICs.*—(i) *QEF.*—A PFIC is a qualified electing fund (QEF) with respect to a shareholder that has elected under section 1295 to be taxed currently on its share of the PFIC's earnings and profits pursuant to section 1293.

(ii) [Withdrawn by REG-113350-13 on December 31, 2013.]

(iii) *Unpedigreed QEF.*—A PFIC is an unpedigreed QEF for a taxable year if—

(A) An election under section 1295 is in effect for that year;

(B) The PFIC has been a QEF with respect to the shareholder for at least one, but not all, of the taxable years that are included wholly or partly in the shareholder's holding period of the PFIC stock and during which the corporation was a PFIC; and

(C) The shareholder has not made an election under section 1291(d)(2) and §1.1291-9 or 1.1291-10 with respect to the PFIC to purge the prior PFIC years from the shareholder's holding period.

For the effect on a shareholder's holding period of an election under section 1291(d)(2), *see* §§1.1291-9(f) and 1.1291-10(f).

(iv) *Nonqualified fund.*—A PFIC is a nonqualified fund with respect to a shareholder if the shareholder has not elected under section 1295 to treat the PFIC as a QEF.

(v) [Withdrawn by REG-113350-13 on December 31, 2013.]

(3) *PrePFIC year and day.*—A prePFIC year is a taxable year (or portion thereof) of the shareholder, included in its holding period of the stock of a corporation, during which the corporation was not a PFIC within the meaning of paragraph (b)(1) of this section. A prePFIC day is a day in a prePFIC year of the shareholder. Thus, the days in a taxable year of a shareholder beginning after 1986 that are included in a taxable year of the corporation that began before 1987 are prePFIC days.

(4) *Prior PFIC year and day.*—A prior PFIC year is a taxable year (or portion thereof) of a shareholder, other than the current shareholder year, included in its holding period of stock of a corporation during which the corporation was a section 1291 fund. A prior PFIC day is a day in a prior PFIC year of a shareholder.

(5) *Current shareholder year.*—The current shareholder year is the taxable year of the shareholder in which occurs a distribution by, or disposition of stock of, a section 1291 fund.

(6) *Stock.*—The term stock includes any equity interest in a corporation, without regard to whether there is a certificate or other representation of the equity interest in the corporation. For a rule that treats an option holder as a shareholder of a section 1291 fund, *see* §1.1291-1(d).

(7) [Withdrawn by REG-113350-13 on December 31, 2013.]

(8) [Withdrawn by REG-113350-13 on December 31, 2013.]

(c) *Coordination with QEF rules.*—(1) *Pedigreed QEFs.*—Section 1291 and these regulations do not apply to direct and indirect distributions by, and direct and indirect dispositions of stock of, a PFIC that, with respect to the shareholder, is a pedigreed QEF as defined in paragraph (b)(2)(ii) of this section.

(2) *Unpedigreed QEFs.*—Section 1291 and these regulations apply to direct and indirect distributions by, and direct and indirect dispositions of stock of, a PFIC that, with respect to the shareholder, is an unpedigreed QEF, as defined in paragraph (b)(2)(iii) of this section. For the treatment under section 1291 and these regulations of inclusions in income under section 1293(a) and distributions of amounts not includible in income by reason of section 1293(c), *see* §1.1291-2(b)(2).

(d) *Option holder as shareholder.*—If a U.S. person has an option to acquire stock of a PFIC (other than stock with respect to which the PFIC is a pedigreed QEF), such option is considered to be stock of a section 1291 fund for purposes of applying section 1291 and these regulations to a disposition of the option. For purposes of this paragraph (d), the exercise of an option is not a disposition to which section 1291 applies. For purposes of this paragraph (d), an option to acquire an option, and each one of a series of such options, are considered an option to acquire stock. For the holding period of stock acquired upon the exercise of an option, *see* §1.1291-1(h)(3).

(e) *Exempt organization as shareholder.*—If the shareholder of a section 1291 fund is an organization exempt from tax under this chapter, section 1291 and these regulations apply to such shareholder only if a dividend from the section 1291 fund would be taxable to the organization under subchapter F.

(f) *Excess distribution from sources within Puerto Rico.*—A deferred tax amount, as defined in §1.1291-4, will be determined under section 1291 and these regulations on amounts derived from sources within Puerto Rico (within the meaning of section 933(1)) by an individual shareholder who is a bona fide resident of Puerto Rico, but only to the extent such amounts are allocated under §1.1291-2(e)(2) to a taxable year in the shareholder's holding period during which the shareholder was not entitled to the benefits of section 933.

(g) *Regulated investment companies and real estate investment trusts.*—A regulated investment company, as defined in section 851, and a real estate investment trust, as defined in section 856, that are shareholders of a section 1291 fund are taxable under section 1291 and these regulations on direct or indirect distributions from a section 1291 fund and on direct or indirect dispositions of the stock of a section 1291 fund, and are therefore liable for the deferred tax amount, as defined in section 1291(c) and §1.1291-4. For a mark-to-market election that may be made by a regulated investment company that is a shareholder of a section 1291 fund, *see* §1.1291-8.

(h) *Holding period.*—(1) *In general.*—Except as otherwise provided in this paragraph (h), §1.1291-6(b)(5), 1.1291-9(f), or 1.1291-10(f), a shareholder's holding period of stock of a PFIC is determined under the general rules of the Code and regulations concerning the holding period of stock. The following example illustrates the rule of this paragraph (h)(1).

Example. T purchased the stock of FC, a foreign corporation, on December 31, 1985. FC has qualified as a PFIC since its taxable year beginning January 1, 1987. For purposes of sections 1291 through 1297 and the regulations under those sections, as well as other provisions of the Code and regulations, T's holding period of the FC stock began on January 1, 1986.

(2) *Stock acquired from U.S. decedent or domestic estate.*—For purposes of section 1291 and these regulations, a shareholder's holding period of a share of stock of a PFIC includes the period the share was held by another U.S. person if the shareholder acquired the share by reason of the death of that other U.S. person (the decedent), the PFIC was a section 1291 fund with respect to the decedent, and the decedent did not recognize

gain pursuant to § 1.1291-6(c)(2)(iii) (or would not have recognized gain had there been any) on the transfer to the shareholder.

(3) *Stock acquired upon exercise of option.*—The holding period of a share of stock of a PFIC acquired upon the exercise of an option includes the period the option was held. The following example illustrates the rule of this paragraph (h)(3).

Example. X is a domestic corporation that owns all of the stock of Y, a PFIC. On January 1, 1993, X issues a debt instrument to G, a U.S. person. Under the terms of the instrument, G may convert the debt instrument into 20 shares of the stock of Y on any date prior to the maturity date of December 31, 2002. On August 14, 1997, G exercises the conversion right and receives 20 shares of Y stock. Pursuant to § 1.1291-1(h)(3), G's holding period of the Y stock begins at the time of the acquisition of the debt instrument, not at the time of acquisition of the Y stock.

(4) *Stock owned directly and indirectly.*—(i) *In general.*—Except as provided in paragraph (h)(2), (3), (4)(ii), (5), or (6) of this section, 1.1291-6(b)(5), 1.1291-9(f), or 1.1291-10(f), a shareholder's holding period of stock of a PFIC owned indirectly begins on the first day that a shareholder is considered to own stock of the PFIC (or of another PFIC that was a predecessor of that PFIC) under § 1.1291-1(b)(8). If a shareholder has owned a share of stock of a PFIC both directly and indirectly, the shareholder's holding period of that share begins on the earlier of—

(A) The first day that the shareholder owned the stock of the PFIC directly; or

(B) The first day that the shareholder was an indirect shareholder with respect to the share of stock of the PFIC (or of another PFIC that was a predecessor of that PFIC).

(ii) *Examples.*—The following examples illustrate the operation of the rule of paragraph (h)(4)(i) of this section.

Example 1. A's holding period of stock of X began on August 14, 1990. X is a corporation that always has been an S corporation. At the time A acquired the X stock, X held stock of FC, a PFIC. For purposes of sections 1291 through 1297, A's holding period of the FC stock began on August 14, 1990, even though X's holding period of that stock began on an earlier day.

Example 2. B, a U.S. person, owns all the stock of FP, a foreign corporation that is not a PFIC; under section 1223, B's holding period of the FP stock began on August 1, 1987. FP owns 50 percent of the stock of FS, a foreign corporation that is not a PFIC; FP's holding period of the FS stock began on December 13, 1987. FS owns 10 percent of FC, a PFIC; under section 1223, FS's holding period of the FC stock began on November 20, 1986. For purposes of section 1291, B's holding period of the FC stock began on December 13, 1987, the first day that ownership of the FC stock is attributed to B under § 1.1291-1(b)(8).

(iii) *Section 1291 fund stock held by former C corporation.*—For purposes of § 1.1291-2(e)(2)(i), if an S corporation's holding period of stock of a section 1291 fund includes any period during which the S corporation was a C corporation, the S corporation shareholder's holding period is the S corporation's holding period of such stock.

(5) *New holding period.*—If a shareholder recognizes all of the gain realized on a direct or indirect disposition of stock of a section 1291 fund, within the meaning of § 1.1291-3(c), (d), or (e), but continues to be a shareholder with respect to such stock immediately after such disposition, the shareholder's holding period for such stock will be treated as beginning on the day after the disposition. For an illustration of this rule as applied to a disposition pursuant to § 1.1291-3(d) (regarding pledged stock), *see* § 1.1291-3(d)(7), *Example 1.*

(6) *Stock transferred to a member of a consolidated return group.*—For the holding period of stock of a section 1291 fund transferred from one member of a consolidated return group to another member of the group for purposes of § 1.1291-2(e)(2)(i), *see* § 1.1291-3(f).

(7) *PFIC character of holding period.*—(i) *In general.*—If a shareholder's holding period of stock of a PFIC includes a period described in section 1223(1), the character of the days in such latter period as prePFIC or prior PFIC days is determined by reference to the character of those days in the shareholder's holding period immediately prior to the exchange. If a shareholder's holding period of stock of a PFIC includes a period described in section 1223(2), the character of the days in such latter period as prePFIC or prior PFIC days is determined by reference to the character, immediately prior to the transfer, of those days in the holding period of the person from whom the stock was acquired.

(ii) *Anti-avoidance rule.*—If a shareholder's holding period of stock of a PFIC includes a period described in section 1223(1), the character of the days in such latter period will be deemed to be prior PFIC days if a purpose for the exchange described in section 1223(1) was avoidance of the interest charge rules under section 1291.

(i) [Withdrawn by REG-113350-13 on December 31, 2013.]

(j) *Effective date.*—(1) *In general.*—Except as otherwise provided in this paragraph (j), §§ 1.1291-1 through 1.1291-9 and the new parts of § 1.1291-10 are effective on April 11, 1992. However, sections 1291 through 1297, inclusive, are effective for taxable years of foreign corporations beginning after December 31, 1986. Accordingly, shareholders of PFICs are subject to sections 1291 through 1297 with respect to transactions occurring within those taxable years. Shareholders of section 1291 funds, in determining their liability under sections 1291 through 1297 during those years, must apply reasonable interpretations of the statute and legislative history and employ reasonable methods to preserve the interest charge.

(2) *Section 1.1291-3(d)(6).*—For purposes of applying section 1297(b)(6), concerning a disposition resulting from the use of PFIC stock as security for a loan, the transition rule provided in § 1.1291-3(d)(6) is effective for taxable years of foreign corporations beginning after 1986.

(3) *Section 1.1291-8.*—Section 1.1291-8 is effective for taxable years of RICs ending after [*INSERT DATE OF PUBLICATION OF THIS DOCUMENT AS A FINAL REGULATION*]. [Reg. § 1.1291-1.]

Passive Foreign Investment Companies: Qualified Electing Funds: Shareholders

Passive Foreign Investment Companies: Qualified Electing Funds: Shareholders.—Reproduced below are the texts of proposed Reg. §§1.1291-2—1.1291-7, relating to the taxation of shareholders of certain passive foreign investment companies (PFICs) upon payment of distributions by such companies or upon the disposition of stock of such companies (published in the Federal Register on April 1, 1992) (INTL-941-86; INTL-656-87; INTL-704-87). Reg. §§1.1291-0, 1.1291-9 and 1.1291-10 were adopted by T.D. 8701 on December 26, 1996. Proposed Reg. §1.1291-8 was withdrawn on February 2, 1999.

☐ Par. 5. Sections 1.1291-2 through 1.1291-8 [1.1291-7]are added to read as follows:

§1.1291-2. Taxation of distributions by section 1291 funds.—(a) *In general.*—Notwithstanding section 301 and the regulations under that section, a shareholder is subject to the rules of section 1291, this section, and §1.1291-4 with respect to a distribution (including an indirect distribution as defined in paragraph (f) of this section) by a section 1291 fund, if any portion of such distribution is an excess distribution. An excess distribution is defined in paragraph (c)(1) of this section. Under paragraph (e)(2)(i) of this section, the excess distribution is allocated ratably over the shareholder's holding period of the stock of the section 1291 fund. The portions of the excess distribution allocated to the current shareholder year and to prePFIC years are included in the shareholder's gross income as ordinary income in the current shareholder year under paragraph (e)(2)(ii) of this section. The portions of the excess distribution allocated to prior PFIC years are not included in the shareholder's gross income pursuant to paragraph (e)(2)(iii) of this section. Instead, the shareholder incurs tax plus interest (the deferred tax amount) on those portions of the excess distribution, as provided in §1.1291-4.

(b) *Distribution.*—(1) *In general.*—For purposes of section 1291 and these regulations, unless otherwise provided in this paragraph (b), a distribution is any actual or constructive transfer of money or property by a section 1291 fund with respect to its stock. For example, a distribution includes a transfer of stock taxable pursuant to section 305(b) and (c), a transfer in redemption of stock taxable under section 301 pursuant to section 302(d), and an amount treated as a dividend under section 78. A distribution, however, does not include a transfer that qualifies under section 305(a) or 355(a). Transfers with respect to stock that are treated as dispositions of the stock under §1.1291-3 are not treated as distributions under this section. For transfers with respect to stock (including transfers that qualify under section 355(a)) that are treated as dispositions, *see* §1.1291-3.

(2) *Coordination with current inclusion rules.*—(i) *Deemed dividend or income inclusions; distributions of previously taxed amounts.*—Amounts included in gross income under section 551(a), 951(a), or 1293(a), and transfers of amounts not included in gross income by reason of section 551(d), 959, or 1293(c), are not treated as distributions for purposes of this section. The following example illustrates the rule of this paragraph (b)(2)(i).

Example. USP, a domestic corporation, purchased in 1989 10 percent of the stock of FC, a section 1291 fund that also is a CFC. Both USP and FC use the calendar year as their taxable year. In 1989, USP, pursuant to section 951(a)(1), included in income $100 of subpart F income of FC, none of which was distributed in 1989. The $100 of subpart F income is not treated as a distribution taxable under section 1291. In 1990, FC did not have any subpart F income. In that year, FC distributed $200 to USP. Of the $200 distribution, $100 had been previously taxed to USP. Because $100 of the $200 distribution is not included in gross income by reason of section 959, pursuant to §1.1291-2(b)(2) that amount is not treated as a distribution for purposes of §1.1291-2(c)(2)(i). Therefore, the total distribution, for purposes of calculating the excess distribution for 1990, is $100.

(ii) *Other rules.*—For treatment of amounts that would be taxable in the same taxable year under section 951(a) or 1293(a) and section 1291, *see* §§1.1291-2(f)(3) and 1.1291-3(e)(4)(ii).

(3) *Section 304 transactions.*—(i) *In general.*—If, in a transaction described in section 304(a), the issuing corporation is a section 1291 fund, any amount treated as paid out of the earnings and profits of such section 1291 fund by virtue of section 304(b)(2) is treated as an excess distribution by such fund for purposes of section 1291 and this section. In addition, the transfer of the stock of such fund will be treated as a disposition to which §§1.1291-3 and 1.1291-6 apply. If, in a transaction described in section 304(a), the acquiring corporation is a section 1291 fund, any amount paid by such corporation to the transferor is treated as a distribution by such fund (notwithstanding the provisions of section 304(b)(2)), and the transferor is treated for purposes of section 1291 and this section as the owner of any stock of the fund that it owns directly or constructively under section 304(c). The following example illustrates the rule of this paragraph (b)(3)(i).

Example. USP, a domestic corporation, owns all the stock of FS1 and FS2. FS1 and FS2 each have accumulated earnings and profits of $100 that were not previously taxed under any other section of the Code. FS1, but not FS2, is a PFIC. USP has not elected under section 1295 to treat FS1 as a QEF. However, USP plans to make a section 1295 election to treat FS1 as a QEF, as well as the deemed dividend election under section 1291(d)(2)(B) to purge USP's holding period of the FS1 stock of its prior PFIC years. Before it makes those elections, USP plans to sell the stock of FS1 to FS2 for its fair market value of $200. The transfer of the FS1 stock to FS2 is a transaction to which section 304 applies. Section 304(b)(2) provides that $100 of the $200 payment to USP is treated as paid directly by FS1 out of its earnings and profits. Pursuant to §1.1291-2(b)(3)(i), the $100 distribution to USP is taxable as an excess distribution. The transfer will not be a taxable disposition under §1.1291-3 because USP's interest in FS1 is not reduced as a result of the transfer. *See* section 304(a)(1) and § 1.1291-6(c)(1)(i).

(ii) *Limitation.*—[Reserved]

(c) *Excess distribution and nonexcess distribution.*—(1) *Excess distribution.*—An excess distribution is that portion of any direct or indirect distribution with respect to a share of stock of a section 1291 fund during the current shareholder year that is the ratable portion (as defined in paragraph (c)(4) of this section) of the total excess distribution (as defined in paragraph (c)(3) of this section), if any. Except as provided in § 1.1291-5, an excess distribution and the taxation thereof are determined without regard to the amount or character of the earnings and profits of the section 1291 fund. Except as provided in paragraph (d)(2) of this section (concerning shares of stock having the same holding period), the excess distribution is calculated separately for each share of stock held.

(2) *Nonexcess distribution.*—(i) *In general.*—A nonexcess distribution with respect to a share of section 1291 stock is the portion of the total amount of all distributions during the current shareholder year with respect to the share that does not exceed 125 percent of the average amount of the distributions with respect to the share during the three taxable years of the shareholder's holding period (or during the lesser number of taxable years in the shareholder's holding period) that immediately precede the current shareholder year. Distributions in any of the preceding three (or fewer) taxable years of the shareholder included in the shareholder's holding period that began before 1987 are included in determining the nonexcess distribution.

(ii) *Amount not included in income.*—The portion of an excess distribution in a prior taxable year that was not included in income pursuant to § 1.1291-2 (e)(2)(iii) is not treated as a distribution in that prior year for purposes of paragraph (c)(2)(i) or (iii) of this section. For an illustration of the rule of this paragraph (c)(2)(ii), *see* paragraph (e)(4), *Example 1*, of this section.

(iii) *Distributions received by predecessors.*—If a shareholder's holding period of the stock of a section 1291 fund includes the period the stock was held by another person, distributions made during the holding period of such other person with respect to the stock will be treated as if they had been received by the shareholder for purposes of paragraph (c)(2)(i) of this section.

(3) *Total excess distribution.*—(i) *In general.*—The total excess distribution with respect to a share of stock of a section 1291 fund is the excess, if any, of—

(A) The total amount of all distributions during the current shareholder year with respect to the share, over

(B) The nonexcess distribution with respect to that stock.

(ii) *Exception.*—Notwithstanding paragraph (c)(3)(i) of this section, the total excess distribution is zero for the taxable year of the shareholder in which the shareholder's holding period of the stock begins. The following example illustrates the rule of this paragraph (c)(3)(ii).

Example. On January 1, 1989, X, a U.S. person, gave his son Y, also a U.S. person, one share of stock of FC, a section 1291 fund, that X had purchased in 1986. Y purchased another share of FC stock on January 3, 1989. Y did not make the section 1295 election with respect to FC. In 1989, FC distributed $100 for each outstanding share of its stock. Pursuant to § 1.1291-2(c)(3)(ii), no portion of the distribution in respect of the share Y purchased in 1989 is treated as an excess distribution. However, the distribution paid to Y with respect to the stock given to him by his father may be wholly or partly an excess distribution. Although Y first held that share of FC stock in 1989, Y's holding period includes the period X held that share of stock, as provided in section 1223(2), and therefore does not begin in 1989.

(4) *Ratable portion.*—The total excess distribution is allocated ratably to each distribution received with respect to a share of stock during the current shareholder year. A distribution's ratable portion of the total excess distribution is the product of the total excess distribution and the ratio of the distribution to the total distribution with respect to the share of stock during the current shareholder year. Each ratable portion of the total excess distribution is an excess distribution.

(d) *Special rules.*—The following rules apply for purposes of calculating the nonexcess distribution and the total excess distribution—

(1) *Stock acquired during the year.*—In general, a distribution in a prior taxable year with respect to a share of stock may only be taken into account in determining a nonexcess distribution under paragraph (c)(2)(i) of this section if the shareholder was a shareholder at the time of such distribution, or the distribution was received by a person whose holding period of the stock is included in the shareholder's holding period. However, with respect to a prior taxable year during which a person became a shareholder, the shareholder may instead take into account the total amount (or portion thereof) that the shareholder determines was actually paid by the section 1291 fund with respect to that share of stock during that taxable year. No other annualization rule will apply under section 1291(b)(3)(C). The following example illustrates the rule of this paragraph (d)(1).

Example. R, a U.S. person, became an indirect shareholder of one share of FC stock on August 1, 1991. R did not elect under section 1295 to treat FC, a PFIC, as a QEF. R and FC both use the calendar year as their taxable years. R determines, based on dividend information provided in FC's 1991 annual report, that FC distributed $100 with respect to each outstanding share of its stock at the end of each quarter during that year. For purposes of calculating nonexcess distributions in 1992, 1993, and 1994, R may treat $400 as the amount received in 1991. If R had been unable to determine the amount distributed in 1991 before August 1, the 1991 distribution would have been limited to the $200 actually distributed after August 1 with respect to the one share of FC stock attributed to R.

(2) *Calculations for shares with same holding period.*—The calculation of the nonexcess distribution and the total excess distribution may be made on an aggregate basis for shares of stock having the same holding period (block of stock). The following example illustrates the rule of this paragraph (d)(2).

Example. (i) *Facts.* X, a U.S. person that is a calendar year taxpayer, owns 12 shares of stock of FC, a PFIC. X has not elected under section 1295 to treat FC as a QEF. X acquired two of the 12 shares on December 31, 1986 (Block #1), four shares on December 31, 1987 (Block #2), and six shares on December 31, 1988 (Block #3). On June 30 of 1987 and 1988, FC distributed $10 in respect of each outstanding share of its stock; no portion of either distribution was an excess distribution. On June 30, 1989, FC distributed $30 in respect of each outstanding share of its stock. For purposes of determining the taxation of the 1989 distribution, the excess distribution may be calculated for each of the three blocks of stock held by X instead of on a share-by-share basis.

(ii) *Block #1 excess distribution.* The nonexcess distribution for Block #1 is $25 (125% times $20 [($20 + $20)/2]). The total excess distribution for Block #1 is $35 ($60 – $25).

(iii) *Block #2 excess distribution.* The nonexcess distribution for Block #2 is $50 (125% × $40, the distribution made in the only preceding taxable year in the holding period of the Block #2 shares). The total excess distribution for Block #2 is $70 ($120 – $50).

(iv) *Block #3.* There is no excess distribution with respect to the Block #3 stock because the first taxable year of the holding period of that block of stock is 1989, the taxable year of the distribution.

(3) *Effect of nontaxable distribution or exchange.*—(i) *Tax-free distributions of stock.*—A distribution with respect to a share of stock, made during the shareholder's holding period for the share but before a distribution of stock under section 305(a) with respect to that share, will be treated ratably as a distribution with respect to the shares in the block of stock composed of the original share and the shares distributed with respect to that share pursuant to the stock distribution.

(ii) *Nontaxable exchange of stock.*—Distributions with respect to stock include distributions with respect to stock exchanged therefor in a nonrecognition transfer in which gain was not recognized pursuant to § 1.1291-6(c).

(iii) *Example.*—The following example illustrates the rule of paragraph (d)(3) of this section.

Example. On December 31, 1985, X, a U.S. person, purchased one share of stock of FC, a corporation. FC has been a section 1291 fund with respect to X since FC's taxable year that began January 1, 1987. In both 1986 and 1987, FC distributed $6 with respect to each share of its stock. FC transferred all its assets and liabilities to F, a PFIC, in a transaction that qualified as a reorganization defined in section 368(a)(1)(C) and that was effective on January 1, 1988. X exchanged his share of FC stock for one share of stock of F in an exchange to which section 354 applied and no gain was recognized pursuant to § 1.1291-6(c)(1). On December 31, 1988, F distributed $3 with respect to each share of its stock. No part of the 1986, 1987, and 1988 distributions was an excess distribution. On December 31, 1989, F distributed $10 with respect to each share of its stock. In calculating the total excess distribution for 1989, the $6 distributions paid in 1986 and 1987 by FC with respect to the FC stock held by X, as well as the $3 distribution paid by F in 1988 on the F stock received in exchange for the FC stock, are taken into account. Accordingly, the total excess distribution for 1989 is $3.75 ($10 – [125% × $5 (the average distribution for the three preceding taxable years)]).

(4) *Distributions in a foreign currency.*—(i) *In general.*—Except as provided in paragraph (d)(4)(ii) of this section, the nonexcess distribution and the total excess distribution are determined in U.S. dollars. Each distribution that must be taken into account for purposes of the calculation is translated into the U.S. dollar at the spot rate (within the meaning of § 1.988-1T (d)) on the date on which such distribution was made. The following example illustrates the rule of this paragraph (d)(4)(i).

Example. USP, a domestic corporation, purchased on December 31, 1986, five percent of the stock of FC, a country X corporation that is a section 1291 fund with respect to USP. The functional currency of FC is the "LC", the currency of country X. FC made no distributions during 1987. FC distributed $100 to USP on August 1, 1988; LC20 on November 20, 1989; and 100 units of country Y currency on December 13, 1990. In order to calculate the 1989 and 1990 excess distributions, USP must convert the 1989 distribution of LC20 into U.S. dollars at the spot rate on November 20, 1989, and the 1990 distribution of 100 units of country Y currency into U.S. dollars at the spot rate on December 13, 1990.

(ii) *Exception.*—If all distributions that must be taken into account for purposes of calculating the nonexcess distribution and the total excess distribution for the current shareholder year were made in a single currency (other than the U.S. dollar), the nonexcess distribution and total excess distribution will be determined in the currency in which the distributions were made. Each ratable portion of a total excess distribution determined in a foreign currency is translated into U.S. dollars at the spot rate on the date of the distribution to which the ratable portion is allocated.

(5) *Adjustments for section 642(c) charitable deduction.*—(i) *In general.*—A trust that is permitted to deduct the amount of its fixed annual charitable obligation from gross income pursuant to section 642(c)(1) (the section 642(c) deduction) generally may adjust an excess distribution from a section 1291 fund as provided in this paragraph (d)(5) by the amount of the section 642(c) deduction. Except as otherwise provided in this paragraph (d)(5), the trust may adjust an excess distribution if, in satisfaction of its fixed annual obligation, it distributes—

(A) amounts received from the section 1291 fund;

(B) the stock of a section 1291 fund; or

(C) the proceeds from the sale thereof, to an organization described in section 170(c), as required under the terms of the governing instrument of the trust.

The adjustment provided in this paragraph (d)(5) is limited to the amount of the trust's fixed annual charitable obligation.

(ii) *Exception.*—This paragraph (d)(5) does not apply to a grantor of a trust if the grantor deducted from income, as provided in section 170(f)(2)(B), the value of an interest in any share of stock of the section 1291 fund upon its transfer to the trust.

(iii) *Adjustments.*—(A) *Corpus consisting only of section 1291 fund stock.*—Where the assets of the trust consist only of stock of one or more section 1291 funds, the section 642(c) deduction first reduces the nonexcess distributions, if any, determined under paragraph (c)(2)(i) of this section. The amount of the section 642(c) deduction remaining after reduction of the nonexcess distributions reduces the portions of the excess distributions allocated to the prePFIC and current shareholder years. Finally, the amount of the section 642(c) deduction remaining after the prior two reductions reduces pro rata the portions of the excess distributions allocated to the prior PFIC years. The deferred tax amount, as defined in § 1.1291-4, is determined with respect to the adjusted allocations of the excess distributions.

(B) *Corpus consisting of section 1291 fund stock and other propertyz.*—*(1) Income from both section 1291 fund stock and other property.*—A distribution of income in satisfaction of a fixed annual charitable obligation is treated as distributed out of income, if any, derived from the trust property other than the stock of a section 1291 fund to the extent thereof, before being treated as distributed out of amounts received from a section 1291 fund. An adjustment will be permitted in the manner provided in paragraph (d)(5)(iii)(A) of this section only after the deduction permitted under section 642(c) has reduced income from other property to zero.

(2) Use of corpus to satisfy obligation.—The trust will not be entitled to the adjustment permitted under this paragraph (d)(5) if the trust uses stock of a section 1291 fund instead of its other property to satisfy its fixed annual charitable obligation.

(6) *PFIC for part of current shareholder year.*—This paragraph (d)(6) applies if the section 1291 fund first qualified as a PFIC for its taxable year beginning after the first day of the current shareholder year and therefore is a section 1291 fund for only a portion of the current shareholder year. Distributions during the portion of the current shareholder year before the corporation qualified as a PFIC are taken into account for purposes of calculating the nonexcess distribution and the total excess distribution. However, those distributions are taxable under the general rules applicable to distributions by a corporation to its shareholder with respect to its stock, notwithstanding that a ratable portion thereof may be an excess distribution within the meaning of paragraph (c)(1) of this section. The following example illustrates the rule of this paragraph (d)(6).

Example. X, a U.S. person, purchased one share of stock of FC, a corporation, on December 31, 1986. X uses the calendar year as its taxable year; FC's taxable year ends November 30. FC first qualified as a PFIC for its taxable year that began December 1, 1990. X did not elect under section 1295 to treat FC as a QEF. X received a distribution of $100 in 1987, but did not receive another distribution from FC until August 1, 1990, when FC distributed $100 per share. On December 13, 1990, FC made another $100 per share distribution. The August distribution is taken into account for purposes of calculating the nonexcess distribution and total excess distribution for 1990 and the ratable portion of the December 13 distribution that is an excess distribution. However, pursuant to § 1.1291-2(d)(6), the August distribution is not subject to section 1291 notwithstanding that a ratable portion of that distribution is an excess distribution within the meaning of § 1.1291-2(c)(1). The August distribution is included in X's 1990 gross income to the extent provided in section 301(c).

(e) *Taxation of a distribution and effect on earnings and profits.*—(1) *Nonexcess distribution.*—A nonexcess distribution, as defined in paragraph (c)(2)(i) of this section, is taxable to a shareholder according to the general rules of taxation applicable to distributions made by a corporation to a shareholder with respect to its stock. *See, e.g.,* section 301 and the regulations under that section.

(2) *Excess distribution.*—(i) *In general.*—To determine the taxation of an excess distribution, the excess distribution is first allocated pro rata to each day in the shareholder's holding period (as determined under § 1.1291-1(h)) of the share of stock with respect to which the distribution was made. The holding period of a share of stock of a section 1291 fund is treated as ending on (and including) the date of each excess distribution solely for purposes of allocating the excess distribution.

(ii) *Allocations included in income.*—The portions of an excess distribution allocated to prePFIC years and the current shareholder year are included in the shareholder's gross income for the current shareholder year as ordinary income.

(iii) *Allocations not included in income.*—The portions of an excess distribution allocated to prior PFIC years are not included in the shareholder's gross income for purposes of this title. These amounts are subject to the deferred tax amount. The deferred tax amount is an additional liability of the shareholder for tax and interest for the current shareholder year. For the calculation of the deferred tax amount and the foreign tax credit that may be taken to reduce the deferred tax amount, *see* §§ 1.1291-4 and 1.1291-5.

(3) *Allocation of earnings and profits.*—For purposes of determining the taxation of a nonexcess distribution and calculating the foreign tax credit under § 1.1291-5, the earnings and profits of a section 1291 fund are allocated proportionately between the nonexcess distribution (as defined in paragraph (c)(2)(i) of this section) and the total excess distribution (as defined in paragraph (c)(3) of this section) and reduced (but not below zero) by the amounts thereof.

(4) *Examples.*—The following examples illustrate the operation of paragraphs (c), (d), and (e) of this section.

Example 1. (i) *Facts.* X, a U.S. person, purchased a share of stock of FC, a corporation, on December 31, 1985. FC has been a section 1291 fund since its taxable year that began January 1, 1987. X received distributions from FC of $50 on December 31, 1987, $80 on December 31, 1988, and $150 on December 31, 1989. FC made no distributions in 1986.

(ii) *1987 excess distribution.* Because X did not receive a distribution from FC during 1986, the only preceding taxable year in its holding period, the total distribution of $50 is the total excess distribution for 1987. That amount is allocated pro rata over X's two-year holding period, as provided in § 1.1291-2(e)(2)(i): $25 is allocated to 1986, a prePFIC year, and $25 to 1987, the current shareholder year. The entire $50 therefore is included in X's gross income for 1987 as ordinary income.

(iii) *1988 excess distribution*. In 1988, of the $80 total distribution, $31.25 (125% × $25 [(0 + $50) / 2]) is the nonexcess distribution, and is taxable as a corporate distribution as provided in section 301(c). The total excess distribution for 1988, $48.75 ($80 – $31.25), is allocated over X's three-year holding period; $16.25 is allocated to each year. The portions of the excess distribution allocated to the prePFIC year (1986) and the current shareholder year (1988) total $32.50; that amount is included in X's gross income as ordinary income. The $16.25 portion of the excess distribution allocated to 1987, the prior PFIC year, is not included in X's gross income, but is subject to the deferred tax amount. Of the $80 distribution, $63.75 ($31.25 + $32.50) is included in X's gross income in 1988.

(iv) *1989 excess distribution*. In 1989, of the $150 total distribution, $47.40 (125% × $37.90 [(0 + $50 + $63.75) / 3]) is the nonexcess distribution, and is taxable as a corporate distribution as provided in section 301(c). The total excess distribution for 1989, $102.60 ($150 –$47.40), is allocated over X's four-year holding period; $25.65 is allocated to each year. The portions of the excess distribution allocated to the prePFIC year (1986) and the current shareholder year (1989) total $51.30; that amount is included in X's gross income as ordinary income. The portions of the excess distribution allocated to the prior PFIC years (1987 and 1988) total $51.30; that amount is not included in X's gross income but is subject to the deferred tax amount. Of the total $150 distribution, $98.70 ($47.40 + $51.30) is included in X's gross income in 1989.

Example 2. (i) *Facts*. X, a U.S. person with a calendar taxable year, purchased 1,000 shares of stock of FC, a corporation, on December 31, 1985. FC has been a section 1291 fund since its taxable year that began January 1, 1987. FC distributed $100,000 to X on January 31, 1989, and $200,000 to X on July 31, 1989. X determined the total excess distribution for 1989 to be $150,000.

(ii) *January 31 distribution*. The excess distribution allocated to the January 31 distribution, which is the ratable portion of the total excess distribution allocated to the $100,000 distribution made on that date, is $50,000 [$150,000 × ($100,000 / $300,000)]. For purposes of allocating the $50,000 excess distribution over X's holding period, X's holding period is treated as ending on (and including) January 31, 1989. X thus held the stock for 1,127 days (365 days in both 1986 and 1987, 366 days in 1988, and 31 days in 1989) at the time of the January 31 distribution. The $50,000 excess distribution allocated to the January 31 distribution is allocated pro rata to the 1,127 days; approximately $44.37 is allocated to each day in the holding period. The total allocations to each of the taxable years in X's holding period are as follows:

TAXABLE YEAR	*TOTAL ALLOCATION PER YEAR*
1986	$16,193.70
1987	$16,193.70
1988	$16,237.70
1989	$1,374.90
Excess distribution:	$50,000.00

The allocation to 1986, the prePFIC year, and the allocation to 1989, the current shareholder year, are included in X's gross income for 1989 as ordinary income. The allocations to 1987 and 1988, the prior PFIC years, are not included in X's gross income in 1989, but are subject to the deferred tax amount.

(iii) *July 31 distribution*. The excess distribution allocated to the July 31 distribution, which is the ratable portion of the total excess distribution allocated to the distribution made on that date, is $100,000 [$150,000 × ($200,000 / $300,000)]. For purposes of the allocation of this excess distribution, X's holding period is treated as ending on July 31, 1989. X thus held the stock for 1,308 days (365 days in both 1986 and 1987, 366 days in 1988, and 212 days in 1989) at the time of the July 31 distribution. The $100,000 excess distribution allocated to the July 31 excess distribution is allocated pro rata to the 1,308 days; approximately $76.45 is allocated to each day in the holding period. The total allocations of the July 31 excess distribution to each of the taxable years in X's holding period are as follows:

TAXABLE YEAR	*TOTAL ALLOCATION PER YEAR*
1986	$27,905.20
1987	$27,905.20
1988	$27,981.65
1989	$16,207.95
Excess distribution:	$100,000.00

The portions of the excess distribution allocated to 1986, the prePFIC year, and to 1989, the current shareholder year, are included as ordinary income in X's gross income for 1989. The portions of the excess distribution allocated to 1987 and 1988, the prior PFIC years, are not included in X's gross income in 1989, but are subject to the deferred tax amount.

Example 3. (i) *Facts*. X, a U.S. person, holds six shares of the stock of FC, a section 1291 fund. Two shares were purchased on December 31, 1986 (Block #1), and four shares were purchased on December 31, 1987 (Block #2). On June 30 of 1987 and 1988, FC distributed $10,000 in respect of each outstanding share of its stock. No portion of the distributions in either year was an excess distribution. On June 30, 1989, FC distributed $30,000 in respect of each outstanding share of its stock.

(ii) *Calculation of the 1989 excess distributions*. The excess distribution is determined separately for each block of stock.

(A) *Block #1 excess distribution*. The nonexcess distribution for Block #1 is $25,000 [125% times ($20,000 + $20,000) / 2]. The total excess distribution for Block #1 is $35,000 ($60,000 – $25,000).

(B) *Block #2 excess distribution*. The nonexcess distribution for Block #2 is $50,000 [125% times $40,000 (the distribution received in the only preceding taxable year included in X's holding period]. The total excess distribution for Block #2 is $70,000 ($120,000 – $50,000).

(iii) *Block #1 allocation*. The holding period of the Block #1 stock began on January 1, 1987, and ended, for purposes of section 1291, on June 30, 1989, for a total of 912 days (365 days in 1987, 366 days in 1988 and 181 days in 1989). The $35,000 excess distribution for Block #1 is allocated pro rata to each of the 912 days. Accordingly, approximately $38.38 is allocated to each day. The total allocations to each of the taxable years in X's holding period are as follows:

TAXABLE YEAR	*TOTAL ALLOCATION PER YEAR*
1987	$14,007.70
1988	$14,046.10
1989	$6,946.20
Excess distribution:	$35,000.00

The portion of the excess distribution allocated to 1989, the current shareholder year, of $6,946.20, is included as ordinary income in X's gross income for 1989. The portions of the excess distribution allocated to the prior PFIC years, 1987 and 1988, an aggregate of $28,053.80, are not included in X's gross income in 1989, but are subject to the deferred tax amount.

(iv) *Block #2 allocation*. The holding period of the Block #2 stock began on January 1, 1988, and ended, for purposes of section 1291, on June 30, 1989, for a total of 547 days (366 days in 1988 and 181 days in 1989). The excess distribution of $70,000 in respect of the Block #2 stock is allocated pro rata to each of the 547 days. Accordingly, approximately $127.97 is allocated to each day. The total allocations to each of the taxable years in X's holding period are as follows:

TAXABLE YEAR	*TOTAL ALLOCATION PER YEAR*
1988	$46,837.40
1989	$23,162.60
Excess distribution:	$70,000.00

The portion of the excess distribution allocated to 1989, the current shareholder year, of $23,162.60, is included as ordinary income in X's gross income for 1989. The portion of the excess distribution allocated to 1988, $46,837.40, is not included in X's gross income in 1989, but is subject to the deferred tax amount.

Example 4. X is a U.S. person that owns all the stock of FC, a section 1291 fund. At the end of its 1991 taxable year, FC has accumulated earnings and profits, before reduction for distributions made during the year, of $100, none of which was previously taxed to X under section 951 or 1293. FC distributes $200 to X on the last day of FC's taxable year. X determines that, of the $200 distribution, $50 is a nonexcess distribution, and $150 is the total excess distribution. FC's earnings and profits of $100 are allocated proportionately between the nonexcess distribution of $50 and the excess distribution of $150, and reduced to zero. Accordingly, $25 of FC's earnings and profits are allocated to the nonexcess distribution and $75 of FC's earnings and profits are allocated to the excess distribution. Therefore, $25 of the $50 nonexcess distribution is taxable as a dividend under section 301(c)(1), and the remaining $25 is taxable to the extent provided in section 301(c)(2) and (3). The excess distribution of $150 is taxable as provided in § 1.1291-2(e)(2).

(f) *Indirect distributions*.—(1) *In general*.—A distribution (as defined in § 1.1291-2(b)) by a section 1291 fund to the actual owner of stock of the section 1291 fund is an indirect distribution if such stock is considered owned by a U.S. person pursuant to § 1.1291-1(b)(8). Except as otherwise provided in this paragraph (f), an indirect shareholder is taxable on the total distribution paid by the section 1291 fund with respect to the stock attributed to the indirect shareholder, as if the indirect shareholder had actually received that amount. The following example illustrates the rule of this paragraph (f)(1).

Example. (i) X, an S corporation under section 1361, purchased 100 shares of stock of FC, a corporation, on December 31, 1985. FC has been a section 1291 fund since its taxable year that began January 1, 1987. A purchased 10 percent of the stock of X on December 31, 1986, and thus became an indirect shareholder of 10 shares of FC stock. Pursuant to § 1.1291-1(h)(4)(i), A's holding period of the FC stock began on January 1, 1987.

(ii) FC distributed $5 per share of stock to its shareholders in 1986, and $8 per share in 1987. In 1987 A is treated as receiving a distribution of $80 from FC. A did not have a total excess distribution in 1987, the taxable year in which A's holding period of the FC stock began.

(iii) FC distributed $12 per share in 1988, all of which was paid on June 30, 1988. A therefore is treated as receiving a distribution of $120 from FC. The nonexcess distribution is $100 [125% times $80]. Accordingly, the excess distribution is $20 ($120 – $100). That amount is allocated under § 1.1291-2(e)(2)(i) to each day in A's holding period of the FC stock, which began on January 1, 1987, and ended, for purposes of the allocation of the excess distribution, on June 30, 1988.

(2) *Pass-through entities*.—(i) *Taxation of trusts, estates, and their beneficiaries*.—[Reserved]

(ii) *Information reporting*.—(A) *In general*.—A domestic partnership that is a direct or indirect shareholder of a section 1291 fund must separately state the total distribution as a distribution from a section 1291 fund on its federal income tax return (if any) and on any Schedule

K-1 filed by the partnership or provided to a partner to which a distributive share of the distribution from the section 1291 fund is allocated pursuant to section 704. In addition, the partnership must state on the Schedule K-1 the information needed by the partner to compute its excess distribution with respect to such total distribution, and provide the name, address and stock basis, where appropriate, of the actual owner of the section 1291 fund that paid the distribution (or whose stock was transferred in an indirect disposition). Any partner receiving such a Schedule K-1 that is itself a domestic partnership is in turn obligated to separately state such information according to the same rules. Similar rules apply to S corporations.

(B) *Trusts and estates*.—[Reserved]

(3) *Coordination with subpart F*.—If, but for this paragraph (f)(3), an indirect distribution would be taxable to an indirect shareholder under this section and also included in the gross income of the indirect shareholder under section 551(a), 951(a)(1), or 1293(a), the indirect distribution is taxable only under this section.

(4) *Exceptions*.—(i) *Distribution to sole shareholder*.—A distribution by a section 1291 fund (distributing fund) to another section 1291 fund (distributee fund) will not be taxable to the direct shareholder of the distributee fund if—

(A) The distributee fund owns all the stock of the distributing fund; and

(B) The distributing fund distributed all its earnings and profits in the current shareholder year and annually distributed all its earnings and profits for each year that is included in the shareholder's holding period of the distributing fund.

(ii) *Other exceptions*.—[Reserved]

(5) *Adjustment to basis*.—The shareholder's adjusted basis of the stock or other property that is owned directly by the shareholder and through which ownership of the section 1291 fund is attributed to the shareholder is increased by the amount of the indirect distribution taxed to the shareholder pursuant to paragraph (f)(1) of this section.

(6) *Treatment of previously taxed amounts*.—The principles of sections 959 and 961 apply with respect to amounts previously taxed under this paragraph (f). The following example illustrates the rule of this paragraph (f)(6).

Example. USP owns 50% of CFC1. CFC1 and its wholly owned subsidiary, CFC2, are both controlled foreign corporations within the meaning of section 957(a), but are not PFICs. CFC2 owns 10% of the stock of NQF, a PFIC. USP is an indirect shareholder of NQF pursuant to § 1.1291-1(b)(8)(ii). USP has not elected to treated NQF as a QEF. In 1992, NQF distributes $100 to CFC2, and CFC1 distributes $100 to USP, but CFC2 makes no distributions to CFC1. At the end of 1992, CFC1 has accumulated earnings and profits of $200, none of which was previously taxed to USP under section 951(a)(1). USP is taxable pursuant to § 1.1291-2(f) on its pro rata share of the indirect distribution paid to CFC2, and also is taxable on CFC1's distribution pursuant to section 301(c). No part of the distribution by CFC1 to USP is attributable to the amount taxed to USP under § 1.1291-2(f) because no part of the distribution can be attributed to NQF's distribution to CFC2. [Reg. § 1.1291-2.]

§ 1.1291-3. Dispositions.—(a) *Purpose and scope*.—Any direct or indirect disposition of stock of a section 1291 fund within the meaning of paragraphs (b), (c), (d), and (e) of this section is taxable to the extent provided in section 1291, this section, and § 1.1291-6. For dispositions of stock of a section 1291 fund that qualify for nonrecognition treatment, *see* § 1.1291-6. Gain is determined on a share-by-share basis and is taxed as an excess distribution as provided in § 1.1291-2(e)(2). Unless otherwise provided under another provision of the Code, a loss realized on a disposition of stock of a section 1291 fund is not recognized.

(b) *Disposition*.—(1) *In general*.—For purposes of this section, a disposition is any transaction or event that constitutes an actual or deemed transfer of property for any purpose of the Code and the regulations thereunder, including (but not limited to) a sale, exchange, gift, or transfer at death, an exchange pursuant to a liquidation or section 302(a) redemption, or a distribution described in section 311, 336, 337, 355(c) or 361(c). For purposes of this paragraph (b), any person receiving a distribution that qualifies under section 355 will be treated as disposing of all of its stock in the distributing corporation (whether or not there is an actual disposition of such stock) in exchange for stock of the distributing corporation, the controlled corporation, or both, as the case may be.

(2) *Change of U.S. residence or citizenship*.—If a shareholder of a section 1291 fund becomes a nonresident alien for U.S. tax purposes, the shareholder will be treated as having disposed of the shareholder's stock in the section 1291 fund for purposes of section 1291 on the last day that the shareholder is a U.S. person. Termination of an election under section 6013(g) is treated as a change of residence (within the meaning of this paragraph (b)(2)) of the spouse who was a resident solely by reason of the section 6013(g) election.

(c) *Direct disposition of stock of a section 1291 fund*.—Except to the extent provided in § 1.1291-6, a direct shareholder of a section 1291 fund recognizes all gain that it realizes on a disposition of the stock of such fund.

(d) *Stock of a section 1291 fund used as security for an obligation*.—(1) *In general*.—Except to the extent provided in paragraphs (d)(3) and (6) of this section, the use of stock of a section 1291 fund as security for the performance of an obligation of a direct or indirect shareholder (or of a person related within the meaning of section 267(b) to that shareholder), in connection with a loan, guarantee, margin account, or otherwise (a pledge of stock), is a transaction that results in a disposition of the stock of the section 1291 fund within the meaning of paragraph (b) of this section. Such pledged stock will be treated as having been disposed of on the later of the date when such stock is first used as security with respect to such obligation, or the first day of the first taxable year of the foreign corporation as a PFIC. Such pledged stock will be treated as having been disposed of for consideration equal to the lesser of—

(i) The unpaid principal of the obligation secured by the stock on the date of disposition; or

(ii) The fair market value of the stock immediately before such disposition.

(2) *Indirect pledge.*—A pledge of stock of a section 1291 fund, as described in paragraph (d)(1) of this section, will be deemed to occur if such stock serves indirectly as security for the performance of an obligation described in that paragraph, and a principal purpose for the structure of the security arrangement was to avoid the rule of that paragraph.

(3) *Requirement of gain realized.*—This paragraph (d) does not apply if the shareholder would realize a loss on an actual disposition of the stock of the section 1291 fund at the time the obligation was secured by the stock.

(4) *Increase in value of pledged stock.*—An increase in the value of stock being used to secure the performance of an obligation will not be treated as a disposition of the stock unless the pledged stock is used to secure additional principal or new indebtedness.

(5) *Adjustment to basis; holding period.*—If stock of a section 1291 fund is treated as disposed of under this paragraph (d), adjustments to basis will be made in accordance with rules similar to those in § 1.1291-6(b)(4). For the holding period of pledged stock, *see* § 1.1291-1(h)(5).

(6) *Transition rule.*—Stock of a section 1291 fund that secured an obligation within the meaning of paragraph (d)(1) of this section as of the effective date of section 1297(b)(6) is not treated as disposed of as of the first day of the first taxable year of the foreign corporation as a PFIC, unless such stock continued to secure such obligation 180 days after the effective date. For a special effective date pertaining to this rule, *see* § 1.1291-1(j)(2).

(7) *Examples.*—The following examples illustrate the operation of this paragraph (d).

Example 1. On November 20, 1995, X, a U.S. person that was a shareholder of FC, a section 1291 fund, used its stock in FC, valued immediately before the loan at $120,000, as security for a $100,000 loan. X's basis in the stock is $70,000. The pledge is treated as a disposition of the stock for $100,000, which is the lesser of the loan principal secured by the stock and the fair market value of the stock. S recognizes $30,000 on the disposition, which gain is taxed as an excess distribution under section 1291 and § 1.1291-2(e)(2). X's basis in the FC stock is increased by $30,000, the amount of gain recognized on the deemed disposition. The holding period of the pledged stock is not adjusted to reflect the disposition because the full amount of the gain inherent in the stock was not recognized (*see* § 1.1291-1(h)(5)).

Example 2. The facts are the same as in *Example 1.* In addition, on August 12, 1996, X borrows an additional $30,000 (for a total outstanding loan balance on that day of $130,000). The value of the FC stock immediately before the additional loan is $130,000. Pursuant to § 1.1291-3(d)(4), there is a disposition within the meaning of § 1.1291-3(d)(1) to the extent the value of the FC stock secures additional indebtedness. The FC stock first secured a loan of $100,000, which was less than its full value. The second loan results in a disposition to the extent that the previously unrecognized appreciation and any additional appreciation secure additional indebtedness. Accordingly, there is an excess distribution of $30,000. X's basis in its FC stock is increased by $30,000, the amount of gain recognized. X's holding period in the FC stock for section 1291 purposes is treated as beginning on the day after the effective date of the second borrowing (*see* § 1.1291-1(h)(5)).

(e) *Indirect dispositions.*—(1) *In general.*—Except as otherwise provided in this paragraph (e) and § 1.1291-6, an indirect shareholder of a section 1291 fund is taxable under section 1291 and this section on an indirect disposition of stock of the section 1291 fund.

(2) *Indirect disposition defined.*—An indirect disposition is—

(i) Any disposition of stock of a section 1291 fund by its actual owner if such stock is attributed to an indirect shareholder under § 1.1291-1(b)(8);

(ii) Any disposition, by an indirect shareholder or any other person, of any interest in a person, if by virtue of such interest the indirect shareholder was treated as owning stock of a section 1291 fund under § 1.1291-1(b)(8); or

(iii) Any other transaction as a result of which an indirect shareholder's ownership of a section 1291 fund is reduced or terminated.

Paragraph (e)(2)(i) of this section applies without regard to whether the indirect shareholder's ownership of a section 1291 fund is changed by the disposition. However, paragraph (e)(2)(ii) of this section does not apply if the disposition does not result in a reduction in the indirect shareholder's ownership of the fund or an increase in the basis of the stock of the fund in the hands of the actual owner.

(3) *Examples.*—The following examples illustrate paragraph (e)(2) of this section.

Example 1. T, a U.S. person, and M, a foreign person, are equal partners of FP, a foreign partnership that owns 10 shares of stock of FC, a PFIC. Pursuant to § 1.1291-1(b)(8)(iii), T is an indirect shareholder of one-half of the shares of FC stock held by FP. T did not elect under section 1295 to treat FC as a QEF. On August 14, 1994, H, a U.S. person, joins the partnership as an equal partner. As a result of H's acquisition of one-third of FP, H is an indirect shareholder of one-third of the FC stock held by FP. H's acquisition of the FP interest is a disposition pursuant to § 1.1291-3(e)(2)(iii), taxable to T, of one-third of T's interest in the FC stock.

Example 2. E, a U.S. person, and R, a foreign person, each own 50% of the outstanding stock of Distributing, a foreign corporation that is not a PFIC or a controlled foreign corporation within the meaning of section 957(a). Distributing owns all the stock of Controlled, a PFIC. Pursuant to § 1.1291-1(b)(8)(ii)(A), E is an indirect shareholder of Controlled. E did not elect under section 1295 to treat Controlled as a QEF. In a transaction that qualifies under section 355(a), Distributing distributes all the Controlled stock to R. As a result of the distribution, E's interest in Controlled is terminated. The distribution is an indirect disposition of E's ownership of Controlled, within the meaning of § 1.1291-3(e)(2)(i), taxable to E under § 1.1291-3(e).

Example 3. C, a U.S. person, owns 51% of the stock of CFC, a foreign corporation that is not a PFIC. Several foreign persons own the remaining 49% of CFC. CFC owns 100 shares of FYZ, a PFIC. Pursuant to § 1.1291-1(b)(8)(ii)(A), C is an indirect shareholder of 51 shares of the FYZ stock held by CFC. C did not elect under section 1295 to treat FYZ as a QEF. To raise capital, CFC makes a public offering of its stock. After the offering, C owns only 35% of the CFC stock. The reduction of C's ownership of CFC terminated C's indirect ownership of the FYZ stock, and therefore is an indirect disposition of the FYZ stock, pursuant to § 1.1291-3(e)(2)(iii), taxable to C under § 1.1291-3(e).

(4) *General rules.*—(i) *Amount and treatment of gain.*—If a shareholder with respect to a share of stock of a section 1291 fund is taxable on an indirect disposition of that share, the shareholder is treated as recognizing an amount of gain with respect to that share equal to the shareholder's pro rata share of the gain realized by the actual owner of that share (in the case of a disposition described in paragraph (e)(2)(i) of this section), or the gain the actual owner would have realized on an actual disposition of such stock (in the case of other dispositions). The gain taxable to the shareholder is an excess distribution, taxable in the manner provided in § 1.1291-2(e)(2). The gain is allocated over the shareholder's holding period of the stock of the section 1291 fund as determined in § 1.1291-1(h)(4).

(ii) *Coordination with current inclusion rules.*—If gain from an indirect disposition would be taxable to a shareholder under this section, and would, but for this paragraph (e)(4)(ii), also be included in the gross income of the shareholder under section 551(a), 951(a)(1), or 1293(a), the indirect disposition is taxable only under this section.

(iii) *Adjustment to basis; holding period.*—The shareholder's adjusted basis of the stock or other property that is owned directly by the shareholder and through which ownership of the section 1291 fund is attributed to the shareholder is increased by the amount of gain recognized by the shareholder pursuant to paragraph (e)(4)(i) of this section. In addition, solely for purposes of determining the subsequent treatment under the Code of a direct or indirect shareholder of the stock of the section 1291 fund treated as transferred in an indirect disposition, the adjusted basis of the actual owner of the stock of the section 1291 fund is increased by the amount of gain recognized by the shareholder. For the holding period rule for stock that is treated as disposed of under paragraph (e)(2) of this section, *see* § 1.1291-1(h)(5).

(iv) *Treatment of previously taxed amounts.*—The principles of sections 959 and 961 apply with respect to distributions by a foreign corporation through which a shareholder was considered to own stock of a section 1291 fund, to the extent that such distributions are attributable to amounts previously taxed under this paragraph (e) on a disposition of the stock of such fund.

(5) *Pass-through entities.*—(i) *Section 1291 fund stock held by former C corporation.*—Solely for purposes of calculating the aggregate amount of interest under § 1.1291-4(d)(1), the S corporation shareholder's gain is determined without regard to section 1366(f)(2). Accordingly, the excess distribution for this purpose includes the amount of the S corporation's liability for tax attributable to the built-in gain in the stock of the section 1291 fund pursuant to section 1374. For an illustration of the rule of this paragraph (e)(5)(i), *see* § 1.1291-4(e), *Example 2*. For the taxation of the S corporation on the disposition of the stock of a section 1291 fund, *see* section 1374.

(ii) *Taxation of trusts, estates, and their beneficiaries.*—[Reserved]

(iii) *Information reporting.*—The information reporting obligations to which pass-through entities are subject with respect to indirect distributions also apply with respect to indirect dispositions. *See* § 1.1291-2(f)(2)(ii).

(6) *Exceptions.*—(i) *Disposition of PFIC's wholly-owned PFIC.*—A direct shareholder of a section 1291 fund (first-tier fund) will not be taxable on an indirect disposition of a section 1291 fund (second-tier fund) that is a wholly owned subsidiary of the first-tier fund if the second-tier fund annually distributed all its earnings and profits for each year that is included in the shareholder's holding period of the second-tier fund.

(ii) *Other exceptions.*—[Reserved]

(f) *Transfers within a consolidated group.*—For purposes of applying sections 1291 through 1297 to the stock of a PFIC, transfers by one member of a consolidated group to another member are ignored. Thus, the basis of the transferred stock in the hands of the transferee is the adjusted basis of such stock in the hands of the transferor, and the holding period of such stock held by a member of the consolidated group includes the holding period of all members of the group that have transferred the stock.

(g) *Installment sales.*—If the gain from a disposition of a share of stock of a section 1291 fund is reported on the installment basis, there is an excess distribution on the receipt of each installment or portion thereof in the amount of the gain to be reported in accordance with section 453 with respect to such share. For purposes of allocating each excess distribution under § 1.1291-2(e)(2)(i), the holding period of the transferred stock, which begins on the date determined under § 1.1291-1(h), is treated as ending on the date of each installment.

(h) *Series of liquidation distributions.*—For purposes of allocating the gain recognized on a distribution of property that is one of a series of distributions in liquidation of a section 1291 fund, the holding period of the stock of the liquidating corporation, which begins on the date determined under § 1.1291-1(h), is treated as ending on the date of each liquidation distribution with respect to which gain is recognized.

(i) *Sections 1246 and 1248 inapplicable.*—Sections 1246 and 1248 do not apply to the disposition of stock of a section 1291 fund that is taxable under section 1291. *See* sections 1246(g) and 1248(g)(2).

(j) *Estate tax deduction.*—If a shareholder acquired the stock of a section 1291 fund from a decedent (other than a decedent who was a nonresident alien at all times during the holding period of the stock), and the decedent did not recognize any gain on the transfer of his or her stock at death pursuant to § 1.1291-6(c)(2)(iii)(A), the shareholder may deduct from gross income, for the taxable year of the disposition of the stock of the section 1291 fund that is taxable to the shareholder, an amount equal to that portion of the decedent's estate tax deemed paid which is attributable to the excess of (A) the value at which such stock was taken into account for purposes of determining the value of the decedent's gross estate, over (B) the value at which it would have been so taken into account if such value had been the basis of the stock in the hands of the shareholder determined under § 1.1291-6(b)(4)(iii). [Reg. § 1.1291-3.]

§ 1.1291-4. The deferred tax amount.—(a) *In general.*—The deferred tax amount is the sum of the aggregate increases in taxes (defined in paragraph (c)(5) of this section) and the aggregate amount of interest (defined in paragraph (d) of this section) determined with respect to the aggregate increases in taxes. The deferred tax amount is computed for the portions of each excess distribution allocated to different prior PFIC years, as defined in § 1.1291-1(b)(4).

(b) *Character of deferred tax amount.*—The aggregate increases in taxes are an additional amount of tax imposed on the shareholder for the current shareholder year. The aggregate increases in taxes are treated as an income tax for purposes of subtitle F (Procedure and Administration), and therefore will be assessed, collected, paid, and subject to penalties and interest in the same manner as other taxes on income. The aggregate amount of interest is treated as interest under section 6601. To determine the extent to which such interest may be deducted for federal income tax purposes, *see* section 163 and the regulations under that section.

(c) *Increase in tax.*—(1) *In general.*—An increase in tax is determined for each portion of an excess distribution allocated to a prior PFIC year. Each increase in tax is determined by multiplying the amount of the excess distribution allocated to the prior PFIC year by the highest statutory rate of tax in effect under either section 1 or section 11, as applicable, for that prior PFIC year.

(2) *Rate of tax in effect.*—The highest statutory rate of tax is determined without regard to the actual rate of tax to which the shareholder was subject in that prior PFIC year. The rate of tax in effect in the case of a distribution or disposition taxable to an indirect shareholder is the rate in effect for the indirect shareholder. For taxable years of the shareholder beginning after 1987 and before January 1, 1991, the highest statutory rate of tax in effect under section 1 is 28 percent. If there was a change of tax rates during a taxable year, the highest rate of tax is determined in the manner described in section 15(e) using the highest statutory rates of tax in effect before and after the change of rates.

(3) *Reduction for foreign taxes.*—To the extent provided in section 1291(g) and § 1.1291-5, each increase in tax is reduced by the foreign tax credit calculated with respect to the increase in tax.

(4) *Net increase in tax.*—The net increase in tax is the amount of the increase in tax after reduction for creditable foreign taxes. *See* paragraph (d) of this section.

(5) *Aggregate increases in taxes.*—The term aggregate increases in taxes means the sum of all net increases in tax calculated for an excess distribution.

(d) *Aggregate amount of interest.*—(1) *In general.* The aggregate amount of interest is the sum of the interest charges computed on all net increases in tax calculated for an excess distribution. An interest charge is computed separately for the interest period of each net increase in tax by using the applicable rates and method under section 6621. The interest period for a net increase in tax is the period beginning on the due date of the income tax return for the prior PFIC year for which the net increase in tax was computed and ending on the due date for the income tax return for the current shareholder year. For purposes of this paragraph, the term due date means the date prescribed by law, determined without regard to extensions, for filing the income tax return for the taxable year of the shareholder.

(2) *Reduction for interest paid under section 453A(c).*—A disposition may be subject to both sections 1291 and 453A(c). The aggregate amount of interest determined in paragraph (d)(1) of this section is reduced by the amount of interest paid under section 453A(c) that is attributable to an excess distribution arising from the disposition. The shareholder may use any reasonable method of determining the amount of the reduction.

(e) *Examples.*—The following examples illustrate the rules of this section.

Example 1. (i) *Facts.* X is a domestic corporation that is a calendar year taxpayer. The due date (without regard to extensions) for its federal income tax return is March 15. X acquired a share of stock of FC, a corporation, on December 31, 1986, for $500. FC has been a section 1291 fund with respect to X since FC's taxable year that began January 1, 1987. On December 31, 1990, X sold the FC stock for $1000. X did not incur any foreign tax on the disposition of the FC stock. X's gain on the sale, $500, is taxed as an excess distribution. The excess distribution is allocated pro rata over X's four-year holding period. Accordingly, $125 is allocated to each year in X's holding period. The $125 allocated to 1990, the current shareholder year, is included in X's ordinary income for that year. The allocations to 1987, 1988 and 1989, the prior PFIC years, are subject to the deferred tax amount under § 1.1291-4.

(ii) *Calculation of the 1987 increase in tax.* The increase in tax for the $125 allocated to 1987 is determined in the manner described in section 15(e) by using a weighted average rate. The weighted average rate is 40 percent:

46% rate: 181/365 × 46% =	22.81%
34% rate: 184/365 × 34% =	17.14%
	39.95% .

The increase in tax for 1987 is $49.94 ($125 × 39.95%).

(iii) *Calculation of the other increases in tax.* The highest statutory rate of tax applicable to X that was in effect for both 1988 and 1989 was 34 percent. The increase in tax for each of 1988 and 1989 is $42.50 ($125 × 34%).

(iv) *Aggregate increases in taxes.* The aggregate increases in taxes are $134.94 ($49.94 + $42.50 + $42.50).

(v) *Interest charge.* Interest on each of the three increases in tax ($49.94, $42.50, and $42.50) is computed using the rates and method provided in section 6621 for the respective interest period. The following are the interest periods:

Year of Allocation	Increase in Tax	Interest Period	
		Beginning on	Ending on
1987	$49.94	March 15, 1988	March 15, 1991
1988	42.50	March 15, 1989	March 15, 1991
1989	42.50	March 15, 1990	March 15, 1991

Example 2. (i) *Facts.* The facts are the same as in *Example 1* except that X was a C corporation until it elected to be treated as an S corporation effective for its taxable year beginning January 1, 1988. A is a U.S. person who has been a shareholder of X since January 1, 1988. A's holding period of the FC stock began on January 1, 1988, pursuant to § 1.1291-1(h)(4)(i). As of January 1, 1988, the FC stock had appreciated in value to $800; X therefore had $300 of built-in gain within the meaning of section 1374. Assume X pays a built-in gain tax of $102 because of the sale of the FC stock in 1990.

(ii) *Calculation of the aggregate increases in taxes owed by A.* The $500 gain recognized, reduced as provided in section 1366(f)(2) by the amount of built-in gain tax of $102 paid by X pursuant to section 1374 to $398, is taxable to A as an excess distribution as provided in § 1.1291-2(e)(2). The $398 excess distribution is allocated pro rata over X's four-year holding period (not A's three-year holding period) as provided in § 1.1291-3(e)(5). The allocation of $99.50 to 1990, the current shareholder year, is included in A's ordinary income. The allocations of $99.50 to 1987, 1988, and 1989 are not included in income, but are subject to the deferred tax amount. The aggregate increases in taxes are determined based on those $99.50 allocations.

(A) *Calculation of the 1987 increase in tax.* The highest statutory rate of tax applicable to A that was in effect in 1987 was 38.5 percent. The increase in tax for the portion of the excess distribution allocated to 1987 is $38.31 ($99.50 × 38.5%).

(B) *Calculation of the other increases in tax.* The highest statutory rate of tax applicable to A that was in effect for both 1988 and 1989 is 28 percent. The increase in tax for each of 1988 and 1989 is $27.86 ($99.50 × 28%).

(C) *Calculation of the aggregate increases in taxes.* The aggregate increases in taxes are $94.03 ($38.31 + 27.86 + 27.86).

(iii) *Calculation of the aggregate amount of interest.* For purposes of calculating the aggregate amount of interest, the reduction provided under section 1366(f)(2) is disregarded and the excess distribution is $500. Accordingly, for purposes of calculating the aggregate amount of interest, $125 is allocated to 1987, 1988, and 1989.

(A) *Calculation of the 1987 hypothetical increase in tax.* The highest statutory rate of tax applicable to A that was in effect in 1987 was 38.5 percent. The hypothetical increase in tax for the portion of the excess distribution allocated to 1987 is $48.12 ($125 × 38.5%).

(B) *Calculation of the other hypothetical increases in tax.* The highest statutory rate of tax applicable to A that was in effect for both 1988 and 1989 is 28 percent. The hypothetical increase in tax for each of 1988 and 1989 is $35.00 ($125 × 28%).

(C) *Interest charge.* Interest on each of the three hypothetical increases in tax ($48.12, $35, and $35) is computed using the rates and method provided in section 6621 for the respective interest period. The following are the interest periods:

Year of Allocation	Increase in Tax	Interest Period	
		Beginning on	Ending on
1987	$48.12	April 15, 1988	April 15, 1991
1988	35.00	April 15, 1989	April 15, 1991
1989	35.00	April 15, 1990	April 15, 1991.

(iv) *The deferred tax amount.* The deferred tax amount is the sum of the aggregate increases in taxes determined in (ii) and the aggregate amount of interest determined in (iii). [Reg. § 1.1291-4.]

§ 1.1291-5. Coordination with the foreign tax credit rules.—(a) *Scope.*—This section provides rules for determining the amount of foreign tax credit that a shareholder may claim on a distribution from a section 1291 fund, and in certain cases, on a disposition of stock of a section 1291 fund. This section applies to a shareholder that has chosen under section 901 for the current shareholder year to claim a credit for foreign taxes paid. The rules of this section apply separately with respect to each section 1291 fund in which the shareholder directly or indirectly owns stock. For purposes of this section, an S corporation is treated as a partnership, and its shareholders as partners of the partnership. *See* section 1373.

(b) *Distributions from section 1291 funds to shareholders that are not entitled to a foreign tax credit for foreign taxes deemed paid.*—(1) *Rule.*—If a section 1291 fund makes a distribution with respect to which a shareholder (other than a shareholder described in paragraph (c) of this section) is subject to tax under § 1.1291-2, and the shareholder would be entitled to a foreign tax credit for foreign taxes paid (including withholding taxes) with respect to such distribution, but not for foreign taxes deemed paid with respect to such distribution (determined in both cases without regard to section 1291 and this section), the foreign tax credit with respect to that distribution is determined under the steps provided in this paragraph (b). The excess distribution is treated as foreign source income described in section 904(d)(1)(A).

(i) *Step 1.*—The shareholder determines the total excess distribution under § 1.1291-2 (c)(3), and the excess distribution taxes. The excess distribution taxes are the creditable foreign taxes (within the meaning of section 1291(g)(2)(A)), paid or accrued with respect to the total distribution for the current shareholder year, allocated to the total excess distribution as follows:

$$\text{Foreign taxes paid with respect to the total distribution} \times \frac{\text{Total excess distribution}}{\text{Total distribution}}$$

The remainder of the creditable foreign taxes are allocated to the nonexcess distribution.

(ii) *Step 2.*—The shareholder allocates the total excess distribution and the excess distribution taxes ratably to each distribution received during the shareholder's taxable year in the manner provided in § 1.1291-2 (c)(4). The shareholder then allocates each excess distribution and the excess distribution taxes allocated to that distribution to each taxable year included in the shareholder's holding period based on the number of days in each such taxable year.

(iii) *Step 3.*—The shareholder determines the tentative increase in tax for each prior PFIC year. The term tentative increase in tax means the increase in tax determined in the manner provided in § 1.1291-4(c) for each prior PFIC year. The tentative increase in tax for a prior PFIC year is the foreign tax credit limitation for the excess distribution taxes allocated to that prior PFIC year.

(iv) *Step 4.*—The shareholder claims as a foreign tax credit with respect to an increase in tax for a prior PFIC year the lesser of the tentative increase in tax for that year determined in *Step 3* or the excess distribution taxes allocated to that prior PFIC year in *Step 2.*

(v) *Step 5.*—The shareholder determines the net increase in tax for each prior PFIC year by reducing the tentative increase in tax for a prior PFIC year determined in *Step 3* by the foreign tax credit determined for that year in *Step 4.* For the calculation of the interest charge for each net increase in tax, *see* § 1.1291-4(d).

(vi) *Step 6.*—The portions of the excess distribution and excess distribution taxes allocated to the current shareholder year and pre-PFIC years, if any, as well as the creditable foreign taxes allocated to the nonexcess distribution, are taken into account in the current shareholder year under the general foreign tax credit rules.

(2) *Carryovers disallowed.*—The amount by which the excess distribution taxes allocated to a prior PFIC year exceed the tentative increase in tax for that year may not be claimed as a foreign tax credit against any federal income tax.

(c) *Distributions from section 1291 funds that are CFCs.*—(1) *Rule.*—If a controlled foreign corporation (CFC) (as defined in section 904(d)(4)) that is a section 1291 fund makes a distribution with respect to which a United States shareholder (also as defined in section 904(d)(4)) is subject to tax under § 1.1291-2, the foreign tax credit with respect to that excess distribution is determined by applying the rules of section 1291(g) on a separate category basis within the meaning of section 904. *See* section 904(d)(3)(A) and the regulations under that section. A distribution described in this paragraph (c) from a section 1291 fund is foreign source income except to the extent the distribution is determined to be derived from U.S. sources pursuant to section 904(g). The foreign tax credit of a United States shareholder with respect to a distribution by a CFC that is taxable as an excess distribution to the shareholder under § 1.1291-2(e)(2) is determined according to the following steps.

(i) *Step 1.*—The shareholder determines—

(A) The separate category or categories (as defined in § 1.904-5(a)(1)) to which the total distribution (including the amount of the gross-up determined under section 78) for the taxable year is allocable under the rules of section 904(d)(3) and the regulations under that section (*see* § 1.904-5(c)(4));

(B) The creditable foreign taxes, which are the foreign taxes paid or deemed paid on the distribution (determined without regard to section 1291 and this section) with respect to each separate category under the rules of sections 901, 902, 904, and 960 and the regulations under those sections (*see* § 1.904-6(b)(3)); and

(C) The portion of the total distribution (including the gross-up) in each separate category that is from U.S. sources pursuant to section 904(g) (*see* § 1.904-5(m)(4) and (6)).

Solely for purposes of section 1291, any portion of the total excess distribution that would not be allocated to a separate category under normally applicable rules because it exceeds the fund's earnings and profits is deemed to be foreign source income allocated to the separate category defined in section 904(d)(1)(A).

(ii) *Step 2.*—The shareholder determines—

(A) The total excess distribution under § 1.1291-2(c)(3) with respect to the total distribution (including the gross-up); and

(B) The portion of the total excess distribution allocable to each separate category (the separate category excess distribution).

Each separate category excess distribution is calculated as follows:

$$\frac{\text{Distribution allocable to a separate category (including gross-up) (Step 1(A))}}{\text{Total distribution (including gross-up)}} \times \text{Total excess distribution}(\textit{Step 2 (A)})$$

(iii) *Step 3.*—The shareholder determines the U.S. source portion of each separate category excess distribution as follows:

$$\frac{\text{U.S. source portion of distribution allocable to a separate category (Step 1(C))}}{\text{Total distribution allocable to that category } (\textit{Step 1 (A)})} \times \text{Separate category excess distribution } (\textit{Step 2 (B)})$$

(iv) *Step 4.*—The shareholder determines the excess distribution taxes with respect to each separate category (separate category excess distribution taxes) as follows:

$$\text{Creditable foreign taxes with respect to the distribution and allocable to the separate category } (\textit{Step 1}\text{ (B)}) \times \frac{\text{Separate category excess distribution } (\textit{Step 2}\text{ (B)})}{\text{Total distribution allocable to that category } (\textit{Step 1}\text{ (A)})}$$

(v) *Step 5.*—(A) The shareholder allocates—

(1) The separate category excess distribution;

(2) The separate category excess distribution taxes; and

(3) The U.S. source portion of the separate category excess distribution ratably to each distribution received during the shareholder's taxable year in the manner provided in § 1.1291-2(c)(4).

(B) The shareholder then allocates—

(1) The amount determined in *Step* 5 (A)*(1)* for each distribution to each taxable year included in the shareholder's holding period based on the number of days in each such taxable year;

(2) The amount determined in *Step* 5 (A)*(2)* for each distribution to each taxable year included in the shareholder's holding period based on the number of days in each such taxable year; and

(3) The amount determined in *Step* 5 (A)*(3)* for each distribution to each taxable year included in the shareholder's holding period based on the number of days in each such taxable year.

Solely for purposes of determining the foreign tax credit limitation for the current shareholder year, the portion of an excess distribution that is allocated to the current shareholder year and prePFIC years, and included in income, is treated as a dividend from a CFC that is not a PFIC. The excess distribution taxes allocated to that portion of the excess distribution are treated as foreign taxes paid with respect to a dividend from a CFC that is not a PFIC and taken into account in the current shareholder year under general foreign tax credit rules.

(vi) *Step 6.*—The shareholder determines a tentative increase in tax for each prior PFIC year for each allocation of a separate category excess distribution determined under *Step 5* (B)*(1)* (separate category tentative increase in tax).

(vii) *Step 7.*—The shareholder determines a foreign tax credit limitation for each prior PFIC year to which the separate category excess distribution is allocated. The limitation is determined as follows:

$$\text{Separate category tentative increase in tax for prior PFIC year } (\textit{Step 6}) \times \frac{\text{Foreign source separate category excess distribution allocated to that prior PFIC year } (\textit{Step 5}\text{ (B)(1)} - \textit{Step 5}\text{ (B)(3)})}{\text{Separate category excess distribution allocated to that prior PFIC year } (\textit{Step 5}\text{ (B)(1)})}$$

(viii) *Step 8.*—The shareholder may claim a foreign tax credit for each separate category tentative increase in tax. The foreign tax credit for a prior PFIC year is the lesser of the foreign tax credit limitation determined in *Step 7* for the prior PFIC year or the amount of the separate category excess distribution taxes allocated to that prior PFIC year under *Step 5* (B)(2).

(ix) *Step 9.*—The shareholder determines the separate category net increase in tax for each prior PFIC year by reducing the separate category tentative increase in tax determined for that year in *Step 6* by the amount of the foreign tax credit determined for that year in *Step 8.* For the calculation of the interest charge on each net increase in tax, *see* § 1.1291-4(d).

(2) *Carryovers disallowed.*—The amount by which the excess distribution taxes allocated to a prior PFIC year exceed the separate category tentative increase in tax for that year may not be claimed as a foreign tax credit against any federal income tax.

(3) *Example.*—The following example illustrates the rules of paragraph (c) of this section.

Example. (i) *Facts.* USP, a domestic corporation, has been a United States shareholder of FC, a CFC that is a section 1291 fund, since December 31, 1986. USP and FC both use the calendar year as their taxable year. USP has not included any amount in income under section 951 with respect to FC. On March 31, 1989, FC distributed $1000 to USP. As of that date, USP had held the FC stock for 821 days (365 days in 1987, 366 days in 1988, and 90 days in 1989). USP elects to credit foreign taxes for 1989, and determines the total creditable taxes with respect to the distribution from FC to be $485, $425 of which are deemed paid taxes and $60 of which are withholding taxes. The total distribution for 1989, including the section 78 gross-up, is $1425.

(ii) *Step 1: Determination of separate category income, U.S. source portions, and foreign taxes.* Applying the look through rules of section 904(d)(3), USP determines that $1125 of the total distribution of $1425 is allocable to distributions from a noncontrolled section 902 corporation, and that the remaining $300 is allocable to general limitation income. USP determines that $390 of creditable foreign taxes were paid and deemed paid with respect to the distributions from the noncontrolled section 902 corporation, and $95 were paid and deemed paid with respect to the general limitation income. USP determines that the distributions from the noncontrolled section 902 corporation and the general limitation income are from foreign sources. Accordingly, *Steps 3* and 5 (A)(3) will not be performed.

(iii) *Step 2: Calculation of total excess distribution and separate category excess distributions.* USP determines, based on FC distributions during the preceding three taxable years, that the total excess distribution for the current taxable year is $800. Of that amount, $631.58 [[$1125 (distribution allocable to distributions from a noncontrolled section 902 corporation)/$1425 (total distribution)] × $800 (total excess distribution)] is allocable to distributions from a noncontrolled section 902 corporation, and $168.42 [[$300 (distribution allocable to general limitation income)/$1425 (total distribution)] × $800 (total excess distribution)] is allocable to general limitation income.

(iv) *Step 4: Calculation of separate category excess distribution taxes.* USP calculates the excess distribution taxes (EDT) allocable to the separate category excess distributions. The noncontrolled section 902 corporation excess distribution taxes are $218.95 [$390 (creditable foreign taxes paid and deemed paid with respect to distributions from a noncontrolled section 902 corporation) × [$631.58 (noncontrolled section 902 corporation excess distribution)/$1125 (distribution from noncontrolled section 902 corporation)]], and the general limitation excess distribution taxes are $53.33 [$95 (creditable foreign taxes paid and deemed paid with respect to general limitation income) × [$168.42 (general limitation income excess distribution)/$300 (distribution allocable to general limitation income)]].

(v) *Step 5: Allocations of separate category excess distributions and excess distribution taxes over holding period.* The separate category excess distributions and the separate category EDT are allocated to each taxable year in USP's holding period based on the number of days in each such taxable year. (Discrepancies may be observed in the following presentation. These discrepancies reflect rounding to the nearest penny of the different calculations performed.)

(A) *Noncontrolled section 902 corporation excess distribution:* $.77 of the noncontrolled section 902 corporation excess distribution ($631.58/821 days) and $.27 of EDT ($218.95/821 days) are allocated to each day. The allocations to each taxable year are as follows:

	Allocations to taxable year	
Taxable year in holding period	*Excess distribution*	*EDT*
1987 (365 days)	$281.05	$98.55
1988 (366 days)	281.82	98.82
1989 (90 days)	69.30	24.30

(B) General limitation excess distribution: $.21 of the general limitation excess distribution ($168.42/821 days) and $.065 of EDT ($53.33/821 days) are allocated to each day. The allocations to each taxable year are as follows:

	Allocations to taxable year	
Taxable year in holding period	*Excess distribution*	*EDT*
1987 (365 days)	$76.65	$23.73
1988 (366 days)	76.86	23.79
1989 (90 days)	18.90	5.85 .

(vi) *Step 6: Calculation of separate category tentative increases in taxes.* USP determines the tentative increases in tax (TIIT) for the allocations of each separate category excess distribution to 1987 and 1988, the prior PFIC years in USP's holding period. The noncontrolled section 902 corporation excess distribution TIIT for 1987 is $112.28 [$281.05 (allocation of noncontrolled section 902 corporation excess distribution to 1987) × 39.95% (the highest corporate tax rate in effect in 1987)], and for 1988, $95.82 [$281.82 (allocation of noncontrolled section 902 corporation excess distribution to 1988) × 34% (highest corporate tax rate in effect in 1988)]. The general limitation excess distribution TIIT for 1987 is $30.62 [$76.65 (allocation of general limitation income excess distribution to 1987) × 39.95% (highest corporate tax rate in effect in 1987)], and for 1988, $26.13 [$76.86 (allocation of general limitation income excess distribution to 1988) × 34% (highest corporate tax rate in effect in 1988)].

(vii) *Step 7: Calculation of the foreign tax credit limitations.* USP determines the foreign tax credit (FTC) limitations for each prior PFIC year on a separate category basis. The FTC limitations are the same as the tentative increases in tax because none of the separate category distributions are from U.S. sources. Therefore, the FTC limitation for the noncontrolled section 902 corporation excess distribution for 1987 is $112.28, and for 1988, $95.82. The FTC limitation for the general limitation excess distribution for 1987 is $30.62, and for 1988, $26.13.

(viii) *Step 8: Calculation of the foreign tax credit.* The FTC for the noncontrolled section 902 corporation excess distribution for 1987 is $98.55 [lower of $112.28 (1987 noncontrolled section 902 corporation FTC limitation) and $98.55 (1987 noncontrolled section 902 corporation EDT)], and for 1988, $95.82 [lower of $95.82 (1988 noncontrolled section 902 corporation FTC limitation) and $98.82 (1988 noncontrolled section 902 corporation EDT)]. The FTC for the general limitation excess distribution for 1987 is $23.73 [lower of $30.62 (1987 general limitation FTC limitation) and $23.73 (1987 general limitation income EDT)], and for 1988 is $23.79 [lower of $26.13 (1988 general limitation income FTC limitation) and $23.79 (1988 general limitation EDT)].

(ix) *Step 9: Calculation of the separate category net increases in taxes.* As provided in § 1.1291-4(c)(3), USP determines the net increase in tax (NIIT) for each separate category excess distribution allocated to a prior PFIC year. The noncontrolled section 902 corporation NIIT for 1987 is $13.73 [$112.28 (1987 noncontrolled section 902 corporation TIIT) less $98.55 (1987 noncontrolled section 902 corporation FTC)], and the noncontrolled section 902 corporation NIIT for 1988 is 0 [$95.82 (1988 noncontrolled section 902 corporation TIIT) less $95.82 (1988 noncontrolled section 902 corporation FTC)]. The general limitation income NIIT for 1987 is $6.89 [$30.62 (1987 general limitation income TIIT) less $23.73 (1987 general limitation income FTC)], and the general limitation NIIT for 1988 is $2.34 [$26.13 (1988 general limitation income TIIT) less $23.79 (1988 general limitation income FTC)]. An interest charge is calculated for each NIIT as provided in § 1.1291-4(d). The $3 excess of noncontrolled section 902 EDT allocated to 1988 ($98.82) over the FTC limitation calculated for the 1988 allocation of the noncontrolled section 902 excess distribution ($95.82) may not be used to reduce any federal income tax. The calculations of *Steps 5* through *9* are summarized as follows:

(A) *Noncontrolled section 902 corporation excess distribution—*

Taxable year (days) in holding period	Allocations to taxable year—Step 5: Excess distribution	EDT	Step 6: TIIT	Step 8: FTC	Step 9: NIIT
1987 (365)	$281.05	$98.55	$112.28	$98.55	$13.73
1988 (366)	281.82	98.82	95.82	95.82	0
1989 (90)	69.30	24.30			

(B) *General limitation income excess distribution—*

Taxable year (days) in holding period	Allocations to taxable year—Step 5: Excess distribution	EDT	Step 6: TIIT	Step 8: FTC	Step 9: NIIT
1987 (365)	$76.65	$23.73	$30.62	$23.73	$6.89
1988 (366)	76.86	23.79	26.13	23.79	2.34
1989 (90)	69.30	24.30			

(x) *Current shareholder year foreign tax credit.* The allocations of the separate category excess distributions to 1989, the current shareholder year, are included in USP's ordinary income. Such income is treated as a dividend from a CFC that is not a PFIC, and the EDT allocated to that income are treated as foreign taxes paid with respect to a dividend from a CFC that is not a PFIC.

(d) *Distributions from section 1291 funds that are noncontrolled section 902 corporations.*—If a noncontrolled section 902 corporation (as defined in section 904(d)(2)(E) and the regulations under that section) that is a section 1291 fund makes a distribution with respect to which a domestic shareholder (as defined in section 902 and the regulations under that section) is subject to tax under § 1.1291-2, the rules of paragraph (c) of this section apply for purposes of determining the amount of the foreign tax credit with respect to that distribution; however, the only separate category is described in section 904(d)(1)(E). This paragraph (d) does not apply to a United States shareholder of a CFC to whom paragraph (c) of this section applies.

(e) *Section 1248 gain.*—For purposes of determining the foreign tax credit under this section, a shareholder treats gain from a disposition of stock of a section 1291 fund as a distribution only to the extent that the gain would be, but for section 1291, includible in gross income as a dividend under section 1248. [Reg. § 1.1291-5.]

§ 1.1291-6. Nonrecognition transfers of stock of section 1291 funds.—(a) *In general.*—(1) *Scope.*—This section provides rules concerning the recognition of gain by a shareholder on a direct or indirect disposition of stock of a section 1291 fund that results from a transaction in which, but for section 1291 and these regulations, there would not be full recognition of gain under the Code and regulations (the transaction hereinafter referred to as a nonrecognition transfer). This section also provides coordination between section 1291 and other provisions of the Code and regulations under which gain must be recognized in transactions that would otherwise be entitled to nonrecognition.

(2) *Nonrecognition transfers.*—A nonrecognition transfer includes, but is not limited to, a gift, a transfer by reason of death, a distribution to a beneficiary by a trust or estate (other than a distribution to which section 643(e)(3) applies), and a transfer in which gain or loss is not fully recognized pursuant to any of the following provisions: Sections 311(a), 332, 336(e), 337, 351, 354, 355, 361, 721, 731, 852(b)(6), 1036, and 1041.

(3) *Application of section to transfer of stock of a pedigreed QEF.*—This section does not apply to a nonrecognition transfer of stock of a pedigreed QEF. The following example illustrates the rule of this paragraph (a)(3).

Example. X is a U.S. person that is a shareholder of FC, a corporation. FC owns all the stock of FS. Both FC and FS are pedigreed QEFs with respect to X. Pursuant to a plan of complete liquidation, satisfying the requirements of section 332, FS distributes all its assets and liabilities to FC. No gain or loss will be recognized to FC, FS, or X under section 1291(f) or 1297(b)(5).

(b) *Recognition of gain or loss.*—(1) *In general.*—Unless otherwise provided in paragraph (c) of this section, a shareholder recognizes gain on any direct or indirect disposition of stock of a section 1291 fund in accordance with the rules of § 1.1291-3, without regard to whether the disposition is a result of a nonrecognition transfer as defined in paragraph (a)(2) of this section.

(2) *Coordination with other recognition provisions.*—A direct or indirect disposition of stock to which an exception to the gain recognition rule of paragraph (b)(1) of this section applies will nevertheless be a disposition taxable under § 1.1291-3 if the gain must be recognized pursuant to another provision of the Code or regulations. For coordination with section 367, *see* paragraph (d)(1) of this section.

(3) *No recognition of loss.*—This section does not permit or require the recognition of loss on a direct or indirect disposition of stock of a section 1291 fund if such loss would not otherwise be recognized under another section of the Code or regulations. For the effect on the holding period of a disposition resulting from a nonrecognition transfer that would be subject to the gain recognition rule but for the fact that a loss is realized, *see* paragraph (b)(5) of this section.

(4) *Special basis rules.*—(i) *Direct shareholders.*—If the gain recognition rule of paragraph (b)(1) of this section applies to a nonrecognition transfer in which a direct shareholder transfers stock of a section 1291 fund, proper adjustment is made to the basis of such stock in the hands of the transferee, as well as to the basis of the property, if any, received by the shareholder in the transaction.

(ii) *Indirect shareholders.*—If the gain recognition rule of paragraph (b)(1) of this section applies to a disposition by an indirect shareholder that results from a nonrecognition transfer, the shareholder's adjusted basis of the stock or other property owned directly by the shareholder through which ownership of the section 1291 fund is attributed to the shareholder is increased by the amount of gain recognized by the shareholder. In addition, solely for purposes of determining the subsequent treatment under the Code and regulations of a direct or indirect shareholder of the stock of the section 1291 fund treated as disposed of, the adjusted basis of the actual owner of the stock of the section 1291 fund is increased by the amount of gain recognized by the shareholder.

(iii) *Stock acquired by reason of death.*—Unless all of the gain is recognized to a shareholder (the decedent) pursuant to paragraph (c)(2)(iii)(B) of this section, the basis of stock received on the death of the decedent by the decedent's estate (other than a foreign estate within the meaning of section 7701(a)(31)), or directly by another U.S. person, is the lower of the fair market value or adjusted basis of the transferred stock in the hands of the shareholder immediately before death. If gain is recognized by the decedent, the decedent's adjusted basis of the stock of the section 1291 fund is increased by the gain recognized with respect thereto.

(iv) *Assets distributed in certain subsidiary liquidations.*—The bases of the assets of a section 1291 fund distributed to an 80 percent corporate distributee (within the meaning of section 337(c)), in complete liquidation of the section 1291 fund pursuant to section 332, is increased by the amount by which the gain recognized by the shareholder exceeds the amount that would have been taxed as a dividend under section 367(b). Except as otherwise provided in this paragraph (b)(4)(iv), the adjusted basis of each distributed asset is increased (but not in excess of its fair market value) by a pro rata portion of the excess described in the preceding sentence, based on the realized but unrecognized gain with respect to such asset relative to the realized but unrecognized gain with respect to all distributed assets. For purposes of the preceding sentence, money is not treated as an asset. The adjusted basis of a receivable may not be increased pursuant to this paragraph (b)(4)(iv) to an amount that exceeds the receivable's face amount.

(5) *Special holding period rule for transfers subject to gain recognition rule.*—If a loss is realized on a direct or indirect disposition of stock of a section 1291 fund in a transaction in which any gain, if realized, would have been recognized under this section, the shareholder's holding period for stock received in the transaction, if any, as well as the transferee's holding period of the transferred stock, begins on the day after the disposition, but only for purposes of applying sections 1291 through 1297 to the shareholder or the transferee with respect to such stock, as appropriate.

(c) *Exceptions to general rule.*—(1) *Transfer of section 1291 fund stock for PFIC stock.*—Gain is not recognized on a direct or indirect disposition of stock of a section 1291 fund that results from a nonrecognition transfer if in the transfer, stock of the section 1291 fund, or an interest in another person that causes the shareholder to be an indirect shareholder, is exchanged solely for either—

(i) Stock of the same or another corporation that either qualifies under section 1296(a) as a PFIC for its taxable year that includes the day after the nonrecognition transfer or is the acquiring foreign corporation in a section 368(a)(1)(F) reorganization; or

(ii) An interest in another person that owns directly or indirectly stock of the transferred section 1291 fund or of another PFIC, but only to the extent (by value) that the shareholder is treated under § 1.1291-1(b)(8) as owning after the transfer at least as great an interest in the section 1291 fund or other PFIC that the indirect shareholder owned before the transfer. Stock in another PFIC owned before the transfer is not taken into account for purposes of the preceding sentence. For the definition of an indirect disposition, *see* generally § 1.1291-3(e)(2).

(2) *Transfer to U.S. person.*—(i) *In general.*—Unless otherwise provided, a shareholder does not recognize gain on a direct or indirect disposition of stock of a section 1291 fund that results from a nonrecognition transfer if immediately after the transfer such stock is owned or considered owned by a U.S. person (U.S. transferee), provided that—

(A) The basis of the stock that is the subject of the disposition, in the hands of its actual owner immediately after the transfer, is no greater than the basis of such stock in the hands of its actual owner immediately before the transfer;

(B) The U.S. transferee's holding period for the transferred stock is at least as long as the holding period of the shareholder immediately before the transfer; and

(C) The aggregate ownership (determined under § 1.1291-1(b)(8)) of the shareholder and the U.S. transferee immediately after the transfer (determined without regard to stock held by the U.S. transferee prior to the transfer) is the same as or greater than the shareholder's proportionate ownership immediately before the transfer.

This paragraph (c)(2)(i) does not apply to a transfer to a partnership, S corporation, trust or estate. For those rules, *see* paragraph (c)(3) of this section.

(ii) *Transitory ownership.*—Gain is not recognized to a domestic corporation that is a party to a reorganization within the meaning of section 368(b) if, pursuant to a plan of reorganization, the corporation acquires stock of a PFIC that is a party to the reorganization in exchange for the domestic corporation's assets, and transfers the PFIC stock under section 361(c) to a shareholder that is a U.S. person in exchange for the shareholder's stock of the domestic corporation.

(iii) *Transfer by reason of death.*—(A) *In general.*—Except as provided in paragraph (c)(2)(iii)(B) of this section, gain is not recognized to a shareholder upon a disposition of stock of a section 1291 fund that results from a nonrecognition transfer to the shareholder's domestic estate or directly to another U.S. person upon the death of the shareholder.

(B) *Exception.*—Gain is recognized to a shareholder on the transfer of stock of a section 1291 fund to the shareholder's domestic estate if, pursuant to the terms of the will, the section 1291 fund stock may be transferred to either a foreign beneficiary or a trust established in the will.

(iv) *Section 355 distribution of stock of section 1291 fund.*—Gain is not recognized to a shareholder that is the distributing corporation upon a direct or indirect disposition of stock of a section 1291 fund that results from the distribution of stock of a controlled corporation to another U.S. person (the distributee) in a transaction qualifying under section 355(a) if the distributee is a shareholder with respect to such stock immediately after the distribution. The distributee in such a transaction takes a holding period in the stock of the controlled corporation equal to the longer of the holding period determined under section 1223(1) or the distributing corporation's holding period of the stock of the controlled corporation. If the controlled corporation is itself the section 1291 fund, the distributee in such a transaction takes a basis in the stock of the controlled corporation equal to the lesser of the adjusted basis determined under section 358 or the distributing corporation's adjusted basis of the stock of the controlled corporation immediately prior to the distribution.

(v) *Gifts incurring gift tax.*—If a shareholder makes a gift of stock of a section 1291 fund to a U.S. person and thereby incurs gift tax, the shareholder will not recognize gain, but will be liable for the deferred tax amount as if the shareholder recognized gain in the amount of the gift tax that is added to the basis of the transferred stock under section 1015(d). The adjusted basis of the transferred stock may only be increased, to the extent provided in section 1015(d), by the amount of gift tax paid. The following example illustrates the rule of this paragraph (c)(2)(v).

Example. M, a U.S. person, purchased 1,000 shares of NQF, a PFIC, on December 31, 1989. M did not elect to treat NQF as a QEF. M gave the NQF stock to her daughter, H, also a U.S. person, on December 31, 1993. M paid $100x of gift tax. As provided in section 1015(a) and (d)(6), H's adjusted basis in the NQF stock is M's adjusted basis, increased by $60x of gift tax paid. As a result, pursuant to §1.1291-6(c)(2)(v), M is liable for the deferred tax amount that M would have owed if M recognized $60x of gain on a taxable transfer of the NQF stock. For purposes of calculating the deferred tax amount, the $60x is allocated over M's four-year holding period, with the deferred tax amount calculated with respect to the $45x allocated to 1991, 1992, and 1993. Other than for the $60x of gift tax paid, there are no further adjustments to H's basis in the NQF.

(vi) *Exception inapplicable.*—Paragraph (c)(2) of this section does not apply to a disposition of stock of a section 1291 fund that results from a nonrecognition transfer of stock of a section 1291 fund if the U.S. transferee is—

(A) An organization that will not be subject to section 1291 and these regulations pursuant to § 1.1291-1(e) with respect to that section 1291 fund; or

(B) A trust, including a testamentary trust or other irrevocable trust, that is not a grantor trust or beneficiary-owned section 678 trust to which paragraph (c)(3)(iv) of this section applies.

(3) *Transfers involving pass-through entities.*—(i) *Section 721 transfer to partnership.*—Gain is not recognized to a shareholder on a disposition of stock of a section 1291 fund that results from a transfer to a partnership under section 721, but only to the extent that the shareholder is treated as owning such stock immediately after the transfer pursuant to § 1.1291-1(b)(8)(iii)(A).

(ii) *Section 731 distribution by partnership.*—Gain is not recognized to a partner on a disposition of stock of a section 1291 fund that results from a distribution under section 731, but only to the extent that the partner is treated as owning such stock immediately after the distribution pursuant to § 1.1291-1(b)(8).

(iii) *Transfer to S corporation.*—Gain is not recognized to a shareholder on a disposition of stock of a section 1291 fund that results from a transfer to an S corporation under section 351, but only to the extent that the shareholder is treated as owning such stock immediately after the transfer pursuant to § 1.1291-1(b)(8)(iii)(B).

(iv) *Transfer to grantor trust.*—Gain is not recognized on a disposition of stock of a section 1291 fund that results from a nonrecognition transfer to a trust by the grantor of the trust if the grantor is treated as owning the portion of the trust that includes both the income and corpus portions of the stock that is disposed of. If a person other than the grantor is treated as the owner of the portion of a beneficiary-owned section 678 trust that includes the income and corpus portions of the stock transferred to the trust, that person is treated as acquiring the stock by gift from the grantor, which is a transfer subject to the general rules of this section. Stock owned directly or indirectly by a grantor of a grantor trust or by a beneficiary of a beneficiary-owned section 678 trust will be treated as transferred by the grantor or other person considered the owner thereof for purposes of this section at the time the grantor or beneficiary is no longer considered the owner of both the income and corpus portions of the stock of the section 1291 fund. For special rules applicable to a grantor or beneficiary-owned section 678 trust, *see* sections 671 through 679 and the regulations under those sections.

(4) *Transfer to nonresident alien spouse who files joint return.*—Gain is not recognized on a disposition of stock of a section 1291 fund that results from a nonrecognition transfer to the shareholder's nonresident alien spouse who has made the election under section 6013(g) and is treated as a resident for purposes of chapter 1 of the Code. A termination of the election pursuant to section 6013(g)(4) will be treated as a disposition of the stock by the transferee spouse as provided in § 1.1291-3(b)(2).

(d) *Special rules.*—(1) *Section 367 or 1492 transfer.*—(i) *Gain recognition transfer.*—If the gain recognition rule of paragraph (b)(1) of this section applies to a disposition of stock of a section 1291 fund that results from a transfer with respect to which section 367 or 1492 requires the shareholder to recognize gain or include an amount in income as a distribution under section 301, the gain realized on the transfer is taxable as an excess distribution as provided in § 1.1291-2(e)(2). The excess, if any, of the amount to be included in income pursuant to section 367(b) over the gain realized is taxable as provided in the regulations under section 367(b).

(ii) *Disposition to which exception applies.*—If an exception to the gain recognition rule of paragraph (b)(1) of this section applies to a disposition to which section 367(b) applies, and section 367(b) requires the shareholder to include an amount in income as a distribution taxable under section 301, that amount is an excess distribution taxable as provided in § 1.1291-2(e)(2).

(2) *Taxable year of disposition by reason of death.*—A disposition of stock of a section 1291

fund by reason of a shareholder's death, to which the gain recognition rule of paragraph (b)(1) or (c)(2)(iii)(B) of this section applies, will be treated as a disposition by the shareholder effected immediately before death and taxable to the shareholder in the shareholder's last taxable year.

(3) *Section 643(e)(3) election.*—An election by a foreign estate or trust under section 643(e)(3) will not apply to stock of a section 1291 fund distributed to a U.S. person if the gain recognized by reason of the election is not taxable in the United States.

(e) *Receipt of nonqualifying property.*—If a nonrecognition transfer results in a disposition of stock of a section 1291 fund to which an exception to the gain recognition rule of paragraph (b)(1) of this section would apply but for the fact that the property received in the transfer includes money or property (nonqualifying property) in addition to property permitted to be received pursuant to paragraph (c) of this section, gain is recognized only to the extent of the nonqualifying property. If such nonqualifying property is treated as a distribution by the section 1291 fund under otherwise applicable provisions of the Code, the distribution will be taxable on an excess distribution as provided in §1.1291-2(e)(2).

(f) *Examples.*—The following examples illustrate the operation of this section.

Example 1. A is a shareholder of PFIC, a corporation organized under the laws of Country X. PFIC is a section 1291 fund with respect to A. To avoid expropriation of the assets of PFIC by the government of Country X, PFIC's management has decided to relocate to Country Y. To effect the relocation, PFIC adopted a plan of reorganization pursuant to which PFIC will transfer all of its assets to Newco, a newly organized Country Y corporation, in exchange for Newco stock and the assumption of PFIC's liabilities in a transaction that will qualify as a reorganization described in section 368(a)(1)(F). PFIC will distribute the Newco stock to its shareholders in exchange for its stock. A will transfer all of its PFIC stock in exchange for Newco stock of equal value. A will not recognize gain on the transfer of PFIC stock in exchange for Newco stock pursuant to section 354 and §1.1291-6(c)(1)(i), and the days in A's holding period of the Newco stock will retain the prePFIC and prior PFIC character of the days in A's holding period of the PFIC stock pursuant to §1.1291-1(h)(7). *See* §1.1291-1(b)(1)(ii).

Example 2. X is a domestic corporation that owns 75 percent of F, a foreign corporation that is not a PFIC. F owns 100 percent of the stock of FS, a PFIC. X is treated under §1.1291-1(b)(8)(ii)(A) as owning 75 percent of the stock of FS. X has not elected under section 1295 to treat FS as a QEF. FC, a foreign corporation, will acquire substantially all the assets of F in exchange for FC stock and the assumption of the liabilities of F in a transaction that will qualify as a reorganization described in section 368(a)(1)(C). FC never qualified as a PFIC and will not qualify as a PFIC at the beginning of the day after the transaction. F will distribute the FC stock to its shareholders in exchange for their F stock. X will transfer all its F stock to F in exchange for FC stock of equal value. After the reorganization, X will hold 49 percent of the outstanding FC stock, and therefore will no longer be treated under §1.1291-1(b)(8)(ii)(A) as owning stock of FS. Pursuant to §§1.1291-6(b)(1) and 1.1291-3(e)(1), X will be taxed on the indirect disposition of the FS stock.

Example 3. X, a domestic corporation, owns stock of PFIC, a corporation that is a section 1291 fund with respect to X. Pursuant to a plan of reorganization, X will transfer to FC, a foreign corporation, substantially all of its assets in exchange for FC voting stock and FC's assumption of the liabilities of X in a transaction that will qualify as a reorganization described in section 368(a)(1)(C). It is assumed that the transaction is not taxable under section 367(a) (including section 367(a)(5)). X will distribute the FC stock to its shareholders in exchange for their X stock. FC is not a PFIC and will not qualify as a PFIC for the taxable year that includes the day after the transfer. In addition, after the reorganization, no U.S. person will own 50 percent or more of FC. Pursuant to §1.1291-6(b)(1), section 361(a) will not apply to X's transfer of the PFIC stock to FC. X therefore will recognize the gain realized on the transfer of the stock of PFIC. The gain will be taxed to X as an excess distribution pursuant to §1.1291-3.

Example 4. X, a domestic corporation, satisfies the stock ownership requirements specified in section 332(b) with respect to PFIC, a corporation that is a section 1291 fund with respect to X. Pursuant to a plan of complete liquidation, PFIC will distribute all its assets and liabilities to X in exchange for its stock and liquidate. Pursuant to §1.1291-6(b)(1) and (d)(1)(i), section 332(a) will not apply to the complete liquidation of PFIC. X therefore will recognize gain on the disposition of the stock of PFIC, which gain will be taxed as an excess distribution pursuant to §1.1291-3. The adjusted basis of the assets of X will be increased as provided in §1.1291-6(b)(4)(iv).

Example 5. USP, a domestic corporation, owns all the stock of USS, also a domestic corporation. USS owns stock of FS, a corporation that is a section 1291 fund with respect to USS. Pursuant to a plan of reorganization that will qualify under section 368(a)(1)(C), USS will transfer substantially all its assets to FC, a PFIC, in exchange for FC stock and the assumption by FC of the liabilities of USS. USS will transfer the FC stock to USP in exchange for its stock. Pursuant to §1.1291-6(c)(1), section 361 applies to USS's transfer to FC of the FS stock. As provided in §1.1291-6(c)(2)(ii), USS will not recognize any gain on the transfer of the FC stock to USP in exchange for its stock.

Example 6. A, a U.S. person, owns all the stock of FC, a corporation that is both a controlled foreign corporation and a section 1291 fund with respect to A. Pursuant to a reorganization plan, FC will transfer all its assets to F, a foreign corporation that is a PFIC but not a controlled foreign corporation after the transfer, in exchange for F stock and the assumption of FC's liabilities in a transaction that will qualify as a reorganization described in section 368(a)(1)(C). FC will distribute the F stock to A in exchange for A's FC stock. A will not recognize gain on the transfer of FC stock in exchange for F stock pursuant to section 354 and §1.1291-6(c)(1). However, the regulations under section 367(b) require A to include a certain amount in gross income as a distribution taxable under section

301. As provided in §1.1291-6(d)(1)(ii), A will treat that amount as an excess distribution taxable as provided in §1.1291-2(e)(2).

Example 7. M, a U.S. person, purchased 100 shares of the stock of NQF on December 31, 1989, for $100. NQF is a corporation that is a section 1291 fund with respect to M. On January 1, 1992, when the 100 shares of NQF stock had a fair market value of $200, M transferred its NQF stock to P, a domestic partnership, of which M and N, also a U.S. person, are equal partners. After the transfer to P, M will be considered to own only 50 shares of the NQF stock pursuant to §1.1291-1(b)(8)(iii)(A), notwithstanding that gain recognized with respect to all 100 shares would be allocated to M pursuant to section 704(c). M therefore is taxable on the disposition of 50 shares of NQF stock in accordance with §1.1291-6(c)(3)(i).

(g) *Reporting requirements for transfers entitled to nonrecognition treatment under this section.*—If an exception to the gain recognition rule of paragraph (b)(1) of this section applies wholly or partly to a disposition of stock of a section 1291 fund that results from a nonrecognition transfer, the shareholder must provide the following information in an attachment to Form 8621, which must be filed with the shareholder's federal income tax return for the taxable year in which the transfer occurs:

(1) A complete description of the transfer, including a complete description of the stock, securities or other property received directly or indirectly in the transfer.

(2) The name, address, and taxpayer identification number (if available) of the transferor and transferee of the transferred property.

(3) A statement citing the applicable exception to the gain recognition rule and stating why the exception is applicable.

(h) *Transfers involving QEF stock.*—For rules concerning the effect of a transfer of stock of a QEF on the section 1295 election, *see* §1.1295-1. [Reg. §1.1291-6.]

§1.1291-7. Section 1291(e) rules similar to section 1246.—[Reserved]

Passive Foreign Investment Companies: Qualified Electing Funds: Shareholders

Passive Foreign Investment Companies: Qualified Electing Funds: Shareholders.—Reproduced below is the text of proposed Reg. §1.1293-1, relating to the taxation of shareholders of certain passive foreign investment companies (PFICs) upon payment of distributions by such companies or upon the disposition of stock of such companies (published in the Federal Register on April 1, 1992) (INTL-941-86; INTL-656-87; INTL-704-87). Reg. §§1.1291-0, 1.1291-9 and 1.1291-10 were adopted by T.D. 8701 on December 26, 1996. Proposed Reg. §1.1291-8 was withdrawn on February 2, 1999.

☐ Par. 6. Section 1.1293-1 is added to read as follows:

§1.1293-1. Current taxation of income from qualified electing funds.—(a) *In general.*—Pursuant to section 1293(a)(1), every U.S. person that is a direct or indirect shareholder of a PFIC during a taxable year of the PFIC for which the shareholder has in effect a section 1295 election (within the meaning of §1.1295-1(a)) includes in gross income the shareholder's pro rata share of the ordinary earnings and net capital gain of such fund for that taxable year. Such amounts are included in income in the taxable year of the shareholder in which or with which the taxable year of the PFIC ends. Section 1293 applies to a shareholder of a pedigreed QEF (as defined in §1.1291-1(b)(2)(ii)) only for those taxable years during which the corporation qualifies as a PFIC under section 1296(a). Section 1293 applies to a shareholder of an unpedigreed QEF (as defined in §1.1291-1(b)(2)(iii)) for those taxable years during which the corporation is a PFIC (as defined in §1.1291-1(b)(1)).

(b) *Other rules.*—[Reserved][Reg. §1.1293-1.]

PFICs: Shareholders: Qualified Electing Fund Elections

PFICs: Shareholders: Qualified Electing Fund Elections.—Reg. §1.1293-2, relating to permitting certain shareholders to make a special election under Code Sec. 1295, in lieu of the election currently provided for under that section, with respect to certain preferred shares of a passive foreign investment company (PFIC), is proposed (published in the Federal Register on December 24, 1996) (REG-209040-88).

☐ Par. 2. Section 1.1293-2 is added to read as follows:

§1.1293-2. Special inclusion rules for special preferred QEF election.—(a) *In general.*—A shareholder (including a shareholder that is a pass-through entity, as described in §1.1295-2(c)(1)) that makes a special preferred QEF election under §1.1295-2 must, regardless of the shareholder's method of accounting, include in income in respect of each share subject to the election, an annual amount (preferred QEF amount) determined according to the rules of paragraph (b) of this section. A shareholder that makes a special preferred QEF election must include the preferred QEF amount in income under this section for each year in which the taxpayer continues to hold a share that is subject to the election. The rules of this section apply in lieu of the general rules of section 1293 and §1.1293-1.[1]

(b) *Preferred QEF amount.*—(1) *In general.*—The preferred QEF amount for any share subject

[1] This proposed regulation was published on April 1, 1992, at 57 Fed. Reg. 11024.

to a special preferred QEF election is the sum of the ratable daily portion of each periodic dividend amount (as described in paragraph (b)(2) of this section) on the share for the taxable year of the shareholder to which that portion relates, plus the preferred discount amount (as defined below), if any, for the taxable year. For purposes of this section, the preferred discount amount for a taxable year is the amount that bears the same ratio to the total amount of preferred discount (as described in § 1.1295-2(b)(2)(i)) on the share as the number of days that the taxpayer held the share in the taxable year bears to the number of days after the date the taxpayer acquired the share and up to (and including) the share's redemption date as established under the principles of § 1.305-5(b). Notwithstanding the preceding sentence, the preferred discount amount for a taxable year is zero if the preferred discount on the share at the time of its acquisition by the shareholder was less than an amount equal to 1/4 of 1 percent of the redemption price of the stock, multiplied by the number of complete years from the date of acquisition of the stock to the redemption date of the stock.

(2) *Periodic dividend amount.*—A periodic dividend amount is the amount payable with respect to a share, whether on a cumulative or noncumulative basis, for a period (wholly or partly within the shareholder's taxable year) for which dividends on the share are calculated based upon the redemption or liquidation price of the share multiplied by a fixed percentage rate.

(c) *Special rules of application.*—(1) *Earnings and profits disregarded.*—The amounts to be included in income pursuant to this section are determined without regard to the earnings and profits of the foreign corporation with respect to which the special preferred QEF election applies.

(2) *Year of inclusion.*—The shareholder includes the preferred QEF amount in its taxable year without regard to the taxable year of the foreign corporation with respect to which the special preferred QEF election applies.

(3) *Character of inclusions.*—The shareholder includes all preferred QEF amounts in income as ordinary earnings.

(4) *Treatment of distributions.*—Distributions received by a shareholder on shares subject to a special preferred QEF election that are paid out of earnings and profits of the foreign corporation are not included in gross income of the shareholder to the extent the distributions do not exceed the preferred QEF amounts (other than any portion of preferred QEF amounts consisting of preferred discount amounts) previously includible in income pursuant to this section. These distributions will, however, be treated as dividends for all other purposes of the Code and regulations. Amounts distributed to a shareholder with respect to shares subject to a special preferred QEF election that exceed amounts previously included in income under this section with respect to such shares are treated for all purposes of the Code and regulations as a distribution of property subject to the rules of section 301.

(5) *Basis adjustment rules.*—The adjusted basis of a shareholder in shares that are subject to a special preferred QEF election shall be—

(i) Increased by any amount that is included in the gross income of the shareholder under paragraph (a) of this section; and

(ii) Decreased by any dividends (not to exceed the amount included in gross income under paragraph (a) of this section) actually paid to the shareholder in respect of such shares.

(6) *Effect limited to electing shareholder.*—This section does not apply to the foreign corporation with respect to which a special preferred QEF election applies. Accordingly, the provisions of this section will not affect the foreign corporation's calculation of its earnings and profits for any purpose of the Code or regulations. In addition, the rules of this section apply only for purposes of determining the tax consequences for holders of shares subject to the election. Thus, the election shall have no effect on the application of the Code or regulations with respect to the tax consequences of the ownership of shares that are not subject to the election, including for purposes of determining whether any distributions from the foreign corporation with respect to such shares should be treated as having been included in the income of any United States person pursuant to section 1293(c) or section 959.

(d) *Examples.*—The following examples illustrate the rules of paragraphs (a), (b) and (c) of this section. Although these examples assume a 30-day month, 360-day year, any reasonable counting method may be used to compute the length of accrual periods. For purposes of simplicity, the relevant amounts as stated are rounded to two decimal places. However, the computations do not reflect any such rounding convention. The examples are as follows:

Example 1. Preferred QEF amount—(i) *Facts.* (A) On May 1, 1998, A, an individual who files his returns on a calendar year basis, purchased for $10,000 in a single secondary market transaction 100 shares of nonconvertible Class A $100 par value preferred stock (the Class A Stock) of FC, a foreign corporation with a taxable year ending on March 31.

(B) The terms of the Class A Stock provide for a mandatory redemption of the Class A Stock by the issuer at par on June 1, 2012. The Class A Stock is not redeemable pursuant to an issuer call or holder put on any other date. Each share of Class A Stock provides for a semi-annual cumulative distribution payable in dollars on June 1 and December 1 equal to one-half the product of the par value of the Class A Stock and the applicable annual dollar LIBOR in effect on the distribution date immediately prior to the relevant distribution date. The shares of the Class A stock are qualified preferred shares in the hands of A. A purchases no other qualified preferred shares of FC during its 1998 or 1999 taxable years.

(C) A made a special preferred QEF election for A's taxable year ended December 31, 1998, which applies to the Class A Stock acquired by A on May 1, 1998. FC is a PFIC under section 1296 for its taxable year ending March 31, 1999, but FC is not a PFIC for its taxable year ending March 31, 2000. FC paid no current dividends on June 1, 1998, and December 1, 1998, paid the June 1, 1999, dividend currently on June 1, 1999, together with accumulated distributions from June 1, 1998, and December 1, 1998, and paid the December 1, 1999, dividend currently on December 1, 1999. The applicable annual LIBOR is 8 percent on December 1, 1997, 7 percent on June 1, 1998, 9 percent on December 1, 1998, 10 percent on June 1, 1999, and 9 percent on December 1, 1999. FC had sufficient earnings and profits, within the meaning of section 312, for its taxable year ending on March 31, 2000, so that actual distributions to all shareholders of Class A Stock in that year were treated as paid out of earnings and profits of FC.

(ii) *Tax consequences to A for A's taxable year ending December 31, 1998*. As required under paragraph (a) of this section, A must include in gross income for its 1998 taxable year the 1998 preferred QEF amount. The preferred QEF amount, as determined under paragraph (b) of this section, for A's 1998 taxable year is the ratable portion of each periodic dividend amount for that year. For 1998, there are three periodic dividend amounts: The periodic dividend amount for the period from December 1, 1997, to June 1, 1998 (periodic dividend amount 1), the periodic dividend amount for the period from June 1, 1998, to December 1, 1998 (periodic dividend amount 2), and the periodic dividend amount for the period from December 1, 1998, to June 1, 1999 (periodic dividend amount 3). Periodic dividend amount 1 in respect of each share owned by A is $4 (1/2 multiplied by the applicable annual LIBOR of 8 percent set on December 1, 1997, multiplied by the $100 amount payable on redemption). Because A acquired the shares on May 1, 1998, A's ratable portion of periodic dividend amount 1 for 1998 is approximately $.67 (30/180 multiplied by $4) per share. Periodic dividend amount 2 in respect of each share owned by A is $3.50 (1/2 multiplied by the applicable annual LIBOR of 7 percent set on June 1, 1998, multiplied by $100). Because A owned the shares for the entire period associated with periodic dividend amount 2, A's ratable portion of periodic dividend amount 2 for 1998 is the full $3.50 per share. Periodic dividend amount 3 in respect of each share owned by A is $4.50 (1/2 multiplied by the applicable annual LIBOR of 9 percent set on December 1, 1998, multiplied by $100). Because the portion of 1998 associated with periodic dividend amount 3 is only the month of December, 1998, A's ratable portion of periodic dividend amount 3 for 1998 is approximately $.75 (30/180 multiplied by $4.50). Accordingly, A's preferred QEF amount for 1998 is approximately $4.92 ($.67 + $3.5 + $.75) per share. A must include approximately $492 (approximately $4.92 per share, multiplied by 100 shares) in income as ordinary earnings for its 1998 tax year even though FC paid no actual dividend to shareholders of Class A Stock for the period in 1998 during which A held the Class A Stock.

(iii) *Tax consequences to A for A's taxable year ending December 31, 1999*. As required under paragraph (a) of this section, A includes in gross income for its 1999 taxable year its preferred QEF amount for 1999. The preferred QEF amount, as determined under paragraph (b) of this section, for A's 1999 taxable year is the ratable portion of each periodic dividend amount for that year. For 1999, there are three periodic dividend amounts: The periodic dividend amount for the period from December 1, 1998, to June 1, 1999 (periodic dividend amount 1), the periodic dividend amount for the period from June 1, 1999, to December 1, 1999 (periodic dividend amount 2), and the periodic dividend amount for the period from December 1, 1999, to June 1, 2000 (periodic dividend amount 3). Periodic dividend amount 1 in respect of each share owned by A is $4.50 (1/2 multiplied by the applicable annual LIBOR of 9 percent set on December 1, 1998, multiplied by $100). Because A held each share of Class A Stock for five months in 1999 for the period associated with periodic dividend amount 1, A's ratable portion of periodic dividend amount 1 for 1999 is approximately $3.75 (150/180 multiplied by $4.50). Periodic dividend amount 2 in respect of each share owned by A is $5 (1/2 multiplied by the applicable annual LIBOR of 10 percent set on June 1, 1999, multiplied by $100). Because A owned the share for the entire period associated with periodic dividend amount 2, A's ratable portion of periodic dividend amount 2 for 1999 is the full $5. Periodic dividend amount 3 in respect of each share owned by A is $4.50 (1/2 multiplied by the applicable annual LIBOR of 9 percent set on December 1, 1999, multiplied by $100). Because A held each share of Class A Stock for one month in 1999 for the period associated with periodic dividend amount 3, A's ratable portion of periodic dividend amount 3 for 1999 is approximately $.75 (30/180 multiplied by $4.50). Accordingly, A's preferred QEF amount for 1998 is approximately $9.50 ($3.75 + $5 + $.75). A must include approximately $950 ($9.50 per share, multiplied by 100 shares) in income as ordinary income for its 1999 taxable year even though FC was not a PFIC for FC's taxable year ending in 2000. The current distributions and arrearages actually paid to A with respect to the Class A Stock are not includible in income by A under paragraph (c)(4) of this section because they constitute amounts previously included in income.

Example 2. Preferred Discount—(i) *Facts*. The facts are the same as in *Example 1* except that A acquired the 100 shares of Class A Stock for $9000.

(ii) *Tax Consequences to A for A's taxable year ending December 31, 1998*. (A) Because the Class A Stock is fixed term preferred stock (as described in § 1.1295-2(b)(1)(vii)) and A acquired each share of the Class A stock with $10 of preferred discount, as described in § 1.1295-2(b)(2), A's preferred QEF amount to be included by A for the taxable year consists of the sum of the ratable daily portion of each periodic dividend amount, as calculated in paragraph (d)(ii) of *Example 1* of this section, plus the preferred discount amount described in paragraph (b)(1) of this section.

(B) The preferred discount amount with respect to each share is approximately $.47 ($10 multiplied by 240 days/5070 days to maturity). A must include approximately $47 ($.47 per share, multiplied by 100 shares), together with the amount calculated in paragraph (d)(ii) of *Example 1* of this section, in income as ordinary earnings for its 1998 tax year even though FC paid no actual dividend to shareholders of Class A Shares for the period in 1998 during which A held the Class A Stock.

(iii) *Tax consequences to A for A's taxable year ending December 31, 1999*. The portion of the preferred discount on each share includible under paragraph (a) of this section is approximately

$.71 ($10 multiplied by 360 days/5070 days to maturity). A must include this amount, together with the amount calculated in paragraph (d)(iii) of *Example 1* of this section, in income as ordinary earnings for its 1999 tax year even though FC was not a PFIC for FC's taxable year ending in 2000. The current distributions and arrearages actually paid to A in 1999 with respect to the Class A Stock are not includible in income by A under paragraph (c)(4) of this section, because they constitute amounts previously included in income.

(e) *Effective date.*—The rules under this section apply with respect to qualified preferred stock subject to a special preferred QEF election made after the date that is 30 days after the date of publication of this document as a final regulation. [Reg. § 1.1293-2.]

Passive Foreign Investment Companies

Passive Foreign Investment Companies: Elections.—Temporary Reg. § 1.1294-1T, relating to requirements for making certain elections by passive foreign investment companies and their shareholders that are United States persons, is also proposed as a final regulation and, when adopted, would become Reg. § 1.1294-1 (published in the Federal Register on March 2, 1988). Temporary Reg. § 1.1295-1T was removed by T.D. 8404, March 31, 1992. Temporary Reg. § 1.1291-0T was reserved by T.D. 8750, December 31, 1997. Temporary Reg. § 1.1297-3T was adopted by T.D. 9231, December 7, 2005.

§ 1.1294-1. Extension to extend the time for payment of tax on undistributed earnings of a qualified electing fund.

Passive Foreign Investment Companies: Qualified Electing Funds: Shareholders

Passive Foreign Investment Companies: Qualified Electing Funds: Shareholders.—Reproduced below is the text of proposed Reg. § 1.1295-1, relating to the taxation of shareholders of certain passive foreign investment companies (PFICs) upon payment of distributions by such companies or upon the disposition of stock of such companies (published in the Federal Register on April 1, 1992) (INTL-941-86; INTL-656-87; INTL-704-87). Reg. §§ 1.1291-0, 1.1291-9 and 1.1291-10 were adopted by T.D. 8701 on December 26, 1996. Proposed Reg. § 1.1291-8 was withdrawn on February 2, 1999.

☐ Par. 7. Section 1.1295-1 is added to read as follows:

§ 1.1295-1. Qualified electing funds.—(a) *In general.*—This section provides certain rules under section 1295 applicable to a U.S. person that has elected to treat a PFIC (as defined in § 1.1291-1(b)(1)) as a QEF (as defined in § 1.1291-1(b)(2)(i)). A U.S. person that has elected to treat a PFIC as a QEF is taxable annually, pursuant to section 1293, on its pro rata share of the ordinary earnings and net capital gain of the QEF.

(b) *Application of section 1295 election.*—(1) *Election personal to shareholder.*—An election under section 1295 and this section (section 1295 election) applies only to the shareholder that makes the election. Accordingly, a shareholder's section 1295 election will not apply to a U.S. transferee (as defined in § 1.1291-6(c)(2)(i)) of stock of a PFIC with respect to which the shareholder made a section 1295 election. A section 1295 election made by a common parent of a consolidated group as agent for members of the group is considered made by each member of the group that owns stock of the PFIC at the time of the election and at any time thereafter.

(2) *Election applicable to specific corporation only.*—(i) *In general.*—Only a corporation with respect to which a shareholder makes a section 1295 election is a QEF. The shareholder's section 1295 election applies to all the stock of the QEF that the shareholder owns at the time of the election or acquires thereafter. Except as provided in paragraph (b)(2)(ii) of this section, if a shareholder transfers stock of a QEF in exchange for stock of another PFIC, the latter PFIC is not a QEF unless the shareholder makes a section 1295 election to treat it as a QEF. If a shareholder disposes of stock of a QEF in exchange for stock of another PFIC in a nonrecognition transfer (as defined in § 1.1291-6(a)(2)) effected prior to April 1, 1992, and the shareholder has consistently treated the other PFIC as a QEF, the shareholder may make a section 1295 election with respect to the other PFIC whose stock was received for the taxable year of the PFIC that includes the day the transfer was effected. Such election must be made by the later of—

(A) The due date provided in section 1295(b); or

(B) The due date for the return for the taxable year of the shareholder that includes April 1, 1992.

For the deadline for making the section 1295 election in the case of nonrecognition transfers effected after April 1, 1992, *see* section 1295(b).

(ii) *Stock of QEF received in a nonrecognition transfer.*—If a U.S. person is a U.S. transferee (as defined in § 1.1291-6(c)(2)(i)) of stock of a PFIC in a nonrecognition transfer in which the shareholder disposing of such stock does not fully recognize the gain with respect to such stock, and the U.S. transferee, at the time of the transaction, has in effect a section 1295 election with respect to that PFIC, the section 1295 election will apply to the newly acquired stock on the day after the transaction. The newly acquired stock will be treated as stock of an unpedigreed QEF for which an election under section 1291(d)(2) and § 1.1291-9 or 1.1291-10 may be made. For purposes of making a section 1291(d)(2) election pursuant to this paragraph (b)(2)(ii), the qualification date is the day after the nonrecognition transaction. The following example illustrates the rule of this paragraph (b)(2)(ii).

Example. (i) X, a domestic corporation, owns stock of NQF, a section 1291 fund with respect to X, and stock of FC, a pedigreed QEF with respect to X. Pursuant to a plan of reorganization, X and the other shareholders of NQF exchange their NQF stock for voting stock of FC in a transaction that qualifies as a reorganization described in section 368(a)(1)(C). Pursuant to §1.1291-6(c)(1), the gain recognition rule of §1.1291-6(b)(1) does not apply to X's disposition of NQF stock. X therefore does not recognize gain on the exchange of NQF stock for FC stock. X's adjusted basis in the FC stock received in the reorganization is equal to X's adjusted basis in the NQF stock immediately prior to the transfer. The holding period of the FC stock received includes the period during which X held the NQF stock, and, as provided in §1.1291-1(h)(7), the character of the days during that period as prePFIC and prior PFIC carry over to the FC stock.

(ii) As provided in §1.1295-1(b)(2)(ii), the section 1295 election that X made with respect to FC applies to the FC stock received in the reorganization. However, because the holding period of the FC stock received in exchange for the NQF stock includes days that are treated as prior PFIC days, the FC stock received in the reorganization is treated as stock of an unpedigreed QEF. X may make an election under section 1291(d)(2) to purge the holding period of the FC stock received of the prior PFIC days carried over with the NQF holding period. [Reg. §1.1295-1.]

PFICs: Shareholders: Qualified Electing Fund Elections

PFICs: Shareholders: Qualified Electing Fund Elections.—Reg. §1.1295-2, relating to permitting certain shareholders to make a special election under Code Sec. 1295, in lieu of the election currently provided for under that section, with respect to certain preferred shares of a passive foreign investment company (PFIC), is proposed (published in the Federal Register on December 24, 1996) (REG-209040-88).

☐ Par. 3. Section 1.1295-2 is added to read as follows:

§1.1295-2. Special preferred QEF election.—(a) *In general.*—This section provides rules permitting certain shareholders to make a special election under section 1295 (special preferred QEF election) in lieu of the election described in §1.1295-1[1] and Notice 88-125, 1988-2 C.B. 535 (see §601.601(d)(2)(ii)(*b*) of this chapter), with respect to certain preferred shares (qualified preferred shares) of a foreign corporation that certifies either that it is a PFIC (as defined in §1.1291-1(b)(1)(i))[1] or that it reasonably believes that it is a PFIC. In order to make a special preferred QEF election, a shareholder must satisfy the stock ownership requirement of paragraph (c)(2) of this section. A special preferred QEF election of a shareholder applies only to those qualified preferred shares acquired and held directly by the shareholder in the taxable year of the shareholder for which the election is made. A shareholder making a special preferred QEF election must account for dividend income on shares subject to the election under the special income inclusion rules described in §1.1293-2, rather than under the general income inclusion rules of section 1293 and §1.1293-1. In addition, for purposes of determining the tax consequences of owning shares subject to the special preferred QEF election, an electing shareholder must treat the foreign corporation as a PFIC for the entire period during which the shareholder continues to hold any of such shares. Paragraph (b) of this section defines qualified preferred share. Paragraph (c) of this section provides rules for determining who may make the special preferred QEF election. Paragraph (d) of this section provides rules concerning the effect of the election. Paragraph (e) of this section provides rules for the time and manner of making the election. Paragraph (f) of this section sets forth the annual reporting requirement for the election. Paragraph (g) of this section provides rules concerning the possible termination or invalidation of the election. For the applicability date of this section, see paragraph (h) of this section.

(b) *Qualified preferred share defined.*—(1) *In general.*—For purposes of this section, a share of a foreign corporation is a qualified preferred share only if—

(i) The share was originally issued for cash or in exchange for qualified preferred shares of the foreign corporation in a transaction to which section 354(a)(1) applied;

(ii) If the share were to constitute a debt obligation, the share would be in registered form within the meaning of §5f.103-1(c) of this chapter;

(iii) All amounts payable with respect to the share are denominated in U.S. dollars and are not determined by reference to the value of a currency other than the U.S. dollar;

(iv) The share is limited and preferred as to dividends and does not participate in corporate growth to any significant extent within the meaning of section 1504(a)(4)(B);

(v) The share has a fixed redemption or liquidation price;

(vi) The share provides for cumulative or noncumulative dividend rights that are limited to an annual (or shorter period) amount computed by multiplying either the redemption or liquidation price of the share by a specified index described in §1.446-3(c)(2)(i), (iii), or (iv) (specified index), or by a specified index periodically re-established pursuant to an auction reset mechanism, set in advance of the period with respect to which the specified index applies;

(vii) If the share may be redeemed under circumstances described in §1.305-5(b) such that redemption premium (as described in §1.305-5(b)) could be treated under section 305(c) as a constructive distribution (fixed term preferred stock), the share was not issued with redemption premium exceeding the de minimis

[1] This proposed regulation was published on April 1, 1992, at 57 Fed. Reg. 11024.

amount described in section 305(c)(1) and § 1.305-5(b)(1);

(viii) If the share may not be redeemed under circumstances described in § 1.305-5(b) such that redemption premium would not be treated under section 305 as a constructive distribution (perpetual preferred stock), the share does not provide shareholders with the right to receive an amount upon liquidation or redemption that exceeds the issue price of the share (as determined under the principles of section 1273(b)) by an amount in excess of 5 percent of such liquidation or redemption amount;

(ix) If redeemable, the share is redeemable only in whole and not in part and is not subject to mandatory redemption within five years of the issue date of the share. Further, the share is not subject to a holder put or issuer call that, based on all the facts and circumstances as of the issue date of the share, is more likely than not to be exercised at a time within five years of the issue date;

(x) If convertible, the share is not convertible into a share other than a share meeting all the conditions set forth in paragraphs (b)(1)(i) through (b)(1)(ix) of this section; and

(xi) The issuer of the share has indicated in an offering document relating to the original issuance of the share or in a written statement available to U.S. holders that the issuer has no current intention or belief that it will not pay dividends on the share on a current basis and that the share meets the conditions set forth in paragraphs (b)(1)(i) through (b)(1)(x) of this section and this paragraph (b)(1)(xi).

(2) *Special rules for shares acquired in secondary market transactions.*—(i) *Fixed term preferred stock.*—A share of fixed term preferred stock (as described in paragraph (b)(1)(vii) of this section) that satisfies the conditions set forth in paragraph (b)(1) of this section and that is acquired in a transaction other than in connection with the initial issuance of the share (a secondary market transaction), shall constitute a qualified preferred share with respect to a shareholder, but only if the shareholder acquires the share for cash and the share has preferred discount (as defined below) that is less than or equal to an amount equal to 1 percent of the redemption price, multiplied by the number of complete years from the date of acquisition of the share to the redemption date as established under the principles of § 1.305-5(b). Sales of shares to bond houses, brokers, or similar persons or organizations acting in the capacity as underwriters, placement agents, or wholesalers are ignored for purposes of determining whether a share is acquired in connection with the initial issuance of the share. For purposes of this section, the preferred discount for a share is the excess of the redemption price of the share payable on the redemption date over the shareholder's acquisition cost for the share.

(ii) *Perpetual preferred stock.*—A share of perpetual preferred stock, within the meaning of paragraph (b)(1)(viii) of this section, that satisfies the conditions set forth in paragraph (b)(1) of this section and that is acquired in a secondary market transaction, shall constitute a qualified preferred share with respect to the shareholder, but only if the shareholder acquires the share for cash and the amount payable upon liquidation of the share exceeds the shareholder's acquisition cost for the share by an amount less than or equal to 10 percent of such liquidation amount.

(iii) *Examples.*—The following examples illustrate the rules of this paragraph (b)(2).

Example 1—(i) *Facts.* On May 1, 1998, A, an individual who files her return on a calendar year basis, purchases for $9000 cash in a single secondary market transaction (as defined in paragraph (b)(2)(i) of this section) 100 shares of nonconvertible Class A $100 par value preferred stock (Class A Stock) of FC, a foreign corporation with a taxable year ending March 31. The terms of the Class A Stock satisfy all the conditions described in paragraph (b)(1) of this section and provide for a mandatory redemption of the Class A Stock by the issuer in U.S. dollars at par on June 1, 2012. The Class A Stock is not redeemable pursuant to an issuer call or holder put on any other date.

(ii) *Analysis.* In order for A to make a special preferred QEF election with respect to the Class A Stock acquired by A, the Class A Stock acquired must constitute qualified preferred shares. Although the Class A Stock meets the requirements for qualified preferred shares set forth in paragraph (b)(1) of this section, the stock also must satisfy the requirements described in paragraph (b)(2) because A acquired the stock in a secondary market transaction. Because the terms of the Class A Stock provide that the stock will be redeemed by the issuer on June 1, 2012, the stock constitutes fixed term preferred stock within the meaning of paragraph (b)(1)(vii) of this section. A purchased the Class A Stock for $90 per share, representing a $10 discount ($100 June 1, 2012, per share redemption price less $90 acquisition cost). Because this $10 discount, which constitutes preferred discount within the meaning of paragraph (b)(2)(i) of this section, is less than $14 (1 percent of the redemption price multiplied by 14 (the number of complete years until the mandatory redemption date)), the Class A Stock acquired by A satisfies the conditions of paragraph (b)(2)(i) of this section and therefore constitutes qualified preferred shares.

Example 2—(i) *Facts.* The facts are the same as in *Example 1*, except that A acquires the 100 shares of Class A Stock for $8000.

(ii) *Analysis.* In this case, A purchased the Class A Stock for $80 per share, representing a $20 discount ($100 June 1, 2012, redemption price less $80 acquisition cost). Because this $20 of preferred discount is greater than $14 (1 percent of the redemption price multiplied by 14 (the number of complete years until the mandatory redemption date)), the Class A Stock fails to satisfy the conditions of paragraph (b)(2)(i) of this section and therefore fails to qualify as qualified preferred shares.

(c) *Who may make the election.*—(1) *In general.*—A U.S. person that acquires qualified preferred shares for cash or in a nonrecognition transaction described in § 1.1291-6(a)[2] (nonrecognition transaction) and that holds such shares directly may make a special preferred QEF elec-

[2] This proposed regulation was published on April 1, 1992, at 57 Fed. Reg. 11024.

tion, provided that, in the case of shares acquired in a nonrecognition transaction, either the qualified preferred shares are treated as stock of a pedigreed QEF, as defined in § 1.1291-1(b)(2)(ii), immediately prior to the nonrecognition transaction, or the gain, if any, realized on the transaction would be recognized under § 1.1291-6(b) with respect to the nonrecognition transaction. A special preferred QEF election will not apply to any shares with respect to which the electing shareholder is an indirect shareholder, within the meaning of § 1.1291-1(b)(8). Solely for purposes of this section, partnerships, S corporations, trusts and estates (pass-through entities) that directly own qualified preferred shares are treated as shareholders that may make a special preferred QEF election. A shareholder may not make a special preferred QEF election if at any time the shareholder made a section 1295 election (other than a special preferred QEF election) with respect to the foreign corporation. A shareholder may not make a special preferred QEF election unless the shareholder satisfies the stock ownership requirements set forth in paragraph (c)(2) of this section, and the shareholder receives from the foreign corporation the statement described in paragraph (c)(3) of this section.

(2) *Ownership requirement*.—A holder of qualified preferred shares of a foreign corporation may make a special preferred QEF election only if, at all times during the taxable year of the shareholder, the shareholder does not own, directly, indirectly, or constructively, within the meaning of section 958, five percent or more of the vote or value of any class of stock of the foreign corporation. The five percent vote or value limitation must be satisfied for each taxable year of the shareholder during which the shareholder continues to hold shares subject to the special preferred QEF election.

(3) *Statement from corporation*.—A shareholder may make the special preferred QEF election only if the foreign corporation has provided a written statement relating to the taxable year of the corporation that ends with or within the taxable year of the shareholder for which the election is made certifying either that the foreign corporation is, or that it reasonably believes that it is, a PFIC, and that it is not a controlled foreign corporation within the meaning of section 957(a) for such taxable year of the corporation. The statement must be provided directly to the electing shareholder or in a disclosure or other document generally available to all U.S. holders. Electing shareholders must retain a copy of the statement for their records.

(d) *Effect of election*.—(1) *In general*.—Unless terminated or invalidated pursuant to paragraph (g) of this section, shares subject to a special preferred QEF election will be treated as shares of a pedigreed QEF (as defined in § 1.1291-1(b)(2)(ii)) for all taxable years of the foreign corporation that are included wholly or partly in the shareholder's holding period of the shares. A special preferred QEF election applies to all qualified preferred shares owned directly by the shareholder that are acquired in the taxable year of the election. Separate special preferred QEF elections may be made for qualified preferred shares acquired in other taxable years of the taxpayer. A special preferred QEF election is personal to the shareholder that made the election and does not apply to a transferee of the shares. A shareholder that has made a special preferred QEF election may not make, with respect to the foreign corporation, any other election permitted under sections 1291 through 1297 and the regulations under those sections, including a section 1295 election as described in § 1.1295-1 and Notice 88-125, 1988-2 C.B. 535 (see § 601.601(d)(2)(ii)(*b*) of this chapter), for any period during which the special preferred QEF election remains in effect with respect to any shares of the shareholder.

(2) *Continued PFIC Characterization*.—By making the special preferred QEF election, the shareholder agrees to treat the foreign corporation as a PFIC with respect to qualified preferred shares subject to the election at all times during its holding period for such shares, without regard to whether the foreign corporation is a PFIC for any taxable year of the foreign corporation during which the preferred QEF election remains in effect.

(3) *Section 1293 inclusions*.—For each taxable year of the shareholder to which an election under this section applies, the shareholder must include in income the preferred QEF amount, as defined in § 1.1293-2, in the manner and under the rules provided in that section.

(e) *Time for and manner of making the special preferred QEF election*.—(1) *Time for making the election*.—A special preferred QEF election must be made on or before the due date, as extended, for filing the shareholder's return for the taxable year during which the shareholder acquired the qualified preferred shares for which the election is being made. A special preferred QEF election may not be made for those shares at any other time pursuant to any other provision of the Code or regulations.

(2) *Manner of making the election*.—(i) *In general*.—A shareholder makes the special preferred QEF election under this section for all qualified preferred shares of a foreign corporation acquired during the shareholder's taxable year by checking the appropriate box in Form 8621 (Return by a Shareholder of a Passive Foreign Investment Company or Qualified Electing Fund), Part I, for making the section 1295 election, and indicating in the margin of Part I that the shareholder is making a special preferred QEF election with respect to certain specified shares. The shareholder also must report the preferred QEF amount for the taxable year of the election on Line 6a of Part II of Form 8621. In addition, the shareholder must attach to Form 8621 the statement (preferred QEF statement) described in paragraph (e)(2)(ii) of this section, signed by the shareholder under penalties of perjury, stating that the information and representations provided in the preferred QEF statement are true, correct, and complete to the best of the shareholder's knowledge and belief.

(ii) *Preferred QEF statement contents*.—The preferred QEF statement must include the following information and representations:

(A) The first taxable year of the shareholder for which the special preferred QEF election is made;

(B) The number of shares subject to the election, their acquisition date(s) and acquisition price(s), and the class designation(s) of the shares;

(C) A representation by the shareholder that it did not at any time during its taxable year own directly, indirectly, or constructively, within the meaning of section 958, five percent or more of the vote or value of any class of stock of the foreign corporation with respect to which the election applies;

(D) A representation by the shareholder that it has obtained the written statement described in paragraph (c)(3) of this section; and

(E) A representation by the shareholder that it has never made a section 1295 election other than a special preferred QEF election with respect to the foreign corporation.

(f) *Annual reporting requirement.*—For each taxable year of a shareholder during which the shareholder holds shares of a foreign corporation subject to one or more special preferred QEF elections, the shareholder must file Form 8621 with respect to the foreign corporation regardless of whether the foreign corporation is or is not a PFIC under section 1296 during any portion of the taxable year. The shareholder must indicate in the margin of Part I of Form 8621 the number of special preferred QEF elections of the shareholder that remain in effect with respect to the foreign corporation. In addition, the shareholder must report, on Line 6a of Part II of Form 8621, the aggregate of the preferred QEF amounts for all relevant special preferred QEF elections in effect for the taxable year.

(g) *Termination or invalidation of election.*—(1) *In general.*—A sale, exchange or other disposition of a share that is subject to a special preferred QEF election will terminate the special preferred QEF election with respect to that share. In addition, the Commissioner may, in the Commissioner's discretion, terminate or invalidate a special preferred QEF election if a shareholder that made the election fails to satisfy the initial or ongoing requirements of the election. Once made, a special preferred QEF election may not be terminated or invalidated by the shareholder.

(2) *Effect of termination or invalidation.*—Termination of a special preferred QEF election by the Commissioner will be effective on the first day of the shareholder's first taxable year following the last taxable year of the shareholder for which the requirements of the election are satisfied. For purposes of sections 1291 through 1297 and the regulations thereunder, the holding period of qualified preferred shares subject to an election that has been terminated will be treated as beginning on the effective date of the termination. A shareholder that has made an election that is invalidated by the Commissioner will be treated for purposes of sections 1291 through 1297 and the regulations thereunder as if the shareholder never made the election.

(h) *Effective date.*—An election under this section may only be made with respect to qualified preferred shares that are issued after the date that is 30 days after the date of publication of this document as a final regulation. [Reg. § 1.1295-2.]

Passive Foreign Investment Companies: Passive Income Characterization: Certain Foreign Banks and Securities Dealers: Exceptions To

Passive Foreign Investment Companies: Passive Income Characterization: Certain Foreign Banks and Securities Dealers: Exceptions To.—Reg. §§ 1.1296-4 and 1.1296-6, relating to the application of the exceptions to passive income contained in section 1296(b) for foreign banks, securities dealers and brokers, are proposed (published in the Federal Register on April 28, 1995) (INTL-65-93). See below (REG-115795-97) for a proposed amendment to proposed Reg. § 1.1296-4.

☐ Par. 4. Sections 1.1296-4 and 1.1296-6 are added to read as follows:

§ 1.1296-4. Characterization of certain banking income of foreign banks as nonpassive.—(a) *General rule.*—For purposes of section 1296, banking income earned by an active bank, as defined in either paragraph (b)(1) or (2) of this section, or by a qualified bank affiliate, as defined in paragraph (i) of this section, is nonpassive income.

(b) *Active bank.*—(1) *U.S. licensed banks.*—A corporation (whether domestic or foreign) is an active bank if it is licensed by federal or state bank regulatory authorities to do business as a bank in the United States. A foreign corporation will not satisfy the requirements of this paragraph (b)(1) if, under its federal or state license or licenses, the foreign corporation is permitted to maintain only an office, such as a representative office, that is prohibited by federal or state law from taking deposits or making loans.

(2) *Other foreign banks.*—A foreign corporation is an active bank if it meets the licensing requirement of paragraph (c) of this section and it actively conducts, within the meaning of § 1.367(a)-2T(b)(3), a banking business that is a trade or business within the meaning of § 1.367(a)-2T(b)(2). In order for the business conducted by a foreign corporation to be considered a banking business, the foreign corporation must also meet the deposit-taking requirements of paragraph (d) of this section and the lending requirements of paragraph (e) of this section.

(c) *Licensing requirements.*—To be an active bank under paragraph (b)(2) of this section, a foreign corporation must be licensed or authorized to accept deposits from residents of the country in which it is chartered or incorporated and to conduct, in that country, one or more of the banking activities described in paragraph (f)(2) of this section. However, in no case will a foreign corporation satisfy the requirements of this paragraph (c) if one of the principal purposes for its obtaining a license or authorization was to satisfy the requirements of this section.

(d) *Deposit-taking requirements.*—(1) *General rule.*—To be an active bank under paragraph (b)(2) of this section—

(i) A foreign corporation must, in the ordinary course of the corporation's trade or business, regularly accept deposits from customers who are residents of the country in which it is licensed or authorized; and

(ii) The amount of deposits shown on the corporation's balance sheet must be substantial.

(2) *Deposit.*—Whether a liability constitutes a deposit for purposes of this paragraph (d)

is determined by reference to the characteristics of the relevant instrument and does not depend solely on whether the instrument is designated as a deposit.

(3) *Substantiality of deposits.*—Whether the amount of deposits (including interbank deposits) shown on a corporation's balance sheet is substantial depends on all the facts and circumstances, including whether the corporation's capital structure and funding sources as a whole are similar to that of banking institutions engaged in the same types of activities and subject to the jurisdiction of the same bank regulatory authorities.

(e) *Lending activities test.*—To be an active bank under paragraph (b)(2) of this section, a corporation must regularly make loans to customers in the ordinary course of its trade or business. A note, bond, debenture or other evidence of indebtedness will be treated as a loan for purposes of this section only if the debt instrument is received by the corporation on an extension of credit made pursuant to a loan agreement entered into in the ordinary course of the corporation's banking business. Such debt instruments generally will not be considered loans for purposes of this section if the instruments are not treated as loans (but are classified as securities or other investment assets, for example) for purposes of the foreign corporation's financial statements.

(f) *Banking income.*—(1) *General rule.*—Banking income is the gross income derived from the active conduct (within the meaning of § 1.367(a)-2T(b)(3)) of any banking activity described in paragraph (f)(2) of this section.

(2) *Banking activities.*—For purposes of this section, the following are banking activities—

(i) Lending activities described in paragraph (e) of this section;

(ii) Factoring evidences of indebtedness for customers;

(iii) Purchasing, selling, discounting, or negotiating for customers notes, drafts, checks, bills of exchange, acceptances, or other evidences of indebtedness;

(iv) Issuing letters of credit and negotiating drafts drawn thereunder for customers;

(v) Performing trust services, including activities as a fiduciary, agent or custodian, for customers, provided such trust activities are not performed in connection with services provided by a dealer in stock, securities or similar financial instruments;

(vi) Arranging foreign exchange transactions (including any section 988 transaction within the meaning of section 988(c)(1)) for, or engaging in foreign exchange transactions with, customers;

(vii) Arranging interest rate or currency futures, forwards, options or notional principal contracts for, or entering into such transactions with, customers;

(viii) Underwriting issues of stock, debt instruments or other securities under best efforts or firm commitment agreements for customers;

(ix) Engaging in finance leases, as defined in § 1. 904-4(e)(2)(i)(V);

(x) Providing charge and credit card services for customers or factoring receivables obtained in the course of providing such services;

(xi) Providing traveler's check and money order services for customers;

(xii) Providing correspondent bank services for customers;

(xiii) Providing paying agency and collection agency services for customers;

(xiv) Maintaining restricted reserves (including money or securities) as described in paragraph (g) of this section; and

(xv) Any other activity that the Commissioner determines, through a revenue ruling or other formal published guidance (see § 601.601(d)(2) of this chapter), to be a banking activity generally conducted by active banks in the ordinary course of their banking business.

(g) *Certain restricted reserves.*—A deposit of assets in a reserve is, for purposes of this section, a banking activity if the deposit is maintained in a segregated account in order to satisfy a capital or reserve requirement under the laws of a jurisdiction in which the corporation actively conducts (within the meaning of § 1.367(a)-2T(b)(3)) a banking business that is a trade or business (within the meaning of § 1.367(a)-2T(b)(2)). A deposit of assets into a reserve qualifies under this paragraph (g) if and only to the extent that the assets are not available for use in connection with the corporation's banking business because of significant regulatory restrictions on the investment of such assets. This paragraph (g) does not apply to ordinary working capital, which is available for unrestricted use.

(h) *Customer relationship.*—Whether a customer relationship exists is determined by reference to all the facts and circumstances. Such a relationship does not exist with respect to transactions between members of a related group, as defined in paragraph (i)(4) of this section, or transactions with any shareholders, officers, directors or other employees of any person that would otherwise be treated as an active bank or qualified bank affiliate if one of the principal purposes for such transactions was to satisfy the requirements of this section.

(i) *Income earned by qualified bank affiliates.*—(1) *General rule.*—A foreign corporation that is not an active bank but which derives banking income, as defined in paragraph (f)(1) of this section, is a qualified bank affiliate for purposes of this section if such corporation meets the requirements of paragraph (i)(2) of this section and the related group of which it is a member meets the requirements of paragraph (i)(3) of this section. Banking income earned by a qualified bank affiliate is nonpassive only for purposes of determining whether any member of the related group is a passive foreign investment company or holds stock in a passive foreign investment company or for purposes of applying section 956A(c)(2)(A). However, banking income of a qualified bank affiliate remains passive with respect to persons who own stock in that affiliate but who are not members of the related group of which the affiliate is a member.

(2) *Affiliate income requirement.*—To be a qualified bank affiliate, at least 60 percent of the foreign corporation's total gross income for the taxable year must be banking income, securities income, as defined in § 1.1296-6(e)(1), or gross income described in section 1296(b)(2)(B) (relating to insurance activities). For purposes of ap-

plying this paragraph (i)(2), the look-through rules of sections 1296(b)(2)(C) and 1296(c) do not apply.

(3) *Group income requirements.*—The related group qualifies under this paragraph (i) if—

(i) At least 30 percent of the aggregate gross financial services income, as defined in § 1.904-4(e)(1), earned during the taxable year by members of the related group is banking income earned by active banks who are members of the related group during the current taxable year; and

(ii) At least 70 percent of the aggregate gross financial services income earned during the taxable year by members of the related group is banking income, securities income, or gross income described in section 1296(b)(2)(B) (relating to insurance activities).

(4) *Related group.*—The related group is the group of persons consisting of the entity being tested under this paragraph (i) and all entities that are related within the meaning of section 954(d)(3) to such entity, substituting "person" for "controlled foreign corporation" each time the latter term appears.

(j) *Income from nonbank activities.*—Income derived from the conduct of activities other than banking activities described in paragraph (f)(2) of this section and income from assets held for the conduct of such other activities are nonpassive only to the extent otherwise provided in section 1296.

(k) *Effective date.*—This section is effective for taxable years beginning after December 31, 1994. However, taxpayers may apply this section to a taxable year beginning after December 31, 1986, but must consistently apply this section to such taxable year and all subsequent years. [Reg. § 1.1296-4.]

§ 1.1296-6. Characterization of certain securities income.—(a) *General rule.*—For purposes of section 1296, securities income earned by an active dealer or active broker, as defined in paragraph (b) of this section, or a qualified securities affiliate, as defined in paragraph (j) of this section, is nonpassive income. This section applies only for purposes of determining whether a controlled foreign corporation, as defined in section 957(a), is a passive foreign investment company with respect to its United States shareholders as defined in section 951(b), or for the purpose of determining whether an asset is passive under section 956A(c)(2)(A).

(b) *Active dealer or broker.*—(1) *General rule.*—A securities dealer, as defined in paragraph (c) of this section, or a securities broker, as defined in paragraph (d) of this section, is an active dealer or an active broker for purposes of this section if it meets the requirements of either paragraph (b)(2) or (3) of this section.

(2) *U.S. licensed dealers and brokers.*—A securities dealer or securities broker (whether foreign or domestic) is an active dealer or an active broker if it is registered as a securities dealer or broker under section 15(a) of the Securities Exchange Act of 1934 or is registered as a Government securities dealer or broker under section 15C(a) of such Act.

(3) *Other dealers and brokers.*—(i) *General rule.*—A securities dealer or a securities broker is an active dealer or an active broker if it meets the licensing requirements of paragraph (b)(3)(ii) of this section and actively conducts, within the meaning of § 1.367(a)-2T(b)(3), one or more securities activities, as defined in paragraph (e)(2) of this section, as a trade or business within the meaning of § 1.367(a)-2T(b)(2).

(ii) *Licensing requirements.*—To be an active dealer or an active broker under paragraph (b)(3) of this section, a securities dealer or securities broker must be licensed or authorized in the country in which it is chartered, incorporated or organized to conduct one or more of the securities activities described in paragraph (e)(2) of this section with residents of that country. The conduct of such activities must be subject to *bona fide* regulation, including appropriate reporting, monitoring and prudential (including capital adequacy) requirements, by a securities regulatory authority in that country that regularly enforces compliance with such requirements and prudential standards.

(c) *Securities dealer.*—For purposes of this section, a securities dealer is a dealer (whether foreign or domestic) in securities within the meaning of section 475(c)(1).

(d) *Securities broker.*—For purposes of this section, a securities broker is a corporation (whether domestic or foreign) that, during its taxable year, stands ready, in the ordinary course of its trade or business, to effect transactions in securities and other financial instruments for the account of customers, including the arrangement of loans of securities owned by customers.

(e) *Securities income.*—(1) *General rule.*—Securities income means the gross income (except as provided in paragraph (i) of this section) derived from the active conduct (within the meaning of § 1.367(a)-2T(b)(3)) of any securities activity described in paragraph (e)(2) of this section.

(2) *Securities activities.*—For purposes of this section, the following are securities activities—

(i) Purchasing or selling stock, debt instruments, interest rate or currency futures or other securities or derivative financial products (including notional principal contracts) from or to customers and holding stock, debt instruments and other securities as inventory for sale to customers, unless the relevant securities or derivative financial products (including notional principal contracts) are not held in a dealer capacity;

(ii) Effecting transactions in securities for customers as a securities broker;

(iii) Arranging futures, forwards, options, or notional principal contracts for, or entering into such transactions with, customers;

(iv) Arranging foreign exchange transactions (including any section 988 transaction within the meaning of section 988(c)(1)) for, or engaging in foreign exchange transactions with, customers;

(v) Underwriting issues of stocks, debt instruments, or other securities under best efforts or firm commitment agreements with customers;

(vi) Purchasing, selling, discounting, or negotiating for customers on a regular basis notes, drafts, checks, bills of exchange, acceptances or other evidences of indebtedness;

(vii) Borrowing or lending stocks or securities for customers;

(viii) Engaging in securities repurchase or reverse repurchase transactions with customers;

(ix) Engaging in hedging activities directly related to another securities activity described in this paragraph (e)(2);

(x) Repackaging mortgages and other financial assets into securities and servicing activities with respect to such financial assets (including the accrual of interest incidental to such activities);

(xi) Engaging in financing activities typically provided by an investment bank, such as—

(A) Project financing provided in connection with, for example, construction projects;

(B) Structured finance, including the extension of a loan and the sale of participations or interests in the loan to other financial institutions or investors; and

(C) Leasing activities to the extent incidental to financing activities described in this paragraph (e)(2)(xi) or to advisory services described in paragraph (e)(2)(xii) of this section;

(xii) Providing financial or investment advisory services, investment management services, fiduciary services, trust services or custodial services;

(xiii) Providing margin or any other financing for a customer secured by securities or money market instruments, including repurchase agreements, or providing financing in connection with any of the activities listed in paragraphs (e)(2)(i) through (e)(2)(xii) of this section;

(xiv) Maintaining deposits of capital (including money or securities) described in paragraph (f) of this section; and

(xv) Any other activity that the Commissioner determines, through a revenue ruling or other formal published guidance, to be a securities activity generally conducted by active dealers or active brokers in the ordinary course of their securities business.

(f) *Certain deposits of capital.*—A deposit of capital is, for purposes of this section, a securities activity if the deposit is maintained in a segregated account in order to satisfy a capital requirement for registration as a securities broker or dealer under the laws of a jurisdiction in which the broker or dealer actively conducts (within the meaning of §1.367(a)-2T(b)(3)) a trade or business (within the meaning of §1.367(a)-2T(b)(2)) as a securities broker or dealer. A deposit of capital qualifies under this paragraph (f) if and only to the extent that the assets are not available for use in connection with the controlled foreign corporation's activities as a securities broker or dealer because of significant regulatory restrictions on the investment of such assets. This paragraph (f) does not apply to ordinary working capital, which is available for unrestricted use.

(g) *Dealer-customer relationship.*—Whether a dealer-customer relationship exists is determined by reference to all the facts and circumstances. Such a relationship does not exist with respect to transactions between members of a related group, as defined in paragraph (j)(4) of this section, or transactions with any shareholders, officers, directors or other employees of any person that would otherwise be treated as an active dealer, active broker or qualified securities affiliate if one of the principal purposes for such transactions was to satisfy the requirements of this section.

(h) *Investment income.*—Income earned on any securities held for investment within the meaning of section 475(b)(1)(A) or not held for sale within the meaning of section 475(b)(1)(B), is passive for purposes of sections 1296(a)(1), 1296(a)(2) and 956A(c)(2)(A).

(i) *Calculation of gross income from a matched book.*—Securities income includes only the net (not gross) income from matched transactions. For purposes of this section, a matched transaction is a sale and repurchase agreement with respect to the same security properly treated as offsetting agreements in a matched book.

(j) *Income earned by qualified securities affiliates.*—(1) *General rule.*—A foreign corporation that is not an active dealer or an active broker but which derives securities income described in paragraph (e)(1) of this section is a qualified securities affiliate for purposes of this section if such corporation meets the requirements of paragraph (j)(2) of this section and is a member of a related group that meets the requirements of paragraph (j)(3) of this section. Securities income earned by a qualified securities affiliate is nonpassive only for purposes of determining whether any member of the related group is a passive foreign investment company or holds stock in a passive foreign investment company or for purposes of applying section 956A(c)(2)(A). However, securities income of a qualified securities affiliate remains passive with respect to persons who own stock in that affiliate but who are not members of the related group of which the affiliate is a member.

(2) *Affiliate income requirement.*—To be a qualified securities affiliate, at least 60 percent of the foreign corporation's total gross income for the taxable year must be banking income, as defined in §1.1296-4(f)(1), securities income, as defined in paragraph (e)(1) of this section, or gross income described in section 1296(b)(2)(B) (relating to insurance activities). For purposes of this paragraph (j)(2), the look-through rules of sections 1296(b)(2)(C) and 1296(c) do not apply.

(3) *Group income requirements.*—The related group qualifies under this paragraph (j) if—

(i) At least 30 percent of the aggregate gross financial services income, as defined in §1.904-4(e)(1), earned during the taxable year by members of the related group is securities income earned by active dealers or active brokers who are members of the related group during the current taxable year; and

(ii) At least 70 percent of the aggregate gross financial services income earned during the taxable year by members of the related group is banking income, securities income, or gross income described in section 1296(b)(2)(B) (relating to insurance activities).

(4) *Related group.*—The related group is the group of persons consisting of the entity being tested under this paragraph (j) and all entities that are related within the meaning of section 954(d)(3) to such entity, substituting "person" for "controlled foreign corporation" each time the latter term appears.

(5) *Example*.—The following example illustrates the rules of this paragraph (j).

Example. (i) *Facts*. SD is a country Y corporation that owns 85 percent of the stock of M, a country Z corporation. A, a U.S. person, owns the remaining 15 percent of the stock of M. B, C, and D, all unrelated U.S. persons, own 5, 15, and 36 percent, respectively, of the stock of SD. The rest of SD's stock is publicly held. SD is a securities dealer within the meaning of section 475(c)(1) and satisfies the licensing requirements of paragraph (b)(3)(ii) of this section. Because M's sole activity is conducting a matched book repo business, M is not a securities dealer within the meaning of section 475. For its taxable year ending December 31, 1994, SD earns $100 of gross income from trading profits and interest and dividends on inventory. For its taxable year ending December 31, 1994, M earns $50 of net interest income from its matched book repo business. SD and M earn no other income. All of SD and M's assets are held in connection with their securities businesses and none has been identified as having been held for investment.

(ii) *Securities income earned by SD*. SD is an active dealer under paragraph (b) of this section because it is a securities dealer under section 475 and satisfies the licensing requirements of paragraph (b)(3)(ii) of this section. Therefore, because SD is a controlled foreign corporation, SD's securities income is nonpassive under paragraph (a) of this section.

(iii) *Securities income earned by M*. (A) SD and M are financial services entities that are the only members of a related group as defined in paragraph (j)(4) of this section. The percentage of the SD-M related group's financial services income that is securities income earned by active dealers (SD), is 66.66 percent (($100/$150) × 100). The percentage of the SD-M related group's financial services income that is securities income, banking income (as defined in § 1.1296-4(f)), or insurance income (as defined in section 1296(b)(2)(B)) is 100 percent (($150/$150) × 100). In addition, the percentage of M's income that is securities income is 100 percent (($50/$50) × 100).

(B) M is a qualified securities affiliate because the gross income tests of paragraphs (j)(2) and (3) of this section are satisfied. Accordingly, because M is a controlled foreign corporation, M's securities income is nonpassive for purposes of determining whether C or D own an interest in a PFIC (whether SD or M). M is thus not a PFIC with respect to C or D because it does not meet the income or asset tests of section 1296(a). SD also is not a PFIC with respect to C or D because it does not meet the income or assets tests of section 1296(a), after applying the look-through rule of section 1296(c).

(C) However, because B owns less than 10 percent of the stock of SD, and is therefore not a United States shareholder with respect to SD under section 951(b), M's interest income is passive (even though it is securities income) for purposes of determining whether B's indirect interest in M is an interest in a PFIC. Moreover, M's interest income is passive for purposes of determining whether A owns an interest in a PFIC. As a result, M meets the income and asset tests of section 1296(a) and is therefore a PFIC with respect to A and B.

(k) *Income from nonsecurities activities*.—Income derived from the conduct of activities other than securities activities described in paragraph (e)(2) of this section and income from assets held for the conduct of such other activities are nonpassive only to the extent otherwise provided in section 1296.

(l) *Effective date*.—This section is effective for taxable years beginning after September 30, 1993. [Reg. § 1.1296-6.]

PFICs: Shareholders: Qualified Electing Fund Election: Rules

PFICs: Shareholders: Qualified Electing Fund Elections: Rules.—Amendments to proposed Reg. § 1.1296-4 (see above (INTL-65-93)), relating to rules for a passive foreign investment company shareholder that makes the election under Code Sec. 1295 to treat the passive foreign investment company as a qualified electing fund, are proposed (published in the Federal Register on January 2, 1998) (REG-115795-97).

□ Par. 7. Section 1.1296-4(e) as proposed at 60 FR 20922 (April 28, 1995) is amended by adding a sentence at the end of the paragraph to read as follows:

§ 1.1296-4. Characterization of certain banking income of foreign banks as passive.

* * *

(e) *Lending activities test*.—* * * An interbank deposit made in the ordinary course of a corporation's banking business will be treated as a loan for purposes of this section. For the effective date of this paragraph (e), see paragraph (k) of this section.

Application of the Grantor Trust Rules to Nonexempt Employees' Trusts

Application of the Grantor Trust Rules to Nonexempt Employees' Trusts.—Reg. § 1.1297-4, relating to the application of the grantor trust rules to nonexempt employees' trusts, is proposed (published in the Federal Register on September 27, 1996) (REG-209826-96).

□ Par. 4. Section 1.1297-4 is added to read as follows:

§ 1.1297-4. Application of subpart E of subchapter J with respect to foreign employees' trusts.—(a) *General rules*.—For purposes of part VI of subchapter P, chapter 1 of the Code, a foreign employer that is not a controlled foreign corporation is not treated as the owner of any portion of a foreign employees' trust (as defined in § 1.671-1(h)(2)) except as provided in this paragraph (a), regardless of whether the employer has a power or interest described in sections 673 through 677 over any portion of the trust.

(1) *Principal purpose to avoid classification as a passive foreign investment company*.—If a principal purpose for a transfer of property by any

person to a foreign employees' trust (as defined in §1.671-1(h)(2)) is to avoid classification of a foreign corporation as a passive foreign investment company, then the following rule applies. If the foreign employer has a power or interest described in sections 673 through 677 over the trust, then the grantor trust rules of subpart E of part I of subchapter J, chapter 1 of the Code will apply, for purposes of part VI of subchapter P, to a fixed dollar amount in the trust that is equal to the fair market value of the property that is transferred for the purpose of avoiding classification as a passive foreign investment company. Whether a principal purpose for a transfer is the avoidance of classification as a passive foreign investment company will be determined on the basis of all of the facts and circumstances, including whether the amount of assets held by the foreign employees' trust is reasonably related to the plan's anticipated liabilities, taking into account any local law and practice relating to proper funding levels.

(2) *Principal purpose to reduce or eliminate taxation under section 1291 or 1293.*—If a principal purpose for a transfer of property by any person to a foreign employees' trust (as defined in §1.671-1(h)(2)) is to reduce or eliminate taxation under section 1291 or 1293, then the following rule applies. If the foreign employer has a power or interest described in sections 673 through 677 over the trust, then the provisions of subpart E will apply, for purposes of part VI of subchapter P, to a fixed dollar amount in the trust that is equal to the fair market value of the property transferred for the purpose of reducing or eliminating taxation under section 1291 or 1293. Whether a principal purpose for a transfer is to reduce or eliminate taxation under section 1291 or 1293 will be determined on the basis of all the facts and circumstances, including whether the amount of assets held by the foreign employees' trust is reasonably related to the plan's anticipated liabilities, taking into account any local law and practice relating to proper funding levels.

(3) *Application to employer entity.*—The rules of this section apply to the employer whose employees benefit under the deferred compensation plan funded through the foreign employees' trust, or, in the case of a deferred compensation plan covering independent contractors, the recipient of services performed by those independent contractors, regardless of whether the plan is maintained through another entity. Thus, for example, where a deferred compensation plan benefitting employees of a foreign employer that is not a controlled foreign corporation is funded through a foreign employees' trust, the foreign employer is considered to be the grantor of the foreign employees' trust for purposes of this paragraph (a).

(b) *Effective date.*—This section applies to taxable years of a foreign corporation ending after September 27, 1996. [Reg. §1.1297-4.]

Certain Foreign Insurance Companies: Passive Income

Certain Foreign Insurance Companies: Passive Income.—Reg. §1.1297-4, regarding when a foreign insurance company's income is excluded from the definition of passive income under section 1297(b)(2)(B), is proposed (published in the Federal Register on April 24, 2015) (REG-108214-15).

Par. 2. Section 1.1297-4 is added to read as follows:

§1.1297-4. Exception from the definition of passive income for certain foreign insurance company income.—(a) *Income derived in the active conduct of an insurance business.*—For purposes of section 1297, the term *passive income* does not include income earned by a foreign corporation that would be subject to tax under subchapter L if it were a domestic corporation, but only to the extent the income is derived in the active conduct of an insurance business.

(b) *Definitions.*—The following definitions apply for purposes of paragraph (a) of this section—

(1) *Active conduct.*—The term *active conduct* has the same meaning as in §1.367(a)-2T(b)(3), except that officers and employees are not considered to include the officers and employees of related entities as provided in §1.367(a)-2T(b)(3).

(2) *Insurance business.*—The term *insurance business* means the business of issuing insurance and annuity contracts and the reinsuring of risks underwritten by insurance companies, together with those investment activities and administrative services that are required to support or are substantially related to insurance and annuity contracts issued or reinsured by the foreign corporation. For purposes of the preceding sentence—

(i) An investment activity is any activity engaged in by the foreign corporation to produce income of a kind that would be foreign personal holding company income as defined in section 954(c); and

(ii) Investment activities are required to support or are substantially related to insurance and annuity contracts issued or reinsured by the foreign corporation to the extent that income from the activities is earned from assets held by the foreign corporation to meet obligations under the contracts.

(c) *Effective/applicability date.*—These regulations apply beginning [EFFECTIVE DATE OF FINAL RULE]. [Reg. §1.1297-4.]

TAX TREATMENT OF S CORPORATIONS AND THEIR SHAREHOLDERS

Subchapter S Corporations: Elections

Subchapter S Corporations: Elections, Consents and Refusals.—Temporary Reg. §18.0, relating to the time and manner of making certain elections, consents, and refusals under the Subchapter S Revision Act of 1982, is also proposed as a final regulation (published in the Federal Register on January 26, 1983).

§18.0. Effective date of temporary regulations under the Subchapter S Revision Act of 1982.

Electing Small Business Trusts: Potential Current Beneficiaries: Nonresident Aliens

Electing Small Business Trusts: Potential Current Beneficiaries: Nonresident Aliens.—Amendments to Reg. §1.1361-1, regarding the recent statutory expansion of the class of permissible potential current beneficiaries of an electing small business trust to include nonresident aliens, are proposed (published in the Federal Register on April 19, 2019) (REG-117062-18).

Par. 3. Section 1.1361-1 is amended by:

1. Revising paragraph (m)(1)(ii)(D).

2. Revising paragraph (m)(2)(ii)(E)(2).

3. Adding two sentences to the end of paragraph (m)(4)(i).

4. Revising the second sentence of paragraph (m)(5)(iii).

5. In paragraph (m)(8), designating *Examples 1* through *9* as paragraphs (m)(8)(i) through (ix).

6. Redesignating paragraphs (m)(8)(i)(i) through (iii) as paragraphs (m)(8)(i)(A) through (C).

7. Redesignating paragraphs (m)(8)(ii)(i) and (ii) as paragraphs (m)(8)(ii)(A) and (B) and revising the second sentence of newly redesignated paragraph (m)(8)(ii)(A).

8. In newly redesignated paragraph (m)(8)(ii)(B), removing the language "*Example* 2(i)" and adding "*Example 2* in paragraph (m)(8)(ii)(A) of this section" in its place.

9. Redesignating paragraphs (m)(8)(vi)(i) through (iii) as paragraphs (m)(8)(vi)(A) through (C) and revising the first sentence of newly redesignated paragraph (m)(8)(vi)(B).

10. In newly redesignated paragraph (m)(8)(vi)(C), removing the language "paragraph (i) of this *Example 6*" and adding "*Example 6* in paragraph (m)(8)(vi)(A) of this section" in its place.

11. In paragraph (m)(9):

i. Removing the language "Paragraphs (m)(2)(ii)(A), (m)(4)(iii) and (vi), and (m)(8), *Example 2, Example 5, Example 7, Example 8,* and *Example 9*" and adding "Paragraphs (m)(2)(ii)(A) and (m)(4)(iii) and (vi) of this section and *Examples* 2, 5, and 7 through 9 in paragraphs (m)(8)(ii), (v), and (vii) through (ix)" in its place.

ii. Adding a sentence at the end of the paragraph.

The revisions and additions read as follows:

§1.1361-1. S corporation defined.

* * *

(m) * * *

(1) * * *

(ii) * * *

(D) *Nonresident aliens.*—A nonresident alien (NRA), as defined in section 7701(b)(1)(B), is an eligible beneficiary of an ESBT and an eligible potential current beneficiary.

* * *

(2) * * *

(ii) * * *

(E) * * *

(2) All potential current beneficiaries of the trust meet the shareholder requirements of section 1361(b)(1); for this purpose, an NRA potential current beneficiary does not violate the requirement under section 1361(b)(1)(C) that an S corporation cannot have an NRA as a shareholder.

* * *

(4) * * *

(i) * * * An NRA potential current beneficiary of an ESBT is treated as a shareholder for purposes of the 100-shareholder limit under section 1361(b)(1)(A). However, an NRA potential current beneficiary of an ESBT is not treated as a shareholder in determining whether a corporation is a small business corporation for purposes of the NRA-shareholder prohibition under section 1361(b)(1)(C).

* * *

(5) * * *

(iii) * * * For example, the S corporation election will terminate if a charitable remainder trust becomes a potential current beneficiary of an ESBT. * * *

* * *

(8) * * *

(ii) * * *

(A) * * * On January 1, 2006, A, a partnership, becomes a potential current beneficiary of Trust. * * *

* * *

(vi) * * *

(B) * * * Assume the same facts as *Example 6* in paragraph (m)(8)(vi)(A) of this section except that D is a charitable remainder trust. * * *

* * *

(9) * * * Paragraphs (m)(1)(ii)(D), (m)(2)(ii)(E)(2), (m)(4)(i), (m)(5)(iii), and (m)(8) of this section apply to all ESBTs after December 31, 2017.

Reporting Income and Deductions: Consolidated Group

Reporting Income and Deductions: Consolidated Group.—Amendments to Reg. §§1.1361-5 and 1.1362-3, revising the rules for reporting certain items of income and deduction that are reportable on the day a corporation joins or leaves a consolidated group, are proposed (published in the Federal Register on March 6, 2015) (REG-100400-14).

Par. 2. Section 1.1361-5 is amended:

1. In paragraph (a)(3), by removing "§1.1502-76(b)(1)(ii)(A)(2) (relating to a special rule" and adding "§1.1502-76(b)(1)(ii)(B) (relating to special rules" in its place.

2. In paragraph (a)(4), *Example 4*, by removing "§ 1.1502-76(b)(1)(ii)(A)(*2*)" and adding "§ 1.1502-76(b)(*1*)(ii)(B)(*1*)" in its place..

§ 1.1361-5. Termination of QSub election.

Par. 3. Section 1.1362-3 is amended in paragraph (a) by removing "§ 1.1502-76(b)(1)(ii)(A)(*2*)" and adding "§ 1.1502-76(b)(1)(ii)(B)" in its place.

§ 1.1362-3. Effect of election on corporation.

Subchapter S Corporations: Elections

Subchapter S Corporations: Elections, Consents and Refusals.—Temporary Reg. §§ 18.1379-1 and 18.1379-2, relating to the time and manner of making certain elections, consents, and refusals under the Subchapter S Revision Act of 1982, are also proposed as final regulations (published in the Federal Register on January 26, 1983). Reg. § 18.1377-1 removed by T.D. 8696 on December 20, 1996, and Reg. § 18.1378-1 removed by T.D. 8996, May 16, 2002.

§ 18.1379-1. Transitional rules on enactment.
§ 18.1379-2. Special rules for all elections, consents, and refusals.

TAX ON SELF-EMPLOYMENT INCOME

Qualified Opportunity Funds: Deferred Gains

Qualified Opportunity Funds: Deferred Gains.—Reg. § 1.1400Z-2(a)-1, relating to gains that may be deferred as a result of a taxpayer's investment in a qualified opportunity fund (QOF), is proposed (published in the Federal Register on October 29, 2018) (REG-115420-18).

Par. 2. Section 1.1400Z-2(a)-1 is added to read as follows:

§ 1.1400Z-2(a)-1. Deferring tax on capital gains by investing in opportunity zones.—(a) *In general.*—Under section 1400Z-2(a) of the Internal Revenue Code (Code) and this section, an eligible taxpayer may elect to defer recognition of some or all of its eligible gains to the extent that the taxpayer timely invests (as provided for by section 1400Z-2(a)(1)(A)) in eligible interests of a qualified opportunity fund (QOF), as defined in section 1400Z-2(d)(1). Paragraph (b) of this section defines eligible taxpayers, eligible gains, and eligible interests and contains related operational rules. Paragraph (c) of this section provides rules for applying section 1400Z-2 to a partnership, S corporation, trust, or estate that recognizes an eligible gain or would recognize such a gain if it did not elect to defer the gain under section 1400Z-2(a).

(b) *Definitions and related operating rules.*—The following definitions and rules apply for purposes of section 1400Z-2 and the regulations thereunder:

(1) *Eligible taxpayer.*—An *eligible taxpayer* is a person that may recognize gains for purposes of Federal income tax accounting. Thus, eligible taxpayers include individuals; C corporations, including regulated investment companies (RICs) and real estate investment trusts (REITs); partnerships; S corporations; trusts and estates. An eligible taxpayer may elect to defer recognition of one or more eligible gains in accordance with the requirements of section 1400Z-2.

(2) *Eligible gain.*—(i) *In general.*—An amount of gain is an *eligible gain*, and thus is eligible for deferral under section 1400Z-2(a), if the gain—

(A) Is treated as a capital gain for Federal income tax purposes;

(B) Would be recognized for Federal income tax purposes before January 1, 2027, if section 1400Z-2(a)(1) did not apply to defer recognition of the gain; and

(C) Does not arise from a sale or exchange with a person that, within the meaning of section 1400Z-2(e)(2), is related to the taxpayer that recognizes the gain or that would recognize the gain if section 1400Z-2(a)(1) did not apply to defer recognition of the gain.

(ii) *Gain not already subject to an election.*—In the case of a taxpayer who has made an election under section 1400Z-2(a) with respect to some but not all of an eligible gain, the term "eligible gain" includes the portion of that eligible gain with respect to which no election has yet been made.

(iii) *Gains under section 1256 contracts.*—(A) *General rule.*—The only gain arising from section 1256 contracts that is eligible for deferral under section 1400Z-2(a)(1) is capital gain net income for a taxable year. This net amount is determined by taking into account the capital gains and losses for a taxable year on all of a taxpayer's section 1256 contracts, including all amounts determined under section 1256(a), both those determined on the last business day of a taxable year and those that section 1256(c) requires to be determined under section 1256(a) because of the termination or transfer during the taxable year of the taxpayer's position with respect to a contract. The 180-day period with respect to any capital gain net income from section 1256 contracts for a taxable year begins on the last day of the taxable year, and the character of that gain when it is later included under section 1400Z-2(a)(1)(B) and (b) is determined under the general rule in paragraph (b)(5) of this section. See paragraph (b)(2)(iii)(B) of this section for limitations on the capital gains eligible for deferral under this paragraph (b)(2)(iii)(A).

(B) *Limitation on deferral for gain from 1256 contracts.*—If, at any time during the taxable year, any of the taxpayer's section 1256 contracts was part of an offsetting positions transaction (as defined in paragraph (b)(2)(iv) of this section) and any other position in that transaction was not a section 1256 contract, then no gain from any section 1256 contract is an eligible gain with respect to that taxpayer in that taxable year.

(iv) *No deferral for gain from a position that is or has been part of an offsetting-positions transaction.*—If a capital gain is from a position that is or has been part of an offsetting-positions transaction, the gain is not eligible for deferral under section 1400Z-2(a)(1). For purposes of this paragraph (b)(2)(iv), an offsetting-positions transaction is a transaction in which a taxpayer has substantially diminished the taxpayer's risk of loss from holding one position with respect to personal property by holding one or more other positions with respect to personal property (whether or not of the same kind). It does not matter whether either of the positions is with respect to actively traded personal property. An offsetting-positions transaction includes a straddle as defined in section 1092 and the regulations thereunder, including section 1092(d)(4), which provides rules for positions held by related persons and certain flow-through entities (for example, a partnership). An offsetting-positions transaction also includes a transaction that would be a straddle (taking into account the principles referred to in the preceding sentence) if the straddle definition did not contain the active trading requirement in section 1092(d)(1). For example, an offsetting-positions transaction includes positions in closely held stock or other non-traded personal property and substantially offsetting derivatives.

(3) *Eligible interest.*—(i) *In general.*—For purposes of section 1400Z-2, an *eligible interest* in a QOF is an equity interest issued by the QOF, including preferred stock or a partnership interest with special allocations. Thus, the term eligible interest excludes any debt instrument within the meaning of section 1275(a)(1) and § 1.1275-1(d).

(ii) *Use as collateral permitted.*—Provided that the eligible taxpayer is the owner of the equity interest for Federal income tax purposes, status as an eligible interest is not impaired by using the interest as collateral for a loan, whether as part of a purchase-money borrowing or otherwise.

(iii) *Deemed contributions not constituting investment.*—*See* § 1.1400Z-2(e)-1(a)(2) for rules regarding deemed contributions of money to a partnership pursuant to section 752(a).

(4) *180-day period.*—(i) *In general.*—Except as otherwise provided elsewhere in this section, the 180-day period referred to in section 1400Z-2(a)(1)(A) with respect to any eligible gain (180-day period) begins on the day on which the gain would be recognized for Federal income tax purposes if the taxpayer did not elect under section 1400Z-2 to defer recognition of that gain.

(ii) *Examples.*—The following examples illustrate the principles of paragraph (b)(4)(i) of this section.

Example 1. Regular-way trades of stock. If stock is sold at a gain in a regular-way trade on an exchange, the 180-day period with respect to the gain on the stock begins on the trade date.

Example 2. Capital gain dividends received by RIC and REIT shareholders. If an individual RIC or REIT shareholder receives a capital gain dividend (as described in section 852(b)(3) or section 857(b)(3)), the shareholder's 180-day period with respect to that gain begins on the day on which the dividend is paid.

Example 3. Undistributed capital gains received by RIC and REIT shareholders. If section 852(b)(3)(D) or section 857(b)(3)(D) (concerning undistributed capital gains) requires the holder of shares in a RIC or REIT to include an amount in the shareholder's long-term capital gains, the shareholder's 180-day period with respect to that gain begins on the last day of the RIC or REIT's taxable year.

Example 4. Additional deferral of previously deferred gains—(i) *Facts.* Taxpayer A invested in a QOF and properly elected to defer realized gain. During 2025, taxpayer A disposes of its entire investment in the QOF in a transaction that, under section 1400Z-2(a)(1)(B) and (b), triggers an inclusion of gain in A's gross income. Section 1400Z-2(b) determines the date and amount of the gain included in A's income. That date is the date on which A disposed of its entire interest in the QOF. A wants to elect under section 1400Z-2 to defer the amount that is required to be included in income.

(ii) *Analysis.*—Under paragraph (b)(4)(i) of this section, the 180-day period for making another investment in a QOF begins on the day on which section 1400Z-2(b) requires the prior gain to be included. As prescribed by section 1400Z-2(b)(1)(A), that is the date of the inclusion-triggering disposition. Thus, in order to make a deferral election under section 1400Z-2, A must invest the amount of the inclusion in the original QOF or in another QOF during the 180-day period beginning on the date when A disposed of its entire investment in the QOF.

(5) *Attributes of gains that section 1400Z-2(a)(1)(B) includes in income.*—If section 1400Z-2(a)(1)(B) and (b) require a taxpayer to include in income some or all of a previously deferred gain, the gain so included has the same attributes in the taxable year of inclusion that it would have had if tax on the gain had not been deferred. These attributes include those taken into account by sections 1(h), 1222, 1256, and any other applicable provisions of the Code.

(6) *First-In, First-Out (FIFO) method to identify which interest in a QOF has been disposed of.*—(i) *FIFO requirement.*—If a taxpayer holds investment interests with identical rights (fungible interests) in a QOF that were acquired on different days and if, on a single day, the taxpayer disposes of less than all of these interests, then the first-in-first-out (FIFO) method must be used to identify which interests were disposed of. Fungible interests may be equivalent shares of stock in a corporation or partnership interests with identical rights.

(ii) *Consequences of identification.*—The FIFO method determines—

(A) Whether an investment is described in section 1400Z-2(e)(1)(A)(i)(an investment to which a gain deferral election under section 1400Z-2(a) applies) or section 1400Z-2(e)(1)(A)(ii) (an investment which was not part of a gain deferral election under section 1400Z-2(a));

(B) In the case of investments described in section 1400Z-2(e)(1)(A)(i), the attributes of the gain subject to a deferral election under section 1400Z-2(a), at the time the gain is included in income (the attributes addressed in paragraph (b)(5) of this section); and

(C) The extent, if any, of an increase under section 1400Z-2(b)(2)(B) in the basis of an investment interest that is disposed of.

(7) *Pro-rata method.*—If, after application of the FIFO method, a taxpayer is treated as having disposed of less than all of the investment interests that the taxpayer acquired on one day and if the interests acquired on that day vary with respect to the characteristics described in paragraph (b)(6)(ii) of this section, then a proportionate allocation must be made to determine which interests were disposed of (pro-rata method).

(8) *Examples.*—The following examples illustrate the rules of paragraph (b)(5) through (7) of this section.

Example 1. Short-term gain. For 2018, taxpayer B properly made an election under section 1400Z-2 to defer $100 of gain that, if not deferred, would have been recognized as short-term capital gain, as defined in section 1222(1). In 2022, section 1400Z-2(a)(1)(B) and (b) requires taxpayer B to include the gain in gross income. Under paragraph (b)(5) of this section, the gain included is short-term capital gain.

Example 2. Collectibles gain. For 2018, taxpayer C properly made an election under section 1400Z-2 to defer a gain that, if not deferred, would have been collectibles gain as defined in IRC section 1(h)(5). In a later taxable year, section 1400Z-2(a)(1)(B) and (b) requires some or all of that deferred gain to be included in gross income. The gain included is collectibles gain.

Example 3. Net gains from section 1256 contracts. For 2019, taxpayer D had $100 of capital gain net income from section 1256 contracts. D timely invested $100 in a QOF and properly made an election under section 1400Z-2 to defer that $100 of gain. In 2023, section 1400Z-2(a)(1)(B) and (b) requires taxpayer D to include that deferred gain in gross income. Under paragraph (b)(5) of this section, the character of the inclusion is governed by section 1256(a)(3) (which requires a 40:60 split between short-term and long-term capital gain). Accordingly, $40 of the inclusion is short-term capital gain and $60 of the inclusion is long-term capital gain.

Example 4. FIFO method. For 2018, taxpayer E properly made an election under section 1400Z-2 to defer $300 of short-term capital gain. For 2020, E properly made a second election under section 1400Z-2 to defer $200 of long-term capital gain. In both cases, E properly invested in QOF Q the amount of the gain to be deferred. The two investments are fungible interests and the price of the interests was the same at the time of the two investments. E did not purchase any additional interest in QOF Q or sell any of its interest in QOF Q until 2024, when E sold for a gain 60 percent of its interest in QOF Q. Under paragraph (b)(6)(i) of this section, E must apply the FIFO method to identify which investments in QOF Q that E disposed of. As determined by this identification, E sold the entire 2018 initial investment in QOF Q. Under section 1400Z-2(a)(1)(B) and (b), the sale triggered an inclusion of deferred gain. Because the inclusion has the same character as the gain that had been deferred, the inclusion is short-term capital gain.

Example 5. FIFO method. In 2018, before Corporation R became a QOF, Taxpayer F invested $100 cash to R in exchange for 100 R common shares. Later in 2018, after R was a QOF, F invested $500 cash to R in exchange for 400 R common shares and properly elected under section 1400Z-2 to defer $500 of independently realized short-term capital gain. Even later in 2018, on different days, F realized $300 of short-term capital gain and $700 of long-term capital gain. On a single day that fell during the 180-day period for both of those gains, F invested $1,000 cash in R in exchange for 800 R common shares and properly elected under section 1400Z-2 to defer the two gains. In 2020, F sold 100 R common shares. Under paragraph (b)(6)(i) of this section, F must apply the FIFO method to identify which investments in R F disposed of. As determined by that identification, F sold the initially acquired 100 R common shares, which were not part of a deferral election under section 1400Z-2. R must recognize gain or loss on the sale of its R shares under the generally applicable Federal income tax rules, but the sale does not trigger an inclusion of any deferred gain.

Example 6. FIFO method. The facts are the same as example 5, except that, in addition, during 2021 F sold an additional 400 R common shares. Under paragraph (b)(6)(i) of this section, F must apply the FIFO method to identify which investments in R were disposed of. As determined by this identification, F sold the 400 common shares which were associated with the deferral of $500 of short-term capital gain. Thus, the deferred gain that must be included upon sale of the 400 R common shares is short-term capital gain.

Example 7. Pro-rata method. The facts are the same as in examples 5 and 6, except that, in addition, during 2022 F sold an additional 400 R common shares. Under paragraph (b)(6)(i) of this section, F must apply the FIFO method to identify which investments in R were disposed of. In 2022, F is treated as holding only the 800 R common shares purchased on a single day, and the section 1400Z-2 deferral election associated with these shares applies to gain with different characteristics (described in paragraph (b)(6)(ii) of this section). Under paragraph (b)(7) of this section, therefore, R must use the pro-rata method to determine which of the characteristics pertain to the deferred gain required to be included as a result of the sale of the 400 R common shares. Under the pro-rata method, $150 of the inclusion is short-term capital gain ($300 × 400/800) and $350 is long-term capital gain ($700 × 400/800).

(c) *Special rules for pass-through entities.*—(1) *Eligible gains that a partnership elects to defer.*—A partnership is an eligible taxpayer under paragraph (b)(1) of this section and may elect to defer recognition of some or all of its eligible gains under section 1400Z-2(a)(2).

(i) *Partnership election.*—If a partnership properly makes an election under section 1400Z-2(a)(2), then—

(A) The partnership defers recognition of the gain under the rules of section 1400Z-2 (that is, the partnership does not recognize gain at the time it otherwise would have in the absence of the election to defer gain recognition);

(B) The deferred gain is not included in the distributive shares of the partners under section 702 and is not subject to section 705(a)(1); and

(ii) *Subsequent recognition.*—Absent any additional deferral under section 1400Z-2(a)(1)(A), any amount of deferred gain that an electing partnership subsequently must include in income under sections 1400Z-2(a)(1)(B) and (b) is recognized by the electing partnership at the time of inclusion and is subject to sections 702 and 705(a)(1) in a manner consistent with recognition at that time.

(2) *Eligible gains that the partnership does not defer.*—(i) *Tax treatment of the partnership.*—If a partnership does not elect to defer some, or all, of the gains for which it could make a deferral election under section 1400Z-2, the partnership's treatment of any such amounts is unaffected by the fact that the eligible gain could have been deferred under section 1400Z-2.

(ii) *Tax treatment by the partners.*—If a partnership does not elect to defer some, or all, of the gains for which it could make a deferral election under section 1400Z-2—

(A) The gains for which a deferral election are not made are included in the partners' distributive shares under section 702 and are subject to section 705(a)(1);

(B) If a partner's distributive share includes one or more gains that are eligible gains with respect to the partner, the partner may elect under section 1400Z-2(a)(1)(A) to defer some or all of its eligible gains; and

(C) A gain in a partner's distributive share is an eligible gain with respect to the partner only if it is an eligible gain with respect to the partnership and it did not arise from a sale or exchange with a person that, within the meaning of section 1400Z-2(e)(2), is related to the partner.

(iii) *180-day period for a partner electing deferral.*—(A) *General rule.*—If a partner's distributive share includes a gain that is described in paragraph (c)(2)(ii)(C) of this section (gains that are eligible gains with respect to the partner), the 180-day period with respect to the partner's eligible gains in the partner's distributive share generally begins on the last day of the partnership taxable year in which the partner's allocable share of the partnership's eligible gain is taken into account under section 706(a).

(B) *Elective rule.*—Notwithstanding the general rule in paragraph (c)(2)(iii)(A) of this section, if a partnership does not elect to defer all of its eligible gain, the partner may elect to treat the partner's own 180-day period with respect to the partner's distributive share of that gain as being the same as the partnership's 180-day period.

(C) The following example illustrates the principles of this paragraph (c)(2)(iii).

Example. Five individuals have identical interests in partnership P, there are no other partners, and P's taxable year is the calendar year. On January 17, 2019, P realizes a capital gain of \$1000*x* that it decides not to elect to defer. Two of the partners, however, want to defer their allocable portions of that gain. One of these two partners invests \$200*x* in a QOF during February 2020. Under the general rule in paragraph (c)(2)(iii)(A) of this section, this investment is within the 180-day period for that partner (which begins on December 31, 2019). The fifth partner, on the other hand, decides to make the election provided in paragraph (c)(2)(iii)(B) of this section and invests \$200*x* in a QOF during February 2019. Under that elective rule, this investment is within the 180-day period for that partner (which begins on January 17, 2019).

(3) *Pass-through entities other than partnerships.*—If an S corporation; a trust; or a decedent's estate recognizes an eligible gain, or would recognize an eligible gain if it did not elect to defer recognition of the gain under section 1400Z-2(a), then rules analogous to the rules of paragraph (c)(1) and (2) of this section apply to that entity and to its shareholders or beneficiaries, as the case may be.

(d) *Elections.*—The Commissioner may prescribe in guidance published in the Internal Revenue Bulletin or in forms and instructions (*see* § § 601.601(d)(2) and 601.602 of this chapter), both the time, form, and manner in which an eligible taxpayer may elect to defer eligible gains under section 1400Z-2(a) and also the time, form, and manner in which a partner may elect to apply the elective 180-day period provided in paragraph (c)(2)(iii)(B) of this section.

(e) *Applicability date.*—This section applies to eligible gains that would be recognized in the absence of deferral on or after the date of publication in the **Federal Register** of a Treasury decision adopting these proposed rules as final regulations. An eligible taxpayer, however, may rely on the proposed rules in this section with respect to eligible gains that would be recognized before that date, but only if the taxpayer applies the rules in their entirety and in a consistent manner. [Reg. § 1.1400Z-2(a)-1.]

Qualified Opportunity Funds: Investment

Qualified Opportunity Funds: Investment.—Amendments to Reg. § 1.1400Z2(a)-1, relating to gains that may be deferred as a result of a taxpayer's investment in a qualified opportunity fund, as well as special rules for an investment in a QOF held by a taxpayer for at least 10 years, are proposed (published in the Federal Register on May 1, 2019) (REG-120186-18).

Par. 2. Section 1.1400Z2(a)-1, as proposed to be added by 83 FR 54279, October 29, 2018 is amended by:

1. Redesignating (b)(2)(iii) and (iv) as paragraphs (b)(2)(v) and (vi), respectively.
2. Adding new paragraphs (b)(2)(iii) and (iv) and paragraphs (b)(9) and (10).

The revisions and additions read as follows:

§ 1.1400Z2(a)-1. Deferring tax on capital gains by investing in opportunity zones.

* * *

(b) * * *

(2) * * *

(iii) *Gains from section 1231 property.*—The only gain arising from section 1231 property that is eligible for deferral under section 1400Z-2(a)(1) is capital gain net income for a taxable year. This net amount is determined by taking into account the capital gains and losses for a taxable year on all of the taxpayer's section 1231 property. The 180-day period described in paragraph (b)(4) of this section with respect to any capital gain net income from section 1231 property for a taxable year begins on the last day of the taxable year.

(iv) *No deferral for gain realized upon the acquisition of an eligible interest.*—Gain is not eligible for deferral under section 1400Z-2(a)(1) if such gain is realized upon the sale or other transfer of property to a QOF in exchange for an eligible interest (*see* paragraph (b)(10)(i)(C) of this section) or the transfer of property to an eligible taxpayer in exchange for an eligible interest (*see* paragraph (b)(10)(iii) of this section).

* * *

(9) *Making an investment for purposes of an election under section 1400Z-2(a).*—(i) *Transfer of cash or other property to a QOF.*—A taxpayer makes an investment for purposes of an election under section 1400Z-2(a)(1)(A) (section 1400Z-2(a)(1)(A) investment) by transferring cash or other property to a QOF in exchange for eligible interests in the QOF, regardless of whether the transfer is one in which the transferor would recognize gain or loss on the property transferred.

(ii) *Furnishing services.*—Services rendered to a QOF are not considered the making of a section 1400Z-2(a)(1)(A) investment. Thus, if a taxpayer receives an eligible interest in a QOF for services rendered to the QOF or to a person in which the QOF holds any direct or indirect equity interest, then the interest in the QOF that the taxpayer receives is not a section 1400Z-2(a)(1)(A) investment but is an investment to which section 1400Z-2(e)(1)(A)(ii) applies.

(iii) *Acquisition of eligible interest from person other than QOF.*—A taxpayer may make a section 1400Z-2(a)(1)(A) investment by acquiring an eligible interest in a QOF from a person other than the QOF.

(10) *Amount invested for purposes of section 1400Z-2(a)(1)(A).*—In the case of any investments described in this paragraph (b)(10), the amount of a taxpayer's section 1400Z-2(a)(1)(A) investment cannot exceed the amount of gain to be deferred under the election. If the amount of the taxpayer's investment as determined under this paragraph (b)(10) exceeds the amount of gain to be deferred under the section 1400Z-2(a) election, the amount of the excess is treated as an investment to which section 1400Z-2(e)(1)(A)(ii) applies. See paragraph (b)(10)(ii) of this section for special rules applicable to transfers to QOF partnerships.

(i) *Transfers to a QOF.*—(A) *Cash.*—If a taxpayer makes a section 1400Z-2(a)(1)(A) investment by transferring cash to a QOF, the amount of the taxpayer's section 1400Z-2(a)(1)(A) investment is that amount of cash.

(B) *Property other than cash—Nonrecognition transactions.*—This paragraph (b)(10)(i)(B) applies if a taxpayer makes a section 1400Z-2(a)(1)(A) investment by transferring property other than cash to a QOF and if, but for the application of section 1400Z-2(b)(2)(B), the taxpayer's basis in the resulting investment in the QOF would be determined, in whole or in part, by reference to the taxpayer's basis in the transferred property.

(1) Amount of section 1400Z-2(a)(1)(A) investment.—If paragraph (b)(10)(i)(B) of this section applies, the amount of the taxpayer's section 1400Z-2(a)(1)(A) investment is the lesser of the taxpayer's adjusted basis in the eligible interest received in the transaction, without regard to section 1400Z-2(b)(2)(B), or the fair market value of the eligible interest received in the transaction, both as determined immediately after the contribution. Paragraph (b)(10)(i)(B) of this section applies separately to each item of property contributed to a QOF.

(2) Fair market value of the eligible interest received exceeds its adjusted basis.—If paragraph (b)(10)(i)(B) of this section applies, and if the fair market value of the eligible interest received is in excess of the taxpayer's adjusted basis in the eligible interest received, without regard to section 1400Z-2(b)(2)(B), then the taxpayer's investment is an investment with mixed funds to which section 1400Z-2(e)(1) applies. Paragraph (b)(10)(i)(B)(*1*) of this section determines the amount of the taxpayer's investment to which section 1400Z-2(e)(1)(A)(i) applies. Section 1400Z-2(e)(1)(A)(ii) applies to the excess of the fair market value of the investment to which section 1400Z-2(e)(1)(A)(i) applies over the taxpayer's adjusted basis therein, determined without regard to section 1400Z-2(b)(2)(B).

(3) Transfer of built-in loss property and section 362(e)(2).—If paragraph (b)(10)(i)(B) of this section and section 362(e)(2) both apply to a transaction, the taxpayer is deemed to have made an election under section 362(e)(2)(C).

(C) *Property other than cash—Taxable transactions.*—This paragraph (b)(10)(i)(C) applies if a taxpayer makes a section 1400Z-2(a)(1)(A) investment by transferring property other than cash to a QOF and if, without regard to section 1400Z-2(b)(2)(B), the taxpayer's basis in the eligible interest received would not be determined, in whole or in part, by reference to the taxpayer's basis in the transferred property. If this paragraph (b)(10)(i)(C) applies, the amount of the taxpayer's section 1400Z-2(a)(1)(A) investment is the fair market value of the transferred property, as determined immediately before the transfer. This paragraph (b)(10)(i)(C) applies separately to each item of property transferred to a QOF.

(D) *Basis in an investment with mixed funds.*—If a taxpayer's investment in a QOF is an investment with mixed funds to which section 1400Z-2(e)(1) applies, the taxpayer's basis in the investment to which section 1400Z-2(e)(1)(A)(ii) applies is equal to the taxpayer's basis in all of the QOF interests received, determined without regard to section 1400Z-2(b)(2)(B), and reduced by the basis of the taxpayer's investment to which section 1400Z-2(e)(1)(A)(i) applies, determined without regard to section 1400Z-2(b)(2)(B).

(ii) *Special rules for transfers to QOF partnerships.*—In the case of an investment in a QOF partnership, the following rules apply:

(A) *Amounts not treated as an investment.*—*(1) Non-contributions in general.*—To the extent the transfer of property to a QOF partnership is characterized other than as a contribution (for example, as a sale for purposes of section 707), the transfer is not a section 1400Z-2(a)(1)(A) investment.

(2) *Reductions in investments otherwise treated as contributions.*—To the extent any transfer of cash or other property to a partnership is not disregarded under paragraph (b)(10)(ii)(A)(*1*) of this section (for example, it is not treated as a disguised sale of the property transferred to the partnership under section 707), the transfer to the partnership will not be treated as a section 1400Z-2(a)(1)(A) investment to the extent the partnership makes a distribution to the partner and the transfer to the partnership and the distribution would be recharacterized as a disguised sale under section 707 if:

(*i*) Any cash contributed were non-cash property; and

(*ii*) In the case of a distribution by the partnership to which § 1.707-5(b) (relating to debt-financed distributions) applies, the partner's share of liabilities is zero.

(B) *Amount invested in a QOF partnership.*—(*1*) *Calculation of amount of qualifying and non-qualifying investments.*—To the extent paragraph (b)(10)(ii)(A) of this section does not apply, the amount of the taxpayer's qualifying investment in a QOF partnership is the lesser of the taxpayer's net basis in the property contributed to the QOF partnership, or the net value of the property contributed by the taxpayer to the QOF partnership. The amount of the taxpayer's non-qualifying investment in the partnership is the excess, if any, of the net value of the contribution over the amount treated as a qualifying investment.

(*2*) *Net basis.*—For purposes of paragraph (b)(10)(ii)(B) of this section, net basis is the excess, if any, of—

(*i*) The adjusted basis of the property contributed to the partnership; over

(*ii*) The amount of any debt to which the property is subject or that is assumed by the partnership in the transaction.

(*3*) *Net value.*—For purposes of paragraph (b)(10)(ii)(B) of this section, net value is the excess of—

(*i*) The gross fair market value of the property contributed; over

(*ii*) The amount of the debt described in paragraph (b)(10)(ii)(B)(2)(ii) of this section.

(*4*) *Basis of qualifying and non-qualifying investments.*—The basis of a qualifying investment is the net basis of the property contributed, determined without regard to section 1400Z-2(b)(2)(B) or any share of debt under section 752(a). The basis of a non-qualifying investment (before any section 752 debt allocation) is the remaining net basis. The bases of qualifying and non-qualifying investments are increased by any debt allocated to such investments under the rules of § 1.1400Z2(b)-1(c)(6)(iv)(B).

(*5*) *Rules applicable to mixed-funds investments.*—If one portion of an investment in a QOF partnership is a qualifying investment and another portion is a non-qualifying investment, see § 1.1400Z2(b)-1(c)(6)(iv) for the rules that apply.

(iii) *Acquisitions from another person.*—If a taxpayer makes a section 1400Z-2(a)(1)(A) investment by acquiring an eligible interest in a QOF from a person other than the QOF, then the amount of the taxpayer's section 1400Z-2(a)(1)(A) investment is the amount of the cash, or the fair market value of the other property, as determined immediately before the exchange, that the taxpayer exchanged for the eligible interest in the QOF.

(iv) *Examples.*—The following examples illustrate the rules of paragraph (b)(10) of this section. For purposes of the following examples, B is an individual and Q is a QOF corporation.

(A) *Example 1: Transfer of built-in gain property with basis less than gain to be deferred.* B realizes $100 of eligible gain within the meaning of paragraph (b)(2) of this section. B transfers unencumbered property with a fair market value of $100 and an adjusted basis of $60 to Q in a transaction that is described in section 351(a). Paragraph (b)(10)(i)(B) of this section applies because B transferred property other than cash to Q and, but for the application of section 1400Z-2(b)(2)(B), B's basis in the eligible interests in Q would be determined, in whole or in part, by reference to B's basis in the transferred property. The fair market value of the eligible interest B received is $100, and, without regard to section 1400Z-2(b)(2)(B), B's basis in the eligible interest received would be $60. Thus, pursuant to paragraph (b)(10)(i)(B)(2) of this section, B's investment is an investment with mixed funds to which section 1400Z-2(e)(1) applies. Pursuant to paragraphs (b)(10)(i)(B)(*1*) and (*2*) of this section, B's section 1400Z-2(a)(1)(A) investment is $60 (the lesser of the taxpayer's adjusted basis in the eligible interest, without regard to section 1400Z-2(b)(2)(B), of $60 and the $100 fair market value of the eligible interest received). Pursuant to section 1400Z-2(b)(2)(B)(i), B's basis in the section 1400Z-2(a)(1)(A) investment is $0. Additionally, B's other investment is $40 (the excess of the fair market value of the eligible interest received ($100) over the taxpayer's adjusted basis in the eligible interest, without regard to section 1400Z-2(b)(2)(B) ($60)). B's basis in the other investment is $0 (B's $60 basis in its investment determined without regard to section 1400Z-2(b)(2)(B), reduced by the $60 of adjusted basis allocated to the investment to which section 1400Z-2(e)(1)(A)(i) applies, determined without regard to section 1400Z-2(b)(2)(B)). *See* paragraph (b)(10)(i)(D) of this section. Pursuant to section 362, Q's basis in the transferred property is $60.

(B) *Example 2: Transfer of built-in gain property with basis in excess of eligible gain to be deferred.* The facts are the same as *Example 1* in paragraph (b)(10)(iv)(A) of this section, except that B realizes $50 of eligible gain within the meaning of paragraph (b)(2) of this section. Pursuant to paragraph (b)(10) of this section, B's section 1400Z-2(a)(1)(A) investment cannot exceed the amount of eligible gain to be deferred (that is, the $50 of eligible gain) under the section 1400Z-2(a) election. Therefore, pursuant to paragraph (b)(10)(i)(B)(*1*) of this section, B's section 1400Z-2(a)(1)(A) investment is $50 (the lesser of the taxpayer's adjusted basis in the eligible interest received, without regard to section 1400Z-2(b)(2)(B), of $60 and the $100 fair market value of the eligible interest, limited by the amount of eligible gain to be deferred under the section 1400Z-2(a) election). B's section 1400Z-2(a)(1)(A) investment has an adjusted basis of $0, as provided in section

1400Z-2(b)(2)(B)(i). Additionally, B's other investment is $50 (the excess of the fair market value of the eligible interest received ($100) over the amount ($50) of B's section 1400Z-2(a)(1)(A) investment). B's basis in the other investment is $10 (B's $60 basis in its investment determined without regard to section 1400Z-2(b)(2)(B)), reduced by the $50 of adjusted basis allocated to B's section 1400Z-2(a)(1)(A) investment, determined without regard to section 1400Z-2(b)(2)(B)).

(C) *Example 3: Transfers to QOF partnerships*—(*1*) *Facts.* A and B each realized $100 of eligible gain and each transfers $100 of cash to a QOF partnership. At a later date, the partnership borrows $120 from an unrelated lender and distributes the cash of $120 equally to A and B.

(*2*) *Analysis.* If the contributions had been of property other than cash, the contributions and distributions would have been tested under the disguised sale rules of § 1.707-5(b) by, among other things, determining the timing of the distribution and amount of the debt allocated to each partner. Under paragraph (b)(10)(ii)(A)(*2*) of this section, the cash of $200 ($100 from A and $100 from B) is treated as property that could be sold in a disguised sale transaction and each partner's share of the debt is zero for purposes of determining the amount of the investment. To the extent there would have been a disguised sale applying the rule of paragraph (b)(10)(ii)(A)(2) of this section, the amount of the investment would be reduced by the amount of the contribution so recharacterized.

(*3*) *Property contributed has built-in gain.* The facts are the same as in this *Example 3* in paragraph (b)(10)(iv)(C)(*1*) of this section, except that the property contributed by A had a value of $100 and basis of $20 and the partnership did not borrow money or make a distribution. Under paragraph (b)(10)(ii)(B)(*1*) of this section, the amount of A's qualifying investment is $20 (the lesser of the net value or the net basis of the property that A contributed), and the excess of the $100 contribution over the $20 qualifying investment constitutes a non-qualifying investment. Under paragraph (b)(10)(ii)(B)(*2*) of this section, A's basis in the qualifying investment (determined without regard to section 1400Z-2(b)(2)(B) or section 752(a)) is $20. After the application of section 1400Z-2(b)(2)(B) but before the application of section 752(a), A's basis in the qualifying investment is zero. A's basis in the non-qualifying investment is zero without regard to the application of section 752(a).

(*4*) *Property contributed has built-in gain and is subject to debt.* The facts are the same as in this *Example 3* in paragraph (b)(10)(iv)(C)(*3*) of this section, except that the property contributed by A has a gross value of $130 and is subject to debt of $30. Under paragraph (b)(10)(ii)(B)(*1*) of this section, the amount of A's qualifying investment is zero, the lesser of the property's $100 net value ($130 minus $30) or zero net basis ($20 minus $30, but limited to zero). The entire contribution constitutes a non-qualifying investment.

(*5*) *Property contributed has built-in loss and is subject to debt.* The facts are the same as in this *Example 3* in paragraph (b)(10)(iv)(C)(*4*) of this section, except that the property contributed by A has a basis of $150. Under paragraph (b)(10)(ii)(B)(*1*) of this section, the amount of A's qualifying investment is $100, the lesser of the property's $100 net value ($130 minus $30) or $120 net basis ($150 minus $30). The non-qualifying investment is $0, the excess of the qualifying investment ($100) over the net value ($100). A's basis in the qualifying investment (determined without regard to section 1400Z-2(b)(2)(B) and section 752(a)) is $120, the net basis. After the application of section 1400Z-2(b)(2)(B), A's basis in the qualifying investment is zero, plus its share of partnership debt under section 752(a).

* * *

Qualified Opportunity Funds: Investment

Qualified Opportunity Funds: Investment.—Reg. § 1.1400Z2(b)-1, relating to gains that may be deferred as a result of a taxpayer's investment in a qualified opportunity fund, as well as special rules for an investment in a QOF held by a taxpayer for at least 10 years, is proposed (published in the Federal Register on May 1, 2019) (REG-120186-18).

Par. 3. Section 1.1400Z2(b)-1 is added to read as follows:

§ 1.1400Z2(b)-1. Inclusion of gains that have been deferred under section 1400Z-2(a).—(a) *Scope and definitions.*—(1) *Scope.*—This section provides rules under section 1400Z-2(b) of the Internal Revenue Code regarding the inclusion in income of gain deferred under section 1400Z-2(a)(1)(A). This section applies to a QOF owner only until all of such owner's gain deferred pursuant to section 1400Z-2(a)(1)(A) has been included in income, subject to the limitations described in paragraph (e)(5) of this section. Paragraph (a)(2) of this section provides additional definitions used in this section and §§ 1.1400Z2(c)-1 through 1.1400Z2(g)-1. Paragraph (b) of this section provides general rules under section 1400Z-2(b)(1) regarding the timing of the inclusion in income of the deferred gain. Paragraph (c) of this section provides rules regarding the determination of the extent to which an event triggers the inclusion in income of all, or a portion, of the deferred gain. Paragraph (d) of this section provides rules regarding holding periods for qualifying investments. Paragraph (e) of this section provides rules regarding the amount of deferred gain included in gross income under section 1400Z-2(a)(1)(B) and (b), including special rules for QOF partnerships and QOF S corporations. Paragraph (f) of this section provides examples illustrating the rules of paragraphs (c), (d), and (e) of this section. Paragraph (g) of this section provides rules regarding basis adjustments under section 1400Z-2(b)(2)(B). Paragraph (h) of this section provides special reporting rules applicable to partners, partnerships, and direct or indirect owners of QOF partnerships. Paragraph (i) of this section provides dates of applicability.

(2) *Definitions.*—The following definitions apply for purposes of this section and §§ 1.1400Z2(c)-1 and 1.1400Z2(g)-1:

(i) *Boot.*—The term *boot* means money or other property that section 354 or 355 does not permit to be received without the recognition of gain.

(ii) *Consolidated group.*—The term *consolidated group* has the meaning provided in § 1.1502-1(h).

(iii) *Deferral election.*—The term *deferral election* means an election under section 1400Z-2(a) made before January 1, 2027, with respect to an eligible interest.

(iv) *Inclusion event.*—The term *inclusion event* means an event described in paragraph (c) of this section.

(v) *Mixed-funds investment.*—The term *mixed-funds investment* means an investment a portion of which is a qualifying investment and a portion of which is a non-qualifying investment.

(vi) *Non-qualifying investment.*—The term *non-qualifying investment* means an investment in a QOF described in section 1400Z-2(e)(1)(A)(ii).

(vii) *Property.*—(A) *In general.*—The term *property* means money, securities, or any other property.

(B) *Inclusion events regarding QOF corporation distributions.*—For purposes of paragraph (c) of this section, in the context in which a QOF corporation makes a distribution, the term property does not include stock (or rights to acquire stock) in the QOF corporation that makes the distribution.

(viii) *QOF.*—The term *QOF* means a qualified opportunity fund, as defined in section 1400Z-2(d)(1) and associated regulations.

(ix) *QOF C corporation.*—The term *QOF C corporation* means a QOF corporation other than a QOF S corporation.

(x) *QOF corporation.*—The term *QOF corporation* means a QOF that is classified as a corporation for Federal income tax purposes.

(xi) *QOF owner.*—The term *QOF owner* means a QOF shareholder or a QOF partner.

(xii) *QOF partner.*—The term *QOF partner* means a person that directly owns a qualifying investment in a QOF partnership or a person that owns such a qualifying investment through equity interests solely in one or more partnerships.

(xiii) *QOF partnership.*—The term *QOF partnership* means a QOF that is classified as a partnership for Federal income tax purposes.

(xiv) *QOF S corporation.*—The term *QOF S corporation* means a QOF corporation that has elected under section 1362 to be an S corporation.

(xv) *QOF shareholder.*—The term *QOF shareholder* means a person that directly owns a qualifying investment in a QOF corporation.

(xvi) *Qualifying investment.*—The term *qualifying investment* means an eligible interest (as defined in § 1.1400Z2(a)-1(b)(3)), or portion thereof, in a QOF to the extent that a deferral election applies with respect to such eligible interest or portion thereof.

(xvii) *Qualifying QOF partnership interest.*—The term *qualifying QOF partnership interest* means a direct or indirect interest in a QOF partnership that is a qualifying investment.

(xviii) *Qualifying QOF stock.*—The term *qualifying QOF stock* means stock in a QOF corporation that is a qualifying investment.

(xix) *Qualifying section 355 transaction.*—The term *qualifying section 355 transaction* means a distribution described in paragraph (c)(11)(i)(B) of this section.

(xx) *Qualifying section 381 transaction.*—The term *qualifying section 381 transaction* means a transaction described in section 381(a)(2), except the following transactions:

(A) An acquisition of assets of a QOF by a QOF shareholder that holds a qualifying investment in the QOF;

(B) An acquisition of assets of a QOF by a tax-exempt entity as defined in § 1.337(d)-4(c)(2);

(C) An acquisition of assets of a QOF by an entity operating on a cooperative basis within the meaning of section 1381;

(D) An acquisition by a QOF of assets of a QOF shareholder that holds a qualifying investment in the QOF;

(E) A reorganization of a QOF in a transaction that qualifies under section 368(a)(1)(G);

(F) A transaction, immediately after which one QOF owns an investment in another QOF; and

(G) A triangular reorganization of a QOF within the meaning of § 1.358-6(b)(2)(i), (ii), or (iii).

(xxi) *Remaining deferred gain.*—The term *remaining deferred gain* means the full amount of gain that was deferred under section 1400Z-2(a)(1)(A), reduced by the amount of gain previously included under paragraph (b) of this section..

(b) *General inclusion rule.*—The gain to which a deferral election applies is included in gross income, to the extent provided in paragraph (e) of this section, in the taxable year that includes the earlier of:

(1) The date of an inclusion event; or

(2) December 31, 2026.

(c) *Inclusion events.*—(1) *General rule.*—Except as otherwise provided in this paragraph (c), the following events are inclusion events (which result in the inclusion of gain under paragraph (b) of this section) if, and to the extent that—

(i) *Reduction of interest in QOF.*—A taxpayer's transfer of a qualifying investment reduces the taxpayer's equity interest in the qualifying investment;

(ii) *Distribution of property regardless of whether the taxpayer's direct interest in the QOF is reduced.*—A taxpayer receives property in a transaction that is treated as a distribution for Federal income tax purposes, whether or not the receipt reduces the taxpayer's ownership of the QOF; or

(iii) *Claim of worthlessness.*—A taxpayer claims a loss for worthless stock under section 165(g) or otherwise claims a worthlessness deduction with respect to its qualifying investment.

(2) *Termination or liquidation of QOF or QOF owner.*—(i) *Termination or liquidation of QOF.*—Except as otherwise provided in this paragraph (c), a taxpayer has an inclusion event with respect to all of its qualifying investment if the QOF ceases to exist for Federal income tax purposes.

(ii) *Liquidation of QOF owner.*—(A) *Portion of distribution treated as sale.*—A distribution of a qualifying investment in a complete liquidation of a QOF owner is an inclusion event to the extent that section 336(a) treats the distribution as if the qualifying investment were sold to the distributee at its fair market value, without regard to section 336(d).

(B) *Distribution to 80-percent distributee.*—A distribution of a qualifying investment in a complete liquidation of a QOF owner is not an inclusion event to the extent section 337(a) applies to the distribution.

(3) *Transfer of an investment in a QOF by gift.*—A taxpayer's transfer of a qualifying investment by gift, whether outright or in trust, is an inclusion event, regardless of whether that transfer is a completed gift for Federal gift tax purposes, and regardless of the taxable or tax-exempt status of the donee of the gift.

(4) *Transfer of an investment in a QOF by reason of the taxpayer's death.*—(i) *In general.*—Except as provided in paragraph (c)(4)(ii) of this section, a transfer of a qualifying investment by reason of the taxpayer's death is not an inclusion event. Transfers by reason of death include, for example:

(A) A transfer by reason of death to the deceased owner's estate;

(B) A distribution of a qualifying investment by the deceased owner's estate;

(C) A distribution of a qualifying investment by the deceased owner's trust that is made by reason of the deceased owner's death;

(D) The passing of a jointly owned qualifying investment to the surviving co-owner by operation of law; and

(E) Any other transfer of a qualifying investment at death by operation of law.

(ii) *Exceptions.*—The following transfers are not included as a transfer by reason of the taxpayer's death, and thus are inclusion events, and the amount recognized is includible in the gross income of the transferor as provided in section 691:

(A) A sale, exchange, or other disposition by the deceased taxpayer's estate or trust, other than a distribution described in paragraph (c)(4)(i) of this section;

(B) Any disposition by the legatee, heir, or beneficiary who received the qualifying investment by reason of the taxpayer's death; and

(C) Any disposition by the surviving joint owner or other recipient who received the qualifying investment by operation of law on the taxpayer's death.

(5) *Grantor trusts.*—(i) *Contributions to grantor trusts.*—If the owner of a qualifying investment contributes it to a trust and, under the grantor trust rules, the owner of the investment is the deemed owner of the trust, the contribution is not an inclusion event.

(ii) *Changes in grantor trust status.*—In general, a change in the status of a grantor trust, whether the termination of grantor trust status or the creation of grantor trust status, is an inclusion event. Notwithstanding the previous sentence, the termination of grantor trust status as the result of the death of the owner of a qualifying investment is not an inclusion event, but the provisions of paragraph (c)(4) of this section apply to distributions or dispositions by the trust.

(6) *Special rules for partners and partnerships.*—(i) *Scope.*—Except as otherwise provided in this paragraph (c)(6), in the case of a partnership that is a QOF or, directly or indirectly solely through one or more partnerships, owns an interest in a QOF, the inclusion rules of this paragraph (c) apply to transactions involving any direct or indirect partner of the QOF to the extent of such partner's share of any eligible gain of the QOF.

(ii) *Transactions that are not inclusion events.*—(A) *In general.*—Notwithstanding paragraphs (c)(1) and (2) and (c)(6)(iii) of this section, and except as otherwise provided in paragraph (c)(6) of this section, no transaction described in paragraph (c)(6)(ii) of this section is an inclusion event.

(B) *Section 721 contributions.*—Subject to paragraph (c)(6)(v) of this section, a contribution by a QOF owner, including any contribution by a partner of a partnership that, solely through one or more upper-tier partnerships, owns an interest in a QOF (contributing partner), of its direct or indirect partnership interest in a qualifying investment to a partnership (transferee partnership) in a transaction governed all or in part by section 721(a) is not an inclusion event, provided the interest transfer does not cause a partnership termination of a QOF partnership, or the direct or indirect owner of a QOF, under section 708(b)(1). *See* paragraph (c)(6)(ii)(C) of this section for transactions governed by section 708(b)(2)(A). Notwithstanding the rules in this paragraph (c)(6)(ii)(B), the inclusion rules in paragraph (c) of this section apply to any part of the transaction to which section 721(a) does not apply. The transferee partnership becomes subject to section 1400Z-2 and all section 1400Z-2 regulations in this chapter with respect to the eligible gain associated with the contributed qualifying investment. The transferee partnership must allocate and report the gain that is associated with the contributed qualifying investment to the contributing partner to the same extent that the gain would have been allocated and reported to the contributing partner in the absence of the contribution.

(C) *Section 708(b)(2)(A) mergers or consolidations.*—Subject to paragraph (c)(6)(v) of this section, a merger or consolidation of a partnership holding a qualifying investment, or of a partnership that holds an interest in such partnership solely through one or more partnerships, with another partnership in a transaction to which section 708(b)(2)(A) applies is not an inclusion event. The resulting partnership or new partnership, as determined under § 1.708-1(c)(1), becomes subject to section 1400Z-2, and all section 1400Z-2 regulations in this chapter, to the same extent that the original partnership was so subject prior to the transaction, and must allocate and report any eligible gain to the same extent and to the same partners that the original partnership allocated and reported such items prior to the transaction. Notwithstanding the rules in this paragraph (c)(6)(ii)(C), the general inclusion rules of paragraph (c) of this section apply to the portion of the transaction that is otherwise treated as a sale or exchange under paragraph (c) of this section.

(iii) *Partnership distributions.*—Notwithstanding paragraph (c)(6)(i) of this section, and subject to paragraph (c)(6)(v) of this section, and except as provided in paragraph (c)(6)(ii)(C) of this section, an actual or deemed distribution of property (including cash) by a QOF partnership to a partner with respect to its qualifying investment is an inclusion event only to the extent that the distributed property has a fair market value in excess of the partner's basis in its qualifying investment. Similar rules apply to distributions involving tiered partnerships. *See* paragraph (c)(6)(iv) of this section for special rules relating to mixed-funds investments.

(iv) *Special rules for mixed-funds investments.*—(A) *General rule.*—The rules of paragraph (c)(6)(iv) of this section apply solely for purposes of section 1400Z-2. A partner that holds a mixed-funds investment in a QOF partnership (a mixed-funds partner) shall be treated as holding two separate interests in the QOF partnership, one a qualifying investment and the other a non-qualifying investment (the separate interests). The basis of each separate interest is determined under the rules described in paragraphs (c)(6)(iv)(B) and (g) of this section as if each interest were held by different taxpayers.

(B) *Allocations and distributions.*—All section 704(b) allocations of income, gain, loss, and deduction, all section 752 allocations of debt, and all distributions made to a mixed-funds partner shall be treated as made to the separate interests based on the allocation percentages of such interests as defined in paragraph (c)(6)(iv)(D) of this section. For purposes of this paragraph (c)(6)(iv)(B), in allocating income, gain, loss, or deduction between these separate interests, section 704(c) principles shall apply to account for any value-basis disparities attributable to the qualifying investment or non-qualifying investment. Any distribution (whether actual or deemed) to the holder of a qualifying investment is subject to the rules of paragraphs (c)(6)(iii) and (v) of this section, without regard to the presence or absence of gain under other provisions of subchapter K of chapter 1 of subtitle A of the Code.

(C) *Subsequent contributions.*—In the event of an increase in a partner's qualifying or non-qualifying investment (for example, as in the case of an additional contribution for a qualifying investment or for an interest that is a non-qualifying investment or a change in allocations for services rendered), the partner's interest in the separate interests shall be valued immediately prior to such event and the allocation percentages shall be adjusted to reflect the relative values of these separate interests and the additional contribution, if any.

(D) *Allocation percentages.*—The allocation percentages of the separate interests shall be determined based on the relative capital contributions attributable to the qualifying investment and the non-qualifying investment. In the event a partner receives a profits interest in the partnership for services rendered to or for the benefit of the partnership, the allocation percentages with respect to such partner shall be calculated based on:

(1) With respect to the profits interest received, the highest share of residual profits the mixed-funds partner would receive with respect to that interest; and

(2) With respect to the remaining interest, the percentage interests for the capital interests described in the immediately preceding sentence.

(v) *Remaining deferred gain reduction rule.*—An inclusion event occurs when and to the extent that a transaction has the effect of reducing—

(A) The amount of remaining deferred gain of one or more direct or indirect partners; or

(B) The amount of gain that would be recognized by such partner or partners under paragraph (e)(4)(ii) of this section to the extent that such amount would reduce such gain to an amount that is less than the remaining deferred gain.

(7) *Special rule for S corporations.*—(i) *In general.*—Except as provided in paragraphs (c)(7)(ii), (iii), and (iv) of this section, none of the following is an inclusion event:

(A) An election, revocation, or termination of a corporation's status as an S corporation under section 1362;

(B) A conversion of a qualified subchapter S trust (as defined in section 1361(d)(3)) to an electing small business trust (as defined in section 1361(e)(1));

(C) A conversion of an electing small business trust to a qualified subchapter S trust;

(D) A valid modification of a trust agreement of an S-corporation shareholder whether by an amendment, a decanting, a judicial reformation, or a material modification;

(E) A 25 percent or less aggregate change in ownership pursuant to paragraph (c)(7)(iii) of this section in the equity investment in an S corporation that directly holds a qualifying investment; and

(F) A disposition of assets by a QOF S corporation.

(ii) *Distributions by QOF S corporation.*—(A) *General rule.*—An actual or constructive distribution of property by a QOF S corporation to a shareholder with respect to its qualifying investment is an inclusion event to the extent that the distribution is treated as gain from the sale or exchange of property under section 1368(b)(2) and (c).

(B) *Spill-over rule.*—For purposes of applying paragraph (c)(7)(ii) of this section to the adjusted basis of a qualifying investment, or non-qualifying investment, as appropriate, in a QOF S corporation, the second sentence of §1.1367-1(c)(3) applies—

(1) With regard to multiple qualifying investments, solely to the respective bases of such qualifying investments, and does not take into account the basis of any non-qualifying investment; and

(2) With regard to multiple non-qualifying investments, solely to the respective bases of such non-qualifying investments, and does not take into account the basis of any qualifying investment.

(iii) *Aggregate change in ownership of an S corporation that is a QOF owner.*—(A) *General rule.*—Solely for purposes of section 1400Z-2, an inclusion event occurs when there is an aggregate change in ownership, within the meaning of paragraph (c)(7)(iii)(B) of this section, of an S corporation that directly holds a qualifying investment in a QOF. The S corporation is treated as having disposed of its entire qualifying investment in the QOF, and neither section 1400Z-2(b)(2)(B)(iii) or (iv) nor section 1400Z-2(c) applies to the S corporation's qualifying investment after that date. The disposition under this paragraph (c)(7)(iii)(A) is treated as occurring on the date the requirements of paragraph (c)(7)(iii)(B) of this section are satisfied.

(B) *Aggregate ownership change threshold.*—For purposes of paragraph (c)(7)(iii)(A) of this section, there is an *aggregate change in ownership* of an S corporation if, immediately after any change in ownership of the S corporation, the percentage of the stock of the S corporation owned directly by the shareholders who owned the S corporation at the time of its deferral election has decreased by more than 25 percent. The ownership percentage of each shareholder referred to in this paragraph (c)(7)(iii)(B) is measured separately from the ownership percentage of all other shareholders. Any decrease in ownership is determined with regard to the percentage held by the relevant shareholder at the time of the election under section 1400Z-2(a), and all decreases are then aggregated. Decreases in ownership may result from, for example, the sale of shares, the redemption of shares, the issuance of new shares, or the occurrence of section 381(a) transactions. The aggregate change in ownership is measured separately for each qualifying investment of the S corporation.

(iv) *Conversion from S corporation to partnership or disregarded entity.*—(A) *General rule.*—Notwithstanding paragraph (c)(7)(i) of this section, and except as provided in paragraph (c)(7)(iv)(B) of this section, a conversion of an S corporation to a partnership or an entity disregarded as separate from its owner under § 301.7701-3(b)(1)(ii) of this chapter is an inclusion event.

(B) *Exception for qualifying section 381 transaction.*—A conversion described in paragraph (c)(7)(iv)(A) of this section is not an inclusion event if the conversion comprises a step in a series of related transactions that together qualify as a qualifying section 381 transaction.

(v) *Treatment of separate blocks of stock in mixed-funds investments.*—With regard to a mixed-funds investment in a QOF S corporation, if different blocks of stock are created for otherwise qualifying investments to track basis in such qualifying investments, the separate blocks are not treated as different classes of stock for purposes of S corporation eligibility under section 1361(b)(1).

(vi) *Applicability.*—Paragraph (c)(7) of this section applies regardless of whether the S corporation is a QOF or a QOF shareholder.

(8) *Distributions by a QOF C corporation.*—A distribution of property by a QOF C corporation with respect to a qualifying investment is not an inclusion event except to the extent section 301(c)(3) applies to the distribution. For purposes of this paragraph (c)(8), a distribution of property also includes a distribution of stock by a QOF C corporation that is treated as a distribution of property to which section 301 applies pursuant to section 305(b).

(9) *Dividend-equivalent redemptions.*—(i) *General rule.*—Except as provided in paragraph (c)(9)(ii) or (iii) of this section, a transaction described in section 302(d) is an inclusion event with respect to the full amount of the distribution.

(ii) *Redemption of stock of wholly owned QOF.*—If all stock in a QOF is held directly by a single shareholder, or directly by members of the same consolidated group, and if shares are redeemed in a transaction to which section 302(d) applies, *see* paragraph (c)(8) of this section (applicable to distributions by QOF corporations).

(iii) *S corporations.*—S corporation section 302(d) transactions are an inclusion event to the extent the distribution exceeds basis in the QOF as adjusted under paragraph (c)(7)(ii) of this section.

(10) *Qualifying section 381 transactions.*—(i) *Assets of a QOF are acquired.*—(A) *In general.*—Except to the extent provided in paragraph (c)(10)(i)(C) of this section, if the assets of a QOF corporation are acquired in a qualifying section 381 transaction, and if the acquiring corporation is a QOF immediately after the acquisition, then the transaction is not an inclusion event.

(B) *Determination of acquiring corporation's status as a QOF.*—For purposes of paragraph (c)(10)(i)(A) of this section, the acquiring corporation is treated as a QOF immediately after the qualifying section 381 transaction if the acquiring corporation satisfies the certification requirements in § 1.1400Z2(d)-1 immediately after the transaction and holds at least 90 percent of its assets in qualified opportunity zone property on the first testing date after the transaction (*see* section 1400Z-2(d)(1) and § 1.1400Z2(d)-1).

(C) *Receipt of boot by QOF shareholder in qualifying section 381 transaction.*—*(1) General rule.*—Except as provided in paragraph (c)(10)(i)(C)(*2*) of this section, if assets of a QOF corporation are acquired in a qualifying section 381 transaction and a taxpayer that is a QOF shareholder receives boot with respect to its qualifying investment, the taxpayer has an inclusion event. If the taxpayer realizes a gain on the transaction, the amount that gives rise to the inclusion event is the amount of gain under section 356 that is not treated as a dividend under section 356(a)(2). If the taxpayer realizes a loss on the transaction, the amount that gives rise to the inclusion event is an amount equal to the fair market value of the boot received.

(2) Receipt of boot from wholly owned QOF.—If all stock in both a QOF and the corporation that acquires the QOF's assets in a qualifying section 381 transaction are held directly by a single shareholder, or directly by members of the same consolidated group, and if the shareholder receives (or group members receive) boot with respect to the qualifying investment in the qualifying section 381 transaction, paragraph (c)(8) of this section (applicable to distributions by QOF corporations) applies to the boot as if it were distributed from the QOF to the shareholder(s) in a separate transaction to which section 301 applied.

(ii) *Assets of a QOF shareholder are acquired.*—(A) *In general.*—Except to the extent provided in paragraph (c)(10)(ii)(B) of this section, a qualifying section 381 transaction in which the assets of a QOF shareholder are acquired is not an inclusion event with respect to the qualifying investment. However, if the qualifying section 381 transaction causes a QOF shareholder that is an S corporation to have an aggregate change in ownership within the meaning of paragraph (c)(7)(iii)(B) of this section, *see* paragraph (c)(7)(iii)(A) of this section.

(B) *Qualifying section 381 transaction in which QOF shareholder's qualifying investment is not completely acquired.*—If the assets of a QOF shareholder are acquired in a qualifying section 381 transaction in which the acquiring corporation does not acquire all of the QOF shareholder's qualifying investment, there is an inclusion event to the extent that the QOF shareholder's qualifying investment is not transferred to the acquiring corporation.

(11) *Section 355 transactions.*—(i) *Distribution by a QOF.*—(A) *In general.*—Except as provided in paragraph (c)(11)(i)(B) of this section, if a QOF corporation distributes stock or securities of a controlled corporation to a taxpayer in a transaction to which section 355, or so much of section 356 as relates to section 355, applies, the taxpayer has an inclusion event with respect to its qualifying investment. The amount that gives rise to such inclusion event is equal to the fair market value of the shares of the controlled corporation and the boot received by the taxpayer in the distribution with respect to its qualifying investment.

(B) *Controlled corporation becomes a QOF.*—(*1*) *In general.*—Except as provided in paragraph (c)(11)(i)(B)(*3*) of this section, if a QOF corporation distributes stock or securities of a controlled corporation in a transaction to which section 355, or so much of section 356 as relates to section 355, applies, and if both the distributing corporation and the controlled corporation are QOFs immediately after the final distribution (qualifying section 355 transaction), then the distribution is not an inclusion event with respect to the taxpayer's qualifying investment in the distributing QOF corporation or the controlled QOF corporation. This paragraph (c)(11)(i)(B) does not apply unless the distributing corporation distributes all of the stock and securities in the controlled corporation held by it immediately before the distribution within a 30-day period. For purposes of this paragraph (c)(11)(i)(B), the term *final distribution* means the last distribution that satisfies the preceding sentence.

(*2*) *Determination of distributing corporation's and controlled corporation's status as QOFs.*—For purposes of paragraph (c)(11)(i)(B)(*1*) of this section, each of the distributing corporation and the controlled corporation is treated as a QOF immediately after the final distribution if the corporation satisfies the certification requirements in § 1.1400Z2(d)-1 immediately after the final distribution and holds at least 90 percent of its assets in qualified opportunity zone property on the first testing date after the final distribution (*see* section 1400Z-2(d)(1) and § 1.1400Z2(d)-1)).

(*3*) *Receipt of boot.*—If a taxpayer receives boot in a qualifying section 355 transaction with respect to its qualifying investment, and if section 356(a) applies to the transaction, the taxpayer has an inclusion event, and the amount that gives rise to the inclusion event is the amount of gain under section 356 that is not treated as a dividend under section 356(a)(2). If a taxpayer receives boot in a qualifying section 355 transaction with respect to its qualifying investment, and if section 356(b) applies to the transaction, *see* paragraph (c)(8) of this section (applicable to distributions by QOF corporations).

(*4*) *Treatment of controlled corporation stock as qualified opportunity zone stock.*—If stock or securities of a controlled corporation are distributed in a qualifying section 355 transaction, and if the distributing corporation retains a portion of the controlled corporation stock after the initial distribution, the retained stock will not cease to qualify as qualified opportunity zone stock in the hands of the distributing corporation solely as a result of the qualifying section 355 transaction. This paragraph (c)(11)(i)(B)(*4*) does not apply unless the distributing corporation distributes all of the stock and securities in the controlled corporation held by it immediately before the distribution within a 30-day period.

(ii) *Distribution by a QOF shareholder.*—If a QOF shareholder distributes stock or securities of a controlled QOF corporation in a transaction to which section 355 applies, then for purposes of section 1400Z-2(b)(1) and paragraph (b) of this section, the taxpayer has an inclusion event to the extent the distribution reduces the taxpayer's direct tax ownership of its qualifying QOF stock. For distributions by a QOF shareholder that is an S corporation, *see also* paragraph (c)(7)(iii) of this section.

(12) *Recapitalizations and section 1036 transactions.*—(i) *No reduction in proportionate interest in qualifying QOF stock.*—(A) *In general.*—Except as otherwise provided in paragraph (c)(8) of this section (relating to distributions subject to section 305(b)) or paragraph (c)(12)(i)(B) of this section, if a QOF corporation engages in a transaction that qualifies as a reorganization described in section 368(a)(1)(E), or if a QOF shareholder engages in a transaction that is described in section 1036, and if the transaction does not have the result of decreasing the taxpayer's proportionate interest in the QOF corporation, the transaction is not an inclusion event.

(B) *Receipt of property or boot by QOF shareholder.*—If the taxpayer receives property or boot in a transaction described in paragraph (c)(12)(i)(A) of this section and section 368(a)(1)(E), then the property or boot is treated as property or boot to which section 301 or section 356 applies, as determined under general tax principles. If the taxpayer receives property that is not permitted to be received without the recognition of gain in a transaction described in paragraph (c)(12)(i)(A) of this section and section 1036, then, for purposes of this section, the property is treated in a similar manner as boot in a transaction described in section 368(a)(1)(E). For the treatment of property to which section 301 applies, *see* paragraph (c)(8) of this section. For the treatment of boot to which section 356 applies (including in situations in which the QOF is wholly and directly owned by a single shareholder or by members of the same consolidated group), *see* paragraph (c)(10) of this section.

(ii) *Reduction in proportionate interest in the QOF corporation.*—If a QOF engages in a transaction that qualifies as a reorganization described in section 368(a)(1)(E), or if a QOF shareholder engages in a transaction that is described in section 1036, and if the transaction has the result of decreasing the taxpayer's proportionate qualifying interest in the QOF corporation, then the taxpayer has an inclusion event in an amount equal to the amount of the reduction in the fair market value of the taxpayer's qualifying QOF stock.

(13) *Section 304 transactions.*—A transfer of a qualifying investment in a transaction described in section 304(a) is an inclusion event

with respect to the full amount of the consideration.

(14) *Deduction for worthlessness.*—If a taxpayer claims a loss for worthless stock under section 165(g) or otherwise claims a worthlessness deduction with respect to all or a portion of its qualifying investment, then for purposes of section 1400Z-2 and all section 1400Z-2 regulations in this chapter, the taxpayer is treated as having disposed of that portion of its qualifying investment on the date it became worthless. Thus, the taxpayer has an inclusion event with respect to that portion of its qualifying investment, and neither section 1400Z-2(b)(2)(B)(iii) or (iv) nor section 1400Z-2(c) applies to that portion of the taxpayer's qualifying investment after the date it became worthless.

(15) *Other inclusion and non-inclusion events.*—Notwithstanding any other provision of this paragraph (c), the Commissioner may determine by published guidance that a type of transaction is or is not an inclusion event.

(d) *Holding periods.*—(1) *Holding period for QOF investment.*—(i) *General rule.*—Solely for purposes of sections 1400Z-2(b)(2)(B) and 1400Z-2(c), and except as otherwise provided in this paragraph (d)(1), the length of time a qualifying investment has been held is determined without regard to the period for which the taxpayer had held property exchanged for such investment.

(ii) *Holding period for QOF investment received in a qualifying section 381 transaction, a reorganization described in section 368(a)(1)(E), or a section 1036 exchange.*—For purposes of section 1400Z-2(b)(2)(B) and 1400Z-2(c), the holding period for QOF stock received by a taxpayer in a qualifying section 381 transaction in which the target corporation was a QOF immediately before the acquisition and the acquiring corporation is a QOF immediately after the acquisition, in a reorganization described in section 368(a)(1)(E), or in a section 1036 exchange, is determined by applying the principles of section 1223(1).

(iii) *Holding period for controlled corporation stock.*—For purposes of section 1400Z-2(b)(2)(B) and 1400Z-2(c), the holding period of a qualifying investment in a controlled corporation received by a taxpayer on its qualifying investment in the distributing corporation in a qualifying section 355 transaction is determined by applying the principles of section 1223(1).

(iv) *Tacking with donor or deceased owner.*—For purposes of section 1400Z-2(b)(2)(B) and 1400Z-2(c), the holding period of a qualifying investment held by a taxpayer who received that qualifying investment as a gift that was not an inclusion event, or by reason of the prior owner's death, includes the time during which that qualifying investment was held by the donor or the deceased owner, respectively.

(2) *Determination of original use of QOF assets.*—(i) *Assets acquired in a section 381 transaction.*—For purposes of section 1400Z-2(d), including for purposes of determining whether the original use of qualified opportunity zone business property commences with the acquiring corporation, any qualified opportunity zone property transferred by the transferor QOF to the acquiring corporation in connection with a qualifying section 381 transaction does not lose its status as qualified opportunity zone property solely as a result of its transfer to the acquiring corporation.

(ii) *Assets contributed to a controlled corporation.*—For purposes of section 1400Z-2(d), including for purposes of determining whether the original use of qualified opportunity zone business property commences with the controlled corporation, any qualified opportunity zone property contributed by the distributing corporation to the controlled corporation in connection with a qualifying section 355 transaction does not lose its status as qualified opportunity zone property solely as a result of its contribution to the controlled corporation.

(3) *Application to partnerships.*—The principles of paragraphs (d)(1) and (2) of this section apply to qualifying QOF partnership interests with regard to non-inclusion transactions described in paragraph (c)(6)(ii) of this section.

(e) *Amount includible.*—Except as provided in § 1.1400Z2(a)-1(b)(4), the amount of gain included in gross income under section 1400Z-2(a)(1)(B) on a date described in paragraph (b) of this section is determined under this paragraph (e).

(1) *In general.*—Except as provided in paragraphs (e)(2) and (4) of this section, and subject to paragraph (e)(5) of this section, in the case of an inclusion event, the amount of gain included in gross income is equal to the excess of the amount described in paragraph (e)(1)(i) of this section over the amount described in paragraph (e)(1)(ii) of this section.

(i) The amount described in this paragraph (e)(1)(i) is equal to the lesser of:

(A) An amount which bears the same proportion to the remaining deferred gain, as:

(1) The fair market value of the portion of the qualifying investment that is disposed of in the inclusion event, as determined as of the date of the inclusion event, bears to;

(2) The fair market value of the total qualifying investment immediately before the inclusion event; or

(B) The amount described in paragraph (e)(1)(i)(A)*(1)* of this section.

(ii) The amount described in this paragraph (e)(1)(ii) is the taxpayer's basis in the portion of the qualifying investment that is disposed of in the inclusion event.

(iii) For purposes of paragraph (e)(1)(i)(A)*(1)* of this section, the fair market value of that portion is determined by multiplying the fair market value of the taxpayer's entire qualifying investment in the QOF, valued as of the date of the inclusion event, by the percentage of the taxpayer's qualifying investment that is represented by the portion disposed of in the inclusion event.

(2) *Property received from a QOF in certain transactions.*—In the case of an inclusion event described in paragraph (c)(6)(iii) or (v) or (c)(8), (9), (10), (11), or (12) of this section, the amount of gain included in gross income is equal to the lesser of:

(i) The remaining deferred gain; or

(ii) The amount that gave rise to the inclusion event. *See* paragraph (c) of this section for rules regarding the amount that gave rise to the inclusion event, and *see* paragraph (g) of this section for applicable ordering rules.

(3) *Gain recognized on December 31, 2026.*—The amount of gain included in gross income on December 31, 2026 is equal to the excess of—

(i) The lesser of—

(A) The remaining deferred gain; and

(B) The fair market value of the qualifying investment held on December 31, 2026; over

(ii) The taxpayer's basis in the qualifying investment as of December 31, 2026, taking into account only section 1400Z-2(b)(2)(B).

(4) *Special amount includible rule for partnerships and S corporations.*—For purposes of paragraphs (e)(1) and (3) of this section, in the case of an inclusion event involving a qualifying investment in a QOF partnership or S corporation, or in the case of a qualifying investment in a QOF partnership or S corporation held on December 31, 2026, the amount of gain included in gross income is equal to the lesser of:

(i) The product of:

(A) The percentage of the qualifying investment that gave rise to the inclusion event; and

(B) The remaining deferred gain, less any basis adjustments pursuant to section 1400Z-2(b)(2)(B)(iii) and (iv); or

(ii) The gain that would be recognized on a fully taxable disposition of the qualifying investment that gave rise to the inclusion event.

(5) *Limitation on amount of gain included after statutory five- and seven-year basis increases.*—The total amount of gain included in gross income under this paragraph (e) is limited to the amount deferred under section 1400Z-2(a)(1), reduced by any increase in the basis of the qualifying investment made pursuant to section 1400Z-2(b)(2)(B)(iii) or (iv). *See* paragraph (g)(2) of this section for limitations on the amount of basis adjustments under section 1400Z-2(b)(2)(B)(iii) and (iv).

(f) *Examples.*—The following examples illustrate the rules of paragraphs (c), (d) and (e) of this section. For purposes of the following examples: A, B, C, W, X, Y, and Z are C corporations that do not file a consolidated Federal income tax return; Q is a QOF corporation or a QOF partnership, as specified in each example; and each divisive corporate transaction satisfies the requirements of section 355.

(1) *Example 1: Determination of basis, holding period, and qualifying investment*—(i) *Facts.* A wholly and directly owns Q, a QOF corporation. On May 31, 2019, A sells a capital asset to an unrelated party and realizes $500 of capital gain. On October 31, 2019, A transfers unencumbered asset N to Q in exchange for a qualifying investment. Asset N, which A has held for 10 years, has a basis of $500 and a fair market value of $500. A elects to defer the inclusion of $500 in gross income under section 1400Z-2(a) and § 1.1400Z2(a)-1.

(ii) *Analysis.* Under § 1.1400Z2(a)-1(b)(10)(i)(B)(*1*), A made a qualifying investment of $500. Under section 1400Z-2(b)(2)(B)(i), A's basis in its qualifying investment in Q is $0. For purposes of sections 1400Z-2(b)(2)(B) and 1400Z-2(c), A's holding period in its new investment in Q begins on October 31, 2019. *See* paragraph (d)(1)(i) of this section. Other than for purposes of applying section 1400Z-2, A has a 10-year holding period in its new Q investment as of October 31, 2019.

(iii) *Transfer of built-in gain property.* The facts are the same as in this *Example 1* in paragraph (f)(1)(i) of this section, but A's basis in transferred asset N is $200. Under § 1.1400Z2(a)-1(b)(10)(i)(B)(*1*), A made a qualifying investment of $200 and a non-qualifying investment of $300.

(2) *Example 2: Transfer of qualifying investment*—(i) *Facts.* On May 31, 2019, A sells a capital asset to an unrelated party and realizes $500 of capital gain. On October 31, 2019, A transfers $500 to newly formed Q, a QOF corporation, in exchange for a qualifying investment. On February 29, 2020, A transfers 25 percent of its qualifying investment in Q to newly formed Y in exchange for 100 percent of Y's stock in a transfer to which section 351 applies (the Transfer), at a time when the fair market value of A's qualifying investment in Q is $800.

(ii) *Analysis.* Under § 1.1400Z2(a)-1(b)(10)(i)(A), A made a qualifying investment of $500 on October 31, 2019. In the Transfer, A exchanged 25 percent of its qualifying investment for Federal income tax purposes, which reduced A's direct qualifying investment. Under paragraph (c)(1)(i) of this section, the Transfer is an inclusion event to the extent of the reduction in A's direct qualifying investment. Under paragraph (e)(1) of this section, A therefore includes in income an amount equal to the excess of the amount described in paragraph (e)(1)(i) of this section over A's basis in the portion of the qualifying investment that was disposed of, which in this case is $0. The amount described in paragraph (e)(1)(i) is the lesser of:

(A) $125 ($500 x ($200 / $800)); or

(B) $200. As a result, A must include $125 of its deferred capital gain in income in 2020. After the Transfer, the Q stock is not qualifying Q stock in Y's hands.

(iii) *Disregarded transfer.* The facts are the same as in this *Example 2* in paragraph (f)(2)(i) of this section, except that Y elects to be treated as an entity that is disregarded as an entity separate from its owner for Federal income tax purposes effective prior to the Contribution. Since the Transfer would be disregarded for Federal income tax purposes, A's transfer of its qualifying investment in Q would not be treated as a reduction in direct tax ownership for Federal income tax purposes, and the Transfer would not be an inclusion event with respect to A's qualifying investment in Q for purposes of section 1400Z-2(b)(1) and paragraph (b) of this section. Thus, A would not be required to include in income any portion of its deferred capital gain.

(iv) *Election to be treated as a corporation.* The facts are the same as in this *Example 2* in paragraph (f)(2)(iii) of this section, except that Y (a disregarded entity) subsequently elects to be treated as a corporation for Federal income tax purposes. A's deemed transfer of its qualifying investment in Q to Y under § 301.7701-3(g)(1)(iv) of this chapter is an inclusion event for purposes of section 1400Z-2(b)(1) and paragraph (b) of this section.

(3) *Example 3: Part sale of qualifying QOF partnership interest in Year 6 when value of the QOF interest has increased*—(i) *Facts.* In October 2018, A and B each realize $200 of eligible gain, and C realizes $600 of eligible gain. On January 1, 2019,

A, B, and C form Q, a QOF partnership. A contributes $200 of cash, B contributes $200 of cash, and C contributes $600 of cash to Q in exchange for qualifying QOF partnership interests in Q. A, B, and C hold 20 percent, 20 percent, and 60 percent interests in Q, respectively. On January 30, 2019, Q obtains a nonrecourse loan from a bank for $1,000. Under section 752, the loan is allocated $200 to A, $200 to B, and $600 to C. On February 1, 2019, Q purchases qualified opportunity zone business property for $2,000. On July 31, 2024, A sells 50 percent of its qualifying QOF partnership interest in Q to B for $400 cash. Prior to the sale, there were no inclusion events, distributions, partner changes, income or loss allocations, or changes in the amount or allocation of debt outstanding. At the time of the sale, the fair market value of Q's qualified opportunity zone business property is $5,000.

(ii) *Analysis*. Because A held its qualifying QOF partnership interest for at least five years, A's basis in its partnership interest at the time of the sale is $220 (the original zero basis with respect to the contribution, plus the $200 debt allocation, plus the 10% increase for interests held for five years). The sale of 50 percent of A's qualifying QOF partnership interest to B requires A to recognize $90 of eligible gain, the lesser of 50 percent of the remaining $180 deferred gain ($90) or the gain that would be recognized on a taxable sale of 50 percent of the interest ($390). A also recognizes $300 of gain relating to the appreciation of its interest in Q.

(4) *Example 4: Sale of qualifying QOF partnership interest when value of the QOF interest has decreased*—(i) *Facts*. The facts are the same as in *Example 3* in paragraph (f)(3) of this section, except that A sells 50 percent of its qualifying QOF partnership interest in Q to B for cash of $50, and at the time of the sale, the fair market value of Q's qualified opportunity zone business property is $1,500.

(ii) *Analysis*. Because A held its qualifying QOF partnership interest for at least five years, A's basis at the time of the sale is $220. Under section 1400Z-2(b)(2)(A), the sale of 50 percent of A's qualifying QOF partnership interest to B requires A to recognize $40 of eligible gain, the lesser of $90 (50 percent of A's remaining deferred gain of $180) or $40 (the gain that would be recognized by A on a sale of 50 percent of its QOF interest). A's remaining basis in its qualifying QOF partnership interest is $110.

(5) *Example 5: Amount includible on December 31, 2026*—(i) *Facts*. The facts are the same as in *Example 3* in paragraph (f)(3) of this section, except that no sale of QOF interests takes place in 2024. Prior to December 31, 2026, there were no inclusion events, distributions, partner changes, income or loss allocations, or changes in the amount or allocation of debt outstanding.

(ii) *Analysis*. For purposes of calculating the amount includible on December 31, 2026, each of A's basis and B's basis is increased by $30 to $230, and C's basis is increased by $90 to $690 because they held their qualifying QOF partnership interests for at least seven years. Each of A and B is required to recognize $170 of eligible gain, and C is required to recognize $510 of eligible gain.

(iii) *Sale of qualifying QOF partnership interests*. The facts are the same as in this *Example 5* in paragraph (f)(5)(i) of this section, except that, on March 2, 2030, C sells its entire qualifying QOF partnership interest in Q to an unrelated buyer for cash of $4,200. Assuming an election under section 1400Z-2(c) is made, the basis of C's Q interest is increased to its fair market value immediately before the sale by C. C is treated as purchasing the interest immediately before the sale and the bases of the partnership's assets are increased in the manner they would be if the partnership had an election under section 754 in effect.

(6) *Example 6: Mixed-funds investment*—(i) *Facts*. On January 1, 2019, A and B form Q, a QOF partnership. A contributes $200 to Q, $100 of which is a qualifying investment, and B contributes $200 to Q in exchange for a qualifying investment. All the cash is used to purchase qualified opportunity zone property. Q has no liabilities. On March 30, 2023, when the values and bases of the qualifying investments remain unchanged, Q distributes $50 to A.

(ii) *Analysis*. Under paragraph (c)(6)(iv) of this section, A is a mixed-funds partner holding two separate interests, a qualifying investment and a non-qualifying investment. One half of the $50 distribution is treated under that provision as being made with respect to A's qualifying investment. For the $25 distribution made with respect to the qualifying investment, A is required to recognize $25 of eligible gain.

(iii) *Basis adjustments*. Under paragraph (g)(1)(ii)(B) of this section, prior to determining the tax consequences of the distribution, A increases its basis in its qualifying QOF partnership interest by $25 under section 1400Z-2(b)(2)(B)(ii). The distribution of $25 results in no gain under section 731. After the distribution, A's basis in its qualifying QOF partnership interest is $0 ($25-$25).

(7) *Example 7: Qualifying section 381 transaction of a QOF corporation*—(i) *Facts*. X wholly and directly owns Q, a QOF corporation. On May 31, 2019, X sells a capital asset to an unrelated party and realizes $500 of capital gain. On October 31, 2019, X contributes $500 to Q in exchange for a qualifying investment. In 2020, Q merges with and into unrelated Y (with Y surviving) in a transaction that qualifies as a reorganization under section 368(a)(1)(A) (the Merger). X does not receive any boot in the Merger with respect to its qualifying investment in Q. Immediately after the Merger, Y satisfies the requirements for QOF status under section 1400Z-2(d)(1) (*see* paragraph (c)(10)(i)(B) of this section).

(ii) *Analysis*. The Merger is not an inclusion event for purposes of section 1400Z-2(b)(1) and paragraph (b) of this section. *See* paragraph (c)(10)(i)(A) of this section. Accordingly, X is not required to include in income in 2020 its $500 of deferred capital gain as a result of the Merger. For purposes of section 1400Z-2(b)(2)(B) and 1400Z-2(c), X's holding period for its investment in Y is treated as beginning on October 31, 2019. For purposes of section 1400Z-2(d), Y's holding period in its assets includes Q's holding period in its assets, and Q's qualified opportunity zone business property continues to qualify as such. *See* paragraph (d)(2)(i) of this section.

(iii) *Merger of QOF shareholder*. The facts are the same as in this *Example 7* in paragraph (f)(7)(i) of this section, except that, in 2020, X (rather than Q) merges with and into Y in a section 381 transaction in which Y acquires all of

X's qualifying interest in Q, and Y does not qualify as a QOF immediately after the merger. The merger transaction is not an inclusion event for purposes of section 1400Z-2(b)(1) and paragraph (b) of this section. *See* paragraph (c)(10)(ii) of this section.

(iv) *Receipt of boot*. The facts are the same as in this *Example 7* in paragraph (f)(7)(i) of this section, except that the value of X's qualifying investment immediately before the Merger is $1,000, X receives $100 of cash in addition to Y stock in the Merger in exchange for its qualifying investment, and neither Q nor Y has any earnings and profits. X realizes $1,000 of gain in the Merger. Under paragraphs (c)(10)(i)(C)(*1*) and (e)(2) of this section, X is required to include $100 of its deferred capital gain in income in 2020.

(v) *Realization of loss*. The facts are the same as in this *Example 7* in paragraph (f)(7)(iv) of this section, except that the Merger occurs in 2025, the value of X's qualifying investment immediately before the Merger is $25, and X receives $10 of boot in the Merger. X realizes $25 of loss in the Merger. Under paragraphs (c)(10)(i)(C)(*1*) and (e)(2) of this section, X is required to include $10 of its deferred capital gain in income in 2020.

(8) *Example 8: Section 355 distribution by a QOF*—(i) *Facts*. A wholly and directly owns Q, a QOF corporation, which wholly and directly owns Y, a corporation that is a qualified opportunity zone business. On May 31, 2019, A sells a capital asset to an unrelated party and realizes $500 of capital gain. On October 31, 2019, A contributes $500 to Q in exchange for a qualifying investment. On June 26, 2025, Q distributes all of the stock of Y to A in a transaction in which no gain or loss is recognized under section 355 (the Distribution). Immediately after the Distribution, each of Q and Y satisfies the requirements for QOF status (*see* paragraph (c)(11)(i)(B)(2) of this section).

(ii) *Analysis*. Because each of Q (the distributing corporation) and Y (the controlled corporation) is a QOF immediately after the Distribution, the Distribution is a qualifying section 355 transaction. Thus, the Distribution is not an inclusion event for purposes of section 1400Z-2(b)(1) and paragraph (b) of this section.. *See* paragraph (c)(11)(i)(B) of this section. Accordingly, A is not required to include in income in 2025 any of its $500 of deferred capital gain as a result of the Distribution. For purposes of section 1400Z-2(b)(2)(B) and 1400Z-2(c), A's holding period for its qualifying investment in Y is treated as beginning on October 31, 2019. See paragraph (d)(2)(i) of this section.

(iii) *Section 355 distribution by a QOF shareholder*. The facts are the same as in this *Example 8* in paragraph (f)(8)(i) of this section, except that A distributes 80 percent of the stock of Q (all of which is a qualifying investment in the hands of A) to A's shareholders in a transaction in which no gain or loss is recognized under section 355. The distribution is an inclusion event for purposes of section 1400Z-2(b)(1) and paragraph (b) of this section, and A is required to include in income $400 (80 percent of its $500 of deferred capital gain) as a result of the distribution. *See* paragraphs (c)(1) and (c)(11)(ii) of this section.

(iv) *Distribution of boot*. The facts are the same as in this *Example 8* in paragraph (f)(8)(i) of this section, except that A receives boot in the Distribution. Under paragraphs (c)(8) and (c)(11)(i)(B)(*3*) of this section, the receipt of boot in the Distribution is an inclusion event for purposes of section 1400Z-2(b)(1) and paragraph (b) of this section to the extent of gain recognized pursuant to section 301(c)(3).

(v) *Section 355 split-off*. The facts are the same as in this *Example 8* in paragraph (f)(8)(i) of this section, except that Q stock is directly owned by both A and B (each of which has made a qualifying investment in Q), and Q distributes all of the Y stock to B in exchange for B's Q stock in a transaction in which no gain or loss is recognized under section 355. The distribution is a qualifying section 355 transaction and is not an inclusion event for purposes of section 1400Z-2(b)(1) and paragraph (b) of this section. Neither A nor B is required to include its deferred capital gain in income in 2025 as a result of the distribution.

(vi) *Section 355 split-up*. The facts are the same as in this *Example 8* in paragraph (f)(8)(v) of this section, except that Q wholly and directly owns both Y and Z; Q distributes all of the Y stock to A in exchange for A's Q stock and distributes all of the Z stock to B in exchange for B's Q stock in a transaction in which no gain or loss is recognized under section 355; Q then liquidates; and immediately after the Distribution, each of Y and Z satisfies the requirements for QOF status. The distribution is a qualifying section 355 transaction and is not an inclusion event for purposes of section 1400Z-2(b)(1) and paragraph (b) of this section. Neither A nor B is required to include its deferred capital gain in income in 2025 as a result of the transaction.

(vii) *Section 355 split-off with boot*. The facts are the same as in this *Example 8* in paragraph (f)(8)(v) of this section, except that B also receives boot. Under paragraph (c)(11)(i)(B)(*3*) of this section, B has an inclusion event, and the amount that gives rise to the inclusion event is the amount of gain under section 356 that is not treated as a dividend under section 356(a)(2).

(9) *Example 9: Recapitalization*—(i) *Facts*. On May 31, 2019, each of A and B sells a capital asset to an unrelated party and realizes $500 of capital gain. On October 31, 2019, A contributes $500 to newly formed Q in exchange for 50 shares of Q nonvoting stock (A's qualifying investment) and B contributes $500 to Q in exchange for 50 shares of Q voting stock (B's qualifying investment). A and B are the sole shareholders of Q. In 2020, when A's qualifying investment is worth $600, A exchanges all of its Q non-voting stock for $120 and 40 shares of Q voting stock in a transaction that qualifies as a reorganization under section 368(a)(1)(E).

(ii) *Analysis*. Because A's proportionate interest in Q has decreased in this transaction, the recapitalization is an inclusion event under paragraph (c)(12)(ii) of this section. Thus, A is treated as having reduced its direct tax ownership of its investment in Q to the extent of the reduction in the fair market value of its qualifying QOF stock. The $120 that A received in the reorganization represents the difference in fair market value between its qualifying investment before and after the reorganization. Under paragraphs (c)(12)(i)(B) and (e)(2) of this section, A is required to include $120 of its deferred capital gain in income in 2020. Because B's proportionate interest in Q has not decreased, and because B did not receive any property in the recapitalization, B does not have an inclusion event with respect to its qualifying investment in Q. *See* paragraph (c)(12)(i) of this section. Therefore, B is not required to include any of its deferred gain in income as a result of this transaction.

(10) *Example 10: Debt financed distribution*—(i) *Facts.* On January 1, 2019, A and B form Q, a QOF partnership, each contributing $200 that is deferred under the section 1400Z-2(a) election to Q in exchange for a qualifying investment. On November 18, 2022, Q obtains a nonrecourse loan from a bank for $300. Under section 752, the loan is allocated $150 to A and $150 to B. On November 30, 2022, when the values and bases of the investments remain unchanged, Q distributes $50 to A.

(ii) *Analysis.* A is not required to recognize gain under § 1.1400Z2(b)-1(c) because A's basis in its qualifying investment is $150 (the original zero basis with respect to the contribution, plus the $150 debt allocation). The distribution reduces A's basis to $100.

(11) *Example 11: Debt financed distribution in excess of basis*—(i) *Facts.* The facts are the same as in *Example 10* in paragraph (f)(10) of this section, except that the loan is entirely allocated to B under section 752. On November 30, 2024, when the values of the investments remain unchanged, Q distributes $50 to A.

(ii) *Analysis.* Under § 1.1400Z2(b)-1(c)(6)(iii), A is required to recognize $30 of eligible gain under section § 1.1400Z2(b)-1(c) because the $50 distributed to A exceeds A's $20 basis in its qualifying investment (the original zero basis with respect to its contribution, plus $20 with regard to section 1400Z-2(b)(2)(B)(iii)).

(12) *Example 12: Aggregate ownership change threshold*—(i) *Facts.* On May 31, 2019, B, an S corporation, sells a capital asset to an unrelated party for cash and realizes $500 of capital gain. On July 15, 2019, B makes a deferral election and transfers the $500 to Q, a QOF partnership in exchange for a qualifying investment. On that date, B has outstanding 100 shares, of which each of individuals D, E, F, and G owns 25 shares. On September 30, 2019, D sells 10 shares of its B stock. On September 30, 2020, E sells 16 shares of its B stock.

(ii) *Analysis.* Under paragraph (c)(7)(iii)(A) of this section, the sales of stock by D and E caused an aggregate change in ownership of B because, the percentage of the stock of B owned directly by D, E, F, and G at the time of B's deferral election decreased by more than 25 percent. Solely for purposes of section 1400Z-2, B's qualifying investment in Q would be treated as disposed of. Consequently, B would have an inclusion event with respect to all of B's remaining deferred gain of $500, and neither section 1400Z-2(b)(2)(B)(iii) or (iv), nor section 1400Z-2(c), would apply to B's qualifying investment after that date.

(g) *Basis adjustments.*—(1) *Timing of section 1400Z-2(b)(2)(B)(ii) adjustments.*—(i) *In general.*—Except as provided in paragraph (g)(1)(ii) of this section, basis adjustments under section 1400Z-2(b)(2)(B)(ii) are made immediately after the amount of gain determined under section 1400Z-2(b)(2)(A) is included in income under section 1400Z-2(b)(1). If the basis adjustment under section 1400Z-2(b)(2)(B)(ii) is being made as a result of an inclusion event, then the basis adjustment is made before determining the other tax consequences of the inclusion event.

(ii) *Specific application to section 301(c)(3) gain, S corporation shareholder gain, or partner gain.*—(A) *General rule.*—This paragraph (g)(1)(ii) applies if a QOF makes a distribution to its owner, and if, without regard to any basis adjustment under section 1400Z-2(b)(2)(B)(ii), at least a portion of the distribution would be characterized as gain under section 301(c)(3) or paragraphs (c)(6)(iii) and (c)(7)(ii) of this section with respect to its qualifying investment.

(B) *Ordering rule.*—If paragraph (g)(1)(ii) of this section applies, the taxpayer is treated as having an inclusion event to the extent provided in paragraph (c)(6)(iii) or (c)(7), (8), (9), (10), (11), or (12) of this section, as applicable. Then, the taxpayer increases its basis under section 1400Z-2(b)(2)(B)(ii), before determining the tax consequences of the distribution.

(C) *Example.*—The following example illustrates the rules of this paragraph (g)(1)(ii).

(*1*) *Example 1*—(*i*) *Facts.* On May 31, 2019, A sells a capital asset to an unrelated party and realizes $500 of capital gain. On October 31, 2019, A contributes $500 to Q, a newly formed QOF corporation, in exchange for all of the outstanding Q common stock and elects to defer the recognition of $500 of capital gain under section 1400Z-2(a) and § 1.1400Z2(a)-1. In 2020, when Q has $40 of earnings and profits, Q distributes $100 to A (the Distribution).

(*ii*) *Recognition of gain.* Under paragraph (g)(1)(ii)(A) of this section, the Distribution is first evaluated without regard to any basis adjustment under section 1400Z-2(b)(2)(B)(ii). Of the $100 distribution, $40 is treated as a dividend and $60 is treated as gain from the sale or exchange of property under section 301(c)(3), because A's basis in its Q stock is $0 under section 1400Z-2(b)(2)(B)(i). Under paragraphs (c)(8) and (e)(2) of this section, $60 of A's gain that was deferred under section 1400Z-2(a) and § 1.1400Z2(a)-1 is recognized in 2020.

(*iii*) *Basis adjustments.* Under paragraph (g)(1)(ii)(B) of this section, prior to determining the further tax consequences of the Distribution, A increases its basis in its Q stock by $60 in accordance with section 1400Z-2(b)(2)(B)(ii). As a result, the Distribution is characterized as a dividend of $40 under section 301(c)(1) and a return of basis of $60 under section 301(c)(2). Therefore, after the section 301 distribution, A's basis in Q is $0 ($60 - $60).

(2) [Reserved]

(2) *Amount of basis adjustment.*—The increases in basis under section 1400Z-2(b)(2)(B)(iii) and (iv) only apply to that portion of the qualifying investment that has not been subject to previous gain inclusion under section 1400Z-2(b)(2)(A).

(3) *Special partnership rules.*—(i) *General rule.*—The initial basis under section 1400Z-2(b)(2)(B)(i) of a qualifying investment in a QOF partnership is zero, as adjusted to take into account the contributing partner's share of partnership debt under section 752.

(ii) *Tiered arrangements.*—Any basis adjustment described in section 1400Z-2(b)(2)(B)(iii) and (iv) and section 1400Z-2(c) (the basis adjustment rules) shall be treated as an item of income described in section

705(a)(1) and shall be reported in accordance with the applicable forms and instructions. Any amount to which the basis adjustment rules or to which section 1400Z-2(b)(1) applies shall be allocated to the owners of the QOF, and to the owners of any partnership that directly or indirectly (solely through one or more partnerships) owns such QOF interest, and shall track to such owners' interests, based on their shares of the remaining deferred gain to which such amounts relate.

(4) *Basis adjustments in S corporation stock.*—(i) *S corporation investor in QOF.*—(A) *S corporation.*—If an S corporation is an investor in a QOF, the S corporation must adjust the basis of its qualifying investment as set forth in this paragraph (g). The rule in this paragraph (g)(4)(i)(A) does not affect adjustments to the basis of any other asset of the S corporation.

(B) *S corporation shareholder.*—*(1) In general.*—The S corporation shareholder's pro-rata share of any recognized capital gain that has been deferred at the S corporation level will be separately stated under section 1366 and will adjust the shareholders' stock basis under section 1367.

(2) Basis adjustments to qualifying investments.—Any adjustment made to the basis of an S corporation's qualifying investment under section 1400Z-2(b)(2)(B)(iii) or (iv), or section 1400Z-2(c), will not:

(i) Be separately stated under section 1366; or

(ii) Until the date on which an inclusion event with respect to the S corporation's qualifying investment occurs, adjust the shareholders' stock basis under section 1367.

(3) Basis adjustments resulting from inclusion events.—If the basis adjustment under section 1400Z-2(b)(2)(B)(ii) is being made as a result of an inclusion event, then the basis adjustment is made before determining the other tax consequences of the inclusion event.

(ii) *QOF S corporation.*—(A) *Transferred basis of assets received.*—If a QOF S corporation receives an asset in exchange for a qualifying investment, the basis of the asset shall be the same as it would be in the hands of the transferor, increased by the amount of the gain recognized by the transferor on such transfer.

(B) *Basis adjustments resulting from inclusion events.*—If the basis adjustment under section 1400Z-2(b)(2)(B)(ii) for the shareholder of the QOF S corporation is being made as a result of an inclusion event, then the basis adjustment is made before determining the other tax consequences of the inclusion event.

(h) *Notifications by partners and partnerships, and shareholders and S corporations.*—(1) *Notification of deferral election.*—A partnership that makes a deferral election must notify all of its partners of the deferral election and state each partner's distributive share of the eligible gain in accordance with applicable forms and instructions. A partner that makes a deferral election must notify the partnership in writing of its deferral election, including the amount of the eligible gain deferred.

(2) *Notification of deferred gain recognition by indirect QOF owner.*—If an indirect owner of a QOF partnership or QOF S corporation sells a portion of its partnership interest or S corporation shares in a transaction to which § 1.1400Z2(b)-1(c)(6)(iv) applies, or which is subject to § 1.1400Z2(b)-1(c)(7)(iii), such indirect owner must provide to the QOF owner notification and information sufficient to enable the QOF owner, in a timely manner, to recognize an appropriate amount of deferred gain.

(3) *Notification of section 1400Z-2(c) election by QOF partner or QOF partnership.*—A QOF partner must notify the QOF partnership of an election under section 1400Z-2(c) to adjust the basis of the qualifying QOF partnership interest that is disposed of in a taxable transaction. Notification of the section 1400Z-2(c) election, and the adjustments to the basis of the qualifying QOF partnership interest(s) disposed of or to the QOF partnership asset(s) disposed of, is to be made in accordance with applicable forms and instructions.

(4) *S corporations.*—Similar rules to those in paragraphs (h)(1) and (3) of this section apply to S corporations as appropriate.

(i) *Applicability dates.*—This section applies for taxable years that begin on or after the date of publication in the **Federal Register** of a Treasury decision adopting these proposed rules as final regulations. However, a taxpayer may rely on the proposed rules in this section with respect to taxable years that begin before that date, but only if the taxpayer applies the rules in their entirety and in a consistent manner. [Reg. § 1.1400Z2(b)-1.]

Qualified Opportunity Funds: Deferred Gains

Qualified Opportunity Funds: Deferred Gains.—Reg. § 1.1400Z-2(c)-1, relating to gains that may be deferred as a result of a taxpayer's investment in a qualified opportunity fund (QOF), is proposed (published in the Federal Register on October 29, 2018) (REG-115420-18).

Par. 3. Section 1.1400Z-2(c)-1 is added to read as follows:

§ 1.1400Z-2(c)-1. Investments held for at least 10 years.—(a) *Limitation on the 10-year rule.*—As required by section 1400Z-2(e)(1)(B) (treatment of investments with mixed funds), section 1400Z-2(c) (special rule for investments held for at least 10 years) applies only to the portion of an investment in a QOF with respect to which a proper election to defer gain under section 1400Z-2(a)(1) is in effect.

(b) *Extension of availability of the election described in section 1400Z-2(c).*—The ability to make an election under section 1400Z-2(c) for investments held for at least 10 years is not impaired solely because, under section 1400Z-1(f), the designation of one or more qualified opportunity zones ceases to be in effect. The preceding sentence does not apply to elections under section 1400Z-2(c) that are related to dispositions occurring after December 31, 2047.

(c) *Examples.*—The following examples illustrate the principles of paragraphs (a) and (b) of this section.

Example 1. (i) *Facts.* In 2020, taxpayer G invests $100 in QOF S in exchange for 100 common shares of QOF S and properly makes an election under section 1400Z-2(a) to defer $100 of gain. G also acquires 200 additional common shares in QOF in exchange for $z. G does not make a section 1400Z-2(a) deferral election with respect to any of the $z investments. At the end of 2028, the qualified opportunity zone designation expires for the population census tract in which QOF S primarily conducts its trade or business. In 2031, G sells all of its 300 QOF S shares, realizes gain, and makes an election to increase the qualifying basis in G's QOF S shares to fair market value. But for the expiration of the designated zones in section 1400Z-1(f), QOF S and G's conduct is consistent with continued eligibility to make the election under section 1400Z-2(c).

(ii) *Analysis*. Under paragraph (b) of this section, although the designation expired on December 31, 2028, the expiration of the zone's designation does not, without more, invalidate G's ability to make an election under section 1400Z-2(c). Accordingly, pursuant to that election, G's basis is increased in the one-third portion of G's investment in QOF S with respect to which G made a proper deferral election under section 1400Z-2(a)(2) (100 common shares / 300 common shares). Under section 1400Z-2(e)(1) and paragraph (a) of this section, however, the election under section 1400Z-2(c) is unavailable for the remaining two-thirds portion of G's investment in QOF S because G did not make a deferral election under section 1400Z-2(a)(2) for this portion of its investment in QOF S (200 common shares / 300 common shares).

(d) *Applicability date.*—This section applies to an election under section 1400Z-2(c) related to dispositions made after the date of publication in the **Federal Register** of a Treasury decision adopting these proposed rules as final regulations. A taxpayer, however, may rely on the proposed rules in this section with respect to dispositions of investment interests in QOFs in situations where the investment was made in connection with an election under section 1400Z-2(a) that relates to the deferral of a gain such that the first day of 180-day period for the gain was before the date of applicability of that section. The preceding sentence applies only if the taxpayer applies the rules of this section in their entirety and in a consistent manner. [Reg. § 1.1400Z-2(c)-1.]

Qualified Opportunity Funds: Investment

Qualified Opportunity Funds: Investment.—Amendments to Reg. § 1.1400Z2(c)-1, relating to gains that may be deferred as a result of a taxpayer's investment in a qualified opportunity fund, as well as special rules for an investment in a QOF held by a taxpayer for at least 10 years, are proposed (published in the Federal Register on May 1, 2019) (REG-120186-18).

Par. 4. Section 1.1400Z2(c)-1, as proposed to be added by 83 FR 54279 October 29, 2018, is amended by:

1. Revising paragraph (a).
2. Redesignating paragraphs (b), (c), and (d) as paragraphs (c), (d), and (f) respectively.
3. Adding new paragraph (b).
4. Revising newly redesignated paragraph (d) introductory text.
5. In newly redesignated paragraph (d)(1)(ii), removing the language "paragraph (b) of this section" and adding in its place "paragraph (c) of this section" and removing the language "paragraph (a) of this section" and adding in its place "paragraphs (a) and (b) of this section".
6. Adding paragraph (d)(2).
7. Adding paragraph (e).
8. Revising newly redesignated paragraph (f).

The revisions and additions read as follows:

§ 1.1400Z2(c)-1. Investments held for at least 10 years.—(a) *Scope and definitions.*—(1) *Scope.*—This section provides rules under section 1400Z-2(c) of the Internal Revenue Code regarding the election to adjust the basis in a qualifying investment in a QOF or certain eligible property held by the QOF. *See* § 1.1400Z2(b)-1(d) for purposes of determining the holding period of a qualifying investment for purposes of this section.

(2) *Definitions.*—The definitions provided in § 1.1400Z2(b)-1(a)(2) apply for purposes of this section.

(b) *Investment to which an election can be made.*—(1) *In general.*—(i) *Election by taxpayer.*—If the taxpayer sells or exchanges a qualifying investment that it has held for at least 10 years, then the taxpayer can make an election described in section 1400Z-2(c) on the sale or exchange of the qualifying investment.

(ii) *Limitation on the 10-year rule.*—As required by section 1400Z-2(e)(1)(B) (treatment of investments with mixed funds), section 1400Z-2(c) applies only to the portion of an investment in a QOF with respect to which a proper election to defer gain under section 1400Z-2(a)(1) is in effect. For rules governing the application of section 1400Z-2(c) to the portion of an investment in a QOF for which a loss has been claimed under section 165(g), see § 1.1400Z2(b)-1(c)(14). *See also* § 1.1400Z2(b)-1(c)(7)(iii) for rules governing the application of section 1400Z-2(c) to the portion of an investment in a QOF held by an S corporation QOF owner that has an aggregate change in ownership within the meaning of § 1.1400Z2(b)-1(c)(7)(iii)(B).

(2) *Special election rules for QOF Partnerships and QOF S Corporations.*—(i) *Dispositions of qualifying QOF partnership interests.*—If a QOF partner's basis in a qualifying QOF partnership interest is adjusted under section 1400Z-2(c), then the basis of the partnership interest is adjusted to an amount equal to the fair market value of the interest, including debt, and immediately prior to the sale or exchange, the basis of the QOF partnership assets are also adjusted, such adjustment is calculated in a manner similar to a section 743(b) adjustment had the transferor partner purchased its interest in the QOF partnership for cash equal to fair market value immediately prior to the sale or exchange assuming that a valid section 754 election had been in place. This paragraph (b)(2)(i) applies without

regard to the amount of deferred gain that was included under section 1400Z-2(b)(1), or the timing of that inclusion.

(ii) *Dispositions of QOF property by QOF partnerships or QOF S corporations.*—(A) *Taxpayer election.*—(*1*) *In general.*—For purposes of section 1400Z-2(c), if a taxpayer has held a qualifying investment (as determined under § 1.1400Z2(b)-1(c)(6)(iv)) in a QOF partnership or QOF S corporation for at least 10 years, and the QOF partnership or QOF S corporation disposes of qualified opportunity zone property after such 10 year holding period, the taxpayer may make an election to exclude from gross income some or all of the capital gain arising from such disposition reported on Schedule K-1 of the QOF partnership or QOF S corporation and attributable to the qualifying investment. To the extent that the Schedule K-1 of a QOF partnership or QOF S corporation separately states capital gains arising from the sale or exchange of any particular qualified opportunity zone property, the taxpayer may make an election with respect to such separately stated item.

(*2*) *Section 1231 gains.*—An election described in paragraph (b)(2)(ii)(A)(*1*) of this section may be made only with respect to capital gain net income from section 1231 property for a taxable year to the extent of net gains determined under section 1231(a) reported on Schedule K-1 of a QOF partnership or QOF S corporation.

(B) *Validity of election.*—To be valid, the taxpayer must make an election described in paragraph (b)(2)(ii)(A)(*1*) of this section for the taxable year in which the capital gain from the sale or exchange of QOF property recognized by the QOF partnership or QOF S corporation would be included in the taxpayer's gross income (without regard to the election set forth in this paragraph (b)(2)(ii)), in accordance with applicable forms and instructions.

(C) *Consequences of election.*—If a taxpayer makes a valid election under this paragraph (b)(2)(ii) with respect to some or all of the capital gain reported on Schedule K-1 of a QOF partnership or QOF S corporation, the amount of such capital gain that the taxpayer elects to exclude from gross income is excluded from the taxpayer's income for purposes of the Internal Revenue Code. Such excluded amount is treated as an item of income under sections 705(a)(1) or 1366.

* * *

(d) * * * The following examples illustrate the principles of paragraphs (a) through (c) of this section.

* * *

(2) *Example 2*—.—(i) *Facts*. In 2019, A and B each contribute $100 to a QOF partnership for qualifying QOF partnership interests.

(ii) *Sale of qualifying QOF partnership interest*. In 2030 when the QOF assets have a value of $260 and a bases of $200, A sells its partnership interest, recognizing $30 of gain, $15 of which is attributable to assets described in section 751(c) and (d), and for which sale A makes an election under section 1400Z-2(c) and paragraph (b)(2)(i) of this section. Because A's election under paragraph (b)(2)(i) of this section is in effect, with regard to the sale, the bases of the assets are treated as adjusted to fair market value immediately before A's sale and there is no gain recognized by A.

(iii) *Sale of QOF property*. The facts are the same as in this *Example 2* in paragraph (d)(2)(i) of this section, except that the partnership sells qualified opportunity zone property with a value of $120 and a basis of $100, recognizing $20 of gain, allocable $10 to each partner and A makes an election under section 1400Z-2(c) and paragraph (b)(2)(ii) of this section for the year in which A's allocable share of the partnership's recognized gain would be included in A's gross income. Because A's election under paragraph (b)(2)(ii) of this section is in effect, A will exclude the $10 allocable share of the partnership's $20 of recognized gain.

(e) *Capital gain dividends paid by a QOF REIT that some shareholders may be able to elect to receive tax free under section 1400Z–2(c)*.—(1) *Eligibility*.—For purposes of paragraph (b) of this section, if a shareholder of a QOF REIT receives a capital gain dividend identified with a date, as defined in paragraph (e)(2) of this section, then, to the extent that the shareholder's shares in the QOF REIT paying the capital gain dividend are a qualifying investment in the QOF REIT—

(i) The shareholder may treat the capital gain dividend, or part thereof, as gain from the sale or exchange of a qualifying investment on the date that the QOF REIT identified with the dividend; and

(ii) If, on the date identified, the shareholder had held that qualifying investment in the QOF REIT for at least 10 years, then the shareholder may apply a zero percent tax rate to that capital gain dividend, or part thereof.

(2) *Definition of capital gain dividend identified with a date.*—A *capital gain dividend identified with a date* means an amount of a capital gain dividend, as defined in section 857(b)(3)(B), or part thereof, and a date that the QOF REIT designates in a notice provided to the shareholder not later than one week after the QOF REIT designates the capital gain dividend pursuant to section 857(b)(3)(B). The notice must be mailed to the shareholder unless the shareholder has provided the QOF REIT with an email address to be used for this purpose. In the manner and at the time determined by the Commissioner, the QOF REIT must provide the Commissioner all data that the Commissioner specifies with respect to the amounts of capital gain dividends and the dates designated by the QOF REIT for each shareholder.

(3) *General limitations on the amounts of capital gain with which a date may be identified.*—(i) *No identification in the absence of any capital gains with respect to qualified opportunity zone property.*—If, during its taxable year, the QOF REIT did not realize long-term capital gain on any sale or exchange of qualified opportunity zone property, then no date may be identified with any capital gain dividends, or parts thereof, with respect to that year.

(ii) *Proportionality.*—Under section 857(g)(2), designations of capital gain dividends identified with a date must be proportional for all dividends paid with respect to the taxable year. Greater than *de minimis* violation of proportionality invalidates all of the purported identifications for a taxable year.

(iii) *Undistributed capital gains.*—If section 857(b)(3)(C)(i) requires a shareholder of a

QOF REIT to include a designated amount in the shareholder's long-term capital gain for a taxable year, then inclusion of this amount in this manner is treated as receipt of a capital gain for purposes of this paragraph (e) and may be identified with a date.

(iv) *Gross gains*.—The amount determined under paragraph (e)(4) of this section is determined without regard to any losses that may have been realized on other sales or exchanges of qualified opportunity zone property. The losses do, however, limit the total amount of capital gain dividends that may be designated under section 857(b)(3).

(4) *Determination of the amount of capital gain with which a date may be identified*.—A QOF REIT may choose to identify the date for an amount of capital gain in one of the following manners:

(i) *Simplified determination*.—If, during its taxable year, the QOF REIT realizes long-term capital gain on one or more sales or exchanges of qualified opportunity zone property, then the QOF REIT may identify the first day of that taxable year as the date identified with each designated amount with respect to the capital gain dividends for that taxable year. A designated identification is invalid in its entirety if the amount of gains that the QOF REIT identifies with that date exceeds the aggregate long-term capital gains realized on those sales or exchanges for that taxable year.

(ii) *Sale date determination*.—(A) *In general*.—If, during its taxable year, the QOF REIT realizes long-term capital gain on one or more sales or exchanges of qualified opportunity zone property, then the QOF REIT may identify capital gain dividends, or a part thereof, with the latest date on which there was such a realization. The amount of capital gain dividends so identified must not exceed the aggregate long-term capital gains realized on that date from sales or exchanges of qualified opportunity zone property. A designated identification is invalid in its entirety if the amount of gains that the QOF REIT identifies with that date violates the preceding sentence.

(B) *Iterative application*.—The process described in paragraph (e)(4)(ii) of this section is applied iteratively to increasingly earlier transaction dates (from latest to earliest) until all capital gain dividends are identified with dates or there are no earlier dates in the taxable year on which the QOF REIT realized long-term capital gains with respect to a sale or exchange of qualified opportunity zone property, whichever comes first.

(f) *Applicability date*.—This section applies to taxable years of a taxpayer, QOF Partnership, QOF S corporation, or QOF REIT, as appropriate, that end on or after the date of publication in the **Federal Register** of a Treasury decision adopting these proposed rules as final regulations.

Qualified Opportunity Funds: Deferred Gains

Qualified Opportunity Funds: Deferred Gains.—Reg. §1.1400Z-2(d)-1, relating to gains that may be deferred as a result of a taxpayer's investment in a qualified opportunity fund (QOF), is proposed (published in the Federal Register on October 29, 2018) (REG-115420-18). Proposed amendments to Reg. §1.1400Z2(d)-1(c)(4)(i), (c)(5), (c)(6), (c)(7), (d)(2)(i)(A), (d)(2)(ii), (d)(2)(iii), (d)(5)(i), and (d)(5)(ii)(B) withdrawn by REG-120186-18 on May 1, 2019.

Par. 4. Section 1.1400Z-2(d)-1 is added to read as follows:

§1.1400Z-2(d)-1. Qualified Opportunity Funds.—(a) *Becoming a QOF*.—(1) *Self-certification*.—Except as provided in paragraph (e)(1) of this section, if a taxpayer that is classified as a corporation or partnership for Federal tax purposes is eligible to be a QOF, the taxpayer may self-certify that it is QOF. This section refers to such a taxpayer as an *eligible entity*. The following rules apply to the self-certification:

(i) *Time, form, and manner*.—The self-certification must be effected at such time and in such form and manner as may be prescribed by the Commissioner in IRS forms or instructions or in publications or guidance published in the Internal Revenue Bulletin (*see* §§601.601(d)(2) and 601.602 of this chapter).

(ii) *First taxable year*.—The self-certification must identify the first taxable year that the eligible entity wants to be a QOF.

(iii) *First month*.—The self-certification may identify the first month (in that initial taxable year) in which the eligible entity wants to be a QOF.

(A) *Failure to specify first month*.—If the self-certification fails to specify the month in the initial taxable year that the eligible entity first wants to be a QOF, then the first month of the eligible entity's initial taxable year as a QOF is the first month that the eligible entity is a QOF.

(B) *Investments before first month not eligible for deferral*.—If an investment in eligible interests of an eligible entity occurs prior to the eligible entity's first month as a QOF, any election under section 1400Z-2(a)(1) made for that investment is invalid.

(2) *Becoming a QOF in a month that is not the first month of the taxable year*.—If an eligible entity's self-certification as a QOF is first effective for a month that is not the first month of that entity's taxable year—

(i) For purposes of section 1400Z-2(d)(1)(A) and (B) in the first year of the QOF's existence, the phrase *first 6-month period of the taxable year of the fund* means the first 6 months each of which is in the taxable year and in each of which the entity is a QOF. Thus, if an eligible entity becomes a QOF in the seventh or later month of a 12-month taxable year, the 90-percent test in section 1400Z-2(d)(1) takes into account only the QOF's assets on the last day of the taxable year.

(ii) The computation of any penalty under section 1400Z-2(f)(1) does not take into account any months before the first month in which an eligible entity is a QOF.

(3) *Pre-existing entities*.—There is no legal barrier to a pre-existing eligible entity becoming a QOF, but the eligible entity must satisfy all of the requirements of section 1400Z-2 and the regulations thereunder, including the requirements regarding qualified opportunity zone property, as defined in section 1400Z-2(d)(2). In particular,

that property must be acquired after December 31, 2017.

(b) *Valuation of assets for purposes of the 90-percent asset test.*—(1) *In general.*—For a taxable year, if a QOF has an applicable financial statement within the meaning of § 1.475(a)-4(h), then the value of each asset of the QOF for purposes of the 90-percent asset test in section 1400Z-2(d)(1) is the value of that asset as reported on the QOF's applicable financial statement for the relevant reporting period.

(2) *QOF without an applicable financial statement.*—If paragraph (b)(1) of this section does not apply to a QOF, then the value of each asset of the QOF for purposes of the 90-percent asset test in section 1400Z-2(d)(1) is the QOF's cost of the asset.

(c) *Qualified opportunity zone property.*—(1) *In general.*—Pursuant to section 1400Z-2(d)(2)(A), the following property is *qualified opportunity zone property:*

(i) Qualified opportunity zone stock as defined in paragraph (c)(2) of this section,

(ii) Qualified opportunity zone partnership interest as defined in paragraph (c)(3) of this section, and

(iii) Qualified opportunity zone business property as defined in paragraph (c)(4) of this section.

(2) *Qualified opportunity zone stock.*—(i) *In general.*—Except as provided in paragraphs (c)(2)(ii) and (e)(2) of this section, if an entity is classified as a corporation for Federal tax purposes (corporation), then an equity interest (stock) in the entity is *qualified opportunity zone stock* if—

(A) The stock is acquired by a QOF after December 31, 2017, at its original issue (directly or through an underwriter) from the corporation solely in exchange for cash,

(B) As of the time the stock was issued, the corporation was a qualified opportunity zone business as defined in section 1400Z-2(d)(3) and paragraph (d) of this section (or, in the case of a new corporation, the corporation was being organized for purposes of being such a qualified opportunity zone business), and

(C) During substantially all of the QOF's holding period for the stock, the corporation qualified as a qualified opportunity zone business as defined in section 1400Z-2(d)(3) and paragraph (d) of this section.

(ii) *Redemptions of stock.*—Pursuant to section 1400Z-2(d)(2)(B)(ii), rules similar to the rules of section 1202(c)(3) apply for purposes of determining whether stock in a corporation qualifies as qualified opportunity zone stock.

(A) *Redemptions from taxpayer or related person.*—Stock acquired by a QOF is not treated as qualified opportunity zone stock if, at any time during the 4-year period beginning on the date 2 years before the issuance of the stock, the corporation issuing the stock purchased (directly or indirectly) any of its stock from the QOF or from a person related (within the meaning of section 267(b) or 707(b)) to the QOF. Even if the purchase occurs after the issuance, the stock was never qualified opportunity zone stock.

(B) *Significant redemptions.*—Stock issued by a corporation is not treated as qualified opportunity zone stock if, at any time during the 2-year period beginning on the date 1 year before the issuance of the stock, the corporation made 1 or more purchases of its stock with an aggregate value (as of the time of the respective purchases) exceeding 5 percent of the aggregate value of all of its stock as of the beginning of the 2-year period. Even if one or more of the disqualifying purchases occurs after the issuance, the stock was never qualified opportunity zone stock.

(C) *Treatment of certain transactions.*—If any transaction is treated under section 304(a) as a distribution in redemption of the stock of any corporation, for purposes of paragraphs (c)(2)(ii)(A) and (B) of this section, that corporation is treated as purchasing an amount of its stock equal to the amount that is treated as such a distribution under section 304(a).

(3) *Qualified opportunity zone partnership interest.*—Except as provided in paragraph (e)(2) of this section, if an entity is classified as a partnership for Federal tax purposes (partnership), any capital or profits interest (partnership interest) in the entity is a *qualified opportunity zone partnership interest* if—

(i) The partnership interest is acquired by a QOF after December 31, 2017, from the partnership solely in exchange for cash,

(ii) As of the time the partnership interest was acquired, the partnership was a qualified opportunity zone business as defined in section 1400Z-2(d)(3) and paragraph (d) of this section (or, in the case of a new partnership, the partnership was being organized for purposes of being a qualified opportunity zone business), and

(iii) During substantially all of the QOF's holding period for the partnership interest, the partnership qualified as a qualified opportunity zone business as defined in section 1400Z-2(d)(3) and paragraph (d) of this section.

(4) *Qualified opportunity zone business property of a QOF.*—Tangible property used in a trade or business of a QOF is qualified opportunity zone business property for purposes of paragraph (c)(1)(iii) of this section if—

(i) [Withdrawn by REG-120186-18 on May 1, 2019.]

(ii) The original use of the tangible property in the qualified opportunity zone, within the meaning of paragraph (c)(7) of this section, commences with the QOF, or the QOF substantially improves the tangible property within the meaning of paragraph (c)(8) of this section (which defines substantial improvement in this context); and

(iii) During substantially all of the QOF's holding period for the tangible property, substantially all of the use of the tangible property was in a qualified opportunity zone.

(5) [Withdrawn by REG-120186-18 on May 1, 2019.]

(6) [Withdrawn by REG-120186-18 on May 1, 2019.]

(7) [Withdrawn by REG-120186-18 on May 1, 2019.]

(8) *Substantial improvement of tangible property.*—(i) *In general.*—Except as provided in paragraph (c)(8)(ii) of this section, for purposes of paragraph (c)(4)(ii) of this section, tangible property is treated as substantially improved by a QOF only if, during any 30-month period beginning after the date of acquisition of the property, additions to the basis of the property in the hands of the QOF exceed an amount equal to the

adjusted basis of the property at the beginning of the 30-month period in the hands of the QOF.

(ii) *Special rules for land and improvements on land.*—(A) *Buildings located in the zone.*—If a QOF purchases a building located on land wholly within a QOZ, under section 1400Z-2(d)(2)(D)(ii) a substantial improvement to the purchased tangible property is measured by the QOF's additions to the adjusted basis of the building. Under section 1400Z-2(d), measuring a substantial improvement to the building by additions to the QOF's adjusted basis of the building does not require the QOF to separately substantially improve the land upon which the building is located.

(B) [*Reserved*].

(d) *Qualified opportunity zone business.*—(1) *In general.*—A trade or business is a *qualified opportunity zone business* if—

(i) Substantially all of the tangible property owned or leased by the trade or business is qualified opportunity zone business property as defined in paragraph (d)(2) of this section,

(ii) Pursuant to section 1400Z-2(d)(3)(A)(iii), the trade or business satisfies the requirements of section 1397C(b)(2), (4), and (8) as defined in paragraph (d)(5) of this section, and

(iii) Pursuant to section 1400Z-2(d)(3)(A)(iii), the trade or business is not described in section 144(c)(6)(B) as defined in paragraph (d)(6) of this section.

(2) *Qualified opportunity zone business property of the qualified opportunity zone business for purposes of paragraph (d)(1)(i) of this section.*—(i) *In general.*—The tangible property used in a trade or business of an entity is qualified opportunity zone business property for purposes of paragraph (d)(1)(i) of this section if—

(A) [Withdrawn by REG-120186-18 on May 1, 2019.]

(B) The original use of the tangible property in the qualified opportunity zone commences with the entity or the entity substantially improves the tangible property within the meaning of paragraph (d)(4) of this section (which defines substantial improvement in this context); and

(C) During substantially all of the entity's holding period for the tangible property, substantially all of the use of the tangible property was in a qualified opportunity zone.

(ii) [Withdrawn by REG-120186-18 on May 1, 2019.]

(iii) [Withdrawn by REG-120186-18 on May 1, 2019.]

(3) *Substantially all requirement of paragraph (d)(1)(i) of this section.*—(i) *In general.*—A trade or business of an entity is treated as satisfying the *substantially all* requirement of paragraph (d)(1)(i) of this section if at least 70 percent of the tangible property owned or leased by the trade or business is qualified opportunity zone business property as defined in paragraph (d)(2) of this section.

(ii) *Calculating percent of tangible property owned or leased in a trade or business.*—(A) *In general.*—If an entity has an applicable financial statement within the meaning of § 1.475(a)-4(h), then the value of each asset of the entity as reported on the entity's applicable financial statement for the relevant reporting period is used for determining whether a trade or business of the entity satisfies the first sentence of paragraph (d)(3)(i) of this section (concerning whether the trade or business is a qualified opportunity zone business).

(B) *Entity without an applicable financial statement.*—If paragraph (d)(3)(ii)(A) of this section does not apply to an entity and a taxpayer both holds an equity interest in the entity and has self-certified as a QOF, then that taxpayer may value the entity's assets using the same methodology under paragraph (b) of this section that the taxpayer uses for determining its own compliance with the 90-percent asset requirement of section 1400Z-2(d)(1) (Compliance Methodology), provided that no other equity holder in the entity is a Five-Percent Zone Taxpayer. If paragraph (d)(3)(ii)(A) of this section does not apply to an entity and if two or more taxpayers that have self-certified as QOFs hold equity interests in the entity and at least one of them is a Five-Percent Zone Taxpayer, then the values of the entity's assets may be calculated using the Compliance Methodology that both is used by a Five-Percent Zone Taxpayer and that produces the highest percentage of qualified opportunity zone business property for the entity.

(C) *Five Percent Zone Taxpayer.*—A *Five-Percent Zone Taxpayer* is a taxpayer that has self-certified as a QOF and that holds stock in the entity (if it is a corporation) representing at least 5 percent in voting rights and value or holds an interest of at least 5 percent in the profits and capital of the entity (if it is a partnership).

(iii) *Example.*—The following example illustrates the principles of paragraph (d)(3)(ii) of this section.

Example. Entity ZS is a corporation that has issued only one class of stock and that conducts a trade or business. Taxpayer X holds 94% of the ZS stock, and Taxpayer Y holds the remaining 6% of that stock. (Thus, both X and Y are Five Percent Zone Taxpayers within the meaning of paragraph (d)(3)(ii)(C) of this section.) ZS does not have an applicable financial statement, and, for that reason, a determination of whether ZS is conducting a qualified opportunity zone business may employ the Compliance Methodology of X or Y. X and Y use different Compliance Methodologies permitted under paragraph (d)(3)(ii) (B) of this section for purposes of satisfying the 90-percent asset test of section 1400Z-2(d)(1). Under X's Compliance Methodology (which is based on X's applicable financial statement), 65% of the tangible property owned or leased by ZS's trade or business is qualified opportunity zone business property. Under Y's Compliance Methodology (which is based on Y's cost), 73% of the tangible property owned or leased by ZS's trade or business is qualified opportunity zone business property. Because Y's Compliance Methodology would produce the higher percentage of qualified opportunity zone business property for ZS (73%), both X and Y may use Y's Compliance Methodology to value ZS's owned or leased tangible property. If ZS's trade or business satisfies all additional requirements in section 1400Z-2(d)(3), the trade or business is a qualified opportunity zone business. Thus, if all of the additional requirements in section 1400Z-2(d)(2)(B) are satisfied, stock in ZS is qualified opportunity zone stock in the hands of a taxpayer that has self-certified as a QOF.

(4) *Substantial improvement of tangible property for purposes of paragraph (d)(2)(i)(B) of this section.*—(i) *In general.*—Except as provided in paragraph (d)(4)(ii) of this section, for purposes of paragraph (d)(2)(i)(B) of this section, tangible property is treated as substantially improved by a qualified opportunity zone business only if, during any 30-month period beginning after the date of acquisition of such tangible property, additions to the basis of such tangible property in the hands of the qualified opportunity zone business exceed an amount equal to the adjusted basis of such tangible property at the beginning of such 30-month period in the hands of the qualified opportunity zone business.

(ii) *Special rules for land and improvements on land.*—(A) *Buildings located in the zone.*—If a QOF purchases a building located on land wholly within a QOZ, under section 1400Z-2(d)(2)(D)(ii) a substantial improvement to the purchased tangible property is measured by the QOF's additions to the adjusted basis of the building. Under section 1400Z-2(d), measuring a substantial improvement to the building by additions to the QOF's adjusted basis of the building does not require the QOF to separately substantially improve the land upon which the building is located.

(B) [*Reserved*].

(5) *Operation of section 1397C requirements incorporated by reference.*—(i) [Withdrawn by REG-120186-18 on May 1, 2019.]

(ii) *Use of intangible property requirement.*—(A) *In general.*—Section 1400Z-2(d)(3) incorporates section 1397C(b)(4), requiring that, with respect to any taxable year, a substantial portion of the intangible property of an opportunity zone business is used in the active conduct of a trade or business in the qualified opportunity zone.

(B) [Withdrawn by REG-120186-18 on May 1, 2019.]

(iii) *Nonqualified financial property limitation.*—Section 1400Z-2(d)(3) incorporates section 1397C(b)(8), limiting in each taxable year the average of the aggregate unadjusted bases of the property of a qualified opportunity zone business that may be attributable to nonqualified financial property. Section 1397C(e)(1), which defines the term *nonqualified financial property* for purposes of section 1397C(b)(8), excludes from that term reasonable amounts of working capital held in cash, cash equivalents, or debt instruments with a term of 18 months or less (working capital assets).

(iv) *Safe harbor for reasonable amount of working capital.*—Solely for purposes of applying section 1397C(e)(1) to the definition of a qualified opportunity zone business under section 1400Z-2(d)(3), working capital assets are treated as reasonable in amount for purposes of sections 1397C(b)(2) and 1400Z-2(d)(3)(A)(ii), if all of the following three requirements are satisfied:

(A) *Designated in writing.*—These amounts are designated in writing for the acquisition, construction, and/or substantial improvement of tangible property in a qualified opportunity zone, as defined in section 1400Z-1(a).

(B) *Reasonable written schedule.*—There is a written schedule consistent with the ordinary start-up of a trade or business for the expenditure of the working capital assets. Under the schedule, the working capital assets must be spent within 31 months of the receipt by the business of the assets.

(C) *Property consumption consistent.*—The working capital assets are actually used in a manner that is substantially consistent with paragraph (d)(5)(iv)(A) and (B) of this section.

(v) *Safe harbor for gross income derived from the active conduct of business.*—Solely for purposes of applying the 50-percent test in section 1397C(b)(2) to the definition of a qualified opportunity zone business in section 1400Z-2(d)(3), if any gross income is derived from property that paragraph (d)(5)(iv) of this section treats as a reasonable amount of working capital, then that gross income is counted toward satisfaction of the 50-percent test.

(vi) *Safe harbor for use of intangible property.*—Solely for purposes of applying the use requirement in section 1397C(b)(4) to the definition of a qualified opportunity zone business under section 1400Z-2(d)(3), the use requirement is treated as being satisfied during any period in which the business is proceeding in a manner that is substantially consistent with paragraphs (d)(5)(iv)(A) through (C) of this section.

(vii) *Safe harbor for property on which working capital is being expended.*—If paragraph (d)(5)(iv) of this section treats some financial property as being a reasonable amount of working capital because of compliance with the three requirements of paragraph (d)(5)(iv)(A)-(C) and if the tangible property referred to in paragraph (d)(5)(iv)(A) is expected to satisfy the requirements of section 1400Z-2(d)(2)(D)(1) as a result of the planned expenditure of those working capital assets, then that tangible property is not treated as failing to satisfy those requirements solely because the scheduled consumption of the working capital is not yet complete.

(viii) *Example.*—The following example illustrates the rules of this paragraph (d)(5):

(i) *Facts.* In 2019, Taxpayer H realized $w million of capital gains and within the 180-day period invested $w million in QOF T, a qualified opportunity fund. QOF T immediately acquired from partnership P a partnership interest in P, solely in exchange for $w million of cash. P immediately placed the $w million in working capital assets, which remained in working capital assets until used. P had written plans to acquire land in a qualified opportunity zone on which it planned to construct a commercial building. Of the $w million, $x million was dedicated to the land purchase, $y million to the construction of the building, and $z million to ancillary but necessary expenditures for the project. The written plans provided for purchase of the land within a month of receipt of the cash from QOF T and for the remaining $y and $z million to be spent within the next 30 months on construction of the building and on the ancillary expenditures. All expenditures were made on schedule, consuming the $w million. During the taxable years that overlap with the first 31-month period, P had no gross income other than that derived from the amounts held in those working capital assets. Prior to completion of the building, P's only assets were the land it purchased, the unspent amounts in the working capital assets, and P's work in process as the building was constructed.

(ii) *Analysis of construction*—(A) P met the three requirements of the safe harbor provided in paragraph (d)(5)(iv) of this section. P had a written plan to spend the $w received from QOF T for the acquisition, construction, and/or substantial improvement of tangible property in a qualified opportunity zone, as defined in section 1400Z-1(a). P had a written schedule consistent with the ordinary start-up for a business for the expenditure of the working capital assets. And, finally, P's working capital assets were actually used in a manner that was substantially consistent with its written plan and the ordinary start-up of a business. Therefore, the $x million, the $y million, and the $z million are treated as reasonable in amount for purposes of sections 1397C(b)(2) and 1400Z-2(d)(3)(A)(ii).

(B) Because P had no other gross income during the 31 months at issue, 100 percent of P's gross income during that time is treated as derived from an active trade or business in the qualified opportunity zone for purposes of satisfying the 50-percent test of section 1397C(b)(2).

(C) For purposes of satisfying the requirement of section 1397C(b)(4), during the period of land acquisition and building construction a substantial portion of P's intangible property is treated as being used in the active conduct of a trade or business in the qualified opportunity zone.

(D) All of the facts described are consistent with QOF T's interest in P being a qualified opportunity zone partnership interest for purposes of satisfying the 90-percent test in section 1400Z-2(d)(1).

(iii) *Analysis of substantial improvement.* The above conclusions would also apply if P's plans had been to buy and substantially improve a pre-existing commercial building. In addition, the fact that P's basis in the building has not yet doubled does not cause the building to fail to satisfy section 1400Z-2(d)(2)(D)1)(III).

(6) *Trade or businesses described in section 144(c)(6)(B) not eligible.*—Pursuant to section 1400Z-2(d)(3)(A)(iii), the following trades or businesses described in section 144(c)(6)(B) cannot qualify as a qualified opportunity zone business:

(i) Any private or commercial golf course,

(ii) Country club,

(iii) Massage parlor,

(iv) Hot tub facility,

(v) Suntan facility,

(vi) Racetrack or other facility used for gambling, or

(vii) Any store the principal business of which is the sale of alcoholic beverages for consumption off premises.

(e) *Exceptions based on where an entity is created, formed, or organized.*—(1) *QOFs.*—If a partnership or corporation (an entity) is not organized in one of the 50 states, the District of Columbia, or the U.S. possessions, it is ineligible to be a QOF. If an entity is organized in a U.S. possession but not in one of the 50 States or the District of Columbia, it may be a QOF only if it is organized for the purpose of investing in qualified opportunity zone property that relates to a trade or business operated in the U.S. possession in which the entity is organized.

(2) *Entities that can issue qualified opportunity zone stock or qualified opportunity zone partnership interests.*—If an entity is not organized in one of the 50 states, the District of Columbia, or the U.S. possessions, an equity interest in the entity is neither qualified opportunity zone stock nor a qualified opportunity zone partnership interest. If an entity is organized in a U.S. possession but not in one of the 50 States or the District of Columbia, an equity interest in the entity may be qualified opportunity zone stock or a qualified opportunity zone partnership interest, as the case may be, only if the entity conducts a qualified opportunity zone business in the U.S. possession in which the entity is organized. An entity described in the preceding sentence is treated as satisfying the "domestic" requirement in section 1400Z-2(d)(2)(B)(i) or section 1400Z-2(C)(i).

(3) *U.S. possession defined.*—For purposes of this paragraph (e), a U.S. possession means any jurisdiction other than the 50 States and the District of Columbia where a designated qualified opportunity zone exists under section 1400Z-1.

(f) *Applicability date.*—This section applies for QOF taxable years that begin on or after the date of publication in the **Federal Register** of a Treasury decision adopting these proposed rules as final regulations. A QOF, however, may rely on the proposed rules in this section with respect to taxable years that begin before the date of applicability of this section, but only if the QOF applies the rules in their entirety and in a consistent manner. [Reg. 1.1400Z-2(d)-1.]

Qualified Opportunity Funds: Investment

Qualified Opportunity Funds: Investment.—Amendments to Reg. §1.1400Z2(d)-1, relating to gains that may be deferred as a result of a taxpayer's investment in a qualified opportunity fund, as well as special rules for an investment in a QOF held by a taxpayer for at least 10 years, are proposed (published in the Federal Register on May 1, 2019) (REG-120186-18).

Par. 5. Section 1.1400Z2(d)-1, as proposed to be added by 83 FR 54279, October 29, 2018, is amended by:

1. Revising paragraphs (b) and (c)(4) through (7).
2. Revising the heading of paragraph (c)(8).
3. In paragraph (c)(8)(i), removing "paragraph (c)(4)(ii) of this section" and adding in its place "this paragraph (c)(8)(i)".
4. Adding paragraphs (c)(8)(ii)(B) and (c)(9).
5. Revising paragraph (d)(2)(i)(A) through (C) and adding paragraphs (d)(2)(i)(D) and (E).
6. Redesignating paragraph (d)(2)(iii) as (d)(2)(iv) and revising newly redesignated paragraph (d)(2)(iv).

7. Redesignating paragraphs (d)(2)(ii) as (d)(2)(iii) and revising newly redesignated paragraph (d)(2)(iii).

8. Adding new paragraph (d)(2)(ii).

9. Revising paragraphs (d)(3)(ii)(A) through (C) and (d)(4)(ii) and the heading of paragraph (d)(5).

10. Adding a sentence at the end of paragraph (d)(5)(i) and adding paragraphs (d)(5)(i)(A) through (E).

11. Adding a sentence at the end of paragraph (d)(5)(ii)(A).

12. Revising paragraphs (d)(5)(ii)(B), (d)(5)(iv) introductory text, and (d)(5)(iv)(A) and (C) and adding paragraphs (d)(5)(iv)(D) and (E).

13. Redesignating paragraph (d)(5)(viii) as (d)(5)(ix) and adding a new paragraph (d)(5)(viii).

14. Adding a sentence at the end of paragraph (f).

The revisions and additions read as follows:

§1.1400Z2(d)-1. Qualified Opportunity Funds.

* * *

(b) *Valuation of assets for purposes of the 90-percent asset test.*—(1) *In general.*—For purposes of the 90-percent asset test in section 1400Z-2(d)(1), on an annual basis, a QOF may value its assets using the applicable financial statement valuation method set forth in paragraph (b)(2) of this section, if the QOF has an applicable financial statement within the meaning of §1.475(a)-4(h), or the alternative valuation method set forth in paragraph (b)(3) of this section. During each taxable year, a QOF must apply consistently the valuation method that it selects under this paragraph (b)(1) to all assets valued with respect to the taxable year.

(2) *Applicable financial statement valuation method.*—(i) *In general.*—Under the applicable financial statement valuation method set forth in this paragraph (b)(2), the value of each asset that is owned or leased by the QOF is the value of that asset as reported on the QOF's applicable financial statement for the relevant reporting period.

(ii) *Requirement for selection of method.*—A QOF may select the applicable financial statement valuation method set forth in this paragraph (b)(2) to value an asset leased by the QOF only if the applicable financial statement of the QOF is prepared according to U.S. generally accepted accounting principles (GAAP) and requires an assignment of value to the lease of the asset.

(3) *Alternative valuation method.*—(i) *In general.*—Under the alternative valuation method set forth in this paragraph (b)(3), the value of the assets owned by a QOF is calculated under paragraph (b)(3)(ii) of this section, and the value of the assets leased by a QOF is calculated under paragraph (b)(3)(iii) of this section.

(ii) *Assets that are owned by a QOF.*—The value of each asset that is owned by a QOF is the QOF's unadjusted cost basis of the asset under section 1012.

(iii) *Assets that are leased by a QOF.*—(A) *In general.*—The value of each asset that is leased by a QOF is equal to the present value of the leased asset as defined in paragraph (b)(3)(iii)(C) of this section.

(B) *Discount rate.*—For purposes of calculating present value under paragraph (b)(3)(iii) of this section, the discount rate is the applicable Federal rate under section 1274(d)(1), determined by substituting the term "lease" for "debt instrument."

(C) *Present value.*—For purposes of paragraph (b)(3)(iii) of this section, present value of a leased asset—

(1) Is equal to the sum of the present values of each payment under the lease for the asset;

(2) Is calculated at the time the QOF enters into the lease for the asset; and

(3) Once calculated, is used as the value for the asset by the QOF for all testing dates for purposes of the 90-percent asset test.

(D) *Term of a lease.*—For purposes of paragraph (b)(3)(iii) of this section, the term of a lease includes periods during which the lessee may extend the lease at a predefined rent.

(4) *Option to disregard recently contributed property.*—A QOF may choose to determine compliance with the 90-percent asset test by excluding from both the numerator and denominator of the test any property that satisfies all the criteria in paragraphs (b)(4)(i) through (iii) of this section. A QOF need not be consistent from one semi-annual test to another in whether it avails itself of this option.

(i) As the case may be, the amount of the property was received by the QOF partnership as a contribution or by the QOF corporation solely in exchange for stock of the corporation;

(ii) This contribution or exchange occurred not more than 6 months before the test from which it is being excluded; and

(iii) Between the date of that contribution or exchange and the date of the asset test, the amount was held continuously in cash, cash equivalents, or debt instruments with a term of 18 months or less.

(c) * * *

(4) *Qualified opportunity zone business property of a QOF.*—(i) *In general.*—Tangible property used in a trade or business of a QOF is qualified opportunity zone business property for purposes of paragraph (c)(1)(iii) of this section if the requirements of paragraphs (c)(4)(i)(A) through (E) of this section, as applicable, are satisfied.

(A) In the case of property that the QOF owns, the property was acquired by the QOF after December 31, 2017, by purchase as defined by section 179(d)(2) from a person that is not a related person within the meaning of section 1400Z-2(e)(2).

(B) In the case of property that the QOF leases—

(1) Qualifying acquisition of possession.—The property was acquired by the QOF under a lease entered into after December 31, 2017;

(2) Arms-length terms.—The terms of the lease were market rate (that is, the terms of

the lease reflect common, arms-length market practice in the locale that includes the qualified opportunity zone as determined under section 482 and all section 482 regulations in this chapter) at the time that the lease was entered into; and

(3) *Additional requirements for leases from a related person.*—If the lessee and the lessor are related parties, paragraph (c)(4)(i)(B)(*4*) and (*5*) of this section must be satisfied.

(4) *Prepayments of not more than one year.*—The lessee at no time makes any prepayment in connection with the lease relating to a period of use of the property that exceeds 12 months.

(5) *Purchase of other QOZBP.*—If the original use of leased tangible personal property in a qualified opportunity zone (within the meaning of in paragraph (c)(4)(i)(B)(*6*) of this section) does not commence with the lessee, the property is not qualified opportunity zone business property unless, during the relevant testing period (as defined in paragraph (c)(4)(i)(B)(*7*) of this section), the lessee becomes the owner of tangible property that is qualified opportunity zone business property having a value not less than the value of that leased tangible personal property. There must be substantial overlap of the zone(s) in which the owner of the property so acquired uses it and the zone(s) in which that person uses the leased property.

(6) *Original use of leased tangible property.*—For purposes of paragraph (c)(4)(i)(B)(*5*) of this section, the original use of leased tangible property in a qualified opportunity zone commences on the date any person first places the property in service in the qualified opportunity zone for purposes of depreciation (or first uses it in a manner that would allow depreciation or amortization if that person were the property's owner). For purposes of this paragraph (c)(4)(i)(B)(*6*), if property has been unused or vacant for an uninterrupted period of at least 5 years, original use in the zone commences on the date after that period when any person first uses or places the property in service in the qualified opportunity zone within the meaning of the preceding sentence. Used tangible property satisfies the original use requirement if the property has not been previously so used or placed in service in the qualified opportunity zone.

(7) *Relevant testing period.*—For purposes of paragraph (c)(4)(i)(B)(*5*) of this section, the *relevant testing period* is the period that begins on the date that the lessee receives possession under the lease of the leased tangible personal property and ends on the earlier of—the date 30-months after the date the lessee receives possession of the property under the lease; or the last day of the term of the lease (within the meaning of paragraph (b)(3)(iii)(D) of this section.

(8) *Valuation of owned or leased property.*—For purposes of paragraph (c)(4)(i)(B)(*5*) of this section, the value of owned or leased property is required to be determined in accordance with the valuation methodologies provided in paragraph (b) of this section, and such value in the case of leased tangible personal property is to be determined on the date the lessee receives possession of the property under the lease.

(C) In the case of tangible property owned by the QOF, the original use of the owned tangible property in the qualified opportunity zone, within the meaning of paragraph (c)(7) of this section, commences with the QOF, or the QOF substantially improves the owned tangible property within the meaning of paragraph (c)(8) of this section (which defines substantial improvement in this context).

(D) In the case of tangible property that is owned or leased by the QOF, during substantially all of the QOF's holding period for the tangible property, substantially all of the use of the tangible property was in a qualified opportunity zone.

(E) In the case of real property (other than unimproved land) that is leased by a QOF, if, at the time the lease is entered into, there was a plan, intent, or expectation for the real property to be purchased by the QOF for an amount of consideration other than the fair market value of the real property determined at the time of the purchase without regard to any prior lease payments, the leased real property is not qualified opportunity zone business property at any time.

(ii) *Trade or business of a QOF.*—The term *trade or business* means a trade or business within the meaning of section 162.

(iii) *Safe harbor for inventory in transit.*—In determining whether tangible property is used in a qualified opportunity zone for purposes of section 1400Z-2(d)(2)(D)(i)(III), and of paragraphs (c)(4)(i)(D), (c)(6), (d)(2)(i)(D), and (d)(2)(iv) of this section, inventory (including raw materials) of a trade or business does not fail to be used in a qualified opportunity zone solely because the inventory is in transit—

(A) From a vendor to a facility of the trade or business that is in a qualified opportunity zone; or

(B) From a facility of the trade or business that is in a qualified opportunity zone to customers of the trade or business that are not located in a qualified opportunity zone.

(5) *Substantially all of a QOF's holding period for property described in paragraphs (c)(2) and (3) and (c)(4)(i)(D) of this section.*—For purposes of determining whether the holding period requirements in paragraphs (c)(2) and (3) and (c)(4)(i)(D) of this section are satisfied, the term *substantially all* means at least 90 percent.

(6) *Substantially all of the usage of tangible property by a QOF in a qualified opportunity zone.*—A trade or business of an entity is treated as satisfying the *substantially all* requirement of paragraph (c)(4)(i)(D) of this section if at least 70 percent of the use of the tangible property is in a qualified opportunity zone.

(7) *Original use of tangible property acquired by purchase.*—(i) *In general.*—For purposes of paragraph (c)(4)(i)(C) of this section, the original use of tangible property in a qualified opportunity zone commences on the date any person first places the property in service in the qualified opportunity zone for purposes of depreciation or amortization (or first uses it in a manner that would allow depreciation or amortization if that person were the property's owner). For purposes of this paragraph (c)(7), if property has been unused or vacant for an uninterrupted period of at least 5 years, original use in the qualified opportunity zone commences on the date after that period when any person first so uses or

places the property in service in the qualified opportunity zone. Used tangible property satisfies the original use requirement if the property has not been previously so used or placed in service in the qualified opportunity zone. If the tangible property had been so used or placed in service in the qualified opportunity zone before it is acquired by purchase, it must be substantially improved in order to satisfy the requirements of section 1400Z-2(d)(2)(D)(i)(II).

(ii) *Lessee improvements to leased property.*—Improvements made by a lessee to leased property satisfy the original use requirement in section 1400Z-2(d)(2)(D)(i)(II) as purchased property for the amount of the unadjusted cost basis under section 1012 of such improvements.

(8) *Substantial improvement of tangible property acquired by purchase*— * * *

(ii) * * *

(B) *Unimproved land.*—Unimproved land that is within a qualified opportunity zone and acquired by purchase in accordance with section 1400Z-2(d)(2)(D)(i)(I) is not required to be substantially improved within the meaning of section 1400Z-2(d)(2)(D)(i)(II) and (d)(2)(D)(ii).

(9) *Substantially all of tangible property owned or leased by a QOF.*—(i) *Tangible property owned by a QOF.*—Whether a QOF has satisfied the "substantially all" threshold set forth in paragraph (c)(6) of this section is to be determined by a fraction—

(A) The numerator of which is the total value of all qualified opportunity zone business property owned or leased by the QOF that meets the requirements in paragraph (c)(4)(i) of this section; and

(B) The denominator of which is the total value of all tangible property owned or leased by the QOF, whether located inside or outside of a qualified opportunity zone.

(d) * * *

(2) * * *

(i) * * *

(A) In the case of tangible property that the entity owns, the tangible property was acquired by the entity after December 31, 2017, by purchase as defined by section 179(d)(2) from a person who is not a related person within the meaning of section 1400Z-2(e)(2).

(B) In the case of tangible property that the entity leases—

(1) Qualifying acquisition of possession.—The property was acquired by the entity under a lease entered into after December 31, 2017;

(2) Arms-length terms.—The terms of the lease are market rate (that is, the terms of the lease reflect common, arms-length market practice in the locale that includes the qualified opportunity zone as determined under section 482 and all section 482 regulations in this chapter) at the time that the lease was entered into; and

(3) Additional requirements for leases from a related person.—If the lessee and the lessor are related parties, paragraphs (d)(2)(i)(B)(4) and (5) of this section must be satisfied.

(4) Prepayments of not more than one year.—The lessee at no time makes any prepayment in connection with the lease relating to a period of use of the property that exceeds 12 months.

(5) Purchase of other QOZBP.—If the original use of leased tangible personal property in a qualified opportunity zone (within the meaning of in paragraph (d)(2)(i)(B)(*6*) of this section) does not commence with the lessee, the property is not qualified opportunity zone business property unless, during the relevant testing period (as defined in paragraph (d)(2)(i)(B)(*7*) of this section), the lessee becomes the owner of tangible property that is qualified opportunity zone business property having a value not less than the value of that leased tangible personal property. There must be substantial overlap of the zone(s) in which the owner of the property so acquired uses it and the zone(s) in which that person uses the leased property.

(6) Original use of leased tangible property.—For purposes of paragraph (d)(2)(i)(B)(*5*) of this section, the original use of leased tangible property in a qualified opportunity zone commences on the date any person first places the property in service in the qualified opportunity zone for purposes of depreciation (or first uses it in a manner that would allow depreciation or amortization if that person were the property's owner). For purposes of this paragraph (d)(2)(i)(B)(*6*), if property has been unused or vacant for an uninterrupted period of at least 5 years, original use in the qualified opportunity zone commences on the date after that period when any person first uses or places the property in service in the qualified opportunity zone within the meaning of the preceding sentence. Used tangible property satisfies the original use requirement if the property has not been previously so used or placed in service in the qualified opportunity zone.

(7) Relevant testing period.—For purposes of paragraph (d)(2)(i)(B)(*5*) of this section, the *relevant testing period* is the period that begins on the date that the lessee receives possession under the lease of the leased tangible personal property and ends on the earlier of—the date 30-months after the date the lessee receives possession of the property under the lease; or the last day of the term of the lease (within the meaning of paragraph (b)(3)(iii)(D) of this section).

(8) Valuation of owned or leased property.—For purposes of paragraph (d)(2)(i)(B)(*5*) of this section, the value of owned or leased property is required to be determined in accordance with the valuation methodologies provided in paragraph (b) of this section, and such value in the case of leased tangible personal property is to be determined on the date the lessee receives possession of the property under the lease.

(C) In the case of tangible property owned by the entity, the original use of the owned tangible property in the qualified opportunity zone, within the meaning of paragraph (c)(7) of this section, commences with the entity, or the entity substantially improves the owned tangible property within the meaning of paragraph (d)(4) of this section (which defines substantial improvement in this context).

(D) In the case of tangible property that is owned or leased by the entity, during substantially all of the entity's holding period for the tangible property, substantially all of the use of the tangible property was in a qualified opportunity zone.

(E) In the case of real property (other than unimproved land) that is leased by the entity, if, at the time the lease is entered into, there was a plan, intent, or expectation for the real property to be purchased by the entity for an amount of consideration other than the fair market value of the real property determined at the time of the purchase without regard to any prior lease payments, the leased real property is not qualified opportunity zone business property at any time.

(ii) *Trade or business of an entity.*—The term *trade or business* means a trade or business within the meaning of section 162.

(iii) *Substantially all of a qualified opportunity zone business's holding period for property described in paragraph (d)(2)(i)(D) of this section.*—For purposes of the holding period requirement in paragraph (d)(2)(i)(D) of this section, the term *substantially all* means at least 90 percent.

(iv) *Substantially all of the use of tangible property by a qualified opportunity zone business in a qualified opportunity zone.*—The substantially all of the use requirement of paragraph (d)(2)(i)(D) of this section is satisfied if at least 70 percent of the use of the tangible property is in a qualified opportunity zone.

(3) * * *

(ii) * * *

(A) *In general.*—Whether a trade or business of the entity satisfies the 70-percent "substantially all" threshold set forth in paragraph (d)(3)(i) of this section is to be determined by a fraction—

(1) The numerator of which is the total value of all qualified opportunity zone business property owned or leased by the qualified opportunity zone business that meets the requirements in paragraph (d)(2)(i) of this section; and

(2) The denominator of which is the total value of all tangible property owned or leased by the qualified opportunity zone business, whether located inside or outside of a qualified opportunity zone.

(B) *Value of tangible property owned or leased by a qualified opportunity zone business.*—*(1) In general.*—For purposes of the fraction set forth in paragraph (d)(3)(ii)(A) of this section, on an annual basis, the owned or leased tangible property of a qualified opportunity zone business may be valued using the applicable financial statement valuation method set forth in paragraph (d)(3)(ii)(B)(2) of this section, if the qualified opportunity zone business has an applicable financial statement within the meaning of § 1.475(a)-4(h), or the alternative valuation method set forth in paragraph (d)(3)(ii)(B)(3) of this section. During each taxable year, the valuation method selected under this paragraph (d)(3)(ii)(B)(*1*) must be applied consistently to all tangible property valued with respect to the taxable year.

(2) Applicable financial statement valuation method.—*(i) In general.*—Under the applicable financial statement valuation method set forth in this paragraph (d)(3)(ii)(B)(2), the value of tangible property of the qualified opportunity zone business, whether owned or leased, is the value of that property as reported, or as otherwise would be reported, on the qualified opportunity zone business's applicable financial statement for the relevant reporting period.

(ii) Requirement for selection of method.—A qualified opportunity zone business may select the applicable financial statement valuation method set forth in this paragraph (d)(3)(ii)(B)(2) to value tangible property leased by the qualified opportunity zone business only if the applicable financial statement of the qualified opportunity zone business requires, or would otherwise require, an assignment of value to the lease of the tangible property.

(3) Alternative valuation method.—*(i) In general.*—Under the alternative valuation method set forth in this paragraph (d)(3)(ii)(B)(*3*), the value of tangible property that is owned by the qualified opportunity zone business is calculated under paragraph (d)(3)(ii)(B)(*3*)(*ii*) of this section, and the value of tangible property that is leased by the qualified opportunity zone business is calculated under paragraph (d)(3)(ii)(B)(*4*) of this section.

(ii) Tangible property owned by a qualified opportunity zone business.—The value of tangible property that is owned by the qualified opportunity zone business is the unadjusted cost basis of the property under section 1012 in the hands of the qualified opportunity zone business for each testing date of a QOF during the year.

(4) Tangible property leased by a qualified opportunity zone business.—*(i) In general.*—For purposes of paragraph (d)(3)(ii)(B)(*3*) of this section, the value of tangible property that is leased by the qualified opportunity zone business is equal to the present value of the leased tangible property as defined in paragraph (d)(3)(ii)(B)(*5*) of this section.

(ii) Discount rate.—For purposes of calculating present value under paragraph (d)(3)(ii)(B)(*4*) of this section, the discount rate is the applicable Federal rate under section 1274(d)(1), determined by substituting the term "lease" for "debt instrument."

(5) Present value.—For purposes of paragraph (d)(3)(ii)(B)(4), present value of leased tangible property

(i) Is equal to the sum of the present values of each payment under the lease for such tangible property;

(ii) Is calculated at the time the qualified opportunity zone business enters into the lease for such leased tangible property; and

(iii) Once calculated, is used as the value for such asset by the qualified opportunity zone business for all testing dates for purposes of the 90-percent asset test.

(6) Term of a lease.—For purposes of paragraph (d)(3)(ii)(B)(*4*) of this section, the term of a lease includes periods during which the lessee may extend the lease at a predefined rent.

(C) *Five-Percent Zone Taxpayer.*—If a taxpayer both holds an equity interest in the entity and has self-certified as a QOF, then that taxpayer may value the entity's assets using the same methodology under paragraph (b) of this section that the taxpayer uses for determining its own compliance with the 90-percent asset requirement of section 1400Z-2(d)(1) (Compliance Methodology), provided that no other equity holder in the entity is a Five-Percent Zone Taxpayer. If two or more taxpayers that have self-certified as QOFs hold equity interests in the entity and at least one of them is a Five-Percent Zone Taxpayer, then the values of the entity's assets may be calculated using the Compliance Methodology that both is used by a Five-Percent Zone Taxpayer and that produces the highest percentage of qualified opportunity zone business property for the entity. A *Five-Percent Zone Taxpayer* is a taxpayer that has self-certified as a QOF and that holds stock in the entity (if it is a corporation) representing at least 5 percent in voting rights and value or holds an interest of at least 5 percent in the profits and capital of the entity (if it is a partnership).

* * *

(4) * * *

(ii) *Special rules for land and improvements on land.*—(A) *Buildings located in the qualified opportunity zone.*—If a qualified opportunity zone business purchases a building located on land wholly within a QOZ, under section 1400Z-2(d)(2)(D)(ii) a substantial improvement to the purchased tangible property is measured in relation to the qualified opportunity zone business's additions to the adjusted basis of the building. Under section 1400Z-2(d), measuring a substantial improvement to the building by additions to the qualified opportunity zone business's adjusted basis of the building does not require the qualified opportunity zone business to separately substantially improve the land upon which the building is located.

(B) *Unimproved land.*—Unimproved land that is within a qualified opportunity zone and acquired by purchase in accordance with section 1400Z-2(d)(2)(D)(i)(I) is not required to be substantially improved within the meaning of section 1400Z-2(d)(2)(D)(i)(II) and (d)(2)(D)(ii).

(5) *Operation of section 1397C requirements adopted by reference.*—(i) * * * A trade or business meets the 50-percent gross income requirement in the preceding sentence if the trade or business satisfies any one of the four criteria described in paragraph (d)(5)(i)(A), (B), (C), or (D) of this section, or any criteria identified in published guidance issued by the IRS under § 601.601(d)(2) of this chapter.

(A) *Services performed in qualified opportunity zone based on hours.*—At least 50 percent of the services performed for the trade or business are performed in the qualified opportunity zone, determined by a fraction—

(1) The numerator of which is the total number of hours performed by employees and independent contractors, and employees of independent contractors, for services performed in a qualified opportunity zone during the taxable year; and

(2) The denominator of which is the total number of hours performed by employees and independent contractors, and employees of independent contractors, for services performed during the taxable year.

(B) *Services performed in qualified opportunity zone based on amounts paid for services.*—At least 50 percent of the services performed for the trade or business are performed in the qualified opportunity zone, determined by a fraction—

(1) The numerator of which is the total amount paid by the entity for services performed in a qualified opportunity zone during the taxable year, whether by employees, independent contractors, or employees of independent contractors; and

(2) The denominator of which is the total amount paid by the entity for services performed during the taxable year, whether by employees, independent contractors, or employees of independent contractors.

(C) *Necessary tangible property and business functions.*—The tangible property of the trade or business located in a qualified opportunity zone and the management or operational functions performed in the qualified opportunity zone are each necessary for the generation of at least 50 percent of the gross income of the trade or business.

(D) *Facts and circumstances.*—Based on all the facts and circumstances, at least 50 percent of the gross income of a qualified opportunity zone business is derived from the active conduct of a trade or business in the qualified opportunity zone.

(E) *Examples.*—The following examples illustrate the principles of paragraphs (d)(5)(i)(C) and (D) of this section.

(1) Example 1. A landscaping business has its headquarters in a qualified opportunity zone, its officers and employees manage the daily operations of the business (within and without the qualified opportunity zone) from its headquarters, and all its equipment and supplies are stored in the headquarters facilities. The activities occurring and the storage of equipment and supplies in the qualified opportunity zone are, taken together, a material factor in the generation of the income of the business.

(2) Example 2. A trade or business is formed or organized under the laws of the jurisdiction within which a qualified opportunity zone is located, and the business has a PO Box located in the qualified opportunity zone. The mail received at that PO Box is fundamental to the income of the trade or business, but there is no other basis for concluding that the income of the trade or business is derived from activities in the qualified opportunity zone. The mere location of the PO Box is not a material factor in the generation of gross income by the trade or business.

(3) Example 3. In 2019, Taxpayer X realized $w million of capital gains and within the 180-day period invested $w million in QOF Y, a qualified opportunity fund. QOF Y immediately acquired from partnership P a partnership interest in P, solely in exchange for $w million of cash. P is a real estate developer that has written plans to acquire land in a qualified opportunity zone on which it plans to construct a commercial building for lease to other trades or businesses. In 2023, P's commercial building is placed in service and is fully leased up to other trades or businesses. For the 2023 taxable year, because at least 50 percent of P's gross income is derived from P's rental of its tangible property in the qualified opportunity zone. Thus, under P's facts and circumstances, P satisfies the gross income test under section 1397C(b)(2).

(ii) *Use of intangible property requirement.*—(A) * * * For purposes of section 1400Z-2(d)(3)(ii) and the preceding sentence, the term *substantial portion* means at least 40 percent.

(B) *Active conduct of a trade or business.*—*(1)* [Reserved]

(2) Operating real property.—Solely for the purposes of section 1400Z-2(d)(3)(A), the ownership and operation (including leasing) of

real property is the active conduct of a trade or business. However, merely entering into a triple-net-lease with respect to real property owned by a taxpayer is not the active conduct of a trade or business by such taxpayer.

(3) Trade or business defined.—The term *trade or business* means a trade or business within the meaning of section 162.

* * *

(iv) *Safe harbor for reasonable amount of working capital.*—Solely for purposes of applying section 1397C(e)(1) to the definition of a qualified opportunity zone business under section 1400Z-2(d)(3), working capital assets are treated as reasonable in amount for purposes of sections 1397C(b)(2) and 1400Z-2(d)(3)(A)(ii), if all of the requirements in paragraphs (d)(5)(iv)(A) through (C) of this section are satisfied.

(A) *Designated in writing.*—These amounts are designated in writing for the development of a trade or business in a qualified opportunity zone (as defined in section 1400Z-1(a)), including when appropriate the acquisition, construction, and/or substantial improvement of tangible property in such a zone.

* * *

(C) *Property consumption consistent.*—The working capital assets are actually used in a manner that is substantially consistent with paragraphs (d)(5)(iv)(A) and (B) of this section. If consumption of the working capital assets is delayed by waiting for governmental action the application for which is complete, that delay does not cause a failure of this paragraph (d)(5)(iv)(C).

(D) *Ability of a single business to benefit from more than a single application of the safe harbor.*—A business may benefit from multiple overlapping or sequential applications of the working capital safe harbor, provided that each application independently satisfies all of the requirements in paragraphs (d)(5)(iv)(A) through (C) of this section.

(E) *Examples.*—The following examples illustrate the rules of paragraph (d)(5)(iv) of this section.

(1) *Example 1: General application of working capital safe harbor*—(*i*) *Facts.* QOF F creates a business entity E to open a fast-food restaurant and acquires almost all of the equity of E in exchange for cash. E has a written plan and a 20-month schedule for the use of this cash to establish the restaurant. Among the planned uses for the cash are identification of favorable locations in the qualified opportunity zone, leasing a building suitable for such a restaurant, outfitting the building with appropriate equipment and furniture (both owned and leased), necessary security deposits, obtaining a franchise and local permits, and the hiring and training of kitchen and wait staff. Not-yet-disbursed amounts were held in assets described in section 1397C(e)(1), and these assets were eventually expended in a manner consistent with the plan and schedule.

(*ii*) *Analysis.* E's use of the cash qualifies for the working capital safe harbor described in paragraph (d)(5)(iv) of this section.

(2) *Example 2: Multiple applications of working capital safe harbor*—(*i*) *Facts.* QOF G creates a business entity H to start a new technology company and acquires equity of H in exchange for cash on Date 1. In addition to H's rapid deployment of capital received from other equity investors, H writes a plan with a 30-month schedule for the use of the Date 1 cash. The plan describes use of the cash to research and develop a new technology (Technology), including paying salaries for engineers and other scientists to conduct the research, purchasing, and leasing equipment to be used in research and furnishing office and laboratory space. Approximately a year-and-a-half after Date 1, on Date 2, G acquires additional equity in H for cash, and H writes a second plan. This new plan has a 25-month schedule for the development of a new application of existing software (Application), to be marketed to government agencies. Among the planned uses for the cash received on Date 2 are paying development costs, including salaries for software engineers, other employees, and third-party consultants to assist in developing and marketing the new application to the anticipated customers. Not-yet-disbursed amounts that were scheduled for development of the Technology and the Application were held in assets described in section 1397C(e)(1), and these assets were eventually expended in a manner substantially consistent with the plans and schedules for both the Technology and the Application.

(*ii*) *Analysis.* H's use of both the cash received on Date 1 and the cash received on Date 2 qualifies for the working capital safe harbor described in paragraph (d)(5)(iv) of this section.

* * *

(viii) *Real property straddling a qualified opportunity zone.*—For purposes of satisfying the requirements in this paragraph (d)(5), when it is necessary to determine whether a qualified opportunity zone is the location of services, tangible property, or business functions, section 1397C(f) applies (substituting "qualified opportunity zone" for "empowerment zone"). If the amount of real property based on square footage located within the qualified opportunity zone is substantial as compared to the amount of real property based on square footage outside of the qualified opportunity zone, and the real property outside of the qualified opportunity zone is contiguous to part or all of the real property located inside the qualified opportunity zone, then all of the property is deemed to be located within a qualified opportunity zone.

* * *

(f) *** Notwithstanding the preceding sentence, a QOF may not rely on the proposed rules in paragraphs (c)(8)(ii)(B) and (d)(4)(ii)(B) of this section (which concern the qualification of land as QOZBP) if the land is unimproved or minimally improved and the QOF or the QOZB purchases the land with an expectation, an intention, or a view not to improve the land by more than an insubstantial amount within 30 months after the date of purchase.

Qualified Opportunity Funds: Deferred Gains

Qualified Opportunity Funds: Deferred Gains.—Reg. §1.1400Z-2(e)-1, relating to gains that may be deferred as a result of a taxpayer's investment in a qualified opportunity fund (QOF), is

proposed (published in the Federal Register on October 29, 2018) (corrected December 28, 2018) (REG-115420-18).

Par. 5. Section 1.1400Z-2(e)-1 is added to read as follows:

§1.1400Z-2(e)-1. Applicable rules.—(a) *Treatment of investments with mixed funds.*—(1) *Investments to which no election under section 1400Z-2(a) applies.*—If a taxpayer invests money in a QOF and does not make an election under section 1400Z-2(a) with respect to that investment, the investment is one described in section 1400Z-2(e)(1)(A)(ii)(a separate investment to which section 1400Z-2(a), (b), and (c) do not apply).

(2) *Treatment of deemed contributions of money under 752(a).*—In the case of a QOF classified as a partnership for Federal income tax purposes, the deemed contribution of money described in section 752(a) does not create or increase an investment in the fund described in section 1400Z-2(e)(1)(A)(ii). Thus, any basis increase resulting from a deemed section 752(a) contribution is not taken into account in determining the portion of a partner's investment subject to section 1400Z-2(e)(1)(A)(i) or (ii).

(3) *Example.*—The following example illustrates the rules of this paragraph (a):

(i) Taxpayer A owns a 50 percent capital interest in Partnership P. Under section 1400Z-2(e)(1), 90 percent of A's investment is described in section 1400Z-2(e)(1)(A)(i) (an investment that only includes amounts to which the election under section 1400Z-2(a) applies), and 10 percent is described in section 1400Z-2(e)(1)(A)(ii) (a separate investment consisting of other amounts). Partnership P borrows $8 million. Under section 752 and the regulations thereunder, taking into account the terms of the partnership agreement, $4 million of the $8 million liability is allocated to A. Under section 752(a), A is treated as contributing $4 million to Partnership P. Under paragraph (2) of this section, A's deemed $4 million contribution to Partnership P is ignored for purposes of determining the percentage of A's investment in Partnership P subject to the deferral election under section 1400Z-2(a) or the portion not subject to such the deferral election under section 1400Z-2(a). As a result, after A's section 752(a) deemed contribution, 90 percent of A's investment in Partnership P is described in section 1400Z-2(e)(1)(A)(i) and 10 percent is described in section 1400Z-2(e)(1)(A)(ii).

(ii) [Reserved]

(b) [*Reserved*].

(c) *Applicability date.*—This section applies to investments in, and deemed contributions of money to, a QOF that occur on or after the date of publication in the **Federal Register** of a Treasury decision adopting these proposed rules as final regulations. An eligible taxpayer, however, may rely on the proposed rules in this section with respect to investments, and deemed contributions, before the date of applicability of this section, but only if the taxpayer applies the rules in their entirety and in a consistent manner. [Reg. §1.1400Z-2(e)-1.]

Qualified Opportunity Funds: Investment

Qualified Opportunity Funds: Investment.—Reg. §1.1400Z2(f)-1, relating to gains that may be deferred as a result of a taxpayer's investment in a qualified opportunity fund, as well as special rules for an investment in a QOF held by a taxpayer for at least 10 years, is proposed (published in the Federal Register on May 1, 2019) (REG-120186-18).

Par. 6. Section 1.1400Z2(f)-1 is added to read as follows:

§1.1400Z2(f)-1. Failure of qualified opportunity fund to maintain investment standard.—(a) *In general.*—Except as provided by §1.1400Z2(d)-1(a)(2)(ii) with respect to a taxpayer's first taxable year as a QOF, if a QOF fails to satisfy the 90-percent asset test in section 1400Z-2(d)(1), then the fund must pay the statutory penalty set forth in section 1400Z-2(f) for each month it fails meet the 90-percent asset test.

(b) *Time period for a QOF to reinvest certain proceeds.*—If a QOF receives proceeds from the return of capital or the sale or disposition of some or all of its qualified opportunity zone property within the meaning of section 1400Z-2(d)(2)(A), and if the QOF reinvests some or all of the proceeds in qualified opportunity zone property by the last day of the 12-month period beginning on the date of the distribution, sale, or disposition, then the proceeds, to the extent that they are so reinvested, are treated as qualified opportunity zone property for purposes of the 90-percent asset test in section 1400Z-2(d)(1), but only to the extent that prior to the reinvestment in qualified opportunity zone property the proceeds are continuously held in cash, cash equivalents, or debt instruments with a term of 18 months or less. If reinvestment of the proceeds is delayed by waiting for governmental action the application for which is complete, that delay does not cause a failure of the 12-month requirement in this paragraph (b).

(c) *Anti-abuse rule.*—(1) *In general.*—Pursuant to section 1400Z-2(e)(4)(C), the rules of section 1400Z-2 and §§1.1400Z2(a)-1 through 1.1400Z2(g)-1 must be applied in a manner consistent with the purposes of section 1400Z-2. Accordingly, if a significant purpose of a transaction is to achieve a tax result that is inconsistent with the purposes of section 1400Z-2, the Commissioner can recast a transaction (or series of transactions) for Federal tax purposes as appropriate to achieve tax results that are consistent with the purposes of section 1400Z-2. Whether a tax result is inconsistent with the purposes of section 1400Z-2 must be determined based on all the facts and circumstances.

(2) [Reserved]

(d) *Applicability date.*—This section applies to taxable years of a QOF that end on or after the date of publication in the **Federal Register** of a Treasury decision adopting these proposed rules as final regulations. However, an eligible taxpayer may rely on the proposed rules in this section (other than paragraph (c) of this section) with respect to taxable years before the date of applicability of this section, but only if the eligible taxpayer applies the rules in their entirety and in a consistent manner. An eligible taxpayer may rely on the proposed rules in paragraph (c) of this section with respect to taxable years before the date of applicability of this section, but only if the eligible taxpayer applies the rules of section 1400Z-2 and §§1.1400Z2(a)-1 through 1.1400Z2(g)-1, as applicable, in their entirety and in a consistent manner. [Reg. §1.1400Z2(f)-1.]

Qualified Opportunity Funds: Investment

Qualified Opportunity Funds: Investment.—Reg. §1.1400Z2(g)-1, relating to gains that may be deferred as a result of a taxpayer's investment in a qualified opportunity fund, as well as special rules for an investment in a QOF held by a taxpayer for at least 10 years, is proposed (published in the Federal Register on May 1, 2019) (REG-120186-18).

Par. 7. Section 1.1400Z2(g)-1 is added to read as follows:

§1.1400Z2(g)-1. Application of opportunity zone rules to members of a consolidated group.—(a) *Scope and definitions.*—(1) *Scope.*—This section provides rules regarding the Federal income tax treatment of QOFs owned by members of consolidated groups.

(2) *Definitions.*—The definitions provided in §1.1400Z2(b)-1(a)(2) apply for purposes of this section.

(b) *QOF stock not stock for purposes of affiliation.*—(1) *In general.*—Stock in a QOF corporation (whether qualifying QOF stock or otherwise) is not treated as stock for purposes of determining whether the issuer is a member of an affiliated group within the meaning of section 1504. Therefore, a QOF corporation can be the common parent of a consolidated group, but a QOF corporation cannot be a subsidiary member of a consolidated group.

(2) *Example.*—The following example illustrates the rules of this paragraph (b).

(i) *Facts.* Corporation P wholly owns corporation S, which wholly owns corporation Q. P, S, and Q are members of a U.S. consolidated group (P group). In 2018, S sells an asset to an unrelated party and realizes $500 of capital gain. S contributes $500 to Q and properly elects to defer recognition of the gain under section 1400Z-2. At such time, Q qualifies and elects to be treated as a QOF.

(ii) *Analysis.* Under paragraph (b) of this section, stock of a QOF (qualifying or otherwise) is not treated as stock for purposes of affiliation under section 1504. Thus, once Q becomes a QOF, Q ceases to be affiliated with the P group members under section 1504(a), and it deconsolidates from the P group.

(c) *Qualifying investments by members of a consolidated group.*—Except as otherwise provided in this section or in §1.1400Z2(b)-1, section 1400Z-2 applies separately to each member of a consolidated group. Therefore, for example, the same member of the group must both engage in the sale of a capital asset giving rise to gain and timely invest an amount equal to some or all of such gain in a QOF (as provided in section 1400Z-2(a)(1)) in order to qualify for deferral of such gain under section 1400Z-2.

(d) *Tiering up of investment adjustments provided by section 1400Z-2.*—Basis increases in a qualifying investment in a QOF under sections 1400Z-2(b)(2)(B)(iii), 1400Z-2(b)(2)(B)(iv), and 1400Z-2(c) are treated as satisfying the requirements of §1.1502-32(b)(3)(ii)(A), and thus qualify as tax-exempt income to the QOF owner. Therefore, if the QOF owner is a member of a consolidated group and is owned by other members of the same group (upper-tier members), the group members increase their bases in the shares of the QOF owner under §1.1502-32(b)(2)(ii). However, there is no basis increase under §1.1502-32(b)(2)(ii) in shares of upper-tier members with regard to basis increases under section 1400Z-2(c) and the regulations at §1.1400Z2(c)-1 unless and until the basis of the qualifying investment is increased to its fair market value, as provided in section 1400Z-2(c) and the regulations at §1.1400Z2(c)-1.

(e) *Application of §1.1502-36(d).*—This paragraph (e) clarifies how §1.1502-36(d) applies if a member (M) transfers a loss share of another member (S) and S is a QOF owner that owns a qualifying investment in a QOF. To determine S's attribute reduction amount under §1.1502-36(d)(3), S's basis in its qualifying investment is included in S's net inside attribute amount to compute S's aggregate inside loss under §1.1502-36(d)(3)(iii)(A). However, S's basis in the qualifying investment is not included in S's category D attributes available for attribute reduction under §1.1502-36(d)(4). Thus, S's basis in the qualifying investment cannot be reduced under §1.1502-36(d). If S's attribute reduction amount exceeds S's attributes available for reduction, then to the extent of S's basis in the qualifying investment (limited by the remaining attribute reduction amount), the common parent is treated as making the election under §1.1502-36(d)(6) to reduce M's basis in the transferred loss S shares.

(f) *Examples.*—The following examples illustrate the rules of this section.

(1) *Example 1: Basis adjustment when member owns qualifying QOF stock*—(i) *Facts.* Corporation P is the common parent of a consolidated group (P group), and P wholly owns Corporation S, a member of the P group. In 2018, S sells an asset to an unrelated party and realizes $500 of capital gain. S contributes $500 to Q (a QOF corporation) and properly elects to defer the gain under section 1400Z-2(a) and §1.1400Z2(a)-1. S does not otherwise own stock in Q. In 2029, when S still owns its qualifying investment in Q, P sells all of the stock of S to an unrelated party.

(ii) *Analysis*—(A) *5-year and 7-year basis increase and §1.1502-32 tier-up.* In 2023, when S has held the stock of Q for five years, under section 1400Z-2(b)(2)(B)(iii), S increases its basis in its Q stock by $50 (10 percent of $500, the amount of gain deferred by reason of section 1400Z-2(a)(1)(A)). The 10-percent basis increase qualifies as tax-exempt income to S under paragraph (d) of this section. Thus, P (an upper-tier member) increases its basis in S's stock by $50 under §1.1502-32(b)(2)(ii). Similarly, in 2025, when S has held the stock of Q for seven years, under section 1400Z-2(b)(2)(B)(iv), S increases its basis in its Q stock by an additional $25 (5 percent of $500). The 5 percent basis increase also qualifies as tax-exempt income to S under paragraph (d) of this section, and P increases its basis in S's stock by an additional $25 under § 1.1502-32(b)(2)(ii).

(B) *S's recognition of deferred capital gain in 2026.* S did not dispose of its Q stock prior to December 31, 2026. Therefore, under section 1400Z-2(b)(1)(B) and § 1.1400Z2(b)-1(b)(2), S's deferred capital gain is included in S's income on December 31, 2026. The amount of gain included under section 1400Z-2(b)(2)(A) is $425 ($500 of deferred gain less S's $75 basis in Q). S's basis in Q is increased by $425 to $500, and P's basis in S also is increased by $425.

(C) *P's disposition of S.* P's sale of S stock in 2029 results in the deconsolidation of S. Q remains a non-consolidated subsidiary of S, and S is not treated as selling or exchanging its Q stock for purposes of section 1400Z-2(c). Therefore, no basis adjustments under section 1400Z-2 are made as a result of P's sale of S stock.

(iii) *S sells the stock of Q after 10 years.* The facts are the same as in this *Example 1* in paragraph (f)(1)(i) of this section, except that in 2029, instead of P selling all of the stock of S, S sells all of the stock of Q to an unrelated party for its fair market value of $800. At the time of the sale, S has owned the Q stock for over 10 years, and S elects under section 1400Z-2(c) to increase its stock basis in Q from $500 (*see* the analysis in this *Example 1* in paragraph (f)(1)(ii)(B) of this section) to the fair market value of Q on the date of the sale, $800. As a result of the election, S's basis in Q is $800 and S has no gain on the sale of Q stock. Additionally, the $300 basis increase in Q is treated as tax-exempt income to S pursuant to paragraph (d) of this section. Thus, P increases its basis in P's S stock by $300 under § 1.1502-32(b)(2)(ii).

(2) *Example 2: Computation and application of the attribute reduction amount under § 1.1502-36(d) when S owns a QOF*—(i) *Facts.* Corporation P (the common parent of a consolidated group) wholly owns corporation M, which wholly owns corporation S, which wholly owns Q (a QOF corporation). In 2018, S sells an asset to an unrelated party and realizes $5,000 of capital gain. S contributes $5,000 to Q and properly elects to defer the gain under section 1400Z-2. In 2024, M sells all of its S stock to an unrelated party for fair market value of $100, and M's basis in the stock of S is $300. At the time of sale, S owns the stock of Q with a basis of $500 (S's basis in Q was increased under section 1400Z-2(b)(2)(B)(iii) to $500 in 2023), and S has a net operating loss carryover of $50. M's transfer of the S shares is a transfer of loss shares under § 1.1502-36. Assume that no basis redetermination is required under § 1.1502-36(b) and no basis reduction is required under § 1.1502-36(c).

(ii) *Attribute reduction under § 1.1502-36(d).* Under § 1.1502-36(d), S's attributes are reduced by S's attribute reduction amount. Section 1.1502-36(d)(3) provides that S's attribute reduction amount is the lesser of the net stock loss and S's aggregate inside loss. The net stock loss is the excess of the $300 aggregate basis of the transferred S shares over the $100 aggregate value of those shares, or $200. S's aggregate inside loss, which includes the basis of the stock of Q as provided by paragraph (e) of this section, is the excess of S's net inside attribute amount over the value of the S share. S's net inside attribute amount is $550, computed as the sum of S's $50 loss carryover and its $500 basis in Q. S's aggregate inside loss is therefore $450 ($550 net inside attribute amount over the $100 value of the S share). Accordingly, S's attribute reduction amount is the lesser of the $200 net stock loss and the $450 aggregate inside loss, or $200. Under § 1.1502-36(d)(4), S's $200 attribute reduction is first allocated and applied to reduce S's $50 loss carryover to $0. Under § 1.1502-36(d)(4)(i)(D), S generally would be able to reduce the basis of its category D assets (including stock in other corporations) by the remaining attribute reduction amount ($150). However, paragraph (e) of this section provides that S's basis in the QOF (Q) shares is not included in S's category D attributes that are available for reduction under § 1.1502-36(d)(4), and the remaining $150 of attribute reduction amount cannot be used to reduce the basis of Q shares under § 1.1502-36(d). Rather, under paragraph (e) of this section, P is treated as making the election under § 1.1502-36(d)(6) to reduce M's basis in the transferred loss S shares by $150. As a result, P's basis in its M stock will also be reduced by $150.

(g) *Applicability date.*—Except as otherwise provided in this paragraph (g), this section applies for taxable years that begin on or after the date of publication in the **Federal Register** of a Treasury decision adopting these proposed rules as final regulations. However, a QOF may rely on the proposed rules in this section with respect to taxable years that begin before the applicability date of this section, but only if the QOF applies the rules in their entirety and in a consistent manner. [Reg. § 1.1400Z2(g)-1.]

Self-Employment Tax: Limited Partner: Definition

Self-Employment Tax: Limited Partner: Definition.—Amendments to Reg. § 1.1402(a)-2, relating to the self-employment tax imposed under Code Sec. 1402, are proposed (published in the Federal Register on January 13, 1997) (REG-209824-96).

☐ Par. 2. Section 1.1402(a)-2 is amended by:

1. Revising the first sentence of paragraph (d).
2. Removing the reference "section 702(a)(9)" in the first sentence of paragraph (e) and adding "section 702(a)(8)" in its place.
3. Revising the last sentence of paragraph (f).
4. Revising paragraphs (g) and (h).
5. Adding new paragraphs (i) and (j).

The revisions and additions read as follows:

§1.1402(a)-2. Computation of net earnings from self-employment.

* * *

(d) * * * Except as otherwise provided in section 1402(a) and paragraph (g) of this section, an individual's net earnings from self-employment include the individual's distributive share (whether or not distributed) of income or loss described in section 702(a)(8) from any trade or business carried on by each partnership of which the individual is a partner. * * *

* * *

(f) * * * For rules governing the classification of an organization as a partnership or otherwise, see §§301.7701-1, 301.7701-2, and 301.7701-3 of this chapter.

(g) *Distributive share of limited partner.*—An individual's net earnings from self-employment do not include the individual's distributive share of income or loss as a limited partner described in paragraph (h) of this section. However, guaranteed payments described in section 707(c) made to the individual for services actually rendered to or on behalf of the partnership engaged in a trade or business are included in the individual's net earnings from self-employment.

(h) *Definition of limited partner.*—(1) *In general.*—Solely for purposes of section 1402(a)(13) and paragraph (g) of this section, an individual is considered to be a limited partner to the extent provided in paragraphs (h)(2), (h)(3), (h)(4), and (h)(5) of this section.

(2) *Limited partner.*—An individual is treated as a limited partner under this paragraph (h)(2) unless the individual—

(i) Has personal liability (as defined in §301.7701-3(b)(2)(ii) of this chapter for the debts of or claims against the partnership by reason of being a partner;

(ii) Has authority (under the law of the jurisdiction in which the partnership is formed) to contract on behalf of the partnership; or

(iii) Participates in the partnership's trade or business for more than 500 hours during the partnership's taxable year.

(3) *Exception for holders of more than one class of interest.*—An individual holding more than one class of interest in the partnership who is not treated as a limited partner under paragraph (h)(2) of this section is treated as a limited partner under this paragraph (h)(3) with respect to a specific class of partnership interest held by such individual if, immediately after the individual acquires that class of interest—

(i) Limited partners within the meaning of paragraph (h)(2) of this section own a substantial, continuing interest in that specific class of partnership interest; and,

(ii) The individual's rights and obligations with respect to that specific class of interest are identical to the rights and obligations of that specific class of partnership interest held by the limited partners described in paragraph (h)(3)(i) of this section.

(4) *Exception for holders of only one class of interest.*—An individual who is not treated as a limited partner under paragraph (h)(2) of this section solely because that individual participates in the partnership's trade or business for more than 500 hours during the partnership's taxable year is treated as a limited partner under this paragraph (h)(4) with respect to the individual's partnership interest if, immediately after the individual acquires that interest—

(i) Limited partners within the meaning of paragraph (h)(2) of this section own a substantial, continuing interest in that specific class of partnership interest; and

(ii) The individual's rights and obligations with respect to the specific class of interest are identical to the rights and obligations of the specific class of partnership interest held by the limited partners described in paragraph (h)(4)(i) of this section.

(5) *Exception for service partners in service partnerships.*—An individual who is a service partner in a service partnership may not be a limited partner under paragraphs (h)(2), (h)(3), or (h)(4) of this section.

(6) *Additional definitions.*—Solely for purposes of this paragraph (h)—

(i) A *class of interest* is an interest that grants the holder specific rights and obligations. If a holder's rights and obligations from an interest are different from another holder's rights and obligations, each holder's interest belongs to a separate class of interest. An individual may hold more than one class of interest in the same partnership provided that each class grants the individual different rights or obligations. The existence of a guaranteed payment described in section 707(c) made to an individual for services rendered to or on behalf of a partnership, however, is not a factor in determining the rights and obligations of a class of interest.

(ii) A *service partner* is a partner who provides services to or on behalf of the service partnership's trade or business. A partner is not considered to be a service partner if that partner only provides a de minimis amount of services to or on behalf of the partnership.

(iii) A *service partnership* is a partnership substantially all the activities of which involve the performance of services in the fields of health, law, engineering, architecture, accounting, actuarial science, or consulting.

(iv) A *substantial interest in a class of interest* is determined based on all of the relevant facts and circumstances. In all cases, however, ownership of 20 percent or more of a specific class of interest is considered substantial.

(i) *Example.*—The following example illustrates the principles of paragraphs (g) and (h) of this section:

Example. (i) A, B, and C form LLC, a limited liability company, under the laws of State to engage in a business that is not a service partnership described in paragraph (h)(6)(iii) of this section. LLC, classified as a partnership for federal tax purposes, allocates all items of income, deduction, and credit of LLC to A, B, and C in proportion to their ownership of LLC. A and C each contribute $1x for one LLC unit. B contributes $2x for two LLC units. Each LLC unit entitles its holder to receive 25 percent of LLC's tax items, including profits. A does not perform services for LLC; however, each year B receives a guaranteed payment of $6x for 600 hours of services rendered to LLC and C receives a guaranteed payment of $10x for 1000 hours of services rendered to LLC. C also is elected LLC's manager. Under State's law, C has the authority to contract on behalf of LLC.

(ii) *Application of general rule of paragraph (h)(2) of this section.* A is treated as a limited partner in LLC under paragraph (h)(2) of this section because A is not liable personally for debts of or claims against LLC, A does not have authority to contract for LLC under State's law, and A does not participate in LLC's trade or business for more than 500 hours during the taxable year. Therefore, A's distributive share attributable to A's LLC unit is excluded from A's net earnings from self-employment under section 1402(a)(13).

(iii) *Distributive share not included in net earnings from self-employment under paragraph (h)(4) of this section.* B's guaranteed payment of $6x is included in B's net earnings from self-employment under section 1402(a)(13). B is not treated as a limited partner under paragraph (h)(2) of this section because, although B is not liable for debts of or claims against LLC and B does not have authority to contract for LLC under State's law, B does participates in LLC's trade or business for more than 500 hours during the taxable year. Further, B is not treated as a limited partner under paragraph (h)(3) of this section because B does not hold more than one class of interest in LLC. However, B is treated as a limited partner under paragraph (h)(4) of this section because B is not treated as a limited partner under paragraph (h)(2) of this section solely because B participated in LLC's business for more than 500 hours and because A is a limited partner under paragraph (h)(2) of this section who owns a substantial interest with rights and obligations that are identical to B's rights and obligations. In this example, B's distributive share is deemed to be a return on B's investment in LLC and not remuneration for B's service to LLC. Thus, B's distributive share attributable to B's two LLC units is not net earnings from self-employment under section 1402(a)(13).

(iv) *Distributive share included in net earnings from self-employment.* C's guaranteed payment of $10x is included in C's net earnings from self-employment under section 1402(a). In addition, C's distributive share attributable to C's LLC unit also is net earnings from self-employment under section 1402(a) because C is not a limited partner under paragraphs (h)(2), (h)(3), or (h)(4) of this section. C is not treated as a limited partner under paragraph (h)(2) of this section because C has the authority under State's law to enter into a binding contract on behalf of LLC and because C participates in LLC's trade or business for more than 500 hours during the taxable year. Further, C is not treated as a limited partner under paragraph (h)(3) of this section because C does not hold more than one class of interest in LLC. Finally, C is not treated as a limited partner under paragraph (h)(4) of this section because C has the power to bind LLC. Thus, C's guaranteed payment and distributive share both are included in C's net earnings from self-employment under section 1402(a).

(j) *Effective date.*—Paragraphs (d), (e), (f), (g), (h), and (i) are applicable beginning with the individual's first taxable year beginning on or after the date this section is published as a final regulation in the Federal Register.

UNEARNED INCOME MEDICARE CONTRIBUTION

Net Investment Income Tax: Guidance Under Section 1411

Net Investment Income Tax: Guidance Under Section 1411.—Amendments to Reg. §1.1411-0, providing guidance on the computation of net investment income, are proposed (published in the Federal Register on December 2, 2013) (REG-130843-13).

☐ Par. 2. Section 1.1411-0 is amended by:

1. Revising the entries under §1.1411-3 for paragraphs (d)(2)(ii), (d)(3) and adding entries (d)(3)(i) through (iii).

2. Revising the entries under §1.1411-4 for paragraphs (d)(4)(iii), (e)(3), and (g)(10) through (13).

3. Adding entries to §1.1411-7.

The revisions and additions to read as follows:

§1.1411-0. Table of contents.

* * *

§1.1411-3 Application to estates and trusts.

* * *

(d) * * *

(2) * * *

(ii) Special rules for CRTs with income from certain CFCs or PFICs.

(3) Elective simplified method.

(i) Treatment of annuity or unitrust distributions.

(ii) Properly allocable deductions in excess of gross income.

(iii) Procedural requirements for making election.

* * *

§1.1411-4 Definition of net investment income.

* * *

(d) * * *

(4) * * *

(iii) Adjustment for capital loss carryforwards for previously excluded income

* * *

(e) * * *

(3) Treatment of income from common trust funds.

* * *

(g) * * *

(10) Treatment of section 707(c) guaranteed payments.

(11) Treatment of section 736 payments.

(i) In general.

(ii) Treatment of section 736(a)(1) payments.

(A) General rule.

(B) Examples.

(iii) Treatment of section 736(a)(2) payments.

(A) Payments for unrealized receivables and goodwill.

(B) Payments not for unrealized receivables or goodwill.

(iv) Treatment of section 736(b) payments.

(v) Application of section 1411(c)(4) to section 736 payments.

(12) Income and deductions from certain notional principal contracts.

Net Investment Income Tax: Guidance Under Section 1411

Net Investment Income Tax: Guidance Under Section 1411.—Amendments to Reg. §§1.1411-3 and 1.1411-4, providing guidance on the computation of net investment income, are proposed (published in the Federal Register on December 2, 2013) (REG-130843-13) (corrected February 24, 2014).

☐ Par 3. Section 1.1411-3 is amended by:
1. Revising paragraph (d)(2)(ii).
2. Revising paragraph (d)(2)(iii) by adding *Example 2* through *Example 5*.
3. Revising paragraph (d)(3).
4. Revising paragraph (f).

The revisions and additions read as follows:

§1.1411-3. Application to estates and trusts.

* * *

(d) * * *

(2) * * *

(ii) *Special rules for CRTs with income from certain CFCs or PFICs.*—If a CRT is a trust described in §1.1411-10(a), and the CRT includes an amount in gross income under section 951(a) or section 1293(a) from a CFC or QEF that is not also income derived from a trade or business described in section 1411(c)(2) and §1.1411-5 (except as provided in §1.1411-10(b)(2)) and an election under §1.1411-10(g) is not in effect with respect to the CFC or QEF, or the CRT is treated as receiving an excess distribution within the meaning of section 1291(b) or recognizing gain treated as an excess distribution under section 1291(a)(2), then the following rules apply for purposes of section 1411 with regard to income derived from the CFC, QEF, or PFIC—

(A) Amounts included in gross income for chapter 1 purposes under section 951(a) or section 1293(a) in a calendar year with respect to the CFC or QEF, and in one or more categories described in §1.664-1(d)(1) are considered excluded income in that calendar year;

(B) For the year in which the CRT is treated as receiving any of the items of net investment income described in paragraphs (c)(1)(i), (c)(1)(ii), (c)(2)(i), and (c)(4) of §1.1411-10 that otherwise are not included in gross income for purposes of chapter 1 for that year (*"NII Inclusion Amount"*) with respect to the CFC, QEF, or PFIC, the rules of this paragraph (d)(2)(ii)(B) apply; and

(1) For purposes of determining the character under section 664 of a distribution to the unitrust or annuity recipient of a CRT, the NII Inclusion Amount treated as received by the CRT shall be allocated among the categories described in section 664(b)(1) through (b)(3), and among the classes within each category as described in §1.664-1(d)(1), in the manner described in this paragraph (d)(2)(ii)(B). Specifically, to the extent the CRT has amounts of excluded income in the categories described in section 664(b)(1) (the Ordinary Income Category) or section 664(b)(2) (the Capital Gain Category), the NII Inclusion Amount shall be allocated to the CRT's classes of excluded income in the Ordinary Income Category, and then to the classes of excluded income in the Capital Gain Category, in turn, until exhaustion of each such class, beginning with the class of excluded income within a category with the highest Federal income tax rate.

(2) Any remaining NII Inclusion Amount not so allocated to classes within the Ordinary Income and Capital Gain Categories shall be placed in the category described in section 664(b)(3) (the Other Income Category). To the extent the CRT distributes amounts from this Other Income Category, that distribution shall constitute a distribution described in §1.1411-10(c)(4).

(3) A distribution by the CRT of excluded income first is deemed to carry out net

investment income to the extent of the NII Inclusion Amount that has been allocated to excluded income in that class.

(4) As a result, a distribution of excluded income will carry out to the unitrust or annuity recipient net investment income attributable to the items described in this paragraph (d)(2)(ii)(B).

(C) In the case of a difference between the amount calculated with respect to a disposition under paragraph (c)(2)(iii) or (c)(2)(iv) of § 1.1411-10 and the amount attributable to the relevant disposition for purposes of chapter 1, the following rules apply—

(1) If the amount of the gain from the disposition for purposes of section 1411 is higher (or the loss smaller) than the amount of the gain (or loss) calculated for purposes of chapter 1, such difference shall be considered an NII Inclusion Amount and shall be allocated as described in paragraph (d)(2)(ii)(B) of this section. However, in applying paragraph (d)(2)(ii)(B) of this section to this increase, the order of the classes and categories to which the allocation is made shall be changed as follows: the increase shall be allocated first to the class in the Capital Gain Category that reflects the nature of the increase (short-term or long-term), then to other classes in that category, in turn until exhausted, then to the classes in the Ordinary Income Category, and finally to the Other Income Category.

(2) If the amount of the gain from the disposition for purposes of section 1411 is smaller (or the loss higher) than the amount of the gain (or loss) calculated for purposes of chapter 1, such difference shall reduce accumulated net investment income in the CRT's categories and their respective classes as follows—

(i) To the extent that the CRT has amounts in the Other Income Category by reason of the application of paragraph (d)(2)(ii)(B) or (d)(2)(ii)(C)*(1)* of this section for the current or prior years, to the Other Income Category; and

(ii) Any excess difference in the same order as specified in paragraph (d)(2)(ii)(C)*(1)* of this section.

(iii) * * *

Example 2. (i) In 2010, A creates a net income with makeup CRT (NIMCRUT). A is the sole income beneficiary of the NIMCRUT for 15 years. As of December 31, 2012, the NIMCRUT had $2,000 of dividend income and $180,000 of long-term capital gain within the Ordinary Income and Capital Gain Categories, respectively. Because both of these amounts were received by the NIMCRUT during a taxable year beginning before 2013, both constitute excluded income within the meaning of § 1.1411-1(d). In Year 1, the NIMCRUT acquires an interest in a CFC. The NIMCRUT does not make the § 1.1411-10(g) election with respect to the CFC. In Year 1, the NIMCRUT receives a section 951(a) inclusion of $5,000 and makes no distributions to A. For all years, income derived with respect to the CFC is not income derived in a trade or business described in section 1411(c)(2) and § 1.1411-5.

(ii) In Year 1, § 1.1411-3(d)(2)(ii)(A) treats the section 951 inclusion as excluded income and allocates it to the class of non-NII with a 39.6% tax rate in the Ordinary Income Category under § 1.664-1(d)(1).

Year 1 ending Category and Class Balances

Category	*Class*	*Excluded / NII*	*Tax Rate*	*Amount*
Ordinary Income				
	Interest and Other Income (including section 951 Inclusions)	Excluded	39.6%	$5,000
	Qualified Dividends	Excluded	20.0%	$2,000
Capital Gain				
	Long-Term	NII	23.8%	$ 0
	Long-Term	Excluded	20.0%	$180,000
Other Income				None

(iii) The NIMCRUT makes no distributions to its sole income beneficiary in Year 2. In Year 3, the CFC distributes $4,000 to the NIMCRUT (which constitutes net investment income under § 1.1411-10(c)(1)(i)), the NIMCRUT has a total of $800 of post-2012 interest, and the NIMCRUT distributes $4,000 to the beneficiary.

Category and Class Balances immediately before both the CFC distribution and the NIMCRUT's Year 3 distribution to A

Category	*Class*	*Excluded / NII*	*Tax Rate*	*Amount*
Ordinary Income				
	Interest (post-2012)	NII	43.4%	$800
	Interest and Other Income (including section 951 Inclusions)	Excluded	39.6%	$5,000
	Qualified Dividends	Excluded	20.0%	$2,000
Capital Gain				
	Long-Term	NII	23.8%	$ 0
	Long-Term	Excluded	20.0%	$180,000
Other Income				None

Section 1.1411-3(d)(2)(ii)(B) will cause the $4,000 distribution from the CFC to be allocated first to the class of excluded income within the Ordinary Income Category with the highest Federal tax rate (the Interest and Other Income class). The distribution to A consists of $800 of post-2012 interest (subject to section 1411) and $3,200 from the Interest and Other Income class, of which all $3,200 constitutes NII by reason of the allocation under § 1.1411-3(d)(2)(ii)(B). Of the $1,800 remaining in that category after the distribution to A, $800 will carry out NII to A, and will be includable in A's net investment income, when it is distributed to A in the future. Because

the $3,200 distributed to A from this class is subject to both income tax and tax under section 1411 for Year 3, the timing differential attributable to the rules in § 1.1411-10 has been corrected within the NIMCRUT before the income is distributed to A.

Year 3 ending Category and Class Balances (immediately following the distribution to A)

Category	*Class*	*Excluded / NII*	*Tax Rate*	*Amount*
Ordinary Income				
	Interest (post-2012)	NII	43.4%	$0
	Interest & Other Income (including section 951 Inclusions)	Excluded	39.6%	$1,800*
	Qualified Dividends	Excluded	20.0%	$2,000
Capital Gain				
	Long-Term	NII	23.8%	$0
	Long-Term	Excluded	20.0%	$180,000
Other Income				None

* Of which $800 will carry out NII to A when distributed

Example 3. (i) Assume the same facts as in *Example 2*, except that, in Year 2, the NIMCRUT has a section 951 inclusion in the amount of $4,000, taxable interest income of $800, tax exempt interest of $4,000. Assume the CRT has $1,100 undistributed capital gain from a taxable year ending before December 31, 2012.

Category and Class Balances immediately before the Year 2 distribution to A

Category	*Class*	*Excluded / NII*	*Tax Rate*	*Amount*
Ordinary Income				
	Interest (post-2012)	NII	43.4%	$800
	Interest and Other Income (including section 951 Inclusions)	Excluded	39.6%	$9,000
	Qualified Dividends	Excluded	20.0%	$2,000
Capital Gain				
	Long-Term	NII	23.8%	$ 0
	Long-Term	Excluded	20.0%	$1,100
Other Income		Excluded		$4,000

(ii) In Year 2, the NIMCRUT made a $4,800 distribution to A in that same year (leaving a net balance in the Interest and Other Income class of $5,000 at the end of Year 2).

Category and Class Balances as of December 31, Year 2 (immediately following the distribution to A)

Category	*Class*	*Excluded / NII*	*Tax Rate*	*Amount*
Ordinary Income				
	Interest (post-2012)	NII	43.4%	$0
	Interest and Other Income (including section 951 Inclusions)	Excluded	39.6%	$5,000
	Qualified Dividends	Excluded	20.0%	$2,000
Capital Gain				
	Long-Term	NII	23.8%	$0
	Long-Term	Excluded	20.0%	$1,100
Other Income		Excluded		$4,000

A's net investment income in Year 2 will include $800 of taxable interest income, but will not include the $4,000 of other ordinary income.

(iii) In Year 3, the NIMCRUT received a distribution from the CFC of $9,000, and assume, for purposes of this example, that the NIMCRUT distributes $6,000 to A. Section 1.1411-3(d)(2)(ii)(B) will cause the $9,000 distribution from the CFC to be allocated first to the class of excluded income within the Ordinary Income Category with the highest Federal tax rate (thus, $5,000 to the Other Income class and $2,000 to Qualified Dividends). The $2,000 balance of the Year 3 distribution from the CFC is allocated under § 1.1411-3(d)(2)(ii)(B) as follows: $1,100 to the Long-Term Capital Gain class of non-NII (so the distribution to A from this class in the future will carry out $1,100 of NII to A), and the remaining $900 to the Other Income Category (so the distribution to A from this class in the future will carry out $900 of NII to A).

The distribution to A consists of $5,000 of Interest and Other Income class and $1,000 of Qualified Dividends, all of which constitutes NII by reason of the allocation under § 1.1411-3(d)(2)(ii)(B).

Category and Class Balances as of December 31, Year 3 (immediately following the distribution to A)

Category	*Class*	*Excluded / NII*	*Tax Rate*	*Amount*
Ordinary Income				
	Interest (post-2012)	NII	43.4%	$0
	Interest & Other Income (section 951 inclusion)	Excluded	39.6%	$0
	Qualified Dividends	Excluded	20.0%	$1,000*
Capital Gain				
	Long-Term	NII	23.8%	$0

Category	Class	Excluded / NII	Tax Rate	Amount
	Long-Term	Excluded	20.0%	$1,100*
Other Income		NII	3.8%	$900
Other Income		Excluded	0.0%	$3,100

* All of which will carry out NII to A when distributed in the future

A's net investment income in Year 3 will include $5,000 of other ordinary income and $1,000 of qualified dividend income.

Example 4. (i) Same facts as in *Example 2*, except that the NIMCRUT distributes $7,000 to A in Year 2. This distribution consists of the section 951 inclusion and the accumulated qualified dividends.

(ii) In Year 2, the NIMCRUT will report $5,000 of ordinary income and $2,000 of qualified dividends to A. Both amounts will constitute excluded income to A. In this case, A does not have to adjust MAGI because the section 951 inclusion is treated in the same way as any other type of excluded income within the Ordinary Income Category.

Year 2 ending Category and Class Balances (immediately following the distribution to A)

Category	Class	Excluded / NII	Tax Rate	Amount
Ordinary Income				
	Interest and Other Income (including section 951 Inclusions)	Excluded	39.6%	$0
	Qualified Dividends	Excluded	20.0%	$0
Capital Gain				
	Long-Term	NII	23.8%	$0
	Long-Term	Excluded	20.0%	$180,000
Other Income				None

(iii) When the CFC distributes $4,000 to the NIMCRUT in Year 3, § 1.1411-3(d)(2)(ii)(B)(*1*) requires the NIMCRUT to allocate that $4,000 to the NIMCRUT's accumulated balance of long-term capital gains recognized by the NIMCRUT prior to December 31, 2012, so that the first $4,000 of the NIMCRUT's long-term capital gains distributed to A in the future will carry out NII to A.

Category and Class Balances immediately before the Year 3 distribution to A

Category	Class	Excluded / NII	Tax Rate	Amount
Ordinary Income				
	Interest and Other Income (including section 951 Inclusions)	Excluded	39.6%	$0
	Qualified Dividends	Excluded	20.0%	$0
Capital Gain				
	Long-Term	Excluded	20.0%	$180,000*
Other Income				None

* Of which $4,000 will carry out NII to A when distributed in the future

When the NIMCRUT distributes the $4,000 to A in the future, the NIMCRUT will report $4,000 of long-term capital gain to A that also constitutes net investment income. No MAGI adjustments associated with that distribution will be required by A.

Year 3 ending Category and Class Balances (immediately following the distribution to A)

Category	Class	Excluded / NII	Tax Rate	Amount
Ordinary Income				
	Interest and Other Income (including section 951 Inclusions)	Excluded	39.6%	$0
	Qualified Dividends	Excluded	20.0%	$0
Capital Gain				
	Long-Term	Excluded	20.0%	$176,000
Other Income				None

Example 5. (i) Same facts as in *Example 4*, except that the NIMCRUT's entire balance of accumulated long-term capital gain was received after 2012 and thus is ANII.

(ii) When the CFC distributes $4,000 to the NIMCRUT in Year 3, § 1.1411-3(d)(2)(ii)(B)(*1*) requires the NIMCRUT to allocate that $4,000 to excluded income within the Ordinary Income or Capital Gain Categories. In this case, the NIMCRUT does not have any excluded income remaining within those categories. As a result, § 1.1411-3(d)(2)(ii)(B)(*2*) requires the excess portion of the CFC distribution not allocable to excluded income in the Ordinary Income or Capital Gain Categories ($4,000 in this case) to be allocated to the Other Income Category.

Category and Class Balances immediately before the Year 3 distribution to A

Category	Class	Excluded / NII	Tax Rate	Amount
Ordinary Income				
	Interest and Other Income (including section 951 Inclusions)	Excluded	39.6%	$0
	Qualified Dividends	Excluded	20.0%	$0

Category	*Class*	*Excluded / NII*	*Tax Rate*	*Amount*
Capital Gain				
	Long-Term	NII	23.8%	$180,000
	Long-Term	Excluded	20.0%	$0
Other Income		NII	3.8%	$4,000

When the NIMCRUT distributes the $4,000 to A, the NIMCRUT will report $4,000 of long-term capital gains to A that also constitute net investment income. No MAGI adjustments associated with the distribution are required by A.

Year 3 ending Category and Class Balances (immediately following the distribution to A)

Category	*Class*	*Excluded / NII*	*Tax Rate*	*Amount*
Ordinary Income				
	Interest and Other Income (including section 951 Inclusions)	Excluded	39.6%	$0
	Qualified Dividends	Excluded	20.0%	$0
Capital Gain				
	Long-Term	NII	23.8%	$176,000
	Long-Term	Excluded	20.0%	$0
Other Income		NII	3.8%	$4,000

After the NIMCRUT distributes all income within the Ordinary and Capital Gain categories, the NIMCRUT will distribute the $4,000 of Other Income to A. Such income will have a zero percent tax rate for chapter 1 purposes but will constitute net investment income. In this case, § 1.1411-3(d)(2)(ii)(B)(2) provides that the future distribution will be considered a distribution of net investment income from a trust within the meaning of § 1.1411-10(c)(4). As a result, § 1.1411-10(e) requires A to increase MAGI for the year of that distribution.

(3) *Elective simplified method.*—(i) *Treatment of annuity or unitrust distributions.*—If a CRT makes a valid election under this paragraph (d)(3), the rules of paragraph (d)(2) of this section shall not apply, and the net investment income of the beneficiary attributable to the beneficiary's annuity or unitrust distribution from the CRT shall include an amount equal to the lesser of—

(A) The beneficiary's share of the total amount of the distributions for that year; or

(B) The beneficiary's same share of the accumulated net investment income (as defined in paragraph (d)(1)(iii) of this section) of the CRT.

(ii) *Properly allocable deductions in excess of gross income.*—In computing the amount described in paragraph (d)(3)(i)(B) of this section, notwithstanding § 1.1411-4(f)(1)(ii) (limitations on deductions in excess of income), if in a taxable year a CRT's properly allocable deductions described in section 1411(c)(1)(B) and the regulations thereunder exceed the gross investment income and net gain described in section 1411(c)(1)(A) and the regulations thereunder, then such excess deductions shall reduce the amount described in paragraph (d)(3)(i)(B) of this section for that taxable year and, to the extent of any remaining excess deductions, for subsequent taxable years of the CRT.

(iii) *Procedural requirements for making election.*—In the case of a CRT established after December 31, 2012, a CRT wanting to make the election under paragraph (d)(3) of this section must do so on its income tax return for the taxable year in which the CRT is established. In the case of a CRT established before January 1, 2013, the CRT wanting to make the election under paragraph (d)(3) of this section must do so on the return for its first taxable year beginning on or after January 1, 2013. Once made, the election is irrevocable. In lieu of the relief provisions under § 301.9100-3, the CRT may make the election on an amended return for that year only if the taxable year for which the election is made, and all taxable years that are affected by the election, for both the CRT and its beneficiaries, are not closed by the period of limitations on assessments under section 6501.

* * *

(f) *Effective/applicability date.*—This section applies to taxable years beginning after December 31, 2013, except that paragraphs (d)(1), (d)(2)(i), *Example 1* of (d)(2)(iii), and (d)(3) of this section applies to taxable years of CRTs that begin after December 31, 2012. However, taxpayers may apply this section to taxable years beginning after December 31, 2012, in accordance with § 1.1411-1(f).

* * *

☐ Par 4. Section 1.1411-4 is amended by revising paragraphs (d)(4)(iii), (e)(3), and (g)(10) through (13) to read as follows:

§ 1.1411-4. Definition of net investment income.

* * *

(d) * * *

(4) * * *

(iii) *Adjustment for capital loss carryforwards for previously excluded income.*—(A) *General rule.*—For purposes of calculating net gain in paragraph (d) of this section (and any allowable loss described in paragraph (f)(4) of this section, if applicable), capital losses are reduced by the lesser of—

(1) The amount of capital loss taken into account in the current year by reason of section 1212(b)(1); or

(2) The amount of net capital loss excluded from net investment income in the preceding year by reason of paragraph (d)(4) of this section.

(B) *Example.*—The following example illustrates the provisions of this paragraph (d)(4)(iii). For purposes of this example, assume the taxpayer is a United States citizen, uses a calendar taxable year, and Year 1 and all subsequent years are taxable years in which section 1411 is in effect:

Example. (i)(A) In Year 1, A, an unmarried individual, disposes of 100 shares of publicly traded stock for a short-term capital gain of $4,000. In addition, A disposes of a partnership interest and recognizes a long-term capital loss of $19,000. Assume that the entire amount of $19,000 loss is not allowed against net investment income pursuant to section 1411(c)(4)(B), § 1.1411-7, and paragraph (d)(4)(ii) of this section. A has no capital loss carryovers from the year preceding Year 1.

(B) For purposes of chapter 1, A reports net capital loss of $15,000, of which $3,000 is allowed as a deduction in computing taxable income under section 1211(b)(1), and the remaining $12,000 is carried forward into Year 2 as a long-term capital loss pursuant to section 1212(b)(1).

(C) For purposes of calculating net investment income, A reports $4,000 of net gain. The $19,000 loss taken into account in computing A's taxable income in Year 1 is not taken into account in computing net gain. Therefore, there are no losses in excess of gains in Year 1 for which a deduction is allowed under paragraph (f)(4) of this section.

(ii)(A) In Year 2, A has no capital gain or loss transactions.

(B) For purposes of chapter 1, A reports net capital loss of $12,000, of which $3,000 is allowed as a deduction in computing taxable income under section 1211(b)(1), and the remaining $9,000 is carried forward into Year 3 as a long-term capital loss pursuant to section 1212(b)(1).

(C) For purposes of calculating net investment income, A must adjust the $12,000 capital loss carryover from Year 1 pursuant to paragraph (d)(4)(iii) of this section. The amount of the adjustment is the lesser of—

(*1*) The amount of capital loss taken into account in the current year by reason of section 1212(b)(1) ($12,000), or

(*2*) The amount of net capital loss excluded from net investment income in Year 1 by reason of paragraph (d)(4) of this section ($19,000). The $19,000 loss was the amount disallowed by reason of paragraph (d)(4)(ii) of this section, and there were no other adjustments under paragraphs (d)(4)(i) or (d)(4)(iii) of this section in Year 1.

(D) The amount of capital loss carryover that is taken into account by A in computing net investment income in Year 2 is $0 ($12,000 carryover amount less the adjustment of $12,000). Accordingly, when calculating net investment income, A has no losses in excess of gains, and no deduction is available to A under paragraph (f)(4) of this section.

(iii)(A) In Year 3, A recognizes a $5,000 short-term capital gain from the disposition of property described in paragraph (d)(4)(i) of this section, and a $1,000 short-term capital loss from the disposition of publicly traded stock.

(B) For purposes of chapter 1, A reports net capital loss carryover from Year 2 of $9,000. In addition, the short-term capital gain of $5,000 and $1,000 short-term capital loss net to produce $4,000 of short-term capital gain. A reports a net capital loss of $5,000 ($5,000 - $1,000 - $9,000), of which $3,000 is allowed as a deduction in computing taxable income under section 1211(b)(1), and the remaining $2,000 is carried forward into Year 4 as a long-term capital loss pursuant to section 1212(b)(1).

(C) For purposes of calculating net investment income, A may exclude the $5,000 capital gain from the calculation of net gain pursuant to paragraph (d)(4)(i) of this section. In addition, A must adjust the $9,000 capital loss carryover from Year 2 pursuant to paragraph (d)(4)(iii) of this section. The amount of the adjustment is the lesser of—

(*1*) The amount of capital loss taken into account in the current year by reason of section 1212(b)(1) ($9,000); or

(*2*) The amount of net capital loss excluded from net investment income in Year 2 by reason of paragraph (d)(4) of this section ($12,000). The $12,000 loss was the amount disallowed by reason of paragraph (d)(4)(iii) of this section, and there were no other adjustments under paragraphs (d)(4)(i) or (d)(4)(ii) of this section in Year 2.

(D) The amount of capital loss carryover that is taken into account by A in computing net investment income in Year 3 is $0 ($9,000 carryover amount less the adjustment of $9,000). Accordingly, when calculating net investment income, A excludes $5,000 of gain under paragraph (d)(4)(i) of this section and the $9,000 capital loss carryover under paragraph (d)(4)(iii) of this section. The amount of losses taken into account for purposes of computing net gain is $1,000 (attributable to the $1,000 short-term capital loss from the disposition of publicly traded stock). Pursuant to paragraph (f)(4) of this section, A is entitled to a deduction of $1,000 because the $1,000 capital loss exceeds the gains, and the loss is less than the amount of allowable loss for chapter 1 purposes ($3,000).

(iv)(A) In Year 4, A recognizes a $8,000 long-term capital loss on the disposition of raw land to which paragraph (d)(4)(i) of this section does not apply.

(B) For purposes of chapter 1, A reports net capital loss carryover from Year 3 of $2,000. The $8,000 long-term capital loss is added to the $2,000 capital loss carryforward to produce a $10,000 long-term capital loss, of which $3,000 is allowed as a deduction in computing taxable income under section 1211(b)(1), and the remaining $7,000 is carried forward into Year 5 as a long-term capital loss pursuant to section 1212(b)(1).

(C) For purposes of calculating net investment income, A takes into account the $8,000 capital loss from the sale of the land. In addition, A must adjust the $2,000 capital loss carryover from Year 3 pursuant to paragraph (d)(4)(iii) of this section. The amount of the adjustment is the lesser of—

(*1*) The amount of capital loss taken into account in the current year by reason of section 1212(b)(1) ($2,000); or

(*2*) The amount of net capital loss excluded from net investment income in Year 3 by reason of paragraph (d)(4) of this section ($4,000). The $4,000 loss is the sum of the $5,000 gain disallowed by reason of paragraph (d)(4)(i) of this section and the $9,000 loss disallowed by reason of paragraph (d)(4)(iii) of this section, and there were no other adjustments under paragraph (d)(4)(ii) of this section in Year 3.

(D) The amount of capital loss carryover that is taken into account by A in computing net investment income in Year 3 is $0 ($2,000 carryover amount less the adjustment of $2,000). The amount of losses taken into account for purposes of computing net gain is $8,000 (attributable to the $8,000 capital loss from the disposition of raw land). Pursuant to paragraph (f)(4) of this section, A is entitled to a deduction of $3,000 because the $8,000 capital loss exceeds the gains, and only $3,000 of the loss is allowable for chapter 1 purposes under section 1211(b)(1).

(v)(A) In Year 5, A has no capital gain or loss transactions.

(B) For purposes of chapter 1, A reports net capital loss carryover from Year 4 of $7,000: $3,000 is allowed as a deduction in computing taxable income under section 1211(b)(1), and the remaining $4,000 is carried forward into Year 6 as a long-term capital loss pursuant to section 1212(b)(1).

(C) For purposes of calculating net investment income, A must adjust the $7,000 capital loss carryover from Year 4 pursuant to paragraph (d)(4)(iii) of this section. The amount of the adjustment is the lesser of—

(*1*) The amount of capital loss taken into account in the current year by reason of section 1212(b)(1) ($7,000); or

(*2*) The amount of net capital loss excluded from net investment income in Year 4 by reason of paragraph (d)(4) of this section ($2,000). The $2,000 loss was the amount disallowed by reason of paragraph (d)(4)(iii) of this section, and there were no other adjustments under paragraphs (d)(4)(i) or (d)(4)(ii) of this section in Year 4.

(D) The amount of capital loss carryover that is taken into account by A in computing net investment income in Year 5 is $5,000 ($7,000 carryover amount less the adjustment of $2,000). The amount of losses taken into account for purposes of computing net gain is $5,000 carried over from Year 4. Pursuant to paragraph (f)(4) of this section, A is entitled to a deduction of $3,000 because the $5,000 capital loss exceeds the gains, and only $3,000 of the loss is allowable for chapter 1 purposes under section 1211(b)(1).

(vi)(A) In Year 6, A has no capital gain or loss transactions.

(B) For purposes of chapter 1, A reports net capital loss carryover from Year 5 of $4,000: $3,000 is allowed as a deduction in computing taxable income under section 1211(b)(1), and the remaining $1,000 is carried forward into Year 7 as a long-term capital loss pursuant to section 1212(b)(1).

(C) For purposes of calculating net investment income, A must adjust the $4,000 capital loss carryover from Year 5 pursuant to paragraph (d)(4)(iii) of this section. The amount of the adjustment is the lesser of—

(*1*) The amount of capital loss taken into account in the current year by reason of section 1212(b)(1) ($4,000); or

(*2*) The amount of net capital loss excluded from net investment income in Year 5 by reason of paragraph (d)(4) of this section ($2,000). The $2,000 loss was the amount disallowed by reason of paragraph (d)(4)(iii) of this section, and there were no other adjustments under paragraphs (d)(4)(i) or (d)(4)(ii) of this section in Year 5.

(D) The amount of capital loss carryover that is taken into account by A in computing net investment income in Year 6 is $2,000 ($4,000 carryover amount less the adjustment of $2,000). The amount of losses taken into account for purposes of computing net gain is $2,000 carried over from Year 5. Pursuant to paragraph (f)(4) of this section, A is entitled to a deduction of $2,000 because the $2,000 capital loss exceeds the gains, and the loss is less than the amount of allowable loss for chapter 1 purposes ($3,000). As a result, the entire $8,000 loss from the raw land has been taken into account in computing A's net investment income ($3,000 in Years 4 and 5, and $2,000 in Year 6).

(vii)(A) In Year 7, A has no capital gain or loss transactions.

(B) For purposes of chapter 1, A reports net capital loss carryover from Year 6 of $1,000. The entire $1,000 is allowed as a deduction in computing taxable income under section 1211(b)(1). A has no capital losses to carry over to Year 8.

(C) For purposes of calculating net investment income, A must adjust the $1,000 capital loss carryover from Year 6 pursuant to paragraph (d)(4)(iii) of this section. The amount of the adjustment is the lesser of—

(*1*) The amount of capital loss taken into account in the current year by reason of section 1212(b)(1) ($1,000); or

(*2*) The amount of net capital loss excluded from net investment income in Year 6 by reason of paragraph (d)(4) of this section ($2,000). The $2,000 loss was the amount disallowed by reason of paragraph (d)(4)(iii) of this section, and there were no other adjustments under paragraphs (d)(4)(i) or (d)(4)(ii) of this section in Year 6.

(D) The amount of capital loss carryover that is taken into account by A in computing net investment income in Year 6 is $0 ($1,000 carryover amount less the adjustment of $1,000). Therefore, when calculating net investment income, A has no losses in excess of gains, and no deduction is available to A under paragraph (f)(4) of this section.

(e) * * *

(3) *Treatment of income from common trust funds.*—If a taxpayer is a participant in a common trust fund and the taxpayer includes under section 584 any item of income, deduction, gain, or loss, then section 1411 and the regulations thereunder apply to that item to the same extent as if the participant had made directly the investments of the common trust fund to which the items are attributable.

* * *

(g) * * *

(10) *Treatment of section 707(c) guaranteed payments.*—Net investment income does not include section 707(c) payments received for services. Except to the extent provided in paragraph (g)(11)(iii)(A) of this section, section 707(c) payments received for the use of capital are net investment income within the meaning of section 1411(c)(1)(A)(i) and paragraph (a)(1)(i) of this section.

(11) *Treatment of section 736 payments.*—(i) *In general.*—The treatment of payments received by a retiring partner or a deceased part-

ner's successor in interest described in section 736 is determined under the rules of this paragraph (g)(11). Section 736 payments are not distributions from a plan or arrangement described in section 1411(c)(5) and § 1.1411-8. To the extent that any portion of a section 736 payment is taken into account in computing a taxpayer's net earnings from self-employment (within the meaning of § 1.1411-9), then such amount is not taken into account in computing net investment income by reason of section 1411(c)(6) and § 1.1411-9.

(ii) *Treatment of section 736(a)(1) payments.*—(A) *General rule.*—In the case of a payment described in section 736(a)(1) as a distributive share of partnership income, the items of income, gain, loss, and deduction attributable to such distributive share are taken into account in computing net investment income in section 1411(c) in a manner consistent with the item's character and treatment for chapter 1 purposes. See § 1.469-2(e)(2)(iii) for rules concerning the item's character and treatment for chapter 1.

(B) *Examples.*—The following examples illustrate the provisions of this paragraph (g)(11)(ii). For purposes of these examples, assume the taxpayer is a United States citizen, uses a calendar taxable year, and Year 1 and all subsequent years are taxable years in which section 1411 is in effect:

Example 1. Distributive share for unrealized receivables. (i) A retires from PRS, a business entity classified as a partnership for Federal Income tax purposes for which capital is not a material income producing factor. A is entitled, pursuant to the partnership agreement, to receive 10% of PRS's net income for 60 months commencing immediately following A's retirement in exchange for A's fair market value share of PRS's unrealized receivables. A will provide no services to PRS for the 60-month period following A's retirement. Prior to A's retirement, A materially participated in PRS's trade or business within the meaning of § 1.469-5T. Prior to A's retirement, A materially participated as a general partner in PRS's trade or business within the meaning of § 1.469-5T. For purposes of section 1411, PRS was not a trade or business described in section 1411(c)(2)(A) prior to A's retirement.

(ii) In Year 3, pursuant to the partnership agreement, A received a cash payment of $20,000. A's distributive share of PRS income in Year 3 included $70,000 of gross income from operations and $50,000 of deductions from operations. PRS's status as a passive or nonpassive activity is determined under § 1.469-2(e)(2)(iii) at the time the liquidation of A's partnership interest commenced, and remains fixed for the duration of A's liquidation payments. Therefore, PRS is a nonpassive activity with respect to A in Year 3 pursuant to § 1.469-2(e)(2)(iii). As a result, the gross income is not attributable to a trade or business described in section 1411(c)(2)(A) or § 1.1411-5(a)(1). Accordingly, A's distributive share of $70,000 of gross income and $50,000 of associated deductions are not includable in A's net investment income in Year 3.

(iii) If PRS's distributive share of operational income and deductions was attributable to a trade or business described in section 1411(c)(2)(B) or § 1.1411-5(a)(2), the $70,000 of gross income amounts would be included in A's net investment income under section 1411(c)(1)(A)(ii) and paragraph (c) of this section and the $50,000 of associated deductions would be properly allocable to such income under section 1411(c)(1)(B) and § 1.1411-4(f)(2)(ii).

Example 2. Excess distributive share payments. Assume the same facts as in *Example 1* except that PRS provides A an additional 2% of PRS's net income for 48 months commencing immediately following A's retirement as an incentive for A to retire earlier than planned. In the case of the additional 2% distributive share, the section 736(a) income characterization rule in § 1.469-2(e)(2)(iii) does not apply because the payment exceeds the value of PRS's unrealized receivables (which was established to equal 10% of PRS's income for 60 months in *Example 1*). As a result, A must determine whether PRS is a trade of business described in section 1411(c)(2)(A) and § 1.1411-5(a)(1) in Year 3 in order to determine whether the distributive share of operating income and deductions is includable in net investment income. If PRS is engaged in a trade or business described in section 1411(c)(2)(A) and § 1.1411-5(a)(1) with respect to A in Year 3, then the distributive share will be taken into account in computing A's net investment income.

(iii) *Treatment of section 736(a)(2) payments.*—(A) *Payments for unrealized receivables and goodwill.*—In the case of a payment described in section 736(a)(2), the portion (if any) of the payment that is allocable to the unrealized receivables (within the meaning of section 751(c)) and goodwill of the partnership (as described and calculated in § 1.469-2(e)(2)(iii)(B)) is included in net investment income under section 1411(c)(1)(A)(iii) and paragraphs (a)(1)(iii) and (d) of this section as gain from the disposition of a partnership interest.

(B) *Payments not for unrealized receivables or goodwill.*—In the case of a section 736(a)(2) payment not described in paragraph (g)(11)(iii)(A) of this section, the payment is characterized as a payment for services or as the payment of interest in a manner consistent with the payment's characterization under § 1.469-2(e)(2)(ii). See paragraph (g)(9) of this section.

(iv) *Treatment of section 736(b) payments.*—Gain or loss attributable to section 736(b) payments is included in net investment income under section 1411(c)(1)(A)(iii) and paragraphs (a)(1)(iii) and (d) of this section as gain or loss from the disposition of a partnership interest. A taxpayer who elects under § 1.736-1(b)(6) must apply the principles that are applied to installment sales in § 1.1411-7(d).

(v) *Application of section 1411(c)(4) to section 736 payments.*—Section 1411(c)(4) and § 1.1411-7 apply to gain or loss attributable to section 736 payments described in paragraphs (g)(11)(iii)(A) and (g)(11)(iv) of this section. In the case of section 736 payments that are received in more than one taxable year, the rules for calculating gain or loss under section 1411(c)(4) and § 1.1411-7 are applied at the time the liquidation of the partner's interest commenced. The principles that are applied to installment sales in § 1.1411-7(d) also apply for purposes of this section.

(12) *Income and deductions from certain notional principal contracts.*—(i) *In general.*—Net in-

come for a taxable year taken into account by a taxpayer under § 1.446-3(d) that is attributable to a notional principal contract described in paragraph (g)(12)(ii) of this section is net investment income described in section 1411(c)(1)(A) and paragraph (a)(1) of this section. A net deduction for a taxable year taken into account by a taxpayer under § 1.446-3(d) that is attributable to a notional principal contract described in paragraph (g)(12)(ii) of this section is a properly allocable deduction described in section 1411(c)(1)(B) and paragraph (f) of this section.

(ii) *Notional principal contracts.*—For purposes of paragraph (g)(12)(i) of this section, a notional principal contract is any notional principal contract described in § 1.446-3(c)(1) that is referenced to property (including an index) that produces (or would produce if the property were to produce income) interest, dividends, royalties, or rents if the property were held directly by the taxpayer. For purposes of the preceding sentence, an interest rate swap, cap, or floor is treated as a notional principal contract that is referenced to a debt instrument.

(13) *Treatment of income or loss from REMIC residual interests.*—The daily portion of taxable income determined under section 860C(a)(2) taken into account in determining tax under chapter 1 by the holder of a residual interest in a REMIC and any inducement fee included in income under § 1.446-6(a) are treated as net investment income under section 1411(c)(1)(A) and paragraph (a)(1) of this section. The daily portion of net loss determined under section 860C(a)(2) taken into account in determining tax under Chapter 1 by the holder of a residual interest in a REMIC is a properly allocable deduction described in section 1411(c)(1)(B) and paragraph (f) of this section.

* * *

Net Investment Income Tax: Guidance Under Section 1411

Net Investment Income Tax: Guidance Under Section 1411.—Reg. § 1.1411-7, providing guidance on the computation of net investment income, is proposed (published in the Federal Register on December 2, 2013) (REG-130843-13) (corrected February 24,2014).

☐ Par. 5. Section 1.1411-7 is added to read as follows:

§ 1.1411-7. Exception for dispositions of certain active interests in partnerships and S corporations.—(a) *In general.*—(1) *General application.*—In the case of a transferor that disposes of an interest in a partnership or S corporation described in paragraph (a)(3) of this section (transferor), the gain or loss from the disposition recognized under chapter 1 that is taken into account under § 1.1411-4(a)(1)(iii) shall be calculated in accordance with this section. The calculation in paragraph (b) of this section reflects the net gain or net loss that the transferor would take into account if the partnership or S corporation sold all of its Section 1411 Property (as defined in paragraph (a)(2)(iv) of this section) for fair market value immediately before the disposition of such interest. In certain instances, transferors may qualify to use an alternative calculation described in paragraph (c) of this section in lieu of the calculation described in paragraph (b) of this section. Paragraph (d) of this section contains additional rules for Section 1411(c)(4) Dispositions (as defined in paragraph (a)(2)(ii) of this section) in deferred recognition transactions. Paragraph (f) of this section provides rules for adjusting the amount of gain or loss computed under this paragraph (a)(1) for transferors subject to basis adjustments required by § 1.1411-10(d). Paragraph (g) of this section provides rules for information disclosures by a partnership or S corporation to transferors and for information reporting by individuals, trusts, and estates. If a transferor disposes of an interest in a partnership or S corporation not described in paragraph (a)(3) of this section, then this section does not apply and the full amount of the gain or loss, as computed under chapter 1 and adjusted by § 1.1411-10(d) (if applicable), is taken into account in computing the transferor's net investment income.

(2) *Definitions.*—For purposes of this section—

(i) The term *Passthrough Entity* means an entity taxed as a partnership or an S corporation. For purposes of this section, a reference to an interest in any S corporation shall mean a reference to stock in such S corporation.

(ii) The term *Section 1411(c)(4) Disposition* means a disposition of an interest in a Passthrough Entity described in paragraph (a)(3) of this section.

(iii) The term *Section 1411 Holding Period* means the year of disposition and the transferor's two taxable years preceding the disposition or the time period the transferor held the interest, whichever is less; provided, however, that for purposes of applying this paragraph (a)(2)(iii), the transferor will—

(A) Include the period that a previous owner or owners held the interest transferred if the transferor acquired its interest from another Passthrough Entity in a nonrecognition transaction during the year of disposition or the prior two taxable years;

(B) Include the period that the transferor held an interest in a Subsidiary Passthrough Entity if the transferor transferred that interest to a Passthrough Entity in a nonrecognition transaction during the year of disposition or the prior two taxable years; and

(C) Include the period that a previous owner or owners held the interest transferred if the transferor acquired its interest by gift.

(iv) The term *Section 1411 Property* means property owned by or held through the Passthrough Entity that, if disposed of by the entity, would result in net gain or loss allocable to the transferor of a type that is includable in determining net investment income of the transferor under § 1.1411-4(a)(1)(iii).

(v) The term *Subsidiary Passthrough Entity* means an interest in a Passthrough Entity owned, directly or indirectly, by another Passthrough Entity.

(3) *Section 1411(c)(4) Dispositions.*—(i) *Transfers by individuals, estates, and trusts.*—The disposition by a transferor of an interest in a Passthrough Entity is a Section 1411(c)(4) Disposition only if—

(A) The Passthrough Entity is engaged in one or more trades or businesses (within the meaning of section 162), or owns an interest (directly or indirectly) in a Subsidiary Passthrough Entity that is engaged in one or more trades or businesses (within the meaning of section 162), that is not described in §1.1411-5(a)(2) (trading in financial instruments or commodities); and

(B) One or more of the trades or businesses of the Passthrough Entity described in paragraph (a)(3)(i)(A) of this section is not a §1.1411-5(a)(1) (passive activity) trade or business of the transferor.

(ii) *Transfers by Passthrough Entities.*—Where a Passthrough Entity (the "holder") disposes of an interest in a Subsidiary Passthrough Entity, that disposition qualifies as a Section 1411(c)(4) Disposition with respect to a partner or shareholder of the Passthrough Entity if the partner or shareholder would satisfy the requirements of paragraph (a)(3)(i) of this section if it held the interest in the Subsidiary Passthrough Entity directly. For this purpose, the partner or shareholder shall be treated as owning a proportionate share of any Subsidiary Passthrough Entity in which the partner or shareholder owns an indirect interest through one or more tiers of Passthrough Entities.

(4) *Special rules.*—(i) *Certain liquidations.*—If a fully taxable disposition of all of the Passthrough Entity's assets is followed by the complete liquidation of the Passthrough Entity as part of a single plan, then the disposition will be treated as an asset sale for purposes of section 1411, and no additional gain or loss will be included in net investment income under §1.1411-4(a)(1)(iii) on the subsequent liquidation of the Passthrough Entity by any transferor who would have satisfied paragraph (a)(3) of this section prior to the sale. A sale of stock in an S corporation with respect to which an election under section 336(e) or section 338(h)(10) is made shall be treated as a fully taxable disposition of the Passthrough Entity's assets followed by the liquidation of the Passthrough Entity for purposes of this paragraph (a)(4)(i).

(ii) *Excluded gain or loss.*—The difference between the amount of gain or loss taken into account in computing taxable income for purposes of chapter 1 and the amount of gain or loss taken into account after the application of this section shall constitute excluded income or excluded loss, as applicable, for purposes of §1.1411-4(d)(4)(ii).

(iii) *Rules applicable to S corporation shareholders.*—(A) *Certain S corporation dispositions.*—If the transfer of an interest in an S corporation causes the S election to terminate on the day of the transfer, then the corporation shall continue to be treated as an S corporation for purposes of applying the rules of this section to the transferor notwithstanding that §1.1362-3(a) treats the day of the transfer as the first day of the corporation's C corporation short year (as defined therein).

(B) *S corporations subject to section 1374.*—For purposes of the calculation under paragraph (b) of this section, the amount of gain or loss allocated to the transferor is determined under section 1366(a), and the allocation does not take into account any reduction in the transferor's pro rata share of gains under section 1366(f)(2) resulting from the hypothetical imposition of tax under section 1374 as a result of the deemed sale.

(C) *Treatment of Qualified Subchapter S Trusts (QSSTs).*—In the case of a disposition of S corporation stock by a QSST, the rules of this section are applied by treating the QSST as the owner of the S corporation stock.

(b) *Calculation.*—(1) *In general.*—A transferor of an interest in a Passthrough Entity who disposes of that interest in a Section 1411(c)(4) Disposition may use the simplified calculation in paragraph (c) of this section if it meets the eligibility requirements set forth in paragraph (c)(2) of this section. Any other transferor who disposes of an interest in a Passthrough Entity in a Section 1411(c)(4) Disposition must include gain or loss under §1.1411-4(a)(1)(iii) determined in accordance with this paragraph (b).

(i) *Gain on disposition of interest.*—If the transferor recognized a gain from the disposition, the amount of the net gain included in §1.1411-4(a)(1)(iii) is the lesser of—

(A) the transferor's gain on the disposition of the interest in the Passthrough Entity as determined in accordance with chapter 1; or

(B) the transferor's allocable share of the chapter 1 net gain from a deemed sale of the Passthrough Entity's Section 1411 Property as determined using the principles of §1.469-2T(e)(3) (allocation of gain or loss to activities of the Passthrough Entity) where the net gain is the sum of the amounts of net gain and net loss allocable to the transferor as determined under §§1.469-2T(e)(3)(ii)(B)*(1)(i)* and 1.469-2T(e)(3)(ii)(B)*(2)(i)* that would constitute income to the transferor for purposes of section 1411 if sold by the Passthrough Entity. The general rules of §1.469-2T(e)(3) apply in calculating the transferor's allocable share of the net gain under this section; however, the gain recharacterization rule of §1.469-2T(e)(3)(iii) shall not apply in any case. The calculation of net gain in this paragraph (b)(1)(i) shall not be less than zero.

(ii) *Loss on disposition of interest.*—If the transferor recognizes a loss from the disposition, the amount of the net loss included in §1.1411-4(a)(1)(iii) is the lesser of—

(A) The transferor's loss (expressed as a positive number) on the disposition of the interest in the Passthrough Entity as determined in accordance with chapter 1; or

(B) The transferor's allocable share of the chapter 1 net loss (expressed as a positive number) from the deemed sale of the entity's Section 1411 Property as determined in accordance with §1.469-2T(e)(3) (allocation of gain or loss to activities of the Passthrough Entity) where the net loss is the sum of the amounts of net gain and net loss allocable to the transferor as determined under §§1.469-2T(e)(3)(ii)(B)*(1)(i)* and 1.469-2T(e)(3)(ii)(B)*(2)(i)* that would constitute income or loss to the transferor for purposes of section 1411 if sold by the Passthrough Entity. The general rules of §1.469-2T(e)(3) apply in calculating the transferor's allocable share of the net gain under this section; however, the gain recharacterization rule of §1.469-2T(e)(3)(iii) shall not apply in any case. The calculation of net gain in this paragraph (b)(1)(ii) shall not be less than zero. For purposes of this paragraph (b)(1)(ii), the loss limitation provisions imposed by sections 704(d) and 1366(d) shall not apply.

(2) *Examples*.—The following examples illustrate the principles of paragraph (b)(1) of this section. For purposes of these examples, assume that the taxpayer is a United States citizen, uses a calendar taxable year, and Year 1 and all subsequent years are taxable years in which section 1411 is in effect:

Example 1. (i) *Facts*. A owns a one-half interest in P, a calendar year partnership. In Year 1, A sells its interest for $200,000. A's adjusted basis for the interest sold is $120,000. Thus, A recognizes $80,000 of gain from the sale (chapter 1 gain). P is engaged in three trade or business activities, X, Y, and Z, none of which are § 1.1411-5(a)(2) (trading in financial instruments or commodities) trades or businesses. P also owns marketable securities. For Year 1, A materially participates in activity Z, thus it is not a § 1.1411-5(a)(1) (passive activity) trade or business of A. A, however, does not materially participate in activities X and Y, so these activities are § 1.1411-5(a)(1) trades or businesses of A. Because P is engaged in at least one trade or business and at least one of those trades or businesses is not passive to the transferor A, A determines its amount of § 1.1411-4(a)(1)(iii) gain or loss from net investment income under § 1.1411-7. Assume for purposes of this example, A is not eligible to compute its § 1.1411-4(a)(1)(iii) gain or loss under the optional simplified reporting method discussed in paragraph (c) of this section. The fair market value and adjusted basis of the gross assets used in P's activities are as follows:

	Adjusted basis	Fair market value	Gain/Loss	A's Share Gain/ Loss
X (Passive as to A)	$136,000	$96,000	($40,000)	($20,000)
Y (Passive as to A)	60,000	124,000	64,000	32,000
Z (Non-passive as to A)	40,000	160,000	120,000	60,000
Marketable securities	4,000	20,000	16,000	8,000
Total	240,000	400,000	160,000	80,000

(ii) *Analysis*. Under paragraph (b)(1) of this section, A must determine the portion of gain or loss from the sale of P's Section 1411 Property allocable to A. Under paragraph (b)(1)(ii) of this section, A's allocable share of gain from P's Section 1411 Property is $20,000 (($20,000) from X + $32,000 from Y + $8,000 from the marketable securities). Because the $20,000 allocable to A from a deemed sale of P's Section 1411 Property is less than A's $80,000 chapter 1 gain, A will include $20,000 under § 1.1411-4(a)(1)(iii).

Example 2. Assume the same facts as *Example 1*, but A materially participates in activities Y and Z and does not materially participate in activity X. Under paragraph (b)(1)(i) of this section, A's allocable share of P's Section 1411 Property is ($12,000) (($20,000) from X + $8,000 from the marketable securities). Because A sold its interest for a chapter 1 gain, the amount allocable to A from a deemed sale of P's Section 1411 Property cannot be less than zero. Accordingly, A includes no gain or loss under § 1.1411-4(a)(1)(iii).

(c) *Optional simplified reporting*.—(1) *In general*.—A transferor of an interest in a Passthrough Entity in a Section 1411(c)(4) Disposition may use the simplified reporting rules of paragraph (c)(4) of this section if it satisfies the eligibility requirements set forth in paragraph (c)(2) of this section and is not described in paragraph (c)(3) of this section. All other transferors of interests in Passthrough Entities in Section 1411(c)(4) Dispositions must use the calculation set forth in paragraph (b) of this section. Paragraph (d) of this section contains additional rules for Section 1411(c)(4) Dispositions in deferred recognition transactions.

(2) *Qualifications*.—Unless described in paragraph (c)(3) of this section, a transferor of an interest in a Passthrough Entity in a Section 1411(c)(4) Disposition may determine the amount of net gain or net loss that is taken into account under § 1.1411-4(a)(1)(iii) in accordance with paragraph (c)(4) of this section if either or both of the requirements in paragraph (c)(2)(i) or (c)(2)(ii) of this section are satisfied:

(i) *Five percent threshold*.—The sum of separately stated income, gain, loss, and deduction items (with any separately stated loss and deduction items included as positive numbers) of a type the transferor would take into account in calculating net investment income (as defined in § 1.1411-1(d)) that are allocated to the transferor in respect of the transferred interest is five percent or less of the sum of all separately stated items of income, gain, loss, and deduction (with any separately stated loss and deduction items included as positive numbers) allocated to the transferor in respect of the transferred interest during the Section 1411 Holding Period, and the total amount of chapter 1 gain or loss recognized by the transferor from the disposition of interests in the Passthrough Entity does not exceed $5 million (including gains or losses from multiple dispositions as part of a plan). All dispositions of interests in the Passthrough Entity that occur during the taxable year will be presumed to be part of a plan. In calculating the percentage described in the first sentence of this paragraph (c)(2)(i), if the transferor acquired the transferred interest in a transaction described in paragraph (a)(2)(iii)(A) or (a)(2)(iii)(C) of this section, then items of income, gain, loss, or deduction allocated to the transferor include any such items allocated to the transferor's predecessor (or predecessors) in interest during the Section 1411 Holding Period. If the transferor transferred an interest in a Subsidiary Passthrough Entity to the Passthrough Entity in a transaction described in paragraph (a)(2)(iii)(B) of this section, then items of income, gain, loss or deduction allocated to the transferor include any items allocated to the transferor during the Section 1411 Holding Period in respect of the interest in the Subsidiary Passthrough Entity.

(ii) *$250,000 gain or loss threshold*.—The total amount of chapter 1 gain or loss recognized by the transferor from the disposition of interests in the Passthrough Entity does not exceed

$250,000 (including gains or losses from multiple dispositions as part of a plan). All dispositions of interests in the Passthrough Entity that occur during the taxable year will be presumed to be part of a plan.

(3) *Nonapplicability.*—A transferor is not eligible to use the simplified reporting method of paragraph (c)(4) of this section if any of the following conditions are met:

(i) The transferor has held directly the interest in the Passthrough Entity (or held the interest indirectly in the case of a Subsidiary Passthrough Entity) for less than twelve months preceding the Section 1411(c)(4) Disposition.

(ii) The transferor transferred, directly or indirectly, Section 1411 Property (other than cash or cash equivalents) to the Passthrough Entity (or a Subsidiary Passthrough Entity described in paragraph (a)(2)(v) of this section), or received a distribution of property (other than Section 1411 property) from the Passthrough Entity (or a Subsidiary Passthrough Entity described in paragraph (a)(2)(v) of this section), during the Section 1411 Holding Period as part of a plan that includes the transfer of the transferor's interest in the Passthrough Entity. A transferor who contributed, directly or indirectly, Section 1411 Property (other than cash or cash equivalents) within 120 days of the disposition of the interest in the Passthrough Entity is presumed to have made the contribution as part of a plan that includes the transfer of the interest in the Passthrough Entity.

(iii) The Passthrough Entity is a partnership, and the transferor transfers a partial interest that represents other than a proportionate share of all of the transferring partner's economic rights in the partnership.

(iv) The transferor knows or has reason to know that the percentage of the Passthrough Entity's gross assets that consist of Section 1411 Property has increased or decreased by 25 percentage points or more during the transferor's Section 1411 Holding Period due to contributions, distributions, or asset acquisitions or dispositions in taxable or nonrecognition transactions.

(v) The Passthrough Entity, which is the subject of the Section 1411(c)(4) Disposition, was taxable as a C corporation during the Section 1411 Holding Period, but during that period elects under section 1362 to be taxable as an S corporation under section 1361.

(4) *Optional simplified reporting calculation.*—The amount of net gain or loss from the transferor's Section 1411(c)(4) Disposition that is includable in § 1.1411-4(a)(1)(iii) is determined by multiplying the transferor's chapter 1 gain or loss on the disposition by a fraction, the numerator of which is the sum of income, gain, loss, and deduction items (with any separately stated loss and deduction items netted as negative numbers) of a type that are taken into account in the calculation of net investment income (as defined in § 1.1411-1(d)) that are allocated to the transferor during the Section 1411 Holding Period and the denominator of which is the sum of all items of income, gain, loss, and deduction allocated to the transferor during the Section 1411 Holding Period (with any separately stated loss and deduction items netted as negative numbers). If the quotient of the fraction is either greater than one or less than zero, then the fraction shall be one; provided, however, that if the numerator is a negative amount in connection with a computation of overall chapter 1 gain on the sale or a positive amount in connection with a computation of overall chapter 1 loss on the sale, then the fraction shall be zero. In calculating the fraction described in the first sentence of this paragraph (c)(4), if the transferor acquired the transferred interest in a transaction described in paragraph (a)(2)(iii)(A) or (C) of this section, then items of income, gain, loss, or deduction allocated to the transferor include any such items allocated to the transferor's predecessor (or predecessors) in interest during the Section 1411 Holding Period. If the transferor transferred an interest in a Subsidiary Passthrough Entity to the Passthrough Entity in a transaction described in paragraph (a)(2)(iii)(B) of this section, then items of income, gain, loss or deduction allocated to the transferor include any items allocated to the transferor during the Section 1411 Holding Period in respect of the interest in the Subsidiary Passthrough Entity.

(5) *Examples.*—The following examples illustrate the principles of paragraph (c)(4) of this section. For purposes of these examples, assume that the taxpayer is a United States citizen, uses a calendar taxable year, and Year 1 and all subsequent years are taxable years in which section 1411 is in effect:

Example 1. Facts. A owns a one-half interest in P, a partnership. In Year 1, A sells the interest for $2,000,000. A's adjusted basis for the interest sold is $1,100,000. Because P is engaged in at least one trade or business and at least one of those trades or businesses is not passive to the transferor A, A determines its amount of § 1.1411-4(a)(1)(iii) gain or loss from net investment income under § 1.1411-7. None of the nonapplicability conditions set forth in section 1.1411-7(c)(3) apply. The aggregate net income from P's activities allocable to A for the year of disposition and the two preceding tax years are as follows:

	Aggregate Income/(loss)
X (Non-Passive as to A)	$1,800,000
Y (Passive as to A)	(10,000)
Marketable securities	20,000

(ii) *Analysis.* During A's Section 1411 Holding Period, A was allocated $30,000 of gross items of a type taken into account in the calculation of net investment income ($10,000 of loss from activity Y and $20,000 of income from marketable securities). The total amount of A's allocated net items during the Section 1411 Holding Period equals $1,830,000 ($1,800,000 income from activity X, $10,000 loss from activity Y, and $20,000 income from marketable securities). Thus, less than 5% ($30,000/1,830,000) of A's allocations during the Section 1411 Holding Period are of a type that are taken into account in the computation of net investment income, and because A's chapter 1 gain recognized of $900,000 is less than $5,000,000, A qualifies under § 1.1411-7(c)(2)(ii) to use the optional simplified method.

(iii) Under paragraph (c)(4) of this section, A's percentage of Section 1411 Property is determined by dividing A's allocable shares of income and loss of a type that are taken into account in the calculation of net investment income (as defined in § 1.1411-1(d)) that are allocated to the transferor by the Passthrough Entity during the Section 1411 Holding Period is $10,000 ($10,000 loss from Y + $20,000 income from marketable securities) by $1,810,000, which is the sum of A's share of income and loss from all of P's activities ($1,800,000 + ($10,000) + 20,000). Thus, A's gain for purposes of § 1.1411-4(a)(1)(iii) is $4,972.32 ($900,000 chapter 1 gain multiplied by the fraction 10,000/1,810,000).

Example 2. Assume the same facts as *Example 1,* but A sells the interest in P for $900,000. Under paragraph (c)(4) of this section, A's percentage of Section 1411 Property is determined by dividing A's allocable share of income and loss of a type that are taken into account in the calculation of a net investment income (as defined in § 1.1411-1(d)) that are allocated to the transferor by the Passthrough Entity during the Section 1411 Holding Period is $10,000 ($10,000 loss from Y + $20,000 income from marketable securities) by $1,810,000, which is the sum of A's share of income and loss from all of P's activates ($1,800,000 + ($10,000) + 20,000). Because A's allocable share during the Section 1411 Holding Period of income and loss of a type that is taken into account in calculating net investment income was a positive amount, and A sells its interest for an overall chapter 1 loss, A uses a fraction of 0 to compute its net investment income under paragraph (c)(4) of this section. Thus, A has no gain or loss for purposes of § 1.1411-4(a)(1)(iii) ($200,000 chapter 1 loss multiplied by a fraction of 0).

(d) *Deferred recognition transactions.*—In the case of a disposition of a Passthrough Entity in an installment sale under section 453 (or in exchange for an annuity contract), the calculations described in paragraphs (b) and (c) of this section shall be applied in the year of the disposition as if the entire amount of gain recognized for chapter 1 is taken into account by the transferor in the year of the disposition. For this purpose, it is assumed that any contingencies potentially affecting consideration to the transferor that are reasonably expected to occur will occur, and in the case of annuities based on the life expectancy of one or more individuals, the present value of the annuity (using existing Federal tax valuation methods) is used to determine the estimated gain. If the calculations in this section result in a transferor excluding only a portion of the chapter 1 gain from net investment income, the amount of excluded gain will constitute an addition to basis for purposes of applying section 453 to determine the amount of gain is includable in net investment income under § 1.1411-4(a)(1)(iii) as payments are received.

(e) *Disposition of tiered Passthrough Entities.*—[Reserved]

(f) *Adjustment to net gain or loss.*—In the case of a disposition of an interest in a Passthrough Entity where the transferor's basis in the interest for section 1411 purposes does not equal the transferor's basis for chapter 1 purposes due to basis adjustments required by § 1.1411-10(d), then the following rules apply:

(i) If the transferor's basis for section 1411 purposes is higher than the transferor's basis for chapter 1 purposes, then the difference reduces the amount of gain or increases the amount of loss, as applicable, that is includable in net investment income under this section.

(ii) If the transferor's basis for section 1411 purposes is lower than the transferor's basis for chapter 1 purposes, then the difference increases the amount of gain or reduces the amount of loss, as applicable, that is includable in net investment income under this section.

(iii) The adjustments to gain or loss includable in net investment income under this paragraph (f) are taken into account by the transferor immediately following the calculation of gain or loss under paragraphs (a)(4)(i), (b)(1) or (c)(4) of this section, as applicable.

(g) *Information reporting.*—(1) *Information to be provided by passthrough entity to transferor.*—Where the Passthrough Entity knows, or has reason to know, that the transferor satisfies paragraph (a)(3)(i) of this section but does not satisfy paragraph (c) of this section, then the Passthrough Entity shall provide the transferor with information as to the transferor's allocable share of the net gain or loss from the deemed sale of the Passthrough Entity's Section 1411 Property as described in paragraph (b)(1) of this section and such other information as may be required by forms, instructions, or in other guidance to allow the transferor to compute gain or loss under this section.

(2) *Information reporting by transferors.*—Any transferor making a calculation under this section must attach a statement to the transferor's return for the year of disposition containing certain information as required by this paragraph (g)(2) and any other information required by guidance and applicable forms and instructions issued by the Commissioner to allow the transferor to compute gain or loss under this section. In the case of a disposition in a transaction described in paragraph (d) of this section, the information required by this paragraph (g)(2) shall apply in the year of the disposition, or in the first year the taxpayer is subject to section 1411 (determined without regard to the effect of this section), whichever is later. The statement must include—

(i) The name and taxpayer identification number of the Passthrough Entity of which the interest was transferred;

(ii) The amount of the transferor's gain or loss on the disposition of the interest for purposes of chapter 1;

(iii) The information provided by the Passthrough Entity to the transferor by reason of paragraph (g)(1) of this section; and

(iv) The amount of adjustment to gain or loss by reason of paragraph (f) of this section, if any.

(h) *Effective/applicability date.*—This section applies to taxable years beginning after December 31, 2013. However, taxpayers may apply this section to taxable years beginning after December 31, 2012 in accordance with § 1.1411-1(f). [Reg. § 1.1411-7.]

WITHHOLDING OF TAX ON NONRESIDENT ALIENS AND FOREIGN CORPORATIONS

Withholding: Nonresident Aliens: Form W-8: Electronic Transmission

Withholding: Nonresident Aliens: Form W-8: Electronic Transmission.—Amendments to Reg. §1.1441-1, relating to the establishment by withholding agents and payors of an electronic system for use by beneficial owners or payees in furnishing Form W-8 (Certificate of Foreign Status), are proposed (published in the Federal Register on October 14, 1997) (REG-107872-97).

□ Par. 2. In §1.1441-1, paragraph (e)(4)(iv) is revised to read as follows:

§1.1441-1. Requirement for the deduction and withholding of tax on payments to foreign persons.

* * *

(e) * * *

(4) * * *

(iv) *Electronic transmission of information.*—(A) *In general.*—A withholding agent may establish a system for beneficial owners or payees to furnish electronically Forms W-8 (or such other form as the Internal Revenue Service may prescribe). The system also may enable the withholding agent to electronically transmit Forms W-8 to another person. The system must meet the requirements described in paragraph (e)(4)(iv)(B) of this section.

(B) *Requirements.*—(1) *In general.*—The electronic system must ensure that the information received is the information sent, and must document all occasions of user access that result in the submission, renewal, or modification of a Form W-8. In addition, the design and operation of the electronic system, including access procedures, must make it reasonably certain that the person accessing the system and furnishing Form W-8 is the person named in the form.

(2) *Same information as paper Form W-8.*—The electronic transmission must provide the withholding agent or payor with exactly the same information as the paper Form W-8.

(3) *Perjury statement and signature requirements.*—The electronic transmission must be signed by way of an electronic signature by the person whose name is on the Form W-8 and the signature must be under penalties of perjury in the manner described in this paragraph (e)(4)(iv)(B)(3).

(i) *Perjury statement.*—The perjury statement must contain the language that appears on the paper Form W-8. The electronic system must inform the person whose name is on the Form W-8 that the person must make the declaration contained in the perjury statement and that the declaration is made by signing the Form W-8. The instructions and the language of the perjury statement must immediately follow the person's certifying statements and immediately precede the person's electronic signature.

(ii) *Electronic signature.*—The act of the electronic signature must be effected by the person whose name is on the electronic Form W-8. The signature must also authenticate and verify the submission. For this purpose, the terms *authenticate* and *verify* have the same meanings as they do when applied to a written signature on a paper Form W-8. An electronic signature can be in any form that satisfies the foregoing requirements. The electronic signature must be the final entry in the person's Form W-8 submission.

(4) *Requests for electronic Forms W-8 data.*—Upon request by the Internal Revenue Service during an examination, the withholding agent must supply a hard copy of the electronic Form W-8 and a statement that, to the best of the withholding agent's knowledge, the electronic Form W-8 was filed by the person whose name is on the form. The hard copy of the electronic Form W-8 must provide exactly the same information as, but need not be a facsimile of, the paper Form W-8.

(C) *Special requirements for transmission of Forms W-8 by an intermediary.*—[Reserved].

* * *

Withholding: Reducing Burden under FATCA

Withholding: Reducing Burden under FATCA.—Amendments to Reg. §1.1441-1, eliminating withholding on payments of gross proceeds, deferring withholding on foreign passthru payments, eliminating withholding on certain insurance premiums, and clarifying the definition of investment entity, are proposed (published in the Federal Register on December 18, 2018) (REG-132881-17).

Par. 2. Section 1.1441-1 is amended by revising paragraphs (c)(38) and (e)(4)(ii)(A)(2) to read as follows:

§1.1441-1. Requirement for the deduction and withholding of tax on payments to foreign persons.

* * *

(c) * * *

(38) *Permanent residence address.*—(i) *In general.*—The term *permanent residence address* is the address in the country of which the person claims to be a resident for purposes of that country's income tax. In the case of a withholding certificate furnished in order to claim a reduced rate of withholding under an income tax treaty, whether a person is a resident of a treaty country must be determined in the manner prescribed under the applicable treaty. See §1.1441-6(b). The address of a financial institution with which the person maintains an account, a post office box, or an address used solely for mailing purposes is not a permanent residence address unless such address is the only address used by the person and appears as the person's registered address in the person's organizational documents. Further, an address that is provided subject to a hold mail instruction (as defined in §1.1471-1(b)(62)) is not a permanent residence address unless the person provides the docu-

mentary evidence described in paragraph (c)(38)(ii) of this section. If, after a withholding certificate is provided, a person's permanent residence address is subsequently subject to a hold mail instruction, the addition of the hold mail instruction is a change in circumstances requiring the person to provide the documentary evidence described in paragraph (c)(38)(ii) of this section in order for a withholding agent to use the address as a permanent residence address. If the person is an individual who does not have a tax residence in any country, the permanent residence address is the place at which the person normally resides. If the person is an entity and does not have a tax residence in any country, then the permanent residence address of the entity is the place at which the person maintains its principal office.

(ii) *Hold mail instruction.*—An address that is subject to a hold mail instruction (as defined in § 1.1471-1(b)(62)) can be used by a withholding agent as a permanent residence address if the person has provided the withholding agent with documentary evidence described in § 1.1471-3(c)(5)(i) (without regard to the requirement in § 1.1471-3(c)(5)(i) that the documentary evidence contain a permanent residence address). The documentary evidence described in § 1.1471-3(c)(5)(i) must support the person's claim of foreign status or, in the case of a person that is claiming treaty benefits, must support residence in the country where the person is claiming a reduced rate of withholding under an income tax treaty.

* * *

(e) * * *

(4) * * *

(ii) * * *

(A) * * *

(*2*) *Documentary evidence for treaty claims and treaty statements.*—Documentary evidence described in § 1.1441-6(c)(3) or (4) shall remain valid until the last day of the third calendar year following the year in which the documentary evidence is provided to the withholding agent, except as provided in paragraph (e)(4)(ii)(B) of this section. A statement regarding entitlement to treaty benefits described in § 1.1441-6(c)(5) (treaty statement) shall remain valid until the last day of the third calendar year following the year in which the treaty statement is provided to the withholding agent except as provided in this paragraph (e)(4)(ii)(A)(*2*). A treaty statement provided by an entity that identifies a limitation on benefits provision for a publicly traded corporation shall not expire at the time provided in the preceding sentence if a withholding agent determines, based on publicly available information at each time for which the treaty statement would otherwise be renewed, that the entity is publicly traded. A withholding agent described in the preceding sentence must retain a record of the information relied upon (to confirm that the entity is publicly traded) for as long as it may be relevant to the determination of the withholding agent's tax liability under section 1461 and § 1.1461-1. Notwithstanding the second sentence of this paragraph (e)(4)(ii)(A)(*2*), a treaty statement provided by an entity that identifies a limitation on benefits provision for a government or tax-exempt organization (other than a tax-exempt pension trust or pension fund) shall remain valid indefinitely. Notwithstanding the validity periods (or exceptions thereto) prescribed in this paragraph (e)(4)(ii)(A)(*2*), a treaty statement will cease to be valid if a change in circumstances makes the information on the statement unreliable or incorrect. For accounts opened and treaty statements obtained prior to January 6, 2017 (including those from publicly traded corporations, governments, and tax-exempt organizations), the treaty statement will expire January 1, 2020.

* * *

Tax on Certain U.S. Source Income: Withholding

Tax on Certain U.S. Source Income: Withholding.—Amendments to Reg. §§1.1441-1 and 1.1441-2, regarding withholding of tax on certain U.S. source income paid to foreign persons and requirements for certain claims for refund or credit of income tax made by foreign persons, are proposed (published in the Federal Register on January 6, 2017) (REG-134247-16).

Par. 2. Section 1.1441-1 is amended by:

1. Adding paragraphs (b)(7)(ii)(B) and (c)(2)(ii).
2. Revising paragraph (c)(3)(ii).
3. Adding paragraphs (c)(38)(ii), (e)(2)(ii)(B), (e)(3)(iv)(C)(*3*), (e)(4)(i)(B), (e)(4)(ii)(A)(*2*), (e)(4)(iv)(D), and (e)(4)(iv)(E).

The revisions and additions read as follows:

§ 1.1441-1. Requirement for the deduction and withholding of tax on payments to foreign persons.

* * *

(b) * * *

(7) * * *

(ii) * * *

(B) [The text of the proposed amendment to § 1.1441-1(b)(7)(ii)(B) is the same as the text of § 1.1441-1T(b)(7)(ii)(B) as added by T.D. 9808.]

* * *

(c) * * *

(2) * * *

(ii) [The text of the proposed amendment to § 1.1441-1(c)(2)(ii) is the same as the text of § 1.1441-1T(c)(2)(ii) as added by T.D. 9808.]

(3) * * *

(ii) [The text of the proposed amendment to § 1.1441-1(c)(3)(ii) is the same as the text of § 1.1441-1T(c)(3)(ii) as added by T.D. 9808.]

* * *

(38) * * *

(ii) [The text of the proposed amendment to § 1.1441-1(c)(38)(ii) is the same as the text of § 1.1441-1T(c)(38)(ii) as added by T.D. 9808.]

* * *

(e) * * *

(2) * * *

(ii) * * *

(B) [The text of the proposed amendment to § 1.1441-1(e)(2)(ii)(B) is the same as the text of §1.1441-1T(e)(2)(ii)(B) as added by T.D. 9808.]

* * *

(3) * * *

(iv) * * *

(C) * * *

(3) [The text of the proposed amendment to §1.1441-1(e)(3)(iv)(C)*(3)* is the same as the text of §1.1441-1T(e)(3)(iv)(C)*(3)* as added by T.D. 9808.]

* * *

(4) * * *

(i) * * *

(B) [The text of the proposed amendment to §1.1441-1(e)(4)(i)(B) is the same as the text of §1.1441-1T(e)(4)(i)(B) as added by T.D. 9808.]

(ii) * * *

(A) * * *

(2) [The text of the proposed amendment to §1.1441-1(e)(4)(ii)(A)*(2)* is the same as the text of §1.1441-1T(e)(4)(ii)(A) as added by T.D. 9808.]

* * *

(iv) * * *

(D) [The text of the proposed amendment to §1.1441-1(e)(4)(iv)(D) is the same as the text of §1.1441-1T(e)(4)(iv)(D) as added by T.D. 9808.]

(E) [The text of the proposed amendment to §1.1441-1(e)(4)(iv)(E) is the same as the text of §1.1441-1(e)(4)(iv)(E) as added by T.D. 9808.]

* * *

Par. 3. Section 1.1441-2 is amended by adding paragraph (a)(8) to read as follows:

§1.1441-2. Amounts subject to withholding.—(a) * * *

(8) [The text of the proposed amendment to §1.1441-2(a)(8) is the same as the text of §1.1441-2T(a)(8) as added by T.D. 9808.]

* * *

Stock and Rights to Acquire Stock: Deemed Distributions

Stock and Rights to Acquire Stock: Deemed Distributions.—Amendments to Reg. §§1.1441-2 and 1.1441-3, regarding deemed distributions of stock and rights to acquire stock and resolving ambiguities concerning the amount and timing of deemed distributions that are or result from adjustments to rights to acquire stock, are proposed (published in the Federal Register on April 13, 2016) (REG-133673-15).

Par. 7. Section 1.1441-2 is amended by:

1. Revising paragraphs (d)(1) and (4).

2. Amending paragraph (f) by removing the language "(d)(4)" in the second sentence and adding in its place "(d)(1)(ii)(C)," and adding a fourth and fifth sentence.

The revisions and addition read as follows:

§1.1441-2. Amounts subject to withholding.

* * *

(d) * * *

(1) *General rule.*—(i) *Control or custody and knowledge.*—Except as provided in paragraph (d)(1)(ii) of this section, a withholding agent has an obligation to withhold under section 1441 only to the extent that, at any time between the date that the obligation to withhold would arise (but for the provisions of this paragraph (d)) and the due date (including extensions) for filing Form 1042 with respect to the calendar year in which the payment occurs, it has—

(A) Control over, or custody of, money or property owned by the recipient or beneficial owner from which to withhold an amount; and

(B) Knowledge of the facts that give rise to the payment.

(ii) *Exception not available.*—The exception from the obligation to withhold under paragraph (d)(1)(i) of this section does not apply if—

(A) The withholding agent is related (within the meaning of section 482) to the recipient or the beneficial owner of the payment;

(B) The payment is a distribution with respect to stock (including a deemed distribution (as defined in §1.305-1(d)(7)) of stock or a right to acquire stock); *see*, however, paragraph (d)(4) of this section, which provides a limited exception from the obligation to withhold on a deemed distribution;

(C) The amounts are described in §1.860G-3(b)(1) (regarding certain partnership allocations of REMIC net income with respect to a REMIC residual interest);

(D) The lack of control over or custody of money or property from which to withhold is part of a pre-arranged plan known to the withholding agent to avoid withholding under section 1441, 1442, or 1443; or

(E) The payment is a deemed payment (as defined in §1.861-3(a)(6)); *see*, however, paragraph (d)(4) of this section, which provides a limited exception from the obligation to withhold on a deemed payment.

(iii) *Documentation.*—Any exception from withholding pursuant to paragraph (d)(1)(i) of this section applies without a requirement that documentation be furnished to the withholding agent. However, documentation may have to be furnished for purposes of the information reporting provisions under chapter 61 of the Code and backup withholding under section 3406.

(iv) *Scope of exception.*—The exception from withholding under this paragraph (d) is not a determination that the amounts are not fixed or determinable annual or periodical income, nor is it an exception from reporting the amount under §1.1461-1(b) and (c).

(v) *Lack of money or property or lack of knowledge.*—A withholding agent does not lack control over money or property for purposes of this paragraph (d)(1) if the withholding agent directs another party to make the payment. Thus, for example, a principal does not cease to have control over a payment when it contracts with a paying agent to make the payments to its account holders in lieu of paying the account holders directly. Further, a withholding agent does not lack knowledge of the facts that give rise to a payment merely because the withholding agent does not know the character or source of the payment for U.S. tax purposes. *See* § 1.1441-3(d)(1) for rules addressing a withholding agent's obligations when the withholding agent has knowledge of the facts that give rise to the payment, but the character or source of the payment is not known.

(vi) *Example.*—A, an individual, owns stock in DC, a domestic corporation, through a custodian, Bank 1. A also has a money market account at Bank 2. DC pays a dividend of $1,000 that is deposited in A's custodial account at Bank 1. A then directs Bank 1 to transfer $1,000 to A's money market account at Bank 2. With respect to the payment of the dividend into A's custodial account with Bank 1, both DC and Bank 1 are withholding agents making a payment of an amount subject to withholding for which they have custody, control, and knowledge. *See* §§ 1.1441-2(b)(1) and 1.1441-7(a)(1). Therefore, both DC and Bank 1 have an obligation to withhold on the payment unless they can reliably associate the payment with documentation sufficient to treat the respective payees as not subject to withholding under chapter 3. With respect to the wire transfer of $1,000 from A's account at Bank 1 to A's account at Bank 2, neither Bank 1 nor Bank 2 is required to withhold on the transfer because neither bank has knowledge of the facts that gave rise to the payment. Even though Bank 1 is a custodian for A's stock in DC and has knowledge regarding the $1,000 dividend paid to A, once Bank 1 credits the $1,000 dividend to A's account, the $1,000 becomes A's property. When A transfers the $1,000 to its account at Bank 2, this is a separate transfer about which Bank 1 has no knowledge regarding the type of payment made. Further, Bank 2 only has knowledge that it receives $1,000 to be credited to A's account but has no knowledge regarding the type of payment made. Accordingly, Bank 1 and Bank 2 have no withholding obligation with respect to the transfer from A's custodial account at Bank 1 to A's money market account at Bank 2.

* * *

(4) *Deemed distributions under section 305(c) and deemed payments.*—(i) *General rule.*—Subject to the rules in this paragraph (d)(4)(i) and paragraph (d)(4)(iii) of this section, and any other exception to withholding (for example, under § 1.1441-4), a withholding agent has an obligation to withhold on a deemed distribution (as defined in § 1.305-1(d)(7)) or a deemed payment (as defined in § 1.861-3(a)(6)) on a security. However, a withholding agent other than the issuer of a specified security (as defined in § 1.6045-1(a)(14)) has an obligation to withhold on a deemed distribution (as defined in § 1.305-1(d)(7)) on a specified security or a deemed payment (as defined in § 1.861-3(a)(6)) that is determined with respect to a deemed distribution on a specified security only if:

(A) The issuer of the specified security reports the information required under § 1.6045B-1 regarding the deemed distribution before the due date (not including extensions) for the withholding agent to file Form 1042 for the calendar year in which the deemed distribution or the deemed payment occurred; or

(B) The withholding agent has actual knowledge of the deemed distribution before the due date (not including extensions) for it to file Form 1042 for the calendar year in which the deemed distribution or the deemed payment occurred, but in such case the requirements of this paragraph (d)(4)(i) will not be considered to be met until January 15 of the year following the calendar year in which the deemed distribution or the deemed payment occurred.

(ii) *Time to withhold on a deemed distribution or deemed payment.*—After the requirements of paragraph (d)(4)(i) of this section have been met, except as provided in § 1.1441-5 regarding the time to withhold for partnerships and trusts, a withholding agent must withhold on a deemed distribution (as defined in § 1.305-1(d)(7)) or a deemed payment (as defined in § 1.861-3(a)(6)) on the earliest of:

(A) The date on which a payment of cash is made with respect to the security or the securities lending or sales-repurchase transaction;

(B) The date on which the security is sold, exchanged, or otherwise disposed of (including a transfer of the security to a separate account not maintained by the withholding agent or a termination of the account relationship); or

(C) The due date (not including extensions) for the withholding agent to file Form 1042 for the calendar year in which the deemed distribution or the deemed payment occurred.

(iii) *Treatment of foreign entities assuming withholding responsibilities.*—Notwithstanding § 1.1441-1(b)(1), a withholding agent may not treat a foreign entity as having assumed primary withholding responsibility under § 1.1441-1(e)(5), § 1.1441-1(b)(2)(iv), § 1.1441-5(c)(2)(i), or § 1.1441-5(e)(5)(v) for a deemed distribution (as defined in § 1.305-1(d)(7)) on a specified security (as defined in § 1.6045-1(a)(14)) or a deemed payment (as defined in § 1.861-3(a)(6)) that is determined with respect to a deemed distribution on a specified security unless the withholding agent has provided the foreign entity a copy of the issuer statement described in § 1.6045B-1(b)(1) within 10 days of the issuer furnishing the statement to the holder of record (or its nominee), or the issuer has met the public reporting requirements described in § 1.6045B-1(a)(3). A foreign entity described in the preceding sentence has an obligation to withhold on the deemed distribution or the deemed payment (unless an exception to withholding under section 1441 applies) if it receives a copy of the statement described in § 1.6045B-1(b)(1) or the issuer has met the public reporting requirements described in § 1.6045B-1(a)(3) by the due date (not including extensions) for filing Form 1042 with respect to the calendar year in which the deemed distribution or the deemed payment occurred. *See* § 1.1441-3(c)(5)(i) for when the foreign entity may rely on the copy of the issuer statement that it receives to determine the amount to withhold.

(iv) *Examples.*—The following examples illustrate when a withholding agent must satisfy its obligation to withhold under paragraph (d)(4) of this section on a deemed distribution.

Example 1 (i) *Facts.* WA is a U.S. custodian that holds a convertible debt instrument (CDI) of Corporation X that is a specified security (as defined in § 1.6045-1(a)(14)) on behalf of A, a foreign person. On March 1 of Year 1, there is a change in the conversion ratio of the CDI that is treated as a deemed distribution under § 1.305-7(b) and (c). On March 15 of Year 1, Corporation X makes an interest payment on the CDI to WA as custodian for A. On April 1 of Year 1, Corporation X reports the information required under § 1.6045B-1 regarding the deemed distribution on its public website. On April 15 of Year 1, Corporation X makes another interest payment on the CDI to WA as custodian for A.

(ii) *Analysis.* Under paragraph (d)(4)(i) of this section, WA does not have an obligation to withhold on the deemed distribution on the CDI that it holds on behalf of A until April 1 of Year 1, the date on which Corporation X satisfied its reporting requirements under § 1.6045B-1 regarding the deemed distribution. WA must withhold on the April 15 cash payment, which is the earliest of the dates specified in paragraph (d)(4)(ii) of this section for withholding on the deemed distribution.

Example 2 (i) *Facts.* The facts are the same as in Example 1, except that an interest payment is not made on the Corporation X CDI on April 15 of Year 1, and the CDI is transferred to a separate account of A that is not maintained by WA on April 15 of Year 1.

(ii) *Analysis.* Because WA is a withholding agent under § 1.1441-7(a)(4) with respect to the deemed distribution on March 1 of Year 1 and Corporation X reports the information required under § 1.6045B-1, WA is required to satisfy the withholding obligation even though the CDI was transferred before a cash payment is made with respect to the CDI. WA does not have an obligation to withhold on the deemed distribution until April 1 of Year 1, the date on which Corporation X reported the conversion ratio adjustment as required by § 1.6045B-1 regarding the deemed distribution. WA must withhold upon the transfer of the CDI to an account not maintained by WA on April 15 of Year 1, which is the earliest of the dates specified in paragraph (d)(4)(ii) of this section for withholding.

Example 3 (i) *Facts.* The facts are the same as in Example 2, except that the CDI is transferred to a separate account of A that is not maintained by WA on March 30 of Year 1.

(ii) *Analysis.* Because WA is a withholding agent under § 1.1441-7(a)(4) with respect to the deemed distribution on March 1 of Year 1 and Corporation X has satisfied its reporting requirements with respect to the deemed distribution, WA is required to satisfy the withholding obligation even though the CDI was transferred before WA received the issuer reporting from Corporation X under § 1.6045B-1 regarding the deemed distribution. WA does not have an obligation to withhold on the deemed distribution until April 1 of Year 1, the date on which Corporation X satisfied its reporting requirements under § 1.6045B-1 regarding the deemed distribution. Because neither of the events specified in paragraphs (d)(4)(ii)(A) and (B) of this section occurred after April 1 of Year 1, WA must satisfy its withholding obligation by the due date (not including extensions) for filing Form 1042 (that is, by March 15 of Year 2), as provided in paragraph (d)(4)(ii)(C) of this section. WA may apply § 1.1461-2(b) in order to collect the underwithheld amount.

* * *

(f) *Effective/applicability date.*—* * * Paragraphs (d)(1) and (d)(4) of this section apply to payments made on or after the date of publication of the Treasury decision adopting these rules as final regulations in the **Federal Register**. A withholding agent may, however, rely on the rules in paragraphs (d)(1) and (d)(4) of this section for all deemed distributions (as defined in § 1.305-1(d)(7)) or deemed payments (as defined in § 1.861-3(a)(6)) occurring on or after January 1, 2016, until the date of publication of a Treasury decision adopting these rules as final regulations in the **Federal Register**.

Par. 8. Section 1.1441-3 is amended by:

1. Adding paragraph (c)(5).

2. Amending paragraph (i) by removing the language "paragraphs (g) and (h)" and adding in its place "paragraphs (c)(5), (g), and (h)".

The addition reads as follows:

§ 1.1441-3. Determination of amounts to be withheld.

* * *

(c) * * *

(5) *Reliance rule for applicable adjustments.*—(i) *In general.*—For purposes of determining the amount of a deemed distribution (as defined in § 1.305-1(d)(7)) on a specified security (as defined in § 1.6045-1(a)(14)) or a deemed payment (as defined in § 1.861-3(a)(6)) that is determined with respect to a deemed distribution on a specified security, a withholding agent other than the issuer of the specified security (as defined in § 1.6045-1(a)(14)) may rely on the information provided by the issuer under § 1.6045B-1 (or a copy of the issuer statement in the circumstances described in § 1.1441-2(d)(4)(iii)) unless it knows that such information is incorrect or unreliable. *See* § 1.1441-2(d)(4) for a withholding agent's obligation to withhold on a deemed distribution or a deemed payment.

(ii) *Effective/applicability date.*—Paragraph (c)(5)(i) of this section applies to payments made on or after the date of publication of the Treasury decision adopting these rules as final regulations in the **Federal Register**. A withholding agent may, however, rely on the rules in paragraph (c)(5)(i) of this section for all deemed distributions (as defined in § 1.305-1(d)(7)) or deemed payments (as defined in § 1.861-3(a)(6)) occurring on or after January 1, 2016, until the date of publication of a Treasury decision adopting these rules as final regulations in the **Federal Register**.

* * *

Withholding: Nonresident Aliens: Sale of Obligations: Between Interest Payment Dates

Withholding: Nonresident Aliens: Sale of Obligations: Between Interest Payment Dates.—Amendments to Reg. §1.1441-3, relating to the obligation to withhold on interest paid with respect to obligations in the case of sales of obligations between interest payment dates, are proposed (published in the Federal Register on October 14, 1997) (REG-114000-97).

□ Par. 2. In §1.1441-3, paragraph (b) is revised to read as follows:

§1.1441-3. Determination of amount to be withheld.

* * *

(b) *Withholding on payments on certain obligations.*—(1) *Withholding at time of payment of interest.*—When making a payment on an interest-bearing obligation, a withholding agent must withhold under §1.1441-1 upon the gross amount of stated interest payable on the interest payment date, regardless of whether the payment constitutes a return of capital or the payment of income within the meaning of section 61, unless the withholding agent has knowledge of the actual amount of interest paid. For this purpose, the withholding agent may rely on information provided by the issuer (or its paying agent), on a representation from the beneficial owner, or on information that the withholding agent has in its records. To the extent an amount was withheld on an amount of capital rather than interest, see rules for adjustments, refunds, or credits under §1.1441-1(b)(8).

(2) *No withholding between interest payment dates.*—(i) *General rule.*—A withholding agent is not required to withhold under §1.1441-1 upon interest accrued on the date of a sale of debt obligations when that sale occurs between two interest payment dates (even though the amount is treated as interest under §1.61-7(c) or (d) and is subject to tax under section 871(a) or 881(a)), unless the withholding agent has knowledge of the amount paid as interest. For purposes of this paragraph (b)(2)(i), a withholding agent is treated as having knowledge in the same manner as a withholding agent has knowledge for purposes of §1.1441-2(b)(3)(ii), dealing with withholding on original issue discount. In addition, notwithstanding lack of knowledge (within the meaning of §1.1441-2(b)(3)(ii)), withholding is required on the entire amount of stated interest paid with respect to the obligation as determined as of the date of original issue if the withholding agent, pursuant to the provisions in §1.1441-1(b)(3), treats the payment as made to a foreign payee because it cannot associate the payment with required documentation and the amount would qualify as portfolio interest. See §1.1441-1(b)(8) for adjustments to any amount that has been overwithheld as a result of this provision.

(ii) *Applicable rules.*—Any exemption from withholding pursuant to paragraph (b)(2)(i) of this section applies without a requirement that documentation be furnished to the withholding agent. However, documentation may have to be furnished for purposes of the information reporting provisions under section 6049 and backup withholding under section 3406. See §1.6045-1(c) for reporting requirements by brokers with respect to sale proceeds. Any exemption from withholding under paragraph (b)(2)(i) of this section is not a determination that the accrued interest is not fixed or determinable annual or periodical income. See §1.61-7(c) regarding the character of payments received by the acquirer of an obligation subsequent to such acquisition (that is, as a return of capital or interest accrued after the acquisition).

* * *

Withholding: Distributions in Redemption of Stock

Withholding: Distributions in Redemption of Stock.—Amendments to Reg. §1.1441-3, providing an escrow procedure that a withholding agent must apply while making the determination under Code Sec. 302 as to whether the distribution in redemption of the stock held by a foreign shareholder is treated as a dividend subject to withholding or a distribution in part or full payment in exchange for stock, are proposed (published in the Federal Register on October 17, 2007) (REG-140206-06).

□ Par. 2. Section 1.1441-3 is amended as follows:

1. A sentence is added at the end of paragraph (c)(2)(i)(B).

2. Paragraph (c)(5) is added.

3. A sentence is added at the end of paragraph (d)(1).

The additions read as follows.

§1.1441-3. Determination of amounts to be withheld.

* * *

(c) * * *

(2) * * *

(i) * * *

(B) * * * The preceding sentence shall not apply to a public section 302 distribution to which paragraph (c)(5) applies.

* * *

(5) *Special rules for certain distributions to which section 302 applies.*—(i) *Withholding responsibility.*—(A) *General rule.*—A corporation that makes a public section 302 distribution, or any intermediary (described in §1.1441-1(c)(13)) making a payment of such a distribution, is required to withhold under section 1441, 1442 or 1443 on the entire amount of the distribution unless the provisions of paragraph (c)(5)(iii) of this section have been applied. The provisions of paragraph (c)(2)(i)(B) or (d)(1) of this section do not apply to a public section 302 distribution.

(B) *Effective/applicability date.*—The rules of this paragraph (c)(5) apply to public section 302 distributions made after December 31, 2008.

(ii) *Definitions.*—Solely for purposes of this paragraph (c)(5), the following definitions shall apply:

(A) *Public section 302 distribution* means a distribution by a corporation in redemption of its stock for which there is an established financial market within the meaning of §1.1092(d)-1.

(B) *Section 302 payment* means payment of a public section 302 distribution.

(C) *Distributing corporation* means a corporation making or treated as making a public section 302 distribution.

(iii) *Escrow procedure.*—(A) *Application.*—*(1) In general.*—The escrow procedure in this paragraph (c)(5)(iii) may be applied only by an intermediary (described in §1.1441-1(c)(13)) that is a U.S. financial institution. A U.S. financial institution making a section 302 payment to a foreign account holder, and applying this escrow procedure, is not required to withhold on the entire amount of a section 302 payment under the general rule of paragraph (c)(5)(i).

(B) *Escrow account.*—*(1) In general.*—A U.S. financial institution shall set aside in an escrow account on the date it receives a section 302 payment from a distributing corporation with respect to stock of a foreign account holder 30 percent (or the applicable dividend rate provided by a tax treaty for a qualifying foreign account holder) of the amount and shall credit the foreign account holder's account with the balance of the section 302 payment.

(2) Qualified intermediaries.—The amount set aside, under paragraph (c)(5)(iii)(B)(1) of this section shall include 30 percent (or the applicable dividend rate provided by a treaty) of the amount paid to any qualified intermediary (QI) (whether or not the QI has assumed primary withholding responsibility) and to any withholding foreign partnership or withholding foreign trust (WP/WT).

(C) *Request for section 302 payment certification.*—On or before the date it receives the section 302 payment, the U.S. financial institution shall provide the following information and instructions, in writing, to the foreign beneficial owner—

(1) The total number of distributing corporation's shares outstanding before and after the public section 302 distribution;

(2) An explanation of the conditions under which the section 302 payment will be treated as a dividend or a payment in exchange for stock for Federal income tax purposes (including an explanation of any applicable constructive ownership rules); and

(3) A request that the beneficial owner of the account provide a certification (section 302 payment certification), within 60 days of the section 302 payment, stating whether the section 302 payment is either a dividend or a payment in exchange for stock under the Internal Revenue Code.

(D) *Content of section 302 payment certification.*—The section 302 payment certification must include the following information:

(1) The beneficial owner's name and account number.

(2) The distributing corporation's name.

(3) The total shares of the distributing corporation outstanding immediately before and immediately after the public section 302 distribution.

(4) A certification from the beneficial owner that either—

(i) The section 302 payment is a payment in exchange for stock because the beneficial owner's proportionate interest has been reduced but not completely terminated;

(ii) The section 302 payment is a payment in exchange for stock because the beneficial owner's interest in the distributing corporation is completely terminated; or

(iii) The section 302 payment is a dividend.

(5) With respect to the certifications in paragraph (c)(5)(iii)(D)(4)(i) and (ii) of this section, the number of shares actually and constructively owned by the beneficial owner before and after the distribution and the beneficial owner's percentage ownership before and after the distribution.

(6) A penalties of perjury statement.

(7) The signature of the beneficial owner and date of signature.

(E) *Receipt of section 302 payment certification.*—*(1) Payment in exchange for stock.*—If, within the 60-day period described in paragraph (c)(5)(iii)(C)(3), the U.S. financial institution receives from the foreign beneficial owner a section 302 payment certification stating that the section 302 payment is a payment in exchange for stock, and if the U.S. financial institution does not know or have reason to know that the information in the section 302 payment certification is unreliable or incorrect, the U.S. financial institution shall credit the account with the amount set aside with respect to the beneficial owner who provides the certification. The entire amount paid (including the amount initially set aside) shall be reported as capital gains on Form 1042-S Foreign Person's U.S. Source Income Subject to Withholding.

(2) Unreliable or incorrect exchange certification.—If the U.S. financial institution knows or has reason to know that the information in the section 3 02 payment certification is unreliable or incorrect, the U.S. financial institution shall treat the payment as a payment for which no section 302 payment certification has been received and shall follow the withholding and reporting procedures in paragraph (c)(5)(iii)(E)(4) of this section.

(3) Dividend.—If, within the 60-day period, the U.S. financial institution receives a section 302 payment certification from the foreign beneficial owner stating that the section 302 payment is a dividend, the U.S. financial institution shall treat the amount set aside as tax withheld as of the time it receives the section 302 payment certification, and shall deposit that amount pursuant to the applicable regulations. The entire amount paid shall be reported on Form 1042-S as dividends.

(4) No timely certification received.—If, within the 60-day period, the U.S. financial institution does not receive a section 302 payment certification, or is treated under paragraph (c)(5)(iii)(E)(2) of this section as not receiving a section 302 payment certification, the U.S. financial institution shall treat the amount set aside as

tax withheld as of the 61st day, and shall deposit that amount pursuant to the applicable regulations. The entire amount paid shall be reported on Form 1042-S as dividends.

(5) Late certification.—If, after the 60-day period has expired, the U.S. financial institution receives a section 3 02 payment certification from a foreign beneficial owner that the section 302 payment is a payment in exchange for stock and the conditions stated in §1.1461-2(a) are satisfied, the U.S. financial institution may apply the refund or offset procedures of that paragraph.

(6) Determination of incorrect treatment.—If, after the 60-day period has expired, the U.S. financial institution determines that the section 302 payment was incorrectly treated as a distribution in exchange for stock, the procedures set forth regarding underwithholding in §1.1461-2(b) are applicable.

(7) Undocumented beneficial owners.—The U.S. financial institution shall withhold at 30 percent on the entire amount paid to a beneficial owner that is not properly documented under §§1.1441-1, 1.1441-5, etc. and that is presumed to be a foreign person, whether or not the U.S. financial institution has received a section 302 payment certification from such beneficial owner. The U.S. financial institution shall report the entire amount paid on Form 1042-S as dividends.

(F) *Amounts in excess of section 302 payment.*—If the amount the U.S. financial institution credits to the account of the foreign beneficial owner from the escrow account includes an amount in excess of the section 302 payment, such as interest accrued on the escrowed funds, the U.S. financial institution shall report and withhold on such excess amount in accordance with the rules under Chapter 3 of the Internal Revenue Code.

(G) *U.S. non-exempt recipients.*—The U.S. financial institution shall treat beneficial owners that are U.S. non-exempt recipients, and that hold stock in the distributing corporation through QIs, WPs/WTs, NQIs and flow-throughs, in accordance with the section 302 payment certifications obtained from those U.S. non-exempt recipients and shall instruct foreign intermediaries and foreign flow-through entities to do the same.

(H) *Notice to distributing corporation.*—The U.S. financial institution shall notify the distributing corporation, in writing, by the filing date of Form 1042-S, of the aggregate amount of the section 302 payment that the U.S. financial institution has reported on Forms 1042-S as capital gains, and the aggregate amount of the section 302 payment that it has reported on Forms 1042-S as dividends.

(I) *Application of Escrow Procedure to Qualified Intermediaries.*—As provided in paragraph (c)(5)(iii)(A) of this section, only the U.S. financial institution may establish an escrow account and the amounts set aside in the escrow account shall include 30 percent (or the applicable treaty rate applicable to dividends) on payments made to a direct account holder that is a QI (including a QI that has assumed primary withholding responsibility). Under the procedure described in paragraph (c)(5)(iii)(I)(3), a QI shall provide the U.S. financial institution with a withholding statement as required in the QI Agreement. If there is a chain of QIs, each QI in the chain shall apply the procedure. The procedures described in this paragraph (I) shall be applied to withholding foreign partnerships and withholding foreign trusts within the meaning of §§1.1441-5(c)(2) and (e)(5)(v), respectively, in the same manner as the procedures apply to a QI.

(1) Request for section 302 payment certification.—The U.S. financial institution shall provide the information and instructions described in paragraph (c)(5)(iii)(C) of this section to the QI, and the QI shall provide the same information and instructions to its account holders including account holders that are U.S. non-exempt recipients.

(2) Content of section 302 payment certification.—The content of the section 302 payment certification shall include the information described in paragraph (c)(5)(iii)(D) of this section.

(3) Receipt of section 302 payment certification.—*(i) Payment in exchange for stock.*—If, within the 60-day period described in paragraph (c)(5)(iii)(C), the QI receives from the beneficial owner a section 302 payment certification stating that the section 302 payment is a payment in exchange for stock and if the QI does not know or have reason to know that the information in the section 302 payment certification is unreliable or incorrect, the QI shall reflect such treatment in its withholding statement provided to the U.S. financial institution, and, based upon the withholding statement, the U.S. financial institution shall release payment from its escrow and the QI shall credit the beneficial owner's account with the amount set aside by the U.S. financial institution with respect to the beneficial owner who provided the certification. The entire amount paid (including the amount initially set aside) shall be reported on the QI's pooled basis Form 1042-S as capital gains.

(ii) Unreliable or incorrect exchange certification.—If the QI knows or has reason to know that the information in the section 302 payment certification is unreliable or incorrect, the QI shall treat the payment as a payment for which no section 302 payment certification has been received and shall follow the withholding and reporting procedures in paragraph (c)(5)(iii)(I)(3)(iv) of this section.

(iii) Dividend.—If, within the 60-day period, QI receives a section 302 payment certification stating that the section 302 payment is a dividend, the QI shall reflect such treatment in its withholding statement and shall treat the payment as a dividend for purposes of its reporting and withholding responsibilities under the QI agreement. The entire amount paid shall be reported on its pooled basis Form 1042-S as dividends.

(iv) No timely certification received.—If, within the 60-day period, the QI does not receive a section 302 payment certification, or is treated under paragraph (c)(5)(iii)(I)(3)(ii) of this section as not receiving a section 302 payment certification, the QI shall reflect such treatment in its withholding statement provided to the U.S. financial institution and shall treat the payment as a dividend for purposes of its reporting and withholding responsibilities under the QI agreement. The entire amount paid shall be

reported on its pooled basis Form 1042-S as dividends.

(v) Late certification.—If, after the 60-day period has expired, the QI receives a section 302 payment certification from a beneficial owner that the section 302 payment is a payment in exchange for stock and the conditions stated in the QI agreement regarding the refund and offset procedures are satisfied, the QI may apply such refund or offset procedures.

(vi) Determination of incorrect treatment.—If, after the 60-day period has expired, the QI determines that the section 302 payment was incorrectly treated as a distribution in exchange for stock, the procedures set forth regarding adjustments for underwithholding in the QI agreement are applicable.

(vii) Undocumented beneficial owners.—The QI shall withhold at 30 percent on the entire amount paid to a beneficial owner that is not properly documented and that is presumed to be a foreign person, whether or not the QI has received a section 302 payment certification from such beneficial owner. The QI shall report the entire amount paid on its pooled basis Form 1042-S as dividends.

(4) U.S. non-exempt recipients.—The QI shall treat direct account holders that are U.S. non-exempt recipients, and that hold stock in the distributing corporation, in accordance with the section 302 payment certifications obtained from those U.S. non-exempt recipients and shall instruct foreign intermediaries and foreign flow-through entities to do the same.

(J) *Intermediaries that are not qualified intermediaries.*—If the U.S. financial institution has an account holder that is an intermediary that is not a QI ("NQI"), the U.S. financial institution shall apply the rules of paragraph (c)(5)(iii)(J)(1) through (4) of this section. Where the provisions of this paragraph (J) refer only to the U.S. financial institution, they shall apply in the same manner to a QI or WP/WT and where they refer to an NQI, they shall apply in the same manner to a flow-through that is not a WP or WT.

(1) The U.S. financial institution shall provide the information and instructions described in paragraph (c)(5)(iii)(C) of this section to the NQI and the NQI shall provide the same information and instructions to its account holders.

(2) The content of the section 302 payment certification shall include the information described in paragraph (c)(5)(iii)(D) of this section.

(3) The NQI shall provide the section 302 payment certification to the U.S. financial institution together with the otherwise required documentation and a withholding statement made in accordance with the section 302 payment certification.

(4) The U.S. financial institution shall treat the section 3 02 payment as a dividend or a payment in exchange for stock based on the information and documentation provided to it under paragraph (c)(5)(iii)(J)(3) of this section. The U.S. financial institution shall withhold and report on a specific payee basis in accordance with this information.

(d) * * *

(1) * * * This paragraph does not apply to a public section 302 distribution to which paragraph (c)(5) applies.

* * *

Withholding: Reducing Burden under FATCA

Withholding: Reducing Burden under FATCA.—Amendments to Reg. §1.1441-6, eliminating withholding on payments of gross proceeds, deferring withholding on foreign passthru payments, eliminating withholding on certain insurance premiums, and clarifying the definition of investment entity, are proposed (published in the Federal Register on December 18, 2018) (REG-132881-17).

Par. 3. Section 1.1441-6 is amended by adding a sentence at the end of paragraph (c)(5)(i) to read as follows:

§1.1441-6. Claim of reduced withholding under an income tax treaty.

* * *

(c) * * *

(5) * * *

(i) * * * A withholding agent may rely on the taxpayer's claim on a treaty statement regarding its reliance on a specific limitation on benefits provision absent actual knowledge that such claim is unreliable or incorrect.

* * *

Tax on Certain U.S. Source Income: Withholding

Tax on Certain U.S. Source Income: Withholding.—Amendments to Reg. §§1.1441-6 and 1.1441-7, regarding withholding of tax on certain U.S. source income paid to foreign persons and requirements for certain claims for refund or credit of income tax made by foreign persons, are proposed (published in the Federal Register on January 6, 2017) (REG-134247-16).

Par. 4. Section 1.1441-6 is amended by:

1. Adding paragraphs (b)(1)(i) and (b)(1)(ii).
2. Revising paragraphs (c)(1) and (c)(5)(i).

The additions and revision read as follows:

§1.1441-6. Claim of reduced withholding under an income tax treaty.

* * *

(b) * * *

(1) * * *

(i) [The text of the proposed amendment to §1.1441-6(b)(1)(i) is the same as the text of §1.1441-6T(b)(1)(i) as added by T.D. 9808.]

(ii) [The text of the proposed amendment to §1.1441-6(b)(1)(ii) is the same as the text of §1.1441-6T(b)(1)(ii) as added by T.D. 9808.]

* * *

(c) * * *

(1) [The text of the proposed amendment to § 1.1441-6(c)(1) is the same as the text of § 1.1441-6T(c)(1) as added by T.D. 9808.]

* * *

(5) * * *

(i) [The text of the proposed amendment to § 1.1441-6(c)(5)(i) is the same as the text of § 1.1441-6T(c)(5)(i) as added by T.D. 9808.]

* * *

Par. 5. Section 1.1441-7 is amended by adding paragraph (b)(10)(iv) to read as follows:

§ 1.1441-7. General provisions relating to withholding agents.

* * *

(b) * * *

(10) * * *

(iv) [The text of the proposed amendment to § 1.1441-7(b)(10)(iv) is the same as the text of § 1.1441-7T(b)(10)(iv) as added by T.D. 9808.]

* * *

Stock and Rights to Acquire Stock: Deemed Distributions

Stock and Rights to Acquire Stock: Deemed Distributions.—Amendments to Reg. § 1.1441-7, regarding deemed distributions of stock and rights to acquire stock and resolving ambiguities concerning the amount and timing of deemed distributions that are or result from adjustments to rights to acquire stock, are proposed (published in the Federal Register on April 13, 2016) (REG-133673-15).

Par. 9. Section 1.1441-7 is amended by:

1. Redesignating paragraph (a)(4) as (a)(5) and adding a second and third sentence to newly redesignated (a)(5).
2. Adding a new paragraph (a)(4).
3. Amending paragraph (g) by removing the language "paragraphs (a)(4)" and adding in its place "paragraphs (a)(5)."

The addition reads as follows:

§ 1.1441-7. General provisions relating to withholding agents.—(a) * * *

(4) *Withholding agent with respect to deemed distributions under section 305(c).*—Any person that issues or holds directly or indirectly (for example, through an account maintained for another intermediary) on behalf of a beneficial owner, or a flow through entity that owns directly or indirectly (through another flow-through entity), a security upon which a deemed distribution (as defined in § 1.305-1(d)(7)) is made has custody of or control over the deemed distribution. *See* § 1.1441-2(d)(4) for a withholding agent's obligation to withhold on the deemed distribution and § 1.1441-3(c)(5)(i) for when a withholding agent may rely on the information reported by the issuer under § 1.6045B-1 to determine the amount to withhold.

(5) * * * Paragraph (a)(4) of this section applies to payments made on or after the date of publication of the Treasury decision adopting these rules as final regulations in the **Federal Register**. A withholding agent may, however, rely on the rules in paragraph (a)(4) of this section for all deemed distributions (as defined in § 1.305-1(d)(7)) occurring on or after January 1, 2016, until the date of publication of a Treasury decision adopting these rules as final regulations in the **Federal Register**.

Disposition of Investment in U.S. Real Property

Nonresident Aliens and Foreign Corporations: Disposition of Investment in U.S. Real Property.—Temporary Reg. §§ 1.1445-10T and 1.1445-11T, relating to dispositions of U.S. real property interests by nonresident aliens and foreign corporations, are also proposed as final regulations and, when adopted, would become Reg. §§ 1.1445-10 and 1.1445-11 (published in the Federal Register on May 5, 1988). Temporary Reg. § 1.1445-9T was removed by T.D. 9082 on August 4, 2003.

§ 1.1445-10. Special rule for foreign governments.

§ 1.1445-11. Special rules requiring withholding under § 1.1445-5.

Return and Extended Due Date: Changes

Return Due Extended Due Date: Changes.—Amendments to Reg. § 1.1446-3, updating the due dates and extensions of time to file certain tax returns and information returns, are proposed (published in the Federal Register on July 20, 2017) (REG-128483-15).

Par. 2. Revise paragraph (b)(2)(v)(C) and add paragraph (g) to § 1.1446-3 to read as follows:

§ 1.1446-3. Time and manner of calculating and paying over the 1446 tax.

* * *

(b) * * *

(2) * * *

(v) * * *

(C) [The text of proposed § 1.1446-3(b)(2)(v)(C) is the same as the text of § 1.1446-3T(b)(2)(v)(C) as added by T.D. 9821].

* * *

(g) *Applicability date.*—The requirements of paragraph (b)(2)(v)(C) of this section are applicable for returns filed on or after the date a Treasury Decision incorporating these amendments as final regulations is published in the **Federal Register**.

Withholding: Reducing Burden under FATCA

Withholding: Reducing Burden under FATCA.—Amendments to Reg. §§1.1461-1 and 1.1461-2, eliminating withholding on payments of gross proceeds, deferring withholding on foreign passthru payments, eliminating withholding on certain insurance premiums, and clarifying the definition of investment entity, are proposed (published in the Federal Register on December 18, 2018) (REG-132881-17).

Par. 4. Section 1.1461-1 is amended by:

1. Adding two sentences after the first sentence in paragraph (a)(1).

2. Redesignating paragraph (c)(1)(i) as paragraph (c)(1)(i)(A) and adding paragraphs (c)(1)(i) introductory text and (c)(1)(i)(B).

3. Adding a sentence at the end of paragraph (c)(4)(iv).

The additions read as follows:

§1.1461-1. Payment and returns of tax withheld.—(a) * * *

(1) * * * In a case in which a withholding agent is permitted to withhold on an amount subject to reporting (as defined in paragraph (c)(2) of this section) in a calendar year (subsequent year) following the calendar year (preceding year) in which the withholding agent paid such amount (or, for a partnership or trust withholding with respect to a foreign partner, beneficiary, or owner, the year the partnership or trust received such amount), the withholding agent shall designate the deposit of the withholding as made for the preceding year and report the tax liability on Form 1042 for the preceding year. In the case of a partnership that withholds as described in the preceding sentence and does not file its federal income tax return on a calendar-year basis, however, such partnership may instead designate the deposit as made for the subsequent year and report the tax liability on Form 1042 for the subsequent year. * * *

* * *

(c) * * *

(1) * * *

(i) *Withholding agent information reporting.*—This paragraph (c)(1)(i) describes the general requirements for a withholding agent to file an information return on Form 1042-S and describes a special rule for a withholding agent that withholds in a subsequent year as described in paragraph (a)(1) of this section.

* * *

(B) *Special reporting by withholding agents that withhold in a subsequent year.*—Notwithstanding the first sentence of paragraph (c)(1)(i)(A) of this section, if a withholding agent designates the deposit of such withholding as made for the preceding calendar year as described in paragraph (a)(1) of this section, the withholding agent is required to report the amount on Form 1042-S for the preceding year. With respect to a withholding agent described in the previous sentence that is a partnership and that withholds after March 15 of the subsequent year, such partnership may file and furnish the Form 1042-S on or before September 15 of that year. In the case of a partnership that designates the deposit of such withholding as made for the subsequent year as permitted in paragraph (a)(1) of this section, however, the partnership shall report the amount on Form 1042-S for the subsequent year.

* * *

(4) * * *

(iv) * * * If a nonqualified intermediary that is a participating FFI or a registered deemed-compliant FFI receives a payment that has been withheld upon at a 30-percent rate under chapter 4 by another withholding agent and that is reported as made to an unknown recipient on Form 1042-S provided to the nonqualified intermediary, the nonqualified intermediary may report the payment (or portion of the payment) on Form 1042-S as made to a recipient that has been withheld upon under chapter 3 when the payment is not an amount for which withholding is required under chapter 4 based on the payee's chapter 4 status and the nonqualified intermediary reports the correct withholding rate for the recipient.

* * *

Par. 5. Section 1.1461-2 is amended by:

1. Revising the second sentence of paragraph (a)(2)(i) introductory text.

2. Revising paragraphs (a)(2)(i)(A) and (B).

3. Adding paragraph (a)(2)(i)(C).

4. Revising paragraph (a)(3).

The revisions and addition read as follows:

§1.1461-2. Adjustments for overwithholding or underwithholding of tax.—(a) * * *

(2) * * *

(i) * * * In such a case, the withholding agent may reimburse itself by reducing, by the amount of tax actually repaid to the beneficial owner or payee, the amount of any deposit of withholding tax otherwise required to be made by the withholding agent under §1.6302-2(a)(1)(iii) for any subsequent payment period occurring before the end of the calendar year following the calendar year of overwithholding. * * *

(A) The repayment to the beneficial owner or payee occurs before the earliest of the due date (including extensions) for filing the Form 1042-S for the calendar year of overwithholding, the date the Form 1042-S is actually filed with the IRS, or the date the Form 1042-S is furnished to the beneficial owner or payee;

(B) The withholding agent states on a timely filed (including extensions) Form 1042-S for the calendar year of overwithholding the amount of tax withheld and the amount of any actual repayment; and

(C) The withholding agent states on a timely filed (including extensions) Form 1042 for the calendar year of overwithholding the amount of adjustments made to overwithholding under paragraph (a)(1) of this section and the amount of any credit claimed under § 1.6414-1.

* * *

(3) *Set-off.*—Under the set-off procedure, the withholding agent may repay the beneficial owner or payee by applying the amount overwithheld against any amount of tax which otherwise would be required under chapter 3 or 4 of the Internal Revenue Code or the regulations under part 1 of this chapter to be withheld from income paid by the withholding agent to such person. Any such set-off that occurs for a payment period in the calendar year following the calendar year of overwithholding shall be allowed only if—

(i) The repayment to the beneficial owner or payee occurs before the earliest of the due date (including extensions) for filing the Form 1042-S for the calendar year of overwithholding, the date the Form 1042-S is actually filed with the IRS, or the date the Form 1042-S is furnished to the beneficial owner or payee;

(ii) The withholding agent states on a timely filed (including extensions) Form 1042-S for the calendar year of overwithholding the amount of tax withheld and the amount of any repayment made through set-off; and

(iii) The withholding agent states on a timely filed (including extensions) Form 1042 for the calendar year of overwithholding the amount of adjustments made to overwithholding under paragraph (a)(1) of this section and the amount of any credit claimed under § 1.6414-1.

* * *

Stock and Rights to Acquire Stock: Deemed Distributions

Stock and Rights to Acquire Stock: Deemed Distributions.—Amendments to Reg. § 1.1461-2, regarding deemed distributions of stock and rights to acquire stock and resolving ambiguities concerning the amount and timing of deemed distributions that are or result from adjustments to rights to acquire stock, are proposed (published in the Federal Register on April 13, 2016) (REG-133673-15).

Par. 10. Section 1.1461-2 is amended by revising the second sentence to paragraph (b), adding a fourth sentence to paragraph (b), and adding a second and third sentence to paragraph (d) to read as follows:

§ 1.1461-2. Adjustments for overwithholding or underwithholding of tax.

* * *

(b) *Withholding of additional tax when underwithholding occurs.*—* * * In the alternative, the withholding agent may satisfy the tax from property that it holds in custody for the beneficial owner, property over which it has control, or additional contributions of property obtained directly or indirectly from the beneficial owner. * * * A withholding agent that adjusts its underwithholding under the procedure described in this paragraph (b) will not be subject to any penalties or additions to tax described in § 1.1461-1(a)(2) if it timely deposits the amounts that it withholds from future payments, proceeds from the liquidation of property, or additional contributions of property obtained directly or indirectly from the beneficial owner. * * *

(d) * * * Paragraph (b) of this section applies to payments made on or after the date of publication of the Treasury decision adopting these rules as final regulations in the **Federal Register**. A withholding agent may, however, rely on the rules in paragraph (b) of this section for payments occurring on or after January 1, 2016, until the date of publication of a Treasury decision adopting these rules as final regulations in the **Federal Register**.

Stock and Rights to Acquire Stock: Deemed Distributions

Stock and Rights to Acquire Stock: Deemed Distributions.—Amendments to Reg. § 1.1471-2, regarding deemed distributions of stock and rights to acquire stock and resolving ambiguities concerning the amount and timing of deemed distributions that are or result from adjustments to rights to acquire stock, are proposed (published in the Federal Register on April 13, 2016) (REG-133673-15).

Par. 11. Section 1.1471-2 is amended by:

1. Revising paragraph (a)(4)(i)(A), redesignating paragraph (B) as new paragraph (E), and adding new paragraphs (B) through (D).
2. Amending paragraph (c) by adding a third and fourth sentence.

The revisions and addition read as follows:

§ 1.1471-2. Requirement to deduct and withhold tax on withholdable payments to certain FFIs.

* * *

(a) * * *

(4) * * *

(i) * * *

(A) *In general.*—Except as provided in paragraph (a)(4)(i)(B) of this section, a withholding agent has an obligation to withhold under chapter 4 only to the extent that, at any time between the date that the obligation to withhold would arise (but for the provisions of this paragraph (a)(4)(i)(A)) and the due date (including extensions) for filing Form 1042 (including extensions) with respect to the calendar year in which the payment occurs, it has—

(1) Control over, or custody of, money or property owned by the recipient or beneficial owner from which to withhold an amount, and

(2) Knowledge of the facts that give rise to the payment.

(B) *Exception not available.*—The exception from the obligation to withhold under paragraph (a)(4)(i)(A) of this section does not apply if—

(1) The withholding agent is related (within the meaning of section 482) to the recipient or the beneficial owner of the payment;

(2) The payment is with respect to stock (including a deemed distribution (as defined in §1.305-1(d)(7)) of stock or a right to acquire stock) or other securities; however, the limited exception from the obligation to withhold on a deemed distribution provided in §1.1441-2(d)(4) also applies to a deemed distribution that is a withholdable payment under chapter 4;

(3) The lack of control over or custody of money or property from which to withhold is part of a pre-arranged plan known to the withholding agent to avoid withholding under section 1471 or 1472;

(4) The amounts are described in §1.860G-3(b)(1) (regarding certain partnership allocations of REMIC net income with respect to a REMIC residual interest);

(5) Any of the special rules described in §1.1441-2(d)(2) or (3), regarding the obligation of a withholding agent with respect to cancellation of debt or the satisfaction of tax liability following underwithholding by a withholding agent, apply with respect to the payment (by applying such rules to payments that are withholdable payments under chapter 4); or

(6) The payment is a deemed payment (as defined in §1.861-3(a)(6)); however, the limited exception from the obligation to withhold on a deemed payment provided in §1.1441-2(d)(4) also applies to a deemed payment that is determined with respect to a deemed distribution on a specified security and that is a withholdable payment under chapter 4.

(C) *Documentation.*—Any exception from withholding pursuant to paragraph (a)(4)(i)(A) of this section applies without a requirement that documentation be furnished to the withholding agent. However, documentation may have to be furnished for purposes of the information reporting provisions under chapter 61 of the Code and backup withholding under section 3406.

(D) *Lack of money or property or lack of knowledge.*—A withholding agent does not lack control over money or property for purposes of this paragraph (a)(4)(i)(A) if the withholding agent directs another party to make the payment. Thus, for example, a principal does not cease to have control over a payment when it contracts with a paying agent to make the payments to its account holders in lieu of paying the account holders directly. Further, a withholding agent does not lack knowledge of the facts that give rise to a payment merely because the withholding agent does not know the character or source of the payment for U.S. tax purposes. *See* paragraph (a)(5) of this section for rules addressing a withholding agent's obligations when the withholding agent has knowledge of the facts that give rise to the payment, but the character or source of the payment is not known.

* * *

(c) * * * Paragraph (a)(4)(i) of this section applies to payments made on or after the date of publication of the Treasury decision adopting these rules as final regulations in the **Federal Register**. A withholding agent may, however, rely on the rules in paragraph (a)(4)(i) of this section (together with the rules in §1.1441-2(d)(4)), for all deemed distributions (as defined in §1.305-1(d)(7)) or deemed payments (as defined in §1.861-3(a)(6)) that are withholdable payments occurring on or after January 1, 2016, until the date of publication of a Treasury decision adopting these rules as final regulations in the **Federal Register**.

Foreign Financial Institutions: Certain Entities: Verification and Certification Requirements

Foreign Financial Institutions: Certain Entities: Verification and Certification Requirements.—Amendments to Reg. §§1.1471-1 and 1.1471-3—1.1471-4, describing the verification requirements (including certifications of compliance) and events of default for entities that agree to perform the chapter 4 due diligence, withholding, and reporting requirements on behalf of certain foreign financial institutions (FFIs) or the chapter 4 due diligence and reporting obligations on behalf of certain nonfinancial foreign entities, are proposed (published in the Federal Register on January 6, 2017) (REG-103477-14).

Par. 2. Section 1.1471-1 is amended by revising paragraphs (b)(99), (b)(116), and (b)(121) to read as follows:

§1.1471-1. Scope of chapter 4 and definitions.

* * *

(b) * * *

(99) [The text of proposed §1.1471-1(b)(99) is the same as the text of §1.1471-1T(b)(99) as added by T.D. 9809].

* * *

(116) [Proposed amendments adopted by T.D. 9852 on 3/21/2019.]

(121) [Proposed amendments adopted by T.D. 9852 on 3/21/2019.]

Par. 3. Section 1.1471-3 is amended by:

1. Revising paragraph (c)(1).
2. Adding paragraphs (c)(3)(iii)(B)(*5*) and (c)(6)(ii)(E)(*4*).
3. Revising paragraphs (c)(7)(ii) and (d)(6)(i)(F).

The revisions and additions read as follows:

§1.1471-3. Identification of payee.

* * *

(c) * * *

(1) [The text of proposed §1.1471-3(c)(1) is the same as the text of §1.1471-3T(c)(1) as added by T.D. 9809].

* * *

(3) * * *

(iii) * * *

(B) * * *

(5) [The text of proposed §1.1471-3(c)(3)(iii)(B)(*5*) is the same as the text of §1.1471-3T(c)(3)(iii)(B)(*5*) as added by T.D. 9809].

* * *

(6) * * *

(ii) * * *

(E) * * *

(4) [The text of proposed §1.1471-3(c)(6)(ii)(E)(*4*) is the same as the text of §1.1471-3T(c)(6)(ii)(E)(*4*) as added by T.D. 9809].

* * *

(7) * * *

(ii) [The text of proposed §1.1471-3(c)(7)(ii) is the same as the text of §1.1471-3T(c)(7)(ii) as added by T.D. 9809].

* * *

(d) * * *

(6) * * *

(i) * * *

(F) [The text of proposed §1.1471-3(d)(6)(i)(F) is the same as the text of §1.1471-3T(d)(6)(i)(F) as added by T.D. 9809].

* * *

Par. 4. Section 1.1471-4 is amended by:

1. Revising paragraphs (c)(2)(ii)(B)(*2*)(*iii*), (d)(4)(iv)(C) and (D), (f)(2)(ii)(A), (f)(3)(i), and (g)(2).

2. Adding paragraphs (d)(2)(ii)(G) and (f)(2)(ii)(B)(*1*) and (2).

The revisions and additions read as follows:

§1.1471-4. FFI agreement.

* * *

(c) * * *

(2) * * *

(ii) * * *

(B) * * *

(2) * * *

(iii) [The text of proposed §1.1471-4(c)(2)(ii)(B)(*2*)(*iii*) is the same as the text of §1.1471-4T(c)(2)(ii)(B)(*2*)(*iii*) as added by T.D. 9809].

* * *

(d) * * *

(2) * * *

(ii) * * *

(G) [The text of proposed §1.1471-4(d)(2)(ii)(G) is the same as the text of §1.1471-4T(d)(2)(ii)(G) as added by T.D. 9809].

* * *

(4) * * *

(iv) * * *

(C) [The text of proposed §1.1471-4(d)(4)(iv)(C) is the same as the text of §1.1471-4T(d)(4)(iv)(C) as added by T.D. 9809].

(D) [The text of proposed §1.1471-4(d)(4)(iv)(D) is the same as the text of §1.1471-4T(d)(4)(iv)(D) as added by T.D. 9809].

* * *

(f) * * *

(2) * * *

(ii) * * *

(A) [Proposed amendments adopted by T.D. 9852 on 3/21/2019.]

(B) * * *

(1) [Proposed amendments adopted by T.D. 9852 on 3/21/2019.]

(2) [Proposed amendments adopted by T.D. 9852 on 3/21/2019.]

(3) * * *

(i) [Proposed amendments adopted by T.D. 9852 on 3/21/2019.]

* * *

(g) * * *

(2) [Proposed amendments adopted by T.D. 9852 on 3/21/2019.]

* * *

Withholding: Reducing Burden under FATCA

Withholding: Reducing Burden under FATCA.—Amendments to Reg. §§1.1471-1—1.1471-5, eliminating withholding on payments of gross proceeds, deferring withholding on foreign passthru payments, eliminating withholding on certain insurance premiums, and clarifying the definition of investment entity, are proposed (published in the Federal Register on December 18, 2018) (REG-132881-17).

Par. 6. Section 1.1471-1 is amended by:

1. Removing paragraph (b)(60) and redesignating paragraphs (b)(61) and (b)(62) as new paragraphs (b)(60) and (b)(61).

2. Adding new paragraph (b)(62).

3. Revising paragraph (b)(99).

The addition and revision read as follows:

§1.1471-1. Scope of chapter 4 and definitions.

* * *

(b) * * *

(62) *Hold mail instruction.*—The term *hold mail instruction* means a current instruction by a person to keep the person's mail until such instruction is amended. An instruction to send all correspondence electronically is not a hold mail instruction.

* * *

(99) *Permanent residence address.*—The term *permanent residence address* has the meaning set forth in §1.1441-1(c)(38).

* * *

Par. 7. Section 1.1471-2 is amended by:

1. Removing the language "or constitutes gross proceeds from the disposition of such an obligation" from the first sentence of paragraph (a)(1).

2. Removing and reserving paragraph (a)(2)(iii)(B).

3. Removing paragraph (a)(2)(vi).

4. Removing the language ", or any gross proceeds from the disposition of such an obligation" from the first and second sentences of paragraph (b)(1).

5. Removing the language "and the gross proceeds allocated to a partner from the disposition of such obligation as determined under § 1.1473-1(a)(5)(vii)" from paragraph (b)(3)(i).

6. Removing the language "and further includes a beneficiary's share of the gross proceeds from a disposition of such obligation as determined under § 1.1473-1(a)(5)(vii)" from paragraph (b)(3)(ii).

7. Removing the language "and the gross proceeds from the disposition of such obligation to the extent such owner is treated as owning the portion of the trust that consists of the obligation" from paragraph (b)(3)(iii).

The revision reads as follows:

§ 1.1471-2. Requirement to deduct and withhold tax on withholdable payments to certain FFIs.—(a) * * *

(2) * * *

(iii) * * *

(B) [Reserved]

* * *

Par. 8. Section 1.1471-3 is amended by:

1. Removing the language that reads "and that is excluded from the definition of a withholdable payment under § 1.1473-1(a)(4)" from paragraph (a)(3)(ii)(A)(*4*).

2. Removing paragraph (c)(8)(iv) and redesignating paragraph (c)(8)(v) as new paragraph (c)(8)(iv).

§ 1.1471-3. Identification of payee.

Par. 9. Section 1.1471-4 is amended by:

1. Removing the language "or the gross proceeds from the disposition of such an obligation" from the seventh sentence of paragraph (b)(1).

2. Revising paragraph (b)(4).

The revision reads as follows:

§ 1.1471-4. FFI agreement.

* * *

(b) * * *

(4) *Foreign passthru payments.*—A participating FFI is not required to deduct and withhold tax on a foreign passthru payment made by such participating FFI to an account held by a recalcitrant account holder or to a nonparticipating FFI before the date that is two years after the date of publication in the **Federal Register** of final regulations defining the term *foreign passthru payment*.

* * *

Par. 10. Section 1.1471-5 is amended by adding a sentence at the end of paragraph (e)(4)(i)(B) to read as follows:

§ 1.1471-5. Definitions applicable to section 1471.

* * *

(e) * * *

(4) * * *

(i) * * *

(B) * * * Notwithstanding the preceding sentence, an entity is not managed by another entity for purposes of this paragraph (e)(4)(i)(B) solely because the first-mentioned entity invests all or a portion of its assets in such other entity, if such other entity is a mutual fund, exchange traded fund, or a collective investment entity that is widely-held and is subject to investor protection regulation.

* * *

Stock and Rights to Acquire Stock: Deemed Distributions

Stock and Rights to Acquire Stock: Deemed Distributions.—Amendments to Reg. § 1.1473-1, regarding deemed distributions of stock and rights to acquire stock and resolving ambiguities concerning the amount and timing of deemed distributions that are or result from adjustments to rights to acquire stock, are proposed (published in the Federal Register on April 13, 2016) (corrected July 5, 2016) (REG-133673-15).

Par. 12. Section 1.1473-1 is amended by:

1. Amending paragraph (a)(2)(vii)(A) by adding a sentence to the end of the paragraph.

2. Adding paragraph (d)(7).

3. Amending paragraph (f) by adding a third and fourth sentence.

The additions read as follows:

§ 1.1473-1. Section 1473 definitions.—(a) * * *

(2) * * *

(vii) * * *

(A) * * * For purposes of determining the amount of a deemed distribution (as defined in § 1.305-1(d)(7)) on a specified security (as defined in § 1.6045-1(a)(14)) or a deemed payment (as defined in § 1.861-3(a)(6)) that is determined with respect to a deemed distribution on a specified security, a withholding agent other than the issuer of the specified security may rely on issuer reporting by applying the rule under

§1.1441-3(c)(5)(i) to deemed distributions or deemed payments that are withholdable payments under chapter 4.

* * *

(d) * * *

(7) *Withholding agent with respect to deemed distributions under section 305(c).*—Any person that issues or holds directly or indirectly (for example, through an account maintained for another intermediary) on behalf of a beneficial owner, or a flow through entity that owns directly or indirectly (through another flow-through entity), a security upon which a deemed distribution (as defined in §1.305-1(d)(7)) is made has custody of or control over the deemed distribution.

* * *

(f) * * * Paragraphs (a)(2)(vii) and (d)(7) of this section apply to payments made on or after the date of publication of the Treasury decision adopting these rules as final regulations in the **Federal Register**. A withholding agent may, however, rely on the rules in paragraphs (a)(2)(vii) and (d)(7) of this section for all deemed distributions (as defined in §1.305-1(d)(7)) or deemed payments (as defined in §1.861-3(a)(6)) that are withholdable payments occurring on or after January 1, 2016, until the date of publication of a Treasury decision adopting these rules as final regulations in the **Federal Register**.

Withholding: Reducing Burden under FATCA

Withholding: Reducing Burden under FATCA.—Amendments to Reg. §1.1473-1, eliminating withholding on payments of gross proceeds, deferring withholding on foreign passthru payments, eliminating withholding on certain insurance premiums, and clarifying the definition of investment entity, are proposed (published in the Federal Register on December 18, 2018) (REG-132881-17).

Par. 11. Section 1.1473-1 is amended by:

1. Revising paragraph (a)(1).
2. Removing the fourth sentence of paragraph (a)(2)(vii)(A).
3. Removing and reserving paragraph (a)(3).
4. Revising paragraph (a)(4)(iii).
5. Removing paragraph (a)(4)(iv) and redesignating paragraphs (a)(4)(v) through (viii) as new paragraphs (a)(4)(iv) through (vii).
6. Removing paragraph (a)(5)(vii).

The revisions read as follows:

§1.1473-1. Section 1473 definitions.—(a) *Definition of withholdable payment.*—(1) *In general.*—Except as otherwise provided in this paragraph (a) and §1.1471-2(b) (regarding grandfathered obligations), the term *withholdable payment* means any payment of U.S. source FDAP income (as defined in paragraph (a)(2) of this section).

* * *

(3) [Reserved]

(4) * * *

(iii) *Excluded nonfinancial payments.*—Payments for the following: services (including wages and other forms of employee compensation (such as stock options)), the use of property, office and equipment leases, software licenses, transportation, freight, gambling winnings, awards, prizes, scholarships, interest on outstanding accounts payable arising from the acquisition of goods or services, and premiums for insurance contracts that do not have cash value (as defined in §1.1471-5(b)(3)(vii)(B)). Notwithstanding the preceding sentence, excluded nonfinancial payments do not include the following: payments in connection with a lending transaction (including loans of securities), a forward, futures, option, or notional principal contract, or a similar financial instrument; premiums for cash value insurance contracts or annuity contracts; amounts paid under cash value insurance or annuity contracts; dividends; interest (including substitute interest described in §1.861-2(a)(7)) other than interest described in the preceding sentence; investment advisory fees; custodial fees; and bank or brokerage fees.

* * *

Foreign Financial Institutions: Certain Entities: Verification and Certification Requirements

Foreign Financial Institutions: Certain Entities: Verification and Certification Requirements.—Amendments to Reg. §1.1474-1, describing the verification requirements (including certifications of compliance) and events of default for entities that agree to perform the chapter 4 due diligence, withholding, and reporting requirements on behalf of certain foreign financial institutions (FFIs) or the chapter 4 due diligence and reporting obligations on behalf of certain nonfinancial foreign entities, are proposed (published in the Federal Register on January 6, 2017) (REG-103477-14).

Par. 7. Section 1.1474-1 is amended by adding paragraph (d)(4)(vii) to read as follows:

§1.1474-1. Liability for withheld tax and withholding agent reporting.

* * *

(d) * * *

(4) * * *

(vii) [The text of proposed §1.1474-1(d)(4)(vii) is the same as the text of §1.1474-1T(d)(4)(vii) as added by T.D. 9809].

* * *

Withholding: Reducing Burden under FATCA

Withholding: Reducing Burden under FATCA.—Amendments to Reg. §§1.1474-1 and 1.1474-2, eliminating withholding on payments of gross proceeds, deferring withholding on foreign passthru payments, eliminating withholding on certain insurance premiums, and clarifying the definition of investment entity, are proposed (published in the Federal Register on December 18, 2018) (REG-132881-17).

Par. 12. Section 1.1474-1 is amended by:

1. Adding two sentences after the first sentence in paragraph (b)(1).
2. Revising paragraph (b)(2).
3. Redesignating paragraph (d)(1)(i) as paragraph (d)(1)(i)(A) and adding paragraphs (d)(1)(i) introductory text and (d)(1)(i)(B).
4. Adding a sentence after the first sentence in paragraph (d)(2)(ii).

The revisions and additions read as follows:

§1.1474-1. Liability for withheld tax and withholding agent reporting.

* * *

(b) * * *

(1) * * * In a case in which a withholding agent is permitted to withhold on a chapter 4 reportable amount (as defined in paragraph (d)(2) of this section) in a calendar year (subsequent year) following the calendar year (preceding year) in which the withholding agent paid such amount (or, for a partnership or trust withholding with respect to a foreign partner, beneficiary, or owner, the year the partnership or trust received such amount), the withholding agent shall designate the deposit of the withholding as made for the preceding year and shall report the tax liability on Form 1042 for the preceding year. In the case of a partnership that withholds as described in the preceding sentence and does not file its federal income tax return on a calendar-year basis, however, such partnership may instead designate the deposit as made for the subsequent year and report the tax liability on Form 1042 for the subsequent year.* * *

(2) *Special rule for foreign passthru payments that include an undetermined amount of income subject to tax.*—[Reserved]

* * *

(d) * * *

(1) * * *

(i) *Withholding agent information reporting.*—This paragraph (d)(1)(i) describes the general requirements for a withholding agent to file an information return on Form 1042-S and describes a special rule for a withholding agent that withholds in a subsequent year as described in paragraph (b)(1) of this section.

* * *

(B) *Special reporting by withholding agents that withhold in a subsequent year.*—Notwithstanding the first sentence of paragraph (d)(1)(i)(A) of this section, if a withholding agent designates the deposit of such withholding as made for the preceding calendar year as described in paragraph (b)(1) of this section, the withholding agent is required to report the amount on Form 1042-S for the preceding year. With respect to a withholding agent described in the previous sentence that is a partnership and that withholds after March 15 of the subsequent year, such partnership may file and furnish the Form 1042-S on or before September 15 of that year. In the case of a partnership that designates the deposit of such withholding as made for the subsequent year as permitted in paragraph (b)(1) of this section, however, the partnership shall report the chapter 4 reportable amount on Form 1042-S for the subsequent year.

* * *

(2) * * *

(ii) * * * A chapter 4 reportable amount also does not include an amount received by a nonqualified intermediary that is a participating FFI or a registered deemed-compliant FFI if the nonqualified intermediary reports such amount as having been withheld upon under chapter 3 to the extent permitted under § 1.1461-1(c)(4)(iv). * * *

* * *

Par. 13. Section 1.1474-2 is amended by revising the second sentence of paragraph (a)(3)(i) introductory text, paragraphs (a)(3)(i)(A) through (C), and paragraph (a)(4) to read as follows:

§1.1474-2. Adjustments for overwithholding or underwithholding of tax.—(a) * * *

(3) * * *

(i) * * * In such a case, the withholding agent may reimburse itself by reducing, by the amount of tax actually repaid to the beneficial owner or payee, the amount of any deposit of withholding tax otherwise required to be made by the withholding agent under § 1.6302-2(a)(1)(iii) for any subsequent payment period occurring before the end of the calendar year following the calendar year of overwithholding. * * *

(A) The repayment to the beneficial owner or payee occurs before the earliest of the due date (including extensions) for filing the Form 1042-S for the calendar year of overwithholding, the date the Form 1042-S is actually filed with the IRS, or the date the Form 1042-S is furnished to the beneficial owner or payee;

(B) The withholding agent states on a timely filed (including extensions) Form 1042-S for the calendar year of overwithholding the amount of tax withheld and the amount of any actual repayment; and

(C) The withholding agent states on a timely filed (including extensions) Form 1042 for the calendar year of overwithholding the amount of adjustments made to overwithholding under paragraph (a)(1) of this section and the amount of any credit claimed under § 1.6414-1.

* * *

(4) *Set-off.*—Under the set-off procedure, the withholding agent may repay the beneficial owner or payee by applying the amount overwithheld against any amount of tax which otherwise would be required under chapter 3 or

4 of the Internal Revenue Code or the regulations under part 1 of this chapter to be withheld from income paid by the withholding agent to such person. Any such set-off that occurs for a payment period in the calendar year following the calendar year of overwithholding shall be allowed only if—

(i) The repayment to the beneficial owner or payee occurs before the earliest of the due date (including extensions) for filing the Form 1042-S for the calendar year of overwithholding, the date the Form 1042-S is actually filed with the IRS, or the date the Form 1042-S is furnished to the beneficial owner or payee;

(ii) The withholding agent states on a timely filed (including extensions) Form 1042-S for the calendar year of overwithholding the amount of tax withheld and the amount of any repayment made through set-off; and

(iii) The withholding agent states on a timely filed (including extensions) Form 1042 for the calendar year of overwithholding the amount of adjustments made to overwithholding under paragraph (a)(1) of this section and the amount of any credit claimed under § 1.6414-1.

* * *

CONSOLIDATED RETURNS

Consolidated Returns: AMT: Definitions

Consolidated Returns: Alternative Minimum Tax.—Reproduced below is the text of a proposed amendment to Reg. § 1.1502-1, relating to the computation of the alternative minimum tax by consolidated groups (published in the Federal Register on December 30, 1992).

☐ Par. 3. Section 1.1502-1 is amended by reserving paragraph (i) and adding paragraph (j) to read as follows:

§ 1.1502-1. Definitions.

* * *

(i) [Reserved]

(j) *Tax liability.*—Except as provided otherwise, references relating to the "tax liability" of a consolidated group are to the consolidated tax liability determined in accordance with § 1.1502-2. However, references in § 1.1552-1 (a) through (f) (relating to the computation of earnings and profits) to the tax liability of a consolidated group are to the regular tax liability of the group, determined in accordance with section 26 (b), reduced by the credits allowable under part IV of subchapter A of the Internal Revenue Code (other than the consolidated minimum tax credit under § 1.1502-55(h)). Similarly, references to a member's tax liability determined as if it had filed separate returns under § 1.1502-33(d), or the separate return tax liability of a member under § 1.1552-1(a)(3)(ii)(*b*), are to the regular tax liability of the member under section 26(b), reduced by the above-referenced credits.

Base Erosion and Anti-Abuse Tax: Guidance

Base Erosion and Anti-Abuse Tax: Guidance.—Amendments to Reg. § 1.1502-2, regarding the tax on base erosion payments of taxpayers with substantial gross receipts and reporting requirements thereunder, are proposed (published in the Federal Register on December 21, 2018) (REG-104259-18).

Par. 4. Section 1.1502-2 is revised to read as follows:

§ 1.1502-2. Computation of tax liability.—(a) *Taxes imposed.*—The tax liability of a group for a consolidated return year is determined by adding together—

(1) The tax imposed by section 11(a) in the amount described in section 11(b) on the consolidated taxable income for the year (reduced by the taxable income of a member described in paragraphs (a)(5) through (8) of this section);

(2) The tax imposed by section 541 on the consolidated undistributed personal holding company income;

(3) If paragraph (a)(2) of this section does not apply, the aggregate of the taxes imposed by section 541 on the separate undistributed personal holding company income of the members which are personal holding companies;

(4) If neither paragraph (a)(2) nor (3) of this section apply, the tax imposed by section 531 on the consolidated accumulated taxable income (see § 1.1502–43);

(5) The tax imposed by section 594(a) in lieu of the taxes imposed by section 11 on the taxable income of a life insurance department of the common parent of a group which is a mutual savings bank;

(6) The tax imposed by section 801 on consolidated life insurance company taxable income;

(7) The tax imposed by section 831(a) on consolidated insurance company taxable income of the members which are subject to such tax;

(8) Any increase in tax described in section 1351(d)(1) (relating to recoveries of foreign expropriation losses); and

(9) The tax imposed by section 59A on base erosion payments of taxpayers with substantial gross receipts.

(b) *Credits.*—A group is allowed as a credit against the taxes described in paragraph (a) (except for paragraph (a)(9) of this section) of this section: the general business credit under section 38 (see § 1.1502-3), the foreign tax credit under section 27 (see § 1.1502-4), and any other applicable credits provided under the Internal Revenue Code. Any increase in tax due to the recapture of a tax credit will be taken into account. See section 59A and the regulations thereunder for credits allowed against the tax described in paragraph (a)(9) of this section.

(c) *Allocation of dollar amounts.*—For purposes of this section, if a member or members of the consolidated group are also members of a controlled group that includes corporations that are not members of the consolidated group, any dollar amount described in any section of the Internal Revenue Code is apportioned among all members of the controlled group in accordance with the provisions of the applicable section and the regulations thereunder.

(d) *Applicability date.*—(1) Except as provided in paragraph (d)(2) of this section, this section applies to any consolidated return year for which the due date of the income tax return (without regard to extensions) is on or after the date of publication of the Treasury Decision adopting these rules as final regulations in the **Federal Register.**

(2) Paragraph (a)(9) of this section applies to consolidated return years beginning after December 31, 2017.

Base Erosion and Anti-Abuse Tax: Guidance

Base Erosion and Anti-Abuse Tax: Guidance.—Amendments to Reg. §1.1502-4, regarding the tax on base erosion payments of taxpayers with substantial gross receipts and reporting requirements thereunder, are proposed (published in the Federal Register on December 21, 2018) (REG-104259-18).

Par. 5. Section 1.1502-4 is amended by revising paragraph (d)(3) to read as follows:

§1.1502-4. Consolidated foreign tax credit.

* * *

(d) * * *

(3) *Computation of tax against which credit is taken.*—The tax against which the limiting fraction under section 904(a) is applied will be the consolidated tax liability of the group determined under §1.1502-2, but without regard to paragraphs (a)(2), (3), (4), (8), and (9) of that section, and without regard to any credit against such liability.

* * *

Consolidated Returns: AMT: Estimated Tax

Consolidated Returns: Alternative Minimum Tax.—Reproduced below is the text of a proposed amendment to Reg. §1.1502-5, relating to the computation of the alternative minimum tax by consolidated groups (published in the Federal Register on December 30, 1992).

☐ Par. 5. Section 1.1502-5 is revised to read as follows:

§1.1502-5. Estimated tax.—(a) *General rule.*—(1) *Consolidated estimated tax.*—If a group files a consolidated return for two consecutive taxable years, it must make payments of estimated tax on a consolidated basis for each subsequent taxable year, until separate returns are filed. When filing on a consolidated basis, the group is generally treated as a single corporation for purposes of section 6655 (relating to payment of estimated tax by corporations). If separate returns are filed by the members for a taxable year, the amount of any estimated tax payments made with respect to a consolidated estimated tax for the year is credited against the separate tax liabilities of the members in any reasonable manner designated by the common parent. Consolidated payments of estimated tax must be deposited with the authorized commercial depositary or Federal Reserve Bank with which the common parent deposits its estimated tax payments. A statement must be attached to the payment setting forth the name, address, employer identification number, and Internal Revenue Service Center of each member.

(2) *First two consolidated return years.*—For its first two consolidated return years, a group may make payments of estimated tax on either a consolidated or a separate member basis, and the amount of any separate estimated tax payments is credited against the consolidated tax liability of the group.

(b) *Addition to tax for failure to pay estimated tax under section 6655.*—(1) *Consolidated return filed.*—For its first two consolidated return years, a group may compute the amount of the penalty (if any) under section 6655 on a consolidated basis or a separate member basis, regardless of the method of payment. Thereafter, the group must compute the penalty for any consolidated return year on a consolidated basis.

(2) *Computation of penalty on consolidated basis.*—(i) This paragraph (b)(2) provides rules for computing the penalty under section 6655 on a consolidated basis.

(ii) The tax shown on the return for the preceding taxable year referred to in section 6655(d)(1)(B)(ii) is, if a consolidated return was filed for that preceding year, the tax shown on the consolidated return for that preceding year or, if a consolidated return was not filed for that preceding year, the aggregate of the taxes shown on the separate returns of the common parent and any other corporation that was a member of the same affiliated group as the common parent for that preceding year.

(iii) If estimated tax was not paid on a consolidated basis, the amount of the group's payments of estimated tax for the taxable year is the aggregate of the payments made by all members for the year.

(iv) If the common parent is otherwise eligible to use the section 6655(d)(1)(B)(ii) required annual payment rule, that rule applies only if the group's consolidated return, or each member's separate return if the group did not file a consolidated return, for the preceding taxable year was a taxable year of 12 months.

(3) *Computation of penalty on separate member basis.*—To compute any penalty under section 6655 on a separate member basis, for purposes of section 6655(d)(1)(B)(i), the "tax shown on the return" for the taxable year is the portion of the tax shown on the consolidated return allocable to the member under paragraph (b)(6) of this section. If the member was included in the consolidated return filed by the group for the preceding taxable year, for purposes of section 6655(d)(1)(B) (ii), the "tax shown on the return" for the preceding taxable year for any member is the portion of the tax shown on the consolidated return for the preceding year allocable to the member under paragraph (b)(6) of this section.

(4) *Consolidated payments if separate returns filed.*—If the group does not file a consolidated

return for the taxable year but makes payments of estimated tax on a consolidated basis, for purposes of section 6655(b)(1)(B), the "amount (if any) of the installment paid" by any member is an amount apportioned to the member in any reasonable manner designated by the common parent. If a member was included in the consolidated return filed by the group for the preceding taxable year, the amount of the member's penalty under section 6655 is computed on the separate member basis described in paragraph (b)(3) of this section.

(5) *Tax defined*.—For purposes of this section, "tax" means the excess of—

(i) The sum of—

(A) The consolidated tax imposed by section 11, section 1201(a), or subchapter L of chapter 1, whichever applies;

(B) The consolidated AMT determined under § 1.1502-55; and

(C) The consolidated environmental tax defined under § 1.1552-1(h)(2); over

(ii) The credits allowable under part IV of subchapter A of chapter 1 of the Internal Revenue Code against the consolidated taxes in paragraphs (b)(5)(i)(A), (B), and (C) of this section.

(6) *Rules for allocation of consolidated tax liability*.—For purposes of this section, the tax shown on a consolidated return shall be allocated to the members of the group by allocating—

(i) Any tax described in paragraph (b)(5)(i)(A) of this section, net of allowable credits under paragraph (b)(5)(ii) (other than the allowable consolidated MTC defined in § 1.1502-55(h)), under the method that the group has elected pursuant to section 1552 and § 1.1502-33(d);

(ii) Any allowable consolidated MTC (as defined in § 1.1502-55(h)) in accordance with the requirements of § 1.1552-1(g);

(iii) Any consolidated AMT described in paragraph (b)(5)(i)(B) of this section in accordance with the requirements of § 1.1552-1(g); and

(iv) Any consolidated environmental tax described in paragraph (b)(5)(i)(C) of this section in accordance with the requirements of § 1.1552-1(h).

(c) *Examples*. The provisions of this section are illustrated by the following examples.

Example 1. Corporations P and S1 file a consolidated return for the first time for calendar year 1992. P and S1 also file consolidated returns for 1993 and 1994. Under paragraph (a)(2) of this section, for 1992 and 1993 P and S1 may pay estimated tax on either a separate or consolidated basis. Under paragraph (a)(1) of this section, for 1994 the group must pay its estimated tax on a consolidated basis. In determining whether P and S1 come within the exception provided in section 6655(d)(1)(B)(ii) for 1994, the "tax shown on the return" is the tax shown on the consolidated return for 1993.

Example 2. Corporations P, S1, and S2 file a consolidated return for the first time for calendar year 1992 and file their second consolidated return in 1993. S2 ceases to be a member of the group on September 15, 1994. Under paragraph (b)(2) of this section, in determining whether the group (which no longer includes S2) comes within the exception provided in section 6655(d)(1)(B)(ii) for 1994, the "tax shown on the return" is the tax shown on the consolidated return for 1993.

Example 3. Corporations P and S1 file a consolidated return for the first time for calendar year 1992 and file their second consolidated return in 1993. Corporation S2 becomes a member of the group on July 1, 1994, and joins in the filing of the consolidated return for 1994. Under paragraph (b)(2) of this section, in determining whether the group (which now includes S2) comes within the exception provided in section 6655(d)(1)(B)(ii) for 1994, the "tax shown on the return" is the tax shown on the consolidated return for 1993. Any tax of S2 for any separate return year is not included as a part of the "tax shown on the return" for purposes of applying section 6655(d)(1)(B)(ii).

Example 4. Corporations X and Y file consolidated returns for the calendar years 1992 and 1993 and separate returns for 1994. Under paragraph (b)(3) of this section, in determining whether X or Y comes within the exception provided in section 6655(d)(1)(B)(ii) for 1994, the "tax shown on the return" is the amount of tax shown on the consolidated return for 1993 allocable to X and to Y in accordance with paragraph (b)(6) of this section.

(d) *Cross reference*.—For provisions relating to quick refunds of corporate estimated tax payments, *see* § 1.1502-78 and §§ 1.6425-1 through 1.6425-3.

(e) *Effective date*.—This section applies to any taxable year for which the due date of the income tax return (without regard to extensions) is on or after [the date that is sixty days after final regulations are filed with the Federal Register]. For prior years, *see* § 1.1502-5 (as contained in the 26 CFR edition revised as of April 1, 1992).

Elimination of Circular Adjustments to Basis: Absorption of Losses

Elimination of Circular Adjustments to Basis: Absorption of Losses.—Amendments to Reg. §§ 1.1502-11 and 1.1502-12, revising the rules concerning the use of a consolidated group's losses in a consolidated return year in which stock of a subsidiary is disposed of, are proposed (published in the Federal Register on June 11, 2015) (REG-101652-10).

Par. 2. Section 1.1502-11 is amended by:

1. Revising paragraphs (a) introductory text, (a)(2), (a)(3), and (a)(4).
2. Removing and reserving paragraph (a)(6).
3. Revising paragraphs (b), (c)(2)(i), and (c)(2)(ii).
4. Removing in paragraph (c)(2)(vi) the phrase "unlimited deductions and losses that are absorbed" and adding "S's absorbed amount of losses" in its place.
5. Revising paragraph (c)(4).
6. Revising the heading of paragraph (c)(7) and adding a sentence at the end of the paragraph.
7. Adding paragraph (e).

The revisions and additions read as follows:

§1.1502-11. Consolidated taxable income.—(a) *In general.*—The consolidated taxable income (CTI) for a consolidated return year shall be determined by taking into account—

* * *

(2) Any consolidated net operating loss (CNOL) deduction (see §1.1502-21 for the computation of the CNOL deduction);

(3) Any consolidated capital gain net income (see §1.1502–22 for the computation of the consolidated capital gain net income);

(4) Any consolidated section 1231 net loss (see §1.1502–23 for the computation of the consolidated section 1231 net loss);

* * *

(6) [Reserved]

* * *

(b) *Elimination of circular basis adjustments if there is no excluded COD income.*—(1) *In general.*—If a member (P) disposes of a share of stock of one or more subsidiaries (S), this paragraph (b) applies to determine the amount of S's losses that will be used in the consolidated return year of disposition and in a carryback year. The purpose of these rules is to prevent P's income, gain, deduction, or loss from the disposition of a share of S's stock from affecting the amount of S's deductions and losses that are absorbed. A change to the amount of S's absorbed losses would affect P's basis in S's stock under §1.1502-32, which in turn affects P's gain or loss on the disposition of S's stock. For purposes of this section, P is treated as disposing of a share of a subsidiary's stock if any event described in §1.1502-19(c) occurs or, if for any reason, a member recognizes gain or loss (including an excess loss account included in income) with respect to the share. However, to the extent income, gain, deduction, or loss from a disposition of a share of S's stock is deferred under any rule of law (for example, §1.1502-13 and section 267(f)), the taxable year in which the deferred amount is taken into account is treated as the taxable year of disposition. This paragraph (b) does not apply if any member realizes discharge of indebtedness income that is excluded from gross income under section 108(a) during the consolidated return year of the disposition. If a member realizes such income, see paragraph (c) of this section. For purposes of this section, S's ordinary loss means its separate net operating loss (as defined in §1.1502-21(b)(2)(iv)(B)). Solely for purposes of this section, any reference to a member's capital gain includes amounts treated as capital gain. Furthermore, for those purposes, a member's capital loss means a consolidated net capital loss determined by reference to only that member's capital gain and capital loss items.

(2) *Deductions and losses of disposed subsidiaries.*—(i) *Determination of absorbed amounts.*—If P disposes of a share of S's stock in a transaction to which this paragraph (b) applies, the extent to which S's ordinary loss and capital loss (including losses carried over from a prior year) that are absorbed in the consolidated return year of the disposition or in a prior year as a carryback (the absorbed amount) is determined under this paragraph (b)(2). S's absorbed amount is the amount that would be absorbed in a computation of the group's consolidated taxable income (CTI) for the consolidated return year of the disposition (and any taxable year to which losses may be carried back) without taking into account any member's income, gain, deduction, or loss from the disposition of any share of any subsidiary's stock in that year. S's absorbed amount is determined after first applying other applicable limitations and ordering rules (for example, limitations imposed by section 382(a) and §1.1502-21 and the ordering rules of section 382(l)(2)) to S's deductions and losses. Any election that the group makes on its actual return for the consolidated return year (for example, an election to relinquish a carryback under §1.1502-21(b)(3)) must be used in this computation. Once S's absorbed amount is determined, that amount is not redetermined. Except as provided in paragraph (b)(2)(iii)(B)(*1*) of this section, the amount determined under this paragraph (b)(2)(i) fixes only the amount of S's losses that will be absorbed. Thus, under paragraph (b)(2)(iii)(A) of this section, the character of the losses that are absorbed in the actual computation of the group's CTI for the year (or as a carryback to a prior year) may not be the same as the character of the losses that are absorbed in determining the absorbed amount. However, if the alternative computation of paragraph (b)(2)(iii)(B)(*1*) of this section is required, the character of the absorbed amount as determined under this paragraph (b)(2)(i) is retained.

(ii) *Stock basis reduction and gain or loss on disposition.*—After the determination of S's absorbed amount, P reduces its basis in S's stock under the investment adjustment rules of §1.1502-32(b)(2) by the absorbed amount. If any share is a loss share, P then adjusts its basis in S's stock by applying paragraphs (b) and (c) of §1.1502-36, and, if an election is actually made under §1.1502-36(d)(6), by applying §1.1502-36(d) to the extent necessary to give effect to the election. P then computes its gain or loss on the disposed of shares after taking into account those adjustments.

(iii) *Actual computation of CTI.*—(A) *In general.*—The group's CTI and any carryback of a portion of a CNOL are determined under applicable provisions of the Internal Revenue Code (Code) and regulations, taking into account gain or loss on any subsidiary's stock, and taking into account losses of disposed of subsidiaries equal to each such subsidiary's absorbed amount.

(B) *Alternative computation.*—If the computation of the group's CTI under paragraph (b)(2)(iii)(A) of this section would result in an absorption of less than all of any disposed of subsidiary's absorbed amount, then the group's CTI is computed by applying the following steps, rather than the computation under that paragraph:

(*1*) First, losses of each disposed of subsidiary equal in both amount and character and from the same taxable years as losses used in the computation of its absorbed amount under paragraph (b)(2)(i) of this section offset income and gain of other members without taking into account any gain or loss on any share of subsidiary stock and without regard to net losses of other members.

(*2*) Second, a disposing member offsets its gain on subsidiary stock with its losses on subsidiary stock of the same character. For this purpose, a loss on subsidiary stock is determined after applying §1.1502-36(b) and (c), and so much of §1.1502-36(d) as is necessary to give effect to an election actually made under

§1.1502-36(d)(6). If the disposing member has net income or gain on subsidiary stock, and if the member also has a loss of the same character (determined without regard to the net income, gain, deduction or loss on subsidiary stock), the loss offsets that net income or gain and any remaining income or gain is added to the amount determined after the application of paragraph (b)(2)(ii)(B)(*1*) of this section. For example, if P has a net capital loss on portfolio stock, that net loss is not taken into account in applying paragraph (b)(2)(iii)(B)(*1*). However, under this paragraph (b)(2)(iii)(B)(*2*), that net capital loss is absorbed to the extent of that member's net capital gain on subsidiary stock.

(*3*) Third, if, after the application of paragraph (b)(2)(iii)(B)(*2*) of this section, the group has remaining income or gain and a disposing member has a net loss on subsidiary stock (determined after applying §1.1502-36(b) and (c), and so much of §1.1502-36(d) as is necessary to give effect to an election actually made under §1.1502-36(d)(6)), that remaining income or gain is then offset by a loss on the disposition of subsidiary stock, subject to the applicable rules of the Code and regulations. The amount of the offset, however, is limited to the lesser of the total remaining ordinary income or capital gain of the group (determined after the application of paragraph (b)(2)(iii)(B)(*2*) of this section), or the amount of the disposing member's ordinary income or capital gain of the same character (determined without regard to the stock loss). If the preceding sentence applies to more than one disposing member, and the sum of the amounts determined under that sentence exceeds the group's remaining ordinary or capital gain, the amounts offset capital gain or ordinary income on a pro rata basis under the principles of paragraph (e) of this section.

(*4*) Fourth, if, after application of paragraph (b)(2)(iii)(B)(*3*) of this section, the group has remaining ordinary income or capital gain, those amounts are offset by the unused losses of all members on a pro rata basis under paragraph (e) of this section.

(C) *Priority of rules.*—The computation of CTI under this paragraph (b)(2)(iii) applies notwithstanding other rules for the absorption of a portion of a member's current year loss, such as paragraphs (a) and (e) of this section, §§1.1502-12 and 1.1502-22(a), and the absorption of a member's portion of a CNOL or consolidated net capital loss carryover from a prior year under §§1.1502-21(b) and 1.1502-22(b), respectively. For example, in some circumstances, an ordinary loss of a disposed of subsidiary may offset capital gain of another member notwithstanding that under general rules a capital loss of another member would be allowed to the extent of capital gains before an ordinary loss is taken into account. Similarly, an ordinary loss with respect to a subsidiary's stock, which would generally offset ordinary income of the owning member and be included in determining that member's separate taxable income, may become a loss carryover if use of that loss would cause less than all of a disposed of subsidiary's absorbed amount to be used.

(D) *Deductions determined by reference to CTI.*—In the case of any deduction of any member that is determined by reference to or limited by the amount of CTI (for example, a charitable contribution deduction under §1.1502-24(c) and a percentage depletion deduction under §1.1502-44(b)), the amount of the deduction is determined without regard to any gain or loss on subsidiary stock.

(iv) *Losses not absorbed.*—To the extent S's losses in the consolidated return year of the disposition of its stock do not offset income or gain by reason of the rules of this paragraph (b), S ceases to be a member, and S's losses are not reattributed under §1.1502-36(d)(6), the losses are carried over to its separate return years (if any) under the applicable principles of the Code and regulations thereunder. Those losses are not taken into account in determining the percentage of CNOL or consolidated net capital loss attributable to members under §1.1502-21(b)(2)(iv) or §1.1502-22(b)(3), respectively. If S remains a member, its unused losses are included in the CNOL or consolidated net capital loss carryovers and are subject to the allocation rules of those sections.

(v) *Disposition of stock of a higher-tier subsidiary.*—If a subsidiary (T) is a lower-tier subsidiary (as described in §1.1502-36(f)(4)) of a higher-tier subsidiary (S), and S's stock is disposed of during a consolidated return year, T's losses are subject to this paragraph (b) as if T's stock had been disposed of. Thus, T's absorbed amount is determined by disregarding any gain or loss (for example, an excess loss account taken into account under §1.1502-19(b)) on a deemed disposition of T's stock as provided under this paragraph (b), as well as any gain or loss on the disposition of a share of any other subsidiary's stock.

(vi) *Examples.*—For purposes of the examples in this paragraph (b)(2)(vi), unless otherwise stated, P is the common parent of a calendar-year consolidated group and owns all of the only class of stock of subsidiaries S, S1, S2, M, M1, and M2 for the entire year; S, S1, S2, M, M1, M2, and T own no stock of lower-tier subsidiaries; all persons use the accrual method of accounting; the facts set forth the only corporate activity; all transactions are between unrelated persons; tax liabilities are disregarded; and §1.1502-36 will not cause P to adjust its basis in S's stock immediately before a disposition. The rules of this paragraph (b)(2) are illustrated by the following examples:

Example 1. Absorption of disposed of subsidiary's losses. (i) *Facts.* P has a $500 basis in S's stock. P sells S's stock for $520 at the close of Year 1. For Year 1, P has ordinary income of $30 (determined without taking into account P's gain or loss from the disposition of S's stock) and S an $80 ordinary loss.

(ii) *Determination of absorbed amount.* To determine S's absorbed amount and the effect of the absorption of its losses under §1.1502-32(b)(2) on P's basis in S's stock, the group's taxable income is computed without taking into account P's gain or loss from the disposition of S's stock. The P group is treated as having a CNOL of $50 (P's $30 of income minus S's $80 separate net operating loss). Accordingly, S's absorbed amount determined under paragraph (b)(2)(i) of this section is $30.

(iii) *Loss absorption and basis reduction.* Under paragraph (b)(2)(ii) of this section, P's basis in S's stock is reduced by S's $30 absorbed amount from $500 to $470 immediately before the disposition. Consequently, P recognizes a $50 gain from the sale of S's stock, and the P group has CTI of $50 for Year 1 (P's $30 of ordinary income plus its $50 of gain from the sale of S's stock, minus $30 of S's ordinary loss equal to its absorbed amount). In addition, S's $50 of unabsorbed loss is carried to S's first separate return year.

Example 2. Carrybacks and carryovers. (i) *Facts.* For Year 1, the P group has CTI of $30 (all of which is attributable to P) and a consolidated net capital loss of $100 ($50 attributable to P and $50 to S), which cannot be carried back. At the beginning of Year 2, P has a $300 basis in S's stock. P sells S's stock for $280 at the close of Year 2. For Year 2, P has ordinary income of $30, and a $20 capital gain (determined without taking into account the consolidated net capital loss carryover from Year 1 or P's gain or loss from the disposition of S's stock), and S has a $100 ordinary loss.

(ii) *Determination of absorbed amount.* To determine S's absorbed amount and the effect of the absorption of its losses under § 1.1502-32(b)(2) on P's basis in S's stock, the group's taxable income for Year 2 is computed without taking into account P's gain or loss from the disposition of S's stock. Under section 1212(a)(1)(B), P's $20 capital gain for Year 2 would be offset by $20 of the group's consolidated capital loss carryover from Year 1 ($10 attributable to P and $10 attributable to S). P's $30 of ordinary income in Year 2 would be offset by $30 of S's $100 ordinary loss in that year. P's $30 of ordinary income in Year 1 would be offset by a $30 CNOL carryback from Year 2, all of which is attributable to S. Accordingly, S's absorbed amount under paragraph (b)(2)(i) of this section is $70 ($10 of S's portion of the consolidated capital loss carryover from Year 1 plus $60 of S's loss from Year 2).

(iii) *Loss absorption and basis reduction.* Under paragraph (b)(2)(ii) of this section, P's basis in S's stock is reduced by S's $70 absorbed amount from $300 to $230, immediately before the disposition, resulting in $50 of capital gain to P from the sale of S's stock for $280 in Year 2. Thus, for Year 2 P will have $70 of capital gain ($50 from the stock sale plus $20 from its other capital gain for that year), which will be offset by $70 of the consolidated capital loss carryover from Year 1, $35 of which is attributable to P and $35 of which is attributable to S. Another $30 of S's ordinary loss offsets P's $30 of ordinary income in Year 2. An amount of S's ordinary loss equal to its remaining $5 absorbed amount may be carried back to Year 1 to offset $5 of the group's CTI in that year. P will have a $15 ($50 - $35) capital loss carryover from Year 1, and S will carry over a $15 ($50 - $35) capital loss from Year 1 and a $65 ($100 - $35) NOL to its first separate return year.

Example 3. Chain of subsidiaries. (i) *Facts.* P has a $500 basis in the stock of S and S has a $500 basis in the stock of T, its wholly owned subsidiary. P sells all of its S stock for $520 at the close of Year 1. For Year 1, P has ordinary income of $30, S has no income or loss, and T has an $80 ordinary loss.

(ii) *Determination of absorbed amount, basis reduction, and loss absorption.* Under § 1.1502-19(c)(1)(ii), T's stock is treated as disposed of when it becomes a nonmember, and its losses are subject to paragraph (b) of this section. Thus, T's absorbed amount is determined by taking into account P's $30 of ordinary income but without taking into account any gain or loss on P's disposition of S's stock. Accordingly, T's absorbed amount determined under paragraph (b)(2)(i) of this section is $30. Under paragraph (b)(2)(ii) of this section, S's basis in T's stock is reduced by $30, from $500 to $470. Furthermore, under § 1.1502-32(a)(3)(iii), P's basis in S's stock is reduced by $30, from $500 to $470, immediately before the sale. Consequently, P recognizes a $50 gain from the sale of S's stock ($520 - $470), and T will have a $50 ($80 - $30) NOL carryover to its first separate return year.

(iii) *Excess loss account in lower-tier stock.* The facts are the same as in paragraph (i) of this *Example 3*, except that S has a $10 excess loss account (ELA) in T's stock (rather than a $500 basis). Under paragraph (b)(1) of this section, T's stock is treated as disposed of and its absorbed amount is determined under paragraph (b)(2)(i) of this section. Thus, T's absorbed amount is determined by taking into account P's $30 of ordinary income but without taking into account P's gain or loss on the disposition of S's stock and S's inclusion of its ELA with respect to T's stock under § 1.1502-19(b)(1). Accordingly, T's absorbed amount determined under paragraph (b)(2)(i) of this section is $30. Under paragraph (b)(2)(ii) of this section, S's ELA in its T stock is increased by $30, from $10 to $40, immediately before the disposition of T's stock. Under § 1.1502-19(b), the ELA is included in S's income. Moreover, under § 1.1502-32(b)(2), P's basis in S's stock is increased immediately before the sale by a net $10 (S's $40 inclusion of T's ELA under § 1.1502-19(b) minus T's $30 absorbed loss that tiers up under § 1.1502-32(a)(3)(iii)) from $500 to $510. Thus, P recognizes $10 of gain on the sale of S's stock ($520 - $510), and S takes into account $40 of gain from the inclusion of its ELA in T's stock. T will have a $50 ($80 - $30) NOL carryover to its first separate return year.

Example 4. Sale of S's stock and S remains in the group. (i) *Facts.* For Year 1, the P group has CTI of $100 (all of which is attributable to P). At the beginning of Year 2, P has a $40 basis in each of the 10 shares of S's stock. P sells 2 shares of S's stock for $85 each at the close of Year 2. For Year 2, P has an $80 ordinary loss (determined without taking into account P's gain or loss from the sale of S's stock), and S has an $80 ordinary loss.

(ii) *Determination of absorbed amount.* To determine S's absorbed amount and the effect of the absorption of its losses under § 1.1502-32(b)(2) on P's basis in S's stock, the group's CTI for Year 2 is computed without taking into account P's gain or loss from the sale of S's stock. Thus, the group would have a $160 CNOL for Year 2, $100 of which is carried back to Year 1 ($50 attributable to S and $50 attributable to P) and offsets $100 of CTI in that year. Accordingly, S's absorbed amount determined under paragraph (b)(2)(i) of this section is $50.

(iii) *Loss absorption and basis reduction.* Under paragraph (b)(2)(ii) of this section, P's basis in all of S's stock is reduced by $50. Each of P's 10 shares of S stock is reduced by $5 from $40 to $35. Consequently, on the sale of each of the 2 shares of S's stock, P recognizes a $50 gain ($85 - $35). The losses available to offset the $100 gain on the sale of S's 2 shares consist of P's $80 ordinary loss and $50 of S's ordinary loss equal its absorbed amount. Under paragraph (e) of this section, P's and S's losses are absorbed on a pro rata basis. Therefore, the group absorbs approximately $62 ($100 x 80/80 + 50) of P's ordinary loss from Year 2, and approximately $38 ($100 x 50/80 + 50) of S's ordinary loss in that year. P's remaining $18 ($80 - $62) of ordinary loss in Year 2 and S's remaining $12 ($50 - $38) of ordinary loss equal to its remaining absorbed amount may be carried back to Year 1 to offset $30 of the $100 of CTI in that year. For Year 2, the P group has $30 remaining of its CNOL (all of which is attributable to S) which is carried to the P group's Year 3 consolidated return year.

(iv) *Lower-tier subsidiary*. The facts are the same as in paragraph (i) of this *Example 4*, except that S has no income or loss for Year 2, but S's wholly owned subsidiary, T, has an $80 ordinary loss. Under paragraph (b)(2)(v) of this section, T's loss is subject to paragraph (b) of this section as if T's stock had been disposed of. To determine T's absorbed amount, and the effect of the absorption of its losses under § 1.1502-32 on S's basis in its T stock and P's basis in its S stock, the group's taxable income is computed without taking into account P's gain or loss from the sale of S's stock. Of the group's $160 CNOL for Year 2, $100 is carried back to Year 1 ($50 attributable to P and $50 attributable to T) and offsets $100 of CTI in that year. Accordingly, T's absorbed amount determined under paragraph (b)(2)(i) of this section is $50. Under paragraph (b)(2)(ii) of this section, S's basis in T's stock is reduced by $50. Under § 1.1502-32(a)(3)(iii), the $50 reduction to S's basis in T's stock tiers up and reduces P's basis in its 10 shares of S stock by $50. Consequently, P's basis in each of the 10 shares of S stock will be decreased by $5 from $40 to $35. On the sale of each of the 2 shares of S's stock, P recognizes a $50 gain ($85 - $35). Under the actual computation, the group has P's $80 ordinary loss and $50 of T's $80 ordinary loss (limited by its absorbed amount) available to offset P's $100 gain on the sale of S's stock. Under paragraph (e) of this section, P's gain is offset on a pro rata basis by approximately $62 ($100 x 80/($80 + $50)) of P's ordinary loss in Year 2, and approximately $38 ($100 x ($50/($80 + $50)) of T's ordinary loss in that year. P's remaining $18 of ordinary loss in Year 2 and $12 of T's ordinary loss equal to its remaining absorbed amount may be carried back to Year 1 to offset $30 of the $100 of CTI in that year. For Year 2, the P group has $30 remaining of its CNOL (all of which is attributable to T) which is carried to the P group's Year 3 consolidated return year.

Example 5. Alternative Computation. (i) *Facts*. At the beginning of Year 1, P has a $200 basis in S's stock. P sells all of its S stock for $100 at the close of Year 1. For Year 1, P has $10 capital gain on portfolio stock. In addition to S, P has two other subsidiaries, M1 and M2. M1 has capital gain of $50; M2 has a capital loss of $30, and S has a capital loss of $60.

(ii) *Determination of absorbed amount*. To determine S's absorbed amounts and the effect of the absorption of its loss under § 1.1502-32(b)(2) on P's basis in S's stock, the group's taxable income is computed without taking into account P's gain or loss from the disposition of S's stock. Under that computation, S's capital loss would offset $40 ($60 x $60/$90) of the group's $60 of capital gain. Accordingly, S's absorbed amount is $40.

(iii) *Basis reduction*. Under paragraph (b)(2)(ii) of this section, S's $40 absorbed amount reduces P's basis in S's stock by $40 from $200 to $160. On the sale of S's stock, P recognizes a capital loss of $60 ($100 - $160).

(iv) *Computation of CTI under generally applicable rules*. In the actual computation under paragraph (b)(2)(iii)(A) of this section, P is treated as having a $50 capital loss ($60 capital loss on the sale of S's stock plus $10 capital gain). Therefore, the only capital gain in the actual computation is M1's $50. There is a total of $120 of capital loss in the computation: S's $40 of capital loss (equal to its absorbed amount), as well as P's $50 and M2's $30 capital losses. M1's $50 of capital gain would be offset on a pro rata basis by approximately $16.50 of S's loss ($50 x $40/$120), approximately $21.00 ($50 x $50/$120) of P's $50 capital loss, and $12.50 ($50 x $30/$120) of M2's capital loss. Because less than all of S's absorbed amount of $40 would be used, the group's CTI is determined under the alternative computation of paragraph (b)(2)(iii)(B) of this section.

(v) *Alternative computation of CTI*. Under paragraph (b)(2)(iii)(B)(*1*) of this section, S's $40 capital loss (the amount and character of S's absorbed amount) first offsets $40 of the $60 of capital gain (determined without taking into account any gain or loss on P's sale of S stock and without regard to M2's capital loss of $30) generated by other members. Accordingly, $20 of capital gain (P's $10 capital gain determined without regard to its loss on S's stock plus M1's $50 capital gain minus S's $40 absorbed amount) remains. Because P has no net stock gain, paragraph (b)(2)(iii)(B)(*2*) of this section is inapplicable. Under paragraph (b)(2)(iii)(B)(*3*) of this section, $10 (the amount of P's capital loss on S's stock limited by the amount of its income included in the computation under paragraph (b)(2)(i) of this section) of P's capital loss offsets the group's $20 remaining capital gain. Under paragraph (b)(2)(iii)(B)(*4*) of this section, capital losses of members other than S offset the group's remaining $10 of capital gain on a pro rata basis. Therefore, the group will use $3.75 of M2's $30 capital loss ($10 x $30/$80) and $6.25 of P's $50 remaining capital loss ($10 x $50/$80). The group will have a $70 consolidated net capital loss carryover to Year 2 ($43.75 attributable to P and $26.25 attributable to M2). Paragraphs (b), (c), and (d)(6) of § 1.1502-36 will not cause P to adjust its basis in S's stock immediately before P's sale of the S stock. However, S's $20 unabsorbed capital loss that may be carried to its first separate return year may be reduced under the attribute reduction rule of § 1.1502-36(d)(2).

Example 6. Loss disposition. (i) *Facts*. For Year 1, the P group has a consolidated net capital loss of $100, all of which is attributable to S, and P and M have no income or loss. At the beginning of Year 2, P has a $300 basis in S's stock. P sells all of S's stock for $100 at the close of Year 2. For Year 2, P and S have no income or loss (determined without taking into account P's gain or loss from the disposition of S's stock) and the group has consolidated capital gain net income of $100 attributable solely to M.

(ii) *Determination of absorbed amount*. To determine S's absorbed amount and the effect of the absorption of its losses under §1.1502-32(b)(2) on P's basis in S's stock, the group's taxable income for Year 2 is computed without taking into account P's gain or loss from the disposition of S's stock. The $100 consolidated net capital loss carryover from Year 1 attributable to S offsets the group's $100 of consolidated capital gain net income in Year 2. Accordingly, S's absorbed amount determined under paragraph (b)(2)(i) of this section is $100.

(iii) *Loss absorption and basis reduction.* Under paragraph (b)(2)(ii) of this section, P's basis in S's stock is reduced from $300 to $200 immediately before the disposition. Consequently, P recognizes a $100 capital loss on the sale of S's stock. In an actual computation of CTI, P's $100 capital loss on S's stock in Year 2 would offset M's $100 capital gain in Year 2 before the consolidated capital loss carryover from Year 1 and, as a result, S's $100 absorbed amount would not be used. Because less than all of S's absorbed amount of $100 would be used, the group's CTI is determined under the alternative computation of paragraph (b)(2)(iii)(B) of this section.

(iv) *Alternative Computation of CTI.* Under paragraph (b)(2)(iii)(B)(*1*) of section, S's $100 consolidated net capital loss carryover from Year 1 first offsets M's $100 of capital gain in Year 2. Because P has no net stock gain to be added to the computation, the amount under paragraph (b)(2)(iii)(B)(2) of this section is zero. Because there is no remaining income to offset, paragraphs (b)(2)(iii)(B)(3) and (b)(2)(iii)(B)(4) of this section are inapplicable. Therefore, P's $100 loss on S's stock becomes a consolidated net capital loss carryover to the group's Year 3 consolidated return year.

Example 7. Netting of Disposing Member's Gains and Losses. (i) *Facts.* At the beginning of Year 1, P has a $120 basis in S's stock. P sells all of S's stock for $80 at the close of Year 1. In addition, P has $60 capital loss on the sale of portfolio stock. S has a capital loss of $180. M1 has a capital gain of $100 and M2 has a capital loss of $120.

(ii) *Determination of absorbed amount.* To determine S's absorbed amount and the effect of the absorption of its loss under §1.1502-32(b)(2) on P's basis in S's stock, the group's taxable income is computed without taking into account P's gain or loss from the disposition of S's stock. Under that computation, S's capital loss would offset $50 ($100 x $180/($180 + $120 + $60)) of M1's $100 capital gain. Accordingly, S's absorbed amount is $50.

(iii) *Basis reduction and computation of CTI under generally applicable rules.* Under paragraph (b)(2)(ii) of this section, P's basis in S's stock is reduced by $50 from $120 to $70 immediately before the sale. Consequently, P recognizes a $10 capital gain on the sale of S's stock. In an actual computation of CTI, P's $10 capital gain on the sale of S's stock would be offset by $10 of P's $60 capital loss. M1's $100 capital gain would be offset by $22.73 ($100 x $50/($50 + $120 + $50)) of P's $50 of net capital loss, $ 54.54 ($100 x $120/$220) of M2's $120 capital loss and $22.73 ($100 x $50/$220) of S's $50 capital loss. Because less than all of S's absorbed amount of $50 would be used, the group's CTI is determined under the alternative computation of paragraph (b)(2)(iii)(B) of this section.

(iv) *Alternative computation of CTI.* Under paragraph (b)(2)(iii)(B)(*1*) of this section, $50 of S's capital loss (the amount and character of S's absorbed amount) first offsets $50 of the $100 capital gain (determined without taking into account any gain or loss on P's sale of S stock and without regard to P's and M2's capital losses). Therefore, after the absorption of S's loss equal to its absorbed amount, there is $50 of remaining capital gain. P will have a $10 capital gain on the sale of S's stock, a $60 capital loss on portfolio stock, and M2 will have a $120 capital loss. Under paragraph (b)(2)(iii)(B)(2) of this section, $10 of P's $60 loss on portfolio stock offsets its $10 gain on S's stock before M2's $120 capital loss is taken into account. No member has a net loss on subsidiary stock, and therefore paragraph (b)(2)(iii)(B)(3) of this section does not apply. Under paragraph (b)(2)(iii)(B)(4) of this section, the remaining capital gain of $50 after the application of paragraph (b)(2)(iii)(B)(3) is offset pro rata by $14.70 ($50 x $50/($50 + $120)) of P's capital loss and $35.30 ($50 x $120/$170) of M2's capital loss. P's unused capital loss of $35.30 and M2's unused capital loss of $84.70 become a $120 consolidated net capital loss carryover to the group's Year 2 consolidated return year.

Example 8. Character of Absorbed Amount. (i) *Facts.* At the beginning of Year 1, P has a $550 basis in S's stock. P sells all of S's stock for $50 at the close of Year 1. In addition, P has a capital gain of $200 (without regard to gain or loss on the sale of S's stock). S has an ordinary loss of $50 and M has an ordinary loss of $25.

(ii) *Determination of absorbed amount.* To determine S's absorbed amount and the effect of the absorption of its losses under §1.1502-32(b)(2) on P's basis in S's stock, the group's taxable income is computed without taking into account P's gain or loss from the disposition of S's stock. Under that computation, S's $50 ordinary loss and M's $25 ordinary loss offset $75 of P's $200 capital gain. Accordingly, S's absorbed amount determined under paragraph (b)(2)(i) of this section is $50.

(iii) *Basis reduction and computation of CTI under generally applicable rules.* Under paragraph (b)(2)(ii) of this section, P's basis in S's stock is reduced by $50 from $550 to $500 immediately before the sale. Consequently, P recognizes a $450 capital loss on the sale of S's stock. In an actual computation of CTI, $200 of P's $450 capital loss on its sale of S's stock would offset its $200 capital gain and none of S's absorbed amount would be used. Because less than all of S's absorbed amount of $50 would be used, the group's CTI is determined under the alternative computation of paragraph (b)(2)(iii)(B) of this section.

(iv) *Alternative computation of CTI.* Under paragraph (b)(2)(iii)(B)(*1*) of this section, S's $50 ordinary loss first offsets $50 of P's $200 capital gain. Therefore, after the absorption of S's loss equal to its absorbed amount, the group will have $150 ($200 - $50) of remaining capital gain. Because P has no net stock gain to be added to the computation, paragraph (b)(2)(iii)(B)(2) of this section is inapplicable. Under paragraph (b)(2)(iii)(B)(3) of this section, $150 of P's $450 loss on S's stock (the lesser of P's $200 capital gain or the group's $150 remaining capital gain) offsets the group's remaining $150 of capital gain. Because there is no more income in the group for M's loss to offset, the amount under paragraph (b)(2)(iii)(B)(*4*) of this section is zero. Therefore, P's remaining unused capital loss on S's stock of $300 and M's $25 ordinary loss become carryovers to the group's Year 2 consolidated return year.

Example 9. Worthless Stock Loss. (i) *Facts.* At the beginning of Year 1, P has a $120 basis in S's stock. For Year 1, P has $100 of ordinary income (determined without taking into account P's gain or loss on the disposition of S's stock) and S generates an $80 ordinary loss. At the close of Year 1, S issues stock to its creditors in a bankruptcy proceeding, and P's stock in S is canceled. The aggregate of S's historic gross receipts meets the requirements of section 165(g)(3)(B), which allows P to claim an ordinary loss with respect to S's stock.

(ii) *Determination of absorbed amount.* To determine S's absorbed amount and the effect of the absorption under § 1.1502-32(b)(2) on P's basis in S's stock, the group's CTI is computed without taking into account P's gain or loss from the disposition of S's stock. Under that computation, S's $80 ordinary loss would offset $80 of P's $100 of ordinary income. Accordingly, S's absorbed amount under paragraph (b)(2)(i) of this section is $80.

(iii) *Basis reduction and computation of CTI under generally applicable rules.* Under paragraph (b)(2)(ii) of this section, S's $80 absorbed amount reduces P's basis in S's stock from $120 to $40. Therefore, P's worthless stock deduction with respect to S's stock is $40. In an actual computation of CTI, P's separate taxable income under § 1.1502-12 would be determined by offsetting P's $100 of ordinary income with its $40 worthless stock deduction with respect to S's stock, leaving $60 of ordinary income that would be offset by S's ordinary loss. However, that computation would result in the absorption of only $60 of S's losses. Because less than all of S's absorbed amount of $80 would be used, the group's CTI is determined under the alternative computation of paragraph (b)(2)(iii)(B) of this section.

(iv) *Alternative computation of CTI.* Under paragraph (b)(2)(iii)(B)(*1*) of this section, S's $80 ordinary loss first offsets $80 of P's $100 of ordinary income. Therefore, after the absorption of S's loss equal to its absorbed amount, the group will have $20 of remaining ordinary income. Because P has no net stock gain to be added to the computation, the amount under paragraph (b)(2)(iii)(B)(*2*) of this section is zero. Under paragraph (b)(2)(iii)(B)(*3*) of this section, the group uses $20 of P's $40 ordinary loss on S's stock to offset the remaining $20 income of the group. Because there remains no more income in the group, the amount under paragraph (b)(2)(iii)(B)(*4*) of this section is zero. P's remaining $20 ordinary loss becomes a CNOL carryover to the group's Year 2 consolidated return year.

Example 10. Charitable Contributions. (i) *Facts.* At the beginning of Year 1, P has a $1,000 basis in S's stock. P sells all of its S stock for $900 at the close of Year 1. For Year 1, P has $1,000 of ordinary income (determined without taking into account P's gain or loss on the disposition of S's stock). For Year 1, S makes a $100 charitable contribution and incurs $200 of ordinary and necessary business expenses that are deductible under section 162(a). In addition, P has a subsidiary M, which also makes a $100 charitable contribution.

(ii) *Determination of S's portion of consolidated charitable contributions deduction.* Under § 1.1502-24(a), a group's consolidated charitable contributions deduction is limited to ten percent of its adjusted consolidated taxable income as defined in § 1.1502-24(c). Under paragraph (b)(2)(iii)(D) of this section, S's portion of the group's consolidated charitable contributions deduction is determined by computing the group's taxable income without regard to P's gain or loss on S's stock. Thus, for purposes of determining the consolidated charitable contributions deduction for Year 1, the group's CTI would be $800 (P's $1,000 of income minus S's $200 of section 162 expenses). Accordingly, the consolidated charitable contributions deduction for Year 1 is limited to $80 ($800 x 10%), $40 attributable to S and $40 attributable to M. Accordingly, S's ordinary loss for Year 1 is $240 ($200 + $40).

(iii) *Determination of absorbed amount.* To determine S's absorbed amount and the effect of the absorption of its losses under § 1.1502-32(b)(2) on P's basis in S's stock, the group's CTI is computed without taking into account P's gain or loss from the disposition of S's stock. S's $240 ordinary loss offsets $240 of P's $1,000 of ordinary income. Accordingly, S's absorbed amount is $240.

(iv) *Loss absorption and basis reduction.* Under paragraph (b)(2)(ii) of this section, S's $240 absorbed amount reduces P's basis in S's stock from $1,000 to $760. On the sale of S's stock, P recognizes capital gain of $140 ($900 - $760). P's ordinary income is offset by $240 of S's ordinary loss and $40 of M's portion of the group's consolidated charitable contributions deduction, resulting in CTI of $860 ($1,000 + $140 - $280). Of the group's excess charitable contributions of $120, $60 will be apportioned to S and carried to its first separate return year. The remaining $60 of excess consolidated charitable contributions is the group's consolidated charitable contribution carryover under § 1.1502-24(b).

Example 11. Application of Unified Loss Rule. (i) *Facts.* In Year 1, P purchases the sole share of S's stock for $500. At the time of the purchase, S owns Land with a basis of $420. During Year 1, P incurs a $100 ordinary loss and S earns $100 in rental income, which increases P's basis in S's stock to $600. For Year 2, P has ordinary income of $30 (determined without taking into account P's gain or loss from the disposition of S's stock) and S incurs an ordinary loss of $80. At the close of Year 2, S has $20 of cash in addition to Land. In addition to S, P has another subsidiary M, which has an ordinary loss of $40 for Year 2. At the close of Year 2, when the value of Land has declined, P sells the sole share of S's stock for $480. No election is made under § 1.1502-36(d)(6) to reduce P's basis in S's stock or reattribute S's attributes to P.

(ii) *Determination of absorbed amount.* To determine S's absorbed amount and the effect of the absorption of its losses under § 1.1502-32(b)(2) on P's basis in S's stock, the group's CTI is computed without taking into account P's gain or loss from the disposition of S's stock. Under paragraph (e)(1) of this section, P's $30 of ordinary income would be offset by $10 ($30 x $40/$120) of M's ordinary loss for

Year 2 and $20 ($30 x $80/$120) of S's ordinary loss for Year 2. Accordingly, S's absorbed amount determined under paragraph (b)(2)(i) of this section is $20.

(iii) *Loss absorption and basis reduction.* Under paragraph (b)(2)(ii) of this section, S's $20 absorbed amount reduces P's basis in S's stock from $600 (P's $500 purchase price plus the $100 positive adjustment in Year 1) to $580. After taking into account the effects of all applicable rules of law, including paragraph (b)(2)(ii) of this section, P would recognize a $100 ($480 - $580) loss on the sale of S's stock. Thus, P's sale of the S share is a transfer of a loss share and therefore subject to § 1.1502-36. Under § 1.1502-36(b)(1)(ii), P's basis in its sole share of S's stock is not subject to redetermination. Under § 1.1502-36(c), P's basis in the S share ($580) is reduced, but not below value, by the lesser of the share's net positive adjustment and disconformity amount. The share's net positive adjustment is the greater of zero and the sum of all investment adjustments (as defined in § 1.1502-36(b)(1)(iii)) applied to the basis of the share. The net positive adjustment applied to the basis of the share is $80, S's $100 income for Year 1 and its $20 absorbed amount for Year 2. The share's disconformity amount is the excess, if any, of its basis ($580) over its allocable portion of S's net inside attribute amount. S's net inside attribute amount of $500 is the sum of S's $20 cash, S's basis in Land of $420, and S's $60 loss carryover ($80 - $20). Thus, the share's disconformity amount is $80 ($580 - $500). The lesser of the net positive adjustment ($80) and the share's disconformity amount ($80) is $80. Accordingly, under § 1.1502-36(c), P's basis in S's share is reduced by $80 from $580 to $500, and after taking into account the adjustments under paragraphs (b) and (c) of § 1.1502-36, the transferred S share is still a loss share ($480 sale price minus $500 basis).

(iv) *Computation of CTI.* In an actual computation of CTI, P's $30 of ordinary income would be offset on a pro rata basis by $20 ($30 x $40/$60) of M's ordinary loss and $10 ($30 x $20/$60) of S's ordinary loss. Because less than all of S's absorbed amount of $20 would be used, the group's CTI is determined under the alternative computation of paragraph (b)(2)(iii)(B) of this section. Under paragraph (b)(2)(iii)(B)(*1*) of this section, the computation of CTI is made by first computing the group's taxable income without taking into account P's loss on the disposition of S's stock and using only S's loss equal to its $20 absorbed amount. Accordingly, the group's $30 of ordinary income is reduced by $20 of S's ordinary loss, leaving $10 of remaining ordinary income. Because P has no net stock gain to be added to the computation, paragraph (b)(2)(iii)(B)(*2*) of this section is inapplicable. Under paragraph (b)(2)(iii)(B)(*3*) of this section, the group's remaining $10 of ordinary income is offset by a loss on the disposition of subsidiary stock, subject to applicable principles of the Code and regulations. The group's remaining $10 of income may not be offset by P's capital loss on the sale of S's stock, because P has no income of the same character on its loss on S's stock. Under paragraph (b)(2)(iii)(B)(*4*) of this section, the group's remaining $10 of ordinary income is offset by $10 of M's ordinary loss. M's $30 unabsorbed loss is carried over as a CNOL and P's remaining $20 capital loss from the sale of S's stock is carried over as a consolidated net capital loss to the group's Year 3 consolidated return year. S's $60 unused loss would be carried over to its separate return year subject to § 1.1502-36(d). Under § 1.1502-36(d)(2), S's attributes are reduced by S's attribute reduction amount. Under § 1.1502-36(d)(3), S's attribute reduction amount is the lesser of the net stock loss and S's aggregate inside loss. The net stock loss is $20, the excess of the $500 basis of the transferred share over the $480 value of the transferred share. S's aggregate inside loss is $20, the excess of its $500 net inside attribute amount over the $480 value of the S share. Therefore, the attribute reduction amount is $20, the lesser of the $20 net stock loss and the $20 aggregate inside loss. Accordingly, S's $20 attribute reduction amount is applied to reduce from $60 to $40 the amount of S's NOL carryover to its separate return year.

(v) *Election to reduce stock basis.* The facts are the same as in paragraph (i) of this *Example 11* except that P elects under § 1.1502-36(d)(6)(i)(B) to reattribute S's losses to the full extent of the attribute reduction amount ($20). Accordingly, P is treated as succeeding to $20 of S's losses as if acquired in a transaction described in section 381(a) (see § 1.1502-36(d)(6)(i)(B) and (iv)(A)) and, as a result, P's basis in the S share is reduced from $500 to $480. After giving effect to the election, P will have no loss on S's stock, the group will have a $50 CNOL carryover to Year 3 ($30 attributable to M and $20 attributable to P), and S will have a $40 NOL carryover to its separate return year.

(3) *Effective/applicability date.*—This paragraph (b) applies to dispositions of subsidiary stock occurring in consolidated return years beginning on or after the date these regulations are published as final regulations in the **Federal Register**.

(c) * * *

(2) * * *

(i) *Limitation on deductions and losses to offset income or gain.*—First, the determination of the extent to which S's deductions and losses for the consolidated return year of the disposition (and its deductions and losses carried over from prior years) may offset income and gain is made pursuant to paragraph (b)(2) of this section.

(ii) *Tentative adjustment of stock basis.*—Second, § 1.1502-32 is tentatively applied to adjust the basis of the S stock to reflect the amount of S's income and gain included, and S's absorbed amount of losses, in the computation of consolidated taxable income or loss for the year of disposition (and any prior years) that is made pursuant to paragraph (b)(2) of this section, but not to reflect the realization of excluded COD income and the reduction of attributes in respect thereof.

* * *

(4) *Definition of lower-tier corporation.*—For purposes of this paragraph (c), lower-tier corporation means a lower-tier subsidiary described in § 1.1502-36(f)(4).

* * *

(7) *Effective/applicability date.*—* * * However, paragraphs (c)(2) and (4) of this section apply to consolidated return years beginning on or after the date these regulations are published as final regulations in the **Federal Register**.

* * *

(e) *Absorption rule.*—(1) *Pro rata absorption of ordinary losses.*—If the group has a CNOL for a consolidated return year, the amount of each member's separate net operating loss, as defined in § 1.1502-21(b)(2)(iv)(B)(*1*), for the year that offsets the income or gain of other members is determined on a pro rata basis under the principles of § 1.1502-21(b)(2)(iv). For example, if, for the consolidated return year, P and S1 have a separate net operating loss of $60 and $30, respectively, and S2 (the only other member of the P group) has $21 of income, $14 of P's net operating loss and $7 of S1's net operating loss offset S2's $21 of income and are absorbed in the year.

(2) *Pro-rata absorption of capital losses.*—If the group has a consolidated net capital loss for a consolidated return year and any member has capital gain net income for the year (taking into account only its capital gains and losses), the amount of each member's capital loss (as defined in paragraph (b)(1) of this section) that offsets the sum of the capital gain net income of other members (computed separately for each member) is determined on a pro rata basis under the principles of § 1.1502-21(b)(2)(iv). For purposes of this paragraph (e)(2), the character of each member's gains and losses is first determined on a consolidated basis. See § § 1.1502-22 and 1.1502-23.

(3) *Effective/applicability date.*—This paragraph (e) applies to consolidated return years beginning on or after the date these regulations are published as final regulations in the **Federal Register.**

Par. 3. Section 1.1502-12 is amended by:

1. Revising paragraphs (b) and (e).
2. Removing and reserving paragraph (m).

The revisions read as follows:

§ 1.1502-12. Separate taxable income.

* * *

(b) Any deduction that is disallowed under § 1.1502-15 shall be taken into account as provided in that section;

* * *

(e) If a member disposes of a share of a subsidiary's stock, the member's deduction or loss (if any) on the stock that will be used in the consolidated return year of the disposition and as a carryback to prior years is computed in accordance with § 1.1502-11(b) or (c), as appropriate.

* * *

(m) [Reserved]

* * *

CFCs: Previously Taxed Earnings and Profits: Exclusion from Gross Income: Basis Adjustments

CFCs: Previously Taxed Earnings and Profits: Exclusion from Gross Income: Basis Adjustments.—Amendments to Reg. § 1.1502-12, providing guidance relating to the exclusion from gross income of previously taxed earnings and profits under Code Sec. 959 and related basis adjustments under Code Sec. 961, are proposed (published in the Federal Register on August 29, 2006) (REG-121509-00).

☐ Par. 10. Section 1.1502-12 as amended by adding paragraph (s) to read as follows:

§ 1.1502-12. Separate taxable income.

* * *

(s) The exclusion from gross income of previously taxed earnings and profits shall be determined by the rules of § 1.959-3(g).

Global Intangible Low-Taxed Income: Guidance

Global Intangible Low-Taxed Income: Guidance.—Amendments to Reg. § § 1.1502-12 and 1.1502-13, implementing section 951A of the Internal Revenue Code, which was enacted on December 22, 2017, are proposed (published in the Federal Register on October 10, 2018) (REG-104390-18).

Par. 11. Section 1.1502-12 is amended by adding paragraph (s) to read as follows:

§ 1.1502-12. Separate taxable income.

(s) See § 1.1502-51 for rules relating to the computation of a member's GILTI inclusion amount under section 951A and related basis adjustments.

* * *

Par. 12. Section 1.1502-13 is amended by adding paragraph (c) to *Example 4* in paragraph (f)(7).

The addition reads as follows:

§ 1.1502-13. Intercompany transactions.

* * *

(f) * * *

(7) * * *

Example 4. * * *

(c) *Application of § 1.1502-51(c)(5) to all cash intercompany reorganization under section 368(a)(1)(D).*—The facts are the same as in paragraph (a) of this *Example 4*, except that S's sole asset is stock of a controlled foreign corporation, within the meaning of section 957, with respect to which S has a net used tested loss amount (within the meaning of § 1.1502-51(e)(15)) of $15. As in paragraph (b) of this *Example 4*, S is treated as receiving additional B stock with a fair market value of $100 (in lieu of the $100) and, under section 358, a basis of $25 which S distributes to M in liquidation. Immediately after the sale, pursuant to § 1.1502-51(c)(5), the basis in the B stock received by M is reduced by $15 (the amount of the net used tested loss amount with respect to the controlled foreign corporation) to $10. Following the basis reduction pursuant to §1.1502-51(c)(5), the B stock (with the exception of the nominal share which is still held by M) received by M is treated as redeemed for $100, and the redemption is treated under section 302(d) as a distribution to which section 301 applies. M's basis of $10 in the B stock is reduced under §1.1502-32(b)(3)(v), resulting in an excess loss account of $90 in the nominal share. (See §1.302-2(c).) M's deemed distribution of the nominal share of B stock to P under §1.368-2(l) will result in M generating an intercompany gain under section 311(b) of $90, to be subsequently taken into account under the matching and acceleration rules.

* * *

Foreign-Derived Intangible Income: Global Intangible Low-Taxed Income: Deduction

Foreign-Derived Intangible Income: Global Intangible Low-Taxed Income: Deduction.—Amendments to Reg. §§1.1502-12 and 1.1502-13, providing guidance to determine the amount of the deduction for foreign-derived intangible income and global intangible low-taxed income, are proposed (published in the Federal Register on March 6, 2019) (REG-104464-18).

Par. 4. Section 1.1502-12, as proposed to be amended in 83 FR 51072 (Oct. 10, 2018), is further amended by adding paragraph (t) to read as follows:

§1.1502-12. Separate taxable income.

* * *

(t) See §1.1502-50 for rules relating to the computation of a member's deduction under section 250.

Par. 5. Section 1.1502-13, as proposed to be amended in 83 FR 67490 (Dec. 28, 2018), is further amended:

1. In paragraph (a)(6)(ii), under the heading "Matching rule. (§1.1502-13(c)(7)(ii))", by adding entry (T); and

2. Adding paragraph (c)(7)(ii)(T).

The additions read as follows:

§1.1502-13. Intercompany transactions.—(a) * * *

(6) * * *

(ii) * * *

Matching rule. (§1.1502-13(c)(7)(ii))

* * *

(T) Example 20. Redetermination of attributes for section 250 purposes.

* * *

(c) * * *

(7) * * *

(ii) * * *

(T) *Example 20: Redetermination of attributes for section 250 purposes*—*(1) Facts*. S manufactures equipment in the United States and recognizes $75 of gross income included in gross DEI (as defined in §1.250(b)-1(c)(14)) on the sale of Asset, which is not depreciable property, to B in Year 1 for $100. In Year 2, B sells Asset to X for $125 and recognizes $25 of gross income. The sale is a FDDEI sale (as defined in §1.250(b)-1(c)(8)), and thus the $25 of income is included in B's gross FDDEI (as defined in §1.250(b)-1(c)(15)) for Year 2.

(2) Timing and attributes. S's $75 of intercompany income is taken into account in Year 2 under the matching rule to reflect the $75 difference between B's $25 corresponding item taken into account (based on B's $100 cost basis in Asset) and the recomputed corresponding item (based on the $25 basis that B would have if S and B were divisions of a single corporation and B's basis were determined by reference to S's basis). In determining whether S's gross income included in gross DEI from the sale of Asset is included in gross FDDEI, S and B are treated as divisions of a single corporation. See paragraph (a)(6) of this section. In determining the amount of income included in gross DEI that is included in gross FDDEI, the attributes of S's intercompany item and B's corresponding item may be redetermined to the extent necessary to produce the same effect on consolidated taxable income (and consolidated tax liability) as if S and B were divisions of a single corporation. See paragraph (c)(1)(i) of this section. Applying section 250 and §1.1502-50 on a single entity basis, all $100 of income included in gross DEI would be gross FDDEI. On a separate entity basis, S would have $75 of gross income included in gross DEI that is included in gross non-FDDEI (as defined in §1.250(b)-1(c)(16)) and B would have $25 of gross income included in gross DEI that is included in gross FDDEI. Thus, on a separate entity basis, S and B would have, in the aggregate, $100 of gross income included in gross DEI, of which only $25 is included gross FDDEI. Accordingly, under single entity treatment, $75 that would be treated as gross income included in gross DEI that is included in gross non-FDDEI on a separate entity basis is redetermined to be included in gross FDDEI.

(3) Intercompany sale for loss. The facts are the same as in paragraph (c)(7)(ii)(T)*(1)* (the facts in *Example 20*), except that S recognizes $25 of loss on the sale of Asset. S's $25 of intercompany loss is taken into account under the matching rule to reflect the $25 difference between B's $25 corresponding item taken into account (based on B's $100 cost basis in Asset) and the recomputed corresponding item (based on the $125 basis that B would have if S and B were divisions of a single corporation and B's basis were determined by reference to S's $125 of costs). Applying section 250 and §1.1502-50 on a single entity basis, $0 of income would be included in gross DEI. In order to reflect this result, under the matching rule, S's $25 loss is allocated and apportioned solely to B's $25 of gross income from the sale of Asset for purposes of determining B's DEI and FDDEI. Furthermore, B's $25 of gross income is not taken into account for purposes of apportioning any other

deductions under section 861 and the regulations under that section for purposes of determining any member's DEI or FDDEI.

* * *

Consolidated Returns: Intercompany Obligations: Disallowance of Interest Expense Deductions

Consolidated Returns: Intercompany Obligations: Disallowance of Interest Expense Deductions.—Amendments to Reg. §1.1502-13, affecting corporations filing consolidated returns by providing special rules for the treatment of certain intercompany transactions involving interest on intercompany obligations, are proposed (published in the Federal Register on May 7, 2004) (REG-128590-03).

☐ Par. 3. Section 1.1502-13 is amended by:

1. Adding a sentence after the second sentence of paragraph (c)(6)(ii)(A).
2. Adding paragraph (c)(6)(iii).
3. Revising the first sentence of *Example 1*(d) of paragraph (g)(5).

The revisions and additions read as follows:

§1.1502-13. Intercompany transactions.

* * *

(c) * * *

(6) * * *

(ii) * * *

(A) * * * However, see §1.265-2(c) for special rules related to the application of paragraph (c)(6)(i) of this section to interest income with respect to certain intercompany obligations the interest deduction on which is disallowed under section 265(a)(2). * * *

* * *

(iii) *Effective date*.—The third sentence of paragraph (c)(6)(ii)(A) of this section shall apply to taxable years beginning on or after the date these regulations are published as final regulations in the Federal Register.

* * *

(g) * * *

(5) * * *

Example 1 * * *

(d) *Tax-exempt income*. The facts are the same as in paragraph (a) of this *Example 1*, except that B's borrowing from S is allocable under section 265 to B's purchase of state and local bonds to which section 103 applies and §1.265-2(c) does not apply. * * *

* * *

Partners and Partnerships: American Jobs Creation Act of 2004 and Taxpayer Relief Act of 1997: Guidance

Partners and Partnerships: American Jobs Creation Act of 2004 and Taxpayer Relief Act of 1997: Guidance.—Amendments to Reg. §1.1502-13, providing guidance on certain provisions of the American Jobs Creation Act of 2004, conforming the regulations to statutory changes in the Taxpayer Relief Act of 1997, modifying the basis allocation rules to prevent certain unintended consequences of the current basis allocation rules for substituted basis transactions and providing additional guidance on allocations resulting from revaluations of partnership property, are proposed (published in the Federal Register on January 16, 2014) (REG-144468-05).

☐ Par. 10. Section 1.1502-13 is amended by:

1. Amending paragraph (h)(2), *Example 4*, by removing "Five years" and adding in its place "Seven years".

§1.1502-13. Intercompany transactions.

Reporting Income and Deductions: Consolidated Group

Reporting Income and Deductions: Consolidated Group.—An amendment to Reg. §1.1502-13, revising the rules for reporting certain items of income and deduction that are reportable on the day a corporation joins or leaves a consolidated group, is proposed (published in the Federal Register on March 6, 2015) (REG-100400-14).

Par. 4. Section 1.1502-13 is amended by adding *Example 3(e)* to paragraph (c)(7)(ii) to read as follows:

§1.1502-13. Intercompany transactions.—

* * *

(c) * * *

(7) * * *

(ii) * * *

Example 3. * * *

(e) *Liability in excess of basis*. The facts are the same as in paragraph (a) of this *Example 3*, except that S and B are not members of the same consolidated group immediately before S's transfer of the land to B, and the land is encumbered with an $80 liability. Immediately after the transfer, S and B are members of the same consolidated group. Thus, the transfer is an intercompany transaction to which section 357(c) does not apply pursuant to §1.1502-80(d).

* * *

Deduction for Business Interest Expense: Limitation

Deduction for Business Interest Expense: Limitation.—Amendments to Reg. §1.1502-13, regarding the limitation on the deduction for business interest expense after the enactment of recent

tax legislation, are proposed (published in the Federal Register on December 28, 2018) (REG-106089-18).

Par. 17. Section 1.1502-13 is amended by—

1. In paragraph (a)(6)(ii)—

a. Under the heading "Matching rule. (§ 1.1502-13(c)(7)(ii))":

i. Designating *Examples* 1 through *17* as entries (A) through (Q).

ii. Adding entries (R) and (S).

b. Under the heading "Anti-avoidance rules. (§ 1.1502-13(h)(2))":

i. Designating *Examples 1* through *5* as entries (i) through (v).

ii. Adding an entry (vi).

2. In paragraph (c)(7)(ii):

a. Designating *Examples 1* through *17* as paragraphs (c)(7)(ii)(A) through (Q), respectively.

b. In newly designated paragraphs (c)(7)(ii)(A) through (Q):

i. Redesignating paragraphs (c)(7)(ii)(A)(a) through (i) as paragraphs (c)(7)(ii)(A)(*1*) through (*9*).

ii. Redesignating paragraphs (c)(7)(ii)(B)(a) and (b) as paragraphs (c)(7)(ii)(B)(*1*) and (*2*).

iii. Redesignating paragraphs (c)(7)(ii)(C)(a) through (d) as paragraphs (c)(7)(ii)(C)(*1*) through (*4*).

iv. Redesignating paragraphs (c)(7)(ii)(D)(a) through (e) as paragraphs (c)(7)(ii)(D)(*1*) through (*5*).

v. Redesignating paragraphs (c)(7)(ii)(E)(a) through (f) as paragraphs (c)(7)(ii)(E)(*1*) through (*6*).

vi. Redesignating paragraphs (c)(7)(ii)(F)(a) through (d) as paragraphs (c)(7)(ii)(F)(*1*) through (*4*).

v. Redesignating paragraphs (c)(7)(ii)(G)(a) through (d) as paragraphs (c)(7)(ii)(G)(*1*) through (*4*).

vi. Redesignating paragraphs (c)(7)(ii)(I)(a) through (e) as paragraphs (c)(7)(ii)(I)(*1*) through (*5*).

vii. Redesignating paragraphs (c)(7)(ii)(J)(a) through (d) as paragraphs (c)(7)(ii)(J)(*1*) through (*4*).

viii. Redesignating paragraphs (c)(7)(ii)(K)(a) through (d) as paragraphs (c)(7)(ii)(K)(*1*) through (*4*).

ix. Redesignating paragraphs (c)(7)(ii)(L)(a) and (b) as paragraphs (c)(7)(ii)(L)(*1*) and (*2*).

x. Redesignating paragraphs (c)(7)(ii)(N)(a) through (c) as paragraphs (c)(7)(ii)(N)(*1*) through (*3*).

xi. Redesignating paragraphs (c)(7)(ii)(O)(a) through (d) as paragraphs (c)(7)(ii)(O)(*1*) through (*4*).

xii. Redesignating paragraphs (c)(7)(ii)(P)(a) and (b) as paragraphs (c)(7)(ii)(P)(*1*) and (*2*).

xiii. Redesignating paragraphs (c)(7)(ii)(Q)(a) through (c) as paragraphs (c)(7)(Q)(*1*) through (*3*).

c. In the table below, for each newly redesignated paragraph listed in the "Paragraph" column, remove the text indicated in the "Remove" column and add in its place the text indicated in the "Add" column:

Paragraph	Remove	Add
(c)(7)(ii)(A)(*5*)	paragraph (a) of this *Example 1*	*Example 1* in paragraph (c)(7)(ii)(A)(*1*) of this section
(c)(7)(ii)(A)(*5*)	paragraphs (c) and (d) of this *Example 1*	*Example 1* in paragraphs (c)(7)(ii)(A)(*3*) and (*4*) of this section
(c)(7)(ii)(A)(*6*)	paragraph (a) of this *Example 1*	*Example 1* in paragraph (c)(7)(ii)(A)(*1*) of this section
(c)(7)(ii)(A)(*7*)	paragraph (a) of this *Example 1*	*Example 1* in paragraph (c)(7)(ii)(A)(*1*) of this section
(c)(7)(ii)(A)(*8*)	paragraph (a) of this *Example 1*	*Example 1* in paragraph (c)(7)(ii)(A)(*1*) of this section
(c)(7)(ii)(A)(*9*)	paragraph (a) of this *Example 1*	*Example 1* in paragraph (c)(7)(ii)(A)(*1*) of this section
(c)(7)(ii)(C)(*3*)	paragraph (a) of this *Example 3*	*Example 3* in paragraph (c)(7)(ii)(C)(*1*) of this section
(c)(7)(ii)(C)(*4*)	paragraph (c) of this *Example 3*	*Example 3* in paragraph (c)(7)(ii)(C)(*3*) of this section
(c)(7)(ii)(C)(*4*)	paragraph (b) of this *Example 3*	*Example 3* in paragraph (c)(7)(ii)(C)(*2*) of this section
(c)(7)(ii)(D)(*5*)	paragraph (a) of this *Example 4*	*Example 4* in paragraph (c)(7)(ii)(D)(*1*) of this section
(c)(7)(ii)(D)(*5*)	paragraphs (c) and (d) of this *Example 4*	*Example 4* in paragraphs (c)(7)(ii)(D)(*3*) and (*4*) of this section
(c)(7)(ii)(E)(*3*)	paragraph (a) of this *Example 5*	*Example 5* in paragraph (c)(7)(ii)(E)(*1*) of this section
(c)(7)(ii)(E)(*4*)	paragraph (a) of this *Example 5*	*Example 5* in paragraph (c)(7)(ii)(E)(*1*) of this section
(c)(7)(ii)(E)(*5*)	paragraph (a) of this *Example 5*	*Example 5* in paragraph (c)(7)(ii)(E)(*1*) of this section

Paragraph	Remove	Add
(c)(7)(ii)(E)(*6*)	paragraph (a) of this *Example 5*	*Example 5* in paragraph (c)(7)(ii)(E)(*1*) of this section
(c)(7)(ii)(F)(*3*)	paragraph (a) of this *Example 6*	*Example 6* in paragraph (c)(7)(ii)(F)(*1*) of this section
(c)(7)(ii)(F)(*4*)	paragraph (a) of this *Example 6*	*Example 6* in paragraph (c)(7)(ii)(F)(*1*) of this section
(c)(7)(ii)(G)(*4*)	paragraph (a) of this *Example 7*	*Example 7* in paragraph (c)(7)(ii)(G)(*1*) of this section
(c)(7)(ii)(G)(*4*)	paragraph (c) of this *Example 7*	*Example 7* in paragraph (c)(7)(ii)(G)(*3*) of this section
(c)(7)(ii)(I)(*3*)	paragraph (a) of this *Example 9*	*Example 9* in paragraph (c)(7)(ii)(I)(*1*) of this section
(c)(7)(ii)(I)(*4*)	paragraph (a) of this *Example 9*	*Example 9* in paragraph (c)(7)(ii)(I)(*1*) of this section
(c)(7)(ii)(I)(*5*)	paragraph (d) of this *Example 9*	*Example 9* in paragraph (c)(7)(ii)(I)(*4*) of this section
(c)(7)(ii)(J)(*3*)	paragraph (a) of this *Example 10*	*Example 10* in paragraph (c)(7)(ii)(J)(*1*) of this section
(c)(7)(ii)(J)(*4*)	paragraph (a) of this *Example 10*	*Example 10* in paragraph (c)(7)(ii)(J)(*1*) of this section
(c)(7)(ii)(K)(*4*)	paragraph (a) of this *Example 11*	*Example 11* in paragraph (c)(7)(ii)(K)(*1*) of this section
(c)(7)(ii)(N)(*2*)	paragraph (a) of this *Example 14*	*Example 14* in paragraph (c)(7)(ii)(N)(*1*) of this section
(c)(7)(ii)(O)(*4*)	paragraph (a) of this *Example 15*	*Example 15* in paragraph (c)(7)(ii)(O)(*1*) of this section
(c)(7)(ii)(Q)(*1*)	*Example 16*	*Example 16* in paragraph (c)(7)(ii)(P) of this section
(c)(7)(ii)(Q)(*2*)	paragraph (f)(7), *Example* 2 of this section	*Example 2* in paragraph (f)(7) of this section
(c)(7)(iii)(A)	Paragraphs (c)(6)(ii)(C), (c)(6)(ii)(D), and (c)(7)(ii), Examples 16 and 17 of this section	Paragraphs (c)(6)(ii)(C) and (D) of this section, *Example 16* in paragraph (c)(7)(ii)(P) of this section, and *Example 17* in paragraph (c)(7)(ii)(Q) of this section

d. Adding paragraphs (c)(7)(ii)(R) and (S).
3. In paragraph (h)(2):
a. Designating *Examples 1* through 5 as paragraphs (h)(2)(i) through (v), respectively.
b. In newly designated paragraphs (h)(2)(i) through (v):
i. Redesignating paragraphs (h)(2)(i)(a) and (b) as paragraphs (h)(2)(i)(A) and (B).
ii. Redesignating paragraphs (h)(2)(ii)(a) and (b) as paragraphs (h)(2)(ii)(A) and (B).
iii. Redesignating paragraphs (h)(2)(iii)(a) and (b) as paragraphs (h)(2)(iii)(A) and (B).
iv. Redesignating paragraphs (h)(2)(iv)(a) and (b) as paragraphs (h)(2)(iv)(A) and (B).
v. Redesiganting paragraphs (h)(2)(v)(a) and (b) as paragraphs (h)(2)(iv)(A) and (B).
c. Adding paragraph (h)(2)(vi).
The additions read as follows:

§1.1502-13. Intercompany transactions.—
(a) * * *

(6) * * *

(ii) * * *

Matching rule. (§1.1502-13(c)(7)(ii))

* * *

(R) Example 18. Transfer of partnership interests in an intercompany sale.

(S) Example 19. Intercompany transfer of partnership interests in a non-recognition transaction.

* * *

Anti-avoidance rules. (§1.1502-13(h)(2))

* * *

(vi) Example 6. Section 163 interest limitation.

* * *

(c) * * *

(7) * * *

(ii) * * *

(R) *Example 18: Transfer of partnership interests in an intercompany sale*—(*1*) *Facts*. P wholly owns S and B, both of which are members of the consolidated group of which P is the common parent. S and A (an unrelated third party) are equal partners in PS1, which was formed in Year 1. At the end of Year 1, the fair market value of PS1 is $200x, and S's adjusted basis in its partnership interest is $100x. During

Year 2, PS1 borrows money, pays $100x of business interest expense, and repays the debt. PS1's section 163(j) limitation is $0; thus, the $100x of Year 2 business interest expense is disallowed as a deduction to PS1, is characterized as excess business interest expense, and is allocated proportionally to PS1's partners. S reduces its basis in its PS1 interest under § 1.163(j)-6(h) to reflect the $50x of excess business interest expense allocated to S, but the reduction is not treated as a noncapital, nondeductible expense (see § 1.163(j)-4(d)(4)(ii)). On the last day of Year 2, S sells its PS1 partnership interest to B for $50x. S has not used any of the excess business interest expense allocated from PS1; thus, immediately before the sale, S's basis in its PS1 interest is increased by $50x (to $100x) under § 1.163(j)-6(h). This basis increase is not treated as tax-exempt income (see § 1.163(j)-4(d)(4)(ii)). During Year 3, PS1 earns $50x of income, all of which is reported to the partners as excess taxable income, and $25x of which is allocated to B. B's basis in its PS1 interest is increased accordingly. Additionally, during Year 3, B earns $25x of business interest income and has no business interest expense other than its allocation of business interest expense from PS1. At the close of business on the last day of Year 4, B sells its PS1 partnership interest to Z (an unrelated third party) for $85x. At the time of the sale, B's basis in its PS1 interest is $75x.

(2) *Definitions*. Under paragraph (b)(1) of this section, S's sale of its PS1 interest to B in Year 2 is an intercompany transaction, with S as the selling member and B as the buying member. S's $50x capital loss on the sale is an intercompany item within the meaning of paragraph (b)(2)(i) of this section. B's $25 of ordinary income in Year 3 and its $10x gain on the sale of the PS1 interest to Z in Year 4 are both corresponding items within the meaning of paragraph (b)(3)(i) of this section.

(3) *Timing and attributes*. S takes its $50x loss into account to reflect the difference in each consolidated return year between B's corresponding items taken into account for the year and the recomputed corresponding item for the year. If S and B were divisions of a single corporation and the intercompany sale were a transfer between divisions, the single entity would have had zero income inclusion in Year 3, as the $25x of excess taxable income attributable to the single entity's interest in PS1 would have allowed the single entity to use $25x of the excess business interest expense allocation from PS1 in Year 2. However, on a separate entity basis, B's corresponding item for Year 3 is $25x of ordinary income (the excess taxable income from PS1). As a result, under § 1.1502-13(c)(ii), S takes into account $25x of its loss in Year 3, the difference between the recomputed corresponding item and B's corresponding item in Year 3 ($0 - $25x = - $25x). Under paragraphs (c)(1)(i) and (c)(4)(i)(A) of this section, the $25x is redetermined to be ordinary. The remaining $25x of S's loss continues to be deferred. The recomputed corresponding item in Year 4 is a $15x capital loss ($85x of sales proceeds minus $100x basis (the original $100x basis, minus a $50 reduction in basis under § 1.163(j)-6(h), plus a $25x increase for its allocable share of PS1's income, plus a $25x increase under § 1.163(j)-6(h)). B's corresponding item is a $10x capital gain ($85x sales proceeds minus $75x basis). Accordingly, the remaining $25x of S's $50x Year 2 capital loss is taken into account in Year 4.

(S) *Example 19: Intercompany transfer of partnership interests in a nonrecognition transaction*—(1) *Facts*. P wholly owns B, which is a member of the consolidated group of which P is the common parent. P and A (an unrelated third party) are equal partners in PS1, which was formed in Year 1. At the end of Year 1, the fair market value of PS1 is $200x, and P's adjusted basis in its partnership interest is $100x. At the beginning of Year 2, PS1 borrows money and purchases inventory. During Year 2, PS1 pays $100x of business interest expense, sells inventory for $100x (net of cost of goods sold), and repays the debt in full. PS1's section 163(j) limitation for Year 2 is $30x (30 percent x $100x). Thus, $70x of PS1's Year 2 business interest expense is disallowed as a deduction to PS1, is characterized as excess business interest, and is allocated proportionally to PS1's partners. P reduces its basis in its PS1 interest under § 1.163(j)-6(h) to reflect the $35x of excess business interest allocated to P. P's basis in its PS1 interest also is increased to reflect the $35x of income allocated to P, leaving P with a basis in its PS1 interest of $100x at the end of Year 2. On the first day of Year 3, P contributes its PS1 partnership interest to B in exchange for B stock in a non-recognition exchange under section 351. At the time, P had not used any of the excess business interest expense allocated from PS1. During Year 4, B sells its PS1 partnership interest to Z (an unrelated third party) for $200x.

(2) *Analysis*. P's transfer of its interest in PS1 to B is an intercompany transaction. The transfer also is a disposition for purposes of § 1.163(j)-6(h). Therefore, immediately before the transfer, P increases its $100x basis in its PS1 interest by $35x (the amount of P's unused excess business interest expense). Under section 362, B receives a carryover basis of $135x in the PS1 interest. P has no intercompany item, but B's $65x of capital gain from its sale of the PS1 interest to Z is a corresponding item because the PS1 interest was acquired in an intercompany transaction. B takes the $65x of capital gain into account in Year 4.

* * *

(h) * * *

(2) * * *

(vi) *Example 6: Section163(j) interest limitation*—(A) *Facts*. S1 and S2 are members of a consolidated group of which P is the common parent. S1 is engaged in an excepted trade or business, and S2 is engaged in a non-excepted trade or business. If S1 were to lend funds directly to S2 in an intercompany transaction, under § 1.163(j)-10(a)(4)(i), the intercompany obligation of S2 would not be considered an asset of S1 for purposes of § 1.163(j)-10 (concerning allocations of interest and other taxable items between excepted and non-excepted trades or businesses for purposes of section 163(j)). With a principal purpose of avoiding treatment of a lending transaction between S1 and S2 as an intercompany transaction (and increasing the P group's basis in its assets allocable to excepted trades or businesses), S1 lends funds to X (an unrelated third party). X then on-lends funds to S2 on substantially similar terms.

(B) *Analysis.* A principal purpose of the steps undertaken was to avoid treatment of a lending transaction between S1 and S2 as an intercompany transaction. Therefore, under paragraph (h)(1) of this section, appropriate adjustments are made, and the X obligation in the hands of S1 is not treated as an asset of S1 for purposes of § 1.163(j)-10, to the extent of the loan from X to S2.

* * *

Consolidated Groups: Carryback of Consolidated NOLs: Separate Return Years

Consolidated Groups: Carryback of Consolidated NOLs: Separate Return Years.—Amendments to Reg. § 1.1502-21, permitting certain acquiring consolidated groups to elect to waive all or a portion of the pre-acquisition portion of the 5-year carryback period under Code Sec. 172(b)(1)(H) for certain losses attributable to certain acquired members, are proposed (published in the Federal Register on May 31, 2002) (REG-122564-02).

☐ Par. 2. Section 1.1502-21 is amended by adding paragraph (b)(3)(ii)(C) to read as follows:

§ 1.1502-21. Net operating losses.

[The text of proposed § 1.1502-21(b)(3)(ii)(C) is the same as the text of § 1.1502-21T(b)(3)(ii)(C) as added by T.D. 8997].

Consolidated Group: Extended Carryback of Losses

Consolidated Group: Extended Carryback of Losses.—Amendments to Reg. § 1.1502-21, providing guidance to consolidated groups that implements the revision to section 172(b)(1)(H), are proposed (published in the Federal Register on June 23, 2010) (REG-151605-09).

Par. 2. Section 1.1502-21 is revised to read as follows:

§ 1.1502-21. Net operating losses.—[The text of proposed § 1.1502-21 is the same as the text for § 1.1502-21T(a) through (h)(9)(i) as added by T.D. 9490].

Application of Section 172(h): Regulations: Consolidated Groups

Application of Section 172(h): Regulations: Consolidated Groups.—Amendments to Reg. § 1.1502-21, providing guidance regarding the treatment of corporate equity reduction transactions (CERTs), including the treatment of multiple step plans for the acquisition of stock and CERTs involving members of a consolidated group, are proposed (published in the Federal Register on September 17, 2012) (REG-140668-07).

☐ Par. 3. Section 1.1502-21 is amended by adding paragraphs (b)(2)(iv)(C) and (h)(1)(iv) and revising paragraphs (b)(3)(ii)(B) and (h)(5) to read as follows:

§ 1.1502-21. Net operating losses.

* * *

(b) * * *

(2) * * *

(iv) * * *

(C) *Apportionment of special status losses.*—*(1) In general.*—The amount of the group's CNOL that is determined to constitute a corporate equity reduction interest loss (CERIL) (as defined in section 172(h)(1) and § 1.172(h)-2(a)(2)), specified liability loss (as defined in section 172(f)(1)), or any other net operating loss (NOL) that is subject to special carryback or carryover rules (special status loss), is apportioned to each member separately from the remainder of the CNOL, based on the percentage of CNOL attributable to the member as determined under paragraph (b)(2)(iv)(B) of this section. This apportionment is made without regard to whether a particular member actually incurred specific expenses or engaged in specific activities required by the special status loss provisions. If a consolidated group must apply § 1.172(h)-3(d)(4) to allocate its CERIL for a loss limitation year between multiple corporate equity reduction transactions (CERTs), then the portion of the CERIL allocable to each CERT is treated as a separate CERIL for purposes of applying this paragraph (b)(2)(iv)(C) to apportion special status losses among members of the group.

(2) Example.—The following example illustrates the rules of this paragraph (b)(2)(iv)(C):

Example. (i) *Facts.* P is the parent of a group that includes S and that maintains a calendar taxable year. S has been a member of the group for all relevant years. In Year 3, the P group engages in a CERT. T is included in the P group beginning on January 1, Year 4, as a result of a transaction that does not constitute a CERT. In Year 4, the P group has a CNOL of $1,200. Under the CERT rules (in section 172(b)(1)(E) and (h), §§ 1.172(h)-1 through 1.172(h)-5, and § 1.1502-72), $300 of the CNOL (25%) constitutes a CERIL. Assume that, absent application of this paragraph (b)(2)(iv)(C), under paragraph (b)(2)(iv)(B) of this section, 2/3 of the CNOL ($800) is attributable to T and the remaining 1/3 of the CNOL ($400) is attributable to S.

(ii) *Analysis.* Under this paragraph (b)(2)(iv)(C), the CNOL is divided into its special status (CERIL) component, and its non-special status component. Because T has separate return year carryback years, each component of the CNOL (the non-special status CNOL and the CERIL) is apportioned under paragraph (b)(2)(iv)(B) of this section. Under that apportionment rule, 2/3 of each amount is apportioned to T, and the remainder of the CNOL is attributable to S and can be carried back to prior P group years, subject to any applicable limitations. Therefore, $200 of the $300 CERIL is apportioned to T, and $600 of the $900 non-special status CNOL is also apportioned to T. The $200 CERIL cannot be carried back to certain taxable years of T under the CERT rules. Likewise, $100 of the $300 CERIL is apportioned to S, and $300 of the $900 non-special status CNOL is also apportioned to S. Under the CERT rules, the $100 CERIL cannot be carried back to certain taxable years.

* * *

(3) * * *

(ii) * * *

(B) *Election on acquisition to waive carryback to separate return years.*—*(1) In general.*—A corporation may make one of three mutually exclusive, irrevocable elections to waive carryback of CNOLs to separate return years of acquired members. Any election that is made with regard to an acquired corporation that was a member of a consolidated group (the former group) immediately before becoming a member of an acquiring group must include all other corporations that were members of the former group and that joined the acquiring group during the same consolidated return year of the acquiring group.

(2) Annual election.—If a corporation becomes a member of an acquiring group, the acquiring group may make an irrevocable election to relinquish, with respect to the part of any CNOL attributable to the member, the portion of the carryback period for which the member filed a separate return. This is an annual election, applicable to the CNOL of a single year. The election is made in a separate statement entitled, "THIS IS AN ELECTION UNDER §1.1502-21(b)(3)(ii)(B)*(2)* TO WAIVE THE PRE- [insert the first taxable year in which the member(s) joined the group] CARRYBACK PERIOD FOR THE PORTION OF THE [insert taxable year] CNOL ATTRIBUTABLE TO [insert the name(s) and EIN(s) of the corporation(s)]." The statement must be filed with the acquiring group's timely filed original return for the consolidated return year of the particular CNOL.

(3) Single election.—If a corporation becomes a member of an acquiring group, the acquiring group may make an irrevocable election to relinquish, with respect to all CNOLs attributable to the member, the portion of the carryback period for which the member filed a separate return. The election is not an annual election and applies to all losses that would otherwise be subject to a carryback to separate return years under section 172 or paragraph (b) of this section. The election is made in a separate statement entitled, "THIS IS AN ELECTION UNDER §1.1502-21(b)(3)(ii)(B)*(3)* TO WAIVE THE PRE- [insert the first taxable year in which the member(s) joined the group] CARRYBACK PERIOD FOR THE PORTION FOR ALL NOLs (and ALL CNOLs) ATTRIBUTABLE TO [insert the name(s) and EIN of the corporation(s)]." The statement must be filed with the acquiring group's timely filed original income tax return for the consolidated return year the corporation (or corporations) became a member.

(4) Special one-time election for deconsolidating member.—Section 1.1502-72(e)(1) makes available an election by a deconsolidating member (or its new common parent immediately following deconsolidation) to relinquish in whole the carryback of all NOLs to taxable years of the former group and any preceding taxable year. An election under §1.1502-72(e)(1) will control whether the deconsolidating corporation is treated as an applicable corporation under section 172(b)(1)(E)(iii) and §1.172(h)-1(b)(1) following the deconsolidation with regard to a CERT of the former group. See §1.1502-72(b). Further, an election under §1.1502-72(e)(1) may affect the computation of the CERIL under section 172(h)(1) and §1.172(h)-2(a)(2) with regard to any CERT for which the deconsolidating corporation (or any group of which the deconsolidating corporation is a member) is an applicable corporation under section 172(b)(1)(E)(iii) and §1.172(h)-1(b)(1) following the deconsolidation. See §1.1502-72(c)(4) and (d)(3)(ii).

* * *

(h) * * *

(1) * * *

(iv) Paragraph (b)(2)(iv)(C) of this section applies to taxable years for which the due date of the original return (without extensions) is on or after the date of publication of the Treasury decision adopting these rules as final regulations in the **Federal Register**.

* * *

(5) *Waiver of carrybacks.*—Paragraph (b)(3)(ii)(B) of this section (relating to the waiver of carrybacks to separate return years) applies to acquisitions occurring on or after the date of publication of the Treasury decision adopting these rules as final regulations in the **Federal Register**, except that it does not apply to any acquisition occurring pursuant to a written agreement that is binding before the date of publication of the Treasury decision adopting these rules as final regulations in the **Federal Register**. For original consolidated Federal income tax returns due (without extensions) before the date of the publication of the Treasury decision adopting these rules as final regulations in the **Federal Register,** see paragraph (b)(3)(ii)(B) of this section as contained in 26 CFR part 1 in effect on April 1, 1999.

* * *

Deduction for Business Interest Expense: Limitation

Deduction for Business Interest Expense: Limitation.—Amendments to Reg. §1.1502-21, regarding the limitation on the deduction for business interest expense after the enactment of recent tax legislation, are proposed (published in the Federal Register on December 28, 2018) (REG-106089-18).

Par. 18. Section 1.1502-21 is amended by revising paragraph (d) to read as follows:

§1.1502-21. Net operating losses.

* * *

(d) *Cross-reference.*—For rules governing the application of a SRLY limitation to business interest expense for which a deduction is disallowed under section 163(j), see §1.163(j)-5(d) and (f).

* * *

Reporting Income and Deductions: Consolidated Group

Reporting Income and Deductions: Consolidated Group.—Amendments to Reg. §§1.1502-21, 1.1502-22 and 1.1502-28, revising the rules for reporting certain items of income and deduction that are reportable on the day a corporation joins or leaves a consolidated group, are proposed (published in the Federal Register on March 6, 2015) (REG-100400-14).

Par. 5. Section 1.1502-21 is amended by revising paragraph (b)(3)(iii) and adding paragraph (h)(1)(iv) to read as follows:

§1.1502-21. Net operating losses.

* * *

(b) * * *

(3) * * *

(iii) *Short years in connection with intercompany transactions to which section 381(a) applies.* If a member distributes or transfers assets in an intercompany transaction to which section 381(a) applies, see §1.1502-76(b)(2)(i).

* * *

(h) * * *

(1) * * *

(iv) Paragraph (b)(3)(iii) of this section applies to consolidated return years beginning on or after the date these regulations are published as final regulations in the **Federal Register**. For transactions occurring before the date these regulations are published as final regulations in the **Federal Register**, see §1.1502-21(b) as contained in 26 CFR part 1, revised as of April 1 preceding the date these regulations are published as final regulations in the **Federal Register**.

* * *

Par. 6. Section 1.1502-22 is amended by:

1. Revising paragraph (b)(4)(i).
2. Revising the heading of paragraph (h).
3. Adding paragraph (h)(1)(iii).

The revisions and addition read as follows:

§1.1502-22. Consolidated capital gain and loss.

* * *

(b) * * *

(4) *Special rules.—(i) Short years in connection with intercompany transactions to which section 381(a) applies.*—If a member distributes or transfers assets in an intercompany transaction to which section 381(a) applies, see §1.1502-76(b)(2)(i).

* * *

(h) *Effective/applicability date.*—(1) * * *

(iii) Paragraph (b)(4)(i) of this section applies to consolidated return years beginning on or after the date these regulations are published as final regulations in the **Federal Register**. For transactions occurring before the date these regulations are published as final regulations in the **Federal Register**, see §1.1502-22(b) as contained in 26 CFR part 1, revised as of April 1 preceding the date these regulations are published as final regulations in the **Federal Register**.

* * *

Par. 7. Section 1.1502-28 is amended in paragraph (b)(11) by removing "§1.1502-76(b)(1)(ii)(B)" and adding "§1.1502-76(b)(1)(ii)(A)(2)" in its place.

§1.1502-28. Consolidated section 108.

Elimination of Circular Adjustments to Basis: Absorption of Losses

Elimination of Circular Adjustments to Basis: Absorption of Losses.—Amendments to Reg. §§1.1502-21, 1.1502-21A, 1.1502-22, 1.1502-22A, 1.1502-23A and 1.1502-24, revising the rules concerning the use of a consolidated group's losses in a consolidated return year in which stock of a subsidiary is disposed of, are proposed (published in the Federal Register on June 11, 2015) (REG-101652-10).

Par. 4. Section 1.1502-21 is amended by:

1. Revising paragraph (b)(2)(iv)(B).
2. Adding paragraphs (b)(3)(vi) and (h)(1)(iv).

The revision and additions read as follows:

§1.1502-21. Net operating losses.

* * *

(b) ***

(2) ***

(iv) ***

(B) *Percentage of CNOL attributable to a member.—(1) In general.*—Except as provided in paragraph (b)(2)(iv)(B)(2) of this section, the percentage of the CNOL attributable to a member shall equal the separate net operating loss of the member for the consolidated return year divided by the sum of the separate net operating losses of all members having such losses for that year. For this purpose, the separate net operating loss of a member is determined by computing the CNOL by reference to only the member's items of income, gain, deduction, and loss (excluding capital gains and amounts treated as capital gains), including the member's losses and deductions actually absorbed by the group in the consolidated return year (whether or not absorbed by the member).

(2) *Recomputed percentage.*—If, for any reason, a member's portion of a CNOL is absorbed or reduced on a non pro rata basis (for example, under §§1.1502-11(b) or (c), 1.1502-28, 1.1502-36(d), or as the result of a carryback to a separate return year), the percentage of the CNOL attributable to each member is recomputed. In addition, if a member with a separate

net operating loss ceases to be a member, the percentage of the CNOL attributable to each remaining member is recomputed under paragraph (b)(2)(iv)(B)(*1*) of this section. The recomputed percentage of the CNOL attributable to each member shall equal the remaining CNOL attributable to the member at the time of the recomputation divided by the sum of the remaining CNOL attributable to all of the remaining members at the time of the recomputation.

(vi) *Amount of subsidiary's absorbed deductions and losses if subsidiary's stock is disposed of.*—For special rules regarding the amount of a subsidiary's deductions and losses that is absorbed if a member disposes of a share of the subsidiary's stock, see § 1.1502-11(b) and (c).

* * *

(h) * * *

(1) * * *

(iv) Paragraphs (b)(2)(iv)(B) and (b)(3)(vi) of this section apply to consolidated return years beginning on or after the date these regulations are published as final regulations in the **Federal Register**.

* * *

(3) * * *

Par. 5. Section 1.1502-21A is removed.

§ 1.1502-21A. Consolidated net operating loss deduction generally applicable for consolidated return years beginning before January 1, 1997.

Par. 6. Section 1.1502-22 is amended by:

1. Revising paragraphs (a)(2) and (3).
2. Adding paragraph (a)(4).

The revisions and addition read as follows:

§ 1.1502-22. Payment and returns of tax withheld by the acquiring agency.

* * *

(a) * * *

(2) The consolidated net section 1231 gain for the year (determined under § 1.1502-23);

(3) The net capital loss carryovers or carrybacks to the year; and

(4) Applying the ordering rules of § 1.1502-11(b) if stock of a subsidiary is disposed of.

* * *

Par. 7. Section 1.1502-22A is removed.

§ 1.1502-22A. Consolidated net capital gain or loss generally applicable for consolidated return years beginning before January 1, 1997.

Par. 8. Section 1.1502-23A is removed.

§ 1.1502-23A. Consolidated net section 1231 gain or loss generally applicable for consolidated return years beginning before January 1, 1997.

Par. 9. Section 1.1502-24 is amended by:

1. Removing the words "Five percent" in paragraph (a)(2) and adding "The percentage limitation on the total charitable contribution deduction provided in section 170(b)(2)(A)" in its place.

2. Removing "section 242," and § 1.1502-25," in paragraph (c).

§ 1.1502-24. Consolidated charitable contributions deductions.

CFCs: Previously Taxed Earnings and Profits: Exclusion from Gross Income: Basis Adjustments

CFCs: Previously Taxed Earnings and Profits: Exclusion from Gross Income: Basis Adjustments.—Amendments to Reg. § 1.1502-32, providing guidance relating to the exclusion from gross income of previously taxed earnings and profits under Code Sec. 959 and related basis adjustments under Code Sec. 961, are proposed (published in the Federal Register on August 29, 2006) (REG-121509-00).

☐ Par. 11. In section 1.1502-32, add a sentence after the second sentence in paragraph (b)(3)(ii)(D), add a sentence after the fourth sentence in paragraph (b)(3)(iii)(B) and add *Example 11* in paragraph (b)(5)(ii) to read as follows:

§ 1.1502-32. Investment adjustments.

* * *

(b) * * *

(3) * * *

(ii) * * *

(D) * * * Further, an increase to a member's previously taxed earnings and profits account under § 1.959-3(g)(1)(i)(B) that pursuant to section 961(a) and § 1.961-1(b) results in an increase to a member's basis in the stock in a CFC shall be treated as the receipt of tax exempt income. * * *

(iii) * * *

(B) * * * Also included as a noncapital, nondeductible expense is a decrease to a member's previously taxed earnings and profits account under § 1.959-3(g)(1)(i)(A) that results in a decrease to a member's basis in the stock in a CFC pursuant to section 961(b) and § 1.961-2(a). * * *

* * *

(5) * * *

(ii) * * *

Example 11. (a) *Facts.* P owns all of the stock of S and S1. S, a United States shareholder, owns 50 percent of the stock in FC, a CFC that uses the U.S. dollar as its functional currency. S1, a United States shareholder owns the remaining 50 percent of the stock in FC. Entering year 1, S has a previously taxed earnings and profits account with respect to its stock in FC consisting of $50x of section 959(c)(2) earnings and profits and S1 has a previously taxed earnings and profits account with respect to its stock in FC consisting of $200x of section 959(c)(2) earnings and profits. Entering year 1, FC has section 959(c)(2) earnings and profits of $250x and non-previously taxed earnings and profits of $100x. In year 1, FC generates no earnings and profits and makes a $100x distribution of earnings and profits on FC stock held by S and a $100x distribution of earnings and profits on the FC stock held by S1.

(b) *Analysis.* First, pursuant to § 1.959-3(e)(2)(ii), the section 959(c)(2) earnings and profits in S's previously taxed earnings and profits account with respect to its FC stock are decreased from $50x to $0 and the section 959(c)(2) earnings and profits in S1's previously taxed earnings and profits account with respect to its FC stock are decreased from $200x to $100x. Then, pursuant to § 1.959-2(e)(2)(v) and (g)(1)(i)(A), the section 959(c)(2) earnings and profits in S1's previously taxed earnings and profits account with respect to its FC stock are decreased from $100x to $50x and, pursuant to § 1.959-3(e)(2)(ii)(B) and (g)(1)(i)(B), the section 959(c)(2) earnings and profits in S's previously taxed earnings and profits account with respect to its FC stock are increased from $0 to $50x and then decreased from $50x to $0. Pursuant to § 1.959-1(c) of this section, the entire $100x distribution to S and $100x distribution to S1 are excluded from S's and S1's gross incomes. Pursuant to paragraph (b)(3)(ii)(D) of this section, the $50x increase to the section 959(c)(2) earnings and profits in S's previously taxed earnings and profits account with respect to its FC stock pursuant to § 1.959-3(g)(1)(i)(B) is treated as the receipt of $50x of tax-exempt income by S. Pursuant to paragraph (b)(2)(ii) of this section, P's basis in S's stock is increased by $50x. Pursuant to paragraph (b)(3)(iii)(B) of this section, the $50x decrease to the section 959(c)(2) earnings and profits in S1's previously taxed earnings and profits account with respect to its FC stock pursuant to § 1.959-3(g)(1)(i)(A) is treated as a noncapital nondeductible expense to S1. Pursuant to paragraph (b)(2)(iii) of this section, P's basis in S1's stock is decreased by $50x.

* * *

Global Intangible Low-Taxed Income: Guidance

Global Intangible Low-Taxed Income: Guidance.—Amendments to Reg. § 1.1502-32, implementing section 951A of the Internal Revenue Code, which was enacted on December 22, 2017, are proposed (published in the Federal Register on October 10, 2018) (REG-104390-18).

Par. 13. Section 1.1502-32 is amended by:

1. Adding paragraphs (b)(3)(ii)(E), (b)(3)(ii)(F), and (b)(3)(iii)(C).
2. Revising paragraph (j).

The revision and additions read as follows:

§ 1.1502-32. Investment adjustments.

* * *

(b) * * *

(3) * * *

(ii) * * *

(E) *Adjustment for the offset tested income amount of a controlled foreign corporation in relation to section 951A.*—S's tax-exempt income for a taxable year includes the aggregate of S's offset tested income amounts (within the meaning of § 1.1502-51(c)(3)) with respect to a controlled foreign corporation (within the meaning of section 957) for all of its U.S. shareholder inclusion years (within the meaning of § 1.951A-1(e)(4)), to the extent such aggregate does not exceed the excess (if any) of—

(1) The aggregate of S's used tested loss amounts (within the meaning of § 1.1502-51(c)(2)) with respect to the controlled foreign corporation for all of its U.S. shareholder inclusion years, over

(2) The aggregate of S's offset tested income amounts with respect to the controlled foreign corporation for all of its U.S. shareholder inclusion years previously treated as tax-exempt income pursuant to this paragraph.

(F) *Adjustment for the net offset tested income amount of a controlled foreign corporation in relation to section 951A.*—S will be treated as having tax-exempt income immediately prior to a transaction (*recognition event*) in which another member of the group recognizes income, gain, deduction, or loss with respect to a share of S's stock to the extent provided in this paragraph (b)(3)(ii)(F). S's tax-exempt income is equal to the portion of the allocable amount that would have been characterized as a dividend to which section 245A, but not section 1059, would have applied if the allocable amount had been distributed by a controlled foreign corporation to the owner of the transferred shares immediately before the recognition event. For purposes of this paragraph—

(1) The term *transferred shares* means the shares of a controlled foreign corporation that S owns within the meaning of section 958(a) or is considered to own by applying the rules of ownership of section 958(b) and that are indirectly transferred as part of the recognition event; and

(2) The term *allocable amount* means the net offset tested income amount (within the meaning of § 1.1502-51(e)(14)) allocable to the transferred shares.

(iii) * * *

(C) *Adjustment for the used tested loss amount of a controlled foreign corporation in relation to section 951A.*—S's noncapital, nondeductible expense includes its amount of used tested loss amount (within the meaning of § 1.1502-51(c)(2)) with respect to a controlled foreign corporation (within the meaning of section 957) for a U.S. shareholder inclusion year (within the meaning of § 1.951A-1(e)(4)).

* * *

(j) *Applicability date.*—(1) *In general.*—Paragraph (b)(4)(iv) of this section applies to any original consolidated Federal income tax return due (without extensions) after June 14, 2007. For original consolidated Federal income tax returns due (without extensions) after May 30, 2006, and on or before June 14, 2007, see § 1.1502-32T as contained in 26 CFR part 1 in effect on April 1, 2007. For original consolidated Federal income tax returns due (without extensions) on or before May 30, 2006, see § 1.1502-32 as contained in 26 CFR part 1 in effect on April 1, 2006.

(2) *Adjustment for the offset tested income amount, net offset tested income amount, and used tested loss amount of a controlled foreign corporation.*—Paragraphs (b)(3)(ii)(E), (b)(3)(ii)(F), and (b)(3)(iii)(C) of this section apply to any consolidated Federal income tax return for a taxable year in which or with which the taxable year of a controlled foreign corporation beginning after December 31, 2017, ends.

* * *

Consolidated Returns: AMT: General Computations

Consolidated Returns: Alternative Minimum Tax.—Amendments to Reg. § 1.1502-33, relating to the computation of the alternative minimum tax by consolidated groups, are proposed (published in the Federal Register on December 30, 1992).

☐ Par. 6. Proposed § 1.1502-33, published in the Federal Register on November 12, 1992 (57 FR 53634), is amended by adding the following sentence at the end of paragraph (d)(1)(i) to read as follows:

§ 1.1502-33. Earnings and profits.

* * *

(d) * * *

(1) * * *

(i) * * * *See* paragraphs (g), (h), and (j) of § 1.1552-1 for rules relating to the allocation of the consolidated AMT (as computed under § 1.1502-55), the consolidated environmental tax (defined in § 1.1552-1(h)), and the consolidated additional taxes (defined in § 1.1502-2(b)) among members of the group.

* * *

Deduction for Business Interest Expense: Limitation

Deduction for Business Interest Expense: Limitation.—Amendments to Reg. § 1.1502-36, regarding the limitation on the deduction for business interest expense after the enactment of recent tax legislation, are proposed (published in the Federal Register on December 28, 2018) (REG-106089-18).

Par. 19. Section 1.1502-36 is amended by:

1. Revising the second sentence of paragraph (f)(2);
2. Revising the paragraph (h) heading;
3. Designating the text of paragraph (h) as paragraph (h)(1) and adding a heading to newly designated paragraph (h)(1); and
4. Adding paragraph (h)(2).

The revisions and addition read as follows:

§ 1.1502-36. Unified loss rule.

* * *

(f) * * *

(2) * * * Such provisions include, for example, sections 163(j), 267(f), and 469, and § 1.1502-13. * * *

* * *

(h) *Applicability date.*—(1) *In general.*—* * *

(2) *Definition in paragraph (f)(2) of this section.*—Paragraph (f)(2) of this section applies to taxable years ending after the date of the Treasury decision adopting these regulations as final regulations is published in the **Federal Register**. For taxable years ending before the date of the Treasury decision adopting these regulations as final regulations is published in the **Federal Register**, see § 1.1502-36 as contained in 26 CFR part 1, revised April 1, 2018. However, taxpayers and their related parties, within the meaning of sections 267(b) and 707(b)(1), may apply the rules of this section to a taxable year beginning after December 31, 2017, so long as the taxpayers and their related parties consistently apply the rules of this section, the section 163(j) regulations (within the meaning of § 1.163(j)-1(b)(32)), and if applicable, §§ 1.263A-9, 1.381(c)(20)-1, 1.469-9, 1.882-5, 1.1502-13, 1.1502-21, 1.1502-79, 1.1502-91 through 1.1502-99 (to the extent they effectuate the rules of §§ 1.382-6 and 1.383-1), and 1.1504-4 to those taxable years.

Base Erosion and Anti-Abuse Tax: Guidance

Base Erosion and Anti-Abuse Tax: Guidance.—Amendments to Reg. § 1.1502-43, regarding the tax on base erosion payments of taxpayers with substantial gross receipts and reporting requirements thereunder, are proposed (published in the Federal Register on December 21, 2018) (REG-104259-18).

Par. 6. Section 1.1502-43 is amended by revising paragraph (b)(2)(i)(A) to read as follows:

§ 1.1502-43. Consolidated accumulated earnings tax.

* * *

(b) * * *

(2) * * *

(i) * * *

(A) The consolidated liability for tax determined without § 1.1502-2(a)(2) through (a)(4), and without the foreign tax credit provided by section 27, over

* * *

Base Erosion and Anti-Abuse Tax: Guidance

Base Erosion and Anti-Abuse Tax: Guidance.—Amendments to Reg. §1.1502-47, regarding the tax on base erosion payments of taxpayers with substantial gross receipts and reporting requirements thereunder, are proposed (published in the Federal Register on December 21, 2018) (REG-104259-18).

Par. 7. Section 1.1502-47 is amended by revising paragraph (f)(7)(iii) to read as follows.

§1.1502-47. Consolidated returns by life-nonlife groups.

* * *

(f) * * *

(7) * * *

(iii) Any taxes described in §1.1502-2 (other than by paragraphs (a)(1) and (d)(6) of that section).

* * *

Foreign-Derived Intangible Income: Global Intangible Low-Taxed Income: Deduction

Foreign-Derived Intangible Income: Global Intangible Low-Taxed Income: Deduction.—Reg. §1.1502-50, providing guidance to determine the amount of the deduction for foreign-derived intangible income and global intangible low-taxed income, is proposed (published in the Federal Register on March 6, 2019) (REG-104464-18).

Par. 6. Section 1.1502-50 is added to read as follows:

§1.1502-50. Consolidated section 250.—(a) *In general.*—(1) *Scope.*—This section provides rules for applying section 250 and the regulations thereunder (the *section 250 regulations*, see §§1.250(a)-1 through 1.250(b)-6) to a member of a consolidated group (*member*). Paragraph (b) of this section provides rules for the determination of the amount of the deduction allowed to a member under section 250(a)(1). Paragraph (c) of this section provides rules governing the impact of intercompany transactions on the determination of a member's qualified business asset investment and the effect of intercompany transactions on the determination of a member's foreign-derived deduction eligible income. Paragraph (d) of this section provides rules governing basis adjustments to member stock resulting from the application of paragraph (b)(1) of this section. Paragraph (e) of this section provides definitions. Paragraph (f) of this section provides examples illustrating the rules of this section. Paragraph (g) of this section provides an applicability date.

(2) *Overview.*—The rules of this section ensure that the aggregate amount of deductions allowed under section 250 to members appropriately reflects the income, expenses, gains, losses, and property of all members. Paragraph (b) of this section allocates the consolidated group's overall deduction amount under section 250 to each member on the basis of its contribution to the consolidated foreign-derived deduction eligible income and consolidated global intangible low-taxed income. The definitions in paragraph (e) of this section provide for the aggregation of the deduction eligible income, foreign-derived deduction eligible income, deemed tangible income return, and global intangible low-taxed income of all members in order to calculate the consolidated group's overall deduction amount under section 250.

(b) *Allowance of deduction.*—(1) *In general.*—A member is allowed a deduction for a consolidated return year under section 250. See §1.250(a)-1(b). The amount of the deduction is equal to the sum of—

(i) The product of the consolidated FDII deduction amount and the member's FDII deduction allocation ratio; and

(ii) The product of the consolidated GILTI deduction amount and the member's GILTI deduction allocation ratio.

(2) *Consolidated taxable income limitation.*—For purposes of applying the limitation described in §1.250(a)-1(b)(2) to the determination of the consolidated FDII deduction amount and the consolidated GILTI deduction amount of a consolidated group for a consolidated return year—

(i) The consolidated foreign-derived intangible income (if any) is reduced (but not below zero) by an amount which bears the same ratio to the consolidated section 250(a)(2) amount that such consolidated foreign-derived intangible income bears to the sum of the consolidated foreign-derived intangible income and the consolidated global intangible low-taxed income; and

(ii) The consolidated global intangible low-taxed income (if any) is reduced (but not below zero) by the excess of the consolidated section 250(a)(2) amount over the reduction described in paragraph (b)(2)(i) of this section.

(c) *Impact of intercompany transactions.*—(1) *Impact on qualified business asset investment determination.*—For purposes of determining a member's qualified business asset investment, the basis of specified tangible property does not include an amount equal to any gain or loss realized with respect to such property by another member in an intercompany transaction (as defined in §1.1502-13(b)(1)), whether or not such gain or loss is deferred. Thus, for example, if a selling member owns specified tangible property with an adjusted basis (within the meaning of section 1011) of $60x and an adjusted basis (for purposes of calculating qualified business asset investment) of $80x, and sells it for $50x to the purchasing member, the basis of such property for purposes of computing the purchasing member's qualified business asset investment is $80x.

(2) *Impact on foreign-derived deduction eligible income characterization.*—For purposes of redetermining attributes of members from an intercompany transaction as foreign-derived deduction eligible income, see § 1.1502-13(c)(1)(i) and (c)(7)(ii)(T), *Example 20.*

(d) *Adjustments to the basis of a member.*—For adjustments to the basis of a member related to paragraph (b)(1) of this section, see § 1.1502-32(b)(3)(ii)(B).

(e) *Definitions.*—The following definitions apply for purposes of this section.

(1) *Consolidated deduction eligible income.*—With respect to a consolidated group for a consolidated return year, the term *consolidated deduction eligible income* means the greater of the sum of the deduction eligible income (whether positive or negative) of all members or zero.

(2) *Consolidated deemed intangible income.*—With respect to a consolidated group for a consolidated return year, the term *consolidated deemed intangible income* means the excess (if any) of the consolidated deduction eligible income, over the consolidated deemed tangible income return.

(3) *Consolidated deemed tangible income return.*—With respect to a consolidated group for a consolidated return year, the term *consolidated deemed tangible income return* means the sum of the deemed tangible income return of all members.

(4) *Consolidated FDII deduction amount.*—With respect to a consolidated group for a consolidated return year, the term *consolidated FDII deduction amount* means the product of the FDII deduction rate and the consolidated foreign-derived intangible income, as adjusted by paragraph (b)(2) of this section.

(5) *Consolidated foreign-derived deduction eligible income.*—With respect to a consolidated group for a consolidated return year, the term *consolidated foreign-derived deduction eligible income* means the greater of the sum of the foreign-derived deduction eligible income (whether positive or negative) of all members or zero.

(6) *Consolidated foreign-derived intangible income.*—With respect to a consolidated group for a consolidated return year, the term *consolidated foreign-derived intangible income* means, except as provided in paragraph (e) of this section, the product of the consolidated deemed intangible income and the consolidated foreign-derived ratio.

(7) *Consolidated foreign-derived ratio.*—With respect to a consolidated group for a consolidated return year, the term *consolidated foreign-derived ratio* means the ratio (not to exceed one) of—

(i) The consolidated foreign-derived deduction eligible income; to

(ii) The consolidated deduction eligible income.

(8) *Consolidated GILTI deduction amount.*—With respect to a consolidated group for a consolidated return year, the term *consolidated GILTI deduction amount* means the product of the GILTI deduction rate and the sum of the consolidated global intangible low-taxed income, as adjusted by paragraph (b)(2) of this section, and the amounts treated as dividends received by the members under section 78 which are attributable to their global intangible low-taxed income for the consolidated return year.

(9) *Consolidated global intangible low-taxed income.*—With respect to a consolidated group for a consolidated return year, the term *consolidated global intangible low-taxed income* means the sum of the global intangible low-taxed income of all members.

(10) *Consolidated section 250(a)(2) amount.*—With respect to a consolidated group for a consolidated return year, the term *consolidated section 250(a)(2) amount* means the excess (if any) of the sum of the consolidated foreign-derived intangible income and the consolidated global intangible low-taxed income (determined without regard to section 250(a)(2) and paragraph (b)(2) of this section), over the consolidated taxable income of the consolidated group (within the meaning of § 1.1502-11) determined with regard to all items of income, deductions, or loss, except for the deduction allowed under section 250 and this section. Therefore, for example, consolidated taxable income under this paragraph (f)(10) is determined taking into account the application of sections 163(j) and 172(a).

(11) *Deduction eligible income.*—With respect to a member for a consolidated return year, the term *deduction eligible income* means the member's gross DEI for the year (within the meaning of § 1.250(b)-1(c)(14)) reduced (including below zero) by the deductions properly allocable to gross DEI for the year (as determined under § 1.250(b)-1(d)(2)).

(12) *Deemed tangible income return.*—With respect to a member for a consolidated return year, the term *deemed tangible income return* means an amount equal to 10 percent of the member's qualified business asset investment, as adjusted by paragraph (c)(1) of this section.

(13) *FDII deduction allocation ratio.*—With respect to a member for a consolidated return year, the term *FDII deduction allocation ratio* means the ratio of—

(i) The member's positive foreign-derived deduction eligible income (if any); to

(ii) The sum of the positive foreign-derived deduction eligible income of all members.

(14) *FDII deduction rate.*—The term *FDII deduction rate* means 37.5 percent for consolidated return years beginning before January 1, 2026, and 21.875 percent for consolidated return years beginning after December 31, 2025.

(15) *Foreign-derived deduction eligible income.*—With respect to a member for a consolidated return year, the term *foreign-derived deduction eligible income* means the member's gross FDDEI for the year (within the meaning of § 1.250(b)-1(c)(15)) reduced (including below zero) by the deductions properly allocable to gross FDDEI for the year (as determined under § 1.250(b)-1(d)(2)).

(16) *GILTI deduction allocation ratio.*—With respect to a member for a consolidated return year, the term *GILTI deduction allocation ratio* means the ratio of—

(i) The sum of the member's global intangible low-taxed income and the amount treated as a dividend received by the member under section 78 which is attributable to its global intangible low-taxed income for the consolidated return year; to

(ii) The sum of consolidated global intangible low-taxed income and the amounts treated as dividends received by the members under section 78 which are attributable to their global intangible low-taxed income for the consolidated return year.

(17) *GILTI deduction rate.*—The term *GILTI deduction rate* means 50 percent for consolidated return years beginning before January 1, 2026, and 37.5 percent for consolidated return years beginning after December 31, 2025.

(18) *Global intangible low-taxed income.*—With respect to a member for a consolidated return year, the term *global intangible low-taxed income* means the sum of the member's GILTI inclusion amount under § 1.1502-51(b) and the member's distributive share of any domestic partnership's GILTI inclusion amount under § 1.951A-5(b)(2).

(19) *Qualified business asset investment.*—The term *qualified business asset investment* has the meaning provided in § 1.250(b)-2(b).

(20) *Specified tangible property.*—The term *specified tangible property* has the meaning provided in § 1.250(b)-2(c)(1).

(f) *Examples.*—The following examples illustrate the rules of this section.

(1) *Example 1: Calculation of deduction attributable to foreign-derived intangible income—(i) Facts.* P is the common parent of the P group and owns all of the only class of stock of subsidiaries USS1 and USS2. The consolidated return year of all persons is the calendar year. In 2018, P has deduction eligible income of $400x, foreign-derived deduction eligible income of $0, and qualified business asset investment of $0; USS1 has deduction eligible income of $200x, foreign-derived deduction eligible income of $200x, and qualified business asset investment of $600x; and USS2 has deduction eligible income of -$100x, foreign-derived deduction eligible income of $100x, and qualified business asset investment of $400x. The P group has consolidated taxable income that is sufficient to make inapplicable the limitation in paragraph (b)(2) of this section. No member of the P group has global intangible low-taxed income.

(ii) *Analysis.* (A) *Consolidated deduction eligible income.* Under paragraph (e)(1) of this section, the P group's consolidated deduction eligible income is $500x, the greater of the sum of the deduction eligible income (whether positive or negative) of all members ($400x + $200x - $100x) or zero.

(B) *Consolidated foreign-derived deduction eligible income.* Under paragraph (e)(5) of this section, the P group's consolidated foreign-derived deduction eligible income is $300x, the greater of the sum of the foreign-derived deduction eligible income (whether positive or negative) of all members ($0 + $200x + $100x) or zero.

(C) *Consolidated deemed tangible income return.* Under paragraph (e)(12) of this section, a member's deemed tangible income return is 10% of its qualified business asset investment. Therefore, P's deemed tangible income return is $0 (0.10 x $0), USS1's deemed tangible income return is $60x (0.10 x $600x), and USS2's deemed tangible income return is $40x (0.10 x $400x). Under paragraph (e)(3) of this section, the P group's consolidated deemed tangible income return is $100x, the sum of the deemed tangible income return of all members ($0 + $60x + $40x).

(D) *Consolidated deemed intangible income.* Under paragraph (e)(2) of this section, the P group's consolidated deemed intangible income is $400x, the excess of its consolidated deduction eligible income over its consolidated deemed tangible income return ($500x - $100x).

(E) *Consolidated foreign-derived intangible income.* Under paragraph (e)(7) of this section, the P group's consolidated foreign-derived ratio is 0.60, the ratio of its consolidated foreign-derived deduction eligible income to its consolidated deduction eligible income ($300x / $500x). Under paragraph (e)(6) of this section, the P group's consolidated foreign-derived intangible income is $240x, the product of its consolidated deemed intangible income and its consolidated foreign-derived ratio ($400x x 0.60).

(F) *Consolidated FDII deduction amount.* Under paragraph (e)(4) of this section, the P group's consolidated FDII deduction amount is $90x, the product of the FDII deduction rate and the consolidated foreign-derived intangible income (0.375 x $240x).

(G) *Member's deduction attributable to consolidated FDII deduction amount.* Under paragraph (b)(1) of this section, a member is allowed a deduction equal, in part, to the product of the consolidated FDII deduction amount of the consolidated group to which the member belongs and the member's FDII deduction allocation ratio. Under paragraph (e)(13) of this section, a member's FDII deduction allocation ratio is the ratio of its positive foreign-derived deduction eligible income to the sum of each member's positive foreign-derived deduction eligible income for such consolidated return year. As a result, the FDII deduction allocation ratios of P, USS1, and USS2 are 0 ($0 / $300x), 2/3 ($200x / $300x), and 1/3 ($100x / $300x), respectively. Therefore, P, USS1, and USS2 are permitted deductions under paragraph (b)(1) of this section in the amount of $0 (0 x $90x), $60x (2/3 x $90x), and $30x (1/3 x $90x), respectively.

(2) *Example 2: Limitation on consolidated foreign-derived deduction eligible income—(i) Facts.* The facts are the same as in paragraph (f)(1)(i) of this section (the facts in *Example 1*), except that P's foreign-derived deduction eligible income is $300x.

(ii) *Analysis.* (A) *Consolidated deduction eligible income and consolidated deemed tangible income return.* As in paragraphs (f)(1)(ii)(A) and (C) of this section (the analysis in *Example 1*), the P group's consolidated deduction eligible income is $500x and the P group's consolidated deemed tangible income return is $100x.

(B) *Consolidated foreign-derived deduction eligible income.* Under paragraph (e)(5) of this section, the P group's consolidated foreign-derived deduction eligible income is $600x, the greater of the sum of the foreign-derived deduction eligible income (whether positive or negative) of all members ($300x + $200x + $100x) or zero.

(C) *Consolidated deemed intangible income and consolidated foreign-derived intangible income.* Under paragraph (e)(2) of this section, the P group's consolidated deemed intangible income is $400x ($500x - $100x). Under paragraph (e)(7) of this section, the P group's consolidated foreign-derived ratio is 1.00 ($600x / $500x, but not in excess of one). Under paragraph (e)(6) of this section, the P group's consolidated foreign-derived intangible income is $400x ($400x x 1.00).

(D) *Consolidated FDII deduction amount and member's deduction attributable to consolidated FDII deduction amount.* Under paragraph (e)(4) of this section, the P group's consolidated FDII deduction amount is $150x (0.375 x $400x). Under paragraph (e)(13) of this section, the FDII deduction allocation ratios of P, USS1, and USS2 are 1/2 ($300 / $600x), 1/3 ($200x / $600x), and 1/6 ($100x / $600x), respectively. Therefore, P, USS1, and USS2 are permitted deductions under paragraph (b)(1) of this section in the amounts of $75x (1/2 x $150x), $50x (1/3 x $150x), and $25x (1/6 x $150x), respectively.

(3) *Example 3: Member with negative foreign-derived deduction eligible income*—(i) *Facts.* The facts are the same as in paragraph (f)(1)(i) of this section (the facts in *Example 1*), except that P's foreign-derived deduction eligible income is -$100x.

(ii) *Analysis.* (A) *Consolidated deduction eligible income and consolidated deemed tangible income return.* As in paragraphs (f)(1)(ii)(A) and (C) of this section (the facts in *Example 1*), the P group's consolidated deduction eligible income is $500x and the P group's consolidated deemed tangible income return is $100x.

(B) *Consolidated foreign-derived deduction eligible income.* Under paragraph (e)(5) of this section, the P group's consolidated foreign-derived deduction eligible income is $200x, the greater of the sum of the foreign-derived deduction eligible income (whether positive or negative) of all members (-$100x + $200x + $100x) or zero.

(C) *Consolidated deemed intangible income and consolidated foreign-derived intangible income.* Under paragraphs (e)(2) and (6) of this section, the P group's consolidated deemed intangible income is $400x ($500x - $100x), and the P group's consolidated foreign-derived intangible income is $160x ($400x x ($200x / $500x)).

(D) *Consolidated FDII deduction amount and member's deduction attributable to consolidated FDII deduction amount.* Under paragraph (e)(4) of this section, the P group's consolidated FDII deduction amount is $60x (0.375 x $160x). Under paragraph (e)(13) of this section, the FDII deduction allocation ratios of P, USS1, and USS2 are 0 ($0 / $300x), 2/3 ($200x / $300x), and 1/3 ($100x / $300x), respectively. Therefore, P, USS1, and USS2 are permitted deductions under paragraph (b)(1) of this section in the amounts of $0 (0 x $60x), $40x (2/3 x $60x), and $20x (1/3 x $60x), respectively.

(4) *Example 4: Calculation of deduction attributable to global intangible low-taxed income*—(i) *Facts.* The facts are the same as in paragraph (f)(1)(i) of this section (the facts in *Example 1*), except that USS1 owns CFC1 and USS2 owns CFC2. USS1 and USS2 have global intangible low-taxed income of $65x and $20x, respectively, and amounts treated as dividends received under section 78 attributable to their global intangible low-taxed income of $10x and $5x, respectively.

(ii) *Analysis.* (A) *Consolidated global intangible low-taxed income.* Under paragraph (e)(9) of this section, the P group's consolidated global intangible low-taxed income is $85x, the sum of the global intangible low-taxed income of all members ($0 + $65x + $20x).

(B) *Consolidated GILTI deduction amount.* Under paragraph (e)(8) of this section, the P group's consolidated GILTI deduction amount is $50x, the product of the GILTI deduction rate and the sum of its consolidated global intangible low-taxed income and the amounts treated as dividends received by the members under section 78 which are attributable to their global intangible low-taxed income for the consolidated return year (0.50 x ($85x + $10x + $5x)).

(C) *Member's deduction attributable to consolidated GILTI deduction amount.* Under paragraph (b)(1) of this section, a member is allowed a deduction equal, in part, to the product of the consolidated GILTI deduction amount of the consolidated group to which the member belongs and the member's GILTI deduction allocation ratio. Under paragraph (e)(16) of this section, a member's GILTI deduction allocation ratio is the ratio of the sum of its global intangible low-taxed income and the amount treated as a dividend received by the member under section 78 which is attributable to its global intangible low-taxed income for the consolidated return year to the sum of the consolidated global intangible low-taxed income and the amounts treated as dividends received by the members under section 78 which are attributable to their global intangible low-taxed income for the consolidated return year. As a result, the GILTI deduction allocation ratios of P, USS1, and USS2 are 0 ($0 / ($85x + $10x + $5x)), 3/4 (($65x + $10x) / ($85x + $10x + $5x)), and 1/4 (($20x + $5x) / ($85x + $10x + $5x)), respectively. Therefore, P, USS1, and USS2 are permitted deductions of $0 (0 x $50x), $37.50x (3/4 x $50x), and $12.50x (1/4 x $50x), respectively.

(D) *Member's deduction under section 250.* Under paragraph (b)(1) of this section, a member is allowed a deduction equal to the sum of the member's deduction attributable to the consolidated FDII deduction amount and the member's deduction attributable to the consolidated GILTI deduction amount. As a result P, USS1, and USS2 are entitled to deductions under paragraph (b)(1) of this section of $0 ($0 + $0), $97.50x ($60x + $37.50x), and $42.50x ($30x + $12.50x), respectively.

(5) *Example 5: Taxable income limitation*—(i) *Facts.* The facts are the same as in paragraph (f)(4)(i) of this section (the facts in *Example 4*), except that the P group's consolidated taxable income (within the meaning of paragraph (e)(10) of this section) is $300x.

(ii) *Analysis.* (A) *Determination of whether the limitation described in paragraph (b)(2) of this section applies.* Under paragraph (b)(2) of this section, in the case of a consolidated group with a consolidated section 250(a)(2) amount for a consolidated year, the amount of the consolidated foreign-derived intangible income and the consolidated global intangible low-taxed income otherwise taken into account in the determination of the consolidated FDII deduction amount and the consolidated GILTI deduction amount are subject to reduction. As in paragraph (f)(1)(ii)(E) of this section (the facts in *Example 1*), the P group's consolidated foreign-derived intangible income is $240x. As in paragraph (f)(4)(ii)(A) of this section (the analysis in *Example 4*), the P group's consolidated global intangible low-taxed income is $85x. The P group's consolidated taxable income is $300x. Under paragraph (e)(10) of this section, the P group's consolidated section 250(a)(2) amount is $25x (($240x + $85x) - $300x), the excess of the sum of the consolidated foreign-derived intangible income and the consolidated global intangible low-taxed income, over the P group's consolidated taxable income. Therefore, the limitation described in paragraph (b)(2) of this section applies.

(B) *Allocation of reduction*. Under paragraph (b)(2)(i) of this section, the P group's consolidated foreign-derived intangible income is reduced by an amount which bears the same ratio to the consolidated section 250(a)(2) amount as the consolidated foreign-derived intangible income bears to the sum of the consolidated foreign-derived intangible income and consolidated global intangible low-taxed income, and the P group's consolidated global intangible low-taxed income is reduced by the excess of the consolidated section 250(a)(2) amount over the reduction described in paragraph (b)(2)(i) of this section. Therefore, for purposes of determining the P group's consolidated FDII deduction amount and consolidated GILTI deduction amount, its consolidated foreign-derived intangible income is reduced to $221.54x ($240x - ($25x x ($240x / $325x))) and its consolidated global intangible low-taxed income is reduced to $78.46x ($85x - ($25x - ($25x x ($240x / $325x)))).

(C) *Calculation of consolidated FDII deduction amount and consolidated GILTI deduction amount*. Under paragraph (e)(4) of this section, the P group's consolidated FDII deduction amount is $83.08x ($221.54x x 0.375). Under paragraph (e)(8) of this section, the P group's consolidated GILTI deduction amount is $39.23x ($78.46x x 0.50).

(D) *Member's deduction attributable to the consolidated FDII deduction amount*. As in paragraph (f)(1)(ii)(G) of this section (the analysis in *Example 1*), the FDII deduction allocation ratios of P, USS1, and USS2 are 0, 2/3, and 1/3, respectively. Therefore, P, USS1, and USS2 are permitted deductions attributable to the consolidated FDII deduction amount of $0 (0 x $83.08x), $55.39x (2/3 x $83.08x), and $27.69x (1/3 x $83.08x), respectively.

(E) *Member's deduction attributable to the consolidated GILTI deduction amount*. As in paragraph (f)(4)(ii)(C) of this section (the analysis in *Example 4*), the GILTI deduction allocation ratios of P, USS1, and USS2 are 0, 3/4, and 1/4, respectively. Therefore, P, USS1, and USS2 are permitted deductions attributable to the consolidated GILTI deduction amount of $0 (0 x $39.23x), $29.42x (3/4 x $39.23x), and $9.81x (1/4 x $39.23x), respectively.

(F) *Member's deduction pursuant section 250*. Under paragraph (b)(1) of this section, a member is allowed a deduction equal to the sum of the member's deduction attributable to consolidated FDII deduction amount and the member's deduction attributable to consolidated GILTI deduction amount. As a result P, USS1, and USS2 are entitled to deductions under paragraph (b)(1) of this section of $0 ($0 + $0), $84.81x ($55.39x + $29.42x), and $37.50x ($27.69x + $9.81x), respectively.

(g) *Applicability date*.—This section applies to consolidated return years ending on or after the date of publication of the Treasury decision adopting these rules as final regulations in the **Federal Register**. [Reg. § 1.1502-50.]

Global Intangible Low-Taxed Income: Guidance

Global Intangible Low-Taxed Income: Guidance.—Reg. § 1.1502-51, implementing section 951A of the Internal Revenue Code, which was enacted on December 22, 2017, is proposed (published in the Federal Register on October 10, 2018) (REG-104390-18).

Par. 14. Section 1.1502-51 is added to read as follows:

§ 1.1502-51. Consolidated section 951A.—(a) *In general*.—This section provides rules for applying section 951A and §§ 1.951A-1 through 1.951A-7 (the *section 951A regulations*) to each member of a consolidated group (each, a *member*) that is a United States shareholder of any controlled foreign corporation. Paragraph (b) describes the inclusion of the GILTI inclusion amount by a member of a consolidated group. Paragraph (c) modifies the rules provided in § 1.951A-6(e) for adjustments to basis related to used tested loss amount. Paragraph (d) provides rules governing basis adjustments to member stock resulting from the application of § 1.951A-6(e) and paragraph (c) of this section. Paragraph (e) provides definitions for purposes of this section. Paragraph (f) provides examples illustrating the rules of this section. Paragraph (g) provides an applicability date.

(b) *Calculation of the GILTI inclusion amount for a member of a consolidated group*.—Each member who is a United States shareholder of any controlled foreign corporation includes in gross income in the U.S. shareholder inclusion year the member's GILTI inclusion amount, if any, for the U.S. shareholder inclusion year. See section 951A(a) and § 1.951A-1(b). The GILTI inclusion amount of a member for a U.S. shareholder inclusion year is the excess (if any) of the member's net CFC tested income for the U.S. shareholder inclusion year, over the member's net deemed tangible income return for the U.S. shareholder inclusion year, determined using the definitions provided in paragraph (e) of this section.

(c) *Adjustments to basis related to used tested loss amount*.—(1) *In general*.—The adjusted basis of the section 958(a) stock of a controlled foreign corporation that is owned (directly or indirectly) by a member (*specified stock*) or an interest in a foreign entity other than a controlled foreign corporation by reason of which a domestic corporation owns (within the meaning of section 958(a)(2)) stock of a controlled foreign corporation is adjusted immediately before its disposition pursuant to § 1.951A-6(e). The amount of the adjustment is determined using the rules provided in paragraphs (c)(2), (3), and (4) of this section.

(2) *Determination of used tested loss amount*.—For purposes of the section 951A regulations and this section, the term *used tested loss amount* means, with respect to a member and a tested loss CFC for a U.S. shareholder inclusion year—

(i) In the case of the consolidated group tested income equaling or exceeding the consolidated group tested loss for a U.S. shareholder inclusion year, the member's pro rata share (determined under §1.951A-1(d)(4)) of the tested loss of the tested loss CFC for the U.S. shareholder inclusion year.

(ii) In the case of the consolidated group tested income being less than the consolidated group tested loss for a U.S. shareholder inclusion year, the amount that bears the same ratio to the member's pro rata share (determined under §1.951A-1(d)(4)) of the tested loss of the tested loss CFC for the U.S. shareholder inclusion year as the consolidated group tested income for the U.S. shareholder inclusion year bears to the consolidated group tested loss for the U.S. shareholder inclusion year.

(3) *Determination of offset tested income amount.*—For purposes of the section 951A regulations and this section, the term *offset tested income amount* means, with respect to a member and a tested income CFC for a U.S. shareholder inclusion year—

(i) In the case of the consolidated group tested income exceeding the consolidated group tested loss for a U.S. shareholder inclusion year, the amount that bears the same ratio to the member's pro rata share (determined under §1.951A-1(d)(2)) of the tested income of the tested income CFC for the U.S. shareholder inclusion year as the consolidated group tested loss for the U.S. shareholder inclusion year bears to the consolidated group tested income for the U.S. shareholder inclusion year.

(ii) In the case of the consolidated group tested income equaling or being less than the consolidated group tested loss for a U.S. shareholder inclusion year, the member's pro rata share (determined under §1.951A-1(d)(2)) of the tested income of the tested income CFC for the U.S. shareholder inclusion year.

(4) *Special rule for disposition by a controlled foreign corporation less than 100 percent owned by a single domestic corporation.*—For purposes of determining the application of §1.951A-6(e)(7), the amount of stock in the controlled foreign corporation a member owns, within the meaning of section 958(a), includes any stock that the member is considered as owning by applying the rules of ownership of section 958(b).

(5) *Special rule for intercompany nonrecognition transactions.*—If a member engages in a nonrecognition transaction (within the meaning of section 7701(a)(45)), with another member in which stock of a controlled foreign corporation that has a net used tested loss amount is directly transferred, the adjusted basis of the nonrecognition property (within the meaning of section 358) received in the nonrecognition transaction is immediately reduced by the amount of the net used tested loss amount. In cases of intercompany transactions that are governed by §1.368-2(l), the reduction in basis pursuant to this paragraph (c)(5) is made prior to the application of §1.1502-13(f)(3). See §1.1502-13(f)(7), Example 4(c).

(d) *Adjustments to the basis of a member.*—For adjustments to the basis of a member related to paragraph (c) of this section, see §1.1502-32(b)(3)(ii)(E), (b)(3)(ii)(F), and (b)(3)(iii)(C).

(e) *Definitions.*—The following definitions apply for purposes of the section—

(1) *Aggregate tested income.*—With respect to a member, the term *aggregate tested income* means the aggregate of the member's pro rata share (determined under §1.951A-1(d)(2)) of the tested income of each tested income CFC for a U.S. shareholder inclusion year.

(2) *Aggregate tested loss.*—With respect to a member, the term *aggregate tested loss* means the aggregate of the member's pro rata share (determined under §1.951A-1(d)(4)) of the tested loss of each tested loss CFC for a U.S. shareholder inclusion year.

(3) *Allocable share.*—The term *allocable share* means, with respect to a member that is a United States shareholder and a U.S. shareholder inclusion year—

(i) With respect to consolidated group QBAI, the product of the consolidated group QBAI of the member's consolidated group and the member's GILTI allocation ratio.

(ii) With respect to consolidated group specified interest expense, the product of the consolidated group specified interest expense of the member's consolidated group and the member's GILTI allocation ratio.

(iii) With respect to consolidated group tested loss, the product of the consolidated group tested loss of the member's consolidated group and the member's GILTI allocation ratio.

(4) *Consolidated group QBAI.*—With respect to a consolidated group, the term *consolidated group QBAI* means the sum of each member's pro rata share (determined under §1.951A-1(d)(3)) of the qualified business asset investment of each tested income CFC for a U.S. shareholder inclusion year.

(5) *Consolidated group specified interest expense.*—With respect to a consolidated group, the term *consolidated group specified interest expense* means the excess (if any) of—

(i) The sum of each member's pro rata share (determined under §1.951A-1(d)(5)) of the tested interest expense of each controlled foreign corporation for the U.S. shareholder inclusion year, over

(ii) The sum of each member's pro rata share (determined under §1.951A-1(d)(6)) of the tested interest income of each controlled foreign corporation for the U.S. shareholder inclusion year.

(6) *Consolidated group tested income.*—With respect to a consolidated group, the term *consolidated group tested income* means the sum of each member's aggregate tested income for a U.S. shareholder inclusion year.

(7) *Consolidated group tested loss.*—With respect to a consolidated group, the term *consolidated group tested loss* means the sum of each member's aggregate tested loss for a U.S. shareholder inclusion year.

(8) *Controlled foreign corporation.*—The term *controlled foreign corporation* means a controlled foreign corporation as defined in section 957.

(9) *Deemed tangible income return.*—With respect to a member, the term *deemed tangible income return* means 10 percent of the member's allocable share of the consolidated group QBAI.

(10) *GILTI allocation ratio.*—With respect to a member, the term *GILTI allocation ratio* means the ratio of—

(i) The aggregate tested income of the member for a U.S. shareholder inclusion year, to

(ii) The consolidated group tested income of the consolidated group of which the member is a member for the U.S. shareholder inclusion year.

(11) *GILTI inclusion amount.*—With respect to a member, the term *GILTI inclusion amount* has the meaning provided in paragraph (b) of this section.

(12) *Net CFC tested income.*—With respect to a member, the term *net CFC tested income* means the excess (if any) of—

(i) The member's aggregate tested income, over

(ii) The member's allocable share of the consolidated group tested loss.

(13) *Net deemed tangible income return.*—With respect to a member, the term *net deemed tangible income return* means the excess (if any) of the member's deemed tangible income return over the member's allocable share of the consolidated group specified interest expense.

(14) *Net offset tested income amount.*—The term *net offset tested income amount* means, with respect to a member and a controlled foreign corporation, the excess (if any) of the amount described in paragraph (e)(15)(ii) of this section over the amount described in paragraph (e)(15)(i) of this section.

(15) *Net used tested loss amount.*—The term *net used tested loss amount* means, with respect to a member and a controlled foreign corporation, the excess (if any) of —

(i) The aggregate of the member's pro rata share of each used tested loss amount of the controlled foreign corporation for each U.S. shareholder inclusion year over

(ii) The aggregate of the member's pro rata share of each offset tested income amount of the controlled foreign corporation for each U.S. shareholder inclusion year.

(16) *Offset tested income amount.*—The term *offset tested income amount* has the meaning provided in paragraph (c)(3) of this section.

(17) *Qualified business asset investment.*—The term *qualified business asset investment* has the meaning provided in § 1.951A-3(b).

(18) *Tested income.*—The term *tested income* has the meaning provided in § 1.951A-2(b)(1).

(19) *Tested income CFC.*—The term *tested income CFC* has the meaning provided in § 1.951A-2(b)(1).

(20) *Tested interest expense.*—The term *tested interest expense* has the meaning provided in § 1.951A-4(b)(1).

(21) *Tested interest income.*—The term *tested interest income* has the meaning provided in § 1.951A-4(b)(2).

(22) *Tested loss.*—The term *tested loss* has the meaning provided in § 1.951A-2(b)(2).

(23) *Tested loss CFC.*—The term *tested loss CFC* has the meaning provided in § 1.951A-2(b)(2).

(24) *United States shareholder.*—The term *United States shareholder* has the meaning provided in § 1.951-1(g)(1).

(25) *U.S. shareholder inclusion year.*—The term *U.S. shareholder inclusion year* has the meaning provided in § 1.951A-1(e)(4).

(26) *Used tested loss amount.*—The term *used tested loss amount* has the meaning provided in paragraph (c)(2) of this section.

(f) *Examples.*—The following examples illustrate the rules of this section. For purposes of the examples in this section, unless otherwise stated: P is the common parent of the P consolidated group; P owns all of the single class of stock of subsidiaries USS1, USS2, and USS3, all of whom are members of the P consolidated group; CFC1, CFC2, CFC3, and CFC4 are all controlled foreign corporations (within the meaning of paragraph (e)(8) of this section); and the taxable year of all persons is the calendar year.

(1) *Example 1: calculation of net CFC tested income within a consolidated group when all CFCs are wholly owned by a member*—(i) *Facts.* USS1 owns all of the single class of stock of CFC1. USS2 owns all of the single class of stock of each of CFC2 and CFC3. USS3 owns all of the single class of stock of CFC4. In Year 1, CFC1 has tested loss of $100, CFC2 has tested income of $200x, CFC3 has tested loss of $200x, and CFC4 has tested income of $600x. Neither CFC2 nor CFC4 has qualified business asset investment in Year 1.

(ii) *Analysis*—(A) *Consolidated group tested income and GILTI allocation ratio.* USS1 has no aggregate tested income; USS2's aggregate tested income is $200x, its pro rata share (within the meaning of § 1.951A-1(d)(2)) of CFC2's tested income; and USS3's aggregate tested income is $600x, its pro rata share (within the meaning of § 1.951A-1(d)(2)) of CFC4's tested income. Therefore, under paragraph (e)(6) of this section, the P consolidated group's consolidated group tested income is $800x ($200x + $600x). As a result, the GILTI allocation ratios of USS1, USS2, and USS3 are 0 ($0/$800x), 0.25 ($200x/$800x), and 0.75 ($600x/$800x), respectively.

(B) *Consolidated group tested loss.* Under paragraph (e)(7) of this section, the P consolidated group's consolidated group tested loss is $300x ($100x + $200x), the aggregate of USS1's aggregate tested loss, which is equal to its pro rata share (within the meaning of § 1.951A-1(d)(4)) of CFC1's tested loss ($100x), and USS2's aggregate tested loss, which is equal to its pro rata share (within the meaning of § 1.951A-1(d)(4)) of CFC3's tested loss ($200x). Under paragraph (e)(3)(iii) of this section, a member's allocable share of the consolidated group tested loss is the product of the consolidated group tested loss of the member's consolidated group and the member's GILTI allocation ratio. Therefore, the allocable shares of the consolidated group tested loss of USS1, USS2, and USS3 are $0 (0 x $300x), $75x (0.25 x $300x), and $225x (0.75 x $300x), respectively.

(C) *Calculation of net CFC tested income.* Under paragraph (e)(12) of this section, a member's net CFC tested income is the excess (if any) of the member's aggregate tested income over the member's allocable share of the consolidated group tested loss. As a result, USS1's, USS2's, and USS3's net CFC tested income amounts are $0 ($0 - $0), $125x ($200x - $75x), and $375x ($600x - $225x), respectively.

(2) *Example 2: calculation of net CFC tested income within a consolidated group when ownership of a tested loss CFC is split between members*—(i) *Facts.* The facts are the same as in paragraph (i) of *Example 1,* except that USS2 and USS3 each own 50% of the single class of stock of CFC3.

(ii) *Analysis.* As in paragraph (ii) of *Example 1,* USS1 has no aggregate tested income and a GILTI allocation ratio of 0, USS2 has $200x of aggregate tested income and a GILTI allocation ratio of 0.25, and USS3 has $600x of aggregate tested income and a GILTI allocation ratio of 0.75. Additionally, the P consolidated group's consolidated group tested loss is $300x (the aggregate of USS1's aggregate tested loss, which is equal to its pro rata share (within the meaning of §1.951A-1(d)(4)) of CFC1's tested loss ($100x); USS2's aggregate tested loss, which is equal to its pro rata share (within the meaning of §1.951A-1(d)(4)) of CFC3's tested loss ($100x); and USS3's aggregate tested loss, which is equal to its pro rata share (within the meaning of §1.951A-1(d)(4)) of CFC3's tested loss ($100x)). As a result, under paragraph (e)(12) of this section, as in paragraph (ii)(C) of *Example 1*, USS1's, USS2's, and USS3's net CFC tested income amounts are $0 ($0 - $0), $125x ($200x - $75x), and $375x ($600x - $225x), respectively.

(3) *Example 3: calculation of GILTI inclusion amount*—(i) *Facts*. The facts are the same as in paragraph (i) of *Example 1*, except that CFC2 and CFC4 have qualified business asset investment of $500x and $2000x, respectively, for Year 1. In Year 1, CFC1 and CFC4 each have tested interest expense (within the meaning of §1.951A-4(b)(1)) of $25x, and CFC1, CFC2, CFC3, and CFC4 have $0 of tested interest income (within the meaning of §1.951A-4(b)(2)). CFC1's tested loss of $100x and CFC4's tested income of $600x take into account the interest paid.

(ii) *Analysis*—(A) *GILTI allocation ratio*. As in paragraph (ii) of *Example 1*, the GILTI allocation ratios of USS1, USS2, and USS3 are 0 ($0/$800x), 0.25 ($200x/$800x), and 0.75 ($600x/$800x), respectively.

(B) *Consolidated group QBAI*. Under paragraph (e)(4) of this section, the P consolidated group's consolidated group QBAI is $2,500x ($500x + $2,000x), the aggregate of USS2's pro rata share (determined under §1.951A-1(d)(3)) of the qualified business asset investment of CFC2 and USS3's pro rata share (determined under §1.951A-1(d)(3)) of the qualified business asset investment of CFC4. Under paragraph (e)(3)(i) of this section, a member's allocable share of consolidated group QBAI is the product of the consolidated group QBAI of the member's consolidated group and the member's GILTI allocation ratio. Therefore, the allocable shares of the consolidated group QBAI of each of USS1, USS2, and USS3 are $0 (0 x $2,500x), $625x (0.25 x $2,500x), and $1,875x (0.75 x $2,500x), respectively.

(C) *Consolidated group specified interest expense*—(*1*) *Pro rata share of tested interest expense*. USS1's pro rata share of the tested interest expense of CFC1 is $25x, the amount by which the tested interest expense increases USS1's pro rata share of CFC1's tested loss (from $75x to $100x) for Year 1. USS3's pro rata share of the tested interest expense of CFC4 is also $25x, the amount by which the tested interest expense decreases USS1's pro rata share of CFC4's tested income (from $625x to $600x). See §1.951A-1(d)(5).

(*2*) *Consolidated group specified interest expense*. Under paragraph (e)(5) of this section, the P consolidated group's consolidated group specified interest expense is $50x, the excess of the sum of each member's pro rata share of the tested interest expense of each controlled foreign corporation ($50x, $25x from USS1 + $25x from USS3), over the sum of each member's pro rata share of tested interest income ($0). Under paragraph (e)(3)(ii) of this section, a member's allocable share of consolidated group specified interest expense is the product of the consolidated group specified interest expense of the member's consolidated group and the member's GILTI allocation ratio. Therefore, the allocable shares of consolidated group specified interest expense of USS1, USS2, and USS3 are $0 (0 x $50x), $12.50x (0.25 x $50x), and $37.50x (0.75 x $50x), respectively.

(D) *Calculation of deemed tangible income return*. Under paragraph (e)(9) of this section, a member's deemed tangible income return means 10 percent of the member's allocable share of the consolidated group QBAI. As a result, USS1's, USS2's, and USS3's deemed tangible income returns are $0 (0.1 x $0), $62.50x (0.1 x $625x), and $187.50x (0.1 x $1,875x), respectively.

(E) *Calculation of net deemed tangible income return*. Under paragraph (e)(13) of this section, a member's net deemed tangible income return means the excess (if any) of a member's deemed tangible income return over the member's allocable share of the consolidated group specified interest. As a result, USS1's, USS2's, and USS3's net deemed tangible income returns are $0 ($0 - $0), $50x ($62.50x - $12.50x), and $150x ($187.50x - $37.50x), respectively.

(F) *Calculation of GILTI inclusion amount*. Under paragraph (b) of this section, a member's GILTI inclusion amount for a U.S. shareholder inclusion year is the excess (if any) of the member's net CFC tested income for the U.S. shareholder inclusion year, over the shareholder's net deemed tangible income return for the U.S. shareholder inclusion year. As described in paragraph (ii)(C) of *Example 1*, the amounts of USS1's, USS2's, and USS3's net CFC tested income are $0, $125x, and $375x, respectively. As described in paragraph (ii)(E) of this *Example 3*, the amounts of USS1's, USS2's, and USS3's net deemed tangible income return are $0, $50x, and $150x, respectively. As a result, under paragraph (b) of this section, USS1's, USS2's, and USS3's GILTI inclusion amounts are $0 ($0 - $0), $75x ($125x - $50x), and $225x ($375x - $150x), respectively.

(G) *Calculation of used tested loss amount and offset tested income amount*. As described in paragraph (ii)(A) of *Example 1*, P consolidated group's consolidated group tested income is $800x. As described in paragraph (ii)(B) of *Example 1*, P consolidated group's consolidated group tested loss is $300x. Therefore, the P consolidated group's consolidated group tested income exceeds its consolidated group tested loss. As a result, USS1 has a $100x used tested loss amount with respect to CFC1 and USS2 has a $200x used tested loss amount with respect to CFC3. Additionally, USS2 has a $75x offset tested income amount with respect to CFC2 ($200x x $300x/$800x) and USS3 has a $225x offset tested income amount with respect to CFC3 ($600x x $300x/$800x). See paragraph (c) of this section. P will adjust its basis in USS1 and USS2 pursuant to the rule in §1.1502-32(b)(3)(iii)(C).

(g) *Applicability date.*—This section applies to taxable years of foreign corporations beginning after December 31, 2017, and to taxable years of United States shareholders in which or with which such taxable years of foreign corporations end. [Reg. § 1.1502-51.]

Consolidated Returns: AMT: General Computations

Consolidated Returns: Alternative Minimum Tax.—Reproduced below is the text of proposed Reg. § 1.1502-55, relating to the computation of the alternative minimum tax by consolidated groups (published in the Federal Register on December 30, 1992).

☐ Par. 7. Section 1.1502-55 is added to read as follows:

§ 1.1502-55. Computation of alternative minimum tax of consolidated groups.—(a) *In general.*—(1) *Overview.*—This section provides rules for determining a consolidated group's alternative minimum tax liability (its consolidated AMT) and for allocating various consolidated AMT attributes to members of the group. *See also* section 1561.

(2) *Principles.*—The consolidated AMT is determined under an approach that generally parallels the determination of the group's consolidated regular tax liability. The statutory scheme and definitions in sections 55 through 59 apply in determining consolidated AMT. For example, section 55(b)(1) defines tentative minimum tax (TMT), and that term is modified under this section and referred to as "consolidated TMT." Generally, this section provides further refinements to the "consolidated" AMT terms only where necessary to illustrate the adjustments required to compute the consolidated AMT or to allocate consolidated AMT attributes among members.

(b) *Consolidated AMTI.*—(1) *In general.*—Consolidated alternative minimum taxable income (AMTI), computed in accordance with the principles of §§ 1.1502-11 and 1.1502-12 (relating to the computation of consolidated taxable income), equals consolidated pre-adjustment AMTI—

(i) Increased or decreased by the consolidated adjustment for adjusted current earnings (consolidated ACE adjustment), computed under paragraph (b)(3) of this section; and

(ii) Decreased by the consolidated alternative tax net operating loss deduction (consolidated ATNOL deduction), computed under paragraph (b)(4) of this section.

(2) *Consolidated pre-adjustment AMTI.*—(i) *In general.*—Consolidated pre-adjustment AMTI is determined in accordance with the principles of § 1.1502-11, taking into account the adjustments and preferences provided in sections 56 (excluding the section 56(g) adjustment), 57, and 58. The consolidated NOL deduction, however, is not taken into account in computing consolidated pre-adjustment AMTI. In determining consolidated pre-adjustment AMTI, a consolidated appreciated property charitable deduction preference must be computed. The consolidated appreciated property charitable deduction preference is the amount by which the consolidated charitable contribution deduction determined under the principles of § 1.1502-24, computed by taking into account the adjustments provided in sections 56 (excluding the section 56(g) adjustment) and 58, would be reduced if all capital gain property of the group were taken into account at its adjusted basis.

(ii) *Separate pre-adjustment AMTI.*—(A) *In general.*—In computing consolidated pre-adjustment AMTI, each member must compute its separate pre-adjustment AMTI. The separate preadjustment AMTI of a member is determined in accordance with the principles of § 1.1502-12, taking into account the adjustments and preferences provided in sections 56 (excluding the section 56(g) adjustment), 57, and 58.

(B) *Computation of member's section 57(a)(2) preference for excess IDCs.*—*(1) In general.*—In computing separate pre-adjustment AMTI, a member's preference under section 57(a)(2) is the member's allocable share of the consolidated IDC preference. A member's allocable share of the consolidated IDC preference is determined by multiplying the consolidated IDC preference by a fraction, the numerator of which is the separate IDC preference of the member, and the denominator of which is the sum of the separate IDC preferences of all members that have a separate IDC preference.

(2) Consolidated IDC preference.—The consolidated IDC preference is the excess of—

(i) The aggregate of each member's excess IDCs (as defined in section 57(a)(2)(B)) arising in the consolidated return year; over

(ii) 65 percent of the consolidated net income arising during the consolidated return year from all oil, gas, and geothermal properties (as defined in section 57(a)(2)(C)) of the group's members.

(3) Separate IDC preference.—A member's separate IDC preference is the amount, if any, by which the member's excess IDCs arising in the taxable year from all properties of the member is greater than 65 percent of the net income from oil, gas and geothermal properties of the member for the taxable year.

(iii) *Example.*—The following example illustrates the computation of consolidated pre-adjustment AMTI under this paragraph (b)(2).

Example. (i) P, S1, and S2 file a consolidated return, and have the following items of income and deduction for AMT purposes.

	P	*S1*	*S2*	*Consolidated*
Income	$1,000	$1,000	$1,000	
Depreciation	(300)	(100)	(200)	
Section 57(a)(2) IDC preference	240	—0—	160	
Section 57(a)(5) tax-exempt interest preference	100	50	—0—	
Separate pre-adjustment AMTI	$1,040	$950	$960	$2,950
AMT capital gains	300	150	100	550

	P	S1	S2	Consolidated
Consolidated pre-adjustment AMTI				$3,500

(ii) Under paragraph (b)(2)(ii)(B) of this section, the section 57(a)(2) IDC preference for each of the members is computed as follows:

	P	S1	S2	Consolidated
IDCs	$460	$100	$395	$955
65% of net income from oil, gas, and geothermal properties	(160)	(200)	(195)	(555)
IDC preference	$300	$-0-	$200	$400

(iii) The $400 consolidated IDC preference is allocated among the members that have a separate IDC preference (P and S2). Each member's allocable share of the consolidated IDC preference, which is included in its separate pre-adjustment AMTI, is computed as follows:

P

$400 consolidated IDC preference × ($300, separate IDC preference / $500, sum of separate IDC preferences of all members) = $240

S2

$400 consolidated IDC preference × ($200, separate IDC preference / $500, sum of separate IDC preferences of all members) = $160

(3) *Consolidated ACE adjustment.*—(i) *In general.*—In computing consolidated AMTI, subject to the limitation of paragraph (b)(3)(iii) of this section, consolidated pre-adjustment AMTI is increased (or decreased) by 75 percent of the excess (or deficit) for the consolidated return year of—

(A) The consolidated ACE (as defined in paragraph (b)(3)(ii) of this section) for the year; over

(B) The consolidated pre-adjustment AMTI (as defined in paragraph (b)(2) of this section) for the year.

(ii) *Consolidated ACE.*—(A) *In general.*—Consolidated ACE is determined in accordance with the principles of § 1.1502-11, taking into account the adjustments and preferences provided in sections 56, 57, and 58. The consolidated NOL deduction and the consolidated section 247 deduction, however, are not taken into account in computing consolidated ACE.

(B) *Separate ACE.*—In computing consolidated ACE, each member must compute its separate ACE. The separate ACE of a member is the separate pre-adjustment AMTI of the member, as defined in paragraph (b)(2)(ii) of this section, adjusted as provided in section 56(g) and § 1.56(g)-1.

(iii) *Limitation on consolidated negative ACE adjustments.*—(A) *In general.*—Under the principles of section 56(g)(2)(B), the amount of the consolidated negative ACE adjustment for any consolidated return year is limited to the sum of—

(1) The consolidated return year cumulative ACE adjustment (as defined in paragraph (b)(3)(iii)(B)(*1*) of this section); and

(2) The separate return year cumulative ACE adjustment (as defined in paragraph (b)(3)(iii)(B)(*2*) of this section).

(B) *Definitions.*—*(1) Consolidated return year cumulative ACE adjustment.*—The consolidated return year cumulative ACE adjustment equals the excess, if any, of the consolidated positive ACE adjustments for prior consolidated return years, over the sum of—

(i) Consolidated negative ACE adjustments for prior consolidated return years (other than any portion of those consolidated negative ACE adjustments attributable to separate return year positive ACE adjustments, as determined under paragraph (b)(3)(iii)(C) of this section); and

(ii) Consolidated positive ACE adjustments for prior consolidated return years apportioned to a corporation that ceases to be a member and carried to its separate return years in accordance with paragraph (e)(2) of this section (or, for consolidated return years for which the due date of the income tax return (without regard to extensions) is before [the date that is sixty days after final regulations are filed with the Federal Register], in accordance with any reasonable method used by the group).

(2) Separate return year cumulative ACE adjustment.—The separate return year cumulative ACE adjustment equals the excess, if any, of the separate return year positive ACE adjustments of the members for prior taxable years (as defined in paragraph (b)(3)(iii)(B)(*3*) of this section), over the sum of—

(i) The separate return year negative ACE adjustments of the members for prior taxable years (as defined in paragraph (b)(3)(iii)(B)(*4*) of this section); and

(ii) The portion of the consolidated negative ACE adjustments of the group for prior consolidated return years attributable to prior year separate return year positive ACE adjustments of the members (as determined under paragraph (b)(3)(iii)(C) of this section).

(3) Separate return year positive ACE adjustments.—Separate return year positive ACE adjustments are—

(i) For each member, the increases in AMTI for prior separate return years (other than years for which the member joined in the filing of a consolidated return) due to the ACE adjustment under section 56(g); and

(ii) For any prior separate return years for which a member joined in the filing of a consolidated return with another group, the member's allocable share of that group's consoli-

dated positive ACE adjustments determined under paragraph (e)(2) of this section (or, for taxable years for which the due date of the income tax return (without regard to extensions) is before [the date that is sixty days after final regulations are filed with the Federal Register], determined in accordance with any reasonable method used by that other group).

(4) Separate return year negative ACE adjustments.—Separate return year negative ACE adjustments include the aggregate decreases in AMTI for prior separate return years (other than years for which the member joined in the filing of a consolidated return) due to the ACE adjustment under section 56(g).

(C) *Consolidated negative ACE adjustments attributable to separate return year positive ACE adjustments.*—The portion of a consolidated negative ACE adjustment attributable to separate return year positive ACE adjustments is equal to the consolidated negative ACE adjustment multiplied by a fraction, the numerator of which is the separate return year cumulative ACE adjustment (as of the beginning of the consolidated return year) and the denominator of which is the aggregate of the separate return year cumulative ACE adjustment and the consolidated return year cumulative ACE adjustment (both determined as of the beginning of the consolidated return year).

(4) *Consolidated ATNOL deduction.*—After taking into account the group's consolidated ACE adjustment for the year, the group takes the consolidated ATNOL deduction into account in computing consolidated AMTI. Subject to applicable limitations (*e.g.*, section 382) and the provisions of section 56(d), the consolidated ATNOL deduction is the aggregate of the consolidated ATNOL carryovers and carrybacks determined under the principles of §1.1502-21. The consolidated ATNOL for a consolidated return year is the consolidated net operating loss determined under the principles of §1.1502-21(e) for the year, taking into account the adjustments and preferences provided in sections 56, 57, and 58 for that year.

(5) *Example.*—The following example illustrates certain general principles of this paragraph (b).

Example. (i) *Separate returns.* P and S file separate returns. P's and S's items of income and deduction for regular tax (RT), AMT, and ACE purposes, and P's and S's tax liability are provided below. The effects of the lower section 11 brackets and the section 55(d) AMT exemption amount are ignored.

(A) P has pre-adjustment AMTI of $700 and ACE of $900, resulting in a $150 positive ACE adjustment (75 percent of the difference between P's ACE and P's pre-adjustment AMTI). P's ATNOL deduction ($100) reduces its AMTI to $750. P's TMT is therefore $150 (20 percent of AMTI). Thus, P has an AMT liability of $48, the difference between P's TMT ($150) and P's regular tax ($102).

P	*RT*	*AMT*	*ACE*
Gross income	$1,000	$1,000	$1,000
Depreciation	(500)	(300)	(100)
Pre-adjustment AMTI		$700	
ACE			900
ACE adjustment		150	
NOL deduction	(200)		
ATNOL deduction		(100)	
Taxable income	$300		
AMTI		$750	
TMT (20%)		$150	
RT liability (34%)	$102		
AMT		$48	

(B) S has pre-adjustment AMTI of $900 and ACE of $800, resulting in a $75 negative ACE adjustment (75 percent of the difference between S's pre-adjustment AMTI and S's ACE. (Assume that S may use the negative adjustment because of prior year positive ACE adjustments). S's ATNOL deduction ($200) reduces its AMTI to $625. Thus, S has no AMT liability because S's regular tax ($306) exceeds its TMT ($125).

S	*RT*	*AMT*	*ACE*
Gross income	$1,000	$1,000	$1,000
Depreciation	0	(100)	(200)
Pre-adjustment AMTI		$900	
ACE			$800
ACE adjustment		(75)	
NOL deduction	(100)		
ATNOL deduction		(200)	
Taxable income	$900		
AMTI		$625	
TMT (20%)		$125	
RT liability (34%)	$306		

S	*RT*	*AMT*	*ACE*
AMT		0	

(ii) *Consolidated return filed.* (A) If P and S instead elect to file a consolidated return, the group would have the following results:

P group

RT	*P*	*S*	*Consolidated*
Gross income	$1,000	$1,000	$2,000
Depreciation	(500)	0	(500)
Aggregate separate taxable income	$500	$1,000	$1,500
Consolidated NOL deduction			(300)
Consolidated taxable income			$1,200
Consolidated RT (34%)			$408

AMT	*P*	*S*	*Consolidated*
Gross income	$1,000	$1,000	$2,000
Depreciation	(300)	(100)	(400)
Consolidated pre-adjustment AMTI	$700	$900	$1,600
ACE depreciation adjustment	200	(100)	100
Consolidated ACE	$900	$800	$1,700
Consolidated ACE adjustment			75
Consolidated ATNOL deduction			(300)
Consolidated AMTI			$1,375
Consolidated TMT (20%)			$275
Consolidated AMT			$0

(B) The P group has consolidated pre-adjustment AMTI of $1,600. In addition, the group has consolidated ACE of $1,700, resulting in a $75 positive consolidated ACE adjustment (75 percent of the difference between the group's ACE and the group's pre-adjustment AMTI). The consolidated ATNOL deduction reduces consolidated AMTI to $1,375. The consolidated TMT is $275. Thus, the P group has no consolidated AMT liability because its consolidated regular tax ($408) exceeds its consolidated TMT ($275).

(c) *Consolidated alternative minimum tax foreign tax credit.*—[Reserved]

(d) *Separate return limitation years.*—[Reserved]

(e) *Separate return years.*—(1) *Carryovers and carrybacks of consolidated AMT attributes to separate return years.*—(i) *In general.*—This paragraph (e)(1) provides principles under which various consolidated AMT attributes are allocated among members of a consolidated group, generally for purposes of apportioning the attribute to a corporation that ceases to be a member. The apportionment of consolidated AMT attributes that have regular tax counterparts is based on the principles applicable to the regular tax counterparts. *See, e.g.*, § 1.1502-21(b) (principles applicable to consolidated net operating losses).

(ii) *Examples.*—The following examples illustrate the application of this paragraph (e)(1).

Example 1. Allocation of consolidated ATNOL. (i) P, S1, and S2 are members of a consolidated group. In 1993, the group has a consolidated ATNOL of $100. P has a separate ATNOL of $150, S1 has a separate ATNOL of $50, and S2 has separate AMTI of $100. The separate ATNOLs for P and S1 are determined by computing the consolidated ATNOL, taking into account only the member's income, gain, deduction, and loss, including the member's losses and deductions actually absorbed by the group in the taxable year (whether or not absorbed by the member). *See* § 1.1502-21(b)(2)(iv).

(ii) Under this paragraph (e)(1), the portion of the consolidated ATNOL allocable to each member is determined in accordance with the principles of the regulations relating to the carryover and carryback of the consolidated NOL to separate return years. *See* § 1.1502-21(b). Thus, the portion of the consolidated ATNOL allocable to P and S1 is determined by multiplying the consolidated ATNOL by a fraction, the numerator of which is the member's separate ATNOL and the denominator of which is the sum of all members' separate ATNOLs. The portion of the consolidated ATNOL allocable to P is $75 ($100 multiplied by $150/$200). The portion of the consolidated ATNOL allocable to S1 is $25 ($100 multiplied by $50/$200). S2 is not allocated a portion of the consolidated ATNOL because S2 had no separate ATNOL.

Example 2. Allocation of consolidated ACE net capital loss. (i) P, S1, and S2 are members of a consolidated group. In 1993, the group has a consolidated ACE net capital loss of $210. P has a separate ACE net capital loss of $90, S1 has a separate ACE net capital gain of $60, and S2 has a separate ACE net capital loss of $180. The separate ACE net capital losses for P and S2 are determined by computing the consolidated ACE net capital loss by taking into account only the member's gains and losses, including the member's losses actually absorbed by the group in the taxable year (whether or not absorbed by the member). *See* §§ 1.1502-22(b)(3) and 1.1502-21(b)(2)(iv).

(ii) Under this paragraph (e)(1), the portion of the consolidated ACE net capital loss allocable to each member is determined in accordance with the principles of the regulations relating to the carryover and carryback of the consolidated net capital loss to separate return years. *See* § 1.1502-22(b). Thus, the portion of the consolidated ACE net capital loss allocable to P and S2 is determined by multiplying the consolidated ACE net capital loss by a fraction, the numerator of which is the member's separate ACE net capital loss and the denominator of which is the sum of all members' separate ACE net capital losses. The portion of the consolidated ACE net capital loss allocable to P is $70 ($210 multiplied by $90/$270). The portion of the consolidated ACE net capital loss allocable to S2 is $140 ($210 multiplied by $180/$270). S1 is not allocated a portion of the consolidated ACE net capital loss because S1 had no separate ACE net capital loss.

(2) *Carryover of consolidated positive ACE adjustments to separate return years.*—(i) *In general.*—If a corporation ceases to be a member, the portion of the consolidated positive ACE adjustments allocated to the corporation is taken into account in its separate return years in accordance with the principles of §§ 1.56(g)-1(a)(2) and 1.1502-21(b). Any separate return year cumulative ACE adjustment attributable to a corporation as of the close of the taxable year in which the corporation ceases to be a member is also taken into account in its separate return year.

(ii) *Portion of consolidated positive ACE adjustments allocable to a member.*—(A) *In general.*—The portion of the consolidated positive ACE adjustments allocated to a member is the consolidated return year cumulative ACE adjustment as of the close of the consolidated return year in which the corporation ceases to be a member, multiplied by a fraction. The numerator of the fraction is the separate cumulative ACE adjustment of the member as of the close of the consolidated return year in which the corporation ceases to be a member, and the denominator of the fraction is the sum of the separate cumulative ACE adjustments of all members having separate cumulative ACE adjustments as of the close of the consolidated return year in which the corporation ceases to be a member.

(B) *Separate cumulative ACE adjustment.*—The separate cumulative ACE adjustment of a member is the consolidated return year cumulative ACE adjustment, if any, taking into account only the member's items of income, gain, deduction, and loss, including the member's losses and deductions actually absorbed by the group (whether or not absorbed by the member).

(f) *Deferral and restoration of gain or loss.*—The principles of the Internal Revenue Code and regulations that affect the timing of inclusion of items in consolidated taxable income generally apply for purposes of computing consolidated pre-adjustment AMTI and consolidated ACE. *See, e.g.*, § 1.1502-13. Applicable adjustments and preferences provided in sections 56, 57, and 58 must be taken into account.

(g) *Stock basis adjustments in computing consolidated AMT.*—(1) *Parallel approach.*—The principles set forth in §§ 1.1502-19 and 1.1502-32 for determining the regular tax basis in (or the regular tax excess loss account with respect to) a member's stock generally apply in determining both the corresponding AMT stock basis (or AMT excess loss account) and ACE stock basis (or ACE excess loss account).

(2) *Modifications to regular tax stock basis principles in computing consolidated pre-adjustment AMTI and consolidated ACE.*—The following modifications to the stock basis adjustment principles of §§ 1.1502-19 and 1.1502-32 apply for purposes of computing AMT stock basis (or AMT excess loss account) used in determining consolidated pre-adjustment AMTI and ACE stock basis (or ACE excess loss account) used in determining consolidated ACE—

(i) Adjustments may be determined annually but are required only if a difference between the regular tax and AMT or ACE basis in (or excess loss with respect to) a member's stock will affect the tax liability of any person (*e.g.*, on a sale of the stock);

(ii) The annual reporting requirements of § 1.1502-32(g) do not apply under the AMT or ACE systems;

(iii) In determining the adjustments under § 1.1502-32(b)(3)(i), any section 57 preference items includible in AMTI are not taken into account (while tax-exempt interest described in section 57(a)(5) is not taken into account in determining the adjustments for AMTI under § 1.1502-32(b)(3)(i), it does result in a positive stock basis adjustment under § 1.1502-32(b)(3)(ii));

(iv) A member's portion of any disallowed consolidated negative ACE adjustment for a consolidated return year is treated as a noncapital, non-deductible expense under § 1.1502-32(b)(3)(iii) for purposes of determining the adjustments to another member's AMT basis in (or excess loss account with respect to) the stock of the member; and

(v) Solely for purposes of computing adjustments to the ACE basis in (or ACE excess loss account with respect to) the stock of a member, the member's excess of ACE deductions over ACE income for a consolidated return year is treated as a tax loss under § 1.1502-32(b)(3)(i) that is absorbed in the same year that it arises.

(3) *Tax payments and refunds.*—The amount of any section 275 tax liability or refund of federal income tax taken into account under §§ 1.1502-19 and 1.1502-32 for regular tax purposes is also taken into account in computing AMT and ACE stock basis (or excess loss account).

(4) *Example.*—The following example illustrates the principles of this paragraph (g).

Example. (i) *Background.* (A) Corporations P and S file a consolidated return. On January 1, 1994, P has a $0 basis in S's stock. S has gross income for regular tax, AMT, and ACE purposes of $10,000 in 1994 and a loss from operations (before taking into account its depreciation deduction) for regular tax, AMT, and ACE purposes of $5,000 in 1995. The P group's tax liability (whether attributable to the regular tax or the AMT) is solely attributable to S, and the consolidated regular tax liability and consolidated AMT liability allocations under § 1.1552-1 are the same as the separate liabilities of S. Finally, the effects of the lower section 11 tax rate brackets and the section 55(d) AMT exemption amount are ignored.

(B) On December 31, 1995, P sells a portion of the S stock. Under paragraph (g)(2)(i) of this section, no adjustments to P's basis in S's stock are required for purposes of computing consolidated pre-adjustment AMTI and consolidated ACE in 1994. However, because there was a stock sale in 1995, P's basis in S's stock must be adjusted for AMT and ACE purposes in 1995 as follows:

(ii) *Stock basis adjustments for 1994*—(A) *Adjustments*—

	RT	*AMT*	*ACE*
Gross income	$10,000	$10,000	$10,000
Depreciation	(5,000)	(4,000)	(3,000)
Taxable income	$5,000		
Pre-adjustment AMTI		$6,000	
ACE			$7,000
ACE adjustment		750	
AMTI		$6,750	
TMT (20%)		$1,350	
RT liability (34%)	$1,700		
AMT		$-0-	

(B) *Stock basis adjustments*—

P's basis in S's stock on 1/1/94	$-0-	$-0-	$-0-
§1.1502-32(b)(3)(i)	5,000	6,750	7,000
§1.1502-32(b)(3)(iii)	(1,700)	(1,700)	(1,700)
P's Basis in S stock on 12/31/94	$3,300	$5,050	$5,300

(iii)(A) *Stock basis adjustments for 1995.*

	RT	*AMT*	*ACE*
Gross income	$(5,000)	$(5,000)	$(5,000)
Depreciation	(5,000)	(4,000)	(3,000)
Taxable income	$(10,000)		
Pre-adjustment AMTI		$(9,000)	
ACE			$(8,000)
ACE adjustment		750	
AMTI		$(8,250)	
TMT (20%)		$-0-	
RT liability (34%)	$-0-		
AMT		$-0-	

Because of the section 56(d) 90-percent limitation on the amount of AMTI that may be offset by an ATNOL deduction, only $6,075 of the $8,250 ATNOL for 1995 is carried back to 1994 under the principles of §1.1502-21(b). Thus, since all $5,000 of the 1994 regular taxable income was offset by the 1995 NOL, but only $6,075 of the 1994 AMTI was offset by the 1995 ATNOL, an AMT liability for 1994 of $135 results. Accordingly, only $1,565 of the $1,700 Federal income taxes paid in 1994 is refunded in 1995.

(B) *Stock basis adjustments*—

P's basis in S stock on 12/31/94	$3,300	$5,050	$5,300
§1.1502-32(b)(3)(i)	(5,000)	(6,075)	(8,000)
§1.1502-32(b)(3)(ii)	1,565	1,565	1,565
§1.1502-32(b)(3)(iii)	(-0-)	(-0-)	(-0-)
P's basis (ELA) in S stock when sold on 12/31/95	$(135)	$540	$(1,135)

(h) *Consolidated MTC.*—(1) *Overview.*—A group's consolidated minimum tax credit (MTC) is generally based on the consolidated adjusted net minimum tax for prior years. Adjustments are made to take into account a member's adjusted net minimum tax from prior separate return years. *See* paragraphs (h)(2) through (4) of this section. Adjustments are also made for the portion of the consolidated adjusted net minimum tax that is allocable to a corporation that ceases to be a member (and thus may be carried to the member's separate return years). *See* paragraph (h)(6) of this section.

(2) *Computation of the consolidated MTC.*—The consolidated MTC available as of the beginning of any consolidated return year is the sum of—

(i) The consolidated return year MTC (as defined in paragraph (h)(3) of this section); and

(ii) The separate return year MTC (as defined in paragraph (h)(4) of this section).

(3) *Consolidated return year MTC.*—(i) *General rule.*—The consolidated return year MTC is the excess (if any) of—

(A) The consolidated adjusted net minimum tax (as defined in paragraph (h)(3)(ii) of this section) for all prior consolidated return years beginning after 1986; over

(B) The sum of—

(1) The amount of the consolidated adjusted net minimum tax for prior consolidated return years that is allowable as a consolidated MTC in prior years; and

(2) The amount of the consolidated adjusted minimum tax for prior consolidated return years that is allowed to be carried to a separate return year of a member in accordance with paragraph (h)(6) of this section (or, for consolidated return years for which the due date of the income tax return (without regard to extensions) is before [the date that is sixty days after the final regulations are filed with the Federal Register], in accordance with any reasonable method used by the group).

(ii) *Consolidated adjusted net minimum tax.*—(A) *In general.*—Except as provided in paragraphs (h)(3)(ii)(B) and (C) of this section, consolidated adjusted net minimum tax is the amount of the consolidated AMT.

(B) *Exception for taxable years beginning after 1986 and before 1990.*—For taxable years beginning after December 31, 1986, and before January 1, 1990, consolidated adjusted net minimum tax is the amount of the consolidated AMT, reduced by the amount that would be the consolidated AMT for the taxable year if the only adjustments and tax preference items were those in section 56(c)(3), section 57(a)(1), section 57(a)(5), and section 57(a)(6).

(C) *Special rule for groups with consolidated disallowed section 29 or section 28 credits.*—The amounts determined under paragraphs (h)(3)(ii)(A) and (B) of this section for a taxable year are increased by the amount, if any, of a group's consolidated disallowed section 29 credit or consolidated disallowed section 28 credit for the year. For this purpose, the consolidated disallowed section 29 credit is the sum of the section 29 credits of all the members that are not allowable under section 29 solely by reason of the application of section 29(b)(6)(B). The consolidated disallowed section 28 credit is the sum of the section 28 credits of all the members that are not allowable under section 28 solely by reason of the application of section 28(d)(2)(B).

(4) *Separate return year MTC.*—(i) *In general.*—The separate return year MTC is, subject to applicable limitations (*e.g*, section 383), the excess (if any) of—

(A) The adjusted net minimum tax (as defined in section 53 (d)) for all prior separate return years of the group members beginning after 1986; over

(B) The sum of—

(1) The amount allowable as an MTC for such prior separate return years; and

(2) The amount described in paragraph (h)(4)(i)(A) of this section that is allowable as a consolidated MTC in prior years.

(ii) *Adjusted net minimum tax arising in another consolidated group.*—In the case of a member that filed a consolidated return in a prior year with another group, the amount described in paragraph (h)(4)(i)(A) of this section includes any consolidated MTC of another group that is attributable to that member and that is apportioned to it and available in the consolidated return year in accordance with paragraph (h)(6) of this section (or, for taxable years for which the due date of the income tax return (without regard to extensions) is before [the date that is sixty days after final regulations are filed with the Federal Register], in accordance with any reasonable method used by that other group).

(iii) *Limitation on portion of separate return year MTC arising in separate return limitation years.*—[Reserved]

(5) *Limitation on allowable consolidated MTC.*—(i) *In general.*—The available consolidated MTC allowable under this paragraph (h) for any consolidated return year is limited to the excess (if any) of—

(A) The modified consolidated regular tax liability (as defined in paragraph (h)(5)(ii) of this section) for the year; over

(B) The consolidated TMT for the year.

(ii) *Modified consolidated regular tax liability.*—Modified consolidated regular tax liability is the consolidated regular tax liability, computed in accordance with section 26(b), reduced by the sum of the consolidated credits allowable under subparts A, B, D, E, and F of part III of subchapter A of chapter 1 of the Internal Revenue Code.

(6) *Carryover of the consolidated MTC to separate return years.*—(i) *In general.*—When a corporation ceases to be a member of a group, the group is required to allocate to that corporation a portion of the group's consolidated MTC. The allocation is generally based on the corporation's contributions to the group's consolidated adjusted net minimum tax during the consolidated return years for which the corporation was a member of the group. The amount of the consolidated MTC properly allocable to a departing member is taken into account by the member in its succeeding separate return years.

(ii) *Consolidated MTC allocable to a member.*—(A) *In general.*—The amount of the consolidated MTC allocable to a corporation equals the corporation's allocable share of the consolidated MTC available as of the beginning of the consolidated return year in which the corporation ceases to be a member of a group—

(1) Increased by the corporation's allocable share of the consolidated adjusted net minimum tax, if any, for the consolidated return year in which the corporation ceases to be a member (as determined under paragraph (h)(6)(iii) of this section); and

(2) Decreased by the corporation's allocable share of any allowable consolidated MTC for the consolidated return year in which the corporation ceases to be a member (as determined under paragraphs (h)(6)(vi) and (7) of this section).

(B) *Reference to rules for determining a member's allocable share.*—For purposes of determining a corporation's allocable share of the consolidated MTC available as of the beginning of the consolidated return year in which the corporation ceases to be a member of a group (as described in paragraph (h)(6)(ii)(A) of this section), the rules of paragraph (h)(6)(iii) of this section apply to determine the corporation's allocable share of consolidated adjusted net minimum tax in each prior consolidated return year, and the rules of paragraphs (h)(6)(vi) and (7) of this section apply to determine the corporation's allocable share of any allowable consolidated MTC in prior consolidated return years. The rules of paragraph (h)(7) of this section are also applicable in determining the remaining amount of the departing member's separate return year MTC (from years prior to joining the consolidated group) that is taken into account in succeeding separate return years.

(iii) *Member's allocable share of consolidated adjusted net minimum tax.*—(A) *In general.*—A member's allocable share of the consolidated adjusted net minimum tax for a consolidated return year is determined by multiplying the consolidated AMT for the year by a fraction, the numerator of which is the separate adjusted AMT of the member (as defined in paragraph (h)(6)(iv) of this section) for the year, and the denominator of which is the sum of the separate adjusted AMTs of each member for the year.

(B) *Special allocation rule for groups with consolidated disallowed section 29 or section 28 credits.*—*(1) General rule.*—In a consolidated return year in which the group has a consolidated disallowed section 29 or 28 credit, in addition to the amount determined under paragraph (h)(6)(iii)(A) of this section, a member's allocable share of consolidated adjusted net minimum tax for the year includes its allocable share of the consolidated disallowed section 29 or 28 credit.

(2) Allocable share of disallowed credit.—A member's allocable share of the consolidated disallowed section 29 credit or consolidated disallowed section 28 credit for a consolidated return year is determined by multiplying the consolidated disallowed section 29 credit amount (or the consolidated disallowed section 28 credit amount) for the year by a fraction. The numerator of the fraction is the total section 29 credits (or section 28 credits) of the member for the taxable year, and the denominator is the total section 29 credits (or section 28 credits) of all members for the year.

(iv) *Separate adjusted AMT.*—(A) *In general.*—Subject to paragraph (h)(6)(iv)(B) of this section, the separate adjusted AMT of a member for a consolidated return year is the excess (if any) of—

(1) The consolidated AMT for the year; over

(2) The consolidated AMT for the year, computed by excluding the member's items of income, gain, deduction, and loss, and the member's credits.

(B) *Special rule in computing separate adjusted AMT.*—If, in computing a member's separate adjusted AMT, there is no consolidated AMT computed without that member's items (*i.e.*, the amount in paragraph (h)(6)(iv)(A)(2) of this section is zero), the amount determined under paragraph (h)(6)(iv)(A) of this section must be increased by the excess (if any) of the consolidated regular tax computed without the member's items, over consolidated TMT computed without the member's items.

(v) *Examples.*—The provisions of paragraphs (h)(1) through (6)(iv) of this section are illustrated by the following examples. In the examples, corporations P, S1, and S2 file a consolidated return. In each example, the group has no consolidated disallowed section 28 or section 29 credits for the year. The effects of the lower section 11 brackets and the section 55(d) exemption amount are ignored.

Example 1. (i) *1993 regular tax and AMT computation.*

	P	*S1*	*S2*	*Consolidated*
Taxable income	$1,200	$(200)	$3,000	$4,000
Adjustments and preferences	1,800	100	2,000	3,900
AMTI	$3,000	$(100)	$5,000	$7,900
TMT (20%)				$1,580
RT liability (34%)				1,360
AMT				$220

(ii) *Computation of separate adjusted AMT.*

(A) *Computation of consolidated AMT excluding P's items:*

Taxable income	$2,800
Adjustments and preferences	2,100
AMTI	$4,900
TMT (20%)	$980
RT liability (34%)	952
AMT	$28

Consolidated AMT computed without P's items is $28. Accordingly, P's separate adjusted AMT is $192 ($220 – $28).

(B) *Computation of consolidated AMT excluding S1's items:*

Taxable income	$4,200
Adjustments and preferences	3,800
AMTI	$8,000
TMT (20%)	$1,600
RT liability (34%)	1,428
AMT	$172

Consolidated AMT computed without S1's items is $172. Accordingly, S1's separate adjusted AMT is $48 ($220 – $172).

(C) *Computation of consolidated AMT excluding S2's items:*

Taxable income	$1,000
Adjustments and preferences	1,900
AMTI	$2,900
TMT (20%)	$580
RT liability (34%)	340
AMT	$240

Consolidated AMT computed without S2's items is $240. Because consolidated AMT computed without S2's items more than that amount computed with S2's items, S2 has no separate adjusted AMT.

(iii) *Allocation of 1993 consolidated adjusted net minimum tax to members of group.* Under paragraph (h)(6)(iii)(A) of this section, the amount of the 1993 consolidated adjusted net minimum tax allocable to P and S1 is determined as follows (S2 is allocated no portion of the 1993 consolidated adjusted net minimum tax because S2 has no separate adjusted AMT):

P

$220 consolidated AMT × ($192, P's separate adjusted AMT / $240, the sum of all members' separate adjusted AMTs) = $176

S1

$220 consolidated AMT × ($48, S1's separate adjusted AMT / $240, the sum of all members' separate adjusted AMTs) = $44

Example 2. (i) 1994 regular tax and AMT computation.

	P	*S1*	*S2*	*Consolidated*
Taxable income	$5,000	$-0-	$2,000	$7,000
Adjustments and preferences	(5,000)	8,000	3,400	6,400
AMTI	$-0-	$8,000	$5,400	$13,400
TMT (20%)				$2,680
RT liability (34%)				2,380
AMT				$300

(ii) *Computation of separate adjusted AMT.*

(A) *Computation of consolidated AMT excluding P's items:*

Taxable income	$2,000
Adjustments and preferences	11,400
AMTI	$13,400
TMT (20%)	$2,680
RT liability (34%)	680
AMT	$2,000

Consolidated AMT computed without P's items is $2,000. Because the consolidated AMT with P is only $300, P has no separate adjusted AMT.

(B) *Computation of consolidated AMT excluding S1's items:*

Taxable income	$7,000
Adjustments and preferences	(1,600)
AMTI	$5,400
TMT (20%)	$1,080
RT liability (34%)	2,380
AMT	$ -0-

The group has no consolidated AMT if S2's items are excluded. Accordingly, under paragraph (h)(6)(iv)(B) of this section, S2's separate adjusted AMT is $400, the sum of $300 (consolidated AMT computed with S2's items minus consolidated AMT computed without S2's items), and $100 (the excess of the consolidated regular tax computed without S2's items ($1,700) over the consolidated TMT computed without S2's items ($1,600)).

The group has no consolidated AMT if S1's items are excluded. Accordingly, under paragraph (h)(6)(iv)(B) of this section, S1's separate adjusted AMT is $1,600, the sum of $300 (consolidated AMT computed with S1's items minus consolidated AMT computed without S1's items), and $1,300 (the excess of the consolidated regular tax computed without S1's items ($2,380) over the consolidated TMT computed without S1's items ($1,080)).

(C) *Computation of consolidated AMT excluding S2's items:*

Taxable income	$5,000
Adjustments and preferences	3,000
AMTI	$8,000
TMT (20%)	1,600
RT liability (34%)	1,700
AMT	$-0-

(iii) *Allocation of 1994 consolidated MTC to members of the group.* Under paragraph (h)(6)(iii)(A) of this section, the amount of the 1994 consolidated adjusted net minimum tax allocable to S1 and S2 is determined as follows (P is allocated no portion of the consolidated MTC because P has no separate adjusted AMT):

S1

$300 consolidated AMT × ($1,600, S1's separate adjusted AMT / $2,000, the sum of all members' separate adjusted AMTs) = $225

S2

$300 consolidated AMT × ($400, S2's separate adjusted AMT / $2,000, the sum of all members' separate adjusted AMTs) = $75

(vi) *Member's allocable share of allowable consolidated MTC in a consolidated return year*—(A) *In general.* For purposes of determining the amount of the consolidated MTC allocable to a member under this paragraph (h)(6), a member's allocable share of the consolidated adjusted net minimum tax for a consolidated return year must, as described in paragraph (h)(6)(ii) of this section, be reduced by the member's allocable share of that amount allowable in a subsequent consolidated return year as a consolidated MTC. The member's allocable share of consolidated adjusted net minimum tax for a year that is allowable as a consolidated MTC in a subsequent taxable year is determined by multiplying the consolidated adjusted net minimum tax for the year allowable as a consolidated MTC (taking into account the ordering rules of paragraph (h)(7) of this section) by a fraction, the numerator of which is the member's allocable share of that consolidated adjusted net minimum tax and the denominator of which is the total amount of that consolidated adjusted net minimum tax.

(B) *Example.* The provisions of this paragraph (h)(6)(vi) are illustrated by the following example.

Example. (i) P, S1, and S2 file a consolidated return. In 1994, the group has consolidated adjusted net minimum tax of $100. Pursuant to the allocation method provided in paragraph (h)(6)(iii) of this section, P's, S1's, and S2's allocable shares of the 1994 consolidated adjusted net minimum tax are $60, $30, and $10, respectively. The group has no separate return year MTC as defined in paragraph (h)(4) of this section.

(ii) In 1995, the group has an $80 excess of modified consolidated regular tax over consolidated tentative minimum tax. Accordingly, $80 of the 1994 consolidated adjusted net minimum tax is allowable as a consolidated MTC in 1995 to offset consolidated regular tax.

(iii) As described in paragraph (h)(6)(ii) of this section, each member's allocable share of the 1994 consolidated adjusted net minimum tax is reduced by its allocable share of that $80 amount allowable as a consolidated MTC in 1995. The reduction amount is, under paragraph (h)(6)(vi) of this section, determined by multiplying the consolidated adjusted net minimum tax allowable as a consolidated MTC by a fraction, the numerator of which is the member's allocable share of that consolidated adjusted net minimum tax and the denominator of which is the total amount of that consolidated adjusted net minimum tax. As provided above, P's allocable share of the consolidated adjusted net minimum tax is 60 percent (60/100), S1's allocable share is 30 percent (30/100), and S2's allocable share is 10 percent (10/100). Accordingly, P's allocable share of the consolidated adjusted net minimum tax is reduced by $48 ($80 multiplied by .60). S1's allocable share of the consolidated adjusted net minimum tax is reduced by $24 ($80 multiplied by .30). S2's allocable share of the consolidated adjusted net minimum tax is reduced by $8 ($80 multiplied by .10).

(7) *Amount of adjusted net minimum tax allowable as a consolidated MTC.*—Under the rules provided in paragraphs (h)(3)(i)(B)(*1*), (h)(4)(i)(B)(2), (h)(6)(ii), and (h)(6)(vi) of this section, adjusted net minimum tax, whether consolidated adjusted net minimum tax or adjusted net minimum tax from separate return years, must be reduced by the amount of that adjusted net minimum tax allowable in a subsequent consolidated return year as a consolidated MTC. For purposes of those rules, consolidated adjusted net minimum tax and adjusted net minimum tax from separate return years are allowable as a consolidated MTC in the order of the taxable year in which the adjusted net minimum tax is imposed, with the adjusted net minimum tax imposed in the taxable year with the earliest year end allowable first. Consolidated adjusted net minimum tax and adjusted net minimum tax from separate return years imposed in taxable years ending on the same date are considered to be allowable as a consolidated MTC in proportion to the total consolidated adjusted net minimum tax and adjusted net minimum tax from separate return years incurred in that same taxable year. If, however, there is a limitation on the use of a consolidated MTC (*e.g.*, under section 383), the adjusted net minimum tax unable to be used as a credit because of the limitation is disregarded for purposes of the computation provided in this paragraph (h)(7).

(i) [Reserved].

(j) *Successor and predecessor.*—For purposes of this section any reference to a corporation or member includes, as the context may require, a reference to a successor or predecessor.

(k) *Effective date.*—This section applies to any consolidated return year for which the due date of the income tax return (without regard to extensions) is on or after [the date that is sixty days after final regulations are filed with the Federal Register]. [Reg. § 1.1502-55.]

Base Erosion and Anti-Abuse Tax: Guidance

Base Erosion and Anti-Abuse Tax: Guidance.—Reg. § 1.1502-59A, regarding the tax on base erosion payments of taxpayers with substantial gross receipts and reporting requirements thereunder, is proposed (published in the Federal Register on December 21, 2018) (REG-104259-18).

Par. 8. Section 1.1502-59A is added to read as follows:

§ 1.1502-59A. Payment and returns of tax withheld by the acquiring agency.—(a) *Scope.*—This section provides rules for the application of section 59A and the regulations thereunder (the *section 59A regulations,* see §§ 1.59A-1 through 1.59A-10) to consolidated groups and their members (as defined in § 1.1502-1(h) and (b), respectively). Rules in the section 59A regulations apply to consolidated groups except as modified in this section. Paragraph (b) of this section provides rules treating a consolidated group (rather than each member of the group) as a single taxpayer, and a single applicable taxpayer, as relevant, for certain purposes. Paragraph (c) of this section coordinates the application of the business interest stacking rule under § 1.59A-3(c)(4) to consolidated groups. Paragraph (d) of this section addresses how the base erosion minimum tax amount is allocated among members of the consolidated group. Paragraph (e) of this section sets forth definitions. Paragraph (f) of this section provides examples. Paragraph (g) of this section provides the applicability date and a transition rule.

(b) *Consolidated group as the applicable taxpayer.*—(1) *In general.*—For purposes of determining whether the consolidated group is an applicable taxpayer (within the meaning of § 1.59A-2(b)) and the amount of tax due pursuant to section 59A(a), all members of a consolidated group are treated as a single taxpayer. Thus, for example, members' deductions are aggregated in making the required computations under section 59A. In addition, items resulting from intercompany transactions (as defined in § 1.1502-13(b)(1)(i)) are disregarded for purposes of making the required computations. For example, additional depreciation deductions resulting from intercompany asset sales are not taken into account for purposes of applying the base erosion percentage test under § 1.59A-2(e).

(2) *Consolidated group as member of the aggregate group.*—The consolidated group is treated

as a single member of an aggregate group for purposes of § 1.59A-2(c).

(3) *Related party determination.*—For purposes of section 59A and the section 59A regulations, if a person is a related party with respect to any member of a consolidated group, that person is a related party of the group and of each of its members.

(c) *Coordination of section 59A(c)(3) and section 163(j) in a consolidated group.*—(1) *Overview.*—This paragraph (c) provides rules regarding the application of § 1.59A-3(c)(4) to a consolidated group's section 163(j) interest deduction. The classification rule in paragraph (c)(3) of this section addresses how to determine if, and to what extent, the group's section 163(j) interest deduction is a base erosion tax benefit. These regulations contain a single-entity classification rule with regard to the deduction of the consolidated group's aggregate current year business interest expense ("BIE"), but a separate-entity classification rule for the deduction of the consolidated group's disallowed BIE carryforwards. Paragraph (c)(3) of this section classifies the group's aggregate current year BIE deduction, in conformity with § 1.59A-3(c)(4), as constituting domestic related current year BIE deduction, foreign related current year BIE deduction, or unrelated current year BIE deduction. The allocation rules in paragraph (c)(4) of this section then allocate to specific members of the group the domestic related current year BIE deduction, foreign related current year BIE deduction, and unrelated current year BIE deduction taken in the taxable year. Any member's current year BIE that is carried forward to the succeeding taxable year as a disallowed BIE carryforward is allocated a status as domestic related BIE carryforward, foreign related BIE carryforward, or unrelated BIE carryforward under paragraph (c)(5) of this section. The status of any disallowed BIE carryforward deducted by a member in a later year is classified on a separate-entity basis by the deducting member under paragraph (c)(3) of this section, based on the status allocated to the member's disallowed BIE carryforward under paragraph (c)(5) of this section. This paragraph (c) also provides rules regarding the consequences of the deconsolidation of a corporation that has been allocated a domestic related BIE carryforward status, a foreign related BIE carryforward status, or an unrelated BIE carryforward status; and the consolidation of a corporation with a disallowed BIE carryforward classified as from payments to a domestic related party, foreign related party, or unrelated party.

(2) *Absorption rule for the group's business interest expense.*—To determine the amount of the group's section 163(j) interest deduction, and to determine the year in which the member's business interest expense giving rise to the deduction was incurred or accrued, see §§ 1.163(j)-4(d) and 1.163(j)-5(b)(3).

(3) *Classification of the group's section 163(j) interest deduction.*—(i) *In general.*—Consistent with § 1.59A-3(c)(4)(i) and paragraph (b) of this section, the classification rule of this paragraph (c)(3) determines whether the consolidated group's section 163(j) interest deduction is a base erosion tax benefit. To the extent the consolidated group's business interest expense is permitted as a deduction under section 163(j)(1) in a taxable year, the deduction is classified first as from business interest expense paid or accrued to a foreign related party and business interest expense paid or accrued to a domestic related party (on a pro-rata basis); any remaining deduction is treated as from business interest expense paid or accrued to an unrelated party.

(ii) *Year-by-year application of the classification rule.*—If the consolidated group's section 163(j) interest deduction in any taxable year is attributable to business interest expense paid or accrued in more than one taxable year (for example, the group deducts the group's aggregate current year BIE, the group's disallowed BIE carryforward from year 1, and the group's disallowed BIE carryforward from year 2), the classification rule in paragraph (c)(3)(i) of this section applies separately to each of those years, pursuant to paragraphs (c)(3)(iii) and (iv) of this section.

(iii) *Classification of current year BIE deductions.*—Current year BIE deductions are classified under the section 59A regulations and this paragraph (c) as if the consolidated group were a single taxpayer that had paid or accrued the group's aggregate current year BIE to domestic related parties, foreign related parties, and unrelated parties. The rules of paragraph (c)(4) of this section apply for allocating current year BIE deductions among members of the consolidated group. To the extent the consolidated group's aggregate current year BIE exceeds its section 163(j) limitation, the rules of paragraph (c)(5) of this section apply.

(iv) *Classification of deductions of disallowed BIE carryforwards.*—Each member of the group applies the classification rule in this paragraph (c)(3) to its deduction of any part of a disallowed BIE carryforward from a year, after the group applies paragraph (c)(5) of this section to the consolidated group's disallowed BIE carryforward from that year. Therefore, disallowed BIE carryforward that is actually deducted by a member is classified based on the status of the components of that carryforward, assigned pursuant to paragraph (c)(5) of this section.

(4) *Allocation of domestic related current year BIE deduction status and foreign related current year BIE deduction status among members of the consolidated group.*—(i) *In general.*—This paragraph (c)(4) applies if the group has domestic related current year BIE deductions, foreign related current year BIE deductions, or both, as a result of the application of the classification rule in paragraph (c)(3) of this section. Under this paragraph (c)(4), the domestic related current year BIE, foreign related current year BIE, or both, that is treated as deducted in the current year are deemed to have been incurred pro-rata by all members that have current year BIE deduction in that year, regardless of which member or members actually incurred the current year BIE to a domestic related party or a foreign related party.

(ii) *Domestic related current year BIE deduction.*—(A) *Amount of domestic related current year BIE deduction status allocable to a member.*—The amount of domestic related current year BIE deduction status that is allocated to a member is determined by multiplying the group's domestic related current year BIE deduction (determined pursuant to paragraph (c)(3) of this section) by the percentage of current year BIE deduction allocable to such member in that year.

(B) *Percentage of current year BIE deduction allocable to a member.*—The percentage of current year BIE deduction allocable to a member is equal to the amount of the member's current year BIE deduction divided by the amount of the group's aggregate current year BIE deduction.

(iii) *Amount of foreign related current year BIE deduction status allocable to a member.*—The amount of foreign related current year BIE deduction status that is allocated to a member is determined by multiplying the group's foreign related current year BIE deduction (determined pursuant to paragraph (c)(3) of this section) by the percentage of current year BIE deduction allocable to such member (defined in paragraph (c)(4)(ii)(B) of this section).

(iv) *Treatment of amounts as having unrelated current year BIE deduction status.*—To the extent the amount of a member's current year BIE that is absorbed under paragraph (c)(2) of this section exceeds the domestic related current year BIE deduction status and foreign related current year BIE deduction status allocated to the member under paragraph (c)(4)(ii) and (iii) of this section, such excess amount is treated as from payments or accruals to an unrelated party.

(5) *Allocation of domestic related BIE carryforward status and foreign related BIE carryforward status to members of the group.*—(i) *In general.*—This paragraph (c)(5) applies in any year the consolidated group's aggregate current year BIE exceeds its section 163(j) limitation. After the application of paragraph (c)(4) of this section, any remaining domestic related current year BIE, foreign related current year BIE, and unrelated current year BIE is deemed to have been incurred pro-rata by members of the group pursuant to the rules in paragraph (c)(5)(ii), (iii), and (iv) of this section, regardless of which member or members actually incurred the business interest expense to a domestic related party, foreign related party, or unrelated party.

(ii) *Domestic related BIE carryforward.*—(A) *Amount of domestic related BIE carryforward status allocable to a member.*—The amount of domestic related BIE carryforward status that is allocated to a member equals the group's domestic related BIE carryforward from that year multiplied by the percentage of disallowed BIE carryforward allocable to the member.

(B) *Percentage of disallowed BIE carryforward allocable to a member.*—The percentage of disallowed BIE carryforward allocable to a member for a taxable year equals the member's disallowed BIE carryforward from that year divided by the consolidated group's disallowed BIE carryforwards from that year.

(iii) *Amount of foreign related BIE carryforward status allocable to a member.*—The amount of foreign related BIE carryforward status that is allocated to a member equals the group's foreign related BIE carryforward from that year multiplied by the percentage of disallowed BIE carryforward allocable to the member (as defined in paragraph (c)(5)(ii)(B) of this section).

(iv) *Treatment of amounts as having unrelated BIE carryforward status.*—If a member's disallowed BIE carryforward for a year exceeds the amount of domestic related BIE carryforward status and foreign related BIE carryforward status that is allocated to the member pursuant to paragraphs (c)(5)(ii) and (iii) of this section, respectively, the excess carryforward amount is treated as from payments or accruals to an unrelated party.

(v) *Coordination with section 381.*—If a disallowed BIE carryforward is allocated a status as a domestic related BIE carryforward, foreign related BIE carryforward, or unrelated BIE carryforward under the allocation rule of paragraph (c)(5) of this section, the acquiring corporation in a transaction described in section 381(a) will succeed to and take into account the allocated status of the carryforward for purposes of section 59A. See § 1.381(c)(20)-1.

(6) *Member deconsolidates from a consolidated group.*—When a member deconsolidates from a group (the original group), the member's disallowed BIE carryforwards retain their allocated status, pursuant to paragraph (c)(5) of this section, as a domestic related BIE carryforward, foreign related BIE carryforward, or unrelated BIE carryforward (as applicable). Following the member's deconsolidation, no other member of the original group is treated as possessing the domestic related BIE carryforward status, foreign related BIE carryforward status, or unrelated BIE carryforward status that is carried forward by the departing member.

(7) *Corporation joins a consolidated group.*—If a corporation joins a consolidated group (the acquiring group), and that corporation was allocated a domestic related BIE carryforward status, foreign related BIE carryforward status, or unrelated BIE carryforward status pursuant to paragraph (c)(5) of this section from another consolidated group (the original group), or separately has a disallowed BIE carryforward that is classified as from payments or accruals to a domestic related party, foreign related party, or unrelated party, the status of the carryforward is taken into account in determining the acquiring group's base erosion tax benefit when the corporation's disallowed BIE carryforward is absorbed.

(d) *Allocation of the base erosion minimum tax amount to members of the consolidated group.*—For rules regarding the allocation of the base erosion minimum tax amount, see section 1552. Allocations under section 1552 take into account the classification and allocation provisions of paragraphs (c)(3) through (5) of this section.

(e) *Definitions.*—The following definitions apply for purposes of this section –

(1) *Aggregate current year BIE.*—The consolidated group's *aggregate current year BIE* is the aggregate of all members' current year BIE.

(2) *Aggregate current year BIE deduction.*—The consolidated group's *aggregate current year BIE deduction* is the aggregate of all members' current year BIE deductions.

(3) *Applicable taxpayer.*—The term *applicable taxpayer* has the meaning provided in § 1.59A-2(b).

(4) *Base erosion minimum tax amount.*—The consolidated group's *base erosion minimum tax amount* is the tax imposed under section 59A.

(5) *Base erosion tax benefit.*—The term *base erosion tax benefit* has the meaning provided in § 1.59A-3(c)(1).

(6) *Business interest expense*.—The term *business interest expense*, with respect to a member and a taxable year, has the meaning provided in § 1.163(j)-1(b)(2), and with respect to a consolidated group and a taxable year, has the meaning provided in § 1.163(j)-4(d)(2)(iii).

(7) *Consolidated group's disallowed BIE carryforwards*.—The term *consolidated group's disallowed BIE carryforwards* has the meaning provided in § 1.163(j)-5(b)(3)(i).

(8) *Current year BIE*.—A member's *current year BIE* is the member's business interest expense that would be deductible in the current taxable year without regard to section 163(j) and that is not a disallowed business interest expense carryforward from a prior taxable year.

(9) *Current year BIE deduction*.—A member's *current year BIE deduction* is the member's current year BIE that is permitted as a deduction in the taxable year.

(10) *Domestic related BIE carryforward*.—The consolidated group's *domestic related BIE carryforward* for any taxable year is the excess of the group's domestic related current year BIE over the group's domestic related current year BIE deduction (if any).

(11) *Domestic related current year BIE*.—The consolidated group's *domestic related current year BIE* for any taxable year is the consolidated group's aggregate current year BIE paid or accrued to a domestic related party.

(12) *Domestic related current year BIE deduction*.—The consolidated group's *domestic related current year BIE deduction* for any taxable year is the portion of the group's aggregate current year BIE deduction classified as from interest paid or accrued to a domestic related party under paragraph (c)(3) of this section.

(13) *Domestic related party*.—A *domestic related party* is a related party that is not a foreign related party and is not a member of the same consolidated group.

(14) *Disallowed BIE carryforward*.—The term *disallowed BIE carryforward* has the meaning provided in § 1.163(j)-1(b)(9).

(15) *Foreign related BIE carryforward*.—The consolidated group's *foreign related BIE carryforward* for any taxable year, is the excess of the group's foreign related current year BIE over the group's foreign related current year BIE deduction (if any).

(16) *Foreign related current year BIE*.—The consolidated group's *foreign related current year BIE* for any taxable year is the consolidated group's aggregate current year BIE paid or accrued to a foreign related party.

(17) *Foreign related current year BIE deduction*.—The consolidated group's *foreign related current year BIE deduction* for any taxable year is the portion of the consolidated group's aggregate current year BIE deduction classified as from interest paid or accrued to a foreign related party under paragraph (c)(3) of this section.

(18) *Foreign related party*.—A *foreign related party* has the meaning provided in § 1.59A-1(b)(12).

(19) *Related party*.—The term *related party* has the meaning provided in § 1.59A-1(b)(17), but excludes members of the same consolidated group.

(20) *Section 163(j) interest deduction*.—The term *section 163(j) interest deduction* means, with respect to a taxable year, the amount of the consolidated group's business interest expense permitted as a deduction pursuant to § 1.163(j)-5(b)(3) in the taxable year.

(21) *Section 163(j) limitation*.—The term *section 163(j) limitation* has the meaning provided in § 1.163(j)-1(b)(31).

(22) *Unrelated BIE carryforward*.—The consolidated group's *unrelated BIE carryforward* for any taxable year is the excess of the group's unrelated current year BIE over the group's unrelated current year BIE deduction.

(23) *Unrelated current year BIE*.—The consolidated group's *unrelated current year BIE* for any taxable year is the consolidated group's aggregate current year BIE paid or accrued to an unrelated party.

(24) *Unrelated current year BIE deduction*.—The consolidated group's *unrelated current year BIE deduction* for any taxable year is the portion of the group's aggregate current year BIE deduction classified as from interest paid or accrued to an unrelated party under paragraph (c)(3) of this section.

(25) *Unrelated party*.—An *unrelated party* is a party that is not a related party.

(f) *Examples*.—The following examples illustrate the general application of this section. For purposes of the examples, a foreign corporation (FP) wholly owns domestic corporation (P), which in turn wholly owns S1 and S2. P, S1, and S2 are members of a consolidated group. The consolidated group is a calendar year taxpayer.

(1) *Example 1: Computation of the consolidated group's base erosion minimum tax amount*. (i) *The consolidated group is the applicable taxpayer*. (A) *Facts*. The members have never engaged in intercompany transactions. For the 2019 taxable year, P, S1, and S2 were permitted the following amounts of deductions (within the meaning of section 59A(c)(4)), $2,400x, $1,000x, and $2,600x; those deductions include base erosion tax benefits of $180x, $370x, and $230x. The group's consolidated taxable income for the year is $150x. In addition, the group satisfies the gross receipts test in § 1.59A-2(d).

(B) *Analysis*. Pursuant to paragraph (b) of this section, the receipts and deductions of P, S1, and S2 are aggregated for purposes of making the computations under section 59A. The group's base erosion percentage is 13% (($180x + $370x + $230x)/($2,400x + $1,000x + $2,600x)). The consolidated group is an applicable taxpayer under § 1.59A-2(b) because the group satisfies the gross receipts test and the group's base erosion percentage (13%) is higher than 3%. The consolidated group's modified taxable income is computed by adding back the members' base erosion tax benefits (and, when the consolidated group has consolidated net operating loss available for deduction, the consolidated net operating loss allowed times base erosion percentage) to the consolidated taxable income, $930x ($150x + $180x + $370x + $230x). The group's base erosion minimum tax amount is then computed as 10 percent of the modified taxable income less the regular tax liability, $61.5x ($930x × 10% - $150x × 21%).

(ii) *The consolidated group engages in intercompany transactions*. (A) *Facts*. The facts are the same as in paragraph (f)(1)(i)(A) of this section (the facts in *Example 1(i)*), except that S1 sold various inventory items to S2 during 2019. Such items are depreciable in the hands of S2 (but would not have been depreciable in the hands of S1) and continued to be owned by S2 during 2019.

(B) *Analysis*. The result is the same as paragraph (f)(1)(i)(A) of this section (the facts in *Example 1*(i)),. Pursuant to paragraph (b)(2) of this section, items resulting from the intercompany sale (for example, gross receipts, depreciation deductions) are not taken into account in computing the group's gross receipts under § 1.59A-2(d) and base erosion percentage under § 1.59A-2(e)(3).

(2) *Example 2: Business interest expense subject to section 163(j) and the group's domestic related current year BIE and foreign related current year BIE for the year equals its section 163(j) limitation.* (i) *Facts*. During the current year (Year 1), P incurred $150x of business interest expense to domestic related parties; S1 incurred $150x of business interest expense to foreign related parties; and S2 incurred $150x of business interest expense to unrelated parties. The group's section 163(j) limitation for the year is $300x. After applying the rules in § 1.163(j)-5(b)(3), the group deducts $150x of P's Year 1 business interest expense, and $75x each of S1 and S2's Year 1 business interest expense. Assume the group is an applicable taxpayer for purposes of section 59A.

(ii) *Analysis*—(A) *Application of the absorption rule in paragraph (c)(2) of this section*. Following the rules in section 163(j), the group's section 163(j) interest deduction for Year 1 is $300x, and the entire amount is from members' Year 1 business interest expense.

(B) *Application of the classification rule in paragraph (c)(3) of this section*. Under paragraph (c)(3) of this section, the group's aggregate current year BIE deduction of $300x is first classified as payments or accruals to related parties (pro-rata among domestic related parties and foreign related parties), and second as payments or accruals to unrelated parties. For Year 1, the group has $150x of domestic related current year BIE and $150x of foreign related current year BIE, and the group's aggregate current year BIE deduction will be classified equally among the related party expenses. Therefore, $150x of the group's deduction is classified as domestic related current year BIE deduction and $150x is classified as a foreign related current year BIE deduction.

(C) *Application of the allocation rule in paragraph (c)(4) of this section*. After the application of the classification rule in paragraph (c)(3) of this section, the group has $150x each of domestic related current year BIE deduction and foreign related current year BIE deduction from the group's aggregate current year BIE in Year 1. The domestic related current year BIE deduction and foreign related current year BIE deduction will be allocated to P, S1, and S2 based on each member's deduction of its Year 1 business interest expense.

(*1*) *Allocations to P*. The percentage of current year BIE deduction attributable to P is 50% (P's deduction of its Year 1 current year BIE, $150x, divided by the group's aggregate current year BIE deduction for Year 1, $300x). Thus, the amount of domestic related current year BIE deduction status allocated to P is $75x (the group's domestic related current year BIE deduction, $150x, multiplied by the percentage of current year BIE deduction allocable to P, 50%); and the amount of foreign related current year BIE deduction status allocated to P is $75x (the group's foreign related current year BIE deduction, $150x, multiplied by the percentage of current year BIE deduction allocable to P, 50%).

(*2*) *Allocations to S1 and S2*. The percentage of current year BIE deduction attributable to S1 is 25% (S1's deduction of its Year 1 current year BIE, $75x, divided by the group's aggregate current year BIE deduction for Year 1, $300x). Thus, the amount of domestic related current year BIE deduction status allocated to S1 is $37.5x (the group's domestic related current year BIE deduction, $150x, multiplied by the percentage of current year BIE deduction allocable to S1, 25%); and the amount of foreign related current year BIE deduction status allocated to S1 is $37.5x (the group's foreign related current year BIE deduction, $150x, multiplied by the percentage of current year BIE deduction allocable to S1, 25%). Because S2 also deducted $75 of its Year 1 current year BIE, S2's deductions are allocated the same pro-rata status as those of S1 under this paragraph (f)(2)(ii)(C)(*2*).

(D) *Application of the allocation rule in paragraph (c)(5) of this section*. Although the group will have disallowed BIE carryforwards after Year 1 (the group's aggregate current year BIE of $450x ($150x + $150x + $150x) exceeds the section 163(j) limitation of $300x), all of the domestic related current year BIE and foreign related current year BIE in Year 1 has been taken into account pursuant to the classification rule in paragraph (c)(3) of this section. Thus, under paragraph (c)(5)(iv) of this section, each member's disallowed BIE carryforward is treated as from payments or accruals to unrelated parties.

(3) *Example 3: Business interest expense subject to section 163(j).* (i) *The group's domestic related current year BIE and foreign related current year BIE for the year exceeds its section 163(j) limitation.* (A) *Facts*. During the current year (Year 1), P incurred $60x of business interest expense to domestic related parties; S1 incurred $40x of business interest expense to foreign related parties; and S2 incurred $80x of business interest expense to unrelated parties. The group's section 163(j) limitation for the year is $60x. After applying the rules in § 1.163(j)-5(b)(3), the group deducts $20x each of P, S1, and S2's current year business interest expense. Assume the group is an applicable taxpayer for purposes of section 59A.

(B) *Analysis*—(*1*) *Application of the absorption rule in paragraph (c)(2) of this section*. Following the rules in section 163(j), the group's section 163(j) interest deduction is $60x, and the entire amount is from members' Year 1 business interest expense.

(*2*) *Application of the classification rule in paragraph (c)(3) of this section*. Under paragraph (c)(3) of this section, the group's $60x of aggregate current year BIE deduction is first classified as payments or accruals to related parties (pro-rata among domestic related parties and foreign related parties), and second as payments or accruals from unrelated parties. The group's total related party interest expense in Year 1, $100x (sum of the group's Year 1 domestic related current year BIE, $60x, and the group's Year 1 foreign related current year BIE, $40x), exceeds the group's aggregate current year BIE deduction of

$60x. Thus, the group's aggregate current year BIE deduction will be classified, pro-rata, as from payments or accruals to domestic related parties and foreign related parties. Of the group's aggregate current year BIE deduction in Year 1, $36x is classified as a domestic related current year BIE deduction (the group's aggregate current year BIE deduction, $60x, multiplied by the ratio of domestic related current year BIE over the group's total Year 1 related party interest expense ($60x / ($60x+$40x))); and $24x of the group's aggregate current year BIE deduction is classified as a foreign related current year BIE deduction (the group's section 163(j) interest deduction, $60x, multiplied by the ratio of foreign related current year BIE over the group's total Year 1 related party interest expense ($40x / ($60x+$40x))).

(3) *Application of the allocation rule in paragraph (c)(4) of this section.* After the application of the classification rule in paragraph (c)(3) of this section, the group has $36x of domestic related current year BIE deduction and $24x of foreign related current year BIE deduction from the group's aggregate current year BIE in Year 1. The domestic related current year BIE deduction and foreign related current year BIE deduction will be allocated to P, S1, and S2 based on each member's current year BIE deduction in Year 1.

(*i*) *Allocation of the group's domestic related current year BIE deduction status.* Because each member is deducting $20x of its Year 1 business interest expense, all three members have the same percentage of current year BIE deduction attributable to them. The percentage of current year BIE deduction attributable to each of P, S1, and S2 is 33.33% (each member's current year BIE deduction in Year 1, $20x, divided by the group's aggregate current year BIE deduction for Year 1, $60x). Thus, the amount of domestic related current year BIE deduction status allocable to each member is $12x (the group's domestic related current year BIE deduction, $36x, multiplied by the percentage of current year BIE deduction allocable to each member, 33.33%).

(*ii*) *Allocations of the group's foreign related current year BIE deduction status.* The amount of foreign related current year BIE deduction status allocable to each member is $8x (the group's foreign related current year BIE deduction, $24x, multiplied by the percentage of current year BIE deduction allocable to each member, 33.33%, as computed earlier in paragraph (f)(3) of this section (*Example 3*).

(4) *Application of the allocation rule in paragraph (c)(5) of this section.* In Year 1 the group has $60x of domestic related current year BIE, of which $36x is deducted in the year (by operation of the classification rule). Therefore, the group has $24x of domestic related BIE carryforward. Similarly, the group has $40x of foreign related current year BIE in Year 1, of which $24x is deducted in the year. Therefore, the group has $16x of foreign related BIE carryforward. The $24x domestic related BIE carryforward status and $16x foreign related BIE carryforward status will be allocated to P, S1, and S2 in proportion to the amount of each member's disallowed BIE carryforward.

(*i*) *Allocation to P.* The percentage of disallowed BIE carryforward allocable to P is 33.33% (P's Year 1 disallowed BIE carryforward, $40x ($60x-$20x), divided by the group's Year 1 disallowed BIE carryforward, $120x ($60x + $40x + 80x - $60x)). Thus, the amount of domestic related BIE carryforward status allocated to P is $8x (the group's domestic related BIE carryforward, $24x, multiplied by the percentage of disallowed BIE carryforward allocable to P, 33.33%); and the amount of foreign related BIE carryforward status allocated to P is $5.33x (the group's foreign related BIE carryforward, $16x, multiplied by the percentage of disallowed BIE carryforward allocable to P, 33.33%). Under paragraph (c)(5)(iv) of this section, P's disallowed BIE carryforward that has not been allocated a status as either a domestic related BIE carryforward or a foreign related BIE carryforward will be treated as interest paid or accrued to an unrelated party. Therefore, $26.67x ($40x P's disallowed BIE carryforward - $8x domestic related BIE carryforward status allocated to P - $5.33x foreign related BIE carryforward status allocated to P) is treated as interest paid or accrued to an unrelated party.

(*ii*) *Allocation to S1.* The percentage of disallowed BIE carryforward allocable to S1 is 16.67% (S1's Year 1 disallowed BIE carryforward, $20x ($40x - $20x), divided by the group's Year 1 disallowed BIE carryforward, $120x ($60x + $40x + 80x - $60x). Thus, the amount of domestic related BIE carryforward status allocated to S1 is $4x (the group's domestic related BIE carryforward, $24x, multiplied by the percentage of disallowed BIE carryforward allocable to S1, 16.67%); and the amount of foreign related BIE carryforward status allocated to S1 is $2.67x (the group's foreign related BIE carryforward, $16x, multiplied by the percentage of disallowed BIE carryforward allocable to S1, 16.67%). Under paragraph (c)(5)(iv) of this section, S1's disallowed BIE that has not been allocated a status as either a domestic related BIE carryforward or a foreign related BIE carryforward will be treated as interest paid or accrued to an unrelated party. Therefore, $13.33x ($20x S1's disallowed BIE carryforward - $4x domestic related BIE carryforward status allocated to S1 - $2.67x foreign related BIE carryforward status allocated to S1) is treated as interest paid or accrued to an unrelated party.

(*iii*) *Allocation to S2.* The percentage of disallowed BIE carryforward allocable to S2 is 50% (S2's Year 1 disallowed BIE carryforward, $60x ($80x-$20x), divided by the group's Year 1 disallowed BIE carryforward, $120x ($60x+$40x+80x-$60x). Thus, the amount of domestic related BIE carryforward status allocated to S2 is $12x (the group's domestic related BIE carryforward, $24x, multiplied by the percentage of disallowed BIE carryforward allocable to S2, 50%); and the amount of foreign related BIE carryforward status allocated to S2 is $8x (the group's foreign related BIE carryforward, $16x, multiplied by the percentage of disallowed BIE carryforward allocable to S2, 50%). Under paragraph (c)(5)(iv) of this section, S2's disallowed BIE that has not been allocated a status as either a domestic related BIE carryforward or a foreign related BIE carryforward will be treated as interest paid or accrued to an unrelated party. Therefore, $40x ($60x S2's disallowed BIE carryforward - $12x domestic related BIE carryforward status allocated to S2 - $8x foreign related BIE carryforward status allocated to S2) is treated as interest paid or accrued to an unrelated party.

(ii) *The group deducting its disallowed BIE carryforwards.* (A) *Facts.* The facts are the same as in paragraph (f)(3)(i)(A) of this section (the facts in *Example 3*(i)), and in addition, none of the members incurs any business interest expense in Year 2. The group's section 163(j) limitation for Year 2 is $30x.

(B) *Analysis*—(*1*) *Application of the absorption rule in paragraph (c)(2) of this section.* Following the rules in section 163(j), each member of the group is deducting $10x of its disallowed BIE carryforward from Year 1. Therefore, the group's section 163(j) deduction for Year 2 is $30x.

(*2*) *Application of the classification rule in paragraph (c)(3) of this section.* Under paragraph (c)(3)(iv) of this section, to the extent members are deducting their Year 1 disallowed BIE carryforward in Year 2, the classification rule will apply to the deduction in Year 2 after the allocation rule in paragraph (c)(5) of this section has allocated the related and unrelated party status to the member's disallowed BIE carryforward in Year 1. The allocation required under paragraph (c)(5) of this section is described in paragraph (f)(3)(i)(B)(*4*) of this section.

(*i*) *Use of P's allocated domestic related BIE carryforward status and foreign related BIE carryforward status.* P has $40x of Year 1 disallowed BIE carryforward, and P was allocated $8x of domestic related BIE carryforward status and $5.33x of foreign related BIE carryforward status. In Year 2, P deducts $10x of its Year 1 disallowed BIE carryforward. Under the classification rule of paragraph (c)(3) of this section, P is treated as deducting pro-rata from its allocated status of domestic related BIE carryforward and foreign related BIE carryforward. Therefore, P is treated as deducting $6x of its allocated domestic related BIE carryforward ($10x × $8x / ($8x + $5.33x)), and $4x of its allocated foreign related BIE carryforward ($10x × $5.33x / $8x + $5.33x)). After Year 2, P has remaining $30x of Year 1 disallowed BIE carryforward, of which $2x has a status of domestic related BIE carryforward, $1.33x has the status of foreign related BIE carryforward, and $26.67x of interest treated as paid or accrued to unrelated parties.

(*ii*) *Use of S1's allocated domestic related BIE carryforward status and foreign related BIE carryforward status.* S1 has $20x of Year 1 disallowed BIE carryforward, and S1 was allocated $4x of domestic related BIE carryforward status and $2.67x of foreign related BIE carryforward status. In Year 2, S2 deducts $10x of its Year 1 disallowed BIE carryforward. Because S2's deduction of its Year 1 disallowed BIE carryforward, $10x, exceeds its allocated domestic related BIE carryforward status ($4x) and foreign related BIE carryforward status ($2.67x), all of the allocated related party status are used up. After Year 2, all of S1's Year 1 disallowed BIE carryforward, $10x, is treated as interest paid or accrued to an unrelated party.

(*iii*) *Use of S2's allocated domestic related BIE carryforward status and foreign related BIE carryforward status.* S2 has $60x of Year 1 disallowed BIE carryforward, and S2 was allocated $12x of domestic related BIE carryforward status and $8x of foreign related BIE carryforward status. In Year 2, S2 deducts $10x of its Year 1 disallowed BIE carryforward. Under the classification rule of paragraph (c)(3) of this section, S2 is treated as deducting $6x of its allocated domestic related BIE carryforward ($10x × $12x / ($12x + $8x)), and $4x of its allocated foreign related BIE carryforward ($10x × $8x / $8x + $12x)). After Year 2, P has remaining $50x of Year 1 disallowed BIE carryforward, of which $6x has a status of domestic related BIE carryforward, $4x has the status of foreign related BIE carryforward, and $40x of interest treated as paid or accrued to unrelated parties.

(g) *Applicability date.*—(1) *In general.*—Except as provided in this paragraph (g), this section applies to taxable years beginning after December 31, 2017.

(2) *Application of section 59A if S joins a consolidated group with a taxable year beginning before January 1, 2018.*—If during calendar year 2018 a corporation (S) joins a consolidated group during a consolidated return year beginning before January 1, 2018, then section 59A will not apply to S's short taxable year that is included in the group's consolidated return year, even though S's short taxable year begins after December 31, 2017. [Reg. § 1.1502-59A.]

Application of Section 172(h): Regulations: Consolidated Groups

Application of Section 172(h): Regulations: Consolidated Groups.—Reg. § 1.1502-72, providing guidance regarding the treatment of corporate equity reduction transactions (CERTs), including the treatment of multiple step plans for the acquisition of stock and CERTs involving members of a consolidated group, are proposed (published in the Federal Register on September 17, 2012) (REG-140668-07) (corrected October 23, 2012).

☐ Par. 4. Section 1.1502-72 is added to read as follows:

§ 1.1502-72. Corporate equity reduction transactions.—(a) *In general.*—(1) *Scope.*—Section 172(b)(1)(E) and (h), § § 1.172(h)-1 through 1.172(h)-5, and the rules of this section (the CERT rules) apply to determine whether a corporate equity reduction transaction (CERT) has occurred and to determine the consequences of the CERT, including rules governing the carryback of losses following a CERT, with respect to corporations that become, are, or cease to be members of a consolidated group.

(2) *Single entity treatment.*—(i) *In general.*—All members of a group are treated as a single taxpayer for purposes of the CERT rules. For example, if multiple members of a group acquire in total 50 percent or more (by vote or value) of the stock of another corporation, the group has engaged in a major stock acquisition (MSA) as defined in section 172(h)(3)(B) and § 1.172(h)-1(c)(2). The transactions and expenditures undertaken by a particular group member are generally not separately tracked; instead, the entire group is treated as a single applicable corporation.

(ii) *Debt and interest of group members.*—(A) *In general.*—The computation of a group's corporate equity reduction interest loss (CERIL) under section 172(h)(1) and § 1.172(h)-2(a)(2) for any loss limitation year (as defined in paragraph (a)(3) of this section) that is a consolidated return year includes the debt of all members and all interest deductions that are allowed on the group's consolidated return for that year. This rule applies regardless of whether any particular debt or interest expense is directly related to the CERT, whether any particular member was included in the group on the date of the CERT, or whether any particular debt would not exist in the group if the group had not engaged in the CERT. But see paragraph (a)(2)(iii) of this section (providing that intercompany transactions are generally disregarded).

(B) *Debt of acquired corporation.*—With respect to a corporation that joins a consolidated group (acquired corporation), in applying the CERT rules to consolidated return years that are loss limitation years, any debt of the acquired corporation is treated as debt of the acquiring group for purposes of applying the avoided cost rules of section 263A(f)(2)(A) on any measurement date after the inclusion of the corporation in the group. See section 172(h)(2) and § 1.172(h)-2(b) (applying the principles of section 263A(f)(2)(A)(ii)); see also § 1.263A-9(f)(2) (defining measurement dates).

(iii) *Intercompany transactions.*—In applying the CERT rules, intercompany transactions as defined in § 1.1502-13 are generally disregarded. For example, interest expense attributable to an intercompany obligation is not taken into account in computing the CERIL or three-year average of a group. However, a transaction between group members is not disregarded if a party to the transaction becomes a non-member pursuant to the same plan or arrangement. In such case, any transaction between group members, including a potential excess distribution (ED) as defined in section 172(h)(3)(C), § 1.172(h)-1(c)(3), and paragraph (f)(1) of this section, is tested on a separate entity basis under the CERT rules. It may also be tested as part of a larger, multi-step MSA. See § 1.172(h)-1(d)(2).

(iv) *Applicable corporation status following inclusion of member with preexisting CERT.*—(A) *Acquiring group treated as applicable corporation.*—If a corporation that is an applicable corporation (including by application of paragraph (b) of this section) with regard to a CERT occurring in a separate return year (pre-existing CERT member) joins a consolidated group, the group is treated as a single applicable corporation with regard to that CERT in the consolidated return year of the acquisition and any succeeding year. A corporation is a pre-existing CERT member regardless of whether the transaction at issue is an MSA that constitutes a CERT with respect to both a consolidated return year of the acquiring group and a separate return year of the acquired corporation.

(B) *End of separate tracking of target.*—Beginning on the first day on which a pre-existing CERT member is included in a consolidated group, the member ceases to be separately tracked as an applicable corporation. See paragraph (a)(2)(i) of this section. The CERT rules thereafter apply to the group, rather than to the member, with regard to any CERT for which the member had been an applicable corporation, including an MSA in which the member was acquired by the group. Therefore, beginning on the day on which the pre-existing CERT member is included in the group, no CERIL is computed with regard to the member, independent of the CERIL computed for the group. But see § 1.1502-21(b)(2)(iv)(C) (providing for allocation and apportionment of a group's CERIL to specific group members) and § 1.172(h)-5(b)(1) (relating to prohibition on carryback of a CERIL).

(3) *Loss limitation years.*—(i) *In general.*—This paragraph applies to identify loss limitation years of a consolidated group and corporations that have been members of a consolidated group. The taxable year in which a CERT actually occurs is a loss limitation year. Any other taxable year (potential loss limitation year) of any applicable corporation (including a consolidated group) constitutes a loss limitation year with regard to the CERT only if, under the carryforward rules of sections 172(b)(1)(A)(ii) and 381(c)(1), the potential loss limitation year would constitute the first or second taxable year following the taxable year of the corporation or consolidated group that actually engaged in the CERT that includes the date on which the CERT occurred. Except as otherwise provided in paragraph (a)(3)(ii) of this section, for purposes of this paragraph (a)(3), sections 172 and 381 are applied as if the inclusion of any corporation in a consolidated group or the deconsolidation of any member from a group were a transaction listed in section 381(a).

(ii) *Corporation joins group in an MSA.*—If a corporation joins a group in an MSA, no separate return year of the acquired corporation ending on or before it joined the acquiring group is treated as a loss limitation year for the purpose of determining the loss limitation years of the acquiring group or any corporation that deconsolidates from that group that relate to the MSA.

(iii) *Deconsolidating members.*—Under this paragraph (a)(3)(iii), a corporation that deconsolidates (deconsolidating member) from a group (former group) that is an applicable corporation may have loss limitation years with regard to a CERT of its former group. See paragraphs (b) (relating to postdeconsolidation status as applicable corporation) and (e)(1) of this section (providing for an irrevocable waiver of carrybacks such that a deconsolidating member is not treated as an applicable corporation). If the consolidated return year during which the deconsolidation occurs (year of deconsolidation) is a first or second loss limitation year with regard to the CERT, then certain separate return years of a deconsolidating member that is treated as an applicable corporation will constitute loss limitation years. If the year of deconsolidation is a first loss limitation year with regard to the CERT, the following two separate return years will constitute loss limitation years. If the year of deconsolidation is a second loss limitation year with regard to the CERT, the separate return year that immediately follows the year of deconsolidation will constitute a loss limitation year. If the deconsolidating member joins another consolidated group, the consolidated return years of that group may also constitute loss limitation years with regard to the CERT of the former group. See paragraph (a)(2)(iv) of this section (relating to inclusion of member with pre-existing CERT).

(4) *Application of rules to reverse acquisitions.*—In the case of any acquisition to which

§ 1.1502-75(d)(3) applies (a reverse acquisition), for purposes of applying the CERT rules, the first corporation (as defined in § 1.1502-75(d)(3)(i)) is treated as the corporation the stock of which is acquired, and the second corporation (as defined in § 1.1502-75(d)(3)(i)) is treated as the corporation that acquires stock. In addition, for purposes of § 1.172(h)-2(b)(3)(i) (identifying CERT costs of an MSA) in the case of a reverse acquisition, the fair market value of the stock acquired equals the fair market value of the stock of the first corporation that the stockholders (immediately before the acquisition) of the first corporation own immediately after the acquisition, rather than the fair market value of the stock of the second corporation.

(b) *Applicable corporation status following deconsolidation.*—(1) *In general.*—If a corporation deconsolidates in a loss limitation year from a group that is treated as an applicable corporation with regard to a CERT, the deconsolidating corporation and the former group are both treated as applicable corporations following the deconsolidation. If the corporation joins another consolidated group (acquiring group) following the deconsolidation, the rules of this section apply to the acquiring group, and this paragraph (b) applies with regard to the deconsolidation of any member from the acquiring group during a loss limitation year associated with the CERT. See paragraph (a)(2)(iv) of this section regarding treatment of a group as a single applicable corporation following an acquisition; see also paragraph (a)(3)(ii) of this section for identification of loss limitation years following a deconsolidation. This paragraph (b) applies without regard to whether any particular corporation would on a separate entity basis have constituted an applicable corporation with regard to the CERT under section 172(b)(1)(E)(iii) and § 1.172(h)-1(b), with or without the application of section 172(h)(4)(C) and paragraph (a)(2) of this section, or whether the CERT occurred in a consolidated return year. However, under this paragraph (b), the deconsolidating corporation may be treated as an applicable corporation with regard to a CERT of a former group only if the group engages in the CERT on or before the date of the deconsolidation, or if a pre-existing CERT member, as described in paragraph (a)(2)(iv)(A) of this section, joins the group on or before the date of the deconsolidation.

(2) *Exception if waiver filed.*—In general, a corporation that deconsolidates from a group (or the parent of a group acquiring the deconsolidating member), may, pursuant to paragraph (e)(1) of this section, make an irrevocable election to relinquish the carryback of all net operating losses (NOLs) (and attributable portions of consolidated net operating losses (CNOLs)) to taxable years of the former group and any preceding years. If such an election is made, the deconsolidating member is not treated as an applicable corporation with regard to any CERT of the former group after the deconsolidation. Any group that acquires the deconsolidating member is not treated as an applicable corporation with regard to any CERT of the former group solely as a result of the acquisition of that member. The former group will continue to be treated as an applicable corporation with regard to the CERT.

(3) *Examples.*—The following examples illustrate the rules of paragraph (a) of this section and this paragraph (b). For purposes of these examples, assume that all entities are domestic C corporations unless otherwise stated. Assume that all applicable corporations have substantial NOLs in their loss limitation years:

Example 1. Single entity treatment of acquisition indebtedness. (i) *Facts.* Corporation T is a calendar-year taxpayer that has significant debt outstanding, which was incurred to fund operations. Unrelated P is the common parent of a calendar-year consolidated group. The following steps occur pursuant to an integrated plan. On May 1, Year 5, P acquires 10 percent of the T stock for $100. On June 30, Year 5, T borrows $700 and immediately thereafter uses the money to redeem some of its shares from its shareholders. On the same day, the P group acquires all of the remaining T stock in exchange for $200. Assume that the $700 cash payment from T to the T shareholders is treated as a redemption. T is first included in the P group on July 1, Year 5. Under § 1.172(h)-1(d)(2), the steps of the integrated plan (including the redemption of the former T shareholders) constitute a single MSA.

(ii) *Analysis.* T's short taxable year ending June 30, Year 5 is T's year of the CERT. The P group's consolidated return Year 5 is the taxable year of the CERT for the group. For purposes of allocating to the single MSA interest paid or accrued during the P group's loss limitation years (Years 5, 6, and 7) under § 1.172(h)-2(b), the P group takes into account the debt of all members, including the $700 loan and all of T's other debt. See paragraph (a)(2)(ii)(B) of this section. The allocation of interest also takes into account all deductions for interest paid or accrued that are included in the consolidated return for the relevant loss limitation year. See paragraph (a)(2)(ii)(A) of this section.

Example 2. Loss limitation years if a corporation joins group in an MSA. Corporation T maintains a taxable year ending June 30. Unrelated X is the common parent of a calendar-year consolidated group. On March 31, Year 5, the X group acquires all of the T stock in a CERT, and T is first included in the X group on April 1, Year 5. On the date of the acquisition, both the X group and T constitute applicable corporations with regard to the Year 5 CERT. See § 1.172(h)-1(b) and paragraph (a)(2) of this section. T's short taxable year ending on March 31, Year 5, was T's taxable year in which the CERT occurred. T's only loss limitation year with respect to the Year 5 CERT is its short taxable year ending on March 31, Year 5. See § 1.172(h)-1(e) and paragraph (a)(3) of this section. Beginning on April 1, Year 5, T ceases to be separately tracked as an applicable corporation. See paragraph (a)(2)(i) and (iv)(B) of this section. The X group's year in which the CERT occurred is its consolidated return Year 5. The X group's loss limitation years with respect to the Year 5 CERT are its full taxable calendar Years 5, 6, and 7. See paragraph (a)(3)(i) and (ii) of this section.

Example 3. Loss limitation years of a group and deconsolidating member. (i) *Facts.* P is the common parent of a calendar-year consolidated group that includes S. On June 30, Year 6, a member of the P group engages in an acquisition that constitutes a CERT. S is not a party to the acquisition. On September 30, Year 6, S deconsolidates from the P group. No election under paragraph (e)(1) of this section is made with respect to the deconsolidation of S. Following its deconsolidation, S does not join in the filing of a consolidated return with another group, and it maintains a calendar taxable year.

(ii) *Analysis*. Because no election is made under paragraph (e)(1) of this section, following the deconsolidation, both the P group and S are treated as applicable corporations with regard to the Year 6 CERT. See paragraph (b)(1) of this section. The P group's loss limitation years with regard to the CERT are its consolidated return Years 6, 7, and 8. See section 172(b)(1)(E)(ii) and paragraph (a)(3)(i) of this section. S deconsolidates from the P group during consolidated return Year 6, which is the first loss limitation year with regard to the CERT. See paragraph (a)(3)(i) of this section. For purposes of applying paragraph (a)(3) of this section to identify loss limitation years, S is treated as deconsolidating from the P group in a transaction to which section 381(a) applies. Therefore, S's two taxable years that follow the deconsolidation, the short year ending December 31, Year 6, and the full taxable calendar Year 7, are its additional loss limitation years with regard to the Year 6 CERT. See paragraph (a)(3)(iii) of this section. See section 172(b)(1)(E)(i) and §1.172(h)-5(b)(1) for rules regarding the prohibition on carryback of a CERIL.

Example 4. Loss limitation years if a preexisting CERT member joins the group. (i) *Acquiring group has loss limitation years*. Corporation T maintains a calendar taxable year and does not join in the filing of a consolidated return. On July 1, Year 5, T engages in a CERT (Year 5 CERT). Unrelated X is the common parent of a calendar-year consolidated group that includes S. On December 31, Year 5, the X group acquires all of the outstanding T stock. T is first included in the X group on January 1, Year 6. The first loss limitation year with respect to the Year 5 CERT is T's calendar Year 5. See §1.172(h)-1(e). As a result of the X group's acquisition of T, the X group is treated as a single applicable corporation with respect to the Year 5 CERT. See paragraph (a)(2)(iv) of this section. For purposes of applying paragraph (a)(3) of this section to identify loss limitation years, T is treated as joining the X group in a transaction to which section 381(a) applies. Because T has one loss limitation year with regard to the CERT before it joins the X group, the X group has two loss limitation years with respect to the Year 5 CERT: its calendar Years 6 and 7. See paragraph (a)(3)(i) of this section. However, the X group must test its acquisition of T under the CERT rules.

(ii) *Acquiring group has no loss limitation years*. The facts are the same as in paragraph (i) of this *Example 4*, except that the X group acquires T on January 31, Year 7. Because T has three loss limitation years before it is included in the X group (calendar Years 5 and 6, and a short taxable year ending on January 31, Year 7), none of the X group's consolidated return years are loss limitation years with regard to the Year 5 CERT. See section 172(b)(1)(E)(ii) and paragraph (a)(3)(i) of this section.

(iii) *Member deconsolidates from acquiring group*. The facts are the same as in paragraph (i) of this *Example 4*, except that S deconsolidates from the X group on June 30, Year 6. No election under paragraph (e)(1) of this section is made on the deconsolidation of S. Following its deconsolidation from the X group, S does not join in the filing of a consolidated return. T and the X group's loss limitation years remain the same as in paragraph (i) of this *Example 4*. Because no election is made under paragraph (e)(1) of this section with respect to S's deconsolidation, following the deconsolidation, S and the X group are both treated as applicable corporations with regard to T's Year 5 CERT. See paragraph (b)(1) of this section. S deconsolidates from the P group during consolidated return Year 6, which is the second loss limitation year with regard to the CERT. See paragraph (a)(3)(i) of this section. Therefore, following its deconsolidation, S's only loss limitation year with respect to the Year 5 CERT is its short taxable year July 1, Year 6 through December 31, Year 6. See paragraph (a)(3)(iii) of this section.

Example 5. Deconsolidation before group engages in CERT. Corporation T is a member of the P group, which maintains a calendar taxable year. On February 28, Year 4, T deconsolidates from the P group due to T's acquisition by the X group, which also maintains a calendar taxable year. T is included in the X group as of March 1, Year 4. No election under paragraph (e)(1) of this section is made on the deconsolidation of T from the P group. On March 31, Year 4, the P group engages in a CERT. Because the P group engages in the CERT after the date of the deconsolidation, T is not treated as an applicable corporation following the deconsolidation. See paragraph (b)(1) of this section. However, the X group must apply the CERT rules to the X group's acquisition of T.

Example 6. Member that engages in CERT deconsolidates with a waiver election. (i) *Facts*. P is the common parent of a calendar-year consolidated group. On March 31, Year 4, the P group engages in an MSA, when member T acquires all of the stock of T1. On June 30, Year 4, T and its subsidiaries (including T1) deconsolidate from the P group due to the acquisition of T by the X group. T and its subsidiaries are first included in the X group as of July 1, Year 4. The X group makes an election under paragraph (e)(1) of this section on the deconsolidation.

(ii) *Analysis*. Because an election under paragraph (e)(1) of this section is made on the deconsolidation of T and its subsidiaries from the P group, following the deconsolidation, only the P group is treated as an applicable corporation with regard to the March 31, Year 4 CERT. Neither T, T1, nor the X group is treated as an applicable corporation with regard to the March 31, Year 4 CERT, even though T directly engaged in the MSA, and T1 was the acquired corporation in that MSA. See paragraph (b)(2) of this section. However, the X group must apply the CERT rules to the X group's acquisition of T.

(c) *Identification and allocation of CERT costs*.—(1) *In general*.—The portion of an NOL that is treated as a CERIL is subject to limitation on carryback. See section 172(b)(1)(E)(i) and §1.172(h)-5(b)(1). A CERIL is computed in part by identifying the deductions allowed for interest allocable to the CERT. The computation of interest allocable to a CERT under section 172(h)(2) and §1.172(h)-2(b) takes into account all CERT costs as defined in §1.172(h)-2(b)(3). This paragraph (c) contains rules applicable to the identification and allocation of CERT costs of a consolidated group.

(2) *Single entity treatment of CERT costs.*—The computation of interest allocable to a CERT in any particular loss limitation year of a consolidated group includes CERT costs incurred (including costs deemed incurred under this paragraph (c)) with regard to the CERT by all corporations that are members of a group during the loss limitation year.

(3) *CERT costs of acquired corporation.*—With respect to a corporation that joins a consolidated group (acquired corporation), for purposes of applying the CERT rules, any CERT costs incurred (or treated as incurred under this paragraph (c)) by the acquired corporation during separate return years prior to the acquired corporation's inclusion in the group are attributed to the acquiring group. Such costs are treated as having been incurred by the acquiring group for purposes of applying the avoided cost rules of section 263A(f)(2)(A) to any measurement date after the acquisition of the corporation. Those CERT costs are no longer separately identified as CERT costs incurred by the acquired corporation.

(4) *Allocation of CERT costs on deconsolidation.*—(i) *In general.*—This paragraph (c)(4) applies to determine the CERT costs allocable to a corporation that deconsolidates in a loss limitation year from a group that is treated as an applicable corporation with regard to a CERT. Under this paragraph (c)(4), CERT costs may be allocated to a deconsolidating corporation only if the group engages in the relevant CERT on or before the date of the deconsolidation, or if a pre-existing CERT member, as described in paragraph (a)(2)(iv)(A) of this section, joins the group on or before the date of the deconsolidation. This paragraph (c)(4) applies regardless of whether any particular corporation would have constituted an applicable corporation under section 172(b)(1)(E)(iii) and § 1.172(h)-1(b) without the application of section 172(h)(4)(C) and paragraph (a)(2) of this section, whether the CERT occurred in a consolidated return year, or whether any particular corporation actually incurred CERT costs.

(ii) *No waiver election made.*—If no election under paragraph (e)(1) of this section is made with regard to the deconsolidation, CERT costs incurred by the group (including costs treated as incurred by the group under this paragraph (c)) are allocated between the deconsolidating corporation and the former group, solely for purposes of computing allocable interest deductions of the deconsolidating corporation and the continuing group with regard to the CERT under section 172(h)(2) and § 1.172(h)-2(b). For purposes of computing interest allocable to the CERT under section 172(h)(2) and § 1.172(h)-2(b) during the loss limitation year of the former group that is the year of the deconsolidation, the CERT costs allocated to the deconsolidating member are included in the group's accumulated CERT costs on those measurement dates on which the deconsolidating corporation was included in the group. The portion of the group's total CERT costs that is allocated to a deconsolidating member equals the group's total CERT costs multiplied by a fraction, the numerator of which equals the value of the deconsolidating corporation immediately after its deconsolidation, and the denominator of which equals the value of the entire group immediately prior to the deconsolidation.

(iii) *Waiver election made.*—If an election under paragraph (e)(1) of this section is made with regard to a deconsolidation, no CERT costs are allocated to the deconsolidating corporation. All CERT costs remain with the former group for purposes of identifying its allocable interest deductions under section 172(h)(2) and § 1.172(h)-2(b) with regard to the CERT.

(5) *Examples.*—The following examples illustrate the rules of this paragraph (c). For purposes of the examples in this paragraph (c)(5), assume that all entities are domestic C corporations unless otherwise stated. Assume that all applicable corporations have substantial NOLs in their loss limitation years:

Example 1. Aggregation of CERT costs of consolidated group and target. (i) *Facts.* P is the common parent of a calendar-year consolidated group that includes S1 and S2. On June 30, Year 5, S1 acquires all of the stock of T for $10 million. P incurs CERT costs of $100,000 and $250,000 for work performed by its outside counsel and an investment banker, respectively, that facilitates the acquisition. In addition, T incurs CERT costs of $175,000 for work performed by its outside counsel that facilitates the acquisition. All of these costs are incurred on or before the date of the acquisition. In all relevant years preceding its acquisition, T does not join in the filing of a consolidated return.

(ii) *Analysis.* For purposes of computing the P group's allocable interest deductions under section 172(h)(2) and § 1.172(h)-2(b), the P group's CERT costs include CERT costs incurred by all members of the P group. See paragraph (c)(2) of this section. In addition, when T joins the P group, the CERT costs incurred by T prior to its inclusion in the P group are attributed to the P group and are treated as having been incurred by the P group for purposes of applying the avoided cost rules of section 263A(f)(2)(A) to any measurement date after the acquisition of T. See paragraph (c)(3) of this section. As a result, the P group's accumulated CERT costs on July 1, Year 5, are $10,525,000 [$10,000,000 + $100,000 + $250,000 + $175,000]. See § 1.172(h)-2(b)(3) for rules defining CERT costs.

Example 2. Acquiring group treated as incurring CERT costs associated with unrelated CERT of target. T is a calendar-year taxpayer that does not join in the filing of a consolidated return. P is the common parent of a calendar-year consolidated group. P also owns 70 percent of the only class of T stock. During Year 4, T engages in a CERT. On June 30, Year 5, P acquires the remainder of the stock of T, and T is first included in the P group on July 1, Year 5. Following the acquisition, the P group is treated as an applicable corporation with regard to T's Year 4 CERT. See paragraph (a)(2)(iv) of this section. The P group's consolidated return Year 5 is the third and final loss limitation year with regard to the Year 4 CERT. See paragraph (a)(3)(i) of this section. The P group is treated as having incurred all of T's expenses allocable to the CERT for purposes of computing any CERIL for consolidated return Year 5. Because T was a member of the P group for less than the entire calendar taxable Year 5, T's CERT costs are included in the P group's accumulated CERT costs only on those measurement dates on which T is included in the group (that is, measurement dates on or after July 1, Year 5). See paragraph (c)(3) of this section and §1.172(h)-2(b)(4). See also paragraph (d)(3)(iii) for rules relating to the interest history of a partial-year member.

Example 3. Allocation of CERT costs to deconsolidating member. (i) *Facts.* P is the common parent of a calendar-year consolidated group. P owns 60 percent of the sole class of stock of T, a calendar-year taxpayer. On January 31, Year 5, the P group engages in a CERT. On March 31, Year 5, P acquires the remainder of the stock of T, and T is first included in the P group on April 1, Year 5. On June 30, Year 6, T deconsolidates from the P group, with no election made under paragraph (e)(1) of this section.

(ii) *Analysis.* T is not a member of the P group at the time of the CERT. However, following its deconsolidation, T is treated as an applicable corporation with regard to the Year 5 CERT because the P group engages in the CERT before T deconsolidates, and no election is made under paragraph (e)(1) of this section on the deconsolidation. See paragraph (b)(1) of this section. Further, a portion of the P group's CERT costs is allocated to T for purposes of computing any CERIL of T (or of any group of which T becomes a member following its deconsolidation from the P group) with regard to the Year 5 CERT. See paragraphs (b)(1) and (c)(4)(ii) of this section. However, the CERT costs of the group otherwise allocated to T are included in the P group's accumulated CERT costs on those measurement dates during which T is included in the group (that is, measurement dates before July 1, Year 6). See paragraph (c)(4)(ii) of this section and §1.172(h)-2(b)(4).

(d) *Determining the three-year average of a group.*—(1) *In general.*—Section 172(h)(2)(C) and §1.172(h)-3(a) limit the amount of allocable interest deductions to the excess (if any) of the amount allowable as a deduction for interest paid or accrued by the taxpayer during the loss limitation year, over the average of interest paid or accrued by the taxpayer (the three-year average) for the three taxable years preceding the taxable year in which the CERT occurred (the lookback period). The computation under section 172(h)(2)(C)(ii) and §1.172(h)-3(b) of a group's three-year average for the lookback period that is relevant to any loss limitation year includes interest paid or accrued (or treated as paid or accrued under this paragraph (d)) during the lookback period by all corporations that are members of the consolidated group during the loss limitation year.

(2) *Varying group membership.*—If group membership varies from one loss limitation year to another, a different three-year average is computed with regard to each loss limitation year of the group.

(3) *Interest history.*—(i) *Combination of interest history of acquired member with group history.*—With respect to a corporation that joins a consolidated group (acquired corporation), for purposes of applying the CERT rules, the interest paid or accrued (or treated as paid or accrued under this paragraph (d)) by the acquired corporation during each separate return year prior to its inclusion in the group is apportioned equally to each day within each of its separate return years. The interest apportioned to dates within the lookback period is then combined with the interest paid or accrued by the acquiring group and is treated as interest paid or accrued by the acquiring group during the lookback period for purposes of computing the three-year average that is relevant to any loss limitation year beginning with the consolidated return year during which the acquired corporation is first included in the group. For purposes of the CERT rules, the interest from the separate return years is no longer separately traced as interest paid or accrued by the acquired corporation. But see paragraph (d)(3)(iii) of this section for rules requiring proration of interest history attributable to corporations that are members of a group for less than an entire loss limitation year. The interest paid or accrued by a predecessor (as defined in §1.172(h)-(1)(b)(2)) of a member of the group is similarly combined with the interest paid or accrued by the group. See §1.172(h)-4(c)(2)(ii)(A).

(ii) *Interest treated as paid or accrued by a corporation that deconsolidates.*—(A) *In general.*—This paragraph (d)(3)(ii) provides rules that apply for purposes of determining any three-year average of a corporation that deconsolidates from a group (or a three-year average of any other group of which it becomes a member) and any three-year average of the group from which the corporation deconsolidates (former group). These rules apply to the computation of any three-year average with regard to a CERT of the former group or any other CERT.

(B) *Waiver election made.*—If an election under paragraph (e)(1) of this section is made with respect to the deconsolidation of a corporation from a group, then, following the deconsolidation, the deconsolidating member is treated as having paid or accrued zero interest during the period of its inclusion in the former group and preceding years. The group retains the interest history that would otherwise be allocated and apportioned to the deconsolidating member under this paragraph (d)(3)(ii).

(C) *No waiver election made.*—If no election under paragraph (e)(1) of this section is made with respect to the deconsolidation of a corporation, a portion of the group's amount of interest treated as paid or accrued during the period of the corporation's consolidation and any preceding years is allocated and apportioned to the deconsolidating corporation. The allocated and apportioned interest is subtracted from the group's interest history and is unavailable to the group (or any other group member) for purposes of computing a three-year average with regard to any loss limitation year of the group (or any other group member) after the year of deconsolidation. But see paragraph (d)(3)(iii) of this section for rules requiring proration of interest history attributable to corporations that are members of a group for less than an entire loss limitation year.

(D) *Method of allocation.*—If no election under paragraph (e)(1) of this section is made when a corporation deconsolidates, solely for purposes of the CERT rules, the corporation is treated as having paid or accrued interest equal to the amount of interest paid or accrued by the group in each consolidated return year through the date of the deconsolidation (including any combination of interest history pursuant to paragraph (d)(3)(i) of this section), multiplied by a fraction, the numerator of which equals the value of the deconsolidating corporation immediately after its deconsolidation, and the denominator of which equals the value of the entire group immediately prior to the deconsolidation.

(iii) *Proration of lookback period interest for members that are part of a group for less than the entire loss limitation year.*—If any member is included in the group for less than an entire consolidated return year that is a loss limitation year (partial-year member), then the group takes into account a pro rata portion of the partial-year member's amount of interest paid or accrued during the lookback period for purposes of determining a group's three-year average relevant to that loss limitation year. The amount of interest treated as paid or accrued that is subject to proration under this paragraph (d)(3)(iii) is the interest of the partial-year member that would otherwise be fully combined with the interest history of the acquiring group under paragraph (d)(3)(i) of this section (with regard to corporations acquired during the loss limitation year) or the interest that is otherwise allocated to a deconsolidating member under paragraph (d)(3)(ii) of this section. The pro rata amount equals the partial-year member's interest treated as paid or accrued for the dates of the lookback period, multiplied by a fraction, the numerator of which equals the number of days of the loss limitation year during which the partial-year member was a member of the group, and the denominator of which equals the number of days in the loss limitation year. This proration applies to interest paid or accrued during the entire lookback period, including portions of the lookback period during which the partial-year member was a member of the group.

(4) *Lookback period.*—(i) *In general.*—The lookback period with regard to a CERT is the three taxable years preceding the taxable year in which the CERT occurs. See section 172(h)(2)(C)(ii) and § 1.172(h)-3(a). The lookback period that is relevant to any CERIL of a consolidated group is the three taxable years preceding the taxable year of the group that includes the date on which the CERT occurred. See § 1.172(h)-5(a) (defining the date on which a CERT occurs if the CERT consists of multiple steps). This rule applies whether the group actually engaged in the CERT or is treated as an applicable corporation with regard to a CERT solely by application of paragraph (a)(2)(iv) of this section.

(ii) *Group not in existence for entire lookback period.*—If a group was not in existence for three taxable years prior to the consolidated return year that includes the date of the CERT, the lookback period includes the group's taxable years preceding the year of the CERT plus the preceding taxable years of the corporation that was the common parent of the group on the first day of the group's first consolidated return year (original common parent). If the group and the original common parent together have fewer than three taxable years that precede the consolidated return year that includes the date of the CERT, the lookback period will be deemed to include full 12-month periods that end on the calendar date that is one day prior to the date of organization of the original common parent.

(iii) *Group not in existence on date of CERT.*—If a group was not in existence on the date on which the CERT occurred, for purposes of determining the lookback period, the group's taxable years will be deemed to include the taxable years of the group's original common parent. If the original common parent was not in existence on the date of the CERT, or it does not have three taxable years that precede its taxable year that includes the date of the CERT, the group will be deemed to have additional 12-month taxable periods that end on the calendar date that is one day prior to the date of the original common parent's organization. From these deemed taxable periods, the group will identify the deemed period that includes the date on which the CERT occurred and the three immediately preceding deemed periods that constitute the lookback period. See § 1.172(h)-5(a) regarding date on which CERT occurred in multi-step transaction.

(iv) *Interest history of corporations not in existence.*—If any member of a group is not in existence for the entire lookback period, for purposes of the CERT rules, that member is treated as having paid or accrued zero interest before its organization. But see § 1.172(h)-4(c)(2)(ii) (regarding interest history of successors).

(5) *Examples.*—The following examples illustrate the rules of this paragraph (d). Unless otherwise stated, assume that all entities are domestic C corporations that have full, 12-month taxable years. Assume that all applicable corporations have substantial NOLs in their loss limitation years:

Example 1. Acquired member's interest history combined with interest history of group. (i) *Facts.* P is the common parent of a calendar-year consolidated group that includes S on all relevant dates. On December 31, Year 5, S acquires the stock of T in a CERT, and T is first included in the P group on January 1, Year 6. Membership in the P group is otherwise stable for all relevant years. Prior to joining the P group, T does not join in the filing of a consolidated return and maintains a calendar taxable year. T's amounts of interest paid or accrued in Years 2, 3, and 4, respectively, are $600, $200, and $400. The P group's amounts of interest paid or accrued in Years 2, 3, and 4, respectively, are $1,400, $1,000, and $1,200.

(ii) *Analysis.* The P group's loss limitation years are calendar Years 5, 6, and 7. See paragraph (a)(3)(i) of this section. Year 5 is also a loss limitation year for T. The P group's lookback period with regard to the CERT is calendar Years 2, 3, and 4. See paragraph (d)(4)(i) of this section. For purposes of computing any three-year average of the P group for its lookback period, on the acquisition of T, the interest history of T is generally combined with the interest history of the P group. See paragraph (d)(3)(i) of this section. However, because T is not a member of the P group on any date during consolidated return Year 5, the computation of the P group's three-year average relevant to Year 5 will not include any of T's interest paid or accrued during the lookback period. See paragraph (d)(3)(iii) of this section. Thus, the P group's three-year average for loss limitation Year 5 is $1,200 ([$1,400 + $1,000 + $1,200]/3). Because T is a member of the P group during each day of loss limitation Years 6 and 7, T's history of interest paid or accrued during the lookback period is fully included in the P group's computation of its three-year average relevant to loss limitation Years 6 and 7. See paragraph (d)(3)(i) and (iii) of this section. Thus, the P group's three-year average for loss limitation Years 6 and 7 is $1,600 ([$1,400 + $1,000 + $1,200 + $600 + $200 + $400]/3).

(iii) *Interest combination if acquired member included in group for part of loss limitation year.* The facts are the same as in paragraph (i) of this *Example 1*, except that S acquires the stock of T on March 31, Year 5, and T is included in the P group for 275 days. Because T is a partial-year member of the P group during loss limitation Year 5, the computation of the three-year average relevant to loss limitation Year 5 includes the interest of T for the lookback period, prorated as required under paragraph (d)(3)(iii) of this section. Because T is in the P group for 275 days during Year 5, the computation of the P group's threeyear average relevant to Year 5 takes into account an amount of T's interest history equal to T's actual amount of interest paid or accrued for each year of the lookback period, multiplied by a fraction equal to 275/365 (number of days of the loss limitation year during which T is a member of the P group divided by the number of days in the loss limitation year), or $452 ($600 x [275/365]), $151 ($200 x [275/365]), and $301 ($400 x [275/365]) for Years 2, 3, and 4, respectively.

Example 2. Lookback period if corporation with CERT history joins group. (i) *Facts.* P is the common parent of a calendar-year consolidated group. P also owns 55 percent of the sole class of stock of Corporation T, which maintains a taxable year ending June 30. On September 30, Year 4, T engages in a CERT. On December 31, Year 5, P acquires the remainder of the stock of T, and T is first included in the P group on January 1, Year 6.

(ii) *Analysis.* T's full taxable year ending June 30, Year 5, and its short year ending December 31, Year 5 are loss limitation years with regard to the September Year 4 CERT. The lookback period for the CERT relevant to these two loss limitation years is T's three taxable years ending on June 30, Years 2, 3, and 4. See section 172(h)(2)(C)(ii) and §1.172(h)-3(a). The P group's calendar Year 6 is its sole loss limitation year with regard to T's September Year 4 CERT. See paragraph (a)(3)(i) of this section. In determining any CERIL with regard to the P group's calendar Year 6, the lookback period is the three taxable years prior to the taxable year of the group that includes the date on which the CERT occurred. See paragraph (d)(4)(i) of this section. Therefore, the lookback period with regard to the P group's loss limitation Year 6 is calendar consolidated return Years 1, 2, and 3.

Example 3. Interest history if no waiver election made on member deconsolidation. (i) *Facts.* P is the common parent of a calendar-year consolidated group that includes S. The P group engaged in a CERT on December 27, Year 5. S deconsolidates from the P group on December 31, Year 5. No election under paragraph (e)(1) of this section is made on the deconsolidation of S. S's value immediately after its deconsolidation is $4,000. The P group's value immediately before S's deconsolidation is $10,000. The P group and its members engaged in no prior CERTs.

(ii) *Analysis.* Because the CERT occurs during the P group's calendar consolidated return Year 5, Years 5, 6, and 7 are the P group's loss limitation years. Because no election is made under paragraph (e)(1) of this section with regard to the deconsolidation of S, S is treated as an applicable corporation with regard to the Year 5 CERT under paragraph (b)(1) of this section and the interest history of the P group during the period of S's consolidation and any preceding years is allocated to S and the remaining members of the P group. See paragraph (d)(3)(ii)(C) of this section. The amount of the P group's interest for each year that is allocated to S is the amount of interest paid or accrued by the P group in the relevant consolidated return year multiplied by a fraction equal to 4,000 divided by 10,000 (the value of the deconsolidating corporation immediately after its deconsolidation divided by the value of the entire group immediately prior to the deconsolidation), or 2/5. See paragraph (d)(3)(ii)(D) of this section. The interest allocated to S is subtracted from the interest history of the group and is unavailable to the P group for purposes of computing a threeyear average with regard to any loss limitation year of the P group after the year of the deconsolidation, including Years 6 and 7. The interest history allocated to S will be maintained by S to be used in the computation of any CERIL of S, or any CERIL of any group of which S is later a member. See paragraph (d)(3)(ii)(C) of this section.

(iii) *Waiver election filed.* The facts are the same as in paragraph (i) of this *Example 3*, except that an election under paragraph (e)(1) of this section is filed on the deconsolidation of S. As a result of that election, S is not treated as an applicable corporation with regard to the Year 5 CERT under paragraph (b)(2) of this section and none of the interest history of the P group is allocated to S under paragraph (d)(3)(ii)(B) of this section. Therefore, in any post-deconsolidation year, for purposes of computing a CERIL in connection with any CERT with regard to which S (or of any group of which S is later a member) is an applicable corporation, S is treated as having paid or accrued zero interest for the period of its inclusion in the P group and preceding years. The P group will retain the interest history that would otherwise be allocated to S. See paragraph (d)(3)(ii)(B) of this section.

Example 4. Interest history if no waiver election made for member that deconsolidates prior to CERT. (i) *Facts.* P is the parent of a calendar-year consolidated group that includes S. On December 31, Year 4, S deconsolidates from the P group. No election is made under paragraph (e)(1) of this section with regard to the deconsolidation. On July 1, Year 5, the P group engages in a CERT. The P group and its members engaged in no prior CERTs.

(ii) *Analysis.* Because no election is made under paragraph (e)(1) of this section with regard to the deconsolidation of S, the interest history of the P group is allocated between S and the remaining members of the P group. See paragraph (d)(3)(ii)(C) of this section. This allocation occurs despite the fact that, at the time of the deconsolidation, the P group has not engaged in a CERT. Therefore, for purposes of computing any three-year average for the P group relevant to the Year 5 CERT, the portion of the interest history allocated to S is unavailable to the P group for purposes of computing a three-year average with regard to any loss limitation year of the P group after the year of the deconsolidation. See paragraph (d)(3)(ii)(C) of this section.

Example 5. Interest history if waiver election made for member that deconsolidates and then engages in a CERT. (i) *Facts.* P is the parent of a calendar-year consolidated group that includes X. On December 31, Year 5, X deconsolidates from the P group and makes an election under paragraph (e)(1) of this section. After its deconsolidation, X maintains a calendar taxable year. During Year 7, X engages in a CERT.

(ii) *Analysis.* X's loss limitation years with regard to the Year 7 CERT are Years 7, 8, and 9. X's lookback period with regard to the CERT is comprised of its Years 4 and 5 in the P consolidated group, and X's separate return Year 6. See section 172(h)(2)(C)(ii) and paragraph (d)(4)(i) of this section. As a result of the filing of the election under paragraph (e)(1) of this section, none of the interest history of the P group is allocated to X. Therefore, for purposes of computing X's three-year average for loss limitation Years 7, 8, and 9, X is treated as having paid or accrued zero interest during Years 4 and 5 of the lookback period. See paragraph (d)(3)(ii)(B) of this section.

Example 6. Interest history if member deconsolidates mid-year. (i) *Facts.* P is the common parent of a calendar-year consolidated group that includes S. S deconsolidates from the P group on June 30, Year 5. No election under paragraph (e)(1) of this section is made on the deconsolidation of S. During Year 5, but prior to the deconsolidation, the P group engages in a CERT. S is not a party to the CERT, and, throughout its history in the group, S paid or accrued only nominal interest.

(ii) *Analysis.* The P group's lookback period is calendar Years 2, 3, and 4. Consolidated return Years 5, 6, and 7 are the P group's loss limitation years. Because no election is made under paragraph (e)(1) of this section with regard to the deconsolidation of S, the interest history of the P group is allocated between S and the remaining members of the P group. See paragraph (d)(3)(ii)(C) of this section. This is true although S played no part in the CERT, and it actually paid or accrued only nominal interest. In the consolidated return year of the deconsolidation (here, the P group's Year 5), S was a member for 181 days. Therefore, the P group includes in the computation of its three-year average relevant to Year 5 a pro rata portion of the interest history allocated to S. See paragraph (d)(3)(ii)(C) and (iii) of this section. The pro rata portion equals the group's interest history allocated to S under paragraph (d)(3)(ii)(C) and (D) of this section, multiplied by a fraction equal to 181/365 (number of days of the loss limitation year during which S is a member divided by the number of days in the loss limitation year). See paragraph (d)(3)(iii) of this section. The portion of the interest history allocated to S is excluded in its entirety from the computation of the group's three-year average relevant to Years 6 and 7. The interest history allocated to S will be used in the computation of any CERIL of S, and any CERIL of any group of which S is later a member. See paragraph (d)(3)(ii)(C) of this section.

Example 7. Group not in existence for the entire lookback period. (i) *Facts.* Corporation P is formed on October 1, Year 3, and maintains a calendar taxable year. On January 1, Year 4, P forms S in a transaction meeting the requirements of section 351. Beginning in Year 4, P files consolidated returns with S, its only subsidiary. The P group maintains a calendar taxable year. During Year 5, the P group engages in an ED.

(ii) *Analysis.* For purposes of limiting any CERIL related to the Year 5 CERT, the P group must measure its interest deductions for the three years preceding the taxable year in which the CERT occurs (three-year average). See section 172(h)(2)(C)(ii) and § 1.172(h)-3(a). However, the P group was not in existence for three taxable years before the year that includes the date of the CERT (calendar Year 5). Rather, the P group was in existence for one full calendar taxable year (Year 4). Because the group does not have a three-year history, the lookback period includes the common parent's (P's) short taxable year (October 1 through December 31, Year 3), and is also deemed to include an additional taxable period (October 1, Year 2 through September 30, Year 3). See paragraph (d)(4)(ii) of this section. Further, in computing the three-year average, the P group members are treated as having paid or accrued zero interest for dates on which they did not exist. However, the P group is treated as having paid any interest paid by P during its short taxable year (October 1 through December 31, Year 3). See paragraph (d)(4)(iv) of this section.

Example 8. Group not in existence prior to year of the CERT but target in existence. (i) *Facts.* Corporation P is formed on January 1, Year 4. On the same day, P organizes wholly-owned, special-purpose corporation S. T is an unrelated, calendar-year corporation with a significant tax history. On February 1, Year 4, S merges into T, with T surviving. In the merger, all of T's historic shareholders receive cash in exchange for their shares. Following the merger, P owns all of the outstanding stock of T, and P is treated as acquiring all the stock of T in an MSA. The P group files consolidated returns beginning in Year 4 and maintains a calendar taxable year. T is first included in the P group on February 2, Year 4.

(ii) *Analysis.* Neither P (the original common parent) nor the P group is in existence before the year that includes the date of the CERT (calendar Year 4). Therefore, for purposes of applying the interest allocation limitation of section 172(h)(2)(C) and § 1.172(h)-3(a), the P group's lookback period is deemed to include three additional taxable periods (January 1 through December 31 for Years 1, 2, and 3). See paragraph (d)(4)(ii) of this section. Further in computing the three-year average, P is treated as having paid or accrued zero interest during the deemed years (January 1, Year 1 through December 30, Year 3). See paragraph (d)(4)(iv) of this section. However, with respect to the group's acquisition of T, the interest history of T is combined with the interest history of the P group. Because T is not a member of the P group for each day of loss limitation Year 4, the computation of the three-year average applicable to loss limitation Year 4 will include only a pro rata portion of the interest of T for the lookback period. See paragraph (d)(3)(i), (d)(3)(iii), and paragraph (iii) of Example 1 of paragraph (d)(5) of this section.

(e) *Election to waive carryback from all separate return years.*—(1) *In general.*—In addition to any other elections available under section 172(b)(3) and § 1.1502-21(b)(3), if a member becomes a non-member of a group (former group), the former member may make an irrevocable election to relinquish the carryback of all NOLs (and attributable portions of CNOLs) to taxable years of the former group and any preceding years. If the former member becomes a member of another group (acquiring group) immediately after its deconsolidation from the former group, the election described in this paragraph (e)(1) is available only to the common parent of the acquiring group. The election is not an annual election and applies to all losses that would otherwise be subject to carryback to years of the former group (or preceding years) under section 172 or § 1.1502-21(b). The election is binding on the deconsolidating corporation and any group of which it may become a member. Further, the election is available without regard to whether the former group is treated as an applicable corporation with regard to any CERT at the time of the deconsolidation. Any election under this paragraph (e)(1) by the common parent of an acquiring group must include all deconsolidating corporations that were members of the former group and that joined the acquiring group during the same consolidated return year of the acquiring group. The election is made in a separate statement entitled, "THIS IS AN ELECTION UNDER § 1.1502-72(e)(1) TO WAIVE THE PRE-[insert the first taxable year following the deconsolidation of the former member(s) from the former group] CARRYBACK PERIOD FOR ALL NOLs AND ALL CNOLs ATTRIBUTABLE TO [insert the name(s) and EIN(s) of the corporation(s)]." The statement must be filed with the timely filed original return of the former member or the acquiring group for the first taxable year following the deconsolidation of the former member from the former group. See paragraphs (b)(2), (c)(4)(iii), and (d)(3)(ii)(B) of this section relating to treatment of a deconsolidating member making an election under this paragraph (e)(1).

(2) *Example.*—The following example illustrates the rules of this paragraph (e):

Example. P, a publicly-held corporation, is the common parent of a calendar-year consolidated group that includes T. On July 30, Year 5, the P group engages in a CERT. On December 31, Year 5, T deconsolidates from the P group, and it continues to maintain a calendar taxable year. With respect to its deconsolidation, T makes an election under paragraph (e)(1) of this section. As a result of such election, T is not treated as an applicable corporation with regard to the P group's Year 5 CERT and none of the CERT costs or interest history of the P group are allocated to T. See paragraphs (b)(2), (c)(4)(iii), and (d)(3)(ii)(B) of this section. On March 30, Year 6, the X group acquires all of the stock of T. The X group maintains a calendar taxable year. A portion of the X group's Year 6 CNOL is attributable to T under § 1.1502-21(b)(2)(iv)(B). Because T filed an election under paragraph (e)(1) of this section with respect to its deconsolidation from the P group, no portion of the X group's Year 6 CNOL attributable to T can be carried back to any taxable years of T, of the P group, or any preceding years.

(f) *Excess distribution.*—(1) *Defined.*—Section 172(h)(3)(C) and § 1.172(h)-1(c)(3) provide that an ED means the excess (if any) of the aggregate distributions (including redemptions) made during a taxable year by a corporation with respect to its stock, over the greater of 150 percent of the average of such distributions (three-year distribution average) for the three taxable years immediately preceding such taxable year (distribution lookback period), or 10 percent of the fair market value of the stock of such corporation as of the beginning of such taxable year.

(2) *Determination of an ED by a group.*—(i) *Aggregation of distributions to non-members.*—For purposes of determining whether a group has made an ED during any consolidated return year (potential ED year), distributions by all members of the group to non-members during the potential ED year are aggregated and tested under section 172(h)(3)(C), § 1.172(h)-1(c)(3), and paragraph (f)(1) of this section.

(ii) *Distributions between members of the same group.*—Distributions between members of the same group are generally disregarded for purposes of applying the CERT rules. However, the preceding sentence does not apply if a party to the transaction is deconsolidated pursuant to the same plan or arrangement. See paragraph (a)(2)(iii) of this section.

(3) *Computation of three-year distribution average.*—(i) *In general.*—The computation under section 172(h)(3)(C)(ii)(I) and § 1.172(h)-1(f) of the group's three-year distribution average includes distributions made during the distribution lookback period to non-members by each corporation that is a member of the consolidated group during the potential ED year. Distributions made during the distribution lookback period by predecessors of those members are also included. See § 1.172(h)-4(d). The computation includes distributions made by corporations during separate return years, subject to additional rules of this paragraph (f) and paragraph (a)(2)(iii) of this section. If a corporation was a member of a prior group during a portion of a distribution lookback period, the distribution history of that corporation during taxable years of the prior group includes only distributions made by that corporation to non-members of the prior group.

(ii) *Corporation deconsolidated from a group.*—If a corporation deconsolidates from a group (former group), the corporation's actual distribution history is subtracted from the group's distribution history and is available to the deconsolidating corporation (or any group of which it becomes a member) for purposes of computing any three-year distribution average following the deconsolidation. The deconsolidating member's distribution history will be unavailable to the former group for purposes of computing its three-year distribution average with regard to any potential ED year of the former group after the year of deconsolidation. See § 1.172(h)-1(f)(1) (excluding from three-year distribution average those distributions treated as part of an MSA).

(iii) *Members included in group for less than entire loss limitation year.*—If any member is included in the group for less than an entire potential ED year (partial-year member), then a pro rata portion of the partial-year member's distribution history is computed under the principles of paragraph (d)(3)(iii) of this section and is included for purposes of determining the group's three-year distribution average relevant to that potential ED year.

(4) *Stock value and stock issuances of a group.*—(i) *Stock issuances taken into account in computing distributions.*—Stock issued by a member of a group is taken into account in applying section 172(h)(3)(E)(ii) and § 1.172(h)-5(c)(1) only if the stock is issued to a non-member. Intercompany stock issuances are disregarded. This rule is applicable whether the stock issuance occurred in the current group or a previous group.

(ii) *Value of stock of group.*—For purposes of applying section 172(h)(3)(C)(ii)(II), § 1.172(h)-1(c)(3), and paragraph (f)(1) of this section (relating to the fair market value of the stock of a distributing corporation), the value of the stock of the group is the value of the stock of all members, other than stock that is owned directly or indirectly by another member. But see section 172(h)(3)(E)(i) for rules regarding the exclusion of certain preferred stock for purposes of applying sections 172(h)(3)(C), § 1.172(h)-1(c)(3) and (f), and this paragraph (f). See also paragraphs (a)(2)(iii) and (f)(2)(ii) of this section, requiring separate entity analysis of certain transactions between members of a consolidated group.

(5) *Examples.*—The following examples illustrate the rules of this paragraph (f). For purposes of these examples, assume that all entities are domestic C corporations:

Example 1. Corporation deconsolidates from group. (i) *Facts.* P is the common parent of a calendar-year consolidated group that includes T. P owns 90 percent of the outstanding stock of T, and A (an unrelated party) owns the remaining 10 percent of the outstanding stock of T. T regularly makes distributions to its shareholders, P and A. On December 31, Year 4, X, the common parent of another calendar-year consolidated group, acquires all of the outstanding stock of T, and T deconsolidates from the P group. T is first included in the X group on January 1, Year 5. On March 31, Year 5, X makes a large distribution to its non-member shareholders. X makes no further distributions during its taxable year.

(ii) *Analysis.* The X group's distribution to its non-member shareholders on March 31, Year 5, is tested as a potential ED under section 172(h)(3)(C), § 1.172(h)-1(c)(3) and (f), and paragraph (f) of this section. The X group's distribution lookback period with regard to the potential ED is January 1 through December 31, for each of Years 2, 3, and 4. For purposes of computing the X group's three-year distribution average, the computation includes any distributions made by T to A, its former non-member shareholder, during the distribution lookback period, because T is a member of the X group during the year of the potential ED. See paragraph (f)(3) of this section. Distributions between members of the X group and between members of the P group are disregarded. See paragraph (f)(2)(ii) of this section.

Example 2. Integrated plan to deconsolidate. T is a wholly-owned subsidiary of P, and is a member of the P group. As part of a plan that includes the deconsolidation of T from the P group, T makes a distribution to P. Because T's distribution to P is part of an integrated plan that results in the deconsolidation of T, T's distribution to P is tested on a separate entity basis as a potential ED under section 172(h)(3)(C), § 1.172(h)-1(c)(3) and (f), and paragraph (f) of this section. See paragraphs (a)(2)(iii) and (f)(2)(ii) of this section. Therefore, the rules of section 172(h)(3)(C), § 1.172(h)-1(c)(3) and (f), and paragraph (f) of this section are applied based on the separate entity value and distribution history of T. See § 1.172(h)-1(d)(2) regarding testing of the distribution as part of a plan of major stock acquisition.

(g) *Life-nonlife groups.*—(1) *Scope.*—This paragraph (g) provides rules for applying the CERT rules to a group that elects under section 1504(c)(2) to file a consolidated return (life-nonlife group). See § 1.1502-47 (rules regarding life-nonlife groups).

(2) *Single entity treatment.*—(i) *In general.*—All members of a life-nonlife group are generally treated as a single taxpayer for purposes of the CERT rules. Accordingly, the rules of paragraphs (a) through (f) and (h) of this section and the rules of §§ 1.172(h)-1 through 1.172(h)-5 are applied by treating the life-nonlife group as a single taxpayer, and are not applied on a subgroup basis. For example, all members of a life-nonlife group are treated as a single entity for purposes of determining whether a CERT has occurred under sections 172(h)(3)(B) and (C) and § 1.172(h)-1. See paragraph (a)(2)(i) of this section. Furthermore, all intercompany transactions between and within subgroups are generally disregarded. In addition, if a pre-existing CERT member becomes a member of a life-nonlife group, the life-nonlife group is treated as a single applicable corporation with regard to that CERT in the consolidated return year of the acquisition and any succeeding year. See paragraph (a)(2)(iv) of this section. If it is determined that a CERT exists, the amount of the CERIL is determined for the entire life-nonlife consolidated group as described in paragraph (g)(2)(ii)(A) of this section, and the CERIL is allocated to each subgroup as described in paragraph (g)(3) of this section.

(ii) *CERIL.*—(A) *Single CERIL computation.*—For any loss limitation year, a single CERIL is computed under section 172(h)(1) and § 1.172(h)-2(a)(2) for the life-nonlife group. The computation of the life-nonlife group's CERIL for any loss limitation year includes all life-nonlife group members' CERT costs, debt, and interest paid or accrued for that year.

(B) *Net operating loss.*—For purposes of determining the CERIL of a lifenonlife group under section 172(h)(1) and § 1.172(h)-2(a)(2), the *net operating loss* of the group in any loss limitation year is the sum of the nonlife consolidated net operating loss (nonlife CNOL) (if any) and the consolidated loss from operations (consolidated LO) (if any) for that year. For this purpose, nonlife consolidated taxable income does not offset any LO, and consolidated partial life insurance company taxable income (as used in § 1.1502-47(g)) does not offset any nonlife CNOL.

(iii) *Carryover to separate return years.*—If any nonlife CNOL or consolidated LO that is attributable to a member of a subgroup may be carried to a separate return year (as defined in § 1.1502-47(d)(10)), the CERIL that is associated with the nonlife CNOL or consolidated LO is apportioned to each member, as relevant, under the method provided by § 1.1502-21(b)(2)(iv)(C)(1).

(iv) *Deconsolidation.*—If a member deconsolidates from a life-nonlife group without an election under paragraph (e)(1) of this section, then paragraphs (b)(1), (c)(4)(i) and (ii), and (d)(3)(ii)(A) and (C) of this section (relating to treatment of a deconsolidating member) apply to allocate CERT status, CERT costs, and interest history from the entire life-nonlife group to the deconsolidating member, and not from a specific subgroup.

(3) *Allocation of a CERIL.*—If a CERIL exists under paragraph (g)(2)(ii)(A) of this section, that CERIL is allocated to each subgroup that has a nonlife CNOL or consolidated LO. The amount of the nonlife CNOL and consolidated LO in a loss limitation year that constitutes a CERIL is equal to the total amount of the CERIL for the loss limitation year multiplied by a fraction, the numerator of which equals the nonlife CNOL or consolidated LO (as relevant), and the denominator of which equals the nonlife CNOL plus the consolidated LO.

(h) *Effective/applicability date.*—(1) *In general.*—Other than paragraph (e) of this section, the rules of this section apply to CERTs occurring on or after the date of publication of the Treasury decision adopting these rules as final regulations in the **Federal Register**. The rules of this section also apply to the deconsolidation of a member from, or the acquisition of a corporation by, a consolidated group that occurs on or after the date of publication of the Treasury decision adopting these rules as final regulations in the **Federal Register**. However, in each case, this section does not apply to any CERT, deconsolidation, or acquisition occurring pursuant to a written agreement that is binding before the date of publication of the Treasury decision adopting these rules as final regulations in the **Federal Register**.

(2) *Waiver election.*—Paragraph (e) of this section applies to the deconsolidation of a member from a consolidated group that occurs on or after the date of publication of Treasury decision adopting these rules as final regulations in the **Federal Register**, except that it does not apply to any deconsolidation occurring pursuant to a written agreement that is binding before the date of publication of the Treasury decision adopting these rules as final regulations in the **Federal Register**. [Reg. § 1.1502-72.]

Reporting Income and Deductions: Consolidated Group

Reporting Income and Deductions: Consolidated Group.—Amendments to Reg. § 1.1502-76, revising the rules for reporting certain items of income and deduction that are reportable on the day a corporation joins or leaves a consolidated group, are proposed (published in the Federal Register on March 6, 2015) (REG-100400-14).

Par. 8. Section 1.1502-76 is amended:

1. By adding a sentence at the end of paragraph (b)(1)(i).
2. By revising paragraphs (b)(1)(ii)(A) and (B).
3. By adding paragraph (b)(1)(ii)(D).
4. By adding a sentence at the end of paragraph (b)(2)(i).
5. By revising paragraph (b)(2)(ii)(C)(9).
6. By removing the last sentence of paragraph (b)(2)(iii).
7. By removing the last sentence of paragraph (b)(2)(v).
8. In paragraph (b)(2)(vi)(C) by removing "paragraph (b)(2)(v)" and adding "paragraph (b)(2)(vi)" in its place.
9. By revising paragraph (b)(3).
10. By adding a sentence at the end of paragraph (b)(4).
11. By adding *Examples 8, 9,* and *10* to paragraph (b)(5).
12. By revising paragraph (b)(6).

The revisions and additions read as follows:

§ 1.1502-76. Taxable year of members of group.

* * *

(b) * * *

(1) * * *

(i) * * * If a corporation (S) becomes or ceases to be a member in a stock disposition or purchase for which an election under section 336(e) or section 338 is made, paragraphs (b)(1)(ii), (b)(2)(ii), and (b)(2)(iii) of this section do not apply to the transaction.

(ii) * * *

(A) *In general.—(1) End of the day rule.*—If S becomes or ceases to be a member during a consolidated return year, S's tax year ends, and (except as provided in paragraph (b)(1)(ii)(A)(2) or paragraph (b)(1)(ii)(B) of this section) for purposes of determining the period in which S must report an item of income, gain, deduction, loss, or credit, S is treated as becoming or ceasing to be a member at the end of the day on which its status as a member changes (end of the day rule).

(2) *Next day rule.*—If an extraordinary item (as defined in paragraph (b)(2)(ii)(C) of this section) results from a transaction that occurs on the day of S's change in status as a member, but after the event resulting in the change, and the item would be taken into account by S on that day, the transaction resulting in the extraordinary item is treated as occurring at the beginning of the following day for purposes of determining the period in which S must report the item (next day rule). The next day rule does not apply to any extraordinary item that becomes includible or deductible simultaneously with the event that causes the change in S's status.

(B) *Special rules for former S corporations.—(1) Beginning of the day rule.*—If an election under section 1362(a) is in effect for S immediately before S becomes a member, S is treated as becoming a member at the beginning of the day the termination of its election under section 1362(a) is effective (termination date), and S's taxable year ends at the end of the day preceding the termination date. See § 1.1361-5(a)(3) for the treatment of certain qualified S corporation subsidiaries.

(2) Previous day rule.—If an extraordinary item (as defined in paragraph (b)(2)(ii)(C) of this section) results from a transac-

tion that occurs on the termination date, but before or simultaneously with the event resulting in the termination of S's election under section 1362(a), and the item would be taken into account by S on that day, the transaction resulting in the extraordinary item is treated as occurring at the end of the previous day for purposes of determining the period in which S must report the item (previous day rule). See §1.1361-5(a)(3) for the treatment of certain qualified S corporation subsidiaries.

* * *

(D) *Coordination with sections 382 and 1374.*—If the day of S's change in status is also the date of an ownership change for purposes of section 382, the rules and principles of this section apply in determining the treatment of any item or asset for purposes of section 382(h). Accordingly, if the day of S's change in status is also a change date, the determination of net unrealized built-in gain or loss will reflect the application of both the end of the day rule and the next day rule, to the extent each applies. Moreover, items includible in the taxable year that ends as a result of S's change in status are not treated as occurring in the recognition period described in section 382(h)(7)(A), and items includible in the taxable year that begins as a result of S's change in status are treated as occurring in the recognition period. If S ceases to be a corporation subject to the tax imposed by section 1374 upon becoming a member of a consolidated group, or if S elects to be a corporation that is subject to such tax for its first separate return year after ceasing to be a member, S's items of recognized built-in gain or loss for purposes of section 1374 will include only the amounts reported on S's separate return (including items reported on that return under the previous day rule or the next day rule).

* * *

(2) * * *

(i) * * * If a member distributes or transfers assets in an intercompany transaction to which section 381(a) applies, a short taxable year of the distributor or transferor corporation is not taken into account either for purposes of determining the taxable years to which any tax attribute of the distributor or transferor corporation may be carried or for purposes of determining the taxable years in which an adjustment under section 481(a) is taken into account.

(ii) * * *

(C) * * *

(9) Any compensation-related deduction in connection with S's change in status (including, for example, a deduction for fees for services rendered in connection with S's change in status and for bonus, severance, and option cancellation payments made in connection with S's change in status);

* * *

(3) *Anti-avoidance rule.*—If any person acts with a principal purpose contrary to the purposes of this paragraph (b) to substantially reduce the federal income tax liability of any person (including by modifying an existing contract or other agreement in anticipation of a change in S's status to shift an item between the taxable years that end and begin as a result of S's change in status), adjustments must be made as necessary to carry out the purposes of this section.

(4) * * * In addition, if S ceases to exist in the same consolidated return year in which S becomes a member, the due date for filing S's separate return shall be determined without regard to S's ceasing to exist in that year.

(5) * * *

Example 8. Allocation of certain amounts that become deductible on the day of S's change in status—(a) *Facts.* P purchases all of the stock of S, an accrual-basis, stand-alone C corporation, on June 30 pursuant to a stock purchase agreement. At the time of the stock purchase, S has outstanding nonqualified stock options issued to certain employees. The options did not have a readily ascertainable fair market value when granted, and the options do not provide for a deferral of compensation (as defined in §1.409A-1(b)). Under the option agreements, S is obligated to pay its employees certain amounts in cancellation of their stock options upon a change in control of S. P's purchase of S's stock causes a change in control of S, and S's obligation to make option cancellation payments to its employees becomes fixed and determinable upon the closing of the stock purchase. Several days after the closing of the stock purchase, S pays its employees the amounts required under the option agreements.

(b) *Analysis.* P's purchase of S's stock causes S to become a member of the P group at the end of the day on June 30. Under paragraph (b)(2)(ii)(C)*(9)* of this section, a deduction arising from S's liability to pay its employees in cancellation of their stock options in connection with S's change in status is an extraordinary item that cannot be prorated and must be allocated to June 30. The next day rule is inapplicable to this deduction because S's liability to pay its employees becomes deductible on the day of S's change in status simultaneously with the event that causes S's change in status. Consequently, a deduction for the option cancellation payments must be reported under the end of the day rule on S's tax return for the period ending June 30.

(c) *Success-based fees.* The facts are the same as in paragraph (a) of this *Example 8*, except that S also engages a consulting firm to provide services in connection with P's purchase of S's stock. Under the terms of the engagement letter, S's obligation to pay for these services is contingent upon the successful closing of the stock purchase. The stock purchase closes successfully, and S's obligation to pay its consultants becomes fixed and determinable at closing. To the extent S's payment of a success-based fee to its consultants is otherwise deductible, this item is an extraordinary item that cannot be prorated and must be reported under the end of the day rule on S's return for the period ending June 30. (See paragraph (b)(2)(ii)(C)*(9)* of this section.) The next day rule is inapplicable to the deduction because S's liability to pay its consultants becomes deductible on the day of S's change in status simultaneously with the event that causes S's change in status.

(d) *Unwanted assets.* The facts are the same as in paragraph (a) of this *Example 8*, except that, after closing on June 30, S sells to an unrelated party certain assets used in S's trade or business that are not wanted by the P group. Gain or loss on the sale of these assets is an extraordinary item that results from a transaction that occurs on the day of S's change in status, but after the event resulting in the change. Consequently, under the next day rule, the gain or loss must be reported on S's tax return for the period beginning July 1.

Example 9. Redemption that causes a change in status—(a) *Facts*. P owns 80 shares of S's only class of outstanding stock, and a person whose ownership of S stock is not attributed to P under section 302(c) owns the remaining 20 shares. On June 30, S distributes land with a basis of $100 and a fair market value of $140 to P in redemption of all of P's stock in S.

(b) *Analysis*. As a result of the redemption, S ceases to be a member of P's consolidated group on June 30. S will recognize $40 of gain under section 311(b) on the distribution of the land to P. The next day rule is inapplicable because S's gain becomes includible on the day of S's change in status simultaneously with the event that causes S's change in status. Consequently, S's gain must be reported under the end of the day rule in its taxable year ending June 30, during which S was a member of the P group. Under § 1.1502-32(b)(2)(i), P's basis in its S stock is increased to reflect S's $40 gain immediately before the redemption of S's stock.

(c) *Partial redemption*. The facts are the same as in paragraph (a) of this *Example 9*, except that S distributes the land to P in redemption of 20 shares of P's stock in S. Thus, immediately after the redemption, P owns 75% (60 shares / 80 shares) of S's outstanding stock, and S's minority shareholder owns 25% (20 shares / 80 shares). The redemption does not satisfy the requirements of section 302(b) and is treated under section 302(d) as a distribution to which section 301 applies. The end of the day rule does not apply for purposes of determining whether P and S are members of the same consolidated group immediately after the redemption. Because P owns only 75% of S's stock immediately after the redemption, the distribution is not an intercompany distribution described in § 1.1502-13(f)(2)(i). Thus, P may not exclude any amount of the distribution that is a dividend, and P's basis in S's stock is not reduced under § 1.1502-32(b)(2)(iv). P may be entitled to a dividends received deduction under section 243(c) (but see section 1059(e)). For the reasons discussed in paragraph (b) of this *Example 9*, S's gain under section 311(b) must be reported under the end of the day rule in S's taxable year ending June 30, during which S was a member of the P group.

(d) *Distribution of loss property*. The facts are the same as in paragraph (a) of this *Example 9*, except that the land distributed by S to P has a fair market value of $60 rather than $140. The end of the day rule applies for purposes of determining the taxable year in which S must take into account its realized loss on the distribution of the land. Thus, under the end of the day rule, S's loss on the distribution of the land, which occurs simultaneously with S's ceasing to be a member, is taken into account in S's taxable year that ends as a result of the redemption. However, the end of the day rule does not apply for other purposes; for example, the rule does not apply in determining whether the transaction is an intercompany distribution or in determining the attributes (as defined in § 1.1502-13(b)(6)) of the loss. Therefore, because S is not a member immediately after the distribution, S's loss on the distribution is not recognized under section 311(a). Under the end of the day rule, the loss is taken into account as a noncapital, nondeductible expense on the P group's consolidated return, and under § 1.1502-32(b)(1)(i), P's basis in its S stock is decreased by $40 immediately before S leaves the group.

Example 10. Extraordinary item of S corporation—(a) *Facts*. On July 1, P purchases all the stock of S, an accrual-basis corporation with an election in effect under section 1362(a). Prior to the sale, S had engaged a consulting firm to find a buyer for S's stock, and the consulting firm's fee was contingent upon the successful closing of the sale of S's stock.

(b) *Analysis*. To the extent S's payment of the success-based fee to its consultants is otherwise deductible, this item is an extraordinary item (see paragraph (b)(2)(ii)(C)(*9*) of this section) that becomes deductible on July 1 simultaneously with the event that terminates S's election as an S corporation. Under paragraph (b)(1)(ii)(B)(*2*) of this section, S's obligation to pay the fee is treated as becoming deductible on June 30 under the previous day rule.

(6) *Effective/applicability date*.—Paragraphs (b)(2)(i) and (b)(4) of this section apply to consolidated return years beginning on or after the date these regulations are published as final regulations in the **Federal Register**. Otherwise, this paragraph (b) applies to corporations becoming or ceasing to be members of consolidated groups on or after the date these regulations are published as final regulations in the **Federal Register**.

* * *

Deduction for Business Interest Expense: Limitation

Deduction for Business Interest Expense: Limitation.—Amendments to Reg. § 1.1502-79, regarding the limitation on the deduction for business interest expense after the enactment of recent tax legislation, are proposed (published in the Federal Register on December 28, 2018) (REG-106089-18).

Par. 20. Section 1.1502-79 is amended by adding paragraph (f) to read as follows:

§ 1.1502-79. Separate return years.

* * *

(f) *Disallowed business interest expense carryforwards*.—For the treatment of disallowed business interest expense carryforwards (within the meaning of § 1.163(j)-1) of a member arising in a separate return limitation year, see § 1.163(j)-5(d) and (f).

Consolidated Returns: Nonapplicability of Code Sec. 357(c)

Consolidated Returns: Nonapplicability of Code Sec. 357(c).—Amendments to Reg. § 1.1502-80, clarifying that, in certain transfers described in Code Sec. 351 between members of a consolidated group, a transferee's assumption of certain liabilities described in section 357(c)(3)

will not reduce the transferor's basis in the transferee's stock received in the transfer, are proposed (published in the Federal Register on November 14, 2001) (REG-137519-01).

☐ Par. 2. In § 1.1502-80, paragraph (d) is revised to read as follows:

§ 1.1502-80. Applicability of other provisions of law.

* * *

(d) *Non-applicability of section 357(c).*—(1) *In general.*—Section 357(c) does not apply to cause the transferor to recognize gain in any transaction to which § 1.1502-13 applies, if such transaction occurs in a consolidated return year beginning on or after the date these regulations are published as final regulations in the Federal Register. Notwithstanding the foregoing, for purposes of determining the transferor's basis in property under section 358(a) received in a transfer described in section 351, section 358(d)(2) shall operate to exclude liabilities described in section 357(c)(3)(A), other than those also described in section 357(c)(3)(B), from the computation of the amount of liabilities assumed that is treated as money received under section 358(d)(1), if such transfer occurs in a consolidated return year beginning on or after the date these regulations are published as final regulations in the Federal Register. This paragraph (d)(1) does not apply to a transaction if the transferor or transferee becomes a nonmember as part of the same plan or arrangement. The transferor (or transferee) is treated as becoming a nonmember once it is no longer a member of a consolidated group that includes the transferee (or transferor). For purposes of this paragraph (d)(1), any reference to a transferor or transferee includes, as the context may require, a reference to a successor or predecessor. For rules regarding the application of section 357(c) to transactions occurring in consolidated return years beginning on or after January 1, 1995, but before the date these regulations are published as final regulations in the Federal Register, see § 1.1502-80(d) in effect prior to the date these regulations are published as final regulations in the Federal Register (see 26 CFR part 1 revised April 1, 2001).

(2) *Examples.*—The principles of paragraph (d)(1) of this section are illustrated by the following examples:

Example 1. P, S, and T are members of a consolidated group. P owns all of the stock of S and T with bases of $30 and $20, respectively. S has assets with a total fair market value equal to $100 and an aggregate basis of $30 and liabilities of $40. S merges into T in a transaction described in section 368(a)(1)(A) (and in section 368(a)(1)(D)). Section 357(c) does not apply to cause S to recognize gain in the merger. P's basis in T's stock increases to $50 ($30 plus $20), and T succeeds to S's $30 basis in the assets transferred and the $40 of liabilities.

Example 2. P owns all the stock of S1. S1 has assets with a total fair market value equal to $100 and an aggregate basis of $30. S1 has $40 of liabilities, $5 of which are described in section 357(c)(3)(A), but not section 357(c)(3)(B), and $35 of which are not described in section 357(c)(3)(A). S1 transfers its assets to a newly formed subsidiary, S2, in exchange for stock of S2 and S2's assumption of the liabilities of $40 in a transaction to which section 351 applies. Section 357(c) does not apply to cause S1 to recognize gain in connection with the transfer. For purposes of determining S1's basis in the S2 stock it received in the exchange, section 358(d)(2) operates to exclude $5 of the liabilities from the computation of the amount of liabilities assumed that are treated as money received under section 358(d)(1). S1's basis in the S2 stock received in the exchange is a $5 excess loss account (reflecting its $30 basis in the assets transferred reduced by $35, the amount of liabilities assumed that are not described in section 357(c)(3)(A)).

* * *

Consolidated Groups: Loss Limitation Rules

Consolidated Groups: Loss Limitation Rules.—Amendments to Reg. § 1.1502-80, relating to the deductibility of losses recognized on dispositions of subsidiary stock by members of a consolidated group, the consequences of treating subsidiary stock as worthless, and when stock of a member of a consolidated group may be treated as worthless, are proposed (published in the Federal Register on March 18, 2004) (REG-153172-03).

☐ Par. 4. In § 1.1502-80, paragraph (c) is revised to read as follows:

§ 1.1502-80. Applicability of other provisions of law.

[The text of this proposed § 1.1502-80(c) is the same as the text of § 1.1502-80T(c) as added by T.D. 9118.]

Consolidated Returns: Alaska Native Corporations

Consolidated Returns: Alaska Native Corporations.—Temporary Reg. § 1.1502-81T, relating to corporations included in a consolidated return with a Native Corporation established under the Alaska Native Claims Settlement Act, is also proposed as a final regulation and, when adopted, would become Reg. § 1.1502-81 (published in the Federal Register on March 18, 1987).

§ 1.1502-81. Alaska Native Corporations.

Deduction for Business Interest Expense: Limitation

Deduction for Business Interest Expense: Limitation.—Amendments to Reg. §§ 1.1502-90 and 1.1502-91, regarding the limitation on the deduction for business interest expense after the

enactment of recent tax legislation, are proposed (published in the Federal Register on December 28, 2018) (REG-106089-18).

Par. 21. Section 1.1502-90 is amended by revising the entry for § 1.1502-98 and adding an entry for § 1.1502-99(d) to read as follows:

§ 1.1502-90. Table of contents.

* * *

Par. 22. Section 1.1502-91 is amended by revising paragraph (e)(2) to read as follows:

§ 1.1502-91. Application of section 382 with respect to a consolidated group.

* * *

(e) * * *

(2) *Example*—(i) *Facts*. The L group has a consolidated net operating loss arising in Year 1 that is carried over to Year 2. The L loss group has an ownership change at the beginning of Year 2.

(ii) *Analysis*. The net operating loss carryover of the L loss group from Year 1 is a pre-change consolidated attribute because the L group was entitled to use the loss in Year 2 and therefore the loss was described in paragraph (c)(1)(i) of this section. Under paragraph (a)(2)(i) of this section, the amount of consolidated taxable income of the L group for Year 2 that may be offset by this loss carryover may not exceed the consolidated section 382 limitation of the L group for that year. See § 1.1502-93 for rules relating to the computation of the consolidated section 382 limitation.

(iii) *Business interest expense*. The facts are the same as in the *Example* in paragraph (e)(2)(i) of this section, except that, rather than a consolidated net operating loss, a member of the L group pays or accrues a business interest expense in Year 1 for which a deduction is disallowed in that year under section 163(j) and § 1.163(j)-2(b). The disallowed business interest expense is carried over to Year 2 under section 163(j)(2) and § 1.163(j)-2(c). Thus, the disallowed business interest expense carryforward is a pre-change loss. Under section 163(j), the L loss group is entitled to deduct the carryforward in Year 2; however, the amount of consolidated taxable income of the L group for Year 2 that may be offset by this carryforward may not exceed the consolidated section 382 limitation of the L group for that year. See § 1.1502-98(b) (providing that §§ 1.1502-91 through 1.1502-96 apply section 382 to business interest expense, with appropriate adjustments).

* * *

Consolidated Returns: Redetermination of Unrealized Built-In Gain and Loss

Consolidated Returns: Redetermination of Unrealized Built-In Gain and Loss.—Amendments to Reg. § 1.1502-91, requiring a loss group or loss subgroup to redetermine its consolidated net unrealized built-in gain and loss in certain circumstances, are proposed (published in the Federal Register on October 24, 2011) (REG-133002-10).

☐ Par. 2. Section 1.1502-91 is amended by:

1. Revising paragraph (g)(1).
2. Adding paragraphs (g)(7) and (g)(8).
3. Revising paragraph (h)(2) and the heading of paragraph (h)(4).
4. Adding paragraph (k).

The revisions and additions read as follows:

§ 1.1502-91. Application of section 382 with respect to a consolidated group.

* * *

(g) *Net unrealized built-in gain and loss*.—(1) *In general*.—The determination of whether a loss group or loss subgroup has a net unrealized built-in gain (NUBIG) or loss (NUBIL) under section 382(h)(3) is based on the aggregate amount of the separately determined NUBIGs or NUBILs (including items of built-in income and deduction described in section 382(h)(6)) of each member that is included in the loss group or loss subgroup, as the case may be, under paragraph (g)(2) of this section. The threshold requirement under section 382(h)(3)(B) applies on an aggregate basis.

(i) *Members included in group*.—If a member is not included in the determination of whether a loss group or loss subgroup has a NUBIL under paragraph (g)(2)(ii) or (g)(2)(iv) of this section, that member is not included in the loss group or loss subgroup. See § 1.1502-94(c) (relating to built-in gain or loss of a new loss member) and § 1.1502-96(a) (relating to the end of separate tracking of certain losses).

(ii) *Determination of separate NUBIG or NUBIL*.—For purposes of determining a member's separate NUBIG or NUBIL—

(A) Stock of a subsidiary that is a member of the loss group or loss subgroup (an included subsidiary) is disregarded, except as provided for in paragraph (g)(7) of this section. For this purpose, the term stock includes stock described in section 1504(a)(4) and § 1.382-2T(f)(18)(ii) and (f)(18)(iii);

(B) Intercompany obligations are disregarded; and

(C) Deferred amounts, such as amounts deferred under section 267 or § 1.1502-13, are built-in items unless they are deferred with respect to—

(1) An intercompany obligation; or

(2) A share of stock of an included subsidiary; however, if an amount deferred with respect to a share of such stock is taken into account at any time during the recognition pe-

riod (whether or not any such loss amount is absorbed), NUBIG or NUBIL must be redetermined in accordance with paragraph (g)(7) of this section.

* * *

(7) *Redetermination of NUBIG or NUBIL of a loss group or loss subgroup to reflect unduplicated built-in gain or loss with respect to stock of an included subsidiary.*—(i) *In general.*—This paragraph (g)(7) applies if, during the recognition period, any member of the consolidated group directly or indirectly takes into account any gain or loss with respect to a share of stock of an included subsidiary (S) that was held by another member of the loss group or loss subgroup immediately before the change date, regardless of whether any such loss is absorbed. If this paragraph (g)(7) applies, the loss group or loss subgroup must redetermine its NUBIG or NUBIL to include any unduplicated built-in gain or loss with respect to the S share in accordance with the provisions of paragraphs (g)(7)(ii) and (g)(7)(iii) of this section. The redetermination is given effect immediately before the time the gain or loss on stock of an included subsidiary is taken into account. The redetermined NUBIG or NUBIL does not affect the tax treatment of transactions taken into account prior to the event that causes a redetermination of NUBIG or NUBIL under this paragraph (g)(7). However, the redetermined NUBIG or NUBIL is effective for all purposes immediately before the gain or loss on stock of an included subsidiary is taken into account. Thus, for example, the redetermined NUBIG or NUBIL is used to determine whether the loss group or subgroup is a NUBIG or NUBIL group, as well as whether the group meets the threshold requirement of section 382(h)(3)(B), at the time of the redetermination.

(ii) *Computation of unduplicated built-in gain or loss with respect to shares of S stock that are subject to this paragraph (g)(7).*—The loss group or loss subgroup computes its unduplicated built-in gain or loss with respect to each share of S stock that is subject to this paragraph (g)(7) by first treating the basis in the share as tentatively adjusted immediately before the change date or, in the case of an amount with respect to S stock that was deferred on the change date, as of the date of the transaction that gave rise to the amount, as though the following occurred immediately before the ownership change or the transaction that gave rise to the deferred amount—

(A) *Deemed recognition of built-in gain or loss of lower-tier included subsidiaries.*—The separate NUBIG and NUBIL of S and all included subsidiaries that are lower-tier to S are treated as recognized, taken into account, and absorbed.

(B) *Tiering up of recognized amounts.*—All amounts deemed recognized, taken into account, and absorbed under paragraph (g)(7)(ii)(A) of this section are then deemed to tier up under the principles of §1.1502-32 to tentatively adjust the basis in all of the S shares that are subject to this paragraph (g)(7).

(C) *Unduplicated gain or loss with respect to S stock.*—If the aggregate tentatively adjusted basis in the S shares subject to this paragraph (g)(7) exceeds the aggregate fair market value of those shares immediately before the change date or, in the case of a deferred amount, on the date of the transaction that gave rise to the item, the excess is the unduplicated loss with respect to those shares. Alternatively, if the aggregate fair market value of the S shares subject to this paragraph (g)(7) exceeds the aggregate tentatively adjusted basis in those shares on such date, the excess is the unduplicated gain with respect to those shares.

(iii) *Redetermination of the group's NUBIG or NUBIL.*—The loss group or loss subgroup's redetermined NUBIG or NUBIL is the sum of—

(A) The loss group or loss subgroup's NUBIG or NUBIL as originally determined without regard to the stock of any included subsidiary;

(B) Any unduplicated gain or loss with respect to a share of stock of an included subsidiary that was previously included in the loss group or loss subgroup's NUBIG or NUBIL under this paragraph (g)(7); and

(C) The unduplicated gain or loss on shares of S stock computed under paragraph (g)(7)(ii) of this section.

(iv) *Anti-avoidance rule.*—If any person acts with a principal purpose contrary to the purposes of this paragraph (g), to avoid the effect of the rules of this paragraph (g), or to apply the rules of this paragraph (g) to avoid the effect of any other provision of the consolidated return regulations, adjustments must be made as necessary to carry out the purposes of this paragraph (g).

(8) *Examples.*—The following examples illustrate the application of the provisions of paragraph (g) of this section. Unless otherwise stated, P is the common parent of a consolidated group that is a loss group and all members of the P group are included subsidiaries with respect to the loss group. P can establish that its gains are recognized built-in gains; P cannot establish that its losses are not recognized built-in losses. In addition, the threshold requirement of section 382(h)(3)(B) is satisfied. All other relevant facts are set forth in the examples.

Example 1. Basic application of provision. (i) *Facts.* On January 1, Year 1, P owns the sole outstanding share of S stock (basis $210, value $160) and the sole outstanding share of M stock. S owns the sole outstanding share of S1 stock (basis $100, value $80) and Truck (basis $70, value $80). S1 owns three of the five outstanding shares of S2 common stock (basis $40, value $20 for each share; thus, basis $120, value $60 in the aggregate). S2 owns Truck 2 (basis $70, value $40) and Truck 3 (basis $30, value $40). M owns the fourth of the five outstanding shares of S2 stock. X, a nonmember of the P group, owns the fifth outstanding share of S2 stock. January 1, Year 1, is a change date for the P group.

(ii) *Determination of the separate NUBIG or NUBIL of each member of the P loss group.* (A) *S2's separate NUBIG or NUBIL.* S2's assets are Truck 2 (with a built-in loss of $30) and Truck 3 (with a built-in gain of $10); therefore, S2 has a NUBIL of $20.

(B) *S1's separate NUBIG or NUBIL.* S1's only assets are the shares of S2 stock, which are disregarded under paragraph (g)(1)(ii)(A) of this section; therefore, S1 has a NUBIG or NUBIL of zero.

(C) *S's separate NUBIG or NUBIL.* S's assets are Truck (with a built-in gain of $10) and the share of S1 stock (which is disregarded); therefore, S has a NUBIG of $10.

(D) *M's separate NUBIG or NUBIL.* M's only asset is the share of S2 stock, which is disregarded under paragraph (g)(1)(ii)(A) of this section; therefore, M has a NUBIG or NUBIL of zero.

(E) *P's separate NUBIG or NUBIL.* P's only assets are the shares of M and S stock, which are disregarded; therefore, P has a NUBIG or NUBIL of zero.

(iii) *Determination of the P group's NUBIG or NUBIL.* The P group has a NUBIL of $10, reflecting the sum of S2's $20 NUBIL and S's $10 NUBIG.

Example 2. Transfer of shares of stock of an included subsidiary during recognition period. (i) *Sale to nonmember.* (A) *Facts.* The facts are the same as in *Example 1.* In addition, in Year 4, S sells its share of S1 stock for $65 to an unrelated party. At the time of the sale, S's basis in the share had been reduced to $90 due to adjustments for depreciation on S2's assets that tiered up under § 1.1502-32. (No adjustments are made to S's basis in the S1 share under § 1.1502-36, including by reason of an election to waive stock loss or reattribute losses.) As a result of the sale of the S1 share during the recognition period, the P group must redetermine its NUBIL under paragraph (g)(7) of this section.

(B) *Redetermination of the P group's NUBIG or NUBIL.* (*1*) *Unduplicated built-in gain or loss with respect to S1 share.* Under paragraph (g)(7)(ii)(A) of this section, the unduplicated built-in gain or loss with respect to the S1 share sold in Year 4 is computed by first treating the separate NUBIG or NUBIL of S1 and S2 (the only included subsidiary that is lower-tier to S1) as having been recognized, taken into account, and absorbed immediately before the change date. Under paragraph (g)(7)(ii)(B) of this section, those amounts are then treated as tiering up under the principles of § 1.1502-32 and tentatively adjusting S's basis in its S1 share, in order to identify the unduplicated gain or loss in the basis of the share under paragraph (g)(7)(ii)(C) of this section. S1 has no separate NUBIG or NUBIL to be treated as recognized, taken into account, and absorbed. S2 has a $20 separate NUBIL that is treated as recognized, taken into account, and absorbed and that is then treated as tiering up to adjust S's basis in the S1 share under the principles of § 1.1502-32. As a result, $12 of S2's $20 NUBIL would be treated as tiering up to S1 through the three S2 shares (of the total five outstanding) held by S1, and that $12 would then be treated as tiering up through S1 to tentatively adjust S's basis in the S1 share. S's tentatively reduced basis in the S1 share is therefore $100 - $12, or $88. Because the tentatively reduced basis of the share exceeds the value of the share by $8 ($88 - $80), S has an $8 unduplicated loss in its basis in its S1 stock.

(*2*) *Redetermined NUBIG or NUBIL of the P group.* Immediately before S takes into account the $25 loss on the sale of its share of S1 stock, the P group's NUBIL is redetermined to be $18, the sum of S2's NUBIL of $20, S1's NUBIL of $0, S's NUBIG of $10, P's NUBIG or NUBIL of $0, M's NUBIG or NUBIL of $0, and the $8 unduplicated loss in the S1 stock.

(C) *Effect of redetermination.* Of the $25 loss on the sale of the S1 share, $20 is recognized built-in loss, but the group only has an $18 NUBIL and so only $18 of the recognized built-in loss is subject to limitation under section 382.

(ii) *Nonrecognition transfer to member followed by sale to nonmember.* The facts are the same as in paragraph (i)(A) of this *Example 2*, except that, in Year 3, M1 joined the P group and S transferred its share of S1 stock to M1 in a transaction qualifying under section 351; as a result, it is M1, not S, that sells the S1 share to X in Year 4. The analysis and results are the same as in paragraphs (i)(B) and (i)(C) of this *Example 2* because this section applies when any member of the group recognizes gain or loss with respect to stock of an included subsidiary that was held by a member of the loss group immediately before the change date.

Example 3. Recognition of built-in loss prior to stock sale. (i) *Facts.* The facts are the same as in paragraph (i)(A) of *Example 2* except that, in addition, in Year 2, S2 sold Truck 2 and recognized the $30 built-in loss on Truck 2, and the P group absorbed the $30 loss. The loss is a recognized built-in loss under section 382(h)(2)(B) and thus subject to limitation to the extent of the originally determined $10 NUBIL.

(ii) *Redetermination of the P group's NUBIG or NUBIL.* (A) *Unduplicated built-in gain or loss with respect to the S1 share.* Because unduplicated stock gain or loss is computed immediately before the change date, the unduplicated stock loss is $8 for the reasons set forth in paragraph (i)(B)(*1*) of *Example 2.*

(B) *Redetermined NUBIG or NUBIL of the P group.* The computation of the P group's redetermined NUBIG or NUBIL is the same as in paragraph (i)(B)(*2*) of *Example 2*, except that the $30 of recognized built-in loss in Year 2 reduces the P group's $10 NUBIL (before NUBIL is redetermined under paragraph (g)(7) of this section) to zero. As a result, immediately before the sale of the S1 share, the P group's NUBIL is redetermined to be $8, which is the sum of zero and the $8 unduplicated loss in the S1 stock.

(iii) *Effect of redetermination.* Of the $25 loss on the sale of the S1 share, $20 is recognized built-in loss, but the group only has an $8 NUBIL and so only $8 of the recognized built-in loss is subject to limitation under section 382. The treatment of the loss recognized on the Year 2 sale of Truck 2 is not affected by the Year 4 redetermination.

Example 4. Sale of less than all shares of stock of an included subsidiary. (i) *Facts.* The facts are the same as in paragraph (i)(A) of *Example 2*, except that S1 has ten shares of stock outstanding, designated Share 1 through Share 10, all of which are owned by S. S's basis in Share 1 is $15.50, and S's basis in Share 2 is $4.50. In addition, instead of selling its one share of S1 stock, on January 1, Year 4, S sells Share 1 and Share 2 to an unrelated party for $16 (their aggregate fair market value).

(ii) *Redetermination of the P group's NUBIG or NUBIL.* (A) *Unduplicated built-in gain or loss with respect to S1 Share 1 and S1 Share 2.* The analysis is the same as in paragraph (i)(B)(*1*) of *Example 2* except that the unduplicated loss is $1.60, computed as the excess of $17.60 ($20 aggregate basis in the shares that are sold, tentatively reduced by $2.40, the shares' portion (2/10) of the $12 tentative adjustment that tiered-up from S2) over $16 (the shares' aggregate value).

(B) *Redetermined NUBIG or NUBIL of the P group*. The P group's redetermined NUBIL is $11.60, which is the sum of S2's NUBIL of $20, S1's NUBIL of $0, S's NUBIG of $10, P's NUBIG or NUBIL of $0, M's NUBIG or NUBIL of $0, and the unduplicated stock loss of $1.60.

(C) *Effect of redetermination*. Of the $4 loss recognized on the Year 4 sale of Share 1 and Share 2, all $4 is recognized built-in loss. The group's redetermined NUBIL is $11.60, and thus all $4 of the $4 recognized built-in loss is subject to limitation under section 382.

Example 5. NUBIL redetermined to be NUBIG. (i) *Disposition of stock of included member*. (A) *Facts*. On January 1, Year 1, P owns the sole outstanding share of S stock (basis $10, value $100). S owns Truck 1 (basis $65, value $50) and Truck 2 (basis $45, value $50). January 1, Year 1, is a change date for the P group. In Year 3, P sells its S share for $100.

(B) *Determination of the P group's NUBIG or NUBIL on change date*. S's assets are Truck 1 (with a built-in loss of $15) and Truck 2 (with a built-in gain of $5); therefore S has a separate NUBIL of $10. P's sole asset is the share of S stock, which is disregarded; therefore, P has a separate NUBIG or NUBIL of zero. Accordingly, on the change date, the P group has a NUBIL of $10, reflecting the sum of S's $10 NUBIL and P's $0 NUBIG/NUBIL.

(C) *Redetermination of the P group's NUBIG or NUBIL on disposition of stock of included subsidiary*. (1) *Unduplicated built-in gain or loss with respect to the S share*. Under paragraph (g)(7)(ii)(A) of this section, the unduplicated built-in gain or loss with respect to the S share sold in Year 3 is computed by first treating S's $10 NUBIL as having been recognized, taken into account, and absorbed immediately before the ownership change. Then, under paragraph (g)(7)(ii)(B) of this section, S's $10 NUBIL is treated as tentatively adjusting P's basis in the S share under the principles of § 1.1502-32. Accordingly, P's tentatively reduced basis in the S share is $10 - $10, or $0. Further, the value of the S share was $100 immediately before the change date. The share's $100 value exceeds the $0 tentatively reduced basis in the share by $100, and thus P has a $100 unduplicated gain in its S stock.

(2) *Redetermined NUBIG or NUBIL of the P group*. Immediately before P takes into account the $90 gain on the sale of its share of S stock, the P group's $10 NUBIL is redetermined to be a $90 NUBIG, the sum of S's NUBIL of $10 and the unduplicated gain in the S stock of $100.

(D) *Effect of redetermination*. Of the $90 gain P recognized on the sale of the S share, all $90 is recognized built-in gain and therefore, under section 382(h)(2)(A), the group's section 382 limitation is increased by $90.

(ii) *Disposition of loss asset prior to disposition of stock of included subsidiary*. (A) *Facts*. The facts are the same as in paragraph (i)(A) of this *Example 5*, except that, in addition, in Year 2, S sells Truck 1 for $50, recognizing a $15 loss that is taken into account and absorbed. As a result of the $15 loss absorption, P's basis in the S share is reduced to an excess loss account of $5 in Year 2 and, thus, when P sells the S share in Year 3, P recognizes $105 gain on the sale ($100 sale proceeds + $5 excess loss account recapture).

(B) *Determination of the P group's NUBIG or NUBIL on change date*. For the reasons set forth in paragraph (i)(B) of this *Example 5*, the P group has a NUBIL of $10 on the change date. Accordingly, S's $15 loss on Truck 1 is a recognized built-in loss under section 382(h)(2)(B), and therefore subject to limitation to the extent of the $10 NUBIL.

(C) *Redetermination of the P group's NUBIG or NUBIL on disposition of stock of included subsidiary*. (*1*) *Unduplicated built-in gain or loss with respect to the S share*. For the reasons set forth in paragraph (i)(C)(*1*) of this *Example 5*, the unduplicated builtin gain with respect to the S share is $100.

(*2*) *Redetermined NUBIG or NUBIL of the P group*. For the reasons set forth in paragraph (i)(C)(*2*) of this *Example 5*, the P group's NUBIG is redetermined to be $90. Immediately before P takes into account the $100 gain on the sale of its share of S stock, the P group's $10 NUBIL is redetermined to be a $90 NUBIG, the sum of S's NUBIL of $10 and P's NUBIG of $100.

(D) *Effect of redetermination*. Of the $105 gain P recognized on the sale of the S share, $90 is recognized built-in gain and therefore, under section 382(h)(2)(A), the group's section 382 limitation is increased by $90. The redetermination of P's original $10 NUBIL to a $100 NUBIG in Year 4 has no effect on the treatment of the Year 2 recognized built-in loss from the sale of Truck 1.

(h) * * *

(2) *Disposition of stock or an intercompany obligation of a member*.—Built-in gain or loss recognized by a member on the disposition of stock (including stock described in section 1504(a)(4) and § 1.382-2T(f)(18)(ii) and (f)(18)(iii)) of another member is treated as a recognized gain or loss for purposes of section 382(h)(2) (unless disallowed) without regard to the extent to which such gain or loss was included in the determination of a net unrealized built-in gain or loss under paragraph (g) of this section. Built-in gain or loss recognized by a member with respect to an intercompany obligation is treated as recognized gain or loss only to the extent (if any) that the transaction gives rise to aggregate income or loss within the consolidated group.

* * *

(4) Successor assets. * * *

* * *

(k) *Effective/Applicability date*.—Paragraphs (g)(1), (g)(7), (g)(8), (h)(2) and (h)(4) of this section apply to amounts taken into account with respect to a share of stock of an included subsidiary on or after the date that final regulations are published in the **FEDERAL REGISTER**, but only with respect to ownership changes occurring on or after October 24, 2011. For amounts taken into account with respect to a share of stock of an included subsidiary not described in the preceding sentence, see §§ 1.1502-91(g) and 1.1502-91(h) as contained in 26 CFR part 1 in effect on April 1, 2011.

Deduction for Business Interest Expense: Limitation

Deduction for Business Interest Expense: Limitation.—Amendments to Reg. § 1.1502-95, regarding the limitation on the deduction for business interest expense after the enactment of recent

tax legislation, are proposed (published in the Federal Register on December 28, 2018) (REG-106089-18).

Par. 23. Section 1.1502-95 is amended in paragraph (b)(4) by:

1. Designating *Examples 1* and 2 as paragraphs (b)(4)(i) and (ii), respectively;

2. In newly designated paragraph (b)(4)(i), redesignating paragraphs (b)(4)(i)(i) and (ii) as paragraphs (b)(4)(i)(A) and (B), respectively;

3. In newly designated paragraph (b)(4)(ii), redesignating paragraphs (b)(4)(ii)(i) and (ii) as paragraphs (b)(4)(ii)(A) and (B), respectively; and

4. Adding two sentences at the end of newly redesignated paragraph (b)(4)(ii)(B).

The additions read follows:

§1.1502-95. Rules on ceasing to be a member of a consolidated group (or loss subgroup).

* * *

(b) * * *

(4) * * *

(ii) * * *

(B) * * * The analysis would be similar if the L loss group had an ownership change under §1.1502-92 in Year 2 with respect to disallowed business interest expense paid or accrued by L2 in Year 1 and carried forward under section 163(j)(2) to Year 2 and Year 3. See §1.1502-98(b) (providing that §§1.1502-91 through 1.1502-96 apply section 382 to business interest expense, with appropriate adjustments).

* * *

Deduction for Business Interest Expense: Limitation

Deduction for Business Interest Expense: Limitation.—Amendments to Reg. §§1.1502-98 and 1.1502-99, regarding the limitation on the deduction for business interest expense after the enactment of recent tax legislation, are proposed (published in the Federal Register on December 28, 2018) (REG-106089-18).

Par. 24. Section 1.1502-98 is amended by:

1. Revising the section heading;

2. Designating the undesignated text as paragraph (a) and adding a heading for newly designated paragraph (a); and

3. Adding paragraph (b).

The revision and additions read as follows:

§1.1502-98. Coordination with sections 383 and 163(j).—(a) *Coordination with section 383.*—* * *

(b) *Application to section 163(j).*—(1) *In general.*—The regulations under sections 163(j), 382, and 383 contain rules governing the application of section 382 to interest expense governed by section 163(j) and the regulations thereunder. See, for example, §§1.163(j)-11(b), 1.382-2, 1.382-6, and 1.383-1. The rules contained in §§1.1502-91 through 1.1502-96 apply these rules to members of a consolidated group, or corporations that join or leave a consolidated group, with appropriate adjustments. For example, for purposes of §§1.1502-91 through 1.1502-96, the term *loss group* includes a consolidated group in which any member is entitled to use a disallowed business interest expense carryforward, within the meaning of §1.163(j)-1(b)(9), that did not arise, and is not treated as arising, in a SRLY with regard to that group. Additionally, a reference to net operating loss carryovers in §§1.1502-91 through 1.1502-96 generally includes a reference to disallowed business interest expense carryforwards. References to a loss or losses in §§1.1502-91 through 1.1502-96 include references to disallowed business interest expense carryforwards or section 382 disallowed business interest carryforwards, within the meaning of §1.382-2(a)(7), as appropriate.

(2) *Appropriate adjustments.*—For purposes of applying the rules in §§1.1502-91 through 1.1502-96 to current-year business interest expense (within the meaning of §1.163(j)-5(a)(2)(i)), disallowed business interest expense carryforwards, and section 382 disallowed business interest carryforwards, appropriate adjustments are required.

Par. 25. Section 1.1502-99 is amended by adding paragraph (d) to read as follows:

§1.1502-99. Effective/applicability dates.

* * *

(d) *Application to section 163(j).*—(1) *Sections 1.382-2 and 1.382-5.*—To the extent the rules of §§1.1502-91 through 1.1502-99 effectuate the rules of §§1.382-2 and 1.382-5, the provisions apply with respect to ownership changes occurring on or after the date the Treasury decision adopting these regulations as final regulations is published in the **Federal Register**. For loss corporations that have ownership changes occurring before the date the Treasury decision adopting these regulations as final regulations is published in the **Federal Register**, see §§1.1502-91 through 1.1502-99 as contained in 26 CFR part 1, revised April 1, 2018. However, taxpayers and their related parties, within the meaning of sections 267(b) and 707(b)(1), may apply the rules of §§1.1502-91 through 1.1502-99 to the extent they apply the rules of §§1.382-2 and 1.382-5, to ownership changes occurring during a taxable year beginning after December 31, 2017, as well as consistently applying the rules of the §§1.1502-91 through 1.1502-99 to the extent they effectuate the rules of §§1.382-2, 1.382-5, 1.382-6, and 1.383-1, the section 163(j) regulations (within the meaning of §1.163(j)-1(b)(32)), and if applicable, §§1.263A-9, 1.381(c)(20)-1, 1.469-9, 1.882-5, 1.1502-13, 1.1502-21, 1.1502-36, 1.1502-79, and 1.1504-4 to taxable years beginning after December 31, 2017.

(2) *Sections 1.382-6 and 1.383-1.*—To the extent the rules of §§1.1502-91 through 1.1502-98 effectuate the rules of §§1.382-6 and 1.383-1, the provisions apply with respect to ownership changes occurring during a taxable year ending

after the date the Treasury decision adopting these regulations as final regulations is published in the **Federal Register**. For the application of these rules to an ownership change with respect to an ownership change occurring during a taxable year ending before the date the Treasury decision adopting these regulations as final regulations is published in the **Federal Register**, see §§1.1502-91 through 1.1502-99 as contained in 26 CFR part 1, revised April 1, 2018. However, taxpayers and their related parties, within the meaning of sections 267(b) and 707(b)(1), may apply the rules of §§1.1502-91 through 1.1502-99 (to the extent that those rules effectuate the rules of §§1.382-6 and 1.383-1), to ownership changes occurring during a taxable year beginning after December 31, 2017, so long as the taxpayers and their related parties consistently apply the rules of the section 163(j) regulations (within the meaning of §1.163(j)-1(b)(32)), and if applicable, §§1.263A-9, 1.381(c)(20)-1, 1.469-9, 1.882-5, 1.1502-13, 1.1502-21, 1.1502-36, 1.1502-79, and 1.1504-4 to taxable years beginning after December 31, 2017.

Base Erosion and Anti-Abuse Tax: Guidance

Base Erosion and Anti-Abuse Tax: Guidance.—Amendments to Reg. §1.1502-100, regarding the tax on base erosion payments of taxpayers with substantial gross receipts and reporting requirements thereunder, are proposed (published in the Federal Register on December 21, 2018) (REG-104259-18).

Par. 9. Section 1.1502-100 is amended by revising paragraph (b) to read as follows:

§1.1502-100. Corporations exempt from tax.

* * *

(b) The tax liability for a consolidated return year of an exempt group is the tax imposed by section 511(a) on the consolidated unrelated taxable income for the year (determined under paragraph (c) of this section), and by allowing the credits provided in §1.1502-2(b).

* * *

Hybrid Arrangements: Rules

Hybrid Arrangements: Rules.—Amendments to Reg. §1.1503(d)-1, implementing sections 245A(e) and 267A of the Internal Revenue Code regarding hybrid dividends and certain amounts paid or accrued in hybrid transactions or with hybrid entities, are proposed (published in the Federal Register on December 28, 2018) (REG-104352-18).

Par. 4 Section 1.1503(d)-1 is amended by:

1. In paragraph (b)(2)(i), removing the word "and".
2. In paragraph (b)(2)(ii), removing the second period and adding in its place "; and".
3. Adding paragraph (b)(2)(iii).
4. Redesignating paragraph (c) as paragraph (d).
5. Adding new paragraph (c).
6. In the first sentence of newly-redesignated paragraph (d)(2)(ii), removing the language "(c)(2)(i)" and adding the language "(d)(2)(i)" in its place.

The additions read as follows:

§1.1503(d)-1. Definitions and special rules for filings under section 1503(d).

* * *

(b) * * *

(2) * * *

(iii) A domestic consenting corporation (as defined in §301.7701-3(c)(3)(i) of this chapter), as provided in paragraph (c)(1) of this section. *See* §1.1503(d)-7(c)(41).

* * *

(c) *Treatment of domestic consenting corporation as a dual resident corporation*.—(1) *Rule*.—A domestic consenting corporation is treated as a dual resident corporation under paragraph (b)(2)(iii) of this section for a taxable year if, on any day during the taxable year, the following requirements are satisfied:

(i) Under the tax law of a foreign country where a specified foreign tax resident is tax resident, the specified foreign tax resident derives or incurs (or would derive or incur) items of income, gain, deduction, or loss of the domestic consenting corporation (because, for example, the domestic consenting corporation is fiscally transparent under such tax law).

(ii) The specified foreign tax resident bears a relationship to the domestic consenting corporation that is described in section 267(b) or 707(b). *See* §1.1503(d)-7(c)(41).

(2) *Definitions*.—The following definitions apply for purposes of this paragraph (c).

(i) The term *fiscally transparent* means, with respect to a domestic consenting corporation or an intermediate entity, fiscally transparent as determined under the principles of §1.894-1(d)(3)(ii) and (iii), without regard to whether a specified foreign tax resident is a resident of a country that has an income tax treaty with the United States.

(ii) The term *specified foreign tax resident* means a body corporate or other entity or body of persons liable to tax under the tax law of a foreign country as a resident.

* * *

Hybrid Arrangements: Rules

Hybrid Arrangements: Rules.—Amendments to Reg. §1.1503(d)-3, implementing sections 245A(e) and 267A of the Internal Revenue Code regarding hybrid dividends and certain amounts paid or accrued in hybrid transactions or with hybrid entities, are proposed (published in the Federal Register on December 28, 2018) (REG-104352-18).

Par. 5. Section 1.1503(d)-3 is amended by adding the language "or (e)(3)" after the language "paragraph (e)(2)" in paragraph (e)(1), and adding paragraph (e)(3) to read as follows:

§1.1503(d)-3. Foreign use.

* * *

(e) * * *

(3) *Exception for domestic consenting corporations.*—Paragraph (e)(1) of this section will not apply so as to deem a foreign use of a dual consolidated loss incurred by a domestic consenting corporation that is a dual resident corporation under §1.1503(d)-1(b)(2)(iii).

Hybrid Arrangements: Rules

Hybrid Arrangements: Rules.—Amendments to Reg. §§1.1503(d)-6—1.1503(d)-8, implementing sections 245A(e) and 267A of the Internal Revenue Code regarding hybrid dividends and certain amounts paid or accrued in hybrid transactions or with hybrid entities, are proposed (published in the Federal Register on December 28, 2018) (REG-104352-18).

Par. 6. Section 1.1503(d)-6 is amended by:

1. Removing the language "a foreign government" and "a foreign country" in paragraph (f)(5)(i), and adding the language "a government of a country" and "the country" in their places, respectively.

2. Removing the language "a foreign government" in paragraph (f)(5)(ii), and adding the language "a government of a country" in its place.

3. Removing the language "the foreign government" in paragraph (f)(5)(iii), and adding the language "a government of a country" in its place.

§1.1503(d)-6. Exceptions to the domestic use limitation rule.

Par. 7. Section 1.1503(d)-7 is amended by redesignating Examples 1 through 40 as paragraphs (c)(1) through (40), respectively, and adding paragraph (c)(41) to read as follows:

§1.1503(d)-7. Examples.

* * *

(c) * * *

(41) *Example 41. Domestic consenting corporation—treated as dual resident corporation*—(i) *Facts.* FSZ1, a Country Z entity that is subject to Country Z tax on its worldwide income or on a residence basis and is classified as a foreign corporation for U.S. tax purposes, owns all the interests in DCC, a domestic eligible entity that has filed an election to be classified as an association. Under Country Z tax law, DCC is fiscally transparent. For taxable year 1, DCC's only item of income, gain, deduction, or loss is a $100x deduction and such deduction comprises a $100x net operating loss of DCC. For Country Z tax purposes, FSZ1's only item of income, gain, deduction, or loss, other than the $100x loss attributable to DCC, is $60x of operating income.

(ii) *Result.* DCC is a domestic consenting corporation because by electing to be classified as an association, it consents to be treated as a dual resident corporation for purposes of section 1503(d). *See* §301.7701-3(c)(3) of this chapter. For taxable year 1, DCC is treated as a dual resident corporation under §1.1503(d)-1(b)(2)(iii) because FSZ1 (a specified foreign tax resident that bears a relationship to DCC that is described in section 267(b) or 707(b)) derives or incurs items of income, gain, deduction, or loss of DCC. *See* §1.1503(d)-1(c). FSZ1 derives or incurs items of income, gain, deduction, or loss of DCC because, under Country Z tax law, DCC is fiscally transparent. Thus, DCC has a $100x dual consolidated loss for taxable year 1. *See* §1.1503(d)-1(b)(5). Because the loss is available to, and in fact does, offset income of FSZ1 under Country Z tax law, there is a foreign use of the dual consolidated loss in year 1. Accordingly, the dual consolidated loss is subject to the domestic use limitation rule of §1.1503(d)-4(b). The result would be the same if FSZ1 were to indirectly own its DCC stock through an intermediate entity that is fiscally transparent under Country Z tax law, or if an individual were to wholly own FSZ1 and FSZ1 were a disregarded entity. In addition, the result would be the same if FSZ1 had no items of income, gain, deduction, or loss, other than the $100x loss attributable to DCC.

(iii) *Alternative facts – DCC not treated as a dual resident corporation.* The facts are the same as in paragraph (c)(41)(i) of this section, except that DCC is not fiscally transparent under Country Z tax law and thus under Country Z tax law FSZ1 does not derive or incur items of income, gain, deduction, or loss of DCC. Accordingly, DCC is not treated as a dual resident corporation under §1.1503(d)-1(b)(2)(iii) for year 1 and, consequently, its $100x net operating loss in that year is not a dual consolidated loss.

(iv) *Alternative facts – mirror legislation.* The facts are the same as in paragraph (c)(41)(i) of this section, except that, under provisions of Country Z tax law that constitute mirror legislation under §1.1503(d)-3(e)(1) and that are substantially similar to the recommendations in Chapter 6 of OECD/G-20, *Neutralising the Effects of Hybrid Mismatch Arrangements, Action 2: 2015 Final Report* (October 2015), Country Z tax law prohibits the $100x loss attributable to DCC from offsetting FSZ1's income that is not also subject to U.S. tax. As is the case in paragraph (c)(41)(ii) of this section, DCC is treated as a dual resident corporation under §1.1503(d)-1(b)(2)(iii) for year 1 and its $100x net operating loss is a dual consolidated loss. Pursuant to §1.1503(d)-3(e)(3), however, the dual consolidated loss is not deemed to be put to a foreign use by virtue of the Country Z mirror legislation. Therefore, DCC is eligible to make a domestic use election for the dual consolidated loss.

Par. 8. Section 1.1503(d)-8 is amended by removing the language "§1.1503(d)-1(c)" and adding in its place the language "§1.1503(d)-1(d)" wherever it appears in paragraphs (b)(3)(i) and (iii), and adding paragraphs (b)(6) and (7) to read as follows:

§ 1.1503(d)-8. Effective dates.

* * *

(b) * * *

(6) *Rules regarding domestic consenting corporations.*—Section 1.1503(d)-1(b)(2)(iii), (c), and (d), as well § 1.1503(d)-3(e)(1) and (e)(3), apply to determinations under § § 1.1503(d)-1 through 1.1503(d)-7 relating to taxable years ending on or after December 20, 2018. For taxable years ending before December 20, 2018, see § § 1.1503(d)-1(c) (previous version of § 1.1503(d)-1(d)) and 1.1503(d)-3(e)(1) (previous version of § 1.1503(d)-3(e)(1)) as contained in 26 CFR part 1 revised as of April 1, 2018.

(7) *Compulsory transfer triggering event exception.*—Sections 1.1503(d)-6(f)(5)(i) through (iii) apply to transfers that occur on or after December 20, 2018. For transfers occurring before December 20, 2018, *see* § 1.1503(d)-6(f)(5)(i) through (iii) as contained in 26 CFR part 1 revised as of April 1, 2018. However, taxpayers may consistently apply § 1.1503(d)-6(f)(5)(i) through (iii) to transfers occurring before December 20, 2018.

Deduction for Business Interest Expense: Limitation

Deduction for Business Interest Expense: Limitation.—Amendments to Reg. § 1.1504-4, regarding the limitation on the deduction for business interest expense after the enactment of recent tax legislation, are proposed (published in the Federal Register on December 28, 2018) (REG-106089-18).

Par. 26. Section 1.1504-4 is amended by:

1. Removing "163(j), 864(e)," from paragraph the first sentence of paragraph (a)(2) and adding "864(e)" in its place; and
2. Adding two sentences at the end of paragraph (i).

The addition reads as follows:

§ 1.1504-4. Treatment of warrants, options, convertible obligations, and other similar interests.

* * *

(i) * * * Paragraph (a)(2) of this section applies with respect to taxable years ending after the date the Treasury decision adopting these regulations as final regulations is published in the **Federal Register**. However, taxpayers and their related parties, within the meaning of sections 267(b) and 707(b)(1), may apply the rules of this section to a taxable year beginning after December 31, 2017, so long as the taxpayers and their related parties consistently apply the rules of this section, the section 163(j) regulations (within the meaning of § 1.163(j)-1(b)(32)), and if applicable, § § 1.263A-9, 1.381(c)(20)-1, 1.382-6, 1.383-1, 1.469-9, 1.882-5, 1.1502-13, 1.1502-21, 1.1502-36, 1.1502-79, and 1.1502-91 through 1.1502-99 (to the extent they effectuate the rules of § § 1.382-6, and 1.383-1), to those taxable years.

Consolidated Returns: AMT

Consolidated Returns: Alternative Minimum Tax.—Reproduced below is the text of a proposed amendment to Reg. § 1.1552-1, relating to the computation of the alternative minimum tax by consolidated groups (published in the Federal Register on December 30, 1992).

□ Par. 8. Section 1.1552-1 is amended by adding paragraphs (g) through (j) to read as follows:

§ 1.1552-1. Earnings and profits.

* * *

(g) *Allocation of consolidated AMT and allowable consolidated MTC to members.*—(1) *In general.*—For purposes of determining the earnings and profits of each member of a consolidated group, the consolidated AMT and allowable consolidated MTC (computed under § 1.1502-55) must be allocated among the members in accordance with this paragraph (g).

(2) *Amount of consolidated AMT allocated to a member.*—The amount of consolidated AMT allocated to a member is determined by multiplying the consolidated AMT by a fraction, the numerator of which is the separate adjusted AMT (as defined in § 1.1502-55(h)(6)(iv)) of the member for the year, and the denominator of which is the sum of each member's separate adjusted AMT for the year.

(3) *Amount of allowable consolidated MTC allocated to a member.*—The amount of allowable consolidated MTC in a taxable year must be allocated among the consolidated group members in accordance with the principles of § 1.1502-55(h)(6)(vi) and (7).

(4) *Effective date.*—Paragraph (g) of this section applies to any consolidated return year for which the due date of the income tax return (without regard to extensions) is on or after [the date that is sixty days after final regulations are filed with the Federal Register].

(h) *Allocation of consolidated environmental tax.*—(1) *In general.*—For purposes of determining the earnings and profits of each member of a consolidated group, the consolidated environmental tax (as defined in paragraph (h)(2) of this section) must be allocated among the members in accordance with paragraph (h)(3) of this section.

(2) *Consolidated environmental tax.*—(i) *In general.*—The consolidated environmental tax is equal to 0.12 percent of the excess of—

(A) Consolidated modified AMTI; over

(B) $2,000,000.

(ii) *Consolidated modified AMTI.*—For purposes of determining the consolidated environmental tax, consolidated modified AMTI is equal to the consolidated AMTI (as defined in § 1.1502-55(b)), but determined without taking into account—

(A) The consolidated ATNOL deduction (as defined in § 1.1502-55(b)(4)); and

(B) The deduction for the payment of an environmental tax under section 164(a)(5).

(3) *Amount of consolidated environmental tax to be allocated to a member.*—(i) *In general.*—The amount of consolidated environmental tax

to be allocated to a member is determined by multiplying the consolidated environmental tax by a fraction, the numerator of which is the separate modified AMTI of the member, and denominator of which is the sum of each member's separate modified AMTI.

(ii) *Separate modified AMTI.*—For purposes of the allocation of consolidated environmental tax, separate modified AMTI of a member is the consolidated modified AMTI determined by taking into account only the member's items of income, gain, deduction, and loss, including the member's losses and deductions actually absorbed by the group in the taxable year (whether or not absorbed by the member). For purposes of this allocation, a member is considered to have separate modified AMTI only if the computation in this paragraph (h)(3)(ii) produces a number that is greater than zero.

(4) *Effective date.*—Paragraph (h) of this section applies to any consolidated return year for which the due date of the income tax return (without regard to extensions) is on or after [the date that is sixty days after final regulations are filed with the Federal Register].

(i) [Reserved]

(j) *Allocation of consolidated additional taxes to members.*—For purposes of determining the earnings and profits of each member of a consolidated group, the consolidated additional taxes (as defined in § 1.1502-2(b)) are allocated to the members in accordance with any reasonable method used by the group. This paragraph (j) applies to any consolidated return year for which the due date of the income tax return (without regard to extensions) is on or after [the date that is sixty days after final regulations are filed with the Federal Register].

ESTATE TAX

Estate and Gift Taxes: Basic Exclusion Amount: Difference

Estate and Gift Taxes: Basic Exclusion Amount: Difference.—Amendments to Reg. § 20.2010-1, addressing the effect of recent legislative changes to the basic exclusion amount used in computing Federal gift and estate taxes, are proposed (published in the Federal Register on November 23, 2018) (REG-106706-18).

Par. 2. Section 20.2010-1 is amended by:

1. Redesignating paragraphs (c) through (e) as paragraphs (d) through (f) respectively;
2. Adding a new paragraph (c); and
3. Revising newly redesignated paragraphs (e)(3) and (f).

The addition and revisions read as follows:

§ 20.2010-1. Unified credit against estate tax; in general.

* * *

(c) *Special rule in the case of a difference between the basic exclusion amount applicable to gifts and that applicable at the donor's date of death.*—(1) *Rule.*—Changes in the basic exclusion amount that occur between the date of a donor's gift and the date of the donor's death may cause the basic exclusion amount allowable on the date of a gift to exceed that allowable on the date of death. If the total of the amounts allowable as a credit in computing the gift tax payable on the decedent's post-1976 gifts, within the meaning of section 2001(b)(2), to the extent such credits are based solely on the basic exclusion amount as defined and adjusted in section 2010(c)(3), exceeds the credit allowable within the meaning of section 2010(a) in computing the estate tax, again only to the extent such credit is based solely on such basic exclusion amount, in each case by applying the tax rates in effect at the decedent's death, then the portion of the credit allowable in computing the estate tax on the decedent's taxable estate that is attributable to the basic exclusion amount is the sum of the amounts attributable to the basic exclusion amount allowable as a credit in computing the gift tax payable on the decedent's post-1976 gifts. The amount allowable as a credit in computing gift tax payable for any year may not exceed the tentative tax on the gifts made during that year, and the amount allowable as a credit in computing the estate tax may not exceed the net tentative tax on the taxable estate. Sections 2505(c) and 2010(d).

(2) *Example.*—Individual A (never married) made cumulative post-1976 taxable gifts of $9 million, all of which were sheltered from gift tax by the cumulative total of $10 million in basic exclusion amount allowable on the dates of the gifts. A dies after 2025 and the basic exclusion amount on A's date of death is $5 million. A was not eligible for any restored exclusion amount pursuant to Notice 2017-15. Because the total of the amounts allowable as a credit in computing the gift tax payable on A's post-1976 gifts (based on the $9 million basic exclusion amount used to determine those credits) exceeds the credit based on the $5 million basic exclusion amount applicable on the decedent's date of death, under paragraph (c)(1) of this section, the credit to be applied for purposes of computing the estate tax is based on a basic exclusion amount of $9 million, the amount used to determine the credits allowable in computing the gift tax payable on the post-1976 gifts made by A.

* * *

(e) * * *

(3) *Basic exclusion amount.*—Except to the extent provided in paragraph (e)(3)(iii) of this section, the basic exclusion amount is the sum of the amounts described in paragraphs (e)(3)(i) and (ii) of this section.

(i) For any decedent dying in calendar year 2011 or thereafter, $5,000,000; and

(ii) For any decedent dying after calendar year 2011, $5,000,000 multiplied by the cost-of-living adjustment determined under section 1(f)(3) for the calendar year of decedent's death by substituting "calendar year 2010" for "calendar year 2016" in section 1(f)(3)(A)(ii) and rounded to the nearest multiple of $10,000.

(iii) In the case of the estates of decedents dying after December 31, 2017, and before January 1, 2026, paragraphs (e)(3)(i) and (ii) of this section will be applied by substituting "$10,000,000" for "$5,000,000."

(f) *Applicability dates.*—(1) *In general.*—Except as provided in paragraph (f)(2) of this section, this section applies to the estates of decedents dying after June 11, 2015. For the rules applicable to estates of decedents dying after December 31, 2010, and before June 12, 2015, see § 20.2010-1T, as contained in 26 CFR part 20, revised as of April 1, 2015.

(2) *Exceptions.*—Paragraph (c) of this section applies to estates of decedents dying on and after the date of publication of a Treasury decision adopting these rules as final regulations. Paragraph (e)(3) of this section applies to the estates of decedents dying after December 31, 2017.

Estate and Gift Taxes: Basic Exclusion Amount: Difference

Estate and Gift Taxes: Basic Exclusion Amount: Difference.—Amendments to Reg. § 20.2010-3, addressing the effect of recent legislative changes to the basic exclusion amount used in computing Federal gift and estate taxes, are proposed (published in the Federal Register on November 23, 2018) (REG-106706-18).

Par. 3. Section 20.2010-3 is amended by removing "§ 20.2010-1(d)(5)" wherever it appears and adding in its place "§ 20.2010-1(e)(5)".

§ 20.2010-3. Portability provisions applicable to the surviving spouse's estate.

Below-Market Loans

Below-Market Interest Rate Loans: Tax Reform Act of 1984.—Reproduced below is the text of a proposed amendment of Reg. § 20.2031-4, detailing the estate tax treatment of lenders and borrowers with respect to below-market term loans made after June 6, 1984, and below-market demand loans outstanding after such date (published in the Federal Register on August 20, 1985).

☐ Par. 7. Section 20.2031-4 is amended by adding a new sentence at the end to read as follows:

§ 20.2031-4. Valuation of notes.

* * * See § 20.7872-1 for special rules in the case of gift loans (within the meaning of § 1.7872-4(b)) made after June 6, 1984.

* * *

Annuities: Interests: Valuation: Actuarial Tables

Annuities: Interests: Valuation: Actuarial Tables.—Amendments to Reg. § 20.2032-1, relating to the use of actuarial tables in valuing annuities, interests for life or terms of years, and remainder or reversionary interests, are proposed (published in the Federal Register on May 7, 2009) (REG-107845-08).

Par. 8. Section 20.2032-1 is amended by revising paragraphs (f)(1) and (h) to read as follows:

§ 20.2032-1. Alternate valuation.

* * *

(f) * * *

(1) [The text of this proposed paragraph (f)(1) is the same as the text of § 20.2032-1T(f)(1) as added by T.D. 9448].

* * *

(h) [The text of this proposed paragraph (h) is the same as the text of § 20.2032-1T(h) as added by T.D. 9448].

Estate Tax: Gross Estate: Alternate Valuation Date: Election

Estate Tax: Gross Estate: Alternate Valuation Date: Election.—Amendments to Reg. § 20.2032-1, providing guidance respecting the election to use the alternate valuation method under Code Sec. 2032, are proposed (published in the Federal Register on November 18, 2011) (REG-112196-07).

☐ Par. 2. For each entry in the table, each paragraph in the "Old Paragraph" column is redesignated as indicated in the "New Paragraph" column:

Old Paragraph	New Paragraph
20.2032-1(c)(1)	20.2032-1(c)(1)(i)
20.2032-1(c)(3)	20.2032-1(c)(3)(i)
20.2032-1(c)(3)(i)	20.2032-1(c)(3)(i)(A)
20.2032-1(c)(3)(ii)	20.2032-1(c)(3)(i)(B)
20.2032-1(c)(3)(iii)	20.2032-1(c)(3)(i)(C)
20.2032-1(c)(3)(iv)	20.2032-1(c)(3)(i)(D)
20.2032-1(c)(3)(v)	20.2032-1(c)(3)(i)(E)
20.2032-1(f)	20.2032-1(f)(2)
20.2032-1(f)(1)	20.2032-1(f)(2)(i)
20.2032-1(f)(2)	20.2032-1(f)(2)(ii)

☐ Par. 3. Section 20.2032-1 is amended by:

1. Revising paragraph (a) introductory text.

2. Revising paragraphs (a)(1) and (a)(2).

3. Revising newly-designated paragraph (c)(1)(i), newly-designated paragraph (c)(3)(i)(C), paragraph (e) introductory text, the introductory text of paragraph (e) *Example 1* preceding the table, the last sentence in newly-designated paragraph (f)(2) introductory text, newly-designated paragraph (f)(2)(i), and the second sentence in newly-designated paragraph (f)(2)(ii).

4. Adding new paragraphs (c)(1)(ii), (c)(1)(iii), (c)(1)(iv), (c)(4), (c)(5), (f)(1), and (f)(3).

5. Adding a paragraph heading and a new second sentence in paragraph (c)(2) introductory text.

6. Adding a paragraph heading to paragraph (c)(3).

7. Designating the undesignated language following newly-designated paragraph (c)(3)(i)(E) as paragraph (c)(3)(ii) and adding a paragraph heading to this paragraph.

8. Designating the table in paragraph (e) as *Example 1* and adding paragraph (e) *Example 2* following the table.

9. Revising the paragraph heading and adding two sentences at the end of paragraph (h).

The additions and revisions read as follows.

§20.2032-1. Alternate valuation.—(a) *In general.*—In general, section 2032 provides for the valuation of a decedent's gross estate at a date (alternate valuation date) other than the date of the decedent's death. More specifically, if an executor elects the alternate valuation method under section 2032, the property includible in the decedent's gross estate on the date of death (decedent's interest) is valued as of whichever of the following dates is applicable:

(1) Any property distributed, sold, exchanged, or otherwise disposed of within 6 months (1 year, if the decedent died on or before December 31, 1970) after the decedent's death (alternate valuation period) is valued as of the date on which it is first distributed, sold, exchanged, or otherwise disposed of (transaction date).

(2) Any property not distributed, sold, exchanged, or otherwise disposed of during the alternate valuation period is valued as of the date 6 months (1 year, if the decedent died on or before December 31, 1970) after the date of the decedent's death (6-month date).

* * *

(c) *Meaning of "distributed, sold, exchanged, or otherwise disposed of".*—(1) *In general.*

(i) *Transactions included.*—The phrase "distributed, sold, exchanged, or otherwise disposed of" comprehends all possible ways by which property ceases to form a part of the gross estate. This phrase includes, but is not limited to:

(A) The use of money on hand at the date of the decedent's death to pay funeral or other expenses of the decedent's estate;

(B) The use of money on hand at the date of the decedent's death to invest in other property;

(C) The exercise of employee stock options;

(D) The surrender of stock for corporate assets in partial or complete liquidation of a corporation, and similar transactions involving partnerships or other entities;

(E) The distribution by the estate (or other holder) of included property as defined in paragraph (d) of this section;

(F) The transfer or exchange of property for other property, whether or not gain or loss is currently recognized for income tax purposes;

(G) The contribution of cash or other property to a corporation, partnership, or other entity, whether or not gain or loss is currently recognized for income tax purposes;

(H) The exchange of interests in a corporation, partnership, or other entity (entity) for one or more different interests (for example, a different class of stock) in the same entity or in an acquiring or resulting entity or entities (see, however, paragraph (c)(1)(ii) of this section); and

(I) Any other change in the ownership structure or interests in, or in the assets of, a corporation, partnership, or other entity, an interest in which is includible in the gross estate, such that the included property after the change does not reasonably represent the included property at the decedent's date of death (see, however, paragraph (c)(1)(iii)(A) of this section). Such a change in the ownership structure or interests in or in the assets of an entity includes, without limitation—

(1) The dilution of the decedent's ownership interest in the entity due to the issuance of additional ownership interests in that entity;

(2) An increase in the decedent's ownership interest in the entity due to the entity's redemption of the interest of a different owner;

(3) A reinvestment of the entity's assets; and

(4) A distribution or disbursement of property (other than excluded property as defined in paragraph (d) of this section) by the entity (other than expenses, such as rents and salaries, paid in the ordinary course of the entity's business), with the effect that the fair market value of the entity before the occurrence does not equal the fair market value of the entity immediately thereafter.

(ii) *Exchange of an interest in an existing corporation, partnership, or other entity includible in the gross estate.*—If an interest in a corporation, partnership, or other entity (entity is includible in the gross estate at death and that interest is exchanged as described in paragraph (c)(1)(i)(H) of this section for one or more different interests in the same entity or in an acquiring or resulting entity or entities, the transaction does not result in an exchange or disposition under section 2032(a)(1) and paragraph (c)(1)(i)(H) of this section if, on the date of the exchange, the fair market value of the interest in the entity equals the fair market value of the interest(s) in the same entity or the acquiring or resulting entity or entities. Such transactions may include, without limitation, reorganizations, recapitalizations, mergers, or similar transactions. In determining whether the exchanged properties have the same fair market value, a difference in value equal to or less than 5 percent of the fair market value, as of the transaction date, of the property interest includible in the gross estate on the decedent's date of death is ignored. If the transaction satisfies the requirements of this paragraph, the property to be valued on the 6-month date (or on the transaction date, if any, subsequent to this transaction) is the property received in the exchange, rather than the property includible in the decedent's gross estate at the date of death. This paragraph has no effect on any other provision of the Internal Revenue Code that is applicable to the transaction. For example, even if the transaction does not result in a deemed exchange as a result of satisfying the requirements of this paragraph, the provisions of chapter 14 may be applicable to determine fair market value for Federal estate tax purposes.

(iii) *Distributions from an account or entity in which the decedent held an interest at death.*

(A) *In general.*—If during the alternate valuation period, an estate (or other holder of the decedent's interest) receives a distribution or disbursement (to the extent the distribution or disbursement consists of included property, as defined in paragraph (d) of this section) (payment) from a partnership, corporation, trust (including an IRA, Roth IRA, 403(b), 401(k), Thrift Savings Plan, etc.), bank account or similar asset, or other entity (entity), and an interest in that entity is includible in the gross estate, the payment does not result in a distribution under paragraph (c)(1)(i)(I) of this section. However, this rule applies only if, on the date of the payment, the fair market value of the decedent's interest in the entity before the payment equals the sum of the fair market value of the payment made to the estate (or other holder of the decedent's interest in the entity) and the fair market value of the decedent's interest in the entity, not including any excluded property, after the payment. In this case, the alternate valuation date of the payment is the date of the payment, and the alternate valuation date of the decedent's remaining interest in the entity, if any, is the 6-month date (or the transaction date, if any, subsequent to this payment). If this requirement is not met, the payment is a distribution under paragraph (c)(1)(i) of this section, and the alternate valuation date of the decedent's entire interest in the entity is the date of the payment. For purposes of this section, a distribution or disbursement is deemed to consist first of excluded property, if any, and then of included property, as those terms are defined in paragraph (d) of this section.

(B) *Special rule.*—If the decedent's interest in an entity that is includible in the gross estate consists of the amount needed to produce an annuity, unitrust, remainder, or other such payment valued under section 2036, then assuming the distribution satisfies the general rule set forth in paragraph (c)(1)(iii)(A) of this section, the value of each distribution (to the extent it is deemed to consist of included property) payable (whether or not actually paid) during the alternate valuation period shall be added to the value of the entity on the alternate valuation date. The sum of the fair market value of these distributions when made and the fair market value of the entity on the alternate valuation date shall be used as the fair market value of the entity in computing the amount, valued as of the alternate valuation date, to be included in the decedent's gross estate under section 2036. See *Example* 2 of paragraph (e) of this section.

(iv) *Aggregation.*—For purposes of this section, a special aggregation rule applies in two situations to determine the value to be included in the gross estate pursuant to an alternate valuation election. Those two situations arise when, during the alternate valuation period, less than all of the interest includible in the decedent's gross estate in a particular property is the subject of a transaction described in paragraphs (c)(1)(i), (c)(1)(ii), (c)(1)(iii), or (c)(2) of this section. In one situation, one or more portions of the includible interest are subject to such a transaction and a portion is still held on the 6-month date. In the other situation, the entire interest includible in the gross estate is disposed of in two or more such transactions during the alternate valuation period, so that no part of that interest remains on the 6-month date. In both of these situations, the fair market value of each portion of the interest includible in the gross estate is to be determined as follows. The fair market value of each portion subject to such a transaction, and the portion remaining, if any, on the 6-month date, is the fair market value, as of the transaction date, or the 6-month date for any remaining portion, of the entire interest includible in the gross estate on the decedent's date of death, multiplied by a fraction. The numerator of that fraction is the portion of the interest subject to that transaction, or the portion remaining on the 6-month date, and the denominator is the entire interest includible in the gross estate at the decedent's date of death.

(2) *Property distributed.*—* * * Property is not considered "distributed" merely because property passes directly at death as a result of a beneficiary designation or other contractual arrangement or by operation of law. * * *

(3) *Person able to sell, exchange, or otherwise dispose of property includible in the gross estate.*—(i) * * *

(A) * * *

(B) * * *

(C) An heir, devisee, or other person to whom title to property passes directly on death by reason of a beneficiary designation or other contractual arrangement or by operation of law;

(D) * * *

(E) * * *

(ii) *Binding contracts.*—* * *

(4) *Certain post-death events.*—If the effect of any other provision of the Internal Revenue Code is that a post-death event is deemed to have occurred on the date of death, the post-death event will not be considered a transaction described in paragraph (c)(1)(i) of this section. For example, the grant, during the alternate valuation period, of a qualified conservation easement in accordance with section 2031(c) is not a transaction described in paragraph (c)(1)(i) of this section. Pursuant to section 2031(c), the post-death grant of the easement is effective for Federal estate tax purposes as of the date of the decedent's death. As a result, for purposes of determining both the estate's eligibility to make an election under this section and the value of the property on the alternate valuation date, the fair market value of the property as of the date of death must be compared to the fair market value of that property as of the alternate valuation date, in each case as that value is adjusted by reason of the existence of the section 2031(c) qualified easement.

(5) *Examples.*—The application of paragraph (c) of this section is illustrated in the following examples. In each example, decedent's (D's) estate elects to value D's gross estate under the alternate valuation method, so that the alternate valuation date of the property includible in the gross estate on D's date of death is either the transaction date or the 6-month date. In each example, assume that the only factors affecting value during the alternate valuation period, and the only occurrences described in paragraphs (c)(1)(i) and (c)(2) of this section, are those described in the example.

Example 1. At D's death, D owned property with a fair market value of $100X. Two months after D's death (Date 1), D's executor and D's family members formed a limited partnership. D's executor contributed all of the property to the partnership and received an interest in the partnership in exchange. The investment of the property in the partnership is a transaction described in paragraph (c)(1)(i)(F) and/or (G) of this section. As a result, the alternate valuation date of the property is the date of its contribution and the value to be included in D's gross estate is the fair market value of the property immediately prior to its contribution to the partnership. The result would be the same if D's estate instead had contributed property to a limited partnership formed prior to D's death by D and/or other parties, related or unrelated to D. Further, the result would be the same if D's estate had contributed the property to a corporation, publicly traded or otherwise, or other entity after D's death and prior to the 6-month date.

Example 2. At D's death, D held incentive stock options that were qualified under section 422. D's executor exercised all of the stock options prior to the 6-month date. The exercise of the stock options is a transaction described in paragraph (c)(1)(i)(C) of this section. Thus, the alternate valuation date of the stock options is the date of their exercise and the value to be included in D's gross estate is the fair market value of the stock options immediately prior to their exercise. The result would be the same if the stock options were not qualified under section 422 and were taxable under section 83 upon exercise.

Example 3. D's gross estate includes a controlling interest in Y, a corporation. During the alternate valuation period, Y issued additional shares of stock and awarded them to certain key employees. D's interest in Y was diluted to a non-controlling interest by Y's issuance of the additional stock. Y's issuance of the stock is a transaction described in paragraph (c)(1)(i)(I) of this section. The value to be included in D's gross estate is the fair market value of D's stock immediately prior to Y's issuance of the additional stock. The result would be the same if D's estate included a minority interest in Y on the date of death and that interest became a controlling interest during the alternate valuation period as the result of Y's redemption of the shares of another shareholder.

Example 4. At D's death, D owned stock in Y, a corporation. During the alternate valuation period, the Board of Directors of Y contributed all of Y's assets to a partnership in exchange for interests therein. The contribution is a transaction described in paragraph (c)(1)(i)(I)(*3*) of this section. Therefore, the alternate valuation date of D's stock in Y is the date of the reinvestment of Y's assets and the value to be included in D's gross estate is the fair market value of D's stock in Y immediately prior to the reinvestment. The result would be the same even if the Board of Directors had contributed only a portion of Y's assets to the partnership during the alternate valuation period.

Example 5. (i) At D's death, D owned common stock in Y, a corporation. Two months after D's death (Date 1), there was a reorganization of Y. In the reorganization, D's estate exchanged all of its stock for a new class of stock in X. On the date of the reorganization, the difference between the fair market value of the stock D's estate received and the fair market value on that date of the stock includible in D's gross estate at death was greater than 5% of the fair market value, as of the date of the reorganization, of the stock D held at death. The reorganization is a transaction described in paragraph (c)(1)(i)(H) of this section and does not satisfy the exception described in paragraph (c)(1)(ii) of this section. Thus, the alternate valuation date is the date of the reorganization and the value to be included in D's gross estate is the fair market value of the stock immediately prior to the reorganization. This result is not affected by whether or not the reorganization is a tax-free reorganization for Federal income tax purposes. The result would be the same if the stock had been held, for example, in an IRA with designated beneficiaries. See paragraph (c)(3)(i)(C) of this section.

(ii) If, instead, the difference between the two fair market values as of the date of the reorganization was equal to or less than 5% of the fair market value, as of the date of the reorganization, of the stock D held at death, the reorganization would satisfy the exception provided in paragraph (c)(1)(ii) of this section. Thus, the alternate valuation date would be the 6-month date. The value to be included in D's gross estate would be the fair market value, determined as of the 6-month date, of the new class of stock in Y that D's estate received in the reorganization.

Example 6. (i) At D's death, D owned an interest in Partnership X that is includible in D's gross estate. During the alternate valuation period, X made a cash distribution to each of the partners. The distribution consists entirely of included property as defined in paragraph (d) of this section. The distribution is a transaction described in paragraph (c)(1)(i)(I)(*4*) of this section. On the date of the distribution, the fair market value of D's interest in X before the distribution equaled the sum of the distribution paid to D's estate and the fair market value of D's interest in X immediately after the distribution. Thus, pursuant to paragraph (c)(1)(iii)(A) of this section, the alternate valuation date of the property distributed is the date of the distribution, and the alternate valuation date of D's interest in X is the 6-month date.

(ii) If, instead, the fair market value of D's interest in X before the distribution did not equal the sum of the distribution paid to D's estate and the fair market value of D's interest in X (not including any excluded property) immediately after the distribution, then pursuant to paragraph (c)(1)(i)(I)(*4*) of this section, the alternate valuation date of D's entire interest in X would be the date of the distribution.

Example 7. D died owning 100% of Blackacre. D's will directs that an undivided 70% interest in Blackacre is to pass to Trust A for the benefit of D's surviving spouse, and an undivided 30% interest is to pass to Trust B for the benefit of D's surviving child. Three months after D's death (Date 1), the executor of D's estate distributed a 70% interest in Blackacre to Trust A. Four months after D's death (Date 2), the executor of D's estate distributed a 30% interest in Blackacre to Trust B. The following values are includible in D's gross estate pursuant to paragraphs (c)(1)(i)(E) and (c)(1)(iv): the fair market value of the 70% interest in Blackacre, determined by calculating 70% of the fair market value of all (100%) of Blackacre as of Date 1; and the fair market value of the 30% interest in Blackacre, determined by calculating 30% of the fair market value of all (100%) of Blackacre as of Date 2.

Example 8. At D's death, D owned 100% of the units of a limited liability company (LLC). Two months after D's death (Date 1), D's executor sold 20% of the LLC units to an unrelated third party. Three months after D's death (Date 2), D's executor sold 40% of the LLC units to D's child. On the 6-month date, the estate held the remaining 40% of the units in the LLC. The alternate valuation date of the units sold is their sale date (Date 1 and Date 2, respectively) pursuant to paragraph (a) of this section. The alternate valuation date of the units remaining in the estate is the 6-month date, as these units have not been distributed, sold, exchanged, or otherwise disposed of in a transaction described in paragraphs (c)(1)(i) or (c)(2) of this section prior to this date. Pursuant to paragraph (c)(1)(iv) of this section, the value of the units disposed of on Date 1 and Date 2 is the fair market value of the 20% and 40% interests, determined by calculating 20% and 40% of the fair market value as of Date 1 and Date 2, respectively, of all the units (100%) includible in the gross estate at D's death. Similarly, the value of the units held on the 6-month date to be included in D's gross estate is the fair market value of those units, determined by taking 40% of the fair market value on the 6-month date of all of the units (100%) includible in the gross estate at D's death. As a result, the fact that the partial sales resulted in the creation of three minority interests is not taken into account in valuing under section 2032 any portion of the LLC interests held by D at D's death.

Example 9. Husband died owning an interest in a brokerage account titled in the names of Husband and Wife with rights of survivorship. On Husband's death, the account held marketable securities, corporate bonds, municipal bonds, certificates of deposit, and cash. During the alternate valuation period, Wife's stockbroker advised her that the account could not be held under the social security number of a deceased individual. Accordingly, approximately one month after Husband's death, Wife directed the stockbroker to transfer the account into an account titled in Wife's sole name. Because title to the joint account passes to Wife at the moment of Husband's death by operation of law, the transfer of the joint account into an account in Wife's sole name is not a transaction described in paragraph (c)(1)(i) of this section. Accordingly, the value of the assets held in Wife's solely owned account will be includible in Husband's gross estate at their fair market value on the 6-month date. The result would be the same if the brokerage firm automatically transferred title to the account into Wife's name, or if Wife changed the beneficiary designation for the account. Finally, the result would be the same if, instead of an account with a brokerage firm, the assets were held in Husband's retirement account (IRA or similar trust such as a Roth IRA, 403(b) plan, or 401(k) plan) or Wife's ownership of the account was the result of a contract (a beneficiary designation form) rather than operation of law.

Example 10. Assume the same facts as in *Example 9* except that, during the alternate valuation period, Wife directed the stockbroker to sell a bond in the account. The sale is a transaction described in paragraph (c)(1)(i)(I)(*4*) of this section. Wife is an individual described in paragraph (c)(3)(i)(D) of this section. Thus, the alternate valuation date of the bond is the date of its sale. The values to be included in D's gross estate are the fair market value of the bond on date of its sale, and the fair market value of the balance of the account on the 6-month date. The result would be the same if the bond had matured and was retired during the alternate valuation period. The result also would be the same if the bond was held within a retirement account (IRA or similar trust such as a Roth IRA, 403(b) plan, or 401(k) plan).

Example 11. Assume the same facts as in *Example 9* except that, during the alternate valuation period, Wife withdrew cash from the account or otherwise received income or other disbursements from the account. Each such withdrawal or disbursement from the account (to the extent it consists of included property as defined in paragraph (d) of this section) is a distribution described in paragraph (c)(1)(i)(I)(*4*) of this section. Provided that, on the date of each distribution, the fair market value of the account before the distribution (not including excluded property) equals the sum of the included property distributed and the fair market value of the included property in the account immediately after the distribution in accordance with paragraph (c)(1)(iii)(A) of this section, the alternate valuation date for each distribution is the date of the distribution and the alternate valuation date for the account is the 6-month date. The value to be included in the gross estate is the fair market value of each distribution of included property (determined as of the date of distribution) and the fair market value of the account on the 6-month date. The result would be the same if the assets were held in an IRA or similar trust, such as a Roth IRA, 403(b) plan, or 401(k) plan.

Example 12. Husband died with a retirement account, having named his three children, in specified shares totaling 100%, as the designated beneficiaries of that account. During the alternate valuation period, the account was divided into three separate retirement accounts, each in the name of a different child and funded with that child's designated share. The division of the retirement account is not a transaction described in paragraph (c)(1)(i) of this section by reason of paragraph (c)(2) of this section, so the alternate valuation date for each of the new accounts is the 6-month date.

Example 13. (i) D's gross estate includes real property. During the alternate valuation period, D's executor grants a conservation easement that restricts the property's use under local law but does not satisfy the requirements of section 2031(c). The easement reduces the fair market value of the property. The executor's grant of the conservation easement is a transaction described in paragraph (c)(1)(i)(E) of this section and does not satisfy the exception described in paragraph (c)(4) of this section. Therefore, the alternate valuation date for the property is the date the easement was granted, and the value to be included in D's gross estate is the fair market value of the property immediately prior to the grant.

(ii) Assume, instead, that the easement satisfied the requirements of section 2031(c) and, thus, satisfied the exception described in paragraph (c)(4) of this section. Pursuant to paragraph (c)(4), for purposes of determining both the estate's eligibility to make an election under section 2032 and the value of the property on the 6-month date, the section 2031(c) qualified easement is taken into account in determining both the fair market value of the property on D's date of death and the fair market value of the property on the 6-month date.

***

(e) *Examples.*—The application of paragraph (d) of this section regarding "included property" and "excluded property" is illustrated by the following examples.

Example 1. Assume that the decedent (D) died on January 1, 1955:***

Example 2. (i) At death, D held a qualified interest described in section 2702(b) in the form of an annuity in a grantor retained annuity trust (GRAT) D had created and funded with $150,000. The trust agreement provides for an annual annuity payment of $12,000 per year to D or D's estate for a term of 10 years. At the expiration of the 10-year term, the remainder is to be distributed to D's child. D dies prior to the expiration of the 10-year term. On D's date of death, the fair market value of the property in the GRAT is $325,000.

(ii) The only assets in the GRAT are an apartment building and a bank account. Three months after D's date of death, an annuity payment of $12,000 is paid in cash to D's estate. The monthly rents from the apartment building total $500. After the date of death and prior to the payment date, the GRAT received $1,500 in excluded property in the form of rent. Pursuant to paragraph (c)(1)(iii)(A) of this section, $1,500 of the $12,000 distributed is deemed to be excluded property for purposes of section 2032. The distribution is a transaction described in paragraph (c)(1)(i)(I)(4) of this section. On the date of the distribution, the fair market value of D's interest in the GRAT before the distribution equals the sum of the distribution paid to D's estate and the fair market value of D's interest in the GRAT immediately after the distribution. Thus, pursuant to paragraph (c)(1)(iii)(A) of this section, the alternate valuation date for the $10,500 cash distribution, which is included property, is the date of its distribution, and the alternate valuation date of the GRAT is the 6-month date.

(iii) The calculation of the value of D's interest in the GRAT includible in D's gross estate at D's death pursuant to section 2036 must be computed under the special rule of paragraph (c)(1)(iii)(B) of this section as a result of the estate's election to use the alternate valuation method under section 2032. On the 6-month date, the section 7520 interest rate is 6% and the fair market value of the property in the GRAT is $289,500. Pursuant to paragraph (c)(1)(iii)(B) of this section, the fair market value of the GRAT property deemed to be included property is $300,000 ($289,500 plus $10,500). Accordingly, for purposes of determining the fair market value of the corpus includible in D's gross estate under section 2036(a)(1) as of the 6-month date, see § 20.2036-1(c)(2), using a GRAT corpus of $300,000 and, pursuant to paragraph (f)(2)(i) of this section, a section 7520 rate of 6%.

(f) *Post-death factors and occurrences.*—(1) *In general.*—The election to use the alternate valuation method under section 2032 permits property includible in the gross estate on the decedent's date of death to be valued on the 6-month date, rather than on the date of death. Thus, the election permits a valuation for Federal estate tax purposes that reflects the impact of factors such as economic or market conditions, occurrences described in section 2054 (to the extent not compensated by insurance or otherwise, and not deducted under that section), and other factors or occurrences during the alternate valuation period, as set forth in guidance issued by the Secretary. Those factors and occurrences do not include the mere lapse of time described in paragraph (f)(2) of this section, or transactions described in paragraph (c)(1)(i) or (c)(2) of this section that are not excluded under paragraphs (c)(1)(ii), (c)(1)(iii)(A), and (c)(4) of this section. Generally, management decisions made in the ordinary course of operating a business, such as a corporation, a partnership, or other business entity, are taken into account under this section as occurrences related to economic or market conditions. To the extent, however, that these decisions change the ownership or control structure of the business entity, or otherwise are included in paragraph (c)(1)(i) or (c)(2) of this section and are not excluded by paragraphs (c)(1)(ii), (c)(1)(iii)(A), or (c)(4) of this section, they will be treated as described in paragraph (c)(1)(i) of this section.

(2) *Mere lapse of time.*—*** The application of this paragraph is illustrated in paragraphs (f)(2)(i) and (f)(2)(ii) of this section:

(i) *Life estates, remainders, and similar interests.*—(A) The fair market value of a life estate, remainder, term interest or similar interest as of the alternate valuation date is determined by applying the methodology prescribed in § 20.2031-7, subject to the following two sentences. The age of each person whose life expectancy may affect the fair market value of the interest shall be determined as of the date of the decedent's death. The fair market value of the property and the applicable interest rate under section 7520 shall be determined using values applicable on the alternate valuation date.

(B) *Examples.*—The application of paragraph (f)(2)(i)(A) of this section is illustrated in the following examples.

Example 1. Assume that the decedent (D) or D's estate was entitled to receive certain property upon the death of A, who was entitled to the income from the property for life. At the time of D's death after April 30, 2009, the fair market value of the property was $50,000, and A was 47 years and 5 months old. In the month in which D died, the section 7520 rate was 6.2%, but rose to 7.4% on the 6-month date. The fair market value of D's remainder interest as of D's date of death was $9,336.00 ($50,000 × 0.18672, the single life remainder factor from Table S for a 47 year old at a 6.2% interest rate), as illustrated in *Example 1* of § 20.2031-7T(d)(5). If, because of economic conditions, the property declined in value during the alternate valuation period and was worth only $40,000 on the 6-month date, the fair market value of the remainder interest would be $5,827 ($40,000 X 0.14568, the Table S value for a 47 year old at a 7.4% interest rate), even though A would have been 48 years old on the 6-month date.

Example 2. D created an intervivos charitable remainder annuity trust (CRAT) described in section 664(d)(1). The trust instrument directs the trustee to hold, invest, and reinvest the corpus of the trust and to pay to D for D's life, and then to D's child (C) for C's life, an amount each year equal to 6% of the initial fair market value of the trust. At the termination of the trust, the corpus, together with the accumulated income, is to be distributed to N, a charitable organization described in sections 170(c), 2055(a), and 2522(a). D died, survived by C. D's estate is entitled to a charitable deduction under section 2055 for the present value of N's remainder interest in the CRAT. Pursuant to § 1.664-2(c) and § 20.7520-2, in determining the fair market value of the remainder interest as of the alternate valuation date, D's executor may elect to use the section 7520 rate in effect for either of the two months immediately preceding the month in which the alternate valuation date occurs. Regardless of the section 7520 rate selected, however, the factor to be used to value the remainder interest is the appropriate factor for C's age on the date of D's death.

(2)(ii) *Patents.*—* * * Six months after the date of the decedent's death, the patent was sold for its then fair market value that had decreased to $60,000 because of the lapse of time. * * *

(3) *Examples.* The following examples illustrate the application of this paragraph (f). In each example, decedent's (D's) estate elects to value D's gross estate under the alternate valuation method, so that the alternate valuation date of the property includible in the gross estate on D's date of death is either the transaction date or the 6-month date. In each example, assume that the only factors affecting value, and the only occurrences described in paragraph (c)(1)(i) or (c)(2) of this section, taking place during the alternate valuation period are those described in the example.

Example 1. At D's death, D's gross estate includes a residence. During the alternate valuation period, the fair market value of the residence (as well as the residential market in the area generally) declines due to a reduction in the availability of credit throughout the United States and, consequently, a decline in the availability of mortgages. The decline in the availability of mortgages is an economic or market condition. Therefore, in valuing the residence on the 6-month date, the effect of this decline on the fair market value of the residence is to be taken into account.

Example 2. (i) At D's death, D is the sole shareholder of corporation Y, a manufacturing company. Four months after D's death, Y's physical plant is destroyed as a result of a natural disaster. The disaster affects a large geographic area and, as a result, the economy of that area is negatively affected. Five months after D's death, Y's Board of Directors votes to liquidate and dissolve Y. The liquidation and dissolution proceeding is not completed as of the 6-month date. The natural disaster is a factor that affects economic and market conditions. Therefore, the disaster, to the extent not compensated by insurance or otherwise, is taken into account in valuing the Y stock on the 6-month date.

(ii) Assume instead that Y's plant is severely damaged due to flooding from the failure of pipes in the facility. The damage is an occurrence described in section 2054. Therefore, the damage, to the extent not compensated by insurance or otherwise, is taken into account in valuing the property on the 6-month date.

Example 3. At D's death, D has an interest in an S corporation, W. During the alternate valuation period, it is discovered that an employee of W has embezzled significant assets from W. W does not reasonably expect to recover the funds or any damages from the employee, and insurance proceeds are not sufficient to cover the loss. The theft is an occurrence described in section 2054. Therefore, the theft, to the extent not compensated by insurance or otherwise, is taken into account in valuing D's interest in W on the 6-month date.

(h) *Effective/applicability date.*—* * * All of paragraph (c)(2) of this section except the second sentence of the introductory text, all of paragraph (c)(3) of this section except paragraph (c)(3)(i)(C) of this section, the chart in *Example 1* of paragraph (e) of this section, all of paragraph (f)(2) of this section except the last sentence, and the first and third sentences in paragraph (f)(2)(ii) of this section are applicable to decedents dying after August 16, 1954. All of paragraphs (a) introductory text, (a)(1), (a)(2), (c)(1)(i), (c)(1)(ii), (c)(1)(iii), (c)(1)(iv), (c)(3)(i)(C), (c)(4), (c)(5), (f)(1), (f)(2)(i), and (f)(3) of this section, the second sentence of the introductory text in paragraph (c)(2) of this section, all of paragraph (e) of this section except the chart in *Example 1*, the last sentence in the introductory text of paragraph (f)(2) of this section, and the second sentence in paragraph (f)(2)(ii) of this section are applicable to estates of decedents dying on or after the date of publication of the Treasury decision adopting these rules as final in the **Federal Register**.

Retention of Stock Voting Rights

Gross Estate: Property in Which Decedent Had Interest: Shares of Stock.—Reproduced below is the text of proposed Reg. § 20.2036-2, relating to the estate tax consequences of a decedent's retention of voting rights in a lifetime transfer of stock (published in the Federal Register on August 3, 1983).

☐ Par. There is added immediately after § 20.2036-1 the following new section:

§ 20.2036-2. Special treatment of retained voting rights.—(a) *In general.*—For purposes of section 2036(a)(1) and § 20.2036-1(a), the retention of the right to vote (directly or indirectly) shares of stock of a controlled corporation is a retention of the enjoyment of the transferred property if:

(1) The transfer was made after June 22, 1976;

(2) The corporation was a controlled corporation at any time after transfer of that stock; and

(3) The corporation was a controlled corporation at any time during the three-year period ending on the decedent's death

The rule of this section does not require inclusion of stock in the gross estate if the transferred stock has no voting rights or if the donor has not retained voting rights in the stock transferred. Thus, for example, if a person owning 100 percent of the voting and nonvoting stock of a corporation transfers the nonvoting stock, that person shall not be treated as having retained the enjoyment of the property transferred merely because of voting rights in the stock retained. Stock carrying voting rights that will vest only when conditions occur, such as preferred stock which gains voting rights only if no dividends are paid, is subject to this section. However, if the decedent's right to vote such stock is only in a fiduciary capacity (*e.g.*, because the decedent is trustee of a trust to which the stock has been transferred), such stock is subject to this section only if, after the transfer by the decedent, the conditions occur that give the decedent the right to vote the stock. Stock that possesses voting rights in only extraordinary matters, such as mergers or liquidations shall be subject to this section unless the decedent's retention of voting rights is only in a fiduciary capacity.

(b) *Relinquishment or cessation of voting rights within three years of death.*—In general, the relinquishment or cessation of retained voting rights shall be treated as a "transfer of property" for purposes of section 2035 (transfer within three years of death) if:

(1) The voting rights were retained in a transfer made after June 22, 1976; and

(2) The corporation was a controlled corporation at some point in time occurring after the transfer, before the relinquishment or cessation of voting rights, and within three years of death.

However, to the extent that a relinquishment of voting rights is in exchange for voting rights in another controlled corporation, the relinquishment shall not be treated as a "transfer of property" for purposes of section 2035. See paragraph (e)(3) of this section for the treatment of voting rights in such other corporation.

(c) *Meaning of right to vote.*—For purposes of this section, the term "right to vote" means the power to vote, whether exercisable alone or in conjunction with other persons. The capacity in which the decedent can exercise voting power is immaterial. Accordingly, a fiduciary power exercisable as trustee, co-trustee, or as officer of a corporation is a right to vote stock within the meaning of this section. For purposes of section 2036(b)(1) and § 20.2036-2(a), the constructive ownership rules of section 318 shall not be used to attribute the retention of voting rights to the decedent. Therefore, the fact that a relative of the decedent is trustee of a trust to which the decedent has transferred stock shall not in itself require a finding that the decedent indirectly retained the right to vote that stock. However, any arrangement to shift formal voting power away from the decedent will not be treated for this purpose as a relinquishment of all voting rights if, in substance, the decedent has retained voting power. Moreover, voting power shall be deemed retained in cases where there is any agreement with the decedent, express or implied, that the shareholder, or other holder of the power to vote stock, either will vote the stock in a specified manner or will not vote the stock. If the decedent has the power to obtain the right to vote, such as where he may appoint himself as a trustee of a trust holding the stock, the decedent has retained the right to vote for purposes of section 2036.

(d) *Meaning of controlled corporation.*—(1) *In general.*—For purposes of this section, the term "controlled corporation" means a corporation in which the decedent, with application of the constructive ownership rules of section 318, is deemed to own or have a right to vote stock possessing at least 20 percent of the total combined voting power of all classes of stock.

(2) *Computations.*—(i) *Total combined voting power of all classes of stock.*—For purposes of this paragraph, the total combined voting power of all classes of stock shall include only stock that currently has voting power. Stock that may vote only on extraordinary matters, such as mergers or liquidations, shall be disregarded. Similarly, treasury stock and stock that is authorized but unissued shall be disregarded.

(ii) *Decedent's percentage of total combined voting power.*—For purposes of this paragraph, in determining whether the voting power possessed by the decedent is at least 20 percent of the total combined voting power of all classes of stock, consideration will be given to all the facts and circumstances. Generally, the percentage of voting power possessed by a person in a corporation may be determined by reference to the power of stock to vote for the election of directors. Instruments that do not have voting rights shall be disregarded. Instruments having no voting rights but which may be converted into voting stock shall be disregarded until such conversion occurs. Instruments carrying voting rights that will vest only when conditions, the occurrence of which is indeterminate, have been met will be disregarded until the conditions have occurred which cause the voting rights to vest. An example of such an instrument is preferred stock which gains voting rights only if no dividends are paid.

(iii) *Example.*—The following example illustrates the application of paragraphs (d)(1) through (d)(2)(ii) of this section.

Example. A corporation has three classes of stock outstanding, consisting of 40 shares of class A voting stock, 50 shares of class B voting stock, and 60 shares of class C preferred stock which is nonvoting except for extraordinary matters or unless the arrearages in dividends exceed a specified amount. Assume for purposes of this example that except for extraordinary business matters, the voting stock's only voting power is the right to vote in the election of directors. The class A stockholders are entitled to elect 7 of the 10 corporate directors, and the class B stockholders are entitled to elect the other 3 of the 10 directors. Thus, the class A stock (as a class) possesses 70 percent of the total combined voting power of all classes of stock, and the class B stock (as a class) possesses 30 percent of such voting power. At the time of *D*' s death, *D* has voting rights in 9 shares of class A stock directly; and with the constructive ownership rules of section 318, *D* is deemed to have voting rights in 3 additional shares of class A stock. *D* has no interest in the class B stock and owns all 60 shares of the class C stock. Thus, *D* is deemed to possess 21 percent ((9 + 3) shares/40 shares × 70 percent) of the total combined voting power of all classes of stock. By reason of such voting power, the corporation is a controlled corporation within the meaning of this section.

(e) *Direct versus indirect retention of voting rights*.—(1) *Direct transfers*.—Subject to the limitations contained in paragraph (a) of this section, if the decedent transfers stock of a controlled corporation (except in case of a bona fide sale for adequate and full consideration in money or money's worth), the retention of voting rights in the stock transferred shall require a portion of the fair market value of the stock to be included in the gross estate. For purposes of this paragraph (e)(1), transfers of stock in exchange for, in whole or in part, either property donated by the decedent or property for which the decedent supplied the purchase consideration, will not be considered a bona fide sale for adequate and full consideration. The amount included in the gross estate under this paragraph (e)(1) shall be an amount, not less than zero, equal to the fair market value at death of the stock transferred less the value of any consideration the decedent received in exchange.

(2) *Indirect transfer*.—Section 2036 applies to indirect as well as direct transfers. The acquisition of voting rights in stock acquired through the exercise of other instruments transferred by the decedent (such as through the exercise of warrants or options, or the conversion rights on convertible nonvoting stock or indebtedness) shall cause the stock to be treated as acquired with consideration furnished by the decedent and an indirect transfer by the decedent. If a third party makes a transfer to the trust and the consideration for the transfer was furnished by the decedent, the transfer by the third party to the trust will be treated as a transfer by the decedent to the trust. In addition, if the decedent makes a transfer by gift to a trust, and the trust subsequently acquires stock in which the decedent has voting rights, then for purposes of section 2036(a), the transaction will be treated as an indirect transfer of stock by the decedent (irrespective of whether the acquisition of the stock can be traced to the gift). The amount included in the gross estate in such a case is equal to the fair market value at death of the portion of the stock acquired with funds provided by the decedent. In the case of a purchase of stock from a third party by a trust, the stock shall be treated as purchased with funds provided by the decedent to the extent there are funds in the trust treated as provided by the decedent. For this purpose, the portion of the funds in the trust treated as provided by the decedent shall be determined after each addition to the trust and is equal to a fraction. The numerator of the fraction is the sum of—

(i) The total value of the trust immediately prior to the latest addition multiplied by the fraction of such value treated as provided by the decedent because of prior additions, and

(ii) The amount of the latest addition to the extent provided by the decedent.

The denominator of the fraction is the total value of the trust immediately after the latest addition.

(3) *Exchange of voting rights*.—For purposes of this section, if a decedent is deemed to have retained the right to vote shares of stock of a controlled corporation in a transfer occurring after June 22, 1976, the subsequent relinquishment of those voting rights, in exchange for voting rights in other stock of a controlled corporation, shall be treated as a retention of voting rights in such other stock. Furthermore, for purposes of section 2036(a), such other stock shall be treated as property transferred by the decedent. For example, if a person transfers stock in ABC Corporation (a controlled corporation) after June 22, 1976, to a trust for which that person is a trustee—thus retaining voting rights in a fiduciary capacity—and the trust later sells the ABC Corporation stock, using the proceeds to purchase stock in XYZ Corporation (a controlled corporation), that person will be treated as having retained the right to vote the shares of XYZ Corporation. In such a transaction, the shares of XYZ Corporation shall be treated as transferred by that person. If the stock in XYZ Corporation is acquired directly from the decedent, the amount included in the gross estate shall be determined under paragraph (e)(1) of this section. If the stock in XYZ Corporation is acquired from someone other than the decedent, the amount included in the decedent's gross estate shall be determined under paragraph (e)(2) of this section.

(4) *Examples*.—The following examples illustrate the application of section 2043 and paragraph (e)(1) and (e)(2) of this section.

Example (1). During 1977, *D* transferred by gift $100,000 cash to a trust. During 1979, *D* transferred to the trust 1000 shares of ABC Corporation voting stock worth $100,000. The 1979 transfer was in exchange for $50,000 cash and *D* retained voting rights in all the stock transferred. Assume that at some time after the stock transfer, ABC Corporation is a controlled corporation within the meaning of this section. *D* dies during 1981, at which time the stock is worth $150,000. As a result of the stock transfer, the amount included in *D*' s gross estate under section 2036 is $100,000, computed as follows:

Fair market value of instruments at death	$150,000
Less consideration received by *D*	50,000
Amount included in *D*'s gross estate	$100,000

Example (2). The facts are the same as in *example (1)* except that the 1979 transfer to the trust (1000 shares of ABC Corporation) was in exchange for $100,000 cash. As a result of the stock transfer, the amount included in *D*' s gross estate under section 2036 is $50,000, computed as follows:

Fair market value of instruments at death	$150,000
Less consideration received by *D*	100,000
Amount included in *D*'s gross estate	$50,000

The 1979 transfer is not considered a *bona fide* sale for adequate and full consideration in money or money's worth since *D* provided the consideration by virtue of his 1977 transfer to the trust.

Example (3). During 1979, *D* transferred by gift 1000 shares of ABC Corporation voting stock worth $100,000 to his wife *W*. During 1980, *W* made a gift of the same stock to a trust. Assume that *D* becomes trustee of the trust and hence acquires the right to vote the stock in that capacity. Assume further that, at some time after *D*'s transfer, ABC Corporation is a controlled corporation within the meaning of this section. *D* dies during 1981, at which time the stock is worth $150,000. The full $150,000 is included in *D*'s gross estate under section 2036.

Example (4). During 1979, *D* transferred by gift $90,000 to a trust that already had $90,000 of funds, all of which is attributable to contributions by persons other than *D*. During 1980, the trust purchased at full fair market value 1000 shares of ABC Corporation voting stock worth $100,000, at which time, because of appreciation, the value of the trust was $210,000. Assume that *D* acquires the right to vote the stock as trustee of the trust and that at some time after the stock purchase, ABC Corporation is a controlled corporation within the meaning of this section. *D* dies during 1981, at which time the stock is worth $150,000. Pursuant to paragraph (e)(2) of this section, at the time of the stock purchase, $105,000 (50 percent of $210,000) of funds in the trust were funds supplied by *D*, $100,000 of which are treated as used to purchase the stock. Accordingly, the amount included in *D*'s gross estate under section 2036, $150,000, is the value at death of the portion of the stock acquired with funds provided by *D*.

Qualified Plan Benefits

Gross Estate: Annuities: Exclusion for Qualified Plan and IRA Benefits.—Temporary Reg. § 20.2039-1T, providing guidance with respect to qualified employee benefit plans, welfare benefit funds and employees receiving benefits through such plans, is proposed (published in the Federal Register on January 29, 1986).

§ 20.2039-1T. Limitations and repeal of estate tax exclusion for qualified plans and individual retirement plans (IRAs) (temporary).

Individual Retirement Plans: Simplified Employee Pensions: Qualified Voluntary Employee Contributions

Individual Retirement Plans: Simplified Employee Pensions: Qualified Voluntary Employee Contributions.—Reproduced below are the texts of proposed amendments of Reg. §§ 20.2039-2 and 20.2039-4, relating to individual retirement plans, simplified employee pensions and qualified voluntary employee contributions (published in the Federal Register on January 23, 1984).

□ Par. 10. Section 20.2039-2 is revised by adding a new subdivision (ix) to paragraph (c)(1) to read as follows:

§ 20.2039-2. Annuities under "qualified plans" and section 403(b) annuity contracts.

* * *

(c) *Amounts excludable from the gross estate.*

(1) * * *

(ix) Any deductible employee contributions (within the meaning of section 72(o)(5)) are considered amounts contributed by the employer.

* * *

□ Par. 11. Section 20.2039-4 is revised by adding a new paragraph (h) to read as follows:

§ 20.2039-4. Lump sum distributions from "qualified plans;" decedents dying after December 31, 1978.

* * *

(h) *Accumulated deductible employee contributions.*—For purposes of this section, a lump sum distribution includes an amount attributable to accumulated deductible employee contributions (as defined in section 72(o)(5)(B)) in any qualified plan taken into account for purposes of determining whether any distribution from that qualified plan is a lump sum distribution as determined under paragraph (b) of this section. Thus, amounts attributable to accumulated deductible employee contributions in a qualified plan under which amounts are payable in a lump sum distribution are not excludible from the decedent's gross estate under § 20.2039-2, unless the recipient makes the section 402(a)/403(c) taxation election with respect to a lump sum distribution payable from that qualified plan.

* * *

Charitable Remainder Trusts

Charitable Remainder Trusts: Election: Extended Date.—Reproduced below is the text of a proposed amendment of Reg. § 20.2055-2, relating to the granting of an extension to permit the reformation of charitable remainder trusts (published in the Federal Register on December 19, 1975).

☐ Par. 3. § 20.2055-2 is amended by adding a sentence at the end of paragraph (a) and by adding a new paragraph (g) immediately following § 20.2055-2(f). These added and amended provisions read as follows:

§ 20.2055-2. Transfers not exclusively for charitable purposes.—(a) *Remainders and similar interests.*—* * * See paragraph (g) of this section for special rules relating to certain wills and trusts in existence on September 21, 1974.

* * *

(g) *Special rules applicable in the case of certain wills and trusts in existence on September 21, 1974.*—(1) In general, in the case of a will executed before September 21, 1974, or a trust created (within the meaning of applicable local law) after July 31, 1969, and before September 21, 1974, if—

(i) At the time of the decedent's death a deduction is not allowable solely because of the failure of an interest in property which passes or has passed from the decedent to a person, or for a use, described in section 2055(a) to meet the requirements of section 2055(e)(2)(A), and

(ii) The governing instrument is amended or conformed in accordance with this paragraph so that the interest is in a trust which is a charitable remainder annuity trust or a charitable remainder unitrust (described in section 664) or a pooled income fund (described in section 642(c)(5)), or the governing instrument is treated under paragraph (g)(8) of this section as if it were amended, a deduction shall nevertheless be allowed.

(2) An amendment or conformation pursuant to this paragraph must be made before January 1, 1976, or, if later, on or before the 30th day after the date on which judicial proceedings begun before January 1, 1976 (which are required to amend or conform the governing instrument) become final.

(3) A governing instrument may be amended or conformed under this paragraph only where:

(i) The transfer is not in trust but passes under a will executed before September 21, 1974;

(ii) The transfer is in the form of a testamentary trust created under a will executed before September 21, 1974;

(iii) The transfer was in trust, which was created (within the meaning of applicable local law) after July 31, 1969, and before September 21, 1974, but only if, at the time of the creation of the trust, the governing instrument provides that an organization described in section 170(c) receives an irrevocable remainder interest in such trust;

(iv) Property was transferred inter vivos after July 31, 1969, and before October 18, 1971, to a trust created (within the meaning of applicable local law) before August 1, 1969, which trust provides that an organization described in section 170(c) receives an irrevocable remainder interest in such trust, and the transferred property and any undistributed income therefrom is severed and placed in a separate trust before the applicable date specified in paragraph (g)(2) of this section. An instrument governing a transfer under this subdivision (iv), which is amended pursuant to this paragraph, shall be treated as having made such transfer to a trust deemed created on the date of such transfer;

(v) In the case of a transfer to a pooled income fund made before September 21, 1974 (or a transfer made under a will which was executed before September 21, 1974), the instrument governing the transfer fails to satisfy the requirements of § 1.642(c)-5(b).

However, a governing instrument may not be amended pursuant to this paragraph unless, at the time of the decedent's death, the interest is an irrevocable remainder interest for which a deduction, but for section 2055(e)(2)(A), would be allowable under section 2055(a) and the regulations thereunder. The provisions of section 508(d)(2)(A) (relating to disallowance of certain charitable, etc., deductions) shall not apply to such interest if the governing instrument is amended so as to comply with the requirements of section 508(e) (relating to governing instruments) by the applicable date described in paragraph (g)(2) of this section.

(4) The decree resulting from any judicial proceedings begun to amend a governing instrument pursuant to paragraph (g)(1) of this section must be binding, under local law, on all parties having an interest in the bequest or transfer as well as the fiduciary of the decedent's estate and trustee of the trust to be amended. In the event local law does not require judicial proceedings to amend or conform a governing instrument, a deduction may nevertheless be allowed if the governing instrument is amended or conformed by nonjudicial agreement between all parties having an interest in the bequest or transfer as well as the fiduciary of the decedent's estate and trustee of the trust to be amended, provided that the agreement is binding, under local law, on all such parties. The judicial proceedings or nonjudicial agreement must also account for any distributions made from the deemed date of creation to the date of the amendment in the following manner:

(i) Where the amount of the distributions which would have been made by the trust to a recipient had the amendment pursuant to paragraph (g)(1) of this section been in effect since the creation of the trust exceeds the amount of the distributions made by the trust prior to the amendment, the trust must pay an amount equal to such excess to the recipient;

(ii) Where the amount of the distributions made to the recipient prior to the amendment pursuant to paragraph (g)(1) of this section exceeds the amount of the distributions which would have been made by such trust if the amended provisions of such trust had been in effect from the time of creation of such trust, the recipient must pay an amount equal to such excess to the trust.

See § 1.664-1(d)(4) for rules relating to the year of inclusion in the case of an underpayment to a recipient and the allowance of a deduction in the case of an overpayment to a recipient.

(5) Where a charitable remainder trust (as described in § 1.664-1(a)(1)(iii)(a)) results from an amendment pursuant to this paragraph, the trust will be treated as a charitable remainder trust for all purposes from the date it would be deemed created under § 1.664-1(a)(4) and (5), whether or not such date is after September 20, 1974. Subject

to the limitations imposed by section 6511, the estate tax charitable deduction is allowable and the charitable remainder trust is exempt from Federal income taxation. For the application of certain excise taxes pursuant to section 4947(a)(2) see §53.4947-1(c)(1)(iii) and (c)(6). In amending a governing instrument pursuant to paragraph (g)(1) of this section, the exchange of a noncharitable beneficiary's interest in an unqualified transfer in trust for an interest in a qualified transfer in trust will not be treated as an act of self-dealing (described in section 4941) or a taxable expenditure (described in section 4945).

(6) If, on the due date for filing the estate tax return (including any extensions thereof), proceedings to amend or conform a governing instrument pursuant to paragraph (g)(1) of this section have not become final, such return shall be filed with the tax computed as if no deduction were allowable under this paragraph. When the proceedings to amend or conform such instrument have become final (within the applicable date described in paragraph (g)(2) of this section), a deduction shall be allowed upon the filing of a claim for credit or refund (within the limitations of section 6511). In the case of a credit or refund as a result of an amendment or conformation made pursuant to this paragraph, no interest shall be allowed for the period prior to the expiration of the 180th day after the date on which the claim for credit or refund is filed.

(7) If a governing instrument is amended under this paragraph, then, except as provided in paragraph (g)(8)(ii) of this section, the amount of the deduction allowable under this section shall be the amount that equals the value of the interest which, under the rules of section 2055 (including the rules governing disclaimers) passes to, or for the use of, an organization described in section 2055(a).

(8)(i) In the case of a will executed before September 21, 1974, or a trust created (within the meaning of applicable local law) before such date and after July 31, 1969, that creates an interest for which a deduction would be allowable under section 2055(a) but for section 2055(e)(2)(A), if the date of death of the decedent is prior to January 1, 1976, and if on or before the filing date of the estate tax return (including any extension thereof)—

(A) The interest is in a charitable trust which, if a deduction under section 2055(a) had been allowed, would be in a trust described in section 4947(a)(1), or

(B) Such interest passes directly to a person or for a use described in section 2055(a) (as, for example, by reason of the termination of an intervening interest),

the governing instrument shall be treated as if it were amended or conformed pursuant to paragraph (g)(1) of this section and a deduction shall be allowed. See section 508(d)(2) and §1.508-2(b) for the disallowance of such a deduction in the case of an interest in a trust described in section 4947(a)(1) if the governing instrument fails to meet the requirements of section 508(e) by the end of the taxable year of the trust in which the filing date of the estate tax return occurs. A governing instrument treated as amended under this subdivision (i) may not thereafter be amended. The provisions of this subparagraph shall not apply if the requirements of subdivision (A) or (B) of this subdivision (ii) are satisfied as a result of an amendment of a dispositive provision of the governing instrument occurring since the date of death of the decedent.

(ii) The amount of the deduction for a transfer which is treated under this paragraph as if it were amended will be determined as if the transfer were a charitable remainder annuity trust which provides an annuity of 6 percent of the initial fair market value payable from the date of death—

(A) In the case of a transfer providing a life estate, for the expected lives of the noncharitable beneficiaries as determined on the date of death of the decedent, or

(B) In the case of a transfer providing a term of years, for the term of years as expressed in the governing instrument, but not to exceed 20 years.

Any distributions made to a recipient from the date of death of the decedent to the date on which the transfer is deemed to be amended (*i.e.*, the date the transfer satisfies the requirements of paragraph (g)(8)(i) of this section) must be taken into account under this subdivision (ii) in determining the amount of the deduction, to the extent that the adjustments in such distributions required by paragraph (g)(4) of this section, determined as if the charitable remainder annuity trust were deemed created at the date of death of the decedent, have not been made on or before the filing date of the estate tax return. [Reg. §20.2055-2.]

GIFT TAX

Guidance under Section 529A: Qualified ABLE Programs

Guidance under Section 529A: Qualified ABLE Programs.—Amendments to Reg. §§25.2501-1 and 25.2503-3, regarding programs under The Stephen Beck, Jr., Achieving a Better Life Experience Act of 2014 and rules under which States or State agencies or instrumentalities may establish and maintain a new type of tax-favored savings program through which contributions may be made to the account of an eligible disabled individual to meet qualified disability expenses, are proposed (published in the Federal Register on June 22, 2015) (REG-102837-15).

Par. 6. Section 25.2501-1 is amended by adding a sentence at the end of paragraph (a)(1) to read as follows:

§25.2501-1. Imposition of Tax.—(a) * * *

(1) * * * For gift tax rules related to an ABLE account established under section 529A, *see* regulations promulgated thereunder.

* * *

Par. 7. Section 25.2503-3 is amended by adding a sentence at the end of paragraph (a) to read as follows:

§25.2503-3. Future interests in property.—(a) * * * A contribution to an ABLE account established under section 529A is not a future interest.

* * *

Annual Exclusion for Spousal IRA Transfers

Annual Exclusion: Contributions to Spousal Individual Retirement Accounts.—Reproduced below is the text of proposed Reg. §25.2503-5, providing that contributions by a working spouse to an individual retirement account for the benefit of a nonworking spouse qualify for the annual gift tax exclusion to the extent that they are deductible for income tax purposes (published in the Federal Register on July 14, 1981).

* * *

☐ Par. 13. There is added after §25.2503-4 the following new section:

§25.2503-5. Individual retirement plan for spouse.—(a) *In general.*—For purposes of section 2503(b), any payment made by an individual for the benefit of his or her spouse—

(1) To an individual retirement account described in section 408(a),

(2) To an individual retirement subaccount described in §1.220-1(b)(3),

(3) For an individual retirement annuity described in section 408(b), or

(4) For a retirement bond described in section 409,

shall not be considered a gift of a future interest in property to the extent that such payment is allowable as a deduction under section 220 for the taxable year for which the contribution is made. Thus, for example, if individual A paid $900 to an individual retirement account for 1980 on behalf of A's spouse, B, of which $875 was deductible, $875 would not be a gift of a future interest.

(b) *Effective date.*—Paragraph (a) of this section is effective for transfers made after December 31, 1976.

Guidance under Section 529A: Qualified ABLE Programs

Guidance under Section 529A: Qualified ABLE Programs.—Amendments to Reg. §25.2503-6 regarding programs under The Stephen Beck, Jr., Achieving a Better Life Experience Act of 2014 and rules under which States or State agencies or instrumentalities may establish and maintain a new type of tax-favored savings program through which contributions may be made to the account of an eligible disabled individual to meet qualified disability expenses, are proposed (published in the Federal Register on June 22, 2015) (REG-102837-15).

Par. 8. Section 25.2503-6 is amended by adding a sentence at the end of paragraph (a) to read as follows:

§25.2503-6. Exclusion for certain qualified transfers to tuition or medical expenses.—(a) * * * A contribution to an ABLE account established under section 529A is not a qualified transfer.

* * *

Guidance under Section 529A: Qualified ABLE Programs

Guidance under Section 529A: Qualified ABLE Programs.—Amendments to Reg. §25.2511-2 regarding programs under The Stephen Beck, Jr., Achieving a Better Life Experience Act of 2014 and rules under which States or State agencies or instrumentalities may establish and maintain a new type of tax-favored savings program through which contributions may be made to the account of an eligible disabled individual to meet qualified disability expenses, are proposed (published in the Federal Register on June 22, 2015) (REG-102837-15).

Par. 9. Section 25.2511-2 is amended by adding a sentence at the end of paragraph (a) to read as follows:

§25.2511-2. Cessation of donor's dominion and control.—(a) * * * For gift tax rules related to an ABLE account established under section 529A, *see* regulations promulgated thereunder.

* * *

Imputed Interest: OID: Safe Haven Rates

Imputed Interest: Original Issue Discount: Safe Haven Interest Rates.—Amendments to Reg. §25.2512-4 and 25.2512-8, relating to (1) the tax treatment of debt instruments issued after July 1, 1982, that contain original issue discount, (2) the imputation of and the accounting for interest with respect to sales and exchanges of property occurring after December 31, 1984, and (3) safe haven interest rates for loans or advances between commonly controlled taxpayers and safe haven leases between such taxpayers, are proposed (published in the Federal Register on August 20, 1985; Reg. §25.2512-4 was reproposed in the Federal Register on April 8, 1986).

☐ Par. 43. Section 25.2512-4 is revised to read as follows:

§25.2512-4. Valuation of notes.—The fair market value of notes, secured or unsecured, is presumed to be the amount of unpaid principal, plus accrued interest to the date of the gift, unless the donor establishes a lower value. The fair market value of a debt instrument (as defined in §1.1275-1(b)) whose issue price is determined under section 1273(b)(1), (2), or (3), or section 1274 is presumed to be its revised issue price (as defined in §1.1275-1(h)). Unless returned at this value, it must be shown by satisfactory evidence that the note is worth less than the unpaid amount (because of the interest rate, or date of maturity, or other cause), or that the note is uncollectible in part (by reason of the insolvency of the party or parties liable, or for other cause), and that the property, if any, pledged or mortgaged as security is insufficient to satisfy it. See §25.2512-8 and §1.1012-2 for special rules relating to certain sales or exchanges of property. See §25.7872-1 for special rules in the case of gift loans (within the meaning of §1.7872-4(b)) made after June 6, 1984. [Reg. §25.2512-4.]

☐ Par. 44. Section 25.2512-8 is revised to read as follows:

§25.2512-8. Transfers for insufficient or excessive consideration.—Transfers reached by the gift tax are not confined to those only which, being without a valuable consideration, accord with the common law concept of gifts, but embrace as well sales, exchanges, and other dispositions of property for a consideration to the extent that the value of the property transferred by the donor differs from the value in money or money's worth of the consideration given therefor. However, a sale, exchange, or other transfer of property made in the ordinary course of business (a transaction which is bona fide, at arm's length, and free from any donative intent), will be considered as made for consideration in money or money's worth equal to the value of the property transferred. If the buyer issues one or more debt instruments as all or a part of the consideration for the property, then the property and the debt instruments shall be valued in accordance with the rules set forth in §1.1012-2. A consideration not reducible to a value in money or money's worth, as love and affection, promise of marriage, etc., is to be wholly disregarded, and the entire value of the property transferred contitutes the amount of the gift. Similarly, a relinquishment or promised relinquishment of dower or curtesy, or of a statutory estate created in lieu of dower or curtesy, or of other marital rights in the spouse's property or estate, shall not be considered to any extent a consideration "in money or money's worth." See, however, section 2516 and the regulations thereunder with respect to certain transfers incident to a divorce. [Reg. §25.2512-8.]

TAX ON GENERATION-SKIPPING TRANSFERS

Guidance under Section 529A: Qualified ABLE Programs

Guidance under Section 529A: Qualified ABLE Programs.—Amendments to Reg. §26.2642-1, regarding programs under The Stephen Beck, Jr., Achieving a Better Life Experience Act of 2014 and rules under which States or State agencies or instrumentalities may establish and maintain a new type of tax-favored savings program through which contributions may be made to the account of an eligible disabled individual to meet qualified disability expenses, are proposed (published in the Federal Register on June 22, 2015) (REG-102837-15).

Par. 11. Section 26.2642-1 is amended by adding a sentence at the end of paragraph (a) to read as follows:

§26.2642-1. Inclusion ratio

(a) * * * For generation-skipping transfer tax rules related to an ABLE account established under section 529A, *see* regulations promulgated thereunder.

* * *

GST Exemption: Extension of Time

GST Exemption: Extension of Time.—Reg. §26.2642-7, describing the circumstances and procedures under which an extension of time will be granted under Code Sec. 2642(g)(1), is proposed (published in the Federal Register on April 17, 2008) (REG-147775-06).

☐ Par. 2. Section 26.2642-7 is added to read as follows:

§26.2642-7. Relief under section 2642(g)(1).—(a) *In general.*—Under section 2642(g)(1)(A), the Secretary has the authority to issue regulations describing the circumstances in which a transferor, as defined in section 2652(a), or the executor of a transferor's estate, as defined in section 2203, will be granted an extension of time to allocate generation-skipping transfer (GST) exemption as described in sections 2642(b)(1) and (2). The Secretary also has the authority to issue regulations describing the circumstances under which a transferor or the executor of a transferor's estate will be granted an extension of time to make the elections described in section 2632(b)(3) and (c)(5). Section 2632(b)(3) provides that an election may be made by or on behalf of a transferor not to have the transferor's GST exemption automatically allocated under section 2632(b)(1) to a direct skip, as defined in section 2612(c), made by the transferor during life. Section 2632(c)(5)(A)(i) provides that an election may be made by or on behalf of a transferor not to have the transferor's GST exemption automatically allocated under section 2632(c)(1) to an indirect skip, as defined in section 2632(c)(3)(A), or to any or all transfers made by such transferor to a particular trust. Section 2632(c)(5)(A)(ii) provides that an election may be made by or on behalf of a transferor to treat any trust as a GST trust, as defined in section 2632(c)(3)(B), for purposes of section 2632(c) with respect to any or all transfers made by that transferor to the trust. This section generally describes the factors that the Internal Revenue Service (IRS) will consider when an extension of time is sought by or on behalf of a transferor to timely allocate GST exemption and/or to make an election under section 2632(b)(3) or (c)(5). Relief provided under this section will be granted through the IRS letter ruling program. See paragraph (h) of this section.

(b) *Effect of Relief.*—If an extension of time to allocate GST exemption is granted under this section, the allocation of GST exemption will be considered effective as of the date of the transfer, and the value of the property transferred for purposes of chapter 11 or chapter 12 will determine the amount of GST exemption to be allocated. If an extension of time to elect out of the automatic allocation of GST exemption under section 2632(b)(3) or (c)(5) is granted under this section, the election will be considered effective as of the date of the transfer. If an extension of time to elect to treat any trust as a GST trust under section 2632(c)(5)(A)(ii) is granted under this section, the election will be considered effective as of the date of the first (or each) transfer covered by that election.

(c) *Limitation on relief.*—The amount of GST exemption that may be allocated to a transfer as the result of relief granted under this section is limited to the amount of the transferor's unused GST exemption under section 2631(c) as of the date of the transfer. Thus, if, by the time of the making of the allocation or election pursuant to relief granted under this section, the GST exemption amount under section 2631(c) has increased to an amount in excess of the amount in effect for the date of the transfer, no portion of the increased amount may be applied to that earlier transfer by reason of the relief granted under this section.

(d) *Basis for determination.*—(1) *In general.*—Requests for relief under this section will be granted when the transferor or the executor of the transferor's estate provides evidence (including the affidavits described in paragraph (h) of this section) to establish to the satisfaction of the IRS that the transferor or the executor of the transferor's estate acted reasonably and in good faith, and that the grant of relief will not prejudice the interests of the Government. Paragraphs (d)(2) and (d)(3) of this section set forth nonexclusive lists of factors the IRS will consider in determining whether this standard of reasonableness, good faith, and lack of prejudice to the interests of the Government has been met so that such relief will be granted. In making this determination, IRS will consider these factors, as well as all other relevant facts and circumstances. Paragraph (e) of this section sets forth situations in which this standard has not been met and, as a result, in which relief under this section will not be granted.

(2) *Reasonableness and good faith.*—The following is a nonexclusive list of factors that will be considered to determine whether the transferor or the executor of the transferor's estate acted reasonably and in good faith for purposes of this section:

(i) The intent of the transferor to timely allocate GST exemption to a transfer or to timely make an election under section 2632(b)(3) or (c)(5), as evidenced in the trust instrument, the instrument of transfer, or other relevant documents contemporaneous with the transfer, such as Federal gift and estate tax returns and correspondence. This may include evidence of the intended GST tax status of the transfer or the trust (for example, exempt, non-exempt, or partially exempt), or more explicit evidence of intent with regard to the allocation of GST exemption or the election under section 2632(b)(3) or (c)(5).

(ii) Intervening events beyond the control of the transferor or of the executor of the transferor's estate as the cause of the failure to allocate GST exemption to a transfer or the failure to make an election under section 2632(b)(3) or (c)(5).

(iii) Lack of awareness by the transferor or the executor of the transferor's estate of the need to allocate GST exemption to the transfer, despite the exercise of reasonable diligence, taking into account the experience of the transferor or the executor of the transferor's estate and the complexity of the GST issue, as the cause of the failure to allocate GST exemption to a transfer or to make an election under section 2632(b)(3) or (c)(5).

(iv) Consistency by the transferor with regard to the allocation of the transferor's GST exemption (for example, the transferor's consistent allocation of GST exemption to transfers to skip persons or to a particular trust, or the transferor's consistent election not to have the automatic allocation of GST exemption apply to transfers to one or more trusts or skip persons pursuant to section 2632(b)(3) or (c)(5)). Evidence of consistency may be less relevant if there has been a change of circumstances or change of trust beneficiaries that would otherwise explain a deviation from prior GST exemption allocation decisions.

(v) Reasonable reliance by the transferor or the executor of the transferor's estate on the advice of a qualified tax professional retained or employed by one or both of them and, in reliance on or consistent with that advice, the failure of the transferor or the executor to allocate GST exemption to the transfer or to make an election described in section 2632(b)(3) or (c)(5). Reliance on a qualified tax professional will not be considered to have been reasonable if the transferor or the executor of the transferor's estate knew or should have known that the professional either—

(A) Was not competent to render advice on the GST exemption; or

(B) Was not aware of all relevant facts.

(3) *Prejudice to the interests of the Government.*—The following is a nonexclusive list of factors that will be considered to determine whether the interests of the Government would be prejudiced for purposes of this section:

(i) The interests of the Government would be prejudiced to the extent to which the request for relief is an effort to benefit from hindsight. The interests of the Government would be prejudiced if the IRS determines that the requested relief is an attempt to benefit from hindsight rather than to achieve the result the transferor or the executor of the transferor's estate intended at the time when the transfer was made. A factor relevant to this determination is whether the grant of the requested relief would permit an economic advantage or other benefit that would not have been available if the allocation or election had been timely made. Similarly, there would be prejudice if a grant of the requested relief would permit an economic advantage or other benefit that results from the selection of one out of a number of alternatives (other than whether or not to make an allocation or election) that were available at the time the allocation or election could have been timely made, if hindsight makes the selected alternative more beneficial than the other alternatives. Finally, in a situation where the only choices were whether or not to make a timely allocation or election, prejudice would exist if the transferor failed to make the allocation or election in order to wait to see (thus, with the benefit of hindsight) whether or not the making of the allocation of exemption or election would be more beneficial.

(ii) The timing of the request for relief will be considered in determining whether the interests of the Government would be prejudiced by granting relief under this section. The interests of the Government would be prejudiced if the transferor or the executor of the transferor's estate delayed the filing of the request for relief with the intent to deprive the IRS of sufficient time to challenge the claimed identity of the transferor of the transferred property that is the subject of the request for relief, the value of that transferred property for Federal gift or estate tax purposes, or any other aspect of the transfer that is relevant for Federal gift or estate tax purposes. The fact that any period of limitations on the assessment or collection of transfer taxes has expired prior to the filing of a request for relief under this section, however, will not by itself prohibit a grant of relief under this section. Similarly, the combination of the expiration of any such period of limitations with the fact that the asset or interest was valued for transfer tax purposes with the use of a valuation discount will not by itself prohibit a grant of relief under this section.

(iii) The occurrence and effect of an intervening taxable termination or taxable distribution will be considered in determining whether the interests of the Government would be prejudiced by granting relief under this section. The interests of the Government may be prejudiced if a taxable termination or taxable distribution occurred between the time for making a timely allocation of GST exemption or a timely election described in section 2632(b)(3) or (c)(5) and the time at which the request for relief under this section was filed. The impact of a grant of relief on (and the difficulty of adjusting) the GST tax consequences of that intervening termination or distribution will be considered in determining whether the occurrence of a taxable termination or taxable distribution constitutes prejudice.

(e) *Situations in which the standard of reasonableness, good faith, and lack of prejudice to the interests of the Government has not been met.*—Relief under this section will not be granted if the IRS determines that the transferor or the executor of the transferor's estate has not acted reasonably and in good faith, and/or that the grant of relief would prejudice the interests of the Government. The following situations provide illustrations of some circumstances under which the standard of reasonableness, good faith, and lack of prejudice to the interests of the Government has not been met, and as a result, in which relief under this section will not be granted:

(1) *Timely allocations and elections.*—Relief will not be granted under this section to decrease or revoke a timely allocation of GST exemption as described in §26.2632-1(b)(4)(ii)(A)(*1*), or to revoke an election under section 2632(b)(3) or (c)(5) made on a timely filed Federal gift or estate tax return.

(2) *Timing.*—Relief will not be granted if the transferor or executor delayed the filing of the request for relief with the intent to deprive the IRS of sufficient time to challenge the claimed identity of the transferor or the valuation of the transferred property for Federal gift or estate tax purposes. (However, see paragraph (d)(3)(ii) of this section for examples of facts which alone do not constitute prejudice.)

(3) *Failure after being accurately informed.*—Relief will not be granted under this section if the decision made by the transferor or the executor of the transferor's estate (who had been accurately informed in all material respects by a qualified tax professional retained or employed by either (or both) of them with regard to the allocation of GST exemption or an election described in section 2632(b)(3) or (c)(5)) was reflected or implemented by the action or inaction that is the subject of the request for relief.

(4) *Hindsight.*—Relief under this section will not be granted if the IRS determines that the requested relief is an attempt to benefit from hindsight rather than an attempt to achieve the result the transferor or the executor of the transferor's estate intended when the transfer was made. One factor that will be relevant to this determination is whether the grant of relief will give the transferor the benefit of hindsight by providing an economic advantage that may not have been available if the allocation or election had been timely made. Thus, relief will not be granted if that relief will shift GST exemption from one trust to another trust unless the beneficiaries of the two trusts, and their respective interests in those trusts, are the same. Similarly, relief will not be granted if there is evidence that the transferor or executor had not made a timely allocation of the exemption in order to determine which of the various trusts achieved the greatest asset appreciation before selecting the trust that should have a zero inclusion ratio.

(f) *Period of limitations under section 6501.*—A request for relief under this section does not reopen, suspend, or extend the period of limitations on assessment or collection of any estate, gift, or GST tax under section 6501. Thus, the IRS may request that the transferor or the transferor's executor consent, under section 6501(c)(4), to an extension of the period of limitation on assessment or collection of any or all gift and GST taxes for the transfer(s) that are the subject of the requested relief. The transferor or the transferor's executor has the right to refuse to extend the period of limitations, or to limit such extension to particular issues or to a particular period of time. See section 6501(c)(4)(B).

(g) *Refunds.*—The filing of a request for relief under section 2642(g)(1) with the IRS does not constitute a claim for refund or credit of an overpayment and no implied right to refund will arise from the filing of such a request for relief. Similarly, the filing of such a request for relief does not extend the period of limitations under section 6511 for filing a claim for refund or credit of an overpayment. In the event the grant of relief under section 2642(g)(1) results in a potential claim for refund or credit of an overpayment, no such refund or credit will be allowed to the taxpayer or to the taxpayer's estate if the period of limitations under section 6511 for filing a claim for a refund or credit of the Federal gift, estate, or GST tax that was reduced by the granted relief has expired. The period of limitations under section 6511 is generally the later of three years from the time the original return is filed or two years from the time the tax was paid. If the IRS and the taxpayer agree to extend the period for assessment of tax, the period for filing a claim for refund or credit will be extended. Section 6511(c). The taxpayer or the taxpayer's estate is responsible for preserving any potential claim for refund or credit. A taxpayer who seeks and is granted relief under section 2642(g)(1) will not be regarded as having filed a claim for refund or credit by requesting such relief. In order to preserve a right of refund or credit, the taxpayer or the executor of the taxpayer's estate also must file before the expiration of the period of limitations under section 6511 for filing such a claim any required forms for requesting a refund or credit in accordance with the instructions to such forms and applicable regulations.

(h) *Procedural requirements.*—(1) *Letter ruling program.*—The relief described in this section is provided through the IRS's private letter ruling program. See Revenue Procedure 2008-1 (2008-1 IRB 1), or its successor, (which are available at *www.irs.gov*). Requests for relief under this section that do not meet the requirements of § 301.9100-2 of this chapter must be made under the rules of this section.

(2) *Affidavit and declaration of transferor or the executor of the transferor's estate.*—(i) The transferor or the executor of the transferor's estate must submit a detailed affidavit describing the events that led to the failure to timely allocate GST exemption to a transfer or the failure to timely elect under section 2632(b)(3) or (c)(5), and the events that led to the discovery of the failure. If the transferor or the executor of the transferor's estate relied on a tax professional for advice with respect to the allocation or election, the affidavit must describe—

(A) The scope of the engagement;

(B) The responsibilities the transferor or the executor of the transferor's estate believed the professional had assumed, if any; and

(C) The extent to which the transferor or the executor of the transferor's estate relied on the professional.

(ii) Attached to each affidavit must be copies of any writing (including, without limitation, notes and e-mails) and other contemporaneous documents within the possession of the affiant relevant to the transferor's intent with regard to the application of GST tax to the transaction for which relief under this section is being requested.

(iii) The affidavit must be accompanied by a dated declaration, signed by the transferor or the executor of the transferor's estate that states: "Under penalties of perjury, I declare that I have examined this affidavit, including any attachments thereto, and to the best of my knowledge and belief, this affidavit, including any attachments thereto, is true, correct, and complete. In addition, under penalties of perjury, I declare that I have examined all the documents included as part of this request for relief, and, to the best of my knowledge and belief, these documents collectively contain all the relevant facts relating to the request for relief, and such facts are true, correct, and complete."

(3) *Affidavits and declarations from other parties.*—(i) The transferor or the executor of the transferor's estate must submit detailed affidavits from individuals who have knowledge or information about the events that led to the failure to allocate GST exemption or to elect under section 2632(b)(3) or (c)(5), and/or to the discovery of the failure. These individuals may include individuals whose knowledge or information is not within the personal knowledge of the transferor or the executor of the transferor's estate. The individuals described in paragraph (h)(3)(i) of this section must include—

(A) Each agent or legal representative of the transferor who participated in the transaction and/or the preparation of the return for which relief is being requested;

(B) The preparer of the relevant Federal estate and/or gift tax return(s);

(C) Each individual (including an employee of the transferor or the executor of the transferor's estate) who made a substantial contribution to the preparation of the relevant Federal estate and/or gift tax return(s); and

(D) Each tax professional who advised or was consulted by the transferor or the executor of the transferor's estate with regard to any aspect of the transfer, the trust, the allocation of GST exemption, and/or the election under section 2632(b)(3) or (c)(5).

(ii) Each affidavit must describe the scope of the engagement and the responsibilities of the individual as well as the advice or service(s) the individual provided to the transferor or the executor of the transferor's estate.

(iii) Attached to each affidavit must be copies of any writing (including, without limitation, notes and e-mails) and other contemporaneous documents within the possession of the affiant relevant to the transferor's intent with regard to the application of GST tax to the transaction for which relief under this section is being requested.

(iv) Each affidavit also must include the name, and current address of the individual, and be accompanied by a dated declaration, signed by the individual that states: "Under penalties of perjury, I declare that I have personal knowledge of the information set forth in this affidavit, including any attachments thereto. In addition, under penalties of perjury, I declare that I have examined this affidavit, including any attachments thereto, and, to the best of my knowledge and belief, the affidavit contains all the relevant facts of which I am aware relating to the request for relief filed by or on behalf of [transferor or the executor of the transferor's estate], and such facts are true, correct, and complete."

(v) If an individual who would be required to provide an affidavit under paragraph (h)(3)(i) of this section has died or is not competent, the affidavit required under paragraph (h)(2) of this section must include a statement to that effect, as well as a statement describing the relationship between that individual and the transferor or the executor of the transferor's estate and the information or knowledge the transferor or the executor of the transferor's estate believes that individual had about the transfer, the trust, the allocation of exemption, or the election. If an individual who would be required to provide an affidavit under paragraph (h)(3)(i) of this section refuses to provide the transferor or the executor of the transferor's estate with such an affidavit, the affidavit required under paragraph (h)(2) of this section must include a statement that the individual has refused to provide the affidavit, a description of the efforts made to obtain the affidavit from the individual, the information or knowledge the transferor or the executor of the transferor's estate believes the individual had about the transfer, and the relationship between the individual and the transferor or the executor of the transferor's estate.

(i) *Effective/applicability date.*—Section 26.2642-7 applies to requests for relief filed on or after the date of publication of the Treasury decision adopting these proposed rules as final regulations in the **Federal Register**. [Reg. § 26.2642-7.]

Guidance under Section 529A: Qualified ABLE Programs

Guidance under Section 529A: Qualified ABLE Programs.—An amendment to Reg. § 26.2652-1, regarding programs under The Stephen Beck, Jr., Achieving a Better Life Experience Act of 2014 and rules under which States or State agencies or instrumentalities may establish and maintain a new type of tax-favored savings program through which contributions may be made to the account of an eligible disabled individual to meet qualified disability expenses, is proposed (published in the Federal Register on June 22, 2015) (REG-102837-15).

Par. 12. Section 26.2652-1 is amended by adding a sentence at the end of paragraph (a)(1) to read as follows:

§ 26.2652-1. Transferor defined; other definitions.—(a) * * *

(1) * * * For generation-skipping transfer tax rules related to an ABLE account established under section 529A, *see* regulations promulgated thereunder.

* * *

GIFTS AND BEQUESTS FROM EXPATRIATES

Gifts and Bequests from Covered Expatriates: Imposition of Tax

Gifts and Bequests from Covered Expatriates: Imposition of Tax.—Reg. §§ 28.2801-0—28.2801-7, relating to a tax on United States citizens and residents who receive gifts or bequests from certain individuals who relinquished United States citizenship or ceased to be lawful permanent residents of the United States on or after June 17, 2008, are proposed (published in the Federal Register on September 10, 2015) (REG-112997-10).

Sections 28.2801-0 to 28.2801-7 are added to read as follows:

§ 28.2801-0. Table of contents.—This section lists the captions in §§ 28.2801-1 through 28.2801-7.

(b) Distribution defined.
(c) Amount of distribution attributable to covered gift or covered bequest.
(1) Section 2801 ratio.
(i) In general.
(ii) Computation.
(2) Effect of reported transfer and tax payment.
(3) Inadequate information to calculate section 2801 ratio.
(d) Foreign trust treated as domestic trust.
(1) Election required.
(2) Effect of election.
(3) Time and manner of making the election.
(i) When to make the election.
(ii) Requirements for a valid election.
(iii) Section 2801 tax payable with the election.
(iv) Designation of U.S. agent.
(A) In general.
(B) Role of designated agent.
(C) Effect of appointment of agent.
(4) Annual certification or filing requirement.
(5) Duration of status as electing foreign trust.
(i) In general.
(ii) Termination.
(iii) Subsequent elections.
(6) Dispute as to amount of section 2801 tax owed by electing foreign trust.
(i) Procedure.
(ii) Effect of timely paying the additional section 2801 tax amount.
(iii) Effect of failing to timely pay the additional section 2801 tax amount (imperfect election).
(A) In general.
(B) Notice to permissible beneficiaries.
(C) Reasonable cause.
(D) Interim period.
(7) No overpayment caused solely by virtue of defect in election.
(e) Examples.
(f) Effective/applicability date.

§ 28.2801-6 Special rules and cross-references.
(a) Determination of basis.
(b) Generation-skipping transfer tax.
(c) Information returns.
(1) Gifts and bequests.
(2) Foreign trust distributions.
(3) Penalties and use of information.
(d) Application of penalties.
(1) Accuracy-related penalties on underpayments.
(2) Penalty for substantial and gross valuation misstatements attributable to incorrect appraisals.
(3) Penalty for failure to file a return and to pay tax.
(e) Effective/applicability date.

§ 28.2801-7 Determining responsibility under section 2801.
(a) Responsibility of recipients of gifts and bequests from expatriates.
(b) Disclosure of return and return information.
(1) In general.
(2) Rebuttable presumption.
(c) Effective/applicability date.

[Reg. § 28.2801-0.]

§ 28.2801-1. Tax on certain gifts and bequests from covered expatriates.—(a) *In general.*—Section 2801 of the Internal Revenue Code (Code) imposes a tax (section 2801 tax) on covered gifts and covered bequests, including distributions from foreign trusts attributable to covered gifts or covered bequests, received by a United States citizen or resident (U.S. citizen or resident) from a covered expatriate during a calendar year. Domestic trusts, as well as foreign trusts electing to be treated as domestic trusts for purposes of section 2801, are subject to tax under section 2801 in the same manner as if the trusts were U.S. citizens. See section 2801(e)(4)(A)(i) and (e)(4)(B)(iii). Accordingly, the section 2801 tax is paid by the U.S. citizen or resident, domestic trust, or foreign trust electing to be treated as a domestic trust for purposes of section 2801 that receives the covered gift or covered bequest. For purposes of this part 28, references to a U.S. citizen or U.S. citizens are considered to include a domestic trust and a foreign trust electing to be treated as a domestic trust for purposes of section 2801.

(b) *Effective/applicability date.*—This section applies on and after the date of publication of a Treasury decision adopting these rules as final regulations in the **Federal Register**. Once these regulations have been published as final regulations in the **Federal Register**, taxpayers may rely upon the final rules of this part for the period beginning June 17, 2008, and ending on the date preceding the date these regulations are published as final regulations in the **Federal Register**. [Reg. § 28.2801-1.]

§ 28.2801-2. Definitions.—(a) *Overview.*—This section provides definitions of terms applicable solely for purposes of section 2801 and the corresponding regulations.

(b) *Citizen or resident of the United States.*—A citizen or resident of the United States (U.S. citizen or resident) is an individual who is a citizen or resident of the United States under the rules applicable for purposes of chapter 11 or 12 of the Code, as the case may be, at the time of receipt of the covered gift or covered bequest. Furthermore, for purposes of this part 28, references to U.S. citizens also include domestic trusts, as well as foreign trusts electing to be treated as a domestic trust under § 28.2801-5(d). See § 28.2801-1(a)(1).

(c) *Domestic trust.*—The term *domestic trust* means a trust defined in section 7701(a)(30)(E). For purposes of this part 28, references to a domestic trust include a foreign trust that elects under § 28.2801-5(d) to be treated as a domestic trust solely for purposes of section 2801.

(d) *Foreign trust.*—(1) *In general.*—The term *foreign trust* means a trust defined in section 7701(a)(31).

(2) *Electing foreign trust.*—The term *electing foreign trust* is a foreign trust that has in effect a valid election to be treated as a domestic trust solely for purposes of section 2801. See § 28.2801-5(d).

(e) *U.S. recipient.*—The term *U.S. recipient* means a citizen or resident of the United States, a domestic trust, and an electing foreign trust that receives a covered gift or covered bequest, whether directly or indirectly, during the calendar year. The term U.S. recipient includes U.S.

citizens or residents receiving a distribution from a foreign trust not electing to be treated as a domestic trust for purposes of section 2801 if the distributions are attributable (in whole or in part) to one or more covered gifts or covered bequests received by the foreign trust. This term also includes the U.S. citizen or resident shareholders, partners, members, or other interest-holders, as the case may be (if any), of a domestic entity that receives a covered gift or covered bequest.

(f) *Covered bequest*.—The term *covered bequest* means any property acquired directly or indirectly by reason of the death of a covered expatriate, regardless of its situs and of whether such property was acquired by the covered expatriate before or after expatriation from the United States. The term also includes distributions made by reason of the death of a covered expatriate from a foreign trust that has not elected under §28.2801-5(d) to be treated as a domestic trust for purposes of section 2801 to the extent the distributions are attributable to covered gifts or covered bequests made to the foreign trust. See §28.2801-3 for additional rules and exceptions applicable to the term *covered bequest*.

(g) *Covered gift*.—The term *covered gift* means any property acquired by gift directly or indirectly from an individual who is a covered expatriate at the time the property is received by a U.S. citizen or resident, regardless of its situs and of whether such property was acquired by the covered expatriate before or after expatriation from the United States. The term also includes distributions made, other than by reason of the death of a covered expatriate, from a foreign trust that has not elected under §28.2801-5(d) to be treated as a domestic trust for purposes of section 2801 to the extent the distributions are attributable to covered gifts or covered bequests made to the foreign trust. See §28.2801-3 for additional rules and exceptions applicable to the term *covered gift*.

(h) *Expatriate and covered expatriate*.—The term *expatriate* has the same meaning for purposes of section 2801 as that term has in section 877A(g)(2). The term *covered expatriate* has the same meaning for purposes of section 2801 as that term has in section 877A(g)(1). The determination of whether an individual is a covered expatriate is made as of the expatriation date as defined in section 877A(g)(3), and if an expatriate meets the definition of a covered expatriate, the expatriate is considered a covered expatriate for purposes of section 2801 at all times after the expatriation date. However, an expatriate (as defined in section 877A(g)(2)) is not treated as a covered expatriate for purposes of section 2801 during any period beginning after the expatriation date during which such individual is subject to United States estate or gift tax (chapter 11 or chapter 12 of subtitle B) as a U.S. citizen or resident. See section 877A(g)(1)(C). An individual's status as a covered expatriate will be determined as of the date of the most recent expatriation, if there has been more than one.

(i) *Indirect acquisition of property*.—An indirect acquisition of property, as referred to in the definitions of a covered gift and covered bequest, includes—

(1) Property acquired as a result of a transfer that is a covered gift or covered bequest to a corporation or other entity other than a trust or estate, to the extent of the respective ownership interest of the recipient U.S. citizen or resident in the corporation or other entity;

(2) Property acquired by or on behalf of a U.S. citizen or resident, either from a covered expatriate or from a foreign trust that received a covered gift or covered bequest, through one or more other foreign trusts, other entities, or a person not subject to the section 2801 tax;

(3) Property paid by a covered expatriate, or distributed from a foreign trust that received a covered gift or covered bequest, in satisfaction of a debt or liability of a U.S. citizen or resident, regardless of the payee of that payment or distribution;

(4) Property acquired by or on behalf of a U.S. citizen or resident pursuant to a non-covered expatriate's power of appointment granted by a covered expatriate over property not in trust, unless the property previously was subjected to section 2801 tax upon the grant of the power or the covered expatriate had no more than a non-general power of appointment over that property; and

(5) Property acquired by or on behalf of a U.S. citizen or resident in other transfers not made directly by the covered expatriate to the U.S. citizen or resident.

(j) *Power of appointment*.—The term *power of appointment* refers to both a general and non-general power of appointment. A general power of appointment is as defined in sections 2041(b) and 2514(c) of the Code and a non-general power of appointment is any power of appointment that is not a general power of appointment.

(k) *Effective/applicability date*.—This section applies on and after the date of publication of a Treasury decision adopting these rules as final regulations in the **Federal Register**. Once these regulations have been published as final regulations in the **Federal Register**, taxpayers may rely upon the final rules of this part for the period beginning June 17, 2008, and ending on the date preceding the date these regulations are published as final regulations in the **Federal Register**. [Reg. §28.2801-2.]

§28.2801-3. Rules and exceptions applicable to covered gifts and covered bequests.—(a) *Covered gift*.—Subject to the provisions of paragraphs (c), (d), and (e) of this section, the term *gift* as used in the definition of covered gift in §28.2801-2(g) has the same meaning as in chapter 12 of subtitle B, but without regard to the exceptions in section 2501(a)(2), (a)(4), and (a)(5), the per-donee exclusion under section 2503(b) for certain transfers of a present interest, the exclusion under section 2503(e) for certain educational or medical expenses, and the waiver of certain pension rights under section 2503(f).

(b) *Covered bequest*.—Subject to the provisions of paragraphs (c), (d), and (e) of this section, property acquired "by reason of the death of a covered expatriate" as described in the definition of covered bequest in §28.2801-2(f) includes any property that would have been includible in the gross estate of the covered expatriate under chapter 11 of subtitle B if the covered expatriate had been a U.S. citizen at the time of death. Therefore, in addition to the items described in §28.2801-2(f), the term *covered bequest* includes, without limitation, property or an interest in property acquired by reason of a covered expatriate's death—

(1) By bequest, devise, trust provision, beneficiary designation or other contractual arrangement, or by operation of law;

(2) That was transferred by the covered expatriate during life, either before or after expatriation, and which would have been includible in the covered expatriate's gross estate under section 2036, section 2037, or section 2038 had the covered expatriate been a U.S. citizen at the time of death;

(3) That was received for the benefit of a covered expatriate from such covered expatriate's spouse, or predeceased spouse, for which a valid qualified terminable interest property (QTIP) election was made on such spouse's, or predeceased spouse's, Form 709, "U.S. Gift (and Generation-Skipping Transfer) Tax Return," Form 706, "United States Estate (and Generation-Skipping Transfer) Tax Return," or Form 706-NA, "United States Estate (and Generation-Skipping Transfer) Tax Return, Estate of nonresident not a citizen of the United States," which would have been included in the covered expatriate's gross estate under section 2044 if the covered expatriate was a U.S. citizen at the time of death; or

(4) That otherwise passed from the covered expatriate by reason of death, such as—

(i) Property held by the covered expatriate and another person as joint tenants with right of survivorship or as tenants by the entirety, but only to the extent such property would have been included in the covered expatriate's gross estate under section 2040 if the covered expatriate had been a U.S. citizen at the time of death;

(ii) Any annuity or other payment that would have been includible in the covered expatriate's gross estate if the covered expatriate had been a U.S. citizen at the time of death;

(iii) Property subject to a general power of appointment held by the covered expatriate at death; or

(iv) Life insurance proceeds payable upon the covered expatriate's death that would have been includible in the covered expatriate's gross estate under section 2042 if the covered expatriate had been a U.S. citizen at the time of death.

(c) *Exceptions to covered gift and covered bequest.*—The following transfers from a covered expatriate are exceptions to the definition of covered gift and covered bequest.

(1) *Reported taxable gifts.*—A transfer of property that is a taxable gift under section 2503(a) and is reported on the donor's timely filed Form 709 is not a covered gift, provided that the donor also timely pays the gift tax, if any, shown as due on that return. A transfer excluded from the definition of a taxable gift, such as a transfer of a present interest not in excess of the annual exclusion amount under section 2503(b), is not excluded from the definition of a covered gift under this paragraph (c)(1) even if reported on the donor's Form 709.

(2) *Property reported as subject to estate tax.*—Property that is included in the gross estate of the covered expatriate and is reported on a timely filed Form 706 or Form 706-NA is not a covered bequest, provided that the estate also timely pays the estate tax, if any, shown as due on that return. For this purpose, estate tax imposed on distributions from or on the remainder of a qualified domestic trust (QDOT) are deemed to be reported on a timely filed Form 706, if the tax due thereon was timely paid. Thus, if the covered expatriate's gross estate is not of sufficient value to require the filing of a Form 706-NA, for example, and no Form 706-NA is timely filed, the property passing from that covered expatriate is not excluded from the definition of a covered bequest under the rule of this paragraph (c)(2). Further, this exclusion does not apply to the property not on such a form, whether or not subject to United States estate tax (that is, non U.S.-situs property that passes to U.S. citizens or residents).

(3) *Transfers to charity.*—A gift to a donee described in section 2522(b) or a bequest to a beneficiary described in section 2055(a) is not a covered gift or covered bequest to the extent a charitable deduction under section 2522 or section 2055 would have been allowed if the covered expatriate had been a U.S. citizen or resident at the time of the transfer.

(4) *Transfers to spouse.*—A transfer from a covered expatriate to the covered expatriate's spouse is not a covered gift or covered bequest to the extent a marital deduction under section 2523 or section 2056 would have been allowed if the covered expatriate had been a U.S. citizen or resident at the time of the transfer. To the extent that a gift or bequest to a trust (or to a separate share of the trust) would qualify for the marital deduction, the gift or bequest is not a covered gift or covered bequest. For purposes of this paragraph (c)(4), a marital deduction is deemed not to be allowed for qualified terminable interest property (QTIP) or for property in a qualified domestic trust (QDOT) unless a valid QTIP and/or QDOT election is made. The term *covered bequest* also does not include assets in a QDOT funded for the benefit of a covered expatriate by the covered expatriate's predeceased spouse, but only if a valid election was made on the predeceased spouse's Form 706 or Form 706-NA to treat the trust as a QDOT.

(5) *Qualified disclaimers.*—A transfer pursuant to a covered expatriate's qualified disclaimer, as defined in section 2518(b), is not a covered gift or covered bequest from that covered expatriate.

(d) *Covered gifts and covered bequests made in trust.*—For purposes of section 2801, when a covered expatriate transfers property to a trust in a transfer that is a covered gift or covered bequest as determined under this section, the transfer of property is treated as a covered gift or covered bequest to the trust, without regard to the beneficial interests in the trust or whether any person has a general power of appointment or a power of withdrawal over trust property. Accordingly, the rules in section 2801(e)(4) and § 28.2801-4(a) apply to determine liability for payment of the section 2801 tax. The U.S. recipient of a covered gift or a covered bequest to a domestic trust or an electing foreign trust is the domestic or electing foreign trust, and the U.S. recipient of a covered gift or a covered bequest to a non-electing foreign trust is any U.S. citizen or resident receiving a distribution from the non-electing foreign trust. See § 28.2801-2(e) for the definition of a U.S. recipient.

(e) *Powers of appointment.*—(1) *Covered expatriate as holder of power.*—The exercise or release of a general power of appointment held by a covered expatriate over property, whether or not in trust (even if that covered expatriate was a U.S. citizen or resident when the general power of appointment was granted), for the benefit of a U.S. citizen or resident is a covered gift or covered bequest. The lapse of a general power of appointment is treated as a release to the extent provided in sections 2041(b)(2) and 2514(e). Furthermore, the exercise of a power of appointment by a covered expatriate that creates another power of appointment as described in section 2041(a)(3) or section 2514(d) for the benefit of a U.S. citizen or resident is a covered gift or a covered bequest.

(2) *Covered expatriate as grantor of power*.—The grant by a covered expatriate to an individual who is a U.S. citizen or resident of a general power of appointment over property not transferred in trust by the covered expatriate is a covered gift or covered bequest to the powerholder. For the rule applying to the grant by a covered expatriate of a general power of appointment over property in trust, see paragraph (d) of this section.

(f) *Examples*.—The provisions of this section are illustrated by the following examples:

Example 1. Transfer to spouse. In Year 1, CE, a covered expatriate domiciled in Country F, a foreign country with which the United States does not have a gift tax treaty, gives $300,000 cash to his wife, W, a U.S. resident and citizen of Country F. Under paragraph (c)(4) of this section, the $100,000 exemption for a noncitizen spouse, as indexed for inflation in Year 1, is excluded from the definition of a covered gift under section 2801 because only that amount of the transfer would have qualified for the gift tax marital deduction if CE had been a U.S. citizen at the time of the gift. See sections 2801(e)(3) and 2523(i). The remaining amount ($300,000 less the $100,000 exemption for a noncitizen spouse as indexed for inflation), however, is a covered gift from CE to W. W must timely file Form 708, "U.S. Return of Gifts or Bequests from Covered Expatriates," and timely pay the tax. See §§28.6011-1(a), 28.6071-1(a), and 28.6151-1(a). W also must report the transfer on Form 3520, "Annual Return to Report Transactions with Foreign Trusts and Receipt of Certain Foreign Gifts," and any other required form. See §28.2801-6(c)(1).

Example 2. Reporting property as subject to estate tax. (i) CE, a covered expatriate domiciled in Country F, a foreign country with which the United States does not have an estate tax treaty, owns a condominium in the United States with son, S, a U.S. citizen. CE and S each contributed their actuarial share of the purchase price when purchasing the condominium and own it as joint tenants with rights of survivorship. On December 14, Year 1, CE dies. At the time of CE's death, the fair market value of CE's share of the condominium, $250,000, is included in CE's gross estate under sections 2040 and 2103.

(ii) On September 14 of the following calendar year, Year 2, the executor of CE's estate timely files a Form 4768, "Application for Extension of Time to File a Return and/or Pay U.S. Estate (and Generation-Skipping Transfer) Taxes," requesting a 6-month extension of time to file Form 706-NA, and a 1-year extension of time to pay the estate tax. The IRS grants both extensions but CE's executor fails to file the Form 706-NA until after March 14 of the calendar year immediately following Year 2.

(iii) S learns that the executor of CE's estate did not timely file Form 706-NA. Because CE is a covered expatriate, S received a covered bequest as defined under §28.2801-2(f) and paragraph (b) of this section. S must timely file Form 708 and pay the section 2801 tax. See §§28.6011-1(a), 28.6071-1(a), and 28.6151-1(a). S also must file Form 3520 to report a large gift or bequest from a foreign person, and any other required form. See §28.2801-6(c)(1).

Example 3. Covered gift in trust with grant of general power of appointment over trust property. (i) On October 20, Year 1, CE, a covered expatriate domiciled in Country F, a foreign country with which the United States does not have a gift tax treaty, transfers $500,000 in cash from an account in Country F to an irrevocable foreign trust created on that same date. Under section 2511(a), no gift tax is imposed on the transfer and thus, CE is not required to file a U.S. gift tax return. Under the terms of the foreign trust, A, CE's child and a U.S. resident, and Q, A's child and a U.S. citizen, may receive discretionary distributions of income and principal during life. At A's death, the assets remaining in the foreign trust will be distributed to B, CE's other U.S. resident child, or if B is not living at the time of A's death, then to CE's then-living issue, *per stirpes*. The terms of the foreign trust also allow A to appoint trust principal and/or income to A, A's estate, A's creditors, the creditors of A's estate, or A's issue at any time. On March 5, Year 2, A exercises this power to appoint and causes the trustee to distribute $100,000 to Q.

(ii) On October 20, Year 1, the irrevocable foreign trust receives a covered gift for purposes of section 2801, but no section 2801 tax is imposed at that time. On March 5, Year 2, when Q receives $100,000 from the irrevocable foreign trust pursuant to the exercise of A's power of appointment, Q has received a distribution attributable to a covered gift and section 2801 tax is imposed on Q as of the date of the distribution. *See* §28.2801-4(d). Q must timely file Form 708 to report the covered gift from a foreign person (specifically, from CE). See section 6039F(a) and §§28.6011-1(a), 28.6071-1(a), and 28.6151-1(a). Under section 2501, A makes a taxable gift to Q of $100,000 when A exercises the general power of appointment for Q's benefit. See section 2514(b). Accordingly, A must report A's $100,000 gift to Q on a timely filed Form 709. See section 6019. Because A is considered the transferor of the $100,000 for gift and GST tax purposes, the distribution to Q is not a generation-skipping transfer under chapter 13. See §26.2652-1(a)(1). Furthermore, because the $100,000 is being distributed from a foreign trust, Q must report the gift on a Form 3520 as a distribution from a foreign trust. See §28.2801-6(c)(2).

Example 4. Lapse of power of appointment held by covered expatriate. (i) A, a U.S. citizen, creates an irrevocable domestic trust for the benefit of A's issue, CE, and CE's children. CE is a covered expatriate, but CE's children are U.S. citizens. CE has the right to withdraw $5,000 in each year in which A makes a contribution to the trust, but the withdrawal right lapses 30 days after the date of the contribution. In Year 1, A funds the trust, but CE fails to exercise CE's right to withdraw $5,000 within 30 days of the contribution. The $5,000 lapse is not considered to be a release of the power, so it is neither a gift for U.S. gift tax purposes, nor a covered gift for purposes of section 2801 under paragraph (e)(1) of this section.

(g) *Effective/applicability date.*—This section applies on and after the date of publication of a Treasury decision adopting these rules as final regulations in the **Federal Register**. Once these regulations have been published as final regulations in the **Federal Register**, taxpayers may rely upon the final rules of this part for the period beginning June 17, 2008, and ending on the date preceding the date these regulations are published as final regulations in the **Federal Register**. [Reg. § 28.2801-3.]

§ 28.2801-4. Liability for and payment of tax on covered gifts and covered bequests; computation of tax.—(a) *Liability for tax.*—(1) *U.S. citizen or resident.*—A U.S. citizen or resident who receives a covered gift or covered bequest is liable for payment of the section 2801 tax.

(2) *Domestic trust.*—(i) *In general.*—A domestic trust that receives a covered gift or covered bequest is treated as a U.S. citizen and is liable for payment of the section 2801 tax. See section 2801(e)(4)(A)(i) and § 28.2801-2(b).

(ii) *Generation-skipping transfer tax.*—A trust's payment of the section 2801 tax does not result in a taxable distribution under section 2621 to any trust beneficiary for purposes of the generation-skipping transfer tax to the extent that the trust, rather than the beneficiary, is liable for the section 2801 tax.

(iii) *Charitable remainder trust.*—A domestic trust qualifying as a charitable remainder trust (as that term is defined in § 1.664-1(a)(1)(iii)(*a*)) is subject to section 2801 when it receives a covered gift or covered bequest. Section 2801(e)(3) excepts from the definition of covered gift and covered bequest property with respect to which a deduction under section 2522 or section 2055, respectively, would have been allowed if the covered expatriate had been a U.S. citizen or resident at the time of the transfer. See § 28.2801-3(c)(3). As a result, the charitable remainder interest's share of each transfer to the charitable remainder trust is not a covered gift or covered bequest. To compute the amount of covered gifts and covered bequests taxable to the charitable remainder trust for a calendar year, the charitable remainder trust will (A) calculate, in accordance with the regulations under section 664 and as of the date of the trust's receipt of the contribution, the value of the remainder interest in each contribution received in such calendar year that would have been a covered gift or covered bequest without regard to section 2801(e)(3), (B) subtract the remainder interest in each such contribution from the amount of that contribution to compute the annuity or unitrust (income) interest in that contribution, and (C) add the total of such income interests, each of which is the portion of the contribution that constitutes a covered gift or covered bequest to the trust. The charitable remainder trust then computes its section 2801 tax in accordance with paragraph (b) of this section.

(iv) *Migrated foreign trust.*—A foreign trust (other than one electing to be treated as a domestic trust under § 28.2801-5(d)) that has previously received a covered gift or covered bequest and that subsequently becomes a domestic trust as defined under section 7701(a)(30)(E) (migrated foreign trust), must file a timely Form 708, "U.S. Return of Gifts or Bequests from Covered Expatriates," for the taxable year in which the trust becomes a domestic trust. The section 2801 tax, if any, must be paid by the due date of that Form 708. On that Form 708, the section 2801 tax is calculated in the same manner as if such trust was making an election under § 28.2801-5(d) to be treated as a domestic trust solely for purposes of the section 2801 tax. Accordingly, the trustee must report and pay the section 2801 tax on all covered gifts and covered bequests received by the trust during the year in which the trust becomes a domestic trust, as well as on the portion of the trust's value at the end of the year preceding the year in which the trust becomes a domestic trust that is attributable to all prior covered gifts and covered bequests. Because the migrated foreign trust will be treated solely for purposes of section 2801 as a domestic trust for the entire year during which it became a domestic trust, distributions made to U.S. citizens or residents during that year but before the date on which the trust became a domestic trust will not be subject to section 2801.

(3) *Foreign trust.*—(i) *In general.*—A foreign trust that receives a covered gift or covered bequest is not liable for payment of the section 2801 tax unless the trust makes an election to be treated as a domestic trust solely for purposes of section 2801 as provided in § 28.2801-5(d). Absent such an election, each U.S. recipient is liable for payment of the section 2801 tax on that person's receipt, either directly or indirectly, of a distribution from the foreign trust to the extent that the distribution is attributable to a covered gift or covered bequest made to the foreign trust. See § 28.2801-5(b) and (c) regarding distributions from foreign trusts.

(ii) *Income tax deduction.*—The U.S. recipient of a distribution from a foreign trust is allowed a deduction against income tax under section 164 in the calendar year in which the section 2801 tax is paid or accrued. The amount of the deduction is equal to the portion of the section 2801 tax attributable to such distribution, but only to the extent that portion of the distribution is included in the U.S. recipient's gross income. The amount of the deduction allowed under section 164 is calculated as follows:

(A) First, the U.S. recipient must determine the total amount of distribution(s) from the foreign trust treated as covered gifts and covered bequests received by that U.S. recipient during the calendar year to which the section 2801 tax payment relates.

(B) Second, of the amount determined in paragraph (a)(3)(ii)(A) of this section, the U.S. recipient must determine the amount that also is includable in the U.S. recipient's gross income for that calendar year. For purposes of this paragraph (a)(3)(ii)(B), distributions from foreign trusts includable in the U.S. recipient's gross income are deemed first to consist of the portion of those distributions, if any, that are attributable to covered gifts and covered bequests.

(C) Finally, the U.S. recipient must determine the portion of the section 2801 tax paid for that calendar year that is attributable to the amount determined in paragraph (a)(3)(ii)(B) of this section, the covered gifts and covered bequests received from the foreign trust that are also included in the U.S. recipient's gross income. This amount is the allowable deduction. Thus, for a calendar year taxpayer, the deduction is determined by multiplying the section 2801 tax paid during the calendar year by the ratio of the amount determined in paragraph (a)(3)(ii)(B) of this section to the total covered gifts and covered bequests received by the U.S. recipient during the calendar year to which that tax payment relates (that is, 2801 tax liability x [foreign trust distributions attributable to covered gifts and covered bequests that are also included in gross income / total covered gifts or covered bequests received]).

(b) *Computation of tax.*—(1) *In general.*—The section 2801 tax is computed by multiplying the net covered gifts and covered bequests (as defined in paragraph (b)(2) of this section) received by a U.S. recipient during the calendar year by the greater of—

(i) The highest rate of estate tax under section 2001(c) in effect for that calendar year; or

(ii) The highest rate of gift tax under section 2502(a) in effect for that calendar year. See paragraph (f) of this section, *Example 1.*

(2) *Net covered gifts and covered bequests.*—The net covered gifts and covered bequests received by a U.S. recipient during the calendar year is the total value of all covered gifts and covered bequests received by that U.S. recipient during the calendar year, less the section 2801(c) amount, which is the dollar amount of the per-donee exclusion in effect under section 2503(b) for that calendar year.

(c) *Value of covered gift or covered bequest.*—The value of a covered gift or covered bequest is the fair market value of the property as of the date of its receipt by the U.S. recipient. See paragraph (d) of this section regarding the determination of the date of receipt. As in the case of chapters 11 and 12, the fair market value of a covered gift or covered bequest is the price at which such property would change hands between a willing buyer and a willing seller, neither being under any compulsion to buy or to sell and both having reasonable knowledge of relevant facts. The fair market value of a covered gift is determined in accordance with the federal gift tax valuation principles of section 2512 and chapter 14 and the corresponding regulations. The fair market value of a covered bequest is determined by applying the federal estate tax valuation principles of section 2031 and chapter 14 and the corresponding regulations, but without regard to sections 2032 and 2032A.

(d) *Date of receipt.*—(1) *In general.*—The section 2801 tax is imposed upon the receipt of a covered gift or covered bequest by a U.S. recipient.

(2) *Covered gift.*—The date of receipt of a covered gift is the same as the date of the gift for purposes of chapter 12 as if the covered expatriate had been a U.S. citizen at the time of the transfer. Thus, for a gift of stock, if the covered expatriate delivers a properly endorsed stock certificate to the U.S. recipient, the date of delivery is the date of receipt for purposes of this section. Alternatively, if the covered expatriate delivers the stock certificate to the issuing corporation or its transfer agent in order to transfer title to the U.S. recipient, the date of receipt is the date the stock is transferred on the books of the corporation. For a transfer of assets by a covered expatriate to a domestic revocable trust, the trust receives the transfer on the date the covered expatriate relinquishes the right to revoke the trust. If, before the donor's relinquishment of the right to revoke the trust, the revocable trust distributes property to a U.S. citizen or resident not in discharge of a support or other obligation of the donor, then the U.S. recipient receives a covered gift on the date of that distribution. For an asset subject to a claim of right of another involving a bona fide dispute, the date of receipt is the date on which such claim is extinguished.

(3) *Covered bequest.*—The date of receipt of a covered bequest is the date of distribution from the estate or the decedent's revocable trust rather than the date of death of the covered expatriate. However, the date of receipt is the date of death for property passing on the death of the covered expatriate by operation of law, or by beneficiary designation or other contractual agreement. Notwithstanding the previous sentences, for an asset subject to a claim of right of another involving a bona fide dispute, the date of receipt is the date on which such claim is extinguished.

(4) *Foreign trusts.*—The date of receipt by a U.S. citizen or resident of property from a foreign trust that has not elected to be treated as a domestic trust under § 28.2801-5(d) is the date of its distribution from the foreign trust.

(5) *Powers of appointment.*—(i) *Covered expatriate as holder of power.*—In the case of the exercise, release, or lapse of a power of appointment held by a covered expatriate that is a covered gift pursuant to § 28.2801-3(e)(1), the date of receipt is the date of the exercise, release, or lapse of the power. In the case of the exercise, release, or lapse of a power of appointment held by a covered expatriate that is a covered bequest pursuant to § 28.2801-3(e)(1), the date of receipt is (*A*) the date the property subject to the power is distributed from the decedent's estate or revocable trust when the power of appointment is over property in such estate or trust, or (*B*) the date of the covered expatriate's death when the power of appointment is over property passing on the covered expatriate's death by operation of law, by beneficiary designation, or by other contractual agreement.

(ii) *Covered expatriate as grantor of power.*—The date of receipt of property subject to a general power of appointment granted by a covered expatriate to a U.S. citizen or resident over property not transferred in trust that constitutes a covered gift or covered bequest pursuant to § 28.2801-3(e)(2) is the first date on which both the power is exercisable by the U.S. citizen or resident and the property subject to the general power has been irrevocably transferred by the covered expatriate. The date of receipt of property subject to a general power of appointment over property in a domestic trust or an electing foreign trust is determined in accordance with paragraphs (d)(2) and (d)(3) of this section, and over property in a non-electing foreign trust is determined in accordance with paragraph (d)(4) of this section. See § 28.2801-3(d) for the rule applying to covered gifts and covered bequests made in trust.

(6) *Indirect receipts.*—The date of receipt by a U.S. citizen or resident of a covered gift or covered bequest received indirectly from a cov-

ered expatriate is the date of its receipt, as determined under paragraph (d)(2) or (d)(3) of this section, by the U.S. citizen or resident who is the first recipient of that property from the covered expatriate to be subject to section 2801 with regard to that property. For example, the date of receipt of property (i) subject to a non-general power of appointment over property not held in trust given by a covered expatriate to a foreign person (other than another covered expatriate) is the date that property is received by the U.S. citizen or resident in whose favor the power was exercised, and (ii) received through one or more entities not subject to section 2801 is the date of its receipt by the U.S. citizen or resident from a conduit entity.

(e) *Reduction of tax for foreign estate or gift tax paid.*—The section 2801 tax is reduced by the amount of any gift or estate tax paid to a foreign country with respect to the covered gift or covered bequest. For this purpose, the term *foreign country* includes possessions and political subdivisions of foreign states. However, no reduction is allowable for interest and penalties paid in connection with those foreign taxes. To claim the reduction of section 2801 tax, the U.S. recipient must attach to the Form 708 a copy of the foreign estate or gift tax return and a copy of the receipt or cancelled check for payment of the foreign estate or gift tax. The U.S. recipient also must report, on an attachment to the Form 708:

(1) The amount of foreign estate or gift tax paid with respect to each covered gift or covered bequest and the amount and date of each payment thereof;

(2) A description and the value of the property with respect to which such taxes were imposed;

(3) Whether any refund of part or all of the foreign estate or gift tax has been or will be claimed or allowed, and the amount; and

(4) All other information necessary for the verification and computation of the amount of the reduction of section 2801 tax.

(f) *Examples.*—The provisions of this section are illustrated by the following examples.

Example 1. Computation of tax. In Year 1, A, a U.S. citizen, receives a $50,000 covered gift from B and an $80,000 covered bequest from C. Both B and C are covered expatriates. In Year 1, the highest estate and gift tax rate is 40 percent and the section 2801(c) amount is $14,000. A's section 2801 tax for Year 1 is computed by multiplying A's net covered gifts and covered bequests by 40 percent. A's net covered gifts and covered bequests for Year 1 are $116,000, which is determined by reducing A's total covered gifts and covered bequests received during Year 1, $130,000 ($50,000 + $80,000), by the section 2801(c) amount of $14,000. A's section 2801 tax liability is then reduced by any foreign estate or gift tax paid under paragraph (e) of this section. Assuming A, B, and C paid no foreign estate or gift tax on the transfers, A's section 2801 tax liability for Year 1 is $46,400 ($116,000 x 0.4).

Example 2. Deduction of section 2801 tax for income tax purposes. In Year 1, B receives a covered bequest of $25,000. Also in Year 1, B receives an aggregate $500,000 of distributions from a non-electing foreign trust of which $100,000 was attributable to a covered gift. In Year 1, the highest estate and gift tax rate is 40 percent and the section 2801(c) amount is $14,000. Based on information provided by the trustee of the foreign trust, B includes $50,000 of the aggregate distributions from the foreign trust in B's gross income for Year 1. Under paragraph (a)(3)(ii) of this section, B (a cash basis taxpayer) is entitled to an income tax deduction under section 164 for the calendar year in which the section 2801 tax is paid. In Year 2, B timely reports the distributions from the foreign trust and pays $44,400 in section 2801 tax (($125,000 - $14,000) x 0.4). In Year 2, B is entitled to an income tax deduction because B paid the section 2801 tax in Year 2 on the Year 1 covered gift and covered bequest. B's Year 2 income tax deduction is computed as follows:

(i) $100,000 of B's total covered gifts and covered bequests of $125,000 received in Year 1 consisted of the portion of the distributions from the foreign trust attributable to covered gifts and covered bequests received by the trust. See paragraph (a)(3)(ii)(A) of this section.

(ii) $50,000 of the $500,000 of trust distributions were includable in B's gross income for Year 1. This amount is deemed to consist first of distributions subject to the section 2801 tax ($100,000). Thus, the entire amount included in B's gross income ($50,000) also is subject to the section 2801 tax, and is used in the numerator to determine the income tax deduction available to B. See paragraph (a)(3)(ii)(B) of this section.

(iii) The portion of B's section 2801 tax liability attributable to distributions from a foreign trust is $17,760 ($44,400 x ($50,000/$125,000)). Therefore, B's deduction under section 164 is $17,760. See paragraph (a)(3)(ii)(C) of this section.

Example 3. Date of receipt; bona fide claim. On October 10, Year 1, CE, a covered expatriate, died testate as a resident of Country F, a foreign country with which the United States does not have an estate tax treaty. CE designated his son, S, as the beneficiary of CE's retirement account. S is a U.S. citizen. CE's wife, W, who is a citizen and resident of Country F, elects to take her elective share of CE's estate under local law. S contests whether the retirement account is property subject to the elective share. S and W agree to settle their respective claims by dividing CE's assets equally between them. On December 15 of Year 2, Country F's court enters an order accepting the terms of the settlement agreement and dismissing the case. Under paragraph (d)(3) of this section, S received a covered bequest of one-half of CE's retirement account on December 15, Year 2, when W's claim of right was extinguished.

(g) *Effective/applicability date.*—This section applies on and after the date of publication of a Treasury decision adopting these rules as final regulations in the **Federal Register**. Once these regulations have been published as final regulations in the **Federal Register**, taxpayers may rely upon the final rules of this part for the period beginning June 17, 2008, and ending on the date preceding the date these regulations are published as final regulations in the **Federal Register**. [Reg. § 28.2801-4.]

§ 28.2801-5. Foreign trusts.—(a) *In general.*—The section 2801 tax is imposed on a U.S. recipient who receives distributions, whether of income or principal, from a foreign trust to the extent the distributions are attributable to one or more covered gifts or covered bequests made to that foreign trust. See paragraph (d) of this section regarding a foreign trust's election to be treated as a domestic trust for purposes of section 2801.

(b) *Distribution defined.*—For purposes of determining whether a U.S. recipient has received a distribution from a foreign trust, the term *distribution* means any direct, indirect, or constructive transfer from a foreign trust. This determination is made without regard to whether any portion of the trust is treated as owned by the U.S. recipient or any other person under subpart E of part I, subchapter J, chapter 1 of the Code (pertaining to grantors and others treated as substantial owners) and without regard to whether the U.S. recipient of the transfer is designated as a beneficiary by the terms of the trust. For purposes of section 2801, the term distribution also includes each disbursement from a foreign trust pursuant to the exercise, release, or lapse of a power of appointment, whether or not a general power. In addition to the reporting requirements under this section, see section 6048(c) regarding the information reporting requirement for U.S. persons receiving a distribution or deemed distribution from a foreign trust during the year.

(c) *Amount of distribution attributable to covered gift or covered bequest.*—(1) *Section 2801 ratio.*—(i) *In general.*—A foreign trust may have received covered gifts and covered bequests as well as contributions that were not covered gifts or covered bequests. Under such circumstances, the fair market value of the foreign trust at any time consists in part of a portion of the trust attributable to the covered gifts and covered bequests it has received (covered portion) and in part of a portion of the trust attributable to other contributions (non-covered portion). The covered portion of the trust includes the ratable portion of appreciation and income that has accrued on the foreign trust's assets from the date of the contribution of the covered gifts and covered bequests to the foreign trust. For purposes of section 2801, the amount of each distribution from the foreign trust, whether made from the income or principal of the trust, that is considered attributable to the foreign trust's covered gifts and covered bequests is determined on a proportional basis, by reference to the section 2801 ratio (as described in paragraph (c)(1)(ii) of this section), and not by the identification or tracing of particular trust assets. Specifically, this portion of each distribution is determined by multiplying the distributed amount by the percentage of the trust that consists of its covered portion immediately prior to that distribution (section 2801 ratio). Thus, for example, the section 2801 ratio of a foreign trust whose assets are comprised exclusively of covered gifts or covered bequests and the income and appreciation thereon, would be 1 and the full amount of each distribution from that foreign trust to a U.S. citizen or resident would be subject to section 2801.

(ii) *Computation.*—The section 2801 ratio, which must be redetermined after each contribution to the foreign trust, is computed by using the following fraction:

$$\text{Section 2801 ratio} = \frac{(X + Y)}{Z}$$

where,

X = The value of the trust attributable to covered gifts and covered bequests, if any, immediately before the contribution (pre-contribution value); this value is determined by multiplying the fair market value of the trust assets immediately prior to the contribution by the section 2801 ratio in effect immediately prior to the current contribution. This amount will be zero for all years prior to the year in which the foreign trust receives its first covered gift or covered bequest;

Y = The portion, if any, of the fair market value of the current contribution that constitutes a covered gift or covered bequest; and

Z = The fair market value of the trust immediately after the current contribution. See paragraph (e) of this section, *Example 1*, for an illustration of this computation.

(2) *Effect of reported transfer and tax payment.*—Once a section 2801 tax has been timely paid on property that thereafter remains in a foreign trust, that property is no longer considered to be, or to be attributable to, a covered gift or covered bequest to the foreign trust for purposes of the computation described in paragraph (c)(1)(ii) of this section. For purposes of the prior sentence, a section 2801 tax is deemed to have been timely paid on amounts for which no section 2801 tax was due as long as those amounts were reported as a covered gift or covered bequest on a timely filed Form 708, "U.S. Return of Gifts or Bequests from Covered Expatriates."

(3) *Inadequate information to calculate section 2801 ratio.*—If the trustee of the foreign trust does not have sufficient books and records to calculate the section 2801 ratio, or if the U.S. recipient is unable to obtain the necessary information with regard to the foreign trust, the U.S. recipient must proceed upon the assumption that the entire distribution for purposes of section 2801 is attributable to a covered gift or covered bequest.

(d) *Foreign trust treated as domestic trust.*—(1) *Election required.*—To be considered an electing foreign trust, so that the foreign trust is treated as a domestic trust solely for purposes of the section 2801 tax, a valid election is required.

(2) *Effect of election.*—(i) A valid election subjects the electing foreign trust to the section 2801 tax on (A) all covered gifts and covered bequests received by the foreign trust during that calendar year, (B) the portion of the trust attributable to covered gifts and covered bequests received by the trust in prior years, as determined in paragraph (d)(3)(iii) of this section, and (C) all covered gifts and covered bequests received by the foreign trust during calendar years subsequent to the first year in which the election is effective, unless and until the election is terminated. To the extent that covered gifts and covered bequests are subject to the section 2801 tax under the prior sentence, those trust receipts are no longer treated as a covered gift or covered bequest for purposes of determining the portion of the trust attributable to covered gifts and covered bequests. Therefore, upon making a valid election, the foreign trust's section 2801 ratio described in paragraph (c)(1)(ii) of this section will be zero until the effective date of any termination of the election and the subsequent receipt of any covered gift or covered bequest, and a distribution made from the foreign trust while this election is in effect is not taxable under section 2801 to the recipient trust beneficiary.

(ii) This election has no effect on any distribution from the foreign trust that was made to a U.S. recipient in a calendar year prior to the calendar year for which the election is made. Thus, even after a valid election is made, a distribution to a U.S. recipient in a calendar year prior to the calendar year for which the election is made that was attributable to one or more covered gifts or covered bequests continues to be a distribution attributable to one or more covered gifts or covered bequests and the section 2801 ratio in place at the time of the distribution continues to apply to that distribution. Furthermore, an election under this section does not relieve the U.S. recipient from the information reporting requirements of section 6048(c).

(3) *Time and manner of making the election.*—(i) *When to make the election.*—The election is made on a timely filed Form 708 for the calendar year for which the foreign trust seeks to subject itself to the section 2801 tax as described in paragraph (d)(2)(i) of this section. The election may be made for a calendar year whether or not the foreign trust received a covered gift or covered bequest during that calendar year. See §28.6071-1.

(ii) *Requirements for a valid election.*—To make a valid election to be treated as a domestic trust for purposes of section 2801, the electing foreign trust must timely file a Form 708 and must, on such form—

(A) Make the election, timely pay the section 2801 tax, if any, as determined under paragraph (d)(3)(iii) of this section, and include a computation illustrating how the trustee of the electing foreign trust calculated both the section 2801 ratio described in paragraph (c)(1)(ii) of this section and the section 2801 tax;

(B) Designate and authorize a U.S. agent as provided in paragraph (d)(3)(iv) of this section;

(C) Agree to file Form 708 annually;

(D) List the amount and year of all prior distributions attributable to covered gifts and covered bequests made to a U.S. recipient and provide the name, address, and taxpayer identification number of each U.S. recipient; and

(E) Notify each permissible distributee that the trustee is making the election under this paragraph (d) and provide to the IRS a list of the name, address, and taxpayer identification number of each permissible distributee. For this purpose, a permissible distributee is any U.S. citizen or resident who:

(1) Currently may or must receive distributions from the trust, whether of income or principal;

(2) May withdraw income or principal from the trust, regardless of whether the right arises or lapses upon the occurrence of a future event; or

(3) Would have been described in paragraph (d)(3)(ii)(E)*(1)* of this section if either the interests of all persons described in (d)(3)(ii)(E)*(1)* or (E)*(2)* had just terminated or the trust had just terminated.

(iii) *Section 2801 tax payable with the election.*—To make a valid election to be treated as a domestic trust for purposes of section 2801, the electing foreign trust must timely pay the section 2801 tax on all covered gifts and covered bequests received by the electing foreign trust in the calendar year for which the Form 708 is being filed. In some cases, an electing foreign trust may have received covered gifts or covered bequests in prior calendar years during which no such election was in effect. In those cases, the trustee must also, at the same time, report and pay the tax on the fair market value, determined as of the last day of the calendar year immediately preceding the year for which the Form 708 is being filed, of the portion of the trust attributable to covered gifts and covered bequests received by such trust in prior calendar years (except as provided in paragraph (d)(6)(iii) of this section with regard to an imperfect election). That portion is determined by multiplying the fair market value of the trust, as of the December 31 immediately preceding the year for which the election is made, by the section 2801 ratio in effect on that date, as calculated under paragraph (c)(1)(ii) of this section. If the trustee does not have sufficient books and records to determine what amount of the corpus and undistributed income is attributable to undistributed prior covered gifts and covered bequests, then that amount is deemed to be the entire fair market value of the trust as of that December 31. See paragraph (c)(3) of this section.

(iv) *Designation of U.S. agent.*—(A) *In general.*—The trustee of an electing foreign trust must designate and authorize a U.S. person, as defined in section 7701(a)(30), to act as an agent for the trust solely for purposes of section 2801. By designating a U.S. agent, the trustee of the foreign trust agrees to provide the agent with all information necessary to comply with any information request or summons issued by the Secretary. Such information may include, without limitation, copies of the books and records of the trust, financial statements, and appraisals of trust property.

(B) *Role of designated agent.*—Acting as an agent for the trust for purposes of section 2801 includes serving as the electing foreign trust's agent for purposes of section 7602 ("Examination of books and witnesses"), section 7603 ("Service of summons"), and section 7604 ("Enforcement of summons") with respect to—

(1) Any request by the Secretary to examine records or produce testimony related to the proper identification or treatment of covered gifts or covered bequests contributed to the electing foreign trust and distributions attributable to such contributions; and

(2) Any summons by the Secretary for records or testimony related to the proper identification or treatment of covered gifts or covered bequests contributed to the electing foreign trust and distributions attributable to such contributions.

(C) *Effect of appointment of U.S. agent.*—An electing foreign trust that appoints such an agent is not considered to have an office or a permanent establishment in the United States, or to be engaged in a trade or business in the United States, solely because of the agent's activities as an agent pursuant to this section.

(4) *Annual certification or filing requirement.*—The trustee of an electing foreign trust must file a timely Form 708 annually either to report and pay the section 2801 tax on all covered gifts and covered bequests received by the trust during the calendar year, or to certify that the electing foreign trust did not receive any

covered gifts or covered bequests during the calendar year.

(5) *Duration of status as electing foreign trust.*—(i) *In general.*—A valid election (one that meets all of the requirements of paragraph (d)(3) of this section) is effective as of January 1 of the calendar year for which the Form 708 on which the election is made is filed. The election, once made, applies for all calendar years until the election is terminated as described in paragraph (d)(5)(ii) of this section.

(ii) *Termination.*—An election to be treated as a domestic trust for purposes of section 2801 is terminated either by the failure of the foreign trust to make the annual filing, together with any payment of the section 2801 tax, as required by paragraph (d)(4) of this section, or by the failure of the foreign trust to timely pay any additional amount of section 2801 tax (in accordance with the requirements of paragraph (d)(6)(ii) of this section) with respect to recalculations described in paragraph (d)(6) of this section (a failure that results in an imperfect election). A termination, if any, is effective as of the beginning of the calendar year for which the trustee fails to make the annual filing required by paragraph (d)(4) of this section or for which the trustee fails to pay any of the amounts described in this paragraph (d)(5)(ii). In the case of a terminated election, the trustee should notify promptly each permissible distributee, as defined in paragraph (d)(3)(ii)(E) of this section, that the foreign trust's election was terminated as of January 1 of the applicable year (with the actual year of the termination being set forth in the notice), and that each U.S. recipient of a distribution made from the foreign trust on and after that date is subject to the section 2801 tax on the portion of each such distribution that is attributable to covered gifts and covered bequests. See paragraph (d)(6)(iii)(B) of this section for an additional notification requirement in the case of an imperfect election.

(iii) *Subsequent elections.*—If a foreign trust's election is terminated under paragraph (d)(5)(ii) of this section, the foreign trust is not prohibited from making another election in a future year, subject to the requirements of paragraph (d)(3) of this section.

(6) *Dispute as to amount of section 2801 tax owed by electing foreign trust.*—(i) *Procedure.*—If the Commissioner disputes the value of a covered gift or covered bequest, or otherwise challenges the computation of the section 2801 tax, that is reported on the electing foreign trust's timely filed Form 708 for any calendar year, the Commissioner will issue a letter (but not a notice of deficiency as defined in section 6212) to the trustee of the electing foreign trust and the appointed U.S. agent that details the disputed information and the proper amount of section 2801 tax as recalculated. The foreign trust must pay the additional amount of section 2801 tax including interest and penalties, if any, in accordance with the requirements of paragraph (d)(6)(ii) of this section, on or before the due date specified in the letter to maintain its election.

(ii) *Effect of timely paying the additional section 2801 tax amount.*—If the trustee of the foreign trust timely pays the additional amount(s) specified in the Commissioner's letter, or such other amount as agreed to by the Commissioner, and enters into a closing agreement with the IRS as described in section 7121, then the foreign trust's election to be treated as a domestic trust under paragraph (d) of this section remains in effect. In addition, in the absence of fraud, malfeasance, or misrepresentation of a material fact, that payment, in conjunction with the closing agreement, will be deemed to render any determination of value to which the closing agreement applies as final and binding on both the IRS and the foreign trust. Thus, subsequently, the IRS will not be able to challenge the section 2801 tax due from either the foreign trust or any of its beneficiaries who are U.S. citizens or residents for the year for which that Form 708 was filed by the foreign trust, except with respect to any covered gifts or covered bequests not reported on that return, and neither the foreign trust nor any of its beneficiaries will be able to file a claim for refund with respect to section 2801 tax paid by the foreign trust on the covered gifts and covered bequests reported on that Form 708.

(iii) *Effect of failing to timely pay the additional section 2801 tax amount (imperfect election).*—(A) *In general.*—If the foreign trust fails to timely pay the additional amount of section 2801 tax with interest and penalties, if any, claimed to be due by the IRS in accordance with the requirements of paragraph (d)(6)(ii) of this section, then the foreign trust's valid election is terminated and becomes an imperfect election. The foreign trust's election is terminated, and is converted into an imperfect election, retroactively as of the first day of the calendar year for which was filed the Form 708 with respect to which the additional amount of section 2801 tax is claimed to be due by the IRS. Thus, the value the foreign trust has reported on the Form 708 and on which the trust has paid the section 2801 tax is no longer considered to be attributable to covered gifts or covered bequests when computing the section 2801 ratio described in paragraph (c)(1)(ii) of this section applicable to distributions made by the foreign trust to U.S. recipients during the calendar year for which the Form 708 was filed and thereafter. The U.S. recipients of distributions from the foreign trust, however, should take into consideration the additional value determined by the IRS, on which the foreign trust did not timely pay the section 2801 tax, when computing the section 2801 ratio to be applied to a distribution from the trust. See paragraph (c) of this section. Any disagreement with regard to that additional value will be an issue to be resolved as part of the review of that U.S. recipient's own Form 708 reporting a distribution.

(B) *Notice to permissible beneficiaries.*—If the trustee of the foreign trust fails to remit the additional payment of the section 2801 tax including all interest and penalties, if any, in accordance with the requirements of paragraph (d)(6)(ii) of this section, by the due date stated in the IRS letter, the trustee should notify promptly each permissible distributee, as defined in paragraph (d)(3)(ii)(E) of this section, of the amount of additional value on which the foreign trust did not timely pay the section 2801 tax as determined by the IRS and that:

(*1*) The foreign trust's election was terminated as of January 1 of the applicable year (with the actual year of the termination being set forth in the notice); and

(2) Each U.S. recipient of a distribution made from the foreign trust on and after that termination date is subject to the section 2801 tax on the portion of each such distribution attributable to covered gifts and covered bequests.

(C) *Reasonable cause*.—If a U.S. recipient received a distribution from such trust on or after January 1 of the year for which the election was terminated and the election became an imperfect election, provided the U.S. recipient files a Form 708 and pays the section 2801 tax within a reasonable period of time after being notified by the trustee of the foreign trust or otherwise becoming aware that a valid election was not in effect when the distribution was made, the U.S. recipient's failure to timely file and pay are due to reasonable cause and not willful neglect for purposes of section 6651. For this purpose, a reasonable period of time is not more than six months after the U.S. recipient is notified by the trustee or the U.S. recipient otherwise becomes aware that a valid election is not in effect.

(D) *Interim period*.—If a foreign trust's valid election is terminated and becomes an imperfect election, there is a period of time (interim period) after the effective date of the termination of the election during which both the foreign trust and its U.S. beneficiaries are likely to continue to comply with section 2801 as it applies to an electing foreign trust with a valid election in place. The interim period begins on the effective date of the termination of the foreign trust's election that resulted in an imperfect election as described in paragraph (d)(6)(iii)(A) of this section, and ends on December 31 of the calendar year immediately preceding the calendar year in which the additional section 2801 tax claimed by the IRS is due. As under the rule in paragraph (d)(6)(iii)(A) of this section regarding imperfect elections, the covered gifts and covered bequests received by the foreign trust during this interim period, which the foreign trust has reported on its timely filed Form 708 and on which the foreign trust has timely paid the section 2801 tax, are no longer considered to be covered gifts and covered bequests for purposes of computing the section 2801 ratio described in paragraph (c)(1)(ii) of this section as it applies to distributions made by non-electing foreign trusts to their U.S. beneficiaries. In addition, each distribution made by the foreign trust to a U.S. citizen or resident during this interim period must be reported on that U.S. recipient's Form 708 by applying the section 2801 ratio to that distribution. Once the interim period has ended, the foreign trust has no election in place and the rules of section 2801(e)(4)(B)(i) will apply until the foreign trust subsequently (if ever) makes another valid election to be treated as a domestic trust for purposes of section 2801.

(7) *No overpayment caused solely by virtue of defect in election*.—Any remittance of section 2801 tax made by a foreign trust electing to be treated as a domestic trust does not become an overpayment solely by virtue of a defect in the election. Instead, if at some subsequent time the IRS determines that the election was not in fact a valid election, then the election shall be considered valid only with respect to the covered gifts or covered bequests on which the section 2801 tax was timely paid by the foreign trust and each covered gift and covered bequest on which the section 2801 tax has been timely paid is no longer treated as a covered gift or covered bequest for purposes of determining the portion of the foreign trust attributable to covered gifts and covered bequests. See paragraphs (d)(2)(i) and (d)(6)(iii) of this section.

(e) *Examples*.—The provisions of this section are illustrated by the following examples.

Example 1. Computation of section 2801 ratio. A and B each contribute $100,000 to a foreign trust. A (but not B) is a covered expatriate and A's contribution is a covered gift. The section 2801 ratio immediately after these two contributions is 0.50, computed as follows: the pre-contribution value of the trust ($0) times the pre-contribution section 2801 ratio (-0-), plus the current covered gift ($100,000), divided by the post-contribution fair market value of the trust ($200,000). See § 28.2801-5(c). Therefore, 50 percent of each distribution from the trust is subject to the section 2801 tax until the next contribution is made to the trust. If the trustee distributes $40,000 to C, a U.S. citizen, before the trust receives any other contributions, then $20,000 ($40,000 x 0.5) is a covered gift to C.

Example 2. Computation of section 2801 ratio when multiple contributions are made to foreign trust. (i) In 2005, A, a U.S. citizen, established and funded an irrevocable foreign trust with $200,000 and reported the transfer as a completed gift. On January 1 of each of the following three years (2006 through 2008), A contributed an additional $100,000 to the foreign trust. A reported A's contributions to the foreign trust as completed gifts on timely filed Forms 709, for calendar years 2005 through 2008. On August 8, 2008, a date after the effective date of section 2801 (June 17, 2008), A expatriated and became a covered expatriate. On January 1 of a year after 2008 (Year X), A makes an additional $100,000 contribution to the trust. The aggregate $600,000 contributed to the trust by A, both before and after expatriation, are the only contributions to the trust. Each year, the trustee of the foreign trust provides beneficiary B, a U.S. citizen, with an accounting of the trust showing each receipt and disbursement of the trust during that year, including the date and amount of each contribution by A.

(ii) The fair market value of the trust was $610,000 immediately prior to A's contribution to the trust on January 1, Year X. Therefore, upon the Year X contribution of A's first and only covered gift, the portion of the trust attributable to covered gifts and covered bequests (covered portion) changed from zero to 0.14 ([(section 2801 ratio of 0 x $610,000 fair market value pre-contribution) plus the $100,000 covered gift]/ $710,000 fair market value post-contribution). See paragraph (c) of this section.

(iii) In February of Year X, B received a distribution of $225,000 from the foreign trust. Although A contributed a total of $600,000 to the foreign trust, A contributed only $100,000 while A was a covered expatriate. Under paragraph (c) of this section, the portion of the $225,000 distribution from the foreign trust attributable to a covered gift is $31,500 ($225,000 x 0.14 (section 2801 ratio)) because the distribution is made proportionally from the covered and non-covered portions of the trust. See paragraph (c)(1) of this section. Accordingly, B received a covered gift of $31,500.

(iv) Pursuant to the terms of the foreign trust, the trust made a terminating distribution on August 5, Year X, when B turned 35, and B received the balance of the appreciated trust, $505,000. The portion of this distribution attributable to covered gifts and covered bequests is $70,700 ($505,000 x 0.14). Therefore, B has received covered gifts from the foreign trust during Year X in the total amount of $102,200 ($31,500 + $70,700).

Example 3. Termination of foreign trust election. The trustee of a foreign trust that received a covered gift makes a valid election to be treated as a domestic trust under § 28.2801-5(d) for Year 1. However, the trustee fails to file timely the Form 708 for the next year, Year 2. The foreign trust election is terminated as of January 1, Year 2, under paragraph (d)(5)(ii) of this section. Thus, any distributions made to U.S. recipients during Year 1 have a section 2801 ratio of zero and are not subject to the section 2801 tax. However, any such distributions made during Year 2 are subject to the section 2801 tax to the extent the distributions are attributable to a covered gift or covered bequest received by the trust during Year 2. Unless the trustee makes a new election as described in paragraph (d)(5)(iii) of this section, beginning in Year 2, the foreign trust's section 2801 ratio must be recomputed each time the foreign trust receives a contribution.

Example 4. Imperfect election by foreign trust. (i) In Year 1, CE, a covered expatriate, gives a 20 percent limited partnership interest in a closely held business to a foreign trust created for the benefit of CE's child, A, who is a U.S. citizen. The limited partnership interest is a covered gift. The trustee of the foreign trust makes a valid election to have the trust treated as a domestic trust for purposes of section 2801, trustee timely files a Form 708, and timely pays the section 2801 tax on the reported fair market value of the covered gift ($500,000). Later in Year 1, the trust makes a $100,000 distribution to A.

(ii) In Year 2, CE contributes $200,000 in cash to the foreign trust. The cash is a covered gift. The trustee of the foreign trust timely files a Form 708 reporting the transfer and pays the section 2801 tax. The trust does not make a distribution to any beneficiary during Year 2. Late in Year 3, the IRS disputes the reported value of the partnership interest transferred in Year 1 and determines that the proper valuation on the date of the gift was $800,000. In Year 3, the IRS issues a letter to the trustee of the foreign trust detailing its finding of the increased valuation and of the resulting additional section 2801 tax including accrued interest, if any, due on or before a later date in Year 3 specified in the letter. The foreign trust fails to pay the additional section 2801 tax liability on or before that due date.

(iii) Under paragraph (d)(6)(iii) of this section, the foreign trust's election for Year 1 is an imperfect election; although it timely filed its return reporting the transfer and paid the tax, it failed to timely pay the additional section 2801 tax when the IRS notified the trust of an additional amount of section 2801 tax claimed to be due. Accordingly, the foreign trust's election is deemed to have terminated as of January 1 of Year 1. In computing the foreign trust's section 2801 ratio upon the receipt of the covered gift in Year 1, the $500,000 of value on which the section 2801 tax was timely paid is no longer deemed to be a covered gift. See paragraph (d)(6)(iii) of this section. When the trustee advises A of the letter from the IRS, A must file a late Form 708 reporting the portion of the Year 1 distribution attributable to covered gifts and covered bequests. Although A may owe section 2801 tax and interest, A will not owe any penalties under section 6651 as long as A files the Form 708 and pays the tax within a reasonable period of time after A receives notice of the termination of the election from the trustee of the foreign trust or otherwise becomes aware of the termination of the election. See paragraph (d)(6)(iii)(C) of this section.

(iv) When A files the Form 708, the IRS will verify whether A treated the $300,000 undervaluation claimed by the IRS as a covered gift in computing the section 2801 ratio. As with any other item reported on that return, A has the burden to prove the value of the covered gift to the foreign trust, and the IRS may challenge that value. If A treats the $300,000 as a covered gift to the trust, under paragraph (c)(1)(ii) of this section, the section 2801 ratio after the Year 1 contribution is 0.375 ($0 + ($300,000)/$800,000)). Thus, 37.5 percent of all distributions made to A from the foreign trust during Year 1 are subject to the section 2801 tax.

(v) The foreign trust's timely filing of the Form 708 for Year 2 and the timely payment of the section 2801 tax shown on that return is not a valid election under paragraph (d)(5)(iii) of this section because the trust did not timely pay the section 2801 tax on all covered gifts and covered bequests in prior years as required in paragraph (d)(3) of this section; that is, the tax on the additional $300,000 of value of the Year 1 transfer. However, under paragraph (d)(6)(iii)(D) of this section, because the foreign trust timely filed and paid the section 2801 tax on the Year 2 covered gift of $200,000, and the additional unpaid tax was not due until Year 3, the $200,000 amount is no longer considered a covered gift for purposes of computing the section 2801 ratio.

Example 5. Subsequent election after termination of foreign trust election. The facts are the same as in *Example 4*. In Year 3, the foreign trust does not receive a covered gift or covered bequest. However, the trustee decides that making another election to be treated as a domestic trust would be in the best interests of the trust's beneficiaries. Accordingly, by the due date for the Form 708 for Year 3, the trustee timely files the return and pays the section 2801 tax on the portion of the trust attributable to covered gifts and covered bequests. See paragraph (d)(5)(iii) of this section. The trustee calculates the portion of the trust attributable to covered gifts and covered bequests received by the trust in prior calendar years by multiplying the fair market value of the trust on December 31, Year 2, by the section 2801 ratio in effect on that date. See paragraph (d)(3)(iii) of this section. The foreign trust is an electing foreign trust in Year 3.

(f) *Effective/applicability date.*—This section applies on and after the date of publication of a Treasury decision adopting these rules as final regulations in the **Federal Register**. Once these regulations have been published as final regulations in the **Federal Register**, taxpayers may rely upon the final rules of this part for the period beginning June 17, 2008, and ending on the date preceding the date these regulations are published as final regulations in the **Federal Register**. [Reg. § 28.2801-5.]

§ 28.2801-6. Special rules and cross-references.—(a) *Determination of basis.*—For purposes of determining the U.S. recipient's basis in property received as a covered gift or covered bequest, see sections 1015 and 1014, respectively. However, section 1015(d) does not apply to increase the basis in a covered gift to reflect the tax paid under this section. For purposes of determining a U.S. recipient's basis in property received as a covered bequest from a decedent who died during 2010 and whose executor elected under section 301(c) of the Tax Relief, Unemployment Insurance Reauthorization, and Job Creation Act of 2010 not to have the estate tax provisions apply, see section 1022.

(b) *Generation-skipping transfer tax.*—Transfers made by a nonresident not a citizen of the United States (NRA transferor) are subject to generation-skipping transfer (GST) tax only to the extent those transfers are subject to federal estate or gift tax as defined in § 26.2652-1(a)(2). In applying this rule, taxable distributions from a trust and taxable terminations are subject to the GST tax only to the extent the NRA transferor's contributions to the trust were subject to federal estate or gift tax as defined in § 26.2652-1(a)(2). See § 26.2663-2. A transfer is subject to federal estate or gift tax, regardless of whether a federal estate or gift tax return reporting the transfer is timely filed and regardless of whether chapter 15 applies because of a covered expatriate's failure to timely file and pay the section 2801 tax, if applicable.

(c) *Information returns.*—(1) *Gifts and bequests.*—Pursuant to section 6039F and the corresponding regulations, and to the extent provided in Notice 97-34, 1997-1 CB 422, and Form 3520, Part IV, each U.S. person (other than an organization described in section 501(c) and exempt from tax under section 501(a)) who treats an amount received from a foreign person (other than through a foreign trust) as a gift or bequest (including a covered gift or covered bequest) must report such gift or bequest on Part IV of Form 3520 if the value of the total of such gifts and bequests exceeds a certain threshold. A U.S. citizen or resident, as defined in § 28.2801-2(b) but not including a foreign trust that elects to be treated as a domestic trust, is included within the definition of a U.S. person for purposes of section 6039F.

(2) *Foreign trust distributions.*—Pursuant to section 6048(c) and the corresponding regulations, and to the extent provided in Notice 97-34 and Part III of Form 3520, U.S. persons must report each distribution received during the taxable year from a foreign trust on Part III of Form 3520. Under section 6677(a), a penalty of the greater of $10,000 or 35 percent of the gross value of the distribution may be imposed on a U.S. person who fails to timely report the distribution. A U.S. citizen or resident as defined in § 28.2801-2(b), but not including a foreign trust that elects to be treated as a domestic trust, generally is required to report such a distribution under section 6048(c).

(3) *Penalties and use of information.*—The filing of Form 706, Form 706-NA, Form 708, or Form 709 does not relieve a U.S. citizen or resident who is required to file Form 3520 from any penalties imposed under section 6677(a) for failure to comply with section 6048(c), or from any penalties imposed under section 6039F(c) for failure to comply with section 6039F(a). Pursuant to section 6039F(c)(1)(A), the Secretary may determine the tax consequences of the receipt of a purported foreign gift or bequest.

(d) *Application of penalties.*—(1) *Accuracy-related penalties on underpayments.*—The section 6662 accuracy-related penalty may be imposed upon any underpayment of tax attributable to—

(i) A substantial valuation understatement under section 6662(g) of a covered gift or covered bequest; or

(ii) A gross valuation misstatement under section 6662(h) of a covered gift or covered bequest.

(2) *Penalty for substantial and gross valuation misstatements attributable to incorrect appraisals.*—The section 6695A penalty for substantial and gross valuation misstatements attributable to incorrect appraisals may be imposed upon any person who prepares an appraisal of the value of a covered gift or covered bequest.

(3) *Penalty for failure to file a return and to pay tax.*—See section 6651 for the application of a penalty for the failure to file Form 708, or the failure to pay the section 2801 tax.

(e) *Effective/applicability date.*—This section applies on and after the date of publication of a Treasury decision adopting these rules as final regulations in the **Federal Register**. Once these regulations have been published as final regulations in the **Federal Register**, taxpayers may rely upon the final rules of this part for the period beginning June 17, 2008, and ending on the date preceding the date these regulations are published as final regulations in the **Federal Register**. [Reg. § 28.2801-6.]

§ 28.2801-7. Determining responsibility under section 2801.—(a) *Responsibility of recipients of gifts and bequests from expatriates.*—It is the responsibility of the taxpayer (in this case, the U.S. citizen or resident receiving a gift or bequest from an expatriate or a distribution from a foreign trust funded at least in part by an expatriate) to ascertain the taxpayer's obligations under section 2801, which includes making the determination of whether the transferor is a covered expatriate and whether the transfer is a covered gift or covered bequest.

(b) *Disclosure of return and return information.*—(1) *In general.*—In certain circumstances, the Internal Revenue Service (IRS) may be permitted, upon request of a U.S. citizen or resident in receipt of a gift or bequest from an expatriate, to disclose to the U.S. citizen or resident return or return information of the donor or decedent expatriate that may assist the U.S. citizen or resident in determining whether the donor or decedent was a covered expatriate and whether the transfer was a covered gift or covered bequest. The U.S. citizen or resident may not rely upon this information, however, if the U.S. citizen or resident knows, or has reason to know, that the information received from the IRS is incorrect. The circumstances under which such information may be disclosed to a U.S. citizen or resident, and the procedures for requesting such information from the IRS, will be as provided by publication in the Internal Revenue Bulletin (see § 601.601(d)(2)(ii)(b)).

(2) *Rebuttable presumption.*—Unless a living donor expatriate authorizes the disclosure of his or her relevant return or return information to the U.S. citizen or resident receiving the gift, there is a rebuttable presumption that the donor is a covered expatriate and that the gift is a covered gift. A taxpayer who reasonably concludes that a gift or bequest is not subject to section 2801 may file a protective Form 708 in accordance with §28.6011-1(b) to start the period for the assessment of any section 2801 tax.

(c) *Effective/applicability date.*—This section applies on and after the date of publication of a Treasury decision adopting these rules as final regulations in the **Federal Register**. Once these regulations have been published as final regulations in the **Federal Register**, taxpayers may rely upon the final rules of this part for the period beginning June 17, 2008, and ending on the date preceding the date these regulations are published as final regulations in the **Federal Register**. [Reg. §28.2801-7.]

WITHHOLDING FROM WAGES

Fringe Benefits: Taxability

Fringe Benefits: Taxability.—Reg. §31.3401(a)-1T, relating to the treatment of taxable and nontaxable fringe benefits, is proposed (published in the Federal Register on January 7, 1985) (LR-216-84).

§31.3401(a)-1T. Question and answer relating to the definition of wages in section 3401(a).

Securities: Basis Reporting: Basis Determination

Securities: Basis Reporting: Basis Determination.—Amendments to Reg. §31.3406(b)(3)-2, relating to reporting sales of securities by brokers and determining the basis of securities, are proposed (published in the Federal Register on December 17, 2009) (REG-101896-09).

Par. 16. Section 31.3406(b)(3)-2 is amended by revising paragraph (b)(4) to read as follows:

§31.3406(b)(3)-2. Reportable barter exchanges and gross proceeds of sales of securities or commodities by brokers.

* * *

(b) * * *

(4) *Security short sales.*—(i) *Short sales closed before January 1, 2011.*—(A) *Amount subject to backup withholding.*—The amount subject to withholding under section 3406 with respect to a short sale of securities closed before January 1, 2011, is the gross proceeds (as defined in §1.6045-1(d)(5) of this chapter) of the short sale. At the option of the broker, however, the amount subject to withholding may be the gain upon the closing of the short sale (if any); consequently, the obligation to withhold under section 3406 is deferred until the closing transaction. A broker may use this alternative method of determining the amount subject to withholding under section 3406 for a short sale only if at the time the short sale is initiated, the broker expects that the amount of gain realized upon the closing of the short sale will be determinable from the broker's records. If, due to events unforeseen at the time the short sale was initiated, the broker is unable to determine the basis of the property used to close the short sale, the property is assumed for this purpose to have a basis of zero.

(B) *Time of backup withholding.*—For short sales closed before January 1, 2011, the determination of whether a short seller is subject to withholding under section 3406 must be made on the date of the initiation or closing, as the case may be, or on the date that the initiation or closing, as the case may be, is entered on the broker's books and records.

(ii) *Short sales closed on or after January 1, 2011.*—For short sales closed on or after January 1, 2011, the obligation to withhold under section 3406 is deferred until the short sale is considered closed under section 1233. The determination of whether a short seller is subject to withholding under section 3406 may be made as of either this date or the date that the closing transaction is entered on the broker's books and records. The amount subject to withholding under section 3406 is the gross proceeds (as defined in §1.6045-1(d)(5) of this chapter) of the short sale. At the option of the broker, however, the amount subject to withholding may be the gain upon the closing of the short sale (if any) if the broker reports both the gross proceeds and basis of the securities on the return of information required by section 6045.

* * *

GENERAL PROVISIONS RELATING TO EMPLOYMENT TAXES

Fringe Benefits: Taxability

Fringe Benefits: Taxability.—Reg. §31.3501(a)-1T, relating to the treatment of taxable and nontaxable fringe benefits, is proposed and, when adopted, would become Reg. §31.3501(a)-1 (published in the Federal Register on January 7, 1985) (LR-216-84).

§31.3501(a)-1. Question and answer relting to the time employers must collect and pay the taxes on noncash fringe benefits.

Employment Taxes

Employment Taxes: Real Estate Agents and Direct Sellers: Employer's Liability.—Reproduced below are the texts of proposed Reg. §§31.3508-1 and 31.3509-1, relating to the treatment of qualified real estate agents and direct sellers as nonemployees, to the determination of employer liability for income tax withholding and employee social security taxes where the employer treated an employee as a nonemployee for purposes of such taxes, and to information reporting of direct sales and payments of remuneration for services (published in the Federal Register on January 7, 1986).

☐ Par. 2. There are inserted immediately after §31.3507-2 the following two new sections.

§31.3508-1. Treatment of qualified real estate agents and direct sellers as nonemployees.—(a) *In general.*—For Federal income and employment tax purposes,

(1) An individual who performs services after December 31, 1982, as a qualified real estate agent or as a direct seller shall not be treated as an employee with respect to such services, and

(2) The service-recipient shall not be treated as an employer with respect to such services.

(b) *Qualified real estate agent defined.*—(1) *In general.*—For purposes of section 3508 and this section, the term "qualified real estate agent" means any individual who is a sales person (including an individual who does not personally make sales but who recruits, trains, or supervises other individuals who make sales) if—

(i) Such individual is a licensed real estate agent,

(ii) Substantially all of the remuneration (whether or not paid in cash) for the services performed by such individual as a real estate agent is directly related to sales or other output (including the performance of services) rather than to the number of hours worked, and

(iii) The services performed by such individual as a real estate agent are performed pursuant to a written contract between such individual and the service-recipient and the contract provides that such individual will not be treated as an employee with respect to such services for Federal tax purposes.

(2) *Services performed as a real estate agent.*—For purposes of this section, the services performed by an individual as a real estate agent include any activities that customarily are performed in connection with the sale of an interest in real property. Such services include the advertising or showing of real property, the acquisition of a lease to real property, and the recruitment, training, or supervision of other real estate sales persons. Such services also include the appraisal activities of a licensed real estate agent in connection with the sale of real property. Services performed as a real estate agent do not include the management of property.

(c) *Direct seller defined.*—(1) *In general.*—For purposes of section 3508 and this section, the term "direct seller" means any person if—

(i) Such person—

(A) Is engaged in the trade or business of selling (or soliciting the sale of) consumer products to any buyer on a buy-sell or deposit-commission basis for resale by the buyer or any other person in the home or in some other place that does not constitute a permanent retail establishment, or

(B) Is engaged in the trade or business of selling (or soliciting the sale of) consumer products in the home or in some other place that does not constitute a permanent retail establishment,

(ii) Substantially all the remuneration (whether or not paid in cash) for the performance of the services described in paragraph (c)(2) of this section is directly related to sales or other output (including the performance of services) rather than to the number of hours worked, and

(iii) Such person performs the services described in paragraph (c)(2) of this section pursuant to a written contract between such person and the service-recipient, and the contract provides that such person will not be treated as an employee with respect to such services for Federal tax purposes.

(2) *Services performed as a direct seller.*—(i) *In general.*—The services described in this paragraph (c)(2) are any services that customarily are directly related to the trade or business of selling (or soliciting the sale of) consumer products in the home or in any other location that does not constitute a permanent retail establishment. Such services include any activity to increase the productivity of other individuals engaged in such sales, such as recruiting, training, motivating, and counseling such individuals. Except as provided in paragraph (c)(2)(ii) of this section, such services do not include the installation or construction on the customer's property of a consumer product. See paragraphs (f) and (g)(3) of this section for the inapplicability of section 3508 where the sale or use of consumer products is only incidental to the rendering of services.

(ii) *Installation of consumer product in conjunction with the sale of such product.*—If an individual engaged in the trade or business of selling consumer products performs installation services in conjunction with the sale of a consumer product such services shall be included as services performed as a direct seller only if the value of such installation services is 10 percent or less of the purchase price of such consumer product (including installation). If the value of such installation services exceeds 10 percent of the purchase price of the consumer product (including installation) the installation services shall not be included as services performed as a direct seller. See paragraph (j) of this section for treatment of dual services under section 3508.

(d) *Substantially all remuneration directly related to sales or other output.*—(1) *Substantially all remuneration.*—(i) *In general.*—The requirement of paragraph (b)(1)(ii) or (c)(1)(ii) of this section is satisfied for any calendar year with respect to the services described in such paragraph if at least 90 percent of the total remuneration, including advances and draws (except as provided in paragraph (d)(1)(ii) of this section), received by the individual from the service-recipient for performing such services during that calendar year is directly related to sales or other output rather than to the number of hours worked.

(ii) *Repayment of advances or draws.*—For purposes of paragraph (d)(1)(i) of this section, total remuneration received by an individual does not include any portion of an advance or draw that is repaid directly or indirectly (including repayment by a debit against the individual's account with the service-recipient) pursuant to a binding written agreement which on the date the advance or draw is received requires repayment of the amount by which such advance or draw exceeds the amount which is directly related to sales or other output (as defined in paragraph (d)(2) of this section). The determination of whether any amounts not excluded under this paragraph (d)(1)(ii) from the total remuneration received by an individual is directly related to sales or other output for purposes of paragraph (d)(1)(i) of this section is made on the basis of all the facts and circumstances (see paragraph (d)(2)(i) of this section).

(2) *Directly relating to sales or other output.*—(i) *In general.*—An item of remuneration is directly related to sales or other if that item is paid, awarded, or credited to the individual on the basis of the individual's services with respect to one or more specific sales transactions or the accomplishment of one or more specific tasks rather than on the basis of the number of hours worked. Whether an item of remuneration is directly related to sales or other output shall be determined on the basis of all the facts and circumstances. For purposes of this section an item of remuneration that is in the nature of salary, that is, a fixed periodical compensation paid for services rendered without regard to the amount of services rendered, shall be treated as an item or remuneration that is paid, awarded, or credited on the basis of the number of hours worked.

(ii) *Directly related to sales or output of some other person.*—For purposes of this section, remuneration received by an individual based on the sale or productivity of some other individual shall be treated as directly related to sales or other output if it was paid, awarded, or credited on the basis of such other individual's services with respect to one or more particular sales transactions or the accomplishment of one or more specific tasks.

(iii) *Remuneration received from a pool.*—Remuneration received by an individual under an arrangement whereby a service-recipient pools the remuneration of several individuals and a portion of the aggregate pooled remuneration is periodically distributed to each pool participant shall be treated as directly related to sales or other output only to the extent that the amount of remuneration received by that individual from the pool does not exceed the amount of remuneration that, in the absence of the pool arrangement, such individual would have received on the basis of the individual's services with respect to one or more specific sale transactions or the accomplishment of one or more specific tasks. Amounts received from the pool in excess of the amount that person would have ordinarily received for performing services in connection with such specific sales transactions or specific tasks are not directly related to sales or other output.

(e) *Written contract requirement.*—(1) *In general.*—Except as otherwise provided in paragraph (e)(2) of this section, a written contract that states that the individual will not be treated as an employee without specifically stating "for Federal tax purposes" does not meet the written contract requirements set forth in paragraph (b)(1)(iii) and (c)(1)(iii).

(2) *Existing contracts.*—(i) *In general.*—A contract which—

(A) Is in effect on or before February 28, 1983, and

(B) States that the individual performing the services will not be treated as an employee but does not specifically include the phrase "for Federal tax purposes," will be deemed to satisfy the written contract requirement if the service-recipient furnishes to the individual performing the services a written notice that specifically states that the individual will not be treated as an employee "for Federal tax purposes."

(ii) *Date contract requirement deemed satisfied.*—If the notice described in paragraph (e)(2)(i) of this section is mailed or otherwise furnished on or before February 28, 1983, the written contract requirement shall be deemed satisfied as of the date of the original contract. If the notice is furnished after that date, the written contract requirement is deemed satisfied as of the date the notice is furnished.

(f) *Trade or business of selling consumer products.*—For purposes of section 3508 and this section, a person is not engaged in the trade or business of selling (or soliciting the sale of) consumer products if the sale or use of such products is in an incidental part of a trade or business in which such person primarily renders services to clients. Whether the sale or use of a product is an incidental part of a trade or business that primarily consists of rendering services shall be determined on the basis of all the facts and circumstances, taking into account such factors as the cost of the product in relation to the cost of the service. Generally, the sale or use of a product is an incidental part of a trade or business that primarily consists of rendering services if the use of the product is necessary to the performance of the particular service (*e.g.*, insecticide in a pest control business). See paragraph (c)(2) of this section for the applicability of this section to individuals who install consumer products in conjunction with the sale of such products.

(g) *Definitions.*—(1) *Buy-sell basis.*—A transaction is on a buy-sell basis if the buyer performing the services is entitled to retain part or all of the difference between the price at which the buyer purchases the product and the price at which the buyer sells the product as part or all of the buyer's remuneration for the services.

(2) *Deposit-commission basis.*—A transaction is on a deposit-commission basis if the buyer performing the service is entitled to retain part or all of a purchase deposit paid by the consumer in connection with the transaction as part or all of the buyer's remuneration for the services.

(3) *Consumer product.*—The term "consumer product" means any tangible personal property which is distributed in commerce and which is normally used for personal, family, or household purposes (including any such prop-

erty intended to be attached to or installed in any real property without regard to whether it is so attached or installed). The term "consumer product" does not include any product used in the manufacture of another product to be distributed in commerce or any product used only incidentally in providing a service (*e.g.*, insecticide used in a pest control service, materials used in an appliance repair business).

(4) *Permanent retail establishment*.—A permanent retail establishment is any retail business operating in a structure or facility that remains stationary for a substantial period of time to which consumers go to purchase consumer goods. Examples of these establishments are: grocery stores, hardware stores, clothing stores, hotels, restaurants, drug stores, and newsstands.

In addition, amusement areas, such as amusement parks and sports arenas, at which consumer products are sold are permanent retail establishments. Portable or mobile structures, facilities, or equipment, such as street vendor stands and mobile carts or vehicles, generally do not constitute permanent retail establishments. However, sales of consumer products may occur in a permanent retail establishment for purposes of this section even though portable or mobile structures, facilities, or equipment is used. For example, a vendor who sells consumer products, such as souvenirs or food, in the stands of a sports arena or on the grounds of an amusement park sells consumer products in a permanent retail establishment. Also, a vendor who sells consumer products in a parking lot or other property which is near to and serving a sports arena or other amusement area pursuant to an agreement which grants to the vendor or to the service-recipient the right to sell consumer products on such property sells consumer products in a permanent retail establishment, regardless of whether the sale is made within a permanent structure.

(5) *Service-recipient*.—The term "service-recipient" means the person (other than a client or customer) for whom the services as a qualified real estate agent or direct seller are performed (*e.g.*, a real estate firm or a company whose consumer products are sold door-to-door).

(h) *No inference*.—The fact that an individual does not qualify under section 3508 and this section as a qualified real estate agent or as a direct seller with respect to any services does not create an inference that such individual is an employee or the service-recipient is an employer with respect to such services.

(i) *Application to statutory employees*.—A statutory employee (that is, an individual in one of the categories of workers defined in section 3121(d)(3) or 3306(i) to be employees) who meets the requirements of prargraph (b) or (c) of this section for classification as a qualified real estate agent or as a direct seller shall be treated as a nonemployee for Federal income tax, Federal Insurance Contribution Act (FICA), and Federal Unemployment Tax Act (FUTA) purposes with respect to services performed as a qualified real estate agent or as a direct seller (as described in paragraphs (b)(2) and (c)(2) of this section, respectively).

(j) *Dual services*.—(1) *In general*.—Section 3508 shall apply only with respect to services performed as a qualified real estate agent or a direct seller. Whether an individual is treated as an employee or as a self-employed individual with respect to services other than those performed as a qualified real estate agent or a direct seller shall be determined under common-law principles.

(2) *Examples*.—The following examples illustrate the principles set forth in this paragraph (j).

Example (1). A is a licensed real estate agent who performs services as a real estate agent pursuant to a written contract described in paragraph (b)(1)(iii) of this section. In addition to performing services as a real estate agent A performs general bookkeeping duties for the same service-recipient. All of the remuneration for the services performed as a real estate agent is directly related to sales. A will be treated as a nonemployee under section 3508 only with respect to A's services as a real estate agent. Whether A is treated as an employee or as a self-employed individual with respect to the bookkeeping duties will be determined under common-law principles.

Example (2). B is engaged in the trade or business of selling aluminum siding. B performs services as a direct seller pursuant to a written contract described in paragraph (c)(1)(iii) of this section. All sales are made in the customer's home and the purchase price includes installation. B installs all aluminum siding which he sells and receives a commission based upon the purchase price as compensation for his services with respect to both the sale and the installation. The value of such installation services exceeds 10 percent of the purchase price of the siding. B will be treated as a nonemployee under section 3508 only with respect to his services as a direct seller. Whether B is treated as an employee or as a self-employed individual with respect to services performed in installing the siding will be determined under common-law principles.

Example (3). The facts are the same as in example (2) excepts that B sells and installs personal computers and that the value of the installation services performed by B is less than 10 percent of the purchase price of the computers including installation. B is treated as a nonemployee under section 3508 with respect to both his services in selling the computers and in installing them. See paragraph (c)(2)(ii) of this section.

Example (4). Assume all the requirements of section 3508(b)(1) and paragraph (b) of this section are satisfied with respect to A, a real estate agent, except that A did not obtain a real estate license until March 29. The license was valid for the remainder of the year. A is treated as self-employed under section 3508 for that portion of the year beginning on March 29. Whether for Federal tax purposes A is to be treated as self-employed for the other portion of the year shall be determined under common law.

(k) *Coordination with retirement plans for self-employed*.—This section shall not prevent an individual who is treated as a self-employed under section 3508 from being covered under a qualified retirement plan for self-employed individuals pursuant to section 401(c)(1) of the Code. [Reg. § 31.3508-1.]

§ 31.3509-1. Determination of employer's liability for certain employment taxes.—(a) *In general*.—Except as otherwise provided in this section, if during any calendar year any employer fails to deduct and withhold any tax under chapter 24 (relating to withholding of income tax) or subchapter A of chapter 21 (relating to the social security tax on employees) of the Internal Revenue Code of 1954 with respect to any employee by reason of treating such employee as not being an employee for purposes of such chapter or subchapter, the amount of the employer's liability for such tax with respect to such year shall be determined under this paragraph (a).

(1) *Income tax withholding.*—The employer's liability for tax under chapter 24 for such year with respect to such employee shall be determined as if the amount required to be deducted and withheld were equal to 1.5 percent of the wages (defined in section 3401(a)) paid to such employee for such year.

(2) *Employee social security taxes.*—The employer's liability for employee social security taxes under subchapter A of chapter 21 for such year with respect to such employee shall be determined as if the taxes imposed under such subchapter were 20 percent of the amount imposed under such subchapter for such year without regard to this paragraph (a)(2).

Section 3509 and this section do not affect an employer's liability for taxes under subchapter B of chapter 21 (relating to employer social security taxes) of the Internal Revenue Code of 1954. See paragraph (c) of this section for increased employer liability where an employer fails to meet certain reporting requirements.

(b) *Definitions.*—(1) *Fails to deduct and withhold any tax.*—(i) *In general.*—For purposes of section 3509 and this section, an employer fails to deduct and withhold any tax under chapter 24 or under subchapter A of chapter 21 with respect to an employee for a calendar year if such employer fails to pay over the full amount of such tax required to be deducted and withheld during calendar year (determined without regard to section 3509 and this section) on or before the due date for the return relating to such tax for the final quarter of such calendar year.

(ii) *Example.*—The provisions of this paragraph (b)(1) may be illustrated by the following example:

Example. M, an employer, does not deduct and withhold income and social security taxes with respect to A, an employee, for the first quarter of 1985 because of M's erroneous belief that A is not an employee. On April 1, 1985, M ascertains the error and begins to withhold and deduct the full amount of income and social security taxes with respect to A for the remaining three quarters of 1985. M also makes timely adjustments under section 6205 with respect to the first quarter's taxes not deducted and withheld, and pays over the full amount of income and social security taxes which were required to be deducted and withheld during 1985 on or before the due date for the return for the fourth quarter of 1985. M has not failed to deduct and withhold income and social security taxes with respect to A during 1985 for purposes of section 3509 and this section.

(2) *Treatment of employee as not being an employee.*—For purposes of section 3509 and this section, an employer has treated an employee as not being an employee for purposes of the withholding requirements of chapter 24 or subchapter A of chapter 21 if, because of his belief that the employee was not an employee, the employer (i) has failed to deduct and withhold such tax as defined in paragraph (b)(1) of this section for the calendar year and (ii) has also failed to file one or more employment tax returns (including, where applicable, Forms 940 (Employer's Annual Federal Unemployment (FUTA) Tax Return), 941 (Employer's Quarterly Federal Tax Return), 942 (Employer's Quarterly Tax Return for Household Employees), 943 (Employer's Annual Tax Return for Agricultural Employees), and W-2 (Wage and Tax Statement)) for any period during the calendar year with respect to such employee. For purposes of this paragraph (b)(2) an employer who has filed a delinquent or amended employment tax return as a result of Internal Revenue Service compliance procedures (*i.e.*, examination or collection activities) has failed to file an employment tax return.

(c) *Employer's liability increased where employer fails to meet reporting requirements.*—(1) *In general.*—In the case of an employer who fails to meet the applicable requirements of section 6041(a), 6041A, or 6051 with respect to any employee, unless such failure is due to reasonable cause, paragraph (a) of this section shall be applied with respect to such employee:

(i) By substituting "3 percent" for "1.5 percent" in paragraph (a)(1) of this section; and

(ii) By substituting "40 percent" for "20 percent" in paragraph (a)(2) of this section.

(2) *Applicable requirement.*—For purposes of paragraph (c)(1) of this section, an employer has failed to meet the applicable requirements of section 6041(a), 6041A, or 6051 with respect to an employee if—

(i) The employer has treated such employee as not being an employee for purposes of the withholding requirements of chapter 24 or subchapter A of chapter 21, and

(ii) The employer has failed to satisfy any of the requirements described in sections 6041(a), 6041A, and 6051 and the regulations thereunder (relating to information returns and statements) which would be applicable consistent with the treatment described in paragraph (c)(2)(i) of this section.

An employer who has failed to timely file any return or statement required under section 6041(a), 6041A, or 6051 has failed to meet the applicable requirements of that section.

(d) *Special rules.*—For purposes of section 3509 and this section:

(1) *Determination of liability.*—If the amount of any employer's liability for tax with respect to an employee is determined under section 3509 and this section:

(i) Such employee's liability for income tax or employee social security taxes shall not be affected by the assessment or collection of any tax so determined and any amount assessed or collected as a result of the application of this section shall not be credited against the employee's tax liability;

(ii) Such employer shall not be entitled to recover from such employee any tax determined under this section;

(iii) Sections 3402(d) and 6521 shall not apply with respect to such employer's liability determined under this section, although section 6521 may apply with respect to an employee's liability regardless of whether the employer's liability is determined under section 3509; and

(iv) Tax imposed by section 3101 or 3402 (including amounts determined under section 3509) for any calendar year that the employer has reported and paid over with respect to such employee shall be allowed as a credit against tax determined under section 3509 with respect to such employee for such calendar year. If the amount of such reported and paid over tax exceeds the employer's liability for tax as determined under section 3509, however, such excess does not constitute an overpayment of tax and does not entitle the employer to a refund or credit for the amount of such excess.

(2) *Section not to apply where employer deducts and withholds income tax but not social security taxes.*—Section 3509 and this section shall not apply to any employer with respect to any wages if:

(i) The employer deducted and withheld any amount of the tax imposed by chapter 24 with respect to such wages, but

(ii) Failed to deduct and withhold the amount of the taxes imposed by subchapter A of chapter 21 with respect to such wages.

(3) *Section not to apply to social security tax with respect to certain statutory employees.*—Section 3509 and this section shall not apply to any tax under subchapter A of chapter 21 with respect to an individual described in section 3121(d)(3). For purposes of the preceding sentence, if an individual would be an employee under section 3121(d)(3) but for the fact that such individual is an employee under section 3121(d)(1) or (2), such individual shall be treated as an individual described in section 3121(d)(3).

(4) *Section not to apply in cases of intentional disregard.*—Section 3509 and this section shall not apply to the determination of any employer's liability for tax under chapter 24 or subchapter A of chapter 21 for any calendar year if any part of such liability is due to the employer's intentional disregard of the requirement to deduct and withhold such tax. For purposes of the preceding sentence, an employer has intentionally disregarded the requirement to deduct and withhold a tax if the employer intentionally failed to deduct and withhold the full amount of such tax with respect to any wages paid on or after the date on which the employer ascertained the employee status of a worker.

(5) *Section not to apply to assessments made before January 1, 1983.*—Section 3509 and this section shall not apply to any tax assessed before January 1, 1983.

(6) *Penalties.*—Section 3509 and this section do not relieve an employer from liability for any penalties, additions to tax, or additional amounts otherwise applicable with respect to a failure to deduct and withhold any taxes. However, for purposes of applying any penalty, addition to tax, or additional amount with respect to any tax for which an employer's liability is determined under section 3509, the employer's tax liability as determined under that section shall be treated as the tax the employer should have withheld, deducted, and paid over. [Reg. § 31.3509-1.]

Employment Taxes: Certified Professional Employer Organizations

Employment Taxes: Certified Professional Employer Organizations.—Reg. § 31.3511-1, setting forth the Federal employment tax liabilities and other obligations of persons certified by the IRS as certified professional employer organizations (CPEOs) in accordance with provisions enacted as part of The Stephen Beck, Jr., Achieving a Better Life Experience Act of 2014, is proposed (published in the Federal Register on May 6, 2016) (REG-127561-15).

Par. 2. Section 31.3511-1 is added to subpart F to read as follows:

§ 31.3511-1. Certified professional employer organization.—(a) *Treatment as employer.*—(1) *In general.*—For purposes of the federal employment taxes and other obligations imposed under chapters 21 through 25 of subtitle C of the Internal Revenue Code (federal employment taxes), a certified professional employer organization (CPEO) (as defined in § 301.7705-1T(b)(1) of this chapter) is treated as the employer of any covered employee (as defined in § 301.7705-1(b)(5) of this chapter), but only with respect to remuneration remitted by the CPEO to such covered employee.

(2) *Work site employee.*—In the case of a covered employee who is a work site employee (as defined in § 301.7705-1(b)(17) of this chapter), no person other than the CPEO is treated as the employer of the work site employee for purposes of federal employment taxes imposed on remuneration remitted by the CPEO to the work site employee.

(3) *Non-work site employee.*—In the case of a covered employee who is not a work site employee, a person other than the CPEO is also treated as an employer of the employee for purposes of federal employment taxes imposed on remuneration remitted by the CPEO to the employee if such person is determined to be an employer of the employee without regard to the application of this paragraph (a) and section 3511.

(b) *Exemptions, exclusions, definitions, and other rules.*—(1) *In general.*—Solely for purposes of federal employment taxes imposed on remuneration remitted by a CPEO to a covered employee, the application of exemptions, exclusions, definitions, and other rules that are based on the type of employer is presumed to be based on the type of employer of the customer of the CPEO for whom the covered employee performs services. If a covered employee performs services for more than one customer of the CPEO during the calendar year, the presumption described in the previous sentence applies separately to remuneration remitted by the CPEO to the covered employee for services performed with respect to each such customer.

(2) *Presumption rebutted.*—The presumption set forth in paragraph (b)(1) of this section may be rebutted if either the Commissioner determines, or the CPEO demonstrates by clear and convincing evidence, that the relationship between the customer and the covered employee is not the legal relationship of employer and employee as set forth in § 31.3401(c)-1. If such a determination or demonstration is made, then,

with respect to remuneration remitted by a CPEO to a covered employee, the application of exemptions, exclusions, definitions, and other rules that are based on the type of employer will be based on the type of employer of the person determined by the Commissioner or demonstrated by the CPEO to be the common law employer of the covered employee in accordance with §31.3401(c)-1.

(3) *No inference from presumption.*—The presumption set forth in paragraph (b)(1) of this section does not create any inference with respect to the determination of who is an employer or employee or whether the legal relationship of employer and employee exists for federal tax purposes or for purposes of any other provision of law (other than for paragraph (b)(1) of this section).

(c) *Annual wage limitation, contribution base, and withholding threshold.*—(1) *CPEO has separate taxable wage base, contribution base, and withholding threshold.*—For purposes of applying the annual wage limitations under sections 3121(a)(1) and 3306(b)(1) (relating to the Federal Insurance Contributions Act and the Federal Unemployment Tax Act, respectively), the contribution base under section 3231(e)(2) (relating to the Railroad Retirement Tax Act), and the withholding threshold under section 3102(f)(1) (relating to the Additional Medicare Tax), remuneration received by a covered employee from a CPEO for performing services for a customer of the CPEO within any calendar year is subject to a separate annual wage limitation, contribution base, and withholding threshold that are each computed without regard to any remuneration received by the covered employee during the calendar year from any other employer (including, if applicable, remuneration received directly from the customer receiving services from the employee). Notwithstanding the preceding sentence, a CPEO is treated as a successor or predecessor employer for purposes of the annual wage limitations and contribution base upon entering into or terminating a CPEO contract (as defined in §301.7705-1(b)(3) of this chapter) with respect to a work site employee, as described in paragraph (d) of this section.

(2) *Performance of services for more than one customer.*—If, during a calendar year, a covered employee receives remuneration from a CPEO for services performed by the covered employee for more than one customer of the CPEO, the annual wage limitation, contribution base, and withholding threshold do not apply to the aggregate remuneration received by the covered employee from the CPEO for services performed for all such customers. Rather, the annual wage limitation, contribution base, and withholding threshold apply separately to the remuneration received by the covered employee from the CPEO with respect to services performed for each customer.

(d) *Successor employer status.*—(1) *In general.*—For purposes of sections 3121(a)(1), 3231(e)(2)(C), and 3306(b)(1), a CPEO and its customer are treated as—

(i) A successor and predecessor employer, respectively, upon entering into a CPEO contract with respect to a work site employee who is performing services for the customer; and

(ii) A predecessor and successor employer, respectively, upon termination of the CPEO contract between the CPEO and the customer with respect to the work site employee who is performing services for the customer.

(2) *Non-work site employee.*—A CPEO entering into a CPEO contract with a customer during a calendar quarter with respect to a covered employee who is not a work site employee at any time during that calendar quarter will not be treated as a successor employer (and the customer will not be treated as a predecessor employer) for purposes of paragraph (d)(1)(i) of this section regardless of whether, during the term of the CPEO contract, the covered employee subsequently becomes a work site employee. Similarly, a CPEO terminating a CPEO contract with a customer during a calendar quarter with respect to a covered employee who is not a work site employee at any time during that calendar quarter will not be treated as a predecessor employer (and the customer will not be treated as a successor employer) for purposes of paragraph (d)(1)(ii) of this section regardless of whether, during the term of the CPEO contract, the covered employee had previously been a work site employee.

(e) *Treatment of credits.*—(1) *In general.*—For purposes of the credits specified in paragraph (e)(2) of this section—

(i) The credit with respect to a work site employee performing services for a customer applies to the customer, not to the CPEO; and

(ii) In computing the credit, the customer, and not the CPEO, is to take into account wages and federal employment taxes paid by the CPEO with respect to the work site employee and for which the CPEO receives payment from the customer.

(2) *Credits specified.*—A credit is specified in this paragraph if such credit is allowed under—

(i) Section 41 (credit for increasing research activity);

(ii) Section 45A (Indian employment credit);

(iii) Section 45B (credit for portion of employer social security taxes paid with respect to employee cash tips);

(iv) Section 45C (clinical testing expenses for certain drugs for rare diseases or conditions);

(v) Section 45R (employee health insurance expenses for small employers);

(vi) Section 51 (work opportunity credit);

(vii) Section 1396 (empowerment zone employment credit); and

(viii) Any other section specified by the Commissioner in further guidance (as defined in §301.7705-1T(b)(8) of this chapter).

(f) *Section not applicable to related customers, self-employed individuals, and other circumstances.*—This section does not apply—

(1) In the case of any customer that—

(i) Has a relationship to a CPEO described in section 267(b) (including, by cross-reference, section 267(f)) or section 707(b), except that "10 percent" shall be substituted for "50 percent" wherever it appears in such sections; or

(ii) Has commenced a CPEO contract with the CPEO but such commencement has not been reported to the IRS as described in paragraph (g)(3)(i) of this section; or

(2) To remuneration paid by a CPEO to any self-employed individual (as defined in § 301.7705-1(b)(14) of this chapter);

(3) To any CPEO contract that a CPEO enters into while its certification has been suspended by the IRS; or

(4) To any CPEO whose certification has been revoked or voluntarily terminated.

(g) *Reporting and recordkeeping.*—(1) *Reporting and recordkeeping for employers.*—A CPEO that is treated as an employer of a covered employee pursuant to paragraph (a) of this section must meet all reporting and recordkeeping requirements described in subtitle F of the Code that are applicable to employers in a manner consistent with such treatment.

(2) *Reporting on magnetic media.*—(i) *In general.*—A CPEO must file on magnetic media any Form 940, "Employer's Annual Federal Unemployment (FUTA) Tax Return," and Form 941, "Employer's QUARTERLY Federal Tax Return," and all required accompanying schedules, as well as such other returns, schedules, and other required forms and documents as is required by further guidance.

(ii) *Waiver.*—The Commissioner may waive the requirements of this paragraph (g)(2) in case of undue economic hardship. The principal factor in determining hardship will be the amount, if any, by which the cost of filing the return, schedule, or other required form or document on magnetic media in accordance with this paragraph (g)(2) exceeds the cost of filing on or by other media. A request for a waiver must be made in accordance with applicable guidance. The waiver will specify the type of filing (that is, the name of the form or schedule) and the period to which it applies. In addition, the waiver will be subject to such terms and conditions regarding the method of filing as may be prescribed by the Commissioner.

(iii) *Magnetic media.*—The term magnetic media means any magnetic media permitted under applicable guidance. These generally include electronic filing, as well as other media specifically permitted under the applicable guidance.

(3) *Reporting to the IRS by CPEOs.*—A CPEO must report the following to the IRS in such time and manner, and including such information, as the Commissioner may prescribe in further guidance:

(i) The commencement or termination of any CPEO contract (as defined in § 301.7705-1(b)(3) of this chapter) with a customer, or any service agreement described in § 31.3504-2(b)(2) with a client, and the name and employer identification number (EIN) of such customer or client.

(ii) With any Form 940 and Form 941 that it files, all required schedules, including but not limited to the applicable Schedule R (or any successor form), containing such information as the Commissioner may require about each of its customers under a CPEO contract (as defined in § 301.7705-1(b)(3) of this chapter) and each of its clients under a service agreement described in § 31.3504-2(b)(2). A CPEO must file Form 940 and Form 941, along with all required schedules, on magnetic media, unless the CPEO is granted a waiver by the Commissioner in accordance with paragraph (g)(2)(ii) of this section.

(iii) A periodic verification that it continues to meet the requirements of § 301.7705-2T of this chapter, as described in § 301.7705-2T(j).

(iv) Any change that materially affects the continuing accuracy of any agreement or information that was previously made or provided by the CPEO to the IRS, as described in § 301.7705-2T(k) of this chapter.

(v) A copy of its audited financial statements and an opinion of a certified public accountant regarding such financial statements, as described in § 301.7705-2T(e)(1) of this chapter.

(vi) The quarterly statements, assertions, and attestations regarding those assertions described in § 301.7705-2T(f)(1) of this chapter.

(vii) Any information the IRS determines is necessary to promote compliance with respect to the credits described in paragraph (e)(2) of this section and section 3302.

(viii) Any other information the Commissioner may prescribe in further guidance.

(4) *Reporting to customers by CPEOs.*—A CPEO must meet the following reporting requirements with respect to its customers in such time and manner, and including such information, as the Commissioner may prescribe in further guidance:

(i) Provide each of its customers with the information necessary for the customer to claim the credits described in paragraph (e)(2) of this section.

(ii) Notify any customer if its CPEO contract has been transferred to another person (or if another person will report, withhold, or pay, under such other person's EIN, any applicable federal employment taxes with respect to the wages of any individuals covered by its CPEO contract) and provide the customer with the name and EIN of such other person.

(iii) If the CPEO's certification is suspended or revoked as described in § 301.7705-2T(n) of this chapter, notify each of its current customers of such suspension or revocation.

(iv) If any covered employees are not or cease to be work site employees because they perform services at a location at which the 85 percent threshold described in § 301.7705-1(b)(17) of this chapter is not met, notify the customer that it may also be liable for federal employment taxes imposed on remuneration remitted by the CPEO to such covered employees, as described in paragraph (a)(3) of this section.

(5) *Information and agreements in any contract or agreement between a CPEO and a customer or client.*—Any CPEO contract (as defined in § 301.7705-1(b)(3) of this chapter) between a CPEO and a customer or service agreement described in § 31.3504-2(b)(2) between a CPEO and a client must—

(i) In the case of a contract that is a CPEO contract,—

(A) Contain the name and EIN of the CPEO reporting, withholding, and paying any applicable federal employment taxes with respect to any remuneration paid to individuals covered by the contract or agreement;

(B) Require the CPEO to provide to the customer the notices and information required by paragraph (g)(4) of this section;

(C) Describe the information that the CPEO will provide that is necessary for the customer to claim the credits specified in paragraph (e)(2) of this section; and

(D) Require the CPEO to notify the customer that the customer may also be liable for federal employment taxes on remuneration remitted by the CPEO to covered employees if the work sites at which they perform services do not (or ever cease to) meet the 85 percent threshold described in § 301.7705-1(b)(17) of this chapter; and

(ii) In the case of a service agreement described in § 31.3504-2(b)(2) that is not a CPEO contract (and thus the individuals covered by that contract are not covered employees), or if this section does not apply to the contract under paragraph (f) of this section, notify, or be accompanied by a notification to, the client that the service agreement or contract is not covered by section 3511 and does not alter the client's liability for federal employment taxes on remuneration remitted by the CPEO to the employees covered by the service agreement or contract.

(h) *Penalties.*—(1) *In general.*—A CPEO that is treated as an employer of a covered employee under this section and that is required to meet the reporting requirements of an employer is subject to the same penalties and additions to tax as an employer with respect to such reporting requirements, including but not limited to penalties and additions to tax under sections 6651, 6656, 6672, 6721, 6722, and 6723.

(2) *Failures to timely make reports required under section 3511.*—CPEOs are subject to penalty under section 6652(n) with respect to reports required to be made to the IRS in paragraphs (g)(1) and (g)(3) of this section and reports required to be made to customers in paragraph (g)(4) of this section.

(3) *Failures to attach Schedule R.*—A CPEO is subject to penalty under section 6652(n) for failure to attach Schedule R (or successor form) to Forms 941 or 940 as required by paragraph (g)(3)(ii) of this section. A CPEO is also subject to penalty under section 6723 for failure to include the EIN of each customer on Schedule R of Form 941 or 940. See § 301.6723-1 of this chapter for the application of the section 6723 penalty in the case of multiple failures on a single document.

(4) *Failures to file on magnetic media.*—With respect to the requirement in paragraph (g)(3)(ii) of this section that a CPEO must file Forms 940 and 941, along with all required schedules, on magnetic media, a failure to file on magnetic media does not constitute a failure to file for purposes of section 6651(a)(1) nor does it constitute a failure to make a report for purposes of section 6652(n). Rather, the requirement to file Forms 940 and 941 on magnetic media is a condition of maintaining certification as a CPEO.

(i) *Effective/applicability date.*—These rules are effective on and after the date of publication of the Treasury decision adopting these rules as final or temporary regulations. Taxpayers may rely on these rules beginning July 1, 2016, and until final or temporary regulations are published. [Reg. § 31.3511-1.]

EXCISE TAXES

Retail Excise Taxes on Certain Luxury Items

Luxury Items Tax.—Reproduced below are the texts of proposed Reg. § 48.4001-1 and a proposed amendment to Reg. § 48.0-2, relating to the retailers' excise taxes on certain passenger vehicles (published in the Federal Register on January 2, 1991). The Revenue Reconciliation Act 0f 1993 (P.L. 103-66) repealed the luxury tax on boats, aircraft, jewelry and furs; thus, the text of the proposed regulations under former Code Secs. 4002, 4003, 4004, 4006, 4007, 4011 and 4012 (Reg. §§ 48.4002-1—48.4012-1) are no longer reproduced.

☐ Par. 3. Section 48.0-2 is amended as follows: 1. Sections 48.0-2(a)(6) and (7) are revised as set forth below; and 2. In paragraph (b)(1), the words "For the purposes of this part, the" are removed and the word "The" is added in their place, and new introductory text is added to paragraph (b) to read as set forth below.

§ 48.0-2. General definitions and attachment of tax.

(a) *Meaning of terms.*—* * *

(6) The term "taxable article" means any article taxable under chapter 31 or 32 of the Code.

(7) The term "vendor" or "seller" includes a lessor except that, with respect to the manufacturer's excise taxes, this rule applies only where the lessor is also the manufacturer of the article.

* * *

(b) *Attachment of tax.*—For purposes of this part, unless otherwise expressly indicated:

☐ Par. 4. A new subpart B (only Reg. § 48.4001-1 currently reproduced) is added immediately following § 48.0-3 to read as follows:

§ 48.4001-1. Luxury tax imposed on passenger vehicles.—(a) *In general.*—(1) *Imposition of tax.*—Section 4001 imposes a tax (the luxury automobile tax) on the first retail sale of a passenger vehicle if the sales price of the vehicle exceeds $30,000.

(2) *Amount of tax.*—The luxury automobile tax is equal to 10 percent of the amount by which the sales price of the vehicle exceeds $30,000.

(3) *Liability for tax.*—The luxury automobile tax shall be paid by the person who makes the first retail sale.

(b) *Passenger vehicle defined.*—(1) *In general.*—For purposes of this section, the term "passenger vehicle" means a 4-wheeled vehicle that is manufactured or sold primarily for use on public streets, roads, and highways, and that is—

(i) Rated (except in the case of a truck, van, or limousine) at 6,000 pounds unloaded gross vehicle weight or less;

(ii) A truck or van rated at 6,000 pounds gross vehicle weight or less; or

(iii) A limousine.

(2) *Meaning of terms.*—The following definitions set forth the meanings of certain terms for purposes of this paragraph (b)—

(i) *Unloaded gross vehicle weight.*—The term "unloaded gross vehicle weight" means the curb weight of a vehicle fully equipped for service, but without passengers or cargo.

(ii) *Gross vehicle weight.*—The term "gross vehicle weight" has the meaning given such term by § 145.4051-1(e)(3).

(iii) *Truck or van.*—(A) *Van.*—The term "van" means a vehicle (whether configured to transport cargo or passengers behind the driver's position) that—

(1) Is built on a truck chassis; and

(2) Has an enclosed body.

(B) *Multi-purpose and sport utility vehicles included.*—The term "truck or van" includes vehicles that are commonly known as minivans or sport utility vehicles.

(iv) *Limousines.*—The term "limousine" means any sedan seating four or more passengers behind the driver.

(c) *Exemption from luxury automobile tax for taxicabs. etc.*—The luxury automobile tax is not imposed on the sale of a passenger vehicle for use by the purchaser exclusively (except for incidental and *de minimis* uses) in the active conduct of a trade or business of transporting persons or property for compensation or hire. A person who is otherwise responsible for the payment of the luxury automobile tax must establish the applicability of this exemption by evidence satisfactory to the Commissioner and may, for that purpose, rely upon an exemption certificate received from the purchaser.

(d) *Cross-references.*—(1) *Exemption certificates.*—See § 48.4011-7 for rules relating to exemption certificates.

(2) *Additional exemptions.*—See §§ 48.4004-2 and 48.4011-2 for additional exemptions from the luxury automobile tax.

(3) *First retail sale and sales price.*—See § 48.4011-3 for the definition of the term "first retail sale." See § 48.4011-4 for the definition of the term "sales price."

(4) *Tax imposed on use.*—See § 48.4011-5 for rules relating to the tax imposed on passenger vehicles that are used before there has been a first retail sale.

(5) *Special rules for payment of tax in case of qualified lease or installment sale.*—See § 48.4011-6 for rules relating to the payment of tax on qualified leases and installment sales.

(6) *Procedural rules.*—For rules relating to the requirements for filing returns and for paying and depositing luxury automobile tax, see 26 CFR Part 40.

(7) *Effective date and termination.*—See § 48.4011-8 for the effective date of this section, and § 48.4012-1 for the termination of the luxury automobile tax. [Reg. § 48.4001-1.]

Excise Taxes: Taxable Fuel: Returns: Definitions

Excise Taxes: Taxable Fuel: Returns: Definitions.—Reg. § 48.0-4 and amendments to Reg. § 48.0-1, relating to credits and payments for alcohol mixtures, biodiesel mixtures, renewable diesel mixtures, alternative fuel mixtures, and alternative fuel sold for use or used as a fuel and relating to the definition of gasoline and diesel fuel, are proposed (published in the Federal Register on July 29, 2008) (REG-155087-05).

Par. 8. Section 48.0-1 is amended as follows:

1. In the second sentence, "and related credits, refunds, and payments" is added after "Code".
2. In the third sentence, "certain luxury items," is removed.
3. In the fourth sentence, "aviation fuel," is removed.

§ 48.0-1. Introduction.

Par. 9. Section 48.0-4 is added to read as follows:

§ 48.0-4. Forms.—Any reference to a form in this part is also a reference to any other form designated for the same use by the Commissioner after the date these regulations are published in the **Federal Register** as final regulations. All such forms must be completed in accordance with the instructions for the forms and contain any additional information required by this part.

Excise Tax: Tractors, Trailers, Trucks, and Tires: Highway Vehicle: Definition

Excise Tax: Tractors, Trailers, Trucks, and Tires: Highway Vehicle: Definition.—Reg. § 48.0-4 and amendments to Reg. §§ 48.0-1 and 48.0-2, relating to the excise taxes imposed on the sale of highway tractors, trailers, trucks, and tires, the use of heavy vehicles on the highway, and the definition of highway vehicle related to these and other taxes, are proposed (published in the Federal Register on March 31, 2016) (REG-103380-05).

Par. 4. Section 48.0-1, fourth sentence, is amended by removing the language "highway-type tires" and adding "taxable tires" in its place.

§ 48.0-1. Introduction.

Par. 5. In § 48.0-2, paragraph (b)(5), first sentence, is amended by removing the language "In the case of a lease," and adding "Except as provided in § 48.4052-1(e), in the case of a lease," in its place.

§48.0-2. Introduction.

Par. 6. Section 48.0-4 is added to subpart A to read as follows:

§48.0-4. Introduction.—(a) *Overview.*—(1) The definitions of *highway vehicle* and *mobile machinery* in this section apply for purposes of this part and part 41 of this chapter. See §41.4482(a)-1(a)(2) of this chapter.

(2) The taxes imposed by sections 4051 and 4481 do not apply to mobile machinery (as defined in paragraph (b)(3)(iii) of this section), and the tax imposed by section 4071 does not apply to tires of a type used exclusively on such mobile machinery. In addition, for purposes of determining whether use of a vehicle qualifies as *off-highway business use* under section 6421(e)(2)(C) (relating to uses in mobile machinery), mobile machinery (as defined in this section) satisfies the design-based test of section 6421(e)(2)(C)(iii). To qualify as off-highway business use, however, the use of the vehicle must also satisfy the use-based test of section 6421(e)(2)(C)(iv).

(b) *Highway vehicle.*—(1) *In general.*—Except as otherwise provided in paragraph (b)(3) of this section, *highway vehicle* means any self-propelled vehicle, or any truck trailer or semitrailer, designed to perform a function of transporting a load over public highways.

(2) *Explanation.*—(i) A vehicle consists of a chassis, or a chassis and a body if the vehicle has a body, but does not include the vehicle's load.

(ii) Except as otherwise provided in paragraph (b)(3) of this section, in determining whether a vehicle is a highway vehicle, it is immaterial whether—

(A) The vehicle can perform functions other than transporting a load over the public highways;

(B) The vehicle is designed to perform a highway transportation function for only a particular kind of load, such as passengers, furnishings and personal effects (as in a house, office, or utility trailer), a special type of cargo, goods, supplies, or materials, or machinery or equipment specially designed to perform some off-highway task unrelated to highway transportation; and

(C) In the case of a vehicle specially designed to transport machinery or equipment, such machinery or equipment is permanently mounted on the vehicle.

(iii) Examples of vehicles that are designed to perform a function of transporting a load over the public highways are passenger automobiles, motorcycles, buses, motor homes, and highway-type trucks, truck tractors, trailers, and semitrailers.

(iv) Examples of vehicles that are not designed to perform a function of transporting a load over the public highways are farm tractors, bulldozers, road graders, and forklifts.

(v) The term *public highway* includes any road (whether a federal highway, state highway, city street, or otherwise) in the United States that is not a private roadway.

(vi) The term *transport* includes tow.

(3) *Exceptions.*—(i) *Certain vehicles specially designed for off-highway transportation.*—(A) *In general.*—The term *highway vehicle* does not include a vehicle if the vehicle is specially designed for the primary function of transporting a particular type of load other than over a public highway and because of this special design such vehicle's capability to transport a load over a public highway is substantially limited or impaired.

(B) *Determination of vehicle's design.*—For purposes of paragraph (c)(3)(i)(A) of this section, a vehicle's design is determined solely on the basis of its physical characteristics.

(C) *Determination of substantial limitation or impairment.*—For purposes of paragraph (c)(3)(i)(A) of this section, in determining whether substantial limitation or impairment exists, account may be taken of factors such as the size of the vehicle, whether the vehicle is subject to the licensing, safety, and other requirements applicable to highway vehicles, and whether the vehicle can transport a load at a sustained speed of at least 25 miles per hour. It is immaterial that a vehicle can transport a greater load off the public highway than the vehicle is permitted to transport over the public highway.

(ii) *Nontransportation truck trailers and semitrailers.*—The term *highway vehicle* does not include a truck trailer or semitrailer if it is specially designed to function only as an enclosed stationary shelter for the carrying on of an off-highway function at an off-highway site.

(iii) *Mobile machinery.*—The term highway vehicle does not include any vehicle that consists of a chassis—

(A) To which there has been permanently mounted (by welding, bolting, riveting, or other means) machinery or equipment to perform a construction, manufacturing, processing, farming, mining, drilling, timbering, or similar operation if the operation of the machinery or equipment is unrelated to transportation on or off the public highways;

(B) That has been specially designed to serve only as a mobile carriage and mount (and a power source, where applicable) for the particular machinery or equipment involved, whether or not such machinery or equipment is in operation; and

(C) That, by reason of such special design, could not, without substantial structural modification, be used as a component of a vehicle designed to perform a function of transporting any load other than that particular machinery or equipment or similar machinery or equipment requiring such a specially designed chassis.

(c) *Examples.*—The following examples illustrate the rules of this section:

Example 1; Off-highway transportation. (1) *Facts.* (i) A tri-axle semitrailer that is used in highway construction, maintenance, and repair work also hauls highway construction and repair materials to job sites. The semitrailer's floor is equipped with a continuous rubber belt attached to a steel slatted roller chain that carries payload to the rear tailgate at a controllable discharge rate. The semitrailer has insulated double sidewalls and a baffled hopper. This equipment enables the semitrailer to transport and unload hot-mix asphalt, asphalt-related materials, and low-slump concrete for highway construction and repair. When used as an asphalt transporter, the semitrailer unloads the asphalt at the job site through the rear tailgate into a trailing asphalt paving machine. The semitrailer is designed to perform a function of transporting a load over public highways.

(ii) A highway tractor tows the semitrailer at normal highway speeds. The semitrailer complies with all federal and state regulations governing highway use, may be legally operated on the public highways when loaded within legal weight limits (80,000 pounds), and does not exceed state maximum highway length, width, or height limitations. Loaded to its capacity with asphalt, the combined weight of the semitrailer, the asphalt, and the tractor exceeds 100,000 pounds. Special state permits may be purchased to operate the tractor/semitrailer combination above the legal weight limit on public highways.

(2) *Analysis*. For purposes of the exception provided by paragraph (b)(3)(i) of this section for vehicles specially designed for off-highway transportation, paragraph (b)(3)(i)(B) of this section provides that a vehicle's design is determined solely on the basis of its physical characteristics. The physical characteristics of this semitrailer include insulated double sidewalls, a baffled hopper, and an unloading mechanism on the floor of the trailer that moves hot road building materials to the back of the trailer and delivers these materials into a paving machine at controlled rates. Examples of the type of machinery or equipment that contribute to the highway transportation function are unloading equipment and machinery that contribute to the preservation of the cargo. The semitrailer's conveyor discharge system and insulated walls are designed to contribute to the highway transportation functions of unloading (discharge conveyor system) and preserving (insulated sidewalls) the load. This equipment is not designed for the job-site function of applying asphalt or low-slump concrete.

(3) *Conclusion*. The semitrailer is not a vehicle described in paragraph (b)(3)(i)(A) of this section. The semitrailer's physical characteristics, such as sidewalls, a hopper, and the unloading mechanism, demonstrate that this semitrailer is capable of transporting asphalt or low-slump concrete over a public highway without substantial limitation or impairment.

Example 2; Mobile machinery. (1) *Facts*. A chassis manufacturer built a truck chassis with a reinforced chassis frame, a heavy-duty engine, and a structure to accommodate the manufacturer's mounting of drilling equipment on the chassis and the use of that drilling equipment off the highways. The manufacturer also bolted a pintle-type trailer hitch to a beam that is welded to, and operates as a rear cross member of, the chassis frame rails. The truck is designed to perform a function of transporting a load over public highways.

(2) *Analysis*. This chassis can perform two functions. First, the chassis serves as a mobile carriage and mount for the drilling equipment installed on its bed. Second, the chassis can tow a trailer because it has a pintle-type trailer hitch. These dual capabilities demonstrate that the chassis was not specially designed to serve only as a mobile carriage and mount for its machinery.

(3) *Conclusion*. The chassis fails to meet the test in paragraph (c)(3)(iii) of this section for treatment as mobile machinery because the chassis is not specially designed to serve only as a mobile carriage and mount for the drilling equipment. A similar conclusion would apply if the manufacturer reinforced the chassis to make the chassis capable of towing a trailer, but the manufacturer did not install the pintle hook.

(d) *Effective/applicability date*.—This section applies on and after the date of publication of these regulations in the **Federal Register** as final regulations. [Reg. §48.0-4.]

Excise Tax: Tractors, Trailers, Trucks, and Tires: Highway Vehicle: Definition

Excise Tax: Tractors, Trailers, Trucks, and Tires: Highway Vehicle: Definition.—Amendments to Reg. §48.4041-8, relating to the excise taxes imposed on the sale of highway tractors, trailers, trucks, and tires, the use of heavy vehicles on the highway, and the definition of highway vehicle related to these and other taxes, are proposed (published in the Federal Register on March 31, 2016) (REG-103380-05).

Par. 7. Section 48.4041-8 is amended as follows:

1. Paragraph (b)(2)(ii), first sentence, is amended by removing the language "A self-propelled" and adding "Before January 1, 2005, a self-propelled" in its place.

2. Paragraph (b)(2)(iv) is added.

The addition reads as follows:

§48.4041-8. Definitions.

* * *

(b) * * *

(2) * * *

(iv) *Off-highway transportation vehicles after December 31, 2004*.—For a description of certain vehicles that are not treated as highway vehicles after December 31, 2004, see §48.0-5(b)(3).

* * *

Excise Taxes: Taxable Fuel: Returns: Definitions

Excise Taxes: Taxable Fuel: Returns: Definitions.—Amendments to Reg. §§48.4041-0, 48.4041-18, 48.4041-19 and 48.4041-20, relating to credits and payments for alcohol mixtures, biodiesel mixtures, renewable diesel mixtures, alternative fuel mixtures, and alternative fuel sold for use or used as a fuel and relating to the definition of gasoline and diesel fuel, are proposed (published in the Federal Register on July 29, 2008) (REG-155087-05).

Par. 10. Section 48.4041-0 is amended as follows:

1. In the first sentence, the language "sales or uses of diesel fuel" is removed and "any liquid (other than biodiesel) that is sold for use or used as a fuel in a diesel-powered highway vehicle or diesel-powered train" is added in its place.

2. In the second sentence, the language "diesel fuel tax" is removed and "tax with respect to these liquids" is added in its place.

§48.4041-0. Applicability of regulations relating to diesel fuel after December 31, 1993.

Par. 11. Section 48.4041-18 is removed and reserved.

§48.4041-18. Fuels containing alcohol.

Par. 12. Section 48.4041-19 is revised to read as follows:

§48.4041-19. Reduction in tax for qualified methanol or ethanol fuel and partially exempt methanol or ethanol fuel.—(a) *In general.*—Section 4041(b)(2) provides a reduced rate of tax under sections 4041(a)(2) and (d) for qualified methanol or ethanol fuel. Section 4041(m) provides a reduced rate of tax under section 4041(a)(2) for partially exempt methanol or ethanol fuel.

(b) *Qualified methanol or ethanol fuel and partially exempt methanol or ethanol fuel defined.*—For purposes of section 4041(b)(2) and this section, qualified methanol or ethanol fuel is liquid motor fuel, at least 85 percent of which (by volume) consists of alcohol produced from coal (including peat). For purposes of section 4041(m) and this section, partially exempt methanol or ethanol fuel is a liquid motor fuel, at least 85 percent of which (by volume) consists of alcohol produced from natural gas (including ethanol produced through the process of thermally cracking ethane that is a constituent of natural gas). The actual gallonage of each component of the mixture (without adjustment for temperature) shall be used in determining whether, at the time of the taxable sale or use, the applicable 85 percent alcohol requirement has been met. A mixture containing less than 85 percent alcohol produced from coal (or less than 85 percent alcohol produced from natural gas) may be treated as satisfying the applicable percentage requirement. In determining whether a particular mixture should be so treated, the Commissioner shall take into account the existence of any facts and circumstances establishing that, but for the commercial and operational realities of the blending process, it may reasonably be concluded that the mixture would have contained at least 85 percent alcohol from the appropriate source. The necessary facts and circumstances will not be found to exist if over a period of time the mixtures blended by a blender show a consistent pattern of failing to contain at least 85 percent alcohol from the appropriate source.

(c) *Effective/applicablity date.*—This section is applicable on and after the date of publication of these regulations in the **Federal Register** as final regulations. For provisions applicable to prior periods, see 26 CFR 48.4041-19 (revised as of April 1, 2008). [Reg. §48.4081-19.]

Par. 13. Section 48.4041-20 is removed and reserved.

§48.4041-20. Partially exempt methanol and ethanol fuel.

Excise Tax: Tractors, Trailers, Trucks, and Tires: Highway Vehicle: Definition

Excise Tax: Tractors, Trailers, Trucks, and Tires: Highway Vehicle: Definition.—Reg. §§48.4051-0—48.4051-2 and amendments to Reg. §145.4051-1, relating to the excise taxes imposed on the sale of highway tractors, trailers, trucks, and tires, the use of heavy vehicles on the highway, and the definition of highway vehicle related to these and other taxes, are proposed (published in the Federal Register on March 31, 2016) (REG-103380-05).

Par. 9. New §§48.4051-0, 48.4051-1, and 48.4051-2 are added to subpart H to read as follows:

§48.4051-0. Overview; Heavy trucks, tractors, and trailers sold at retail.—Sections 48.4051-1, 48.4051-2, and 48.4052-1 provide guidance under sections 4051 and 4052 relating to the tax on the first retail sale of certain truck and trailer chassis and bodies and certain tractors. This guidance includes rules relating to the imposition of tax, liability for tax, exclusions, and definitions. For rules under sections 4051 and 4052 on the treatment of leases, uses treated as sales, and the determination of price for which an article is sold, see §145.4052-1 of this chapter. [Reg. §48.4051-0.]

§48.4051-1. Imposition of tax; Heavy trucks, tractors, and trailers sold at retail.—(a) *Imposition of tax.*—Section 4051 imposes a tax on the first retail sale of the following articles (including in each case parts or accessories sold on or in connection with the article or with the sale of the article):

(1) Automobile truck chassis and bodies.

(2) Truck trailer and semitrailer chassis and bodies.

(3) Tractors of the kind chiefly used for highway transportation in combination with a truck trailer or semitrailer.

(b) *Tax base and rate of tax.*—The tax is the applicable percentage of the price for which the article is sold. The applicable percentage is prescribed in section 4051(a)(1). For rules for the determination of price, see paragraph (d)(4) of this section and §145.4052-1(d) of this chapter.

(c) *Liability for tax.*—(1) *In general.*—Except as provided in paragraph (c)(2) of this section, the person that makes the first retail sale (as defined in §48.4052-1(a)) of a taxable article listed in paragraph (a) of this section is liable for the tax imposed by section 4051. This person is referred to as the *retailer* in this section and §48.4051-2.

(2) *Exceptions; cross references.*—For cases in which a person other than the retailer is liable for the tax imposed under paragraph (a) of this section, see §§48.4051-1(d)(2)(ii) and (iii) (relating to chassis and bodies sold for use as a component part of a highway vehicle) and §48.4051-1(e)(6)(ii) (relating to certain chassis completed as tractors).

(d) *Special rules.*—(1) *Separate taxation of chassis and body.*—If a chassis is a component part of a highway vehicle, the taxability of the chassis is determined independently of, and without regard to, the body that is installed on the chassis. If a body is a component part of a highway vehicle, the taxability of the body is determined independently of, and without regard to, the chassis on which the body is installed.

(2) *Chassis and bodies sold for use as a component part of a highway vehicle.*—(i) *In general.*—A chassis or body listed in paragraph (a) of this section is taxable under section 4051 only if such chassis or body is sold for use as a component part of a highway vehicle that is an automobile truck, truck trailer or semitrailer, or a tractor of the kind chiefly used for highway transportation in combination with a trailer or semitrailer. A chassis or body that is not listed in paragraph (a) of this section (for example, a chassis or body of a passenger automobile) is not taxable under section 4051 even though such chassis or body is used as a component part of a highway vehicle.

(ii) *Retailer; conditions for avoidance of liability.*—The retailer is not liable for tax on a chassis or body if, at the time of the first retail sale, the retailer—

(A) Has obtained from the buyer a certificate described in paragraph (d)(2)(iv) of this section stating, among other things, that the buyer will use the chassis or body as a component part of a vehicle that is not a highway vehicle;

(B) Has no reason to believe that any information in the certificate is false; and

(C) Has not received a notification from the IRS under paragraph (d)(2)(iv) of this section with respect to the buyer or the type of chassis or body.

(iii) *Liability of buyer.*—If a buyer that provides a certificate described in paragraph (d)(2)(iv) of this section uses the chassis or body to which the certificate relates as a component part of a highway vehicle, the buyer is liable for the tax imposed on the first retail sale of such chassis or body.

(iv) *Form of certificate.*—The certificate described in this paragraph (d)(2)(iv) consists of a statement that is signed under penalties of perjury by a person with authority to bind the buyer, is in substantially the same form as the model certificate in paragraph (d)(2)(v) of this section, and includes all the information necessary to complete the model certificate. The IRS may withdraw the right of a buyer to provide a certificate under this section if the buyer uses the chassis or body to which a certificate relates other than as stated in the certificate. The IRS may notify any retailer that the buyer's right to provide a certificate has been withdrawn. The IRS may also notify a retailer that sales of a specified type or types of chassis or bodies may not be made tax-free under this paragraph (d)(2) until further notification. The certificate may be included as part of any business records used to document a sale.

(v) *Model Certificate.*

Certificate

(To support the tax-free sale of a chassis or body that is to be used as a component part of a non-highway vehicle)

The undersigned buyer of a chassis or body listed in section 4051 ("Buyer") hereby certifies the following under penalties of perjury:

1. ______________________________

____

____

Seller's name, address, and employer identification number

2. ______________________________

____

____

Buyer's name, address, and employer identification number

3. ______________________________

Date and location of sale to Buyer

4. The article(s) listed below will not be used as a component part of a highway vehicle. If the article is a chassis, Buyer has listed the chassis Vehicle Identification Number. If the article is a body, Buyer has listed the body's identification number.

5. Buyer understands that it must be prepared to establish, by evidence satisfactory to an examining agent, how Buyer used the article.

6. Buyer has not been notified by the Internal Revenue Service that its right to provide a certificate has been withdrawn.

7. Buyer understands that if it uses a chassis or body listed in this certificate as a component part of a highway vehicle, Buyer is liable for the tax imposed by section 4051 of the Internal Revenue Code.
8. Buyer understands that Buyer may be liable for the section 6701 penalty (relating to aiding and abetting an understatement of tax liability) if this is an erroneous certification.
9. Buyer understands that the fraudulent use of this certificate may subject Buyer and all parties making any fraudulent use of this statement to a fine or imprisonment, or both, together with the costs of prosecution.

Printed or typed name of person signing this certificate

Title of person signing

Signature and date signed

(3) *Sale of a completed unit.*—A sale of an automobile truck, truck trailer, or semitrailer is considered a sale of a chassis and of a body listed in paragraph (a) of this section.

(4) *Equipment installed on chassis or bodies.*—For purposes of section 4051, the sale price of a chassis or body includes any amount paid for equipment or machinery that is installed on and is an integral part of the chassis or body. Equipment or machinery is an integral part of a chassis or body if the equipment or machinery contributes to the highway transportation function of the chassis or body. Examples of machinery or equipment that contributes to the highway transportation function of a chassis or body are loading and unloading equipment; towing winches; and all other machinery or equipment that contributes to the maintenance or safety of the vehicle, the preservation of cargo (other than refrigeration units), or the comfort or convenience of the driver or passengers.

(5) *Vehicle use.*—In determining whether a tractor, a truck body or chassis, or a truck trailer or semitrailer chassis or body is subject to the tax imposed by section 4051, the use (whether commercial, personal, recreational, or otherwise) of an article is immaterial.

(e) *Explanation of terms and exclusions; tractors, trucks, trailers.*—(1) *Tractor.*—The term *tractor* means a highway vehicle primarily designed to tow a vehicle, such as a truck trailer or semitrailer. A vehicle equipped with air brakes and/or a towing package will be presumed to be a tractor unless it is established, based on all the vehicle's characteristics, that the vehicle is not primarily designed to tow a vehicle. However, a vehicle that is not equipped with air brakes and/or a towing package is a tractor if the vehicle is primarily designed to tow a vehicle.

(2) *Truck.*—The term *truck* means a highway vehicle primarily designed to transport its load on the same chassis as the engine even if it is also equipped to tow a vehicle, such as a trailer or semitrailer.

(3) *Primarily designed.*—The term *primarily* means principally or of first importance. *Primarily* does not mean exclusively. The function for which a vehicle is primarily designed is evidenced by physical characteristics such as the vehicle's capacity to tow a vehicle, carry cargo, and operate (including brake) safely when towing or carrying cargo. Towing capacity depends on the vehicle's gross vehicle weight (GVW) rating and gross combination weight (GCW) rating and whether the vehicle is configured to tow a trailer or semitrailer. Cargo carrying capacity depends on the vehicle's GVW rating and the configuration of the vehicle's bed or platform. If a vehicle is capable of more than one function, such as towing a vehicle and carrying cargo on the same chassis as the engine, the physical characteristics of the vehicle determine the purpose for which the vehicle is primarily designed. A vehicle that can both carry cargo on its chassis and tow a trailer is either a truck or tractor depending on which function is of greater importance.

(4) *Trailer.*—(i) *In general.*—The term *trailer* means a non-self-propelled vehicle hauled, towed, or drawn by a separate truck or tractor. A trailer consists of a chassis and a body. A chassis is the frame that supports the trailer's suspension, axles, wheels, tires, and brakes. A body is the structure usually installed on the trailer chassis to accommodate the intended load of the trailer. In some instances, the body may itself constitute all or part of the intended load.

(ii) *Truck trailer.*—The term *truck trailer* means a trailer that carries all of its weight and the weight of its load on its own chassis.

(iii) *Semitrailer.*—The term *semitrailer* means a trailer, the front end of which is designed to be attached to, and rest upon, the vehicle that tows it. A portion of the semitrailer's weight and load also rests upon the towing vehicle.

(5) *Incomplete chassis cab; classification as a truck.*—An incomplete chassis cab is classified as a truck at the time of its sale if, at such time—

(i) The incomplete chassis cab is not equipped with any of the features listed in paragraph (e)(7) of this section; and

(ii) The seller—

(A) Has obtained from the buyer a certificate described in paragraph (e)(8) of this section stating, among other things, that the buyer will equip the incomplete chassis cab as a truck;

(B) Has no reason to believe that any information in the certificate is false; and

(C) Has not received a notification under paragraph (e)(8) of this section with respect to the buyer.

(6) *Incomplete chassis cab; classification as a tractor.*—(i) *In general.*—An incomplete chassis cab is classified as a tractor at the time of its sale if, at such time—

(A) The incomplete chassis cab is equipped with any of the features listed in paragraph (e)(7) of this section; or

(B) The seller fails to satisfy one or more of the conditions set forth in paragraph (e)(5)(ii) of this section.

(ii) *Completion as a tractor.*—If no tax is imposed under section 4051(a)(1) on the sale of an incomplete chassis cab classified as a truck under paragraph (e)(5) of this section and the purchaser completes the incomplete chassis cab as a taxable tractor, the purchaser is liable for tax under section 4051(a)(1) on the purchaser's sale or use of the taxable tractor.

(7) *Incomplete chassis cab; features.*—The features referred to in paragraphs (e)(5)(i) and (e)(6)(i)(A) of this section are the following:

(i) A device for supplying air or hydraulic pressure or electric or other power from the incomplete chassis cab to the brake system of a towed vehicle.

(ii) A mechanism for protecting the incomplete chassis cab brake system from the effects of a loss of pressure in the brake system of a towed vehicle.

(iii) A control linking the brake system of the incomplete chassis cab to the brake system of a towed vehicle.

(iv) A control in the incomplete chassis cab for operating a towed vehicle's brakes independently of the incomplete chassis cab's brakes.

(v) Any other equipment designed to establish or enhance the incomplete chassis cab's use as a tractor.

(8) *Incomplete chassis cab; certificate.*—(i) *In general.*—The certificate described in this paragraph (e)(8) consists of a statement that is signed under penalties of perjury by a person with authority to bind the buyer, is in substantially the same form as the model certificate in paragraph (e)(8(ii) of this section, and includes all the information necessary to complete the model certificate. The IRS may withdraw the right of a buyer of vehicles to provide a certificate under this section if the buyer uses the vehicles to which a certificate relates other than as stated in the certificate. The IRS may notify any seller that the buyer's right to provide a certificate has been withdrawn. The certificate may be included as part of any business records normally used to document a sale.

(ii) *Model Certificate.*

Certificate

(To support the completion of an incomplete chassis cab as a truck)

The undersigned buyer of articles listed in section 4051 ("Buyer") hereby certifies the following under penalties of perjury:

1. ____

____

____

Seller's name, address, and employer identification number

2. ____

____

____

Buyer's name, address, and employer identification number

3. ____

Date and location of sale to Buyer

4. Buyer certifies that Buyer will complete these incomplete chassis cabs listed below as trucks:

VIN:	*VIN:*
VIN:	*VIN:*
VIN:	*VIN:*
VIN:	*VIN:*

5. Buyer has not been notified by the Internal Revenue Service that its right to provide a certificate has been withdrawn.

6. Buyer understands that if Buyer completes an incomplete chassis cab listed in this certificate as a taxable tractor described in section 4051(a)(1)(E) and then uses it or sells it, Buyer may be liable for the tax imposed by section 4051 on this sale or use. See 26 CFR 48.4051-1(e)(6)(ii) and 145.4052-1(c).

7. Buyer understands that Buyer may be liable for the section 6701 penalty (relating to aiding and abetting an understatement of tax liability) if this is an erroneous certification.

8. Buyer understands that the fraudulent use of this certificate may subject Buyer and all parties making any fraudulent use of this statement to a fine or imprisonment, or both, together with the costs of prosecution.

____

Printed or typed name of person signing this certificate

____

Title of person signing

____

Signature and date signed

(f) *Exclusions.*—(1) *In general.*—Tax is not imposed by section 4051 on the first retail sale of the following articles:

(i) Automobile truck chassis or bodies that have practical and commercial fitness for use with a vehicle that has a GVW of 33,000 pounds or less.

(ii) Truck trailer and semitrailer chassis or bodies that have practical and commercial fitness for use with a truck trailer or semitrailer that has a GVW of 26,000 pounds or less.

(iii) Tractors that have—

(A) A GVW of 19,500 pounds or less; and

(B) A GCW of 33,000 pounds or less.

(2) *Practical and commercial fitness.*—A chassis or body possesses practical fitness for use with a vehicle if it performs its intended function up to a generally acceptable standard of efficiency with the vehicle, and a chassis or body possesses commercial fitness for use with a vehicle if it is generally available for use with the

vehicle at a price that is reasonably competitive with other articles that may be used for the same purpose. A truck chassis that has practical and commercial fitness for use with a vehicle having a GVW of 33,000 pounds or less is not subject to the tax imposed by section 4051 regardless of the body actually mounted on the chassis. A truck trailer or semitrailer chassis that has practical and commercial fitness for use with a vehicle having a GVW of 26,000 pounds or less is not subject to tax regardless of the body actually mounted on the chassis. A taxable chassis or body, as the case may be, remains subject to tax—

(i) Even if an exempt body is mounted on a taxable chassis or a taxable body is mounted on an exempt chassis; and

(ii) The resulting vehicle is a highway vehicle.

(3) *Gross vehicle weight*.—(i) The term *gross vehicle weight* means the maximum total weight of a loaded vehicle. Except as otherwise provided in this paragraph (f)(3), the maximum total weight is the GVW rating of the article as specified by the manufacturer on the Manufacturer's Statement of Origin (or comparable document) or by the retailer of the completed article on a comparable document. In determining the GVW, the following rules apply:

(A) The GVW rating must take into account, among other things, the strength of the chassis frame, the axle capacity and placement, and, if an article is specially equipped to the buyer's specifications, those specifications.

(B) The manufacturer or retailer of an article listed in paragraph (a) of this section must specify the article's GVW rating at the time the article requires no additional manufacture other than—

(1) The addition of readily attachable articles, such as tire or rim assemblies or minor accessories;

(2) The performance of minor finishing operations, such as painting; or

(3) In the case of a chassis, the addition of a body.

(C) If the IRS finds that a GVW rating by the manufacturer or a later seller is unreasonable in light of the facts and circumstances in a particular case, that GVW rating will not be used for purposes of section 4051.

(D) The IRS may exclude from a GVW rating any readily attachable parts to the extent the IRS finds that the use of such parts in computing the GVW rating results in an inaccurate GVW rating.

(E) If the following or similar ratings are inconsistent, the highest of these ratings is the GVW rating:

(1) The rating indicated in a label or identifying device affixed to an article.

(2) The rating set forth in sales invoice or warranty agreement.

(3) The advertised rating for that article (or identical articles).

(ii) The retailer must keep a record of the GVW rating for each chassis, body, or vehicle it sells. For this purpose, a record of the serial number of each such article is treated as a record of the GVW rating of the article if such rating is indicated by the serial number. The GVW rating must be retained as part of the retailer's records for each of its chassis, bodies, or vehicles.

(4) *Gross combination weight*.—(i) The term *gross combination weight* means the GVW of the tractor plus the GVW of any trailer or semitrailer that the tractor may safely tow. Unless a particular rating is unreasonable in light of the facts and circumstances in a particular case, the IRS will consider the GCW of a tractor to be the highest GCW rating specified on any of the following documents:

(A) The Manufacturer's Statement of Origin (or comparable document) or a comparable document of a seller of the completed tractor.

(B) A label or identifying device affixed to the completed tractor by the manufacturer or the seller.

(C) A sales invoice or warranty agreement.

(D) An advertisement for the tractor (or identical tractors).

(ii) The retailer must keep a record of the GCW rating for each tractor it sells. The GCW rating must be retained as part of the retailer's records for each of its tractors.

(g) *Example*.—The following example illustrates the application of paragraphs (e)(1), (2), (3), and (4) of this section:

Example. (1) *Facts*. (i) A vehicle has the capacity to tow truck trailers and semitrailers (trailers) that have a GVW of 20,000 pounds. The vehicle has a standard chassis cab (4-door with crew cab), accommodating five passengers, and is outfitted with certain luxury features. The cab has an electric trailer brake control that connects to the brakes of a towed trailer and to a hook up for trailer lights. The vehicle has two storage boxes behind the cab that can accommodate incidental items such as small tools and vehicle repair equipment.

(ii) The vehicle has a GVW rating of 23,000 pounds and a GCW rating of 43,000 pounds. The vehicle is equipped with hydraulic disc brakes with a four wheel automatic braking system, a 300 horsepower engine, and a six-speed automatic transmission. The front axle of the vehicle has an 8,000 pound rating and the rear axle has a 15,000 pound rating.

(iii) The vehicle has three types of hitching devices: a removable ball gooseneck hitch, a fifth wheel hitch, and a heavy duty trailer receiver hitch. The vehicle's platform, which is approximately 139 inches long, is designed with a rectangular well to accommodate the gooseneck and fifth wheel hitches (bed hitches). This platform slopes at the rear of the rectangular well and has tie down hooks. Optional removable steel stake rails can be placed around the platform.

(2) *Analysis*. (i) Some characteristics of the vehicle such as its chassis cab with a GVW rating of 23,000 pounds, a 300 horsepower engine, a front axle with an 8,000 pound rating, and a rear axle with a 15,000 pound rating are consistent with either a cargo carrying or a towing function. In this case, however, the vehicle also has a GCW rating of 43,000 pounds and its engine, brakes, transmission, axle ratings, electric trailer brake control, trailer hook up lights, and hitches enable it to tow a trailer that has a GVW rating of 20,000 pounds.

(ii) When the vehicle's bed hitches are used to tow, the cargo carrying capacity of the vehicle is limited to the storage boxes behind the cab and is minimal in comparison to the GVW rating of the towed truck trailer or semitrailer. Neither the steel stake bed rails nor the tie down hooks significantly increase cargo carrying capacity when either of the bed hitches is used. Even if neither of the vehicle's two bed hitches is used, the design of the vehicle significantly reduces its cargo carrying capacity when compared to the cargo carrying capacity of a pickup truck body or a flatbed truck body installed on a comparable chassis. The significant reduction in cargo carrying capacity resulting from the vehicle's platform with its rectangular well and sloping platform at the rear of the rectangular well is evidence that the vehicle is not primarily designed to carry cargo. By accommodating the bed hitches, however, this platform configuration increases the vehicle's towing capacity and, in conjunction with the other features described above, makes it possible to safely tow a trailer with a GVW rating of 20,000 pounds.

(3) *Conclusion.* The vehicle's physical characteristics, which maximize towing capacity at the expense of carrying capacity, establish that the vehicle is primarily designed to tow a vehicle, such as a truck trailer or semitrailer, rather than to carry cargo on its chassis. Thus, the vehicle is a tractor.

(h) *Effective/applicability date.*—This section applies on and after the date of publication of these regulations in the **Federal Register** as final regulations. [Reg. § 48.4051-1.]

§ 48.4051-2. Imposition of tax; parts and accessories.—(a) *Parts or accessories sold on or in connection with the sale of chassis, bodies, and tractors.*—(1) *In general.*—(i) The tax imposed by section 4051 applies to parts or accessories sold on or in connection with, or with the sale of, any article specified in § 48.4051-1(a). The tax applies whether or not the parts or accessories are separately billed by the retailer.

(ii) If a taxable chassis or body is sold by the retailer without parts or accessories that are considered equipment essential for the operation or appearance of the taxable article, the sale of these parts or accessories by the retailer to the buyer of the taxable article will be considered, in the absence of evidence to the contrary, to have been made in connection with the sale of the taxable article even though they are shipped separately, whether at the same time or on a different date.

(iii) Parts and accessories that are spares or replacements are not subject to the tax described in paragraph (a)(1)(i) of this section.

(2) *Example.*—The following example illustrates the application of this paragraph (a):

Example. X buys from Retailer a chassis in a sale subject to the tax imposed by section 4051. At the time of the sale, bumpers were not attached to the chassis; rather, they had been ordered from Retailer and delivered to X at a later date. For purposes of the tax imposed by section 4051, the price of the chassis includes the price of the bumpers, regardless of when the Retailer delivered the bumpers or billed X for the bumpers.

(b) *Parts or accessories not sold on or in connection with the sale of chassis, bodies, and tractors.*—(1) *In general.*—Section 4051(b)(1) imposes a tax on the installation of a part or accessory on a taxable article specified in § 48.4051-1(a) within six months after the article was first placed in service. However, the tax imposed by section 4051(b)(1) does not apply if—

(i) The part or accessory is a replacement part or accessory; or

(ii) The aggregate price of non-replacement parts and accessories (and their installation) for any vehicle does not exceed $1,000.

(2) *Application and rate of tax.*—The tax is the applicable percentage of the price of the part or accessory and its installation. The applicable percentage is prescribed in section 4051(b)(1).

(3) *Liability for tax.*—The owner, lessee, or operator of the vehicle on which the parts or accessories are installed is liable for this tax. The owner(s) of the trade or business that installs the parts or accessories is secondarily liable for this tax.

(4) *Definitions.*—(i) *First placed in service.*—For purposes of this section, a vehicle is *first placed in service* on the date on which the owner of the vehicle took actual possession of the vehicle. This date can be established by the delivery ticket signed by the owner or other comparable document indicating delivery to, and acceptance by, the owner.

(ii) *Replacement part.*—The term *replacement part* means an item that is substantially similar to and intended to take the place of a vehicle part that has worn out or broken down, regardless of when it is ordered.

(5) *Example.*—The following example illustrates the application of this paragraph (b). Assume that during the periods described, the rate of tax is 12 percent of the price of the part or accessory and its installation.

Example. X bought a vehicle in a sale that was subject to the tax imposed by section 4051 and first placed it in service on September 1, 2013. On October 1, 2013, X purchases and has installed non-replacement parts at a cost of $750. On November 1, 2013, X purchases and has installed additional non-replacement parts at a cost of $450. On December 1, 2013, X purchases and has installed additional non-replacement parts and accessories at a cost of $900. Although the price of each separate purchase and installation is less than $1,000, the aggregate price exceeds the $1,000 limit on November 1, 2013. Accordingly, on November 1, 2013, X is liable for tax of $144 (12 percent x ($750 + $450)) on account of the installations on October 1, and November 1, 2013. On December 1, 2013, X is liable for a tax of $108 (12 percent x $900) on account of the installation on that date. To report its liability X must file Form 720, Quarterly Federal Excise Tax Return, for the fourth calendar quarter of 2013 by January 31, 2014.

(c) *Effective/applicability date.*—This section applies on and after the date of publication of these regulations in the **Federal Register** as final regulations. [Reg. § 48.4051-2.]

Par. 28. Section 145.4051-1 is revised to read as follows:

§ 145.4051-1. Imposition of tax on heavy trucks, tractors, and trailers sold at retail.—(a) For rules relating to the imposition of the tax imposed by section 4051 and related rules on the tax base, liability for tax, explanation of terms, and exclusions, see §48.4051-1 through §48.4052-2 of this chapter.

(b) This section applies on and after the date on which these regulations are published as final regulations in the **Federal Register**.

Excise Tax: Tractors, Trailers, Trucks, and Tires: Highway Vehicle: Definition

Excise Tax: Tractors, Trailers, Trucks, and Tires: Highway Vehicle: Definition.—Amendments to Reg. §§48.4052-1 and 145.4052-1, relating to the excise taxes imposed on the sale of highway tractors, trailers, trucks, and tires, the use of heavy vehicles on the highway, and the definition of highway vehicle related to these and other taxes, are proposed (published in the Federal Register on March 31, 2016) (REG-103380-05).

Par. 10. Section 48.4052-1 is revised to read as follows:

§48.4052-1. Definition; first retail sale.—(a) *In general.*—For purposes of the tax imposed by section 4051, *first retail sale* means a taxable sale defined in paragraph (b) of this section.

(b) *Taxable sale; in general.*—A sale of an article described in §48.4051-1(a) is a taxable sale except in the following cases:

(1) The sale is an exempt sale. A sale is an exempt sale if—

(i) The sale is a tax-free sale under section 4221;

(ii) The sale is of a used article that had previously been sold tax-free under section 4221; or

(iii) The article is sold for resale or leasing in a long-term lease and, at the time of sale, the seller—

(A) Has obtained from the buyer a certificate described in paragraph (d) of this section stating, among other things, that the buyer will either resell the vehicle or lease it in a long-term lease;

(B) Has no reason to believe that any information in the certificate is false; and

(C) Has not received a notification from the IRS under paragraph (d)(1) of this section with respect to the buyer.

(2) There has been a prior sale of the article that is not an exempt sale. The previous sentence does not apply if the prior sale is described in paragraph (c)(1) of this section.

(c) *Special rule for trailers and semitrailers.*—(1) *In general.*—A sale is described in this paragraph (c)(1) if the sale—

(i) Is a sale of a chassis or body of a truck trailer or semitrailer ("trailer or semitrailer");

(ii) Is not an exempt sale; and

(iii) Occurs less than six months after the first sale of the trailer or semitrailer that is not an exempt sale.

(2) *Credit.*—In the case of a sale described in paragraph (c)(1) of this section, any tax paid by the prior seller on account of its sale (and not at any time refunded to or credited against any other liability of the prior seller) is treated as a payment on behalf of the person (the subsequent seller) liable for the tax on the sale described in paragraph (c)(1) of this section. The subsequent seller may claim such payment as a credit against its liability for tax on the sale described in paragraph (c)(1) of this section if the following conditions are met:

(i) The claim is made on Form 720, "Quarterly Federal Excise Tax Return" (or such other form as the IRS may designate) in accordance with the instructions for that form.

(ii) The subsequent seller has not been repaid any portion of the tax by the prior seller and has not provided the prior seller with a written consent to the allowance of a credit or refund.

(iii) The subsequent seller has records substantiating the amount of tax paid by the prior seller on its sale of the truck trailer or semitrailer.

(d) *Certificate.*—(1) *In general.*—The certificate referred to in paragraph (b)(1)(iii) of this section is a statement that is signed under penalties of perjury by a person with authority to bind the buyer, is in substantially the same form as the model certificate provided in paragraph (d)(3) of this section, and contains all information necessary to complete the model certificate. The IRS may withdraw the right of a buyer of vehicles to provide a certificate under this section if the buyer uses the vehicles to which a certificate relates other than as stated in the certificate. The IRS may notify any seller that the buyer's right to provide a certificate has been withdrawn. The certificate may be included as part of any business records normally used to document a sale.

(2) *Effect of use other than as stated in certificate.*—If a buyer that provides a certificate described in paragraph (b)(1)(iii)(A) of this section uses or leases (in a short term lease) an article listed in the certificate, the sale of such article to the buyer is treated as the first retail sale of the article and the buyer is liable for the tax imposed on such sale. If the conditions of paragraph (b)(1)(iii)(A), (B), and (C) of this section are satisfied, the seller will not be liable for the tax imposed on such sale.

(3) *Model certificate.*

Certificate

(To support nontaxable sale of articles listed in section 4051 for resale or long term lease under section 4052 of the Internal Revenue Code)

The undersigned buyer of articles listed in section 4051 ("Buyer") hereby certifies the following under penalties of perjury:

1. ____

____

Seller's name, address, and employer identification number
2.

Buyer's name, address, and employer identification number
3.
Date and location of sale to Buyer
4. The articles listed below will be either resold by Buyer or leased on a long term basis by Buyer. If the article is a chassis, Buyer has listed the chassis Vehicle Identification Number. If the article is a body, Buyer has listed the body's identification number.

5. Buyer understands that it must be prepared to establish, by evidence satisfactory to an examining agent, how each article bought under this certificate was used.
6. Buyer has not been notified by the Internal Revenue Service that its right to provide a certificate has been withdrawn.
7. Buyer understands that if it uses or leases (in a short term lease) an article listed in this certificate, Buyer will be liable for the tax imposed by section 4051(a)(1) on the article. See 26 CFR 48.4051-1 and 145.4052-1(c).
8. Buyer understands that Buyer may be liable for the section 6701 penalty (relating to aiding and abetting an understatement of tax liability) if this is an erroneous certification.
9. Buyer understands that the fraudulent use of this certificate may subject Buyer and all parties making any fraudulent use of this statement to a fine or imprisonment, or both, together with the costs of prosecution.

Printed or typed name of person signing this certificate

Title of person signing

Signature and date signed

(e) *No installment payment of tax*.—If a lease is a taxable sale under § 145.4052-1(b) of this chapter or an installment sale (or another form of sale under which the sales price is paid in installments), then the liability for the entire tax arises at the time of the lease or installment sale. No portion of the tax is deferred by reason of the fact that the sales price is paid in installments.

(f) *Effective/applicability date*.—This section applies on and after the date of publication of these regulations in the **Federal Register** as final regulations.

Par. 29. Section 145.4052-1 is amended by:
1. Revising paragraph (a).
2. Adding two sentences after the first sentence in paragraph (d)(1).
3. Removing the last sentence in paragraph (d)(8)(iii).
4. Revising paragraph (g).
The revisions read as follows:

§ 145.4052-1. Special rules and definitions.— (a) *First retail sale*.—For the definition of first retail sale, see § 48.4052-1 of this chapter.

* * *

(d) * * *

(1) * * *. Total consideration paid for a chassis or body includes charges for equipment installed on the chassis or body. See § 48.4051-1(d)(4). * * *

* * *

(g) *Effective/applicability date*.—This section applies on and after the date of publication of these regulations in the **Federal Register** as final regulations.

Par. 31. For each section listed in the tables, remove the language in the "Remove" column and add in its place the language in the "Add" column as set forth below:

Section	Remove	Add
§ 145.4052-1(b)(1) First sentence	§ 145.4051-1	§ 48.4051-1 of this chapter
Second sentence	paragraph (a)(2) of this section	§ 48.4052-1(b) of this chapter
§ 145.4052-1(b)(2)	§ 145.4051-1	§ 48.4051-1 of this chapter
	paragraph (a)(2) of this section	§ 48.4052-1(b) of this chapter
§ 145.4052-1(c)(1)	§ 145.4051-1	§ 48.4051-1 of this chapter
§ 145.4052-1(c)(5)(ii)	4216(a), 4216(f)	4052(b)(1)(A) and (B), 4216(a)
§ 145.4052-1(d)(1) Fourth sentence	Installatioin	installation

Excise Tax: Tractors, Trailers, Trucks, and Tires: Highway Vehicle: Definition

Excise Tax: Tractors, Trailers, Trucks, and Tires: Highway Vehicle: Definition.—Amendments to Reg. §§145.4061-1 and 48.4061(a)-1, relating to the excise taxes imposed on the sale of highway tractors, trailers, trucks, and tires, the use of heavy vehicles on the highway, and the definition of highway vehicle related to these and other taxes, are proposed (published in the Federal Register on March 31, 2016) (REG-103380-05).

Par. 11. Section 48.4061(a)-1 is amended as follows:

1. Paragraph (d)(2)(ii), first sentence, is amended by removing the language "A self-propelled" and adding "Before January 1, 2005, a self-propelled" in its place.

2. Paragraph (d)(2)(iv) is added.

The addition reads as follows:

§48.4061(a)-1. Imposition of tax; exclusion for light-duty trucks, etc.

* * *

(d) * * *

(2) * * *

(iv) *Off-highway transportation vehicles after October 21, 2004.*—For a description of certain vehicles that are not treated as highway vehicles after October 21, 2004, see §48.0-5(b)(3).

* * *

Par. 30. Section 145.4061-1 is removed.

§145.4061-1. Application to manufacturers tax.

Excise Tax: Tractors, Trailers, Trucks, and Tires: Highway Vehicle: Definition

Excise Tax: Tractors, Trailers, Trucks, and Tires: Highway Vehicle: Definition.—Amendments to Reg. §48.4071-1—48.4071-4, relating to the excise taxes imposed on the sale of highway tractors, trailers, trucks, and tires, the use of heavy vehicles on the highway, and the definition of highway vehicle related to these and other taxes, are proposed (published in the Federal Register on March 31, 2016) (REG-103380-05).

Par. 13. Section 48.4071-1 is revised to read as follows:

§48.4071-1. Tires; imposition of tax.—(a) *In general.*—(1) Tax is imposed by section 4071 on the sale by the manufacturer of a taxable tire with a maximum rated load capacity greater than 3,500 pounds.

(2) See §48.4072-1(b) for the definition of the term *taxable tire.*

(b) *Tax base and computation of tax.*—The tax base is equal to the number of 10-pound increments, rounded down to the nearest ten pounds, by which the maximum rated load capacity exceeds 3,500 pounds. The tax is determined by multiplying this tax base by the rate of tax specified in section 4071(a). Thus, for example, a taxable tire with a maximum rated load capacity of 4,005 pounds is treated as having a maximum rated load capacity of 4,000 pounds and a tax base of 50 ((4000 - 3,500) ÷ 10). The tax imposed on the tire is the rate of tax under section 4071(a) times 50.

(c) *Liability for tax.*—The manufacturer of a taxable tire is liable for the tax imposed by section 4071.

(d) *Effective/applicability date.*—This section applies on and after the date of publication of these regulations in the **Federal Register** as final regulations.

Par. 14. Section 48.4071-2 is revised to read as follows:

§48.4071-2. Determination of maximum rated load capacity.—(a) *In general.*—For purposes of the tax imposed by section 4071, the maximum rated load capacity is the maximum rated load rating inscribed on a taxable tire's sidewall provided the inscription meets the standards prescribed by the National Highway Traffic Safety Administration in its regulations. If a taxable tire has multiple maximum load ratings, the taxable tire's highest maximum load rating is the taxable tire's maximum rated load capacity for purposes of the tax.

(b) *Tampering.*—In the event of any tampering with, or the appearance of tampering with, the inscription of a taxable tire's maximum rated load capacity as described in paragraph (a) of this section, the tire's maximum rated load capacity is the maximum rated load capacity of a comparable tire.

(c) *Effective/applicability date.*—This section applies on and after the date of publication of these regulations in the **Federal Register** as final regulations.

Par. 15. Section 48.4071-3 is amended by:

1. Revising the section heading and paragraph (a).
2. Revising paragraph (c)(1).
3. Adding paragraph (e).
4. Removing the undesignated authority citation at the end of the section.

The revisions and addition read as follows:

§ 48.4071-3. Imposition of tax on tires delivered to manufacturer's retail outlet.—(a) *General rule.*—If a tire manufacturer delivers a taxable tire it manufactured to one of its retail outlets, the manufacturer is liable for the tax imposed by section 4071 on this tire in the same manner as if the tire had been sold upon delivery to the retail outlet. The amount of tax is computed under § 48.4071-1.

* * *

(c) * * *

(1) *Delivery.*—(i) *Delivery options.*—A manufacturer of taxable tires may, at its option, treat either of the following events as constituting delivery to a retail outlet:

(A) Delivery of taxable tires to a common carrier (or, where the taxable tires are transported by the manufacturer, the placing of the taxable tires into the manufacturer's highway vehicle) for shipment from the plant in which the taxable tires are manufactured, or from a regional distribution center of taxable tires, to a retail outlet or to a location in the immediate vicinity of a retail outlet primarily for future delivery to the retail outlet.

(B) Arrival of the taxable tires at the retail outlet, or, where shipment is to a location in the immediate vicinity of a retail outlet primarily for future delivery to the retail outlet, the arrival of the taxable tires at such location.

(ii) *Delivery election.*—A manufacturer that has elected to treat one of the events listed in paragraph (c)(1)(i)(A) or (B) of this section as constituting delivery to a retail outlet may not use a different criterion for a later return period unless the manufacturer obtains permission from the IRS in advance.

* * *

(e) *Effective/applicability date.*—This section applies on and after the date of publication of these regulations in the **Federal Register** as final regulations.

Par. 26. For each section listed in the tables, remove the language in the "Remove" column from wherever it appears in the paragraph and add in its place the language in the "Add" column as set forth below:

Section	Remove	Add
§ 48.4071-3(b) Second sentence	tires or tubes	taxable tires
Fourth sentence	tires or inner tubes	taxable tires
Fifth sentence	tires	taxable tires
Sixth sentence	taxable tires and inner tubes	taxable tires
§ 48.4071-3(c)(1) Introductory text	tires or inner tubes	taxable tires
§ 48.4071-3(c)(1)(i)	tires or inner tubes	taxable tires
	tires or tubes	taxable tires
	tires and inner tubes	taxable tires
§ 48.4071-3(c)(2)(i) Second sentence	tires and inner tubes	taxable tires
Third sentence	tires or inner tubes	taxable tires
Fourth sentence	Tires and inner tubes	Taxable tires
	tires and tubes	taxable tires
Seventh sentence	tires and inner tubes tires and tubes tires or tubes	taxable tires
Eighth sentence	tires and inner tubes tire or inner tube	taxable tires
§ 48.4071-3(c)(2)(ii) First sentence (Example)	tires and tubes	taxable tires
Third sentence (Example)	tires and inner tubes	taxable tires
Fourth sentence (Example)	tires or inner tubes tires and tubes	taxable tires
§ 48.4071-3(c)(3)(i)	tire or inner tube	taxable tire
§ 48.4071-3(c)(3)(ii)	tire or inner tube	taxable tire
§ 48.4071-3(d)(1) First sentence	tires and inner tubes	taxable tires
Second sentence	tires or inner tubes	taxable tires
§ 48.4071-3(d)(2)	tires and inner tubes	taxable tires
§ 48.4071-3(d)(3)(i) First sentence	tire or inner tube	taxable tire
Second sentence	tire or inner tube	taxable tire

Section	Remove	Add
§ 48.4071-3(d)(3)(ii) Third sentence (Example)	tires and tubes (each of the two times it appears)	taxable tires
Fourth sentence (Example)	tires or inner tubes	taxable tires

Par. 16. Section 48.4071-4 is removed.

§ 48.4071-4. Original equipment tires on imported articles.

Excise Tax: Tractors, Trailers, Trucks, and Tires: Highway Vehicle: Definition

Excise Tax: Tractors, Trailers, Trucks, and Tires: Highway Vehicle: Definition.—Amendments to Reg. § 48.4072-1, relating to the excise taxes imposed on the sale of highway tractors, trailers, trucks, and tires, the use of heavy vehicles on the highway, and the definition of highway vehicle related to these and other taxes, are proposed (published in the Federal Register on March 31, 2016) (REG-103380-05).

Par. 17. Section 48.4072-1 is amended by:

1. Revising paragraphs (b), (c), and (d).
2. Amending paragraph (e) by removing the second, third, and fourth sentences.
3. Revising paragraphs (f), (g), and (h).
4. Removing the undesignated authority citation at the end of the section. The revisions and addition read as follows:

§ 48.4072-1. Definitions.

* * *

(b) *Taxable tire.*—(1) *In general.*—The term *taxable tire* means a tire—

(i) Of the type used on highway vehicles;

(ii) That is wholly or in part made of rubber; and

(iii) That is marked pursuant to federal regulations for for highway use.

(2) *Recapped and retreaded tires.*—The term *taxable tire* includes a used tire that is recapped or retreaded (whether from shoulder-to-shoulder or bead-to-bead) only if—

(i) The used tire had not previously been sold in the United States;

(ii) The used tire is recapped or retreaded outside the United States; and

(iii) When imported into the United States, the recapped or retreaded tire meets the requirements of section (b)(1) of this section.

(c) *Tires of the type used on highway vehicles.*—The term *tires of the type used on highway vehicles* means tires (other than tires of a type used exclusively on mobile machinery (within the meaning of § 48.0-5(c))) of the type used on—

(1) Highway vehicles; or

(2) Vehicles of the type used in connection with highway vehicles.

(d) *Rated load capacity.*—The term *rated load capacity* means the maximum load a tire is rated to carry at a specified inflation pressure.

* * *

(f) *Super single tire.*—The term *super single tire* means a single tire greater than 13 inches in cross section width designed to replace two tires in a dual fitment. The term does not include any tire designed for steering or an all position tire.

(g) Examples. The following examples illustrate the application of this section.

Example 1. (1) *Facts.* (i) A foreign tire manufacturer manufactures a tire that meets the Federal Motor Vehicle Safety Standard for truck tires prescribed by the DOT. The tire is not of a type used exclusively on mobile machinery (within the meaning of § 48.0-5(c)). This tire is partially made of rubber. The foreign manufacturer marks this tire for highway use pursuant to DOT regulations. The foreign manufacturer sells the tire for use in the foreign country.

(ii) After use in the foreign country, a tire importer buys the tire and imports it into the United States. At the time of importation, the tread on this tire's casing meets the criteria for minimal tread on trucks used in interstate commerce as prescribed by the DOT.

(2) *Analysis.* The imported tire is a taxable tire because the tire is of the type used on a highway vehicle and is not of a type used exclusively on mobile machinery, the tire is wholly or in part made of rubber, and the tire is marked pursuant to federal regulations for highway use.

Example 2. (1) *Facts.* A tire manufacturer pays the tax imposed by section 4071(a) when it sells a tire that is (1) of the type used on highway vehicles; (2) wholly or in part made of rubber; and (3) marked pursuant to federal regulations for highway use. The tire does not have any design features to indicate that it is a tire of a type used exclusively on mobile machinery (within the meaning of § 48.0-5(b)(3)(iii)). The purchaser of this tire puts the tire on mobile machinery described in § 48.0-5(b)(3)(iii).

(2) *Analysis.* A tire that is "of the type used on highway vehicles" and "not of a type used exclusively on mobile machinery" retains those characteristics regardless of how the tire is actually used. Therefore, the characterization of a tire as a taxable tire is not changed because the tire is actually used on a vehicle that is mobile machinery.

(h) *Effective/applicability date.*—This section applies on and after the date of publication of these regulations in the **Federal Register** as final regulations.

Excise Tax: Tractors, Trailers, Trucks, and Tires: Highway Vehicle: Definition

Excise Tax: Tractors, Trailers, Trucks, and Tires: Highway Vehicle: Definition.—Amendments to Reg. §§48.4073-1—48.4073-4, relating to the excise taxes imposed on the sale of highway tractors, trailers, trucks, and tires, the use of heavy vehicles on the highway, and the definition of highway vehicle related to these and other taxes, are proposed (published in the Federal Register on March 31, 2016) (REG-103380-05).

Par. 19. Section 48.4073-1 is revised to read as follows:

§48.4073-1. Exemption for tires sold for the exclusive use of the Department of Defense or the Coast Guard.—(a) *In general.*—Tax is not imposed by section 4071 on the sale of a taxable tire if—

(1) The manufacturer of the taxable tire meets the registration requirements of section 4222; and

(2) The sale of the taxable tire is to the Department of Defense or the Coast Guard for the exclusive use of the Department of Defense or the Coast Guard,

(b) *Sales for resale.*—A manufacturer may sell a taxable tire tax-free under section 4073 and this section only if the sale is directly made to either the Department of Defense or the Coast Guard for such agency's exclusive use. Accordingly, a sale may not be made taxfree to a dealer for resale to the Department of Defense or the Coast Guard for its exclusive use, even though it is known at the time of sale by the manufacturer that the article will be so resold.

(c) *Certificate.*—(1) *Effect of certificate.*—A manufacturer will not be liable for tax on the sale of a taxable tire if, at the time of the sale, the manufacturer has obtained from the buyer an unexpired certificate described in paragraph (c)(2) of this section and has no reason to believe any information in the certificate is false. A buyer that provides an erroneous certificate described in paragraph (c)(2) of this section is liable for any tax imposed on the sale to which the certificate relates.

(2) *Form of certificate.*—The certificate described in this paragraph (c)(2) is a statement by the Department of Defense or the Coast Guard that is signed under penalties of perjury by a person with authority to bind the Department of Defense or the Coast Guard, is in substantially the same form as the model certificate provided in paragraph (c)(3) of this section, and contains all information necessary to complete the model certificate. A new certificate or notice that the current certificate is invalid must be given if any information in the current certificate changes. The certificate may be included as part of any business records normally used to document a sale.

(3) *Model Certificate.*

Certificate

(To support the tax-free sales of tires to the Department of Defense or the Coast Guard under section 4073 of the Internal Revenue Code)

The undersigned buyer of taxable tires ("Buyer") hereby certifies the following under penalties of perjury:

1. ______________________________

____

____

Manufacturer's name, address, and employer identification number

2. ______________________________

____

____

Buyer's name, address, and employer identification number

3. ______________________________

Date and location of sale to Buyer

4. The tire(s) to which this certificate applies will be for the exclusive use of Buyer (that is, the Department of Defense or the Coast Guard).

5. This certificate applies to Buyer's purchases from Manufacturer as follows (complete as applicable):

a. A single purchase on invoice or delivery ticket number ______

b. All purchases between ___(effective date) and ___(expiration date), a period not exceeding 12 calendar quarters after the effective date, under account or order number(s) ___. If this certificate applies only to Buyer's purchases for certain locations, check here ______ and list the locations.

____

____

____

6. Buyer will provide a new certificate to the Manufacturer if any information in this certificate changes.

7. Buyer understands that Buyer may be liable for the section 6701 penalty (relating to aiding and abetting an understatement of tax liability) if this is an erroneous certification.

8. Buyer understands that the fraudulent use of this certificate may subject Buyer and all parties making any fraudulent use of this statement to a fine or imprisonment, or both, together with the costs of prosecution.

Printed or typed name of person signing this certificate

Title of person signing

Signature and date signed

(d) *Effective/applicability date*.—This section applies on and after the date of publication of these regulations in the **Federal Register** as final regulations.

Par. 20. Section 48.4073-2 is revised to read as follows:

§48.4073-2. American National Red Cross.—(a) For the exemption allowed to the American National Red Cross from the tax imposed by section 4071, see the Secretary's Authorization, 1979-1 C.B. 478 (See §601.601(d)(2)(ii)(*b*) of this chapter.)

(b) *Effective/applicability date*.—This section applies on and after the date of publication of these regulations in the **Federal Register** as final regulations.

Par. 21. Sections 48.4073-3 and 48.4073-4 are removed.

§48.4073-3. Exemption of tread rubber used for recapping non-highway tires.

Par. 21. Sections 48.4073-3 and 48.4073-4 are removed.

§48.4073-4. Other tax-free sales.

Excise Taxes: Taxable Fuel: Returns: Definitions

Excise Taxes: Taxable Fuel: Returns: Definitions.—Amendments to Reg. §§48.4081-1, 48.4081-2, 48.4081-3 and 48.4081-6, relating to credits and payments for alcohol mixtures, biodiesel mixtures, renewable diesel mixtures, alternative fuel mixtures, and alternative fuel sold for use or used as a fuel and relating to the definition of gasoline and diesel fuel, are proposed (published in the Federal Register on July 29, 2008) (REG-155087-05) (corrected August 25, 2008).

Par. 14. Section 48.4081-1 is amended as follows:

1. Paragraph (b) is amended by:

a. Revising the definition of Blender.

b. Adding the definition of Diesel-water fuel emulsion in alphabetical order.

c. Adding the language "(other than a mixture as defined in §48.6426-1(b))" after "any liquid" in the introductory text of the definition of Excluded liquid.

d. Revising the definition of Finished gasoline.

e. Revising the definition of Gasoline.

f. Adding the definition of Gasoline blend in alphabetical order.

g. Revising the definition of Refinery.

h. Removing the language "effective January 2, 1998," from the last sentence in the definition of Terminal.

2. Paragraph (c) is amended by:

a. In paragraph (c)(1)(i), removing the language "paragraphs (c)(1)(ii) and (c)(1)(iii)" in the introductory phrase and adding "paragraph (c)(1)(ii)" in its place.

b. In paragraph (c)(1)(ii), removing the language "A mixture" and adding "In calendar quarters beginning before the date of publication of these regulations in the **Federal Register** as final regulations, a mixture" in its place.

c. Removing paragraph (c)(1)(iii).

d. In paragraph (c)(2)(i), first sentence, adding the language "any of the following: a mixture (as defined in §48.6426-1(b)) that contains diesel fuel; renewable diesel as defined in section 40A(f)(3); transmix (as defined in section 4083(a)(3)(B)); and" after "*diesel fuel* means".

e. In paragraph (c)(2)(ii), first sentence, adding the language "biodiesel, alternative fuel (as defined in section 6426(d)(2)), qualified methanol or ethanol fuel (as defined in section 4041(b)(2)(B)), partially exempt methanol or ethanol fuel (as defined in section 4041(m)(2))," after "kerosene,".

f. In paragraph (c)(3)(i)(V) removing the language "gasoline;" and adding "gasoline; and" in its place.

g. In paragraph (c)(3)(i)(W), removing the language "Toluene; and" and adding "Toluene." in its place.

h. Removing paragraph (c)(3)(i)(X).

3. Paragraph (e) is amended by removing the language "48.4081-6(b)," and by adding the language "48.6426-1(b)" after "48.4101-1(b),".

4. Revising paragraph (f).

The revisions and additions read as follows:

§48.4081-1. Taxable fuel; definitions

* * *

(b) * * *

Blender means the person that has title to blended taxable fuel immediately after it is created.

* * *

Diesel-water fuel emulsion means diesel fuel at least 14 percent of which is water and with respect to which the emulsion additive is registered by a United States manufacturer with the Environmental Protection Agency pursuant to section 211 of the Clean Air Act (as in effect on March 31, 2003).

* * *

Finished gasoline means all products that are commonly or commercially known or sold as gasoline and are suitable for use as a motor fuel, other than—

(1) Products that have an ASTM octane number of less than 75 as determined by the motor method; and

(2) Alternative fuel as defined in section 6426(d)(2).

Gasoline means aviation gasoline, finished gasoline, gasoline blends, gasoline blendstocks, and leaded gasoline.

Gasoline blend includes any liquid (other than finished gasoline) that contains at least 0.1 percent (by volume) of finished gasoline and that is suitable for use as a fuel in a motor vehicle or motorboat. However, the term does not include qualified methanol or ethanol fuel (as defined in section 4041(b)(2)(B)), partially exempt methanol or ethanol fuel (as defined in section 4041(m)(2)), or alcohol that is denatured under a formula approved by the Secretary.

* * *

Refinery means a facility used to produce taxable fuel and from which taxable fuel may be removed by pipeline, by vessel, or at a rack. However, the term does not include a facility where only blended taxable fuel, and no other type of taxable fuel, is produced.

* * *

(f) *Effective/applicability date.*—This section is applicable on and after the date of publication of these regulations in the **Federal Register** as final regulations. For provisions applicable to prior periods, see 26 CFR 48.4081-1 (revised as of April 1, 2008).

Par. 15. Section 48.4081-2 is amended by removing the last sentence of paragraph (d).

§48.4081-2. Taxable fuel; tax on removal at a terminal rack.

Par. 16. Section 48.4081-3 is amended as follows:

1. Paragraph (b)(1)(iii) is removed.

2. Removing the last sentence in paragraphs (g)(1) and (h).

§48.4081-3. Taxable fuel; taxable events other than removal at the terminal rack.

Par. 17. Section 48.4081-6 is removed and reserved.

§48.4081-6. Gasoline; gasohol.

Excise Tax: Tractors, Trailers, Trucks, and Tires: Highway Vehicle: Definition

Excise Tax: Tractors, Trailers, Trucks, and Tires: Highway Vehicle: Definition.—Amendments to Reg. §48.4081-1, relating to the excise taxes imposed on the sale of highway tractors, trailers, trucks, and tires, the use of heavy vehicles on the highway, and the definition of highway vehicle related to these and other taxes, are proposed (published in the Federal Register on March 31, 2016) (REG-103380-05).

Par. 22. Section 48.4081-1(b) is amended by removing the language "§48.4061(a)-1(d)" in the definition of *Diesel-powered highway vehicle* and adding "§48.0-5" in its place.

§48.4081-1. Taxable fuel; definitions.

Par. 26. For each section listed in the tables, remove the language in the "Remove" column from wherever it appears in the paragraph and add in its place the language in the "Add" column as set forth below:

Section	Remove	Add
§48.4081-1(b)	48.4061(a)-1(d)	48.0-5 of this chapter

Excise Taxes: Diesel Fuel and Kerosene: Dye Injections

Excise Taxes: Diesel Fuel and Kerosene: Dye Injections.—Amendments to Reg. §§48.4082-1 and 48.4101-1, relating to the mechanical dye injection of diesel fuel and kerosene, are proposed (published in the Federal Register on April 26, 2005) (REG-154000-04).

☐ Par. 2. In §48.4082-1, paragraphs (d) and (e)(2) are revised to read as follows:

§48.4082-1. Diesel fuel and kerosene; exemption for dyed fuel.

* * *

(d) [The text of this proposed paragraph (d) is the same as the text of §48.4082-1T(d) as added by T.D. 9199].

(e) * * *

(e)(2) [The text of this proposed paragraph (e)(2) is the same as the text of §48.4082-1T(e)(2) as added by T.D. 9199].

☐ Par. 3. Section 48.4101-1 is amended by revising paragraph (h)(3)(iv) to read as follows:

§48.4101-1. Taxable fuel; registration.

* * *

(h) * * *

(3) * * *

(iv) [The text of this proposed paragraph (h)(3)(iv) is the same as the text of §48.4101-1T(h)(3)(iv) as added by T.D. 9199].

Excise Taxes: Taxable Fuel: Returns: Definitions

Excise Taxes: Taxable Fuel: Returns: Definitions.—Amendments to Reg. §§48.4082-4 and 48.4101-1, relating to credits and payments for alcohol mixtures, biodiesel mixtures, renewable diesel mixtures, alternative fuel mixtures, and alternative fuel sold for use or used as a fuel and relating to the definition of gasoline and diesel fuel, are proposed (published in the Federal Register on July 29, 2008) (REG-155087-05).

Par. 18. Section 48.4082-4, is amended by adding the language "or biodiesel" after "taxable fuel" in paragraphs (a)(1)(iii) and (b)(1)(iii).

§48.4082-4. Diesel fuel and kerosene; backup tax.

Par. 19. Section 48.4101-1 is amended as follows:

1. Paragraph (a)(1) is amended by removing the language "4081 and" and adding "4081, for certain producers and importers of alcohol, biodiesel, and renewable diesel, and alternative fuelers under sections 6426 and 6427, and for purposes of" in its place.
2. Revising paragraphs (a)(2), (c)(1)(vi), (c)(1)(vii), and adding paragraph (c)(1)(viii).
3. Paragraphs (a)(3) and (b)(3) are removed and reserved.
4. Paragraph (b)(9) is amended by removing the language "48.4081-6(b), 48.4082-5(b), 48.4082-6(b), 48.4082-7(b)" and adding "48.4082-5(b), 48.4082-7(b), 48.6426-1(b)," in its place.
5. Revising paragraph (d)(2) and adding paragraph (d)(7).
6. Paragraph (d)(5) is amended by, removing the language "vendor; or" and adding "vendor;" in its place.
7. Paragraph (d)(6) is amended by removing the language "pump)." and adding "pump); or" in its place.
8. Paragraph (f)(1)(i) is amended by removing from the heading the language "and vessel operators." and adding "vessel operators, alternative fuelers, producers or importers of alcohol, biodiesel, or renewable diesel, and diesel-water fuel emulsion producers." in its place.
9. Paragraph (f)(1)(ii) is amended by removing the language in the heading "and vessel operators" and adding "vessel operators, alternative fuelers, producers or importers of alcohol, biodiesel, or renewable diesel, and dieselwater fuel emulsion producers" in its place.
10. Paragraph (f)(1)(ii) is amended by removing the language in the introductory text "or vessel operator" and adding "vessel operator, alternative fueler, producer or importer of alcohol, biodiesel, or renewable diesel, or dieselwater fuel emulsion producer" in its place.
11. Paragraph (f)(1)(ii)(B) is amended by adding the language "reporting," after "payment,".
12. Paragraph (f)(4)(ii)(A) is amended by removing the language in the introductory text "district director" and adding "Commissioner" in its place.
13. Paragraph (f)(4)(ii)(A)(*1*) is amended by removing the language "district director);" and adding "Commissioner); and" in its place.
14. Paragraph (f)(4) (ii)(A)(*2*) is amended by removing the language "district director); and" and adding "Commissioner." in its place.
15. Removing paragraph (f)(4)(i)(A)(3).
16. Paragraph (f)(4)(iii) is amended by removing the language "deposit, and payment" and adding "deposit, payment, reporting, and claim" in its place.
17. Revising paragraph (h)(2)(iii).
18. Paragraph (j)(2) is amended by removing the language in the introductory text "district director" and adding "Commissioner" in its place.
19. Paragraph (j)(2)(i), is amended by removing the language "district director);" and adding "Commissioner); and" in its place.
20. Paragraph (j)(2)(ii) is amended by removing the language "district director); and" and adding "Commissioner)." in its place.
21. Removing paragraph (j)(2)(iii).
22. Paragraph (k) is amended by adding a new sentence between the existing second and third sentences.
23. Paragraph (l)(5) is added.

The revisions and additions read as follows:

§48.4101-1. Taxable fuel; registration.—(a) * * *

(2) A person is registered under section 4101 only if the Commissioner has issued a registration letter to the person and the registration has not been revoked or suspended or the person is treated under this paragraph (a)(2) as registered under section 4101. The following persons are treated as registered under section 4101:

(i) The United States is treated as registered under section 4101 for all purposes.

(ii) A partner in a partnership is treated as registered under section 4101 for purposes of claims filed under section 34 if the partnership is registered under section 4101 for purposes of filing claims under section 6426 or 6427.

(iii) A taxable fuel registrant is treated as registered under section 4101 as a diesel-water fuel emulsion producer.

(iv) A foreign person is treated as registered under section 4101 as a producer of alcohol, biodiesel, or renewable diesel if—

(A) The person produces alcohol, biodiesel, or renewable diesel outside the United States and does not produce alcohol, biodiesel, or renewable diesel within the United States; and

(B) The alcohol, biodiesel, or renewable diesel is imported into the United States by a person registered under section 4101 as a producer or importer of alcohol, biodiesel, or renewable diesel.

* * *

(c) * * *

(1) * * *

(vi) A terminal operator;

(vii) A vessel operator; or

(viii) A producer or importer of alcohol, biodiesel, or renewable diesel.

* * *

(d) * * *

(2) An alternative fueler;

* * *

(7) A diesel-water fuel emulsion producer.

* * *

(h) * * *

(2) * * *

(iii) Make any false statement on, or violate the terms of, any certificate given to another person to support—

(A) Any claim for credit, refund, or payment; or

(B) An exemption from, or reduced rate of, tax imposed by section 4081; or

* * *

(k) * * * For rules relating to claims with respect to alcohol, biodiesel, renewable diesel and alternative fuel, see §§48.6426-1 through 48.6426-7. * * *

(l) * * *

(5) References in this section to biodiesel and alcohol are applicable after December 31, 2004. References in this section to renewable diesel and diesel-water fuel emulsion are applicable after December 31, 2005. References in this section to alternative fuel are applicable after September 30, 2006.

Excise Tax: Tractors, Trailers, Trucks, and Tires: Highway Vehicle: Definition

Excise Tax: Tractors, Trailers, Trucks, and Tires: Highway Vehicle: Definition.—Amendments to Reg. §§48.4221-7 and 48.4221-8, relating to the excise taxes imposed on the sale of highway tractors, trailers, trucks, and tires, the use of heavy vehicles on the highway, and the definition of highway vehicle related to these and other taxes, are proposed (published in the Federal Register on March 31, 2016) (REG-103380-05).

Par. 23. Section 48.4221-7 is amended by:

1. Revising the section heading and paragraph (a).
2. Removing paragraph (b) and redesignating paragraph (c) as paragraph (b).
3. Revising redesignated paragraph (b)(2).
4. Adding new paragraph (c).

The revisions and addition read as follows:

§48.4221-7. Tax-free sale of tires for use on other articles.—(a) *In general.*—Under section 4221(e)(2), tax is not imposed by section 4071 on the sale of a taxable tire if—

(1) The taxable tire is sold for use by the purchaser for sale on or in connection with the sale of another article manufactured or produced by the purchaser;

(2) The other article is to be sold by the purchaser—

(i) In a tax-free sale for export, for use as supplies for vessels or aircraft, to a state or local government for its exclusive use, or to a nonprofit educational organization for its exclusive use; or

(ii) For any of such purposes in a sale that would be tax-free but for the fact that the other article is not subject to tax under section 4051 or 4064;

(3) The registration requirements of section 4222 and the regulations thereunder are met; and

(4) The proof, described in paragraph (b) of this section, of the disposition of the other article, is timely received by the manufacturer.

(b) * * *

(2) *Required information.*—(i) *In general.*—The information referred to in paragraph (b)(1) of this section is a statement that is signed under penalties of perjury by a person with authority to bind the purchaser, is in substantially the same form as the model certificate provided in paragraph (b)(2)(ii) of this section, and contains all information necessary to complete the model certificate. For purchasers that are not required to be registered under section 4222, the IRS may withdraw the right of a purchaser of a taxable tire to provide a certificate under this section if the purchaser uses the tire to which a certificate relates other than as stated in the certificate. The IRS may notify any manufacturer to whom such purchaser has provided a certificate that the purchaser's right to provide a certificate has been withdrawn. The certificate may be included as part of any business records normally used to document a sale.

(ii) *Model certificate.*

Certificate

(To support the nontaxable sale of taxable tires by the manufacturer when sold for use on or in connection with the sale of another article manufactured or produced by the buyer and sold by the buyer in a sale that meets the requirements of section 4221(e)(2))

The undersigned buyer of taxable tires ("Buyer") hereby certifies the following under penalties of perjury:

1. ______________________________

____

Manufacturer's name, address, employer identification number, and registration number

2. ______________________________

____

Buyer's name, address, employer identification number, and registration number (if required)

3. ______________________________

Date and location of sale to Buyer

4. The taxable tire(s) listed below, by its (their) United States Department of Transportation identification number(s), are covered by this certificate

5. The taxable tire(s) listed in this certificate that were purchased or shipped on the date specified in entry 3 have been used on or in connection with the sale of (describe product sold by Buyer) by Buyer and such sale was—*(complete line (i), (ii), (iii), or (iv), whichever is applicable)*

(i) for export by ____________ (Name of carrier) to ____________ (Name of foreign country or possession) and was so exported on ____________, ________ (Date). (A copy of the bill of lading or other proof of exportation is attached.)

(ii) for use as supplies on ____________ (Name of vessel or aircraft) that is registered in ____________ (Name of country in which vessel or aircraft is registered).

(iii) to ______________________________ (Name of state or local government).

(iv) to ____________________ (Name and address of the nonprofit educational organization).

6. Buyer understands that it must be prepared to establish, by evidence satisfactory to an examining agent, how each tire bought under this certificate was used.

7. Check here _____ if Buyer is not required to be registered with the Internal Revenue Service because Buyer is a state or local government, a foreign person buying for export, or the United States.

8. Buyer understands that Buyer may be liable for the section 6701 penalty (relating to aiding and abetting an understatement of tax liability) if this is an erroneous certification.

9. Buyer understands that the fraudulent use of this certificate may subject Buyer and all parties making any fraudulent use of this statement to a fine or imprisonment, or both, together with the costs of prosecution.

____

Printed or typed name of person signing this certificate

____

Title of person signing

____

Signature and date signed

(c) *Effective/applicability date.*—This section applies on and after the date of publication of these regulations in the **Federal Register** as final regulations.

Par. 26. For each section listed in the tables, remove the language in the "Remove" column from wherever it appears in the paragraph and add in its place the language in the "Add" column as set forth below:

Section	Remove	Add
Redesignated § 48.4221-7 (b)(1)	tire or inner tube	taxable tire
Second sentence	tire or inner tube	taxable tire
Third sentence	tire or inner tube	taxable tire

Par. 24. Section 48.4221-8 is amended by:

1. Revising the section heading and paragraph (a).

2. Removing the second paragraph (b), *Registration requirements for tires, tubes, and tread rubber; vendees purchasing tax-free.*

3. Revising paragraphs (c) and (d).

4. Removing paragraphs (e) and (f).

The revisions read as follows:

§48.4221-8. Tax-free sales of tires used on intercity, local, and school buses.—(a) *In general.*—Under section 4221(e)(3), tax is not imposed by section 4071 on the sale of a taxable tire for use by the buyer on or in connection with a qualified bus, as defined in paragraph (b) of this section, if—

(1) The registration requirements of section 4222 and the regulations thereunder are met;

(2) At the time of sale, the manufacturer of the taxable tire—

(i) Possesses a certificate (in the form described in paragraph (c)(2) of this section) from the buyer of a taxable tire, in which, among other things, the buyer certifies that the buyer will use the taxable tire on or in connection with a qualified bus;

(ii) Has no reason to believe that any information in the certificate described in paragraph (c) of this section is false; and

(iii) Has not received a notification from the IRS under paragraph (c)(2) of this section with respect to the buyer.

* * *

(c) *Certificate.*—(1) *Effect of certificate.*—A manufacturer will not be liable for tax on the sale of a taxable tire if the conditions of paragraph (a)(2) of this section are satisfied. In such a case, a buyer that provides an erroneous certificate described in paragraph (c)(2) of this section is liable for any tax imposed on the sale to which the certificate relates.

(2) *In general.*—The certificate referred to in paragraph (a)(2) of this section is a statement that is signed under penalties of perjury by a person with authority to bind the buyer, is in substantially the same form as the model certificate provided in paragraph (c)(3) of this section, and contains all information necessary to complete the model certificate. For purchasers that are not required to be registered under section 4222, the IRS may withdraw the right of a buyer of a taxable tire to provide a certificate under this section if the buyer uses the tires to which a certificate relates other than as stated in the certificate. The IRS may notify any manufacturer to whom the buyer has provided a certificate that the buyer's right to provide a certificate has been withdrawn. The certificate may be included as part of any business records normally used to document a sale.

(3) *Model certificate.*

Certificate

(To support the nontaxable sale of taxable tires used on intercity, local, and school buses)

The undersigned buyer of taxable tires ("Buyer") hereby certifies the following under penalties of perjury:

1. ______________________________

____

____

Manufacturer's name, address, employer identification number, and registration number

2. ______________________________

____

____

Buyer's name, address, employer identification number, and registration number

3. ______________________________

Date and location of sale to Buyer

4. The taxable tire(s) listed below, by its (their) United States Department of Transportation identification number(s), will be used on intercity, local, and school buses.

5. Buyer understands that it must be prepared to establish, by evidence satisfactory to an examining agent, how each tire bought under this certificate was used.

6. Check here ____ if Buyer is not required to be registered with the Internal Revenue Service because Purchaser is a state or local government or the United States.

7. Buyer understands that Buyer may be liable for the section 6701 penalty (relating to aiding and abetting an understatement of tax liability) if this is an erroneous certification.

8. Buyer understands that the fraudulent use of this certificate may subject Buyer and all parties making any fraudulent use of this statement to a fine or imprisonment, or both, together with the costs of prosecution.

____

Printed or typed name of person signing this certificate

____

Title of person signing

____

Signature and date signed

(d) *Effective/applicability date.*—This section applies on and after the date of publication of these regulations in the **Federal Register** as final regulations.

Communication Excise Tax: Toll Telephone Service: Distance

Communication Excise Tax: Toll Telephone Service: Distance Sensitivity.—Reg. § 49.4252-0, relating to the definition of toll telephone service for purposes of the communications excise tax, is proposed (published in the Federal Register on April 1, 2003) (REG-141097-02).

☐ Par. 2. Section 49.4252-0 is added to read as follows:

§ 49.4252-0. Section 4252(b)(1); distance sensitivity.—(a) *In general.*—For a communications service to constitute toll telephone service described in section 4252(b)(1), the charge for the service need not vary with the distance of each individual communication.

(b) *Effective date.*—This section applies to amounts paid on and after the date of publication of these regulations in the Federal Register as final regulations. [Reg. § 49.4252-0.]

Expatriate Health Plans: Issuers: Excepted Benefits

Expatriate Health Plans: Issuers: Excepted Benefits.—Amendments to Reg. § 46.4377-1, relating to the rules for expatriate health plans, expatriate health plan issuers, and qualified expatriates under the Expatriate Health Coverage Clarification Act of 2014 (EHCCA), are proposed (published in the Federal Register on June 10, 2016) (REG-135702-15).

6. Section 46.4377-1 is amended by redesignating paragraph (c) as paragraph (d) and adding new paragraph (c) to read as follows:

§ 46.4377-1. Definitions and special rules.

* * *

(c) *Treatment of expatriate health plans.*—For policy years and plan years that end after January 1, 2017, the fees imposed by sections 4375 and 4376 do not apply to an expatriate health plan within the meaning of § 54.9831-1(f)(3).

* * *

Excise Tax: Tractors, Trailers, Trucks, and Tires: Highway Vehicle: Definition

Excise Tax: Tractors, Trailers, Trucks, and Tires: Highway Vehicle: Definition.—Amendments to Reg. § 41.4482(a)-1, relating to the excise taxes imposed on the sale of highway tractors, trailers, trucks, and tires, the use of heavy vehicles on the highway, and the definition of highway vehicle related to these and other taxes, are proposed (published in the Federal Register on March 31, 2016) (REG-103380-05).

Par. 2. Section 41.4482(a)-1(a)(2) is amended by removing the language "§ 48.4061(a)-1(d)" and adding "§ 48.0-5" in its place.

§ 41.4482(a)-1. Definition of highway motor vehicle.

REGISTRATION-REQUIRED OBLIGATIONS

Definition of Registered Form: Guidance

Definition of Registered Form: Guidance.—Amendments to Reg. § 46.4701-1, providing guidance on the definitions of registration-required obligation and registered form, including guidance on the issuance of pass-through certificates and participation interests in registered form, are proposed (published in the Federal Register on September 19, 2017) (REG-125374-16).

Par. 16. Section 46.4701-1 is amended by:

1. Revising paragraphs (b)(3), (4), and (5).
2. Redesignating paragraph (e) as paragraph (e)(1).
3. Revising the paragraph heading of newly redesignated paragraph (e)(1).
4. Adding a new paragraph heading for paragraph (e).
5. Adding paragraph (e)(2).

The revisions and additions read as follows:

§ 46.4701-1. Tax on issuer of registration-required obligation not in registered form.

* * *

(b) * * *

(3) *Registration-required obligation.*—The term *registration-required obligation* has the same meaning as in section 163(f) and § 1.163-5(a)(2)(i) of this chapter, except that the term does not include an obligation described in section 4701(b)(1)(B) or any obligation that is required to be registered under section 149(a), such as bonds that are tax-exempt under section 103. For purposes of determining whether an obligation is described in section 4701(b)(1)(B), the rules of § 1.163-5(c) of this chapter apply.

(4) *Registered form.*—The term *registered form* has the same meaning as in § 1.163-5(b) of this chapter.

(5) *Issuer.*—(i) *In general.*—Except as provided in paragraph (b)(5)(ii) of this section, the term *issuer* is the person whose interest deduction would be disallowed solely by reason of section 163(f)(1).

(ii) *Sponsor treated as issuer.*—A pass-through certificate (as defined in § 1.163-5(a)(3)(i)(B) of this chapter), a participation interest described in § 1.163-5(a)(3)(ii) of this chapter, or a regular interest in a REMIC, as defined in sections 860D and 860G and the regulations thereunder, is considered to be issued solely by the recipient of the proceeds from the issuance of the certificate or interest (the *sponsor*). The sponsor is therefore liable for any excise tax under section 4701 that may be imposed with reference to the principal amount of the pass-through certificate, participation interest, or regular interest.

* * *

(e) *Applicability date.*—(1) *In general.*—* * *

(2) *Exception.*—Notwithstanding paragraph (e)(1) of this section, paragraphs (b)(3), (4), and (5) of this section apply to obligations issued after March 18, 2012. For the rules that apply to obligations issued on or before March 18, 2012, see §46.4701-1 as contained in 26 CFR part 46, revised as of the date of the most recent annual revision.

PRIVATE FOUNDATIONS

Below-Market Loans

Below-Market Loans: Interest.—Reproduced below is the text of a proposed amendment of Reg. §53.4941(d)-2, relating to the tax treatment of both lender and borrower in certain below-market interest rate loan transactions (published in the Federal Register on August 20, 1985).

* * *

☐ Par. 10. Section 53.4941(d)-2 is amended by revising paragraph (c)(2) to read as follows:

§53.4941(d)-2. Specific acts of self-dealing.—

* * *

(c) Loans. * * *

(2) *Loans without interest.*—Subparagraph (1) of this paragraph shall not apply to the lending of money or other extension of credit by a disqualified person to a private foundation if the loan or other extension of credit is without interest (determined without regard to foregone interest described in section 7872) or other charge.

QUALIFIED PENSION, ETC., PLANS

Employees' Trusts: Minimum Funding Requirements

Employees' Trusts: Minimum Funding Requirements: Minimum Funding Excise Taxes.—Reproduced below are the texts of proposed Reg. §§54.4971-1—54.4971-3, relating to the minimum funding requirements for employee pension benefit plans, and to excise taxes for failure to meet the minimum funding standards (published in the Federal Register on December 1, 1982).

☐ Par. 8. The Pension Excise Tax Regulations, 26 CFR Part 54, are amended by adding in the appropriate place the following new sections:

§54.4971-1. General rules relating to excise tax on failure to meet minimum funding standards.—(a) [Reserved]

(b) [Reserved]

(c) *Additional tax.*—Section 4971(b) imposes an excise tax in any case in which an initial tax is imposed under section 4971(a) on an accumulated funding deficiency and the accumulated funding deficiency is not corrected within the taxable period (as defined in section 4971(c)(3)). The additional tax is 100 percent of the accumulated funding deficiency to the extent not corrected.

(d) [Reserved]

(e) *Definition of taxable period.*—(1) *In general.*—For purposes of any accumulated funding deficiency, the term "taxable period" means the period beginning with the end of the plan year in which there is an accumulated funding deficiency and ending on the earlier of:

(i) The date of mailing of a notice of deficiency under section 6212 with respect to the tax imposed by section 4971(a), or

(ii) The date on which the tax imposed by section 4971(a) is assessed.

(2) *Special rule.*—Where a notice of deficiency referred to in paragraph (e)(1)(i) of this section is not mailed because a waiver of the restrictions on assessment and collection of a deficiency has been accepted or because the deficiency is paid, the date of filing of the waiver or the date of such payment, respectively, shall be treated as the end of the taxable period. [Reg. §54.4971-1.]

§54.4971-2. Operational rules and special definitions relating to excise tax on failure to meet minimum funding standards.—(a) *Correction.*—(1) *General rule.*—To correct an accumulated funding deficiency for a plan year, a contribution must be made to the plan that reduces the deficiency, as of the end of that plan year, to zero. To reduce the deficiency to zero, the contribution must include interest at the plan's actuarial valuation rate for the period between the end of that plan year and the date of the contribution.

(2) *Corrective effect of certain retroactive amendments.*—Certain retroactive plan amendments that meet the requirements of section 412(c)(8) may reduce an accumulated funding deficiency for a plan year to zero.

(3) *Optional corrective actions when employers withdraw from certain plans.*—See §54.4971-3(e)(2) for correcting deficiencies attributable to certain withdrawing employers.

(b) *No deduction.*—Under section 275(a)(6), no deduction is allowed for a tax imposed under section 4971(a) or (b).

(c) *Waiver of imposition of tax.*—Under section 3002(b) of the Employee Retirement Income Security Act of 1974 (ERISA), the Commissioner may waive the imposition of the additional tax under section 4971(b) in appropriate cases. This authority does not extend to the imposition of the initial tax under section 4971(a).

(d) *Notification of the Secretary of Labor.*—(1) *In general.*—Except as provided in paragraph (d)(2) of this section, before issuing a notice of deficiency with respect to the tax imposed under section 4971(a) or (b), the Commissioner must notify the Secretary of Labor that the Internal Revenue Service proposes to assess the tax. The purpose of this notice is to give the Secretary of Labor a reasonable opportunity to obtain a correction of the accumulated funding deficiency or to comment on the imposition of the tax. (See section 4971(d) and section 3002(b) of ERISA.) The Commissioner may issue a notice of deficiency with respect to the tax imposed under section 4971(a) or (b) 60 days after the mailing of the notice of proposed deficiency to the Secretary of Labor. Any action taken by the Secretary of Labor will not affect the imposition of the 5-percent initial tax imposed by section 4971(a). See paragraph (c) of this section, however, concerning the Commissioner's authority to waive the 100-percent additional tax imposed by section 4971(b).

(2) *Jeopardy assessments.*—The Commissioner may determine that the assessment or collection of the tax imposed under section 4971(a) or (b) will be jeopardized by delay. If the Commissioner makes this determination, the Internal Revenue Service may immediately assess a deficiency under section 6861 without prior notice to the Secretary of Labor. Abatement of the assessment may be granted upon correction of the deficiency. See section 6861 and §301.6861-1 concerning abatement of assessments.

(e) *Request for investigation with respect to tax imposed under section 4971.*—Under section 3002(b) of ERISA, upon receiving a written request from the Secretary of Labor or from the Pension Benefit Guaranty Corporation, the Commissioner will investigate whether the taxes under section 4971(a) and (b) should be imposed on any employer referred to in the request. [Reg. §54.4971-2.]

§54.4971-3. Rules relating to liability for excise tax on failure to meet minimum funding standards.—(a) *General rule.*—(1) *One employer.*—An excise tax imposed under section 4971(a) or (b) with respect to a plan to or under which only one employer is responsible for contributing must be paid by that employer.

(2) *More than one employer.*—An excise tax imposed under section 4971(a) or (b) with respect to a plan to or under which more than one employer is responsible for contributing must be allocated between these employers under paragraph (b) of this section.

(3) *Related employers.*—Related corporations, trades, and businesses described in section 414(b) and (c) are "related employers" for purposes of this section. All related employers are treated as one employer for purposes of paragraph (b) of this section. The tax liability of each such related employer is determined separately by allocations under paragraph (c) of this section.

(b) *Allocation of tax liability.*—(1) *In general.*—Section 413(b)(6) and (c)(5) and section 414(b) and (c) discuss liability for tax under section 4971(a) or (b) with respect to collectively bargained plans and plans of more than one employer. Each employer's tax liability relates to an accumulated funding deficiency under a plan. However, the funding deficiency is determined with respect to a plan as a whole, not with respect to individual employers adopting the plan. Therefore, the deficiency must be allocated among employers adopting or maintaining the plan to determine their individual liability for a tax. Except as otherwise provided in paragraphs (c) and (d) of this section, this liability must be determined in a reasonable manner that is not inconsistent with the requirements of this paragraph (b).

(2) *Failure of individual employer to meet obligation under plan or contract.*—(i) *Single delinquency.*—An accumulated funding deficiency may be attributable, in whole or in part, to a delinquent contribution, that is, the failure of an individual employer to contribute to the plan as required by its terms or by the terms of a collectively bargained agreement pursuant to which the plan is maintained. To the extent that an accumulated funding deficiency is attributable to a delinquent contribution, the delinquent employer is solely liable for the resulting tax imposed under section 4971(a) or (b).

(ii) *Multiple delinquency.*—If an accumulated funding deficiency is attributable to more than one delinquent employer, liability for tax is allocated in proportion to each employer's share of the delinquency.

(iii) *Further liability.*—A delinquent employer may also be liable for the portion of tax determined by an allocation under paragraph (b)(3) of this section.

(3) *Failure of employers in the aggregate to avoid accumulated funding deficiency.*—(i) *Aggregate failure.*—An accumulated funding deficiency may be attributable, in whole or in part, to the failure of employers in the aggregate to contribute to the plan a sufficient amount to avoid an accumulated funding deficiency. To the extent that a deficiency for a plan year is not attributable to a delinquent contribution for that year, the deficiency is attributable to an aggregate failure described in this subparagraph (3). Thus, for example, if 10 percent of the deficiency results from a delinquent contribution described in paragraph (b)(2) of this section, 90 percent results from failures described in this subparagraph (3). The allocation of tax liability to an individual employer for such an aggregate failure to avoid an accumulated funding deficiency is made under paragraph (b)(3)(ii) of this section.

(ii) *Allocation rule for aggregate failure.*—An individual employer's liability for tax attributable to an aggregate failure described in this subparagraph (3) is the product of the tax attributable to the aggregate failure times a fraction. The numerator of this fraction is the contribution the employer is required to make for the plan year under the plan or under the collectively bargained agreement pursuant to which the plan is maintained. The denominator of this fraction is the total contribution all employers are required to make for the plan year under the plan or under the collectively bargained agreement pursuant to which the plan is maintained. Thus, for example, if an employer is responsible for one-half of a plan's required contribution and 90 percent of an accumulated funding deficiency arises under this subparagraph (3), that employer is liable under this subparagraph (3) for 45 percent of the tax under section 4971(a) or (b), as the case may be, with respect to that deficiency.

(c) *Allocation rules for related employers.*—(1) *In general.*—To the extent that an accumulated funding deficiency is attributable to related employers, those employers are jointly and severally liable for an excise tax imposed under section 4971(a) or (b) with respect to that deficiency.

(2) *Plans not solely maintained by related employers.*—A plan that is not solely maintained by related employers first allocates tax liability under paragraph (b) of this section by treating the related employers as a single employer. The related employers are jointly and severally liable for the tax liability so allocated to any of the related employers.

(d) *Effect of plan termination on employer's tax liability.*—No tax is imposed under section 4971(a) for years after the plan year in which a plan terminates. An employer is liable only for unpaid 5-percent initial taxes under section 4971(a) and any additional tax which has been imposed under section 4971(b).

(e) *Effect of employer withdrawal from plan.*—(1) *General rule.*—An employer that withdraws from a plan remains liable for tax imposed with respect to the portion of an accumulated funding deficiency attributable to that employer for plan years before withdrawal.

(2) *Years subsequent to withdrawal.*—For any plan year with an accumulated funding deficiency, the tax is allocated between the employers responsible for contributing to the plan for that plan year in accordance with paragraphs (b) or (c) even if the deficiency in that year is attributable to an uncorrected deficiency from a prior year.

(f) *Examples.*—The provisions of paragraphs (a)-(c) of this section may be illustrated by the following examples:

Example (1). Employers *W, X, Y* and Z maintain a collectively bargained plan. *Y* and Z are related employers under paragraph (a)(3). *W* and *X* are each unrelated to any other employer. For plan year 1982, the employers are obligated, under the collectively bargained agreement, to contribute the following amount: *W*—$10x; *X*—$20x; *Y*—$30x; Z—$40x. As of the last date for making plan contributions, there is a delinquency of $10x attributable to *W* and $30x attributable to *Y*. Under paragraph (b)(2)(ii), *W* is liable for 10/40 of the tax imposed for 1982. Under paragraphs (b)(2)(ii) and (c)(2), *Y* and *Z* are jointly and severally liable for 30/40 of the tax.

Example (2). Assume the same facts as in Example (1). For plan year 1983, the minimum funding requirement is $145x. Contributions totaling $110x are made for 1983 in the amounts provided by the agreement: *W*—$15x; *X*—$20x; *Y*—$30x; *Z*—$45x. Under paragraph (b)(3)(i) of this section, there is an aggregate failure to avoid an accumulated funding deficiency, as the minimum funding requirement exceeds plan contributions by $35x. The tax attributable to the aggregate failure is allocated under paragraphs (b)(3)(ii) and (c)(2) as follows: *W* is liable for 15/110, or 13.6 percent of the tax; *X* is liable for 20/110, or 18.2 percent. *Y* and *Z* are jointly and severally liable for 75/110, or 68.2 percent.

Example (3). Assume the same facts as in Example (1). For 1984, the minimum funding requirement is $210x and employers are obligated under the agreement to contribute $130x: *W*—$15x; *X*—$25x; *Y*—$30x; *Z*—$60x. There is a funding deficiency due in part to a delinquency attributable to *Y*. Under paragraph (b)(3)(i), the remaining deficiency is an aggregate failure. Under paragraphs (b)(2)(i) and (c), *Y* and Z are jointly and severally liable for the 23 percent (30/130) of the excise tax attributable to the delinquency. The remaining 76.9 percent of the tax is allocated as follows: *W*—15/130 (11.5 percent) of the 76.9 percent; *X*—25/130 (19.2 percent) of the aggregate failure tax; *Y* and *Z*, combined under paragraph (c)(2)—90/130 (69.2 percent) of the aggregate failure tax. *Y* and *Z* are jointly and severally liable for approximately 76.3 percent of the total tax under section 4971 for the year: 23.1 percent attributable to *Y*'s delinquency and 53.2 percent (69.2 × 76.9 attributable to the aggregate failure under paragraph (b)(3)). [Reg. § 54.4971-3.]

Individual Retirement Plans: Simplified Employee Pensions

Individual Retirement Plans: Simplified Employee Pensions.—Reproduced below are the texts of proposed Reg. § 54.4973-1 and a proposed amendment of Reg. § 54.4974-1, relating to individual retirement plans and simplified employee pensions (published in the Federal Register on July 14, 1981).

* * *

☐ Par. 16. There is inserted in the appropriate place the following new section:

§ 54.4973-1. Excess contributions to certain accounts, contract and bonds.—(a) *In general.*—Under section 4973, in the case of an individual retirement account (described in section 408(a)), an individual retirement annuity (described in section 408(b)), a custodial account treated as an annuity contract under section 403(b)(7)(A), or an individual retirement bond described in section 409, a tax equal to 6 percent of the amount of excess contributions (as defined in paragraph (c) or (d) of this section) to such account, annuity or bond is imposed.

(b) *Individual liable for tax.*—(1) *Individual retirement plans.*—In the case of an individual retirement account, individual retirement annuity for individual retirement bond the tax imposed by section 4973 shall be paid by the individual to whom a deduction is or would be allowed with respect to contributions for the taxable year under section 219 (determined without regard to subsection (b)(1) thereof) or section 220 (determined without regard to subsection (b)(1) thereof), whichever is appropriate.

(2) *Custodial accounts under section 403(b)(7)(A).*—In the case of a custodial account treated as an annuity contract under section 403(b)(7)(A), the tax imposed by section 4973 shall be paid by the individual for whose benefit the account is maintained.

(c) *Excess contributions defined for individual retirement plans.*—For purposes of section 4973, in the case of individual retirement accounts, individual retirement annuities, or individual retirement bonds, the term "excess contributions" means the sum of—

(1) The excess (if any) of—

(i) The amount contributed for the taxable year to the accounts or for the annuities or bonds (other than a valid rollover contribution described in section 402(a)(5), 402(a)(7), 403(a)(4), 403(b)(8), 408(d)(3) or 409(b)(3)(C)), over

(ii) The amount allowable as a deduction under section 219 or 220 for such contributions, and

(2) The amount determined under this subsection for the preceding taxable year, reduced by the sum of—

(i) The distributions out of the account for the taxable year which were included in the gross income of the payee under section 408(d)(1),

(ii) The distributions out of the account for the taxable year to which section 408(d)(5) applies, and

(iii) The excess (if any) of the maximum amount allowable as a deduction under section 219 or 220 for the taxable year over the amount contributed (determined without regard to sections 219(c)(5) and 220(c)(6)) to the accounts or for the annuities or bonds for the taxable year. For purposes of this paragraph, any contribution which is distributed from the individual retirement account, individual retirement annuity, or bond in a distribution to which section 408(d)(4) applies shall be treated as an amount not contributed.

(d) *Excess contributions defined for custodial accounts under section 403(b)(7)(A).*—For purposes of section 4973, in the case of a custodial account referred to in paragraph (b)(2) of this section, the term "excess contributions" means the sum of—

(1) The excess (if any) of the amount contributed for the taxable year to such account (other than a valid rollover contribution described in section 403(b)(8), 408(d)(3)(A)(iii), or 409(b)(3)(C)), over the lesser of the amount excludable from gross income under section 403(b) or the amount permitted to be contributed under the limitations contained in section 415 (or under whichever such section is applicable, if only one is applicable), and

(2) The amount determined under this subsection for the preceding taxable year, reduced by—

(i) The excess (if any) of the lesser of (A) the amount excludable from gross income under section 403(b) or (B) the amount permitted to be contributed under the limitations contained in section 415 over the amount contributed to the account for the taxable year (or under whichever such section is applicable, if only one is applicable), and

(ii) The sum of the distributions out of the account (for the taxable year) which are included in gross income under section 72(e).

(e) *Special rules.*—(1) The tax imposed by section 4973 cannot exceed 6 percent of the value (determined as of the close of the individual's taxable year) of the account, annuity or bond.

(2) In the case of an endowment contract described in section 408(b), the tax imposed by section 4973 is not applicable to any amount allocable under § 1.219-1(b)(3) to the cost of life insurance under the contract.

(f) *Examples.*—The provisions of this section may be illustrated by the following examples:

Example (1). On April 20, 1979, A, a single individual, establishes an individual retirement account (IRA) and contributes $1,500. On January 11, 1980, A determines he has compensation for 1979 within the meaning of section 219(c) and the regulations thereafter of $8,000. Under section 219, the maximum amount allowable as a deduction for retirement savings available to A is $1,200. On April 15, 1980, A files his income tax return for 1979 taking a deduction of $1,200 for his contribution to his IRA, and as of such date there had been no distribution from the IRA. Under section 4973, A would have $300 of excess contribution in his account for 1979 [($1,500 – $1,200) + 0] and A would be liable for an excise tax of $18 on such excess contribution.

Example (2). Assume the same facts as in Example (1). Assume further that on July 1, 1980, A contributes $1,500 to his account. On January 9, 1981, A determines that he has compensation for 1980 of $12,000. Under section 219, the maximum amount allowable to A as a deduction for retirement savings is $1,500 for 1980. On April 15, 1981, A files his income tax return for 1980 taking a deduction of $1,500 for his contribution to his IRA. As of such date, there had been no distribution from the account. Under section 4973, A would have $300 of excess contributions in his IRA for 1980 [($1,500 – $1,500) + ($300 – $0)] and would be liable for an excise tax of $18 on such excess contribution.

Example (3). Assume the same facts as in Examples (1) and (2). Assume further that on July 1, 1981, A contributes $1,000 to his account. On January 9, 1982, A determines that he has compensation for 1981 of $15,000. Under section 219, the maximum amount allowable as a deduction to A as a deduction for retirement savings is $1,500 for 1981. On April 15, 1982, A files his income tax return for 1981 taking a deduction of $1,000 for his 1981 contribution to his IRA and an additional deduction of $300 under section 219(c)(5). A will have no excess contributions in his IRA for 1981 because he made no excess contributions for 1981 and the previous year's excess contribution has been eliminated by the underutilization (section 4973(b)(2)(C)) of 1981's allowable contribution.

Example (4). Assume the same facts as in Examples (1) and (2). Assume further that on July 1, 1981, A contributes $1,500 to his account. On December 1, 1981, A withdraws $300 from his IRA. On January 9, 1982, A determines that he has compensation for 1981 of $15,000. Under section 219, the maximum amount allowable as a deduction to A as a deduction for retirement savings is $1,500 for 1981. On April 15, 1982, A files his income tax return for 1981 taking a deduction of $1,500 for his 1981 contribution to his IRA. A will have no excess contributions in his IRA for 1981 because he made no excess contributions for 1981 and the previous year's excess contribution has been eliminated in a distribution described in section 408(d)(5).

Example (5). On February 1, 1979, H, an individual, establishes an IRA for himself and one for his nonworking spouse W. He contributes $875 to his account and $775 to his wife's account. On January 31, 1980, H determines that he has compensation for 1979 within the meaning of section 220(c) and the regulations thereunder of $20,000. Under section 220(b)(1), the maximum amount allowable as a deduction for retirement savings to A is $1,550. On April 15, 1980, H files a joint income tax return for 1979 and takes a deduction of $1,550 for his contribution to the IRA of himself and his spouse. As of such date, there had been no distribution from either IRA. Under section 4973, H would have $100 of excess contributions in his account for 1979 [($1,650 – $1,550) + 0] and H would be liable for an excise tax of $6 on such excess contribution.

Example (6). Assume the same facts as in Example (5). Assume further that on June 1, 1980, H contributes $875 to his account and $875 to his wife's account. On January 31, 1981, H determines that he has compensation for 1980 within the meaning of section 220(c) and the regulations thereunder of $20,000. Under section 220(b)(1), the maximum amount allowable as a deduction for retirement savings is $1,750. On April 15, 1981, H files his income tax return for 1980 taking a deduction of $1,750 for his contribution to the individual retirement account of himself and his wife. As of such date, there had been no distribution from either account. Under section 4973, H would have $100 of excess contributions in his account for 1980 and would be liable for an excise tax of $6 for such excess contribution.

Example (7). Assume the same facts as in Example (5). Assume further that on June 1, 1980, A contributes $1,000 to his account and nothing to his wife's account. On January 31, 1981, A determines that he has compensation for 1980 within the meaning of section 219(c) of $22,000. On April 15, 1981, H files his income tax return for 1980 and takes a $1,000 deduction under section 219(a) for the 1980 contribution to his IRA and a $100 deduction under section 219(c)(5) for the 1979 excess contribution. Under section 4973, H would have $0 excess contributions for 1980 because the previous year's excess contribution has been eliminated under section 4973(b)(2)(C).

Example (8). On March 1, 1979, a custodial account under section 403(b)(7)(A) is established for the benefit of T who is otherwise eligible to have such an account established and a contribution of $7,000 is made to such account by A's employer which is a tax-exempt organization described in section 501(c)(3). The amount excludable from T's gross income in 1979 under section 403(b) is $4,000 and the amount permitted to be contributed for 1979 under section 415 is $5,000. Under section 4973, T would have an excess contribution of $3,000 [($7,000 – $4,000) + 0] in his account for 1979 and would be liable for an excise tax of $180. [Reg. § 54.4973-1.]

☐ Par. 17. A new paragraph (d) is added to § 54.4974-1 to read as follows.

§ 54.4974-1. Excise tax on accumulations in individual retirement accounts or annuities.—

* * *

(d) *Waiver of tax in certain cases.*—(1) *In general.*—If the payee described in section 4974(a) establishes to the satisfaction of the Commissioner that—

(i) The shortfall described in section 4974(a) in the amount distributed during any taxable year was due to reasonable error, and

(ii) Reasonable steps are being taken to remedy the shortfall, the tax imposed by section 4974(a) may be waived.

(2) *Reasonable error.*—Examples of reasonable error leading to an underdistribution include: erroneous advice from the sponsoring organization or other pension advisors or organizations which misled the payee, attempts by the payee to apply the required formula which led to a miscalculation, or misunderstanding of the formula.

* * *

Employee Trusts: Effective Dates

Employee Trusts: Tax Reform Act of 1984: Effective Dates.—Temporary Reg. §§ 54.4976-1T and 54.4978-1T are also proposed as final regulations and, when adopted, would become Reg. §§ 54.4976-1 and 54.4978-1 (published in the Federal Register on February 4, 1986).

§ 54.4976-1. Questions and answers relating to taxes with respect to welfare benefit funds.

§ 54.4978-1. Questions and answers relating to the tax on certain dispositions by employee stock ownership plans and certain cooperatives.

Fringe Benefits: Taxability

Fringe Benefits: Taxability.—Reg. § 54.4977-1T, relating to the treatment of taxable and nontaxable fringe benefits, is proposed (published in the Federal Register on January 7, 1985) (LR-216-84).

§ 54.4977-1. Questions and answers relating to the election concerning lines of business in existence on January 1, 1984.

Qualified Plans: Automatic Contribution Arrangements

Qualified Plans: Automatic Contribution Arrangements.—Amendments to Reg. § 54.4979-1, relating to automatic contribution arrangements allowed by certain qualified plans, are proposed (published in the Federal Register on November 8, 2007) (REG-133300-07).

☐ Par. 15. Section 54.4979-1(c)(1) is amended by:

Revising the first and second sentences of paragraph (c)(1) to read as follows:

§ 54.4979-1. Excise tax on certain excess contributions and excess aggregate contributions.

* * *

(c) *No tax when excess distributed within 21/2 months of close of year or additional employer contributions made.*—(1) *General rule.*—No tax is imposed under this section on any excess contribution or excess aggregate contribution, as the case may be, to the extent the contribution (together with any income allocable thereto) is corrected before the close of the first 21/2 months of the following plan year (6 months in the case of a plan that includes an eligible automatic contribution arrangement within the meaning of section 414(w)). Qualified nonelective contributions and qualified matching contributions taken into account under § 1.401(k)-2(a)(6) of this Chapter or qualified nonelective contributions or elective contributions taken into account under § 1.401(m)-2(a)(6) of this Chapter for a plan year may permit a plan to avoid excess contributions or excess aggregate contributions, respectively, even if made after the close of the 21/2 month period (6 months in the case of a plan that includes an eligible automatic contribution arrangement within the meaning of section 414(w)). * * *

* * *

HEALTH INSURANCE PROVIDERS FEE

Expatriate Health Plans: Issuers: Excepted Benefits

Expatriate Health Plans: Issuers: Excepted Benefits.—Amendments to Reg. §§57.2, 57.4 and 57.10, relating to the rules for expatriate health plans, expatriate health plan issuers, and qualified expatriates under the Expatriate Health Coverage Clarification Act of 2014 (EHCCA), are proposed (published in the Federal Register on June 10, 2016) (REG-135702-15).

14. Section 57.2 is amended by revising paragraph (n) to read as follows:

§57.2. Explanation of terms.

* * *

(n) *United States health risk.*—(1) *In general.*—The term *United States health risk* means the health risk of any individual who is—

(i) A United States citizen;

(ii) A resident of the United States (within the meaning of section 7701(b)(1)(A)); or

(iii) Located in the United States (within the meaning of paragraph (i) of this section) during the period such individual is so located.

(2) *Qualified expatriates, spouses, and dependents.*—The term *United States health risk* does not include the health risk of any individual who is a qualified expatriate (within the meaning of §54.9831-1(f)(6)) enrolled in an expatriate health plan (within the meaning of §54.9831-1(f)(3)). For purposes of this paragraph, a qualified expatriate includes any spouse, dependent, or any other individual enrolled in the expatriate health plan.

* * *

15. Section 57.4 is amended by adding a sentence to the end of paragraph (b)(2) and adding paragraph (b)(3) to read as follows:

§57.4. Fee calculation.

* * *

(b) * * *

(2) * * * This presumption does not apply to excluded premiums for qualified expatriates in expatriate health plans as described in §57.2(n)(2).

(3) *Manner of determining excluded premiums for qualified expatriates in expatriate health plans.*—The IRS may specify in other guidance published in the Internal Revenue Bulletin the manner of determining excluded premiums for qualified expatriates in expatriate health plans as described in §57.2(n)(2).

* * *

16. Section 57.10 is amended by revising paragraph (a) and adding paragraph (c) to read as follows:

§57.10. Effective/applicability dates.—(a) *In general.*—Except as provided in paragraphs (b) and (c) of this section, §§57.1 through 57.9 apply to any fee that is due on or after September 30, 2014.

* * *

(c) *Qualified expatriates in expatriate health plans.*—Section 57.2(n)(2), the last sentence of §57.4(b)(2), and §57.4(b)(3) apply to any fee that is due on or after the date the final regulations are published in the Federal Register. Until the date the final regulations are published in the Federal Register, taxpayers may rely on these rules for any fee that is due on or after September 30, 2018.

Health Insurance Providers Fee: Net Premiums Written

Health Insurance Providers Fee: Net Premiums Written.—Amendments to Reg. §57.2, modifying the current definition of "net premiums written" for purposes of the fee imposed by section 9010 of the Patient Protection and Affordable Care Act, as amended, are proposed (published in the Federal Register on December 9, 2010) (REG-134438-15).

2. Section 57.2 is amended by revising paragraph (k) to read as follows:

§57.2. Explanation of terms.

* * *

(k) *Net premiums written.*—(1) *In general.*—The term *net premiums written* means premiums written, adjusted as provided in paragraph (k)(2) of this section.

(2) *Adjustments.*—Net premiums written include adjustments to account for:

(i) *Assumption reinsurance, but not indemnity reinsurance.*—Net premiums written include reinsurance premiums written, reduced by reinsurance ceded, and reduced by ceding commissions with respect to the data *year. Net* premiums written do not include premiums written for indemnity reinsurance and are not reduced by indemnity reinsurance ceded because indemnity reinsurance within the meaning of paragraph (h)(5)(i) of this section is not health insurance under paragraph (h)(1) of this section. However, in the case of assumption reinsurance within the meaning of paragraph (h)(5)(ii) of this section, net premiums written include premiums written for assumption reinsurance, reduced by assumption reinsurance premiums ceded.

(ii) *Medical loss ratio (MLR) rebates.*—Net premiums written are reduced by MLR rebates with respect to the data year. For this purpose, MLR rebates are computed on an accrual basis.

(iii) *Premium adjustments related to retrospectively rated contracts.*—Net premiums written include retrospectively rated contract receipts and are reduced by retrospectively rated contract payments with respect to the data year. For this purpose, net premium adjustments related to retrospectively rated contracts are computed on an accrual basis.

(iv) *Amounts related to the risk adjustment program under section 1343 of the ACA.*—Net premiums written include risk adjustment payments (within the meaning of 42 U.S.C. 18063(b)) received with respect to the data year and are reduced by risk adjustment charges (within the meaning of 42 U.S.C. 18063(a)) paid with respect to the data year. For this purpose, risk adjustment payments and risk adjustment charges are computed on an accrual basis.

(v) *Additional adjustments published in the Internal Revenue Bulletin.*—The IRS may provide rules in guidance published in the Internal Revenue Bulletin (see § 601.601(d)(2) of this chapter) for additional adjustments against premiums written in determining net premiums written.

Electronic Filing: Report of Health Insurance Provider Information

Electronic Filing: Report of Health Insurance Provider Information.—Amendments to Reg. § 57.3, requiring certain covered entities engaged in the business of providing health insurance for United States health risks to electronically file Form 8963, are proposed (published in the Federal Register on December 9, 2016) (REG-123829-16).

Par. 2. Section 57.3 is amended by revising paragraph (a)(2) to read as follows:

§ 57.3. Reporting requirements and associated penalties.

* * *

(a) * * *

(2) *Manner of reporting.*—(i) *In general.*—The IRS may provide rules in guidance published in the Internal Revenue Bulletin for the manner of reporting by a covered entity under this section, including rules for reporting by a designated entity on behalf of a controlled group that is treated as a single covered entity.

(ii) *Electronic filing required.*—Any Form 8963 (including corrected forms) filed pursuant to paragraph (a)(1) of this section reporting more than $25 million in net premiums written must be filed electronically in accordance with the instructions to the form. If a Form 8963 or corrected Form 8963 is required to be filed electronically under this paragraph (a)(2)(ii), any subsequently filed Form 8963 filed for the same fee year must also be filed electronically. For purposes of paragraph (b) of this section, any Form 8963 required to be filed electronically under this section will not be considered filed unless it is filed electronically.

* * *

Electronic Filing: Report of Health Insurance Provider Information

Electronic Filing: Report of Health Insurance Provider Information.—Amendments to Reg. § 57.10, requiring certain covered entities engaged in the business of providing health insurance for United States health risks to electronically file Form 8963, are proposed (published in the Federal Register on December 9, 2016) (REG-123829-16).

Par. 3 Section 57.10 is amended by revising paragraph (a) and adding paragraph (c) to read as follows:

§ 57.10. Effective/applicability date.—(a) Except as provided paragraphs (b) and (c) of this section, § § 57.1 through 57.9 apply to any fee that is due on or after September 30, 2014.

* * *

(c) Section 57.3(a)(2)(ii) applies to Forms 8963, including corrected Forms 8963, filed after December 31, 2017.

Health Insurance Providers Fee: Net Premiums Written

Health Insurance Providers Fee: Net Premiums Written.—Amendments to Reg. § 57.10, modifying the current definition of "net premiums written" for purposes of the fee imposed by section 9010 of the Patient Protection and Affordable Care Act, as amended, are proposed (published in the Federal Register on December 9, 2010) (REG-134438-15).

3. Section 57.10 is amended by revising paragraph (a) and adding paragraph (c) to read as follows:

§ 57.10. Effective/applicability date.—(a) *In general.*—Except as provided in paragraphs (b) and (c) of this section, § § 57.1 through 57.9 apply to any fee that is due on or after September 30, 2014.

* * *

(c) *Paragraph (k) of § 57.2.*—Paragraph (k) of § 57.2 applies to any fee that is due on or after September 30, 2018.

MAINTENANCE OF MINIMUM ESSENTIAL COVERAGE

Expatriate Health Plans: Issuers: Excepted Benefits

Expatriate Health Plans: Issuers: Excepted Benefits.—Amendments to Reg. §1.5000A-2, relating to the rules for expatriate health plans, expatriate health plan issuers, and qualified expatriates under the Expatriate Health Coverage Clarification Act of 2014 (EHCCA), are proposed (published in the Federal Register on June 10, 2016) (REG-135702-15).

3. Section 1.5000A-2 is amended by adding paragraphs (c)(1)(i)(D) and (d)(3) to read as follows:

§1.5000A-2. Minimum essential coverage.

* * *

(c) * * *

(1) * * *

(i) * * *

(D) A group health plan that is an expatriate health plan within the meaning of §54.9831-1(f)(3) of this chapter if the requirements of §54.9831-1(f)(3)(i) of this chapter are met by providing coverage for qualified expatriates described in §54.9831-1(f)(6)(i) or (ii) of this chapter.

* * *

(d) * * *

(3) *Certain expatriate health plans.*—An expatriate health plan within the meaning of §54.9831-1(f)(3) of this chapter that is not an eligible employer-sponsored plan under paragraph (c)(1)(i)(D) of this section is a plan in the individual market.

* * *

Premium Tax Credit: Individual Shared Responsibility

Premium Tax Credit: Individual Shared Responsibility.—Amendments to Reg. §1.5000A-3, relating to the health insurance premium tax credit (premium tax credit) and the individual shared responsibility provision, are proposed (published in the Federal Register on July 8, 2016) (REG-109086-15).

Par. 7. Section 1.5000A-3 is amended by adding a new paragraph (e)(3)(ii)(G) to read as follows:

§1.5000A-3. Exempt individuals.

* * *

(e) * * *

(3) * * *

(ii) * * *

(G) *Opt-out arrangements.*—*(1) In general.*—Except as otherwise provided in this paragraph (e)(3)(ii)(G), the amount of an opt-out payment made available to an employee under an opt-out arrangement increases the employee's (or related individual's) required contribution for purposes of determining the affordability of the eligible employer-sponsored plan to which the opt-out arrangement relates, regardless of whether the employee (or related individual) enrolls in the eligible employer-sponsored plan or declines to enroll in that coverage and is paid the opt-out payment.

(2) Eligible opt-out arrangements.—The amount of an opt-out payment made available to an employee under an eligible opt-out arrangement does not increase the employee's (or related individual's) required contribution for purposes of determining the affordability of the eligible employer-sponsored plan to which the eligible opt-out arrangement relates, regardless of whether the employee (or related individual) enrolls in the eligible employer-sponsored plan or is paid the opt-out payment.

(3) Definitions.—The following definitions apply for purposes of this paragraph (e)(3)(ii)(G):

(A) Opt-out payment.—The term *opt-out payment* means a payment that is available only if an employee declines coverage, including waiving coverage in which the employee would otherwise be enrolled, under an eligible employer-sponsored plan and that is not permitted to be used to pay for coverage under the eligible employer-sponsored plan. An amount provided as an employer contribution to a cafeteria plan that is permitted to be used by the employee to purchase minimum essential coverage is not an opt-out payment, whether or not the employee may receive the amount as a taxable benefit. See paragraph (e)(3)(ii)(E) of this section for the treatment of employer contributions to a cafeteria plan.

(B) Opt-out arrangement.—The term *opt-out arrangement* means the arrangement under which an opt-out payment is made available.

(C) Eligible opt-out arrangement.—The term *eligible opt-out arrangement* means an arrangement under which an employee's right to receive an opt-out payment is conditioned on the employee providing reasonable evidence that the employee and all other individuals for whom the employee reasonably expects to claim a personal exemption deduction for the taxable year or years that begin or end in or with the employer's plan year to which the opt-out arrangement applies (employee's expected tax family) have, or will have, minimum essential coverage (other than coverage in the individual market, whether or not obtained through the Marketplace) during the period of coverage to which the opt-out arrangement applies. For this purpose, reasonable evidence of alternative coverage may include the employee's attestation that the employee and all other members of the employee's expected tax family have, or will have, minimum essential coverage (other than coverage in the individual market, whether or not obtained through the Marketplace) for the relevant period. Regardless of the evidence of alternative coverage required under the arrangement, to be an eligible opt-out arrangement, the arrangement must provide that the opt-out payment will not be made, and the employer in fact must not make the payment, if the employer knows or has reason to know that the employee or any other member of the employee's expected tax family does not have, or will not have, the alternative coverage. The arrangement must also require that the evidence of the alternative coverage be provided no less frequently than every

plan year to which the eligible opt-out arrangement applies, and that it must be provided no earlier than a reasonable period of time before the commencement of the period of coverage to which the eligible opt-out arrangement applies. If the reasonable evidence (such as an attestation) is obtained as part of the regular annual open enrollment period that occurs within a few months before the commencement of the next plan year of employer-sponsored coverage, it will qualify as being provided no earlier than a reasonable period of time before commencement of the applicable period of coverage. An eligible opt-out arrangement is also permitted to require evidence of alternative coverage to be provided at a later date, such as after the plan year starts, which would enable the employer to require evidence that the employee and all other members of the employee's expected tax family have already obtained the alternative coverage. Nothing in this rule prohibits an employer from requiring reasonable evidence of alternative coverage other than an attestation in order for an employee to qualify for an opt-out payment under an eligible opt-out arrangement. Further, provided that the reasonable evidence requirement is met, the amount of an opt-out payment made available under an eligible opt-out arrangement continues to be excluded from the employee's required contribution for the remainder of the period of coverage to which the opt-out payment originally applied even if the alternative coverage subsequently terminates for the employee or for any other member of the employee's expected tax family, regardless of whether the opt-out payment is required to be adjusted or terminated due to the loss of alternative coverage, and regardless of whether the employee is required to provide notice of the loss of alternative coverage to the employer.

* * *

INFORMATION AND RETURNS

Gifts and Bequests from Covered Expatriates: Imposition of Tax

Gifts and Bequests from Covered Expatriates: Imposition of Tax.—Reg. §28.6001-1, relating to a tax on United States citizens and residents who receive gifts or bequests from certain individuals who relinquished United States citizenship or ceased to be lawful permanent residents of the United States on or after June 17, 2008, is proposed (published in the Federal Register on September 10, 2015) (REG-112997-10).

Section 28.6001-1 is added to read as follows:

§28.6001-1. Records required to be kept.— (a) *In general.*—Every U.S. recipient as defined in §28.2801-2(e) subject to taxation under chapter 15 of the Internal Revenue Code must keep, for the purpose of determining the total amount of covered gifts and covered bequests, such permanent books of account or records as are necessary to establish the amount of that person's aggregate covered gifts and covered bequests, and the other information required to be shown on Form 708, "United States Return of Tax for Gifts and Bequests from Covered Expatriates." All documents and vouchers used in preparing the Form 708 must be retained by the person required to file the return so as to be available for inspection whenever required.

(b) *Supplemental information.*—In order that the Internal Revenue Service (IRS) may determine the correct tax, the U.S. recipient as defined in §28.2801-2(e) must furnish such supplemental information as may be deemed necessary by the IRS. Therefore, the U.S. recipient must furnish, upon request, copies of all documents relating to the covered gift or covered bequest, appraisals of any items included in the aggregate amount of covered gifts and covered bequests, copies of balance sheets and other financial statements obtainable by that person relating to the value of stock or other property constituting the covered gift or covered bequest, and any other information obtainable by that person that may be necessary in the determination of the tax. See section 2801 and the corresponding regulations. For every policy of life insurance listed on the return, the U.S. recipient must procure a statement from the insurance company on Form 712 and file it with the IRS office where the return is filed. If specifically requested by the Commissioner, the insurance company must file this statement directly with the Commissioner. [Reg. §28.6001-1.]

Gifts and Bequests from Covered Expatriates: Imposition of Tax

Gifts and Bequests from Covered Expatriates: Imposition of Tax.—Reg. §28.6011-1, relating to a tax on United States citizens and residents who receive gifts or bequests from certain individuals who relinquished United States citizenship or ceased to be lawful permanent residents of the United States on or after June 17, 2008, is proposed (published in the Federal Register on September 10, 2015) (REG-112997-10).

Section 28.6011-1 is added to read as follows:

§28.6011-1. Returns.—(a) *Return required.*— The return of any tax to which this part 28 applies must be made on Form 708, "United States Return of Tax for Gifts and Bequests from Covered Expatriates," according to the instructions applicable to the form. With respect to each covered gift and covered bequest received during the calendar year, the U.S. recipient as defined in §28.2801-2(e) must include on Form 708 the information set forth in §25.6019-4. The U.S. recipient must file Form 708 for each calendar year in which a covered gift or covered bequest is received. The U.S. recipient who receives the covered gift or covered bequest during the calendar year is the person required to file the return. A U.S. recipient is not required to file such form, however, for a calendar year in which the total fair market value of all covered gifts and covered bequests received by that person during that calendar year is less than or equal to the section 2801(c) amount, which is the dollar amount of the per-donee exclusion in effect under section 2503(b) for that calendar year.

(b) *Protective return*.—(i) A U.S. citizen or resident (as defined in § 28.2801-2(b)) that receives a gift or bequest from an expatriate and reasonably concludes that the gift or bequest is not a covered gift or a covered bequest from a covered expatriate may file a protective Form 708 in order to start the period for assessment of tax. To be a protective Form 708, it must provide all of the information otherwise required on Form 708, along with an affidavit, signed under penalties of perjury, setting forth the information on which that U.S. citizen or resident has relied in concluding that the donor or decedent, as the case may be, was not a covered expatriate, or that the transfer was not a covered gift or a covered bequest, as well as that person's efforts to obtain other information that might be relevant to these determinations. If that U.S. citizen or resident has obtained information from the Internal Revenue Service (IRS) (as described in § 28.2801-7(b)(1)), it must attach a copy of such information. The U.S. citizen or resident also must attach a copy of a completed Form 3520, Part III, for all trust distributions, or Part IV for all gifts and bequests, if applicable. If the return meets the requirements of this paragraph (b)(i), and if the IRS does not assess a section 2801 tax liability for that tax year within the limitations period for assessment stated in section 6501, the IRS may not later assess a section 2801 tax with regard to any transfer reported on that Form 708.

(ii) A U.S. citizen or resident who receives a gift or bequest from an expatriate and who files a protective Form 708 meeting the requirements of paragraph (b)(i) of this section showing no tax due, absent fraud or other special factors, will not be subject to any additions to tax for late filing under section 6651(a)(1) or for late payment under section 6651(a)(2), even if the gift or bequest is determined to be a covered gift or covered bequest from a covered expatriate within the limitations period for assessment stated in section 6501. Notwithstanding the foregoing, however, if a U.S. citizen or resident knows, or has reason to know, that the information provided by the IRS or any other source is incorrect or incomplete, that U.S. citizen or resident may not rely on that information, and except as provided in the preceding paragraph (b)(i) of this section, may be subject to all of the generally applicable provisions governing assessment of tax, collection of tax, and penalties. See sections 6501, 6502, 6651 and 6662.

(c) *Effective/applicability dates*.—This section applies on and after the date of publication of a Treasury decision adopting these rules as final regulations in the **Federal Register**. [Reg. § 28.6011-1.]

Qualified Plans: Excise Taxes

Qualified Plans: Excise Taxes.—Temporary Reg. § 54.6011-1T, relating to the payment of excise tax by employers receiving reversions of qualified plan assets required by the Tax Reform Act of 1986, is also proposed as a final regulation and, when adopted, would become Reg. § 54.6011-1 (published in the Federal Register on April 3, 1987).

§ 54.6011-1. General requirement of return, statement, or list.

Domestic International Sales Corporations

Domestic International Sales Corporations: Taxation of Income.—Reproduced below is the text of a proposed amendment of Reg. § 1.6011-2, relating to the taxation of income allocable to a DISC for taxable years beginning after 1984 (published in the Federal Register on February 3, 1987).

* * *

☐ Par. 13. In § 1.6011-2, a new sentence is added immediately after the third sentence in paragraph (a) to read as follows:

§ 1.6011-2. Returns, etc. of DISCs and former DISCs.—(a) *Records and information*.—* * * For taxable years beginning after 1984, every DISC or former DISC shall also disclose on the Schedule K (Form 1120-DISC) the amount of the shareholder's deferred DISC income for the shareholder's taxable year (as defined in section 995(f)(3)). * * *

* * *

Guidance under Section 529A: Qualified ABLE Programs

Guidance under Section 529A: Qualified ABLE Programs.—Amendments to Reg. § 301.6011-2, regarding programs under The Stephen Beck, Jr., Achieving a Better Life Experience Act of 2014 and rules under which States or State agencies or instrumentalities may establish and maintain a new type of tax-favored savings program through which contributions may be made to the account of an eligible disabled individual to meet qualified disability expenses, are proposed (published in the Federal Register on June 22, 2015) (REG-102837-15).

Par. 14. Section 301.6011-2 is amended by adding the word "series" after "5498" in the first sentence of paragraph (b)(1).

§ 301.6011-2. Required use of magnetic media.

Information Returns: Using Magnetic Media

Information Returns: Using Magnetic Media.—Amendments to Reg. §301.6011-2, amending the rules for determining whether information returns must be filed using magnetic media (electronically), are proposed (published in the Federal Register on May 31, 2018) (REG-102951-16).

Par. 2. Section 301.6011-2 is amended as follows:

a. Paragraphs (b)(4) through (6) are added.

b. Paragraphs (c)(1)(iii) and (iv) are removed.

c. Paragraph (g)(2) is revised.

The additions and revisions read as follows:

§301.6011-2. Required use of magnetic media.

* * *

(b) * * *

(4) *Aggregation of returns.*—For purposes of determining whether the number of returns a person is required to file meets the 250-return threshold under paragraph (c)(1)(i) of this section, all types of returns covered by paragraphs (b)(1) and (2) of this section required to be filed during the calendar year are aggregated. Corrected returns are not taken into account in determining whether the 250-return threshold is met.

(5) *Corrected returns.*—Any person required to file returns covered by paragraphs (b)(1) and (2) of this section on magnetic media for a calendar year must file corrected returns covered by paragraphs (b)(1) and (2) of this section for such calendar year on magnetic media.

(6) *Examples.*—The provisions of paragraphs (b)(4) and (5) of this section are illustrated by the following examples:

Example 1. For the 2018 calendar year, Company W is required to file 200 Forms 1099-INT, "Interest Income," and 200 Forms 1099-DIV, "Dividends and Distributions," for a total of 400 returns. Because Company W is required to file 250 or more returns covered by paragraphs (b)(1) and (2) of this section for the calendar year, Company W must file all Forms 1099-INT and Forms 1099-DIV electronically.

Example 2. During the 2018 calendar year, Company X has 200 employees in Puerto Rico and 75 employees in American Samoa, for a total of 275 returns. Because Company X is required to file 250 or more returns covered by paragraphs (b)(1) and (2) of this section for the calendar year, Company X must file Forms 499R-2/W-2PR, "Commonwealth of Puerto Rico Withholding Statement," and Forms W-2AS, "American Samoa Wage and Tax Statement," electronically.

Example 3. For the 2018 calendar year, Company Y files 300 original Forms 1099-MISC, "Miscellaneous Income." Later, Company Y files 70 corrected Forms 1099-MISC for the 2018 calendar year. Because Company Y is required to file 250 or more returns covered by paragraphs (b)(1) and (2) of this section for the calendar year, Company Y must file its original 300 Forms 1099-MISC, as well as its 70 corrected Forms 1099-MISC for the 2018 calendar year, electronically.

* * *

(g) * * *

(2) Paragraphs (a)(1), (b)(1) and (2), (c)(1)(i), (c)(2), (d), (e), and (f) of this section are effective for information returns required to be filed after December 31, 1996. For information returns required to be filed after December 31, 1989, and before January 1, 1997, see section 6011(e) [26 USC 6011(e)]. Paragraph (b)(4) of this section is effective for information returns required to be filed after December 31, 2018. Paragraph (b)(5) of this section is effective for corrected information returns filed after December 31, 2018.

* * *

Reportable Transactions: Disclosure: Patented Transactions

Reportable Transactions: Disclosure: Patented Transactions.—Amendments to Reg. §1.6011-4, providing rules to the disclosure of reportable transactions, including patented transactions, under Code Secs. 6011 and 6111, are proposed (published in the Federal Register on September 26, 2007) (REG-129916-07).

☐ Par. 2. Section 1.6011-4 is amended by:

1. Revising paragraphs (b)(7) and (c)(3)(i)(F).

2. Adding to paragraph (c)(3)(ii) *Examples 4, 5, 6,* and *7*.

3. Revising paragraph (h)(2).

The revisions and additions read as follows:

§1.6011-4. Requirement of statement disclosing participation in certain transactions by taxpayers.

* * *

(b) * * *

(7) *Patented transactions.*—(i) *In general.*—A patented transaction is a transaction for which a taxpayer pays (directly or indirectly) a fee in any amount to a patent holder or the patent holder's agent for the legal right to use a tax planning method that the taxpayer knows or has reason to know is the subject of the patent. A patented transaction also is a transaction for which a taxpayer (the patent holder or the patent holder's agent) has the right to payment for another person's use of a tax planning method that is the subject of the patent.

(ii) *Definitions.*—For purposes of this paragraph (b)(7), the following definitions apply:

(A) *Fee.*—The term *fee* means consideration in whatever form paid, whether in cash or in kind, for the right to use a tax planning method that is the subject of a patent. The term *fee* includes any consideration the taxpayer knows or has reason to know will be paid indirectly to the patent holder or patent holder's agent, such as through a referral fee, fee-sharing arrangement, or license. The term *fee* does not include amounts paid in settlement of, or as the award of damages in, a suit for damages for infringement of the patent.

(B) *Patent*.—The term *patent* means a patent granted under the provisions of title 35 of the United States Code, or any foreign patent granting rights generally similar to those under a United States patent. See § 1.1235-2(a). The term *patent* includes patents that have been applied for but not yet granted.

(C) *Patent holder*.—A person is a patent holder if—

(1) The person is a holder as defined in § 1.1235-2(d) and (e);

(2) The person would be a holder as defined in § 1.1235-2(d)(2) if the phrase *S corporation or trust* was substituted for the word *partnership* and the phrase *shareholder or beneficiary* was substituted for the words *member* and *partner*;

(3) The person is an employer of a holder as defined in § 1.1235-2(d) and the holder transferred to the employer all substantial rights to the patent as defined in § 1.1235-2(b); or

(4) The person receives all substantial rights to the patent as defined in § 1.1235-2(b) in exchange (directly or indirectly) for consideration in any form.

(D) *Patent holder's agent*.—The term *patent holder's agent* means any person who has the permission of the patent holder to offer for sale or exchange, to sell or exchange, or to market a tax planning method that is the subject of a patent. The term *patent holder's agent* also means any person who receives (directly or indirectly) for or on behalf of a patent holder a fee in any amount for a tax planning method that is the subject of a patent.

(E) *Payment*.—The term *payment* includes consideration in whatever form paid, whether in cash or in kind, for the right to use a tax planning method that is the subject of a patent. For example, if a patent holder or patent holder's agent receives payment for a patented transaction and a separate payment for another transaction, part or all of the payment for the other transaction may be treated as payment for the patented transaction if the facts and circumstances indicate that the payment for the other transaction is in consideration for the patented transaction. The term *payment* also includes amounts paid in settlement of, or as the award of damages in, a suit for damages for infringement of the patent.

(F) *Tax planning method*.—The term *tax planning method* means any plan, strategy, technique, or structure designed to affect Federal income, estate, gift, generation skipping transfer, employment, or excise taxes. A patent issued solely for tax preparation software or other tools used to perform or model mathematical calculations or to provide mechanical assistance in the preparation of tax or information returns is not a tax planning method.

(iii) *Related parties*.—For purposes of this paragraph (b)(7), persons who bear a relationship to each other as described in section 267(b) or 707(b) will be treated as the same person.

* * *

(c) * * *

(3) * * *

(i) * * *

(F) *Patented transactions*.—A taxpayer has participated in a patented transaction, as defined in paragraph (b)(7) of this section, if the taxpayer's tax return reflects a tax benefit from the transaction (including a deduction for fees paid in any amount to the patent holder or patent holder's agent). A taxpayer also has participated in a patented transaction, as defined in paragraph (b)(7) of this section, if the taxpayer is the patent holder or patent holder's agent and the taxpayer's tax return reflects a tax benefit in relation to obtaining a patent for a tax planning method (including any deduction for amounts paid to the United States Patent and Trademark Office as required by title 35 of the United States Code and attorney's fees) or reflects income from a payment received from another person for the use of the tax planning method that is the subject of the patent.

* * *

(ii) * * *

Example 4. (i) A, an individual, creates a tax planning method and applies for a U.S. patent. A pays attorney fees in relation to obtaining the patent and A pays the fee required under title 35 of the United States Code for the patent application. Subsequently, C pays a fee to A for the legal right to use the tax planning method that C knows or has reason to know is the subject of A's patent. A's tax return reflects both a deduction for an amount paid in relation to obtaining a patent and income from C's payment to A for the legal right to use the tax planning method that is the subject of the patent. C's tax return reflects a deduction for an amount paid to A for the right to use the tax planning method that is the subject of the patent.

(ii) A is a patent holder under paragraph (b)(7)(ii)(C)*(1)* of this section. The transaction is a reportable transaction for A under paragraph (b)(7) of this section because A has the right to payment for another person's use of the tax planning method that is the subject of the patent. The transaction is a reportable transaction for C under paragraph (b)(7) of this section, because C paid a fee to A for the legal right to use a tax planning method that C knew or had reason to know was the subject of a patent. A has participated in the transaction in the year in which A's tax return reflects a tax benefit in relation to obtaining the patent or reflects income from C's payment to A for the legal right to use the tax planning method that is the subject of the patent. C has participated in the transaction in the year in which C's tax return reflects the deduction for any amount paid to A for the legal right to use the tax planning method that is the subject of the patent. C also participates in the transaction for any years for which any other tax benefit from the transaction is reflected on C's tax return.

Example 5. (i) A, an individual, is the employee of B, a corporation. A creates a tax planning method and applies for a U.S. patent but B pays the fee required under title 35 of the United States Code for A's patent application. Pursuant to A's employment contract with B, B holds all substantial rights to the patent. B's tax return reflects a deduction for the amount paid in relation to obtaining the patent.

(ii) A and B are patent holders under paragraph (b)(7)(ii)(C)*(1)* and *(3)* of this section, respectively. The transaction is not a reportable transaction for A under paragraph (b)(7) of this section because A does not have the right to payment for another person's use of the tax planning method that is the subject of the patent. The transaction is a reportable transaction for B under paragraph (b)(7) of this section because B holds all substantial rights to the patent and has the right to payment for another person's use of the tax planning method that is the subject of the patent. B has participated in the transaction in the year in which B's tax return reflects a tax benefit in relation to obtaining the patent. B also participates in the transaction for any years for which B's tax return reflects income from a payment received from another person for the use of the tax planning method that is the subject of the patent.

Example 6. (i) Assume the facts as in *Example 4*, except that A agrees to license the patent to F, a financial institution. The license agreement between A and F provides that F may offer the tax planning method to its clients and if a client decides to use the tax planning method, F must pay A for each client's use of the tax planning method. F offers the tax planning method to G who uses the tax planning method and knows or has reason to know it is the subject of a patent. F charges G for financial planning services and pays A for G's use of the tax planning method. A's tax return reflects income from the payment received from F. F's tax return reflects income from the payment received from G, and G's tax return reflects a deduction for the fees paid to F.

(ii) F is a patent holder's agent under paragraph (b)(7)(ii)(D) of this section because F has the permission of the patent holder to offer for sale or exchange, to sell or exchange, or to market a tax planning method that is the subject of a patent. F also is a patent holder's agent under paragraph (b)(7)(ii)(D) of this section because F receives (directly or indirectly) a fee in any amount for a tax planning method that is the subject of a patent for or on behalf of a patent holder. The transaction is a reportable transaction for both A and F under paragraph (b)(7) of this section because A and F each have the right to payment for another person's use of the tax planning method that is the subject of the patent. The transaction is a reportable transaction for G under paragraph (b)(7) of this section because G paid a fee (directly or indirectly) to a patent holder or a patent holder's agent for the legal right to use a tax planning method that G knew or had reason to know was the subject of the patent. A has participated in the transaction in the years in which A's tax return reflects income from the payment received from F for G's use of the tax planning method that is the subject of the patent. F has participated in the transaction in the years in which F's tax return reflects income from the payment received from G for use of the tax planning method that is the subject of the patent. G has participated in the transaction in the years in which G's tax return reflects a deduction for the fees paid to F. G also participates in the transaction for any years for which any other tax benefit from the transaction is reflected on G's tax return.

Example 7. Assume the same facts as in *Example 4*. J uses a tax planning method that is the same as the tax planning method that is the subject of A's patent. J does not pay any fees to any patent holder or patent holder's agent with respect to the tax planning method that is the subject of the patent. A sues J for infringement of the patent and J pays A an amount for damages. A's tax return reflects as income the amounts for damages received from J. The transaction is not a reportable transaction for J under paragraph (b)(7) of this section because J did not pay any fees (as defined in paragraph (b)(7)(ii)(A) of this section) (directly or indirectly) to a patent holder or patent holder's agent for the legal right to use a tax planning method that J knew or had reason to know was the subject of the patent. A has participated in a reportable transaction under paragraph (b)(7) of this section in the year in which A's tax return reflects income from a payment (the amount received as an award for damages in a suit for damages for infringement of the patent) received from another person for the use of the tax planning method that is the subject of a patent.

* * *

(h) * * *

(2) *Patented transactions.*—Upon the publication of the Treasury decision adopting these rules as final regulations in the **Federal Register**, paragraphs (b)(7), (c)(3)(i)(F), and (c)(3)(ii) *Examples 4* through *7* of this section will apply to transactions entered into on or after September 26, 2007.

Classification: Cell Companies: Series LLCs

Classification: Cell Companies: Series LLCs.—Reg. §301.6011-6, regarding the classification for Federal tax purposes of a series of a domestic series limited liability company (LLC), a cell of a domestic cell company, or a foreign series or cell that conducts an insurance business, is proposed (published in the Federal Register on September 14, 2010) (REG-119921-09).

Par. 2. Section 301.6011-6 is added to read as follows:

§301.6011-6. Statements of series and series organizations.—(a) *Statement required.*—Each series and series organization (as defined in paragraph (b) of this section) shall file a statement for each taxable year containing the identifying information with respect to the series or series organization as prescribed by the Internal Revenue Service for this purpose and shall include the information required by the statement and its instructions.

(b) *Definitions.*—(1) *Series.*—The term *series* has the same meaning as in §301.7701-1(a)(5)(viii)(C).

(2) *Series organization.*—The term *series organization* has the same meaning as in §301.7701-1(a)(5)(viii)(A).

(c) *Effective/applicability date.*—This section applies to taxable years beginning after the date of publication of the Treasury decision adopting these rules as final regulations in the **Federal Register**.

Information Reporting: Minimum Essential Coverage

Information Reporting: Minimum Essential Coverage.—Reg. § 301.6011-8, affecting health insurance issuers, employers, governments, and other persons that provide minimum essential coverage to individuals, are proposed (published in the Federal Register on September 9, 2013) (REG-132455-11).

☐ Par. 5. Section 301.6011-8 is added to read as follows:

§ 301.6011-8. Required use of magnetic media to report minimum essential coverage.—(a) *Returns reporting minimum essential coverage must be filed on magnetic media.*—A person required to file an information return reporting minimum essential coverage under § 1.6055-1 of this chapter must file the return on magnetic media if the person is required to file to least 250 returns during the calendar year. Returns filed on magnetic media must be made in accordance with applicable publications, forms, instructions, or published guidance, see §§ 601.601(d) and 601.602 of this chapter.

(b) *Magnetic media.*—For purposes of this section, the term *magnetic media* has the same meaning as in § 301.6011-2(a)(1).

(c) *Determination of 250 returns.*—For purposes of this section, a person is required to file at least 250 returns if, during the calendar year, the person is required to file at least 250 returns of any type, including information returns (for example, Forms W-2, Forms 1099), income tax returns, employment tax returns, and excise tax returns.

(d) *Waiver.*—The Commissioner may waive the requirements of this section in cases of hardship in accordance with § 301.6011-2(c)(2)(i).

(e) *Failure to file.*—If a person fails to file an information return on magnetic media when required by this section, the person is deemed to have failed to file the return. See section 6721 for penalties for failure to file returns and see section 6724 and the regulations under section 6721 for failure to file on magnetic media.

(f) *Effective/applicability date.*—This section applies to returns on Form 1095-B or another form the IRS designates required to be filed after December 31, 2015. Reporting entities will not be subject to penalties under section 6721 with respect to the reporting requirements for 2014 (for information returns that would have been required to be filed in 2015 with respect to 2014). [Reg. § 301.6011-8.]

Information Reporting: Health Insurance Coverage: Applicable Large Employers

Information Reporting: Health Insurance Coverage: Applicable Large Employers.—Reg. § 301.6011-9, providing guidance to employers that are subject to the information reporting requirements under section 6056 of the Internal Revenue Code (Code), enacted by the Affordable Care Act, is proposed (published in the Federal Register on September 9, 2013) (REG-136630-12).

☐ Par. 2. Section 301.6011-9 is added to read as follows:

§ 301.6011-9. Electronic filing of section 6056 returns.—(a) *Returns required under section 6056.*—An applicable large employer member, as defined in § 301.6056-1(b)(2), is required to file electronically an information return under section 6056 and § 301.6056-1, except as otherwise provided in paragraph (b) of this section.

(b) *Exceptions.*—(1) *Low-volume filers/250-return threshold.*—(i) *In general.*—An applicable large employer member will not be required to file electronically the section 6056 information return described in paragraph (a) of this section unless it is required to file 250 or more returns during the calendar year. Each section 6056 information return for a full-time employee is a separate return. For purposes of this section, an applicable large employer member is required to file at least 250 returns if, during the calendar year, the applicable large employer member is required to file at least 250 returns of any type, including information returns (for example, Forms W-2, Forms 1099), income tax returns, employment tax returns, and excise tax returns. An applicable large employer member filing fewer than 250 returns during the calendar year may make the returns on the prescribed paper form.

(ii) *Examples.*—The following examples illustrate the provisions of paragraph (b)(1) of this section:

Example 1. Company X is an applicable large employer member. For the calendar year ending December 31, 2015, Company X is required to file 275 section 6056 returns. Company X is required to file section 6056 returns electronically for that calendar year because 275 section 6056 information returns exceed the 250-return threshold.

Example 2. Company Y is an applicable large employer member. For the calendar year ending December 31, 2015, Company Y is required to file 200 returns on Form W-2 and 150 section 6056 returns. Company Y is required to file the section 6056 returns electronically for that calendar year because it is required to file more than 250 returns (that is, the 200 Forms W-2 plus the 150 section 6056 returns).

(2) *Waiver.*—(i) *In general.*—The Commissioner may waive the requirements of this section if hardship is shown in a request for waiver filed in accordance with this paragraph (b)(2)(i). The principal factor in determining hardship will be the amount, if any, by which the cost of filing the section 6056 returns in accordance with this section exceeds the costs of filing the returns on other media. A request for waiver must be made in accordance with applicable revenue procedures or publications (see § 601.601(d)(2)(ii)*(b)* of this chapter). Pursuant to these procedures, a request for waiver should be filed at least 45 days before the due date of the section 6056 return in order for the IRS to have adequate time to respond to the request for waiver. The waiver will specify the type of information return (that is, section 6056 information return) and the period to which it applies and will be subject to

such terms and conditions regarding the method of reporting as may be prescribed by the Commissioner.

(ii) *Supplemental rules.*—The Commissioner may prescribe rules that supplement the provisions of paragraph (b)(2)(i) of this section.

(c) *Effective/applicability date.*—The rules of this section are effective as of the date of publication of the Treasury decision adopting these rules as final regulations in the **Federal Register**. This section applies to returns on "Form 1095-C" or another form the IRS designates required to be filed after December 31, 2014. However, reporting entities will not be subject to penalties under sections 6721 or 6722 with respect to the reporting requirements for 2014 (for information returns filed and for statements furnished to employees in 2015). [Reg. §301:6011-9.]

Excise Taxes: Taxable Fuel: Returns: Definitions

Excise Taxes: Taxable Fuel: Returns: Definitions.—Amendments to Reg. §40.0-1, relating to credits and payments for alcohol mixtures, biodiesel mixtures, renewable diesel mixtures, alternative fuel mixtures, and alternative fuel sold for use or used as a fuel and relating to the definition of gasoline and diesel fuel, are proposed (published in the Federal Register on July 29, 2008) (REG-155087-05).

Par. 5. Section 40.0-1 is amended by revising paragraph (d) and adding paragraph (e) to read as follows:

§40.0-1. Introduction.

* * *

(d) *Person.*—For purposes of this part, each business unit that has, or is required to have, a separate employer identification number is treated as a separate person. Thus, business units (for example, a parent corporation and a subsidiary corporation, a proprietorship and a related partnership, or the various members of a consolidated group), each of which has a different employer identification number, are separate persons.

(e) *Effective/applicability date.*—This part is effective for returns and deposits that relate to calendar quarters beginning after September 30, 2008. For rules applicable to returns and deposits that relate to prior periods, see 26 CFR part 40 (revised as of April 1, 2008).

Return and Extended Due Date: Changes

Return Due Extended Due Date: Changes.—Amendments to Reg. §1.6012-6, updating the due dates and extensions of time to file certain tax returns and information returns, are proposed (published in the Federal Register on July 20, 2017) (REG-128483-15).

Par. 3. Revise paragraph (a)(1) and add paragraph (c) to §1.6012-6 to read as follows:

§1.6012-6. Returns by political organizations.—(a) * * *

(1) [The text of proposed §1.6012-6(a)(1) is the same as the text of §1.6012-6T(a)(1) as added by T.D. 9821]

* * *

(c) *Applicability date.*—The requirements of paragraph (a)(1) of this section are applicable for returns filed on or after the date a Treasury Decision incorporating these amendments as final regulations is published in the **Federal Register**.

Dependency Exemption: Authorized Placement Agency: Definition

Dependency Exemption: Authorized Placement Agency: Definition.—Amendments to Reg. §1.6013-1, relating to the definition of an authorized placement agency for purposes of a dependency exemption for a child placed for adoption that were issued prior to the changes made to the law by the Working Families Tax Relief Act of 2004, are proposed (published in the Federal Register on January 19, 2017) (REG-137604-07).

Par. 18. Section 1.6013-1 is amended by removing paragraph (e).

§1.6013-1. Joint returns.

Tax Liability: Relief from Joint and Several Liability

Tax Liability: Relief from Joint and Several Liability.—Amendments to Reg. §1.6015-0, providing guidance to taxpayers on when and how to request relief under sections 66 and 6015, are proposed (published in the Federal Register on August 13, 2013) (REG-132251-11).

☐ Par. 4. Section 1.6015-0 is amended as follows:

1. In §1.6015-5, revising the entry for paragraph (a) as new entry for paragraph (a)(1) and adding a new entry for paragraph (a)(2); entries for paragraphs (b)(1) through (b)(5) are revised; entries for paragraphs (b)(2)(i) and (b)(2)(ii) are removed; and new entries are added for paragraphs (b)(3)(i), (b)(3)(ii), (b)(6), (c)(1), (c)(2), and (c)(3).

2. Section 1.6015-9 heading is revised.

The additions and revisions read as follows:

§1.6015-0. Table of contents.

* * *

§1.6015-5 Time and manner for requesting relief.

(a) Requesting relief.

(1) In general.

(2) Requesting relief as part of a collection due process hearing.

(b) * * *

(1) Relief other than equitable relief.

(2) Equitable relief.

(3) Definitions.

Tax Liability: Relief from Joint and Several Liability

Tax Liability: Relief from Joint and Several Liability.—Amendments to Reg. §1.6015-5, providing guidance to taxpayers on when and how to request relief under sections 66 and 6015, are proposed (published in the Federal Register on August 13, 2013) (REG-132251-11).

□ Par. 5. Section 1.6015-5 is amended to read as follows:

1. Paragraph (a) is amended by designating the introductory text as (a)(1), adding a new heading for paragraph (a)(1) introductory text, and adding new paragraph (a)(2).

2. Paragraph (b)(1) is revised.

3. Paragraphs (b)(2), (b)(3), (b)(4), and (b)(5) are redesignated as paragraphs (b)(3), (b)(4), (b)(5), and (b)(6).

4. New paragraph (b)(2) is added.

5. Newly-designated paragraphs (b)(3)(ii), (b)(4), (b)(5), and (b)(6) are revised.

6. Paragraph (c)(1) is amended by adding a new sentence at the end of the paragraph.

7. Paragraph (c)(2) is redesignated as paragraph (c)(3) and revised and new paragraph (c)(2) is added.

The revisions and additions read as follows:

§1.6015-5. Time and manner for requesting relief.—(a) *Requesting relief.*—(1) *In general.*—* * *

(2) *Requesting relief as part of a collection due process hearing.*—A requesting spouse may also elect the application of §1.6015-2 or 1.6015-3, or request equitable relief under §1.6015-4, pursuant to the collection due process (CDP) hearing procedures under sections 6320 and 6330, by attaching Form 8857, "Request for Innocent Spouse Relief," or an equivalent written statement to Form 12153, "Request for a Collection Due Process or Equivalent Hearing" (or other specified form).

(b) * * *.—(1) *Relief other than equitable relief.*—To elect the application of §1.6015-2 or 1.6015-3, a requesting spouse must file Form 8857 or other similar statement with the IRS no later than two years from the date of the first collection activity against the requesting spouse after July 22, 1998, with respect to the joint tax liability.

(2) *Equitable relief.*—To request equitable relief under §1.6015-4, a requesting spouse must file Form 8857 or other similar statement with the IRS within the period of limitation on collection of tax in section 6502 or within the period of limitation on credit or refund of tax in section 6511, as applicable to the joint tax liability. If a requesting spouse files a request for equitable relief under §1.6015-4 within the period of limitation on collection of tax, the IRS will consider the request for equitable relief, but the requesting spouse will be eligible for a credit or refund of tax only if the limitation period for credit or refund of tax is open when the request is filed (assuming all other requirements are met, including the limit on amount of credit or refund prescribed in section 6511(b)(2)). Alternatively, if a requesting spouse files a request for equitable relief after the period of limitation on collection of tax has expired but while the limitation period on credit or refund of tax remains open, the IRS will consider the request for equitable relief insofar as tax was paid by or collected from the requesting spouse, and the requesting spouse will be eligible for a potential credit or refund of tax. If neither the section 6502 nor section 6511 limitation period is open when a requesting spouse files a request for equitable relief, the IRS will not consider the request for equitable relief. See §1.6015-1(g).

(3) * * *.—(ii) *Section 6330 notice.*—A section 6330 notice refers to the notice sent, pursuant to section 6330, providing taxpayers notice of the IRS's intent to levy and of their right to a CDP hearing. The mailing of a section 6330 notice by certified mail to the requesting spouse's last known address is sufficient to start the two-year period, described in paragraph (b)(1), regardless of whether the requesting spouse actually receives the notice.

(4) *Requests for relief made before commencement of collection activity.*—Except as provided in paragraph (b)(6) of this section, an election under §1.6015-2 or 1.6015-3 or a request for equitable relief under §1.6015-4 may be made before any collection activity has commenced. For example, an election or request for equitable relief may be made in connection with an examination of a joint Federal income tax return or a demand for payment, or pursuant to the CDP hearing procedures of section 6320 with respect to the filing of a Notice of Federal Tax Lien. A request for equitable relief under §1.6015-4 for a liability that is properly reported on a joint Federal income tax return but not paid with the return or by the due date for payment is properly submitted at any time after the return is filed.

(5) *Examples.*—The following examples illustrate the rules of this paragraph (b):

Example 1. On January 12, 2009, the IRS mailed a section 6330 notice to H and W, by certified mail to their last known address, regarding their 2007 joint Federal income tax liability, which was the result of an understatement. The section 6330 notice was the first collection activity the IRS initiated against H and W to collect the 2007 joint liability. H and W did not request a CDP hearing in response to the section 6330 notice. On June 5, 2009, the IRS issued a levy on W's wages to W's employer. On July 10, 2009, the IRS issued a levy on H's wages to H's employer. To be considered for relief under §1.6015-2 or 1.6015-3, a Form 8857 or other request for relief must be filed on or before January

12, 2011, which is two years after the IRS sent the section 6330 notice. The two-year period for purposes of §§1.6015-2 and 1.6015-3 (not applicable to §1.6015-4) runs from the date the section 6330 notice was mailed and not from the date of the actual levy.

Example 2. On May 5, 2011, the IRS offset W's overpayment from W's 2010 separate Federal income tax return in the amount of $2,000 to H and W's joint tax liability for 2009 of $5,000, for which H and W filed a joint return on April 15, 2010. The offset is the first collection activity the IRS initiated against W to collect the 2009 joint liability. On October 3, 2013, W requests relief under section 6015. W's request is not timely under §§1.6015-2 and 1.6015-3 because the request was made more than two years after the IRS's first collection activity against W - the offset of W's overpayment from 2010. As to equitable relief under §1.6015-4, the period of limitation on collection is open when W files her request, and the request can be considered for equitable relief of the unpaid tax of $3,000. W is not, however, eligible for any credit or refund of the $2,000 amount that the IRS applied against H and W's 2009 joint liability, because the period of limitation on credit or refund of tax for 2009 is no longer open when W files her request for relief. Under section 6511(a), a credit or refund of tax must generally be claimed within three years after the filing date of a tax return for the tax year or two years after payment of the tax, whichever is later. Thus, the last day for W to claim a credit or refund of the $2,000 amount was May 5, 2013, but her request for relief was not filed until October 3, 2013.

Example 3. On June 14, 2011, the IRS offset W's overpayment from her separate Federal income tax return for 2010 against H and W's joint liability for 2009, which was the result of an understatement. On July 5, 2012, the IRS offset H's overpayment from his separate Federal income tax return for 2011 against H and W's joint liability for 2009. The offset is the first collection activity the IRS initiated against H to collect the 2009 joint liability. On November 25, 2013, H requests relief under section 6015 by filing Form 8857. H's request is timely. For purposes of §§1.6015-2 and 1.6015-3, the request was filed within two years of the IRS's first collection activity against H. The IRS's collection activity against W does not start the two-year period for H to request relief. Additionally, for purposes of §1.6015-4, the period of limitation on collection was open when H filed Form 8857, making him eligible for equitable relief from any unpaid liability for 2009, and the period of limitation on a credit or refund of tax for 2009 that was paid through the offset of H's overpayment for 2011 was likewise open when H filed his Form 8857.

Example 4. On April 15, 2008, H and W filed a joint Federal income tax return for tax year 2007. On October 1, 2009, additional liability was assessed against H and W as a result of income attributable to H being omitted from the return. H and W divorced soon after and, in late December 2009, W moved out of the family home without notifying the United States Postal Service or the IRS of her change of address until the end of January 2010. On January 15, 2010, the IRS mailed a section 6330 notice regarding H and W's 2007 joint Federal income tax liability to H and W's last known address (the address on H and W's joint Federal income tax return for tax year 2008, filed on April 15, 2009). H and W did not request a CDP hearing in response to the section 6330 notice. The IRS issued a levy on W's wages to W's employer on June 2, 2010. W filed Form 8857 requesting relief under section 6015 on May 15, 2012. Actual receipt of a section 6330 notice is not required to start the two-year period for purposes of §1.6015-2 or 1.6015-3, as long as the notice is sent to the taxpayer at the taxpayer's last known address by certified or registered mail. The two-year period, therefore, expired on January 15, 2012. Accordingly, W's request for relief is too late to be considered for any relief under §1.6015-2 or 1.6015-3, as the request was filed more than two years after the IRS sent the section 6330 notice. But because the period of limitation on collection was open (generally until October 1, 2019) when W filed the Form 8857, the IRS will consider whether W is entitled to equitable relief under §1.6015- 4. Further, to the extent W's request for equitable relief under §1.6015-4 seeks a refund of tax W paid through the levy, W's Form 8857 is a timely claim for refund because it was filed within the applicable period of limitation for credit or refund of tax (in this case, two years from payment of the tax).

Example 5. H and W timely filed a joint Federal income tax return for tax year 1999. The IRS selected the 1999 return for examination and determined a deficiency in tax of $10,000. The IRS assessed the tax on December 1, 2001. The taxpayers were divorced in 2005. On her separate Federal income tax return for tax year 2005, W reported an overpayment of $2,500, which the IRS applied on May 3, 2006, to the joint liability for 1999. On her separate Federal income tax return for tax year 2009, W reported an overpayment of $1,750, which the IRS applied on May 15, 2010, to the joint liability for 1999. On May 1, 2012, W filed with the IRS a Form 8857 requesting relief under section 6015. The IRS will not consider whether W is entitled to any relief under §1.6015-2 or 1.6015-3 because W's election is untimely as W's Form 8857 was filed after the end of the two-year period running from the offset of W's overpayment from her tax year 2005 return. Although the collection period expired on December 1, 2011, the IRS will consider whether W is entitled to equitable relief under §1.6015-4 for tax year 1999 because W filed Form 8857 within the two-year period for claiming a credit or refund of tax under section 6511(a). Under section 6511(b)(2), the amount of any refund to which W might be entitled is limited to $1,750 (the amount paid within the two years preceding the filing of W's Form 8857), and the $2,500 collected in May 2006 is not available for refund.

Example 6. Assume the same facts as in Example 5, except that W's separate Federal income tax return for tax year 2009 did not report an overpayment, and there was no offset against the joint liability for 1999. The IRS will not consider whether W is entitled to any relief under §1.6015-2 or 1.6015-3 because W's election is untimely as W's Form 8857 was filed after the end of the two-year period running from the offset of W's overpayment from her tax year 2005 return. Further, as the collection period expired on December 1, 2011, and the period for claiming a credit or refund of tax under section 6511(a) expired on May 3, 2008, IRS will not consider whether W is entitled to equitable relief under §1.6015-4 for tax year 1999.

(6) *Premature requests for relief.*—The IRS will not consider for relief under §§1.6015-2, 1.6015-3, or 1.6015-4 any election or request for relief from joint and several liability that is premature. A premature election or request for relief is an election or request, other than a request for relief for a liability that is properly reported on a joint Federal income tax return but not paid, that is filed for a tax year prior to the receipt of a notification of an examination or a letter or notice from the IRS indicating that there may be an outstanding liability with regard to that year. These notices or letters do not include notices issued pursuant to section 6223 relating to Tax Equity and Fiscal Responsibility Act of 1982 (TEFRA) partnership proceedings. A premature request for relief is not considered an election or request under §1.6015-1(h)(5).

(c) * * *.—(1) * * * A requesting spouse who receives a final administrative determination of relief under §1.6015-1 may not later elect the application of §1.6015-2 or 1.6015-3, or request equitable relief under §1.6015-4, including through the CDP hearing procedures under sections 6320 and 6330.

(2) *Reconsideration process.*—Pursuant to §§1.6015-1(h)(5) and 1.6015-5(c)(1), a requesting spouse is generally entitled to submit only one request for relief and receive only one final administrative determination. Nevertheless, if a requesting spouse submits new information (including new facts, evidence, and arguments not previously considered) to the IRS after the IRS issues a final administrative determination to the requesting spouse, the IRS may reconsider the requesting spouse's request for relief under its established reconsideration process. A request for a reconsideration is not a qualifying election under §1.6015-2 or 1.6015-3, or a request under §1.6015-4, for purposes of §1.6015-1(h)(5). Any reconsideration of a final administrative determination by the IRS, and any notice or letter issued to the requesting spouse as a result of the reconsideration (such as Letter 4277C, Letter 5186C, Letter 5187C, or Letter 5188C), is not the IRS's final determination for purposes of section 6015(e) and is not subject to review by the Tax Court under section 6015(e) or §1.6015-7.

(3) *Examples.*—The following examples illustrate the rules of this paragraph (c):

Example 1. In January 2008, W became a limited partner in partnership P, and in February 2009, she started her own business from which she earned $100,000 of gross income for the taxable year 2009. H and W filed a joint Federal income tax return for 2009, on which they claimed $20,000 in losses from the investment in P, and they omitted W's self-employment tax. In March 2011, the IRS commenced an examination under the provisions of the Code for TEFRA partnership proceedings and sent H and W a notice of the proceeding under section 6223(a)(1). In September 2011, the IRS opened an examination of H and W's 2009 joint return regarding the omitted self-employment tax. In 2012, H decides to pursue relief under section 6015. H may file a request for relief as to liability for self-employment tax because he has received a notification of an examination informing him of potential liability. A request for relief regarding the TEFRA partnership proceeding, however, is premature under paragraph (b)(6) of this section. H must wait until the IRS sends him a notice of computational adjustment or assesses any liability resulting from the TEFRA partnership proceeding before he may file a request for relief from that liability. An assessment of tax in the TEFRA partnership proceeding would be separate from an assessment for the self-employment tax. Therefore, a subsequent request from H for relief from any liability resulting from the TEFRA partnership proceeding will not be precluded under this paragraph (c) by a previous request that H filed for relief from self-employment tax liability.

Example 2. On October 21, 2009, H filed a Form 8857 requesting relief under §§1.6015-2, 1.6015-3, and 1.6015-4 for an assessed deficiency relating to his joint income tax return for tax year 2004. On August 11, 2010, the IRS issued a final administrative determination denying H relief from the liability for tax year 2004. Under section 6015(e), H had until November 9, 2010, to file a petition to the Tax Court to challenge the denial of relief. H did not timely file a petition. On October 3, 2011, H submitted information with respect to his claim for relief for tax year 2004 that he did not previously provide. The IRS considered the new information pursuant to its established reconsideration process in IRM 25.15.17 (Rev. 03/08/2013) and informed H on January 25, 2012, via Letter 4277C that he was still not entitled to relief under any subsection of section 6015. Letter 4277C is not a final administrative determination and did not confer any new rights for H to file a petition to the Tax Court to challenge the final administrative determination issued on August 11, 2010, or the denial of relief from the IRS's reconsideration.

Tax Liability: Relief from Joint and Several Liability

Tax Liability: Relief from Joint and Several Liability.—Amendments to Reg. §1.6015-9, providing guidance to taxpayers on when and how to request relief under sections 66 and 6015, are proposed (published in the Federal Register on August 13, 2013) (REG-132251-11).

☐ Par 6. Section 1.6015-9 is revised to read as follows:

§1.6015-9. Effective/applicability date.—(a) *In general.*—Except as provided in paragraph (b) of this section, §§1.6015-0 through 1.6015-9 are applicable for all elections under §1.6015-2 or 1.6015-3 or any requests for relief under §1.6015-4 filed on or after July 18, 2002.

(b) Except for the rules for determining the timeliness of an election under §1.6015-2 or 1.6015-3, or a request for equitable relief under §1.6015-4 in paragraphs (b)(1) and (b)(2) of §1.6015-5, §1.6015-5 is applicable to any election under §1.6015-2 or 1.6015-3, or to any request for equitable relief under §1.6015-4, filed on or after the date of publication of the Treasury decision adopting these rules as final regulations in the **Federal Register**. The rules for determining the timeliness of an election under §1.6015-2 or 1.6015-3, or a request for equitable relief under §1.6015-4 in paragraphs (b)(1) and (b)(2) of §1.6015-5 are applicable to any election under

§ 1.6015-2 or 1.6015-3, or to any request for equitable relief under § 1.6015-4, filed on or after July 25, 2011 (the date that Notice 2011-70, 2011-32 IRB 135, was issued to the public). [Reg. § 1.6015-9.]

Taxable Income: Relief from Joint and Several Liability

Taxable Income: Relief from Joint and Several Liability.—Amendments to Reg. §§ 1.6015-0—1.6015-9, relating to relief from joint and several liability under section 6015 of the Internal Revenue Code and reflecting changes in the law made by the Tax Relief and Health Care Act of 2006 as well as changes in the law arising from litigation, are proposed (published in the Federal Register on November 20, 2015) (REG-134219-08).

Par. 7. Section 1.6015-0 is amended by:

1. In § 1.6015-1, entries for paragraphs (e)(1), (e)(2), (e)(3), (e)(4), (e)(5), (h)(6), (h)(7), (h)(8), (k), (l), (m), (n), (o), and (p) are added and the entry for paragraph (h)(5) is revised.

2. In § 1.6015-2, entries for paragraphs (b), (c), (d), and (e) are revised and the entries for paragraphs (e)(1) and (e)(2) are removed.

3. In § 1.6015-3, entries for paragraphs (a) and (c)(2)(v) are revised and entries for paragraphs (c)(2)(vi), (d)(2)(i)(A), (d)(2)(i)(B), and (e) are added.

4. In § 1.6015-4, an entry for paragraph (d) is added.

5. In § 1.6015-5, an entry for paragraph (d) is added.

6. In § 1.6015-6, an entry for paragraph (d) is added.

7. In § 1.6015-7, entries for paragraphs (c)(1) and (c)(4)(iii) are revised and entries for paragraphs (c)(1)(i), (c)(1)(ii), (c)(1)(iii), and (d) are added.

8. In § 1.6015-8, an entry for paragraph (d) is added.

9. Section 1.6015-9 entry is removed.

The revisions and additions read as follows:

§ 1.6015-0. Table of contents.

* * *

(iii) Assessment to which the request relates.

(d) Effective/applicability date.

§ 1.6015-8 Applicable liabilities.

* * *

(d) Effective/applicability date.

Par. 8. Section 1.6015-1 is amended by:
1. Paragraphs (a)(2), (e), (h)(1), and (h)(5) are revised.
2. The last three sentences of paragraph (h)(4) are removed.
3. Paragraphs (h)(6), (7), and (8) and (k) are added.
4. Paragraph (l) is added and reserved.
5. Paragraphs (m), (n), (o), and (p) are added.
The revisions and additions read as follows:

§ 1.6015-1. Relief from joint and several liability on a joint return.—(a) * * *

(2) A requesting spouse may submit a single request for relief under § § 1.6015-2, 1.6015-3, and 1.6015-4. Upon submitting a request for relief, the IRS will consider whether relief is appropriate under § § 1.6015-2 and 1.6015-3 and, to the extent relief is unavailable under both of those provisions, under § 1.6015-4. Equitable relief under § 1.6015-4 is available only to a requesting spouse who fails to qualify for relief under § § 1.6015-2 and 1.6015-3.

* * *

(e) *Res judicata and collateral estoppel.*—(1) *In general.*—A requesting spouse is barred from relief from joint and several liability under section 6015 by res judicata for any tax year for which a court of competent jurisdiction has rendered a final decision on the requesting spouse's tax liability if relief under section 6015 was at issue in the prior proceeding, or if the requesting spouse meaningfully participated in that proceeding and could have raised the issue of relief under section 6015.

(2) *Situations in which relief under § 1.6015-3 will not be considered to have been at issue in the prior proceeding.*—Relief under § 1.6015-3 will not be considered to have been at issue in a prior proceeding if the requesting spouse only raised the issue of relief under section 6015 in general and did not specify under which subsection relief was being requested, and the requesting spouse was not eligible for relief under § 1.6015-3 during the prior proceeding because the requesting spouse was not divorced, widowed, or legally separated, or had been a member of the same household as the nonrequesting spouse during the prior 12 months.

(3) *Meaningful participation.*—A requesting spouse meaningfully participated in the prior proceeding if the requesting spouse was involved in the proceeding so that the requesting spouse could have raised the issue of relief under section 6015 in that proceeding. Meaningful participation is a facts and circumstances determination. Absent abuse as set forth in paragraph (i) of this section, the following is a nonexclusive list of acts to be considered in making the facts and circumstances determination: whether the requesting spouse participated in the IRS Appeals process while the prior proceeding was docketed; whether the requesting spouse participated in pretrial meetings; whether the requesting spouse participated in discovery; whether the requesting spouse participated in settlement negotiations; whether the requesting spouse signed court documents, such as a petition, a stipulation of facts, motions, briefs, or any other documents; whether the requesting spouse participated at trial (for example, the requesting spouse was present or testified at the prior proceeding); and whether the requesting spouse was represented by counsel in the prior proceeding. No one act necessarily determines the outcome. The degree of importance of each act varies depending on the requesting spouse's facts and circumstances.

(i) Notwithstanding the fact that a requesting spouse performed any of the acts listed in paragraph (e)(3) of this section in the prior proceeding, the requesting spouse will not be considered to have meaningfully participated in the prior proceeding if the requesting spouse establishes that the requesting spouse performed the acts because the nonrequesting spouse abused (as described in paragraph (o) of this section) or maintained control over the requesting spouse, and the requesting spouse did not challenge the nonrequesting spouse for fear of the nonrequesting spouse's retaliation.

(ii) A requesting spouse did not meaningfully participate in a prior proceeding if, due to the effective date of section 6015, relief under section 6015 was not available in that proceeding.

(iii) In a case petitioned from a statutory notice of deficiency under section 6213, the fact that the requesting spouse did not have the ability to effectively contest the underlying deficiency is irrelevant for purposes of determining whether the requesting spouse meaningfully participated in the court proceeding for purposes of paragraph (e)(1) of this section.

(4) *Examples.*—The following examples illustrate the rules of this paragraph (e):

Example 1. In a prior court proceeding involving a petition from a notice of deficiency related to a joint income tax return, H and W were still married and filed a timely joint petition to the United States Tax Court. The petition stated that W was entitled to relief under section 6015 without specifying under which subsection she was requesting relief. Before trial, H negotiates with the IRS Chief Counsel attorney and settles the case. W did not meaningfully participate. A stipulated decision was entered that did not mention relief under section 6015. One year later W files a request for relief under section 6015. While W did not meaningfully participate in the prior court proceeding, because relief under section 6015 was at issue in that case, res judicata applies except with respect to relief under § 1.6015-3. Because W did not specify that she was requesting relief under § 1.6015-3, and W was not eligible to request relief under that section because she was still married to the nonrequesting spouse throughout the court proceeding, relief under § 1.6015-3 is not considered to have been at issue in that case. Thus, W is not barred by res judicata from raising relief under § 1.6015-3 in a later case. However, any later claim from W requesting relief under § 1.6015-2 or § 1.6015-4 would be barred by res judicata.

Example 2. Same facts as in *Example 1* of this paragraph (e)(4) except that H and W are divorced at the time the petition was filed. Because W was eligible to request relief under § 1.6015-3 as she was divorced from H, relief under § 1.6015-3 is considered to be at issue in the prior court proceeding and W is barred by res judicata from raising relief under § 1.6015-3 in a later case. Thus, any later claim from W requesting relief under any subsection of section 6015 would be barred by res judicata.

Example 3. The IRS issued a notice of deficiency to H and W determining a deficiency on H and W's joint income tax return based on H's Schedule C business. H and W timely filed a petition in the United States Tax Court. W signed the petition and numerous other documents, participated in discussions regarding the case with the IRS Chief Counsel attorney, and ultimately agreed to a settlement of the case. W could have raised any issue, but W did not have any access to H's records regarding his Schedule C business, over which H maintained exclusive control. Relief under section 6015 was never raised in the court proceeding. If W were to later file a request for relief under section 6015, W's claim would be barred by res judicata. Considering these facts and circumstances, W meaningfully participated in the prior court proceeding regarding the deficiency. The fact that W could not have effectively contested the underlying deficiency because she had no access to H's Schedule C records is not relevant to the determination of whether W meaningfully participated. Instead the meaningful participation exception looks to W's involvement in the prior court proceeding and her ability to raise relief under section 6015 as a defense.

Example 4. Same facts as *Example 3* of this paragraph (e)(4), except that W's participation in discussions with the IRS Chief Counsel attorney were clearly controlled by H, and W was fearful of H when she agreed to settle the case. In this situation, her involvement in the prior proceeding would not be considered meaningful participation because W was able to establish that H maintained control over her and that she did not challenge H for fear of the H's retaliation. If W were to later file a request for relief under section 6015, her claim would not be barred by res judicata.

Example 5. In March 2014, the IRS issued a notice of deficiency to H and W determining a deficiency on H and W's joint income tax return for tax year 2011. H and W timely filed a pro se petition in the United States Tax Court for redetermination of the deficiency. W signed the petition, but otherwise, H handled the entire litigation, from discussing the case with the IRS Chief Counsel attorney to agreeing to a settlement of the case. Relief under section 6015 was never raised. W signed the decision document that H had agreed to with the IRS Chief Counsel attorney. If W were to later file a claim requesting relief under section 6015, W's claim would not be barred by res judicata. Considering these facts and circumstances, W's involvement in the prior court proceeding regarding the deficiency did not rise to the level of meaningful participation.

Example 6. Same facts as in *Example 5* of this paragraph (e)(4) except that W also participated in settlement negotiations with the IRS Chief Counsel attorney that resulted in the decision document entered in the case. Considering these facts and circumstances—signing the petition and the decision document, along with participating in the negotiations that led to the settlement reflected in the decision document—W meaningfully participated in the prior court proceeding regarding the deficiency because W could have raised relief under section 6015. Any later claim from W requesting relief under section 6015 would be barred by res judicata.

Example 7. In a prior court proceeding involving a petition from a notice of deficiency, H and W hired counsel, C, to represent them in the United States Tax Court. W agreed to C's representation, but otherwise, only H met and communicated with C about the case. C signed and filed the petition, discussed the case with the IRS Chief Counsel attorney, and agreed to a settlement of the case after discussing it with H. Relief under section 6015 was never raised. C signed the decision document on behalf of H and W. If W were to later file a claim requesting relief under section 6015, W's claim would not be barred by res judicata. Even though W was represented by counsel in the prior court proceeding regarding the deficiency, considering all the facts and circumstances, W's involvement in the prior court proceeding did not rise to the level of meaningful participation.

Example 8. In a prior court proceeding involving a petition from a notice of deficiency, H did not sign the petition or other court documents, participate in the Appeals or Counsel settlement negotiations, attend pretrial meetings, or hire separate counsel. H did, however, attend the trial and testify. Considering these facts and circumstances, H's participation in the trial is sufficient to establish that H meaningfully participated in the prior court proceeding regarding the deficiency because H's participation provided H with a definite opportunity to raise relief under section 6015 in that proceeding. Any later claim from H requesting relief under section 6015 would be barred by res judicata.

Example 9. The IRS issued a joint notice of deficiency to H and W determining a deficiency on H and W's joint income tax return based on H's Schedule C business. Only W timely filed a petition in the United States Tax Court. W conceded the deficiency shortly before trial and signed a decision document. W did not raise relief under section 6015. If W were to later file a claim requesting relief under section 6015, W's claim would be barred by res judicata. Because W was the only petitioner in the prior court proceeding, W's participation in that proceeding was meaningful participation.

(5) *Collateral estoppel.*—Any final decisions rendered by a court of competent jurisdiction regarding issues relevant to section 6015 are conclusive, and the requesting spouse may be collaterally estopped from relitigating those issues.

* * *

(h) *Definitions.*—(1) *Requesting spouse.*—A requesting spouse is an individual who filed a joint income tax return and requests relief from Federal income tax liability arising from that return under § 1.6015-2, § 1.6015-3, or § 1.6015-4.

* * *

(5) *Request for relief.*—A qualifying request under § 1.6015-2, § 1.6015-3, or § 1.6015-4 is the first timely request for relief from joint and several liability for the tax year for which relief is sought. A qualifying request also includes a requesting spouse's second request for relief from joint and several liability for the same tax year under § 1.6015-3 when the additional qualifications of paragraphs (h)(5)(i) and (ii) of this section are met—

(i) The requesting spouse did not qualify for relief under § 1.6015-3 at the time of the first request solely because the qualifications of § 1.6015-3(a) were not satisfied; and

(ii) At the time of the second request, the qualifications for relief under § 1.6015-3(a) were satisfied.

(6) *Unpaid tax and underpayment.*—Unpaid tax and underpayment for purposes of § 1.6015-4 means the balance due shown on the joint return, reduced by the tax paid with the joint return. The balance due shown on the joint return is determined after application of the credits for tax withheld under section 31, any amounts paid as estimated income tax, any amounts paid with an extension of time to file, or any other credits applied against the total tax reported on the return. Tax paid with the joint return includes a check or money order remitted with the return or Form 1040-V, "Payment Voucher," or payment by direct debit, credit card, or other commercially acceptable means under section 6311. If the joint return is filed on or before the last day prescribed for filing under section 6072 (determined without regard to any extension of time to file under section 6081), the tax paid with the joint return includes any tax paid on or before the last day prescribed for payment under section 6151. If the joint return is filed after the last day prescribed for filing, the tax paid with the joint return includes any tax paid on or before the date the joint return is filed. A requesting spouse is not entitled to be considered for relief under § 1.6015-4 for any tax paid with the joint return. If the tax paid with the joint return completely satisfies the balance due shown on the return, then there is no unpaid tax for purposes of § 1.6015-4.

(7) *Understatement.*—The term understatement means the excess of the amount of tax required to be shown on the return for the taxable year over the amount of the tax imposed which is shown on the return, reduced by any rebate (within the meaning of section 6211(b)(2)).

(8) *Deficiency.*—The term deficiency has the same meaning given to that term in section 6211 and § 301.6211-1 of this chapter.

* * *

(k) *Credit or refund.*—(1) *In general.*—Except as provided in paragraphs (k)(2) through (5) of this section, a requesting spouse who is eligible for relief can receive a credit or refund of payments made to satisfy the joint income tax liability, whether the liability resulted from an understatement or an underpayment.

(2) *No credit or refund allowed under § 1.6015-3.*—A requesting spouse is not entitled to a credit or refund of any payments made on the joint income tax liability as a result of allocating the deficiency under § 1.6015-3. See section 6015(g)(3) and § 1.6015-3(c)(1).

(3) *No circumvention of §§ 1.6015-1(k)(2) and 1.6015-3(c)(1).*—Section 1.6015-4 may not be used to circumvent the limitation of § 1.6015-3(c)(1) (such as, no refunds under § 1.6015-3). Therefore, relief is not available under this section to obtain a credit or refund of liabilities already paid, for which the requesting spouse would otherwise qualify for relief under § 1.6015-3. For purposes of determining whether the requesting spouse qualifies for relief under § 1.6015-3, the fact that a refund was barred by section 6015(g)(2) and paragraph (k)(2) of this section does not mean that the requesting spouse did not receive full relief. A requesting spouse is entitled to full relief under § 1.6015-3 if the requesting spouse was eligible to allocate the deficiency in full to the nonrequesting spouse.

(4) *Limitations on credit or refund.*—The availability of credit or refund is subject to the limitations provided by sections 6511 and 6512(b). Generally the filing of Form 8857, "Request for Innocent Spouse Relief," will be treated as the filing of a claim for credit or refund even if the requesting spouse does not specifically request a credit or refund. The amount allowable as a credit or refund, assuming the requesting spouse is eligible for relief, includes payments made after the filing of the Form 8857, as well as payments made within the applicable look-back period provided by section 6511(b).

(5) *Requesting spouse limited to credit or refund of payments made by the requesting spouse.*—A requesting spouse is only eligible for a credit or refund of payments to the extent the requesting spouse establishes that he or she provided the funds used to make the payment for which he or she seeks a credit or refund. Thus, a requesting spouse is not eligible for a credit or refund of payments made by the nonrequesting spouse. A requesting spouse is also generally not eligible for a credit or refund of joint payments made with the nonrequesting spouse. A requesting spouse, however, may be eligible for a credit or refund of the requesting spouse's portion of an overpayment from a joint return filed with the nonrequesting spouse that was offset under section 6402 to the spouses' joint income tax liability, to the extent that the requesting spouse can establish his or her contribution to the overpayment.

(l) [Reserved]

(m) *Penalties and interest.*—Generally, a spouse who is entitled to relief under § 1.6015-2, § 1.6015-3, or § 1.6015-4 is also entitled to relief from related penalties, additions to tax, additional amounts, and interest (collectively, penalties and interest). Penalties and interest, however, are not separate erroneous items (as defined in paragraph (h)(4) of this section) from which a requesting spouse can be relieved separate from the tax. Rather relief from penalties and interest related to an understatement or deficiency will generally be determined based on the proportion of the total erroneous items from which the requesting spouse is relieved. For penalties that relate to a particular erroneous item, see § 1.6015-3(d)(4)(iv)(B). Penalties and interest on an underpayment are also not separate items from which a requesting spouse may obtain relief under § 1.6015-4. Relief from penalties and interest on the underpayment will be determined based on the amount of relief from the underpayment to which the requesting spouse is entitled. If the underlying tax liability (whether an assessed deficiency or an underpayment) was paid in full after the joint return was filed but penalties and interest remain unpaid, the requesting spouse may be relieved from the penalties and interest if the requesting spouse is entitled to relief from the underlying tax. The fact that the requesting spouse is entitled to relief from the underlying tax but is not entitled to a refund because of § 1.6015-1(k) does not prevent the requesting spouse from being relieved from liability for the penalties and interest.

(n) *Attribution of understatement or deficiency resulting from an increase to adjusted gross income.*—(1) *In general.*—Any portion of an understatement or deficiency relating to the disallowance of an item (or increase to an amount of tax) separately listed on an individual income tax return solely due to the increase of adjusted gross income (or modified adjusted gross income or other similar phase-out thresholds) as a result of an erroneous item solely attributable to the nonrequesting spouse will also be attributable to the nonrequesting spouse unless the evidence shows that a different result is appropriate. If the increase to adjusted gross income is the result of an erroneous item(s) of both the requesting and nonrequesting spouses, the item disallowed (or increased tax) due to the increase to adjusted gross income will be attributable to the requesting spouse in the same ratio as the amount of the item or items attributable to the requesting spouse over the total amount of the items that resulted in the increase to adjusted gross income.

(2) *Examples.*—The following examples illustrate the rules of this paragraph (n):

Example 1. H and W file a joint Federal income tax return. After applying withholding credits there is a tax liability of $500. Based on the earned income reported on the return and the number of qualifying children, H and W are entitled to an Earned Income Tax Credit (EITC) in the amount of $1,500. The EITC satisfies the $500 in tax due and H and W receive a refund in the amount of $1,000. Later the IRS concludes that H had additional unreported income, which increased the tax liability on the return to $1,000 and resulted in H and W's EITC being reduced to zero due to their adjusted gross income exceeding the maximum amount. The IRS determines a deficiency in the amount of $2,000 – $1,500 of which relates to the EITC and $500 of which relates to H's erroneous item – the omitted income. If W requests relief under section 6015, the entire $2,000 deficiency is attributable to H because the EITC was disallowed solely due to the increase of adjusted gross income as a result of H's omitted income. W satisfies the attribution factor of § 1.6015-2(a)(2) and the threshold condition in section 4.01(7) of Rev. Proc. 2013-34 with respect to the entire deficiency. Under § 1.6015-3(d)(4)(ii), the portion of the deficiency related to the disallowance of the EITC is initially allocated to H.

Example 2. H and W file a joint Federal income tax return reporting a total tax liability of $22,000. Later the IRS concludes that H had additional unreported income in the amount of $20,000, which increased H and W's adjusted gross income and their alternative minimum taxable income. As a result, H and W now owe the Alternative Minimum Tax (AMT). The IRS determines a deficiency in the amount of $5,250 – $250 of which relates to H and W's AMT liability as determined under section 55 and $5,000 of which relates to the increase in H and W's section 1 income tax liability. If W requests relief under section 6015, the entire $5,250 deficiency is attributable to H because H and W owe the AMT solely due to H's erroneous item – the omitted income. W satisfies the attribution factor of § 1.6015-2(a)(2) and the threshold condition in section 4.01(7) of Rev. Proc. 2013-34 with respect to the entire deficiency. Under § 1.6015-3(d)(4)(ii), the portion of the deficiency related to the AMT is initially allocated to H.

Example 3. H and W file a joint Federal income tax return reporting itemized deductions on Schedule A, "Itemized Deductions," in the amount of $50,000. Later the IRS concludes that $10,000 of W's expenses reported on her Schedule C, "Profit or Loss From Business," were not allowable, which increased H and W's adjusted gross income. As a result, H and W's itemized expenses are reduced to $45,000 as their adjusted gross income exceeded the phase-out amount. The IRS determines a deficiency in the amount of $5,000. If H requests relief under section 6015, the entire $5,000 deficiency is attributable to W because the itemized deductions were reduced solely due to the increase of adjusted gross income as a result of W's erroneous item – the Schedule C expenses. H satisfies the attribution factor of § 1.6015-2(a)(2) and the threshold condition in section 4.01(7) of Rev. Proc. 2013-34 with respect to the entire deficiency. Under § 1.6015-3(d)(2)(iv), the portion of the deficiency related to the disallowance of the Schedule A deductions is initially allocated to W.

Example 4. H and W file a joint Federal income tax return reporting itemized deductions on Schedule A in the amount of $50,000. Later the IRS concludes that H had additional unreported income in the amount of $4,000 and W had additional unreported income in the amount of $6,000, which increased H and W's adjusted gross income. As a result, H and W's itemized expenses are reduced to $45,000 as their adjusted gross income exceeded the phase-out amount. The IRS determines a deficiency in the amount of $6,000 – $1,500 of which relates to H's erroneous item, $2,500 of which relates to W's erroneous item, and $2,000 of which relates to the reduced itemized deductions. Assuming the conditions for relief under section 6015 are otherwise satisfied, the $2,500 deficiency from W's omitted income is attributable to W and the $1,500 deficiency from H's omitted income is attributable to H. Because the increase to adjusted gross income as a result of both H and W's erroneous items reduced the itemized deductions, the portion of the deficiency related to the disallowed itemized deductions is partially attributable to both H and W. Of the $2,000 deficiency from the disallowed itemized deductions, $800 is attributable to H because 40 percent ($4,000/$10,000) of the items that resulted in the increase to adjusted gross income are attributable to H, and $1,200 is attributable to W because 60 percent ($6,000/$10,000) of the items that resulted in the increase to adjusted gross income are attributable to W. If both H and W requested relief the most H could be relieved from is $3700, the amount attributable to W ($2500 + $1200), and the most W could be relieved from is $2300, the amount attributable to H ($1500 + $800).

(o) *Abuse by the nonrequesting spouse.*—Abuse comes in many forms and can include physical, psychological, sexual, or emotional abuse, including efforts to control, isolate, humiliate, and intimidate the requesting spouse, or to undermine the requesting spouse's ability to reason independently and be able to do what is required under the tax laws. All the facts and circumstances are considered in determining whether a requesting spouse was abused. The impact of a nonrequesting spouse's alcohol or drug abuse is also considered in determining whether a requesting spouse was abused. Depending on the facts and circumstances, abuse of the requesting spouse's child or other family member living in the household may constitute abuse of the requesting spouse.

(p) *Effective/applicability date.*—This section will be applicable on the date of publication of a Treasury decision adopting these rules as final regulations in the **Federal Register**.

Par. 9. Section 1.6015-2 is amended by:
1. Paragraph (a) introductory text is revised.
2. Paragraph (b) is removed.
3. Paragraphs (c), (d), and (e) are redesignated as paragraphs (b), (c), and (d).
4. Newly designated paragraph (b) is revised.
5. The last sentence of newly designated paragraph (c) is revised.
6. Newly designated paragraph (d) is revised.
7. Paragraph (e) is added.

The revisions and addition read as follows:

§1.6015-2. Relief from liability applicable to all qualifying joint filers.—(a) *In general.*—A requesting spouse may be relieved from joint and several liability for tax (including related additions to tax, additional amounts, penalties, and interest) from an understatement for a taxable year under this section if the requesting spouse requests relief in accordance with §§1.6015-1(h)(5) and 1.6015-5, and—

* * *

(b) *Knowledge or reason to know.*—A requesting spouse has knowledge or reason to know of an understatement if he or she actually knew of the understatement, or if a reasonable person in similar circumstances would have known of the understatement. For rules relating to a requesting spouse's actual knowledge, see §1.6015-3(c)(2). All of the facts and circumstances are considered in determining whether a requesting spouse had reason to know of an understatement. The facts and circumstances that are considered include, but are not limited to, the nature of the erroneous item and the amount of the erroneous item relative to other items; any deceit or evasiveness of the nonrequesting spouse; the couple's financial situation; the requesting spouse's educational background and business experience; the extent of the requesting spouse's participation in the activity that resulted in the erroneous item; the requesting spouse's involvement in business or household financial matters; whether the requesting spouse failed to inquire, at or before the time the return was signed, about items on the return or omitted from the return that a reasonable person would question; any lavish or unusual expenditures compared with past spending levels; and whether the erroneous item represented a departure from a recurring pattern reflected in prior years' returns (for example, omitted income from an investment regularly reported on prior years' returns). A requesting spouse has knowledge or reason to know of the portion of an understatement related to an item attributable to the nonrequesting spouse under §1.6015-1(n) if the requesting spouse knows or has reason to know of the nonrequesting spouse's erroneous item or items that resulted in the increase to adjusted gross income. Depending on the facts and circumstances, if the requesting spouse was abused by the nonrequesting spouse (as described in §1.6015-1(o)), or the nonrequesting spouse maintained control of the household finances by restricting the requesting spouse's access to financial information, and because of the abuse or financial control, the requesting spouse was not able to challenge the treatment of any items on the joint return for fear of the nonrequesting spouse's retaliation, the requesting spouse will be treated as not having knowledge or reason to know of the items giving rise to the understatement. If, however, the requesting spouse involuntarily executed the return, the requesting spouse may choose to establish that the return was signed under duress. In such a case, §1.6013-4(d) applies.

(c) * * * For guidance concerning the criteria to be used in determining whether it is inequitable to hold a requesting spouse jointly and severally liable under this section, see Rev. Proc. 2013-34 (2013-2 CB 397), or other guidance published by the Treasury and IRS (see §601.601(d)(2) of this chapter).

(d) *Partial relief.*—(1) *In general.*—If a requesting spouse had no knowledge or reason to know of a portion of an erroneous item, the requesting spouse may be relieved of the liability attributable to that portion of that item, if all other requirements are met with respect to that portion.

(2) *Example.*—The following example illustrates the rules of this paragraph (d):

Example. H and W are married and file their 2014 joint income tax return in March 2015. In April 2016, H is convicted of embezzling $2 million from his employer during 2014. H kept all of his embezzlement income in an individual bank account, and he used most of the funds to support his gambling habit. H and W had a joint bank account into which H and W deposited all of their reported income. Each month during 2014, H transferred an additional $10,000 from the individual account to H and W's joint bank account. Although H paid the household expenses using this joint account, W regularly received the bank statements relating to the account. W did not know or have reason to know of H's embezzling activities. W did, however, know or have reason to know of $120,000 of the $2 million of H's embezzlement income at the time she signed the joint return because that amount passed through the couple's joint bank account and she regularly received bank statements showing the monthly deposits from H's individual account. Therefore, W may be relieved of the liability arising from $1,880,000 of the unreported embezzlement income, but she may not be relieved of the liability for the deficiency arising from $120,000 of the unreported embezzlement income of which she knew and had reason to know.

(e) *Effective/applicability date.*—This section will be applicable on the date of publication of a Treasury decision adopting these rules as final regulations in the **Federal Register**.

Par. 10. Section 1.6015-3 is amended by:

1. The paragraph heading and first sentence of paragraph (a) are revised.
2. Paragraphs (c)(1) and (c)(2)(iv) are revised.
3. A sentence is added at the end of paragraph (c)(2)(i).
4. Paragraph (c)(2)(v) is redesignated as paragraph (c)(2)(vi) and paragraph (c)(2)(v) is added.
5. Newly redesignated paragraph (c)(2)(vi) is revised.
6. Paragraphs (d)(2)(i) and (d)(5) introductory text are revised.
7. In paragraph (d)(5), *Examples 7, 8, 9, 10,* and *11* are added.
8. Paragraph (e) is added.

The revisions and additions read as follows:

§1.6015-3. Allocation of deficiency for individuals who are no longer married, are legally separated, or are not members of the same household.—(a) *Allocation of deficiency.*—A requesting spouse may allocate a deficiency (as defined in §1.6015-1(h)(8)) if, as defined in paragraph (b) of this section, the requesting spouse is divorced, widowed, or legally separated, or has not been a member of the same household as the nonrequesting spouse at any time during the 12-month period ending on the date the request for relief is filed. * * *

(c) * * * (1) *No refunds.* Although a requesting spouse may be eligible to allocate the deficiency to the nonrequesting spouse, refunds are not authorized under this section. Refunds of paid liabilities for which a requesting spouse was entitled to allocate the deficiency under this section may be considered under §1.6015-2 but not under §1.6015-4. See §1.6015-1(k)(3).

(2) * * * (i) * * * A requesting spouse has actual knowledge of the portion of an understatement related to an item attributable to the nonrequesting spouse under §1.6015-1(n) and allocable to the nonrequesting spouse under paragraph (d) of this section if the requesting spouse has actual knowledge of the nonrequesting spouse's erroneous item or items that resulted in the increase to adjusted gross income.

* * *

(iv) *Factors supporting actual knowledge.*—To demonstrate that a requesting spouse had actual knowledge of an erroneous item at the time the return was signed, the Internal Revenue Service (IRS) will consider all the facts and circumstances, including but not limited to, whether the requesting spouse made a deliberate effort to avoid learning about the item to be shielded from liability; whether the erroneous item would have been allocable to the requesting spouse but for the tax benefit rule in paragraph (d)(2)(i) of this section; and whether the requesting spouse and the nonrequesting spouse jointly owned the property that resulted in the erroneous item. These factors, together with all other facts and circumstances, may demonstrate that the requesting spouse had actual knowledge of the item. If the requesting spouse had actual knowledge of an erroneous item, the portion of the deficiency with respect to that item will not be allocated to the nonrequesting spouse.

(v) *Actual knowledge and community property.*—A requesting spouse will not be considered to have had an ownership interest in an item based solely on the operation of community property law. Rather, a requesting spouse who resided in a community property state at the time the return was signed will be considered to have had an ownership interest in an item only if the requesting spouse's name appeared on the ownership documents, or there otherwise is an indication that the requesting spouse asserted dominion and control over the item. For example, assume H and W live in State A, a community property state. After their marriage, H opens a bank account in his name. Under the operation of the community property laws of State A, W owns one-half of the bank account. Assuming there is no other indication that she asserted dominion and control over the item, W does not have an ownership interest in the account for purposes of this paragraph (c)(2)(v) because she does not hold the account in her name.

(vi) *Abuse exception.*—Depending on the facts and circumstances, if the requesting spouse was abused by the nonrequesting spouse (as described in §1.6015-1(o)), or the nonrequesting spouse maintained control of the household finances by restricting the requesting spouse's access to financial information, and because of the abuse or financial control, the requesting spouse was not able to challenge the treatment of any items on the joint return for fear of the nonrequesting spouse's retaliation, the limitation on the requesting spouse's ability to allocate the deficiency because of actual knowledge will not apply. The requesting spouse will be treated as not having knowledge of the items giving rise to the deficiency. If, however, the requesting spouse involuntarily executed the return, the requesting spouse may choose to establish that the return was signed under duress. In such a case, §1.6013-4(d) applies.

* * *

(d) * * *

(2) * * *

(i) *Benefit on the return.*—(A) *In general.*—An erroneous item that would otherwise be allocated to one spouse is allocated to the second spouse to the extent that the second spouse received a tax benefit on the joint return and the first spouse did not receive a tax benefit. An erroneous item under this paragraph can be allocated to a requesting spouse or a nonrequesting spouse, but only a spouse who requests relief under this section may allocate the deficiency. A spouse who does not request relief under section 6015 remains fully liable for the deficiency. An allocation from a requesting spouse to a nonrequesting spouse reduces the amount for which a requesting spouse remains liable while an allocation from a nonrequesting spouse to a requesting spouse increases the amount for which a requesting spouse remains liable.

(B) *Calculating separate taxable income and tax due.*—Under section 6015(d)(3)(A), the items giving rise to the deficiency must be allocated to each spouse in the same manner as the items would have been allocated if the spouses had filed separate returns. In determining whether a spouse received a tax benefit from the item, it may be necessary to calculate each spouse's hypothetical separate return taxable income, determined without regard to the erroneous items, and taking into consideration adjusted gross income, allowable deductions and losses, and allowable credits against tax.

* * *

(5) *Examples.*—The following examples illustrate the rules of this paragraph (d). In each example, assume that the requesting spouse or spouses qualify to allocate the deficiency, that a request under section 6015 was timely made, and that the deficiency remains unpaid. In addition, unless otherwise stated, assume that neither spouse actually knew of the erroneous items allocable to the other spouse. The examples are as follows:

* * *

Example 7. Calculation of tax benefit based on taxable income. (i) On their joint Federal income tax return for tax year 2009, H reports $60,000 of wage income; W reports $25,000 of wage income; and H and W report joint interest income of $2,000 and joint ordinary income from investments in the amount of $6,000. In addition, H and W properly deduct $30,000 for their two personal exemptions and itemized deductions, and W erroneously reports a loss from her separate investment in a partnership in the amount of $20,000. On May 3, 2012, a $5,000 deficiency is assessed with respect to their 2009 joint return. W dies in November 2012. H requests innocent spouse relief. The deficiency on the joint return results from a disallowance of all of W's $20,000 loss (which is initially allocable to W).

(ii) After taking all sources of income and all allowable deductions into consideration, H's separate taxable income is $49,000 and W's separate taxable income is $14,000, calculated as follows:

	H	W
Wages	$60,000	$25,000
Interest Income	$1,000	$1,000
Investment Income	$3,000	$3,000
Adj. Gross Income	$64,000	$29,000
Exemptions and Deductions	($15,000)	($15,000)
Taxable Income	$49,000	$14,000
W's Disallowed Loss		($20,000)
Tax Benefit Not Used by W		($6,000)
Tax Benefit to W		($14,000)
Tax Benefit to H	($6,000)	

(iii) As W only used $14,000 of her $20,000 loss from her separate investment in a partnership to offset her separate taxable income, H benefited from the other $6,000 of the disallowed loss used to offset his separate taxable income. Therefore, $14,000 of the disallowed $20,000 loss is allocable to W (7/10) and $6,000 of the disallowed loss is allocable to H (3/10). H's liability is limited to $1,500 (3/10 of the $5,000 deficiency).

Example 8. Nonrequesting spouse receives a benefit on the joint return from the requesting spouse's erroneous item. (i) On their joint Federal income tax return for tax year 2008, W reports $40,000 of wage income and H reports $12,000 of wage income. In addition, H and W properly deduct $20,000 for their two personal exemptions and itemized deductions, H erroneously deducts a casualty loss in the amount of $5,000 related to a loss on his separately held property, and W erroneously takes a loss in the amount of $7,000 from an investment in a tax shelter. H and W legally separate in 2010, and on October 21, 2011, a $2,400 deficiency is assessed with respect to their 2008 joint return. H requests innocent spouse relief. The deficiency on the joint return results from a disallowance of all of H's $5,000 loss and all of W's $7,000 loss (which is allocable to W and for which H did not have actual knowledge).

(ii) The $5,000 casualty loss is initially allocated to H. As H's separate taxable income is only $2,000 ($12,000 wage income less $10,000 - 50 percent of the exemptions and itemized deductions), H only used $2,000 of his $5,000 casualty loss to offset his separate taxable income, and W benefited from the other $3,000 of the disallowed loss, which offset a portion of her separate taxable income. Therefore, $3,000 of the disallowed loss is allocable to W even though the loss is H's item, and $2,000 of the loss is allocable to H. The $7,000 tax shelter loss is also allocable to W as H did not have knowledge of the facts that made the tax shelter item unallowable as a loss. H's allocation percentage is 1/6 ($2,000/$12,000) and H's liability is limited to $400 (1/6 of $2,400 deficiency). The IRS may collect up to $400 from H and up to $2,400 from W (although the total amount collected may not exceed $2,400).

(iii) If the IRS could establish that H had knowledge of the facts that made the deduction for his casualty loss unallowable, the entire $5,000 casualty loss would be allocable to H. H's allocation percentage would be 5/12 ($5,000/$12,000) and H's liability would be limited to $1,000 (5/12 of $2,400 deficiency).

(iv) If W also requested innocent spouse relief (and H did not have knowledge of the facts that made his loss unallowable), there would be no remaining joint and several liability, and the IRS would be permitted to collect $400 from H (1/6 ($2,000/$12,000) of the $2,400 deficiency) and $2,000 (5/6 ($10,000/$12,000) of $2,400 deficiency) from W. If the IRS could establish that W had knowledge of the facts that made the deduction for the casualty loss unallowable, W would then be liable for the entire $2,400 deficiency, while H would remain liable for up to $400.

Example 9. Allocation of liability based on joint erroneous loss item. (i) On their joint Federal income tax return for tax year 2009, H reports $100,000 of wage income and W reports $50,000 of wage income. In addition, H and W properly deduct $40,000 for their two personal exemptions and itemized deductions, and erroneously report a loss in the amount of $50,000 from a jointly-held investment in a tax shelter. H and W divorce in 2011, and on August 14, 2012, a $12,000 deficiency is assessed with respect to their 2009 joint return. W requests innocent spouse relief. The deficiency on the joint return results from a disallowance of all of the $50,000 loss.

(ii) Under paragraph (d)(2)(iv) of this section, in the absence of clear and convincing evidence supporting a different allocation, an erroneous deduction item related to a jointly-owned investment is generally allocated 50 percent to each spouse. Thus, $25,000 of the loss is allocated to each spouse. In determining the effect, if any, of the tax benefit rule of § 1.6015-1(d)(2)(i), H's separate taxable income is $80,000: $100,000 wage income minus $20,000, or 50 percent of the exemptions and itemized deductions; and W's separate taxable income is $30,000: $50,000 minus $20,000. As both H's and W's separate taxable income exceeds their allocated share of the disallowed loss, no additional amount is allocated between the spouses. W's allocation percentage is 1/2 ($25,000/$50,000) and W's liability is limited to $6,000 (1/2 of $12,000 deficiency). The IRS may collect up to $6,000 from W and up to $12,000 from H (although the total amount collected may not exceed $12,000).

(iii) If the IRS could establish that W had knowledge of the facts that made the loss unallowable, both H and W would then remain jointly and severally liable for the $12,000 deficiency.

Example 10. Calculation of tax benefit based on joint erroneous item. Assume the same facts as in *Example 9* of this paragraph (d)(5), except that W's wage income is only $40,000. W's separate taxable income would then be only $20,000 ($40,000 wage income minus $20,000 - 50 percent of the exemptions and itemized deductions). W would only be able to use $20,000 of the $25,000 loss from the tax shelter to offset her separate taxable income. Accordingly, H benefited from the other $5,000 of the disallowed loss, which was used to offset a portion of his separate taxable income. Therefore, $20,000 of the disallowed loss is allocable to W, and $30,000 is allocable to H: $25,000 (H's 50 percent of the disallowed loss) plus $5,000 (the portion of W's 50 percent that is allocable to H because H received a tax benefit). W's allocation percentage is 2/5 ($20,000/$50,000) and W's liability is limited to $4,800 (2/5 of $12,000 deficiency). The IRS may collect up to $4,800 from W and up to $12,000 from H (although the total amount collected may not exceed $12,000).

Example 11. Allocation of erroneous item based on fraud of the nonrequesting spouse. During 2009, W fraudulently accesses H's brokerage account to sell stock that H had separately received from an inheritance. W deposits the funds from the sale in a separate bank account to which H did not have access. H and W file a joint Federal income tax return for tax year 2009. The return did not include the income from the sale of the stock. H and W divorce in November 2010. The divorce decree states that W committed forgery and defrauded H with respect to his brokerage account. The IRS commences an audit in March 2011 and determines a deficiency based on the omission of the income from the sale of the stock. H requests innocent spouse relief. Under paragraph (d)(2)(iii) of this section, items of investment income are generally allocated to the spouse who owned the investment, which in this case would be H. Under paragraph (d)(2)(ii) of this section, however, the IRS may allocate any item between the spouses if the IRS determines that the allocation is appropriate due to fraud by one or both spouses. The IRS determines that W committed fraud with respect to H and as a result it is appropriate to allocate the deficiency to W under paragraph (d)(2)(ii).

(e) *Effective/applicability date.*—This section will be applicable on the date of publication of a Treasury decision adopting these rules as final regulations in the **Federal Register.**

Par. 17. For each entry for Section 1.6015-3 in the "Section" column remove the language in the "Remove" column and add the language in the "Add" column in its place.

Section	Remove	Add
1.6015-3(c)(4) *Example 4* (ii), (iii), (iv), and (v), first sentence	*Example 5*	*Example 4*
1.6015-3(c)(4) *Example 5* (ii), (iii), and (iv), first sentence	*Example 6*	*Example 5*

Par. 11. Section 1.6015-4 is revised to read as follows:

§ 1.6015-4. Equitable relief.—(a) A requesting spouse who files a joint return for which an understatement or deficiency (as defined by § 1.6015-1(h)(7) and (8)) was determined or for which there was unpaid tax (as defined by § 1.6015-1(h)(6)), and who does not qualify for full relief under § 1.6015-2 or § 1.6015-3, may be entitled to equitable relief under this section. The Internal Revenue Service (IRS) has the discretion to grant equitable relief from joint and several liability to a requesting spouse when, considering all of the facts and circumstances, it would be inequitable to hold the requesting spouse jointly and severally liable.

(b) This section may not be used to circumvent the limitation of § 1.6015-3(c)(1). Therefore, relief is not available under this section to obtain a refund of liabilities already paid, for which the requesting spouse would otherwise qualify for relief under § 1.6015-3. See § 1.6015-1(k)(3). If the requesting spouse is only eligible for partial relief under § 1.6015-3 (i.e., some portion of the deficiency is allocable to the requesting spouse), then the requesting spouse may be considered for relief under this section with respect to the portion of the deficiency for which the requesting spouse was not entitled to relief.

(c) For guidance concerning the criteria to be used in determining whether it is inequitable to hold a requesting spouse jointly and severally liable under this section, see Rev. Proc. 2013-34 (2013-1 IRB 397), or other guidance published by the Treasury and IRS (see § 601.601(d)(2) of this chapter).

(d) *Effective/applicability date.*—This section will be applicable on the date of publication of a Treasury decision adopting these rules as final regulations in the **Federal Register**.

Par. 12. Section 1.6015-5 is amended by adding paragraph (d) to read as follows:

§ 1.6015-5. Time and manner for requesting relief.

* * *

(d) *Effective/applicability date.*—This section will be applicable on the date of publication of a Treasury decision adopting these rules as final regulations in the **Federal Register**.

Par. 13. Section 1.6015-6 is amended by revising the first sentence of paragraph (a)(1), adding a sentence at the end of paragraph (a)(2), and adding paragraph (d) to read as follows:

§ 1.6015-6. Nonrequesting spouse's notice and opportunity to participate in administrative proceedings.—(a) * * * (1) When the Internal Revenue Service (IRS) receives a request for relief under § 1.6015-2, § 1.6015-3, or § 1.6015-4, the IRS must send a notice to the nonrequesting spouse's last known address that informs the nonrequesting spouse of the requesting spouse's request for relief. * * *

(2) * * * For guidance concerning the nonrequesting spouse's right to appeal the preliminary determination to IRS Appeals, see Rev. Proc. 2003-19 (2003-1 CB 371), or other guidance published by the Treasury Department and the IRS (see § 601.601(d)(2) of this chapter).

* * *

(d) *Effective/applicability date.*—This section will be applicable on the date of publication of a Treasury decision adopting these rules as final regulations in the **Federal Register**.

Par. 14. In § 1.6015-7, paragraphs (b), (c)(1), (c)(3), and (c)(4)(iii) are revised and paragraph (d) is added to read as follows:

§ 1.6015-7. Tax Court review.

* * *

(b) *Time period for petitioning the Tax Court.*—Pursuant to section 6015(e), the requesting spouse may petition the Tax Court to review the denial of relief under § 1.6015-1 within 90 days after the date the Internal Revenue Service's (IRS) final determination is mailed by certified or registered mail (the 90-day period). If the IRS does not mail the requesting spouse a final determination letter within 6 months of the date the requesting spouse files a request for relief under section 6015, the requesting spouse may petition the Tax Court to review the request at any time after the expiration of the 6-month period and before the expiration of the 90-day period. The Tax Court also may review a request for relief if the Tax Court has jurisdiction under another section of the Internal Revenue Code, such as section 6213(a) or section 6330(d). This paragraph (b) applies to liabilities arising on or after December 20, 2006, or arising prior to December 20, 2006, and remaining unpaid as of that date. For liabilities arising prior to December 20, 2006, which were fully paid prior to that date, the requesting spouse may petition the Tax Court to review the denial of relief as discussed above, but only with respect to denials of relief involving understatements under § 1.6015-2, § 1.6015-3, or § 1.6015-4.

(c) *Restrictions on collection and suspension of the running of the period of limitations.*—(1) *Restrictions on collection.*—(i) *Restrictions on collection for requests for relief made on or after December 20, 2006.*—Unless the IRS determines that collection will be jeopardized by delay, no levy or proceeding in court shall be made, begun, or prosecuted against a spouse requesting relief under § 1.6015-2, § 1.6015-3, or § 1.6015-4 (except for certain requests for relief made solely under § 1.6015-4) for the collection of any assessment to which the request relates until the expiration of the 90-day period described in paragraph (b) of this section, or, if a petition is filed with the Tax Court, until the decision of the Tax Court becomes final under section 7481. For requests for relief made solely under § 1.6015-4, the restrictions on collection only apply if the liability arose on or after December 20, 2006, or arose prior to December 20, 2006, and remained unpaid as of that date. The restrictions on collection begin on the date the request is filed.

(ii) *Restriction on collection for requests for relief made before December 20, 2006.*—Unless the IRS determines that collection will be jeopardized by delay, no levy or proceeding in court shall be made, begun, or prosecuted against a requesting spouse requesting relief under § 1.6015-2 or § 1.6015-3 for the collection of any assessment to which the request relates until the expiration of the 90-day period described in paragraph (b) of this section, or if a petition is filed with the Tax Court, until the decision of the Tax Court becomes final under section 7481. The restrictions on collection begin on the date the request is filed with the IRS. For requests for relief made solely under § 1.6015-4, the restrictions on collection do not begin until December 20, 2006, and only apply with respect to liabilities remaining unpaid on or after that date.

(iii) *Rules for determining the period of the restrictions on collection.*—For more information regarding the date on which a decision of the Tax Court becomes final, see section 7481 and the regulations thereunder. Notwithstanding paragraphs (c)(1)(i) and (ii) of this section, if the requesting spouse appeals the Tax Court's decision, the IRS may resume collection of the liability from the requesting spouse on the date the requesting spouse files the notice of appeal, unless the requesting spouse files an appeal bond pursuant to the rules of section 7485. Jeopardy under paragraphs (c)(1)(i) and (ii) of this section means conditions exist that would require an assessment under section 6851 or 6861 and the regulations thereunder.

* * *

(3) *Suspension of the running of the period of limitations.*—The running of the period of limitations in section 6502 on collection against the requesting spouse of the assessment to which the request under § 1.6015-2, § 1.6015-3, or § 1.6015-4 relates is suspended for the period during which the IRS is prohibited by paragraph (c)(1) of this section from collecting by levy or a proceeding in court and for 60 days thereafter. If the requesting spouse, however, signs a waiver of the restrictions on collection in accordance with paragraph (c)(2) of this section, the suspension of the period of limitations in section 6502 on collection against the requesting spouse will terminate on the date that is 60 days after the date the waiver is filed with the IRS.

(4) * * *

(iii) *Assessment to which the request relates.*—For purposes of this paragraph (c), the assessment to which the request relates is the entire assessment of the understatement or the balance due shown on the return to which the request relates, even if the request for relief is made with respect to only part of that understatement or balance due.

(d) *Effective/applicability date.*—This section will be applicable on the date of publication of a Treasury decision adopting these rules as final regulations in the **Federal Register**.

Par. 15. Section 1.6015-8 is amended by adding paragraph (d) to read as follows:

§ 1.6015-8. Applicable liabilities.

* * *

(d) *Effective/applicability date.*—This section will be applicable on the date of publication of a Treasury decision adopting these rules as final regulations in the **Federal Register**.

Par. 17. For each entry for Section 1.6015-8 in the "Section" column remove the language in the "Remove" column and add the language in the "Add" column in its place.

Section	Remove	Add
1.6015-8(c) *Example 1*, fifth sentence	6015(b)	6015

Par. 16. Section 1.6015-9 is removed.

§ 1.6015-9. Effective/applicability date.

Return and Extended Due Date: Changes

Return Due Extended Due Date: Changes.—Amendments to Reg. § 1.6031(a)-1, updating the due dates and extensions of time to file certain tax returns and information returns, are proposed (published in the Federal Register on July 20, 2017) (REG-128483-15).

Par. 4. Revise paragraphs (e)(2) and (f) of § 1.6031(a)-1 to read as follows:

§ 1.6031(a)-1. Return of partnership income.

* * *

(e) * * *

(2) [The text of proposed § 1.6031(a)-1(e)(2) is the same as the text of § 1.6031(a)-1T(e)(2) as added by T.D. 9821].

* * *

(f) *Applicability date.*—The requirements of paragraph (e)(2) of this section are applicable for returns filed on or after the date a Treasury Decision incorporating these amendments as final regulations is published in the **Federal Register**.

Returns: Partnerships: Partnership Information

Returns: Partnerships: Partnership Information.—Temporary Reg. §§ 1.6031(b)-1T and 1.6031(c)-1T, relating to partnership statements and nominee reporting of partnership information, are also proposed as final regulations and, when adopted, would become Reg. §§ 1.6031(b)-1 and 1.6031(c)-1, respectively (published in the Federal Register on September 7, 1988).

§ 1.6031(b)-1. Statements to partners.

§ 1.6031(c)-1. Nominee reporting of partnership infomation.

Return and Extended Due Date: Changes

Return Due Extended Due Date: Changes.—Amendments to Reg. § 1.6032-1, updating the due dates and extensions of time to file certain tax returns and information returns, are proposed (published in the Federal Register on July 20, 2017) (REG-128483-15).

Par. 5. Revise § 1.6032-1 to read as follows:

§ 1.6032-1. Returns of banks with respect to common trust funds.—(a) [The text of proposed § 1.6032-1(a) is the same as the text of § 1.6032-1T(a) as added by T.D. 9821].

(b) The requirements of paragraph (a) of this section are applicable for returns filed on or after the date a Treasury Decision incorporating these amendments as final regulations is published in the **Federal Register**.

Expenditures Incurred in Attempts to Influence Legislation

Business Expenses: Private Foundations, Excise Taxes: Expenditures Incurred in Attempts to Influence Legislation.—Reproduced below is the text of a proposed amendment to Reg. § 1.6033-2, relating to the treatment, for federal income tax purposes, of expenditures incurred in attempts to influence legislation (published in the Federal Register on November 25, 1980).

* * *

☐ Par. 3. Section 1.6033-2 is amended by revising paragraph (k), by redesignating revised paragraph (k) as paragraph (l), and by adding a new paragraph (k). These revised, redesignated, and added provisions read as follows:

§ 1.6033-2. Returns by exempt organizations; taxable years beginning after December 31, 1969.

* * *

(k) *Statements about certain expenditures.*—For years after 1980, every organization which is described in section 501(c)(5) or (6) and any other organization exempt under section 501(a) whose members or contributors may deduct dues or contributions as business expenses under section 162 shall furnish to its members and contributors a statement showing what percentage of its total expenditures during the calendar year were lobbying or political expenditures of a type for which § 1.162-20 denies deductions to taxpayers. The statement required by the preceding sentence shall be furnished on or before January 31 of the following calendar year. This paragraph shall not apply to an organization for any year during which the organization makes no lobbying or political expenditures of a type for which § 1.162-20 denies deductions to taxpayers. Furthermore, an organization is not required under this paragraph to furnish any statement to a member or contributor for any year if the portion of that person's payments to the organization for that year which is allocable to the type of expenditures for which § 1.162-20 denies deductions is

(1) Less than $25, or

(2) Less than $50 and less than 5 percent of the total payments made by that person to the organization for the year.

(l) *Effective date.*—The provisions of this section, other than paragraph (k), shall apply with respect to returns filed for taxable years beginning after December 31, 1969.

Return and Extended Due Date: Changes

Return Due Extended Due Date: Changes.—Amendments to Reg. § 1.6033-2, updating the due dates and extensions of time to file certain tax returns and information returns, are proposed (published in the Federal Register on July 20, 2017) (REG-128483-15).

Par. 6. Revise paragraphs (e) and (k) of § 1.6033-2 to read as follows:

§ 1.6033-2. Returns by exempt organizations (taxable years beginning after December 31, 1969) and returns by certain nonexempt organizations (taxable years beginning after December 31, 1980).

* * *

(e) [The text of proposed § 1.6033-2(e) is the same as the text of § 1.6033-2T(e) as added by T.D. 9821].

* * *

(k) *Applicability date.*—The requirements of paragraph (e) of this section are applicable for returns filed on or after the date a Treasury Decision incorporating these amendments as final regulations is published in the **Federal Register**.

Estate and Person Acquiring Property from Decedent: Consistent Basis Reporting

Estate and Person Acquiring Property from Decedent: Consistent Basis Reporting.—Amendments to Reg. § 1.6035-1, providing guidance regarding the requirement that a recipient's basis in certain property acquired from a decedent be consistent with the value of the property as finally determined for Federal estate tax purposes, are proposed (published in the Federal Register on March 4, 2016) (REG-127923-15). Proposed Reg. § 1.6035-2 has been adopted by T.D. 9797 on December 1, 2016. Proposed Reg. § 1.6035-3 was removed by T.D. 9849 on March 11, 2019.

Par. 3. Section 1.6035-1 is revised to read as follows:

§ 1.6035-1. Basis information to persons acquiring property from decedent.—(a) *Required Information Return and Statement(s).*—(1) *In general.*—An executor (defined in paragraph (g)(1) of this section) required to file a return under section 6018 for an estate must file an Information Return (defined in paragraph (g)(2) of this section) with the Internal Revenue Service (IRS) to report the value of certain property (described in paragraph (b)(1) of this section) included in the decedent's gross estate for purposes of the tax imposed by chapter 11 of subtitle B of the Internal Revenue Code (chapter 11) and other information prescribed by the Information Return and the instructions thereto. The value to be reported is the final value of the property as described in § 1.1014-10(c). This executor also must furnish a Statement (defined in paragraph (g)(3) of this section) to each beneficiary who has (or will) acquire, whether from the decedent or by reason of the death of the decedent, property reported on the Information Return to identify the property the beneficiary is to receive and to report the value of that property and other information prescribed by the Statement and instructions thereto. The Information Return and each Statement are required to be filed and furnished by the date provided in paragraph (d) of this section. If, after the Information Return and Statement are filed and furnished, there are certain changes in the final value and/or the recipient of property as described in paragraph (e) or (f) of this section, the executor must file a supplemental Information Return with the IRS and furnish a supplemental Statement to the beneficiary. Subsequent transfers of all or a portion of property previously reported (or required to be reported) on the Information Return required by paragraph (a) of this section, in transactions in which the transferee acquires the property with the transferor's basis, require additional reporting as described in paragraph (f) of this section.

(2) *Exception*.—Paragraph (a)(1) of this section applies only to the executor of an estate required by section 6018 to file an estate tax return. Accordingly, notwithstanding §20.2010-2(a)(1), the executor does not have to file or furnish the Information Return or Statement(s) referred to in paragraph (a)(1) of this section if the executor is not required by section 6018 to file an estate tax return for the estate, even if the executor does file such a return for other purposes, e.g., to make a generation-skipping transfer tax exemption allocation or election, to make the portability election under section 2010(c)(5), or to make a protective filing to avoid any penalty if an asset value is later determined to cause a return to be required or otherwise.

(b) *Property for which reporting is required*.—(1) *In general*.—The property to which the reporting requirement under paragraph (a)(1) of this section applies is all property reported or required to be reported on a return under section 6018. This includes, for example, any other property whose basis is determined in whole or in part by reference to that property (for example as the result of a like-kind exchange or involuntary conversion). Of the property of a deceased nonresident non-citizen, this includes only the property that is subject to U.S. estate tax; similarly, this includes only the decedent's one-half of community property. Nevertheless, the following property is excepted from the reporting requirements—

(i) Cash (other than a coin collection or other coins or bills with numismatic value);

(ii) Income in respect of a decedent (as defined in section 691);

(iii) Tangible personal property for which an appraisal is not required under §20.2031-6(b); and

(iv) Property sold, exchanged, or otherwise disposed of (and therefore not distributed to a beneficiary) by the estate in a transaction in which capital gain or loss is recognized.

(2) *Examples*.—The following examples illustrate the provisions of paragraph (b)(1) of this section.

Example 1. Included in D's gross estate are the contents of his residence. Pursuant to §20.2031-6(a), the executor attaches to the return required by section 6018 filed for D's estate a room by room itemization of household and personal effects. All articles are named specifically. In each room a number of articles, none of which has a value in excess of $100, are grouped. A value is provided for each named article. Included in the household and personal effects are a painting, a rug, and a clock, each of which has a value in excess of $3,000. Pursuant to §20.2031-6(b), the executor obtains an appraisal from a disinterested, competent appraiser(s) of recognized standing and ability, or a disinterested dealer(s) in the class of personalty involved for the painting, rug, and clock. The executor attaches these appraisals to the estate tax return for D's estate. Pursuant to paragraph (b)(1)(iii) of this section, the reporting requirements of paragraph (a)(1) of this section apply only to the painting, rug, and clock.

Example 2. Included in D's estate are shares in C, a publicly traded company. Shortly after D's death but prior to the filing of the estate tax return for D's estate, C is acquired by T, also a publicly traded company. For the shares in C includible in D's estate, the estate receives new shares in T and cash in a fully taxable transaction. Pursuant to paragraph (b)(1)(iv) of this section, the reporting requirements of paragraph (a)(1) of this section do not apply to the new shares in T or the cash.

(c) *Beneficiaries*.—(1) *In general*.—As provided in paragraph (a)(1) of this section, the executor must furnish to each beneficiary (including a beneficiary who is also an executor) receiving property that must be reported on the Information Return filed with the IRS, the Statement containing the required information regarding that beneficiary's property. For purposes of this provision, the beneficiary of a life estate is the life tenant, the beneficiary of a remainder interest is the remainderman(men) identified as if the life tenant were to die immediately after the decedent, and the beneficiary of a contingent interest is a beneficiary, unless the contingency has occurred prior to the filing of the Form 8971. If the contingency subsequently negates the inheritance of the beneficiary, the executor must do supplemental reporting in accordance with paragraph (e) of this section to report the change of beneficiary.

(2) *Beneficiary not an individual*.—If the beneficiary is a trust or another estate, the executor must furnish the beneficiary's Statement to the trustee or executor of the trust or estate, rather than to the beneficiaries of that trust or estate. If the beneficiary is a business entity, the executor must furnish the Statement to the entity. However, see paragraph (f) of this section for additional reporting requirements in the event the trust, estate, or entity transfers all or a portion of the property in a transaction in which the transferee acquires the basis of the trust, estate, or entity.

(3) *Beneficiary not determined*.—If, by the due date provided in paragraph (d) of this section, the executor has not determined what property will be used to satisfy the interest of each beneficiary, the executor must report on the Statement for each such beneficiary all of the property that the executor could use to satisfy that beneficiary's interest. Once the exact distribution has been determined, the executor may, but is not required to, file and furnish a supplemental Information Return and Statement as provided in paragraph (e)(3) of this section.

(4) *Beneficiary not located.*—An executor must use reasonable due diligence to identify and locate all beneficiaries. If the executor is unable to locate a beneficiary by the due date of the Information Return provided in paragraph (d) of this section, the executor must so report on that Information Return and explain the efforts the executor has taken to locate the beneficiary and to satisfy the obligation of reasonable due diligence. If the executor subsequently locates the beneficiary, the executor must furnish the beneficiary with that beneficiary's Statement and file a supplemental Information Return with the IRS within 30 days of locating the beneficiary. A copy of the beneficiary's Statement must be attached to the supplemental Information Return. If the executor is unable to locate a beneficiary and distributes the property to a different beneficiary who was not identified in the Information Return as the recipient of that property, the executor must file a supplemental Information Return with the IRS and furnish the substitute beneficiary with that beneficiary's Statement within 30 days after the property is distributed. See paragraph (e)(1) of this section. A copy of the substitute beneficiary's Statement must be attached to the supplemental Information Return.

(d) *Due dates.*—(1) *In general.*—Except as provided in § 1.6035-2T, the executor must file the Information Return with the IRS, and must furnish to each beneficiary the Statement with regard to the property to be received by that beneficiary, on or before the earlier of—

(i) The date that is 30 days after the due date of the estate tax return required by section 6018 (including extensions, if any), or

(ii) The date that is 30 days after the date on which that return is filed with the IRS.

(2) *Transition rule.*—If the due date of an estate tax return required to be filed by section 6018 is on or before July 31, 2015, but the executor does not file the return with the IRS until after July 31, 2015, then the Information Return and Statement(s) are due on or before the date that is 30 days after the date on which the estate tax return is filed, except as provided in § 1.6035-2T.

(e) *Duty to supplement.*—(1) *In general.*—In the event of any adjustment to the information required to be reported on the Information Return or any Statement as described in paragraph (e)(2) of this section, the executor must file a supplemental Information Return with the IRS including all supplemental Statements and furnish a corresponding supplemental Statement to each affected beneficiary by the due date described in paragraph (e)(4) of this section.

(2) *Adjustments requiring supplement.*—Except as provided in paragraph (e)(3) of this section, an adjustment to which the duty to supplement applies is any change to the information required to be reported on the Information Return or Statement that causes the information as reported to be incorrect or incomplete. Such changes include, for example, the discovery of property that should have been (but was not) reported on an estate tax return described in section 6018, a change in the value of property pursuant to an examination or litigation, or a change in the identity of the beneficiary to whom the property is to be distributed (pursuant to a death, disclaimer, bankruptcy, or otherwise). Such changes also include the executor's disposition of property acquired from the decedent or as a result of the death of the decedent in a transaction in which the basis of new property received by the estate is determined in whole or in part by reference to the property acquired from the decedent or as a result of the death of the decedent (for example as the result of a like-kind exchange or involuntary conversion). Changes requiring supplement pursuant to this paragraph (e)(2) are not inconsequential errors or omissions within the meaning of § 301.6722-1(b) of this chapter.

(3) *Adjustments not requiring supplement.*—(i) *In general.*—A supplemental Information Return and Statement may but they are not required to be filed or furnished-

(A) To correct an inconsequential error or omission within the meaning of § 301.6722-1(b) of this chapter, or

(B) To specify the actual distribution of property previously reported as being available to satisfy the interests of multiple beneficiaries in the situation described in paragraph (c)(3) of this section.

(ii) *Example.*—Paragraph (e)(3)(i)(B) of this section is illustrated by the following example.

Example 1. D's Will provided for D's residuary estate to be distributed to D's three children (E, F, and G). D's residuary estate included stock in a publicly traded company (X), a personal residence, and three paintings. On the due date of the Information Return and Statement required by paragraph (a)(1) of this section, D's executor had not yet determined which property each child would receive from D's residuary estate in satisfaction of that child's bequest. In accordance with paragraph (c)(3) of this section, D's executor reported on the Information Return filed with the IRS and on each child's own Statement that E, F, and G each might receive an interest in the stock in X, the personal residence, and the three paintings. Several months later, the executor determined that E would receive the stock in X, F would receive the residence, and G would receive the paintings. Paragraph (e)(3)(i)(B) of this section provides that the executor may but is not required to file a supplemental Information Return with the IRS and furnish supplemental Statements to E, F, and G to accurately report which beneficiary received what property.

Example 2. D's Will provided that D's jewelry and household effects (personalty) are to be distributed among D's three children (E, F, and G) as determined by E, F, and G. In accordance with paragraph (c)(3) of this section, D's executor reports on the Information Return filed with the IRS and on each child's own Statement each item of personalty other than items described in paragraph (b)(1)(iii) of this section. Several months later, E, F, and G determine who is to receive each item of personalty. Paragraph (e)(3)(i)(B) of this section provides that the executor may but is not required to file a supplemental Information Return with the IRS and furnish supplemental Statements to E, F, and G to accurately report which beneficiary received which item(s) of personalty.

(4) *Due date of supplemental reporting.*—(i) *In general.*—Except as provided in paragraph (e)(4)(ii) of this section, the supplemental Information Return must be filed and each supple-

mental Statement must be furnished on or before 30 days after—

(A) The final value within the meaning of § 1.1014-10(c)(1) is determined;

(B) The executor discovers that the information reported on the Information Return or Statement is otherwise incorrect or incomplete, except to the extent described in paragraph (e)(3)(i) of this section; or

(C) A supplemental estate tax return under section 6018 is filed reporting property not reported on a previously filed estate tax return pursuant to § 1.1014-10(c)(3)(i). In this case, a copy of the supplemental Statement provided to each beneficiary of an interest in this property must be attached to the supplemental Information Return.

(ii) *Probate property or property from decedent's revocable trust.*—With respect to property in the probate estate or held by a revocable trust at the decedent's death, if an event described in paragraph (e)(4)(i)(A), (B), or (C) of this section occurs after the decedent's date of death but before or on the date the property is distributed to the beneficiary, the due date for the supplemental Information Return and corresponding supplemental Statement is the date that is 30 days after the date the property is distributed to the beneficiary. If the executor chooses to furnish to the beneficiary on the Statement information regarding any changes to the basis of the reported property as described in § 1.1014-10(a)(2) that occurred after the date of death but before or on the date of distribution, that basis adjustment information (which is not part of the requirement under section 6035) must be shown separately from the final value required to be reported on that Statement.

(f) *Subsequent transfers.*—If all or any portion of property that previously was reported or is required to be reported on an Information Return (and thus on the recipient's Statement or supplemental Statement) is distributed or transferred (by gift or otherwise) by the recipient in a transaction in which a related transferee determines its basis, in whole or in part, by reference to the recipient/transferor's basis, the recipient/transferor must, no later than 30 days after the date of the distribution or other transfer, file with the IRS a supplemental Statement and furnish a copy of the same supplemental Statement to the transferee. The requirement to file a supplemental Statement and furnish a copy to the transferee similarly applies to the distribution or transfer of any other property the basis of which is determined in whole or in part by reference to that property (for example as the result of a like-kind exchange or involuntary conversion). In the case of a supplemental Statement filed by the recipient/transferor before the recipient/transferor's receipt of the Statement described in paragraph (a) of this section, the supplemental Statement will report the change in the ownership of the property and need not provide the value information that would otherwise be required on the supplemental Statement. In the event the transfer occurs before the final value is determined within the meaning of proposed § 1.1014-10(c), the transferor must provide the executor with a copy of the supplemental Statement filed with the IRS and furnished to the transferee in order to notify the executor of the change in ownership of the property. When the executor subsequently files any Return and issues any Statement required by paragraphs (a) or (e) of this section, the executor must provide the Statement (or supplemental Statement) to the new transferee instead of to the transferor. For purposes of this provision, a related transferee means any member of the transferor's family as defined in section 2704(c)(2), any controlled entity (a corporation or any other entity in which the transferor and members of the transferor's family (as defined in section 2704(c)(2)), whether directly or indirectly, have control within the meaning of section 2701(b)(2)(A) or (B)), and any trust of which the transferor is a deemed owner for income tax purposes. If the transferor chooses to include on the supplemental Statement provided to the transferee information regarding any changes to the basis of the reported property as described in § 1.1014-10(a)(2) that occurred during the transferor's ownership of the property, that basis adjustment information (which is not part of the requirement under section 6035) must be shown separately from the final value required to be reported on that Statement.

(g) *Definitions.*—For purposes of this section, the following terms are defined as follows—

(1) *Executor* has the same meaning as in section 2203 and includes any other person required under section 6018(b) to file a return.

(2) *Information Return* means the Form 8971, including each beneficiary's Statement as defined in paragraph (g)(3) of this section required to be furnished, or any successor form issued by the IRS for this purpose.

(3) *Statement* means the payee statement described as Schedule A of the Information Return furnished to a beneficiary or any successor form or schedule issued by the IRS for this purpose.

(h) *Penalties.*—(1) *Failure to timely file complete and correct Information Return.*—For provisions relating to the penalty provided for failure to file an Information Return required by section 6035(a)(1) on or before the required filing date, failure to include all of the required information on an Information Return, or the filing of an Information Return that includes incorrect information, see section 6721 and the regulations thereunder. See section 6724 and the regulations thereunder for rules relating to waivers of penalties for certain failures due to reasonable cause.

(2) *Failure to timely furnish correct Statements.*—For provisions relating to the penalty provided for failure to furnish a Statement required by section 6035(a)(2) on or before the prescribed date, failure to include all of the required information on a Statement, or the filing of a Statement that includes incorrect information, see section 6722 and the regulations thereunder. See section 6724 and the regulations thereunder for rules relating to waivers of penalties for certain failures due to reasonable cause.

(i) *Effective/applicability date.*—Upon the publication of the Treasury Decision adopting these rules as final in the **Federal Register**, this section will apply to property acquired from a decedent or by reason of the death of a decedent whose return required by section 6018 is filed after July 31, 2015. Persons may rely upon these rules before the date of publication of the Treasury Decision adopting these rules as final in the **Federal Register**.

Global Intangible Low-Taxed Income: Guidance

Global Intangible Low-Taxed Income: Guidance.—Amendments to Reg. §1.6038-2 implementing section 951A of the Internal Revenue Code, which was enacted on December 22, 2017, are proposed (published in the Federal Register on October 10, 2018) (REG-104390-18).

Par. 15. Section 1.6038-2 is amended by:

1. Revising the section heading.
2. Revising the first sentence in paragraph (a).
3. Revising paragraph (m).

The revisions read as follows:

§1.6038-2. Information returns required of United States persons with respect to annual accounting periods of certain foreign corporations.—(a) *Requirement of return.*—Every U.S. person shall make a separate annual information return with respect to each annual accounting period (described in paragraph (e) of this section) of each foreign corporation which that person controls (as defined in paragraph (b) of this section) at any time during such annual accounting period. * * *

* * *

(m) *Applicability dates.*—This section applies to taxable years of foreign corporations beginning on or after October 3, 2018. See 26 CFR 1.6038-2 (revised as of April 1, 2018) for rules applicable to taxable years of foreign corporations beginning before such date.

Hybrid Arrangements: Rules

Hybrid Arrangements: Rules.—Amendments to Reg. §§1.6038-2 and 1.6038-3, implementing sections 245A(e) and 267A of the Internal Revenue Code regarding hybrid dividends and certain amounts paid or accrued in hybrid transactions or with hybrid entities, are proposed (published in the Federal Register on December 28, 2018) (REG-104352-18).

Par. 9. Section 1.6038-2 is amended by adding paragraphs (f)(13) and (14) and adding a sentence at the end of paragraph (m) to read as follows:

§1.6038-2. Information returns required of United States persons with respect to annual accounting periods of certain foreign corporations beginning after December 31, 1962.

* * *

(f) * * *

(13) *Amounts involving hybrid transactions or hybrid entities under section 267A.*—If for the annual accounting period, the corporation pays or accrues interest or royalties for which a deduction is disallowed under section 267A and the regulations under section 267A as contained in 26 CFR part 1, then Form 5471 (or successor form) must contain such information about the disallowance in the form and manner and to the extent prescribed by the form, instruction, publication, or other guidance published in the Internal Revenue Bulletin.

(14) *Hybrid dividends under section 245A.*—If for the annual accounting period, the corporation pays or receives a hybrid dividend or a tiered hybrid dividend under section 245A and the regulations under section 245A as contained in 26 CFR part 1, then Form 5471 (or successor form) must contain such information about the hybrid dividend or tiered hybrid dividend in the form and manner and to the extent prescribed by the form, instruction, publication, or other guidance published in the Internal Revenue Bulletin.

* * *

(m) *Applicability dates.*—* * * Paragraphs (f)(13) and (14) of this section apply with respect to information for annual accounting periods beginning on or after December 20, 2018.

Par. 10. Section 1.6038-3 is amended by:

1. Adding paragraph (g)(3).
2. Redesignating the final paragraph (1) of the section as paragraph (l), revising the paragraph heading for newly-designated paragraph (l), and adding a sentence to the end of newly-designated paragraph (l).

The additions and revision read as follows:

§1.6038-3. Information returns required of certain United States persons with respect to controlled foreign partnerships (CFPs).

* * *

(g) * * *

(3) *Amounts involving hybrid transactions or hybrid entities under section 267A.*—In addition to the information required pursuant to paragraphs (g)(1) and (2) of this section, if, during the partnership's taxable year for which the Form 8865 is being filed, the partnership paid or accrued interest or royalties for which a deduction is disallowed under section 267A and the regulations under section 267A as contained in 26 CFR part 1, the controlling fifty-percent partners must provide information about the disallowance in the form and manner and to the extent prescribed by Form 8865 (or successor form), instruction, publication, or other guidance published in the Internal Revenue Bulletin.

* * *

(l) *Applicability dates.*—* * * Paragraph (g)(3) of this section applies for taxable years of a foreign partnership beginning on or after December 20, 2018.

Foreign-Derived Intangible Income: Global Intangible Low-Taxed Income: Deduction

Foreign-Derived Intangible Income: Global Intangible Low-Taxed Income: Deduction.—Amendments to Reg. §§1.6038-2 and 1.6038-3, providing guidance to determine the amount of the deduction for foreign-derived intangible income and global intangible low-taxed income, are proposed (published in the Federal Register on March 6, 2019) (REG-104464-18).

Par. 7. Section 1.6038-2, as proposed to be amended at 83 FR 67612 (Dec. 28, 2018), is further amended by adding paragraph (f)(15) and a sentence at the end of paragraph (m) to read as follows:

§1.6038-2. Information returns required of United States persons with respect to annual accounting periods of certain foreign corporations beginning after December 31, 1962.

* * *

(f) * * *

(15) *Information reporting under section 250.*—If the person required to file Form 5471 (or any successor form) claims a deduction under section 250(a) that is determined, in whole or part, by reference to its foreign-derived intangible income, and any amount required to be reported under paragraph (f)(11) of this section is included in its computation of foreign-derived deduction eligible income, such person will provide on Form 5471 (or any successor form) such information that is prescribed by the form, instructions, publication, or other guidance.

* * *

(m) * * * Paragraph (f)(15) of this section applies with respect to information for annual accounting periods beginning on or after March 4, 2019.

Par. 8. Section 1.6038-3, as proposed to be amended at 83 FR 67612 (Dec. 28, 2018), is further amended by adding paragraph (g)(4) and a sentence to the end of paragraph (l) to read as follows:

§1.6038-3. Information returns required of certain United States persons with respect to controlled foreign partnerships (CFPs).

* * *

(g) * * *

(4) *Additional information required to be submitted by a controlling ten-percent or a controlling fifty-percent partner that has a deduction under section 250 by reason of FDII.*—In addition to the information required pursuant to paragraphs (g)(1), (2), and (3) of this section, if, with respect to the partnership's tax year for which the Form 8865 is being filed, a controlling ten-percent partner or a controlling fifty-percent partner has a deduction under section 250 (by reason of having foreign-derived intangible income), determined, in whole or in part, by reference to the income, assets, or activities of the partnership, or transactions between the controlling-ten percent partner or controlling fifty-percent partner and the partnership, the controlling ten-percent partner or controlling fifty-percent partner must provide its share of the partnership's gross DEI, gross FDDEI, deductions that are definitely related to the partnership's gross DEI and gross FDDEI, and partnership QBAI (as those terms are defined in the section 250 regulations) in the form and manner and to the extent prescribed by Form 8865 (or any successor form), instruction, publication, or other guidance.

* * *

(l) * * * Paragraph (g)(4) of this section applies for tax years of a foreign partnership beginning on or after March 4, 2019.

Global Intangible Low-Taxed Income: Guidance

Global Intangible Low-Taxed Income: Guidance.—Reg. §1.6038-5 implementing section 951A of the Internal Revenue Code, which was enacted on December 22, 2017, is proposed (published in the Federal Register on October 10, 2018) (REG-104390-18).

Par. 16. Section 1.6038-5 is added to read as follows:

§1.6038-5. Information returns required of certain United States persons to report amounts determined with respect to certain foreign corporations for global intangible low-taxed income (GILTI) purposes.—(a) *Requirement of return.*—Except as provided in paragraph (d) of this section, each United States person who is a United States shareholder (as defined in section 951(b)) of any controlled foreign corporation must make an annual return on Form 8992, "U.S. Shareholder Calculation of Global Intangible Low-Taxed Income (GILTI)," (or successor form) for each U.S. shareholder inclusion year (as defined in §1.951A-1(e)(4)) setting forth the information with respect to each such controlled foreign corporation, in such form and manner, as Form 8992 (or successor form) prescribes.

(b) *Time and manner for filing.*—Returns on Form 8992 (or successor form) required under paragraph (a) of this section for a taxable year must be filed with the United States person's income tax return on or before the due date (taking into account extensions) for filing that person's income tax return.

(c) *Failure to furnish information.*—(1) *Penalties.*—If any person required to file Form 8992 (or successor form) under section 6038 and this section fails to furnish the information prescribed on Form 8992 within the time prescribed by paragraph (b) of this section, the penalties imposed by section 6038(b) and (c) may apply.

(2) *Increase in penalty.*—If a failure described in paragraph (c)(1) of this section continues for more than 90 days after the date on which the Director of Field Operations, Area Director, or Director of Compliance Campus Operations mails notice of such failure to the person required to file Form 8992, such person shall pay a penalty of $10,000, in addition to the penalty imposed by section 6038(b)(1), for each 30-day period (or a fraction of) during which such failure continues after such 90-day period has expired. The additional penalty imposed by section

6038(b)(2) and this paragraph (c)(2) shall be limited to a maximum of $50,000 for each failure.

(3) *Reasonable cause.*—(i) For purposes of section 6038(b) and (c) and this section, the time prescribed for furnishing information under paragraph (b) of this section, and the beginning of the 90-day period after mailing of notice by the director under paragraph (c)(2) of this section, shall be treated as being not earlier than the last day on which reasonable cause existed for failure to furnish the information.

(ii) To show that reasonable cause existed for failure to furnish information as required by section 6038 and this section, the person required to report such information must make an affirmative showing of all facts alleged as reasonable cause for such failure in a written statement containing a declaration that it is made under the penalties of perjury. The statement must be filed with the director where the return is required to be filed. The director shall determine whether the failure to furnish information was due to reasonable cause, and if so, the period of time for which such reasonable cause existed. In the case of a return that has been filed as required by this section except for an omission of, or error with respect to, some of the information required, if the person who filed the return establishes to the satisfaction of the director that the person has substantially complied with this section, then the omission or error shall not constitute a failure under this section.

(d) *Exception from filing requirement.*—Any United States person that does not own, within the meaning of section 958(a), stock of a controlled foreign corporation in which the United States person is a United States shareholder for a taxable year is not required to file Form 8992. For this purpose, a U.S. shareholder partner (as defined in § 1.951A-5(e)(3)) with respect to a partnership CFC (as defined in § 1.951A-5(e)(2)) is treated as owning, within the meaning of section 958(a), stock of the partnership CFC.

(e) *Applicability date.*—This section applies to taxable years of controlled foreign corporations beginning on or after October 3, 2018. [Reg. § 1.6038-5.]

Base Erosion and Anti-Abuse Tax: Guidance

Base Erosion and Anti-Abuse Tax: Guidance.—Amendments to Reg. §§ 1.6038A-1 and 1.6038A-2, regarding the tax on base erosion payments of taxpayers with substantial gross receipts and reporting requirements thereunder, are proposed (published in the Federal Register on December 21, 2018) (REG-104259-18).

Par. 10. Section 1.6038A-1 is amended by adding a sentence to the end of paragraph (n)(2) and revising the last sentence of paragraph (n)(3) to read as follows:

§ 1.6038A-1. General requirements and definitions.

* * *

(n) * * *

(2) * * * Section 1.6038A-2(a)(3), (b)(6), and (b)(7) apply for taxable years beginning after December 31, 2017.

(3) * * * For taxable years ending on or before December 31, 2017, see § 1.6038A-4 as contained in 26 CFR part 1 revised as of April 1, 2018.

* * *

Par. 11. Section 1.6038A-2 is amended by

1. Revising the headings for paragraphs (a) and (a)(1).
2. Revising paragraph (a)(2).
3. Adding paragraph (a)(3).
4. Revising paragraphs (b)(1)(ii), (b)(2)(iv), and the second sentence of paragraph (b)(3).
5. Redesignating paragraphs (b)(6) through (b)(9) as paragraphs (b)(8) through (b)(11).
6. Adding new paragraphs (b)(6) and (7).
7. Revising paragraph (c) and the first sentence of paragraph (d).
8. Removing the language "Paragraph (b)(8)" from the second sentence of paragraph (g) and adding the language "Paragraph (b)(10)" in its place.
9. Adding two sentences to the end of paragraph (g).

The revisions and additions read as follows:

§ 1.6038A-2. Requirement of return.—(a) *Forms required.*—(1) *Form 5472.*—* * *

(2) *Reportable transaction.*—A reportable transaction is any transaction of the types listed in paragraphs (b)(3) and (4) of this section, and, in the case of a reporting corporation that is an applicable taxpayer, as defined under § 1.59A-2(b), any other arrangement that, to prevent avoidance of the purposes of section 59A, is identified on Form 5472 as a reportable transaction. However, except as the Secretary may prescribe otherwise for an applicable taxpayer, the transaction is not a reportable transaction if neither party to the transaction is a United States person as defined in section 7701(a)(30) (which, for purposes of section 6038A, includes an entity that is a reporting corporation as a result of being treated as a corporation under § 301.7701-2(c)(2)(vi) of this chapter) and the transaction—

(i) Will not generate in any taxable year gross income from sources within the United States or income effectively connected, or treated as effectively connected, with the conduct of a trade or business within the United States, and

(ii) Will not generate in any taxable year any expense, loss, or other deduction that is allocable or apportionable to such income.

(3) *Form 8991.*—Each reporting corporation that is an applicable taxpayer, as defined under § 1.59A-2(b), must make an annual information return on Form 8991. The obligation of an applicable taxpayer to report on Form 8991 does not depend on applicability of tax under section 59A or obligation to file Form 5472.

(b) * * *

(1) * * *

(ii) The name, address, and U.S. taxpayer identification number, if applicable, of all its direct and indirect foreign shareholders (for an indirect 25-percent foreign shareholder, explain the attribution of ownership); whether any 25-percent foreign shareholder is a surrogate foreign corporation under section 7874(a)(2)(B) or a member of an expanded affiliated group as defined in section 7874(c)(1); each country in which each 25-percent foreign shareholder files an income tax return as a resident under the tax laws of that country; the places where each 25-percent shareholder conducts its business; and the country or countries of organization, citizenship, and incorporation of each 25-percent foreign shareholder.

* * *

(2) * * *

(iv) The relationship of the reporting corporation to the related party (including, to the extent the form may prescribe, any intermediate relationships).

(3) * * * The total amount of such transactions, as well as the separate amounts for each type of transaction described below, and, to the extent the form may prescribe, any further description, categorization, or listing of transactions within these types, must be reported on Form 5472, in the manner the form prescribes. * * *

* * *

(6) *Compilation of reportable transactions across multiple related parties.*—A reporting corporation must, to the extent and in the manner Form 5472 may prescribe, include a schedule tabulating information with respect to related parties for which the reporting corporation is required to file Forms 5472. The schedule will not require information (beyond totaling) that is not required for the individual Forms 5472. The schedule may include the following:

(i) The identity and status of the related parties;

(ii) The reporting corporation's relationship to the related parties;

(iii) The reporting corporation's reportable transactions with the related parties; and

(iv) Other items required to be reported on Form 5472.

(7) *Information on Form 5472 and Form 8991 regarding base erosion payments.*—If any reporting corporation is an applicable taxpayer, as defined under § 1.59A-2(b), it must report the information required by Form 8991 and by any Form 5472 it is required to file, regarding:

(i) Determination of whether a taxpayer is an applicable taxpayer;

(ii) Computation of base erosion minimum tax amount, including computation of regular tax liability as adjusted for purposes of computing base erosion minimum tax amount;

(iii) Computation of modified taxable income;

(iv) Base erosion tax benefits;

(v) Base erosion percentage calculation;

(vi) Base erosion payments;

(vii) Amounts with respect to services as described in § 1.59A-3(b)(3)(i), including a breakdown of the amount of the total services cost and any mark-up component;

(viii) Arrangements or transactions described in § 1.59A-9;

(ix) Any qualified derivative payment, including:

(A) The aggregate amount of qualified derivative payments for the taxable year, including as determined by type of derivative contract;

(B) The identity of each counterparty and the aggregate amount of qualified derivative payments made to that counterparty; and

(C) A representation that all payments satisfy the requirements of § 1.59A-6(b)(2), and

(x) Any other information necessary to carry out section 59A.

* * *

(c) *Method of reporting.*—All statements required on or with the Form 5472 or Form 8991 under this section and § 1.6038A-5 must be in the English language. All amounts required to be reported under paragraph (b) of this section must be expressed in United States currency, with a statement of the exchange rates used, and, to the extent the forms may require, must indicate the method by which the amount of a reportable transaction or item was determined.

(d) * * * A Form 5472 and Form 8991 required under this section must be filed with the reporting corporation's income tax return for the taxable year by the due date (including extensions) of that return. * * *

* * *

(g) * * * Paragraph (b)(7)(ix) of this section applies to taxable years beginning one year after final regulations are published in the **Federal Register**. Before these regulations are applicable, a taxpayer will be treated as satisfying the reporting requirement described in § 1.59A-6(b)(2) only to the extent that it reports the aggregate amount of qualified derivative payments on Form 8991.

Hybrid Arrangements: Rules

Hybrid Arrangements: Rules.—Amendments to Reg. § 1.6038A-2, implementing sections 245A(e) and 267A of the Internal Revenue Code regarding hybrid dividends and certain amounts paid or accrued in hybrid transactions or with hybrid entities, are proposed (published in the Federal Register on December 28, 2018) (REG-104352-18).

Par. 11. Section 1.6038A-2 is amended by adding paragraph (b)(5)(iii) and adding a sentence at the end of paragraph (g) to read as follows:

§ 1.6038A-2. Requirement of return.

* * *

(b) * * *

(5) * * *

(iii) If, for the taxable year, a reporting corporation pays or accrues interest or royalties for which a deduction is disallowed under section 267A and the regulations under section 267A as contained in 26 CFR part 1, then the reporting corporation must provide such information about the disallowance in the form and manner and to the extent prescribed by Form

5472 (or successor form), instruction, publication, or other guidance published in the Internal Revenue Bulletin.

* * *

(g) * * * Paragraph (b)(5)(iii) of this section applies with respect to information for annual accounting periods beginning on or after December 20, 2018.

Foreign-Derived Intangible Income: Global Intangible Low-Taxed Income: Deduction

Foreign-Derived Intangible Income: Global Intangible Low-Taxed Income: Deduction.—Amendments to Reg. §1.6038A-2, providing guidance to determine the amount of the deduction for foreign-derived intangible income and global intangible low-taxed income, are proposed (published in the Federal Register on March 6, 2019) (REG-104464-18).

Par. 9. Section 1.6038A-2, as proposed to be amended at 83 FR 67612 (Dec. 28, 2018), is further amended by adding paragraph (b)(5)(iv) and a sentence at the end of paragraph (g) to read as follows:

§1.6038A-2. Requirements of return.

* * *

(b) * * *

(5) * * *

(iv) *Information reporting under section 250.*—If, for the taxable year, the reporting corporation has a deduction under section 250 (by reason of having foreign-derived intangible income) with respect to any amount required to be reported under paragraph (b)(3) or (4) of this section, the reporting corporation will provide on Form 5472 (or any successor form) such information about the deduction in the form and manner and to the extent prescribed by Form 5472 (or any successor form), instruction, publication, or other guidance.

* * *

(g) * * * Paragraph (b)(5)(iv) of this section applies with respect to information for annual accounting periods beginning on or after March 4, 2019.

Base Erosion and Anti-Abuse Tax: Guidance

Base Erosion and Anti-Abuse Tax: Guidance.—Amendments to Reg. §1.6038A-4, regarding the tax on base erosion payments of taxpayers with substantial gross receipts and reporting requirements thereunder, are proposed (published in the Federal Register on December 21, 2018) (REG-104259-18).

Par. 12. For each paragraph listed in the table, remove the language in the "Remove" column from wherever it appears and add in its place the language in the "Add" column as set forth below:

§1.6038A-4. Monetary penalty.

Section	Remove	Add
Section 1.6038A-4(a)(1)	$10,000	$25,000
Section 1.6038A-4(a)(3)	$10,000	$25,000
Section 1.6038A-4(d)(1)	$10,000	$25,000
Section 1.6038A-4(d)(4)	$10,000	$25,000
Section 1.6038A-4(f)	$10,000	$25,000
Section 1.6038A-4(f)	$30,000	$75,000
Section 1.6038A-4(f)	$90,000	$225,000

Foreign Corporations: Transfer of Property

Reorganizations: Foreign Corporations: Transfer of Property.—Temporary Reg. §1.6038B-1T, relating to transfers of property to foreign corporations, is proposed (published in the Federal Register on May 16, 1986) (LR-3-86).

§1.6038B-1T. Reporting of certain transfers to foreign corporations (temporary).

U.S. Persons: Partnerships with Foreign Partners: Transfers of Appreciated Property

U.S. Persons: Partnerships with Foreign Partners: Transfers of Appreciated Property.—Amendments to Reg. §1.6038B-2, addressing transfers of appreciated property by U.S. persons to partnerships with foreign partners related to the transferor, are proposed (published in the Federal Register on January 19, 2017) (REG-127203-15).

Par. 12. Section 1.6038B-2 is amended by:

1. Revising paragraph (a)(3).
2. Adding paragraphs (a)(1)(iii), (c)(8), and (c)(9).
3. Revising paragraph (h)(3).
4. Adding paragraphs (j)(4) and (j)(5).

§ 1.6038B-2. Reporting of certain transfers to foreign partnerships.—(a) * * *

(1) * * *

(iii) [The text of proposed § 1.6038B-2(a)(1)(iii) is the same as the text of § 1.6038B-2T(a)(1)(iii) as added by T.D. 9814].

* * *

(3) [The text of proposed § 1.6038B-2(a)(3) is the same as the text of § 1.6038B-2T(a)(3) as added by T.D. 9814].

* * *

(c) * * *

(8) [The text of proposed § 1.6038B-2(c)(8) is the same as the text of § 1.6038B-2T(c)(8) as added by T.D. 9814].

(9) [The text of proposed § 1.6038B-2(c)(9) is the same as the text of § 1.6038B-2T(c)(9) as added by T.D. 9814].

* * *

(h) * * *

(3) [The text of proposed § 1.6038B-2(h)(3) is the same as the text of § 1.6038B-2T(h)(3) as added by T.D. 9814].

* * *

(j) * * *

(4) [The text of proposed § 1.6038B-2(j)(4) is the same as the text of § 1.6038B-2T(j)(4) as added by T.D. 9814].

(5) [The text of proposed § 1.6038B-2(j)(5) is the same as the text of § 1.6038B-2T(j)(5) as added by T.D. 9814].

Foreign-Owned Corporations: Information Returns

Foreign-Owned Corporations: Information Returns: Records.—Reproduced below is the text of proposed Reg. § 1.6038C-1, relating to foreign-owned corporations (published in the Federal Register on December 10, 1990).

☐ Par. 5. New § 1.6038C-1 is added to read as follows:

§ 1.6038C-1. General rule.—The rules of §§ 1.6038A-1 through 1.6038A-7 generally will apply for purposes of section 6038C.

Return and Extended Due Date: Changes

Return Due Extended Due Date: Changes.—Amendments to Reg. § 1.6041-2, updating the due dates and extensions of time to file certain tax returns and information returns, are proposed (published in the Federal Register on July 20, 2017) (REG-128483-15).

Par. 7. Revise paragraph (a)(3)(ii) and add paragraph (d) to § 1.6041-2 to read as follows:

§ 1.6041-2. Return of information as to payments to employees.—(a) * * *

(3) * * *

(ii) [The text of proposed § 1.6041-2(a)(3)(ii) is the same as the text of § 1.6041-2T(a)(3)(ii) as added by T.D. 9821].

* * *

(d) *Applicability date.*—The requirements of paragraph (a)(3)(ii) of this section are applicable for returns filed on or after the date a Treasury Decision incorporating these amendments as final regulations is published in the **Federal Register**.

Return and Extended Due Date: Changes

Return Due Extended Due Date: Changes.—Amendments to Reg. § 1.6041-6, updating the due dates and extensions of time to file certain tax returns and information returns, are proposed (published in the Federal Register on July 20, 2017) (REG-128483-15).

Par. 8. Revise § 1.6041-6 to read as follows:

§ 1.6041-6. Returns made on Forms 1096 and 1099 under section 6041; contents and time and place for filing.—(a) and (b) [The text of proposed § 1.6041-6(a) and (b) is the same as the text of § 1.6041-6T(a) and (b) as added by T.D. 9821].

(c) *Applicability date.*—The requirements of paragraphs (a) and (b) of this section are applicable for returns filed on or after the date a Treasury Decision incorporating these amendments as final regulations is published in the **Federal Register**.

Employment Taxes

Employment Taxes: Real Estate Agents and Direct Sellers: Employer's Liability.—Reproduced below is the text of proposed Reg. § 1.6041A-1, relating to the treatment of qualified real estate agents and direct sellers as nonemployees, to the determination of employer liability for income tax withholding and employee social security taxes where the employer treated an employee as a nonemployee for purposes of such taxes, and to information reporting of direct sales and payments of remuneration for services (published in the Federal Register on January 7, 1986) (INTL-214-82).

☐ Par. 4. A new § 1.6041A-1 is added immediately after § 1.6041-7 to read as set forth below:

§ 1.6041A-1. Returns regarding payments of remuneration for services and certain direct sales.—(a) *Returns regarding remuneration for services*—

(1) *In general.*—If—

(i) Any service-recipient engaged in a trade or business pays in the course of that trade or business during any calendar year after 1982 remuneration to any person for services performed by that person, and

(ii) The aggregate amount of remuneration paid to such person during such calendar year is $600 or more,

then the service-recipient shall make a return in accordance with paragraph (e) of this section. For purposes of the preceding sentence, the term "service-recipient" means the person for whom the service is performed (*e.g.*, in the case of a real estate agent, the real estate firm for which such agent performs services). For purposes of this paragraph (a)(1) only, the term remuneration does not include amounts paid to any person for services performed by such person if the service-recipient knows that such amounts are excludable from the gross income of the person performing such services. For example, a return is not required with respect to amounts paid to a foster parent which are known by the service-recipient to constitute foster care payments that are excludable from gross income under section 131. For purposes of this paragraph (a)(1), a service-recipient shall be considered to know facts set forth in a written statement provided to the service-recipient, made under the penalties of perjury and signed by the person performing such services, in the absence of knowledge by the service-recipient that such statement is untrue. See section 6041A (d) for rules relating to the application of section 6041A and this section to governmental units (and agencies or instrumentalities thereof).

(2) *Payment attributable to parts and materials.*—For purposes of section 6041A and this section, the aggregate amount of remuneration paid to any person for services rendered includes any payments for parts or materials used by such person in rendering the services unless the trade or business of such person is primarily that of selling parts or materials. Whether a person is engaged primarily in the trade or business of selling parts and materials rather than providing services shall be determined on the basis of all facts and circumstances, taking into account such factors as whether such person holds himself or herself out as a dealer in parts and whether, with respect to the type of services rendered, a service-recipient ordinarily would specify the type or brand of parts or materials to be used.

Example. X Company makes a payment to an unincorporated repair shop for repairs to one of the company's automobiles. The automobile sustained body damage in an accident. The repair contract requires payment of $300 for labor and $400 for new parts that were installed. The repair shop does not hold itself out as a dealer in parts. Generally, customers of the repair shop do not specify the type or brand of replacement parts to be installed. Therefore, the aggregate amount of remuneration that is required to be reported pursuant to section 6041A(a) includes the payment for parts.

(b) *Returns regarding direct sales of $5,000 or more.*—(1) *In general.*—If—

(i) Any person engaged in a trade or business in the course of such trade or business during any calendar year sells consumer products to any buyer on a buy-sell, deposit-commission, or other commission basis for resale (by the buyer or any other person) in the home or otherwise than in a permanent retail establishment, and

(ii) The aggregate amount of such sales made by such person to such buyer during such calendar year is $5,000 or more,

then such person shall make a return with respect to such buyer in accordance with paragraph (e) of this section. This requirement shall apply to sales made in any calendar year after 1982.

(2) *Sale defined.*—For purposes of this paragraph (b), a person will be considered to sell a product to a buyer for resale even though such buyer does not acquire title to the product prior to selling it to the consumer. For example, a company sales person, paid on a commission basis, who does not acquire title to a product before selling it to the consumer is considered to have bought the product for resale for purposes of section 6041A(b) and this paragraph.

(3) *Acquisition for resale in a permanent retail establishment.*—Section 6041A(b) and this paragraph do not apply to sales of a product to a buyer who sells the product only in a permanent retail establishment, as defined in §31.3508-1(g)(4) of this chapter (Employment Tax Regulations). If a buyer acquires consumer products from a person for resale both in the home (or otherwise than in a permanent retail establishment) as well as in a permanent retail establishment, then such person shall, for purposes of determining the aggregate amount of sales made to such buyer under paragraph (b)(1)(i) of this section, take into account all sales of such products made to such buyer during the calendar year.

(4) *Products purchased for personal use or consumption.*—All sales to a buyer of consumer products on a buy-sell, deposit-commission, or other commission basis that are suitable for resale to another person shall be taken into account in determining the aggregate amount of sales made to such buyer under paragraph (b)(1)(i) of this section even if such buyer purchases some of the products for the buyer's personal use or consumption or disposes of some of the products other than by resale (for example, gifts to relatives). Sales of products that cannot be resold, such as samples and catalogues, are not taken into account in determining the aggregate amount of sales to a buyer during the calendar year.

(5) *Consumer product defined.*—For purposes of section 6041A(b) and this paragraph, the term "consumer product" means any tangible personal property which is distributed in commerce and which is normally used for personal, family, or household purposes (including any such property intended to be attached to or installed in any real property without regard to whether it is so attached or installed). The term "consumer product" does not include any product used to manufacture another product to be distributed in commerce or any product used only incidentally in providing a service (*e.g.*, insecticide used in a pest control service, material used in an appliance repair business).

(c) *Engaged in trade or business.*—For purposes of section 6041A(a)(1) or (b)(1) and this section, whether a service-recipient or other person is engaged in a trade or business shall be determined under the rules set forth in §1.6041-1(b).

(d) *Exceptions to return requirement.*—(1) *Return required under another section.*—No return shall be required under paragraph (a) of this section if a statement with respect to the services is required to be furnished under section 6051, 6052, or 6053.

(2) *Transactions exempt from reporting under section 6041.*—No return shall be required under paragraph (a) of this section with respect to a payment which is exempted under § 1.6041-3 from the reporting requirement of section 6041, and no return shall be required under paragraph (b) of this section with respect to sales made to a corporation.

(e) *Time and manner of filing.*—(1) *Form.*—The return required to be filed under section 6041A(a) or (b) and paragraph (a) or (b) of this section shall be filed on Forms 1096 and 1099 in accordance with the instructions accompanying those forms.

(2) *Time for filing.*—The return shall be filed on or before February 28 of the year following the calendar year for which the return is filed.

(3) *Place of filing.*—The return shall be filed with the appropriate Internal Revenue Center, at the address listed in the instructions for Forms 1096 and 1099.

(4) *Contents.*—(i) *In general.*—Unless otherwise provided in the instructions to Form 1099, the return required under section 6041A(a) or (b) and paragraph (a) or (b) of this section shall set forth the information contained in paragraph (e)(4)(ii) or (iii) of this section.

(ii) *Return required under section 6041A(a).*—The return required to be filed under section 6041A(a) and paragraph (a)(1) of this section shall set forth the aggregate amount of remuneration paid to the person with respect to whom the return is made during the calendar year for services rendered, the name, address, and taxpayer identification number of the person making the payment, and the name, address, and taxpayer identification number of the recipient of the remuneration.

(iii) *Return required under section 6041A(b).*—A return required to be filed under section 6041A(b) and paragraph (b)(1) of this section shall set forth the name, address, and taxpayer identification number of the person making the sales, and the name, address, and taxpayer identification number of the buyer.

(f) *Statements to be furnished to persons with respect to whom information is required to be furnished.*—(1) *In general.*—Every person required to file a return pursuant to section 6041A(a) or (b) and paragraph (a) or (b) of this section shall furnish a written statement to each person whose name is required to be set forth in that return.

(2) *Time for furnishing statement.*—The written statement required under paragraph (f)(1) of this section shall be furnished to the person on or before January 31 of the year following the calendar year for which the return under section 6041A(a) or (b) was made.

(3) *Contents of statement.*—The statement shall contain—

(i) The name, address, and taxpayer identification number of the person required to make the return, and

(ii) In the case of a return required to be filed under section 6041A(a) and paragraph (a)(1) of this section, the aggregate amount of payments to the person required to be shown on the return.

(g) *Recipient to furnish name, address, and identification number.*—Any person with respect to whom a return or statement is required to be made pursuant to section 6041A and this section by another person shall furnish to that other person his name, address, and identification number upon demand by the person required to make the return.

(h) *Penalties.*—For provisions relating to the penalties for failure to file a return or to furnish a statement under section 6041A and this section, see sections 6652 and 6678 of the Code. For provisions relating to the penalty for failure to supply identification numbers under this section, see section 6676. [Reg. § 1.6041A-1.]

Consolidated Returns: Dual Consolidated Losses

Consolidated Returns: Dual Consolidated Losses.—Amendments to Reg. § 1.6043-4T, relating to various dual consolidated loss issues, including exceptions to the general prohibition against using a dual consolidated loss to reduce the taxable income of any other member of the affiliated group, are proposed (published in the Federal Register on May 24, 2005) (REG-102144-04).

☐ Par. 4. In § 1.6043-4T, paragraph (a)(1)(iii) is amended by removing the language "§ 1.1503-2(c)(2)" and adding "§ 1.1503(d)-1(b)(2)" in its place.

§ 1.6043-4T. Information returns relating to certain acquisitions of control and changes in capital structure (temporary).

Imputed Interest: Original Issue Discount: Safe Haven Interest Rates

Imputed Interest: Original Issue Discount: Safe Haven Interest Rates.—Reproduced below is the text of a proposed amendment of Reg. § 1.6045-1, relating to (1) the tax treatment of debt instruments issued after July 1, 1982, that contain original issue discount, (2) the imputation of and the accounting for interest with respect to sales and exchanges of property occurring after December 31, 1984, and (3) safe haven interest rates for loans or advances between commonly controlled taxpayers and safe haven leases between such taxpayers (published in the Federal Register on April 8, 1986).

☐ Par. 29. Paragraph (c) of § 1.6045-1 is amended by removing the phrase "section 1232(b)(1)" every place it appears and adding in its place the phrase "section 1273(a)(1)".

§ 1.6045-1. Returns of information of brokers and barter exchanges.

Definition of Registered Form: Guidance

Definition of Registered Form: Guidance.—Amendments to Reg. §1.6045-1, providing guidance on the definitions of registration-required obligation and registered form, including guidance on the issuance of pass-through certificates and participation interests in registered form, are proposed (published in the Federal Register on September 19, 2017) (REG-125374-16).

Par. 10. Section 1.6045-1(n)(2)(ii)(J) is amended by removing the language "§ 1.1471-1(b)(18)" and adding in its place the language "§ 1.1471-1(b)(21)".

§1.6045-1. Returns of information of brokers and barter exchanges.

Correct Payee Statements: Failure to File Correct Information: Penalties

Correct Payee Statements: Failure to File Correct Information: Penalties.—Amendments to Reg. §1.6045-1, relating to penalties for failure to file correct information returns or furnish correct payee statements, are proposed (published in the Federal Register on October 17, 2018) (REG-118826-16).

Par. 2. Section 1.6045-1 is amended by redesignating paragraph (d)(6)(vii) as paragraph (d)(6)(viii), adding paragraphs (d)(6)(vii) and (ix), and revising paragraphs (k)(4), (l), and (q) to read as follows:

§1.6045-1. Returns of information of brokers and barter exchanges.

* * *

(d) * * *

(6) * * *

(vii) *Treatment of de minimis errors.*—For purposes of this section, a customer's adjusted basis shall generally be determined by treating any incorrect dollar amount which is not required to be corrected by reason of section 6721(c)(3) or section 6722(c)(3) as the correct amount. However if a broker, upon identifying a dollar amount as incorrect, voluntarily both files a corrected information return and issues a corrected payee statement showing the correct dollar amount, then regardless of any requirement under section 6721 or section 6722, the adjusted basis shall be the correct dollar amount as reported on the corrected information return and corrected payee statement.

* * *

(ix) *Applicability date.*—Paragraph (d)(6)(vii) of this section applies with respect to information returns required to be filed and payee statements required to be furnished on or after January 1 of the calendar year immediately following the date of publication of a Treasury decision adopting these rules as final regulations in the **Federal Register**.

* * *

(k) * * *

(4) *Cross-reference to penalty.*—For provisions for failure to furnish timely a correct payee statement, see §301.6722-1 of this chapter (Procedure and Administration Regulations). See §301.6724-1 of this chapter for the waiver of a penalty if the failure is due to reasonable cause and is not due to willful neglect.

(l) *Use of magnetic media.*—See §301.6011-2 of this chapter for rules relating to filing information returns on magnetic media and for rules relating to waivers granted for undue hardship. A broker or barter exchange that fails to file a Form 1099 on magnetic media, when required, may be subject to a penalty under section 6721 for each such failure. See paragraph (j) of this section.

* * *

(q) *Applicability date.*—Except as otherwise provided in paragraphs (d)(6)(ix), (m)(2)(ii), and (n)(12)(ii) of this section, and in this paragraph (q), this section applies on or after January 6, 2017. Paragraphs (k)(4) and (l) of this section apply with respect to information returns required to be filed and payee statements required to be furnished on or after January 1 of the calendar year immediately following the date of publication of a Treasury decision adopting these rules as final regulations in the **Federal Register**. (For rules that apply after June 30, 2014, and before January 6, 2017, see this section as in effect and contained in 26 CFR part 1, as revised April 1, 2016.)

Stock and Rights to Acquire Stock: Deemed Distributions

Stock and Rights to Acquire Stock: Deemed Distributions.—Amendments to Reg. §1.6045B-1, regarding deemed distributions of stock and rights to acquire stock and resolving ambiguities concerning the amount and timing of deemed distributions that are or result from adjustments to rights to acquire stock, are proposed (published in the Federal Register on April 13, 2016) (REG-133673-15).

Par. 13. Section 1.6045B-1 is amended by adding paragraph (i) to read as follows:

§1.6045B-1. Returns relating to actions affecting basis of securities.

* * *

(i) *Deemed distribution under section 305(c).*—(1) *In general.*—This paragraph (i) provides special rules for an organizational action resulting in a deemed distribution under section 305(c) that affects the basis of a specified security, including a deemed distribution resulting from an applicable adjustment (for example, a conversion ratio adjustment). *See* paragraph (j) of this section to determine when this section applies to an organizational action that affects the basis of a specified security. For example, under paragraph (j)(4) of this section, this section applies to a deemed distribution under section 305(c) resulting from an applicable adjustment to a convertible debt instrument if the deemed distribution occurs on or after January 1, 2016, and the deemed distribution could affect the basis of the convertible debt instrument.

(2) *Mandatory reporting.*—Notwithstanding any other provision in this section (including the reporting exceptions for exempt recipients in paragraphs (a)(4) and (b)(5) of this section), for an organizational action described in paragraph (i)(1) of this section the issuer must file an issuer return in accordance with paragraphs (a)(1) and (2) of this section and issuer statements in accordance with paragraphs (b)(1), (2), and (3) of this section. However, the requirement to file an issuer return and issuer statement in accordance with the preceding sentence does not apply if the issuer satisfies the public reporting requirements of paragraph (a)(3) of this section.

(3) *Information required to be reported.*—For purposes of paragraph (i)(2) of this section, an issuer must provide the information required under paragraph (a)(1) of this section, including—

(i) The date of the deemed distribution under section 305(c) as determined in accordance with §1.305-7(c)(5) (pursuant to paragraph (a)(1)(iv) of this section); and

(ii) The amount of the deemed distribution under section 305(c) as determined in accordance with §1.305-7(c)(4) (pursuant to paragraph (a)(1)(v) of this section).

(4) *Effective/applicability date.*—Paragraph (i)(2) of this section applies to a deemed distribution under section 305(c) occurring on or after the date of publication of the Treasury decision adopting these rules as final regulations in the **Federal Register**. For purposes of paragraphs (a)(1)(v) and (i)(3)(ii) of this section, an issuer must determine the amount of a deemed distribution under section 305(c) in accordance with §1.305-7(c)(4) for a deemed distribution occurring on or after the date of publication. For purposes of reporting the amount of a deemed distribution occurring prior to the date of publication, an issuer may determine the amount of the deemed distribution by treating such distribution either as a distribution of a right to acquire stock in accordance with §1.305-7(c)(4), or as a distribution of the shares of stock that would be received upon exercise of the right. For purposes of paragraphs (a)(1)(iv) and (i)(3)(i) of this section, an issuer must determine the date of a deemed distribution under section 305(c) occurring on or after the date of publication in accordance with §1.305-7(c)(5). An issuer, however, may rely on §1.305-7(c)(5) to determine the date of a deemed distribution that occurs prior to the date of publication.

* * *

CFCs: Insurance Income: Tax Years After 1986

Controlled Foreign Corporations: Insurance Income: Tax Years After 1986.—Reproduced below is a proposed amendment to Reg. §1.6046-1, relating to the election to expense certain depreciable business assets (published in the Federal Register on April 17, 1991).

☐ Par. 8. Section 1.6046-1 is amended as follows:

1. Paragraph (a)(2)(i) is revised.
2. Paragraph (c)(1)(i) and (c)(1)(ii)(*c*) is revised.
3. New paragraph (c)(1)(iii) is added preceding the concluding text of paragraph (c)(1).
4. The added and revised provisions read as follows:

§1.6046-1. Returns as to organization or reorganization of foreign corporations and as to acquisitions of their stock, on or after January 1, 1963.—(a) *Officers or directors.*—* * *

(2) *When liability arises after January 1, 1963.*—(i) *Requirement of return.*—Each United States citizen or resident who is at any time after January 1, 1963, an officer or director of a foreign corporation shall make a return on Form 5471 setting forth the information described in paragraph (a)(2)(ii) of this section with respect to each United States person who, during the time such citizen or resident is such an officer or director—

(*a*) Acquires (whether in one or more transactions) outstanding stock of such corporation which has, or which when added to any such stock then owned by him (excluding any stock owned by him on January 1, 1963, if on that date he owned 5 percent or more in value of such stock) has, a value equal to 5 percent or more in value of the outstanding stock of such foreign corporation,

(*b*) Acquires (whether in one or more transactions) an additional 5 percent or more in value of the outstanding stock of such foreign corporation, or

(*c*) Is not described in paragraph (a)(2)(i)(*a*) or (*b*) of this section, and who, at any time after January 1, 1987, is treated as a United States shareholder under section 953(c) and §1.953-3(b)(2)(i) with respect to a foreign corporation.

* * *

(c) *Returns required of United States persons when liability to file arises after January 1, 1963.*—(1) *United States persons required to file.*—* * *

(i) Such person acquires (whether in one or more transactions) outstanding stock of such foreign corporation which has, or which when added to any such stock then owned by him (excluding any stock owned by him on January 1, 1963, if on that date he owned 5 percent or more in value of such stock) has, a value equal to 5 percent or more in value of the outstanding stock of such foreign corporation,

(ii) * * *

(*c*) Disposes of sufficient stock in such foreign corporation to reduce his interest to less than 5 percent in value of the outstanding stock of such foreign corporation, or

(iii) Such person is, at any time after January 1, 1987, treated as a United States shareholder under section 953(c) with respect to a foreign corporation.

* * *

Imputed Interest: OID: Safe Haven Rates

Imputed Interest: Original Issue Discount: Safe Haven Interest Rates.—Reproduced below is the text of a proposed amendment of Reg. §1.6049-4, relating to (1) the tax treatment of debt instruments issued after July 1, 1982, that contain original issue discount, (2) the imputation of and the accounting for interest with respect to sales and exchanges of property occurring after December 31, 1984, and (3) safe haven interest rates for loans or advances between commonly controlled taxpayers and safe haven leases between such taxpayers (published in the Federal Register on April 8, 1986).

☐ Par. 30. Paragraph (e)(2) of §1.6049-4 is amended by removing the phrase "section 1232(a)(3)" and adding in its place the phrase "section 1271(a)(3)(A)".

§1.6049-4. Return of information as to interest paid and original issue discount includible in gross income after December 31, 1982.

Imputed Interest: OID: Safe Haven Interest Rates

Imputed Interest: Original Issue Discount: Safe Haven Interest Rates.—Reproduced below is the text of a proposed amendment of Reg. §1.6049-5, relating (1) the tax treatment of debt instruments issued after July 1, 1982, that contain original issue discount, (2) the imputation of and the accounting for interest with respect to sales and exchanges of property occurring after December 31, 1984, and (3) safe haven interest rates for loans or advances between commonly controlled taxpayers and safe haven leases between such taxpayers (published in the Federal Register on April 8, 1986).

☐ Par. 31. Section 1.6049-5 is amended as follows:

1. In paragraph (b)(1)(vi)(B)(4) by removing the phrase "section 1232(b)(1)" and adding in its place the phrase "section 1273(a)(1)".

2. In paragraph (c) by removing the ninth sentence thereof and by revising the second, fourth and seventh sentences to read as follows:

§1.6049-5. Interest and original issue discount subject to reporting after December 31, 1982.

* * *

(c) *Original issue discount treated as payment of interest.*—* * * In the case of an obligation as to which there is during any calendar year an amount of original issue discount includible in the gross income of any holder (as determined under section 1272 and the regulations thereunder), the issuer of the obligation or a middleman (as defined in §1.6049-4(f)(4)) shall be treated as having paid to such holder during such calendar year an amount of interest equal to the amount of original issue discount so includible without regard to any reduction by reason of an acquisition premium under section 1272(a)(6) and (b)(4) or a purchase at a premium under section 1272(c)()1) and §1.1275-1(f). * * * In the case of (1) an obligation to which section 1272 does not apply (for example, a short-term government obligation as defined in section 1271(a)(3)(A)) and (2) an obligation issued on or before December 31, 1982, in bearer form, the amount of original issue discount includible in gross income shall be treated as if paid in the calendar year in which the date of maturity occurs or in which the date of redemption occurs if redemption occurs before maturity. * * * Discount on short term government obligations as defined in section 1271(a)(3)(B), such as Treasury bills, and discount on other obligations with a maturity at the date of issue of not more than 1 year (a short term obligation), including commercial paper, when paid at maturity or redemption if redemption occurs before maturity, shall constitute a payment of interest for purposes of section 6049. * * *

* * *

Information Returns: OID

Information Returns: Original Issue Discount; Brokers.—Temporary Reg. §1.6049-5T, relating to reporting requirements for original issue discount debt instruments, is also proposed as a final regulation and, when adopted, would become Reg. §1.6049-5 (published in the Federal Register on December 17, 1986).

§1.6049-5. Reporting by brokers of interest and original issue discount on and after Janaury 1, 1986.

Definition of Registered Form: Guidance

Definition of Registered Form: Guidance.—Amendments to Reg. §1.6049-5, providing guidance on the definitions of registration-required obligation and registered form, including guidance on the issuance of pass-through certificates and participation interests in registered form, are proposed (published in the Federal Register on September 19, 2017) (REG-125374-16).

Par. 11. Section 1.6049-5 is amended by:

2. Removing "§5f.103-1(c))," and adding in its place "§1.163-5(b));" in paragraph (a)(1)(i).

3. Removing the language "§5f.163-1" and adding in its place the language "§1.163-5(a)(2)" in paragraph (a)(1)(ii).

§1.6049-5. Interest and original issue discount subject to reporting after December 31, 1982.

Imputed Interest: OID: Safe Haven Interest Rates

Imputed Interest: Original Issue Discount: Safe Haven Interest Rates.—Reproduced below is the text of a proposed amendment of Reg. §1.6049-6, relating to (1) the tax treatment of debt instruments issued after July 1, 1982, that contain original issue discount, (2) the imputation of and the accounting for interest with respect to sales and exchanges of property occurring after December 31, 1984, and (3) safe haven interest rates for loans or advances between commonly controlled taxpayers and safe haven leases between such taxpayers (published in the Federal Register on April 8, 1986).

§1.6049-6. Statements to recipients of interest payments and holders of obligations for attributed original issue discount..

☐ Par. 32. Paragraph (d) of §1.6049-6 is amended by removing the phrase "section 1232A" and adding in its place the phrase "section 1272(a)".

* * *

REMICs: Reporting Information: Extension of Time

REMICs: Reporting Information: Extension of Time.—Reproduced below is the text of a proposed amendment to Reg. §1.6049-7, relating to real estate mortgage investment conduits (published in the Federal Register on September 30, 1991).

☐ Par 4. Section 1.6049-7 is amended by revising paragraphs (e)(3)(ii)(A) and (f)(7)(ii) to read as follows:

§1.6049-7. Returns of information with respect to REMIC regular interests and collateralized debt obligations.

* * *

(e) * * *

(3) * * *

(ii) * * *

(A) The 41st day after the close of the calendar quarter for which the information was requested, or

* * *

(f) * * *

(7) * * *

(ii) *Time for furnishing information.*—The statement required in paragraph (f)(7)(i) of this section must be furnished on or before the later of—

(A) The 45th day after receipt of the request,

(B) The 55th day after the close of the calendar quarter for which the information was requested, or

(C) If the information is requested for the last calendar quarter in a calendar year, March 15 of the year following the calendar quarter for which the information was requested.

* * *

Returns: Foreclosures: Abandonment of Security

Information Returns: Loan Security: Abandonments, Foreclosure and Other Acquisitions.—Temporary Reg. §1.6050J-1T, relating to the requirement of reporting abandonments, foreclosures, and other acquisitions of property securing indebtedness, is also proposed as a final regulation and, when adopted, would become Reg. §1.6050J-1 (published in the Federal Register on August 31, 1984).

§1.6050J-1. Questions and answers concerning information returns relating to foreclosures and abandonments of security.

Partners and Partnerships: Sales or Exchanges: Certain Distributions

Partners and Partnerships: Sales or Exchanges: Certain Distributions.—Amendments to Reg. §1.6050K-1, prescribing how a partner should measure its interest in a partnership's unrealized receivables and inventory items, and that provide guidance regarding the tax consequences of a distribution that causes a reduction in that interest, are proposed (published in the Federal Register on November 3, 2014) (REG-151416-06).

☐ Par. 17. Section 1.6050K-1 is amended by revising paragraph (a)(4)(ii) and adding a new sentence after the third sentence of paragraph (c) introductory text to read as follows:

§1.6050K-1. Returns relating to sales or exchanges of certain partnership interests.—(a) * * *

(4) * * *

(ii) *Section 751 property.*—For purposes of this section, the term "section 751 property" means unrealized receivables, as defined in section 751(c) and the regulations, and inventory items, as defined in section 751(d) and the regulations.

* * *

(c) * * * With respect to any statement required to be furnished to a transferor, the statement shall, in addition to the other information required, include the amount of any gain or loss attributable to section 751 property that is required to be recognized pursuant to paragraph (a)(2) of § 1.751-1. * * *

* * *

Qualified Tuition: Related Expenses: Reporting

Qualified Tuition: Related Expenses: Reporting.—Amendments to Reg. §§ 1.6050S-0 and 1.6050S-1, revising the rules for reporting qualified tuition and related expenses under section 6050S on a Form 1098-T, "Tuition Statement," and conforming the regulations to changes made to section 6050S by the Protecting Americans from Tax Hikes Act of 2015, are proposed (published in the Federal Register on August 2, 2016) (corrected September 26, 2016) (REG-131418-14).

Par. 6. Section 1.6050S-0 is amended by:

1. Revising the entry for § 1.6050S-1(a)(2)(i).
2. Removing the entries for § 1.6050S-1(a)(2)(iii) and (iv).
3. Revising the entries for § 1.6050S-1(b)(2) introductory text and (b)(2)(ii).
4. Revising the entry for § 1.6050S-1(b)(3) introductory text.
5. Removing the entries for § 1.6050S-1(b)(3)(iii), (iv) and (v).
6. Revising the entry for § 1.6050S-1(b)(4).
7. Removing the entry for § 1.6050S-1(b)(5).
8. Redesignating the entry for § 1.6050S-1(b)(6) as § 1.6050S-1(b)(5).
9. Adding entries for § 1.6050S-1(c)(1)(i), (ii) and (iii).
10. Removing the entry for § 1.6050S-1(c)(2)(ii).
11. Redesignating the entry for § 1.6050S-1(c)(2)(iii) as § 1.6050S-1(c)(2)(ii).
12. Redesignating the entries for § 1.6050S-1(e) and § 1.6050S-1(f) as § 1.6050S-1(f) and § 1.6050S-1(g), respectively.
13. Adding a new entry for § 1.6050S-1(e).
14. Revising the newly redesignated entry for § 1.6050S-1(f)(4).
15. Adding a new entry for § 1.6050S-1(f)(5).

The revisions and additions to read as follows:

§ 1.6050S-0. Table of Contents.

* * *

(5) Failure to furnish TIN.

Par. 7. Section 1.6050S-1 is amended by:

1. Revising paragraph (a)(2)(i) and removing paragraphs (a)(2)(iii) and (iv).
2. Revising paragraphs (b)(1), (b)(2)(i), and (b)(2)(ii)(D), (E), (G) and (H).
3. Redesignating paragraphs (b)(2)(ii)(I) and (J) as paragraphs (b)(2)(ii)(J) and (K), respectively, and adding a new paragraph (b)(2)(ii)(I).
4. Revising newly redesignated paragraph (b)(2)(ii)(J).
5. Revising paragraphs (b)(2)(iv), (v), (vi) and *Example 1, 2, 3,* and 4 in paragraph (b)(2)(vii).
6. In paragraph (b)(2)(vii), adding *Example 5* and 6.
7. Removing paragraph (b)(3) and redesignating paragraphs (b)(4), (5) and (6) as paragraphs (b)(3), (4) and (5), respectively.
8. Revising newly redesignated paragraph (b)(4)(i).
9. Removing newly redesignated paragraph (b)(4)(ii) and further redesignating paragraph (b)(4)(iii) as paragraph (b)(4)(ii).
10. Revising paragraphs (c)(1)(iii)(A), (B) and (C).
11. Redesignating paragraphs (c)(1)(iii)(D), (E), (F), and (G) as paragraphs (c)(1)(iii)(E), (F), (G), and (H), respectively.
12. Revising newly re-designated paragraphs (c)(1)(iii)(E), (F), (G), and (H).
13. Adding a new paragraph (c)(1)(iii)(D).
14. Revising paragraph (c)(2)(i).
15. Removing paragraph (c)(2)(ii) and redesignating paragraph (c)(2)(iii) as paragraph (c)(2)(ii).
16. Redesignating paragraphs (e) and (f) as paragraphs (f) and (g), respectively.
17. Adding a new paragraph (e).
18. In newly redesignated paragraph (f):

i. Revising paragraph (f)(3)(ii).
ii. In paragraph (f)(3)(iii), removing the language "(e)(3)(iii)" and adding "(f)(3)(iii)" in its place.
iii. Further redesignating paragraph (f)(4) as paragraph (f)(5).
iv. Adding new paragraph (f)(4).

19. Revising newly redesignated paragraph (g).

The revisions and additions read as follows:

§1.6050S-1. Information reporting for qualified tuition and related expenses.—(a) * * *

(2) * * *

(i) *No reporting of amounts for books, supplies and equipment unless the amount is a fee required to be paid to the institution.*—(A) *In general.*—The information reporting requirements of this section do not apply to amounts paid for books, supplies, and equipment unless the amount is a fee that must be paid to the eligible educational institution as a condition of enrollment or attendance under §1.25A-2(d)(2)(ii).

(B) *Examples.*—The following examples illustrates the rules of this paragraph (a)(2):

Example 1. First-year students at College W are required to obtain books and other materials used in its mandatory first-year curriculum. The books and other materials are not required to be purchased from College W and may be borrowed from other students or purchased from off-campus bookstores, as well as from College W's bookstore. College W bills students for any books and materials purchased from College W's bookstore. Because the first-year books and materials may be purchased from any vendor, the amount is not a fee that must be paid to the eligible educational institution as a condition of enrollment or attendance and, therefore, is not subject to reporting under paragraph (a)(2)(i) of this section. No amount is reportable even if a first-year student pays College W for the required books and other materials purchased from College W's bookstore.

Example 2. Assume the same facts as *Example 1* of this paragraph (a)(2), except College W furnishes the books and other materials to each first-year student and the books may not be borrowed or purchased from other sources. College W charges a separate fee for books and materials to all first-year students for these items as part of the bill required to be paid to attend the institution. Under paragraph (a)(2)(i) of this section, because the amount is a fee that must be paid to the eligible educational institution as a condition of enrollment or attendance, the fee, if paid by or on behalf of the student, must be reported on the Form 1098-T as part of the qualified tuition and related expenses.

* * *

(b) *Requirement to file return.*—(1) *In general.*—Eligible educational institutions must report the information described in paragraph (b)(2) of this section, which requires institutions to report, among other information, the amount of payments received during the calendar year for qualified tuition and related expenses. Institutions must report separately adjustments made during the calendar year that relate to payments received for qualified tuition and related expenses that were reported for a prior calendar year. For purposes of paragraph (b)(2) of this section, an adjustment made to payments received means a reimbursement or refund. Insurers must report the information described in paragraph (b)(3) of this section.

(2) *Information reporting requirements.*—(i) *In general.*—Except as provided in paragraph (a)(2) of this section (regarding exceptions where no information reporting is required), an eligible educational institution must file an information return with the IRS on Form 1098–T, "Tuition Statement," with respect to each individual enrolled (as determined in paragraph (d)(1) of this section) for an academic period beginning during the calendar year (including an academic period beginning during the first three months of the next calendar year) or during a prior calendar year and for whom a transaction described in paragraph (b)(2)(ii)(C), (E), (F), or (G)

of this section is made during the calendar year. An eligible educational institution may use a substitute Form 1098–T if the substitute form complies with applicable revenue procedures relating to substitute forms (see § 601.601(d)(2) of this chapter).

(ii) * * *

(D) An indication by the institution whether any payments received for qualified tuition and related expenses reported for the calendar year relate to an academic period that begins during the first three months of the next calendar year and the amount of such payments;

(E) The amount of any scholarships or grants for the payment of the individual's cost of attendance (as defined in paragraph (e)(2) of this section) that the institution administered and processed (as defined in paragraph (e)(1) of this section) during the calendar year;

* * *

(G) The amount of any reductions to the amount of scholarships or grants for the payment of the individual's cost of attendance (as defined in paragraph (e)(2) of this section) that were reported by the eligible educational institution with respect to the individual for a prior calendar year;

(H) A statement or other indication showing whether the individual was enrolled for at least half of the normal full-time work load for the course of study the individual is pursuing for at least one academic period that begins during the calendar year (see section 25A and the regulations thereunder for more information regarding workload requirements);

(I) A statement or other indication showing the number of months (for this purpose, one day in a month is treated as an entire month) during the calendar year that the individual was enrolled for the normal full-time workload for the course of study the individual is pursuing at the institution;

(J) A statement or other indication showing whether the individual was enrolled in a program leading to a graduate-level degree, graduate-level certificate, or other recognized graduate-level educational credential, unless the student is enrolled in both a graduate-level program and an undergraduate level program during the same calendar year at the same institution in which case no statement or indication is required; and

* * *

(iv) *Separate reporting of reimbursements or refunds of payments of qualified tuition and related expenses that were reported for a prior calendar year.*—An institution must separately report on Form 1098–T any reimbursements or refunds (as defined in paragraph (b)(2)(vi) of this section) made during the current calendar year that relate to payments of qualified tuition and related expenses that were reported by the institution for a prior calendar year. Such reimbursements or refunds are not netted against the payments received for qualified tuition and related expenses during the current calendar year.

(v) *Payments received for qualified tuition and related expenses determined.*—For purposes of determining the amount of payments received for qualified tuition and related expenses during a calendar year, payments received with respect to an individual during the calendar year from any source (except for any scholarship or grant that, by its terms, must be applied to expenses other than qualified tuition and related expenses, such as room and board) are treated first as payments of qualified tuition and related expenses up to the total amount billed by the institution for qualified tuition and related expenses for enrollment during the calendar year, and then as payments of expenses other than qualified tuition and related expenses for enrollment during the calendar year. Payments received with respect to an amount billed for enrollment during an academic period beginning in the first 3 months of the following calendar year in which the payment is made are treated as payment of qualified tuition and related expenses in the calendar year during which the payment is received by the institution. For purposes of this section, a payment includes any positive account balance (such as any reimbursement or refund credited to an individual's account) that an institution applies toward current charges.

(vi) *Reimbursements or refunds of payments for qualified tuition and related expenses determined.*—For purposes of determining the amount of reimbursements or refunds made of payments received for qualified tuition and related expenses, any reimbursement or refund made with respect to an individual during a calendar year (except for any refund of a scholarship or grant that, by its terms, was required to be applied to expenses other than qualified tuition and related expenses, such as room and board) is treated as a reimbursement or refund of payments for qualified tuition and related expenses up to the amount of any reduction in charges for qualified tuition and related expenses. For purposes of this section, a reimbursement or refund includes amounts that an institution credits to an individual's account, as well as amounts disbursed to, or on behalf of, the individual.

(vii) * * *

Example 1. (i) Student A enrolls in University X as a full-time student for the 2016 fall semester. In early August 2016, University X sends a bill to Student A for $16,000 for the 2016 fall semester breaking out the current charges as follows: $10,000 for qualified tuition and related expenses and $6,000 for room and board. In late August 2016, Student A pays $11,000 to University X, leaving a remaining balance to be paid of $5,000. In early September 2016, Student A drops to half-time enrollment for the 2016 fall semester but remains in on-campus housing. In late September 2016, University X credits $5,000 to Student A's account, reflecting a $5,000 reduction in the $10,000 charge for qualified tuition and related expenses as a result of dropping from full-time to half-time status. No other transactions occur with respect to Student A's account with University X. In late September 2016, University X applies the $5,000 credit toward Student A's current charges, eliminating any outstanding balance on Student A's account with University X.

(ii) Under paragraph (b)(2)(v) of this section, the $11,000 payment is treated as a payment of qualified tuition and related expenses up to the $10,000 billed for qualified tuition and related expenses. Under paragraph (b)(2)(vi) of this section, the $5,000 credited to the student's account is treated as a reimbursement or refund of payments for qualified tuition and related expenses because there is a reduction in charges for qualified tuition and related expenses equal to the $5,000 credit due to Student A dropping to half-time for the 2016 fall semester. Under paragraph (b)(2)(iii) of this section, the $10,000 payment received for qualified tuition and related expenses during 2016 is reduced by the $5,000 reimbursement or refund of payments received for qualified tuition and related expenses during 2016. Therefore, University X is required to report $5,000 of payments received for qualified tuition and related expenses during 2016 on a 2016 Form 1098-T.

Example 2. (i) The facts are the same as in *Example 1* of this paragraph (b)(2)(vii), except that Student A pays the full $16,000 in late August 2016. In late September 2016, University X reduces the tuition charges by $5,000 and issues a $5,000 refund to Student A.

(ii) Under paragraph (b)(2)(v) of this section, the $16,000 payment is treated as a payment of qualified tuition and related expenses up to the $10,000 billed for qualified tuition and related expenses. Under paragraph (b)(2)(vi) of this section, the $5,000 refund is treated as reimbursement or refund of payments for qualified tuition and related expenses because University X reduced the charges for qualified tuition and related expenses equal to the $5,000 refund disbursed to the student due to dropping to half-time for the 2016 fall semester. Under paragraph (b)(2)(iii) of this section, the $10,000 payment received for qualified tuition and related expenses during 2016 is reduced by the $5,000 reimbursement or refund of payments received for qualified tuition and related expenses during 2016. Therefore, University X is required to report $5,000 of payments received for qualified tuition and related expenses during 2016 on a 2016 Form 1098-T.

Example 3. (i) The facts are the same as in *Example 1* of this paragraph (b)(2)(vii), except that Student A is enrolled full-time, and, in early September 2016, Student A decides to live at home with her parents. In late September 2016, University X adjusts Student A's account to eliminate room and board charges and issues a $1,000 refund to Student A.

(ii) Under paragraph (b)(2)(v) of this section, the $11,000 payment is treated as a payment of qualified tuition and related expenses up to the $10,000 billed for qualified tuition and related expenses. Under paragraph (b)(2)(vi) of this section, the $1,000 refund is not treated as reimbursement or refund of payments for qualified tuition and related expenses because University X has reduced room and board charges for the 2016 fall semester, rather than reducing charges for qualified tuition and related expenses for the 2016 fall semester. Therefore, under paragraph (b)(2)(iii) of this section, University X is required to report $10,000 of payments received for qualified tuition and related expenses during 2016 on a 2016 Form 1098-T.

Example 4. (i) Student B enrolls in College Y as a full-time student for the 2017 spring semester. In early December 2016, College Y sends a bill to Student B for $16,000 for the 2017 spring semester breaking out current charges as follows: $10,000 for qualified tuition and related expenses and $6,000 for room and board. In late December 2016, College Y receives a payment of $16,000 from Student B. In mid-January 2017, after the 2017 spring semester classes begin, Student B drops to halftime enrollment. In mid-January 2017, College Y credits Student B's account with $5,000, reflecting a $5,000 reduction in charges for qualified tuition and related expenses, but does not issue a refund to Student B. Thereafter, Student B's account reflects a positive balance of $5,000 due to the credit and there is no other activity on Student B's account until early August when College Y sends a bill for $16,000 for the 2017 fall semester breaking out the current charges as follows: $10,000 for qualified tuition and related expenses and $6,000 for room and board. In early September 2017, College Y applies the $5,000 positive account balance (credit) toward Student B's $16,000 bill for the 2017 fall semester. In late September 2017, Student B pays $6,000 towards the charges for the 2017 fall semester.

(ii) For calendar year 2016, under paragraph (b)(2)(v) of this section, $10,000 of the $16,000 payment received by College Y in December 2016 is treated as a payment of qualified tuition and related expenses. Therefore, College Y is required to report $10,000 of payments received for qualified tuition and related expenses during 2016 on a 2016 Form 1098-T. In addition, College Y is required to indicate that $10,000 of the payments reported on the 2016 Form 1098-T relate to an academic period that begins during the first three months of the next calendar year.

(iii) Under paragraph (b)(2)(vi) of this section, the $5,000 credited to Student B's account in January 2017 is treated as a reimbursement or refund of qualified tuition and related expenses because there is a reduction in charges for qualified tuition and related expenses of $5,000 for the 2017 spring semester. Under paragraph (b)(2)(iv) of this section, however, this reduction is a reimbursement or refund of qualified tuition and related expenses made during 2017 and, therefore, must be separately reported on the 2017 Form 1098–T. The 2016 Form 1098-T reporting $10,000 of qualified tuition and related expenses for 2016 is unchanged.

(iv) Under paragraph (b)(2)(v) of this section, the $5,000 positive account balance that is applied toward charges for the 2017 fall semester is treated as a payment made in 2017. Therefore, College Y received total payments of $11,000 during 2017 (the $5,000 credit plus the $6,000 payment). Under paragraph (b)(2)(v) of this section, the $11,000 of total payments made during 2017 are treated as a payment of qualified tuition and related expenses up to the $10,000 billed for qualified tuition and related expenses for the 2017 fall semester. Therefore, for 2017, College Y is required to report $10,000 of payments received for qualified tuition and related expenses during 2017 and a $5,000 refund of payments of qualified tuition and related expenses reported for 2016 on the 2017 Form 1098-T.

Example 5. (i) Student C enrolls in College Z as a full-time student for the 2016 fall semester and the 2017 spring semester. Student C was not enrolled in, and did not attend, any institution of higher education prior to the 2016 fall semester. In August 2016, College Z sends a bill to Student C for $11,000 for the 2016 fall semester. In December 2016, College Z sends a bill to Student C for $11,000 for the 2017 spring semester. Qualified tuition and related expenses billed for each semester is $6,000 and room and board billed for each semester is $5,000. In September 2016, College Z receives a payment of $11,000 which is applied toward the amount billed for Student C's attendance during the 2016 fall semester. In December 2016, College Z receives a payment of $4,500 which is applied toward the amount billed for Student C's attendance during the 2017 spring semester. In February 2017, College Z receives a payment of $6,500, the remainder of the amount billed for enrollment during the 2017 spring semester.

(ii) On the 2016 Form 1098-T, College Z reports the payment of $10,500 of qualified tuition and related expenses determined as follows: $6,000 for the payment received in September 2016 with respect to the amount billed for qualified tuition and related expenses for the 2016 fall semester and $4,500 for the payment received in December 2016 with respect to the amount billed for qualified tuition and related expenses for the 2017 spring semester. On the 2017 Form 1098-T, College Z reports the payment of $1,500 of qualified tuition and related expenses received in February 2017 with respect to the amount billed for qualified tuition and related expenses for the 2017 spring semester.

Example 6. The facts are the same as *Example 5* of this paragraph (b)(2)(vii) except in January 2017 College Z receives payment of $11,000 for the entire amount billed for the 2017 spring semester. On the 2016 Form 1098-T, College Z reports the payment of $6,000 for the payment received in September 2016 with respect to the amount billed for qualified tuition and related expenses for the 2016 fall semester. On the 2017 Form 1098-T, College Z reports the payment of $6,000 of qualified tuition and related expenses received in January 2017 with respect to the amount billed for qualified tuition and related expenses for the 2017 spring semester.

* * *

(4) *Time and place for filing return.*—(i) *In general.*—Except as provided in paragraph (b)(4)(ii) of this section, Form 1098-T must be filed on or before February 28 (March 31 if filed electronically) of the year following the calendar year in which payments were received for qualified tuition or related expenses, or reimbursements, refunds, or reductions of such amounts were made. An institution or insurer must file Form 1098-T with the IRS according to the instructions for Form 1098-T.

* * *

(c) * * *

(1) * * *

(iii) * * *

(A) State that the statement reports total payments received by the institution for qualified tuition and related expenses during the calendar year, or the total reimbursements or refunds made by the insurer;

(B) State that, under section 25A and the regulations thereunder, the taxpayer may claim an education tax credit only with respect to qualified tuition and related expenses actually paid during the calendar year; and that the taxpayer may not be able to claim an education tax credit with respect to the entire amount of payments received for qualified tuition and related expenses reported on the Form 1098-T for the calendar year;

(C) State that the amount of any scholarships or grants reported on the Form 1098-T for the calendar year and other similar amounts not reported on the Form 1098-T (because they are not administered and processed by the eligible educational institution as defined in paragraph (e)(1) of this section) that are allocated by the student to pay qualified tuition and related expenses may reduce the amount of any allowable education tax credit for the taxable year;

(D) State that even if the eligible educational institution applies scholarships or grants reported on the Form 1098-T for the calendar year to qualified tuition and related expenses, the student may, for tax purposes, be able to allocate all or a portion of the scholarships or grants to expenses other than qualified tuition and related expenses (and, therefore, forego having to reduce the amount of the education tax credit the student may claim) if the terms of the scholarship or grant permit it to be used for expenses other than qualified tuition and related expenses and the student includes the amount in income on his federal income tax return.

* * *

(E) State that the amount of any reimbursements or refunds of payments received, or reductions in charges, for qualified tuition and related expenses, or any reductions to the amount of scholarships or grants, reported by the eligible educational institution with respect to the individual for a prior calendar year on Form 1098-T may affect the amount of any allowable education tax credit for the prior calendar year (and may result in an increase in tax liability for the year of the refund);

(F) State that the amount of any reimbursements or refunds of qualified tuition and related expenses reported on a Form 1098-T by an eligible educational institution or insurer may reduce the amount of an allowable education tax credit for a taxable year (and may result in an increase in tax liability for the year of the refund);

(G) State that the taxpayer should refer to relevant IRS forms and publications, such as Publication 970, "Tax Benefits for Education," and should not refer to the institution or the insurer, for explanations relating to the eligibility requirements for, and calculation of, any allowable education tax credit; and

(H) Include the name, address, and phone number of the information contact of the eligible educational institution or insurer that filed the Form 1098–T.

(2) *Time and manner for furnishing statement.*—(i) *In general.*—Except as provided in paragraph (c)(2)(ii) of this section, an institution or insurer must furnish the statement described in paragraph (c)(1) of this section to each individual for whom it is required to file a return, on or before January 31 of the year following the calendar year in which payments were received for qualified tuition and related expenses, or reimbursements, refunds or reductions of such amounts were made. If mailed, the statement must be sent to the individual's permanent address or the individual's temporary address if the institution or insurer does not know the individual's permanent address. If furnished electronically, the statement must be furnished in accordance with applicable regulations.

* * *

(e) *Definitions.*—The following definitions apply with respect to this section:

(1) *Administered and processed.*—(i) *In general.*—A scholarship or grant is "administered and processed" by an eligible educational institution if the institution receives payment of an amount (whether by cash, check, or other means of payment) that the institution knows or reasonably should know, is a scholarship or grant, regardless of whether the institution is named payee or co-payee of such amount and regardless of whether, in the case of a payment other than in cash, the student endorses the check or other means of payment for the benefit of the institution. For instance, Pell Grants, described in the Higher Education Act of 1965 (20 U.S.C. 1070), as amended, are administered and processed by an institution in all cases.

(ii) *Examples.*—The following examples illustrate the definition in this paragraph (e)(1):

Example 1. University M received a Pell Grant on behalf of Student B, a student enrolled in a degree program at University M. University M provides all required notifications to and obtains all the necessary paperwork from Student B and applies the Pell Grant to Student B's account. Because University M received the Pell Grant and University M knows or should know that the Pell Grant is a scholarship or grant, under paragraph (e)(1)(i) of this section, the Pell Grant is administered and processed by University M.

Example 2. University N receives a check from Organization Y made out to Student C. University N is not named as a payee on the check. The cover letter accompanying the check provides University N with sufficient information to reasonably know that the check represents payment of a scholarship that may be used to pay Student C's qualified tuition and related expenses. Under paragraph (e)(1)(i) of this section, the scholarship from Organization Y is administered and processed by University N. This is the case even though University N is not named on the check as a payee and regardless of whether Student C endorses the check over to University N.

(2) *Cost of attendance.*—The term "cost of attendance" has the same meaning as section 472 of the Higher Education Act of 1965, 20 U.S.C. 1087ll.

(f) * * *

(3) * * *

(ii) *Acting in a responsible manner.*—An institution or insurer must request the TIN of each individual for whom it is required to file a return if it does not already have a record of the individual's correct TIN. If the institution or insurer does not have a record of the individual's correct TIN, then it must solicit the TIN in the manner described in paragraph (f)(3)(iii) of this section on or before December 31 of each year during which it receives payments of qualified tuition and related expenses or makes reimbursements, refunds, or reductions of such amounts with respect to the individual. If an individual refuses to provide his or her TIN upon request, the institution or insurer must file the return and furnish the statement required by this section without the individual's TIN, but with all other required information. The specific solicitation requirements of paragraph (f)(3)(iii) of this section apply in lieu of the solicitation requirements of § 301.6724-1(e) and (f) of this chapter for the purpose of determining whether an institution or insurer acted in a responsible manner in attempting to obtain a correct TIN. An institution or insurer that complies with the requirements of this paragraph (f)(3) will be considered to have acted in a responsible manner within the meaning of § 301.6724-1(d) of this chapter with respect to any failure to include the correct TIN of an individual on a return or statement required by section 6050S and this section.

* * *

(4) *No penalty imposed on eligible educational institutions that certify compliance with paragraph (f)(3) of this section at the time of filing the return.*—In the case of returns required to be filed and statements required to be furnished after December 31, 2015, the IRS will not impose a penalty against an eligible educational institution under section 6721 or 6722 for failure to include the individual's correct TIN on the return or statement if the institution makes a true and accurate certification to the IRS under penalties of perjury (in the form and manner prescribed by the Secretary in publications, forms and instructions, or other published guidance) at the time of filing of the return that the institution complied with the requirements in paragraphs (f)(3)(ii) and (iii) of this section. Nothing in this paragraph (f)(4) prevents the IRS from imposing a penalty under section 6721 or 6722 if after the IRS receives the certification described in this paragraph (f)(4) the IRS determines that the requirements of paragraph (f)(3) of this section are not satisfied or the failure is unrelated to an incorrect or missing TIN for the individual for whom the institution is required to file a return or statement.

* * *

(g) *Applicability date.*—The rules in this section apply to information returns required to be filed, and statements required to be furnished, after December 31, 2003, except that paragraphs (a)(2), (b)(1), (b)(2)(i), (b)(2)(ii)(D), (E), and (G) through (K), (b)(2)(iv) through (vii), (b)(4)(i) and (ii), (c)(1)(iii)(B) through (H), (e), and (f)(4) apply to information returns required to be filed, and statements required to be furnished, after the date of publication of the Treasury decision adopting these rules as final regulations in the **Federal Register**. For information returns required to be filed, and statements required to be furnished, on or before the date of publication of the Treasury decision adopting these rules as final regulations in the **Federal Register**, § 1.6050S-1 (as contained in 26 CFR part 1, revised April 2014) applies.

Life Insurance Contracts: Information Reporting

Life Insurance Contracts: Information Reporting.—Reg. §§ 1.6050Y-1—1.6050Y-4, providing guidance on new information reporting obligations under section 6050Y related to reportable policy sales of life insurance contracts and payments of reportable death benefits, are proposed (published in the Federal Register on March 25, 2019) (REG-103083-18).

Par. 4. Section 1.6050Y-1 is added to read as follows:

§1.6050Y-1. Information reporting for reportable policy sales, transfers of life insurance contracts to foreign persons, and reportable death benefits.—(a) *Definitions.*—The following definitions apply for purposes of this section and §§1.6050Y-2 through 1.6050Y-4:

(1) *Acquirer.*—The term *acquirer* means any person that acquires an interest in a life insurance contract (through a direct acquisition or indirect acquisition of the interest) in a reportable policy sale.

(2) *Buyer.*—The term *buyer* means, with respect to any interest in a life insurance contract that has been transferred in a reportable policy sale, the person that was the most recent acquirer of that interest in a reportable policy sale as of the date reportable death benefits are paid under the contract.

(3) *Direct acquisition of an interest in a life insurance contract.*—The term *direct acquisition of an interest in a life insurance contract* has the meaning given to it in §1.101-1(e)(3)(i).

(4) *Foreign person.*—The term *foreign person* means a person that is not a United States person, as defined in section 7701(a)(30).

(5) *Indirect acquisition of an interest in a life insurance contract.*—The term *indirect acquisition of an interest in a life insurance contract* has the meaning given to it in §1.101-1(e)(3)(ii).

(6) *Interest in a life insurance contract.*—The term *interest in a life insurance contract* has the meaning given to it in §1.101-1(e)(1).

(7) *Investment in the contract.*—(i) *Definition of investment in the contract.*—With respect to the original policyholder of a life insurance contract, the term *investment in the contract* on any date means that person's investment in the contract under section 72(e)(6) on that date. With respect to any other person, the term *investment in the contract* on any date means the *estimate of investment in the contract* on that date.

(ii) *Definition of estimate of investment in the contract.*—The term *estimate of investment in the contract* with respect to any person, other than the original policyholder, means, on any date, the aggregate amount of premiums paid for the contract by that person before that date, less the aggregate amount received under the contract by that person before that date to the extent such information is known to or can reasonably be estimated by the issuer or payor.

(8) *Issuer.*—(i) *In general.*—Except as provided in paragraphs (a)(8)(ii) and (iii) of this section, the term *issuer* generally means, on any date, with respect to any interest in a life insurance contract, any person that bears any part of the risk with respect to the life insurance contract on that date and any person responsible on that date for administering the contract, including collecting premiums and paying death benefits. For instance, if a reinsurer reinsures on an indemnity basis all or a portion of the risks that the original issuer (and continuing contract administrator) might otherwise have incurred with respect to a life insurance contract, both the reinsurer and the original issuer of the contract are issuers of the life insurance contract for purposes of this paragraph (a)(8)(i). Any designee of an issuer is also considered an issuer for purposes of this paragraph (a)(8)(i).

(ii) *6050Y(a) issuer.*—For purposes of information reporting under section 6050Y(a) and §1.6050Y-2, the 6050Y(a) issuer is the issuer that is responsible for administering the life insurance contract, including collecting premiums and paying death benefits under the contract, on the date of the reportable policy sale.

(iii) *6050Y(b) issuer.*—For purposes of information reporting under section 6050Y(b) and §1.6050Y-3, a 6050Y(b) issuer is:

(A) Any person that receives a RPSS with respect to a life insurance contract or interest therein (or, in the case of a designee, receives notice that the issuer for whom it serves as designee received a RPSS), and is or was, on or before the date of receipt of the RPSS, an issuer with respect to the life insurance contract; or

(B) Any person that receives notice of a transfer to a foreign person of the life insurance contract and is or was, on the date of transfer or on the date of receipt of the notice, an issuer with respect to the life insurance contract, unless:

(1) That person (or, in the case of a designee, the issuer for whom it serves as designee) is not responsible for administering the life insurance contract, including collecting premiums and paying death benefits under the contract, on the date the notice of a transfer to a foreign person of a life insurance contract is received; and

(2) That person, or its designee, provides the issuer that is responsible on that date for administering the life insurance contract, including collecting premiums and paying death benefits under the contract, with such notice and with any available information necessary to accomplish reporting under section 6050Y(b) and §1.6050Y-3.

(iv) *Designee.*—A person is treated as the designee of an issuer for purposes of this paragraph (a)(8) only if so designated in writing, including electronically. The designation must be signed and acknowledged, in writing or electronically, by the person named as designee, or that person's representative, and by the issuer making the designation, or its representative.

(9) *Life insurance contract.*—The term *life insurance contract* has the meaning given to it in section 7702(a). A life insurance contract may also be referred to as a life insurance policy.

(10) *Notice of a transfer to a foreign person.*—The term *notice of a transfer to a foreign person* means any notice of a transfer of title to, possession of, or legal ownership of a life insurance contract received by a 6050Y(b) issuer, including information provided for nontax purposes such as a change of address notice for purposes of sending statements or for other purposes, and information relating to loans, premiums, or death benefits with respect to the contract unless the 6050Y(b) issuer knows that no transfer of the life insurance contract has occurred or knows that the transferee is a United States person. For this purpose, a 6050Y(b) issuer may rely on a Form W-9, Request for Taxpayer Identification Number and Certification, or a valid substitute form, that meets the requirements of §1.1441-1(d)(2) (substituting "6050Y(b) issuer" for "withholding agent"), that indicates the transferee is a United States person. For in-

stance, a change of address notice that changes the address to a foreign address or other updates to the information relating to the payment of premiums that includes foreign banking or other foreign financial institution information is notice of a transfer to a foreign person unless the 6050Y(b) issuer knows that no transfer has occurred or the transferee is a United States person.

(11) *Payor*.—The term *payor* means any person making a payment of reportable death benefits.

(12) *Reportable death benefits*.—The term *reportable death benefits* means amounts paid by reason of the death of the insured under a life insurance contract that are attributable to an interest in the life insurance contract that was transferred in a reportable policy sale.

(13) *Reportable death benefits payment recipient*.—The term *reportable death benefits payment recipient* means any person that receives reportable death benefits as a beneficiary under a life insurance contract or as the holder of an interest in a life insurance contract.

(14) *Reportable policy sale*.—The term *reportable policy sale* has the meaning given to it in §1.101-1(c).

(15) *Reportable policy sale payment*.—The term *reportable policy sale payment* generally means the total amount of cash and the fair market value of any other consideration transferred, or to be transferred, in a reportable policy sale, including any amount of a reportable policy sale payment recipient's debt assumed by the acquirer in a reportable policy sale. In the case of an indirect acquisition of an interest in a life insurance contract that is a reportable policy sale, the reportable policy sale payment is the amount of cash and the fair market value of any other consideration transferred for the ownership interest in the entity, including the amount of any debt assumed by the acquirer, that is appropriately allocable to the interest in the life insurance contract held by the entity.

(16) *Reportable policy sale payment recipient*.—The term *reportable policy sale payment recipient* means any person that receives a reportable policy sale payment in a reportable policy sale. A broker or other intermediary that retains a portion of the cash or other consideration transferred in a reportable policy sale is also a reportable policy sale payment recipient.

(17) *Reportable policy sale statement*.—The term *reportable policy sale statement (RPSS)* means a statement furnished by an acquirer to an issuer under section 6050Y(a)(2) and §1.6050Y-2(d)(2)(i).

(18) *Seller*.—The term *seller* means any person that—

(i) Holds an interest in a life insurance contract and transfers that interest, or any part of that interest, to an acquirer in a reportable policy sale; or

(ii) Owns a life insurance contract and transfers title to, possession of, or legal ownership of that life insurance contract to a foreign person.

(19) *Transfer of an interest in a life insurance contract*.—The term *transfer of an interest in a life insurance contract* has the meaning given to it in §1.101-1(e)(2).

(20) *United States person*.—The term *United States person* has the meaning given to it in section 7701(a)(30).

(b) *Applicability date*.—This section and §§1.6050Y-2 through 1.6050Y-3 apply to reportable policy sales made after December 31, 2017. This section and §1.6050Y-4 apply to reportable death benefits paid after December 31, 2017. However, for reportable policy sales and payments of reportable death benefits occurring after December 31, 2017, and before the date final regulations are published in the **Federal Register**, transition relief will be provided as follows:

(1) For reportable policy sales occurring after December 31, 2017, and before the date final regulations are published in the **Federal Register**, statements required to be furnished to issuers under section 6050Y(a)(2) and §1.6050Y-2 must be furnished by the later of the applicable deadline set forth in final regulations or 60 days after the date final regulations are published in the **Federal Register**.

(2) For reportable policy sales occurring after December 31, 2017, and before the date final regulations are published in the **Federal Register**, returns required to be filed under section 6050Y(a)(1) and (b)(1), §1.6050Y-2, and §1.6050Y-3 and statements required to be furnished to payment recipients and sellers under section 6050Y(a)(2) and (b)(2), §1.6050Y-2, and §1.6050Y-3 must be filed or furnished by the later of the applicable deadline set forth in final regulations or 90 days after the date final regulations are published in the **Federal Register**.

(3) For payments of reportable death benefits paid after December 31, 2017, and before the date final regulations are published in the **Federal Register**, returns required to be filed under section 6050Y(c)(1) and §1.6050Y-4 and statements required to be furnished to payment recipients under section 6050Y(c)(2) and §1.6050Y-4 must be filed or furnished by the later of the applicable deadline set forth in final regulations or 90 days after the date final regulations are published in the **Federal Register**. [Reg. §1.6050Y-1.]

Par. 5. Section 1.6050Y-2 is added to read as follows:

§1.6050Y-2. Information reporting by acquirers for reportable policy sale payments.—(a) *Requirement of reporting*.—Except as provided in paragraph (f) of this section, every person that is an acquirer in a reportable policy sale during any calendar year must file a separate information return with the Internal Revenue Service (IRS) in the form and manner as required by the IRS for each reportable policy sale payment recipient, including any seller that is a reportable policy sale payment recipient. Each return must include the following information with respect to the seller or other reportable policy sale payment recipient to which the return relates:

(1) The name, address, and taxpayer identification number (TIN) of the acquirer;

(2) The name, address, and TIN of the seller or other reportable policy sale payment recipient to which the return relates;

(3) The date of the reportable policy sale;

(4) The name of the 6050Y(a) issuer of the life insurance contract acquired and the policy number of the life insurance contract;

(5) The aggregate amount of reportable policy sale payments made, or to be made, to the seller or other reportable policy sale payment recipient to which the return relates with respect to the reportable policy sale; and

(6) Any other information that is required by the form or its instructions.

(b) *Unified reporting.*—The information reporting requirement of paragraph (a) of this section applies to each acquirer in a series of prearranged transfers of an interest in a life insurance contract. In a series of prearranged transfers, an acquirer's reporting obligation is deemed satisfied if the information required by paragraph (a) of this section with respect to that acquirer is timely reported on behalf of that acquirer in a manner that is consistent with forms, instructions, and other IRS guidance by one or more other acquirers or by a third party information reporting contractor.

(c) *Time and place for filing.*—Returns required to be made under paragraph (a) of this section must be filed with the Internal Revenue Service Center designated on the prescribed form or in its instructions on or before February 28 (March 31 if filed electronically) of the year following the calendar year in which the reportable policy sale occurred. However, see §1.6050Y-1(b)(2) for transition rules.

(d) *Requirement of and time for furnishing statements.*—(1) *Statements to reportable policy sale payment recipients.*—(i) *Requirement of furnishing statement.*—Every person required to file an information return under paragraph (a) of this section with respect to a reportable policy sale payment recipient must furnish in the form and manner prescribed by the IRS to the reportable policy sale payment recipient whose name is set forth in that return a written statement showing the information required by paragraph (a) of this section with respect to the reportable policy sale payment recipient and the name, address, and phone number of the information contact of the person furnishing the written statement. The contact information of the person furnishing the written statement must provide direct access to a person that can answer questions about the statement. The statement is not required to include information with respect to any other reportable policy sale payment recipient in the reportable policy sale or information about reportable policy sale payments to any other reportable policy sale payment recipient.

(ii) *Time for furnishing statement.*—Each statement required by paragraph (d)(1)(i) of this section to be furnished to any reportable policy sale payment recipient must be furnished on or before February 15 of the year following the calendar year in which the reportable policy sale occurred. However, see §1.6050Y-1(b)(2) for transition rules.

(2) *Statements to 6050Y(a) issuers.*—(i) *Requirement of furnishing RPSS.*—(A) *In general.*—Except as provided in paragraph (d)(2)(i)(B) of this section, every person required to file a return under paragraph (a) of this section must furnish in the form and manner prescribed by the IRS to the 6050Y(a) issuer whose name is required to be set forth in the return a RPSS with respect to each reportable policy sale payment recipient that is also a seller. Each RPSS must show the information required by paragraph (a) of this section with respect to the seller named therein, except that the RPSS is not required to set forth the amount of any reportable policy sale payment. Each RPSS must also show the name, address, and phone number of the information contact of the person furnishing the RPSS. This contact information must provide direct access to a person that can answer questions about the RPSS.

(B) *Exception from reporting.*—A RPSS is not required to be furnished to the 6050Y(a) issuer by an acquirer acquiring an interest in a life insurance contract in an indirect acquisition.

(ii) *Time for furnishing RPSS.*—Except as otherwise provided in this paragraph (d)(2)(ii), each RPSS required by paragraph (d)(2)(i) of this section to be furnished to a 6050Y(a) issuer must be furnished by the later of 20 calendar days after the reportable policy sale, or 5 calendar days after the end of the applicable state law rescission period. However, if the later date is after January 15 of the year following the calendar year in which the reportable policy sale occurred, the RPSS must be furnished by January 15 of the year following the calendar year in which the reportable policy sale occurred. See §1.6050Y-1(b)(1) for transition rules.

(3) *Unified reporting.*—The information reporting requirements of paragraphs (d)(1)(i) and (d)(2)(i) of this section apply to each acquirer in a series of prearranged transfers of an interest in a life insurance contract, as described in paragraph (b) of this section. In a series of prearranged transfers of an interest in a life insurance contract, an acquirer's obligation to furnish statements is deemed satisfied if the information required by paragraphs (d)(1)(i) and (d)(2)(i) of this section with respect to that acquirer is timely reported on behalf of that acquirer consistent with forms, instructions, and other IRS guidance by one or more other acquirers or by a third party information reporting contractor.

(e) *Notice of rescission of a reportable policy sale.*—Any person that has filed a return required by section 6050Y(a)(1) and this section with respect to a reportable policy sale must file a corrected return within 15 calendar days of the receipt of notice of the rescission of the reportable policy sale. Any person that has furnished a written statement under section 6050Y(a)(2) and this section with respect to the reportable policy sale must furnish the recipient of that statement with a corrected statement within 15 calendar days of the receipt of notice of the rescission of the reportable policy sale.

(f) *Exceptions to requirement to file.*—An acquirer that is a foreign person is not required to file an information return under paragraph (a) of this section with respect to a reportable policy sale unless—

(1) The life insurance contract (or interest therein) transferred in the sale is on the life of an insured who is a United States person at the time of the sale; or

(2) The sale is subject to the laws of one or more States of the United States that pertain to acquisitions or sales of life insurance contracts (or interests therein).

(g) *Cross-reference to penalty provisions.*—(1) *Failure to file correct information return.*—For provisions relating to the penalty provided for failure to file timely a correct information return required under section 6050Y(a)(1) and this section, see section 6721 and §301.6721-1 of this chapter. See §301.6724-1 of this chapter for the waiver of a penalty if the failure is due to reasonable cause and is not due to willful neglect.

(2) *Failure to furnish correct statement.*—For provisions relating to the penalty provided for failure to furnish a correct statement to identified persons under section 6050Y(a)(2) and this section, see section 6722 and §301.6722-2 of this chapter. See §301.6724-1 of this chapter for the waiver of a penalty if the failure is due to reasonable cause and is not due to willful neglect. [Reg. §1.6050Y-2.]

Par. 6. Section 1.6050Y-3 is added to read as follows:

§1.6050Y-3. Information reporting by 6050Y(b) issuers for reportable policy sales and transfers of life insurance contracts to foreign persons.—(a) *Requirement of reporting.*—Except as provided in paragraph (f) of this section, each 6050Y(b) issuer, that receives a RPSS or any notice of a transfer to a foreign person must file an information return with the Internal Revenue Service (IRS) with respect to each seller in the form and manner prescribed by the IRS. The return must include the following information with respect to the seller:

(1) The name, address, and taxpayer identification number (TIN) of the seller;

(2) The investment in the contract with respect to the seller;

(3) The amount the seller would have received if the seller had surrendered the life insurance contract on the date of the reportable policy sale or the transfer of the contract to a foreign person, or if the date of the transfer to a foreign person is not known to the 6050Y(b) issuer, the date the 6050Y(b) issuer received notice of the transfer; and

(4) Any other information that is required by the form or its instructions.

(b) *Unified reporting.*—Each 6050Y(b) issuer subject to the information reporting requirement of paragraph (a) of this section must satisfy that requirement, but a 6050Y(b) issuer's reporting obligation is deemed satisfied if the information required by paragraph (a) of this section with respect to that 6050Y(b) issuer is timely reported on behalf of that 6050Y(b) issuer in a manner that is consistent with forms, instructions, and other IRS guidance by one or more other 6050Y(b) issuers or by a third party information reporting contractor.

(c) *Time and place for filing.*—Except as otherwise provided in this paragraph (c), returns required to be made under paragraph (a) of this section must be filed with the Internal Revenue Service Center designated on the prescribed form or in its instructions on or before February 28 (March 31 if filed electronically) of the year following the calendar year in which the reportable policy sale or the transfer of the contract to a foreign person occurred. If the 6050Y(b) issuer does not receive notice of a transfer to a foreign person until after January 31 of the calendar year following the year in which the transfer occurred, returns required to be made under paragraph (a) of this section must be filed by the later of February 28 (March 31 if filed electronically) of the calendar year following the year in which the transfer occurred or thirty days after the date notice is received. See §1.6050Y-1(b)(2) for transition rules.

(d) *Requirement of and time for furnishing statements.*—(1) *Requirement of furnishing statement.*—Every 6050Y(b) issuer filing a return required by paragraph (a) of this section must furnish to each seller that is a reportable policy sale payment recipient or makes a transfer to a foreign person and whose name is required to be set forth in the return a written statement showing the information required by paragraph (a) of this section with respect to that seller and the name, address, and phone number of the information contact of the person filing the return. This contact information must provide direct access to a person that can answer questions about the statement.

(2) *Time for furnishing statement.*—Except as otherwise provided in this paragraph (d)(2), each statement required by paragraph (d)(1) of this section to be furnished to any seller must be furnished on or before February 15 of the year following the calendar year in which the reportable policy sale or transfer to a foreign person occurred. If a 6050Y(b) issuer does not receive notice of a transfer to a foreign person until after January 31 of the calendar year following the year in which the transfer occurred, each statement required to be made under paragraph (d) of this section must be furnished by the date thirty days after the date notice is received. See §1.6050Y-1(b)(2) for transition rules.

(3) *Unified reporting.*—Each 6050Y(b) issuer subject to the information reporting requirement of paragraph (d)(1) of this section must satisfy that requirement, but a 6050Y(b) issuer's reporting obligation is deemed satisfied if the information required by paragraph (d)(1) of this section with respect to that 6050Y(b) issuer is timely reported on behalf of that 6050Y(b) issuer consistent with forms, instructions, and other IRS guidance by one or more other 6050Y(b) issuers or by a third party information reporting contractor.

(e) *Notice of rescission of a reportable policy sale or transfer of an insurance contract to a foreign person.*—Any 6050Y(b) issuer that has filed a return required by section 6050Y(b)(1) and this section with respect to a reportable policy sale or transfer of an insurance contract to a foreign person must file a corrected return within 15 calendar days of the receipt of notice of the rescission of the reportable policy sale or transfer of the insurance contract to a foreign person. Any 6050Y(b) issuer that has furnished a written statement under section 6050Y(b)(2) and this section with respect to the reportable policy sale or transfer of the insurance contract to a foreign person must furnish the recipient of that statement with a corrected statement within 15 calendar days of the receipt of notice of the rescission of the reportable policy sale or transfer of the insurance contract to a foreign person.

(f) *Exceptions to requirement to file.*—A 6050Y(b) issuer is not required to file an information return under paragraph (a) of this section when either paragraph (f)(1) or (2) of this section applies.

(1) Except as otherwise provided in this paragraph (f)(1), the 6050Y(b) issuer obtains documentation upon which it may rely to treat a seller of the contract as a foreign beneficial owner in accordance with §1.1441-1(e)(1)(ii), applying in such case the provisions of §1.1441-1 by substituting the term "6050Y(b) issuer" for the term "withholding agent" and without regard to the fact that that these provisions apply only to amounts subject to withholding under chapter 3 of subtitle A of the Internal Revenue Code. A 6050Y(b) issuer may also obtain from a seller that is a partnership or trust, in addition to documentation establishing the entity's foreign status, a written certification from the entity that no beneficial owner of any portion of the proceeds of the sale is a United States person. In such a case, the issuer may rely upon the written certification to treat the partnership or trust as a foreign beneficial owner for purposes of this paragraph (f)(1) provided that the seller does not have actual knowledge that a United States person is the beneficial owner of all or a portion of the proceeds of the sale. See §1.1441-1(c)(6)(ii) for the definition of beneficial owner that applies for purposes of this paragraph (f)(1). Additionally, for certifying its status as a foreign beneficial owner (as applicable) for purposes of this paragraph (f)(1), a seller that is required to report any of the income from the sale as effectively connected with the conduct of a trade or business in the United States under section 864(b) is required to provide to the 6050Y(b) issuer a Form W-8ECI, Certificate of Foreign Person's Claim that Income is Effectively Connected with the Conduct of a Trade or Business in the United States. If a 6050Y(b) issuer obtains a Form W-8ECI from a seller with respect to the sale or has reason to know that income from the sale is effectively connected with the conduct of a trade or business in the United States under section 864(b), the exception to reporting described in this paragraph (f)(1) does not apply.

(2) The 6050Y(b) issuer receives notice of a transfer to a foreign person, but does not receive a RPSS with respect to the transfer, provided that, at the time the notice is received—

(i) The 6050Y(b) issuer is not a United States person;

(ii) The life insurance contract (or interest therein) transferred is not on the life of a United States person; and

(iii) The 6050Y(b) issuer has not classified the seller as a United States person in its books and records.

(g) *Cross-reference to penalty provisions.*—(1) *Failure to file correct information return.*—For provisions relating to the penalty provided for failure to file timely a correct information return required under section 6050Y(b)(1) and this section, see section 6721 and §301.6721-1 of this chapter. See §301.6724-1 of this chapter for the waiver of a penalty if the failure is due to reasonable cause and is not due to willful neglect.

(2) *Failure to furnish correct statement.*—For provisions relating to the penalty provided for failure to furnish a correct statement to identified persons under section 6050Y(b)(2) and this section, see section 6722 and §301.6722-2 of this chapter. See §301.6724-1 of this chapter for the waiver of a penalty if the failure is due to reasonable cause and is not due to willful neglect. [Reg. §1.6050Y-3.]

Par. 7. Section 1.6050Y-4 is added to read as follows:

§1.6050Y-4. Information reporting by payors for reportable death benefits.—(a) *Requirement of reporting.*—Except as provided in paragraph (e) of this section, every person that is a payor of reportable death benefits during any calendar year must file a separate information return for such calendar year with the Internal Revenue Service (IRS) for each reportable death benefits payment recipient in the form and manner prescribed by the IRS. The return must include the following information with respect to the reportable death benefits payment recipient to which the return relates:

(1) The name, address, and taxpayer identification number (TIN) of the payor;

(2) The name, address, and TIN of the reportable death benefits payment recipient;

(3) The date of the payment;

(4) The gross amount of payments made to the reportable death benefits payment recipient during the taxable year;

(5) The payor's estimate of the investment in the contract with respect to the buyer, limited to the payor's estimate of the buyer's investment in the contract with respect to the interest for which the reportable death benefits payment recipient was paid; and

(6) Any other information that is required by the form or its instructions.

(b) *Time and place for filing.*—Except as otherwise provided in §1.6050Y-1(b)(3), returns required to be made under this section must be filed with the Internal Revenue Service Center designated in the instructions for the form on or before February 28 (March 31 if filed electronically) of the year following the calendar year in which the payment of reportable death benefits was made.

(c) *Requirement of and time for furnishing statements.*—(1) *Requirement of furnishing statement.*—Every person required to file an information return under paragraph (a) of this section must furnish to each reportable death benefits payment recipient whose name is required to be set forth in that return a written statement showing the information required by paragraph (a) of this section with respect to that reportable death benefits payment recipient and the name, address, and phone number of the information contact of the payor. This contact information must provide direct access to a person that can answer questions about the statement.

(2) *Time for furnishing statement.*—Each statement required by paragraph (c)(1) of this section to be furnished to any reportable death benefits payment recipient must be furnished on or before January 31 of the year following the calendar year in which the payment of reportable death benefits was made. However, see §1.6050Y-1(b)(3) for transition rules.

(d) *Notice of rescission of a reportable policy sale.*—Any person that has filed a return required by section 6050Y(c) and this section with respect to a payment of reportable death benefits must file a corrected return within 15 calendar days of the receipt of notice of the rescission of the buyer's reportable policy sale. Any person that has furnished a written statement under section 6050Y(c)(2) and this section with respect to a payment of reportable death benefits must furnish the recipient of that statement with a corrected statement within 15 calendar days of the receipt of notice of the rescission of the buyer's reportable policy sale.

(e) *Exceptions to requirement to file.*—A payor is not required to file an information return under paragraph (a) of this section with respect to a payment of reportable death benefits when either paragraph (e)(1) or (2) of this section applies.

(1) Except as otherwise provided in this paragraph (e)(1), the payor obtains documentation in accordance with § 1.1441-1(e)(1)(ii) upon which it may rely to treat the reportable death benefits payment recipient as a foreign beneficial owner of the reportable death benefits, applying in such case the provisions of § 1.1441-1 by substituting the term "payor" for the term "withholding agent" and without regard to the fact that the provisions apply only to amounts subject to withholding under chapter 3 of subtitle A of the Internal Revenue Code. A payor may also obtain from a partnership or trust that is a reportable death benefits recipient, in addition to documentation establishing the entity's foreign status, a written certification from the entity that no beneficial owner of any portion of the reportable death benefits payment is a United States person. In such a case, a payor may rely upon the written certification to treat the partnership or trust as a foreign beneficial owner for purposes of this paragraph (e)(1) provided that the payor does not have actual knowledge that a United States person is the beneficial owner of all or a portion of the reportable death benefits payment. See § 1.1441-1(c)(6)(ii) for the definition of beneficial owner that applies for purposes of this paragraph (e)(1). Additionally, for certifying its status as a foreign beneficial owner (as applicable) for purposes of this paragraph (e)(1), a reportable death benefits payment recipient that is required to report any of the income from the sale as effectively connected with the conduct of a trade or business in the United States under section 864(b) is required to provide to the payor a Form W-8ECI, Certificate of Foreign Person's Claim that Income is Effectively Connected with the Conduct of a Trade or Business in the United States. If a payor obtains a Form W-8ECI from a reportable death benefits payment recipient with respect to the payment of reportable death benefits or has reason to know that the payment is effectively connected with the conduct of a trade or business of the recipient in the United States under section 864(b), the exception to reporting described in this paragraph (e)(1) does not apply.

(2) The buyer obtained the life insurance contract (or interest therein) under which reportable death benefits are paid in a reportable policy sale to which the exception to reporting described in § 1.6050Y-3(f)(2) applies.

(f) *Cross-reference to penalty provisions.*—(1) *Failure to file correct information return.*—For provisions relating to the penalty provided for failure to file timely a correct information return required under section 6050Y(c)(1) and this section, see section 6721 and § 301.6721-1 of this chapter. See § 301.6724-1 of this chapter for the waiver of a penalty if the failure is due to reasonable cause and is not due to willful neglect.

(2) *Failure to furnish correct statement.*—For provisions relating to the penalty provided for failure to furnish a correct statement to identified persons under section 6050Y(c)(2) and this section, see section 6722 and § 301.6722-2 of this chapter. See § 301.6724-1 of this chapter for the waiver of a penalty if the failure is due to reasonable cause and is not due to willful neglect. [Reg. § 1.6050Y-4.]

Forms W-2: Use of Truncated Taxpayer Identification Numbers

Forms W-2: Use of Truncated Taxpayer Identification Numbers.—Amendments to Reg. §§ 31.6051-1—31.6051-3, permitting employers to voluntarily truncate employees' social security numbers on copies of Forms W-2, Wage and Tax Statement, that are furnished to employees so that the truncated SSNs appear in the form of IRS truncated taxpayer identification numbers, are proposed (published in the Federal Register on September 20, 2017) (REG-105004-16).

Par. 4. Section 31.6051-1 is amended by:

1. Revising paragraphs (a)(1)(i)(*b*) and (b)(1)(ii).
2. Removing paragraph (d)(1)(ii)(C).
3. Revising paragraphs (f), (h)(2), and (i).
4. Removing paragraph (j)(8).
5. Adding paragraph (k).

The revisions and addition read as follows:

§ 31.6051-1. Statements for employees.—(a) * * *

(1) * * *

(i) * * *

(*b*) The name, address, and social security number of the employee, which may be truncated to appear in the form of an IRS truncated taxpayer identification number (TTIN) on copies of Forms W-2 that are furnished to the employee (for provisions relating to the use of TTINs, see § 301.6109-4 of this chapter (Procedure and Administration Regulations)), if wages as defined in section 3121(a) have been paid or if the Form W–2 is required to be furnished to the employee,

* * *

(b) * * *

(1) * * *

(ii) The name, address, and social security number of the employee, which may be truncated to appear in the form of an IRS truncated taxpayer identification number (TTIN) on copies of Forms W-2 that are furnished to the employee (for provisions relating to the use of TTINs, see § 301.6109-4 of this chapter (Procedure and Administration Regulations)),

* * *

(f) *Statements with respect to compensation, as defined in the Railroad Retirement Tax Act.*—(1) *Notification of possible credit or refund.*—With respect to compensation (as defined in section 3231(e)), every employer (as defined in section 3231(a)) who is required to deduct and withhold from an employee (as defined in section 3231(b)) a tax under section 3201, shall include on or with the statement required to be furnished to such employee under section 6051(a), a notice concerning the provisions of this title with respect to the allowance of a credit or refund of the tax on wages imposed by section 3101(b) and the tax on compensation imposed by section 3201 or 3211 which is treated as a tax on wages imposed by section 3101(b).

(2) *Information to be supplied to employees upon request.*—With respect to compensation (as defined in section 3231(e)), every employer (as defined in section 3231(a)) who is required to deduct and withhold tax under section 3201 from an employee (as defined in section 3231(b)) who has also received wages during such year subject to the tax imposed by section 3101(b), shall upon request of such employee furnish to him or her a written statement showing—

(i) The total amount of compensation with respect to which the tax imposed by section 3101(b) was deducted;

(ii) The total amount of employee tax under section 3201 deducted and withheld (increased by any adjustment in the calendar year for overcollection, or decreased by any adjustment in such year for undercollection, of such tax during any prior year); and

(iii) The proportion thereof (expressed either as a dollar amount, or a percentage of the total amount of compensation as defined in section 3231(e), or as a percentage of the total amount of employee tax under section 3201) withheld as tax under section 3201 for financing the cost of hospital insurance benefits.

* * *

(h) * * *

(2) *Time for furnishing statement.*—The statement required by this paragraph (h) for a calendar year shall be furnished—

(i) In the case of an employee who is required to be furnished a Form W-2, Wage and Tax Statement, for the calendar year, within one week of (before or after) the date that the employee is furnished a timely Form W-2 for the calendar year (or, if a Form W-2 is not so furnished, on or before the date by which it is required to be furnished); and

(ii) In the case of an employee who is not required to be furnished a Form W-2 for the calendar year, on or before February 7 of the year succeeding the calendar year.

* * *

(i) *Cross references.*—For provisions relating to the penalties provided for the willful furnishing of a false or fraudulent statement, or for the willful failure to furnish a statement, see §31.6674-1 and section 7204. For additional provisions relating to the inclusion of identification numbers and account numbers in statements on Form W-2, see §§31.6109-1 and 31.6109-4. For the penalties applicable to information returns and payee statements, see sections 6721-6724 and the regulations thereunder.

* * *

(k) *Applicability date.*—This section is applicable for statements required to be furnished under section 6051 after December 31, 2018.

Par. 5. Section 31.6051-2 is amended by revising paragraphs (a) and (c) and adding paragraph (d) to read as follows:

§31.6051-2. Information returns on Form W-3 and Social Security Administration copies of Forms W-2.—(a) *In general.*—Every employer who is required to make a return of tax under §31.6011(a)-1 (relating to returns under the Federal Insurance Contributions Act), §31.6011(a)-4 (relating to returns of income tax withheld from wages), or §31.6011(a)-5 (relating to monthly returns) for a calendar year or any period therein, shall file the Social Security Administration copy of each Form W-2 required under §31.6051-1 to be furnished by the employer with respect to wages paid during the calendar year. An employer may not truncate an employee's social security number to appear in the form of an IRS truncated taxpayer identification number (TTIN) on copies of Form W-2 filed with the Social Security Administration. Each Form W-2 and the transmittal Form W-3 shall together constitute an information return to be filed with the Social Security Administration as indicated on the instructions to such forms. For the requirement to submit the information on Form W-2 on magnetic media, see section 6011(e) and §301.6011-2 of this chapter (Procedure and Administration Regulations).

* * *

(c) *Cross references.*—For provisions relating to the time for filing the information returns required by this section and to extensions of the time for filing, see sections 6071 and 6081 and the regulations thereunder. For the penalties applicable to information returns and payee statements, see sections 6721 through 6724 and the regulations thereunder.

(d) *Applicability date.*—This section is applicable for statements required to be filed under section 6051 after December 31, 2018.

Par. 6. Section 31.6051-3 is amended by revising paragraphs (a)(1)(i), (b)(1), (e)(3), and (f) and removing paragraph (g) to read as follows:

§31.6051-3. Statements required in case of sick pay paid by third parties.—(a) * * *

(1) * * *

(i) The name and, if there is withholding from sick pay under section 3402(o) and the regulations thereunder, the social security account number of the payee (the payee's social security number may not be truncated to appear in the form of an IRS truncated taxpayer identification number (TTIN)),

(b) * * *

(1) All of the information required to be furnished under paragraph (a) of this section, but the employer may truncate the payee's social security number to appear in the form of an IRS truncated taxpayer identification number (TTIN) on copies of Forms W-2 that are furnished to the

payee (for provisions relating to the use of TTINs, see § 301.6109-4 of this chapter (Procedure and Administration Regulations)),

* * *

(e) * * *

(3) The provisions of section 6109 (relating to identifying numbers) and the regulations thereunder shall be applicable to Form W-2 and to any payee of sick pay to whom a statement on Form W-2 is required by this section to be furnished. The employer must include the social security number of the payee on all copies of Forms W-2. The employer may truncate the payee's social security number to appear in the form of an IRS truncated taxpayer identification number (TTIN) on copies of Forms W-2 that are furnished to the payee. For provisions relating to the use of truncated taxpayer identification numbers (TTINs), see § 301.6109-4 of this chapter (Procedure and Administration Regulations).

* * *

(f) *Applicability date.*—This section is applicable for statements required to be furnished under section 6051 after December 31, 2018.

Forms W-2: Use of Truncated Taxpayer Identification Numbers

Forms W-2: Use of Truncated Taxpayer Identification Numbers.—Amendments to Reg. § 1.6052-2, permitting employers to voluntarily truncate employees' social security numbers on copies of Forms W-2, Wage and Tax Statement, that are furnished to employees so that the truncated SSNs appear in the form of IRS truncated taxpayer identification numbers, are proposed (published in the Federal Register on September 20, 2017) (REG-105004-16).

Par. 2. Section 1.6052-2 is amended by:

1. Revising paragraph (a).
2. Removing paragraph (b).
3. Redesignating paragraph (e) as new paragraph (b).
4. Revising paragraphs (c) and (d).
5. Removing paragraphs (f) and (g).

The revisions read as follows:

§ 1.6052-2. Statements to be furnished employees with respect to wages paid in the form of group-term life insurance.—(a) *Requirement.*—Every employer filing a return under section 6052(a) and § 1.6052-1, with respect to group-term life insurance on the life of an employee, shall furnish to the employee whose name is set forth in such return the tax return copy and the employee's copy of Form W-2. Each copy of Form W-2 must show the information required to be shown on the Form W-2 filed under § 1.6052-1. An employer may truncate an employee's social security number to appear in the form of an IRS truncated taxpayer identification number (TTIN) on copies of Form W-2 furnished to the employee. For provisions relating to the use of TTINs, see § 301.6109-4 of this chapter (Procedure and Administration Regulations). The rules in § 31.6051-1 of this chapter (Employment Taxes and Collection of Income Tax at Source Regulations) shall apply with respect to the means and time (including extensions thereof) for furnishing the employee's copy of Form W-2 required by this section to the employee and making corrections to such form.

* * *

(c) *Penalty.*—For provisions relating to the penalty provided for failure to furnish a statement under this section, see section 6722 and the regulations thereunder.

(d) *Applicability date.*—This section is applicable for statements required to be furnished under section 6052 after December 31, 2018.

Catastrophic Health Coverage: Information Reporting

Catastrophic Health Coverage: Information Reporting.—Amendments to Reg. § 1.6055-1, relating to information reporting of minimum essential coverage under section 6055 of the Internal Revenue Code, are proposed (published in the Federal Register on August 2, 2016) (REG-103058-16).

Par. 2. Section 1.6055-1 is amended by:

1. Adding paragraphs (b)(13) and (14).
2. Redesignating paragraph (c)(1)(iv) as (c)(1)(v) and adding a new paragraph (c)(1)(iv).
3. Revising paragraphs (d)(1) and (2).
4. Redesignating paragraph (d)(3) as (d)(5) and adding a new paragraph (d)(3).
5. Adding paragraphs (d)(4) and (6).
6. Revising paragraph (g)(3).
7. Revising paragraph (h)(1).
8. Adding paragraph (h)(3).
9. Revising paragraph (j).

The revisions and additions read as follows:

§ 1.6055-1. Information reporting for minimum essential coverage.

* * *

(b) * * *

(13) *Catastrophic plan.*—The term catastrophic plan has the same meaning as in section 1302(e) of the Affordable Care Act (42 U.S.C. 18022(e)).

(14) *Basic health program.*—The term basic health program means a basic health program established under section 1331 of the Affordable Care Act (42 U.S.C. 18051).

(c) * * *

(1) * * *

(iv) The state agency that administers a Basic Health Program;

* * *

(d) *Reporting not required.*—(1) *Qualified health plans.*—Except for coverage under a catastrophic plan, a health insurance issuer is not required to file a return or furnish a report under this section for coverage in a qualified health plan in the individual market enrolled in through an Exchange.

(2) *Duplicative coverage.*—If an individual is covered for a month by more than one minimum essential coverage plan or program provided by the same reporting entity, reporting is required for only one of the plans or programs for that month.

(3) *Supplemental coverage.*—Reporting is not required for minimum essential coverage of an individual for a month if that individual is eligible for that coverage only if enrolled in other minimum essential coverage for which section 6055 reporting is required and is not waived under this paragraph (d)(3). This paragraph (d)(3) applies with respect to eligible employer-sponsored coverage only if the supplemental coverage is offered by the same employer that offered the eligible employer-sponsored coverage for which reporting is required. For this purpose, an employer is treated as offering minimum essential coverage offered by any other person that is a member of a controlled group of entities under section 414(b) or (c), an affiliated service group under section 414(m), or an entity in an arrangement described under section 414(o) of which the employer is also a member.

(4) *Certain coverage provided by Territories and Possessions.*—The agencies that administer Medicaid and the Children's Health Insurance Program in American Samoa, the Commonwealth of the Northern Mariana Islands, Guam, Puerto Rico, and the United States Virgin Islands are not required to report that coverage under section 6055.

* * *

(6) *Examples.*—The following examples illustrate the rules of this paragraph (d).

Example 1. Upon being hired, Taxpayer A enrolls in a self-insured major medical group health plan and a health reimbursement arrangement (HRA), both offered by A's employer, V. Both the group health plan and the HRA are minimum essential coverage, and V is the reporting entity for both. Because V is the reporting entity for both the self-insured major medical group health plan and the HRA, under paragraph (d)(2) of this section V must report under paragraph (a) of this section for either its self-insured major medical group health plan or its HRA for A for the months in which A is enrolled in both plans.

Example 2. Taxpayer B is enrolled in an insured employer-sponsored group health plan offered by B's employer, W. B is also covered by an HRA offered by W. Under the terms of the HRA, B is eligible for the HRA because B is enrolled in W's insured employer-sponsored group health plan. W's insured employer-sponsored group health plan is minimum essential coverage and, under paragraphs (a) and (c)(1)(i) of this section, the issuer of the insured employer-sponsored group health plan must report coverage under the plan. Therefore, for the months in which B is enrolled in both plans, under paragraph (d)(3) of this section, W does not need to report the HRA for B because the issuer is required to report on coverage for B in the insured employer-sponsored group health plan offered by W for those months.

Example 3. Taxpayer C enrolls in a Medicare Savings Program administered by X, a state Medicaid agency, which provides financial assistance with Medicare Part A premiums. Only individuals enrolled in Medicare Part A are offered coverage in this Medicare Savings Program. Medicare Part A is government-sponsored minimum essential coverage and, under paragraphs (a) and (c)(1)(iii) of this section, Medicare must report coverage under the program. Therefore, under paragraph (d)(3) of this section, X does not need to report under paragraph (a) of this section for C's coverage under the Medicare Savings Program.

Example 4. Taxpayer E obtains a Medicare supplemental insurance (Medigap) policy that provides financial assistance with costs not covered by Medicare Part A from Z, a health insurance issuer. Only individuals enrolled in Medicare Part A are offered coverage under this Medigap policy. Medicare Part A is minimum essential coverage and, under paragraphs (a) and (c)(1)(iii) of this section, Medicare is required to report E's coverage under Medicare Part A. Therefore, under paragraph (d)(3) of this section, Z does not need to report E's coverage under the Medigap policy.

Example 5. Taxpayer F is covered by an HRA offered by F's employer, P. F is also enrolled in a non-HRA group health plan that is self-insured and sponsored by F's spouse's employer, Q. P and Q are not treated as one employer under section 414(b), (c), (m), or (o). Under the terms of the HRA, F is eligible for the HRA only because F is enrolled in a non-HRA group health plan, which in this case is the group health plan offered by Q. However, because the HRA and the non-HRA group health plan are offered by different employers, paragraph (d)(3) of this section does not apply. Accordingly, under paragraphs (a) and (c)(2)(i)(A) of this section, P must report F's enrollment in the HRA, and Q must report F's (and F's spouse's) enrollment in the non-HRA group health plan.

* * *

(g) * * *

(3) *Form of the statement.*—A statement required under this paragraph (g) may be made either by furnishing to the responsible individual a copy of the return filed with the Internal Revenue Service or on a substitute statement. A substitute statement must include the information required to be shown on the return filed with the Internal Revenue Service and must comply with requirements in published guidance (see §601.601(d)(2) of this chapter) relating to substitute statements. An individual's identifying number may be truncated to appear in the form of an IRS truncated taxpayer identification number (TTIN) on the statement furnished to the responsible individual. The identifying number of the employer may also be truncated to appear in the form of a TTIN on the statement furnished to the responsible individual. For provisions relating to the use of TTINs, see §301.6109-4 of this chapter (Procedure and Administration Regulations).

* * *

(h) * * *

(1) *In general.*—For provisions relating to the penalty for failure to file timely a correct information return required under section 6055, see section 6721 and the regulations under that section. For provisions relating to the penalty for failure to furnish timely a correct statement to responsible individuals required under section 6055, see section 6722 and the regulations under that section. See section 6724, and the regulations thereunder, and paragraph (h)(3) of this section for provisions relating to the waiver of penalties if a failure to file or furnish timely or accurately is due to reasonable cause and not due to willful neglect.

* * *

(3) *Application of section 6724 waiver of penalties to section 6055 reporting.*—(i) *In general.*—Paragraphs (e) and (f) of §301.6724-1 of this chapter, as modified by this paragraph (h)(3), apply to reasonable cause waivers of penalties under sections 6721 and 6722 for failure to file timely or accurate information returns or to furnish individual statements required to be filed or furnished under section 6055.

(ii) *Account opened.*—For purposes of section 6055 reporting and the solicitation rules contained in paragraphs (i), (ii), (iii), and (v) of §301.6724-1(e)(1) of this chapter and paragraph (i) of §301.6724-1(f)(1) of this chapter, an account is considered opened at the time the reporting entity receives a substantially complete application for coverage (including an application to add an individual to existing coverage) from or on behalf of an individual for whom the reporting entity does not already provide coverage.

(iii) *First annual solicitation deadline for missing TINs.*—In lieu of the deadline for the first annual solicitation contained in paragraph (ii) of §301.6724-1(e)(1) of this chapter, the first annual solicitation must be made on or before the seventy-fifth day after the date on which an account is opened (or, in the case of retroactive coverage, the seventy-fifth day after the determination of retroactive coverage is made). The period from the date on which the reporting entity receives an application for coverage to the last day on which the first annual solicitation may be made is the first annual solicitation period.

(iv) *Failures to which a solicitation relates.*—(A) *Missing TIN.*—For purposes of reporting under section 6055 and the solicitation rules contained in paragraph (1) of §301.6724-1(e) of this chapter, the initial and first annual solicitations relate to failures on returns required to be filed for the year which includes the first effective date of coverage for a covered individual. The second annual solicitation relates to failures on returns filed for the year immediately following the year to which the first annual solicitation relates and for succeeding calendar years.

(B) *Incorrect TIN.*—For purposes of reporting under section 6055 and the solicitation rules contained in paragraph (i) of §301.6724-1(f)(1) of this chapter, the initial solicitation relates to failures on returns required to be filed for the year which includes the first effective date of coverage for a covered individual.

(v) *Solicitations made to responsible individual.*—For purposes of reporting under section 6055 and the solicitation rules contained in §301.6724-1(e) and (f) of this chapter, an initial or annual solicitation made to the responsible individual is treated as a solicitation made to a covered individual.

* * *

(j) *Applicability date.*—(1) Except as provided in paragraphs (j)(2) and (3) of this section, this section applies for calendar years ending after December 31, 2014.

(2) Paragraphs (b)(14), (c)(1)(v), (d)(2) through (6), and (g)(3) of this section apply to calendar years ending after December 31, 2015. Paragraphs (d)(2), (d)(3), and (g)(3) of §1.6055-1 as contained in 26 CFR part 1 edition revision as of April 1, 2016, apply to calendar years ending after December 31, 2014 and beginning before January 1, 2016.

(3) Paragraphs (b)(13) and (d)(1) of this section apply to calendar years beginning after December 31, 2016. Paragraph (d)(1) of §1.6055-1 as contained in 26 CFR part 1 edition revised as of April 1, 2016, applies to calendar years ending after December 31, 2015 and beginning before January 1, 2017.

Expatriate Health Plans: Issuers: Excepted Benefits

Expatriate Health Plans: Issuers: Excepted Benefits.—Amendments to Reg. §1.6055-2, relating to the rules for expatriate health plans, expatriate health plan issuers, and qualified expatriates under the Expatriate Health Coverage Clarification Act of 2014 (EHCCA), are proposed (published in the Federal Register on June 10, 2016) (REG-135702-15).

4. Section 1.6055-2 is amended by adding paragraph (a)(8) to read as follows:

§1.6055-2. Electronic furnishing of statements.—(a) * * *

(8) *Special rule for expatriate health plan coverage.*—(i) *In general.*—In the case of an individual covered under an expatriate health plan (within the meaning of §54.9831-1(f)(3) of this chapter), the recipient is treated as having consented under paragraph (a)(2) of this section unless the recipient has explicitly refused to consent to receive the statement in an electronic format. The refusal to consent may be made electronically or in a paper document. A recipient's request for a paper statement is treated as an explicit refusal to receive the statement in electronic format. A furnisher relying on this paragraph (a)(8) must satisfy the requirements of paragraphs (a)(3) through (7) of this section, except that the statement required under paragraph (a)(3) must be provided at least 30 days prior to the time for furnishing under §1.6055-1(g)(4)(i)(A) of this chapter of the first statement that the furnisher intends to furnish electronically to the recipient, and the other requirements of paragraph (a)(3) are modified to reflect that the statement will be furnished electronically unless the recipient explicitly refuses to consent to receive the statement in an electronic format.

(ii) *Manner and time of notifying recipient.*—The IRS may specify in other guidance published in the Internal Revenue Bulletin the manner and timing for the initial notification of recipients that the statement required under paragraph (a)(3) of this section will be furnished electronically unless the recipient explicitly refuses to consent to receive the statement in an electronic format. See § 601.601(d)(2)(ii)(B) of this chapter.

(iii) *Effective/applicability date.*—The provisions of this paragraph (a)(8) apply as of January 1, 2017.

* * *

Expatriate Health Plans: Issuers: Excepted Benefits

Expatriate Health Plans: Issuers: Excepted Benefits.—Amendments to Reg. § 301.6056-2, relating to the rules for expatriate health plans, expatriate health plan issuers, and qualified expatriates under the Expatriate Health Coverage Clarification Act of 2014 (EHCCA), are proposed (published in the Federal Register on June 10, 2016) (REG-135702-15).

18. Section 301.6056-2 is amended by adding paragraph (a)(8) to read as follows:

§ 301.6056-2. Electronic furnishing of statements.—(a) * * *

(8) *Special rule for expatriate health plan coverage.*—(i) *In general.*—In the case of an individual covered under an expatriate health plan (within the meaning of § 54.9831-1(f)(3) of this chapter), the recipient is treated as having consented under paragraph (a)(2) of this section unless the recipient has explicitly refused to consent to receive the statement in an electronic format. The refusal to consent may be made electronically or in a paper document. A recipient's request for a paper statement is treated as an explicit refusal to receive the statement in electronic format. A furnisher relying on this paragraph (a)(8) must satisfy the requirements of paragraphs (a)(3) through (7) of this section, except that the statement required under paragraph (a)(3) must be provided at least 30 days prior to the time for furnishing under § 301.6056-1(g)(4)(i)(A) of this chapter of the first statement that the furnisher intends to furnish electronically to the recipient, and the other requirements of paragraph (a)(3) are modified to reflect that the statement will be furnished electronically unless the recipient explicitly refuses consent to receive the statement in an electronic format.

(ii) *Manner and time of notifying recipient.*—The IRS may specify in other guidance published in the Internal Revenue Bulletin the manner and timing for the initial notification of recipients that the statement required under paragraph (a)(3) of this section will be furnished electronically unless the recipient explicitly refuses to consent to receive the statement in an electronic format. See § 601.601(d)(2)(ii)(B) of this chapter.

(iii) *Effective/applicability date.*—The provisions of this paragraph (a)(8) apply as of January 1, 2017.

* * *

Deferred Vested Benefits: Reporting and Notice Requirements

Deferred Vested Benefits: Reporting and Notice Requirements.—Amendments to Reg. §§ 301.6057-1 and 301.6057-2, relating to automatic extensions of time for filing certain employee plan returns by adding the Form 8955-SSA, "Annual Registration Statement Identifying Separated Participants With Deferred Vested Benefits," to the list of forms that are covered by the Income Tax Regulations on automatic extensions, are proposed (published in the Federal Register on June 21, 2012) (REG-153627-08).

☐ Par. 4. Section 301.6057-1 is amended by:

1. Revising paragraphs (a)(4) and (a)(5)(ii).
2. Removing paragraph (b)(2)(iii) and redesignating paragraph (b)(2)(iv) as (b)(2)(iii).
3. Revising newly designated paragraph (b)(2)(iii).
4. Revising paragraphs (b)(3)(ii), (b)(3)(iii), (c), (d), (f), and (g).

☐ Par. 5. Section 301.6057-1 is amended by removing the language "schedule SSA" and adding "Form 8955-SSA" in its place.

The revisions read as follows:

§ 301.6057-1. Employee retirement benefit plans; identification of participant with deferred vested retirement benefit.—

(a) * * *

(4) *Filing requirements.*—(i) *In general.*—Information relating to the deferred vested retirement benefit of a plan participant must be filed on Form 8955-SSA, "Annual Registration Statement Identifying Separated Participants With Deferred Vested Benefits." Form 8955-SSA shall be filed on behalf of an employee retirement benefit plan for each plan year for which information relating to the deferred vested retirement benefit of a plan participant is filed under paragraph (a)(5) or (b)(2) of this section. There shall be reported on Form 8955-SSA the name and Social Security number of the participant, a description of the nature, form and amount of the deferred vested retirement benefit to which the participant is entitled, and such other information as is required by section 6057(a) or Form 8955-SSA and the accompanying instructions. The form of the benefit reported on Form 8955-SSA shall be the normal form of benefit under the plan, or, if the plan administrator (within the meaning of section 414(g)) considers it more appropriate, any other form of benefit.

(ii) *General due date for filing.*—The forms prescribed by section 6057(a), including Form 8955-SSA, shall be filed in the manner and at the time as required by the forms and related instructions applicable to the annual period.

(iii) *Delegation of authority to Commissioner.*—The Commissioner may provide special rules under section 6057 (including designating the form used to comply with section 6057) in revenue rulings, notices, or other guidance published in the Internal Revenue Bulletin (see

§601.601(d)(2)(ii)(b) of this chapter) that the Commissioner determines to be necessary or appropriate with respect to the filing requirements under section 6057.

(5) * * *

(ii) *Exception.*—Nothwithstanding paragraph (a)(5)(i) of this section, no information relating to the deferred vested retirement benefit of a separated participant is required to be filed on Form 8955-SSA if, before the date such Form 8955-SSA is required to be filed (including any extension of time for filing granted pursuant to section 6081), the participant—

(A) Is paid some or all of the deferred vested retirement benefit under the plan;

(B) Returns to service covered under the plan; or

(C) Forfeits all of the deferred vested retirement benefit under the plan.

(b) * * *

(2) * * *

(iii) *Exception.*—Notwithstanding paragraph (b)(2)(i) of this section, no information relating to a participant's deferred vested retirement benefit is required to be filed on Form 8955-SSA if, before the date such Form 8955-SSA is required to be filed (including any extension of time for filing granted pursuant to section 6081), the participant—

(A) Is paid some or all of the deferred vested retirement benefit under the plan;

(B) Accrues additional retirement benefits under the plan; or

(C) Forfeits all of the deferred vested retirement benefit under the plan.

(3) * * *

(ii) *Inability to determine correct amount of participant's deferred vested retirement benefit.*—The plan administrator must indicate on Form 8955-SSA that the amount of a participant's deferred vested retirement benefit showed therein may be other than that to which the participant is actually entitled if such amount is computed on the basis of plan records that the plan administrator maintains and such records—

(A) Are incomplete with respect to the participant's service covered by the plan (as described in paragraph (b)(3)(i) of this section); or

(B) Fail to account for the participant's service not covered by the plan which is relevant to a determination of the participant's deferred vested retirement benefit under the plan (as described in paragraph (b)(3)(i) of this section).

(iii) *Inability to determine whether participant vested in deferred retirement benefit.*—Where, as described in paragraph (b)(3)(i) of this section, information to be reported on Form 8955-SSA is to be based upon records which are incomplete with respect to a participant's service covered by the plan or which fail to take into account relevant service not covered by the plan, the plan administrator may be unable to determine whether or not the participant is vested in any deferred retirement benefit. If, in view of information provided either by the incomplete records or the plan participant, there is a significant likelihood that the plan participant is vested in a deferred retirement benefit under the plan, information relating to the participant must be filed on Form 8955-SSA with the notation that the participant may be entitled to a deferred vested benefit under the plan, but information relating to the amount of the benefit may be omitted. This paragraph (b)(3)(iii) does not apply in a case in which it can be determined from plan records maintained by the plan administrator that the participant is vested in a deferred retirement benefit. Paragraph (b)(3)(ii) of this section, however, may apply in such a case.

(c) *Voluntary filing.*—(1) *In general.*—The plan administrator of an employee retirement benefit plan described in paragraph (a)(3) of this section, or any other employee retirement benefit plan (including a governmental plan within the meaning of section 414(d) or a church plan within the meaning of section 414(e)), may, at its option, file on Form 8955-SSA information relating to the deferred vested retirement benefit of any plan participant who separates at any time from service covered by the plan.

(2) *Deleting previously filed information.*—If, after information relating to the deferred vested retirement benefit of a plan participant is filed on Form 8955-SSA (or a predecessor to Form 8955-SSA), the plan participant is paid some or all of the deferred vested retirement benefit under the plan or forfeits all of the deferred vested retirement benefit under the plan, the plan administrator may, at its option, file on Form 8955-SSA (or such other form as may be provided for this purpose) the name and Social Security number of the plan participant with the notation that information previously filed relating to the participant's deferred vested retirement benefit should be deleted.

(d) *Filing incident to cessation of payment of benefits.*—(1) *In general.*

No information relating to the deferred vested retirement benefit of a plan participant is required to be filed on Form 8955-SSA if before the date such Form 8955-SSA is required to be filed, some of the deferred vested retirement benefit is paid to the participant, and information relating to a participant's deferred vested retirement benefit which was previously filed on Form 8955-SSA (or a predecessor to Form 8955-SSA) may be deleted if the participant is paid some of the deferred vested retirement benefit. If payment of the deferred vested retirement benefit ceases before all of the benefit to which the participant is entitled is paid to the participant, information relating to the deferred vested retirement benefit to which the participant remains entitled shall be filed on the Form 8955-SSA filed for the plan year following the last plan year within which a portion of the benefit is paid to the participant.

(2) *Exception.*—Notwithstanding paragraph (d)(1) of this section, no information relating to the deferred vested retirement benefit to which the participant remains entitled is required to be filed on Form 8955-SSA if, before the date such Form 8955-SSA is required to be filed (including any extension of time for filing granted pursuant to section 6081), the participant—

(i) Returns to service covered by the plan;

(ii) Accrues additional retirement benefits under the plan; or

(iii) Forfeits the benefit under the plan.

* * *

(f) *Penalties.*—For amounts imposed in the case of failure to file the report of deferred vested retirement benefits required by section 6057(a) and paragraph (a) or (b) of this section, see section 6652(d)(1).

(g) *Effective/applicability date.*—(1) *In general.*—Except as otherwise provided in this paragraph (g), this section is applicable for filings on or after June 21, 2012.

(2) *Special effective date rules for periods before the general effective date.*—Section 301.6057-1 of this chapter, as it appeared in the April 1, 2008 edition of 26 CFR part 301, applies for periods before the general effective date.

□ Par. 6. Section 301.6057-2 is amended by revising paragraph (c) as follows:

§ 301.6057-2. Employee retirement benefit plans; notification of change in plan status.

* * *

(c) *Penalty.*—For amounts imposed in the case of failure to file a notification of a change in plan status required by section 6057(b) and this section, see section 6652(d)(2).

* * *

Gifts and Bequests from Covered Expatriates: Imposition of Tax

Gifts and Bequests from Covered Expatriates: Imposition of Tax.—Reg. § 28.6060-1, relating to a tax on United States citizens and residents who receive gifts or bequests from certain individuals who relinquished United States citizenship or ceased to be lawful permanent residents of the United States on or after June 17, 2008, is proposed (published in the Federal Register on September 10, 2015) (REG-112997-10).

Section 28.6060-1 is added to read as follows:

§ 28.6060-1. Reporting requirements for tax return preparers.—(a) *In general.*—A person that employs one or more signing tax return preparers to prepare a return or claim for refund of any tax to which this part 28 applies, other than for the person, at any time during a return period, must satisfy the recordkeeping and inspection requirements in the manner stated in § 1.6060-1 of this chapter.

(b) *Effective/applicability date.*—This section applies to returns and claims for refund filed on or after the date of publication of a Treasury decision adopting these rules as final regulations in the **Federal Register**. [Reg. § 28.6060-1.]

Gifts and Bequests from Covered Expatriates: Imposition of Tax

Gifts and Bequests from Covered Expatriates: Imposition of Tax.—Reg. § 28.6071-1, relating to a tax on United States citizens and residents who receive gifts or bequests from certain individuals who relinquished United States citizenship or ceased to be lawful permanent residents of the United States on or after June 17, 2008, is proposed (published in the Federal Register on September 10, 2015) (REG-112997-10).

Section 28.6071-1 is added to read as follows:

§ 28.6071-1. Time for filing returns.—(a) *In general.*—(1) A U.S. recipient as defined in § 28.2801-2(e) must file Form 708, "U.S. Return of Gifts or Bequests from Covered Expatriates," on or before the fifteenth day of the eighteenth calendar month following the close of the calendar year in which the covered gift or covered bequest was received. Notwithstanding the preceding sentence, the due date for a Form 708 reporting a covered bequest that is not received on the decedent's date of death under § 28.2801-4(d)(3) is the later of—

(i) The fifteenth day of the eighteenth calendar month following the close of the calendar year in which the covered expatriate died; or

(ii) The fifteenth day of the sixth month of the calendar year following the close of the calendar year in which the covered bequest was received.

(2) If a U.S. recipient receives multiple covered gifts and covered bequests during the same calendar year, the rule in paragraph (a)(1) of this section may result in different due dates and the filing of multiple returns reporting the different transfers received during the same calendar year.

(b) *Migrated foreign trust.*—The due date for a Form 708 for the year in which a foreign trust becomes a domestic trust is the fifteenth day of the sixth month of the calendar year following the close of the calendar year in which the foreign trust becomes a domestic trust.

(c) *Certain returns by foreign trusts.*—(1) *Election under § 28.2801-5(d) for calendar year in which no covered gift or covered bequest received.*—A foreign trust making an election to be treated as a domestic trust for purposes of section 2801 under § 28.2801-5(d) for a calendar year in which the foreign trust received no covered gifts or covered bequests must file a Form 708 on or before the fifteenth day of the sixth month of the calendar year following the close of the calendar year for which the election is made.

(2) *Certification to maintain election under § 28.2801-5(d) for calendar year in which no covered gift or covered bequest received.*—An electing foreign trust filing a Form 708 to certify that the electing foreign trust did not receive any covered gifts or covered bequests during the calendar year must file the Form 708 on or before the fifteenth day of the sixth month of the calendar year following the close of that calendar year. See § 28.2801-5(d)(4).

(d) *Transition period.*—The Form 708 reporting covered gifts or covered bequests received on or after June 17, 2008, and before the date of publication of a Treasury decision adopting these rules as final regulations in the **Federal Register**, will be due within a reasonable period of time after the date of that publication as specified in the final regulations, but in no event before the due date of the first return required under the final regulations for covered gifts or covered bequests received after the final regulations are published.

(e) *Effective/applicability dates.*—This section applies to each Form 708 filed on or after the date on which a Treasury decision is published adopting these rules as final regulations in the **Federal Register**. [Reg. § 28.6071-1.]

Classification: Cell Companies: Series LLCs

Classification: Cell Companies: Series LLCs.—Reg. § 301.6071-2, regarding the classification for Federal tax purposes of a series of a domestic series limited liability company (LLC), a cell of a domestic cell company, or a foreign series or cell that conducts an insurance business, is proposed (published in the Federal Register on September 14, 2010) (REG-119921-09).

Par. 3. Section 301.6071-2 is added to read as follows:

§ 301.6071-2. Time for filing statements of series and series organizations.—(a) *In general.*—Statements required by § 301.6011-6 must be filed on or before March 15 of the year following the period for which the return is made.

(b) *Effective/applicability date.*—This section applies to taxable years beginning after the date of publication of the Treasury decision adopting these rules as final regulations in the **Federal Register**.

Return and Extended Due Date: Changes

Return Due Extended Due Date: Changes.—Amendments to Reg. § 31.6071(a)-1, updating the due dates and extensions of time to file certain tax returns and information returns, are proposed (published in the Federal Register on July 20, 2017) (REG-128483-15).

Par. 17. Revise paragraph (a)(3) and add paragraph (g) to § 31.6071(a)-1 to read as follows:

§ 31.6071(a)-1. Time for filing returns and other documents.—(a) * * *

(3) [The text of proposed § 31.6071(a)-1(a)(3) is the same as the text of § 31.6071(a)-1T(a)(3) as added by T.D. 9821].

* * *

(g) *Applicability date.*—The requirements of paragraph (a)(3) of this section are applicable for returns filed on or after the date a Treasury Decision incorporating these amendments as final regulations is published in the **Federal Register**.

Return and Extended Due Date: Changes

Return Due Extended Due Date: Changes.—Amendments to Reg. § 1.6072-2, updating the due dates and extensions of time to file certain tax returns and information returns, are proposed (published in the Federal Register on July 20, 2017) (REG-128483-15).

Par. 9. Revise paragraphs (a) and (d)(1) and (2) and add paragraph (g) to § 1.6072-2 to read as follows:

§ 1.6072-2. Time for filing returns of corporations.—(a) [The text of proposed § 1.6072-2(a) is the same as the text of § 1.6072-2T(a) as added by T.D. 9821].

* * *

(d) * * *

(1) and (2) [The text of proposed § 1.6072-2(d)(1) and (2) is the same as the text of § 1.6072-2T(d)(1) and (2) as added by T.D. 9821].

* * *

(g) *Applicability date.*—The requirements of paragraphs (a) and (d)(1) and (2) of this section are applicable for returns filed on or after the date a Treasury Decision incorporating these amendments as final regulations is published in the **Federal Register**.

Return and Extended Due Date: Changes

Return Due Extended Due Date: Changes.—Amendments to Reg. §§ 1.6081-1—1.6081-3, 1.6081-5 and 1.6081-6 updating the due dates and extensions of time to file certain tax returns and information returns, are proposed (published in the Federal Register on July 20, 2017) (REG-128483-15).

Par. 10. Revise paragraphs (a) and (c) of § 1.6081-1 to read as follows:

§ 1.6081-1. Extension of time for filing returns.—(a) [The text of proposed § 1.6081-1(a) is the same as the text of § 1.6081-1T(a) as added by T.D. 9821].

* * *

(c) *Applicability dates.*—The requirements of paragraph (a) of this section are applicable for returns filed on or after the date a Treasury Decision incorporating these amendments as final regulations is published in the **Federal Register**.

Par. 11. Revise paragraphs (a)(1) and (h) of § 1.6081-2 to read as follows:

§ 1.6081-2. Automatic extension of time to file certain returns filed by partnerships.—(a) * * *

(1) [The text of proposed § 1.6081-2(a)(1) is the same as the text of § 1.6081-2T(a)(1) as added by T.D. 9821].

* * *

(h) *Applicability date.*—The requirements of paragraph (a)(1) of this section are applicable for returns filed on or after the date a Treasury Decision incorporating these amendments as final regulations is published in the **Federal Register**.

Par. 12. Revise the introductory text of paragraph (a), redesignate paragraph (e) as paragraph (g), revise newly redesignated paragraph (g), and add paragraphs (e) and (f) to §1.6081-3 to read as follows:

§1.6081-3. Automatic extension of time for filing corporation income tax returns.—(a) [The text of the introductory text of proposed §1.6081-3(a) is the same as the text of the introductory text of §1.6081-3T(a) as added by T.D. 9821].

* * *

(e) and (f) [The text of proposed §1.6081-3(e) and (f) is the same as the text of §1.6081-3T(e) and (f) as added by T.D. 9821].

(g) *Applicability date.*—The requirements of paragraphs (a), (e), and (f) of this section are applicable for returns filed on or after the date a Treasury Decision incorporating these amendments as final regulations is published in the **Federal Register**.

Par. 13. Revise paragraphs (a)(1) and (f) of §1.6081-5 to read as follows:

§1.6081-5. Extensions of time in the case of certain partnerships, corporations and U.S. citizens and residents.—(a) * * *

(1) [The text of proposed §1.6081-5(a)(1) is the same as the text of §1.6081-5T(a)(1) as added by T.D. 9821].

* * *

(f) *Applicability date.*—The requirements of paragraph (a)(1) of this section are applicable for returns filed on or after the date a Treasury Decision incorporating these amendments as final regulations is published in the **Federal Register**.

Par. 14. Revise paragraphs (a)(1) and (g) of §1.6081-6 to read as follows:

§1.6081-6. Automatic extension of time to file estate or trust income tax return.—(a) * * *

(1) [The text of proposed §1.6081-6(a)(1) is the same as the text of §1.6081-6T(a)(1) as added by T.D. 9821].

* * *

(g) *Applicability date.*—The requirements of paragraph (a)(1) of this section are applicable for returns filed on or after the date a Treasury Decision incorporating these amendments as final regulations is published in the **Federal Register**.

Gifts and Bequests from Covered Expatriates: Imposition of Tax

Gifts and Bequests from Covered Expatriates: Imposition of Tax.—Reg. §28.6081-1, relating to a tax on United States citizens and residents who receive gifts or bequests from certain individuals who relinquished United States citizenship or ceased to be lawful permanent residents of the United States on or after June 17, 2008, is proposed (published in the Federal Register on September 10, 2015) (REG-112997-10).

Section 28.6081-1 is added to read as follows:

§28.6081-1. Automatic extension of time for filing returns reporting gifts and bequests from covered expatriates.—(a) *In general.*—A U.S. recipient as defined in §28.2801-2(e) may request an extension of time to file a Form 708, "U.S. Return of Gifts or Bequests from Covered Expatriates," by filing Form 7004, "Application for Automatic Extension of Time to file Certain Business Income Tax, Information, and Other Returns." A U.S. recipient must include on Form 7004 an estimate of the amount of section 2801 tax liability and must file Form 7004 with the Internal Revenue Service office designated in the Form's instructions (except as provided in §301.6091-1(b) of this chapter for hand-carried documents).

(b) *Automatic extension.*—A U.S. recipient as defined in §28.2801-2(e) will be allowed an automatic six-month extension of time beyond the date prescribed in §28.6071-1 to file Form 708 if Form 7004 is filed on or before the due date for filing Form 708 in accordance with the procedures under paragraph (a) of this section.

(c) *No extension of time for the payment of tax.*—An automatic extension of time for filing a return granted under paragraph (b) of this section will not extend the time for payment of any tax due with such return.

(d) *Penalties.*—See section 6651 regarding penalties for failure to file the required tax return or failure to pay the amount shown as tax on the return.

(e) *Effective/applicability dates.*—This section applies to applications for an extension of time to file Form 708 filed on or after the date of publication of a Treasury decision adopting these rules as final regulations in the **Federal Register**. [Reg. §28.6081-1.]

Return and Extended Due Date: Changes

Return Due Extended Due Date: Changes.—Amendments to Reg. §1.6081-9, updating the due dates and extensions of time to file certain tax returns and information returns, are proposed (published in the Federal Register on July 20, 2017) (REG-128483-15).

Par. 15. Revise the section heading and paragraphs (a), (b)(1) and (3), and (c) through (f) of §1.6081-9 to read as follows:

§1.6081-9. Automatic extension of time to file exempt or political organization returns.—(a) [The text of proposed §1.6081-9(a) is the same as the text of §1.6081-9T(a) as added by T.D. 9821].

(b) * * *

(1) [The text of proposed §1.6081-9(b)(1) is the same as the text of §1.6081-9T(b)(1) as added by T.D. 9821].

* * *

(3) [The text of proposed §1.6081-9(b)(3) is the same as the text of §1.6081-9T(b)(3) as added by T.D. 9821].

* * *

(c) through (e) [The text of proposed §1.6081-9(c) through (e) is the same as the text of §1.6081-9T(c) through (e) as added by T.D. 9821].

(f) *Applicability date.*—The requirements of paragraphs (a), (b)(1) and (3), and (c) through (e) of this section are applicable for returns filed on or after the date a Treasury Decision incorporating these amendments as final regulations is published in the **Federal Register**.

Deferred Vested Benefits: Reporting and Notice Requirements

Deferred Vested Benefits: Reporting and Notice Requirements.—Amendments to Reg. §1.6081-11, relating to automatic extensions of time for filing certain employee plan returns by adding the Form 8955-SSA, "Annual Registration Statement Identifying Separated Participants With Deferred Vested Benefits," to the list of forms that are covered by the Income Tax Regulations on automatic extensions, are proposed (published in the Federal Register on June 21, 2012) (REG-153627-08).

☐ Par. 2. Section 1.6081-11 is amended by:

1. Revising paragraph (a).
2. Adding paragraph (b)(3).
3. Revising the paragraph heading of paragraph (d) and adding paragraph (d)(2).
4. Revising the paragraph heading of paragraph (e) and adding paragraph (e)(2).

The revisions and additions read as follows:

§1.6081-11. Automatic extension of time for filing certain employee plan returns.—(a) *In general.*—An administrator or sponsor of an employee benefit plan required to file a return under the provisions of subpart E of part III of chapter 61 or the regulations under that chapter on Form 5500 (series), "Annual Return/Report of Employee Benefit Plan" or Form 8955-SSA, "Annual Registration Statement Identifying Separated Participants with Deferred Vested Benefits," will be allowed an automatic extension of time to file the return until the 15th day of the third month following the date prescribed for filing the return if the administrator or sponsor files an application under this section in accordance with paragraph (b) of this section.

(b) * * *

(3) A signature is not required for an automatic extension of time to file Form 5500 (series) and Form 8955-SSA.

* * *

(d) *Penalties.*—(1) *Form 5500.*—* * *

(2) *Form 8955-SSA.*—See section 6652 for penalties for failure to file a timely and complete Form 8955-SSA.

(e) *Effective/Applicability dates.*—(1) *Form 5500.*—* * *

(2) *Form 8955-SSA.*—This section is applicable for applications for an automatic extension of time to file Form 8955-SSA filed after June 21, 2012.

Gifts and Bequests from Covered Expatriates: Imposition of Tax

Gifts and Bequests from Covered Expatriates: Imposition of Tax.—Reg. §28.6091-1, relating to a tax on United States citizens and residents who receive gifts or bequests from certain individuals who relinquished United States citizenship or ceased to be lawful permanent residents of the United States on or after June 17, 2008, is proposed (published in the Federal Register on September 10, 2015) (REG-112997-10).

Section 28.6091-1 is added to read as follows:

§28.6091-1. Place for filing returns.—A U.S. recipient as defined in §28.2801-2(e) must file Form 708, "U.S. Return of Gifts and Bequests from Covered Expatriates," with the Internal Revenue Service office designated in the instructions applicable to the Form. [Reg. §28.6091-1.]

Gifts and Bequests from Covered Expatriates: Imposition of Tax

Gifts and Bequests from Covered Expatriates: Imposition of Tax.—Reg. §28.6101-1, relating to a tax on United States citizens and residents who receive gifts or bequests from certain individuals who relinquished United States citizenship or ceased to be lawful permanent residents of the United States on or after June 17, 2008, is proposed (published in the Federal Register on September 10, 2015) (REG-112997-10).

Section 28.6101-1 is added to read as follows:

§28.6101-1. Period covered by returns.—See §28.6011-1 for the rules relating to the period covered by the return. [Reg. §28.6101-1.]

Disclosure of Returns and Return Information: Contractors

Disclosure of Returns and Return Information: Contractors.—Amendments to Reg. §301.6103(n)-1, authorizing the Department of State to disclose returns and return information to its contractors who assist the Department of State in carrying out its responsibilities under section

32101 of the Fixing America's Surface Transportation Act, are proposed (published in the Federal Register on March 13, 2018) (REG-129260-16).

Par. 2. Sections [301.]6103(n)-1(a)(1) and (e)(4)(i) are amended by removing the language "or the Department of Justice" and adding the language "the Department of Justice, or the Department of State" in its place.

Par. 3. Section 301.6103(n)-1(g) is amended to read as follows:

§ 301.6103(n)-1. Disclosure of returns and return information in connection with written contracts or agreements for the acquisition of property or services for tax administration purposes.

* * *

(g) *Applicability date.*—This section is applicable on June 5, 2007, except that paragraphs (a) and (e)(4)(i) of this section apply to the Department of State on or after March 12, 2018.

Disclosure of Information: Tax-Exempt Organizations

Disclosure of Information: Tax-Exempt Organizations.—Amendments to Reg. § 301.6104(c)-1, providing guidance to states regarding the process by which they may obtain or inspect certain returns and return information (including information about final and proposed denials and revocations of tax-exempt status) for the purpose of administering state laws governing certain tax-exempt organizations and their activities, are proposed (published in the Federal Register on March 15, 2011) (REG-140108-08).

☐ Par. 2. Section 301.6104(c)-1 is revised to read as follows:

§ 301.6104(c)-1. Disclosure of certain information to state officials.—(a) *In general.*—(1) Subject to the disclosure, recordkeeping, and safeguard provisions of section 6103, and upon written request by an appropriate state officer (ASO, as defined in paragraph (i)(1) of this section), the IRS may disclose or make available to the ASO the returns and return information described in paragraph (c) of this section with respect to—

(i) any organization described or formerly described in section 501(c)(3) and exempt or formerly exempt from taxation under section 501(a) (a charitable organization); or

(ii) any organization that has applied for recognition as an organization described in section 501(c)(3) (an applicant). Such information shall be disclosed or made available only as necessary to administer state laws regulating charitable organizations.

(2) Subject to the disclosure, recordkeeping, and safeguard provisions of section 6103, and upon written request by an ASO, the IRS may disclose or make available to the ASO returns and return information regarding any organization described or formerly described in section 501(c) other than section 501(c)(1) or (c)(3). Such information shall be disclosed or made available only as necessary to administer state laws regulating the solicitation or administration of the charitable funds or charitable assets of these organizations.

(b) *Disclosure agreement.*—The IRS may require an ASO to execute a disclosure agreement or similar document specifying the procedures, terms, and conditions for the disclosure or inspection of information under section 6104(c), including compliance with the safeguards prescribed by section 6103(p)(4), as well as specifying the information to be disclosed. Such an agreement or similar document shall constitute the request for disclosure required by section 6104(c)(1)(C), as well as the written request required by section 6104(c)(2)(C)(i) and (c)(3). For security guidelines and other safeguards for protecting returns and return information, see guidance published by the IRS. See, for example, IRS Publication 1075, "Tax Information Security Guidelines for Federal, State and Local Agencies and Entities."

(c) *Disclosures regarding charitable organizations and applicants.*—(1) With respect to any organization described in paragraph (d) of this section, the IRS may disclose or make available for inspection under section 6104(c)(1) and (c)(2) to an ASO the following returns and return information with respect to a charitable organization or applicant:

(i) A refusal or proposed refusal to recognize an organization's exemption as a charitable organization (a final or proposed denial letter).

(ii) Information regarding a grant of exemption following a proposed denial.

(iii) A revocation of exemption as a charitable organization (a final revocation letter), including a notice of termination or dissolution.

(iv) A proposed revocation of recognition of exemption as a charitable organization (a proposed revocation letter).

(v) Information regarding the final disposition of a proposed revocation of recognition other than by final revocation.

(vi) A notice of deficiency or proposed notice of deficiency of tax imposed under section 507 or chapter 41 or 42 on the organization or a taxable person (as described in paragraph (i)(4) of this section).

(vii) Information regarding the final disposition of a proposed notice of deficiency of tax imposed under section 507 or chapter 41 or 42 on the organization other than by issuance of a final notice of deficiency.

(viii) The names, addresses, and taxpayer identification numbers of applicants for charitable status, provided on an applicant-by-applicant basis or by periodic lists of applicants. Under this provision the IRS may respond to inquiries from an ASO as to whether a particular organization has applied for recognition of exemption as a charitable organization.

(ix) Information regarding the final disposition of an application for recognition of exemption where no proposed denial letter is issued, including whether the application was withdrawn or whether the applicant failed to establish its exemption.

(x) Returns and other return information relating to the return information described in this paragraph (c)(1), except for returns and return information relating to proposed notices of deficiency described in paragraph (c)(1)(vi) of this section with respect to taxable persons.

(2) The IRS may disclose or make available for inspection returns and return information of a charitable organization or applicant, if the IRS determines that such information might constitute evidence of noncompliance with the laws under the jurisdiction of the ASO regulating charitable organizations and applicants. Such information may be disclosed on the IRS' own initiative. Disclosures under this paragraph (c)(2) may be made before the IRS issues a proposed determination (denial of recognition, revocation, or notice of deficiency) or any other action by the IRS described in this section.

(d) *Organizations to which disclosure applies.*—Regarding the information described in paragraphs (a)(2) and (c) of this section, the IRS will disclose or make available for inspection to an ASO such information only with respect to—

(1) an organization formed under the laws of the ASO's state;

(2) an organization, the principal office of which is located in the ASO's state;

(3) an organization that, as determined by the IRS, is or might be subject to the laws of the ASO's state regulating charitable organizations or the solicitation or administration of charitable funds or charitable assets; or

(4) a private foundation required by §1.6033-2(a)(iv) to list the ASO's state on any of the foundation's returns filed for its last five years.

(e) *Disclosure limitations.*—Notwithstanding any other provision of this section, the IRS will not disclose or make available for inspection under section 6104(c) any information, the disclosure of which it determines would seriously impair federal tax administration, including, but not limited to—

(1) identification of a confidential informant or interference with a civil or criminal tax investigation; and

(2) information obtained pursuant to a tax convention between the United States and a foreign government (see section 6105(c)(2) for the definition of *tax convention*).

(f) *Disclosure recipients.*—(1) *In general.*—The IRS may disclose returns and return information under section 6104(c) to, or make it available for inspection by—

(i) an ASO, as defined in paragraph (i)(1) of this section, or

(ii) a person other than an ASO, but only if that person is a state officer or employee designated by the ASO to receive information under section 6104(c) on behalf of the ASO, as specified in paragraph (f)(2) of this section.

(2) *Designation by ASO.*—An ASO may designate state officers or employees to receive information under section 6104(c) on the ASO's behalf by specifying in writing each person's name and job title, and the name and address of the person's office. The ASO must promptly notify the IRS in writing of any additions, deletions, or other changes to the list of designated persons.

(g) *Redisclosure.*—An ASO to whom a return or return information has been disclosed may thereafter disclose such information—

(1) to another state officer or employee only as necessary to administer state laws governing charitable organizations or state laws regulating the solicitation or administration of charitable funds or charitable assets of noncharitable exempt organizations; or

(2) except as provided in paragraph (h)(1) of this section, to another state officer or employee who is personally and directly preparing for a civil proceeding before a state administrative body or court in a matter involving the enforcement of state laws regulating organizations with respect to which information can be disclosed under this section, solely for use in such a proceeding, but only if—

(i) the organization or a taxable person is a party to the proceeding, or the proceeding arose out of, or in connection with, determining the civil liability of the organization or a taxable person, or collecting such civil liability, under state laws governing organizations with respect to which information can be disclosed under this section;

(ii) the treatment of an item reflected on such a return is directly related to the resolution of an issue in the proceeding; or

(iii) the return or return information directly relates to a transactional relationship between the organization or a taxable person and a person who is a party to the proceeding that directly affects the resolution of an issue in the proceeding.

(h) *Redisclosure limitations.*—(1) Before disclosing in a state administrative or judicial proceeding, or to any party as provided by paragraph (g)(2) of this section, any return or return information received under section 6104(c), the ASO shall notify the IRS of the intention to make such a disclosure. No state officer or employee shall make such a disclosure except in accordance with any conditions the IRS might impose in response to the ASO's notice of intent. No such disclosure shall be made if the IRS determines that the disclosure would seriously impair federal tax administration.

(2) An ASO to whom a return or return information has been disclosed shall not disclose that information to an agent or contractor.

(i) *Definitions.*—(1) *Appropriate state officer* means—

(i) the state attorney general;

(ii) the state tax officer;

(iii) with respect to a charitable organization or applicant, any state officer other than the attorney general or tax officer charged with overseeing charitable organizations; and

(iv) with respect to a section 501(c) organization that is not described in section 501(c)(1) or (c)(3), the head of the agency designated by the state attorney general as having primary responsibility for overseeing the solicitation of funds for charitable purposes. A state officer described in paragraph (i)(1)(iii) or (i)(1)(iv) of this section must show that the officer is an ASO by presenting a letter from the state attorney general describing the functions and authority of the officer under state law, with sufficient facts for the IRS to determine that the officer is an ASO.

(2) *Return* has the same meaning as in section 6103(b)(1).

(3) *Return information* has the same meaning as in section 6103(b)(2).

(4) *Taxable person* means any person who is liable or potentially liable for excise taxes under chapter 41 or 42. Such a person includes—

(i) a disqualified person described in section 4946(a)(1), 4951(e)(4), or 4958(f);

(ii) a foundation manager described in section 4946(b);

(iii) an organization manager described in section 4955(f)(2) or 4958(f)(2);

(iv) a person described in section 4958(c)(3)(B);

(v) an entity manager described in section 4965(d); and

(vi) a fund manager described in section 4966(d)(3).

(j) *Failure to comply.*—Upon a determination that an ASO has failed to comply with the requirements of section 6103(p)(4), the IRS may take the actions it deems necessary to ensure compliance, including the refusal to disclose any further returns or return information to the ASO until the IRS determines that the requirements have been met. For procedures for the administrative review of a determination that an authorized recipient has failed to safeguard returns or return information, see § 301.6103(p)(7)-1.

(k) *Effective/applicability date.*—The rules of this section apply to taxable years beginning on or after the date of publication in the **Federal Register** of the Treasury decision adopting these rules as final regulations. [Reg. § 301.6104(c)-1.]

Gifts and Bequests from Covered Expatriates: Imposition of Tax

Gifts and Bequests from Covered Expatriates: Imposition of Tax.—Reg. § 28.6107-1, relating to a tax on United States citizens and residents who receive gifts or bequests from certain individuals who relinquished United States citizenship or ceased to be lawful permanent residents of the United States on or after June 17, 2008, is proposed (published in the Federal Register on September 10, 2015) (REG-112997-10).

Section 28.6107-1 is added to read as follows:

§ 28.6107-1. Tax return preparer must furnish copy of return or claim for refund to taxpayer and must retain a copy or record.—(a) *In general.*—A person who is a signing tax return preparer of any return or claim for refund of any tax to which this part 28 applies must furnish a completed copy of the return or claim for refund to the taxpayer and retain a completed copy or record in the manner stated in § 1.6107-1 of this chapter.

(b) *Effective/applicability dates.*—This section applies to returns and claims for refund filed on or after the date of publication of a Treasury decision adopting these rules as final regulations in the **Federal Register**. [Reg. § 28.6107-1.]

Gifts and Bequests from Covered Expatriates: Imposition of Tax

Gifts and Bequests from Covered Expatriates: Imposition of Tax.—Reg. § 28.6109-1, relating to a tax on United States citizens and residents who receive gifts or bequests from certain individuals who relinquished United States citizenship or ceased to be lawful permanent residents of the United States on or after June 17, 2008, is proposed (published in the Federal Register on September 10, 2015) (REG-112997-10).

Section 28.6109-1 is added to read as follows:

§ 28.6109-1. Tax return preparers furnishing identifying numbers for returns or claims for refund.—(a) *In general.*—Each tax return or claim for refund of the tax under chapter 15 of subtitle B of the Internal Revenue Code prepared by one or more signing tax return preparers must include the identifying number of the preparer required by § 1.6695-1(b) of this chapter to sign the return or claim for refund in the manner stated in § 1.6109-2 of this chapter.

(b) *Effective/applicability date.*—This section applies on and after the date of publication of a Treasury decision adopting these rules as final regulations in the **Federal Register**. [Reg. § 28.6109-1.]

Tax Return Preparer: Furnishing Identifying Number

Tax Return Preparer: Furnishing Identifying Number.—Amendments to Reg. § 1.6109-2, providing guidance on the eligibility of tax return preparers to obtain a preparer tax identification number (PTIN), are proposed (published in the Federal Register on February 15, 2012) (REG-124791-11).

☐ Par. 2. Section 1.6109-2 is amended by adding a new sentence to the end of paragraph (a)(1) and revising paragraphs (d), (f), (h) and (i) to read as follows:

§ 1.6109-2. Tax return preparers furnishing identifying numbers for returns or claims for refund and related requirements.

(a) * * *

(1) * * * For purposes of this section only, the terms *tax return* and *claim for refund of tax* include all tax forms submitted to the Internal Revenue Service unless specifically excluded by the Internal Revenue Service in other appropriate guidance.

* * *

(d)(1) Beginning after December 31, 2010, all tax return preparers must have a preparer tax identification number or other prescribed identifying number that was applied for and received at the time and in the manner, including the payment of a user fee, as may be prescribed by the Internal Revenue Service in forms, instructions, or other appropriate guidance.

(2) Except as provided in paragraph (h) of this section, to obtain a preparer tax identification number or other prescribed identifying number, a tax return preparer must be one of the following:

(i) An attorney;

(ii) A certified public accountant;

(iii) An enrolled agent;

(iv) A registered tax return preparer authorized to practice before the Internal Revenue Service under 31 U.S.C. 330 and the regulations thereunder;

(v) An individual 18 years of age or older who is supervised, in the manner the Internal Revenue Service prescribes in forms, instructions, or other appropriate guidance, as a tax return preparer by an attorney, certified public accountant, enrolled agent, enrolled retirement plan agent, or enrolled actuary authorized to practice before the Internal Revenue Service under 31 U.S.C. 330 and the regulations thereunder; or

(vi) An individual 18 years of age or older who certifies that the individual is a tax return preparer exclusively with respect to tax returns and claims for refund of tax that are not covered, at the time the tax return preparer applies for or renews the number, by a minimum competency examination prescribed by the Internal Revenue Service in forms, instructions, or other appropriate guidance. An individual must comply with any requirements at the time and in the manner that the Internal Revenue Service may prescribe in forms, instructions, or other appropriate guidance.

* * *

(f) As may be prescribed in forms, instructions, or other appropriate guidance, the Internal Revenue Service may conduct a Federal tax compliance check and a suitability check on a tax return preparer who applies for or renews a preparer tax identification number or other prescribed identifying number.

* * *

(h) The Internal Revenue Service, through forms, instructions, or other appropriate guidance, may prescribe exceptions to the requirements of this section, including the requirement that an individual be authorized to practice before the Internal Revenue Service before receiving a preparer tax identification number or other prescribed identifying number, as necessary in the interest of effective tax administration.

(i) *Effective/applicability date*.—Paragraph (a)(1) of this section applies to tax returns and claims for refund filed after December 31, 2008, except the last sentence of paragraph (a)(1), which applies to tax returns and claims for refund filed on or after the date that final regulations are published in the **Federal Register**. Paragraph (a)(2)(i) of this section applies to tax returns and claims for refund filed on or before December 31, 2010. Paragraph (a)(2)(ii) of this section applies to tax returns and claims for refund filed after December 31, 2010. Paragraph (d)(1) of this section applies to tax return preparers after December 31, 2010. Paragraph (d)(2) of this section applies to tax return preparers on or after the date that final regulations are published in the **Federal Register**. Paragraph (e) of this section applies after September 30, 2010. Paragraph (f) of this section applies on or after the date that final regulations are published in the **Federal Register**. Paragraphs (g) and (h) of this section apply after September 30, 2010.

Dependency Exemption: Authorized Placement Agency: Definition

Dependency Exemption: Authorized Placement Agency: Definition.—Amendments to Reg. §301.6109-3, relating to the definition of an authorized placement agency for purposes of a dependency exemption for a child placed for adoption that were issued prior to the changes made to the law by the Working Families Tax Relief Act of 2004, are proposed (published in the Federal Register on January 19, 2017) (REG-137604-07).

Par. 20. Section 301.6109-3 is amended by:

1. Revising the first sentence and adding a sentence to the end of the paragraph in paragraph (a)(1).

2. Revising paragraphs (b), (c)(1)(ii), the fourth and fifth sentences of (c)(2) introductory text, and paragraph (d).

The revisions and addition read as follows:

§301.6109-3. IRS adoption taxpayer identification numbers.—(a) *In general*.—(1) *Definition*.—An IRS adoption taxpayer identification number (ATIN) is a temporary taxpayer identifying number assigned by the Internal Revenue Service (IRS) to a child (other than an alien individual as defined in §301.6109-1(d)(3)(i)) who has been placed lawfully with a prospective adoptive parent for legal adoption by that person. * * * A child lawfully placed with a prospective adoptive parent for legal adoption includes a child placed for legal adoption by the child's parent or parents by blood, an authorized placement agency, or any other person authorized by State law to place a child for legal adoption.

* * *

(b) *Definitions*.—(1) Authorized placement agency has the same meaning as in §1.152-1(b)(1)(iv).

(2) *Child* means a child who has not been adopted but has been placed lawfully with a prospective adoptive parent for legal adoption by that person.

(3) *Prospective adoptive parent* means a person in whose household a child has been placed lawfully for legal adoption by that person.

(c) * * *

(1) * * *

(ii) The child has been placed lawfully with the prospective adoptive parent for legal adoption by that person;

* * *

(2) * * * In addition, the application must include documentary evidence the IRS prescribes to establish that a child has been placed lawfully with the prospective adoptive parent for legal adoption by that person. Examples of acceptable documentary evidence estab-

lishing lawful placement for a legal adoption may include—

* * *

(d) *Applicability date.*—(1) *In general.*—Except as otherwise provided in paragraph (d)(2) of this section, the provisions of this section apply to income tax returns due (without regard to extension) on or after April 15, 1998.

(2) *Exception.*—Paragraphs (a)(1), (b), (c)(1)(ii), and (c)(2) of this section apply to income tax returns due (without regard to extension) on or after the date these regulations are published as final regulations in the **Federal Register**.

Forms W-2: Use of Truncated Taxpayer Identification Numbers

Forms W-2: Use of Truncated Taxpayer Identification Numbers.—Amendments to Reg. §301.6109-4, permitting employers to voluntarily truncate employees' social security numbers on copies of Forms W-2, Wage and Tax Statement, that are furnished to employees so that the truncated SSNs appear in the form of IRS truncated taxpayer identification numbers, are proposed (published in the Federal Register on September 20, 2017) (REG-105004-16).

Par. 8. Section 301.6109-4 is amended by revising paragraphs (b)(2)(ii) and (iii), (b)(3), and (c) to read as follows:

§301.6109-4. Payment and returns of tax withheld by the acquiring agency.

* * *

(b) * * *

(2) * * *

(ii) A TTIN may not be used on a statement or document if a statute, regulation, other guidance published in the Internal Revenue Bulletin, form, or instructions, specifically requires use of a SSN, ITIN, ATIN, or EIN and does not specifically state that the taxpayer identifying number may be truncated. For example, a TTIN may not be used on a Form W–8ECI or Form W–8IMY because the forms and/or form instructions specifically prescribe use of an SSN, EIN, or ITIN for the U.S. taxpayer identification number.

(iii) A TTIN may not be used on any return, statement, or other document that is required to be filed with or furnished to the Internal Revenue Service or the Social Security Administration in the case of forms required to be filed with the Social Security Administration under the internal revenue laws.

* * *

(3) *Examples.*—The provisions of this paragraph (b) are illustrated by the following examples:

(i) *Example 1.*—Pursuant to section 6051(d) and §31.6051-2(a) of this chapter, Employer files the Social Security Administration copy of Employee's Form W-2, Wage and Tax Statement, with the Social Security Administration. Employer may not truncate any identifying number on the Social Security Administration copy. Pursuant to section 6051(a) and §31.6051-1(a)(1)(i) of this chapter, Employer furnishes copies of Form W-2 to Employee. There are no applicable statutes, regulations, other published guidance, forms, or instructions that prohibit use of a TTIN on Form W-2, and §31.6051-1(a)(1)(i) specifically permits truncating employees' SSNs. Accordingly, Employer may truncate Employee's SSN to appear in the form of a TTIN on copies of Form W-2 furnished to Employee. Employer may not truncate its own EIN on copies of Form W-2 furnished to Employee.

(ii) *Example 2.*—On April 5, year 1, Donor contributes a used car with a blue book value of $1100 to Charitable Organization. On April 20, year 1, Charitable Organization sends Donor copies B and C of the Form 1098-C as a contemporaneous written acknowledgement of the $1100 contribution as required by section 170(f)(12). In late - February, year 2, Charitable Organization prepares and files copy A of Form 1098-C with the IRS, reporting Donor's donation of a qualified vehicle in year 1. Charitable Organization may truncate Donor's SSN to appear in the form of a TTIN in the Donor's Identification Number box on copies B and C of the Form 1098-C because copies B and C of the Form 1098-C are documents required by the Internal Revenue Code and regulations to be furnished to another person; there are no applicable statutes, regulations, other published guidance, forms or instructions that prohibit the use of a TTIN on those copies; and there are no applicable statutes, regulations, other published guidance, forms, or instructions that specifically require use of an SSN or other identifying number on those copies. Charitable Organization may not truncate its own EIN on copies B and C of the Form 1098-C because a person cannot truncate its own taxpayer identifying number on any statement or other document the person furnishes to another person. Charitable Organization may not truncate any identifying number on copy A of the Form 1098-C because copy A is required to be filed with the IRS.

(c) *Applicability date.*—This section is applicable to returns, statements and other documents required to be filed or furnished after December 31, 2018.

Tax Shelter Registration: Questions and Answers

Tax Shelter Registration: Questions and Answers.—Temporary Reg. §301.6111-1T, relating to tax shelter registration, is also proposed as a final regulation and, when adopted, would become Reg. §301.6111-1 (published in the Federal Register on August 15, 1984).

§301.6111-1. Questions and answers relating to tax shelter registration.

Tax Shelter Registration: Abusers: Lists

Tax Shelter Registration: List of Potential Abusers.—An amendment to Temporary Reg. § 301.6111-1T, relating to tax shelter registration and the requirement to maintain lists of investors in potentially abusive tax shelters, is also proposed as final (published in the Federal Register on October 31, 1984).

§ 301.6111-1. Questions and answers relating to tax shelter registration.

Tax Shelter Registration: Amended Application

Registration of Tax Shelters: Amended Application.—An amendment to Temporary Reg. § 301.6111-1T, relating to the registration of tax shelters, is also proposed as final (published in the Federal Register on March 4, 1986).

§ 301.6111-1. Questions and answers relating to tax shelter registration.

Reportable Transactions: Disclosure: Patented Transactions

Reportable Transactions: Disclosure: Patented Transactions.—Amendments to Reg. § 301.6111-3, providing rules to the disclosure of reportable transactions, including patented transactions, under Code Secs. 6011 and 6111, are proposed (published in the Federal Register on September 26, 2007) (REG-129916-07).

☐ Par. 4. Section 301.6111-3 is amended by revising paragraphs (b)(2)(ii)(E), (b)(3)(i)(C), and (i)(2) to read as follows:

§ 301.6111-3. Disclosures of reportable transactions.

* * *

(b) * * *

(2) * * *

(ii) * * *

(E) *Patented transactions.*—A statement relates to a tax aspect of a transaction that causes it to be a patented transaction if the statement is made or provided by the patent holder or by the patent holder's agent, as defined in § 1.6011-4(b)(7)(ii)(C) or (D) of this chapter, and concerns the tax planning method that is the subject of the patent.

* * *

(3) * * *

(i) * * *

(C) *Patented transactions.*—For patented transactions described in § 1.6011-4(b)(7) of this chapter, the threshold amounts in § 301.6111-3(b)(3)(i)(A) are reduced from $50,000 to $250 and from $250,000 to $500.

* * *

(i) * * *

(2) *Patented transactions.*—Upon the publication of the Treasury decision adopting these rules as final regulations in the Federal Register, paragraphs (b)(2)(ii)(E) and (b)(3)(i)(C) of this section will apply to transactions with respect to which a material advisor makes a tax statement on or after September 26, 2007.

TIME AND PLACE FOR PAYING TAX

Gifts and Bequests from Covered Expatriates: Imposition of Tax

Gifts and Bequests from Covered Expatriates: Imposition of Tax.—Reg. § 28.6151-1, relating to a tax on United States citizens and residents who receive gifts or bequests from certain individuals who relinquished United States citizenship or ceased to be lawful permanent residents of the United States on or after June 17, 2008, is proposed (published in the Federal Register on September 10, 2015) (REG-112997-10).

Section 28.6151-1 is added to read as follows:

§ 28.6151-1. Time and place for paying tax shown on returns.—The tax due under this part 28 must be paid at the time prescribed in § 28.6071-1 for filing the return, and at the place prescribed in § 28.6091-1 for filing the return. [Reg. § 28.6151-1.]

Enrolled and Enrolled Retirement Plan Agents: Fees

Enrolled and Enrolled Retirement Plan Agents: Fees.—Amendments to Reg. § 300.0, relating to imposing user fees for enrolled agents and enrolled retirement plan agents, are proposed (published in the Federal Register on November 19, 2018) (REG-122898-17).

Par. 2. Section 300.0 is amended by removing paragraph (b)(10) and redesignating paragraphs (b)(11) through (13) as paragraphs (b)(10) through (12).

§ 300.0. User fees; in general.

User Fees: Offers in Compromise

User Fees: Offers in Compromise.—Amendments to Reg. § 300.3, affecting taxpayers who wish to pay their liabilities through offers in compromise, are proposed (published in the Federal Register on October 13, 2016) (REG-108934-16).

Par 2. In § 300.3, paragraphs (b)(1) introductory text and (d) are revised to read as follows:

§ 300.3. Offer to compromise fee.

* * *

(b) *Fee.*—(1) The fee for processing an offer to compromise submitted before February 27, 2017, is $186. The fee for processing an offer to compromise submitted on or after February 27, 2017, is $300. No fee will be charged if an offer is—* * *

* * *

(d) *Effective/applicability date.*—This section is applicable beginning February 27, 2017.

Enrolled and Enrolled Retirement Plan Agents: Fees

Enrolled and Enrolled Retirement Plan Agents: Fees.—Amendments to Reg. §§ 300.5 and 300.6, relating to imposing user fees for enrolled agents and enrolled retirement plan agents, are proposed (published in the Federal Register on November 19, 2018) (REG-122898-17).

Par. 3. Section 300.5 is amended by revising paragraphs (b) and (d) to read as follows:

§ 300.5. Enrollment of enrolled agent fee.

* * *

(b) *Fee.*—The fee for initially enrolling as an enrolled agent with the IRS is $67.

* * *

(d) *Applicability date.*—This section applies 30 days after the date of publication of a Treasury Decision adopting this rule as a final regulation in the Federal Register.

Par. 4. Section 300.6 is amended by revising paragraphs (b) and (d) to read as follows:

§ 300.6. Renewal of enrollment of enrolled agent fee.

* * *

(b) *Fee.*—The fee for renewal of enrollment as an enrolled agent with the IRS is $67.

* * *

(d) *Applicability date.*—This section applies 30 days after the date of publication of a Treasury Decision adopting this rule as a final regulation in the Federal Register.

Enrolled and Enrolled Retirement Plan Agents: Fees

Enrolled and Enrolled Retirement Plan Agents: Fees.—Amendments to Reg. §§ 300.10—300.13, relating to imposing user fees for enrolled agents and enrolled retirement plan agents, are proposed (published in the Federal Register on November 19, 2018) (REG-122898-17).

Par. 5. Section 300.10 is removed.

§ 300.10. Enrolled retirement plan agent special enrollment examination fee.

Par. 6. Redesignate § 300.11 as § 300.10 and revise newly-redesignated § 300.10 to read as follows:

§ 300.10. Renewal of enrollment of enrolled retirement plan agent fee.

* * *

(b) *Fee.*—The fee for renewal of enrollment as an enrolled retirement plan agent with the IRS is $67.

* * *

(d) *Applicability date.*—This section applies 30 days after the date of publication of a Treasury Decision adopting this rule as a final regulation in the Federal Register.

Par. 7. Redesignate § § 300.12 and 300.13 as § § 300.11 and 300.12.

§ 300.11. Registered tax return preparer competency examination fee.

Par. 7. Redesignate § § 300.12 and 300.13 as § § 300.11 and 300.12.

§ 300.12. Fee for obtaining a preparer tax identification number.

Estimated Tax: Corporations

Estimated Tax: Corporations.—Reproduced below are the texts of proposed amendments to Reg. §§ 1.6164-4 and 1.6164-8, relating to estimated tax requirements for corporations (published in the Federal Register on March 26, 1984).

☐ Par. 2. Paragraph (a) of § 1.6164-4 is revised to read as follows:

§ 1.6164-4. Payment of remainder of tax where extension relates only to part of the tax.—(a) *Time for payment.*—If an extension of time relates only to part of the tax, the time for payment of the remainder of the tax shall be considered to be the date on which payment would have been required if such remainder had been the tax.

* * *

☐ Par. 3. Paragraph (a) of § 1.6164-8 is revised to read as follows:

§1.6164-8. Payments on termination.—(a) *In general.*—If an extension of time under section 6164 is terminated with respect to any amount either (1) by the filing of a new statement by the taxpayer under section 6164(e) extending the time for payment of a lesser amount than was extended in a prior statement, or (2) by action of the district director under section 6164(f) after making an examination of the statement filed by the corporation, no further extension of time may be made under section 6164 with respect to such amount. The time for payment of such amount shall be the date on which payment would have been required if there had been no extension with respect to such amount.

* * *

ASSESSMENT

Partnerships: Centralized Partnership Audit Regime

Partnerships: Centralized Partnership Audit Regime.—Reg. 301.6225-4, implementing the centralized partnership audit regime that have not been finalized to reflect the changes made by the Technical Corrections Act of 2018, contained in Title II of the Consolidated Appropriations Act of 2018 (TTCA), is proposed (published in the Federal Register on August 17, 2018) (REG-136118-15; REG-119337-17; REG-118067-17; REG-120232-17 and REG-120233-17).

Par. 11. Section 301.6225-4 is added to read as follows:

§301.6225-4. Effect of a partnership adjustment on specified tax attributes of partnerships and their partners.—(a) *Adjustments to specified tax attributes.*—(1) *In general.*—When there is a partnership adjustment (as defined in §301.6241-1(a)(6)), the partnership and its adjustment year partners (as defined in §301.6241-1(a)(2)) generally must adjust their specified tax attributes (as defined in paragraph (a)(2) of this section) in accordance with the rules in this section. For a partnership adjustment that results in an imputed underpayment (as defined in §301.6241-1(a)(3)), specified tax attributes are generally adjusted by making appropriate adjustments to the book value and basis of partnership property under paragraph (b)(2) of this section, creating notional items based on the partnership adjustment under paragraph (b)(3) of this section, allocating those notional items as described in paragraph (b)(5) of this section, and determining the effect of those notional items for the partnership and its reviewed year partners (as defined in §301.6241-1(a)(9)) or their successors (as defined in §1.704-1(b)(1)(viii)(*b*) of this chapter) under paragraph (b)(6) of this section. Paragraph (c) of this section describes how to treat an expenditure for any payment required to be made by a partnership under subchapter C of chapter 63 of the Internal Revenue Code (subchapter C of chapter 63) including any imputed underpayment. Paragraph (d) of this section describes adjustments to tax attributes of a partnership and its partners in the case of a partnership adjustment that does not result in an imputed underpayment (as described in §301.6225-1(f)).

(2) *Specified tax attributes.*—Specified tax attributes are the tax basis and book value of a partnership's property, amounts determined under section 704(c), adjustment year partners' bases in their partnership interests, adjustment year partners' capital accounts determined and maintained in accordance with §1.704-1(b)(2) of this chapter, and earnings and profits under section 312.

(3) *Timing.*—Adjustments to specified tax attributes under this section are made in the adjustment year (as defined in §301.6241-1(a)(1)). Thus, to the extent that an adjustment to a specified tax attribute under this section is reflected on a federal tax return, the partnership adjustment is generally first reflected on any return filed with respect to the adjustment year.

(4) *Effect of other sections.*—The determination of specified tax attributes under this section is not conclusive as to tax attributes of a partnership or its partners determined under other sections of the Internal Revenue Code (Code), including the subchapter C of chapter 63. For example, a partnership that files an administrative adjustment request (AAR) under section 6227 adjusts partnership tax attributes as appropriate. Further, to the extent a partner or partnership appropriately adjusted its tax attributes prior to a final determination under subchapter C of chapter 63 with respect to a partnership adjustment (for example, in the context of an amended return modification described in §301.6225-2(d)(2), the alternative procedure to filing amended returns as described in §301.6225-2(d)(2)(x), or a closing agreement described in §301.6225-2(d)(8)), those tax attributes are not adjusted under this section. Similarly, to the extent a partner filed a return inconsistent with the treatment of items on a partnership return, a reviewed year partner (or its successor) does not adjust its tax attributes to the extent the partner's prior return was consistent with the partnership adjustment. For the rules regarding consistent treatment by partners, see §301.6222-1.

(5) *Election under section 6226.*—(i) *In general.*—Except as otherwise provided in paragraph (a)(5)(ii) of this section, tax attributes of a partnership and its partners are adjusted for a partnership adjustment that results in an imputed underpayment with respect to which an election is made under §301.6226-1 in accordance with §301.6226-4, and not the rules of this section.

(ii) *Pass-through partners and indirect partners.*—A pass-through partner (as defined in §301.6241-1(a)(5)) that is a partnership and pays an imputed underpayment under §301.6226-3(e)(4) treats its share of each partnership adjustment reflected on the relevant statement as a partnership adjustment described in paragraph (a)(1) of this section, treats the imputed underpayment under §301.6226-3(e)(4)(iii) as an imputed underpayment determined under §301.6225-1 for purposes of §1.704-1(b)(2)(iii)(*a*) and (*f*) of this chapter, treats items arising from an adjustment that does not result in an imputed underpayment as an item under paragraph (d) of this section, and finally treats amounts with respect to any penalties, additions to tax, and additional amounts and interest computed as an amount described in §1.704-1(b)(2)(iii)(*f*)(*3*) of this chapter.

(6) *Reflection of economic arrangement.*—This section and the rules in §1.704-1(b)(1)(viii), (b)(2)(iii)(*a*) and (*f*), (b)(2)(iv)(*i*)(*4*), and (b)(4)(xi), (xii), (xiii), (xiv), and (xv) of this chapter must be interpreted in a manner that reflects the economic arrangement of the parties and the principles of subchapter K of the Code, taking into account the rules of the centralized partnership audit regime.

(b) *Adjusting specified tax attributes in the case of a partnership adjustment that results in an imputed underpayment.*—(1) *In general.*—This paragraph (b) applies with respect to each partnership adjustment that was taken into account in the determination of the imputed underpayment under §301.6225-1, except to the extent partner or partnership tax attributes were already adjusted as part of the partnership adjustment.

(2) *Book value and basis of partnership property.*—Partnership-level specified tax attributes must be adjusted under this paragraph (b)(2). Specifically, the partnership must make appropriate adjustments to the book value and basis of property to take into account any partnership adjustment. No adjustments are made with respect to property that was held by the partnership in the reviewed year but is no longer held by the partnership in the adjustment year. Amounts determined under section 704(c) must also be adjusted to take into account the partnership adjustment.

(3) *Creation of notional items based on partnership adjustment.*—(i) *In general.*—In order to give appropriate effect to each partnership adjustment for partner-level specified tax attributes, notional items are created with respect to each partnership adjustment, except as provided in paragraph (b)(4) of this section.

(ii) *Increase in income or gain.*—In the case of a partnership adjustment that is an increase to income or gain, a notional item of income or gain is created in an amount equal to the partnership adjustment.

(iii) *Increase in expense or loss.*—In the case of a partnership adjustment that is an increase to an expense or a loss, a notional item of an expense or loss is created in an amount equal to the partnership adjustment.

(iv) *Decrease in income or gain.*—In the case of a partnership adjustment that is a decrease to income or gain, a notional item of expense or loss is created in an amount equal to the partnership adjustment.

(v) *Decrease in expense or loss.*—In the case of a partnership adjustment that is a decrease to an expense or to a loss, a notional item of income or gain is created in an amount equal to the partnership adjustment.

(vi) *Credits.*—If a partnership adjustment reflects a net increase or net decrease in credits as determined in accordance with §301.6225-1, the partnership may have one or more notional items of income, gain, loss, or deduction that reflects the change in the item that gives rise to the credit, and those items are treated as items in paragraph (b)(3)(ii), (iii), (iv), or (v) of this section. For example, if a partnership adjustment is to a credit, a notional item of deduction may be created when appropriate. See section 280C.

(4) *Situations in which notional items are not created.*—(i) *In general.*—In the case of a partnership adjustment described in this paragraph (b)(4), or when the creation of a notional item would duplicate a specified tax attribute or an actual item already taken into account, notional items are not created. Nevertheless, in these situations specified tax attributes are adjusted for the partnership and its reviewed year partners or their successors (as defined in §1.704-1(b)(i)(viii)(*b*) of this chapter) in a manner that is consistent with how the partnership adjustment would have been taken into account under the partnership agreement in effect for the reviewed year taking into account all facts and circumstances. See §1.704-1(b)(2)(iii)(*f*)(*4*) of this chapter for rules for allocating the expenditure for an imputed underpayment in these circumstances.

(ii) *Adjustments for non-section 704(b) items.*—Notional items are not created for a partnership adjustment that does not derive from items that would have been allocated in the reviewed year under section 704(b). See paragraph (e) of this section, *Example 5*.

(iii) *Section 705(a)(2)(B) expenditures.*—Notional items are not created for a partnership adjustment that is a change of an item of deduction to a section 705(a)(2)(B) expenditure.

(iv) *Tax-exempt income.*—Notional items are not created for a partnership adjustment to an item of income of a partnership exempt from tax under subtitle A of the Code.

(5) *Allocation of the notional items.*—Notional items are allocated to the reviewed year partners or their successors under §1.704-1(b)(4)(xi) of this chapter.

(6) *Effect of notional items.*—(i) *In general.*—The partnership creates notional items of income, gain, loss, deduction, or credit in order to make appropriate adjustments to specified tax attributes. See paragraph (e), *Example 1* of this section.

(ii) *Partner capital accounts.*—For purposes of capital accounts determined and maintained in accordance with §1.704-1(b)(2) of this chapter, a notional item of income, gain, loss, deduction or credit is treated as an item of income, gain, loss, deduction or credit (including for purposes of determining book value). Similar adjustments may be appropriate for partnerships that do not determine and maintain capital accounts in accordance with §1.704-1(b)(2) of this chapter.

(iii) *Partner's basis in its interest.*—(A) *In general.*—Except as otherwise provided, the basis of a partner's interest in a partnership is adjusted (but not below zero) to reflect any notional item allocated to the partner by treating the notional item as an item described in section 705(a).

(B) *Special basis rules.*—The basis of a partner's interest in a partnership is not adjusted for any notional items allocated to the partner —

(*1*) When a partner that is not a tax-exempt entity (as defined in §301.6225-2(d)(3)(ii)) is a successor under §1.704-1(b)(1)(viii)(*b*) of this chapter to a reviewed year tax-exempt partner, to the extent that the IRS approved a modification under

§ 301.6225-2 because the tax-exempt partner was not subject to tax; or

(2) When the notional item would be allocated to a successor that is related (within the meaning of sections 267(b) or 707(b)) to the reviewed year partner, the successor acquired its interest from the reviewed year partner in a transaction (or series of transactions) in which not all gain or loss is recognized during an administrative adjustment proceeding with respect to the partnership's reviewed year under subchapter C of chapter 63, and a principal purpose of the interest transfer (or transfers) was to shift the economic burden of the imputed underpayment among the related parties.

(c) *Determining a partner's share of an expenditure for any payment required to be made by a partnership under subchapter C of chapter 63.*—Payment by a partnership of any amount required to be paid under subchapter C of chapter 63 as described in § 301.6241-4(a) is treated as an expenditure described in section 705(a)(2)(B). Rules for determining whether the economic effect of an allocation of these expenses is substantial are provided in § 1.704-1(b)(2)(iii)(*f*) of this chapter and rules for determining whether an allocation of these expenses is deemed to be in accordance with the partners' interests in the partnership are provided in § 1.704-1(b)(4)(xii) of this chapter.

(d) *Adjusting tax attributes for a partnership adjustment that does not result in an imputed underpayment.*—The rules under subchapter K of the Code apply in the case of a partnership adjustment that does not result in an imputed underpayment. See § 301.6225-3(c). Accordingly, tax attributes (as defined in § 301.6241-1(a)(10)) of a partnership and its partners are adjusted under those rules. An item arising from a partnership adjustment that does not result in an imputed underpayment (as defined in § 301.6225-1(f)) is allocated under § 1.704-1(b)(4)(xiii) of this chapter.

(e) *Examples.*—The following examples illustrate the rules of this section. For purposes of these examples, unless otherwise stated, Partnership is subject to the provisions of subchapter C of chapter 63, Partnership and its partners are calendar year taxpayers, all partners are U.S. persons, and the highest rate of income tax in effect for all taxpayers is 20 percent for all relevant periods.

Example 1. (i) In 2019, A, B, and C are individuals that form Partnership. A contributes Whiteacre, which is unimproved land with an adjusted basis of $400 and a fair market value of $1000, and B and C each contribute $1000 in cash. The partnership agreement provides that all income, gain, loss, and deduction will be allocated in equal 1/3 shares among the partners. The partnership agreement also provides that the partners' capital accounts will be determined and maintained in accordance with § 1.704-1(b)(2)(iv) of this chapter, distributions in liquidation of the partnership (or any partner's interest) will be made in accordance with the partners' positive capital account balances, and any partner with a deficit balance in his capital account following the liquidation of his interest must restore that deficit to the partnership (as provided in § 1.704-1(b)(2)(ii)(*b*)(*2*) and *(3)* of this chapter).

(ii) Upon formation, Partnership has the following assets and capital accounts:

	Partnership Basis	*Book*	*Value*
Cash	$2000	$2000	$2000
Whiteacre	400	1000	1000
Totals	2400	3000	3000

	Outside Basis	*Book*	*Value*
A	$400	$1000	$1000
B	1000	1000	1000
C	1000	1000	1000
	2400	3000	3000

(iii) In 2019, Partnership makes a $120 payment for Asset that it treats as a deductible expense on its partnership return.

	Partnership Basis	*Book*	*Value*
Cash	$1880	$1880	$1880
Whiteacre	400	1000	1000
Asset	0	0	120
Totals	2280	2880	3000

	Outside Basis	*Book*	*Value*
A	$360	$960	$1000
B	960	960	1000
C	960	960	1000
	2280	2880	3000

(iv) Partnership does not file an AAR for 2020. In 2021 (the adjustment year) it is finally determined that Partnership's $120 expenditure was not allowed as a deduction in 2019 (the reviewed year), but rather was the acquisition of an asset for which cost recovery deductions are unavailable. Accordingly, the IRS makes a partnership adjustment that disallows the entire $120 deduction, which results in an imputed underpayment of $48 ($120 x 40 percent). Partnership did not request modification under § 301.6225-2. Partnership pays the $48 imputed underpayment.

(v) Partnership first determines its tax attribute adjustments resulting from the partnership adjustment by applying paragraph (b) of this section. Pursuant to paragraph (b)(2) of this section, Partnership must re-state the basis and book value of Asset to $120. Further, pursuant to paragraph (b)(3)(v) of this section, a $120 notional item of income is created. The $120 item of notional income is allocated in equal shares ($40) to A, B, and C in 2021 under § 1.704-1(b)(4)(xi) of this chapter. Accordingly, in 2021 Partnership increases the capital accounts of A, B, and C by $40 each, and increases A, B, and C's outside bases by $40 each under paragraph (b)(6)(ii) and (iii) of this section, respectively.

(vi) As described in paragraph (c) of this section, Partnership's payment of the $48 imputed underpayment is treated as an expenditure described in section 705(a)(2)(B) under § 301.6241-4. Under § 1.704-1(b)(4)(xii) of this chapter, Partnership determines each partner's properly allocable share of this expenditure in 2021 by allocating the expenditure in proportion to the allocations of the notional item to which the expenditure relates. Accordingly, each of A, B, and C have a properly allocable share of $16 each, which is the same proportion (1/3 each) in which A, B, and C share the $120 item of notional income. Thus, A, B and C's capital accounts are each decreased by $16 in 2021 and A, B and C's outside bases are each decreased by $16 in 2021. The allocation of the expenditure under the partnership agreement has economic effect under § 1.704-1(b)(2)(ii) of this chapter and, because the allocation of the expenditure is determined in accordance with § 1.704-1(b)(2)(iii)(*f*) of this chapter, the economic effect of these allocations is deemed to be substantial.

(vii) The payment is also reflected by a $48 decrease in partnership cash for book purposes under § 1.704-1(b)(4)(ii) of this chapter. Therefore, in 2021, A's basis in Partnership is $384 and his capital account is $984. B and C each have a basis and capital account of $984.

	Partnership Basis	*Book*	*Value*
Cash	$1832	$1832	$1832
Whiteacre	400	1000	1000
Asset	120	120	120
Totals	2352	2952	2952

	Outside Basis	*Book*	*Value*
A	$384	$984	$984
B	984	984	984
C	984	984	984
	2352	2952	2952

Example 2. (i) The facts are the same as in *Example 1* of this paragraph (e), except the IRS approves modification under § 301.6225-2(d)(3) with respect to A, which is a tax-exempt entity, and under § 301.6225-2(d)(4) with respect to C, which is a corporation subject to a tax rate of 20 percent. These modifications reduce Partnership's overall imputed underpayment from $48 to $30.

(ii) As in *Example 1* of this paragraph (e), Partnership determines its tax attribute adjustments resulting from the partnership adjustment by applying paragraph (b) of this section. Pursuant to paragraph (b)(3)(v) of this section, a $120 notional item of income is created. The $120 item of notional income is allocated in equal shares ($40) to A, B, and C in 2021 under § 1.704-1(b)(4)(xi) of this chapter. Accordingly, in 2021 Partnership increases the capital accounts of A, B, and C by $40 each, and increases A, B, and C's outside bases by $40 each under paragraph (b)(6)(ii) and (iii) of this section, respectively.

(iii) However, the modifications affect how Partnership must allocate the imputed underpayment expenditure among A, B, and C in 2021 (the adjustment year) pursuant to § 1.704-1(b)(2)(iii)(*f*) of this chapter. Specifically, Partnership allocates the $24 expenditure in 2021 in proportion to the allocation of the notional item to which it relates (which is 1/3 each as in *Example 1* of this paragraph (e)), but it must also take into account modifications attributable to each partner. Accordingly, B's allocation is $16 (its share of the imputed underpayment, for which no modification occurred), and A and C have properly allocable shares of $0 and $8, respectively (their shares, taking into account modification). Thus, A's capital account is decreased by $0, B's capital account is decreased by $16, and C's capital account is decreased by $8 in 2021 and their respective outside bases are decreased by the same amounts in 2021.

(iv) The payment is also reflected by a $24 decrease in partnership cash for book purposes. Therefore, in 2021, A's basis in Partnership is $400 and his capital account is $1000, B's basis and capital account are both $984, and C's basis and capital account are both $992.

	Partnership Basis	*Book*	*Value*
Cash	$1856	$1856	$1856
Whiteacre	400	1000	1000
Asset	120	120	120
Totals	2376	2976	2976

	Outside Basis	*Book*	*Value*
A	$400	$1000	$1000
B	984	984	984
C	992	992	992
Totals	2376	2976	2976

Example 3. The facts are the same as in *Example 1* of this paragraph (e). However, in 2020, C transfers its entire interest in Partnership to D (an individual) for cash. Under § 1.704-1(b)(2)(iv)(l) of this chapter, C's capital account carries over to D. In 2021, the year the IRS determines that Partnership's $120 expense is not allowed as a deduction, D is C's successor under § 1.704-1(b)(1)(viii)(*b*)(2) of this chapter with respect to specified tax attributes and the payment of the imputed underpayment treated as an expenditure under section 705(a)(2)(B).

Example 4. The facts are the same as in *Example 1* of this paragraph (e), except that the partnership agreement provides that the section 705(a)(2)(B) expenditure for imputed underpayments made by the partnership are specially allocated to A (all other items continue to be allocated in equal shares). Accordingly, in 2021, the section 705(a)(2)(B) expenditure is allocated entirely to A, which reduces its capital account by $48, which has economic effect under § 1.704-1(b)(2)(ii) of this chapter. However, the economic effect of this allocation is not substantial under § 1.704-1(b)(2)(iii)(*a*) of this chapter because it is not allocated in the manner described in § 1.704-1(b)(2)(iii)(*f*) of this chapter. The allocation will also not be deemed to be in accordance with the partners' interests in the partnership under § 1.704-1(b)(3)(ix) of this chapter because it is not allocated pursuant to the rules under § 1.704-1(b)(4)(xii) of this chapter.

Example 5. (i) In 2019, Partnership has two partners, A and B. Both A and B have a $0 basis in their interests in Partnership. Further, Partnership has a $200 liability as defined in § 1.752-1(a)(4) of this chapter. The liability is treated as a nonrecourse liability as defined in § 1.752-1(a)(2) of this chapter so that A and B both are treated as having a $100 share of the liability under § 1.752-3 of this chapter. In 2021 (the adjustment year), the IRS determines that the liability was inappropriately classified as a nonrecourse liability, should have been classified as a recourse liability as defined in § 1.752-1(a)(1) of this chapter, and that A should have no share of the recourse liability under § 1.752-2 of this chapter. The recharacterization of the liability from nonrecourse to recourse and the decrease in A's share of partnership liabilities are adjustments that are not allocated under section 704(b) under § 301.6225-1(c)(5)(ii). As a result of the adjustments, the IRS includes in the residual grouping $100 of increased income to account for the cumulative effects of these adjustments to reflect the $100 decrease in A's share of partnership liabilities under §§ 1.752-1(c) and 1.731-1(a)(1)(i) of this chapter and determines an imputed underpayment of $40 ($100 x 40 percent). Partnership does not request modification under § 301.6225-2. Partnership pays the $40 imputed underpayment.

(ii) Pursuant to paragraph (b)(4)(ii) of this of this section, notional items are not created with respect to this partnership adjustment. Instead, under paragraph (b)(4)(i) of this section, specified tax attributes are adjusted in a manner that is consistent with how the partnership adjustment would have been taken into account under the partnership agreement in effect for the reviewed year taking into account all facts and circumstances. In this case, no specified tax attributes are adjusted.

(iii) However, because A would have borne the economic burden of the partnership adjustment if the partnership and its partners had originally reported in a manner consistent with the partnership adjustment, the $40 imputed underpayment section 705(a)(2)(B) expenditure is allocated to A under § 1.704-1(b)(2)(iii)(*f*)(*4*) of this chapter.

(f) *Applicability date.*—(1) *In general.*—Except as provided in paragraph (f)(2) of this section, this section applies to partnership taxable years beginning after December 31, 2017.

(2) *Election under § 301.9100-22 in effect.*—This section applies to any partnership taxable year beginning after November 2, 2015 and before January 1, 2018 for which a valid election under § 301.9100-22 is in effect. [Reg. § 301.6225-4.]

Partnerships: Centralized Partnership Audit Regime

Partnerships: Centralized Partnership Audit Regime.—Reg. § 301.6226-4, implementing the centralized partnership audit regime that have not been finalized to reflect the changes made by the Technical Corrections Act of 2018, contained in Title II of the Consolidated Appropriations Act of 2018 (TTCA), is proposed (published in the Federal Register on August 17, 2018) (REG-136118-15; REG-119337-17; REG-118067-17; REG-120232-17 and REG-120233-17).

Par. 15. Section 301.6226-4 is added to read as follows:

§ 301.6226-4. Effect of a partnership adjustment on tax attributes of partnerships and their partners.—(a) *Adjustments to tax attributes.*—(1) *In general.*—When a partnership adjustment (as defined in § 301.6241-1(a)(6)) is taken into account by the reviewed year partners (as defined in § 301.6241-1(a)(9)) or affected partners (as described in § 301.6226-3(e)(3)(i)) pursuant to an election made by a partnership under § 301.6226-1, the partnership and its reviewed year partners or affected partners must adjust their tax attributes (as defined in § 301.6241-1(a)(10)) in accordance with the rules in this section.

(2) *Application to pass-through partners and indirect partners.*—To the extent a pass-through partner (as defined in § 301.6241-1(a)(5)) pays an imputed underpayment under § 301.6226-3(e)(4)(iii), such pass-through partner and its affected partners or their successors must make adjustments to their tax attributes in accordance with the rules in § 301.6225-4.

(3) *Allocation of partnership adjustments.*—Partnership adjustments are allocated to the reviewed year partners or affected partners under § 1.704-1(b)(4)(xiv) of this chapter.

(b) *Adjusting tax attributes of a partnership and its partners when an election under section 6226 is made.*—For partnership adjustments that are taken into account by the reviewed year partners or affected partners because an election is made under § 301.6226-1, the partnership adjustments to be taken into account by each partner are determined under § 301.6226-2(f). Accordingly, the reviewed year partners or affected partners must take into account the partnership adjustments as reflected on the statements described in § 301.6226-2 or § 301.6226-3(e)(3) in accordance with § 301.6226-3. The reviewed year partners or affected partners and the partnership adjust partnership tax attributes affected by reason of an adjustment reflected on the statements described in § 301.6226-2 or § 301.6226-3(e)(3) with respect to the reviewed year (as defined in § 301.6241-1(a)(8)), except to the extent partner or partnership tax attributes were already adjusted as part of the partnership adjustment. Additionally, reviewed year partners or affected partners adjust their partner tax attributes that are affected by the adjustments reflected on the statements described in § 301.6226-2 or § 301.6226-3(e)(3), but these adjustments to partner tax attributes are calculated with respect to each year beginning with the first affected year (as defined in § 301.6226-3(b)(2)(i)), followed by any intervening years (as defined in § 301.6226-3(b)(3)(i)), concluding with the reporting year (as defined in § 301.6226-3(a)).

(c) *Example.*—The following example illustrates the rules of this section. For purposes of this example, Partnership is subject to the provisions of subchapter C of chapter 63 of the Internal Revenue Code, Partnership and its partners are calendar year taxpayers, all partners are U.S. persons, and the highest rate of income tax in effect for all taxpayers is 40 percent for all relevant periods.

Example. (i) In 2021, J, K and L form Partnership by each contributing $500 in exchange for partnership interests that share all items of income, gain, loss and deduction in identical shares. Partnership immediately purchases Asset on January 1, 2021 for $1,500, which it depreciates using the straight-line method with a

10-year recovery period beginning in 2021 ($150) so that each partner has a $50 distributive share of the depreciation, resulting in an outside basis of $450 for each partner. Accordingly, at the end of 2022, J, K and L have an outside basis and capital account of $400 each ($500 less $50 of their respective allocable shares of depreciation in 2021 and $50 in 2022).

	Partnership Basis	*Book*	*Value*
Asset	$1200	$1200	$1500
Totals	1200	1200	1500

	Outside Basis	*Book*	*Value*
J	$400	$400	$500
K	400	400	500
L	400	400	500
	1200	1200	1500

(ii) The IRS initiates an administrative proceeding with respect to Partnership's 2021 taxable year (reviewed year) and in 2023 (adjustment year) finally determines that Asset should have been depreciated with a 20-year recovery period beginning in 2021, resulting in a $75 partnership adjustment that results in an imputed underpayment. The IRS does not initiate an administrative proceeding with respect to Partnership's 2022 taxable year, and Partnership does not file an administrative adjustment request for that taxable year. Partnership makes an election under § 301.6226-1 with respect to the imputed underpayment. Therefore, J, K and L each are furnished a statement described in § 301.6226-2 by Partnership reflecting the $25 income adjustment for 2021.

(iii) Tax attributes of the partners must be adjusted to reflect the $75 partnership adjustment reflected on the statements described in § 301.6226-2 that is taken into account in equal shares ($25) by J, K, and L with respect to 2021. Specifically, J, K and L's outside bases and capital accounts must be increased $25 each with respect to the 2021 tax year. As a result, J, K and L each have an outside basis and capital account of $425 ($400 plus $25 of income realized with respect to 2021). Asset's basis and book value must also be changed in 2023. Thus, after adjusting tax attributes of the partners to take into account the election under § 301.6226-1 and taking into account other activities of Partnership in 2023, accounts are stated as follows:

	Partnership Basis	*Book*	*Value*
Asset	$1275	$1275	$1500
Totals	1275	1275	1500

	Outside Basis	*Book*	*Value*
J	$425	$425	$500
K	425	425	500
L	425	425	500
	1275	1275	1500

(d) *Applicability date.*—(1) *In general.*—Except as provided in paragraph (d)(2) of this section, this section applies to partnership taxable years beginning after December 31, 2017.

(2) *Election under § 301.9100-22 in effect.*—This section applies to any partnership taxable year beginning after November 2, 2015 and before January 1, 2018 for which a valid election under § 301.9100-22 is in effect. [Reg. § 301.6226-4.]

COLLECTION

Excise Taxes: Taxable Fuel: Returns: Definitions

Excise Taxes: Taxable Fuel: Returns: Definitions.—Amendments to Reg. § 40.6302(c)-1, relating to credits and payments for alcohol mixtures, biodiesel mixtures, renewable diesel mixtures, alternative fuel mixtures, and alternative fuel sold for use or used as a fuel and relating to the definition of gasoline and diesel fuel, are proposed (published in the Federal Register on July 29, 2008) (REG-155087-05).

Par. 6. Section 40.6302(c)-1 is amended as follows:

1. Paragraph (e)(1)(ii) is amended by removing the language "components);" and adding "components); and" in its place.
2. Paragraph (e)(1)(iii) is amended by removing the language "chemicals); and" and adding "chemicals)." in its place.
3. Paragraph (e)(1)(iv) is removed.

§ 40.6302(c)-1. Use of Government depositaries.

ABATEMENTS, CREDITS, AND REFUNDS

Elimination of Circular Adjustments to Basis: Absorption of Losses

Elimination of Circular Adjustments to Basis: Absorption of Losses.—Amendments to Reg. § 301.6402-7, revising the rules concerning the use of a consolidated group's losses in a consolidated return year in which stock of a subsidiary is disposed of, are proposed (published in the Federal Register on June 11, 2015) (REG-101652-10).

Par. 11. Section 301.6402-7 is amended by revising the last sentence of paragraph (g)(2)(ii) and paragraph (l) to read as follows:

§ 301.6402-7. Claims for refund and applications for tentative carryback adjustments involving consolidated groups that include insolvent financial institutions.

* * *

(g) * * *

(2) * * *

(ii) * * * For this purpose, the separate net operating loss of a member is determined by computing the consolidated net operating loss by reference to only the member's items of income, gain, deduction, and loss (excluding capital gains and amounts treated as capital gains), including the member's losses and deductions actually absorbed by the group in the consolidated return year (whether or not absorbed by the member).

* * *

(l) *Effective/applicability dates.*—This section applies to refunds and tentative carryback adjustments paid after December 30, 1991. However, the last sentence of paragraph (g)(2)(ii) of this section applies to separate net operating losses of members incurred in consolidated return years beginning on or after the date these regulations are published as final regulations in the **Federal Register.**

Excise Tax: Tractors, Trailers, Trucks, and Tires: Highway Vehicle: Definition

Excise Tax: Tractors, Trailers, Trucks, and Tires: Highway Vehicle: Definition.—Amendments to Reg. §48.6416(c)-1, relating to the excise taxes imposed on the sale of highway tractors, trailers, trucks, and tires, the use of heavy vehicles on the highway, and the definition of highway vehicle related to these and other taxes, are proposed (published in the Federal Register on March 31, 2016) (REG-103380-05).

Par. 25. Section 48.6416(c)-1 is removed.

§48.6416(c)-1. Credit for tax paid on tires or, prior to January 1, 1984, inner tubes.

Excise Tax: Tractors, Trailers, Trucks, and Tires: Highway Vehicle: Definition

Excise Tax: Tractors, Trailers, Trucks, and Tires: Highway Vehicle: Definition.—Amendments to Reg. §48.6421-4,relating to the excise taxes imposed on the sale of highway tractors, trailers, trucks, and tires, the use of heavy vehicles on the highway, and the definition of highway vehicle related to these and other taxes, are proposed (published in the Federal Register on March 31, 2016) (REG-103380-05).

Par. 26. For each section listed in the tables, remove the language in the "Remove" column from wherever it appears in the paragraph and add in its place the language in the "Add" column as set forth below:

§48.6421-4. Meaning of terms.

Section	Remove	Add
§48.6421-4(c)	48.4061(a)-1(d)	48.0-5

Excise Taxes: Taxable Fuel: Returns: Definitions

Excise Taxes: Taxable Fuel: Returns: Definitions.—Reg. §§48.6426-1—48.6426-7, relating to credits and payments for alcohol mixtures, biodiesel mixtures, renewable diesel mixtures, alternative fuel mixtures, and alternative fuel sold for use or used as a fuel and relating to the definition of gasoline and diesel fuel, are proposed (published in the Federal Register on July 29, 2008) (REG-155087-05).

Par. 20. Sections 48.6426-1 through 48.6426-7 are added to read as follows:

§48.6426-1. Renewable and alternative fuels; explanation of terms.—(a) *Overview.*—This section provides an explanation of terms for purposes of the credits allowed by sections 34 and 6426 and the payments allowed by section 6427(e). The definition of *alcohol* in paragraph (c) of this section is also applicable for purposes of the credits allowed by section 40. The definitions of *biodiesel* and *renewable diesel* in paragraph (b) of this section are also applicable for purposes of the credits allowed by section 40A.

(b) *Explanation of terms.*

Agri-biodiesel means biodiesel derived solely from virgin oils. Virgin oils include virgin vegetable oils from the sources listed in section 40A(d)(2), as well as virgin oils not listed, such as palm oil and fish oil. Biodiesel produced from a feedstock that includes any recycled oils (such as recycled cooking oils) is not agri-biodiesel because it is not derived solely from virgin oils.

Alcohol is defined in paragraph (c) of this section.

Alcohol fuel mixture means a mixture of alcohol and taxable fuel that contains at least 0.1 percent (by volume) of taxable fuel.

Alternative fuel means, except as otherwise provided in the following sentence, liquefied petroleum gas, P Series Fuels (as defined by the Secretary of Energy under 42 U.S.C. 13211(2)), compressed or liquefied natural gas, liquefied hydrogen, any liquid fuel derived from coal (including peat) through the Fischer-Tropsch process, and liquid fuel derived from biomass (as defined in section 0.45K(c)(3)). The term does not include ethanol, methanol, biodiesel, or renewable diesel.

Alternative fuel mixture means a mixture of alternative fuel and taxable fuel that contains at least 0.1 percent (by volume) of taxable fuel.

Alternative fueler means a person that—

(1) Is an alternative fueler (unmixed fuel); or

(2) Produces alternative fuel mixtures for sale or use in its trade or business.

Alternative fueler (unmixed fuel) with respect to any alternative fuel that is sold for use or used as a fuel in a motor vehicle or motorboat is—

(1) In the case of alternative fuel on which tax is imposed by section 4041(a)(2) or (3), the person liable for such tax (determined in the case of compressed natural gas after the application of § 48.4041-21 and in the case of any other alternative fuel after the application of rules similar to the rules of § § 48.4041-3 and 48.4041-5);

(2) In the case of alternative fuel that is not described in paragraph (1) or (3) of this definition, the person that would be so liable for such tax but for the application of an exemption provided by section 4041(a)(3)(B), (b), (f), (g), or (h); and

(3) In the case of liquefied natural gas (LNG) that is sold in bulk for the exclusive use of a State that provides the written waiver described in § 48.6426-6(c)(4) and is delivered into a bulk supply tank that can only fuel motor vehicles and motorboats of the State, the person that sells the alternative fuel to the State.

Biodiesel means biodiesel as defined in section 40A(d)(1). Biodiesel may be produced either within or outside the United States. Fuel meets the Environmental Protection Agency (EPA) registration requirements described in section 40A(d)(1)(A) if the EPA does not require the fuel to be registered.

Biodiesel mixture means a mixture of biodiesel and diesel fuel that contains at least at least 0.1 percent (by volume) of diesel fuel. The kerosene in a biodiesel mixture is not included in either the overall volume of the mixture or the volume of diesel fuel in the mixture for purposes of determining whether the biodiesel mixture satisfies the 0.1 percent requirement. The diesel fuel in a biodiesel mixture may be dyed or undyed. See, however, section 6715 for the penalty for willful alteration of the strength or composition of any dye in dyed fuel and § 48.6715-1 for related rules.

Commingled biodiesel means biodiesel that is held by—

(1) Its producer in a storage tank at a time when the tank is used only for the storage of biodiesel and is used to store both biodiesel (other than agribiodiesel) and agri-biodiesel; or

(2) A person other than its producer in a storage tank at a time when the tank is used only for the storage of biodiesel and is used to store biodiesel to which more than a single Certificate for Biodiesel applies.

Commingled renewable diesel means renewable diesel held by a person other than its producer in a storage tank at a time when the tank is used only for the storage of renewable diesel and is used to store renewable diesel to which more than a single Certificate for Renewable Diesel applies.

Mixture means an alcohol fuel mixture, a biodiesel mixture, a renewable diesel mixture, or an alternative fuel mixture.

Mixture producer is the person that has title to the mixture immediately after it is created.

Motor vehicle has the meaning given to the term by § 48.4041-8(c). Thus, for example, the term includes forklift trucks used to carry loads at industrial plants and warehouses.

Producer means the person that produces alcohol, biodiesel, or renewable diesel.

Registered biodiesel producer means a biodiesel producer that is registered under section 4101 as a producer of biodiesel.

Registered renewable diesel producer means a renewable diesel producer that is registered under section 4101 as a producer of renewable diesel.

Renewable diesel means renewable diesel as defined in section 40A(f)(3). For this purpose, a fuel meets the Environmental Protection Agency's (EPA) registration requirements described in section 40A(f)(3)(A) if the EPA does not require the fuel to be registered or if diesel fuel coproduced from renewable diesel and petroleum feedstocks is registered. Renewable diesel may be produced either within or outside the United States.

Renewable diesel mixture is defined in paragraph (d) of this section.

Reseller means, with respect to any biodiesel or renewable diesel, a person that buys and subsequently sells such fuel without using the fuel to produce a biodiesel or renewable diesel mixture.

Thermal depolymerization process means, for purposes of the definition of *renewable diesel* in section 40A(f)(3), a process for the reduction of complex organic materials through the use of pressure and heat to decompose long chain polymers of hydrogen, oxygen, and carbon into short-chain petroleum hydrocarbons with a maximum length of around 18 carbons. A process may qualify as thermal depolymerization even if catalysts are used in the process.

Use as a fuel is defined in paragraph (e) of this section.

(c) *Alcohol; definition.*—(1) *In general.*—Except as otherwise provided in this paragraph (c), *alcohol* means any alcohol, including methanol and ethanol, that is not a derivative product of petroleum, natural gas, or coal (including peat). Thus, for example, the term does not include an ethanol by-product produced from a derivative of petroleum or natural gas. However, the term does include alcohol made from renewable resources, such as agricultural or forestry products. The term also includes alcohol made from urban wastes, such as methanol made from methane gas formed at waste disposal sites.

(2) *Source of the alcohol.*—Alcohol may be produced either within or outside the United States.

(3) *Proof and denaturants.*—Except for purposes of section 40, alcohol does not include alcohol with a proof of less than 190 degrees (determined without regard to added denaturants). For purposes of section 40, alcohol does not include alcohol with a proof of less than 150 degrees (determined without regard to added denaturants). If alcohol includes impurities or denaturants, the volume of alcohol is determined under the following rules:

(i) Except for purposes of section 40, the volume of alcohol includes the volume of any impurities (other than added denaturants and any fuel with which the alcohol is mixed) that reduce the purity of the alcohol to not less than 190 proof (determined without regard to added denaturants and any fuel with which the alcohol is mixed).

(ii) For purposes of section 40, the volume of alcohol includes the volume of any impurities (other than added denaturants and any fuel with which the alcohol is mixed) that reduce the purity of the alcohol to not less than 150 proof (determined without regard to added denaturants and any fuel with which the alcohol is mixed).

(iii) The volume of alcohol includes the volume of any approved denaturants that reduce the purity of the alcohol, but only to the extent that the volume of the approved denaturants does not exceed five percent of the unadjusted volume of the alcohol. The unadjusted volume of the alcohol is determined for this purpose by including in unadjusted volume the approved denaturants and the impurities included in volume under paragraph (c)(3)(i) or (ii) of this section. If the volume of the approved denaturants exceeds five percent of the unadjusted volume of the alcohol, the excess over five percent is not considered alcohol.

(iv) For purposes of this paragraph (c)(3), approved denaturants are any denaturants (including gasoline and other nonalcohol fuel denaturants) that reduce the purity of the alcohol and are added to such alcohol under a formula approved by the Secretary.

(4) *ETBE*.—Ethyl tertiary butyl ether (ETBE) and other ethers produced from alcohol are treated as alcohol. The ether is treated as alcohol of the same type as the alcohol used to produce the ether and the volume of alcohol resulting from such treatment is the volume of alcohol of such type with an energy content equal to the energy content of the ether.

(d) *Renewable diesel mixture; definition*.—(1) *In general*.—*Renewable diesel mixture* means—

(i) A mixture of renewable diesel and diesel fuel (other than renewable diesel) that contains at least 0.1 percent (by volume) of diesel fuel (other than renewable diesel); and

(ii) Fuel produced from biomass (as defined in section 45K(c)(3)) and petroleum feedstocks using a thermal depolyermization process if such fuel has been registered by the Environmental Protection Agency (EPA) under section 211 of the Clean Air Act (42 U.S.C. 7545) and meets the requirements of ASTM D975 or D396.

(2) *Special rules*.—The kerosene in a renewable diesel mixture is not included in either the overall volume of the mixture or the volume of diesel fuel in the mixture for purposes of determining whether the renewable diesel mixture satisfies the 0.1 percent requirement. The diesel fuel in the renewable diesel mixture may be dyed or undyed. See, however, section 6715 for the penalty for willful alteration of the strength or composition of any dye in dyed fuel and § 48.6715-1 for related rules. For availability for ASTM specifications, see § 48.4081-1(d).

(e) *Use as a fuel; definitions*.—(1) A mixture is *used as a fuel* when it is consumed in the production of energy. Thus, for example, a mixture is used as a fuel when it is consumed in an internal combustion engine to power a vehicle or in a furnace to produce heat. However, a mixture that is destroyed in a fire or other casualty loss is not used as a fuel.

(2) A mixture is *sold for use as a fuel* if the producer sells the fuel and has reason to believe that the mixture will be used as a fuel by either the producer's buyer or any later buyer of the mixture.

(3) Alternative fuel (not in a mixture) is sold for use or used as a fuel in a motor vehicle or motorboat when the alternative fueler (unmixed fuel) with respect to the fuel delivers it into the fuel supply tank of a motor vehicle or motor boat or sells it in bulk for use by the buyer as a fuel in a motor vehicle or motorboat.

(f) *Other definitions*.—For the definitions of taxable fuel and diesel fuel, see § 48.4081-1.

(g) *Effective/applicability date*.—This section is applicable on and after the date these regulations are published as final regulations in the **Federal Register**. [Reg. § 48.6426-1.]

§ 48.6426-2. Alcohol fuel mixtures.—(a) *Overview*.—This section provides rules under which an alcohol fuel mixture producer may claim an excise tax credit under section 6426, a payment under section 6427, or an income tax credit under section 34. These claims relate to the mixture producer's sale or use of an alcohol fuel mixture and are based on the amount of alcohol used to produce the alcohol fuel mixture. For the applicable claim rate, see section 6426.

(b) *Conditions to allowance*.—(1) *Excise tax credit*.—A claim for the alcohol fuel mixture credit with respect to an alcohol fuel mixture is allowed under section 6426 only if each of the following conditions is satisfied:

(i) The claimant produced the alcohol fuel mixture for sale or use in the trade or business of the claimant.

(ii) The claimant sold the alcohol fuel mixture for use as a fuel or used the alcohol fuel mixture as a fuel.

(iii) The claimant has made no other claim with respect to the alcohol in the mixture or, if another claim has been made, such other claim is disregarded under this paragraph (b)(1)(iii). A claim is disregarded under this paragraph (b)(1)(iii) if it is—

(A) A claim for the small ethanol producer credit under section 40; or

(B) An erroneous claim under section 6427 and either the claim has been disallowed or the claimant has repaid the government the amount received under section 6427 with interest.

(iv) The claimant has filed a timely claim on Form 720, "Quarterly Federal Excise Tax Return," that contains all the information required in paragraph (c) of this section.

(2) *Payment or income tax credit*.—A claim for an alcohol fuel mixture payment under section 6427 or an income tax credit under section 34 is allowed only if—

(i) The conditions of paragraphs (b)(1)(i) and (ii) of this section are met; and

(ii) The claimant has filed a timely claim for payment on Form 720 or Form 8849, "Claim for Refund of Excise Taxes," or for a credit on Form 4136, "Credit for Federal Tax Paid on Fuels," that contains all the information required by paragraph (c) of this section.

(3) *ETBE; sold for use or used as a fuel*.—An alcohol fuel mixture that is produced at a refinery and that includes ethyl tertiary butyl ether or other ethers produced from alcohol is treated as

meeting the requirement of paragraph (b)(1)(ii) of this section when the mixture is removed from the refinery and any subsequent sale or use of the mixture is disregarded for purposes of this section.

(4) *Overall limitations on credits and payments.*—See § 48.6426-7(a) for overall limitations on credits and payments allowed with respect to mixtures under sections 34, 6426, and 6427.

(c) *Content of claim.*—Each claim for an alcohol fuel mixture credit or payment must contain the following information with respect to the mixture covered by the claim:

(1) The amount of alcohol in the alcohol fuel mixture.

(2) A statement that the conditions to allowance described in paragraph (b) of this section have been met.

(3) A statement that the claimant either—

(i) Produced the alcohol it used in the mixture; or

(ii) Has in its possession a record of the name, address, and employer identification number of the person(s) that sold the alcohol to the claimant and the date of purchase.

(d) *Effective/applicability date.*—This section is applicable on and after the date these regulations are published as final regulations in the **Federal Register**. [Reg. § 48.6426-2.]

§ 48.6426-3. Biodiesel mixtures.—(a) *Overview.*—This section provides rules under which a biodiesel mixture producer may claim an excise tax credit under section 6426, a payment under section 6427, or an income tax credit under section 34. These claims relate to the mixture producer's sale or use of a biodiesel mixture and are based on the amount of biodiesel used to produce the biodiesel mixture. For the applicable claim rate, see section 6426.

(b) *Conditions to allowance.*—(1) *Excise tax credit.*—A claim for the biodiesel mixture credit with respect to a biodiesel mixture is allowed under section 6426 only if each of the following conditions is satisfied:

(i) The claimant produced the biodiesel mixture for sale or use in the trade or business of the claimant.

(ii) The claimant sold the biodiesel mixture for use as a fuel or used the biodiesel mixture as a fuel.

(iii) The claimant—

(A) Produced the biodiesel in the mixture; or

(B) Has obtained a certificate from the registered biodiesel producer as described in paragraph (e) of this section and, if applicable, a statement described in paragraph (f) of this section, for such biodiesel and has no reason to believe any information in the certificate and statement is false.

(iv) The claimant has made no other claim with respect to the biodiesel in the mixture or, if another claim has been made, such other claim is disregarded under this paragraph (b)(1)(iv). A claim is disregarded under this paragraph (b)(1)(iv) if it is—

(A) A claim for the small agri-biodiesel producer credit under section 40A; or

(B) An erroneous claim under section 6427 and either the claim has been disallowed or the claimant has repaid the government the amount received under section 6427 with interest.

(v) The claimant has filed a timely claim on Form 720, "Quarterly Federal Excise Tax Return," that contains all the information required in paragraph (c) of this section.

(2) *Payment or income tax credit.*—A claim for a biodiesel mixture payment under section 6427 or an income tax credit under section 34 is allowed only if—

(i) The conditions of paragraphs (b)(1)(i), (ii), and (iii) of this section are met; and

(ii) The claimant has filed a timely claim for payment on Form 720 or Form 8849, "Claim for Refund of Excise Tax," or for a credit on Form 4136, "Credit for Federal Tax Paid on Fuels," that contains all the information required by paragraph (c) of this section.

(3) *Overall limitations on credits and payments.*—See § 48.6426-7(a) for overall limitations on credits and payments allowed with respect to mixtures under sections 34, 6426, and 6427.

(c) *Content of claim.*—Each claim for a biodiesel mixture credit or payment must contain the following information with respect to the mixture covered by the claim:

(1) The amount of agri-biodiesel and biodiesel other than agri-biodiesel in the biodiesel mixture.

(2) Unless the claimant is the producer of the biodiesel in the biodiesel mixture, a copy of the applicable Certificate for Biodiesel described in paragraph (e) of this section and Statement(s) of Biodiesel Reseller described in paragraph (f) of this section. In the case of a certificate and statement that support a claim made on more than one claim form, the certificate and statement are to be included with the first claim and the claimant is to provide information related to the certificate and statement on any subsequent claim in accordance with the instructions applicable to the claim form.

(3) A statement that the conditions to allowance described in paragraph (b) of this section have been met.

(4) A statement that the claimant either—

(i) Is a registered biodiesel producer and produced the biodiesel it used in the mixture; or

(ii) Has in its possession a record of the name, address, and employer identification number of the person(s) that sold the biodiesel to the claimant and the date of purchase.

(d) *Commingled biodiesel; accounting method.*—For purposes of determining the certificate applicable to commingled biodiesel, a person that holds commingled biodiesel may identify the biodiesel it sells or uses by any reasonable method, including the first-in, first-out method applied either on a tank-by-tank basis or on an aggregate basis to all commingled biodiesel the person holds.

(e) *Certificate for Biodiesel.*—(1) *In general.*—The certificate to be obtained by the claimant is a statement that is signed under penalties of perjury by a person with authority to bind the registered biodiesel producer, is in substantially the same form as the model certificate in paragraph (e)(4) of this section, and contains all the information necessary to complete such model certificate.

(2) *Certificate identification number.*—The certificate identification number is determined by the producer and must be unique to each certificate.

(3) *Multiple certificates for single sale.*—A registered biodiesel producer may, with respect to a particular sale of biodiesel, provide multiple separate certificates, each applicable to a portion of the total volume of biodiesel sold. Thus, for example, a biodiesel producer that sells 5,000 gallons of biodiesel may provide its buyer with five certificates for 1,000 gallons each. The multiple certificates may be provided either to the buyer at or after the time of sale or to a reseller in the circumstances described in paragraph (f)(2) of this section.

(4) *Model certificate.*

CERTIFICATE FOR BIODIESEL

Certificate Identification Number: ______________

(To support a claim related to biodiesel or a biodiesel mixture under the Internal Revenue Code)

The undersigned biodiesel producer ("Producer") hereby certifies the following under penalties of perjury:

1. ______________________________

____

____

Producer's name, address, and employer identification number

2. ______________________________

____

____

Name, address, and employer identification number of person buying the biodiesel from Producer

3. ______________________________

Date and location of sale to buyer

4. This certificate applies to ____gallons of biodiesel.

5. Producer certifies that the biodiesel to which this certificate relates is:

____% Agri-biodiesel (derived solely from virgin oils)

____% Biodiesel other than agri-biodiesel

6. This certificate applies to the following sale:

____Invoice or delivery ticket number

____Total number of gallons of biodiesel sold under that invoice or delivery ticket number (including biodiesel not covered by this certificate)

7. ____Total number of certificates issued for that invoice or delivery ticket number

8. ______________________________

____

____

Name, address, and employer identification number of reseller to whom certificate is issued (only in the case of certificates reissued to a reseller after the return of the original certificate)

9. ____Original Certificate Identification Number (only in the case of certificates reissued to a reseller after return of the original certificate)

10. Producer is registered as a biodiesel producer with registration number ____. Producer's registration has not been suspended or revoked by the Internal Revenue Service.

Producer certifies that the biodiesel to which this certificate relates is monoalkyl esters of long chain fatty acids derived from plant or animal matter and that it meets the requirements of the American Society of Testing and Materials D6751 and the registration requirements for fuels and fuel additives established by EPA under section 211 of the Clean Air Act (42 U.S.C. 7545).

Producer understands that the fraudulent use of this certificate may subject Producer and all parties making any fraudulent use of this certificate to a fine or imprisonment, or both, together with the costs of prosecution.

____

Printed or typed name of person signing this certificate

____

Title of person signing

____

Signature and date signed

(f) *Statement of Biodiesel Reseller.*—(1) *In general.*—A person that receives a Certificate for Biodiesel, and subsequently sells the biodiesel without producing a biodiesel mixture, is to give the certificate and a statement that satisfies the requirements of this paragraph (f) to its buyer. The statement must contain all of the information necessary to complete the model statement in paragraph (f)(4) of this section and be attached to the Certificate for Biodiesel. A reseller cannot make multiple copies of a Certificate for Biodiesel to divide the certificate between multiple buyers.

(2) *Multiple resales.*—If a single Certificate for Biodiesel applies to biodiesel that a reseller expects to sell to multiple buyers, the reseller should return the certificate (together with any statements provided by intervening resellers) to the producer who may reissue to the reseller multiple Certificates for Biodiesel in the appropriate volumes. The reissued certificates must

include the Certificate Identification Number from the certificate that has been returned.

(3) *Withdrawal of the right to provide a certificate.*—The Internal Revenue Service may withdraw the right of a reseller of biodiesel to provide the certificate and a statement under this section if the Internal Revenue Service cannot verify the accuracy of the reseller's statements. The Internal Revenue Service may notify any person to whom the buyer has provided a statement that the reseller's right to provide the certificate and a statement has been withdrawn.

(4) *Model statement of biodiesel reseller.*

STATEMENT OF BIODIESEL RESELLER

(To support a claim related to biodiesel or a biodiesel mixture under the Internal Revenue Code)

The undersigned biodiesel reseller ("Reseller") hereby certifies the following under penalties of perjury:

1. ____________________

Reseller's name, address, and employer identification number

2. ____________________

Name, address, and employer identification number of Reseller's buyer

3. ____________________

Date and location of sale to buyer

4. ____________________

Volume of biodiesel sold

5. ____________________

Certificate Identification Number on the Certificate for Biodiesel

Reseller has bought the biodiesel described in the accompanying Certificate for Biodiesel and Reseller has no reason to believe that any information in the certificate is false.

Reseller has not been notified by the Internal Revenue Service that its right to provide a certificate and a statement has been withdrawn.

Reseller understands that the fraudulent use of this statement may subject Reseller and all parties making any fraudulent use of this statement to a fine or imprisonment, or both, together with the costs of prosecution.

____

Printed or typed name of person signing this certificate

____

Title of person signing

____

Signature and date signed

(g) *Erroneous certificates; reasonable cause.*—If a claim for credit or payment described in this section is based on erroneous information in a certificate or statement described in paragraph (e)(4) or (f)(4) of this section, the claim is not allowed. Thus, for example, if a producer identifies a product as agribiodiesel on a Certificate for Biodiesel and the product does not meet the registration requirements established by EPA, a claim for a biodiesel mixture credit based on the certificate is not allowed. However, if the claimant has met the conditions of paragraph (b)(1)(iii)(B) of this section with respect to the certificate or statement, reliance on the certificate or statement will be treated as reasonable cause for purposes of the penalties imposed by sections 6651 (relating to failure to pay) and 6675 (relating to excessive claims).

(h) *Effective/applicability date.*—This section is applicable on and after the date of publication of these regulations as final regulations in the **Federal Register**. [Reg. § 48.6426-3.]

§ 48.6426-4. Renewable diesel mixtures.—(a) *Overview.*—This section provides rules under which a renewable diesel mixture producer may claim an excise tax credit under section 6426, a payment under section 6427, or an income tax credit under section 34. These claims relate to the mixture producer's sale or use of a renewable diesel mixture and are based on the amount of renewable diesel used to produce the renewable diesel mixture. For the applicable claim rate, see section 40A(f)(2).

(b) *Conditions to allowance.*—(1) *Excise tax credit.*—A claim for the renewable diesel mixture credit with respect to a renewable diesel mixture is allowed under section 6426 only if each of the following conditions is satisfied:

(i) The claimant produced the renewable diesel mixture for sale or use in the trade or business of the claimant.

(ii) The claimant sold the renewable diesel mixture for use as a fuel or used the renewable diesel mixture as a fuel.

(iii) The claimant—

(A) Produced the renewable diesel in the mixture; or

(B) Has obtained a certificate from the registered renewable diesel producer as described in paragraph (e) of this section and, if applicable, a statement described in paragraph (f) of this section, for such renewable diesel and has no reason to believe any information in the certificate and statement is false.

(iv) The claimant has made no other claim with respect to the renewable diesel in the mixture or, if another claim has been made, such other claim is disregarded under this paragraph (b)(1)(iv). A claim is disregarded under this paragraph (b)(1)(iv) if it is an erroneous claim under section 6427 and either the claim has been disallowed or the claimant has repaid the government the amount received under section 6427 with interest.

(v) The claimant has filed a timely claim on Form 720, "Quarterly Federal Excise Tax Return," that contains all the information required in paragraph (c) of this section.

(2) *Payment or income tax credit.*—A claim for a renewable diesel mixture payment under section 6427 or an income tax credit under section 34 is allowed only if—

(i) The conditions of paragraphs (b)(1)(i), (ii), and (iii) of this section are met; and

(ii) The claimant has filed a timely claim for payment on Form 720 or Form 8849, "Claim for Refund of Excise Taxes," or for a credit on Form 4136, "Credit for Federal Tax Paid on Fuels," that contains all the information required by paragraph (c) of this section.

(3) *Overall limitations on credits and payments.*—See §48.6426-7(a) for overall limitations on credits and payments allowed with respect to mixtures under sections 34, 6426, and 6427.

(c) *Content of claim.*—Each claim for a renewable diesel mixture credit or payment must contain the following information with respect to the mixture covered by the claim:

(1) The amount of renewable diesel in the renewable diesel mixture.

(2) Unless the claimant is the producer of the renewable diesel in the renewable diesel mixture, a copy of the applicable Certificate for Renewable Diesel described in paragraph (e) of this section and Statement(s) of Renewable Diesel Reseller described in paragraph (f) of this section. In the case of a certificate and statement that support a claim made on more than one claim form, the certificate and statement are to be included with the first claim and the claimant is to provide information related to the certificate and statement on any subsequent claim in accordance with the instructions applicable to the claim form.

(3) A statement that the conditions to allowance described in paragraph (b) of this section have been met.

(4) A statement that the claimant either—

(i) Is a registered renewable diesel producer and produced the renewable diesel it used in the mixture; or

(ii) Has in its possession a record of the name, address, and employer identification number of the person(s) that sold the renewable diesel to the claimant and the date of purchase.

(d) *Commingled renewable diesel; accounting method.*—For purposes of determining the certificate applicable to commingled renewable diesel, a person that holds commingled renewable diesel may identify the renewable diesel it sells or uses by any reasonable method, including the first-in, first-out method applied either on a tank-by-tank basis or on an aggregate basis to all commingled renewable diesel the person holds.

(e) *Certificate for Renewable Diesel.*—(1) *In general.*—The certificate to be obtained by the claimant is a statement that is signed under penalties of perjury by a person with authority to bind the registered renewable diesel producer, is substantially in the same form as the model certificate in paragraph (e)(4) of this section, and contains all the information necessary to complete such model certificate.

(2) *Certificate identification number.*—The certificate identification number is determined by the producer and must be unique to each certificate.

(3) *Multiple certificates for single sale.*—A registered renewable diesel producer may, with respect to a particular sale of renewable diesel, provide multiple separate certificates, each applicable to a portion of the total volume of renewable diesel sold. Thus, for example, a renewable diesel producer that sells 5,000 gallons of renewable diesel may provide its buyer with five certificates for 1,000 gallons each. The multiple certificates may be provided either to the buyer at or after the time of sale or to a reseller in the circumstances described in paragraph (f)(2) of this section.

(4) *Model certificate.*

CERTIFICATE FOR RENEWABLE DIESEL

Certificate Identification Number: ____________

(To support a claim related to renewable diesel or a renewable diesel mixture under the Internal Revenue Code)

The undersigned renewable diesel producer ("Producer") hereby certifies the following under penalties of perjury:

1. ____

Producer's name, address, and employer identification number

2. ____

Name, address, and employer identification number of person buying the renewable diesel from Producer

3. ____

Date and location of sale to buyer

4. This certificate applies to ____gallons of renewable diesel.

5. This certificate applies to the following sale:

____Invoice or delivery ticket number

____Total number of gallons of renewable diesel sold under that invoice or delivery ticket number (including renewable diesel not covered by this certificate)

6. ____Total number of certificates issued for that invoice or delivery ticket number

7. ____

Name, address, and employer identification number of reseller to whom certificate is issued (only in the case of certificates reissued to a reseller after the return of the original certificate)

8. _____Original Certificate Identification Number (only in the case of certificates reissued to a reseller after return of the original certificate)

9. Producer is registered as a renewable diesel producer with registration number _____. Producer's registration has not been suspended or revoked by the Internal Revenue Service.

Producer certifies that the renewable diesel to which this certificate relates is diesel fuel derived from biomass (as defined in section 45K(c)(3) of the Internal Revenue Code) using a thermal depolymerization process and that it meets the requirements of the American Society of Testing and Materials D975 or D396 and the registration requirements for fuels and fuel additives established by EPA under section 211 of the Clean Air Act (42 U.S.C. 7545).

Producer understands that the fraudulent use of this certificate may subject Producer and all parties making any fraudulent use of this certificate to a fine or imprisonment, or both, together with the costs of prosecution.

Printed or typed name of person signing this certificate

Title of person signing

Signature and date signed

(f) *Statement of Renewable Diesel Reseller.*—(1) *In general.*—A person that receives a Certificate for Renewable Diesel, and subsequently sells the renewable diesel without producing a renewable diesel mixture, is to give the certificate and a statement that satisfies the requirements of this paragraph (f) to its buyer. The statement must contain all of the information necessary to complete the model statement in paragraph (f)(4) of this section and be attached to the Certificate for Renewable Diesel. A reseller cannot make multiple copies of a Certificate for Renewable Diesel to divide the certificate between multiple buyers.

(2) *Multiple resales.*—If a single Certificate for Renewable Diesel applies to renewable diesel that a reseller expects to sell to multiple buyers, the reseller should return the certificate (together with any statements provided by intervening resellers) to the producer who may reissue to the reseller multiple Certificates for Renewable Diesel in the appropriate volumes. The reissued certificates must include the Certificate Identification Number from the certificate that has been returned.

(3) *Withdrawal of the right to provide a certificate.*—The Internal Revenue Service may withdraw the right of a reseller of renewable diesel to provide the certificate and a statement under this section if the Internal Revenue Service cannot verify the accuracy of the reseller's statements. The Internal Revenue Service may notify any person to whom the buyer has provided a statement that the reseller's right to provide the certificate and a statement has been withdrawn.

(4) *Model statement of renewable diesel reseller.*

STATEMENT OF RENEWABLE DIESEL RESELLER

(To support a claim related to renewable diesel or a renewable diesel mixture under the Internal Revenue Code)

The undersigned renewable diesel reseller ("Reseller") hereby certifies the following under penalties of perjury:

1. _____

Reseller's name, address, and employer identification number

2. _____

Name, address, and employer identification number of Reseller's buyer

3. _____

Date and location of sale to buyer

4. _____

Volume of renewable diesel sold

5. _____

Certificate Identification Number on the Certificate for Renewable Diesel

Reseller has bought the renewable diesel described in the accompanying Certificate for Renewable Diesel and Reseller has no reason to believe that any information in the certificate is false.

Reseller has not been notified by the Internal Revenue Service that its right to provide a certificate and a statement has been withdrawn.

Reseller understands that the fraudulent use of this statement may subject Reseller and all parties making any fraudulent use of this statement to a fine or imprisonment, or both, together with the costs of prosecution.

Printed or typed name of person signing this certificate

Title of person signing

Signature and date signed

(g) *Erroneous certificates; reasonable cause.*—If a claim for credit or payment described in this section is based on erroneous information in a certificate or statement described in paragraph (e)(4) or (f)(4) of this section, the claim is not allowed. Thus, for example, if a producer identifies a product as renewable diesel on a Certificate for Renewable Diesel and the product does not meet the registration requirements established by EPA, a claim for a renewable diesel mixture credit based on the certificate is not allowed. However, if the claimant has met the conditions of paragraph (b)(1)(iii)(B) of this section with respect to the certificate or statement, reliance on the certificate or statement will be treated as reasonable cause for purposes of the penalties imposed by sections 6651 (relating to failure to pay) and 6675 (relating to excessive claims).

(h) *Effective/applicability date.*—This section is applicable on and after the date these regulations are published as final regulations in the **Federal Register**. [Reg. § 48.6426-4.]

§ 48.6426-5. Alternative fuel mixtures.—(a) *Overview.*—This section provides rules under which an alternative fueler that produces an alternative fuel mixture may claim an excise tax credit under section 6426, a payment under section 6427, or an income tax credit under section 34. These claims relate to the mixture producer's sale or use of an alternative fuel mixture and are based on the amount of alternative fuel used to produce the alternative fuel mixture. For the applicable claim rate, see section 6426.

(b) *Conditions to allowance.*—(1) *Excise tax credit.*—A claim for the alternative fuel mixture credit with respect to an alternative fuel mixture is allowed under section 6426 only if each of the following conditions is satisfied:

(i) The claimant produced the alternative fuel mixture for sale or use in the trade or business of the claimant.

(ii) The claimant sold the alternative fuel mixture for use as a fuel or used the alternative fuel mixture as a fuel.

(iii) The claimant is registered under section 4101 as an alternative fueler.

(iv) The claimant has made no other claim with respect to the alternative fuel in the mixture or, if another claim has been made, such other claim is disregarded under this paragraph (b)(1)(iv). A claim is disregarded under this paragraph (b)(1)(iv) if it is an erroneous claim under section 6427 and either the claim has been disallowed or the claimant has repaid the government the amount received under section 6427 with interest.

(v) The claimant has filed a timely claim on Form 720, "Quarterly Federal Excise Tax Return," that contains all the information required by the claim form described in paragraph (c) of this section.

(2) *Payment or income tax credit.*—A claim for an alternative fuel mixture payment under section 6427 or an alternative fuel mixture credit under sections 34 and 6427 is allowed only if—

(i) The conditions of paragraphs (b)(1)(i), (ii), and (iii) of this section are met; and

(ii) The claimant has filed a timely claim for payment on Form 720 or Form 8849, "Claim for Refund of Excise Taxes," or for a credit on Form 4136, "Credit for Fuel Tax Paid on Fuels," that contains all the information required by the claim form described in paragraph (c) of this section.

(3) *Overall limitations on credits and payments.*—See § 48.6426-7(a) for overall limitations on credits and payments allowed with respect to mixtures under sections 34, 6426, and 6427.

(c) *Content of claim.*—Each claim for an alternative fuel mixture credit or payment must contain the following information with respect to the mixture covered by the claim:

(1) The amount of alternative fuel in the alternative fuel mixture.

(2) A statement that the conditions to allowance described in paragraph (b) of this section have been met.

(3) A statement that the claimant either—

(i) Produced the alternative fuel it used in the mixture; or

(ii) Has in its possession—

(A) A record of the name, address, and employer identification number of the person(s) that sold the alternative fuel to the claimant and the date of purchase; and

(B) An invoice or other purchase documentation identifying the alternative fuel.

(d) *Effective/applicability date.*—This section is applicable on and after the date these regulations are published as final regulations in the **Federal Register**. [Reg. § 48.6426-5.]

§ 48.6426-6. Alternative fuel.—(a) *Overview.*—This section provides rules under which an alternative fueler (unmixed fuel) may claim an excise tax credit under section 6426, a payment under section 6427, or an income tax credit under section 34. These claims are based on the amount of alternative fuel sold or used. For the applicable claim rate, see section 6426.

(b) *Conditions to allowance.*—(1) *Excise tax credit.*—A claim for the alternative fuel excise tax credit with respect to alternative fuel sold for use or used as a fuel in a motor vehicle or motorboat is allowed under section 6426 only if each of the following conditions is satisfied:

(i) The claimant is the alternative fueler (unmixed fuel) with respect to the fuel.

(ii) The claimant is registered under section 4101 as an alternative fueler (unmixed fuel).

(iii) The claimant has made no other claim with respect to the alternative fuel or, if another claim has been made, such other claim is disregarded under this paragraph (b)(1)(iii). A claim is disregarded under this paragraph (b)(1)(iii) if it is an erroneous claim under section

6427 and either the claim has been disallowed or the claimant has repaid the government the amount received under section 6427 with interest.

(iv) The claimant has filed a timely claim on Form 720, "Quarterly Federal Excise Tax Return," that contains all the information required by the claim form described in paragraph (c) of this section.

(2) *Payment or income tax credit.*—A claim for an alternative fuel payment under section 6427 or an income tax credit under section 34 is allowed only if—

(i) The conditions of paragraphs (b)(1)(i) and (ii) of this section are met;

(ii) The sale or use is in the claimant's trade or business; and

(iii) The claimant has filed a timely claim for payment on Form 8849, "Claim for Refund of Excise Taxes," or for a credit on Form 4136, "Credit for Fuel Tax Paid on Fuels," that contains all the information required by paragraph (c) of this section.

(3) *Overall limitations on credits and payments.*—See §48.6426-7(b) for overall limitations on credits and payments allowed with respect to alternative fuel under sections 34, 6426, and 6427.

(c) *Content of claim.*—Each claim for an alternative fuel credit or payment must contain the following information with respect to the alternative fuel covered by the claim:

(1) The amount of alternative fuel sold or used.

(2) A statement that the conditions to allowance described in paragraph (b) of this section have been met.

(3) A statement that the claimant either—

(i) Produced the alternative fuel it sold or used; or

(ii) Has in its possession—

(A) A record of the name, address, and employer identification number of the person(s) that sold the alternative fuel to the claimant and the date of purchase; and

(B) An invoice or other purchase documentation identifying the alternative fuel.

(4) In the case of liquefied natural gas (LNG) that the claimant sold in bulk for the exclusive use of the State and delivered into a bulk supply tank that can only fuel motor vehicles or motorboats of the State, a statement that the claimant has in its possession a written waiver, signed under penalties of perjury by a person with authority to bind the State, stating that the LNG is delivered in bulk for the exclusive use of the State in a motor vehicle or motorboat and that the State gives up its right to claim any alternative fuel credit for such LNG.

(d) *Effective/applicability date.*—This section is applicable on and after the date these regulations are published as final regulations in the **Federal Register**. [Reg. §48.6426-6.]

§48.6426-7. Overall limitations on credits and payments.—(a) *Limitations applicable to mixtures.*—In the case of mixtures, the following limitations apply:

(1) The aggregate amount that, but for the coordination rules in sections 6426(g) and 6427(e)(3), would be allowable to a claimant either as a credit under section 6426 or a payment under section 6427 with respect to sales and uses of mixtures during a calendar quarter is allowed only as a credit under section 6426 to the extent such amount does not exceed the claimant's tax liability under section 4081 for the calendar quarter.

(2) The aggregate amount allowed to a claimant as a payment under section 6427 or an income tax credit under section 34 with respect to sales and uses of mixtures during a calendar quarter shall not exceed the amount that, but for the coordination rules in sections 6426(g) and 6427(e)(3), would be allowable to the claimant with respect to such sales and uses reduced by the claimant's tax liability under section 4081 for the calendar quarter.

(b) *Limitations applicable to alternative fuel.*—In the case of alternative fuel, the following limitations apply:

(1) The aggregate amount that, but for the coordination rules in sections 6426(g) and 6427(e)(3), would be allowable to a claimant either as a credit under section 6426 or a payment under section 6427 with respect to sales and uses of alternative fuel during a calendar quarter is allowed only as a credit under section 6426 to the extent such amount does not exceed the claimant's tax liability under section 4041 for the calendar quarter.

(2) The aggregate amount allowed to a claimant as a payment under section 6427 or an income tax credit under section 34 with respect to sales and uses of alternative fuel during a calendar quarter shall not exceed the amount that, but for the coordination rules in sections 6426(g) and 6427(e)(3), would be allowable to the claimant with respect to such sales and uses reduced by the claimant's tax liability under section 4041 for the calendar quarter.

(c) *Effective/applicability dates.*—This section is applicable on and after the date of publication of these regulations as final regulations in the **Federal Register**. [Reg. §48.6426-7.]

Excise Taxes: Taxable Fuel: Returns: Definitions

Excise Taxes: Taxable Fuel: Returns: Definitions.—Amendments to Reg. §48.6427-8, relating to credits and payments for alcohol mixtures, biodiesel mixtures, renewable diesel mixtures, alternative fuel mixtures, and alternative fuel sold for use or used as a fuel and relating to the definition of gasoline and diesel fuel, are proposed (published in the Federal Register on July 29, 2008) (REG-155087-05).

Par. 21. Section 48.6427-8 is amended as follows:

1. Revising paragraph (b)(1)(v) and adding (b)(1)(vii)(E).

2. Paragraph (b)(1)(vii)(C) is amended by removing the language "vehicle; or" and adding "vehicle;" in its place.

3. Paragraph (b)(1)(vii)(D) is amended by removing the language "6427(b)(3))." and adding "6427(b)(3)); or" in its place.

4. Paragraph (f) is amended by removing the language from the first sentence "1994." and adding "1994, and paragraph (b)(1)(vii)(E), which is applicable after the date these regulations are published as final regulations in the **Federal Register**." in its place."

The revision and addition read as follows:

§48.6427-8. Diesel fuel and kerosene; claims by ultimate purchasers.

* * *

(b) * * *

(1) * * *

(v) The diesel fuel or kerosene was not used on a farm for farming purposes (as defined in § 48.6420-4) or, except in the case of fuel described in paragraph (b)(1)(vii)(E) of the section, by a State;

* * *

(vii) * * *

(E) For the exclusive use, in the case of blended taxable fuel that is produced by a State and is both diesel fuel and a mixture (as defined in §48.6426-1(b)), of the State that produced the blended taxable fuel.

* * *

Gasoline and Diesel Fuel Excise Tax: Rules Relating to Gasohol: Tax on Compressed Natural Gas

Gasoline and Diesel Fuel Excise Tax: Rules Relating to Gasohol: Tax on Compressed Natural Gas.—Reg. §48.6427-10, relating to gasohol blending and the taxes on diesel fuel and compressed natural gas, is proposed (published in the Federal Register on October 19, 1994).

☐ Par. 29. Section 48.6427-10 is added to read as follows:

§48.6427-10. Credit or payment with respect to gasoline used to produce gasohol.—(a) *Conditions to allowance of credit or payment*.—A claim for credit or payment with respect to gasoline is allowed under section 6427(f) only if—

(1) The gasoline to which the claim relates was taxed at the aggregate rate of tax imposed by section 4081 without regard to section 4081(c);

(2) The claimant used the gasoline to produce gasohol (as defined in §48.4081-6(b)(2)) that was sold or used in the claimant's trade or business; and

(3) The claimant has filed a timely claim for a credit or payment that contains the information required under paragraph (c) of this section.

(b) *Form of claim.*—Each claim for a payment under section 6427(f) must be made on Form 8849 (or such other form as the Commissioner may designate) in accordance with the instructions for that form. Each claim for a credit under section 6427(f) must be made on Form 4136 (or such other form as the Commissioner may designate) in accordance with the instructions for that form.

(c) *Content of claim.*—Each claim for credit or payment under section 6427(f) must contain the following information with respect to each batch of gasohol that contains the gasoline covered by the claim:

(1) The claimant's registration number, if the claimant is a registered gasohol blender (as defined in §48.4081-6(b)(4)).

(2) The name, address, and employer identification number of the person that sold the claimant the gasoline.

(3) The date and location of the sale of the gasoline.

(4) The volume of the gasoline.

(5) The name, address, and employer identification number of the person that sold the claimant the alcohol.

(6) The date and location of the sale of the alcohol.

(7) The volume and type of the alcohol.

(8) In the case of a claim for a payment, a copy of the invoice or other record of sale relating to each purchase of alcohol.

(9) The written or typed name of the individual signing the claim and the telephone number of that individual.

(10) The amount of credit or payment claimed.

(d) *Time for filing claim.*—For rules relating to the time for filing a claim under section 6427(f), see section 6427(i). A claim under section 6427(f) is not considered to be filed unless it contains all the information required by paragraph (c) of this section and received at the place required by the form.

(e) *Effective date.*—This section is effective with respect to claims relating to gasohol produced after December 31, 1994. [Reg. §48.6427-10.]

Excise Taxes: Taxable Fuel: Returns: Definitions

Excise Taxes: Taxable Fuel: Returns: Definitions.—Reg. §48.6427-12, relating to credits and payments for alcohol mixtures, biodiesel mixtures, renewable diesel mixtures, alternative fuel mixtures, and alternative fuel sold for use or used as a fuel and relating to the definition of gasoline and diesel fuel, is proposed (published in the Federal Register on July 29, 2008) (REG-155087-05).

Par. 22. Section 48.6427-12 is added to read as follows:

§48.6427-12. Alcohol, alternative fuel, biodiesel, and renewable diesel.—(a) *In general.*—This section contains special rules for payments related to fuels containing alcohol, alternative fuel, biodiesel, and renewable diesel. Other rules for these payments are in §§48.6426-1 through 48.6426-7.

(b) *Coordination with excise tax credit.*—If the aggregate amount a person receives as a payment under section 6427(e) with respect to sales and uses of mixtures during a calendar quarter exceeds the amount allowed under § 48.6426-7(a), the excess constitutes an excessive amount for purposes of section 6206 and such amount, as well as the civil penalty under section 6675, may be assessed as if it were a tax imposed by section 4081. If the excessive amount is repaid to the government, with interest from the date of the payment (section 6602), on or before the due date of the Form 720, "Quarterly Federal Excise Tax Return," for the calendar quarter, the claim for the excessive amount will be treated as due to reasonable cause and the penalty under section 6675 will not be imposed with respect to the claim. If a person claims an income tax credit under section 34 in lieu of a payment under section 6427(e) with respect to sales and uses of mixtures during a calendar quarter and the aggregate amount claimed as an income tax credit with respect to such sales and uses exceeds the amount allowed under § 48.6426-7(a)(2), the income tax rules related to assessing an underpayment of income tax liability apply. The section 6675 penalty for excessive claims with respect to fuels does not apply in the case of section 34 income tax credits. Similar rules apply to excessive claims under sections 34 or 6427 with respect to sales and uses of alternative fuel.

(c) *Payment computation for certain blenders*.—(1) *In general*.—This paragraph (c) applies to a blender for any calendar quarter in which the blender's entire tax liability under section 4081 is based solely on the volume of alcohol in alcohol fuel mixtures, biodiesel in biodiesel mixtures, renewable diesel in renewable diesel mixtures, or alternative fuel in alternative fuel mixtures. If this paragraph (c) applies for a calendar quarter, the blender may use the following procedure to determine the amount it may claim as an income tax credit under section 34 or a payment under section 6427(e) with respect to each mixture that it sells or uses during the quarter:

(i) First, determine the amount allowed under section 6426 as a credit on Form 720 by multiplying the volume of untaxed liquid used to produce the mixture by the tax imposed per gallon on the untaxed liquid.

(ii) Then, determine the total credit and payment allowable by multiplying the volume of untaxed liquid used to produce the mixture by the tax credit rate per gallon.

(iii) Then, subtract the amount determined in paragraph (c)(1)(i) of this section (the section 6426 credit amount) from the amount determined in paragraph (c)(1)(ii) of this section. This difference is the amount of the payment or income tax credit that may be claimed with respect to that mixture.

(2) *Example*.—The following example illustrates the provisions of this paragraph (c):

(i) P is a biodiesel mixture producer. P produces blended taxable fuel outside of the bulk transfer/terminal system by adding biodiesel that is agribiodiesel to taxed diesel fuel. See §§ 48.4081-1(c)(1) and 48.4081-3(g). P has no § 4081 liability other than its liability as a blender on its sale of the biodiesel mixture. During the period August 1 through August 10 (at which time the tax rate on diesel fuel is $0.244 per gallon and the claim amount on agri-biodiesel is $1.00 per gallon), P uses 5,000 gallons of agri-biodiesel to produce a biodiesel mixture. P determines that it may claim $3,780 as a payment under section 6427(e) with respect to this mixture. P computes this amount by—

(A) Multiplying 5,000 (gallons of agri-biodiesel) × $0.244 (tax imposed per gallon) = $1,220;

(B) Multiplying 5,000 (gallons of agri-biodiesel) × $1.00 (tax credit rate per gallon) = $5,000; and

(C) Subtracting $1,220 from $5,000 = $3,780.

(ii) On August 11, P files Form 8849 for the period August 1 - August 10. To avoid an excessive claim, P limits the claim on Form 8849 to $3,780 reporting 3,780 gallons of agri-biodiesel.

(iii) On Form 720 P reports liability for IRS No. 60(c) of $1,220 (5,000 gallons × $.244) and claims a credit on Schedule C for $1,220 for period August 1 -August 10, reporting on Schedule C 1,220 gallons of agri-biodiesel.

(d) *Effective/applicability date*.—This section is applicable on and after the date these regulations are published as final regulations in the **Federal Register**. [Reg. § 48.6427-12.]

INTEREST

Modification of Interest Payments for Certain Periods

Modification of Interest Payments for Certain Periods.—Reproduced below is the text of proposed amendments to Reg. § 301.6601-1, relating to the accrual of interest on overpayments and underpayments of tax (published in the Federal Register on October 9, 1984).

☐ Paragraph 1. Section 301.6601-1 is amended as follows:

1. Paragraph (d) is revised to read as set forth below.
2. Paragraphs (e)(1) and (e)(3) are revised to read as set forth below.
3. New paragraphs (e)(4) and (e)(5) are added as set forth below.

§ 301.6601-1. Interest on underpayments.

* * *

(d) *Suspension of interest; waiver of restrictions on assessment*.—In the case of a deficiency determined by a district director (or an assistant regional commissioner, appellate) with respect to any income, estate, gift tax, or excise tax imposed by chapters 41, 42, 43, 44, and 45, if the taxpayer files with such internal revenue officer an agreement waiving the restrictions on assessment of such deficiency, and if notice and demand for payment of such deficiency is not made within 30 days after the filing of such waiver, no interest shall be imposed on the deficiency for the period beginning immediately after such 30th day and ending on the date notice and demand is made. In the case of an agreement with respect to a portion of the deficiency, the rules as set forth in this paragraph are applicable only to that portion of the deficiency to which the agreement relates.

(e) *Income tax reduced by carryback.*—(1)(i) The carryback of a net operating loss, net capital loss, or a credit carryback as defined by § 301.6611-1(f)(1) shall not affect the computation of interest on any income tax for the period commencing with the last day prescribed for the payment of such tax and ending with the filing date, as defined in paragraph (e)(4) of this section, for the taxable year in which the loss or credit arises. For example, if the carryback of a net operating loss, a net capital loss, or a credit carryback to a prior taxable period eliminates or reduces a deficiency in income tax for that period, the full amount of the deficiency will bear interest at the annual rate established under section 6621 from the last date prescribed for payment of such tax until the filing date for the taxable year in which the loss or credit arose. Interest will continue to run beyond such filing date on any portion of the deficiency which is not eliminated by the carryback. With respect to any portion of a credit carryback from a taxable year attributable to a net operating loss carryback, a capital loss carryback or other credit carryback from a subsequent taxable year, such credit carryback shall not affect the computation of interest on any income tax for the period commencing with the last day prescribed for the payment of such tax and ending with the filing date for such subsequent taxable year.

(ii) The provisions of paragraph (e)(1)(i) of this section are illustrated by the following examples.

Example (1). Corporation L is a calendar year taxpayer. For taxable years 1980 and 1981, L reported no income tax liability. For 1982, L has an underpayment of income tax of $500. In 1983, L has a net operating loss which L carries back to 1982, reducing the underpayment to $200. For purposes of computing the interest on the underpayment of income tax for 1982, interest will accrue on the $500 beginning on March 15, 1983. Beginning on March 16, 1984, interest on the 1982 income tax underpayment will accrue on only $200.

Example (2). Corporation R is a calendar year taxpayer. For taxable years 1980, 1981 and 1982, R reported no income tax liability. In 1983, R had a net operating loss which could not be carried forward to 1984 because R had reported no income tax liability for 1984. As a result of an audit conducted on R in 1985, a $500 deficiency is assessed on R for taxable year 1982. R applied the 1983 net operating loss to the $500 assessed deficiency, thus reducing the deficiency to $200. Interest begins accruing on the $500 deficiency on March 15, 1983. Beginning on March 16, 1984, interest on the 1982 deficiency will accrue on only $200.

* * *

(3) Where there has been an allowance of an overpayment attributable to a net operating loss carryback, a capital loss carryback or a credit carryback as defined by § 301.6611-1(f)(1) and all or part of such allowance is later determined to be excessive, interest shall be computed on the excessive amount from the filing date for the year in which the net operating loss, net capital loss, or credit arose until the date on which the repayment of such excessive amount is received. Where there has been an allowance of an overpayment with respect to any portion of a credit carryback from a taxable year attributable to a net operating loss carryback or a capital loss carryback from a subsequent taxable year and all or part of such allowance is later determined to be excessive, interest shall be computed on the excessive amount from the filing date for such subsequent taxable year until the date on which the repayment of such excessive amount is received.

(4) For purposes of paragraph (e) of this section, the term "filing date" means the last day fixed by law or regulation for filing the return of income tax for the taxable year (determined without regard to any extension of time).

(5) Section 301.6601-1(e)(1), (3) and (4) apply to interest accruing after October 3, 1982. See 26 CFR 301.6601-1(e) (revised as of April 1, 1982) for rules applicable to interest accruing before October 4, 1982.

Modification of Interest Payments for Certain Periods

Modification of Interest Payments for Certain Periods.—Reproduced below is the text of proposed amendments to Reg. § 301.6611-1, relating to the accrual of interest on overpayments and underpayments of tax (published in the Federal Register on October 9, 1984).

☐ Par. 2. Section 301.6611-1 is revised to read as follows:

§ 301.6611-1. Interest on overpayments.—(a) *General rule.*—Except as otherwise provided, interest shall be allowed on any overpayment of any tax at the annual rate established under section 6621 from the date of overpayment of the tax.

(b) *Date of overpayment.*—(1) *In general.*—Except as provided in section 6401(a), relating to assessment and collection after the expiration of the applicable period of limitation, there can be no overpayment of tax until the entire tax liability has been satisfied. Therefore, the dates of overpayment of any tax are the date of payment of the first amount which (when added to previous payments) is in excess of the tax liability (including any interest, addition to the tax, or additional amount) and the dates of payment of all amounts subsequently paid with respect to such tax liability. For rules relating to the determination of the date of payment in the case of an advance payment of tax, a payment of estimated tax, and a credit for income tax withholding, see paragraph (d) of this section.

(2) *Period for which interest is allowable in the case of credits of overpayment.*—(i) *General rule.*—If an overpayment of tax is credited, interest shall be allowed from the date of overpayment to the due date (as determined under paragraph (b)(2)(ii) of this section) of the amount against which such overpayment is credited. See paragraph (b)(4) of this section for late returns.

(ii) *Determination of due date.*—(A) *In general.*—The term "due date", as used in this section, means the last day fixed by law or regulations for the payment of the tax (determined without regard to any extension of time), and not the date on which the district director or the director of the regional service center makes demand for the payment of the tax. Therefore, the due date of a tax is the date fixed for the payment of the tax or the several installments thereof.

(B) *Tax payable in installments.—(1) In general.*—In the case of a credit against a tax, where the taxpayer had properly elected to pay the tax in installments, the due date is the date prescribed for the payment of the installment against which the credit is applied.

(2) Delinquent installment.—If the taxpayer is delinquent in payment of an installment of tax and a notice and demand has been issued for the payment of the delinquent installment and the remaining installments, the due date of each remaining installment shall then be the date of such notice and demand.

(C) *Tax or installment not yet due.*—If a taxpayer agrees to the crediting of an overpayment against tax or an installment of tax and the schedule of allowance is signed prior to the date on which such tax or installment would otherwise become due, then the due date of such tax or installment shall be the date on which such schedule is signed.

(D) *Assessed interest.*—In the case of a credit against assessed interest, the due date is the date of the assessment of such interest.

(E) *Additional amount, addition to the tax, or assessable penalty.*—In the case of a credit against an amount assessed as an additional amount, addition to the tax, or assessable penalty, the due date is the date of the assessment.

(F) *Estimated income tax for succeeding year.*—If the taxpayer elects to have all or part of the overpayment shown by his return applied to his estimated tax for his succeeding taxable year, no interest shall be allowed on such portion of the overpayment credited and such amount shall be applied as a payment on account of the estimated tax for such year or the installments thereof.

(3) *Period for which interest is allowable in the case of refunds of overpayment.*—If an overpayment of tax is refunded, interest shall be allowed from the date of the overpayment to a date determined by the district director or the director of the regional service center, which shall be not more than 30 days prior to the date of the refund check. The acceptance of a refund check shall not deprive the taxpayer of the right to make a claim for any additional overpayment and interest thereon, provided the claim is made within the applicable period of limitation. However, if a taxpayer does not accept a refund check, no additional interest on the amount of the overpayment included in such check shall be allowed. See paragraph (b)(4) of this section for late returns.

(4) *Late returns.*—For the purpose of paragraphs (b)(2), (b)(3) and (f) of this section, if, after October 3, 1982, a return is filed after the last date prescribed for filing such return (including any extension of time for filing the return), no interest shall be allowed or paid for any day before the date on which the return is filed. A return will not be treated as filed until it is filed in processible form. For rules relating to the processible form requirement, see paragraph (h)(1) of this section.

(c) *Examples.*—The provisions of paragraph (b) of this section may be illustrated by the following examples:

Example (1). Corporation X files an income tax return on March 15, 1955, for the calendar year 1954 disclosing a tax liability of $1,000 and elects to pay the tax in installments. Subsequent to payment of the final installment, the correct tax liability is determined to be $900.

Tax liability

Assessed	$1,000
Correct liability	900
Overassessment	100

Record of payments

Mar. 15, 1955	500
June 15, 1955	500

Since the correct liability in this case is $900, the payment of $500 made on March 15, 1955, and $400 of the payment made on June 15, 1955, are applied in satisfaction of the tax liability. The balance of the payment made on June 15, 1955 ($100) constitutes the amount of the overpayment, and the date on which such payment was made would be the date of the overpayment from which interest would be computed.

Example (2). Corporation Y files an income tax return for the calendar year 1954 on March 15, 1955, disclosing a tax liability of $50,000, and elects to pay the tax in installments. On October 15, 1956, a deficiency in the amount of $10,000 is assessed and is paid in equal amounts on November 15 and November 26, 1956. On April 15, 1957, it is determined that the correct tax liability of the taxpayer for 1954 is only $35,000.

Tax liability

Original assessment	$50,000
Deficiency assessment	10,000
Total assessed	60,000
Correct liability	35,000
Overassessment	25,000

Record of payments

Mar. 15, 1955	25,000
June 15, 1955	25,000
Nov. 15, 1956	5,000
Nov. 26, 1956	5,000

Since the correct liability in this case is $35,000, the entire payment of $25,000 made on March 15, 1955, and $10,000 of the payment made on June 15, 1955, are applied in satisfaction of the tax liability. The balance of the payment made on June 15, 1955 ($15,000), plus the amounts paid on

November 15 ($5,000), and November 26, 1956 ($5,000), constitute the amount of the overpayment. The dates of the overpayments from which interest would be computed are as follows:

Date	Amount of overpayment
June 15, 1955	$15,000
Nov. 15, 1956	5,000
Nov. 26, 1956	5,000

The amount of any interest paid with respect to the deficiency of $10,000 is also an overpayment.

Example (3). Corporation Z failed to file a timely income tax return for the calendar year 1982. Z filed the 1982 return on November 20, 1983, disclosing a tax liability of $50,000 which was paid in full on March 15, 1983. On October 15, 1984, a deficiency in the amount of $10,000 is assessed and is paid on November 15, 1984. On April 15, 1985, it is determined that the correct tax liability of the taxpayer for 1982 is only $35,000.

TAX LIABILITY	
Original assessment	$50,000
Deficiency assessment	10,000
Total assessed	$60,000
Correct liability	35,000
Overassessment	$25,000
RECORD OF PAYMENTS	
March 15, 1983	$50,000
Nov. 15, 1984	10,000

Since the correct liability in this case is $35,000, only $35,000 of the $50,000 payment made on March 15, 1983 is applied in satisfaction of the tax liability. The balance of the payment made on March 15, 1983 ($15,000), plus the amount paid on November 15, 1984 ($10,000), constitute the amount of the overpayment. The dates of the overpayment from which interest would be computed are as follows:

Date	Amount of overpayment
Nov. 20, 1983	$15,000
Nov. 15, 1984	10,000

The amount of any interest paid with respect to the deficiency of $10,000 is also an overpayment.

(d) *Advance payment of tax, payment of estimated tax, and credit for income tax withholding.*—In the case of an advance payment of tax, a payment of estimated income tax, or a credit for income tax withholding, the provisions of section 6513 (except the provisions of subsection (c) thereof), applicable in determining the date of payment of tax for purposes of the period of limitations on credit or refund, shall apply in determining the date of overpayment for purposes of computing interest thereon.

(e) *Refund of overpayment within 45 days after return is filed.*—No interest shall be allowed on any overpayment of tax imposed by subtitle A of the Code if such overpayment is refunded—

(1) In the case of a return filed on or before the last date prescribed for filing the return of such tax (determined without regard to any extension of time for filing such return), within 45 days after such last date, or

(2) After December 17, 1966, in the case of a return filed after the last day prescribed for filing the return, within 45 days after the date on which the return is filed.

For the purpose of this paragraph (e), a return filed after October 3, 1982, will not be considered filed until it is filed in processible form, (as determined under paragraph (h)(1) of this section).

(f) *Refund of income tax caused by carrybacks.*—(1) *In general.*—If any overpayment of tax imposed by subtitle A of the Code results from the carryback of net operating loss, a net capital loss, or a credit carryback, such overpayment, for purposes of this section, shall be deemed not to have been made prior to the filing date for the taxable year in which the loss or credit arises, or, with respect to any portion of a credit carryback from a taxable year attributable to a net operating loss carryback, a capital loss carryback, or other credit carryback from a subsequent taxable year, such overpayment shall be deemed not to have been made prior to the close of the filing date for such subsequent taxable year. The term "credit carryback" means any investment credit carryback, work incentive program credit carryback, new employee credit carryback, research credit carryback, or employee stock ownership credit carryback. The term "filing date" means the last day fixed by law or regulation for filing the return of tax imposed by subtitle A for the taxable year (determined without regard to any extension of time).

(2) *Special rules for carrybacks.*—(i) *In general.*—An overpayment of tax described in paragraph (f)(1) of this section is treated as an overpayment for the loss year (as defined in paragraph (f)(2)(ii) of this section). In applying sections 6611(e) and 6611(f)(3)(B), and solely for purposes of those sections, the following rules apply:

(A) No interest is payable if the overpayment for the loss year is refunded within 45 days after the later of the filing of the claim for refund of the overpayment or the filing date of the return of tax imposed by subtitle A for that year. For this purpose, if an application for tentative carryback adjustment (an application under section 6411(a)) with respect to a particular overpayment is filed after the filing of a claim for refund for the overpayment, the claim for refund is treated as filed on the date the application for tentative carryback adjustment is filed;

(B) A claim for refund of the overpayment will not be treated as filed unless it is filed in processible form (as described in paragraph (h)(1) of this section);

(C) The term "claim" includes claim for credit or refund (*e.g.*, an amended tax return (the Form 1040X or Form 1120X for individuals or corporations, respectively)) and an application for a tentative carryback adjustment; and

(D) The filing date of the return of tax imposed by subtitle A may not be earlier than the last date prescribed for filing such return (determined without extensions).

(ii) *Loss year*.—The term "loss year" means—

(A) In the case of a carryback of a net operating loss or net capital loss, the taxable year in which such loss arises;

(B) In the case of a credit carryback (as defined by paragraph (f)(1) of this section), the taxable year in which such credit carryback arises; and

(C) In the case of any portion of a credit carryback from a taxable year to which a net operating loss, a net capital loss, or any other credit carryback was carried from a subsequent taxable year, the subsequent taxable year.

(iii) *Cross references*.—See section 6611(i) which treats the return of tax imposed by subtitle A for the loss year as not filed for purposes of section 6611(e) unless it is filed in processible form. Also see section 6611(b)(3) and paragraph (b)(4) of this section for rules that apply to late returns.

(iv) *Effective date*.—Section 301.6611-1(f) applies to interest accruing after October 3, 1982. See 26 CFR 301.6611-1(f) (revised as of April 1, 1982) for rules applicable to interest accruing before October 4, 1982.

(v) *Examples*.—The provisions of this section may be illustrated by the following examples:

Example (1). Corporation Q is a calendar year taxpayer. For taxable years 1978, 1979, and 1980, net capital gains were reported. However, for 1981 Q had a net capital loss which Q could carry back to 1978, resulting in an overpayment for that year. Q properly filed the 1981 tax return on March 15, 1982. Q properly filed the claim for refund of the overpayment resulting from the carryback on November 15, 1982.

(a) If the refund is made within 45 days after filing the claim then interest will accrue between January 1, 1982 and October 3, 1982.

(b) If the refund is made more than 45 days after filing the claim then interest will accrue from January 1, 1982.

Example (2). Corporation R reports income on a fiscal year ending August 31. For taxable years ending August 31, 1979, 1980, and 1981, net capital gains were reported. However, for the taxable year ending August 31, 1982, R had a net capital loss which R could carry back to 1979, resulting in an overpayment for that year. R properly filed the 1982 tax return on October 15, 1982. R properly filed the claim for refund of the overpayment on November 10, 1982.

(a) If the refund is made within 45 days after November 15, 1982, then interest will accrue from September 1, 1982 until October 3, 1982.

(b) If the refund is made more than 45 days after November 15, 1982, then interest will accrue from September 1, 1982 until October 3, 1982 and from November 15, 1982.

Example (3). Corporation S is a calendar year taxpayer. For taxable years 1979, 1980, and 1981, net capital gains were reported. However, for 1982, S had a net capital loss which S could carry back to 1979, resulting in an overpayment for that year. S properly filed the 1982 tax return on February 4, 1983. S properly filed the claim for refund of the overpayment on February 15, 1983.

(a) If the refund is made within 45 days after March 15, 1983, then no interest will accrue on the overpayment.

(b) If the refund is made after 45 days of March 15, 1983, then interest will accrue from March 15, 1983.

Example (4). Corporation Y is a calendar year taxpayer. For taxable years 1979, 1980, and 1981 net capital gains were reported. However, for 1982, Y had a net capital loss which Y could carry back to 1979, resulting in an overpayment for that year. Y properly filed the 1982 tax return on March 1, 1983. Y properly filed the claim for refund of the overpayment on May 15, 1983.

(a) If the refund is made within 45 days after May 15, 1983, then no interest will accrue on the overpayment.

(b) If the refund is made more than 45 days after May 15, 1983, then interest will accrue from March 15, 1983.

Example (5). Corporation Z is a calendar year taxpayer. For taxable years 1979, 1980, and 1981, net capital gains were reported. However, for 1982, Z had a net capital loss which Z could carry back to 1979, resulting in an overpayment for that year. Z filed the 1982 tax return late, on November 1, 1983. Z properly filed the claim for refund for overpayment on November 15, 1983.

(a) If the refund is made within 45 days after November 15, 1983, then no interest will accrue on the overpayment.

(b) If the refund is made more than 45 days after November 15, 1983, then interest will accrue from November 1, 1983.

(g) *Refund of income tax caused by carryback of foreign taxes*.—(1) *In general*.—For purposes of paragraph (a) of this section, any overpayment of tax resulting from a carryback of tax paid or accrued to foreign countries or possessions of the United States shall be deemed not to have been paid or accrued before the filing date (as defined in section 6611(f)(3)) for the taxable year under subtitle F of the Code in which such taxes were in fact paid or accrued.

(2) *Effective date*.—Section 301.6611-1(g) applies to interest accruing after October 3, 1982. See 26 CFR 301.6611-1(g) (revised as of April 1, 1982) for rules applicable to interest accruing before October 4, 1982.

(h) *Processible form*.—(1) *In general*.—A return is in processible form if—

(i) The return is filed on a form permitted under the Code or regulations (see paragraph (h)(2) of this section), and

(ii) The return contains the required information described in paragraph (h)(3) of this section.

(2) *Return on permitted form; components of return.*—In applying paragraph (h)(1)(i) of this section, the term "return" includes all components of the return. A component of the return is a required attachment, supporting document, or schedule required by the return, whether or not the information from the document or schedule appears on the return itself. Supporting documents and schedules include, for example, Form W-2, relating to wages; Schedule D, relating to capital gain or loss; Form 3903, relating to moving expenses; Schedule G, relating to income averaging; Form 3468, relating to investment credit; and Form 4625, relating to minimum tax. The term "form permitted under the Code or regulations" includes a substitute form, schedule, or chart containing the same general provisions as the proper form, so long as the taxpayer complies with all revenue procedures relating to substitute forms in effect at that time.

(3) *Information required.*—The return must contain—

(i) The taxpayer's name, address, identifying number, and authorized signature, and

(ii) Sufficient required information on the return and its components (as defined in paragraph (h)(2) of this section) to permit the mathematical verification of the tax liability as shown on the return.

However, the information required by subdivisions (i) and (ii) is required in the case of a component of the return (within the meaning of paragraph (h)(2) of this section) only to the extent required by that component.

(4) *Examples.*—The provisions of paragraph (h) of this section may be illustrated by the following examples:

Example (1). A, an individual calendar year taxpayer, filed A's 1982 tax return on the due date, April 15, 1983. The return was properly completed except for A's failure to include schedule D, relating to capital gains or losses, with the filed return. On June 17, 1983, A's schedule D was filed. Because A did not file schedule D until June 17, 1983, there was insufficient information to mathematically verify the tax liability. Therefore, A's return is treated as filed on June 17, 1983 for purposes of section 6611(b)(3) and (e).

Example (2). B, an individual calendar year taxpayer, filed B's 1982 tax return on the due date, April 15, 1983. The return was completed properly except for B's mathematical error in totaling B's sources of income resulting in an incorrect computation of liability. The error was discovered, and on July 24, 1983, B paid the additional tax. There was sufficient information filed with the return to compute the proper tax liability. Therefore, the return is treated as filed on April 15, 1983.

Example (3). Corporation X, a calendar year taxpayer, filed its 1982 tax return on the due date, March 15, 1983. The return was properly completed except that X did not use schedule A for cost of goods sold. However, X did include with the filed return its own schedule of cost of goods sold drafted on a substitute form and containing provisions identical with schedule A as required by the revenue procedures relating to substitute forms in effect at the time. Therefore, the return will be treated as filed on March 15, 1983.

Example (4). C, an individual calendar year taxpayer, filed C's 1982 tax return on the due date, April 15, 1983. The return was properly completed except for C's failure to include Schedule A, relating to itemized deductions, with the filed return. Because C's 1040 return reflects C's choice to utilize Schedule A, and C failed to file Schedule A, there was insufficient information for mathematically verifying the tax liability. Therefore, for purposes of sections 611(b)(3) and (e), C's return is not treated as filed. The return will be treated as filed when either Schedule A is filed or an amended return, reflecting C's election not to itemize, is filed.

(5) *Application.*—The requirements of section 6611(i) and this paragraph (h), relating to the processible form requirement, apply to sections 6611(b)(3), relating to late returns, 6611(e), relating to income tax refund within 45 days of a return, and 6611(h), relating to the windfall profit tax. See also, paragraph (f)(2)(i)(B) of this section (relating to interest on overpayments relating to certain carrybacks).

Interest Rate: Overpayments and Underpayments

Interest Rate: Overpayments and Underpayments: Determination.—Temporary Reg. §301.6621-2T, relating to the increased rate of interest on substantial underpayments attributable to tax motivated transactions, is also proposed as a final regulation and, when adopted, will become Reg. §301.6621-2 (published in the Federal Register on December 28, 1984).

§301.6621-2. Questions and answers relating to the increased rate of interest on substantial underpayments attributable to certain tax motivated transactions.

ADDITIONS TO TAX, ADDITIONAL AMOUNTS, ASSESSABLE PENALTIES

Individual Retirement Plans: Simplified Employee Pensions: Qualified Voluntary Employee Contributions

Individual Retirement Plans: Simplified Employee Pensions: Qualified Voluntary Employee Contributions.—Reproduced below is the text of proposed Reg. §301.6652-4, relating to individual retirement plans, simplified employee pensions and qualified voluntary employee contributions (published in the Federal Register on January 23, 1984).

* * *

☐ Par. 13. There is added after §301.6652-3 the following new section:

§301.6652-4. Failure to file information with respect to qualified voluntary employee contributions.—(a) *Failure to make annual reports to employees.*—In the case of a failure to make an annual report required by §1.219(a)-5(g) which contains the information required by such section on the date prescribed therefor, there shall be paid (on notice and demand by the Secretary and in the same manner as tax) by the person failing to make such annual report an amount equal to $25 for each participant with respect to when there was a failure to make such report, multiplied by the number of years during which such failure continues.

(b) *Limitation.*—The total amount imposed under this section on any person shall not exceed $10,000 with respect to any calendar year.

Advance Payments for Goods and Long-Term Contracts: Existing Regulations Removed

Advance Payments for Goods and Long-Term Contracts: Existing Regulations Removed.—Amendments to Reg. §1.6655-0, removing regulations regarding advance payments for goods and long-term contracts that are no longer necessary after the enactment of recent tax legislation, are proposed (published in the Federal Register on October 15, 2018) (REG-104872-18).

Par. 6. Section 1.6655-0 is amended by removing the entries for §1.6655-2(f)(3)(i) and (f)(3)(i)(A) and redesignating the entry for §1.6655-2(f)(3)(i)(B) as §1.6655-2(f)(3)(i).

§1.6655-0. Table of contents.

Advance Payments for Goods and Long-Term Contracts: Existing Regulations Removed

Advance Payments for Goods and Long-Term Contracts: Existing Regulations Removed.—Amendments to Reg. §1.6655-2, removing regulations regarding advance payments for goods and long-term contracts that are no longer necessary after the enactment of recent tax legislation, are proposed (published in the Federal Register on October 15, 2018) (REG-104872-18).

Par. 7. Section 1.6655-2 is amended by removing paragraphs (f)(3)(i) heading and (f)(3)(i)(A) and redesignating (f)(3)(i)(B) as (f)(3)(i).

§1.6655-2. Annualized income installment method.

Base Erosion and Anti-Abuse Tax: Guidance

Base Erosion and Anti-Abuse Tax: Guidance.—Amendments to Reg. §1.6655-5, regarding the tax on base erosion payments of taxpayers with substantial gross receipts and reporting requirements thereunder, are proposed (published in the Federal Register on December 21, 2018) (REG-104259-18).

Par. 13. Section 1.6655-5 is amended by removing the language "§1.1502-2(h)" in paragraph (e) *Example 10* and adding the language "§1.1502-1(h)" in its place.

§1.6655-5. Short taxable year.

Advance Payments for Goods and Long-Term Contracts: Existing Regulations Removed

Advance Payments for Goods and Long-Term Contracts: Existing Regulations Removed.—Amendments to Reg. §1.6655-6, removing regulations regarding advance payments for goods and long-term contracts that are no longer necessary after the enactment of recent tax legislation, are proposed (published in the Federal Register on October 15, 2018) (REG-104872-18).

Par. 8. Section 1.6655-6 is amended in paragraph (c) by:

1. Revising the heading and introductory text;

2. Removing *Example 1;*

3. Designating *Example 2* as paragraph (c)(1) and revising the heading of newly designated paragraph (c)(1); and

3. Adding a reserved paragraph (c)(2).

The revisions read as follows:

§1.6655-6. Methods of accounting.

* * *

(c) *Example.*—The following example illustrates the rules of this section:

(1) *Example.*—* * *

* * *

Estate and Person Acquiring Property from Decedent: Consistent Basis Reporting

Estate and Person Acquiring Property from Decedent: Consistent Basis Reporting—Reg. §1.6662-8, providing guidance regarding the requirement that a recipient's basis in certain property acquired from a decedent be consistent with the value of the property as finally determined

for Federal estate tax purposes, is proposed (published in the Federal Register on March 4, 2016) (REG-127923-15).

Par. 6. Section 1.6662-8 is added to read as follows:

§1.6662-8. Inconsistent estate basis reporting.—(a) *In general.*—Section 6662(a) and (b)(8) impose an accuracy-related penalty on the portion of any underpayment of tax required to be shown on a return that is attributable to an inconsistent estate basis.

(b) *Inconsistent estate basis.*—In accordance with section 6662(k), there is an *inconsistent estate basis* to the extent that a taxpayer claims a basis, without regard to the adjustments described in §1.1014-10(a)(2), in property described in paragraph (c) of this section that exceeds that property's final value as determined under §1.1014-10(c).

(c) *Applicable property.*—The property to which this section applies is property described in §1.1014-10(b) that is reported or required to be reported on a return required by section 6018 filed after July 31, 2015.

(d) *Effective/applicability date.*—Upon the publication of the Treasury Decision adopting these rules as final in the **Federal Register**, this section will apply to property described in §1.1014-10(b) acquired from a decedent or by reason of the death of a decedent whose return required by section 6018 is filed after July 31, 2015. Persons may rely upon these rules before the date of publication of the Treasury Decision adopting these rules as final in the **Federal Register**. [Reg. §1.6662-8.]

Foreign Tax Credits

Foreign Tax Credits: Foreign Tax Redeterminations: Notifications.—Temporary Reg. §301.6689-1T, relating to a taxpayer's obligation to file notification of a foreign tax redetermination, to make adjustments to a taxpayer's pools of foreign taxes and earnings and profits, and the imposition of the civil penalty for failure to file such notice or report such adjustments, is also proposed as a final regulation and, when adopted, would become Reg. §301.6689-1 (published in the Federal Register on June 23, 1988).

§301.6689-1. Failure to file notice of redetermination of foreign tax.

Foreign Tax Credit: Foreign Tax Redeterminations

Foreign Tax Credit: Foreign Tax Redeterminations.—Reg. §301.6689-1, relating to a taxpayer's obligation under Code Sec. 905(c) to notify the IRS of a foreign tax redetermination, is proposed (published in the Federal Register on November 7, 2007) (REG-209020-86).

☐ Par. 5. Section 301.6689-1 is added to read as follows:

§301.6689-1. Failure to file notice of redetermination of foreign tax.—(a) [The text of the proposed amendments to §301.6689-1(a) is the same as the text of §301.6689-1T(a) as added by T.D. 9362].

(b) through (d) [Reserved]. For further guidance, see §301.6689-1T(b) through (d).

(e) [The text of the proposed amendments to §301.6689-1(e)(1) is the same as the text of §301.6689-1T(e)(1) as added by T.D. 9362].

Individual Retirement Plans: Simplified Employee Pensions

Individual Retirement Plans: Simplified Employee Pensions.—Reproduced below is the text of a proposed amendment to Reg. §301.6693-1, relating to individual retirement plans and simplified employee pensions (published in the Federal Register on July 14, 1981).

☐ Par. 18. Section 301.6693-1 is revised by changing its title, adding after paragraph (a)(2) a new paragraph (a)(3), and amending paragraph (e). Section 301.6693-1, as revised, reads as follows:

§301.6693-1. Penalty for failure to provide reports and documents concerning individual retirement accounts, individual retirement annuities and simplified employee pensions.—(a) *In general.*—* * *

(3) *Simplified employee pensions.*—An employer who makes a contribution on behalf of an employee to a simplified employee pension who fails to furnish or file a report or any other document required under section 408(1) or §1.408-9 within the time and in the manner prescribed for furnishing or filing such item shall pay a penalty of $10 for each failure unless it is shown that such failure is due to reasonable cause.

* * *

(e) *Effective date.*—This section shall take effect on January 1, 1975, except for paragraph (a)(3) which is effective for years beginning after December 31, 1978.

Gifts and Bequests from Covered Expatriates: Imposition of Tax

Gifts and Bequests from Covered Expatriates: Imposition of Tax.—Reg. §§28.6694-1—28.6694-4, relating to a tax on United States citizens and residents who receive gifts or bequests from certain individuals who relinquished United States citizenship or ceased to be lawful permanent residents of the United States on or after June 17, 2008, is proposed (published in the Federal Register on September 10, 2015) (REG-112997-10).

Sections 28.6694-1 to 28.6694-4 are added to read as follows:

§28.6694-1. Section 6694 penalties applicable to return preparer.—(a) *In general.*—For general rules regarding section 6694 penalties applicable to preparers of returns or claims for refund of the tax under chapter 15 of subtitle B of the Internal Revenue Code (Code), see §1.6694-1 of this chapter.

(b) *Effective/applicability date.*—This section applies to returns and claims for refund filed, and advice provided, on or after the date of publication of a Treasury decision adopting these rules as final regulations in the **Federal Register.** [Reg. §28.6694-1.]

§28.6694-2. Penalties for understatement due to an unreasonable position.—(a) *In general.*—A person who is a tax return preparer of any return or claim for refund of any tax under chapter 15 of subtitle B of the Code is subject to penalties under section 6694(a) in the manner stated in §1.6694-2 of this chapter.

(b) *Effective/applicability date.*—This section applies to returns and claims for refund filed, and advice provided, on or after the date of publication of a Treasury decision adopting these rules as final regulations in the **Federal Register.** [Reg. §28.6694-2.]

§28.6694-3. Penalties for understatement due to an unreasonable position.—(a) *In general.*—A person who is a tax return preparer of any return or claim for refund of any tax under chapter 15 of subtitle B of the Code is subject to penalties under section 6694(b) in the manner stated in §1.6694-3 of this chapter.

(b) *Effective/applicability date.*—This section applies to returns and claims for refund filed, and advice provided, on or after the date of publication of a Treasury decision adopting these rules as final regulations in the **Federal Register.** [Reg. §28.6694-3.]

§28.6694-4. Extension of period of collection when tax return preparer pays 15 percent of a penalty for understatement of taxpayer's liability and certain other procedural matters.—(a) *In general.*—For rules relating to the extension of the period of collection when a tax return preparer who prepared a return or claim for refund of tax under chapter 15 of subtitle B of the Code pays 15 percent of a penalty for understatement of taxpayer's liability, and for procedural matters relating to the investigation, assessment, and collection of the penalties under section 6694(a) and (b), the rules under §1.6694-4 of this chapter apply.

(b) *Effective/applicability date.*—This section applies to returns and claims for refund filed, and advice provided, on or after the date of publication of a Treasury decision adopting these rules as final regulations in the **Federal Register.** [Reg. §28.6694-4.]

Gifts and Bequests from Covered Expatriates: Imposition of Tax

Gifts and Bequests from Covered Expatriates: Imposition of Tax.—Reg. §§28.6695-1 and 28.6696-1, relating to a tax on United States citizens and residents who receive gifts or bequests from certain individuals who relinquished United States citizenship or ceased to be lawful permanent residents of the United States on or after June 17, 2008, is proposed (published in the Federal Register on September 10, 2015) (REG-112997-10).

Section 28.6695-1 is added to read as follows:

§28.6695-1. Other assessable penalties with respect to the preparation of tax returns for other persons.—(a) *In general.*—A person who is a tax return preparer of any return or claim for refund of any tax under chapter 15 of subtitle B of the Internal Revenue Code (Code) is subject to penalties for failure to furnish a copy to the taxpayer under section 6695(a) of the Code, failure to sign the return under section 6695(b) of the Code, failure to furnish an identification number under section 6695(c) of the Code, failure to retain a copy or list under section 6695(d) of the Code, failure to file a correct information return under section 6695(e) of the Code, and negotiation of a check under section 6695(f) of the Code, in the manner stated in §1.6695-1 of this chapter.

(b) *Effective/applicability date.*—This section applies to returns and claims for refund filed on or after the date of publication of a Treasury decision adopting these rules as final regulations in the **Federal Register.**[Reg. §28.6695-1.]

Section 28.6696-1 is added to read as follows:

§28.6696-1. Claims for credit or refund by tax return preparers and appraisers.—(a) *In general.*—For rules regarding claims for credit or refund by a tax return preparer who prepared a return or claim for refund for any tax under chapter 15 of subtitle B of the Internal Revenue Code (Code), or by an appraiser that prepared an appraisal in connection with such a return or claim for refund under section 6695A of the Code, the rules under §1.6696-1 of this chapter will apply.

(b) *Effective/applicability date.*—This section applies to returns and claims for refund filed, appraisals, and advice provided, on or after the date of publication of a Treasury decision adopting these rules as final regulations in the **Federal Register.** [Reg. §28.6696-1.]

Tax Shelters: List of Investors

Tax Shelters: List of Investors.—Temporary Reg. §301.6708-1T, relating to the requirement to maintain a list of investors in potentially abusive tax shelters, is also proposed as a final regulation and, when adopted, would become Reg. §301.6708-1 (published in the Federal Register on August 29, 1984).

§301.6708-1. Failure to maintain list of investors in potentially abusive tax shelters.

Mortgage Credit Certificates

Mortgage Credit Certificates: Issuance Penalties.—Temporary Reg. § 1.6709-1T, relating to the issuance of mortgage credit certificates, is also proposed as final and, when adopted, would become Reg. § 1.6709-1 (published in the Federal Register on May 8, 1985).

§ 301.6709-1. Penalties with respect to mortgage credit certificates.

Correct Payee Statements: Failure to File Correct Information: Penalties

Correct Payee Statements: Failure to File Correct Information: Penalties.—Amendments to Reg. §§ 301.6721-0 and 301.6721-1, relating to penalties for failure to file correct information returns or furnish correct payee statements, are proposed (published in the Federal Register on October 17, 2018) (REG-118826-16).

Par. 4. Section 301.6721-0 is revised to read as follows:

§ 301.6721-0. Table of Contents.—In order to facilitate the use of §§ 301.6721-1 through 6724-1, this section lists the paragraph headings contained in these sections.

(4) Specified information reporting requirement defined.
(b) Examples.
§ 301.6724-1 *Reasonable cause.*
(a) Waiver of the penalty.
(1) General rule.
(2) Reasonable cause defined.
(b) Significant mitigating factors.
(c) Events beyond the filer's control.
(1) In general.
(2) Unavailability of the relevant business records.
(3) Undue economic hardship relating to filing on magnetic media.
(4) Actions of the Internal Revenue Service.
(5) Actions of agent—imputed reasonable cause.
(6) Actions of the payee or any other person.
(d) Responsible manner.
(1) In general.
(2) Special rule for filers seeking a waiver pursuant to paragraph (c)(6) of this section.
(e) Acting in a responsible manner—special rules for missing TINs.
(1) In general.
(i) Initial solicitation.
(ii) First annual solicitation.
(iii) Second annual solicitation.
(iv) Additional requirements.
(v) Failures to which a solicitation relates.
(vi) Exceptions and limitations.
(2) Manner of making annual solicitations—by mail or telephone.
(i) By mail.
(ii) By telephone.
(f) Acting in a responsible manner—special rules for incorrect TINs.
(1) In general.
(i) Initial solicitation.
(ii) First annual solicitation.
(iii) Second annual solicitation.
(iv) Additional requirements.
(2) Manner of making annual solicitation if notified pursuant to section 3406(a)(1)(B) and the regulations thereunder.
(3) Manner of making annual solicitation if notified pursuant to section 6721.
(4) Failures to which a solicitation relates.
(5) Exceptions and limitations.
(g) Due diligence safe harbor.
(1) In general.
(2) Special rules relating to TINs.
(3) Effective dates.
(h) Reasonable cause safe harbor after election under section 6722(c)(3)(B).
(i) [Reserved]
(j) Failures to which this section relates.
(k) Examples.
(l) [Reserved]
(m) Procedure for seeking a waiver.
(n) Manner of payment.
(o) Applicability date.

Par. 5. Section 301.6721-1 is amended by:
1. Revising paragraph (a)(1).
2. Revising the ninth sentence of paragraph (a)(2)(ii).
3. Revising paragraphs (b)(1), (2), (5), and (6), (c)(1), (c)(2)(iii), (c)(3), and (d).
4. Redesignating paragraphs (e), (f), and (g) as paragraphs (f), (g), and (h).
5. Adding a new paragraph (e).
6. Revising newly redesignated paragraphs (f)(1), (g)(1) and (4) through (6), (h)(1), and (h)(2)(x) and (xi) and adding paragraph (h)(2)(xii).
7. Revising newly redesignated paragraphs (h)(3)(xvii), (xviii), (xxiv), and (xxv) and adding paragraph (h)(3)(xxvi).
8. Revising newly redesignated paragraphs (h)(4) and (6).
9. Adding paragraphs (i) and (j).
The revisions and additions read as follows:

§ 301.6721-1. Failure to file correct information returns.—(a) *Imposition of penalty.*—(1) *General rule.*—A penalty of $250 is imposed for each information return (as defined in section 6724(d)(1) and paragraph (h) of this section) with respect to which a failure (as defined in section 6721(a)(2) and paragraph (a)(2) of this section) occurs. No more than one penalty will be imposed under this paragraph (a)(1) with respect to a single information return even though there may be more than one failure with respect to such return. The total amount imposed on any person for all failures during any calendar year with respect to all information returns shall not exceed $3,000,000. See paragraph (b) of this section for a reduction in the penalty when the failures are corrected within specified periods. See paragraph (c) of this section for an exception to the penalty for inconsequential errors or omissions. See paragraph (d) of this section for an exception to the penalty for a de minimis number of failures. See paragraph (e) of this section for a safe harbor exception for certain de minimis errors. See paragraph (f) of this section for lower limitations to the $3,000,000 maximum penalty. See paragraph (g) of this section for higher penalties when a failure is due to intentional disregard of the requirement to file timely correct information returns. See paragraph (i) of this section for inflation adjustments to penalty amounts. See § 301.6724–1(a)(1) for waiver of the penalty for a failure that is due to reasonable cause.

(2) * * *

(ii) * * * Except as provided in paragraph (c)(1) or (e)(1) of this section, a failure to include correct information encompasses a failure to include the information required by applicable information reporting statutes or by any administrative pronouncements issued thereunder (such as regulations, revenue rulings, revenue procedures, or information reporting forms and form instructions). * * *

(b) *Reduction in the penalty when a correction is made within specified periods.*—(1) *Correction within 30 days.*—The penalty imposed under section 6721(a) for a failure to file timely or for a failure to include correct information shall be $50 in lieu of $250 if the failure is corrected on or before the 30th day after the required filing date ("within 30 days"). The total amount imposed on a person for all failures during any calendar year that are corrected within 30 days shall not exceed $500,000.

(2) *Correction after 30 days but on or before August 1*.—The penalty imposed under section 6721(a) for a failure to file timely or for a failure to include correct information shall be $100 in lieu of $250 if the failure is corrected after the 30–day period described in paragraph (b)(1) of this section but on or before August 1 of the year in which the required filing date occurs ("after 30 days but on or before August 1"). See paragraph (b)(6) of this section for an exception to the provisions of this paragraph (b)(2) for returns that are not due on January 31, February 28, or March 15. The total amount imposed on a person for all failures during any calendar year corrected after 30 days but on or before August 1 shall not exceed $1,500,000.

* * *

(5) *Examples*.—The provisions of paragraphs (a) and (b)(1) through (4) of this section may be illustrated by the following examples. These examples do not take into account any possible application of the de minimis exception under paragraph (d) of this section, the safe harbor exception for certain de minimis errors under paragraph (e) of this section, the lower small business limitations under paragraph (f) of this section, the penalty for intentional disregard under paragraph (g) of this section, any adjustments for inflation under paragraph (i) of this section, or the reasonable cause waiver under § 301.6724-1(a):

(i) *Example 1*.—Corporation R fails to file timely 23,000 Forms 1099–MISC (relating to miscellaneous income) for the 2018 calendar year. Five thousand of these returns are filed with correct information within 30 days, and 18,000 after 30 days but on or before August 1, 2019. For the same year R fails to file timely 400 Forms 1099–INT (relating to payments of interest) which R eventually files on September 28, 2019, after the period for reduction of the penalty has elapsed. R is subject to a penalty of $100,000 for the 400 forms which were not filed by August 1 ($250 x 400 = $100,000), $1,500,000 for the 18,000 forms filed after 30 days ($100 x 18,000 = $1,800,000, limited to $1,500,000 under paragraph (b)(2) of this section), and $250,000 for the 5,000 forms filed within 30 days ($50 x 5,000 = $250,000), for a total penalty of $1,850,000.

(ii) *Example 2*.—Corporation T fails to file timely 14,000 Forms 1099–MISC for the 2018 calendar year. T files the 14,000 Forms 1099–MISC on September 1, 2019. Because T does not correct the failure by August 1, 2019, T is subject to a penalty of $3,000,000, the maximum penalty under paragraph (a) of this section. Without the limitation of paragraph (a), T would be subject to a $3,500,000 penalty ($250 x 14,000 = $3,500,000).

(iii) *Example 3*.—Corporation U files timely 300 Forms 1099–MISC on paper for the 2018 calendar year with correct information. Under section 6011(e)(2) a person required to file at least 250 returns during a calendar year must file those returns on magnetic media. U does not correct its failures to file these returns on magnetic media by August 1, 2019. It is therefore subject to a penalty for a failure to file timely under paragraph (a)(2) of this section. However, pursuant to section 6724(c) and paragraph (a)(2) of this section, the penalty for a failure to file timely on magnetic media applies only to the extent the number of returns exceeds 250. As U was required to file 300 returns on magnetic media, U is subject to a penalty of $12,500 for 50 returns ($250 x 50 = $12,500).

(iv) *Example 4*.—Corporation V files 300 Forms 1099–B (relating to proceeds from broker and barter exchange transactions) on paper for the 2018 calendar year. The forms were filed on March 15, 2019, rather than on the required filing date of February 28, 2019. Under section 6011(e)(2), a person required to file at least 250 returns during a calendar year must file those returns on magnetic media. V does not correctly file these returns on magnetic media by August 1, 2019. V is subject to a penalty of $12,500 for filing 250 of the returns late ($50 x 250) and $12,500 for failing to file 50 returns on magnetic media ($250 x 50) for a total penalty of $25,000.

(6) *Application to returns not due on January 31, February 28, or March 15*.—For returns that are not due on January 31, February 28, or March 15 (for example, Forms 8300 reporting certain cash payments of $10,000 or more), the penalty is $50 if the failure is corrected within 30 days. If the failure is corrected after 30 days, the penalty is $250 rather than $100. There is no period during which the penalty is reduced to $100 under paragraph (b)(2) of this section.

(c) *Exception for inconsequential errors or omissions*.—(1) *In general*.—An inconsequential error or omission is not considered a failure to include correct information. For purposes of this paragraph (c)(1), the term "inconsequential error or omission" means any failure that does not prevent or hinder the Internal Revenue Service from processing the return, from correlating the information required to be shown on the return with the information shown on the payee's tax return, or from otherwise putting the return to its intended use. See paragraph (h)(5) of this section for the definition of "payee."

(2) * * *

(iii) Any monetary amounts, except as provided in paragraph (e) of this section. The Internal Revenue Service may, by administrative pronouncement, specify other types of errors or omissions that are never inconsequential.

(3) *Examples*.—The provisions of this paragraph (c) may be illustrated by the following examples, which do not take into account any possible application of the penalty for intentional disregard under paragraph (g) of this section or the reasonable cause waiver under § 301.6724-1(a):

(i) *Example 1*.—A filer files a Form 1099–MISC (relating to miscellaneous income) with the Internal Revenue Service. The Form 1099–MISC is complete and correct except that the word "street" is misspelled in the payee's address. The error does not prevent or hinder the Internal Revenue Service from processing the return, from correlating the information required to be shown on the return with the information shown on the payee's tax return, or from otherwise putting the return to its intended use. Therefore, no penalty is imposed under paragraph (a) of this section.

(ii) *Example 2*.—A filer files a Form 1099–MISC with the Internal Revenue Service.

The Form 1099–MISC is complete and correct except that the payee's first name, William, is misspelled as "Willaim." The error does not prevent or hinder the Internal Revenue Service from processing the return, from correlating the information required to be shown on the return with the information shown on the payee's tax return, or from otherwise putting the return to its intended use. See paragraph (c)(2) of this section. Therefore, no penalty is imposed under paragraph (a) of this section.

(iii) *Example 3.*—A filer files a Form 1099–MISC with the Internal Revenue Service. The Form 1099–MISC is complete and correct except that the payee's name, "John Doe," is misspelled as "John Ode." Under paragraph (c)(2) of this section, supplying an incorrect surname for a payee is never considered an inconsequential error. Therefore, a penalty is imposed under paragraph (a) of this section.

(d) *Exception for a de minimis number of failures.*—(1) *Requirements.*—The penalty under paragraph (a) of this section is not imposed for a de minimis number of failures to include correct information if the filer corrects such failures on or before August 1 of the year in which the required filing date occurs. See paragraph (d)(4) of this section for special rules relating to returns that are not due on January 31, February 28, or March 15.

(2) *Calculation of the de minimis exception.*—The number of returns to which the de minimis exception applies for any calendar year shall not exceed the greater of 10 or one-half of one percent of the total number of all information returns the filer is required to file during the year. If the number of returns on which the filer fails to include correct information exceeds the number of returns to which the de minimis exception applies, the de minimis exception applies to those returns that will afford the filer the greatest reduction in penalty. The de minimis exception applies to failures to include correct information that exist after the application (if any) of the safe harbor exception for certain de minimis errors under paragraph (e) of this section and after the application (if any) of the waiver for reasonable cause under section 6724(a) and § 301.6724-1. Returns to which the de minimis exception applies are treated as having been originally filed with correct information.

(3) *Examples.*—The provisions of this paragraph (d) may be illustrated by the following examples. In each of the examples, the failures to file and to include correct information are subject to penalty under paragraph (a) of this section. The examples do not take into account any possible application of the safe harbor exception for certain de minimis errors under paragraph (e) of this section, the lower small business limitations under paragraph (f) of this section, the penalty for intentional disregard under paragraph (g) of this section, any adjustment for inflation under paragraph (i) of this section, or the reasonable cause waiver under § 301.6724-1(a).

(i) *Example 1.*—Corporation T files timely 10,000 Forms 1099–INT (relating to payments of interest) for 2018 by February 28, 2019. The 10,000 returns are all the information returns that T is required to file during the 2019 calendar year. Of the returns filed, 70 contained incorrect information. T corrects the failures on July 12, 2019. No penalty is imposed for 50 of the failures (that is, the greater of 10 or .005 x 10,000 = 50) even though the total failures, 70, exceed the number to which the de minimis exception may apply. The $100 penalty under paragraph (b)(2) of this section is imposed, in lieu of $250, for the remaining 20 failures, which were corrected after 30 days but on or before August 1, resulting in a total penalty of $2000 ($100 x 20 = $2000).

(ii) *Example 2.*—Corporation U files timely 9,500 Forms 1099–INT for 2018 by February 28, 2019. Fifty of these returns contain incorrect information with respect to which U files correct information on August 1, 2019. U also files 500 Forms 1099–INT for 2018 on August 30, 2019, after the required filing date. The 10,000 returns are all the information returns that U is required to file during the 2019 calendar year. The calculation of the de minimis exception is based on the 10,000 returns required to be filed during the 2019 calendar year even though 500 of the returns filed during the year were not filed timely. Therefore, the number of failures for which the de minimis exception applies is 50, and accordingly no penalty is imposed for the 50 Forms 1099–INT that were corrected on August 1, 2019. However, the $250 penalty under paragraph (a)(1) of this section is imposed for each failure to file timely, resulting in a total penalty of $125,000 ($250 x 500 = $125,000).

(iii) *Example 3.*—Corporation V files timely 9,950 Forms 1099–INT for 2018 by February 28, 2019. However, V fails to file timely 50 of its Forms 1099–INT. The 10,000 returns are all the information returns that V is required to file during the 2019 calendar year. Upon discovering the error, V files the 50 returns within 30 days of February 28, 2019. The 50 returns are complete and correct except that V fails to include the taxpayer identification numbers of the payees on the returns. V files corrected returns on August 1, 2019. Absent application of the de minimis exception, the penalty imposed for the failure to include correct information would be $5,000 ($100 x 50 = $5,000). Because the incorrect returns are corrected on August 1, the 50 forms are treated under the de minimis exception as originally filed with correct information, and therefore no penalty is imposed under paragraph (a) of this section for the failure to include correct information. Nevertheless, the penalty under paragraph (a) of this section is imposed for the failure to file timely the 50 returns because the de minimis exception does not apply to the penalty for the failure to file timely. Hence, a penalty of $2,500 ($50 x 50 = $2500) is imposed.

(iv) *Example 4.*—Corporation W files timely 100 Forms 1099–DIV and files an additional 50 Forms 1099–DIV late, but within 30 days of February 28, 2019. These are all the information returns that W was required to file during the 2019 calendar year. W discovers errors on 10 of the returns that were filed timely, and on 5 of the returns that were filed late. W corrects all the errors on August 1. The de minimis exception applies to 10 of the corrected returns. The exception will be allocated to the 10 returns that were filed timely with incorrect information, because that allocation is most favorable to W (that is, applying the exception to a return filed late with incorrect information would save W $50, by reducing the penalty on that return from $100 to $50, but applying the exception to a return filed timely would save W $100, by reducing the penalty on that return from $100 to $0). (See paragraph (b)(4) of this section.)

(4) *Nonapplication to returns not due on January 31, February 28, or March 15.*—The exception for a de minimis number of failures provided in paragraph (d)(1) of this section does not apply to failures with respect to returns that are not due on January 31, February 28, or March 15 (for example, Forms 8300 reporting certain cash payments of $10,000 or more). Nevertheless, the returns that are not due on January 31, February 28, or March 15 are included in the total number of all information returns that the filer is required to file during a year for purposes of calculating the number of the returns subject to the de minimis exception under paragraph (d)(2) of this section.

(e) *Safe harbor exception for certain de minimis errors.*—(1) *In general.*—Except as provided in paragraph (e)(3) or (g)(4) of this section, the penalty under section 6721(a) and paragraph (a) of this section is not imposed for a failure described in section 6721(a)(2)(B) and paragraph (a)(2)(ii) of this section (failure to include correct information on information return) when the failure relates to an incorrect dollar amount and is a de minimis error. When this safe harbor applies to an information return and the information return was otherwise correct and timely filed, no correction is required and, for purposes of this section, the information return is treated as having been filed with all of the correct required information.

(2) *Definition of de minimis error.*—For the definition of de minimis error, see § 301.6722-1(d)(2).

(3) *Election to override the safe harbor exception.*—The safe harbor exception provided for by paragraph (e)(1) of this section does not apply to any information return if the incorrect dollar amount that would qualify as a de minimis error for purposes of this paragraph (e) relates to an amount with respect to which an election has been made (and has not been revoked) under section 6722(c)(3)(B) and § 301.6722-1(d)(3). See § 301.6722-1(d)(3) for additional rules relating to the election under section 6722(c)(3)(B) and § 301.6722-1(d)(3), including rules relating to the revocation of the election and the inapplicability of the election to certain information. See § 301.6724-1(h) for rules relating to waiver of the section 6721 penalty in cases where the safe harbor exception provided for by paragraph (e)(1) of this section does not apply because of an election under § 301.6722-1(d)(3).

(f) *Lower limitations on the $3,000,000 maximum penalty amount with respect to persons with gross receipts of not more than $5,000,000.*—(1) *In general.*—If a person meets the gross receipts test (as defined in paragraph (f)(2) of this section) for any calendar year, the total amount of the penalty imposed on such person for all failures described in section 6721(a)(2) and paragraph (a)(2) of this section during such calendar year shall not exceed $1,000,000. The total amount of the penalty imposed under paragraph (b)(1) of this section for failures corrected within 30 days shall not exceed $175,000 for such calendar year. The total amount of the penalty imposed under paragraph (b)(2) of this section for failures corrected after 30 days but on or before August 1 shall not exceed $500,000 for such calendar year.

* * *

(g) *Higher penalty for intentional disregard of requirement to file timely correct information returns.*—(1) *Application of section 6721(e).*—If a failure is due to intentional disregard of the requirement to file timely or to include correct information on a return as described in paragraph (h) of this section, the amount of the penalty imposed under paragraph (a) of this section shall be determined under paragraph (g)(4) of this section.

* * *

(4) *Amount of the penalty.*—If one or more failures to file timely or to include correct information are due to intentional disregard of the requirement to file timely or to include correct information, then, with respect to each such failure determined under this paragraph (g)—

(i) Paragraphs (b), (d), (e), and (f) of this section shall not apply;

(ii) The $3,000,000 limitation under paragraph (a) of this section shall not apply, and the penalty under this paragraph (g) shall not be taken into account in applying the $3,000,000 limitation (or any similar limitation under paragraph (b) or (f) of this section) to penalties not determined under this paragraph (g);

(iii) The penalty imposed under paragraph (a) of this section shall be $500 or, if greater, the statutory percentage; and

(iv) The term "statutory percentage" means—

(A) In the case of a return other than a return required under section 6045(a), 6041A(b), 6050H, 6050I, 6050J, 6050K, 6050L, or 6050V, 10 percent of the aggregate dollar amount of the items required to be reported correctly;

(B) In the case of a return required to be filed by section 6045(a), 6050K, or 6050L, 5 percent of the aggregate dollar amount of the items required to be reported correctly;

(C) In the case of a return required to be filed under section 6050I(a), for any transaction (or related transactions), the greater of $25,000 or the amount of cash (within the meaning of section 6050I(d)) received in such transaction to the extent the amount of such cash does not exceed $100,000; or

(D) In the case of a return required to be filed under section 6050V, 10 percent of the value of the benefit of any contract with respect to which information is required to be included on the return.

(5) *Computation of the penalty; aggregate dollar amount of the items required to be reported correctly.*—The aggregate dollar amount used in computing the penalty under this paragraph (g) is the amount that is not reported or is reported incorrectly. If the intentional disregard relates to a dollar amount, the statutory percentage is applied to the difference between the dollar amount reported and the amount required to be reported correctly. If the intentional disregard relates to any other item on the return, the statutory percentage is applied to the aggregate amount of items required to be reported correctly. In determining the aggregate amount of items required to be reported correctly, no item shall be taken into account more than once. For example, if a filer willfully fails to file a Form 1099–INT on which $800 of interest and $160 of Federal income tax withheld (that is, backup withholding) is required to be reported, only the

$800 amount is taken into account in computing the penalty.

(6) *Examples*.—The provisions of this paragraph (g) may be illustrated by the following examples, which do not take into account any adjustments for inflation under paragraph (i) of this section:

(i) *Example 1*.—On December 1, 2018, Automobile dealer P receives $55,000 from an individual for the purchase of an automobile in a transaction subject to reporting under section 6050I. The individual presents documents to P that identify him as "John Doe." However, P completes the Form 8300 (relating to cash received in a trade or business) and reflects the name of a cartoon character as the filer. Because P knew at the time of filing the Form 8300 that the filer's name was not the name of the cartoon character, he willfully failed to include correct information as described under paragraph (g)(2) of this section. Therefore, the penalty under paragraph (g)(4) of this section is imposed for the intentional disregard of the requirement to include correct information. The amount used in computing the penalty under paragraph (g)(5) of this section is $55,000 (that is, the amount required to be reported on the return with respect to which the payee is not correctly identified). The amount of the penalty determined under paragraph (g)(4)(iv)(C) of this section is $55,000 (that is, the greater of $25,000 or the amount of cash received in the transaction up to $100,000).

(ii) *Example 2*.—On December 1, 2018, Individual B contacts his agent, F, to act as his intermediary in the purchase of an automobile. B gives F $20,000 and requests F to purchase the automobile in F's name, which F does. F prepares the Form 8300 as required under section 6050I, but in the area designated for the name of the filer, F writes "confidential." Because F knew at the time the return was filed that it contained incomplete information, the penalty under paragraph (g)(4) of this section is imposed for the intentional disregard of the requirement to include correct information. The amount used in computing the penalty under paragraph (g)(5) of this section is $20,000 (that is, the amount required to be reported on the return with respect to which the payee is not correctly identified). The amount of the penalty determined under paragraph (g)(4)(iv)(C) of this section is $25,000 (that is, the greater of $25,000 or the amount of cash received in the transaction up to $100,000).

(iii) *Example 3*.—Corporation M deliberately does not include $5,000 of dividends on a Form 1099–DIV (relating to payments of dividends) on which a total of $200,000 (including the $5,000 dividends) is required to be reported under section 6042(a). Because the failure was deliberate, Corporation M's failure is due to intentional disregard of the requirement to include correct information. Accordingly, the amount of the penalty imposed under paragraph (a) is determined under paragraph (g)(4) of this section. Because the Form 1099–DIV is required to be filed under section 6042(a), under paragraph (g)(4)(iv)(A) the amount of the penalty with respect to such failure is 10 percent of the aggregate dollar amount of the items that were required to be but that were not reported correctly. Under paragraph (g)(5) of this section, $5,000 is the difference between the dollar amount reported and the amount required to be reported correctly. Therefore, the amount of the penalty is $500 ($5,000 x .10 = $500).

(iv) *Example 4*.—Form 8027 requires certain large food and beverage establishments to report certain information with respect to tips. The form requires (among other things) that the establishment report its gross receipts from food and beverage operations. Establishment A, in intentional disregard of the information reporting requirement, reported gross receipts of $1,000,000, when the correct amount was $1,500,000. The significance of the gross receipts reporting requirement is that section 6053(c)(3)(A) requires an establishment to allocate as tips among its employees the excess of 8 percent of its gross receipts over the aggregate amount reported by employees to the establishment as tips under section 6053(a). A's misstatement of its gross receipts caused A to show $80,000 on the Form 8027 as 8 percent of its gross receipts, rather than the correct amount of $120,000. A correctly reported the amount of tips reported to it by employees under section 6053(a) as $80,000. Thus A reported the excess of 8 percent of its gross receipts over tips reported to it as zero, rather than as the correct amount of $40,000. The requirement of reporting gross receipts is considered merely a step in the computation of the excess of 8 percent of gross receipts over tips reported to A under section 6053(a), so that the penalty for intentional disregard will be $4,000 (that is, 10 percent of the difference between the $40,000 required to be reported as the excess of 8 percent of gross receipts over tips reported under section 6053(a), and the zero amount actually reported).

(h) *Definitions*.—(1) *Information return*.—For purposes of this section, the term "information return" has the same meaning as "information return" as defined in section 6724(d)(1), including any statement described in paragraph (h)(2) of this section, any return described in paragraph (h)(3) of this section, and any other items described in paragraph (h)(4) of this section.

(2) * * *

(x) Section 408(i) (relating to reports with respect to individual retirement accounts or annuities on Form 1099-R, "Distributions From Pensions, Annuities, Retirement or Profit-Sharing Plans, IRAs, Insurance Contracts, etc.");

(xi) Section 6047(d) (relating to reports by employers, plan administrators, etc., on Form 1099–R); or

(xii) Section 6035 (relating to basis information with respect to property acquired from decedents, generally Form 8971, "Information Regarding Beneficiaries Acquiring Property From a Decedent" and the Schedule(s) A required to be filed along with it).

(3) * * *

(xvii) Section 1060(b) (relating to reporting requirements of transferors and transferees in certain asset acquisitions, generally reported on Form 8594, "Asset Acquisition Statement"), or section 1060(e) (relating to information required in the case of certain transfers of interests in entities);

(xviii) Section 4101(d) (relating to information reporting with respect to fuel oils);

* * *

(xxiv) Section 6055 (relating to information returns reporting minimum essential coverage);

(xxv) Section 6056 (relating to information returns reporting on offers of health insurance coverage by applicable large employer members); or

(xxvi) Section 6050Y (relating to returns relating to certain life insurance contract transactions).

(4) *Other items.*—The term information return also includes any form, statement, or schedule required to be filed with the Internal Revenue Service with respect to any amount from which tax is required to be deducted and withheld under chapter 3 of the Internal Revenue Code (or from which tax would be required to be so deducted and withheld but for an exemption under the Internal Revenue Code or any treaty obligation of the United States), generally Forms 1042–S, "Foreign Person's U.S. Source Income Subject to Withholding," and 8805, "Foreign Partner's Information Statement of Section 1446 Withholding Tax." The provisions of this paragraph (h)(4) referring to Form 8805, shall apply to partnership taxable years beginning after May 18, 2005, or such earlier time as the regulations under §§1.1446-1 through 1.1446-5 of this chapter apply by reason of an election under §1.1446-7 of this chapter.

* * *

(6) *Filer.*—For purposes of this section the term "filer" means a person that is required to file an information return as defined in paragraph (h)(1) of this section under the applicable information reporting section described in paragraphs (h)(2) through (4) of this section.

(i) *Adjustment for inflation.*—Each of the dollar amounts under paragraphs (a), (b), (f) (other than (f)(2)), and (g) of this section and paragraphs (a), (b), (d) (other than paragraph (2)(A)), and (e) of section 6721 shall be adjusted for inflation pursuant to section 6721(f).

(j) *Applicability date.*—This section applies with respect to information returns required to be filed on or after January 1 of the calendar year immediately following the date of publication of a Treasury decision adopting these rules as final regulations in the **Federal Register**.

Estate and Person Acquiring Property from Decedent: Consistent Basis Reporting

Estate and Person Acquiring Property from Decedent: Consistent Basis Reporting.—Amendments to Reg. §§301.6721-1 and 301.6722-1, providing guidance regarding the requirement that a recipient's basis in certain property acquired from a decedent be consistent with the value of the property as finally determined for Federal estate tax purposes, are proposed (published in the Federal Register on March 4, 2016) (REG-127923-15).

Par. 8. Section 301.6721-1 is amended by removing the word "or" at the end of paragraph (g)(2)(x), removing the period and adding "; or" at the end of paragraph (g)(2)(xi), and adding paragraph (g)(2)(xii).

The addition reads as follows:

§301.6721-1. Failure to file correct information returns.

* * *

(g) * * *

(2) * * *

(xii) Section 6035 (relating to basis of property acquired from decedents).

* * *

Par. 9. Section 301.6722-1 is amended by removing the word "or" at the end of paragraph (d)(2)(xxxiii), removing the period and adding a semi-colon in its place followed by the word "or" at the end of paragraph (d)(2)(xxxiv), and adding paragraph (d)(2)(xxxv).

The addition reads as follows:

§301.6722-1. Failure to furnish correct payee statements.

* * *

(d) * * *

(2) * * *

(xxxv) Section 6035 (relating to basis of property acquired from decedents).

* * *

Information Returns: Using Magnetic Media

Information Returns: Using Magnetic Media.—Amendments to Reg. §301.6721-1, amending the rules for determining whether information returns must be filed using magnetic media (electronically), are proposed (published in the Federal Register on May 31, 2018) (REG-102951-16).

Par. 3. Section 301.6721-1 is amended as follows:

a. By removing the fifth through seventh sentences in paragraph (a)(2)(ii).

b. Adding paragraph (h).

The revisions and addition reads as follows:

§301.6721-1. Failure to file correct information returns.

* * *

(h) *Effective dates.*—Paragraph (a)(2)(ii) of this section is effective for information returns required to be filed after December 31, 2018.

Correct Payee Statements: Failure to File Correct Information: Penalties

Correct Payee Statements: Failure to File Correct Information: Penalties.—Amendments to Reg. § 301.6722-1, relating to penalties for failure to file correct information returns or furnish correct payee statements, are proposed (published in the Federal Register on October 17, 2018) (REG-118826-16).

Par. 6. Section 301.6722-1 is amended by:

1. Revising paragraphs (a)(1), (a)(2)(ii), and (b)(2)(i).
2. In paragraphs (b)(2)(ii) and (iii), removing the comma at the end of each paragraph and adding a semicolon in its place.
3. Revising paragraph (b)(3) introductory text.
4. In paragraph (b)(3), designate *Examples 1* and 2 as paragraphs (b)(3)(i) and (ii).
5. Revising paragraph (c)(1).
6. Redesignating paragraphs (c)(2)(i), (ii), and (iii) as paragraphs (c)(2)(ii), (iii), and (iv).
7. Adding a new paragraph (c)(2)(i).
8. Revising newly redesignated paragraphs (c)(2)(ii) and (iii).
9. Redesignating paragraphs (d) and (e) as paragraphs (e) and (g).
10. Adding a new paragraph (d).
11. Revising newly redesignated paragraphs (e)(1), (e)(2) introductory text, and (e)(2)(xxxiii) and (xxxiv).
12. Adding paragraphs (e)(2)(xxxv), (xxxvi), and (xxxvii), (e)(4), and (f).
13. Revising newly redesignated paragraph (g).

The revisions and additions read as follows:

§ 301.6722-1. Failure to furnish correct payee statements.—(a) *Imposition of penalty.*—(1) *General rule.*—A penalty of $250 is imposed for each payee statement (as defined in section 6724(d)(2) and paragraph (e)(2) of this section) with respect to which a failure (as defined in section 6722(a) and paragraph (a)(2) of this section) occurs. No more than one penalty will be imposed under this paragraph (a) with respect to a single payee statement even though there may be more than one failure with respect to such statement. However, the penalty shall apply to failures on composite substitute payee statements as though each type of payment and other required information were furnished on separate statements. A "composite substitute payee statement" is a single document created by a filer to reflect several types of payments made to the same payee. The total amount imposed on any person for all failures during any calendar year with respect to all payee statements shall not exceed $3,000,000. See section 6722(e) and paragraph (c) of this section for higher penalties when a failure is due to intentional disregard of the requirement to furnish timely correct payee statements. See paragraph (d) of this section for a safe harbor exception for certain de minimis errors. See paragraph (f) of this section for inflation adjustments to penalty amounts. See § 301.6724-1(a)(1) for a waiver of the penalty for a failure that is due to reasonable cause.

(2) * * *

(ii) A failure to include all of the information required to be shown on a payee statement or the inclusion of incorrect information ("failure to include correct information"). A failure to furnish timely includes a failure to furnish a written statement to the payee in a statement mailing as required under sections 6042(c), 6044(e), 6049(c), and 6050N(b), as well as a failure to furnish the statement on a form acceptable to the Internal Revenue Service. Except as provided in paragraph (b) or (d) of this section, a failure to include correct information encompasses a failure to include the information required by applicable information reporting statutes or by any administrative pronouncements issued thereunder (such as regulations, revenue rulings, revenue procedures, or information reporting forms).

(b) * * *

(2) * * *

(i) A dollar amount, except as provided in paragraph (d) of this section;

* * *

(3) *Examples.*—The provisions of this paragraph (b) may be illustrated by the following examples which do not take into account any possible application of the penalty for intentional disregard under paragraph (c) of this section, the safe harbor exception for certain de minimis errors under paragraph (d) of this section, or the reasonable cause waiver under § 301.6724-1(a):

* * *

(c) *Higher penalty for intentional disregard of requirement to furnish timely correct payee statements.*—(1) *Application of section 6722(e).*—If a failure is due to intentional disregard of the requirement to furnish timely correct payee statements, the amount of the penalty shall be determined under paragraph (c)(2) of this section. Whether a failure is due to intentional disregard of the requirement to furnish timely correct payee statements is based upon the facts and circumstances surrounding the failure. The facts and circumstances considered include those under § 301.6721-1(g)(3), which shall apply in determining whether a failure under this section is due to intentional disregard.

(2) * * *

(i) Paragraph (d) of this section shall not apply;

(ii) The $3,000,000 limitation under paragraph (a) of this section shall not apply and the penalty under this paragraph (c)(2) shall not be taken into account in applying the $3,000,000 limitation to penalties not determined under this paragraph (c)(2);

(iii) The penalty imposed under paragraph (a) of this section shall be $500 or, if greater, the statutory percentage; and

* * *

(d) *Safe harbor exception for certain de minimis errors.*—(1) *In general.*—Except as provided in paragraphs (c) and (d)(3) of this section, the penalty under section 6722(a) and paragraph (a) of this section is not imposed for a failure described in section 6722(a)(2)(B) and paragraph (a)(2)(ii) of this section (failure to include correct information on payee statement) when the failure relates to an incorrect dollar amount and is a de minimis error. When this safe harbor applies to a payee statement and the payee statement was otherwise correct and timely furnished no correction is required and, for purposes of this section, the payee statement is treated as having been furnished with all of the correct required information.

(2) *Definition of de minimis error*.—For purposes of paragraph (d) of this section, an error in a dollar amount is de minimis if the difference between any single amount in error and the correct amount is not more than $100, and, if the difference is with respect to an amount of tax withheld, it is not more than $25. For purposes of this paragraph (d)(2), tax withheld includes any amount required to be shown on an information return or payee statement (as defined in section 6724(d)(1) and (d)(2), respectively) withheld under section 3402, as well as any such amount that is creditable under sections 27, 31, 33, or 1474.

(3) *Election to override the safe harbor exception*.—(i) *In general*.—Except as provided in paragraphs (d)(3)(vi) and (vii) of this section, the safe harbor exception provided for by this paragraph (d) does not apply to any payee statement if the person to whom the statement is required to be furnished (the payee) makes an election that the safe harbor not apply with respect to the statement.

(ii) *Timing of election*.—The payee must elect no later than the later of 30 days after the date on which the payee statement is required to be furnished to the payee, or October 15 of the calendar year, to receive a correct payee statement required to be furnished in that calendar year without having the safe harbor under paragraph (d)(1) of this section apply. The date of an election is the date the election is received by the filer. For purposes of this section, the provisions of section 7502 relating to timely mailing treated as timely delivery apply in determining the date an election is considered to be received by the filer, treating delivery to the filer as if the filer were an agency, officer, or office under such section. The election shall remain in effect for all subsequent years unless revoked under paragraph (d)(3)(vii) of this section.

(iii) *Manner for making the election*.—Except as provided in paragraph (d)(3)(v) of this section, the payee must make the election by delivering the election in writing to the filer. Except as provided in paragraph (d)(3)(v) of this section, the written election must be made in writing on paper. The payee may deliver the election in person, by mail by United States Postal Service, or by a designated delivery service as defined under section 7502(f)(2). If the filer has not otherwise provided an address under paragraph (d)(3)(v) of this section, the payee shall send the written election to the filer's address appearing on the payee statement furnished by the filer to the payee with respect to which the election is being made or as directed by that person upon appropriate inquiry by the payee. The written election must:

(A) Clearly state that the payee is making the election;

(B) Provide the payee's name, address, and taxpayer identification number (TIN) (as defined in section 7701(a)(41) of the Internal Revenue Code) to the filer;

(C) If the payee wants the election to apply only to specific types of statements, identify the type of payee statement(s) and account number(s), if applicable, to which the election applies (for example, Form 1099-DIV, "Dividends and Distributions"); and

(D) Provide any other information required by the Internal Revenue Service in forms, instructions, or publications.

(iv) *Payee statements to which the election applies*.—An election by a payee under paragraph (d)(3)(i) of this section applies to all types of payee statements the filer is required to furnish to the payee, unless the payee specifies otherwise on the election under paragraph (d)(3)(iii)(C) of this section.

(v) *Reasonable alternative manner for making the election in cases of notification by the filer*.—(A) *In general*.—If the filer satisfies the requirements of paragraph (d)(3)(v)(B) of this section, and provides for a reasonable alternative manner as described in paragraph (d)(3)(v)(E) of this section, a payee may decide to make the election under paragraph (d)(3)(i) of this section pursuant to that reasonable alternative manner.

(B) *Notification of payee of reasonable alternative manner for making election*.—The filer may elect to provide notification to the payee of a reasonable alternative manner to make the election under paragraph (d)(3)(i) of this section, as described in paragraph (d)(3)(v)(E) of this section. To provide a valid notification under this paragraph (d)(3)(v)(B), the filer must provide notification to the payee that:

(1) Is in writing (either on paper or in electronic format);

(2) Is timely provided to the payee under paragraph (d)(3)(v)(D) of this section;

(3) Explains to the payee to whom that filer is required to furnish a payee statement of the payee's ability to elect, under paragraph (d)(3)(i) of this section, that the safe harbor exceptions for de minimis errors not apply, and of the payee's ability to choose to make the election using the default method under paragraph (d)(3)(iii) of this section;

(4) Provides an address to which the payee may send an election under paragraphs (d)(3)(i) and (iii) of this section;

(5) Provides any reasonable alternative manner or manners, as described in paragraph (d)(3)(v)(E) of this section, that the filer is making available for the payee to make the election under paragraph (d)(3)(i) of this section; and

(6) Describes the information required for making the election described by paragraphs (d)(3)(iii)(A) through (D) of this section. Solely for purposes of the reasonable alternative manner, the notification may provide that some or all of the information described in paragraph (d)(3)(iii)(B) of this section is not required and may provide that the provision of an account number as referenced in paragraph (d)(3)(iii)(C) of this section is required if the payee decides to use the reasonable alternative manner for the election.

(C) *Notification of revocation procedures.*—A notification under this paragraph (d)(3)(v) may also provide the procedures for making a revocation of an election under paragraph (d)(3)(vii) of this section. Solely for purposes of the reasonable alternative manner, the notification may provide that some or all of the information described in paragraph (d)(3)(vii)(B) of this section is not required and may provide that the provision of an account number as referenced in paragraph (d)(3)(vii)(E) of this section is required if the payee decides to use a reasonable alternative manner for making a revocation.

(D) *Time for providing notification of reasonable alternative manner for making payee election.*—A notification under this paragraph (d)(3)(v) will be timely under paragraph (d)(3)(v)(B)(2) of this section if:

(1) The notification is provided with, or at the time of, the furnishing of the payee statement; or

(2) The filer previously provided a valid notification under paragraph (d)(3)(v) of this section to the payee with, or at the time of, the furnishing of a payee statement associated with a particular account, in which case notification will be considered to have been timely provided with respect to subsequent payee statements associated with that particular account. If the filer wishes to provide for a different reasonable alternative manner than a previous reasonable alternative manner, the filer must provide new notification in compliance with the timeliness rule of paragraph (d)(3)(v)(D)(*1*) of this section, and must accept payee elections under the previous reasonable alternative manner for a period of at least 60 days after the receipt of the new notification by the payee.

(E) *Reasonable alternative manner.*—A reasonable alternative manner described in a notification under paragraph (d)(3)(v)(B) of this section may include that a payee election under paragraph (d)(3)(i) of this section may be made electronically (for example, via e-mail or web site) or telephonically. The reasonable alternative manner may not impose any prerequisite, condition, or time limitation on, or otherwise limit, the payee's ability to make an election under paragraph (d)(3)(iii) of this section, except as described in paragraphs (d)(3)(ii) and (iii) of this section; it may only offer a reasonable alternative manner or manners for making this election under this paragraph (d)(3)(v).

(vi) *Election not available for certain information.*—The election to override the safe harbor exception provided for by paragraph (d)(3)(i) of this section is not available with respect to information that may not be altered under specific information reporting rules. See, for example, § 1.6045-4(i)(5) of this chapter.

(vii) *Revocation of election.*—The payee may revoke a prior election by submitting a revocation to the filer. The effect of a revocation of a prior election is that the safe harbor for certain de minimis errors will apply to the payee statements that the payee identifies and that are furnished or are due to be furnished after the revocation is received. The revocation will remain in effect until the payee makes a valid and timely election under paragraph (d)(3)(i) of this section. The date of a revocation is the date the revocation is received by the filer. For purposes of this section, the provisions of section 7502 relating to timely mailing treated as timely delivery apply in determining the date a revocation is considered to be received by the filer, treating delivery to the filer as if the filer were an agency, officer, or office under such section. The revocation must be made in the same manner or manners described for making the election, that is pursuant to either paragraph (d)(3)(iii) or (v) of this section, as the payee chooses if paragraph (d)(3)(v) of this section is applicable. Except as provided under paragraph (d)(3)(v)(B)(*6*) of this section, the revocation must:

(A) Clearly state that the payee is revoking the payee's prior election;

(B) Provide the payee's name, address, and TIN to the filer;

(C) Provide the name of the filer;

(D) Identify the type of payee statement(s) (for example, Form 1099-DIV)

to which the revocation applies;

(E) Identify the account number(s), if applicable, to which the revocation applies; and

(F) Provide any other information required by the Internal Revenue Service in forms, instructions or publications.

(viii) *Reasonable cause.*—See § 301.6724-1(h) for rules relating to waiver of the section 6722 penalty in cases where the safe harbor exception provided for by paragraph (d)(1) of this section does not apply because of an election under paragraph (d)(3)(i) of this section.

(4) *Record retention.*—To facilitate proof of compliance with reporting and other obligations under the internal revenue laws, filers must retain records of any election or revocation by the payee under paragraph (d)(3)(i) or (vii) of this section, respectively, and any notification made under paragraph (d)(3)(v) of this section for as long as the contents of the election, revocation, or notification may be material in the administration of any internal revenue law. For rules regarding record retention, see section 6001 and § 1.6001-1 of this chapter. For additional procedures applicable to record retention in the context of electronic storage, see Rev. Proc. 97-22, 1997-1 C.B. 652, Rev. Proc. 98-25, 1998-1 C.B. 689, and any subsequently published guidance.

(5) *Examples.*—The provisions of paragraphs (d)(1) through (4) of this section may be illustrated by the following examples, which do not address any possible application of the penalty for intentional disregard under paragraph (c) of this section or the reasonable cause waiver under § 301.6724-1(a):

(i) *Example 1.* (A) Filer W is required to file with the IRS by February 28, 2019, and furnish to Payee A by February 15, 2019, Form 1099-B "Proceeds From Broker and Barter Exchange Transactions," because Filer W is a broker who sold stocks on behalf of Payee A resulting in proceeds of $5000 during calendar year 2018. Filer W properly withheld an amount of $1736 under applicable backup withholding rules because Payee A failed to furnish Payee A's TIN to Filer W. On the Form 1099-B, Filer W reports as follows: Box 1d, Proceeds, $4900; and Box 4, Federal income tax withheld, $1761. Filer W otherwise correctly and timely files and furnishes the Form 1099-B. Payee A does not make an election under paragraph (d)(3)(i) of this section.

(B) The safe harbor exception for de minimis errors provided for by paragraph (d)(1) of this section applies, because the differences between each of the amounts reported in error and the correct amounts are not more than the applicable limits. The error in the dollar amount reported in Box 1d, Proceeds, is de minimis because the difference between the amount in error ($4900) and the correct amount ($5000) is not more than $100; it is exactly $100. The error in the dollar amount reported in Box 4, Federal income tax withheld, is de minimis because the $25 difference between the amount in error ($1761) and the correct amount ($1736) is not more than $25, the limit for an error with respect to an amount reported for tax withheld.

(ii) *Example 2.* (A) The facts are the same as in *Example 1* in paragraph (d)(5)(i) of this section, except that Filer W reports $1710 as the amount in Box 4, Federal income tax withheld.

(B) The safe harbor exception for de minimis errors provided for by paragraph (d)(1) of this section does not apply because the Form 1099-B contains a failure that is not a de minimis error. The difference between the amount in error ($1710) and the correct amount ($1736) is $26, which is more than the $25 limit for de minimis errors with respect to an amount reported for tax withheld.

(iii) *Example 3.* (A) In 2019, Filer X provides Payee B with valid notification of a reasonable alternative manner under paragraph (d)(3)(v) of this section for making the payee election under paragraph (d)(3)(i) of this section. Payee B timely elects pursuant to the reasonable alternative manner during 2019. Payee B elects with respect to all payee statements that Filer X is required to furnish to Payee B. In January 2020, Filer X decides to provide for a different, but also valid, reasonable alternative manner; Filer X provides notification of this different reasonable alternative manner to Payee B, and Payee B receives notification of this different reasonable alternative manner, pursuant to paragraph (d)(3)(v)(B) of this section, on January 16, 2020.

(B) Payee B decides to revoke Payee B's prior election, with respect to the Forms 1099-DIV that Filer X is required to furnish to Payee B. Under paragraph (d)(3)(vii) of this section, Payee B may provide the revocation to Filer X in any of three different manners. First, Payee B may provide the revocation to Filer X in the same manner as if Payee B were making an election under the default manner of paragraph (d)(3)(iii) of this section; Payee B may do so at any time. Second, having received notification from Filer X of the different reasonable alternative manner on January 16, 2020, Payee B may provide the revocation to Filer X in the same manner as if Payee B were making an election under the different reasonable alternative manner pursuant to paragraph (d)(3)(v) of this section. Third, because Filer X previously provided notification of a reasonable alternative manner (2019 alternative) before providing notification of a different reasonable alternative manner on January 16, 2020, (2020 alternative), Payee B may provide the revocation to Filer X in the same manner as if Payee B were making an election under the previous reasonable alternative manner (2019 alternative); Payee B may do so for a period of 60 days after January 16, 2020, pursuant to paragraph (d)(3)(v)(D)(2) of this section.

(e) *Definitions.*—(1) *Payee.*—See §301.6721-1(h)(5) for the definition of "payee."

(2) *Payee statement.*—For purposes of this section the term "payee statement" has the same meaning as payee statement as defined by section 6724(d)(2), including any statement required to be furnished under—

* * *

(xxxiii) Section 6055 (relating to information returns reporting minimum essential coverage);

(xxxiv) Section 6056 (relating to information returns reporting on offers of health insurance coverage by applicable large employer members);

(xxxv) Section 6035, other than a statement described in section 6724(d)(1)(D), (relating to basis information with respect to property acquired from decedents, generally Schedule A of Form 8971, "Information Regarding Beneficiaries Acquiring Property From a Decedent");

(xxxvi) Section 6050Y(a)(2), 6050Y(b)(2), or 6050Y(c)(2) (relating to certain life insurance contract transactions); or

(xxxvii) Section 6226(a)(2) (regarding statements relating to alternative to payment of imputed underpayment by a partnership) or under any other provision of this title which provides for the application of rules similar to section 6226(a)(2).

* * *

(4) *Filer.*—For purposes of this section the term "filer" means a person that is required to furnish a payee statement as defined in paragraphs (e)(2) and (3) of this section under the applicable information reporting section described in paragraphs (e)(2) and (3) of this section.

(f) *Adjustment for inflation.*—Each of the dollar amounts under paragraphs (a), (b), and (c) of this section and paragraphs (a), (b), (d)(1), and (e) of section 6722 shall be adjusted for inflation pursuant to section 6722(f).

(g) *Applicability date.*—This section applies with respect to payee statements required to be furnished on or after January 1 of the calendar year immediately following the date of publication of a Treasury decision adopting these rules as final regulations in the **Federal Register**.

Information Reporting: Waiver of Penalty: Prompt Correction

Information Reporting: Waiver of Penalty: Prompt Correction.—Amendments to Reg. §301.6724-1, relating to waiver under Code Sec. 6724 of a penalty imposed by Code Sec. 6721 for failure to file a correct information return and providing guidance on the requirement of prompt correction of the failure to file or file correctly, are proposed (published in the Federal Register on July 9, 2003) (REG-141669-02).

☐ Par. 2. Section 301.6724-1 is amended by:

1. Revising paragraph (d)(1)(ii)(D).
2. Adding paragraph (d)(3).

The revision and addition read as follows:

§301.6724-1. Reasonable cause.

* * *

(d) * * *

(1) * * *

(ii) * * *

(D) Correcting the failure as promptly as possible upon removal of the impediment or discovery of the failure. A person may correct a failure by filing or correcting the information return, by furnishing or correcting the payee statement, or by providing or correcting the information to satisfy the specified information reporting requirement with respect to which the failure occurs. This paragraph (d)(1)(ii)(D) does not apply with respect to information that specific information reporting rules prohibit the filer from altering. See §1.6045-4(i)(5) of this chapter. In the case of a waiver of a penalty imposed by section 6722 or 6723 of the Internal Revenue Code, correction is prompt if it is made within 30 days after the date of removal of the impediment or discovery of the failure. For purposes of section 6721 of the Internal Revenue Code, a correction is prompt if the Internal Revenue Service receives the correction—

(i) On or before 30 days after the required filing date;

(ii) On or before August 1 following that required filing date;

(iii) On or before the date or dates announced in guidance governing the electronic or magnetic filing of information returns;

(iv) On or before the date or dates announced in other guidance including forms and instructions; or

(v) Within 30 days after the date the impediment is removed or the failure is discovered if the correction is not submitted within the time frames set forth in paragraphs (d)(1)(ii)(D)(*i*) through (*iv*).

* * *

(3) [Reserved]For further guidance, see §301.6724-1T(d)(3).

* * *

Catastrophic Health Coverage: Information Reporting

Catastrophic Health Coverage: Information Reporting.—Amendments to Reg. §301.6724-1, relating to information reporting of minimum essential coverage under section 6055 of the Internal Revenue Code, are proposed (published in the Federal Register on August 2, 2016) (REG-103058-16).

Par. 4. Section 301.6724-1 is amended by adding a sentence to the end of paragraph (e)(1)(vi)(A) to read as follows:

§301.6724-1. Reasonable cause.

* * *

(e) * * *

(1) * * *

(vi) *Exceptions and limitations.*—(A) * * * See §1.6055-1(h)(3) of this chapter, which provides rules on the time, form, and manner in which a TIN must be provided for information returns required to be filed and individual statements required to be furnished under section 6055.

* * *

Qualified Tuition: Related Expenses: Reporting

Qualified Tuition: Related Expenses: Reporting.—Amendments to Reg. §301.6724-1, revising the rules for reporting qualified tuition and related expenses under section 6050S on a Form 1098-T, "Tuition Statement," and conforming the regulations to changes made to section 6050S by the Protecting Americans from Tax Hikes Act of 2015, are proposed (published in the Federal Register on August 2, 2016) (REG-131418-14).

Par. 9. Section 301.6724-1 is amended by adding a sentence at the end of paragraph (a)(1) to read as follows:

§301.6724-1. Reasonable cause.—(a) * * *

(1) * * * For waiver in the case of eligible educational institutions required to report information under section 6050S with respect to qualified tuition and related expenses, see §1.6050S-1(f) of this chapter.

* * *

Correct Payee Statements: Failure to File Correct Information: Penalties

Correct Payee Statements: Failure to File Correct Information: Penalties.—Amendments to Reg. §301.6724-1, relating to penalties for failure to file correct information returns or furnish correct payee statements, are proposed (published in the Federal Register on October 17, 2018) (REG-118826-16).

Par. 7. Section 301.6724-1 is amended by:

1. Revising paragraphs (a)(1) and (a)(2)(ii).

2. Designating the undesignated paragraph following paragraph (a)(2)(ii) as paragraph (a)(2)(iii) and revising newly designated paragraph (a)(2)(iii).

3. Revising paragraphs (b) introductory text and (b)(2)(i) and (ii).

4. Designating the undesignated paragraph following paragraph (b)(2)(ii) as paragraph (b)(3).

5. Revising paragraphs (c)(3)(ii), (e)(1) introductory text, (e)(1)(i), (e)(1)(vi)(E) and (F), (f)(1) introductory text, (f)(1)(i), (f)(5)(i) and (ii), (g), (h), (k), (m) introductory text, and (m)(1).

6. Adding paragraph (o).

The revisions and additions read as follows:

§ 301.6724-1. Reasonable cause.—(a) *Waiver of the penalty.*—(1) *General rule.*—The penalty for a failure relating to an information reporting requirement as defined in paragraph (j) of this section is waived if the failure is due to reasonable cause and is not due to willful neglect.

(2) * * *

(ii) The failure arose from events beyond the filer's control ("impediment"), as described in paragraph (c) of this section.

(iii) Moreover, the filer must establish that the filer acted in a responsible manner, as described in paragraph (d) of this section, both before and after the failure occurred. Thus, if the filer establishes that there are significant mitigating factors for a failure but is unable to establish that the filer acted in a responsible manner, the mitigating factors will not be sufficient to obtain a waiver of the penalty. Similarly, if the filer establishes that a failure arose from an impediment but is unable to establish that the filer acted in a responsible manner, the impediment will not be sufficient to obtain a waiver of the penalty. See paragraph (g) of this section for the reasonable cause safe harbor for persons who exercise due diligence. See paragraph (h) of this section for the reasonable cause safe harbor after an election under section 6722(c)(3)(B) and § 301.6722-1(d)(3).

(b) *Significant mitigating factors.*—In order to establish reasonable cause under this paragraph (b), the filer must satisfy paragraph (d) of this section and must show that there are significant mitigating factors for the failure. See paragraph (c)(5) of this section for the application of this paragraph (b) to failures attributable to the actions of a filer's agent. The applicable mitigating factors include, but are not limited to—

* * *

(2) * * *

(i) Whether the filer has incurred any penalty under § 301.6721-1, § 301.6722-1, or § 301.6723-1 in prior years for the failure; and

(ii) If the filer has incurred any such penalty in prior years, the extent of the filer's success in lessening its error rate from year to year.

* * *

(c) * * *

(3) * * *

(ii) The cost of filing on magnetic media was prohibitive as determined at least 45 days before the due date of the returns (without regard to extensions);

* * *

(e) *Acting in a responsible manner—special rules for missing TINs.*—(1) *In general.*—A filer that is seeking a waiver for reasonable cause under paragraph (c)(6) of this section will satisfy paragraph (d)(2) of this section with respect to establishing that a failure to include a TIN on an information return resulted from the failure of the payee to provide information to the filer (that is, a missing TIN) only if the filer makes the initial and, if required, the annual solicitations described in this paragraph (e) ("required solicitations"). For purposes of this section, a number is treated as a "missing TIN" if the number does not contain nine digits or includes one or more alpha characters (a character or symbol other than an Arabic numeral) as one of the nine digits. A solicitation means a request by the filer for the payee to furnish a correct TIN. See paragraph (f) of this section for the rules that a filer must follow to establish that the filer acted in a responsible manner with respect to providing incorrect TINs on information returns. See paragraph (e)(1)(vi)(A) of this section for alternative solicitation requirements. See paragraph (g) of this section for the safe harbor due diligence rules.

(i) *Initial solicitation.*—An initial solicitation for a payee's correct TIN must be made at the time an account is opened. The term "account" includes accounts, relationships, and other transactions. However, a filer is not required to make an initial solicitation under this paragraph (e)(1)(i) with respect to a new account if the filer has the payee's TIN and uses that TIN for all accounts of the payee. For example, see § 31.3406(h)-3(a) of this chapter. If the account is opened in person, the initial solicitation may be made by oral or written request, such as on an account creation document. If the account is opened by mail, telephone, or other electronic means, the TIN may be requested through such communications. If the account is opened by the payee's completing and mailing an application furnished by the filer that requests the payee's TIN, the initial solicitation requirement is considered met. If a TIN is not received as a result of an initial solicitation, the filer may be required to make additional solicitations ("annual solicitations").

* * *

(vi) * * *

(E) A filer is not required to make annual solicitations by mail on accounts with respect to which the filer has an undeliverable address, that is, where other mailings to that address have been returned to the filer because the address was incorrect and no new address has been provided to the filer.

(F) Except as provided in paragraphs (e)(1)(vi) (A) and (C) of this section, no more than two annual solicitations are required under this paragraph (e) in order for a filer to establish reasonable cause.

* * *

(f) *Acting in a responsible manner—special rules for incorrect TINs.*—(1) *In general.*—A filer that is seeking a waiver for reasonable cause under paragraph (c)(6) of this section will satisfy paragraph (d)(2) of this section with respect to establishing that a failure resulted from incorrect information provided by the payee or any other person (that is, inclusion of an incorrect TIN) on an information return only if the filer makes the initial and annual solicitations described in this paragraph (f). See paragraph (e)(1) of this section for the definition of the term "solicitation." See paragraph (f)(5)(i) of this section for alternative solicitation requirements. See paragraph (g) of this section for the safe harbor due diligence rules.

(i) *Initial solicitation.*—An initial solicitation for a payee's correct TIN must be made at the time the account is opened. The term "account" includes accounts, relationships, and other transactions. However, a filer is not required to make an initial solicitation under this paragraph (f)(1)(i) with respect to a new account if the filer has the payee's TIN and uses that TIN for all accounts of the payee. For example, see § 31.3406(h)-3(a) of this chapter. No additional solicitation is required after the filer receives the TIN unless the Internal Revenue Service or, in some cases, a broker notifies the filer that the TIN is incorrect. Following such notification the filer may be required to make an annual solicitation to obtain the correct TIN as provided in paragraphs (f)(1)(ii) and (iii) of this section.

* * *

(5) *Exceptions and limitations..*—(i) The solicitation requirements under this paragraph (f) do not apply to the extent that an information reporting provision under which a return, as defined in § 301.6721-1(h), is filed provides specific requirements relating to the manner or the time period in which a TIN must be solicited. In that event, the requirements of this paragraph (f) will be satisfied only if the filer complies with the manner and time period requirement under the specific information reporting provisions and this paragraph (f), to the extent applicable.

(ii) An annual solicitation is not required to be made for a year under this paragraph (f) with respect to an account if no payments are made to the account for such year or if no return as defined in § 301.6721-1(h) is required to be filed for the account for such year.

* * *

(g) *Due diligence safe harbor.*—(1) *In general.*—A filer may establish reasonable cause with respect to a failure relating to an information reporting requirement as described in paragraph (j) of this section if the filer exercises due diligence with respect to failures described in sections 6721 through 6723.

(2) *Special rules relating to TINs.*—(i) *Questions and answers.*—The following questions and answers provide guidance on the exercise of due diligence for an exception to a penalty under sections 6721 through 6723 for a failure to provide a correct TIN on any information return as defined in § 301.6721-1(h), payee statement as defined in § 301.6722-1(e), document as described in § 301.6723-1(a)(4), or the failure merely to provide a TIN as described in § 301.6723-1(a)(4)(ii).

(ii) *General rule.*—(A) *Q-1.*—Is a filer subject to a penalty for a failure to provide a correct TIN on an information return with respect to a reportable interest or dividend payment if the payee has certified, under penalties of perjury, that the TIN furnished to the filer is the payee's correct number, the filer provided that number on an information return, and the number is later determined not to be the payee's correct number?

(B) *A-1.*—A filer is not subject to a penalty for failure to provide the payee's correct TIN on an information return, if the payee has certified, under penalties of perjury, that the TIN provided to the filer was his correct number, and the filer included such number on the information return before being notified by the Internal Revenue Service (IRS) (or a broker) that the number is incorrect.

(iii) *Due Diligence Defined for Accounts Opened and Instruments Acquired After December 31, 1983.*—(A)*(1) Q-2.*—In order for a filer of a reportable interest or dividend payment (other than in a window transaction) to be considered to have exercised due diligence in furnishing the correct TIN of a payee with respect to an account opened or an instrument acquired after December 31, 1983, what actions must the filer take?

(2) *A-2.*—*(i)* In general, the filer of an account or instrument that is not a pre-1984 account nor a window transaction must use a TIN provided by the payee under penalties of perjury on information returns filed with the IRS to satisfy the due diligence requirement. Therefore, if a filer permits a payee to open an account without obtaining the payee's TIN under penalties of perjury and files an information return with the IRS with a missing or an incorrect TIN, the filer will be liable for the $250 penalty for the year with respect to which such information return is filed. However, in its administrative discretion, the IRS will not enforce the penalty with respect to a calendar year if the certified TIN is obtained after the account is opened and before December 31 of such year, provided that the filer exercises due diligence in processing such number, that is, the filer uses the same care in processing the TIN provided by the payee that a reasonably prudent filer would use in the course of the filer's business in handling account information such as account numbers and balances.

(ii) Once notified by the IRS (or a broker) that a number is incorrect, a filer is liable for the penalty for all prior years in which an information return was filed with that particular incorrect number if the filer has not exercised due diligence with respect to such years. A pre-existing certified TIN does not constitute an exercise of due diligence after the IRS or a broker notifies the filer that the number is incorrect unless the filer undertakes the actions described in § 31.3406(d)-5(d)(2)(i) of this chapter with respect to accounts receiving reportable payments described in section 3406(b)(1) and reported on information returns described in sections 6724(d)(1)(A)(i) through (iv).

(B)*(1) Q-3.*—Is a filer as described in paragraph (g)(2)(iii)(A)(2) of this section liable for the penalty if the filer obtained a certified TIN from a payee but inadvertently processed the name or number incorrectly on the information return?

(2) A-3.—Yes. The filer is liable for the penalty unless the filer exercised that degree of care in processing the TIN and name and in furnishing it on the information return that a reasonably prudent filer would use in the course of the filer's business in handling account information, such as account numbers and account balances.

(iv) *Special rules.*—(A)*(1) Q-4.*—With respect to an instrument transferred without the assistance of a broker, is a filer liable for the penalty for filing an information return with a missing or an incorrect TIN if the filer records on its books a transfer of a readily tradable instrument in a transaction in which the filer was not a party?

(2) A-4.—Generally, a filer as described in paragraph (g)(2)(iv)(A)*(1)* of this section will be considered to have exercised due diligence with respect to a readily tradable instrument that is not part of a pre-1984 account with the filer if the filer records on its books a transfer in which the filer was not a party. This exception applies until the calendar year in which the filer receives a certified TIN from the payee.

(B)*(1) Q–5.*—Is the filer described in paragraph (g)(2)(iv)(A)(2) of this section required to solicit the TIN of a payee of an account with a missing TIN in order to be considered as having exercised due diligence in a subsequent calendar year?

(2) A–5.—There is no requirement on the filer to solicit the TIN in order to be considered to have exercised due diligence in a subsequent calendar year under the rule set forth in paragraph (g)(2)(iv)(A)(2) of this section.

(C)*(1) Q–6.*—Is a filer as described in paragraph (g)(2)(iv)(A)(*1*) of this section considered to have exercised due diligence if the payee provides a TIN to the filer (whether or not certified), the filer uses that number on the information return filed for the payee, and the number is later determined to be incorrect?

(2) A–6.—A filer as described in paragraph (g)(2)(iv)(A)(*1*) of this section who records on its books a transfer in which it was not a party is considered to have exercised due diligence under the rule set forth in paragraph (g)(2)(iv)(A)(2) of this section where the transfer is accompanied with a TIN provided that the filer uses the same care in processing the TIN provided by a payee that a reasonably prudent filer would use in the course of the filer's business in handling account information, such as account numbers and account balances. Thus, a filer will not be liable for the penalty if the filer uses the TIN provided by the payee on information returns that it files, even if the TIN provided by the payee is later determined to be incorrect. However, a filer will not be considered as having exercised due diligence under paragraph (g)(2)(iv)(A)(2) of this section after the IRS or a broker notifies the filer that the number is incorrect unless the filer undertakes the required additional actions described in paragraph (g)(2)(iii)(A)(*2*)(*ii*) of this section.

(D)*(1) Q–7.*—Is a filer liable for a penalty for filing an information return with a missing or an incorrect TIN with respect to a post-1983 account or instrument if the filer could have met the due diligence requirements but for the fact that the filer incurred an undue hardship?

(2) A–7.—A filer of a post-1983 account or instrument is not liable for a penalty under section 6721(a) for filing an information return with a missing or an incorrect TIN if the IRS determines that the filer could have satisfied the due diligence requirements but for the fact that the filer incurred an undue hardship. An undue hardship is an extraordinary or unexpected event such as the destruction of records or place of business of the filer by fire or other casualty (or the place of business of the filer's agent who under a pre-existing written contract had agreed to fulfill the filer's due diligence obligations with respect to the account subject to the penalty and there was no means for the obligations to be performed by another agent or the filer). Undue hardship will also be found to exist if the filer could have met the due diligence requirements only by incurring an extraordinary cost.

(E)*(1) Q–8.*—How does a filer obtain a determination from the IRS that the filer has met the undue hardship exception to the penalty under section 6721(a) for the failure to include the correct TIN on an information return for the year with respect to which the filer is subject to the penalty?

(2) A–8.—A determination of undue hardship may be established only by submitting a written statement to the IRS signed under penalties of perjury that sets forth all the facts and circumstances that make an affirmative showing that the filer could have satisfied the due diligence requirements but for the occurrence of an undue hardship. Thus, the statement must describe the undue hardship and make an affirmative showing that the filer either was in the process of exercising or stood ready to exercise due diligence when the undue hardship occurred. A filer may request an undue hardship determination by submitting a written statement to the address provided with the notice proposing penalty assessment (for example, Notice 972CG) or the notice of penalty assessment (for example, CP15 or CP215), or as otherwise directed by the Internal Revenue Service in forms, instructions or publications.

(F)*(1) Q–9.*—Is a pre-1984 account or instrument of a filer that is exchanged for an account or instrument of another filer as a result of a merger of the other filer or acquisition of the accounts or instruments of such filer transformed into a post-1983 account or instrument if the merger or acquisition occurs after December 31, 1983?

(2) A–9.—No. A pre-1984 account or instrument that is exchanged for another account or instrument pursuant to a statutory merger or the acquisition of accounts or instruments is not transformed into a post-1983 account or instrument because the exchange occurs without the participation of the payee.

(G)*(1) Q–10.*—May the acquiring taxpayer described in paragraph (g)(2)(iv)(F)(2) of this section rely upon the business records and past procedures of the merged filer or the filer whose accounts or instruments were acquired in order to establish that due diligence has been exercised on the acquired pre-1984 and post-1983 accounts or instruments?

(2) A–10.—Yes. The acquiring filer may rely upon the business records and past procedures of the merged filer or of the filer whose accounts or instruments were acquired in order to establish due diligence to avoid the penalty under section 6721(a) with respect to information returns that have been or will be filed.

(H)*(1) Q–11.*—To what extent may a filer rely on the due diligence rules set forth in §§35a.9999-1, 35a.9999-2, and 35a.9999-3 of this chapter in effect prior to January 1, 2001 (see §§35a.9999-1, 35a.9999-2, and 35a.9999-3 as contained in 26 CFR part 35a, revised April 1, 1999).

(2) A–11.—A filer may rely on the due diligence rules set forth in §§35a.9999-1, 35a.9999-2, and 35a.9999-3 of this chapter in effect prior to January 1, 2001 (see §§35a.9999-1, 35a.9999-2, and 35a.9999-3 as contained in 26 CFR part 35a, revised April 1, 1999) solely for the definitions of terms or phrases used in this paragraph (g)(2).

(3) *Effective dates.*—This paragraph (g) is effective for information returns as defined in section 6724(d)(1) required to be filed, payee statements as defined in section 6724(d)(2) required to be furnished, and specified informa-

tion as described in section 6724(d)(3) required to be reported on or after January 1 of the calendar year immediately following the date of publication of a Treasury decision adopting these rules as final regulations in the **Federal Register**. See § 301.6724-1(g) in effect prior to January 1 of the calendar year immediately following the date of publication of a Treasury decision adopting these rules as final regulations in the **Federal Register** for substantially similar rules applicable prior to January 1 of the calendar year immediately following the date of publication of a Treasury decision adopting these rules as final regulations in the **Federal Register**.

(h) *Reasonable cause safe harbor after election under section 6722(c)(3)(B).*—A filer may establish reasonable cause with respect to a failure relating to an information reporting requirement as described in paragraph (j) of this section under this paragraph (h) if the failure is a result of an election under § 301.6722-1(d)(3)(i) and the presence of a de minimis error or errors as described in sections 6721(c)(3) and 6722(c)(3) and §§ 301.6721-1(e) and 301.6722-1(d) on a filed information return or furnished payee statement. This paragraph (h) applies only when the safe harbor exceptions provided for by § 301.6721-1(e)(1) or § 301.6722-1(d)(1) would have applied, but for an election under § 301.6722-1(d)(3)(i). To establish reasonable cause and not willful neglect under this paragraph (h), the filer must file a corrected information return or furnish a corrected payee statement, or both, as applicable, within 30 days of the date of the election under § 301.6722-1(d)(3)(i). Where specific rules provide for additional time in which to furnish a corrected payee statement and file a corrected information return, the 30-day rule does not apply and the specific rules will apply. See for example §§ 31.6051-1(c) through (d) and 31.6051-2(b). If the filer rectifies the failure outside of this 30-day period, the determination of reasonable cause will be on a case-by-case basis.

* * *

(k) *Examples.*—The provisions of this section may be illustrated by the following examples:

(1) *Example 1.* (i) On August 1, 2015, Individual A, an independent contractor, establishes a relationship ("an account") with Institution L, which pays A amounts reportable under section 6041. When A opens the account L requests that A supply his TIN on the account creation document. A fails to provide his TIN. On October 1, 2015, L mails a solicitation for A's TIN that satisfies the requirement of paragraph (e)(1)(ii) of this section. A does not provide a TIN to L during 2015. L timely files an information return subject to section 6721, that does not contain A's TIN, for payments made during the 2015 calendar year with respect to A's account. A penalty is imposed on L pursuant to § 301.6721-1(a)(2) for L's failure to file a correct information return because A's TIN was not shown on the return. The penalty will be waived, however, if L establishes that the failure was due to reasonable cause as defined in this section.

(ii) To establish reasonable cause under this section, L must satisfy both paragraphs (c)(6) and (d) of this section. The criteria for obtaining a waiver under these paragraphs are as follows:

(A) L acted in a responsible manner in attempting to satisfy the information reporting requirement as described in paragraph (d) of this section; and

(B) L demonstrates that the failure arose from events beyond L's control, as described in paragraph (c)(6) of this section.

(iii) Pursuant to paragraph (d)(2) of this section, L may demonstrate that it acted in a responsible manner only by complying with paragraph (e) of this section. Paragraph (e) of this section requires a filer to request a TIN at the time the account is opened (the initial solicitation) and, if the filer does not receive the TIN at that time, to solicit the TIN on or before December 31 of the year the account is opened (for accounts opened before December) or January 31 of the following year (for accounts in the preceding December) (the annual solicitation). Because L has performed these solicitations within the time and in the manner prescribed by paragraph (e) of this section, L has acted in a responsible manner as described in paragraph (d) of this section. L satisfies paragraph (c)(6) of this section because under the facts, L can show that the failure was caused by A's failure to provide a TIN, an event beyond L's control. As a result, L has established reasonable cause under paragraph (a)(2) of this section. Therefore, the penalty imposed under § 301.6721-1(a)(2) for the failure on the 2015 information return is waived. See section 3406(a)(1)(A) which requires L to impose backup withholding on reportable payments to A if L has not received A's TIN.

(2) *Example 2.* (i) On August 1, 2015, Individual B opens an account with Bank M, which pays B interest reportable under section 6049. When B opens the account, M requests that B supply his TIN on the account creation document. B provides his TIN to M. On February 29, 2016, M includes the TIN that B provided on the Form 1099–INT for the 2015 calendar year. In October 2016 the Internal Revenue Service, pursuant to section 3406(a)(1)(B), notifies M that the 2015 return filed for B contains an incorrect TIN. In April 2017 a penalty is imposed on M pursuant to § 301.6721-1(a)(2) for M's failure to file a correct information return for the 2015 calendar year, that is, the return did not contain B's correct TIN. The penalty will be waived, however, if M establishes that the failure was due to reasonable cause as defined in this section.

(ii) To establish reasonable cause under this section, M must satisfy the criteria in both paragraphs (c)(6) and (d) of this section. Pursuant to paragraph (d)(2) of this section, M can demonstrate that it acted in a responsible manner only if M complies with paragraph (f) of this section. Paragraph (f) of this section requires a filer to request a TIN at the time the account is opened, an initial solicitation. Under paragraph (f)(4) of this section the initial solicitation relates to failures on returns filed for the year an account is opened. Because M performed the initial solicitation in 2015 in the time and manner prescribed in paragraph (f)(1)(i) of this section and reflected the TIN received from B on the 2015 return as required by paragraph (f)(1)(iv) of this section, M has acted in a responsible manner as described in paragraph (d) of this section. M satisfies paragraph (c)(6) of this section because, under the facts, M can show that the failure was caused by B's failure to provide a correct TIN, an event beyond M's control. As a result, M has established reasonable cause under paragraph (a)(2) of this section. Therefore, the penalty imposed under § 301.6721-1(a)(2) for the failure on the 2015 information return is waived. See section 3406(a)(1)(B) which requires M to impose backup withholding on reportable payments to B if M has not received B's correct TIN.

(3) *Example 3.* (i) *Table.*

Table 1 to Paragraph (k)(3)(i)

2015	2/2016	10/2016	2/2017
Account opened (solicits TIN)	2015 return	B-notice w/respect to 2015 return	2016 return filed.

4/2017	10/2017	2/2018	4/2018
6721 penalty notice for 2015 return	B-notice w/respect to 2016 return	2017 return filed	6721 penalty notice for 2016

(ii) The facts are the same as in Example 2 in paragraph (k)(2) of this section. Under § 31.3406(d)-5(d)(2)(i) of this chapter and paragraph (f)(3) of this section, within 15 days of the October 2016 notification of the incorrect TIN from the Internal Revenue Service, M solicits the correct TIN from B. B fails to respond. M timely files the return for 2016 with respect to the account setting forth B's incorrect TIN. In October 2017 the Internal Revenue Service notifies M pursuant to section 3406(a)(1)(B) that the 2016 return contains an incorrect TIN. In April 2018, a penalty is imposed on M pursuant to § 301.6721-1(a)(2) for M's failure to include B's correct TIN on the return for 2016. The penalty will be waived, if M establishes that the failure was due to reasonable cause as defined in this section.

(iii) M must satisfy the reasonable cause criteria in paragraphs (c)(6) and (d) of this section. M may demonstrate that it acted in a responsible manner as required under paragraph (d) of this section only by complying with paragraph (f) of this section. Paragraph (f) of this section requires a filer to make an initial solicitation for a TIN when an account is opened. Further, a filer must make an annual solicitation for a TIN by mail within 15 business days after the date that the Internal Revenue Service notifies the filer of an incorrect TIN pursuant to section 3406(a)(1)(B). M made the initial solicitation for the TIN in 2015 and, after being notified of the incorrect TIN in October 2016, the first annual solicitation within the time and manner prescribed by § 31.3406(d)-5(d)(2)(i) of this chapter and paragraphs (f)(1)(ii) and (f)(2) of this section. M acted in a responsible manner. M satisfies paragraph (c)(6) of this section because, under the facts, M can show that the failure was caused by B's failure to provide his correct TIN, an event beyond M's control. As a result M has established reasonable cause under paragraph (a)(2) of this section. Therefore, the penalty imposed under § 301.6721-1(a)(2) for the failure on the 2016 return is waived due to reasonable cause.

(4) *Example 4.* (i) *Table.*

Table 2 to Paragraph (k)(2)(i)

2015	2/2016	10/2016	2/2017
Account opened (solicits TIN)	2015 return filed	B-notice w/respect to 2015 return	2016 return filed.

4/2017	10/2017	2/2018	4/2018
6721 penalty notice for 2015 return	B-notice w/respect to 2016 return	2017 return filed	6721 penalty notice for 2016 return.

(ii) The facts are the same as in Example 3 in paragraph (k)(3) of this section. M timely solicits B's TIN in October 2017, which B fails to provide. M files the return for 2017 with the incorrect TIN. In April 2019 the Internal Revenue Service informs M that the 2017 return contains an incorrect TIN. M does not solicit a TIN from B in 2018 and files a return for 2018 with B's incorrect TIN. M seeks a waiver of the penalty under § 301.6721-1(a)(2) for reasonable cause. M must satisfy the reasonable cause criteria in paragraphs (c)(6) and (d) of this section. Because M made the initial and two annual solicitations as required by paragraph (f) of this section, M has demonstrated that it acted in a responsible manner and is not required to solicit B's TIN in 2018. See paragraph (f)(5)(iv) of this section. M satisfies paragraph (c)(6) of this section because, under the facts, M can show that the failure was caused by B's failure to provide his correct TIN, an event beyond M's control. Therefore, M has established reasonable cause under paragraph (a)(2) of this section.

(5) *Example 5.* In 2016, Mortgage Finance Company N lends money to C to purchase property in a transaction subject to reporting under section 6050H and to section 6721. As part of the transaction, C gives N a promissory note providing for repayment of principal and the payment of interest. At the time C incurs the obligation N requests C's TIN, as required under § 1.6050H-2(f) of this chapter. C fails to provide the TIN as required by § 1.6050H-2(f) of this chapter. N sends solicitations by mail in 2016 and 2017 for the missing TIN, which C fails to provide. However, for 2018 M fails to send the solicitation required by § 1.6050H–2(f) of this chapter. N files returns for the 2016, 2017, and 2018 calendar years pursuant to section 6050H without C's TIN. Although N made the initial and the first annual solicitations in 2016 and the second annual solicitation in 2017, N did not

solicit the TIN in 2018 as required under section 6050H, which requires continued annual solicitations until the TIN is obtained. Therefore, under paragraph (e)(1)(vi)(A) of this section the penalty imposed under § 301.6721-1(a) for the 2018 information return is not waived.

(6) *Example 6*. (i) *Table*.

Table 3 to Paragraph (k)(6)(i)

10/2015	2/2016	10/2016	2/2017
Account opened. (solicits TIN)	2015 return filed	B-notice w/respect to 2015 return	2016 return filed.
4/2017	**10/2017**	**02/2018**	**4/2018**
6721 penalty notice for 2015 return	B-notice w/respect to 2016 return	2017 return filed	6721 penalty notice for 2016 return

(ii) On October 1, 2015, Individual E opens an account with Institution R, which pays E amounts reportable under section 6049. When E opens the account, R requests that E supply his TIN on an account creation document, which E does. Pursuant to paragraph (f)(1)(iv) of this section, R uses the TIN furnished by E on the information return filed for the 2015 calendar year. In October 2016 the Internal Revenue Service notifies R pursuant to section 3406(a)(1)(B) that the information return filed for E for the 2015 calendar year contained an incorrect TIN. At the time R receives this notification, E's account contains the incorrect TIN. On December 31, 2016, R telephones E pursuant to paragraphs (f)(2) and (e)(2)(ii) of this section and receives different TIN information from E. R uses this information on the return that it files timely for E for the 2016 calendar year, that is, in February 2017.

(iii) In April 2017, the Internal Revenue Service notifies R pursuant to § 301.6721-1(a)(2) that the information return filed for the 2015 calendar year contains an incorrect TIN. The penalty will be waived, however, if R establishes the failure was due to reasonable cause as defined in this section.

(iv) To establish reasonable cause under this section, R must satisfy the criteria in both paragraphs (c)(6) and (d)(2) of this section. Pursuant to paragraph (d)(2) of this section, R can demonstrate that it acted in a responsible manner only if it complies with paragraph (f) of this section. R solicited E's TIN at the time the account was opened (initial solicitation). Under paragraphs (d)(2) and (f)(4) of this section, the initial solicitation relates to failures on returns filed for the year in which an account is opened (that is, 2015) and for subsequent years until the calendar year in which the filer receives a notification of an incorrect TIN pursuant to section 3406. Because E failed to provide the correct TIN upon request, the failure arose from events beyond R's control as described in paragraph (c)(6) of this section. Therefore, the penalty with respect to the failure on the 2015 calendar year information return is waived due to reasonable cause.

(7) *Example 7*. (i) The facts are the same as in Example 6 in paragraph (k)(6) of this section. In April 2018 the Internal Revenue Service notifies R pursuant to § 301.6721-1(a)(2) that the information return filed for the 2016 calendar year for E contained an incorrect TIN.

(ii) To establish reasonable cause for the failure under this section, R must satisfy the criteria in both paragraphs (c)(6) and (d)(2) of this section. Pursuant to paragraph (d)(2) of this section R may establish that it acted in a responsible manner only by complying with paragraph (f) of this section. Pursuant to paragraph (f)(1)(ii) of this section, R must make an annual solicitation after being notified of an incorrect TIN if the payee's account contains the incorrect TIN at the time of the notification. Paragraph (f)(3) of this section provides that if the filer is notified pursuant to section 3406(a)(1)(B) the time and manner of making an annual solicitation is that required under § 31.3406(d)-5(g)(1)(ii) of this chapter. Section 31.3406(d)-5(g)(1)(ii) of this chapter requires R to notify E by mail within 15 business days after the date of the notice from the Internal Revenue Service, which R failed to do. As a result, R has failed to act in a responsible manner with respect to the failure on the 2016 information return, and the penalty will not be waived due to reasonable cause.

(8) *Example 8*. (i) On January 31, 2017, Institution Q timely furnishes Form 1099-MISC to Individual F. Also on January 31, 2017, Q timely files a corresponding Form 1099-MISC with the Internal Revenue Service. On March 15, 2017, Q becomes aware of de minimis errors (within the meaning of § 301.6722-1(d)(2)) made on the Form 1099-MISC furnished to F and filed with the Internal Revenue Service. On March 20, 2017, F makes an election under § 301.6722-1(d)(3)(i) with respect to the Form 1099-MISC that Q furnished to F. Q furnishes a corrected Form 1099-MISC to F and files a corrected Form 1099-MISC with the Internal Revenue Service by April 19, 2017, which date is 30 days from March 20, 2017.

(ii) The election by F and the presence of de minimis errors on the Forms 1099-MISC make the penalties under sections 6721 and 6722 applicable to Q. See §§ 301.6721-1(e)(3) and 301.6722-1(d)(3). Q, however, rectified the failures within 30 days of March 20, 2017, the date F made the election under § 301.6722-1(d)(3)(i) with respect to the Form 1099-MISC that Q furnished to F. Therefore, under paragraph (h) of this section, Q is considered to have established reasonable cause, and under section 6724 and paragraph (a)(1) of this section the penalties under sections 6721 and 6722 are inapplicable.

(9) *Example 9*. (i) The facts are the same as in Example 8 in paragraph (k)(8) of this section, except that Q does not become aware of de minimis errors made on the Form 1099-MISC furnished to F and filed with the Internal Revenue Service until June 28, 2017. Additionally, Q furnishes the corrected Form 1099-MISC to F and files the corrected Form 1099-MISC with the Internal Revenue Service after June 28, 2017, but by

July 28, 2017, which date is 30 days from June 28, 2017.

(ii) As in the example in paragraph (k)(9)(i), the election by F and the presence of de minimis errors on the Forms 1099-MISC make the penalties under sections 6721 and 6722 applicable to Q. Additionally, because Q did not furnish a corrected Form 1099-MISC to F and file a corrected Form 1099-MISC with the Internal Revenue Service within 30 days of the date of F's election under § 301.6722-1(d)(3)(i), paragraph (h) of this section does not apply. However, Q may be able to demonstrate reasonable cause under the provisions of paragraph (a) of this paragraph. As part of this demonstration, for example, Q may be able to demonstrate that Q acted in a responsible manner under paragraph (d)(1) of this section by rectifying the failure (the de minimis errors) within 30 days of discovery.

* * *

(m) *Procedure for seeking a waiver.*—In seeking an administrative determination that the failure was due to reasonable cause and not willful neglect, the filer must submit a written statement to the address provided with the notice proposing penalty assessment (for example, Notice 972CG) or the notice of penalty assessment (for example, CP15 or CP215), or as otherwise directed by the Internal Revenue Service in forms, instructions or publications. The statement must—

(1) State the specific provision under which the waiver is being requested, that is, paragraph (b) or under paragraphs (c)(2) through (6) or paragraph (h);

* * *

(o) *Applicability date.*—In general, this section applies with respect to information returns required to be filed and payee statements required to be furnished on or after January 1 of the calendar year immediately following the date of publication of a Treasury decision adopting these rules as final regulations in the **Federal Register**. See paragraph (g)(3) of this section for effective dates applicable to paragraph (g) of this section. Paragraph (h) of this section applies with respect to information returns required to be filed and payee statements required to be furnished on or after January 1, 2017. See I.R.C. section 7805(b)(1)(C) and section 4 of Notice 2017-09, IRB-2017-4 (January 23, 2017).

MISCELLANEOUS PROVISIONS

Taxable Year: Partnerships, S Corporations, Personal Service Corporations

Taxable Year: Election: Partnership: S Corporation: Personal Service Corporation.—Temporary Reg. §§1.7519-0T—1.7519-3T, relating to the election of a taxable year by a partnership, S corporation or personal service corporation, are also proposed as final regulations and, when adopted, would become Reg. §§1.7519-0—1.7519-3 (published in the Federal Register on May 27, 1988).

§1.7519-0. Table of contents.

§1.7519-1. Required payments for entities electing not to have required year.

§1.7519-2. Required payments—procedures and administration.

§1.7519-3. Effective date.

DISCOVERY OF LIABILITY AND ENFORCEMENT OF TITLE

Administrative Proceedings: Excluding Non-Government Attorneys

Administrative Proceedings: Excluding Non-Government Attorneys.—Amendments to Reg. §301.7602-1, relating to administrative proceedings by generally excluding non-government attorneys from receiving summoned books, paper, records, or other data or from participating in the interview of a witness summoned by the IRS to provide testimony under oath, are proposed (published in the Federal Register on March 28, 2018) (REG-132434-17).

Par. 2. Section 301.7602-1 is amended by revising paragraphs(b)(3) and (d) to read as follows:

§301.7602-1. Examination of books and witnesses.

* * *

(b) * * *

(3) *Participation of a person described in section 6103(n).*—(i) *In general.*—Except as provided in paragraph (b)(3)(ii) of this section, for purposes of this paragraph (b), a person authorized to receive returns or return information under section 6103(n) and §301.6103(n)-1(a) of the regulations may receive and review books, papers, records, or other data produced in compliance with a summons, and, in the presence and under the guidance of an IRS officer or employee, participate fully in the interview of a witness summoned by the IRS to provide testimony under oath. Fully participating in an interview includes, but is not limited to, receipt, review, and use of summoned books, papers, records, or other data; being present during summons interviews; and questioning the person providing testimony under oath.

(ii) *Exception for certain non-governmental attorneys.*—An attorney who is not an officer or employee of the United States may not be hired by the IRS to perform the activities described in paragraph (b)(3)(i) of this section unless the attorney is hired by the IRS as a specialist in foreign, state, or local law, including tax law, or in non-tax substantive law that is relevant to an issue in the examination, such as patent law, property law, or environmental law, or is hired for knowledge, skills, or abilities other than providing legal services as an attorney.

* * *

(d) *Applicability date.*—This section is applicable after September 3, 1982, except for paragraphs (b)(1) and (2) of this section which are applicable on and after April 1, 2005 and paragraph (b)(3) of this section which applies to examinations begun or administrative summonses served by the IRS on or after March 27, 2018. For rules under paragraphs (b)(1) and (2) of this section that are applicable to summonses issued on or after September 10, 2002 or under paragraph (b)(3) of this section that are applicable to summons interviews conducted on or after June 18, 2014 and before July 14, 2016, see 26 CFR 301.7602-1T (revised as of April 1, 2016). For rules under paragraph (b)(3) of this section that are applicable to administrative summonses served by the IRS before March 27, 2018, see 26 CFR 301.7602-1 (revised as of April 1, 2017).

Church Tax: Inquiries and Examinations: Questions and Answers

Church Tax: Inquiries and Examinations: Questions and Answers.—Amendments to Reg. §301.7611-1, relating to the questions and answers relating to church tax inquiries and examinations, are proposed (published in the Federal Register on August 5, 2009) (REG-112756-09).

☐ Par. 2. In §301.7611-1, each entry in the table, undesignated paragraphs in the "Old Paragraph" column are designated as new paragraphs in the "New Paragraph" column to read as follows:

§301.7611-1. Questions and answer relating to church tax inquiries and examinations.

Old Paragraph	*New Paragraph*
§301.7611-1 A-5 first undesignated paragraph	§301.7611-1 A-5 paragraph (a)
§301.7611-1 A-5 second undesignated paragraph	§301.7611-1 A-5 paragraph (b)
§301.7611-1 A-6 first undesignated paragraph	§301.7611-1 A-6 paragraph (a)
§301.7611-1 A-9 first undesignated paragraph	§301.7611-1 A-9 paragraph (a)
§301.7611-1 A-9 second undesignated paragraph	§301.7611-1 A-9 paragraph (b)
§301.7611-1 A-10 first undesignated paragraph	§301.7611-1 A-10 paragraph (a)
§301.7611-1 A-10 second undesignated paragraph	§301.7611-1 A-10 paragraph (b)
§301.7611-1 A-10 third undesignated paragraph	§301.7611-1 A-10 paragraph (c)
§301.7611-1 A-10 fourth undesignated paragraph	§301.7611-1 A-10 paragraph (d)
§301.7611-1 A-10 fifth undesignated paragraph	§301.7611-1 A-10 paragraph (e)
§301.7611-1 A-11 first undesignated paragraph	§301.7611-1 A-11 paragraph (a)
§301.7611-1 A-11 second undesignated paragraph	§301.7611-1 A-11 paragraph (b)

Old Paragraph	New Paragraph
§ 301.7611-1 A-11 third undesignated paragraph	§ 301.7611-1 A-11 paragraph (c)
§ 301.7611-1 A-13 first undesignated paragraph	§ 301.7611-1 A-13 paragraph (a)
§ 301.7611-1 A-13a first undesignated paragraph	§ 301.7611-1 A-13a paragraph (a)
§ 301.7611-1 A-14 first undesignated paragraph	§ 301.7611-1 A-14 paragraph (a)
§ 301.7611-1 A-14 second undesignated paragraph	§ 301.7611-1 A-14 paragraph (b)
§ 301.7611-1 A-15 first undesignated paragraph	§ 301.7611-1 A-15 paragraph (a)
§ 301.7611-1 A-15 second undesignated paragraph	§ 301.7611-1 A-15 paragraph (b)
§ 301.7611-1 A-15 third undesignated paragraph	§ 301.7611-1 A-15 paragraph (c)
§ 301.7611-1 A-15 fourth undesignated paragraph	§ 301.7611-1 A-15 paragraph (d)
§ 301.7611-1 A-15 fifth undesignated paragraph	§ 301.7611-1 A-15 paragraph (e)
§ 301.7611-1 A-15 sixth undesignated paragraph	§ 301.7611-1 A-15 paragraph (f)
§ 301.7611-1 A-15 seventh undesignated paragraph	§ 301.7611-1 A-15 paragraph (g)
§ 301.7611-1 A-16 first undesignated paragraph	§ 301.7611-1 A-16 paragraph (a)
§ 301.7611-1 A-17 first undesignated paragraph	§ 301.7611-1 A-17 paragraph (a)

Par. 3. For each section listed in the table, remove the language in the "Remove" column and add in its place the language in the "Add" column as set forth below:

Section	Remove	Add
§ 301.7611-1 A-1 first sentence	appropriate Regional Commissioner (or higher Treasury official)	Director, Exempt Organizations
§ 301.7611-1 A-7 first sentence	appropriate Internal Revenue Service Regional Commissioner	Director, Exempt Organizations
§ 301.7611-1 A-9 first sentence	appropriate Regional Commissioner	Director, Exempt Organizations
§ 301.7611-1 A-10 first sentence	appropriate Regional Counsel	Division Counsel/Associate Chief Counsel, Tax Exempt and Government Entities
§ 301.7611-1 A-10 paragraph (b) first sentence	At the time the notice of examination (second notice) is provided to the church, a copy of the same notice will be provided to the appropriate Regional Counsel.	Before the notice of examination (second notice) is provided to the church, a copy of the same notice will be provided to the Division Counsel / Associate Chief Counsel, Tax Exempt and Government Entities.
§ 301.7611-1 A-10 paragraph (b) second sentence	Regional Counsel	Division Counsel/Associate Chief Counsel, Tax Exempt and Government Entities
§ 301.7611-1 A-11 paragraph (c) first, second and third sentences	Regional Counsel	Division Counsel/Associate Chief Counsel, Tax Exempt and Government Entities
§ 301.7611-1 A-15 paragraph (c) first and third sentences	appropriate Regional Commissioner	Director, Exempt Organizations
§ 301.7611-1 A-15 paragraph (c) second sentence	Regional Commissioner	Director, Exempt Organizations

Section	Remove	Add
§301.7611-1 A-16 first sentence	Assistant Commissioner (Employee Plans and Exempt Organizations)	Commissioner, Tax Exempt and Government Entities or the Deputy Commissioner, Tax Exempt and Government Entities
§301.7611-1 A-16 second sentence	Assistant Commissioner's approval	approval of the Commissioner, Tax Exempt and Government Entities or the Deputy Commissioner, Tax Exempt and Government Entities
§301.7611-1 A-16 paragraph (a) second sentence	Assistant Commissioner (Employee Plans and Exempt Organizations)	Commissioner, Tax Exempt and Government Entities or the Deputy Commissioner, Tax Exempt and Government Entities
§301.7611-1 A-17 first sentence	Regional Commissioner	Director, Exempt Organizations
§301.7611-1 A-17 paragraph(a) third sentence	Regional Commissioner	Director, Exempt Organizations
§301.7611-1 A-17 paragraph (a) fourth sentence	appropriate Regional Commissioner's belief	belief of the Director, Exempt Organizations

DEFINITIONS

Gifts and Bequests from Covered Expatriates: Imposition of Tax

Gifts and Bequests from Covered Expatriates: Imposition of Tax.—Reg. §28.7701-1, relating to a tax on United States citizens and residents who receive gifts or bequests from certain individuals who relinquished United States citizenship or ceased to be lawful permanent residents of the United States on or after June 17, 2008, is proposed (published in the Federal Register on September 10, 2015) (REG-112997-10).

Section 28.7701-1 is added to read as follows:

§28.7701-1. Tax return preparer.—For the definition of the term *tax return preparer,* see §301.7701-15 of this chapter.

Classification: Cell Companies: Series LLCs

Classification: Cell Companies: Series LLCs.—Amendments to Reg. §301.7701-1, regarding the classification for Federal tax purposes of a series of a domestic series limited liability company (LLC), a cell of a domestic cell company, or a foreign series or cell that conducts an insurance business, are proposed (published in the Federal Register on September 14, 2010) (REG-119921-09).

Par. 4. Section 301.7701-1 is amended by:

1. Adding paragraph (a)(5).
2. Revising paragraphs (e) and (f).

The additions and revisions read as follows:

§301.7701-1. Classification of organizations for Federal tax purposes.—(a) * * *

(5) *Series and series organizations.*—(i) *Entity status of a domestic series.*—For Federal tax purposes, except as provided in paragraph (a)(5)(ix) of this section, a series (as defined in paragraph (a)(5)(viii)(C) of this section) organized or established under the laws of the United States or of any State, whether or not a juridical person for local law purposes, is treated as an entity formed under local law.

(ii) *Certain foreign series conducting an insurance business.*—For Federal tax purposes, except as provided in paragraph (a)(5)(ix) of this section, a series organized or established under the laws of a foreign jurisdiction is treated as an entity formed under local law if the arrangements and other activities of the series, if conducted by a domestic company, would result in classification as an insurance company within the meaning of section 816(a) or section 831(c).

(iii) *Recognition of entity status.*—Whether a series that is treated as a local law entity under paragraph (a)(5)(i) or (ii) of this section is recognized as a separate entity for Federal tax purposes is determined under this section and general tax principles.

(iv) *Classification of series.*—The classification of a series that is recognized as a separate entity for Federal tax purposes is determined under paragraph (b) of this section.

(v) *Jurisdiction in which series is organized or established.*—A series is treated as created or organized under the laws of a State or foreign jurisdiction if the series is established under the laws of such jurisdiction. See §301.7701-5 for rules that determine whether a business entity is domestic or foreign.

(vi) *Ownership of series and the assets of series.*—For Federal tax purposes, the ownership of interests in a series and of the assets associated with a series is determined under general tax principles. A series organization is not treated as the owner for Federal tax purposes of a series or of the assets associated with a series merely because the series organization holds legal title to the assets associated with the series.

(vii) *Effect of Federal and local law treatment.*—To the extent that, pursuant to the provisions of this paragraph (a)(5), a series is a taxpayer against whom tax may be assessed under Chapter 63 of Title 26, then any tax assessed against the series may be collected by the Internal Revenue Service from the series in the same manner the assessment could be collected by the Internal Revenue Service from any other taxpayer. In addition, to the extent Federal or local law permits a debt attributable to the series to be collected from the series organization or other series of the series organization, then, notwithstanding any other provision of this paragraph (a)(5), and consistent with the provisions of Federal or local law, the series organization and other series of the series organization may also be considered the taxpayer from whom the tax assessed against the series may be administratively or judicially collected. Further, when a creditor is permitted to collect a liability attributable to a series organization from any series of the series organization, a tax liability assessed against the series organization may be collected directly from a series of the series organization by administrative or judicial means.

(viii) *Definitions.*—(A) *Series organization.*—A *series organization* is a juridical entity that establishes and maintains, or under which is established and maintained, a series (as defined in paragraph (a)(5)(viii)(C) of this section). A series organization includes a series limited liability company, series partnership, series trust, protected cell company, segregated cell company, segregated portfolio company, or segregated account company.

(B) *Series statute.*—A *series statute* is a statute of a State or foreign jurisdiction that explicitly provides for the organization or establishment of a series of a juridical person and explicitly permits—

(1) Members or participants of a series organization to have rights, powers, or duties with respect to the series;

(2) A series to have separate rights, powers, or duties with respect to specified property or obligations; and

(3) The segregation of assets and liabilities such that none of the debts and liabilities of the series organization (other than liabilities to the State or foreign jurisdiction related to the organization or operation of the series organization, such as franchise fees or administrative costs) or of any other series of the series organization are enforceable against the assets of a particular series of the series organization.

(C) *Series.*—A *series* is a segregated group of assets and liabilities that is established pursuant to a series statute (as defined in paragraph (a)(5)(viii)(B) of this section) by agreement of a series organization (as defined in paragraph (a)(5)(viii)(A) of this section). A series includes a series, cell, segregated account, or segregated portfolio, including a cell, segregated account, or segregated portfolio that is formed under the insurance code of a jurisdiction or is engaged in an insurance business. However, the term *series* does not include a segregated asset account of a life insurance company. See section 817(d)(1); § 1.817-5(e). An election, agreement, or other arrangement that permits debts and liabilities of other series or the series organization to be enforceable against the assets of a particular series, or a failure to comply with the record keeping requirements for the limitation on liability available under the relevant series statute, will be disregarded for purposes of this paragraph (a)(5)(viii)(C).

(ix) *Treatment of series and series organizations under Subtitle C - Employment Taxes and Collection of Income Tax (Chapters 21, 22, 23, 23A, 24 and 25 of the Internal Revenue Code).*—[Reserved.]

(x) *Examples.*—The following examples illustrate the principles of this paragraph (a)(5):

Example 1. Domestic Series LLC. (i) *Facts.* Series LLC is a series organization (within the meaning of paragraph (a)(5)(viii)(A) of this section). Series LLC has three members (1, 2, and 3). Series LLC establishes two series (A and B) pursuant to the LLC statute of state Y, a series statute within the meaning of paragraph (a)(5)(viii)(B) of this section. Under general tax principles, Members 1 and 2 are the owners of Series A, and Member 3 is the owner of Series B. Series A and B are not described in § 301.7701-2(b) or paragraph (a)(3) of this section and are not trusts within the meaning of § 301.7701-4.

(ii) *Analysis.* Under paragraph (a)(5)(i) of this section, Series A and Series B are each treated as an entity formed under local law. The classification of Series A and Series B is determined under paragraph (b) of this section. The default classification under § 301.7701-3 of Series A is a partnership and of Series B is a disregarded entity.

Example 2. Foreign Insurance Cell. (i) *Facts.* Insurance CellCo is a series organization (within the meaning of paragraph (a)(5)(viii)(A) of this section) organized under the laws of foreign Country X. Insurance CellCo has established one cell, Cell A, pursuant to a Country X law that is a series statute (within the meaning of paragraph (a)(5)(viii)(B) of this section). More than half the business of Cell A during the taxable year is the issuing of insurance or annuity contracts or the reinsuring of risks underwritten by insurance companies. If the activities of Cell A were conducted by a domestic company, that company would qualify as an insurance company within the meaning of sections 816(a) and 831(c).

(ii) *Analysis.* Under paragraph (a)(5)(ii) of this section, Cell A is treated as an entity formed under local law. Because Cell A is an insurance company, it is classified as a corporation under § 301.7701-2(b)(4).

* * *

(e) *State.*—For purposes of this section and §§ 301.7701-2 and 301.7701-4, the term *State* includes the District of Columbia.

(f) *Effective/applicability dates.*—(1) *In general.*—Except as provided in paragraphs (f)(2) and (f)(3) of this section, the rules of this section are applicable as of January 1, 1997.

(2) *Cost sharing arrangements.*—The rules of paragraph (c) of this section are applicable on January 5, 2009.

(3) *Series and series organizations.*—(i) *In general.*—Except as otherwise provided in this paragraph (f)(3), paragraph (a)(5) of this section applies on and after the date final regulations are published in the **Federal Register**.

(ii) *Transition rule.*—(A) *In general.*—Except as provided in paragraph (f)(3)(ii)(B) of this section, a taxpayer's treatment of a series in a manner inconsistent with the final regulations will be respected on and after the date final regulations are published in the **Federal Register**, provided that—

(1) The series was established prior to September 14, 2010;

(2) The series (independent of the series organization or other series of the series organization) conducted business or investment activity, or, in the case of a series established pursuant to a foreign statute, more than half the business of the series was the issuing of insurance or annuity contracts or the reinsuring of risks underwritten by insurance companies, on and prior to September 14, 2010;

(3) If the series was established pursuant to a foreign statute, the series' classification was relevant (as defined in §301.7701-3(d)), and more than half the business of the series was the issuing of insurance or annuity contracts or the reinsuring of risks underwritten by insurance companies for all taxable years beginning with the taxable year that includes September 14, 2010;

(4) No owner of the series treats the series as an entity separate from any other series of the series organization or from the series organization for purposes of filing any Federal income tax returns, information returns, or withholding documents in any taxable year;

(5) The series and series organization had a reasonable basis (within the meaning of section 6662) for their claimed classification; and

(6) Neither the series nor any owner of the series nor the series organization was notified in writing on or before the date final regulations are published in the **Federal Register** that classification of the series was under examination (in which case the series' classification will be determined in the examination).

(B) *Exception to transition rule.*—Paragraph (f)(3)(ii)(A) of this section will not apply on and after the date any person or persons who were not owners of the series organization (or series) prior to September 14, 2010 own, in the aggregate, a fifty percent or greater interest in the series organization (or series). For purposes of the preceding sentence, the term interest means—

(1) In the case of a partnership, a capital or profits interest; and

(2) In the case of a corporation, an equity interest measured by vote or value.

Indian Tribal Governments

Indian Tribal Governments: Treatment as States.—Temporary Reg. §305.7701-1, relating to the treatment of Indian tribal governments as states, is also proposed as a final regulation and, when adopted, would become Reg. §305.7701-1 (published in the Federal Register on May 7, 1984).

§305.7701-1. Definition of Indian tribal government.

Partners and Partnerships: Self-Employment Tax: Disregarded Entity

Partners and Partnerships: Self-Employment Tax: Disregarded Entity.—Amendments to Reg. §301.7701-2, clarifying the employment tax treatment of partners in a partnership that owns a disregarded entity, are proposed (published in the Federal Register on May 4, 2016) (REG-114307-15).

Par. 2. Section 301.7701-2 is amended by revising paragraphs (c)(2)(iv)(C)(2) and adding paragraph (e)(8)(i) to read as follows:

§301.7701-2. Business entities; definitions.

* * *

(c) * * *

(2) * * *

(iv) * * *

(C) * * *

(2) [The text of the proposed amendment to §301.7701-2(c)(2)(iv)(C)(2) is the same as the text of §301.7701-2T(c)(2)(iv)(C)(2) as added by T.D. 9766].

* * *

(e) * * *

(8)(i) [The text of the proposed amendments to §301.7701-2(e)(8)(i) is the same as the text of §301.7701-2T(e)(8)(i) as added by T.D. 9766].

Hybrid Arrangements: Rules

Hybrid Arrangements: Rules.—Amendments to Reg. §301.7701-3, implementing sections 245A(e) and 267A of the Internal Revenue Code regarding hybrid dividends and certain amounts paid or accrued in hybrid transactions or with hybrid entities, are proposed (published in the Federal Register on December 28, 2018) (REG-104352-18).

Par. 13. Section 301.7701-3 is amended by revising the sixth sentence of paragraph (a) and adding paragraph (c)(3) to read as follows:

§301.7701-3. Classification of certain business entities.—(a) *In general.*—* * * Paragraph (c) of this section provides rules for making express elections, including a rule under which a domestic eligible entity that elects to be classified as an association consents to be subject to the dual consolidated loss rules of section 1503(d).

* * *

(c) * * *

(3) *Consent to be subject to section 1503(d).*—(i) *Rule.*—A domestic eligible entity that elects to be classified as an association consents to be treated as a dual resident corporation for purposes of section 1503(d) (such an entity, a *domestic consenting corporation*), for any taxable year for which it is classified as an association and the condition set forth in §1.1503(d)-1(c)(1) of this chapter is satisfied.

(ii) *Transition rule — deemed consent.*—If, as a result of the applicability date relating to paragraph (c)(3)(i) of this section, a domestic eligible entity that is classified as an association has not consented to be treated as a domestic consenting corporation pursuant to paragraph (c)(3)(i) of this section, then the domestic eligible entity is deemed to consent to be so treated as of its first taxable year beginning on or after December 20, 2019. The first sentence of this paragraph (c)(3)(ii) does not apply if the domestic eligible entity elects, on or after December 20, 2018 and effective before its first taxable year beginning on or after December 20, 2019, to be classified as a partnership or disregarded entity such that it ceases to be a domestic eligible entity that is classified as an association. For purposes of the election described in the second sentence of this paragraph (c)(3)(ii), the sixty month limitation under paragraph (c)(1)(iv) of this section is waived.

(iii) *Applicability date.*—The sixth sentence of paragraph (a) of this section and paragraph (c)(3)(i) of this section apply to a domestic eligible entity that on or after December 20, 2018 files an election to be classified as an association (regardless of whether the election is effective before December 20, 2018). Paragraph (c)(3)(ii) of this section applies as of December 20, 2018.

* * *

Employee Trusts: Effective Dates

Employee Trusts: Tax Reform Act of 1984: Effective Dates.—Temporary Reg. §301.7701-17T is also proposed as a final regulation and, when adopted, would become Reg. §301.7701-17 (published in the Federal Register on February 4, 1986).

§301.7701-17. Collective-bargaining plans and agreements.

Treaty-Based Return Positions

Treaty-Based Return Positions: Dual Status Alien.—Reproduced below is the text of proposed amendments to Reg. §301.7701(b)-7, relating to treaty-based return positions (published in the Federal Register on April 27, 1992). The proposed amendment to Reg. §301.7701(b)-7(c)(2) was adopted by T.D. 8733 on October 6, 1997.

☐ Par. 3. Section 301.7701(b)-7 is amended as follows:

1. By adding text in paragraph (a)(4).
2. By adding text in paragraphs (c)(2) [see above regarding adoption of this amendment] and (3).
3. By adding a new *Example 5* to paragraph (e).
4. The additions read as follows.

§301.7701(b)-7. Coordination with income tax treaties.—(a) * * *

(4) *Special rules for S corporations.*—(i) *In general.*—Notwithstanding paragraph (a)(3) of this section, for purposes of determining whether a domestic corporation meets the definition of a small business corporation under section 1361(b)(1), the following rules in paragraphs (a)(4)(ii) through (v) of this section shall apply with respect to a dual resident taxpayer.

(ii) *Dual resident not claiming treaty benefits.*—A dual resident taxpayer who does not claim any treaty benefits (as a nonresident of the United States) so as to reduce the individual's United States income tax liability shall be treated as a United States resident for purposes of section 1361(b)(1)(C). Accordingly, the dual resident taxpayer may be or become a shareholder in an S corporation without thereby causing the S corporation to have a nonresident alien as a shareholder for purposes of section 1361(b)(1)(C).

(iii) *Dual resident claiming treaty benefits.*—A dual resident taxpayer who claims any treaty benefit (as a nonresident of the United States) so as to reduce the individual's United States income tax liability shall be treated as a nonresident alien of the United States for purposes of section 1361(b)(1)(C). Accordingly, if the dual resident taxpayer is a shareholder in an S corporation for any portion of a taxable year with respect to which the taxpayer claims a treaty benefit, then the corporation's election under section 1362(a) shall be terminated pursuant to section 1362(d)(2) effective as of the first day of the taxable year of the dual resident in which the dual resident is an S corporation shareholder and claims treaty benefits as a nonresident of the United States. See §301.7701(b)-7(b) and (c) for reporting requirements that apply to dual resident taxpayers.

(iv) *Special exception.*—Notwithstanding paragraph (a)(4)(iii) of this section, a dual resident taxpayer who claims a treaty benefit (as a nonresident of the United States) shall be treated as a United States resident for purposes of section 1361(b)(1)(C) if the conditions of paragraphs (a)(4)(iv) (A), (B), and (C) of this section are satisfied. This paragraph (a)(4)(iv) shall not apply if the S corporation was a C corporation, the S corporation is a successor to a C corporation, or the S corporation is a successor to an S corporation that itself was a successor (direct or indirect) to a C corporation.

(A) *S corporation income.*—*(1)* Except as otherwise provided in this section, in determining the dual resident taxpayer's United States income tax liability, in accordance with section 1366(b), the character and source of any item included in the dual resident's income shall be determined as if such item were realized by the dual resident taxpayer.

(2) The dual resident taxpayer shall be considered as carrying on a business within the United States through a permanent establishment if the S corporation of which the dual resident taxpayer is a shareholder carries on such business. For this purpose, the S corporation shall be treated as a foreign corporation resident in the foreign country in which the dual resident is a resident.

(3) Procedures similar to those provided under section 1446 relating to withholding requirements applicable to partnerships with foreign partners shall apply as if the S corporation were a partnership (other than a publicly traded partnership) and the dual resident taxpayer were a foreign partner in that partnership.

(B) *Dispositions of S corporation stock.*—Except as otherwise provided in this section, for purposes of determining the taxation of the dual resident taxpayer on the disposition of the individual's shares in the S corporation, the S corporation shall be treated as a partnership (other than a publicly traded partnership) and the dual resident taxpayer shall be treated as a foreign partner in that partnership.

(C) *Withholding agreement.*—The dual resident taxpayer and the S corporation of which the taxpayer is a shareholder must enter into an agreement, pursuant to procedures prescribed by the Commissioner, to withhold income tax with respect to the shareholder's pro rata share of items of income described in section 1366(a)(1) and gain from the disposition of his or her shares in the S corporation.

(v) *Effective date.*—(A) *In general.*—The rules described in this paragraph (a)(4) shall be effective for taxable years of S corporations beginning on or after July 27, 1992.

(B) *Effect on prior years.*—For taxable years of S corporations beginning before July 27, 1992, a dual resident S corporation shareholder that previously claimed or will claim a treaty benefit on a U.S. income tax return (as a nonresident of the United States) must either—

(1) Waive the treaty benefit claimed and file an amended return as a resident of the United States; or

(2) Determine the character of his or her pro rata share of S corporation items according to a reasonable method consistent with the principles of section 1366. A method that satisfies the requirements of paragraphs (a)(4)(iv)(A)(*1*) and (*2*) and (B) of this section is a reasonable method. A method under which the taxable income of the S corporation is not taxed to the dual resident shareholder under section 881 is not a reasonable method.

* * *

(c) * * *

(3) *S corporation shareholders.*—If the taxpayer who claims a treaty benefit as a nonresident of the United States is a shareholder in an S corporation (as defined in section 1361(a)(1)) then, for purposes of paragraph (c)(1) of this section, the statement shall also indicate that the taxpayer understands that claiming a treaty benefit as a nonresident of the United States shall, unless a withholding agreement is entered into pursuant to paragraph (a)(4)(iv) of this section and the procedures prescribed by the Commissioner, terminate the S corporation's election under section 1362(a).

* * *

(e) * * *

Example 5. D, an alien individual, is a resident of foreign country Z, under Z's internal law. D is also a resident of the United States under the Internal Revenue Code and a shareholder in Corp E, an S corporation within the meaning of section 1361(a)(1). Country Z is a party to an income tax convention with the United States. Under the convention D is considered to be a resident of country Z. If Corp E were a foreign corporation resident in country Z, Corp E (under the convention) would be deemed to be carrying on a business within the United States through a permanent establishment. D chooses to file in the United States as a nonresident in order to claim treaty benefits with respect to certain items of income covered by the convention. Pursuant to § 301.7701(b)-7(a)(4)(iii), D will be considered a nonresident of the United States for purposes of section 1361(b)(1)(C). Accordingly, Corp E will cease to qualify as a "small business corporation" within the meaning of section 1361(b)(1). However, if D and Corp E enter into a withholding agreement in accordance with the procedures prescribed by the Commissioner, Corp E will continue to qualify as a small business corporation. Pursuant to § 301.7701(b)-7(a)(4)(iv)(A), to the extent that Corp E's items of income, loss, deduction and credit would be considered to be attributable to a permanent establishment within the United States under the convention, D's pro rata share of Corp E items shall, pursuant to section 1366(b), be deemed to be attributable to a permanent establishment within the United States for purposes of determining D's United States tax liability.

Life Insurance Contracts: Reasonable Mortality Charges

Life Insurance Contracts: Reasonable Mortality Charges.—Reg. § 1.7702-1, relating to the required use of reasonable mortality charges in determining whether a contract qualifies as a life insurance contract, is proposed (published in the Federal Register on July 5, 1991).

§ 1.7702-1. Mortality charges. [1].—(a) *General rule.*—Reasonable mortality charges must be used in determining the "net single premium," the "guideline single premium," and the "guideline level premium" under section 7702 for a life insurance contract. For purposes of this paragraph, mortality charges are "reasonable mortality charges" if they do not exceed the lesser of (1) the charges described in paragraph (b) of this section or in one of the safe harbors contained in paragraph (c) of this section, or (2) the mortality charges specified in the contract.[1]

(b) *Reasonable mortality charges.*—(1) *Actually expected to be imposed.*—Except as limited by paragraph (b)(2) of this section, mortality charges described in this paragraph are those amounts that the insurance company actually expects to impose as consideration for its assuming the risk of the insured's death (regardless of the designation used for those charges), taking into account any relevant characteristics of the insured of which the company is aware. Every insurance company to which this paragraph applies must be prepared to establish to the satisfaction of the district director that the mortality charges are actually expected to be imposed, taking into account the likelihood of the surrender of the contract.

(2) *Limit on charges.*—If mortality charges described in paragraph (b)(1) of this section exceed the mortality charges derived from the prevailing commissioners' standard tables in effect as of the time the contract is issued, they are not described in this paragraph (b). Notwithstanding the preceding sentence, mortality charges that are imposed with regard to a substandard risk (as defined in paragraph (d)(2) of this section) or imposed with regard to a nonparticipating contract (as defined in paragraph (d)(3) of this section) do not fail to be described in this paragraph (b) solely on the grounds that the charges exceed the applicable mortality charges specified in the prevailing commissioners' standard tables as of the time the contract is issued.

(c) *Safe harbors.*—(1) *1980 C.S.O. Basic Mortality Tables.*—For contracts that provide a death benefit that is payable upon the death of one insured, mortality charges are reasonable mortality charges if they do not exceed the applicable mortality charges set forth in the 1980 Standard Ordinary Mortality Tables of the National Association of Insurance Commissioners for male or female insureds, without select factors (the "1980 C.S.O. Basic Mortality Tables").

(2) *Unisex tables and smoker/nonsmoker tables.*—Mortality charges exceeding those specified in the 1980 C.S.O. Basic Mortality Tables are reasonable mortality charges if the contract using the charges has only one insured and is issued under a plan of insurance (as defined in paragraph (d)(5) of this section) that meets the following requirements:

(i) The nonforfeiture values for all contracts issued under the plan of insurance are determined under either 1980 C.S.O. Gender-Blended Mortality Tables (unisex tables) or 1980 C.S.O. Smoker and Nonsmoker Mortality Tables (smoker/nonsmoker tables), as appropriate; and

(ii) No contract issued under the plan of insurance calls for mortality charges which exceed the applicable charges specified in either the unisex or smoker/nonsmoker tables, as the case may be. That is, for any plan of insurance, if unisex tables are used to determine the mortality charges for female insureds, then the same tables must be used to determine the mortality charges for male insureds; if separate smoker tables are used to determine the mortality charges for smokers, then separate nonsmoker tables must be used to determine the mortality charges for nonsmokers.

(3) *Certain contracts based on 1958 C.S.O. table.*—Mortality charges exceeding those specified in the 1980 C.S.O. Basic Mortality Tables are reasonable mortality charges if the contract using the charges has only one insured and is issued under a plan of insurance that meets all of the following requirements:

(i) The mortality charge is imposed under a contract that is not a modified endowment contract, within the meaning of section 7702A, determined using the applicable mortality charges derived from the 1958 standard ordinary mortality and morbidity table of the National Association of Insurance Commissioners (1958 C.S.O. table);

(ii) The contract was issued on or before December 31, 1988, pursuant to a plan of insurance or policy blank that was based on the 1958 C.S.O. table;

(iii) The mortality charges for the contract do not exceed the charges specified in the 1958 C.S.O. table; and

(iv) The plan or policy blank was approved by the appropriate state regulatory authority on or before October 21, 1988.

(d) *Definitions.*—For purposes of this regulation the following terms have the following meaning.

(1) *Prevailing commissioners' standard tables.*—The term "prevailing commissioners' standard tables" means the tables containing the higher of—

(i) The charges in the tables defined by section 807(d)(5)(A), or

(ii) The charges in any other tables that sections 807(d)(5)(B) or 807(d)(5)(C) allow to be used with respect to the contract for purposes of section 807(d)(2)(C). For this purpose the limitation of section 807(d)(5)(E) shall not apply.

(2) *Substandard risk.*—"Substandard risk" means a risk of death that exceeds the standards set for normal or regular risks. Whether any particular insured person presents a substandard risk must be determined by taking into account all relevant facts and circumstances including the insured's medical history and laws that increase the potential unknown insurance risk with respect to an insured by limiting a company's ability to inquire into certain aspects of the insured's medical history.

(3) *Nonparticipating contract.*—"Nonparticipating contract" means a contract other than a "variable contract" defined in section 817(d) that provides no right to the policyholder to participate in the issuer's divisible surplus, if any, and that contains no charge reduction mechanism.

(4) *Charge reduction mechanism.*—"Charge reduction mechanism" means any dividend or similar distribution to the holder of the contract in his or her capacity as holder. A charge reduction mechanism includes—

(i) Any amount paid or credited (including an increase in benefits) if the amount is not fixed in the contract but depends on the

[1] The tables referenced in this section are available for public inspection during normal business hours at the Internal Revenue Service FOIA Reading Room, Room 1569, 1111 Constitution Avenue, N.W., Washington, D.C. 20224.

experience of the company or the discretion of management,

(ii) Any amount in the nature of interest paid or credited to the extent the amount is in excess of interest determined at the minimum rate guaranteed under the contract,

(iii) Any amount by which the premium is reduced that (but for the reduction) would have been required to be paid under the contract, and

(iv) Any refund or credit based on the experience of the contract or group involved.

(5) *Plan of insurance.*—"Plan of insurance" refers to those life insurance contracts sold by the company to a targeted market group which is not defined, directly or indirectly, on the basis of either the gender or the smoking habits of the insureds.

(e) *Effective date.*—This section applies to life insurance contracts entered into on or after October 21, 1988. [Reg. § 1.7702-1.]

Life Insurance Contracts: Qualified Accelerated Death Benefits

Life Insurance Contracts: Qualified Accelerated Death Benefits.—Reproduced below are the texts of proposed Reg. §§1.7702-2 and 1.7702A-1, relating to the definition of a life insurance contract for federal tax purposes and the tax treatment of amounts received as qualified accelerated death benefits (published in the Federal Register on December 15, 1992).

☐ Par. 4. Sections 1.7702-2 and 1.7702A-1 are added to read as follows:

§1.7702-2. Definitions.—(a) *In general.*—Paragraphs (b) through (i) of this section provide definitions and other rules only for purposes of section 7702.

(b) *Cash value.*—(1) *In general.*—Except as otherwise provided in paragraph (b)(2) of this section, the cash value of a contract is the greater of—

(i) The maximum amount payable under the contract (determined without regard to any surrender charge or policy loan); or

(ii) The maximum amount that the policyholder can borrow under the contract.

(2) *Amounts excluded from cash value.*—The cash value of a contract does not include—

(i) The amount of any death benefit (as defined in paragraph (c) of this section);

(ii) The amount of any qualified additional benefit;

(iii) The amount of any other benefit described in paragraph (f) of this section;

(iv) An amount returned to the insured upon termination of a credit life insurance contract due to a full repayment of the debt covered by the contract; or

(v) A reasonable termination dividend not in excess of $35 for each $1,000 of the face amount of the contract.

(c) *Death benefit.*—(1) *In general.*—A death benefit is the amount payable by reason of the death of the insured (determined without regard to any qualified additional benefits).

(2) *Qualified accelerated death benefit treated as death benefit.*—For purposes of paragraph (b)(2)(i) of this section, the amount payable as a qualified accelerated death benefit as defined in paragraph (d) of this section (but determined without regard to any reduction for discounting) is treated as a death benefit.

(d) *Qualified accelerated death benefit.*—(1) *In general.*—A benefit payable prior to death (accelerated benefit) is a qualified accelerated death benefit if, under the contract, the following conditions are satisfied—

(i) The accelerated benefit is payable only if the insured becomes terminally ill (as defined in paragraph (e) of this section);

(ii) The amount of the accelerated benefit is equal to or more than the present value of the reduction in the death benefit otherwise payable in the event of the death of the insured (without regard to any qualified additional benefits); and

(iii) The ratio of the cash surrender value of the contract immediately after the payment of the accelerated benefit to the cash surrender value of the contract immediately before the payment of the accelerated benefit is equal to or greater than the ratio of the death benefit immediately after the payment of the accelerated benefit to the death benefit immediately before the payment of the accelerated benefit.

(2) *Determination of present value of the reduction in death benefit.*—For purposes of paragraph (d)(1)(ii) of this section, the present value of the reduction in death benefit occurring upon payment of an qualified accelerated death benefit must be determined by—

(i) Using as the discount rate the greater of—

(A) The applicable federal interest rate determined under section 846(c)(2); or

(B) The interest rate applicable to policy loans under the contract; and

(ii) Assuming that the death benefit (or the portion thereof) would have been paid 12 months after the date of the payment of the accelerated benefit.

(3) *Examples.*—The following examples illustrate the provisions of this paragraph (d).

Example 1. *B* owns an insurance contract with a death benefit of $100,000 and a cash value of $30,000. In 1994, the insured becomes terminally ill (as defined in paragraph (e) of this section). In 1994, *B* receives an accelerated benefit equal to forty percent of the death benefit under the contract (discounted in accordance with to the rules of paragraph (d)(2) of this section). As a result of the payment of the accelerated benefit, the amount that *B* is entitled to receive upon the surrender of the contract is reduced by $12,000 (forty percent of $30,000) to $18,000. The ratio of the cash surrender value of the contract immediately after the payment of the accelerated benefit to the cash surrender value of the contract immediately before the payment of the accelerated benefit (18:30) is equal to the ratio of the death benefit immediately after the payment of the accelerated benefit to the death benefit immediately before the payment of the accelerated benefit (60:100). The accelerated benefit constitutes a qualified accelerated death benefit.

Example 2. *C* owns an insurance contract with a death benefit of $100,000. In 1994, the insured becomes terminally ill (as defined in paragraph (e) of this section). The policy loan rate specified in the contract is 10 percent and exceeds the federal applicable rate determined under section 846(c). In 1994, C receives an accelerated benefit equal to the entire death benefit of the policy discounted by 10 percent for 12 months from the date of payment and the contract terminates. The accelerated benefit is a qualified accelerated death benefit.

Example 3. The facts are the same as in *Example 2* except that C receives an accelerated benefit equal to the entire death benefit of the policy discounted by 20 percent for 12 months from the date of payment and the contract terminates. The accelerated benefit is not a qualified accelerated death benefit.

(e) *Terminally ill defined.*—An individual is terminally ill if the insurer determines that the individual has an illness or physical condition that, notwithstanding appropriate medical care, is reasonably expected to result in death within 12 months from the date of payment of the accelerated death benefit.

(f) *Certain other additional benefits.*—(1) *In general.*—An additional benefit is described in this paragraph (f) if the following conditions are satisfied—

(i) The benefit is payable solely upon the occurrence of a morbidity risk;

(ii) The charges for the benefit are separately stated and currently imposed by the terms of the contract; and

(iii) The charges for the benefit are not included in premiums taken into account in the determination of the investment in the contract under section 72(c)(1) or 72(e)(6) and are not taken into account in the determination of premiums paid under section 7702(f)(1).

(2) *Examples.*—The following examples illustrate the provisions of this paragraph (f):

Example 1. A owns an insurance contract with a death benefit of $100,000. The contract contains a provision that upon the occurrence of a morbidity risk, the insurance company will pay to *A* a morbidity benefit equal to 70 percent of the contract's death benefit in complete termination of *A*'s rights under the contract. Upon surrender of the contract prior to the occurrence of the morbidity risk, *A* currently would be entitled to receive $40,000. The morbidity benefit is payable solely upon the occurrence of a morbidity risk. The charges for the morbidity benefit are separately stated and currently imposed under the contract. The charges for the morbidity benefit are not included in premiums taken into account in the determination of the investment in the contract under section 72(c)(1) or 72(e)(6) and are not taken into account in the determination of premiums paid under section 7702(f)(1). The excess of the $70,000 (70 percent of $100,000) payable to *A* upon the occurrence of the morbidity risk over $40,000 is an additional benefit which is not a qualified additional benefit. The additional benefit is described in this paragraph (f). Under paragraph (b)(2)(iii) of this section, the amount of the additional benefit (the $30,000 payable by reason of the occurrence of a morbidity risk) is not included in the contract's cash value. Accordingly, $40,000 is treated as cash value payable upon complete surrender of the contract while the remaining $30,000 is treated as a morbidity benefit under the contract.

Example 2. The facts are the same as in *Example 1* except that the charges for the morbidity benefit are not separately stated and currently imposed. The benefit is not described in this paragraph (f) and consequently the benefit is not excluded from the cash value of the contract. Under paragraph (b)(2)(iii) of this section, the contract's cash value includes the amounts payable by reason of the occurrence of a morbidity risk.

Example 3. The facts are the same as in *Example 1* except that the charges for the morbidity benefit are included in premiums taken into account in the determination of the investment in the contract under section 72(c)(1) or 72(e)(6). The benefit is not described in this paragraph (f) and consequently the benefit is not excluded from the cash value of the contract. Under paragraph (b)(2)(iii) of this section, the contract's cash value includes the amounts payable by reason of the occurrence of a morbidity risk.

(g) *Adjustments under section 7702(f)(7).*—If a life insurance contract is not terminated upon the payment of a qualified accelerated death benefit or an additional benefit described in paragraph (f) of this section, any change in the benefits under (or in other terms of) the contract is a change not reflected in any previous determination or adjustment under section 7702 and is an adjustment event under section 7702(f)(7).

(h) *Cash surrender value.*—(1) *In general.*—Except as provided in paragraph (h)(2) of this section, cash surrender value of a contract is its cash value, as determined under paragraph (b) of this section.

(2) *For purposes of section 7702(f)(7).*—For purposes of determining the recapture ceiling under section 7702(f)(7), cash surrender value is the amount that would be payable under the contract (determined without regard to any surrender charge, policy loan, or reasonable termination dividends) if the contract were terminated immediately prior to the change in the benefits under (or in other terms of) the contract.

(i) *Net surrender value.*—For purposes of section 7702(g), the net surrender value of a contract at any time is the amount that would be payable under the contract (determined with regard to surrender charges but without regard to any policy loan) if the contract were terminated at that time.

(j) *Effective date and special rules.*—(1) *In general.*—Except as otherwise provided in this paragraph (j), this section applies only with respect to contracts issued or entered into after June 30, 1993.

(2) *Provision of certain benefits before July 1, 1993.*—(i) *Not treated as cash value.*—If a benefit or loan payable only in the event the insured becomes terminally ill (as defined in paragraph (e) of this section), or an additional benefit (other than a qualified additional benefit) or loan payable solely upon the occurrence of a morbidity risk, is provided in a life insurance contract before July 1, 1993, the benefit or loan is not treated as cash value under section 7702.

(ii) *No effect on date of issuance.*—If a benefit or loan provision described in paragraph (j)(2)(i) of this section is added to a life insurance contract before July 1, 1993, the addition of the benefit or loan has no effect on the date that the contract was issued or entered into for purposes of section 7702.

(iii) *Special rule for addition of benefit or loan provision after December 15, 1992.*—This paragraph (j)(2) applies with respect to a benefit or loan provision added to a life insurance contract after December 15, 1992, only if the insurer can demonstrate that the benefit or loan provision was available under a life insurance contract issued in the United States as of December 15, 1992.

(3) *Addition of qualified accelerated death benefit.*—If a qualified accelerated death benefit (as defined in paragraph (d) of this section) is added to a life insurance contract at any time—

(i) The addition of the benefit has no effect on the date that the contract was issued or entered into for purposes of section 7702; and

(ii) Paragraph (b)(2)(i) of this section shall apply to the qualified accelerated death benefit.

(4) *Addition of other additional benefits.*—If an additional benefit described in paragraph (f) of this section is added to a life insurance contract at any time—

(i) The addition of the benefit has no effect on the date that the contract was issued or entered into for purposes of section 7702; and

(ii) The benefit is not treated as cash value under section 7702. [Reg. § 1.7702-2.]

§ 1.7702A-1. Addition of certain benefits.—(a) *Addition of certain benefits before July 1, 1993.*—(1) *No effect on date of issuance.*—If a benefit or loan payable only in the event the insured becomes terminally ill (as defined in § 1.7702-2(e)), or an additional benefit (other than a qualified additional benefit) or loan payable solely upon the occurrence of a morbidity risk, is added to a life insurance contract before July 1, 1993, the addition of the benefit or loan provision has no effect on the date that the contract was issued or entered into for purposes of section 7702A.

(2) *No material change.*—If a benefit or loan provision described in paragraph (a)(1) of this section is added to a life insurance contract before July 1, 1993, the addition of the benefit is not treated as a material change under section 7702A(c)(3).

(3) *Special rule for addition of benefit or loan provision after December 15, 1992.*—This paragraph (a) applies with respect to a benefit or loan provision added to a life insurance contract after December 15, 1992, only if the insurer can demonstrate that the benefit or loan provision was available under a life insurance contract issued within the United States as of December 15, 1992.

(b) *Addition of qualified accelerated death benefit.*—If a qualified accelerated death benefit (as defined in § 1.7702-2(d)) is added to a life insurance contract at any time—

(1) The addition of the benefit has no effect on the date that the contract was issued or entered into for purposes of section 7702A; and

(2) The addition of the benefit is not treated as a material change under section 7702A(c)(3).

(c) *Addition of other additional benefits.*—If an additional benefit described in § 1.7702-2(f) is added to a life insurance contract at any time—

(1) The addition of the benefit has no effect on the date that the contract was issued or entered into for purposes of section 7702A; and

(2) The addition of the benefit is not treated as a material change under section 7702A(c)(3). [Reg. § 1.7702A-1.]

Employment Taxes: Certified Professional Employer Organizations

Employment Taxes: Certified Professional Employer Organizations.—Reg. §§ 301.7705-1 and 301.7705-2, setting forth the Federal employment tax liabilities and other obligations of persons certified by the IRS as certified professional employer organizations (CPEOs) in accordance with provisions enacted as part of The Stephen Beck, Jr., Achieving a Better Life Experience Act of 2014, are proposed (published in the Federal Register on May 6, 2016) (REG-127561-15).

Par. 4. Sections 301.7705-1 and 301.7705-2 are added to read as follows:

§ 301.7705-1. Certified professional employer organization.—(a) The definitions set forth in this section apply for purposes of this section, §§ 31.3511-1 and 301.7705-2, and sections 3302(h), 3303(a)(4), 6053(c)(8), and 7528(b)(4).

(b) [The text of proposed § 301.7705-1(b)(1) through (2) is the same as the text of § 301.7705-1T(b)(1) through (2) as added by T.D. 9768].

(3) *CPEO contract* means a service contract between a CPEO and a customer that is in writing and provides that, with respect to an individual providing services to the customer, the CPEO will—

(i) Assume responsibility for payment of wages to the individual, without regard to the receipt or adequacy of payment from the customer for the services;

(ii) Assume responsibility for reporting, withholding, and paying any applicable federal employment taxes with respect to the individual's wages, without regard to the receipt or adequacy of payment from the customer for the services;

(iii) Assume responsibility for any employee benefits that the service contract may require the CPEO to provide to the individual, without regard to the receipt or adequacy of payment from the customer for such benefits;

(iv) Assume responsibility for recruiting, hiring, and firing the individual in addition to the customer's responsibility for recruiting, hiring, and firing the individual;

(v) Maintain employee records relating to the individual; and

(vi) Agree to be treated as a CPEO for purposes of section 3511 with respect to the individual.

(4) [The text of proposed § 301.7705-1(b)(4) is the same as the text of § 301.7705-1T(b)(4) as added by T.D. 9768].

(5) *Covered employee* means, with respect to a customer, any individual (other than a self-employed individual, as defined in paragraph (b)(14) of this section) who performs services for the customer and who is covered by a CPEO contract between the CPEO and the customer.

(6) *Customer.*—(i) *In general.*—Except as provided in paragraph (b)(6)(ii) of this section, a customer is any person who enters into a CPEO contract with a CPEO.

(ii) *Persons who are not customers.*—A provider of employment-related services that uses its own EIN for filing federal employment tax returns on behalf of its clients (or who used its own EIN immediately prior to entering into a CPEO contract with the CPEO) is not a customer, even if it has entered into a CPEO contract with the CPEO.

(7) [The text of proposed §301.7705-1(b)(7) through (13) is the same as the text of §301.7705-1T(b)(7) through (13) as added by T.D. 9768].

(14) *Self-employed individual* means an individual with net earnings from self-employment (as defined in section 1402(a) and without regard to the exceptions thereunder) derived from providing services covered by a CPEO contract, whether such net earnings from self-employment are derived from providing services as a non-employee to a customer of the CPEO, from the individual's own trade or business as a sole proprietor customer of the CPEO, or as an individual who is a partner in a partnership that is a customer of the CPEO, but only with regard to such net earnings.

(15) [The text of proposed §301.7705-1(b)(15) is the same as the text of §301.7705-1T(b)(15) as added by T.D. 9768].

(16) *Work site* means a physical location at which an individual regularly performs services for a customer of a CPEO or, if there is no such location, the location from which the customer assigns work to the individual. A work site may not be the individual's residence or a telework site unless the customer requires the individual to work at that site. For purposes of this paragraph (b)(16), work sites that are contiguous locations will be treated as a single physical location and thus a single work site, and noncontiguous locations that are not reasonably proximate will be treated as separate physical locations and thus separate work sites. A CPEO may treat noncontiguous locations that are reasonably proximate as a single physical location and thus a single work site. Any two work sites that are separated by 35 or more miles or that operate in a different industry or industries will not be treated as reasonably proximate for purposes of this paragraph (b)(16).

(17) *Work site employee.*—(i) *In general.*—A work site employee means, with respect to a customer, a covered employee who performs services for such customer at a work site where at least 85 percent of the individuals performing services for the customer are covered employees of the customer.

(ii) *Self-employed individuals.*—Solely for purposes of determining whether the 85 percent threshold described in paragraph (b)(17)(i) of this section is met, a self-employed individual described in paragraph (b)(14) of this section is treated as a covered employee if such individual would be a covered employee but for the exclusion of self-employed individuals from the definition of covered employee in paragraph (b)(5) of this section.

(iii) *Excluded employees.*—In determining whether the 85 percent threshold described in paragraph (b)(17)(i) of this section is met, an individual that is an excluded employee described in section 414(q)(5) is not treated either as an individual providing services or a covered employee.

(iv) *Treatment for calendar quarter.*—A covered employee will be considered a work site employee for the entirety of a calendar quarter if the employee qualifies as a work site employee at any time during that quarter.

(v) *Separate determination for each work site.*—The determination of whether a covered employee is a work site employee is made separately with regard to each work site at which the covered employee regularly provides services and for each customer for which the covered employee is providing services. A covered employee may be determined to be a work site employee of more than one work site during a calendar quarter.

(c) [The text of proposed §301.7705-1(c)(1) is the same as the text of §301.7705-1T(c)(1) as added by T.D. 9768].

(2) *Definitions related to section 3511.*—Paragraphs (b)(3), (5), (6), (14), (16), and (17) of this section are applicable on the date of publication of the Treasury decision adopting these rules as final or temporary regulations. [Reg. §301.7705-1.]

§301.7705-2. CPEO certification process.—[The text of proposed §301.7705-2 is the same as the text of §301.7705-2T as added by T.D. 9768]. [Reg. §301.7705-2.]

GENERAL RULES

Indian Tribal Governments

Indian Tribal Governments: Treatment as States.—Temporary Reg. §305.7871-1, relating to the treatment of Indian tribal governments as states, is also proposed as a final regulation (published in the Federal Register on May 7, 1984).

§305.7871-1. Indian tribal governments treated as States for certain purposes.

Below Market Loans

Below Market Loans: Interest.—Reproduced below are the texts of proposed Reg. §§1.7872-1—1.7872-14, 20.7872-1 and 25.7872-1, relating to the tax treatment of both lender and borrower in certain below-market interest rate loan transactions (published in the Federal Register on August 20, 1985; proposed Reg. §1.7872-4(e) was reproposed in the Federal Register on April 8, 1986).

☐ New §1.7872-1 is added in the appropriate place. This new section reads as follows:

§1.7872-1. Introduction.—(a) *Statement of purpose.*—Section 7872 generally treats certain loans in which the interest rate charged is less than the applicable Federal rate as economically equivalent to loans bearing interest at the applicable Federal rate, coupled with a payment by the lender to the borrower sufficient to fund all or part of the payment of interest by the borrower. Such loans are referred to as "below-market loans." See §1.7872-3 for detailed definitions of below-market loans and the determination of the applicable Federal rate.

Accordingly, section 7872 recharacterizes a below-market loan as two transactions:

(1) An arm's-length transaction in which the lender makes a loan to the borrower in exchange for a note requiring the payment of interest at the applicable Federal rate; and

(2) A transfer of funds by the lender to the borrower ("imputed transfer").

The timing and the characterization of the amount of the imputed transfer by the lender to the borrower are determined in accordance with the substance of the transaction. The timing and the amount of the imputed interest payment (the excess of the amount of interest required to be paid using the applicable Federal rate, *over* the amount of interest required to be paid according to the loan agreement) by the borrower to the lender depend on the character of the imputed transfer by the lender to the borrower and whether the loan is a term loan or a demand loan. If the imputed transfer by the lender is characterized as a gift, the provisions of chapter 12 of the Internal Revenue Code, relating to gift tax, also apply. All imputed transfers under section 7872 (*e.g.*, interest, compensation, gift) are characterized in accordance with the substance of the transaction, and, except as otherwise provided in the regulations under section 7872, are treated as so characterized for all purposes of the Code. For example, for purposes of section 170, an interest-free loan to a charity referred to in section 170 for which interest is imputed under section 7872, is treated as an interest bearing loan coupled with periodic gifts to the charity in the amount of the imputed transfer, for purposes of section 170. In addition, all applicable information and reporting requirements (*e.g.*, reporting on W-2 and Form 1099) must be satisfied.

(b) *Effective date.*—(1) *In general.*—The provisions of section 7872 generally apply, for periods after June 6, 1984, to demand loans outstanding after that date and to loans other than demand loans made after that date.

(2) *Demand loans repaid before September 17, 1984.*—If a demand loan which was outstanding on June 6, 1984, is repaid before September 17, 1984, section 7872 does not apply to the loan. For purposes of this paragraph (b)(2) only, a loan is treated as repaid if it is repaid, cancelled, forgiven, modified, or otherwise retired. For example, if the loan agreement for an interest-free demand loan, which is outstanding on June 6, 1984, is modified on September 10, 1984, to require the borrower to pay a 5 percent simple rate of interest, then for purposes of this paragraph (b)(2) the original loan is treated as repaid on September 10, 1984, and section 7872 applies to the modified loan beginning on that date.

(3) *Change in loan agreement.*—For purposes of section 7872, any loan which is renegotiated, extended, or revised after June 6, 1984, is treated as a loan made after June 6, 1984. Accordingly, for purposes of the effective date provisions of this paragraph (b) in the case of such a loan, the provisions of section 7872 apply as if the loan were a new loan made on the day the lender and borrower enter into a binding agreement to change the provisions of the loan.

(4) *Other Federal tax consequences.*—Section 7872 does not alter the law applicable to below-market loans for periods prior to the effective date of section 7872. Accordingly, below-market interest rate loans which are not subject to section 7872 by reason of the effective date provisions of this paragraph (b), including loans which are repaid under the rule described in paragraph (b)(2) of this section, may still have Federal tax consequences. See, *e.g.*, *Dickman v. Commissioner*, 465 U.S. — (1984), 104 S. Ct. 1086.

(c) *Key to Code provisions.*—The following key is intended to facilitate research with respect to specific Code provisions. The key identifies the regulations section in which the principal discussion of a particular Code provision appears. As a result of the interrelationship among Code provisions, other regulation sections may also discuss the particular Code provision. Section 1.7872-2 deals with the definition of the term "loan" for purposes of section 7872. The following table identifies the provisions of section 7872 that are dealt with in §§1.7872-2 through 1.7872-14 and lists each provision of Code section 7872 below the regulation section in which it is covered.

§1.7872-2		
(f)	(8)	

§1.7872-3		
(e)	(1)	
(f)	(2)	
(g)	(1)	(A)

§1.7872-4		
(c)	(1)	
(f)	(3)	

§1.7872-5		
(g)	(1)	(C)

§1.7872-6	
(a)	
(d)	(2)

§1.7872-7	
(b)	
(d)	(2)
(f)	(1)
(f)	(4)
(f)	(10)

§1.7872-8	
(c)	(2)
(d)	(1)

§1.7872-9	
(c)	(3)
(f)	(10)

§1.7872-10	
(f)	(5)
(f)	(6)

§1.7872-11		
(f)	(7)	
(f)	(9)	
(g)	(1)	(A)
(g)	(1)	(B)

§1.7872-12			§1.7872-13		§1.7872-14		
(e)	(1)	(A)	(e)	(2)	(e)	(1)	(B)
					(f)	(1)	

See §20.7872-1 for regulations under section 7872(g)(2).

See §25.7872-1 for gift tax regulations.

See §53.4941(d)-2 for interest-free loans between private foundations and disqualified persons. [Reg. §1.7872-1.]

☐ New §20.7872-1 is added in the appropriate place to read as follows:

§20.7872-1. Certain below-market loans.—For purposes of chapter 11 of the Internal Revenue Code, relating to estate tax, a gift term loan (within the meaning of §1.7872-4(b)) that is made after June 6, 1984, shall be valued at the lesser of:

(a) the unpaid stated principal, plus accrued interest; or

(b) the sum of the present value of all payments due under the note (including accrual interest), using the applicable Federal rate for loans of a term equal to the remaining term of the loan in effect at the date of death.

No discount is allowed based on evidence that the loan is uncollectible unless the facts concerning collectibility of the loan have changed significantly since the time the loan was made. This section applies with respect to any term loan made with donative intent after June 6, 1984, regardless of the interest rate under the loan agreement, and regardless of whether that interest rate exceeds the applicable Federal rate in effect on the day on which the loan was made. [Reg. §20.7872-1.]

☐ New §25.7872-1 is added in the appropriate place to read as follows:

§25.7872-1. Certain below-market loans.—For purposes of Chapter 12 of the Internal Revenue Code, relating to gift tax, if a taxpayer makes a gift loan (within the meaning of §1.7872-4(b)) that is a term loan (within the meaning of §1.7872-10(a)(2)) and that is made after June 6, 1984, the excess of the amount loaned over the present value of all payments which are required to be made under the terms of the loan agreement shall be treated as a gift from the lender to the borrower on the date the loan is made. If a taxpayer makes a gift loan that is a demand loan (within the meaning of §1.7872-10(a)(1)) and that is outstanding during any calendar period after June 6, 1984, and not repaid before September 17, 1984, the amount of foregone interest (within the meaning of section 7872(e)(2)) attributable to that calendar period shall be treated as a gift from the lender to the borrower. The *de minimis* exception described in section 7872(c)(2) applies to the gift tax treatment of a gift loan. In the case of a term gift loan, however, once section 7872 applies to the loan, the *de minimis* exception will not apply to the loan at some later date regardless of whether the aggregate outstanding amount of loans does not continue to exceed the limitation amount. For a detailed analysis of section 7872, see the income tax regulations under section 7872, §1.7872-1 through §1.7872-14. [Reg. §25.7872-1.]

☐ New §§1.7872-2 through 1.7872-14 are added in the appropriate place. These new sections read as follows:

§1.7872-2. Definition of loan.—(a) *In general.*—(1) *"Loan" interpreted broadly.*—For purposes of section 7872, the term "loan" includes generally any extension of credit (including, for example, a purchase money mortgage) and any transaction under which the owner of money permits another person to use the money for a period of time after which the money is to be transferred to the owner or applied according to an express or implied agreement with the onwer. The term "loan" is interpreted broadly to implement the anti-abuse intent of the statute. An integrated series of transactions which is the equivalent of a loan is treated as a loan. A payment for property, goods, or services under a contract, however, is not a loan merely because one of the payor's remedies for breach of the contract is recovery of the payment. Similarly, a bona fide prepayment made in a manner consistent with normal commercial practices for services, property, or the use of property, generally, is not a loan; see section 461 and the regulations thereunder for the treatment of certain prepaid expenses and for the special rules of sections 461(h) and (i). However, a taxpayer's characterization of a transaction as a prepayment or as a loan is not conclusive. Transactions will be characterized for tax purposes according to their economic substance, rather than the terms used to describe them. Thus, for example, receipt by a partner from a partnership of money is treated as a loan if it is so characterized under §1.731-1(c)(2).

(2) *Limitations on applicability of section 7872.*—(i) *In general.*—Section 7872 applies only to certain below-market loans (as defined in section 7872(e)(1)). Section 1.7872-4 lists the categories of below-market loans to which section 7872 generally applies. Certain below-market loans within these categories, however, are exempt from the provisions of section 7872. See §1.7872-5 for specific exemptions from the rules.

(ii) *Loans to which section 483 or 1274 applies.*—Generally, section 7872 does not apply to any loan which is given in consideration for the sale or exchange of property (within the meaning of section 1274(c)(1)) or paid on account of the sale or exchange of property (within the meaning of section 483(c)(1)), even if the rules of those sections do not apply by reason of exceptions or safe harbor provisions. Any transaction, however, which otherwise is described in section 7872(c)(1)(A), (B), or (C), and is—

(A) a debt instrument that is issued in exchange for property and that is payable on demand.

(B) A debt instrument described in section 1273(b)(3), or

(C) A debt instrument described in section 1275(b), unless the transaction is described in § 1.7872-5(b)(1),

not subject to sections 483 and 1274 and is subject to section 7872.

(iii) *Relation to section 482.*—If a below-market loan subject to section 7872 would also be subject to section 482 if the Commissioner chose to apply section 482 to the loan transaction, then section 7872 will be applied first. If the Commissioner chooses to apply section 482, then the loan transaction is subject to section 482 in addition to section 7872.

(3) *Loan proceeds transferred over time.*—In general, each extension of credit or transfer of money by a lender to a borrower is treated as a separate loan. Accordingly, if the loan agreement provides that the lender will transfer the loan proceeds to the borrower in installments, each installment payment is treated as a separate loan. Similarly, in the case of a loan in which the transfer of the loan proceeds to the borrower is subject to a draw-down restriction, each draw-down of loan proceeds is treated as a separate loan.

(b) *Examples of transactions treated as loans.*—(1) *Refundable deposits.*—(i) *In general.*—If an amount is treated for Federal tax purposes as a deposit rather than as a prepayment or an advance payment, the amount is treated as a loan for purposes of section 7872.

(ii) *Partially refundable deposits.*—If an amount is treated for Federal tax purposes as a deposit rather than as a prepayment or an advance payment and the amount is refundable only for a certain period of time or is only partially refundable, then the deposit is treated as a loan only to the extent that it is refundable and only for the period of time that it is refundable.

(iii) *Exception.*—Paragraph (b)(1)(i) does not apply if the deposit is custodial in nature or is held in trust for the benefit of the transferor. The deposit is treated as custodial in nature if the transferee is not entitled to the beneficial enjoyment of the amount deposited including interest thereon (except as security for an obligation of the transferor). Thus, if an amount is placed in escrow to secure a contractual obligation of the transferor, and the escrow agreement provides that all interest earned is paid to the transferor and that the transferee has no rights to or interest in the escrowed amount unless and until the transferor defaults on the obligation, then, in the absence of any facts which indicate that the transaction was entered into for tax avoidance purposes, the deposit is not a loan.

(2) *Permitting agent or intermediary to retain funds.*—An agreement under which an agent or intermediary is permitted to retain possession of money for a period of time before transferring the money to his or her principal is treated as a loan for purposes of section 7872. For example, a taxpayer who enters into an agreement with a broker under which the broker may retain possession of the proceeds from the sale of the taxpayer's property (*e.g.*, securities issued by the taxpayer) for a period of time and uses or invests those funds (other than for the taxpayer's account) is treated as making a loan to the broker for the period of time that the broker retains possession of the proceeds.

(3) *Advances.*—An advance of money to a employee, salesman, or other similar person to defray anticipated expenditures is not treated as a loan for purposes of section 7872 if the amount of money advanced is reasonably calculated not to exceed the anticipated expenditures and if the advance of money is made on a day within a reasonable period of time of the day that the anticipated expenditure will be incurred. An advance or draw of money against a partner's distributive share of income which is treated in the manner described in § 1.731-1(a)(1)(ii) is not a loan for purposes of section 7872. [Reg. § 1.7872-2.]

§ 1.7872-3. Definition of below-market loans.—(a) *In general.*—Section 7872 does not impute interest on loans which require the payment of interest at the applicable Federal rate. This section defines the applicable Federal rate and provides rules for determining whether an interest-bearing loan provides sufficient stated interest to avoid classification as a below-market loan. The term "below-market loan" means any loan if—

(1) In the case of a demand loan, interest is payable at a rate less than the applicable Federal rate; or

(2) In the case of a term loan, the amount loaned exceeds the present value of all payments due under the loan, determined as of the day the loan is made, using a discount rate equal to the applicable Federal rate in effect on the day the loan is made.

Sections 1.7872-13 and 1.7872-14 contain the computations necessary for determining the amount of imputed interest on a below-market loan which is subject to section 7872.

(b) *Applicable Federal rate.*—(1) *In general.*—The applicable Federal rate is an annual stated rate of interest based on semiannual compounding. In addition, the Commissioner may prescribe equivalent rates based on compounding periods other than semiannual compounding (for example, annual compounding, quarterly compounding, and monthly compounding), to facilitate application of this section to loans other than those involving semiannual payments or compounding. Thus, loans providing for annual payments or annual compounding of interest over the entire life of the loan will use the applicable Federal rates based on annual compounding; loans providing for quarterly payments or quarterly compounding over the entire life of the loan will use the applicable Federal rates based on quarterly compounding; and loans providing for monthly payments or monthly compounding over the entire life of the loan will use the applicable Federal rates based on monthly compounding. The shorter of the compounding period or the payment interval determines which rate is appropriate. Loans providing for payments or compounding of interest at other intervals (*e.g.*, daily, weekly, bi-monthly) may use the applicable Federal rates published by the Commissioner based on the shortest compounding period that is longer than the shorter of the compounding period or the payment interval provided for over the entire life of the loan. Thus, loans providing for daily or weekly payments or compounding of interest may use the applicable Federal rate based on monthly compounding; loans providing for bi-monthly payments or compounding of interest will use the applicable Federal rates based on quarterly compounding; etc. Alternatively, taxpayers may compute and use interest rates other than those published by the Commissioner for other interest payment or compounding periods if such rates are equivalent to the applicable Federal rates. Any reference to the applicable Federal rate in the regulations under section 7872 includes the equivalent rates based on different compounding or payment periods.

(2) *Determination of applicable Federal rate.*—(i) *In general.*—The applicable Federal rate for loans described in paragraphs (b)(3), (4), and (5) of this section is defined by reference to Federal statutory rates and alternate Federal rates.

(ii) *Definition of Federal statutory rate.*—The Federal statutory rates are the short-, mid-, and long-term rates in effect under section 1274(d) and their equivalent rates based on different compounding assumptions. These rates are published by the Commissioner for each semiannual period January 1 through June 30 and July 1 through December 31.

(iii) *Definition of alternate Federal rate.*—The alternate Federal rates are the short-, mid-, and long-term rates established by the Commissioner on a monthly basis, and their equivalent rates based on different compounding assumptions. These rates are published by the Commissioner on a monthly basis.

(iv) *Definition of semiannual period.*—For purposes of section 7872 and the regulations thereunder, the first semiannual period means the period in any calendar year beginning on January 1 and ending on June 30, and the second semiannual period means the period in any calendar year beginning on July 1 and ending on December 31.

(3) *Demand loans.*—(i) *In general.*—In the case of a demand loan, the applicable Federal rate for a semiannual period (January 1 through June 30 or July 1 through December 31), is the lower of:

(A) The Federal statutory short-term rate in effect for the semiannual period; or

(B) The special rate for demand loans described in paragraph (b)(3)(ii) of this section.

(ii) *Special rate for demand loans.*—The special rate for demand loans is—

(A) For the semiannual period in which the loan is made, the alternate Federal short-term rate which is in effect on the day the loan is made; and

(B) For each subsequent semiannual period in which the loan is outstanding, the alternate Federal short-term rate which is in effect for the first month of that semiannual period (*i.e.,* January or July).

For a special safe harbor rule for certain variable interest rate demand loans, see paragraph (c)(2) of this section.

(4) *Term loans.*—In the case of a term loan, including a gift term loan or a term loan that is treated as a demand loan as provided in § 1.7872-10(a)(5), the applicable Federal rate is the lower of:

(i) The Federal statutory rate for loans of that term in effect on the day the loan is made; or

(ii) The alternate Federal rate for loans of that term in effect on the day the loan is made.

(5) *Loans conditioned on future services.*—In the case of a term loan that is treated as a demand loan as provided in § 1.7872-10(a)(5), on the date the condition to perform substantial services is removed or lapses, the demand loan is treated as terminated and a new term loan is created. The applicable Federal rate for the new term loan is the lower of the following:

(i) The applicable Federal rate in effect on the day the original loan was made; or

(ii) The applicable Federal rate in effect on the day the condition lapses or is removed.

(6) *Periods before January 1, 1985.*—For term loans made and demand loans outstanding after June 6, 1984, and before January 1, 1985, the applicable Federal rate under section 7872(f)(2) is as follows:

(i) 10.25 percent, compounded annually;

(ii) 10.00 percent, compounded semiannually;

(iii) 9.88 percent, compounded quarterly; and

(iv) 9.80 percent, compounded monthly.

(c) *Loans having sufficient stated interest.*—(1) *In general.*—Section 7872 does not apply to any loan which has sufficient stated interest. A loan has sufficient stated interest if it provides for interest on the outstanding loan balance at a rate no lower than the applicable Federal rate based on a compounding period appropriate for that loan. See paragraph (b)(1) of this section for a description of appropriate compounding periods. See § 1.7872-11(a) for rules relating to waiver of interest.

(2) *Safe harbor for demand loans.*—If the interest rate on a demand loan is changed, either under the terms of the original loan agreement, or subsequently, the loan will be treated as a new loan for purposes of determining the applicable Federal rate for that loan. Thus, the loan will have sufficient stated interest for the remainder of the semiannual period following such change of interest rate if the new interest rate is not less than the lower of the Federal statutory short-term rate in effect for the semiannual period or the alternate Federal short-term rate in effect on the day the new interest rate takes effect.

(3) *Examples.*—The provisions of this paragraph (c) may be illustrated by the following examples.

Example (1). On December 1, 1984, A makes a $100,000 5-year gift term loan to B, requiring 10 interest payments of $5,000 each, payable on May 31 and November 30 of each year the loan is outstanding. Since the loan requires semiannual interest payments, the appropriate compounding assumption is semiannual compounding. For term loans made during 1984, the applicable Federal rate based on semiannual compounding is 10 percent. The loan is not a below-market loan because it provides for interest at a rate of 10 percent, payable semiannually.

Example (2). Assume the same facts as in Example (1), except the loan requires 5 annual interest payments of $10,000 each, payable on November 30 of each year the loan is outstanding. Since the loan requires annual interest payments, the appropriate compounding assumption is annual compounding. The loan is a below-market loan because, although interest is stated at a rate of 10 percent, a rate that reflects semiannual compounding is not appropriate for a loan with annual payments.

Example (3). Assume the same facts as in Example (2), except that the loan requires 5 annual interest payments of $10,250 each, payable on November 30 of each year that the loan is outstanding. Since the loan requires annual interest payments, the appropriate compounding assumption is annual compounding. For term loans made during 1984, the applicable Federal rate based on annual compounding is 10.25 percent. The loan is not a below-market loan because it provides for interest at a rate of 10.25 percent, compounded annually.

Example (4). Assume the same facts as in Example (1), except that the loan requires 120 monthly interest payments of $816.67 each, payable on the last calendar day of each month that the loan is outstanding. Since the loan requires monthly interest payments, the appropriate compounding assumption is monthly compounding. The loan is not a below-market loan because it requires monthly payments of interest based on a rate of 9.80 percent, the applicable Federal rate of interest on monthly compounding.

Example (5). (i) A makes a demand loan to her son, B, on April 1, 1985. The loan requires quarterly interest payments due at the end of each calendar quarter at a rate of 10 percent. Assume that on April 1, 1985, the Federal statutory short-term rate in effect is 12 percent, compounded quarterly, and that the alternate Federal short-term rate in effect for the month of April is 10 percent, compounded quarterly. The loan is not a below-market loan for the period April 1, 1985, through June 30, 1985.

(ii) Assume that on July 1, 1985, the Federal sttutory short-term rate in effect is 11 percent, compounded quarterly, and the alternate Federal short-term rate in effect for the month of July is 10.20 percent, compounded quarterly. The loan no longer has sufficient stated interest. If A raises the interest rate to at least 10.20 percent, the loan will have sufficient stated interest and will not be a below-market loan for the period of July 1 through December 31, 1985.

(iii) Assume that on July 1, 1985, A increases the interest rate on the loan to 10.20 percent, a rate equal to the alternate Federal short-term rate in effect for July. Further assume that the alternate Federal short-term rate subsequently decreases so that such rate in effect for the month of August decreases to 10 percent. On August 1, 1985, A lowers the interest rate on this loan to 10 percent and does not change that rate for the remainder of the semiannual period. The loan has sufficient stated interest and will not be a below-market loan for the semiannual period beginning on July 1, 1985, even if the alternate Federal rate is greater than 10 percent for any or all of the four remaining months in the semiannual period ending on December 31, 1985.

(d) *Short periods.*—The rules for determining whether a loan has sufficient stated interest also apply to short periods (*e.g.*, a period that is shorter than the interval between interest payments or interest compounding under the loan which may occur at the beginning or end of the loan). For special computational rules and examples relating to short periods, see § 1.7872-12.

(e) *Variable rates of interest.*—(1) *In general.*— If a loan requires payments of interest calculated at a rate of interest based in whole or in part on an objective index or combination of indices of market interest rates (*e.g.*, a prime rate, the applicable Federal rate, the average yield on government securities as reflected in the weekly Treasury bill rate, the Treasury constant maturity series, or LIBOR (London interbank offered rate)), the loan will be treated as having sufficient stated interest if—

(i) In the case of a term loan, the rate fixed by the index or indices is no lower than the applicable Federal rate, as determined under paragraph (b)(4) of this section (as modified by paragraph (e)(2) of this section), on the date the loan is made; or

(ii) In the case of a demand loan, the interest rate fixed by the index or indices is no lower than the applicable Federal rate, as determined under paragraph (b)(3) of this section, for each semiannual period that the loan is outstanding. See paragraph (e)(2)(i) of this section for rules relating to variable interest rate demand loans the interest rates of which are tied to the applicable Federal rate.

(2) *Special rules.*—(i) *Demand loans tied to the applicable Federal rate.*—A variable rate demand loan will be treated as having sufficient stated interest if, by the terms of the loan agreement, the interest rate cannot be less than the lower of the Federal statutory short-term rate or the alternate Federal short-term rate in effect at the beginning (or, if the agreement so provides, at the end) of the payment or compounding period (whichever is shorter).

(ii) *Applicable Federal rate for variable interest rate term loans.*—For purposes of determining the applicable Federal rate, if a term loan requires payments or compounding of interest based on a variable rate (within the meaning of paragraph (e)(1) of this section), the term of the loan shall be treated as being equal to the longest period of time that exists between the dates that, under the loan agreement, the interest rate charged on the loan is required to be recomputed (whether or not the recomputation results in a rate different from the immediately preceding rate). Thus, for example, in the case of a 10 year term loan that charges interest at a variable rate equal to a rate 2 points above the prime rate, and that requires that the interest rate be adjusted every 18 months to reflect any changes in the prime rate, the applicable Federal rate is determined by treating the loan as having a term of 18 months rather than a term of 10 years. Accordingly, the applicable Federal short-term rate rather than the applicable Federal long-term rate shall apply.

(3) The provisions of paragraph (e)(1) of this section may be illustrated by the following examples:

Example (1). On April 1, 1985, A loans $200,000 to B, repayable on demand. The note calls for interest to be paid semiannually on September 30 and March 31 of each year at a rate equal to the alternate Federal short-term rate (based on semiannual compounding) for the month in which the payment is made. The loan has sufficient stated interest.

Example (2). Assume the same facts as in *Example (1)* except that the note calls for interest at a rate equal to the lower of the alternate

Federal short-term rate or the statutory Federal short-term rate (in each case, based on semiannual compounding) for the month in which the payment is made. The loan has sufficient stated interest.

Example (3). Assume the same facts as in *Example (1)* except that interest is computed and compounded at the end of each month at a rate equal to the lower of the alternate Federal short-term rate or the statutory Federal short-term rate (in each case, based on monthly compounding) in effect for that month. Accrued interest is payable semiannually on September 30 and March 31 of each year. The loan has sufficient stated interest.

Example (4). Assume the same facts as in *Example (1)* except that interest is payable at the prime rate of a major lending institution at the time each payment is made. The prime rate is not an index which by its terms cannot be less than the lower of the statutory Federal short-term rate or the alternate Federal short-term rate. Therefore, the loan will be tested for sufficient stated interest in each semiannual period under the rules of paragraph (b)(3) of this section.

(f) *Contingent interest.*—[RESERVED] [Reg. § 1.7872-3.]

§ 1.7872-4. Types of below-market loans.—(a) *In general.*—Section 7872 applies only to certain categories of below-market loans. These categories are gift loans, compensation-related loans, corporation-shareholder loans, tax avoidance loans, and certain other loans classified in the regulations under section 7872 as significant tax effect loans (*i.e.,* loans whose interest arrangements have a significant effect on any Federal tax liability of the lender or the borrower).

(b) *Gift loans.*—(1) *In general.*—The term "gift loan" means any below-market loan in which the foregoing of interest is in the nature of a gift within the meaning of Chapter 12 of the Internal Revenue Code (whether or not the lender is a natural person).

(2) *Cross reference.*—See § 1.7872-8 for special rules limiting the application of section 7872 to gift loans. See paragraph (g) of this section for rules with respect to below-market loans which are indirectly gift loans.

(c) *Compensation-related loans.*—(1) *In general.*—A compensation-related loan is a below-market loan that is made in connection with the performance of services, directly or indirectly, between—

(i) An employer and an employee,

(ii) An independent contractor and a person for whom such independent contractor provides services, or

(iii) A partnership and a partner if the loan is made in consideration for services performed by the partner acting other than in his capacity as a member of the partnership.

The imputed transfer (amount of money treated as transferred) by the lender to the borrower is compensation. For purposes of this section, the term "in connection with the performance of services" has the same meaning as the term has for purposes of section 83. A loan from a qualified pension, profit-sharing, or stock bonus plan to a participant of the plan is not, directly or indirectly, a compensation-related loan.

(2) *Loan in part in exchange for services.*—Except as provided in paragraph (d)(2) of this section (relating to a loan from a corporation to an employee who is also a shareholder of the corporation), a loan which is made in part in exchange for services and in part for other reasons is treated as a compensation-related loan for purposes of section 7872(c)(3) only if more than 25 percent of the amount loaned is attributable to the performance of services. If 25 percent or less of the amount loaned is attributable to the performance of services, the loan is not subject to section 7872 by reason of being a compensation-related loan. The loan may, however, be subject to section 7872 by reason of being a below-market loan characterized other than as a compensation-related loan (*e.g.,* corporation-shareholder loan or tax avoidance loan). If—

(i) a loan is characterized as a "compensation-related" loan under this paragraph (c),

(ii) less than 100 percent of the amount loaned is attributable to the performance of services, and

(iii) the portion of the amount loaned that is not attributable to the performance of services is not subject to section 7872,

then the amounts of imputed transfer (as defined in § 1.7872-1(a)(2)) and imputed interest (as defined in § 1.7872-1(a)) are determined only with respect to that part of the loan which is attributable to services. All of the facts and circumstances surrounding the loan agreement and the relationship between the lender and the borrower are taken into account in determining the portion of the loan made in exchange for services.

(3) *Third-party lender as agent.*—A below-market loan by an unrelated third-party lender to an employee is treated as attributable to the performance of services if, taking into account all the facts and circumstances, the transaction is in substance a loan by the employer made with the aid of a third-party lender acting as an agent of the employer. Among the facts and circumstances which indicate whether such a loan has been made is whether the employer bears the risk of default at and immediately after the time the loan is made. The principles of this paragraph (c)(3) also apply with respect to a below-market loan by an unrelated third-party lender to an independent contractor.

(4) *Special rule for continuing care facilities.*—Any loan to a continuing care facility will not be treated, in whole or in part, as a compensation-related loan.

(5) *Cross-references.*—For a special rule in the case of a below-market loan that could be characterized as both a compensation-related loan and a corporation-shareholder loan, see paragraph (d)(2) of this section. See paragraph (g) of this section for rules with respect to below-market loans which are indirectly compensation-related loans.

(d) *Corporation-shareholder loans.*—(1) *In general.*—A below-market loan is a corporation-shareholder loan if the loan is made directly or indirectly between a corporation and any shareholder of the corporation. The amount of money treated as transferred by the lender to the borrower is a distribution of money (characterized according to section 301 or, in the case of an S corporation, section 1368) if the corporation is the lender, or a contribution to capital if the shareholder is the lender.

(2) *Special rule.*—A below-market loan—

(i) from a publicly held corporation to an employee of the corporation who is also a shareholder owning directly or indirectly more than 0.5 percent of the total voting power of all classes of stock entitled to vote or more than 0.5 percent of the total value of shares of all other classes of stock or 0.5 percent of the total value of shares of all other classes of stock or 5 percent of the total value of shares of all classes of stock (including voting stock) of the corporation; or

(ii) from a corporation that is not a publicly held corporation to an employee of the corporation who is also a shareholder owning directly or indirectly more than 5 percent of the total voting power of all classes of stock entitled to vote or more than 5 percent of the total number of shares of all other classes of stock or 5 percent of the total value of shares of all classes of stock (including voting stock) of the corporation;

will be presumed to be a corporation-shareholder loan, in the absence of clear and convincing evidence that the loan is made solely in connection with the performance of services. For purposes of determining the percentage of direct and indirect stock ownership, the constructive ownership rules of section 267(c) apply.

(3) *Cross-reference.*—See paragraph (g) of this section for rules with respect to below-market loans which are indirectly corporation-shareholder loans.

(e) *Tax avoidance loans.*—(1) *In general.*—A tax avoidance loan is any below-market loan one of the principal purposes for the interest arrangements of which is the avoidance of Federal tax with respect to either the borrower or the lender, or both. For purposes of this rule, tax avoidance is a principal purpose of the interest arrangements if a principal factor in the decision to structure the transaction as a below-market loan (rather than, for example, as a market interest rate loan and a payment by the lender to the borrower) is to reduce the Federal tax liability of the borrower or the lender or both. The purpose for entering into the transaction (for example, to make a gift or to pay compensation) is irrelevant in determining whether a principal purpose of the interest arrangements of the loan is the avoidance of Federal tax.

(2) *Certain loans incident to sales or exchanges.*—If, pursuant to a plan that is incident to a sale or exchange of property, a party who is related (within the meaning of section 168(e)(4)(D)) to the seller—

(i) Makes a below-market loan to the buyer of the property, or

(ii) Makes a below-market loan to the seller that is assumed by the buyer in connection with the sale or exchange,

then the loan shall be treated as a tax avoidance loan within the meaning of paragraph (e)(1) of this section. There shall be an irrebuttable presumption that such a plan exists if such a loan is made within one year of the sale or exchange.

(3) *Examples.*—The provisions of paragraph (e) of this section may be illustrated by the following examples:

Example (1). (i) S and T are each wholly-owned subsidiaries of P. S sells property to an individual, A, for cash of $3,000,000. Three months after the sale, T loans to A $2,000,000 for 10 years at an interest rate of 6%, payable semiannually. On the date the loan is made, the Federal long-term rate is 12%, compounded semiannually.

(ii) The loan from T to A is a tax avoidance loan pursuant to paragraph (e)(2) of this section. The issue price of the debt instrument given in exchange for the loan is $1,311,805, and the total amount of foregone interest is $688,195. On the date the loan is made, A is treated as having received a refund of $688,195 of the purchase price of the property from S, thereby reducing A's basis in the property by this amount. T is treated as having paid a dividend of $688,195 to P, and P is treated as having made a contribution to the capital of S in the same amount.

Example (2). The facts are the same as in example (1), except that T loans the $2,000,000 to S immediately before the sale. A purchases the property for cash of $1,000,000 and assumes S's debt to T. On the date of the sale, the Federal long-term rate is 12%, compounded semiannually. The loan from T to S is a tax-avoidance loan. The issue price of the debt instrument and the amount of foregone interest are the same as in example (1). A's basis in the property is limited to $2,311,805 (see § 1.1274-7(d)). T is treated as having paid a dividend of $688,195 to P, and P is treated as having made a contribution to the capital of S in the same amount.

(f) *Certain below-market loans with significant effect on tax liability ("significant-effect" loans).*—[RESERVED].

(g) *Indirect loans.*—(1) *In general.*—If a below-market loan is made between two persons and, based on all the facts and circumstances, the effect of the loan is to make a gift or a capital contribution or a distribution of money (under section 301 or in the case of an S corporation, section 1368), or to pay compensation to a third person ("indirect participant"), or is otherwise attributable to the relationship of the lender or borrower to the indirect participant, the loan is restructured as two or more successive below-market loans ("deemed loans") for purposes of section 7872, as follows:

(i) A deemed below-market loan made by the named lender to the indirect participant; and

(ii) A deemed below-market loan made by the indirect participant to the borrower.

Section 7872 is applied separately to each deemed loan, and each deemed loan is treated as having the same provisions as the original loan between the lender and the borrower. Thus, for example, if a father makes an interest-free loan to his daughter's corporation, the loan is restructured as a below-market loan from father to daughter (deemed gift loan) and a second below-market loan from daughter to corporation (deemed corporation-shareholder loan). Similarly, if a corporation makes an interest-free loan to another commonly controlled corporation, the loan is restructured as a below-market loan from the lending corporation to the common parent corporation and a second below-market loan from the parent corporation to the borrowing corporation.

(2) *Special rule for intermediaries.*—If a lender and a borrower use another person, such as an individual, a trust, a partnership, or a corporation, as an intermediary or middleman in a loan transaction and a purpose for such use is to avoid the application of section 7872(c)(1)(A),

(B), or (C), the intermediary will be ignored and the loan will be treated as made directly between the lender and the borrower. Thus, for example, if a father and a son arrange their below-market loan transaction by having the father make a below-market loan to the father's partnership, followed by a second below-market loan (with substantially identical terms and conditions as the first loan) made by the partnership to the son, the two below-market loans will be restructured as one below-market loan from the father to the son. [Reg. § 1.7872-4.]

§ 1.7872-5. Exempted loans.—(a) *In general.*—(1) *General rule.*—Except as provided in paragraph (a)(2) of this section, notwithstanding any other provision of section 7872 and the regulations thereunder, section 7872 does not apply to the loans listed in paragraph (b) of this section because the interest arrangements do not have a significant effect on the Federal tax liability of the borrower or the lender.

(2) *No exemption for tax avoidance loans.*—If a taxpayer structures a transaction to be a loan described in paragraph (b) of this section and one of the principal purposes of so structuring the transaction is the avoidance of Federal tax, then the transaction will be recharacterized as a tax avoidance loan as defined in section 7872(c)(1)(D).

(b) *List of exemptions.*—Except as provided in paragraph (a) of this section, the following transactions are exempt from section 7872:

(1) Loans which are made available by the lender to the general public on the same terms and conditions and which are consistent with the lender's customary business practices;

(2) Accounts or withdrawable shares with a bank (as defined in section 581), or an institution to which section 591 applies, or a credit union, made in the ordinary course of its business;

(3) Acquisitions of publicly traded debt obligations for an amount equal to the public trading price at the time of acquisition;

(4) Loans made by a life insurance company (as defined in section 816(a)), in the ordinary course of its business, to an insured, under a loan right contained in a life insurance policy and in which the cash surrender values are used as collateral for the loans;

(5) Loans subsidized by the Federal, State (including the District of Columbia), or Municipal government (or any agency or instrumentality thereof), and which are made available under a program of general application to the public;

(6) Employee-relocation loans that meet the requirements of paragraph (c)(1) of this section;

(7) Obligations the interest on which is excluded from gross income under section 103;

(8) Obligations of the United States government;

(9) Loans to a charitable organization (described in section 170(c)), but only if at no time during the taxable year will the aggregate outstanding amount of loans by the lender to all such organizations exceed $10,000;

(10) Loans made to or from a foreign person that meet the requirements of paragraph (c)(2) of this section;

(11) Loans made by a private foundation or other organization described in section 170(c), the primary purpose of which is to accomplish one or more of the purposes described in section 170(c)(2)(B);

(12) Loans made prior to July 1, 1986, to the extent excepted from the application of section 482 for the 6-month (or longer) period referred to in § 1.482-2(a)(3);

(13) For periods prior to July 1, 1986, all money, securities, and property received by a futures commission merchant or by a clearing organization (i) to margin, guarantee or secure contracts for future delivery on or subject to the rules of a qualified board or exchange (as defined in section 1256(g)(7)), or (ii) to purchase, margin, guarantee or secure options contracts traded on or subject to the rules of a qualified board or exchange, and all money accruing to account holders as the result of such futures and options contracts;

(14) Loans where the taxpayer can show that the below market interest arrangements have no significant effect on any Federal tax liability of the lender or the borrower, as described in paragraph (c)(3) of this section; and

(15) Loans, described in revenue rulings or revenue procedures issued under section 7872(g)(1)(C), if the Commissioner finds that the factors justifying an exemption for such loans are sufficiently similar to the factors justifying the exemptions contained in this section.

(c) *Special rules.*—(1) *Employee-relocation loans.*—(i) *Mortgage loans.*—In the case of a compensation-related loan to an employee, where such loan is secured by a mortgage on the new principal residence (within the meaning of section 217 and the regulations thereunder) of the employee, acquired in connection with the transfer of that employee to a new principal place of work (which meets the requirements in section 217(c) and the regulations thereunder), the loan will be exempt from section 7872 if the following conditions are satisfied:

(A) The loan is a demand loan or is a term loan the benefits of the interest arrangements of which are not transferable by the employee and are conditioned on the future performance of substantial services by the employee;

(B) The employee certifies to the employer that the employee reasonably expects to be entitled to and will itemize deductions for each year the loan is outstanding; and

(C) The loan agreement requires that the loan proceeds be used only to purchase the new principal residence of the employee.

(ii) *Bridge loans.*—In the case of a compensation-related loan to an employee which is not described in paragraph (c)(1)(i) of this section, and which is used to purchase a new principal residence (within the meaning of section 217 and the regulations thereunder) of the employee acquired in connection with the transfer of that employee to a new principal place of work (which meets the requirements in section 217(c) and the regulations thereunder), the loan will be exempt from section 7872 if the following conditions are satisfied:

(A) The conditions contained in paragraphs (c)(1)(i)(A), (B), and (C) of this section;

(B) The loan agreement provides that the loan is payable in full within 15 days after the date of the sale of the employee's immediately former principal residence;

(C) The aggregate principal amount of all outstanding loans described in this paragraph (c)(1)(ii) to an employee is no greater than the employer's reasonable estimate of the amount of the equity of the employee and the employee's spouse in the employee's immediately former principal residence, and

(D) The employee's immediately former principal residence is not converted to business or investment use.

(2) *Below-market loans involving foreign persons.*—(i) Section 7872 shall not apply to a below-market loan (other than a compensation-related loan or a corporation-shareholder loan where the borrower is a shareholder that is not a C corporation as defined in section 1361(a)(2)) if the lender is a foreign person and the borrower is a U.S. person, unless the interest income imputed to the foreign lender (without regard to this paragraph) would be effectively connected with the conduct of a U.S. trade or business within the meaning of section 864(c) and the regulations thereunder and not exempt from U.S. income taxation under an applicable income tax treaty.

(ii) Section 7872 shall not apply to a below-market loan where both the lender and the borrower are foreign persons unless the interest income imputed to the lender (without regard to this paragraph) would be effectively connected with the conduct of a U.S. trade or business within the meaning of section 864(c) and the regulations thereunder and not exempt from U.S. income taxation under an applicable income tax treaty.

(iii) For purposes of this section, the term "foreign person" means any person that is not a U.S. person.

(3) *Loans without significant tax effect.*—Whether a loan will be considered to be a loan the interest arrangements of which have a significant effect on any Federal tax liability of the lender or the borrower will be determined according to all of the facts and circumstances. Among the factors to be considered are—

(i) whether items of income and deduction generated by the loan offset each other;

(ii) the amount of such items;

(iii) the cost to the taxpayer of complying with the provisions of section 7872 if such section were applied, and

(iv) any non-tax reasons for deciding to structure the transaction as a below-market loan rather than a loan with interest at a rate equal to or greater than the applicable Federal rate and a payment by the lender to the borrower. [Reg. § 1.7872-5.]

§ 1.7872-6. Timing and amount of transfers in connection with gift loans and demand loans.—(a) *In general.*—Section 7872(a) and the provisions of this section govern the timing and the amount of the imputed transfer by the lender to the borrower and the imputed interest payment by the borrower to the lender in the case of a below-market demand loan. Section 7872(a) and this section also govern the timing and the amount of the imputed transfer by the lender to the borrower and the imputed interest payment by the borrower to the lender for income tax purposes in the case of term gift loans. (See section 7872(b), 7872(d)(2), and § 1.7872-7 for rules governing the timing and the amount of the imputed transfer by the lender to the borrower in the case of term gift loans for gift tax purposes.) Section 7872(d)(1) and § 1.7872-8 limit the amount of the imputed interest payment with respect to certain gift loans. See § 1.7872-10(a) for rules for distinguishing demand loans from term loans. See § 1.7872-11(f) for special rules governing loans repayable in foreign currency, which apply notwithstanding any contrary rules set forth in this section.

(b) *Time of transfer.*—(1) *In general.*—Except as otherwise provided in paragraphs (b)(3), (4), and (5) of this section, the foregone interest (as defined in section 7872(e)(2) and paragraph (c) of this section) attributable to periods during any calendar year is treated as transferred by the lender to the borrower (and retransferred by the borrower to the lender) on December 31 of that calendar year and shall be treated for tax purposes in a manner consistent with the taxpayer's method of accounting.

(2) *Example.*—Paragraph (b)(1) of this section may be illustrated by the following example.

Example. On January 1, 1985, E makes a $200,000 interest-free demand loan to F, an employee of E. The loan remains outstanding for the entire 1985 calendar year. E has a taxable year ending September 30. F is a calendar year taxpayer. For 1985, the imputed compensation payment and the imputed interest payment (as computed under paragraph (c) of this section) are treated as made on December 31.

(3) *Gift loans between natural persons.*—In the case of gift loans directly between natural persons within the meaning of § 1.7872-8(a)(2), any imputed transfer and any imputed interest payment to which this section applies during the borrower's taxable year is treated, for both the lender and the borrower, as occurring on the last day of the borrower's taxable year.

(4) *Death, liquidation or termination of borrower.*—If the borrower dies (in the case of a borrower who is a natural person) or is liquidated or otherwise terminated (in the case of a borrower other than a natural person), any imputed transfer and any imputed interest payment arising during the borrower's final taxable year are treated, for both the lender and the borrower, as occurring on the last day of the borrower's final taxable year.

(5) *Repayment of loan.*—If a below-market loan is repaid, any imputed transfer and any imputed interest payment arising during the borrower's taxable year which includes the date of repayment is treated, for both the lender and the borrower, as occurring on the day the loan is repaid.

(c) *Amount of transfer.*—In the case of a below-market loan to which section 7872 applies and which is a demand loan (including a term loan that is treated as a demand loan as provided in § 1.7872-10(a)(5)) or a gift term loan, the foregone interest (as computed under the provisions of § 1.7872-13) with respect to the loan is treated as transferred by the lender to the borrower and retransferred as interest by the borrower to the lender. Generally, for any calendar year the term "foregone interest" means the excess of—

(1) The amount of interest that would have been payable in that year if interest had accrued at the applicable Federal rate (as determined in § 1.7872-13); over

(2) Any interest payable on the loan properly allocable to that year. The amount of foregone interest is computed for each day during the period for which section 7872(a) applies to the loan and is treated as transferred and retransferred on the date specified in paragraph (b) of this section. [Reg. § 1.7872-6.]

§ 1.7872-7. Timing and amount of transfers in connection with below-market term loans.—(a) *In general.*—This section governs the Federal income tax consequences of below-market term loans, other than gift term loans or term loans treated as demand loans under the provisions of § 1.7872-10(a)(5), to which section 7872 applies. It also governs the Federal gift tax consequences of below-market gift term loans. See § 1.7872-11(f) for special rules which govern loans repayable in foreign currency and which apply notwithstanding any contrary rules set forth in this section.

(1) *Timing and amount of transfer from lender to borrower.*—In the case of term loans to which this section applies, the amount of the imputed transfer by the lender to the borrower—

(i) is treated as transferred at the time the loan is made and is treated for tax purposes in a manner consistent with the taxpayer's method of accounting; and

(ii) is equal to the excess of—

(A) The amount loaned (as defined in paragraph (a)(4) of this section); over

(B) The present value (as determined in paragraph (a)(5) of this section and § 1.7872-14) of all payments which are required to be made under the terms of the loan agreement, whether express or implied.

(2) *Gift term loans.*—In the case of a gift term loan, the rules of paragraph (a)(1) of this section apply for gift tax purposes only. For rules governing the income tax consequences of gift term loans, see § 1.7872-6.

(3) *Treatment of amount equal to imputed transfer as original issue discount.*—(i) *In general.*—Any below-market loan to which paragraph (a)(1) of this section applies shall be treated as having original issue discount in an amount equal to the amount of the imputed transfer determined under paragraph (a)(1) of this section. This imputed original issue discount is in addition to any other original issue discount on the loan (determined without regard to section 7872(b) or this paragraph). For purposes of applying section 1272 to a loan described in this paragraph, the issue price shall be treated as equal to the stated principal reduced by the amount of the imputed transfer and the yield to maturity is the applicable Federal rate.

(ii) *Example.*—The provisions of this paragraph (a)(3) may be illustrated by the following example.

Example. (i) On June 10, 1984, L lends $45,000 to B, a corporation in which L is a shareholder, for five years in exchange for a $50,000 note bearing interest at a below-market rate. Assume that the present value of all payments that B must make to L is $42,000. This loan is a corporation-shareholder term loan under section 7872(c)(1)(C). Accordingly, the amount of the imputed transfer by L to B is determined under the provisions of section 7872(b).

(ii) On June 10, 1984, L is treated as transferring $3,000 (the excess of $45,000 (amount loaned) over $42,000 (present value of all payments)), in accordance with section 7872(b)(1). This imputed transfer is treated as a contribution to B's capital by L. An amount equal to the imputed transfer is treated as original issue discount. This original issue discount is in addition to the $5,000 ($50,000, the state redemption price, less $45,000, the issue price) of original issue discount otherwise determined under section 1273. As a result, the loan is treated as having a total $8,000 of original issue discount.

(4) *Amount loaned.*—The term "amount loaned" means the amount received by the borrower (determined without regard to section 7872). See § 1.7872-2(a)(3) for the treatment of the transfer of the loan proceeds to the borrower in installments or subject to draw-down restrictions.

(5) *Present value.*—The present value of all payments which are required to be made under the provisions of the loan agreement is computed as of the date the loan is made (or, if later, as of the day the loan first becomes subject to the provisions of section 7872). The discount rate for the present value computation is the applicable Federal rate as defined in § 1.7872-3(b) in effect on the day on which the loan is made. For rules governing the computation of present value, see § 1.7872-14. See also *Example (3)* in § 1.7872-8(b)(5).

(6) *Basis.*—In the case of a term loan the lender's basis in the note received in exchange for lending money is equal to the present value of all payments which are required to be made under the terms of the loan agreement, whether express or implied, with adjustments as provided for in section 1272(d)(2).

(b) *Special rule for the de minimis provisions.*—(1) *In general.*—If as a result of the application of the *de minimis* provisions of section 7872(c)(2) or (3), a loan becomes subject to section 7872 and this section on a day after the day on which the loan is made, the provisions of this section generally apply to the loan as if the loan were made on that later day. The applicable Federal rate applied to this loan (including for purposes of computing the present value of the loan), however, is the applicable Federal rate (as defined in § 1.7872-3(b)) in effect on the day on which the loan is first made. The present value computation described in paragraph (a)(1)(ii)(B) of this section is made as of the day on which section 7872 and this section first apply to the loan. For purposes of making this computation, the term of the loan is equal to the period beginning on the day that section 7872 first applies to the loan and ending on the day on which the loan is to be repaid according to the loan agreement. Any payments payable acording to the loan agreement before the day on which section 7872 and this section first apply to the loans are disregarded.

(2) *Continuing application of section 7872.*—Once section 7872 and this section apply to a term loan, they continue to apply to the loan regardless of whether the *de minimis* provisions of section 7872(c)(2) or (3) apply at some later date. In the case of a gift term loan, this paragraph applies only for gift tax purposes and does not apply for income tax purposes. [Reg. § 1.7872-7.]

§ 1.7872-8. Special rules for gift loans directly between natural persons.—(a) *Special rules for gift loans directly between natural per-*

sons.—(1) *In general*.—Section 7872 (c)(2) and (d) apply special rules to gift loans directly between natural persons if the aggregate outstanding amount of loans (as determined in paragraph (b)(2) of this section) between those natural persons does not exceed specified limitations.

(2) *Loans directly between natural persons*.—(i) For purposes of this section, a loan is made directly between natural persons only if both the lender and borrower are natural persons. For this purpose, a loan by a natural person lender to the guardian (or custodian, in the case of a gift made pursuant to the Uniform Gift to Minors Act) of a natural person is treated as a loan directly between natural persons. If, however, a parent lends money to a trust of which the child is the sole beneficiary, the loan is not treated as directly between natural persons for purposes of this section.

(ii) A gift loan which results from restructuring an indirect loan as two or more loans (as described in § 1.7872-4(g)) and in which natural persons are deemed to be the lender and the borrower is treated as a loan directly between natural persons. Thus, for example, if an employer makes a below-market loan to an employee's child, the loan is restructured as one loan from the employer to the employee, and a second loan from the employee to his child. The deemed gift loan between the employee and the employee's child is treated as directly between natural persons.

(b) *De minimis exception*.—(1) *In general*.—Except as otherwise provided in paragraph (b)(3) of this section or in § 1.7872-7(a) (with respect to the gift tax consequences of a gift term loan to which the provisions of section 7872 have already been applied), in the case of any gift loan directly between natural persons, the provisions of section 7872 do not apply to any loan outstanding on any day in which the aggregate outstanding amount of loans between the lender and borrower does not exceed $10,000. The *de minimis* rule of this paragraph (b)(1) applies with respect to a gift loan even though that loan could also be characterized as a tax avoidance loan within the meaning of section 7872(c)(1)(D) and § 1.7872-4(e).

(2) *Aggregate outstanding amount of loans*.—The aggregate outstanding amount of loans between natural persons is the sum of the principal amounts of outstanding loans directly between the individuals, regardless of the character of the loans, regardless of the interest rate charged on the loans, and regardless of the date on which the loans were made. For this purpose, the principal amount of a loan which is also subject to section 1272 (without applying the limitation of section 1273(a)(3)) is the "adjusted issue price" as that term is defined in section 1272(a)(4). See § 1.7872-7(a)(3)(i) for the determination of the issue price of a loan which is also subject to section 1272.

(3) *Loans attributable to acquisition or carrying of income-producing assets*.—The *de minimis* exception described in paragraph (b)(1) of this section does not apply to any gift loan directly attributable to the purchase or carrying of the income-producing assets. A gift loan is directly attributable to the purchase or carrying of income-producing assets, for example, if the loan proceeds are directly traceable to the purchase of the income-producing assets, the assets are used as collateral for the loan, or there is direct evidence that the loan was made to avoid disposition of the assets.

(4) *Income-producing assets*.—For purposes of this paragraph (b), the term "income-producing asset" means (i) an asset of a type that generates ordinary income, or, (ii) a market discount bond issued before July 19, 1984. Accordingly, an income-producing asset includes, but is not limited to, a business, a certificate of deposit, a savings account, stock (whether or not dividends are paid), bonds and rental property.

(5) *Examples*.—The provisions of this paragraph (b) may be illustrated by the following examples.

Example (1). (i) As of January 1, 1985, the total aggregate outstanding amount of loans by Parent P, to child, C, is $6,000. None of these loans is a below-market loan. On February 1, 1985, P makes a $3,000 below-market demand loan to C. On March 1, 1985, P makes a $2,000 below-market demand loan to C. On November 1, 1985, C repays $1,500 of principal of the market-rate loans to P; all of the other loans remain outstanding as of December 31, 1985. The below-market loans are gift loans and are the only new loans between P and C for calendar year 1985.

(ii) For the periods January 1, 1985, through February 28, 1985, and November 1, 1985, through December 31, 1985, section 7872 does not apply to the loans between P and C because the outstanding loan balance between P and C does not exceed $10,000 during these periods. For the period beginning on March 1, 1985, and ending on October 31, 1985, however, the aggregate outstanding amount of loans directly between P and C exceeds $10,000. Accordingly, the provisions of section 7872(a) apply to the $3,000 gift loan and $2,000 gift loan during that period.

Example (2). (i) Assume the same facts as in Example (1) except that the $2,000 gift loan made on March 1, 1985, is a term loan for a period of five years. The Federal gift tax and income tax consequences of the $3,000 gift demand loan made on February 1, 1985, are the same as in Example (1).

(ii) With respect to the $2,000 gift term loan, section 7872(b)(1) applies beginning on March 1, 1985, for purposes of computing the amount of the imputed gift by P to C. For the period beginning on March 1, 1985, and ending on October 31, 1985, section 7872(a) applies to the $2,000 gift term loan for purposes of determining the amount and the timing of the imputed interest payment by C to P. For the two-monthly period beginning on November 1, 1985, section 7872(a) does not apply to the $2,000 loan for Federal income tax purposes because the outstanding loan balance between P and C does not exceed $10,000 during this period.

Example (3). (i) Assume the same facts as in Example (1) except that the $3,000 gift loan made on February 1, 1985, is a term loan for a period of five years. The Federal gift tax and income tax consequences of the $2,000 demand gift loan made on March 1, 1985, are identical to those in Example (1).

(ii) On February 1, 1985, section 7872 does not apply to the $3,000 loan because the outstanding loan balance between P and C does not exceed $10,000. On March 1, 1985, however, the aggregate outstanding amount of loans between

P and C exceeds $10,000. For Federal gift tax purposes, section 7872(b)(1) applies to the $3,000 loan beginning on March 1, 1985. Under § 1.7872-7(b), the provisions of section 7872 apply to the $3,000 loan for gift and income tax purposes as if the loan had been made on March 1, 1985. See § 1.7872-7(a)(5) for special rules for computing the present value of payments due on the loan. For the eight-month period beginning on March 1, 1985, section 7872(a) applies to the $3,000 loan for purposes of determining the imputed interest payment by C to P. For the two-month period beginning on November 1, 1985, section 7872(a) does not apply to the $3,000 loan for Federal income tax purposes because of the application of the *de minimis* provisions.

Example (4). On June 10, 1984, parent, L, makes an $8,000 interest-free gift term loan to L's child, B. This is the only loan outstanding between L and B during 1984. On June 11, 1984, B invests the $8,000 in corporate stock. The $10,000 *de minimis* provision does not apply to the loan, because the loan proceeds are directly attributable to the purchase of corporate stock, an income-producing asset.

(c) *Limitation on amount of imputed interest payment.*—(1) *In general.*—In the case of a loan between a borrower and a lender both of whom are natural persons (within the meaning of paragraph (a)(2) of this section), for all days during the borrower's taxable year on which the aggregate outstanding amount of loans (within the meaning of paragraph (b)(2) of this section) between the borrower and the lender, is $100,000 or less, the amount of the imputed interest payment by the borrower to the lender with respect to any gift loan is limited to the borrower's net investment income (as determined under paragraph (c)(7) of this section) for the taxable year. This paragraph (c) does not affect the gift tax consequences of any loan under section 7872.

(2) *Tax avoidance loan.*—Paragraph (c)(1) of this section does not apply to any loan which is a tax avoidance loan within the meaning of § 1.7872-4(e).

(3) *No limitation if investment income is manipulated.*—Paragraph (c)(1) of this section does not apply if a borrower can control the timing of the receipt of investment income and actually does manipulate the timing to accelerate or defer the receipt of investment income. For example, if the borrower can, and actually does, control the timing of dividends paid by a closely held corporation, the limitation on the amount of the imputed interest payment does not apply.

(4) *Net investment income of $1,000 or less disregarded.*—If paragraph (c)(1) of this section applies and if the borrower's net investment income (as determined under paragraph (c)(7) of this section) for a taxable year is $1,000 or less, the borrower's net investment income for that year is deemed to be zero for purposes of this paragraph (c).

(5) *No proration of net investment income.*—The entire amount of the borrower's net investment income for a taxable year (as determined under paragraph (c)(7) of this section) is taken into account in determining the maximum imputed interest payment for those days during the year on which the net investment income limitation applies. Accordingly, the amount of net investment income is not allocated among the days of the borrower's taxable year. Further, for a taxable year of a borrower which ends after June 6, 1984, and includes any day or days before June 7, 1984, the entire amount of net investment income for the taxable year is taken into account in determining the maximum imputed interest payment for the days during that year on which the limitation applies.

(6) *Allocation among gift loans.*—In the case of a borrower who has more than one gift loan outstanding during a taxable year, the borrower's net investment income for that year is allocated among the gift loans in proportion to the respective amounts which would be treated as imputed interest payments by the borrower to the lender or lenders with respect to those loans without regard to this paragraph (c). (See Example (2) of paragraph (c)(9) of this section.) No amount of the net investment income is allocable to any gift loan between the lender and the borrower for periods during which the aggregate outstanding amount of loans (within the meaning of paragraph (b)(2) of this section) between the borrower and that lender exceeds $100,000.

(7) *Amounts included in net investment income.*—For purposes of section 7872, net investment income for a taxable year equals the sum of—

(i) Net investment income for that year as determined under section 163(d)(3), excluding any item of income on a deferred payment obligation which is treated under section 7872(d)(1)(E)(iii) and paragraph (c)(7)(ii) of this section as interest received in a prior taxable year ending after June 6, 1984, and

(ii) The amount that is treated under section 7872(d)(1)(E)(iii) as interest received for that year on a deferred payment obligation.

(8) *Deferred payment obligation.*—The term "deferred payment obligation" means a market discount bond issued before July 18, 1984, or an obligation that, if held to maturity, would produce a predictable and regular flow of ordinary income which, under applicable tax rules, is not recognized until a subsequent period. Accordingly, deferred payment obligations include, but are not limited to, those obligations listed in section 7872(d)(1)(E)(iv).

(9) *Examples.*—The provisions of this paragraph (c) may be illustrated by the following examples.

Example (1). On January 1, 1985, parent P makes a $50,000 below-market gift loan to C, P's child, who uses the calendar year as the taxable year. On March 1, 1985, P makes an additional $75,000 market-rate loan to C. On October 1, 1985, C repays $30,000 of the market-rate loan. Assume that C's net investment income (as determined under paragraph (c)(7) of this section) for 1985 is $2,400. The limitation under section 7872(d)(1) on the amount of imputed interest payment applies to the $50,000 loan for the two-month period beginning on January 1, 1985, and the three-month period beginning on October 1, 1985. Accordingly, the imputed interest payment on the $50,000 loan for 1985 may not exceed $2,400.

Example (2). During 1985, natural person borrower B has three gift loans outstanding, each from a different lender. Each loan is eligible for the entire year for the special limitation on the amount of imputed interest payments under section 7872(d)(1) but none of the loans is eligible for the de minimis exception of paragraph (b) of this section. B's net investment income for 1985 is $6,000. The aggregate imputed interest payments on these loans (determined without regard to section 7872(d)(1)) would be $9,000. The amount of imputed interest payment attributable to each loan after application of section 7872(d)(1) is computed as follows:

Loan	Imputed interest payments (before application of section 7872(d)(1))	Relative share of net investment income (imputed interest payment after application of section 7872(d)(1))	
1	$3,000	$2,000	$6,000 × $3,000/$9,000)
2	4,000	2,667	(6,000 × 4,000/9,000)
3	2,000	1,333	(6,000 × 2,000/9,000)
Total	$9,000	$6,000	

Consequently, the imputed interest payment to lender 1 cannot exceed $2,000; the imputed interest payment to lender 2 cannot exceed $2,667; and, the imputed interest payment to lender 3 cannot exceed $1,333. [Reg. § 1.7872-8.]

§ 1.7872-9. *De minimis* exception for compensation-related or corporation-shareholder loans.—(a) *In general.*—In the case of any demand loan described in section 7872(c)(1)(B) or (C), the provisions of section 7872 do not apply to any day on which the aggregate outstanding amount of loans between the lender and the borrower does not exceed $10,000. In the case of any term loan described in section 7872(c)(1)(B) or (C) (relating to the *de minimis* rules), the provisions of section 7872 apply to the loan as of the first day on which the aggregate outstanding amount of loans between the lender and the borrower exceeds $10,000. Once section 7872 applies to a term loan, section 7872 continues to apply to the loan regardless of whether the $10,000 limitation applies at some later date.

(b) *Aggregate outstanding amount of loans.*—The aggregate outstanding amount of loans between the lender and the borrower is the sum of the principal amounts of outstanding loans directly between the parties, regardless of the character of the loans, regardless of the interest rate charged on the loans, and regardless of the date on which the loans were made. For this purpose, the principal amount of a loan which is also subject to section 1272 (without applying the limitation of section 1273(a)(3)) is the "adjusted issue price" as that term is defined in section 1272(a)(4). See § 1.7872(a)(3)(i) for the determination of the issue price of a loan which is also subject to section 7872.

(c) *Tax avoidance loan.*—This section does not apply to any loan which is a tax avoidance loan within the meaning of § 1.7872-4(e).

(d) *Example.*—The provisions of this section may be illustrated by the following example:

Example. (i) On January 1, 1985, L made a $4,000 four-year term loan to B, a corporation in which L is a shareholder. On October 15, 1986, L made a $7,000 five-year term loan to B. Both loans are interest-free and are payable on the last day of the loan term. There are no other outstanding loans between L and B. Neither loan is a tax avoidance loan.

(ii) For the period beginning on January 1, 1985 and ending on October 14, 1986, the provisions of section 7872 do not apply to the $4,000 loan because the outstanding loan balance between L and B does not exceed $10,000. On October 15, 1986, however, the aggregate amount of loans between L and B exceeds $10,000. Accordingly, the provisions of section 7872(b) apply to both loans. See § 1.7872-4(d) for the proper Federal tax treatment of the imputed transfer by L to B. For purposes of computing the present value of all payments to be made under the loan agreements, the applicable Federal rate for the $4,000 loan is the applicable Federal rate in effect on January 1, 1985, for loans with a term of 4 years (even though less than three years remain before the loan ends). Under § 1.7872-7(b), the present value of the payment to be made under the $4,000 loan agreement is determined as of October 15, 1986 (the date on which section 7872 first applies to the $4,000 loan) for a loan with a term which begins on October 15, 1986, and ends on January 1, 1989. [Reg. § 1.7872-9.]

§ 1.7872-10. Other definitions.—(a) *"Term" and "demand" loans distinguished.*—For purposes of section 7872—

(1) *Demand loan.*—Any loan which is payable in full at any time on the demand of the lender (or within a reasonable time after the lender's demand), is a "demand loan."

(2) *Term loan.*—A loan is treated as a "term loan" if the loan agreement specifies an ascertainable period of time during which the loan is to be outstanding. For purposes of this rule, a period of time is treated as being ascertainable if the period may be determined actuarially. Thus, a loan agreement which provides that D loans E $16,000 for E's life will be treated as a term loan because the life expectancy of E may be determined actuarially.

(3) *Acceleration and extension clauses.*—Acceleration clauses and similar provisions that would make a loan due before the time otherwise specified including provisions permitting prepayment of a loan or accelerating the maturity date on disposition of collateral ("due on sale" clauses) are disregarded for purposes of section 7872. Thus, a loan for a term of 15 years is a term loan for 15 years even if it is subject to acceleration upon some action of the borrower. If the loan agreement specifies an ascertainable period of time during which the loan is to be outstanding but contains an extension clause or similar provision that would make the loan due after the time otherwise specified, the loan is a term loan during the ascertainable period and a second demand or term loan thereafter; the classification of the second loan as term or demand depends upon the terms of the extension clause.

(4) *Loans for a period of time not ascertainable.*—[Reserved]

(5) *Certain loans conditioned on future services.*—For all purposes of section 7872 other than determining the applicable Federal rate (see, § 1.7872-3(b)), if the benefits of the interest arrangements of a term loan are not transferable by the individual borrower and are conditioned on the future performance of substantial services by the individual borrower (within the meaning

of section 83), the loan is treated as a demand loan. All facts and circumstances must be examined to determine whether the future services to be performed are substantial.

(6) *Revolving credit loans.*—For purposes of section 7872, an extension of credit by reason of the use of a credit card that is available to a broad segment of the general public is treated as a demand loan, and the provisions of section 7872 may apply if the loan is described in one of the categories set forth in § 1.7872-4. The period during which the loan is outstanding begins on the first day on which a finance charge would be assessed if payment of the outstanding balance is not made. For rules governing the computation of foregone interest for demand loans with variable balances, see § 1.7872-13(c).

(b) [Reserved for further definitions as needed.] [Reg. § 1.7872-10.]

§ 1.7872-11. Special rules.—(a) *Waiver, cancellation or forgiveness of interest payments.*—If a loan is made requiring the payment of stated interest and the accrued but unpaid interest is subsequently waived, cancelled, or forgiven by the lender, such waiver, cancellation, or forgiveness is treated as if the interest had in fact been paid to the lender and then retransferred by the lender to the borrower but only if—

(1) the loan initially would have been subject to section 7872 had it been made without interest;

(2) the waiver, cancellation or forgiveness does not include in substantial part the loan principal; and

(3) a principal purpose of the waiver, cancellation, or forgiveness is to confer a benefit on the borrower, such as to pay compensation or make a gift, a capital contribution, a distribution of money under section 301, or a similar payment to the borrower.

The retransferred amount is characterized for Federal tax purposes in accordance with the substance of the transaction. The requisite purpose described in paragraph (a)(iii) of this section is presumed in the case of loans between family members, corporations and shareholders, employers and employees, or an independent contractor and a person for whom such independent contractor provides services unless the taxpayer can show by clear and convincing evidence that the interest obligation was waived, cancelled, or forgiven for a legitimate business purpose of the lender who is acting in the capacity as a creditor seeking to maximize satisfaction of a claim, such as in the case of a borrower's insolvency.

(b) *Disposition of interest or obligation in loan.*—[RESERVED]

(c) *Husband and wife treated as 1 person.*—Section 7872(f)(7) provides that a husband and wife shall be treated as 1 person. Accordingly, all loans to or from the husband will be combined with all loans to or from the wife for purposes of applying section 7872. All loans between a husband and a wife are disregarded for purposes of section 7872.

(d) *Withholding.*—In the case of any loan (term or demand) subject to section 7872, no amount is required to be withheld under chapter 24, relating to the collection of income tax at the source on wages and back-up withholding, with respect to any amount treated as transferred or retransferred under section 7872(a) or (b). Withholding is required where appropriate, however, for purposes of chapter 21, relating to the Federal Insurance Contributions Act, and Chapter 22, relating to the Railroad Retirement Tax Act, on any amount of money treated as transferred and retransferred between the lender and borrower because of the application of section 7872.

(e) *Treatment of renegotiations.*—[RESERVED]

(f) *Loans denominated in foreign currencies.*—(1) *Applicable rate.*—If a loan is denominated in a currency other than the U.S. dollar, then for purposes of section 7872 and the regulations thereunder, a rate that constitutes a market interest rate in the currency in which the loan is denominated shall be substituted for the applicable Federal rate.

(2) *Treatment of imputed transfer as interest.*—(i) *In general.*—If a loan is denominated in a currency other than the U.S. dollar then, notwithstanding section 7872(a)(1)(B), § 1.7872-6, and § 1.7872-7, the amount of imputed interest treated as retransferred by the borrower to the lender shall only be treated as interest to the extent consistent with other principles of tax law regarding foreign currency lending transactions and to the extent provided in this paragraph (f)(2).

(ii) *Loans denominated in appreciating currencies.*—[Reserved]

(iii) *Loans denominated in depreciating currencies.*—[Reserved]

(3) *Example.*—The provisions of this paragraph (f)(1) may be illustrated by the following example.

Example. A lends her daughter B thse sum of 100,000 foreign currency units, repayable in 5 years with interest payable semiannually at a rate of 12 percent. Assume that the market rate of interest for loans denominated in that foreign currency at the time of the transaction is 30 percent, compounded semiannually, and that the current exchange rate is 5 foreign currency units to the dollar. A has made a below-market gift loan to B. The amount of A's gift to B is the excess of 100,000 foreign currency units (or $20,000) over the present value of all payments to be made under the loan, using a discount rate of 30 percent, which is 54,831 foreign units (or $10,966). Thus, the amount of A's gift is $9,034.

(g) *Reporting requirements.*—(1) *Lender.*—A lender must attach a statement to the lender's income tax return for any taxable year in which the lender either has interest imputed under section 7872 or claims a deduction for an amount deemed to be transferred to a borrower under section 7872. The statement must—

(i) Explain that it relates to an amount includible in income or deductible by reason of section 7872,

(ii) Provide the name, address, and taxpayer identification number of each borrower.

(iii) Specify the amount of imputed interest income and the amount and character of any item deductible by reason of section 7872 attributable to each borrower.

(iv) Specify the mathematical assumptions used (*e.g.*, 360 day calendar year, the exact method or the approximate method for computing interest for a short period (see, § 1.7872-13)) for computing the amounts imputed under section 7872, and

(v) Include any other information required by the return or the instructions thereto.

(2) *Borrower.*—A borrower must attach a statement to the borrower's income tax return for any taxable year in which the borrower either has income from an imputed transfer under section 7872 or claims a deduction for an amount of interest expenst imputed under section 7872. The statement must—

(i) Explain that it relates to an amount includible in income or deductible by reason of section 7872,

(ii) Provide the name, address, and taxpayer identification number of each lender,

(iii) Specify the amount of imputed interest expense and the amount and character of any income imputed under section 7872 attributable to each lender,

(iv) Specify the mathematical assumptions used (*e.g.*, 360 day calendar year, the exact method or the approximate method for computing interest for a short period (see, § 1.7872-13)) for computing the amounts imputed under section 7872, and

(v) Include any other information required by the return or the instructions thereto.

(3) *Special rule for gift loans.*—In the case of a gift loan directly between natural persons, the lender must recognize the entire amount of interest income imputed under section 7872 (determined without regard to section 7872(d)(1)) unless the borrower notifies the lender, in a signed statement, of the amount of the borrower's net investment income properly allocable to the loan according to the provisions of section 7872(d)(1) and § 1.7872-8(c)(6).

(4) *Information and reporting.*—All amounts imputed under section 7872 (*e.g.*, interest, compensation, gift) are characterized in accordance with the substance of the transaction and, except as otherwise provided in the regulations under section 7872, are treated as so characterized for all purposes of the Code. Accordingly, all applicable information and reporting requirements (*e.g.*, reporting on Form W-2 and Form 1099) must be satisfied. [Reg. § 1.7872-11.]

§ 1.7872-12. Computational rules to determine sufficient stated interest for short periods.—(a) *Scope.*—This section provides computational rules only for the purpose of determining whether the interest payable on a loan during a short period is sufficient to prevent characterization of the loan as a below-market loan under § 1.7872-3. For rules for the calculation of the amount of interest to be imputed on a below-market loan, including rules for short periods, see § 1.7872-13 and § 1.7872-14.

(b) *Short period defined.*—(1) *In general.*—A short period (as referred to in § 1.7872-3(d)) for a loan is any period shorter than the regular compounding period or regular payment interval required under the loan agreement. Generally, a short period will arise at the beginning or the end of a loan (or at the time the loan first becomes subject to section 7872 because of the application of the *de minimis* provisions). For example, a loan made on January 17, 1985, and calling for semiannual payments of interest on June 30 and December 31 of each year will have a short period beginning on January 17, 1985, and ending on June 30, 1985.

(2) *Special short periods in the case of demand loans.*—In the case of a demand loan, in addition to any short periods described in paragraph (b)(1) of this section, additional short periods may also arise because of the need to adjust the applicable Federal rate on January 1 and July 1 of each year. These short periods arise in cases when the dates January 1 or July 1 fall within the compounding periods or payment intervals required under the loan agreement. For example, a below-market demand loan made on April 1, 1985, that is outstanding throughout 1985 and that calls for semiannual interest payments on September 30 and March 31 of each year will have 3 short periods in 1985. The first short period begins on April 1, 1985, and ends on June 30, 1985. The second short period begins on July 1, 1985, and ends on September 30, 1985. The third short period begins on October 1, 1985, and ends on December 31, 1985.

(c) *Interest payable for a short period.*—(1) *Exact method.*—The smallest amount of interest that must be paid for a short period in order to prevent the loan from being a below-market loan is determined by the exact method. The exact method assumes daily compounding of interest.

(2) *Approximate method.*—The approximate method is also provided for the convenience of taxpayers who do not wish to use the exact method. The approximate method assumes simple interest within any compounding period and will always produce an amount of interest for the short period that is slightly higher than that produced under the exact method. Under this method, a sufficient amount of interest for any short period is determined by multiplying the amount that would constitute sufficient stated interest for a full period by a fraction the numerator of which is equal to the length of the short period and the denominator of which is the length of a full period.

(3) *Counting convention.*—In computing the length of a short period, any reasonable convention may be used. Common conventions are "30 days per month/360 days per year", "actual days per month/actual days per year", and "actual days per month/360 days per year". The examples in the regulations under section 7872 all use the "30 days per month/360 days per year" convention.

(d) *Examples.*—This section may be illustrated by the following examples.

Example (1). On February 1, 1986, A makes a $100,000 loan to B for a term of 4 months. The loan is repaid on May 31, 1986. Assume that the applicable Federal rate on February 1, 1986, for a loan of this term is 10 percent, compounded semiannually. Using the exact method, the amount of interest that must be paid on May 31, 1986, if the loan is not to be a below-market loan is $3,306.16, calculated as follows:

$\$100{,}000 \times [(1 + .10/2)^{4/6} - 1] = \$3{,}306.16$

Example (2). Assume the same facts as in Example (1). Using the approximate method, a sufficient amount of interest is stated on the loan if $3,333.33 of interest is payable on May 31, 1986, calculated as follows:

$\$100{,}000 \times [(.10/2) \times (4/6)] = \$3{,}333.33$

[Reg. § 1.7872-12.]

§ 1.7872-13. Computation of foregone interest.—(a) *Demand loans outstanding for an entire calendar year.*—(1) *In general.*—In the case of a below-market demand loan of a fixed principal amount that remains outstanding for an entire calendar year, the amount of foregone interest (as referred to in § 1.7872-6(c)) shall be the excess of—

(i) The result produced when the "blended annual rate" is multiplied by the principal amount of the loan, over

(ii) The sum of all amounts payable as interest on the loan properly allocable to the calendar year (including all amounts of original issue discount allocated to that year under section 1272).

The "blended annual rate" will be published annually by the Commissioner and is determined generally by blending the applicable Federal rates for demand loans outstanding for the entire year.

(2) *Example.*—Paragraph (a)(1) may be illustrated by the following example.

Example. On January 1, 1985, A makes a $100,000 demand loan to B with stated interest equal to 9 percent. Interest is payable semiannually on June 30, and December 31. The loan remains outstanding for the entire year. On both June 30, and December 31, 1985, B makes a $4,500 payment of interest to A. Assume that the blended annual rate for 1985 is 10.45 percent. The amount of foregone interest is $1,450, computed as follows:

$10,450 = $100,000 × 10.45 percent

$1,450 = $10,450 – $9,000

(b) *Demand loans outstanding for less than an entire calendar year.*—(1) *In general.*—In the case of any below-market demand loan outstanding for less than the calendar year, the amount of foregone interest shall be the excess of—

(i) The amount of interest ("I") which would have been payable on the loan for the year if interest accrued on the loan at the applicable Federal rate and were payable on the date specified in section 7872(a)(2) and § 1.7872-6(b), over

(ii) The sum of all amounts payable as interest on the loan properly allocable to the calendar year (including all amounts of original issue discount allocated to that year under section 1272).

In general, "I" is determined by assuming daily compounding of interest. However, individual taxpayers who are parties to below-market loans in the aggregate of $250,000 or less may choose (see, § 1.7872-11(g)) to compute and report foregone interest under the approximate method set forth in paragraph (b)(2) of this section. If the taxpayer chooses the approximate method but fails to properly compute the amount of foregone interest under that method, the correct amount of foregone interest will be recomputed under the approximate method.

(2) *Approximate method.*—Under the approximate method, "I" is calculated as follows:

(i) *Loan outstanding during one semiannual period only.*—If a loan is outstanding only during one semiannual period of a calendar year, to determine "I", multiply the principal amount of the loan by one-half the applicable Federal rate based on semiannual compounding in effect for that loan, then multiply the result by a fraction representing the portion of the semiannual period during which the loan was outstanding.

(ii) *Example.*—Paragraph (b)(2)(i) of this section may be illustrated by the following example.

Example. A $200,000 interest-free demand loan is outstanding on January 1, 1986, and is repaid on March 31, 1986. Assume that the applicable Federal rate (based on semiannual compounding) for demand loans made in January 1986 is 10 percent. The amount of interest that would have been payable on the loan for the year if the loan provided for interest at the applicable Federal rate determined under the approximate method is $5,000, computed as follows:

$5,000 = $200,000 × (.10/2) × (3/6)

Because no interest is payable on the loan, this amount is also the amount of foregone interest.

(iii) *Loans outstanding during both semiannual periods.*—If a loan is outstanding for at least part of each semiannual period (but less than the full calendar year), then, under the approximate method, "I" must be calculated in two steps. First, calculate an amount of interest for the first semiannual period by treating the loan as if it were repaid on June 30, using the approach described in paragraph (b)(3)(i) of this section. Second, add this amount of interest to the principal of the loan, and then calculate an amount of interest for the second semiannual period as if the loan of this higher amount were made on July 1, again using the approach described in paragraph (b)(3)(i) of this section. The sum of these two interest amounts is the value for "I" calculated under the approximate method.

(3) *Examples.*—Paragraph (b)(2) of this sectioon may be illustrated by the following examples.

Example (1). On March 1, 1986, A makes a $100,000 interest-free demand loan to B. The loan remains outstanding on December 31, 1986. Assume that the applicable Federal rate for a demand loan made in March 1986, based on semiannual compounding, for the first semiannual period in 1986 is 9.89 percent and that the applicable Federal rate, based on semiannual compounding, for a demand loan outstanding in July 1986 is 10.50 percent. The amount of foregone interest under the exact method is $8,691.76, calculated as follows:

$100,000 × [(1 + .0989/2) 4/6 (1 + .1050/2) – 1] = $8,691.76

Example (2). (i) Assume the same facts as in Example (1).

The amount of foregone interest under the approximate method is $8,719.92, calculated as follows:

(ii) For the short period March 1 to June 30, 1986, the amount of foregone interest is $3,296.67, calculated as follows:

$3,296.67 = $100,000 × (.0989/2) × (4/6)

(iii) For the second semiannual period in 1986, the amount of foregone interest is computed by first adding the interest for the first semiannual period ($3,296.67) to the original principal amount to obtain a new principal amount of $103,296.67. Foregone interest for the second semiannual period is then $5,423.08, computed as follows:

$5,423.08 = $103,296.67 × (.1050/2)

(iv) Using the approximate method, the amount of foregone interest for 1986 is $8,719.75 ($3,296.67 + $5,423.08).

(c) *Demand loans with fluctuating loan balances.*—If a demand loan does not have a constant outstanding principal amount during a period, the amount of foregone interest shall be computed according to the principles set forth in paragraph (b) of this section, with each increase in the outstanding loan balance being treated as a new loan and each decrease being treated as first a repayment of accrued but unpaid interest (if any), and then a repayment of principal.

(d) *Examples*.—This provisions of paragraph (c) of this section may be illustrated by the following examples.

Example (1). (i) On October 1, 1984, C makes a $50,000 interest-free demand loan to D. On October 1, 1985, C makes an additional interest-free demand loan of $25,000 to D. Assume that section 7872 applies to both loans, that the blended annual rate for 1985 is 10.45 percent, and that the applicable Federal rate based on semiannual compounding for demand loans made in October 1985, is 10.50 percent. The amount of foregone interest for 1985 is calculated as follows:

(ii) $50,000 is outstanding for the entire year. The foregone interest on this amount is ($5,000 × .1045) = $5,225.00

(iii) $25,000 is outstanding for the last three months of 1985. Under the exact method, the amount of foregone interest on this portion of the loan is $647.86, computed as follows:

$\$25,000 \times [(1 + .1050/2)^{3/6} - 1] = \$647.86$

Under the approximate method, the amount of foregone interest is $656.25, computed as follows:

$\$25,000 \times (.1050/2) \times (3/6) = \$656.25$

(iv) The total amount of foregone interest is $5,872.86 ($5,225.00 + $647.86) under the exact method, and $5,881.25 ($5,225.00 + $656.25) under the approximate method.

Example (2). (i) On September 1, 1985, E makes a $100,000 interest-free demand loan to F. The loan agreement requires F to repay $10,000 of the principal amount of the loan at the end of each month that the loan is outstanding. Assume that section 7872 applies to the loan and that the applicable Federal rate based on semiannual compounding for demand loans made in September 1985, is 10.50 percent. The amount of foregone interest for 1985 is calculated as follows:

(ii) $70,000 is outstanding for four months. Under the exact method, the amount of foregone interest on this portion of the loan is $2,429.05, computed as follows:

$\$70,000 \times [(1 + .1050/2)^{4/6} - 1] = \$2,429.05$

Under the approximate method, the amount of foregone interest on this protion of the loan is $2,450.00, computed as follows:

$\$70,000 \times (.1050/2) \times (4/6) = \$2,450.00$

(iii) $10,000 is outstanding for 3 months. Under the exact method, the amount of foregone interest on this portion of the loan is $259.14, computed as follows:

$\$10,000 \times [(1 + .1050/2)^{3/6} - 1] = \$259.14$

Under the approximate method, the amount of foregone interest on this portion of the loan is $262.50, computed as follows:

$\$10,000 \times (.1050/2) \times (3/6) = \$262.50$

(iv) An additional $10,000 is outstanding 2 months. Under the exact method, the amount of foregone interest on this portion of the loan is $172.02, computed as follows:

$\$10,000 \times [(1 + .1050/2)^{2/6} - 1] = \$172.02$

Under the approximate method, the amount of foregone interest on this portion of the loan is $175.00, computed as follows:

$\$10,000 \times (.1050/2) \times (2/6) = \$175.00$

(v) A final $10,000 is outstanding for 1 month. Under the exact method, the amount of foregone interest on this portion of the loan is $85.65, computed as follows:

$\$10,000 \times [1 + 1050/2)^{1/6} - 1] = \$85.65$

Under the approximate method, the amount of foregone interest on this portion of the loan is $87.50, computed as follows:

$\$10,000 \times (.1050/2) \times (1/6) = \$87.50$

(vi) The total amount of foregone interest is $2,945.86 under the exact method, and $2,975.00 under the approximate method.

(e) *Gift term loans and certain loans conditioned on future services*.—(1) *In general*.—In the case of any gift term loan or any term loan that is treated as a demand loan as provided in § 1.7872-10(a)(5), the amount of foregone interest for income tax purposes shall be computed as if the loan were a demand loan, except that:

(i) In applying paragraph (a)(1)(i), use the applicable Federal rate based on annual compounding in effect on the day the loan is made instead of the blended annual rate, and

(ii) In applying paragraph (b), use the applicable Federal rate based on semiannual compounding in effect on the day the loan is made instead of the applicable Federal rate for demand loans in effect during the period for which foregone interest is being computed.

(2) *Example*.—The provisions of this paragraph (e) may be illustrated by the following examples:

Example (1). On January 1, 1986, parent P makes a $200,000 gift term loan to child C. The loan agreement provides that the term of the loan is four years and that 5 percent simple interest is payable annually. Both P and C are calendar year taxpayers, and both are still living on December 31, 1986. Assume that the Federal mid-term rate based on annual compounding in effect on January 1, 1986, is 11.83 percent. The loan is a below-market loan. The amount of foregone interest for each year is $13,660.00, computed as follows:

($200,000) × .1183 = $23,660.00

$23,660.00 – $10,000.00 = $13,660.00

For gift tax purposes, an imputed gift is treated as made on January 1, 1986, and is equal to the excess of the amount loaned ($200,000) over the present value of all payments due under the loan, discounted at 11.83 percent compounded annually ($153,360.82), or $41,639.82. For rules for determining the computation of present value, see § 1.7872-14.

Example (2). Assume the same facts as in Example (1) except that C repays the loan on September 30, 1987, along with an interest payment of $7,500. For income tax purposes, the imputed payments are treated as transferred on December 31, 1986 and September 30, 1987. The amount of the imputed payments for 1986 are the same as in Example (1). For 1987, under the exact method the amount of foregone interest is $9,994.73, computed as follows:

$\$17,494.73 = \$200,000 \times [(1 + .1183)^{9/12} - 1]$

$17,494.73 – $ 7,500 = $9,994.73

For gift tax purposes, the imputed gift is treated as made January 1, 1986, and is the same as in Example (1).

(f) *Allocation of stated interest*.—If interest that is payable on a demand loan is properly allocable to a period which includes more than one calendar year, the amount of interest to be allocated to each calendar year is determined by using any reasonable method of allocation.

(g) *Counting conventions.*—(1) *Whole periods.*—All whole periods, whether expressed annually, semi-annually, quarterly, or monthly, shall be treated as having equal length. For example, a leap year shall be treated as having the same number of days as a non-leap year; all months shall be treated as having the same number of days.

(2) *Short periods.*—In computing the length of a short period, any reasonable convention may be used. See § 1.7872-12(c)(2) for a list of conventions commonly used. [Reg. § 1.7872-13.]

§ 1.7872-14. Determination of present value.—(a) *In general.*—This section provides rules for computing the present value of a payment (as referred to in § 1.7872-7(a)(1)) to be made in the future. In general, for purposes of section 7872, the present value of a loan payment to be made in the future is the amount of that payment discounted at the applicable Federal rate from the date in the future that the payment is due to the date on which the computation is made. For this purpose, the computation date is the date the loan first becomes subject to section 7872. To determine the present value of a payment, use the applicable Federal rate in effect on the day the loan is made that reflects the compounding assumption (*i.e.,* annual, semiannual, quarterly, or monthly) that is appropriate for the loan. See § 1.7872-3(b).

(b) *Examples.*—The provisions of this section may be illustrated by the following examples:

Example (1). (i) On July 1, 1984, corporation A makes a $200,000 interest-free three-year term loan to shareholder B. The applicable Federal rate is 10-percent, compounded semiannually.

(ii) The present value of this payment is $149.243.08, determined as follows:

$$\$149{,}243.08 = \frac{\$200{,}000}{[1 + (.10/2)]^{6}}$$

(iii) The excess of the amount loaned over the present value of all payments on the loan ($200,000 – $149,243.08), or $50,756.92, is treated as a distribution of property (characterized according to section 301) paid to B on July 1, 1984. The same amount, $50,756.92, is treated as original issue discount under sections 1272 and 163(e).

Example (2). (i) On July 1, 1984, Employer E makes a $3,000 interest-free three year compensation-related term loan to employee W. On December 1, 1984, E makes an $9,000 interest-free compensation-related demand loan to W. The demand loan remains outstanding throughout December 1984. The two loans are the only loans outstanding between E and W during 1984, and neither is characterized under section 7872(c)(1)(D) as a tax avoidance loan. The applicable Federal rate for all loans for periods before January 1, 1985, is 10 percent, compounded semiannually.

(ii) For the period beginning on July 1, 1984, and ending on November 30, 1984, the provisions of section 7872 do not apply to the $3,000 loan because of the application of the *de minimis* rules of section 7872(c)(3).

(iii) On December 1, 1984, however, the aggregate amount of loans outstanding between E and W exceeds $10,000. As a result, section 7872 applies to both loans for December 1984. Both the imputed transfer and the imputed interest payment with respect to the $9,000 demand loan are determined under section 7872(a). The amount of the imputed transfer by E to W with respect to the $3,000 term loan is determined under section 7872(b)(1). An amount equal to the amount of the imputed transfer with respect to the $3,000 term loan is treated as original issue discount.

(iv) With respect to the $3,000 term loan, the amount of the imputed transfer is equal to the excess of the amount loaned, over the present value of all payments which are required to be made under the $3,000 two-year term loan agreement, determined as of December 1, 1984 (the day section 7872 first applies to the $3,000 loan). The present value of $3,000 payable on June 30, 1987, determined as of December 1, 1984, is $2,331.54, computed as follows:

$$\$2{,}331.54 = \frac{\$3{,}000}{(1 + .10/2)^{5+1/6}}$$

The imputed transfer on the $3,000 loan is $668.46 ($3,000.00 – $2,331.54).

(v) The foregone interest on the $9,000 demand loan is determined as of December 31, 1984, with respect to the one month during 1984 to which section 7872 applies to the loan. The amount of foregone interest for 1984 under the exact method is $73.48, computed as follows:

$\$73.48 = \$9{,}000 \times [(1 + .10/2)^{1/6} - 1]$

Example (3). (i) Assume the same facts as in Example (2) except that the provisions of the $3,000 three-year term loan require W to make annual payments of interest at a 5 percent simple rate and except that E makes W the $9,000 loan on November 27, 1985.

(ii) Under the agreement W pays $150 (5 percent of $3,000) on June 30, 1985, June 30, 1986, and June 30, 1987. Since the first of these payments is payable prior to November 27, 1985, only the second and third $150 payments are taken into account. W is treated as paying $150 on June 30, 1986 and $3,150 ($3,000 principal and $150 interest) on June 30, 1987.

(iii) The present value as of November 27, 1984 of the $150 payable on June 30, 1986, is $128.39, computed as follows:

$$\$128.39 = \frac{\$150.00}{(1 + .10/2)^{3+34/180}}$$

(iv) The present value as of November 27, 1984 of the $3,150 payable on June 30, 1987, is $2,445.47, computed as follows:

$$\$2{,}445.47 = \frac{\$3{,}150.00}{(1 + .10/2)^{5+34/180}}$$

The sum of these two present values is $2,573.86 ($128.39 + $2,445.47). Therefore, the amount of the imputed transfer with respect to the $3,000 loan is $426.14 ($3,000.00 – $2,573.86).

(v) The foregone interest on the $9,000 demand loan under the exact method is $83.33 ($\$9{,}000 \times [(1 + .10/2)^{34/180} - 1]$). [Reg. § 1.7872-14.]

ELECTIONS UNDER ECONOMIC RECOVERY TAX ACT OF 1981

GST Exemption: Extension of Time

GST Exemption: Extension of Time.—Amendments to Reg. §301.9100-3, describing the circumstances and procedures under which an extension of time will be granted under Code Sec. 2642(g)(1), are proposed (published in the Federal Register on April 17, 2008) (REG-147775-06).

☐ Par. 4. Section 301.9100-3 is amended by adding a newparagraph (g) to read as follows:

§301.9100-3. Other extensions.

* * *

(g) *Relief under section 2642(g)(1).*—(1) *Procedures.*—The procedures set forth in this section are not applicable for requests for relief under section 2642(g)(1). For requests for reflief under section 2642(g)(1), see §26.2642-7.

(2) *Effective/applicability date.*—Paragraph (g) of this section applies to requests for relief under section 2642(g)(1) filed on or after the date of publication of the Treasury decision adopting these rules as final regulations in the **Federal Register.**

GROUP HEALTH PLAN REQUIREMENTS

Group Health Plans: Portability Requirements

Group Health Plans: Portability Requirements.—Reg. §54.9801-7 and amendments to Reg. §§54.9801-1, 54.9801-2, 54.9801-4, 54.9801-5 and 54.9801-6, clarifying certain portability requirements for group health plans and issuers of health insurance coverage offered in connection with a group health plans, are proposed (published in the Federal Register on December 30, 2004) (REG-130370-04).

☐ Par. 2. Section 54.9801-1 is amended in paragraph (a)(1) by removing the language "54.9801-6" and adding "54.9801-7" in its place.

§54.9801-1. Basis and scope.

☐ Par. 3. Section 54.9801-2 is amended in the first sentence by removing the language "54.9801-6" and adding "54.9801-7" in its place.

§54.9801-2. Definitions.

☐ Par. 4. Section 54.9801-4 is amended by:

a. Revising paragraphs (b)(2)(iii) and (b)(2)(iv).

b. Adding *Examples 4* and *6* in paragraph (b)(2)(v).

The revisions and additions read as follows:

§54.9801-4. Rules relating to creditable coverage.

* * *

(b) *Standard method.*—* * *

(2) *Counting creditable coverage.*—* * *

(iii) *Significant break in coverage defined.*—A *significant break in coverage* means a period of 63 consecutive days during each of which an individual does not have any creditable coverage, except that periods described in paragraph (b)(2)(iv) of this section are not taken into account in determining a significant break in coverage. (See section 731(b)(2)(iii) of ERISA and section 2723(b)(2)(iii) of the PHS Act, which exclude from preemption state insurance laws that require a break of more than 63 days before an individual has a significant break in coverage for purposes of state law.)

(iv) *Periods that toll a significant break.*—Days in a waiting period and days in an affiliation period are not taken into account in determining whether a significant break in coverage has occurred. In addition, for an individual who elects COBRA continuation coverage during the second election period provided under the Trade Act of 2002, the days between the date the individual lost group health plan coverage and the first day of the second COBRA election period are not taken into account in determining whether a significant break in coverage has occurred. Moreover, in the case of an individual whose coverage ceases, if a certificate of creditable coverage with respect to that cessation is not provided on or before the date coverage ceases, then the period that begins on the first date that an individual has no creditable coverage and that continues through the earlier of the following two dates is not taken into account in determining whether a significant break in coverage has occurred:

(A) The date that a certificate of creditable coverage with respect to that cessation is provided; or

(B) The date 44 days after coverage ceases.

(v) *Examples.*—* * *

Example 4. (i) *Facts.* Individual *B* terminates coverage under a group health plan, and a certificate of creditable coverage is provided 10 days later. *B* begins employment with Employer *R* and begins enrollment in *R*'s plan 60 days after the certificate is provided.

(ii) *Conclusion.* In this *Example 4*, even though *B* had no coverage for 69 days, the 10 days before the certificate of creditable coverage is provided are not taken into account in determining a significant break in coverage. Therefore, *B*'s break in coverage is only 59 days and is not a significant break in coverage. Accordingly, *B*'s prior coverage must be counted by *R*' s plan.

* * *

Example 6. (i) *Facts.* Employer *V* sponsors a group health plan. Under the terms of the plan, the only benefits provided are those provided under an insurance policy. Individual *D* works for *V* and has creditable coverage under *V*'s plan. *V* fails to pay the issuer the premiums for the coverage period beginning March 1. Consistent with applicable state law, the issuer terminates the policy so that the last day of coverage is April 30. *V* goes out of business on July 31. On August 15 *D* begins employment with Employer *W* and enrolls in *W*'s group health plan. *W*'s plan imposes a 12-month preexisting condition exclusion on all enrollees. *D* never receives a certificate of creditable coverage for coverage under *V*'s plan.

(ii) *Conclusion.* In this *Example 6*, the period from May 1 (the first day without coverage) through June 13 (the date 44 days after coverage under *V*'s plan ceases) is not taken into account in determining a 63-day break in coverage. This is because, in cases in which a certificate of creditable coverage is not provided by the date coverage is lost, the break begins on the date the certificate is provided, or the date 44 days after coverage ceases, if earlier. Therefore, even though *D*'s actual period without coverage was 106 days (May 1 through August 14), because the period from May 1 through June 13 is not taken into account, *D*'s break in coverage is only 62 days (June 14 through August 14). Thus, *D* has not experienced a significant break in coverage, and *D*'s prior coverage must be counted by *W*'s plan.

* * *

☐ Par. 5. Section 54.9801-5 is amended by:

a. Redesignating paragraphs (a)(3)(ii)(H)(*5*) and (*6*) as paragraphs (a)(3)(ii)(H)(*6*) and (*7*), respectively.

b. Adding a new paragraph (a)(3)(ii)(H)(*5*).

The addition reads as follows:

§ 54.9801-5. Evidence of creditable coverage.

(a) *Certificate of creditable coverage.*—* * *

(3) *Form and content of certificate.*—* * *

(ii) *Required information.*—* * *

(H) * * *

(*5*) The interaction with the Family and Medical Leave Act;

* * *

☐ Par. 6. Section 54.9801-6 is amended by:

a. Revising paragraph (a)(1).

b. Revising paragraph (a)(4).

c. Revising paragraph (b)(1).

d. Revising paragraph (b)(3).

e. Revising *Example* 2 in paragraph (b)(4).

f. Adding *Examples 3, 4,* and *5* in paragraph (b)(4).

The additions and revisions read as follows:

§ 54.9801-6. Special enrollment periods.—(a) *Special enrollment for certain individuals who lose coverage.*—(1) *In general.*—A group health plan is required to permit current employees and dependents (as defined in § 54.9801-2) who are described in paragraph (a)(2) of this section to enroll for coverage under the terms of the plan if the conditions in paragraph (a)(3) of this section are satisfied. Paragraph (a)(4) of this section describes procedures that a plan may require an employee to follow and describes the date by which coverage must begin. The special enrollment rights under this paragraph (a) apply without regard to the dates on which an individual would otherwise be able to enroll under the plan. (See section 701(f)(1) of ERISA and section 2701(f)(1) of the PHS Act, under which this obligation is also imposed on a health insurance issuer offering group health insurance coverage.)

* * *

(4) *Applying for special enrollment and effective date of coverage.*—(i) *Request.*—A plan must allow an employee a period of at least 30 days after an event described in paragraph (a)(3) of this section (loss of eligibility for coverage, termination of employer contributions, or exhaustion of COBRA continuation coverage) to request enrollment (for the employee or the employee's dependent). For this purpose, any written or oral request made to any of the following constitutes a request for enrollment —

(A) The plan administrator;

(B) An issuer offering health insurance coverage under the plan;

(C) A person who customarily handles claims for the plan (such as a third party administrator); or

(D) Any other designated representative.

(ii) *Tolling of period for requesting special enrollment.*—(A) In the case of an individual whose coverage ceases, if a certificate of creditable coverage with respect to that cessation is not provided on or before the date coverage ceases, then the period for requesting special enrollment described in paragraph (a)(4)(i) of this section does not end until 30 days after the earlier of —

(*1*) The date that a certificate of creditable coverage with respect to that cessation is provided; or

(*2*) The date 44 days after coverage ceases.

(B) For purposes of this paragraph (a)(4), if an individual's coverage ceases due to the operation of a lifetime limit on all benefits, coverage is considered to cease on the earliest date that a claim is denied due to the operation of the lifetime limit. (Nonetheless, the date of a loss of eligibility for coverage is determined under the rules of paragraph (a)(3) of this section, which provides that a loss of eligibility occurs when a claim that would meet or exceed a lifetime limit on all benefits is incurred, not when it is denied.)

(C) The rules of this paragraph (a)(4)(ii) are illustrated by the following examples:

Example 1. (i) *Facts.* Employer *V* provides group health coverage through a policy provided by Issuer *M*. Individual *D* works for *V* and is covered under *V*'s plan. *V* fails to pay *M* the premiums for the coverage period beginning March 1. Consistent with applicable state law, *M* terminates the policy so that the last day of coverage is April 30. On May 15, *M* provides *D* with a certificate of creditable coverage with respect to *D*'s cessation of coverage under *V*'s plan.

(ii) *Conclusion*. In this *Example 1*, the period to request special enrollment ends no earlier than June 14 (which is 30 days after May 15, the day a certificate of creditable coverage is provided with respect to *D*).

Example 2. (i) *Facts*. Same facts as *Example 1*, except *D* is never provided with a certificate of creditable coverage.

(ii) *Conclusion*. In this *Example 2*, the period to request special enrollment ends no earlier than July 13. (July 13 is 74 days after April 30, the date coverage ceases. That is, July 13 is 30 days after the end of the 44-day maximum tolling period.)

Example 3. (i) *Facts*. Individual *E* works for Employer *W* and has coverage under *W*'s plan. *W*'s plan has a lifetime limit of $1 million on all benefits under the plan. On September 13, *E* incurs a claim that would exceed the plan's lifetime limit. On September 28, *W* denies the claim due to the operation of the lifetime limit and a certificate of creditable coverage is provided on October 3. *E* is otherwise eligible to enroll in the group health plan of the employer of *E*'s spouse.

(ii) *Conclusion*. In this *Example 3*, the period to request special enrollment in the plan of the employer of *E*'s spouse ends no earlier than November 2 (30 days after the date the certificate is provided) and begins not later than September 13, the date *E* lost eligibility for coverage.

(iii) *Reasonable procedures for special enrollment*. After an individual has requested enrollment under paragraph (a)(4)(i) of this section, a plan may require the individual to complete enrollment materials within a reasonable time after the end of the 30-day period described in paragraph (a)(4)(i) of this section. In these enrollment materials, the plan may require the individual only to provide information required of individuals who enroll when first eligible and information about the event giving rise to the special enrollment right. A plan may establish a deadline for receiving completed enrollment materials, but such a deadline must be extended for information that an individual making reasonable efforts does not obtain by that deadline.

(iv) *Date coverage must begin*. If the plan requires completion of additional enrollment materials in accordance with paragraph (a)(4)(iii) of this section, coverage must begin no later than the first day of the first calendar month beginning after the date the plan receives enrollment materials that are substantially complete. If the plan does not require completion of additional enrollment materials, coverage must begin no later than the first day of the first calendar month beginning after the date the plan receives the request for special enrollment under paragraph (a)(4)(i) of this section.

(b) *Special enrollment with respect to certain dependent beneficiaries*.—(1) *In general*.—A group health plan that makes coverage available with respect to dependents is required to permit individuals described in paragraph (b)(2) of this section to be enrolled for coverage in a benefit package under the terms of the plan. Paragraph (b)(3) of this section describes procedures that a plan may require an individual to follow and describes the date by which coverage must begin. The special enrollment rights under this paragraph (b) apply without regard to the dates on which an individual would otherwise be able to enroll under the plan. (See 29 CFR 2590.701-6(b) and 45 CFR 146.117(b), under which this obligation is also imposed on a health insurance issuer offering group health insurance coverage.)

* * *

(3) *Applying for special enrollment and effective date of coverage*.—(i) *Request*.—A plan must allow an individual a period of at least 30 days after the date of the marriage, birth, adoption, or placement for adoption (or, if dependent coverage is not generally made available at the time of the marriage, birth, adoption, or placement for adoption, a period of at least 30 days after the date the plan makes dependent coverage generally available) to request enrollment (for the individual or the individual's dependent). For this purpose, any written or oral request made to any of the following constitutes a request for enrollment —

(A) The plan administrator;

(B) An issuer offering health insurance coverage under the plan;

(C) A person who customarily handles claims for the plan (such as a third party administrator); or

(D) Any other designated representative.

(ii) *Reasonable procedures for special enrollment*.—After an individual has requested enrollment under paragraph (b)(3)(i) of this section, a plan may require the individual to complete enrollment materials within a reasonable time after the end of the 30-day period described in paragraph (b)(3)(i) of this section. In these enrollment materials, the plan may require the individual only to provide information required of individuals who enroll when first eligible and information about the event giving rise to the special enrollment right. A plan may establish a deadline for receiving completed enrollment materials, but such a deadline must be extended for information that an individual making reasonable efforts does not obtain by that deadline.

(iii) *Date coverage must begin*.—(A) *Marriage*.—In the case of marriage, if the plan requires completion of additional enrollment materials in accordance with paragraph (b)(3)(ii) of this section, coverage must begin no later than the first day of the first calendar month beginning after the date the plan receives enrollment materials that are substantially complete. If the plan does not require such additional enrollment materials, coverage must begin no later than the first day of the first calendar month beginning after the date the plan receives the request for special enrollment under paragraph (b)(3)(i) of this section.

(B) *Birth, adoption, or placement for adoption*.—Coverage must begin in the case of a dependent's birth on the date of birth and in the case of a dependent's adoption or placement for adoption no later than the date of such adoption or placement for adoption (or, if dependent coverage is not made generally available at the time of the birth, adoption, or placement for adoption, the date the plan makes dependent coverage available). If the plan requires completion of additional enrollment materials in accordance with paragraph (b)(3)(ii) of this section, the plan must provide benefits (including benefits retroactively to the date of birth, adoption, or placement for adoption) once the plan receives enrollment materials that are substantially complete.

(4) *Examples.*—* * *

Example 2. (i) *Facts.* Individual *D* works for Employer *X*. *X* maintains a group health plan with two benefit packages — an HMO option and an indemnity option. Self-only and family coverage are available under both options. *D* enrolls for self-only coverage in the HMO option. Then, a child, *E*, is placed for adoption with *D*. Within 30 days of the placement of *E* for adoption, *D* requests enrollment for *D* and *E* under the plan's indemnity option and submits completed enrollment materials timely.

(ii) *Conclusion.* In this *Example 2*, *D* and *E* satisfy the conditions for special enrollment under paragraphs (b)(2)(v) and (b)(3) of this section. Therefore, the plan must allow *D* and *E* to enroll in the indemnity coverage, effective as of the date of the placement for adoption.

Example 3. (i) *Facts.* Same facts as *Example 1*. On March 17 (two days after the birth of C), *A* telephones the plan administrator and requests special enrollment of *A*, *B*, and *C*. The plan administrator sends *A* an enrollment form. Under the terms of the plan, enrollment is denied unless a completed form is submitted within 30 days of the event giving rise to the special enrollment right (in this case, *C*'s birth).

(ii) *Conclusion.* In this *Example 3*, the plan does not satisfy paragraph (b)(3) of this section. The plan may require only that *A* request enrollment during the 30-day period after *C*'s birth. *A* did so by telephoning the plan administrator. The plan may not condition special enrollment on filing additional enrollment materials during the 30-day period. To comply with paragraph (b)(3) of this section, the plan must allow *A* a reasonable time after the end of the 30-day period to submit any additional enrollment materials. Once these enrollment materials are received, the plan must allow whatever coverage is chosen to begin on March 15, the date of *C*'s birth.

Example 4. (i) *Facts.* Same facts as *Example 3*, except that *A* telephones the plan administrator to request enrollment on April 13 (29 days after *C*'s birth). Also, under the terms of the plan, the deadline for submitting the enrollment form is 14 days after the end of the 30-day period for requesting special enrollment (thus, in this case, April 28, which is 44 days after *C*'s birth). The form requests the same information for *A*, *B*, and *C* (name, date of birth, and place of birth) as well as a copy of *C*'s birth certificate. *A* fills out the enrollment form and delivers it to the plan administrator on April 28. At that time *A* does not have a birth certificate for *C* but applies on that day for one from the appropriate government office. *A* receives the birth certificate on June 1 and furnishes a copy of the birth certificate to the plan administrator shortly thereafter.

(ii) *Conclusion.* In this *Example 4*, *A*, *B*, and *C* are entitled to special enrollment under the plan even though *A* did not satisfy the plan's requirement of providing a copy of *C*'s birth certificate by the plan's 14-day deadline. While a plan may establish such a deadline, the plan must extend the deadline for information that an individual making reasonable efforts does not obtain by that deadline. *A* delivered the enrollment form to the plan administrator by the deadline and made reasonable efforts to furnish the birth certificate that the plan requires.

Example 5. (i) *Facts.* Same facts as *Example 4*. On May 3 (after *A* has delivered the enrollment form to the plan administrator but before *A* provides the birth certificate) *A* submits claims for all medical expenses incurred for *B* and *C* from the date of *C*'s birth.

(ii) *Conclusion.* In this *Example 5*, the plan must pay all of the claims submitted by *A*. Because the plan requires that individuals seeking special enrollment complete additional enrollment materials, it is required to provide benefits once it receives enrollment materials that are substantially complete. The form that A submitted on April 28 was substantially complete. Because *C*'s birth is the event giving rise to the special enrollment right, on April 28 *A*, *B*, and *C* become entitled to benefits under the plan retroactive to the date of *C*'s birth.

* * *

☐ Par. 7. A new § 54.9801-7 is added to read as follows:

§ 54.9801-7. Interaction with the Family and Medical Leave Act.—(a) *In general.*—The rules of §§ 54.9801-1 through 54.9801-6 apply with respect to an individual on leave under the Family and Medical Leave Act of 1993 (29 U.S.C. 2601) (FMLA), and apply with respect to a dependent of such an individual, except to the extent otherwise provided in this section.

(b) *Tolling of significant break in coverage during FMLA leave.*—In the case of an individual (or a dependent of the individual) who is covered under a group health plan, if the individual takes FMLA leave and does not continue group health coverage for any period of FMLA leave, that period is not taken into account in determining whether a significant break in coverage has occurred under § 54.9801-4(b)(2)(iii).

(c) *Application of certification provisions.*—(1) *Timing of issuance of certificate.*—(i) In the case of an individual (or a dependent of the individual) who is covered under a group health plan, if the individual takes FMLA leave and the individual's group health coverage is terminated during FMLA leave, an automatic certificate must be provided in accordance with the timing rules set forth in § 54.9801-5(a)(2)(ii)(B) (which generally require plans to provide certificates within a reasonable time after coverage ceases).

(ii) In the case of an individual (or a dependent of the individual) who is covered under a group health plan, if the individual takes FMLA leave and continues group health coverage for the period of FMLA leave, but then ceases coverage under the plan at the end of FMLA leave, an automatic certificate must be provided in accordance with the timing rules set forth in § 54.9801-5(a)(2)(ii)(A) (which generally require plans to provide a certificate no later than the time a notice is required to be furnished for a qualifying event under a COBRA continuation provision).

(2) *Demonstrating FMLA leave.*—(i) A plan is required to take into account all information about FMLA leave that it obtains or that is presented on behalf of an individual. A plan must treat the individual as having been on FMLA leave for a period if —

(A) The individual attests to the period of FMLA leave; and

(B) The individual cooperates with the plan's efforts to verify the individual's FMLA leave.

(ii) Nothing in this section prevents a plan from modifying its initial determination of FMLA leave if it determines that the individual did not have the claimed FMLA leave, provided that the plan follows procedures for reconsideration similar to those set forth in § 54.9801-3(f).

(d) *Relationship to loss of eligibility special enrollment rules.*—In the case of an individual (or a dependent of the individual) who is covered under a group health plan and who takes FMLA leave, a loss of eligibility for coverage under § 54.9801-6(a) occurs when the period of FMLA leave ends if —

(1) The individual's group health coverage is terminated at any time during FMLA leave; and

(2) The individual does not return to work for the employer at the end of FMLA leave.

[Reg. § 54.9801-7.]

Expatriate Health Plans: Issuers: Excepted Benefits

Expatriate Health Plans: Issuers: Excepted Benefits.—Amendments to Reg. § 54.9801-2, relating to the rules for expatriate health plans, expatriate health plan issuers, and qualified expatriates under the Expatriate Health Coverage Clarification Act of 2014 (EHCCA), are proposed (published in the Federal Register on June 10, 2016) (REG-135702-15).

8. Section 54.9801-2 is amended by:

a. Adding in alphabetical order definitions for "expatriate health insurance issuer", "expatriate health plan", and "qualified expatriate;"

b. Revising the definition of "short-term, limited-duration insurance"; and

c. Adding in alphabetical order a definition for "travel insurance".

The additions and revisions read as follows:

§ 54.9801-2. Definitions.

* * *

Expatriate health insurance issuer means an expatriate health insurance issuer within the meaning of § 54.9831-1(f)(2).

Expatriate health plan means an expatriate health plan within the meaning of § 54.9831-1(f)(3).

* * *

Qualified expatriate means a qualified expatriate within the meaning of § 54.9831-1(f)(6).

* * *

[The definitions of *Short term, limited-duration insurance* and *Travel insurance* were adopted by T.D. 9791 on 10/28/2016.]

* * *

Insurance Coverage: Health Reimbursement Arrangements

Insurance Coverage: Health Reimbursement Arrangements.—Amendments to Reg. § 54.9801-2, regarding health reimbursement arrangements (HRAs) and other account-based group health plans, are proposed (published in the Federal Register on October 29, 2018) (REG-136724-17).

Par. 4. Section 54.9801-2 is amended by revising the definition of "Group health insurance coverage" to read as follows:

§ 54.9801-2. Definitions.

* * *

Group health insurance coverage means health insurance coverage offered in connection with a group health plan. Individual health insurance coverage reimbursed by the arrangements described in 29 CFR 2510.3-1(l) is not offered in connection with a group health plan, and is not group health insurance coverage, provided all the conditions in 29 CFR 2510.3-1(l) are satisfied.

* * *

Group Health Plans: Genetic Information Nondiscrimination Act

Group Health Plans: Genetic Information Nondiscrimination Act.—Reg. § 54.9802-3, governing the provisions of the Genetic Information Nondiscrimination Act prohibiting discrimination based on genetic information for group health plans, is proposed (published in the Federal Register on October 7, 2009) (REG-123829-08).

Par. 2. Section 54.9802-3 is added to read as follows:

§ 54.9802-3. Additional requirements prohibiting discrimination based on genetic information.

[The text of proposed § 54.9802-3 is the same as the text of § 54.9802-3T as added by T.D. 9464.]

Insurance Coverage: Health Reimbursement Arrangements

Insurance Coverage: Health Reimbursement Arrangements.—Reg. § 54.9802-4, regarding health reimbursement arrangements (HRAs) and other account-based group health plans, is proposed (published in the Federal Register on October 29, 2018) (REG-136724-17).

Par. 5. Section 54.9802-4 is added to read as follows:

§ 54.9802-4. Special rule allowing integration of health reimbursement arrangements (HRAs) and other account-based group health plans with individual health insurance coverage and prohibiting discrimination in HRAs and other account-based group health plans.—(a) *Scope.*—This section applies to health reimbursement arrangements (HRAs) and other account-based group health plans, as defined in § 54.9815-2711(d)(6)(i) of this part. For ease of reference, the term "HRA" is used in this section to include other account-based group health plans.

(b) *Purpose.*—This section provides the conditions that an HRA must satisfy in order to be integrated with individual health insurance coverage for purposes of Public Health Service Act (PHS Act) sections 2711 and 2713 and § 54.9815-2711(d)(4) of this part. Some of the conditions set forth in this section specifically relate to compliance with PHS Act sections 2711 and 2713 and some relate to the effect of having or being offered an HRA on eligibility for the premium tax credit under section 36B. In addition, this section provides conditions that an HRA integrated with individual health insurance coverage must satisfy in order to comply with the nondiscrimination provisions in section 9802 and section 2705 of the PHS Act (which is incorporated in section 9815) and that are consistent with the provisions of the Patient Protection and Affordable Care Act, Public Law 111–148 (124 Stat. 119 (2010)), and the Health Care and Education Reconciliation Act of 2010, Public Law 111–152 (124 Stat. 1029 (2010)), each as amended, that are designed to create a competitive individual market. These conditions are intended to prevent an HRA plan sponsor from intentionally or unintentionally, directly or indirectly, steering any participants or dependents with adverse health factors away from its traditional group health plan, if any, and toward individual health insurance coverage.

(c) *General rule.*—An HRA will be considered to be integrated with individual health insurance coverage for purposes of PHS Act sections 2711 and 2713 and § 54.9815-2711(d)(4) of this part and will not be considered to discriminate in violation of section 9802 and PHS Act section 2705 solely because it offers an HRA integrated with individual health insurance coverage, provided that the conditions of this paragraph (c) are satisfied.

(1) *Enrollment in individual health insurance coverage.*—The HRA must require that the participant and any dependent(s) are enrolled in individual health insurance coverage that is subject to and complies with the requirements in PHS Act sections 2711 and 2713 for each month that the individual(s) are covered by the HRA. For this purpose, all individual health insurance coverage, except for individual health insurance coverage that consists solely of excepted benefits, is treated as being subject to and complying with PHS Act sections 2711 and 2713. References to individual health insurance coverage in this paragraph (c) do not include individual health insurance coverage that consists solely of excepted benefits. The HRA must also provide that, subject to applicable COBRA or other continuation of coverage requirements, if any individual covered by the HRA ceases to be covered by such individual health insurance coverage, the individual may not seek reimbursement under the HRA for claims that are incurred after the individual health insurance coverage ceases. In addition, subject to applicable COBRA or other continuation of coverage requirements, if the participant and all of the dependents covered by the participant's HRA cease to be covered by such individual health insurance coverage, the participant must forfeit the HRA.

(2) *No traditional group health plan may be offered to same participants.*—To the extent a plan sponsor offers any class of employees (as defined in paragraph (d) of this section) an HRA integrated with individual health insurance coverage, the plan sponsor may not also offer a traditional group health plan to the same class of employees. For this purpose, a traditional group health plan is any group health plan other than either an account-based group health plan or a group health plan that consists solely of excepted benefits. Therefore, a plan sponsor may not offer a choice between an HRA integrated with individual health insurance coverage or a traditional group health plan to any participant.

(3) *Same terms requirement.*—To the extent a plan sponsor offers an HRA integrated with individual health insurance coverage to a class of employees described in paragraph (d) of this section, the HRA must be offered on the same terms to all participants within the class, except as provided in paragraphs (c)(3)(i) and (ii) of this section and except that the HRA will not fail to be treated as provided on the same terms even if the plan sponsor offers the HRA to some, but not all, former employees within a class of employees. However, if a plan sponsor offers the HRA to one or more former employees within a class of employees, the HRA must be offered to the former employee(s) on the same terms as to all other employees within the class. Also, amounts that are not used to reimburse medical care expenses (as defined in § 54.9815-2711(d)(6)(ii) of this part) for any plan year that are made available to participants in later plan years are disregarded for purposes of determining whether an HRA is offered on the same terms, provided that the method for determining whether participants have access to unused amounts in future years, and the methodology and formula for determining the amounts of unused funds which they may access in future years, is the same for all participants in a class of employees. In addition, the ability to pay the portion of the premium for individual health insurance coverage that is not covered by the HRA, if any, by using a salary reduction arrangement under section 125 is considered to be a term of the HRA for purposes of this paragraph; therefore, an HRA shall fail to be treated as provided on the same

terms unless such a salary reduction arrangement, if made available to any participant in a class of employees, is made available on the same terms to all participants (other than former employees) in the class of employees. Further, the HRA shall not fail to be treated as provided on the same terms because the maximum dollar amount made available to participants in a class of employees to reimburse medical care expenses for any plan year increases:

(i) As the age of the participant increases, so long as the same maximum dollar amount attributable to the increase in age is made available to all participants in that class of employees who are the same age; or

(ii) As the number of the participant's dependents who are covered under the HRA increases, so long as the same maximum dollar amount attributable to the increase in family size is made available to all participants in that class of employees with the same number of dependents covered by the HRA.

(4) *Opt out.*—Under the terms of the HRA, a participant who is otherwise eligible for coverage must be permitted to opt out of and waive future reimbursements from the HRA at least annually, and, upon termination of employment, either the remaining amounts in the HRA are forfeited or the participant is permitted to permanently opt out of and waive future reimbursements from the HRA.

(5) *Reasonable procedures for verification and substantiation.*—(i) *General rule for verification of individual health insurance coverage for the plan year.*—The HRA must implement, and comply with, reasonable procedures to verify that participants and dependents are, or will be, enrolled in individual health insurance coverage for the plan year. The reasonable procedures may include a requirement that a participant substantiate enrollment by providing either:

(A) A document from a third party (for example, the issuer) showing that the participant and any dependents covered by the HRA are, or will be, enrolled in individual health insurance coverage (for example, an insurance card or an explanation of benefits document pertaining to the relevant time period); or

(B) An attestation by the participant stating that the participant and dependent(s) covered by the HRA are or will be enrolled in individual health insurance coverage, the date coverage began or will begin, and the name of the provider of the coverage.

(ii) *Coverage substantiation with each request for reimbursement of medical care expenses.*—Following the initial verification of coverage, with each new request for reimbursement of an incurred medical care expense for the same plan year, the HRA may not reimburse participants for any medical care expenses unless, prior to each reimbursement, the participant provides substantiation (which may be in the form of a written attestation) that the participant and if applicable, the dependent whose medical care expenses are requested to be reimbursed continue to be enrolled in individual health insurance coverage for the month during which the medical care expenses were incurred. The attestation may be part of the form used for requesting reimbursement.

(iii) *Reliance on substantiation.*—For purposes of this paragraph (c)(5), an HRA may rely on the participant's documentation or attestation unless the HRA has actual knowledge that any individual covered by the HRA is not, or will not be, enrolled in individual health insurance coverage for the plan year or the month, as applicable.

(6) *Notice requirement.*—(i) *Timing.*—The HRA must provide a written notice to each participant at least 90 days before the beginning of each plan year or, for a participant who is not eligible to participate at the beginning of the plan year (or who is not eligible to participate at the time the notice is provided at least 90 days before the beginning of the plan year), no later than the date on which the participant is first eligible to participate in the HRA.

(ii) *Content.*—The notice must include all the information described in this paragraph (c)(6)(ii) (and may include any additional information as long as it does not conflict with the required information set forth in paragraph (c)(6)(ii)(A) through (H) of this section).

(A) A description of the terms of the HRA, including the maximum dollar amount available for each participant (including the self-only HRA amount available for the plan year (or the maximum dollar amount available for the plan year if the HRA provides for reimbursements up to a single dollar amount regardless of whether a participant has self-only or family coverage)), any rules regarding the proration of the maximum dollar amount applicable to any participant who is not eligible to participate in the HRA for the entire plan year, whether the participant's family members are eligible for the HRA, a statement that the HRA is not a qualified small employer health reimbursement arrangement, a statement that the HRA requires the participant and any dependents to be enrolled in individual health insurance coverage, a statement that the participant is required to substantiate the existence of such enrollment, a statement that the coverage enrolled in cannot be short-term, limited-duration insurance or excepted benefits, and, if the requirements under 29 CFR 2510.3-1(l) are met, a statement that the individual health insurance coverage enrolled in is not subject to the Employee Retirement Income Security Act (ERISA).

(B) A statement of the right of the participant to opt out of and waive future reimbursements from the HRA, as set forth under paragraph (c)(4) of this section.

(C) A description of the potential availability of the premium tax credit if the participant opts out of and waives future reimbursements from the HRA and the HRA is not affordable for one or more months under § 1.36B-2(c)(5) of this chapter, a statement that even if the participant opts out of and waives future reimbursements from an HRA, the offer will prohibit the participant (and, potentially, the participant's dependents) from receiving a premium tax credit for the participant's coverage (or the dependent's coverage, if applicable) on the Exchange (as defined in 45 CFR 155.20) for any month that the HRA is affordable under § 1.36B-2(c)(5) of this chapter, and a statement that, if the participant is a former employee, the offer of the HRA does not render the participant ineligible for the premium tax credit regardless of whether it is affordable under § 1.36B-2(c)(5) of this chapter;

(D) A statement that if the participant accepts the HRA, the participant may not claim a premium tax credit for the participant's Exchange coverage for any month the HRA may be used to reimburse medical care expenses of the participant and a premium tax credit may not be claimed for the Exchange coverage of the participant's dependents for any month the HRA may be used to reimburse medical care expenses of the dependents.

(E) A statement that the participant must inform any Exchange to which the participant applies for advance payments of the premium tax credit of the availability of the HRA, the self-only HRA amount available for the plan year (or the maximum dollar amount available for the plan year if the HRA provides for reimbursements up to a single dollar amount regardless of whether a participant has self-only or family coverage) as set forth in the written notice in accordance with paragraph (c)(6)(ii)(A) of this section, the number of months in the plan year the HRA is available to the participant, whether the HRA is also available to the participant's dependents, and whether the participant is a current employee or former employee.

(F) A statement that the participant should retain the written notice because it may be needed to determine whether the participant is allowed a premium tax credit on the participant's individual income tax return and, if so, the months the participant is allowed the premium tax credit.

(G) A statement that the HRA may not reimburse any medical care expense unless the substantiation requirement set forth in paragraph (c)(5) of this section is satisfied.

(H) A statement that it is the responsibility of the participant to inform the HRA if the participant or any dependent whose medical care expenses are reimbursable by the HRA is no longer enrolled in individual health insurance coverage.

(d) *Classes of employees.*—(1) *List of classes.*—Participants may be treated as belonging to a class of employees based on whether they are, or are not, included in the classes described in this paragraph (d)(1). If the HRA is offered to former employees, former employees are considered to be in the same class in which they were in immediately before separation from service. (See paragraph (d)(2) of this section for additional rules regarding the definition of "full-time employees," "part-time employees," and "seasonal employees.")

(i) Full-time employees, defined to mean either full-time employees under section 4980H and the regulations thereunder (§54.4980H-1(a)(21) of this part) or employees who are not part-time employees (as described in §1.105-11(c)(2)(iii)(C) of this chapter);

(ii) Part-time employees, defined to mean either employees who are not full-time employees under section 4980H and §54.4980H-1 and -3 of this part or part-time employees as described in §1.105-11(c)(2)(iii)(C) of this chapter;

(iii) Seasonal employees, defined to mean seasonal employees as described in either §54.4980H-1(a)(38) of this part or §1.105-11(c)(2)(iii)(C) of this chapter;

(iv) Employees included in a unit of employees covered by a collective bargaining agreement in which the plan sponsor participates (as described in §1.105-11(c)(2)(iii)(D) of this chapter);

(v) Employees who have not satisfied a waiting period for coverage (if the waiting period complies with §54.9815-2708 of this part);

(vi) Employees who have not attained age 25 prior to the beginning of the plan year (as described in §1.105-11(c)(2)(iii)(B) of this chapter);

(vii) Non-resident aliens with no U.S.-based income (as described in §1.105-11(c)(2)(iii)(E) of this chapter);

(viii) Employees whose primary site of employment is in the same rating area as defined in 45 CFR 147.102(b); or

(ix) A group of participants described as a combination of two or more of the classes of employees set forth in paragraphs (d)(1)(i) through (viii) of this section. (For example, part-time employees included in a unit of employees covered by a collective bargaining agreement could be one class of employees and full-time employees included in a unit of employees covered by the same collective bargaining agreement could be another class of employees.)

(2) *Consistency requirement.*—For any plan year, a plan sponsor may define "full-time employee," "part-time employee," and "seasonal employee" in accordance with the relevant provisions of section 105(h) and §1.105-11 of this chapter or of section 4980H and §54.4980H-1 and -3 of this part if:

(i) To the extent applicable under the HRA for the plan year, each of the three classes of employees are defined in accordance with either section 105(h) or section 4980H for the plan year; and

(ii) The HRA plan document sets forth the applicable definitions prior to the beginning of the plan year in which the definitions will apply.

(e) *Examples.*—The following examples illustrate the provisions of paragraphs (c)(2) and (3) of this section. In each example, the HRA may reimburse any medical care expenses, including premiums for individual health insurance coverage.

(1) *Example 1.* (i) *Facts.* For 2020, Plan Sponsor X offers the following to its employees. Full-time employees in rating area A are offered $2,000 each in an HRA. Part-time employees in rating area A are offered $500 each in an HRA. All employees in rating area B are offered a traditional group health plan.

(ii) *Conclusion.* The requirements of paragraphs (c)(2) and (3) of this section are satisfied in this *Example 1.*

(2) *Example 2.* (i) *Facts.* For 2020, Plan Sponsor Y offers the following to its employees. Employees covered by a collective bargaining agreement in which Plan Sponsor Y participates are offered a traditional group health plan (as required by the collective bargaining agreement). All other employees (non-collectively bargained employees) are offered the following amounts in an HRA: $1,000 each for employees age 25 to 35; $2,000 each for employees age 36 to 45; $2,500 each for employees age 46 to 55; and $4,000 each for employees over age 55. Non-collectively bargained employees who have not attained age 25 by January 1, 2020 are not offered an HRA or a traditional group health plan.

(ii) *Conclusion*. The requirements of paragraphs (c)(2) and (3) of this section are satisfied in this *Example 2*.

(3) *Example 3*. (i) *Facts*. For 2020, Plan Sponsor Z offers the following amounts in an HRA to its employees who have completed the plan's waiting period, which complies with the requirements for waiting periods in § 54.9815-2708 of this part: $1,500, if the employee is the only individual covered by the HRA; $3,500, if the employee and one additional family member are covered by the HRA; and $5,000, if the employee and more than one additional family member are covered by the HRA.

(ii) *Conclusion*. The requirements of paragraphs (c)(2) and (3) of this section are satisfied in this *Example 3*.

(f) *Applicability date*.—This section applies to plan years beginning on or after January 1, 2020. [Reg. § 54.9802-4.]

Insurance Coverage: Health Reimbursement Arrangements

Insurance Coverage: Health Reimbursement Arrangements.—Amendments to Reg. § 54.9815-2711, regarding health reimbursement arrangements (HRAs) and other account-based group health plans, are proposed (published in the Federal Register on October 29, 2018) (REG-136724-17).

Par. 6. Section 54.9815-2711 is amended by revising paragraphs (c), (d), and (e) to read as follows:

§ 54.9815-2711. No lifetime or annual limits.

* * *

(c) *Definition of essential health benefits*.—The term "essential health benefits" means essential health benefits under section 1302(b) of the Patient Protection and Affordable Care Act. For this purpose, a group health plan or a health insurance issuer that is not required to provide essential health benefits under section 1302(b) must define "essential health benefits" in a manner that is consistent with the following paragraphs (c)(1) or (2):

(1) For plan years beginning before January 1, 2020, one of the EHB-benchmark plans applicable in a State under 45 CFR 156.110, and including coverage of any additional required benefits that are considered essential health benefits consistent with 45 CFR 155.170(a)(2), or one of the three Federal Employee Health Benefits Program (FEHBP) plan options as defined by 45 CFR 156.100(a)(3), and including coverage of additional required benefits under 45 CFR 156.110; or

(2) For plan years beginning on or after January 1, 2020, an EHB-benchmark plan selected by a State in accordance with the available options and requirements for EHB-benchmark plan selection at 45 CFR 156.111, including an EHB-benchmark plan in a State that takes no action to change its EHB-benchmark plan and thus retains the EHB-benchmark plan applicable in that State for the prior year in accordance with 45 CFR 156.111(d)(1), and including coverage of any additional required benefits that are considered essential health benefits consistent with 45 CFR 155.170(a)(2).

(d) *Health reimbursement arrangements (HRAs) and other account-based group health plans*.—(1) *In general*.—If an HRA or other account-based group health plan is integrated with another group health plan or individual health insurance coverage and the other group health plan or individual health insurance coverage, as applicable, separately is subject to and satisfies the requirements in PHS Act section 2711 and paragraph (a)(2) of this section, the fact that the benefits under the HRA or other account-based group health plan are limited does not cause the HRA or other account-based group health plan to fail to meet the requirements of PHS Act section 2711 and paragraph (a)(2) of this section. Similarly, if an HRA or other account-based group health plan is integrated with another group health plan or individual health insurance coverage and the other group health plan or individual health insurance coverage, as applicable, separately is subject to and satisfies the requirements in PHS Act section 2713 and § 54.9815-2713(a)(1) of this part, the fact that the benefits under the HRA or other account-based group health plan are limited does not cause the HRA or other account-based group health plan to fail to meet the requirements of PHS Act section 2713 and § 54.9815-2713(a)(1) of this part. For this purpose, all individual health insurance coverage, except for coverage that consists solely of excepted benefits, is treated as being subject to and complying with PHS Act sections 2711 and 2713.

(2) *Requirements for an HRA or other account-based group health plan to be integrated with another group health plan*.—An HRA or other account-based group health plan is integrated with another group health plan for purposes of PHS Act section 2711 and paragraph (a)(2) of this section if it meets the requirements under one of the integration methods set forth in paragraph (d)(2)(i) or (ii) of this section. For purposes of the integration methods under which an HRA or other account-based group health plan is integrated with another group health plan, integration does not require that the HRA or other account-based group health plan and the other group health plan with which it is integrated share the same plan sponsor, the same plan document or governing instruments, or file a single Form 5500, if applicable. An HRA or other account-based group health plan integrated with another group health plan for purposes of PHS Act section 2711 and paragraph (a)(2) of this section may not be used to purchase individual health insurance coverage unless that coverage consists solely of excepted benefits, as defined in 45 CFR 148.220.

(i) *Method for integration with a group health plan: Minimum value not required*.—An HRA or other account-based group health plan is integrated with another group health plan for purposes of this paragraph if:

(A) The plan sponsor offers a group health plan (other than the HRA or other account-based group health plan) to the employee that does not consist solely of excepted benefits;

(B) The employee receiving the HRA or other account-based group health plan is actually enrolled in a group health plan (other than the HRA or other account-based group health plan) that does not consist solely of excepted benefits, regardless of whether the plan is offered by the same plan sponsor (referred to as non-HRA group coverage);

(C) The HRA or other account-based group health plan is available only to employees who are enrolled in non-HRA group coverage, regardless of whether the non-HRA group coverage is offered by the plan sponsor of the HRA or other account-based group health plan (for example, the HRA may be offered only to employees who do not enroll in an employer's group health plan but are enrolled in other non-HRA group coverage, such as a group health plan maintained by the employer of the employee's spouse);

(D) The benefits under the HRA or other account-based group health plan are limited to reimbursement of one or more of the following — co-payments, co-insurance, deductibles, and premiums under the non-HRA group coverage, as well as medical care expenses that do not constitute essential health benefits as defined in paragraph (c) of this section; and

(E) Under the terms of the HRA or other account-based group health plan, an employee (or former employee) is permitted to permanently opt out of and waive future reimbursements from the HRA or other account-based group health plan at least annually and, upon termination of employment, either the remaining amounts in the HRA or other account-based group health plan are forfeited or the employee is permitted to permanently opt out of and waive future reimbursements from the HRA or other account-based group health plan (see paragraph (d)(3) of this section for additional rules regarding forfeiture and waiver).

(ii) *Method for integration with another group health plan: Minimum value required.*—An HRA or other account-based group health plan is integrated with another group health plan for purposes of this paragraph if:

(A) The plan sponsor offers a group health plan (other than the HRA or other account-based group health plan) to the employee that provides minimum value pursuant to section 36B(c)(2)(C)(ii) and § 1.36B-6 of this chapter;

(B) The employee receiving the HRA or other account-based group health plan is actually enrolled in a group health plan (other than the HRA or other account-based group health plan) that provides minimum value pursuant to section 36B(c)(2)(C)(ii) and § 1.36B-6 of this chapter regardless of whether the plan is offered by the plan sponsor of the HRA or other account-based group health plan (referred to as non-HRA MV group coverage);

(C) The HRA or other account-based group health plan is available only to employees who are actually enrolled in non-HRA MV group coverage, regardless of whether the non-HRA MV group coverage is offered by the plan sponsor of the HRA or other account-based group health plan (for example, the HRA may be offered only to employees who do not enroll in an employer's group health plan but are enrolled in other non-HRA MV group coverage, such as a group health plan maintained by an employer of the employee's spouse); and

(D) Under the terms of the HRA or other account-based group health plan, an employee (or former employee) is permitted to permanently opt out of and waive future reimbursements from the HRA or other account-based group health plan at least annually, and, upon termination of employment, either the remaining amounts in the HRA or other account-based group health plan are forfeited or the employee is permitted to permanently opt out of and waive future reimbursements from the HRA or other account-based group health plan (see paragraph (d)(3) of this section for additional rules regarding forfeiture and waiver).

(3) *Forfeiture.*—For purposes of integration under paragraphs (d)(2)(i)(E) and (d)(2)(ii)(D) of this section, forfeiture or waiver occurs even if the forfeited or waived amounts may be reinstated upon a fixed date, a participant's death, or the earlier of the two events (the reinstatement event). For this purpose, coverage under an HRA or other account-based group health plan is considered forfeited or waived prior to a reinstatement event only if the participant's election to forfeit or waive is irrevocable, meaning that, beginning on the effective date of the election and through the date of the reinstatement event, the participant and the participant's beneficiaries have no access to amounts credited to the HRA or other account-based group health plan. This means that upon and after reinstatement, the reinstated amounts under the HRA or other account-based group health plan may not be used to reimburse or pay medical care expenses incurred during the period after forfeiture and prior to reinstatement.

(4) *Requirements for an HRA or other account-based group health plan to be integrated with individual health insurance coverage.*—An HRA or other account-based group health plan is integrated with individual health insurance coverage (and treated as complying with PHS Act sections 2711 and 2713) if the HRA or other account-based group health plan meets the requirements of § 54.9802-4(c) of this part.

(5) *Integration with Medicare parts B and D.*—For employers that are not required to offer their non-HRA group health plan coverage to employees who are Medicare beneficiaries, an HRA or other account-based group health plan that may be used to reimburse premiums under Medicare part B or D may be integrated with Medicare (and deemed to comply with PHS Act sections 2711 and 2713) if the requirements of this paragraph (d)(5) are satisfied with respect to employees who would be eligible for the employer's non-HRA group health plan but for their eligibility for Medicare (and the integration rules under paragraphs (d)(2)(i) and (ii) of this section continue to apply to employees who are not eligible for Medicare):

(i) The plan sponsor offers a group health plan (other than the HRA or other account-based group health plan and that does not consist solely of excepted benefits) to employees who are not eligible for Medicare;

(ii) The employee receiving the HRA or other account-based group health plan is actually enrolled in Medicare part B or D;

(iii) The HRA or other account-based group health plan is available only to employees who are enrolled in Medicare part B or D; and

(iv) The HRA or other account-based group health plan complies with paragraphs (d)(2)(i)(E) and (d)(2)(ii)(D) of this section.

(6) *Definitions.*—The following definitions apply for purposes of this section.

(i) *Account-based group health plan.*—An account-based group health plan is an employer-provided group health plan that provides reimbursements of medical care expenses with the reimbursement subject to a maximum fixed dollar amount for a period. An HRA is a type of account-based group health plan. An account-based group health plan does not include a qualified small employer health reimbursement arrangement, as defined in section 9831(d)(2).

(ii) *Medical care expenses.*—Medical care expenses means expenses for medical care as defined under section 213(d).

(e) *Applicability date.*—The provisions of this section are applicable to group health plans and health insurance issuers for plan years beginning on or after January 1, 2020. Until [APPLICABILITY DATE OF FINAL RULE], plans and issuers are required to continue to comply with the corresponding sections of 26 CFR part 54, contained in the 26 CFR subchapter D, revised as of April 1, 2018.

Group Health Plans: Portability Requirements

Group Health Plans: Portability Requirements.—Amendments to Reg. § 54.9831-1, clarifying certain portability requirements for group health plans and issuers of health insurance coverage offered in connection with a group health plans, are proposed (published in the Federal Register on December 30, 2004) (REG-130370-04).

☐ Par. 8. Section 54.9831-1 is amended by:

a. Adding paragraph (a)(2).

b. Revising paragraph (b).

c. Adding paragraph (e).

d. Revising paragraph (c)(1).

The additions and revisions read as follows:

§ 54.9831-1. Special rules relating to group health plans.—(a) *Group health plan.*—* * *

(2) *Determination of number of plans.*—The number of group health plans that an employer or employee organization (including for this purpose a joint board of trustees of a multiemployer trust affiliated with one or more multiemployer plans) maintains is determined under the rules of this paragraph (a)(2).

(i) Except as provided in paragraph (a)(2)(ii) or (iii) of this section, health care benefits provided by a corporation, partnership, or other entity or trade or business, or by an employee organization, constitute one group health plan, unless —

(A) It is clear from the instruments governing the arrangement or arrangements to provide health care benefits that the benefits are being provided under separate plans; and

(B) The arrangement or arrangements are operated pursuant to such instruments as separate plans.

(ii) A multiemployer plan and a nonmultiemployer plan are always separate plans.

(iii) If a principal purpose of establishing separate plans is to evade any requirement of law, then the separate plans will be considered a single plan to the extent necessary to prevent the evasion.

(b) *General exception for certain small group health plans.*—The requirements of § § 54.9801-1 through 54.9801-7, 54.9802-1, 54.9802-2, 54.9811-1T, 54.9812-1T, and 54.9833-1 do not apply to any group health plan for any plan year if, on the first day of the plan year, the plan has fewer than two participants who are current employees.

(c) *Excepted benefits.*—(1) *In general.*—The requirements of § § 54.9801-1 through 54.9801-7, 54.9802-1, 54.9802-2, 54.9811-1T, 54.9812-1T, and 54.9833-1 do not apply to any group health plan in relation to its provision of the benefits described in paragraph (c)(2), (3), (4), or (5) of this section (or any combination of these benefits).

* * *

(e) *Determining the average number of employees.*—(1) *Scope.*—Whenever the application of a rule in this part depends upon the average number of employees employed by an employer, the determination of that number is made in accordance with the rules of this paragraph (e).

(2) *Full-time equivalents.*—The average number of employees is determined by calculating the average number of full-time equivalents on business days during the preceding calendar year.

(3) *Methodology.*—For the preceding calendar year, the average number of full-time equivalents is determined by —

(i) Determining the number of employees who were employed full-time by the employer throughout the entire calendar year;

(ii) Totaling all employment hours (not to exceed 40 hours per week) for each part-time employee, and for each full-time employee who was not employed full-time with the employer throughout the entire calendar year;

(iii) Dividing the total determined under paragraph (e)(3)(ii) of this section by a figure that represents the annual full-time hours under the employer's general employment practices, such as 2,080 hours (although for this purpose not more than 40 hours per week may be used); and

(iv) Adding the quotient determined under paragraph (e)(3)(iii) of this section to the number determined under paragraph (e)(3)(i).

(4) *Rounding.*—For purposes of paragraph (e)(3)(iv) of this section, all fractions are disregarded. For instance, a figure of 50.9 is deemed to be 50.

(5) *Employers not in existence in the preceding year.*—In the case of an employer that was in existence for less than the entire preceding calendar year (including an employer that was not in existence at all), a determination of the average number of employees that the employer employs is based on the average number of employees that it is reasonably expected the employer will employ on business days in the current calendar year.

(6) *Scope of the term "employer".*—For purposes of this paragraph (e), employer includes any predecessor of the employer. In addition, all persons treated as a single employer under section 414(b), (c), (m), or (o) are treated as one employer.

(7) *Special rule for multiemployer plans.*—(i) With respect to the application of a rule in this part to a multiemployer plan (as defined in section 3(37) of ERISA), each employer with at least one employee participating in the plan is considered to employ the same average number of employees. That number is the highest number that results by applying the rules of paragraphs (e)(1) through (6) of this section separately to each of the employers.

(ii) The rules of this paragraph (e)(7) are illustrated by the following example:

Example. (i) *Facts.* Twenty five employers have at least one employee who participates in Multiemployer Plan *M*. Among these 25 employers, Employer *K* has 51 employees, determined under the rules of paragraphs (e)(1) through (6) of this section. Each of the other 24 employers has fewer than 50 employees.

(ii) *Conclusion.* With respect to the application of a rule in this part to *M*, each of the 25 employers is considered to employ 51 employees.

Expatriate Health Plans: Issuers: Excepted Benefits

Expatriate Health Plans: Issuers: Excepted Benefits.—Amendments to Reg. §54.9831-1, relating to the rules for expatriate health plans, expatriate health plan issuers, and qualified expatriates under the Expatriate Health Coverage Clarification Act of 2014 (EHCCA), are proposed (published in the Federal Register on June 10, 2016) (REG-135702-15).

11. Section 54.9831-1 is amended:

a. In paragraph (c)(2)(vii) by removing "and" at the end;

b. In paragraph (c)(2)(viii) by adding "and" at the end;

c. Adding paragraph (c)(2)(ix);

d. Revising paragraph (c)(4)(i);

e. Adding paragraph (c)(4)(ii)(D);

f. Revising paragraphs (c)(4)(iii) and (c)(5)(i)(C); and

g. Adding paragraph (f).

The revisions and additions read as follows:

§54.9831-1. Special rules relating to group health plans.

* * *

(c) * * *

(2) * * *

(ix) [Amendment adopted by T.D. 9791 on 10/28/2016.]

* * *

(4) *Noncoordinated benefits.*—(i) *Excepted benefits that are not coordinated.*—Coverage for only a specified disease or illness (for example, cancer-only policies) or hospital indemnity or other fixed indemnity insurance is excepted only if the coverage meets each of the conditions specified in paragraph (c)(4)(ii) of this section.

(ii) * * *

(D) To be hospital indemnity or other fixed indemnity insurance, the insurance must pay a fixed dollar amount per day (or per other time period, such as per week) of hospitalization or illness (for example, $100/day) without regard to the amount of expenses incurred or the type of items or services received and —

(1) The plan or issuer must provide, in any application or enrollment materials provided to participants at or before the time participants are given the opportunity to enroll in the coverage, a notice that prominently displays in at least 14 point type the following language: "THIS IS A SUPPLEMENT TO HEALTH INSURANCE AND IS NOT A SUBSTITUTE FOR MAJOR MEDICAL COVERAGE. THIS IS NOT QUALIFYING HEALTH COVERAGE ('MINIMUM ESSENTIAL COVERAGE') THAT SATISFIES THE HEALTH COVERAGE REQUIREMENT OF THE AFFORDABLE CARE ACT. IF YOU DON'T HAVE MINIMUM ESSENTIAL COVERAGE, YOU MAY OWE AN ADDITIONAL PAYMENT WITH YOUR TAXES."

(2) If participants are required to reenroll (in either paper or electronic form) for renewal or reissuance, the notice described in paragraph (c)(4)(ii)(D)*(1)* of this section must be displayed in the reenrollment materials that are provided to the participants at or before the time participants are given the opportunity to reenroll in the coverage.

(3) If a notice satisfying the requirements of this paragraph (c)(4)(ii)(D) is timely provided to a participant, the obligation to provide the notice is satisfied for both the plan and the issuer.

(iii) *Examples.*—The rules of this paragraph (c)(4) are illustrated by the following examples:

Example 1. (i) *Facts.* An employer sponsors a group health plan that provides coverage through an insurance policy. The policy provides benefits only for hospital stays at a fixed percentage of hospital expenses up to a maximum of $100 a day.

(ii) *Conclusion.* In this *Example 1*, because the policy pays a percentage of expenses incurred rather than a fixed dollar amount per day (or per other time period, such as per week), the policy is not hospital indemnity or other fixed indemnity insurance that is an excepted benefit under this paragraph (c)(4). This is the result even if, in practice, the policy pays the maximum of $100 for every day of hospitalization.

Example 2. (i) *Facts.* An employer sponsors a group health plan that provides coverage through an insurance policy. The policy provides benefits for doctors' visits at $50 per visit, hospitalization at $100 per day, various surgical procedures at different dollar rates per procedure, and prescription drugs at $15 per prescription.

(ii) *Conclusion.* In this *Example 2*, for doctors' visits, surgery, and prescription drugs, payment is not made on a per-period basis, but instead is based on whether a procedure or item is provided, such as whether an individual has surgery or a doctor visit or is prescribed a drug, and the amount of payment varies based on the type of procedure or item. Because benefits related to office visits, surgery, and prescription drugs are not paid based on a fixed dollar amount per day (or per other time period, such as per week), as required under paragraph (c)(4) of this section, the policy is not hospital indemnity or other fixed indemnity insurance that is an excepted benefit under this paragraph (c)(4).

Example 3. (i) *Facts*. An employer sponsors a group health plan that provides coverage through an insurance policy. The policy provides benefits for certain services at a fixed dollar amount per day, but the dollar amount varies by the type of service.

(ii) *Conclusion*. In this *Example 3*, because the policy provides benefits in a different amount per day depending on the type of service, rather than one specific dollar amount per day regardless of the type of service, the policy is not hospital indemnity or other fixed indemnity insurance that is an excepted benefit under this paragraph (c)(4).

(5) * * *

(i) * * *

(C) [Amendment adopted by T.D. 9791 on 10/28/2016.]

* * *

(f) *Expatriate health plans and expatriate health insurance issuers*.—(1) *In general*.—With respect to coverage under an expatriate health plan, the requirements of section 9815 of the Code and implementing rules and regulations (incorporating sections 2701 through 2728 of the Public Health Service Act) do not apply to—

(i) An expatriate health plan (as defined in paragraph (f)(3) of this section),

(ii) An employer, solely in its capacity as plan sponsor of an expatriate health plan, and

(iii) An expatriate health insurance issuer (as defined in paragraph (f)(2) of this section) with respect to coverage under an expatriate health plan.

(2) *Definition of expatriate health insurance issuer*.—(i) *In general*.—Expatriate health insurance issuer means a health insurance issuer, within the meaning of §54.9801-2, that issues expatriate health plans and that in the course of its normal business operations—

(A) Maintains network provider agreements that provide for direct claims payments, with health care providers in eight or more countries;

(B) Maintains call centers in three or more countries, and accepts calls from customers in eight or more languages;

(C) Processed at least $1 million in claims in foreign currency equivalents during the preceding calendar year, determined using the Treasury Department's currency exchange rate in effect on the last day of the preceding calendar year;

(D) Makes global evacuation/repatriation coverage available;

(E) Maintains legal and compliance resources in three or more countries; and

(F) Has licenses or other authority to sell insurance in more than two countries, including in the United States.

(ii) *Additional rules*.—For purposes of meeting the requirements of this paragraph (f)(2), two or more entities, including one entity that is the expatriate health insurance issuer, that are members of the expatriate health insurance issuer's controlled group (as determined under §57.2(c) of this chapter) are treated as one expatriate health insurance issuer. Alternatively, the requirements of this paragraph (f)(2) may be satisfied through contracts between an expatriate health insurance issuer and third parties.

(3) *Definition of expatriate health plan*.—Expatriate health plan means a plan that satisfies the requirements of paragraphs (f)(3)(i) through (iii) of this section.

(i) *Substantially all qualified expatriates requirement*.—Substantially all primary enrollees in the expatriate health plan must be qualified expatriates. For purposes of this paragraph (f)(3)(i), the primary enrollee is the individual covered by the plan or policy whose eligibility for coverage is not due to that individual's status as the spouse, dependent, or other beneficiary of another covered individual. Notwithstanding the foregoing, an individual is not a primary enrollee if the individual is not a national of the United States and the individual resides in his or her country of citizenship. A plan satisfies the requirement of this paragraph (f)(3)(i) for a plan or policy year only if, on the first day of the plan or policy year, less than 5 percent of the primary enrollees (or less than 5 primary enrollees if greater) are not qualified expatriates.

(ii) *Substantially all benefits not excepted benefits requirement*.—Substantially all of the benefits provided under the plan or coverage must be benefits that are not excepted benefits described in §54.9831-1(c).

(iii) *Additional requirements*.—To qualify as an expatriate health plan, the plan or coverage must also meet the following requirements:

(A) The plan or coverage provides coverage for inpatient hospital services, outpatient facility services, physician services, and emergency services (comparable to emergency services coverage that was described in and offered under section 8903(1) of title 5, United States Code for plan year 2009) in the following locations—

(1) In the case of individuals described in paragraph (f)(6)(i) of this section, in the United States and in the country or countries from which the individual was transferred or assigned, and such other country or countries the Secretary of Health and Human Services, in consultation with the Secretary of the Treasury and Secretary of Labor, may designate;

(2) In the case of individuals described in paragraph (f)(6)(ii) of this section, in the country or countries in which the individual is present in connection with his employment, and such other country or countries the Secretary of Health and Human Services, in consultation with the Secretary of the Treasury and Secretary of Labor, may designate; or

(3) In the case of individuals described in paragraph (f)(6)(iii) of this section, in the country or countries the Secretary of Health and Human Services, in consultation with the Secretary of the Treasury and Secretary of Labor, may designate.

(B) The plan sponsor reasonably believes that benefits provided by the plan or coverage satisfy the minimum value requirements of section 36B(c)(2)(C)(ii). For this purpose, a plan sponsor is permitted to rely on the reasonable representations of the issuer or administrator regarding whether benefits offered by the issuer or group health plan satisfy the minimum value requirements unless the plan sponsor knows or has reason to know that the benefits fail to satisfy the minimum value requirements.

(C) In the case of a plan or coverage that provides dependent coverage of children, such coverage must be available until an individual attains age 26, unless an individual is the child of a child receiving dependent coverage.

(D) The plan or coverage is:

(1) In the case of individuals described in paragraph (f)(6)(i) or (ii) of this section, a group health plan (including health insurance coverage offered in connection with a group health plan), issued by an expatriate health insurance issuer or administered by an expatriate health plan administrator. A group health plan will not fail to be an expatriate health plan merely because any portion of the coverage is provided through a self-insured arrangement.

(2) In the case of individuals described in paragraph (f)(6)(iii) of this section, health insurance coverage issued by an expatriate health insurance issuer.

(E) The plan or coverage offers reimbursements for items or services in local currency in eight or more countries.

(F) The plan or coverage satisfies the provisions of Chapter 100 and regulations thereunder as in effect on March 22, 2010. For this purpose, the plan or coverage is not required to comply with section 9801(e) (relating to certification of creditable coverage) and underlying regulations. However, to the extent the plan or coverage imposes a preexisting condition exclusion, the plan or coverage must ensure that individuals with prior creditable coverage who enroll in the plan or coverage have an opportunity to demonstrate that they have creditable coverage offsetting the preexisting condition exclusion.

(iv) *Example.*—The rule of paragraph (f)(3)(i) of this section is illustrated by the following example:

Example. (i) *Facts.* Business has health plan X for 250 U.S. citizens working outside of the United States in Country Y. All of the U.S. citizens working in Country Y satisfy the requirements to be qualified expatriates under §54.9831-1(f)(6)(ii). In addition to the 250 U.S. citizens, Business employs 100 citizens of Country Y who reside in Country Y and do not satisfy the requirements to be qualified expatriates under §54.9831-1(f)(6)(ii). Health plan X covers both the U.S. citizens and citizens of Country Y.

(ii) *Conclusion.* Health plan X satisfies the requirement of §54.9831-1(f)(3)(i) that substantially all primary enrollees of an expatriate health plan be qualified expatriates because 100 percent of the primary enrollees are qualified expatriates. The 100 citizens of Country Y who reside in Country Y are not treated as primary enrollees for purposes of the substantially all requirement of §54.9831-1(f)(3)(i) because they are not nationals of the United States and they reside in the country of their citizenship.

(4) *Definition of expatriate health plan administrator.*—(i) *In general.*—Expatriate health plan administrator means an administrator that in the course of its regular business operations—

(A) Maintains network provider agreements that provide for direct claims payments, with health care providers in eight or more countries,

(B) Maintains call centers, in three or more countries, and accepts calls from customers in eight or more languages,

(C) Processed at least $1 million in claims in foreign currency equivalents during the preceding calendar year, determined using the Treasury Department's currency exchange rate in effect on the last day of the preceding calendar year,

(D) Makes global evacuation/repatriation coverage available,

(E) Maintains legal and compliance resources in three or more countries, and

(F) Has licenses or other authority to sell insurance in more than two countries, including in the United States.

(ii) *Additional rules.*—For purposes of meeting the requirements of this paragraph (f)(4), two or more entities, including one entity that is the expatriate health plan administrator, that are members of the expatriate health plan administrator's controlled group (as determined under §57.2(c) of this chapter) are treated as one expatriate health plan administrator. Alternatively, the requirements of this paragraph (f)(4) may be satisfied through contracts between an expatriate health plan administrator and third parties.

(5) *Definition of group health plan.*—Group health plan, for purposes of this section, means a group health plan as defined in §54.9831-1(a).

(6) *Definition of qualified expatriate.*—Qualified expatriate, for purposes of this section, means an individual who is described in paragraph (f)(6)(i), (ii), or (iii) of this section.

(i) *Individuals transferred or assigned by their employer to work in the United States.*—An individual is described in this paragraph (f)(6)(i) only if such individual has the skills, qualifications, job duties, or expertise that has caused the individual's employer to transfer or assign the individual to the United States for a specific and temporary purpose or assignment that is tied to the individual's employment with such employer. This paragraph (f)(6)(i) applies only to an individual who the plan sponsor has reasonably determined requires access to health coverage and other related services and support in multiple countries, and is offered other multinational benefits on a periodic basis (such as tax equalization, compensation for cross-border moving expenses, or compensation to enable the individual to return to the individual's home country), and does not apply to any individual who is a national of the United States. For purposes of this paragraph (f)(6)(i), an individual who is not expected to travel outside the United States at least one time per year during the coverage period would not reasonably require access to health coverage and other related services and support in multiple countries. Furthermore, the offer of a one-time *de minimis* benefit would not meet the standard for the offer of other multinational benefits on a periodic basis.

(ii) *Individuals working outside the United States.*—An individual is described in this paragraph (f)(6)(ii) only if the individual is a national of the United States who is working outside the United States for at least 180 days in a consecutive 12-month period that overlaps with a single plan year, or across two consecutive plan years.

(iii) *Individuals within a group of similarly situated individuals.*—(A) An individual is described in this paragraph (f)(6)(iii) only if:

(1) The individual is a member of a group of similarly situated individuals that is formed for the purpose of traveling or relocating internationally in service of one or more of the purposes listed in section 501(c)(3) or (4), or similarly situated organizations or groups. For example, a group of students that is formed for purposes of traveling and studying abroad for a 6-month period is described in this paragraph (f)(6)(iii);

(2) In the case of a group organized to travel or relocate outside the United States, the individual is expected to travel or reside outside the United States for at least 180 days in a consecutive 12-month period that overlaps with the policy year (or in the case of a policy year that is less than 12 months, at least half the policy year);

(3) In the case of a group organized to travel or relocate within the United States, the individual is expected to travel or reside in the United States for not more than 12 months;

(4) The individual is not traveling or relocating internationally in connection with an employment-related purpose; and

(5) The group meets the test for having associational ties under section 2791(d)(3)(B) through (F) of the PHS Act (42 U.S.C. 300gg-91(d)(3)(B) through (F)).

(B) This paragraph (f)(6)(iii) does not apply to a group that is formed primarily for the sale or purchase of health insurance coverage.

(C) If a group of similarly situated individuals satisfies the requirements of this paragraph (f)(6)(iii), the Secretary of Health and Human Services, in consultation with the Secretary and the Secretary of Labor, has determined that the group requires access to health coverage and other related services and support in multiple countries.

(7) *Definition of United States.*—Solely for purposes of this paragraph (f), United States means the 50 States, the District of Columbia, and Puerto Rico.

(8) *National of the United States.*—For purposes of this paragraph (f), national of the United States, when referring to an individual, has the meaning used in the Immigration and Nationality Act (8 U.S.C. 1101 et. seq.) and includes U.S. citizens and non-citizen nationals. Thus, for example, an individual born in American Samoa is a national of the United States at birth.

Insurance Coverage: Health Reimbursement Arrangements

Insurance Coverage: Health Reimbursement Arrangements.—Amendments to Reg. § 54.9831-1, regarding health reimbursement arrangements (HRAs) and other account-based group health plans, are proposed (published in the Federal Register on October 29, 2018) (REG-136724-17).

Par 7. Section 54.9831-1 is amended by revising paragraph (c)(3)(i) and adding paragraph (c)(3)(viii) to read as follows:

§ 54.9831-1. Special rules relating to group health plans.

* * *

(c) * * *

(3) * * *

(i) *In general.*—Limited-scope dental benefits, limited-scope vision benefits, or long-term care benefits are excepted if they are provided under a separate policy, certificate, or contract of insurance, or are otherwise not an integral part of a group health plan as described in paragraph (c)(3)(ii) of this section. In addition, benefits provided under a health flexible spending arrangement (health FSA) are excepted benefits if they satisfy the requirements of paragraph (c)(3)(v) of this section; benefits provided under an employee assistance program are excepted benefits if they satisfy the requirements of paragraph (c)(3)(vi) of this section; benefits provided under limited wraparound coverage are excepted benefits if they satisfy the requirements of paragraph (c)(3)(vii) of this section; and benefits provided under a health reimbursement arrangement or other account-based group health plan, other than a health FSA, are excepted benefits if they satisfy the requirements of paragraph (c)(3)(viii) of this section.

* * *

(viii) *Health reimbursement arrangements (HRAs) and other account-based group health plans.*—Benefits provided under an HRA or other account-based group health plan, other than a health FSA, are excepted if they satisfy all of the requirements of this paragraph (c)(3)(viii). See paragraph (c)(3)(v) of this section of these regulations for the circumstances in which benefits provided under a health FSA are excepted benefits. For purposes of this paragraph, the term "HRA or other account-based group health plan" has the same meaning as "account based group health plan" set forth in § 54.9815-2711(d)(6)(i) of this part, except that the term does not include health FSAs.

(A) *Otherwise not an integral part of the plan.*—Other group health plan coverage that is not limited to excepted benefits and that is not an HRA or other account-based group health plan must be made available by the same plan sponsor for the plan year to the participant.

(B) *Benefits are limited in amount.*—*(1) Limit on annual amounts made available.*—The amounts newly made available for each plan year under the HRA or other account-based group health plan do not exceed $1,800. In the case of any plan year beginning after December 31, 2020, the dollar amount in the preceding sentence shall be increased by an amount equal to such dollar amount multiplied by the cost-of-living adjustment. The cost of living adjustment is the percentage (if any) by which the C-CPI-U for the preceding calendar year exceeds the C-CPI-U for calendar year 2019. The term "C-CPI-U" means the Chained Consumer Price Index for All Urban Consumers as published by the Bureau of Labor Statistics of the Department of Labor. The C-CPI-U for any calendar year is the average of the C-CPI-U as of the close of the 12-month period ending on August 31 of such calendar year. The values of the C-CPI-U used for any calendar year shall be the latest values so published as of the date on which the Bureau publishes the initial value of the C-CPI-U for the month of August for the preceding calendar year. Any such increase that is not a multiple of $50 shall be rounded to the next lowest multiple of $50.

(2) *Carryover amounts*.—If the terms of the HRA or other account-based group health plan allow unused amounts to be made available to participants and dependents in later plan years, such carryover amounts are disregarded for purposes of determining whether benefits are limited in amount.

(3) *Multiple HRAs or other account-based group health plans*.—If the plan sponsor provides more than one HRA or other account-based group health plan to the participant for the same time period, the amounts made available under all such plans are aggregated to determine whether the benefits are limited in amount.

(C) *Prohibition on reimbursement of certain health insurance premiums*.—The HRA or other account-based group health plan must not reimburse premiums for individual health insurance coverage, group health plan coverage (other than COBRA continuation coverage or other continuation coverage), or Medicare parts B or D, except that the HRA or other account-based group health plan may reimburse premiums for such coverage that consists solely of excepted benefits.

(D) *Uniform availability*.—The HRA or other account-based group health plan is made available under the same terms to all similarly situated individuals, as defined in § 54.9802-1(d) of this part, regardless of any health factor (as described in § 54.9802-1(a)).

STATEMENT OF PROCEDURAL RULES

Statement of Procedural Rules: Liability for Tax: Taxpayer Appeals

Statement of Procedural Rules: Liability for Tax: Taxpayer Appeals.—Amendments to Reg. § 601.106, relating to how a taxpayer may appeal, without going to court, adjustments affecting a taxpayer's tax liability, are proposed (published in the Federal Register on September 20, 1993) (IA-85-91).

Par. 4. Section 601.106 is amended as follows:

1. Paragraphs (a) through (f) are revised.
2. Paragraph (g)(1) is revised.
3. Paragraph (h) is amended by:
   a. Redesignating the text of paragraph (h)(1) as paragraph (h)(1)(i).
   b. Adding paragraph headings for (h)(1) and newly designated paragraph (h)(1)(i).
   c. Redesignating the text of paragraph (h)(2) as paragraph (h)(1)(ii) and revising it.
   d. Redesignating the text of paragraph (h)(3) as paragraph (h)(2)(i).
   e. Adding headings for newly designated paragraphs (h)(2) and (h)(2)(i).
   f. Adding the word "original" immediately before the word "disposition" in newly designated paragraph (h)(2)(i).
   g. Redesignating the text of paragraph (h)(4) as paragraph (h)(2)(ii).
   h. Adding a heading to newly designated paragraph (h)(2)(ii).
4. Paragraph (i) is revised.
5. The revised and added provisions read as follows:

§ 601.106. Appeals functions.—(a) *General.*—(1) *Purpose.*—Appeals is the administrative appeals office of the Internal Revenue Service. Its purpose is to resolve tax controversies without litigation, to the extent possible. Appeals is to approach these controversies in a fair and impartial manner to both the taxpayer and the government.

(2) *Authorization.*—(i) *For the Appeals function.*—Appeals authority on non-docketed cases has been delegated by the Commissioner while Appeals authority on docketed cases has been delegated by the Chief Counsel.

(ii) *For an Appeals office.*—Each region contains Appeals offices with local office facilities within the region. An Appeals office has jurisdiction over cases originating in the office of any District Director, Service Center/Compliance Center Director, or the Assistant Commissioner (International) situated in the region, or in any case in which jurisdiction has been transferred to the region. A taxpayer residing or located outside the United States uses the facilities of the Washington, D.C. Appeals Office of the Mid-Atlantic Region or any other Appeals office that the taxpayer specifies when initiating the appeal.

(iii) *For settlement by Appeals personnel.*—Unless settlement authority has been delegated to other employees, settlements with a taxpayer must be approved by the Chief, an Associate Chief, or a Team Chief in the Appeals office.

(3) *Subject matter jurisdiction; in general.*—Appeals offices have exclusive settlement jurisdiction and final authority within the Internal Revenue Service for the determination of the following types of tax liability and other items—

(i) Federal income tax, estate tax (including extensions for payment under section 6161(a)(2) of the Internal Revenue Code), gift tax, generation-skipping transfer tax, or miscellaneous excise taxes under chapter 41, 42, 43, 44, or 45 of subtitle D of the Internal Revenue Code, all of which are subject to the deficiency procedures (Chapter 45 was repealed for oil removed on or after August 23, 1988.);

(ii) Any other tax which is subject to the deficiency procedures;

(iii) Employment tax or certain miscellaneous excise tax under subtitle D of the Internal Revenue Code (which are not subject to the deficiency procedures except as noted in paragraph (a)(3)(i)(A) of this section);

(iv) Liability for additions to the tax, additional amounts, and assessable penalties provided under chapter 68 of the Internal Revenue Code (collectively referred to in this section as penalties);

(v) The initial or continuing recognition of the tax exempt or foundation status of an organization;

(vi) The initial or continuing determination of employee plan qualification under subchapter D of chapter 1 of the Internal Revenue Code;

(vii) The adjustment or readjustment of partnership items;

(viii) Offers in compromise under section 7122 of the Internal Revenue Code;

(ix) Abatement of interest under section 6404(e)(1) of the Internal Revenue Code; and

(x) Any other disputed tax issues that the Internal Revenue Service determines are administratively appealable.

(4) *Limitations on authority.*—The authority described in paragraphs (a)(2) and (a)(3) of this section does not include the authority to:

(i)(A) Consider any case involving the qualification of an employee plan or the tax exempt or foundation status of an organization if such consideration has already been given in a National Office ruling or technical advice (but only to the extent the case involves qualification or the tax exempt or foundation status). In such a case the decision of the National Office is final. The plan or organization has no right of administrative appeal to Appeals or elsewhere;

(B) If a case is already under Appeals' jurisdiction and Appeals' proposed disposition is contrary to either a National Office ruling concerning tax exempt or foundation status, or a National Office technical advice concerning either qualification or tax exempt or foundation status (issued before the case went to Appeals), the Appeals determination is not final. In such a case Appeals' proposed disposition will be submitted to the Assistant Commissioner (Employee Plans and Exempt Organizations) through the Office of the Regional Director of Appeals. However, in a section 521 case, the proposed disposition will be submitted to the Associate Chief Counsel (Domestic) through the Office of the Regional Director of Appeals. The decision of the Assistant Commissioner or the Associate Chief Counsel will be followed by Appeals;

(ii) Consider any case that was docketed under section 6110 of the Internal Revenue Code concerning the public inspection of written documents or section 7428, 7476, 7477 (repealed after December 31, 1984) or 7478 of the Internal Revenue Code concerning declaratory judgements;

(iii) Eliminate the fraud penalty in a tax year or period for which criminal prosecution against the taxpayer (or related taxpayer involving the same transaction) has been recommended to the Department of Justice for a willful attempt to evade or defeat tax, or for a willful failure to file a return, except upon the recommendation or concurrence of Counsel. Similarly, an Appeals office has no authority to eliminate the fraud penalty in a tax year or period that relates to or affects the year or period described in this paragraph (4)(iii);

(iv) Consider any case in which a recommendation for criminal prosecution is pending, except with the concurrence of Counsel;

(v) Determine alcohol, tobacco, and certain other excise tax liability under subtitle E of the Internal Revenue Code or under subchapter D, chapter 78 of subtitle F of the Internal Revenue Code, insofar as subchapter D relates to taxes imposed under subtitle E;

(vi) Consider a Trust Fund Recovery Penalty case (formerly referred to as a 100 percent penalty case) if the assessment is to be made because of Chief Counsel's request to support a third-party action in a pending refund suit. See Rev. Proc. 84-78, 1984-2 C.B. 754;

(vii) Consider any case solely involving the failure or refusal to comply with the tax laws because of moral, religious, political, constitutional, conscientious, or similar grounds; or

(viii) Consider an issue or a case that is designated for litigation by Chief Counsel.

(b) *Appeal rights of the taxpayer.*—(1) *In general.*—The Appeals process is initiated at the request of the taxpayer. The procedures for initiating an appeal are described below.

(2) *When an organization, rather than each member, is treated as the taxpayer.*—Labor unions, trade associations, and other organizations whose members' dues have been disallowed as a deduction to each member because the organization spent amounts for lobbying, promoting or defeating legislation, political campaigning, or for propaganda related to those activities, are afforded rights of administrative appeal similar to those rights afforded to taxpayers generally.

(3) *Situations in which a taxpayer may request an appeal.*—(i) *Letter proposing adjustments.*—A taxpayer may request an appeal in any case in which a District Director, Service Center/Compliance Center Director, or the Assistant Commissioner (International) has issued a letter proposing adjustments (commonly referred to as the 30 day letter) concerning an item described in paragraph (a)(3) of this section. (The taxpayer will be informed of the right to an administrative appeal in this letter.)

(ii) *After issuance of a statutory notice of deficiency.*—A taxpayer who has been issued a statutory notice of deficiency (commonly referred to as the 90 day letter) will not be granted a conference by Appeals during the 90 day period (150 day period if the notice is addressed to a person outside the United States) following the mailing of the notice if the taxpayer had a conference or was offered a conference prior to the issuance, unless unusual circumstances exist.

(iii) *Penalties.*—Certain chapter 68 penalties that have been assessed may be appealed before payment is made. (These penalties may also be appealed after payment is made but before the filing of a claim for refund.) This post-assessment appeal procedure applies to all but the following chapter 68 penalties—

(A) Penalties that are not subject to a reasonable cause or reasonable basis determination (e.g., the penalty for failure to pay estimated income tax under section 6655 of the Internal Revenue Code);

(B) Penalties that are subject to the deficiency procedures of subchapter B of chapter 63 of the Internal Revenue Code (e.g., the accuracy-related penalty and the fraud penalty under sections 6662 and 6663 of the Internal Revenue Code, respectively). Taxpayers have the right to appeal these penalties prior to assessment;

(C) Penalties that are subject to an administratively granted pre-assessment appeal procedure (such as that provided in §1.6694-2(a)(1) of this chapter for return preparers);

(D) The penalties provided in sections 6700 and 6701 of the Internal Revenue Code for promoting abusive tax shelters, and for aiding and abetting, respectively. These penalties are subject to the procedural rules of section 6703 of the Internal Revenue Code which provides for an extension of the period of collection of the penalty when a person pays not less than 15 percent of the amount of such penalty; and

(E) The Trust Fund Recovery Penalty (formerly referred to as the 100 percent penalty) provided under section 6672 of the Internal Revenue Code. The taxpayer generally has the opportunity to appeal this penalty prior to assessment.

(4) *Initiation of an appeal.*—(i) *General rules.*—An appeal is initiated by filing a protest. See paragraph (b)(4)(iii) of this section for a simplified procedure for small cases.

(ii) *Contents of a protest.*—A protest provides the reasons in writing why the taxpayer does not agree with the disputed adjustments to tax liability. In addition, a protest should contain identifying information, which is described in the letter (or in other information enclosed with the letter) that offers the taxpayer the opportunity to appeal. Examples of items that should be in a protest are as follows:

(A) If the disagreement concerns factual matters, the protest should include a statement in writing of the taxpayer's view of the facts. Factual matters concern, for example, evidence of the date when income was received and the existence of records proving the payment of an expense.

(B) If the disagreement concerns whether or how an item should be taxed, the protest should include a reason or reasons in writing for the taxpayer's position. Such disagreements concern, for example, whether the law requires that certain proceeds be included in gross income. The reasoning may be based simply on what the taxpayer believes is logical and fair. Inclusion of references to supporting authorities such as the Internal Revenue Code, Treasury regulations, court cases, revenue rulings and revenue procedures will facilitate consideration of the appeal. Reference may also be made to Internal Revenue Service publications.

(iii) *Small case request.*—(A) *In general.*—If the total amount (described in paragraph (b)(4)(iii)(B) of this section) is not more than $25,000 for any tax period, the taxpayer may initiate an appeal by requesting Appeals consideration, indicating the unagreed adjustments to tax liability and stating the reason for disagreement. A taxpayer may provide any additional information that he or she feels is pertinent.

(B) *Total amount defined.*—(1) *In general.*—The total amount includes the entire amount of additional tax and penalties proposed by the Internal Revenue Service, not just the portion of additional tax or penalties that the taxpayer disputes. The total amount also includes the entire amount of a refund or credit claimed by the taxpayer. Where the Service determines that an overassessment was made, the total amount is the amount proposed by the Internal Revenue Service. Interest is not included in any of these amounts.

(2) *Offer in compromise.*—In an offer in compromise, the total amount includes the assessed tax, penalties, and interest sought to be compromised.

(3) *Penalties.*—In the case of penalties that are assessed before a taxpayer is given the opportunity to dispute the penalties (a post-assessment penalty case), the total amount is the amount of the disputed penalties for any tax period.

(C) *Subjects always requiring a protest.*—A protest is required to obtain Appeals consideration in all employee plan and exempt organization cases. (If corporate or individual returns are adjusted in connection with employee plan or exempt organization cases, these returns are not subject to this paragraph (b)(4)(iii)(C).) A protest is also required in all partnership and S corporation cases.

(iv) *Where to file a protest or a small case request.*—Filing instructions are in the letter (or in other information enclosed with the letter) that offers the taxpayer the opportunity to appeal. The receiving office will review the protest or small case request for the purpose of deciding whether further development or action is required prior to referring the case to Appeals.

(c) *Nature of Appeals' proceedings.*—(1) *In general.*—Appeals' proceedings are informal. Testimony is not taken under oath, although matters alleged as facts may be required to be submitted later in the form of affidavits, or declared to be true under penalties of perjury.

(2) *Presentation of new information at Appeals.*—(i) *Newly discovered information.*—If newly discovered evidence is presented to Appeals in a case pending in non-docketed status, Appeals may send the new information to the originating function (the District Director, Service Center/Compliance Center Director, or Assistant Commissioner (International)) for consideration and comment.

(ii) *Withheld information.*—A taxpayer cannot withhold information from the District Director, Service Center/Compliance Center Director, or Assistant Commissioner (International) and expect to present it for the first time before Appeals at a conference in non-docketed status. If such information is presented to Appeals, generally, the case will be returned to the originating function for reconsideration.

(3) *Taxpayer representatives.*—Taxpayers may represent themselves or may designate a qualified representative to act for them. If a taxpayer engages a representative to present the appeal, the taxpayer and representative must follow the practice and conference procedures in Treasury Department Circular 230 as amended (31 CFR part 10), and in subpart E of this part.

(d) *Consideration of cases by Appeals.*—(1) *In general.*—Appeals will follow the law and the recognized standards of legal construction in determining facts and applying the law. Appeals will determine the correct amount of the tax with strict impartiality as between the taxpayer and the Government, and without favoritism or discrimination between taxpayers.

(2) *Factors considered by Appeals.*—Appeals will ordinarily consider the relative merits of the opposing views in light of the hazards which would exist if the case was litigated. However, no settlement will be made based upon the nuisance value of the case to either party. If the taxpayer makes an unacceptable settlement proposal under circumstances indicating a good faith attempt to reach an agreement on a basis that is fair to both the Government and the taxpayer, then, generally, the Appeals officer should indicate to the taxpayer the kind of settlement that the officer would recommend for acceptance. Appeals may defer action on, or may decline to settle, certain cases or issues in order to achieve greater uniformity and enhance overall voluntary compliance with the tax laws.

(3) *Making a taxpayer's return.*—In cases under Appeals jurisdiction, the Appeals official has the authority to make and subscribe to a return under the provisions of section 6020 of the Internal Revenue Code where a taxpayer fails to make a required return.

(4) *When an Appeals officer's proposed settlement is not approved.*—An Appeals officer may recommend acceptance of the taxpayer's proposal of settlement, or may recommend other action favorable to the taxpayer. However, as stated in paragraph (a)(2)(iii) of this section, generally, settlements with a taxpayer must be approved by the Chief, an Associate Chief, or a Team Chief in the Appeals office. If the Appeals officer's recommendation is disapproved in whole or in part by a reviewing officer, then, generally, the reviewing officer will advise the taxpayer of the decision and will offer the taxpayer a conference (with the reviewing officer), which the taxpayer may accept by written confirmation. However, a conference will not be offered if the interest of the Government would be injured by delay, as, for example, in a case involving the imminent expiration of the period of limitations or the dissipation of assets.

(5) *Related taxpayer.*—The District Director, the Service Center/Compliance Center Director, and the Assistant Commissioner (International) are responsible for assembling the return of a related taxpayer for an examination. Ordinarily, a case concerning a related taxpayer is not requested from the examining office by Appeals unless this action is necessary to ensure consistency. If the action is necessary, Appeals contacts the examining office to determine what action should be taken by both offices. Appeals may assume jurisdiction in a related taxpayer case with the concurrence of the related taxpayer after the examining office has completed any necessary action. The related taxpayer does not have to file a protest. If the need for assuming jurisdiction over a related taxpayer case becomes apparent after a conference has been held, Appeals may contact the related taxpayer. In the absence of any objection, Appeals assumes jurisdiction after requesting that the examining office complete action on the case.

(6) *Assistance from Counsel.*—(i) *In general.*—Appeals may use Counsel as a resource on non-docketed cases when advice is needed concerning the hazards of litigation, interpretation of law, or evaluation of evidence. This advice will be provided through informal arrangements between each Counsel and Appeals office.

(ii) *Counsel attendance at conference.*—Appeals generally does not ask Counsel to attend settlement conferences. However, in certain cases Counsel may attend an appeals settlement conference. For example, Counsel may attend a conference for a case involving the fraud penalty for which criminal prosecution against the taxpayer (or a related taxpayer involving the same transaction) has been recommended to the Department of Justice for a willful attempt to evade or defeat tax, or for a willful failure to file a return.

(iii) *Technical advice from the National Office.*—(A) *Definition.*—Technical advice means advice or guidance as to the interpretation and proper application of internal revenue laws, related statutes, and regulations, to a specific set of facts, furnished by the National Office upon Appeals' request in connection with the processing and consideration of a non-docketed case. It is furnished as a means of assisting Internal Revenue Service personnel in closing cases and establishing and maintaining consistent holdings in the various regions. It does not include memoranda on matters of general technical application furnished to Appeals where the issues are not raised in connection with the consideration and handling of a specific taxpayer's case.

(B) *Procedures for technical advice.*—General procedures for technical advice are found in § 601.105(b)(5). In addition, the technical advice rules are not applicable to an appeal of penalties described in paragraph (b)(3)(iv) of this section.

(e) *Settlement of a case before Appeals.*—(1) *In general; new issue.*—During consideration of a case, the Appeals office should neither reopen an issue as to which the taxpayer and the office of the District Director, Service Center/Compliance Center Director, or Assistant Commissioner (International) are in agreement, nor raise a new issue, unless the ground for such action is a substantial one and the potential effect upon the tax liability is material. If Appeals raises a new issue, the taxpayer or the taxpayer's representative should be so advised and should be offered an opportunity for discussion before taking any formal action, such as the issuance of a statutory notice of deficiency (commonly referred to as the 90 day letter).

(2) *Case not docketed in the Tax Court.*—(i) *Agreed issues.*—If settlement of some or all of the issues is reached with the taxpayer by Appeals, the taxpayer will be requested to sign the appropriate agreement form for the agreed issue or issues.

(ii) *Unagreed Issues.*—(A) *In general.*—*(1) Case subject to the deficiency procedures.*—To the extent that the taxpayer does not agree with a proposed deficiency, a statutory notice of deficiency (commonly referred to as the 90 day letter) will be issued by Appeals as prescribed in sections 6212 and 6861 of the Internal Revenue Code. (The statutory notice is issued for deficiencies in income, estate, gift, generation-skipping transfer, or certain miscellaneous excise taxes (under chapter 41, 42, 43, 44, or 45 of the Internal Revenue Code). Each Chief, Associate Chief, or Team Chief of an Appeals office is authorized to issue the statutory notice of deficiency. The taxpayer may file a petition with the U.S. Tax Court for a redetermination of the deficiency. The petition must be filed within 90 days (150 days if the notice is addressed to a person outside of the United States) after the statutory notice of deficiency is mailed (not counting Saturday, Sunday, or a legal holiday in the District of Columbia as the last day).

(2) Case not subject to the deficiency procedures.—If the unagreed case is not subject to the deficiency procedures, the case and its administrative file will be forwarded to the appropriate Internal Revenue Service function with instructions to take action on the unagreed tax liability determined by Appeals.

(B) *Refund claimed by a Taxpayer.*—If a claim for refund is disallowed in full or in part by Appeals and the taxpayer does not sign Form 2297, Waiver of Statutory Notification of Claim Disallowance, Appeals will issue a statutory notice of claim disallowance.

(3) *Case docketed in Tax Court.*—(i) *Appeals jurisdiction.*—(A) *In general.*—Except in unusual cases, a docketed case is referred by Counsel to Appeals to reach a settlement with the taxpayer (even if Appeals issued the statutory notice of deficiency). If Appeals has the case under consideration at the time it is docketed, then it retains the case. See Rev. Proc. 87-24, 1987-1 C.B. 720.

(B) *Period of jurisdiction.—(1) Deficiency of more than $10,000.*—Appeals has exclusive jurisdiction of a docketed case involving a deficiency of more than $10,000 per period (including taxes and penalties) as long as Appeals believes there is a reasonable likelihood of settlement, or until the case appears on a trial calendar. Counsel may extend the period of Appeals consideration of the case when it appears on the trial calendar.

(2) Deficiency of $10,000 or less.—In general, Appeals has exclusive jurisdiction of a docketed case involving a deficiency of $10,000 or less per period (including tax and penalties) for a period of six months, except that jurisdiction ends one month before the trial calendar call. In a Small Tax Case (S case), Appeals' jurisdiction ends 15 days before the trial calendar call. Appeals and Counsel may agree to extend the period of consideration. A case is designated as an S case by the Court upon request of the petitioner and includes the letter S as part of the docket number. An S case is given expeditious consideration.

(C) *Exclusive jurisdiction.*—In general, Appeals has sole settlement authority over docketed cases referred to, or retained by, Appeals pursuant to these procedures until the case is returned to Counsel. However, a case or an issue in a case may be reserved by Counsel. Upon request, Appeals will return a case to Counsel to allow adequate trial preparation. Whenever a docketed case is returned to Counsel, sole authority to try or to settle the case will revert to Counsel, unless Counsel and Appeals agree that settlement authority over some or all of the issues will be retained by Appeals. Thus, in some situations Counsel will prepare a case for trial while Appeals simultaneously negotiates for a settlement.

(D) *Transfer of jurisdiction to and from Counsel.*—By agreement between Counsel and Appeals, any docketed case (or portions thereof) may be transferred from Counsel to Appeals or from Appeals to Counsel, notwithstanding the fact that the case was previously considered by the receiving function. This authority is to be utilized to promote more efficient disposition of the case.

(E) *Assisting Counsel.*—For cases or issues over which Counsel has jurisdiction, Appeals may assist Counsel with settlement negotiations, with trial preparation, or at trial.

(F) *Coordination of settlements in related cases.*—Unless both offices agree that the offer is acceptable, no settlement offer will be accepted by Appeals if there is a related case in Counsel. (Related cases may involve different tax years of the same taxpayer or different taxpayers engaging in a similar transaction.) Disagreements between Appeals and Counsel on whether the offer should be accepted will be resolved by the Regional Counsel, with the advice and assistance of the Regional Director of Appeals and the Deputy Regional Counsel (Tax Litigation).

(ii) *Agreed issues.*—If some or all of the issues in a docketed case are settled by the taxpayer and Appeals, Appeals generally prepares a document reflecting settlement of these issues. The agreement is recorded in a decision document or stipulation of settlement. This document stipulates to the agreed deficiency or overpayment (or to the disposition of agreed issues if less than all issues are agreed) and is signed by the taxpayer. Appeals forwards the document, along with any necessary computations, to Counsel who signs and files the document with the Tax Court. If the court signs the document, it is entered as a decision of the court (or, if the settlement resolves only some of the issues in the case, as a part of the record of the case). No settlement of a docketed case is binding on either the taxpayer or the government until it is entered as a decision (or filed as part of the record in the case).

(iii) *Unagreed issues.*—To the extent issues in a docketed case remain unsettled after consideration and conference in Appeals, the case will be returned to Counsel.

(f) *Transfer of a case to another Appeals office.*—(1) *Non-docketed case.*—(i) *Routine.*—An Appeals office may transfer jurisdiction in a non-docketed case to an office that is closer to the taxpayer's residence or place of business if the taxpayer's books and records are available there.

(ii) *Hardship.*—An Appeals office may transfer jurisdiction in a non-docketed case to another office to relieve the taxpayer of hardship. The request is made to the transferring office which will determine whether hardship exists. If hardship exists, the transfer will be made if the taxpayer's books and records are available to the receiving office, and if both offices agree that the transfer is not an attempt to obtain a more favorable resolution of the disputed issues.

(iii) *Special situations.*—From time to time special transfer rules will be published in the Internal Revenue Manual for certain types of cases.

(iv) *Approval needed.*—Transfers within a region for reasons other than those listed in paragraphs (f)(1)(i), (ii) and (iii) of this section must be approved by both the transferring and receiving Regional Directors of Appeals. If the directors cannot agree, the proposed transfer may be referred to the National Director of Appeals for decision.

(2) *Docketed case.*—(i) *In general.*—A docketed case under Appeals jurisdiction will be transferred to the Appeals office serving the locality designated by the Tax Court for trial unless that locality is Washington, D.C. Docketed cases set for a Tax Court trial should be transferred to the Washington, D.C., office only if the taxpayer resides in the area and the books and records are available there. Otherwise the case should be transferred to the Appeals office serving the taxpayer's residence or place of business.

(ii) *Special situations.*—From time to time special transfer rules will be published in the Internal Revenue Manual for certain types of docketed cases.

(iii) *Approval needed.*—Transfers within a region for reasons other than those listed in paragraphs (f)(2)(i) and (ii) of this section must be approved by both the transferring and receiving Regional Directors of Appeals. If the directors cannot agree, the proposed transfer may be referred to the National Director of Appeals for decision.

(iv) *Coordination with Counsel.*—All transfers of docketed cases must be coordinated with Counsel.

(g) *Limitation on the jurisdiction and function of Appeals.*—(1) *Overpayment of more than $1,000,000.*—If Appeals determines that there is an overpayment of income, estate, generation-skipping transfer, gift or certain miscellaneous excise taxes (under chapter 41, 42, 43, 44, or 45 of the Internal Revenue Code), including penalties and interest, in excess of $1,000,000, such determination will be reviewed by the Joint Committee on Taxation. See § 601.108.

* * *

(h) * * *

(1) *Closed with mutual concessions.*—(i) *Service initiated opening.*—* * *

(ii) *Taxpayer initiated opening.*—Under certain unusual circumstances favorable to the taxpayer, such as retroactive legislation, a case not docketed in the Tax Court and closed by Appeals on the basis of concessions made by both Appeals and the taxpayer may be reopened upon written application from the taxpayer, and only with the approval of the Regional Director of Appeals. The processing of an application for a tentative carryback adjustment or a claim for refund or credit for an overassessment (for a year involved in the prior closing) attributable to a claimed deduction or credit for a carryback provided by law, and not included in a previous Appeals determination, does not constitute a reopening requiring approval. A subsequent assessment of an excessive tentative allowance also does not constitute such a reopening. The National Director of Appeals may authorize, in advance, the reopening of similar classes of cases if legislative enactments or compelling administrative reasons require such advance approval.

(2) *Closed without mutual concessions.*—(i) *Service initiated opening.*—* * *

(ii) *Taxpayer initiated opening.*—* * *

(i) *Effective dates.*—In general, the rules will be effective on the date of publication of the final rules in the Federal Register. The rules in § 601.106(b)(4), which describe how a taxpayer initiates an appeal, will be effective 60 days after the date of publication of the final rules in the Federal Register. However, if the letter (or other information enclosed with the letter) offering the taxpayer the opportunity to appeal refers to rules predating the rules in § 601.106(b)(4), then the taxpayer may follow either the old rules or new rules. [Reg. § 601.106.]

[The next page is 92,101.]

Income Tax Proposed Regulations—Preambles

[¶49,003] **Proposed Regulations and Proposed Amendments of Regulations,** published in the Federal Register on April 30, 1975.

Employee plans: Lump-sum distributions.—Reg. §§1.402(e)-2 and 1.402(e)-3 and amendments of Reg. §§1.72-4, 1.72-13, 1.101-2, 1.122-1, 1.402(a)-1, 1.403(a)-1, 1.403(a)-2, 1.652(b)-1, and 1.1304-2 (Code Sec. 1304 was repealed by the Tax Reform Act of 1986), relating to the treatment of lump-sum distributions, have been proposed. Reg. §§1.62-1 was removed 3/5/88 by T.D. 8189. Reg. §1.405-3 was removed by T.D. 9849 on 3/11/2019.

Notice is hereby given that the regulations set forth in tentative form in the attached appendix are proposed to be prescribed by the Commissioner of Internal Revenue, with the approval of the Secretary of the Treasury or his delegate. Prior to the final adoption of such regulations, consideration will be given to any comments pertaining thereto which are submitted in writing (preferably six copies) to the Commissioner of Internal Revenue, Attention: CC:LR:T, Washington, D.C. 20224, by June 16, 1975. Pursuant to 26 CFR 601.601(b), designations of material as confidential or not to be disclosed, contained in such comments, will not be accepted. Thus, a person submitting written comments should not include therein material that he considers to be confidential or inappropriate for disclosure to the public. It will be presumed by the Internal Revenue Service that every written comment submitted to it in response to this notice of proposed rule making is intended by the person submitting it to be subject in its entirety to public inspection and copying in accordance with the procedures of 26 CFR 601.702(d)(9). Any person submitting written comments who desires an opportunity to comment orally at a public hearing on these proposed regulations should submit his request, in writing, to the Commissioner by June 16, 1975. In such case, a public hearing will be held, and notice of the time, place, and date will be published in a subsequent issue of the FEDERAL REGISTER, unless the person or persons who have requested a hearing withdraw their requests for a hearing before notice of the hearing has been filed with the Office of the Federal Register. The proposed regulations are to be issued under the authority contained in sections 402(a)(2), 402(e), and 7805 of the Internal Revenue Code of 1954 (88 Stat. 990, 987 and 68A Stat. 917; 26 U.S.C. 402(a)(2), 402(e), 7805).

DONALD C. ALEXANDER,
Commissioner of Internal Revenue.

This document proposes amendments to the Income Tax Regulations (26 CFR Part 1) in order to conform the regulations under sections 62, 72, 101, 122, 402, 403, 405, 652, and 1304 of the Internal Revenue Code of 1954 to the provisions of section 2005 of the Employee Retirement Income Security Act of 1974 (Pub. L. 93-406, 88 Stat. 987), relating to taxation of certain lump sum distributions.

The amendments proposed relating to sections 62, 72, 101, 122, ¶403, ¶405, 652, and 1304 of the Code merely conform the regulations under those sections to the changes in the taxation of a lump sum distribution under section 402 of the Code, as amended by section 2005(a) of the Act.

Under section 402(a)(2) of the Code, as amended, a method of computing the capital gain portion of a lump sum distribution is provided. In general, the capital gain portion of a lump sum distribution will be an amount equal to the product of the total taxable amount of the lump sum distribution and a fraction, the numerator of which is the number of calendar years of active participation before January 1, 1974, and the denominator of which is the total number of calendar years of active participation.

Under section 402(e)(1) of the Code, as amended, a separate tax is imposed on the ordinary income portion of a lump sum distribution.

Under section 402(e)(2) of the Code, as amended, a special rule is provided for computing the separate tax on the ordinary income portion of a lump sum distribution if there have been one or more lump sum distributions after December 31, 1973, made with respect to the recipient within the 6-taxable-year period ending on the last day of the taxable year of the recipient in which the distribution is made.

Under section 402(e)(3) of the Code, as amended, a deduction is allowed from gross income equal to the amount of the ordinary income portion of the distribution included in the recipient's gross income.

Under section 402(e)(4) of the Code, as amended, definitions and special rules are provided for computing the separate tax, including the definition of a lump sum distribution and the computation of the ordinary income portion of a lump sum distribution.

Under proposed §1.402(e)-2(c)(1), a special method for computing the separate tax on a distribution including an annuity contract is provided. In such a case, the adjusted total taxable amount must be determined. For taxable years beginning before January 1, 1975, the adjusted total taxable amount is defined as the sum of the total taxable amount of the lump sum distribution for the taxable year, and the current actuarial value of annuity contracts distributed to the recipient reduced by the portion of the net amount contributed by the employee which is allocable to the annuity contract. For taxable years beginning after December 31, 1974, the adjusted total taxable amount is defined as the sum of the total taxable amount of the lump sum distribution for the taxable year, and the current actuarial value of annuity contracts distributed to the recipient reduced by the excess of the net amount contributed by the employee over the cash and other property distributed.

Under proposed §1.402(e)-2(d)(1), a distribution to multiple recipients (except a payment or distribution solely to two or more trusts) cannot qualify as a lump sum distribution unless the amount of the distribution is otherwise includible in the income of the individual in respect of whom the distribution was made under the judicial doctrines of assignment of income or constructive receipt of income.

Under proposed § 1.402(e)-2(d)(3), the term "active participation" is defined so that active participation commences with the first month in which an employee becomes a participant under the plan and ends with the earliest of (1) the month in which the employee receives a lump sum distribution under the plan, (2) in the case of an employee without regard to section 401(e)(1), the month in which the employee separates from the service of the employer, (3) the month in which the employee dies, or (4) in the case of a self-employed individual who receives a lump sum distribution on account of disability, the first month in which he becomes disabled.

It is contemplated that upon adoption of the proposed amendments the Temporary Income Tax Regulations under section 402(e)(4)(B)(§ 11.402(e)(4)(B)-1) will be revoked.

Proposed amendments to the regulations. In order to conform the Income Tax Regulations (26 CFR Part 1) to the provisions of section 2005 of the Employee Retirement Income Security Act of 1974 (Pub. L. 93-406, 88 Stat. 987), such regulations are amended.

[¶ 49,007] Proposed Regulations (LR-194-77), published in the Federal Register on February 3, 1978.

Gross income: Deferred: Compensation reduction plans or arrangements.—Reg. § 1.61-16, relating to amounts of payments which are deferred under compensation reduction plans or arrangements, is proposed.

AGENCY: Internal Revenue Service, Treasury.

ACTION: Notice of proposed rulemaking.

SUMMARY: This document contains proposed regulations relating to the tax treatment of amounts of compensatory payments which are deferred under certain nonqualified compensation reduction plans or arrangements. The regulations would reflect a change in the Internal Revenue Service position relating to these plans or arrangements and provide the public with needed guidance.

DATES: Written comments and requests for a public hearing must be delivered or mailed by April 4, 1978. The amendments are proposed to be effective in the case of compensatory payments which the taxpayer has chosen to defer if the amount would have been payable, but for the taxpayer's exercise of the option to defer receipt, on or after a date 30 days following publication of this regulation as a Treasury Decision in the Federal Register.

ADDRESS: Send comments and requests for a public hearing to: Commissioner of Internal Revenue, Attention: CC:LR:T (LR-194-77), Washington, D.C. 20224.

FOR FURTHER INFORMATION CONTACT: William E. Mantle of the Legislation and Regulations Division, Office of the Chief Counsel, Internal Revenue Service, 1111 Constitution Avenue, NW., Washington D.C. 20224 (Attention: CC:LR:T) (202-566-3734).

SUPPLEMENTARY INFORMATION:

BACKGROUND

This document contains a proposed amendment to the Income Tax Regulations (26 CFR Part 1) under section 61 of the Internal Revenue Code of 1954. The amendment is proposed in order to change the Internal Revenue Service position on certain nonqualified compensation reduction plans or arrangements and is to be issued under the authority contained in section 7805 of the Internal Revenue Code of 1954 (68A Stat. 917; 26 U.S.C. 7805).

GENERAL RULE

The new regulation provides that if a taxpayer (whether or not an employee) individually chooses to have payment of some portion of his current compensation or an amount of an increase in compensation deferred and paid in a later year, the amount will nevertheless be treated as received by the taxpayer in the earlier taxable year. The taxpayer's exercise of the option to defer payment must be under a plan or arrangement other than one described in sections 401(a), 403(a) or (b), or 405(a) of the Internal Revenue Code of 1954 (relating respectively to qualified pension, profit-sharing, and stock bonus plans; taxation of employee annuities; and qualified bond purchase plans).

DEFINITION OF COMPENSATION

Under the proposed amendment, a taxpayer's compensation includes, in addition to basic or regular compensation fixed by contract, statute, or otherwise, a supplement, such as a bonus, and increases in basic or regular compensation.

EXCEPTION

An exception to the general rule is proposed to provide that it does not apply to the amount of any payment which the taxpayer has chosen to defer under an existing plan or arrangement if the amount would have been payable, but for the taxpayer's exercise of the option to defer receipt, before a date 30 days following publication of this regulation as a Treasury decision in the FEDERAL REGISTER.

EFFECT ON PRESENT IRS PUBLISHED POSITIONS

If this regulation is published as a Treasury decision, Rev. Rul. 67-449, 1967-2 C.B. 173, Rev. Rul. 68-86, 1968-1 C.B. 184, Rev. Rul. 69-650 1969-2 C.B. 106, and Rev. Rul. 71-419, 1971-2 C.B. 220 would no longer be applied and present Service acquiescences in the decisions in *James F. Oates*, 18 T.C. 570 (1952) and *Ray S. Robinson*, 44 T.C. 20 (1965) would be reconsidered. Further, it would be necessary to examine the facts and circumstances of cases similar to those described in several other published revenue rulings (such as Examples (1) and (3) of Rev. Rul. 60-31, 1960-1 C.B. 174, Rev. Rul. 68-99, 1968-1 C.B. 193, and Rev. Rul. 72-25, 1972-1 C.B. 127) to determine whether the deferral of payment of compensation was in fact at the individual option of the taxpayer who earned the compensation.

On September 7, 1977, the Service announced in IR-1881 that it had suspended the issuance of rulings dealing with the income tax treatment of certain non-qualified deferred compensation plans established by State and local governments and other employers pending completion of a review of this area. The plans reviewed permit the employee to individually elect to defer a portion of his or her salary. This proposed amendment represents conclusions reached as a result of this review.

COMMENTS AND REQUESTS FOR A PUBLIC HEARING

Before adopting these proposed regulations, consideration will be given to any written comments that are submitted (preferably six copies) to the Commissioner of Internal Revenue. All comments will be available for public inspection and copying. A public hearing will be held upon written request to the Commissioner by any person who has submitted written comments. If a public hearing is held, notice of the time and place will be published in the FEDERAL REGISTER.

DRAFTING INFORMATION

The principal author of these proposed regulations was William E. Mantle of the Legislation and Regulations Division of the Office of Chief Counsel, Internal Revenue Service. However, personnel from other offices of the Internal Revenue Service and Treasury Department participated in developing the regulation, both on matters of substance and style.

[¶ 49,008] Proposed Regulations and Proposed Amendments of Regulations (EE-16-78), published in the Federal Register on May 31, 1979.

Employee plans: Lump-sum distributions.—Reg. § 1.402(e)-14 and amendments of Reg. §§ 1.402(a)-1, 1.402(e)-2 and 1.403(a)-2, relating to the election to treat no portion of a lump-sum distribution from an employee plan as long-term capital gain, are proposed.

AGENCY: Internal Revenue Service, Treasury.

ACTION: Notice of proposed rulemaking.

SUMMARY: This document contains proposed regulations relating to the election to treat no portion of a lump sum distribution from an employee benefit plan as long-term capital gain. Changes in the applicable tax law were made by the Tax Reform Act of 1976. The regulations would provide the public with the guidance needed to comply with that Act and would affect any recipient of a lump sum distribution.

DATES: Written comments and requests for a public hearing must be delivered or mailed by July 30, 1979. The amendments are proposed to be effective for distributions received in taxable years of the recipient beginning after December 31, 1975.

ADDRESS: Send comments and requests for a public hearing to: Commissioner of Internal Revenue, Attention: CC:LR:T:EE-16-78, Washington, D.C. 20224.

FOR FURTHER INFORMATION CONTACT: Richard L. Johnson of the Employee Plans and Exempt Organizations Division, Office of the Chief Counsel, Internal Revenue Service, 1111 Constitution Avenue, N.W., Washington, D.C. 20224. Attention: CC:LR:T, 202-566-3544 (not a toll-free number).

SUPPLEMENTARY INFORMATION:

BACKGROUND

On April 30, 1975, the Federal Register published at 40 F.R. 18798 proposed amendments to the Income Tax Regulations (26 CFR Part 1) under sections 402(a), 402(e), 403(a) and other sections of the Internal Revenue Code of 1954, relating to the taxation of lump sum distributions from qualified pension, profit-sharing, stock bonus and annuity plans. A correction notice was published in the Federal Register on May 23, 1975, at 40 F.R. 22548. The amendments were proposed to conform the regulations to section 2005 of the Employee Retirement Income Security Act of 1974 (88 Stat. 987). Proposed amendments contained in paragraphs 1 and 2 of the appendix to that notice of proposed rulemaking were adopted by Treasury decision 7399 published in the Federal Register on February 3, 1976, at 41 F.R. 5099. The remainder of the amendments proposed in the appendix to the notice of proposed rulemaking of April 30, 1975, have not yet been adopted.

This document contains further proposed amendments to the Income Tax Regulations (26 CFR Part 1) under Code sections 402(a)(2), ¶ 402(e) and ¶ 403(a)(2) to conform the regulations to Code section 402(e)(4)(L), as added by section 1512 of the Tax Reform Act of 1976 (90 Stat. 1742). The proposed regulations are to be issued under the authority contained in sections 402(e)(4)(L) and 7805 of the Internal Revenue Code of 1954 (90 Stat. 1742, 68A Stat. 917; 26 U.S.C. 402(e)(4)(L), 7805).

PRE-1974 AND POST-1973 PLAN PARTICIPATION

Under Code section 402(a)(2) or ¶ 403(a)(2), a portion of a lump sum distribution from a qualified pension, profit sharing, stock bonus or annuity plan is taxable as long-term capital gain. If the employee has been a participant in the plan for at least 5 years, and if the recipient is eligible to make the required election, the portion of the distribution not taxable as long-term capital gain is taxable under the 10-year averaging provisions of Code section 402(e). The portion of a lump sum distribution taxable as long-term capital gain is determined by taking into account the number of calendar years of participation by the employee in the plan before January 1, 1974. The portion taxable under Code section 402(e) represents participation in the plan after December 31, 1973.

ORDINARY INCOME ELECTION

Under Code section 402(e)(4)(L), a recipient may elect, under certain circumstances, to treat all calendar years of the employee's participation in all plans before January 1, 1974, as calendar years of participation after December 31, 1973. In such a case, no portion of the lump sum distribution is taxable as long-term capital gain. If the distribution is otherwise eligible for application of Code section 402(e), the total taxable amount of the distribution is taxable under the 10-year averaging provisions.

COMMENTS AND REQUESTS FOR A PUBLIC HEARING

Before adopting these proposed regulations, consideration will have to be given to any written comments that are submitted (preferably eight copies) to the Commissioner of Internal Revenue. All comments will be available for public inspection and copying. A public hearing will be held upon written request to the Commissioner by any person who has submitted written comments. If a public hearing is held, notice of the time and place will be published in the FEDERAL REGISTER.

DRAFTING INFORMATION

The principal author of these proposed regulations is Richard L. Johnson of the Employee Plans and Exempt Organizations Division of the Office of Chief Counsel, Internal Revenue Service. However, personnel from other offices of the Internal Revenue Service and Treasury Department participated in developing the regulation, both on matters of substance and style.

[¶49,009] **Proposed Regulations (LR-168-76),** published in the Federal Register on June 5, 1979.

Deductions limited to amount at risk.—Reg. §§1.465-1—1.465-7, Reg. 1.465-9—1.469-13, 1.465-22—1.465-26, 1.465-38, 1.465-39, 1.465-41—1.465-45, 1.465-66—1.465-69, 1.465-75—1.465-79 and 1.465-95, relating to determination of amounts at risk with respect to certain activities, are proposed. Proposed Reg. §§1.465-8 and 1.465-20 were adopted by T.D. 9124 on April 30, 2004.

AGENCY: Internal Revenue Service, Treasury.

ACTION: Notice of proposed rulemaking.

SUMMARY: This document contains proposed regulations relating to the determination of amounts at risk with respect to certain activities. Changes to the applicable tax law were made by the Tax Reform Act of 1976. The regulations would provide the public with the guidance needed to determine the amount of allowable deductions incurred with respect to activities covered by the at risk rules.

DATES: Written comments and requests for a public hearing must be delivered or mailed by August 6, 1979. The amendments are proposed to be effective for amounts paid or incurred in taxable years beginning after December 31, 1975, except as otherwise provided.

ADDRESS: Send comments and requests for a public hearing to: Commissioner of Internal Revenue, Attention: CC:LR:T (LR-168-76), Washington, D.C. 20224.

FOR FURTHER INFORMATION CONTACT: David Jacobson of the Legislation and Regulations Division, Office of the Chief Counsel, Internal Revenue Service, 1111 Constitution Avenue, N.W., Washington, D.C. 20224, 202-566-3923, not a toll-free call.

SUPPLEMENTARY INFORMATION:

BACKGROUND

This document contains proposed amendments to the Income Tax Regulations (26 CFR Part 1) and the Temporary Income Tax Regulations under the Tax Reform Act of 1976 (26 CFR Part 7) undersection 465 of the Internal Revenue Code of 1954. These amendments are proposed to conform the regulations to section 204 of the Tax Reform Act of 1976 (90 Stat. 1531) and are to be issued under the authority contained in section 7805 of the Internal Revenue Code of 1954 (68A Stat. 917; 26 U.S.C. 7805).

EXPLANATION OF THE REGULATIONS

Section 465 provides a limit on the amount of loss deductions taxpayers engaged in certain activities will be allowed. The activities for which the limits will apply are holding, producing or distributing motion picture films or videotapes; farming; leasing section 1245 property; and exploring for or exploiting oil and gas resources. Section 465 applies to all noncorporate taxpayers engaged in one or more of these activities. In addition, section 465 applies to electing small business corporations and personal holding companies if engaged in one or more of these activities.

Taxpayers to which section 465 applies are not permitted to deduct losses from the listed activities in excess of the amount they are at risk. The proposed regulations provide rules for determining the amount which a taxpayer is at risk. In general, a taxpayer is at risk for cash contributed to the activity as well as for amounts borrowed for use in the activity for which the taxpayer is personally liable. Amounts borrowed on a nonrecourse basis generally will not increase the amount a taxpayer is at risk. However, if property not used in the activity is pledged as security, the amount at risk may be increased to the extent of the net fair market value of the security.

Section 465 also provides that amounts borrowed from persons with an interest in the activity other than that of a creditor will not increase the amount at risk. The proposed regulations provide rules for determining who has an interest in the activity other than that of a creditor as well as providing other rules illustrating the applicability of section 465. The proposed regulations contain references to amendments to section 465 made by the Revenue Act of 1978 and the Energy Tax Act of 1978. These references have been added to the proposed regulations in order to alert taxpayers that section 465 has been amended since the time it was originally enacted. However, the proposed regulations do not provide guidance with respect to these amendments. This guidance will be provided in a later regulations project.

COMMENTS AND REQUESTS FOR A PUBLIC HEARING

Before adopting these proposed regulations, consideration will be given to any written comments that are submitted (preferably six copies) to the Commissioner of Internal Revenue. All comments will be available for public inspection and copying. A public hearing will be held upon written request to the Commissioner by any person who has submitted written comments. If a public hearing is held, notice of the time and place will be published in the FEDERAL REGISTER.

DRAFTING INFORMATION

The principal author of these proposed regulations is David Jacobson of the Legislation and Regulations Division of the Office of Chief Counsel, Internal Revenue Service. However, personnel from other offices of the Internal Revenue Service and Treasury Department participated in developing the regulation, both on matters of substance and style.

[¶49,010] Proposed Regulations (EE-164-78), published in the Federal Register on April 9, 1980.

Employee trusts: Vesting schedule: Discrimination.—Reg. §1.411(d)-1, relating to a determination if the vesting schedule of a qualified plan discriminates in favor of employees who are officers, shareholders, or highly compensated, is proposed.

AGENCY: Internal Revenue Service, Treasury.

ACTION: Notice of proposed rulemaking.

SUMMARY: This document contains proposed regulations prescribing rules for determining if the vesting schedule of a qualified plan discriminates in favor of employees who are officers, shareholders, or highly compensated. Changes to the applicable tax law were made by the Employee Retirement Income Security Act of 1974. The regulations would provide the public with additional guidance needed to comply with the Act and would affect all employers maintaining qualified plans.

DATES: Written comments and requests for a public hearing must be delivered or mailed by June 9, 1980. The amendments are proposed to be effective for plan years beginning 30 days after the publication of this regulation in the FEDERAL REGISTER as a Treasury decision.

ADDRESS: Send comments and requests for a public hearing to: Commissioner of Internal Revenue, Attention: CC:LR:T (EE-164-78), Washington, D.C. 20224.

FOR FURTHER INFORMATION CONTACT: Kirk F. Maldonado of the Employee Plans and Exempt Organizations Division, Office of the Chief Counsel, Internal Revenue Service, 1111 Constitution Avenue, N.W., Washington, D.C. 20224 (Attention: CC:LR:T) (202-566-3430) (not a toll-free number).

SUPPLEMENTARY INFORMATION:

BACKGROUND

This document contains proposed amendments to the Income Tax Regulations (26 CFR Part 1) under section 411(d)(1) of the Internal Revenue Code of 1954. These amendments are proposed to conform the regulations to section 1012(a) of the Employee Retirement Income Security Act of 1974 (88 Stat. 901) and these regulations are to be issued under the authority contained in section 7805 of the Internal Revenue Code of 1954 (68A Stat. 917; 26 U.S.C. 7805).

STATUTORY PROVISIONS

Section 401(a)(4) of the Code provides that a plan which discriminates in favor of employees who are officers, shareholders, or highly compensated (hereinafter referred to as "prohibited group") is not a qualified plan under section 401(a). Section 411(d)(1) provides that the vesting schedule of a plan which satisfies the requirements of section 411 shall be considered as satisfying any vesting requirements resulting from the application of section 401(a)(4) except in two situations. One situation, as set forth in section 411(d)(1)(A) is a pattern of abuse under the plan which tends to discriminate in favor of the prohibited group (pattern of abuse). The other situation, as detailed in section 411(d)(1)(B)), is where there have been, or there is reason to believe there will be, an accrual of benefits or forfeitures tending to discriminate in favor of the prohibited group (hereinafter referred to as "discriminatory vesting").

PRIOR GUIDELINES

Initial guidelines under section 411(d)(1) were set forth in Revenue Procedure 75-49, 1975-2 C.B. 584. That procedure established several alternative tests, with respect to vesting, that a plan must satisfy to secure a favorable advance determination letter. If a plan fails to satisfy these tests, a favorable advance determination letter will not be issued unless the plan adopts accelerated vesting (so-called "4/40 vesting").

Revenue Procedure 75-49 was modified in Revenue Procedure 76-11, 1976-1 C.B. 550. That procedure adopted alternative ways of satisfying the requirements of section 411(d)(1) in order to secure a favorable advance determination letter, in addition to the tests contained in Revenue Procedure 75-49.

The tests of Revenue Procedures 75-49 and 76-11 were applied only with respect to whether a plan could receive a favorable advance determination letter. The determination letter by its terms provided that the approval of the plan's qualified status by the Service did not extend to the plan in operation. Therefore, separate tests for determining discrimination in vesting were necessary with respect to the issuance of a determination letter and with respect to testing the operation of the plan's vesting schedule.

In addition, the tests described in Revenue Procedures 75-49 and 76-11 were generally mechanical. Objections were raised by plan administrators and sponsors when they were required to accept 4/40 vesting as a minimum schedule, and yet 4/40 vesting did not reflect the policies of ERISA if applied as a maximum vesting schedule. At the same time, it is recognized that there is a value in allowing safe harbors for plan administrators who seek a determination letter with respect to the qualified status of a plan. Therefore, although a facts and circumstances test more accurately reflects the vesting antidiscrimination provisions of the Code, and the policies of ERISA, it is recognized that some forms of safe harbor are appropriate for certainty purposes.

The rules contained in the proposed regulations attempt to accommodate both goals. On the one hand, a facts and circumstances test is described. This description is amplified by a list of factors which may be included in applying the test. It is anticipated that these factors will offer substantial guidance to plan administrators in reviewing the vesting provisions applicable both with respect to a determination letter application and with respect to the status of a plan in operation. On the other hand, two safe harbor tests are provided which would insulate a plan against a finding of discriminatory vesting under the plan.

After this regulation is adopted, it is anticipated that the tests and vesting schedule contained in Revenue Procedures 75-49 and 76-11 will no longer be applied. While plans having determination letters based on 4/40 vesting need not apply for a new determination letter on the basis of the plan's vesting schedule, plan administrators should be aware that the tests included in these regulations will be applied in testing the operation of each plan's vesting schedule and are cautioned to review each plan accordingly. Because of the guidance to be provided by this regulation after it is adopted, the concerns voiced by plan administrators under prior rules regarding how a plan's operation with respect to vesting would be judged should be alleviated. In addition, when a plan is submitted to the Internal Revenue Service for a determination letter it is anticipated that the rules in these regulations will be applied for purposes of issuing such letters.

DISCRIMINATION IN VESTING

The proposed rules provide that the determination of whether there is a pattern of abuse or discriminatory vesting under a plan shall be determined on the facts and circumstances of each case. Several criteria are set forth as factors to be used in making such a determination.

Two safe harbors are provided against a finding of discriminatory vesting under the plan. One safe harbor requires full vesting after an employee has three years of service. The other safe harbor requires full vesting after ten years of service, and the sum of the vested percentages for the employee's service prior to the completion of ten years of service must equal or exceed 700.

COMMENTS AND REQUESTS FOR A PUBLIC HEARING

Before adopting these proposed regulations, consideration will be given to any written comments that are submitted (preferably eight copies) to the Commissioner of Internal Revenue. All comments will be available for public inspection and copying. A public hearing will be held upon written request to the Commissioner by any person who has submitted written comments. If a public hearing is held, notice of the time and place will be published in the FEDERAL REGISTER.

DRAFTING INFORMATION

The principal author of these proposed regulation is Kirk F. Maldonado of the Employee Plans and Exempt Organizations Division of the Office of Chief Counsel, Internal Revenue Service. However, personnel from other offices of the Internal Revenue Service and Treasury Department participated in developing these regulations, both on matters of substance and style.

[¶49,012] Proposed Amendment of Regulation (EE-164-78), published in the Federal Register on June 12, 1980.

Employees' trusts: Antidiscrimination rules: Coordination of vesting and discrimination requirements.—An amendment of proposed Reg. §1.411(d)-1, relating to coordination of vesting and discrimination requirements for employees' trusts, is proposed.

AGENCY: Internal Revenue Service, Treasury.

ACTION: Notice of proposed rulemaking.

SUMMARY: This document contains modifications to proposed regulations, published in the FEDERAL REGISTER for April 9, 1980 (45 FR 24201), relating to coordination of vesting and discrimination requirements for qualified pension, etc. plans. These modifications to the proposed regulations have been prepared in response to the comments received on the proposed regulation. The test for determining the existence of discriminatory vesting is reproposed in modified form and the "safe harbors" against a finding of discriminatory vesting are withdrawn.

DATES: A public hearing on the notice of proposed rulemaking published April 9, 1980, has been scheduled for July 10, 1980. A notice of the public hearing was published in the FEDERAL REGISTER on May 2, 1980. Outlines of oral comments for the public hearing must be delivered or mailed by June 26, 1980. Written comments on the modifications set forth in this notice must be delivered or mailed by August 11, 1980.

ADDRESS: Send comments to: Commissioner of Internal Revenue, Attention: CC:LR:T (EE-164-78), Washington, D.C. 20224.

FOR FURTHER INFORMATION CONTACT: Kirk F. Maldonado of the Employee Plans and Exempt Organizations Division, Office of the Chief Counsel, Internal Revenue Service, 1111 Constitution Avenue, N.W., Washington, D.C. 20224 (Attention: CC:LR:T) (202-566-3430) (not a toll-free number).

SUPPLEMENTARY INFORMATION:

BACKGROUND

This document contains modifications to proposed regulations under section 411(d)(1) of the Internal Revenue Code of 1954. Section 411(d)(1) was added by section 1012(a) of the Employee Retirement Income Security Act of 1974 (88 Stat. 901). The amendments are to be issued under the authority contained in section 7805 of the Internal Revenue Code of 1954 (68A Stat. 917; 26 U.S.C. 7805).

STATUTORY PROVISIONS

Section 401(a)(4) of the Code provides that a plan which discriminates in favor of employees who are officers, shareholders, or highly compensated (hereinafter referred to as "prohibited group") is not a qualified plan under section 401(a). Section 411(d)(1) provides that the vesting schedule of a plan which satisfies the requirements of section 411 shall be considered as satisfying any vesting requirements resulting from the application of section 401(a)(4) except in two situations. One situation, as set forth in section ¶411(d)(1)(A), is a pattern of abuse under the plan which tends to discriminate in favor of the prohibited group (pattern of abuse). The other situation, as detailed in section 411(d)(1)(B), is where there have been, or there is reason to believe there will be, an accrual of benefits or forfeitures tending to discriminate in favor of the prohibited group (hereinafter referred to as "discriminatory vesting").

PRIOR DETERMINATION LETTERS

Initial guidelines under section 411(d)(1) were set forth in Revenue Procedure 75-49, 1975-2 C.B. 584. That Procedure established several alternative tests, with respect to vesting, that a plan must satisfy to secure a favorable advance determination letter. If a plan failed to satisfy these tests, a favorable determination letter was not issued unless the plan adopted the accelerated vesting schedule set forth in the Procedure (so-called "4/40 vesting").

Revenue Procedure 76-11, 1976-1 C.B. 550, was issued pending reconsideration of Revenue Procedure 75-49. That Procedure adopted two new alternative means of satisfying the requirements of section 411(d)(1) in order to secure a favorable advance determination letter, in addition to the tests contained in Revenue Procedure 75-49.

One of the new alternatives contained in Revenue Procedure 76-11 is to establish that the plan had previously received a favorable advance determination letter which had not been revoked, and that the percentage of vesting of each participant under the plan as amended is not less (at every point) than that provided under the vesting schedule of the plan when it received the most recent favorable prior determination letter.

The other new alternative contained in Revenue Procedure 76-11 is a demonstration, on the basis of all of the facts and circumstances that there has not been, and that there is no reason to believe there will be, any discriminatory accruals.

Revenue Procedure 76-11 also provided that a plan could secure a favorable determination letter without regard to whether the vesting is nondiscriminatory.

However, the determination letters processed in this manner contained a caveat to the effect that such letter is not a determination as to whether the vesting provisions of the plan satisfy the nondiscrimination requirements of section 401(a)(4).

The tests of Revenue Procedures 75-49 and 76-11 are applied only with respect to whether a plan could receive a favorable advance determination letter. The determination letter, by its terms, provided that the approval of the plan's qualified status by the Internal Revenue Service did not extend to the plan in operation. Therefore, separate tests for determining discrimination in vesting were necessary with respect to the issuance of a determination letter and with respect to testing the operation of the plan's vesting schedule.

Thus, an employer could receive a favorable advance determination letter, but would have no protection against a finding that the plan's vesting schedule was discriminatory in operation. The proposed rules remove this separate testing of form and operation, and provide that the test for discriminatory vesting shall be made, in both situations, on the basis of the facts and circumstances. Thus, if a plan has a favorable advance determination letter based on the facts and circumstances test of the proposed rules, this determination will protect the plan from a finding of discriminatory vesting in operation, provided the facts and circumstances have not materially changed since the determination letter was issued.

Additionally, plans which currently possess certain types of favorable determination letters will be treated as if their determination letter was processed under the facts and circumstances test contained in the proposed rules. The plans which will be given this treatment are those which received their favorable determination letter based on their satisfying one or more of the following tests:

1. the key employee and/or the turnover test of Revenue Procedure 75-49;
2. the prior letter test of Revenue Procedure 76-11; or
3. the facts and circumstances test of Revenue Procedure 76-11.

Thus, a plan described above would also be protected against a finding of discriminatory vesting in operation, based on its outstanding favorable determination letter, provided the facts and circumstances have not materially changed.

SAFE HARBORS

Paragraph (d) of proposed regulation § 1.411(d)-1, as published in the FEDERAL REGISTER on April 9, 1980, set forth two safe harbors against a finding of discriminatory vesting. Both of the safe harbors required the adoption of a vesting schedule substantially more rapid than 4/40 vesting. Many of the commentators viewed this as an attempt to require that all plans adopt either one of these accelerated vesting schedules. Because that was not the intent of those proposed rules, the portion of the proposed regulation containing the safe harbors is withdrawn.

However, this deletion should not be interpreted as meaning that 4/40 vesting is a safe harbor. Comments are requested from the public as to the desirability of reinstating a safe harbor and, if so, on what basis.

TEST FOR DISCRIMINATORY VESTING

Paragraph (c)(2) of proposed regulation § 1.411(d)-1, as published in the FEDERAL REGISTER on April 9, 1980, set forth certain factors to be considered in applying the facts and circumstances test for discriminatory vesting. These factors were included simply to reflect current Internal Revenue Service practice and to provide greater guidance to both employers and to Internal Revenue Service personnel. The factors were not intended to create new standards.

Nevertheless, many commentators interpreted the recital of specific factors as substantially increasing their burden of establishing that the plan's vesting schedule is nondiscriminatory. Accordingly, the list of specific factors is deleted in the reproposed test for discriminatory vesting.

The determination of whether the vesting schedule of a plan is discriminatory, under the reproposed rules, shall be made on the basis of the facts and circumstances of each case. The reproposed rules now specifically provide that a plan's vesting schedule is nondiscriminatory if the disparity between the vested benefits provided to the prohibited group and the vested benefits provided to all other employees is reasonable.

ADDITIONAL GUIDANCE

It is anticipated that additional guidance regarding the application of the facts and circumstances test for discriminatory vesting will be provided in revenue rulings and procedures issued at the time the regulations are published in final form. Accordingly, comments are requested as to whether the following examples are appropriate for this purpose:

Example 1. A plan has the "10 year cliff" vesting schedule described in section 411(a)(2)(A) for all employees. Employment turnover among members of the prohibited group is less than that for all other employees because the prohibited group tends to stay longer with the company. Nevertheless, the present value of the vested benefits for the officers and 5% shareholders (determined using the attribution rules of section 1563(e), without regard to section 1563(e)(3)(C)), is less than the present value of the vested benefits of all other employees. Because the vested benefits provided employees who are not officers or shareholders are greater than that provided officers and shareholders, the plan's vesting schedule is not considered to be discriminatory.

Example 2. The facts are the same as in *Example 1*, except that there has been no comparison of the present values of the vested benefits of each group of employees. However, it is clear that the class of employees who have vested benefits, considering those employees alone and not any nonvested employees, would satisfy the nondiscriminatory classification test of section 410(b)(1)(B) by covering a reasonable cross section. Because a reasonable cross section of all employees under the plan have vested benefits, the vesting schedule of the plan is not considered to be discriminatory. [When the example is published, specific facts along the lines of Revenue Ruling 70-200, 1970-1 C.B. 101, Revenue Ruling 74-255, 1974-1 C.B. 93, and Revenue Ruling 74-256, 1974-1 C.B. 94, will be included to illustrate the reasonable cross section test.]

Example 3. Company B has a plan that satisfies the minimum participation requirements of section 410. The plan provides for 4/40 vesting. In its six years of operation the plan has always covered five employees. Because of the high rate of employee turnover, the only employee, past or present, to earn a vested benefit under the plan is X. X is the sole shareholder of Company B. Absent a showing of other facts and circumstances, the vesting schedule of the plan is discriminatory.

COMMENTS AND PUBLIC HEARING

Before adopting these proposed regulations, consideration will be given to any written comments that are submitted (preferably eight copies) to the Commissioner of Internal Revenue. All comments will be available for public inspection and copying. As indicated above, a public hearing has already been scheduled on the proposed regulations published April 9, 1980. Anyone wishing to comment on these modifications may do so at that hearing.

DRAFTING INFORMATION

The principal author of this regulation is Kirk F. Maldonado of the Employee Plans and Exempt Organizations Division of the Office of Chief Counsel, Internal Revenue Service. However, personnel from other offices of the Internal Revenue Service and the Treasury Department participated in developing the regulation, both on matters of substance and style.

[¶ 49,018] **Proposed Regulations and Proposed Amendments of Regulations (EE-7-78)**, published in the Federal Register on July 14, 1981.

Individual retirement plans: Simplified employee pensions.—Reg. §§ 1.219-3, 1.220-1, 1.404(h)-1, 1.408-7, 1.408-8, 1.408-9 and 54.4973-1 and proposed amendments of Reg. §§ 1.219-1, 1.219-2, 1.408-2, 1.408-3, 1.408-4, 1.408-6, 54.4974-1 and 301.6693-1, relating to individual retirement plans and simplified employee pensions, are proposed. Reg. § 1.62-1 was removed on 3/25/1988 by T.D. 8189 and Reg. § 1.415-8 was removed on 4/4/2007 by T.D. 9319. Reg. § 1.408-4(b)(4)(ii) was withdrawn on 7/11/2014 by REG-209459-78.

AGENCY: Internal Revenue Service, Treasury.

ACTION: Notice of proposed rulemaking.

SUMMARY: This document contains proposed regulations relating to individual retirement plans and simplified employee pensions. Changes to the applicable law were made by the Employee Retirement Income Security Act of 1974, the Tax Reform Act of 1976, the Revenue Act of 1978 and the Technical Corrections Act of 1979. The regulations would provide the public with the guidance needed to comply with these Acts and would affect institutions which sponsor individual retirement plans and simplified employee pensions. The regulations also affect employers and individuals who use these plans for retirement income.

DATES: Written comments and requests for a public hearing must be delivered or mailed by September 14, 1981. The amendments have varying effective dates. The provisions relating to spousal individual retirement plans are generally effective for taxable years beginning after December 31, 1976. The provisions relating to simplified employee pensions are generally effective for taxable years beginning after December 31, 1978. The provisions defining "active participant" for individuals covered by defined benefit offset plans are effective for taxable years beginning after December 31, 1980.

ADDRESS: Send comments and requests for a public hearing to: Commissioner of Internal Revenue, Attention: CC:LR:T (EE-7-78), Washington, D.C. 20224.

FOR FURTHER INFORMATION CONTACT: William D. Gibbs of the Employee Plans and Exempt Organizations Division, Office of the Chief Counsel, Internal Revenue Service, 1111 Constitution Avenue, N.W., Washington, D.C. 20224 (Attention: CC:LR:T) (202-566-3430) (not a toll-free number).

SUPPLEMENTARY INFORMATION:

BACKGROUND

This document contains proposed amendments to the Income Tax Regulations (26 CFR Part 1), the Gift Tax Regulations (26 CFR Part 25), the Employment Tax Regulations (26 CFR Part 31), the Regulations on Pension Excise Taxes (26 CFR Part 54) and the Procedure and Administration Regulations (26 CFR Part 301) under sections 62, 219, 220, 404, 408, 409, 2503, 3121, 3306, 4973, 4974, and 6693 of the Internal Revenue Code of 1954. These amendments are proposed to conform the regulations to section 2002(d) of the Employee Retirement Income Security Act of 1974 (88 Stat. 966), section 1501 of the Tax Reform Act of 1976 (90 Stat. 1734), sections 152, 156(c) and 157 of the Revenue Act of 1978 (92 Stat. 2797, 2802, 2803), and sections 101(a)(10), 101(a)(14)(A), 101(a)(14)(B), and 101(a)(14)(E)(ii) of the Technical Corrections Act of 1979 (94 Stat. 201-205). These regulations are to be issued under the authority contained in section 7805 of the Internal Revenue Code of 1954 (68A Stat. 917; 26 U.S.C. 7805).

On August 8, 1980, the Federal Register published final regulations relating to individual retirement plans under the Income Tax Regulations (26 CFR Part 1) under sections 219, 408, 409 and under the Pension Excise Taxes (26 CFR Part 54) under section 4974 (45 FR 52782). Also, because of subsequent statutory provisions, some of the proposed regulations published on February 21, 1975 (40 FR 7661) were withdrawn in connection with those final regulations. The preamble to those final regulations indicated that regulations under other statutory provisions relating to retirement plans would be reproposed at a later date. This document contains these reproposed amendments, other than those relating to the rollover rules under Code sections 402 and ¶ 403. The Service intends to repropose these rules at a later date in connection with the regulations under Code sections 402(a)(5), (6) and (7), and 403(a)(4), (6) and (8).

SPOUSAL INDIVIDUAL RETIREMENT PLANS

Internal Revenue Code section 220 allows an individual to deduct amounts contributed to an individual retirement plan maintained for the individual's benefit and an individual retirement plan maintained for the benefit of the individual's nonemployed spouse. The proposed regulations set forth the type of funding arrangements which must be used and additional limitations and restrictions the individual and spouse must meet in order for the individual to obtain this deduction.

SIMPLIFIED EMPLOYEE PENSIONS

Internal Revenue Code section 408(k) sets forth rules for simplified employee pension ("SEP's"). The proposed regulations, §§ 1.408-7 through -9, indicate to employers and sponsoring institutions what requirements these arrangements must meet. Section 1.404(h)-1 of the proposed regulations sets forth the special deduction limitations for employers under Code section 404(h). Sections 1.219-1(d)(4) and 1.219-3 of the proposed regulations set forth the rules governing the inclusion/deduction rules for employees for employer contributions to SEP's.

An employee will be allowed to deduct an employer contribution to a simplified employee pension. In general, the maximum amount the employee will be allowed to deduct is the lesser of 15 percent of compensation includible in gross income or $7,500. Proposed § 1.219-3 makes it clear that the deduction and the compensation are computed separately with respect to each employer's arrangement. Thus, an employee who has two or more employers can use only the compensation from the employer maintaining the simplified employee pension arrangement in computing the section 219(b)(7) limitation. On the other hand, if two or more employers of an employee each maintain a simplified employee pension arrangement, the employee will be allowed to deduct each employer's contribution, up to the compensation and dollar limit applied separately to each employer. Special limitations apply to certain related employers under Code section 414(b) and (c) and to self-employed individuals.

Certain rules have been included to make SEP arrangements more administrable by employers and the Service. Under proposed § 1.408-7(d)(1)(iii) an employer is not required to make a contribution to the SEP of an otherwise eligible employee who receives less than $200 compensation for a calendar year. This relieves employers of the burden of setting up SEP's to which very small amounts of money will be contributed (the maximum deductible contribution would equal $30 (15% of $200)). This rule was published by the Service in Announcement 80-112, 1980-36 I.R.B. 35.

Further, under proposed § 1.408-7(d)(2), employers may execute necessary documents on behalf of employees who are unwilling or unable to execute those documents or whom the employer is unable to locate. This remedial rule prevents an employer's SEP arrangement from being disqualified because of a recalcitrant employee or one who has left the employer's service and is unable to be located by the employer. (See also proposed § 1.408-9(c) for possible reporting requirements in this instance.) Comments are requested as to what alternative remedial action, in lieu of execution on behalf of employees, employers would wish to take to avoid disqualification of their SEP arrangements. Comments also are requested on this proposed rule as to whether in a particular State there is any law that would preclude this action by the employer on the employee's behalf.

Employer contributions which exceed the amounts called for under the written allocation formula for the SEP arrangement are treated as if made to the employee's individual retirement account or individual retirement annuity, maintained outside the employee's SEP. It is contemplated that the employer, when it discovers the erroneous contribution, will notify the employee of the amount of the non-SEP contribution made in excess of the allocation formula. Because this amount may result in an excess contribution when made the employee may wish to take appropriate action in order to avoid IRA penalties. The normal IRA rules under Code section 219 apply in such a situation. This rule is proposed in order to prevent the entire SEP arrangement from being disqualified due to an inadvertent error on the part of the employer, such as an incorrect calculation of employee compensation. Under Code section 408(k), the entire SEP arrangement could be disqualified on account of the excess contribution. This rule is proposed to provide relief in such cases. See proposed § 1.408-7(f) and the example of how the rule would operate in a particular case.

Proposed § 1.408-7(c)(2) contains a special rule clarifying the relationship between SEP's and salary reduction agreements. This rule makes it clear that employer contributions to an employee's individual retirement account or annuity that are made under a salary reduction agreement between the employer and employee are not treated as employer contributions to an employee's simplified employee pension. Thus, if the employee may elect either a contribution or current compensation, the contribution is treated as an employee contribution and, therefore, is not eligible for the favorable SEP arrangement rules.

Similarly, other contributions such as voluntary contributions made by the employee, or on behalf of the employee by the employer as the agent for the employee (such as by payroll withholding), are treated as employee contributions.

Even though the employer picks the institution or substantially influences the employee's choice of the institution to which the employer makes the SEP contribution and which serves as trustee or sponsor for the employee's SEP, the SEP arrangement remains qualified under the Code. Further, this action by the employer is not a prohibition on withdrawal of funds within the meaning of Code section 408(k)(4)(B). The employer should, however, be aware that the Department of Labor may require special reporting for such action. (See 29 C.F.R. § 2520.104-48 (1980) and 29 C.F.R. § 2520.104-49 (1981).)

Proposed § 1.408-9 contains reporting requirements for SEP's. Employers who use the Service's Model Simplified Employee Pension Arrangement (Form 5305-SEP) and furnish the Model to their employees will satisfy the disclosure requirements relating to adoption of the SEP arrangement. Further, if the employer reports the amount of the SEP contribution on an employee's W-2, the annual reporting requirements will be satisfied. The Department of Labor also has reporting requirements for SEP's, which are in addition to the requirements of the Internal Revenue Service. (See 29 C.F.R. § 2520.104-48 (1980) and 29 C.F.R. § 2520.104-49 (1981).)

Employers who failed to make required contributions on behalf of employees for calendar year 1979 because the employees were no longer employed at the end of the employer's taxable year may make such "make up" contributions before January 1, 1981. This conforms to Announcement 80-112, 1980-36 I.R.B. 35. This relief is given because employers may not have anticipated the rules contained in that announcement and § 1.408-7(d)(1), (2) and (3), relating to which employees are entitled to receive an allocation. It is expected that employers who make such contributions will comply with the reporting requirements of § 1.408-9(b) and file amended tax returns. Likewise, employees who receive such contributions are expected to file amended tax returns.

OTHER AMENDMENTS

Conforming and technical amendments made by the Tax Reform Act of 1976, the Revenue Act of 1978, and the Technical Corrections Act of 1979 have been made to the regulations under Code sections 62, 219, 220, 404, 408, 409, 415, 3121, 3306, 4973, 4974, and 6693.

Also, regulations are proposed which define "active participant" under section 219(b)(2) for individuals who are covered by defined benefit offset plans integrated with Federal or State benefits such as social security benefits. These rules were requested by commentators at the public hearing held July 19, 1979, on the reproposed active participant rules, and in other written comments on those proposed regulations published in the FEDERAL REGISTER on March 23, 1979 (44 FR 17754). This proposed rule allows employees to make IRA contributions when, in effect, they get no benefit from their employers' plans.

REGULATORY FLEXIBILITY ACT

Although this document is a notice of proposed rulemaking which solicits public comment, the Internal Revenue Service has concluded that the regulations proposed herein are interpretative and that the notice and public procedure requirements of 5 U.S.C. 553 do not apply. Accordingly, these proposed regulations do not constitute regulations subject to the Regulatory Flexibility Act (5 U.S.C. chapter 6).

COMMENTS AND REQUESTS FOR A PUBLIC HEARING

Before adopting these proposed regulations, consideration will be given to any written comments that are submitted (preferably six copies) to the Commissioner of Internal Revenue. All comments will be available for public inspection and copying. A public hearing will be held upon written request to the Commissioner by any person who has submitted written comments. If a public hearing is held, notice of the time and place will be published in the FEDERAL REGISTER.

DRAFTING INFORMATION

The principal author of these proposed regulations is William D. Gibbs of the Employee Plans and Exempt Organizations Division of the Office of Chief Counsel, Internal Revenue Service. However, personnel from other offices of the Internal Revenue Service and Treasury Department participated in developing the regulations, both on matters of substance and style.

[¶49,022] Proposed Regulations and Proposed Amendments of Regulations (EE-99-78), published in the Federal Register on December 1, 1982.

Employees' trusts: Minimum funding requirements: Minimum funding excise taxes.—Reg. §§1.412(a)-1, 1.412(b)-1, 1.412(b)-4, 1.412(c)(2)-2, 1.412(c)(4)-1—1.412(c)(10)-1, 1.412(g)-1, and 54.4971-2—54.4971-3, amendments of Reg. §§1.413-1 and 1.413-2, and the deletions of Reg. §§11.412(c)-7, 11.412(c)-11, and 11.412(c)-12, relating to the minimum funding requirements for employee pension benefit plans, and to excise taxes for failure to meet the minimum funding standards, are proposed.

AGENCY: Internal Revenue Service, Treasury.

ACTION: Notice of proposed rulemaking.

SUMMARY: This document contains proposed regulations relating to the minimum funding requirements for employee pension benefit plans, and to excise taxes for failure to meet the minimum funding standards. Changes to the applicable tax law were made by the Employee Retirement Income Security Act of 1974. The regulations would provide the public with guidance needed to comply with that Act and would affect all pension plans subject to the provisions of the Act.

DATES: Written comments and requests for public hearing must be delivered or mailed by January 28, 1983. The proposed amendments would apply generally for plan years beginning after 1975, but earlier (or later) in the case of some plans as provided for meeting the minimum funding requirements under the Act. The proposed rules pertaining to the frequency of actuarial valuations, and to the time for making contributions, generally would not be effective prior to the publication of final regulations.

ADDRESS: Send comments and requests for a public hearing to: Commissioner of Internal Revenue, Attention: CC:LR:T (EE-99-78), Washington, D.C. 20224.

FOR FURTHER INFORMATION CONTACT: Eric A. Raps of the Employee Plans and Exempt Organizations Division, Office of the Chief Counsel, Internal Revenue Service, 1111 Constitution Avenue, N.W., Washington, D.C. 20224 (Attention: CC:LR:T) (202-566-6212, not a toll-free call).

SUPPLEMENTARY INFORMATION:

BACKGROUND

This document contains proposed amendments to the Income Tax Regulations (26 CFR Part 1) under section 412 of the Internal Revenue Code of 1954. These amendments are proposed to conform the regulations to section 1013(a) of the Employee Retirement Income Security Act of 1974 (ERISA) (88 Stat. 914). The proposed amendments would also apply for purposes of sections 302 and 305 of ERISA (88 Stat. 869, 873).

The proposed amendments would be issued under the authority of section 302(b)(4), (b)(5), (c)(2)(B), (c)(9) and (c)(10) of ERISA (88 Stat. 870, 871, and 872; 29 U.S.C. 1082) and sections 412(b)(4), (b)(5), (c)(2)(B), (c)(9) and (c)(10) and 7805 of the Internal Revenue Code of 1954 (88 Stat. 915, 916, and 917; 68A Stat. 917; 26 U.S.C. 412(b)(4), (b)(5), (c)(2)(B), (c)(9), and (c)(10) and 7805).

This document also contains proposed amendments to the Income Tax Regulations (26 CFR Part 1) and the Pension Excise Tax Regulations (26 CFR Part 54) under section 413(b)(6) and (c)(5) and section 4971 of the Internal Revenue Code of 1954. These regulations are proposed primarily to conform the regulations to section 1013(b) of the Employee Retirement Income Security Act of 1974 (ERISA) (88 Stat. 920). They are to be issued under the authority of section 413(b)(6) and (c)(5) and section 7805 of the Internal Revenue Code of 1954 (88 Stat. 924, 925, 68A Stat. 917; 26 U.S.C. 413(b)(6) and (c)(5), 7805).

The proposed regulations do not reflect changes to the second-level excise tax made by the Act of Dec. 24, 1980, Pub. L. 96-596 (94 Stat. 3469), or amendments to sections 412 and 4971 made by the Multiemployer Pension Plan Amendments Act of 1980, Pub. L. 96-364 (94 Stat. 1208).

PURPOSE AND SCOPE

The proposed amendments address the remaining statutory provisions not yet addressed by regulations relating to the minimum funding requirements with respect to which either regulatory guidance is required by law or interpretative assistance would be helpful in applying the law. These proposed amendments, together with proposed or final regulations previously issued under section 412 of the Code, generally constitute the regulatory guidance to be provided with respect to the minimum funding requirements, with the exception of rules relating to mergers. However, comments noting additional issues with respect to which regulatory guidance might be helpful will be considered along with comments addressing issues that arise under the proposed amendments.

The provisions under section 4971 of the Code contain sanctions for enforcing the minimum funding requirements. The sanctions are two excise taxes. The initial tax is 5 percent of an accumulated funding deficiency, and an additional tax of 100 percent is imposed if the deficiency is not corrected. Generally, the employer responsible for contributing to the plan is liable for these taxes.

Section 3002(b) of ERISA provides special rules regarding the section 4971 taxes and coordination of matters regarding these taxes with the Secretary of Labor.

FUNDING STANDARD ACCOUNT

Under section 412(b) of the Code, a plan must maintain a funding standard account. The mechanics for reflecting charges and credits to the account appear in section 412(b)(2) and (3). The proposed amendments address a number of key issues arising under the funding standard account provisions.

MONEY PURCHASE PLANS

Under the proposed amendments, a money purchase pension plan is, like other plans, required to maintain a funding standard account. However, the accounting under such a plan for funding purposes is limited to charges for the contribution required under the formula provided by the plan, credits for amounts actually contributed, and charges and credits to amortize certain bases.

Normally, the need to create an amortization base does not exist under a money purchase plan. However, such a base would be created, for example, with the issuance of a waiver of the minimum funding standard for a plan.

COMBINING AND OFFSETTING

The proposed amendments would provide rules, as required under section 412(b)(4) of the Code, for combining and offsetting amortization amounts determined under the funding standard account. The proposed method for combining and offsetting these amounts is described in the legislative history of ERISA. (See H.R. Rep. No. 93-807, 93d Cong., 2d Sess. 86-87 (1974), 1974-3 C.B. Supp. 321-322.)

TREATMENT OF INTEREST

The proposed amendments would provide rules, as required by section 412(b)(5) of the Code, for treating interest charges and credits under the funding standard account.

Generally under the proposed amendments, charges and credits are made as of an assumed accounting date under the plan. There must be an interest charge or credit, as the case may be, for the period between this assumed date and the end of the plan year.

A contribution made during the "grace period" between the last day of a plan year and the day determined under section 412(c)(10) is treated as having been made on the last day of the plan year.

RETROACTIVE CHANGES

The proposed amendments provide for reflecting in the funding standard account retroactive changes required by the Commissioner to adjust for the use of unreasonable assumptions or funding methods.

PLAN TERMINATION

The proposed amendments relating to the effect of plan termination on the funding standard account are substantially identical to the provisions of Rev. Rul. 79-237, 1979-2 C.B. 190.

BOND VALUATION ELECTION

The proposed amendments would provide rules, as required by section 412(c)(2)(B) of the Code, for the election of a special valuation rule applicable to bonds and other evidences of indebtedness. The proposed amendments would be substantially identical to temporary regulations published in 1974 with respect to the bond valuation election. However, the proposed amendments would clarify the temporary rules by providing that certain convertible debt instruments are treated as debt until converted into equity securities. The rules concerning valuation of convertible debt would be effective only for debt instruments acquired after the date on which the proposal is adopted as a final regulation. For debt instruments acquired before that date, a valuation method will be considered acceptable if it is applied on a consistent basis.

ACTUARIAL VALUATION

The proposed amendments would provide rules, as required by section 412(c)(9) of the Code, relating to the frequency of actuarial valuations for plans. These rules would identify situations in which valuations may be required more frequently than once every 3 years. Comments are requested as to the appropriateness of requiring more frequent valuations under the situations described in the proposed amendments. Comments are also requested as to any additional circumstances where valuations should be required more frequently than once every 3 years. The rules also would describe how the funding standard account is to be maintained for years when there is no valuation.

TIMING OF CONTRIBUTIONS

The proposed amendments would provide rules, as required by section 412(c)(10) of the Code, relating to the time for making contributions for purposes of section 412. Unlike the temporary regulations published in 1976, these rules would not contain an automatic six-month extension of the two and one-half month grace period set forth as a general rule under the statute for meeting the minimum funding requirements. The Commissioner may approve applications for an extension of the grace period of up to six months. This more restrictive approach would be applied prospectively from a date after the publication of final regulations. However, a transitional rule is provided to phase in the two and one-half month period over the first three plan years following a date after publication of final regulations, and extensions may be approved by the Commissioner.

ALTERNATIVE FUNDING STANDARD ACCOUNT

The proposed amendments contain rules that would apply to plans maintaining the alternative minimum funding standard account. These rules would reflect section 412(g)(1) by limiting the use of the alternative account to plans using a funding method that requires contributions in all years at least equal to those required under the entry age normal funding method. Thus, only plans that use the entry age normal funding method may use the alternative account.

ALLOCATION OF EXCISE TAX LIABILITY

The proposed amendments would contain rules to allocate excise tax liability under section 4971 of more than one employer, but they would permit allocation in a reasonable manner that is not inconsistent with the rules provided.

Under the proposed amendments, the tax liability of each employer would generally be based on the obligation of each employer to contribute to the plan. To the extent that a funding deficiency would be attributable to the delinquent contribution of an individual employer, that employer would be liable for the tax. To the extent that a funding deficiency is not attributable to a delinquent contribution, each employer would share liability in proportion to its share of required contributions to the plan.

ALLOCATIONS FOR RELATED EMPLOYERS

The general rules for allocating tax liability would not apply to certain related employers. To the extent that an accumulated funding deficiency is attributable to related employers, those employers would be jointly and severally liable for the excise tax with respect to that deficiency. This rule would apply to related employers maintaining a plan of their own or in conjunction with other employers.

EMPLOYER WITHDRAWAL

The proposed amendments would generally provide that an employer withdrawing from a plan remains liable for tax imposed with respect to the portion of an accumulated funding deficiency attributable to that employer for years before withdrawal. The remaining employers would be liable for the tax attributable to the accumulated funding deficiency for years after an employer's withdrawal, even if the deficiency is attributable to prior years.

TEMPORARY REGULATIONS SUPERSEDED

The proposed amendments contain rules that would supersede the following temporary regulations: § 11.412(c)-7, relating to the election to treat certain retroactive plan amendments as made on the first day of the plan year; § 11.412(c)-11, relating to the election with respect to bonds; and § 11.412(c)-12, relating to the extension of time to make contributions to satisfy requirements of section 412.

EXECUTIVE ORDER 12291 AND REGULATORY FLEXIBILITY ACT

The Commissioner of Internal Revenue has determined that this proposed regulation is not a major regulation for purposes of Executive Order 12291. Accordingly, a regulatory impact analysis is not required.

Although this document is a notice of proposed rulemaking which solicits public comments, the Internal Revenue Service has concluded that the regulations proposed herein are interpretative and that the notice and public procedure requirements of 5 U.S.C. 553 do not apply. Accordingly, these proposed regulations do not constitute regulations subject to the Regulatory Flexibility Act (5 U.S.C. chapter 6).

COMMENTS AND REQUESTS FOR A PUBLIC HEARING

Before adopting these proposed regulations, consideration will be given to any written comments that are submitted (preferably eight copies) to the Commissioner of Internal Revenue. It is requested that persons submitting comments use professional letterhead stationery only if the comment represents the position of the firm or a named client, rather than the views of the writer. All comments are available for public inspection and copying. A public hearing will be held upon written request to the Commission by any person who has submitted written comments. If a public hearing is held, notice of the time and place will be published in the Federal Register.

DRAFTING INFORMATION

The principal author of these proposed regulations is Joe E. Horowitz of the Employee Plans and Exempt Organizations Division of the Office of Chief Counsel, Internal Revenue Service. However, personnel from other offices of the Internal Revenue Service and Treasury Department participated in developing the regulations, both on matters of substance and style.

[¶49,024] **Proposed Amendment of Regulation (LR-254-81),** published in the Federal Register on February 10, 1983.

Inventories: Last-in, first-out rule: Increase in value: Three-year averaging method.—Amendment of Reg. §1.472-2, relating to three-year averaging for increases in inventory value, is proposed.

AGENCY: Internal Revenue Service, Treasury.

ACTION: Notice of proposed rulemaking.

SUMMARY: This document contains proposed regulations under section 472 of the Code relating to 3-year averaging for increases in inventory value. Changes in the applicable tax law were made by the Economic Recovery Tax Act of 1981. These regulations would provide the public with guidance needed to comply with the act and would affect taxpayers first adopting the LIFO inventory method for taxable years beginning after December 31, 1981.

DATES: Written comments and requests for a public hearing must be delivered or mailed by April 11, 1983. The amendments are proposed to be effective with respect to taxable years beginning after December 31, 1981.

ADDRESS: Send comments and requests for a public hearing to: Commissioner of Internal Revenue, Attention: CC:LR:T, (LR-254-81), Washington, D.C. 20224.

FOR FURTHER INFORMATION CONTACT: Mr. Gregory A. Roth of the Legislation and Regulations Division, Office of Chief Counsel, Internal Revenue Service, 1111 Constitution Avenue, N.W., Washington, D.C. 20224 (Attention: CC:LR:T) (202-566-3238, not a toll-free number).

SUPPLEMENTARY INFORMATION:

BACKGROUND

This document contains proposed amendments to the Income Tax Regulations (26 CFR Part 1) under section 472(d) of the Internal Revenue Code of 1954. These amendments are proposed to conform the regulations to section 236 of the Economic Recovery Tax Act of 1981 (95 Stat. 172) and are to be issued under the authority contained in sections 472(d) and 7805 of the Internal Revenue Code of 1954 (26 U.S.C. 472(d) and 7805).

INVENTORY VALUATION

Section 472(d) requires opening inventory of the taxable year for which the LIFO method is first used to be valued at cost. Restoration shall be made with respect to any writedown to market values resulting from the pricing of former inventories. Such restoration amount shall be taken into account ratably in each of the three taxable years beginning with the first taxable year for which the LIFO method is used.

COMMENTS AND REQUESTS FOR A PUBLIC HEARING

Before adopting these proposed regulations consideration will be given to any written comments that are submitted (preferably six copies) to the Commissioner of Internal Revenue. All comments will be available for public inspection and copying. A public hearing will be held on written request to the Commissioner by any person who has submitted written comments. If a public hearing is held, notice of the time and place will be published in the *FEDERAL REGISTER*.

SPECIAL ANALYSES

The Commissioner of Internal Revenue has determined that this proposed rule is not a major rule as defined in Executive Order 12291. Accordingly a Regulatory Impact Analysis is not required. Although this document is a notice of proposed rulemaking that solicits public comment, the Internal Revenue Service has concluded that the notice and public procedure requirements of 5 U.S.C. 553 do not apply because the rules proposed are interpretative. Accordingly, a Regulatory Flexibility Analysis is not required.

DRAFTING INFORMATION

The principal author of these proposed regulations is Gregory A. Roth of the Legislation and Regulations Division of the Office of Chief Counsel, Internal Revenue Service. However, personnel from other offices of the Internal Revenue Service and Treasury Department participated in developing the regulations, both on matters of substance and style.

[¶49,025] **Proposed Regulations and Amendments (EE-3-81),** published in the Federal Register on February 25, 1983.

Employees' trusts: Affiliated service groups.—Reg. §§1.414(m)-1—1.414(m)-4 and amendments of Reg. §1.105-11, which prescribe rules for determining whether two or more separate service organizations constitute an affiliated group and which detail how certain requirements are

satisfied by a qualified retirement plan maintained by a member of an affiliated service group, are proposed. Reg. § 1.415-8 was removed 4/4/2007 by T.D. 9319.

AGENCY: Internal Revenue Service, Treasury.

ACTION: Notice of proposed rulemaking.

SUMMARY: This document contains proposed regulations prescribing rules for determining whether two or more separate service organizations constitute an affiliated service group, and detailing how certain requirements are satisfied by a qualified retirement plan maintained by a member of an affiliated service group. Changes to the applicable tax law were made by the Miscellaneous Revenue Act of 1980. The regulations would provide the public with additional guidance needed to comply with that Act and would affect all employers that maintain qualified retirement plans and that are members of an affiliated service group.

DATES: Written comments and requests for a public hearing must be delivered or mailed by April 26, 1983. For plans that were not in existence on November 30, 1980, the amendments are effective for plan years ending after that date. For plans in existence on November 30, 1980, the amendments are effective for plan years beginning after that date.

ADDRESS: Send comments and requests for a public hearing to: Commissioner of Internal Revenue, Attention: CC:LR:T (EE-3-81), Washington, D.C. 20224.

FOR FURTHER INFORMATION CONTACT: Patricia K. Keesler of the Employee Plans and Exempt Organizations Division, Office of Chief Counsel, Internal Revenue Service, 1111 Constitution Avenue, N.W., Washington, D.C. 20224 (Attention: CC:LR:T) (202/566-3430) (not a toll-free number).

SUPPLEMENTARY INFORMATION:

BACKGROUND

This document contains proposed amendments to the Income Tax Regulations (26 CFR Part 1) under section 414(m) of the Internal Revenue Code of 1954. These amendments are proposed to conform the regulations to section 201 of the Miscellaneous Revenue Act of 1980 (94 Stat. 3526) and section 5 of Public Law 96-613 (94 Stat. 3580). These regulations do not reflect amendments made to section 414(m) under the Tax Equity and Fiscal Responsibility Act of 1982. These regulations are to be issued under the authority contained in section 414(m) and in section 7805 of the Internal Revenue Code of 1954 (94 Stat. 3526, 94 Stat. 3580, 68A Stat. 917; 26 U.S.C. 414(m), 7805).

STATUTORY PROVISIONS

Section 414(m)(1) of the Code provides that, for purposes of certain employee benefit requirements listed in section 414(m)(4), except to the extent otherwise provided in regulations, all employees of the members of an affiliated service group shall be treated as employed by a single employer.

Section 414(m)(2) defines an affiliated service group as a First Service Organization and one or more of the following: (A) any service organization (A Organization) that is a shareholder or partner in the First Service Organization and that regularly performs services for the First Service Organization or is regularly associated with the First Service Organization in performing services for third persons; and (B) any other organization (B Organization) if a significant portion of the business of that organization is the performance of services for the First Service Organization, for A Organizations, or both, of a type historically performed by employees in the service field of the First Service Organization or the A Organizations, and ten percent or more of the interests in the organization is held by persons who are officers, highly compensated employees, or owners of the First Service Organization or of the A Organizations.

Section 414(m)(3) defines a service organization as an organization the principal business of which is the performance of services.

Section 414(m)(5)(A) provides that the term "organization" means a corporation, partnership, or other organization. Section 414(m)(5)(B) provides that the principles of section 267(c) apply in determining ownership.

Section 414(m)(6) provides that the Secretary of the Treasury or his delegate shall prescribe such regulations as may be necessary to prevent the avoidance of the employee benefit requirements listed in section 414(m)(4) through the use of separate service organizations.

PRIOR GUIDELINES

Initial guidelines under section 414(m) were set forth in Revenue Ruling 81-105, 1981-1 C.B. 256. Rev. Rul. 81-105 provided illustrations of how the provisions of section 414(m) operate by way of three examples. The rules set forth in Rev. Rul. 81-105 remain operative and are not affected by the promulgation of these proposed regulations.

Revenue Procedure 81-12, 1981-1 C.B. 652, prescribes procedures for (1) obtaining a ruling on whether two or more organizations are members of an affiliated service group, and (2) obtaining determination letters on the qualification, under section 401(a) or 403(a), of an employees' pension, profit-sharing, stock bonus, annuity, or bond purchase plan established by a member of an affiliated service group.

ADMINISTRATIVE EXEMPTIONS

Several parties have expressed concern that aggregation may be required under the rules of section 414(m)(2)(A) and (B) in situations where there has been no attempt to avoid the employee benefit requirements listed in section 414(m)(4).

Those parties noted that an organization qualifies as an A Organization whenever it is a shareholder or partner in the First Service Organization and regularly performs services for the First

Service Organization or is regularly associated with the First Service Organization in performing services for third persons. Thus, aggregation will be required regardless of how small the interest is that the A Organization holds in the First Service Organization, irrespective of whether the services performed by the A Organization are of a type historically performed by employees in the service field of the First Service Organization, and even if the services performed for the First Service Organization only constitute an insignificant portion of the business of the A Organization.

However, section 414(m)(1) grants authority to promulgate regulations that specify when all the employees of an affiliated service group will not be treated as employed by a single employer. Accordingly, proposed Treasury Regulation § 1.414(m)-1(c) provides that a corporation, other than a professional service corporation, will not be treated as a First Service Organization for purposes of section 414(m)(2)(A). Professional service corporations are not excepted from treatment as First Service Organizations for purposes of section 414(m)(2)(A) because the legislative history indicates that such corporations were intended to be covered. A special definition of professional service corporations is provided in the proposed regulation.

A corporation will still be treated as a First Service Organization for purposes of section 414(m)(2)(B). Thus, two corporations, neither of which is a professional service organization, will be aggregated only if one of the corporations satisfies the more stringent tests to be classified as a B Organization.

However, the Commissioner may determine that, in practice, the exception in the A Organization test for corporations, other than professional service corporations, results in an avoidance of the requirements of section 414(m) that circumvents Congressional intent. If such avoidance is found in a significant number of cases, this exception may be removed from the regulations.

Similarly, several parties have mentioned that aggregation may be required under section 414(m)(2)(B) whenever the owner of the potential B Organization acquires an interest in the First Service Organization (or in an A Organization), even though this interest is minimal and even though the owner does not have any other significant connection with the First Service Organization (*i.e.*, the owner is not an officer or highly compensated employee of the First Service Organization).

Pursuant to the authority contained in section 414(m)(1), a special rule is provided for determining whether ten percent or more of the interests in the potential B Organization is held by officers, highly compensated employees, or owners of the First Service Organization (or of an A Organization). For this purpose, the interests held by persons who are owners of the First Service Organization and the B Organization (but who are not also officers or highly compensated employees of the First Service Organization), will be taken into account as owners of the First Service Organization only if they hold, in the aggregate, three percent or more of the interests in such First Service Organization.

There may be other situations, not covered by the special rules of the regulations, where aggregation should not be required although the organizations are described in the literal language of either section 414(m)(2)(A) or (B). Comments are solicited from the public as to what these rules should be.

SIGNIFICANT PORTION

Proposed Treasury Regulation § 1.414(m)-2(c)(2) provides that the determination of whether providing services for the First Service Organization, for one or more A Organizations determined with respect to the First Service Organization, or for both, is a significant portion of the business of the potential B Organization will generally be based on the facts and circumstances. However, two specific rules are provided.

A safe harbor rule is provided under which the performance of services for the First Service Organization, for one or more A Organizations, or for both, will not be considered a significant portion of the business of a potential B Organization if the Service Receipts Percentage is less than five percent. The Service Receipts Percentage is the ratio of the gross receipts of the organization derived from performing services for the First Service Organization, for one or more A Organizations, or for both, to the total gross receipts of the organization derived from performing services. This ratio is the greater of the ratio for the year for which the determination is being made or for the three year period including that year and the two preceding years (or the period of existence of the organization, if less).

Except for a situation described in the preceding paragraph, the performance of services for the First Service Organization, for one or more A Organizations, or for both, will be considered a significant portion of the business of the potential B Organization if the Total Receipts Percentage is ten percent or more. The Total Receipts Percentage is calculated in the same manner as the Service Receipts Percentage, except that gross receipts in the denominator are determined without regard to whether they were derived from performing services.

Comments from the public are requested regarding these significant portion tests.

HISTORICALLY PERFORMED

Proposed Treasury Regulation § 1.414(m)-2(c)(3) provides that services will be considered of a type historically performed by employees in a particular service field if it was not unusual for the services to be performed by employees of organizations in that service field in the United States on December 13, 1980 (the date of enactment of section 414(m)).

CONSTRUCTIVE OWNERSHIP

Proposed Treasury Regulation § 1.414(m)-2(d)(2) provides that in determining ownership for purposes of section 414(m), an individual's interest under a plan that qualifies under section 401(a) will be taken into account. Comments from the public are requested concerning the appropriateness of this rule in cases in which the investment in employer securities by the plan results from an independent decision of the plan trustee.

ORGANIZATION

Proposed Treasury Regulation § 1.414(m)-2(e) provides that the term "organization" includes a sole proprietorship. The proposed regulations do not consider the impact of sections 414(b) (controlled group of corporations) or 414(c) (group of trades or businesses under common control) on the definition of "organization" in § 1.414(m)-2(e)(1). Specifically, the regulations do not consider the situation in which a particular organization is potentially part of both an affiliated service group and either a controlled group of corporations or a group of trades or businesses under common control. In such a situation, issues arise as to the order in which the determinations are made as to what constitutes a single employer. For example, whereas an individual corporation may be a service organization, the controlled group of which that corporation is a part may not be a service organization (or vice versa). Comments from the public are requested regarding the treatment of a controlled group of corporations or a group of trades or businesses under common control in this respect.

SERVICE ORGANIZATION

Proposed Treasury Regulation § 1.414(m)-2(f) provides that the principal business of an organization will be considered the performance of services if capital is not a material income-producing factor for the organization. The test for determining whether or not capital is a material income-producing factor is similar to the test in Treasury Regulation § 1.1348-3(a)(3)(ii), as in effect on February 25, 1983.

Numerous fields are listed in proposed Treasury Regulation § 1.414(m)-2(f) as being service fields. Organizations engaged in a field not listed therein and in which capital is a material income-producing factor will not be considered to be service organizations until the first day of the first plan year beginning at least 180 days after the date of the publication of an official document (such as a revenue ruling) giving notice to the contrary. The Commissioner of Internal Revenue is granted authority to determine that certain organizations, or types of organizations, should not be considered as being subject to the requirements of section 414(m) even though the organizations are engaged in a field listed in the proposed regulation. Comments are requested from the public as to examples of organizations that should or should not be considered as being service organizations subject to the provisions of section 414(m).

MULTIPLE AFFILIATED SERVICE GROUPS

Proposed Treasury Regulation § 1.414(m)-2(g) provides rules for multiple affiliated service groups. Two or more affiliated service groups will not be aggregated simply because an organization is an A Organization or a B Organization with respect to each affiliated service group. However, if an organization is a First Service Organization with respect to two or more A Organizations or two or more B Organizations, or both, all of the organizations will be considered to constitute a single affiliated service group.

SPECIAL QUALIFICATION REQUIREMENTS

Pursuant to the authority granted in section 414(m)(6), proposed Treasury Regulation § 1.414(m)-3(b) provides that if a plan maintained by a member of an affiliated service group covers an employee described in section 401(c)(1) (self-employed individual), an owner-employee (as described in section 401(c)(3)), or a shareholder-employee (as described in section 1379(d)) the plan must also satisfy the special requirements relating to plans that cover those types of employees, to the extent those requirements apply, even though that individual is not employed by the member maintaining the plan. This provision only applies if such an employee's earned income or compensation received as a shareholder-employee is taken into account in computing contributions or benefits under the plan.

MULTIPLE EMPLOYER PLANS

Proposed Treasury Regulation § 1.414(m)-3(c) provides that if a plan maintained by a member of an affiliated service group covers an individual who is not an employee of that member, but who is an employee of another member of that affiliated service group, the plan will be considered to be maintained by more than one employer for purposes of several provisions of section 413(c) (relating to plans maintained by more than one employer). This rule allows a member of the affiliated service group to deduct contributions on behalf of individuals who are not employed by that member.

However, this multiple employer plan rule does not apply in the case of a controlled group of corporations (as described in section 414(b)) or a group of trades or businesses under common control (as described in section 414(c)). Those situations will be governed by the special rules of section 414(b) or (c), respectively.

DISCRIMINATION

Proposed Treasury Regulation § 1.414(m)-3(d) provides that in testing for discrimination under section 401(a)(4) (requiring that contributions or benefits do not discriminate in favor of employees who are officers, shareholders, or highly compensated), all of the compensation paid to an individual must be considered in determining the contributions or benefits on behalf of the individual under a plan maintained by a member of an affiliated service group, without regard to the percentage of the organization employing the individual owned by the member maintaining the plan.

EFFECTIVE DATES

In the case of a plan that was not in existence on November 30, 1980, section 414(m) applies to plan years ending after that date. In the case of a plan that was in existence on November 30, 1980, section 414(m) applies to plan years beginning after that date.

Proposed Treasury Regulation § 1.414(m)-4(b)(1) provides that a defined contribution plan in existence on November 30, 1980 that fails to satisfy the requirements for qualification under section 401(a) solely because of the application of section 414(m) will be treated as continuing to satisfy the requirements of section 401(a) after the effective date of section 414(m) if the plan is terminated and all amounts are distributed to participants within 180 days after the latest of:

(i) [insert the date of the publication of this regulation in the Federal Register as a Treasury decision],

(ii) The date on which notice of the final determination with respect to a request for a determination letter is issued by the Internal Revenue Service, such request is withdrawn, or such request is finally disposed of by the Internal Revenue Service, provided the request for a determination letter was pending on [insert the date of the publication of this regulation in the Federal Register as a Treasury decision] or, in the case of a request for a determination letter on the plan termination, was made within 60 days after [insert the date of the publication of this regulation in the Federal Register as a Treasury decision], or

(iii) If a petition is timely filed with the United States Tax Court for a declaratory judgment under section 7476 with respect to the final determination (or the failure of the Internal Revenue Service to make a final determination) in response to such request, the date on which the decision of the United States Tax Court in such proceeding becomes final.

Proposed Treasury Regulation § 1.414(m)-4(b)(2) provides that a defined benefit plan in existence on November 30, 1980 that fails to satisfy the requirements for qualification under section 401(a) solely because of the application of section 414(m) will be treated as continuing to satisfy the requirements of section 401(a) after the effective date of section 414(m) if the plan is terminated and all amounts are distributed within the same period as that provided for defined contribution plans. However, deductions for contributions to the plan for plan years after the effective date of section 414(m) are limited to those necessary to satisfy the minimum funding standards of section 412.

RELIANCE ON PROPOSED REGULATIONS

Pending the adoption of final regulations, taxpayers may rely on the rules contained in this notice of proposed rulemaking and the Internal Revenue Service will issue determination, opinion, and ruling letters based on these rules. If any provisions of the final regulations are less favorable to taxpayers than these proposed rules, those provisions only will be effective for periods after adoption of the final regulations.

COMMENTS AND REQUESTS FOR A PUBLIC HEARING

Before adopting these proposed regulations, consideration will be given to any written comments that are submitted (preferably six copies) to the Commissioner of Internal Revenue. All comments will be available for public inspection and copying. A public hearing will be held upon written request to the Commissioner by any person who has submitted written comments. If a public hearing is held, notice of the time and place will be published in the FEDERAL REGISTER.

EXECUTIVE ORDER 12291AND
REGULATORY FLEXIBILITY ACT

The Commissioner has determined that this proposed regulation is not a major regulation for purposes of Executive Order 12291. Accordingly, a regulatory impact analysis is not required.

Although this document is a notice of proposed rulemaking which solicits public comments, the Internal Revenue Service has concluded that the regulations proposed herein are interpretative and that the notice and public procedure requirements of 5 U.S.C. 553 do not apply. Accordingly, these proposed regulations do not constitute regulations subject to the Regulatory Flexibility Act (5 U.S.C. chapter 6).

DRAFTING INFORMATION

The principal authors of these proposed regulations are Kirk F. Maldonado and Mary M. Levontin of the Employee Plans and Exempt Organizations Division of the Office of Chief Counsel, Internal Revenue Service. However, personnel from other offices of the Internal Revenue Service and Treasury Department participated in developing these regulations, both on matters of substance and style.

[¶ 49,031] Proposed Regulations and Proposed Amendments of Regulations (EE-148-81), published in the Federal Register on January 23, 1984.

Individual retirement plans: Simplified employee pensions: Qualified voluntary employee contributions.—Reg. § § 1.219(a)-1—1.219(a)-6, 1.408-10 and 301.6652-4 and amendments of Reg. § § 1.408-2 and 1.408-3, relating to individual retirement plans, simplified employee pensions and qualified voluntary employee contributions, are proposed. Reg. § 1.409-1 was withdrawn on 1/8/96 by EE-148-81. Reg. § § 1.415-1, 1.415-2, 1.415-6 and 1.415-7 were removed 4/4/2007 by T.D. 9319.

AGENCY: Internal Revenue Service, Treasury.

ACTION: Notice of proposed rulemaking.

SUMMARY: This document contains proposed regulations relating to individual retirement plans, simplified employee pensions, and qualified voluntary employee contributions. Changes to the applicable law were made by the Economic Recovery Tax Act of 1981. The regulations would provide the public with the guidance needed to comply with the Act. The regulations would affect: institutions which sponsor individual retirement plans and simplified employee pensions, employers and individuals who use individual retirement plans and simplified employee pensions for retirement income, employers who maintain plans which accept qualified voluntary employee contributions and employees who make qualified voluntary employee contributions.

DATES: Written comments and requests for a public hearing must be delivered or mailed by March 23, 1984. The regulations are generally effective for taxable years beginning after December 31, 1981.

ADDRESS: Send comments and requests for a public hearing to: Commissioner of Internal Revenue, Attention: CC:LR:T (EE-148-81), Washington, D.C. 20224.

FOR FURTHER INFORMATION CONTACT: William D. Gibbs of the Employee Plans and Exempt Organizations Division, Office of the Chief Counsel, Internal Revenue Service, 1111 Constitution Avenue, N.W., Washington, D.C. 20224 (Attention: CC:LR:T) (202-566-3430) (not a toll-free number).

SUPPLEMENTARY INFORMATION:

BACKGROUND

This document contains proposed amendments to the Income Tax Regulations (26 CFR Part 1), the Estate Tax Regulations (26 CFR Part 20), the Gift Tax Regulations (26 CFR Part 25), and the Procedure and Administration Regulations (26 CFR Part 301) under sections 219, 408, 409, 415, 2039, 2517, and 6652 of the Internal Revenue Code of 1954. These amendments are proposed to conform the regulations to sections 311 (except subsection (b)) and 314(b) of the Economic Recovery Tax Act of 1981 (95 Stat. 274, 286). These regulations are to be issued under the authority contained in section 7805 of the Internal Revenue Code of 1954 (68A Stat. 917; 26 U.S.C. 7805).

INDIVIDUAL RETIREMENT PLANS

Section 219, as amended by the Economic Recovery Tax Act of 1981, allows an individual a deduction of up to the lesser of $2,000 or compensation includible in gross income for contributions to an individual retirement plan. Unlike old section 219, an individual is allowed this deduction whether or not he is an "active participant" in an employer's plan. The deduction for individual retirement plan contributions is reduced, however, by amounts which the employee contributes to an employer's plan and treats as qualified voluntary employee contributions. The remainder of the individual retirement plan rules are similar to those under prior law.

SPOUSAL INDIVIDUAL RETIREMENT ACCOUNTS

Code section 220 was deleted by the Economic Recovery Tax Act of 1981. In its place is new section 219(c), which allows an individual and his nonworking spouse to contribute up to the lesser of compensation includible in the working spouse's gross income or $2,250 to individual retirement accounts. The spouses must file a joint return to obtain this additional $250 deduction. No deduction is allowed if the spouse for whose benefit the individual retirement plan is maintained has attained age 70½ before the close of the taxable year.

There is no requirement, as under old law, that equal amounts be contributed to the individual retirement accounts of both spouses. However, no more than $2,000 may be contributed to the individual retirement account of either spouse.

SIMPLIFIED EMPLOYEE PENSIONS

The Economic Recovery Tax Act of 1981 increased the maximum deduction for contributions to simplified employee pensions to the lesser of 15% of compensation from the employer maintaining the simplified employee pension arrangement or the amount contributed by the employer to the simplified employee pension and included in gross income (but not in excess of $15,000). An employee may also contribute and deduct the lesser of $2,000 or compensation includible in gross income regardless of the employer's contribution to the simplified employee pension.

QUALIFIED VOLUNTARY EMPLOYEE CONTRIBUTIONS

Section 219, as amended by the Economic Recovery Tax Act of 1981, allows an individual a deduction for qualified voluntary employee contributions (QVEC's). QVEC's are voluntary contributions made by an individual as an employee under an employer's plan. The employer's plan must allow employees to make contributions which may be treated as QVEC's.

The maximum amount which can be deducted as a QVEC is the lesser of $2,000 or the compensation includible in gross income from the employer which maintains the plan which accepts the QVEC's.

Proposed § 1.219(a)-5(a) sets forth the type of plans which can accept qualified voluntary employee contributions.

Proposed § 1.219(a)-5(c) sets forth the rules a plan must follow to receive qualified voluntary employee contributions.

Additional rules for QVEC's are set forth in proposed § 1.219(a)-5(d), (e), and (f).

The reporting rules for qualified voluntary employee contributions are in proposed § 1.219(a)-5(g). This provision gives the Commissioner discretionary authority to modify the reporting requirements for these contributions. Any such modification of the reporting requirements would be subject to review by the Office of Management and Budget under the Paperwork Reduction Act of 1980.

OTHER AMENDMENTS

Conforming and technical amendments made by the Economic Recovery Tax Act of 1981 have been made to the regulations under Code sections 408, 409, 415, 2039, 2517, and 6652.

Although the Treasury Department stopped selling retirement bonds in early 1982, the regulations contain references to Code sections 405 and 409. These references apply to retirement bonds sold through early 1982 and to retirement bonds that may be sold subsequently.

These proposed regulations do not reflect amendments made to the Code by the Tax Equity and Fiscal Responsibility Act of 1982. These proposed regulations reflect changes in the applicable statutory provisions made by the Technical Corrections Act of 1982.

EXECUTIVE ORDER 12291 AND REGULATORY FLEXIBILITY ACT

The Commissioner has determined that this proposed regulation is not a major regulation for purposes of Executive Order 12291. Accordingly, a regulatory impact analysis is not required.

Although this document is a notice of proposed rulemaking which solicits public comment, the Internal Revenue Service has concluded that the regulations proposed herein are interpretative and that the notice and public procedure requirements of 5 U.S.C. 553 do not apply. Accordingly, these proposed regulations do not constitute regulations subject to the Regulatory Flexibility Act (5 U.S.C. chapter 6).

COMMENTS AND REQUESTS FOR A PUBLIC HEARING

Before adopting these proposed regulations, consideration will be given to any written comments that are submitted (preferably seven copies) to the Commissioner of Internal Revenue. All comments will be available for public inspection and copying. A public hearing will be held upon written request to the Commissioner by any person who has submitted written comments. If a public hearing is held, notice of the time and place will be published in the *Federal Register*.

The collection of information requirements contained in this notice of proposed rulemaking have been submitted to the Office of Management and Budget (OMB) for review under section 3504(h) of the Paperwork Reduction Act of 1980. Comments on these requirements should be sent to the Office of Information and Regulatory Affairs of OMB, Attention: Desk Office for Internal Revenue Service, New Executive Office Building, Washington, D.C. 20503. The Internal Revenue Service requests that persons submitting comments on these requirements to OMB also send copies of those comments to the Service.

DRAFTING INFORMATION

The principal author of these proposed regulations is William D. Gibbs of the Employee Plans and Exempt Organizations Division of the Office of Chief Counsel, Internal Revenue Service. However, personnel from other offices of the Internal Revenue Service and Treasury Department participated in developing the regulation, both on matters of substance and style.

[¶49,032] Proposed Regulations and Proposed Amendments of Regulations (LR-185-81), published in the Federal Register on February 16, 1984.

Accelerated cost recovery system.—Reg. §§1.168-1—1.168-6 and amendments of Reg. §§1.167(a)-11, 1.178-1, 1.1016-3 and 1.1016-4, relating to the Accelerated Cost Recovery System for recovering capital costs of eligible property, are proposed. Reg. §1.168-5(a) was adopted 12/23/86 by T.D. 8116. Reg. §1.168-2(n) was withdrawn on 1/29/98.

AGENCY: Internal Revenue Service, Treasury.

ACTION: Notice of proposed rulemaking.

SUMMARY: This document contains proposed regulations relating to the Accelerated Cost Recovery System (hereinafter referred to as ACRS) for recovering capital costs of eligible property. Changes to the applicable tax law were made by the Economic Recovery Tax Act of 1981 (hereinafter referred to as ERTA), the Tax Equity and Fiscal Responsibility Act of 1982 (hereinafter referred to as TEFRA) and the Technical Corrections Act of 1982. Prior law allowed as a depreciation deduction a reasonable allowance for exhaustion, wear and tear, or obsolescence of eligible property. ERTA replaced this prior law depreciation system with ACRS. Generally, under ACRS cost recovery deductions are determined by the use of tables which reflect the use of accelerated methods of cost recovery over predetermined recovery periods. These recovery periods are generally unrelated to, and shorter than, prior law "useful lives." TEFRA repealed the more accelerated tables for personal property which were to be effective for property placed in service after 1984. These regulations would provide taxpayers with the guidance needed to comply with the Acts.

DATES: Written comments must be delivered or mailed by May 16, 1984. In general, these regulations apply to eligible property placed in service after December 31, 1980.

ADDRESS: Send comments to: Commissioner of Internal Revenue, Attention: CC:LR:T (LR-185-81), Washington, D.C. 20224.

FOR FURTHER INFORMATION CONTACT: John A. Tolleris (with respect to §1.168-4 (202-566-3590)), Joseph M. Rosenthal (with respect to the repair allowance, §1.167(a)-11(d)(2) (202-566-3288)), or George T. Magnatta (with respect to all other provisions (202-566-3294)), of the Legislation and Regulations Division, Office of the Chief Counsel, Internal Revenue Service, 1111 Constitution Avenue, N.W., Washington, D.C. 20224 (Attention: CC:LR:T).

SUPPLEMENTARY INFORMATION:

BACKGROUND

This document contains proposed amendments to the Income Tax Regulations (26 CFR Part 1) under sections 167, 168, 178, and 1016 of the Internal Revenue Code of 1954. These amendments are proposed to conform the regulations to sections 201 and 203 of the Economic Recovery Tax Act of

1981 (Pub. L. 97-34; 95 Stat. 203, 221), sections 205 and 206 of the Tax Equity and Fiscal Responsibility Act of 1982 (Pub. L. 97-248; 96 Stat. 427, 431), and section 102 of the Technical Corrections Act of 1982 (Pub. L. 97-448; 96 Stat. 2367). These amendments are to be issued under the authority contained in section 168 (95 Stat. 203; 26 U.S.C. 168) and section 7805 (68A Stat. 917; 26 U.S.C. 7805) of the Internal Revenue Code of 1954.

ACCELERATED COST RECOVERY SYSTEM

Section 168, as added by ERTA, is a replacement for the prior law depreciation system for recovering the capital costs of trade or business assets or investment assets. Generally, this new Accelerated Cost Recovery System (ACRS), added by section 168, provides for the recovery of capital costs of eligible property by the use of tables, which reflect the use of accelerated methods of cost recovery over predetermined recovery periods. These recovery periods are generally unrelated to, and shorter than, those under prior law. Unlike prior law, ACRS does not make any distinction between new and used property. This new capital cost recovery system is mandatory for all eligible property, hereinafter referred to as "recovery property." Recovery property includes both real and personal property. Generally, to be eligible for ACRS property must be (1) tangible property of a character subject to the allowance for depreciation, (2) used in a trade or business or held for the production of income, and (3) placed in service by the taxpayer after December 31, 1980. Recovery property does not include (1) tangible depreciable property the taxpayer properly elects to depreciate under a method not expressed in terms of years, (2) public utility property where the taxpayer does not use a normalization method of accounting, and (3) certain pre-1981 property involved in post-1980 "churning" transactions to obtain the benefits of ACRS.

In addition, recovery property does not include intangible property. The Internal Revenue Service is continuing to examine the extent to which certain types of property, such as computer software and master motion picture negatives, may constitute intangible property that is ineligible for ACRS. The Internal Revenue Service is also examining the manner in which other provisions of the Code (such as section 48(k)) may apply if such property is considered eligible for ACRS. Accordingly, these issues have been reserved in these proposed regulations and are the subject of a recently opened project, under which regulations will be issued as soon as possible. In the meantime, the Service will continue to administer the area in accordance with its current position. Comments on these questions from interested persons are welcome.

The allowable ACRS deduction is generally determined by multiplying the unadjusted basis of the property by the applicable percentage contained in the relevant ACRS tables. The prior law concept of salvage value is abolished in determining deductions under this new system. Thus, the entire cost or other basis of the property is recovered under ACRS. The proposed regulations provide rules for determining the allowable deduction when the basis of the property is redetermined (*e.g.*, where there is a readjustment of the purchase price).

Under ACRS, the cost of personal property must be recovered over a 3-year, 5-year, 10-year, or 15-year recovery period (unless the taxpayer elects a longer recovery period under rules described below). Real property is recovered over a 15-year recovery period (unless a longer period is elected). With respect to personal property, a full year's recovery deduction is allowed in the first recovery year regardless of when the asset is placed in service during that taxable year. No recovery deduction is allowed in the taxable year in which personal property is disposed of. The proposed regulations provide rules for computing the allowable deduction where the taxpayer has a taxable year of less than 12 months. In addition, for real property, the recovery for the year the asset is placed in service or is disposed of is based on the number of months the property is in service during the year, regardless of whether the taxpayer has a normal or short taxable year.

Taxpayers may elect to recover the cost of eligible property using the straight line method over the applicable recovery period or over a longer optional recovery period. For example, taxpayers may recover the capital costs of 5-year recovery property over a 5-year, 12-year, or 25-year period or the cost of real property over a 15-year, 35-year, or 45-year period, using the straight line method. Except for real property, the election applies to all recovery property of the particular class placed in service in the same taxable year. Generally, this election is irrevocable. The proposed regulations provide tables containing the applicable percentages when an optional straight line election is made.

Taxpayers may, under certain conditions, elect to recover the capital costs of certain recovery property in a mass asset account. If the election is made, mass assets which have the same asset depreciation range (ADR) midpoint life as of January 1, 1981, and which are placed in service in the same taxable year, will be accounted for in a single account. As a consequence of the election, upon the disposition of an asset from that account, the taxpayer will generally include in income the full amount realized on the disposition. The unadjusted basis of the asset disposed of will continue to be included in determining the recovery deduction for the account. The proposed regulations define mass assets, provide rules for determining when dispositions occur for purposes of investment tax credit recapture, and provide rules for recovering any increase in basis resulting from such recapture. The proposed regulations also provide rules relating to the recognition of gain or loss on the disposition of recovery property other than from a mass asset account.

Under ACRS, component cost recovery is not permitted. Thus, the same recovery period and method generally must be used for a building and all structural components. The recovery period for a component generally begins at the later of the time the component or the building is placed in service.

Under the proposed regulations, a building is considered placed in service when a significant portion is made available for use in a finished condition. The taxpayer at that time begins recovery of so much of the capitalized costs as are properly allocable to the portion of the building in service. Similarly, as portions of the building are later made available, recovery of the properly allocable costs will commence.

Capitalized expenditures, which are section 1250 property, paid or incurred after the building is completed are recovered under the same period and method as are used for the building, recovery beginning when the improvement is placed in service. However, if a capitalized expenditure qualifies as a "substantial improvement," a new recovery period and method are permitted, recovery beginning when the improvement is placed in service.

Similarly, with respect to personal property, amounts paid or incurred after the property is placed in service, which are properly chargeable to capital account, are treated as newly-purchased property for ACRS purposes. That property is assigned to the same recovery class as the property to which the expenditure relates. Any applicable recovery period and method may be selected for such improvement, recovery beginning when the improvement is placed in service.

Rules are also provided clarifying the results when a lessee makes improvements on leased property.

The proposed regulations clarify the rules which prevent taxpayers from converting pre-1981 property into post-1980 recovery property. Under those rules, if the taxpayer enters into certain "churning" transactions, the methods of cost recovery provided under ACRS are not available with respect to the property.

ACRS contains special rules for property which is used predominantly outside the United States. The proposed regulations define this type of property and also provide guidance for property which ceases or begins to be used predominantly outside the United States after having been placed in service in a prior taxable year.

Similarly, the proposed regulations provide rules for determining the deductions for other property which changes status under ACRS (*e.g.*, property which ceases to be used in connection with research and experimentation, property converted from personal to business use). Additionally, the proposed regulations provide rules for determining the deductions for property which is used both for personal and business purposes.

ACRS provides special rules for recovery property which is involved in certain nonrecognition and other transactions (section 168(f)(7),(10)). Generally, in these transactions the transferee is bound by the transferor's recovery period and method with respect to so much of the basis of the property in the hands of the transferee as does not exceed its basis in the hands of the transferor. The proposed regulations clarify the class of transactions subject to the rules and the manner of computing the deductions available to the transferor and transferee.

The proposed regulations also clarify the rules with respect to property involved in a transaction to which section 1031 or 1033 applies (section 168(f)(7)). Additionally, the proposed regulations clarify the deductions available with respect to property transferred by gift or bequest and with respect to partnership property to which basis adjustments are made.

The proposed regulations also provide the guidance necessary for making the various elections under section 168.

Since Congress made no change to certain provisions of the Code which require (or allow) a taxpayer to compute depreciation by use of the straight line method over the property's useful life (*e.g.*, section 163(d)(3)(C), 1016(a)(3)), the proposed regulations contain no special rules in that regard. As a result, the rules under prior law continue to apply.

Section 203(b) of ERTA terminated the class life asset depreciation range (ADR) system, authorized by section 167(m) of the Code, for recovery property placed in service after 1980. Additionally, section 201(c) of ERTA repealed the asset guideline class repair allowance, authorized by section 263(e), effective for property placed in service after December 31, 1980. The proposed regulations implement these statutory changes by amending § 1.167(a)-11(a)(1) and (d)(2) and by making other conforming amendments. The proposed regulations also clarify that the repair allowance is continued in effect for expenditures made after December 31, 1980, for the repair, maintenance, rehabilitation, or improvement of property placed in service before January 1, 1981.

The proposed regulations provide that the taxpayer may elect the repair allowance for a taxable year by (a) making the election to apply ADR for the taxable year (even if all the property placed in service during the taxable year is recovery property to which the ADR system does not apply), and (b) making an election to apply the asset guideline class repair allowance for the taxable year.

For periods after December 31, 1980, the proposed regulations provide that expenditures that are property improvements or excluded additions under the repair allowance rules shall generally be treated as separate items of recovery property, as described above.

These regulations concerning ACRS are effective for property placed in service after December 31, 1980. A taxpayer who has filed a return and who either did not claim allowable ACRS deductions, or did not claim the full amount allowable (*e.g.*, because the taxpayer used a different rule for years following a short taxable year than is provided in these regulations), should file an amended return.

NON-APPLICABILITY OF EXECUTIVE ORDER 12291

It has been determined that this notice of proposed rulemaking is not subject to review under Executive Order 12291 or the Treasury and OMB implementation of the order dated April 29, 1983.

REGULATORY FLEXIBILITY ACT

Although this document is a notice of proposed rulemaking which solicits public comment, the Internal Revenue Service has concluded that the regulations proposed herein are interpretative and that the notice and public procedure requirements of 5 U.S.C. 553 do not apply. Accordingly, these proposed regulations do not constitute regulations subject to the Regulatory Flexibility Act (5 U.S.C. chapter 6).

COMMENTS—PUBLIC HEARING

Before adopting these proposed regulations, consideration will be given to any written comments that are submitted (preferably seven copies) to the Commissioner of Internal Revenue. All comments will be available for public inspection and copying. A public hearing will be held in accordance with the notice of hearing published in this issue of the FEDERAL REGISTER.

PAPERWORK REDUCTION ACT

The collection of information requirements contained in this notice of proposed rulemaking have been submitted to the Office of Management and Budget (OMB) for review under section 3504(h) of the Paperwork Reduction Act. Comments on these requirements should be sent to the Office of Information and Regulatory Affairs of OMB, Attention: Desk Officer for Internal Revenue Service, New Executive Office Building, Washington, D.C. 20503. The Internal Revenue Service requests that persons submitting comments on these requirements to OMB also send copies of those comments to the Service.

DRAFTING INFORMATION

The principal authors of these regulations are John A. Tolleris, George T. Magnatta, Harold T. Flanagan, and Joseph M. Rosenthal of the Legislation and Regulations Division of the Office of Chief Counsel, Internal Revenue Service. However, personnel from other offices of the Internal Revenue Service and Treasury Department participated in developing the regulations, both on matters of substance and style.

[¶ 49,056] Proposed Regulations (EE-66-84), published in the Federal Register on July 3, 1985.

Welfare benefit fund: Collective bargaining: Limits on contributions and reserves.—Reg. §1.419A-2T, relating to welfare benefit funds maintained pursuant to collective bargaining agreements, is proposed.

AGENCY: Internal Revenue Service, Treasury.

ACTION: Notice of proposed rulemaking by cross reference to temporary regulations.

SUMMARY: In the Rules and Regulations portion of this issue of the *Federal Register*, the Internal Revenue Service is issuing temporary regulations relating to contributions to and reserves of welfare benefit funds maintained pursuant to a collective bargaining agreement. The text of those temporary regulations also serves as the comment document for this notice of proposed rulemaking.

DATES: Written comments and requests for a public hearing must be delivered or mailed by September 3, 1985. The regulations are proposed to be effective for contributions paid or accrued after December 31, 1985.

ADDRESS: Send comments and requests for a public hearing to Commissioner of Internal Revenue, Attn: CC:LR:T (EE-66-84), 1111 Constitution Avenue NW., Washington, D.C. 20224.

FOR FURTHER INFORMATION CONTACT: John T. Ricotta of the Employee Plans and Exempt Organizations Division, Office of Chief Counsel, Internal Revenue Service, 1111 Constitution Avenue NW., Washington, D.C. 20224, Attention: CC:LR:T (EE-66-84), telephone: 202-566-4396 (not a toll-free number).

SUPPLEMENTARY INFORMATION:

Background

The temporary regulations provide guidance concerning the limits on contributions to and the reserves of welfare benefit funds maintained pursuant to a collective bargaining agreement under section 419A(f)(5) of the Internal Revenue Code of 1954 (Code), as added to the Code by section 511 of the Tax Reform Act of 1984 (26 U.S.C. 419A). The proposed regulations are issued under the authority contained in section 7805 of the Code (26 U.S.C. 7805). For the text of the temporary regulations, see FR Doc. 85-15940 published in the Rules and Regulations portion of this issue of the *Federal Register.*

Special Analyses

The Commissioner of Internal Revenue has determined that this proposed rule is not a major rule as defined in Executive Order 12291and that a Regulatory Impact Analysis is therefore not required. Although this document is a notice of proposed rulemaking which solicits public comment, the Internal Revenue has concluded that the regulations proposed herein are interpretative and that the notice and public procedure requirements of 5 U.S.C. 553 do not apply. Accordingly, these proposed regulations do not constitute regulations subject to the Regulatory Flexibility Act (5 U.S.C. Chapter 6).

Comments and Requests for a Public Hearing

Before adopting the temporary regulations referred to in this document as final regulations, consideration will be given to any written comments that are submitted (preferably 8 copies) to the Commissioner of Internal Revenue. All comments will be available for public inspection and copying. A public hearing will be held upon written request to the Commissioner by any person who has submitted written comments. If a public hearing is held, notice of the time and place will be published in the *Federal Register*.

[¶ 49,059] Proposed Amendments to Regulations (LR-114-85), published in the Federal Register on September 3, 1985.

Mortgage credit certificates: Information reporting.—Amendments to Reg. § 1.25-4T, dealing with information reporting and policy statement requirements, are proposed.

AGENCY: Internal Revenue Service, Treasury.

ACTION: Notice of proposed rulemaking by cross-reference to temporary regulations.

SUMMARY: This document provides proposed regulations that relate to mortgage credit certificates. Changes to the applicable tax law were made by the Tax Reform Act of 1984. These regulations affect all holders and issuers of mortgage credit certificates. In addition, in the Rules and Regulations portion of this FEDERAL REGISTER, the Internal Revenue Service is issuing temporary regulations that relate to mortgage credit certificates. The text of those temporary regulations also serves as the comment document for this proposed rulemaking.

DATES: Written comments and requests for a public hearing must be delivered or mailed by November 4, 1985. These regulations are proposed to be effective with respect to mortgage credit certificates issued after September 30, 1985.

ADDRESS: Send comments and requests for a public hearing to: Commissioner of Internal Revenue, Attention: CC:LR:T (LR-114-85), Washington, D.C. 20224.

FOR FURTHER INFORMATION CONTACT: Mitchell H. Rapaport of the Legislation and Regulations Division, Office of Chief Counsel, Internal Revenue Service, 1111 Constitution Avenue, N.W., Washington, D.C. 20224 (Attention: CC:LR:T) (202-566-3740).

SUPPLEMENTARY INFORMATION:

BACKGROUND

The temporary regulations in the Rules and Regulations portion of this issue of the FEDERAL REGISTER amend § 1.25-4T of Title 26 of the Code of Federal Regulations. The final regulations, which this document proposes to be based on those temporary regulations, would be added to Part 1 of Title 26 of the Code of Federal Regulations. For the text of the Temporary Regulations, see FR Doc. (T.D. 8048) published in the Rules and Regulations portion of this issue of the FEDERAL REGISTER. The preamble to the temporary regulations explains the addition to the regulations.

On May 8, 1985, temporary and proposed regulations with respect to mortgage credit certificates were published in the FEDERAL REGISTER (50 FR 19344; 50 FR 19383). Those regulations reserved § 1.25-4T(e), relating to the information reporting requirement, and § 1.25-4T(f), relating to the policy statement requirement. The Service received numerous written comments responding to a notice of proposed rulemaking published in the FEDERAL REGISTER on December 12, 1984 (49 FR 48323), with respect to the reporting and policy statement requirements as they apply to qualified mortgage bonds and qualified veterans' mortgage bonds, and a public hearing was held on April 30, 1985. After consideration of all comments regarding those proposed regulations, temporary and proposed regulations relating to the information reporting and policy statement requirements applicable to mortgage credit certificates are being provided.

The regulations interpret the provisions of section 25(g) of the Code, which add certain information reporting requirements to the requirements that mortgage credit certificate programs must meet.

These regulations are proposed to be issued under the authority of section 25(g) and section 7805 of the Internal Revenue Code (98 Stat. 911, 26 U.S.C. 25(g); 68A Stat. 917, 26 U.S.C. 7805).

NON-APPLICABILITY OF EXECUTIVE ORDER 12291

The Commissioner of Internal Revenue has determined that this proposed rule is not a major rule as defined in Executive Order 12291and that a regulatory impact analysis therefore is not required.

REGULATORY FLEXIBILITY ANALYSIS

Although this document is a notice of proposed rulemaking that solicits public comment, the Internal Revenue Service has concluded that the regulations proposed herein are interpretative and that the notice and public procedure requirements of 5 U.S.C. 553 do not apply. Accordingly, these proposed regulations do not constitute regulations subject to the Regulatory Flexibility Act (5 U.S.C. chapter 6).

DRAFTING INFORMATION

The principal author of these proposed regulations is Mitchell H. Rapaport of the Legislation and Regulations Division of the Office of Chief Counsel, Internal Revenue Service. However, personnel from other offices of the Internal Revenue Service and Treasury Department participated in developing the regulations, on matters of both substance and style.

COMMENTS AND REQUESTS FOR A PUBLIC HEARING

Before the adoption of these proposed regulations, consideration will be given to any written comments that are submitted (preferably seven copies) to the Commissioner of Internal Revenue. All comments will be available for public inspection and copying. A public hearing will be held upon written request to the Commissioner by any person who has submitted written comments. If a public hearing is held, notice of the time and place will be published in the FEDERAL REGISTER. The collection of information requirements contained herein have been submitted to the Office of Management and Budget (OMB) for review under section 3504(h) of the Paperwork Reduction Act.

Comments on the requirements should be sent to the Office of Information and Regulatory Affairs of OMB, Attention: Desk Officer for Internal Revenue Service, New Executive Office Building, Washington, D.C. 20503. The Internal Revenue Service requests persons submitting comments to OMB also to send copies of the comments to the Service.

[¶49,064] Proposed Regulations (LR-214-82), published in the Federal Register on January 7, 1986.

Employment taxes: Real estate agents and direct sellers: Employer's liability.—Reg. §§31.3508-1, 31.3509-1 and 1.6041A-1, relating to the treatment of qualified real estate agents and direct sellers as nonemployees, to the determination of employer liability for income tax withholding and employee social security taxes where the employer treated an employee as a nonemployee for purposes of such taxes, and to information reporting of direct sales and payments of remuneration for services, are proposed.

AGENCY: Internal Revenue Service, Treasury

ACTION: Notice of proposed rulemaking.

SUMMARY: This document contains proposed amendments to the Employment Tax Regulations under sections 3508, relating to the treatment of qualified real estate agents and direct sellers as nonemployees for Federal income and employment tax purposes, and under section 3509, relating to the determination of employer liability for income tax withholding and employee social security taxes where the employer treated an employee as a nonemployee for purposes of such taxes. It also contains proposed amendments to the Income Tax Regulations under section 6041A, relating to information reporting of direct sales and payments of remuneration for services. Sections 3508, 3509, and 6041A were added to the tax law by sections 269, 270, and 312, respectively, of the Tax Equity and Fiscal Responsibility Act of 1982 (96 Stat. 551, 553, 601). The regulations would provide the public with the guidance needed to comply with the applicable tax law.

DATES: Written comments and requests for a public hearing must be delivered or mailed by March 10, 1986. The regulations under section 3508 are proposed to be effective for services performed after December 31, 1982, and the regulations under section 6041A are proposed to be effective for payments and sales made after December 31, 1982. The regulations under section 3509 are proposed to be effective for any income and employee social security taxes required to be deducted and withheld, except with respect to assessments made before January 1, 1983.

ADDRESS: Send comments and requests for a public hearing to: Commissioner of Internal Revenue, Attention: CC:LR:T (LR-214-82), Washington, D.C. 20224.

FOR FURTHER INFORMATION CONTACT: Robert E. Shaw of the Legislation and Regulations Division, Office of Chief Counsel, Internal Revenue Service, 1111 Constitution Avenue, N.W., Washington, D. C. 20224 (Attention: CC:LR:T) (202-566-3297, not a toll-free call).

SUPPLEMENTARY INFORMATION:

BACKGROUND

The determination of whether an individual is an employee or independent contractor for Federal tax purposes is important for several reasons. Wages paid to employees generally are subject to social security taxes imposed on the employer and the employee under the Federal Insurance Contributions Act (FICA) and to unemployment taxes imposed on the employer under the Federal Unemployment Tax Act (FUTA). Compensation paid to independent contractors is subject to the tax on self-employment income (SECA), but not to FICA or FUTA taxes. The SECA is generally paid only by self-employed individuals. In additon, Federal income tax must generally be withheld from compensation paid to employees but not from compensation paid to independent contractors.

Except for sections 3121(d)(3) and 3306(i), which establish categories of statutory employees for social security and Federal unemployment tax purposes, prior to the enactment of the Tax Equity and Fiscal Responsibility Act of 1982, the determination of an individual's status as an employee or independent contractor generally was made under common-law (*i.e.,* nonstatutory) rules. Under the common-law test, an individual generally is an employee if the person for whom the individual performs services has the right to control and direct that individual, not only as to the result to be accomplished by the work but also as to the details and means by which that result is accomplished. Thus, the most important factor under the common law is the degree of control, or right of control, which the employer has over the manner in which the work is to be performed.

The Service applies various factors that have evolved from the common law to determine whether the requisite control exists. Because of the difficulty that often arises in applying these factors, several bills introduced in both the House and the Senate during 1982 set forth statutory "safe-harbor" tests which, if satisfied with respect to an individual, would result in that individual being classified as an independent contractor. The proposed safe-harbor requirements, generally applicable to post-1982 services, related to (1) control of hours worked, (2) place of business, (3) investment or income fluctuation, (4) written contract and notice of tax responsibilities, and (5) the filing of required returns. S.Rep. No. 97-494, 97 Cong., 2d Sess. 364 (1982). Workers who did not meet the safe-harbor tests still would have had their employment tax status determined under the common-law rules.

In enacting the Tax Equity and Fiscal Responsibility Act of 1982 (P.L. 97-248), Congress rejected the broader safe-harbor tests proposed by these bills and instead partially resolved the employee-independent contractor controversy by creating two categories of statutory nonemployees—qualified real estate agents and direct sellers. Thus, notwithstanding the common-law rules, an individual is an independent contractor for services that satisfy the statutory requirements of section 3508. Other employment situations generally must continue to be evaluated under common-law principles.

In response to the serious tax deficiencies that may arise when a worker erroneously treated as an independent contractor is reclassified as an employee, Congress enacted section 3509, which fixes an employer's liability for income tax withholding and employee social security taxes generally at a fraction of the amount of taxes which should have been deducted and withheld. Section 3509 provides relief to employers who would otherwise be liable for the full amount of such taxes which should have been deducted and withheld and provides a sanction for an employer's erroneous treatment of a worker in situations in which the employer would otherwise be able to escape liability for such taxes under the statutory offset provisions of sections 3402(d) and 6521.

To assure increased compliance by direct sellers with the income tax law, Congress added section 6041A (section 312 of the Tax Equity and Fiscal Responsibility Act of 1982) which, in addition to other requirements, imposes an obligation on direct sellers of consumer products to report gross sales totalling $5,000 or more in a calendar year to any buyer for resale in the home or some place other than a permanent retail establishment. Congress also provided a penalty for failure to file this return (section 6652) and a penalty for failure to furnish certain statements (section 6678).

EXPLANATION OF PROVISIONS

In general

The proposed regulations provide that an individual performing services as a qualified real estate agent or a direct seller will not be treated as an employee and the service-recipient will not be treated as an employer for Federal income and employment tax purposes. In order to qualify for such treatment substantially all the remuneration paid by a service-recipient to an individual for services as a real estate agent or direct seller must be directly related to sales or other output and such services must be performed pursuant to a written contract providing that such individual will not be treated as an employee for Federal tax purposes.

The proposed regulations make clear that a statutory employee (that is, an individual treated as an employee under section 3121(d)(3) of the Code) who also qualifies as a nonemployee under section 3508 will be treated as a nonemployee for FICA, FUTA and Federal income tax withholding purposes with respect to services described in section 3508. For example, an agent-driver (statutory employee) who qualifies as a direct seller (statutory nonemployee) will be treated as a nonemployee for FICA, FUTA, and income tax withholding purposes with respect to services performed as a direct seller. The regulations also make clear that the written contract requirement is not met unless the contract specifically states that the individual will not be treated as an employee for Federal tax purposes. For this purpose, it is not sufficient that the contract merely states that the individual will not be treated as an employee.

"Substantially all" remuneration requirement

Section 3508 requires that in order for an individual to be treated as a qualified real estate agent or a direct seller substantially all of the remuneration received for services as a real estate agent or direct seller must be directly related to sales or other output. The proposed regulations provide that the "substantially all remuneration" test is satisfied with respect to services performed as a real estate agent or direct seller if at least 90 percent of the total remuneration received during the calendar year by the individual for services performed as a real estate agent or direct seller is directly related to sales or other output rather than to the number of hours worked. The proposed regulations also provide rules for applying the "directly related to sales or other output" requirement to pooled remuneration arrangements, remuneration received in advance of sales or performance, and remuneration dependent on the productivity of others.

Direct sellers

A direct seller is any salesperson who, in addition to meeting the "substantially all" remuneration and written contract requirements, sells consumer products, either directly or though a middleperson (*i.e.*, a buyer) for ultimate resale, in the home or in a place other than in a permanent retail establishment. The proposed regulations define "consumer product" as any tangible personal property which is distributed in commerce and which is normally used for personal, family, or household purposes (including any such property intended to be attached to or installed in any real property without regard to whether it is so attached or installed). This definition corresponds to the definition provided in 15 U.S.C. § 2301, and the limitation to tangible property is consistent with other definitions of consumer products found in the United States Code (15 U.S.C. § 2052; 18 U.S.C. § 1365; 42 U.S.C. § 6291). The proposed regulations define "permanent retail establishment" as any business operating in or from a structure or facility which remains stationary for a substantial period of time to which consumers go to purchase consumer goods. The proposed regulations also clarify that vendors operating within, or on the grounds of, a permanent structure or facility such as a sports arena or amusement park are considered to operate in a permanent retail establishment for purposes of section 3508. Thus, the term "direct seller" may include door-to-door salespersons of not only products traditionally thought of as consumer products (*e.g.*, personal toiletry items, vacuum cleaners, kitchen products) but also products which require installation or construction on the consumer's property (*e.g.*, residential swimming pools, aluminum siding, kitchen cabinets, storm windows, insulation, carpeting) and products not used in or around the home. The term also includes salespersons who sell consumer goods directly to consumers through an exchange medium other than a permanent retail establishment (*e.g.*, mobile meal wagons or street vendors). The term does not include door-to-door salespersons of intangible products (*e.g.*, insurance, cable television subscription).

Persons who provide services generally are not direct sellers. For example, persons who provide services that do not involve the use of a product (*e.g.*, polltakers) or services that involve parts or materials which are incidental to providing services (*e.g.*, painting, carpet cleaning, septic tank cleaning, lawn care, pest control services, or appliance repair) are considered service providers rather than direct sellers.

Services of real estate agent and direct seller

The proposed regulations provide that the services performed as a direct seller are activities generally associated with the sale of consumer products in the home or otherwise than in a permanent retail establishment. These services include activities that are necessary to increase the sales efforts of other individuals, such as providing motivation, encouragement, training, recruitment, or counseling. Installation services performed by a direct seller in connection with the sale of a consumer product generally are not services performed by a direct seller. However, the proposed regulations provide that installation services rendered by a seller in conjunction with the sale of a consumer product will be services performed as a direct seller if the value of the installation services is 10 percent or less of the purchase price of the product (including installation).

The services performed as a real estate agent are those activities generally associated with the sale of real property. Such services include appraising property, advertising and showing property, closing sales, acquiring a lease to the property, and recruiting, training and supervising other salespersons. The services performed as a real estate agent do not include the management of property.

Retirement plans for self-employed individuals

The proposed regulations make clear that the fact that an individual is treated as a nonemployee under section 3508 for employment tax purposes will not prevent the individual from being covered under a qualified retirement plan for self-employed individuals.

Employer liability under section 3509.

An employer's liability for failure to deduct and withhold income tax or employee social security taxes by reason of treating an employee as a nonemployee for purposes of such taxes is generally determined under section 3509. The employer's liability for income tax withholding is determined as if the amount required to be deducted and withheld was equal to 1.5 percent (3 percent where the employer disregards certain reporting requirements) of the wages paid to the individual erroneously treated as a nonemployee. The employer's liability for employee social security taxes is determined as if such taxes imposed were 20 percent (40 percent where the employer disregards certain reporting requirements) of the amount imposed without regard to section 3509. The increased percentages are applicable where an employer fails to timely file any return or statement under sections 6041 (a), 6041A, or 6051 that would be required consistent with the employer's treatment of the worker as a nonemployee.

The proposed regulations clarify that, for purposes of section 3509, an employer fails to withhold taxes when the employer fails to pay over the full amount of tax required to be deducted and withheld during a calendar year on or before the due date for the return relating to such taxes for the final quarter of such calendar year. Thus, section 3509 is generally applied with respect to each calendar year as a unit.

Under section 3509 and the proposed regulations, if an employer's liability for any tax is determined under section 3509 the employer (i) may not collect from the employee any amount of tax so determined, and (ii) is not entitled to any offset of liability under section 3402 (d) or 6521. An employee's liability for taxes is not affected by application of section 3509 to the employer and the offset provisions of section 6521 may, where applicable, apply with respect to the employee's liability for employee social security taxes. An employer's liability for employer social security taxes is not affected by section 3509.

Section 3509 does not apply where an employer deducts income tax but not employee social security taxes or where the employer intentionally disregards the requirements to withhold and deduct Federal income tax or employee social security taxes. Section 3509 does not apply to employee social security taxes with respect to statutory employees described in section 3121(d)(3). The proposed regulations clarify that if an employer's liability for any tax is determined under section 3509 the employer may still be liable for penalties with respect to his or her failure to deduct and withhold such tax. The amount of such penalties, however, is based on the amount of the employer's liability for such tax under section 3509.

The proposed regulations also clarify that the amount of an employer's liability for tax determined under section 3509 will be considered satisfied to the extent of the amount of such tax which was actually withheld and deducted from the employee and paid. If the amount withheld, deducted, and paid exceeds the employer's liability as computed under section 3509, however, the employer may not claim a refund or credit of such excess amount.

New reporting requirements

Section 6041A added two reporting requirements relating to payments as remuneration for services and gross sales of consumer products to a buyer for resale in the home or otherwise than in a permanent retail establishment. Section 6041A(a) requires that a service-recipient engaged in a trade or business, who, in the course of that trade or business, makes payments to a person as remuneration for services, report such payments if the total remuneration paid to that person by the service-recipient during the calendar year is $600 or more. The proposed regulations provide that such remuneration does not include any amounts which the service-recipient knows are excludable from the gross income of the person performing services (*e.g.*, qualified foster care payments under section 131). Section 6041A(b) requires a direct seller to report gross sales of consumer products totalling $5,000 or more in a calendar year to any buyer who resells the product in the home or any place other than a permanent retail establishment. All sales of consumer products to a buyer for resale to another person are taken into account in determining the aggregate amount of sales to that buyer during the calendar year, even if the buyer resells some of the products in a permanent retail establishment.

The proposed regulations clarify that the aggregate amount of sales of consumer products to a buyer during a calendar year includes the sale of products used by the buyer for the buyer's personal use or consumption (including products disposed of in a manner other than resale such as gifts to friends or relatives). However, the aggregate amount of sales does not include the sale of goods that cannot be resold, such as catalogs and samples.

The proposed regulations make clear that an information return is required with respect to any person who sells consumer products in the home or otherwise than in a permanent retail establishment regardless of whether that person purchases the product from the company and resells it to the consumer or is a company salesperson (other than an employee) who does not acquire title to a product before selling it.

The proposed regulations provide that the regulatory exceptions to the reporting requirement under section 6041, as set forth in § 1.6041-3, are applicable to the reporting requirement under section 6041A(a).

COMMENTS AND PUBLIC HEARING

Before adoption of these proposed regulations, consideration will be given to any written comments that are submitted (preferably eight copies) to the Commissioner of Internal Revenue. All comments will be available for public inspection and copying. A public hearing will be held upon written request to the Commissioner by any person who has submitted written comments. If a public hearing is held, notice of the time and place will be published in the Federal Register.

The collection of information requirements contained in this notice of proposed rulemaking have been submitted to the Office of Management and Budget (OMB) for review under section 3504(h) of the Paperwork Reduction Act. Comments on these requirements should be sent to the Office of Information and Regulatory Affairs of OMB, Attention: Desk Officer for Internal Revenue Service, New Executive Office Building, Washington, D.C. 20530. The Internal Revenue Service requests that persons submitting comments on these requirements to OMB also send copies of those comments to the Service.

SPECIAL ANALYSES

The Commissioner of Internal Revenue has determined that this proposed rule is not a major rule as defined in Executive Order 12291and that a Regulatory Impact Analysis is therefore not required.

Although this document is a notice of proposed rulemaking which solicits public comment, the Internal Revenue Service has concluded that the regulations proposed herein are interpretative and that the notice and public comment requirements of 5 U.S.C. 553 do not apply. Accordingly, these proposed regulations do not constitute regulations subject to the Regulatory Flexibility Act (5 U.S.C. Chapter 6).

DRAFTING INFORMATION

The principal authors of these proposed regulations are Robert E. Shaw of the Legislation and Regulations Division of the Office of Chief Counsel, Internal Revenue Service, and Donald W. Stevenson, formerly of that Division. However, personnel from other offices of the Internal Revenue Service and Treasury Department participated in developing the regulations, both on matters of substance and style.

[¶ 49,065] Proposed Regulations (LR-106-77), published in the Federal Register on January 21, 1986.

Possessions corporations credit: Qualified possession source investment income.—Reg. §§ 1.936-2, 1.936-3 and 1.936-3A and amendments of Reg. § 7.936-1, defining the term "qualified possession source investment income," are proposed.

AGENCY: Internal Revenue Service, Treasury.

ACTION: Notice of proposed rulemaking.

SUMMARY: This document contains proposed regulations defining the term "qualified possession source investment income" for purposes of the Puerto Rico and possession tax credit enacted by the Tax Reform Act of 1976.

DATES: Written comments and requests for a public hearing must be delivered or mailed by March 24, 1986. The regulations are proposed to apply generally to taxable years beginning after December 31, 1975.

ADDRESS: Send comments and requests for a public hearing to: Commissioner of Internal Revenue, Attention: CC:LR:T (LR-106-77), Washington, D.C. 20224.

FOR FURTHER INFORMATION CONTACT: Jacob Feldman of the Legislation and Regulations Division, Office of the Chief Counsel, Internal Revenue Service, 1111 Constitution Avenue, N.W., Washington, D.C. 20224, Attention: CC:LR:T, 202-566-3289, not a toll-free call.

SUPPLEMENTARY INFORMATION:

BACKGROUND

This document contains proposed amendments to the Income Tax Regulations (26 CFR Part 1) under section 936 of the Internal Revenue Code of 1954, and deletes Temporary Regulations (26 CFR Part 7) under section 936. Section 936 was added to the Code by section 1051(b) of the Tax Reform Act of 1976 and was amended by section 701(u)(11) of the Revenue Act of 1978.

EXPLANATION OF PROVISIONS

A domestic corporation that elects the application of section 936 may qualify for the Puerto Rico and possession tax credit. This credit is equal to the Federal income tax attributable to *inter alia* the corporation's qualified possession source investment income. Section 936(d)(2) defines qualified possession source investment income as gross income (less the properly apportioned or allocated deductions) that is—

(1) From sources within a possession of the United States in which a trade or business is actively conducted;

(2) Attributable to investment in that possession (for use therein); and

(3) Attributable to the investment of funds initially derived from the active conduct of a trade or business in that possession or from such investment.

Source of Income

Proposed § 1.936-2(a) provides that generally the source of income for purposes of section 936 is to be determined in accordance with § 1.863-6. Special rules are provided for determining the source of certain interest and dividends (proposed § 1.936-2(b)).

Investment in a Possession (for use therein)

Proposed § 1.936-3 takes the position that interest and certain dividends derived by a U.S. corporation which conducts an active trade or business in Puerto Rico will be treated as attributable to investment in Puerto Rico (for use therein) as required under section 936(d)(2) if the interest or certain dividends qualify for exemption from Puerto Rican income tax. To qualify for exemption from Puerto Rican income tax, a taxpayer must satisfy criteria in the Puerto Rican income tax statute and regulations thereunder that the funds invested are in fact used in Puerto Rico. This is the position taken in temporary regulation § 7.936-1. The present proposed regulations, however, reflect the updating of the Puerto Rican regulations on April 17, 1984. In addition, for investments made by the U.S. corporation more than 30 days after publication of the regulation by Treasury decision, the U.S. corporation must obtain at the time it makes the investment the written agreement of the institution receiving the funds that the investment of the funds by the institution will qualify for the exemption under Puerto Rican regulations.

Reliance on the Puerto Rico regulatory system for satisfaction of this requirement is based on the rules in existence as a result of the April 17, 1984, amendments. Changes in those rules, or in the method of operation of the Puerto Rico government's regulatory or investment authority, may require the development and application of a separate set of rules for determining when investment income is attributable to investment in Puerto Rico (for use therein).

Proposed § 1.936-3 deals only with the application of section 936(d)(2) to investment in Puerto Rico. The credit provided by section 936 is also available with respect to certain investment income derived from other possessions of the United States (not including the Virgin Islands), if such income is attributable to investment of funds in the possession "for use therein" and if the other requirements of section 936(d)(2) are met.

Initially Derived from a Possession

Proposed § 1.936-3A takes the position that funds are treated as initially derived from a possession if such funds represent an investment of taxable income from sources without the United States derived from the active conduct of a trade or business in a possession or a reinvestment of qualified possession source investment income. Such funds are treated as qualified funds and the amount which may be invested is determined on an annual basis. Losses as well as distributions with respect to these funds will reduce the amount of qualified funds. Therefore, an investment which is treated as made from qualified funds in one year might no longer qualify if a loss or a distribution of income reduces the amount of qualified funds. The proposed regulation also takes the position that an investment of funds derived from a capital contribution does not qualify.

COMMENTS AND REQUESTS FOR A PUBLIC HEARING

Before adopting these proposed regulations, consideration will be given to any written comments that are submitted (preferably eight copies) to the Commissioner of Internal Revenue. All comments will be available for public inspection and copying. A public hearing will be held upon written request to the Commissioner by any person who has submitted written comments. If a public hearing is held, notice of the time and place will be published in the FEDERAL REGISTER.

REGULATORY FLEXIBILITY ACT AND EXECUTIVE ORDER 12291

Although this document is a notice of proposed rulemaking which solicits public comment, the Internal Revenue Service has concluded that the regulations proposed herein are interpretative and that the notice and public procedure requirements of 5 U.S.C. 553 do not apply. Accordingly, these proposed regulations do not constitute regulations subject to the Regulatory Flexibility Act (5 U.S.C. chapter 6). The Commissioner of Internal Revenue has determined that this proposed rule is not subject to Executive Order 12291, and, accordingly, a regulatory impact analysis is not required.

DRAFTING INFORMATION

The principal author of these proposed regulations is Jacob Feldman of the Legislation and Regulations Division of the Office of Chief Counsel, Internal Revenue Service. However, personnel from other offices of the Internal Revenue Service and Treasury Department participated in developing the regulation, both on matters of substance and style.

[¶49,066] Proposed Regulations (EE-96-85), published in the Federal Register on February 4, 1986.

Employee trusts: Tax Reform Act of 1984: Effective dates.—Reg. §§1.72(e)-1T, 1.79-4T, 1.133-1T, 1.162-10T, 1.402(a)(5)-1T, 1.404(a)-1T, 1.404(b)-1T, 1.404(d)-1T, 1.404(k)-1T, 1.419-1T, 1.419A-1T, 1.505(c)-1T, 1.1042-1T, 54.4976-1T, 54.4978-1T and 301.7701-17T are proposed.

AGENCY: Internal Revenue Service, Treasury.

ACTION: Notice of proposed rulemaking by cross reference to temporary regulations.

SUMMARY: In the Rules and Regulations portion of this issue of the Federal Register, the Internal Revenue Service is issuing temporary regulations relating to effective dates and certain other issues arising under the employee benefit provisions of the Tax Reform Act of 1984. The text of those temporary regulations also serves as the comment document for this notice of proposed rulemaking.

DATES: Written comments and requests for a public hearing must be delivered or mailed by April 7, 1986. The regulations are proposed to be effective on varying dates provided in the temporary regulations.

ADDRESS: Send comments and requests for a public hearing to Commissioner of Internal Revenue, Attn: CC:LR:T (EE-96-85), 1111 Constitution Avenue N.W., Washington, D.C. 20224. FOR FURTHER INFORMATION CONTACT: John T. Ricotta of the Employee Plans and Exempt Organizations Division, Office of Chief Counsel, Internal Revenue Service, 1111 Constitution Ave., N.W., Washington, D.C. 20224, Attention: CC:LR:T (EE-96-85), telephone: 202-566-3544 (not a toll-free number).

SUPPLEMENTARY INFORMATION:

BACKGROUND

The temporary regulations provide guidance concerning the economic performance requirement for certain employee benefits under section 461(h) of the Internal Revenue Code of 1954 (Code), as added by section 91 of the Tax Reform Act of 1984 (Act) (P.L. 98-369, 98 Stat. 598); the transitional rule for vested accrued vacation pay under section 463 of the Code, as amended by section 91(i) of the Act (P.L. 98-369, 98 Stat. 609); the treatment of group-term life insurance purchased for employees under section 79 of the Code, as amended by section 223 of the Act (P.L. 98-369, 98 Stat. 775); the treatment of funded welfare benefit plans under sections 419 and 419A of the Code, as added by section 511 of the Act (P.L. 98-369, 98 Stat. 854); the treatment of unfunded deferred benefits under sections 404(b) and 162 of the Code, as amended by section 512 of the Act (P.L. 98-369, 98 Stat. 862); additional requirements for tax-exempt status of certain organizations under section 505 of the Code, as added by section 513 of the Act (P.L. 98-369, 98 Stat. 863); rollovers of partial distributions under sections 402 and 403 of the Code, as amended by section 522 of the Act (P.L. 98-369, 98 Stat. 868); distributions where substantially all contributions are employee contributions under section 72 of the Code, as amended by section 523 of the Act (P.L. 98-369, 98 Stat. 871); repeal of the estate tax exclusion for qualified plan benefits under section 2039 of the Code, as amended by section 525 of the Act (P.L. 98-369, 98 Stat. 873); determination of whether there is a collective bargaining agreement under section 7701(a)(46) of the Code, as added by section 526(c) of the Act (P.L. 98-369, 98 Stat. 881); nonrecognition of gain on stock sold to an employee stock ownership plan (ESOP) under section 1042 of the Code, as added by section 541 of the Act (P.L. 98-369, 98 Stat. 887); deductibility of dividends relating to ESOPs under sections 404 and 3405 of the Code, as amended by section 542 of the Act (P.L. 98-369, 98 Stat. 890); exclusion of interest on ESOP loans under section 133 of the Code, as added by section 543 of the Act (P.L. 98-369, 98 Stat. 894); treatment of an employer and an employee benefit association as related under section 1239 of the Code, as amended by section 557 of the Act (P.L. 98-369, 98 Stat. 898); and technical corrections to the pension provisions of the Tax Equity and Fiscal Responsibility Act of 1982 under sections 713 and 715 of the Act (P.L. 98-369, 98 Stat. 955, 966). The proposed regulations are issued under the authority contained in section 7805 of the Code (26 U.S.C. §7805). For the text of the temporary regulations, see F.R. Doc. published in the Rules and Regulations portion of this issue of the FEDERAL REGISTER.

SPECIAL ANALYSES

The Commissioner of Internal Revenue has determined that this proposed rule is not a major rule as defined in Executive Order 12291and that a Regulatory Impact Analysis is therefore not required. Although this document is a notice of proposed rulemaking which solicits public comment, the Internal Revenue Service has concluded that the regulations proposed herein are interpretative and that the notice and public procedure requirements of 5 U.S.C. 553 do not apply. Accordingly, these proposed regulations do not constitute regulations subject to the Regulatory Flexibility Act (5 U.S.C. Chapter 6).

COMMENTS AND REQUESTS FOR A PUBLIC HEARING

Before the adoption of these proposed regulations, consideration will be given to any written comments that are submitted (preferably eight copies) to the Commissioner of Internal Revenue. All comments will be available for public inspection and copying. A public hearing will be held upon written request to the Commissioner by any person who has submitted written comments. If a public hearing is held, notice of the time and place will be published in the Federal Register. The collection of information requirements contained herein have been submitted to the Office of Management and Budget (OMB) for review under section 3504(h) of the Paperwork Reduction Act. Comments on the requirements should be sent to the Office of Information and Regulatory Affairs, of OMB, Attention: Desk Officer for Internal Revenue Service, New Executive Office Building, Washington, D.C. 20503. The Internal Revenue Service requests persons submitting comments to OMB also to send copies of the comments to the Service.

[¶ 49,067] Proposed Amendments of Regulations (LR-59-74), published in the Federal Register on February 21, 1986.

Interest received: Governmental obligations: Industrial development bonds: Principal user.—Amendment of Reg. § 1.103-10, which would define the term "principal user" for purposes of Code Sec. 103(b)(6), (15), is proposed.

AGENCY: Internal Revenue Service, Treasury.

ACTION: Notice of proposed rulemaking.

SUMMARY: This document contains proposed regulations which would define the term "principal user" for purposes of paragraphs (6) and (15) of section 103(b) of the Internal Revenue Code of 1954. The regulations would affect issuers, holders, and recipients of the proceeds of industrial development bonds issued under section 103(b)(6) of the Code.

DATES: Written comments must be delivered or mailed by April 22, 1986. The amendments are proposed to be effective after August 20, 1986, in determining the tax-exempt status of obligations issued after August 20, 1986.

ADDRESS: Send comments to: Commissioner of Internal Revenue, Attention: CC:LR:T (LR-59-74), Washington, D.C. 20224.

FOR FURTHER INFORMATION CONTACT: John A. Tolleris of the Legislation and Regulations Division, Office of the Chief Counsel, Internal Revenue Service, 1111 Constitution Avenue, N.W., Washington, D.C. 20224 (Attention: CC:LR:T) (Telephone: 202-566-3590, not a toll-free number).

SUPPLEMENTARY INFORMATION:

BACKGROUND

This document contains proposed clarifying amendments to the Income Tax Regulations (26 CFR Part 1) under section 103(b)(6) of the Internal Revenue Code of 1954.

EXPLANATION OF PROVISIONS

The amendments clarify the term "principal user" for purposes of applying the provisions of Code section 103(b)(6) and (15) and the regulations thereunder with respect to small issues of industrial development bonds. Section 103(b)(6) provides, among other things, that an issue of $1 million or less of industrial development bonds financing the acquisition, construction, reconstruction, or improvement of land or property of a character subject to the depreciation allowance (or an issue to redeem such a prior issue) is not exempt from Federal taxation when the issue in question combined with the outstanding face amount of prior issues financing certain similar facilities exceeds $1 million; the facilities which are taken into account for this purpose are those the "principal user" of which is or will be the same or two or more related persons, and which are located within the same county or incorporated municipality.

Section 103(b)(6) also provides that, if an issuer makes the necessary election, the limit for an exempt small issue of industrial development bonds is increased from $1 million to $10 million. In such case, however, certain other amounts must also be aggregated with the issue of obligations in question for purposes of determining whether the $10 million limitation has been exceeded and whether the interest upon the issue of obligations in question is thus subject to Federal income taxation. The additional amounts to be taken into account are certain capital expenditures, made within a 6-year period beginning 3 years before the date of issue of the obligations in question and ending 3 years after the date of issue, with respect not only to the facility financed by the issue in question, but also with respect to other facilities within the same county or incorporated municipality of which the "principal user" is or will be the same person or a person related to the "principal user" of the facility financed with the issue of obligations in question.

The proposed regulations provide, in general, that the principal users are persons who for tax purposes currently hold more than a 10-percent ownership interest in a facility. In addition, lessees or sublessees who use a sufficiently valuable portion of the facility pursuant to a sufficiently long-term lease are also principal users. Persons with interests comparable to that of an owner or lessee who is a principal user and some purchasers of the output of certain facilities are also treated as principal users.

The proposed regulations provide that, when a facility has more than one principal user, certain issues of obligations with respect to all principal users must be aggregated with the issue of obligations in question for purposes of determining whether the $1 million or $10 million limitation has been exceeded. Similarly, if the $10 million limitation has been elected by the issuer, certain capital expenditures with respect to all principal users must also be aggregated to determine whether the $10 million limitation has been exceeded.

For purposes of aggregating issues of obligations or capital expenditures of persons who are principal users, only issues and capital expenditures with respect to persons who are principal users of the facility before the expiration of the test period described in section 103(b)(15)(D) are aggregated. Accordingly, if a person who is a principal user of a facility financed by an exempt small issue becomes the principal user of another facility financed by a second exempt small issue more than 3 years after the later of the date of the second issue or the date the facility financed by the second issue was placed in service, the two issues are not aggregated. Similarly, capital expenditures during the 6-year period described in section 103(b)(6)(D)(ii) with respect to a principal user are not taken into account if that person does not become a principal user of the facility until more than 3 years after the later of the date of the issue or the date the facility financed by the issue is first placed in service.

The test-period concept was adopted for purposes of section 103(b)(6) for reasons of administrative convenience. The statutory reference to a person who "is or will be" a principal user could be construed as referring to a person who at any time is a principal user; as referring only to a person who is or is about to be a principal user on the date of issuance; or as referring to a person who becomes a principal user within some intermediate time period. In adopting the test-period concept, the Service attempted to reach a result which gives effect to the statutory language while also being administrable. Adoption of the test period described in section 103(b)(15)(D) serves the additional function of limiting the period for determination of the principal user status to a single period for purposes of both paragraphs (6) and (15) of section 103(b).

The proposed regulations provide special rules for exempt persons, *i.e.*, State and local governments and organizations that are tax-exempt under section 501(c)(3), that are principal users of facilities financed with exempt small issues of industrial development bonds. For purposes of determining whether the small-issue limitation has been exceeded with respect to any facility of which an exempt person is a principal user, certain industrial development bonds issued with respect to the exempt person and, for purposes of the $10 million limitation, certain capital expenditures must be aggregated with the issue in question. This does not include capital expenditures with respect to other facilities used by the exempt person in an activity other than an unrelated trade or business (as defined by section 513).

REGULATORY FLEXIBILITY ACT

The Secretary of the Treasury has certified that this proposed rule will not have a significant impact on a substantial number of small entities because the economic and any other secondary or incidental impact flows directly from the underlying statute. A regulatory flexibility analysis, therefore, is not required under the Regulatory Flexibility Act (5 U.S.C. chapter 6).

NON-APPLICABILITY OF EXECUTIVE ORDER 12291

The Commissioner of Internal Revenue has determined that this proposed rule is not a major rule as defined in Executive Order 12291and that a regulatory impact analysis therefore is not required.

COMMENTS—PUBLIC HEARING

Before adoption of these proposed regulations, consideration will be given to any written comments that are submitted (preferably seven copies) to the Commissioner of Internal Revenue. All comments will be available for public inspection and copying. A public hearing will be held in accordance with the notice of hearing published in this issue of the FEDERAL REGISTER.

DRAFTING INFORMATION

The principal author of these proposed regulations is John A. Tolleris of the Legislation and Regulations Division of the Office of Chief Counsel, Internal Revenue Service. However, personnel from other offices of the Internal Revenue Service and Treasury Department participated in developing the regulations, both on matters of substance and style.

[¶49,068] Proposed Amendments of Regulations (LR-157-84), published in the Federal Register on February 21, 1986.

Interest received: Governmental obligations: Limitation on beneficiaries.—Amendments of Reg. §1.103-10, relating to industrial development bonds and the beneficiaries of such bond issues, are proposed.

AGENCY: Internal Revenue Service, Treasury.

ACTION: Notice of proposed rulemaking.

SUMMARY: This document contains proposed regulations that relate to certain industrial development tax-exempt bonds and to certain beneficiaries of such bond issues. Changes to the applicable tax law were made by the Tax Reform Act of 1984 that generally deny Federal income tax exemption for a small issue of industrial development bonds if any of its test-period beneficiaries is allocated more than $40 million of outstanding industrial development bonds, including its allocated portion of the small issue in question. This provision restricts the amount of small issues of industrial development bonds that may be issued for a beneficiary when that person already benefits from a significant amount of tax-exempt industrial development bonds.

DATES: Written comments must be delivered or mailed by April 22, 1986. These regulations are proposed to be effective after August 20, 1986, in determining the tax-exempt status of obligations issued after August 20, 1986. However, these regulations would not apply to certain obligations described in section 631(f) of the Tax Reform Act of 1984 and to certain obligations with respect to facilities described in section 631(c)(3) of the Tax Reform Act of 1984. The provisions of §1.103-10(i)(4)(vi) are generally proposed to be effective after December 31, 1983, in determining the tax-exempt status of obligations issued after December 31, 1983.

ADDRESS: Please mail or deliver comments to: Commissioner of Internal Revenue, Attention: CC:LR:T (LR-157-84), 1111 Constitution Avenue, N.W., Washington, D.C. 20224.

FOR FURTHER INFORMATION CONTACT: John A. Tolleris of the Legislation and Regulations Division, Office of Chief Counsel, 1111 Constitution Avenue, N.W., Washington, D.C. 20224 (Attention: CC:LR:T) (Telephone: 202-566-3590, not a toll-free number).

SUPPLEMENTARY INFORMATION:

BACKGROUND

This document contains proposed amendments to the Income Tax Regulations (26 CFR Part 1) under section 103(b)(15) of the Internal Revenue Code of 1954. These proposed amendments provide needed guidance regarding the provisions of section 103(b)(15) concerning the $40 million limitation which were enacted by section 623 of the Tax Reform Act of 1984 (Pub. L. 98-369; 98 Stat. 921).

EXPLANATION OF PROVISIONS

The $40 million limitation applicable to small issues of tax-exempt industrial development bonds was enacted in the Tax Reform Act of 1984. This limitation generally denies Federal income tax exemption for a small issue of industrial development bonds if any test-period beneficiary is allocated more than $40 million of outstanding industrial development bonds, including its allocated portion of the issue in question. A person is a "test-period beneficiary" of the bond-financed facility, if he is an owner or a principal user of a facility financed by the issue at any time during the 3-year period after the issue is issued, or after the facility is placed in service, whichever occurs later. A person who is related to a principal user at any time during the test period is also a test-period beneficiary, unless the principal user ceased using the facility before the two persons became related.

These proposed regulations provide guidance on the allocation of the proceeds of an issue of industrial development bonds among test-period beneficiaries. In determining whether the $40 million limitation has been exceeded with respect to a test-period beneficiary, the portions of the outstanding amounts of all industrial development bonds (not just small issues) allocable to the beneficiary are aggregated.

NONAPPLICABILITY OF EXECUTIVE ORDER 12291

The Commissioner of Internal Revenue has determined that this proposed rule is not a major rule as defined in Executive Order 12291and that a regulatory impact analysis therefore is not required.

REGULATORY FLEXIBILITY ACT

The Secretary of the Treasury has certified that this proposed rule will not have a significant impact on a substantial number of small entities because the economic and any other secondary or incidental impact flows directly from the underlying statute. A regulatory flexibility analysis, therefore, is not required under the Regulatory Flexibility Act (5 U.S.C. chapter 6).

DRAFTING INFORMATION

The principal author of these proposed regulations is John A. Tolleris of the Legislation and Regulations Division of the Office of Chief Counsel, Internal Revenue Service. However, personnel from other offices of the Internal Revenue Service and the Treasury Department participated in developing the regulations, on matters of both substance and style.

COMMENTS—PUBLIC HEARING

Before adoption of these proposed regulations, consideration will be given to any written comments that are submitted (preferably seven copies) to the Commissioner of Internal Revenue. All comments will be available for public inspection and copying. A public hearing will be held in accordance with the notice of hearing published in this issue of the FEDERAL REGISTER.

Income taxes, Taxable income, Deductions, Exemptions.

[¶49,069] Proposed Amendment of Regulations (LR-66-85), published in the Federal Register on March 4, 1986.

Registration of tax shelters: Amended application.—Amendments of Reg. §301.6111-1, relating to the registration of tax shelters, are proposed.

AGENCY: Internal Revenue Service, Treasury.

ACTION: Notice of proposed rulemaking by cross-reference to temporary regulations.

SUMMARY: In the Rules and Regulations portion of this issue of the FEDERAL REGISTER, the Internal Revenue Service is issuing temporary regulations relating to tax shelter registration. The text of those temporary regulations also serves as the comment document for this proposed rulemaking.

DATES: Written comments and requests for a public hearing must be delivered by [SIXTY DAYS AFTER PUBLICATION OF THIS DOCUMENT IN THE FEDERAL REGISTER]. The amendments are proposed to be effective generally with respect to tax shelters in which any interest is first sold after August 31, 1984.

ADDRESS: Send comments and requests for a public hearing to: Commissioner of Internal Revenue, Attention: CC:LR:T (LR-66-85), Washington, D.C. 20224.

FOR FURTHER INFORMATION CONTACT: Paulette Chernyshev, Office of Chief Counsel, Internal Revenue Service, 1111 Constitution Avenue, N.W., Washington, D.C. 20224 (Attention: CC:LR:T) telephone 202-566-3288 (not a toll-free call).

SUPPLEMENTARY INFORMATION:

BACKGROUND

The temporary regulations (designated by a "T" following the section citation) in the Rules and Regulations portion of this issue of the FEDERAL REGISTER amend Parts 301 and 602 of Title 26 of the Code of Federal Regulations. These amendments change the rules relating to tax shelter registration under section 6111 of the Internal Revenue Code of 1954, as added by section 141 of the Tax Reform Act of 1984 (Pub. L. 98-369, 98 Stat. 678). For the text of the temporary regulations, see FR Doc. (T.D. 8078) published in the Rules and Regulations portion of this issue of the FEDERAL REGISTER. The preamble to the temporary regulations provides a discussion of the rules. The final regulations, which this document proposes to base on those temporary regulations, would amend Parts 301 and 602 of Title 26 of the Code of Federal Regulations.

EXECUTIVE ORDER 12291; REGULATORY FLEXIBILITY ACT

The Commissioner of Internal Revenue has determined that this proposed rule is not a major rule as defined in Executive Order 12291and that a Regulatory Impact Analysis is therefore not required.

Although this document is a notice of proposed rulemaking that solicits public comments, the Internal Revenue Service has concluded that the regulations proposed herein are interpretative and that the notice and public procedure requirements of 5 U.S.C. 553 do not apply. Accordingly, these proposed regulations do not constitute regulations subject to the regulatory Flexibility Act (5 U.S.C. Chapter 6).

COMMENTS AND REQUESTS FOR A PUBLIC HEARING

Before adopting these proposed regulations, consideration will be given to any written comments that are submitted (preferably eight copies) to the Commissioner of Internal Revenue. All comments will be available for public inspection and copying. A public hearing will be held upon written request to the Commissioner by any person who has submitted written comments. If a public hearing is held, notice of the time and place will be published in the FEDERAL REGISTER.

The collection of information requirements contained in this notice of proposed rulemaking have been submitted to the Office of Management and Budget (OMB) for review under section 3504(h) of the Paperwork Reduction Act. Comments on these requirements should be sent to the Office of Information and Regulatory Affairs of OMB, Attention: Desk Officer for Internal Revenue Service, New Executive Office Building, Washington, D.C. 20503. The Internal Revenue Service requests that persons submitting comments on these requirements to OMB also send copies of those comments to the Service.

DRAFTING INFORMATION

The principal author of these regulations is Paulette Chernyshev of the Legislation and Regulations Division of the Office of Chief Counsel, Internal Revenue Service. However, personnel from other offices of the Internal Revenue Service and Treasury Department participated in developing the regulations on matters of both substance and style.

[¶49,070] Proposed Regulations and Proposed Amendments of Regulations (LR-189-84), published in the Federal Register on April 8, 1986.

Imputed interest: Original issue discount: Safe haven interest rates.—Amendments of Reg. §§1.61-6, 1.61-7, 6a.103A-2, 1.163-4, 1.249-1, 1.582-1, 1.636-1, 1.818-3, 1.861-2, 1.993-1, 1.1012-2, 1.1016-5, 1.1037-1, 1.1232-1, 1.1232-2, 1.1232-3, 1.1232-3A, 1.6045-1, 1.6049-4—1.6049-6, 1.7872-4, 3.2 and 3.3, relating to (1) the tax treatment of debt instruments issued after July 1, 1982, that contain original issue discount, (2) the imputation of and the accounting for interest with respect to sales and exchanges of property occurring after December 31, 1984, and (3) safe haven interest rates for loans or advances between commonly controlled taxpayers and safe haven leases between such taxpayers, are proposed. Proposed Reg. §§1.163-7, 1.446-2, 1.483-3, 1.1271-1—1.1271-3, 1.1272-1, 1.1273-1, 1.1273-2, 1.1274-1, 1.1274-7, 1.1274A-1, 1.1275-1, 1.1275-2, 1.1275-3 and 1.1275-5 and proposed amendments of Reg. §§1.483-1, 1.483-2,1.1001-1 and 1.1012-1 were substantially revised on 12/22/92 by FI-189-84 and subsequently adopted on 1/27/94 by T.D. 8517. Proposed Reg. §1.1275-4, which was superseded on 12/16/94 by FI-59-91, was adopted on 6/11/96 by T.D. 8674.

AGENCY: Internal Revenue Service, Treasury.

ACTION: Notice of proposed rulemaking.

SUMMARY: This document contains proposed regulations relating to (1) the tax treatment of debt instruments issued after July 1, 1982, that contain original issue discount, (2) the imputation of and the accounting for interest with respect to sales and exchanges of property occurring after December 31, 1984, and (3) safe haven interest rates for loans or advances between commonly controlled taxpayers and safe haven leases between such taxpayers. Changes to the applicable law were made by the Tax Equity and Fiscal Responsibility Act of 1982 as amended by the Technical Corrections Act of 1982, and the Tax Reform Act of 1984 as amended by Pub. L. No. 98-612 and Pub. L. No. 99-121. The regulations would provide needed guidance to taxpayers who must comply with these provisions of the law.

DATES:

PROPOSED EFFECTIVE DATE

Generally, the regulations contained in this document are proposed to be effective as follows:

§ 1.163-7 § § 1.1271-1—1.1273-2 § § 1.1275-1—1.1275-5	Debt instruments issued after July 1, 1982
§ § 1.483-1—1.483-5 § § 1.1274-1—1.1274-7	Sales or exchanges of property occurring after December 31, 1984
§ 1.1274A-1	Certain sales or exchanges of property occurring after June 30, 1985
§ 1.446-2	Lending transactions occurring after May 8, 1986, and certain sales or exchanges of property occurring after December 31, 1984
§ 1.482-2	Term loans and advances entered into after May 8, 1986, and demand loans and advances after such date

DATES FOR COMMENTS AND REQUEST FOR A PUBLIC HEARING

Written comments and request for a public hearing must be delivered or mailed by [60 DAYS AFTER THIS IS PUBLISHED IN THE FEDERAL REGISTER]. June 9, 1986.

ADDRESS: Send comments (preferably eight copies) and request for a public hearing to: Commissioner of Internal Revenue, Attention: CC:LR:T, (LR-189-84), 1111 Constitution Avenue, N.W., Washington, D.C. 20224.

FOR FURTHER INFORMATION CONTACT: Theresa E. Bearman (sections 163, 1271, 1272, 1273, 1275 and related matters), Ewan D. Purkiss (sections 446, 483, 1274 and related matters), Susan T. Baker (all matters other than those relating to sections 446, 482 and 483), or Joseph M. Rosenthal (section 482 and related matters) of the Legislation and Regulations Division, Office of Chief Counsel, Internal Revenue Service, 1111 Constitution Avenue, N.W., Washington, D.C. 20224 (Attention: CC:LR:T LR-189-84). Telephone 202-566-3829 (Bearman), 202-566-3238 (Purkiss), 202-566-3294 (Baker), 202-566-3289 (Rosenthal) (not a toll-free call).

SUPPLEMENTARY INFORMATION:

I. BACKGROUND

This document contains proposed amendments to the Income Tax Regulations (26 CFR Part 1) under sections 163(e), 446, 482, 483 and 1271 through 1275 of the Internal Revenue Code of 1954. With the exception of the amendments to the regulations under section 446, these amendments are proposed to conform the regulations to section 231 of the Tax Equity and Fiscal Responsibility Act of 1982 (96 Stat. 324, 496), as amended by section 306 of the Technical Corrections Act of 1982 (97 Stat. 448), and sections 41, 42 and 44 of the Tax Reform Act of 1984 (98 Stat. 494, 531) as amended by Pub. L. No. 98-612 (98 Stat. 3180) and Pub. L. No. 99-121 (99 Stat. 505). The amendments to the regulations under section 446 are proposed to provide rules to account for interest in transactions outside the scope of the original issue discount rules.

II. INTRODUCTION

The regulations under sections 163(e), 483, and 1271 through 1275 provide two principal sets of rules: the imputed interest rules and the original issue discount rules. The imputed interest rules are prescribed by sections 1274 and 483, and the original issue discount rules by sections 163(e), 1271, 1272, 1273 and 1275.

The imputed interest rules of sections 1274 and 483 relate to the measurement of interest and principal for tax purposes in a sale or exchange of property (other than publicly traded property) involving deferred payments. For transactions subject to the imputed interest rules, interest will be imputed to the transaction if a minimum amount of interest is not stated. If a transaction states at least the minimum amount of interest, it is said to provide for adequate stated interest. When interest is imputed to a transaction, a portion of the stated principal amount of the debt instrument is recharacterized as interest for tax purposes. The imputed interest rules do not require an increase in the total amount of payments agreed to by the parties to a transaction. These rules merely recharacterize as interest for Federal tax purposes a portion of the payments denominated as principal by the parties. In the case of transactions to which section 1274 applies, imputed interest is treated as original issue discount and is accounted for under those rules. In the case of transactions subject to section 483, imputed interest (and any stated interest) is subject to a new set of rules provided under section 446 and is accounted for under those rules.

In general, under the original issue discount rules, a portion of the original issue discount on a debt instrument is required to be included in income by the holder and deducted from income by the issuer annually without regard to their regular accounting methods. The total amount of original issue discount is defined as the difference between the debt instrument's stated redemption price at maturity and its issue price and arises in one of three ways. First, in the case of a debt instrument subject to section 1274 that does not provide for adequate stated interest, interest is imputed and is treated as original issue discount. Second, in the case of a debt instrument issued for cash or publicly traded property, original issue discount arises if the debt instrument is issued for less than its face amount. Third, in the case of all debt instruments, original issue discount arises if the debt instrument does not call for interest that is payable currently at a single constant rate over its entire term.

III. THE IMPUTED INTEREST RULES

A. APPLICABILITY

1. SECTION 1274

Section 1274 applies to any debt instrument issued in exchange for property if neither the debt instrument nor the property is publicly traded and if one or more of the payments under the debt instrument are due more than 6 months after the date of the sale or exchange. Section 1274, however, does not apply to the following:

(a) Certain sales or exchanges by an individual, estate, testamentary trust, or small corporation or partnership of a farm if the sales price of the farm does not exceed $1,000,000;

(b) Any sale or exchange by an individual of the individual's principal residence, regardless of the amount of the sales price;

(c) Any sale or exchange of property if the sum of all the payments (including principal and interest) under any debt instrument and the value of any other consideration does not exceed $250,000;

(d) Any debt instrument issued in a qualified sale within the meaning of section 483(e) if the stated principal amount of the debt instrument does not exceed $500,000; and

(e) Any cash method debt instrument within the meaning of section 1274A(c).

2. SECTION 483

Section 483 applies to sales or exchanges of nonpublicly traded property excepted from the provisions of section 1274. Thus, section 483 applies to: the sale or exchange of a farm if the sales price does not exceed $1,000,000, sales involving total payments of $250,000 or less, sales of principal residences, qualified sales of land, and cash method debt instruments. Unlike section 1274, however, section 483 applies only if the contract for the sale or exchange calls for payments due more than one year from the date of the sale or exchange. Section 483 does not apply to the following:

(a) Any sale or exchange of property if the sales price does not exceed $3,000; and

(b) In the case of a purchaser, any amount that is treated as containing interest under section 163(b).

3. EXCEPTIONS FROM BOTH SECTIONS 1274 AND 483

The imputed interest rules of sections 1274 and 483 do not apply to the following:

(a) Any transaction to the extent any amount is contingent upon the productivity, use, or disposition of property and entitled to capital gain treatment under section 1235, relating to sales or exchanges of patents.

(b) Any annuity under section 72 that is not a debt instrument within the meaning of section 1275(a).

(c) Any issuer (obligor) of a debt instrument issued for property that is personal use property in the hands of the issuer. The imputed interest rules, however, apply to any holder (obligee) of the debt instrument unless the loan incurred in the transaction is a below-market loan of the type described in section 7872(c)(1)(A)—(C). The treatment of the latter class of debt instruments is governed by the provisions of section 7872.

(d) Any debt instrument that evidences demand loan (within the meaning of section 7872(f)(5)) and is a below-market loan of the type described in section 7872(c)(1)(A)—(C). The treatment of these debt instruments is governed by the provisions of section 7872.

B. STATING ADEQUATE INTEREST TO AVOID THE IMPUTATION OF INTEREST

1. IN GENERAL

To prevent the imputation of interest, a debt instrument must provide for adequate stated interest. For this purpose, a debt instrument generally provides for adequate stated interest if it calls for interest over its entire term at a rate no lower than the test rate of interest applicable to the debt instrument. If a debt instrument does not provide for a fixed rate of interest at least equal to the test rate of interest, the adequacy of interest is determined by comparing the stated principal amount involved in the transaction with the sum of present values of all payments due under the debt instrument, determined by discounting the payments at a rate equal to the test rate of interest. A debt instrument generally has adequate stated interest if the stated principal amount of the debt instrument is less than or equal to the sum of these present values. However, in the case of a potentially abusive situation as discussed below, the debt instrument does not have adequate stated interest unless the stated principal amount is less than or equal to the fair market value of the property sold or exchanged.

The test rate of interest applicable to a debt instrument generally depends on the amount of seller financing (based on stated principal) involved in the transaction. For sales or exchanges of property (other than new section 38 property) involving seller financing of $2,800,000 or less, the test rate of interest is the lower of the applicable Federal rate or 9 percent, compounded semiannually (or an equivalent rate based on an appropriate compounding period). If the sales price is contingent, the 9 percent rate is not available unless the sales price cannot exceed $2,800,000. For sales or exchanges of property with seller financing in excess of $2,800,000, and all sales or exchanges of new section 38 property, the test rate of interest is 100 percent of the applicable Federal rate. For sales or exchanges of property involved in sale-leaseback transactions, the test rate of interest is 110 percent of the applicable Federal rate. These rules also apply to transactions subject to section 483. Sales or exchanges that are qualified sales, however, are subject to a special lower test rate of interest as discussed below. For sales or exchanges occurring before July 1, 1985, special test rates of interest apply.

The applicable Federal rate is either the Federal short-term rate (for debt instruments with terms not over 3 years), the Federal mid-term rate (for debt instruments with terms over 3 years but not over 9 years), or the Federal long-term rate (for debt instruments with terms over 9 years). The Federal rates are annual stated rates of interest based on semiannual compounding. The Federal rates are published monthly by the Commissioner in Revenue Rulings along with equivalent annual, quarterly and monthly rates. In general, the appropriate compounding period depends on the intervals between payments. In general, the applicable Federal rate is the lowest of the rates in effect for the first month in which there is a binding written contract or the two preceding two months.

The applicable Federal rates are determined monthly. The Federal rates are based on the yields to maturity of outstanding marketable obligations of the United States of similar maturities (for example, maturities up to 3 years for the Federal short-term rate) for the one-month period ending on the 14th day of the month preceding the month for which the rates are applicable. In certain cases, the applicable Federal rate may be a lower rate based on certain allowable Treasury index rates.

2. SPECIAL RULES

a. TEST RATE FOR INSTALLMENT OBLIGATIONS

The proposed regulations provide special rules for determining whether an installment obligation provides for adequate stated interest. For self-amortizing installment and level-principal obligations, tables are provided under which the test rate of interest may be computed as a blended rate equal to a weighted average of the Federal rates. In general, the rules are designed to allow taxpayers to receive the benefit of the short-term and mid-term rates (which are generally lower than the long-term rate) without having to provide three separate debt instruments.

b. CONTINGENT PAYMENTS

In general, contingent interest payments are not taken into account in applying the imputed interest rules. Thus, whether a debt instrument states adequate interest will be determined by ignoring any contingent interest payments.

Under a special rule proposed by the regulations, however, the stated principal amount of a debt instrument calling for contingent payments of interest will be respected in certain cases. To qualify for the special rule, the contingent payments of interest must be conditioned on a return from the use of the property. In addition, the debt instrument must call for fixed payments of interest equal to at least 80 percent of the test rate of interest applicable to the debt instrument, and it must be reasonable to expect that the payments of contingent interest will raise the yield on the debt instrument to at least the test rate of interest. If the property acquired for the debt instrument is depreciable or inventoriable property, then, in addition to the requirements noted above, the term of the debt instrument cannot exceed 4 years in the case of 3-year or 5-year property or inventoriable property, or 12 years in the case of any other depreciable property that is not inventoriable property.

The contingent payment rules do not affect whether rights to receive contingent payments constitute debt or equity for Federal tax purposes or whether an instrument evidences a valid indebtedness.

c. VARIABLE RATE DEBT INSTRUMENTS

For purposes of determining whether a debt instrument calling for variable interest based on current values of an objective interest index provides for adequate stated interest, the proposed regulations generally treat the debt instrument as if it called for interest at a fixed rate equal to the rate established by the index on the date the test rate of interest is determined. Examples of objective indices include the prime rate, the applicable Federal rate, the average yield on Treasury securities, and LIBOR (London Interbank Offered Rate). If the rate of interest determined by the index is no lower than the test rate of interest, the debt instrument has adequate stated interest. Interest payments based on an index other than an objective interest index are generally treated as contingent payments.

Under the proposed regulations, the applicable Federal rate for a variable rate debt instrument that calls for variable interest payments based on current values of an objective interest index is the Federal rate corresponding to the adjustment interval of the debt instrument. Thus, for example, if the interest rate on a debt instrument is tied to a bank's prime rate and adjusted annually, the adequacy of interest is determined by testing the rate of interest as determined by the index against the Federal short-term rate.

d. QUALIFIED SALES OF LAND

In the case of a debt instrument issued in a qualified sale of land and subject to the rules of section 483(e), the test rate of interest is 6 percent, compounded semiannually. A qualified sale is a sale or exchange of land by an individual to a member of the individual's family. A debt instrument issued in a qualified sale is subject to the rules of section 483(e) if the face amount (stated principal amount) of the debt instrument issued for the land does not exceed $500,000, regardless of the amount of the sales price, and if certain other conditions are satisfied. Thus, the parties are free to structure a sale with two debt instruments, the first having a face amount of $500,000 and a 6 percent interest rate, and the second subject to the rules of section 1274 or section 483, whichever is applicable. If, however, a single debt instrument is issued with a face amount in excess of $500,000, the 6 percent test rate does not apply.

The proposed regulations contain this rule because the Service is concerned with the complexity of rules that would be necessary to apply two different accounting rules to a single debt instrument. The Service invites comments on this proposed rule.

3. POTENTIALLY ABUSIVE TRANSACTIONS

Regardless of the amount of interest stated in a sale or exchange, if the transaction is a potentially abusive transaction, the adequacy of interest is determined by comparing the stated principal amount of the debt instrument with the fair market value of the property sold or exchanged as discussed above. A potentially abusive situation includes any transaction that is a tax shelter (within the meaning of section 6661(b)(2)(C)(ii)), and any situation involving recent sales transactions, nonrecourse financing, and financing with a term in excess of the economic life of the property. In addition, under regulatory authority, the proposed regulations categorize as potentially abusive situations transactions involving foreign currency. The potentially abusive situation rules also may apply to cash method debt instruments (which are described in greater detail below) subject to section 483.

4. ASSUMPTIONS AND MODIFICATIONS

Sections 1274 and 483 do not apply to a debt instrument assumed or taken subject to in a sale or exchange occurring after June 30, 1985, or a debt instrument issued before October 16, 1985, assumed or taken subject to in a sale or exchange involving a sales price of $100,000,000 or less occurring after December 31, 1984, and before July 1, 1985, unless the debt instrument is modified. The proposed regulations provide special rules for a debt instrument issued after October 15, 1984, or any debt instrument involved in a transaction with a sales price in excess of $100,000,000 that is assumed or taken subject to in a sale or exchange occurring after December 31, 1984, and before July 1, 1985, and that is not modified as part of the sale or exchange.

If a debt instrument assumed or taken subject to is modified, the modification is treated as a separate transaction. In general, a modified debt instrument is treated as a new debt instrument given in exchange for the old debt instrument in a transaction to which section 1274 applies. If a modification is attributable to the seller the modification is treated as occurring immediately before the sale or exchange, and the buyer is treated as assuming the modified debt instrument. Modifications are attributable to the seller unless the seller neither consents to nor participates in the modification. If a modification is attributable to the buyer, the modification is treated as occurring immediately after the sale or exchange.

With certain exceptions, sections 1274 and 483 apply to a debt instrument issued after October 15, 1984, or a debt instrument involved in a transaction with a sales price in excess of $100,000,000 that is assumed or taken subject to and that is not modified as part of a sale or exchange occurring after December 31, 1984, and before July 1, 1985. In these cases, sections 1274 and 483 apply only for purposes of determining the tax consequences of the sale or exchange to the buyer.

C. IMPUTATION OF INTEREST

Under section 1274, if a debt instrument does not provide for adequate stated interest, the issue price of the debt instrument is its imputed principal amount. Except in the case of potentially abusive situations, the imputed principal amount of a debt instrument is the sum of the present values of all the payments due under the instrument determined by discounting the payments at the imputed rate of interest. Generally, for purposes of imputing interest, the imputed rate of interest is the same as the test rate of interest. For sales or exchanges occurring before July 1, 1985, special imputed rates of interest apply.

When interest is imputed, the imputed principal amount becomes the issue price. This issue price is lower than the stated principal amount of the debt instrument, since it reflects the fact that a portion of the stated principal is recharacterized as interest. Thus, the imputed interest is treated as original issue discount. In potentially abusive situations, the imputed principal amount of the debt instrument is the fair market value of the property sold or exchanged.

Under section 483, imputed interest is referred to as unstated interest. Unstated interest is defined as the excess of the deferred payments (all payments of the sales price due more than 6 months after the date of the sale or exchange) over the sum of the present values of the deferred payments and any stated interest. For this purpose, the present values are determined by discounting the payments at the imputed rate of interest. In the case of cash method debt instruments to which the potentially abusive rules apply, the fair market value of the property sold or exchanged is used in place of the present value of the deferred payments and any stated interest.

IV. ACCOUNTING FOR ORIGINAL ISSUE DISCOUNT

A. IN GENERAL

Original issue discount is defined as the excess of a debt instrument's stated redemption price at maturity over its issue price. A portion of the original issue discount on a debt instrument is accounted for on a current basis by both the issuer and the holder. The amount of original issue discount that is accounted for on a current basis is the amount that accrues on a constant interest or economic accrual basis, regardless of whether the issuer or holder is an accrual basis taxpayer.

For purposes of determining the accrual of original issue discount, the term of a debt instrument generally is divided into accrual periods of equal length as discussed in greater detail below. Original issue discount is allocated to each accrual period according to a formula based upon the adjusted issue price of the debt instrument at the beginning of the accrual period, the yield of the debt instrument, and the actual interest payments (if any) for that period. To determine the holder's annual inclusion under section 1272, the original issue discount allocated to each accrual period is then apportioned ratably among the days within the accrual period to produce the daily portion of original issue discount for each day during that accrual period. The total amount of original issue discount includible for any taxable year is the sum of the daily portions of original issue discount for each day during the taxable year that the taxpayer held the debt instrument.

Debt instruments excepted from the current inclusion rule are debt instruments with a term of one year or less, tax-exempt obligations, debt instruments issued by a natural person before March 2, 1984, debt instruments purchased at a premium, U.S. savings bonds, certain loans made between natural persons, and debt instruments issued before January 1, 1985, which are not capital assets in the hands of the holder.

In general, the amount of original issue discount deductible by an issuer under section 163(e) is determined in the same manner as the amount includible by the holder under section 1272. The regulations contain several exceptions to this general rule.

B. PAYING INTEREST CURRENTLY AT CONSTANT RATE TO AVOID THE ORIGINAL ISSUE DISCOUNT RULES

In the case of any debt instrument subject to section 1274 that provides for adequate stated interest, or in the case of any debt instrument issued at par for cash of publicly traded property, the original issue discount rules do not apply if all interest is payable currently at a constant rate over the entire term of the debt instrument. For this purpose, interest is considered payable currently if the interest is payable unconditionally and at regular intervals of one year or less. Interest is not considered payable at a constant rate if the debt instrument involves deferred interest (if the debt instrument has a lower initial rate of interest or an interest holiday for an initial period) or prepaid interest (if it has a higher initial rate of interest).

C. DETERMINING THE TOTAL AMOUNT OF ORIGINAL ISSUE DISCOUNT

1. STATED REDEMPTION PRICE AT MATURITY

Except in the case of installment obligations, the stated redemption price at maturity of a debt instrument is defined as the amount fixed by the last modification of the purchase agreement including interest and other amounts payable at that time. The stated redemption price at maturity does not include any interest based on a fixed or variable rate that is actually and unconditionally payable at intervals of one year or less over the entire term of the debt instrument. These amounts are referred to as qualified periodic interest payments. In the case of an installment obligation, the stated redemption price at maturity equals the sum of all payments under the debt instrument less any qualified periodic interest payments.

2. DETERMINATION OF ISSUE PRICE

If a debt instrument subject to section 1274 states adequate interest, the issue price is the stated principal amount of the debt instrument. If the debt instrument does not state adequate interest as discussed above, the issue price is the imputed principal amount determined according to the provisions of section 1274.

The issue price of a debt instrument not subject to section 1274 is determined as follows:

(a) A debt instrument that is part of an issue of debt instruments publicly offered and issued for cash—the initial price at which a substantial portion of the issue is sold to the public;

(b) A debt instrument that is part of an issue of debt instruments not publicly offered and issued for cash—the price paid by the first buyer;

(c) A debt instrument that is issued for property and is part of an issue of debt instruments a portion of which is traded on an established securities market—the fair market value of that debt instrument determined as of the first trading date after the date of issue of the debt instrument;

(d) A nonpublicly traded debt instrument issued in exchange for publicly traded property—the fair market value of the property; and

(e) A debt instrument that does not fall within the first four categories set forth above and that is not governed by section 1274—its stated redemption price at maturity.

3. DE MINIMIS RULES

In the case of the holder, a debt instrument having a *de minimis* amount of original issue discount is treated as if the original issue discount were zero. Except in the case of an installment obligation, discount is considered *de minimis* if it is less than one-quarter of one percent of the stated redemption price at maturity multiplied by the number of complete years to maturity.

Special rules are provided for installment obligations. To compute the *de minimis* amount of original issue discount allowable on installment obligations generally, taxpayers must utilize a weighted average maturity in lieu of the number of full years from the issue date to final maturity. For debt instruments which are self-amortizing obligations, the proposed regulations provide a safe harbor which allows taxpayers to treat one-sixth of one percent of the stated redemption price at maturity multiplied by the number of complete years to final maturity as *de minimis* original issue discount.

D. ALLOCATION OF ORIGINAL ISSUE DISCOUNT TO AN ACCRUAL PERIOD

1. IN GENERAL

The amount of original issue discount allocable to an accrual period generally is equal to the product of the adjusted issue price at the beginning of the accrual period and the yield of the debt instrument, less amounts of stated interest payable during the accrual period. Each of the terms used in this calculation is defined under section 1272 and the proposed regulations as described in the succeeding discussion.

2. ACCRUAL PERIOD

Generally, for debt instruments issued after December 31, 1984, the accrual period is the interval between payment or compounding dates provided by the debt instrument (but in no event longer than one year), with the final accrual period ending on the maturity date of the debt instrument. Rules are provided for debt instruments with irregular payment or compounding intervals. For debt instruments that provide for a single payment at maturity and that have no other payment or compounding dates, the accrual period is the six-month period ending on the date in each calendar year that corresponds to the maturity date of the debt instrument or the date that is six months prior to that date. For debt instruments issued after July 1, 1982, and before January 1, 1985, the accrual period is the one-year period beginning on the issue date and on the corresponding day in each calendar year throughout the term of the debt instrument.

3. ADJUSTED ISSUE PRICE

The adjusted issue price at the beginning of the first accrual period is the issue price. The adjusted issue price at the beginning of each succeeding accrual period is equal to the adjusted issue price at the beginning of the immediately preceding accrual period increased by the amount of original issue discount accrued during that period. In the case of an installment obligation, the adjusted issue price at the beginning of an accrual period is reduced by any payments of principal or interest that are included in the stated redemption price at maturity and that are made during the immediately preceding accrual period.

4. YIELD

The yield of a debt instrument is that rate of interest that, when used to determine the present value of all payments of principal and interest to be made under the debt instrument, provides an amount equal to the issue price of the debt instrument. Yield is expressed as an annual interest rate and is determined by compounding at the end of the accrual period. Special rules are provided for certain debt instruments that provide a variable rate of interest with a resulting variable yield as discussed in greater detail below.

5. ACQUISITION PREMIUM

In determining the amount a holder must include in income, the daily portion of original issue discount is reduced by an appropriate share of any acquisition premium paid by that holder. Acquisition premium arises when a person purchases a debt instrument at a price which is in excess of the revised issue price on the date of purchase, but which is less than the stated redemption price at maturity. For debt instruments issued after July 1, 1982, and purchased before July 19, 1984, the daily portion is reduced ratably by an amount equal to the total acquisition premium divided by the number of days from the date of purchase up to (but not including) the stated maturity date. For debt instruments issued after July 1, 1982, and purchased after July 18, 1984, the daily portion is reduced by a constant fraction equal to the total acquisition premium divided by the total unaccrued original issue discount on the date of purchase.

E. SPECIAL RULES

1. SERIAL MATURITY AND INSTALLMENT OBLIGATIONS

Under regulations published under section 1232 of prior law, single obligations that provided for payments prior to maturity (other than payments of interest at fixed, periodic intervals of one year or less over the entire term of the obligation) were treated as a serial issue with each installment payment representing a separate obligation with its own issue price and stated redemption price at maturity. Original issue discount with respect to a serial issue, where independent issue prices could not be established for each individual series, was apportioned among the series based upon a linear ("bond-years") formula.

Because the OID rules now apply to a much broader class of obligations, including mortgages involving as many as 360 separate payments of principal, the proposed regulations eliminate the prior law treatment of each payment of principal under an installment obligations as a separate debt instrument. Instead, the regulations treat all installment obligations and certain serial maturity obligations as a single installment obligation for all purposes under sections 1271 through 1275. For this purpose, an installment obligation is defined as a debt instrument that provides for payments prior to maturity other than qualified periodic interest payments. Stated redemption price at maturity of an installment obligation is defined as the sum of all payments to be made under the obligation other than qualified periodic interest payments. This rule is effective for installment obligations issued after December 31, 1984 and for debt instruments maturing serially issued after May 8, 1986; the issuer and holder may, however, elect jointly to change this treatment.

2. VARIABLE RATE DEBT INSTRUMENTS

The proposed regulations provide rules for the determination of the amount of original issue discount on debt instruments that provide for a variable rate of interest based on current values of an objective interest rate index. Generally, original issue discount attributable to deferred payments of interest made under these debt instruments is accounted for based upon a variable yield equal to the variable rate fixed by the debt instrument. Any other original issue discount on these debt instruments is determined on the issue date by assuming that the interest rate in effect on that date remains constant over the entire term of the debt instrument and is accounted for on that basis, regardless of the actual interest rate under the debt instrument.

3. CONTINGENT PAYMENTS

Under the proposed regulations, contingent payments are generally not taken into account in applying the original issue discount and imputed interest rules. Instead, contingent payments are segregated from noncontingent payments and are accounted for separately. In determining whether a payment is contingent, the Commissioner may disregard remote and incidental contingencies. The parties to a transaction are, however, bound by its form and must treat a payment subject to a stated contingency as contingent. The contingent payment rules do not affect whether rights to receive contingent payments constitute debt or equity for Federal tax purposes or whether an instrument evidences a valid indebtedness.

Under the separate accounting rules for contingent payments, contingent payments may be recharacterized in certain situations. First, any payment of principal made on account of a sale or exchange of nonpublicly traded property that is not accompanied by a payment of adequate stated interest will be recharacterized in part as interest. Second, in the case of a debt instrument that does not provide for adequate stated interest and that accordingly has imputed interest, certain contingent interest payments may be recharacterized in part as principal to restore to basis amounts previously recharacterized as imputed interest. In these cases, a payment subject to recharacterization is treated as a payment of principal in an amount equal to the present value of the payment and as a payment of interest to the extent of the difference between the amount of the payment and the present value of the payment. The amount of all payments characterized as principal, however, cannot exceed the amount of the fixed or maximum stated principal amount under a debt instrument.

Third, a contingent payment made under a debt instrument issued for cash or publicly traded property may be recharacterized in a case in which the issue price of the debt instrument exceeds the sum of all the noncontingent payments due under the debt instrument. In such a case, the noncontingent payments under the debt instrument are treated entirely as principal. Each contingent payment is treated as a payment of interest to the extent of the total interest deemed accrued and not allocated to prior payments, and a payment of principal to the extent of the excess of the amount of the payment over the portion of the payment treated as interest. The total interest deemed accrued for any accrual period is based on an assumed yield to maturity equal to the applicable Federal rate which would have applied had the debt instrument been issued for nonpublicly traded property. Once the sum of all the portions of the contingent payments that are treated as principal under this rule reaches the difference between the issue price of the debt instrument and the sum of all the noncontingent payments under the debt instrument, any additional contingent payments are treated as interest.

If a contingent payment is paid within six months of the date it becomes fixed, the portion of the payment recharacterized as interest is accounted for by both the issuer and the holder when the payment becomes fixed. The proposed regulations provide, however, that if a contingent payment is not paid within six months of the date it becomes fixed, the buyer is treated as having issued a separate debt instrument on the date the payment becomes fixed. The issue price of this deemed debt instrument is determined under section 1274 (regardless of whether the payment arose under a debt instrument that was issued for cash or publicly traded property). An amount equal to the issue price is characterized as principal and interest as discussed above.

In the case of a debt instrument subject to section 1274, special rules are provided for the treatment of payments contingent only with respect to due date but which are payable within a fixed period. Under these rules, the buyer's initial basis and the allocation of interest to accrual periods are determined by assuming that all payments under the debt instrument are made at the latest possible date and in the smallest amount permitted. When payments are made before the end of the fixed period, basis and interest accrual adjustments are made.

4. PUT OR CALL OPTIONS

The proposed regulations provide a special rule for the determination of yield, maturity date, and stated redemption price at maturity of a debt instrument that provides for a put or call option or an option to extend the term of the debt instrument. Yield of such a debt instrument is determined as of the issue date by assuming that the holder of the particular option will act in accordance with his own economic interest (as viewed from the issue date) in deciding whether to exercise the option. For example, if the issuer of a debt instrument has a call right and if the yield to the call date (assuming exercise of the call option) would be less than the yield to maturity assuming no exercise of the call, it will be assumed as of the date of issue that the call option will be exercised. The maturity date and the stated redemption price at maturity are then determined according to the presumption of exercise. Special rules are provided for debt instruments issued in a transaction governed by section 1274 that contain such options.

5. REORGANIZATIONS

In the case of debt instruments issued after December 13, 1982, in exchange for other debt instruments in a reorganization (within the meaning of section 368(a)), a special rule limits the original issue discount created upon the exchange. If the issue price of the new debt instrument would be less than the adjusted issue price of the old debt instrument but for this rule, then the issue price of the new debt instrument is equal to the adjusted issue price of the old debt instrument.

F. INFORMATION REPORTING REQUIREMENTS

Section 1275(c)(1) requires an issuer of publicly offered debt instruments issued after the date of publication of these regulations in final form having original issue discount to set forth on the face of the debt instrument the amount of original issue discount and the issue date. In addition, the proposed regulations require the yield to maturity, the method selected to determine yield for a short accrual period, and the amount of original issue discount allocable to a short accrual period to be set forth on the face of the debt instrument. Similar requirements apply to the first holder of a nonpublicly offered debt instrument, if such holder disposes of the debt instrument before maturity.

Section 1275(c)(2) requires the issuer of a publicly offered debt instrument having original issue discount to furnish the Secretary with certain information. The temporary regulations issued under this section require certain additional items to be furnished to the Secretary and are proposed herein as a part of these regulations with the following amendment: Section 1275(c)(2) shall not apply to issuers of publicly offered debt instruments that are: (1) certificates of deposit, or (2) stripped bonds and coupons within the meaning of section 1286.

G. TREATMENT OF AMOUNTS RECEIVED ON SALE, EXCHANGE OR REDEMPTION OF DEBT INSTRUMENTS

Under the law in effect prior to the Tax Reform Act of 1984, amounts received upon retirement of certain debt instruments held as capital assets were considered to have been received in exchange therefor. Gain on sale, exchange, or retirement was treated as capital gain in the absence of an intention to call the bond before maturity. In the case of a short-term obligation, a portion of the gain was treated as ordinary interest income to the extent of accrued discount in the hands of the holder.

The rules of prior law relating to the characterization of gain upon sale, exchange or retirement of a debt instrument issued at a discount have been retained, except that the requirement that the debt instrument be a capital asset in the hands of the holder has been repealed for debt instruments issued at a discount after July 18, 1984.

V. ACCOUNTING FOR INTEREST

Under the revised section 483, unstated interest is required to be accounted for on an economic accrual basis consistent with the allocation of original issue discount under section 1272(a) and Rev. Rul. 83-84, 1983-1 C.B. 97. Unlike original issue discount, however, unstated interest is not subject to annual periodic inclusion or deduction. The proposed regulations prescribe rules under section 446 governing the method of accounting for interest in lending and deferred payment transactions outside the scope of the original issue discount rules. Thus, these rules apply to the accounting for unstated interest (and any stated interest) in transactions to which section 483 applies. Under the proposed section 446 regulations, interest accrues in generally the same manner as original issue discount. For purposes of determining how accrued interest is allocated to payments under a debt instrument, a payment is treated: first, as a payment of interest to the extent interest has accrued and remains unpaid as of the date of the payment; second, as a prepayment of interest to the extent the parties have allocated more interest to payments than the amount of interest that has accrued as of the date of the payment; and third, as a payment of principal to the extent of the excess of the payment over the sum of the accrued and the prepaid interest. In certain small transactions, however, the allocation of the parties of less interest to a payment than the amount of accrued interest that remains unpaid as of the date of the payment will be respected.

VI. CASH METHOD DEBT INSTRUMENTS

As noted above, section 483 rather than section 1274 applies to cash method debt instruments. Interest on a cash method debt instrument is accounted for under the cash receipts and disbursements method of accounting. In general, a debt instrument is a cash method debt instrument if the stated principal amount of the debt instrument does not exceed $2,000,000, the lender is neither an accrual method taxpayer nor a dealer with respect to the property, and the borrower and the lender jointly elect the cash method treatment. However, a debt instrument issued in exchange for new section 38 property or a debt instrument issued in a sale-leaseback transaction does not qualify for the cash method treatment. The cash method election is generally binding on successors of the lender and the borrower. If, however, the lender (or a successor thereof) transfers the cash method debt instrument to an accrual method taxpayer, the election does not apply to the successor for any period after the transfer and section 1272 will apply to the successor.

VII. AMENDMENTS TO SECTION 482 REGULATIONS

1. IN GENERAL

In section 44(b)(2) of the Tax Reform Act of 1984, Congress directed the Treasury to amend the safe haven interest rates under the section 482 regulations to provide floating rates consistent with the rates applicable under sections 483 and 1274. These proposed regulations are in response to that directive. In addition, these proposed regulations would make certain other changes to the section 482 regulations. The proposed regulations would reduce the interest-free period on certain intercompany balances between controlled taxpayers under existing § 1.482-2(a)(3) from six months to 60 days. The proposed regulations would also delete the formula method for determining a safe-haven rental charge for leases of tangible depreciable property between related taxpayers under § 1.482-2(c)(2)(ii).

2. EXPLANATION OF THE PROPOSED REGULATIONS

a. SAFE HAVEN INTEREST RATES

Section 1.482-2(a)(2)(iii) of the proposed regulations provides generally that the range of safe haven interest rates on loans or advances between controlled entities will be between 100 percent and 130 percent of the applicable Federal rate (AFR) corresponding to the term of the loan, with adjustments for inadequate interest made at 100 percent of the AFR, compounded semiannually, and adjustments for excessive interest made at 130 percent of the AFR, compounded semiannually. The upper limit of 130 percent of the AFR approximates the interest yield on bonds with a Moody's rating of BAA. Consistent with section 1274(e), the lower limit is 110 percent of the AFR in the case of sale-leaseback transactions. The effective dates of the proposed regulations are described in § 1.482-2(a)(2)(iii)(A) of the proposed regulations.

The proposed regulations continue the rule of the existing regulations that controlled taxpayers may demonstrate that a rate outside the safe haven range is a more appropriate rate under all the facts and circumstances.

Section 1.482-2(a)(3) of the proposed regulations provides that where the interest rate on a loan or advance is subject to adjustment both under section 482 and some other Code section (for example, sections 467, 483, 1274, or 7872), the other Code section is to be applied first, and the provisions of section 482 may then be applied to the loan or advance, as adjusted by the other Code section. If the other Code section does not apply to the loan or advance because of an exception, limitation, or *de minimis* rule contained in the other Code section, the provisions of the section 482 regulations may still be applied to the loan or advance by the district director. Under this arrangement it would be unlikely that actual adjustments would be required under both section 482 and the other Code section. Under certain circumstances, however, both section 482 and the other Code section may apply. For example, if the AFR exceeds 9 percent, and if the related taxpayers use the special 9 percent rate prescribed in section 1274A(a), the transaction may be subject to further adjustment under section 482.

Under proposed § 1.482-2(a)(1)(iii), the interest-free period on certain intercompany balances (six months under the existing regulations) is reduced to 60 days. The proposed regulations continue the rule of the existing regulations that the taxpayer is permitted to use a longer interest-free period if it can demonstrate that it regularly grants uncontrolled parties a longer interest-free period on similar transactions in its trade or business.

b. LEASES

Section 1.482-2(c) of the existing regulations provides a formula method for determining a safe haven rental charge for certain leases of tangible depreciable property between controlled entities. There is no minimum or maximum lease period for which the safe haven rental charge can be used. Under the existing regulation taxpayers are never required to use the safe haven formula rental if the taxpayer can establish a more appropriate rental charge. However, in cases where the taxpayer may use the safe haven rental amount, the IRS may not challenge the safe haven amount, even if the amount does not clearly reflect income. Because of these deficiencies in the operation of the safe haven formula, it would be deleted under the proposed regulations. The safe haven rule for subleases under § 1.482-2(c)(2)(iii) would be retained. The effective dates of the proposed regulations are described in § 1.482-2(c)(2)(ii).

VIII. QUESTIONS RESERVED

The proposed regulations do not revise the definition of intention to call before maturity nor do they address the application of the intention to call rules in the case of debt instruments with indefinite maturities. The Internal Revenue Service is actively considering and welcomes comments specifically directed toward these reserved issues, as well as those directed to the following:

1. How the original issue discount rules should apply to foreign currency transactions, and

2. Whether a portion of the issue price of a debt instrument providing for a conversion feature should properly be allocated to that conversion feature in a manner similar to the allocation of issue price for investment units under section 1273(c)(2).

REGULATORY FLEXIBILITY ACT

Although this document is a notice of proposed rulemaking that solicits public comment, the Internal Revenue Service has concluded that the regulations proposed herein are interpretative and that the notice and public procedure requirements of 5 U.S.C 553 do not apply. Accordingly, these proposed regulations do not constitute regulations subject to the Regulatory Flexibility Act (5 U.S.C. chapter 6).

NON-APPLICATION OF EXECUTIVE ORDER 12291

The Commissioner of Internal Revenue has determined that this proposed rule is not a major rule as defined in Executive Order 12291 and that a regulatory impact analysis therefore is not required.

COMMENTS AND REQUEST FOR A PUBLIC HEARING

Before these proposed regulations are adopted, consideration will be given to any written comments that are submitted (preferably eight copies) to the Commissioner of Internal Revenue. All comments will be available for public inspection and copying. A public hearing will be held upon written request to the Commissioner by any person who has submitted written comments. If a public hearing is held, notice of the time and place will be published in the FEDERAL REGISTER. The collection of information requirements contained herein have been submitted to the Office of Management and Budget (OMB) for review under section 3504(h) of the Paperwork Reduction Act. Comments on the requirements should be sent to the Office of Information and Regulatory Affairs of OMB, Attention: Desk Officer for Internal Revenue Service, New Executive Office Building, Washington, D.C. 20503. The Internal Revenue Service requests that persons submitting comments to OMB also send copies of the comments to the Service.

DRAFTING INFORMATION

The principal author of the proposed regulations under sections 163, 1271, 1272, 1273, and 1275 is Theresa E. Bearman of the Legislation and Regulations Division of the Office of Chief Counsel, Internal Revenue Service; the principal author of the regulations under sections 446, 483 and 1274 is Ewan D. Purkiss of the Legislation and Regulations Division of the Office of Chief Counsel, Internal Revenue Service; and the principal author of the regulations under section 482 is Joseph M. Rosenthal of the Legislation and Regulations Division of the Office of Chief Counsel, Internal Revenue Service. However, personnel from other offices of the Internal Revenue Service and the Treasury Department participated in developing the regulations on matters of both substance and style.

[¶49,071] Proposed Regulations (LR-3-86), published in the Federal Register on May 16, 1986.

Reorganizations: Foreign corporations: Transfer of property.—Reg. §§1.367(a)-1T, 1.367(a)-6T, 1.367(d)-1T and 1.6038B-1T, relating to transfers of property to foreign corporations, are proposed. Temporary Reg. §1.367(a)-3T was adopted as Reg. §1.367(a)-3 by T.D. 8702 on December 27, 1996. Temporary Reg. §§1.367(a)-2T and 1.367(a)-4T were adopted and Reg. §§1.367(a)-5T was removed by T.D. 9803 on December 15, 2016.

AGENCY: Internal Revenue Service, Treasury.

ACTION: Notice of proposed rulemaking cross-reference to temporary regulations.

SUMMARY: In the Rules and Regulations portion of this issue of the Federal Register, the Internal Revenue Service is issuing temporary regulations that add new §§1.367(a)-1T through 1.367(a)-6T, relating to transfers of property by U.S. persons to foreign corporations, new §1.367(d)-1T, relating to transfers of intangible property by U.S. persons to foreign corporations, and new §1.6038B-1T, relating to reporting of transactions described in section 367. The text of the new sections also serves as the comment document for this notice of proposed rulemaking.

DATES: Written comments and requests for a public hearing must be delivered or mailed before July 15, 1986. The regulations are proposed generally to apply to transfers made after December 31, 1984.

ADDRESS: Send comments and requests for a public hearing to: Commissioner of Internal Revenue, Attention: CC:LR:T [LR-3-86], Washington, DC 20224.

FOR FURTHER INFORMATION CONTACT: Charles W. Culmer of the Legislation and Regulations Division, Office of Chief Counsel, Internal Revenue Service, 1111 Constitution Avenue, N.W., Washington, DC 20224, (Attention: CC:LR:T) (202-566-4336, not a toll-free call).

SUPPLEMENTARY INFORMATION:

BACKGROUND

The temporary regulations published in the Rules and Regulations portion of this issue of the FEDERAL REGISTER add new §§1.367(a)-1T, 1.367(a)-2T, 1.367(a)-3T, 1.367(a)-4T, 1.367(a)-5T, 1.367(a)-6T, 1.367(d)-1T, and 1.6038B-1T to 26 CFR Part 1. The final regulations that are proposed to be based on these temporary regulations would amend 26 CFR Part 1 by adding these new temporary regulation sections as final regulation sections under sections 367 and 6038B of the Internal Revenue Code of 1954. For the text of the temporary regulations, see FR Doc.—[T.D. 8087]published in the Rules and Regulations portion of this issue of the FEDERAL REGISTER.

REGULATORY FLEXIBILITY ACT AND EXECUTIVE ORDER 12291

The Commissioner of Internal Revenue has determined that this proposed rule is not a major rule as defined in Executive Order 12291 and that a Regulatory Impact Analysis is therefore not required. The Secretary of the Treasury has certified that this rule will not have a significant impact on a substantial number of small entities. Few small entities would be affected by these regulations. A regulatory flexibility analysis, therefore, is not required under the Regulatory Flexibility Act (5 U.S.C. chapter 6).

COMMENTS AND REQUESTS FOR A PUBLIC HEARING

Before adopting these proposed regulations, consideration will be given to any written comments that are submitted (preferably eight copies) to the Commissioner of Internal Revenue. All comments will be available for public inspection and copying. A public hearing will be held upon written request to the Commissioner by any person who has submitted written comments. If a public hearing is held, notice of the time and place will be published in the FEDERAL REGISTER. The collection of information requirements contained herein have been submitted to the Office of Management and Budget (OMB) for review under section 3504(h) of the Paperwork Reduction Act. Comments on the requirements should be sent to the Office of Information and Regulatory Affairs of OMB, Attention: Desk Officer for Internal Revenue Service, New Executive Office Building, Washington, DC 20503.

The Internal Revenue Service requests persons submitting comments to OMB to also send copies of the comments to the Service.

DRAFTING INFORMATION

The principal author of this regulation is Charles W. Culmer of the Legislation and Regulations Division of the Office of Chief Counsel, Internal Revenue Service. However, personnel from other offices of the Internal Revenue Service and Treasury Department participated in developing the regulations on matters of substance and style.

[¶49,072] Proposed Regulations (LR-144-85), published in the Federal Register on December 17, 1986.

Information returns: Original issue discount: Brokers.—Reg. § 1.6049-5T, relating to reporting requirements for original issue discount debt instruments, is proposed.

AGENCY: Internal Revenue Service, Treasury.

ACTION: Notice of proposed rulemaking and cross-reference to temporary regulations.

SUMMARY: In the Rules and Regulations portion of this issue of the FEDERAL REGISTER, the Internal Revenue Service is issuing temporary regulations concerning the reporting requirements under section 6049 of the Internal Revenue Code of 1954 for original issue discount debt instruments. The temporary regulations also serve as the text for this notice of proposed rulemaking.

DATES: Written comments and requests for a public hearing must be delivered or mailed by February 17, 1987. The regulations are proposed to be effective on or after January 1, 1986.

ADDRESS: Send comments and requests for a public hearing to: Commissioner of Internal Revenue, Attention: CC:LR:T (LR-144-85), 1111 Constitution Avenue, N.W., Washington, D.C. 20224.

FOR FURTHER INFORMATION CONTACT: Susan T. Baker of the Legislation and Regulations Division, Office of the Chief Counsel, Internal Revenue Service, 1111 Constitution Avenue, N.W., Washington, D.C. 20224 (Attention: CC:LR:T) (LR-144-85) (202-566-3829, not a toll-free call).

SUPPLEMENTARY INFORMATION:

BACKGROUND

The temporary regulations published in the Rules and Regulations portion of this issue of the FEDERAL REGISTER amend 26 CFR Parts 1 and 602. The final regulations which are proposed to be based on the temporary regulations would amend 26 CFR Parts 1 and 602 to add new regulations under section 6049 of the Internal Revenue Code of 1954 relating to original issue discount reporting requirements as they apply to certain brokers and other middlemen.

DESCRIPTION OF PROPOSED REGULATIONS

For a description of the subject matter of these proposed regulations relating to the reporting requirements for brokers and other middlemen under section 6049 of the Internal Revenue Code of 1954, see the description and text of the temporary regulations incorporated in F.R. Doc. [T.D.—]published in the Rules and Regulations portion of this issue of the FEDERAL REGISTER.

NON-APPLICABILITY OF EXECUTIVE ORDER 12291

The Commissioner of Internal Revenue has determined that this proposed rule is not a major rule as defined in Executive Order 12291. Accordingly, a Regulatory Impact Analysis is not required.

REGULATORY FLEXIBILITY ACT

The Internal Revenue Service has concluded that although this document is a notice of proposed rulemaking that solicits public comment, the regulations proposed herein are interpretative and the notice and public procedure requirements of 5 U.S.C. 553 do not apply. Accordingly, no Regulatory Flexibility Analysis is required for this rule.

DRAFTING INFORMATION

The principal author of these proposed regulations is Theresa E. Bearman of the Legislation and Regulations Division of the Office of Chief Counsel, Internal Revenue Service. However, personnel from other offices of the Internal Revenue Service and Treasury Department participated in developing the regulations, on matters of both substance and style.

COMMENTS AND REQUESTS FOR A PUBLIC HEARING

Before these proposed regulations are adopted, consideration will be given to any written comments that are submitted (preferably eight copies) to the Commissioner of Internal Revenue. All comments will be available for public inspection and copying. A public hearing will be held upon written request to the Commissioner by any person who has submitted written comments. If a public hearing is held, notice of the time and place will be published in the FEDERAL REGISTER. The collection of information requirements contained herein have been submitted to the Office of Management and Budget (OMB) for review under section 3504(h) of the Paperwork Reduction Act. Comments on the requirements should be sent to the Office of Information and Regulatory Affairs of OMB, Attention: Desk Officer for Internal Revenue Service, New Executive Office Building, Washington, D.C. 20503. The Internal Revenue Service requests persons submitting comments to OMB to also send copies of the comments to the Service.

[¶49,073] Proposed Amendments of Regulations (INTL-53-86), published in the Federal Register on December 19, 1986.

Registration-required obligations: Withholding.—Amendments of Reg. §5f.103-1, relating to the definition of the term "registration-required" with respect to certain types of obligations and to the repeal of the 30 percent withholding tax on certain types of interest, are proposed. Reg. §35a.9999-5 was removed by T.D. 8734 on October 6, 1997.

AGENCY: Internal Revenue Service, Treasury.

ACTION: Notice of proposed rulemaking by cross reference to temporary regulations.

SUMMARY: This document provides notice of proposed rulemaking relating to the definition of the term "registration-required" with respect to certain types of obligations, and relating to the repeal of the 30 percent withholding tax on certain types of interest by the Tax Reform Act of 1984. In the Rules and Regulations portion of this Federal Register, the Internal Revenue Service is issuing temporary income tax regulations relating to the definition of the term "registration-required" with respect to certain obligations, and the repeal of 30 percent withholding by the Tax Reform Act of 1984. The text of those temporary regulations serves as the comment document for this notice of proposed rulemaking.

DATE: Written comments and requests for a public hearing must be delivered or mailed before [DATE WHICH IS 60 DAYS AFTER PUBLICATION OF THIS DOCUMENT IN THE FEDERAL REGISTER].

ADDRESS: Send comments and requests for a public hearing to: Commissioner of Internal Revenue, Attention: CC:LR:T (INTL-53-86).

FOR FURTHER INFORMATION CONTACT: Carl Cooper of the Office of the Associate Chief Counsel (International) within the Office of Chief Counsel, Internal Revenue Service, 1111 Constitution Avenue, N.W., Washington, D.C. 20224, Attention: CC:LR:T [INTL-53-86], (202-566-3388).

SUPPLEMENTARY INFORMATION:

BACKGROUND

The temporary regulations published in the Rules and Regulations portion of this issue of the Federal Register amend existing temporary regulations. Section 5f.103-1 is amended by revising paragraph (c)(1), by adding a new paragraph (e), by revising example (2) of paragraph (f), and by adding examples to paragraph (f). Section 35a.9999-5 is amended by revising Q & As-1, 8, 18 and 20, by inserting new Q & As-19 and 22 through 28, and by renumbering existing Q & A-20 as Q & A-21. For the text of the temporary regulations, see FR Doc. [T.D. 8111] published in the rules and regulations portion of this issue of the Federal Register.

REGULATORY FLEXIBILITY ACT AND EXECUTIVE ORDER 12291

The Commissioner of Internal Revenue has determined that this proposed rule is not a major rule as defined in Executive Order 12291 and that a Regulatory Impact Analysis is therefore not required. Although this document is a notice of a proposed rulemaking which solicits public comment, the Internal Revenue Service has concluded that the regulations proposed herein are interpretative and that the notice and public procedure requirements of 5 U.S.C. 553 do not apply. Accordingly, these text of the temporary regulations, see FR Doc. [T.D. 8111]published in the rules and regulations portion of this issue of the Federal Register.

REGULATORY FLEXIBILITY ACT AND EXECUTIVE ORDER 12291

The Commissioner of Internal Revenue has determined that this proposed rule is not a major rule as defined in Executive Order 12291 and that a Regulatory Impact Analysis is therefore not required. Although this document is a notice of a proposed rulemaking which solicits public comment, the Internal Revenue Service has concluded that the regulations proposed herein are interpretative and that the notice and public procedure requirements of 5 U.S.C. 553 do not apply. Accordingly, these proposed regulations do not constitute regulations subject to the Regulatory Flexibility Act (5 U.S.C. chapter 6).

COMMENTS AND REQUESTS FOR A PUBLIC HEARING

Before adopting these proposed regulations as final regulations, consideration will be given to any written comments that are submitted (preferably eight copies) to the Commissioner of Internal Revenue. All comments will be available for public inspection and copying. A public hearing will be held upon written request to the Commissioner by any person who has submitted written comments. If a public hearing is held, notice of the time and place will be published in the Federal Register. The collection of information requirements contained herein have been submitted to OMB for review under the Paperwork Reduction Act, and comments on them should be sent to the Office of Information and Regulatory Affairs of OMB, Attn: Desk Officer for the Internal Revenue Service, New Executive Office Building, Washington, DC 20503. The Internal Revenue Service requests persons submitting comments to OMB to also send copies of the comments to the Service.

DRAFTING INFORMATION

The principal authors of this regulation are P. Ann Fisher and Carl Cooper of the Office of the Associate Chief Counsel (International) within the office of the Office of Chief Counsel, Internal Revenue Service. However, personnel from other Offices of the Internal Revenue Service and Treasury Department participated in developing the regulations on matters of substance and style.

[¶49,074] Proposed Regulations and Amendments of Regulations (INTL-43-86), published in the Federal Register on February 3, 1987.

Domestic International Sales Corporations: Taxation of income.—Reg. §§1.995-2A, 1.995-8, 1.995(f)-1 and 1.996-9 and amendments of Reg. §§1.921-1T, 1.991-1, 1.992-1, 1.992-2, 1.995-2, 1.995-7, 1.996-1 and 1.6011-2, relating to the taxation of income allocable to a DISC for taxable years beginning after 1984, are proposed. Reg. §1.995-7 was removed 1/5/96 by T.D. 8655.

AGENCY: Internal Revenue Service, Treasury.

ACTION: Notice of proposed rulemaking.

SUMMARY: This document contains proposed regulations relating to the taxation of income allocable to a Domestic International Sales Corporation (DISC) for taxable years beginning after 1984. Changes to the applicable tax law were made by the Tax Reform Act of 1984 and the Technical Corrections Title of the Tax Reform Act of 1986. The proposed regulations would provide DISCs and DISC shareholders with guidance needed to comply with the Act and would affect all DISCs and DISC shareholders.

DATES: Written comments and requests for a public hearing must be delivered or mailed by April 3, 1987. The regulations are proposed to be effective for transactions after December 31, 1984, in taxable years ending after December 31, 1984.

ADDRESS: Send comments and requests for a public hearing to: Commissioner of Internal Revenue, Attn: CC:LR:T (Intl-43-86), Washington, D.C. 20224.

FOR FURTHER INFORMATION CONTACT: Joseph M. Rosenthal of the Office of the Associate Chief Counsel (International), Internal Revenue Service, 1111 Constitution Avenue, N.W., Washington, D.C. 20224 (Attn: CC:LR:T). Telephone 202-566-6276 (not a toll-free call.)

SUPPLEMENTARY INFORMATION:

BACKGROUND

This document contains proposed amendments to the Income Tax Regulations (26 CFR Part 1) under sections 441, 991, 992, 995, 996 and 6011 of the Internal Revenue Code of 1954. These amendments are proposed to provide regulations under sections 441(h), 995(b)(1)(E), 995(f) and 996 which were added to the Code by sections 803 and 802 of the Tax Reform Act of 1984 (Pub. L. 98-369, 98 Stat. 672) or amended by the Technical Corrections Title of the Tax Reform Act of 1986 (Pub. L. 99-514, 100 Stat. 2085).

EXPLANATION OF THE PROPOSED REGULATIONS TERMINATION OF DISC ELECTION AND EXEMPTION OF DISC INCOME FROM TAX

Under section 805(b) of the Tax Reform Act of 1984, the last taxable year of each DISC which began before January 1, 1985, ended on December 31, 1984. The termination of a DISC's taxable year on that date is treated under §1.921-1T(a) as a revocation of the corporation's DISC election. All corporations which wish to be treated as a DISC for any period after 1984 must make a new DISC election on Form 4876A. Regulations providing for the time and manner of making the new DISC election were provided by §1.921-1T(b)(1) Q&A-1. Those regulations generally require that the election of a corporation to be treated as an interest charge DISC for the corporation's first taxable year beginning after December 31, 1984, must be filed on Form 4876A within 90 days after the beginning of such year. The Service has learned that many corporations which were DISCs on December 31, 1984, and which intended to continue to be treated as an interest charge DISC may have failed to re-elect DISC status in a timely manner. Accordingly, section 1.992-2(a)(3) of these proposed regulations extends the time for re-electing DISC status for 1985 and subsequent taxable years for corporations which were treated as a DISC for the taxable year ending December 31, 1984, to June 3, 1987. Forms 4876A filed by such corporations within this time will be accepted by the Service as a timely DISC election for the DISC's taxable year beginning January 1, 1985, based on these proposed regulations.

In addition, under section 805(b) of the Tax Reform Act of 1984, generally all corportions which qualified as DISCs on December 31, 1984, are permitted to treat their accumulated DISC income as previously taxed income when distributed after that date. Temporary regulations relating to the treatment of such distributions were provided by §1.921-1T and are contained in §1.996-9 of the proposed regulations. That section of the proposed regulations also provides that any net operating loss or capital loss carryforward of a DISC as of December 31, 1984, is to be reduced by the amount of accumulated DISC income that was exempted from tax. In addition, that section also provides that no foreign tax credit shall be allowed with respect to any foreign taxes paid with respect to the amount of accumulated DISC income that was exempted from tax.

NEW DISC RULES

The Tax Reform Act of 1984 also changed many of the rules applicable to DISCs effective for taxable years ending after 1984.

Taxable year of the DISC

A DISC is required to use the same taxable year as its principal shareholder. The same rule also applies to Foreign Sales Corporations (FSCs) and to small FSCs. Section 1.441-1(h) of the proposed regulations provides rules relating to this requirement. The DISC must change its taxable year if the principal shareholder changes its taxable year, or if a different shareholder having a different taxable year becomes the principal shareholder of the DISC. If the DISC must change its taxable year to conform to the taxable year of a new principal shareholder, §1.441-1(h)(3)(iii) of the proposed regulations provides that the short period required to effect the change shall end with the close of the new principal shareholder's taxable year within which the change in ownership occurs. This provision would amend the rule for determining the short period contained in § 1.921-1T(b)(6) of the Temporary Regulations (under which the short period is the taxable year of the DISC following the DISC's taxable year in which the change of ownership occurs), and is proposed to be effective for changes in ownership occurring after 30 days after the date the proposed regulations are finalized.

Controlled groups

A DISC and a FSC or a small FSC cannot be members of the same greater-than-50-percent controlled group. Rules relating to this requirement are contained in § 1.992-1(j) of the proposed regulations. In general, the DISC election of a corporation is treated as revoked if a FSC or a small FSC election becomes effective for any other member of the controlled group. A special transitional rule is provided if a DISC and a FSC or small FSC become members of the same controlled group by reason of an acquisition of a shareholder in either the DISC, the FSC or the small FSC.

Deemed distributions

The deemed distribution relating to base period export gross receipts (the incremental rule) is eliminated for taxable years beginning after 1984, and is replaced with a deemed distribution of the DISC's taxable income attributable to qualified export receipts that exceed $10 million. Section 1.995-8 of the proposed regulations provides rules relating to this new deemed distribution. In general, the $10 million amount may be allocated to qualified gross receipts on a transaction-by-transaction basis. Section 1.995-8(b)(2) of the proposed regulations provides a special rule for the allocation of qualified gross receipts attributable to related and subsidiary services. Section 1.995-8(f) of the proposed regulations provides a method for allocating the $10 million amount among DISCs which are members of the same controlled group. Under section 1.995-8(a), the $10 million amount is to be prorated on a daily basis in the case of a DISC having a short taxable year.

The deemed distribution of 50 percent of the DISC's taxable income to a non-C corporation DISC shareholder is eliminated, and the deemed distribution of 57.5 percent of the DISC's taxable income to a C corporation DISC shareholder is reduced to a deemed distribution of 1/17th of the amount of the DISC's taxable income for the taxable year in excess of the other deemed distributions. See § 1.995-2A of the proposed regulations.

INTEREST CHARGE

In general

The Tax Reform Act of 1984 also provides for an annual interest charge on the shareholders of the DISC. Section 1.995(f)-1 of the proposed regulations provides rules relating to this requirement. In general, the amount of the interest charge is based on the additional income tax that would otherwise be due on the accumulated DISC income deferred by the DISC in taxable years beginning after 1984 computed as if the deferred income were distributed to the shareholder. The rate of interest charged is tied to the rate of interest on 52-week Treasury bills (the "base period T-bill rate"), as described below. The interest charge is not imposed on the accumulated DISC income for the taxable year in which it is earned. Thus, a DISC shareholder will not have an interest charge for the shareholder's taxable year ending with or including the last day of the DISC's first taxable year for which its new DISC election is made. Section 1.995(f)-1(f) contains rules for determining the amount of the deferred DISC income.

DISC-related deferred tax liability

The tax that would otherwise be due on the deferred DISC income, the "shareholder's DISC-related deferred tax liability", for a taxable year of the shareholder is the excess of the shareholder's tax liability computed as if the deferred DISC income were included in the shareholder's gross income over the shareholder's actual tax liability for the taxable year. Sections 1.995(f)-1(d) and (e) of the proposed regulations provide rules relating to this computation. Under section 995(f)(2), the computation is to be made without regard to carrybacks to the taxable year from a later taxable year. Under § 1.995(f)-1(d)(4) of the proposed regulations, the computation is also to be made without regard to carryforwards to the taxable year or to any other item that may be carried by the shareholder to another taxable year. Thus, the treatment of carrybacks and carryovers of deductions and credits in the computation of the amount of the shareholder's DISC-related deferred tax liability is similar to the treatment of such items under section 644(a) of the Code. Section 644(a) provides a special rule for determining the tax imposed on a trust's gain on the sale of property contributed to the trust within two years by reference to the additional tax that would have been imposed on the grantor if the property had been sold by the grantor.

Base period T-bill rate

The rate of interest charged on the shareholder's DISC-related deferred tax liability for a taxable year is equal to the "base period T-bill rate." This rate is equivalent to the average investment yield on 52 week T-bills auctioned during the one-year period ending on September 30 of the calendar year ending with or within the taxable year of the shareholder. The base period T-bill rate, as determined above, is then compounded daily for the number of days in the shareholder's taxable year for which the interest charge is being determined. Under section 6622, the amount of any interest required to be paid under the Code is determined by daily compounding.

The base period T-bill rate for each one-year period ending September 30 shall be published in a revenue ruling in the Internal Revenue Bulletin. That revenue ruling shall also contain a table of factors reflecting daily compounding of the base period T-bill rate. Revenue Ruling 86-132, 1986-46

I.R.B. 5 published the base period T-bill rates for the periods September 30, 1984, 1985 and 1986, together with tables of factors reflecting daily compounding.

To compute the amount of the interest charge for the shareholder's taxable year, the shareholder shall multiply the DISC-related deferred tax liability by the base period T-bill rate factor corresponding to the number of days in the shareholder's taxable year for which the interest charge is being determined. Generally, the shareholder will use the base period T-bill rate factor for a 365 day year. The factor to be used will be other than the factor for 365 days if the shareholder's taxable year is a short taxable year, if the shareholder uses the 52-53 week taxable year, or if the shareholder's taxable year is a leap year.

Paragraph (g) of § 1.995(f)-1 of the proposed regulations provides rules for determining the amount of the interest charge for a taxable year in which stock in the DISC is transferred. In general, the transferor and the transferee shareholders compute their DISC-related deferred tax liability as if they each held the stock for the entire taxable year and then multiply that amount by the base period T-bill rate factor for the number of days in the year that each shareholder held the stock. A reduction in the amount of deferred DISC income (and thus of the interest charge) is made for any gain recognized on the transfer under section 995(c).

Section 1.995(f)-1(h) of the proposed regulations provides for pass-through treatment of the interest charge in the case of DISC stock held by a partnership or an S corporation. If stock in a DISC is held by an estate or trust, however, the interest charge is imposed on the estate or trust.

Payment, collection and assessment of the interest charge

Section 995(f)(6) provides that the amount of the interest charge for a taxable year is treated as interest imposed on an underpayment of tax under section 6601. Thus, the interest charge may be deducted by the DISC shareholder only to the extent that the shareholder may deduct interest on an underpayment of tax. The interest charge is due at the same time the shareholder's income tax return for the taxable year is required to be filed, without regard to extensions. No payments of estimated tax under section 6154 or 6654 are required with respect to the interest charge.

The interest charge is to be computed on Form 8404. To assist the IRS in properly processing the shareholder's Form 8404 and crediting the payment to the shareholder's account, the Form 8404, together with the shareholder's payment of the interest charge, is *not* to be included with or attached to the shareholder's income tax return for the taxable year.

Technical corrections

The Technical Corrections Title of the Tax Reform Act of 1986 made several amendments to the DISC and FSC rules. The proposed regulations incorporate those amendments, but do not address any issues that may be raised by other substantive provisions of the Tax Reform Act of 1986.

EXECUTIVE ORDER 12291 AND REGULATORY FLEXIBILITY ACT

The Commissioner of Internal Revenue has determined that this proposed rule is not a major rule as defined in Executive Order 12291 and that a Regulatory Impact Analysis is therefore not required. Although this document is a notice of proposed rulemaking which solicits public comment, the Internal Revenue Service has determined that the regulations proposed herein are interpretative and that the notice and public procedure requirements of 5 U.S.C. § 553 do not apply. Accordingly, these proposed regulations do not constitute regulations subject to the Regulatory Flexibility Act (5 U.S.C. Chapter 6).

COMMENTS AND REQUESTS FOR A PUBLIC HEARING

Before adopting these proposed regulations, consideration will be given to any written comments that are submitted (preferably eight copies) to the Commissioner of Internal Revenue. All comments will be available for public inspection and copying. A public hearing will be held upon written request to the Commissioner by any person who has submitted written comments. If a public hearing is held, notice of the time and place will be published in the FEDERAL REGISTER.

PAPERWORK REDUCTION ACT

The collection of information requirements contained in this notice of proposed rulemaking have been submitted to the Office of Management and Budget (OMB) for review under section 3504(h) of the Paperwork Reduction Act. Comments on these requirements should be sent to the Office of Regulatory Affairs of OMB, Attention: Desk Officer for Internal Revenue Service, New Executive Office Building, Washington, D.C. 20503. The Internal Revenue Service requests that persons submitting comments to these requirements to the OMB also send copies of those comments to the IRS.

DRAFTING INFORMATION

The principal author of the proposed regulations is Joseph M. Rosenthal of the Office of the Associate Chief Counsel (International), Internal Revenue Service. However, personnel from other offices of the Internal Revenue Service and the Treasury Department participated in developing these regulations on matters of substance and style.

[¶ 49,075] Proposed Regulations (REG-209015-86) [originally issued as INTL-153-86], published in the Federal Register on March 3, 1987.

Foreign sales corporations.—Reg. § § 1.927(a)-1T and 1.927(d)-2T, relating to foreign sales corporations, are proposed. Reg. § 1.927(e)-1 was adopted 9/17/98 by T.D. 8782. Temporary Reg. § § 1.921-3T, 1.923-1T, 1.924(a)-1T, 1.925(a)-1T, 1.925(b)-1T, 1.926(a)-1T, 1.927(b)-1T and 1.927(e)-2T were removed by T.D. 9849 on 3/11/2019.

AGENCY: Internal Revenue Service, Treasury.

ACTION: Notice of proposed rulemaking by cross-reference to temporary regulations.

SUMMARY: This document provides proposed Income Tax Regulations relating to rules for application of the foreign sales corporation (FSC) transfer pricing rules, for distributions from a FSC, for treatment of losses of a FSC, for sourcing and classification of a FSC's income, for computation of exempt foreign trade income, for computation of the FSC's and the FSC's United States shareholder's foreign tax credits, for definitions of foreign trading gross receipts, export property and gross receipts, for effect of boycott participation on FSC benefits, and for sourcing a related supplier's income if the transfer pricing rules are used to compute the FSC's profit. In the Rules and Regulations portion of this FEDERAL REGISTER, the Internal Revenue Service is issuing temporary regulations relating to these matters. The text of those temporary regulations also serves as the comment document for this proposed rulemaking.

DATES: Written comments and requests for a public hearing must be delivered or mailed before May 4, 1987. These rules would apply to taxable years beginning after December 31, 1984.

ADDRESS: Send comments and requests for a public hearing to Commissioner of Internal Revenue, Attention: CC: LR:T (INTL-153-86), Washington, D.C. 20224.

FOR FURTHER INFORMATION CONTACT: Richard Chewning, of the Office of Associate Chief Counsel (International), within the Office of Chief Counsel, Internal Revenue Service, 1111 Constitution Avenue, N.W., Washington, D.C. 20224 (Attention: CC:LR:T (INTL-153-86)) (202-566-6384, not a toll-free call).

SUPPLEMENTARY INFORMATION:

BACKGROUND

The temporary regulations published in the Rules and Regulations portion of this issue of the FEDERAL REGISTER add new §§1.921-3T, 1.923-1T, 1.924(a)-1T, 1.925(a)-1T, 1.925(b)-1T, 1.926(a)-1T, 1.927(a)-1T, 1.927(b)-1T, 1.927(d)-2T, 1.927(e)-1T and 1.927(e)-2T to 26 CFR Part 1. The final regulations that are proposed to be based on the temporary regulations would amend 26 CFR Part 1. For the text of the temporary regulations, see [INSERT FEDERAL REGISTER REFERENCE] [T.D. 8126]published in the Rules and Regulations portion of this issue of the FEDERAL REGISTER.

EXECUTIVE ORDER 12291 AND REGULATORY FLEXIBILITY ACT

The Commissioner of Internal Revenue has determined that these proposed rules are not major rules as defined in Executive Order 12291 and that a Regulatory Impact Analysis is therefore not required. Although this document is a notice of a proposed rulemaking which solicits public comment, the Internal Revenue Service has concluded that the regulations proposed herein are interpretative and that the notice and public procedure requirements of 5 U.S.C. 553 do not apply. Accordingly, these proposed regulations do not constitute regulations subject to the Regulatory Flexibility Act (5 U.S.C. chapter 6).

PAPERWORK REDUCTION ACT

The collection of information requirements contained in this notice of proposed rulemaking have been submitted to the Office of Management and Budget (OMB) for review under section 3504(h) of the Paperwork Reduction Act. Comments on these collection of information requirements may be sent to the Office of Information and Regulatory Affairs of OMB, Attention: Desk Officer for Internal Revenue Service, New Executive Office Building, Washington, D.C. 20503. The Internal Revenue Service requests that persons submitting comments on these requirements to OMB also send copies of those comments to the Internal Revenue Service.

COMMENTS AND REQUESTS FOR A PUBLIC HEARING

Before adopting these proposed regulations, consideration will be given to any written comments that are submitted (preferably eight copies) to the Commissioner of Internal Revenue. All comments will be available for public inspection and copying. A public hearing will be held upon written request to the Commissioner by any person who has submitted written comments. If a public hearing is held, notice of the time and place will be published in the FEDERAL REGISTER.

DRAFTING INFORMATION

The principal author of these regulations is Richard Chewning, of the Office of Associate Chief Counsel (International), within the Office of Chief Counsel, Internal Revenue Service. Personnel from other offices of the Internal Revenue Service and Treasury Department participated in developing the regulations.

[¶49,076] Proposed Regulations (CO-23-87), published in the Federal Register on March 18, 1987.

Consolidated returns: Alaska Native Corporations.—Reg. §1.1502-81T, relating to corporations included in a consolidated return with a Native Corporation established under the Alaska Native Claims Settlement Act, is proposed.

AGENCY: Internal Revenue Service, Treasury.

ACTION: Notice of proposed rulemaking by cross-reference to temporary regulations.

SUMMARY: In the Rules and Regulations portion of this issue of the FEDERAL REGISTER, the Internal Revenue Service is issuing temporary regulations that add new §1.1502-81T to provide rules relating to certain corporations included in a consolidated return with a Native Corporation established under the Alaska Native Claims Settlement Act. The text of the new section also serves as the comment document for this notice of proposed rulemaking.

PROPOSED EFFECTIVE DATE

The regulations are proposed to apply generally to taxable years beginning after December 31, 1984.

DATE FOR COMMENTS AND REQUESTS FOR A PUBLIC HEARING

Written comments and requests for a public hearing must be delivered or mailed by [60 DAYS AFTER DATE OF PUBLICATION OF THIS DOCUMENT IN THE FEDERAL REGISTER.]

ADDRESS: Send comments and requests for a public hearing to: Commissioner of Internal Revenue, Attention: CC:LR:T [LR-23-87], Washington, D.C. 20224.

FOR FURTHER INFORMATION CONTACT: Mark S. Jennings of the Legislation and Regulations Division, Office of Chief Counsel, Internal Revenue Service, 1111 Constitution Avenue, N.W., Washington, D.C. 20224 (Attention: CC:LR:T) or telephone 202-566-3458 (not a toll-free number).

SUPPLEMENTARY INFORMATION:

BACKGROUND

Temporary regulations published in the Rules and Regulations portion of this issue of the FEDERAL REGISTER add new temporary regulation § 1.1502-81T to Part 1 of Title 26 of the Code of Federal Regulations ("CFR"). The final regulations that are proposed to be based on the new temporary regulation would be added to Part 1 of Title 26 of the CFR. Those final regulations would make clear that the rules provided by section 60(b)(5) of the Tax Reform Act of 1984 and section 1804(e)(4) of the Tax Reform Act of 1986 result in no tax saving, tax benefit, or tax loss to any person, other than the use of the losses and credits of an Alaska Native Corporation and its wholly owned subsidiaries. For the text of the new temporary regulations, see T.D. 8130, published in the Rules and Regulations portion of this issue of the Federal Register. The preamble to the temporary regulations explains the additions to the regulations.

REGULATORY FLEXIBILITY ACT AND EXECUTIVE ORDER 12291

Although this document is a notice of proposed rulemaking that solicits public comment, the Secretary of the Treasury has certified that this rule will not have a significant impact on a substantial number of small entities because the economic and any other secondary or incidental impact flows directly from the underlying statute. A regulatory flexibility analysis is therefore not required under the Regulatory Flexibility Act (5 U.S.C. chapter 6). The Commissioner of Internal Revenue has determined that this proposed rule is not a major rule as defined in Executive Order 12291 and that a Regulatory Impact Analysis is therefore not required.

COMMENTS AND REQUESTS FOR A PUBLIC HEARING

Before these proposed regulations are adopted, consideration will be given to any written comments that are submitted (preferably eight copies) to the Commissioner of Internal Revenue. All comments will be available for public inspection and copying. A public hearing will be held upon written request to the Commissioner by any person who has submitted written comments. If a public hearing is held, notice of the time and place will be published in the FEDERAL REGISTER.

DRAFTING INFORMATION

The principal author of these proposed regulations is Mark S. Jennings of the Legislation and Regulations Division of the Office of Chief Counsel, Internal Revenue Service. However, personnel from other offices of the Internal Revenue Service and Treasury Department participated in developing the regulations, both on matters of substance and style.

[¶ 49,077] Proposed Regulations (EE-151-86), published in the Federal Register on April 3, 1987.

Excise tax: Retirement plans: Qualified plan assets: Reversion of.—Reg. §§ 54.6011-1T and 54.6071-1T, relating to the payment of excise tax by employers receiving reversions of qualified plan assets required by the Tax Reform Act of 1986, are proposed. Reg. § 54.6071-1T was withdrawn 4/26/93 by T.D. 8474.

AGENCY: Internal Revenue Service, Treasury.

ACTION: Notice of proposed rulemaking by cross reference to temporary regulations.

SUMMARY: This document provides regulations regarding the payment of the excise tax by employers receiving (directly or indirectly) reversions of qualified plan assets required by the Tax Reform Act of 1986. In the Rules and Regulations portion of this FEDERAL REGISTER, the Internal Revenue Service is issuing temporary regulations relating to the payment of the excise tax; the text of these temporary regulations also serves as the comment document for this notice of proposed rulemaking.

DATES: Written comments and requests for a public hearing must be delivered or mailed by June 2, 1987. These amendments are proposed to be applicable to reversions occurring after December 31, 1985.

ADDRESS: Please mail or deliver comments to: Commissioner of Internal Revenue, Attention: CC:LR:T (EE-151-86), 1111 Constitution Avenue, N.W., Washington, D.C. 20224.

FOR FURTHER INFORMATION CONTACT: Suzanne K. Tank of the Employee Plans and Exempt Organizations Division, Office of Chief Counsel, Internal Revenue Service, 1111 Constitution Avenue, N.W., Washington, D.C. 20224 (Attention: CC:LR:T) (202-566-3938, not a toll-free number).

SUPPLEMENTARY INFORMATION:

BACKGROUND

The temporary regulations in the Rules and Regulations portion of this issue of the FEDERAL REGISTER amend Part 54 of the Code of Federal Regulations. New § 54.6011-1T and new § 54.6071-1T are added to Part 54 of Title 26 of the Code of Federal Regulations. When § 54.6011-1T is promulgated as final regulations, § 54.6011-1 will be revised to reflect the new provision. For the text of the temporary regulations, see FR Doc. (TD 8133) published in the Rules and Regulations portion of this issue of the FEDERAL REGISTER. The preamble to the temporary regulations explains this addition to the Pension Excise Tax Regulations.

NONAPPLICABILITY OF EXECUTIVE ORDER 12291

The Commissioner of Internal Revenue has determined that this proposed rule is not a major rule as defined in Executive Order 12291 and that a regulatory impact analysis therefore is not required.

REGULATORY FLEXIBILITY ACT

The Secretary of the Treasury has certified that this rule will not have a significant impact on a substantial number of small entities. First, most small businesses maintain defined contribution plans. The regulations do not generally affect defined contribution plans. Hence, small businesses would not generally be affected by the regulation. Second, very few businesses with defined benefit plans will be terminating their plans and receiving a reversion in any calendar quarter or year. A Regulatory Flexibility Analysis, therefore, is not required under the Regulatory Flexibility Act (5 U.S.C. 605(b)).

PAPERWORK REDUCTION ACT

The collection of information requirements contained in this regulation have been submitted to the Office of Management and Budget (OMB) for review under section 3504(h) of the Paperwork Reduction Act of 1980. Comments on these requirements should be sent to the Office of Information and Regulatory Affairs of OMB, Attention: Desk Officer for Internal Revenue Service, New Executive Office Building, Washington, D.C. 20503. The Internal Revenue Service requests that persons submitting comments on the requirements to OMB also send copies of these comments to the Service.

DRAFTING INFORMATION

The principal author of these proposed regulations is Suzanne K. Tank of the Employee Plans and Exempt Organizations Division of the Office of Chief Counsel, Internal Revenue Service. However, personnel from other offices of the Internal Revenue Service and the Treasury Department participated in developing the regulations, on matters of both substance and style.

COMMENTS AND REQUESTS FOR A PUBLIC HEARING

Before adoption of these proposed regulations, consideration will be given to any written comments that are submitted (preferably eight copies) to the Commissioner of Internal Revenue. All comments will be available for public inspection and copying. A public hearing will be held upon written request to the Commissioner by any person who has submitted written comments. If a public hearing is held, notice of the time and place will be published in the FEDERAL REGISTER.

[¶ 49,078] Proposed Regulations and Amendments of Regulations (EE-143-86), published in the Federal Register on June 15, 1987.

Business expenses: Sickness and disability payments: Group health plan.—Amendments of Reg. § 1.106-1, relating to the requirement that a group health plan offer continuation coverage to people who would otherwise lose coverage as a result of certain events, are proposed. Reg. § 1.162-26 was adopted by T.D. 8812 (see Reg. §§ 54.4980B-0—54.4980B-8), applicable to qualifying events occurring in plan years beginning on or after January 1, 2000.

AGENCY: Internal Revenue Service, Treasury.

ACTION: Notice of proposed rulemaking.

SUMMARY: This document contains proposed regulations relating to the requirement that a group health plan offer continuation coverage to people who would otherwise lose coverage as a result of certain events. They reflect changes made by the Consolidated Omnibus Budget Reconciliation Act of 1985 (COBRA) and the Tax Reform Act of 1986. The regulations will generally affect sponsors of and participants in group health plans, and they provide plan sponsors with guidance necessary to comply with the law.

DATES: Written comments and requests for a public hearing must be delivered or mailed [60 DAYS AFTER DATE OF PUBLICATION OF NOTICE OF PROPOSED RULEMAKING]. These regulations are proposed to be effective when final regulations are published in the FEDERAL REGISTER as a Treasury decision.

ADDRESS: Send comments and requests for a public hearing to: Commissioner of Internal Revenue, Attention: CC:LR:T (EE-143-86) Washington, D.C. 20224.

FOR FURTHER INFORMATION CONTACT: Mark Schwimmer of the Employee Plans and Exempt Organizations Division, Office of Chief Counsel, Internal Revenue Service, 1111 Constitution Avenue, N.W., Washington, D.C. 20224 (Attention: CC:LR:T). Telephone 202-566-6212 (not a toll-free number).

SUPPLEMENTARY INFORMATION:

BACKGROUND

This document contains proposed amendments to the Income Tax Regulations (26 CFR Part 1) under sections 106(b), 162(i)(2), and 162(k) of the Internal Revenue Code of 1986 (Code). The proposed regulations conform the regulations to section 10001 of the Consolidated Omnibus Budget Reconcilation Act of 1985 (COBRA) (100 Stat. 222) and to section 1895(d) of the Tax Reform Act of 1986 (100 Stat. 2936), which made technical corrections to the COBRA provisions.

COBRA added a new section 162(k) of the Code to specify continuation coverage requirements for employer-provided group health plans. In general, a group health plan must offer each "qualified beneficiary" who would otherwise lose coverage under the plan as a result of a "qualifying event" an opportunity to elect continuation of the coverage being received immediately before the qualifying event. A qualified beneficiary who properly elects continuation coverage can be charged an amount no greater than 102 percent of the "applicable premium." The "applicable premium" is based on the plan's cost of providing coverage.

If a group health plan fails to comply with these continuation coverage requirements, the employer will be unable to deduct contributions made to that or any other group health plan (section 162(i)(2)), and certain highly compensated individuals will be unable to exclude from income any employer-provided coverage under that or any other group health plan (section 106(b)).

In addition, there may be non-tax consequences if a group health plan fails to comply with parallel requirements that section 10002 of COBRA added to Title I of the Employee Retirement Income Security Act of 1974 (ERISA). Title I of ERISA is administered by the Department of Labor. Governmental plans (as defined in section 414(d) of the Code) are exempt from both the tax and ERISA provisions. However, State and local governmental group health plans are subject to parallel requirements that section 10003 of COBRA added to the Public Health Service Act, which is administered by the Department of Health and Human Services.

The proposed regulations do not reflect section 9501 of the Omnibus Budget Reconciliation Act of 1986, which extended the COBRA continuation coverage requirements to certain individuals receiving retiree medical benefits from employers that are involved in bankruptcy proceedings. The changes made by that act will be addressed in a later issuance.

The proposed regulations clarify which plans must offer COBRA continuation coverage and the tax consequences of failing to do so. They also provide guidance on a variety of details, including the scope of the continuation coverage, who is a qualified beneficiary, what is a qualifying event, how elections are made, and when payment must be made. Rules regarding computation of the applicable premium under section 162(k)(4) will be addressed in a later issuance.

Section 414(t) as added by the Tax Reform Act of 1986 extends the employer aggregation rules of sections 414(b), (c), (m), and (o) to a variety of employee benefit provisions. The list of those provisions includes section 106 (denying an income exclusion to highly compensated employees of an employer maintaining a group health plan that fails to comply with section 162(k)), but does not include section 162(i)(2) (denying deductions to such an employer) or section 162(k) itself. A technical correction to add sections 162(i)(2) and 162(k) to the list was included in H.Con.Res. 395. Although the 99th Congress adjourned without enacting that concurrent resolution, the correction was identical in both House and Senate versions. Accordingly, the proposed regulations set forth employer aggregation rules that anticipate a similar technical correction with retroactive effect being enacted in the current session of Congress.

There is no connection between the proposed regulations and section 89 of the Code. For example, the definitions set forth in the proposed regulations will not affect the meaning of "core benefits," "non-core benefits," or any other terms for purposes of section 89. Also, the computation of applicable premiums for COBRA continuation coverage will not affect the determination of the value of group health plan benefits for purposes of section 89.

EFFECTIVE DATE

The regulations are proposed to be effective when final regulations are published in the FEDERAL REGISTER as a Treasury decision. Group health plans become subject to the COBRA continuation coverage requirements at different times, however, depending on the plan year of a plan and whether the plan is a collectively bargained plan. With respect to qualifying events that occur on or after the date that a plan became or becomes subject to those requirements and before the effective date of final regulations, the plan and the employer must operate in good faith compliance with a reasonable interpretation of the statutory requirements (i.e., title X of COBRA). For the period before the effective date of final regulations, the Internal Revenue Service will consider compliance with the terms of these proposed regulations to constitute good faith compliance with a reasonable interpretation of the statutory requirements (other than the statutory requirements regarding the computation of the applicable premium or the treatment, under section 9501 of the Omnibus Budget Reconciliation Act of 1986, of certain bankruptcies as qualifying events, which are not addressed in these proposed regulations). Moreover, plans and employers will be considered to be in compliance with the terms of these proposed regulations if, between [DATE OF PUBLICATION OF NOTICE OF PROPOSED RULEMAKING] and [90 DAYS AFTER DATE OF PUBLICATION OF NOTICE OF PROPOSED RULEMAKING], they operate in good faith compliance with a reasonable interpretation of the statutory requirements and, from [91 DAYS AFTER DATE OF PUBLICATION OF NOTICE OF PROPOSED RULEMAKING] until the effective date of final regulations, they operate in compliance with the terms of these proposed regulations. In addition, the Internal Revenue Service will not consider actions inconsistent with the terms of these proposed regulations necessarily to constitute a lack of good faith compliance with a reasonable interpretation of the statutory requirements; whether there has been good faith compliance with a reasonable interpretation of the statutory requirements will depend on all the facts and circumstances of each case.

SPECIAL ANALYSES

The Commissioner of Internal Revenue has determined that this proposed rule is not a major rule as defined in Executive Order 12291. Therefore, a Regulatory Impact Analysis is not required. Although this document is a notice of proposed rulemaking which solicits public comment, the Internal Revenue Service has concluded that the regulations proposed herein are interpretative and that the notice and public procedure requirements of 5 U.S.C. 553 do not apply. Accordingly, these proposed regulations do not constitute regulations subject to the Regulatory Flexibility Act (5 U.S.C. chapter 6).

COMMENTS AND REQUESTS FOR PUBLIC HEARING

Before adopting these proposed regulations, consideration will be given to any written comments that are submitted (preferably eight copies) to the Commissioner of Internal Revenue. All comments will be available for public inspection and copying. A public hearing will be held upon written request to the Commissioner by any person who has submitted written comments. If a public hearing is held, notice of the time and place will be published in the FEDERAL REGISTER.

DRAFTING INFORMATION

The principal author of these proposed regulations is Mark Schwimmer of the Employee Plans and Exempt Organizations Division of the Office of Chief Counsel, Internal Revenue Service. However, personnel from other offices of the Internal Revenue Service and Treasury Department participated in developing the regulations, both on matters of substance and style.

[¶49,079] Proposed Regulations (LR-122-86), published in the Federal Register on June 16, 1987.

Accounting methods: Cash method: Limitations.—Reg. §§1.448-1T, relating to the limitation on the use of the cash method of accounting, is proposed. Reg. §1.448-2T was adopted on 8/31/2006 by T.D. 9285.

AGENCY: Internal Revenue Service, Treasury.

ACTION: Notice of proposed rulemaking by cross-reference to temporary regulations.

SUMMARY: In the Rules and Regulations portion of this issue of the FEDERAL REGISTER, the Internal Revenue Service is issuing temporary amendments to the income tax regulations relating to the limitation on the use of the cash method of accounting. Changes to the law were made by the Tax Reform Act of 1986. The text of those temporary regulations also serves as the comment document for this proposed rulemaking.

DATES: Written comments and requests for a public hearing must be delivered or mailed by [60 DAYS AFTER PUBLICATION OF THIS PROPOSED RULE IN THE FEDERAL REGISTER].

ADDRESS: Send comments and requests for public hearing to: Commissioner of Internal Revenue, Attention: CC:LR:T (LR-122-86), Washington, D.C. 20224.

FOR FURTHER INFORMATION CONTACT: Ewan D. Purkiss of the Legislation and Regulations Division, Office of Chief Counsel, Internal Revenue Service, 1111 Constitution Avenue, N.W., Washington, D.C. 20224 (Attention: CC:LR:T) (202-566-3238, not a toll-free call).

SUPPLEMENTARY INFORMATION:

BACKGROUND

The temporary regulations (designated by a T following the section citation) in the Rules and Regulations portion of this issue of the FEDERAL REGISTER amend Part 1 of Title 26 of the Code of Federal Regulations. These amendments reflect the provisions of section 448 of the Internal Revenue Code of 1986 as added by section 801 of the Tax Reform Act of 1986 (Pub. L. 99-514, 100 Stat. 2085). For the text of the temporary regulations, see FR Doc. (T.D. 8143) published in the Rules and Regulations portion of this issue of the FEDERAL REGISTER. A general discussion of the temporary regulations is contained in the preamble to the regulations. The final regulations, which this document proposes to base on the temporary regulations, would amend Part 1 of Title 26 of the Code of Federal Regulations.

SPECIAL ANALYSIS

The Commissioner of Internal Revenue has determined that this proposed rule is not a major rule as defined in Executive Order 12291. Accordingly, a Regulatory Impact Analysis is not required. Although this document is a notice of proposed rulemaking that solicits public comments, the Internal Revenue Service has concluded that the proposed regulations are interpretative and that the notice and public procedure requirements of 5 U.S.C. 553 do not apply. Accordingly, a regulatory flexibility analysis is not required under the Regulatory Flexibility Act (5 U.S.C. chapter 6).

COMMENTS AND REQUESTS FOR A PUBLIC HEARING

Before adopting these proposed regulations, consideration will be given to any written comments that are submitted (preferably eight copies) to the Commissioner of Internal Revenue. All comments will be available for public inspection and copying. A public hearing will be held upon written request to the Commissioner by any person who submitted comments. If a public hearing is held, notice of the time and place will be published in the FEDERAL REGISTER.

The collection of information requirements contained in this notice of proposed rulemaking have been submitted to the Office of Management and Budget (OMB) for review under section 3504(h) of the Paperwork Reduction Act. Comments on the requirements should be sent to the Office of Information and Regulatory Affairs of OMB, Attention: Desk Officer for Internal Revenue Service, New Executive Office Building, Washington, D.C. 20503. The Internal Revenue Service requests that persons submitting comments on these requirements to OMB also send copies of those comments to the Service.

DRAFTING INFORMATION

The principal author of these proposed regulations is Ewan D. Purkiss of the Legislation and Regulations Division, Office of Chief Counsel, Internal Revenue Service. However, personnel from other offices of the Internal Revenue Service and Treasury participated in developing the regulations on matters of both substance and style.

[¶49,080] Proposed Regulations (LR-83-86), published in the Federal Register on June 22, 1987.

Low-income housing credit.—Reg. §1.42-1T, relating to the low-income housing credit, is proposed.

AGENCY: Internal Revenue Service, Treasury.

ACTION: Notice of proposed rulemaking by cross reference to temporary regulations.

SUMMARY: In the Rules and Regulations portion of this issue of the FEDERAL REGISTER, the Internal Revenue Service is issuing temporary regulations relating to the low-income housing credit under section 42 of the Internal Revenue Code of 1986, as enacted by the Tax Reform Act of 1986 (Pub. L. 99-514). The text of those temporary regulations also serves as the comment document for this notice of proposed rulemaking.

DATES: Written comments and requests for a public hearing must be delivered or mailed by August 21, 1987. In general, the regulations are proposed to be effective after December 31, 1986, for buildings placed in service after December 31, 1986, in taxable years ending after that date.

ADDRESS: Send comments and requests for a public hearing to: Commissioner of Internal Revenue, Attention: CC:LR:T (LR-83-86), 1111 Constitution Avenue, N.W., Washington, D.C. 20224.

FOR FURTHER INFORMATION CONTACT: Robert Beatson of the Legislation and Regulations Division, Office of Chief Counsel, Internal Revenue Service, 1111 Constitution Avenue N.W., Washington, D.C. 20224 (Attention: CC:LR:T) (202-566-3829, not a toll-free call).

SUPPLEMENTARY INFORMATION:

BACKGROUND

The temporary regulations in the Rules and Regulations portion of this issue of the FEDERAL REGISTER amend 26 CFR Parts 1 and 602. The temporary regulations add new §1.42-1T to Part 1 of Title 26 of the Code of Federal Regulations. The final regulations, which this document proposes to be based on those temporary regulations, would amend 26 CFR Parts 1 and 602 and would add new §1.42-1 to Part 1 of Title 26 of the Code of Federal Regulations. For the text of the temporary regulations, see FR Doc. (T.D. 8144) published in the Rules and Regulations portion of this issue of the FEDERAL REGISTER. The preamble to the temporary regulations explains the additions to the Income Tax Regulations.

The proposed regulations provide needed guidance regarding the provisions of section 42, as enacted by section 252 of the Tax Reform Act of 1986.

NON-APPLICABILITY OF EXECUTIVE ORDER 12291

The Commissioner of Internal Revenue has determined that this proposed rule is not a major rule as defined in Executive Order 12291 and that a regulatory impact analysis therefore is not required.

REGULATORY FLEXIBILITY ACT

Although this document is a notice of proposed rulemaking that solicits public comment, the Internal Revenue Service has concluded that the regulations proposed herein are interpretative and that the notice and public procedure requirements of 5 U.S.C. 553 do not apply. Accordingly, this proposed regulation does not constitute a regulation subject to the Regulatory Flexibility Act (5 U.S.C. chapter 6).

DRAFTING INFORMATION

The principal author of these proposed regulations is Robert Beatson of the Legislation and Regulations Division of the Office of Chief Counsel, Internal Revenue Service. However, personnel from other offices of the Internal Revenue Service and the Treasury Department participated in developing the regulations both on matters of substance and style.

COMMENTS AND REQUESTS FOR A PUBLIC HEARING

Before adoption of these proposed regulations, consideration will be given to any written comments that are submitted (preferably eight copies) to the Commissioner of Internal Revenue. Comments are encouraged both with respect to the matters addressed in these proposed regulations and any other issues arising under section 42 with respect to which guidance is needed. All comments will be available for public inspection and copying. A public hearing will be held upon written request to the Commissioner by any person who has submitted written comments. If a public hearing is held, notice of the time and place will be published in the FEDERAL REGISTER. The collection of information requirements contained herein have been submitted to the Office of Management and

Budget (OMB) for review under section 3504(h) of the Paperwork Reduction Act. Comments on the requirements should be sent to the Office of Information and Regulatory Affairs of OMB, Attention: Desk Officer for Internal Revenue Service, New Executive Office Building, Washington, DC 20503. The Internal Revenue Service requests persons submitting comments to OBM to also send copies of the comments to the Service.

[¶49,081] Proposed Regulations (LR-10-87), published in the Federal Register on July 2, 1987.

Interest paid or payable: Allocation.—Reg. §1.163-8T, relating to the allocation of interest expense among a taxpayer's expenditures, is proposed.

AGENCY: Internal Revenue Service, Treasury.

ACTION: Notice of proposed rulemaking by cross-reference to temporary regulations.

SUMMARY: In the Rules and Regulations portion of this issue of the FEDERAL REGISTER, the Internal Revenue Service is issuing temporary regulations relating to the allocation of interest expense among expenditures. The text of those temporary regulations also serves as the comment document for this proposed rulemaking.

DATE: The amendments to the regulations are proposed to be effective with respect to interest expense paid or accrued in taxable years beginning after December 31, 1986. Written comments and requests for a public hearing must be delivered or mailed by August 31, 1987.

ADDRESS: Send comments and requests for a public hearing to:

Commissioner of Internal Revenue, Attention: CC:LR:T (LR-10-87), Washington, D.C. 20224.

FOR FURTHER INFORMATION CONTACT: Michael J. Grace of the Legislation and Regulations Division, Office of Chief Counsel, Internal Revenue Service, 1111 Constitution Avenue, N.W., Washington, D.C. 20224, Attention: CC:LR:T, (202) 566-3288 (not a toll-free call).

SUPPLEMENTARY INFORMATION:

BACKGROUND

The temporary regulations (designated by a T following the section citation) in the Rules and Regulations portion of this issue of the FEDERAL REGISTER amend the Income Tax Regulations (26 CFR Part 1) to provide rules relating to the allocation of interest expense for purposes of applying the limitations on passive activity losses and credits, investment interest, and personal interest. The temporary regulations reflect the amendment of the Internal Revenue Code of 1986 by sections 501 and 511 of the Act (100 Stat. 2233 and 2244), which added sections 469 (relating to the limitation on passive activity losses and credits) and 163(h) (relating to the disallowance of deductions for personal interest) and amended section 163(d) (relating to the limitation on investment interest). This document proposes to adopt the temporary regulations as final regulations. Accordingly, the text of the temporary regulations serves as the comment document for this notice of proposed rulemaking. In addition, the preamble to the temporary regulations explains the proposed and temporary rules.

For the text of the temporary regulations, see FR Doc. (T.D.) published in the Rules and Regulations portion of this issue of the FEDERAL REGISTER.

SPECIAL ANALYSES

The Commissioner of Internal Revenue has determined that this proposed rule is not a major rule as defined in Executive Order 12291 and that a regulatory impact analysis is not required. Although this document is a notice of proposed rulemaking that solicits public comments, the Internal Revenue Service has concluded that the proposed regulations are interpretative and that the notice and public procedure requirements of 5 U.S.C. 553 do not apply. Accordingly, these proposed regulations are not subject to the Regulatory Flexibility Act (5 U.S.C. chapter 6).

COMMENTS AND REQUESTS FOR A PUBLIC HEARING

Before these proposed regulations are adopted, consideration will be given to any written comments that are submitted (preferably eight copies) to the Commissioner of Internal Revenue. All comments will be available for public inspection and copying. A public hearing will be held upon written request to the Commissioner by any person who submitted comments. If a public hearing is held, notice of the time and place will be published in the FEDERAL REGISTER.

The collection of information requirements contained herein have been submitted to the Office of Management and Budget (OMB) for review under section 3504(h) of the Paperwork Reduction Act. Comments on the requirements should be sent to the Office of Information and Regulatory Affairs of OMB, Attention: Desk Officer for Internal Revenue Service, New Executive Office Building, Washington, D.C. 20503. The Internal Revenue Service requests that persons submitting comments to OMB also send copies of the comments to the Service.

DRAFTING INFORMATION

The principal author of these proposed regulations is Michael J. Grace of the Legislation and Regulations Division, Office of Chief Counsel, Internal Revenue Service. However, personnel from other offices of the Internal Revenue Service and Treasury participated in developing the regulations on matters of both substance and style.

[¶49,083] Proposed Regulations (LR-106-86), published in the Federal Register on August 11, 1987.

Carryforwards: Ownership change: Limitations.—Reg. §1.382-2T, relating to the limitation on net operating loss carryforwards and certain built-in losses following ownership changes, is proposed. Reg. §1.382-1T was redesignated as Reg. §1.382-1 on 10/2/92 by T.D. 8440.

AGENCY: Internal Revenue Service, Treasury.

ACTION: Notice of proposed rulemaking by cross-reference to temporary regulations.

SUMMARY: In the Rules and Regulations portion of this issue of the FEDERAL REGISTER, the Internal Revenue Service is adding temporary regulations pertaining to section 382 of the Internal Revenue Code of 1986 ("Code"), which was amended by section 621 of the Tax Reform Act of 1986. The temporary regulations provide the necessary guidance for determining when there is an ownership change resulting in a limitation on corporate net operating loss carryforwards under section 382. The text of the temporary regulations also serves as the comment document for this notice of proposed rulemaking.

DATES FOR COMMENTS AND REQUESTS FOR A PUBLIC HEARING

Written comments and requests for a public hearing must be delivered or mailed by [60 DAYS AFTER DATE OF PUBLICATION OF THIS DOCUMENT IN THE FEDERAL REGISTER].

ADDRESS: Send comments or requests for a public hearing to: Commissioner of Internal Revenue, Attention: CC:LR:T [LR-106-86], 1111 Constitution Avenue, N.W., Washington, D.C. 20224.

FOR FURTHER INFORMATION CONTACT: Keith E. Stanley of the Legislation and Regulations Division, Office of Chief Counsel, Internal Revenue Service, 1111 Constitution Avenue, N.W., Washington, D.C. 20224 (Attention: CC:LR:T) or telephone (202) 566-3458 (not a toll-free number).

SUPPLEMENTARY INFORMATION:

BACKGROUND

Temporary regulations published in the Rules and Regulations portion of this issue of the FEDERAL REGISTER add temporary regulations §§1.382-1T and 1.382-2T to Part 1 of Title 26 of the Code of Federal Regulations ("CFR"). The final regulations which are proposed to be based on the temporary regulations would be added to Part 1 of Title 26 of the CFR. The final regulations would provide the necessary guidance with respect to the determination of when there is an ownership change that results in a limitation on corporate net operating loss carryforwards under section 382. Section 382 of the Code was amended by section 621 of the Tax Reform Act of 1986 (Pub. L. No. 99-514, 100 Stat. 2085). For the text of the temporary regulations, see T.D. 8149 published in the Rules and Regulations portion of this issue of the FEDERAL REGISTER. The preamble to the temporary regulations explains the added regulations.

REGULATORY FLEXIBILITY ACT AND EXECUTIVE ORDER 12291

Although this document is a notice of proposed rulemaking that solicits public comment, the Internal Revenue Service has concluded that the notice and public procedure requirements of 5 U.S.C. 553 do not apply because the rules provided herein are interpretative. Accordingly, these proposed regulations do not constitute regulations subject to the Regulatory Flexibility Act (5 U.S.C. chapter 6). The Commissioner of Internal Revenue has determined that this proposed rule is not a major rule as defined in Executive Order 12291 and that a Regulatory Impact Analysis therefore is not required.

COMMENTS AND REQUESTS FOR A PUBLIC HEARING

Before adopting these proposed regulations, consideration will be given to any written comments that are submitted (preferably eight copies) to the Commissioner of Internal Revenue. All comments will be available for public inspection and copying. A public hearing will be held upon written request to the Commissioner by any person who has submitted written comments. If a public hearing is held, notice of time and place will be published in the FEDERAL REGISTER. The collection of information requirements contained herein have been submitted to the Office of Management and Budget (OMB) for review under section 3504(h) of the Paperwork Reduction Act. Comments on the requirements should be sent to the Office of Information and Regulatory Affairs of OMB, Attention: Desk Officer for Internal Revenue Service, New Executive Office Building, Washington, D.C. 20503. The Internal Revenue Service requests persons submitting comments to OMB also send copies of the comments to the Service.

DRAFTING INFORMATION

The principal author of these regulations is Keith E. Stanley of the Legislation and Regulations Division of the Office of Chief Counsel, Internal Revenue Service. However, personnel from other offices of the Internal Revenue Service and Treasury Department participated in developing the regulations, both in matters of substance and style.

[¶49,084] Proposed Regulations (EE-111-82), published in the Federal Register on August 27, 1987.

Employee trusts: Affiliated service groups, employee leasing and other arrangements.—Reg. §1.414(o)-1, relating to affiliated service groups, employee leasing and other arrangements, is proposed. Reg. §§1.414(m)-5, 1.414(m)-6, 1.414(n)—1.414(n)-4 and portions of Reg. §1.414(o)-1 were withdrawn 4/27/93 by CO-53-92.

AGENCY: Internal Revenue Service, Treasury.
ACTION: Notice of proposed rulemaking.
SUMMARY: This document provides proposed regulations prescribing rules for determining: (1) when a management organization and the organization for which the management organization performs management services constitute an affiliated service group; (2) when leased employees are treated as employees of the lessee organization for purposes of certain employee benefit provisions; and (3) when arrangements involving separate organizations, employee leasing, or other arrangements will be ignored in order to prevent the avoidance of certain employee benefit requirements.
Changes to the applicable tax law were made by the Tax Equity and Fiscal Responsibility Act of 1982, the Tax Reform Act of 1984, and the Tax Reform Act of 1986. The regulations provide the public with guidance needed to comply with those Acts and would affect employers that maintain, and participants in, qualified plans.
DATES: Written comments and requests for a public hearing must be delivered or mailed by October 26, 1987. The regulations provided by this document are proposed to be generally effective for tax years beginning after December 31, 1983.
ADDRESS: Send comments and requests for a public hearing to: Commissioner of Internal Revenue, Attention: CC:LR:T (EE-111-82), Washington, D.C. 20224.
FOR FURTHER INFORMATION CONTACT: Michael Garvey of the Employee Plans and Exempt Organizations Division, Office of Chief Counsel, Internal Revenue Service, 1111 Constitution Avenue, N.W., Washington, D.C. 20224, Attention: CC:LR:T, (202) 566-3903, not a toll-free call.
SUPPLEMENTARY INFORMATION:

BACKGROUND

This document contains proposed amendments to the Income Tax Regulations (26 CFR Part 1) under sections 414(m)(5), 414(n), and 414(o) of the Internal Revenue Code. These amendments are proposed to conform the regulations to sections 246 and 248 of the Tax Equity and Fiscal Responsibility Act of 1982 (26 USC §§414(m)(5), 414(n)), section 526 of the Tax Reform Act of 1984 (26 USC §§414(n)(2), 414 (o)), and section 1146 of the Tax Reform Act of 1986 (26 USC §§414(n), 414(o)). Other sections of the Tax Reform Act of 1986 that relate to section 414(n) are not reflected in this document.

ORGANIZATIONS PERFORMING MANAGEMENT FUNCTIONS

Section 414(m)(5) of the Code expands the definition of an affiliated service group that is to be treated as a single employer under section 414(m) for purposes of certain employee benefit requirements. Pursuant to section 414(m)(5), an affiliated service group includes a management oganization and a recipient organization (i.e., the organization (and related organizations) for which the management organization performs management functions). An organization is a management organization if the principal business of the organization is the performing of, on a regular and continuing basis, management functions for a recipient organization.

EMPLOYEE LEASING

Section 414(n) provides that, under certain circumstances, an individual ("leased employee") who performs services for a person ("recipient") through another person ("leasing organization") shall be treated as the employee of the recipient for purposes of certain employee benefit requirements. If the services being provided by an individual to a recipient are pursuant to an agreement between the recipient and the leasing organization, and the individual performs such services for the recipient on a substantially full-time basis for a period of at least one year, and the services are of a type historically performed by employees, then the individual is a leased employee and, therefore, shall be treated as an employee of the recipient.

Section 414(n)(5) provides, however, that if the leasing organization maintains a safe-harbor plan with respect to a leased employee, such individual will generally not be treated as an employee of the recipient. Section 414(n)(5), as originally enacted, required that a safe-harbor plan must be a qualified money purchase pension plan with provision for nonintegrated employer contributions of at least $7^1/_2$ percent, immediate participation, and full and immediate vesting.

The Tax Reform Act of 1986 amended several provisions relating to sections 414(n) and 414(o). These amendments include the following:

(1) The definition of a safe-harbor plan under section 414(n)(5) has been amended to require a contribution rate of 10 percent and to require that the plan must cover all employees of the leasing organization (other than employees who perform substantially all of their services for the leasing organization (and not for recipients) and employees whose compensation from the leasing organization is less than $1,000 during the plan year and during each of the 3 prior plan years).

(2) Under section 414(n)(5), a leased employee will be treated as an employee of the recipient, regardless of the existence of a safe-harbor plan, if more than 20 percent of the recipient's nonhighly compensated workforce are leased employees (as specially defined for this purpose).

(3) A recordkeeping exception from the section 414(n) employee leasing provisions is provided under section 414(o) in the case of an employer that has no section 416(g) top-heavy plans and that uses the services of nonemployees only for an insignificant percentage of the employer's total workload.

(4) The scope of the section 414(n) employee leasing provisions has been expanded to include a number of non-pension employee benefit requirements (listed under section 414(n)(3)), including group-term life insurance, accident and health plans, qualified group legal services, cafeteria plans,

etc. In addition, the employee leasing provisions will apply to these non-pension employee benefit requirements regardless of the existence of a safe-harbor plan.

Except for the amendments relating to the non-pension employee benefit requirements, the proposed regulations reflect the Tax Reform Act of 1986 amendments described above. Guidance relating to the non-pension employee benefit requirements, and other relevant amendments made by the Tax Reform Act of 1986, will be forthcoming.

AVOIDANCE OF CERTAIN EMPLOYEE BENEFITS REQUIREMENTS

Section 414(o) provides that the Secretary shall prescribe such regulations as may be necessary to prevent the avoidance of any employee benefit requirement listed in sections 414(m)(4) or 414(n)(3) through the use of separate organizations, employee leasing, or other arrangements. Specifically, the Secretary has the authority to provide rules in addition to the rules contained in sections 414(m) and 414(n).

Pursuant to section 414(o), the proposed regulations provide rules relating to several arrangements that may result in the avoidance of the listed employee benefit requirements. These arrangements include the leasing of certain owners, the leasing of certain managers, the creation of successive organizations in time, expense sharing arrangements, plans maintained by certain corporate directors, and plans covering certain five-percent owners.

EFFECTIVE DATES

The amendments made to section 414 by the Tax Equity and Fiscal Responsibility Act of 1982 are effective for tax years of a recipient or of a member of an affiliated service group that begin after December 31, 1983.

The amendments made to section 414 by the Tax Reform Act of 1984 are effective as of July 18, 1984. The regulations promulgated under section 414(o), however, are variously effective for (1) plan years beginning more than six months after this document is published in the FEDERAL REGISTER, (2) plan years beginning more than sixty days after this document is published in the FEDERAL REGISTER as a Treasury decision, and (3) plan years beginning during or after the first tax year of a recipient beginning after December 31, 1983. (To the extent that the regulations under section 414(o) aggregate plans for purposes of section 415 that were not previously aggregated, the rules of § 1.415-10 apply.)

The amendments made to section 414 by the Tax Reform Act of 1986 are generally effective with respect to services performed after December 31, 1986. The recordkeeping exception from section 414(n), provided under section 414(o), and certain clarifying amendments under section 414(n) are effective as if originally enacted as part of the section 414 amendments made by the Tax Equity and Fiscal Responsibility Act of 1982. The section 414(n)(3) amendments relating to the non-pension employee benefit requirements are generally effective when section 89 applies to such non-pension employee benefits (see section 1151(k) of the Tax Reform Act of 1986).

SPECIAL ANALYSIS

The Commissioner of Internal Revenue has determined this rule is not a major rule as defined in Executive Order 12291. Therefore, a Regulatory Impact Analysis is not required. Although this document is a notice of proposed rulemaking that solicits public comment, the Internal Revenue Service has concluded that the regulations proposed are interpretative and that the notice and public procedure requirements of 5 USC 553(b) do not apply. Accordingly, these proposed regulations do not constitute regulations subject to the Regulatory Flexibility Act (5 USC chapter 6).

COMMENTS AND REQUESTS FOR A PUBLIC HEARING

Before adopting these proposed regulations, consideration will be given to any written comments that are submitted (preferably eight copies) to the Commissioner of Internal Revenue. All comments will be available for public inspection and copying. A public hearing will be held upon written request to the Commissioner by any person who has submitted written comments. If a public hearing is held, notice of the time and place will be published in the FEDERAL REGISTER.

DRAFTING INFORMATION

The principal author of these proposed regulations is Philip R. Bosco of the Employee Plans and Exempt Organizations Division of the Office of Chief Counsel, Internal Revenue Service. However, personnel from other offices of the Internal Revenue Service and Treasury participated in developing the regulations, both on matters of substance and style.

[¶ 49,086] Proposed Regulations (LR-45-870), published in the Federal Register on December 23, 1987.

Personal service corporations: Partnerships: S corporations: Taxable years.—Reg. § 1.702-3T is proposed. Reg. § 18.1366-5 was removed by T.D. 8600 on July 20, 1995. Reg. §§ 1.441-1T, 1.441-2T and 1.441-4T were removed by T.D. 8996 on May 16, 2002.

AGENCY: Internal Revenue Service, Treasury.

ACTION: Notice of proposed rulemaking by cross-reference to temporary regulations.

SUMMARY: In the Rules and Regulations portion of this issue of the *Federal Register*, the Internal Revenue Service is issuing temporary regulations relating to taxable years of personal service corporations, partnerships and S corporations (and owners of those entities). Changes to the applicable law were made by the Tax Reform Act of 1986. The text of those temporary regulations also serves as the comment document for this proposed rulemaking.

DATES: Written comments and requests for a public hearing must be mailed or delivered by February 22, 1988. The amendments are proposed to be effective for taxable years beginning after December 31, 1986.

ADDRESS: Send comments and requests for public hearing to: Commissioner of Internal Revenue, Attention: CC:LR:T (LR-45-87) Washington, D.C. 20224.

FOR FURTHER INFORMATION CONTACT: Arthur E. Davis III of the Legislation and Regulations Division, Office of Chief Counsel, Internal Revenue Service, 1111 Constitution Avenue, N.W., Washington, D.C. 20224 (Attention: CC:LR:T), (202) 566-3238, not a toll-free call.

SUPPLEMENTARY INFORMATION:

BACKGROUND

The temporary regulations (designated by a "T" following the section citation) in the Rules and Regulations portion of this issue of the Federal Register amend Part 1 of Title 26 of the Code of Federal Regulations. These amendments are proposed to conform the regulations to the requirements of section 806 of the Tax Reform Act of 1986 (Pub. L. 99-514), 100 Stat. 2362. For the text of the temporary regulations, see FR Doc. (T.D. 8167) published in the Rules and Regulations portion of this issue of the *Federal Register*. The preamble to the temporary regulations provides a discussion of the rules. The final regulations, which this document proposes to base on those temporary regulations, would amend Part 1 of Title 26 of the Code of Federal Regulations.

SPECIAL ANALYSES

The Commissioner of Internal Revenue has determined that this proposed rule is not a major rule as defined in Executive Order 12291. Accordingly, a Regulatory Impact Analysis is not required. Although this document is a notice of proposed rulemaking that solicits public comments, the Internal Revenue Service has concluded that the regulations proposed herein are interpretative and that the notice and public procedure requirements of 5 U.S.C. 553 do not apply. Accordingly, a regulatory flexibility analysis is not required under the Regulatory Flexibility Act (5 U.S.C. chapter 6).

COMMENTS AND REQUESTS FOR A PUBLIC HEARING

Before adopting these proposed regulations, consideration will be given to any written comments that are submitted (preferably eight copies) to the Commissioner of Internal Revenue. All comments will be available for public inspection and copying. A public hearing will be held upon written request to the Commissioner by any person who has submitted comments. If a public hearing is held, notice of the time and place will be published in the *Federal Register*.

DRAFTING INFORMATION

The principal author of these regulations is Arthur E. Davis III of the Legislation and Regulations Division, Office of Chief Counsel, Internal Revenue Service. However, personnel from other offices of the Internal Revenue Service and Treasury Department participated in developing the regulations on matters of both substance and style.

[¶ 49,087] Proposed Regulations (LR-137-86), published in the Federal Register on December 22, 1987.

Personal interest: Paid or accrued: Qualified residence interest.—Reg. §§ 1.163-9T and 1.163-10T, relating to the treatment of personal interest and the treatment and determination of qualified residence interest, are proposed.

AGENCY: Internal Revenue Service, Treasury.

ACTION: Notice of proposed rulemaking by cross-reference to temporary regulations.

SUMMARY: In the Rules and Regulations portion of this issue of the *Federal Register*, the Internal Revenue Service is issuing temporary amendments to the income tax regulations relating to the treatment of personal interest and the treatment and determination of qualified residence interest. Changes to the law were made by the Tax Reform Act of 1986. The text of those temporary regulations also serves as the comment document for this proposed rulemaking.

DATES: The regulations contained in this document are proposed to be effective for taxable years beginning after December 31, 1986. Written comments and requests for a public hearing must be delivered or mailed by [60 DAYS AFTER PUBLICATION OF THIS PROPOSED RULE IN THE FEDERAL REGISTER].

ADDRESS: Send comments and requests for public hearing to: Commissioner of Internal Revenue, Attention: CC:LR:T (LR-137-86), Washington, D.C. 20224.

FOR FURTHER INFORMATION CONTACT: Sharon L. Hall of the Legislation and Regulations Division, Office of Chief Counsel, Internal Revenue Service, 111 Constitution Avenue, N.W., Washington, D.C. 20224 (Attention: CC:LR:T) (202-566-3288, not a toll-free call).

SUPPLEMENTARY INFORMATION:

BACKGROUND

The temporary regulations (designated by a T following the section citation) in the Rules and Regulations portion of this issue of the Federal Register amend Part 1 of Title 26 of the Code of Federal Regulations. These amendments reflect the provisions of section 163(h) of the Internal Revenue Code of 1986 as added by section 511(b) of the Tax Reform Act of 1986 (Pub. L. 99-514, 100 Stat. 2246). For the text of the temporary regulations, see FR Doc. (T.D. 8168) published in the Rules and Regulations portion of this issue of the *Federal Register*. A general discussion of the temporary regulations is contained in the preamble to the regulations. The final regulations, which this document proposes to base on the temporary regulations, would amend Part 1 of Title 26 of the Code of Federal Regulations.

SPECIAL ANALYSES

The Commissioner of Internal Revenue has determined that this proposed rule is not a major rule as defined in Executive Order 12291. Accordingly, a Regulatory Impact Analysis is not required. Although this document is a notice of proposed rulemaking that solicits public comments, the Internal Revenue Service has concluded that the proposed regulations are interpretative and that the notice and public procedure requirements of 5 U.S.C. 553 do not apply. Accordingly, a regulatory flexibility analysis is not required under the Regulatory Flexibility Act (5 U.S.C. chapter 6).

The collection of information requirements contained in this notice of proposed rulemaking have been submitted to the Office of Management and Budget (OMB) for review under section 3504(h) of the Paperwork Reduction Act. Comments on the requirements should be sent to the Office of Information and Regulatory Affairs of OMB, Attention: Desk Officer for Internal Revenue Service, New Executive Office Building, Washington, D.C. 20503. The Internal Revenue Service requests that persons submitting comments on these requirements to OMB also send copies of those comments to the Service.

COMMENTS AND REQUESTS FOR A PUBLIC HEARING

Before adopting these proposed regulations, consideration will be given to any written comments that are submitted (preferably eight copies) to the Commissioner of Internal Revenue. All comments will be available for public inspection and copying. A public hearing will be held upon written request to the Commissioner by any person who submitted comments. If a public hearing is held, notice of the time and place will be published in the *Federal Register.*

DRAFTING INFORMATION

The principal author of these proposed regulations is Sharon L. Hall of the Legislation and Regulations Division, Office of Chief Counsel, Internal Revenue Service. However, personnel from other offices of the Internal Revenue Service and Treasury participated in developing the regulations on matters of both substance and style.

[¶ 49,088] Proposed regulations (EE-167-86), published in the Federal Register on January 6, 1988.

Qualified employee plans: Minimum vesting standards.—Reg. §§ 1.410(a)-3, 1.410(a)-8, 1.410(a)-9, 1.411(a)-3, 1.411(a)-4 and 1.411(a)-8, relating to minimum vesting standards for qualified employee plans, are proposed.

AGENCY: Internal Revenue Service, Treasury.

ACTION: Notice of proposed rulemaking by cross-reference to temporary regulations.

SUMMARY: This document provides proposed regulations relating to the minimum vesting standards for qualified employee plans. Changes to the applicable laws were made by the Tax Reform Act of 1986. These proposed regulations amend the current regulations to reflect the changes. In the Rules and Regulations portion of this issue of the FEDERAL REGISTER, the Internal Revenue Service is issuing temporary regulations relating to the minimum vesting standards. The text of these temporary regulations also serves as the comment document for this notice of proposed rulemaking.

DATES: Written comments and requests for a public hearing must be delivered or mailed by March 7, 1988. The amendments are proposed to be generally effective for plan years beginning after December 31, 1988.

ADDRESS: Send comments and requests for a public hearing to: Commissioner of Internal Revenue, Attention: CC:LR:T (EE-167-86), 1111 Constitution Avenue, N.W., Washington, D.C. 20224.

FOR FURTHER INFORMATION CONTACT: V. Moore of the Employee Plans and Exempt Organizations Division, Office of Chief Counsel, Internal Revenue Service, 1111 Constitution Avenue, N.W., Washington, D.C. 20224 (Attention: CC:LR:T) (202-566-3938, not a toll-free call).

SUPPLEMENTARY INFORMATION:

BACKGROUND

The temporary regulations in the Rules and Regulations portion of this issue of the FEDERAL REGISTER amend Part 1 of the Code of Federal Regulations. New § 1.410(a)-3T, § 1.410(a)-8T, § 1.410(a)-9T, § 1.411(a)-3T, § 1.411(a)-4T, and § 1.411(a)-8T are added to Part 1 of Title 26 of the Code of Federal Regulations. When these temporary regulations are promulgated as final regulations, § 1.410(a)-3, § 1.410(a)-5, § 1.410(a)-7, § 1.411(a)-3, § 1.411(a)-4, and § 1.411(a)-8 will be revised to reflect the new provisions. For the text of the temporary regulations, see T.D. 8170 published in the Rules and Regulations portion of this issue of the FEDERAL REGISTER. The preamble to the temporary regulations explains the amendments to the Income Tax Regulations.

REGULATORY FLEXIBILITY ACT AND EXECUTIVE ORDER 12291

Although this document is a notice of proposed rulemaking which solicits public comment, the Internal Revenue Service has concluded that the regulations proposed herein are interpretative and that the notice and public procedure requirements of 5 U.S.C. 553 do not apply. Accordingly, these proposed regulations do not constitute regulations subject to the Regulatory Flexibility Act (5 U.S.C. chapter 6).

The Commissioner of Internal Revenue has determined that this proposed rule is not a major rule as defined in Executive Order 12291 and that a regulatory impact analysis therefore is not required.

COMMENTS AND REQUESTS FOR A PUBLIC HEARING

Before adopting these proposed regulations, consideration will be given to any written comments that are submitted (preferably eight copies) to the Commissioner of Internal Revenue. All comments will be available for public inspection and copying. A public hearing will be held upon written request to the Commissioner by any person who has submitted written comments. If a public hearing is held, notice of the time and place will be published in the FEDERAL REGISTER.

DRAFTING INFORMATION

The principal author of these proposed regulations is V. Moore of the Employee Plans and Exempt Organizations Division of the Office of Chief Counsel. Other offices of the Internal Revenue Service and Treasury Department participated in developing the regulations, both on matters of substance and style.

[¶ 49,089] Proposed regulations (EE-129-86), published in the Federal Register on February 19, 1988.

Employee benefit plans: Highly compensated employee: Compensation: Definition.—Reg. § 1.414(q)-1T, relating to the scope and meaning of the terms "highly compensated employee" and "compensation," are proposed.

AGENCY: Internal Revenue Service, Treasury.

ACTION: Notice of proposed rulemaking by cross-reference to temporary regulations.

SUMMARY: In the Rules and Regulations portion of this issue of the Federal Register, the Internal Revenue Service is issuing temporary regulations relating to the scope and meaning of the terms "highly compensated employee" in section 414(q) and "compensation" in section 414(s) of the Internal Revenue Code of 1986. They reflect changes made by the Tax Reform Act of 1986 (TRA '86). The text of those temporary regulations also serves as the text for this Notice of Proposed Rulemaking. These regulations will provide the public with guidance necessary to comply with the law and would affect sponsors of, and participants in, pension, profit-sharing and stock bonus plans, and certain other employee benefit plans.

DATES: Written comments and requests for a public hearing must be delivered or mailed April 19, 1988. In general, these regulations apply to years beginning on or after January 1, 1987, except as otherwise specified in TRA '86.

ADDRESS: Send comments and requests for a public hearing to: Commissioner of Internal Revenue, Attention: CC:LR:T (EE-129-86) Washington, D.C. 20224.

FOR FURTHER INFORMATION CONTACT: Nancy J. Marks of the Employee Plans and Exempt Organizations Division, Office of the Chief Counsel, Internal Revenue Service, 1111 Constitution Avenue, N.W., Washington, D.C. 20224 (Attention: CC:LR:T). (202-566-3938) (not a toll-free number).

SUPPLEMENTARY INFORMATION:

BACKGROUND

The temporary regulations in the Rules and Regulations portion of this issue of the Federal Register amend 26 CFR by adding a new section 1.414(q)-1T under Part 1 to provide guidance with respect to the definitions of highly compensated employee and compensation within the meaning of Code section 414(q) and (s). The regulations are proposed to be issued under the authority contained in sections 414(s) and 7805 of the Code (100 Stat. 2453, 68A Stat. 917; 26 U.S.C. 414(s), 7805). For the text of the temporary regulations, see F.R. Doc. (T.D.) published in the Rules and Regulations portion of this issue of the Federal Register.

SPECIAL ANALYSES

The Commissioner of Internal Revenue has determined that this proposed rule is not a major rule as defined in Executive Order 12291 and that a regulatory impact analysis is not required.

Although this document is a notice of proposed rulemaking which solicits public comment, the Internal Revenue Service has concluded that the regulations proposed herein are interpretative and that the notice and public procedure requirements of 5 U.S.C. 553 do not apply. Accordingly, these proposed regulations do not constitute regulations subject to the Regulatory Flexibility Act (5 U.S.C. chapter 6).

COMMENTS AND REQUESTS FOR PUBLIC HEARING

Before adopting these proposed regulations, consideration will be given to any written comments that are submitted (preferably eight copies) to the Commissioner of Internal Revenue. All comments will be available for public inspection and copying. A public hearing will be held upon written request to the Commissioner by any person who has submitted written comments. If a public hearing is held, notice of the time and place will be published in the FEDERAL REGISTER.

DRAFTING INFORMATION

The principal author of these proposed regulations is Nancy J. Marks of the Employee Plans and Exempt Organizations Division of the Office of Chief Counsel, Internal Revenue Service. However, personnel from other offices of the Internal Revenue Service and Treasury Department participated in developing the regulations, both on matters of substance and style.

[¶49,090] Proposed Regulations (LR-14-88), published in the Federal Register on February 24, 1988.

Passive activity losses and credits: Limitations.—Reg. §§1.469-1T, 1.469-2T, 1.469-3T, and 1.469-5T, relating to the limitations on passive activity losses and passive activity credits, are proposed. Reg. §1.469-11T was adopted 5/11/92 by T.D. 8417.

AGENCY: Internal Revenue Service, Treasury.

ACTION: Notice of proposed rulemaking by cross-reference to temporary regulations.

SUMMARY: In the Rules and Regulations portion of this issue of the Federal Register, the Internal Revenue Service is issuing temporary regulations relating to the limitations on passive activity losses and passive activity credits. Changes to the applicable tax law were made by the Tax Reform Act of 1986. The text of those temporary regulations also serves as the comment document for this notice of proposed rulemaking.

DATE: Except as otherwise provided in §1.469-11T, the amendments to the regulations are proposed to be effective for taxable years beginning after December 31, 1986. Written comments and requests for a public hearing must be delivered or mailed by [60 DAYS AFTER PUBLICATION OF THIS PROPOSED RULE IN THE FEDERAL REGISTER].

ADDRESS: Send comments and requests for a public hearing to: Commissioner of Internal Revenue, Attention: CC:LR:T (LR-14-88), Washington, D.C. 20224.

FOR FURTHER INFORMATION CONTACT: Michael J. Grace of the Legislation and Regulations Division, Office of Chief Counsel, Internal Revenue Service, 1111 Constitution Avenue, N.W., Washington, D.C. 20224, Attention: CC:LR:T, (202) 566-3288 (not a toll-free call).

SUPPLEMENTARY INFORMATION:

BACKGROUND

The temporary regulations (designated by a T following the section citations) in the Rules and Regulations portion of this issue of the Federal Register amend the Income Tax Regulations (26 CFR Part 1) to provide rules relating to the limitations on passive activity losses and passive activity credits. The temporary regulations reflect the amendment of the Internal Revenue Code of 1986 by sections 501 and 502 of the Tax Reform Act of 1986 (Pub. L. 99-514, 100 Stat. 2233 and 2241), which added section 469 (relating to the limitations on passive activity losses and passive activity credits). This document proposes to adopt the temporary regulations as final regulations. Accordingly, the text of the temporary regulations serves as the comment document for this notice of proposed rulemaking. In addition, the preamble to the temporary regulations explains the proposed and temporary rules.

For the text of the temporary regulations, see FR Doc. (T.D. 8175) published in the Rules and Regulations portion of this issue of the Federal Register.

SPECIAL ANALYSES

The Commissioner of Internal Revenue has determined that this proposed rule is not a major rule as defined in Executive Order 12291 and that a regulatory impact analysis is not required. Although this document is a notice of proposed rulemaking that solicits public comments, the Internal Revenue Service has concluded that the proposed regulations are interpretative and that the notice and public procedure requirements of 5 U.S.C. 553 do not apply. Accordingly, these proposed regulations are not subject to the Regulatory Flexibility Act (5 U.S.C. chapter 6).

COMMENTS AND REQUESTS FOR A PUBLIC HEARING

Before these proposed regulations are adopted, consideration will be given to any written comments that are submitted (preferably eight copies) to the Commissioner of Internal Revenue. All comments will be available for public inspection and copying. A public hearing will be held upon written request to the Commissioner by any person who submitted comments. If a public hearing is held, notice of the time and place will be published in the Federal Register.

DRAFTING INFORMATION

The principal author of these proposed regulations is Michael J. Grace of the Legislation and Regulations Division, Office of Chief Counsel, Internal Revenue Service. However, personnel from other offices of the Internal Revenue Service and Treasury Department participated in developing the regulations on matters of both substance and style.

[¶49,091] Proposed Regulations (INTL-941-86), published in the Federal Register on March 2, 1988.

Passive foreign investment companies: Elections.—Reg. §§1.1291-0T, 1.1294-1T and 1.1297-3T, relating to requirements for making certain elections by passive foreign investment companies and their shareholders that are United States persons, are proposed. Reg. §1.1295-1T was removed 3/31/92 by T.D. 8404. Reg. §1.1291-10 was adopted 12/26/96 by T.D. 8701.

AGENCY: Internal Revenue Service, Treasury.

ACTION: Notice of proposed rulemaking by cross-reference to temporary regulations.

SUMMARY: In the Rules and Regulations portion of this issue of the FEDERAL REGISTER, the Internal Revenue Service is issuing temporary income tax regulations relating to elections by passive foreign investment companies and their shareholders who are United States persons. The text of the temporary regulations also serves as the comment document for this notice of proposed rulemaking.

DATES: The regulations are proposed to be effective for taxable years beginning after December 31, 1986. Written comments and requests for a public hearing must be delivered or mailed by May 5, 1988.
ADDRESS: Send comments and requests for a public hearing to Commissioner of Internal Revenue, Attention: CC:LR:T (CC:INTL-941-86), Washington, DC 20224.
FOR FURTHER INFORMATION CONTACT: Gayle E. Novig of the Office of the Associate Chief Counsel (International), within the Office of Chief Counsel, Internal Revenue Service, 1111 Constitution Avenue N.W., Washington, DC 20224 (Attention: CC:LR:T) (202-634-5423, not a toll free number).
SUPPLEMENTARY INFORMATION:

BACKGROUND

This document provides proposed income tax regulations (26 CFR Part 1) under sections 1291(d)(2), 1294, 1295, and 1297(b)(1) of the Internal Revenue Code of 1986. These provisions were added to the Internal Revenue Code by section 1235 of the Tax Reform Act of 1986 (Pub. L. 99-514). The regulations will be effective for taxable years beginning after 1986. For the text of the temporary regulations, see T.D. 8178 published in the Rules and Regulations portion of this FEDERAL REGISTER. The preamble to the temporary regulations provides a discussion of the rules.

SPECIAL ANALYSES

It has been determined that this proposed rule is not a major rule as defined in Executive Order 12291. Therefore, a Regulatory Impact Analysis is not required and has not been prepared. Although this document is a notice of proposed rulemaking that solicits public comment, it has been concluded that the notice and public procedure requirements of 5 U.S.C. 553 do not apply. Accordingly, these proposed regulations do not constitute regulations subject to the Regulatory Flexibility Act (5 U.S.C. chapter 6).

COMMENTS AND REQUESTS FOR A PUBLIC HEARING

Before these temporary and proposed regulations are adopted as final regulations, consideration will be given to any written comments that are submitted (preferably seven copies) to the Commissioner of Internal Revenue. All comments will be available for public inspection and copying. A public hearing will be held upon written request to the Commissioner by any person who has submitted written comments. If a public hearing is held, notice of the time and place will be published in the FEDERAL REGISTER. The collection of information requirements contained herein have been submitted to the Office of Management and Budget (OMB) for review under section 3504(h) of the Paperwork Reduction Act. Comments on the requirements should be sent to the Office of Information and Regulatory Affairs of OMB,

Attention: Desk Officer for Internal Revenue Service, New Executive Office Building, Washington, DC 20503. The Internal Revenue Service requests persons submitting comments to OMB to also send copies of the comments to the Service.

DRAFTING INFORMATION

The principal author of these temporary regulations is Gayle E. Novig of the Office of the Associate Chief Counsel (International), within the Office of Chief Counsel, Internal Revenue Service. However, personnel from other offices of the Internal Revenue Service and Treasury Department participated in developing the regulations, on matters of both substance and style.

[¶ 49,092] Proposed Regulations (LR-97-86), published in the Federal Register on March 28, 1988.

Itemized deductions: Two-percent floor.—Reg. §§ 1.62-1T, 1.67-1T and 1.67-2T, relating to the two-percent floor on miscellaneous itemized deductions, are proposed.
AGENCY: Internal Revenue Service, Treasury.
ACTION: Notice of proposed rulemaking by cross-reference to temporary regulations.
SUMMARY: In the Rules and Regulations portion of this issue of the FEDERAL REGISTER, the Internal Revenue Service is issuing temporary income tax regulations relating to the 2-percent floor on miscellaneous itemized deductions. The text of the temporary regulations also serves as the comment document for this notice of proposed rulemaking.
DATES:

PROPOSED EFFECTIVE DATE

The regulations are proposed to be effective for taxable years beginning after December 31, 1986.

DATES FOR COMMENTS AND REQUESTS FOR A PUBLIC HEARING

Written comments and requests for a public hearing must be delivered or mailed by May 27, 1988.

ADDRESS: Send comments and requests for a public hearing to: Commissioner of Internal Revenue, Attention: CC:LR:T (LR-97-86) Washington, D.C. 20224.

FOR FURTHER INFORMATION CONTACT: Beverly A. Baughman of the Legislation and Regulations Division, Office of Chief Counsel, Internal Revenue Service, 1111 Constitution Ave., N.W., Washington, D.C. 20224 (Attention: CC:LR:T) (202-566-3297, not a toll-free call).
SUPPLEMENTARY INFORMATION:

BACKGROUND

The temporary regulations in the Rules and Regulations portion of this issue of the FEDERAL REGISTER amend the Income Tax Regulations (26 CFR Part 1) to provide rules under section 67.

For the text of the temporary regulations, see T.D. 8189, published in the Rules and Regulations portion of this issue of the FEDERAL REGISTER. The preamble to the temporary regulations explains the addition to the regulations.

SPECIAL ANALYSES

The Commissioner of Internal Revenue has determined that this proposed rule is not a major rule as defined in Executive Order 12291 and that a Regulatory Impact Analysis is therefore not required. Although this document is a notice of proposed rulemaking that solicits public comment, the Internal Revenue Service has concluded that the regulations proposed herein are interpretative and that the notice and public procedure requirements of 5 U.S.C. 553 do not apply. Accordingly, these proposed regulations do not constitute regulations subject to the Regulatory Flexibility Act (5 U.S.C. chapter 6).

COMMENTS AND REQUESTS FOR A PUBLIC HEARING

Before adopting these proposed regulations, consideration will be given to any written comments that are submitted (preferably seven copies) to the Commissioner of Internal Revenue. All comments will be available for public inspection and copying. A public hearing will be held upon written request to the Commissioner by any person who has submitted written comments. If public hearing is held, notice of time and place will be published in the FEDERAL REGISTER. The collection of information requirements contained herein have been submitted for OMB review under the Paperwork Reduction Act, and comments on them should be sent to the Office of Information and Regulatory Affairs of OMB, ATTN: Desk Office for Internal Revenue Service, New Executive Office Bldg., Washington, D.C. 20503. The Internal Revenue Service requests persons submitting comments to OMB to also send copies of the comments to the Service.

DRAFTING INFORMATION

The principal author of these proposed regulations is Beverly A. Baughman of the Legislation and Regulations Divisions of the Office of Chief Counsel, Internal Revenue Service. However, personnel from other offices of the Internal Revenue Service and Treasury Department participated in developing the regulations, both on matters of substance and style.

[¶49,093] Proposed Regulations and Amendments of Regulations (EE-184-86), published in the Federal Register on April 11, 1988.

Pension plans: Accruals: Retirement age.—Reg. §§1.410(a)-4A and 1.411(b)-2 and amendments of Reg. §§1.411(a)-1, 1.411(a)-7 and 1.411(c)-1, relating to the requirement for continued accruals beyond normal retirement age under employee pension plans, are proposed.

AGENCY: Internal Revenue Service, Treasury.

ACTION: Notice of proposed rulemaking.

SUMMARY: This document contains proposed regulations relating to the requirement for continued accruals beyond normal retirement age under employee pension benefit plans. Changes to the applicable tax law were made by the Omnibus Budget Reconciliation Act of 1986. These regulations will provide the public with guidance needed to comply with the minimum participation and vesting standards and affect employers maintaining employee retirement plans.

DATES: Written comments and requests for a public hearing must be delivered or mailed by [60 DAYS AFTER PUBLICATION OF NOTICE OF PROPOSED RULEMAKING]. These amendments generally apply to plan years beginning after December 31, 1987, except as otherwise specified in the Omnibus Budget Reconciliation Act of 1986.

ADDRESS: Send comments and requests for a public hearing to: Commissioner of Internal Revenue, Attention: CC:LR:T (EE-184-86) Washington, D.C. 20224.

FOR FURTHER INFORMATION CONTACT: Michael C. Garvey of the Employee Benefits and Exempt Organizations Division, Office of Chief Counsel, Internal Revenue Service, 1111 Constitution Avenue, N.W., Washington, D.C. 20224 (Attention: CC:LR:T) (202-566-6271) (not a toll-free number).

SUPPLEMENTARY INFORMATION:

BACKGROUND

This document contains proposed amendments to the Income Tax Regulations (26 CFR Part 1) under sections 410 and 411 of the Internal Revenue Code of 1986. These amendments are proposed to conform the regulations to sections 9201 through 9204, Subtitle C (Older Americans Pension Benefits) of Title IX of the Omnibus Budget Reconciliation Act of 1986 (Pub. L. 99-509) (OBRA 1986) (100 Stat. 1874, 1973).

EXPLANATION OF PROVISIONS

Section 9202(b)(1) of OBRA 1986 added subparagraph (H) to section 411(b)(1) of the Internal Revenue Code (Code) to provide rules for continued benefit accruals under defined benefit plans without regard to the attainment of any age. Section 9202(b)(2) of OBRA 1986 redesignated paragraphs (2) and (3) of Code section 411(b) as paragraphs (3) and (4) and added a new paragraph (2) to Code section 411(b) to provide rules for allocations to the accounts of employees in defined contribution plans without regard to the attainment of any age.

Effective with respect to plan years beginning after December 31, 1987, section 411(b)(1)(H)(i) provides the general rule that a defined benefit plan will not be treated as meeting the minimum vesting standards of section 411 (and, accordingly, will not constitute a qualified plan under section 401(a)) if under the plan an employee's benefit accrual is ceased, or the rate of an employee's benefit accrual is reduced, because of the attainment of any age. Effective for plan years beginning after

December 31, 1987, section 411(b)(2) provides that a defined contribution plan will not be treated as satisfying the minimum vesting standards of section 411 (and, accordingly, will not constitute a qualified plan under section 401(a)) if allocations to an employee's account are ceased, or the rate of allocations to an employee's account is reduced, because of the attainment of any age.

The proposed regulations provide that reductions or cessations of account allocations or benefit accruals that are based on factors other than age will not affect the qualification of the plan under section 411(b)(1)(H) or (b)(2). The proposed regulations also provide that benefits under a defined benefit plan may accrue at different rates without violating section 411(b)(1)(H), provided the difference in the rate of benefit accrual is determined without regard to the attainment of any age.

Section 411(b)(1)(H)(ii) provides that a plan will not be treated as failing to satisfy the general rule in section 411(b)(1)(H)(i) merely because the plan contains a limitation (determined without regard to age) on the maximum number of years of service or participation that are taken into account in determining benefits under the plan or merely because the plan contains a limitation on the amount of benefits an employee will receive under the plan. The proposed regulations provide that these limitations are permitted in both defined benefit plans and defined contribution plans (including target benefit plans).

Section 411(b)(1)(H)(iii) provides that, with respect to an employee who, as of the end of a plan year, has attained normal retirement age under a defined benefit plan, certain adjustments may be made to the benefit accrual for the plan year if the plan distributes benefits to the employee or if the plan adjusts the amount of the benefits payable to take into account delayed payment. The continued benefit accrual rules of section 411(b)(1)(H) operate in conjunction with the suspension of benefit payment rules under section 203(a)(3)(B) of the Employee Retirement Income Security Act of 1974 (ERISA) and the proposed regulations do not change the rules relating to the suspension of pension benefit payments under section 203(a)(3)(B) of ERISA and the regulations thereunder issued by the Department of Labor. However, the proposed regulations provide rules under which benefit accruals required under section 411(b)(1)(H)(i) may be reduced or offset either by the value of actuarial adjustments in an employee's normal retirement benefit or by the value of benefit distributions made to an employee.

Section 411(b)(1)(H)(iv) provides that a defined benefit plan will not be treated as failing to satisfy the general rule of section 411(b)(1)(H)(i) merely because the subsidized portion of an early retirement benefit provided under the plan (whether provided on a permanent or temporary basis) is disregarded in determining benefit accruals under the plan. The proposed regulations also provide that a plan will not be treated as failing to satisfy the general rule of section 411(b)(1)(H)(i) merely because a social security supplemental benefit or a qualified disability benefit is disregarded in determining benefit accruals under the plan.

The proposed regulations provide that the rate of an employee's benefit accrual under a defined benefit plan or the rate of allocations to an employee's account under a defined contribution plan will be considered to be reduced on account of the attainment of a specified age if optional forms of benefits, ancillary benefits or other benefits, rights or features under a plan that are provided with respect to benefits or allocations prior to such age are not provided (on terms that are at least as favorable to employees) with respect to benefits or allocations after such age. Thus, for example, under the proposed regulations, a plan may not make a lump sum option available only with respect to benefits or allocations attributable to service prior to a specified age. Similarly, a plan may not use actuarial assumptions that are less favorable to employees for determining lump sum benefits payable after a specified age than are used for determining lump sum benefits payable prior to such age. However, the proposed regulations provide that the accrual rate under a defined benefit plan will not be considered to be reduced merely because the subsidized portion of an early retirement benefit, a qualified disability benefit or a social security supplemental benefit provided under the plan ceases to be provided to an employee or is provided on a reduced basis to an employee by a plan on account of the employee's attainment of a specified age.

Section 411(b)(1)(H)(v) and (b)(2)(D) provide that the Secretary shall prescribe regulations coordinating the requirements of section 411(b)(1)(H) and (b)(2) with the requirements of sections 411(a), 404, 410, 415 and the antidiscrimination provisions of subchapter D of Chapter 1 (Code sections 401 through ¶425). The proposed regulations provide that no allocation to the account of an employee in a defined contribution plan and no benefit accrual on behalf of an employee in a defined benefit plan are required under section 411(b)(1)(H) or (b)(2) if such allocation or benefit accrual would cause the plan to (1) exceed the section 415 limitations on benefits and contributions, or (2) discriminate in favor of highly compensated employees within the meaning of section 401(a)(4).

Section 9203(a)(2) of OBRA 1986 amended Code section 410(a)(2) to provide that a plan will not constitute a qualified plan under section 401(a) if the plan excludes from participation (on the basis of age) an employee who has attained a specified age. The proposed regulations provide that, effective for plan years beginning after December 31, 1987, a plan may not apply a maximum age provision to any employee who has at least one hour of service for the employer on or after January 1, 1988, regardless of when the employee first performed an hour of service for the employer.

In the case of an employee who was ineligible to participate in a plan before the effective date of amended Code section 410(a)(2) because of a maximum age condition and who is eligible to participate in the plan on or after the effective date of such section, hours of service and years of service credited to the employee before the first plan year beginning on or after January 1, 1988, shall be taken into account in accordance with section 411 and the regulations thereunder and in accordance with 29 CFR Part 2530 for purposes of determining the employee's nonforfeitable right to the employee's accrued benefit. However, with respect to an employee described in the preceding sentence, hours of service and years of service credited to the employee before the first plan year beginning on or after January 1, 1988, are not required to be taken into account for purposes of determining the employee's accrued benefit under the plan for plan years beginning on or after January 1, 1988. See, also, section 411(a)(4) and § 1.411(a)-5 for rules relating to service that must be taken into account in determining an employee's nonforfeitable right to the employee's accrued benefit.

Section 9203(b)(2) of OBRA 1986 amended Code section 411(a)(8)(B) to provide rules relating to the determination of a participant's normal retirement age under a defined benefit plan and a defined contribution plan. Because section 203(e) of the pending Technical Corrections Act of 1987 (H.R. 2636) would change the definition of normal retirement age from the definition now set forth in section 411(a)(8)(B) (as amended by OBRA 1986), the proposed regulations do not set forth any rules under section 411(a)(8)(B) (as amended by OBRA 1986).

Section 9202(b) of OBRA 1986 amended Code section 411(b)(2)(C) to require the Secretary to provide by regulations for the application of the continued allocation rules of section 411(b)(2) to target benefit plans. The proposed regulations do not provide detailed special rules applicable to target benefit plans. Target benefit plans are subject to the rules applicable to defined contribution plans. The Commissioner will prescribe such additional rules relating to the continued allocation of contributions and accrual of benefits under target benefit plans as may be necessary or appropriate.

EFFECTIVE DATE

Section 9204(a)(1) of OBRA 1986 provides that the amendments made with regard to section 411(b)(1)(H) and (b)(2) "shall apply only with respect to plan years beginning on or after January 1, 1988, and only to employees who have 1 hour of service in any plan year to which such amendments apply." The proposed regulations provide that section 411(b)(1)(H) and (b)(2) does not apply to an employee who does not have at least 1 hour of service for the employer in a plan year beginning on or after January 1, 1988.

However, the proposed regulations provide that section 411(b)(1)(H) and (b)(2) applies with respect to all years of service completed by an employee who has at least 1 hour of service in a plan year beginning on or after January 1, 1988. Accordingly, under section 411(b)(1)(H)(i), the proposed regulations provide that, for plan years beginning on or after January 1, 1988, in determining the benefit payable under a defined benefit plan to a participant who has at least 1 hour of service in a plan year beginning on or after January 1, 1988, the plan does not satisfy section 411(a) if the plan disregards, because of the participant's attainment of any age, any year of service completed by the participant or any compensation earned by the participant after attaining such age, including years of service completed and compensation earned before the first plan year beginning on or after January 1, 1988. Under the proposed regulations, section 411(b)(2) does not require allocations to the accounts of employees under a defined contribution plan for any plan year beginning before January 1, 1988. However, the proposed regulations provide that, for plan years beginning on or after January 1, 1988, in determining the allocation to the account of a participant (who has at least 1 hour of service in a plan year beginning on or after January 1, 1988) under a defined contribution plan that determines allocations under a service related allocation formula, the plan does not satisfy section 411(a) if the plan disregards, because of the participant's attainment of any age, any year of service completed by the participant.

Under the proposed regulations, a defined benefit plan and a defined contribution plan will not be treated as impermissibly disregarding, because of the participant's attainment of any age, a year of service completed by the participant before the first plan year beginning before January 1, 1988, merely because the participant was not eligible under the plan to make mandatory or voluntary employee contributions (as well as contributions under a cash or deferred arrangement described in section 401(k)) for such year.

TITLE I OF ERISA AND OBRA 1986

Under section 101 of Reorganization Plan No. 4 of 1978 (43 FR 47713), the Secretary of the Treasury has jurisdiction over the subject matter addressed in the OBRA 1986 regulations. Therefore, under section 104 of the Reorganization Plan, these regulations apply when the Secretary of Labor exercises authority under Title I of ERISA (as amended, including the amendments made by Title IX of OBRA 1986 and the amendments by the Tax Reform Act of 1986). Thus, the requirements also apply to employee plans subject to Part 2 of Title I of ERISA.

Under section 9201 of OBRA 1986, these regulations also apply for purposes of applying comparable provisions under section 4(i)(7) of the Age Discrimination in Employment Act of 1967 (29 U.S.C. 623) as amended. No inference is intended under the proposed regulations as to the application of the Age Discrimination in Employment Act of 1967, as in effect prior to its amendment by OBRA 1986, to employees who are not credited with at least 1 hour of service in a plan year beginning on or after January 1, 1988.

RELIANCE ON THESE PROPOSED REGULATIONS

Taxpayers may rely on these proposed regulations for guidance pending the issuance of final regulations. Because these regulations are generally effective for plan years beginning after 1987, the Service will apply these proposed regulations in issuing rulings and in examining returns with respect to taxpayers and plans. If future guidance is more restrictive, such guidance will be applied without retroactive effect.

TIME OF PLAN AMENDMENTS

The proposed regulations provide rules relating to the postponement of the deadline for amending plans to comply with the provisions of OBRA 1986. Plan amendments required to conform the plan to the changes contained in OBRA 1986 need not be made until the dates specified in section 1140 of the Tax Reform Act of 1986 (in general, the last day of the first plan year commencing on or after January 1, 1989). This deferred amendment date is available only if: (1) the plan is operated in accordance with the applicable provisions of OBRA 1986 for the period beginning with the effective date of the provision with respect to the plan; (2) the plan amendments adopted are retroactive to such effective date; and (3) the plan amendments adopted are consistent with plan operation during the retroactive effective period.

SPECIAL ANALYSES

The Commissioner of Internal Revenue has determined that this proposed rule is not a major rule as defined in Executive Order 12291 and that a regulatory impact analysis is not required.

Although this document is a notice of proposed rulemaking which solicits public comments, the Internal Revenue Service has concluded that the regulations proposed herein are interpretative and that the notice and public procedure requirements of 5 U.S.C. 553 do not apply. Accordingly, these proposed regulations do not constitute regulations subject to the Regulatory Flexibility Act (5 U.S.C. Chapter 6).

COMMENTS AND REQUESTS FOR A PUBLIC HEARING

Before adopting these proposed regulations, consideration will be given to any written comments that are submitted (preferably eight copies) to the Commissioner of Internal Revenue. All comments will be available for public inspection and copying. A public hearing will be held upon written request to the Commissioner by any person who has submitted comments. If a public hearing is held, notice of the time and place will be published in the FEDERAL REGISTER.

DRAFTING INFORMATION

The principal author of these proposed regulations is Michael C. Garvey of the Employee Benefits and Exempt Organizations Division of the Office of Chief Counsel, Internal Revenue Service. However, personnel from other offices of the Internal Revenue Service and Treasury Department participated in developing the regulations, both on matters of substance and style.

[¶49,095] Proposed Regulations (REG-209039-87) [originally issued as INTL-491-87], published in the Federal Register on May 5, 1988.

Nonresident aliens and foreign corporations: Disposition of investment in U.S. real property.—Reg. §§1.897-4AT, 1.897-5T, 1.897-6T, 1.897-7T, 1.897-8T, 1.897-9T, 1.1445-10T and 1.1445-11T, relating to dispositions of U.S. real property interests by nonresident aliens and foreign corporations, are proposed. Temporary Reg. §1.1445-9T was removed by T.D. 9082.

AGENCY: Internal Revenue Service, Treasury.

ACTION: Notice of proposed rulemaking by cross-reference to temporary regulations.

SUMMARY: In the Rules and Regulations portion of this issue, the Internal Revenue Service is issuing temporary regulations that add new §§1.897-4AT, 1.897-5T, 1.897-6T, 1.897-7T, 1.897-8T and 1.897-9T relating to corporate distributions and certain nonrecognition exchanges, and new §§1.1445-9T and 1.1445-10T relating to certain withholding provisions, all in the context of the Foreign Investment in Real Property Tax Act (FIRPTA). In addition, the regulations provide rules with respect to the treatment of interests in publicly traded corporations. The text of the temporary regulations also serves as the comment document for this notice of proposed rulemaking.

DATES: Written comments and requests for a public hearing must be delivered or mailed before July 5, 1988. Except as otherwise specifically provided, these rules are proposed to apply to exchanges, distributions, or transfers of U.S. real property interests occurring after June 18, 1980. Although these regulations are proposed to be applied as of June 18, 1980, it is anticipated that any taxpayer desiring to apply the temporary regulations in lieu of the final regulations for the period prior to the adoption of the final regulations will be allowed to so choose. All changes and additions to portions of the existing regulations under sections 897 and 1445 are proposed to be generally effective after June 6, 1988. Paragraph (e) of §1.897-9T dealing with foreign governments and international organizations is effective July 1, 1986. The special rules under section 1445 for section 1034 nonrecognition are effective after August 3, 1988.

ADDRESS: Send comments and requests for a public hearing to Commissioner of Internal Revenue, Attention: CC:LR:T (INTL-491-87), Washington, DC 20224.

FOR FURTHER INFORMATION CONTACT: Charles P. Besecky of the Office of Associate Chief Counsel (International) within the Office of Chief Counsel, Internal Revenue Service, 1111 Constitution Avenue, N.W., Washington, DC 20224 (Attn: CC:LR:T). Telephone 202-566-3319, (not a toll-free call).

SUPPLEMENTARY INFORMATION:

BACKGROUND

The temporary regulations published in the Rules and Regulations portion of this issue of the Federal Register add §§1.897-4AT, 1.897-5T, 1.897-6T, 1.897-7T, 1.897-8T, 1.897-9T, 1.1445-9T and

1.1445-10T to 26 CFR Part 1. The final regulations that are proposed to be based on these temporary regulations would amend 26 CFR Part 1 by adding these temporary regulations sections as final regulations under section 897(c), (d), (e), (g), and (j), under the authority of section 367(e)(2), and under section 1445 of the Internal Revenue Code of 1986. For the text of the temporary regulations, see FR Doc.—[T.D. 8198] published in the Rules and Regulations portion of this issue of the Federal Register.

SPECIAL ANALYSES

It has been determined that this proposed rule is not a major rule as defined in Executive Order 12291 and that a Regulatory Impact Analysis is therefore not required. It has also been determined that this rule will not have a significant impact on a substantial number of small entities. Few small entities would be affected by these regulations. A regulatory flexibility analysis, therefore, is not required under the Regulatory Flexibility Act (5 U.S.C. chapter 6).

COMMENTS AND REQUESTS FOR A PUBLIC HEARING

Before adopting these proposed regulations, consideration will be given to any written comments that are submitted (preferably eight copies) to the Commissioner of Internal Revenue. All comments will be available for public inspection and copying. A public hearing will be held upon written request to the Commissioner by any person who has submitted written comments. If a public hearing is held, notice of the time and place will be published in the FEDERAL REGISTER.

The collection of information requirements contained herein have been submitted to the Office of Management and Budget (OMB) for review under section 3504(h) of the Paperwork Reduction Act. Comments on the requirements should be sent to the Office of Information and Regulatory Affairs of OMB, Attention: Desk Office for Internal Revenue Service, New Executive Office Building, Washington, DC 20503. The Internal Revenue Service requests persons submitting comments to OMB to also send copies of the comments to the Service.

DRAFTING INFORMATION

The principal author of this regulation is Charles P. Besecky of the Office of Associate Chief Counsel, (International), within the Office of Chief Counsel, Internal Revenue Service. However, personnel from other offices of the Internal Revenue Service and Treasury Department participated in developing the regulations on matters of substance and style.

[¶49,096] Proposed Amendments of Regulations (LR-83-87), published in the Federal Register on May 5, 1988.

Charitable contributions: Substantiation requirements.—Amendments of Reg. §§1.642(c)-1 and 1.642(c)-2, relating to deductions in excess of $5,000 claimed for charitable contributions of property, are proposed. Proposed amendments of Reg. §1.170A-13 was withdrawn on August 7, 2008 by REG-140029-07.

AGENCY: Internal Revenue Service, Treasury.

ACTION: Notice of proposed rulemaking.

SUMMARY: This document contains proposed amendments to the income tax regulations relating to deductions in excess of $5,000 claimed for charitable contributions of certain property. The proposed regulations would provide substantiation requirements with which all donors must comply with respect to charitable contributions of certain property if the amount claimed or reported as a deduction with respect to the contribution exceeds $5,000.

DATES:

PROPOSED EFFECTIVE DATES

The regulations are proposed to be effective for certain charitable contributions of property made after the date that is 30 days after a Treasury decision on this subject is published in the FEDERAL REGISTER.

DATES FOR COMMENTS AND REQUESTS FOR A PUBLIC HEARING

Written comments and requests for a public hearing must be delivered or mailed by July 6, 1988.

ADDRESS: Send comments and requests for a public hearing to: Commissioner of Internal Revenue, Attention: CC:LR:T (LR-83-87), Washington, D.C. 20224.

FOR FURTHER INFORMATION CONTACT: Beverly A. Baughman of the Legislation and Regulations Division, Office of Chief Counsel, Internal Revenue Service, 1111 Constitution Ave., N.W., Washington, D.C. 20224 (Attention: CC:LR:T) (202-566-3297, not a toll-free call.)

SUPPLEMENTARY INFORMATION:

BACKGROUND

On December 31, 1984, the FEDERAL REGISTER published proposed amendments to the Income Tax Regulations (26 CFR Part 1) under sections 170(a) and 6050L of the Internal Revenue Code of 1954, as well as temporary regulations (T.D. 8003) containing the same rules. The temporary regulations set forth substantiation requirements with which individuals, closely held corporations, personal service corporations, partnerships, and S corporations must comply with respect to charitable contributions of certain property made after December 31, 1984, if the amount claimed or reported as a deduction with respect to the contribution exceeds $5,000. Treasury decision [8199], which is contained in the Rules and Regulations portion of this issue of the FEDERAL REGISTER, finalizes the temporary and proposed regulations. The final regulations add the requirement that C corporations (as defined in section 1361 (a)(2)) must comply with some of the substantiation requirements contained in the regulations with respect to contributions of certain property made after June 6, 1988.

This document contains proposed amendments to § 1.170A-13 of the Income Tax Regulations (26 CFR Part 1), as amended by T.D. [INSERT T.D. NUMBER]

EXPLANATION OF PROVISIONS

The proposed regulations would apply all the substantiation requirements contained in § 1.170A-13 (c) to all donors (including C corporations, trusts, estates, and pooled income funds) with respect to contributions of certain property made after the date that is 30 days after a Treasury decision on the subject of this notice of proposed rulemaking is published in the FEDERAL REGISTER.

SPECIAL ANALYSES

The Commissioner of Internal Revenue has determined that this proposed rule is not a major rule as defined in Executive Order 12291 and that a Regulatory Impact Analysis is therefore not required. Although this document is a notice of proposed rulemaking that solicits public comment, the Internal Revenue Service has concluded that the regulations proposed herein are interpretative and that the notice and public procedure requirements of 5 U.S.C. 553 do not apply. Accordingly, the proposed regulations do not constitute regulations subject to the Regulatory Flexibility Act (5 U.S.C. chapter 6).

COMMENTS AND REQUESTS FOR A PUBLIC HEARING

Before adopting these proposed regulations consideration will be given to any written comments that are submitted (preferably seven copies) to the Commissioner of Internal Revenue. All comments will be available for public inspection and copying. A public hearing will be held upon written request to the Commissioner by any person who has submitted written comments. If a public hearing is held, notice of the time and place will be published in the FEDERAL REGISTER. The collection of information requirements contained herein have been submitted to the Office of Management and Budget (OMB) for review under section 3504 (h) of the Paperwork Reduction Act. Comments on the requirements should be sent to the Office of Information and Regulatory Affairs for OMB, Attention: Desk Officer for Internal Revenue Service, New Executive Office Building, Washington, D.C. 20503. The Internal Revenue Service requests persons submitting comments to OMB to also send copies of the comments to the Service.

DRAFTING INFORMATION

The principal author of there proposed regulations is Beverly A. Baughman of the Legislation and Regulations Division of the Office of Chief Counsel, Internal Revenue Service. However, personnel from other offices of the Internal Revenue Service and Treasury Department participated in developing the regulations, on matters of both substance and style.

[¶ 49,097] Proposed Regulations (INTL-990-86), published in the Federal Register on May 19, 1988.

Interest paid: Pass-through certificates: Registration requirements.—Reg. § 1.163-5T, relating to registration requirements with respect to certain debt obligations and sanctions on issuers of registration-required obligations not in registered form, is proposed.

AGENCY: Internal Revenue Service, Treasury.

ACTION: Notice of proposed rulemaking by cross-reference to temporary regulations.

SUMMARY: This document provides a notice of proposed rulemaking relating to the definition of the term "registration-required obligations" with respect to pass-through certificates and the application of the sanctions on issuers of "registration-required obligations" not in registered form to the issuers of such certificates. In the Rules and Regulations portion of this Federal Register, the Internal Revenue Service is issuing temporary income tax regulations with respect to this subject. The text of these temporary regulations serves as the comment document for this notice of proposed rulemaking.

DATE: Written comments and requests for a public hearing must be delivered or mailed by July 18, 1988.

ADDRESS: Send comments and requests for public hearing to: Commissioner of Internal Revenue, Attention: CC:LR:T (INTL-990-86), Washington, D.C. 20224.

FOR FURTHER INFORMATION CONTACT: Carl M. Cooper of the Office of Associate Chief Counsel (International), within the Office of Chief Counsel, Internal Revenue Service, 1111 Constitution Avenue, N.W., Washington, D.C. 20224, Attention: CC:LR:T [INTL-990-86], telephone 202-566-3388, (not a toll-free number).

SUPPLEMENTARY INFORMATION:

BACKGROUND

Section 1.163-5T(d) was deleted by T.D. 8110, which was published on December 19, 1986, in the Federal Register at 51 FR 45453 when all of § 1.163-5T was removed. Paragraph (d) is being replaced retroactively into the regulations as § 1.163-5T(d) (with prior paragraphs reserved) through temporary regulations published in the Rules and Regulations portion of this issue of the Federal Register.

REGULATORY FLEXIBILITY ACT AND EXECUTIVE ORDER 12291

The Commissioner of Internal Revenue has determined that this proposed rule is not a major rule as defined in Executive Order 12291 and that a Regulatory Impact Analysis is therefore not required. Although this document is a notice of proposed rulemaking which solicits public comment, the Internal Revenue Service has concluded that the regulations proposed herein are interpretative and that the notice and public procedure requirements of 5 U.S.C. 553 do not apply. Accordingly, these proposed regulations do not constitute regulations subject to the Regulatory Flexibility Act (5 U.S.C. chapter 6).

COMMENTS AND REQUESTS FOR A PUBLIC HEARING

Before adopting these proposed regulations as final regulations, consideration will be given to any written comments that are submitted (preferably eight copies) to the Commissioner of Internal Revenue. All comments will be available for public inspection and copying. A public hearing will be held **upon written request to the Commissioner by any person who has submitted written comments. If a public hearing is held, notice of the time and place will be published in the Federal Register.**

DRAFTING INFORMATION

The principal author of this regulation is Carl M. Cooper of the Office of Associate Chief Counsel (International), within the Office of Chief Counsel, Internal Revenue Service. However, personnel from other offices of the Internal Revenue Service and Treasury Department participated in developing the regulations on matters of substance and style.

LIST OF SUBJECTS IN 26 CFR 1.61 through 1.281-4

Income taxes, Taxable income, Deductions, Exemptions

Proposal of Regulations

The temporary regulations, FR Doc. [T.D. 8202]published in the Rules and Regulations portion of this issue of the Federal Register, are hereby also proposed as final regulations under section 163 of the Internal Revenue Code of 1954.

[¶49,098] Proposed Amendment of Regulations (INTL-905-87), published in the Federal Register on May 19, 1988.

Interest paid: Pass-through certificates: Registration requirements.—Amendments of Reg. §1.163-5T, relating to registration requirements with respect to certain debt obligations and sanctions on issuers of registration-required obligations not in registered form, are proposed.

AGENCY: Internal Revenue Service, Treasury.

ACTION: Notice of proposed rulemaking.

SUMMARY: This document provides a notice of proposed rulemaking relating to the application of the sanctions on issuers of registration required obligations not in registered form. These regulations would provide the public with guidance necessary to comply with the Tax Equity and Fiscal Responsibility Act of 1982.

DATES: Written comments and requests for a public hearing must be delivered or mailed before July 18, 1988. These regulations are proposed to be applicable to the transfers of obligations occurring after August 17, 1988.

ADDRESS: Send comments and request for a public hearing to: Commissioner of Internal Revenue, Attention: CC:LR:T (INTL-905-87), Washington, DC 20224.

FOR FURTHER INFORMATION CONTACT: Carl M. Cooper of the Office of Associate Chief Counsel (International), within the Office of Chief Counsel, Internal Revenue Service, 1111 Constitution Avenue, N.W., Washington, DC 20224 (Attn: CC:LR:T). Telephone 202-566-3388, (not a toll-free call).

SUPPLEMENTARY INFORMATION:

BACKGROUND

Section 4701 imposes a tax on issuers of "registration-required obligations" not in registered form. Section 5f.103-1(c)(1) provides generally that an obligation is in registered form if it is registered with the issuer (or its agent) and may be transferred by surrender and reissuance by the issuer (or its agent), or through a book entry system maintained by the issuer (or its agent), or through both of these methods.

EXPLANATION OF PROVISIONS

An issuer or its agent may have no knowledge or control over the method of transfer of an obligation that is held by a nominee. A new paragraph (d)(7) of §1.163-5T has been proposed to provide explicitly for the application of section 4701 to circumstances in which a holder transfers an obligation through a method not described in §5f.103-1(c)(1).

Section 1.163-5T(d)(7) of these proposed regulations provides, pursuant to §46.4701-1(a)(5), that any person who holds a registration required obligation that is in registered form within the meaning of §5f.103-1(c)(1) and who transfers the obligation through a method not described in §5f.103-1(c)(1) is considered the issuer of the obligations transferred for purposes of section 4701. Such transferor is therefore subject to the tax imposed under section 4701, even though he may not be the person whose interest deduction would be disallowed by reason of section 163(f)(1). Such transferor is considered to have issued the obligation on the date of the transfer in the principal amount of the obligation transferred. Section 1.163-5T(d)(7) would apply to transfers occurring after August 17, 1988.

SPECIAL ANALYSES

It has been determined that this proposed rule is not a major rule as defined in Executive Order 12291 and that a Regulatory Impact Analysis is therefore not required. Although this document is a notice of proposed rulemaking that solicits public comments, it has been determined that the regulations proposed herein are interpretative and that the notice and public procedure requirements of 5 U.S.C. 553 do not apply. Accordingly, these proposed regulations do not constitute regulations subject to the Regulatory Flexibility Act (5 U.S.C. chapter 6) and a Regulatory Flexibility Analysis has not been prepared.

COMMENTS AND REQUESTS FOR A PUBLIC HEARING

Before adopting final regulations, consideration will be given to any written comments that are submitted (preferably eight copies) to the Commissioner of Internal Revenue. All comments will be available for public inspection and copying. A public hearing will be held upon written request to the Commissioner by any person who has submitted written comments. If a public hearing is held, notice of the time and place will be published in the FEDERAL REGISTER.

DRAFTING INFORMATION

The principal author of these regulations is Carl M. Cooper of the Office of Associate Chief Counsel (International), within the Office of Chief Counsel, Internal Revenue Service. However, personnel from other offices of the Internal Revenue Service and the Treasury Department participated in developing these regulations, both in matters of substance and style.

[¶49,099] **Proposed Regulations (LR-53-880), published in the Federal Register** on May 27, 1988.

Taxable year: Election: Partnership: S corporation: Personal service corporation.—Reg. §§1.280H-0T, 1.280H-1T, 1.444-0T—1.444-3T and 1.7519-0T—1.7519-3T, relating to the election of a taxable year by a partnership, S corporation or personal service corporation, are proposed. Reg. §1.706-1T was removed by T.D. 8996 on 5/16/2002. Reg. §1.706-3T was adopted as amendments to Reg. §1.706-1 by T.D. 9009 on 7/22/2002.

AGENCY: Internal Revenue Service, Treasury.

ACTION: Notice of proposed rulemaking.

SUMMARY: In the rules and regulations portion of this issue of the FEDERAL REGISTER, the Internal Revenue Service is issuing temporary regulations relating to the election of a taxable year other than the required year by a partnership, S corporation or personal service corporation. Changes to the applicable law were made by the Revenue Act of 1987. In addition, the regulations include conforming and clarifying rules regarding the determination of the taxable year of a partnership undersection 706. The text of these temporary regulations also serves as the comment document for this notice of proposed rulemaking.

DATES: The amendments to the regulations are proposed to be effective generally for taxable years beginning after December 31, 1986. Written comments and requests for a public hearing must be delivered or mailed by July 26, 1988.

ADDRESS: Send comments and requests for a public hearing to: Commissioner of Internal Revenue, Attention: CC:LR:T (LR-53-88), Washington, D.C. 20224.

FOR FURTHER INFORMATION CONTACT: Arthur E. Davis III of the Legislation and Regulations Division, Office of Chief Counsel, Internal Revenue Service, 1111 Constitution Avenue N.W., Washington, D.C. 20224, Attention: CC:LR:T, (202) 566-3918 (not a toll-free call).

SUPPLEMENTARY INFORMATION:

BACKGROUND

The temporary regulations (designated by a "T" following the section citations) in the Rules and Regulations portion of this issue of the FEDERAL REGISTER amend the Income Tax Regulations (26 CFR Part 1) to provide temporary rules relating to the election by a partnership, S corporation, or personal service corporation to use a taxable year other than the year required (the "required year") under the applicable provision of the Internal Revenue Code of 1986 (the "Code"). The temporary regulations reflect the amendment of the Code by section 10206 of the Revenue Act of 1987 (Pub. L. 100-203, 101 Stat. 1330), which added sections 444, 7519 and 280H. Section 444 provides for the election (a "section 444 election") to use a taxable year other than the required year. A partnership or S corporation that makes or continues a section 444 election must make the payment required by section 7519. A personal service corporation that makes or continues a section 444 election is subject to the deduction limitations imposed by section 280H. This document proposes to adopt the temporary regulations as final regulations. Accordingly, the text of the temporary regulations serves as the comment document for this notice of proposed rulemaking. In addition, the preamble to the temporary regulations explains the proposed and temporary rules.

For the text of the temporary regulations, see FR Doc. (T.D. 8205) published in the Rules and Regulations portion of this issue of the FEDERAL REGISTER.

SPECIAL ANALYSES

The Commissioner of Internal Revenue has determined that this proposed rule is not a major rule as defined in Executive Order 12291 and that a regulatory impact analysis therefore is not required. Although this document is a notice of proposed rulemaking that solicits public comments, the Internal Revenue Service has concluded that the proposed regulations are interpretative and that the notice and public procedure requirements of 5 U.S.C. 553 do not apply. Accordingly, these proposed regulations are not subject to the Regulatory Flexibility Act (5 U.S.C. chapter 6).

The reporting requirements contained in this notice of proposed rulemaking have been submitted in accordance with the requirements of the Paperwork Reduction Act of 1980 to the Office of Management and Budget (OMB) for review. OMB has approved these requirements (control number 1545-1036).

COMMENTS AND REQUESTS FOR A PUBLIC HEARING

Before these proposed regulations are adopted, consideration will be given to any written comments that are submitted (preferably eight copies) to the Commissioner of Internal Revenue. All comments will be available for public inspection and copying. A public hearing will be held upon written request to the Commissioner by any person who submitted written comments. If a public hearing is held, notice of the time and place will be published in the Federal Register.

DRAFTING INFORMATION

The principal author of these proposed regulations is Arthur E. Davis III of the Legislation and Regulations Division of the Office of Chief Counsel, Internal Revenue Service. However, personnel from other offices of the Internal Revenue Service and Treasury Department participated in developing the regulations on matters of both substance and style.

[¶49,100] Proposed Regulations and Amendments of Regulations (LR-3-87), published in the Federal Register on June 9, 1988.

Exclusions: Scholarships: Payment for services.—Reg. §§1.117-0 and 1.117-6 and amendments of Reg. §§1.117-1—1.117-5, relating to the exclusion from gross income of qualified scholarships, are proposed. On 10/6/97, T.D. 8734 adopted the proposal to withdraw amendments to §1.6041-3.

AGENCY: Internal Revenue Service, Treasury.

ACTION: Notice of proposed rulemaking.

SUMMARY: This document contains proposed regulations relating to the exclusion from gross income of qualified scholarships. Changes to the applicable law were made by the Tax Reform Act of 1986. These regulations would provide necessary guidance to Internal Revenue Service personnel who administer the Internal Revenue Code and members of the public who are subject to these laws.

DATES: Written comments and requests for a public hearing must be delivered or mailed by [SIXTY DAYS AFTER DATE OF PUBLICATION IN THE FEDERAL REGISTER]. These amendments are proposed to be generally effective for taxable years beginning after December 31, 1986.

ADDRESS: Send comments and requests for a public hearing to: Commissioner of Internal Revenue, Attention: CC:LR:T (LR-3-87) Washington, D.C. 20224.

FOR FURTHER INFORMATION CONTACT: Ruth Hoffman of the Legislation and Regulations Division, Office of Chief Counsel, Internal Revenue Service, 1111 Constitution Avenue, N.W., Washington, D.C. 20224 (Attention CC:LR:T) (202-566-3287) (not a toll-free number).

SUPPLEMENTARY INFORMATION:

BACKGROUND

This document contains proposed amendments to the Income Tax Regulations (26 CFR Part 1) under sections 117 and 6041 of the Internal Revenue Code of 1986 (Code). These amendments are proposed to conform the regulations under section 117 and section 6041 to the changes made by section 123(a) of the Tax Reform Act of 1986 (1986 Act) (Pub. L. 99-514, 100 Stat. 2112).

IN GENERAL

The 1986 Act amended section 117 of the Code, relating to the exclusion from gross income of scholarships or fellowship grants. Section 117(a) provides that gross income does not include any amount received as a qualified scholarship by an individual who is a candidate for a degree at an educational organization described in section 170(b)(1)(A)(ii). An individual who is not a candidate for a degree must include in gross income any amount received as a scholarship or fellowship grant. Proposed §1.117-6(c)(4) defines the term candidate for a degree. Proposed §1.117-6(c)(1) provides that a qualified scholarship is any amount received by an individual as a scholarship or fellowship grant and used for qualified tuition and related expenses. As defined in proposed §1.117-6(c)(2), qualified tuition and related expenses are tuition and fees required for enrollment or attendance at an educational organization, and fees, books, supplies, and equipment required for courses of instruction. Qualified tuition and related expenses do not include any amount received as a scholarship or fellowship grant and used for room and board or incidental expenses such as travel, research, or clerical help. Thus, any such amount is not excludable from gross income.

Under proposed §1.117-6(h), any amount of a scholarship or fellowship grant in excess of the amount permitted to be excluded from gross income under proposed §1.117-6(b) is considered earned income for purposes of section 63(c)(5) (relating to the standard deduction for dependents) and section 6012(a)(1)(C)(i) (relating to dependents required to make returns of income).

Section 117(d) provides that gross income does not include any amount received as a qualified tuition reduction. This document does not provide proposed regulations with respect to section 117(d). Proposed regulations addressing matters relating to section 117(d) are expected to be provided by another regulations project.

SCHOLARSHIPS REPRESENTING PAYMENT FOR SERVICES

The general rule providing for an exclusion from gross income of qualified scholarships is limited under section 117(c) to qualified scholarship amounts that do not represent payment for teaching, research, or other services by the recipient required as a condition to receiving the qualified scholarship. Section 117(c) also applies to qualified tuition reductions (as defined under section 117(d)).

Under proposed § 1.117-6(d)(1), that portion of a scholarship or fellowship grant that represents payment for services is included in gross income, regardless of whether such services are required of all candidates for the degree as a condition to receiving the degree.

Proposed § 1.117-6(d)(2) provides that a scholarship or fellowship grant represents payment for services when the grantor requires the recipient to perform services in return for the granting of the scholarship or fellowship. A requirement that the recipient pursue studies, research, or other activities primarily for the benefit of the grantor is treated as a requirement to perform services. The granting of a scholarship or fellowship is considered to be in return for services whether such services are required to be performed before, concurrent with, or after receiving the scholarship or fellowship grant.

If only a portion of a scholarship or fellowship grant represents payment for services, the grantor must determine the amount of the scholarship or fellowship grant (including any reduction in tuition or related expenses) to be allocated to payment for services. Proposed § 1.117-6(d)(3) provides rules for determining what portion of the scholarship or fellowship grant must be allocated by the grantor to payment for services, and indicates some of the factors to be considered in making that allocation. If the recipient includes in gross income the amount allocated by the grantor to payment for services and such amount represents reasonable compensation for those services, then any additional amount of a scholarship or fellowship grant received from the same grantor that meets the requirements of proposed § 1.117-6(b) is excludable from gross income.

EFFECTIVE DATE RULES

Section 117, as amended by the 1986 Act, generally applies to taxable years beginning on or after January 1, 1987. However, under proposed § 1.117-6(f), section 117, as in effect prior to its amendment by the 1986 Act, continues to apply to a scholarship or fellowship granted before August 17, 1986, whenever received. In addition, section 117, as in effect prior to its amendment by the 1986 Act, applies in the case of a scholarship or fellowship granted after August 16, 1986, and before January 1, 1987, to the extent of any amount received prior to January 1, 1987, that is attributable to expenditures incurred before January 1, 1987.

For purposes of the effective date rules, proposed § 1.117-6(f)(2) provides that a scholarship or fellowship is granted when the grantor either notifies the recipient of the award or notifies an organization or institution acting on behalf of a specified recipient of the award to be provided to such recipient. If the notification is sent by mail, notification occurs as of the date the notice is postmarked. If evidence of a postmark does not exist, the date on the award letter is treated as the notification date.

Under proposed § 1.117-6(f)(3), a scholarship or fellowship is considered granted before August 17, 1986, to the extent that, in a notice of award made before that date, the grantor made a firm commitment to provide the recipient with a fixed cash amount or a readily determinable amount. For purposes of this section, a condition that the recipient remain in good standing or maintain a specific grade point average, or a requirement that the recipient show continuing financial need is not taken into account in determining whether the grantor made a firm commitment to provide the scholarship or fellowship grant for more than one academic period.

Under proposed § 1.117-6(f)(3)(i), amounts treated as a scholarship or fellowship granted before August 17, 1986, must be applied against qualified tuition and related expenses before any amount treated as a scholarship or fellowship granted after August 16, 1986, may be eligible for exclusion as a qualified scholarship.

In addition, proposed § 1.117-6(f)(3)(i) provides that if a scholarship or fellowship initially awarded before August 17, 1986, is granted for a period exceeding one academic period (for example, a semester), amounts received in subsequent academic periods are treated as granted before August 17, 1986, only if: (a) the amount awarded for the first academic period is described in the original notice of award as a fixed cash amount or readily determinable amount; (b) the original notice of award contains a firm commitment by the grantor to provide the scholarship or fellowship grant for more than one academic period; and (c) the recipient is not required to reapply to the grantor in order to receive the scholarship or fellowship grant in future academic periods.

Proposed § 1.117-6(f)(3)(ii) provides that amounts received in subsequent academic periods that were not initially described in the notice of award as either fixed cash amounts or readily determinable amounts are treated as granted before August 17, 1986, but only to the extent of the amount granted for the initial academic period.

REPORTING AND WITHHOLDING REQUIREMENTS

Under proposed § 1.6041-3(q), unless a scholarship or fellowship grant represents payment for services by the recipient, neither the grantor nor the educational organization attended by the recipient is required to file a return of information with respect to such grant. However, there are reporting and withholding requirements for scholarship or fellowship grants to nonresident aliens under section 1441 of the Code.

Under proposed § 1.117-6(d)(4), any amount of a scholarship or fellowship grant that represents payment for services is considered wages for purposes of section 3401(a). Therefore, such amounts are subject to section 3402 (relating to withholding for income taxes) and the grantor is subject to section 6051 (relating to reporting wages of employees) and is required to file Form W-2 with respect to scholarship or fellowship amounts representing payment for services. However, according to the rules set forth in sections 3121(b), 3306(c), and the regulations thereunder, the application of sections

3101 and 3111 (relating to the Federal Insurance Contributions Act (FICA)), or section 3301 (relating to the Federal Unemployment Tax Act (FUTA)) depends upon the nature of the employment and the status of the organization. When only a portion of a scholarship or fellowship grant represents payment for services, the grantor is subject to the reporting and withholding requirements only with respect to the portion that represents such payments.

SPECIAL ANALYSES

The Commissioner of Internal Revenue has determined that this proposed rule is not a major rule as defined in Executive Order 12291 and that a Regulatory Impact Analysis is therefore not required. Although this document is a notice of proposed rulemaking that solicits public comment, the Internal Revenue Service has concluded that the notice and public procedure requirements of 5 U.S.C. 553 do not apply. Accordingly, these proposed regulations do not constitute regulations subject to the Regulatory Flexibility Act (5 U.S.C. chapter 6).

COMMENTS AND REQUEST FOR A PUBLIC HEARING

Before adopting these proposed regulations, consideration will be given to any written comments that are submitted (preferably eight copies) to the Commissioner of Internal Revenue. All comments will be available for public inspection and copying. A public hearing will be held upon written request to the Commissioner by any person who has submitted written comments. If a public hearing is held, notice of the time and place will be published in the FEDERAL REGISTER. The collection of information requirements contained herein have been submitted to the Office of Management and Budget (OMB) for review under section 3504(h) of the Paperwork Reduction Act. Comments on the requirements should be sent to the Office of Information and Regulatory Affairs of OMB, Attention: Desk Officer for Internal Revenue Service, New Executive Office Building, Washington, D.C. 20503. The Internal Revenue Service requests that persons submitting comments to OMB also send copies of those comments to the Service.

DRAFTING INFORMATION

The principal author of these proposed regulations is Ruth Hoffman of the Legislation and Regulations Division of the Office of Chief Counsel, Internal Revenue Service. However, personnel from other offices of the Internal Revenue Service and Treasury Department participated in developing the regulations, on matters of both substance and style.

[¶49,101] Proposed Regulations and Amendments of Regulations (REG-209001-86) [originally issued as INTL-49-86], published in the Federal Register on June 14, 1988.

Controlled foreign corporations: Investment of earnings in U.S. property: Related person factoring income.—Reg. §1.864-8T and amendments to Reg. §§1.956-1T and 1.956-2T, relating to the treatment of related person factoring income, are proposed. Reg. §1.304-4T was reproposed by REG-132232-08 on December 30, 2009. Reg. §1.956-3 adopted by T.D. 9792 on November 2, 2016. Proposed Reg. §§1.956-1(b)(4), 1.956-2(d)(2) and 1.956-3(b)(2)(ii) withdrawn by REG-122387-16 on November 3, 2016.

AGENCY: Internal Revenue Service, Treasury.

ACTION: Notice of proposed rulemaking by cross-reference to temporary regulations.

SUMMARY: This document provides proposed regulations relating to the treatment of related person factoring income, as well as proposed changes to regulations relating to the determination of the amount of earnings of a controlled foreign corporation invested in United States property. Also included is a proposed regulation relating to redemptions of stock through the use of related corporations. In the Rules and Regulations portion of this issue of the FEDERAL REGISTER, the Internal Revenue Service is issuing temporary Income Tax Regulations relating to the treatment of related person factoring income, investments in United States property and redemptions through the use of related corporations. The text of the temporary regulations also serves as the comment document for this notice of proposed rulemaking.

DATES: The regulations under §§1.864-8T and 1.956-3T are proposed to be effective July 14, 1988, and are proposed to be applicable, as of their dates of transfer, with respect to accounts receivable and evidences of indebtedness transferred after March 1, 1984. The regulations under §§1.956-1T, and 1.956-2T are proposed to be effective July 14, 1988, with respect to investments in U.S. property made on or after June 14, 1988. The regulations under §1.304-4T are proposed to be effective June 14, 1988, with respect to acquisitions of stock occurring on or after June 14, 1988.

Written comments and requests for a public hearing must be delivered or mailed by August 15, 1988.

ADDRESS: Send comments and requests for a public hearing to: Commissioner of Internal Revenue, Attention: CC:LR:T (INTL-49-86), Washington, D.C. 20224.

FOR FURTHER INFORMATION CONTACT: Regarding §§1.864-8T and 1.956-3T, contact Barbara Allen Felker of the Office of the Associate Chief Counsel (International) within the Office of Chief Counsel, Internal Revenue Service, 1111 Constitution Avenue, N.W., Washington, D.C. 20224, Attention: CC:LR:T (INTL-49-86). Telephone (202) 634-5406 (not a toll-free call). Regarding §§1.304-4T, 1.956-1T, and 1.956-2T, contact Riea M. Lainoff of the Office of the Associate Chief Counsel (International), within the Office of Chief Counsel, Internal Revenue Service, 1111 Constitution Avenue, N.W., Washington, D.C. 20224, Attention: CC:LR:T (INTL-49-86). Telephone (202) 566-6645 (not a toll-free call).

SUPPLEMENTARY INFORMATION:

BACKGROUND

The temporary regulations published in the Rules and Regulations portion of this issue of the FEDERAL REGISTER add new §§1.864-8T and 1.956-3T to Part 1 of the Title 26 of the Code of Federal Regulations. These regulations implement sections 864(d) and 956(b)(3), which were added to the Internal Revenue Code of 1954 by section 123 of the Tax Reform Act of 1984 (Pub. L. 98-369, 98 Stat. 644, 646) and amended by sections 1201(d)(4), 1221(a)(2),1223(b)(1),1275(c)(7) and 1810(c) of the Tax Reform Act of 1986 (Pub. L. 99-514, 100 Stat. 2085, 2525, 2550, 2558, 2599, 2824). New §§1.956-1T, and 1.956-2T amend §§1.956-1(b)(4), 1.956-1(e), and §1.956-2(d)(2), respectively, under section 956 of the Internal Revenue Code of 1986. The temporary regulations published in the Rules and Regulations portion of this issue of the FEDERAL REGISTER also add new §1.304-4T to Part 1 of Title 26 of the Code of Federal Regulations. The preamble to the temporary regulations explains these additions to the Income Tax Regulations.

COMMENTS AND REQUESTS FOR A PUBLIC HEARING

Before adopting these proposed regulations, consideration will be given to any written comments that are submitted (preferably eight copies) to the Commissioner of Internal Revenue. All comments will be available for public inspection and copying. A public hearing will be held upon written request to the Commissioner by any person who has submitted written comments. If a public hearing is held, notice of the time and place will be published in the FEDERAL REGISTER.

SPECIAL ANALYSES

It has been determined that these proposed rules are not major rules as defined in Executive Order 12291 and that a Regulatory Impact Analysis is therefore not required. Although this document is a notice of a proposed rulemaking which solicits public comment, the Internal Revenue Service has concluded that the regulations proposed herein are interpretative and that the notice and public procedure requirements of 5 U.S.C. §553 do not apply. Accordingly, these proposed regulations do not constitute regulations subject to the Regulatory Flexibility Act (5 U.S.C. chapter 6).

DRAFTING INFORMATION

The principal authors of these proposed regulations are Barbara Allen Felker, Riea M. Lainoff, Marnie J. Carro, and Ann Zukas of the Office of the Associate Chief Counsel (International) within the Office of Chief Counsel, Internal Revenue Service. However, personnel from other offices of the Internal Revenue Service and Treasury Department participated in developing the regulations on matters of both substance and style.

[¶49,102] Proposed Regulations (REG-209020-86) [originally issued as INTL-061-86], published in the Federal Register on June 23, 1988.

Foreign tax credits: Foreign tax redeterminations: Notification.—Reg. §§1.905-3T, 1.905-4T, 1.905-5T, and 301.6689-1T, relating to a taxpayer's obligation to file notification of a foreign tax redetermination, to make adjustments to a taxpayer's pools of foreign taxes and earnings and profits, and the imposition of the civil penalty for failure to file such notice or report such adjustments, are proposed.

AGENCY: Internal Revenue Service, Treasury.

ACTION: Notice of proposed rulemaking by cross-reference to temporary regulations.

SUMMARY: This document provides proposed Income Tax Regulations and Regulations on Procedure and Administration relating to a taxpayer's obligation under section 905(c) of the Internal Revenue Code of 1986 to file notification of a foreign tax redetermination, to make adjustments to a taxpayer's pools of foreign taxes and earnings and profits, and the imposition of the civil penalty for failure to file such notice or report such adjustments. In the Rules and Regulations portion of this issue of the FEDERAL REGISTER, the Internal Revenue Service is issuing temporary regulations relating to these matters. The text of those temporary regulations also serves as the comment document for this proposed rulemaking.

DATES: Written comments and requests for a public hearing must be delivered or mailed before August 22, 1988. These rules would generally apply to taxable years beginning after December 31, 1986.

ADDRESS: Send comments and requests for a public hearing to Commissioner of Internal Revenue, Attention: CC:LR:T (INTL-061-86), Washington, D.C. 20224.

FOR FURTHER INFORMATION CONTACT: Eli J. Dicker, of the Office of Associate Chief Counsel (International), within the Office of Chief Counsel, Internal Revenue Service, 1111 Constitution Avenue, N.W., Washington, D.C. 20224 (Attention: CC:LR:T (INTL-061-86)) (202-566-3490, not a toll-free call).

SUPPLEMENTARY INFORMATION:

PAPERWORK REDUCTION ACT

The collection of information contained in this notice of proposed rulemaking has been submitted to the Office of Management and Budget for review in accordance with the Paperwork Reduction Act of 1980 (44 U.S.C. 3504(h)). Comments on the collection of information should be sent to the Office of Information and Regulatory Affairs, Office of Management and Budget, Washington, D.C. 20503, Attention: Desk Officer for Internal Revenue Service, with copies to the Internal Revenue Service, Washington, D.C. 20224, Attention: IRS Reports Clearance Officer TR:FP.

The collection of information in this regulation is in §§1.905-3T, 1.905-4T, and 1.905-5T. This information is required by the Internal Revenue Service to enable it to effectively administer the provisions of section 905(c). The information is needed by the Service to verify pooling adjustments to account for the effect of foreign tax redeterminations and to recompute a United States taxpayer's United States tax liability when a foreign tax redetermination requires such a recomputation. The likely respondents are individuals, households, businesses, and other for-profit institutions. Estimated total annual reporting burden: 10,000 hours. Estimated average annual burden per respondent: one hour. Estimated number of respondents: 10,000. Estimated annual frequency of responses: as necessary to comply with the provisions of section 905(c).

BACKGROUND

The temporary regulations published in the Rules and Regulations portion of this issue of the FEDERAL REGISTER add new §§1.905-3T, 1.905-4T, and 1.905-5T to 26 CFR Part 1. They also add §301.6689-1T to 26 CFR Part 301. The final regulations that are proposed to be based on the temporary regulations would amend 26 CFR Parts 1, 301, and 602. For the text of the temporary regulations, see [T.D. 8210]published in the Rules and Regulations portion of this issue of the FEDERAL REGISTER.

SPECIAL ANALYSES

These proposed rules are not major rules as defined in Executive Order 12291. Therefore, a Regulatory Impact Analysis is not required. Although this document is a notice of proposed rulemaking that solicits public comments, the notice and public procedure requirements of 5 U.S.C. §553 do not apply because the regulations proposed herein are interpretative. Therefore, an initial Regulatory Flexibility Analysis is not required by the Regulatory Flexibility Act (5 U.S.C. Chapter 6).

COMMENTS AND REQUESTS FOR A PUBLIC HEARING

Before adopting these proposed regulations, consideration will be given to any written comments that are submitted (preferably eight copies) to the Commissioner of Internal Revenue. All comments will be available for public inspection and copying. A public hearing will be held upon written request to the Commissioner by any person who has submitted written comments. If a public hearing is held, notice of the time and place will be published in the FEDERAL REGISTER.

DRAFTING INFORMATION

The principal author of these regulations is Eli J. Dicker, of the Office of Associate Chief Counsel (International), within the Office of Chief Counsel, Internal Revenue Service. Other personnel from offices of the Internal Revenue Service and Treasury Department participated in developing the regulations both on matters of substance and style.

[¶49,103] Proposed Regulations (REG-209024-88) [originally issued as INTL-285-88], published in the Federal Register on June 27, 1988.

Income of foreign governments and international organizations.—Reg. §§1.892-1T—1.892-7, relating to current taxation of income of foreign governments from investment sources within the United States, are proposed. Reg. §1.1441-8T was adopted as Reg. §1.1441-8 by T.D. 8734, effective 1/1/2001 (per T.D. 8856).

Income of Foreign Governments and International Organizations

AGENCY: Internal Revenue Service, Treasury.

ACTION: Notice of proposed rulemaking by cross-reference to temporary regulations.

SUMMARY: This document contains proposed income tax regulations relating to current taxation of income of foreign governments from investment sources within the United States. This action is necessary because of changes to the applicable tax law made by the Tax Reform Act of 1986. In the Rules and Regulations portion of this FEDERAL REGISTER, the Internal Revenue Service is issuing temporary regulations relating to these matters. The text of those temporary regulations also serves as the comment document for this proposed rulemaking.

DATES: These regulations are proposed to be effective for taxable years beginning after June 30, 1986. Written comments and request for a public hearing must be delivered or mailed by August 26, 1988.

ADDRESS: Send comments and requests for a public hearing to: Commissioner of Internal Revenue, (Attention: CC:LR:T, INTL-285-88), Washington, DC 20224.

FOR FURTHER INFORMATION CONTACT: David A. Juster of the Office of Associate Chief Counsel (International), within the Office of Chief Counsel, Internal Revenue Service, 1111 Constitution Avenue, N.W., Washington, DC 20224 (Attention: CC:LR:T (INTL-285-88)) (202-566-6384, not a toll-free call).

SUPPLEMENTARY INFORMATION:

PAPERWORK REDUCTION ACT

The collection of information contained in this notice of proposed rulemaking has been submitted to the Office of Management and Budget for review in accordance with the Paperwork Reduction Act of 1980 (44 U.S.C. 3504(h)). Comments on the collection of information should be sent to the Office of Information and Regulatory Affairs, Office of Management and Budget, Washington, D.C. 20503, attention: Desk Officer for Internal Revenue Service, with copies to the Internal Revenue Service, Washington, D.C. 20224, Attention: IRS Reports Clearance Officer TR:FP.

The collection of information in this regulation is in §1.1441-8T(b). This information is required by Internal Revenue Service to avoid withholding of tax at source with regard to specific types of income received by foreign governments and international organizations. This information will be used by withholding agents to verify that specific items of income received by such foreign governments or international organizations are excluded from gross income by reason of section 892 and are therefore exempt from withholding under section 1441. The likely respondents are foreign governments or international organizations.

Estimated total annual reporting burden: 45,000 hours.

Estimated average annual burden per respondent: 15 hours.

Estimated number of respondents: 3000.

Estimated annual frequency of responses: Annually.

BACKGROUND

The temporary regulations published in the Rules and Regulations portion of this issue of the FEDERAL REGISTER add new §§1.892-1T through 1.892-7T and 1441-8T. The final regulations that are proposed to be based on the temporary regulations would amend 26 CFR Parts 1 and 602. For the text of the temporary regulations, see [T.D. 8277]published in the Rules and Regulations portion of this issue of the FEDERAL REGISTER.

SPECIAL ANALYSES

These proposed rules are not major rules as defined in Executive Order 12291. Therefore, a Regulatory Impact Analysis is not required. Although this document is a notice of proposed rulemaking that solicits public comments, the notice and public procedure requirements of 5 U.S.C. §553 do not apply because the regulations proposed herein are interpretative. Therefore, an initial Regulatory Flexibility Analysis is not required by the Regulatory Flexibility Act (5 U.S.C. Chapter 6).

COMMENTS AND REQUEST FOR A PUBLIC HEARING

Before adopting as final regulations these proposed regulations, consideration will be given to any written comments that are submitted (preferably a signed original and seven copies) to the Commissioner of Internal Revenue. All comments will be available for public inspection and copying. A public hearing will be held upon written request to the Commissioner by any person who has submitted written comments. If a public hearing is to be held, notice of the time and place will be published in the FEDERAL REGISTER.

DRAFTING INFORMATION

The principal author of these regulations is David A. Juster of the Office of Associate Chief Counsel (International), within the Office of Chief Counsel, Internal Revenue Service. However, personnel from other offices of the Internal Revenue Service and Treasury Department participated in developing the regulations on matters of substance and style.

[¶49,105] Proposed Regulations and Amendments of Regulations (LR-119-86), published in the Federal Register on July 18, 1988.

Gains and losses: Asset acquisitions: Allocation rules.—Reg. §§1.167(a)-5T and 1.1031(d)-1T, relating to allocation rules for certain asset acquisitions under Code Sec. 1060, are proposed. Reg. §1.1060-1T was removed 2/12/2001 by T.D. 8940 and Reg. §1.755-2T was removed 6/6/2003 by T.D. 9059.

AGENCY: Internal Revenue Service, Treasury.

ACTION: Notice of proposed rulemaking by cross-reference to temporary regulations.

SUMMARY: In the Rules and Regulations portion of this issue of the FEDERAL REGISTER, the Internal Revenue Service is issuing temporary regulations to provide guidance to taxpayers concerning the application of the allocation rules for certain asset acquisitions under section 1060 to taxpayers generally and to partnerships. The text of the new sections also serves as the comment document for this notice of proposed rulemaking.

DATES:

PROPOSED EFFECTIVE DATE

The regulations are proposed to apply generally to any applicable asset acquisition made after May 6, 1986, unless such acquisition is pursuant to a binding contract which was in effect on May 6, 1986, and at all times thereafter. The reporting requirements apply to asset acquisitions (and to certain adjustments of consideration) occurring in a taxable year for which the due date (including extensions of time) of the income tax return or return of income is on or after September 13, 1988.

DATE FOR COMMENTS AND REQUESTS FOR A PUBLIC HEARING

Written comments and requests for a public hearing must be delivered or mailed by September 16, 1988.

ADDRESS: Send comments and requests for a public hearing to: Commissioner of Internal Revenue, Attention: CC:LR:T [LR-119-86], Washington, D.C. 20224.

FOR FURTHER INFORMATION CONTACT: Judith C. Winkler of the Legislation and Regulations Division, Office of Chief Counsel, Internal Revenue Service, 1111 Constitution Avenue, N.W., Washington, D.C. 20224 (Attention: CC:LR:T) or telephone 202-566-3458 (not a toll-free number). For information concerning the temporary regulations under section 755, contact Robert E. Shaw of the Legislation and Regulations Division, Office of Chief Counsel, Internal Revenue Service, 1111 Constitution Avenue, N.W., Washington, D.C. 20224, (Attention: CC:LR:T) or telephone 202-566-3297 (not a toll-free number).

SUPPLEMENTARY INFORMATION:

PAPERWORK REDUCTION ACT

The collection of information contained in this notice of proposed rulemaking has been submitted to the Office of Management and Budget for review in accordance with the Paperwork Reduction Act of 1980 (44 U.S.C. 3504(h)). Comments on the collection of information should be sent to the Office of Information and Regulatory Affairs, Office of Management and Budget, Washington, D.C. 20503, Attention: Desk Officer for the Internal Revenue Service, with copies to the Internal Revenue Service at the address previously specified.

The collection of information in this regulation is in section 26 CFR 1.1060-1T(h). This information is required by the Internal Revenue Service pursuant to section 1060. This information will be used to verify that the purchaser and the seller are complying with section 1060 by allocating the consideration among the assets pursuant to the residual method of allocation. The likely respondents are businesses or other for-profit institutions and small businesses or organizations.

Estimated total annual reporting and/or recordkeeping burden: 21,053 hours.

Estimated average annual burden hours per respondent and/or recordkeeper: 1.05 hours.

Estimated number of respondents and/or recordkeepers: 20,000.

Estimated annual frequency of responses: One time generally.

BACKGROUND

Temporary regulations published in the Rules and Regulations portion of this issue of the FEDERAL REGISTER add new temporary regulations §§1.167(a)-5T, 1.755-2T, 1.1031(d)-1T, and 1.1060-1T, to Part 1 of Title 26 of the Code of Federal Regulations (CFR), and amend §1.338(b)-3T. The final regulations that are proposed to be based on these temporary regulations would be added to Part 1 of Title 26 of the CFR. Those final regulations would provide guidance on the allocation of consideration among the assets transferred in an applicable asset acquisition. Section 1060 was added by section 641 of the Tax Reform Act of 1986 (Pub. L. No. 99-514; 100 Stat. 2085). For the text of the new temporary regulations, see T.D. 8215, published in the Rules and Regulations portion of this issue of the FEDERAL REGISTER. The preamble to the temporary regulations explains the regulations.

SPECIAL ANALYSES

Although this document is a notice of proposed rulemaking that solicits public comment, the Internal Revenue Service has concluded that the regulations proposed herein are interpretative and the notice and public procedure requirements of 5 U.S.C. 553 do not apply. Accordingly, these proposed regulations do not constitute regulations subject to the Regulatory Flexibility Act (5 U.S.C. chapter 6). The Commissioner of Internal Revenue has determined that this proposed rule is not a major rule as defined in Executive Order 12291 and that a Regulatory Impact Analysis therefore is not required.

COMMENTS AND REQUESTS FOR A PUBLIC HEARING

Before these proposed regulations are adopted, consideration will be given to any written comments that are submitted (preferably eight copies) to the Commissioner of Internal Revenue. All comments will be available for public inspection and copying. A public hearing will be held upon written request to the Commissioner by any person who has submitted written comments. If a public hearing is held, notice of the time and place will be published in the FEDERAL REGISTER.

DRAFTING INFORMATION

The principal author of the proposed regulations under sections 167, 338, 1031 and 1060 is Judith C. Winkler of the Legislation and Regulations Division of the Office of Chief Counsel, Internal Revenue Service. The principal author of the proposed regulations under section 755 is Robert Shaw of the Legislation and Regulations Division of the Office of Chief Counsel, Internal Revenue Service. However, personnel from other offices of the Internal Revenue Service and Treasury Department participated in developing the regulations, on matters of both substance and style.

[¶49,106] Proposed Regulations (INTL-934-86), published in the Federal Register on September 2, 1988.

Foreign corporations: Branch profits tax.—Reg. §§1.884-0T—1.884-5T, relating to the branch profits tax, are proposed. Reg. §§1.884-0, 1.884-1, 1.884-4 and 1.884-5 were adopted 9/10/92 by T.D. 8432.

AGENCY: Internal Revenue Service, Treasury.

ACTION: Notice of proposed rulemaking by cross-reference to temporary regulations.

SUMMARY: This document contains proposed Income Tax Regulations relating to the branch tax. In the Rules and Regulations portion of this FEDERAL REGISTER, the Internal Revenue Service is issuing temporary regulations relating to these matters. The text of these temporary regulations also serves as the comment document for this proposed rulemaking.

DATES: These regulations are proposed to be effective for taxable years beginning after December 31, 1986. Written comments and requests for a public hearing must be delivered or mailed by November 1, 1988.

ADDRESS: Send comments and requests for a public hearing to: Commissioner of Internal Revenue, (Attention: CC:LR:T, INTL-934-86), Washington, DC 20224.

FOR FURTHER INFORMATION CONTACT: Richard M. Elliott of the Office of Associate Chief Counsel (International), within the Office of the Chief Counsel, Internal Revenue Service, 1111 Constitution Avenue, N.W., Washington, DC 20224 (Attn: CC:LR:T, INTL-934-86) (202-566-6457, not a toll-free call).

SUPPLEMENTARY INFORMATION:

PAPERWORK REDUCTION ACT

The collection of information contained in this notice of proposed rulemaking has been submitted to the Office of Management and Budget for review in accordance with the Paperwork Reduction Act of 1980 (44 U.S.C. 3504(h)). Comments on the collection of information should be sent to the Office of Information and Regulatory Affairs, Office of Management and Budget, Washington, DC 20503, Attention: Desk Officer for Internal Revenue Service, with copies to the Internal Revenue Service, Washington, DC 20224, Attention: IRS Reports Clearance Officer TR:FP.

The collection of information in this regulation is in §§1.884-1T(d)(11), 1.884-2T(a)(2), 1.884-2T(b), 1.884-2T(c)(2), 1.884-2T(d)(1), 1.884-2T(d)(4), 1.884-2T(d)(5), 1.884-4T(b)(7), 1.884-4T(c)(1), 1.884-5T(b)(3) through (7), 1.884-5T(d)(6), and 1.884-5T(f). This information is required by the Internal Revenue Service to ensure the correct computation of tax under section 884. This information will be used in audits of taxpayers. The likely respondents are business or other for-profit institutions.

Estimated total annual reporting and/or recordkeeping burden: 20,500 hours.

The estimated annual burden per respondent/recordkeeper varies from .5 to 10.5 hours depending on individual circumstances, with an estimated average of 6.5 hours.

Estimated number of respondents and/or recordkeepers: 3000.

Estimated annual frequency of responses: Annually.

BACKGROUND

The temporary regulations published in the Rules and Regulations portion of this issue of the FEDERAL REGISTER add new §§1.884-0T through 1.884-2T, 1.884-4T, and 1.884-5T. The final regulations that are proposed to be based on the temporary regulations would amend 26 CFR Parts 1 and 602. For the text of the temporary regulations, see [INSERT FEDERAL REGISTER REFERENCE] [T.D. 8223] published in the Rules and Regulations portion of this issue of the FEDERAL REGISTER.

SPECIAL ANALYSES

These proposed rules are not major rules as defined in Executive Order 12291. Therefore, a Regulatory Impact Analysis is not required. Although this document is a notice of proposed rulemaking that solicits public comments, the notice and public procedure requirements of 5 U.S.C. §553 do not apply because the regulations proposed herein are interpretative. Therefore, an initial Regulatory Flexibility Analysis is not required by the Regulatory Flexibility Act (5 U.S.C. Chapter 6).

COMMENTS AND REQUEST FOR A PUBLIC HEARING

Before adopting as final regulations these proposed regulations, consideration will be given to any written comments that are submitted (preferably a signed original and seven copies) to the Commissioner of Internal Revenue. All comments will be available for public inspection and copying. A public hearing will be held upon written request to the Commissioner by any person who has submitted written comments. If a public hearing is to be held, notice of the time and place will be published in the FEDERAL REGISTER.

DRAFTING INFORMATION

The principal author of these regulations is Richard M. Elliott of the Office of the Associate Chief Counsel (International), within the Office of the Chief Counsel, Internal Revenue Service. However, personnel from other offices of the Internal Revenue Service and Treasury Department participated in developing the regulations.

[¶49,107] **Proposed Regulations (LR-156-86),** published in the Federal Register on September 6, 1988.

Returns: Partnerships: Partnership information.—Reg. §§1.6031(b)-1T and 1.6031(c)-1T, relating to partnership statements and nominee reporting of partnership information, are proposed.

AGENCY: Internal Revenue Service, Treasury.

ACTION: Notice of proposed rulemaking by cross-reference to temporary regulations.

SUMMARY: In the Rules and Regulations portion of this issue of the FEDERAL REGISTER, the Internal Revenue Service is issuing temporary regulations relating to partnership statements and nominee reporting of partnership information. The text of the temporary regulations serves as the comment document for this notice of proposed rulemaking.

DATES: Written comments and requests for a public hearing must be delivered or mailed by [60 DAYS AFTER DATE OF PUBLICATION OF THIS DOCUMENT IN THE FEDERAL REGISTER]. Except as otherwise provided, the text of §1.6031(b)-1T is proposed to be effective for partnership taxable years beginning after September 3, 1982. Except as otherwise provided, the text of §1.6031(c)-1T is proposed to be effective for partnership taxable years beginning after October 22, 1986.

ADDRESS: Send comments and requests for a public hearing to: Commissioner of Internal Revenue, 1111 Constitution Avenue, N.W., Attention: CC:LR:T (LR-156-86), Washington, D.C. 20224.

FOR FURTHER INFORMATION CONTACT: Stuart G. Wessler of the Legislation and Regulations Division, Office of the Chief Counsel, Internal Revenue Service, 1111 Constitution Avenue, N.W., Washington, D.C. 20224 (Attention: CC:LR:T LR-1556-86). Telephone 202-566-3297 (not a toll-free call).

SUPPLEMENTARY INFORMATION:

PAPERWORK REDUCTION ACT

The collection of information contained in this notice of proposed rulemaking has been submitted to the Office of Management and Budget for review in accordance with the Paperwork Reduction Act of 1980 (44 U.S.C. 3504(h)). Comments on the collection of information should be sent to the Office of Information and Regulatory Affairs, Office of Management and Budget, Washington, D.C. 20503, attention: Desk Officer for the Internal Revenue Service, with copies to the Internal Revenue Service at the address previously specified.

The collection of information in this regulation are in §§1.6031(b)-1T (a) and 1.6031(c)-1T (a) and (h). This information is required by the Internal Revenue Service pursuant to section 6031. This information will be used to verify that a taxpayer is reporting the correct amount of income or gain or claiming the correct amount of losses, deductions, or credits with respect to that taxpayer's interest in the partnership. The likely respondents are individuals or households, State or local governments, farms, business or other for-profit institutions, non-profit institutions, and small businesses or organizations.

These estimates are an approximation of the average time expected to be necessary for a collection of information. They are based on such information as is available to the Internal Revenue Service. Individual respondents/recordkeepers may require greater or less time, depending on their particular circumstances.

Estimated total annual reporting and recordkeeping burden: 6,374 hours.

Estimated average annual burden hours per respondent and recordkeeper varies from .02 to .627 hours, depending on individual circumstances, with an estimated average of .06 hours.

Estimated number of respondents and recordkeepers: 105,000.

Estimated annual frequency of response: On occasion.

BACKGROUND

The temporary regulations (designated by a "T" following the section citation) in the Rules and Regulations section of this issue of the FEDERAL REGISTER amend Part 1 of Title 26 of the Code of Federal Regulations to provide rules under section 6031(b) of the Internal Revenue Code of 1986, as added by section 403 of the Tax Equity end Fiscal Responsibility Act of 1982 (96 Stat. 669) and amended by sections 1501(c)(16) and 1811(b)(1)(A)(i) of the Tax Reform Act of 1986 (100 Stat. 2740, 2832), and under section 6031(c), as added by section 1811(b)(1)(A)(ii) of the Tax Reform Act of 1986 (100 Stat. 2832). This document proposes to adopt those temporary regulations as final regulations; accordingly, the text of the temporary regulations serves as the comment document for this notice of proposed rulemaking. In addition, the preamble to the temporary regulations provides a discussion of the proposed and temporary rules.

For the text of the temporary regulations, see T.D. 8225 published in the Rules and Regulations section of this issue of the FEDERAL REGISTER.

SPECIAL ANALYSES

The Commissioner of Internal Revenue has determined that the proposed rule is not a major rule as defined in Executive Order 12291 and that a Regulatory Impact Analysis is therefore not required.

The Secretary of the Treasury has certified that this rule will not have a significant impact on a substantial number of small entities because the number of significantly affected small entities is not substantial. A regulatory flexibility analysis, therefore, is not required under the Regulatory Flexibility Act (5 U.S.C. chapter 6).

COMMENTS AND REQUESTS FOR A PUBLIC HEARING

Before adopting these proposed regulations, consideration will be given to any written comments that are submitted (preferably eight copies) to the Commissioner of Internal Revenue. All comments will be available for public inspection and copying. A public hearing will be held upon written request of any person who has submitted written comments. If a public hearing is held, notice of the time and place will be published in the FEDERAL REGISTER.

DRAFTING INFORMATION

The principal author of these proposed regulations is Stuart G. Wessler of the Legislation and Regulations Division of the Office of Chief Counsel, Internal Revenue Service. However, personnel from other offices of the Internal Revenue Service and Treasury Department participated in developing the regulations, both on matters of substance and style.

[¶49,109] Proposed Regulations (INTL-952-86), published in the Federal Register on September 14, 1988.

Income from U.S. sources: Allocation and apportionment of expenses.—Reg. §§1.861-8T—1.861-12T, 1.861-14T and 1.863-3T (redesignated as Temporary Reg. §1.863-3AT by T.D. 8687), relating to the allocation and apportionment of interest expense and certain other expenses for purposes of the foreign tax credit rules and certain other international tax provisions, are proposed. Temporary Reg. §1.861-9T(e)(2) and (e)(3) were adopted on 7/15/2014 by T.D. 9676.

AGENCY: Internal Revenue Service, Treasury.

ACTION: Notice of proposed rulemaking by cross-reference to temporary regulations.

SUMMARY: This document provides proposed Income Tax Regulations relating to the allocation and apportionment of interest expense and certain other expenses for purposes of the foreign tax credit rules and certain other international tax provisions. In the rules and regulations portion of this FEDERAL REGISTER, the Internal Revenue Service is issuing temporary regulations relating to these matters. The text of those temporary regulations also serves as the comment document for this notice of proposed rulemaking. This document also withdraws the notice of proposed rulemaking relating to the same subject that appeared in the FEDERAL REGISTER on September 11, 1987 (52 FR 34580).

DATES: In general, these regulations would be applicable to the allocation and apportionment of interest expense and certain other expenses for taxable years beginning after December 31, 1986. Comments and requests for a public hearing must be delivered or mailed before December 13, 1988.

ADDRESS: Send comments and requests for a public hearing to: Commissioner of Internal Revenue, (Attention: CC:LR:T, INTL-952-86), Washington, D.C. 20224.

FOR FURTHER INFORMATION CONTACT: David Merrick, regarding the allocation and apportionment of interest expense, and Carl Cooper, regarding the allocation and apportionment of other expenses, both of the Office of Associate Chief Counsel (International), within the Office of Chief Counsel, Internal Revenue Service, 1111 Constitution Avenue, NW, Washington, D.C. 20224 (Attention: CC:LR:T (INTL-952-86)) (David Merrick 202-566-6276, Carl Cooper 202-634-5406, not a toll-free call).

SUPPLEMENTARY INFORMATION:

PAPERWORK REDUCTION ACT

The collection of information contained in this notice of proposed rulemaking has been submitted to the Office of Management and Budget for review in accordance with the Paperwork Reduction Act of 1980 (44 U.S.C. §3504(h)). Comments on the collection of information should be sent to the Office of Information and Regulatory Affairs, Office of Management and Budget, Washington, DC 20503, Attention: Desk Officer for Internal Revenue Service, with copies to the Internal Revenue Service at the address previously specified.

The affirmative elections in this regulation are in §1.861-9T(g)(1)(ii), which requires taxpayers affirmatively to elect either the gross income or the asset method of apportionment in the case of a controlled foreign corporation, and in §1.861-12T(c)(4)(ii), which permits taxpayers to elect under certain circumstances to reallocate interest expense that is allocated to a noncontrolled section 902 corporation. This information will be used in audits of taxpayers. The likely respondents are businesses and other for-profit institutions.

Estimated total annual reporting burden: 2,500 hours.

Estimated annual burden per respondent: 10 minutes.

Estimated number of respondents: 15,000.

Estimated annual frequency of responses: On occasion.

BACKGROUND

The temporary regulations published in the rules and regulations portion of this issue of the FEDERAL REGISTER add new temporary regulations §§1.861-8T through 1.861-14T. For the text of the temporary regulations, see [INSERT FEDERAL REGISTER REFERENCE]

[T.D. 8228] published in the rules and regulations portion of this issue of the FEDERAL REGISTER.

SPECIAL ANALYSES

It has been determined that these proposed rules are not major rules as defined in Executive Order 12291. Therefore, a Regulatory Impact Analysis is not required. Although this document is a notice of proposed rulemaking that solicits public comment, the notice and public procedure requirements of 5 U.S.C. §553 do not apply because it has been determined that these proposed regulations will not have a significant impact on a substantial number of small entities. Therefore, an initial Regulatory Flexibility Analysis is not required by Regulatory Flexibility Act (5 U.S.C. Chapter 6).

COMMENTS AND REQUESTS FOR A PUBLIC HEARING

Before adopting these proposed regulations, consideration will be given to any written comments that are submitted (preferably a signed original and seven copies) to the Commissioner of Internal Revenue. All comments will be available for public inspection and copying. A public hearing will be held upon written request by any person who submits written comments on the proposed rules. Notice of the time and place for the hearing will be published in the FEDERAL REGISTER.

DRAFTING INFORMATION

The principal author of the proposed regulations relating to the allocation and apportionment of interest expense is David Merrick, and the principal author of the proposed regulations relating to the allocation and apportionment of other expenses is Carl Cooper, both of the Office of Associate Chief Counsel (International), within the Office of Chief Counsel, Internal Revenue Service. Other personnel from offices of the Internal Revenue Service and Treasury Department participated in developing these regulations.

[¶49,110] Proposed Regulations and Amendments (IA-111-86), published in the Federal Register on January 9, 1989.

Exclusions: Prizes and awards: Employee achievement awards.—Reg. §§1.74-2 and 1.274-8 and amendments of Reg. §§1.74-1, 1.102-1, 1.274-1 and 1.274-3, relating to prizes and awards and employee achievement awards, are proposed.

AGENCY: Internal Revenue Service.

ACTION: Notice of proposed rulemaking.

SUMMARY: This document contains proposed amendments to the regulations relating to the excludability of certain prizes and awards and to the deductibility of certain employee awards. Changes to the applicable tax law were made by the Tax Reform Act of 1986. These amendments, if adopted, will provide the public with the guidance needed to comply with this Act.

DATES: Written comments and requests for a public hearing must be delivered or mailed by Mar. 10, 1989. The amendments are proposed to be effective after December 31, 1986.

ADDRESS: Send comments and requests for a public hearing to: Commissioner of Internal Revenue, Internal Revenue Service, 1111 Constitution Avenue, N.W., Washington, D.C. 20224; Attention: CC:CORP:T:R, IA-111-86.

FOR FURTHER INFORMATION CONTACT: Johnnel St. Germain of the Office of Assistant Chief Counsel (Income Tax and Accounting), Internal Revenue Service, 1111 Constitution Avenue, N.W., Washington, D.C. 20224; Attention: CC:CORP:T:R, IA-111-86. Telephone 202-566-4509 (not a toll-free call).

SUPPLEMENTARY INFORMATION:

PAPERWORK REDUCTION ACT

The collections of information contained in this notice of proposed rulemaking have been submitted to the Office of Management and Budget for review in accordance with the Paperwork Reduction Act of 1980 (44 U.S.C. 3504(h)). Comments on the collections of information should be sent to the Office of Information and Regulatory Affairs, Office of Management and Budget, Washington, D.C. 20503, attention: Desk Officer for the Internal Revenue Service. Copies of comments should also be sent to the Internal Revenue Service at the address previously specified.

The collections of information in this regulation are in 26 CFR §§1.74-1(c). This information is required by the Internal Revenue Service in order to verify that the proper amount of income is reported by taxpayers on their returns of tax. The likely respondents are individuals.

Estimated total annual reporting burden: 1,275 hours.

Estimated average annual burden per respondent: 15 minutes.

Estimated number of respondents: 5,100.

BACKGROUND

This document contains proposed amendments to the Income Tax Regulations (26 CFR Part 1) under sections 74, 102, and 274 of the Internal Revenue Code (Code). The amendments are proposed to conform the regulations to section 122 of the Tax Reform Act of 1986 (Pub. L. 99-514). The proposed amendments, if adopted, will be issued under the authority contained in section 7805 of the Code (68A Stat. 917; 26 U.S.C. 7805).

GENERAL INFORMATION

Prior to the 1986 Code, section 74 stated that prizes and awards, other than certain types of fellowship grants and scholarships, were includible in gross income unless they were made primarily in recognition of religious, charitable, scientific, educational, artistic, literary, or civic achievement. To qualify for the exclusion, the recipient must have been selected without any action on his part and could not be required to render substantial services as a condition to receiving the prize or award.

Within the context of a business relationship, prizes and awards that would otherwise be includible in a recipient's gross income were excludable if they qualified as gifts under section 102. In general, section 274(b) disallowed an employer a business deduction for gifts to an employee to the extent that the total cost of all gifts of cash, tangible personal property, and other items to the same individual during the taxable year exceeded $25. A special exception to the $25 limitation was allowed for items of tangible personal property awarded to an employee for length of service, safety achievement, or productivity. The employer could deduct the cost of such an award up to $400. If the item was provided under a qualified award plan, the deductibility limitation was increased to $1600, provided the average cost of all plan awards made during the year did not exceed $400. A de minimis fringe benefit under section 132(e) was, and continues to be, excludable from gross income and is not subject to the requirements imposed upon prizes and awards under sections 74 and 274.

EXPLANATION OF PROVISIONS

These proposed amendments relate to the excludability of certain prizes and awards and to the deductibility of certain employee awards and reflect the substantial changes made by the Tax Reform Act of 1986 (the Act) to sections 74, 102 and 274 of the Internal Revenue Code (Code). Changes to the applicable sections of the Code and regulations, amended or newly incorporated by this document, are effective for awards made after December 31, 1986.

Under the Act, the section 74(b) exclusion for prizes or awards received in recognition of charitable achievement is available only if the payor transfers the prize or award to one or more entities described in paragraph (1) and/or (2) of section 170(c), pursuant to the direction of the recipient.

Section 1.74-1(c) of the proposed regulations requires that recipients of prizes and awards clearly designate, in writing, within 45 days of the date the item is granted that they wish to have the prize or award transferred to one or more qualifying donee organizations. The proposed regulations set forth requirements which, in certain instances, determine whether a qualifying designation has been made.

Section 1.74-1(d) of the proposed regulations clarifies that the exclusion under section 74(b) will not be available unless the prize or award is transferred by the payor to one or more qualified donee organizations before the recipient, or any person other than the grantor or a qualified donee organization, uses the item. In general, a transfer may be accomplished by any method that results in receipt of the prize or award by, or on behalf of, one or more qualified donee organizations.

Section 1.74-1(e) further clarifies the requirements of section 74(b) by defining certain terms. Definitions are included which determine what constitutes a "qualified donee organization," when a "disqualifying use" has taken place, and when an item is considered "granted."

Section 1.74-1(f) provides that neither the payor nor the recipient of the prize or award may claim a charitable contribution deduction for the value of any prize or award for which an exclusion is allowed under section 74(b).

All of the requirements of section 74(b) in existence prior to passage of the Act remain in effect and must be met in order for the award recipient to be eligible for the exclusion. Accordingly, rules and regulations governing these additional requirements, to the extent they are not inconsistent with the proposed regulations, will remain in effect.

New Code section 74(c) excludes certain employee achievement awards from gross income. The exclusion applies, subject to certain limitations, to the value of awards made by the employer for safety achievement or length of service achievement. The amount of the exclusion generally corresponds with the deduction given the employer under new section 274(j) for these "employee achievement awards." Thus, in general, the employee must include these awards in income to the extent that the fair market value of the award, or, if greater, the cost of the award to the employer, exceeds the amount deductible under section 274(j). The exclusion allows an employee to exclude the full fair market value of the award where the cost of the award is fully deductible by the employer.

Section 1.74-2(d) of the proposed regulations provides special rules for employee achievement awards applicable to sole-proprietors and tax-exempt employers.

Section 1.74-2(e) clarifies that an employee award, whether or not an employee achievement award, may be excludible from gross income as a de minimis fringe benefit under section 132(e).

Section 102(c) of the Code clarifies that, with the exception of employee achievement awards under section 74(c) and de minimis fringe benefits under section 132(e), an employee shall not exclude from gross income any amount transferred to the employee (or for the employee's benefit) by, or on behalf of, the employer in the form of a gift, bequest, devise, or inheritance. Therefore, while awards satisfying the requirements of section 74(c) and de minimis fringe benefits qualifying under section 132(e) will be excluded from gross income under those sections, no amounts (except in certain narrowly defined circumstances) transferred by, or on behalf of, an individual's employer will be excludable from gross income under section 102.

Section 1.102-1(f)(2) of the proposed regulations provides that for purposes of section 102(c), extraordinary transfers to the natural objects of one's bounty will not be considered transfers for the benefit of an employee if it can be shown that the transfer was not made in recognition of the transferee's employment. Thus, the rules set out in *Comm. v. Duberstein*, 363 U.S. 278 (1960), formerly applicable in the determination of whether all property transferred inter-vivos from an employer to an employee constitutes a gift, will only be applicable where the transferee employee would be the natural object of the employer's bounty.

From an employer's perspective, the Act substantially modifies an employer's ability to deduct the cost of certain employee awards. New section 274(j) defines deductible "employee achievement awards" to include only those awards made for length of service achievement award or safety achievement. In addition, an employee achievement award must be an item of tangible personal property awarded as part of a meaningful presentation and made under conditions and circumstances that do not create a significant likelihood of the payment of disguised compensation.

Section 274(j) also establishes a limit on the amount that may be deducted by an employer. The annual deduction limitation per employee is $400 for employee achievement awards that are not awarded as part of a qualified award plan. The annual deduction limitation per employee is $1,600 for employee achievement awards that are awarded as part of a qualified award plan. In no event may an employer deduct more than $1,600 per employee for all employee achievement awards made during the year. An award is not a qualified plan award where the average cost of all employee achievement awards made by the employer pursuant to a plan exceeds $400 during the taxable year.

Section 1.274-8(b) of the proposed regulations clarifies that the $1,600 deduction limitation applies in the aggregate, so that the $1,600 limitation for qualified plan awards and the $400 limitation for employee achievement awards that are not qualified plan awards cannot be added together to allow deductions exceeding $1,600 for employee achievement awards made to an employee in a taxable year.

Section 1.274-8(c)(2) of the proposed regulations provides that tangible personal property does not include cash or any gift certificate other than a nonnegotiable gift certificate conferring only the right to receive tangible personal property. The proposed regulations also give examples of what will be considered to create a significant likelihood of the payment of disguised compensation. For example, the providing of employee achievement awards in a manner that discriminates in favor of highly paid employees will be considered to be payment of disguised compensation.

Section 1.274-8(c)(5) of the proposed regulations defines a "qualified plan award" as an employee achievement award presented pursuant to an established written award plan or program of the employer that does not discriminate as to eligibility or benefits.

Section 1.274-8(d)(1) of the proposed regulations states that the deduction limitations shall apply to a partnership as well as to each member of the partnership. Paragraph (d)(2) provides that the cost of length of service achievement awards (other than awards excludable under section 132(e)) may only be deducted by the employer if the employee has at least 5 years of service with the employer and has not received a length of service achievement award during that year or any of the 4 prior years. In addition, this paragraph clarifies that although a retirement award will be treated as having been provided for length of service achievement, it may also qualify for treatment as a de minimis fringe benefit under § 132(e) of the Code. Paragraph (d)(3) provides guidance with respect to safety achievement awards. An employer may deduct the cost of safety achievement awards only when presented to no more than 10% of an employer's eligible employees. Eligible employees include any employee who has worked for the employer in a full time capacity for at least one year and who is not a manager, administrator, clerical employee, or other professional employee. Special rules clarify that in the case where more than 10% of an employer's eligible employees receive a safety achievement award, no award will be considered to be awarded for safety achievement if it cannot be determined that that award was presented before the 10% limitation was exceeded.

The Act specifically excludes awards qualifying as de minimis fringe benefits under section 132(e) from the requirements for length of service achievement and safety achievement. As a result, employers are not required to consider section 132(e) awards in determining whether employee achievement awards comply with the 5 year limitations for length of service achievement and the 10% eligible employee limitations for safety achievement.

SPECIAL ANALYSES

The Commissioner of Internal Revenue has determined that this proposed rule is not a major rule as defined in Executive Order 12291. Accordingly, a Regulatory Impact Analysis is not required. The Internal Revenue Service has concluded that although this document is a notice of proposed rulemaking that solicits public comment, the regulations proposed herein are interpretative and the notice and public procedure requirements of 5 U.S.C. 553 do not apply. Accordingly, no Regulatory Flexibility Analysis is required for this rule.

COMMENTS AND REQUESTS FOR A PUBLIC HEARING

Before adopting these proposed regulations, consideration will be given to any written comments that are submitted (preferably eight copies) to the Commissioner of Internal Revenue. All comments will be available for public inspection and copying. A public hearing will be held upon written request to the Commissioner by any person who has submitted written comments. If a public hearing is held, notice of time and place will be published in the FEDERAL REGISTER.

DRAFTING INFORMATION

The principal author of these proposed regulations is Christopher J. Wilson, formerly of the Legislation and Regulations Division of the Office of Chief Counsel, Internal Revenue Service. However, personnel from other offices of the Internal Revenue Service and Treasury Department participated in developing the regulations, on matters of both substance and style.

[¶ 49,111] Proposed Regulations (INTL-304-89), published in the Federal Register on August 2, 1989.

Income from source: Interest expense allocation.—Reg. §§ 1.861-9T and 1.861-13T, relating to transition rules for the allocation and apportionment of interest expense for the purposes of the foreign tax credit rules and certain other international tax provisions, are proposed.

AGENCY: Internal Revenue Service, Treasury.

ACTION: Notice of proposed rulemaking by cross-reference to temporary regulations.

SUMMARY: This document provides proposed Income Tax Regulations relating to transition rules for the allocation and apportionment of interest expense for purposes of the foreign tax credit rules and certain other international tax provisions. This document also provides rules concerning the treatment of financial products that alter effective interest expense. Changes to the transition rules were made by the Technical and Miscellaneous Revenue Act of 1988. These regulations are necessary to provide guidance needed by taxpayers engaging in international transactions in order to comply with these changes. In the rules and regulations portion of this FEDERAL REGISTER, the Internal Revenue Service is issuing temporary regulations relating to these matters. The text of those temporary regulations also serves as the comment document for this notice of proposed rulemaking. Certain additional regulations are also proposed by this document.

DATES: These regulations are proposed to be effective for taxable years beginning after December 31, 1986. These regulations would be applicable to the allocation and apportionment of interest expense for taxable years beginning after December 31, 1986, except for § 1.861-9T(b)(6), which is effective for transactions entered into after September 14, 1988. Comments and requests for a public hearing must be delivered or mailed before August 31, 1989.

ADDRESS: Send comments and requests for a public hearing to: Commissioner of Internal Revenue, Attention: CC:CORP:T:R (INTL-952-86), Room 4429, Washington, D.C. 20224.
FOR FURTHER INFORMATION CONTACT: Charles Plambeck of the office of Associate Chief Counsel (International), within the Office of Chief Counsel, Internal Revenue Service, 1111 Constitution Avenue, NW, Washington, D.C. 20224 (Attention: CC:CORP:T:R. (INTL-952-86)) (202-566-6284), not a toll-free call).
SUPPLEMENTARY INFORMATION:

BACKGROUND

The temporary regulations published in the rules and regulations portion of this issue of the FEDERAL REGISTER add new temporary regulations §1.861-13T and a new paragraph (b)(6) to §1.861-9T. For the text of the temporary regulations, see T.D. 8257 published in the rules and regulations portion of this issue of the FEDERAL REGISTER. Certain additional regulations are also proposed by this document.

SPECIAL ANALYSES

It has been determined that these rules are not major rules as defined in Executive Order 12291. Therefore, a Regulatory Impact Analysis is not required. It has also been determined that section 553(b) of the Administrative Procedure Act (5 U.S.C. Chapter 5) and the Regulatory Flexibility Act (5 U.S.C. Chapter 6) do not apply to these regulations, and, therefore, an initial Regulatory Flexibility Analysis is not required. Pursuant to section 7805(f) of the Internal Revenue Code, the notice of proposed rulemaking for the regulations was submitted to the Administrator of the Small Business Administration for comment on their impact on small business.

COMMENTS AND REQUESTS FOR A PUBLIC HEARING

Before adopting these proposed regulations, consideration will be given to any written comments that are submitted (preferably a signed original and eight copies) to the Commissioner of Internal Revenue. All comments will be available for public inspection and copying. A public hearing will be held upon written request by any person who submits written comments on the proposed rules. Notice of the time and place for the hearing will be published in the FEDERAL REGISTER.

DRAFTING INFORMATION

The principal author of these proposed regulations is David Merrick of the Office of Associate Chief Counsel (International), within the Office of Chief Counsel, Internal Revenue Service. Other personnel from offices of the Internal Revenue Service and Treasury Department participated in developing these regulations.

[¶49,112] Proposed Regulations and Amendments of Regulations (CO-69-87), published in the Federal Register on September 20, 1989.

Carryovers: Excess credits: Use of pre-change attributes.—Amendments of Reg. §1.382-2T, relating to the manner and method of absorbing the Code Sec. 382 limitation with respect to certain capital losses and excess credits after there has been an ownership change of a corporation, are proposed. Reg. §§1.383-1 and 1.383-2 were adopted by T.D. 8352 on 6/26/91.
AGENCY: Internal Revenue Service, Treasury.
ACTION: Notice of proposed rulemaking by cross-reference to temporary regulations.
SUMMARY: In the Rules and Regulations portion of this issue of the Federal Register, the Internal Revenue Service is adding temporary regulations pertaining to section 383 of the Internal Revenue Code of 1986 ("Code"), which was amended by the Tax Reform Act of 1986. The temporary regulations provide guidance under section 383 relating to the manner and method of absorbing the section 382 limitation with respect to certain capital losses and excess credits after there has been an ownership change of a corporation within the meaning of section 382. The temporary regulations also contain amendments to the temporary regulations under section 382. The text of the temporary regulations also serves as the comment document for this notice of proposed rulemaking.
DATES: Written comments and requests for a public hearing must be mailed by Nov 20, 1989. The proposed regulations would apply generally to any ownership change, as defined under section 382, occurring after December 31, 1986.
ADDRESS: Send comments or requests for a public hearing to: Internal Revenue Service, Attention: CC:CORP:T:R [CO-69-87], Room 4429, 1111 Constitution Avenue, N.W., Washington, D.C. 20224.
FOR FURTHER INFORMATION CONTACT: Lori J. Jones of the Office of Assistant Chief Counsel (Corporate), Office of Chief Counsel, (202) 566-3205 (not a toll-free number).
SUPPLEMENTARY INFORMATION:

Paperwork Reduction Act

The collections of information contained in this notice of proposed rulemaking have been submitted to the Office of Management and Budget for review in accordance with the Paperwork Reduction Act of 1980 (44 U.S.C. 3504(h)). Comments on the collections of information should be sent to the Office of Management and Budget, Paperwork Reduction Project, Washington, D.C. 20503, with copies to the Internal Revenue Service, ATTN: IRS Reports Clearances Officer TR:FP, Washington, D.C. 20224.

The collections of information in this regulation are in 26 CFR 1.382-2T(a) and 1.383-1T(j). This information is required by the Internal Revenue Service to help ensure that loss corporations report the proper amount of certain capital losses and excess credits on their income tax returns. The information will be used by the Internal Revenue Service to more readily verify compliance with sections 382 and 383.

These estimates are an approximation of the average time expected to be necessary for a collection of information. They are based on such information as is available to the Internal Revenue Service. Individual respondents may require greater or less time, depending on their particular circumstances. Estimated total annual reporting burden: 247,500 hours. The estimated annual burden per respondent varies from 6 minutes to 30 minutes, depending on individual circumstances, with an estimated average of 18 minutes.

Estimated number of respondents: 750,000

Estimated frequency of respondents: annually.

Background

Temporary regulations published in the Rules and Regulations portion of this issue of the Federal Register add temporary regulations §1.383-1T and 2T to Part 1 of Title 26 of the Code of the Federal Regulations ("CFR") and amend §1.382-2T of that part. The final regulations which are proposed to be based on the temporary regulations would be added to Part 1 of Title 26 of CFR. The final regulations would provide guidance under sections 382 and 383 relating to the manner and method of absorbing the section 382 limitation with respect to certain capital losses and excess credits after there has been an ownership change of a corporation within the meaning of section 382. Sections 382 and 383 of the Code were amended by section 621 of the Tax Reform Act of 1986 (Pub. L. No. 99-514, 100 Stat. 2085). Section 382 was further amended by section 10225 of the Revenue Act of 1987 (Pub. L. No. 100-203; 101 Stat. 1330-413) and by sections 1006, 4012, and 5077 of the Technical and Miscellaneous Revenue Act of 1988 (Pub. L. No. 100-647). For the text of the temporary regulations, see T.D. [8264] published in the Rules and Regulations portion of this issue of the Federal Register. The preamble to the temporary regulations explains the added regulations.

Special Analyses

It has been determined that these proposed rules are not major rules as defined in Executive Order 12291. Therefore, a Regulatory Impact Analysis is not required. It has also been determined that section 553(b) of the Administrative Procedure Act (5 U.S.C. Chapter 5) and the Regulatory Flexibility Act (5 U.S.C. Chapter 6) do not apply to these regulations and, therefore, an initial Regulatory Flexibility Analysis is not required. Pursuant to section 7805(f) of the Internal Revenue Code, these regulations will be submitted to the Administrator of the Small Business Administration for comment on their impact on small business.

Comments and Requests for a Public Hearing

Before adopting these proposed regulations, consideration will be given to any written comments that are submitted (preferably eight copies) to the Internal Revenue Service. All comments will be available for public inspection and copying. A public hearing will be held upon written request by any person who has submitted written comments. If a public hearing is held, notice of time and place will be published in the Federal Register.

Drafting Information

The principal author of these proposed regulations is Lori J. Jones, Office of the Assistant Chief Counsel (Corporate), Office of Chief Counsel, Internal Revenue Service. However, personnel from other offices of the Internal Revenue Service and Treasury Department participated in developing the regulations, in matters of both substance and style.

[¶49,115] Proposed Regulations and Amendments of Regulations (INTL-704-87), published in the Federal Register on January 16, 1990.

Corporate distributions: Foreign corporation.—Amendments of Reg. §1.367(a)-1T, relating to the distribution of stock and securities by a domestic corporation to a person who is not a United States person, and also relating to a liquidating distribution of property by a domestic or foreign corporation to a foreign corporation, are proposed as final. Reg. §§1.367(e)-0 and 1.367(e)-1 were adopted 1/15/93 by T.D. 8472 and removed 8/9/96 by T.D. 8682. Reg. §1.367(e)-2 was adopted 8/6/99 by T.D. 8834. Reg. §7.367(b)-1 was removed 1/21/2000 by T.D. 8862.

AGENCY: Internal Revenue Service, Treasury.

ACTION: Notice of proposed rulemaking by cross-reference to temporary regulations.

SUMMARY: In the Rules and Regulations portion of this issue, the Internal Revenue Service is issuing temporary Income Tax Regulations that add new sections necessary to implementing section 367(e)(1) and (2) of the Internal Revenue Code of 1986, relating to certain corporate distributions to foreign shareholders. These provisions affect the taxability of both corporate distributors and shareholder distributees. The regulations also add certain provisions under section 367(a) and (b) concerning reorganizations under section 368(a)(1)(F) involving foreign corporations. The text of the temporary regulations also serves as the comment document for this notice of proposed rulemaking.

DATES: Written comments and requests for a public hearing must be delivered or mailed before March 19, 1990.

Except as set forth below, these regulations are proposed to be effective with respect to distributions after July 31, 1986. The following provisions have the following special proposed effective dates:

§1.367(a)-1(e) . . . . April 1, 1987
§1.367(a)-1(f) . . . . January 1, 1985

§1.367(e)-1 . . . . February 16, 1990
§1.367(b)-1(e) . . . . April 1, 1987
§1.367(b)-1(f) . . . . January 1, 1985

ADDRESS: Send comments and requests for a public hearing to Commissioner of Internal Revenue, (Attention: CC:CORP:T:R INTL-704-87), Room 4429, Washington, DC 20224.

FOR FURTHER INFORMATION CONTACT: Charles P. Besecky of the Office of Associate Chief Counsel (International) within the Office of Chief Counsel, Internal Revenue Service, 1111 Constitution Avenue, N.W., Washington, DC 20224 (Attention: CC:LR:T) (202-566-6444, not a toll-free call).

SUPPLEMENTARY INFORMATION:

PAPERWORK REDUCTION ACT

The collection of information contained in this notice of proposed rulemaking has been submitted to the Office of Management and Budget for review in accordance with the Paperwork Reduction Act of 1980 (44 U.S.C. §3504(h)). Comments on the collection of information should be sent to the Office of Management and Budget, Paperwork Reduction Project (1545-1124), Washington, D.C. 20503, with copies to the Internal Revenue Service, Attention: IRS Reports Clearance Officer TR:FP, Washington, DC 20224.

The collection of information in this regulation is in section 1.367(e)-1T(c)(2) and section 1.367(e)-2T(b)(2)(i) and (c)(2)(i). This information is required by the Internal Revenue Service to ensure that gains recognized by the distributing and distributee corporations are reported on the appropriate income tax return. This information will be used to assure compliance with the provisions of the regulation. The likely respondents are business or other for-profit institutions.

These estimates are an approximation of the average time expected to be necessary for a collection of information. They are based on such information as is available to the Internal Revenue Service. Individual respondents/recordkeepers may require greater or less time, depending upon their particular circumstances.

Estimated total annual reporting and/or recordkeeping burden: 3,200 hours.

Estimated average annual burden per respondent: 8 hours.

Estimated number of respondents: 400.

Estimated annual frequency of responses: 1.

BACKGROUND

The temporary regulations published in the Rules and Regulations portion of this issue of the FEDERAL REGISTER add §§1.367(a)-1T(e) and (f), 1.367(a)-0T, 1.367(e)-1T, and 1.367(e)-2T to 26 CFR Part 1, and add new paragraphs (e) and (f) to §7.367(b)-1 of 26 CFR Part 7. The final regulations that are proposed to be based on these temporary regulations would amend 26 CFR Parts 1, 7 and 602 by adding these temporary regulations as final regulations under section 367(a), (b) and (e) of the Internal Revenue Code of 1986. For the text of the temporary regulations, see T.D. 8280 published in the Rules and Regulations portion of this issue of the FEDERAL REGISTER.

SPECIAL ANALYSES

It has been determined that this proposed rule is not a major rule as defined in Executive Order 12291. Therefore, a Regulatory Impact Analysis is not required. It is hereby certified that the proposed rule will not have a significant impact on a substantial number of small entities. Few small entities would be affected by these regulations. A regulatory flexibility analysis, therefore, is not required under the Regulatory Flexibility Act (5 U.S.C. chapter 6). Pursuant to section 7805(f) of the Internal Revenue Code, these regulations will be submitted to the Administrator of the Small Business Administration for comment on their impact on small business.

COMMENTS AND REQUESTS FOR A PUBLIC HEARING

Before adopting these proposed regulations, consideration will be given to any written comments that are submitted (preferably a signed original and eight copies) to the Commissioner of Internal Revenue. All comments will be available for public inspection and copying. A public hearing will be held upon written request to the Commissioner by any person who has submitted written comments. If a public hearing is held, notice of the time and place will be published in the FEDERAL REGISTER.

DRAFTING INFORMATION

The principal author of these regulations is Charles P. Besecky of the Office of Associate Chief Counsel (International), within the Office of Chief Counsel, Internal Revenue Service. However, personnel from other offices of the Internal Revenue Service and Treasury Department participated in developing the regulations on matters of substance and style.

[¶49,118] **Proposed Regulations and Proposed Amendments of Regulations (IL-868-89),** published in the Federal Register on December 10, 1990.

Foreign-owned corporations: Information returns: Records.—Reg. §1.6038C-1, relating to foreign-owned corporations, is proposed. Reg. §§1.6038A-0—1.6038A-7 are adopted.

AGENCY: Internal Revenue Service, Treasury.

ACTION: Notice of proposed rulemaking.

SUMMARY: This document contains proposed Income Tax Regulations relating to information which must be reported and records which must be maintained by certain foreign-owned corporations under sections 6038A and 6038C of the Internal Revenue Code. These regulations will provide appropriate guidance for affected reporting corporations and related parties. The regulations will affect any reporting corporation, that is, certain domestic corporations or foreign corporations, as well as certain related parties of the reporting corporation.

DATES: Written comments, requests to appear, and outlines of oral comments to be presented at a public hearing scheduled for Friday, February 22, 1991, at 10:00 a.m., must be received by Friday, February 8, 1991. See notice of hearing published elsewhere in this issue of the Federal Register.

FOR FURTHER INFORMATION CONTACT: Concerning the hearing on the proposed rulemaking, Felicia Daniels, Regulations Unit, 202-566-3935 (not a toll-free call); concerning a particular regulation section, Carol P. Tello or Grace Perez-Navarro of the Office of Associate Chief Counsel (International), within the Office of Chief Counsel, (202-377-9493 (Ms. Tello), 202-287-4851 (Ms. Perez-Navarro), not toll-free calls).

SUPPLEMENTARY INFORMATION:

Paperwork Reduction Act

The collection of information contained in this notice of proposed rulemaking has been submitted to the Office of Management and Budget in accordance with the Paperwork Reduction Act of 1980 (44 U.S.C. 3504(h)). Comments on the collection of information should be sent to the Office of Management and Budget, Attention: Desk Officer for the Department of the Treasury, Office of Information and Regulatory Affairs, Washington, D. C. 20503, with copies to the Internal Revenue Service, Attention: IRS Reports Clearance Officer T:FP, Washington, D. C. 20224. The collection of information in this regulation is in §§1.6038A-2 and 1.6038A-3. This information is required by the Internal Revenue Service to determine the correct tax treatment of transactions between 25-percent foreign-owned corporations engaged in a U.S. trade or business and related parties. The likely respondents for Form 5472 are corporations.

These estimates are an approximation of the average time expected to be necessary for record maintenance and collection of information. They are based upon such information as is available to the Internal Revenue Service. Individual respondents and recordkeepers may require greater or less time, depending on their particular circumstances.

Estimated total annual reporting and recordkeeping burden: 1,539,000 hours

The estimated average annual reporting burden per respondent is 14 hours and 26 minutes.

The estimated average annual recordkeeping burden per recordkeeper is 10 hours.

Estimated number of respondents/recordkeepers: 63,000.

Estimated annual frequency of responses: 1.

Background

This document contains proposed Income Tax Regulations (26 CFR Part 1) under sections 6038A and 6038C of the Internal Revenue Code of 1986. These regulations are generally proposed to be effective for taxable years beginning after July 10, 1989. However, special effective date rules are proposed to provide that certain provisions sections will be effective as of, except as follows:

§1.6038A-1(c)	July 10, 1989
§1.6038A-2	July 10, 1989
§1.6038A-3	March 20, 1990
§1. 6038A-4	July 10, 1989
§1. 6038A-6	November 5, 1990

Explanation of Provisions

Prior Law

Prior to the enactment of the Revenue Reconciliation Act of 1989, section 6038A required an annual filing of an information return, Form 5472, by a domestic corporation (or a foreign corporation engaged in trade or business within the United States) that is controlled by a foreign person. A person controlled a corporation if that person owned stock possessing more than 50 percent of the total voting power of all classes of stock entitled to vote or more than 50 percent of the total value of shares of all classes of stock. If a corporation failed to furnish the information required under the statute, a penalty of $1000 was imposed for each taxable year with respect to which such failure occurred. An additional penalty of $1000 was imposed for each 30-day period during which such failure continued after the expiration of a 90-day period following the mailing of a notice of failure. The increase in the additional penalty was limited to $24,000.

Statutory Provision

The Revenue Reconciliation Act of 1989 amended section 6038A in several significant ways. First, the threshold of foreign ownership subjecting a corporation to the application of section 6038A was lowered from 50 percent to 25 percent. Second, amended section 6038A requires the maintenance of records as prescribed by regulations.

The penalty for the failure either to file timely the annual information return or to maintain (or to cause another to maintain) the prescribed records is $10,000 for each taxable year with respect to which such failure occurs. The former maximum additional penalty of $24,000 has been deleted. If the failure continues for more than 90 days after the day on which notice is given by the Service of such failure, an additional penalty of $10,000 is assessed for each 30-day period or part thereof that the failure continues.

In addition to the above changes, the 1989 Act added a new section, section 6038A(e)(1), requiring a foreign related party that engages in transactions with a reporting corporation to authorize the reporting corporation to act as its agent solely for purposes of sections 7602, 7603, and 7604.

If the related party does not authorize the reporting corporation to act as its agent, the Secretary shall apply the noncompliance penalty with respect to transactions between the related party and the reporting corporation.

If the noncompliance penalty applies, the amount allowed as a deduction for amounts paid or incurred to the related party and for the cost of goods purchased from the related party or sold by the reporting corporation to the related party is determined by the Secretary in his sole discretion based upon such probative information as the Secretary may choose to obtain. *See* H.R. Conf. Rep. 386, 101st Cong., 1st Sess. 593-595 (1989).

The noncompliance penalty may also be applied to a transaction between the related party and the reporting corporation if the reporting corporation does not substantially comply with a summons for records or testimony relating to such transaction.

The Omnibus Budget Reconciliation Act of 1990 (the 1990 Act) added section 6038C to the Internal Revenue Code. Foreign corporations engaged in U.S. trade or business are subject to the provisions of section 6038C, which are similar to the provisions of section 6038A. Additional regulations under section 6038C will be issued at a later time which will reflect the 1990 Act changes with respect to such corporations.

Comments

Comments are solicited with respect to ways to permit related foreign corporations to file a single agency designation, in a manner similar to the rules contained in paragraph (g) of § 1.6038A-1 regarding the ability of the common parent of an affiliated group to file a consolidated Form 5472 for all related party transactions of the U.S. consolidated return group and to be designated as agent for related parties.

The *de minimis* rule of § 1.6038A-1(h) was developed after consideration of case studies submitted by international examiners. Comments from taxpayers are solicited.

Comments and case studies are also solicited on whether the various tests for determining material profit and loss statements under § 1.6038A-3(c)(3) are appropriate. In particular, comments regarding the existing accounting and business practices for maintaining profit and loss statements are requested. Objections to the profit and loss statement standards set forth in these regulations should be accompanied by proposed alternatives. Comments also are solicited on when a profit margin analysis, rather than a return on assets analysis, might be appropriate for the high profit test under paragraph (c)(6) of section 1.6038A-3.

Explanation of Proposed Regulations

General requirement and definitions

Section 1.6038A-1 provides the general rule that certain foreign-owned U.S. corporations and foreign corporations engaged in trade or business within the United States (reporting corporations) must furnish certain information annually on an information return, Form 5472, and maintain records relating to transactions between the reporting corporation and a foreign related party as described in § 1.6038A-3. Definitions are provided for the terms reporting corporation, 25-percent foreign-owned, 25-percent foreign shareholder, related party, foreign person, and foreign related party. Special rules are provided for U.S. consolidated return groups.

Requirement of return

Section 1.6038A-2 describes the information that must be furnished annually on Form 5472. Reporting corporations whose sole trade or business in the United States is a banking, financing, or similar business as defined in § 1.864-4(c)(5)(i) (formerly excepted from filing Form 5472) will be subject to the information filing requirement of § 1.6038A-2.

Record maintenance

Section 1.6038A-3 provides the general rule that records to be maintained by a reporting corporation are those records sufficient to establish the correctness of the federal income tax return (including the correct treatment of transactions with related parties) of the reporting corporation. Records prepared, maintained, or possessed by a foreign related party relating to transactions between the reporting corporation and any related parties must be maintained in the United States, except where an election is in effect under paragraph (f) of § 1.6038A-3. A record may be maintained in the United States by a party other than the reporting corporation; however, the reporting corporation remains liable for the proper compilation and maintenance of such records.

The regulations generally are based upon the view that the requirement to "maintain" records does not require their creation. However, basic accounting records and material profit and loss statements must be created if they are not otherwise maintained. In connection with record maintenance and production, labels placed upon documents by the taxpayer shall not control.

Some reporting corporations may be unfamiliar with record maintenance practices generally adopted in the United States under the guidance of section 6001, its regulations, and longstanding administrative practice developed thereunder. In addition, such corporations may not be aware of the specific information that would be relevant to an examination of their related party transactions. In the absence of detailed guidance, such reporting corporations might not retain the information that is required for U.S. tax purposes. Therefore, six general categories of records with respect to related party transactions are provided as a safe harbor. Reporting corporations that maintain records in the categories that apply to the particular industry or business of the reporting corporation, to the extent such records may be relevant to the correct U.S. tax treatment of the transactions between related parties, are deemed to meet the record maintenance requirements of section 6038A.

Reporting corporations may enter into agreements with the District Director or the Assistant Commissioner (International) specifying what records must be maintained to satisfy the maintenance requirements for such reporting corporations under this section. Agreements with respect to retention of machine-sensible records under Rev. Proc. 86-19 may also be executed. An annual election to maintain records outside the United States is provided if the reporting corporation agrees to produce the records as prescribed by the regulations. The District Director or the Assistant Commissioner (International) may invalidate the election to maintain records outside the United States under certain circumstances.

Monetary penalty

Section 1.6038A-4 provides for the imposition of a monetary penalty of $10,000 for each taxable year in which a reporting corporation fails to timely file Form 5472, fails to maintain or cause another to maintain the records described in §1.6038A-3, or fails to produce the records within the time prescribed in §1.6038A-3. A rule permitting a reporting corporation to show reasonable cause as to why the failure occurred is provided. The reasonable cause exception is to be interpreted in accordance with the legislative history. *See* S. Prt. 101- [ ], 101st Cong., 1st Sess. 117 (1989) and H. Conf. Rep. No. 386, 101st Cong., 1st Sess. 593 (1989). Failure to maintain records is determined upon the basis of the overall compliance with the records maintenance requirement by a reporting corporation. Finally, rules relating to the increase in the penalty where the failure continues after notification are provided.

Authorization of agent

Section 1.6038A-5 provides that the noncompliance penalty in §1.6038A-7 shall apply to any transaction between a related party and a reporting corporation, unless the related party authorizes the reporting corporation to act as its limited agent solely for purposes of sections 7602, 7603, and 7604. When the proposed regulations become final, a related party annually shall authorize the reporting corporation to act as its limited agent on Form 5472 or within 30 days of a request from the Service. Until official Internal Revenue Service forms are available, the authorization as set forth in the regulations should be utilized. A procedure is provided for the retroactive authorization of an agent with respect to inadvertent transactions with related parties when the relationship is attenuated and certain other requirements are met. Additionally, a provision allows for the authorization by a foreign related party to be deemed under certain circumstances. A deemed authorization is effective only for transactions entered into prior to the time when the reporting corporation knew or had reason to know that the related party was in fact related.

Failure to furnish information

Section 1.6038A-6 provides that the noncompliance penalty contained in §1.6038A-7 may be applied under certain circumstances when information requested by the Service is not produced. A special rule permits the District Director or the Assistant Commissioner (International) to choose not to apply the noncompliance penalty when, in the discretion of the District Director or the Assistant Commissioner (International), the failure to furnish information is *de minimis*.

Noncompliance penalty

Section 1.6038A-7 provides that if a foreign related party does not authorize the reporting corporation to act as its agent as required by §1.6038A-5 or, if following a failure to furnish information as required by §1.6038A-6, the District Director or the Assistant Commissioner (International) determines that §1.6038A-7 should apply, the District Director or the Assistant Commissioner (International) shall determine the amount of deductions allowed for any amount paid or incurred by the reporting corporation to the related party in connection with such transaction and the cost to the reporting corporation of any property acquired in such transaction from the related party or transferred to the related party. The amount of the deduction or cost to the reporting corporation shall be determined in the sole discretion of the District Director or the Assistant Commissioner (International). *See* H. Conf. Rep. 386, 101st Cong., 1st Sess. 593-95 (1989).

Section 6038C

Corporations subject to section 6038C generally will be subject to the rules contained in §§1.6038A-1 through 1.6038A-7.

Special Analyses

It has been determined that these proposed rules are not major rules as defined in Executive Order 12291. Therefore, a Regulatory Impact Analysis is not required. It also has been determined that section 553(b) of the Administrative Procedure Act (5 U.S.C. Chapter 5) and the Regulatory Flexibility Act (5 U.S.C. Chapter 6) do not apply to these regulations, and, therefore, a final Regulatory Flexibility Analysis is not required. Pursuant to section 7805(f) of the Internal Revenue Code, these regulations will be submitted to the Administrator of the Small Business Administration for comments on their impact on small business.

Comments and Request for a Public Hearing

Before adopting these proposed regulations, consideration will be given to any written comments that are submitted (preferably a signed original and eight copies) to the Internal Revenue Service. All comments will be available for public inspection and copying. A public hearing will be held on Friday, February 22, 1991.

Drafting Information

The principal authors of these regulations are Carol P. Tello and Grace Perez-Navarro of the Office of Associate Chief Counsel (International), within the Office of Chief Counsel, Internal Revenue Service. Other personnel from the Internal Revenue Service and Treasury Department participated in developing these regulations.

[¶ 49,119] Proposed Regulations and Proposed Amendments of Regulations (REG-208289-86) [originally issued as INTL-939-86], published in the Federal Register on April 17, 1991.

Controlled foreign corporations: Insurance income: Tax years after 1986.—Reg. §§ 1.953-0—1.953-7 and amendments to Reg. §§ 1.953-1—1.953-6, 1.954-1T, 1.964-1, 1.1248-1 and 1.6046-1, relating to the definition and computation of the insurance income of controlled foreign corporations, have been proposed.

AGENCY: Internal Revenue Service, Treasury.

ACTION: Notice of proposed rulemaking.

SUMMARY: This document contains proposed Income Tax Regulations relating to the definition and computation of the insurance income of a controlled foreign corporation. The proposed regulations also contain definitions and rules applicable to certain captive insurance companies. This action is necessary because of changes to the applicable tax law made by the Tax Reform Act of 1986 and by the Technical and Miscellaneous Revenue Act of 1988. These regulations would provide guidance needed to comply with these changes and would affect controlled foreign corporations with income derived from insurance operations.

DATES: Written comments must be received by June 17, 1991.

A public hearing on these proposed regulations will be held Monday, June 24, 1991, beginning at 10 a.m. See the notice of public hearing on these proposed regulations elsewhere in this issue of the Federal Register.

ADDRESSES: Send comments to: Commissioner of Internal Revenue, P.O. Box 7604, Ben Franklin Station, Attention: CC:CORP:T:R (INTL-939-86), Room 4429, Washington, DC 20044.

FOR FURTHER INFORMATION CONTACT: David R. Cooper of the Office of Associate Chief Counsel (International), within the Office of Chief Counsel, Internal Revenue Service, 1111 Constitution Avenue, N.W., Washington, DC 20224, Attention: CC:INTL:Br2 (INTL-939-86) (202-566-6645, not a toll-free call).

SUPPLEMENTARY INFORMATION:

Paperwork Reduction Act

The collection of information contained in this notice of proposed rulemaking has been submitted to the Office of Management and Budget for review in accordance with the Paperwork Reduction Act of 1980 (44 U.S.C. § 3504(h)). Comments on the collection of information should be sent to the Office of Management and Budget, Attention: Desk Officer for the Department of the Treasury, Office of Information and Regulatory Affairs, Washington, DC 20503, with copies to the Internal Revenue Service, Attention: IRS Reports Clearance Officer T:FP, Washington, DC 20224.

The collection of information in these regulations is in §§ 1.953-2(e)(3)(iii), 1.953-4(b), 1.953-5(a), 1.953-6(a), 1.953-7(c)(8), 1.6046-1(a)(2)(i)(c), and 1.6046-1(c)(1)(iii). This information is required by the Internal Revenue Service in order for taxpayers to elect to locate risks with respect to movable property by reference to the location of the property in a prior period; to allocate investment income to a particular category of insurance income; to allocate deductions to a particular category of insurance income; to determine the amount of those items, such as reserves, which are computed with reference to an insurance company's annual statement; to elect to have related person insurance income treated as income effectively connected with the conduct of a United States trade or business; and to collect the information required by section 6046 relating to controlled foreign corporations as defined in section 953(c). The information will be used to verify that locating movable property on the basis of where the property is located in a prior period does not result in a material distortion when compared to where the property is actually located during a current period; to verify the connection between certain items of investment income and a specific category of insurance income; to verify the connection between deductions and a specific category of insurance income; to verify the accuracy of those items which are determined by reference to an insurance company's annual statement; to permit related person insurance income to be taxed at the corporate level as income effectively connected with the conduct of a United States trade or business rather than at the shareholder level as subpart F income; and to ensure compliance with the Internal Revenue Code as it relates to controlled foreign corporations as defined in section 953(c). The likely respondents are business or other for-profit institutions.

These estimates are an approximation of the average time expected to be necessary for a collection of information. They are based on information as is available to the Internal Revenue Service. Individual respondents/recordkeepers may require greater or less time, depending on their particular circumstances.

Estimated total annual reporting and recordkeeping burden: 14,100 hours.

The estimated annual burden per respondent and/or recordkeeper varies from 20 to 60 hours, depending on individual circumstances, with an estimated average of 28.2 hours.

Estimated number of respondents and/or recordkeepers: 500.

Estimated annual frequency of responses: Annually.

Background

This document contains proposed amendments to the Income Tax Regulations (26 CFR Part 1) under sections 953, 954, 964, 1248, and 6046 of the Internal Revenue Code of 1986. These amendments are proposed to conform the regulations to section 1221(b) of the Tax Reform Act of 1986 (Pub. L. 99-514, 100 Stat. 2085, 2551) and to section 1012(i) of the Technical and Miscellaneous Revenue Act of 1988 (Pub. L. 100-647, 102 Stat. 3342).

Explanation of Provisions

Statutory Provisions

A United States shareholder of a controlled foreign corporation is subject to current United States taxation on the subpart F income of the foreign corporation. Subpart F income is defined under section 952 and consists of several types of income, one of which is "insurance income," as defined in section 953. Insurance income exists only with respect to bona fide contracts of insurance (or reinsurance) or annuity contracts. This regulation does not address the issue of what constitutes insurance. Whether a payment is considered an insurance premium or a contribution to capital can, however, affect both the characterization of receipts as "insurance income" and the value of stock in a controlled foreign corporation owned by United States persons. Therefore, the characterization of payments as insurance premiums or contributions to capital must be considered carefully.

Insurance income is income (including investment income) attributable to the issuing or reinsuring of any insurance or annuity contract in connection with risks located in a country other than the country under the laws of which the controlled foreign corporation is created or organized and which would be taxed under subchapter L of the Code if the income were the income of a domestic insurance company. Although not within the definition of insurance income under section 953, the investment income attributable to insurance, reinsurance, or annuity contracts covering risks located in the controlled foreign corporation's country of incorporation may be subject to subpart F as foreign personal holding company income under sections 954(a)(1) and 954(c) of the Code.

Section 953(c) provides special definitions of the terms "United States shareholder" and "controlled foreign corporation" for the purpose of taking into account related person insurance income. Related person insurance income is any insurance income attributable to a policy of insurance or reinsurance under which the insured is a United States shareholder of the controlled foreign corporation or a related person to such a shareholder. For purposes of taking into account related person insurance income, the term "United States shareholder" means any United States person (as defined in section 957(c)) who owns, within the meaning of section 958(a), any stock of the foreign corporation, and the term "controlled foreign corporation" means any foreign corporation if 25 percent or more of the total combined voting power of all classes of stock of the foreign corporation entitled to vote, or 25 percent or more of the total value of the stock of the foreign corporation, is owned (within the meaning of section 958(a)), or is considered as owned by applying the rules of ownership of section 958(b), by United States shareholders on any day during the taxable year of the foreign corporation. A person is related to a United States shareholder if such person is related within the meaning of section 954(d)(3) to the United States shareholder. In addition, in the case of a policy covering liabilities arising from services performed as a director, officer, or employee of a corporation, or as a partner or employee of a partnership, the person performing the services and the entity for which the services are performed are related persons.

Section 953(c) contains certain exceptions which, if applicable, relieve United States shareholders (other than United States shareholders as defined in section 951(b)) from having to include related person insurance income in their gross income. Section 953(c) also provides special rules for determining a United States shareholder's pro rata share of related person insurance income and provides for the application of section 1248 to persons who are United States shareholders solely by virtue of section 953(c)(1)(A).

Finally, the statute provides for certain rules preventing the application of certain provisions of subchapter L of the Code in computing insurance income, and provides regulatory authority to prescribe rules for the allocation and apportionment of income, expenses, losses, and deductions, as well as rules to carry out the purpose of the related person insurance income provisions of section 953(c).

The proposed regulations do not address section 953(d), which permits a foreign insurance company that is a controlled foreign corporation to elect to be treated as a domestic corporation, or section 964(d), which permits a qualified insurance branch of a controlled foreign corporation to be treated as a separate foreign corporation created under the laws of the foreign country. Guidance will be provided under those sections as part of another regulation project. *See* Notice 89-79, 1989-2 C.B. 392, for interim guidance under section 953(d).

Consideration has been given to whether the definition of the term "life insurance contract" under section 7702(a), the diversification requirements for variable contracts under section 817(h), and the distribution requirements of section 72(s) should be considered applicable for subpart F purposes to contracts issued by controlled foreign corporations conducting insurance operations with nonresident aliens. The proposed regulations contain a reservation on these issues. Comments are invited on them.

Summary of Regulations

Because of the substantial modification of the provisions of section 953 by the Tax Reform Act of 1986, the proposed regulations redraft the current regulations under section 953 in their entirety. In addition, several conforming modifications in the form of proposed regulations are made to the final regulations under sections 954, 964(a), 1248(a), and 6046(a). The regulations are proposed to be applicable to taxable years of controlled foreign corporations beginning after December 31, 1986. However, the amendments to sections 953(c)(2) and 953(c)(3) by sections 1012(i)(3)(A) and 1012(i)(3)(B)(i) and (ii) of the Technical and Miscellaneous Revenue Act of 1988 are proposed to apply to taxable years beginning after December 31, 1987 to the extent such amendments add the phrase "(directly or indirectly)." Further, the rsisk location rules of § 1.953-2 are proposed to apply only to periods of coverage that begin on or after June 17, 1991. Prior to the effective date of § 1.953-2, taxpayers may determine the location of risks by using the principles of § 1.953-2 of the current regulations, but those principles shall be applied to determine whether risks are located in or outside the controlled foreign corporation's country of incorporation rather than in or outside the United States. Comments are invited on whether other transitional rules would be appropriate.

Upon adoption of the proposed regulations as temporary or final regulations, the current regulations under section 953 will be retained (although redesignated as §§ 1.953-1A through 1.953-6A) because they remain applicable with respect to taxable years of controlled foreign corporations beginning before January 1, 1987. Similarly, several conforming modifications in the form of proposed regulations are made to the final regulations under sections 954, 964(a), 1248(a), and 6046(a).

Section 1.953-1(a) provides definitions of the different categories of insurance income of a controlled foreign corporation that issues insurance, reinsurance, or annuity contracts. Income from a contract covering risks outside the controlled foreign corporation's country of incorporation (the "home country") constitutes insurance income within the meaning of section 953. Income from a contract covering risks in the controlled foreign corporation's home country is income within the same-country insurance category (the "SCI category"). Premiums within the SCI category are generally not considered to be section 953 insurance income and are not includable in the gross income of United States shareholders of a controlled foreign corporation. However, investment income within the SCI category may be subject to inclusion in the gross income of United States shareholders of the controlled foreign corporation as foreign personal holding company income under sections 954(a)(1) and 954(c). Section 1.953-1(a) also defines two categories of section 953 insurance income: income within the RPII category, which is income that constitutes related person insurance income, and income within the nonRPII category, which is all section 953 insurance income other than related person insurance income.

Section 1.953-1(b) provides the procedures that are used to determine the amount of a controlled foreign corporation's section 953 insurance income and its foreign personal holding company income derived from insurance, reinsurance, and annuity contracts. The first step in the procedure is to determine whether premiums constitute section 953 insurance income or SCI income. The second step is to determine whether premiums that constitute section 953 insurance income are attributable to the RPII or nonRPII categories. The third step is to allocate and apportion investment income to the RPII, nonRPII, and SCI categories. The last step is to allocate and apportion expenses, losses, and other deductions among the RPII, nonRPII, and SCI categories, and to allocate and apportion deductions within the SCI category, and in certain circumstances within the RPII category, between premium and investment income.

Section 1.953-2 provides rules for determining whether premiums are attributable to the section 953 insurance income or SCI income categories. That determination is made by locating the risks covered by an insurance, reinsurance, or annuity contract during the period of coverage to which the premiums under the contract relate. Premiums written before the first taxable year of a controlled foreign corporation beginning after December 31, 1986 that become earned under section 832(b)(4) in such taxable year or succeeding taxable years must be classified as either section 953 insurance income or SCI income.

Section 1.953-2(d) provides general rules of allocation and apportionment of premiums to or between the section 953 insurance income category and the SCI income category where an insurance, reinsurance, or annuity contract covers risks both in and outside the home country. Section 1.953-2(d) also provides that if 80 percent or more of the premiums under a contract of insurance or reinsurance or an annuity contract are apportioned to risks in or outside the home country, then all of the premiums are attributed to risks in or outside the home country, respectively.

Section 1.953-2(e) sets forth specific rules for locating risks in connection with property. Such risks are generally located where the property is located during the period or periods of coverage under the contract of insurance or reinsurance that are applicable to a taxable year. Specific rules are provided for determining the location of commercial transportation property, noncommercial transportation property, property exported or imported by railroad or motor vehicle, property exported or imported by ship or aircraft, and shipments originating and terminating in or outside the home country. Specific rules are also provided for allocating and apportioning premiums when the contract of insurance or reinsurance covers many related items of property, such as inventory, which may be both in and outside the home country. In order to aid a controlled foreign corporation that is not able to determine the location of moveable property as of the close of its taxable year, a specific rule is also set forth for locating risks in connection with such property.

Section 1.953-2(f) provides specific rules for locating risks in connection with liability arising out of activities. Generally, such risks are located where the activities that could give rise to the liability are performed. Specific rules are provided for locating activities with respect to liabilities arising from the use or consumption of property that is manufactured, produced, constructed, or assembled by the insured. Specific rules are also provided for determining the location of activities in connection with transportation property and selling activities.

Section 1.953-2(g) sets forth rules for locating risks in connection with contracts of insurance or reinsurance covering life or health. This section also covers the location of risks under annuity contracts, whether life annuities or annuities certain. Such risks are generally located in the country of the residence of the person with the "determining life." For a contract of insurance or reinsurance providing protection against loss of life or health, the determining life is the person whose life or health is covered by the contract. For a life annuity, or a contract reinsuring life annuities, the determining life is the person by whose life the annuity payments are measured. For an annuity certain, or a contract reinsuring annuities certain, both the purchaser of the annuity and the beneficiary of the annuity payments are the appropriate determining lives. If either the purchaser or beneficiary of an annuity certain resides outside the home country, the premiums received with respect to the annuity constitute section 953 insurance income. The residence of the person with the determining life is generally determined by the address of such person that is provided to the insurer. Finally, section 1.953-2(h) provides rules for determining the location of risks in certain direct or indirect cross-insurance arrangements.

Section 1.953-3 contains the rules for distinguishing RPII premiums from non-RPII premiums. Section 1.953-3(a) states that RPII premiums are section 953 insurance income premiums that constitute related person insurance income.

Section 1.953-3(b) defines related person insurance income. Related person insurance income is included within the meaning of the term "insurance income" as that term is used in section 953 of the Code. Related person insurance income is defined as premium and investment income attributable to a policy of insurance or reinsurance that provides insurance coverage to a related insured on risks located outside the controlled foreign corporation's country of incorporation, or premium and investment income attributable to any annuity contract that is purchased by, or for the benefit of, a related insured if the determining life is located outside the controlled foreign corporation's country of incorporation. For this purpose, a related insured is any insured, purchaser of an annuity contract, or beneficiary under an annuity contract that is a United States shareholder of the controlled foreign corporation or a related person (within the meaning of section 954(d)(3)) to a United States shareholder. In addition, in the case of any policy of insurance covering liability arising from services performed as a director, officer, or employee of a corporation, or as a partner or employee of a partnership, the person performing such services and the entity for which such services are performed shall be treated as related persons. Related person insurance income also includes income attributable to contracts reinsuring and contracts indirectly insuring related insureds if the risks under the contract are located outside the controlled foreign corporation's country of incorporation.

For purposes only of taking related person insurance income into account, the terms "United States shareholder" and "controlled foreign corporation" are specially defined in § 1.953-3(b). An exception from the modified definition of United States shareholder is provided for persons who would be United States shareholders of an insuring foreign corporation as a result of their ownership of stock in another foreign corporation if the stock of the other foreign corporation is publicly traded, the United States person owns less than five percent of such foreign corporation's stock and the stock of the insuring foreign corporation constitutes less than five percent of the total value of all assets of such foreign corporation. Section 1.953-3(b) also provides that related person insurance income includes insurance income attributable to certain direct or indirect cross-insurance arrangements.

Section 1.953-3(b) also provides rules for determining whether premiums constitute related person insurance premiums under certain specific circumstances. Premiums received prior to December 31, 1986 which become earned in the controlled foreign corporation's first taxable year beginning after December 31, 1986, or any succeeding taxable year, may constitute related person insurance income. Rules are also provided for computing RPII premiums when the related insured owns stock for less than the entire taxable year. An anti-abuse rule states that capital contributions may be recharacterized as premiums in certain circumstances.

Section 1.953-4 provides guidance concerning the allocation and apportionment of items of investment income to or among the RPII, nonRPII, and SCI categories. An item of investment income is allocated to a particular category of income if it directly relates to a contract which gives rise to premiums allocable to that category. An item of investment income is considered directly related to a contract which gives rise to premiums within a particular category if the income is derived from an asset which is identified on the controlled foreign corporation's books and records as an asset relating to RPII, nonRPII, or SCI contracts and the controlled foreign corporation separately accounts for the various income, exclusion, deduction, reserve, and other liability items properly attributable to such contracts. If investment income cannot be allocated, it is apportioned among the various categories of income in accordance with apportionment formulas provided in § 1.953-4(c).

Section 1.953-5(a) provides rules for allocating expenses, losses, and other deductions among the RPII, nonRPII, and SCI categories. Allocation of deductions generally is made in accordance with §§1.861-8, 1.861-8T, 1.861-9T, 1.861-10T, and 1.861-12T of the regulations. Specific rules are provided to allocate reserve deductions and deductions for claims, benefits, and losses. Deductions that cannot be allocated are apportioned among the various categories in accordance with the rules provided in §1.953-5(b), which are generally consistent with the principles of §§1.861-8, 1.861-8T, 1.861-9T, 1.861-10T, and 1.861-12T. Under §1.953-5(b), deductions that are allocated or apportioned to investment income pursuant to the regulations under section 861 are apportioned among the various income categories in the same manner as investment income. Other deductions that are not allocated or apportioned to investment income pursuant to the regulations under section 861 are apportioned among the various income categories in accordance with the amount of premium income, adjusted by increases or decreases in reserves, in each category.

Section 1.953-5(c) provides rules for allocating and apportioning deductions to or between premium and investment income within the SCI and, in certain circumstances, within the RPII categories. Although deductions other than those for reserves, losses, and specified policy acquisition expenses are allocated and apportioned between investment and premium income by following the principles of §§1.861-8, 1.861-8T, 1.861-9T, 1.861-10T, and 1.861-12T, specific rules are provided under §1.953-5(c)(3) for apportioning reserves, losses, and specified policy acquisition expenses between investment and premium income for taxable years beginning on or after April 17, 1991. The method prescribed for apportioning reserves between premium and investment income is based on the assumptions that premiums are received and losses paid at mid-year, and that the investment income portion of the increase in reserves can be calculated by assuming the reserves earn investment income at the interest rate used to calculate tax reserves. For taxable years beginning prior to April 17, 1991, taxpayers may use a reasonable apportionment formula. However, in most cases, a method that apportions reserves and losses between premium and investment income based on the ratio of premium or investment income to total income will not be considered a reasonable apportionment.

Section 1.953-6 contains provisions relating to the application of subchapter L and certain sections of subchapter N of the Code. Section 1.953-6(a) states that the provisions of subchapter L are generally applicable in determining the amount of a controlled foreign corporation's section 953 insurance income and SCI investment income to be included in gross income. Section 1.953-6(b) lists the provisions of subchapter L which are not applicable. Section 1.953-6(c) contains rules for making the election under section 831(b) to be taxed on investment income only. A section 831(b) election is a corporate level election and therefore can be made only by a controlled foreign corporation that has made the election under §1.953-7(c) to have its related person insurance income taxed as income effectively connected with the conduct of a trade or business within the United States. Section 1.953-6(d) contains rules necessary to determine whether a controlled foreign corporation is subject to the rules of part I of subchapter L of the Code relating to life insurance companies. Section 1.953-6(e) provides specific rules relating to the computation of the reserves of a controlled foreign corporation. Section 1.953-6(f) states that a controlled foreign corporation that would not be taxable as an insurance company if it were a domestic corporation is nevertheless subject to section 953 and prescribes rules for determining the insurance income of such a corporation. Section 1.953-6(g) describes the relationship between sections 953 and 954. Section 1.953-6(h) provides rules for computing a United States shareholder's pro rata share of section 953 insurance income. Section 1.953-6(i) states that section 959 (exclusion from gross income of previously taxed earnings and profits), section 961 (adjustment to basis in stock in controlled foreign corporations and of other property), and section 1248 (gains from certain sales or exchanges of stock in certain foreign corporations) are applicable to persons who would not be United States shareholders but for section 953(c) and §1.953-3(b)(2)(i). Section 1.953-6(k) provides that income that is subject to subpart F solely by virtue of the full inclusion rule of section 954(b)(3)(B) is not considered related person insurance income and need not be included in the gross income of persons that are not United States shareholders within the meaning of section 951(b).

Section 1.953-7 sets forth the exceptions to inclusion of related person insurance income by persons who are not United States shareholders under section 951(b). Section 1.953-7(a) provides rules relating to the exception that applies if less than 20 percent of the stock of a controlled foreign corporation is owned by insureds. Section 1.953-7(b) relates to the exception for a controlled foreign corporation with a de minimis amount of related person insurance income. Section 1.953-7(c) provides rules and procedures for an election by a corporation that is a controlled foreign corporation solely by virtue of section 953(c) to have its related person insurance income treated as if it were effectively connected with a United States trade or business. To make an election, the controlled foreign corporation must waive treaty benefits, except for benefits with respect to section 884, must timely file an election statement, must enter a closing agreement with the Internal Revenue Service, and must provide an adequate letter of credit.

These proposed regulations would amend the temporary regulations under §1.954-1T(c) to state that a controlled foreign corporation with foreign base company income derived from insurance operations allocates and apportions deductions in accordance with §1.953-5. These proposed regulations also would amend §1.964-1(c)(5) to identify those shareholders who are the controlling United States shareholders of a foreign corporation that is a controlled foreign corporation solely by virtue of section 953(c)(1) for purposes of making elections on behalf of the controlled foreign corporation. In addition, these proposed regulations would amend the final regulations under section 1248(a) to make clear the application of section 1248 to persons that are United States shareholders by virtue of section 953(c). Finally, these proposed regulations also would amend the regulations under section 6046(a) to make the reporting requirements of that section applicable to persons that are United States shareholders by virtue of section 953(c).

With certain exceptions, the proposed regulations do not draw a distinction between mutual insurance companies and stock insurance companies. However, the Internal Revenue Service is interested in receiving comments relating to application of the rules of this regulation with respect to mutual insurance companies and, in particular, whether certain mutual insurance companies should be excluded from the provisions of section 953 and the criteria for such an exclusion.

Special Analyses

It has been determined that these proposed rules are not major rules as defined in Executive Order 12291. Therefore, a Regulatory Impact Analysis is not required. It has also been determined that section 553(b) of the Administrative Procedure Act (5 U.S.C. Chapter 5) and the Regulatory Flexibility Act (5 U.S.C. Chapter 6) do not apply to these regulations, and, therefore, an initial Regulatory Flexibility Analysis is not required. Pursuant to section 7805(f) of the Internal Revenue Code, these regulations will be submitted to the Chief Counsel for Advocacy of the Small Business Administration for comment on their impact on small business.

Comments and Public Hearing

Before adopting these proposed regulations, consideration will be given to any written comments that are submitted (preferably a signed original and eight copies) to the Internal Revenue Service. All comments will be available for public inspection and copying.

A public hearing will be held on Monday, June 24, 1991, beginning at 10 a.m., in the Internal Revenue Service Auditorium, Seventh Floor, 7400 Corridor, Internal Revenue Building, 1111 Constitution Avenue, N.W., Washington, DC. For further information, see the notice of public hearing on these proposed regulations in the Proposed Rules section of this issue of the Federal Register.

Drafting Information

The principal author of these proposed regulations is Philip L. Garlett, formerly of the Office of Associate Chief Counsel (International), within the Office of Chief Counsel, Internal Revenue Service. Other personnel from the Internal Revenue Service and Treasury Department participated in developing the regulations.

[¶49,120] Proposed Amendments of Regulations (REG-209014-89) [originally issued as INTL-088-89], published in the Federal Register on May 13, 1991.

Qualified Caribbean Basin Countries: Investments: Requirements.—Amendments to Reg. §1.936-10, relating to the use of Code Sec. 936 funds to finance an investment that qualifies as a privatization, are proposed.

AGENCY: Internal Revenue Service, Treasury.

ACTION: Notice of proposed rulemaking.

SUMMARY: This document contains proposed regulations relating to the use of section 936 funds to finance an investment that qualifies as a privatization. The regulations prescribe conditions for such an investment to qualify as for use in Puerto Rico under section 936(d)(4). These regulations are necessary to give guidance as to whether the use of section 936 funds in a privatization transaction will qualify as for use in Puerto Rico under section 936(d)(4).

DATES: Written comments, requests to appear, and outlines of oral comments to be presented at a public hearing scheduled for Friday, July 12, 1991, at 10:00 a.m., must be received by Friday, June 28, 1991. See notice of hearing published elsewhere in this issue of the Federal Register.

Addresses: Send comments, requests to appear and outline of oral comments to be presented to: Internal Revenue Service, P. O. Box 7604, Ben Franklin Station, Atten: CC:CORP:T:R (INTL-88-89), Room 5228, Washington, D.C. 20044.

FOR FURTHER INFORMATION CONTACT: Concerning the hearing on the proposed rulemaking, Felicia Daniels, Regulations Unit, 202-566-3935; concerning a particular provision of this proposed regulation, Christine Halphen (202-377-9493, not a toll-free call) or W. Edward Williams (202-287-4851, not a toll-free call) of the Office of Associate Chief Counsel (International) within the Office of Chief Counsel, Internal Revenue Service.

SUPPLEMENTARY INFORMATION:

Background

This document contains proposed amendments to the Income Tax Regulations (26 CFR Part 1). These regulations are proposed to be issued under the authority contained in section 7805 of the Internal Revenue Code of 1986 (68A Stat. 917, 26 U.S.C. 7805).

On September 22, 1989, the Federal Register published proposed and temporary Income Tax Regulations (26 CFR part 1) [T.D. 8268, 1989-2 C.B. 134] under section 936(d)(4) of the Internal Revenue Code of 1986, which section was enacted by section 1231(c) of the Tax Reform Act of 1986 (100 Stat. 2085). The proposed and temporary regulations reserved on the issue of privatization. The final regulations published in the Rules and Regulations portion of this Federal Register also reserve on this issue.

Explanation of Provision

In general, the proposed regulations provide that a financing transaction effecting a privatization will be a qualified investment for purposes of section 936(d)(4) if the investment involves a transfer of ownership from a government entity to the private sector and has a positive developmental impact on the economy of a qualified CBI country. Section 1.936-10(c)(5)(v) of the proposed regulations lists six requirements for a qualified privatization. One of these requirements is that the United States Agency for International Development, or the Overseas Private Investment Corporation if it is sponsoring a transaction, certifies that the acquisition is expected to have a significant positive developmental impact in the qualified Caribbean Basin country where the privatization occurs. The regulations are proposed to be effective 30 days after their publication in the Federal Register as final regulations.

Regulatory Flexibility Act and Executive Order 12291

Although this document is a notice of proposed rulemaking which solicits public comment, it has been determined that the regulations proposed herein are interpretative and that the notice and public procedure requirements of 5 U.S.C. 553 do not apply. Accordingly, these proposed regulations do not constitute regulations subject to the Regulatory Flexibility Act (5 U.S.C. chapter 6).

It has also been determined that this proposed rule is not a major rule as defined in Executive Order 12291 and that a regulatory impact analysis therefore is not required.

Drafting Information

The principal authors of these proposed regulations are Christine Halphen and W. Edward Williams of the Office of the Associate Chief Counsel (International) within the Office of Chief Counsel, Internal Revenue Service. Other personnel from offices of the Internal Revenue Service and the Treasury Department participated in developing these proposed regulations.

[¶49,122] Proposed Regulations (FI-069-89), published in the Federal Register on July 5, 1991.

Life insurance contracts: Reasonable mortality charges.—Proposed Reg. §1.7702-1, relating to the required use of reasonable mortality charges in determining whether a contract qualifies as a life insurance contract, are proposed. Reg. §1.7702 was adopted by T.D. 9287 on September 12, 2006.

AGENCY: Internal Revenue Service, Treasury.

ACTION: Notice of proposed rulemaking.

SUMMARY: This document provides proposed regulations relating to the required use of reasonable mortality charges in determining whether a contract qualifies as a life insurance contract and, by cross-reference, whether the contract is a modified endowment contract for federal tax purposes. Changes were made to this requirement by the Technical and Miscellaneous Revenue Act of 1988. These regulations are necessary to provide guidance to insurance companies attempting to qualify their products as life insurance contracts.

DATES: Written comments must be received by September 4, 1991. Requests to speak (with outlines of oral comments) at a public hearing scheduled for September 25, 1991, at 10 a.m. must be received by September 11, 1991. See notice of hearing published elsewhere in this issue of the Federal Register.

ADDRESSES: Send comments, requests to appear at the public hearing, and outlines of comments to be presented to: Internal Revenue Service, P.O. Box 7604, Ben Franklin Station, Atten: CC:CORP:T:R (FI-69-89), Room 5228, Washington, D.C. 20044.

FOR FURTHER INFORMATION CONTACT: Concerning the regulations, Donald J. Drees, Jr., 202-566-3350 (not a toll-free number). Concerning the hearing, Carol Savage of the Regulations Unit, 202-377-9236 (not a toll-free number).

SUPPLEMENTARY INFORMATION:

Background

This document sets forth proposed income tax regulations under section 7702(c)(3)(B)(i) of the Internal Revenue Code relating to the required use of reasonable mortality charges in determining whether a contract qualifies as a life insurance contract for purposes of the Code. Section 7702(c)(3)(B)(i) was amended by the Technical and Miscellaneous Revenue Act of 1988, 102 Stat. 3342. In Notice 88-128, 1988-2 C.B. 540, the Internal Revenue Service provided interim rules interpreting the reasonable mortality charge requirement.

Explanation of Provisions

Section 7702, which was enacted by the Tax Reform Act of 1984, section 221(a), defines the term "life insurance contract" for purposes of the Code as any contract that is a life insurance contract under applicable law, but only if the contract either (1) meets the cash value accumulation test of section 7702(b), or (2) both meets the guideline premium requirements of section 7702(c) and falls within the cash value corridor of section 7702(d).

Section 7702(c)(3)(B)(i) provides that reasonable mortality charges are those which meet the requirements (if any) prescribed in regulations and which (except as provided in regulations) do not exceed the mortality charges specified in the prevailing commissioners' standard tables (as defined in section 807(d)(5)) as of the time the contract is issued. The mortality charges specified in section 7702(c)(3)(B)(i) are used to determine the "net single premium" (for the cash value accumulation test) and the "guideline single premium" and the "guideline level premium" (for the guideline premium test). *See* sections 7702(b)(2)(B) and 7702(c)(4).

These proposed regulations define "reasonable mortality charges" as those amounts that an insurance company actually expects to impose as consideration for assuming the risk of the insured's death (regardless of the designation used for those charges), taking into account any relevant characteristics of the insured of which the company is aware. Except as provided in the proposed regulations, reasonable mortality charges cannot exceed the lesser of the applicable mortality charges specified in the prevailing commissioners' standard tables in effect at the time the contract is issued or the mortality charges specified in the contract at issuance.

The proposed regulations provide three safe harbors under which mortality charges for contracts with only one insured are deemed to be reasonable mortality charges. The first safe harbor provides that mortality charges that do not exceed the applicable charges set forth in the Commissioners' 1980 Standard Ordinary Mortality Table for male or female insureds ("1980 C.S.O. Basic Mortality Tables") are treated as reasonable mortality charges. (These tables are gender specific but do not contain other selection factors.) There is statistical evidence that mortality charges provided in these tables exceed charges actually imposed by insurance companies. As a result, contracts qualifying as life insurance under the safe harbor can be more investment-oriented than contracts that are tested under an "actually imposed" mortality charge standard. Nevertheless, this safe harbor is created in recognition of state minimum nonforfeiture laws which may require cash values based on these higher mortality charges.

The second safe harbor treats mortality charges that do not exceed the applicable charges in certain variations of the 1980 C.S.O. Mortality Tables as reasonable mortality charges, provided certain requirements are satisfied. Thus, if a state permits minimum nonforfeiture values for all contracts issued under a plan of insurance to be determined using the 1980 C.S.O. Gender-Blended Mortality Tables ("unisex tables"), then the applicable mortality charges in those tables are treated as reasonable mortality charges for female insureds (provided the same tables are used to determine mortality charges for male insureds) even though the charges exceed the charges applicable for female insureds specified in the 1980 C.S.O. Basic Mortality Tables. Similarly, if a state permits minimum nonforfeiture values for all contracts issued under a plan of insurance to be determined using the 1980 C.S.O. Smoker and Nonsmoker Mortality Tables ("smoker/nonsmoker tables"), then the applicable mortality charges in those tables for smoker insureds are treated as reasonable mortality charges (provided nonsmoker tables are used to determine nonsmoker mortality charges) even though the charges exceed the applicable charges specified in the 1980 C.S.O. Basic Mortality Tables. The third safe harbor treats mortality charges as reasonable if they are not in excess of the applicable charges specified in the 1958 C.S.O. Mortality Table provided that the applicable contracts are not "modified endowment contracts" and were issued on or before December 31, 1988, pursuant to a plan of insurance or policy blank that was based on the 1958 C.S.O. Mortality Tables and that was approved by the appropriate state regulatory authority on or before October 21, 1988.

The proposed regulations also provide special rules for contracts involving substandard risks and for nonparticipating contracts. Although reasonable mortality charges generally may not exceed the applicable charges specified in the prevailing commissioners' standard tables, the special rules permit mortality charges for contracts involving substandard risks and for nonparticipating contracts to exceed the charges set forth in the prevailing tables if the insurance company actually expects to impose those higher charges. For this purpose, the term "substandard risk" is defined to mean a risk of death that exceeds the standards set for normal or regular risks. In determining whether any particular insured presents a substandard risk, a company must take into account relevant facts and circumstances such as the insured person's medical history and any law that prohibits or limits the company's inquiry into some or all aspects of the insured's medical history (thereby increasing the potential unknown insurance risk with respect to insureds). The term "nonparticipating contract" is defined as a contract that contains no right to participate in the issuer's divisible surplus, if any, and that contains no "charge reduction mechanism."

The proposed regulations define the term "prevailing commissioners' standard tables" to mean the tables containing the higher of the charges in the tables described in section 807(d)(5)(A) or the charges in any other tables that section 807(d)(5) allows to be used with respect to contracts for purposes of section 807(d)(2)(C) (relating to the computation of life insurance reserves). (For this purpose, the limitation of section 807(d)(5)(E) does not apply.) Thus, for example, if the prevailing commissioners' standard tables as of the beginning of any calendar year (hereinafter referred to as the year of change) is different from the prevailing commissioners' standard tables as of the beginning of the preceding calendar year, then except as provided in the temporary regulations, the reasonable mortality charges for contracts issued after the change and before the close of the 3-year period beginning on the first day of the year of change cannot exceed the higher of the applicable mortality charges specified in the old tables or those specified in the new tables.

The proposed regulations apply to life insurance contracts entered into on or after October 21, 1988.

Special Analyses

It has been determined that these proposed rules are not major rules as defined in Executive Order 12291. Therefore, a Regulatory Impact Analysis is not required. It has also been determined that section 553(b) of the Administrative Procedure Act (5 U.S.C. chapter 5) and the Regulatory Flexibility Act (5 U.S.C. chapter 6) do not apply to these regulations, and, therefore, an initial Regulatory Flexibility Analysis is not required. Pursuant to section 7805(f) of the Internal Revenue Code, the proposed regulations will be submitted to the Chief Counsel for Advocacy of the Small Business Administration for comment on their impact on small business.

Comments and Request for a Public Hearing

Before the adoption of these proposed regulations, consideration will be given to any written comments that are submitted (preferably a signed original and eight copies) to the Internal Revenue Service. Comments are specifically requested on the appropriateness of using mortality charges that are less than those in the 1980 C.S.O. tables either to define reasonable mortality charges or to establish a safe harbor. Comments are also specifically requested on (1) whether or not the 1980 C.S.O. tables, which are a safe harbor under these proposed regulations, generally contain mortality charges high enough to cover the charges actually imposed with respect to the most common substandard risk cases, and (2) any appropriate safe harbors or methodologies for computing mortality charges for contracts involving more than one insured.

All comments will be available for public inspection and copying in their entirety. A public hearing has been scheduled for September 25, 1991. See notice of hearing published elsewhere in this issue of the Federal Register.

Drafting Information

The principal author of these proposed regulations is Donald J. Drees, Jr., Office of the Assistant Chief Counsel (Financial Institutions and Products), Office of Chief Counsel, Internal Revenue Service. However, personnel from other offices of the Service and the Treasury Department participated in developing the regulations, in matters of both substance and style.

[¶49,123] **Proposed Regulations and Proposed Amendments of Regulations (FI-16-89)**, published in the Federal Register on July 10, 1991.

Notional principal contracts: Timing of income and deductions.—Reg. §1.446-3 relating to notional principal contracts, is proposed. T.D. 8491 adopted Reg §§1.446-3 (except (e)(4)(iv)) and 1.1092(d)-1 and amendments of Reg. §§1.61-14, 1.162-1, 1.451-1, 1.461-4 and 1.988-2 on October 8, 1993. On October 14, 1993, proposed Reg. §1.446-4 was withdrawn. On December 16, 1994, proposed Reg. §1.1275-4 was superseded.

AGENCY: Internal Revenue Service, Treasury.

ACTION: Notice of proposed rulemaking.

SUMMARY: These proposed regulations relate to the timing of income and deductions with respect to notional principal contracts. The regulations will provide taxpayers and Internal Revenue Service personnel with guidance necessary to account for notional principal contracts. The proposed regulations also permit dealers and traders in derivative financial instruments to elect, subject to certain conditions, to mark those instruments to market. Finally, the proposed regulations define actively traded personal property under section 1092(d).

DATES: Written comments, requests to appear, and outlines of oral comments to be presented at the public hearing scheduled for October 7, 1991 must be received by September 23, 1991. See notice of hearing published elsewhere in this issue of the Federal Register.

ADDRESSES: Send comments, requests to appear, and outlines of oral comments to: Internal Revenue Service, P.O. Box 7604, Ben Franklin Station, Attn: CC:CORP:T:R (FI-16-89), Room 5228, Washington, D.C. 20044.

FOR FURTHER INFORMATION CONTACT: Karl T. Walli, (202) 566-3516 (not a toll-free number).

SUPPLEMENTARY INFORMATION:

Background

This document contains proposed amendments to the Income Tax Regulations (26 CFR part 1) under sections 446(b) (relating to general rules for methods of accounting) and 1092(d) (relating to definitions and special rules with respect to straddles) of the Internal Revenue Code of 1986. These regulations are cross-referenced in new proposed regulations §§1.61-14, 1.162-1, 1.451-1, 1.461-4, 1.988-2T, and 1.1275-4, which are also added to part 1 of title 26 of the CFR.

Except as noted below, these regulations are proposed to be effective for notional principal contracts entered into after the date a Treasury Decision based on these proposed regulations is published in the Federal Register. For contracts entered into prior to the effective date of the proposed regulations, the Commissioner generally will treat a method of accounting as clearly reflecting income if it takes payments into account over the life of the contract under a reasonable amortization method, whether or not the method satisfies the rules in the proposed regulations. See Notice 89-21, 1989-1 C.B. 651, 652. Proposed regulation section 1.446-4 is proposed to be effective for taxable years ending on or after the date a Treasury Decision based on these proposed regulations is published in the Federal Register. Proposed regulation section 1.1092(d)-1 is proposed to be effective for notional principal contracts entered into on or after July 8, 1991.

Explanation of Provisions

A. Overview

The term "notional principal contract" generally describes an agreement between two parties to exchange payments calculated by reference to a notional principal amount. The term typically encompasses interest rate swap agreements, commodity swap agreements, interest rate cap and floor agreements, currency swap agreements, and other similar contracts. Financial institutions and corporations use these products to minimize exposure to adverse changes in interest rates, commodity prices, and currency exchange rates.

In a typical interest rate swap agreement, one party agrees to make periodic payments based on a fixed rate while the counterparty agrees to make periodic payments based on a floating rate. Payments are calculated on the basis of a hypothetical or "notional" principal amount, and payment amounts are typically netted when payments are due on common dates. A commodity swap is like an interest rate swap except that a commodity price index is used instead of an interest rate index, and the notional principal amount is measured in units of a commodity, rather than in dollars. A typical interest rate cap agreement involves an initial cash payment by one party (the purchaser) to a counterparty (the seller, usually a financial institution) in exchange for an agreement by the seller to make cash payments to the purchaser at specified future times if interest rates (as determined by a specified interest rate index) exceed a specified level. Under an interest rate floor agreement, the seller of the floor agrees to pay the purchaser if interest rates fall below a specified level.

Because the notional principal amount is not exchanged by the parties, the payments due under a typical interest rate swap, cap, or floor are not compensation for the use or forbearance of money and therefore are not "interest." On the other hand, a lump-sum payment under one of these contracts may be economically identical to a loan. In this case, the party making the lump-sum payment receives a return, part of which is properly characterized as interest under section 61(a)(4) because it represents compensation for the use or forbearance of money.

A notional principal contract may be entered into directly with another principal end-user. More commonly, however, the counterparty to the contract is a commercial or investment bank that acts as a "dealer" in such contracts. The dealer typically creates a portfolio of notional principal contracts and seeks to maintain a balanced market position. Notional principal contract dealers provide liquidity for the market by standing ready to enter into these contracts with any qualified party at any time.

As described in part B below, these proposed regulations prescribe rules for the timing of income and deductions with respect to notional principal contracts. Except in limited circumstances where amounts are recharacterized as interest, these regulations do not address the character of income, loss, or deductions with respect to notional principal contracts.

The Service is aware of the fact that many notional principal contracts are used to hedge assets or liabilities, and it is considering whether to permit taxpayers to account for a notional principal contract and the asset or liability that the notional principal contract hedges on an integrated basis. Comments on this subject are welcome. At this time, however, the proposed regulations do not permit taxpayers to determine the timing of income or deductions with respect to a notional principal contract by integrating that contract with any other asset or liability.

B. Specific Provisions

Section 1.446-3(b) states that the purpose of these proposed regulations is to clearly reflect the income and deductions from notional principal contracts. The Internal Revenue Service believes that the income from a notional principal contract can only be reflected clearly by applying accounting methods that reflect the economic substance of that contract. The proposed regulations prescribe accounting methods that are intended to reflect the economic substance of notional principal contracts without creating unnecessary complexity.

Section 1.446-3(c) defines a notional principal contract as a financial instrument that provides for payments by one party to another at specified intervals calculated by reference to a specified index upon a notional principal amount in exchange for specified consideration or a promise to pay similar amounts. The term "specified index" includes fixed interest rates and prices, interest rate indices, stock indices, and commodity indices, as well as amounts derived from arithmetic operations on these indices, such as fixed multiples and averages. Thus, notional principal contracts governed by this section include interest rate swaps, basis swaps, interest rate caps and floors, commodity swaps, equity swaps, equity index swaps, and similar agreements. The Internal Revenue Service is currently considering whether equity and equity index swaps should be treated in the same manner as interest rate and commodity swaps for sourcing and withholding tax purposes.

Section 1.446-3(d) describes several of the common notional principal contracts that are governed by the regulations, including interest rate swaps, interest rate caps, interest rate floors, and commodity swaps. Options and forwards that entitle or obligate a party to enter into, extend, cancel, or change the terms of a notional principal contract are not notional principal contracts, although a payment made or received in connection with such an agreement is treated as a nonperiodic payment with respect to a notional principal contract if and when the notional principal contract is entered into.

Section 1.446-3(e)(1) provides that net income or deduction from a notional principal contract for a taxable year is included in or deducted from gross income for that taxable year. The net income or deduction from a notional principal contract for a taxable year equals the sum of all of the periodic payments that are recognized from that contract for the taxable year and all of the nonperiodic payments that are recognized from that contract for the taxable year.

A periodic payment is defined in section 1.446-3(e)(2) as a payment that generally is payable at fixed periodic intervals of one year or less during the entire term of a notional principal contract. Periodic payments are included in income or deducted in the taxable year to which they relate.

Section 1.446-3(e)(3) defines a nonperiodic payment as any payment made or received pursuant to a notional principal contract that is not a periodic payment or a termination payment. Nonperiodic payments must be included in income or deducted over the life of the notional principal contract in a manner that reflects the economic substance of the payment. Thus, a nonperiodic payment for a swap must be amortized in a manner consistent with the values of a series of cash-settled forward contracts that reflect the specified index and the notional principal amount. In the case of an interest rate swap, the taxpayer may elect to amortize nonperiodic payments over the term of the swap assuming a constant yield to maturity. The premium paid for a cap or floor must be amortized in a manner consistent with the values of a series of cash-settled options that reflect the specified index and the notional principal amount.

Because the Service is concerned that some taxpayers may not have access to information or expertise about option pricing, the Service intends to issue a revenue procedure to provide taxpayers with an alternative method of amortizing payments for interest rate caps and floors. The revenue procedure will be issued at the time of publication of the Treasury Decision that promulgates final regulations based upon these proposed regulations. The proposed text of this revenue procedure is set out below. Comments are requested concerning the factors contained in Tables 1 and 2 of this proposed revenue procedure, and concerning the feasibility of, and need for, similar revenue procedures covering other notional principal contracts, such as commodity caps and floors.

Rev. Proc. **-**

SECTION 1. PURPOSE

This revenue procedure sets out optional amortization tables to compute the amount of a nonperiodic payment that is to be included in income or deducted over the life of an interest rate cap or floor agreement under section 1.446-3(e)(3)(ii)(D)(2) of the Income Tax Regulations.

SEC. 2. BACKGROUND AND OBJECTIVE

Section 1.446-3(e)(3)(ii)(A) of the regulations provides that premium payments made to purchase caps and floors are to be amortized in a manner that reflects the economic substance of the instruments. Section 1.446-3(e)(3)(ii)(D)(2) provides that the Commissioner may prescribe by revenue procedure an alternative method for allocating the premium paid or received for an interest rate cap or floor to each year of the agreement. Pursuant to that section, this revenue procedure sets out tables that taxpayers may use to amortize interest rate cap and floor premiums if they so elect. The tables set out in section 4 are derived from standard option pricing formulas, incorporating volatility assumptions that are intended to be consistent with representative pricing for interest rate caps and floors.

SEC. 3. SCOPE

.01 *In general*. The election provided in this revenue procedure applies only to interest rate caps and floors that are based on a specified index that—

(1) meets the conditions in section 1.446-3(c)(2)(ii) or (iii) of the regulations,

(2) is an average of specified indices described in paragraph (1) above, or

(3) is a specified index described in paragraph (1) or (2) above plus or minus a fixed number of basis points.

Taxpayers may not make the election for any interest rate cap or floor with a cap or floor rate that, at the inception of the contract, falls outside of the range of rates specified in the cap table or the floor table, respectively.

.02 *Dealers and traders*. This election is not available for any taxpayer that is a dealer or trader in any derivative financial instruments within the meaning of section 1.446-4(b) of the regulations.

SEC. 4. PROCEDURE

.01 *Annual election*. For each taxable year in which the taxpayer enters into an interest rate cap or floor agreement, the taxpayer may elect to use the method provided in this revenue procedure for all interest rate cap and floor agreements entered into in that year. As to those agreements, the election is irrevocable.

.02 *Method of election*. The election is made by attaching to the timely filed (including extensions) federal income tax return a statement that the taxpayer is making an election under this revenue procedure for the taxable year that the cap or floor agreement is entered into.

SEC. 5. USE OF THE TABLES

The amortization tables set forth in section 6 below may be used to derive a schedule of annual amortization rates to be applied to the unadjusted amount of the premium paid or received for an interest rate cap or floor agreement. Table 1 lists a series of factors corresponding to the years covered by the interest rate cap agreement and the number of basis points by which the cap rate differs from the specified interest rate index. Table 2 lists a series of factors corresponding to the years covered by the interest rate floor agreement and the number of basis points by which the specified interest rate index differs from the floor rate. The annual amortization amount for a year covered by an interest rate cap or floor agreement is calculated as follows:

First, obtain the sum of the factors for all years covered by the agreement.

Second, divide that year's factor by the sum of the factors for all years covered by the agreement.

Third, multiply that result by the premium to be amortized.

Taxpayers may use any reasonable method of interpolation to determine the appropriate factors for a particular cap or floor if a period covered by the agreement is less than 12 months long or the number of basis points by which the current rate differs from the cap or floor rate is between two amounts that are shown on the table.

SEC. 6. CAP AND FLOOR TABLES

TABLE 1
Factors to Be Used in Amortizing Interest Rate Cap Agreements

Excess of cap rate over current rate in basis points	*Term of interest rate cap agreement in years*				
	1	2	3	4	5
500	0.0	2.7	15.8	31.3	50.1
450	0.0	4.4	19.8	41.3	60.0
400	0.0	8.1	26.8	49.2	70.7
350	0.3	11.5	37.2	64.3	83.7
300	0.9	19.4	52.4	80.3	104.5
250	2.6	28.3	67.9	100.7	124.7
200	5.4	45.1	88.9	122.9	151.4
150	11.8	68.3	121.2	157.2	183.8
100	25.3	101.3	159.2	195.2	224.1
50	53.1	158.5	207.3	242.6	256.7
0	100.0	216.8	264.0	295.2	311.4
(25)	139.5	261.8	301.5	322.7	341.7
	6	7	8	9	10
500	64.8	79.4	91.2	100.9	109.8
450	77.0	91.1	104.5	115.6	121.8
400	90.1	103.5	115.8	128.3	135.5
350	105.8	120.9	134.7	144.1	152.2
300	124.5	139.9	152.0	161.0	168.4
250	146.9	162.1	173.6	181.7	189.5
200	173.6	187.9	196.8	206.5	210.2
150	203.2	217.8	223.3	229.9	234.6
100	239.4	249.8	251.4	256.1	256.4
50	271.5	283.2	287.4	288.2	288.8
0	320.4	326.6	327.3	327.7	323.9
(25)	349.6	351.6	353.1	347.2	341.7

TABLE 2
Factors to Be Used in Amortizing Interest Rate Floor Agreements

Excess of current rate over floor rate in basis points	*Term of interest rate floor agreement in years*				
	1	2	3	4	5
350	0.0	0.1	1.9	6.3	11.4
300	0.0	1.0	7.0	16.0	26.2
250	0.1	5.5	19.1	33.2	48.2
200	0.9	16.4	41.9	61.6	79.3
150	4.9	39.4	73.7	102.2	126.1
100	18.1	79.1	125.8	155.1	180.6
50	46.6	140.9	190.6	219.7	235.0
0	100.0	216.8	264.0	295.2	311.4
(25)	143.1	267.2	308.5	339.1	352.8
	6	7	8	9	10
350	17.9	23.3	28.3	33.2	37.4
300	34.9	42.4	49.7	55.9	59.6
250	60.0	69.6	76.6	83.8	89.2
200	95.0	105.9	114.5	120.7	126.7
150	140.6	151.7	160.8	163.6	167.4
100	194.4	205.5	211.6	209.6	210.5
50	250.6	260.0	264.1	266.4	264.6
0	320.4	326.6	327.3	327.7	323.9
(25)	361.1	364.9	363.4	360.3	353.2

SEC. 7. EXAMPLE

At a time when the three-month London Interbank Offered Rate ("LIBOR") is 8%, a taxpayer purchases a three year interest rate cap agreement under which a bank is obligated to make quarterly payments to the taxpayer equal to a $25 million notional principal amount times one-quarter of the excess, if any, of three-month LIBOR over 9%. The taxpayer pays the bank a premium of $600,000 at the inception of the contract, and elects to amortize the cap premium using the method provided in this revenue procedure.

An interest rate cap agreement using LIBOR as an interest rate index qualifies under section 3.01 of this revenue procedure, and the taxpayer makes the election as required in section 4.01 of this revenue procedure for all interest rate caps and floors entered into during that taxable year.

Table 1 applies to interest rate cap agreements. Table 1 lists the following factors for a three year interest rate cap that is 100 basis points over the current LIBOR rate: 25.3, 101.3, and 159.2, for years 1, 2, and 3, respectively. The sum of these three factors is 285.8. Thus, the amortization ratio for the first 12-month period covered by the agreement is 8.85% (the ratio of the first year factor, 25.3, to the total of all factors, 285.8). The amortization ratio for the second 12-month period is 35.44% (101.3/285.8), and the amortization ratio for the third 12-month period is 55.71% (159.2/285.8). Applying these amortization ratios to the $600,000 cap premium, the taxpayer's deductions with respect to this nonperiodic payment are $53,100 for the first period (8.85% × $600,000), $212,640 for the second period (35.44% × $600,000), and $334,260 for the third period (55.71% × $600,000).

SEC. 8. EFFECTIVE DATE

The election provided by this revenue procedure may be made for interest rate cap and floor agreements entered into in tax years ending on or after [Insert date a Treasury Decision based on these proposed regulations is published in the Federal Register].

Section 1.446-3(e)(4) of the proposed regulations provides special rules for compound and disguised notional principal contracts, notional principal contracts that are hedged with other financial instruments, swaps with significant nonperiodic payments, and caps and floors that are significantly in-the-money. Because swaps with significant nonperiodic payments and caps and floors that are significantly in-the-money include a significant loan component, income is not clearly reflected unless the parties to these contracts account for the interest income and expense. The Service is aware of the withholding tax consequences that may arise from interest recharacterization. These rules are not intended to disrupt typical market transactions, and the Service solicits comments on the standards for recharacterization set out in the proposed regulations (including the examples).

Section 1.446-3(e)(5) treats payments made with respect to options and forward contracts that entitle or obligate a person to enter into a notional principal contract as nonperiodic payments if and when the notional principal contract is entered into.

Section 1.446-3(e)(6) requires all parties to a notional principal contract to recognize gain or loss from the termination of a notional principal contract in the year of termination. A termination includes both an extinguishment and an assignment of a notional principal contract.

Section 1.446-3(f) sets forth an anti-abuse rule that is intended to prevent a taxpayer from applying the accounting methods that are prescribed by the proposed regulations to a notional principal contract that is not a customary commercial transaction if applying those methods to that contract would produce a material distortion of income and the taxpayer would not have entered into the transaction but for that material distortion of income. In such a case, the Commissioner has the discretion to apply accounting methods that reflect the economic substance of the transaction. This anti-abuse rule is included so that the overall purpose of the proposed regulations, which is to clearly reflect the income from a transaction by prescribing accounting methods that reflect the economic substance of the transaction, can be fulfilled with respect to all notional principal contracts.

Subject to certain conditions, section 1.446-4 permits dealers and traders in derivative financial instruments to elect a mark-to-market method of accounting in computing their taxable income. The mark-to-market election is invalid if the dealer or trader or any related party uses a lower-of-cost-or-market method (LCM) to account for securities or commodities held in a capacity as a dealer or trader (or as hedges of such securities or commodities). A "derivative financial instrument" includes notional principal contracts as well as futures, forwards, options, and short positions in commodities and securities.

The mark-to-market election is proposed to be available for taxable years ending on or after the date a Treasury Decision based on these proposed regulations is published in the Federal Register. The Service anticipates issuing a revenue procedure that will waive the 180-day rule contained in section 1.446-1(e)(3)(i) of the regulations so that dealers and traders can change their method of accounting for derivative financial instruments by making the mark-to-market election for their first taxable year ending on or after publication of the Treasury Decision. The Service anticipates issuing a second revenue procedure for electing taxpayers that are required to change their method of accounting for securities and commodities from the LCM method. The revenue procedures will describe how to obtain the Commissioner's consent for these changes and will set forth the terms and conditions that will be imposed for consent to be granted.

The Service anticipates that the revenue procedure governing the mark-to-market election under section 1.446-4 for derivative financial instruments will impose terms and conditions (including the section 481(a) adjustment period) similar to those applicable to Category B methods of accounting. See Rev. Proc. 84-74, 1984-2 C.B. 736. The Service further anticipates that the revenue procedure governing the change from the LCM method for securities and commodities will employ a cut-off transition. Under this cut-off transition, the taxpayer's old method of accounting will continue to apply to inventory acquired prior to the year of change. The Service invites comments on appropriate terms and conditions for these revenue procedures.

Section 1.1092(d)-1(a) of the proposed regulations clarifies the definition of "actively traded" personal property. Generally, actively traded personal property includes any personal property for which brokers or dealers provide regular pricing information in an established financial market. Section 1.1092(d)-1(b) enumerates several categories of established financial markets.

The proposed regulations under section 1092 also address the application of that section to notional principal contracts. There has been some question whether a financial product such as an interest rate swap, which may be either an asset or a liability depending upon the movement of interest rates, constitutes an interest in personal property that is subject to section 1092 and section 1234A. Under section 1.1092(d)-1(c)(1), notional principal contracts are generally actively traded personal property. Thus, under the proposed regulations, a loss realized with respect to a notional principal contract would not be recognized under section 1092(a) to the extent the taxpayer has an unrecognized gain in one or more offsetting positions. Further, the gain or loss realized through the termination (through extinguishment or assignment) of a taxpayer's rights and obligations under a notional principal contract would generally be treated as gain or loss from the sale of a capital asset under section 1234A.

Special Analyses

It has been determined that these proposed rules are not major rules as defined in Executive Order 12291. Therefore, a Regulatory Impact Analysis is not required. Although this document is a notice of proposed rulemaking that solicits public comments, the notice and public comment procedure requirements of 5 U.S.C. section 553(b) do not apply because the regulations proposed herein are interpretative. Therefore, an initial Regulatory Flexibility Analysis is not required by the Regulatory Flexibility Act (5 U.S.C. chapter 6). Pursuant to section 7805(f)(1) of the Internal Revenue Code, these regulations will be submitted to the Chief Counsel for Advocacy of the Small Business Administration for comment on their impact on small business.

Comments and Public Hearing

Before adopting these proposed regulations, consideration will be given to any written comments that are submitted (preferably a signed original and eight copies) to the Internal Revenue Service. All comments will be available for public inspection and copying in their entirety. A public hearing is scheduled for October 7, 1991. See Notice of Public Hearing published elsewhere in this issue of the Federal Register.

Drafting Information

The principal author of these proposed regulations is Karl T. Walli, Office of the Assistant Chief Counsel (Financial Institutions and Products), Office of Chief Counsel, Internal Revenue Service. However, other personnel from the Service and the Treasury Department participated in their development.

[¶ 49,124] Proposed Regulations and Proposed Amendments of Regulations (FI-38-91), published in the Federal Register on September 30, 1991.

REMICs: Reporting information: Extension of time.—Reg. §§ 1.67-3T, 1.860F-4 and 1.6049-7, relating to real estate mortgage investment conduits, are proposed.

AGENCY: Internal Revenue Service, Treasury

ACTION: Notice of proposed rulemaking.

SUMMARY: This document contains proposed income tax regulations relating to real estate mortgage investment conduits (REMICs). The relevant provisions in the Internal Revenue Code were added or amended by the Tax Reform Act of 1986 and by the Technical and Miscellaneous Revenue Act of 1988. These regulations extend the time for REMICs and certain other issuers to provide financial information to brokers, middlemen, and certain holders of REMIC interests or other debt instruments.

DATES: Written comments must be received by (*Insert date that is 45 days after date of publication in the Federal Register*). A public hearing has been scheduled for December 5, 1991. Requests to speak at the hearing, along with outlines of oral comments, must be received by (*Insert date that is 45 days after date of publication in the Federal Register*). See the notice of hearing published elsewhere in this issue of the Federal Register.

ADDRESSES: Send comments and requests to speak at the public hearing, along with outlines of oral comments, to: Internal Revenue Service, P.O. Box 7604, Ben Franklin Station, Attention: CC:CORP:T:R (FI-38-91), Room 5228, Washington, D.C. 20044.

FOR FURTHER INFORMATION CONTACT: Felicia Daniels, with respect to the public hearing, telephone 202-566-3935, and James W.C. Canup, with respect to the proposed regulations, telephone 202-566-6624. These are not toll-free numbers.

SUPPLEMENTARY INFORMATION:

Background

Section 671 of the Tax Reform Act of 1986 (the 1986 Act) added to the Internal Revenue Code (Code) new sections 860A through 860G to provide rules relating to real estate mortgage investment conduits. Section 674 of the 1986 Act amended section 6049 to impose certain information reporting requirements with respect to REMIC interests and certain other debt instruments. Section 1006(t) of the Technical and Miscellaneous Revenue Act of 1988 (TAMRA) amended certain provisions in sections 860A through 860G and section 6049.

In the Rules and Regulations portion of this Federal Register, the Internal Revenue Service is issuing final and temporary regulations under sections 67, 860D, 860F, and 6049 of the Code. Those regulations generally govern the filing of REMIC tax returns and require notice of income and other information to be provided to investors in REMICs and other collateralized debt obligations. This document proposes amendments to those final and temporary regulations.

Explanation of Provisions

Sections 1.67-3T(f), 1.860F-4(e)(2), and 1.6049-7(e)(3) and (f)(7) generally require certain financial information concerning REMIC interests and collateralized debt obligations to be furnished on or before the 30th day after the close of a calendar quarter or calendar year (the 45th day in the case of a non-calendar year taxpayer requesting information from a broker or middleman). The information must be furnished to persons specified in §1.6049-7(e)(4), which includes certain brokers and middlemen. These brokers and middlemen are required by §1.6049-7(b)(2) to file information returns with the Internal Revenue Service by February 28 of the following year (absent any extensions of time) and by §1.6049-7(f) to furnish the holder with a written statement by March 15 of the following year.

Commentators have indicated that in many instances the 30-day time period allotted for REMICs and issuers of collateralized debt obligations to obtain, process, and report the financial information on the underlying mortgages or obligations is not sufficient.

In response to this concern, the proposed regulations would amend the existing regulations to require the financial information to be reported on or before the 41st day after the close of a calendar quarter or calendar year (the 55th day in the case of a non-calendar year taxpayer requesting information from a broker or middleman). The dates by which brokers and middlemen must report to the Service and holders, however, would not be extended. The proposed regulations would not change the information to be reported.

These regulations are proposed to be effective for calendar quarters and calendar years ending after (*Insert date that is 60 days after the date a Treasury Decision based on these proposed regulations is published in the Federal Register*).

Special Analyses

It has been determined that these proposed regulations will not be major regulations as defined in Executive Order 12291. Therefore, a Regulatory Impact Analysis is not required. It has also been determined that section 553(b) of the Administrative Procedure Act (5 U.S.C. chapter 5) and the Regulatory Flexibility Act (5 U.S.C. chapter 6) do not apply to these regulations, and, therefore, an initial Regulatory Flexibility Analysis is not required. Pursuant to section 7805(f) of the Internal Revenue Code, the proposed regulations are being sent to the Chief Counsel for Advocacy of the Small Business Administration for comment on their impact on small business.

Comments and Requests to Appear at the Public Hearing

Before adopting these proposed regulations, consideration will be given to any written comments that are submitted (preferably a signed original and eight copies) to the Internal Revenue Service. All comments will be available for public inspection and copying in their entirety. A public hearing has been scheduled for December 5, 1991. See the notice of hearing published elsewhere in this issue of the Federal Register.

Drafting Information

The principal author of these proposed regulations is James W.C. Canup, Office of the Assistant Chief Counsel (Financial Institutions and Products), Internal Revenue Service. However, personnel from other offices of the IRS and Treasury Department participated in their development.

[¶49,125] Proposed Amendments of Regulations (REG-208202-91) [originally issued as INTL-0015-91], published in the Federal Register on March 17, 1992.

Gain or loss: Nonfunctional currency transactions.—Amendments of Reg. §§1.988-1, 1.988-2 and 1.988-5, relating to the taxation of gain or loss from certain foreign currency transactions, are proposed. Amendments of Reg. §1.988-2(b)(15), (d)(5), (e)(3)(iv) and (e)(7) were adopted 1/12/2000 by T.D. 8860. Amendments of Reg. §1.6045-1 were adopted 10/6/97 by T.D. 8734. Proposed amendments of Reg. §1.988-1(a)(3), (4) and (5) were withdrawn 8/29/2003.

AGENCY: Internal Revenue Service, Treasury.

ACTION: Notice of proposed rulemaking.

SUMMARY: This document contains proposed Income Tax Regulations relating to the taxation of gain or loss from certain foreign currency transactions and applies to taxpayers engaging in such transactions. This action is necessary because of changes to the applicable tax law made by the Tax Reform Act of 1986.

DATES: Comments and requests for a public hearing must be received by May 18, 1992.

ADDRESSES: Send comments and requests for a public hearing to: Internal Revenue Service, P.O. Box 7604, Ben Franklin Station, Attention: CC:CORP:T:R (INTL-O015-91), Room 5228, Washington, D.C. 20044.

FOR FURTHER INFORMATION CONTACT: Jeffrey L. Dorfman of the Office of Associate Chief Counsel (International), within the Office of Chief Counsel, Internal Revenue Service, 1111 Constitution Avenue, N. W., Washington, DC 20224 (Attention: CC:CORP:T:R (INTL-O015-91) (202-377-9059 (Dorfman), not toll-free calls).

SUPPLEMENTARY INFORMATION:

Paperwork Reduction Act

The collection of information contained in this notice of proposed rulemaking has been submitted to the Office of Management and Budget for review in accordance with the Paperwork Reduction Act of 1980 (44 U.S.C. 3504(h)). Comments on the collection of information should be sent to the Office of Management and Budget, Attn: Desk Officer for the Department of the Treasury, Office of Information and Regulatory Affairs, Washington, D.C. 20503, with copies to the Internal Revenue Service, Attention: IRS Reports Clearance Officer T:FP, Washington, DC 20224.

The collection of information in these regulations is in § 1.988-5(d) and (f). This information is required by the Internal Revenue Service to verify various elections made by the taxpayer. The likely respondents are businesses or other for-profit institutions.

These estimates are an approximation of the average time expected to be necessary for a collection of information. They are based on information as is available to the Internal Revenue Service. Individual respondents/recordkeepers may require greater or less time, depending on their particular circumstances.

Estimated total annual reporting and/or recordkeeping burden: 1,000 hours.

The estimated annual burden per respondent/recordkeeper varies from 30 minutes to 60 minutes, depending on individual circumstances, with an estimated average of 40 minutes.

Estimated number of respondents and/or recordkeepers: 1,500.

Background

This document contains proposed amendments to the Income Tax Regulations (26 CFR part 1) under section 988 of the Internal Revenue Code.

Explanation of Provisions

Section 1.988-1.

Section 1.988-1(a)(3) coordinates section 988 with § 1.1275-4(g) of the proposed regulations. Section 1.988-1(a)(3) provides that § 1.1275-4(g) applies prior to section 988 to separate a contingent payment debt instrument into contingent and noncontingent components. To the extent applicable, section 988 applies to the distinct components.

Section 1.988-1(a)(4) provides rules for the treatment of dual currency debt instruments. Section 1.988-1(a)(4) provides that a dual currency debt instrument is separated into two hypothetical instruments—a zero coupon bond denominated in the currency of the stated redemption price at maturity (discounted as provided in § 1.1273-2(d)(2)(iv) of the proposed regulations), and an installment obligation, as defined in § 1.1273-1(b)(2) of the proposed regulations, denominated in the currency of the qualified periodic interest payments of the dual currency debt instrument. To the extent applicable, section 988 applies to the distinct instruments.

Section 1.988-1(a)(5) provides rules for multi-currency debt instruments similar to the rules applicable to dual currency debt instruments.

Section 1.988-2.

Pursuant to section 989(c)(5), § 1.988-2(b)(14) provides special rules regarding nonfunctional currency related person debt. If a debt instrument denominated in a nonfunctional currency is entered into between related persons as defined in sections 267(b) and 707(b), and the taxpayer disposes of or terminates such instrument prior to maturity in a transaction in which exchange gain or loss would be recognized, the District Director or the Assistant Commissioner (International) may defer such gain or loss if he determines that the debt has in effect been replaced with debt denominated in a different currency (replacement debt) entered into with a related person (regardless of whether the replacement currency is the taxpayer's functional currency). Such deferral, however, shall not exceed the earlier of the date the replacement debt is terminated in a transaction in which gain or loss is recognized or the maturity date of the replacement debt (so long as such debt is not replaced with related person debt denominated in a different currency). The rule set forth in § 1.988-2(b)(14) does not apply to debt for debt exchanges in the same nonfunctional currency. The Service solicits comments regarding issues raised by debt for debt exchanges in the same nonfunctional currency.

Section 1.988-2(b)(15) provides rules addressing debt instruments denominated in hyperinflationary currencies. Generally, exchange gain or loss is recognized at the close of each taxable year and is treated as a offset to interest income or expense.

Section 1.988-2(d)(4) and (e)(7) provides rules addressing forward contracts, futures contracts, option contracts and currency swaps where payments to be made or received are denominated in hyperinflationary currencies (hereafter referred to as hyperinflationary contracts). Section 1.988-2(d)(4) and (e)(7) generally provides that a taxpayer's position in a hyperinflationary contract is to be marked to market on the last day of the taxable year and any exchange gain or loss realized on such date.

Section 1.988-2(e)(3)(iv) coordinates section 988 with the rules of § 1.446-3(e)(4)(iii) of the proposed regulations regarding currency swaps with significant nonperiodic payments.

Section 1.988-5.

Section 1.988-5(d) provides integration rules for hedged qualified payments patterned after the rules in § 1.988-5(b) of the final regulations regarding hedged executory contracts. A qualified payment is—(1) a declared but unpaid dividend denominated in a nonfunctional currency with respect to the recipient of such dividend, or (2) an unaccrued rent or royalty payment denominated in a nonfunctional currency of the taxpayer the amount of which is fixed on the date the hedge is entered into. The term hedge is defined in §1.988-5(d)(2)(iii). If a qualified payment and a hedge satisfy the rules of §1.988-5(d)(2)(i), the qualified payment and hedge are integrated. The effect of integrating a qualified payment and hedge is to treat amounts paid or received under the hedge as paid or received under the qualified payment or any subsequent account payable or receivable, or that portion thereof to which the hedge relates.

Mark to market method of accounting.

Pursuant to §1.988-5(f), certain taxpayers may elect to realize for the taxable year exchange gain or loss on section 988 transactions that results from changes in exchange rates between the date a financial accounting period begins and the date a financial accounting period closes (but no less frequently than quarterly), provided such treatment is consistent with the taxpayer's method of accounting for financial reporting purposes (and that method conforms to U.S. generally accepted accounting principles). If a taxpayer makes the mark to market election under §1.988-5(f), it must use the mark to market method to account for all section 988 transactions, other than those subject to the special hedging rules of §1.988-5. Designation of a transaction as a hedging transaction for financial accounting (which generally precludes such transaction from being marked to market under the financial accounting rules) is irrelevant.

The time and manner of making a mark to market election is prescribed in §1.988-5(f)(4). Such election cannot be revoked without the consent of the Commissioner and related person conformity rules apply.

If there is a Treasury Decision based on these proposed regulations, the Service anticipates issuing a revenue procedure setting forth the terms and conditions under which a change of method of accounting will be granted. The Service solicits comments regarding the terms and conditions of the revenue procedure, including the character of the adjustments for purposes of sections 904 and 954, and the appropriate period during which the section 481(a) adjustment should be taken into account.

§1.6045-1(d)(6)(iii)

Proposed §1.6045-1(d)(6)(iii) is in response to a comment which suggested conforming the section 6045 broker reporting rules and section 988(d) hedging rules where the sale of stock or securities for nonfunctional currency and the hedge are effected through the same broker.

Special Analyses

It has been determined that these rules are not major rules as defined in Executive Order 12291. Therefore, a Regulatory Impact Analysis is not required. It also has been determined that section 553(b) of the Administrative Procedure Act (5 U.S.C. chapter 5) and the Regulatory Flexibility Act (5 U.S.C. chapter 6) do not apply to these regulations, and, therefore, an initial Regulatory Flexibility Analysis is not required. Pursuant to section 7805(f) of the Internal Revenue Code, these regulations will be submitted to the Chief Counsel for Advocacy of the Small Business Administration for comment on their impact on small business.

Comments and Request for a Public Hearing

Before adopting these regulations, consideration will be given to any written comments that are submitted (preferably a signed original and eight copies) to the Internal Revenue Service. All comments will be available for public inspection and copying. A public hearing will be held upon written request by any person who submits timely written comments on the proposed rules. Notice of the time, place and date for the hearing will be published in the Federal Register.

Drafting Information

The principal authors of these regulations are Jeffrey Dorfman and Charles T. Plambeck. Messrs. Dorfman and Plambeck are of the Office of Chief Counsel, Internal Revenue Service. Other personnel from the Internal Revenue Service and Treasury Department participated in developing the regulations.

[¶49,126] Proposed Regulations and Proposed Amendments of Regulations (INTL-941-86, INTL-656-87, INTL-704-87), published in the Federal Register on April 1, 1992.

Passive foreign investment companies: Qualified electing funds: Shareholders.—Reg. §§1.1291-1—1.1291-7, 1.1293-1 and 1.1295-1, relating to the taxation of shareholders of certain passive foreign investment companies (PFICs) upon payment of distributions by such companies or upon the disposition of stock of such companies, are proposed. Reg. §§1.1291-0, 1.1291-9 and 1.1291-10 were adopted 12/26/1996 by T.D. 8701. Reg. §1.1291-8 was withdrawn on 2/1/1999. Reg. §1.367(e)-1T was adopted as Reg. §1.367(e)-1 on 1/15/1993 by T.D. 8472 and removed on 8/9/1996 by T.D. 8682. Reg. §1.367(e)-2T was removed on 8/6/1999 by T.D. 8834. Reg. §1.1291-1(b)(2)(ii), (b)(2)(v), (b)(7), (b)(8), and (i) was withdrawn on 12/31/2013 by REG-113350-13.

AGENCY: Internal Revenue Service, Treasury.

ACTION: Notice of proposed rulemaking.

SUMMARY: This document contains proposed income tax regulations concerning the taxation of shareholders of certain passive foreign investment companies (PFICs) upon payment of distributions by such companies or upon disposition of the stock of such companies. These rules were enacted by the Tax Reform Act of 1986, and amended by the Technical and Miscellaneous Revenue Act of 1988.

DATES: Written comments and requests for a public hearing must be received by July 30, 1992.

ADDRESSES: Send written comments and requests for a public hearing to Internal Revenue Service, P.O. Box 7604, Ben Franklin Station, Attention: CC:CORP:T:R (INTL-656-87), room 5228, Washington, DC 20044.

FOR FURTHER INFORMATION CONTACT: Gayle E. Novig of the Office of Associate Chief Counsel (International), within the Office of Chief Counsel, Internal Revenue Service, 1111 Constitution Avenue, NW, Washington, DC 20224 (Attention: CC:CORP:T:R (INTL-656-87)) (202-377-9059, not a toll free number).

SUPPLEMENTARY INFORMATION:

Paperwork Reduction Act

The collections of information contained in this notice of proposed rulemaking have been submitted to the Office of Management and Budget for review in accordance with the Paperwork Reduction Act of 1980 (44 U.S.C. 3504(h)). Comments on the collections of information should be sent to the Office of Management and Budget, Attention: Desk Officer for the Department of the Treasury, Office of Information and Regulatory Affairs, Washington, DC 20503, with copies to the Internal Revenue Service, Attention: IRS Reports Clearance Officer T:FP, Washington, DC 20224.

The collections of information in these regulations are in 26 CFR sections 1.1291-1(i), 1.1291-2(f)(2)(ii), 1.1291-3(e)(5)(iii), 1.1291-6(g), 1.1291-8(g), 1.1291-9(d), and 1.1291-10(d)(2)(vii). The collections of information found in 26 CFR section 1.1291-9(d) and 1.1291-10(d)(2)(vii) are also being published as temporary rules in the Rules and Regulations section of this issue of the Federal Register. This information is required by the Internal Revenue Service to identify PFICs and their shareholders, administer shareholder elections, verify amounts reported, and track transfers of stock of certain PFICs. The likely respondents and/or recordkeepers are individuals or households, business or other for-profit institutions, non-profit institutions, and small businesses or organizations.

These estimates are an approximation of the average time expected to be necessary for a collection of information. They are based on such information as is available to the Internal Revenue Service. Individual respondents/recordkeepers may require greater or less time, depending on their particular circumstances.

Estimated total annual reporting and/or recordkeeping burden for filing Form 8621 reported in OMB No. 1545-1002: 31,680 hours.

The estimated total annual burden per respondent/recordkeeper for the other requirements in this regulation is 8,750 hours, with an estimated average of one hour.

Estimated number of respondents and/or recordkeepers: 8,750.

Estimated frequency of responses: Annually.

Background

This document contains proposed Income Tax Regulations (26 CFR part 1) under sections 1291, 1293, 1295, and 1297 of the Internal Revenue Code of 1986. These provisions were added to the Internal Revenue Code of 1986 by section 1235 of the Tax Reform Act of 1986 (Pub. L. 99-514, 100 Stat. 2320), and amended by section 1012(p) of the Technical and Miscellaneous Revenue Act of 1988 (Pub. L. 100-647, 102 Stat. 3342). With the exceptions of different effective dates for the rules concerning certain pledges of PFIC stock outstanding on the effective date of the statute (§ 1.1291-3(d)(6)), and the mark-to-market election available to regulated investment companies (§ 1.1291-8), these regulations are proposed to be effective April 1, 1992. However, as sections 1291 through 1297 of the Code are effective for taxable years of foreign corporations beginning after 1986, shareholders of PFICs are subject to those provisions with respect to transactions occurring during those taxable years.

Explanation of Provisions

Overview of Statute

The Tax Reform Act of 1986, as amended by the Technical and Miscellaneous Revenue Act of 1988, established special rules for the taxation of U.S. persons that are shareholders of PFICs. For taxable years beginning after December 31, 1986, a foreign corporation will be classified as a PFIC if either 75 percent or more of its gross income for the taxable year is passive, or the average percentage of its assets (by value) for the taxable year that produce passive income or are held for the production of passive income is at least 50 percent. Subject to certain exceptions, passive income for these purposes generally is foreign personal holding company income as defined in section 954(c) of the Internal Revenue Code of 1986.

Sections 1291 through 1297 provide two different and sometimes overlapping sets of rules for taxing U.S. persons that are shareholders of a PFIC. In general, shareholders are subject to a special tax regime under section 1291 that applies to distributions by the PFIC and dispositions of PFIC stock. In the proposed regulations, if section 1291 applies to a particular shareholder with respect to a PFIC, the PFIC is referred to as a section 1291 fund with respect to the shareholder. A significant consequence of being treated as a section 1291 fund is that the foreign corporation will continue to be treated as a PFIC, and therefore the shareholder will continue to be subject to section 1291, even after the corporation ceases to satisfy either the income or the asset test for PFIC status under section 1296.

Each shareholder, however, may elect under section 1295 to treat a PFIC as a qualified electing fund (QEF); if such an election is made, the shareholder will be taxed currently under section 1293 on its pro rata share of the earnings of the QEF. A shareholder that makes a QEF election may or may not continue to be subject to the special tax regime under section 1291. Stated differently, a PFIC that is a QEF with respect to a particular shareholder may or may not continue to be a section 1291 fund with respect to that shareholder. If the shareholder makes the QEF election for the foreign corporation's first taxable year as a PFIC that is included in the shareholder's holding period for the stock of the PFIC, section 1291 will not apply to the shareholder. If the shareholder makes the QEF election at a later time, but also makes an election under section 1291(d)(2) to purge the PFIC stock that it holds of its taint as a section 1291 fund, the shareholder will accelerate the application of section 1291 to the PFIC stock that it holds, and section 1291 will not apply to the shareholder thereafter. In both cases, the proposed regulations refer to such a PFIC as a pedigreed QEF with respect to the electing shareholder, and the PFIC is not considered to be a section 1291 fund with respect to that shareholder.

On the other hand, if the shareholder makes the QEF election at a later time and does not make a purging election, section 1291 will continue to apply to the shareholder notwithstanding the application of section 1293. The proposed regulations refer to such a PFIC as an unpedigreed QEF in respect of the shareholder. Because section 1291 applies to the shareholder of an unpedigreed QEF, the QEF continues to be a section 1291 fund.

Pursuant to section 1291, a U.S. person that is a shareholder of a section 1291 fund pays tax and an interest charge on receipt of certain distributions and upon disposition of stock of the section 1291 fund. Under this rule, gain from a disposition or the portion of any distribution that is an excess distribution (defined in section 1291(b)) is treated as ordinary income earned ratably over the shareholder's holding period of the stock of the section 1291 fund. The portion allocated to the current year, and to years when the corporation was not a PFIC, are included in the shareholder's gross income for the year of the distribution; the remainder is not included in gross income, but the shareholder must pay a deferred tax amount (defined in section 1291(c)) with respect to that portion. The deferred tax amount is, in general, the amount of tax that would have been owed if the allocated amount had been included in income in the earlier year, plus interest.

Section 1291(f) provides regulatory authority for taxing transfers of stock of a section 1291 fund notwithstanding an otherwise applicable nonrecognition provision of the Code or regulations. Accordingly, gifts, transfers at death, and exchanges of stock pursuant to nonrecognition provisions will be taxable to the extent provided in the regulations.

Section 1297(a) provides attribution rules for determining whether a U.S. person is an indirect shareholder of a PFIC. Section 1297(b)(5) provides that, under regulations, a U.S. person treated as an indirect shareholder of a PFIC under section 1297(a) will be taxable on any distribution paid by the PFIC to the actual owner of the PFIC stock (indirect distribution), and on any disposition by the U.S. person or the actual owner if, as a result of the disposition, the U.S. person is no longer treated under section 1297(a) as owning the stock of the PFIC (indirect disposition).

Section 1297(d) grants authority to the Secretary to prescribe such regulations as may be necessary or appropriate to carry out the purposes of sections 1291 through 1297.

Explanation of Proposed Regulations

Definitions and general rules

Section 1.1291-1(b) defines the terms PFIC, QEF, pedigreed QEF, unpedigreed QEF, nonqualified fund, and section 1291 fund. As explained above, whether a corporation is a PFIC, QEF (pedigreed or unpedigreed), nonqualified fund, or section 1291 fund is determined on a shareholder by shareholder basis. In general, section 1291 and the proposed regulations under that section do not apply to determine the taxation of a shareholder of a pedigreed QEF with respect to a distribution paid by the pedigreed QEF or a disposition of its stock.

It should be noted that the definition of the term nonqualified fund in the proposed regulations differs from the definition of the same term in the current Form 8621, Return by a Shareholder of a Passive Foreign Investment Company or Qualified Electing Fund. (In the form, the term has the same meaning as the term section 1291 fund in the proposed regulations.) The form will be revised to eliminate this difference.

Section 1.1291-1(b)(3), (4), and (5) define the terms prePFIC year, prior PFIC year, and current shareholder year, terms relevant to the determination of the tax consequences under section 1291 of a distribution by, or a disposition of, a section 1291 fund. A prePFIC year is a taxable year (or portion thereof) of the shareholder included wholly or partly in the shareholder's holding period, either before the shareholder became a United States person (within the meaning of section 7701(a)(30)), or before the section 1291 fund qualified as a PFIC. A prior PFIC year is a taxable year (or portion thereof), other than the current shareholder year, included in the shareholder's holding period during which the section 1291 fund was a PFIC. The term current shareholder year refers to the shareholder's taxable year in which the taxable event occurs.

The term shareholder includes any person that owns an equity interest in the PFIC directly or indirectly, as provided in § 1.1291-1(b)(8). Section 1.1291-1(b)(8) defines the term indirect shareholder as a U.S. person that indirectly owns stock of a PFIC, and provides attribution rules for ownership of a PFIC through a person other than an individual.

Stock directly or indirectly owned by a U.S. person generally is not attributed to another U.S. person. However, pursuant to section 1297(a) and (d), stock owned directly or indirectly by an S corporation or domestic partnership, trust or estate is treated as owned proportionately by its shareholders, partners or beneficiaries. Moreover, stock may be attributed through a domestic C corporation in some circumstances if, absent such attribution, the stock of a PFIC would not be treated as owned by any U.S. person.

As described above, under the proposed regulations a beneficiary of a trust or estate is a shareholder of a proportionate amount of the PFIC stock owned directly or indirectly by the trust or estate. Comment is solicited whether different attribution rules, such as the indirect ownership rules in § 25.2701-6 (relating to special valuation rules for purposes of estate and gift taxes), should be adopted for purposes of determining whether a beneficiary of a trust or estate is an indirect shareholder of a PFIC.

Stock of a section 1291 fund owned directly or indirectly by a regulated investment company (RIC) or a real estate investment trust (REIT) is not attributed to the shareholders of the RIC or REIT. A RIC or REIT that is a shareholder of a section 1291 fund is taxable on direct or indirect distributions and dispositions. For a special mark-to-market rule applicable to RICs, *see* § 1.1291-8.

Under section 1297(a)(4) and the regulations, a person that holds an option to acquire PFIC stock is treated as a shareholder of PFIC stock. Section 1.1291-1(d) provides that such a person will be treated as a shareholder of a section 1291 fund subject to section 1291 on a disposition (other than by exercise) of that option. For purposes of sections 1291 through 1297, the holding period of stock of a PFIC acquired upon exercise of an option will include the period that the option was held. If the shareholder elects to treat the PFIC as a QEF, the PFIC will be an unpedigreed QEF because of the PFIC years in the shareholder's holding period attributable to the period the person held the option. The shareholder may make a section 1291(d)(2) election to purge those years from its holding period in order for the PFIC to be a pedigreed QEF.

In limited circumstances, an exempt organization that is a direct or indirect shareholder of a section 1291 fund may be subject to tax under section 1291 and these regulations. Section 1.1291-1(e) provides that an exempt organization will be taxable under section 1291 and the regulations with respect to a distribution from a section 1291 fund or a disposition of its stock if a dividend from that corporation would be taxable to the exempt organization pursuant to subchapter F.

With certain exceptions, the general Code and regulatory rules apply for purposes of determining a shareholder's holding period of PFIC stock. The proposed regulations also provide that generally, unless a shareholder previously held the stock directly, an indirect shareholder's holding period of stock of a PFIC begins on the first day that ownership of the stock of the PFIC is attributed to the person under section 1297(a). A shareholder will get a new holding period in the stock of a PFIC only after the shareholder recognizes all the gain with respect to the stock. If stock of a section 1291 fund is acquired in a transaction to which section 1223(1) or 1223(2) applies, the character of the years in the shareholder's tacked holding period as prePFIC or prior PFIC is determined by reference to the character of the holding period of the property transferred in the exchange (section 1223(1)) or received from the transferor (section 1223(2)).

Section 1.1291-1(i) sets forth the annual reporting requirements of direct and indirect shareholders of all PFICs.

Section 1.1291-2—Taxation of Excess Distributions

In general. Section 1.1291-2 provides rules for taxing a direct or indirect shareholder of a section 1291 fund on a distribution by the fund. Section 1.1291-2(b) defines the term distribution for purposes of section 1291. The term does not include a nontaxable distribution that qualifies under section 305(a) or 355(a). In addition, distributions that are treated as in exchange for stock, such as liquidation distributions and section 302(a) redemptions, are not distributions to which § 1.1291-2 applies. Those distributions are treated as dispositions subject to § 1.1291-3.

The proposed regulations at § 1.1291-2(b)(3) provide that the shareholder has an excess distribution to the extent section 304(b)(2) treats the distribution as being paid out of the earnings and profits of an issuing corporation that is a section 1291 fund. In addition, the section 304 transaction will be a taxable disposition of stock of a section 1291 fund to the extent the shareholder's interest in the issuing corporation that is a section 1291 fund is reduced as a result of the transaction. Finally, the regulations provide that an amount paid by an acquiring corporation that is a section 1291 fund will be an excess distribution. It is possible that there may be multiple taxation under these rules. Comments are therefore solicited about how to better coordinate sections 304 and 1291, without permitting avoidance of section 1291.

Section 1.1291-2(c) provides rules for determining the nonexcess distribution and the total excess distribution for the current shareholder year. These amounts are calculated on a per share basis without regard to the earnings and profits of the section 1291 fund. The total excess distribution is the amount by which the total distribution for the current shareholder year, with certain adjustments, exceeds the nonexcess distribution. The nonexcess distribution is defined as the portion of the total distribution that does not exceed 125 percent of the average of the distributions made with respect to the stock during the preceding three taxable years included in the shareholder's holding period. For purposes of calculating the excess distribution, the portion of a prior year's excess distribution that was not included in income (the portion subject to the deferred tax amount) is not considered a distribution made in a prior year. If the section 1291 fund makes more than one distribution during the current shareholder year, and there is a total excess distribution for the year, a ratable portion of each distribution is an excess distribution.

Section 1.1291-2(c)(3)(ii) provides that the total excess distribution is zero in the taxable year of the shareholder in which the shareholder's holding period begins. This rule applies only to distributions, and not to excess distributions arising from dispositions of section 1291 fund stock.

The excess distribution is calculated using the U.S. dollar. In general, each distribution in a foreign currency is converted into U.S. dollars at the spot rate on the date of the distribution. However, if all relevant distributions have been made in a single foreign currency, the excess distribution is calculated in that currency and then converted into the U.S. dollar at the spot rate on the date of the current shareholder year distribution.

The earnings and profits of a section 1291 fund are generally irrelevant for purposes of section 1291. For that reason, as stated above, the excess distribution is calculated without regard to the earnings and profits of the section 1291 fund. If the earnings and profits can be calculated, the shareholder can avoid the interest charge and other disadvantages under section 1291 by making the QEF election.

However, the earnings and profits of a section 1291 fund are relevant for purposes of claiming the foreign tax credit for deemed paid taxes and determining the taxation of a nonexcess distribution. For these purposes, § 1.1291-2(e)(3) provides that earnings and profits are allocated proportionately between the nonexcess distribution and the total excess distribution.

Special rules. Pursuant to proposed § 1.1291-2(b)(2), neither an inclusion of income under section 951(a)(1), 551(b) or 1293(a), nor an actual distribution of an amount previously taxed under one of those sections, is a distribution for purposes of section 1291. Accordingly, an inclusion in income under section 951, 551 or 1293 is neither subject to section 1291 in the year of inclusion nor treated as a distribution made in a prior year when calculating a nonexcess distribution. In addition, distributions of previously taxed amounts are not taken into account when calculating the nonexcess distribution. Therefore, the total distribution for the current year is first reduced by the amount that is not included in gross income by reason of section 959, 551(d), or 1293(c). In developing these rules, treatment of inclusions in income under section 951, 551, or 1293 in prior years as distributions was considered. However, such a rule was not adopted because such amounts were not subject to section 1291 in the year of inclusion.

Proposed regulation § 1.1291-2(d)(1) provides that, for purposes of calculating the average of distributions made during the preceding three taxable years, a shareholder whose holding period begins after the first day of the shareholder's taxable year may take into account distributions paid during that year but before the shareholder's holding period began. Consideration was given to other methods of annualizing distributions (for example, extrapolation from distributions actually received), but such methods were rejected because they tended to produce distorted results.

Pursuant to section 1291(b)(3)(G), § 1.1291-2(d)(5) provides rules for adjusting an excess distribution received by a trust that is entitled to deduct the amount of its fixed annual charitable obligation from gross income under section 642(c).

The proposed regulations at § 1.1291-2(d)(6) provide a rule for calculating the excess distribution in a taxable year of the shareholder during which the foreign corporation was a PFIC for only part of that year. Under this rule, all distributions paid during the year with respect to the stock owned or treated as owned by the shareholder are taken into account for purposes of calculating the excess distribution, but only those distributions made after the foreign corporation became a PFIC are taxed under section 1291.

Taxation of a distribution. Section 1.1291-2(e) provides the rules for the taxation of a nonexcess distribution and an excess distribution. A nonexcess distribution is taxed according to the general rules applicable to corporate distributions. To determine the taxation of an excess distribution, the excess distribution is allocated pro rata to each day in the shareholder's holding period (treated as ending on the date of the distribution) without regard to whether the corporation actually derived earnings and profits during the years to which the excess distribution is allocated.

The portions of an excess distribution allocated to the current shareholder year and to the prePFIC years are included in the shareholder's ordinary income and are not subject to the deferred tax amount. The portions of an excess distribution allocated to the prior PFIC years are not included, or treated as included, in gross income for any purpose. Therefore, any losses in the current shareholder year or prior years may not offset the portions of an excess distribution allocated to the prior PFIC years. The amounts allocated to prior PFIC years are subject to the deferred tax amount, determined under § 1.1291-4, which includes an interest charge.

Indirect distributions. An indirect distribution is a distribution by a section 1291 fund to the actual shareholder of stock of a section 1291 fund that a shareholder is considered to own under § 1.1291-1(b)(8). Generally, a shareholder is taxable on its pro rata share of the total distribution paid by the section 1291 fund. The nonexcess distribution and total excess distribution are calculated at the indirect shareholder level.

The proposed regulations provide an exception to the general rule that all indirect distributions are taxable. A shareholder is not taxable on an indirect distribution paid by a section 1291 fund to its sole shareholder that is a section 1291 fund owned directly by the shareholder, provided the distributing fund has distributed all its earnings each year included in the shareholder's holding period of the distributing fund. Comment is solicited on whether there are additional circumstances in which an indirect shareholder of a section 1291 fund should not be taxed on distributions by, or dispositions of the stock of, a section 1291 fund.

The proposed regulations require partnerships and S corporations to provide information to their partners and shareholders. This information is intended to assist the indirect shareholders in calculating their excess distributions. Information reporting obligations of trusts and estates are reserved.

Other than the guidance provided in § 1.1291-2(f)(6) (adjustments for trusts permitted to take the section 642(c) deduction) and § 1.1291-6(d)(3) (section 643(e)(3) election), the regulations do not provide explicit rules for determining the tax consequences to a trust or estate (or a beneficiary thereof) that directly or indirectly owns stock of a section 1291 fund. Until such rules are issued, the shareholder must apply the PFIC rules and subchapter J in a reasonable manner that triggers or preserves the interest charge. Comments are invited about the manner in which excess distributions paid with respect to stock directly or indirectly owned by trusts or estates should be taxed under section 1291.

Dispositions of stock of section 1291 funds

Section 1.1291-3 provides general rules for determining the tax consequences of transfers of stock of section 1291 funds. Unless otherwise provided, gain recognized on a direct or indirect disposition of a share of stock of a section 1291 fund is taxed as an excess distribution in the manner provided in § 1.1291-2(e)(2).

A loss that is recognized on the disposition of a share of stock of a section 1291 fund does not offset the gain recognized on another share. The general rules applicable to losses recognized on a disposition of stock apply to losses realized and recognized on the disposition of stock of a section 1291 fund.

Definition of disposition. Section 1.1291-3(b)(1) defines the term disposition for purposes of section 1291. A disposition includes a gift, a transfer by reason of death, and a transfer that qualifies for nonrecognition treatment under another provision of the Code. Paragraphs (b)(2) and (d) of proposed § 1.1291-3 contain special rules providing that the change of residence or citizenship status of a U.S. resident alien or citizen to nonresident alien status, and a pledge of section 1291 fund stock constitute dispositions. Under § 1.1291-3(c), (d), and (e), dispositions of stock of a section 1291 fund are generally taxable unless an exception applies.

Indirect dispositions. An indirect disposition includes a disposition of the stock of a section 1291 fund by its actual owner and a disposition by the indirect shareholder or other person of any interest in a person if by virtue of such interest a U.S. person is treated as an owner of the stock of the section 1291 fund. The former rule applies without regard to whether the disposition reduces or terminates the shareholder's interest in the PFIC. The latter rule, however, does not apply if the transaction does not affect the shareholder's interest in the PFIC or the actual owner's basis in the PFIC. The proposed regulations also provide that an indirect disposition includes a transaction that reduces or eliminates the indirect shareholder's interest in the PFIC.

The scope of the indirect disposition rules in the proposed regulations is broader than the scope of the rule in section 1297(b)(5). The rules have been expanded under the authority of section 1297(d) to prevent avoidance of section 1291 (for example, through transactions between affiliated foreign companies).

In the case of an indirect disposition, the gain that is treated as an excess distribution to the indirect shareholder is the shareholder's proportionate share of the actual owner's gain with respect to the stock of the fund (whether or not such gain is realized by the actual owner). Thus, the amount taxable to the indirect shareholder is determined without regard to the amount the shareholder would recognize on a disposition of the interest through which the shareholder is considered to own the stock of the section 1291 fund.

Generally, the excess distribution is allocated over the indirect shareholder's holding period. However, § 1.1291-1(h)(4)(iii) provides that an S corporation shareholder uses the holding period of the S corporation if the S corporation directly or indirectly owned the stock of the PFIC prior to its election under section 1362. In addition, the deferred tax amount owed by the S corporation shareholders is calculated using the applicable rate of tax under section 1, even for years during which the S corporation was a C corporation that are included in the shareholders' holding period, pursuant to § 1.1291-4(c)(2).

The S corporation also may be taxable on a disposition of section 1291 fund stock as provided in section 1374. If the S corporation pays built-in gain tax pursuant to section 1374 on the disposition of the section 1291 fund, the S corporation shareholders' excess distribution, pursuant to section 1366(f)(2), does not include the built-in gain tax paid by the S corporation. However, the proposed regulations provide that the section 1366(f)(2) deduction is disregarded when calculating the aggregate amount of interest under section 1291(c)(3).

Transfers within a consolidated group. Proposed regulation § 1.1291-3(f) provides a special rule for transfers of stock of a section 1291 fund between members of a consolidated return group. Comments are solicited on how to coordinate this rule with the consolidated return regulations.

Installment sales. Section 1.1291-3(g) provides rules for applying section 1291 to installment sales of section 1291 fund stock. The gain portion of each installment is an excess distribution. For purposes of allocating each excess distribution under § 1.1291-2(e), the holding period of the transferred stock is treated as ending on the date the installment payment is received. A deferred tax amount is owed for each installment received. This rule applies section 1291(a)(3), which provides that the holding period ends on the date of each excess distribution.

Coordination with sections 1246 and 1248. Section 1.1291-3(i) provides that neither section 1246 nor section 1248 applies to the disposition of stock of a section 1291 fund. However, as provided in

§1.1291-5(e), a shareholder may calculate a foreign tax credit on a disposition of stock of a section 1291 fund taking into account the indirect foreign tax credits to which the shareholder would have been entitled if section 1248 would have applied to the disposition of the section 1291 fund stock but for section 1291.

Deferred Tax Amount

Section 1.1291-4 provides the rules for determining the deferred tax amount. The deferred tax amount is calculated with respect to that portion of the excess distribution that is allocated to prior PFIC years and not included in income. It is the sum of the aggregate increases in taxes and the aggregate amount of interest determined with respect to the increases in taxes.

An increase in tax is calculated for each portion of an excess distribution allocated to a prior PFIC year. It is the product of the portion of the excess distribution allocated to a prior PFIC year and the highest rate of tax in effect in that prior year under section 1 or 11, as applicable. The aggregate increases in taxes are the sum of all increases in tax calculated with respect to an excess distribution. The aggregate increases in taxes are additional taxes owed in the current shareholder year regardless of the shareholder's tax position in that year or any of the prior PFIC years. Therefore, if unpaid, they will result in penalties and interest in the same manner as other taxes on income.

The aggregate amount of interest, the interest charge component of the deferred tax amount, is interest under section 6601 for the underpayment of tax. Interest is owed on each increase in tax calculated for a prior PFIC year (reduced by foreign tax credits pursuant to §1.1291-5) as if the portion of the excess distribution allocated to that prior PFIC year was distributed in that year but the tax thereon was not paid until the return due date for the current shareholder year. The interest charge is calculated, using the rates and method provided in section 6621, for the period beginning on the due date (without regard to extensions) for the shareholder's return for the prior PFIC year, and ending on the due date (without regard to extensions) for the shareholder's return for the current shareholder year.

Coordination with the Foreign Tax Credit Rules

Section 1.1291-5 provides the steps for determining the foreign tax credit a shareholder may claim against the increases in tax on an excess distribution, including in certain cases the excess distribution on a disposition of stock of a section 1291 fund. The foreign tax credit under these steps is determined separately for distributions received from different section 1291 funds and for each excess distribution. Excess foreign tax credits calculated with respect to an increase in tax may not be used to offset any other increase in tax or any other federal income tax. The calculation of the foreign tax credit for foreign taxes paid on the portion of the excess distribution subject to the deferred tax amount is separate from the calculation of the credit for other foreign taxes paid during the current shareholder year.

Nonrecognition Transfers of Stock of Section 1291 funds

In general. Section 1.1291-6 provides rules for the recognition of gain by a shareholder on a direct or indirect disposition of stock of a section 1291 fund that results from a transaction in which, but for section 1291(f), there would not be full recognition of gain. The general rule of §1.1291-6 is that the U.S. person recognizes gain unless an exception set forth in §1.1291-6(c) applies. Gain from the disposition therefore is generally recognized and taxed as an excess distribution notwithstanding any other provision of the Code or regulations.

Exceptions to the gain recognition rule. Generally, a shareholder will not be required to recognize gain if the shareholder receives a direct or indirect interest of equivalent value in a PFIC in exchange for the PFIC stock transferred. In addition, a shareholder will not be required to recognize gain if, immediately after the transfer, the transferred stock is owned by a U.S. person (the U.S. transferee) that will be taxed under section 1291 on subsequent distributions and dispositions of the transferred stock, provided the U.S. transferee's adjusted basis in the stock is less than or equal to the shareholder's basis, and the U.S. transferee's holding period of the stock is at least as long as the shareholder's holding period.

Nothing in §1.1291-6 is to be interpreted as overriding any other provision of the Code or regulations requiring recognition of gain or loss. If, under §1.1291-6(c), an exception to the gain recognition rule applies to a transfer that is taxable under another provision, such as section 367 and the regulations under that section, the gain is taxable as a distribution or disposition, as appropriate, under section 1291. Section 1.1291-6 also does not require or permit the recognition of loss unless the loss is recognized under another section of the Code or regulations.

Basis and holding period rules. If gain is recognized under the gain recognition rule of §1.1291-6, the basis of the transferred stock and the basis of any stock received in exchange therefor are increased by the amount of gain recognized. If all gain realized is recognized, the holding period of such stock begins on the day after the transfer. If a shareholder realizes a loss on a transfer to which the gain recognition rule would have applied had a gain been realized, the shareholder does not recognize the loss, but the shareholder's holding period begins on the day after the transfer. If stock is transferred at death to a U.S. person and gain is not recognized, the basis of the transferred stock is the lower of the fair market value or adjusted basis of the transferred stock in the hands of the decedent shareholder on the date of death. The U.S. beneficiary's holding period of that stock includes the period the decedent held the stock. The days in the holding period of stock received by a shareholder or transferee in a transfer to which an exception to the gain recognition rule applies retain the PFIC character those days had with respect to the stock transferred.

Mark-to-market election by a regulated investment company

In general. Section 1.1291-8 of the proposed regulations permits a RIC to make a mark-to-market election with respect to the stock of section 1291 funds of which it is a direct or indirect shareholder. Because RICs in many instances have not been able to obtain the information necessary to make the QEF election under section 1295, the election under § 1.1291-8 is needed as a means to coordinate the rules of section 1291 with the rules of sections 851 through 855.

The deferred tax amount generally will be avoided with respect to stock of section 1291 funds because stock that was marked to market at the end of a year gets a new holding period at the beginning of the following year. Any excess distribution with respect to stock subject to the election thereafter will be allocated under § 1.1291-2(e)(2) only to days in the current year.

Nothing in the proposed regulation precludes a RIC from electing under section 1295 to treat as a QEF a section 1291 fund whose stock was previously marked to market under § 1.1291-8.

Scope. The mark-to-market election is only available to a RIC that is either an open-end RIC or a closed-end RIC that determines and publishes weekly its net asset value. In such cases, the election will apply to all section 1291 fund stock of which the RIC is a shareholder. Comment is solicited on whether, and how, the election should be extended to other RICs.

Effect of the election. The election applies to the year in which made and to each succeeding year unless revoked with the consent of the Commissioner. At the end of each of the RIC's taxable years to which the election applies, the RIC recognizes, on a share-by-share basis, the amount by which the fair market value of the section 1291 fund stock exceeds its adjusted basis. No loss may be recognized as a result of making the election. The holding period of stock that was marked to market, including stock of a section 1291 fund with respect to which there was no mark-to-market gain, begins on the first day of each taxable year of the RIC. The proposed regulations also provide for basis adjustments to avoid double taxation of the mark-to-market gain.

Except as provided in § 1.1291-8, the election otherwise has no effect on the manner in which a distribution by a section 1291 fund or a disposition of its stock is taxed to the electing RIC. Accordingly, distributions by a section 1291 fund will be taxable to the RIC pursuant to the general rules of the proposed regulations. Similarly, gain from the disposition of stock of the section 1291 fund will be treated as an excess distribution.

The proposed regulations provide a transition rule pursuant to which a RIC that makes the mark-to-market election in the first taxable year ending after [*INSERT DATE THIS DOCUMENT IS PUBLISHED AS FINAL REGULATIONS*] must include as ordinary income in that year all appreciation in the section 1291 fund stock as of the beginning of that year and pay a nondeductible interest charge. In addition, if the RIC failed to make a mark-to-market election in a prior year because it reasonably believed that it was not a shareholder of a section 1291 fund or did not apply a previously made election to a corporation because it reasonably believed that the corporation was not a section 1291 fund, the proposed regulations permit the RIC to elect to recognize the mark-to-market gains for the prior years with respect to the discovered stock in the year of discovery. All the mark-to market gain is included in income in the year of discovery, subject to a nondeductible interest charge.

Although the objective of the mark-to-market election is to eliminate the RIC's liability for the deferred tax amount, the RIC may nevertheless owe such tax in the first year in which the election applies with respect to stock with a holding period that includes a prior PFIC year if it did not make the election in the first year in which it is permitted to do so. In that case, the transition rule will not apply to the RIC if it makes the election in a subsequent year; any gain recognized will be allocated over the entire holding period, triggering the deferred tax amount. Similarly, if the RIC does not elect the remedy in § 1.1291-8(e) of the proposed regulations in the year of discovery, the RIC may be liable for the deferred tax amount arising from excess distributions with respect to the discovered stock.

Purging Elections

Deemed Dividend Election. Section 1.1291-9 specifies the time and manner for making the election under section 1291(d)(2)(B). This election may be made by a U.S. person that is a direct or indirect shareholder of an unpedigreed QEF that also is a CFC. A shareholder that makes the section 1291(d)(2)(B) election is treated as receiving a dividend on the first day of its taxable year in which it makes the QEF election (qualification date).

The fact that the qualification date falls on a day other than the first day of the CFC's first taxable year as a QEF will have no effect on the amount that the shareholder must include in income pursuant to section 1293(a) for that first QEF year. As provided in section 1293, the shareholder includes in income its pro rata share of the ordinary earnings and net capital gain of the QEF for the taxable year of the QEF that ends during the shareholder's taxable year. However, the amount of the deemed dividend will not include the portion of the current earnings that the shareholder demonstrates are included in the shareholder's income that year under section 1293(a).

Section 1.1291-9(h)(2) provides that a shareholder may not make the deemed dividend election of section 1291(d)(2)(B) if the CFC will not qualify as a PFIC under section 1296(a) for the first taxable year for which the QEF election was made. In that case, the shareholder of an unpedigreed QEF that no longer qualifies as a PFIC under section 1296(a) may make only the deemed sale election provided in section 1297(b)(1) and § 1.1297-3T.

Deemed sale election. The proposed regulations differ from § 1.1291-10, as proposed, in two significant respects. First, the proposed regulations change the qualification date for deemed sale elections made after May 1, 1992. This change is consistent with the definition of qualification date for the deemed dividend election described above.

Secondly, the proposed regulations clarify the amount of gain a shareholder recognizes when it makes a deemed sale election with respect to a PFIC of which it is an indirect shareholder. An indirect shareholder recognizes the amount of gain the actual shareholder of the stock would realize if the actual owner sold or otherwise disposed of the PFIC stock that the shareholder is considered to own.

Section 1293

Proposed § 1.1293-1(a) provides that section 1293 applies to pedigreed QEF shareholders only with respect to taxable years of the QEF in which the QEF satisfies either the income test or the asset test of section 1296(a). The proposed regulation also provides that if the PFIC is an unpedigreed QEF with respect to the shareholder, section 1293 applies to the shareholder in all years that the PFIC is a section 1291 fund, including those years in which the corporation does not satisfy either the income or asset test.

Application of section 1295 election

Section 1.1295-1 of the proposed regulations provides specific rules concerning the application of the section 1295 election to the electing shareholder, transferees of the shareholder, stock acquired after the election was made, stock received in exchange for the QEF stock, and corporations that are successors of QEFs. The proposed regulations, however, do not provide guidance for making the section 1295 election. Until publication of regulations providing such guidance, taxpayers wishing to make the section 1295 election may continue to rely on Notice 88-125, 1988-2 C.B. 535.

The QEF election applies only to the shareholder that makes the election and not to any other shareholder of the PFIC or to a transferee of the QEF stock. Furthermore, the QEF election only applies to the corporation for which the shareholder makes the election and not to a successor corporation. Nevertheless, proposed regulation § 1.1295-1(b)(2)(i) permits a shareholder who transferred stock of a QEF in a nonrecognition transaction before a certain date to make a retroactive section 1295 election to treat the successor corporation as a QEF.

Distributions described in section 367(e)

The proposed regulations amend proposed § § 1.367(e)-(1) and 1.367(e)-2 to provide that § 1.1291-3 and, in certain cases, § 1.1291-6 apply to determine the taxation of distributions of stock of a section 1291 fund described in section 367(e)(1) and (2). The proposed regulations also amend proposed § 1.367(e)-2(c)(3)(iv) to cross-reference to the rule that provides that the liquidation of a section 1291 fund may be an indirect disposition taxable to the indirect shareholder.

Effective dates. Proposed § 1.1291-1(j) provides that, with certain exceptions, the regulations are effective April 1, 1992. Although the regulations are proposed to be effective prospectively, sections 1291 through 1297 are nevertheless effective for taxable years of foreign corporations beginning after December 31, 1986. Shareholders of corporations that qualified as PFICs after that date therefore must apply the statute in determining the tax consequences of distributions by section 1291 funds and dispositions of stock of section 1291 funds that were effected before the effective date of the proposed regulations. Such shareholders must apply reasonable interpretations of the Code. The Department of the Treasury and the Internal Revenue Service regard these regulations as a reasonable interpretation of the Code.

Certain provisions of the proposed regulations have other effective dates. Section 1.1291-3(d)(6) of the proposed regulations, which concerns pledges of PFIC stock outstanding on the effective date of the statute, will be effective retroactively to taxable years of PFICs beginning after December 31, 1986. Section 1.1291-8 permits regulated investment companies to make a mark-to-market election with respect to their section 1291 fund stock in taxable years ending after [*INSERT DATE THIS DOCUMENT IS PUBLISHED AS A FINAL REGULATION*].

Special Analyses

It has been determined that these proposed rules are not major rules as defined in Executive Order 12291. Therefore, a Regulatory Impact Analysis is not required. It has also been determined that section 553(b) of the Administrative Procedure Act (5 U.S.C. chapter 5) and the Regulatory Flexibility Act (5 U.S.C. chapter 6) do not apply to these regulations, and, therefore, an initial Regulatory Flexibility Analysis is not required. Pursuant to section 7805(f) of the Internal Revenue Code, these regulations will be submitted to the Chief Counsel for Advocacy of the Small Business Administration for comment on their impact on small business.

Comments and Request for a Public Hearing

Before adopting these proposed regulations, consideration will be given to any written comments that are submitted timely (preferably a signed original and eight copies) to the Internal Revenue Service. All comments will be available for public inspection and copying. A public hearing will be held upon written request by any person who submits written comments as prescribed in the proposed rules. Notice of the time and place for the hearing will be published in the Federal Register.

Drafting Information

The principal author of these proposed regulations is Gayle E. Novig of the Office of Associate Chief Counsel (International), within the Office of Chief Counsel, Internal Revenue Service. Other personnel from the IRS and Treasury Department participated in developing the regulations.

[¶49,127] **Proposed Amendments of Regulations (INTL-121-90)**, published in the Federal Register on April 27, 1992.

Treaty-based return positions: Dual status alien.—Amendments of Reg. §301.7701(b)-7 (except (c)(2)), relating to treaty-based return positions, are proposed. Amendments to Reg. §§301.6114-1 and 301.7701(b)-7(c)(2) were adopted 10/6/97 by T.D. 8733.

AGENCY: Internal Revenue Service, Treasury.

ACTION: Notice of proposed rulemaking.

SUMMARY: This document contains proposed Income Tax Regulations relating to sections 6114 and 7701(b) of the Internal Revenue Code of 1986 (the Code). The proposed regulations under section 6114 provide that reporting is specifically required if the residency of an individual is determined under a treaty and apart from the Code. This action is necessary to implement section 6114 of the Internal Revenue Code of 1986 in cases in which a resident alien, who claims treaty benefits as a resident of the other treaty partner's country ("dual status alien"), fails to file a statement as required by the regulations under section 7701(b). The proposed regulations under section 7701(b) provide that for purposes of determining the U.S. income tax liability of a dual status alien who is a shareholder of an S corporation, the trade or business or permanent establishment of the S corporation shall be passed through to the dual status alien pursuant to section 1366(b).

DATES: Written comments and requests for a public hearing must be received by June 26, 1992.

ADDRESSES: Send comments and requests for a public hearing to: Internal Revenue Service, P. O. Box 7604, Ben Franklin Station, Attn: CC:CORP:T:R, (INTL-121-90), room 5228, Washington, DC 20044.

FOR FURTHER INFORMATION CONTACT: David A. Juster of the Office of Associate Chief Counsel (International), within the Office of Chief Counsel, Internal Revenue Service, 1111 Constitution Avenue, N.W., Washington, DC 20224, Attention: CC:CORP:T:R (INTL-121-90) (202-566-3452, not a toll-free call).

SUPPLEMENTARY INFORMATION:

Paperwork Reduction Act

The collections of information contained in this notice of proposed rulemaking has been submitted to the Office of Management and Budget for review in accordance with the Paperwork Reduction Act of 1980 (44 U.S.C. 3504(h)). Comments on the collections of information should be sent to the Office of Management and Budget, Attn: Desk Officer for the Department of the Treasury, Office of Information and Regulatory Affairs, Washington, DC 20503, with copies to the Internal Revenue Service, Attention: IRS Reports Clearance Officer T:FP, Washington, D.C. 20224.

The collections of information in these regulations are in §§301.6114-1(b)(8) and 301.7701(b)-7(a)(4)(iv)(C). The information required by §301.6114-1(b)(8) will be used by the Internal Revenue Service to identify taxpayers taking a treaty-based return position and the specific income for which such treaty-position is taken. The information required by §301.7701(b)-7(a)(4)(iv)(C) will be used by the Internal Revenue Service to identify dual resident S corporation shareholders taking treaty-based return positions in order to ensure that at least one level of U.S. tax is paid on an S corporation's earnings.

These estimates are an approximation of the average time expected to be necessary for a collection of information. They are based on such information as is available to the Internal Revenue Service. Individual respondents may require greater or less time, depending on their particular circumstances.

§301.6114-1(b)(8) Reporting requirement.

Estimated total annual reporting burden: 1,000 hours.

The estimated annual burden per respondent varies from 1/2 hour to 3 hours, depending on individual circumstances, with an estimated average of 1 hour.

Estimated number of respondents: 1,000.

Estimated frequency of responses: Annually.

§301.7701(b)-7(a)(4)(iv)(C) Reporting requirement.

Estimated total annual reporting burden: 15 hours.

The estimated annual burden per respondent varies from 1/2 hour to 1 hour, depending on individual circumstances, with an estimated average of 3/4 hour.

Estimated number of respondents: 20.

Estimated frequency of responses: Annually.

Background

This document contains proposed amendments to the final Income Tax Regulations (26 CFR §301.6114-1), published in the Federal Register on March 14, 1990 (55 FR 9438) and on July 12, 1990 (55 FR 28608). The proposed amendments relate to paragraphs (b) and (c) of §301.6114-1. The regulations under section 6114 are proposed to be effective after [insert the date that is 60 days after the date these regulations are published in the Federal Register as final regulations]. Also contained in this document are proposed amendments to the final Income Tax Regulations (26 CFR 301.7701(b)-7), published elsewhere in this issue of the Federal Register. The proposed amendments which relate to paragraphs (a)(4) and (c)(3) of §301.7701(b)-7 are proposed to be effective for S corporation taxable years beginning on or after July 27, 1992. The proposed amendments to paragraph (c)(2) of §301.7701(b)-7 are proposed to be effective after [insert the date that is 60 days after the date these regulations are published in the Federal Register as final regulations].

Explanation of Provisions

Section 6114 requires each taxpayer who, with respect to any tax imposed by the Code, takes a position that a treaty of the United States overrules, or modifies, an internal revenue law of the United States to disclose that position on a return of tax for that tax or in such other form as the Secretary may prescribe. Section 6712 provides penalties for the failure to comply with the disclosure requirement of section 6114.

Currently, paragraph (c)(2) of § 301.6114-1 provides that if the residency of an individual is determined under a treaty and apart from the Code, then the section 6114 treaty-based return reporting requirement is waived. The waiver was originally provided because it was contemplated, at the time of the promulgation of regulations under section 6114, that the regulations under section 7701(b), being drafted at that time, would include a reporting requirement and penalty provision. In the process of completing the regulations under section 7701(b), the Service concluded that the rules of section 6114 should apply to individuals determining their residence under a treaty.

This document contains proposed regulations which add new paragraph (b)(8) and amend paragraph (c) of § 301.6114-1. New paragraph (b)(8) of § 301.6114-1 is proposed to provide that, for returns relating to taxable years for which the due date for filing returns (without extensions) is after [the date that is 60 days after the date these regulations are published in the Federal Register as final regulations], reporting is required under section 6114 if the residency of an individual is determined under a treaty and apart from the Code. Proposed paragraph (b)(8) also provides that the taxpayer shall disclose the treaty-based return position on a statement (in the form required by § 301.7701(b)-7(c)) attached to his or her return. This proposed change will not result in duplicative reporting under section 6114 because a statement in the form required in § 301.7701(b)-7(c) will be considered disclosure for purposes of section 6114 and the regulations thereunder. The proposed amendment to paragraph (c)(2) of § 301.6114-1 provides that, for returns relating to earlier taxable years not subject to this change, reporting is waived under section 6114 if the residency of an individual is determined under a treaty and apart from the Code. In addition, a proposed amendment to the end flush language of paragraph (c) provides that the reporting requirements under new paragraph (b)(8) of § 301.6114-1, are waived if payments or income items received by the individual during the course of the taxable year do not exceed $100,000 in the aggregate.

This document also contains proposed revisions to § 301.7701(b)-7 of the final regulations published elsewhere in this issue of the Federal Register. Section 301.7701(b)-7 of the regulations provides, in general, that if a dual resident taxpayer (an alien individual who is a resident of both the United States and a foreign country with which the United States has an income tax convention) claims a treaty benefit as a nonresident alien with respect to an item of income covered by the treaty, the individual will be treated as a nonresident for purposes of computing the individual's United States income tax liability under the Internal Revenue Code. Congress has made it clear (by the enactment of section 1361(b)(2)(C)) that nonresident aliens may not be shareholders of an S corporation. In order to ensure that at least one level of U.S. tax is paid on an S corporation's earnings, paragraph (a)(4)(iii) of § 301.7701(b)-7 is proposed to provide that for purposes of determining whether a domestic corporation meets the definition of an S corporation under section 1361(a)(1), a dual resident taxpayer who claims a treaty benefit (as a nonresident of the United States) so as to reduce the individual's United States income tax liability shall be treated as a nonresident alien of the United States. Accordingly, if the dual resident taxpayer is a shareholder in an S corporation for any portion of a taxable year with respect to which the taxpayer claims a treaty benefit, then the corporation's election under section 1362(a) shall be terminated pursuant to section 1362(d)(2) effective on the first day of the dual resident's taxable year with respect to which the dual resident taxpayer claims a treaty benefit. A dual resident who does not claim treaty benefits to reduce U.S. tax will not be subject this rule, and thus, may be or become a shareholder in an S corporation.

Proposed paragraph (a)(4)(iv) of § 301.7701(b)-7 provides a special exception (if certain specified conditions are satisfied) that permits a dual resident taxpayer to be treated as United States resident for purposes of section 1361(a)(1) even if the taxpayer claims treaty benefits. The special exception will apply if a dual resident S corporation shareholder and the S corporation enter into an agreement to be subject to tax and withholding as if the dual resident were a nonresident alien partner in a partnership. The character and source of the S corporation items included in the dual resident shareholder's income will be determined as if realized by the shareholder. The dual resident shareholder will be considered as carrying on a business within the United States through a permanent establishment if the S corporation carries on such a business. The Service intends to publish a revenue procedure that will provide additional detail concerning the manner of applying these rules and the contents of the withholding agreement. For example, the revenue procedure will prescribe the withholding requirements on current income (income attributable to a permanent establishment, income that is fixed or determinable, annual or periodical income, and income attributable to U.S. real property interests), and gain on sale of S corporation stock (including gain attributable to U.S. real property interests). A dual resident shareholder of an S corporation that was a C corporation, or a successor to a C corporation or a successor to an S corporation that itself was a successor (direct or indirect) to a C corporation is not eligible for the exception.

For years to which this special exception does not apply, an individual who has claimed treaty benefits so as to reduce his or her United States income tax liability will not be considered a nonresident alien for purposes of section 1361(b)(1)(C) provided the individual has reasonably taken into account for United States income tax purposes his or her share of S corporation income, gain, loss, deduction, and credit in accordance with section 1366 of the Code.

Under paragraph (b) of § 301.7701(b)-7, a dual resident taxpayer who claims a treaty benefit as a nonresident alien must attach a statement (in the form required by paragraph (c)) to his or her Form 1040NR. Proposed paragraph (c)(3) of § 301.7701(b)-7 provides that an additional declaration must be included in the statement disclosing a treaty-based return position that is filed by a dual resident taxpayer who is a shareholder in an S corporation.

Proposed paragraph (c)(2) of § 301.7701(b)-7 also provides that for purposes of stating the approximate amount of subpart F income to be included in the statement filed by a dual resident taxpayer who is a shareholder in a controlled foreign corporation (as defined in section 957), the approximate amount of income may be based on the audited foreign financial statements of the CFC if there are no other United States shareholders in that CFC.

Special Analyses

It has been determined that these rules are not major rules as defined in Executive Order 12291. Therefore, a Regulatory Impact Analysis is not required. It has also been determined that § 553(b) of the Administrative Procedure Act (5 U.S.C. chapter 5) and the Regulatory Flexibility Act (5 U.S.C. chapter 6) do not apply to these regulations, and therefore, an initial Regulatory Flexibility Analysis is not required. Pursuant to section 7805(f) of the Internal Revenue Code, these regulations will be submitted to the Chief Counsel for Advocacy of the Small Business Administration for comment on their impact on small business.

Comments and Request for a Public Hearing

Before adopting these proposed regulations, consideration will be given to any written comments that are timely submitted (preferably a signed original and eight copies) to the Internal Revenue Service. All comments will be available for public inspection and copying. A public hearing will be held upon written request by any person who submits timely written comments on the proposed rules. Notice of the time, place and date for the hearing will be published in the Federal Register.

Drafting Information

Various personnel from the Office of Associate Chief Counsel (International), within the Office of Chief Counsel, Internal Revenue Service and the Treasury Department participated in developing the regulations.

[¶ 49,129] Proposed Amendments of Regulations (EE-23-92), published in the Federal Register on August 7, 1992.

Exemption from tax: VEBA: Geographic locale restriction.—Amendments to Reg. § 1.501(c)(9)-2, relating to the qualification of voluntary employees' beneficiary associations under Code Sec. 501(c)(9), are proposed.

AGENCY: Internal Revenue Service, Treasury.

ACTION: Notice of proposed rulemaking and notice of public hearing.

SUMMARY: This document contains proposed regulations about the qualification of voluntary employees' beneficiary associations (VEBAs) under section 501(c)(9) of the Internal Revenue Code (Code). The proposed regulations supplement the existing regulations with rules for determining whether the membership of an organization consists of employees of employers engaged in the same line of business in the same geographic locale. The proposed regulations will provide the public with guidance necessary to comply with the law in the case of an organization that does not consist exclusively of the employees of a single employer or the members of a single labor union. They will affect entities seeking to sponsor VEBAs covering the employees of more than one unrelated employer, as well as those employees.

DATES: Written comments must be received by October 6, 1992. Requests to speak (with outlines of oral comments) at a public hearing scheduled for December 3, 1992, at 1:00 p.m. must be received by November 12, 1992.

ADDRESSES: Send all submissions to: Internal Revenue Service, P.O. Box 7604, Ben Franklin Station, Attention: CC:CORP:T:R (EE-23-92) Washington, D.C. 20044.

FOR FURTHER INFORMATION CONTACT: Michael J. Roach at 202-622-6060 concerning the regulations; Carol Savage at 202-622-8452 concerning the hearing (not toll-free numbers).

SUPPLEMENTARY INFORMATION:

Background

The existing regulations at § 1.501(c)(9)-2(a)(1) contain general rules for determining when an association qualifies as a voluntary employees' beneficiary association (VEBA) eligible for exemption from income tax under section 501(c)(9) of the Internal Revenue Code. Under those regulations, the members of the association must share an employment-related common bond. The members are deemed to share an employment-related common bond if membership in the association is open only to persons whose eligibility for membership is based on employment by a single employer or affiliated group of employers, or is based on membership in one or more locals of a national or international labor union, or is based on coverage under one or more collective bargaining agreements. In addition, under the existing regulations, employees of one or more employers engaged in the same line of business in the same geographic locale are considered to share an employment-related common bond.

Questions have arisen about the geographic extent of a single "geographic locale." In its report on the Deficit Reduction Act of 1984, Pub. L. No. 98-369, 98 Stat. 494, the House Ways and Means Committee described the effect of the geographic locale restriction affecting VEBAs as follows:

> Under [the] standards [prescribed in the regulations], for example, a group of car dealers in the same city or other similarly restricted geographical locale could form a VEBA to provide permissible benefits to their employees.

H.R. Rep. No. 432, Part II, 98th Cong., 2d Sess. 1285.

Administratively, the Internal Revenue Service has treated employers located in any one state as located in the same geographic locale. The Service has also treated a single standard metropolitan statistical area (SMSA), as defined by the Bureau of the Census, as a single geographic locale, even though the boundaries of some SMSAs include portions of more than one state.

In 1986, the United States Court of Appeals for the Seventh Circuit held the geographic locale restriction invalid in *Water Quality Association Employees' Benefit Corp. v. United States*, 795 F.2d 1303 (7th Cir. 1986). The court agreed with the Government's argument that the existence of an employment-related common bond is the essential factor that distinguishes a tax-exempt VEBA from a taxable insurance company, but concluded that restricting VEBAs covering employees of unrelated employers to those employers located in the same geographic locale did not enhance the employment-related bond of the employees participating in the organization.

The preamble to the final regulations published as T.D. 7750, 1981-1 C.B. 338 (46 F. R. 1719 (January 7, 1981)), explains the reason why the Secretary decided to retain the geographic locale restriction despite comments from the public requesting its deletion from the final regulations. In relevant part, the preamble states:

> First, section 501(c)(9) provides for the exemption of associations of employees who enjoy some employment related bond. Allowing section 501(c)(9) to be used as a tax-exempt vehicle for offering insurance products to unrelated individuals scattered throughout the country would undermine those provisions of the Internal Revenue Code that prescribe the income tax treatment of insurance companies. Second, it is the position of the Internal Revenue Service that where an organization such as a national trade association or business league exempt from taxation under section 501(c)(6) operates a group insurance program for its members, the organization is engaged in an unrelated trade or business. *See* Rev. Rul. 66-151, 1966-1 C.B. 152; Rev. Rul. 73-386, 1973-2 C.B. 191; Rev. Rul. 78-52, 1978-1 C.B. 166. To allow trade associations to provide insurance benefits through a trust exempt under section 501(c)(9) would simply facilitate circumvention of the unrelated trade or business income tax otherwise applicable to such organizations.

These restrictions are consistent with the history of section 501(c)(9) of the Code. As Kenneth W. Gideon, then Assistant Secretary of the Treasury for Tax Policy, said in testimony before the Subcommittee on Taxation of the Senate Finance Committee on September 10, 1991, the VEBA tax exemption was originally intended to benefit associations formed and managed by employees of a single employer, or of small local groups of employers, to provide certain welfare benefits to their members in situations where such benefits would not otherwise have been available. *Tax Simplification Bills: Hearings on S. 1364, S. 1394, and H.R. 2777 Before the Subcommittee on Taxation of the Senate Committee on Finance*, 102d Cong., 1st Sess., 260-261. In 1928, when the predecessor of section 501(c)(9) of the Code was enacted as section 103(16) of the Revenue Act of 1928, 45 Stat; 791, ch. 852, the prevalent form of "mutual benefit association" that provided welfare benefits to employees was an organization providing benefits to the employees of a single establishment, such as an industrial plant. National Industrial Conference Board, *The Present Status of Mutual Benefit Associations*, 1-2, 50-51 (1931). At the time, there was concern that, although these organizations performed valuable social functions, they might not be able to continue to exist without a tax exemption. By contrast, larger associations covering employees of unrelated employers in different geographic areas are more likely to be viable without a tax exemption, and the benefits they provide are more likely to be available through commercial insurance. *Tax Simplification Bills, supra*, at 260. In general, when Congress exempts a class of organizations from income tax, it is deemed to have referred to the existing organizations of that class at the time the exemption was adopted. *United States v. Cambridge Loan and Building Co.*, 278 U.S. 55, 58 (1928). Thus, the absence of large regional or national organizations among the class of organizations known as VEBAs or "mutual benefit associations" that were dedicated to providing welfare benefits to employees in 1928 is relevant in determining the proper scope of the exemption granted by section 501(c)(9) of the Code.

The factors cited in the preamble to the 1981 regulations for imposing a geographic locale restriction on the membership of VEBAs that include employees of unrelated employers are matters of continuing concern today. Because of these factors and the history of section 501(c)(9), the proposed regulations limit the geographic region within which unrelated employers must be engaged in the same line of business in order for employees of those lines of business to participate in a single VEBA to the minimum area that is consistent with enabling all employees of employers engaged in a particular line of business to participate in an economically feasible VEBA. If VEBA participation were always limited to employees of employers located in the same state or SMSA, however, the diversity of regional population density and employment patterns in the United States could make it infeasible in many cases for benefits to be provided through a VEBA. Accordingly, the proposed regulations afford a safe harbor that treats any three contiguous states as a single geographic locale, and they authorize the Commissioner of Internal Revenue to recognize larger areas as a single geographic locale on a case-by-case basis upon application by an organization seeking recognition as a VEBA. Thus, the Commissioner may recognize an organization as a VEBA under section 501(c)(9), even though its members are employed by unrelated employers engaged in the same line of business located in any number of states, whether or not contiguous. To obtain recognition as a VEBA under this discretionary authority, the applicant must show (1) that it would not be economically feasible to cover employees of employers engaged in that line of business in the states to be included in the proposed VEBA under two or more separate VEBAs, and (2) either that the states to be included are all contiguous, or that there are legitimate reasons supporting the inclusion of those particular states.

During the drafting of these proposed regulations consideration was given to a rule that would allow an area to be treated as a single geographic locale even though it included areas outside the United States. It is not clear, however, whether it is necessary or desirable to include such a rule. Comments are invited about the extent, if any, to which the regulations should allow the inclusion of areas outside the United States in a single geographic locale.

Proposed Effective Date

These regulations are proposed to be effective on August 7, 1992; however, taxpayers may treat the rules as applicable to prior years.

Special Analyses

It has been determined that these rules are not major rules as defined in Executive Order 12291. Therefore, a Regulatory Impact Analysis is not required. It has also been determined that section 553(b) of the Administrative Procedure Act (5 U.S.C. chapter 5) and the Regulatory Flexibility Act (5 U.S.C. chapter 6) do not apply to these proposed regulations and, therefore, an initial Regulatory Flexibility Analysis is not required. Pursuant to section 7805(f) of the Internal Revenue Code, these regulations will be submitted to the Chief Counsel for Advocacy of the Small Business Administration for comment on their impact on small business.

Comments and Public Hearing

Before these proposed regulations are adopted as final regulations, consideration will be given to any written comments that are submitted timely (preferably an original and eight copies) to the Internal Revenue Service. All comments will be available for public inspection and copying.

A public hearing will be held on Thursday, December 3, 1992, at 1:00 p.m. in the Internal Revenue Service Auditorium, Internal Revenue Building, 1111 Constitution Avenue, N.W. Washington, DC. The rules of § 601.601(a)(3) of the "Statement of Procedural Rules" (26 CFR part 601) shall apply to the public hearing.

Persons who have submitted written comments by October 6, 1992, and who also desire to present oral comments at the hearing on the proposed regulations, should submit, not later than November 12, 1992, a request to speak and an outline of the oral comments to be presented at the hearing stating the time they wish to devote to each subject.

Each speaker (or group of speakers representing a single entity) will be limited to 10 minutes for an oral presentation exclusive of the time consumed by the questions from the panel for the government and answers thereto.

Because of controlled access restrictions, attendees cannot be admitted beyond the lobby of the Internal Revenue Building before 12:45 p.m.

An agenda showing the scheduling of the speakers will be made after outlines are received from the persons testifying. Copies of the agenda will be available free of charge at the hearing.

Drafting Information

The principal author of these proposed regulations is Michael J. Roach, Office of the Associate Chief Counsel (Employee Benefits and Exempt Organizations), Internal Revenue Service. However, personnel from other offices of the Service and the Treasury Department participated in their development.

[¶ 49,130] Proposed Regulations (PS-55-89), published in the Federal Register on August 31, 1992.

MACRS: General asset accounts.—Amendments to Reg. § 1.56(g)-1, relating to the election to maintain general asset accounts for depreciable assets to which Code Sec. 168 applies, are proposed. Reg. §§ 1.168(i)-0 and 1.168(i)-1 adopted by T.D. 8566 on October 7, 1994.

AGENCY: Internal Revenue Service, Treasury.

ACTION: Notice of proposed rulemaking.

SUMMARY: This document contains proposed regulations on the election to maintain general asset accounts for depreciable assets to which section 168 of the Internal Revenue Code applies. Changes to the applicable tax law were made by the Tax Reform Act of 1986. The regulations will simplify certain depreciation calculations.

DATES: Written comments must be received by October 15, 1992. Requests to speak (with outlines of oral comments to be presented) at a public hearing scheduled for 10 a.m. on November 4, 1992, must be received by October 14, 1992.

ADDRESSES: Send comments and requests to speak (with outlines of oral comments to be presented) at the public hearing to: Internal Revenue Service, P.O. Box 7604, Ben Franklin Station, Washington, D.C. 20044 (Attn: CC:CORP:T:R (PS-55-89), Room 5228).

FOR FURTHER INFORMATION CONTACT: Concerning the hearing, Carol Savage at (202) 622-8452 (not a toll-free number); concerning the regulations, Kathleen Reed at (202) 622-3110 (not a toll-free number).

SUPPLEMENTARY INFORMATION:

Paperwork Reduction Act

The collection of information requirement contained in this notice of proposed rulemaking has been submitted to the Office of Management and Budget for review in accordance with the Paperwork Reduction Act of 1980 (44 U.S.C 3504(h)). Comments on the collection of information should be sent to the Office of Management and Budget, Attention: Desk Officer for the Department of the Treasury, Office of Information and Regulatory Affairs, Washington, D.C. 20503, with copies to the Internal Revenue Service, Attention: IRS Reports Clearance Officer T:FP, Washington, D.C. 20224.

The collection of information in this regulation is in proposed regulation § 1.168(i)-1(g)(3). This information is required by the Internal Revenue Service to monitor compliance with the election requirement of section 168(i)(4) of the Internal Revenue Code. The likely respondents or recordkeepers are individuals, businesses, and other for-profit institutions.

These estimates are an approximation of the average time expected to be necessary for a collection of information. They are based on such information as is available to the Internal Revenue Service. Individual respondents or recordkeepers may require more or less time depending on their particular circumstances. Estimated total annual reporting and recordkeeping burden: 250 hours.

The estimated annual burden per respondent or recordkeeper varies from .20 to .30 hours, depending on individual circumstances, with an estimated average of .25 hours. Estimated number of respondents and recordkeepers: *1,000.*

Estimated annual frequency of responses: One.

Background

This document contains proposed amendments to the Income Tax Regulations (26 CFR 1) under section 168(i)(4) of the Internal Revenue Code (Code) reflecting amendments made by section 201 of the Tax Reform Act of 1986. The amendments are to be issued under the authority contained in sections 168(i)(4) and 7805 of the Code.

Explanation of Provisions

The proposed regulations would simplify the computation of depreciation by allowing taxpayers to elect to group assets in one or more general asset accounts under section 168(i)(4) of the Code. The assets in any particular general asset account are depreciated as a single asset.

The proposed regulations provide that a general asset account includes assets that have the same asset class, depreciation method, recovery period, and convention and that are placed in service in the same taxable year. Assets subject to the general depreciation system of section 168(a) of the Code or the alternative depreciation system of section 168(g) may be accounted for in general asset accounts. Unlike the rules under section 168 as in existence before enactment of the Tax Reform Act of 1986, general asset account treatment is not limited to "mass assets."

An asset may not be placed in a general asset account if a credit is determined under section 47 or 48 of the Code or if the asset initially is used both in a trade or business (or for the production of income) and in a personal activity. If investment credit assets were included, additional rules would be required to redetermine the basis of the general asset account for any recapture amount determined under section 50. The Service concluded that the added complexity of these rules is not warranted under the circumstances; however, taxpayers are invited to comment on this matter.

In addition, assets that are used predominantly outside the United States or that give rise to depreciation deductions that are apportioned in whole or in part to foreign source income may not be placed in a general asset account. The inclusion of such assets would present substantial difficulties in applying other provisions of the Code, such as the rules of section 864(e) of the Code for apportioning the deduction for interest expense and the rules of section 865(c) for determining the source of gain from the disposition of depreciable personal property. The Service invites comments on how the issues presented by including such assets in a general asset account might be resolved in a manner that would not be unduly burdensome.

As required by section 168(i)(4) of the Code, the proposed regulations provide generally that the amount realized upon the disposition of an asset from a general asset account is recognized as ordinary income. The ordinary income treatment, however, is limited to the unadjusted depreciable basis of the account (determined by disregarding any election made under section 179 or 190 with respect to assets in the account) less any amounts previously recognized as ordinary income at the time of disposition. Any excess amount realized is subject to all other applicable provisions of the Code relating to recognition and character of gain (except the recapture provisions). In computing the depreciation allowance for the account, the unadjusted depreciable basis and the depreciation reserve of the general asset account are not reduced as a result of the disposition.

A special rule is provided for the disposition of all the assets or the last asset from the general asset account. Moreover, the taxpayer may terminate general asset account treatment for a particular asset if the asset is disposed of as the result of a casualty, a charitable contribution, the cessation of a business, or in transactions to which certain nonrecognition sections of the Code apply. For transactions described in section 168(i)(7)(B) of the Code, the transferee generally is bound by the transferor's general asset account election.

The proposed regulations include an anti-abuse rule providing that if an asset in a general asset account is disposed of in certain transactions one of the principal purposes of which is to avoid the limitations imposed under the Code with respect to a net operating loss deduction or the utilization of any credit, the disposition of the asset is treated as though an election under section 168(i)(4) of the Code had never been made for the asset.

The proposed regulations further provide the time and manner in which to make the election to establish general asset accounts. The election generally is irrevocable and is binding on the taxpayer for computing taxable income as well as computing alternative minimum taxable income.

Finally, the proposed regulations provide that these regulations apply to assets placed in service in taxable years ending on or after [the date of publication of the final regulations in the Federal Register]. For prior taxable years, the Service will allow the use of any reasonable method that clearly reflects income and is consistently applied to the general asset accounts.

Special Analyses

It has been determined that these proposed rules are not major rules as defined in Executive Order 12291. Therefore, a Regulatory Impact Analysis is not required. It has also been determined that section 553(b) of the Administrative Procedure Act (5 U.S.C. chapter 5) and the Regulatory Flexibility Act (5 U.S.C. chapter 6) do not apply to these proposed regulations. Therefore, an initial Regulatory Flexibility Analysis is not required. Pursuant to section 7805(f) of the Code, a copy of the rules will be submitted to the Chief Counsel for Advocacy of the Small Business Administration for comment on their impact on small business.

Written Comments and Public Hearing

Before adopting these proposed regulations, consideration will be given to any written comments that are submitted (preferably a signed original and eight copies) to the Internal Revenue Service. All comments will be available for public inspection and copying. The public hearing will be held at 10 a.m. on November 4, 1992. See the notice of public hearing published elsewhere in this issue of the Federal Register.

Drafting Information

The principal author of these proposed regulations is Kathleen Reed, Office of Assistant Chief Counsel (Passthroughs and Special Industries), Internal Revenue Service. However, personnel from other offices of the Internal Revenue Service and Treasury Department participated in their development and style.

[¶ 49,131] Proposed Regulations (FI-61-91), published in the Federal Register on September 3, 1992.

REMICs: Reporting requirements: Allocable investment expenses.—Reg. § 1.67-3T, relating to reporting requirements with respect to real estate mortgage investment conduits, is proposed.

AGENCY: Internal Revenue Service, Treasury.

ACTION: Notice of proposed rulemaking.

SUMMARY: On March 9, 1988, the Internal Revenue Service issued temporary regulations [T.D. 8186] under section 67 of the Internal Revenue Code relating to reporting requirements with respect to Real Estate Mortgage Investment Conduits (REMICs) that were published in the Rules and Regulations portion of the Federal Register (53 FR 7504). These regulations propose to adopt as final regulations that portion of the temporary regulations under § 1.67-3T(a) through (e) (as contained in the CFR edition revised as of April 1, 1992), relating to reporting requirements under section 67 with respect to REMICs. The text of the temporary regulations serves as the comment document for this notice of proposed rulemaking.

DATES: Written comments and requests to speak (with outlines of oral comments) at the public hearing that is scheduled for November 9, 1992, must be received by October 19, 1992. See notice of hearing published elsewhere in this issue of the Federal Register.

ADDRESSES: Send comments, requests to speak at the public hearing, and outlines of oral comments, to: Internal Revenue Service, P.O. Box 7604, Ben Franklin Station, Washington, D.C. 20044, Attn: CC:CORP:T:R (FI-61-91), Room 5228.

FOR FURTHER INFORMATION CONTACT: James W.C. Canup, 202-622-3950 (not a toll-free number).

SUPPLEMENTARY INFORMATION:

Background

On March 9, 1988, temporary regulations [T.D. 8186] under section 67 were published in the Federal Register (53 FR 7504). Section 1.67-3T(f) of those regulations was amended on September 7, 1989 [T.D. 8259](54 FR 37098). Section 1.67-3T(f) of those regulations was also revised on September 30, 1991 [T.D. 8366] (56 FR 49512). In the Rules and Regulations portion of this issue of the Federal Register, the Internal Revenue Service is issuing final regulations under § 1.67-3(f). These regulations propose to adopt as final regulations that portion of the temporary regulations under § 1.67-3T(a) through (e) (as contained in the CFR edition revised as of April 1, 1992).

Section 132 of the Tax Reform Act of 1986 (the 1986 Act) added to the Internal Revenue Code section 67, which disallows certain miscellaneous itemized deductions in computing the taxable income of an individual to the extent that the aggregate of those deductions does not exceed two percent of the individual's adjusted gross income. Section 67(c) directs that regulations be issued to prohibit the indirect deduction through pass-through entities of amounts that are not allowable as a deduction if paid or incurred directly by an individual. Section 67(c) also directs that regulations provide any necessary reporting requirements. The regulations under section 67 that are contained in this document fulfill the requirements of section 67(c) as it applies to REMICs.

Explanation of Provisions

In general, a REMIC is a fixed pool of mortgages in which multiple classes of interests are held by investors and which elects to be taxed as a REMIC. The regulations under section 67 require notice of income and other information to be provided to REMIC investors and the Internal Revenue Service.

Treatment of allocable investment expenses

Section 1.67-3T(a)(1) requires a REMIC to allocate to each of its pass-through interest holders the holder's proportionate share of the aggregate amount of allocable investment expenses of the REMIC for the calendar quarter. In general, a pass-through interest holder (as defined in § 1.67-3T(a)(2)(i)(A)) is any holder of a residual interest that is either an individual (other than certain nonresident aliens), a person that computes its taxable income in the same manner as would an individual, or a pass-through entity, interests in which are owned by either an individual or a person that computes its taxable income in the same manner as would an individual.

The term "pass-through entity" includes, pursuant to § 1.67-2T(g), a grantor trust, a partnership, an S corporation, a common trust fund, a nonpublicly offered regulated investment company, and a REMIC. It does not include an estate, a nongrantor trust, a cooperative, a real estate investment trust, or other entities such as a qualified pension plan, an individual retirement account, or an insurance company holding assets in a separate asset account to fund certain variable contracts. The term "allocable investment expenses" (as defined in § 1.67-3T(a)(3)) means the aggregate amount of the expenses paid or accrued in the calendar quarter for which a deduction is allowable under section 212 in determining the taxable income of the REMIC for the calendar quarter.

Pursuant to § 1.67-3T(b)(1) a pass-through interest holder is treated both as having received or accrued income and as having paid or incurred an expense described in section 212 (or section 162 in the case of a pass-through interest holder that is a regulated investment company) in an amount equal to the pass-through interest holder's proportionate share of the allocable investment expenses of the REMIC.

Under § 1.67-3T(b)(1)(i), a pass-through interest holder whose taxable year is the calendar year or ends with a calendar quarter takes into account the amounts in those calendar quarters that fall within the holder's taxable year. Separate inclusion rules apply under § 1.67-3T(b)(1)(ii) to a holder whose taxable year does not end with a calendar quarter. An interest holder in a REMIC that is not a pass-through interest holder does not take into account in computing its taxable income any amount of its proportionate share of allocable investment expenses. Under § 1.67-3T(c)(1), a REMIC generally computes a pass-through interest holder's proportionate share of its allocable investment expenses by determining the daily amount of such expenses and allocating this daily amount to the pass-through interest holder in proportion to its respective holdings on that day. Generally, a pass-through interest holder's proportionate share of the daily amount of the allocable investment expenses is determined by taking into account all holders of REMIC residual interests, whether or not those holders are pass-through interest holders.

Single-class REMICs

In the case of a single-class REMIC (as described in § 1.67-3T(a)(2)(ii)), the term "pass-through interest holder" is defined more broadly to include any regular or residual interest holder that is either an individual (other than certain nonresident aliens), a person that computes its taxable income in the same manner as would an individual, or a pass-through entity, interests in which are owned by certain types of holders. Under § 1.67-3T(c)(3), a single-class REMIC allocates its investment expenses for a calendar quarter to each holder in proportion to the amount of income that accrues to the holder for that quarter.

Special Analyses

It has been determined that these proposed rules are not major rules as defined in Executive Order 12291. Therefore, a Regulatory Impact Analysis is not required. It has also been determined that section 553(b) of the Administrative Procedure Act (5 U.S.C. chapter 5) and the Regulatory Flexibility Act (5 U.S.C. chapter 6) do not apply to this regulation, and, therefore, an initial Regulatory Flexibility Analysis is not required. Pursuant to section 7805(f) of the Internal Revenue Code, this regulation will be submitted to the Chief Counsel for Advocacy of the Small Business Administration for comment on its impact on small business.

Comments and Requests to Appear at the Public Hearing

Before this proposed regulation is adopted, consideration will be given to any written comments that are timely submitted (preferably a signed original and eight copies) to the Internal Revenue Service. All comments will be available for public inspection and copying in their entirety. A public hearing will be held on November 9, 1992. See the notice of public hearing published elsewhere in this issue of the Federal Register.

Drafting Information

The principal author of the proposed regulation is James W. C. Canup, Office of the Assistant Chief Counsel (Financial Institutions and Products), Internal Revenue Service. However, other personnel from the Service and Treasury Department participated in their development.

Proposal of Regulations

The portion of the temporary regulations (T.D. 8186) under § 1.67-3T(a) through (e) (as contained in the CFR edition revised as of April 1, 1992), is hereby also proposed as final regulations under section 67 of the Internal Revenue Code of 1986.

[¶ 49,132] Proposed Amendments of Regulations (EE-101-91), published in the Federal Register on October 9, 1992.

Fringe benefits: Employer-provided vehicle and fuel: Lease valuation rule.—Amendments to Reg. § 1.61-21, relating to the valuation of an employee's personal use of employer-provided fuel when an employer-provided automobile is valued pursuant to the automobile lease valuation rule, are proposed.

AGENCY: Internal Revenue Service, Treasury.

ACTION: Notice of proposed rulemaking

SUMMARY: This document contains proposed amendments relating to the taxation and valuation of fringe benefits under section 61 of the Internal Revenue Code. These proposed amendments update previous guidance concerning the valuation of an employee's personal use of employer-provided fuel when an employer-provided automobile is valued pursuant to the automobile lease valuation rule. The proposed regulations affect employees receiving this fringe benefit and provide guidance to employers and employees to help determine their federal tax liability.

DATES: Written comments and requests for a public hearing must be received by November 9, 1992.

ADDRESSES: Send comments and requests for a public hearing to: Internal Revenue Service, P.O. Box 7604, Ben Franklin Station, Attention: CC:CORP:T:R (EE-lOl-91), Room 5228, Washington, D.C. 20044.

FOR FURTHER INFORMATION CONTACT: Marianna Dyson, at 202-622-4606 (not a toll-free number).

SUPPLEMENTARY INFORMATION:

Background

This document contains proposed amendments to the Income Tax Regulations (26 CFR part 1) under section 61 of the Internal Revenue Code of 1986 (Code). The amendments pertain to the valuation of employer-provided fuel under the automobile lease valuation rule of § 1.61-21(d) of the regulations.

Explanation of Provisions

The final fringe benefit regulations issued in July 1989 and effective for benefits furnished on or after January 1, 1989, provide that in valuing the personal use of automobiles under § 1.61-21(d) of the regulations, the Annual Lease Values do not include the fair market value of fuel provided by the employer. Thus, fuel consumed for any personal miles driven must be valued separately for inclusion in income. Section 1.61-21(d)(3)(ii)(A).

Under § 1.61-21(d)(3)(ii)(B), employer-paid fuel provided *in kind* to employees for personal use may be valued at fair market value or, in the alternative, at 5.5 cents per mile. If the cost of the fuel is reimbursed by or charged to an employer, the value of the fuel is its fair market value, which is generally the amount of the actual reimbursement or amount charged, provided the purchase of the fuel is at arm's-length. Section 1.61-21(d)(3)(ii)(C).

For employers with fleets of at least 20 automobiles, § 1.61-21(d)(3)(ii)(D) sets forth two additional methods for valuing fuel for personal use. The general method provides that employers who reimburse employees for the cost of fuel or allow employees to charge the employer for the cost of fuel may value the fuel by reference to the employer's "fleet-average cents-per-mile fuel cost." The fleet-average cents-per-mile fuel cost is equal to the fleet-average per-gallon fuel cost divided by the fleet-average miles-per-gallon rate. The average per-gallon fuel cost and the miles-per-gallon rate are determined by averaging the per-gallon fuel costs and miles-per-gallon rates of a representative sample of the automobiles in the fleet equal to the greater of ten percent of the automobiles in the fleet or 20 automobiles for a representative period. Section 1.61-21(d)(3)(ii)(D).

In lieu of calculating the "fleet-average cents-per-mile fuel cost" under the general method of paragraph (d)(3)(ii)(D) of § 1.61-21, employers with fleets of at least 20 automobiles that use the fleet-average valuation rule of paragraph (d)(5)(D) may use the 5.5 cents-per-mile option of paragraph (d)(3)(ii)(B), if determining the amount of the actual reimbursement or the amount charged for the purchase of fuel would impose unreasonable administrative burdens on the employer ("the alternative method").

In no event, however, may an employer with a fleet of at least 20 automobiles use either the general or alternative method of paragraph (d)(3)(ii)(D) of § 1.61-21 unless the requirements of paragraph (d)(5)(v)(D) are also met. This paragraph contains the rules for using a fleet-average value in calculating the Annual Lease Values of the automobiles in the fleet. In particular, it specifies that the fair market value of each vehicle in the fleet may not exceed $16,500 (as adjusted pursuant to section 280F(d)(7) of the Code).

For calendar years prior to 1991, Notice 89-110, 1989-2 C.B. 447, expanded the availability of the 5.5 cents-per-mile option to employers with fleets of at least 20 automobiles that satisfy the requirements of paragraph (d)(5)(v)(D), regardless of whether they are actually using the fleet-average valuation rule of paragraph (d)(5)(v). Notice 91-41, 1991-51 I.R.B. 63, provides that the 5.5 cents-per-mile option as provided in Notice 89-110 is available in calendar year 1991.

Notice 89-110 did not eliminate the requirement that the employer must demonstrate that it is using the 5.5 cents-per-mile option because determining the amount of the actual reimbursement or the amount charged for the purchase of fuel would impose unreasonable administrative burdens on the employer. As a practical matter, however, it is believed that fleet operators with at least 20 automobiles would have little difficulty in demonstrating the existence of unreasonable administrative burdens.

The proposed amendments to § 1.61-21(d)(3)(ii) provide that, for calendar year 1992, employers with fleets of at least 20 automobiles may continue to use the 5.5 cents-per-mile rate as provided in Notice 89-110 and extended in Notice 91-41. In addition, the proposed amendments provide that employers with fleets of at least 20 automobiles may value fuel that is reimbursed by or charged to the employer by reference to the alternative cents-per-mile rate without regard to the rules in paragraph (d)(5)(v)(D) concerning the value of automobiles in the fleet, and without the necessity of demonstrating the existence of administrative burdens.

Finally, the proposed amendments provide that for calendar years subsequent to 1992 the Service will announce the appropriate cents-per-mile rate for valuing fuel that is provided in kind or that is reimbursed by or charged to employers with fleets of at least 20 automobiles. The announcement will appear in the annual revenue procedure concerning the optional standard mileage rates used in computing deductible costs of operating a passenger automobile for business.

The rules under paragraph (d)(3)(ii) of § 1.61-21, as amended by this Notice, will enable employers with fleets of at least 20 automobiles to value the personal use of employer-paid fuel in any of the following ways: (1) fuel provided in kind may be valued at fair market value based on all the facts and circumstances; (2) fuel that is provided in kind may be valued at the cents-per-mile rate applicable to the particular year; (3) fuel, the cost of which is reimbursed by or charged to the employer, may be valued based on the amount of the actual reimbursement or the amount charged; (4) fuel, the cost of which is reimbursed by or charged to the employer, may be valued based on the fleet-average cents-per-mile fuel cost; or (5) fuel, the cost of which is reimbursed by or charged to the employer, may be valued based on the applicable cents-per-mile rate without regard to the fair market value of any automobile in the fleet or the administrative burdens requirement.

The amendments are proposed to be effective for benefits provided in calendar years beginning after December 31, 1992. However, because of the number of inquiries the Service has received from taxpayers expressing uncertainty as to the scope of the guidance in Notice 89-110 concerning employer-provided fuel, the amendments may be relied upon as if they had been included in the final regulations published on July 6, 1989.

Special Analyses

It has been determined that these rules are not major rules as defined in Executive Order 12291. Therefore, a Regulatory Impact Analysis is not required. It has also been determined that section 553(b) of the Administrative Procedure Act (5 U.S.C. chapter 5) and the Regulatory Flexibility Act (5 U.S.C. chapter 6) do not apply to these regulations, and, therefore, an initial Regulatory Flexibility Analysis is not required. Pursuant to section 7805(f) of the Internal Revenue Code, these regulations will be submitted to the Chief Counsel for Advocacy of the Small Business Administration for comment on their impact on small business.

Comments and Requests to Appear at a Public Hearing

Before adopting these proposed regulations, consideration will be given to any written comments that are submitted (preferably a signed original and eight copies) to the Internal Revenue Service. All comments will be available for public inspection and copying in their entirety. A public hearing will be held upon written request to the Commissioner by any person who has submitted written comments. Written comments and requests for a hearing must be received by November 9, 1992. If a public hearing is held, notice of the time and place will be published in the Federal Register.

Drafting Information

The principal author of these regulations is Marianna Dyson, Office of the Associate Chief Counsel (Employee Benefits and Exempt Organizations), Internal Revenue Service. However, personnel from other offices of the Service and Treasury Department participated in their development.

[¶ 49,134] Proposed Regulations (FI-25-92), published in the Federal Register on December 15, 1992.

Life insurance contracts: Qualified accelerated death benefits.—Reg. §§ 1.101-8, 1.7702-0, 1.7702-2, and 1.7702A-1, relating to the definition of a life insurance contract for federal tax purposes and the tax treatment of amounts received as qualified accelerated death benefits, are proposed.

AGENCY: Internal Revenue Service, Treasury.

ACTION: Notice of proposed rulemaking.

SUMMARY: This document provides proposed regulations relating to the definition of a life insurance contract for federal tax purposes and to the federal income tax treatment of amounts received as qualified accelerated death benefits. These proposed regulations are necessary to provide guidance to insurance companies and their policyholders.

DATES: Written comments, requests to speak, and outlines of oral arguments to be presented at the hearing scheduled for March 19, 1993, at 10:00 a.m. in the Internal Revenue Service Auditorium, must be received by February 26, 1993. See notice of hearing published elsewhere in this issue of the **Federal Register.**

ADDRESSES: Send submissions to: Internal Revenue Service, P.O. Box 7604, Ben Franklin Station, Attention: CC:CORP:T:R (FI-25-92), Room 5228, Washington, D.C. 20044.

FOR FURTHER INFORMATION CONTACT: Concerning the regulations, Ann H. Logan, 202-622-3970 (not a toll-free number). Concerning the hearing, Mike Slaughter of the Regulations Unit, 202-622-7190 (not a toll-free number).

SUPPLEMENTARY INFORMATION:

Background

This document sets forth proposed amendments to the Income Tax Regulations (26 CFR part 1) under sections 101, 7702, and 7702A of the Internal Revenue Code (Code). The proposed rules relate to the definition of a life insurance contract under section 7702 of the Internal Revenue Code, to the treatment of a life insurance contract under section 7702A, and to the federal income tax treatment of amounts received as qualified accelerated death benefits under section 101. The proposed regulations reflect the addition of section 7702 to the Code by section 221(a) of the Tax Reform Act of 1984, Pub. L. 98-369, and the addition of section 7702A to the Code by section 5012 of the Technical and Miscellaneous Revenue Act of 1988, Pub. L. 100-647.

Purpose of Regulations

The proposed regulations provide insurers with the standards needed to design and market insurance contracts that provide both death benefits and morbidity benefits without subjecting policyholders to taxation on the inside build-up of the life insurance contracts.

In recognition of the needs of individuals who become terminally ill, the proposed regulations also allow the payment of benefits prior to death without any income tax liability to the recipient if death is expected to occur within 12 months.

For insurance contracts that, prior to July 1, 1993, provide for a benefit or loan for terminally ill individuals or a morbidity benefit, the proposed regulations provide transition rules that prevent the benefit or loan from resulting in adverse federal tax consequences to the policyholders and avoid the reporting and withholding requirements that would be imposed upon the insurers if the contracts were to fail to qualify as life insurance contracts. *See* Rev. Rul. 91-17, 1991-1 C.B. 190.

Summary of Relevant Statutory Provisions

Section 7702 defines a "life insurance contract" as any contract that is a life insurance contract under applicable law, but only if the contract either (1) meets the cash value accumulation test of section 7702(b), or (2) meets the guideline premium requirements of section 7702(c) and falls within the cash value corridor of section 7702(d).

The cash value accumulation test of section 7702(b) requires that, by the terms of the contract, the cash surrender value of the contract may not at any time exceed the net single premium that would have to be paid at that time to fund the future benefits under the contract. "Cash surrender value" for purposes of section 7702 is defined in section 7702(f)(2)(A) as the cash value of the contract determined without regard to any surrender charge, policy loan, or reasonable termination dividends. The "net single premium" must be determined using the assumptions, computational rules, definitions, and special rules contained in section 7702.

The guideline premium limitation of section 7702(c) provides that the premiums paid under the contract at any time must not exceed the greater of the guideline single premium or the sum of the guideline level premiums to that date. Contracts qualifying as life insurance under the guideline premium test also must satisfy the cash value corridor of section 7702(d). The corridor specifies a minimum ratio of death benefits to cash surrender values.

Section 7702(f)(7) provides for adjustments in determinations made under section 7702 if there is a change in the benefits under (or in other terms of) the contract which was not reflected in any previous determination or adjustment. A reduction in death benefits is an adjustment event under section 7702(f)(7). Qualification as a life insurance contract after an adjustment event requires redetermination of values under the contract, including the net single premium, the guideline premium limitation, and the cash value corridor, depending on the test under which the contract qualifies as life insurance.

Section 7702(g) governs the federal income tax treatment of a life insurance contract under applicable law that fails to meet the definition of a life insurance contract under section 7702(a), either at inception or at a later date. In general, under section 7702(g)(1)(A), the "income on the contract" is treated as ordinary income that is received or accrued annually by the policyholder.

Section 7702A(a) defines a modified endowment contract as a life insurance contract meeting the requirements of section 7702 which is entered into on or after June 21, 1988 and which fails to meet the 7-pay test of section 7702A(b) or a life insurance contract which is received in exchange for a modified endowment contract.

Section 7702A(c)(3)(A)(i) provides that, if there is a "material change" within the meaning of section 7702A(c)(3) to a life insurance contract that is subject to section 7702A, the contract is treated as entered into on the day that the material change takes effect. A material change in the benefits under (or in other terms of) the contract includes any increase in the death benefit under the contract or any increase in, or addition of, a qualified additional benefit under the contract.

Section 101(a) provides in part that gross income does not include amounts received (whether in a single sum or otherwise) under a life insurance contract, if the amounts are paid by reason of the death of the insured.

Section 72(c)(1) defines investment in the contract for purposes of determining the exclusion ratio for amounts received as an annuity under an annuity, endowment, or life insurance contract. Section 72(e)(6) defines investment in the contract for amounts received under an annuity, endowment, or life insurance contract if the amount is not received as an annuity and no other income tax provision applies. *See* Rev. Rul. 55-349, 1955-1 C.B. 232, (premiums for supplementary benefits excluded from the investment in the contract).

New Insurance Contracts

Insurance companies have developed insurance contracts which provide both death benefits and "living benefits" designed to assist policyholders with the rising costs of medical care, particularly medical care in the later years of life. Living benefits generally may be divided into two types of benefits. The first type of living benefit, an "accelerated death benefit," addresses the needs of terminally ill individuals who may incur substantial medical and living expenses prior to death. This benefit allows the policyholder, under a life insurance contract insuring a terminally ill individual, to "accelerate" the death benefit paid under the contract. Generally, the accelerated death benefit is equal to all or a portion of the death benefit discounted for the remaining life expectancy (generally 12 months or less) of the terminally ill individual. The payment of a benefit is conditioned upon the policyholder surrendering all or a portion of the policyholder's rights under the life insurance contract.

A second type of living benefit provides accident and health benefits upon the occurrence of certain morbidity risks, for example, a condition requiring a long-term stay in a nursing home or certain dread diseases. The living benefit is a specified amount which is determined by reference to all or a portion of the death benefit otherwise payable. As with accelerated death benefits, the payment of a benefit is conditioned upon the policyholder surrendering all or a portion of the policyholder's rights under the life insurance contract.

Explanation of Provisions

The proposed regulations are being promulgated to provide guidance concerning the tax treatment to the owners and issuers of insurance contracts that provide living benefits by addressing the application of sections 72, 101, 7702, and 7702A to those insurance contracts.

The proposed regulations allow qualified accelerated death benefits under an insurance contract to be treated as amounts paid by reason of the death of the insured for purposes of sections 101(a) and 7702. This proposed treatment allows an insurance contract including these benefits to continue to meet the definition of a life insurance contract under section 7702. The proposed regulations also permit a person who receives a qualified accelerated death benefit to exclude, under section 101(a), the benefit from gross income.

A qualified accelerated death benefit is defined in the proposed regulations as a benefit payable under a contract on the life of an insured who becomes terminally ill, where the amount of the death benefit made available cannot be discounted by more than 12 months at the rate of interest specified in the regulations. Under the proposed regulations an individual is terminally ill if the individual has an illness or physical condition that, notwithstanding appropriate medical care, is reasonably expected to result in death within 12 months from the date of payment of the accelerated death benefit. As the 12 month determination is necessarily subjective to some extent, it is expected that the insurer will act prudently in its determination of whether the person is terminally ill. The Service is considering whether to develop further guidance that would create a presumption of terminal illness in certain circumstances.

The proposed regulations also address the treatment, under section 7702, of other living benefits that provide payments upon the occurrence of a morbidity risk of an amount determined by reference to all or a portion of the death benefit otherwise payable under an insurance contract. For purposes of section 7702, the benefit could be viewed as an amount paid upon surrender of a contract and accordingly would be included in the cash surrender value of the contract. The impact of this characterization would be to disqualify as life insurance under section 7702 many contracts providing these benefits. Contracts with large cash surrender values would no longer qualify under the cash value accumulation test of section 7702(b) while contracts qualifying under the guideline premium test of section 7702(c) would fail the cash value corridor test of section 7702(d). For example, a policyholder, age 37, might own an insurance contract with a $100,000 face amount, that also provides for a payment of $70,000 upon surrender of the contract if the policyholder is hospitalized for a specified number of days. The $70,000 hospital benefit could result in the failure of the contract to qualify as a life insurance contract under section 7702.

To enable policyholders to avoid this result, the proposed regulations adopt an approach which assumes that a life insurance contract and an accident and health insurance contract which could be sold separately should be allowed to be sold together without endangering the qualification of the contract offering both benefits as a life insurance contract under section 7702. To preserve qualification of the contract offering both benefits as a life insurance contract, the proposed regulations exclude amounts payable as additional benefits (other than qualified additional benefits) from cash value if the following conditions are satisfied: (1) the benefits are paid solely upon the occurrence of a morbidity risk, (2) the charges for the benefits are separately stated and currently imposed by the insurer, and (3) the charges are not included in premiums taken into account in the determination of the investment in the contract under section 72 and are not taken into account in the determination of premiums paid under section 7702(f)(1).

If the three conditions are met, the proposed regulations treat a life insurance contract with an additional accident and health benefit as providing both a potential death benefit and a potential living benefit which is paid upon the occurrence of a morbidity risk. The living benefit is treated as being comprised of two elements: (1) a payment upon the partial or full surrender of the life insurance contract for part or all of the cash value, and (2) a payment upon the occurrence of a morbidity event of an additional accident and health benefit equal to the difference between the total payment received and the amount received by the policyholder on the full or partial surrender of the contract. If, however, the three conditions are not satisfied, the additional benefit will not be excluded from cash value under section 7702.

The requirement that morbidity risk charges for living benefits be separately stated and currently imposed by the terms of the life insurance contract is necessary if section 7702 is to operate in the manner intended by Congress. Providing for the proper allocation and treatment of charges for these contracts assures the appropriate treatment of amounts paid into the contract and benefits paid.

The approach in the proposed regulations is intended to level the playing field between contracts that provide accident and health benefits in conjunction with life insurance benefits and contracts that provide only accident and health benefits. Thus, the approach of the proposed regulations will allow a contract providing both accident and health and life insurance benefits to continue to qualify as a life insurance contract under section 7702 so long as the contract provides appropriate treatment of the charges for the accident and health benefits.

The proposed regulations also exclude from cash value qualified additional benefits, certain amounts returned upon termination of a credit life insurance contract, and reasonable termination dividend.

The proposed regulations define cash surrender value, net surrender value, and death benefit for purposes of section 7702.

Proposed Effective Dates

The proposed regulations under section 7702, relating to the definition of cash value and the tax treatment of certain benefits, would be effective generally for contracts issued or entered into after June 30, 1993.

Under the proposed regulations, the provision of certain benefits or loans in a life insurance contract before July 1, 1993, does not increase the cash value of the contract. The proposed regulations also provide that the addition to a life insurance contract, before July 1, 1993, of certain benefits or loans has no effect on the date that the contract was issued or entered into for purposes of section 7702 and 7702A, and does not cause a material change in the contract under section 7702A.

The addition of a qualified accelerated death benefit (or an additional benefit satisfying the three conditions specified in proposed § 1.7702-2(f)) to a life insurance contract at any time has no effect on the date that the contract was issued or entered into for purposes of section 7702 and 7702A, and does not cause a material change in the contract under section 7702A.

The section 101 exclusion provided by the proposed regulations for qualified accelerated death benefits would be effective for amounts received on or after the date on which final regulations defining a qualified accelerated death benefit are published in the Federal Register.

Special Analyses

It has been determined that these proposed rules are not major rules as defined in Executive Order 12291. Therefore, a Regulatory Impact Analysis is not required. It has also been determined that section 553(b) of the Administrative Procedure Act (5 U.S.C. chapter 5) and the Regulatory Flexibility Act (5 U.S.C. chapter 6) do not apply to these regulations, and, therefore, an initial Regulatory Flexibility Analysis is not required. Pursuant to section 7805(f) of the Internal Revenue Code, the proposed regulations will be submitted to the Chief Counsel for Advocacy of the Small Business Administration for comment on their impact on small business.

Comments and Request for a Public Hearing

Before the adoption of these proposed regulations, consideration will be given to any written comments that are timely submitted (preferably a signed original and eight copies) to the Internal Revenue Service.

Comments are specifically requested on the need for special rules under section 7702(f)(7) for contracts that do not terminate upon payment of a morbidity benefit or a qualified accelerated death benefit. Comments are also requested on whether the proposed regulations treat additional benefits insuring morbidity risks that are attached to a life insurance contract in the same fashion as contracts which provide similar benefits that are not attached to a life insurance contract. Finally, comments are requested on whether the regulations should specify how premiums and charges should be allocated among the various benefits provided under a life insurance contract.

All comments will be available for public inspection and copying in their entirety. A public hearing has been scheduled for March 19, 1993. See notice of hearing published elsewhere in this issue of the Federal Register.

Drafting Information

The principal author of these proposed regulations is Ann H. Logan, Office of the Assistant Chief Counsel (Financial Institutions and Products), Office of Chief Counsel, Internal Revenue Service. However, personnel from other offices of the Service and the Treasury Department participated in developing the regulations, in matters of both substance and style.

[¶ 49,136] **Proposed Regulations and Proposed Amendments of Regulations (FI-189-84)**, published in the Federal Register on December 22, 1992.

Debt instruments: Imputed interest: Original issue discount: Sale or exchange of property.—Reg. §§1.163-7, 1.446-2, 1.483-1—1.483-3, 1.1271-1,1.1272-1,1.1272-2, 1.1272-3, 1.1273-1, 1.1273-2, 1.1274-1, 1.1274-2, 1.1274-3, 1.1274-4, 1.1274-5, 1.1274A-1, 1.1275-1, 1.1275-2, 1.1275-3 and 1.1275-5, and amendments of Reg. §§1.1001-1 and 1.1012-1, relating to the tax treatment of debt instruments with original issue discount and the imputation of interest on deferred payments under certain contracts for the sale or exchange of property, were adopted on 1/27/94 by T.D. 8517. Reg. §1.446-2(e)(3) is still proposed.

AGENCY: Internal Revenue Service, Treasury.

ACTION: Notice of proposed rulemaking.

SUMMARY: This document contains proposed regulations relating to the tax treatment of debt instruments with original issue discount and the imputation of interest on deferred payments under certain contracts for the sale or exchange of property. The proposed regulations in this document revise some of the proposed regulations that were published in the Federal Register on April 8, 1986. The proposed regulations would provide needed guidance to holders and issuers of debt instruments with original issue discount and to buyers and sellers of property.

DATES: A public hearing on these proposed regulations is scheduled for 10:00 a.m. on February 16, 1993, in room 3313 at 1111 Constitution Ave., N.W., Washington, D.C. Requests to appear at the public hearing and outlines of oral comments must be received by January 26, 1993. Written comments must be received by January 26, 1993. See notice of hearing published elsewhere in this issue of the Federal Register.

ADDRESSES: Send comments, requests to appear, and outlines of oral comments to: Internal Revenue Service, P.O. Box 7604, Ben Franklin Station, Attn: CC:CORP:T:R (FI-189-84), Room 5228, Washington, D.C. 20044.

FOR FURTHER INFORMATION CONTACT: Frederick S. Campbell-Mohn, 202-622-3940 (not a toll-free number), William E. Blanchard, 202-622-3950 (not a toll-free number), or Andrew C. Kittler, 202-622-3940 (not a toll-free number).

SUPPLEMENTARY INFORMATION:

Paperwork Reduction Act

The collection of information requirements contained in this notice of proposed rulemaking has been submitted to the Office of Management and Budget for review in accordance with the Paperwork Reduction Act of 1980 (44 U.S.C. 3504(h)). Comments on the collection of information should be sent to the Office of Management and Budget, Attn: Desk Officer for the Department of the Treasury, Office of Information and Regulatory Affairs, Washington, D.C. 20503, with copies to the Internal Revenue Service, Attn: IRS Reports Clearance Officer T:FP, Washington, D.C. 20224.

The required collections of information in this regulation are in §§1.1272-1(d)(2)(iii), 1.1272-3, 1.1273-2(f)(2), 1.1274-3(d), 1.1274-5(b), 1.1274A-1(c), and 1.1275-3(b). This information is required by the Internal Revenue Service in connection with tracking the accrual of original issue discount. This information will be used for audit and examination purposes. The likely respondents are businesses or other for-profit institutions.

These estimates are an approximation of the average time expected to be necessary for a collection of information. They are based on such information as is available to the Internal Revenue Service. Individual respondents may require more or less time, depending on their particular circumstances.

Estimated total reporting burden: 289,500 hours.

The estimated burden per respondent varies from .3 to .5 hours, depending on individual circumstances, with an estimated average of .4 hours.

Estimated number of respondents: 750,000.

Estimated annual frequency of responses: 1.

Background

On April 8, 1986, the Federal Register published a notice of proposed rulemaking (51 FR 12022) relating to original issue discount (OID) under section 163(e) and sections 1271 through 1275, unstated interest under section 483, and the accrual of interest under section 446. The notice also included proposed amendments to the regulations under related provisions of the Internal Revenue Code. The proposed regulations were subsequently amended on September 7, 1989 (54 FR 37125), February 28, 1991 (56 FR 8308), May 7, 1991 (56 FR 21112) and July 12, 1991 (56 FR 31887). The proposed regulations that were issued in 1986, as amended in 1989 and 1991, are hereinafter referred to as the 1986 proposed regulations.

Explanation of Provisions

Numerous written comments were made on the 1986 proposed regulations. In addition, on November 17, 1986, the Internal Revenue Service held a public hearing on the 1986 proposed regulations. In general, commentators criticized the complexity and length of the 1986 proposed regulations, as well as the narrow definitions of certain terms, including the definitions of accrual period, qualified periodic interest payment, variable rate debt instrument, and de minimis OID.

In response to these comments, the proposed regulations simplify the rules that were in the 1986 proposed regulations and, as explained below, provide more flexible definitions of certain terms for purposes of these rules. The proposed regulations attempt to conform the rules to normal commercial practices and to exclude from their application debt instruments with limited potential to defer or accelerate interest.

The proposed regulations are significantly shorter in length than the 1986 proposed regulations. The shorter length is generally attributable to the simplification of the rules and the elimination of rules that are also in the statute. In addition, because the proposed regulations are proposed to be effective for debt instruments issued on or after the date that is 60 days after the date the regulations are finalized, the proposed regulations do not include the numerous transitional rules that were in the 1986 proposed regulations.

The proposed regulations do not amend the rules for contingent payments that are in § 1.1275-4 of the 1986 proposed regulations. These rules will be addressed in future regulations.

In general, the major changes from the 1986 proposed regulations are noted as follows:

Section 1.163-7 Deduction for OID on certain debt instruments.

The proposed regulations allow the issuer of a debt instrument with a de minimis amount of OID to deduct the OID using a straight line method rather than a constant yield method. In addition, if an issuer redeems a debt instrument for the issuer's newly issued debt instrument, the proposed regulations provide rules to determine the amount of the repurchase premium, if any, on the redemption and the timing of the issuer's deduction for the repurchase premium. To determine the amount of the repurchase premium, the issuer's repurchase price for the debt instrument is the issue price of the newly issued debt instrument (reduced by any unstated interest). However, if the issue price of the newly issued debt instrument is determined under either section 1273(b)(4) or section 1274, any repurchase premium on the redemption is amortized by the issuer over the term of the newly issued instrument in the same manner as if it were OID on the instrument.

Section 1.446-2 Method of accounting for interest.

The proposed regulations clarify that unstated interest, as determined under section 483, is taken into account by the buyer and the seller based on their respective methods of accounting for stated interest.

Request for comments: In general, the proposed regulations require the use of the constant yield method to determine interest accruals. However, the proposed regulations generally respect the allocation of payments under a lending or sales contract if (1) the aggregate amount of payments due under the contract does not exceed $250,000, (2) the contract does not have unstated interest, and (3) the debt instrument evidencing the contract is not issued at a discount. This small transaction exception was also in the 1986 proposed regulations. The exception, however, has a limited scope, and taxpayers must still determine whether interest is prepaid under their allocation. Comments are requested as to whether the final regulations should keep this exception. Comments are also requested as to whether the final regulations should allow the use of the Rule of 78's (or any other method) to allocate interest on consumer loans that are not within the small transaction exception, including loans issued for cash.

Section 1.483-1 through 1.483-3 Unstated interest.

For purposes of the lower test rate under section 483(e) for certain sales or exchanges of land between related individuals, the proposed regulations allow the use of the lower rate for a single debt instrument to the extent the stated principal amount of the instrument does not exceed $500,000. For example, if the stated principal amount of the debt instrument is $700,000, the proposed regulations treat the instrument as two instruments: a $500,000 debt instrument, which is eligible for the lower test rate, and a $200,000 debt instrument. The 1986 proposed regulations only allowed the lower rate if a separate debt instrument was issued for the principal amount in excess of $500,000.

Sections 1.1001-1(g) and 1.1012-1(g) Amount realized and basis.

The proposed regulations provide that the issue price of a debt instrument issued in a sale or exchange of property determines the seller's amount realized and the buyer's basis in the property. However, the proposed regulations provide that if the issue price of the debt instrument equals the instrument's stated redemption price at maturity under section 1273(b)(4), the issue price is reduced by any unstated interest for purposes of sections 1001 and 1012.

Section 1.1271-1 Special rules applicable to amounts received on retirement, sale or exchange of debt instruments.

Under section 1271, if there is an intention to call a debt instrument prior to maturity, the gain on the sale, exchange, or retirement of the debt instrument is treated as ordinary income to the extent of any unaccrued OID. The proposed regulations add rules to determine when there is an intention to call the debt instrument prior to maturity. An intention to call exists only if there is an agreement not provided for in the debt instrument that the issuer will redeem the instrument prior to maturity. For example, a mandatory sinking fund provision or call option is not evidence of an intention to call under section 1271. The proposed regulations also provide that the intention to call rules do not apply to publicly offered debt instruments or to debt instruments subject to section 1272(a)(6).

Section 1.1272-1 Current inclusion in income of OID.

The proposed regulations provide that the amount of OID that accrues during an accrual period is determined using the constant yield method. For purposes of this determination, the 1986 proposed regulations required that all accrual periods on a debt instrument (other than a short initial or final accrual period) be of equal length. The proposed regulations, however, allow the use of accrual periods of different lengths of not more than one year. In determining the amount of OID accruals, the yield of the debt instrument must be adjusted to take into account the length of the particular accrual period if accrual periods of different lengths are used.

The proposed regulations also provide new rules to determine the yield and maturity of a debt instrument with a stated contingency that could result in the acceleration or deferral of payments if the amounts payable upon the occurrence of the contingency are fixed. In general, the contingency is ignored. However, if, based on all the facts and circumstances, the contingency is more likely than not to occur, it is assumed that the contingency will occur. In addition, special rules that were in the 1986 proposed regulations for a debt instrument with a put option, call option, or option to extend are retained, and extended to a debt instrument with an option to pay interest in the form of additional debt instruments of the issuer.

If a debt instrument is partially prepaid, the proposed regulations provide that the payment is subject to the payment ordering rule under § 1.1275-2. In general, the payment reduces the adjusted issue price of the debt instrument. For purposes of OID accruals after the prepayment, the yield of the debt instrument is not adjusted for the prepayment. However, any shortfall created as a result of the prepayment is treated as OID and allocated to the final accrual period. *See* § 1.1272-1(c)(2).

Section 1.1272-2 Treatment of debt instruments purchased at a premium.

The proposed regulations define the term purchase as any acquisition of a debt instrument. In addition, the proposed regulations provide new rules to determine the adjusted basis of a debt instrument for purposes of determining whether a holder has acquired a debt instrument at a premium or at an acquisition premium.

Section 1.1272-3 Election by accrual method holder to treat all interest on a debt instrument as OID.

Under the proposed regulations, a holder that uses an accrual method of accounting may elect to treat all interest on a debt instrument as OID. For purposes of the election, interest includes stated interest, OID, market discount, de minimis OID and market discount, acquisition discount, and unstated interest, as adjusted for any acquisition premium or amortizable bond premium. In effect, the election simplifies the calculation of interest income for the holder by applying a single method (constant yield method) to determine the timing and amount of interest income on the debt instrument (*e.g.*, a holder that acquires a debt instrument with acquisition premium need not calculate and use the acquisition premium fraction).

Request for comments: The proposed regulations impose certain conditions on the use of the election. In general, the conditions are similar to those in the market discount and amortizable bond premium rules. For example, if the election is made for a debt instrument with amortizable bond premium or with market discount, the holder becomes subject to the conformity requirements of section 171 or section 1278(b), whichever is applicable. Comments are requested as to whether the final regulations should retain the conformity requirements and other conditions.

Section 1.1273-1 Definition of OID.

OID is defined as the excess of a debt instrument's stated redemption price at maturity over the instrument's issue price. Under the 1986 proposed regulations, a debt instrument's stated redemption price at maturity was defined as the sum of all payments due under the instrument other than qualified periodic interest payments. In general, qualified periodic interest payments were defined as a series of payments equal to the product of the outstanding principal balance of the debt instrument and a single fixed rate of interest that is actually and unconditionally payable at fixed periodic intervals of one year or less during the entire term of the debt instrument (including short periods).

The proposed regulations, by providing a more flexible approach to the treatment of stated interest, generally exclude from their application debt instruments with limited potential to defer or accelerate interest. Under the proposed regulations, "qualified stated interest" is the term used to refer to stated interest that is not includible in the debt instrument's stated redemption price at maturity. Qualified stated interest for a fixed-rate debt instrument is stated interest that is unconditionally payable in cash or in property (other than debt instruments of the issuer) at least annually at a single fixed rate. Interest is payable at a single fixed rate only if the rate appropriately takes into account the length of the interval between payments.

The proposed regulations provide that no stated interest on a short-term obligation is qualified stated interest. Therefore, all stated interest payments on a short-term obligation are included in its stated redemption price at maturity. In response to comments made on the 1986 proposed regulations, which had the same rule, the rule applies for purposes of sections 871 and 881.

The proposed regulations provide an additional rule to determine when a debt instrument with an interest holiday or a teaser rate has a de minimis amount of OID. Under this rule, the amount of OID resulting from an interest holiday or a teaser rate is generally the amount of interest foregone during the holiday or teaser period. The instrument is then tested under the general de minimis rules to determine whether the debt instrument has de minimis OID. For example, under this rule, a 30-year self-amortizing mortgage loan with a fixed interest rate of 8.5 percent, compounded monthly, but a 2-year teaser rate of 6 percent, compounded monthly, would have only a de minimis amount of OID.

The proposed regulations also add rules for the treatment of de minimis OID by the holder. A holder includes de minimis OID in income on a pro rata basis as principal payments are made on the debt instrument. In addition, any gain attributable to de minimis OID that is recognized upon the sale or exchange of a debt instrument is capital gain if the instrument is a capital asset in the hands of the holder. A similar rule was provided in § 1.1232-3(b)(1)(ii).

Section 1.1273-2 Determination of issue price.

The proposed regulations provide new rules to determine when a debt instrument is publicly traded or is issued for property that is publicly traded for purposes of determining the issue price of the debt instrument. In general, a debt instrument or property (stock, security, contract, commodity, or currency) is publicly traded if, at any time during a 60-day period ending 30 days after the issue date of the debt instrument, the debt instrument or property is traded on an established market. A debt instrument or property is traded on an established market if (1) it is listed on certain securities exchanges, interdealer quotation systems, or designated foreign exchanges or boards of trade, (2) it is traded on a designated contract market or an interbank market, (3) it appears on a system of general circulation that provides a reasonable basis to determine fair market value by disseminating either recent price quotations of identified brokers and dealers or actual prices of recent sales transactions, or (4) price quotations with respect to the debt instrument are readily available from dealers and brokers. Price quotations are deemed not readily available if (1) no other outstanding debt of the issuer is traded on an established market, (2) the original stated principal amount of the issue is less than $25 million, (3) all other issues of the issuer's debt that are traded on an established market impose materially more restrictive covenants or conditions on the issuer, or (4) the maturity date of the debt instrument is more than 3 years after the latest maturity date of all other issues of the issuer that are traded on an established market.

The proposed regulations allocate the issue price of an investment unit between the components of the unit based on their relative fair market values. The 1986 proposed regulations provided allocation rules that generally restated common law valuation principles. Unlike the 1986 proposed regulations, the proposed regulations do not provide specific allocation rules. Under the proposed regulations, however, the holder of an investment unit must use the issuer's allocation unless the holder discloses on its Federal income tax return that it plans to use an allocation that is inconsistent with the issuer's allocation.

The 1986 proposed regulations provided that no portion of the issue price of a debt instrument is allocated to a right to convert the instrument into stock of the issuer. However, after the amendments proposed on February 28, 1991, if the conversion right could be satisfied in cash, the 1986 proposed regulations allocated a portion of the issue price of the debt instrument to the conversion right. The proposed regulations modify these rules by providing that no portion of the issue price of a debt instrument is allocated to a right to convert the instrument into stock of the issuer or a party related to the issuer, even if the conversion right may be satisfied in cash.

The proposed regulations change the lender's treatment of a payment of points made incident to a lending transaction. Under the proposed regulations, a payment of points (including a payment of points that is deductible by the borrower under section 461(g)(2)) reduces the issue price of the debt instrument, thereby creating OID on the instrument. If the amount of OID created under this rule is de minimis, the proposed regulations treat the OID in the same manner as any other amount of de minimis OID. By contrast, the 1986 proposed regulations required that the lender include the payment in income when received, regardless of the lender's method of accounting. *See* § 1.446-2(e) of the 1986 proposed regulations.

Sections 1.1274-1 through 1.1274-5 Determination of issue price in the case of certain debt instruments issued for property.

The proposed regulations restructure and simplify the rules that were in §§ 1.1274-1 through 1.1274-7 of the 1986 proposed regulations.

The proposed regulations modify the 1986 proposed regulations by providing that the issue price of a debt instrument issued for nonpublicly traded property in a potentially abusive situation is the fair market value of the property. In addition, the proposed regulations treat a debt instrument with clearly excessive interest as issued in a potentially abusive situation. The proposed regulations also provide that, for purposes of the potentially abusive rules, the term nonrecourse financing does not include a sale or exchange of a real property interest financed by a nonrecourse debt instrument, if, in addition to the instrument, the purchaser provides a down payment that is at least 20 percent of the total stated purchase price of the interest.

The proposed regulations provide new rules to determine the imputed principal amount of a debt instrument if the instrument provides for contingent payments. Under the proposed regulations, the imputed principal amount generally is the sum of the present values of the noncontingent payments and the fair market value of the contingent payments. If the fair market value of the contingent payments cannot be determined when separated from the noncontingent payments, the imputed principal amount is the fair market value of the debt instrument. Only in rare and extraordinary cases will the fair market value of the debt instrument be treated as not reasonably ascertainable.

The proposed regulations provide new rules to determine the test rate of interest for an installment obligation. Unlike the 1986 proposed regulations, which had three alternative rules, the proposed regulations use a single rule that uses the weighted average maturity of the debt instrument to determine the test rate.

The proposed regulations no longer contain the transitional rule in the 1986 proposed regulations that provided that section 1274 applied to a modified debt instrument only if the original debt instrument was subject to section 1274.

The proposed regulations limit the use of a test rate that is lower than the applicable Federal rate to debt instruments having a maturity of six months or less (or to debt instruments with a qualified floating rate of interest that is reset at least every six months). For debt instruments having a maturity of less than three months, the proposed regulations modify the 1986 proposed regulations and provide that the allowable Treasury index rate is the market yield on U.S. Treasury bills with the same maturity as the debt instrument.

The proposed regulations provide new rules for debt instruments that are materially modified in connection with an assumption of a debt instrument as part of a sale or exchange of property. In general, the modification is treated as a separate transaction that takes place immediately before the sale or exchange and is attributed to the seller. The seller and buyer, however, may jointly elect to treat the transaction as one in which the buyer first assumed the unmodified debt instrument and subsequently modified the debt instrument.

Request for comments: The proposed regulations provide rules to determine the issue price of a debt instrument subject to an option that allows a holder or issuer the unconditional right to accelerate or defer payments (including a put option, call option, or option to extend the maturity of an instrument). These rules are similar to rules contained in the 1986 proposed regulations. Comments are requested regarding the appropriateness of these rules and regarding whether these rules should be extended to options subject to contingencies that affect the right to exercise or the amounts payable in the event of exercise.

The proposed regulations do not provide any limitations on "recent sales transactions" that are subject to the potentially abusive situation rules. Comments are requested on the limitations, if any, that should be included in the final regulations.

Section 1.1274A-1 Special rules for certain transactions where stated principal amount does not exceed $2,800,000.

The proposed regulations revise the rules for making a cash method election. The proposed regulations also allow a cash method election for a debt instrument that was issued in a debt-for-debt exchange, subject to an anti-abuse rule, if the instrument otherwise qualifies as a cash method debt instrument. The 1986 proposed regulations only allowed the election if the "old" debt instrument was a cash method debt instrument. In addition, the proposed regulations disallow interest deductions for a debt instrument that is incurred or continued to purchase or carry a cash method debt instrument.

Section 1.1275-1 Definitions.

The term "debt instrument" is defined as any instrument or contractual arrangement that constitutes indebtedness under general principles of Federal income tax law. Based on this definition, the proposed regulations treat a payment of stock pursuant to a contingent stock payout under section 483, rather than under the OID provisions. *See Example 3* in § 1.446-2(h).

Section 1.1275-2 Special rules relating to debt instruments.

The proposed regulations revise the aggregation rules that were in the 1986 proposed regulations. In general, only debt instruments that are issued by a single issuer to a single holder are aggregated. The Commissioner, however, may aggregate debt instruments that are issued by more than one issuer or that are issued to more than one holder if the debt instruments are issued in an arrangement that is designed to avoid the aggregation rule. In addition, if under the terms of a debt instrument the holder may receive one or more additional debt instruments of the issuer, the additional debt instruments are aggregated with the original debt instrument.

The proposed regulations also provide a specific payment ordering rule for purposes of the OID provisions. In addition, the proposed regulations add rules for qualified reopenings of Treasury securities.

Section 1.1275-3 OID information reporting requirements.

The 1986 proposed regulations generally required an issuer of a debt instrument with OID to legend the instrument with certain information. The proposed regulations provide that debt instruments do not have to be legended if the instruments are publicly offered or are issued by individuals. In addition, the proposed regulations except a debt instrument from legending if the instrument is not evidenced by a physical document. In the case of a debt instrument that has to be legended, the proposed regulations provide new rules that should simplify compliance with the legending requirement. As an alternative to detailed legending of OID information, the proposed regulations permit the issuer to provide the address or telephone number of a representative of the issuer who will promptly give the OID information to the holder upon request.

Section 1.1275-5 Variable rate debt instruments.

The proposed regulations substantially expand the definition of the term "variable rate debt instrument." In general, a variable rate debt instrument is a debt instrument that provides for stated interest (compounded or paid at least annually) at a qualified floating rate, an objective rate, a fixed rate followed by a qualified floating rate, or a qualified floating rate followed by another qualified floating rate. A qualified floating rate generally is an interest-like rate, such as the applicable Federal rate or LIBOR. An objective rate generally is a rate based on the price of property that is actively traded (other than foreign currency) or an index of the prices of such property. An objective rate is also a rate that is based on one or more qualified floating rates (unless the rate itself is a qualified floating rate). For example, a multiple of a qualified floating rate is an objective rate.

For purposes of determining whether a variable rate debt instrument has OID, the proposed regulations generally treat all stated interest on the instrument that is unconditionally payable at least annually as qualified stated interest. If, however, the debt instrument provides for stated interest at a fixed rate followed by a qualified floating rate or a qualified floating rate followed by a different qualified floating rate, the instrument may have accelerated or deferred interest, which is not qualified stated interest. For example, if a ten-year debt instrument provides for annual interest payments for the first five years equal to the value of one-year LIBOR on each payment date and for the last five years equal to the value of one-year LIBOR on each payment date plus 200 basis points, the 200 basis points in the last five years is deferred interest.

The proposed regulations also provide rules for the accrual of OID on variable rate debt instruments. In general, if the OID is attributable to accelerated or deferred interest or to "true discount" (the excess of a debt instrument's stated principal amount over its issue price), the OID is allocated to an accrual period under the rules of section 1272. The allocation, however, is determined by assuming that the debt instrument provided for qualified stated interest payments at the end of each accrual period based on a reasonable fixed rate.

The proposed regulations provide a special rule for certain tax-exempt debt instruments that provide for stated interest at an objective rate. If the issuer of a tax-exempt debt instrument, contemporaneously with the issuance, enters into one or more financial contracts that substantially offset the variations in the objective rate, the debt instrument is not a variable rate debt instrument. The Treasury Department and the Internal Revenue Service are considering the appropriate treatment of tax-exempt debt instruments with embedded options, forwards, and swaps.

Request for comments: The 1986 proposed regulations did not provide clear guidance on the treatment of a debt instrument that provided for one or more variable interest rates or a combination of a fixed and a variable interest rate. The proposed regulations provide guidance for the treatment of these debt instruments. In general, the proposed regulations attempt to provide rules that reflect the economics of these debt instruments and limit the acceleration or deferral of interest. Comments are requested on the appropriateness of these rules, including the rules for accelerated and deferred interest.

As noted above, the proposed regulations provide a special rule for certain tax-exempt debt instruments with stated interest at an objective rate. Comments are requested on the appropriateness of this rule.

Comments are requested on whether there should be a consistency rule for debt instruments with accelerated interest or deferred interest.

Effective dates

The proposed regulations are proposed to be effective for debt instruments issued on or after the date that is 60 days after the date the regulations are finalized. The proposed regulations are also proposed to be effective for lending transactions, sales and exchanges that occur on or after the date that is 60 days after the date the regulations are finalized. The rules for qualified reopenings of Treasury securities, however, will be effective for reopenings on or after March 25, 1992.

The Internal Revenue Service intends to treat the 1986 proposed regulations that are withdrawn in this document as authority under section 6662 for debt instruments issued prior to their withdrawal and for lending transactions, sales and exchanges that occurred prior to their withdrawal.

Special Analyses

It has been determined that these proposed rules are not major rules as defined in Executive Order 12291. Therefore, a Regulatory Impact Analysis is not required. It also has been determined that section 553(b) of the Administrative Procedure Act (5 U.S.C. chapter 5) and the Regulatory Flexibility Act (5 U.S.C. chapter 6) do not apply to these regulations, and, therefore, an initial Regulatory Flexibility Analysis is not required. Pursuant to section 7805(f) of the Internal Revenue Code, these proposed regulations will be submitted to the Chief Counsel for Advocacy of the Small Business Administration for comment on their impact on small business.

Comments and Public Hearing

Before these proposed regulations are adopted, consideration will be given to any written comments that are timely submitted (preferably a signed original and eight copies) to the Internal Revenue Service. All comments will be available for public inspection and copying in their entirety.

A public hearing on these proposed regulations will be held on February 16, 1993, at 10:00 a.m. See the notice of public hearing published elsewhere in this issue of the Federal Register.

Drafting Information

The principal authors of these regulations are Frederick S. Campbell-Mohn, William E. Blanchard, and Andrew C. Kittler of the Office of Assistant Chief Counsel (Financial Institutions and Products), Internal Revenue Service. However, other personnel from the Service and Treasury Department participated in their development.

[¶ 49,138] **Proposed Regulations and Proposed Amendments of Regulations (IA-57-89)**, published in the Federal Register on December 30, 1992.

Consolidated returns: Alternative minimum tax.—Reg. §§1.1502-55 and amendments of Reg. §§1.56(g)-1, 1.1502-1, 1.1502-5, 1.1502-33 and 1.1552-1, relating to the computation of the alternative minimum tax by consolidated groups, are proposed. Proposed amendments of Reg. §1.1502-2 is withdrawn on December 13, 2018 by REG-104259-18.

AGENCY: Internal Revenue Service, Treasury.

ACTION: Notice of Proposed Rulemaking.

SUMMARY: This document proposes regulations under sections 53 through 59, 1502, and 1552 of the Internal Revenue Code relating to the computation of the alternative minimum tax by consolidated groups. The regulations also provide rules for allocating items such as the consolidated alternative minimum tax liability and the consolidated minimum tax credit among the members of a consolidated group. In addition, certain conforming amendments are proposed for related regulations dealing with the computation of adjusted current earnings.

DATES: Written comments and requests to speak (with outlines of oral comments to be presented) at the public hearing scheduled for April 6, 1993, at 10:00 a.m., must be received by March 1, 1993.

ADDRESSES: Send submissions to: Internal Revenue Service, P.O. Box 7604, Ben Franklin Station, Attn: CC:CORP:TR (IA-57-89), Room 5228, Washington, D.C. 20044.

FOR FURTHER INFORMATION CONTACT: Martin Scully, Jr. of the Office of the Assistant Chief Counsel, Income Tax and Accounting, (202) 622-4960 (not a toll-free number).

SUPPLEMENTARY INFORMATION:

Background

For taxable years beginning after December 31, 1986, corporations are subject to both the regular tax and the alternative minimum tax (AMT). These proposed regulations apply the AMT to consolidated groups. The Internal Revenue Service recognizes that application of the statutory AMT provisions to consolidated groups is complex and requests comments on how these proposed regulations might be further simplified.

Explanation of Provisions

I. *Computation of Consolidated AMT*

A. *In general*

The Service believes that Congress generally intended the AMT and adjusted current earnings (ACE) systems to be separate from, and parallel to, the regular tax system. *See, e.g*, § 1.56(g)-1(a)(5). Accordingly, under the separate and parallel principle, all of the provisions of the Internal Revenue Code (Code) and regulations apply in determining consolidated alternative minimum taxable income (AMTI) and consolidated ACE unless the Service provides otherwise in regulations or other guidance.

The proposed regulations apply the separate and parallel principle to consolidated groups. They do not, however, illustrate how this principle applies in all cases. For example, although not discussed in the regulations, the loss disallowance rules of § 1.1502-20 and the life/non-life consolidation rules of § 1.1502-47 apply to consolidated groups under the AMT and ACE systems. Unless an exception to the separate and parallel principle is provided, the separate and parallel principle governs the treatment of all consolidated AMT and ACE items.

The proposed regulations provide rules for (a) computing the AMT liability of a consolidated group (consolidated AMT) and (b) allocating various consolidated AMT attributes to members as necessary (*e.g.*, to determine the allocation of the attributes when a corporation ceases to be a member). The statutory scheme and definitions in sections 53 through 59 of the Code generally apply in determining consolidated AMT, as modified in the proposed regulations to clarify their application to consolidated groups. Thus, consolidated AMT is the excess of consolidated tentative minimum tax (TMT) for the taxable year over consolidated regular tax for the taxable year. Consolidated TMT is determined by first computing 20 percent of the excess of consolidated AMTI for the taxable year over a consolidated exemption amount. That amount is then reduced by the consolidated AMT foreign tax credit in arriving at consolidated TMT. Consolidated regular tax is computed in accordance with the principles of section 55(c) of the Code.

Consolidated AMTI is equal to consolidated pre-adjustment AMTI, increased or decreased by the consolidated ACE adjustment, and then decreased by the consolidated alternative tax net operating loss (ATNOL) deduction, which is the consolidated NOL deduction taking into account the AMT adjustments and preferences.

Under the separate and parallel principle, a consolidated group generally computes its AMT liability in much the same way as its regular tax liability. For example, consolidated pre-adjustment AMTI is computed in accordance with §§ 1.1502-11 and 1.1502-12 principles. The separate pre-adjustment AMTI of each member is calculated under § 1.1502-12, determined by taking into account the adjustments and preferences in sections 56 (excluding the ACE adjustment under section 56(g)), 57, and 58. The separate pre-adjustment AMTIs of the members are then aggregated under § 1.1502-11 principles. Next, the consolidated items listed in § 1.1502-11 (other than the consolidated NOL deduction), determined by taking into account the adjustments and preferences of sections 56 (excluding the section 56(g) ACE adjustment), 57, and 58, are added to that aggregate amount to arrive at consolidated pre-adjustment AMTI. Consolidated ACE is calculated in a similar manner.

Under the method proposed for calculating consolidated AMT, separate member data will be available to calculate each member's allocable share of the group's consolidated AMT for purposes of determining annual stock basis adjustments under proposed § § 1.1502-19 and 1.1502-32 and annual adjustments to earnings and profits under § 1.1502-33. In addition, the proposed method will provide groups with the separate corporation data necessary for various other computations required under the consolidated return regulations. *See, e.g.*, proposed § 1.1502-76(b) (allocating a subsidiary's income between separate and consolidated returns). Finally, because the proposed method parallels the computation of consolidated regular taxable income, it should be familiar to taxpayers.

To implement the proposed approach to the computation of consolidated AMT, certain conforming amendments are necessary. At present, § 1.56(g)-1(n)(3) of the ACE regulations provides that consolidated pre-adjustment AMTI is the consolidated taxable income (as defined in § 1.1502-11) of a consolidated group determined with appropriate adjustments and preferences. The Service proposes to amend the ACE regulations to specify that under the separate and parallel principle a consolidated group computes its consolidated ACE in accordance with the rules for computing consolidated regular taxable income in § § 1.1502-11 and 1.1502-12, as modified in these proposed regulations.

B. *Treatment of adjustments and preferences*

In most cases, the amount of a preference or adjustment is not affected by whether the item is computed separately by each member or on a consolidated basis. The Service has, however, identified three preference items that are affected by whether they are computed on a consolidated basis: (a) the preference for excess intangible drilling costs (IDCs); (b) the preference for charitable contributions of appreciated property; and (c) the preference for bad debt reserves of financial institutions. As discussed below, the proposed regulations apply a consolidated approach to compute the preferences for excess IDCs and charitable contributions, and a separate member approach to compute the preference for bad debt reserves.

1. *Section 57(a)(2) preference for excess IDCs*

Section 57(a)(2) provides a preference equal to the amount by which excess IDCs are greater than 65 percent of net income from all oil, gas, and geothermal properties of the taxpayer. Because section 57(a)(2) applies with respect to *all* such properties of the taxpayer, "excess net income" from one property (*i.e.*, where 65 percent of the property's net income is greater than the excess IDCs) can offset a section 57(a)(2) preference that would otherwise be generated by other properties held by the taxpayer. Similarly, the proposed regulations provide that the section 57(a)(2) IDC preference is computed using a consolidated approach. Thus, one member's section 57(a)(2) preference may be offset by another member's excess net income from oil, gas, and geothermal properties.

Although the IDC preference is computed using a consolidated approach, it is nevertheless allocated back to the members and included in the computation of separate pre-adjustment AMTI. This treatment is consistent with the regular tax treatment of the limitation on percentage depletion deductions under § 1.1502-44, which is computed using a consolidated approach but is included in separate taxable income under § 1.1502-12(p).

2. *Section 57(a)(6) preference for charitable contributions of appreciated property*

Section 57(a)(6) provides a preference equal to the amount by which the section 170 charitable contribution deduction would be reduced if all capital gain property (as defined in section 57 (a)(6)(B)) were taken into account at its adjusted basis. Under § § 1.1502-11(a)(5) and 1.1502-24, a consolidated section 170 deduction is computed. Therefore, to be consistent with the single entity principles of § § 1.1502-11 and 1.1502-24, the section 57(a)(6) preference is computed on a consolidated basis. The proposed regulations provide that the consolidated section 57(a)(6) preference is the amount by which the consolidated charitable contribution deduction would be reduced if all capital gain property of the group were taken into account at its adjusted basis.

3. *Section 57(a)(4) preference for bad debt reserves of financial institutions*

Section 57(a)(4) provides a preference equal to the amount by which a financial institution's allowable section 593 deduction for a reasonable addition to a reserve for bad debts (the section 593 deduction) exceeds the amount that would have been allowable under section 585(b) had the financial institution maintained its bad debt reserve for all taxable years on the basis of actual experience (the hypothetical section 585 deduction).

Section 593 does not specifically set forth the amount to be deducted. For example, for qualifying real property loans, a financial institution subject to section 593 may generally deduct an amount equal to the amount determined under section 593(b)(2) (the percentage of taxable income method), an amount equal to the amount determined under section 585(b), or some lesser amount. Thus, each section 593 financial institution makes an election regarding its reasonable addition to its reserve for bad debts for the taxable year. The Service believes that, because each member's section 593 deduction is determined separately based on elections made and methods of accounting employed by that member, the section 57(a)(4) preference should also be determined separately by each member.

In addition, if the section 57(a)(4) preference were computed on a consolidated basis, an undue double benefit to taxpayers could result. If a financial institution chooses under section 593 to deduct an amount that is less than its hypothetical section 585(b) deduction, the next year's hypothetical section 585(b) deduction is increased by the difference between the institution's hypothetical section 585(b) deduction and its section 593 deduction. This increase in the hypothetical section 585(b) deduction in the next year potentially lowers the section 57(a)(4) preference in that year. If, in addition to lowering the next year's preference, the difference between the institution's hypothetical section 585(b) deduction and its section 593 deduction were to offset the current year preferences of other group members, the group could obtain a double benefit.

C. *Rules relating to separate return limitation years*

The proposed regulations do not limit a consolidated group's use of net positive ACE adjustments arising in a separate return limitation year (SRLY). Although a negative ACE adjustment may be used only to the extent of prior net positive ACE adjustments, the Service has concluded that the increased compliance burden of applying the SRLY rules to net positive ACE adjustments is not warranted.

The proposed regulations reserve, however, on other applications of the SRLY limitations.

D. *Carryovers and carrybacks of consolidated AMT items to separate return years*

The proposed regulations provide rules for the carryover and carryback of consolidated AMT items—items for which there are regular tax counterparts, as well as the consolidated ACE adjustment—to separate return years of a member. In the case of consolidated AMT items for which there are regular tax counterparts (*e.g.*, consolidated ATNOLs and consolidated AMT and ACE net capital losses), the portion of the item that is allocated to a corporation ceasing to be a member and carried to its separate return years is determined in accordance with the regular tax principles relating to the parallel regular tax item. In general, a consolidated item is allocated to a member based on its proportionate share of the separately determined items of all members. *See, e.g.*, proposed § 1.1502-21(b)(2) (carryovers and carrybacks of consolidated net operating losses to separate return years).

The proposed regulations also provide rules for allocating consolidated positive ACE adjustments (*i.e.*, the increases in consolidated AMTI of the group in prior years due to the consolidated ACE adjustment) to members. Because a current year negative ACE adjustment is allowable only to the extent that prior year positive ACE adjustments exceed prior year negative ACE adjustments, positive ACE adjustments from prior years could be valuable to a corporation ceasing to be a member.

The proposed regulations provide that a member's portion of the consolidated positive ACE adjustments is taken into account in the member's separate return years under the principles of § 1.56(g)-1(a)(2) and proposed § 1.1502-21(b). The member's portion of the consolidated positive ACE adjustments is based on the member's proportionate share of the separate cumulative ACE adjustments of all members (the consolidated cumulative ACE adjustment taking into account only the member's items). Because of the potentially burdensome nature of the cumulative allocation method, and the required recordkeeping, the Service considered not allocating the consolidated ACE adjustment to departing members. Under this alternative approach, the group's prior consolidated ACE adjustments would remain entirely with the group even when corporations responsible for that adjustment cease to be members. However, each member already must calculate its separate ACE and its separate pre-adjustment AMTI in computing consolidated AMTI. Further, even corporations filing separate returns must track their cumulative ACE history to determine whether a negative ACE adjustment may offset AMTI. The proposed regulations, therefore, do not adopt this non-allocation approach. The Service, however, solicits comments on whether the final regulations should provide that no allocations of the consolidated ACE adjustment should be made to departing members. These comments should address issues that would arise if no allocations were made, including acquisitions of groups and groups ceasing to exist as consolidated groups.

E. *Deferral and restoration of AMT items*

The proposed regulations provide rules relating to the deferral and restoration of AMT items. Under the separate and parallel approach, the regular tax principles used in computing consolidated taxable income are applied in computing consolidated pre-adjustment AMTI and consolidated ACE. *See, e.g.*, § 1.1502-13.

F. *Stock basis adjustments*

Proposed regulations modifying the determination of stock basis adjustments under § 1.1502-32 (and excess loss accounts under § 1.1502-19) were filed with the Federal Register on November 10, 1992. *See* CO-30-92 (57 FR 53634, 1992-48 I.R.B. 27). Based on those proposed regulations, this document proposes rules for adjusting stock basis (and excess loss accounts) in computing consolidated pre-adjustment AMTI and consolidated ACE. Under the separate and parallel approach, the principles of proposed §§ 1.1502-19 and 1.1502-32 for determining the regular tax basis in (or the regular tax excess loss account with respect to) a member's stock are generally applied in computing consolidated pre-adjustment AMTI and consolidated ACE.

Certain modifications to the general principles are provided, however. For example, while recently-issued proposed regulations ordinarily require basis adjustments to be determined as of the close of each consolidated return year and as of any other time necessary to determine the tax liability of any person, basis adjustments in computing consolidated pre-adjustment AMTI and consolidated ACE are required only if a difference between the regular tax and AMT or ACE basis in a member's stock will affect the tax liability of any person (*e.g.*, on the sale of the stock). Thus, the annual reporting requirements of proposed § 1.1502-32(g) are not applied under the AMT system.

II. *Consolidated Minimum Tax Credit*

A. *General rules*

Under the proposed regulations, a group's consolidated minimum tax credit (MTC) is equal to the sum of (a) the consolidated return year MTC, and (b) the separate return year MTC. The proposed regulations provide rules for computing the consolidated return year MTC and the separate return year MTC. The consolidated MTC allowable for any consolidated return year is limited to the excess (if any) of modified consolidated regular tax for the year, over consolidated TMT for the year. Modified consolidated regular tax is the consolidated regular tax determined under the principles of section 26(b) reduced by all allowable credits (other than the consolidated MTC).

B. *Carryover of consolidated MTC to separate return years*

The proposed regulations provide rules for the carryover of the consolidated MTC to the separate return years of corporations that cease to be members. Specifically, the portion of the consolidated MTC that is allocated to a member and carried over to a separate return year is determined in accordance with the principles of section 53, § 1.1502-3(c), and proposed § 1.1502-21(b).

The amount of the consolidated MTC allocated to a member is generally the member's share of the group's consolidated adjusted net minimum tax for each consolidated return year, reduced by the member's share of the consolidated adjusted net minimum tax allowable as a consolidated MTC during consolidated return years for which the member was included in the group. A member's allocable share of the consolidated adjusted net minimum tax is based on its proportionate share of the separate adjusted AMT of the members for the year. The separate adjusted AMT of a member is, in general, the excess of the consolidated AMT for the year over the consolidated AMT for the year computed by excluding the member's items.

The method provided in the proposed regulations for computing the separate adjusted AMT of each member takes into account not only the member's separate AMT, but also other contributions the member makes to consolidated AMT. For example, if a member has a regular tax net operating loss (NOL) on a separate basis that reduces consolidated regular tax, the NOL may increase consolidated AMT (unless the member's corresponding ATNOL reduces consolidated TMT by at least the same amount). Under the proposed regulations, if the member's NOL (considering its relationship to the ATNOL) increases consolidated AMT, that increase is taken into account in allocating consolidated MTC.

The Service is aware that, under the proposed allocation method, it is possible for a member with regular tax in excess of TMT on a separate company basis to receive an allocation of the consolidated MTC. Consider the following example:

	P	*S*	*Consolidated*
Taxable income	$(100)	$100	$- 0 -
AMTI	100	50	150
TMT	20	10	30
Regular tax (34% rate)	- 0 -	34	- 0 -
AMT	$20	$0	$30

Consolidated AMT computed with S's items is $30, but consolidated AMT computed without S's items is only $20. Thus, under the proposed allocation method S would be allocated consolidated MTC even though S's regular tax exceeded its TMT on a separate basis. This result is appropriate because S's $100 of taxable income did not increase the consolidated regular tax, while its $50 of AMTI did increase consolidated TMT by $10. The inclusion of S's items therefore increased consolidated AMT by $10.

The Service considered other methods for allocating the consolidated MTC. Under one alternative, the group's consolidated MTC would be allocated to each member based on that member's proportionate share of the group's total adjustments and preferences. This method was rejected because it takes into account only one component that contributes to the consolidated MTC and it could lead to distortions. For example, a member with adjustments and preferences may actually reduce consolidated AMT if the member's items increase consolidated regular tax more than they increase consolidated TMT. Nevertheless, the member would be allocated an amount of the consolidated MTC under this method.

Another alternative would allocate consolidated MTC based on the separate AMT liability of each member. The separate AMT liability of a member would be the consolidated AMT taking into account only that member's items. Under this method, each member with a separate AMT liability would be allocated a proportionate share of the consolidated MTC. This method was also rejected because it could lead to inappropriate results and would fail to make any allocation of the consolidated MTC in certain cases. For example, a group could have an AMT liability, even though none of its members has a separate AMT liability. In such a case, no member of the group would receive an allocation under this method.

The Service invites suggestions about other ways to allocate the consolidated MTC that are either simpler or more accurate than the method in the proposed regulations.

III. *Proposed amendments to the existing consolidated return regulations*

The proposed regulations generally provide that references in the consolidated return regulations to the tax liability of a consolidated group are to the tax liability determined under § 1.1502-2(a). Under § 1.1502-2(a), as proposed to be amended by these regulations, consolidated tax liability is the sum of (a) the consolidated regular tax, (b) the consolidated AMT, (c) the consolidated environmental tax, and (d) the aggregate of the additional taxes provided under section 26(b)(2) (other than the taxes under sections 55 and 59A) imposed on members. However, references to the consolidated tax liability (or the tax liability of a consolidated group) in § 1.1552-1(a) through (f) are generally references to the group's regular tax liability determined in accordance with section 26(b). Similar references in § 1.1502-33(d) have already been clarified in recently-issued proposed regulations. *See* CO-30-92 (57 FR 53634, 1992-48 I.R.B. 27).

Section 1.1502-5, dealing with estimated tax payments by a consolidated group, is amended to reflect recent law changes with respect to the estimated tax underpayment exceptions and to add the consolidated AMT to the estimated tax payment requirements.

Comments are solicited as to additional conforming changes to the existing consolidated return regulations that should be included in the final regulations to take into account the definition of the term "tax" under these proposed regulations.

IV. *Allocations in determining earnings and profits*

A. *Allocation of consolidated AMT*

The proposed regulations allocate consolidated AMT among the members for purposes of determining earnings and profits. Additionally, if modified consolidated regular tax exceeds consolidated TMT, the proposed regulations require that the earnings and profits of a member be increased for the member's allocable share of any consolidated MTC allowable.

The proposed regulations provide only one method for determining the amount of consolidated AMT allocated to each member of a consolidated group. The method selected for allocating the consolidated AMT among members considers the benefits that one member's AMT and ACE attributes provide in offsetting the consolidated AMT liability that would otherwise result if the member were not included in the consolidated group. For this reason, and because each member's decrease in earnings and profits based on its allocable share of the consolidated AMT is ultimately reversed by the member's allocable share of any consolidated MTC allowable in a consolidated return year, the proposed regulations do not provide for § 1.1502-33(d) AMT liability allocations.

The Service invites comments regarding its conclusion that § 1.1502-33(d) allocation rules are not necessary given the method provided in the proposed regulations for allocating the consolidated AMT liability. Comments should recommend any specific alternatives to the approach taken in the proposed regulations and should consider the appropriate treatment of departing group members under any such alternatives.

B. *Allocation of consolidated environmental tax*

The proposed regulations allocate the consolidated environmental tax based on a member's proportionate share of the separate modified AMTI of the members for the year. Separate modified AMTI is the consolidated modified AMTI taking into account only the member's items of income, gain, deduction, and loss.

C. *Allocation of consolidated additional taxes*

The proposed regulations provide that the consolidated additional taxes (defined in § 1.1502-2(b)) are allocated to members in accordance with any reasonable method used by the group. *See, e.g.*, the taxes under sections 531 and 541.

V. *References to proposed regulations*

References in the amendatory paragraphs of this Notice of Proposed Rulemaking to §§ 1.1502-19, 1.1502-21, 1.1502-22, 1.1502-32, and 1.1502-33, (or any of the paragraphs thereunder) are intended as references to those sections, as proposed to be amended by previously issued Notices of Proposed Rulemaking.

Special Analyses

It has been determined that these proposed rules are not major rules as defined in Executive Order 12291. Therefore, a Regulatory Impact Analysis is not required. It has also been determined that section 553(b) of the Administrative Procedure Act (5 U.S.C. chapter 5) and the Regulatory Flexibility Act (5 U.S.C. chapter 6) do not apply to these proposed rules, and therefore, an initial Regulatory Flexibility Analysis is not required. Pursuant to section 7805(f) of the Internal Revenue Code, these proposed rules will be submitted to the Chief Counsel for Advocacy of the Small Business Administration for comment on their impact on small businesses.

Written Comments and Public Hearing

Before these proposed regulations are adopted, consideration will be given to any written comments that are submitted timely (preferably a signed original and eight copies) to the Internal Revenue Service. All comments will be available for public inspection and copying in their entirety. Written comments, requests to appear at the public hearing, and outlines of oral comments to be presented at a public hearing scheduled for April 6, 1993, must be received by March 16, 1993. See notice of hearing published elsewhere in this issue of the Federal Register.

Drafting Information

The principal author of these proposed regulations is Martin Scully, Jr. of the Office of Assistant Chief Counsel, Income Tax and Accounting, Internal Revenue Service. However, other personnel from the Service and the Treasury assisted in their development.

[¶ 49,139] Proposed Regulations and Proposed Amendments of Regulations (REG-208985-89) [originally issued as INTL-0848-89], published in the Federal Register on January 5, 1993.

Foreign corporations: Tax years.—Reg. §§ 1.563-3 and 1.898-0—1.898-4, and amendments of Reg. §§ 1.442-1, and 1.563-3, relating to the required taxable year of those foreign corporations beginning after July 10, 1989, are proposed. Amendments to Proposed Reg. § 1.898-4 were proposed on 6/13/2001. Reg. §§ 1.441-1T and 1.442-2T were removed by T.D. 8996 on May 16, 2002.

AGENCY: Internal Revenue Service, Treasury.
ACTION: Notice of proposed rulemaking.
SUMMARY: This document contains proposed Income Tax Regulations setting forth the required taxable year for specified foreign corporations for taxable years of those foreign corporations beginning after July 10, 1989. This action is necessary because of changes to the applicable tax law made by the Omnibus Budget Reconciliation Act of 1989, which added section 898 to the Internal Revenue Code. The regulations will give guidance on which foreign corporations must change their taxable year and how to effect the change in taxable year.
DATES: Written comments and requests for a public hearing must be received by March 8, 1993.
ADDRESSES: Send written comments and requests for a public hearing to: Internal Revenue Service, P.O. Box 7604, Ben Franklin Station, Attention: CC:CORP:T:R (INTL-0848-89), room 5228, Washington, DC 20044.
FOR FURTHER INFORMATION CONTACT: Bill Lundeen of the Office of Associate Chief Counsel (International), within the Office of Chief Counsel, Internal Revenue Service, 1111 Constitution Avenue, N.W., Washington, DC 20224 (Attention: CC:CORP:T:R (202-622-3870 (INTL-0848-89), not a toll-free call).
SUPPLEMENTARY INFORMATION:
A. *Paperwork Reduction Act*

The collection of information contained in this notice of proposed rulemaking has been submitted to the Office of Management and Budget for review in accordance with the Paperwork Reduction Act of 1980 (44 U.S.C. 3504(h)). Comments on the collection of information should be sent to the Office of Management and Budget, Attn: Desk Officer for the Department of the Treasury, Office of Information and Regulatory Affairs, Washington, D.C. 20503, with copies to the Internal Revenue Service, Attn: IRS Reports Clearance Officer, T:FP, Washington, DC 20224.

The collection of information in these proposed regulations is in § § 1.563-3, 1.898-3 and 1.898-4. The Internal Revenue Service requires this information to verify compliance with section 898 of the Internal Revenue Code. The respondents will be certain United States shareholders of specified foreign corporations.

The estimates are an approximation of the average time expected to be necessary for a collection of information.

They are based on information as is available to the Internal Revenue Service. Individual respondents may require greater or lesser time, depending on their particular circumstances.

Estimated total annual reporting burden: 600 hours.

Estimated burden per respondent varies from .5 hours to 1.5 hour, depending on individual circumstances, with an estimated average of 1 hour.

Estimated number of respondents: 600.

Estimated frequency of responses: Once every three years.

B. *Background*

This document contains proposed regulations under sections 441, 442, 563 and 898 of the Internal Revenue Code (Code). Sections 1.898-1 through 1.898-4 are proposed to be effective for taxable years of specified foreign corporations beginning after July 10, 1989. However, § § 1.898-3 (a)(4)(regarding situations in which inconsistent majority U.S. shareholder years exist) and 1.898-3 (a)(5)(iii)(regarding situations in which additional testing days are required) are proposed to be effective for taxable years beginning after [INSERT DATE 120 DAYS AFTER DATE OF PUBLICATION OF FINAL REGULATIONS IN THE FEDERAL REGISTER], and section 1.898-4 (b) is proposed to be effective for changes in the required year of a specified foreign corporation subsequent to its first taxable year beginning after July 10, 1989.

C. *Explanation of Provisions*

Introduction

Section 7401(a) of the Omnibus Budget Reconciliation Act of 1989, Pub. L. No. 101-239, 103 Stat. 2106 ("the Act"), added section 898 to the Code. The purpose of section 898 is to eliminate the deferral of income and, therefore, the understatement in income, by United States shareholders of certain controlled foreign corporations and foreign personal holding companies, referred to in the statute as specified foreign corporations. Deferral results when certain income earned by these corporations is subject to United States income tax in a taxable year of the United States shareholder subsequent to the taxable year during which it was earned. The elimination of deferral is accomplished by requiring a specified foreign corporation to conform its taxable year to the required year, which is generally the majority U.S. shareholder year, for taxable years of specified foreign corporations beginning after July 10, 1989.

Section 1.898-1.

Section 1.898-I provides the general rule that, for purposes of the Internal Revenue Code, the taxable year of any specified foreign corporation shall be the required year determined under section 898(c) and § 1.898-3. In addition, § 1.898-1 (b) sets forth the effective dates of the regulations under section 898.

The regulations at paragraph (c) exempt certain specified foreign corporations from section 898 in three circumstances. First, a specified foreign corporation is exempt from section 898 so long as its United States shareholders do not have any amount includible in gross income pursuant to section

951(a) and do not receive any actual or deemed distributions attributable to amounts described in section 553 with respect to that corporation. Once any United States shareholder has such amounts, however, section 898 applies to the specified foreign corporation. Second, a specified foreign corporation that is a foreign insurance company and elects to be treated as a domestic corporation pursuant to section 953(d) is exempt from section 898. Likewise, a specified foreign corporation described in section 1504(d) for which an election has been made to treat it as a domestic corporation is exempt from section 898.

Section 1.898-2.

Section 1.898-2(a) defines specified foreign corporation. Generally, a specified foreign corporation is defined to include controlled foreign corporations and foreign personal holding companies. However, specified foreign corporations include only those controlled foreign corporations and foreign personal holding companies that meet certain ownership requirements. Paragraphs (b)(1) and (b)(2) set forth the ownership requirements of a specified foreign corporation and paragraph (b)(3) defines United States shareholder for purposes of these rules. Paragraph (c) provides a special rule for foreign personal holding companies that are specified foreign corporations.

There is an inconsistency in the legislative history of section 898 between the Senate Print and the Conference Report. The conference agreement generally follows the Senate amendment, but misstates the Senate amendment in reporting that section 898 applies only to a controlled foreign corporation or foreign personal holding company, more than 50 percent of the total voting power or value of the *U.S.-owned* stock of which is treated as owned by a United States shareholder, and that section 898 takes into account only the taxable years of those United States shareholders (and certain related persons) in determining the majority U.S. shareholder year. The words "U.S.-owned" did not appear in the Senate amendment, which is the version of the bill that Congress enacted and which became public law. Accordingly, specified foreign corporations include controlled foreign corporations and foreign personal holding companies in which a United States shareholder owns (or is considered to own) more than 50 percent of the voting power of all classes of stock of the corporation entitled to vote, or more than 50 percent of the total value of all classes of stock of the corporation.

Section 1.898-3.

Section 1.898-3(a)(1) provides the general rule that the required year of a specified foreign corporation means the majority U.S. shareholder year. Paragraph (a)(2) provides that a specified foreign corporation that is a controlled foreign corporation may elect, in lieu of the required year, a taxable year beginning one month earlier than the majority U.S. shareholder year. Paragraph (a)(3) defines majority U.S. shareholder year, and paragraph (a) (4) provides rules for situations in which more than one majority U.S. shareholder year exists. Paragraph (a)(5) defines testing days which are the days on which a specified foreign corporation must determine whether it is using the required year. Paragraph (b) provides special rules for foreign personal holding companies that are specified foreign corporations.

Section 1.898-4.

Section 1.898-4 provides special rules applicable to specified foreign corporations. Paragraph (a) sets forth rules for changes to the required year of a specified foreign corporation for its first taxable year beginning after July 10, 1989, and paragraph (b) provides rules for changes in the required year of a specified foreign corporation during a taxable year subsequent to its first taxable year beginning after July 10, 1989.

Paragraph (c) provides rules for situations in which a specified foreign corporation maintains a foreign taxable year (for purposes of computing income tax liabilities due a foreign country) that is different from its required year, including rules relating to the computation of income and earnings and profits of the corporation and rules for the situation in which the U.S. majority shareholder year is a 52-53-week taxable year and the specified foreign corporation's taxable year is not, or in which the specified foreign corporation's taxable year is a 52-53-week taxable year and the U.S. majority shareholder year is not.

A foreign income tax accrues only when the liability for it is fixed and the amount of the liability can be determined. This event generally occurs at the end of the foreign taxable year with respect to a foreign income tax that is imposed on that year's income. Consequently, with the enactment of section 898, a mismatch may arise between the income that comprises a subpart F or foreign personal holding company inclusion and the creditable foreign taxes related to the inclusion when the foreign taxable year of a specified foreign corporation ends later than the corporation's United States taxable year.

Adherence to the foreign tax accrual rule in the context of section 898 may result in income being taxed under subpart F without the associated foreign income taxes being available as a credit under section 960. While we considered several options to address the effect of the foreign tax accrual rule in this context, we believe that adherence to the foreign tax accrual rule is justified for several reasons. First, unlike section 338(i), there is no direct authority in section 898 to modify the rule. Second, rules that require the pooling of post-1986 undistributed earnings and foreign taxes mitigate the effect of the foreign tax accrual rule. Third, determining the foreign taxes on a specified foreign corporation's taxable income prior to the end of the foreign taxable year may not be possible, especially where that foreign taxable year has not ended by the filing date of the applicable U.S. tax return. Accordingly, modifying the foreign tax accrual rule for specified foreign corporations that have foreign taxable years which differ from their required year would result in speculative foreign tax accruals, necessitating a corrective mechanism, and would result in a set of highly complex rules which would be difficult to administer. Such an approach would place additional pressure on the foreign tax credit rules, in particular, on the section 905(c) rules. Finally, the potential mismatch resulting from adherence to the foreign tax accrual rule is mitigated by the rule, discussed below, that applies to the first taxable year after section 898 was enacted and that spreads over four taxable years the recognition of certain income otherwise required to be recognized in one year as a result of section 898.

Section 1.898-4(d) provides rules to implement section 7401(d)(2)(C) of the Act. That section of the Act provides that if, because of the change in taxable year, any United States person would be required to include in gross income for its taxable year amounts attributable to two taxable years of the specified foreign corporation, the amount of income reported for the short taxable year of the specified foreign corporation shall be included in the United States person's gross income ratably over its next four taxable years beginning with its taxable year in which amounts attributable to two taxable years of the specified foreign corporation would have been included.

The foregoing four-year rule applies only when a United States person would otherwise be required to include deemed distributions of income from more than one taxable year of the specified foreign corporation in any one of its own taxable years, and only if the short taxable year of the specified foreign corporation was its first taxable year beginning after July 10, 1989. If a specified foreign corporation that changed its taxable year in accordance with section 898 derived subpart F income in its first taxable year, but not in its second (short) taxable year, which ended within the one taxable year of the United States person, then the ratable four-year inclusion would not be applicable. Finally, any United States person who would otherwise be subject to the four-year rule may not waive that rule and accelerate an income inclusion due to the application of section 898.

Section 1.563-3.

Section 7401(b)(1) of the Act amended section 563 of the Code by adding a new subsection (c) which generally requires that, in determining the dividends paid deduction for purposes of the foreign personal holding company provisions of the Code, a dividend paid after the close of any taxable year, and on or before the 15th day of the third month following the close of that taxable year, will be considered as paid during that taxable year to the extent the foreign personal holding company designates the dividend as being taken into account under section 563(c). Section 1.563-3 provides rules to implement section 7401(b)(1).

D. *Special Analyses*

It has been determined that these rules are not major rules as defined in Executive Order 12291. Therefore, a Regulatory Impact Analysis is not required. It has also been determined that section 553(b) of the Administrative Procedure Act (5 U.S.C. chapter 5) and the Regulatory Flexibility Act (5 U.S.C. chapter 6) do not apply to these regulations, and therefore, an initial Regulatory Flexibility Analysis is not required. Pursuant to section 7805(f) of the Internal Revenue Code, these regulations will be submitted to the Chief Counsel for Advocacy of the Small Business Administration for comment on the impact of the rules on small business.

E. *Comments and Requests for a Public Hearing*

Before adopting these regulations, consideration will be given to any written comments that are submitted (preferably a signed original and eight copies) to the Internal Revenue Service. All comments will be available for public inspection and copying. A public hearing will be held upon written request by any person who submits timely written comments on the proposed rules. Notice of the time, place and date for the hearing will be published in the Federal Register.

F. *Drafting Information*

The principal author of this regulation is Bill Lundeen of the Office of Associate Chief Counsel (International), within the Office of Chief Counsel, Internal Revenue Service. Other personnel from the Internal Revenue Service and Treasury Department participated in developing the regulations.

[¶49,142] Proposed Regulations (REG-245935-96) [originally issued as EE-14-81], published in the Federal Register on May 7, 1993.

Foreign deferred compensation plans: Limitations: Deductions: Adjustments: Earnings and profits.—Reg. §§1.404A-0—1.404A-7, relating to the limitations on deductions and adjustments to earnings and profits with respect to certain foreign deferred compensation plans, are proposed. The proposed regulations issued under Code Sec. 404A on April 8, 1985, have been withdrawn.

AGENCY: Internal Revenue Service, Treasury.

ACTION: Withdrawal of previous proposed rules and notice of proposed rulemaking.

SUMMARY: This document contains proposed regulations relating to the limitations on deductions and adjustments to earnings and profits (or accumulated profits) with respect to certain foreign deferred compensation plans. These new proposed regulations reflect changes to the applicable law made by the Act of December 28, 1980, as amended by the Technical Corrections Act of 1982, by the Tax Reform Act of 1986, and by the Technical and Miscellaneous Revenue Act of 1988. The new proposed regulations will affect employers (and shareholders of employers) that provide deferred compensation directly or indirectly to foreign employees and will provide the public and Internal Revenue Service personnel with the guidance needed to comply with section 404A of the Internal

Revenue Code of 1986. These new proposed regulations supersede the prior proposed regulations published in the Federal Register on April 8, 1985 (50 FR 13821).

DATES: Written comments must be received by [*INSERT DATE THAT IS 60 DAYS AFTER THE DATE OF PUBLICATION OF THESE PROPOSED REGULATIONS IN THE FEDERAL REGISTER*]. Requests to speak (with outlines of oral comments) at a public hearing scheduled for October 5, 1993, at 10:00 a.m., must be received by September 14, 1993. See notice of hearing published elsewhere in this issue of the Federal Register.

ADDRESSES: Send comments, requests to appear at the public hearing, and outlines of comments to be presented to: Internal Revenue Service, P.O. Box 7604, Ben Franklin Station, Attention: CC:CORP:T:R (EE-14-81), Room 5228, Washington, D.C. 20044.

FOR FURTHER INFORMATION CONTACT: Concerning the proposed regulations, Elizabeth A. Purcell, Office of the Associate Chief Counsel (Employee Benefits and Exempt Organizations) at (202) 622-6080 (not a toll-free number). Concerning the hearing, Carol Savage, Regulations Unit, at (202) 622-8452 (not a toll-free number).

SUPPLEMENTARY INFORMATION:

Statutory Authority.

This document contains proposed amendments to the Income Tax Regulations (26 CFR part 1) under sections 404A and 7805(a) of the Internal Revenue Code (Code).

Paperwork Reduction Act.

The collection of information requirement contained in this notice of proposed rulemaking has been submitted to the Office of Management and Budget for review in accordance with the Paperwork Reduction Act of 1980 (44 U.S.C. 3504(h)). Comments on the collection of information should be sent to the Office of Management and Budget, Attention: Desk Officer for the Department of the Treasury, Office of Information and Regulatory Affairs, Washington, D.C. 20503, with copies to the Internal Revenue Service, Attention: IRS Reports Clearance Officer T:FP, Washington, D.C. 20224.

The collection of information requirement in these regulations is in §§1.404A-5, 1.404A-6 and 1.404A-7. This information is required by the Internal Revenue Service to determine accurately the correct deductions and reductions in earnings and profits for foreign deferred compensation. The likely respondents are businesses or other for-profit institutions.

These estimates are an approximation of the average time expected to be necessary for a collection of information. They are based on such information as is available to the Internal Revenue Service. Individual respondents may require greater or less time, depending on their particular circumstances. The estimated total annual reporting burden is 633,200 hours. The estimated annual reporting burden per respondent varies from 5 hours to 1,000 hours, depending on individual circumstances, with an estimated average of 506 hours. The estimated number of respondents is 1,250. The estimated annual frequency: once.

Background.

On April 8, 1985, the Internal Revenue Service published in the Federal Register proposed amendments to the Income Tax Regulations under section 404A of the Internal Revenue Code of 1954 (now 1986) (50 FR 13821). Comments were requested and received, and a public hearing was held on September 20, 1985. After consideration of the comments received, the Service has determined that, rather than promulgate final regulations, it is more appropriate to withdraw the original proposed regulations and propose new regulations. This determination is based on a number of factors, including the number of significant substantive changes made to the prior proposed rules, changes to the underlying statute and other relevant Code provisions, and a need to reorganize the regulations. For a general discussion of section 404A and description of the prior proposed regulations, see the preamble to the prior proposed regulations published in the Federal Register on April 8, 1985.

The significant differences (or, where appropriate, the significant similarities) between these new proposed regulations and the prior proposed regulations are discussed, section by section, in the remainder of this preamble. Prior proposed §1.404A-1 remains new proposed §1.404A-1. However, the rules found in §1.404A-2 of the prior proposed regulations are now incorporated in new proposed §§1.404A-6 and 1.404A-7. Prior proposed §§1.404A-3, 1.404A-4, 1.404A-5 and 1.404A-6 are redesignated §§1.404A-2, 1.404A-3, 1.404A-4 and 1.404A-5, respectively.

Section 1.404A-1: General rules concerning deductions and adjustments to earnings and profits for foreign deferred compensation plans.

90-percent test

As a condition to electing treatment as a qualified foreign plan, section 404A(e)(2) requires that 90 percent or more of the amounts taken into account for a taxable year under the plan be attributable to services performed by nonresident aliens, the compensation for which is not subject to United States federal income tax. Prior proposed §1.404A-1(c) provided that, in determining whether the 90-percent test is satisfied, accrued benefits may be calculated under any reasonable method. It also provided that the rules for calculating the present value of accrued benefits at normal retirement age (except for the actuarial assumption safe harbor) under §1.416-1 (concerning the determination whether a retirement plan is top-heavy) are presumed to be reasonable for this purpose.

Many commentators suggested that these rules for calculating accrued benefits for purposes of the 90-percent test are extremely burdensome and disproportionately expensive. They also suggested that the calculations require a degree of precision and accuracy that in many cases is unwarranted by the circumstances (i.e., where very few plan participants are United States citizens or residents and little compensation of the plan participants is subject to United States federal income tax). To give taxpayers in those cases a less burdensome and less expensive means of demonstrating compliance with the 90-percent requirement, a safe harbor provision has been provided in paragraph (c)(2) of new proposed § 1.404A-1. It provides that the 90-percent requirement of § 1.404A-1(a)(3) will be deemed satisfied with respect to a plan if the participants' benefits under the plan increase generally in proportion to their compensation taken into account under the plan, and the sum of (1) the compensation of United States citizens and residents taken into account under the plan, and (2) any other compensation subject to United States federal income tax taken into account under the plan, does not exceed five percent of all compensation taken into account under the plan for the plan year. This safe harbor provision does not apply, however, if the Commissioner determines that a significant purpose of the plan is to provide benefits not otherwise eligible for tax benefits under the Internal Revenue Code for participants who are United States citizens or residents. An example is provided in new proposed § 1.404A-1(c)(4) to illustrate the application of this safe harbor provision.

Termination indemnity plans

Many commentators suggested that the regulations be revised to provide specifically that certain termination indemnity plans are considered deferred compensation plans for purposes of section 404A. The laws of many countries require employers to maintain termination indemnity plans to pay termination benefits. Some of these termination indemnities are payable solely upon involuntary discharge (other than by reason of mandatory retirement) and thus may be viewed as dismissal wage plans under United States tax principles. However, other termination indemnity plans are akin to deferred compensation plans. For example, one commentator noted that, in one European country, employers are required by law to provide severance benefits equal to one month's pay (final pay) for each year of service. These benefits are fully vested and payable upon all events of termination, including retirement.

Because the provisions of termination indemnity plans may vary widely, paragraph (iii) of the definition of deferred compensation in paragraph (e) of new proposed § 1.404A-1 provides guidelines for determining whether such a plan provides deferred compensation. A termination indemnity plan is considered to provide deferred compensation if: (1) a major purpose of the plan is to provide for the payment of retirement benefits, (2) it has a benefit formula providing for payment based at least in part upon length of service, (3) it provides for the payment of benefits to employees (or their beneficiaries) after the employee's retirement, death or other termination of employment, and (4) it meets such other requirements as may be prescribed by the Commissioner with respect to termination indemnity plans. An example is provided under the definition of deferred compensation in paragraph (e) of new proposed § 1.404A-1 to illustrate this provision. Any plan that meets these requirements is treated as providing deferred compensation, whether or not it is called a termination indemnity plan.

Equivalent of a trust

Section 404A(b)(5)(A) provides that, in order for a contribution to be taken into account in the case of a qualified funded plan, it must be paid to a trust or the "equivalent of a trust". The reference to the equivalent of a trust recognizes that, in some foreign countries, the common law concept of a trust does not exist. Thus, in those countries, the arrangement used to fund deferred compensation benefits for purposes of section 404A(b)(5)(A) must be functionally equivalent to a trust. The essential function of a trust in the context of a United States deferred compensation plan is to provide an entity separate from an employer through which deferred compensation benefits may be secured and liabilities funded. The four elements necessary to accomplish this function are provided in the definition of "equivalent of a trust" in paragraph (e) of new proposed § 1.404A-1. These elements have been revised to allow an employer some latitude to insulate corpus and income from the claims of an employer's creditors, and to remove the concept of legal and beneficial ownership. Finally, the concept of fiduciary duty has been replaced with legally enforceable duty.

Some commentators urged the Service to endorse as the equivalent of a trust the so-called "Security Contract" or "Security Concept" developed in Germany. As explained by those commentators, the Security Contract combines a book reserve commitment by an employer with a pledge and guaranty. First, an employer establishes a book reserve for its pension liabilities for which it receives a tax deduction under German law. It then establishes a wholly-owned subsidiary to which it transfers assets to fund its pension liabilities. As such, the corpus and income of the subsidiary are separately identifiable from an employer's general assets. This arrangement, without more, would not satisfy the requirements of the equivalent of a trust because the assets held by the subsidiary are not protected from the claims of an employer's creditors in the event of bankruptcy or receivership. Under the Security Contract concept, however, the subsidiary also pledges its assets irrevocably to a custodian who then gives a guaranty to the employees to pay the benefits up to the assets pledged to the custodian in the event an employer declares bankruptcy or goes into receivership. The custodian's guaranty is intended to place a prior lien on the assets pledged and protect them from the claims of an employer's creditors in the event of bankruptcy or receivership.

As one commentator asserted, however, it is unclear under German law that the arrangement provides such protection. According to that commentator, in the event of bankruptcy or receivership, the German Pension Guaranty Corporation is required by law to settle an employer's book reserve commitment. The Pension Guaranty Corporation then becomes a non-privileged creditor in the bankruptcy process and exercises any rights the employees have under the plan. As a non-privileged creditor, the Pension Guaranty Corporation is not entitled to all the assets pledged to the custodian, but is limited to a percentage of employer assets that is consistent with its general bankruptcy quota. Thus, it appears that the subsidiary's assets may be subject to the claims of an employer's creditors before all claims of the Pension Guaranty Corporation, exercising the rights of the employees under the plan, are settled.

Until the Service is satisfied that the corpus and income of the subsidiary are to be used to satisfy the claims of the employees and their beneficiaries (or those exercising their rights under the plan) before those of an employer's creditors, the Service cannot endorse this arrangement as the equivalent of a trust.

Exclusive means for deduction or reduction in earnings and profits

For foreign plans that fail to satisfy the requirements of section 404A, section 404 governs deductions for deferred compensation expense. For plans that are not qualified under section 401, section 404(a)(5) generally provides that the employer's deduction for contributions is delayed until amounts attributable to the employer's contribution are includible in the plan participant's gross income. In addition, under section 404(a)(5), deductions are denied altogether unless separate accounts are maintained for each participant. The Service took this position with respect to a foreign plan in Private Letter Ruling 7904042 (Oct. 25, 1978), available in the Freedom of Information Reading Room, Room 1569, Internal Revenue Service, 1111 Constitution Avenue, N.W., Washington, D.C. 20224. This position is reflected, in part, in paragraph (a) of new proposed § 1.404A-1.

Prior proposed § 1.404A-1(e) provided that earnings and profits (or accumulated profits) may be reduced with respect to payments by an employer to a funded foreign deferred compensation plan that are not deductible under section 404(a) even where an election under section 404A has not been made. Upon reexamination of the Congressional intent underlying the enactment of section 404A, however, the Service now believes that the position reflected in the prior proposed regulations is inconsistent with the purposes of section 404A (and the limitations thereunder). Thus, in accordance with the Secretary's section 404A(h) authority to prescribe regulations necessary to carry out the purposes of section 404A, paragraph (a) of new proposed § 1.404A-1 provides that section 404A provides the exclusive means by which an employer may reduce earnings and profits for deferred compensation in situations other than those in which a reduction of earnings and profits is permitted under section 404. See also the discussion below of the relevance of sections 61, 671 through 679, and 1001 in this context.

Request for comments concerning foreign corporations that are not controlled

The Service is considering whether simplified or alternative methods of determining allowable earnings and profits reductions under section 404A might be appropriate for foreign corporations that are not controlled. Suggestions are invited on this matter.

Section 1.404A-2: Rules for qualified funded plans.

Substantiality of payments to trust

A commentator suggested that the focus of the flush language of paragraph (b) of prior proposed § 1.404A-3 (requiring a trust to have "substantiality") should be on the substantiality of payments to a trust (or the equivalent of a trust) rather than on the substantiality of a trust (or the equivalent of a trust), because the determination with respect to the latter can be made under the standards set forth in prior proposed § 1.404A-1(g)(9). Accordingly, new proposed § 1.404A-2(b)(2)(i) provides that employer contributions must have substance. For example, contributions may not be made in the form of a promissory note. This also means that the contributions must be accumulated in the trust (or the equivalent of a trust) in order to be distributed as benefits under a deferred compensation plan. Whether contributions are being accumulated in the trust (or the equivalent of a trust) to be distributed as benefits will depend on the facts and circumstances. The example in paragraph (b)(5) of new proposed § 1.404A-2 reflects this change.

Exclusive benefit rule

Section 404A(b)(5)(A) provides that, in the case of a qualified funded plan, a contribution is taken into account only if it is paid to a trust (or the equivalent of a trust) that meets the requirements of section 401(a)(2). Section 401(a)(2) provides generally that it must be impossible, at any time prior to the satisfaction of all liabilities with respect to employees and their beneficiaries under the trust, for any part of the corpus or income to be used for, or diverted to, purposes other than the exclusive benefit of the employees or their beneficiaries. Thus, in effect, section 404A(b)(5)(A) reemphasizes, with regard to qualified funded plans, the general rule found in section 404A(e) that any "qualified foreign plan" must be for the exclusive benefit of an employer's employees or their beneficiaries. (As stated in the Senate Finance Committee Report, "[f]irst, the plan must be for the exclusive benefit of an employer's employees or their beneficiaries." S. Rep. No. 1039, 96th Cong., 2d Sess. 13 (1980).)

To reflect this emphasis, new proposed § 1.404A-2(b)(2) provides that one important factor that is taken into account in determining whether a trust has or has not been operated in a manner consistent with the exclusive benefit rule is whether it has not or has been involved in a transaction that would be described in section 4975(c)(1) if the plan were the type of plan subject to those rules. For example, a loan from the trust to an employer, on any terms, ordinarily would be a circumstance that strongly suggests noncompliance with section 404A(b)(5)(A). Similarly, a sale, exchange, or lease of any property between the trust and an employer would generally violate this provision. These rules, as set forth in new proposed § 1.404A-2(b)(2), apply prospectively.

Contributions deemed made before payment

Paragraph (c) of new proposed § 1.404A-2 clarifies the circumstances under which a payment made after the last day of an employer's taxable year is deemed to have been made on that last day.

Frequency of actuarial valuations

The new proposed regulations generally continue the requirement in the prior proposed regulations that an actuarial valuation be made no less frequently than once every three years for a qualified funded plan. However, for interim years, they require a reasonable actuarial determination to be made of whether the full funding limit in § 1.404A-5(c)(2) applies to the plan, and provide that the Commissioner may require an actuarial valuation in interim years under appropriate circumstances. It is anticipated that the Commissioner will not exercise this authority except in situations similar to those described in § 1.412(c)(9)-1(d) of the proposed regulations.

Shareholder-level consequences

A sentence in paragraph (d)(1) of prior proposed § 1.404A-3 provided that, where a foreign corporation maintained a qualified funded plan, the deductible amount was taken into account for the shareholder's taxable year in which or with which an employer's taxable year ended. This sentence has been deleted because section 404A does not govern the time at which adjustments to earnings and profits of a foreign employer corporation for a particular year are taken into account at the shareholder level.

Section 1.404A-3: Rules for qualified reserve plans.

The new proposed regulations have modified in several ways the guidance on the calculation of the amount that may be taken into account under a qualified reserve plan. First, the presentation has been changed in order to parallel the components of net periodic pension cost used in Statement of Financial Accounting Standards No. 87 "Employer's Accounting for Pensions" (1985), available from the Financial Accounting Standards Board, 401 Merritt 7, Norwalk, CT 06856. Thus, the amount taken into account for a year is based on the sum of a type of "service cost", "interest cost" and the amortization of the increase or decrease in the reserve from other sources. As part of this change, the steps for determining the actuarial gain or loss have been made explicit. In addition, as discussed below, certain increases or decreases in the reserve that were subject to amortization under the old proposed regulations are now included in the reasonable addition to the reserve.

Ten-Year amortization

Section 404A(c)(4) provides for the spreading over ten years of certain increases and decreases in reserves on account of various events including a catch-all category of "such other factors as may be prescribed by regulations". The Senate Finance Committee Report includes two suggestions of possible items that could be included in this category: "adjustments in the reserve resulting from changes in levels of compensation on which benefits depend or the vesting in one year of a benefit which was accrued in a prior year." S. Rep. No. 1039, 96th Cong. 2d. Sess. 14 (1980).

Some commentators criticized the rule in paragraph (d) of prior proposed § 1.404A-4 providing for the amortization of changes in the reserve arising from these two sources. They suggested that the ten-year amortization requirement for increases or decreases to the reserve on account of changes in the level of compensation upon which plan benefits depend, and for vesting of benefits accrued in prior years, was unnecessary because those items are ongoing costs of the plan that are specifically contemplated by the plan and will arise periodically as each participant's circumstances dictate. Thus, those increases or decreases can be expected to occur regularly in the aggregate and will not create the "bunching" that section 404A(c)(4) was designed to avoid.

The new proposed regulations respond to commentators' concerns by incorporating certain increases in the reserve (as described below) into the definition of the reasonable addition to a reserve, subject to an anti-abuse rule. The effect of this change is to allow immediate recognition, rather than ten-year amortization, of these changes. Under normal circumstances this immediate recognition will not result in significant bunching of income or deductions. Further, to the extent bunching occurs, abuse potential is limited because the bunching is the result of a deferral of deductions rather than the recognition of these items. Finally, as discussed below, for taxable years beginning after December 31, 1986, the indirect foreign tax credit is determined using post-1986 earnings and profits (i.e., aggregated for all post-1986 years). Use of a multi-year earnings and profits pool diminishes the effect of bunching on the foreign tax credit.

The increases in reserve that are now included in the reasonable addition to the reserve are those increases that result from expected changes in compensation and from the increase in vesting for employees whose liabilities were included in the reserve as of the beginning of the year. Thus, for example, the reasonable addition to the reserve may reflect an expected increase in compensation of five percent and expected changes in the vesting percentage in the current year for all employees in the reserve as of the beginning of the year. By contrast, any increase in reserve that results from compensation changes that are greater than expected or from the inclusion of newly-vested employees who were not included in the prior year's reserve are categorized as actuarial losses subject to ten-year amortization.

Section 1.404A-4: United States and foreign law limitations on amounts taken into account for qualified foreign plans.

Section 404A(d) limitation—pooling of earnings and profits

Section 404A(d)(3) provides that, in determining the earnings and profits (and accumulated profits) of any foreign corporation with respect to a qualified foreign plan, the amount determined under section 404A with respect to any plan for any taxable year must not exceed the amount allowed as a deduction under the appropriate foreign law for such taxable year. As the legislative history makes clear, this limitation was imposed in response to "the possibilities for distortion of a taxpayer's indirect foreign tax credit which are presented by the present annual system for determining the amount of the foreign taxes paid by a subsidiary which are attributable to dividends paid to U.S. shareholders." S. Rep. No. 1039, 96th Cong., 2d Sess. 15 (1980). The legislative history further makes clear that "[t]his potential for distortion might be eliminated if the indirect credit were computed with reference to the subsidiary's accumulated foreign taxes and undistributed accumulated profits for all years." *Id.*

Section 1202(a) of the Tax Reform Act of 1986 amended section 902 to provide for computation of the indirect foreign tax credit by pooling all post-1986 earnings and profits and all post-1986 creditable foreign taxes. These amendments to section 902 prevent the distortion at which section 404A(d)(3) was aimed. Section 1012(b)(4) of the Technical and Miscellaneous Revenue Act of 1988 added specific regulatory authority to section 404A(d)(3) (retroactive to enactment of the Tax Reform Act of 1986), to take this change in the law into account. Accordingly, pursuant to that grant of regulatory authority, new proposed § 1.404A-4 provides that, for taxable years beginning after December 31, 1986, the reduction of earnings and profits of a foreign corporation with respect to a qualified foreign plan is determined without regard to the tax deduction under foreign law for that year. This new rule allows any amount that is disallowed for a year (because the foreign tax deduction for that year is greater than the amount allowed under section 404A(b) or (c)) to be carried forward to a future year, in which it may increase the amount allowable under section 404A.

Section 404A(d) limitation

Section 404A(d)(1) provides that the annual amount allowable under section 404A "shall equal" the lesser of the cumulative United States amount or the cumulative foreign amount, reduced by the aggregate amount. Prior proposed § 1.404A-5 (a) provided that the annual amount allowable "shall not exceed" these cumulative amounts. The new proposed regulations adopt the language of the statute. See new proposed § 1.404A-4 (b).

Foreign currency rules

One commentator requested guidance with respect to a number of foreign currency issues. Sections 985-989 were subsequently enacted by the Tax Reform Act of 1986. These sections, effective for taxable years beginning after December 31, 1986, address many of the problems identified by the commentator. Paragraph (d)(1) in new proposed § 1.404A-4 clarifies that, for taxable years beginning after December 31, 1986, income or loss of foreign branches and earnings and profits (or deficits in earnings and profits) of foreign corporations are determined in functional currency as defined in section 985. For taxable years beginning before January 1, 1987, paragraph (d)(2) in new proposed § 1.404A-4 provides that the rules in effect for those taxable years determine the amount of income or loss or earnings and profits (or deficit in earnings and profits) for the foreign branch or subsidiary. A new paragraph (d)(3) provides special rules for those circumstances where the net worth method of accounting is used.

Section 1.404A-5: Additional limitations on amounts taken into account for qualified foreign plans.

New proposed § 1.404A-5 clarifies the evidentiary requirements and rules on actuarial assumptions. No significant changes are made to the rules in prior proposed § 1.404A-6, which are now contained in new proposed § 1.404A-5.

Section 1.404A-6: Elections under section 404A and other changes in accounting method.

Time and manner for making elections

Paragraph (b)(5) of prior proposed § 1.404A-2 provided that elections made under section 404A must be made no later than the time prescribed by law for filing the United States tax return for a United States taxpayer's taxable year. For a qualified foreign plan maintained by a foreign corporation, the regulations have been modified to conform the filing requirements to the general rules applicable to tax accounting elections on behalf of foreign corporations under section 964. For example, under the new proposed regulations, a section 404A election need not be made before the United States shareholder's tax liability is affected by the earnings and profits of the foreign corporation. Such an effect on the United States shareholder's tax liability may occur as the result of any of the following: a dividend distribution, an income inclusion under section 951(a), a section 1248 transaction, a section 864(e) basis adjustment by earnings and profits, or an inclusion in income of the earnings of a qualified electing fund under section 1293(a)(1).

The prior proposed regulations provided that, in order for "protective" or "Method (2)" elections to be effective, taxpayers who made those elections had to file amended returns no later than 90 days after the date on which the final regulations were published in the Federal Register. See Ann. 81-114, Ann. 81-148 and Ann. 82-128, reproduced as an appendix to this preamble. Otherwise, the elections would have no effect. Numerous commentators suggested that the 90-day period is inadequate for taxpayers to evaluate the final regulations, collect the required data, make the appropriate actuarial calculations, decide whether the election is beneficial, and file the required returns. Thus, the deadlines for perfecting retroactive elections and making or perfecting certain other elections in new proposed § 1.404A-7 have generally been extended to 365 days after the publication of final regulations.

Single plan

As originally proposed, § 1.404A-2(b)(6)(i) provided that an election may be made with respect to each plan that qualifies as a "single plan". The term "single plan" has for this purpose the same definition as it has in § 1.414(l)-1(b). Commentators asked for an illustration of the application of this single plan rule to an existing deferred compensation plan that is split into two single plans for purposes of section 404A. Thus, a new example has been added in paragraph (a)(2) of new proposed § 1.404A-6.

Section 481(a) adjustment

New proposed § 1.404A-6(a) addresses the adoption of methods of accounting and changes in methods of accounting with respect to a foreign deferred compensation plan for which an election under section 404A has been made. It clarifies, for example, that an initial election with respect to a pre-existing plan, termination of an election, revocation of an election, and a change in actuarial funding method, constitute changes in methods of accounting under section 446(e) and section 481(a). To compute the section 481(a) adjustment upon a change in method of accounting under section 404A, § 1.404A-6(f)(6) of the prior proposed regulations required a historical computation. Taxpayers were to compute contributions, deductions or reductions in earnings and profits from the establishment of the plan to the first day of the first year in which a section 404A election was made. Commentators argued that this historical approach was unduly burdensome.

The new proposed regulations respond to commentators' concerns by generally replacing the historical computation requirement with a "snapshot" approach to determining the amount of the section 481(a) adjustment for purposes of section 404A. As illustrated below, the snapshot approach is adopted in the proposed regulations in an effort to reduce substantially taxpayers' recordkeeping and compliance burdens.

The snapshot approach is generally intended to compare (i) the extent to which an employer has accelerated deductions (or reductions in earnings and profits) under its old method of accounting for deferred compensation with (ii) the acceleration (if any) that would have been allowed under its new method of accounting. In the interest of avoiding historical calculations and other complexities, the snapshot approach generally attempts to compare the old and new methods of accounting based, to the extent possible, on actual reserve or fund balances existing at the time of the change. These balances generally have been reduced for amounts actually paid to plan participants and beneficiaries. However, amounts actually paid to participants and beneficiaries would be the same under both an employer's old method and its new method of accounting. Therefore, deductions attributable to such payments can be eliminated from consideration in determining both the old and the new method amounts that are compared.

In other words, in the case of both the old method and the new method of accounting, the extent of acceleration is measured by reference to a common baseline: the amount actually paid to plan participants and beneficiaries (i.e., a pay-as-you-go method). Thus, the snapshot approach generally measures the extent to which an employer, under its old method of accounting, has claimed deductions (or reductions in earnings and profits) that exceed the amount actually paid to plan participants and beneficiaries as of the change in accounting method. This amount (generally referred to as the "Old Method Closing Amount") is then compared to the deductions (or reductions in earnings and profits) in excess of the amount actually paid to plan participants and beneficiaries that the employer would have claimed for the same period under its new method of accounting (generally referred to as the "New Method Opening Amount"). The section 481(a) adjustment is equal to the difference between the Old Method Closing Amount and the New Method Opening Amount. The comparison is based on the status of the plan as of the beginning of the year of a change in accounting method.

To illustrate, if the employer has used a funded method of accounting for deferred compensation, the Old Method Closing Amount equals the amount of the fund balance as of the beginning of the year that the accounting method is changed. In determining the amount of the section 481(a) adjustment for purposes of section 404A, this fund balance is compared with a New Method Opening Amount. The New Method Opening Amount will depend on which new method of accounting the employer elects. If the employer makes a qualified funded plan election, the New Method Opening Amount generally will equal the amount of the fund balance, adjusted as appropriate to reflect the limitations in section 404A(b) and (d) on prior contributions to the fund that could have been taken into account under section 404A. If, however, the employer makes a qualified reserve plan election, the New Method Opening Amount generally will be the amount of the reserve under section 404A(c). Alternatively, if the new method of accounting is a non-section 404A method (i.e., a pay-as-you-go method), the New Method Opening Amount generally will be zero.

As the foregoing discussion indicates, the new method will not necessarily be a section 404A method (a qualified funded plan method or qualified reserve plan method), and the old method will not necessarily be a non-section 404A method. The section 481(a) adjustment and the proposed snapshot approach to computing the adjustment apply whether the employer is changing to or from a section 404A method or from one section 404A method to another. For example, assume that a foreign branch has a qualified funded plan with a trust fund balance of 15 of functional currency (as defined in section 985(b)). Assume that this fund balance resulted from FC10 of deductible contributions to the fund under section 404A, plus FC5 of net investment income earned within the fund. Under the snapshot approach, the Old Method Closing Amount upon a change to qualified reserve plan treatment is FC15. Assuming that the reserve under the qualified reserve plan method is FC20 as of the date of the method change, the New Method Opening Amount is FC20, and the amount of the section 481(a) adjustment under section 404A is a negative FC5.

By using the amount of the fund balance in determining both the Old Method Closing Amount and the New Method Opening Amount, the proposed regulations require consideration of both the deductions previously taken by the employer and the accumulated net income (or inside build-up) of a fund in calculating the amount of the section 481(a) adjustment for purposes of section 404A. The Service believes that, in addition to permitting the adoption of a simplified method for determining the section 481(a) adjustment, consideration of a fund's accumulated net income under the snapshot approach avoids additional complexities that might result from the application of sections 61 and 1001 at the time of an election under section 404A. For example, consider an employer that makes a qualified funded plan election after having used a funded method of accounting for a foreign deferred compensation plan that is not a qualified funded plan. Ordinarily, the value of the fund (which is used to satisfy the employer's plan liabilities) will exceed the employer's contributions to the fund (net of the fund's previous payments to plan participants and beneficiaries). If the snapshot method were not applied, arguably sections 61 and 1001 would result in a recognition of income (or increase in earnings and profits) by the employer at the time of the election equal to the excess of the value of the fund over the employer's basis in the fund. This result is consistent with the treatment of a change in method of accounting that consists of a qualified funded plan election as involving a change in the status of the fund from a grantor trust (defined and treated in accordance with sections 671 through 679) to a non-grantor trust (treated in a manner analogous to the treatment of a trust under a section 401(a) tax- qualified plan). The Service solicits comments from interested parties on this analysis and on the utility of the snapshot approach in reducing taxpayer burden.

Effect of section 404A(d)(1) limits on section 481(a) adjustment computation

Since the limitations of section 404A(d)(1) are part of the section 404A method of accounting under the new proposed regulations, the snapshot section 481(a) adjustment calculation must take into account the cumulative foreign amount limitation in section 404A(d) and new proposed § 1.404A-4. This is a departure from § 1.404A-6(f)(9) in the prior proposed regulations. The snapshot approach includes a simplified method to make this adjustment in computing the section 481(a) adjustment. More specifically, paragraph (g) of new proposed § 1.404A-6 allows taxpayers to use the snapshot approach to compute the initial cumulative United States and foreign law limitations under section 404A(d) as of the beginning of a year of change in method of accounting. The rules to initialize the cumulative United States amount, cumulative foreign amount and the aggregate amount rely on the constant relationship between these three amounts (i.e., the aggregate amount always equals the lesser of the two cumulative amounts).

Section 481(a) adjustment period

As required by section 404A(g)(5), the period for taking into account the section 481(a) adjustment arising from an election or a re-election under section 404A is 15 years. Additionally, new proposed § 1.404A-6(e)(2)(iii) provides for a six-year section 481(a) adjustment period for a change in method of accounting arising from the termination or revocation of an election under section 404A, and for any other change in accounting method under section 404A. This new paragraph also requires netting of any section 481(a) adjustment remaining from a previous change in method in determining the amount to be taken into account during the six-year section 481(a) adjustment period. The example in new proposed § 1.404A-6(e)(4) illustrates this netting rule.

Examples in the new proposed regulations illustrate the principle under section 446(e) and its underlying administrative procedures that the District Director may modify a taxpayer's calculated section 481(a) adjustment under section 404A if the District Director (1) determines that the taxpayer used an erroneous method of accounting in an open year prior to the year in which the taxpayer's qualified funded plan or qualified reserve plan election is effective, and (2) requires the taxpayer to change its erroneous method of accounting in that earlier open year. For example, if a taxpayer erroneously deducted FC100 for amounts accrued under a reserve plan in an open year prior to the effective date of a qualified reserve plan election under section 404A, the District Director could require the taxpayer to change its method of accounting in that earlier open year and to take a positive FC100 section 481(a) adjustment into account entirely in that earlier open year (rather than permitting the positive FC100 amount to be netted against any New Method Opening Amount under the snapshot approach and spread prospectively over a 15-year section 481(a) adjustment period). See section 2.02 of Rev. Proc. 92-20, 1992-1 C.B. 685.

Section 1.404A-7: Effective date and retroactive application.

Prior proposed § 1.404A-2(c), relating to retroactive elections, has been moved to § 1.404A-7. This change was made because the rules relating to retroactive elections are relatively discrete and thus logically should be set apart from the general election rules. Because the importance of these rules will greatly diminish within a few years, their placement at the end of the regulations will improve the clarity of the remainder of the regulations for the future. Other specific changes to the retroactive election rules are discussed below.

All-or-nothing rule

Many commentators criticized the rule in paragraph (c)(2)(ii) of prior proposed § 1.404A-2 as an improper interpretation of section 2(e)(2) of the Act of December 28, 1980 (Pub. L. 96-603). Prior proposed § 1.404A-2(c)(2)(i) provided that a taxpayer could elect, during its "open period," for section 404A to apply to a qualified foreign plan maintained by a foreign subsidiary. However, prior proposed §1.404A-2(c)(2)(i) conditioned that election for any plan on a taxpayer electing to apply section 404A with respect to all written plans of every foreign subsidiary (whether or not wholly owned) that defer the receipt of compensation and that satisfy the requirements of section 404A(e)(1) and (2). Commentators argued that the "all-or-nothing rule" of section 2(e)(2) of the Act of December 28, 1980, simply provides that a taxpayer may elect to have section 404A apply for certain prior years, and that such an election must be made for all of a taxpayer's foreign subsidiaries. It does not, however, require that a taxpayer make an election under section 404A for any of its foreign subsidiaries' plans. According to this view, once the election is made to have section 404A apply to the foreign subsidiaries for prior years, the consequences of making or not making an election under section 404A will be determined as though section 404A had been in effect for those years.

After further consideration, the proposed regulations adopt the commentators' view of section 2(e)(2) of the Act of December 28, 1980. Thus, if a taxpayer makes an election to have section 404A apply retroactively to its foreign subsidiaries during its open period, the election to have section 404A apply must be made for all of a taxpayer's foreign subsidiaries (whether or not wholly owned) during a taxpayer's open period. Accordingly, if a taxpayer elects to have section 404A apply during a taxpayer's open period, it may not rely on any other law or rule of law to reduce earnings and profits (or accumulated profits) of any foreign subsidiary with respect to deferred compensation expenses, regardless of whether the taxpayer elects to apply section 404A to any specific deferred compensation plan. Paragraph (b) of new §1.404A-7 reflects this view, and paragraph (c)(5) illustrates this rule with an example.

Making, perfecting and revoking retroactive elections

New proposed §1.404A-7 provides rules for making, perfecting and revoking retroactive effective date elections as well as retroactive plan-by-plan elections for qualified foreign plans maintained by foreign subsidiaries and for qualified funded plans maintained by foreign branches. Taxpayers are afforded 365 days after publication of the final regulations to decide whether to perfect or revoke retroactive elections or to make, revoke or re-elect in intervals of six or more years, effective for taxable years in the open period (as defined in new proposed §1.404A-7(g)(6)) and continuing after taxable years beginning after December 31, 1979. Taxpayers must file amended returns and attach statements in order to perfect a retroactive election and to conform all items to the treatment consistent with election or revocation. If the amended returns and statements are not timely filed, the retroactive elections will be deemed revoked.

Alternative to contemporaneous evidence requirement

Many commentators criticized the rule in prior proposed §1.404A-2(c)(4)(iii) prohibiting a retroactive election if a taxpayer was unable to calculate the requisite section 481(a) adjustment based upon actual data, because, in effect, it unduly restricted taxpayers' ability to make retroactive elections. The commentators were concerned that many taxpayers would lack "actual data", and thus be unable to make the election, and that, even if such data were technically available, its retrieval would be prohibitively burdensome. After further consideration, the Service has altered this requirement. Accordingly, new proposed §1.404A-7(f) provides that the section 481(a) adjustment must be made based upon contemporaneous substantiation quality data. If contemporaneous substantiation quality data is not readily available, however, the adjustment may be based on data which are combinations of actual contemporaneous evidence and reasonable actuarial backward projections of substantiation quality data.

For the convenience of taxpayers, Ann. 81-114, 1981 I.R.B. 21, Ann. 81-148, 1981-39 I.R.B. 15, and Ann. 82-128, 1982-39 I.R.B. 103, concerning Method (1) and Method (2) elections, are reproduced below.

APPENDIX

ANNOUNCEMENT 81-114, 1981-28 I.R.B. 21

This announcement provides guidance relating to section 404A of the Internal Revenue Code. Until proposed regulations are published, taxpayers may rely on the guidance provided below.

Section 404A, added by the Act of December 28, 1980, Pub. L. 96-603 (1981-5 I.R.B. 31), allows taxpayers to make certain elections concerning deductions for amounts paid or accrued by an employer under qualified foreign plans. The two types of qualified foreign plans are qualified funded plans and qualified reserve plans. A qualified foreign plan is any written plan which defers the receipt of compensation and which satisfies two requirements. First, the plan must be for the exclusive benefit of the employer's employees or their beneficiaries. Second, 90 percent or more of the amounts taken into account for the taxable year under the plan must be attributable to services performed by nonresident aliens, the compensation for which is not subject to federal income tax. In addition, the employer must properly elect to have section 404A apply to such plan. If an employer does not make such an election, deductions (or reductions in earnings and profits) are allowed only as provided under section 404 for plans and trusts meeting the requirements of that section.

The rules of section 404A are applicable for taxable years beginning after December 31, 1979, and for certain prior years to the extent the taxpayer elects to have the provisions of section 404A of the Code apply retroactively. Pending the issuance of regulations relating to such elections, the elections referred to in section 404A(e)(3) and (f)(2) of the Code may be made either by (1) claiming the permissible deduction or credit on the taxpayer's income tax return for the first taxable year ending on or after December 31, 1980, including extensions (or an amended return that is filed no later than the end of the extended time period prescribed in section 6081, whether or not such time is actually extended for filing the taxpayer's return), or (2) attaching a statement of election to the taxpayer's income tax return within the time period described in the first method. If the election is made by attaching a statement of election under method (2), the taxpayer's current return would not include deductions or in the case of foreign subsidiaries, take into account reductions in earnings and profits that relate to foreign deferred compensation plans. Deductions or credits consistent with the election would be included on an amended return, to be filed no later than the deadline (described below) for revoking the election. Under either method, the taxpayer must attach to the return a list of plans with respect to which the elections are made. Method (1) or method (2) may also be used for the elections described in section 2(e) of Pub. L. 96-603. When method (2) is used in connection with section 2(e) of Pub. L. 96-603, taxpayers need not amend past returns until regulations are issued.

A taxpayer must determine the amount deductible under section 404A(d) based, in part, on the cumulative foreign amount as defined in section 404A(d)(2)(B). No deduction is allowable under section 404A unless the cumulative foreign amount is established in one of the documents described in section 404A(g)(2)(A)(i), (ii) or (iii) of the Code. Section 404A(g)(2)(A)(iii) authorizes the Secretary to promulgate regulations that would accept certain unspecified statements or evidence as being sufficient to establish the amount of the deduction under foreign law. Until such time as regulations are promulgated under section 404A(g)(2)(A)(iii), the requirements of that section will be considered to be satisfied by a statement prepared at or before the time the return is filed, which lists separately for each plan the cumulative foreign amount and which states that such cumulative foreign amount has been determined pursuant to the requirements of the appropriate foreign tax law. The statement must be prepared by the U.S. taxpayer or a person authorized to practice before the Service. While a taxpayer need not attach any of these documents to its tax return, the taxpayer must furnish the documents for examination upon request of the Internal Revenue Service.

Taxpayers that have made the elections described in section 404A and/or section 2 (e) of Pub. L. 96-603 under method (2) need not prepare the statement, described in the immediately preceding paragraph, until they amend their returns. In addition, taxpayers that have made the election described in section 404A for taxable years beginning after December 31, 1979, under Method (1), and have made the election described in section 2 (e) of Pub. L. 96-603 under method (2) will satisfy section 404A(g)(2)(A)(iii) if the cumulative foreign amount in the statement reflects the aggregate foreign deductions allowed under foreign law for taxable years commencing after December 31, 1979.

Taxpayers that have already made an election, referred to in this announcement, that does not conform with the requirements stated herein may perfect that election on an amended return filed by the later of September 23, 1981 or by the due date of the taxpayer's income tax return for the first taxable year beginning after December 31, 1979, including extensions. These taxpayers may also satisfy section 404A(g)(2)(A)(iii), to the extent applicable as previously described in this announcement, by preparing the required statement within the same time limits for perfecting the elections under sections 404A(e)(3) and (f)(2).

The qualified reserve plan election, including any retroactive election described in section 2(e)(2) of Pub. L. 96-603, may be revoked on an amended return for the first taxable year ending on or after December 31, 1980, without the consent of the Commissioner until 90 days after the publication of final regulations regarding such elections. Similarly, the qualified foreign plan election and the retroactive election described in section 2(e)(3) may be revoked within the same period.

It is anticipated that the effective date of the final regulations generally will be for taxable years beginning after December 31, 1979, and such prior years as may be affected by an election under section 2(e) of Pub. L. 96-603. Accordingly, taxpayers may be required to amend their tax returns to the extent that deductions or credits claimed are inconsistent with final regulations.

ANNOUNCEMENT 81-148, 1981-39 I.R.B. 15

On June 24, 1981, the Internal Revenue Service issued Announcement 81-114, 1981-28 I.R.B. 21. The announcement was intended to provide pre-regulation guidance to taxpayers concerning recent legislation under section 404A. Taxpayers have expressed concern with respect to a statement in that announcement, with respect to reductions of earnings and profits if section 404A is not elected. Announcement 81-114 is clarified as follows:

The decision not to elect section 404A will not affect the computation of earnings and profits with respect to contributions to plans as allowed under prior law. In the case of an accrued liability to a reserve plan, however, such accrued liability reduces earnings and profits only as provided in section 404A with respect to the taxable years described in section 2 (e) of Pub. L. 96-603, 1980-2 C.B. 684.

ANNOUNCEMENT 82-128, 1982-39 I.R.B. 103

Taxpayers that are interested in making the elections referred to in section 404A(e)(3) and (f)(2) of the Internal Revenue Code may continue to use the "method (1)" or "method (2)" election described in Announcement 81-114, 1981-28 I.R.B. 21 for taxable years beginning after December 31, 1979, until further guidance is made available. Pending the issuance of regulations under section 404A, qualified foreign plans must comply with the reporting requirements and other rules contained in Announcement 81-114.

Effective dates.

The amendments are proposed generally to apply to taxable years beginning after December 31, 1979. The prohibited transaction rules in § 1.404A-2 (a) are proposed to be effective May 6, 1993. If a taxpayer elected pursuant to section 2(e)(2) of the Act of December 28, 1980, the amendments are proposed to apply to certain prior taxable years beginning after December 31, 1970.

Special Analyses.

It has been determined that these proposed rules are not major rules as defined in Executive Order 12291. Therefore, a Regulatory Impact Analysis is not required. It has also been determined that section 553(b) of the Administrative Procedure Act (5 U.S.C. chapter 5) and the Regulatory Flexibility Act (5 U.S.C. chapter 6) do not apply to these proposed regulations and, therefore, an initial Regulatory Flexibility Analysis is not required. Pursuant to section 7805(f) of the Internal Revenue Code, these proposed regulations will be submitted to the Chief Counsel for Advocacy of the Small Business Administration for comment on their impact on small business.

Comments and Requests to Appear at the Public Hearing.

Before adopting these proposed regulations, consideration will be given to any written comments that are submitted (preferably a signed original and eight copies) to the Commissioner of Internal Revenue. All comments will be available for public inspection and copying in their entirety. Because the Treasury Department expects to issue final regulations on this matter as soon as possible, a public hearing will be held at 10:00 a.m. on October 5, 1993, in Room 2615, Internal Revenue Building, 1111 Constitution Ave., N.W., Washington, D.C. Written comments must be received by July 6, 1993. Requests to speak (with outlines of oral comments) at the public hearing must be received by September 14, 1993. See notice of hearing published elsewhere in this issue of the Federal Register.

Drafting Information.

The principal author of these proposed regulations is Elizabeth A. Purcell of the Office of the Associate Chief Counsel (Employee Benefits and Exempt Organizations), Internal Revenue Service. However, personnel from other offices of the Service and Treasury Department participated in their development.

[¶ 49,143] Proposed Amendments of Regulation (IA-85-91), published in the Federal Register on September 20, 1993.

Statement of Procedural Rules: Liability for tax: Taxpayer appeals.—Amendments to Reg. § 601.106, relating to how a taxpayer may appeal, without going to court, adjustments affecting a taxpayer's tax liability, are proposed.

AGENCY: Internal Revenue Service (IRS), Treasury.

ACTION: Proposed Amendments to Statement of Procedural Rules and Notice of Public Hearing.

SUMMARY: This document proposes to amend the Statement of Procedural Rules relating to how a taxpayer may appeal, without going to court, adjustments affecting a taxpayer's tax liability. This document clarifies, updates, reorders, and revises the existing rules.

DATES: Written comments, requests to speak and outlines of oral comments to be presented at the public hearing scheduled for November 23, 1993, must be received by November 4, 1993.

ADDRESSES: Send submissions to: Internal Revenue Service, P.O. Box 7604, Ben Franklin Station, Attn: CC:DOM:CORP:T:R (IA-85-91), room 5228, Washington, DC 20044. In the alternative, submissions may be hand delivered to: CC:DOM:CORP:T:R (IA-85-91), room 5228, Internal Revenue Service, 1111 Constitution Avenue, NW, Washington, DC 20224. The public hearing will be held in room 2615, Internal Revenue Service Building, 1111 Constitution Avenue, NW, Washington, DC.

FOR FURTHER INFORMATION CONTACT: Cheryl Revier at telephone (202) 401-5202 (not a toll-free number).

SUPPLEMENTARY INFORMATION:

Paperwork Reduction Act

The collection of information contained in this proposed amendment is not subject to the Paperwork Reduction Act of 1980 (44 U.S.C. 3504(h)) because it concerns information collected during an administrative action.

Background

Statements of Procedural Rules inform the public of the procedures to be followed by a government agency and the public in their dealings with each other. Government agencies are required to file Statements of Procedural Rules in the Federal Register by the Administrative Procedure Act of 1946, 5 U.S.C. 552(a)(1)(c). The Statement of Procedural Rules for the Appeals function of the Internal Revenue Service is codified in § 601.106 of title 26 of the Code of Federal Regulations.

This document concerns the subpart of the Statement of Procedural Rules that describes how a taxpayer may appeal, without going to court, adjustments affecting a taxpayer's tax liability. These adjustments generally result from letters from the Internal Revenue Service, office interviews or field examinations. The appeal is made to the taxpayer's local Appeals Office of the Internal Revenue Service, which is independent of the local District Director, Service Center/Compliance Center Director, or Assistant Commissioner (International) that made the adjustments.

This document, for the most part, simply clarifies, updates, and reorders the existing rules. However, this document also changes the rules in § 601.106(b)(4) prescribing the information that a taxpayer provides to initiate an appeal (the protest rules). This document also revises the rules in § 601.106(e)(3) for disposition and settlement of cases docketed in the Tax Court to reflect Rev. Proc. 87-24, 1987-1 C.B. 720.

These rules are procedural, and, therefore, are exempt from the general notice of rulemaking requirements (5 U.S.C. 553(b)(3)(A)). However, public comment is being sought on the procedural rules because of the change in the protest rules. Comments are particularly sought on the protest rules to ensure they are both simple and effective.

Explanation of Provision

Information that a taxpayer provides to initiate an appeal

Presently, the information a taxpayer must provide to initiate an appeal varies depending on which Internal Revenue Service function has proposed the adjustments to the taxpayer's tax liability. Under the proposed general protest rule, the information would not vary in this manner.

Under proposed § 601.106(b)(4) the information to be provided to initiate an appeal varies only with the dollar amount of the adjustments to the taxpayer's liability. If the proposed change in tax for the period is not more than $25,000, a "small case request" is used to initiate an appeal. For greater amounts, a "protest" is used to initiate the appeal. (In certain cases described in § 601.106(b)(4)(iii)(C) involving $25,000 or less, however, a protest was required under the old rules and continues to be required.) A small case request should indicate the unagreed adjustments and provide the reasons for the disagreement. Generally, more detail and formality is required in a protest than in a small case request. In addition to the items in a small case request, a protest should provide the taxpayer's view of any disputed facts. The protest should also provide references to any materials the taxpayer would like to bring to Appeal's attention in support of the reasons for disagreement. Complete protest requirements are described in Publication 5, the Internal Revenue Service publication concerning taxpayers' appeal rights and protest rules.

Disposition and settlement of cases docketed in the Tax Court

Rev. Proc. 87-24, 1987-1 C.B. 720, facilitates the effective use of Appeals in Tax Court cases and the earlier development and disposition of such cases either by settlement or by trial. These rules are now fully reflected in § 601.106(e)(3).

Among other items, the following items have been clarified or have been updated in the statement of procedural rules to reflect current Appeals practice:

• Certain references to offices or positions have been changed to reflect various reorganizations within the Service.

• The positions to whom settlement authority in Appeals has been or could be delegated are clarified by specific references to the Chief, an Associate Chief, or a Team Chief in the Appeals office and to other employees specifically delegated such authority.

• The list of items for Appeals' subject matter jurisdiction is updated to include, among others, the following items: (1) any tax that is subject to the deficiency procedures; (2) partnership items that are adjusted or readjusted; (3) offers in compromise under section 7122 of the Internal Revenue Code; (4) abatement of interest under section 6404(e)(1) of the Internal Revenue Code; and (5) any other disputed tax issues that the Internal Revenue Service determines are administratively appealable.

• The regulations clarify that Appeals' may accept jurisdiction of the following docketed cases: (1) cases for which Appeals issued the notice of deficiency, liability, or other determination, and (2) cases for which the Employee Plans/Exempt Organization function issued such notice after all petitioned issues were considered by Appeals.

• The regulations make clear that Appeals' authority does not extend to include issues designated for litigation by Chief Counsel.

• Because the technical advice procedures are published annually in a revenue procedure the technical advice rules have been removed from these regulations. See, Rev. Proc. 93-2, 1993-1 I.R.B. 50.

• The procedure for settlement of docketed cases is clarified to provide that no settlement of a docketed case is binding on either the government or the taxpayer until it is entered as a decision.

• The procedure for transferring a case to another Appeals office is updated to reflect that a case may be transferred to relieve the taxpayer of hardship.

Proposed effective dates

In general, the rules will be effective on the date of publication of the final rules in the Federal Register. The rules in § 601.106(b)(4), which describe how a taxpayer initiates an appeal, will be effective 60 days after the date of publication of the final rules in the Federal Register. However, if the letter (or other information enclosed with the letter) offering the taxpayer the opportunity to appeal refers to rules predating the rules in § 601.106(b)(4), then the taxpayer may follow either the old rules or new rules.

Special Analyses

It has been determined that these proposed rules are not major rules as defined in Executive Order 12291. Therefore, a Regulatory Impact Analysis is not required. It has also been determined that section 553(b) of the Administrative Procedure Act (5 U.S.C. chapter 5) and the Regulatory Flexibility Act (5 U.S.C. chapter 6) do not apply to these rules, and, therefore, a Regulatory Flexibility Analysis is not required. Pursuant to section 7805(f) of the Internal Revenue Code, a copy of these proposed amendments will be submitted to the Chief Counsel for Advocacy of the Small Business Administration for comment on their impact on small business.

Comments and Public Hearing

Before these proposed amendments are adopted as final, consideration will be given to any written comments that are timely submitted (preferably an original and eight copies) to the Internal Revenue Service. All comments will be available for public inspection and copying in their entirety.

A public hearing will be held on Tuesday, November 23, 1993, at 10:00 a.m. in Room 2615, Internal Revenue Service Building, 1111 Constitution Avenue, NW, Washington, DC. The rules of § 601.601(a)(3) of the Statement of Procedural Rules apply to the public hearing.

Any person who has submitted timely written comments, and who desires to present oral comments at the public hearing on the proposed amendments, should submit, not later than November 4, 1993, a request to speak and an outline of the oral comments to be presented at the hearing stating the time the person wishes to devote to each subject.

Each speaker (or group of speakers representing a single entity) will be limited to 10 minutes for an oral presentation exclusive of the time consumed by questions from the panel for the government and answers thereto.

Because of controlled access restrictions, attendees cannot be admitted beyond the lobby of the Internal Revenue Service Building before 9:45 a.m.

An agenda showing the scheduling of the speakers will be made after the outlines are received from persons testifying. Copies of the agenda will be available free of charge at the hearing.

Drafting Information

The principal author of these rules is Cheryl Revier, Office of Field Services, National Director of Appeals, Internal Revenue Service. However, personnel from other offices of the Internal Revenue Service participated in their development.

[¶ 49,144] Proposed Regulations (PS-55-93), published in the Federal Register on March 15, 1994.

Deductions: Elections: Depreciation: Intangible property.—Reg. §§ 1.167(a)-13 and 1.197-1, relating to the procedures for making elections under the intangibles provisions of the Omnibus Budget Reconciliation Act of 1993 (P.L. 103-66), are proposed.

AGENCY: Internal Revenue Service (IRS), Treasury.

ACTION: Notice of proposed rulemaking by cross-reference to temporary regulations.

SUMMARY: In the Rules and Regulations section of this issue of the Federal Register, the IRS is issuing temporary regulations relating to the procedures for making elections regarding the amortization of certain intangible property. The temporary regulations reflect changes to the law made by the Omnibus Budget Reconciliation Act of 1993 (OBRA '93) and affect electing taxpayers who acquired intangible property after July 25, 1991, or who acquired intangibles under a written binding contract in effect on August 10, 1993. The text of the temporary regulations also serves as the text of these proposed regulations.

DATES: Written comments must be received by May 16, 1994.

ADDRESSES: Send submissions to: CC:DOM:CORP:T:R (PS-55-93), room 5228, Internal Revenue Service, P.O. Box 7604, Ben Franklin Station, Washington, DC 20044. In the alternative, comments and requests may be hand delivered to: CC:DOM:CORP:T:R (PS-55-93), Internal Revenue Service, room 5228, 1111 Constitution Avenue NW, Washington, DC 20224.

FOR FURTHER INFORMATION CONTACT: John Huffman, (202) 622-3110 (not toll-free number).

SUPPLEMENTARY INFORMATION:

Paperwork Reduction Act

The collection of information contained in this notice of proposed rulemaking has been submitted to the Office of Management and Budget for review in accordance with the Paperwork Reduction Act (44 U.S.C. 3504(h)). Comments on the collection of information should be sent to the Office of Management and Budget, Attn: Desk Officer for the Department of the Treasury, Office of Information and Regulatory Affairs, Washington, DC 20503, with copies to the Internal Revenue Service, Attn: IRS Reports Clearance Officer, PC:FP, Washington, DC 20224.

The collection of information is in § 1.197-1T(e). This information is required by the IRS in order to verify that electing taxpayers have properly determined amortization and depreciation deductions allowable under sections 167(f) and 197. The likely reporting entities are businesses and other for-profit institutions.

Estimated total annual reporting burden: 10,000 hours.

The estimated annual burden per respondent varies from 30 minutes to 75 minutes, depending on individual circumstances, with an estimated average of 1 hour.

Estimated number of respondents: 10,000.

Estimated annual frequency of responses: One time.

Background

Temporary regulations in the Rules and Regulations section of this issue of the Federal Register amend the Income Tax Regulations (26 CFR part 1) relating to sections 167(f) and 197 by adding §§ 1.167(a)-13T and 1.197-1T. The temporary regulations contain rules relating to the depreciation and amortization of certain intangible property.

The text of those temporary regulations also serves as the text of these proposed regulations. The preamble to the temporary regulations explains the temporary and proposed regulations.

Special Analyses

It has been determined that this notice of proposed rulemaking is not a significant regulatory action as defined in Executive Order 12866. Therefore, a regulatory assessment is not required. It also has been determined that section 553(b) of the Administrative Procedure Act (5 U.S.C. chapter 5) and the Regulatory Flexibility Act (5 U.S.C. chapter 6) do not apply to these regulations, and, therefore, a Regulatory Flexibility Analysis is not required. Pursuant to section 7805(f) of the Internal Revenue Code, this notice of proposed rulemaking will be submitted to the Chief Counsel for Advocacy of the Small Business Administration for comment on its impact on small business.

Comments and Requests for a Public Hearing

Before these proposed regulations are adopted as final regulations, consideration will be given to any written comments that are submitted timely (preferably a signed original and eight copies) to the IRS. All comments will be available for public inspection and copying. A public hearing may be scheduled if requested in writing by a person that timely submits written comments. If a public hearing is scheduled, notice of the date, time, and place for the hearing will be published in the Federal Register.

Drafting Information

The principal author of these regulations is John Huffman, Office of Assistant Chief Counsel (Passthroughs and Special Industries). However, other personnel from the IRS and Treasury Department participated in their development.

[¶49,145] Proposed Regulations and Proposed Amendments of Regulations (REG-209724-94) [originally issued as FI-42-94], published in the Federal Register on January 4, 1995.

Methods of accounting: Mark-to-market method: Dealers in securities.—Reg. §§1.475(a)-1, 1.475(a)-2 and 1.475(b)-3, relating to the mark-to-market method of accounting for securities that is required to be used by a dealer in securities, are proposed. Reg. §1.475-0, 1.475(a)-3 and 1.475(b)-4 and amendments of Reg. §§1.475(c)-1, 1.475(c)-2 and 1.475(e)-1 were adopted 12/23/96 by T.D. 8700.

AGENCY: Internal Revenue Service (IRS), Treasury.

ACTION: Notice of proposed rulemaking and notice of public hearing.

SUMMARY: This document contains proposed regulations relating to the mark-to-market method of accounting for securities that is required to be used by a dealer in securities. The proposed regulations address the relationship between mark-to-market accounting and the accrual of stated interest and discount and the amortization of premium and between mark-to-market accounting and the tax treatment of bad debts. They also provide rules relating to certain dispositions and acquisitions of securities required to be marked to market, the exemption from mark-to-market treatment of securities in certain securitization transactions, and the identification requirements for obtaining exemption from mark-to-market treatment. Finally, these proposed regulations provide guidance relating to the exclusion of REMIC residual interests from the definition of security and to the relationship between the mark-to-market provisions and the integrated transaction rules in the proposed regulations on debt instruments with contingent payments. This document also provides notice of a public hearing on these proposed regulations.

DATES: Written comments must be received by April 3, 1995. Outlines of oral comments to be presented at a public hearing scheduled for May 3, 1995, at 10 a.m. must be received by April 3, 1995.

ADDRESSES: Send submissions to: CC:DOM:CORP:T:R (FI-42-94), room 5228, Internal Revenue Service, POB 7604, Ben Franklin Station, Washington, DC 20044. In the alternative, submissions may be hand delivered between the hours of 8 a.m. and 5 p.m. to: CC:DOM:CORP:T:R (FI-42-94), Courier's Desk, Internal Revenue Service, 1111 Constitution Avenue NW, Washington, DC.

The public hearing will be held in the Internal Revenue Auditorium, 7400 corridor, Internal Revenue Building, 1111 Constitution Avenue NW, Washington, DC 20224.

FOR FURTHER INFORMATION CONTACT: Concerning §1.475(c)-2(a)(4), Carol A. Schwartz, (202) 622-3920; concerning other sections of the regulations, Robert B. Williams, (202) 622-3960, or JoLynn Ricks, (202) 622-3920; concerning submissions and the hearing, Michael Slaughter, (202) 622-7190 (not toll-free numbers).

SUPPLEMENTARY INFORMATION:

Paperwork Reduction Act

The collection of information contained in this notice of proposed rulemaking has been submitted to the Office of Management and Budget for review in accordance with the Paperwork Reduction Act (44 U.S.C. 3504(h)). Comments on the collection of information should be sent to the Office of Management and Budget, Attn: Desk Officer for the Department of the Treasury, Office of Information and Regulatory Affairs, Washington, DC 20503, with copies to the Internal Revenue Service, Attn: IRS Reports Clearance Officer, PC:FP, Washington, DC 20224.

The collection of information is in §1.475(b)-4. The information required to be recorded under §1.475(b)-4 is required by the IRS to determine whether exemption from mark-to-market treatment is properly claimed. This information will be used to make that determination upon audit of taxpayers' books and records. The likely recordkeepers are businesses or other for-profit institutions.

Estimated total annual recordkeeping burden: 2,500 hours.

The estimated annual burden per recordkeeper varies from 15 minutes to 3 hours, depending on individual circumstances, with an estimated average of 1 hour.

Estimated number of recordkeepers: 2,500.

Background

Section 475 of the Internal Revenue Code requires mark-to-market accounting for dealers in securities, broadly defined. Section 475 was added by section 13223 of the Revenue Reconciliation Act of 1993, Pub. L. 103-66, 107 Stat. 481, and is effective for all taxable years ending on or after December 31, 1993.

On December 29, 1993, temporary regulations (T.D. 8505, 58 FR 68747) and cross-reference proposed regulations (FI-72-93, 58 FR 68798) were published to furnish guidance on several issues, including the scope of exemptions from the mark-to-market requirements, certain transitional issues relating to the scope of exemptions, and the meaning of the statutory terms "dealer in securities" and "held for investment." This notice contains proposed regulations that supplement, and in a few cases revise, the proposed regulations that were published last December.

Explanation of Provisions

Stated Interest, Discount, and Premium

The proposed regulations contained in this notice provide rules for taking into account interest (including original issue discount (OID) and market discount), premium, and certain gains and losses on securities that are debt instruments. In general, immediately before a debt instrument is marked to market, Code provisions related to calculating interest must be applied, and basis must be correspondingly adjusted. The mark-to-market computations do not affect either the amount treated as interest earned from a debt instrument or the taxable years in which that interest is taken into account.

For example, immediately before a debt instrument is marked to market, accruals of unpaid qualified stated interest (QSI) must be taken into account, and basis must be correspondingly increased. This is true regardless of the taxpayer's regular method of accounting. Marking a debt instrument to market under section 475(a) precludes the deferral that a cash-basis taxpayer might have experienced in the absence of the statutory provision, and the current accrual under the proposed regulations is needed in order to preserve the interest character of the QSI.

For debt instruments acquired with original issue discount or market discount, the proposed regulations require that, immediately before the mark-to-market gain or loss is computed under section 475(a), any OID or market discount accrued through the date of computation must be taken into account, and basis must be correspondingly increased. The amount of discount attributable to a particular period of time is computed under sections 1272 through 1275 (in the case of OID) and sections 1276 through 1278 (in the case of market discount). Thus, for example, the computation of OID attributable to a particular period takes into account any reduction for acquisition premium under section 1272(a)(7).

As indicated in the preceding paragraph, the proposed regulations provide that, in the case of a market discount bond to which section 475(a) applies, the holder must take market discount into account as it accrues, regardless of whether the holder elected under section 1278(b) to do so for all of its bonds. This rule is necessary to prevent market discount from producing gain on the mark instead of interest income. This provision, however, does not impose a section 1278(b) election on the taxpayer, because it does not apply to bonds that are not marked to market under section 475.

For taxable debt instruments acquired with amortizable bond premium, the proposed regulations provide that, if a dealer has made an election to amortize premium under section 171, any amortization for the taxable year (or for the portion of the taxable year during which the instrument is held by the dealer) must be taken into account (and basis must be appropriately reduced) before the mark-to-market gain or loss is computed under section 475. Because section 171 applies only to instruments not held primarily for sale to customers in the ordinary course of the taxpayer's trade or business, this proposed regulatory provision is applicable only to premium instruments described in section 475(b)(1) for which the taxpayer has not made the identification described in section 475(b)(2).

In the case of tax-exempt bonds, the proposed regulations require basis to be reduced as required by section 1016(a)(5) or (6) before mark-to-market gain or loss is computed.

If a dealer acquires a bond with premium and a section 171 election first applies to the bond in a taxable year after the year of acquisition, the proposed regulations require the dealer to amortize premium based on the original basis, without regard to any mark-to-market adjustments that may have been taken into account before the section 171 election became effective, but with regard to the adjustments required under section 171(b)(1). Thus, for example, if a dealer acquires in year 1 an instrument that is subject to section 475(a) and that has $10 of amortizable premium and if the dealer makes an election to amortize premium that is first effective in year 4 (when unamortized premium attributable to years 1 through 3 is $4), the dealer takes into account the appropriate portion of the remaining $6 of amortizable bond premium (as required under section 171(b)(3)) each taxable year before computing the mark-to-market adjustment on the instrument. Any mark-to-market basis adjustments in taxable years 1 through 3 are ignored in determining the amount of amortizable bond premium to which the election applies.

Under section 475(a)(2), a dealer in securities recognizes mark-to-market gain or loss on a security, other than inventory, as if the security were sold on the last business day of the taxable year. Although there may be circumstances under which marking a security to market produces results similar to the actual sale of the security, the statutory reference to the deemed sale prescribes the amount of gain or loss to be taken into account and does not trigger all of the consequences of a sale and reacquisition under the Code. For example, when a dealer in securities marks a bond (or other security) to market and takes recognized gain or loss into account, the dealer has not actually sold and reacquired the bond. Thus, under the proposed regulations, marking a debt instrument does not create, increase, or reduce market discount, acquisition premium, or bond premium.

The proposed regulations also contain a special rule to provide the proper character for mark-to-market gains or losses on a market discount instrument that was originally identified as held for investment by the dealer. This rule is necessary to ensure that all market discount is ultimately characterized as interest income and not as gain from the sale of a security.

Worthless Debts

The proposed regulations provide rules for marking a partially or wholly worthless debt to market. These rules coordinate the mark-to-market rules with the bad debt rules under the Code. The amount of gain or loss recognized under section 475(a)(2) when a debt instrument is marked to market generally is the difference between the adjusted basis and the fair market value of the debt. Under the proposed regulations, if a debt becomes partially or wholly worthless during a taxable year, the amount of any gain or loss required to be taken into account under section 475(a) is determined using a basis that reflects the worthlessness. The basis of the marked-to-market debt is treated as having been reduced by the amount of any book or regulatory charge-off (including the establishment of a specific allowance for a loan loss) for which a deduction could have been taken, without regard to whether any portion of the charge-off is, in fact, deducted or charged to a tax reserve for bad debts. The difference between this adjusted basis and the fair market value of the debt is the amount of gain or loss to be taken into account under section 475(a)(2). Thus, if the debt is wholly worthless, its basis would be reduced to zero and no gain or loss would be taken into account under section 475(a)(2).

This proposed treatment preserves the longstanding distinctions between losses due to the worthlessness of debts and other losses on debt instruments held by a taxpayer. See § 1.166-1(a), which requires bad debts to be taken into account either as a specific deduction in respect of debts or as a deduction for a reasonable addition to a reserve for bad debts. See also § § 1.585-3 and 1.593-7(c), which require a reserve-method taxpayer to charge bad debts to the reserve for bad debts. In addition, computing the mark-to-market adjustment as if the debt's basis had been adjusted to reflect worthlessness preserves a taxpayer's ability to postpone claiming a deduction for partial worthlessness until the debt becomes wholly worthless. To the extent that a debt has been previously charged off, mark-to-market gain is treated as a recovery.

The rules that are provided for bad debts in the proposed regulations do not apply to debts accounted for by a dealer as inventory under section 475(a)(1). Although it is possible for a debt that is in inventory to become partially worthless prior to sale, the likelihood or frequency of such an occurrence is difficult to ascertain given the speed with which inventory is sold. Comments are requested, however, concerning whether similar rules are necessary for partially worthless debt that is accounted for as inventory of the dealer.

Dispositions

Section 475(a) states that regulations may provide for securities held by a dealer to be marked to market at times other than the end of the dealer's taxable year. In general, the proposed regulations provide that, if a dealer in securities ceases to be the owner of a security for tax purposes, and if the security would have been marked to market under section 475(a) if the dealer's taxable year had ended immediately before the dealer ceases to own it, then (whether or not the security is inventory in the hands of the dealer) the dealer must recognize gain or loss as if the security had been sold for its fair market value immediately before the dealer ceases to own it. Any gain or loss so recognized is taken into account at that time.

In the absence of a mark upon disposition, a gain on a security held by a dealer could be deferred by transferring the security before the end of the taxable year to a related non-dealer in an intercompany transaction or in a non-recognition, carry-over-basis transaction. This potential for abuse is avoided if marking to market is required in every case in which a dealer ceases to be the owner of a security for tax purposes. The proposed requirement is analogous to the requirement that applies to dispositions of securities that are required to be marked to market under section 1256.

Transfers to which the proposed rule applies include the following: (a) Transfers to a controlled corporation under section 351; (b) Transfers to a trust (other than a grantor trust); (c) Transfers by gift to a charitable or non-charitable donee; (d) Transfers to other members of the same controlled group; (e) Transfers to a partnership under section 721; and (f) Transfers of mortgages to a REMIC under section 860F(b).

In the case of a transfer by a dealer to a partnership, the basis of a security transferred is generally its fair market value, because the security is marked to market immediately before the transfer. Thus, no special allocation issues arise. If there is any difference between a transferred security's basis after the mark and its fair market value (because, for example, the security transferred had been properly identified as held for investment but ceased to be so held at some time prior to the date of transfer), any special allocation of built-in gain or loss with respect to that security in the hands of the partnership will be made under section 704 and the regulations thereunder.

The mark to market immediately before disposition is separate and distinct from the disposition transaction. Thus, for example, the gain or loss from the mark is not gain or loss from a deferred intercompany transaction under § 1.1502-13.

Securities Acquired with Substituted Basis

The proposed regulations provide rules for situations where a dealer in securities receives a security with a basis in its hands that is determined, in whole or in part, either by reference to the basis of the security in the hands of the transferor or by reference to other property held at any time by the dealer. In these cases, section 475(a) applies only to post-acquisition gain and loss with respect to the security. That is, section 475(a) applies only to changes in value of the security occurring after its acquisition. See section 475(b)(3). The character of the mark-to-market gain or loss is determined as provided under section 475(d)(3). The character of pre-acquisition gain or loss (that is, the built-in gain or loss at the date the dealer acquires the security) and the time for taking that gain or loss into account are determined without regard to section 475. The fact that a security has a substituted basis in the dealer's hands does not affect the security's date of acquisition for purposes of determining the timeliness of an identification under section 475(b).

The proposed regulations provide rules for the identification of securities contributed and received in securitization transactions. Under the proposed regulations, a taxpayer that expects to contribute securities to a trust or other entity in exchange for interests therein may identify the contributed securities as held for investment (within the meaning of section 475(b)(1)(A)) or not held for sale (within the meaning of section 475(b)(1)(B)) only if it expects each of the interests received (whether or not a security within the meaning of section 475(c)(2)) to be either held for investment or not held for sale to customers in the ordinary course of the taxpayer's business. Thus, for example, if a mortgage banker securitizes its loans and does not intend to hold for investment (or for other than sale to customers) all of the interests received in the securitization transaction, the mortgage banker will be required to account for its inventory of mortgages at fair market value under section 475(a)(1), regardless of whether the mortgages are to be sold to a trust or contributed to a REMIC.

Under the proposed regulations, if a dealer engages in a securitization transaction that results in dispositions of only partial interests in the contributed securities, the dealer is not permitted to identify the contributed securities as exempt under section 475(b)(1)(A) or (B). As a result, all of the contributed securities must be accounted for under section 475(a). Moreover, under the mark-on-disposition rule of these proposed regulations, the dealer is required to mark the securities to market immediately before the securitization transaction. The Service invites comments on whether there are other administrable approaches that reflect the fact that only a partial disposition of the securities has occurred.

In other securitization transactions, a taxpayer transfers securities to a trust (or other entity) in a transaction that is not a disposition of the securities for tax purposes. The trust issues certificates (or other forms of interest) that represent secured debt of the taxpayer rather than debt of the trust or ownership of the underlying securities. In these cases, if the taxpayer retains the full ownership of the contributed securities for tax purposes and if the contributed securities otherwise qualify to be identified as held for investment or not held for sales then the taxpayer may identify the securities as held for investment or not held for sale notwithstanding the transfer.

Further, if a transfer of securities is a disposition, a taxpayer may identify the interests received in a securitization transaction as exempt from mark-to-market if the interests are described in section 475(b)(1) and are not treated for tax purposes as continuing ownership of the securities transferred. This identification is permitted even if the securitized assets were marked to market under section 475. For example, a taxpayer may identify some of the REMIC regular interests received on the transfer of mortgage securities to a REMIC, even if the mortgages were subject to section 475(a). Conversely, a taxpayer that has marked mortgages to market but subsequently contributes those mortgages to a grantor trust and receives beneficial interests therein may not identify the beneficial interests as exempt from mark-to-market treatment, because the beneficial interests represent continued ownership of the contributed securities, whose eligibility for exemption was determined when they were acquired.

The proposed regulations clarify that an identification of a security as exempt must specify the subparagraph of section 475(b)(1) under which the exemption is claimed and that the time by which a dealer must identify a security as exempt is not affected by whether the dealer has a substituted basis in the security. The proposed regulations also provide rules for determining whether an identification of a security as exempt is timely where a dealer engages in certain integrated transactions described in § 1.1275-6 as proposed on December 16, 1994 (FI-59-91, 59 FR 64884, 64905).

Definition of Dealer in Securities

Section 475(c)(1) defines a dealer in securities as a taxpayer who regularly purchases securities from, or sells securities to, customers in the ordinary course of a trade or business or who regularly offers to enter into, assume, offset, assign or otherwise terminate positions in securities with customers in the ordinary course of a trade or business.

The proposed regulations provide that whether a taxpayer is transacting business with customers is determined based on all of the facts and circumstances.

Under section 475(c)(1)(B) and the proposed regulations, the term dealer in securities includes a taxpayer that, in the ordinary course of its trade or business, regularly holds itself out as being willing and able to enter into either side of a transaction enumerated in section 475(c)(1)(B). For instance, if a taxpayer regularly holds itself out as being willing to enter a swap in which it is either the fixed or the floating payor, the taxpayer is a swaps dealer.

The proposed regulations clarify that a life insurance company does not become a dealer in securities solely by selling annuity, endowment, or life insurance policies to its customers. Under the temporary regulations published on December 29, 1993 (T.D. 8505), a contract that is treated for federal income tax purposes as an annuity, endowment, or life insurance contract is deemed to have been identified as held for investment, and is therefore not marked to market by the policy holder. This was necessary because variable life and annuity products fall within the literal language of section 475(c)(2)(E). Because many life insurance companies sell these insurance contracts to their customers, some commentators asked whether these life insurance companies were dealers in securities. There is no indication that Congress intended for a life insurance company that was not otherwise a dealer in securities to be characterized as a dealer merely because it sells life insurance policies to its customers. These proposed regulations provide the appropriate clarification.

Definition of Security

The temporary regulations that were published on December 29, 1993 (T.D. 8505), exclude certain items from the definition of security. Among the excluded items are liabilities of the taxpayer and negative value residual interests (NVRIs) in a REMIC and other arrangements that are determined to have substantially the same economic effect as NVRIs (for example, a widely held partnership that holds noneconomic REMIC residual interests). Those rules are needed to carry out the purposes of section 475 and other Code provisions, including section 860E.

These proposed regulations clarify that a liability of the taxpayer means a debt issued by the taxpayer. Also, for the reasons given below, these proposed regulations exclude all REMIC residual interests from the definition of security.

A typical REMIC holds a pool of long-term, real estate mortgages originated at a "blended" interest rate. These mortgages are used to support the issuance of regular interests, which are treated as debt, with varied maturities and interest rates. The REMIC takes cash flows on the mortgages and redirects them to holders of the regular interests. As a result, there is generally a mismatch in the recognition of interest income from the mortgages and the interest expense attributable to the regular interests. This mismatch of interest income and interest deductions results in taxable income or loss that does not represent economic gain or loss. Some commentators refer to this as "phantom" income or loss.

Phantom income or loss is allocated to the holders of the residual interests in a REMIC even though that income or loss does not represent any economic benefit or detriment to those holders. Further, sections 860C and 860E require a residual interest holder to pay taxes on a portion of phantom income (called "excess inclusion") and to increase the basis of the residual interest by the amount of phantom income. Because this basis increase does not represent economic value, a subsequent mark to market is likely to result in a loss. Permitting taxpayers to take this loss into account currently under the mark-to-market provisions effectively undermines the Congressional mandate embodied in section 860E to require current taxation of phantom income.

Although the adverse effect of section 475 on section 860E is most apparent when the residual interests being considered are NVRIs, residual interests with positive value present the same issue. Many residual interests with positive value, in spite of being entitled to REMIC distributions, have substantially the same economic effect as NVRIs and thus are already excluded by the temporary regulations from the definition of "security." The IRS is concerned, however, that residual interests may be structured in a way that avoids embodying substantially the same economic effects as an NVRI but that still undermines the purposes of section 860E. The proposed regulations, therefore, contain a rule that would remove from the category of securities subject to section 475 all residual interests that are acquired after January 4, 1995. Also removed are arrangements that are acquired after that date and are determined to have substantially the same economic effect as a REMIC residual interest (for instance, an interest in a widely held partnership holding residual interests). The temporary regulations continue to apply to all residual interests described therein for all taxable years ending on or after December 31, 1993.

In addition, the Commissioner has determined that, if a residual interest, or an interest or arrangement that has substantially the same economic effect, is not a security within the meaning of section 475, it should not be treated as inventory under other provisions. Additional guidance on this matter will be issued.

Comments are requested concerning whether there are any residual interests that do not undermine section 860E upon being marked to market. If comments are received that describe any such interests, subsequent guidance may provide that they are included in the mark-to-market regime. In this regard, it is important that any mechanism for identifying these interests not impose an undue burden on either taxpayers or the IRS.

Additional Comments Requested

The provisions of section 475 generally apply in determining the taxable income of a dealer that may also be subject to various international provisions of the Code. The Service is considering the possibility of using the definitions contained in section 475 and the regulations thereunder for purposes of various international provisions, except where a modification of the provisions is necessary to carry out the purposes of those international provisions. Comments on this issue also are welcome.

Finally, the Service is considering whether there are additional situations in which securities should not be accounted for under section 475(a). (The temporary and proposed regulations that were published on December 29, 1993, listed some such situations.) For example, a dealer in securities may acquire at original issue and in exchange for property certain non-interest-bearing debt instruments that are not subject to the interest imputation provisions of section 1274 or 483. Because these instruments will seldom appreciate in value, it may be inappropriate to subject them to the mark-to-market regime.

Dates of Applicability

The proposed regulations will apply to identifications made, securities acquired, or events occurring, on or after January 4, 1995, or to taxable years beginning on or after January 1, 1995, as appropriate.

Special Analyses

It has been determined that this notice of proposed rulemaking is not a significant regulatory action as defined in EO 12866. Therefore, a regulatory assessment is not required. It also has been determined that section 553(b) of the Administrative Procedure Act (5 U.S.C. chapter 5) and the Regulatory Flexibility Act (5 U.S.C. chapter 6) do not apply to these regulations, and, therefore, a Regulatory Flexibility Analysis is not required. Pursuant to section 7805(f) of the Code, this notice of proposed rulemaking will be submitted to the Chief Counsel for Advocacy of the Small Business Administration for comment on its impact on small business.

Comments and Public Hearing

Before these proposed regulations are adopted as final regulations, consideration will be given to any written comments (a signed original and eight (8) copies) that are submitted timely to the IRS. All comments will be available for public inspection and copying.

A public hearing has been scheduled for Wednesday, May 3, 1995 at 10 a.m. The public hearing will be held in the Internal Revenue Auditorium, 7400 corridor, Internal Revenue Building, 1111 Constitution Avenue NW, Washington, DC 20224. Because of access restrictions, visitors will not be admitted beyond the Internal Revenue Building lobby more than 15 minutes before the hearing starts.

The rules of 26 CFR 601.601(a)(3) apply to the hearing.

Persons that wish to present oral comments at the hearing must submit written comments by April 3, 1995, and submit an outline of the topics to be discussed and the time to be devoted to each topic (signed original and eight (8) copies) by April 3, 1995.

A period of 10 minutes will be allotted to each person for making comments.

An agenda showing the scheduling of the speakers will be prepared after the deadline for receiving outlines has passed. Copies of the agenda will be available free of charge at the hearing.

Drafting Information

The principal authors of these regulations are Robert B. Williams and JoLynn Ricks, Office of Assistant Chief Counsel (Financial Institutions & Products). However, other personnel from the IRS and Treasury Department participated in their development.

[¶49,147] Proposed Regulations and Proposed Amendments of Regulations (INTL-65-93), published in the Federal Register on April 28, 1995.

Passive foreign investment companies: Passive income characterization: Certain foreign banks and securities dealers: Exceptions to.—Reg. §§1.1296-4 and 1.1296-6 and amendments of Reg. §1.1291-0, relating to the application of the exceptions to passive income contained in section 1296(b) for foreign banks, securities dealers and brokers, are proposed. On 1/2/98, amendments of proposed Reg. §1.1296-4 were proposed (¶49,242). A public hearing on this proposal is scheduled for August 31, 1995.

AGENCY: Internal Revenue Service (IRS), Treasury.

ACTION: Notice of proposed rulemaking and notice of public hearing.

SUMMARY: This document provides guidance concerning the application of the exceptions to passive income contained in section 1296(b) for foreign banks, securities dealers and brokers. This document affects persons who own direct or indirect interests in certain foreign corporations. This document also provides notice of a public hearing on these proposed regulations.

DATES: Written comments must be received by August 10, 1995. Outlines of oral comments to be presented at the public hearing scheduled for August 31, 1995 at 10 a.m. must be received by August 10, 1995.

ADDRESSES: Send submissions to: CC:DOM:CORP:T:R (INTL-0065-93), room 5228, Internal Revenue Service, POB 7604, Ben Franklin Station, Washington, DC 20044. In the alternative, submissions may be hand delivered between the hours of 8 a.m. and 5 p.m. to: CC:DOM:CORP:T:R (INTL-0065-93), Courier's Desk, Internal Revenue Building, 1111 Constitution Avenue, NW, Washington, DC.

FOR FURTHER INFORMATION CONTACT: Concerning the regulations, Ramon Camacho at (202) 622-3870; concerning submissions and the hearing, Ms. Christina Vasquez, (202) 622-7180 (not toll-free numbers).

SUPPLEMENTARY INFORMATION

Background

A passive foreign investment company (PFIC) is any foreign corporation that satisfies either the income test or asset test in section 1296(a) of the Internal Revenue Code (Code). Under the income test, a foreign corporation is a PFIC if 75 percent or more of its gross income for the year is passive income. Sec. 1296(a)(1). Alternatively, a foreign corporation is a PFIC if 50 percent or more of the average value of its assets for the taxable year produce passive income or are held for the production of passive income. Sec. 1296(a)(2). Under section 1296(b)(1), passive income is foreign personal holding company income as defined in section 954(c) of the Code, and includes dividends, interest, certain rents and royalties, and gain from certain property transactions, including gain from the sale of assets that produce passive income.

Under section 1296(b)(2)(A), income earned in the active conduct of a banking business by a foreign corporation licensed to do business as a bank in the United States and, to the extent provided in regulations, by other corporations engaged in the banking business is not passive. Notice 89-81, 1989-2 CB 399, (Notice) described rules to be incorporated into subsequent regulations that would expand this exception to certain foreign banks not licensed to do a banking business in the United States. The rules contained in § 1.1296-4 of the proposed regulations would implement section 1296(b)(2)(A) for banking activities conducted by foreign corporations.

In 1993, Congress added section 1296(b)(3)(A) to the Code, effective for taxable years beginning after September 30, 1993. See Omnibus Budget Reconciliation Act of 1993 (1993 Act), Pub. L. 103-66, section 13231(d), 107 Stat. 312, 499. The provision treats as nonpassive any income derived in the active conduct of a securities business by a controlled foreign corporation (CFC) if the CFC is a U.S. registered dealer or broker and, to the extent provided in regulations, a CFC not so registered. The rules contained in § 1.1296-6 would implement section 1296(b)(3)(A).

Section 956A, added by the 1993 Act, requires each U.S. shareholder of a CFC to include in income its pro rata share of the CFC's excess passive assets. Under section 956A(c)(2), a passive asset is any asset that produces passive income as defined in section 1296(b). An asset that generates nonpassive income under § 1.1296-4 or § 1.1296-6 of the proposed regulations will be nonpassive for purposes of section 956A.

Explanation of Provisions.

I. *Description of Proposed Rules for Foreign Banks.*

A. *General Rule.*

Section 1.1296-4(a) of the proposed regulations provides generally that, for purposes of section 1296(a)(1), passive income does not include banking income earned by an active bank or by a qualified affiliate of such a bank. For this purpose, an active bank is either a corporation that possesses a license issued under federal or state law to do business as a bank in the United States, or a foreign corporation that meets the licensing, deposit-taking, and lending requirements of paragraphs (c), (d), and (e), respectively, of § 1.1296-4.

The proposed rules generally adopt the deposit, lending, and licensing standards contained in the Notice. These standards are consistent with the provisions of the Code that define a bank as an institution that accepts deposits from and makes loans to the public and is licensed under state or federal law to conduct banking activities. See e.g., sec. 581. The IRS and Treasury believe that Congress intended to grant the banking exception only to corporations that conform to a traditional U.S. banking model.

However, the proposed rules liberalize the approach taken in the Notice in several ways. Most significantly, the proposed rules adopt subjective tests to measure whether the corporation meets the deposit-taking and lending requirements. The IRS and Treasury rejected reliance on objective tests such as those in the Notice after learning, through several ruling requests pursuant to the Notice, that objective standards may cause legitimate banks to be treated as nonbanks.

Because of the rigidity of the objective tests, the Notice permitted the IRS to rule in rare and unusual circumstances that a foreign corporation was an active bank even though it failed to satisfy the requirements of the Notice. The proposed regulations do not adopt this procedure because the IRS and Treasury believe that the enhanced flexibility of the proposed rules should permit all foreign corporations actively conducting a licensed banking business (whether directly or through affiliates) to qualify for the bank exception.

B. *Licensing Requirement*

A foreign corporation that is not licensed in the United States satisfies the licensing requirements of § 1.1296-4(c) if it is licensed or authorized to accept deposits from residents of the country in which it is chartered or incorporated, and to conduct, in such country, any of the banking activities described in the proposed regulations. However, a corporation fails this licensing test if one of the principal purposes for its obtaining a license was compliance with the requirements of this section.

The IRS and Treasury believe that being licensed as a bank by a bank regulatory authority is strong evidence that a corporation is a bank. The proposed regulations therefore adopt a licensing test to distinguish banks from investment funds.

C. *Deposit-taking Test.*

A foreign corporation satisfies the deposit-taking test of § 1.1296-4(d) if it regularly accepts deposits in the ordinary course of its trade or business from customers who are residents of the country in which it is licensed or authorized. In addition, the amount of deposits shown on the corporation's balance sheet must be substantial. Section 1.1296-4(d)(3) provides that whether the amount of deposits on a corporation's balance sheet is substantial depends on all the facts and circumstances, including whether the capital structure and funding of the bank as a whole are similar to that of comparable banking institutions engaged in the same types of activities and subject to regulation by the same banking authorities.

The proposed regulations adopt this deposit-taking test in part to distinguish banks from finance companies, which do not accept deposits. This distinction between finance companies and banks is required by Congress. H.R. Conf. Rep. No. 213, 103d Cong., 1st Sess. 641 (1993) (noting that the banking, insurance, and securities exemptions "do not apply to income derived in the conduct of financing and credit services businesses"). Although the IRS and Treasury believe that deposit-taking is a key attribute of all active banks, they also recognize that subjective tests will better accommodate the various types of banks that have developed as a result of different banking systems and regulatory frameworks.

The proposed regulations introduce flexibility to the deposit-taking requirements in several ways. First, the requirement that the amount of deposits be substantial is more flexible than the Notice requirement that deposits constitute at least 50 percent of the total liabilities of the bank. The IRS and Treasury recognize that a bank's funding preferences may be affected by market conditions and regulatory requirements and believes that an institution may be properly treated as an active bank even if deposits do not constitute the institution's primary source of funding.

Second, unlike the Notice, the proposed regulations do not include any special rules for interbank deposits but treat them like any other deposit, regardless of whether they are received from persons who are members of a related group as defined in § 1.1296-4(i)(4). The IRS and Treasury believe this change is appropriate because the acceptance of interbank deposits from related or unrelated persons on an arm's length basis is a banking activity normally engaged in by banks. In addition, the impact of a rule that distinguishes between interbank deposits received from related persons and those received from unrelated persons is diminished where deposit-taking activity is not measured with a bright-line test.

Finally, the proposed rules change the Notice requirement that a corporation must hold deposits from at least 1,000 persons who are bona fide residents of the country that issued the corporation's banking license because this requirement proved troublesome for certain private banks with clientele from several countries. The requirement was intended to address cases where a bank is licensed by a country but not allowed to accept deposits from its residents. In the IRS and Treasury's view, such an entity should not be treated as an active bank for purposes of section 1296 because it is not accorded full bank status by the bank authorities that issued its banking license. However, the IRS and Treasury believe that a bright-line deposit standard is not necessary to address this concern. Instead, the proposed regulations require that a corporation regularly accept deposits from residents of the country in which it is licensed.

D. *Lending Test.*

A foreign corporation satisfies the lending test of § 1.1296-4(e) if it regularly makes loans to customers in the ordinary course of its trade or business. This is a change from the Notice's requirement that loans to unrelated persons make up more than 50 percent of the corporation's loan portfolio. The lending test is necessary to distinguish banks, which extend credit to customers, from corporations that merely invest. However, such a distinction can be drawn without relying on a bright-line standard such as that contained in the Notice.

In order to distinguish loans from investments for purposes of these rules, the proposed regulations provide that a note, bond, debenture or other evidence of indebtedness is a loan only if it is received by the corporation on an extension of credit made pursuant to a loan agreement entered into in the ordinary course of the corporation's banking business. Debt instruments treated as securities for purposes of the corporation's financial statements generally are not loans.

E. *Banking Income and Activities.*

Section 1.1296-4(f)(1) provides that banking income is gross income derived from the active conduct of any banking activity as defined in § 1.1296-4(f)(2). These activities include all of the activities treated as banking activities in the Notice, with no material changes, except that finance leasing is included as a banking activity.

The proposed regulations do not adopt the Notice's rule that all of the U.S. effectively connected income earned by a foreign corporation in the active conduct of a trade or business pursuant to a U.S. bank license automatically is nonpassive. One effect of this rule was that effectively connected income earned by a U.S.-licensed bank from transactions with related parties would have been banking income, while income earned by non-U.S.-licensed banks from similar related-party transactions would not have been banking income. Because the proposed regulations generally do not differentiate between related party and non-related party transactions in the same way as the Notice, the only effect of the rule would have been to treat, in the case of U.S. licensed banks only, as banking income the income earned on transactions with related parties who are not customers and income earned from activities (such as securities activities) that are not banking activities described in § 1.1296-4(f). The IRS and Treasury believe that the standards for determining whether income is derived in the active conduct of a banking business should be the same for all corporations that are either active banks or qualified bank affiliates.

The IRS and Treasury are aware that many bank activities may also be considered securities activities. Under the proposed regulations, an entity that performs an activity that is both a banking activity and a securities activity must satisfy only the requirements of the bank rules to treat income from such activity as nonpassive. For example, an entity that derives income from dealing in foreign exchange may treat such income as nonpassive if it is an active bank (or a qualified bank affiliate) even though it is not a controlled foreign corporation.

Dealing in securities, however, is not included as both a banking activity and a securities activity. The IRS and Treasury believe that Congress intended that income from dealing in securities should be nonpassive only if it is earned by a controlled foreign corporation that actively conducts a securities business and meets the other requirements of section 1296(b)(3)(A).

The IRS and Treasury have become aware that certain developing country economies impose high deposit reserve requirements as a tool for implementing monetary policy. Because the central banks of these countries require the maintenance of such reserves as a prerequisite to conducting a banking business, the earnings on such assets, if any, should appropriately be excluded from passive income.

F. *Customer Relationship.*

Under the proposed regulations, a bank satisfies the deposit and lending tests only if it carries on such activities with customers. Moreover, only the income from its banking activities (and those of its qualified bank affiliates) conducted with, or for, customers will produce nonpassive income. This is a change from the Notice requirement, under which activities qualified only if they were conducted with unrelated parties. Under the proposed regulations, a customer may be any person, related or unrelated, if that person has a customer relationship with the bank. Whether such a relationship exists depends on all the facts and circumstances. However, persons who are related to, or who are shareholders, officers, directors, or other employees of, the corporation will not be treated as customers of the corporation if one of the principal purposes for the corporation's transacting business with such persons was to qualify the corporation as an active bank or qualified bank affiliate.

G. *Affiliates of Active Banks*

The IRS and Treasury recognize that many active banks conduct one or more banking activities through separately incorporated affiliates that may not individually qualify as active banks. Accordingly, the proposed regulations provide rules under which income from banking activities may be treated as nonpassive if earned by a corporation that does not qualify as an active bank but is a member of a related group of which an active bank is also a member. However, such income is nonpassive only for purposes of determining whether any member of the related group is a passive foreign investment company or for purposes of applying the excess passive asset rules of section 956A(c)(2)(A). In addition, such income remains passive with respect to persons who own stock in the affiliate but who are not members of the related group of which the affiliate is a member.

For purposes of these rules, a related group is any group of persons related within the meaning of section 954(d)(3), substituting person for controlled foreign corporation. This definition is a departure from the affiliated group definition of the Notice because it permits noncorporate entities (such as partnerships) to count as members of the group for purposes of satisfying the groupwide gross income test.

Section 1.1296-4(i)(2) requires the bank affiliate to generate more than 60 percent of its income from banking, insurance and securities activities (but not other financial services). For purposes of this test, the look-through rules of sections 1296(c) and 1296(b)(2)(C) do not apply. This requirement ensures that a bank affiliate's eligibility for the bank exception depends upon the business activities conducted directly by the affiliate, and is not influenced by activities conducted by related persons. However, a bank affiliate may nevertheless apply sections 1296(c) and 1296(b)(2)(A) to determine whether it is a PFIC under the income or asset tests of section 1296(a).

In addition, the related group must meet two gross income tests for the exception to apply. First, under § 1.1296-4(i)(3)(i), income from banking activities derived by active banks must constitute at least 30 percent of the financial services income earned by group members. Second, under § 1.1296-4(i)(3)(ii), income earned by group members from banking activities, securities activities, and insurance activities must constitute at least 70 percent of the financial services income earned by group members that are financial services entities. The regulations adopt the definition of financial services income contained in § 1.904-4(e), which includes only income earned by financial services entities.

These affiliate rules are structurally similar to the affiliate rules contained in the Notice, but have been modified in several respects to respond to taxpayer comments. For example, the 80 percent stock ownership threshold of the Notice caused many corporations to be treated as PFICs solely because the gross income of subsidiaries in which the group owned less than an 80 percent interest was excluded for purposes of the Notice's gross income tests, even though the group had voting control of such subsidiaries. The adoption of a lower 50 percent ownership threshold for group membership in the proposed regulations recognizes that international groups are not organized to meet the 80 percent threshold required for consolidation under U.S. tax law.

In addition, the gross income tests were changed in several ways to deal with problems encountered by diversified affiliated groups. First, the denominators of the fractions now include only financial services income, which by its terms includes only income earned by financial services entities. This change prevents foreign corporations that are part of a banking group from being disqualified solely because the group is a subgroup of a larger group that does not perform solely financial services.

Second, the numerator of the fraction for the groupwide gross income test now includes gross income from securities and insurance activities in addition to banking activities. This change prevents a foreign corporation engaged in banking activities that is part of a banking subgroup from being disqualified solely because it is part of a larger group that provides a broad range of financial services.

Finally, the proposed rules drop the Notice requirement that an active bank be a group member for 5 years before its income may count towards satisfaction of the gross income tests. Since PFIC status is determined annually, the IRS and Treasury believe that whether a group is a banking group should depend only on its status during the current taxable year.

H. *Income from Nonbanking Activities.*

As in the Notice, § 1.1296-4(j) of the proposed regulations provides that income derived from the conduct of activities other than banking activities described in § 1.1296-4(f)(2) and income from assets held for the conduct of such activities are nonpassive only to the extent provided in section 1296.

J. *Effective Date.*

Section 1.1296-4 is proposed to be effective for all taxable years beginning after December 31, 1994. However, taxpayers may apply § 1.1296-4 to a taxable year beginning after December 31, 1986, but must consistently apply § 1.1296-4 to such taxable year and all subsequent years. While application of § 1.1296-4 to a year beginning after December 31, 1986, cannot affect the tax liability of a taxpayer for any closed taxable year, a taxpayer may apply § 1.1296-4 to a closed taxable year for the purpose of determining whether a foreign corporation is a PFIC in calculating the taxpayer's liability for an open taxable year.

II. *Exception for Income Earned in a Securities Business.*

A. *General Rule.*

Section 1.1296-6(a) of the proposed regulations provides generally that securities income earned by an active securities dealer, active securities broker or qualified securities affiliate is nonpassive. As required by section 1296(b)(3)(C), the rules apply only for purposes of determining whether a controlled foreign corporation (as defined in section 957(a)) is a PFIC with respect to its United States shareholders (as defined in section 951(b)), or for purposes of determining whether an asset is passive under section 956A(c)(2).

B. *Active Securities Dealer and Active Securities Broker.*

Under § 1.1296-6(b)(1), an active dealer or broker is a dealer or broker that meets certain licensing requirements. Section 1.1296-6(c) defines a securities dealer as a dealer in securities within the meaning of section 475(c)(1). Under § 1.1296-6(d), a securities broker is a foreign corporation that stands ready to effect transactions in securities and other financial instruments for the account of customers in the ordinary course of its trade or business during the taxable year. A securities dealer or broker is licensed under § 1.1296-6(b) if it possesses a U.S. license to do business as a securities dealer or broker in the United States or if it is licensed or authorized in the country in which it is chartered or incorporated to conduct one or more securities activities described in § 1.1296-6(e)(2) with residents of that country. The conduct of such activities must be subject to bona fide regulation, including appropriate reporting, monitoring and prudential requirements, by a Securities regulatory authority that regularly enforces compliance with such standards.

C. *Securities Income & Securities Activities.*

Section 1.1296-6(e)(1) provides generally that securities income means the gross income derived from the active conduct of any securities activity that constitutes a trade or business. The list of securities activities contained in § 1.1296-6(e)(2) generally is consistent with the legislative history to section 1296(b)(3)(A). See H.R. Rep. No. 111, 103d Cong., 1st Sess. 704 (1993).

Section 1.1296-6(e)(2)(iv) includes as an additional securities activity the maintenance of a capital deposit required under foreign law as a prerequisite to acting as a broker in that jurisdiction. Without this rule, a broker that is not also a dealer could be a PFIC under section 1296(a)(2) even though the majority of its income is commission income. This rule applies only if significant restrictions exist on the use of its capital. Thus, working capital will not qualify as a deposit for purposes of this rule.

In general, only income from transactions entered into with, or on behalf of, persons with whom the corporation has a dealer-customer relationship may be treated as nonpassive. Section 1.1296-6(g) adopts without change the definition of dealer-customer relationship contained in the bank rules.

Under § 1.1296-6(h) of the proposed regulations, income and gain from a security identified as held for investment under section 475(b)(1)(A) or which is not held for sale within the meaning of section 475(b)(1)(B) is passive. Because the identification rules of sections 475(b) and 1.475(b)-1T and 1.475(b)-2T apply, the rules governing identification of inventory securities in Notice 88-22, 1988-1 CB 489 and Notice 89-81, 1989-2 CB 399 do not apply with respect to taxable years beginning after September 30, 1993. However, the inventory identification rules of Notice 89-81 and Notice 88-22 will continue to apply for taxable years beginning before October 1, 1993.

D. *Matched Book Income*

Section 1.1296-6(i) of the proposed regulations provides special rules for determining a securities dealer's income from certain matched transactions. These rules are adopted in order to eliminate a potential opportunity for abuse that arises from the manner in which a matched book repo business is conducted by securities dealers.

A matched transaction is defined as a sale and repurchase agreement with respect to the same security, entered into by the controlled foreign corporation in the active conduct of its trade or business and properly treated as offsetting agreements in a matched book. In a typical repurchase agreement a taxpayer sells a security and, at the same time, agrees to repurchase an identical security from the purchaser at a price in excess of the taxpayer's sales price. In a reverse repurchase agreement, a taxpayer purchases a security and concurrently agrees to sell an identical security to the seller at a price in excess of the taxpayer's purchase price. A taxpayer who keeps a matched book generally enters into offsetting repurchase and reverse repurchase agreements involving identical securities. Such taxpayers act as intermediaries by matching persons who need cash for a short period with those who need securities for the same period.

Under the proposed regulations, securities income includes only the net (not gross) income from matched transactions. Without the proposed regulation's netting rule, related groups that are predominantly engaged in passive activities could easily meet the gross income tests contained in the qualified affiliate rules because a CFC conducting a matched book business will earn large amounts of gross income, even though net economic income from matched book activities is comparatively small.

E. *Affiliates of Dealers or Brokers.*

Like banks, securities dealers and brokers frequently operate through separately incorporated subsidiaries that may not qualify independently as active securities dealers or brokers but which form part of an integrated securities business conducted by an active dealer or broker. Accordingly, the proposed regulations contain rules that extend the securities dealer/broker exception to certain qualified affiliates of active securities dealers or brokers. These rules generally mirror the qualified bank affiliate rules contained in § 1.1296-4(i), except that they extend the securities dealer/broker exception only to qualified securities affiliates that are CFCs, as required by section 1296(b)(3)(A).

F. *Income from Nonsecurities Activities.*

Section 1.1296-6(k) of the proposed regulations provides that income derived from the conduct of activities other than securities activities described in § 1.1296-6(e)(2) and income from assets held for the conduct of such activities are nonpassive only to the extent provided in section 1296.

G. *Effective Date.*

The rules contained in § 1.1296-6 are proposed to be effectivefor taxable years beginning after September 30, 1993.

III. *Look-Through Rules.*

The proposed regulations do not contain guidance regarding the look-through rules of sections 1296(c) and 1296(b)(2)(C) or the grouping rules of section 956A(d). In general, the proposed regulations also do not address whether, and to what extent, look-through principles may apply to characterize income from a partnership as nonpassive and an interest in a partnership as a nonpassive asset, except to the extent that section 475 may treat a partnership as a securities dealer. Because these issues are not unique to financial institutions, the IRS and Treasury will address them in future regulations of more general application. The IRS and Treasury solicit comments on the proper scope and application of look-through and grouping concepts to banks, securities dealers and securities brokers.

Special Analyses

It has been determined that this notice of proposed rulemaking is not a significant regulatory action as defined in EO 12866. Therefore, a regulatory assessment is not required. It also has been determined that section 553(b) of the Administrative Procedure Act (5 U.S.C. chapter 5) and the Regulatory Flexibility Act (5 U.S.C. chapter 6) do not apply to these regulations, and, therefore, a Regulatory Flexibility Analysis is not required. Pursuant to section 7805(f) of the Internal Revenue Code, this notice of proposed rulemaking will be submitted to the Chief Counsel for Advocacy of the Small Business Administration for comment on its impact on small business.

Comments and Public Hearing

Before these proposed regulations are adopted as final regulations, consideration will be given to any written comments (a signed original and eight (8) copies) that are submitted timely to the IRS. All comments will be available for public inspection and copying.

A public hearing has been scheduled for August 31, 1995, at 10 a.m., in the Internal Revenue Service Auditorium, 7400 corridor. Because of access restrictions, visitors will not be admitted beyond the Internal Revenue Building lobby more than 15 minutes before the hearing starts.

The rules of 26 CFR 601.601(a)(3) apply to the hearing.

Persons that wish to present oral comments at the hearing must submit written comments and an outline of the topics to be discussed and the time to be devoted to each topic (signed original and eight (8) copies) by August 10, 1995.

A period of 10 minutes will be allotted to each person for making comments.

An agenda showing the scheduling of the speakers will be prepared after the deadline for receiving outlines has passed. Copies of the agenda will be available free of charge at the hearing.

Drafting Information

The principal author of these regulations is Ramon Camacho, Office of the Associate Chief Counsel (International). However, other personnel from the IRS and Treasury Department participated in their development.

[¶49,148] Proposed Amendments of Regulations (FI-21-95), published in the Federal Register on May 2, 1995.

Straddles: Personal property defined.—Amendments of Reg. §1.1092(d)-2, relating to the definition of personal property for purposes of the straddle rules, are proposed. A public hearing on this proposal is scheduled for August 30, 1995.

AGENCY: Internal Revenue Service (IRS), Treasury.

ACTION: Notice of proposed rulemaking and notice of public hearing.

SUMMARY: This document contains proposed regulations relating to the definition of personal property for purposes of the straddle rules. This action is necessary to reflect changes in the law made by the Tax Reform Act of 1984. The regulations provide guidance to persons who enter into straddle transactions.

DATES: Written comments must be received by July 31, 1995. Requests to appear and outlines of topics to be discussed at the public hearing scheduled for August 30, 1995, must be submitted by August 9, 1995.

ADDRESSES: Send submissions to: CC:DOM:CORP:T:R (FI-21-95), room 5228, Internal Revenue Service, POB 7604, Ben Franklin Station, Washington, DC 20044. In the alternative, submissions may be hand delivered between the hours of 8 a.m. and 5 p.m. to: CC:DOM:CORP:T:R (FI-21-95), Courier's Desk, Internal Revenue Service, 1111 Constitution Avenue, NW., Washington, DC. A public hearing has been scheduled for Wednesday, August 30, 1995, at 10 a.m. in the Auditorium, Internal Revenue Building, 1111 Constitution Avenue, NW., Washington, DC.

FOR FURTHER INFORMATION CONTACT: Concerning the regulations, Robert B. Williams, (202) 622-3960; concerning submissions and the hearing, Michael Slaughter, (202) 622-7190 (not toll-free numbers).

SUPPLEMENTARY INFORMATION:

Background

Section 1092(d) of the Internal Revenue Code provides definitions and special rules relating to straddles. Under section 1092(d)(3)(B)(i)(II), an ownership interest in stock, which generally is not treated as personal property subject to the straddle rules, may be personal property if it is part of a straddle at least one of the offsetting positions of which is, under regulations, a position with respect to substantially similar or related property (other than stock). On March 20, 1995, the IRS published final regulations (§1.1092(d)-2) under section 1092(d)(3)(B). Those regulations generally apply the rules of §1.246-5 to determine whether an offsetting position is a position with respect to substantially similar or related property (other than stock) within the meaning of section 1092(d)(3)(B)(i)(II).

Explanation of Provisions

The proposed regulations clarify the definition of the term *personal property* under section 1092(d)(1) as it applies to stock. The proposed regulations provide that personal property includes any stock of a type that is actively traded and that is part of a straddle at least one of the offsetting positions of which is a position with respect to substantially similar or related property (other than stock). For this purpose, a position with respect to substantially similar or related property (other than stock) does not include direct ownership of stock or a short sale of stock but includes any other position with respect to substantially similar or related property. These proposed regulations thus clarify that, for example, stock and an equity swap with respect to property that is substantially similar or related to that stock can constitute a straddle for purposes of section 1092.

The proposed regulations also address the scope of section 1092(d)(3)(B)(i), which provides that stock that is offset by an option with respect to that stock or substantially identical stock or by a position with respect to substantially similar or related property (other than stock) is treated as personal property under section 1092(d)(3)(B). Although this provision does not contain an explicit active trading requirement, the legislative history of the Tax Reform Act of 1984 indicates that Congress contemplated that the stock would be treated as personal property under this test only if it is of a type that is actively traded. H.R. Conf. Rep. No. 861, 98th Cong., 2d Sess. 907 (1984). The regulations, therefore, include this requirement. In contrast, the regulations clarify that, for purposes of section 1092(d)(3)(B)(ii), if a corporation is formed or availed of to take positions in personal property that offset positions taken by any shareholder, stock of the corporation may be treated as personal property under section 1092(d)(3)(B) even if it is not actively traded.

The proposed regulations generally are effective for positions established on or after May 1, 1995. The IRS believes, however, that the regulations merely clarify the rule that applied once §1.1092(d)-2 was promulgated. There is no implication that the results reached under these proposed regulations would not also be reached for positions established on or after March 17, 1995, and before May 1, 1995.

Special Analyses

It has been determined that this notice of proposed rulemaking is not a significant regulatory action as defined in EO 12866. Therefore, a regulatory assessment is not required. It also has been determined that section 553(b) of the Administrative Procedure Act (5 U.S.C. chapter 5) and the Regulatory Flexibility Act (5 U.S.C. chapter 6) do not apply to these regulations, and, therefore, a Regulatory Flexibility Analysis is not required. Pursuant to section 7805(f) of the Internal Revenue Code, this notice of proposed rulemaking will be submitted to the Chief Counsel for Advocacy of the Small Business Administration for comment on its impact on small business.

Comments and Public Hearing

Before these proposed regulations are adopted as final regulations, consideration will be given to any written comments (a signed original and eight (8) copies) that are submitted timely to the IRS. All comments will be available for public inspection and copying.

A public hearing has been scheduled for Wednesday, August 30, 1995, at 10 a.m. The public hearing will be held in the IRS Auditorium, 7th Floor, 1111 Constitution Avenue, NW, Washington DC 20224. Because of access restrictions, visitors will not be admitted beyond the Internal Revenue Building lobby more than 15 minutes before the hearing starts.

The rules of 26 CFR 601.601(a)(3) apply to the hearing.

Persons that wish to present oral comments at the hearing must submit written comments by July 31, 1995, and submit an outline of the topics to be discussed and the time to be devoted to each topic (signed original and eight (8) copies) by August 9, 1995.

A period of 10 minutes will be allotted to each person for making comments.

An agenda showing the scheduling of the speakers will be prepared after the deadline for receiving outlines has passed. Copies of the agenda will be available free of charge at the hearing.

Drafting Information

The principal author of these regulations is Robert B. Williams, Office of Assistant Chief Counsel (Financial Institutions and Products). However, other personnel from the IRS and Treasury Department participated in their development.

[¶ 49,151] Proposed Amendments of Regulations (EE-35-95), published in the Federal Register on December 26, 1995.

Employers-Employees: Retirement plans: Contributions: Allocation: Accrued benefits.—Amendments of Reg. §1.411(c)-1, relating to guidance on calculation of an employee's accrued benefit derived from the employee's contributions to a qualified defined benefit pension plan, is proposed.

AGENCY: Internal Revenue Service (IRS), Treasury.

ACTION: Notice of proposed rulemaking.

SUMMARY: This document contains proposed regulations that provide guidance on calculation of an employee's accrued benefit derived from the employee's contributions to a qualified defined benefit pension plan. These regulations are issued to reflect changes to the applicable law made by the Omnibus Budget Reconciliation Act of 1987 (OBRA `87) and the Omnibus Budget Reconciliation Act of 1989 (OBRA '89). OBRA '87 and OBRA '89 amended the law to change the accumulation of employee contributions and the conversion of those accumulated contributions to employee-derived accrued benefits.

DATES: Written comments and requests for a public hearing must be received by March 21, 1996.

ADDRESSES: Send submissions to: CC:DOM:CORP:R (EE-35-95), room 5228, Internal Revenue Service, POB 7604, Ben Franklin Station, Washington, DC 20044. In the alternative, submissions may be hand delivered between the hours of 8 a.m. and 5 p.m. to: CC:DOM:CORP:R (EE-35-95), Courier's Desk, Internal Revenue Service, 1111 Constitution Avenue, NW., Washington, DC.

FOR FURTHER INFORMATION CONTACT: Concerning the regulations, Janet A. Laufer, (202) 622-4606, concerning submissions, Michael Slaughter, (202) 622-7190 (not toll-free numbers).

SUPPLEMENTARY INFORMATION:

Background

This document contains proposed amendments to regulations containing rules for computing an employee's accrued benefit derived from the employee's contributions to a qualified defined benefit pension plan. The proposed amendments reflect changes made to section 411(c)(2) by the Omnibus Budget Reconciliation Act of 1987, Public Law 100-203 (OBRA `87), and the Omnibus Budget Reconciliation Act of 1989, Public Law 101-239 (OBRA '89). OBRA `87 and OBRA `89 changed the interest rates used to accumulate an employee's contributions to normal retirement age. OBRA `89 also changed the manner in which the accumulated contributions are converted to an annual benefit payable at normal retirement age, and removed a limitation on the employee-derived accrued benefit contained in prior law.

Section 411(c)(1) provides that an employee's accrued benefit derived from employer contributions as of any applicable date is the excess, if any, of the accrued benefit for the employee as of that date over the accrued benefit derived from contributions made by the employee as of that date. Section 411(c)(2)(B) provides that in the case of a defined benefit plan, the accrued benefit derived from contributions made by an employee as of any applicable date is the amount equal to the employee's contributions accumulated to normal retirement age using the interest rate(s) specified in section 411(c)(2)(C), expressed as an actuarially equivalent annual benefit commencing at normal retirement age using an interest rate which would be used by the plan under section 417(e)(3), as of the determination date. If the employee-derived accrued benefit is determined with respect to a benefit other than an annual benefit in the form of a single life annuity (without ancillary benefits) commencing at normal retirement age, section 411(c)(3) requires that the employee-derived accrued benefit be the actuarial equivalent of the benefit determined under section 411(c)(2).

Under section 411(c)(2)(C)(iii)(I), effective for plan years beginning after December 31, 1987, the interest rate used to accumulate an employee's contributions until the determination date is 120 percent of the Federal mid-term rate under section 1274 of the Internal Revenue Code (Code). For the period between the determination date and normal retirement age, section 411(c)(2)(C)(iii)(II) provides that the interest rate used to accumulate an employee's contributions is the interest rate which would be used under the plan under section 417(e)(3) as of the determination date. As noted above, section 411(c)(2)(B) provides that the interest rate which would be used under the plan under section 417(e)(3) as of the determination date also applies for purposes of converting the accumulated contributions to an annual benefit commencing at normal retirement age. The Retirement Protection Act of 1994, Public Law 103-465 (RPA `94) amended section 417(e) to change the applicable interest rate under section 417(e)(3) and to specify the applicable mortality table under that section. Examples contained in § 1.411(c)-1(c)(6) of these proposed regulations reflect a plan that has been amended to comply with the interest rate and mortality table specifications enacted in RPA '94.

Explanation of Provisions

1. *Conversion calculation*

Prior to OBRA `89, section 411(c)(2)(B) specified that the conversion factor to be used for purposes of computing the employee-derived accrued benefit was 10 percent for a straight life annuity commencing at normal retirement age of 65 (i.e., multiply the accumulated contributions by .10), and that for other normal retirement ages the conversion factor was to be determined in accordance with regulations prescribed by the Secretary. Section 1.411(c)-1(c)(2) of the existing regulations provides that for normal retirement ages other than age 65, the conversion factor shall be the factor as determined by the Commissioner.

Rev. Rul. 76-47 (1976-1 C.B. 109) sets forth in tabular form the conversion factors to be used for determining the accrued benefit derived from employee contributions when the normal retirement age under the plan is other than age 65 or when the normal form of benefit is other than a single life annuity (without ancillary benefits). Rev. Rul. 76-47 further provides that where no standard factor is available, a conversion factor must be determined using an interest rate of 5 percent and the UP-1984 mortality table (without age setback).

OBRA `89 deleted the ten percent conversion factor in section 411(c)(2)(B) and replaced it with the requirement that the accumulated contributions at normal retirement age be expressed as an annual benefit commencing at normal retirement age using an interest rate which would be used under the plan under section 417(e)(3) (as of the determination date). This change was effective retroactively to the effective date of the OBRA '87 provision relating to section 411(c)(2)(C) (the first day of the first plan year beginning after December 31, 1987).

To reflect the OBRA `89 amendments, these proposed regulations define *appropriate conversion factor* with respect to an accrued benefit expressed in the form of an annual benefit that is nondecreasing for the life of the participant as the present value of an annuity in the form of that annual benefit commencing at normal retirement age at a rate of $1 per year. This amount is to be computed using the interest rate and mortality table which would be used under the plan under section 417(e)(3) and § 1.417(e)-1T. To reflect the post-OBRA '89 conversion factor definition and to conform to common actuarial practice, these proposed regulations would change the *multiplied by* language in § 1.411(c)-1(c)(1) to *divided by*.

2. *Accumulated contributions*

As added by the Employee Retirement Income Security Act of 1974 (ERISA), section 411(c)(2)(C) provided that employee contributions were to be accumulated using a standard interest rate of 5 percent for years beginning on or after the effective date of that section. OBRA `87 changed the interest rate under section 411(c)(2)(C) to 120 percent of the applicable Federal mid-term rate under section 1274 for plan years after 1987. OBRA '89 again amended section 411(c)(2)(C) to provide that 120 percent of the applicable Federal mid-term rate under section 1274 is to be used for accumulating contributions only up to the *determination date*. For the period from the determination date to normal retirement age, the interest rate which would be used under the plan under section 417(e)(3) (as of the determination date) must be used for accumulating contributions for the period from the determination date to normal retirement age. Accordingly, these proposed regulations would amend paragraph (3) of § 1.411(c)-1(c) to reflect those rates. As stated above, RPA '94 amended section 417(e)(3) to change the applicable interest rate. See § 1.417(e)-1T.

3. *Determination date*

Section 1.411(c)-1(c)(5)(i) defines the term determination date for purposes of section 411(c)(2)(C)(iii), in a case in which a participant will receive his or her entire accrued benefit derived from employee contributions in any one of the following forms (described in paragraph (c)(5)(ii)): an annuity that is substantially nonincreasing, substantially nonincreasing installment payments for a fixed number of years, or a single sum distribution. In such a case, the term determination date means the date on which distribution of such benefit commences. For this purpose, an annuity that is nonincreasing except for automatic increases to reflect increases in the consumer price index is considered to be an annuity that is substantially nonincreasing.

Thus, for example, for purposes of section 411(c)(2)(C)(iii), in the case of a distribution of the employee's entire accrued benefit (or the employee's entire employee-derived accrued benefit) in the form of a nonincreasing single life annuity payable commencing either at normal retirement age or at early retirement age, the determination date is the date the annuity commences. Similarly, in the case of a single sum distribution of accumulated employee contributions (i.e., employee contributions plus interest computed at or above the section 411(c) required rates) upon termination of employment with a deferred annuity benefit derived solely from employer contributions, the determination date is the date of distribution of the single sum of accumulated employee contributions.

Alternatively, the plan may provide that the determination date is the annuity starting date, as defined in § 1.401(a)-20, Q&A-10.

Under § 1.411(c)-1(c)(5)(iii) of these regulations, where a participant will receive a distribution that is not described in paragraph (c)(5)(i), the determination date will be as provided by the Commissioner.

4. *Elimination of limitation on employee-derived accrued benefit*

Prior to OBRA `89, section 411(c)(2)(E) of the Code limited the accrued benefit derived from employee contributions to the greater of (1) the employee's accrued benefit under the plan, or (2) the sum of the employee's mandatory contributions, without interest. Section 7881(m)(1)(C) of OBRA `89 deleted that provision. Section 7881(m)(1)(D) of OBRA '89 added section 411(a)(7)(D) to the Code, which provides that the accrued benefit of an employee shall not be less than the amount determined under section 411(c)(2)(B) with respect to the employee's accumulated contributions. Accordingly, these proposed regulations delete the rule included in § 1.411(c)-1(d) of the existing regulations, which reflects the pre-OBRA `89 rule.

5. *Delegation of authority*

Section 1.411(c)-1(d) of these proposed regulations provides that the Commissioner may prescribe additional guidance on calculating the accrued benefit derived from employer or employee contributions under a defined benefit plan.

Effective Date

These amendments are proposed to be effective for plan years beginning on or after January 1, 1997. For example, assume that under a plan the employee's date of termination of employment is treated as the determination date, and distribution of the employee's entire employee-derived accrued benefit (as determined under the terms of the plan then in effect) occurs or commences prior to the first day of the plan year beginning in 1997. In that case, with respect to interest credits under section 411(c)(2)(C)(iii) for plan years beginning after 1987, the Service will not treat the plan as having failed to satisfy the requirements of section 411(c), nor will it require that additional amounts be credited in the calculation of the employee-derived accrued benefit in order to satisfy the requirements of section 411(c) after final regulations become effective, merely because the date the employee's employment terminated was treated as the determination date, provided that interest is credited in accordance with section 411(c)(2)(C)(iii)(I) for the period before the date the employee terminated employment and in accordance with section 411(c)(2)(C)(iii)(II) thereafter.

Once amendments to the regulations under § 1.411(c)-1 are adopted in final form, the Service will obsolete or modify Rev. Rul. 76-47, Rev. Rul. 78-202 (1978-2 C.B. 124) and Rev. Rul. 89-60 (1989-1 C.B. 113) as necessary or appropriate.

Taxpayers may rely on these proposed regulations for guidance pending the issuance of final regulations.

Special Analyses

It has been determined that this notice of proposed rulemaking is not a significant regulatory action as defined in EO 12866. Therefore, a regulatory assessment is not required. It also has been determined that section 553(b) of the Administrative Procedure Act (5 U.S.C. chapter 5) and the Regulatory Flexibility Act (5 U.S.C. chapter 6) do not apply to these regulations, and, therefore, a Regulatory Flexibility Analysis is not required. Pursuant to section 7805(f) of the Internal Revenue Code, this notice of proposed rulemaking will be submitted to the Chief Counsel for Advocacy of the Small Business Administration for comment on its impact on small business.

Comments and Requests for a Public Hearing

Before these proposed regulations are adopted as final regulations, consideration will be given to any written comments (a signed original and eight (8) copies) that are submitted timely to the IRS. All comments will be available for public inspection and copying. A public hearing may be scheduled if requested in writing by a person that timely submits written comments. If a public hearing is scheduled, notice of the date, time, and place for the hearing will be published in the Federal Register.

Drafting Information

The principal author of these regulations is Janet A. Laufer, Office of the Associate Chief Counsel (Employee Benefits and Exempt Organizations). However, other personnel from the IRS and Treasury Department participated in their development.

[¶ 49,152] Proposed Amendments of Regulations (INTL-0054-95), published in the Federal Register on March 8, 1996.

Foreign corporations: Determination of interest expense deduction: Branch profits tax.—Amendments of Reg. §§ 1.882-5 and 1.884-1, relating to the determination of the interest expense deduction of foreign corporations and the branch profits tax, are proposed. A public hearing on this proposal is scheduled for June 6, 1996.

AGENCY: Internal Revenue Service (IRS), Treasury.

ACTION: Notice of proposed rulemaking and notice of public hearing.

SUMMARY: This document contains proposed Income Tax Regulations relating to the determination of the interest expense deduction of foreign corporations under section 882 and the branch profits tax under section 884 of the Internal Revenue Code of 1986. These proposed regulations are necessary to provide guidance that coordinates with guidance provided in final regulations under sections 882 and 884 published elsewhere in this issue of the Federal Register. These regulations will affect foreign corporations engaged in a U.S. trade or business. This document also provides notice of a public hearing on these proposed regulations.

DATES: Written comments must be received by June 6, 1996. Outlines of topics to be discussed at the public hearing scheduled for Thursday, June 6, 1996, at 10:00 a.m. must be received by May 23, 1996.

ADDRESSES: Send submissions to: CC:DOM:CORP:R (INTL-0054-95), room 5228, Internal Revenue Service, POB 7604, Ben Franklin Station, Washington DC 20044. In the alternative, submissions may be hand delivered between the hours of 8 a.m. and 5 p.m. to CC:DOM:CORP:R (INTL-0054-95), Courier's Desk, Internal Revenue Service, 1111 Constitution Avenue NW., Washington DC. The public hearing will be held in the Auditorium, Internal Revenue Building, 1111 Constitution Avenue NW., Washington DC.

FOR FURTHER INFORMATION CONTACT: Concerning the regulations, Ahmad Pirasteh or Richard Hoge, (202) 622-3870; and the hearing, Michael Slaughter (202) 622-7190 (not toll-free numbers).

SUPPLEMENTARY INFORMATION:

Background

This document contains proposed regulations amending the Income Tax Regulations (26 CFR Part 1) under sections 882 and 884 of the Internal Revenue Code. In final regulations under sections 882 and 884, published elsewhere in this issue of the Federal Register, various sections were reserved. These proposed regulations would provide guidance under those reserved sections, as well as amend other sections, to coordinate with the final regulations.

Explanation of the Provisions

I. *Financial products.*

The proposed regulations include several provisions that take into account recent developments in the tax treatment of financial instruments, such as the enactment of section 475, the development of hedging rules and the introduction of profit split methodologies in global trading Advance Pricing Agreements. The IRS and Treasury intend to issue regulations under section 864 that will address these recent developments as they affect the determination of a foreign corporation's effectively connected income. Comments are solicited on these proposed regulations as they relate to financial products and on their interaction with the determination of effectively connected income.

A. *"Split asset" rule for section 475 securities and section 1256 contracts.* Currently § 1.884-1(d)(2)(vii) provides a "split asset" rule for certain securities described in § 1.864-4(c)(5)(ii)(*b*)(*3*) that produce income only a portion of which is treated as effectively connected with the conduct of a U.S. trade or business. Since other securities may also produce income split between effectively connected and non-effectively connected income, the rule has been broadened to cover all financial instruments that meet the definition of a security under section 475(c)(2), as well as section 1256 contracts, that may produce such split income. Accordingly, a foreign corporation that, under an Advance Pricing Agreement, is permitted to apply a "profit split" methodology to determine the portion of its income from a portfolio of securities that is effectively connected with the conduct of a U.S. trade or business would apply this rule. This rule will also apply to determine the portion of a foreign corporation's portfolio of securities that is a U.S. asset for purposes of § 1.882-5.

B. *Hedging transactions.* Proposed § 1.884-1(c)(2)(ii) introduces a new rule for hedging transactions for purposes of section 884. The new rule requires that a taxpayer increase or decrease, as the case may be, the amount of its U.S. assets by the amount of any gain or loss on any transaction that hedges the U.S. assets. If the hedging transaction is undertaken outside the United States, perhaps as part of a global hedging strategy of the foreign corporation, then the hedging transaction is only taken into account to the extent that income from the transaction would be treated as income effectively connected with the U.S. trade or business of the taxpayer. If, however, the hedging transaction is entered into by the U.S. branch, it will only affect the amount of U.S. assets if it is contemporaneously identified as a hedging transaction in accordance with the provisions of § 1.1221-2.

In response to comments, hedging rules also have been added to the interest allocation rules of § 1.882-5. These rules provide that a transaction that hedges a U.S. booked liability will be taken into account in determining the amount, currency denomination, and interest rate associated with that liability for purposes of performing the second and third steps of the interest expense calculation.

C. *Securities marked-to-market.* Section 1.884-1(d)(6), which provides "E&P basis" rules for specific types of U.S. assets, has been clarified to provide rules for securities subject to mark-to-market accounting. The new provision in § 1.884-1(d)(6)(v) specifies that securities subject to section 475, as well as section 1256 contracts, have an E&P basis equal to their mark-to-market value as of the determination date. Proposed § 1.882-5(b)(2)(iv) provides a basis adjustment rule under which such assets are treated as having been marked-to-market on each determination date. Examples are contained in the proposed regulations that illustrate the effect of these rules on the calculation of worldwide assets and liabilities.

II. *Transactions between partners and partnerships.*

Example 4 in proposed § 1.882-5(c)(5) would clarify that an obligation of a partnership to make payments to its partner for the use of capital, which gives rise to guaranteed payments under section 707(c), is not a liability for purposes of § 1.882-5. The Service and Treasury solicit comments on the treatment of loans between partners and partnerships as part of Treasury's review of the international tax aspects of pass-through entities.

Special Analyses

It has been determined that this notice of proposed rulemaking is not a significant regulatory action as defined in EO 12866. Therefore, a regulatory assessment is not required. It has also been determined that section 553(b) of the Administrative Procedures Act (5 U.S.C. chapter 5) and the Regulatory Flexibility Act (5 U.S.C. chapter 6) do not apply to these regulations, and, therefore, a Regulatory Flexibility Analysis is not required. Pursuant to section 7805(f) of the Internal Revenue Code, this notice of proposed rulemaking will be submitted to the Chief Counsel for Advocacy of the Small Business Administration for comment on its impact on small business.

Comments and Request for a Public Hearing

Before these proposed regulations are adopted as final regulations, consideration will be given to any written comments (signed original and eight (8) copies) that are timely submitted to the IRS. All comments will be available for public inspection and copying.

A public hearing has been scheduled for Thursday, June 6, 1996, at 10:00 a.m. in the Auditorium, Internal Revenue Building, 1111 Constitution Avenue NW., Washington, DC. Because of access restrictions, visitors will not be admitted beyond the building lobby more than 15 minutes before the hearing starts.

The rules of 26 CFR 601.601(a)(3) apply to the hearing. Persons that wish to present oral comments at the hearing must submit written comments by June 6, 1996, and submit an outline of topics to be discussed and time to be devoted to each topic (signed original and eight (8) copies) by May 23, 1996.

A period of 10 minutes will be allotted to each person for making comments.

An agenda showing the scheduling of the speakers will be prepared after the deadline for receiving outlines has passed. Copies of the agenda will be available free of charge at the hearing.

Drafting Information

Several persons from the Office of Chief Counsel and the Treasury Department participated in drafting these regulations.

[¶ 49,154] Proposed Regulations and Proposed Amendments of Regulations (REG-209826-96), published in the Federal Register on September 27, 1996.

Trusts: Nonexempt employees': Grantor trust rules: Application of.—Reg. § 1.1297-4 and amendments of Reg. §§ 1.671-1 and 1.671-2, relating to the application of the grantor trust rules to nonexempt employees' trusts, are proposed. A public hearing on this proposal is scheduled for January 15, 1997.

AGENCY: Internal Revenue Service (IRS), Treasury.

ACTION: Notice of proposed rulemaking and notice of public hearing.

SUMMARY: This document contains proposed regulations relating to the application of the grantor trust rules to nonexempt employees' trusts. The proposed regulations clarify that the grantor trust rules generally do not apply to domestic nonexempt employees' trusts, and clarify the interaction between the grantor trust rules, the rules generally governing the taxation of nonqualified deferred compensation arrangements, and the antideferral rules for United States persons holding interests in foreign entities. The proposed regulations affect nonexempt employees' trusts funding deferred compensation arrangements, as well as U.S. persons holding interests in certain foreign corporations and foreign partnerships with deferred compensation arrangements funded through foreign nonexempt employees' trusts. In addition, the proposed regulations affect U.S. persons that have deferred compensation arrangements funded through certain foreign nonexempt employees' trusts. This document also provides notice of a public hearing on these proposed regulations.

DATES: Written comments must be received by December 26, 1996. Requests to speak (with outlines of oral comments to be discussed) at the public hearing scheduled for January 15, 1997, at 10:00 a.m. must be submitted by December 24, 1996.

ADDRESSES: Send submissions to: CC:DOM:CORP:R (REG-209826-96), room 5226, Internal Revenue Service, POB 7604, Ben Franklin Station, Washington, DC 20044. Submissions may be hand delivered between the hours of 8 a.m. and 5 p.m. to: CC:DOM:CORP:R (REG-209826-96), Courier's Desk, Internal Revenue Service, 1111 Constitution Avenue, NW., Washington, DC. The public hearing will be held in room 2615, Internal Revenue Building, 1111 Constitution Avenue, NW., Washington, DC. Alternatively, taxpayers may submit comments electronically via the Internet by selecting the "Tax Regs" option on the IRS Home Page, or by submitting comments directly to the IRS Internet site at http://www.irs.ustreas.gov/prod/tax>regs/comments.html.

FOR FURTHER INFORMATION CONTACT: Concerning the regulations, James A. Quinn, (202) 622-3060; Linda S. F. Marshall, (202) 622-6030; Kristine K. Schlaman (202) 622-3840; and M. Grace Fleeman (202) 622-3850; concerning submissions and the hearing, Michael Slaughter, (202) 622-7190 (not toll-free numbers).

SUPPLEMENTARY INFORMATION:

Paperwork Reduction Act

The collection of information contained in this notice of proposed rulemaking has been submitted to the Office of Management and Budget for review in accordance with the Paperwork Reduction Act of 1995 (44 U.S.C. 3507(d)). Comments on the collection of information should be sent to the Office of Management and Budget, Attn: Desk Officer for the Department of the Treasury, Office of Information and Regulatory Affairs, Washington, DC 20503, with copies to the Internal Revenue Service, Attn: IRS Reports Clearance Officer, T:FP, Washington, DC 20224. Comments on the collection of information should be received by November 26, 1996. Comments are specifically requested concerning:

Whether the proposed collection of information is necessary for the proper performance of the functions of the Internal Revenue Service, including whether the information will have practical utility;

The accuracy of the estimated burden associated with the proposed collection of information (see below);

How the quality, utility, and clarity of the information to be collected may be enhanced;

How the burden of complying with the proposed collection of information may be minimized, including through the application of automated collection techniques or other forms of information technology; and

Estimates of capital or start-up costs and costs of operation, maintenance, and purchase of services to provide information.

The collection of information in this proposed regulation is in § 1.671-1(h)(3)(iii). This information is required by the IRS to determine accurately the portion of certain foreign employees' trusts properly treated as owned by the employer. This information will be used to notify the Commissioner that certain entities are relying on an exception for reasonable funding. The collection of information is mandatory. The likely respondents are businesses or other for-profit organizations.

Estimated total annual reporting burden: 1,000 hours.

The estimated annual burden per respondent varies from .5 hours to 1.5 hours, depending on individual circumstances, with an estimated average of 1 hour.

Estimated number of respondents: 1,000.

Estimated annual frequency of responses: On occasion.

An agency may not conduct or sponsor, and a person is not required to respond to, a collection of information unless the collection of information displays a valid control number assigned by the Office of Management and Budget.

Books or records relating to a collection of information must be retained as long as their contents may become material in the administration of any internal revenue law. Generally, tax returns and tax return information are confidential, as required by 26 U.S.C. 6103.

Background

On May 7, 1993, the IRS issued proposed regulations under section 404A (58 FR 27219). The section 404A proposed regulations provide that section 404A is the exclusive means by which an employer may take a deduction or reduce earnings and profits for amounts used to fund deferred compensation in situations other than those in which a deduction or reduction of earnings and profits is permitted under section 404 (the "exclusive means" rule).

The section 404A proposed regulations do not provide rules regarding the treatment of income and ownership of assets of foreign trusts established to fund deferred compensation arrangements, but refer to "other applicable provisions," including the grantor trust rules of subpart E of the Internal Revenue Code of 1986, as amended. Thus, the 1993 proposed section 404A regulations imply that, if an employer cannot or does not elect section 404A treatment for a foreign trust established to fund the employer's deferred compensation arrangements, the employer may be treated as the owner of the entire trust for purposes of subtitle A of the Code under sections 671 through 679 even though all or part of the trust assets are set aside for purposes of satisfying liabilities under the plan. Conversely, some commentators believe that, for U.S. tax purposes, a foreign employer would not be treated as the owner of any portion of a foreign trust established to fund a section 404A qualified foreign plan even though all or part of the trust assets might be used for purposes other than satisfying liabilities under the plan. A number of different rules, in addition to the grantor trust rules, potentially affect the taxation of foreign trusts established to fund deferred compensation arrangements. These rules include: the nonexempt deferred compensation trust rules of sections 402(b) and 404(a)(5); the partnership rules of subchapter K; and the antideferral rules, which include subpart F and the passive foreign investment company (PFIC) rules (sections 1291 through 1297).

Following publication of the proposed 1993 regulations and enactment of section 956A in August of 1993, comments were received concerning both the asset ownership rules for foreign employees' trusts and the "exclusive means" rule for deductions or reductions in earnings and profits. These proposed regulations address only comments concerning income and asset ownership rules for foreign employees' trusts for federal income tax purposes. A foreign employees' trust is a nonexempt employees' trust described in section 402(b) that is part of a deferred compensation plan, and that is a foreign trust within the meaning of section 7701(a)(31). Comments concerning the "exclusive means" rule will be addressed in future regulations.

Statutory Background

1. Transfers of Property Not Complete for Tax Purposes

In certain situations, assets that are owned by a trust as a legal matter may be treated as owned by another person for tax purposes. Thus, assets may be treated as owned by a pension trust for non-tax legal purposes but not for tax purposes. This occurs, for example, if the person who has purportedly transferred assets to the trust retains the benefits and burdens of ownership. *See, e.g., Frank Lyon Co. v. United States*, 435 U.S. 561 (1978); *Corliss v. Bowers*, 281 U.S. 376 (1930); *Grodt & McKay Realty, Inc. v. Commissioner*, 77 T.C. 1221 (1981); Rev. Proc. 75-21 (1975-1 C.B. 715). If, under these principles, no assets have been transferred to an employees' trust for federal tax purposes, these proposed regulations do not apply.

2. Subpart E—Grantors and others treated as substantial owners

Even if there has been a completed transfer of trust assets, the subpart E rules may apply to treat the grantor as the owner of a portion of the trust for federal income tax purposes. Subpart E of part I of subchapter J, chapter 1 of the Code (sections 671 through 679) taxes income of a trust to the grantor or another person notwithstanding that the grantor or other person may not be a beneficiary of the trust. Under section 671, a grantor or another person includes in computing taxable income and credits those items of income, deduction, and credit against tax that are attributable to or included in any portion of a trust of which that person is treated as the owner.

Sections 673 through 679 set forth the rules for determining when the grantor or another person is treated as the owner of a portion of a trust for federal income tax purposes. Under sections 673 through 678, the grantor trust rules apply only if the grantor or other person has certain powers or interests. For example, section 676 provides that the grantor is treated as the owner of a portion of a trust where, at any time, the power to revest in the grantor title to that portion is exercisable by the grantor or a nonadverse party, or both. A grantor who is the owner of a trust under subpart E is treated as the owner of the trust property for federal income tax purposes. See Rev. Rul. 85-13 (1985-1 C.B. 184). This document is made available by the Superintendent of Documents, U.S. Government Printing Office, Washington, DC 20402.

Section 679 generally applies to a U.S. person who directly or indirectly transfers property to a foreign trust, subject to certain exceptions described below. Section 679 generally treats a U.S. person transferring property to a foreign trust as the owner of the portion of the trust attributable to the transferred property for any taxable year of that person for which there is a U.S. beneficiary of any portion of the trust. In general, a trust is treated as having a U.S. beneficiary for a taxable year of the U.S. transferor unless, under the terms of the trust, no part of the income or corpus of the trust may be paid or accumulated during the taxable year to or for the benefit of a U.S. person, and unless no part of the income or corpus of the trust could be paid to or for the benefit of a U.S. person if the trust were terminated at any time during the taxable year. A U.S. person is treated as having made an indirect transfer to the foreign trust of property if a non-U.S. person acts as a conduit with respect to the transfer or if the U.S. person has sufficient control over the non-U.S. person to direct the transfer by the non-U.S. person rather than itself.

Section 679(a) provides several exceptions from the application of section 679 for certain compensatory trusts. Under these exceptions, section 679 does not apply to a trust described in section 404(a)(4) or section 404A. Pursuant to amendments made in section 1903(b) of the Small Business Job Protection Act of 1996 (SBJPA), section 679 also does not apply to any transfer of property after February 6, 1995, to a trust described in section 402(b).

3. Taxability of beneficiary of nonexempt employees' trust

Section 402(b) provides rules for the taxability of beneficiaries of a nonexempt employees' trust. Under section 402(b)(1), employer contributions to a nonexempt employees' trust generally are included in the gross income of the employee in accordance with section 83. Section 402(b)(2) provides that amounts distributed or made available from a nonexempt employees' trust generally are taxable to the distributee under the rules of section 72 in the taxable year in which distributed or made available. Section 402(b)(4) provides that, under certain circumstances, a highly compensated employee is taxed each year on the employee's vested accrued benefit (other than the employee's investment in the contract) in a nonexempt employees' trust. Under section 402(b)(3), a beneficiary of a nonexempt employees' trust generally is not treated as the owner of any portion of the trust under subpart E. The rules of section 402(b) apply to a beneficiary of a nonexempt employees' trust regardless of whether the trust is a domestic trust or a foreign trust.

4. Employer deduction for contributions to a nonexempt employees' trust

Section 404(a)(5) provides rules regarding the deductibility of contributions to a nonqualified deferred compensation plan. Under section 404(a)(5), any contribution paid by an employer under a deferred compensation plan, if otherwise deductible under chapter 1 of the Code, is deductible only in the taxable year in which an amount attributable to the contribution is includible in the gross income of employees participating in the plan, and only if separate accounts are maintained for each employee. Section 1.404(a)-12(b)(1) clarifies that an employer's deduction for contributions to a nonexempt employees' trust is restricted to the amount of the contribution, and excludes any income received by the trust with respect to contributed amounts.

5. The partnership rules of subchapter K

A partnership is not subject to income taxation. However, a partner must take into account separately on its return its distributive share of the partnership's income, gain, loss, deduction, or credit. A U.S. partner of a foreign partnership is subject to U.S. tax on its distributive share of partnership income. In addition, a foreign partnership may have a controlled foreign corporation (CFC) partner which must take into account its distributive share of partnership income, gain, loss, or deduction in determining its taxable income. These distributive share inclusions of the CFC may result in subpart F income and thus income to a U.S. shareholder of the CFC. If the grantor trust rules do not apply to any portion of a foreign employees' trust, a foreign partnership could fund a foreign employees' trust in excess of the amount needed to meet its obligations to its employees under its deferred compensation plan and yet retain control over the excess amount. As a result, the foreign partnership would not have to include items in taxable income attributable to the excess amount, and consequently the U.S. partner or CFC would not have to include those items in its income.

6. The antideferral rules of subpart F, including section 956A, and PFIC

A U.S. person that owns stock in a foreign corporation generally pays no U.S. tax currently on income earned by the foreign corporation. Instead, the United States defers taxation of that income until it is distributed to the U.S. person. The antideferral rules, however, which include subpart F and the PFIC rules, limit this deferral in certain situations.

Subpart F of part III of Subchapter N (sections 951 through 964) applies to CFCs. A foreign corporation is a CFC if more than 50 percent of the total voting power of all classes of stock entitled to vote, or the total value of the stock in the corporation, is owned by "U.S. shareholders" (defined as U.S. persons who own ten percent or more of the voting power of all classes of stock entitled to vote) on any day during the foreign corporation's taxable year. The United States generally taxes U.S. shareholders of the CFC currently on their pro rata share of the CFC's subpart F income and sections 956 and 956A amounts. In effect, the U.S. shareholders are treated as having received a distribution out of the earnings and profits (E&P) of the CFC.

The types of income earned by a foreign employees' trust (dividends, interest, income equivalent to interest, rents and royalties, and annuities) are generally subpart F income. The inclusion under section 956 is based on the CFC's investment in U.S. property, which generally includes stock of a U.S. shareholder of the CFC. A U.S. shareholder's section 956A amount for a taxable year is the lesser of two amounts. The first amount is the excess of the U.S. shareholder's pro rata share of the CFC's "excess passive assets" over the portion of the CFC's E&P treated as previously included in gross income by the U.S. shareholder under section 956A. For purposes of section 956A, "passive asset" includes any asset which produces (or is held for the production of) passive income, and generally includes property that produces dividends, interest, income equivalent to interest, rents and royalties, and annuities, subject to exceptions that generally are not relevant in this context. The second amount is the U.S. shareholder's pro rata share of the CFC's "applicable earnings" to the extent accumulated in taxable years beginning after September 30, 1993.

Section 1501(a)(2) of SBJPA repeals section 956A. The repeal is effective for taxable years of foreign corporations beginning after December 31, 1996, and for taxable years of U.S. shareholders with or within which such taxable years of foreign corporations end.

If a CFC employer is not treated for federal income tax purposes as the owner of any portion of a foreign employees' trust under the grantor trust rules, then to the extent that passive assets contributed by a CFC to a nonexempt employees' trust would otherwise result in subpart F consequences for the CFC and its shareholders, the CFC's contribution could allow those consequences to be avoided. For example, a contribution by a CFC of passive assets to its foreign employees' trust could reduce the CFC's subpart F earnings and profits, and its applicable earnings or passive assets for section 956A purposes, and could affect the CFC's increase in investment in U.S. property for purposes of section 956, all of which could affect a U.S. shareholder's pro rata subpart F inclusions for the taxable year.

In contrast to the subpart F rules, the PFIC rules apply to any U.S. person who directly or indirectly owns any stock in a foreign corporation that is a PFIC under either an income or asset test. A foreign corporation, including a CFC, is a PFIC if either (1) 75 percent or more of its gross income for the taxable year is passive income or (2) at least 50 percent of the value of the corporation's assets produce passive income or are held for the production of passive income. For this purpose, passive income generally is the same type of income (dividends, interest, income equivalent to interest, rents and royalties, and annuities) that would be earned by a foreign employees' trust.

Under the PFIC rules, a U.S. person who is a direct or indirect shareholder of a PFIC is subject to a special tax regime upon either disposition of the PFIC's stock or receipt of certain distributions (excess distributions) from the PFIC. A shareholder, however, may avoid the application of this special regime by electing to include its pro rata share of certain of the PFIC's passive income in the year in which the foreign corporation earns it.

If the grantor trust rules did not apply to any portion of a foreign employees' trust, a contribution by a foreign corporation of passive assets to a nonexempt employees' trust would enable a U.S. person to avoid the PFIC rules if those assets would otherwise generate PFIC consequences for the foreign corporation and its shareholders. For example, by transferring passive assets to its nonexempt employees' trust in excess of the amount needed to meet obligations to its employees under its deferred compensation plan while retaining control over the excess amount, a foreign corporation could divest itself of a sufficient amount of passive assets and the passive income they produce to avoid meeting the income and asset tests. Furthermore, a foreign corporation that is a PFIC could minimize income inclusions for a U.S. shareholder that has made an election to include PFIC income currently by transferring income-producing assets to a foreign employees' trust.

Overview of proposed regulations

Under the proposed regulations, an employer is not treated as an owner of any portion of a domestic nonexempt employees' trust described in section 402(b) for federal income tax purposes. Section 404(a)(5) and § 1.404(a)-12(b) provide a deduction to the employer solely for contributions to a nonexempt employees' trust, and not for any income of the trust. This rule is inconsistent with treating the employer as owning any portion of a nonexempt employees' trust, which would require the employer to recognize the trust's income that it may not deduct under section 404(a)(5). Accordingly, such a trust is treated as a separate taxable trust that is taxed under the rules of section 641 et seq. The rule in the proposed regulations is consistent with the holdings of a number of private letter rulings with respect to nonexempt employees' trusts and with the Service's treatment of trusts that no longer qualify as exempt under 501(a) (because they are no longer described in section 401(a)) as separate taxable trusts rather than as grantor trusts. See also Rev. Rul. 74-299 (1974-1 C.B. 154). This document is made available by the Superintendent of Documents, U.S. Government Printing Office, Washington, DC 20402.

Under the proposed regulations, an employer generally is not treated as the owner of any portion of a foreign nonexempt employees' trust for federal income tax purposes, except as provided under section 679. The proposed regulations, however, also provide that the grantor trust rules apply to determine whether an employer that is a CFC or a U.S. employer is treated as the owner of a specified "fractional interest" in a foreign employees' trust. This rule applies whether or not the employer elects section 404A treatment for the trust. Under the proposed regulations, this rule also applies in the case of an employer that is a foreign partnership with one or more partners that are U.S. persons or CFCs (U.S.- related partnership). Such an employer is treated as the owner of a portion of a foreign employees' trust under these proposed regulations only if the employer retains a grantor trust power or interest over a foreign employees' trust and has a specified "fractional interest" in the trust.

Under these proposed regulations, the grantor trust rules of subpart E do not apply to a foreign employees' trust with respect to a foreign employer other than a CFC or a U.S.-related foreign partnership, except for cases in which assets are transferred to a foreign employees' trust with a principal purpose of avoiding the PFIC rules. The IRS and Treasury will continue to consider whether these regulations should provide additional antiabuse rules that may be necessary for other purposes, including for purposes of calculating earnings and profits, determining the foreign tax credit limitation, and applying the interest allocation rules of § 1.882-5.

Explanation of provisions

1. § 1.671-1(g): Domestic nonexempt employees' trusts

The proposed regulations provide that an employer is not treated for federal income tax purposes as an owner of any portion of a nonexempt employees' trust described in section 402(b) that is part of a deferred compensation plan, and that is not a foreign trust within the meaning of section 7701(a)(31), regardless of whether the employer has a power or interest described in sections 673 through 677 over any portion of the trust. This rule is analogous to the rule set forth in § 1.641(a)-0, which provides that subchapter J, including the grantor trust rules, does not apply to tax-exempt employees' trusts.

2. § 1.671-1(h): Subpart E rules for certain foreign employees' trusts

The proposed regulations provide Subpart E rules for foreign employees' trusts of CFCs, foreign partnerships, and U.S. employers that apply for all federal income tax purposes. Under the proposed regulations, except as provided under section 679 or the proposed regulations (as described below), an employer is not treated as an owner of any portion of a foreign employees' trust for federal income tax purposes. If an employer is treated as the owner of a portion of a foreign employees' trust for federal income tax purposes as described below, then the employer is considered to own the trust assets attributable to that portion of the trust for all federal income tax purposes. Thus, for example, if an employer is treated as the owner of a portion of a foreign employees' trust for federal income tax purposes as described below, then income of the trust that is attributable to that portion of the trust increases the employer's earnings and profits for purposes of sections 312 and 964.

A foreign employees' trust is a nonexempt employees' trust described in section 402(b) that is part of a deferred compensation plan, and that is a foreign trust within the meaning of section 7701(a)(31). The proposed regulations apply to any foreign employees' trust of a CFC or U.S.-related foreign partnership, whether or not a trust funds a qualified foreign plan (as defined in section 404A(e)). The proposed regulations clarify that the income inclusion and asset ownership rules apply to the entity whose employees or independent contractors are covered under the deferred compensation plan.

A. Plan of CFC employer

The proposed regulations provide that, if a CFC maintains a deferred compensation plan funded through a foreign employees' trust, then, with respect to the CFC, the provisions of subpart E apply to the portion of the trust that is the fractional interest of the trust described in the proposed regulations.

B. Plan of U.S. employer

The proposed regulations provide that if a U.S. person maintains a deferred compensation plan funded through a foreign employees' trust, then, with respect to the U.S. person, the provisions of subpart E apply to the portion of the trust that is the fractional interest of the trust described in the proposed regulations.

C. Plan of U.S.-related foreign partnership employer

The proposed regulations provide that, if a U.S.-related foreign partnership maintains a deferred compensation plan funded through a foreign employees' trust, then, with respect to the U.S.-related foreign partnership, the provisions of subpart E apply to the portion of the trust that is the fractional interest of the trust described in the proposed regulations. The IRS and Treasury solicit comments on whether these regulations should provide a safe harbor rule for a U.S.-related foreign partnership that maintains a deferred compensation plan funded through a foreign employees' trust if U.S. or CFC partnership interests are de minimis. The IRS and Treasury specifically solicit comments concerning the amount of U.S. or CFC partnership interests that would qualify as "de minimis."

D. Plan of non-CFC foreign employer

The proposed regulations provide that a foreign employer that is not a CFC is treated as an owner of a portion of a foreign employees' trust only as provided in the antiabuse rule of § 1.1297-4.

E. Fractional interest

The fractional interest of a foreign employees' trust described above is defined in the proposed regulations as an undivided fractional interest in the trust for which the fraction is equal to the relevant amount determined for the employer's taxable year divided by the fair market value of trust assets determined for the employer's taxable year.

F. Relevant amount

The relevant amount for the employer's taxable year is defined in the proposed regulations as the amount, if any, by which the fair market value of trust assets, plus the fair market value of any assets available to pay plan liabilities (including any amount held under an annuity contract that exceeds the amount that is needed to satisfy the liabilities provided for under the contract) that are held in the equivalent of a trust within the meaning of section 404A(b)(5)(A), exceed the plan's accrued liability, determined using a projected unit credit funding method.

The relevant amount is reduced to the extent the taxpayer demonstrates to the Commissioner that the relevant amount is attributable to amounts that were properly contributed to the trust pursuant to a reasonable funding method, or experience that is favorable relative to any actuarial assumptions used that the Commissioner determines to be reasonable. In addition, if an employer that is a controlled foreign corporation otherwise would be treated as the owner of a fractional interest in a foreign employees' trust, the taxpayer may rely on this rule only if it so indicates on a statement attached to a timely filed Form 5471. The IRS and Treasury solicit comments regarding the most appropriate way in which to extend a filing requirement to partners in U.S.-related foreign partnerships and other affected taxpayers.

G. Plan's accrued liability

Under the proposed regulations, the plan's accrued liability for a taxable year of the employer is computed as of the plan's measurement date for the employer's taxable year. The plan's accrued liability is determined using a projected unit credit funding method, taking into account only liabilities relating to services performed for the employer or a predecessor employer. In addition, the plan's accrued liability is reduced (but not below zero) by any liabilities that are provided for under annuity contracts held to satisfy plan liabilities.

Because CFCs generally are required to determine their taxable income by reference to U.S. tax principles, the definition of a plan's "accrued liability" refers to § 1.412(c)(3)-1. This definition generally is intended to track the method used for calculating pension costs under Statement of Financial Accounting Standards No. 87, Employers' Accounting for Pensions (FAS 87), available from the Financial Accounting Standards Board, 401 Merritt 7, Norwalk, CT 06856. Under the method required to be used to calculate FAS 87's projected benefit obligation (PBO), plan costs are based on projected salary levels. Because many taxpayers already compute PBO annually to determine the pension costs of their nonexempt employees' trusts for financial reporting, the timing, interval and method to compute plan liabilities under § 1.671-1(h) should minimize taxpayer burden. The IRS and Treasury solicit comments regarding the extent to which the proposed regulations conform to existing procedures under FAS 87 and applicable foreign law, and regarding appropriate conforming adjustments.

H. Fair market value of trust assets

Under the proposed regulations, for a taxable year of the employer, the fair market value of trust assets, and the fair market value of retirement annuities or other assets held in the equivalent of a trust, equals the fair market value of those assets, as of the measurement date for the employer's taxable year. The fair market value of these assets is adjusted to include contributions made between the measurement date and the end of the employer's taxable year.

I. De minimis exception

The proposed regulations provide an exception to the general rule for determining the relevant amount. If the relevant amount would not otherwise be greater than the plan's normal cost for the plan year ending with or within the employer's taxable year, then the relevant amount is considered to be zero.

J. Proposed effective date and transition rules

The proposed regulations are proposed to be prospective. For taxable years ending prior to September 27, 1996, employers generally would not be treated for federal income tax purposes as owning the assets of foreign nonexempt employees' trusts (except as provided under section 679), consistent with the rules applying to domestic nonexempt employees' trusts. A transition rule, for purposes of § 1.671-1(h), exempts certain amounts from the application of the proposed regulations. This exemption is phased out over a ten-year period. There is a special transition rule for any foreign corporation that becomes a CFC after September 27, 1996. In addition, there is a special transition rule for certain entities that become U.S.-related foreign partnerships after September 27, 1996.

3. § 1.671-2: General asset ownership rules

The proposed regulations provide that a person who is treated as the owner of any portion of a trust under subpart E is considered to own the trust assets attributable to that portion of the trust for all federal income tax purposes.

4. § 1.1297-4: Subpart E rules for foreign employers that are not controlled foreign corporations

Under the proposed regulations, a foreign employer other than a CFC is not treated as the owner of any portion of a foreign nonexempt employees' trust for purposes of sections 1291 through 1297, except for cases in which a principal purpose for transferring property to the trust is to avoid classification of a foreign corporation as a PFIC (as defined in section 1296) or, if the foreign corporation is classified as a PFIC, in cases in which a principal purpose for transferring property to the trust is to avoid or to reduce taxation of U.S. shareholders of the PFIC under section 1291 or 1293. The effective date of this rule is September 27, 1996.

Income inclusion and related asset ownership rules for foreign welfare benefit plans

The IRS and Treasury solicit comments on the need for (and content of) income inclusion and asset ownership rules for foreign welfare benefit trusts.

Special Analyses

It has been determined that this notice of proposed rulemaking is not a significant regulatory action as defined in Executive Order 12866. Therefore, a regulatory assessment is not required. It is hereby certified that these regulations do not have a significant economic impact on a substantial number of small entities. This certification is based on the fact that these regulations will primarily affect U.S. owners of significant interests in foreign entities, which owners generally are large multinational corporations. This certification is also based on the fact that the burden imposed by the collection of information in the regulation, which is a requirement that certain entities may rely on an exception for reasonable funding only if they indicate such reliance on a statement attached to a timely filed Form 5471, is minimal, and, therefore, the collection of information will not impose a significant economic impact on such entities. Therefore, a Regulatory Flexibility Analysis under the Regulatory Flexibility Act (5 U.S.C. chapter 6) is not required. Pursuant to section 7805(f) of the Internal Revenue Code, this notice of proposed rulemaking will be submitted to the Chief Counsel for Advocacy of the Small Business Administration for comment on its impact on small business.

Comments and Public Hearing

Before these proposed regulations are adopted as final regulations, consideration will be given to any written comments (a signed original and eight (8) copies) that are submitted timely to the IRS. All comments will be available for public inspection and copying.

A public hearing has been scheduled for January 15, 1997, at 10:00 a.m. in room 2615, Internal Revenue Building, 1111 Constitution Avenue, NW., Washington DC. Because of access restrictions, visitors will not be admitted beyond the Internal Revenue Building lobby more than 15 minutes before the hearing starts.

The rules of 26 CFR 601.601(a)(3) apply to the hearing.

Persons that wish to present oral comments at the hearing must submit written comments by December 26, 1996, and submit an outline of the topics to be discussed and the time to be devoted to each topic (signed original and eight (8) copies) by December 24, 1996.

A period of 10 minutes will be allotted to each person for making comments.

An agenda showing the scheduling of the speakers will be prepared after the deadline for receiving outlines has passed. Copies of the agenda will be available free of charge at the hearing.

Drafting Information

The principal authors of these regulations are James A. Quinn of the Office of Assistant Chief Counsel (Passthroughs and Special Industries), Linda S. F. Marshall of the Office of Associate Chief Counsel (Employee Benefits and Exempt Organizations), and Kristine K. Schlaman and M. Grace Fleeman of the Office of Associate Chief Counsel (International). However, other personnel from the IRS and Treasury Department participated in their development.

[¶ 49,155] Proposed Regulations (REG-209040-88), published in the Federal Register on December 24, 1996.

PFICs: Shareholders: Qualified electing fund elections.—Reg. §§ 1.1293-2 and 1.1295-2, relating to permitting certain shareholders to make a special election under Code Sec. 1295, in lieu of the election currently provided for under that section, with respect to certain preferred shares of a passive foreign investment company (PFIC), are proposed. A public hearing has been scheduled for May 8, 1997.

AGENCY: Internal Revenue Service (IRS), Treasury

ACTION: Notice of proposed rulemaking and notice of public hearing.

SUMMARY: This document contains proposed regulations permitting certain shareholders to make a special election under section 1295, in lieu of the election currently provided for under that section, with respect to certain preferred shares of a passive foreign investment company (PFIC). A shareholder that makes a special election must account for dividend income on the shares subject to the special election under special income inclusion rules, rather than under the general income inclusion rules of section 1293. This document also provides notice of a public hearing on these proposed regulations.

DATES: Written comments must be received by March 24, 1997. Requests to speak and outlines of oral comments to be discussed at the public hearing scheduled for May 8, 1997, at 10:00 a.m. must be received by April 17, 1997.

ADDRESSES: Send submissions to: CC:DOM:CORP:R (REG-209040-88), room 5226, Internal Revenue Service, POB 7604, Ben Franklin Station, Washington, DC 20044. Submissions may be hand delivered between the hours of 8 a.m. and 5 p.m. to: CC:DOM:CORP:R (REG-209040-88), Courier's Desk, Internal Revenue Service, 1111 Constitution Avenue, NW., Washington, DC. Alternatively, taxpayers may submit comments electronically via the Internet by selecting the "Tax Regs" option on the IRS Home Page, or by submitting comments directly to the IRS Internet site at http://www.irs.ustreas.gov/prod/tax>regs/comments.html. The public hearing will be held in room 3313, Internal Revenue Building, 1111 Constitution Avenue, NW., Washington, DC.

FOR FURTHER INFORMATION CONTACT: Concerning the regulations, Judith Cavell Cohen, (202) 622-3880; concerning submissions and the hearing, Evangelista Lee, (202) 622-7190 (not toll-free numbers).

SUPPLEMENTARY INFORMATION:

Paperwork Reduction Act

The collection of information contained in this notice of proposed rulemaking has been submitted to the Office of Management and Budget for review in accordance with the Paperwork Reduction Act of 1995 (44 U.S.C. 3507(d)). Comments on the collection of information should be sent to the Office of Management and Budget, Attn: Desk Officer for the Department of the Treasury, Office of Information and Regulatory Affairs, Washington, DC 20503, with copies to the Internal Revenue Service, Attn: IRS Reports Clearance Officer, T:FP, Washington, DC 20224. Comments on the collection of information should be received by February 24, 1997. Comments are specifically requested concerning:

Whether the proposed collection of information is necessary for the proper performance of the functions of the Internal Revenue Service, including whether the information will have practical utility;

The accuracy of the estimated burden associated with the proposed collection of information (see below);

How the quality, utility, and clarity of the information to be collected may be enhanced;

How the burden of complying with the proposed collection of information may be minimized, including through the application of automated collection techniques or other forms of information technology; and

Estimates of capital or start-up costs and costs of operation, maintenance, and purchase of services to provide information.

The collection of information in this proposed regulation is in proposed regulation § 1.1295-2(c)(3) and proposed regulation § 1.1295-2(e) and (f). This information will notify the Commissioner that certain shareholders have made the special election. In addition, this information will enable the IRS to determine if a shareholder qualifies for the special election and is satisfying the income inclusion requirements of proposed regulation § 1.1293-2. The collection of information is mandatory. The likely respondents are individuals, businesses, and other for-profit organizations.

Estimated total annual reporting/recordkeeping burden: 600 hours. The estimated annual burden per respondent varies from 21 minutes to 8.3 hours, depending on individual circumstances, with an estimated average of 35 minutes.

Estimated number of respondents: 1030.

Estimated annual frequency of responses: On occasion.

An agency may not conduct or sponsor, and a person is not required to respond to, a collection of information unless the collection of information displays a valid control number assigned by the Office of Management and Budget.

Books or records relating to a collection of information must be retained as long as their contents may become material in the administration of any internal revenue law. Generally, tax returns and tax return information are confidential, as required by 26 U.S.C. 6103.

Background

This document contains proposed Income Tax Regulations (26 CFR part 1) under sections 1293 and 1295 of the Internal Revenue Code. Sections 1293 and 1295 were added by the Tax Reform Act of 1986 (the Act) and were amended by the Technical and Miscellaneous Revenue Act of 1988 (TAMRA). The sections, as amended, were effective for taxable years of foreign corporations beginning after December 31, 1986. Section 1293 also was amended by the Omnibus Reconciliation Act of 1993

(OBRA). Guidance for making the section 1295 election was provided in proposed regulation § 1.1295-1 and Notice 88-125, 1988-2 C.B. 535. Guidance regarding the annual income inclusion rule for shareholders making a section 1295 election was provided in proposed regulation § 1.1293-1.

Explanation of Provisions

Special Preferred Section 1295 Election

1. Introduction.

The passive foreign investment company (PFIC) rules of the Code are designed to eliminate potential tax deferral opportunities associated with equity investments by United States persons in foreign corporations that have substantial levels of passive income or assets. The PFIC rules eliminate tax deferral opportunities by applying the section 1291 interest charge regime to PFIC shareholders that fail to make a section 1295 annual income inclusion election (section 1295 election). In general, the section 1291 interest charge regime applies to the "extraordinary" portion of any distribution received by the shareholder, and any gain recognized on a disposition of shares.

The PFIC rules apply to investments in both common and preferred shares of a PFIC. Preferred shares, unlike common shares, generally provide for limited dividend and liquidation or redemption rights, and thus do not participate significantly in corporate growth. Accordingly, preferred shares of a PFIC generally do not afford U.S. investors with the same potential for U.S. tax deferral as common shares of a PFIC.

Preferred shareholders, like common shareholders, may make the section 1295 election to avoid the interest charge regime of section 1291. Shareholders that make the section 1295 election are required under section 1293 to include in income annually, as ordinary income, their pro rata share of the PFIC's ordinary earnings and, as long-term capital gain, their pro rata share of the PFIC's net capital gain for the year. In order to determine their pro rata share of ordinary earnings and net capital gain, shareholders that have made a section 1295 election must obtain certain U.S. tax accounting information from the PFIC regarding the PFIC's earnings. If this information is not available, the shareholders cannot make the section 1295 election. If the requisite information is available, the annual information reporting and collection requirements associated with the section 1295 election may render the election impractical for smaller investors. Because preferred shares often do not afford investors with significant tax-deferral opportunity, commenters have suggested that the current section 1295 election regime should be simplified for certain types of preferred shares.

The proposed regulations adopt a special section 1295 election regime that would require holders of certain preferred shares of a PFIC that elect to be subject to the regime to accrue annually ordinary dividend income with respect to the preferred shares regardless of the holder's pro rata share of ordinary earnings or net capital gain of the PFIC for the year. Because shareholders would accrue income regardless of the earnings and net capital gain of the PFIC, shareholders that elect to be subject to the regime would not have to report and collect any U.S. tax accounting information regarding the PFIC in order to make the special section 1295 election.

The proposed regulations are issued under two sections of the Code. Section 1.1295-2 of the proposed regulations provides rules for making a QEF election under the special proposed section 1295 election regime (special preferred QEF election). Section 1.1293-2 describes the annual income inclusion rules for shareholders that have made the special preferred QEF election. The proposed regulations would apply only with respect to qualifying preferred shares issued after the date the proposed regulations are finalized.

2. Rules for making the special preferred QEF election.

Under proposed regulation § 1.1295-2(a), the special preferred QEF election may be made in lieu of the section 1295 election described in proposed regulation § 1.1295-1 and Notice 88-125, 1988-2 C.B. 535 (regular section 1295 election), with respect to certain types of preferred shares (qualified preferred shares) by certain holders satisfying prescribed ownership requirements.

The special preferred QEF election may only be made with respect to qualified preferred shares as defined in proposed regulation § 1.1295-2(b). To ensure that the special preferred QEF election cannot be used for tax avoidance purposes and to reduce complexity, the proposed regulations define qualified preferred shares narrowly to include only a limited class of preferred shares likely to be marketed to U.S. retail investors. Although the definition of qualified preferred shares includes both cumulative and non-cumulative preferred shares, the definition excludes various types of preferred shares, including preferred shares denominated in a foreign currency and preferred shares issued at a significant discount to their liquidation or redemption amounts. The PFIC issuing the preferred shares must represent that it intends to pay dividends currently. Proposed regulation § 1.1295-2(b) provides additional restrictions with respect to preferred shares acquired in secondary market transactions.

Proposed regulation § 1.1295-2(c) describes shareholders who may make the election. Under proposed regulation § 1.1295-2(c)(1), any United States person that acquires qualified preferred shares for cash or in certain nonrecognition transactions and that holds such shares directly may make the election. United States persons that are pass-through entities, including partnerships, S corporations, trusts and estates, may qualify as shareholders.

The special preferred QEF election regime is narrowly targeted to eliminate certain of the information reporting and collection requirements associated with the existing section 1295 election and annual inclusion rules for U.S. retail investors in preferred shares of PFICs. Treasury and the Service believe that the special preferred QEF election regime should only apply with respect to foreign corporations that are not expected to be in a position to provide U.S. tax accounting information to shareholders. Accordingly, proposed regulation § 1.1295-2(c)(2) provides that the special preferred QEF election does not apply to holders of preferred shares in a PFIC that is a controlled foreign corporation. Further, proposed regulation § 1.1295-2(c)(3) provides that the special preferred QEF election does not apply to holders that own 5 percent or more of the vote or value of any class of shares of the PFIC. Holders of five percent or more of the vote or value of any class of shares generally are not the type of retail investor that the proposed regulations are designed to assist. Such holders may only make the section 1295 election provided under current rules.

Proposed regulation § 1.1295-2(c)(3) requires the corporation to provide to electing shareholders a statement, directly or in a disclosure document generally available to all U.S. shareholders, either that it is or that it reasonably believes that it is a PFIC and that it is not a controlled foreign corporation. Shareholders that fail to receive such a statement are not permitted to make a special preferred QEF election

Proposed regulation § 1.1295-2(d) describes the effect of the special preferred QEF election. Proposed regulation § 1.1295-2(d)(1) provides that shares subject to a special preferred QEF election will be treated as shares of a pedigreed QEF (as defined in proposed regulation § 1.1291-1(b)(2)(ii)) for all taxable years of the foreign corporation that are included wholly or partly in the shareholder's holding period of the shares. Under the proposed regulations, the election will apply to all qualified preferred shares of a foreign corporation owned directly by the shareholder that are acquired in the taxable year with respect to which the election is made. Although a special preferred QEF election will not apply automatically to qualified preferred shares acquired in subsequent taxable years of a shareholder, the proposed regulations permit the shareholder to make separate special preferred QEF elections with respect to qualified preferred shares acquired in later years.

Proposed regulation § 1.1295-2(d)(2) provides that the special preferred QEF election regime applies whether or not the foreign corporation is a PFIC in any year subsequent to the year of the election. Accordingly, shareholders that make the special preferred QEF election must make annual § 1.1293-2 income inclusions, as provided in proposed regulation § 1.1295-2(d)(3), even if the foreign corporation does not qualify as a PFIC for a particular year.

Proposed regulation § 1.1295-2(e) specifies the time and manner of making the special preferred QEF election. In order to make the special preferred QEF election, a shareholder files Form 8621 (Return by a Shareholder of a Passive Foreign Investment Company or Qualified Electing Fund), for the taxable year of the election, checking the appropriate box in Form 8621, Part I, for making the section 1295 election, and indicating in the margin of Part I that the shareholder is making a special preferred QEF election with respect to certain specified shares. In addition, the shareholder must attach to Form 8621 a brief statement containing the information and representations contained in proposed regulation § 1.1295-2(e)(2)(ii). Under proposed regulation § 1.1295-2(f), in subsequent years, the shareholder must file Form 8621 with respect to the foreign corporation but need not attach any statement to the form. For all taxable years covered by the election, the shareholder must report on Line 6a of Part II of Form 8621 the amount includible under proposed regulation § 1.1293-2 with respect to qualified preferred shares subject to a special preferred QEF election.

Proposed regulation § 1.1293-2(g) states that a sale, exchange or other disposition of shares subject to a special preferred QEF election terminates the election with respect to those shares. Also, the Commissioner may terminate or invalidate an election if a shareholder fails to satisfy the initial or ongoing requirements of the election. For example, the Commissioner may terminate or invalidate a special preferred QEF election if the shareholder owns five percent or more of the vote or value of any class of shares of the PFIC at any time during the period that the shareholder owns qualified preferred shares subject to the election. A shareholder may not itself terminate a special preferred QEF election.

3. *Annual inclusion rules for electing shareholders.*

Under proposed regulation § 1.1293-2(a), a shareholder that has made a special preferred QEF election must make annual income inclusions with respect to qualified preferred shares subject to the election. Unlike the annual income inclusions provided under section 1293 and proposed regulation § 1.1293-1, the annual inclusions under the special preferred QEF election regime are determined without regard to the shareholder's pro rata share of the foreign corporation's ordinary earnings or net capital gains.

Proposed regulation § 1.1293-2(b) provides rules for determining the amount that a shareholder must include in income annually under the special preferred QEF election regime. Under the proposed regulations, this annual amount consists of two components. The first component is an annual inclusion amount based on a ratable daily portion of dividend income that accrues on the qualified preferred shares (annual dividend amount). This ratable inclusion rule for the annual dividend amount is analogous to the rule for inclusion of income with respect to periodic payments on notional principal contracts under § 1.446-3. The second component of the preferred QEF amount arises only in respect of fixed term preferred shares, as described proposed regulation § 1.1295-2(b)(vii), acquired in a secondary market transaction, and is calculated based on the ratable inclusion of the excess, if any, of the redemption price of the shares over the acquisition cost of the shares (preferred discount amount). This ratable inclusion rule for the preferred discount amount is analogous to the rule for the ratable inclusion of market discount on certain debt under section 1276(b)(1). The Service and Treasury solicit comments regarding the income inclusion rules of the proposed regulations, including comments as to whether foreign corporations and their agents could effectively assist holders in complying with the income inclusion rules applicable to preferred discount.

Proposed regulation § 1.1293-2(c) provides certain special rules regarding the annual income inclusion required under proposed regulation § 1.1293-2(a). Under § 1.1293-2(c)(1), annual amounts are included in income by shareholders irrespective of the PFIC's earnings and profits. In this regard, the special preferred QEF election differs from the regular section 1295 election in that shareholders making the special preferred QEF election must accrue the annual amount as ordinary income even if the amount exceeds the shareholder's pro rata share of the foreign corporation's earnings and profits. Proposed regulation § 1.1293-2(c)(3) requires the shareholder to include the annual dividend amount as ordinary income regardless of whether any portion of the PFIC's earnings for the year represents net capital gain. Proposed regulation § 1.1293-2(c)(4) provides rules for the tax-free distribution of previously taxed amounts. Proposed regulation § 1.1293-2(c)(5) provides certain basis adjustment rules similar to the basis adjustment rule of section 1293(d). Finally, proposed regulation § 1.1293-2(c)(6) provides rules intended to limit the effect of a special preferred QEF election to the shareholder making the election. Accordingly, a special preferred QEF election will not affect the foreign corporation's calculation of its earnings and profits, and will have no consequences for shareholders that have not made a special preferred QEF election.

Special Analyses

It has been determined that this notice of proposed rulemaking is not a significant regulatory action as defined in Executive Order 12866. Therefore, a regulatory assessment is not required. It is hereby certified that these regulations do not have a significant economic impact on a substantial number of small entities. This certification is based on the fact that these regulations represent a wholly elective simpler alternative to the section 1295 election described in § 1.1295-1 and Notice 88-125, 1988-2 C.B. 535, and impose a lighter collection of information burden. Further, the requirement that electing shareholders indicate their special election on Form 8621 annually and attach a statement, providing certain information in the first year of the election only, is minimal and will not impose a significant economic impact on electing shareholders. Therefore, a Regulatory Flexibility Analysis under the Regulatory Flexibility Act (5 U.S.C. chapter 6) is not required. Pursuant to section 7805(f) of the Internal Revenue Code, this notice of proposed rulemaking will be submitted to the Chief Counsel for Advocacy of the Small Business Administration for comment on its impact on small business.

Comments and Public Hearing

Before these proposed regulations are adopted as final regulations, consideration will be given to any written comments (a signed original and eight (8) copies) that are submitted timely to the IRS. All comments will be available for public inspection and copying.

A public hearing has been scheduled for May 8, 1997, at 10:00 a.m. in room 3313, Internal Revenue Building, 1111 Constitution Avenue, NW., Washington DC. Because of access restrictions, visitors will not be admitted beyond the Internal Revenue Building lobby more than 15 minutes before the hearing starts.

The rules of 26 CFR 601.601(a)(3) apply to the hearing.

Persons that wish to present oral comments at the hearing must submit written comments by March 24, 1997, and submit an outline of the topics to be discussed and the time to be devoted to each topic (signed original and eight (8) copies) by April 17, 1997.

A period of 10 minutes will be allotted to each person for making comments.

An agenda showing the schedule of speakers will be prepared after the deadline for receiving outlines has passed. Copies of the agenda will be available free of charge at the hearing.

Drafting Information

The principal author of these regulations is Judith Cavell Cohen of the Office of Associate Chief Counsel (International). However, other personnel from the IRS and Treasury Department participated in their development.

[¶ 49,156] Proposed Amendments of Regulations (REG-246018-96), published in the Federal Register on January 2, 1997.

Life insurance companies: Property and casualty insurance companies: Life insurance reserves.—Amendments of Reg. § 1.801-4, permitting the recomputation of certain life insurance reserves if such reserves were initially computed or estimated on other than an actuarial basis, are proposed. A public hearing on this proposal is scheduled for April 17, 1997.

AGENCY: Internal Revenue Service (IRS), Treasury.

ACTION: Notice of proposed rulemaking and notice of public hearing.

SUMMARY: This document contains proposed regulations relating to the definition of life insurance reserves. The proposed regulations permit the taxpayer or the IRS to recompute certain reserves if those reserves were initially computed or estimated on other than an actuarial basis. The proposed regulations affect both life insurance companies and property and casualty insurance companies. This document also contains a notice of a public hearing on the proposed regulations.

DATES: Written comments must be received by April 2, 1997. Requests to speak and outlines of oral comments to be discussed at the public hearing scheduled for Thursday, April 17, 1997, at 10 a.m. must be received by Thursday, March 27, 1997.

ADDRESSES: Send submissions to: CC:DOM:CORP:R (REG-246018-96), room 5226, Internal Revenue Service, POB 7604, Ben Franklin Station, Washington, DC 20044. Submissions may be hand delivered between the hours of 8 a.m. and 5 p.m. to: CC:DOM:CORP:R (REG-246018-96), Courier's Desk, Internal Revenue Service, 1111 Constitution Avenue NW, Washington, DC. Alternatively, taxpayers may submit comments electronically via the Internet by selecting the "Tax Regs" option on the IRS Home Page, or by submitting comments directly to the IRS Internet site at http://www.irs.ustreas.gov/prod/tax>regs/comments.html. The public hearing will be held in the Commissioner's conference room, room 3313, Internal Revenue Service Building, 1111 Constitution Avenue, N.W. Washington, D.C.

FOR FURTHER INFORMATION CONTACT: Concerning the regulations, Ann Cammack, (202) 622-3970; concerning submissions and the hearing, Evangelista Lee, (202) 622-7190 (not toll-free numbers).

SUPPLEMENTARY INFORMATION:

Background

To qualify as a life insurance reserve for purposes of Part I of subchapter L of the Internal Revenue Code, a reserve must satisfy various requirements, including the requirement in section 816(b)(1)(A) and § 1.801-4(a)(1) that it be "computed or estimated on the basis of recognized mortality or morbidity tables and assumed rates of interest." Qualifying as a life reserve under section 816(b) has various consequences. Life reserves are included in the numerator and denominator of the reserve ratio test of section 816(a), which is used to determine when an insurance company is taxed as a life insurance companyunder Part I of subchapter L. Increases in life reserves as defined in section 816(b) are taken into account under section 807(c)(1). In addition, life reserves as defined in section 816(b) are considered part of a nonlife company's unearned premiums under section 832(b)(4).

Two circuits have construed former section 801(b)(1)(A), which was recodified as section 816(b)(1)(A) in 1984, to prevent reserves held with respect to life, annuity or noncancellable accident and health policies but not computed or estimated using actuarial tables from qualifying as life reserves. The IRS also has held that life reserves must be computed or estimated using actuarial tables under former section 801(b)(1)(A). *See, e.g.,* Rev. Rul. 69-302 (1969-2 C.B. 186). The Claims Court, in contrast, has concluded that the statute and regulation do not necessarily require the insurance company to compute its life reserves using actuarial tables, when a different method results in reserves that "reasonably approximate" actuarial reserves.

Rev. Rul. 69-302 held that not only were life reserves required to be computed or estimated on the basis of recognized mortality or morbidity tables and assumed rates of interest, but that reserves for credit life insurance contracts could not be retroactively recomputed in a manner that would enable them to qualify as life reserves. Neither of the cases cited in Rev. Rul. 69-302, however, addressed the question of whether taxpayers or the Commissioner could recompute reserves based on information that was available at the end of the applicable taxable year. Two subsequent cases came to opposite conclusions on this issue.

The reserve ratio test of section 816(a) was intended to distinguish between life and nonlife insurance companies based on the nature of each company's business, as measured by its reserves. This purpose is not achieved, however, if a company that only issues life insurance, annuity or noncancellable accident and health contracts can elect to be taxed as a nonlife company by failing to use mortality and morbidity tables and assumed rates of interest in computing or estimating its reserves for some of those contracts.

Explanation of Provisions

Proposed § 1.801-4(g)(1) provides that if an insurance company does not compute or estimate its reserves for certain contracts on the basis of mortality or morbidity tables and assumed rates of interest, then the taxpayer or the Commissioner may recompute those reserves on the basis of mortality or morbidity tables and assumed rates of interest. This regulation will apply to reserves for contracts involving, at the time with respect to which the reserves are computed, life, accident or health contingencies, if such reserves were not initially computed in accordance with the requirements of section 816(b)(1)(A).

Proposed § 1.801-4(g)(2) provides that if the taxpayer or the Commissioner recomputes reserves pursuant to § 1.801-4(g)(1), the reserves satisfy the section 816(b)(1)(A) requirement that a life reserve be computed or estimated using actuarial tables and assumed rates of interest. Assuming that these amounts satisfy the other requirements of section 816(b), the recomputed amounts will be considered life insurance reserves under section 816(b), and the recomputed reserves will be included in both the numerator and the denominator of the reserve ratio test under section 816(a). In addition, the reserves for such contracts will be taken into account under section 807(c)(1) and will be used to compute a nonlife company's unearned premiums under section 832(b)(4).

Proposed § 1.801-4(g)(3) provides that for purposes of section 816(b)(4) and § 1.801-3(i), which provide that the mean of the beginning and end of year reserves will be used for purposes of section 816(a), (b) and (c), the reserves on a life insurance, annuity or noncancellable accident and health contract must be recomputed for both the beginning and the end of the year.

Proposed § 1.801-4(g)(4) requires that no information acquired after the date as of which the beginning of year reserves were initially computed or estimated may be taken into account in recomputing those reserves under paragraph (g)(1). It also requires that no information acquired after the date as of which the end of year reserves were initially computed or estimated may be taken into account in recomputing those reserves under paragraph (g)(1).

The IRS is considering whether to issue guidance under section 816, including regulations regarding the definition of "total reserves" under section 816(c) as well as redesignating and revising the regulations issued under prior law section 801. The IRS invites comments on this matter.

Proposed Effective Date

Proposed §1.801-4(g) would be effective with respect to returns filed for taxable years beginning after the publication of the final regulations.

Effect on Other Documents

The IRS will modify, clarify, or obsolete publications as necessary to conform with this regulation as of the date of publication in the Federal Register of the final regulations. *See e.g.*, Rev. Rul. 69-302 (1969-2 C.B. 186). The IRS solicits comments as to whether other publications should be modified or obsoleted.

Special Analyses

It has been determined that this notice of proposed rulemaking is not a significant regulatory action as defined in EO 12866. Therefore, a regulatory assessment is not required. It also has been determined that section 553(b) of the Administrative Procedure Act (5 U.S.C. chapter 5) does not apply to these regulations, and because the regulations do not impose a collection of information on small entities, the Regulatory Flexibility Act (5 U.S.C. chapter 6) does not apply. Pursuant to section 7805(f) of the Internal Revenue Code, this notice of proposed rulemaking will be submitted to the Chief Counsel for Advocacy of the Small Business Administration for comment on its impact on small business.

Comments and Public Hearing

Before these proposed regulations are adopted as final regulations, consideration will be given to any written comments (a signed original and 8 copies) that are submitted timely to the IRS. All comments will be available for public inspection and copying.

A public hearing has been scheduled for Thursday, April 17, 1997 in the Commissioner's conference room, room 3313, Internal Revenue Service Building at 10:00 a.m. Because of access restrictions, visitors will not be admitted beyond the Internal Revenue Building lobby more than 15 minutes before the hearing starts.

The rules of 26 CFR 601.601(a)(3) apply to the hearing.

Persons that wish to present oral comments at the hearing must submit written comments by March 27, 1997 and submit an outline of the topics to be discussed and the time to be devoted to each topic (a signed original and 8 copies) by March 27, 1997.

A period of 10 minutes will be allotted to each person for making comments.

An agenda showing the scheduling of the speakers will be prepared after the deadline for receiving outlines has passed. Copies of the agenda will be available free of charge at the hearing.

Drafting Information

The principal author of this regulation is Ann B. Cammack, Office of Assistant Chief Counsel (Financial Institutions and Products). However, other personnel from the IRS and Treasury Department participated in their development.

[¶49,157] Proposed Amendments of Regulations (REG-209824-96), published in the Federal Register on January 13, 1997.

Limited partner for self-employment tax purposes: Definition of.—Amendments of Reg. §1.1402(a)-2, relating to the self-employment income tax imposed under Code Sec. 1402, are proposed. A public hearing on this proposal is scheduled for May 21, 1997.

AGENCY: Internal Revenue Service (IRS), Treasury.

ACTION: Notice of proposed rulemaking and notice of public hearing.

SUMMARY: This document contains proposed amendments to the regulations relating to the self-employment income tax imposed under section 1402 of the Internal Revenue Code of 1986. These regulations permit individuals to determine whether they are limited partners for purposes of section 1402(a)(13), eliminating the uncertainty in calculating an individual's net earnings from self-employment under existing law. This document also contains a notice of public hearing on the proposed regulations.

DATES: Written comments must be received by April 14, 1997. Requests to speak and outlines of oral comments to be discussed at the public hearing scheduled for May 21, 1997, at 10 a.m. must be received by April 30, 1997.

ADDRESSES: Send submissions to: CC:DOM:CORP:R (REG-209824-96), room 5226, Internal Revenue Service, POB 7604, Ben Franklin Station, Washington, DC 20044. Submissions may be hand delivered between the hours of 8 a.m. and 5 p.m. to: CC:DOM:CORP:R (REG-209824-96), Courier's Desk, Internal Revenue Service, 1111 Constitution Avenue, NW, Washington, DC. Alternatively, taxpayers may submit comments electronically via the Internet by selecting the "Tax Regs" option on the IRS Home Page, or by submitting comments directly to the IRS Internet site at http://www.irs.ustreas.gov/prod/tax>regs/comments.html. The public hearing will be held in the Auditorium, Internal Revenue Service building, 1111 Constitution Avenue, NW, Washington, DC.

FOR FURTHER INFORMATION CONTACT: Concerning the regulation, Robert Honigman, (202) 622-3050; concerning submissions and the hearing, Christina Vasquez, (202) 622-6808 (not toll-free numbers).

SUPPLEMENTARY INFORMATION:

Background

This document contains proposed amendments to the Income Tax Regulations (26 CFR part 1) under section 1402 of the Internal Revenue Code and replaces the notice of proposed rulemaking published in the Federal Register on December 29, 1994, at 59 FR 67253, that treated certain members of a limited liability company (LLC) as limited partners for self-employment tax purposes. Written comments responding to the proposed regulations were received, and a public hearing was held on June 23, 1995.

Under the 1994 proposed regulations, an individual owning an interest in an LLC was treated as a limited partner if (1) the individual lacked the authority to make management decisions necessary to conduct the LLC's business (the management test), and (2) the LLC could have been formed as a limited partnership rather than an LLC in the same jurisdiction, and the member could have qualified as a limited partner in the limited partnership under applicable law (the limited partner equivalence test). The intent of the 1994 proposed regulations was to treat owners of an LLC interest in the same manner as similarly situated partners in a state law partnership.

Public comments on the 1994 proposed regulations were mixed. While some commentators were pleased with the proposed regulations for attempting to conform the treatment of LLCs with state law partnerships, others criticized the 1994 proposed regulations based on a variety of arguments.

A number of commentators discussed administrative and compliance problems with the 1994 proposed regulations. For example, it was noted that both the management test and the limited partner equivalence test depend upon legal or factual determinations that may be difficult for taxpayers or the IRS to make with certainty.

Another commentator pointed out that basing the self-employment tax treatment of LLC members on state law limited partnership rules would lead to disparate treatment between members of different LLCs with identical rights based solely on differences in the limited partnership statutes of the states in which the members form their LLC. For example, State A's limited partnership act may allow a limited partner to participate in a partnership's business while State B's limited partnership act may not. Thus, an LLC member, who is not a manager, that participates in the LLC's business would be a limited partner under the proposed regulations if the LLC is formed in State A, but not if the LLC is formed in State B. Commentators asserted that this disparate treatment is inherently unfair for federal tax purposes.

Some commentators argued for a "material participation" test to determine whether an LLC member's distributive share is included in the individual's net earnings from self-employment. The proposed regulations did not contain a participation test. Commentators advocating a participation test stressed that such a test would eliminate uncertainty concerning many LLC members' limited partner status and would better implement the self-employment tax goal of taxing compensation for services.

Other commentators argued for a more uniform approach, stating that a single test should govern all business entities (i.e., partnerships, LLCs, LLPs, sole proprietorships, et al.) whose members may be subject to self-employment tax. These commentators generally recognized, however, that a change in the treatment of a sole proprietorship or an entity that is not characterized as a partnership for federal tax purposes would be beyond the scope of regulations to be issued under section 1402(a)(13).

Finally, some commentators focused on whether the Service would respect the ownership of more than one class of partnership interest for self-employment tax purposes (bifurcation of interests). The proposed regulations treated an LLC member as a limited partner with respect to his or her entire interest (if the member was not a manager and satisfied the limited partner equivalence test), or not at all (if either the management test or limited partner equivalence test was not satisfied). Commentators, however, pointed to the legislative history of section 1402(a)(13) to support their argument that Congress only intended to tax a partner's distributive share attributable to a general partner interest. Under this argument, a partner that holds both a general partner interest and a limited partner interest is only subject to self-employment tax on the distributive share attributable to the partner's general partner interest. This intent also may be inferred from the statutory language of section 1402(a)(13) that the self-employment tax does not apply to " . . . the distributive share of any item of income or loss of a limited partner, as such . . . ." Based on this evidence, these commentators requested that the proposed regulations be revised to allow the bifurcation of interests for self-employment tax purposes.

After considering the comments received, the IRS and Treasury have decided to withdraw the 1994 notice of proposed rulemaking and to re-propose amendments to the Income Tax Regulations (26 CFR part 1) under section 1402 of the Code.

Explanation of Provisions

The proposed regulations contained in this document define which partners of a federal tax partnership are considered limited partners for section 1402(a)(13) purposes. These proposed regulations apply to all entities classified as a partnership for federal tax purposes, regardless of the state law characterization of the entity. Thus, the same standards apply when determining the status of an individual owning an interest in a state law limited partnership or the status of an individual owning an interest in an LLC. In order to achieve this conformity, the proposed regulations adopt an approach which depends on the relationship between the partner, the partnership, and the partnership's business. State law characterizations of an individual as a "limited partner" or otherwise are not determinative.

Generally, an individual will be treated as a limited partner under the proposed regulations unless the individual (1) has personal liability (as defined in § 301.7701-3(b)(2)(ii) of the Procedure and Administration Regulations) for the debts of or claims against the partnership by reason of being a partner; (2) has authority to contract on behalf of the partnership under the statute or law pursuant to which the partnership is organized; or, (3) participates in the partnership's trade or business for more than 500 hours during the taxable year. If, however, substantially all of the activities of a partnership involve the performance of services in the fields of health, law, engineering, architecture, accounting, actuarial science, or consulting, any individual who provides services as part of that trade or business will not be considered a limited partner.

By adopting these functional tests, the proposed regulations ensure that similarly situated individuals owning interests in entities formed under different statutes or in different jurisdictions will be treated similarly. The need for a functional approach results not only from the proliferation of new business entities such as LLCs, but also from the evolution of state limited partnership statutes. When Congress enacted the limited partner exclusion found in section 1402(a)(13), state laws generally did not allow limited partners to participate in the partnership's trade or business to the extent that state laws allow limited partners to participate today. Thus, even in the case of a state law limited partnership, a functional approach is necessary to ensure that the self-employment tax consequences to similarly situated taxpayers do not differ depending upon where the partnership organized.

The proposed regulations allow an individual who is not a limited partner for section 1402(a)(13) purposes to nonetheless exclude from net earnings from self-employment a portion of that individual's distributive share if the individual holds more than one class of interest in the partnership. Similarly, the proposed regulations permit an individual that participates in the trade or business of the partnership to bifurcate his or her distributive share by disregarding guaranteed payments for services. In each case, however, such bifurcation of interests is permitted only to the extent the individual's distributive share is identical to the distributive share of partners who qualify as limited partners under the proposed regulation (without regard to the bifurcation rules) and who own a substantial interest in the partnership. Together, these rules exclude from an individual's net earnings from self-employment amounts that are demonstrably returns on capital invested in the partnership.

Proposed Effective Date

These regulations are proposed to be effective beginning with the individual's first taxable year beginning on or after the date these regulations are published as final regulations in the Federal Register.

Special Analyses

It has been determined that this notice of proposed rulemaking is not a significant regulatory action as defined in EO 12866. Therefore, a regulatory assessment is not required. It also has been determined that section 553(b) of the Administrative Procedure Act (5 U.S.C. chapter 5) does not apply to these regulations, and, because the regulations do not impose a collection of information on small entities, the Regulatory Flexibility Act (5 U.S.C. chapter 6) does not apply. Pursuant to section 7805(f) of the Internal Revenue Code, this notice of proposed rulemaking will be submitted to the Chief Counsel for Advocacy of the Small Business Administration for comment on its impact on small business.

Comments and Public Hearing

Before these proposed regulations are adopted as final regulations, consideration will be given to any written comments (a signed original and eight (8) copies) that are submitted timely to the IRS. All comments will be available for public inspection and copying.

A public hearing has been scheduled for Wednesday, May 21, 1997, at 10 a.m. in the Auditorium, Internal Revenue Service building, 1111 Constitution Avenue, NW, Washington, DC. Because of access restrictions, visitors will not be admitted beyond the Internal Revenue Service building lobby more than 15 minutes before the hearing starts.

The rules of 26 CFR 601.601(a)(3) apply to the hearing.

Persons that wish to present oral comments at the hearing must submit written comments by April 14, 1997, and submit an outline of the topics to be discussed and the time to be devoted to each topic (signed original and eight (8) copies) by April 30, 1997.

A period of 10 minutes will be allotted to each person for making comments.

An agenda showing the scheduling of the speakers will be prepared after the deadline for receiving outlines has passed. Copies of the agenda will be available free of charge at the hearing.

Drafting Information

The principal author of these regulations is Robert Honigman of the Office of Assistant Chief Counsel (Passthroughs & Special Industries). However, other personnel from the IRS and Treasury Department participated in their development.

[¶49,160] Proposed Amendments of Regulations (REG-107872-97), published in the Federal Register on October 14, 1997.

Withholding: Nonresident aliens: Form W-8: Electronic transmission.—Amendments of Reg. §1.1441-1, relating to the establishment by withholding agents and payors of an electronic system for use by beneficial owners or payees in furnishing Form W-8 (Certificate of Foreign Status), are proposed.

AGENCY: Internal Revenue Service (IRS), Treasury.

ACTION: Notice of proposed rulemaking.

SUMMARY: This document contains proposed regulations relating to the submission of Form W-8, a withholding certificate, needed for purposes of chapters 3 and 61 of the Internal Revenue Code (Code) and other withholding or reporting provisions of the Code, such as section 3402, 3405, or 3406. The proposed regulations provide guidance to withholding agents and payors who wish to establish an electronic system for use by beneficial owners or payees in furnishing Form W-8. The proposed regulations state the general requirements that such an electronic system must satisfy so that a withholding agent or payor may rely on a Form W-8 transmitted through such a system. These regulations affect withholding agents and payors that establish electronic systems and beneficial owners and payees who use these systems.

DATES: Written comments and requests for a public hearing must be received by [INSERT DATE 90 DAYS AFTER DATE OF PUBLICATION OF THIS DOCUMENT IN THE FEDERAL REGISTER].

ADDRESSES: Send submissions to: CC:DOM:CORP:R (REG-107872-97), room 5228, Internal Revenue Service, POB 7604, Ben Franklin Station, Washington, DC 20044. Submissions may be hand delivered between the hours of 8 a.m. and 5 p.m. to: CC:DOM:CORP:R (REG-107872-97), Courier's Desk, Internal Revenue Service, 1111 Constitution Avenue, NW., Washington, DC. Alternatively, taxpayers may submit comments electronically via the Internet by selecting the "Tax Regs" option on the IRS Home Page, or by submitting comments directly to the IRS Internet site at www.irs.ustreas.gov/prod/tax_regs/comments.html.

FOR FURTHER INFORMATION CONTACT: Concerning the regulations, Lilo Hester, 202-622-3840; concerning submissions, Evangelista Lee, 202-622-8452 (not toll-free numbers).

SUPPLEMENTARY INFORMATION:

Background

This document contains proposed amendments to the Income Tax Regulations (26 CFR part 1) under section 1441 of the Internal Revenue Code (Code). These amendments are proposed to provide general procedures for withholding agents and payors to establish acceptable electronic systems.

Final regulations published in the Rules and Regulations section of this issue of the Federal Register add §1.1441-1(e)(4)(iv) which authorizes the electronic transmission of a Form W-8 described in §1.1441-1(e)(1)(i). In addition, by cross-reference contained in §1.6049-5(c)(2) (published as a final rule in the Rules and Regulations section of this issue of the Federal Register), the regulation authorizes electronic transmission of a Form W-8 furnished for purposes of chapter 61 of the Code (i.e., information reporting) or for purposes of another income tax withholding provision of the Code, such as section 3406.

Pursuant to chapter 3 (or, in certain cases, chapter 61) of the Code, a beneficial owner or a payee (i.e., a person who receives a payment) must furnish a withholding certificate to a withholding agent or payor in order to establish its status as a foreign person and entitlement to a reduced rate of withholding. By establishing foreign status, and other relevant characteristics, a beneficial owner or payee may be entitled to a reduction or exemption in the amount of withholding under chapter 3 of the Code or an exemption from information reporting under chapter 61 of the Code or from backup withholding under section 3406. The receipt of a withholding certificate affects the amount of tax that the withholding agent or payor may be required to withhold from the payment, and the type and form of information that it must provide to the IRS. The regulations under sections 1441 and 1443 specifically identify Form W-8 (or an acceptable substitute form) as the required form of the withholding certificate.

These proposed regulations apply to electronic transmission of Forms W-8. The regulations do not apply to Form 8233 for use by individuals who claim a reduced rate of withholding under an income tax convention for services performed in the United States. See §1.1441-4(b)(2). In addition, the regulations do not apply to documentary evidence (described in §1.6049-5(c)(1)) that may be substituted for the Form W-8 with respect to certain payments made to accounts maintained outside of the United States. However, the IRS and Treasury invite comments on any computer technology (e.g., imaging) that could make electronic transmission of documentary evidence possible.

Explanation of Provisions

1. Type and Design of System Determined by Withholding Agent or Payor Subject to Specific Requirements.

Under the proposed regulations, a withholding agent or payor may choose to establish an electronic system to receive or transmit Forms W-8 (or such other form as the IRS may prescribe), including a payor or withholding agent that is an intermediary. The withholding agent or payor may determine the type of system (such as telephone or computer) available for that purpose. The system must, however, (1) reliably identify the user, (2) ensure that the information received is the information sent, and (3) document occasions of user access that result in a submission, renewal, or modification of the withholding certificate. The proposed regulations envision that implementation of these specific requirements necessitates a direct relationship between the withholding agent or payor and the beneficial owner or payee. The proposed regulations reserve on applicable standards for systems used by intermediaries to transmit forms received from another payor or withholding agent. The IRS and Treasury recognize the importance of allowing the electronic transmission of Forms W-8 through one or more intermediaries (i.e., persons not acting for their own account). Therefore, comments are solicited regarding the logistical operation of an electronic transmission system for use by an intermediary satisfying the IRS requirements that the integrity, accuracy, and reliability of the original electronic transmission through an intermediary system is adequately protected.

2. Relationship Between Paper and Electronic Withholding Certificate.

The electronic transmission must contain exactly the same information as the paper Form W-8 (or such other form as the IRS may prescribe). Any guidance, such as regulations or instructions, that applies to the paper Form W-8 also applies to electronically transmitted forms.

3. Electronic Filing Optional.

Section 1.1441-1(e)(4)(iv) authorizing the use of electronic systems was promulgated to assist in reducing burdens (in terms of cost and time) on withholding agents, payors, payees, and beneficial owners. The use of an electronic system for the transmission of Form W-8 is merely an alternative to the use of a paper form. Electronic transmission of Form W-8 is not mandatory. A withholding agent or payor may not mandate the use of electronic systems to receive or transmit the forms. Thus, a payee or beneficial owner may furnish a Form W-8 to the withholding agent or payor on paper.

4. Signature Under Penalties of Perjury.

Section 6061 generally provides that any return, statement, or other document required to be made under any provision of the internal revenue laws or regulations shall be signed in accordance with forms or regulations prescribed by the Secretary. Section 301.6061-1(b) provides that the Secretary may prescribe in forms, instructions, or other appropriate guidance the method of signing any return, statement, or other document required to be made under any provision of the internal revenue laws or regulations. Section 6065 provides that, except as provided by the Secretary, any return, statement or other document shall contain or be verified by a written declaration that it is made under the penalties of perjury. These requirements apply to a Form W-8 (or such other form as the Internal Revenue Service may prescribe), including one that is filed electronically, as provided in § 1.1441-1(e)(2)(ii), (3)(ii), (3)(iii), and (3)(v), and § 1.1441-5(c)(2)(iv) and (3)(iii) of the final regulations. The proposed regulations, therefore, include guidance on the perjury statement and the signature requirements for Forms W-8 that are filed electronically.

5. IRS Requests for Electronic Data.

Upon request by the IRS in the course of an examination, a withholding agent or payor must supply a hard copy of the information contained on the electronically transmitted Form W-8 and a statement that, to the best of the withholding agent's knowledge, the electronic Form W-8 was furnished by the person whose name is on the form. The printout of the Form W-8 information must be provided to the IRS in English.

Proposed Effective Date

These regulations are proposed to become effective January 1, 1999.

Special Analyses

It has been determined that this Treasury decision is not a significant regulatory action as defined in EO 12866. Therefore, a regulatory assessment is not required. It also has been determined that section 553(b) of the Administrative Procedure Act (5 U.S.C. chapter 5) does not apply to these regulations, and, because the proposed regulations do not impose a collection of information on small entities, the Regulatory Flexibility Act (5 U.S.C. chapter 6) does not apply. Pursuant to section 7805(f) of the Code, this notice of proposed rulemaking will be submitted to the Small Business Administration for comment on its impact on small business.

Comments and Requests for a Public Hearing

Before these proposed regulations are adopted as final regulations, consideration will be given to any written comments (a signed original and eight copies) that are submitted timely (in the manner described in the ADDRESSES portion of this preamble) to the IRS. All comments will be available for public inspection and copying.

A public hearing may be scheduled if requested in writing by any person that submits written comments. If a public hearing is scheduled, notice of the date, time, and place for the hearing will be published in the Federal Register.

Drafting Information

The principal author of these regulations is Lilo A. Hester, Office of the Associate Chief Counsel (International), IRS. However, other personnel from the IRS and Treasury Department participated in their development.

[¶ 49,161] Proposed Amendments of Regulations (REG-114000-97), published in the Federal Register on October 14, 1997.

Withholding: Nonresident aliens: Sale of obligations: Interest: Between interest payment dates.—Amendments of Reg. § 1.1441-3, relating to the obligation to withhold on interest paid

with respect to obligations in the case of sales of obligations between interest payment dates, are proposed. A public hearing on this proposal is scheduled for January 26, 1998.

AGENCY: Internal Revenue Service (IRS), Treasury.

ACTION: Notice of proposed rulemaking and notice of public hearing.

SUMMARY: This notice of proposed rulemaking provides guidance regarding the obligation to withhold on interest paid with respect to obligations in the case of the sale of obligations between interest payment dates. These regulations would affect United States and foreign withholding agents and recipients. This document also provides notice of a public hearing on these proposed regulations.

DATES: Comments and outlines of oral comments to be presented at the public hearing scheduled for January 26, 1998, at 10 a.m. must be received by January 5, 1998.

ADDRESSES: Send submission to: CC:DOM:CORP:R (REG-114000-97), room 5226, Internal Revenue Service, POB 7604, Ben Franklin Station, Washington DC 20224. Submissions may be hand delivered between the hours of 8 a.m. and 5 p.m. to: CC:DOM:CORP:R (Reg-114000-97), Courier desk, Internal Revenue Service, 1111 Constitution Avenue, NW., Washington DC. Alternatively, taxpayers may submit comments electronically via the internet by selecting the "Tax Regs" option on the IRS Home Page, or by submitting comments directly to the IRS internet site at http://www.irs.ustreas.gov/prod/tax>regs/comments.html. The hearing scheduled for January 26, 1998, will be held in the Commissioner's Conference Room, room 3313, Internal Revenue Service, 1111 Constitution Avenue, NW., Washington, DC.

FOR FURTHER INFORMATION CONTACT: Concerning the regulations, Lilo Hester at (202) 622-3840 (not a toll-free number); concerning submissions and the hearing, Evangelista Lee, (202) 622-7180 (not a toll-free number).

SUPPLEMENTARY INFORMATION

Background

In this issue of the Federal Register, the IRS and Treasury are publishing final withholding and reporting regulations under chapter 3 of the Internal Revenue Code (Code) and other sections of the Code. Section 1.1441-3(b)(2) of the final regulations provides that no withholding is required upon interest accrued on the date of a sale of debt obligations when the sale occurs between two interest payment dates, even though the amount is treated as interest under § 1.61-7(c) or (d) and is subject to tax under section 871 or 881. In contrast, § 1.1441-2(b)(3) of the final regulations provides that withholding is required on amounts of original issue discount in the event of a sale of an original issue discount obligation or a payment on such an obligation, subject to certain exceptions. The IRS and Treasury believe that, in view of these provisions, the exemption from withholding on non-OID amounts is no longer justified. A withholding agent that pays amounts to a foreign person in connection with the sale of an obligation between interest payments dates is in the same position as a withholding agent that pays amounts to a foreign person in connection with the sale of an original issue discount obligation. The withholding exemption for sale of debt obligations between interest payment dates provides an easy avenue for the avoidance of the documentation requirements imposed under sections 871(h) and 881(c) for purposes of qualifying interest on registered debt obligations as portfolio interest. For this reason, and in order to create parity with the tax treatment of original issue discount obligations under chapter 3 of the Code, it is no longer appropriate to continue this exemption.

Under § 1.1441-2(b)(3), a withholding agent must withhold on an amount of original issue discount to the extent that it has actual knowledge of the proportion of the amount of the payment that is taxable to the beneficial owner under section 871(a)(1)(C) or 881(a)(3)(A). A withholding agent has actual knowledge if it knows how long the beneficial owner has held the obligation, the terms of the obligation, and the extent to which the beneficial owner purchased the obligation at a premium. A withholding agent is treated as having knowledge if the information is reasonably available. Special rules are provided for withholding agents with which the beneficial owner does not maintain a direct account relationship. Further, the regulations under § 1.1441-2(b)(3) dealing with original issue discount provide that, in the case of an obligation that would qualify as portfolio interest if documentation were provided to the withholding agent, withholding is required on the entire amount of stated interest, if any, and original issue discount, if no such documentation is provided, irrespective of whether the withholding agent has knowledge of the portion of the payment representing taxable original issue discount. For this purpose, the withholding agent may rely upon the IRS List of Original issue Discount Instruments contained in IRS Publication 1212 (available from the IRS Distribution Centers).

In response to comments, the provisions in § 1.1441-3(b)(1) are proposed to be modified to reduce the amount upon which withholding is required. No obligation to withhold is imposed under current law on the payment of stated interest on an obligation that was purchased between interest payment dates. Under § 1.61-7(c), interest received on the interest payment date is treated as a return of basis to the extent it represents accrued unpaid interest as of the date of purchase as reflected in the new holder's basis for the obligation. Therefore, when the new holder receives a payment of the stated interest, the holder's tax liability is limited to the amount of interest accrued after the date of purchase (subject to additional adjustments reflecting possible acquisition premiums or market discounts). Because of the difficulty for a withholding agent to determine the amount accrued to the holder and other adjustments affecting the actual amount taxable to the holder, withholding on the entire amount of stated interest is required under the current withholding regulations under §1.1441-3(b)(1).

Commentators have asked that the withholding agent be permitted to withhold on the amount that it knows is taxable. The final withholding regulations did not modify the proposed regulations on this point because the Treasury and IRS consider that withholding on the entire amount is justified if withholding on sales of obligations between interest payment dates is not required. However, because these proposed regulations require withholding, the regulations permit a withholding agent to adjust the amount of withholding at the time of payment of stated interest to account for earlier withholding.

Special Analyses

It has been determined that this notice of proposed rulemaking is not a significant regulatory action as defined in EO 12866. Therefore, a regulatory assessment is not required. It also has been determined that section 553(b) of the Administrative Procedure Act (5 U.S.C. chapter 5) does not apply to these regulations, and because the regulation does not impose a collection of information on small entities, the Regulatory Flexibility Act (5 U.S.C. chapter 6) does not apply. Pursuant to section 7805(f) of the Internal Revenue Code, this notice of proposed rulemaking will be submitted to the Chief Counsel for Advocacy of the Small Business Administration for comment on its impact on small business.

Comments and Public Hearing

Before these proposed regulations are adopted as final regulations, consideration will be given to any comments that are submitted timely to the IRS. All comments will be available for public inspection and copying.

A public hearing has been scheduled for January 26, 1998, at 10 a.m. in the Commissioner's Conference Room, room 3313, Internal Revenue Building, 1111 Constitution Ave, NW., Washington DC. Because of access restrictions, visitors will not be admitted beyond the Internal Revenue Building lobby more than 15 minutes before the hearing starts.

The rules of 26 CFR 601.601(a)(3) apply to the hearing.

Persons who wish to present oral comments at the hearing must submit comments and an outline of the topics to be discussed and the time to be devoted to each topic by January 5, 1998.

A period of 10 minutes will be allotted to each person for making comments.

An agenda showing the scheduling of the speakers will be prepared after the deadline for receiving outlines has passed. Copies of the agenda will be available free of charge at the hearing.

[¶49,164] Proposed Regulations and Proposed Amendments of Regulations (REG-115795-97), published in the Federal Register on January 2, 1998.

Passive foreign investment companies: Shareholders: Qualified electing fund election.—Amendments of proposed Reg. §1.1296-4 (as proposed on 4/28/95 by INTL-65-93 (¶49,203)) and Reg. §1.1297-3, relating to rules for a passive foreign investment company shareholder that makes the election under Code Sec. 1295 to treat the passive foreign investment company as a qualified electing fund, are proposed. Reg. §§1.1291-1, 1.1293-1, 1.1295-1 and 1.1295-3 were adopted 2/4/2000 by T.D. 8870.

AGENCY: Internal Revenue Service (IRS), Treasury

ACTION: Notice of proposed rulemaking by cross-reference to temporary regulations and notice of public hearing.

SUMMARY: In the Rules and Regulations section of this issue of the Federal Register, the IRS is issuing temporary regulations that provide guidance to a passive foreign investment company (PFIC) shareholder that makes the election under section 1295 (section 1295 election) to treat the PFIC as a qualified electing fund (QEF). The temporary regulations also provide guidance for shareholders that wish to make a section 1295 election that will apply on a retroactive basis (retroactive election). The temporary regulations also include a rule concerning the taxation under section 1291 of an exempt organization that is a shareholder of a PFIC that is not a pedigreed QEF. This rule was originally proposed in 1992. The text of the temporary regulations also serves as the text of these proposed regulations. In addition, this document proposes amendments to proposed regulation §1.1296-4(e), concerning the treatment of interbank deposits as loans for purposes of the exception to passive income characterization of income derived in the active conduct of a banking business. This document also provides notice of a public hearing on these proposed regulations.

DATES: Written comments must be received by April 2, 1998. Requests to speak and outlines of oral comments to be discussed at the public hearing scheduled for April 16, 1998, must be received by March 26, 1998.

ADDRESSES: Send submissions to: CC:DOM:CORP:R (REG-115795-97), room 5226, Internal Revenue Service, POB 7604, Ben Franklin Station, Washington, DC 20044. Submissions may be hand delivered between the hours of 8 a.m. and 5 p.m. to: CC:DOM:CORP:R (REG-115795-97), Courier's Desk, Internal Revenue Service, 1111 Constitution Avenue, NW, Washington, DC. Alternatively, taxpayers may submit comments electronically via the Internet by selecting the "Tax Regs" option on the IRS Home Page, or by submitting comments directly to the IRS Internet site at http://www.irs.ustreas.gov/prod/tax>regs/comments.html. The public hearing will be held in Room 3313, Internal Revenue Service, 1111 Constitution Avenue, NW, Washington, DC.

FOR FURTHER INFORMATION CONTACT: Concerning the regulations, Gayle Novig, (202) 622-3840; concerning submissions and the hearing, Evangelista Lee, (202) 622-7190 (not toll-free numbers).

SUPPLEMENTARY INFORMATION:

Paperwork Reduction Act

The collection of information contained in this notice of proposed rulemaking has been submitted to the Office of Management and Budget for review in accordance with the Paperwork Reduction Act of 1995 (44 U.S.C. 3507(d)).

Comments on the collection of information should be sent to the Office of Management and Budget, Attn: Desk Officer for the Department of the Treasury, Office of Information and Regulatory Affairs, Washington, DC 20503, with copies to the Internal Revenue Service, Attn: IRS Reports Clearance Officer, T:FP, Washington, DC 20224. Comments on the collection of information should be received by March 3, 1998. Comments are specifically requested concerning:

Whether the proposed collection of information is necessary for the proper performance of the functions of the Internal Revenue Service, including whether the information will have practical utility;

The accuracy of the estimated burden associated with the proposed collection of information (see below);

How the quality, utility, and clarity of the information to be collected may be enhanced;

How the burden of complying with the proposed collection of information may be minimized, including through the application of automated collection techniques or other forms of information technology; and

Estimates of capital or start-up costs and costs of operation, maintenance, and purchase of services to provide information.

The collection of information in this proposed regulation is in proposed regulation §§1.1295-1(f), 1.1295-1(g), 1.1295-3(c), and 1.1295-3(g). The information required in §1.1295-1(f) and (g) will notify the Internal Revenue Service that certain shareholders have made the section 1295 election, and will enable the Internal Revenue Service to determine if a shareholder is satisfying the election and annual reporting requirements and is reporting income as required under section 1293.

The information required in proposed regulation §1.1295-3(c) will notify the IRS that certain shareholders of foreign corporations have filed a Protective Statement to preserve their ability to make a retroactive section 1295 election, and that those shareholders have extended the periods of limitations for their taxable years to which the Protective Statement will apply. The information will enable the IRS to verify that the shareholders filing the Protective Statement had the requisite reasonable belief at the time they filed the statement. The information required in proposed regulation §1.1295-3(g) will notify the IRS that a shareholder has made the retroactive election and, in the case of a shareholder that filed a Protective Statement, that the shareholder's waiver of the periods of limitations will terminate within three years of making the election. The information will enable the Service to verify that the requirements for making a retroactive election have been satisfied.

The collection of information and responses to these collections of information are mandatory. The likely respondents are individuals, businesses, and other for-profit organizations.

An agency may not conduct or sponsor, and a person is not required to respond to, a collection of information unless the collection of information displays a valid control number assigned by the Office of Management and Budget.

Books or records relating to a collection of information must be retained as long as their contents may become material in the administration of any internal revenue law. Generally, tax returns and tax return information are confidential, as required by 26 U.S.C. 6103.

Estimated total annual reporting/recordkeeping burden: 623 hours. The estimated annual burden per respondent varies from 15 minutes to three hours, depending on individual circumstances, with an estimated average of 29 minutes.

Estimated number of respondents: 1,290.

Estimated annual frequency of responses: Annually or one time only.

Background

Sections 1291, 1293, 1295, and 1297.

Temporary regulations in the Rules and Regulations section of this issue of the Federal Register amend the Income Tax Regulations (26 CFR part 1) relating to sections 1291, 1293, 1295, and 1297. The temporary regulations contain rules concerning the taxation of exempt organizations under section 1291, elections under section 1295 to treat passive foreign investment companies as qualified electing funds (QEFs), the calculation of net capital gain for purposes of section 1293, and the inclusion of the pro rata shares of the earnings and profits of QEFs held through pass through entities. The temporary regulations amend §1.1297-3T, permitting in certain cases the application of the rules of section 1291(d)(2)(B) to an election made under section 1297(b)(1).

The text of those temporary regulations also serves as the text of these proposed regulations. The preamble to the temporary regulations explains the temporary regulations.

Section 1296.

On April 28, 1995, proposed regulations were published providing guidance for the exceptions to passive income characterization of certain income derived by active foreign banks and foreign security dealers provided in section 1296(b)(2)(A) and (b)(3), respectively. The proposed section 1296 regulations reflect comments received with respect to Notice 89-81, 1989-2 C.B. 399. That notice established tests for determining whether a foreign corporation qualified for the active foreign bank exception. The notice specifically stated that interbank deposits would not be treated as loans made in the ordinary course of a banking business.

After consideration of the comments received with respect to the Notice, the IRS and Treasury determined that interbank deposits were made and accepted in the ordinary course of a banking business, and therefore should be treated as such for purposes of section 1296(b)(2)(A). Accordingly, proposed regulation § 1.1296-4(d)(3) specifically includes interbank deposits with other deposits for purposes of determining whether the foreign corporation satisfies the deposit-taking requirements of § 1.1296-4(d). Also in response to comments, proposed regulation § 1.1296-4(e) is clarified to specifically provide that interbank deposits made with banks in the ordinary course of business constitute loans for purposes of § 1.1296-4. This clarification is favorable to taxpayers, and is proposed to be effective for taxable years beginning after December 31, 1994. It is also proposed that taxpayers may apply it to a taxable year beginning after December 31, 1986, provided it is consistently applied to that taxable year and all subsequent taxable years. The dates for applying proposed regulation § 1.1296-4(e) coincide with the dates for which § 1.1296-4 is proposed to be effective. See proposed regulation § 1.1296-4(k).

Special Analyses

It has been determined that this notice of proposed rulemaking is not a significant regulatory action as defined in Executive Order 12866. Therefore, a regulatory assessment is not required. Pursuant to section 7805(f) of the Internal Revenue Code, this notice of proposed rulemaking will be submitted to the Chief Counsel for Advocacy of the Small Business Administration for comment on its impact on small business. It has been determined that an initial regulatory flexibility analysis is required for the collection of information in this notice of proposed rulemaking under 5 U.S.C. § 603. This analysis is set forth below under the heading 'Initial Regulatory Flexibility Analysis.'

Initial Regulatory Flexibility Analysis. This initial analysis is provided pursuant to the Regulatory Flexibility Act (5 U.S.C. chapter 6). The major objective of the proposed regulations is to provide guidance to PFIC shareholders that wish to elect under section 1295 to treat their PFICs as QEFs, and provide guidance to those PFICs about the requirements imposed on them. The legal basis for these requirements is contained in sections 1293, 1294, and 1295. The IRS and Treasury are not aware of any federal rules that duplicate, overlap, or conflict with the proposed regulations.

The recordkeeping and reporting requirements of the proposed regulations enable the Internal Revenue Service to identify those taxpayers that are treating their PFICs as QEFs; to verify that those U.S. taxpayers are currently including their shares of QEF earnings in income, as required in section 1293 of the Internal Revenue Code; to be informed of those QEF shareholders that are not paying their section 1293 tax liability because they made the section 1294 election to defer the time for payment; to identify those shareholders of foreign corporations that are preserving their right to make a retroactive section 1295 election; to identify those shareholders making retroactive elections and verify that they are satisfying the requirements of a retroactive election; and, in the case of shareholders that have filed Protective Statements, the dates by which the shareholders' extensions of periods of limitations will terminate.

These proposed regulations will affect those small entities that are PFICs, at least one shareholder of which makes the section 1295 election. The proposed regulations also will affect those small entities that are PFIC shareholders that make the section 1295 election. The IRS and Treasury believe that affected small entities generally will be small businesses, as local governments are not likely to invest in PFICs. Also, few, if any, affected small entities likely will be tax exempt organizations, because only a tax exempt entity that is taxable under subchapter F on dividends received from the PFIC generally would need to consider making the section 1295 election.

The collections of information in these proposed regulations would impact a small entity that is treated as a QEF principally by requiring the entity to calculate annually its ordinary earnings and net capital gain according to federal income tax accounting principles, as required by section 1293, and report that information to its shareholders that are U.S. persons. With the enactment of section 1(h), the QEF also must calculate each type of long term capital gain that it derived and the applicable rates of tax for proper inclusion of the QEF's net capital gain by the QEF shareholders. Alternatively, the regulations permit the QEF to provide its shareholders with its books, records and other documents necessary for the shareholders to calculate the ordinary earnings and net capital gain amounts. This alternative will enable a small entity that is a QEF to avoid the burden of calculating its net capital gain by providing its shareholders with information with which the shareholders can make the calculations.

The economic impact of other collections of information contained in these proposed regulations would fall on a small entity that is a shareholder of a PFIC for which it has made the section 1295 election or that is a pass through entity to which an interest holder transferred stock subject to a section 1295 election. The economic impact would result primarily from the reporting and recordkeeping requirements pertaining to (1) the manner for making the section 1295 election and the annual election requirements; (2) the calculation by the shareholder (rather than the QEF) of the QEF's ordinary earnings and net capital gain according to federal income tax principles, and its pro rata shares thereof; (3) a request for consent to revoke a section 1295 election; (4) the preservation of the right to make a retroactive election under section 1295; (5) a request for consent to make a retroactive election; (6) making a retroactive election, including filing amended returns for the affected taxable years; and (7) providing interest holders with PFIC statements and other information received by an intermediary shareholder.

The proposed regulations reduce the burden under existing rules for making the section 1295 election for all taxpayers, including small businesses and other small entities. Unlike the current requirements provided in Notice 88-125, the proposed regulations only require electing shareholders to file Form 8621 to make the section 1295 election, thereby eliminating the shareholder election statement as well as the requirement to file a copy of the PFIC Annual Information Statement. The proposed regulations only require shareholders to retain the PFIC Annual Information Statement or the Annual Intermediary Statement received as well as a copy of their filings for each year to which the section 1295 election applies. In addition, the proposed regulations impose a lesser burden on small shareholders, typically individuals and small entities, to preserve their right to make a retroactive election and a lesser burden of making a retroactive election. A small entity that owns less than five percent of each class of stock of a foreign corporation and satisfies other requirements is not required to file a Protective Statement to preserve its right to make a retroactive election with respect to the foreign corporation. Similarly, a small entity potentially has fewer amended returns to file to make a retroactive election than a shareholder that filed a Protective Statement. These changes in election requirements are illustrative of IRS efforts to minimize burden, particularly with respect to small entities.

An estimate of the number of small entities that would be affected by these regulations is unavailable. In any event, the enactment in 1997 of the mark-to-market election for PFIC shareholders and the elimination of the overlap in certain cases of subpart F and the PFIC provisions, will reduce the number of small entities that would be affected by these regulations.

None of the significant alternatives considered in drafting these regulations would have significantly altered the economic impact of the collections of information on small entities. In considering the significant alternatives that would be permissible under the Code and would enable the IRS to ensure compliance with the Code, the IRS and Treasury concluded that the alternatives generally would impose equal or greater burdens.

Comments and Public Hearing

Before these proposed regulations are adopted as final regulations, consideration will be given to any written comments (a signed original and eight (8) copies) that are submitted timely to the IRS. All comments will be available for public inspection and copying.

A public hearing has been scheduled for April 16, 1998, at 10 a.m., in room 2615, Internal Revenue Building, 1111 Constitution Avenue, NW, Washington, DC. Because of access restrictions, visitors will not be admitted beyond the Internal Revenue lobby more than 15 minutes before the hearing starts.

The rules of 26 CFR 601.601(a)(3) apply to the hearing.

Persons that wish to present oral comments at the hearing must submit written comments by April 2, 1998, and submit an outline of the topics to be discussed and the time to be devoted to each topic (signed original and eight (8) copies) by March 26, 1998.

A period of 10 minutes will be allotted to each person for making comments.

An agenda showing the schedule of speakers will be prepared after the deadline for receiving outlines has passed. Copies of the agenda will be available free of charge at the hearing.

Drafting Information

The principal authors of the proposed regulations are Gayle Novig and Judith Cavell Cohen, of the Office of the Associate Chief Counsel (International). Other personnel from the IRS and Treasury Department also participated in the development of these regulations.

[¶49,165] Proposed Regulations and Proposed Amendments of Regulations (REG-208299-90), published in the Federal Register on March 6, 1998 (corrected 4/21/98).

Global dealing operations: Allocation and sourcing of income and deductions.—Reg. §§1.475(g)-2 and 1.482-8 and amendments of Reg. §§1.482-0—1.482-2, 1.482-8, 1.863-3, 1.863-7, 1.864-4, 1.864-6, 1.894-1 and 1.988-4, relating to the allocation and sourcing of income, deductions, gains and losses from a global dealing operation, are proposed. A public hearing on this proposal is scheduled for July 14, 1998.

AGENCY: Internal Revenue Service (IRS), Treasury.

ACTION: Notice of proposed rulemaking and notice of public hearing.

SUMMARY: This document contains proposed rules for the allocation among controlled taxpayers and sourcing of income, deductions, gains and losses from a global dealing operation; rules applying these allocation and sourcing rules to foreign currency transactions and to foreign corporations engaged in a U.S. trade or business; and rules concerning the mark-to-market treatment resulting from hedging activities of a global dealing operation. These proposed rules affect foreign and domestic persons that are participants in such operations either directly or indirectly through subsidiaries or partnerships. These proposed rules are necessary to enable participants in a global dealing operation to determine their arm's length contribution to a global dealing operation. This document also provides notice of a public hearing on these proposed regulations.

DATES: Written comments must be received by June 4, 1998. Outlines of oral comments to be discussed at the public hearing scheduled for July 14, 1998, must be received by June 18, 1998.

ADDRESSES: Send submissions to: CC:DOM:CORP:R (REG-208299-90), room 5226, Internal Revenue Service, POB 7604, Ben Franklin Station, Washington, DC 20044. Submissions may be hand delivered between the hours of 8 a.m. and 5 p.m. to: CC:DOM:CORP:R (REG-208299-90), Courier's Desk, Internal Revenue Service, 1111 Constitution Avenue, N.W., Washington, D.C. Alternatively, taxpayers may submit comments electronically via the Internet by selecting the "Tax Regs" option on the IRS Home Page, or by submitting comments directly to the IRS Internet site at http://www.irs.ustreas.gov/prod/tax>regs/comments.html. The public hearing will be held in room 2615, Internal Revenue Building, 1111 Constitution Avenue, NW, Washington, DC.

FOR FURTHER INFORMATION CONTACT: Concerning the regulations in general, Ginny Chung of the Office of Associate Chief Counsel (International), (202) 622-3870; concerning the mark-to-market treatment of global dealing operations, Richard Hoge or JoLynn Ricks of the Office of Assistant Chief Counsel (Financial Institutions & Products), (202) 622-3920; concerning submissions and the hearing, Michael Slaughter, (202) 622-7190 (not toll-free numbers).

SUPPLEMENTARY INFORMATION:

Paperwork Reduction Act

The collections of information contained in this notice of proposed rulemaking have been submitted to the Office of Management and Budget for review in accordance with the Paperwork Reduction Act of 1995 (44 U.S.C. 3507(d)). Comments on the collections of information should be sent to the Office of Management and Budget, Attn: Desk Officer for the Department of the Treasury, Office of Information and Regulatory Affairs, Washington, DC 20503, with copies to the Internal Revenue Service, Attn: IRS Reports Clearance officer, T:FS:FP, Washington, DC 20224. Comments on the collections of information should be received by May 5, 1998.

Comments are specifically requested concerning:

Whether the proposed collections of information are necessary for the proper performance of the functions of the Internal Revenue Service, including whether the information will have practical utility;

The accuracy of the estimated burden associated with the proposed collections of information (see below);

How the quality, utility, and clarity of the information to be collected may be enhanced;

How the burden of complying with the proposed collections of information may be minimized, including through the application of automated collection techniques or other forms of information technology; and

Estimates of capital or start-up costs and costs of operation, maintenance, and purchase of services to provide information.

The collections of information in these proposed regulations are in §§1.475(g)-2(b), 1.482-8(b)(3), 1.482-8(c)(3), 1.482-8(d)(3), 1.482-8(e)(5), 1.482-8(e)(6), and 1.863-3(h). The information is required to determine an arm's length price. The collections of information are mandatory. The likely recordkeepers are business or other for-profit institutions.

An agency may not conduct or sponsor, and a person is not required to respond to, a collection of information unless the collection of information displays a valid control number assigned by the Office of Management and Budget.

Books or records relating to a collection of information must be retained as long as their contents may become material in the administration of any internal revenue law. Generally, tax returns and tax return information are confidential, as required by 26 U.S.C. 6103.

Estimated total annual recordkeeping burden: 20,000 hours. Estimated average annual burden per recordkeeper is 40 hours. Estimated number of recordkeepers: 500.

Background

In 1990, the IRS issued Announcement 90-106, 1990-38 IRB 29, requesting comments on how the regulations under sections 482, 864 and other sections of the Internal Revenue Code could be improved to address the taxation issues raised by global trading of financial instruments. Section 482 concerns the allocation of income, deductions, credits and allowances among related parties. Section 864 provides rules for determining the income of a foreign person that is "effectively connected" with the conduct of a U.S. trade or business and therefore can be taxed on a net income basis in the United States. Provisions under sections 864(c)(2) and (3) provide rules for determining when U.S. source income is effectively connected income (ECI); section 864(c)(4) provides rules for determining when foreign source income is ECI.

The rules for determining the source of income generally are in sections 861, 862, 863 and 865, and the regulations promulgated under those sections. Section 1.863-7 provides a special rule for income from notional principal contracts, under which such income will be treated as U.S.-source ECI if it arises from the conduct of a U.S. trade or business under principles similar to those that apply under section 864(c)(2). An identical rule applies for determining U.S. source ECI under §1.988-4(c) from foreign exchange gain or loss from certain transactions denominated in a foreign currency.

Because no regulations were issued in response to the comments that were received after Announcement 90-106, there remain a number of uncertainties regarding the manner in which the existing regulations described above apply to financial institutions that deal in financial instruments through one or more entities or trading locations. Many financial institutions have sought to resolve these problems by negotiating advance pricing agreements (APAs) with the IRS. In 1994, the IRS published Notice 94-40, 1994-1 CB 351, which provided a generic description of the IRS's experience with global dealing operations conducted in a functionally fully integrated manner. Notice 94-40 specified that it was not intended to prescribe rules for future APAs or for taxpayers that did not enter into APAs. Moreover, Notice 94-40 provided no guidance of any kind for financial institutions that do not conduct their global dealing operations in a functionally fully integrated manner.

Explanation of Provisions

1. *Introduction*

This document contains proposed regulations relating to the determination of an arm's length allocation of income among participants engaged in a global dealing operation. For purposes of these regulations, the terms "global dealing operation" and "participant" are specifically defined. The purpose of these regulations is to provide guidance on applying the arm's length principle to transactions between participants in a global dealing operation. The general rules in the final regulations under section 482 that provide the best method rule, comparability analysis, and the arm's length range are generally adopted with some modifications to conform these principles to the global dealing environment. In addition, the proposed regulations contain new specified methods with respect to global dealing operations that replace the specified methods in §§1.482-3 through 1.482-6.

This document also contains proposed regulations addressing the source of income earned in a global dealing operation and the circumstances under which such income is effectively connected to a foreign corporation's U.S. trade or business. The regulations proposed under section 863 generally source income earned in a global dealing operation by reference to the residence of the participant. For these purposes, residence is defined under section 988(a)(3)(B) such that global dealing income may be sourced between separate qualified business units (QBUs) of a single taxpayer or among separate taxpayers who are participants, as the case may be. Exceptions to this general rule are discussed in further detail below.

Proposed amendments to the regulations under section 864 provide that the principles of the proposed section 482 regulations may be applied to determine the amount of income, gain or loss from a foreign corporation's global dealing operation that is effectively connected to a U.S. trade or business of a participant. Similar rules apply to foreign currency transactions that are part of a global dealing operation.

The combination of these allocation, sourcing, and effectively connected income rules is intended to enable taxpayers to establish and recognize on an arm's length basis the contributions provided by separate QBUs to a global dealing operation.

This document also contains proposed regulations under section 475 to coordinate the accounting rules governing the timing of income with the allocation, sourcing, and effectively connected income rules proposed in this document and discussed above.

2. *Explanation of Specific Provisions*

A. *§1.482-1(a)(1)*

Section 1.482-1(a)(1) has been amended to include expressly transactions undertaken in the course of a global dealing operation between controlled taxpayers within the scope of transactions covered by section 482. The purpose of this amendment is to clarify that the principles of section 482 apply to evaluate whether global dealing transactions entered into between controlled taxpayers are at arm's length.

B. *§1.482-8(a)—General Requirements*

Section 1.482-8(a)(1) lists specified methods that may be used to determine if global dealing transactions entered into between controlled taxpayers are at arm's length. The enumerated methods must be applied in accordance with all of the provisions of §1.482-1, including the best method rule of §1.482-1(c), the comparability analysis of §1.482-1(d), and the arm's length range rule of §1.482-1(e). The section further requires that any modifications or supplemental considerations applicable to a global dealing operation set forth in §1.482-8(a)(3) be taken into account when applying any of the transfer pricing methods. Specific modifications to the factors for determining comparability and the arm's length range rule are provided in §1.482-8(a)(3). These modifications and special considerations are discussed in more detail under their respective headings below.

C. *§1.482-8(a)(2)—Definitions Applicable to a Global Dealing Operation*

Section 1.482-8(a)(2) defines "global dealing operation," "participant," "regular dealer in securities," and other terms that apply for purposes of these regulations. These definitions supplement the general definitions provided in §1.482-1(i).

The rules of §1.482-8 apply only to a global dealing operation. A "global dealing operation" consists of the execution of customer transactions (including marketing, sales, pricing and risk management activities) in a particular financial product or line of financial products, in multiple tax jurisdictions and/or through multiple participants. The taking of proprietary positions is not included within the definition of a global dealing operation unless the proprietary positions are entered into by a regular dealer in securities in connection with its activities as such a dealer. Thus, a hedge fund that does not have customers is not covered by these regulations. Positions held in inventory by a regular dealer in securities, however, are covered by these regulations even if the positions are unhedged because the dealer is taking a view as to future market changes.

Similarly, lending activities are not included within the definition of a global dealing operation. However, if a person makes a market in, by buying and selling, asset-backed securities, the income from that activity may be covered by these regulations, regardless of whether the dealer was a party to the loans backing the securities. Therefore, income earned from such lending activities or from securities held for investment is not income from a global dealing operation and is not governed by this section. A security may be held for investment for purposes of this section even though it is not identified as held for investment under section 475.

Activities unrelated to the conduct of a global dealing operation are not covered by these regulations, even if they are accounted for on a mark-to-market basis. Accordingly, income from proprietary trading that is not undertaken in connection with a global dealing operation, and other financial transactions that are not entered into in a dealing capacity are not covered by these proposed regulations. The regulations require that participants engaged in dealing and nondealing activities and/or multiple dealing activities segregate income and expense attributable to each separate dealing operation so that the best method may be used to evaluate whether controlled transactions entered into in connection with a particular dealing activity are priced at arm's length. The regulations also require that taxpayers segregate their dealer activities from their lending, proprietary trading or other investment activities not entered into in connection with a global dealing operation. Comments are solicited on whether the proposed regulations issued under section 475 in this notice of proposed rulemaking are sufficient to facilitate identification of the amount of income that should be subject to allocation under the global dealing regulations.

The term "participant" is defined as a controlled taxpayer that is either a regular dealer in securities within the meaning of § 1.482-8(a)(2)(iii), or a member of a group of controlled taxpayers which includes a regular dealer in securities, so long as that member conducts one or more activities related to the activities of such dealer. For these purposes, such related activities are the marketing, sales, pricing, and risk management activities necessary to the definition of a global dealing operation. Additionally, brokering is a related activity that may give rise to participant status. Related activities do not include credit analysis, accounting services, back office services, or the provision of a guarantee of one or more transactions entered into by a regular dealer in securities or other participant. This definition is significant because the transfer pricing methods contained in this section can only be used by participants, and only to evaluate whether compensation attributable to a regular dealer in securities or a marketing, sales, pricing, risk management or brokering function is at arm's length. Whether the compensation paid for other functions performed in the course of a global dealing operation (including certain services and development of intangibles) is at arm's length is determined under the appropriate section 482 regulations applicable to those transactions.

The definition of a global dealing operation does not require that the global dealing operation be conducted around the world or on a twenty-four hour basis. These regulations will apply if the controlled taxpayers, or QBUs of a single taxpayer, operate in the aggregate in more than one tax jurisdiction. It is not necessary, however, for the participants to conduct the global dealing operation in more than one tax jurisdiction. For example, a participant that is resident in one tax jurisdiction may conduct its participant activities in the global dealing operation through a trade or business in another jurisdiction that is the same jurisdiction where the dealer activity of a separate controlled taxpayer takes place. In this situation, the rules of this section apply to determine the allocation of income, gain or loss between the two controlled taxpayers even if all of the income, gain or loss is allocable within the same tax jurisdiction.

The term "regular dealer in securities" is specifically defined in this regulation consistently with the definition of a regular dealer under § 1.954-2(a)(4)(iv). Under these proposed regulations, a dealer in physical securities or currencies is a regular dealer in securities if it regularly and actively offers to, and in fact does, purchase securities or currencies from and sell securities or currencies to customers who are not controlled taxpayers in the ordinary course of a trade or business. In addition, a dealer in derivatives is a regular dealer in securities if it regularly and actively offers to, and in fact does, enter into, assume, offset, assign or otherwise terminate positions in securities with customers who are not controlled entities in the ordinary course of a trade or business. The IRS solicits comments on whether these regulations should be extended to cover dealers in commodities and/or persons trading for their own account that are not dealers.

D. *Best Method and Comparability*

Consistent with the general principles of section 482, the best method rule applies to evaluate the most appropriate method for determining whether the controlled transactions are priced at arm's length. New specified methods which replace the specified methods of § § 1.482-2 through 1.482-6 for a global dealing operation are set forth in § § 1.482-8(b) through 1.482-8(f). The comparable profits method of § 1.482-5 has been excluded as a specified method for a global dealing operation because of the high variability in profits from company to company and year to year due to differences in business strategies and fluctuations in the financial markets.

The proposed regulations do not apply specific methods to certain trading models, such as those commonly referred to in the financial services industry as "separate enterprise," "natural home," "centralized product management," or "integrated trading." Rather, the proposed regulations adopt the best method rule of § 1.482-1(c) to determine the most appropriate transfer pricing methodology, taking into account all of the facts and circumstances of a particular taxpayer's trading structure. Consistent with the best method rule, there is no priority of methods.

Application of the best method rule will depend on the structure and organization of the individual taxpayer's global dealing operation and the nature of the transaction at issue. Where a taxpayer is engaged in more than one global dealing operation, it will be necessary to segregate each activity and determine on a transaction-by-transaction basis within each activity which method provides the most reliable measure of an arm's length price. It may be appropriate to apply the same method to multiple transactions of the same type within a single business activity entered into as part of a global dealing operation. For example, if a taxpayer operates its global dealing activity in notional principal contracts differently than its foreign exchange trading activity, then the income from notional principal contracts may be allocated using a different methodology than the income from foreign exchange trading. Moreover, the best method rule may require that different methods be used to determine whether different controlled transactions are priced at arm's length even within the same product line. For example, one method may be the most appropriate to determine if a controlled transaction between a global dealing operation and another business activity is at arm's length, while a different method may be the most appropriate to determine if the allocation of income and expenses among participants in a global dealing operation is at arm's length.

Section 1.482-8(a)(3) reiterates that the principle of comparability in § 1.482-1(d) applies to transactions entered into by a global dealing operation. The comparability factors provided in § 1.482-8(a)(3) (functional analysis, risk, and economic conditions), however, must be applied in place of the comparability factors discussed in § 1.482-1(d)(3). The comparability factors for contractual terms in § 1.482-8(a)(3) supplement the comparability factors for contractual terms in § 1.482-1(d)(3)(ii). The comparability factors in this section have been included to provide guidance on the factors that may be most relevant in assessing comparability in the context of a global dealing operation.

E. *Arm's Length Range*

In determining the arm's length range, § 1.482-1(e) will apply except as modified by these proposed regulations. In determining the reliability of an arm's length range, the IRS believes that it is necessary to consider the fact that the market for financial products is highly volatile and participants in a global dealing operation frequently earn only thin profit margins. The reliability of using a statistical range in establishing a comparable price of a financial product in a global dealing operation is based on facts and circumstances. In a global dealing operation, close proximity in time between a controlled transaction and an uncontrolled transaction may be a relevant factor in determining the reliability of the uncontrolled transaction as a measure of the arm's length price. The relevant time period will depend on the price volatility of the particular product.

The district director may, notwithstanding § 1.482-1(e)(1), adjust a taxpayer's results under a method applied on a transaction-by-transaction basis if a valid statistical analysis demonstrates that the taxpayer's controlled prices, when analyzed on an aggregate basis, provide results that are not arm's length. See § 1.482-1(f)(2)(iv). This may occur, for example, when there is a pattern of prices in controlled transactions that are higher or lower than the prices of comparable uncontrolled transactions.

Comments are solicited on the types of analyses and factors that may be relevant for pricing controlled financial transactions in a global dealing operation. Section 1.482-1(e) continues to apply in its entirety to transactions among participants that are common to businesses other than a global dealing operation. In this regard, the existing rules continue to apply to pricing of certain services from a participant to a regular dealer in securities other than services that give rise to participant status.

F. *Comparable Uncontrolled Financial Transaction Method*

The comparable uncontrolled financial transaction (CUFT) method is set forth in § 1.482-8(b). The CUFT method evaluates whether controlled transactions satisfy the arm's length standard by comparing the price of a controlled financial transaction with the price of a comparable uncontrolled financial transaction. Similarity in the contractual terms and risks assumed in entering into the financial transaction are the most important comparability factors under this method.

Ordinarily, in global dealing operations, proprietary pricing models are used to calculate a financial product's price based upon market data, such as interest rates, currency rates, and market risks. The regulations contemplate that indirect evidence of the price of a CUFT may be derived from a proprietary pricing model if the data used in the model is widely and routinely used in the ordinary course of the taxpayer's business to price uncontrolled transactions, and adjustments are made to the amount charged to reflect differences in the factors that affect the price to which uncontrolled taxpayers would agree. In addition, the proprietary pricing model must be used in the same manner to price transactions with controlled and uncontrolled parties. If a taxpayer uses its internal pricing model as evidence of a CUFT, it must, upon request, furnish the pricing model to the district director in order to substantiate its use.

G. *Gross Margin Method*

The gross margin method is set forth in § 1.482-8(c) and should be considered in situations where a taxpayer performs only a routine marketing or sales function as part of a global dealing operation. Frequently, taxpayers that perform the sales function in these circumstances participate in the dealing of a variety of, rather than solely identical, financial products. In such a case, the variety of financial products sold within a relevant time period may limit the availability of comparable uncontrolled financial transactions. Where the taxpayer has performed a similar function for a variety of products, however, the cross margin method can be used to determine if controlled transactions are priced at arm's length by reference to the amount earned by the taxpayer for performing similar functions with respect to uncontrolled transactions.

The gross margin method determines if the gross profit realized on sales of financial products acquired from controlled parties is at arm's length by comparing that profit to the gross profit earned on uncontrolled transactions. Since comparability under this method depends on the similarity of functions performed and risks assumed, adjustments must be made for differences between the functions performed in the disposition of financial products acquired in controlled transactions and the functions performed in the disposition of financial products acquired in uncontrolled transactions. Although close product similarity will tend to improve the reliability of the gross margin method, the reliability of this method is not as dependent on product similarity as the CUFT method.

Participants in a global dealing operation may act simply as brokers, or they may participate in structuring complex products. As the role of the participant exceeds the brokerage function, it becomes more difficult to find comparable functions because the contributions made in structuring one complex financial product are not likely to be comparable to the contributions made in structuring a different complex financial product. Accordingly, the regulations provide that the reliability of this method is decreased where a participant is substantially involved in developing a financial product or in tailoring the product to the unique requirements of a customer prior to resale.

H. *Gross Markup Method*

Like the gross margin method, the gross markup method set forth in § 1.482-8(d) should generally be considered in situations where a taxpayer performs only a routine marketing or sales function as part of a global dealing operation, and, as is often the case, handles a variety of financial products within a relevant time period. The gross markup method is generally appropriate in cases where the taxpayer performs a routine sales function in buying a financial product from an uncontrolled party and reselling or transferring the product to a controlled party.

The gross markup method determines if the gross profit earned on the purchase of financial products from uncontrolled parties and sold to controlled taxpayers is at arm's length by comparing that profit to the gross profit earned on uncontrolled transactions. Like the gross margin method, comparability under this method depends on the similarity of the functions performed and risks assumed in the controlled and uncontrolled transactions. Accordingly, adjustments should be made for differences between the functions performed in the sale or transfer of financial products to controlled parties, and the functions performed with respect to the sale or transfer of financial products to uncontrolled parties. Although close product similarity will tend to improve the reliability of the gross markup method, the reliability of this method is not as dependent on product similarity as the CUFT method.

As in the gross margin method, the regulations provide that the reliability of this method generally is decreased where a participant is substantially involved in developing a financial product or in tailoring the product to the unique requirements of a customer prior to resale.

I. *Profit Split Methods*

New profit split methods are proposed for global dealing participants under § 1.482-8(e). Global dealing by its nature involves a certain degree of integration among the participants in the global dealing operation. The structure of some global dealing operations may make it difficult to apply a traditional transactional method to determine if income is allocated among participants on an arm's length basis. Two profit split methods, the total profit split method and the residual profit split method, have been included as specified methods for determining if global dealing income is allocated at arm's length.

Profit split methods may be used to evaluate if the allocation of operating profit from a global dealing operation compensates the participants at arm's length for their contribution by evaluating if the allocation is one which uncontrolled parties would agree to. Accordingly, the reliability of this method is cependent upon clear identification of the respective contributions of each participant to the global dealing operation.

In general, the profit split methods must be based on objective market benchmarks that provide a high degree of reliability, i.e., comparable arrangements between unrelated parties that allocate profits in the same manner and on the same basis. Even if such comparable uncontrolled transactions are not available, however, the taxpayer may be able to demonstrate that a total profit split provides arm's length results that reflect the economic value of the contribution of each participant, by reference to other objective factors that provide reliability due to their arm's length nature. For example, an allocation of income based on trader bonuses may be reliable, under the particular facts and circumstances of a given case, if the taxpayer can demonstrate that such bonuses are based on the value added by the individual traders. By contrast, an allocation based on headcount or gross expenses may be unreliable, because the respective participants might, for example, have large differences in efficiency or cost control practices, which would tend to make such factors poor reflections of the economic value of the functions contributed by each participant.

The proposed regulations define gross profit as gross income earned by the global dealing operation. Operating expenses are those not applicable to the determination of gross income earned by the global dealing operation. The operating expenses are global expenses of the global dealing operation and are subtracted from gross profit to determine the operating profit. Taxpayers may need to allocate operating expenses that relate to more than one global dealing activity.

The regulations state that in appropriate circumstances a multi-factor formula may be used to determine whether an allocation is at arm's length. Use of a multi-factor formula is permitted so long as the formula allocates the operating profit or loss based upon the factors that uncontrolled taxpayers would consider. The regulations do not prescribe specific factors to be used in the formula since the appropriateness of any one factor will depend on all the facts and circumstances associated with the global dealing operation. However, the regulations require that the multi-factor formula take into account all of the functions performed and risks assumed by a participant, and attribute the appropriate amount of income or loss to each function. The IRS also solicits comments concerning which factors may be appropriate (for example, initial net present value of derivatives contracts) and the circumstances under which specific factors may be appropriately applied.

The purpose of the factors is to measure the relative value contributed by each participant. Thus, adjustments must be made for any circumstances other than the relative value contributed by a participant that influence the amount of a factor so that the factor does not allocate income to a participant based on circumstances that are not relevant to the value of the function or activity being measured. For example, if trader compensation is used to allocate income among participants, and the traders in two different jurisdictions would be paid different amounts (for example, due to cost of living differences) to contribute the same value, adjustments should be made for the difference so that the factors accurately measure the value contributed by the trading function. The IRS solicits comments regarding the types of adjustments that should be made, how to make such adjustments, and the need for further guidance on this point.

The total profit split method entails a one step process whereby the operating profit is allocated among the participants based on their relative contributions to the profitability of the global dealing operation. No distinction is made between routine and nonroutine contributions. The total profit split method may be useful to allocate income earned by a highly integrated global dealing operation where all routine and nonroutine dealer functions are performed by each participant in each location. Accordingly, total profit or loss of the global dealing operation may be allocated among various jurisdictions based on the relative performance of equivalent functions in each jurisdiction.

The residual profit split method entails a two step process. In the first step, the routine functions are compensated with a market return based upon the best transfer pricing method applicable to that transaction. Routine functions may include, but are not limited to, functions that would not give rise to participant status and which should be evaluated under § § 1.482-3 through 1.482-6. After compensating the routine functions, the remaining operating profit (the "residual profit") is allocated among the participants based upon their respective nonroutine contributions.

It should be noted that, while in appropriate cases a profit split method may be used to determine if a participant is compensated at arm's length, use of the profit split method does not change the contractual relationship between participants, nor does it affect the character of intercompany payments. For example, if a controlled taxpayer provides solely trading services to a global dealing operation in a particular jurisdiction, any payment it receives as compensation for services retains its character as payment for services and, under the regulations, is not converted into a pro rata share of each item of gross income earned by the global dealing operation.

J. *Unspecified Methods*

Consistent with the principles underlying the best method rule, the regulations provide the option to use an unspecified method if it is determined to be the best method. The IRS solicits comments on the extent to which the variety of methods on which specific guidance has been provided is adequate.

Guidance on the use of a comparable profits method has specifically not been included as a specified method in the proposed regulations because use of that method depends on the existence of arrangements between uncontrolled taxpayers that perform comparable functions and assume comparable risks. Global dealing frequently involves the use of unique intangibles such as trader know-how. Additionally, anticipated profit is often influenced by the amount of risk a participant is willing to bear. Accordingly, the IRS believes it is unlikely that the comparability of these important functions can be measured and adjusted for accurately in a global dealing operation.

K. *Source of Global Dealing Income*

Under current final regulations in § 1.863-7(a), all of the income attributable to a notional principal contract is sourced by reference to the taxpayer's residence. Exceptions are provided for effectively connected notional principal contract income, and for income earned by a foreign QBU of a U.S. resident taxpayer if the notional principal contract is properly reflected on the books of the foreign QBU. Attribution of all of the income from a notional principal contract to a single location has generally been referred to as the "all or nothing" rule. The current final regulations do not provide for multi-location sourcing of notional principal contract income among the QBUs that have participated in the acquisition or risk management of a notional principal contract and therefore do not recognize that significant activities, including structuring or risk managing derivatives, often occur through QBUs in more than one jurisdiction.

Recognizing the need for multi-location sourcing of income earned in a global dealing operation, the proposed regulations provide a new rule under § 1.863-3(h) which sources income from a global dealing operation in the same manner as the income would be allocated under § 1.482-8 if each QBU were a separate entity. However, the rules must be applied differently to take into account the economic differences between acting through a single legal entity and through separate legal entities.

Accordingly, income from a single transaction may be split-sourced to more than one location, so long as the allocation methodology satisfies the arm's length standard. The all or nothing rule of § 1.863-7(a) continues to apply to notional principal contract income attributable to activities not related to a global dealing operation. Corresponding changes have been made in proposed § 1.988-4(h) to exclude exchange gain or loss derived in the conduct of a global dealing operation from the general source rules in § 1.988-4(b) and (c).

These special source rules apply only with respect to participants that perform a dealing, marketing, sales, pricing, risk management or brokering function. Moreover, these rules do not apply to income, such as fees for services, for which a specific source rule is provided in section 861, 862 or 865 of the Code. Accordingly, if a controlled taxpayer provides back office services, the amount and source of an intercompany payment for such services is determined under existing transfer pricing and sourcing rules applicable to those services without regard to whether the controlled taxpayer is also a participant in a global dealing operation.

If an entity directly bears the risk assumed by the global dealing operation, it should be compensated for that function. In providing, however, that the source (and effectively connected status) of global dealing income is determined by reference to where the dealing, marketing, sales, pricing, risk management or brokering function that gave rise to the income occurred, the regulations effectively provide that compensation for risk bearing should be sourced by reference to where the capital is employed by traders, marketers and salespeople, rather than the residence of the capital provider. This principle applies where a taxpayer directly bears risk arising from the conduct of a global dealing operation, such as when it acts as a counterparty without performing other global dealing functions. A special rule provides that the activities of a dependent agent may give rise to participant status through a deemed QBU that performs its participant functions in the same location where the dependent agent performs its participant functions. The deemed QBU may be created without regard to the books and records requirement of § 1.989-1(b).

As indicated, accounting, back office, credit analysis, and general supervision and policy control functions do not give rise to participant status in a global dealing operation but are services that should be remunerated and sourced separately under existing rules. This principle also applies where a taxpayer bears risk indirectly, such as through the extension of a guarantee. Accordingly, the sourcing rule of § 1.863-3(h) does not apply to interest, dividend, or guarantee fee income received by an owner or guarantor of a global dealing operation that is conducted by another controlled taxpayer. The source of interest, dividend and guarantee fee income, substitute interost and substitute dividend payments sourced under §§ 1.861-2(a)(7) and 1.861-3(a)(6), and other income sourced by section 861, 862 or 865 continues to be governed by the source rules applicable to those transactions.

The proposed regulations provide, consistent with U.S. tax principles, that an agreement between two QBUs of a single taxpayer does not give rise to a transaction because a taxpayer cannot enter into nor profit from a "transaction" with itself. See, e.g., § 1.446-3(c)(1). The IRS believes, however, that these agreements between QBUs of a single taxpayer may provide evidence of how income from the taxpayer's transactions with third parties should be allocated among QBUs. It is a common practice for taxpayers to allocate income or loss from transactions with third parties among QBUs for internal control and risk management purposes. Accordingly, the proposed regulations specifically provide that such allocations may be used to source income to the same extent and in the same manner as they may be used to allocate income between related persons. Conversely, such transactions may not be used to the extent they do not provide an arm's length result.

L. *Determination of Global Dealing Income Effectively Connected with a U.S. Business*

After determining the source of income, it is necessary to determine the extent to which such income is ECI. Under current law, the general rule is that all of the income, gain or loss from a global dealing operation is effectively connected with a U.S. trade or business if the U.S. trade or business materially participates in the acquisition of the asset that gives rise to the income, gain or loss, or property is held for use in the active conduct of a U.S. trade or business, or the business activities conducted by the U.S. trade or business are a material factor in the realization of income, gain or loss. As noted above, the current final regulations do not permit the attribution of income, gain or loss from a global dealing operation that is allocated and sourced to a U.S. trade or business under § 1.863-3(h) shall be effectively connected. In this regard, an asset used in a global dealing operation is treated as an asset used in a U.S. trade or business to the extent that an allocation is made to a U.S. QBU. Similarly, the U.S. trade or business is also treated as a material factor in the realization of income, gain or loss for which an allocation is made to a U.S. QBU. A special rule for U.S. source interest and dividend income, including substitute interest and substitute dividends, earned by a foreign banking or similar financial institution in a global dealing operation treats such income as attributable to a U.S. trade or business to the extent such income would be sourced to the United States under § 1.863-3(h). Any foreign source income allocated to the United States under the principles of § 1.863-3(h) is also treated as attributable to the U.S. trade or business.

The proposed regulations also limit an entity's effectively connected income from a global dealing operation to that portion of an item of income, gain or loss that would be sourced to the U.S. trade or business if the rules of § 1.863-3(h) were to apply. These rules are intended to ensure that income for which a specific source rule is provided in section 861, 862 or 865 does not produce effectively connected income unless it was earned through functions performed by a U.S. QBU of the taxpayer.

With respect to notional principal contract income and foreign exchange gain or loss, proposed §§1.863-3(h) and 1.988-4(h) also provide that such income, gain or loss is effectively connected with the conduct of a U.S. trade or business to the extent that it is sourced to the United States under §1.863-3(h).

In certain circumstances, the global dealing activities of an entity acting as the agent of a foreign taxpayer in the United States may cause the foreign taxpayer to be engaged in a U.S. trade or business. Any income effectively connected with the U.S. trade or business must be reported by the foreign corporation on a timely filed U.S. tax return in order for the foreign corporation to be eligible for deductions and credits attributable to such income. See §1.882-4. In addition, the agent must also report any income earned in its capacity as agent on its own tax return. The provisions governing the time and manner for foreign corporations to make elections under §§1.882-5 and 1.884-1 remain in force as promulgated. Under current rules, these formalities must be observed even if all of the global dealing income would be allocated between a U.S. corporation and a foreign corporation's U.S. trade or business. The IRS believes that these requirements are justified because of potential differences that might occur with respect to the realization of losses and between actual dividend remittances of a U.S. corporation and deemed dividend remittances under the branch profits tax. The IRS, however, solicits comments regarding whether these filing requirements can be simplified, taking into consideration the policies underlying the filing requirements of §1.882-4.

The Business Profits article contained in U.S. income tax treaties requires the United States to attribute to a permanent establishment that portion of the income earned by the entity from transactions with third parties that the permanent establishment might be expected to earn if it were an independent enterprise. Because the proposed regulations contained in this document allocate global trading income among permanent establishments under the arm's length principle of the Associated Enterprises article of U.S. income tax treaties, such rules are consistent with our obligations under the Business Profits article. Accordingly, a proposed rule under section 894 provides that, if a taxpayer is engaged in a global dealing operation through a U.S. permanent establishment, the proposed regulations will apply to determine the income attributable to that U.S. permanent establishment under the applicable U.S. income tax treaty.

M. *Relationship to Other Regulations*

The allocation rules contained herein do not apply to the allocation of interest expense. As discussed in the preamble to §1.882-5 (TD 8658, 1996-1 CB 161, 162, 61 FR 9326, March 5, 1996), the rules contained in §1.882-5 are the exclusive rules for allocating interest expense, including under U.S. income tax treaties.

Proposed regulations have been issued under sections 882 and 884 (INTL-0054-95, 1996-1 CB 844, 61 FR 9377, March 5, 1996) for purposes of allocating interest expense and determining the U.S. assets and/or liabilities reflected on the books of a foreign corporation's U.S. trade or business that are attributable to its activities as a dealer under section 475. The proposed regulations (and similar final regulations) under section 884 address the treatment of assets which give rise to both effectively connected and non-effectively connected income. Those rules thus address a situation analogous to the split-sourcing situation addressed in these proposed regulations. The IRS anticipates issuing proposed regulations under section 861 that provide a similar rule for purposes of allocating interest expense of a U.S. corporation that has assets that give rise to split-sourced income. Comments are solicited on the compatibility of the proposed regulations contained in this document with the principles of the proposed regulations that address a foreign corporation's allocation of interest expense, including its computation of U.S. assets included in step 1 of the §1.882-5 formula and component liabilities included in steps 2 and 3 of the §1.882-5 formula.

The IRS believes that the transfer pricing compliance issues associated with a global dealing operation are substantially similar to those raised by related party transactions generally. The IRS also believes that the existing regulations under section 6662 adequately address these issues. Accordingly, amendments have not been proposed to the regulations under section 6662. Section 6662 may not in certain circumstances, however, apply to the computation of effectively connected income in accordance with proposed regulations under section 475, 863, 864 or 988 contained in this document. The IRS will propose regulations under section 6038C regarding the information reporting and recordkeeping requirements applicable to foreign corporations engaged in a global dealing operation. It is anticipated that these regulations will coordinate the application of sections 6662 and 6038C where necessary.

No inference should be drawn from the examples in these proposed regulations concerning the treatment or significance of liquidity and creditworthiness or the effect of such items on the valuation of a security. The purpose of the proposed regulations under section 482 is not to provide guidance on the valuation of a security, but rather to determine whether the prices of controlled transactions satisfy the arm's length standard. Section 475 and the regulations thereunder continue to govern exclusively the valuation of securities.

N. *Section 475*

A dealer in securities as defined in section 475 is generally required to mark its securities to market. Securities are exempt from mark-to-market accounting if the securities are held for investment or not held for sale to customers and are properly identified on the taxpayer's books and records. Additionally, securities that hedge positions that are not subject to mark-to-market accounting are exempt from mark-to-market accounting if they are properly identified.

Under the current regulations, a taxpayer may not take into account an agreement between separate business units within the same entity that transfers risk management responsibility from a non-dealing business unit to a dealing business unit. Moreover, such an agreement may not be used to allocate income, expense, gain or loss between activities that are accounted for on a mark-to-market basis and activities that are accounted for on a non-mark-to-market basis. In contrast, the regulations proposed in this document under sections 482, 863, 864, 894, and 988 allow a taxpayer to take into account records of internal transfers when allocating global dealing income earned from third parties for purposes of determining source and effectively connected income. This may cause a mismatch in the timing of income, expense, gain, or loss.

For example, if a taxpayer's lending desk enters into a third-party transaction that exposes the lending desk to currency or interest rate risk, the lending desk may transfer responsibility for managing the risk for that particular transaction toanother business activity that can manage the risk more efficiently (e.g., the desk that deals in currency or interest rate derivatives). The dealing desk then, in the ordinary course of its business, may enter into a transaction such as a swap with a third party to hedge the aggregate risk of the dealing desk and, indirectly, the risk incurred by the lending desk with respect to the original transaction. Where, as is generally the case, the dealing desk has a large volume of transactions, it is not possible as a practical matter to associate the aggregate hedge with the risk of the lending desk. Since the transactions entered into by the dealing desk must generally be marked to market, the third-party transaction that hedges the aggregate risk of the dealing desk (which includes the risk transferred from the lending desk) must generally also be marked. To the extent that a portion of the income, expense, gain, or loss from the aggregate hedging transaction is allocated to the lending desk under the proposed global dealing regulations, the potential timing mismatch described above will occur if the lending desk accounts for its positions on a non-mark-to-market basis. This mismatch could occur because the portion of the income, expense, gain, or loss from the hedging transaction, although allocated to the lending desk for sourcing and effectively connected income purposes, will be accounted for on a mark-to-market basis under the dealing desk's method of accounting. Entirely exempting the aggregate hedging transaction from mark-to-market accounting does not adequately solve this problem, because it results in the portion of the income, expense, gain or loss from the aggregate hedging transaction that is allocated to the dealing desk being accounted for on other than a mark-to-market method.

As the example shows, respecting records of internal transfers for purposes of sourcing without respecting these same records for purposes of timing could produce unpredictable and arbitrary results. Accordingly, the proposed regulations permit participants in a global dealing operation to respect records of internal transfers in applying the timing rules of section 475. Because the need to reconcile sourcing and timing exists only in the context of a cross-border operation, the proposed regulations have a limited scope. In particular, for the proposed regulations to apply, income of the global dealing desk must be subject to allocation among two or more jurisdictions or be sourced to two or more jurisdictions.

The purpose of the proposed regulations under section 475 is to coordinate section 475 with the proposed global dealing regulations and to facilitate identification of the amount of income, expense, gain or loss from third party transactions that is subject to mark-to-market accounting. This rule is not intended to allow a shifting of income inconsistent with the arm's length standard.

Under the proposed section 475 regulations, an interdesk agreement or "risk transfer agreement" (RTA) includes a transfer of responsibility for risk management between a business unit that is hedging some of its risk (the hedging QBU) and another business unit of the same taxpayer that uses mark-to-market accounting (the marking QBU). If the marking QBU, the hedging QBU, and the RTA satisfy certain requirements, the RTA is taken into account for purposes of determining the timing of income allocated by the proposed global dealing regulations to the separate business units of a taxpayer.

The proposed amendments to the section 475 regulations require that the marking QBU must be a dealer within the meaning of proposed § 1.482-8(a)(2)(iii) and that its income must be allocated to at least two jurisdictions under proposed § 1.482-8 or sourced to at least two jurisdictions under proposed § 1.863-3(h). Additionally, the RTA qualifies only if the marking QBU would mark its side of the RTA to market under section 475 if the transaction were with an unrelated third party. Thus, if the marking QBU were to identify the RTA as a hedge of a position that is not subject to mark-to-market accounting (such as debt issued by the marking QBU), the RTA would not qualify. The IRS requests comments on whether the marking QBU should ever be able to exempt its position in the RTA from mark-to-market treatment and account for its position in the RTA.

The proposed amendments to the section 475 regulations are intended to address situations where the hedging QBU transfers responsibility for the management of risk arising from a transaction with a third party. Accordingly, the proposed regulations require that the hedging QBU's position in the RTA would be a hedge within the meaning of § 1.1221-2(b) if the transaction were entered into with an unrelated entity. The IRS solicits comments on whether this requirement is broad enough to address the business needs of entities engaged in global dealing and nondealing activities. Comments suggesting that the requirement should be broadened (e.g., to include risk reduction with respect to capital assets) should address how such a regime could be coordinated with other relevant rules (e.g., the straddle rules). Additionally, if a taxpayer suggests changes to the section 475 rules proposed in this notice, the IRS requests additional comments addressing whether or not corresponding changes should be made to § 1.1221-2(d).

The proposed regulations also require that the RTA be recorded on the books and records of the QBU no later than the time the RTA is effective. RTAs that are not timely recorded do not qualify under the proposed regulations. Additionally, the RTA must be accounted for in a manner that is consistent with the QBU's usual accounting practices.

If all of the requirements of the proposed regulations are satisfied, then for purposes of determining the timing of income, expense, gain, or loss allocated to a QBU under the global dealing regulations, the marking QBU and the hedging QBU account for their respective positions in the RTA as if the position were entered into with an unrelated third part.

Special Analyses

It has been determined that this notice of proposed rulemaking is not a significant regulatory action as defined in Executive Order 12866. Therefore, a regulatory impact analysis is not required. It is hereby certified that these regulations do not have a significant economic impact on a substantial number or small entities. This certification is based upon the fact that these regulations affect entities who participate in cross-border global dealing of stocks and securities. These regulations affect the source of income and allocation of income, deductions, credits, and allowances among such entities. The primary participants who engage in cross-border global dealing activities are large regulated commercial banks and brokerage firms, and investment banks. Accordingly, the IRS does not believe that a substantial number of small entities engage in cross-border global dealing activities covered by these regulation. Therefore, a Regulatory Flexibility Analysis under the Regulatory Flexibility Act (5 U.S.C. Chapter 6) is not required. Pursuant to section 7805(f) of the Code, this notice of proposed rulemaking will be submitted to the Chief Counsel for Advocacy of the Small Business Administration for comment on their impact on small business.

Comments and Public Hearing

Before these proposed regulations are adopted as final regulations, consideration will be given to any written. comments that are submitted timely to the IRS (a signed original and eight (8) copies). All comments will be available for public inspection and copying.

A public hearing has been scheduled for July 14, 1998, at 10 a.m. in room 2615, Internal Revenue Building, 1111 Constitution Avenue NW, Washington, DC. Because of access restrictions, visitors will not be admitted beyond the Internal Revenue Building lobby more than 15 minutes before the hearing starts.

The rules of 26 CFR 601.601(a)(3) apply to the hearing.

Persons that wish to present oral comments at the hearing must submit written comments by June 4, 1998, and submit an outline of the topics to be discussed and the time to be devoted to each topic by June 18, 1998.

A period of 10 minutes will be allotted to each person for making comments.

An agenda showing the scheduling of the speakers will be prepared after the deadline for receiving outlines has passed. Copies of the agenda will be available free of charge at the hearing.

Proposed Effective Date

These regulations are proposed to be effective for. taxable years beginning after the date final regulations are published in the Federal Register.

Drafting Information

The principal authors of these regulations are Ginny Chung of the Office of Associate Chief Counsel (International) and Richard Hoge of the Office of Assistant Chief Counsel (Financial Institutions & Products). However, other personnel from the IRS and Treasury Department participated in their development.

[¶ 49,166] Proposed Regulation (REG-106031-98), published in the Federal Register on June 12, 1998.

Foreign taxpayers: Derivative financial instruments: Safe harbors.—Reg. § 1.864(b)-1, providing that foreign taxpayers who effect transactions in derivative financial instruments for their own accounts are not thereby engaged in a trade or business in the United States if they are not dealers in stocks, securities, commodities or derivatives, is proposed. A public hearing on this proposal is scheduled for September 9, 1998.

ACTION: Notice of proposed rulemaking and notice of public hearing.

SUMMARY: This document contains proposed rules for the treatment of foreign taxpayers trading in derivative financial instruments for their own account. These proposed rules provide that foreign taxpayers who effect transactions in derivative financial instruments for their own accounts are not thereby engaged in a trade or business in the United States if they are not dealers in stocks, securities, commodities or derivatives. These proposed rules affect foreign persons that conduct such trading for their own account either directly through U.S. offices or indirectly through partnerships or other agents. This document also provides notice of a public hearing on these proposed regulations.

DATES: Written comments must be received by September 10, 1998. Outlines of oral comments to be discussed at the public hearing scheduled for September 9, 1998, must be received by August 19, 1998.

ADDRESSES: Send submissions to: CC:DOM:CORP:R (REG-106031-98), room 5226, Internal Revenue Service, POB 7604, Ben Franklin Station, Washington, DC 20044. Submissions may be hand delivered between the hours of 8 a.m. and 5 p.m. to: CC:DOM:CORP:R (REG-106031-98), Courier's Desk, Internal Revenue Service, 1111 Constitution Avenue NW., Washington, DC. Alternatively, taxpayers may submit comments electronically via the Internet by selecting the "Tax Regs" option on the IRS Home Page, or by submitting comments directly to the IRS Internet site at http://www.irs.ustreas.gov/prod/tax>regs/comments.html. The public hearing will be held in room 2615, Internal Revenue Building, 1111 Constitution Avenue NW., Washington, DC.

FOR FURTHER INFORMATION CONTACT: Milton Cahn of the Office of Associate Chief Counsel (International), (202) 622-3870; concerning submissions and the hearing, LaNita Van Dyke, (202) 622-7190 (not toll-free numbers).

SUPPLEMENTARY INFORMATION:

Background

Section 864(b) of the Code provides that the phrase "trade or business within the United States" generally includes the performance of personal services within the United States at any time during the taxable year but, under certain circumstances, does not include trading in stocks, securities, or commodities through an independent agent or for a taxpayer's own account (the "trading safe harbors").

Regulations regarding certain aspects of the trading safe harbors were promulgated in 1968. Since the promulgation of these regulations, the use of derivative financial instruments has increased significantly. This is due in large measure to the overall expansion and growing sophistication of global capital markets. Although guidance concerning the tax treatment of derivatives and notional principal contracts has been issued under other provisions of the Code (see, e.g., §§1.446-3, 1.863-7(b)), the section 864(b) regulations have not been modernized to take into account the manner in which taxpayers customarily use derivative transactions.

Explanation of Provisions

1. *In General*

These proposed regulations provide that foreign taxpayers who are not dealers with respect to any derivative transactions, who are not otherwise dealers in stocks, securities, or commodities, and who enter into derivative transactions for their own accounts are not engaged in trade or business within the United States solely by reason of those transactions. The term "derivative" is defined as an interest rate, currency, equity or commodity notional principal contract or an evidence of an interest in, or derivative financial instrument in, any commodity, currency, or any of the items described in Code section 475(c)(2)(A)-(D).

For purposes of these proposed regulations, the term "currency" is limited to those currencies that are of a kind customarily dealt in on an organized commodity exchange. No inference is intended, however, as to whether currencies that are not traded on an organized commodity exchange are "of a kind" customarily dealt in on an organized commodity exchange. Comments are solicited on this issue.

Under the statutory safe harbors, taxpayers who are dealers in stocks and securities but not commodities may avail themselves of the commodities trading safe harbor of section 864(b)(2)(B)(ii), and likewise, dealers in commodities but not stocks and securities may avail themselves of the stocks and securities trading safe harbor of section 864(b)(2)(A)(ii). The proposed regulations, however, do not specify into which statutory safe harbor any particular derivative transaction falls. Accordingly, dealers in stocks, securities, commodities, or derivatives may not avail themselves of the benefits of these proposed regulations.

Treasury and the IRS are considering the appropriate application of both the stocks and securities safe harbor of section 864(b)(2)(A)(ii) and the commodities safe harbor of section 864(b)(2)(B)(ii) with respect to a dealer in a derivative which arguably might be classified as both a security and a commodity. Treasury and the IRS are also considering the appropriate application of the section 864(b)(2)(A)(ii) and (B)(ii) safe harbors to dealers in either stocks and securities or commodities who enter into a derivative transaction which arguably might be classified within both sections. Comments are solicited on these points including the classification of specific derivatives for purposes of the safe harbors.

Comments are also solicited regarding whether the final regulations should include derivative transactions in either the stocks and securities, or commodities trading safe harbors under sections 864(b)(2)(A)(i) and (B)(i). In particular, the IRS solicits comments as to whether certain dealers could inappropriately avoid the limitations of section 864(b)(2)(C) with respect to derivative transactions effected through independent agents in the United States.

2. *Eligible Nondealer*

Until Treasury and the IRS determine whether particular derivative transactions should be classified under the stocks and securities or commodities safe harbors, the proposed regulations provide that derivative transactions (including hedging transactions) do not constitute a U.S. trade or business if the taxpayer meets the newly proposed definition of an "eligible nondealer."

An eligible nondealer is defined as a foreign resident taxpayer who is not a dealer in stocks, securities, commodities or derivatives at any time during the taxable year. Dealer status is determined on a worldwide basis and disqualifies a taxpayer from the safe harbor of the proposed regulations even if no dealing activities are conducted in the United States. For example, if a taxpayer is a dealer in commodities through its home country office and conducts no dealing activities through its U.S. office, but enters into derivative transactions for its own account through the U.S. office, the taxpayer fails to be an eligible nondealer.

Under the proposed regulations, the definition of dealer in stocks or securities refers to § 1.864-2(c)(2)(iv) and the definition of dealer in commodities refers to the use of that term in § 1.864-2(d). The definition of eligible nondealer contains language based on the definition of dealer in securities in section 475(c)(1)(B), including regularly holding oneself out, in the ordinary course of one's trade or business, as being willing and able to enter into either side of a derivative transaction. See § 1.475(c)-1(a)(2).

Treasury and the IRS are considering issuing additional guidance with respect to the definition of a dealer for purposes of applying the trading safe harbors generally. Comments are solicited regarding the definition of a dealer, including the adequacy of the present rules in § 1.864-2(c)(2)(iv) and § 1.864-2(d), possible rules for identifying derivative transactions entered into with customers in the "ordinary course," and the appropriateness of adopting a definition similar to that provided in section 475(c)(1).

3. *Swaps on U.S. Equities*

Treasury and the IRS are aware that in order to avoid the tax imposed on U.S. source dividends under sections 871 and 881 and Chapter 3 of the Code, some foreign investors use notional principal contract transactions based on U.S. equities ("U.S. based equity swaps"). Accordingly, Treasury and the IRS are considering whether rules should be developed to preserve the withholding tax with respect to such transactions. Specifically, Treasury and the IRS are evaluating whether conduit (e.g., section 7701(l)) or other principles should be invoked in regulations, to characterize payments made with respect to U.S. based equity swaps as subject to U.S. withholding tax.

Treasury and the IRS are considering whether or not finalization of the proposed regulations as they relate to U.S. based equity swaps should await guidance concerning the application of the withholding rules to such transactions. Broadening the section 864(b)(2)(A)(ii) and (B)(ii) safe harbors to include derivatives could impair the ability of the United States to tax U.S. source dividend payments.

Congress enacted the stocks and securities trading safe harbor in 1936 to provide certainty that foreign persons who merely trade stocks and securities would not be subject to the net income tax regime. Section 211(b), Revenue Act of 1936, Pub. L. 74-740, 49 Stat. 1648, 1714-15 (1936); S. Rep. No. 2156, 74th Cong., 2d Sess. 21 (1936). Congress' decision to include the safe harbor was premised on the fundamental assumption that ordinary income from U.S. stocks and securities would be appropriately subject to U.S. taxation through the withholding tax on fixed and determinable or annual and periodic income ("FDAP"), and that activities beyond the scope of the safe harbor would remain subject to net tax if the taxpayer was engaged in a trade or business or had an office in the United States. Id. The Foreign Investors Tax Act of 1966, which expanded the trading safe harbors to include trading activities conducted by or on behalf of a non-U.S. resident taxpayer through a U.S. office for the foreign taxpayer's own account, built upon the same principles reflected in the Revenue Act of 1936. See Section 102(d), Foreign Investors Tax Act of 1966, Pub. L. 89-809, 80 Stat. 1539, 1544 (1966); S. Rep. No. 1701, 99th Cong., 2d Sess. 16-17, 22-23, 32-33 (1966).

Treasury and the IRS request comments regarding the U.S. taxation of non-U.S. persons investing in derivatives generally in addition to the treatment of derivatives under the trading safe harbors. Comments are also solicited concerning the appropriate source of payments made pursuant to U.S. based equity swaps and whether conduit or other principles should be invoked for purposes of sections 871, 881 and Chapter 3 of the Code, including the circumstances under which such payments between non-U.S. resident counterparties (i.e., foreign-to-foreign payments) may be included in such regulations. In addition, comments are also solicited concerning the appropriate treatment of swaps or other derivative transactions on property (other than stocks and securities) that produce FDAP income, e.g., rents and royalties.

Special Analyses

It has been determined that this notice of proposed rulemaking is not a significant regulatory action as defined in EO 12866. Therefore, a regulatory impact analysis is not required. It also has been determined that section 553(b) of the Administrative Procedure Act (5 U.S.C. chapter 5) does not apply to these regulations, and because the regulation does not impose a collection of information on small entities, the Regulatory Flexibility Act (5 U.S.C. chapter 6) does not apply. Therefore, a Regulatory Flexibility Analysis under the Regulatory Flexibility Act (5 U.S.C. Chapter 6) is not required. Pursuant to section 7805(f) of the Code, this notice of proposed rulemaking will be submitted to the Chief Counsel for Advocacy of the Small Business Administration for comment on their impact on small business.

Comments and Public Hearing

Before these proposed regulations are adopted as final regulations, consideration will be given to any written comments that are submitted timely to the IRS (a signed original and eight (8) copies). All comments will be available for public inspection and copying.

A public hearing has been scheduled for September 9, 1998, at 10:00 A.M., in room 2615, Internal Revenue Building, 1111 Constitution Avenue NW, Washington, DC. Because of access restrictions, visitors will not be admitted beyond the Internal Revenue Building lobby more than 15 minutes before the hearing starts.

The rules of 26 CFR 601.601(a)(3) apply to the hearing. Persons that wish to present oral comments at the hearing must submit written comments by September 10, 1998, and submit an outline of the topics to be discussed and the time to be devoted to each topic by August 19, 1998.

A period of 10 minutes will be allotted to each person for making comments.

An agenda showing the scheduling of the speakers will be prepared after the deadline for receiving outlines has passed. Copies of the agenda will be available free of charge at the hearing.

Proposed Effective Date

These regulations are proposed to be effective for taxable years beginning 30 days after the date final regulations are published in the Federal Register. Taxpayers may elect to apply the provisions of the final regulations to taxable years beginning before the date which is 30 days after these regulations are published as final in the Federal Register. No inference is intended regarding the treatment of derivative transactions under sections 864(b)(2)(A)(ii) and (B)(ii) and the current regulations. For periods prior to the effective date, taxpayers engaged in derivative transactions may take any reasonable position with regard to the section 864(b)(2)(A)(ii) and (B)(ii) safe harbors. Positions consistent with these proposed regulations will be considered reasonable.

Drafting Information

The principal author of these regulations is Milton Cahn of the Office of Associate Chief Counsel (International). However, other personnel from the IRS and Treasury Department participated in their development.

[¶ 49,167] **Proposed Regulations (REG-106177-97)**, published in the Federal Register on August 24, 1998.

Qualified state tuition programs: Distributions: Reporting requirements.—Reg. §§1.529-0—1.529-6, relating to qualified state tuition programs (QSTPs) and affecting QSTPs established and maintained by a state, or an agency or instrumentality of a state, and individuals receiving distributions from QSTPs, are proposed. A public hearing on this proposal has been scheduled for January 6, 1999.

AGENCY: Internal Revenue Service (IRS), Treasury.

ACTION: Notice of proposed rulemaking and notice of public hearing.

SUMMARY: This document contains proposed regulations relating to qualified State tuition programs (QSTPs). These proposed regulations reflect changes to the law made by the Small Business Job Protection Act of 1996 and the Taxpayer Relief Act of 1997. The proposed regulations affect QSTPs established and maintained by a State or agency or instrumentality of a State, and individuals receiving distributions from QSTPs. This document also provides notice of a public hearing on these proposed regulations.

DATES: Written comments must be received by November 23, 1998. Outlines of topics to be discussed at the public hearing scheduled for Wednesday, January 6, 1999, at 10 a.m. must be received by December 16, 1998.

ADDRESSES: Send submissions to CC:DOM:CORP:R (REG-106177-97), room 5226, Internal Revenue Service, POB 7604, Ben Franklin Station, Washington, DC 20044. Submissions may be hand delivered between the hours of 8 a.m. and 5 p.m. to: CC:DOM:CORP:R (REG106177-97), Courier's Desk, Internal Revenue Service, 1111 Constitution Avenue, NW., Washington DC. Alternatively, taxpayers may submit comments electronically via the Internet by selecting the "Tax Regs" option on the IRS Home Page, or by submitting comments directly to the IRS Internet site at http://www.irs.ustreas.gov/prod/tax>regs/comments.html. The public hearing will be held in room 2615, Internal Revenue Building, 1111 Constitution Avenue, NW., Washington, DC.

FOR FURTHER INFORMATION CONTACT: Concerning the proposed regulations, Monice Rosenbaum, (202) 622-6070; concerning the proposed estate and gift tax regulations, Susan Hurwitz (202) 622-3090; concerning submissions and the hearing, Michael Slaughter, (202) 622-7190 (not toll-free numbers).

SUPPLEMENTARY INFORMATION:

Paperwork Reduction Act

The collection of information contained in this notice of proposed rulemaking has been submitted to the Office of Management and Budget for review in accordance with the Paperwork Reduction Act of 1995 (44 U.S.C. 3507(d)). Comments on the collection of information should be sent to the Office of Management and Budget, Attn: Desk Officer for the Department of the Treasury, Office of Information and Regulatory Affairs, Washington DC 20503, with copies to the Internal Revenue Service, Attn: IRS Reports Clearance Officer, OP:FS:FP, Washington, DC 20224. Comments on the collection of information should be received by October 23, 1998. Comments are specifically requested concerning:

Whether the proposed collection of information is necessary for the proper performance of the functions of the Internal Revenue Service, including whether the information will have practical utility;

The accuracy of the estimated burden associated with the proposed collection of information;

How the quality, utility, and clarity of the information to be collected may be enhanced;

How the burden of complying with the proposed collection of information may be minimized, including through the application of automated collection techniques or other forms of information technology; and

Estimates of capital or start-up costs and costs of operation, maintenance, and purchase or services to provide information.

The collection of information in this proposed regulation is in §§1.529-2(e)(4), 1.529-2(f) and (i), 1.529-4, and 1.529-5(b)(2). This information is required by the IRS to verify compliance with sections 529(b)(3), (4), (7) and (d). This information will be used by the IRS and individuals receiving distributions from QSTPs to determine that the taxable amount of the distribution has been computed correctly. The collection of information is required to obtain the benefit of being a QSTP described in section 529. The likely respondents and/or recordkeepers are state governments and distributees who receive distributions under the programs. The burden for reporting distributions is reflected in the burden for Form 1099-G, Certain Government Payments. The burden for electing to take certain contributions to a QSTP into account ratably over a five year period in determining the amount of gifts made during the calendar year is reflected in the burden for Form 709, Federal Gift Tax Return.

Estimated total annual reporting/recordkeeping burden: 705,000 hours

Estimated average annual burden per respondent/recordkeeper: 35 hours, 10 minutes

Estimated number of respondents/recordkeepers: 20,051

Estimated annual frequency of responses: On occasion

An agency may not conduct or sponsor, and a person is not required to respond to, a collection of information unless it displays a valid control number assigned by the Office of Management and Budget.

Books or records relating to a collection of information must be retained as long as their contents may become material in the administration of any internal revenue law. Generally, tax returns and tax return information are confidential, as required by 26 U.S.C. 6103.

Background

This document contains proposed amendments to the Income Tax Regulations (26 CFR part 1) relating to qualified State tuition programs described in section 529. Section 529 was added to the Internal Revenue Code by section 1806 of the Small Business Job Protection Act of 1996, Public Law 104-188, 110 Stat. 1895. Section 529 was modified by sections 211 and 1601(h) of the Taxpayer Relief Act of 1997, Public Law 105-34, 111 Stat. 810 and 1092.

Section 529 provides tax-exempt status to qualified State tuition programs (QSTPs) established and maintained by a State (or agency or instrumentality thereof) under which persons may (1) purchase tuition credits or certificates on behalf of a designated beneficiary entitling the beneficiary to a waiver or payment of qualified higher education expenses, or (2) contribute to an account established exclusively for the purpose of meeting qualified higher education expenses of the designated beneficiary. Qualified higher education expenses, for purposes of section 529, are tuition, fees, books, supplies, and equipment required for enrollment or attendance at an eligible educational institution, as well as certain room and board expenses for students who attend an eligible educational institution at least half-time. An eligible educational institution is an accredited post-secondary educational institution offering credit toward a bachelor's degree, an associate's degree, a graduate-level or professional degree, or another recognized post-secondary credential. The institution must be eligible to participate in Department of Education student aid programs.

QSTPs established and maintained by a State (or agency or instrumentality thereof) must require all contributions to the program be made only in cash. Neither contributors nor designated beneficiaries may direct the investment of any contributions or any earnings on contributions. No interest in the program may be pledged as security for a loan. A separate accounting must be provided to each designated beneficiary in the program. A program must impose a more than de minimis penalty on refunds that are not used for qualified higher education expenses, not made on account of death or disability of the designated beneficiary, or not made on account of a scholarship or certain other educational allowances. A program must provide adequate safeguards to prevent contributions in excess of those necessary to provide for the qualified higher education expenses of the beneficiary. A specified individual must be designated as the beneficiary at the commencement of participation in a QSTP, unless the interests in the program are purchased by a State or local government or a tax-exempt organization described in section 501(c)(3) as part of a scholarship program operated by such government or organization under which beneficiaries to be named in the future will receive the interests as scholarships.

Distributions under a QSTP are includible in the gross income of the distributee in the manner as provided under section 72 to the extent not excluded from gross income under any other provision. Distributions include in-kind benefits furnished to a designated beneficiary under a QSTP. Any distribution, or portion of a distribution, that is transferred within 60 days under a QSTP to the credit of a new designated beneficiary who is a member of the family of the old designated beneficiary shall not be treated as a distribution. A change in the designated beneficiary of an interest in a QSTP shall not be treated as a distribution if the new beneficiary is a member of the family of the old beneficiary. A member of the family means the spouse of the designated beneficiary or an individual who is related to the designated beneficiary as described in section 152(a)(1) through (8) or is the spouse of any of these individuals.

Section 529, as added to the Code by the Small Business Job Protection Act of 1996 (1996 Act), contained provisions addressing the estate, gift, and generation-skipping transfer tax. The provisions were significantly revised, effective prospectively, by the Taxpayer Relief Act of 1997 (1997 Act).

A contribution on behalf of a designated beneficiary to a QSTP which is made after August 20, 1996, and before August 6, 1997, is not treated as a taxable gift. Rather, the subsequent waiver (or payment) of qualified higher education expenses of a designated beneficiary by (or to) an educational institution under the QSTP is treated as a qualified transfer under section 2503(e) and is not treated as a transfer of property by gift for purposes of section 2501. As such, the contribution is not subject to the generation-skipping transfer tax imposed by section 2601.

In contrast, under section 529 as amended by the 1997 Act, a contribution on behalf of a designated beneficiary to a QSTP after August 5, 1997, is a completed gift of a present interest in property under section 2503(b) from the contributor to the designated beneficiary and is not a qualified transfer within themeaning of section 2503(e). The portion of a contribution excludible from taxable gifts under section 2503(b) also satisfies the requirements of section 2642(c)(2) and, therefore, is also excludible for purposes of the generation-skipping transfer tax imposed under section 2601. For purposes of the annual exclusion, a contributor may elect to take certain contributions to a QSTP into account ratably over a five-year period in determining the amount of gifts made during the calendar year. Under section 529 as amended by the 1997 Act, a transfer which occurs by reason of a change in the designated beneficiary of a QSTP, or a rollover from the account of one beneficiary to the account of another beneficiary in a QSTP, is not a taxable gift if the new beneficiary is a member of the family, as defined in section 529(e)(2), of the old beneficiary, and is assigned to the same generation, as defined in section 2651, as the old beneficiary. If the new beneficiary is assigned to a lower generation than the old beneficiary, the transfer is a taxable gift from the old beneficiary to the new beneficiary regardless of whether the new beneficiary is a member of the family of the old beneficiary. In addition, the transfer will be subject to the generation-skipping transfer tax if the new beneficiary is assigned to a generation which is two or more levels lower than the generation assignment of the old beneficiary. The five-year averaging election for purposes of the gift tax annual exclusion may be applied to the transfer.

Regarding the application of the estate tax, the value of any interest in any QSTP which is attributable to contributions made by a decedent who died after August 20, 1996, and before June 9, 1997, is includible in the decedent's gross estate. In contrast, pursuant to the 1997 Act amendments to section 529, the value of such an interest is not includible in the gross estate of a decedent who dies after June 8, 1997, unless the decedent had elected the five-year averaging rule for purposes of the gift tax annual exclusion and died before the close of the five-year period. In that case, the portion of the contribution allocable to calendar years beginning after the decedent's date of death is includible in his gross estate.

Also, pursuant to the 1997 Act amendments to section 529, the value of any interest in a QSTP held for a designated beneficiary who dies after June 8, 1997, is includible in the designated beneficiary's gross estate.

The Federal estate and gift tax treatment of QSTP interests has no effect on the actual rights and obligations of the parties pursuant to the terms of the contracts under State law. In addition, the estate and gift tax treatment of contributions to a QSTP and interests in a QSTP is generally different from the treatment that would otherwise apply under generally applicable estate and gift tax principles. For example, under most contracts, the contributor may retain the right to change the designated beneficiary of an account, to designate any person other than the designated beneficiary to whom funds may be paid from the account, or to receive distributions from the account if no such other person is designated. Such rights would ordinarily cause the transfer to the account to fail to be a completed gift and mandate inclusion of the value of the undistributed interest in the QSTP in the gross estate of the contributor under sections 2036 and/or 2038. However, under section 529, the gross estate of a contributor who dies after June 8, 1997, does not include the value of any interest in a QSTP attributable to contributions from the contributor (except amounts attributable to calendar years after death where the five-year averaging rule has been elected). Also, because a contribution after August 5, 1997, is a completed gift from the contributor to the designated beneficiary, any subsequent transfer which occurs by reason of a change in the designated beneficiary or a rollover from the account of the original designated beneficiary to the account of another beneficiary is treated, to the extent it is subject to the gift and/or generation-skipping transfer tax, as a transfer from the original designated beneficiary to the new beneficiary. This is the result even though the change in beneficiary or the rollover is made at the direction of the contributor under the terms of the contract.

Comments from Notice 96-58

In Notice 96-58, 1996-2 C.B. 226, the Internal Revenue Service invited comments on section 529 including the requirements for reporting distributions by QSTPs, the requirements for qualification and operation of programs, and the treatment of distributions made by programs for federal tax purposes. Eighteen comments were received. The comments addressed a broad range of issues, including but not limited to, those outlined by Notice 96-58, the concept of account ownership and gift tax rules, enforcement of penalties, accounting and recordkeeping, and transition relief for programs in existence on August 20, 1996. The summary below is not intended to be a complete discussion of the comments. However, all matters presented in the comments were considered in the drafting of this notice of proposed rulemaking.

One commenter discussed in detail the requirements that a QSTP be "established and maintained" by a State or agency or instrumentality of a State. The commenter recommended a list of factors to be considered in determining whether a State maintains the program. This commenter and others urged that the use of outside contractors or the holding of program deposits at a private financial institution selected by the State not be determinative of whether the program was maintained by the State.

One commenter was endorsed by several others for suggesting two specific safe harbors to satisfy the requirement that a program impose more than a de minimis penalty on refunds. The first safe harbor was a 5 percent of earnings penalty on refunds of earnings prior to the designated beneficiary matriculating, reduced to at least a 1 percent penalty on refunds of earnings only after the age of matriculation. The second safe harbor was a fixed-rate safe harbor equal to the lesser of $50 or 1 percent of the assets distributed. Another commenter suggested an additional safe harbor based on the return of Series EE savings bonds. That commenter also suggested that safe harbors are not necessarily the minimum acceptable penalties and that all facts and circumstances should be taken into account in determining the adequacy of penalties that are less than the safe harbor penalties.

Commenters urged that regulations limit or avoid rules requiring programs to enforce penalties or require substantiation to ensure that disbursements are used to pay for qualified higher education expenses. Recognizing however that there may be some misuse in this area, commenters recommended that checks from QSTPs be marked with a special endorsement or be payable to both the educational institution and the designated beneficiary.

Commenters suggested that the prohibition on investment direction not include a choice between a prepaid tuition program and a savings program (established and maintained in one State), a choice among options in a prepaid tuition program, a choice among options for the initial contribution to the program, or an opportunity to change investment strategies. One commenter suggested that the prohibition on investment direction not apply to prevent participation in the program by program board and staff members.

Commenters suggested several approaches for satisfying the prohibition on excess contributions. Two safe harbors were proposed; one was based upon eight times the average annual undergraduate tuition and required fees at private four-year universities; the other was based upon five years of tuition, fees, books, supplies, and equipment at the highest cost institution allowed by the State's program. Other approaches proposed allowing the provision of adequate safeguards to prevent excess contributions to be left to the discretion of the program or allowing the contributor to certify that no attempt would be made to overfund the account.

Commenters made suggestions and raised concerns regarding: separate accounting rules including, but not limited to, the valuation and tracking of tuition units; the operating rules treating all programs in which an individual is a designated beneficiary as one program, and treating all distributions during a taxable year as one distribution; the application of section 72 to calculate distributions; and, income tax consequences relating to account ownership, penalties, and withholding.

The modifications made to section 529 by the Taxpayer Relief Act of 1997 have addressed, in large part, the issues raised by commenters concerning transition relief for programs in existence on August 20, 1996, estate and gift tax consequences for contributors and designated beneficiaries, and definitions pertaining to family members and eligible educational institutions.

Explanation of Provisions

Qualification as Qualified State Tuition Program (QSTP): Unrelated Business Income Tax and Filing Requirements

The proposed regulations provide guidance on the requirements a program must satisfy in order to be a QSTP described in section 529. A program that meets these requirements generally is exempt from income taxation. However, a QSTP is subject to the taxes imposed by section 511 relating to imposition of tax on unrelated business income. For purposes of section 529 and these regulations, an interest in a QSTP shall not be treated as debt for purposes of section 514; consequently, investment income earned on contributions to the program by purchasers will not constitute debt-financed income subject to the unrelated business income tax. However, investment income of the QSTP shall be subject to the unrelated business income tax to the extent the program incurs indebtedness when acquiring or improving income-producing property. Earnings forfeited on educational contracts or savings, amounts collected as penalties on refunds or excess contributions, and certain administrative and other fees are not unrelated business income to the QSTP. A QSTP is not required to file Form 990, Return of Organization Exempt From Income Tax, however, this does not affect the obligation of a QSTP to file Form 990-T, Exempt Organization Business Income Tax Return.

Established and Maintained

The proposed regulations provide that a program is established by a State or agency or instrumentality of the State if the program is initiated by State statute or regulation, or by an act of a State official or agency with the authority to act on behalf of the State. A program is maintained by a State or agency or instrumentality of a State if all the terms and conditions of the program are set by the State or agency or instrumentality and the State or agency or instrumentality is actively involved on an ongoing basis in the administration of the program, including supervising all decisions relating to the investment of assets contributed to the program. The proposed regulations set forth factors that are relevant in determining whether a State, agency or instrumentality is actively involved in the administration of the program. Included in the factors is the manner and extent to which it is permissible for the program to contract out for professional and financial services.

Penalties and Substantiation—Safe Harbors

As required by section 529(b)(3), a more than de minimis penalty must be imposed on the earnings portion of any distribution from the program that is not used for the qualified higher education expenses of the designated beneficiary, not made on account of the death or disability of the designated beneficiary, or not made on account of a scholarship or certain other payments described in sections 135(d)(1)(B) and (C) that are received by the designated beneficiary to the extent the amount of the refund does not exceed the amount of the scholarship, allowance, or payment. The penalty shall also not apply to rollover distributions described in section 529(c)(3)(C) which are discussed in the section titled *Income Tax Treatment of Distributees*, below. The proposed regulations provide that a penalty is more than de minimis if it is consistent with a program intended to assist individuals in saving exclusively for qualified higher education expenses. Whether any penalty is more than de minimis will depend upon the facts and circumstance of the particular program, including the extent to which the penalty offsets the federal income tax benefit from having deferred income tax liability on the earnings portion of any distribution. The proposed regulations provide a safe harbor penalty that a program may adopt for satisfying this requirement. For purposes of the safe harbor, a penalty imposed on the earnings portion of a distribution is more than de minimis if it is equal to or greater than 10 percent of the earnings.

To be treated as imposing a more than de minimis penalty as required by section 529(b)(3) a program must implement practices and procedures for identifying whether a distribution is subject to a penalty and collecting any penalty that is due. The proposed regulations, in the form of a safe harbor, set forth practices and procedures that may be implemented by a program. The safe harbor provides that distributions are treated as payments of qualified higher education expenses if the distribution is made directly to an eligible educational institution; the distribution is made in the form of a check payable to both the designated beneficiary and the eligible educational institution; the distribution is made after the designated beneficiary submits substantiation showing that the qualified higher education expenses were paid and the program reviews the substantiation; or the designated beneficiary certifies prior to distribution the amount to be used for qualified higher education expenses and the program requires substantiation of payment within 30 days of making the distribution, the program reviews the substantiation, and the program retains an amount necessary to collect the penalty owed on the distribution if valid substantiation is not produced.

The safe harbor procedure provides that a penalty be collected on all other distributions except where prior to distribution the program receives written third party confirmation that the designated beneficiary has died or become disabled or has received a scholarship or allowance or payment described in section 135(d)(1)(B) or (C). Alternatively, distributions may be made upon the certification of the account owner that the designated beneficiary has died or become disabled or has received a scholarship or allowance or payment described above, if the program withholds a portion of the distribution as a penalty. The penalty may be refunded after receipt of third party confirmation of the certification made by the account owner.

The safe harbor procedure provides that a program may document amounts refunded from eligible educational institutions that were not used for qualified higher education expenses by requiring a signed written statement from the distributee identifying the amount of any refund received from an eligible educational institution at the end of each year in which distributions for qualified higher education expenses were made and of the next year. A program must also have procedures to collect the penalty either by retaining a sufficient balance in the account to pay the penalty, withholding an amount equal to the penalty from a distribution, or collecting the penalty on a State income tax return.

Other Requirements for QSTP Qualification

As described in section 529(b)(1)(A), the proposed regulations provide that contributions to the program can be placed into either a prepaid educational arrangement or contract, or an educational savings account, or both, but cannot be placed into any other type of account. Contributions may be made only in cash and not in property as provided in section 529(b)(2), however, the proposed regulations provide that a program may accept payment in cash, or by check, money order, credit card, or similar methods.

Section 529(b)(4) requires that a program provide separate accounting for each designated beneficiary. Separate accounting requires that contributions for the benefit of a designated beneficiary and earning attributable to those contributions are allocated to the appropriate account. The proposed regulations provide that if a program does not ordinarily provide each account owner an annual account statement showing the transactions related to the account, the program must give this information to the account owner or designated beneficiary upon request.

Section 529(b)(5) states that a program shall not be treated as a QSTP unless it provides that any contributor to, or designated beneficiary under, such program may not directly or indirectly direct the investment of any contributions to the program or any earnings thereon. A program will not violate the requirement of this paragraph if it permits a person who establishes an account to select between a prepaid educational services account and an educational savings account, or to select among different investment strategies designed exclusively by the program, at the time that an educational savings account is established. However, the proposed regulations clarify that a program will violate this requirement if, after an account with the program initially is established, the account owner, a contributor, or the designated beneficiary subsequently is permitted to select among different investment options or strategies. A program will not violate this requirement merely because it permits its board members, its employees, or the board members or employees of a contractor it hires to perform administrative services to purchase tuition credits or certificates or make contributions.

Section 529(b)(6) provides that a program may not allow any interest in the program, or any portion of an interest in the program, to be used as security for a loan. The proposed regulations clarify that this restriction includes, but is not limited to, a prohibition on the use of any interest in the program as security for a loan used to purchase the interest in the program.

Section 529(b)(7) requires a program to establish adequate safeguards to prevent contributions for the benefit of a designated beneficiary in excess of those necessary to provide for the qualified higher education expenses of the designated beneficiary. The proposed regulations provide a safe harbor that permits a program to satisfy this requirement if the program will bar any additional contributions to an account as soon as the account reaches a specified limit applicable to all accounts of designated beneficiaries with the same expected year of enrollment. The total contributions may not exceed the amount determined by actuarial estimates that is necessary to pay tuition, required fees, and room and board expenses of the designated beneficiary for five years of undergraduate enrollment at the highest cost institution allowed by the program. The safe harbor in the proposed regulations applies only to the program. Despite the fact that a program has met the safe harbor, a particular account established under the program may have a balance that exceeds the amount actually needed to cover the particular designated beneficiary's qualified higher education expenses. Distributions made that are not used for qualified higher education expenses of the designated beneficiary are subject to the penalty provisions of section 529(b)(3).

Income Tax Treatment of Distributees

In accordance with section 529(c)(3), the proposed regulations provide that distributions made by a QSTP, including any benefit furnished in-kind, must be included in the gross income of the distributee to the extent that the distribution consists of earnings. The proposed regulations clarify that term "distributee" refers to the designated beneficiary or the account owner who receives or is treated as receiving a distribution from a QSTP. As required by section 529(c)(3)(A), distributions under a QSTP must be included in income in the manner as provided under section 72. Therefore, deposits or contributions made into an account under a QSTP are recovered ratably over the period of time distributions are made. The amount of taxable earnings shall be determined by applying an earnings ratio, generally the earnings allocable to the account as of the close of the calendar year divided by the total account balance as of the close of the calendar year, to the distribution. In the case of a prepaid educational services account, this method of calculating taxable earnings utilizes an average value for each unit of education (e.g., credit, hour, semester, or other unit of education) that is distributed rather than the recovery of the cost of any particular unit of education.

In accordance with section 529(c)(3)(C), the proposed regulations permit nontaxable rollover distributions. A rollover consists of a distribution or transfer from an account of a designated beneficiary that is transferred to or deposited within 60 days of the distribution into an account of another individual who is a member of the family of the designated beneficiary. A distribution is not a rollover distribution unless there is a change in beneficiary. The new designated beneficiary's account may be in a QSTP established or maintained by the same State or by another State. A transfer from the designated beneficiary to himself or herself, regardless of whether the transfer is to an account within the same QSTP or another QSTP in the same or another State, is not a rollover distribution and is taxable under the general rule. The Internal Revenue Service is concerned about the use of multiple rollovers to circumvent the restriction on investment direction. In particular, the Internal Revenue Service requests comments on this issue, including whether limits should be placed on the number of rollovers permitted within a certain time period or rollovers back to the original designated beneficiary. No taxable distribution will result from a change in designated beneficiary of an interest in a QSTP purchased by a State or local government or an organization described in section 501(c)(3) as part of a scholarship program.

Reporting Requirements

The proposed regulations set forth recordkeeping and reporting requirements. A QSTP must maintain records that enable the program to produce an annual account balance for each account. See, requirements related to section 529(b)(4) above. A QSTP must report taxable earnings on Form 1099-G, Certain Government Payments, to distributees. Any reporting requirements promulgated under section 529(d) apply in lieu of any other reporting requirement for a program that may apply with respect to information returns or payee statements or distributions. The proposed regulations contain more detail on how the information must be reported.

Estate and Gift Tax

The proposed regulations provide guidance on the gift and generation-skipping transfer tax consequences of contributions to a QSTP, a change in the designated beneficiary of a QSTP, and a rollover from the account of one beneficiary to the account of another beneficiary under a QSTP. The proposed regulations also provide guidance on whether and to what extent the value of an interest in a QSTP is includible in the gross estate of a contributor to a QSTP or the gross estate of a designated beneficiary of a QSTP. Because of the amendments to section 529 made by the Taxpayer Relief Act of 1997, different gift tax rules apply to contributions made after August 20, 1996, and before August 6, 1997, than apply to contributions made after August 5, 1997. Also, estates of decedents dying after August 20, 1996, and before June 9, 1997, are treated differently from estates of decedents dying after June 8, 1997. Comments are requested specifically on whether there is a need for more detailed guidance with respect to the estate, gift, and generation-skipping transfer tax provisions.

Transition Rules

In accordance with section 1806(c) of the Small Business Job Protection Act of 1996 and section 1601(h) of the Taxpayer Relief Act of 1997, special transition rules apply to programs in existence on August 20, 1996. The proposed regulations provide that no income tax liability will be asserted against a QSTP for any period before the program meets the requirements of section 529 and these regulations if the program qualifies for the transition relief. A program shall be treated as meeting the transition rule if it conforms to the requirements of section 529 and these regulations by the date of final regulations.

The proposed regulations provide transition rules that grandfather certain provisions in contracts issued and accounts opened before August 20, 1996. These contracts may be honored without regard to the definitions of "member of the family" and "eligible educational institution" used in section 529(e)(2) and (3), and without regard to section 529(b)(6) which prohibits the pledging of a QSTP interest as security for a loan. However, regardless of the terms of any agreement executed before August 20, 1996, distributions made by the QSTP are subject to tax according to the rules of § 1.529-3 and subject to the reporting requirements of § 1.529-4.

Proposed Effective Date

These regulations are proposed to be effective on the date they are published in the Federal Register as final regulations. Taxpayers may, however, rely on the proposed regulations for taxable years ending after August 20, 1996. Programs that were in existence on August 20, 1996, may also rely upon the transition rules provided.

Special Analyses

It has been determined that this notice of proposed rulemaking is not a significant regulatory action as defined in Executive Order 12866. Therefore, a regulatory assessment is not required. It has also been determined that section 553(b) of the Administrative Procedure Act (5 U.S.C. chapter 5) does not apply to these regulations, and, because the regulations do not impose a collection of information on small entities, the Regulatory Flexibility Act (5 U.S.C. chapter 6) does not apply. Pursuant to section 7805(f) of the Internal Revenue Code, this notice of proposed rulemaking will be submitted to the Chief counsel for Advocacy of the Small Business Administration for comment on its impact on small business.

Comments and Public Hearing

Before these proposed regulations are adopted as final regulations, consideration will be given to any written comments (a signed original and eight (8) copies) that are submitted timely to the IRS. All comments will be available for public inspection and copying.

A public hearing has been scheduled for Wednesday, January 6, 1999, beginning at 10 a.m. in room 2615 of the Internal Revenue Building, 1111 Constitution Avenue, NW., Washington, DC. Because of access restrictions, visitors will not be admitted beyond the Internal Revenue Building lobby more than 15 minutes before the hearing starts.

The rules of 26 CFR 601.601(a)(3) apply to the hearing.

Persons who wish to present oral comments at the hearing must submit written comments and an outline of the topics to be discussed and the time to be devoted to each topic (signed original and eight (8) copies) by December 16, 1998.

A period of 10 minutes will be allotted to each person for making comments.

An agenda showing the scheduling of the speakers will be prepared after the deadline for receiving outlines has passed. Copies of the agenda will be available free of charge at the hearing.

Drafting Information

The principal authors of these proposed regulations are Monice Rosenbaum, Office of Associate Chief Counsel (Employee Benefits and Exempt Organizations) and Susan Hurwitz, Office of the Associate Chief Counsel (Passthroughs and Special Industries). However, other personnel from the IRS and Treasury Department participated in their development.

[¶ 49,169] Proposed Regulations and Proposed Amendments of Regulations (REG-104924-98), published in the Federal Register on January 28, 1999.

Commodities: Securities: Mark-to-market accounting.—Reg. §§ 1.471-12, 1.475(e)-1, 1.475(f)-1 and 1.475(f)-2 and amendments of Reg. §§ 1.446-1, 1.475(c)-1, 1.475(c)-2, 1.475(e)-1 and 1.475(g)-1, regarding the election to use the mark-to-market method of accounting for dealers in commodities and traders in securities or commodities, are proposed. A public hearing on this proposal has been scheduled for June 3, 1999.

AGENCY: Internal Revenue Service (IRS), Treasury.

ACTION: Notice of proposed rulemaking and notice of public hearing.

SUMMARY: This document contains proposed regulations for dealers in commodities and traders in securities or commodities regarding the election to use the mark-to-market method of accounting for their businesses. Section 1001(b) of the Taxpayer Relief Act of 1997 amended the applicable tax law for these taxpayers. This document also contains proposed regulations providing guidance on statutory changes to section 475 contained in the Internal Revenue Service Restructuring and Reform Act of 1998 (IRS Restructuring Act). This guidance is necessary because section 7003 of the IRS Restructuring Act generally prohibited the application of mark-to-market accounting to nonfinancial customer paper. Among other things, the proposed regulations provide guidance to taxpayers who are using mark-to-market accounting for nonfinancial customer paper. This document also provides notice of a public hearing on these proposed regulations.

DATES: Written comments and outlines of topics to be discussed at the public hearing scheduled for June 3, 1999, at 10 a.m. must be received by May 13, 1999.

ADDRESSES: Send submissions to CC:DOM:CORP:R (REG-104924-98), room 5226, Internal Revenue Service, POB 7604, Ben Franklin Station, Washington, DC 20044. Submissions may be hand delivered Monday through Friday between the hours of 8 a.m. and 5 p.m. to: CC:DOM:CORP:R (REG-104924-98), Courier's Desk, Internal Revenue Service, 1111 Constitution Avenue, NW., Washington, DC. Alternatively, taxpayers may submit comments electronically via the Internet by selecting the "Tax Regs" option on the IRS Home Page, or by submitting comments directly to the IRS Internet site at http://www.irs.ustreas.gov/prod/tax>regs/comments.html. The public hearing will be held in room 2615, Internal Revenue Building, 1111 Constitution Avenue, NW., Washington, DC.

FOR FURTHER INFORMATION CONTACT: Concerning the regulations about elections by commodities dealers and securities and commodities traders, Jo Lynn Ricks, 202-622-3920; concerning the regulations about nonfinancial customer paper, Pamela Lew, 202-622-3950; concerning submissions and the hearing, Michael L. Slaughter, Jr., 202-622-7190 (not toll-free numbers).

SUPPLEMENTARY INFORMATION:

Paperwork Reduction Act

The collection of information contained in this notice of proposed rulemaking has been submitted to the Office of Management and Budget for review in accordance with the Paperwork Reduction Act of 1995 (44 U.S.C. 3507(d)). Comments on the collection of information should be sent to the Office of Management and Budget, Attn: Desk Officer for the Department of Treasury, Office of Information and Regulatory Affairs, Washington, DC, 20503, with copies to the Internal Revenue Service, Attn: IRS Reports Clearance Officer, OP:FS:FP, Washington, DC 20224. Comments concerning the collection of information must be received by March 29, 1999.

The first collection of information in this proposed regulation is described in the Explanation of Provisions section of this document (rather than being included in the text of the proposed regulations). That description indicates that the elections under section 475(e)(1) and (f)(1) and (2) may be required to be made on a form to be developed by the IRS. This burden will be reflected on that new form.

The second collection of information in this proposed regulation is in §§1.475(e)-1 and 1.475(f)-2. The information required to be recorded under §§1.475(e)-1 and 1.475(f)-2 is required by the IRS to determine whether an exemption from mark-to-market accounting is properly claimed. This information will be used to make that determination upon audit of taxpayers' books and records. The likely recordkeepers are businesses or other for-profit institutions.

Estimated total annual recordkeeping burden: 1,000 hours.

The estimated annual burden per recordkeeper varies from 15 minutes to 3 hours, depending on individual circumstances, with an estimated average of 1 hour.

Estimated number of recordkeepers: 1,000.

An agency may not conduct or sponsor, and a person is not required to respond to, a collection of information unless it displays a valid control number assigned by the Office of Management and Budget.

Books or records relating to a collection of information must be retained as long as their contents may become material in the administration of any internal revenue law. Generally, tax returns and tax return information are confidential, as required by 26 U.S.C. 6103.

Background

Section 475 provides that dealers in securities generally must use mark-to-market accounting for all securities. Exceptions from the mark-to-market requirement are generally provided for securities not held for sale to customers and certain securities held as a hedge, provided that the securities are identified as exempt in a proper and timely manner.

For purposes of section 475, a security includes any note, bond, debenture, or other evidence of indebtedness. Revenue Ruling 97-37 (1997-39 I.R.B. 4), clarified that "other evidence of indebtedness" includes customer paper, commonly referred to as trade accounts receivable. The IRS provided procedures for a taxpayer to change its method of accounting for customer paper in Revenue Procedure 97-43 (1997-39 I.R.B. 12).

The IRS Restructuring Act modified the definition of security for purposes of section 475 to exclude nonfinancial customer paper. For this purpose, nonfinancial customer paper is any receivable arising out of the sale of nonfinancial goods or services by a person the principal activity of which is the selling or providing of nonfinancial goods or services if the receivable is held by that person (or a related person) at all times since its issuance. Section 475(c)(4), added by the IRS Restructuring Act, precludes a taxpayer from using mark-to-market accounting under section 475 for nonfinancial customer paper. In addition, the legislative history of the IRS Restructuring Act indicates that taxpayers may not account for nonfinancial customer paper using a mark-to-market or lower-of-cost-or-market method of accounting under other sections of the Code. See H.R. Conf. Rep. No. 599, 105th Cong., 2d Sess. 353-54 (1998). Congress, however, authorized the Secretary to issue regulations describing situations where taxpayers must use mark-to-market accounting for nonfinancial customer paper in order to prevent taxpayers from using the exclusion in section 475(c)(4) to avoid marking to market receivables that are inventory in the hands of the taxpayer or a related person.

Section 475(e) and (f), added by section 1001(b) of the Taxpayer Relief Act of 1997, allows securities traders and commodities traders and dealers to elect mark-to-market accounting similar to that currently required for securities dealers. These provisions are effective for all taxable years ending after August 5, 1997, the date of enactment of the Taxpayer Relief Act. The proposed regulations clarify several issues relating to these elections, including the identification of securities and commodities as exempt from mark-to-market accounting, the character of marked securities and commodities, and the time and manner for making the elections.

Explanation of Provisions

Nonfinancial Customer Paper

Sections 1.446-1(c)(2)(iii), 1.471-12, and 1.475(c)-2(d) of the proposed regulations provide that taxpayers may not use mark-to-market or lower-of-cost-or-market accounting for any nonfinancial customer paper unless a regulation affirmatively provides that the nonfinancial customer paper is to be marked to market as inventory.

The remaining proposed regulations pertaining to section 475(c)(4) are cross references or minor technical changes required by the addition of § 1.475(c)-2(d).

Dealers in Commodities

The proposed regulations generally provide that, except as provided in guidance prescribed by the Commissioner, the rules for mark-to-market accounting for securities dealers apply to commodities dealers that make an election under section 475(e)(1) (electing commodities dealers). Comments are requested whether there are circumstances where the specific rules applicable to securities dealers should not be applied to electing commodities dealers.

Under the proposed regulations, unless the Commissioner otherwise provides in a revenue ruling, revenue procedure, or letter ruling, the exemption from mark-to-market accounting for assets held for investment does not apply to a commodity derivative held by an electing dealer in commodities. If the rule described in the preceding sentence applies (and consequently requires a commodity derivative to be marked to market), the gain or loss is ordinary. The IRS and the Treasury Department believe that it would be extremely rare for a commodity derivative held by a commodities derivative dealer to be acquired other than in a dealer capacity. See § 1.475(c)-1(a)(2). Moreover, the IRS and the Treasury Department believe that a dealer in physical commodities generally engages in derivatives activities that are virtually indistinguishable from its dealings in physical commodities. This situation invokes many of the practical concerns that led Congress to enact section 475(b)(4). The IRS and the Treasury Department welcome comments on whether, and under what circumstances, it may be appropriate for a dealer in physical commodities to identify commodity derivatives as held for investment.

The proposed regulations also provide that, in all cases, if a dealer in commodities identifies a commodity as exempt from mark-to-market accounting under section 475(b)(2), the identification is ineffective unless it is made before the close of the day on which the commodity was acquired, originated, or entered into. Thus, a rule similar to the 30-day identification rule for certain securities in Holding 8 of Rev. Rul. 97-39 (1997-39 I.R.B. 4), does not apply to commodities dealers.

Traders in Securities or Commodities

The proposed regulations provide that the principles underlying the rules and administrative interpretations applicable to securities dealers also apply to electing traders, unless the proposed regulations or the Commissioner provides otherwise. The IRS and the Treasury Department request comments on whether there are circumstances under which a specific rule applicable to securities dealers should not apply to electing securities traders.

The proposed regulations provide rules for the identification of investment securities as exempt from mark-to-market accounting. The proposed regulations clarify that a trader in securities who elects mark-to-market accounting under section 475(f)(1) for its trading business (an electing trader) must identify, in accordance with section 475(f)(1)(B)(ii), any security held other than in connection with the trading business. If the electing trader is also a dealer in securities, the trader need only identify under section 475(f)(1)(B)(ii) securities that are not held in connection with the trading business and that are also described in section 475(b)(1) (without regard to section 475(b)(2)). That is, the trader need not identify securities that could not properly be identified as being exempt from section 475(a).

The IRS and the Treasury Department believe that in making the section 475 election available to securities traders, Congress did not want taxpayers selectively to mark to market some securities but selectively to identify other securities as exempt from this treatment. Congress addressed this concern by establishing a higher burden of proof for electing securities traders to identify securities as not subject to section 475 than is applicable to securities dealers. The IRS and the Treasury Department share this concern, particularly because it traditionally has been easier to distinguish investment securities from dealer securities than to distinguish investment securities from trading securities.

Accordingly, the proposed regulations provide that in no event is the requirement of section 475(f)(1)(B)(i) satisfied unless the electing trader demonstrates by clear and convincing evidence that a security has no connection to its trading activities. The IRS and Treasury Department request comments on whether any trader of securities could meet this burden and under what circumstances.

In addition, the IRS and the Treasury Department seek comments on the manner in which securities are identified as not held in connection with trading activities and, in particular, comments that focus on the administrability of rules in this area.

Because of the fungible nature of certain securities, the proposed regulations provide a special rule for identifying securities held other than in connection with the electing trader's trading business when the electing trader also trades other of the same or substantially similar securities. In this circumstance, the electing trader does not satisfy section 475(f)(1)(B)(i) unless the security is held in a separate, nontrading account maintained with a third party. The IRS and the Treasury Department are considering extending this special identification rule to all securities, rather than solely to those that are fungible, and request comments on the advisability of doing so.

Under the proposed regulations, all identifications under section 475(f)(1)(B)(ii) must be made on the same day the electing trader acquires, originates, or enters into the security. Thus, a rule similar to the 30-day identification rule for certain securities in Holding 8 of Rev. Rul. 97-39 does not apply to electing traders.

Because the principles of the rules and administrative interpretations applicable to securities dealers apply to electing traders, if an electing trader improperly identifies as exempt a security that is actually held in connection with that business, the gain or loss with respect to the security is ordinary, and the consequences described in section 475(d)(2) apply to the security (i.e., the security is marked to market and any losses realized with respect to the security prior to its disposition are recognized only to the extent of gain previously recognized with respect to the security). Similarly, under the proposed regulations, if an electing trader fails to identify a security that is not held in connection with its trading business, the consequences of section 475(d)(2) apply to the security, and the gain or loss with respect to the security is ordinary. Moreover, in the event of this failure, the Commissioner may nevertheless treat the security as if the requirements for exemption from mark-to-market accounting were satisfied.

The proposed regulations further provide that the gain or loss with respect to a security that is marked to market under section 475(f)(1)(A) is ordinary. Under this rule, if an electing trader disposes of a security before the close of the taxable year, proposed § 1.475(a)-2 applies, and the gain or loss is ordinary income or loss. See sections 475(f)(1)(D) and 475(d)(3) and the legislative history to section 475(f). H.R. Rep. No. 148, 105th Cong., 1st Sess. 445 (1997).

Under the proposed regulations, the above rules for electing securities traders also apply to electing commodities traders. In addition, the proposed regulations provide a special character rule for traders in section 1256 commodity contracts who elect mark-to-market accounting for their businesses. For these traders, the proposed regulations clarify that the capital character rule of section 1256 does not apply to these contracts and, thus, the gain or loss with respect to such contracts is ordinary.

Making the Elections

The proposed regulations clarify that if a dealer in securities also has a securities or commodities trading business or a commodities dealing business, the dealer may make an election for that business.

The proposed regulations also provide that the mark-to-market elections for dealers in commodities and for traders in securities or commodities must be made in the time and manner prescribed by the Commissioner. The IRS and the Treasury Department anticipate requiring taxpayers to make the election by filing a form, to be developed by the IRS, not later than 22 months after the beginning of the taxable year for which the election is made. (See the Paperwork Reduction Act section of this preamble, which requests comments on the burden that may be imposed by this requirement.) Interim procedures are being provided in a revenue procedure.

Proposed Effective Dates

The proposed regulations in § 1.475(c)-2(d)(1) apply to every taxpayer who is required by section 475(c)(4) to cease using mark-to-market accounting for nonfinancial customer paper. These regulations are applicable for all taxable years ending after July 22, 1998. Proposed §§ 1.446-1(c)(2)(iii), 1.471-12, and 1.475(c)-2(d)(2) are applicable for all taxable years ending on or after January 28, 1999. The proposed regulations in §§ 1.475(e)-1 and 1.475(f)-2 generally apply to securities or commodities acquired on or after March 1, 1999. The rules concerning the time and manner for making the mark-to-market elections for commodities dealers and securities and commodities traders are generally applicable for taxable years ending on or after January 28, 1999.

Special Analyses

It has been determined that this notice of proposed rulemaking is not a significant regulatory action as defined in EO 12866. Therefore, a regulatory impact analysis is not required. It is hereby certified that the collection of information in these regulations will not have a significant economic impact on a substantial number of small entities. As previously noted, in those instances where a small entity elects to apply the rules in these regulations, the burden of the collection of information is not significant. Accordingly, a Regulatory Flexibility Analysis is not required. Pursuant to section 7805(f), this notice of proposed rulemaking will be submitted to the Chief Counsel for Advocacy of the Small Business Administration for comment on its impact on small business.

Comments and Public Hearing

Before these proposed regulations are adopted as final regulations, consideration will be given to any written comments (a signed original and eight (8) copies) that are submitted timely to the IRS. The IRS and the Treasury Department specifically request comments on the clarity of the proposed regulations and how they can be made easier to understand. All comments will be available for public inspection and copying.

A public hearing has been scheduled for June 3, 1999, beginning at 10 a.m. in room 2615 of the Internal Revenue Building, 1111 Constitution Avenue, NW., Washington, DC. Due to building security procedures, visitors must enter at the 10th Street entrance, located between Constitution and Pennsylvania Avenues, NW. In addition, all visitors must present photo identification to enter the building. Because of access restrictions, visitors will not be admitted beyond the immediate entrance area more than 15 minutes before the hearing starts. For information about having your name placed on the building access list to attend the hearing, see the "FOR FURTHER INFORMATION CONTACT" section of this preamble.

The rules of 26 CFR 601.601(a)(3) apply to the hearing. Persons who wish to present oral comments at the hearing must submit written comments and an outline of the topics to be discussed and the time to be devoted to each topic (signed original and eight (8) copies) by May 13, 1999. A period of 10 minutes will be allotted to each person for making comments. An agenda showing the scheduling of the speakers will be prepared after the deadline for receiving outlines has passed. Copies of the agenda will be available free of charge at the hearing.

Drafting Information

The principal authors of these regulations are Jo Lynn Ricks and Pamela Lew of the Office of Assistant Chief Counsel (Financial Institutions & Products). However, other personnel from the IRS and the Treasury Department participated in their development.

[¶49,170] Proposed Regulation and Proposed Amendments of Regulations (REG-113909-98), published in the Federal Register on July 13, 1999.

Controlled foreign corporations: Hybrid branches: Subpart F income.—Reg. §1.954-9 and amendments of Reg. §§1.904-5 and 1.954-0—1.954-2, relating to the treatment under subpart F of certain payments involving branches of a controlled foreign corporation that are treated as separate entities for foreign tax purposes or partnerships in which controlled foreign corporations are partners, are proposed. Proposed regulations (REG-104537-97) published on March 26, 1998, are withdrawn. A public hearing on this proposal is scheduled for December 1, 1999.

AGENCY: Internal Revenue Service (IRS), Treasury.

ACTION: Withdrawal; Notice of proposed rulemaking; and notice of public hearing.

SUMMARY: This document withdraws the notice of proposed rulemaking and notice of proposed rulemaking by cross-reference to temporary regulations that was published in the Federal Register on March 26, 1998, providing guidance under subpart F relating to partnerships and branches. This document contains new proposed regulations relating to the treatment under subpart F of certain transactions involving hybrid branches. These regulations are necessary to provide guidance on transactions relating to such entities. This document also provides notice of a public hearing on these proposed regulations.

DATES: Written comments, and outlines of oral comments to be discussed at the public hearing scheduled for December 1, 1999, must be received by November 10, 1999.

ADDRESSES: Send submissions to: CC:DOM:CORP:R (REG-113909-98), room 5226, Internal Revenue Service, POB 7604, Ben Franklin Station, Washington DC 20044. Submissions may be hand delivered Monday through Friday between the hours of 8 a.m. and 5 p.m. to: CC:DOM:CORP:R (REG-113909-98), Courier's Desk, Internal Revenue Service, 1111 Constitution Avenue, NW., Washington DC. Alternatively, taxpayers may submit comments electronically via the Internet by selecting the "Tax Regs" option on the IRS Home Page, or by submitting comments directly to the IRS Internet site at http://www.irs.ustreas.gov/prod/tax>regs/regslist.html. The public hearing will be held in room 2615, Internal Revenue Building, 1111 Constitution Avenue NW., Washington, DC 20224.

FOR FURTHER INFORMATION CONTACT: Concerning the regulations, Valerie Mark, (202) 622-3840; concerning submissions of comments, the hearing, and/or to be placed on the building access list to attend the hearing, LaNita Van Dyke (202) 622-7180 (not toll-free numbers).

SUPPLEMENTARY INFORMATION:

Background

On March 23, 1998 (63 FR 14669, March 26, 1998), the IRS issued proposed regulations (REG-104537-97) relating to the treatment under subpart F of certain partnership and hybrid branch transactions. The provisions of the proposed regulations relating to hybrid branch transactions were also issued as temporary regulations (TD 8767) (63 FR 14613, March 26, 1998). Certain members of Congress and taxpayers raised concerns about the proposed and temporary regulations relating to hybrid branch transactions. On June 19, 1998, the Treasury announced in Notice 98-35 (1998-27 I.R.B. 35) that the temporary regulations would be removed and that the proposed regulations relating to hybrid transactions would be re-proposed with new dates of applicability to give Congress the opportunity to consider in greater depth the issues raised by hybrid transactions.

As provided in Notice 98-35, these proposed regulations substantially restate the regulations relating to hybrid transactions issued in March of 1998. These proposed regulations, however, contain certain clarifications requested by taxpayers. Further, as described in greater detail below, unlike the effective date rules announced in Notice 98-35, these regulations are proposed to be effective only for payments made in taxable years commencing after the date that is five years after the date of finalization of these regulations. The permanent grandfather relief described in Notice 98-35 remains unchanged.

These proposed regulations represent the IRS and Treasury's views of how current law should be enforced. Treasury is currently undertaking a comprehensive study of subpart F. These proposed regulations will not control the results of the study. For example, an objective analysis of the policies and goals of subpart F may lead to the conclusion that subpart F should be significantly restructured.

To the extent, however, that Congress does not restructure subpart F in a manner that would alter the rules enforced by these regulations, Treasury and the IRS believe that these regulations will be necessary to preserve the integrity of the current statutory scheme. The use of hybrid arrangements, which is greatly facilitated by the "check-the-box" entity classification regulations (§§301.7701-1 through 301.7701-3), would otherwise give rise to the following inconsistency: if sales income is shifted from one CFC to a related CFC in a different jurisdiction, subpart F income may arise; if sales income is shifted from one CFC to its branch in a different jurisdiction, subpart F income may arise; if income is shifted through interest payments from one CFC to a related CFC in a different jurisdiction, subpart F income may arise; however, if income is shifted through interest payments from one CFC to its hybrid branch in a different jurisdiction, subpart F income will not arise. This final result does not seem an appropriate policy outcome within the framework of current subpart F, and is almost certainly inconsistent with the Congressional intent underlying the rules being interpreted here.

Treasury anticipates that taxpayers will comment both on the appropriateness of these proposed regulations under current law, and on the contents of its subpart F study, including any conclusions that the study might draw about potential changes to subpart F. To allow proper time to consider all these issues, Treasury and the IRS have significantly modified and liberalized the effective date rules set forth in Notice 98-35. New regulations regarding the treatment of a controlled foreign corporation's distributive share of partnership income will be proposed at a later date.

Explanation of Provisions

I. *In General*

In these proposed regulations, Treasury and the IRS set forth a framework for dealing with issues arising under subpart F (sections 951 through 964) that relate to the use of certain entities that are regarded as fiscally transparent for purposes of U.S. tax law.

II. *Hybrid Branches*

Treasury and the IRS understand that certain taxpayers are using arrangements involving hybrid branches to circumvent the purposes of subpart F. These arrangements generally involve the use of deductible payments to reduce the taxable income of a CFC under foreign law, thereby reducing that CFC's foreign tax and, also under foreign law, the corresponding creation in another entity of low-taxed, passive income of the type to which subpart F was intended to apply. Because of the structure of these arrangements, however, taxpayers take the position that this income is not taxed under subpart F. Treasury and the IRS have concluded that use of these hybrid branch arrangements is contrary to the policies and rules of subpart F.

Under these proposed regulations, hybrid branch payments, as defined in the regulations, between a CFC and its hybrid branch, or between hybrid branches of the CFC may give rise to subpart F income. When certain conditions are present, the non-subpart F income of the CFC, in the amount of the hybrid branch payment, is recharacterized as subpart F income of the CFC. Those conditions include that: the hybrid branch payment reduces the foreign tax of the payor; the hybrid branch payment would have been foreign personal holding company income if made between separate CFCs; and there is a disparity between the effective rate of tax on the payment in the hands of the payee and the hypothetical rate of tax that would have applied if the payment had been taxed in the hands of the payor.

The proposed regulations would make clear that the CFC and the hybrid branch, or the hybrid branches, are treated as separate corporations only to recharacterize non-subpart F income as subpart F income in the amount of the hybrid branch payment, and to apply the tax disparity rule of §1.954-9(a)(5)(iv). For all other purposes (e.g., for purposes of the earnings and profits limitation of section 952), a CFC and its hybrid branch, or hybrid branches, would not be treated as separate corporations.

The proposed regulations would provide that the amount recharacterized as subpart F income is the gross amount of the hybrid branch payment limited by the amount of the CFC's earnings and profits attributable to non-subpart F income. This amount is the excess of current earnings and profits over subpart F income, determined after the application of the rules of sections 954(b) and 952(c) and before the application of these proposed regulations. To the extent that the full amount required to be recharacterized under this provision cannot be recharacterized because it exceeds earnings and profits attributable to non-subpart F income, there is no requirement to carry such amounts back or forward to another year.

The proposed regulations would provide that, under certain circumstances, the recharacterization rules will also apply to a CFC's proportionate share of any hybrid branch payment made between a partnership in which the CFC is a partner and a hybrid branch of the partnership, or between hybrid branches of such a partnership. When the partnership is treated as fiscally transparent by the CFC's taxing jurisdiction, the. recharacterization rules are applied by treating the hybrid branch payment as if it had been made directly between the CFC and the hybrid branch, or as though the hybrid branches of the partnership had been hybrid branches of the CFC, as applicable. If the partnership is treated as a separate entity by the CFC's taxing jurisdiction, the recharacterization rules are applied to the partnership as if it were a CFC.

The proposed regulations would provide that income will not be recharacterized unless there is a disparity between the effective rate at which the hybrid branch payment is taxed to the payee and a hypothetical tax rate that measures the tax savings to the payor from the deductible payment. This provision is similar to the rule in § 1.954-3(b), and adopts the same percentage tests as contained in that provision. The regulations also provide a special high tax exception applicable to the hybrid branch payment that is similar to the one contained in section 954(b)(4).

For purposes of determining the amount of taxes deemed paid under section 960, the amount of non-subpart F income recharacterized as subpart F income is treated as attributable to income in separate foreign tax credit baskets in proportion to the ratio of non-subpart F income in each basket to the total amount of non-subpart F income of the CFC for the taxable year.

III. *Related Provisions*

These proposed regulations would provide rules, contained in § 1.954-1(c)(1)(i)(B), to prevent expenses, including related person interest expense that would normally be allocable under section 954(b)(5) to subpart F income of a CFC, from being allocated to a payment from which the expense arises. The allocation limit applies: (i) to the extent such payment is included in the subpart F income of the CFC; (ii) if the expense arises from any payment between the CFC and ahybrid partnership in which the CFC is a partner; and (iii) if the payment reduces foreign tax and there is a significant disparity in tax rates between the payor and payee jurisdictions.

These proposed regulations also would address the application of the related person exceptions to the foreign personal holding company income rules in the context of partnership distributive shares and transactions involving hybrid branches. Under section 954(c)(3), foreign personal holding company income does not include certain interest, dividends, rents and royalties received from related corporations. These exceptions apply, in the case of interest and dividends, when the related corporate payor is organized in the country in which the CFC is organized and uses a substantial part of its assets in a trade or business in that country and, in the case of rents and royalties, when the rent or royalty payment is made for the use or privilege of using property within the CFC's country of incorporation.

Under these proposed regulations, if the partnership receives an item of income that reduces the foreign income tax of the payor, the related person exceptions of section 954(c)(3) would apply to exclude the income from the foreign personal holding company income of the CFC partner only where: the exception would have applied if the CFC earned the income directly (testing relatedness and country of incorporation at the CFC partner level); and either the partnership is organized and operates in the CFC's country of incorporation, the partnership is treated as fiscally transparent in the CFC's countries of incorporation and operation, or there is no significant disparity between the effective rate of tax imposed on the income and the rate of tax that would be imposed on the income if earned directly by the CFC partner.

In addition, these proposed regulations contain rules that would apply the related person exceptions to certain payments involving hybrid branches. These rules would apply to payments by a CFC to a hybrid branch of a related CFC. Under these rules, the related person exceptions would apply to exclude the payments from the foreign personal holding company income of the recipient CFC only if the payment would have qualified for the exception if the hybrid branch had been a separate CFC incorporated in the jurisdiction in which the payment is subject to tax (other than a withholding tax).

IV. *Request for Comments*

Comments on policy issues that relate to subpart F and deferral, generally, including comments on legislative modifications to the current rules, and comments solicited on the broad policy issues mentioned in Notice 98-35, can be submitted in response to the study mentioned above. Treasury and the IRS invite comments on the appropriateness of these regulations under the current subpart F rules.

Proposed Effective Date

These proposed regulations will not be finalized before July 1, 2000. It is proposed that, when finalized, these regulations would be effective only for payments made in taxable years of a controlled foreign corporation commencing after the date that is five years after the date of finalization of these regulations. These regulations would not, however, apply to any payments made under hybrid arrangements entered into before June 19, 1998. This exception is permanent so long as the arrangement is not substantially modified on or after June 19, 1998. An illustrative list of events that would and would not constitute "substantial modification" of an arrangement is included in these regulations.

Special Analyses

It has been determined that this notice of proposed rulemaking is not a significant regulatory action as defined in Executive Order 12866. Therefore, a regulatory assessment is not required. It has also been determined that section 553(b) of the Administrative Procedures Act (5 U.S.C. chapter 5) does not apply to these regulations, and, because the regulation does not impose a collection of information on small entities, the Regulatory Flexibility Act (5 U.S.C. chapter 6) does not apply. Pursuant to section 7805(f) of the Internal Revenue Code, this notice of proposed rulemaking will be submitted to the Chief Counsel for Advocacy of the Small Business Administration for comment on its impact on small business.

Request for Comments

Before these proposed regulations are adopted as final regulations, consideration will be given to any written comments (a signed original and eight (8) copies) that are submitted timely to the IRS. The IRS and Treasury specifically request comments on the clarity of these proposed regulations and how they may be made easier to understand. All comments will be available for public inspection and copying.

A public hearing has been scheduled for December 1, 1999, at 10 a.m., in room 2615, Internal Revenue Building, 1111 Constitution Avenue NW., Washington, DC. Due to building security procedures, visitors must enter at the 10th Street entrance, located between Constitution and Pennsylvania Avenues, NW. In addition, all visitors must present photo identification to enter the building. Because of access restrictions, visitors will not be admitted beyond the immediate entrance area more than 15 minutes before the hearing starts. For information about having your name placed on the building access list to attend the hearing, see the "FOR FURTHER INFORMATION CONTACT" section of this preamble.

The rules of 26 CFR 601.601(a)(3) apply to the hearing.

Persons that wish to present oral comments at the hearing must submit written comments and an outline of topics to be discussed and time to be devoted to each topic (signed original and eight (8) copies) by November 10, 1999.

A period of 10 minutes will be allotted to each person for making comments.

An agenda showing the scheduling of the speakers will be prepared after the deadline for receiving outlines has passed. Copies of the agenda will be available free of charge at the hearing.

Drafting Information

The principal author of these regulations is Valerie Mark, of the Office of the Associate Chief Counsel (International). Other personnel from the IRS and Treasury Department also participated in the development of these regulations.

[¶ 49,172] Proposed Amendments of Regulation (REG-103882-99), published in the Federal Register on February 8, 2000.

Depletion: Lease of mineral property: Uniform capitalization rules: Delay rental, treatment of.—Amendments of Reg. § 1.612-3, conforming regulations relating to delay rental to the requirements of Code Sec. 263A relating to capitalization and inclusion in inventory of costs of certain expenses, are proposed. A public hearing on this proposal is scheduled for May 26, 2000.

AGENCY: Internal Revenue Service (IRS), Treasury.

ACTION: Notice of proposed rulemaking and notice of public hearing.

SUMMARY: This document contains proposed amendments conforming regulations relating to delay rental to the requirements of section 263A relating to capitalization and inclusion in inventory of costs of certain expenses. Changes to the applicable law were made by the Tax Reform Act of 1986 and the Technical and Miscellaneous Revenue Act of 1988. The proposed regulations provide the public with guidance concerning the application of section 263A to delay rental.

DATES: Written comments must be received by May 8, 2000. Outlines of topics to be discussed at the public hearing scheduled for May 26, 2000, at 10 a.m. must be received by May 5, 2000.

ADDRESSES: Send submissions to: CC:DOM:CORP:R (REG-103882-99), room 5226, Internal Revenue Service, POB 7604, Ben Franklin Station, Washington, DC 20044. Submissions may be hand delivered between the hours of 8 a.m. and 5 p.m. to: CC:DOM:CORP:R (REG-103882-99), Courier's Desk, Internal Revenue Service, 1111 Constitution Avenue, NW., Washington, DC. Alternatively, taxpayers may submit comments electronically via the Internet by selecting the "Tax Regs" option on the IRS Home Page, or by submitting comments directly to the IRS Internet site at http://www.irs.ustreas.gov/prod/tax_regs/regslist.html. The public hearing will be held in room 2615, Internal Revenue Building, 1111 Constitution Avenue, NW., Washington, DC.

FOR FURTHER INFORMATION CONTACT: Concerning the regulation, Brenda M. Stewart, (202) 622-3120; concerning submissions and the hearing, LaNita Van Dyke, (202) 622-7180 (not toll-free numbers).

SUPPLEMENTARY INFORMATION:

Background

This document contains proposed amendments to the Income Tax Regulations (26 CFR part 1) under section 612 to conform them to the requirements of section 263A. Section 263A was enacted by the Tax Reform Act of 1986, Public Law 99-514 (100 Stat. 2085), and amended by the Technical and Miscellaneous Revenue Act of 1988, Public Law 100-647 (102 Stat. 3342).

Explanation of Provisions

Under the terms of a lease of mineral property, the lessee acquires, for a stated term, the right and obligation to obtain production of minerals from the property. A lease may provide that for each year that the lessee fails to make efforts to obtain production, the lessee must pay a "delay rental" to the lessor.

Section 1.612-3(c)(1) of the final regulations defines a delay rental as an amount paid for the privilege of deferring development of the property and which could have been avoided by abandonment of the lease, or by commencement of development operations, or by obtaining production. Section 1.612-3(c)(2) of the final regulations provides that since a delay rental is in the nature of rent, it is ordinary income to the payee and not subject to depletion. The payor may at his election deduct the delay rental as an expense, or charge it to depletable capital account under section 266.

Section 263A was enacted subsequent to the issuance of § 1.612-3(c) of the final regulations. The uniform capitalization rules of section 263A generally require the capitalization of all direct costs and certain indirect costs properly allocable to property produced by the taxpayer. Capitalization may be required even though production (development) has not yet begun. § 1.263A-2(a)(3)(ii). In some situations, a delay rental may be required to be capitalized under section 263A. Accordingly, the proposed regulation clarifies that subsequent to the enactment of section 263A, the payor of a delay rental may elect to expense currently the delay rental or charge it to depletable capital account under section 266 to the extent that the delay rental is not required to be capitalized under section 263A and the regulations thereunder.

Special Analyses

It has been determined that this notice of proposed rulemaking is not a significant regulatory action as defined in Executive Order 12866. Therefore, a regulatory assessment is not required. It has also been determined that section 553(b) of the Administrative Procedure Act (5 U.S.C. chapter 5) does not apply to these regulations, and because the regulations do not impose a collection of information on small entities, a Regulatory Flexibility Analysis is not required. Pursuant to section 7805(f) of the Internal Revenue Code, this notice of proposed rulemaking will be submitted to the Chief Counsel for Advocacy of the Small Business Administration for comment on its impact on small business.

Comments and Public Hearing

Before these proposed regulations are adopted as final regulations, consideration will be given to any written comments that are submitted timely (a signed original and eight copies) to the IRS. The IRS and Treasury request comments on the clarity of the proposed regulations and they may be made easier to understand. All comments will be made available for public inspection and copying.

A public hearing has been scheduled for May 26, 2000, at 10 a.m. in room 2615, Internal Revenue Building, 1111 Constitution Avenue NW., Washington, DC. Because of access restrictions, visitors will not be admitted beyond the Internal Revenue Building lobby more than 15 minutes before the hearing starts.

The rules of 26 CFR 601.601(a)(3) apply to the hearing.

Persons that wish to present oral comments at the hearing must submit written comments (a signed original and eight (8) copies) by May 8, 2000. The outline of topics to be discussed at the hearing must be received by May 5, 2000.

A period of 10 minutes will be allotted for each person for making comments.

An agenda showing the scheduling of the speakers will be prepared after the deadline for receiving outlines has passed. Copies of the agenda will be available free of charge at the hearing.

Drafting Information

The principal author of this proposed regulation is Brenda M. Stewart of the Office of Assistant Chief Counsel (Passthroughs and Special Industries), Internal Revenue Service. However, other personnel from the IRS and Treasury Department participated in its development.

[¶ 49,175] Proposed Regulations and Proposed Amendments of Regulations (REG-116050-99), published in the Federal Register on November 15, 2000.

Corporate reorganizations: Foreign corporations: Stock transfer rules: Carryovers.—Reg. § 1.367(b)-8 and amendments of Reg. §§ 1.312-10, 1.367(b)-5 and 1.367(e)-1, addressing the carryover of certain tax attributes such as earnings and profits and foreign income tax accounts when two corporations combine in a section 367(b) transaction, are proposed. Reg. §§ 1.367(b)-7 and 1.367(b)-9 and amendments to Reg. §§ 1.367(b)-0—1.367(b)-6 and 1.381(a)-1 were adopted by T.D. 9273 on August 7, 2006.

AGENCY: Internal Revenue Service (IRS), Treasury.

ACTION: Notice of proposed rulemaking and notice of public hearing.

SUMMARY: This document contains proposed regulations addressing transactions described in section 367(b) of the Internal Revenue Code (section 367(b) transactions). A section 367(b) transaction includes a corporate reorganization, liquidation, or division involving one or more foreign corporations. The proposed regulations address the carryover of certain tax attributes, such as earnings and profits and foreign income tax accounts, when two corporations combine in a section 367(b) transaction. The proposed regulations also address the allocation of certain tax attributes when a corporation distributes stock of another corporation in a section 367(b) transaction. This document also provides notice of a public hearing on the proposed regulations.

DATES: Written or electronic comments and requests to speak (with outlines of oral comments) at a public hearing scheduled for March 13, 2001 must be received by February 20, 2001.

ADDRESSES: Send submissions to: CC:M&SP:RU (REG-116050-99), room 5226, Internal Revenue Service, POB 7604, Ben Franklin Station, Washington, DC 20044. Submissions may be hand delivered Monday through Friday between the hours of 8 a.m. and 5 p.m. to: CC:M&SP:RU (REG-116050-99), Courier's Desk, Internal Revenue Service, 1111 Constitution Avenue, NW., Washington, DC. Alternatively, taxpayers may submit comments electronically via the Internet by selecting the "Tax Regs" option on the IRS Home Page, or by submitting comments directly to the IRS Internet site at http://www.irs.gov/tax>regs/regslist.html. The public hearing will be held in room 7218, Internal Revenue Building, 1111 Constitution Avenue, NW., Washington DC.

FOR FURTHER INFORMATION CONTACT: Concerning the proposed regulations, Anne O'Connell Devereaux, at (202) 622-3850; concerning submissions of comments, the hearing, and/or to be placed on the building access list to attend the hearing, Guy Traynor, at (202) 622-7180 (not toll-free numbers).

SUPPLEMENTARY INFORMATION:

Paperwork Reduction Act

The collection of information contained in this notice of proposed rulemaking has been submitted to the Office of Management and Budget for review in accordance with the Paperwork Reduction Act of 1995 (44 U.S.C. 3507(d)). Comments on the collection of information should be sent to the Office of Management and Budget, Attn: Desk Officer for the Department of the Treasury, Office of Information and Regulatory Affairs, Washington, DC 20503, with copies to the Internal Revenue Service, Attn: IRS Reports Clearance Officer, W:CAR:MP:FP:S:O, Washington, DC 20224. Comments on the collection of information should be received by January 16, 2001. Comments are specifically requested concerning:

—Whether the proposed collection of information is necessary for the proper performance of the functions of the IRS, including whether the information will have practical utility;

—The accuracy of the estimated burden associated with the proposed collection of information (see below);

—How the quality, utility, and clarity of the information to be collected may be enhanced;

—How the burden of complying with the proposed collection of information may be minimized, including through the application of automated collection techniques or other forms of information technology; and

—Estimates of capital or start-up costs and costs of operation, maintenance, and purchase of services to provide information.

The collection of information in this proposed regulation is in §1.367(b)-1. This collection of information is required by the IRS to verify compliance with the regulations under section 367(b) relating to exchanges described therein. The likely respondents are corporations that are affected by such exchanges.

Estimated total annual reporting burden: 1,800 hours.

The estimated annual burden per respondent: 3 hours.

Estimated number of respondents: 600.

Estimated annual frequency of responses: One.

An agency may not conduct or sponsor, and a person is not required to respond to, a collection of information unless it displays a valid control number assigned by the Office of Management and Budget.

Books or records relating to a collection of information must be retained as long as their contents may become material in the administration of any internal revenue law. Generally, tax returns and tax return information are confidential, as required by 26 U.S.C. 6103.

Background

On December 27, 1977, the IRS and Treasury issued proposed and temporary regulations under section 367(b) of the Code. Subsequent guidance updated and amended the 1977 temporary regulations several times over the next 14 years. On August 26, 1991, the IRS and Treasury issued proposed regulations §§1.367(b)-1 through 1.367(b)-6 (the 1991 proposed regulations). Final regulations under section 367(b) of the Internal Revenue Code (Code) were issued in June 1998 and January 2000 and the 1977 temporary regulations and the 1991 proposed regulations were generally removed. The preamble to the January 2000 final regulations refers to proposed regulations that would be issued at a later date to address the carryover of certain corporate tax attributes in transactions involving one or more foreign corporations. Those proposed regulations are set forth in this document.

Overview

A. *General Policies of Section 367(b)*

In general, section 367 governs corporate restructurings under sections 332, 351, 354, 355, 356, and 361 (Subchapter C nonrecognition transactions) in which the status of a foreign corporation as a "corporation" is necessary for the application of the relevant nonrecognition provisions. Other provisions in Subchapter C (Subchapter C carryover provisions) apply to such transactions in conjunction with the enumerated provisions and detail additional consequences that occur in connection with the transactions. For example, sections 362 and 381 govern the carryover of basis and earnings and profits from the transferor corporation to the transferee corporation in applicable transactions and section 312 governs the allocation of earnings and profits from a distributing corporation in a transaction described in section 355.

The Subchapter C carryover provisions generally have been drafted to apply to domestic corporations and U.S. shareholders, and thus do not fully take into account the cross-border aspects of U.S. taxation. For example, sections 381 and 312 do not take into account source and foreign tax credit issues that arise when earnings and profits move from one corporation to another.

Congress enacted section 367(b) to ensure that international tax considerations in the Code are adequately addressed when the Subchapter C provisions apply to an exchange involving a foreign corporation in order to prevent the avoidance of U.S. taxation. Because determining the proper interaction of the Code's international and Subchapter C provisions is "necessarily highly technical," Congress granted the Secretary broad regulatory authority to provide the "necessary or appropriate" rules rather than enacting a complex statutory regime. H.R. Rep. No. 658, 94th Cong., 1st Sess. 241 (1975). Thus, section 367(b)(2) provides in part that the regulations "shall include (but shall not be limited to) regulations . . . providing . . . the extent to which adjustments shall be made to earnings and profits, basis of stock or securities, and basis of assets."

The proposed regulations provide rules regarding the movement of certain corporate tax attributes between corporations in a Subchapter C nonrecognition transaction involving one or more foreign corporations. Generally, the regulations continue to apply the principles of the Subchapter C carryover provisions with modifications as necessary or appropriate to preserve international tax policies of the Code and to prevent material distortions of income.

The remainder of the Overview section is divided by specific categories of section 367(b) transactions and describes the relevant Subchapter C and international policies and provisions. The "Details of Provisions" portion of this preamble describes the proposed regulations' principal operative rules that implement the policies and reconcile the provisions described in the Overview portion of this preamble. The IRS and Treasury welcome comments regarding both the general approach and the specific provisions of the proposed regulations.

B. *Specific Policies Related to Inbound Nonrecognition Transactions (Prop. Reg. § 1.367(b)-3)*

Proposed § 1.367(b)-3 addresses acquisitions by a domestic corporation (domestic acquiring corporation) of the assets of a foreign corporation (foreign acquired corporation) in a section 332 liquidation or an asset acquisition described in section 368(a)(1), such as a C, D, or F reorganization (inbound nonrecognition transaction).

The preamble to the January 2000 final regulations generally describes international policy issues that can arise in an inbound nonrecognition transaction. The preamble states that the "principal policy consideration of section 367(b) with respect to inbound nonrecognition transactions is the appropriate carryover of attributes from foreign to domestic corporations. This consideration has interrelated shareholder-level and corporate-level components." The final regulations address the carryover of certain attributes, such as the carryover of foreign taxes, earnings and profits, and basis. However, the carryover of earnings and profits, and basis are addressed only to the extent attributable to earnings and profits accumulated during a U.S. shareholder's holding period, i.e., "the all earnings and profits amount," as defined in § 1.367(b)-2(d).

The preamble to the final regulations also notes that it would be consistent with the policy considerations of section 367(b) for future regulations to provide further rules with respect to the extent to which attributes carry over from a foreign corporation to a U.S. corporation. The proposed regulations do not comprehensively address this issue. Compare Modify Treatment of Built-In Losses and Other Attribute Trafficking, General Explanations of the Administration's Fiscal Year 2001 Revenue Proposals at 205. However, the proposed regulations do provide additional rules concerning several attributes, specifically net operating loss and capital loss carryovers, and earnings and profits that are not included in income as an all earnings and profits amount (or a deficit in earnings and profits). The proposed regulations generally provide that these tax attributes carry over from a foreign acquired corporation to a domestic acquiring corporation only to the extent that they are effectively connected to a U.S. trade or business (or attributable to a permanent establishment, in the case of an applicable U.S. income tax treaty).

C. *Specific Policies Related to Foreign 381 Transactions (Prop. Reg. § 1. 367(b)-7)*

Proposed regulation § 1.367(b)-7 applies to an acquisition by a foreign corporation (foreign acquiring corporation) of the assets of another foreign corporation (foreign target corporation) in a transaction described in section 381 (foreign 381 transaction) and addresses the manner in which earnings and profits and foreign income taxes of the foreign acquiring corporation and foreign target corporation carry over to the surviving foreign corporation (foreign surviving corporation). This would include, for example, a C, D, or F reorganization or a section 332 liquidation between two foreign corporations.

The international provisions of the Code distinguish between categories of foreign corporations. A foreign acquiring, target, or surviving corporation can be a controlled foreign corporation as defined in section 953 or 957 (CFC), a noncontrolled section 902 corporation as defined in section 904(d)(2)(E) after 2003, the effective date of section 1105(b) of Public Law 105-34 (111 Stat. 788) (the 1997 Act) (look-through 10/50 corporation and, together with CFCs, look-through corporations), a noncontrolled section 902 corporation before 2003 (non-look-through 10/50 corporation and, together with look-through 10/50 corporations, 10/50 corporations), or a foreign corporation that is neither a CFC nor a 10/50 corporation (less-than-10%-U.S.-owned foreign corporation).

The principal Code sections implicated by the carryover of earnings and profits and foreign income taxes in a foreign 381 transaction are sections 381, 902, 904, and 959. Section 381 generally permits earnings and profits (or deficit in earnings and profits) to carry over to a surviving corporation, thus enabling "the successor corporation to step into the 'tax shoes' of its predecessor . . . . [and] represents the economic integration of two or more separate businesses into a unified business enterprise." H. Rep. No. 1337, 83rd Cong., 2nd Sess. 41 (1954). However, a deficit in earnings and profits of either the transferee or transferor corporation can only be used to offset earnings and profits accumulated after the date of transfer (hovering deficit rule). Section 381(c)(2)(B). The hovering deficit rule is a legislative mechanism designed to deter the trafficking in favorable tax attributes that the IRS and courts had repeatedly encountered. See, e.g., *Commissioner v. Phipps*, 336 U.S. 410 (1949). The proposed regulations adopt the principles of section 381 but adapt its operation in consideration of the international provisions that address foreign corporations' earnings and profits and their related foreign income taxes, such as sections 902, 904, and 959.

Section 902 generally provides that a deemed paid foreign tax credit is available to a domestic corporation that receives a dividend from a foreign corporation in which it owns 10 percent or more of the voting stock (i.e., a look-through corporation or non-look-through 10/50 corporation). The Code modifies the general last-in, first-out (LIFO) rule of section 316 and provides that look-through corporations and non-look-through 10/50 corporations pay dividends out of multi-year pools of earnings and profits and foreign income taxes for earnings and profits accumulated (and related foreign income taxes paid or deemed paid) in taxable years beginning after December 31, 1986, or the first day after which a domestic corporation owns 10 percent or more of the voting stock of a foreign corporation, whichever is later. Section 902(c). (The Code and regulations refer to pooled earnings and profits and foreign income taxes as post-1986 undistributed earnings and post-1986 foreign income taxes even though a particular corporation may begin to pool after 1986. Sections 902(c)(1) and (2), § 1.902-1(a) (8) and (9).)

Congress enacted the pooling rules because it believed that averaging of foreign income taxes was fairer than distributions out of annual layers. Joint Committee on Taxation, General Explanation of the Tax Reform Act of 1986 (Public Law 99-514) (1986 Bluebook) at 870. Averaging prevents taxpayers from inflating their foreign income tax rate for a particular year in order to obtain artificially enhanced foreign tax credits. Id. Averaging also prevents the trapping of foreign income taxes in years in which a taxpayer may have no earnings and profits. Id.

However, Congress enacted pooling on a limited basis. Earnings and profits accumulated (and related foreign income taxes paid or deemed paid) while a foreign corporation is a less-than-10%-U.S.-owned foreign corporation and pre-1987 earnings and profits accumulated (and related foreign income taxes paid or deemed paid) by a look-through corporation or non-look-through 10/50 corporation are not pooled. Rather, such earnings and profits (and related foreign income taxes) are maintained in separate annual layers. Section 902(c)(6). (The Code and regulations refer to earnings and profits and foreign income taxes in annual layers as pre-1987 accumulated profits and pre-1987 foreign income taxes even though a particular corporation may have annual layers for years after 1986. Section 902(c)(6); § 1.902-1(a)(10).)

A distribution of earnings and profits is first out of pooled earnings and profits and then, only after all pooled earnings and profits have been distributed, out of annual layers of earnings and profits on a LIFO basis. Section 902(a) and (c). The retention of annual layers beneath pooled earnings and profits limits the need to recreate tax histories, an administrative burden that is more significant for periods during which a corporation had limited nexus to the U.S. taxing jurisdiction and for pre-1987 earnings and profits when pooling was not required.

The section 904 foreign tax credit limitation ensures that taxpayers can use foreign tax credits only to offset U.S. tax on foreign source income. The limitation is computed separately with respect to different categories of income (baskets). The purpose of the baskets is to limit taxpayers' ability to cross-credit taxes from different categories of foreign source income. Congress was concerned that, without separate limitations, cross-crediting opportunities would distort economic incentives to invest in the United States versus abroad. 1986 Bluebook at 862.

A dividend received by a U.S. shareholder that owns less than 10 percent of the stock of a foreign corporation is categorized as passive income because such a dividend is in the nature of a portfolio investment. 1986 Bluebook at 866.

A dividend received by a U.S. shareholder that owns 10 percent or more of a foreign corporation is subject to other limitations. Dividends paid by a non-look-through 10/50 corporation to a 10 percent or greater U.S. corporate shareholder are currently subject to a separate basket limitation on a corporation-by-corporation basis. Congress initially separately basketed dividends from each 10/50 corporation because it believed a minority investment in a foreign corporation did not create sufficient identity of interest to justify look-through treatment and that cross-crediting of taxes among investments in 10/50 corporations was inappropriate because the foreign companies were not parts of a single economic unit. 1986 Bluebook at 868. In addition, Congress was concerned about the administrability of applying the look-through rules to 10/50 corporations. 1986 Bluebook at 868.

In 1997, Congress amended the Code's treatment of dividends from 10/50 corporations to provide that dividends paid after taxable years beginning after December 31, 2002 by a look-through 10/50 corporation out of earnings and profits accumulated before 2003 are subject to a single separate basket limitation for all 10/50 corporations, while dividends paid out of earnings and profits accumulated after 2003 are treated as income in a basket based on the ratio of the earnings and profits attributable to income in such basket to the foreign corporation's total earnings and profits (the so-called "look-through" approach). Earnings and profits accumulated after 2003 by a look-through 10/50 corporation are distributed before earnings and profits accumulated by that same foreign corporation before 2003. Joint Committee on Taxation, General Explanation of Tax Legislation Enacted in 1997 (1997 Bluebook) at 303.

The legislative history indicates that Congress changed its view with respect to 10/50 corporations because the separate basket limitation for dividends from each 10/50 corporation imposed a substantial recordkeeping burden and discouraged minority investments in foreign joint ventures. 1997 Bluebook at 302. However, as described above, the 1997 Act enacted look-through treatment for 10/50 corporation dividends only on a limited basis. Furthermore, Congress provided regulatory authority regarding the treatment of distributions out of earnings and profits for periods prior to a taxpayer's acquisition of stock in a look-through 10/50 corporation because of concerns that look-through treatment could provide inappropriate opportunities to traffic in foreign taxes.

Dividends paid by a CFC out of earnings and profits accumulated while the corporation was not a CFC are treated as a distribution from a 10/50 corporation while dividends paid out of earnings and profits accumulated while the corporation was a CFC are eligible for look-through treatment. Section 904(d)(2)(E)(i) and (d)(3). As in the case of a look-through 10/50 corporation, pooled earnings and profits of a CFC that are eligible for look-through treatment are distributed before other pooled earnings and profits. Prop. Reg. § 1.904-4(g)(3)(iii). Congress provided look-through treatment for dividends paid by CFCs in order to provide greater parity between the treatment of income earned through a branch and a subsidiary. 1986 Bluebook at 866.

Before 1997, except as otherwise provided in regulations, dividend distributions to a 10 percent U.S. shareholder of a CFC did not obtain look-through treatment unless the distributed earnings and profits accrued while the shareholder was a 10 percent U.S. shareholder and the corporation was a CFC. Section 904(d)(2)(E)(i), as in effect before the 1997 Act. This rule was intended to prevent trafficking in foreign income taxes related to preacquisition earnings and profits. However, because of the administrative issues presented by maintaining shareholder-level earnings and profits accounts, Congress modified the rule in 1997 to provide that look-through treatment applies with respect to CFC earnings and profits without regard to whether a 10 percent U.S. shareholder was a shareholder at the time accumulated. However, pre-CFC earnings and profits continue to be treated as earnings and profits of a 10/50 corporation because of foreign tax credit trafficking concerns.

The section 904 basketing rules reflect Congress' concern with respect to cross-crediting opportunities and its intent to limit the benefit of look-through treatment to appropriate circumstances. Where Congress determined that look-through is inappropriate, a dividend is treated as passive income or is subject to a separate limitation for 10/50 corporations (whether separately or collectively). Regulations have not yet been issued with respect to preacquisition earnings and profits of a look-through 10/50 corporation and the effect, if any, on the treatment of pre-CFC earnings and profits described in section 904(d)(2)(E)(i). The IRS and Treasury solicit comments as to the appropriate treatment of such earnings and profits after 2003 in light of Congress' anti-trafficking concerns, as well as the impact that such rules should have on the section 367(b) regulations.

Another international provision implicated by the movement of earnings and profits in foreign 381 transactions is section 959. Section 959 governs the distribution of earnings and profits that have been previously taxed to U.S. shareholders under section 951(a) (PTI). After studying the interaction of section 367(b) and the PTI rules, the IRS and Treasury determined that more guidance under section 959 would be useful before issuing regulations to address PTI issues that arise under section 367(b). Accordingly, the IRS and Treasury have opened a separate regulations project under section 959 and expect to issue regulations that address PTI issues under section 959 as well as section 367(b) in the future. The fundamental issue under consideration in that project is whether earnings and profits that are treated as PTI should be distributable to another shareholder, as well as the various implications that result from that determination. The IRS and Treasury invite comments with respect to these issues. Accordingly, the proposed regulations reserve on section 367(b) issues related to PTI.

Other sections may have also applied to characterize pre-transaction earnings of a foreign acquiring corporation or a foreign target corporation for certain purposes of the Code. For example, certain earnings may have been subject to characterization as U.S. source earnings under section 904(g), effectively connected earnings and profits under section 884, or post-1986 undistributed U.S. earnings under section 245. The characterization of such earnings carry over to the foreign surviving corporation for purposes of applying the relevant Code sections. See *Georday Enterprises v. Commissioner*, 126 F.2d 384 (4th Cir. 1942).

D. *Specific Policies Related to Foreign Divisive Transactions (Prop. Req. § 1.367(b)-8)*

Proposed regulation § 1.367(b)-8 addresses the allocation of earnings and profits and foreign income taxes in a transaction described in section 312(h) (that is, a section 355 distribution whether or not in connection with a section 368(a)(1)(D) reorganization) in which either or both the distributing or the controlled corporation is a foreign corporation (foreign divisive transaction). The scope of proposed § 1.367(b)-8 thus encompasses three situations: a domestic distributing corporation that distributes stock of a foreign controlled corporation, a foreign distributing corporation that distributes stock of a domestic controlled corporation, and a foreign distributing corporation that distributes stock of a foreign controlled corporation. The proposed regulations generally adopt the principles embodied in the regulations under section 312(h) but modify their application in consideration of the international provisions such as the source and foreign tax credit rules.

Regulations under section 312(h) reflect the principle that a pro rata portion of a distributing corporation's earnings and profits should be reduced to account for the distribution of a portion of its assets. § 1.312-10. Furthermore, the earnings and profits of a controlled corporation should include the portion of the distributing corporation's earnings and profits allocable to any assets transferred to the controlled corporation in connection with a section 368(a)(1)(D) reorganization (D reorganization) that immediately precedes the section 355 distribution (together with a D reorganization, a D/355 distribution). § 1.312-10(a). If a section 355 distribution is not preceded by a D reorganization, the earnings and profits of the controlled corporation are at least equal to the amount of the reduction in the distributing corporation's earnings and profits. § 1.312-10(b). It is likely that this rule was included to prevent taxpayers from using a section 355 distribution as a device to facilitate a bailout of earnings and profits through the controlled corporation. (The § 1.312-10 rules are derived from the Senate's directions to the IRS and Treasury in implementing the regulatory authority in section 312(h); the Senate Report does not, however, explain its reasons for these rules. Senate Finance Committee, Report on H.R. 8300 (1954), at 249.)

The application of the § 1.312-10 rules to foreign divisive transactions implicates the Code's international provisions because earnings and profits are moving in the cross-border context and because the earnings and profits of controlled foreign corporations are being adjusted. In transactions involving a domestic distributing corporation and a foreign controlled corporation, the foreign controlled corporation may succeed to earnings and profits of the domestic distributing corporation. A post-transaction distribution by the foreign controlled corporation out of earnings and profits it receives from the domestic distributing corporation is generally eligible for the dividends received deduction and treated as U.S. source income under sections 243(e) and 861(a)(2)(C). This treatment is appropriate because the earnings and profits have already been subject to U.S. corporate taxation and should not be subject to a second level of U.S. corporate tax upon repatriation if the earnings and profits would have qualified for the dividends received deduction if distributed before the section 355 distribution. H.R. Rep. No. 2101, at 3 (1960). In addition, such earnings and profits should not increase a domestic distributee's foreign tax credit limitation under section 904.

In circumstances where the foreign controlled corporation makes a post-transaction distribution to foreign shareholders, the foreign divisive transaction should not alter the character of earnings and profits allocated from the domestic distributing corporation. Otherwise, the section 355 distribution may serve as a vehicle to avoid U.S. tax, including U.S. withholding tax. Accordingly, the proposed regulations provide that a post-transaction distribution out of earnings and profits of a distributing corporation that carry over to a foreign controlled corporation is generally treated as a U.S. source dividend for purposes of Chapter 3 of subtitle A of the Code. See *Georday Enterprises v. Commissioner*, 126 F.2d 384 (4th Cir. 1942).

Foreign divisive transactions involving a foreign distributing corporation and a domestic controlled corporation are similar to inbound nonrecognition transactions to the extent the domestic controlled corporation receives assets of a foreign corporation. Current regulations under § 1.367(b)-3 require direct and indirect U.S. shareholders in an inbound asset reorganization to include an all earnings and profits amount in income in order to ensure, in part, that the bases of assets repatriated to the United States reflect an after-tax amount. Section 1.367(b)-3(d) and proposed § 1.367(b)-3(f) provide further rules regarding the carryover of earnings and profits and foreign income taxes from a foreign corporation to a domestic corporation. Those rules should also apply to a section 355 distribution involving a foreign distributing corporation and a domestic controlled corporation. These transactions also implicate the current rules under § 1.367(b)-5, because a reduction in a foreign distributing corporation's earnings and profits can directly affect the post-transaction application of section 1248 with respect to U.S. shareholders of the distributing corporation.

Foreign divisive transactions involving a foreign distributing corporation and a foreign controlled corporation raise issues similar to those raised in the context of a foreign 381 transaction described in § 1.367(b)-7, to the extent the controlled corporation succeeds to earnings and profits (and related foreign income taxes) of the distributing corporation. Accordingly, the proposed regulations adopt the principles of § 1.367(b)-7 to determine the manner in which the foreign controlled corporation succeeds to the earnings and profits (and related foreign income taxes) of a foreign distributing corporation. These transactions also implicate the § 1.367(b)-5 rules concerning diminutions in U.S. shareholders' section 1248 amounts.

The proposed regulations under § 1.367(b)-8 balance the § 1.312-10 rules and policies with the interests and concerns of the relevant international provisions of the Code. However, the IRS and Treasury recognize that the mechanics of § 1.312-10 as applied in the international context can be cumbersome and complex. The IRS and Treasury solicit comments as to whether the mechanical difficulties of applying the section 312 rules in the cross-border context outweigh the benefits and, if so, whether there are simpler alternative regimes that would address the international policy concerns without compromising the Subchapter C policies embodied in § 1.312-10.

Details of Provisions

A. *Prop. Reg. § 1.367(b)-1*

The proposed regulations supplement the current § 1.367(b)-1 notice requirements in consideration of the transactions addressed by proposed § § 1.367(b)-7 and 1.367(b)-8. Accordingly, foreign surviving corporations described in proposed § 1.367(b)-7 and distributing and controlled corporations involved in transactions described in proposed § 1.367(b)-8 are included within the scope of the § 1.367(b)-1 notice requirement.

B. *Prop. Reg. § 1.367(b)-3*

The proposed regulations address the carryover of net operating loss and capital loss carryovers, and earnings and profits that are not included in income as an all earnings and profits amount (or a deficit in earnings and profits). The proposed regulations generally provide that these tax attributes do not carry over from a foreign acquired corporation to a domestic acquiring corporation unless they are effectively connected to a U.S. trade or business (or attributable to a permanent establishment, in the context of a relevant U.S. income tax treaty).

The limitations on the carryover of these attributes prevent inappropriate or anomalous results. For example, net operating loss and capital loss carryovers are eligible to carry over from a foreign acquired corporation to a domestic acquiring corporation only to the extent the underlying deductions or losses were allowable under Chapter 1 of subtitle A of the Code. Thus, only a net operating loss or capital loss carryover that is effectively connected to a U.S. trade or business (or attributable to a permanent establishment) may carry over. Inappropriate or anomalous results are thus avoided because losses incurred by a foreign acquired corporation outside the U.S. taxing jurisdiction should not be available to offset the future U.S. tax liability of a domestic acquiring corporation. Otherwise, a taxpayer would have an incentive to import losses into the United States in order to shelter future income from U.S. tax.

The carryover of earnings and profits (or a deficit in earnings and profits) of the foreign acquired corporation can create similarly inappropriate results. For example, the policies underlying the section 243(a) dividends received deduction are not present with respect to a subsequent distribution by the domestic acquiring corporation out of earnings and profits accumulated by the foreign acquired corporation because those earnings and profits are not generally subject to a U.S. corporate level of tax. On the other hand, if the foreign acquired corporation has PTI, those earnings should not be taxed again when distributed to U.S. shareholders to whom the PTI is attributable regardless of whether or not the U.S. shareholder is eligible for the dividends received deduction. A deficit in earnings and profits can also be used to avoid tax, such as in the case of a foreign shareholder of a domestic acquiring corporation that imports a deficit and therefore is not subject to U.S. withholding tax on subsequent corporate distributions.

As a result of the issues raised by a carryover of earnings and profits and given that § 1.367(b)-3 already requires U.S. shareholders to include in income as a deemed dividend the all earnings and profits amount, the proposed regulations provide that earnings and profits (or deficit in earnings and profits) of the foreign acquired corporation do not carry over to the domestic acquiring corporation except to the extent effectively connected to a U.S. trade or business (or attributable to a permanent establishment, in the context of a relevant U.S. income tax treaty).

C. *Prop. Reg. § 1.367(b)-7*

Proposed § 1.367(b)-7 provides the manner in which a foreign surviving corporation succeeds to and takes into account the earnings and profits and foreign income taxes of a foreign acquiring corporation and a foreign target corporation. The proposed regulation attempts to preserve the character of earnings and profits and foreign income taxes to the extent possible in light of the applicable statutory limitations, as well as the relevant policy and administrative concerns. Compare § 1.381(c)(2)-1(a)(3) (ensuring that earnings and profits accumulated before March 1, 1913 retain their character as pre-1913 earnings and profits after a section 381 transaction). Accordingly, the proposed rules provide that, to the extent possible, pooled earnings and profits (and foreign income taxes) remain pooled, earnings and profits (and foreign income taxes) in annual layers remain in annual layers, foreign income taxes trapped before the transaction remain trapped after the transaction, and earnings and profits (and foreign income taxes) remain in the same basket before and after the transaction.

The proposed regulation also respects the section 902 preference for distributing pooled earnings and profits before earnings and profits in annual layers. Accordingly, proposed § 1.367(b)-7 provides that a foreign surviving corporation's pooled earnings and profits are distributed first (even though earnings and profits in the annual layers may have been accumulated after earnings and profits in the pool) and annual layers are distributed on a LIFO basis. Similarly, the proposed regulation also incorporates the section 904 preference for distributing pooled earnings and profits eligible for look-through before other pooled earnings and profits.

However, in certain cases, an overriding statutory policy requires that the proposed regulation modify the character of earnings and profits (and related foreign income taxes). For example, if a CFC combines with a non-look-through 10/50 corporation in a foreign 381 transaction and the foreign surviving corporation is a non-look-through 10/50 corporation, dividends paid by the surviving non-look-through 10/50 corporation are required to be separately basketed and do not obtain the benefit of look-through. Thus, earnings and profits of a CFC that would have obtained the benefit of look-through if distributed before the foreign 381 transaction are not eligible for look-through after the transaction. (The loss of look-through in connection with this type of foreign 381 transaction is somewhat ameliorated by a U.S. shareholder's section 1248 amount inclusion under § 1.367(b)-4 with respect to earnings and profits that accrued during its holding period.)

Proposed regulation § 1.367(b)-7 also provides rules regarding the carryover of deficits in earnings and profits from one foreign corporation to another. The purpose of the hovering deficit rule in the domestic context is to prevent the trafficking of deficits in earnings and profits. Otherwise, a corporation with positive earnings and profits may acquire or be acquired by another corporation with a deficit in earnings and profits and make distributions out of capital rather than earnings and profits.

In transactions involving foreign corporations, similar concerns exist regarding the trafficking of deficits in earnings and profits. The ability to benefit from combining positive and deficit earnings and profits among foreign corporations is different than in the domestic context, however, because of the nature of the foreign tax credit rules. In a reorganization involving two domestic corporations, the hovering deficit rule applies to a corporation with a net accumulated deficit in earnings and profits because the relevant statutory rules do not distinguish among classes of earnings and profits. In contrast, the foreign tax credit rules require further subcategorization of earnings and profits according to the pooling and basketing rules. Because of these distinctions, taxpayers may inappropriately benefit by trafficking in an earnings and profits deficit in a basket, pool, or particular annual layer, even though a corporation may have net positive earnings and profits. Accordingly, the proposed regulations apply the hovering deficit principle to the relevant subcategories of earnings and profits and provide that foreign income taxes related to the deficit are not added to the foreign surviving corporation's foreign income tax accounts until all of the deficit has been offset with post-transaction earnings. (Under proposed § 1.367(b)-9 (which is described below), these hovering deficit rules do not apply to F reorganizations and foreign 381 transactions in which either the foreign target corporation or the foreign acquiring corporation is newly created.)

Because the treatment of distributions by a foreign surviving corporation depends on whether it is a look-through corporation, a non-look-through 10/50 corporation, or a less-than-10%-U.S.-owned foreign corporation, proposed § 1.367(b)-7 is divided according to these categories. The proposed regulation uses the term surviving corporation in order to prevent confusion between the acquiring corporation and the foreign surviving entity. In addition, the term highlights the proposed regulation's general approach that provides the same results regardless of whether a corporation is the ostensible acquiring or target corporation.

1. *Look-through surviving corporation*

Where the foreign surviving corporation is a look-through corporation, the proposed regulation generally preserves the character of earnings and profits and foreign income taxes. For example, if a CFC (CFC1) acquires the assets of another CFC (CFC2) in a foreign 381 transaction and the surviving corporation is a CFC, then the corporations' positive amounts of earnings and profits and foreign income taxes would carry over in a manner that combines the look-through earnings and profits pools (and related foreign income taxes) of each corporation on a basket-by-basket basis. Thus, for example, CFC1's passive basket would be combined with CFC2's passive basket, CFC1's general basket would be combined with CFC2's general basket, and so forth.

If CFC1 or CFC2 has pooled earnings and profits or foreign income taxes that do not qualify for look-through treatment (non-look-through pool) (for example, earnings and profits accumulated during a period when the corporation was not a CFC and that are subject to a separate 10/50 limitation), such earnings and profits and foreign income taxes would be distributed only after all of the look-through earnings and profits pool has been distributed. This rule is consistent with the ordering rule in Prop. Reg. § 1.904-4(g)(3)(iii), which provides that when a 10/50 corporation becomes a CFC, pooled earnings and profits accumulated and foreign income taxes paid or accrued while the corporation is a CFC are distributed before pooled earnings and profits accumulated and foreign income taxes paid or accrued while the corporation was a 10/50 corporation. (If the foreign surviving corporation is instead a look-through 10/50 corporation, this rule is also consistent with the earnings and profits in the look-through pool being distributed before earnings and profits in the non-look-through pool.)

When earnings and profits from the non-look-through pool are distributed, the earnings and profits will be distributed pro rata out of the non-look-through pools of CFC1 and CFC2 (if any) and placed in two separate baskets under section 904(d)(1)(E). This preserves the character of the earnings and profits and related foreign income taxes and is consistent with the policy of section 904(d)(1)(E) to maintain separate baskets for each 10/50 corporation. After 2003, these earnings and profits will continue to be distributed pro rata from separate non-look-through pools but will be combined into a single 10/50 basket in the hands of the distributee. Maintaining separate pools prevents the refreshing of foreign income taxes that would have been trapped had the foreign 381 transaction not occurred. (The same rules apply in the case of a foreign surviving corporation that is a look-through 10/50 corporation.)

If CFC1 or CFC2 has pre-1987 accumulated profits (i.e., annual layers of earnings and profits) or foreign income taxes, then those earnings and profits are distributed only after the distribution of all pooled earnings and profits and taxes, regardless of whether those earnings and profits may have been accumulated after the pooled earnings and profits of the other corporation. Such earnings and profits are distributed on a LIFO basis and pro rata out of the respective corporation's annual layers if both companies have earnings and profits in the same year that are treated as pre-1987 accumulated profits and foreign income taxes. This rule respects two international policies. First, pooled earnings and profits are distributed before earnings and profits in annual layers. Second, earnings and profits in annual layers should not be pooled unless they are distributed to an upper-tier entity. Compare § 1.902-1(a)(8)(ii) (providing that distributions out of pre-1987 earnings and profits by a lower-tier corporation are included in the post-1986 earnings and profits of an upper-tier corporation). This rule is also consistent with the section 902 rule that traps foreign income taxes in annual layers in which there are no earnings and profits.

These results preserve the character of earnings and profits and taxes because pooled earnings and profits and taxes remain pooled, earnings and profits and taxes retain the same character under the look-through provisions, and foreign income taxes that were trapped before the foreign 381 transaction remain trapped. The rules are also consistent with concerns about limiting the administrative burden of requiring taxpayers to recreate tax histories.

Because of the foreign tax credit considerations presented by foreign 381 transactions, § 1.367(b)-7 applies the hovering deficit rule to subcategories of earnings and profits. Thus, deficits in the look-through pool, non-look-through pool, and net deficits in annual layers can offset only future earnings and profits of the foreign surviving corporation. In addition, a hovering deficit cannot be used to reduce current earnings and profits of the foreign surviving corporation and, as a result, does not reduce subpart F income. Foreign income taxes related to a hovering deficit do not enter the foreign income tax accounts of the surviving corporation until the entire hovering deficit offsets post-transaction earnings and profits. However, foreign income taxes related to the post-transaction earnings that are offset by the hovering deficit immediately enter the foreign income tax accounts of the foreign surviving corporation.

2. *Non-look-through 10/50 surviving corporation*

The proposed regulation's rules with respect to a non-look-through 10/50 corporation apply if the foreign surviving corporation is a 10/50 corporation before 2003. The principal statutory limitation of a non-look-through 10/50 corporation is that a dividend distribution is not eligible for look-through treatment and is instead separately basketed for each 10/50 corporation. As a result, earnings and profits of an acquiring or target corporation that would have been eligible for look-through (assuming the corporation qualified under the look-through rule) if distributed before the foreign 381 transaction lose their look-through character after the transaction.

For example, suppose a CFC combines with a non-look-through 10/50 corporation in a foreign 381 transaction in 2001 and the surviving entity is a non-look-through 10/50 corporation. Prior to the transaction, the CFC maintained earnings and profits and foreign income tax accounts expecting that the look-through rules would apply on a distribution of earnings and profits to U.S. shareholders. However, after the foreign 381 transaction, section 904(d)(1)(E) requires that a distribution from the surviving 10/50 corporation will be deemed to be paid out of a single pool of earnings and profits that will be separately basketed. In order to address the carryover of attributes to a non-look-through 10/50 corporation in a manner consistent with section 904(d)(1)(E), the proposed regulations combine the net positive earnings and profits and foreign income taxes in the respective pools of the acquiring and target corporations. (Thus, the separate baskets of pooled earnings and profits and foreign income taxes of the CFC would be netted into a single pool along with the non-look-through 10/50 corporation's pooled earnings and profits and foreign income taxes.)

Annual layers of the acquiring and target corporations are carried over to the foreign surviving corporation under the same rules as described above with respect to look-through corporations. Hovering deficit rules similar to those described with respect to a look-through corporation's non-look-through pool and annual layers also apply to surviving non-look-through 10/50 corporations.

Look-through treatment of earnings and profits and foreign income taxes does not re-emerge if the corporation later becomes a look-through corporation. For example, if the surviving non-look-through 10/50 corporation becomes a CFC, all of the earnings and profits and foreign income taxes of the surviving non-look-through 10/50 corporation remain as earnings and profits to which the look-through rules do not apply. Look-through only applies to earnings and profits accumulated after the corporation becomes a CFC. The IRS and Treasury believe that this rule is appropriate because of the administrative difficulties posed by recreating tax histories. In addition, earnings and profits and foreign income taxes of a CFC accumulated during a U.S. shareholder's holding period are generally deemed distributed (and the look-through rules apply) if a U.S. shareholder includes a section 1248 amount in income under § 1.367(b)-4 in connection with the foreign 381 transaction.

3. *Less-than-10%-U.S.-owned foreign surviving corporation*

Proposed § 1.367(b)-7 also determines the manner in which earnings and profits and foreign income taxes of the acquiring and target corporation are combined if the foreign surviving corporation is a less-than-10%-U.S.-owned foreign corporation. Generally, rules similar to the rules provided for annual layers of look-through corporations and non-look-through 10/50 corporations apply with respect to the annual layers of the acquiring and target corporation, but the rules take into account the possibility that one of the corporations may have been a CFC or 10/50 corporation immediately prior to the foreign 381 transaction.

If either the acquiring or target corporation is a CFC or a 10/50 corporation, its pooled earnings and profits and foreign income taxes are treated as earnings and profits and foreign income taxes accumulated in the annual layer of the applicable corporation immediately before the foreign 381 transaction. For example, suppose a less-than-10%-U.S.-owned foreign corporation combines with a 10/50 corporation and the foreign surviving corporation is a less-than-10%-U.S.-owned foreign corporation. The foreign surviving corporation is an entity that has never been required to pool earnings and profits and foreign income taxes under section 902(c)(3). Accordingly, distributions from the foreign surviving corporation are out of annual layers on a LIFO basis. Rather than recreating the tax history of the acquired 10/50 corporation for each year, the proposed regulation places all pooled earnings and profits and foreign income taxes of the 10/50 corporation into a single annual layer that closes immediately before the foreign 381 transaction. This rule is intended to ameliorate administrative burdens while respecting the policy that earnings and profits and foreign income taxes are distributed from annual layers for a less-than-10%-U.S.-owned foreign corporation. Because of concerns about neutrality, the same result applies regardless of whether the 10/50 corporation is the ostensible acquiring or target corporation.

If the surviving less-than-10%-U.S.-owned foreign corporation later becomes a non-look-through 10/50 corporation or a look-through corporation, earnings and profits and foreign income taxes that were pooled or obtained the benefit of look-through prior to the foreign 381 transaction are not recreated. Instead, those earnings and profits and foreign income taxes remain as earnings and profits accumulated and foreign income taxes paid or deemed paid while the corporation was a less-than-10%-U.S.-owned foreign corporation. As in the case of a surviving non-look-through 10/50 corporation that later becomes a look-through corporation, this rule is provided because of administrative issues associated with recreating tax histories. In addition, earnings and profits and foreign income taxes of a CFC accumulated during a shareholder's holding period generally would have been deemed distributed (and the look-through rules would have applied) if the shareholder was required to include a section 1248 amount in income under § 1.367(b)-4 in connection with the foreign 381 transaction.

D. *Prop. Reg. § 1.367(b)-8*

Section 1.367(b)-8 provides rules applicable to foreign divisive transactions. The regulation is divided into four sections. Section 1.367(b)-8(b) provides rules that are generally applicable to foreign divisive transactions. The other three sections describe the application of the general rules to specific situations. Section 1.367(b)-8(c) applies to a distribution by a domestic distributing corporation of the stock of a foreign controlled corporation, § 1.367(b)-8(d) applies to a distribution by a foreign distributing corporation of the stock of a domestic controlled corporation, and § 1.367(b)-8(e) applies to a distribution by a foreign distributing corporation of the stock of a foreign controlled corporation.

1. *General rules applicable to foreign divisive transactions*

Section 1.367(b)-8(b) provides that the rules of § 1.312-10 generally apply to determine the allocation of earnings and profits between a distributing and a controlled corporation, as well as to determine the reduction in the earnings and profits of a distributing corporation. The rules of § 1.312-10 are, however, subject to certain modifications.

In a D/355 distribution involving a controlled corporation that is newly created as part of the transaction, § 1.312-10(a) allocates the pre-transaction earnings and profits of the distributing corporation between the distributing and controlled corporations based upon a comparison of the fair market values of the assets received by the controlled corporation and the assets retained by the distributing corporation after the D reorganization. Section 1.312-10(a) provides that, "in a proper case," this allocation should be based on the relative net bases of the assets transferred and retained by the distributing corporation, or based on another "appropriate" method.

The proposed regulations generally adopt the rule of § 1.312-10(a), except that the allocation is based upon relative net adjusted bases of assets transferred and retained in all cases. This rule reflects the view that net basis is the most accurate measure of the appropriate amount of earnings and profits that should be allocated to the assets transferred by a distributing corporation in the D reorganization. For example, in cases where the controlled corporation recognizes gain on a later sale or distribution of appreciated property that it receives from the distributing corporation an allocation based upon relative bases prevents a misallocation of earnings and profits to the controlled corporation.

In a section 355 distribution that is not preceded by a D reorganization, § 1.312-10(b) provides that the earnings and profits of the distributing corporation are decreased by an amount equal to the lesser of (i) the amount by which the earnings and profits of the distributing corporation would have been decreased if it had transferred the stock of the controlled corporation to a new corporation in a D/355 distribution, and (ii) the net worth of the controlled corporation. For this purpose, net worth is defined as "the sum of the bases of all of the properties plus cash minus all liabilities." If "the earnings and profits of the controlled corporation immediately before the transaction are less than the amount of the decrease in earnings and profits of the distributing corporation . . . the earnings and profits of the controlled corporation, immediately after the transaction, shall be equal to the amount of such decrease. If the earnings and profits of the controlled corporation immediately before the transaction are more than the amount of the decrease in the earnings and profits of the distributing corporation, they shall remain the same."

Section 1.312-10(b) reflects the principle that a pro rata portion of a distributing corporation's earnings and profits should be reduced to account for the distribution of the controlled corporation. In addition, the requirement that the earnings and profits of the controlled corporation at least equal the reduction in the distributing corporation's earnings and profits appears intended to prevent a bailout of earnings and profits through the controlled corporation, while preventing the potential double counting of earnings and profits in situations where the distributing corporation did not organize the controlled corporation.

In consideration of the complexities raised by the cross-border application of the § 1.312-10(b) adjustment to the controlled corporation's earnings and profits, taken together with the current rules that prevent the potential bailout of earnings and profits in the international context (such as the § 1.367(b)-5 requirement that a shareholder include in income a reduction in its section 1248 amount), the IRS and Treasury have concluded that the § 1.312-10(b) rules should be modified when applied to section 367(b) transactions. Accordingly, the proposed regulations provide that the earnings and profits of the distributing corporation are decreased in an amount equal to the amount by which the earnings and profits of the distributing corporation would have been decreased if it had transferred the stock of the controlled corporation to a new corporation in a D/355 distribution. However, the earnings and profits of the controlled corporation are not increased or replaced. The reduction in earnings and profits (and related foreign income taxes) of the distributing corporation disappears unless otherwise included in income, such as under § 1.367(b)-5.

Section 1.312-10 does not specifically address the allocation and reduction of earnings and profits in connection with a D/355 distribution that involves a preexisting controlled corporation. The proposed regulations provide that, in such a case, the distributing corporation's earnings and profits are reduced in a manner that incorporates both the rules applicable to a D/355 distribution with a newly created controlled corporation and a section 355 distribution that is not preceded by a D reorganization. The rule thus accounts for a decrease in earnings and profits attributable to assets transferred to the controlled corporation as part of the D reorganization as well as a decrease in earnings and profits attributable to the distribution of stock of a preexisting controlled corporation (without regard to the D reorganization). The controlled corporation succeeds only to those earnings and profits allocable to the property it receives in the D reorganization.

In consideration of the international provisions' distinctions among classes and categories of earnings and profits, proposed § 1.367(b)-8(b) specifically addresses the determination of which earnings and profits of the distributing corporation are affected by a foreign divisive transaction. The proposed regulation provides that an allocation or reduction in earnings and profits shall generally be pro rata out of a cross-section of the distributing corporation's tax history (except to the extent it is included in income as a deemed dividend such as under § 1.367(b)-3 or § 1.367(b)-5). This rule determines the earnings and profits (and related foreign income taxes, where applicable) that remain in the distributing corporation after the transaction as well as any earnings and profits (and related foreign income taxes, where applicable) to which the controlled corporation succeeds in a D reorganization.

The proposed § 1.367(b)-8(b) cross-section rule decreases the earnings and profits of a distributing corporation without regard to the type of income generated by the assets of the controlled corporation. This is consistent with the general assumption in § 1.312-10 and the proposed regulations that the earnings and profits of the distributing corporation should be decreased proportionately to reflect the transfer or distribution of assets, rather than by some other measure, such as by determining the earnings and profits attributable to the income generated by assets transferred or distributed (a tracing model) or by decreasing most recently accumulated earnings and profits to the extent of assets transferred or distributed (a dividend model).

2. *Branch profits tax considerations*

Notwithstanding the above-described rules, the proposed regulations provide that an allocation or reduction in a distributing corporation's earnings and profits shall not reduce the distributing corporation's effectively connected earnings and profits or non-previously taxed accumulated effectively connected earnings and profits, as defined in the branch profits rule in section 884 (branch earnings). Both a domestic or foreign distributing corporation can potentially have branch earnings that are subject to the branch profits tax.

In the case of a foreign divisive transaction that does not include a D reorganization, a U.S. branch of a foreign distributing corporation would be retained by the foreign distributing corporation. Accordingly, § 1.367(b)-8 should not reduce the foreign distributing corporation's branch earnings because such a reduction would improperly decrease the earnings subject to the branch profits tax upon the section 355 distribution (which would trigger the branch profits tax under section 884). The same issues arise in the case of a D/355 distribution in which a foreign distributing corporation transfers the assets that are not part of a U.S. branch to a controlled corporation. The IRS and Treasury do not believe that it is appropriate to reduce the earnings that could give rise to a subsequent branch profits tax under these circumstances.

Different issues arise in a foreign divisive transaction in which a foreign distributing corporation transfers the assets of a U.S. branch to a controlled corporation as part of a D/355 distribution. While the branch profits rules permit a deferral of the branch profits tax in certain instances (by allowing branch earnings to be allocated to the domestic transferee in proportion to the assets transferred when a branch is incorporated in a section 351 exchange in a domestic corporation (see § 1.884-2T(d)(1)), the branch profits tax is triggered in any event if stock of the incorporated branch is later distributed to its shareholders. See § 1.884-2T(d)(5). Accordingly, because foreign divisive transactions include a section 355 distribution immediately following the D reorganization, it would be unnecessary and inappropriate to attribute branch earnings to a domestic controlled corporation under proposed § 1.367(b)-8.

Similar branch profits issues can arise with respect to a domestic distributing corporation. While branch earnings are accumulated by a foreign corporation, such earnings may have been carried over to a domestic corporation in a prior section 351 or 381 transaction. See § 1.884-2T(c)(4). Accordingly, the proposed regulations treat domestic distributing corporation in the same manner as foreign distributing corporations with respect to branch earnings.

3. *Domestic corporation distributes stock of a foreign corporation*

In foreign divisive transactions involving a domestic distributing corporation and a foreign controlled corporation, the foreign controlled corporation may succeed to earnings and profits of the domestic distributing corporation. The regulations provide that sections 243(e) and 861(a)(2)(C) apply to earnings and profits allocated to the foreign controlled corporation that were accumulated by a domestic corporation. In addition, a post-transaction distribution out of earnings and profits allocated to the foreign controlled corporation is generally treated as a U.S. source dividend under section 904(g) and for purposes of Chapter 3 of subtitle A of the Code. See *Georday Enterprises v. Commissioner*, 126 F.2d 384 (4th Cir. 1942).

4. *Foreign corporation distributes stock of a domestic corporation*

In foreign divisive transactions involving a foreign distributing corporation and a domestic controlled corporation, two issues arise in determining the appropriate reduction in the foreign distributing corporation's earnings and profits and its effects on the earnings and profits of the domestic controlled corporation. First, it should be determined whether it is appropriate to reduce PTI of the foreign distributing corporation and, if so, in what manner (e.g., if the foreign distributing corporation has earnings and profits that are PTI and not PTI, should the reduction in earnings and profits be out of PTI first, last, pro rata, or depending on the identity of the controlled corporation's shareholders). As in the case of § 1.367(b)-7, § 1.367(b)-8 reserves on PTI issues, and the IRS and Treasury solicit comments with respect to the appropriate treatment of these amounts.

Second, a domestic corporation succeeds to the earnings and profits of a foreign corporation if the section 355 distribution is preceded by a D reorganization. Because earnings and profits are allocable from foreign corporate solution to U.S. corporate solution, U.S. shareholders are required to include in income the all earnings and profits amount attributable to earnings and profits that carry over to the controlled corporation. The proposed regulations provide rules that coordinate the proposed § 1.367(b)-8 and the current § 1.367(b)-3 regimes. The regulations, however, reserve with respect to the treatment of U.S. persons that own foreign distributing corporation stock after a non pro rata distribution. The IRS and Treasury invite comments as to whether U.S. shareholders should have an all earnings and profits amount inclusion in connection with a non pro rata foreign divisive transaction in which they do not receive stock of the domestic controlled corporation.

5. *Foreign corporation distributes stock of a foreign corporation*

In foreign divisive transactions involving a foreign distributing corporation and a foreign controlled corporation, the foreign controlled corporation may succeed to earnings and profits of the foreign distributing corporation. Because such earnings and profits are allocated from one foreign corporation to another foreign corporation, the transaction raises issues similar to those in a foreign 381 transaction. Accordingly, the proposed regulations adopt and apply the principles in proposed regulation § 1.367(b)-7 to these transactions.

E. *Prop. Reg. § 1.367(b)-9*

Proposed § 1.367(b)-9 provides special rules applicable to foreign-to-foreign F reorganizations and foreign 381 transactions in which either the foreign target corporation or the foreign acquiring corporation is newly created. Proposed § 1.367(b)-9 also applies to foreign divisive transactions that involve a foreign distributing and a foreign controlled corporation, either of which is newly created.

Under proposed § 1.367(b)-9, a foreign surviving corporation succeeds to earnings and profits, deficits in earnings and profits, and foreign income taxes without regard to the proposed § 1.367(b)-7 hovering deficit rules. See section 1.381(b)-1(a)(2) (providing an analogous rule with respect to domestic F reorganizations).

This rule prevents inappropriate tax consequences. For example, under the generally applicable hovering deficit rules, a foreign corporation with significant deficits in earnings and profits could combine with a newly created foreign corporation and thereafter distribute dividends (along with deemed paid foreign income taxes under section 902), despite the presence of a significant deficit that would have precluded a dividend distribution before the transaction. Proposed § 1.367(b)-7 provides the Commissioner discretion to apply the principles of proposed § 1.367(b)-9 to circumstances where a principal purpose of the foreign 381 transaction is to affirmatively use the hovering deficit rule in order to gain a tax benefit.

Proposed Effective Dates

These regulations are proposed to apply to section 367(b) exchanges that occur on or after 30 days after these regulations are published as final regulations in the Federal Register.

Special Analyses

It has been determined that this notice of proposed rulemaking is not a significant regulatory action as defined in Executive Order 12866. Therefore, a regulatory assessment is not required. It has also been determined that section 553(b) of the Administrative Procedure Act (5 U.S.C. chapter 5) does not apply to these regulations, and because the regulation does not impose a collection of information on small entities, the Regulatory Flexibility Act (5 U.S.C. chapter 6) does not apply.

Comments and Public Hearing

Before these proposed regulations are adopted as final regulations, consideration will be given to any electronic or written comments (a signed original and eight (8) copies) that are submitted timely to the IRS. The IRS and Treasury Department request comments on the clarity of the proposed rules and how they can be made easier to understand. All comments will be available for public inspection and copying.

A public hearing has been scheduled for March 13, 2001, beginning at 10 a.m., in room 7218 of the Internal Revenue Building, 1111 Constitution Avenue, NW., Washington, DC. Due to building security procedures, visitors must enter at the 10th Street entrace, located between Constitution and Pennsylvania Avenues, NW. In addition, all visitors must present photo identification to enter the building. Because of access restrictions, visitors will not be admitted beyond the immediate entrance area more than 15 minutes before the hearing starts. For information about having your name placed on the building access list to attend the hearing, see the "FOR FURTHER INFORMATION CONTACT" section of this preamble.

The rules of 26 CFR 601.601(a)(3) apply to the hearing. Persons who wish to present oral comments at the hearing must submit electronic or written comments and an outline of the topics to be discussed and the time to be devoted to each topic (signed original and eight (8) copies) by February 20, 2001. A period of 10 minutes will be allotted to each person for making comments. An agenda showing the scheduling of the speakers will be prepared after the deadline for receiving outlines has passed. Copies of the agenda will be available free of charge at the hearing.

Drafting Information

The principal author of these regulations is Anne O'Connell Devereaux, Office of Associate Chief Counsel (International). However, other personnel from the IRS and Treasury Department participated in their development.

[¶49,181] Proposed Amendments of Regulations (REG-105801-00), published in the Federal Register on January 18, 2001.

Straddle rules: Capitalization of interest: Carrying charges: Personal property.—Reg. §§1.263(g)-1—1.263(g)-5, clarifying the application of the straddle rules to a variety of financial instruments, are proposed. A public hearing on this proposal is scheduled for May 22, 2001. Proposed amendments of Reg. §1.1092(d)-1 adopted as Temporary Reg. §1.1092(d)-1T by T.D. 9635 on 9/4/2013.

AGENCY: Internal Revenue Service (IRS), Treasury.

ACTION: Notice of proposed rulemaking and notice of public hearing.

SUMMARY: This document contains proposed regulations that clarify the application of the straddle rules to a variety of financial instruments. The proposed regulations clarify what constitutes interest and carrying charges and when interest and carrying charges are properly allocable to personal property that is part of a straddle. The proposed regulations also clarify that a taxpayer's obligation under a debt instrument can be a position in personal property that is part of a straddle. The proposed regulations provide guidance to taxpayers that enter into straddle transactions. This document provides notice of a public hearing on these proposed regulations.

DATES: Written and electronic comments and requests to appear and outlines of topics to be discussed at the public hearing scheduled for May 22, 2001, at 10 a.m., must be submitted by May 1, 2001.

ADDRESSES: Send submissions to: CC:M&SP:RU (REG-105801-00), room 5226, Internal Revenue Service, POB 7604, Ben Franklin Station, Washington, DC 20044. Submissions may be hand delivered between the hours of 8 a.m. and 5 p.m. to: CC:M&SP:RU (REG-105801-00), Courier's Desk, Internal Revenue Service, 1111 Constitution Avenue NW., Washington, DC. Alternatively, taxpayers may submit comments electronically via the Internet by submitting comments directly to the IRS Internet site at http://www.irs.gov/tax_regs/regslist.html. The public hearing will be held in the Auditorium, Internal Revenue Building, 1111 Constitution Avenue, NW., Washington, DC.

FOR FURTHER INFORMATION CONTACT: Concerning the proposed regulations, Kenneth Christman (202) 622-3950; concerning submission and delivery of comments and the public hearing, Treena Garrett, (202) 622-7180 (not toll-free numbers).

SUPPLEMENTARY INFORMATION:

Background

Sections 501 and 502 of the Economic Recovery Tax Act of 1981 (Public Law 97-34, 95 Stat. 172) added sections 1092 and 263(g), respectively, to the Internal Revenue Code to address certain deferral and conversion strategies involving economically offsetting positions in actively traded personal property. These economically offsetting positions are called straddles. Section 1092(c)(1).

In general, under section 1092, a taxpayer that realizes a loss on a position in actively traded personal property must defer the recognition of the loss to the extent the taxpayer has unrecognized gain on an economically offsetting position in the property. This deferral rule matches the recognition of loss with the recognition of the economically offsetting income. Section 263(g) addresses interest and carrying charges properly allocable to personal property that is part of a straddle. Under this section, these otherwise deductible expenses are not currently deductible. Instead, they must be capitalized into the basis of the property. By requiring capitalization, section 263(g) prevents: (1) a taxpayer from gaining a timing advantage by accruing deductions associated with carrying the straddle transaction before recognizing income from a position in personal property that is part of the straddle; and (2) the deductions from having a character different from that of the income.

These proposed regulations provide certain rules with respect to the application of section 263(g) and section 1092.

Explanation of Provisions

The proposed regulations consist of §1.263(g)-1, which provides a general introduction, and §§1.263(g)-2, 1.263(g)-3, 1.263(g)-4, and 1.263(g)-5, described below. The proposed regulations also include a new paragraph 1.1092(d)-1(d).

The proposed regulations generally address four issues: (1) the definition of *personal property* as such term is used in section 263(g) (in §1.263(g)-2); (2) the type of payments that are subject to the capitalization rules of section 263(g) (in §1.263(g)-3); (3) the operation of the capitalization rules of section 263(g) (in §1.263(g)-4); and (4) the circumstances under which an issuer's obligation under a debt instrument can be a position in actively traded personal property and, therefore, part of a straddle (in §1.1092(d)-1(d)). These issues are discussed in more detail below.

Definition of the Term Personal Property for Purposes of Section 263(g)

Section 263(g)(1) requires capitalization of interest and carrying charges properly allocable to personal property that is part of a straddle (as defined in section 1092(c)). Section 1092(d)(1) defines personal property for purposes of section 1092, as personal property of a type that is actively traded. Commentators have suggested that because sections 263(g) and 1092 were enacted at the same time, the term *personal property* as used in section 263(g) should be given the same definition under section 1092(d)(1). This would limit the definition of personal property in section 263(g) to personal property of a type that is actively traded.

Despite this suggestion, the proposed regulations provide that personal property has its common law meaning in section 263(g) for two reasons. First, the definition in section 1092(d)(1) by its terms applies only for purposes of section 1092. Second, the broader, common law interpretation of personal property more closely accords with the purposes of section 263(g). Application of the limited definition in section 1092(d)(1) for purposes of section 263(g) could result in dissimilar tax treatment of economically similar transactions. For example, adoption of the narrower definition would cause section 263(g) to apply to a transaction in which a taxpayer borrows to purchase actively traded personal property that is a part of a straddle but not to a similar transaction in which the taxpayer borrows to purchase a derivative instrument that is not itself actively traded but is a position in actively traded property.

Consequently, proposed §1.263(g)-2 defines personal property as a property right, whether or not actively traded, other than a right in real property. This definition includes both financial positions that provide substantial rights but do not impose substantial obligations on the holder (e.g., common stock or a purchased option) and executory contracts that impose both rights and obligations on the holder (e.g., notional principal contracts (NPC's) and forward transactions). However, the definition excludes straddles comprised only of financial positions that impose only obligations on the holder (e.g., the obligor's position in a debt instrument or a writer's position in an option).

Payments That Are Subject to the Capitalization Rules of Section 263(g)

Section 263(g)(1) provides for the capitalization of interest and carrying charges. For this purpose, *interest and carrying charges* are collectively defined in section 263(g)(2) as "interest incurred or continued to purchase or carry the personal property" and "all other amounts (including charges to insure, store, or transport) paid or incurred to carry the personal property," less certain types of income from the personal property.

The phrase "incurred or continued to purchase or carry" also appears in section 265(a)(2), which disallows interest expense on indebtedness incurred or continued to purchase or carry tax-exempt debt. Rev. Proc. 72-18 (1972-1 C.B. 740) sets out rules for determining when this standard is met for purposes of section 265(a)(2). Under that revenue procedure, indebtedness issued by a taxpayer that is not a dealer in tax-exempt obligations meets this standard if (1) the proceeds of the indebtedness are directly traceable to the purchase of the tax-exempt obligations, (2) the tax-exempt obligations are used as collateral for the borrowing, or (3) the totality of the facts and circumstances supports a reasonable inference that the purpose of the borrowing was to purchase or carry tax-exempt obligations. In general, the facts-and-circumstances test is met if there is a "sufficiently direct relationship" between the borrowing and the investment in the tax-exempt obligations. Similarly, the proposed regulations provide that a sufficiently direct relationship between indebtedness or other financing and personal property that is part of a straddle exists if payments on the indebtedness or other financing are determined by reference to the value or change in value of the personal property. See §1.263(g)-3(c).

Section 263(g) also applies to "all other amounts (including charges to insure, store or transport the personal property)" paid or incurred to carry personal property that is part of a straddle. As noted by one commentator, "taxpayers should not be permitted to deduct items incurred in connection with protecting or preserving the value of assets" that are part of a straddle. Therefore, the term, *to carry* in the context of section 263(g) includes the reduction of the risk of holding an asset. Because straddles necessarily involve positions that offset each other, the positions "carry" each other.

Accordingly, under §1.263(g)-3(b) of the proposed regulations, interest and carrying charges subject to capitalization under section 263(g) include: (I) otherwise deductible payments or accruals (including interest and original issue discount) on indebtedness or other financing issued or continued to purchase or carry personal property that is part of a straddle; (2) otherwise deductible fees or expenses paid or incurred in connection with the taxpayer's acquiring or holding personal property that is part of a straddle, including, but not limited to, fees or expenses incurred to purchase, insure, store, maintain, or transport the personal property; and (3) other otherwise deductible payments or accruals on financial instruments that are part of a straddle or that carry part of a straddle.

Section 263(g) requires capitalization of interest and carrying charges that exceed certain specified income inclusions (allowable offsets) listed in section 263(g)(2)(B). Section 1.263(g)-3(e) sets forth the allowable offsets, including amounts that are receipts or accruals on financial instruments that are part of a straddle or carry part of a straddle. The Treasury Department and the IRS solicit comments regarding whether other amounts should be treated as allowable offsets for purposes of section 263(g).

Operation of the Capitalization Rules of Section 263(g)

Generally, section 263(g) coordinates the character and timing of items of income and loss attributable to a taxpayer's position in a straddle by allocating interest and carrying charges to the capital account of a position in personal property that is part of the straddle. Proposed regulation § 1.263(g)-4 provides a set of allocation rules governing the "capitalization" of interest and carrying charges.

In many cases, certain allocation rules readily suggest themselves.

Congress was aware of "cash and carry" transactions in adopting section 263(g). See H.R. Rep. No. 201, 97th Cong. 1st Sess. 203-04 (1981). In a typical transaction, a taxpayer borrows to purchase personal property and sells the property forward. The debt instrument generates ordinary deductions (interest expense) that precede predictable (and approximately equal) capital gains on the sale of the personal property. Coordination of the amount and timing of income and loss in a cash and carry transaction is achieved under the proposed regulation by allocating the interest expense to the capital account of the personal property. This rule applies to all transactions in which a taxpayer has borrowed to purchase personal property that is part of a straddle.

If the proceeds of a borrowing are not used to purchase personal property, a second allocation rule allocates interest expense to personal property when the personal property collateralizes the borrowing. See Rev. Proc. 72-18, § 3.03 (disallowing interest deduction for debt secured by tax-exempt obligations); Rev. Rul. 78-348 (1978-2 C.B. 95) (applying yield restrictions to investments pledged by person benefitting from tax-exempt bond financing).

A third allocation rule of the proposed regulations allocates interest on indebtedness to personal property when payments on the indebtedness are determined by reference to the value, or change in value, of the personal property that is part of a straddle.

Fees and charges related to the maintenance of the personal property, such as charges to insure, store, or transport the personal property, are allocated to the capital account of that personal property. See S. Rep. No. 144, 97th Cong. 1st Sess. 154 (1981).

In other cases, the appropriate method for allocating capitalized interest and carrying charges is less obvious. This may be true of payments or accruals on a financial instrument, such as a NPC, described in proposed § 1.263(g)-3(d). For example, the proposed rules would apply to a taxpayer that holds stock and enters into an equity swap that is a short position with respect to the stock. In such a case, both the stock and the equity swap may be personal property that is part of a straddle, and payments on the equity swap could be capitalized with respect to the capital account of either the stock or the equity swap. However, it may not be clear how a capitalization rule would apply in conjunction with the rules under § 1.446-3 with respect to payments on NPCs. Accordingly, the proposed rules provide that, in cases to which a specific allocation rule is not applicable, interest and carrying charges will be allocated to personal property that is part of a straddle in the manner that is most appropriate under all the facts and circumstances. Proposed regulations § 1.263(g)-4(c) *Example 7* (relating to a straddle consisting of stock and an equity swap) illustrate one application of this facts and circumstances rule. The Treasury Department and the IRS invite comments and suggestions regarding both the proposed specific allocation rules and the general facts and circumstances allocation rule.

The regulations under section 263(g) are proposed to be effective for expenses paid, incurred, or accrued after the date the regulations are adopted as final for straddles established on or after January 18, 2001. See § 1.263(g)-5.

Obligation Under a Debt Instrument as a Position in Personal Property

If a taxpayer is the obligor under a debt instrument that provides for one or more payments linked to the value of actively traded personal property, the value of the taxpayer's obligation under the debt instrument changes as the value of the referenced property changes. For this reason, the taxpayer's position as obligor under the debt instrument functions as a position in the referenced property.

Some commentators have suggested that a debt instrument (other than one denominated in an actively traded foreign currency) cannot be a position of the obligor in personal property that is part of a straddle. Section 1092(d)(7) provides that an obligor's interest in a nonfunctional-currency-denominated debt instrument is treated under section 1092(d)(2) as a position in the nonfunctional currency. From this, the commentators infer that an obligor's interest in a debt instrument may never be treated as an interest in personal property other than a nonfunctional currency.

However, neither the legislative history nor the express language of section 1092(d)(7) indicates that Congress intended to exclude interests in personal property from the definition of *position* in section 1092(d)(2). A rule that a debt instrument can be a position in currency does not establish that a debt instrument is a position only in currency. This interpretation of section 1092(d)(7) has already been rejected by the IRS and Treasury in § 1.1275-4(b)(9)(vi), which provides that increased interest expense on a contingent payment debt instrument issued by a taxpayer may be a straddle loss subject to section 1092 deferral.

To clarify the definition of *position* under section 1092(d)(2), § 1.1092(d)-1(d) of the proposed regulations explicitly provides that an obligation under a debt instrument may be a position in personal property that is part of a straddle. This provision is proposed to be effective for straddles established on or after January 18, 2001. However, no inference is intended with respect to straddles established prior to January 18, 2001. Thus, in appropriate cases, the IRS may take the position under section 1092(d)(2) that, even in the absence of a regulation, an obligation under a debt instrument was part of a straddle prior to the effective date of § 1.1092(d)-1(d) if the debt instrument functioned economically as an interest in actively traded personal property.

In 1995, the IRS published proposed regulation § 1.1092(d)-(2). See 60 F.R.21482; FI-21-95, 1995-1 C.B. 935. The proposed regulations clarify the circumstances in which common stock may be personal property for the purposes of section 1092. Because proposed regulation § § 1.1092(d)-2 and 1.1092(d)-1(d) address similar issues, the IRS proposes to finalize both regulations simultaneously. The Treasury Department and the IRS, therefore, invite additional comment on proposed § 1.1092(d)-(2).

In addition, in 1985, the Treasury Department and the IRS adopted Temporary Regulation § 1.1092(d)-5T(d), which defines the term *loss* for purposes of § § 1.1092(b)-1T through 1.1092(b)-4T as a loss otherwise allowable under section 165(a). The Treasury Department and the IRS request comments on whether that definition should be expanded to include expenses such as interest and carrying charges or payments on notional principal contracts. If so, how should such a change be coordinated with the proposed regulations in this document?

Special Analyses

It has been determined that this notice of proposed rulemaking is not a significant regulatory action as defined in Executive Order 12866. Therefore, a regulatory assessment is not required. It also has been determined that section 553(b) of the Administrative Procedure Act (5 U.S.C. chapter 5) does not apply to these regulations, and because the regulation does not impose a collection of information on small entities, the Regulatory Flexibility Act (5 U.S.C. chapter 6) does not apply. Pursuant to section 7805(f) of the Internal Revenue Code, this notice of proposed rulemaking will be submitted to the Chief Counsel for Advocacy of the Small Business Administration for comment on its impact on small business.

Comments and Public Hearing

Before these proposed regulations are adopted as final regulations, consideration will be given to any written or electronic comments (a signed original and eight (8) copies, if written) that are submitted timely (in the manner described in the ADDRESSES portion of this preamble) to the IRS. The IRS and Treasury request comments on the clarity of the proposed regulations and how they may be made easier to understand. All comments will be available for public inspection and copying.

A public hearing has been scheduled for May 22, 2001, at 10 a.m. in the Auditorium, Internal Revenue Building, 1111 Constitution Avenue NW., Washington DC. Due to building security procedures, visitors must enter at the 10th Street entrance located between Constitution and Pennsylvania Avenues, NW. In addition, all visitors must present photo identifications to enter the building. Because of access restrictions, visitors will not be admitted beyond the immediate entrance area more than 15 minutes before the hearing starts. For information about having your name placed on the building access list to attend the hearing, see the "FOR FURTHER INFORMATION CONTACT" section of this preamble.

The rules of 26 CFR 601.601(a)(3) apply to the hearing. Persons who wish to present oral comments at the hearing must submit and an outline of the topics to be discussed and the time to be devoted to each topic (signed original and eight (8) copies) by May 1, 2001. A period of 10 minutes will be allotted to each person for making comments. An agenda showing the scheduling of the speakers will be prepared after the deadline for receiving outlines has passed. Copies of the agenda will be available free of charge at the hearing.

Drafting Information

The principal author of these regulations is Kenneth Christman, Office of Associate Chief Counsel (Financial Institutions and Products). However, other personnel from the IRS and Treasury Department participated in their development.

[¶ 49,183] Proposed Amendments of Regulation (REG-137519-01), published in the Federal Register on November 14, 2001.

Consolidated returns: Applicability of other provisions of law: Non-applicability of Code Sec. 357(c).—Amendments of Reg. § 1.1502-80, relating to the consolidated return regulations dealing with the non-applicability of Code Sec. 357(c) in a consolidated group, are proposed. A public hearing on this proposal is scheduled for March 21, 2002.

AGENCY: Internal Revenue Service (IRS), Treasury.

ACTION: Notice of proposed rule-making and notice of public hearing.

SUMMARY: This document proposes amendments relating to the consolidated return regulations dealing with the non-applicability of section 357(c) in a consolidated group. The proposed amendments clarify that, in certain transfers described in section 351 between members of a consolidated group, a transferee's assumption of certain liabilities described in section 357(c)(3) will not reduce the transferor's basis in the transferee's stock received in the transfer. This document also provides notice of a public hearing on these proposed regulations.

DATES: Written or electronic comments and requests to speak (with outlines of oral comments to be discussed) at the public hearing scheduled for March 21, 2002, must be submitted by February 28, 2002.

ADDRESSES: Send submissions to: CC:ITA:RU (REG-137519-01), room 5226, Internal Revenue Service, POB 7604, Ben Franklin Station, Washington, DC 20044. Submissions may be hand delivered Monday through Friday between the hours of 8 a.m. and 5 p.m. to: CC:ITA:RU (REG-137519-01), Courier's Desk, Internal Revenue Service, 1111 Constitution Avenue, NW., Washington, DC. Alternatively, taxpayers may submit comments electronically via the internet by selecting the "Tax Regs" option on the IRS Home Page, or by submitting comments directly to the IRS internet site at *http://www.irs.ustreas.gov/tax_regs/reglist.html.* The public hearing will be held in room 4718, Internal Revenue Building, 1111 Constitution Avenue, NW., Washington, DC.

FOR FURTHER INFORMATION CONTACT: Concerning the regulations, T. Ian Russell of the Office of Associate Chief Counsel (Corporate), (202) 622-7930; concerning submissions, the hearing, and/or to be placed on the building access list to attend the hearing, Donna M. Poindexter (202-622-7180) (not toll-free numbers).

SUPPLEMENTARY INFORMATION:

Background

Section 357(c)(1) generally provides that, in the case of certain exchanges described in section 351, if the sum of the amount of the liabilities assumed by the transferee corporation exceeds the total of the adjusted basis of the property transferred pursuant to such exchange, then such excess shall be considered as gain from the sale or exchange of a capital asset or of property that is not a capital asset. Section 357(c)(3), however, excludes from the computation of liabilities assumed liabilities the payment of which would give rise to a deduction, provided that the incurrence of such liabilities did not result in the creation of, or an increase in, the basis of any property.

Section 358(a) generally provides that, in the case of an exchange to which section 351 applies, the basis of the property permitted to be received without the recognition of gain or loss is decreased by the amount of any money received by the transferor. For this purpose, under section 358(d)(1), the transferee's assumption of a liability of the transferor is treated as money received by the transferor on the exchange. Section 358(d)(2), however, provides an exception for liabilities excluded under section 357(c)(3).

On August 15, 1994, final regulations (TD 8560) adding paragraph (d) to § 1.1502-80 were published in the Federal Register (59 FR 41666). A correcting amendment adding a sentence to the end of paragraph (d) of § 1.1502-80 was published in the Federal Register for March 14, 1997 (62 FR 12096). As currently in effect, § 1.1502-80(d) provides that "[s]ection 357(c) does not apply to any transaction to which § 1.1502-13, § 1.1502-13T, § 1.1502-14, or § 1.1502-14T applies, if it occurs in a consolidated return year beginning on or after January 1, 1995." The example in that regulation contemplates that, to the extent that the transferor does not recognize gain under section 357(c) by reason of the rule of § 1.1502-80(d), the transferor's basis in the stock of the transferee that it receives in the exchange is reduced, with the result that an excess loss account may arise.

A concern has been raised that, as currently drafted, § 1.1502-80(d) may produce an unintended basis result in certain intragroup transfers described in section 351. In particular, it is possible that one might conclude that, because § 1.1502-80(d) provides that section 357(c) does not apply to certain intragroup section 351 exchanges, no liabilities can technically be excluded under section 357(c)(3). If that analysis were correct, in the case of a transfer described in section 351 between members of a consolidated group, the transferor's basis in the stock of the transferee received in the transfer would be reduced by liabilities assumed by the transferee, including those liabilities described in section 357(c)(3) that would not have reduced basis had section 357(c) applied. Assuming the transferor and the transferee are members of the consolidated group at the time the liability does in fact give rise to a deduction on the part of the transferee and is taken into account on the consolidated return, the transferor's basis in the stock of the transferee would be reduced a second time under the principles of § 1.1502-32. This duplicated basis reduction, i.e., once at the time of the transfer described in section 351 and again at the time the liability is taken into account by the consolidated group, may ultimately cause the transferor to recognize an amount of gain on the sale of the stock of the transferee that does not clearly reflect income.

Explanation of Provisions

These proposed regulations clarify that, in certain transfers described in section 351 between members of a consolidated group, a transferee's assumption of liabilities described in section 357(c)(3)(A), other than those also described in section 357(c)(3)(B), will not reduce the transferor's basis in the transferee's stock received in the exchange.

Proposed Effective Date

These regulations are proposed to apply to transactions occurring in consolidated return years beginning on or after the date these regulations are published as final regulations in the Federal Register.

Special Analyses

It has been determined that this notice of proposed rulemaking is not a significant regulatory action as defined in Executive Order 12866. Therefore, a regulatory assessment is not required. It is hereby certified that these regulations do not have a significant economic impact on a substantial number of small entities. This certification is based on the fact that these regulations will affect affiliated groups of corporations that have elected to file consolidated returns, which tend to be larger businesses. Therefore, a Regulatory Flexibility Analysis under the Regulatory Flexibility Act (5 U.S.C. chapter 6) is not required. Pursuant to section 7805(f) of the Internal Revenue Code, these regulations will be submitted to the Chief Counsel for Advocacy of the Small Business Administration for comment on their impact on small business.

Comments and Public Hearing

Before these proposed regulations are adopted as final regulations, consideration will be given to any written comments (preferably a signed original and eight (8) copies) that are submitted timely to the IRS. The IRS and Treasury request comments on the clarity of the proposed regulations and how it may be made easier to understand. All comments will be available for public inspection and copying.

A public hearing has been scheduled for March 21, 2002, beginning at 10 a.m., in room 4718, Internal Revenue Building, 1111 Constitution Avenue NW., Washington, DC.

Because of access restrictions, visitors will not be admitted beyond the Internal Revenue Building lobby more than 15 minutes before the hearing starts.

The rules of 26 CFR 601.601(a)(3) apply to the hearing.

Persons that wish to present oral comments at the hearing must submit timely written comments and an outline of the topics to be discussed and the time to be devoted to each topic (preferably a signed original and eight (8) copies) by February 28, 2002.

A period of 10 minutes will be allotted to each person for making comments.

An agenda showing the scheduling of the speakers will be prepared after the deadline for receiving outlines has passed. Copies of the agenda will be available free of charge at the hearing.

Drafting Information

The principal author of these regulations is T. Ian Russell, Office of Associate Chief Counsel (Corporate). However, other personnel from the IRS and Treasury Department participated in their development.

[¶49,187] Proposed Amendments of Regulation (REG-165706-01), published in the Federal Register on April 10, 2002.

Tax-exempt bonds: Refunding issue, definition of.—Amendments of Reg. §1.150-1, modifying to the definition of refunding issue applicable to tax-exempt bonds issued by States and local governments, are proposed. A public hearing on this proposal is scheduled for July 30, 2002.

AGENCY: Internal Revenue Service (IRS), Treasury.

ACTION: Notice of proposed rulemaking and notice of public hearing.

SUMMARY: This document contains proposed regulations on the definition of refunding issue applicable to tax-exempt bonds issued by States and local governments. This document provides a notice of public hearing on these proposed regulations.

DATES: Written or electronic comments must be received by July 9, 2002. Outlines of topics to be discussed at the public hearing scheduled for July 30, 2002, at 10 a.m., must be received by July 9, 2002.

ADDRESSES: Send submissions to: CC:ITA:RU (REG-165706-01), room 5226, Internal Revenue Service, POB 7604, Ben Franklin Station, Washington, DC 20044. Submissions may be hand delivered between the hours of 8 a.m. and 5 p.m. to: CC:ITA:RU (REG-165706-01), courier's desk, Internal Revenue Service, 1111 Constitution Avenue NW., Washington, DC. Alternatively, submissions may be made electronically to the IRS Internet site at www.irs.gov/regs. The public hearing will be held in the Auditorium, Internal Revenue Building, 1111 Constitution Avenue NW., Washington, DC.

FOR FURTHER INFORMATION CONTACT: Concerning the regulations, Michael P. Brewer, (202) 622-3980; concerning submissions and the hearing, Treena Garrett, (202) 622-7190 (not toll-free numbers).

SUPPLEMENTARY INFORMATION:

Background

Section 150 of the Internal Revenue Code (Code) provides certain definitions and special rules for purposes of applying the tax-exempt bond limitations contained in sections 103 and 141 through 150. On June 18, 1993, final regulations (TD 8476) under section 150 were published in the Federal Register (58 FR 33510). On May 9, 1997, additional final regulations (TD 8718) under section 150 were published in the Federal Register (62 FR 25502). This document proposes to modify the definition of refunding issue under §1.150-1(d).

Explanation of Provisions

Section 1.150-1(d) of the current regulations provides a definition of *refunding issue*. In general, a refunding issue is an issue of obligations the proceeds of which are used to pay principal, interest, or redemption price on another issue. The current regulations contain certain exceptions to this general rule. One exception (the *change in obligor exception*) provides that an issue is not a refunding issue to the extent that the obligor of one issue is neither the obligor of the other issue nor a related party with respect to the obligor of the other issue. Another exception (the *six-month exception*) provides that if a person assumes (including taking subject to) obligations of an unrelated party in connection with an asset acquisition (other than a transaction to which section 381(a) applies if the person assuming the obligation is the acquiring corporation within the meaning of section 381(a)), and the assumed issue is refinanced within six-months before or after the date of the debt assumption, the refinancing issue is not treated as a refunding issue.

Section 1.150-1(b) of the current regulations provides that the term *related party* means, in reference to a governmental unit or a 501(c)(3) organization, any member of the same controlled group. Section 1.150-1(e) of the current regulations provides that the term *controlled group* means a group of entities controlled directly or indirectly by the same entity or group of entities. The determination of control is made on the basis of all the relevant facts and circumstances. One entity or group of entities (the *controlling entity*) generally controls another entity or group of entities (the *controlled entity*) if the controlling entity possesses either of the following rights or powers and the rights or powers are discretionary and non-ministerial: (i) the right or power both to approve and to remove without cause a controlling portion of the governing body of the controlled entity; or (ii) the right or power to require the use of funds or assets of the controlled entity for any purpose of the controlling entity.

Recently, questions have arisen regarding the application of these provisions with respect to certain issuances of bonds for 501(c)(3) organizations that operate hospital systems. In question generally is whether bonds issued in connection with the combination of two or more 501(c)(3) organizations to refinance outstanding bonds should be characterized as refunding bonds. One question is how the change in obligor exception and the six-month exception should be applied when the obligor of the new issue becomes related to the obligor of the other issue as part of the refinancing transaction. Another question is whether the acquisition by a 501(c)(3) organization of the sole membership interest in another 501(c)(3) organization should be treated as an asset acquisition for purposes of the six-month exception. A third question is what assets should be treated as financed by the new bonds under both the change in obligor exception and the six-month exception.

In general, the proposed regulations retain the change in obligor exception and the six-month exception, with certain modifications. The proposed regulations clarify that the determination of whether persons are related for purposes of the change in obligor exception and the six-month exception is generally made immediately before the transaction. However, a refinancing issue is a refunding issue under the proposed regulations if the obligor of the refinanced issue (or any person that is related to the obligor of the refinanced issue immediately before the transaction) has or obtains in the transaction the right to appoint the majority of the members of the governing body of the obligor of the refinancing issue (or any person that controls the obligor of the refinancing issue).

The proposed regulations state that the six-month exception applies to *acquistion transactions*. An acquistion transaction is a transaction is a transaction in which a person acquires from an unrelated party: (i) assets, other than an equity interest in an entity, if the acquirer is treated as acquiring such assets for all Federal income tax purposes; (ii) stock of a corporation with respect to which a valid election under section 338 is made; or (iii) control of a governmental unit or a 501(c)(3) organization through the acquisition of stock, membership interests or otherwise.

The proposed regulations retain the exclusion under which the six-month exception does not apply to transactions to which section 381(a) applies, and broaden its scope. In particular, under the proposed regulations the exclusion may apply even if the person assuming the obligations is not the acquiring corporation within the meaning of section 381(a) (for example, a transaction in which a corporation assumes the obligations of a target corporation in a transaction to which section 381(a) applies and then contributes all of the assets of the target corporation to a controlled subsidiary). The proposed regulations also extend the application of this rule for section 381(a) transactions to the change in obligor exception.

The proposed regulations provide two new, additional requirements for purposes of the change in obligor exception and the six-month exception. In certain circumstances where the obligors of the issues are affiliated before the transaction or become affiliated as part of the transaction, the proposed regulations provide that an issue will be treated as a refunding issue unless: (i) the refinanced issue is redeemed on the earliest date on which the issue may be redeemed, and (ii) the new issue is treated as being used to finance the assets that were financed with the proceeds of the refinanced issue. These new requirements are intended to further the Congressional policy against overburdening the tax-exempt bond market, as expressed in sections 148 and 149(d). In particular, they are intended to prevent overburdening in the case of transactions between affiliated persons that contain certain economic characteristics of a refunding.

Proposed Effective Date

The proposed regulations will apply to bonds sold on or after the date of publication of final regulations in the Federal Register. However, issuers may apply the proposed regulations in whole, but not in part, to any issue that is sold on or after the date the proposed regulations are published in the Federal Register and before the applicability date of the final regulations.

Special Analyses

It has been determined that this notice of proposed rulemaking is not a significant regulatory action as defined in Executive Order 12866. Therefore, a regulatory assessment is not required. It has also been determined that section 553(b) of the Administrative Procedure Act (5 U.S.C. chapter 5) does not apply to these regulations, and because the regulations do not impose a collection of information on small entities, the Regulatory Flexibility Act (5 U.S.C. chapter 6) does not apply. Pursuant to section 7805(f) of the Internal Revenue Code, this notice of proposed rulemaking will be submitted to the Chief Counsel for Advocacy of the Small Business Administration for comment on its impact on small business.

Comments and Public Hearing

Before these proposed regulations are adopted as final regulations, consideration will be given to any written comments that are submitted timely (preferably a signed original and eight copies) to the IRS. All comments will be available for public inspection and copying.

A public hearing has been scheduled for July 30, 2002, at 10:00 a.m. in the Auditorium, Internal Revenue Building, 1111 Constitution Avenue, NW., Washington, DC. Because of access restrictions, visitors will not be admitted beyond the lobby more than 15 minutes before the hearing starts.

The rules of 26 CFR 601.601(a)(3) apply to the hearing.

Persons who wish to present oral comments at the hearing must submit written comments by July 9, 2002, and submit an outline of the topics to be discussed and the amount of time to be devoted to each topic by July 9, 2002.

A period of 10 minutes will be allotted to each person for making comments.

An agenda showing the scheduling of the speakers will be prepared after the deadline for receiving outlines has passed. Copies of the agenda will be available free of charge at the hearing.

Drafting Information

The principal authors of these regulations are Bruce M. Serchuk, Office of Chief Counsel (Tax-exempt and Government Entities), Internal Revenue Service and Stephen J. Watson, Office of Tax Legislative Counsel, Department of the Treasury. However, other personnel from the IRS and Treasury Department participated in their development.

[¶49,189] Proposed Amendments of Regulation (REG-122564-02), published in the Federal Register on May 31, 2002.

Consolidated returns: Net operating losses: 5-year carryback period.—Amendments of Reg. §1.1502-21, permitting certain acquiring consolidated groups to elect to waive all or a portion of the pre-acquisition portion of the 5-year carryback period under Code Sec. 172(b)(1)(H) for certain losses attributable to certain acquired members, are proposed.

AGENCY: Internal Revenue Service (IRS), Treasury.

ACTION: Notice of proposed rulemaking.

SUMMARY: This document contains proposed regulations under section 1502 that affect corporations filing consolidated returns. In the Rules and Regulations section of this issue of the Federal Register, the IRS is issuing temporary regulations permitting certain acquiring consolidated groups to elect to waive all or a portion of the pre-acquisition portion of the 5-year carryback period under section 172(b)(1)(H) for certain losses attributable to certain acquired members. The text of those regulations also serves as the text of these proposed regulations.

DATES: Written or electronic comments and requests for a public hearing must be received by July 30, 2002.

ADDRESSES: Send submissions to: CC:ITA:RU, room 5226 (REG-122564-02), Internal Revenue Service, POB 7604, Ben Franklin Station, Washington, DC 20044. Submissions may also be hand delivered Monday through Friday between the hours of 8 a.m. and 5 p.m. to: CC:ITA:RU, room 5226 (REG-122564-02), Courier's Desk, Internal Revenue Service, 1111 Constitution Avenue, NW, Washington, DC. Alternatively, taxpayers may submit comments electronically via the Internet directly to the IRS Internet site at www.irs.gov/regs.

FOR FURTHER INFORMATION CONTACT: Concerning the regulation, Marie C. Milnes-Vasquez (202) 622-7770; concerning submissions and/or requests for a public hearing, Guy Traynor, (202) 622-7180 (not toll-free numbers).

SUPPLEMENTARY INFORMATION:

Paperwork Reduction Act

The collection of information contained in this notice of proposed rulemaking has been submitted to the Office of Management and Budget for review in accordance with the Paperwork Reduction Act of 1995 (44 U.S.C. 3507(d)). Comments on the collection of information should be sent to the **Office of Management and Budget,** Attn: Desk Officer for the Department of the Treasury, Office of Information and Regulatory Affairs, Washington, DC 20503, with copies to the **Internal Revenue Service,** Attn: IRS Reports Clearance Officer, W:CAR:MP:FP:S, Washington, DC 20224. Comments on the collection of information should be received by July 30, 2002. Comments are specifically requested concerning:

Whether the proposed collection of information is necessary for the proper performance of the functions of the Internal Revenue Service, including whether the information will have practical utility;

The accuracy of the estimated burden associated with the proposed collection of information (see below);

How the quality, utility, and clarity of the information to be collected may be enhanced;

How the burden of complying with the proposed collections of information may be minimized, including through the application of automated collection techniques or other forms of information technology; and

Estimates of capital or start-up costs and costs of operation, maintenance, and purchase of service to provide information.

The collection of information in this proposed regulation is in § 1.1502-21(b)(3)(ii)(C). This information is required to document the taxpayer's election to relinquish portions of its carryback period for 2001 and 2002 losses attributable to acquired members. The data will be used by the Internal Revenue Service to ensure that taxpayers are preparing their returns in accordance with their elections. The collection of information is required to obtain a benefit. The likely respondents are businesses.

Estimated total annual reporting burden: 1,000 hours.

Estimated average annual burden hours per respondent: 15 minutes.

Estimated number of respondents: 4,000.

Estimated annual frequency of responses: Once.

An agency may not conduct or sponsor, and a person is not required to respond to, a collection of information unless it displays a valid control number assigned by the Office of Management and Budget.

Books or records relating to a collection of information must be retained as long as their contents may become material in the administration of any internal revenue law. Generally, tax returns and tax return information are confidential, as required by 26 U.S.C. 6103.

Background and Explanation

Temporary regulations in the Rules and Regulations section of this issue of the Federal Register amend the Income Tax Regulations (26 CFR part 1) relating to section 1502. The temporary regulations provide rules permitting certain acquiring consolidated groups to elect to waive all or a portion of the pre-acquisition portion of the 5-year carryback period under section 172(b)(1)(H) for certain losses attributable to certain acquired members. The text of those regulations also serves as the text of these proposed regulations. The preamble to the temporary regulations explains the amendments.

Special Analyses

It has been determined that this notice of proposed rulemaking is not a significant regulatory action as defined in Executive Order 12866. Therefore, a regulatory assessment is not required. It is hereby certified that these regulations do not have a significant economic impact on a substantial number of small entities. This certification is based on the fact that these regulations principally affect persons filing consolidated Federal income tax returns. Available data indicates that most consolidated return filers are large companies (not small businesses). Therefore, a Regulatory Flexibility Analysis under the Regulatory Flexibility Act (5 U.S.C. chapter 6) is not required. Pursuant to section 7805(f) of the Internal Revenue Code, these regulations will be submitted to the Chief Counsel for Advocacy of the Small Business Administration for comment on their impact on small business.

Comments and Public Hearing

Before these proposed regulations are adopted as final regulations, consideration will be given to any written comments (a signed original and eight (8) copies) or electronic comments that are timely submitted to the IRS. All comments will be made available for public inspection and copying. A public hearing may be scheduled if requested in writing by any person that timely submits written comments. If a public hearing is scheduled, notice of the date, time, and place for the hearing will be published in the Federal Register.

Drafting Information

The principal author of these proposed regulations is Marie C. Milnes-Vasquez, Office of the Associate Chief Counsel (Corporate). However, other personnel from the IRS and Treasury Department participated in their development.

[¶ 49,190] Proposed Regulations (REG-103823-99), published in the Federal Register on May 31, 2002.

Depreciation methods: Income forecast method: Cost recovery.—Reg. §§ 1.167(n)-0—1.167(n)-7, relating to deductions available to taxpayers using the income forecast method of depreciation under Code Sec. 167(g), are proposed. A public hearing on this proposal is scheduled for September 4, 2002.

AGENCY: Internal Revenue Service (IRS), Treasury.

ACTION: Notice of proposed rulemaking and notice of public hearing.

SUMMARY: This document contains proposed regulations relating to deductions available to taxpayers using the income forecast method of depreciation under section 167(g). These proposed regulations reflect changes to the law made by the Small Business Job Protection Act of 1996 and the

Taxpayer Relief Act of 1997 and affect taxpayers that produce, own, or license films, videos, sound recordings, books, copyrights, patents, and certain other similar properties. This document also provides notice of a public hearing on these regulations.

DATES: Written comments must be received by August 29, 2002. Requests to speak and outlines of topics to be discussed at the public hearing scheduled for September 4, 2002, at 10 a.m., must be received by August 13, 2002.

ADDRESSES: Send submissions to: CC:IT&A:RU (REG-103823-99), room 5226, Internal Revenue Service, POB 7604, Ben Franklin Station, Washington, DC 20044. Submissions may be hand delivered between the hours of 8 a.m. and 5 p.m. to: CC:IT&A:RU (REG-103823-99), Courier's Desk, Internal Revenue Service, 1111 Constitution Avenue NW., Washington, DC. Alternatively, taxpayers may submit comments directly to the IRS Internet site at www.irs.gov/regs. A public hearing will be held in room 2615, Internal Revenue Building, 1111 Constitution Avenue NW., Washington, DC.

FOR FURTHER INFORMATION CONTACT: Concerning the regulations, Bernard P. Harvey, (202) 622-3110; concerning submissions and, the hearing and/or to be placed on the building access list to attend the hearing, Guy R. Traynor, (202) 622-7180 (not toll-free numbers).

SUPPLEMENTARY INFORMATION:

Background

This document contains proposed amendments to 26 CFR part 1 to provide regulations under section 167(g) of the Internal Revenue Code of 1986 (Code). Section 167(g) was added to the Code by the Small Business Job Protection Act of 1996, Public Law 104-188, 1604 (110 Stat. 1755, 1836) (Aug. 20, 1996), and significant amendments were made to the provision by the Taxpayer Relief Act of 1997, Public Law 105-34, 1086 (111 Stat. 788, 957) (Aug. 5, 1997).

Explanation of Provisions

The income forecast method of depreciation has been a permissible method for certain properties since the early 1960s. The income forecast method permits taxpayers to recover the depreciable basis in property over the anticipated income to be earned from the property. The income forecast method is available for interests (including interests involving limited rights in property) in motion picture films, video tapes, sound recordings, copyrights, books, and patents. See Rev. Rul. 60-358 (1960-2 C.B. 68); Rev. Rul. 64-273 (1964-2 C.B. 62); Rev. Rul. 79-285 (1979-2 C.B. 91); and Rev. Rul. 89-62 (1989-1 C.B. 78). The income forecast method is appropriate for these types of property because they possess unique income earning characteristics (for example, the income earning potential of a film may vary as a direct result of the film's popularity) and, therefore, the economic usefulness of these properties cannot be measured adequately by the property's physical condition or by the passage of time. In 1996, Congress enacted statutory income forecast rules to ensure that, for certain properties, the allowances for depreciation appropriately match the basis of an income forecast property with the income derived therefrom. In 1997, Congress placed limitations on the type of property that could be depreciated using the income forecast method.

Computation of Allowances for Depreciation

The proposed regulations provide that, under the income forecast method, a taxpayer's allowance for depreciation for a given year for an income forecast property generally is an amount that bears the same relationship to the depreciable basis of the property that the "current year income" for that year bears to the "forecasted total income" for the property. The proposed regulations provide a revised computation for computing a taxpayer's allowance for depreciation in years when conditions necessitate using a revised forecasted total income that differs from the forecasted total income used in computing depreciation allowances in previous years. Pursuant to these rules, taxpayers may revise forecasted total income and use the revised computation in taxable years after income forecast property is placed in service when information becomes available that indicates that forecasted total income (or revised forecasted total income) previously used to compute income forecast depreciation is inaccurate. Under the revised computation, a taxpayer's allowance for depreciation for the current and all future years for an income forecast property is an amount that bears the same relationship to the unrecovered depreciable basis of the property that the current year income for that year bears to the result obtained by subtracting from revised forecasted total income for the property the amounts of current year income for prior taxable years. Taxpayers are required to use the revised computation in certain situations (discussed in this preamble under the heading of *Income From the Property*).

The proposed regulations also provide several special rules for computing allowances for depreciation under the income forecast method. A special rule applies for certain basis redeterminations whereby an additional "catch up" allowance for depreciation is allowed in the year that basis is redetermined. Under this special rule, the additional depreciation allowance is an amount equal to the cumulative allowances for depreciation that would have been permitted in previous years had the basis redetermination amount been included in basis in the year the property was placed in service. It is intended that this additional allowance will ameliorate the potential back-loading of depreciation deductions that may otherwise occur if the additional amount were taken into account over the remaining income from the property and diminish the amount of look-back interest that may otherwise accrue. This special rule does not apply if the additional basis is treated as separate property.

Pursuant to section 167(g)(1)(C), a taxpayer's adjusted basis in an income forecast property is to be recovered by the end of the tenth taxable year following the taxable year in which the income forecast property is placed in service. The proposed regulations also provide that generally a taxpayer may deduct the adjusted basis in income forecast property in the year income from the property ceases completely and permanently (unless the income cessation arises in connection with the disposition of income forecast property). If additional amounts are paid or incurred with respect to income forecast property in taxable years after either of these special rules is applied, the additional amounts may be deducted when paid or incurred unless such amounts give rise to separate property.

Use of the income forecast method is elected on a property-by-property basis. Once elected, the income forecast method is a method of accounting that may not be changed without the consent of the Commissioner. Modifications to forecasted total income to take into account information that becomes available after the property is placed in service in accordance with these proposed regulations is not a change in a method of accounting requiring the Commissioner's consent.

Section 167(g) sets forth rules for the use of the income forecast method and any similar method. Thus, any method that calculates depreciation based on the flow of income generated by a property (or group of properties) is a "similar method" subject to the requirements of this regulation, including, e.g., the requirement that the look-back method be applied in certain circumstances. Congress did not identify any method that should be treated as a similar method. Treasury and the IRS seek comments on other methods that should be treated as coming within the scope of the term *any similar method*.

Commentators suggested that we specifically approve a method of depreciation based on the application of percentages derived from historical patterns of income for similar properties as a similar method because to do so would simplify the computation of depreciation deductions for large groupings of properties. This suggestion has not been adopted because it is not clear that the historical patterns of income used to apply the suggested approach will accurately reflect the income from any particular income forecast property. Moreover, this suggested approach is not predicated upon the unique income earning characteristics of an income forecast property.

Basis Rules

The cost of producing income forecast property is capitalized and recovered through an allowance for depreciation. The proposed regulations follow the general principles set forth in the regulations under sections 263, 263A, 446, and 461 for determining the basis of income forecast property. Commentators have written to Treasury and the IRS requesting guidance on various issues involving the timing of inclusion in basis of direct costs of income forecast property that are contingent upon the amount of income earned from the property (or other similar factors) and the means by which those costs may be deducted. In accordance with these requests, and in light of section 167(g)(1)(B), the proposed regulations address certain basis issues that are peculiar to the income forecast method of computing depreciation allowances.

Section 263A applies to income forecast property produced by the taxpayer. Section 1.263A-1(c)(2)(ii) provides that an amount required to be capitalized under section 263A may not be included in basis any earlier than the taxable year during which the amount is incurred within the meaning of § 1.446-1(c)(1)(ii). Section 1.446-1(c)(1)(ii) provides that under an accrual method of accounting a liability is incurred, and generally is taken into account for Federal income tax purposes, in the taxable year in which the "all events test" is satisfied. Sections 1.446-1(c)(1)(ii) and 1.461-1(a)(2) set forth the "all events test" which provides that a liability is incurred in the taxable year in which: (1) all the events have occurred that establish the fact of liability; (2) the amount of the liability can be determined with reasonable accuracy; and (3) economic performance has occurred with respect to the liability. Because section 167(g)(1)(B) provides that the adjusted basis of income forecast property depreciated using the income forecast method includes only amounts with respect to which the requirements of section 461(h) are satisfied, these rules are specifically restated in the proposed regulations.

The proposed regulations reiterate that contingent amounts that are either direct costs of the production of income forecast property or indirect costs properly allocable to the production of income forecast property are not added to basis until the taxable year in which the all events test, including the economic performance requirement of section 461(h), is satisfied. Under the proposed rules, the timing of the inclusion of certain of these costs in basis may be affected by § 1.461-1(a)(2)(iii)(A), § 1.461-1(a)(2)(iii)(D) and section 404.

Thus, the proposed regulations provide that contingent basis amounts that are either direct costs of income forecast property or indirect costs properly allocable to income forecast property are generally treated as basis redetermination amounts which increase the basis of income forecast property in the year paid or incurred. As noted above, the proposed regulations provide a special allowance applicable to certain basis redetermination amounts.

Commentators have also suggested that *Transamerica Corp. v. United States*, 999 F.2d 1362 (9th Cir. 1993), supports including contingent amounts in the basis of income forecast property beginning in the year the property is placed in service. In *Transamerica*, the Ninth Circuit interpreted Rev. Rul. 60-358, supra, as it applied in taxable years prior to the enactment of section 167(g), the economic performance requirements of section 461(h), the uniform capitalization requirement of section 263A, and other changes. The Ninth Circuit held that contingent basis amounts may be included in the basis of income forecast property in the year that the property is placed in service so long as the forecasted total income used in the computation of depreciation under the income forecast method includes an amount of income from the property sufficient to indicate that the contingency will be satisfied. Commentators urge the continuing application of the *Transamerica* approach because this approach matches most closely the costs of creating an income forecast property with the income earned thereform. Treasury and the IRS recognize that it may appear to be reasonable to include estimated amounts in the basis of income forecast property when the operation of the income forecast formula requires the use of estimated amounts in the forecasts of income that are used to determine the amount of income forecast depreciation, particularly where the income forecasts indicate that the contingencies will be resolved, and resolved relatively quickly, after the property is placed in service. Treasury and the IRS also recognize that the historic operation of the income forecast formula deters taxpayers from increasing their forecast of income in order to increase the contingent basis amounts includible in the basis of income forecast property because the increases in forecasted total income operate to increase the denominator of the income forecast formula and thus diminish the amount of depreciation of the income forecast property. This deterrent effect operates in most (but not all) situations to prevent the cumulative amount of income forecast depreciation deductions in any given taxable year from exceeding the total amount actually incurred in any given taxable year, which is the primary concern with the inclusion of contingent amounts in basis. However, because Congress specifically provided in section 167(g)(1)(B) that the adjusted basis of income forecast property includes only those amounts which satisfy the requirements of section 461(h) and because all events that establish the fact of the liability for contingent amounts have not occurred, the proposed regulations do not follow the *Transamerica* approach.

Commentators have also argued that *Associated Patentees, Inc. v. Commissioner*, 4 T.C. 979 (1945), supports an immediate deduction for contingent basis amounts arising from the provision of either property or services in the production of income forecast property that are paid or incurred in years after the year in which income forecast property is placed in service. The proposed regulations do not adopt this interpretation of *Associated Patentees* because providing a more favorable cost recovery rule for contingent basis amounts than for fixed amounts would create an unwarranted incentive for characterizing costs as contingent amounts. Contingent basis amounts arising from the provision of either property or services in the production of income forecast property must be capitalized into the basis of income forecast property in accordance with § 1.263A-1(e).

Salvage Value

The proposed regulations do not provide that the basis upon which depreciation is computed under the income forecast method is reduced for salvage value. The unique statutory scheme Congress adopted for income forecast property requires this departure from the rules generally applicable to property depreciated under section 167, and from the provisions of Rev. Rul. 60-358, supra, which had governed income forecast depreciation prior to the enactment of section 167(g). Based on the provisions of section 167(g), Congress intended that taxpayers be able to recover their entire basis in income forecast property within the period beginning with the year income forecast property is placed in service and ending with the 10th taxable year after the year the property is placed in service and that basis be recovered over the total income earned in connection with the property within that same time frame.

Section 167(g)(1)(C) requires taxpayers to recover the adjusted basis of income forecast property as of the beginning of the 10th taxable year after the property is placed in service as an allowance for depreciation in such year. The term *adjusted basis* refers to the basis of property for purposes of determining gain or loss, which is determined generally by adjusting the cost or other basis in property prescribed by section 1012 by the adjustments required by section 1016. See § 1.1011-1. The use of this term in section 167(g)(1)(C) indicates that Congress intended that the entire basis of an income forecast property be recovered within the period beginning with the year income forecast property is placed in service and ending with the 10th taxable year after the year the property is placed in service. The legislative history confirms this reading of the provision, stating that "(a)ny costs that are not recovered by the end of the tenth taxable year after the property was placed in service may be taken into account as depreciation in such year." H.R. Conf. Rep. No. 737, 104th Cong., 2d Sess. 299 (1996).

Consistent with this rule, the estimated income from the property is all the income projected to be earned over the first eleven taxable years the property is used by any taxpayer. Under section 167(g)(1)(A), the adjusted basis of income forecast property is to be recovered through allowances for income forecast depreciation over the "amount of income earned in connection with the property" through the end of the tenth taxable year after the year in which the income forecast property is placed in service. The legislative history to section 167(g)(1)(A) states that "income to be taken into account under the income forecast method includes all estimated income generated by the property." H.R. Conf. Rep. No. 737, at 297. By referring to income generated by the property, and not to income to be earned by the taxpayer, Congress established a regime whereby a taxpayer using the income forecast method must include within forecasted total income amounts that are to be earned not only by the taxpayer, but also by any subsequent owner during the eleven year period.

Income From the Property

The income forecast formula uses the ratio of current year income to forecasted total income from the property to determine the current allowance for depreciation. Both current year income and forecasted total income are to be computed in accordance with a taxpayer's method of accounting. Pursuant to Code section 167(g)(1)(A) and (g)(5)(C), forecasted total income is to include all anticipated income from any source through the end of the tenth taxable year following the year in which the income forecast property is placed in service (except, as discussed below, in the year of disposition of income forecast property). Thus, for example, in the case of a film, such income includes income from foreign and domestic theatrical, television, and other releases and syndications; income from video tape releases, sales, rentals, and syndications; and incidental income associated with the property such as income from the financial exploitation of characters, designs, titles, scripts, and scores, but only to the extent that such incidental income is earned in connection with the ultimate use of such items by, or the ultimate sale of merchandise to, persons who are not related to the taxpayer (within the meaning of section 267(b)). Apportionment rules are provided for situations when income from the exploitation of characters, designs, titles, scripts, scores, and other incidental income may relate to more than one income forecast property.

Under the proposed regulations, taxpayers are required at the end of the taxable year in which income forecast property is placed in service to make an accurate projection of all anticipated income to be earned from the income forecast property based on the conditions known to exist at that time. This estimate is referred to as forecasted total income. As discussed above, forecasted total income includes not only the income that the taxpayer forecasts it will earn by the end of the tenth taxable year after the year in which the income forecast property is placed in service, but also income that may be earned by other owners of the income forecast property during that same period.

The proposed regulations also require taxpayers to evaluate the accuracy of their forecasts annually. In order to perform these evaluations of forecasted total income, taxpayers must compute revised forecasted total income. Revised forecasted total income is the sum of current year income for the current taxable year and all prior taxable years, plus all income from the income forecast property that the taxpayer reasonably believes will be includible in current year income in taxable years after the current taxable year up to and including the 10th taxable year after the year in which the income forecast property is placed in service. Taxpayers are required to use the revised computation if forecasted total income in the immediately preceding taxable year falls outside a range bounded on the low end by 90 percent of revised forecasted total income for the current taxable year, and on the upper end by 110 percent of revised forecasted total income for the current taxable year. (In the situation where revised forecasted total income was used to compute income forecast depreciation in the immediately preceding taxable year, this comparison is made by comparing the revised forecasted total income for the current taxable year to revised forecasted total income for the immediately preceding taxable year.) Taxpayers may elect to alter their computations of income forecast depreciation (using the revised computation detailed below) when revised forecasted total income differs from forecasted total income.

Pursuant to Code section 167(g)(5)(B), income from the syndication of a television series need not be included in the income forecast computation prior to the fourth taxable year beginning after the date the first episode of the series is placed in service, unless an arrangement relating to future syndication exists. In such a case, syndication income is included in the income forecast computation at the time the arrangement relating to future syndication is made. This special rule also applies for purposes of applying the look-back method.

Special rules apply if income forecast property is disposed of prior to the end of the 10th taxable year after the year the property is placed in service. In such a case, section 167(g)(5)(E) requires that for purposes of applying the look-back method, income from the disposition of the property is to be taken into account. Failure to apply a similar rule for purposes of computing income forecast depreciation in the year of disposition may permit a depreciation differential that would not be corrected through the operation of the look-back method (because the differential would arise in a year for which the period of time to which look-back interest would apply would be zero). Accordingly, the proposed regulations require taxpayers to take income from the disposition of income forecast property into account in the year of disposition in computing revised forecasted total income both for purposes of computing its income forecast depreciation and for purposes of applying the look-back method.

Income Forecast Property

Section 167(g)(6) limits the types of property for which the income forecast method may be utilized. The income forecast method is available for interests (including interests involving limited rights in property) in motion picture films, video tapes, sound recordings, copyrights, books, and patents. In addition, section 167(g)(6)(E) provides the authority for Treasury and the IRS to extend the income forecast method to other types of property. The proposed regulations extend the method to theatrical productions and authorize the Commissioner to publish guidance designating other properties.

The proposed regulations generally require the income forecast method to be applied on a property-by-property basis. In certain limited circumstances, interests in multiple properties may be grouped together and treated as a single income forecast property. The ability to treat multiple income forecast properties as a single property for purposes of applying the income forecast method of depreciation is limited, however, to certain episodes of a television series or to multiple interests in specified income forecast properties acquired for broadcast pursuant to a single contract. The special allowance applicable to certain basis redetermination amounts is not available to basis redetermination amounts associated with interests in multiple income forecast properties treated as a single income forecast property under these rules. Commentators have requested that broad groupings of dissimilar properties be permitted in accordance with historic financial accounting practices. Because it is not clear that income would be clearly reflected if broader groupings of properties were permitted, this suggestion has not been incorporated into the proposed regulations. Treasury and the

IRS request comments on whether the proposed permitted groupings are appropriate and whether additional groupings should be allowed.

Under section 167(g)(5)(A)(ii), an amount incurred after income forecast property is placed in service that is significant and that gives rise to a significant increase in income when compared to the previous amount of forecasted total income is treated as a separate income forecast property and depreciated accordingly. Under the proposed regulations, an amount that does not exceed the lesser of 5 percent of the depreciable basis of the income forecast property with which the amount is associated or $100,000 is not considered significant for this purpose. An amount incurred after income forecast property is placed in service that is not significant or that does not give rise to a significant increase in income is subject to the general rules and is treated as a basis redetermination amount.

In addition, a cost incurred in a taxable year following the year in which the taxpayer has recovered through depreciation the entire adjusted basis of an income forecast property is treated as a separate income forecast property. If it is expected to give rise to a significant increase in income, the amount of the cost is treated as income forecast property that is newly placed in service. Otherwise, it is deductible in the year paid or incurred.

Look-back

In general, the look-back method applies any time property is depreciated using the income forecast method. A taxpayer using the income forecast method is required to pay, or is entitled to receive, interest computed under the look-back method for any year to which the look-back requirement applies. A taxpayer must pay look-back interest if deductions are accelerated due to the underestimation of total income expected to be earned with respect to the property. Conversely, a taxpayer is entitled to receive look-back interest if deductions are delayed as a result of overestimating total income expected to be earned with respect to the property. The look-back method applies separately to each income forecast property, unless properties are aggregated pursuant to special rules contained in the proposed regulations.

Generally, the look-back method is applied in the third and tenth taxable years following the year in which the income forecast property is placed in service. The look-back method also applies in the year income from the income forecast property ceases with respect to the taxpayer (and with respect to all persons who would be treated as a single taxpayer with the taxpayer under rules similar to those in section 41(f)(1)).

The look-back method does not apply to any income forecast property the basis of which is $100,000 or less in the year the look-back method would otherwise apply (redetermined without any reduction for depreciation allowed or allowable). In addition, the look-back method is not applicable for any year which would otherwise be a recomputation year if a 10 percent test is satisfied. The 10 percent test is met if forecasted total income (and, if applicable, revised forecasted total income) for each prior year is greater than 90 percent of revised forecasted total income for the year which would otherwise be a recomputation year and is less than 110 percent of revised forecasted total income for the year which would otherwise be a recomputation year. If the look-back method is applied for the third taxable year following the year in which income forecast property is placed in service, a special rule applies in determining whether the 10 percent test is satisfied in any subsequent year. Under the special rule, the amount of the forecasted total income or the revised forecasted total income for each taxable year up to and including the third taxable year following the year in which income forecast property is placed in service is deemed to be equal to the revised forecasted total income that was used for purposes of applying the look-back method in the third taxable year following the year in which income forecast property is placed in service.

In order to apply the look-back method, prior year allowances for depreciation for income forecast property are recomputed using revised forecasted total income for the recomputation year in lieu of forecasted total income (or, if appropriate, revised forecasted income) from the property that was used in the computation of depreciation under the income forecast method in the prior year. If a taxpayer sells or otherwise disposes of income forecast property, the amount realized upon the disposition of the property is included in determining revised forecasted total income from the property in the year of disposition. These recomputed depreciation allowances are then used to determine either a hypothetical overpayment of tax or a hypothetical underpayment of tax.

Generally, taxpayers must determine the hypothetical overpayment or underpayment of tax arising from the change in depreciation allowances by recomputing their tax liability. Thus, a taxpayer's tax liability for each prior year is recomputed by substituting the recomputed depreciation allowances for the depreciation allowances originally claimed. The recomputed tax liability is then compared to the taxpayer's actual liability. For purposes of this comparison, the taxpayer must determine the actual tax liability for each prior year based on the information available on the later of (1) the due date of the return, including extensions, (2) the date of an amended return, (3) the date a return is adjusted by examination, or (4) the date of any previous application of the look-back requirement for the income forecast property. The result of this comparison is a hypothetical overpayment or underpayment of tax for each prior year in which allowances for depreciation were claimed for income forecast property subject to the look-back method.

Pass-through entities that are not closely-held pass-through entities must use a simplified method to compute their hypothetical overpayment or underpayment for each prior year in which allowances for depreciation were claimed for income forecast property subject to the look-back method. Under the simplified method, taxpayers apply a set rate (i.e., the highest rate applicable under section 1 or

11) to the net changes in depreciation allowances for each year. Treasury and the IRS considered, but did not provide, an election for other taxpayers to use the simplified method similar to the election set forth in § 1.460-6(d)(4)(ii). Treasury and the IRS request comments on whether the use of the simplified method should be extended to taxpayers other than those required to use the simplified method, and if so, whether additional safeguards beyond the consistency rules for related taxpayers, the rules precluding changes from the simplified method without permission, and the overpayment ceiling would be appropriate.

Regardless of the method used, the resulting hypothetical overpayments or underpayments are then used to compute interest that is to be charged or credited on each of these amounts. Interest is generally computed from the due date of the return (not including extensions) for the years in which changes in depreciation allowances occur to the due date of the recomputation year (not including extensions). Special rules are provided for taxpayers who do not use the simplified method where changes in depreciation allowances affect tax liability in years other than the year in which the changes in depreciation allowances occur. Interest is computed using the overpayment rate under section 6621. The amounts resulting from these computations are netted to arrive at look-back interest due to the taxpayer or payable to the government for the recomputation year. For purposes of computing taxable income, look-back interest is treated as interest on an overpayment or underpayment of tax. Under section 167(g)(5)(D), look-back interest required to be paid is treated as a tax liability for penalty purposes.

Proposed Effective Date

The regulations are proposed to apply to property placed in service on or after the date that final regulations are published in the Federal Register.

Special Analyses

It has been determined that this Treasury decision is not a significant regulatory action as defined in Executive Order 12866. Therefore, a regulatory assessment is not required. It also has been determined that section 553(b) of the Administrative Procedure Act (5 U.S.C. chapter 5) does not apply to these regulations and, because these regulations do not impose on small entities a collection of information requirement, the Regulatory Flexibility Act (5 U.S.C. chapter 6) does not apply. Therefore, a Regulatory Flexibility Analysis is not required. Pursuant to section 7805(f) of the Code, this notice of proposed rulemaking will be submitted to the Chief Counsel for Advocacy of the Small Business Administration for comment on its impact on small business.

Comments and Public Hearing

Before these proposed regulations are adopted as final regulations, consideration will be given to any written or electronic comments (a signed original and eight (8) copies, if written) that are submitted timely (in the manner described in the ADDRESSES portion of this preamble) to the IRS. The IRS and the Treasury Department specifically request comments on the clarity of the proposed regulations and how they may be made easier to understand. All comments will be available for public inspection and copying.

A public hearing has been scheduled for September 4, 2002, at 10 a.m. in the Internal Revenue Service Auditorium, Internal Revenue Building, 1111 Constitution Avenue NW, Washington, DC. All visitors must present photo identification to enter the building. Because of access restrictions, visitors will not be admitted beyond the immediate entrance area more than 30 minutes before the hearing starts at the Constitution Avenue entrance. For information about having your name placed on the building access list to attend the hearing, see the "FOR FURTHER INFORMATION CONTACT" section of this preamble.

The rules of 26 CFR 601.601(a)(3) apply to this hearing. Persons that wish to present oral comments at the hearing must submit timely written comments and an outline of the topics to be discussed and the time to be devoted to each topic (preferably a signed original and eight (8) copies) by August 13, 2002.

A period of 10 minutes will be allotted to each person for making comments.

An agenda showing the scheduling of the speakers will be prepared after the deadline for receiving outlines has passed. Copies of the agenda will be available free of charge at the hearing.

Drafting Information

The principal author of these regulations is Bernard P. Harvey, Office of Associate Chief Counsel (Passthroughs and Special Industries). However, other personnel from the IRS and Treasury Department participated in their development.

[¶ 49,206] Proposed Amendments of Regulations (REG-141669-02), published in the Federal Register on July 9, 2003.

Penalties, civil: Failure to file a correct information return: Waiver.—Amendments of Reg. § 301.6724-1, relating to waiver of a penalty imposed by Code Sec. 6721 for failure to file a correct information return, are proposed. A public hearing on this proposal is scheduled for October 21, 2003.

AGENCY: Internal Revenue Service (IRS), Treasury.

ACTION: Notice of proposed rulemaking and notice of public hearing.

SUMMARY: This document contains proposed regulations relating to waiver under section 6724 of the Internal Revenue Code (Code) of a penalty imposed by section 6721 for failure to file a correct information return. The proposed regulations provide guidance on the requirement of prompt correction of the failure to file or file correctly. The proposed regulations provide that the IRS will deem information returns promptly corrected if corrected within 30 days of the required filing date, or by August 1 following that required filing date. After August 1, a correction is prompt if made by the time announced by the IRS in published guidance. The proposed regulations do not change the rules for determining reasonable cause for waiving the penalty for failure to furnish correct payee statements under section 6722 or the time to comply with other information reporting requirements under section 6723.

DATES: Written and electronic comments are due by October 7, 2003. Requests to speak (with outlines of topics to be discussed) at the public hearing scheduled for October 21, 2003, are due by September 30, 2003.

ADDRESSES: Send submissions to: CC:PA:RU (REG-141669-02), Room 5526, Internal Revenue Service, POB 7604, Ben Franklin Station, Washington, DC 20044. Commenters may hand deliver submissions Monday through Friday between the hours of 8 a.m. and 4 p.m. to: CC:PA:RU (REG-141669-02), Courier's Desk, Internal Revenue Service, 1111 Constitution Avenue, NW., Washington, DC. Alternatively, commenters may submit comments electronically to the IRS Internet site at *www.irs.gov/regs.* The public hearing will be held in the IRS Auditorium, Internal Revenue Building, 1111 Constitution Avenue, NW., Washington, DC.

FOR FURTHER INFORMATION CONTACT: Concerning the proposed regulations, contact Robert A. Desilets, Jr. at (202) 622-4910; concerning submissions of comments, the hearing, and/or to be placed on the building access list to attend the hearing, Treena Garrett at (202) 622-7180 (not toll-free numbers).

SUPPLEMENTARY INFORMATION:

Background

This document contains proposed amendments to the Procedure and Administration Regulations (26 CFR part 301) under section 6724(a) of the Code. Section 301.6724-1(d)(1)(ii)(D) of the proposed regulations will clarify when a correction of an information return is prompt for purposes of establishing reasonable cause to waive the penalty under section 6721 of the Code. Existing § 301.6724-1(d)(1)(ii)(D), adopted on December 31, 1991 (56 FR 67178), provides in pertinent part that a correction is prompt if it occurs on the earliest date of a regular submission of corrections, defining regular submissions as occurring at intervals of 30 or fewer days. Many information return filers have urged the IRS to replace the 30-day correction interval with an interval corresponding to the schedule for tiered penalties.

Explanation of Provisions

I. Section 6721

Section 6721 imposes penalties on failures to file, or file correct, information returns. Section 6721 creates a threetiered penalty structure to encourage timely filing and prompt correction of errors in previously filed returns. Congress enacted the three-tiered penalty structure in the Omnibus Budget Reconciliation Act of 1989 (Public Law 101-239, 103 Stat. 2388, 2389). Section 6721 generally imposes a penalty in the amount of $50 for each return with respect to which a failure occurs, but not to exceed $250,000 per person per calendar year. However, if a filer corrects a failure within 30 days after the required filing date, the penalty with respect to such return shall be $15 in lieu of $50, but not to exceed $75,000 per filer per calendar year. Moreover, if a filer corrects a failure more than 30 days after the required filing date, but before August 1 of the calendar year in which the required filing date occurs, the penalty with respect to each return shall be $30 in lieu of $50, but not to exceed $150,000 per filer per calendar year. Section 6721 provides these penalties to encourage prompt corrections of failures to file, or file correct, information returns. H.R. Rep. 101-386, at 648-649 (1989).

II. Section 6724

Section 6724(a) provides for a waiver of information reporting penalties under sections 6721 through 6723 if the failure giving rise to such penalties was due to reasonable cause and not willful neglect. Under § 301.6724-1(a) of the regulations, to prove reasonable cause for a failure, the filer must establish either that there are significant mitigating factors with respect to the failure or that the failure arose from an event beyond the filer's control (an impediment). In addition, the filer must have acted in a responsible manner both before and after the failure.

Under § 301.6724-1(d) of the regulations, a filer is considered as acting in a responsible manner if the filer exercises reasonable care, i.e., the care that a reasonably prudent person would use under the circumstances in the course of business in determining filing obligations and in handling account information such as account numbers and balances. Section 301.6724-1(d) of the regulations also refers to the promptness of correction, i.e., when the filer undertook significant steps to avoid or mitigate the failure.

Section 301.6724-1(d)(1)(ii)(D) currently provides, in part, that a correction is considered prompt if it is made within 30 days after the date of removal of an impediment or discovery of a failure, or on the earliest date thereafter on which a regular submission of corrections occurs. Submissions are regular only if they occur at intervals of 30 days or fewer. Under the 30-day rule, a filer of a large number of information returns that discovers errors over a period of several months would be required to submit multiple corrections in a series of filings. Information return filers have urged the IRS to allow filers to "bundle" their corrections, i.e., submit the corrected information returns less frequently according to a defined timetable. The IRS agrees that the current rule may be burdensome and that bundling should be permitted.

The proposed regulations provide that a correction of an information return is prompt if the filer makes the correction within 30 days of the required filing date, or by August 1 following that required filing date. After August 1, a correction is prompt if the filer makes the correction by the date or dates announced in guidance governing the electronic or magnetic filing of information returns, or in other guidance including forms and instructions. It is anticipated that the date or dates will be in November and/or December of the calendar year in which the required filing date occurs. After the dates announced in the guidance, the proposed regulations provide that a correction is prompt if it is made within 30 days after the date the impediment is removed or the failure is discovered.

The proposed regulations apply solely for the purpose of determining whether there is reasonable cause for waiving the penalty for failure to file correct information returns imposed by section 6721. The proposed regulations do not apply for the purpose of determining whether there is reasonable cause for waiving the penalties imposed by sections 6722 and 6723. The IRS and Treasury Department believe that a filer should correct promptly a failure to furnish a correct payee statement or a failure to satisfy the reporting requirements described in section 6724(d)(2) and (3) with regard to sections 6722 and 6723, respectively. Therefore, the proposed regulations retain the 30-day correction period for waiving the penalties imposed by sections 6722 and 6723.

The proposed regulations do not affect or alter the tiered penalty rate schedule of section 6721. To ensure that a reduced penalty amount under section 6721 will apply, in the event that the IRS does not grant a reasonable cause waiver, a filer should file correct information returns with the IRS within 30 days after the required filing date, or before August 1 of the calendar year in which the required filing date occurs.

Proposed Effective Date

The proposed regulations apply to corrections of information returns made after the date of publication of a Treasury decision adopting the proposed regulations as final regulations in the **Federal Register**. However, filers may cite these rules for purposes of requesting a reasonable cause waiver prior to the date that the proposed regulations become final.

Special Analyses

It has been determined that this notice of proposed rulemaking is not a significant regulatory action as defined in Executive Order 12866. Therefore, a regulatory assessment is not required. It has also been determined that section 553(b) of the Administrative Procedure Act (5 U.S.C. chapter 5) does not apply to these proposed regulations, and because the proposed regulations do not impose a collection of information on small entities, the Regulatory Flexibility Act (5 U.S.C. chapter 6) does not apply. Pursuant to section 7805(f) of the Code, this notice of proposed rulemaking will be submitted to the Chief Counsel for Advocacy of the Small Business Administration for comment on its impact on small business.

Comments and Public Hearing

Before adoption of these proposed regulations as final regulations, the IRS will consider any electronic or written comments (a signed original and eight (8) copies) that a commenter submits timely (in the manner described in the ADDRESSES portion of this preamble) to the IRS. The IRS and the Treasury Department request comments on the clarity of the proposed regulations and how they can be easier to understand. All comments will be available for public inspection and copying. Written comments on the proposed regulations are due by October 7, 2003.

A public hearing has been scheduled for October 21, 2003, beginning at 10 a.m. in the IRS Auditorium, Internal Revenue Building, 1111 Constitution Avenue, NW., Washington, DC. All visitors must present photo identification to enter the building. Because of access restrictions, visitors will not be admitted beyond the immediate entrance area more than 30 minutes before the hearing starts. For information about having your name placed on the building access list to attend the hearing, see the FOR FURTHER INFORMATION CONTACT portion of this preamble.

The rules of 26 CFR 601.601(a)(3) apply to the hearing. Persons who wish to present oral comments must submit electronic or written comments and an outline of the topics for discussion and the time for each topic (a signed original and eight (8) copies) by September 30, 2003. Each person making comments will have 10 minutes to present comments. The IRS will prepare an agenda showing the scheduling of the speakers after the deadline for reviewing outlines has passed. Copies of the agenda will be available free of charge at the hearing.

Drafting Information

The principal author of these proposed regulations is Robert A. Desilets, Jr., Office of the Associate Chief Counsel (Procedure and Administration), Administrative Provisions and Judicial Practice Division. However, other personnel from the IRS and the Treasury Department participated in their development.

[¶ 49,208] Proposed Amendments of Regulations (REG-121122-03), published in the Federal Register on July 9, 2003.

Proposed regulations: Nonrecognition of gain on stock sold to employee organizations: Reporting requirements: Notarized statement of purchase requirements.—Amendments of Reg.

§1.1042-1T, relating to notarized statements of purchase and taxpayers making an election to defer recognition of gain on the sale of stock to an employee stock ownership plan, are proposed.

AGENCY: Internal Revenue Service (IRS), Treasury.

ACTION: Notice of proposed rulemaking.

SUMMARY: This document contains proposed amendments to the temporary regulations relating to notarized statements of purchase under section 1042 of the Internal Revenue Code of 1986. The proposed regulations would affect taxpayers making an election to defer the recognition of gain under section 1042 on the sale of stock to an employee stock ownership plan. The proposed regulations provide guidance on the notarization requirements of the temporary regulations.

DATES: Written and electronic comments and requests for a public hearing must be received by October 8, 2003.

ADDRESSES: Send submissions to: CC:PA:RU (REG-121122-03), room 5226, Internal Revenue Service, POB 7604, Ben Franklin Station, Washington, DC 20044. Submissions may be hand delivered Monday through Friday between the hours of 8 a.m. and 4 p.m. to: CC:PA:RU (REG-121122-03), Courier's Desk, Internal Revenue Service, 1111 Constitution Avenue, NW., Washington, DC. Alternatively, taxpayers may submit comments electronically directly to the IRS Internet site at *www.irs.gov/regs*.

FOR FURTHER INFORMATION CONTACT: Concerning the regulations, John T. Ricotta at (202) 622-6060 (not a toll-free number); concerning submissions or hearing requests, Sonya Cruse, (202) 622-7180 (not a toll-free number).

SUPPLEMENTARY INFORMATION:

Background

This document contains proposed amendments to the requirement of §1.1042-1T, A-3(b) of the Temporary Income Tax regulations that a statement of purchase for qualified replacement property be notarized within 30 days of the date of purchase of the property (30-day notarization requirement).

The temporary regulations under section 1042 were published in TD 8073 on February 4, 1986 (EE-63-84) (51 FR 4312) as part of a package of temporary regulations addressing effective dates and other issues under the Tax Reform Act of 1984. The text of the temporary regulations also served as a notice of proposed rulemaking (EE-96-85) (51 FR 4391). A public hearing was held on June 26, 1986, concerning the proposed regulations.

Explanation of Provisions

Overview

Section 1042(a) provides that a taxpayer or executor may elect in certain cases not to recognize long-term capital gain on the sale of *qualified securities* to an employee stock ownership plan (ESOP) (as defined in section 4975(e)(7)) or eligible worker owned cooperative (as defined in section 1042(c)(2)) if the taxpayer purchases *qualified replacement property* (as defined in section 1042(c)(4)) within the replacement period of section 1042(c)(3) and the requirements of section 1042(b) and §1.1042-1T of the Temporary Income Tax Regulations are satisfied.

Section 1042(c)(1) provides that the term *qualified securities* means employer securities (as defined in section 409(l)) which are issued by a domestic C corporation that has no stock outstanding that is readily tradable on an established securities market and which were not received by the taxpayer in a distribution from a plan described in section 401(a) or in a transfer pursuant to an option or other right to acquire stock to which section 83, 422, or 423 applied.

A sale of *qualified securities* meets the requirements of section 1042(b) if: (1) the qualified securities are sold to an ESOP (as defined in section 4975(e)(7)), or an eligible worker owned cooperative; (2) the plan or cooperative owns (after application of section 318(a)(4)), immediately after the sale, at least 30 percent of (a) each class of outstanding stock of the corporation (other than stock described in section 1504(a)(4)) which issued the securities or (b) the total value of all outstanding stock of the corporation (other than stock described in section 1504(a)(4)); (3) the taxpayer files with the Secretary a verified written statement of the employer whose employees are covered by the ESOP or an authorized officer of the cooperative consenting to the application of sections 4978 and 4979A (which provide for excise taxes on certain dispositions or allocations of securities acquired in a sale to which section 1042 applies) with respect to such employer or cooperative; and (4) the taxpayer's holding period with respect to the qualified securities is at least three years (determined as of the time of the sale).

The taxpayer must purchase *qualified replacement property* within the *replacement period*, which is defined in section 1042(c)(3) as the period which begins three months before the date on which the sale of qualified securities occurs and ends 12 months after the date of such sale.

Section 1042(c)(4)(A) defines *qualified replacement property* as any security issued by a domestic operating corporation which did not, for the taxable year preceding the taxable year in which such security was purchased, have passive investment income (as defined in section 1362(d)(3)(C)) in excess of 25 percent of the gross receipts of such corporation for such preceding taxable year, and is not the corporation which issued the qualified securities which such security is replacing or a member of the same controlled group of corporations (within the meaning of section 1563(a)(1)) as such corporation.

Section 1042(c)(4)(B) defines an *operating corporation* as a corporation more than 50 percent of the assets of which, at the time the security was purchased or before the close of the replacement period, were used in the active conduct of a trade or business.

Section 1.1042-1T A-3(a) of the Temporary Income Tax Regulations states that the election is to be made in a *statement of election* attached to the taxpayer's income tax return filed on or before the due date (including extensions of time) for the taxable year in which the sale occurs.

Section 1.1042-1T A-3(b) states that the *statement of election* must provide that the taxpayer elects to treat the sale of securities as a sale of qualified securities under section 1042(a) and must contain the following information: (1) A description of the qualified securities sold, including the type and number of shares; (2) The date of the sale of the qualified securities; (3) The adjusted basis of the qualified securities; (4) The amount realized upon the sale of the qualified securities; (5) The identity of the ESOP or eligible worker-owned cooperative to which the qualified securities were sold; and (6) If the sale was part of a single interrelated transaction under a prearranged agreement between taxpayers involving other sales of qualified securities, the names and taxpayer identification numbers of the other taxpayers under the agreement and the number of shares sold by the other taxpayers.

Section 1.1042-1T, A-3(b) further provides that, if the taxpayer has purchased qualified replacement property at the time of the election, the taxpayer must attach as part of the statement of election a *statement of purchase* describing the qualified replacement property, the date of the purchase, and the cost of the property, and declaring such property to be qualified replacement property with respect to the sale of qualified securities.

The statement of purchase must be notarized no later than 30 days after the purchase. The purpose of the statement of purchase is to identify qualified replacement property with respect to a sale of qualified securities. The qualified replacement property will have its cost basis reduced under section 1042(d) to reflect the gain on the sale of qualified securities that is being deferred by the taxpayer. Upon subsequent disposition of the qualified replacement property by the taxpayer, the deferred gain will be recognized by the taxpayer under section 1042(e). Under section 1042(f), the filing of the statement of purchase of qualified replacement property (or a statement of the taxpayer's intention not to purchase replacement property) will begin the statutory period for assessment of any deficiency with respect to gain arising from the sale of the qualified securities. The purpose of the 30-day notarization requirement is to provide a contemporaneous identification of replacement property.

However, the 30-day notarization requirement leads to frequent mistakes by taxpayers and their advisors. Taxpayers are often unaware of this requirement and become aware of it only when they prepare their tax returns for the year of sale to the ESOP. By this time, the 30-day period is typically past because purchases of replacement property may have been made up to one year before. A number of private letter rulings have been issued granting relief to taxpayers in these situations as long as the statements were notarized shortly after the taxpayer became aware of the requirement and it was represented that the property listed was the only replacement property purchased for this sale.

A number of commentators on the temporary and proposed regulations criticized this requirement as without statutory authority, a trap for the unwary, and inconsistent with the definition of the qualified replacement period in section 1042(c)(3).

Proposed Amendment to the Regulations

In order to facilitate taxpayer compliance with the temporary regulations concerning identification of qualified replacement property through notarization of the statements of purchase, the proposed amendment to the temporary regulations would modify § 1.1042-1T, A-3(b) to provide that the notarization requirements for the *statement of purchase* are satisfied if the taxpayer's statement of purchase is notarized not later than the time the taxpayer files the income tax return for the taxable year in which the sale of qualified securities occurred in any case in which any qualified replacement property was purchased by such time and during the qualified replacement period. If qualified replacement property was purchased after such filing date and during the qualified replacement period, the statement of purchase must be notarized not later than the time the taxpayer's income tax return is filed for the taxable year following the year for which the election under section 1042(a) was made.

Proposed Effective Date

The proposed amendments to the temporary regulations would apply to taxable years of sellers ending on or after the date of publication of the Treasury decision adopting these amendments as final regulations in the **Federal Register**. However, taxpayers may rely upon these proposed regulations for guidance with respect to all open taxable years pending the issuance of final regulations. If, and to the extent, future guidance is more restrictive than the guidance in these proposed regulations, the future guidance will be applied without retroactive effect.

Special Analyses

It has been determined that this notice of proposed rulemaking is not a significant regulatory action as defined in Executive Order 12866. Therefore, a regulatory assessment is not required. It also has been determined that section 553(b) of the Administrative Procedure Act (5 U.S.C. chapter 5) does not apply to these regulations, and because these regulations do not impose a collection of information on small entities, the Regulatory Flexibility Act (5 U.S.C. chapter 6) does not apply. Pursuant to section 7805(f) of the Internal Revenue Code, these proposed regulations will be submitted to the Chief Counsel for Advocacy of the Small Business Administration for comment on its impact on small business.

Comments and Public Hearing

Before these proposed regulations are adopted as final regulations, consideration will be given to any written (a signed original and 8 copies) or electronic comments that are submitted timely to the IRS. The IRS and Treasury Department request comments on the clarity of the proposed rules and how they can be made easier to understand. All comments will be available for public inspection and copying. A public hearing will be scheduled if requested in writing by any person that timely submits written comments. If a public hearing is scheduled, notice of the date, time, and place for the public hearing will be published in the **Federal Register**.

Drafting Information

The principal author of these regulations is John T. Ricotta of the Office of the Division Counsel/Associate Chief Counsel (Tax Exempt and Government Entities). However, other personnel from The IRS and Treasury participated in their development.

[¶49,216] **Proposed Regulations and Proposed Amendments of Regulations (REG-166012-02)**, published in the Federal Register on February 26, 2004.

Sales or exchanges: Notional principal contracts: Contingent nonperiodic payments: Inclusion in income: Deduction: Accounting methods: Proposed regulations.—Reg. §§1.162-30 and 1.1234A-1 and amendments of Reg. §§1.212-1 and 1.446-3, relating to the inclusion into income or deduction of a contingent nonperiodic payment provided for under a notional principal contract (NPC), are proposed. A public hearing on this proposal is scheduled for May 25, 2004.

AGENCY: Internal Revenue Service (IRS), Treasury.

ACTION: Notice of proposed rulemaking and notice of public hearing.

SUMMARY: This document contains proposed regulations relating to the inclusion into income or deduction of a contingent nonperiodic payment provided for under a notional principal contract (NPC). This document also provides guidance relating to the character of payments made pursuant to an NPC. These regulations will affect taxpayers that enter into NPCs. This document also provides a notice of a public hearing on these proposed regulations.

DATES: Written or electronically transmitted comments and requests to speak (with outlines of oral comments to be discussed) at the public hearing scheduled for May 25, 2004, at 10 a.m., must be received by May 4, 2004. Comments on the collection of information should be received by April 26, 2004.

ADDRESSES: Send submissions to CC:PA:LPD:PR (REG-166012-02), room 5203, Internal Revenue Service, POB 7604, Ben Franklin Station, Washington, DC 20044. Submissions may be hand-delivered Monday through Friday between the hours of 8 a.m. and 4 p.m. to CC:PA:LPD:PR (REG-166012-02), Courier's Desk, Internal Revenue Service, 1111 Constitution Avenue, NW., Washington, DC. Alternatively, taxpayers may submit electronic comments directly to the IRS Internet site at: *www.irs.gov/regs*. The public hearing will be held in the IRS Auditorium, Seventh Floor, Internal Revenue Service, 1111 Constitution Avenue, NW., Washington, DC.

FOR FURTHER INFORMATION CONTACT: Concerning submissions of comments, the hearing, or to be placed on the building access list to attend the hearing, Sonya Cruse, (202) 622-7180; concerning the regulations, Kate Sleeth, (202) 622-3920 (not toll-free numbers).

SUPPLEMENTARY INFORMATION:

Paperwork Reduction Act

The collection of information contained in this notice of proposed rulemaking has been submitted to the Office of Management and Budget for review in accordance with the Paperwork Reduction Act of 1995 (44 U.S.C. 3507(d)). Comments on the collection of information should be sent to the **Office of Management and Budget,** Attn: Desk Officer for the Department of the Treasury, Office of Information and Regulatory Affairs, Washington, DC 20503, with copies to the **Internal Revenue Service,** Attn: IRS Reports Clearance Officer, SE:W:CAR:MP:T:T:SP, Washington, DC 20224. Comments on the collection of information should be received by April 26, 2004. Comments are specifically requested concerning:

Whether the proposed collection of information is necessary for the proper performance of the functions of the IRS, including whether the information will have practical utility;

The accuracy of the estimated burden associated with the proposed collection of information (see below);

How the quality, utility, and clarity of the information to be collected may be enhanced;

How the burden of complying with the proposed collection of information may be minimized, including through the application of automated collection techniques or other forms of information technology; and

Estimates of capital or start-up costs and costs of operation, maintenance, and purchase of services to provide information.

The collection of information in these proposed regulations is in §1.446-3(g)(6)(vii). This information is required by the IRS to verify compliance with section 446 and the method of accounting described in §1.446-3(g)(6). This information will be used to determine whether the amount of tax has been calculated correctly. The collection of information is required to properly determine the amount of income or deduction to be taken into account. The respondents are sophisticated investors that enter into notional principal contracts with contingent nonperiodic payments.

Estimated total annual recordkeeping burden: 25,500 hours.

Estimated average annual burden per recordkeeper: 6 hours.

Estimated number of recordkeepers: 4,250.

An agency may not conduct or sponsor, and a person is not required to respond to, a collection of information unless it displays a valid control number assigned by the Office of Management and Budget.

Books or records relating to a collection of information must be retained as long as their contents may become material in the administration of any internal revenue law. Generally, tax returns and tax return information are confidential, as required by 26 U.S.C. 6103.

Background

This document contains proposed amendments to 26 CFR Part 1 under section 446(b) of the Internal Revenue Code (Code). This document also contains proposed amendments under sections 162, 212 and 1234A of the Code.

In 1989, the IRS issued Notice 89-21 (1989-1 C.B. 651), to provide guidance with respect to the tax treatment of lump-sum payments received in connection with NPCs. The Notice stated that a method of accounting that properly recognizes a lump-sum payment over the life of the contract clearly reflects income and indicated that regulations would be issued to provide specific rules regarding the manner in which a taxpayer must take into account over the life of an NPC payments made or received with respect to the contract. The Notice further stated that "for contracts entered into prior to the effective date of the regulations, the Commissioner will generally treat a method of accounting as clearly reflecting income if it takes such payments into account over the life of the contract under a reasonable amortization method, whether or not the method satisfies the specific rules in the forthcoming regulations." (1989-1 C.B. 652).

On October 14, 1993, the IRS published in the **Federal Register** final regulations (TD 8491; 1993-2 C.B. 215 [58 FR 53125]) under section 446(b) relating to the timing of income and deductions for amounts paid or received pursuant to NPCs. §1.446-3. In this preamble, the final regulations published in 1993 are referred to as the 1993 Treasury regulations.

The 1993 Treasury regulations define an NPC as a "financial instrument that provides for the payment of amounts by one party to another at specified intervals calculated by reference to a specified index upon a notional principal amount in exchange for specified consideration or a promise to pay similar amounts." §1.446-3(c)(1)(i). Payments made pursuant to NPCs are divided into three categories (periodic, nonperiodic, and termination payments), and the 1993 Treasury regulations provide timing regimes for each. The 1993 Treasury regulations require all taxpayers, regardless of their method of accounting, to recognize the ratable daily portion of a nonperiodic payment for the taxable year to which that portion relates. Nonperiodic payments generally must be recognized over the term of an NPC in a manner that reflects the economic substance of the contract. §1.446-3(f)(2)(i). Although §1.446-3 does not distinguish between noncontingent and contingent nonperiodic payments, the specific rules and examples in the 1993 Treasury regulations address only noncontingent nonperiodic payments. The Preamble to the 1993 Treasury regulations states that "the IRS expects to address contingent payments in future regulations, and welcomes comment on the treatment of those payments." (1993-2 C.B. 216). In addition, neither §1.446-3 nor any other section provides specific rules governing the character of the various types of NPC payments.

On July 23, 2001, the IRS published Notice 2001-44 (2001-2 C.B. 77), soliciting comments on the appropriate method for the inclusion or deduction of contingent nonperiodic payments made pursuant to NPCs and the proper character treatment of payments made pursuant to an NPC. The Notice set forth four different methods under consideration by the IRS and Treasury and asked the public to comment on the extent to which each method reflects certain fundamental tax policy principles, including certainty, clarity, administrability, and neutrality. Several comments were received from the public, which expressed diverse views regarding the relative advantages and disadvantages of the different methods. Included in the four methods were the noncontingent swap method and a mark-to-market method, versions of which are adopted in the proposed regulations.

The Notice also solicited comments on the proper character of payments on NPCs and bullet swaps. The comments received on this issue also reflected differing views.

Explanation of Provisions

A. *Overview*

The IRS and Treasury understand that some taxpayers take into account contingent nonperiodic payments on an NPC only when the payment becomes fixed and determinable (the open transaction or wait-and-see method of accounting). The wait-and-see method, however, is inconsistent with the existing specific timing rules for periodic and nonperiodic payments and with the general rule in §1.446-3(f)(2)(i) respecting recognition of nonperiodic payments over the term of the contract. For example, if the amount of a periodic payment is set in arrears at the end of an accrual period that spans taxable years, the parties cannot use a wait-and-see method for the portion of the accrual period in the first taxable year. Instead, the parties must use a reasonable estimate of the payment for determining taxable income in the year before the payment is fixed. §1.446-3(e)(2)(ii). In addition, some NPCs are structured to provide for nonperiodic payments consisting of a noncontingent component and a contingent component, which the parties to the contract treat as a single contingent payment that they account for under the wait-and-see method. The attempted application of the wait-

and-see method to these contracts highlights the potential for abuse present in the method. See Rev. Rul. 2002-30 (2002-1 C.B. 971).

The back-loaded timing of tax consequences that results from the wait-and-see method is also inconsistent with the timing regime that § 1.1275-4(b) provides for contingent debt instruments subject to the noncontingent bond method. Under the noncontingent bond method, the parties to a contingent payment debt instrument must determine the yield at which a comparable noncontingent debt instrument would be issued and then project a fixed amount for each contingent payment and each noncontingent payment. The projected amounts are accounted for over the term of the debt instrument. The difference, if any, between the projected amount of a contingent payment and the actual amount of the payment generally is accounted for when payment is made.

The proposed regulations adopt a variation on the noncontingent swap regime described in Notice 2001-44, as well as an elective mark-to-market regime. The 1993 Treasury regulations reflect an underlying principle that nonperiodic payments should be spread over the term of an NPC in a manner that properly reflects the economic substance of the contract. The proposed regulations build upon this principle. Furthermore, the IRS and Treasury believe that the proposed regulations provide a timing regime for contingent nonperiodic payments that clearly reflects the economics of the underlying contracts. The requirement that nonperiodic payments be spread over the term of an NPC results in substantially similar treatment for all NPCs without regard to whether payment obligations are settled on a current basis through periodic payments or are either pre-paid or deferred through nonperiodic payments. Adopting this approach for contingent payment NPCs achieves symmetry between fixed payment NPCs and contingent payment NPCs.

The proposed noncontingent swap method requires taxpayers to project the expected amount of contingent payments, to take into account annually the appropriate portions of the projected contingent amounts, to reproject the contingent amounts annually, and to reflect the differences between projected amounts and reprojected amounts through adjustments. The IRS and Treasury recognize that annual reprojections will require additional effort by taxpayers and the IRS. The IRS and Treasury believe, however, that the annual reprojection requirement is essential to ensure clear reflection of income with respect to NPCs with one or more contingent nonperiodic payments. Moreover, reprojections, and the resulting adjustments to current inclusion and deduction amounts, are especially important for the income and deductions generated by these types of contracts because otherwise, taxpayers might be more likely to attempt to manipulate the character of the income or deductions from the contract.

In developing the proposed regulations, the IRS and Treasury have taken into account comments received in response to Notice 2001-44, as well as the following considerations. First, although many comments advocated the wait-and-see method of accounting for contingent nonperiodic payments, this method encourages the creation of NPCs that provide such payments. As a result of the adoption of guidelines for taking contingent nonperiodic payments into account over the term of an NPC, the tax treatment of payments with respect to an NPC should no longer provide an incentive for structuring payments in a particular manner. Second, taxpayers using swaps with contingent nonperiodic payments are sophisticated investors. Many of these taxpayers will be making similar projections and reprojections for their own purposes in evaluating the results of their derivative investments and taking actions to manage the risks created by their derivative investments. Third, the proposed regulations also provide an elective mark-to-market method as an alternative to the noncontingent swap method. Taxpayers who use a mark-to-market method for financial reporting purposes may adopt the elective mark-to-market method to reduce their tax and accounting administrative burden for NPCs.

The IRS and Treasury understand that similar timing issues exist for other types of derivative investments, like bullet swaps and prepaid forward contracts. Although the application of the proposed regulations to these types of transactions may achieve appropriate timing, the application of these rules to investments other than NPCs could present a number of issues not directly addressed by the rules contained in these proposed regulations. The expansion of the scope of these proposed regulations to contracts other than NPCs is not being proposed at this time so as not to delay the publication of the proposed regulations.

With respect to character, the proposed regulations under sections 162 and 212 provide that both periodic and nonperiodic payments with respect to NPCs are generally ordinary in character. This is because neither periodic nor nonperiodic payments (whenever made) involve a sale or exchange within the meaning of section 1222, and no other section of the Code provides otherwise. The proposed regulations issued under section 1234A provide capital treatment for termination payments. Under the proposed regulations, however, even nonperiodic payments made at the maturity of an NPC are not termination payments under section 1234A.

Because of their recurring nature, periodic payments should be treated as ordinary income items, whether or not the payments are made at the expiration of an NPC. The same rationale applies to nonperiodic payments, which are required to be spread over the term of an NPC. Even if a nonperiodic payment is made at the expiration or termination of an NPC, only the final portion is taken into account on the termination date for the contract, and that portion should be treated in the same way as a periodic payment.

B. *Specific Provisions*

Adjustments

Paragraph (d) (2) of the proposed regulations provides for adjustments to be made in the gain or loss realized on the sale, exchange, or termination of an NPC, to account for inclusions into income and deductions provided for in the 1993 Treasury regulations and the proposed regulations, as well as for any payments made or received on the NPC. These adjustments are expected to produce consequences similar to the consequences that would result if basis were increased or decreased for these items. Using adjustments for this purpose avoids the issue of negative basis.

Significant nonperiodic payments

Paragraph (g)(4) of the proposed regulations clarifies the rules for the treatment of an NPC with a significant upfront nonperiodic payment and provides additional rules for the treatment of a significant nonperiodic payment that is not paid upfront. The 1993 Treasury regulations provide that a significant nonperiodic payment on an NPC is treated as two separate transactions - an on-market level payment NPC and a loan. § 1.446-3(g)(4). The proposed regulations clarify that the parties to an NPC with one or more significant nonperiodic payments must treat the contract as two or more separate transactions consisting of an on-market NPC and one or more loans. In some cases, the on-market NPC payments for a party making a significant nonperiodic upfront payment will be level payments that may be constructed through a combination of the actual payments on the NPC and level payments computed under the level payment method described in § 1.446-3(f)(2)(iii)(A).

The proposed regulations also provide that an NPC with a significant nonperiodic payment that is not paid upfront is treated as if the party receiving the significant nonperiodic payment paid a series of annual level payment loan advances, equal to the present value of the nonperiodic payment, to the party owing the significant nonperiodic payment. The interest component of the level payments is treated as interest for all purposes of the Code and is not taken into account in determining the income and deductions on the NPC. The principal component of the level payments is calculated solely to determine the interest amount. The party owing the significant nonperiodic payment is then treated as using the level payment loan advances to make annual level payment NPC payments, which are included in income and deducted as provided in § 1.446-3(d).

Contingent nonperiodic payments

The 1993 Treasury regulations define both periodic and nonperiodic payments but do not distinguish between contingent and noncontingent nonperiodic payments. Paragraph (g)(6)(i)(B) of the proposed regulations defines a contingent nonperiodic payment as any nonperiodic payment other than a noncontingent nonperiodic payment. A noncontingent nonperiodic payment is defined in paragraph (g)(6)(i)(A) of the proposed regulations as a nonperiodic payment that either is fixed on or before the end of the taxable year in which a contract commences or is equal to the sum of amounts that would be periodic payments if they are paid when they become fixed, including amounts determined as interest accruals.

Paragraph (g)(6)(ii) of the proposed regulations sets forth the noncontingent swap method for the inclusion into income and deduction of contingent nonperiodic payments. The noncontingent swap method requires taxpayers to project the reasonably expected amount of the contingent nonperiodic payment and to apply the level payment method and, as appropriate, the rules for significant nonperiodic payments, to the projected amount as if it were a noncontingent nonperiodic payment. The risk-free rate of return, which is defined in the proposed regulations, is used in applying the level payment method.

Paragraphs (g)(6)(iii)(A) through (C) of the proposed regulations provide the methods for projecting the reasonably expected amount. If the contingent payment is determined by reference to the value of a specified index at a designated future date, the projected amount may be determined by reference to the future value of the specified index in actively traded futures or forward contracts providing for delivery or settlement on the designated future date. If no actively traded contract exists for the designated future date, the value may be derived from actively traded futures or forward contracts providing for delivery or settlement within three months of the designated future date.

The projected amount may also be determined based on the projected future value of the current market price of the specified index. The future value is determined using a constant yield method at the risk-free interest rate with appropriate compounding and making appropriate adjustments for expected cash payments on the property underlying the specified index. The proposed regulations use the applicable federal rate under section 1274(d)(1) as the risk-free rate for this purpose. Comments are requested on whether this rate is appropriate.

If neither of the two methods described above results in a reasonable estimate of the future value of the specified index, the taxpayer must use another method that does result in a reasonable estimate of the amount of the contingent payment and that is based on objective financial information, and must consistently use the method from year to year.

The proposed regulations require annual adjustments to the projected amounts of the contingent payment. Paragraphs (g)(6)(iv) through (vi) of the proposed regulations provide rules for the redetermination of the projected amount of the contingent payment and the subsequent adjustments to the recognition of income and deductions under a contract based on the reprojected amount.

Paragraph (g)(6)(iv) of the proposed regulations provides that the projected amount must be redetermined on each successive anniversary date (redetermination date) and on each special redetermination date as described below. On each redetermination date, the taxpayer must reproject the amount of the contingent payment using the same method used at the commencement of the NPC but applied to the new current value of the specified index. Once the contingent payment is reprojected, the level payment method (and the rules for significant nonperiodic payments, if applicable) are applied again using the new projected amount.

Comments are requested as to how the reprojection process should respond to changes in the availability of market data during the life of an NPC. Suppose, for example, that the initial projection is made when there are no actively traded futures or forward contracts in the specified index but that these contracts come into existence before the time of one of the reprojections. Should the reprojections be made using the newly available futures data rather than the method employed for the first projection?

Paragraph (g)(6)(v) of the proposed regulations provides rules for adjustments following the redetermination of the projected amount of the contingent payment. The amounts determined for the redetermined projected amount under the level payment method and, as applicable, the rules for significant nonperiodic payments, are recognized in the current and subsequent taxable years. In addition, any difference between the newly determined amounts for prior periods and the amounts determined and previously taken into account using the previously projected contingent payment are recognized ratably over the one-year period beginning with the redetermination date. Any difference in amounts that would have been treated as interest under the rules for significant nonperiodic payments is also treated as interest for all purposes of the Code.

Paragraph (g)(6)(iv)(B) of the proposed regulations provides a special rule for a contingent nonperiodic payment that is fixed more than six months before it is due. If the date on which the payment becomes fixed is in a different taxable year from the date it is due, the date on which the payment becomes fixed is a special redetermination date. In such a case, the fixed amount is treated as the reprojected amount, and the rules described above for redeterminations and adjustments apply.

In general, under paragraph (g)(6)(vi) of the proposed regulations, when a contingent payment is made, the parties must make appropriate adjustments to the amount of income or deduction attributable to the NPC for any differences between the projected amount of the contingent payment and the actual amount of the contingent payment.

Paragraph (g)(6)(vii) of the proposed regulations provides a recordkeeping requirement with respect to the noncontingent swap method. Taxpayers must maintain in their books and records a description of the method used to determine the projected amount of the contingent payment, the projected payment schedules, and the adjustments taken into account under the proposed regulations.

The IRS and Treasury are considering whether to provide an alternative to the noncontingent swap method that would permit a taxpayer to use a current inclusion method for certain NPCs that provide for periodic calculations of amounts due under the terms of the NPC, but provide for deferred payment of the amounts. The IRS and Treasury are considering permitting current inclusion of income and deduction for the amounts so calculated, provided the NPC also provides for accrual of interest at a qualified rate until the periodically determined amounts are paid or offset against other amounts due under the NPC. The purpose of providing a current inclusion method for the deferred payment NPC described above is to provide tax treatment for NPCs with contingent nonperiodic payments that is economically equivalent to the tax treatment of NPCs providing only for periodic payments while avoiding the necessity of using projected amounts for contingent payments. The IRS and Treasury request comments concerning whether an NPC like the deferred payment NPC described above would be a viable transaction for market participants, whether a current inclusion method would be an appropriate substitute for the noncontingent swap method for deferred payment NPCs, and whether that method should require separate computation of interest accruals.

Elective mark-to-market methodology

Paragraph (i) of the proposed regulations provides an elective mark-to-market methodology for certain NPCs providing for nonperiodic payments. If an election is made, the specific accounting rules for nonperiodic payments in § 1.446-3(f)(2) (other than (f)(2)(i)) are not applicable. Instead, for any contract that is held at the close of the taxable year, the taxpayer determines income inclusions and deductions by reference to the gain or loss that would be realized if the contract were sold for its fair market value on the last business day of the taxable year. Because the determination of fair market value takes into account the expected value of future nonperiodic payments, the mark-to-market methodology constitutes a reasonable basis for amortizing the nonperiodic payments over the term of the contract as required by § 1.446-3(f)(2)(i).

Proper adjustments are made in the amount of gain or loss subsequently realized (or calculated) for income inclusions and deductions taken into account in marking the contract to fair market value. Furthermore, under paragraph (i)(5) of the proposed regulations, if an election is made for a contract providing for a significant nonperiodic payment, paragraph (g)(4) continues to apply and proper adjustments must be made to the income inclusions and deductions recognized under the mark-to-market methodology to take into account amounts recognized as interest and the payment or receipt of the significant nonperiodic payment, subject to the special rule set forth below.

The proposed regulations set forth a special rule for contracts providing for significant contingent nonperiodic payments that are subject to the mark-to-market election. If a contract provides for a significant contingent nonperiodic payment, the taxpayer must apply the noncontingent swap method to determine the amounts recognized as interest under paragraph (g)(4). However, the taxpayer is not required to reproject the amount of the contingent payment each year. The interest amounts for subsequent years are the interest amounts as determined using the initial projection of the contingent payment. Furthermore, an alternative deemed equivalent value method may be used to determine the projected amount of the contingent payment. The deemed equivalent value method may be applied when the contract fixes the timing and amount of all of the payments under the contract, except for the significant contingent nonperiodic payment. The amount of the significant contingent nonperiodic payment is deemed to be the amount that causes the present value of all the payments by the taxpayer to equal the present value of all of the payments of the counterparty to the contract.

The inclusion of an elective mark-to-market methodology is intended to provide taxpayers with an alternative to the provisions of paragraphs (f) of the 1993 Treasury regulations and (g)(6) of the proposed regulations respecting nonperiodic payments. With respect to significant nonperiodic payments, however, the proposed regulations preserve certain features of those provisions for purposes of computing an interest component of swap payments. Such a calculation is necessary to preserve the characterization of an accrual as interest. The IRS and Treasury request comments on the appropriateness of requiring taxpayers to compute an interest amount for significant nonperiodic payments under the elective mark-to-market methodology and, in particular, on any effect that requirement may have on the relative usefulness and administrability of the mark-to-market methodology.

Paragraph (i)(2) of the proposed regulations provides the scope of the election. The election is available to contracts that are: (1) actively traded within the meaning of § 1.1092(d)-1(c) (determined without regard to the limitation in § 1.1092(d)-1(c)(2)); (2) marked to market for purposes of the taxpayer's financial statements provided the taxpayer satisfies the requirements in paragraph (i)(4) of the proposed regulations; (3) subject to an agreement by a party to the contract that is a person to whom section 475 applies to supply to the taxpayer the value that it uses in applying section 475(a)(2); or (4) marked to market by a regulated investment company (RIC) described in section 1296(e)(2). Paragraphs (i)(3)(i) through (iv) of the proposed regulations provide the acceptable methods for determining fair market value. If the contract is actively traded, the fair market value is determined based on the mean between the bid and asked prices quoted for the contract. If a contract is not actively traded, but is marked to market for financial statement purposes, and the valuations used for those purposes comply with the requirements of paragraph (i)(4), the fair market value is deemed to be the value used for the financial statements. For a contract that is subject to an agreement with a dealer in securities to provide a value, the value that is provided by the dealer is the fair market value. Finally, for a contract marked to market by a RIC, the fair market value is equal to the value used for purposes of determining the RIC's net asset value.

Paragraph (i)(6) of the proposed regulations provides that the mark-to-market election shall be made in the time and manner prescribed by the Commissioner and is effective for the taxable year in which it is made and all subsequent years unless revoked with the consent of the Commissioner.

The proposed regulations indicate that a taxpayer will be permitted to elect the mark-to-market method for NPCs that are marked to market for purposes of the taxpayer's financial statements and that the values used on the financial statements may be used as fair market value under the mark-to-market election. However, the proposed regulations also indicate that an election to use financial statement values will be subject to further requirements. On May 5, 2003, the IRS and Treasury published in the **Federal Register** an Advance Notice of Proposed Rule Making (REG-100420-03) requesting comments regarding appropriate rules for the use of financial statement values under the mark-to-market provisions of section 475 applicable to securities dealers and electing commodities dealers and securities and commodities traders. The IRS and Treasury will take into account the comments received in response to that Advance Notice in developing the rules to be established for use of financial statement values under the mark-to-market method set forth in paragraph (i) of the proposed regulations. In addition, unlike other mark-to-market regimes, the mark-to-market method proposed in paragraph (i) does not require a mark immediately before disposition in either a recognition or nonrecognition context. *Cf.* section 1256(c) and proposed regulations § 1.475(a)-2. The IRS and Treasury request comments regarding this aspect of the proposed regulations and whether taxpayers who are eligible to elect a mark-to-market method under section 475 but do not do so should be eligible to make the paragraph (i) election for NPCs.

Anti-abuse rule

Paragraph (i) of the 1993 Treasury regulations provides that if a taxpayer "enters into a transaction with a principal purpose of applying the rules of [§ 1.446-3] to produce a material distortion of income," the IRS may depart from those rules "as necessary to reflect the appropriate timing of income and deductions from the transaction." In light of the comprehensive rules in the proposed regulations prescribing methods of accounting for NPCs, the IRS and Treasury have determined that a general anti-abuse rule is not necessary to prevent these methods being used in a manner that fails to clearly reflect income. Accordingly, the proposed regulations delete this rule.

Proposed dates of applicability

These proposed regulations contain both new substantive rules as well as clarifying changes to the 1993 Treasury regulations. The new substantive rules, which are contained in paragraph (g)(6) (the noncontingent swap method) (except (g)(6)(i)) and paragraph (i) (the mark-to-market election), are proposed to apply to NPCs entered into on or after 30 days after the date of publication of the final regulations in the **Federal Register**. Paragraphs (c) (definitions), (d) (taxable year of inclusion and deduction), (f) (nonperiodic payments), (g)(4) (significant nonperiodic payments), and (g)(6)(i) (definition of contingent and noncontingent nonperiodic payments) are proposed to be integrated into the 1993 Treasury regulations which apply to NPCs entered into on or after December 13, 1993. Because of their purely clarifying nature, these proposed changes will apply to the same transactions that are governed by the 1993 Treasury regulations.

With respect to NPCs that provide for contingent nonperiodic payments and that are in effect or entered into on or after 30 days after the date of publication of these proposed regulations in the **Federal Register**, if a taxpayer has not adopted a method of accounting for these NPCs, the taxpayer must adopt a method that takes contingent nonperiodic payments into account over the life of the contract under a reasonable amortization method, which may be, but need not be, a method that satisfies the specific rules in these proposed regulations. If a taxpayer has adopted a method of accounting for these NPCs, the Commissioner generally will not require a change in the accounting method earlier than the first year ending on or after 30 days after the date of publication of the final regulations in the **Federal Register**. The preceding sentence does not apply to transactions described in Rev. Rul. 2002-30 (2002-1 C.B. 971) or other published guidance.

The proposed regulations do not contain a specific consistency requirement. Nevertheless, under the general rules governing accounting methods, once a taxpayer adopts a method of accounting for an item, the taxpayer must use the same method from year to year unless the taxpayer obtains the Commissioner's consent to change to another method of accounting.

Character

The proposed regulations under § 1.162-30 provide that in general, the net periodic and nonperiodic payments (including mark-to-market deductions) are deductible by the payor under section 162 as ordinary and necessary business expenses. However, payments representing interest under the rules for significant nonperiodic payments as well as termination payments are not deductible under section 162. A similar rule is provided for individuals in the proposed regulations under § 1.212-1(q). These regulations under sections 162 and 212 are proposed to apply to NPCs entered into on or after 30 days after the date of publication of the final regulations in the **Federal Register**.

Any gain or loss arising from a termination payment, however, is treated as capital gain or loss pursuant to the proposed regulations under section 1234A. These proposed regulations clarify that periodic payments, noncontingent nonperiodic payments, and contingent nonperiodic payments are not termination payments.

The proposed regulations under section 1234A also apply to any gain or loss arising from the settlement of obligations under a bullet swap or forward contract. A payment in settlement of obligations under a bullet swap or forward contract, including a payment pursuant to the terms of the bullet swap or forward contract, is treated as gain or loss from a termination of the bullet swap or forward contract.

For purposes of these proposed regulations, a bullet swap is defined as a financial instrument that is not an excluded contract as defined in § 1.446-3(c)(1)(ii), that provides for the computation of an amount or amounts due from one party to another by reference to a specified index upon a notional principal amount, and that provides for settlement of all the parties' obligations at or close to maturity of the contract, rather than for the payment of the specified amounts at specific intervals. The definition of bullet swap is intended to cover a contract that obligates each party to make a payment at the end of the contract, although only one net payment will actually be paid. For example, party A is obligated to pay at the end of three years a fixed rate multiplied by the notional amount. Also at the end of three years, party B is obligated to pay a variable rate multiplied by the same notional amount. At the end of three years, only one party makes a net payment equal to the difference between the fixed rate multiplied by the notional amount and the variable rate multiplied by the notional amount.

These regulations under section 1234A are proposed to apply to NPCs entered into on or after 30 days after the date of publication of the final regulations in the **Federal Register.**

Special Analyses

It has been determined that this notice of proposed rulemaking is not a significant regulatory action as defined in Executive Order 12866. Therefore, a regulatory assessment is not required. It is hereby certified that these regulations will not have a significant economic impact on a substantial number of small entities. This certification is based on the fact that very few small businesses enter into NPCs with contingent nonperiodic payments because these contracts are costly and complex and because they require constant monitoring and a sophisticated understanding of the capital markets. Therefore, a Regulatory Flexibility Analysis is not required. Pursuant to section 7805(f) of the Code, this notice of proposed rulemaking will be submitted to the Chief Counsel for Advocacy of the Small Business Administration for comment on its impact on small businesses.

Comments and Public Hearing

Before these proposed regulations are adopted as final regulations, consideration will be given to any written comments (a signed original and eight (8) copies) or electronic comments that are submitted timely to the IRS. The IRS and Treasury specifically request comments on the clarity of the proposed rules and how they may be made easier to understand. All comments will be available for public inspection and copying.

A public hearing has been scheduled for May 25, 2004, beginning at 10 a.m., in the IRS Auditorium, Seventh Floor, Internal Revenue Building, 1111 Constitution Avenue, NW., Washington, DC. Due to building security procedures, visitors must enter at the Constitution Avenue entrance. In addition, all visitors must present photo identification to enter the building. Because of access restrictions, visitors will not be admitted beyond the immediate entrance area more than 30 minutes before the hearing starts. For information about having your name placed on the building access list to attend the hearing, see "FOR FURTHER INFORMATION CONTACT" section of this preamble.

The rules of 26 CFR 601.601(a)(3) apply to the hearing. Persons who wish to present oral comments at the hearing must submit written comments or electronic comments and an outline of topics to be discussed and the time to be devoted to each topic (a signed original and eight (8) copies) by May 4, 2004. A period of 10 minutes will be allotted to each person making comments. An agenda showing the scheduling of the speakers will be prepared after the deadline for receiving outlines has passed. Copies of the agenda will be available free of charge at the hearing.

Drafting Information

The principal author of these regulations is Kate Sleeth, Office of the Associate Chief Counsel (Financial Institutions and Products). However, other personnel from the IRS and Treasury participated in their development.

[¶49,217] Proposed Amendments of Regulations (REG-153172-03), published in the Federal Register on March 18, 2004.

Consolidated returns: Regulations covering consolidated returns: Losses: Disposition of subsidiary stock: Proposed regulations.—Amendments of Reg. §1.1502-80, relating to the deductibility of losses recognized on dispositions of subsidiary stock by members of a consolidated group, the consequences of treating subsidiary stock as worthless, and when stock of a member of a consolidated group may be treated as worthless, are proposed. Amendments of Reg. §1.337(d)-2 were adopted by T.D. 9187 on 3/2/2005. Amendments of Reg. §1.1502-35 were adopted by T.D. 9254 on 3/9/2006..

AGENCY: Internal Revenue Service (IRS), Treasury.

ACTION: Notice of proposed rulemaking by cross-reference to temporary regulations.

SUMMARY: In the Rules and Regulations section of this issue of the **Federal Register**, the IRS is issuing temporary regulations under sections 337(d) and 1502 of the Internal Revenue Code relating to the deductibility of losses recognized on dispositions of subsidiary stock by members of a consolidated group, the consequences of treating subsidiary stock as worthless, and when stock of a member of a consolidated group may be treated as worthless. The temporary regulations apply to corporations filing consolidated returns. The text of the temporary regulations published in this issue of the **Federal Register** also serves as the text of these proposed regulations.

DATES: Written or electronic comments must be received by June 16, 2004.

ADDRESSES: Send submissions to: CC:PA:LPD:PR (REG-153172-03), room 5203, Internal Revenue Service, POB 7604, Ben Franklin Station, Washington, DC 20044. Submissions may be hand delivered Monday through Friday between the hours of 8 a.m. and 4 p.m. to CC:PA:LPD:PR (REG-153172-03), Courier's Desk, Internal Revenue Service, 1111 Constitution Avenue, NW., Washington, DC 20044. Alternatively, taxpayers may submit electronic comments directly to the IRS Internet site at *www.irs.gov/regs*.

FOR FURTHER INFORMATION CONTACT: Regarding the regulations under section 337(d), Mark Weiss (202-622-7790) of the Office of Associate Chief Counsel (Corporate), and regarding the regulations under section 1502, Lola L. Johnson (202-622-7550) of the Office of Associate Chief Counsel (Corporate); regarding submission of comments and/or requests for a hearing, Sonya M. Cruse (202-622-4693) of the Office of Procedure and Administration (not toll-free numbers).

SUPPLEMENTARY INFORMATION:

Background and Explanation of Provisions

Temporary regulations in the Rules and Regulations section of this issue of the **Federal Register** amend the Income Tax Regulations (26 CFR part 1) relating to section 337(d) and section 1502. The text of those regulations also serves as the text of these proposed regulations. The preamble to the temporary regulations explains the amendments.

Special Analyses

It has been determined that this notice of proposed rulemaking is not a significant regulatory action as defined in Executive Order 12866. Therefore, a regulatory assessment is not required. It is hereby certified that these regulations will not have a significant economic impact on a substantial number of small entities. This certification is based on the fact that these regulations will primarily affect affiliated groups of corporations, which tend to be larger businesses. Therefore a Regulatory Flexibility Analysis is not required. Pursuant to section 7805(f) of the Internal Revenue Code, this notice of proposed rulemaking will be submitted to the Chief Counsel for Advocacy of the Small Business Administration for comment on its impact on small business.

Comments and Requests for a Public Hearing

Before these proposed regulations are adopted as final regulations, consideration will be given to any written comments (a signed original and eight (8) copies) or electronic comments that are submitted timely to the IRS. The IRS and the Treasury Department request comments on the clarity of the proposed regulations and how they may be made easier to understand. All comments will be available for public inspection and copying. A public hearing may be scheduled if requested by any person who timely submits comments. If a public hearing is scheduled, notice of the date, time and place for the hearing will be published in the **Federal Register**.

Drafting Information

The principal author of the regulations under section 337(d) is Mark Weiss, Office of Associate Chief Counsel (Corporate). The principal author of the regulations under section 1502 is Lola L. Johnson, Office of Associate Chief Counsel (Corporate). However, other personnel from the IRS and Treasury participated in their development.

[¶49,219] Proposed Amendments of Regulations (REG-128590-03), published in the Federal Register on May 7, 2004.

Deductions: Expenses: Interest: Tax-exempt obligations: Related entities: Consolidated groups: Income exclusion.—Amendments of Reg. §§1.265-2 and 1.1502-13, affecting corporations filing consolidated returns and providing special rules for the treatment of certain intercompany transactions involving interest on intercompany obligations, are proposed..

AGENCY: Internal Revenue Service (IRS), Treasury.

ACTION: Notice of proposed rulemaking.

SUMMARY: This document contains proposed regulations under section 265(a)(2) that affect corporations filing consolidated returns. These regulations provide special rules for the treatment of certain intercompany transactions involving interest on intercompany obligations.

DATES: Written or electronic comments and requests for a public hearing must be received by August 5, 2004.

ADDRESSES: Send submissions to: CC:PA:LPD:PR (REG-128590-03), room 5203, Internal Revenue Service, POB 7604, Ben Franklin Station, Washington, DC 20044. Submissions may be hand delivered Monday through Friday between the hours of 8 a.m. and 4 p.m. to CC:PA:LPD:PR (REG-128590-03), Courier's Desk, Internal Revenue Service, 1111 Constitution Avenue, NW., Washington, DC. Alternatively, taxpayers may submit comments electronically via the IRS Internet site at *www.irs.gov/regs* or via the Federal eRulemaking Portal at *www.regulations.gov* (indicate IRS and REG-128590-03).

FOR FURTHER INFORMATION CONTACT: Concerning the proposed regulations, Frances L. Kelly, (202) 622-7770; concerning submissions of comments and/or requests for a public hearing, Guy Traynor, (202) 622-7180 (not toll-free numbers).

SUPPLEMENTARY INFORMATION:

Background

Section 265(a)(2)

Section 163(a) generally allows a deduction for all interest paid or accrued within the taxable year on indebtedness. Under section 265(a)(2), however, no deduction is allowed for interest on indebtedness incurred or continued to purchase or carry obligations the interest on which is wholly exempt from Federal income taxes.

Rev. Proc. 72-18 (1972-1 C.B. 740) provides guidelines for the application of section 265(a)(2) to taxpayers holding tax-exempt obligations. Section 3.01 of the revenue procedure states that the application of section 265(a)(2) requires a determination, based upon all the facts and circumstances, of the taxpayer's purpose in incurring or continuing each item of indebtedness. Such purpose may be established by either direct or circumstantial evidence. Direct evidence includes direct tracing of borrowed funds to investments in tax-exempt obligations and the pledging of tax-exempt obligations as security for the indebtedness. To the extent that there is direct evidence establishing a purpose to purchase or carry tax-exempt obligations, the interest paid or incurred on such indebtedness may not be deducted. In certain other cases when an interest deduction is disallowed (for example, when amounts borrowed by a dealer in tax-exempt obligations are not directly traceable to tax-exempt obligations), section 7 of Rev. Proc. 72-18 sets forth a formula to calculate the disallowed interest deduction. That formula provides that the amount of the disallowed interest deduction is determined by multiplying the total interest on the indebtedness by a fraction, the numerator of which is the average amount during the taxable year of the taxpayer's tax-exempt obligations (valued at their adjusted bases), and the denominator of which is the average amount during the taxable year of the taxpayer's total assets (valued at their adjusted bases) minus the amount of any indebtedness the interest deduction on which is not subject to disallowance to any extent under Rev. Proc. 72-18.

In *H Enterprises International, Inc. v. Commissioner*, 75 T.C.M. (CCH) 1948 (1998), *aff'd*, 183 F.3d 907 (8th Cir. 1999), a parent and a subsidiary were members of the same consolidated group of corporations. The subsidiary declared a dividend and, a few days later, borrowed funds and immediately used part of those funds to make the dividend distribution to the parent. A portion of the distributed funds was disbursed to two investment divisions of the parent, which used the funds to acquire investments including tax-exempt obligations.

The court held that a portion of the subsidiary's indebtedness was incurred for the purpose of purchasing or carrying tax-exempt obligations (held in the parent's investment divisions) and, therefore, no deduction was allowed for the interest on this portion of the indebtedness under section 265(a)(2). To establish the required purposive connection under section 265(a)(2), the court reasoned that the activities of the parent corporation were relevant in determining the subsidiary's purpose for borrowing the funds. The court stated that if the analysis only focused on the borrower and not the transferee, then the purpose of the borrower corporation would always be acceptable, frustrating the legislative intent of section 265(a)(2).

Rev. Rul. 2004-47 (2004-21 I.R.B.) provides guidance on the application of section 265(a)(2) in a number of situations in which a member of an affiliated group borrows money from an unrelated party and transfers funds to another member of the group that is a dealer in tax-exempt obligations. In *Situation 4*, P and S are members of the same affiliated group but file separate tax returns. P borrows funds from L, an unrelated bank, and lends the borrowed funds to S, a dealer in tax-exempt obligations. S uses the borrowed funds in its business. The ruling examines the obligation from L to P and the obligation from P to S for the application of section 265(a)(2). With regard to the loan from L to P, P uses the borrowed funds to make a loan to S, and P separately accounts for the taxable interest income from the obligation. The ruling concludes that P does not have a purpose of using the borrowed funds to purchase or carry tax-exempt obligations within the meaning of section 265(a)(2). With regard to the loan from P to S, although the borrowed funds are not directly traceable to S's purchase or carry of tax-exempt obligations, the ruling concludes that section 265(a)(2) applies to disallow a deduction for a portion of S's interest expense. The portion of S's interest deduction that is disallowed is determined pursuant to the formula of section 7 of Rev. Proc. 72-18.

The Intercompany Transaction Regulations

Section 1.1502-13 prescribes rules relating to the treatment of transactions between members of a consolidated group. With respect to intercompany obligations, the intercompany transaction rules generally operate to match the debtor member's items with the lending member's items from the intercompany obligation.

Under § 1.1502-13(c)(6)(i), if section 265(a)(2) permanently and explicitly disallows a debtor member's interest deduction with respect to a debt to another member, the lending member's interest income is treated as excluded from gross income. See § 1.1502-13(g)(5), *Example 1*(d). In cases when a member of the group borrows from another member to purchase or carry tax-exempt obligations, and the lending member has not borrowed from sources outside of the group to fund the intercompany obligation, the result reached under the § 1.1502-13(c)(6)(i) exclusion rule is appropriate in that it reflects that intercompany lending transactions do not alter the net worth of the group and, thus, should not affect consolidated taxable income.

However, when the lending member borrows from a nonmember, the lending member lends those funds to the debtor member, and the debtor member uses those funds to purchase or carry tax-exempt obligations, the application of the § 1.1502-13(c)(6)(i) exclusion rule may produce inappropriate results. For example, assume P borrows $100 from L, a nonmember, for the purpose of lending the $100 to S under the same terms, and S's purpose for borrowing $60 of the intercompany loan from P is to purchase $60 of tax-exempt obligations. Under section 265(a)(2), a deduction would be disallowed for a portion of S's interest expense on the intercompany obligation and a portion of P's interest income would be excluded from P's gross income under § 1.1502-13(c)(6)(i). Accordingly, section 265(a)(2) may have no effect on the group's taxable income, even though the group has borrowed to purchase tax-exempt obligations.

Explanation of Provisions

The IRS and Treasury Department believe that, when a member's indebtedness to a nonmember is directly traceable to an intercompany obligation and another member of the group uses the funds borrowed from the nonmember to purchase or carry tax-exempt obligations, the net tax effect of these transactions for the group should be a disallowance of a deduction for interest under section 265(a)(2).

These proposed regulations reflect that when a member (P) borrows funds from a nonmember and lends all of those funds to another member (S) that uses those funds to purchase tax-exempt obligations, section 265(a)(2) will apply to disallow a deduction for the interest on S's obligation to P, not P's obligation to the nonmember. These proposed regulations provide that, if a member of a consolidated group incurs or continues indebtedness to a nonmember, that indebtedness to the nonmember is directly traceable to all or a portion of an intercompany obligation extended to a member of the group (the borrowing member) by another member of the group (the lending member), and section 265(a)(2) applies to disallow a deduction for all or a portion of the borrowing member's interest expense incurred with respect to the intercompany obligation, then § 1.1502-13(c)(6)(i) will not apply to exclude an amount of the lending member's interest income with respect to the intercompany obligation that equals the amount of the borrowing member's disallowed interest deduction. This override of the exclusion rule is subject, however, to a limitation. In particular, the amount of interest income not excluded cannot exceed the interest expense on the portion of the nonmember indebtedness that is directly traceable to the intercompany obligation. This limitation ensures that applying section 265(a)(2) to disallow an interest deduction with respect to an intercompany obligation that can be directly traced to nonmember indebtedness does not result in a worse overall tax position for the group than applying section 265(a)(2) to disallow a deduction for the interest paid to the nonmember.

Therefore, subject to the limitation discussed above, if the proceeds of P's borrowing from a nonmember can be directly traced to a P-S intercompany obligation and all or a portion of S's interest expense on the P-S intercompany obligation is disallowed as a deduction under section 265(a)(2), these proposed regulations require that all or a portion of P's interest income on the intercompany obligation not be excluded under § 1.1502-13(c)(6)(i).

In an Advance Notice of Proposed Rulemaking (REG-128572-03) in this issue of the **Federal Register**, the IRS and Treasury Department are soliciting comments regarding whether regulations under section 7701(f) should address the application of sections 265(a)(2) and 246A in transactions involving related parties, pass-thru entities, or other intermediaries, and suggestions as to the approach that should be taken by those regulations. It is possible that those comments and any regulations proposed under section 7701(f) will result in amendments to the rules set forth in these proposed regulations.

Proposed Effective Date

These regulations are proposed to apply to taxable years beginning on or after the date these regulations are published as final regulations in the **Federal Register.**

Special Analysis

It has been determined that this notice of proposed rulemaking is not a significant regulatory action as defined in Executive Order 12866. Therefore, a regulatory assessment is not required. It is hereby certified that these regulations will not have a significant economic impact on a substantial number of small entities. This certification is based upon the fact that these regulations will primarily affect affiliated groups of corporations that have elected to file consolidated returns, which tend to be larger businesses. Therefore, a Regulatory Flexibility Analysis under the Regulatory Flexibility Act (5 U.S.C. chapter 6) is not required. Pursuant to section 7805(f) of the Internal Revenue Code, these regulations will be submitted to the Chief Counsel for Advocacy of the Small Business Administration for comment on their impact on small business.

Comments and Requests for a Public Hearing

Before these proposed regulations are adopted as final regulations, consideration will be given to any written (a signed original and eight (8) copies) or electronic comments that are submitted timely to the IRS. The IRS and Treasury Department request comments on the clarity of the proposed rules and how they can be made easier to understand. All comments will be available for public inspection and copying. A public hearing will be scheduled if requested in writing by any person that timely submits written comments. If a public hearing is scheduled, notice of the date, time, and place for the public hearing will be published in the **Federal Register.**

Drafting Information

The principal author of these proposed regulations is Frances L. Kelly, Office of the Associate Chief Counsel (Corporate). However, other personnel from the IRS and Treasury Department participated in their development.

[¶ 49,226] Proposed Amendments of Regulations (REG-108637-03), published in the Federal Register on August 25, 2004.

Original issue discount: Accrual: REMICs.—Amendments of Reg. §§ 1.1271-0 and 1.1275-2, relating to the accrual of original issue discount (OID) on certain real estate mortgage investment conduit (REMIC) regular interests, are proposed. A public hearing on this proposal is scheduled for November 17, 2004.

AGENCY: Internal Revenue Service (IRS), Treasury.

ACTION: Notice of proposed rulemaking and notice of public hearing.

SUMMARY: This document contains proposed regulations relating to the accrual of original issue discount (OID) on certain real estate mortgage investment conduit (REMIC) regular interests. The proposed regulations are necessary to provide guidance to REMICs, REMIC regular interest holders and information reporters regarding the accrual of OID. This document also provides notice of a public hearing on the proposed regulations.

DATES: Written or electronic comments must be received by November 23, 2004. Outlines of topics to be discussed at the public hearing scheduled for November 17, 2004, must be received by October 27, 2004.

ADDRESSES: Send submissions to: CC:PA:LPD:PR (REG-108637-03), room 5203, Internal Revenue Service, PO Box 7604, Ben Franklin Station, Washington, DC 20044. Submissions may be hand-delivered Monday through Friday between the hours of 8 a.m. and 4 p.m. to CC:PA:LPD:PR (REG-108637-03), Courier's Desk, Internal Revenue Service, 1111 Constitution Avenue, NW., Washington, DC, or sent electronically, via the IRS Internet site at *www.irs.gov/regs* or via the Federal eRulemaking Portal at *www.regulations.gov* (IRS—REG-108637-03). The public hearing will be held in the Auditorium, Internal Revenue Building, 1111 Constitution Avenue, NW., Washington, DC.

FOR FURTHER INFORMATION CONTACT: Concerning the regulations, contact Rebecca Asta at (202) 622-3930. To be placed on the building access list for the hearing, contact Sonya Cruse at (202) 622-7180.

SUPPLEMENTARY INFORMATION:

Background and Explanation of Provisions

1. *General Background*

A debt instrument may provide for qualified stated interest (QSI) (that is, certain periodic payments of stated interest), OID, or both. Sections 163(e) and 1271 through 1275 provide rules for the treatment of OID on debt instruments. In general, the holder of a debt instrument includes OID in income as it accrues, even if the holder generally uses a cash method of accounting. A holder of a REMIC regular interest includes QSI in income under an accrual method of accounting because section 860B(b) requires that amounts includible in gross income with respect to a REMIC regular interest be determined under an accrual method.

For many debt instruments, only one or two days separate the date on which the holder becomes entitled to a payment (the record date) from the date on which the holder receives payment (the payment date). For REMIC regular interests, however, the record date may precede the payment date by 15 to 30 days.

2. *Current REMIC Accrual Practice*

Under the governing contract provisions, REMIC regular interests generally accrue interest from the issue date to the final record date, and holders become entitled to receive interest payments based on month-end record dates. The IRS and the Treasury Department understand, however, that, in general, REMIC servicers have interpreted the OID rules to require or permit holders' OID to accrue for tax purposes over the period from payment date to payment date and have treated QSI as accruing over the same periods. To compensate for accruing QSI and OID beyond the final record date to the final payment date, the servicers have treated QSI and OID on REMIC regular interests as not accruing from the date of issue for a period equal to the number of days between the record date and payment date. In effect, for tax purposes, the tax accrual of QSI and OID lags the legal accrual of interest by the delayed payment period.

For tax purposes, as of the date a REMIC regular interest is purchased in the secondary market, the purchaser begins to accrue QSI and OID, and the seller ceases to accrue QSI and OID. A purchaser that holds the instrument until the final payment date or redemption accrues QSI and OID past the final record date as long as it holds the instrument. A purchaser that begins to accrue QSI and OID on the purchase date gives up the benefit of the lag in the beginning of the accrual period. As a result, the delayed accrual system causes the last secondary market purchaser of a REMIC regular interest to accrue for tax purposes an additional number of days of QSI and OID equal to the number of days between the record and payment dates, and too much QSI and OID is allocated to the last secondary purchaser of the REMIC regular interest. Moreover, because of principal payments, the holder will earn interest on a declining principal balance, while the lagging tax accruals will be based on a higher principal amount between record dates and payment dates in many instances. Consequently, a secondary market purchaser that is not the last secondary market purchaser will experience tax accruals in excess of legal entitlements if the regular interest has significant stated principal and bears interest at a stated rate.

3. *Overview of the Proposed Regulations*

The proposed rules address the misallocation of QSI and OID by creating a special rule for accruing OID on REMIC regular interests that provide for a delay between record and payment dates. Under the proposed regulations, the period over which OID accrues generally coincides with the period over which the holder's right to interest payments accrues under the governing contract provisions.

Generally, under the proposed regulations, if the terms of a REMIC regular interest provide for a delay between the record and payment dates, the initial accrual period begins on the date of issuance of the regular interest, and the final accrual period ends on the final record date of that REMIC regular interest. By shifting the entire tax accrual schedule, this special rule allocates all QSI and OID to the period between the issue date and the final record date of the instrument and none to the period between the final record date and final payment date. For purposes of calculating OID in the final accrual period with the methodology described in section 1272(a)(6), but for no other purpose, payments on the REMIC regular interest after the end of that accrual period that are included in the stated redemption price at maturity of the instrument (such as the payment on the final payment date) are treated as being made during the final accrual period.

The IRS and Treasury Department recognize that, although the proposed regulations result in a more accurate allocation of QSI and OID among REMIC regular interest holders, some economic accuracy may be sacrificed by ending the accrual of OID before final payments are made on the regular interests. Therefore, the proposed regulations are limited to REMIC regular interests with delayed payment periods of fewer than 32 days. The regulation regarding REMIC regular interests with delayed payment periods of more than 31 days is reserved. The IRS and Treasury Department request comments on whether additional guidance is needed for these REMIC regular interests.

4. *Accrual of Qualified Stated Interest*

Section 1.1272-1(a) requires a holder to include QSI in income under the holder's regular method of accounting. Section 1.446-2(b) requires a holder, as well as the issuer, to accrue QSI ratably over the accrual period to which it is attributable. In addition, section 860B(b) requires a holder of a regular interest to accrue amounts into gross income regardless of the holder's overall method of accounting. The amounts that must be so accrued include QSI. The Treasury Department and the IRS understand that many REMIC servicers have accrued QSI over the same period as OID. It is intended that, with respect to the accrual periods referenced in § 1.446-2(b), the initial accrual period for QSI will begin on the date of issuance and the final accrual period for QSI will end on the final record date. As a result, the QSI accrues over the same period as the OID.

Proposed Effective Date

These regulations are proposed to apply to any REMIC regular interest issued after the date the final regulations are published in the **Federal Register.** The proposed regulations provide automatic consent for the holder of a REMIC regular interest to change its method of accounting for OID under the final regulations. The change is proposed to be made on a cut-off basis and, thus, does not affect REMIC regular interests issued before the date the final regulations are published in the **Federal Register.**

The Treasury Department and the IRS are concerned regarding the extent to which holders of REMIC regular interests will be aware that changes in accounting methods for QSI may be necessary to comply with the special rule in the proposed regulations. If a holder of REMIC regular interests relies on data provided on behalf of the REMIC rather than performing its own computations, the holder may be unaware that these rules will have required newly issued REMICs to alter the accrual periods over which interest reported to holders is computed. The Treasury Department and the IRS request comments on the way in which a change in accounting method for QSI should be effected.

The Treasury Department and the IRS request comments concerning the extent to which any other debt instruments provide for a significant delay between record and payment dates and, if some do, whether rules like those in the proposed regulations should be extended to them. Any comments received will be considered in connection with the publication of final regulations in the **Federal Register.**

Special Analyses

It has been determined that this notice of proposed rulemaking is not a significant regulatory action as defined in Executive Order 12866. Therefore, a regulatory flexibility assessment is not required. It has also been determined that section 553(b) of the Administrative Procedures Act (5 U.S.C. chapter 5) does not apply to these regulations, and because the regulation does not impose a collection of information on small entities, the Regulatory Flexibility Act (5 U.S.C. chapter 6) does not apply. Pursuant to section 7805(f) of the Internal Revenue Code, this notice of proposed rulemaking will be submitted to the Chief Counsel for Advocacy of the Small Business Administration for comment on its impact on small businesses.

Comments and Public Hearing

Before these proposed regulations are adopted as final regulations, consideration will be given to any written comments (a signed original and eight (8) copies) or electronic comments that are submitted timely to the IRS. The Treasury Department and IRS specifically request comments on the clarity of the proposed rules and how they may be made easier to understand. All comments will be available for public inspection and copying.

A public hearing has been scheduled for November 17, 2004, beginning at 10 a.m. in the Auditorium of the Internal Revenue Building, 1111 Constitution Avenue, NW., Washington, DC. Due to building security procedures, visitors must enter at the Constitution Avenue entrance. All visitors must present photo identification to enter the building. Because of access restrictions, visitors will not be admitted beyond the immediate entrance area more than 30 minutes before the hearing starts. For information about having your name placed on the building access list to attend the hearing, see the "FOR FURTHER INFORMATION CONTACT" section of this preamble.

The rules of 26 CFR 601.601(a)(3) apply to the hearing. Persons who wish to present oral comments at the hearing must submit written or electronic comments by November 23, 2004, and an outline of the topics to be discussed and the time to be devoted to each topic (signed original and eight (8) copies) by October 27, 2004. A period of 10 minutes will be allotted to each person for making comments. An agenda showing the schedule of speakers will be prepared after the deadline for receiving outlines has passed. Copies of the agenda will be available free of charge at the hearing.

Drafting Information

The principal author of these proposed regulations is Rebecca Asta of the Office of Associate Chief Counsel (Financial Institutions and Products). However, other personnel from the IRS and Treasury Department participated in their development.

[¶ 49,228] Proposed Regulation and Proposed Amendments of Regulations (REG-114726-04), published in the Federal Register on November 10, 2004 (corrected 12/28/2004).

Pension plans: Phased retirement: Partial retirement: Benefits paid: Benefit accrual: Testing: Retirement age.—Reg. § 1.401(a)-3 and amendments of Reg. § 1.401(a)-1, providing rules permitting distributions to be made from a pension plan under a phased retirement program, are proposed. Amendments to Reg. § 1.401(a)-1 were adopted 5/21/2007 by T.D. 9325.

AGENCY: Internal Revenue Service (IRS), Treasury.

ACTION: Notice of proposed rulemaking.

SUMMARY: This notice of proposed rulemaking contains proposed amendments to the Income Tax Regulations under section 401(a) of the Internal Revenue Code. These proposed regulations provide rules permitting distributions to be made from a pension plan under a phased retirement program and set forth requirements for a bona fide phased retirement program. The proposed regulations will provide the public with guidance regarding distributions from qualified pension plans and will affect administrators of, and participants in, such plans.

DATES: Written or electronic comments and requests for a public hearing must be received by February 8, 2005.

ADDRESSES: Send submissions to: CC:PA:LPD:PR (REG-114726-04), room 5203, Internal Revenue Service, PO Box 7604, Ben Franklin Station, Washington, DC 20044. Submissions may be hand-delivered Monday through Friday between the hours of 8 a.m. and 4 p.m. to CC:PA:LPD:PR (REG-114726-04), Courier's Desk, Internal Revenue Service, 1111 Constitution Avenue, NW., Washington, DC, or sent electronically, via the IRS Internet site at *www.irs.gov/regs* or via the Federal eRulemaking Portal at *www.regulations.gov* (indicate IRS and REG-114726-04).

FOR FURTHER INFORMATION CONTACT: Concerning the regulations, Cathy A. Vohs, 202-622-6090; concerning submissions and requests for a public hearing, contact Sonya Cruse, 202-622-7180 (not toll-free numbers).

SUPPLEMENTARY INFORMATION:

Background

As people are living longer, healthier lives, there is a greater risk that individuals may outlive their retirement savings. In addition, employers have expressed interest in encouraging older, more experienced workers to stay in the workforce. One approach that some employers have implemented is to offer employees the opportunity for phased retirement."

While there is no single approach to phased retirement, these arrangements generally provide employees who are at or near eligibility for retirement with the opportunity for a reduced schedule or workload, thereby providing a smoother transition from full-time employment to retirement. These arrangements permit the employer to retain the services of an experienced employee and provide the employee with the opportunity to continue active employment at a level that also allows greater flexibility and time away from work.

During such a transition arrangement, employees may wish to supplement their part-time income with a portion of their retirement savings. However, phased retirement can also increase the risk of outliving retirement savings for employees who begin drawing upon their retirement savings before normal retirement age. Even though the annuity distribution options offered by defined benefit plans preclude outliving benefits, early distribution of a portion of the employee's benefit will reduce the benefits available after full retirement. On the other hand, phased retirement also can provide employees additional time to save for retirement because employees continue working while they are able to do so, and can accrue additional benefits and reduce or forgo early spending of their retirement savings.

In light of this background, Treasury and the IRS issued Notice 2002-43 in the Cumulative Bulletin (2002-27 C.B. 38 (July 8, 2002)), in which comments were requested regarding phased retirement. Notice 2002-43 specifically requested comments on a wide variety of issues, including the following:

! Under what circumstances, if any, would permitting distributions from a defined benefit plan before an employee attains normal retirement age be consistent with the requirement that a defined benefit plan be established and maintained primarily for purposes of providing benefits after retirement, such as the extent to which an employee has actually reduced his or her workload?

! If there are such circumstances, how should any early retirement subsidy be treated?

Comments Received

Sixteen written comments were formally submitted in response to Notice 2002-43. These comments are in addition to the substantial number of articles and other published materials addressing phased retirement.[1]

While some of the comments expressed concerns over the potential for both dissipation of retirement funds and violation of age discrimination laws, commentators generally responded favorably to the proposal to provide guidance on facilitating phased retirement arrangements. These commentators noted that permitting pension distributions during phased retirement would be attractive to both employers and employees. Commentators also indicated that any guidance issued should provide that establishment of phased retirement arrangements be optional on the part of the employer and that participation in any such arrangement be voluntary on the part of the employee.

Most of the comments recommended that eligibility to participate in a phased retirement program be limited to employees who are eligible for immediately commencing retirement benefits under the plan (including those eligible for early retirement benefits). Other comments recommended that retirement benefits be permitted to start at a specific age or combination of age and service; however,

---

[1] See, for example, Pension & Welfare Benefits Administration, U.S. Department of Labor, "Report on Working Group on Phased Retirement to the Advisory Council on Employee Welfare & Pension Benefit Plans," 2000; Forman, Jonathan Barry, "How Federal Pension Laws Influence Individual Work and Retirement Decisions," 54 Tax Law. 143 (2000); Littler Mendelson, "Employers Consider 'Phased Retirement' to Retain Employees," Maryland Employment Law Letter, Vol 10, Issue 6 (April, 2000); Geisel, Jerry, "Rethinking Phased Retirement; IRS Call for Comment May Signal Pension Law Changes," Business Insurance (June 24, 2002); Flahaven, Brian, "Please Don't Go! Why Phased Retirement May Make Sense For Your Government," 18 Gov't Finance Review 24 (Oct. 1, 2002); NPR, Morning Edition, "Older Workers Turn to 'Phased' Retirement," (May 18, 2004) at *www.npr.org/features/feature.php?wfId=1900465*

they noted that current legislative constraints, notably the section 72(t) 10 percent additional income tax on early distributions, may limit the desirability of this option.

Some commentators advocated that any phased retirement arrangement should be cost neutral and not create additional funding obligations for employers. Others recommended that any early retirement subsidy available to an employee upon full retirement continue to be available if the employee participates in phased retirement. For example, one such commentator recommended not only that any early retirement subsidy be available upon phased retirement, but also that the subsidy so paid not be permitted to be applied to reduce the remainder of the benefit that is earned by the employee, particularly if the employee continues working past normal retirement age.

The comments were divided over what constituted phased retirement. Several recommended that phased retirement benefits be limited to cases in which there is a reduction in hours worked. Others recommended that a reduction in hours not be required and that a transition to a less stressful job also be considered phased retirement or that the full retirement benefit be payable after the attainment of a specified age or years of service without regard to any change in work.

The commentators who recommended that phased retirement benefits be limited to cases in which there is a reduction in hours worked generally recommended that the phased retirement benefits payable be proportionate to the reduction in work, based on a "dual status" approach. Under this dual status approach, an employee who reduces his or her work schedule to, for example, 80 percent of full-time would be considered to be 20 percent retired and thus entitled to 20 percent of his or her retirement benefit. The employee would continue to accrue additional benefits based on the actual hours he or she continues to work.

Several of the commentators discussed the implications of phased retirement benefits for purposes of the nondiscrimination rules of section 401(a)(4) and the anti-cutback rules of section 411(d)(6). Many of the comments said that phased retirement arrangements must be flexible and that it would be important for employers to be able to adopt a phased retirement arrangement on a temporary (even experimental) basis.

Many commentators expressed concern over the effect that a reduction in hours and the corresponding reduction in compensation would have on the final average pay of an individual for purposes of the benefit calculation when the employee fully retires. These comments generally requested guidance on this issue, including clarification as to whether an employee's final average pay is permitted to decline as a result of the employee's reduction in hours pursuant to participation in a phased retirement arrangement.

Explanation of Provisions

Overview

The proposed regulations would amend § 1.401(a)-1(b) and add § 1.401(a)-3 in order to permit a pro rata share of an employee's accrued benefit to be paid under a bona fide phased retirement program. The pro rata share is based on the extent to which the employee has reduced hours under the program. Under this pro rata approach, an employee maintains a dual status (i.e., partially retired and partially in service) during the phased retirement period. This pro rata or dual status approach to phased retirement was one of the approaches recommended by commentators.

While all approaches suggested by commentators were considered, the pro rata approach is the most consistent with the requirement that benefits be maintained primarily for retirement. Other approaches, such as permitting benefits to be fully available if an employee works reduced hours as part of phased retirement or permitting distributions of the entire accrued benefit to be paid as of a specified age prior to normal retirement age, are fundamentally inconsistent with the § 1.401(a)-1(b) principle that benefits be paid only after retirement. In addition, although a number of commentators suggested that guidance address the practice of terminating an employee with a prearranged rehiring of the employee (or similar sham transactions), the proposed regulations do not address this topic because it involves additional issues outside the scope of this project.

Rules Relating to Phased Retirement

Under the proposed regulations, a plan would be permitted to pay a pro rata portion of the employee's benefits under a bona fide phased retirement program before attainment of normal retirement age. The proposed regulations define a bona fide phased retirement program as a written, employer-adopted program pursuant to which employees may reduce the number of hours they customarily work beginning on or after a retirement date specified under the program and receive phased retirement benefits. Payment of phased retirement benefits is permitted only if the program meets certain conditions, including that employee participation is voluntary and the employee and employer expect the employee to reduce, by 20 percent or more, the number of hours the employee works during the phased retirement period.

Consistent with the pro rata approach discussed above, the maximum amount that is permitted to be paid is limited to the portion of the employee's accrued benefit equal to the product of the employee's total accrued benefit on the date the employee commences phased retirement (or any earlier date selected by the plan for administrative ease) and the employee's reduction in work. The reduction in work is based on the employee's work schedule fraction, which is the ratio of the hours that the employee is reasonably expected to work during the phased retirement period to the hours that would be worked if the employee were full-time. Based in part on commentators' concerns regarding early retirement subsidies, the proposed regulations generally require that all early retirement benefits, retirement-type subsidies, and optional forms of benefit that would be available upon full retirement be available with respect to the phased retirement accrued benefit. However, the proposed regulations would not permit payment to be made in the form of a single-sum distribution (or other eligible rollover distribution) in order to prevent the premature distribution of retirement benefits. The phased retirement benefit is an optional form of benefit protected by section 411(d)(6) and the election of a phased retirement benefit is subject to the provisions of section 417, including the required explanation of the qualified joint and survivor annuity.

Some comments suggested that phased retirement be limited to employees who have attained an age or service (or combination thereof) that is customary for retirement, e.g., where the employer has reasonably determined in good faith that participants who cease employment with the employer after that age or service combination are typically not expected to continue to perform further services of a generally comparable nature elsewhere in the workforce. Such a retirement age might be considerably lower than age 65 in certain occupations (such as police or firefighters). As discussed further below (under the heading *Application to Plans Other Than Qualified Pension Plans*), the Treasury and IRS have concluded that they do not have the authority to permit payments to begin from a section 401(k) plan under a bona fide phased retirement program before the employee attains age 59 1/2 or has a severance from employment.[2] Further, section 72(t)(3)(B) provides an additional income tax on early distributions if annuity distributions are made before the earlier of age 59 1/2 or separation from service. Accordingly, in lieu of a customary retirement age, the proposed regulations adopt a rule that is consistent with section 401(k) and section 72(t)(3)(B), under which phased retirement benefits may not be paid before an employee attains age 59 1/2.

Additional Accruals During Phased Retirement

The regulations provide that, during the phased retirement period, in addition to being entitled to the phased retirement benefit, the employee must be entitled to participate in the plan in the same manner as if the employee were still maintaining a full-time work schedule (including calculation of average earnings) and must be entitled to the same benefits (including early retirement benefits, retirement-type subsidies, and optional forms of benefits) upon full retirement as a similarly situated employee who has not elected phased retirement, except that the years of service credited under the plan for any plan year during the phased retirement period is multiplied by the ratio of the employee's actual hours of service during the year to the employee's full-time work schedule, or by the ratio of the employee's compensation to the compensation that would be paid for full-time work. Thus, for example, under a plan with a 1,000 hours of service requirement to accrue a benefit, an employee participating in a phased retirement program will accrue proportionate additional benefits, even if the employee works fewer than 1,000 hours of service.

The requirement that full-time compensation be imputed, with a proportionate reduction based on an employee's actual service, is intended to ensure that a participant is not disadvantaged by reason of choosing phased retirement. This rule precludes the need for extensive disclosure requirements, e.g., disclosure to alert participants to rights that may be lost as a result of participating in a phased retirement program. To be consistent with the requirement to use full-time compensation, the proposed regulations require an employee who was a highly compensated employee before commencing phased retirement to be treated as a highly compensated employee during phased retirement. See also § 1.414(q)-1T, A-4 & A-5.

Under the proposed regulations, the employee's final retirement benefit is comprised of the phased retirement benefit and the balance of the employee's accrued benefit under the plan (i.e., the excess of the total plan formula benefit over the portion of the accrued benefit paid as a phased retirement benefit). Upon full retirement, the phased retirement benefit can continue unchanged or the plan is permitted to offer a new election with respect to that benefit.

This bifurcation is consistent with commentators' recommendation that an employee who is in a phased retirement program has a dual status, under which the employee is treated as retired to the extent of the reduction in hours and is treated as working to the extent of the employee's continued work with the employer. This approach also ensures that a phased retirement program offers an early retirement subsidy to the extent the employee has reduced his or her hours, and that the remainder of the employee's benefit rights is not adversely affected by participation in the phased retirement program.

Testing and Adjustment of Payments

Subject to certain exceptions, the proposed regulations require periodic testing to ensure that employees in phased retirement are in fact working at the reduced schedule, as expected. Thus, unless an exception applies, a plan must provide for an annual comparison between the number of hours actually worked by an employee during a testing period and the number of hours the employee was reasonably expected to work. If the actual hours worked during the testing period are materially greater than the expected number of hours, then the employee's phased retirement benefit must be reduced prospectively. For this purpose, the employee's hours worked are materially greater than the employee's work schedule if they exceed either percent of the work schedule or 90 percent of the hours that the employee would work under a full-time schedule.

---

[2] Cf., *Edwards v. Commissioner*, T.C. Memo. 1989-409, *aff'd*, 906 F.2d 114 (4th Cir. 1990).

This annual comparison is not required after the employee is within 3 months of attaining normal retirement age or if the amount of compensation paid to the employee by the employer during the phased retirement testing period does not exceed the compensation that would be paid to the employee if he or she had worked full time multiplied by the employee's work schedule fraction. Further, no comparison is required during the first year of an employee's phased retirement or if the employee has entered into an agreement with the employer that the employee will retire within 2 years.

In the event that the employer and employee agree to increase prospectively the hours that the employee will work, then the employee's phased retirement benefit must be adjusted based on a new work schedule. The date of the agreement to increase the employee's hours is treated as a comparison date for testing purposes.

In calculating the employee's benefit at full retirement, if an employee's phased retirement benefits have been reduced during phased retirement, the employee's accrued benefit under the plan is offset by an amount that is actuarially equivalent to the additional payments made before the reduction. The potential for this offset, like other material features of the phased retirement optional form of benefit, must be disclosed as part of the QJSA explanation as required under § 1.401(a)-20, Q&A-36, and § 1.417(a)(3)-1(c)(1)(v) and (d)(1).

If the employee's phased retirement benefit is less than the maximum amount permitted or the employee's work schedule is further reduced at a later date, the proposed regulations allow a plan to provide one or more additional phased retirement benefits to the employee. The additional phased retirement benefit, commencing at a later annuity starting date, provides flexibility to reflect future reductions in the employee's work hours.

Provisions Relating to Payment After Normal Retirement Age

The proposed regulations clarify that a pension plan (i.e., a defined benefit plan or money purchase pension plan) is permitted to pay benefits upon an employee's attainment of normal retirement age. However, normal retirement age cannot be set so low as to be a subterfuge to avoid the requirements of section 401(a), and, accordingly, normal retirement age cannot be earlier than the earliest age that is reasonably representative of a typical retirement age for the covered workforce.[3]

Application to Plans Other Than Qualified Pension Plans

The regulations that limit distributions that are modified by these proposed regulations only apply to pension plans (i.e., defined benefit or money purchase pension plans). Other types of plans may be subject to less restrictive rules regarding in-service distributions, including amounts held in or attributable to: (1) qualified profit sharing and stock bonus plans to the extent not attributable to elective deferrals under section 401(k); (2) insurance annuities under section 403(b)(1), and retirement income accounts under section 403(b)(9), to the extent not attributable to elective deferrals; (3) custodial accounts under section 403(b)(7) to the extent not attributable to elective deferrals; and (4) elective deferrals under section 401(k) or 403(b). In general, these types of plans are permitted to provide for distributions after attainment of age 59 $^1/_2$, without regard to whether the employee has retired or had a severance from employment. Accordingly, they may either provide for the same phased retirement rules that are proposed in these regulations or may provide for other partial or full in-service distributions to be available after attainment of age 59 $^1/_2$. However, eligible governmental plans under section 457(b) are not generally permitted to provide for payments to be made before the earlier of severance from employment or attainment of age 70 $^1/_2$. See generally § 1.457-6.

Other Issues

The proposed regulations also authorize the Commissioner to issue additional rules in guidance of general applicability regarding the coordination of partial retirement under a phased retirement program and the plan qualification rules under section 401(a).

These proposed regulations do not address all of the issues that commentators raised in response to Notice 2002-43. Thus, as noted above, the proposed regulations do not address when a full retirement occurs and specifically do not endorse a prearranged termination and rehire as constituting a full retirement. Further, the proposed regulations only address certain tax issues. For example, although commentators pointed out that the continued availability of health coverage would be an important feature for employees in deciding whether to participate in phased retirement, the proposed regulations do not include any rules relating to health coverage. Similarly, the proposed regulations do not address any potential age discrimination issues, other than through the requirement that participation in a bona fide phased retirement program be voluntary.

Proposed Effective Date

The rules in these regulations are proposed to apply to plan years beginning on or after the date of publication of the Treasury decision adopting these rules as final regulations in the **Federal Register**. These proposed regulations cannot be relied on before they are adopted as final regulations.

Special Analyses

It has been determined that this notice of proposed rulemaking is not a significant regulatory action as defined in Executive Order 12866. Therefore, a regulatory assessment is not required. It also has been determined that section 553(b) of the Administrative Procedure Act (5 U.S.C. chapter 5) does not

---

[3] While a low normal retirement age may have a significant cost effect on a traditional defined benefit plan, this effect is not as significant for defined contribution plans or for hybrid defined benefit plans.

apply to these proposed regulations, and, because these regulations do not impose a collection of information on small entities, the Regulatory Flexibility Act (5 U.S.C. chapter 6) does not apply. Pursuant to section 7805(f) of the Internal Revenue Code, this notice of proposed rulemaking will be submitted to the Chief Counsel for Advocacy of the Small Business Administration for comment on its impact on small business.

Comments and Requests for a Public Hearing

Before these proposed regulations are adopted as final regulations, consideration will be given to any written comments (a signed original and eight (8) copies) or electronic comments that are submitted timely to the IRS. All comments will be available for public inspection and copying.

Comments are specifically requested on the following issues:

- Should eligibility to participate in a phased retirement program be extended to employees that reduce their workload using a standard, other than counting hours, to identify the reduction, and, if so, are there administrable methods for measuring the reduction?
- The proposed regulations require periodic testing of the hours an employee actually works during phased retirement, and if the hours are materially greater than the employee's phased retirement work schedule, the phased retirement benefit must be adjusted. As discussed above (under the heading *Testing*), there are a number of exceptions to this requirement. Are there other, less complex alternatives that also would ensure that phased retirement benefits correspond to the employee's reduction in hours?
- The proposed regulations require an offset for the actuarial value of additional payments made before a reduction in phased retirement benefits. Should the regulations permit this offset to be calculated without regard to any early retirement subsidy and, if so, how should a subsidy be quantified?
- The proposed regulations clarify that the right to receive a phased retirement benefit as a partial payment is a separate optional form of benefit for purposes of section 411(d)(6) and, thus, is a benefit, right, or feature for purposes of the special nondiscrimination rules at § 1.401(a)(4)-4. Comments are requested on whether there are facts and circumstances under which the age and service conditions for a particular employer's phased retirement program should be disregarded in applying § 1.401(a)(4)-4 (even if the program may only be in place for a temporary period), or under which the rules at § 1.401(a)(4)-4 should otherwise be modified with respect to phased retirement.
- Should any special rules be adopted to coordinate the rules regarding distributions and continued accruals during phased retirement with a plan's provisions regarding employment after normal retirement age, such as suspension of benefits?

A public hearing may be scheduled if requested in writing by a person that timely submits written comments. If a public hearing is scheduled, notice of the date, time and place for the hearing will be published in the **Federal Register**.

Drafting Information

The principal author of these proposed regulations is Cathy A. Vohs of the Office of the Division Counsel/Associate Chief Counsel (Tax Exempt and Government Entities). However, other personnel from the IRS and Treasury participated in their development.

[¶ 49,234] Proposed Regulations (REG-130370-04), published in the Federal Register on December 30, 2004.

Group health plan requirements: Portability: Regulations.—Reg. § 54.9801-7 and amendments of Reg. §§ 54.9801-1, 54.9801-2, 54.9801-4—54.9801-6 and 54.9831-1, relating to the portability requirements for group health plans and issuers of health insurance coverage offered in connection with a group health plan, are proposed.

AGENCIES: Internal Revenue Service, Department of the Treasury; Employee Benefits Security Administration, Department of Labor; Centers for Medicare & Medicaid Services, Department of Health and Human Services.

ACTION: Notice of proposed rulemaking and request for comments.

SUMMARY: These proposed rules would clarify certain portability requirements for group health plans and issuers of health insurance coverage offered in connection with a group health plan. These rules propose to implement changes made to the Internal Revenue Code, the Employee Retirement Income Security Act, and the Public Health Service Act enacted as part of the Health Insurance Portability and Accountability Act of 1996.

DATES : Written comments on this notice of proposed rulemaking are invited and must be received by the Departments on or before March 30, 2005.

ADDRESSES: Written comments should be submitted with a signed original and three copies (except for electronic submissions) to any of the addresses specified below. Any comment that is submitted to any Department will be shared with the other Departments.

Comments to the IRS can be addressed to:

CC:PA:LPD:PR (REG-130370-04)
Room 5203
Internal Revenue Service
POB 7604, Ben Franklin Station

Washington, DC 20044
In the alternative, comments may be hand-delivered between the hours of 8 a.m. and 4 p.m. to:
CC:PA:LPD:PR (REG-130370-04)
Courier's Desk
Internal Revenue Service
1111 Constitution Avenue, NW.
Washington, DC 20224
Alternatively, comments may be transmitted electronically via the IRS Internet site at: *www.irs.gov/regs* or via the Federal eRulemaking Portal at *www.regulations.gov* (IRS - REG-130370-04).

Comments to the Department of Labor can be addressed to:
U.S. Department of Labor
Employee Benefits Security Administration
200 Constitution Avenue NW., Room C-5331
Washington, DC 20210
Attention : Proposed Portability Requirements
Alternatively, comments may be hand-delivered between the hours of 9:00 a.m. and 5:00 p.m. to the same address. Comments may also be transmitted by e-mail to: e-ohpsca.ebsa@dol.gov.

Comments to HHS can be submitted as described below:
In commenting, please refer to file code CMS-2158-P. Because of staff and resource limitations, we cannot accept comments by facsimile (FAX) transmission.

You may submit comments in one of three ways (no duplicates, please):

1. *Electronically*. You may submit electronic comments on specific issues in this regulation to *http://www.cms.hhs.gov/regulations/ecomments*. (Attachments should be in Microsoft Word, WordPerfect, or Excel; however, we prefer Microsoft Word.)

2. *By mail*. You may mail written comments (one original and two copies) to the following address ONLY:

Centers for Medicare & Medicaid Services,
Department of Health and Human Services,
Attention: CMS-2158-P,
P.O. Box 8017,
Baltimore, MD 21244-8010.

Please allow sufficient time for mailed comments to be received before the close of the comment period.

3. *By hand or courier*. If you prefer, you may deliver (by hand or courier) your written comments (one original and two copies) before the close of the comment period to one of the following addresses. If you intend to deliver your comments to the Baltimore address, please call telephone number (410) 786-7195 in advance to schedule your arrival with one of our staff members.

Room 445-G, Hubert H. Humphrey Building,
200 Independence Avenue, SW.,
Washington, DC 20201; or
7500 Security Boulevard,
Baltimore, MD 21244-1850.

(Because access to the interior of the HHH Building is not readily available to persons without Federal Government identification, commenters are encouraged to leave their comments in the CMS drop slots located in the main lobby of the building. A stamp-in clock is available for persons wishing to retain a proof of filing by stamping in and retaining an extra copy of the comments being filed.)

Comments mailed to the addresses indicated as appropriate for hand or courier delivery may be delayed and received after the comment period.

Submission of comments on paperwork requirements. You may submit comments on this document's paperwork requirements by mailing your comments to the addresses provided at the end of the "Collection of Information Requirements" section in this document.

All submissions to the IRS will be open to public inspection and copying in room 1621, 1111 Constitution Avenue, NW., Washington, DC from 9 a.m. to 4 p.m.

All submissions to the Department of Labor will be open to public inspection and copying in the Public Disclosure Room, Employee Benefits Security Administration, U.S. Department of Labor, Room N-1513, 200 Constitution Avenue, NW., Washington, DC from 8:30 a.m. to 4:30 p.m.

All submissions timely submitted to HHS will be available for public inspection as they are received, generally beginning approximately three weeks after publication of a document, at the headquarters for the Centers for Medicare & Medicaid Services, 7500 Security Boulevard, Baltimore, MD 21244, Monday through Friday of each week from 8:30 a.m. to 4:00 p.m. To schedule an appointment to view public comments, phone 410-786-7195.

FOR FURTHER INFORMATION CONTACT: Dave Mlawsky, Centers for Medicare & Medicaid Services (CMS), Department of Health and Human Services, at 1-877-267-2323 ext. 61565; Amy Turner, Employee Benefits Security Administration, Department of Labor, at (202) 693-8335; or Russ Weinheimer, Internal Revenue Service, Department of the Treasury, at (202) 622-6080.

SUPPLEMENTARY INFORMATION:

Customer Service Information

To assist consumers and the regulated community, the Departments have issued questions and answers concerning HIPAA. Individuals interested in obtaining copies of Department of Labor publications concerning changes in health care law may call a toll free number, 1-866-444-EBSA (3272), or access the publications on-line at www.dol.gov/ebsa, the Department of Labor's website. These regulations as well as other information on the new health care laws are also available on the Department of Labor's interactive web pages, Health *E* laws. In addition, CMS's publication entitled "Protecting Your Health Insurance Coverage" is available by calling 1-800-633-4227 or on the Department of Health and Human Services' website (www.cms.hhs.gov/hipaa1), which includes the interactive webpages, HIPAA Online. Copies of the HIPAA regulations, as well as notices and press releases related to HIPAA and other health care laws, are also available at the above-referenced websites.

A. Background

The Health Insurance Portability and Accountability Act of 1996 (HIPAA), Public Law 104-191, was enacted on August 21, 1996. HIPAA amended the Internal Revenue Code of 1986 (Code), the Employee Retirement Income Security Act of 1974 (ERISA), and the Public Health Service Act (PHS Act) to provide for, among other things, improved portability and continuity of health coverage. Interim final regulations implementing the HIPAA provisions were first made available to the public on April 1, 1997 (published in the **Federal Register** on April 8, 1997, 62 FR 16894) (April 1997 interim rules). On December 29, 1997, the Departments published a clarification of the April 1997 interim rules as they relate to excepted benefits. On October 25, 1999, the Departments published a notice in the **Federal Register** (64 FR 57520) soliciting additional comments on the portability requirements based on the experience of plans and issuers operating under the April 1997 interim rules.

After consideration of all the comments received on the portability provisions, the Departments are publishing final regulations elsewhere in this issue of the **Federal Register**. These proposed rules address additional and discrete issues for which the Departments are soliciting further comment before promulgating final regulations.

B. Overview of the Proposed Regulations

1. *Rules Relating to Creditable Coverage - 26 CFR 54.9801-4, 29 CFR 2590.701-4, 45 CFR 146.113*

Tolling of the 63-day break-in-coverage rule

These proposed rules would modify the 63-day break-in-coverage rules with one significant substantive change. Under the proposed rules, the beginning of the period that is used for determining whether a significant break in coverage has occurred (generally 63 days) is tolled in cases in which a certificate of creditable coverage is not provided on or before the day coverage ceases. In those cases, the significant-break-in-coverage period is tolled until a certificate is provided but not beyond 44 days after the coverage ceases.

The Departments have fashioned this tolling rule (and a similar tolling rule for the 30-day period for requesting special enrollment) in an effort to address the inequity of individuals' losing coverage without being aware that the coverage has ended while minimizing the burdens on subsequent plans and issuers that are not responsible for providing the missing or untimely certificates. Numerous situations have come to the attention of the Departments in which an individual's health coverage is terminated but in which the individual does not learn of the termination of coverage until well after it occurs. The statute generally requires that a certificate of creditable coverage be provided at the time an individual ceases to be covered under a plan. The statute, the April 1997 interim rules, and the final regulations (published elsewhere in this issue of the **Federal Register**) all permit a plan or issuer to provide the certificate at a later date if it is provided at a time consistent with notices required under a COBRA continuation provision. The statute also directs the Secretaries to establish rules to prevent a plan or issuer's failure to provide a certificate timely from adversely affecting the individual's subsequent coverage. If a plan or issuer chooses to provide a certificate later than the date an individual loses coverage, as the regulations permit in certain circumstances, these proposed rules provide that an individual should not suffer from this rule of convenience for the plan or issuer. However, to prevent the abuse that might result from an open-ended tolling rule, an outside limit of 44 days is placed on this relief. This reflects the fact that, in most cases, plans and issuers are required to provide certificates within 44 days (although some plans and issuers may be required to provide certificates sooner than 44 days after coverage ceases and some entities are not required to provide certificates at all). The Departments have adopted this uniform limit on the tolling rule for purposes of consistency. New examples have been added to illustrate the tolling rule.

2. *Evidence of Creditable Coverage - 26 CFR 54.9801-5, 29 CFR 2590.701-5, 45 CFR 146.115*

Information in certificate and model certificate

These proposed rules would modify the required elements for the educational statement in certificates of creditable coverage to require a disclosure about the Family and Medical Leave Act. Use of the first model certificate below by group health plans and group health insurance issuers, or use of the appropriate model certificate that appears in the preamble to the related final regulations published elsewhere in this issue of the **Federal Register**, will satisfy the requirements of paragraph (a)(3)(ii) in this section of the final regulations. Similarly, for purposes of complying with those final regulations, State Medicaid programs may use the second version below, or may use the appropriate model certificate that appears in the preamble to those final regulations. Thus, until this proposed regulation is published as a final regulation, entities may use either the model certificates published below, or those published elsewhere in this issue of the **Federal Register**. For entities that choose not to use the model certificates below until this proposed regulation is published as a final regulation, we welcome comments as to the applicability date for using them.

CERTIFICATE OF GROUP HEALTH PLAN COVERAGE

1. Date of this certificate:__________
2. Name of group health plan:__________

____

3. Name of participant:__________
4. Identification number of participant:__________

5 Name of individuals to whom this certificate applies:__________

____

6. Name, address, and telephone number of plan administrator or issuer responsible for providing this certificate:__________

____

____

7. For further information, call:__________
8. If the individual(s) identified in line 5 has (have) at least 18 months of creditable coverage (disregarding periods of coverage before a 63-day break), check here and skip lines 9 and 10:______
9. Date waiting period or affiliation period (if any) began:__________
10. Date coverage began:__________
11. Date coverage ended (or if coverage has not ended, enter "continuing"):__________

[Note: separate certificates will be furnished if information is not identical for the participant and each beneficiary.]

Statement of HIPAA Portability Rights

IMPORTANT—KEEP THIS CERTIFICATE. This certificate is evidence of your coverage under this plan. Under a federal law known as HIPAA, you may need evidence of your coverage to reduce a preexisting condition exclusion period under another plan, to help you get special enrollment in another plan, or to get certain types of individual health coverage even if you have health problems.

Preexisting condition exclusions. Some group health plans restrict coverage for medical conditions present before an individual's enrollment. These restrictions are known as "preexisting condition exclusions." A preexisting condition exclusion can apply only to conditions for which medical advice, diagnosis, care, or treatment was recommended or received within the 6 months before your "enrollment date." Your enrollment date is your first day of coverage under the plan, or, if there is a waiting period, the first day of your waiting period (typically, your first day of work). In addition, a preexisting condition exclusion cannot last for more than 12 months after your enrollment date (18 months if you are a late enrollee). Finally, a preexisting condition exclusion cannot apply to pregnancy and cannot apply to a child who is enrolled in health coverage within 30 days after birth, adoption, or placement for adoption.

If a plan imposes a preexisting condition exclusion, the length of the exclusion must be reduced by the amount of your prior creditable coverage. Most health coverage is creditable coverage, including group health plan coverage, COBRA continuation coverage, coverage under an individual health policy, Medicare, Medicaid, State Children's Health Insurance Program (SCHIP), and coverage through high-risk pools and the Peace Corps. Not all forms of creditable coverage are required to provide certificates like this one. If you do not receive a certificate for past coverage, talk to your new plan administrator.

You can add up any creditable coverage you have, including the coverage shown on this certificate. However, if at any time you went for 63 days or more without any coverage (called a break in coverage) a plan may not have to count the coverage you had before the break.

—Therefore, once your coverage ends, you should try to obtain alternative coverage as soon as possible to avoid a 63-day break. You may use this certificate as evidence of your creditable coverage to reduce the length of any preexisting condition exclusion if you enroll in another plan.

Right to get special enrollment in another plan. Under HIPAA, if you lose your group health plan coverage, you may be able to get into another group health plan for which you are eligible (such as a spouse's plan), even if the plan generally does not accept late enrollees, if you request enrollment within 30 days. (Additional special enrollment rights are triggered by marriage, birth, adoption, and placement for adoption.)

—Therefore, once your coverage ends, if you are eligible for coverage in another plan (such as a spouse's plan), you should request special enrollment as soon as possible.

Prohibition against discrimination based on a health factor . Under HIPAA, a group health plan may not keep you (or your dependents) out of the plan based on anything related to your health. Also, a group health plan may not charge you (or your dependents) more for coverage, based on health, than the amount charged a similarly situated individual.

Right to individual health coverage. Under HIPAA, if you are an "eligible individual," you have a right to buy certain individual health policies (or in some states, to buy coverage through a high-risk pool) without a preexisting condition exclusion. To be an eligible individual, you must meet the following requirements:

- You have had coverage for at least 18 months without a break in coverage of 63 days or more;
- Your most recent coverage was under a group health plan (which can be shown by this certificate);

• Your group coverage was not terminated because of fraud or nonpayment of premiums;

• You are not eligible for COBRA continuation coverage or you have exhausted your COBRA benefits (or continuation coverage under a similar state provision); and

• You are not eligible for another group health plan, Medicare, or Medicaid, and do not have any other health insurance coverage.

The right to buy individual coverage is the same whether you are laid off, fired, or quit your job.

—Therefore, if you are interested in obtaining individual coverage and you meet the other criteria to be an eligible individual, you should apply for this coverage as soon as possible to avoid losing your eligible individual status due to a 63-day break.

Special information for people on FMLA leave. If you are taking leave under the Family and Medical Leave Act (FMLA) and you drop health coverage during your leave, any days without health coverage while on FMLA leave will not count towards a 63-day break in coverage. In addition, if you do not return from leave, the 30-day period to request special enrollment in another plan will not start before your FMLA leave ends.

—Therefore, when you apply for other health coverage, you should tell your plan administrator or health insurer about any prior FMLA leave.

State flexibility . This certificate describes minimum HIPAA protections under federal law. States may require insurers and HMOs to provide additional protections to individuals in that state.

For more information. If you have questions about your HIPAA rights, you may contact your state insurance department or the U.S. Department of Labor, Employee Benefits Security Administration (EBSA) toll-free at 1-866-444-3272 (for free HIPAA publications ask for publications concerning changes in health care laws). You may also contact the CMS publication hotline at 1-800-633-4227 (ask for "Protecting Your Health Insurance Coverage"). These publications and other useful information are also available on the Internet at: *http://www.dol.gov/ebsa,* the DOL's interactive web pages - Health E laws, or *http://www.cms.hhs.gov/hipaa1*.

CERTIFICATE OF MEDICAID COVERAGE

1. Date of this certificate:____________

2. Name of state Medicaid program:____________

3. Name of recipient:____________

4. Identification number of recipient:____________

5 Name of individuals to whom this certificate applies:____________

6. Name, address, and telephone number of state Medicaid agency responsible for providing this certificate:____________

7. For further information, call:____________

8. If the individual(s) identified in line 5 has (have) at least 18 months of creditable coverage (disregarding periods of coverage before a 63-day break), check here and skip line 9.____

9. Date coverage began:____________

10. Date coverage ended (or if coverage has not ended, enter "continuing"):____________

[Note: separate certificates will be furnished if information is not identical for the recipient and each dependant]

Statement of HIPAA Portability Rights

IMPORTANT—KEEP THIS CERTIFICATE. This certificate is evidence of your coverage under this state Medicaid program. Under a federal law known as HIPAA, you may need evidence of your coverage to reduce a preexisting condition exclusion period under a group health plan, to help you get special enrollment in a group health plan, or to get certain types of individual health coverage even if you have health problems.

Preexisting condition exclusions. Some group health plans restrict coverage for medical conditions present before an individual's enrollment. These restrictions are known as "preexisting condition exclusions." A preexisting condition exclusion can apply only to conditions for which medical advice, diagnosis, care, or treatment was recommended or received within the 6 months before your "enrollment date." Your enrollment date is your first day of coverage under the plan, or, if there is a waiting period, the first day of your waiting period (typically, your first day of work). In addition, a preexisting condition exclusion cannot last for more than 12 months after your enrollment date (18 months if you are a late enrollee). Finally, a preexisting condition exclusion cannot apply to pregnancy and cannot apply to a child who is enrolled in health coverage within 30 days after birth, adoption, or placement for adoption.

If a plan imposes a preexisting condition exclusion, the length of the exclusion must be reduced by the amount of your prior creditable coverage. Most health coverage is creditable coverage, including group health plan coverage, COBRA continuation coverage, coverage under an individual health policy, Medicare, Medicaid, State Children's Health Insurance Program (SCHIP), and coverage through high-risk pools and the Peace Corps. Not all forms of creditable coverage are required to provide certificates like this one. If you do not receive a certificate for past coverage, talk to your new plan administrator.

You can add up any creditable coverage you have, including the coverage shown on this certificate. However, if at any time you went for 63 days or more without any coverage (called a break in coverage) a plan may not have to count the coverage you had before the break.

—Therefore, once your coverage ends, you should try to obtain alternative coverage as soon as possible to avoid a 63-day break. You may use this certificate as evidence of your creditable coverage to reduce the length of any preexisting condition exclusion if you enroll in a group health plan.

Right to get special enrollment in another plan. Under HIPAA, if you lose your group health plan coverage, you may be able to get into another group health plan for which you are eligible (such as a spouse's plan), even if the plan generally does not accept late enrollees, if you request enrollment within 30 days. (Additional special enrollment rights are triggered by marriage, birth, adoption, and placement for adoption.)

—Therefore, once your coverage in a group health plan ends, if you are eligible for coverage in another plan (such as a spouse's plan), you should request special enrollment as soon as possible.

Prohibition against discrimination based on a health factor . Under HIPAA, a group health plan may not keep you (or your dependents) out of the plan based on anything related to your health. Also, a group health plan may not charge you (or your dependents) more for coverage, based on health, than the amount charged a similarly situated individual.

Right to individual health coverage. Under HIPAA, if you are an "eligible individual," you have a right to buy certain individual health policies (or in some states, to buy coverage through a high-risk pool) without a preexisting condition exclusion. To be an eligible individual, you must meet the following requirements:

- You have had coverage for at least 18 months without a break in coverage of 63 days or more;
- Your most recent coverage was under a group health plan;
- Your group coverage was not terminated because of fraud or nonpayment of premiums;
- You are not eligible for COBRA continuation coverage or you have exhausted your COBRA benefits (or continuation coverage under a similar state provision); and
- You are not eligible for another group health plan, Medicare, or Medicaid, and do not have any other health insurance coverage.

The right to buy individual coverage is the same whether you are laid off, fired, or quit your job.

—Therefore, if you are interested in obtaining individual coverage and you meet the other criteria to be an eligible individual, you should apply for this coverage as soon as possible to avoid losing your eligible individual status due to a 63-day break.

Special information for people on FMLA leave. If you are taking leave under the Family and Medical Leave Act (FMLA) and you drop health coverage during your leave, any days without health coverage while on FMLA leave will not count towards a 63-day break in coverage. In addition, if you do not return from leave, the 30-day period to request special enrollment in another plan will not start before your FMLA leave ends.

—Therefore, when you apply for other health coverage, you should tell your plan administrator or health insurer about any prior FMLA leave.

State flexibility . This certificate describes minimum HIPAA protections under federal law. States may require insurers and HMOs to provide additional protections to individuals in that state.

For more information. If you have questions about your HIPAA rights, you may contact your state insurance department or the U.S. Department of Labor, Employee Benefits Security Administration (EBSA) toll-free at 1-866-444-3272 (for free HIPAA publications ask for publications concerning changes in health care laws). You may also contact the CMS publication hotline at 1-800-633-4227 (ask for "Protecting Your Health Insurance Coverage"). These publications and other useful information are also available on the Internet at: *http://www.dol.gov/ebsa* or *http://www.cms.hhs.gov/hipaa1*.

3. *Special Enrollment Periods - 26 CFR 54.9801-6, 29 CFR 2590.701-6, 45 CFR 146.117*

Tolling of the special enrollment period

Under HIPAA, the April 1997 interim rules, and the final regulations, an individual wishing to special enroll following a loss of coverage is generally required to request enrollment not later than 30 days after the loss of eligibility, termination of employer contributions, or exhaustion of COBRA continuation coverage. For individuals whose coverage ceases and a certificate of creditable coverage is not provided on or before the date coverage ceases, this regulation provides for proposed tolling rules similar to those described above for determining a significant break. That is, the special enrollment period terminates at the end of the 30-day period that begins on the first day after the earlier of the date that a certificate of creditable coverage is provided or the date 44 days after coverage ceases.

Modification of special enrollment procedures and when coverage begins under special enrollment

The April 1997 interim rules did not establish procedures for processing requests for special enrollment beyond affirming the statutory requirement that requests be made not later than 30 days after the event giving rise to the special enrollment right and providing that the same requirements could be imposed on special enrollees that were imposed on other enrollees (e.g., that the request be made in writing). Some examples in the April 1997 interim rules could be read to suggest that plans and issuers could require individuals requesting special enrollment to file completed applications for health coverage by the end of the special enrollment period.

It has been brought to the Departments' attention that some plans and issuers were imposing application requirements that could not reasonably be completed within the special enrollment period (for example, requiring the social security number of a newborn within 30 days of the birth), effectively denying individuals their right to special enroll their dependents. In this regard, the statute merely requires an employee to request special enrollment, or an individual to seek to enroll, during the special enrollment period. These proposed regulations preserve individuals' access to special enrollment by clarifying that during the special enrollment period individuals are only required to make an oral or written request for special enrollment.

The proposed regulations provide further that after a timely request, the plan or issuer may require the individual to complete all enrollment materials within a reasonable time after the end of the special enrollment period. However, the enrollment procedure may only require information required from individuals who enroll when first eligible and information about the event giving rise to the special enrollment right. While a plan can impose a deadline for submitting the completed enrollment materials, the deadline must be extended for information that an individual making reasonable efforts cannot obtain within that deadline.

Thus, even where a plan requires social security numbers from individuals who enroll when first eligible, the plan must provide an extended deadline for receiving the social security number in the case of a newborn. In no event could a plan deny special enrollment for newborns because an employee could not provide a social security number for the newborn within the special enrollment period.

As regards the effective date of coverage for special enrollments, the proposed rules generally follow the statute, the April 1997 interim final rules, and the final regulations being published elsewhere in this issue of the **Federal Register**. However clarifications of the effective date of coverage are added to conform to the clarification of the special enrollment procedures. Where the special enrollment right results from a loss of eligibility for coverage or marriage, coverage generally must begin no later than the first day of the first calendar month after the date the plan or issuer receives the request for special enrollment. However, if the plan or issuer requires completion of additional enrollment materials, coverage must begin no later than the first day of the first calendar month after the plan or issuer receives enrollment materials that are substantially complete.

Where the special enrollment right results from a birth, coverage must begin on the date of birth. In the case of adoption or placement for adoption, coverage must begin no later than the date of such adoption or placement for adoption. If a plan or issuer requires completion of additional enrollment materials, the plan or issuer must provide benefits once the plan or issuer receives substantially complete enrollment materials. However, the benefits provided at that time must be retroactive to the date of birth, adoption, or placement for adoption.

The Departments welcome comments on these aspects of the proposed rule.

4. *Interaction with the Family and Medical Leave Act -26 CFR 54.9801-7, 29 CFR 701-8, 45 CFR 146.120*

The proposed rules address how the HIPAA portability requirements apply in situations where a person is on leave under the Family and Medical Leave Act of 1993 (FMLA). A general principle of FMLA is that an employee returning from leave under FMLA should generally be in the same position the employee was in before taking leave. At issue is how to reconcile that principle of FMLA with the HIPAA rights and requirements that are triggered by an individual ending coverage under a group health plan. These proposed regulations provide specific rules that clarify how HIPAA and FMLA interact when the coverage of an employee or an employee's dependent ends in connection with an employee taking leave under FMLA.

With respect to the rules concerning a significant break in coverage, if an employee takes FMLA leave and does not continue group health coverage for any part of the leave, the period of FMLA leave without coverage is not taken into account in determining whether a significant break in coverage has occurred for the employee or any dependents. To the extent an individual needs to demonstrate that coverage ceased in connection with FMLA leave (which would toll any significant break with respect to another plan or issuer), these regulations provide that a plan or issuer must take into account all information that it obtains about an employee's FMLA leave. Further, if an individual attests to the period of FMLA leave and the individual cooperates with a plan's or issuer's efforts to verify the individual's FMLA leave, the plan or issuer must treat the individual as having been on FMLA leave for the period attested to for purposes of determining if the individual had a significant break in coverage. Nonetheless, a plan or issuer is not prevented from modifying its initial determination of FMLA leave if it determines that the individual did not have the claimed FMLA leave, provided that the plan or issuer follows procedures for reconsideration similar to those set forth in the final rules governing determinations of creditable coverage.

The question has arisen whether it would be appropriate to waive the general requirement to provide automatic certificates of creditable coverage in the case of an individual who declines coverage when electing FMLA leave if the individual will be reinstated at the end of FMLA leave. At the time an employee elects FMLA leave, the employer (as well as the employee) may not know if the employee will later return from FMLA leave and elect to be reinstated. Requiring plans and issuers to provide certificates when individuals cease health coverage in connection with FMLA leave may result in some certificates being issued when individuals ceasing coverage will not need the certificates as evidence of coverage (because of later reinstatement). However, automatic issuance likely imposes less burden because the plan or issuer does not need to determine whether a certificate is required. Moreover, automatic issuance eliminates the need for remedial measures if an individual expected to be reinstated in fact is not later reinstated. Thus, these proposed regulations clarify there is no exception to the general rule requiring automatic certificates when coverage ends and provide that if an individual covered under a group health plan takes FMLA leave and ceases coverage under the plan, an automatic certificate must be provided.

With respect to the special enrollment rules, an individual (or a dependent of the individual) who is covered under a group health plan and who takes FMLA leave has a loss of eligibility that results in a special enrollment period if the individual's group health coverage is terminated at any time during FMLA leave and the individual does not return to work for the employer at the end of FMLA leave. This special enrollment period begins when the period of FMLA leave ends. Moreover, the rules that delay the start of the special enrollment period until the receipt of a certificate of creditable coverage continue to operate.

5. *Special rules—Excepted plans and excepted benefits—26 CFR 54.9831-1, 29 CFR 2590.732, 45 CFR 146.145*

Determination of number of plans

Various provisions in Chapter 100 of the Code, Part 7 of Subtitle B of Title I of ERISA, and Title XXVII of the PHS Act apply when an individual commences coverage or terminates coverage under a group health plan. For example, a certificate of creditable coverage must be provided when an individual ceases to be covered under a group health plan. Under the April 1997 interim rules, it was not always clear whether an individual changing benefit elections among those offered by an employer or employee organization was merely switching between benefit packages under a single plan or was switching from one plan to another. These proposed regulations add rules to remove this uncertainty.

Under these proposed regulations, all medical care benefits made available by an employer or employee organization (including a board of trustees of a multiemployer trust) are generally considered to constitute one group health plan (the default rule). However, the employer or employee organization can establish more than one group health plan if it is clear from the instruments governing the arrangements to provide medical care benefits that the benefits are being provided under separate plans and if the arrangements are operated pursuant to the instruments as separate plans. A multiemployer plan and a nonmultiemployer plan are always separate plans. Under an anti-abuse rule, separate plans are aggregated to the extent necessary to prevent the evasion of any legal requirement.

These rules provide plan sponsors great flexibility while minimizing the burden of making decisions about how many plans to maintain. For example, many employers may wish to minimize the number of certificates of creditable coverage required to be furnished to continuing employees. Under the default rule, because all health benefits provided by an employer are considered a single group health plan, there is no need to furnish a certificate of creditable coverage when an employee merely switches coverage among the options made available by the employer. This need would arise only if the employer designated separate benefit packages as separate plans in the plan documents and only if the benefit packages were also operated pursuant to the plan documents as separate plans.

The anti-abuse rule limits the flexibility of these rules to prevent evasions. For example, a plan sponsor might design an arrangement under which the participation of each of many employees in the arrangement would be considered a separate plan. On the face of it, such an arrangement might appear to satisfy the requirement for a plan being exempt from the requirements of Chapter 100 of the Code, Part 7 of ERISA, and Title XXVII of the PHS Act because on the first day of the plan year each plan would have fewer than two participants who are current employees. This would give the impression that the plans would not have to comply with the prohibitions against discriminating based on one or more health factors, with the restrictions on preexisting condition exclusions, nor with any of the other requirements of Chapter 100 of the Code, Part 7 of ERISA, and Title XXVII of the PHS Act. The anti-abuse rule would require the aggregation of plans under such an arrangement to the extent necessary to make the plans subject to the requirements of Chapter 100 of the Code, Part 7 of ERISA, and Title XXVII of the PHS Act. The anti-abuse rule would apply in similar fashion to prevent the evasion of any other law that applies to group health plans or to the parties administering them or providing benefits under them.

Counting the average number of employees

These proposed regulations add rules for counting the average number of employees employed by an employer during a year.[1] Various rules in Chapter 100 of the Code, Part 7 of ERISA, and Title XXVII of the PHS Act require the determination of such an average number, including the Mental Health Parity Act provisions, the guaranteed access provisions under the PHS Act for small employers, and the exemption from the excise tax under the Code for certain small employers.

Under these proposed regulations, the average number of employees employed by an employer is determined by using a full-time equivalents method. Each full-time employee employed for the entire previous calendar year counts as one employee. Full-time employees employed less than the entire previous calendar year and part-time employees are counted by totaling their employment hours in the previous calendar year (but not to exceed 40 hours for any week) and dividing that number by the annual full-time hours under the employer's general employment practices (but not exceeding 40

---

[1] The rules for determining the average number of employees employed by an employer during a year are not used for counting the number employed by the employer on a given day, such as the first day of a plan year.

hours per week). Any resulting fraction is disregarded. For example, if these calculations produce a result of 50.9, the average number of employees is considered to be 50. If an employer existed for less than the entire previous calendar year (including not being in existence at all), then the determination of the average number of employees is made by estimating the average number of employees that it is reasonably expected that the employer will employ on business days in the current calendar year. For a multiemployer plan, the number of employees employed by the employer with the most employees is attributed to each employer with at least one employee participating in the plan.

C. Economic Impact and Paperwork Burden

Summary—Department of Labor and Department of Health and Human Services

HIPAA's group market portability provisions, which limit the scope and application of preexisting condition exclusions and establish special enrollment rights, provide a minimum standard of protection designed to increase access to health coverage. The Departments crafted these proposed regulations to secure these protections under certain special circumstances, consistent with the intent of Congress, and to do so in a manner that is economically efficient. The Departments are unable to quantify the regulations' economic benefits and costs, but believe that their benefits will justify their costs.

HIPAA's primary economic effects ensue directly from its statutory provisions. HIPAA's statutory group market portability provisions extend coverage to certain individuals and preexisting conditions not otherwise covered. This extension of coverage entails both benefits and costs. Individuals enjoying expanded coverage will realize benefits, sometimes including improvements in health and relief from so-called "job lock." The costs of HIPAA's portability provisions generally include the cost of extending coverage, as well as certain attendant administrative costs. The Departments believe that the benefits of HIPAA are concentrated in a relatively small population, while the costs are distributed broadly across group plan enrollees. The economic effects of HIPAA's statutory portability provisions are discussed in detail in the preamble to the final regulation under the "Effects of the Statute" of the "Basis for Assessment of Economic Impact" section, published elsewhere in this issue of the **Federal Register**.

By clarifying and securing HIPAA's statutory portability protections, these proposed regulations will help ensure that HIPAA rights are fully realized. The result is likely to be a small increase at the margin in the economic effects of HIPAA's statutory portability provisions.

These proposed regulations are intended to secure and implement HIPAA's group market portability and special enrollment provisions under certain special circumstances. The regulations will secure HIPAA's portability rights for individuals who are not timely notified that their coverage has ended and for individuals whose coverage ends in connection with the taking of leave that is guaranteed under FMLA. The regulations also will clarify and thereby secure individuals' special enrollment rights under HIPAA, and clarify the methodologies to be used by employers to determine the number of plans offered and the average number of individuals employed during a given year.

Additional economic benefits derive from the regulations' clarifications of HIPAA requirements. The regulations will reduce uncertainty and costly disputes between employees, employers and issuers, and promote confidence among employees in health benefits' value, thereby promoting labor market efficiency and fostering the establishment and continuation by employers of group health plans.

Benefits under these regulations will be concentrated among a small number of affected individuals while costs will be spread thinly across group plan enrollees.

Affected individuals will generally include those who would have lost access to coverage for needed medical care after being denied HIPAA portability and/or special enrollment rights due to time spent without coverage prior to receiving a certificate or while on FMLA-guaranteed leave. The benefits of these regulations for any particular affected individual may be significant. As noted above and under "Effects of the Statute" in the "Basis for Assessment of Economic Impact" section of the preamble to the final regulation, published elsewhere in this issue of the **Federal Register**, access to coverage for needed medical care is important to individuals' health and productivity. However, the number of affected individuals, and therefore the aggregate cost of extended access to coverage under these regulations, is expected to be small, for several reasons. First, these regulations extend HIPAA rights only in instances where individuals are not timely notified that their coverage has ended or their coverage ends in connection with the taking of FMLA-guaranteed leave. Second, the period over which this regulation extends rights will often be short, insofar as certificates are often provided promptly after coverage ends and many family leave periods are far shorter than the guaranteed 12 weeks. Third, it is generally in individuals' interest to minimize periods of uninsurance. Individuals are likely to exercise their portability and special enrollment rights as soon as possible after coverage ends, which will often be before any extension of such rights under these regulations becomes effective. Fourth, only a portion of individuals who enroll in health plans in circumstances where these regulations alone guarantee their special enrollment or portability rights would otherwise have been denied such rights. Fifth, only a small minority of individuals who avoid a significant break in coverage as a direct result of these regulations would otherwise have lost coverage for needed medical care. (The affected minority would be those who suffer from preexisting conditions, join health plans that exclude coverage for such conditions, and require treatment of such conditions during the exclusion periods.)

Affected individuals may also include some who would have been denied special enrollment rights if plans or issuers failed to recognize their requests for special enrollment or imposed unreasonable deadlines or requirements for completion of enrollment materials.

As noted above, the Departments expect that these regulations will increase at the margin the economic effects of HIPAA's statutory portability provisions. For the reasons stated immediately above, the Departments believe that these increases will be small on aggregate, adding only a small increment to the costs attributable to HIPAA's statutory portability provisions, which themselves amount to a small fraction of one percent of health plan expenditures. Additionally, as with the cost of HIPAA's statutory portability provisions, the majority of these costs will be borne by group plan enrollees. The Departments expect these regulations to have little or no perceptible negative impact on employers' propensity to offer health benefit plans or on the generosity of those plans. In sum, the Departments expect that the benefits of these regulations, which can be very large for a particular affected individual, will justify their costs. The basis for the Departments' conclusions is detailed below.

The Departments solicit comments on their conclusions and their basis for them, and empirical data or other information that would support a fuller or more accurate analysis.

Executive Order 12866—Department of Labor and Department of Health and Human Services

Under Executive Order 12866 (58 FR 551735, Oct. 4, 1993), the Departments must determine whether a regulatory action is "significant" and therefore subject to the requirements of the Executive Order and subject to review by the Office of Management and Budget (OMB). Under section 3(f), the order defines a "significant regulatory action" as an action that is likely to result in a rule: (1) having an annual effect on the economy of $100 million or more, or adversely and materially affecting a sector of the economy, productivity, competition, jobs, the environment, public health or safety, or state, local or tribal governments or communities (also referred to as "economically significant"); (2) creating serious inconsistency or otherwise interfering with an action taken or planned by another agency; (3) materially altering the budgetary impacts of entitlement grants, user fees, or loan programs or the rights and obligations of recipients thereof; or (4) raising novel legal or policy issues arising out of legal mandates, the President's priorities, or the principles set forth in the Executive Order.

Pursuant to the terms of the Executive Order, the Departments have determined that this action raises novel policy issues arising out of legal mandates. Therefore, this notice is "significant" and subject to OMB review under Section 3(f)(4) of the Executive Order. Consistent with the Executive Order, the Departments have assessed the costs and benefits of this regulatory action. The Departments' assessment, and the analysis underlying that assessment, is detailed below. The Departments performed a comprehensive, unified analysis to estimate the costs and benefits attributable to the regulations for purposes of compliance with Executive Order 12866, the Regulatory Flexibility Act, and the Paperwork Reduction Act.

Statement of need for proposed action

These proposed regulations clarify and interpret the HIPAA portability provisions under Section 701 of the Employee Retirement Income Security Act of 1974 (ERISA), Section 2701 of the Public Health Service Act, and Section 9801 of the Internal Revenue Code of 1986. The regulations are needed to secure and implement HIPAA's portability rights for individuals who are not timely notified that their coverage has ended and for individuals whose coverage ends in connection with the taking of leave that is guaranteed under FMLA, and to clarify and secure individuals' special enrollment rights under HIPAA.

Economic effects

As noted above, HIPAA's primary economic effects ensue directly from its statutory provisions. HIPAA's statutory group market portability provisions extend coverage to certain individuals and preexisting conditions not otherwise covered. This extension of coverage entails both benefits and costs. The economic effects of HIPAA's statutory portability provisions is summarized above and discussed in detail under the "Basis for Assessment of Economic Impact" section of the preamble to the final regulation, published elsewhere in this issue of the **Federal Register**

Also as noted above, by clarifying and securing HIPAA's statutory portability protections, these regulations will help ensure that HIPAA rights are fully realized. The result is likely to be a small increase at the margin in the economic effects of HIPAA's statutory portability provisions. The benefits of these regulations will be concentrated among a small number of affected individuals, while their costs will be spread thinly across plans and issuers. The regulations also will reduce uncertainty about health benefits' scope and value, thereby promoting employee health benefit coverage and labor market efficiency. The Departments believe that the regulations' benefits will justify their cost. The Departments assessment of the expected economic effects of the regulation are summarized above and discussed in detail below.

Regulatory Flexibility Act—The Department of Labor and Department of Health and Human Services

The Regulatory Flexibility Act (5 U.S.C. 601 *et seq.*) (RFA), imposes certain requirements with respect to Federal rules that are subject to the notice and comment requirements of section 553(b) of the Administrative Procedure Act (5 U.S.C. 551 *et seq.*) and which are likely to have a significant economic impact on a substantial number of small entities. Section 603 of the RFA stipulates that an agency, unless it certifies that a proposed rule will not have a significant economic impact on a substantial number of small entities, must present an initial regulatory flexibility analysis at the time of publication of the notice of proposed rulemaking that describes the impact of the rule on small entities and seeks public comment on such impact. Small entities include small businesses, organizations, and governmental jurisdictions.

For purposes of analysis under the RFA, the Departments consider a small entity to be an employee benefit plan with fewer than 100 participants. The basis for this definition is found in section 104(a)(2) of ERISA, which permits the Secretary of Labor to prescribe simplified annual reports for pension plans which cover fewer than 100 participants. Under section 104(a)(3), the Secretary may also provide for simplified annual reporting and disclosure if the statutory requirements of part 1 of Title I of ERISA would otherwise be inappropriate for welfare benefit plans. Pursuant to the authority of section 104(a)(3), the Department of Labor has previously issued at 29 CFR 2520.104-20, 2520.104-21, 2520.104-41, 2520.104-46 and 2520.104b-10 certain simplified reporting provisions and limited exemptions from reporting and disclosure requirements for small plans, including unfunded or insured welfare plans covering fewer than 100 participants and which satisfy certain other requirements.

Further, while some small plans are maintained by large employers, most are maintained by small employers. Both small and large plans may enlist small third party service providers to perform administrative functions, but it is generally understood that third party service providers transfer their costs to their plan clients in the form of fees. Thus, the Departments believe that assessing the impact of this rule on small plans is an appropriate substitute for evaluating the effect on small entities. The definition of small entity considered appropriate for this purpose differs, however, from a definition of small business based on size standards promulgated by the Small Business Administration (SBA) (13 CFR 121.201) pursuant to the Small Business Act (5 U.S.C. 631 *et seq.*). The Department of Labor solicited comments on the use of this standard for evaluating the effects of the proposal on small entities. No comments were received with respect to the standard. Therefore, a summary of the initial regulatory flexibility analysis based on the 100 participant size standard is presented below.

The economic effects of HIPAA's statutory provisions on small plans are discussed extensively under the "Regulatory Flexibility Act—Department of Labor and Department of Health and Human Services" section of the preamble to the final regulation, published elsewhere in this issue of the **Federal Register**.

By clarifying and securing HIPAA's statutory portability protections, these regulations will help ensure that these benefits are fully realized. The result is likely to be a small increase in the economic effects of HIPAA's statutory provisions. The Departments were unable to estimate the amount of this increase. However, the direct financial value of coverage extensions pursuant to HIPAA's statutory portability provisions are estimated to be approximately $180 million for small plans, or a small fraction of one percent of total small plan expenditures.[2]

The regulations also will reduce uncertainty about health benefits' scope and value, thereby promoting employee health benefit coverage, including coverage under small plans, and labor market efficiency.

The benefits of these regulations will be concentrated among a small number of affected small group plan enrollees, while their costs will be spread thinly across small group plans enrollees. The benefits of these regulations for any particular affected individual, which may include improved health and productivity, may be significant. However, as previously noted, the number of affected individuals, and therefore the aggregate cost of these regulations, is expected to be small. The Departments believe that the benefits to affected individuals of the application of these regulations to small plans justify the cost to small plans of such application. The basis for the Departments' conclusions is detailed below.

The Departments generally expect the impact of the regulations on any particular small plan to be small. A very large majority of small plans are fully insured, so the cost will fall nominally on issuers rather than from plans. Issuers are expected to pass this cost back to plans and enrollees, but will spread much of it across a large number of plans, thereby minimizing the impact on any particular plan. However, it is possible that small plans that self-insure, or fully insured small plans whose premiums are tied closely to their particular claims experience, might bear all or most of the cost associated with extensions of coverage attributable directly to these regulations. The Departments have no way to quantify the incidence or magnitude of such costs, and solicit comments on such incidence and magnitude, and on whether these regulations would have a significant impact on a substantial number of small plans.

Special Analyses—Department of the Treasury

Notwithstanding the determinations of the Departments of Labor and of Health and Human Services, for purposes of the Department of the Treasury this notice of proposed rulemaking is not a significant regulatory action. Because this notice of proposed rulemaking does not impose a collection of information on small entities and is not subject to section 553(b) of the Administrative Procedure Act (5 U.S.C. chapter 5), the Regulatory Flexibility Act (5 U.S.C. chapter 6) does not apply pursuant to

[2] Computer runs using Medical Expenditure Survey Household Component (MEPS-HC) and the Robert Wood Johnson Employer Health Benefits Survey determined that the share of covered private-sector job leavers at small firms average 35 percent of all covered private sector job leavers. From this, we inferred that the financial burden borne by small plans is approximately 35 percent of the total expenditures by private-sector group health plans which was estimated to be $515 million.

5 U.S.C. 603(a), which exempts from the Regulatory Flexibility Act's requirements certain rules involving the internal revenue laws. Pursuant to section 7805(f) of the Internal Revenue Code, this notice of proposed rulemaking will be submitted to the Chief Counsel for Advocacy of the Small Business Administration for comment on its impact on small business.

Paperwork Reduction Act

Department of Labor

These final regulations include three separate collections of information as that term is defined in the Paperwork Reduction Act of 1995 (PRA 95), 44 U.S.C. 3502(3): the Notice of Enrollment Rights, Notice of Preexisting Condition Exclusion, and Certificate of Creditable Coverage. Each of these disclosures is currently approved by the Office of Management and Budget (OMB) through October 31, 2006 in accordance with PRA 95 under control numbers 1210-0101, 1210-0102, and 1210-0103.

Department of the Treasury

These final regulations include a collection of information as that term is defined in PRA 95: the Notice of Enrollment Rights, Notice of Preexisting Condition Exclusion, and Certificate of Creditable Coverage. Each of these disclosures is currently approved by OMB under control number 1545-1537.

Department of Health and Human Services

These final regulations include three separate collections of information as that term is defined in PRA 95: the Notice of Enrollment Rights, Notice of Preexisting Condition Exclusion, and Certificate of Creditable Coverage. Each of these disclosures is currently approved by OMB through June 30, 2006 in accordance with PRA 95 under control number 0938-0702.

Small Business Regulatory Enforcement Fairness Act

The rule being issued here is subject to the provisions of the Small Business Regulatory Enforcement Fairness Act of 1996 (5 U.S.C. 801 *et seq.*) and, if finalized, will be transmitted to Congress and the Comptroller General for review. The rule is not a "major rule" as that term is defined in 5 U.S.C. 804, because it is not likely to result in (1) an annual effect on the economy of $100 million or more; (2) a major increase in costs or prices for consumers, individual industries, or federal, state, or local government agencies, or geographic regions; or (3) significant adverse effects on competition, employment, investment, productivity, innovation, or on the ability of United States-based enterprises to compete with foreign-based enterprises in domestic or export markets.

Unfunded Mandates Reform Act

Section 202 of the Unfunded Mandates Reform Act of 1995 requires that agencies assess anticipated costs and benefits before issuing any rule that may result in an expenditure in any 1 year by state, local, or tribal governments, in the aggregate, or by the private sector, of $100 million. These proposed regulations have no such mandated consequential effect on state, local, or tribal governments, or on the private sector.

Federalism Statement Under Executive Order 13132—Department of Labor and Department of Health and Human Services

Executive Order 13132 outlines fundamental principles of federalism. It requires adherence to specific criteria by federal agencies in formulating and implementing policies that have "substantial direct effects" on the States, the relationship between the national government and States, or on the distribution of power and responsibilities among the various levels of government. Federal agencies promulgating regulations that have these federalism implications must consult with State and local officials, and describe the extent of their consultation and the nature of the concerns of State and local officials in the preamble to the regulation.

In the Departments' view, these proposed regulations have federalism implications because they may have substantial direct effects on the States, the relationship between the national government and States, or on the distribution of power and responsibilities among the various levels of government. However, in the Departments' view, the federalism implications of these proposed regulations are substantially mitigated because, with respect to health insurance issuers, the vast majority of States have enacted laws which meet or exceed the federal HIPAA portability standards.

In general, through section 514, ERISA supersedes State laws to the extent that they relate to any covered employee benefit plan, and preserves State laws that regulate insurance, banking or securities. While ERISA prohibits States from regulating a plan as an insurance or investment company or bank, HIPAA added a new section to ERISA (as well as to the PHS Act) narrowly preempting State requirements for issuers of group health insurance coverage. Specifically, with respect to seven provisions of the HIPAA portability rules, states may impose stricter obligations on health insurance issuers.[3] Moreover, with respect to other requirements for health insurance issuers, states may continue to apply state law requirements except to the extent that such requirements prevent the application of HIPAA's portability, access, and renewability provisions.

---

[3] States may shorten the six-month look-back period prior to the enrollment date; shorten the 12-month and 18-month maximum preexisting condition exclusion periods; increase the 63-day significant break in coverage period; increase the 30-day period for newborns, adopted children, and children placed for adoption to enroll in the plan with no preexisting condition exclusion; further limit the circumstances in which a preexisting condition exclusion may be applied (beyond the federal exceptions for certain newborns, adopted children, children placed for adoption, pregnancy, and genetic information in the absence of a diagnosis; require additional special enrollment periods; and reduce the HMO affiliation period to less than 2 months (3 months for late enrollees).

In enacting these new preemption provisions, Congress intended to preempt State insurance requirements only to the extent that they prevent the application of the basic protections set forth in HIPAA. HIPAA's conference report states that the conferees intended the narrowest preemption of State laws with regard to health insurance issuers. H.R. Conf. Rep. No. 736, 104\th/ Cong. 2d Session 205 (1996). State insurance laws that are more stringent than the federal requirements are unlikely to "prevent the application of" the HIPAA portability provisions, and be preempted. Accordingly, States have significant latitude to impose requirements on health insurance insurers that are more restrictive than the federal law.

Guidance conveying this interpretation of HIPAA's preemption provisions was published in the Federal Register on April 8, 1997, 62 F.R. 16904. These proposed regulations clarify and implement the statute's minimum standards and do not significantly reduce the discretion given the States by the statute. Moreover, the Departments understand that the vast majority of States have requirements that meet or exceed the minimum requirements of the HIPAA portability provisions.

HIPAA provides that the States may enforce the provisions of HIPAA as they pertain to issuers, but that the Secretary of Health and Human Services must enforce any provisions that a State fails to substantially enforce. To date, CMS enforces the HIPAA portability provisions in only one State in accordance with that State's specific request to do so. When exercising its responsibility to enforce the provisions of HIPAA, CMS works cooperatively with the State for the purpose of addressing the State's concerns and avoiding conflicts with the exercise of State authority. CMS has developed procedures to implement its enforcement responsibilities, and to afford the States the maximum opportunity to enforce HIPAA's requirements in the first instance. CMS's procedures address the handling of reports that States may not be enforcing HIPAA's requirements, and the mechanism for allocating responsibility between the States and CMS. In compliance with Executive Order 13132's requirement that agencies examine closely any policies that may have federalism implications or limit the policymaking discretion of the States, the Department of Labor and CMS have engaged in numerous efforts to consult and work cooperatively with affected State and local officials.

For example, the Departments sought and received input from State insurance regulators and the National Association of Insurance Commissioners (NAIC). The NAIC is a non-profit corporation established by the insurance commissioners of the 50 States, the District of Columbia, and the four U.S. territories. In most States the Insurance Commissioner is appointed by the Governor, in approximately 14 States, the insurance commissioner is an elected official. Among other activities, it provides a forum for the development of uniform policy when uniformity is appropriate. Its members meet, discuss and offer solutions to mutual problems. The NAIC sponsors quarterly meetings to provide a forum for the exchange of ideas and in-depth consideration of insurance issues by regulators, industry representatives and consumers. CMS and the Department of Labor staff have consistently attended these quarterly meetings to listen to the concerns of the State Insurance Departments regarding HIPAA portability issues. In addition to the general discussions, committee meetings, and task groups, the NAIC sponsors the standing CMS/DOL meeting on HIPAA issues for members during the quarterly conferences. This meeting provides CMS and the Department of Labor with the opportunity to provide updates on regulations, bulletins, enforcement actions, and outreach efforts regarding HIPAA.

The Departments received written comments on the interim regulation from the NAIC and from ten States. In general, these comments raised technical issues that the Departments considered in conjunction with similar issues raised by other commenters. In a letter sent before issuance of the interim regulation, the NAIC expressed concerns that the Departments interpret the new preemption provisions of HIPAA narrowly so as to give the States flexibility to impose more stringent requirements. As discussed above, the Departments address this concern in the preamble to the interim regulation.

In addition, the Departments specifically consulted with the NAIC in developing these proposed regulations. Through the NAIC, the Departments sought and received the input of State insurance departments regarding certain insurance industry definitions, enrollment procedures and standard coverage terms. This input is generally reflected in the discussion of comments received and changes made in Section B - Overview of the Regulations of the preamble to the final regulations published elsewhere in this issue of the **Federal Register**.

The Departments have also cooperated with the States in several ongoing outreach initiatives, through which information on HIPAA is shared among federal regulators, State regulators and the regulated community. In particular, the Department of Labor has established a Health Benefits Education Campaign with more than 70 partners, including CMS, NAIC and many business and consumer groups. CMS has sponsored conferences with the States - the Consumer Outreach and Advocacy conferences in March 1999 and June 2000, and the Implementation and Enforcement of HIPAA National State-Federal Conferences in August 1999, 2000, 2001, 2002, and 2003. Furthermore, both the Department of Labor and CMS websites offer links to important State websites and other resources, facilitating coordination between the State and federal regulators and the regulated community.

Throughout the process of developing these regulations, to the extent feasible within the specific preemption provisions of HIPAA, the Departments have attempted to balance the States' interests in regulating health insurance issuers, and the Congress' intent to provide uniform minimum protections to consumers in every State. By doing so, it is the Departments' view that they have complied with the requirements of Executive Order 13132.

Pursuant to the requirements set forth in Section 8(a) of Executive Order 13132, and by the signatures affixed to proposed final regulations, the Departments certify that the Employee Benefits Security Administration and the Centers for Medicare & Medicaid Services have complied with the requirements of Executive Order 13132 for the attached proposed regulation, Notice of Proposed Rulemaking for Health Coverage Portability: Tolling and Certain Time Periods and Interaction with the Family and Medical Leave Act under HIPAA Titles I & IV (RIN 1210-AA54 and RIN 0938-AL88), in a meaningful and timely manner.

Basis for Assessment of Economic Impact—Department of Labor and Department of Health and Human Services

As noted above, the primary economic effects of HIPAA's portability provisions ensue directly from the statute. The Department's assessment of the economic effects of HIPAA's statutory portability provisions and the basis for the assessment is presented in detail under the "Basis for Assessment of Economic Impact" section of the preamble to the final regulation, published elsewhere in this issue of the **Federal Register**. By clarifying and securing HIPAA's statutory portability protections, these regulations will help ensure that HIPAA rights are fully realized. The result is likely to be a small increase in the economic effects of HIPAA's statutory portability provisions.

Additional economic benefits derive from the regulations' clarifications of HIPAA's portability requirements. The regulations provide clarity through both their provisions and their examples of how those provisions apply in various circumstances. By clarifying employees' rights and plan sponsors' obligations under HIPAA's portability provisions, the regulations will reduce uncertainty and costly disputes over these rights and obligations. They will promote employers' and employees' common understanding of the value of group health plan benefits and confidence in the security and predictability of those benefits, thereby improving labor market efficiency and fostering the establishment and continuation of group health plans by employers.[4]

These proposed regulations are intended to secure and implement HIPAA's group market portability provisions under certain special circumstances. The regulations will secure HIPAA's portability rights for individuals who are not timely notified that their coverage has ended and for individuals whose coverage ends in connection with the taking of leave that is guaranteed under FMLA. The regulations also will clarify and thereby secure individuals' special enrollment rights under HIPAA, and clarify the methodologies to be used by employers to determine the number of plans offered and the average number of individuals employed during a given year.

The benefits of these regulations will be concentrated among a small number of affected individuals.

Affected individuals will generally include those who would have lost access to coverage for needed medical care after forfeiting HIPAA portability and/or special enrollment rights due to time spent without coverage prior to receiving a certificate or while on FMLA-guaranteed leave. Affected individuals may also include some who would have been denied special enrollment rights if plans or issuers failed to recognize their requests for special enrollment or imposed unreasonable deadlines or requirements for completion of enrollment materials. The benefits of these regulations for any particular affected individual may be large. As noted above, access to coverage for needed medical care is important to individuals' health and productivity. However, the number of affected individuals, and therefore the aggregate cost of extended access to coverage under these regulations, is expected to be small, for several reasons.

First, these regulations extend HIPAA rights only in instances where individuals do not receive certificates immediately when coverage ends or their coverage ends in connection with the taking of FMLA-guaranteed leave. The Departments know of no source of data on the timeliness with which certificates are typically provided. The final regulations that accompany these proposed regulations

---

[4] The voluntary nature of the employment-based health benefit system in conjunction with the open and dynamic character of labor markets make explicit as well as implicit negotiations on compensation a key determinant of the prevalence of employee benefits coverage. It is likely that 80% to 100% of the cost of employee benefits is borne by workers through reduced wages (see for example Jonathan Gruber and Alan B. Krueger, "The Incidence of Mandated Employer-Provided Insurance: Lessons from Workers Compensation Insurance," in, David Bradford, ed., *Tax Policy and Economy*, pp:111-143 (Cambridge, MA: MIT Press, 1991); Jonathan Gruber, "The Incidence of Mandated Maternity Benefits," *American Economic Review*, Vol. 84 no. 3 (June 1994), pp. 622-641; Lawrence H. Summers, "Some Simple Economics of Mandated Benefits," *American Economic Review*, Vol. 79, No. 2 (May 1989), pp:177-183; Louise Sheiner, "Health Care Costs, Wages, and Aging," Federal Reserve Board of Governors working paper, April 1999; Mark Pauly and Brad Herring, *Pooling Health Insurance Risks* (Washington, DC: AEI Press, 1999), Gail A. Jensen and Michael A. Morrisey, "Endogenous Fringe Benefits, Compensating Wage Differentials and Older Workers," *International Journal of Health Care Finance and Economics* Vol 1, No. 3-4 (forthcoming), and Edward Montgomery, Kathryn Shaw, and Mary Ellen Benedict, "Pensions and Wages: An Hedonic Price Theory Approach," *International Economic Review*, Vol. 33 No. 1 (Feb. 1992.), pp:111-128.) The prevalence of benefits is therefore largely dependent on the efficacy of this exchange. If workers perceive that there is the potential for inappropriate denial of benefits they will discount their value to adjust for this risk. This discount drives a wedge in the compensation negotiation, limiting its efficiency. With workers unwilling to bear the full cost of the benefit, fewer benefits will be provided. The extent to which workers perceive a federal regulation supported by enforcement authority to improve the security and quality of benefits, the differential between the employers costs and workers willingness top accept wage offsets is minimized.

permit plans to provide certificates with COBRA notices, up to 44 days after coverage ends. Plans, however, often do have the option of providing certificates immediately when coverage ends or even in advance, for example as part of exit packages given to terminating employees or in mailings to covered dependents in advance of birthdays that will end their eligibility for coverage. With respect to FMLA-protected leave, data provided in a 1996 report to Congress suggests that the number of employees who lose coverage in connection with FMLA-protected leave is likely to be small. The report notes that over an 18-month period just 1.2 percent of surveyed employees took what they reported to be FMLA leave. A similar survey of employers found that 3.6 percent of employees took such leave. Nearly all of those taking leave continued their health coverage. (This is not surprising, given that FMLA requires covered employers to extend eligibility for health insurance to employees on FMLA-protected leave on the same terms that applied when the employees were not on leave.) Just 9 percent of leave-takers reported that they lost some kind of employee benefit, with one-third of these reporting that they lost health insurance.[5] Putting these numbers together and converting to an annual basis, in a given year between 0.02 percent and 0.07 percent of employees, or well under one in one thousand, might lose health coverage in connection with FMLA-protected leave. Many of these will ultimately exercise their right to be reinstated in the job from which they took leave and to exercise their FMLA-guaranteed right to resume their previous health coverage. Therefore, the number of employees who will lose coverage and then, later and at the conclusion of FMLA-protected leave, enjoy extended portability rights under HIPAA as a result of these regulations, is likely to be very small.

Second, the period over which this regulation extends rights will often be short, insofar as certificates are often provided promptly after coverage ends and many family leave periods are far shorter than the guaranteed 12 weeks. As noted above, plans generally are required to provide certificates no later than 44 days after coverage ends and may provide them sooner. According to the aforementioned report to Congress on FMLA-protected leave, 41 percent of employees taking FMLA-protected leave did so for less than 8 days. Fifty-eight percent were on leave for less than 15 days, and two-thirds were on leave for less than 29 days. (FMLA protects leaves of up to 12 weeks, or 84 days.)

Third, it is generally in individuals' interest to minimize periods of uninsurance. Individuals are likely to exercise their portability and special enrollment rights as soon as possible after coverage ends, which will often be before any extension of such rights under these regulations becomes effective. Over one 36-month period prior to HIPAA, 71 percent of Americans had continuous coverage - that is, incurred not even a single, one-month break in coverage. Just 4 percent were uninsured for the entire period. About one-half of observed spells without insurance lasted less than 5 months. As noted above, few employees taking FMLA-protected leave had a lapse in health coverage.

Fourth, only a portion of individuals who enroll in health plans in circumstances where these regulations alone guarantee their special enrollment or portability rights would otherwise have been denied such rights. HIPAA special enrollment and portability requirements, both as specified under the final regulations and as modified under these proposed regulations, are minimum standards. Plans are free to provide additional enrollment opportunities.

Fifth, only a small minority of individuals who avoid a significant break in coverage solely as a direct result of these regulations would otherwise have lost coverage for needed medical care. The affected minority would be those who suffer from preexisting conditions, join health plans that exclude coverage for such conditions, and require treatment of such conditions during the exclusion periods. GAO estimated that HIPAA could ensure continued coverage for up to 25 million Americans.[6] More recent estimates suggest that the number of individual policy holders and their dependents which could be helped by HIPAA's portability provisions are more in the 14 million range.[7] As noted above, however, the number of workers and dependents actually gaining coverage for a preexisting condition due to credit for prior coverage following a job change under HIPAA will be smaller than this. Both GAO's and our estimates of people who could benefit include all job changers with prior coverage and their dependents, irrespective of whether their new employer offers a plan, whether their new plan imposed a preexisting condition exclusion period, and whether they actually suffer from a preexisting condition. Accounting for these narrower criteria, CBO estimated that, at any point in time, about 100,000 individuals would have a preexisting condition exclusion reduced for prior creditable coverage. An additional 45,000 would gain added coverage in the individual market. The CBO estimate demonstrates that the number of individuals actually gaining coverage for needed medical services will be a small fraction of all those whose right to such coverage HIPAA's

---

[5] Commission on Family and Medical Leave and U.S. Department of Labor, *A Workable Balance: Report to Congress on Family and Medical Leave Policies*, transmitted April 30, 1996.

[6] U.S. General Accounting Office, Report HEHS-95-257, "Health Insurance Portability: Reform Could Ensure Continued Coverage for up to 25 Million Americans," September 1995.

[7] We calculated these estimates using internal runs off the MEPS-HC. These runs gave the number of total job changers, total job changers that had employer-sponsored insurance (ESI), and whether this coverage had been for less than 12 months or not. Estimates for dependents were based off the ratio of policy-holders to total dependents from the March 2003 Current Population Survey (March CPS). It should be noted, however, that the EBSA estimate of 14 million does not include estimate of individuals no longer eligible for COBRA continuation coverage or individuals facing job lock, while the GAO numbers do.

portability provisions guarantee. Accordingly, the Departments expect that the number gaining coverage for needed services as a direct result of these regulations will be a small fraction of the already small number whose right to such coverage these regulations would establish.

The Departments attempted to estimate the number of individuals who might avoid a break in coverage because of the provision of these proposed regulations that tolls the break until the individual receives a certification but not more than 44 days. The Departments examined coverage patterns evident in the Survey of Income and Program Participation (SIPP), a longitudinal household survey that tracks transitions in coverage. SIPP interviews households once every four months. The Departments estimate that, in a given year, about 7 million individuals have breaks in coverage lasting 4 months or less. The survey data suffer from so-called "seam bias" - respondents tend to report that status as unchanged over 4-month increments. Of the 7 million reporting breaks of 4 months or less, 6.5 million report breaks of exactly 4 months. This finding is consistent with the more general finding that breaks of 4 months or less are far more common than longer breaks. It seems likely that the 7 million breaks of 4 months or less actually included proportionate or disproportionately large share of breaks of 1 or 2 months. Assuming the breaks are actually distributed evenly by length between 1 day and 4 months, then about one-half of the breaks, or 3.5 million breaks, would have lasted less than 63 days and therefore would not have constituted breaks for purposes of HIPAA's portability protections even without reference to the provision of this proposed regulation that tolls the break until the individual receives a certification but not more than 44 days. Approximately three-fourths of the remaining breaks or about 2.6 million breaks, would have lasted between 1 and 44 additional days and thereby potentially have been tolled until the individuals received their certifications but not more than 44 days. Thus 2.6 million provides a reasonable upper bound on the number of individuals who might avoid a break in coverage in a given year because of this tolling provision. It is not known what fraction of these would subsequently join group health plans that include preexisting condition exclusions while suffering from and requiring additional care for preexisting conditions. Comparing GAO's (20 million or more) and our (14 million) estimates of the number of individuals who could potentially benefit from HIPAA's portability protections (individuals with prior creditable coverage who join new health plans in a given year) with the CBO estimate of the number who might actually have added group coverage for needed care (100,000) produces a ratio of about 1 percent. If this proportion holds for group health plan enrollees who avoid breaks because of this tolling provision, then an upper bound of about 26,000 individuals annually might gain coverage for needed care under the proposed regulation's provision treating coverage under such programs as creditable coverage.

The Departments considered whether certain individuals whose HIPAA portability rights these proposed regulations would extend may be disproportionately likely to be in (or have dependents who are in) poor health. Specifically, individuals taking FMLA-protected leave, especially those who elect not to be reinstated in their prior jobs following FMLA-protected leave, may be so likely. On the other hand, individuals in such circumstances are also particularly unlikely to allow their health insurance from their prior job to lapse while they are on leave. Accordingly, most such individuals' special enrollment periods and countable breaks in coverage (if any) would probably have begun at the conclusion of the FMLA-protected leave even in absence of these proposed regulations. The Departments are therefore uncertain whether individuals who would exercise HIPAA portability rights extended solely by these regulations would be more costly to insure than others exercising HIPAA portability rights, and solicit comments on this question.

Affected individuals may also include some who would have been denied special enrollment rights if plans or issuers failed to recognize their requests for special enrollment or imposed unreasonable deadlines or requirements for completion of enrollment materials.

As noted above, the Departments expect that these regulations will result in a small increase the economic effects of HIPAA's statutory provisions. For the reasons stated immediately above, the Departments believe that this increase will be small on aggregate, adding only a small increment to the cost attributable to HIPAA's statutory portability provisions, which themselves amount to a small fraction of one percent of health plan expenditures. Thus the increase will be negligible relative to typical year-to-year increases in premiums charged by issuers, which can amount to several percentage points or more. Therefore, the Departments expect these regulations to have little or no perceptible negative impact on employers' propensity to offer health benefit plans or on the generosity of those plans. In sum, the Departments expect that the benefits of these regulations, which can be very large for a particular affected individual, will justify their costs.

[¶49,239] Proposed Regulations and Proposed Amendments of Regulations (REG-102144-04), published in the Federal Register on May 24, 2005.

Consolidated returns: Dual consolidated losses: Dual resident corporation: Separate unit.—Amendments of Reg. §1.6043-4T, relating to dual consolidated losses, are proposed. A public hearing on this proposal is scheduled for September 7, 2005. Reg. §§1.1503(d)-0—1.1503(d)-6 and amendments of Reg. §§1.1502-21, are adopted.

AGENCY: Internal Revenue Service (IRS), Treasury.

ACTION: Notice of proposed rule making and notice of public hearing.

SUMMARY: This document contains proposed regulations under section 1503(d) of the Internal Revenue Code (Code) regarding dual consolidated losses. Section 1503(d) generally provides that a dual consolidated loss of a dual resident corporation cannot reduce the taxable income of any other member of the affiliated group unless, to the extent provided in regulations, such loss does not offset the income of any foreign corporation. Similar rules apply to losses of separate units of domestic corporations. The proposed regulations address various dual consolidated loss issues, including exceptions to the general prohibition against using a dual consolidated loss to reduce the taxable income of any other member of the affiliated group.

DATES: Written and electronic comments and outlines of topics to be discussed at the public hearing scheduled for September 7, 2005, at 10:00 a.m., must be received by May 24, 2005

ADDRESSES: Send submissions to CC:PA:LPD:PR (REG-102144-04), room 5203, Internal Revenue Service, P.O. Box 7604, Washington, DC 20044. Submissions may be hand delivered between the hours of 8 a.m. and 4 p.m. to CC:PA:LPD:PR (REG-102144-04), Courier's Desk, Internal Revenue Service, 1111 Constitution Avenue, NW., Washington, DC, or sent electronically via the IRS Internet site at *www.irs.gov/regs* or via the Federal eRulemaking Portal at *www.regulations.gov/* (IRS and REG-102144-04). The public hearing will be held in the Auditorium of the Internal Revenue Building, 1111 Constitution Avenue, NW., Washington, DC.

FOR FURTHER INFORMATION CONTACT: Concerning the proposed regulations, Kathryn T. Holman, (202) 622-3840 (not a toll-free number); concerning submissions and the hearing, Robin Jones, (202) 622-3521 (not a toll-free number).

SUPPLEMENTARY INFORMATION:

Paperwork Reduction Act

The collection of information contained in this notice of proposed rulemaking has been submitted to the Office of Management and Budget in accordance with the Paperwork Reduction Act of 1995 (44 USC 3507(d)). Comments on the collection of information should be sent to the **Office of Management and Budget,** Attn: Desk Officer for the Department of the Treasury, Office of Information and Regulatory Affairs, Washington, DC 20503, with copies to the **Internal Revenue Service,** Attn: IRS Reports Clearance Officer, W:CAR:MP:FP:S Washington, DC 20224. Comments on the collection of information should be received by July 22, 2005. Comments are specifically requested concerning:

Whether the proposed collection of information is necessary for the proper performance of the functions of the IRS, including whether the information will have practical utility;

The accuracy of the estimated burden associated with the proposed collection of information (see below);

How the quality, utility, and clarity of the information to be collected may be enhanced;

How the burden of complying with the proposed collection of information may be minimized, including through the application of automated collection techniques or other forms of information technology; and

Estimates of capital or start-up costs and costs of operation, maintenance, and purchase of service to provide information.

The collections of information in these proposed regulations are in §§1.1503(d)-1(b)(14), 1.1503(d)-1(c)(1), 1.1503(d)-2(d), 1.1503(d)-4(c)(2), 1.1503(d)-4(d), 1.1503(d)-4(e)(2), 1.1503(d)-4(f)(2), 1.1503(d)-4(g), 1.1503(d)-4(h) and 1.1503(d)-4(i). The various information is required. First, it notifies the IRS when the taxpayer asserts that it had reasonable cause for failing to comply with certain filing requirements under the regulations. Second, it indicates when the taxpayer attempts to rebut the amount of presumed tainted income. Finally, it provides the IRS various information regarding exceptions to the domestic use limitation, including domestic use elections, domestic use agreements, triggering events and recapture.

The collection of information is in certain cases required and in certain cases voluntary. The likely respondents will be domestic corporations with foreign operations that generate losses.

Estimated total annual reporting and/or recordkeeping burden: 2,665 hours.

Estimated average annual burden hours per respondent and/or recordkeeper: 1.5 hours.

Estimated number of respondents and/or recordkeepers: 1,765.

Estimated annual frequency of responses: Annually.

An agency may not conduct or sponsor, and a person is not required to respond to, a collection of information unless it displays a valid control number assigned by the Office of Management and Budget.

Books or records relating to a collection of information must be retained as long as their contents may become material in the administration of any internal revenue law. Generally, tax returns and tax return information are confidential, as required by 26 USC 6103.

Background

The United States taxes the worldwide income of domestic corporations. A domestic corporation is a corporation created or organized in the United States or under the law of the United States or of any State. The United States allows certain domestic corporations to file consolidated returns with other affiliated domestic corporations. When two or more domestic corporations file a consolidated return, losses that one corporation incurs generally may reduce or eliminate tax on income that another corporation earns.

Some countries use criteria other than place of incorporation or organization to determine whether corporations are residents for tax purposes. For example, some countries treat corporations as residents for tax purposes if they are managed or controlled in that country. If one of these countries determines a corporation to be a resident, the corporation is generally subject to income tax of that foreign country on a residence basis. As a result, if such a corporation is a domestic corporation for U.S. tax purposes, it is a dual resident corporation and is subject to the income tax of both the foreign country and the United States on a residence basis.

Prior to the Tax Reform Act of 1986, if a corporation was a resident of both a foreign country and the United States, and the foreign country permitted the losses of the corporation to be used to offset the income of another person (for example, as a result of consolidation), then the dual resident corporation could use any losses it generated twice: once to offset income that was subject to U.S. tax, but not foreign tax, and a second time to offset income subject to foreign tax, but not U.S. tax (double-dip).

Congress was concerned that this double-dip of a single economic loss could result in an undue tax advantage to certain foreign investors that made investments in domestic corporations, and could create an undue incentive for certain foreign corporations to acquire domestic corporations and for domestic corporations to acquire foreign rather than domestic assets. Staff of Joint Committee on Taxation, 99th Cong., 2nd Sess., General Explanation of the Tax Reform Act of 1986, at 1064 - 1065 (1987). Through such double-dipping, worldwide economic income could be rendered partially or fully exempt from current taxation. Moreover, even if the foreign income against which the loss was used would eventually be subject to U.S. tax (upon a repatriation of earnings), there were timing benefits of double dipping that the statute was intended to prevent. Congress responded to this concern by enacting section 1503(d) as part of the Tax Reform Act of 1986.

Section 1503(d) provides that a dual consolidated loss of a corporation cannot reduce the taxable income of any other member of the corporation's affiliated group. The statute defines a dual consolidated loss as a net operating loss of a domestic corporation that is subject to an income tax of a foreign country on its income without regard to the source of its income, or is subject to tax on a residence basis. The statute authorizes the issuance of regulations permitting the use of a dual consolidated loss to offset the income of a domestic affiliate if the loss does not offset the income of a foreign corporation under foreign law.

Section 1503(d) further states that, to the extent provided in regulations, similar rules apply to any loss of a *separate unit* of a domestic corporation as if such unit were a wholly owned subsidiary of the corporation. Although the statute does not define the term separate unit, the legislative history to the provision refers to the loss of any separate and clearly identifiable unit of a trade or business of a taxpayer and cites as an example a foreign branch of a domestic corporation. See H.R. Rep. No. 795, 100th Cong., 2d Sess. July 26, 1988) at 293.

The IRS and Treasury issued temporary regulations under section 1503(d) in 1989 (TD 8261, 1989-2 C.B. 220). The temporary regulations generally provided that, unless one of three limited exceptions applied, a dual consolidated loss of a dual resident corporation could not offset the income of any other member of the dual resident corporation's affiliated group. The temporary regulations contained similar rules for losses incurred by separate units.

In response to comments that the temporary regulations were unnecessarily restrictive, the IRS and Treasury issued final regulations under section 1503(d) in 1992 (TD 8434, 1992-2 C.B. 240). These final regulations were updated and amended over the next 11 years (current regulations). The current regulations apply the section 1503(d) limitation more narrowly than the temporary regulations. The current regulations adopt an *actual use* standard for permitting a dual consolidated loss to offset income of members of the affiliated group. This standard, which applies to both dual resident corporations and separate units, requires taxpayers to certify that no portion of the dual consolidated loss has been or will be used to offset the income of any other person under the income tax laws of a foreign country. If such a certification is made and a subsequent *triggering event* occurs, the dual consolidated loss must be recaptured in the year of the event (plus an applicable interest charge).

This document proposes amendments to the current regulations under section 1503(d). Conforming amendments are also proposed to related regulations under sections 1502 and 6043.

Overview

In general, the proposed regulations address three fundamental concerns that arise in connection with the current regulations. First, the IRS and Treasury believe that the scope of application of the current regulations should be modified. For example, the current regulations may apply to certain structures where there is little likelihood of a double-dip. Moreover, the IRS and Treasury understand that some taxpayers have taken the position that the current regulations do not apply to certain structures that provide taxpayers the benefits of the type of double-dip that section 1503(d) is intended to deny. Accordingly, the proposed regulations are designed to minimize these cases of potential over- and under-application.

Second, the IRS and Treasury recognize that there are many unresolved issues that arise when applying the current regulations, particularly in light of the adoption of the entity classification regulations under §§301.7701-1 through 301.7701-3. Thus, the proposed regulations modernize the dual consolidated loss regime to take into account the entity classification regulations and to resolve the related issues so that the rules can be applied by taxpayers and the Commissioner with greater certainty.

Finally, the IRS and Treasury believe that, in many cases, the current regulations are administratively burdensome to both taxpayers and the Commissioner. Accordingly, the proposed regulations reduce, to the extent possible, the administrative burden imposed on taxpayers and the Commissioner.

Explanation of Provisions

A. *Structure of the Proposed Regulations*

The proposed regulations are set forth in six sections. Section 1.1503(d)-1 contains definitions and special rules for filings. Section 1.1503(d)-2 sets forth operating rules, which include the general rule that prohibits the domestic use of a dual consolidated loss (subject to certain exceptions discussed below), a rule that limits the use of dual consolidated losses following certain transactions, an anti-avoidance provision that prevents dual consolidated losses from offsetting income from assets acquired in certain nonrecognition transactions or contributions to capital, and rules for computing foreign tax credit limitations. Section 1.1503(d)-3 contains special rules for accounting for dual consolidated losses. These special rules determine the amount of a dual consolidated loss, determine the effect of a dual consolidated loss on domestic affiliates, and provide special basis adjustments. Section 1.1503(d)-4 provides exceptions to the general rule that prohibits the domestic use of a dual consolidated loss, including a domestic use election. Section 1.1503(d)-5 contains examples that illustrate the application of the proposed regulations. Finally, § 1.1503(d)-6 contains the proposed effective date of the proposed regulations.

In addition to the proposed regulatory amendments under section 1503(d), the proposed regulations also include conforming proposed amendments to § 1.1502-21 and § 1.6043-4T.

B. *Definitions and Special Rules for Filings under Section 1503(d)—§ 1.1503(d)-1*

1. *Treatment of a separate unit as a domestic corporation and a dual resident corporation*

Section 1.1503-2(c)(3) and (4) of the current regulations defines a separate unit of a domestic corporation as a foreign branch, within the meaning of § 1.367(a)-6T(g), (foreign branch separate unit) and an interest in a partnership, trust or hybrid entity. The current regulations also provide that any separate unit of a domestic corporation is treated as a separate domestic corporation for purposes of applying the dual consolidated loss rules. Section 1.1503-2(c)(2). In addition, the current regulations provide that, unless otherwise indicated, any reference to a dual resident corporation refers also to a separate unit. As a result of these rules, certain provisions of the current regulations only refer to dual resident corporations, and therefore apply to separate units because they are treated as domestic corporations and dual resident corporations. However, other provisions of the current regulations refer to both dual resident corporations and separate units (for example, see § 1.1503-2(g)(2)(iii)(A)).

The IRS and Treasury believe that, in certain cases, treating separate units as domestic corporations creates uncertainty in applying the current regulations. This may occur, for example, as a result of certain rules applying to separate units because they are treated as domestic corporations or dual resident corporations, while other rules apply explicitly to separate units themselves. Accordingly, the proposed regulations do not contain a general rule that treats separate units as domestic corporations or dual resident corporations for all purposes of applying the dual consolidated loss regulations. Instead, the proposed regulations explicitly refer to dual resident corporations and separate units where appropriate, treat separate units as domestic corporations only for limited purposes, and modify the operative rules where necessary to take into account differences between dual resident corporations and separate units.

2. *Application of section 1503(d) to S corporations*

Section 1.1503-2(c)(2) of the current regulations provides that an S corporation, as defined in section 1361, is not a dual resident corporation. The preamble to the current regulations explains that S corporations are so excluded because an S corporation cannot have a domestic corporation as one of its shareholders. The current regulations do not, however, explicitly exclude separate units owned by an S corporation from the definition of a dual resident corporation. As a result, the current regulations can be read to provide that an S corporation, although it cannot itself be a dual resident corporation, could own a separate unit that would be a dual resident corporation.

The IRS and Treasury believe that such a result is inappropriate because an S corporation cannot have a domestic corporation as one of its shareholders and generally is not taxable at the entity level. Accordingly, the proposed regulations provide that for purposes of the dual consolidated loss rules, an S corporation is not treated as a domestic corporation. This modification clarifies that the dual consolidated loss regulations do not apply to the S corporation itself, or to foreign branches or interests in certain flow-through entities owned by an S corporation.

The IRS and Treasury request comments as to whether regulated investment companies (as defined in section 851) or real estate investment trusts (as defined in section 856) should be similarly excluded from the application of the dual consolidated loss rules.

3. *Losses of a foreign insurance company treated as a domestic corporation*

Section 953(d) generally provides that a foreign corporation that would qualify to be taxed as an insurance company if it were a domestic corporation may, under certain circumstances, elect to be treated as a domestic corporation. Section 953(d)(3) provides that if a corporation elects to be treated as a domestic corporation pursuant to section 953(d) and is treated as a member of an affiliated group, any loss of such corporation is treated as a dual consolidated loss for purposes of section 1503(d), without regard to section 1503(d)(2)(B) (grant of regulatory authority to exclude losses which do not offset the income of foreign corporations from the definition of a dual consolidated loss). Therefore, losses of such corporations are treated as dual consolidated losses regardless of whether the corporation is subject to an income tax of a foreign country on its worldwide income or on a residence basis.

The current regulations do not address the application of section 953(d)(3). However, the definition of a dual resident corporation contained in the proposed regulations includes a foreign insurance company that makes an election to be treated as a domestic corporation pursuant to section 953(d) and is a member of an affiliated group, regardless of how such entity is taxed by the foreign country.

4. *Definition of a separate unit*

(a) *Interests in Non-Hybrid Entity Partnerships and Interests in Non-Hybrid Entity Grantor Trusts*

Section 1.1503-2(c)(4) of the current regulations defines a separate unit to include an interest in a hybrid entity (hybrid entity separate unit). The current regulations define a hybrid entity as an entity that is not taxable as an association for U.S. income tax purposes, but is subject to income tax in a foreign jurisdiction as a corporation (or otherwise at the entity level) either on its worldwide income or on a residence basis. This definition includes an interest in such an entity that is treated for U.S. tax purposes as a partnership (hybrid entity partnership) or as a grantor trust (hybrid entity grantor trust). An interest in an entity that is treated as a partnership or a grantor trust for both U.S. and foreign tax purposes (non-hybrid entity partnership and non-hybrid entity grantor trust, respectively) also is treated as a separate unit under the current regulations. § 1.1503-2(c)(3)(i).

The current regulations also apply to a separate unit owned indirectly through a partnership or grantor trust. Thus, for example, if a partnership owns a foreign branch within the meaning of § 1.367(a)-6T(g), a domestic corporate partner's interest in such partnership, and its indirect interest in a portion of the foreign branch owned through the partnership, each constitutes a separate unit.

Under the current regulations, an interest in a non-hybrid entity partnership or a non-hybrid entity grantor trust is also treated as a separate unit, regardless of whether the partnership or grantor trust has any nexus with a foreign jurisdiction. This rule can result in the application of the dual consolidated loss rules when there may be little opportunity for a double-dip. For example, if two domestic corporations each own 50 percent of a domestic partnership that generates losses attributable to activities conducted solely in the United States, the corporate partners would be technically subject to the dual consolidated loss rules and therefore would not be allowed to offset their income with such losses, unless an exception applied. In such a case, however, it may be unlikely that the losses would be available to offset income of another person under the income tax laws of a foreign country.

The IRS and Treasury believe that including an interest in a non-hybrid entity partnership and an interest in a non-hybrid entity grantor trust in the definition of a separate unit may not be necessary and is administratively burdensome. In such cases, it may be unlikely that deductions and losses solely attributable to activities of the partnership or grantor trust, that do not rise to the level of a taxable presence in a foreign jurisdiction, can be used to offset income of another person under the income tax laws of a foreign country. As a result, the proposed regulations eliminate from the definition of a separate unit an interest in a non-hybrid entity partnership and an interest in a non-hybrid entity grantor trust. It should be noted, however, that the proposed regulations retain the rule contained in the current regulations that a domestic corporation can own a separate unit indirectly through both hybrid entity and non-hybrid entity partnerships, and through both hybrid entity and non-hybrid entity grantor trusts.

(b) *Separate Unit Combination Rule*

Section 1.1503-2(c)(3)(ii) of the current regulations provides that if two or more foreign branches located in the same foreign country are owned by a single domestic corporation and the losses of each branch are made available to offset the income of the other branches under the tax laws of the foreign country, then the branches are treated as one separate unit. The combination rule in the current regulations does not apply to interests in hybrid entity separate units or to dual resident corporations.

Although a disregarded entity is treated as a branch of its owner for various purposes of the Code, the current regulations distinguish a hybrid entity separate unit that is disregarded as an entity separate from its owner from a foreign branch separate unit. Compare § 1.1503-2(c)(3)(i)(A) and (c)(4); see also § 1.1503-2(g)(2)(vi)(C). Accordingly, the combination rule under the current regulations does not apply to an interest in a hybrid entity separate unit, even if the hybrid entity is disregarded as an entity separate from its owner.

The combination rule in the current regulations also requires the foreign branches to be owned by a single domestic corporation. Thus, for example, the current regulations do not permit the combination of foreign branches owned by different domestic corporations, even if such corporations are members of the same consolidated group. In addition, in some cases the current regulations do not allow the combination of foreign branches that are owned indirectly by a single domestic corporation through other separate units because, as discussed above, such other separate units are generally treated as domestic corporations for purposes of applying the dual consolidated loss regulations. As a result, such foreign branches are not treated as being owned by a single domestic corporation.

The IRS and Treasury believe that the application of the combination rule should not be restricted to foreign branch separate units. In addition, the IRS and Treasury believe that the combination rule should not be limited to those cases where the domestic corporation owns the separate units directly. Therefore, provided certain requirements are satisfied, the proposed regulations adopt a broader combination rule that combines all separate units that are directly or indirectly owned by a single domestic corporation.

In order for separate units to be combined under the proposed regulations, the losses of each separate unit must be made available to offset the income of the other separate units under the tax laws of a single foreign country. In addition, if the separate unit is a foreign branch separate unit, it must be located in the foreign country that allows its losses to be made available to offset income of each separate unit; if the separate unit is a hybrid entity separate unit, the hybrid entity must be subject to tax in the foreign country that allows losses to be made available to each separate unit either on its worldwide income or on a residence basis.

The combination rule in the proposed regulations does not combine separate units owned by different domestic corporations, even if the domestic corporations are included in the same consolidated group. The IRS and Treasury believe this approach is consistent with section 1503(d)(3), which provides that, to the extent provided in regulations, a loss of a separate unit of a domestic corporation is subject to the dual consolidated loss rules as if it were a wholly owned subsidiary of such domestic corporation. In addition, the combination rule contained in the proposed regulations only applies to separate units and therefore does not apply to dual resident corporations.

The IRS and Treasury, however, request comments as to whether there is authority to expand the combination rule and, if so, whether the combination rule should be expanded to include separate units that are owned directly or indirectly by domestic corporations that are members of the same consolidated group. Similarly, comments are requested as to whether the combination rule should be extended to apply to dual resident corporations. Further, the IRS and Treasury request comments on the application of the operative provisions of the proposed regulations to combined separate units owned by different domestic corporations (for example, the SRLY limitation under § 1.1503(d)-3(c)).

5. *Exception to the definition of a dual consolidated loss*

Section 1.1503-2(c)(5)(ii)(A) of the current regulations provides a very limited exception to the definition of a dual consolidated loss where the income tax laws of a foreign country do not permit the dual resident corporation to either: (1) use its losses, expenses, or deductions to offset the income of any other person in the same taxable year; or (2) carry over or carry back its losses, expenses, or deductions to be used, by any means, to offset the income of any other person in other taxable years. This exception only applies in rare and unusual cases where the income tax laws of the foreign country do not allow any portion of the dual consolidated loss to be used to offset income of another person under any circumstances.

The IRS and Treasury understand that some taxpayers have improperly interpreted this provision in a manner inconsistent with the policies of the dual consolidated loss rules. As a result, the proposed regulations eliminate this exception to the definition of a dual consolidated loss. As discussed below, however, the proposed regulations contain a new exception to the general rule restricting the use of a dual consolidated loss to offset income of a domestic affiliate. In general, this new exception applies when there is no possibility that any portion of the dual consolidated loss can be double-dipped, and operates in a manner that is similar to the manner in which the exception to the definition of a dual consolidated loss contained in the current regulations operates.

6. *Partnership special allocations*

Section 1.1503-2(c)(5)(iii) of the current regulations reserves on the treatment of dual consolidated losses of separate units that are partnership interests, including interests in hybrid entities. The preamble to the current regulations explains that the reservation was principally the result of concerns regarding partnership special allocations.

The proposed regulations no longer reserve on the treatment of separate units that are partnership interests. However, the IRS will continue to challenge structures that attempt to use special allocations in a manner that is inconsistent with the principles of section 1503(d).

7. *Domestic use of a dual consolidated loss*

Section 1.1503-2(b)(1) of the current regulations states that, except as otherwise provided, a dual consolidated loss cannot offset the taxable income of any domestic affiliate, regardless of whether the loss offsets income of another person under the income tax laws of a foreign country, and regardless of whether the income that the loss may offset in the foreign country is, has been, or will be subject to tax in the United States. Section 1.1503-2(c)(13) defines the term domestic affiliate to mean any member of an affiliated group, without regard to exceptions contained in section 1504(b) (other than section 1504(b)(3)) relating to includible corporations.

The proposed regulations retain the general prohibition against using a dual consolidated loss to offset income of domestic affiliates contained in the current regulations, with modifications, and refer to such usage as a *domestic use* of a dual consolidated loss. This general prohibition is subject to a number of exceptions, discussed below. In addition, because the proposed regulations do not treat separate units as domestic corporations and dual resident corporations (other than for limited purposes) the proposed regulations expand the definition of a domestic affiliate to include separate units. This expanded definition is necessary for purposes of applying the domestic use limitation rule.

8. *Foreign use of a dual consolidated loss*

(a) *General Rule*

Section 1.1503-2T(g)(2)(i) of the current regulations provides that, in order to elect relief from the general limitation on the use of a dual consolidated loss to offset income of a domestic affiliate with respect to a dual consolidated loss ((g)(2)(i) election), the taxpayer must, among other things, certify that no portion of the losses, expenses, or deductions taken into account in computing the dual consolidated loss has been, or will be, used to offset the income of any other person under the income tax laws of a foreign country. If, contrary to this certification, there is such a *use*, the dual consolidated loss subject to the (g)(2)(i) election generally must be recaptured and reported as gross income.

The IRS and Treasury understand that issues arise involving the application of the use rule contained in the current regulations. For example, issues may arise where items of income, gain, deduction and loss are treated as being generated or incurred by different persons under U.S. and foreign law. Similarly, issues may arise due to different definitions of a *person* under U.S. and foreign law. These issues have become more prevalent since the adoption of the entity classification regulations under § § 301.7701-1 through 301.7701-3.

The IRS and Treasury also understand that taxpayers have taken positions under the current regulations regarding the use of a dual consolidated loss that are inconsistent with the policies underlying section 1503(d). On the other hand, the IRS and Treasury believe that, under the current regulations, a use can be deemed to occur in certain cases where there may be little likelihood of the type of double-dip that section 1503(d) was intended to prevent.

For the reasons discussed above, the proposed regulations modify the definition of *use* and provide a rule based on *foreign use*. These modifications are intended to minimize the potential over- and under-application of the dual consolidated loss rules that can occur under the current regulations. Under the proposed regulations, the foreign use definition is intended to minimize the opportunity for a double-dip. However, the new definition is also intended to minimize the situations in which a foreign use will occur in cases where there may be little likelihood of a double-dip.

The proposed regulations provide that a foreign use is deemed to occur only if two conditions are satisfied. The first condition is satisfied if any portion of a loss or deduction taken into account in computing the dual consolidated loss is made available under the income tax laws of a foreign country to offset or reduce, directly or indirectly, any item that is recognized as income or gain under such laws (including items of income or gain generated by the dual resident corporation or separate unit itself), regardless of whether income or gain is actually offset, and regardless of whether such items are recognized under U.S. tax principles. This condition ensures that there will not be a foreign use unless all or a portion of the dual consolidated loss offsets or reduces, or is made available to offset or reduce, income or gain for foreign tax purposes.

The second condition is satisfied if items that are (or could be) offset pursuant to the first condition are considered, under U.S. tax principles, to be items of: (1) a foreign corporation; or (2) a direct or indirect (for example, through a partnership) owner of an interest in a hybrid entity, provided such interest is not a separate unit. This condition is intended to limit a foreign use to situations where the foreign income that is (or could be) offset by the dual consolidated loss is not currently subject to U.S. corporate income tax. In general, if the foreign income that is offset is currently subject to U.S. corporate income tax, there is no double-dip of the dual consolidated loss.

(b) *Exception to Foreign Use if no Dilution of an Interest in a Separate Unit*

Section 1.1503-2(c)(15) of the current regulations employs a so-called *actual use* standard for determining whether there has been a use of a dual consolidated loss to offset the income of another person under the laws of a foreign country. Although referred to as an *actual use* standard, this rule provides that a use is considered to occur in the year in which a loss, expense or deduction taken into account in computing the dual consolidated loss is made available for such an offset, unless an exception applies. The fact that the other person does not have sufficient income in that year to benefit from such an offset is not taken into account.

The *available* component of the actual use standard was adopted because of the administrative complexity that would result from having a use occur only when income is actually offset. For example, if in the year that a portion of the dual consolidated loss is made available to be used by another person, the other person itself generates a loss (or has a loss carryover), then in many cases the portion of the dual consolidated loss would become part of the loss carryover. Such loss therefore would be available to be carried forward or carried back to offset income in different taxable years. Under this approach, the portion of the loss carryforward or carryback that was taken into account in computing the dual consolidated loss would need to be identified and tracked, which would require detailed ordering rules for determining when such losses were used. Timing and base differences between the U.S. and foreign jurisdiction would further complicate such an approach.

Because of the administrative complexities discussed above, the foreign use definition contained in the proposed regulations retains the available for use standard. However, because the available for use standard is retained, there are many cases in which a foreign use of a dual consolidated loss attributable to interests in hybrid entity partnerships and hybrid entity grantor trusts, and separate units owned indirectly through partnerships and grantor trusts, occurs, even though no portion of any item of deduction or loss comprising the dual consolidated loss is double-dipped. In the case of interests in hybrid entity partnerships and hybrid entity grantor trusts, a portion of the dual consolidated loss attributable to an interest in such entity in many cases would be made available to offset income or gain of a direct or indirect owner of an interest in such hybrid entity, provided such interest is not a separate unit. This typically would occur because under foreign law the hybrid entity is taxed as a corporation (or otherwise at the entity level) and its net losses may be carried forward or carried back. A similar result may occur in the case of a separate unit owned indirectly through a non-hybrid entity partnership or a non-hybrid entity grantor trust because of timing and base differences between the laws of the United States and the foreign jurisdiction.

The IRS and Treasury believe this is an inappropriate result in many cases. For example, the IRS and Treasury believe that if there is no dilution of the domestic owner's interest in the separate unit, it is unlikely that any portion of the dual consolidated loss attributable to such separate unit can be put to a foreign use (other than through an election to consolidate or similar method, discussed below). Therefore, the proposed regulations include three new exceptions to the definition of a foreign use where there is no dilution of an interest in a separate unit. The new exceptions to foreign use apply to dual consolidated losses attributable to two types of separate units: (1) interests in hybrid entity partnerships and interests in hybrid entity grantor trusts; and (2) separate units owned indirectly through partnerships and grantor trusts.

The first exception to foreign use provides that, in general, no foreign use shall be considered to occur with respect to a dual consolidated loss attributable to an interest in a hybrid entity partnership or a hybrid entity grantor trust, solely because an item of deduction or loss taken into account in computing such dual consolidated loss is made available, under the income tax laws of a foreign country, to offset or reduce, directly or indirectly, any item that is recognized as income or gain under such laws and is considered under U.S. tax principles to be an item of the direct or indirect owner of an interest in such hybrid entity that is not a separate unit.

The second exception to foreign use provides that, in general, no foreign use shall be considered to occur with respect to a dual consolidated loss attributable to or taken into account by a separate unit owned indirectly through a partnership or grantor trust solely because an item of deduction or loss taken into account in computing such dual consolidated loss is made available, under the income tax laws of a foreign country, to offset or reduce, directly or indirectly, any item that is recognized as income or gain under such laws and is considered under U.S. tax principles to be an item of a direct or indirect owner of an interest in such partnership or trust.

Finally, the proposed regulations provide a similar exception for combined separate units that include individual separate units to which one of the other dilution exceptions would apply, but for the separate unit combination rule.

The new exceptions to foreign use are subject to certain limitations, however. First, the exceptions will not apply if there has been a dilution of the interest in the separate unit. That is, the exception will not apply if during any taxable year the domestic owner's percentage interest in the separate unit, as compared to its interest in the separate unit as of the last day of the taxable year in which such dual consolidated loss was incurred, is reduced as a result of another person acquiring through sale, exchange, contribution or other means an interest in such partnership or grantor trust, unless the taxpayer demonstrates, to the satisfaction of the Commissioner, that the other person that acquired the interest in the partnership or grantor trust was a domestic corporation. The exceptions to foreign use should not apply when a person (other than a domestic corporation) acquires an interest in the separate unit because the dilution would typically result in an actual foreign use.

Second, the exceptions do not apply if the availability does not arise solely from the ownership in such partnership or trust and the allocation of the item of deduction or loss, or the offsetting by such deduction or loss, of an item of income or gain of the partnership or trust. For example, the exception does not apply in the case where the item of loss or deduction is made available through a foreign consolidation regime.

The IRS and Treasury request comments on the issues discussed above in connection with the availability component of the foreign use definition. Comments are specifically requested as to whether the dilution rules are appropriate and, if so, whether a *de minimis* exception should be provided.

9. *Mirror legislation rule*

Section 1.1503-2(c)(15)(iv) of the current regulations contains a *mirror legislation rule* that addresses legislation enacted by foreign jurisdictions that operates in a manner similar to the dual consolidated loss rules. This rule was designed to prevent the revenue gain resulting from the disallowance of the double-dip benefit of a dual consolidated loss from inuring solely to the foreign jurisdiction (to the detriment of the United States). Staff of the Joint Committee on Taxation, General Explanation of the Tax Reform Act of 1986, at 1065-66 (J. Comm. Print 1987).

Congress recognized that mirror legislation in a foreign jurisdiction, in conjunction with a mirror legislation rule such as that contained in the current regulations, could result in the disallowance of a dual consolidated loss in both the United States and in the foreign jurisdiction. In such a case, Congress intended that Treasury pursue with the appropriate authorities in the foreign jurisdiction a bilateral agreement that would allow the use of the loss of a dual resident corporation to offset income of an affiliate in only one country. Staff of the Joint Committee on Taxation, General Explanation of the Tax Reform Act of 1986, at 1066. The mirror rule was specifically held to be valid by the Court of Appeals for the Federal Circuit. *British Car Auctions, Inc. v. United States*, 35 Fed. Cl. 123 (1996), *aff'd without op.*, 116 F.3d 1497 (Fed. Cir. 1997).

The mirror legislation rule contained in the current regulations provides that if the laws of a foreign country deny the use of a loss of a dual resident corporation (or separate unit) to offset the income of another person because the dual resident corporation (or separate unit) is also subject to tax by another country on its worldwide income or on a residence basis, the loss is deemed to be used against the income of another person in such foreign country such that no (g)(2)(i) election can be made with respect to such loss. This rule is intended to prevent the foreign jurisdiction from enacting legislation that gives taxpayers no choice but to use the dual consolidated loss to offset income in the United States. This result is contrary to the general policy underlying the structure of the current regulations that provides taxpayers the choice of using the dual consolidated loss to either offset income in the United States or income in the foreign jurisdiction (but not both).

As a result of the consistency rule (discussed below), the deemed use of a dual consolidated loss pursuant to the mirror legislation rule may also restrict the ability to use other dual consolidated losses to offset the income of domestic affiliates, even if such losses are not subject to the mirror legislation.

Subsequent to the issuance of the current regulations, several foreign jurisdictions enacted various forms of mirror legislation that, absent the mirror legislation rule, would have the effect of forcing certain taxpayers to use dual consolidated losses to offset income of domestic affiliates.

Given the relevant legislative history and *British Car Auctions*, the IRS and Treasury believe that the mirror legislation rule remains necessary. This is particularly true in light of the prevalence of mirror legislation in foreign jurisdictions. As a result, the proposed regulations retain the mirror legislation rule. The proposed regulations modify the mirror legislation rule, however, to address its proper application with respect to mirror legislation enacted subsequent to the issuance of the current regulations, and to modify its application to better take into account the policies underlying the consistency rule.

In general, the mirror legislation rule contained in the proposed regulations applies when the opportunity for a foreign use is denied because: (1) the loss is incurred by a dual resident corporation that is subject to income taxation by another country on its worldwide income or on a residence basis; (2) the loss may be available to offset income other than income of the dual resident corporation or separate unit under the laws of another country; or (3) the deductibility of any portion of a loss or deduction taken into account in computing the dual consolidated loss depends on whether such amount is deductible under the laws of another country.

The IRS and Treasury understand that there may be uncertainty as to the application of the mirror legislation rule in a given case when the mirror legislation is limited in its application. Mirror legislation may or may not apply to a particular dual resident corporation or separate unit depending on various factors, including the type of entity or structure that generates the loss, the ownership of the operation or entity that generates the loss, the manner in which the operation or entity is taxed in another jurisdiction, or the ability of the losses to be deducted in another jurisdiction. As a result, the proposed regulations clarify that the mere existence of mirror legislation, regardless of whether it applies to the particular dual resident corporation, may not result in a deemed foreign use. For example, see § 1.1503(d)-5(c) *Example 23*.

The proposed regulations also clarify that the absence of an affiliate in the foreign jurisdiction, or the failure to make an election to enable a foreign use, does not prevent the opportunity for a foreign use. Thus, for example, the mirror legislation rule may apply even if there are no affiliates of the dual resident corporation in the foreign jurisdiction or, even where there is such an affiliate, no election is made to consolidate.

As discussed below, the consistency rule is intended to promote uniformity and reduce administrative burdens. The IRS and Treasury believe that these concerns may not be significant, however, where there is only a deemed foreign use of a dual consolidated loss as a result of the mirror legislation rule. Accordingly, the mirror legislation rule contained in the proposed regulations provides that a deemed foreign use is not treated as a foreign use for purposes of applying the consistency rule.

10. *Reasonable cause exception*

The current regulations require various filings to be included on a timely filed tax return. In addition, taxpayers that fail to include such filings on a timely filed tax return must request an extension of time to file under § 301.9100-3.

The IRS and Treasury believe that requiring taxpayers to request relief for an extension of time to file under § 301.9100-3 results in an unnecessary administrative burden on both taxpayers and the Commissioner. The IRS and Treasury believe that a reasonable cause standard, similar to that used in other international provisions of the Code (such as sections 367(a) and 6038B), is a more appropriate and less burdensome means for taxpayers to cure compliance defects under section 1503(d). As a result, the proposed regulations adopt a reasonable cause standard. Moreover, extensions of time under § 301.9100-3 will not be granted for filings under these proposed regulations. See § 301.9100-1(d).

Under the reasonable cause standard, if a person that is permitted or required to file an election, agreement, statement, rebuttal, computation, or other information under the regulations fails to make such a filing in a timely manner, such person shall be considered to have satisfied the timeliness requirement with respect to such filing if the person is able to demonstrate, to the satisfaction of the Director of Field Operations having jurisdiction of the taxpayer's tax return for the taxable year, that such failure was due to reasonable cause and not willful neglect. Once the person becomes aware of the failure, the person must make this demonstration and comply by attaching all the necessary filings to an amended tax return (that amends the tax return to which the filings should have been attached), and including a written statement explaining the reasons for the failure to comply.

In determining whether the taxpayer has reasonable cause, the Director of Field Operations shall consider whether the taxpayer acted reasonably and in good faith. Whether the taxpayer acted reasonably and in good faith will be determined after considering all the facts and circumstances. The Director of Field Operations shall notify the person in writing within 120 days of the filing if it is determined that the failure to comply was not due to reasonable cause, or if additional time will be needed to make such determination.

C. *Operating Rules—§1.1503(d)-2*

1. *Application of rules to multiple tiers of separate units*

Section 1.1503-2(b)(3) of the current regulations provides that if a separate unit of a domestic corporation is owned indirectly through another separate unit, limitations on the dual consolidated losses of the separate units apply as if the upper-tier separate unit were a subsidiary of the domestic corporation, and the lower-tier separate unit were a lower-tier subsidiary. In light of changes made to other provisions of the proposed regulations, this rule is no longer necessary. As a result, the proposed regulations do not contain this provision.

2. *Tainted income*

Section 1.1503-2(e) of the current regulations prevents the dual consolidated loss of a dual resident corporation that ceases being a dual resident corporation from offsetting tainted income of such corporation. Subject to certain exceptions, tainted income is defined as income derived from assets that are acquired by a dual resident corporation in a nonrecognition transaction, or as a contribution to capital, at any time during the three taxable years immediately preceding the tax year in which the corporation ceases to be a dual resident corporation, or at any time thereafter. The current regulations also contain a rule that, absent proof to the contrary, presumes an amount of income generated during a taxable year as being tainted income. Such amount is the corporation's taxable income for the year multiplied by a fraction, the numerator of which is the fair market value of the tainted assets at the end of the year, and the denominator of which is the fair market value of the total assets owned by each domestic corporation at the end of each year.

The tainted income rule is intended to prevent taxpayers from obtaining a double-dip with respect to a dual consolidated loss by stuffing assets into a dual resident corporation after, or in certain cases before, it terminates its status as a dual resident corporation. A double-dip may be obtained in such case because the income that offsets the dual consolidated loss generally would not be subject to tax in the foreign jurisdiction after the dual resident status of the corporation terminates.

The proposed regulations retain the tainted income rule, subject to the following modifications. The proposed regulations clarify that tainted income includes both income or gain recognized on the sale or other disposition of tainted assets and income derived as a result of holding tainted assets. The proposed regulations also modify the rule defining the amount of income presumed to be tainted income. The proposed regulations clarify that the presumptive rule only applies to income derived as a result of holding tainted assets; income or gain recognized on the sale or other disposition of tainted assets should be readily determinable such that the presumptive rule need not apply. The proposed regulations also provide that the numerator in the presumptive income fraction is the fair market value of tainted assets determined at the time such assets were acquired by the corporation, as opposed to being determined at the end of the taxable year. The IRS and Treasury believe that this approach is more administrable because value should be more readily determinable on the acquisition date. In addition, this approach does not require tainted assets to be traced over time.

D. *Special Rules for Accounting for Dual Consolidated Losses—§1.1503(d)-3*

1. *Items attributable to a separate unit*

(a) *Overview*

Section 1.1503-2(d)(1)(ii) of the current regulations provides a rule for determining whether a separate unit has a dual consolidated loss. Under this rule, the separate unit must compute its taxable income as if it were a separate domestic corporation that is a dual resident corporation, using only those items of income, expense, deduction, and loss that are *otherwise attributable to* such separate unit.

The current regulations do not provide any guidance for determining the items of income, gain, deduction and loss that are otherwise attributable to a separate unit. The IRS and Treasury understand that the absence of such guidance has resulted in considerable uncertainty. For example, commentators have questioned whether all or any portion of the interest expense of a domestic owner is attributable to a separate unit.

It is also unclear the extent to which a separate unit is treated as a separate domestic corporation under this rule. For example, commentators have questioned whether a transaction between a separate unit and its owner that is generally disregarded for federal tax purposes (for example, interest paid by a disregarded entity on an obligation held by its owner) can create an item of income, gain, deduction or loss for purposes of calculating a dual consolidated loss.

Commentators have also questioned whether each separate unit in a tiered separate unit structure (that is, where one separate unit owns another separate unit) must separately determine whether it has a dual consolidated loss, or whether such separate units are combined for this purpose.

The proposed regulations provide more definitive rules for determining the amount of a dual consolidated loss (or income) of a separate unit. These rules apply solely for purposes of section 1503(d) and, therefore, do not apply for other purposes of the Code (for example, section 987). The proposed regulations first provide general rules that apply for purposes of calculating dual consolidated losses (or income) for both foreign branch separate units and hybrid entity separate units. The proposed regulations provide additional rules for calculating the dual consolidated losses (or income) of foreign branch separate units, hybrid entity separate units, and separate units owned indirectly through other separate units, non-hybrid entity partnerships, or non-hybrid entity grantor trusts. Finally, the proposed regulations provide special rules that apply to tiered separate units, combined separate units, dispositions of separate units, and the treatment of certain income inclusions on stock.

(b) *General Rules*

The proposed regulations clarify that only existing tax accounting items of income, gain, deduction and loss (translated into U.S. dollars) should be taken into account for purposes of calculating the dual consolidated loss of a separate unit. In other words, treating a separate unit as a separate domestic corporation does not cause items that are disregarded for U.S. tax purposes (for example, interest paid by a disregarded entity on an obligation held by its owner) to be regarded for purposes of calculating a separate unit's dual consolidated loss.

The proposed regulations also clarify that in the case of tiered separate units, each separate unit must calculate its own dual consolidated loss and no item of income, gain, deduction and loss may be taken into account in determining the taxable income or loss of more than one separate unit. Similarly, the proposed regulations clarify that items of one separate unit cannot offset or otherwise be taken into account by another separate unit for purposes of calculating a dual consolidated loss (unless the separate unit combination rule applies). These rules ensure that the dual consolidated loss calculation is computed separately for each separate unit, which is necessary to prevent deductions and losses from being double-dipped.

(c) *Foreign Branch Separate Unit*

The proposed regulations provide that the asset use and business activities principles of section 864(c) apply for purposes of determining the items of income, gain, deduction (other than interest) and loss that are taken into account in determining the taxable income or loss of a foreign branch separate unit. For this purpose, the trading safe harbors of section 864(b) do not apply for purposes of determining whether a trade or business exists within a foreign country or whether income may be treated as effectively connected to a foreign branch separate unit. In addition, the limitations on effectively connected treatment of foreign source related-party income under section 864(c)(4)(D) do not apply.

The proposed regulations further provide that the principles of §1.882-5, as modified, apply for purposes of determining the items of interest expense that are taken into account in determining the taxable income or loss of a foreign branch separate unit. The rules provide that a taxpayer must use U.S. tax principles to determine both the classification and amounts of the assets and liabilities when the actual worldwide ratio is used. The valuation of assets must be determined under the same methodology the taxpayer uses under §1.861-9T(g) for purposes of allocating and apportioning interest expense under section 864(e). Further, and solely for these purposes, the domestic owner of the foreign branch separate unit is treated as a foreign corporation, the foreign branch separate unit is treated as a trade or business within the United States, and assets other than those of the foreign branch separate unit are treated as assets that are not U.S. assets. Accordingly, only the interest expense of the domestic owner of the foreign branch separate unit is subject to allocation for purposes of computing the dual consolidated loss. The IRS and Treasury believe that the application of these principles will better harmonize the borrowing rate and effective interest costs that both the United States and the foreign country take into account in determining the dual consolidated loss, as compared to the use of §1.861-9T.

The IRS and Treasury believe that taking items into account in determining the taxable income or loss of a foreign branch separate unit under these standards is administrable because of the existing guidance provided under these provisions. In addition, the IRS and Treasury believe that this approach furthers the policy underlying section 1503(d) because it serves as a reasonable approximation of the items that the foreign jurisdiction may recognize as being taken into account in determining the taxable income or loss of a branch or permanent establishment of a non-resident corporation in such jurisdiction. Nevertheless, the IRS and Treasury solicit comments on these provisions and whether other administrable approaches (that approximate the items taken into account by the foreign jurisdiction) should be considered.

(d) *Hybrid Entity*

The proposed regulations provide rules for attributing items of income, gain, deduction and loss to a hybrid entity. These rules are necessary to determine the items that are attributable to an interest in a hybrid entity that constitutes a separate unit.

The proposed regulations provide that, in general, the items of income, gain, deduction and loss that are attributable to a hybrid entity are those items that are properly reflected on its books and records, as adjusted to conform to U.S. tax principles. The principles of §1.988-4(b)(2) apply for purposes of making this determination. These principles generally provide that the determination is a question of fact and must be consistently applied. These principles also provide that the Commissioner may allocate items of income, gain, deduction and loss between the domestic corporation (and intervening entities, if any) that own the hybrid entity separate unit, and the hybrid entity separate unit, if such items are not properly reflected on the books and records of the hybrid entity.

The proposed regulations also provide that if a hybrid entity owns an interest in either a non-hybrid entity partnership or a non-hybrid entity grantor trust, items of income, gain, deduction and loss that are properly reflected on the books and records of such partnership or grantor trust (under the principles of § 1.988-4(b)(2), as adjusted to conform to U.S. tax principles), are treated as being properly reflected on the books and records of the hybrid entity. However, such items are treated as being properly reflected on the books and records of the hybrid entity only to the extent they are taken into account by the hybrid entity under principles of subchapter K, chapter 1 of the Code, or the principles of subpart E, subchapter J, chapter 1 of the Code, as the case may be.

The IRS and Treasury believe that attributing items to a hybrid entity under this standard is administrable because it is generally consistent with the accounting treatment of the items. The IRS and Treasury also believe that this standard furthers the policy underlying section 1503(d) because the items that are properly reflected on the books and records of the hybrid entity (as adjusted to conform to U.S. tax principles) represent the best approximation of items that the foreign jurisdiction would recognize as being attributable to the entity. For example, it is likely that a foreign jurisdiction would recognize and take into account as being attributable to a hybrid entity the interest expense properly reflected on the books and records of the hybrid entity; however, it is unlikely that a foreign jurisdiction would recognize, and take into account as being attributable to a hybrid entity, interest expense of a domestic corporation that owns an interest in the hybrid entity.

(e) *Interest in a Disregarded Hybrid Entity*

The proposed regulations provide that, except to the extent otherwise provided under special rules (discussed below), items that are attributable to an interest in a hybrid entity that is disregarded as an entity separate from its owner are those items that are attributable to such hybrid entity itself.

(f) *Interests in Hybrid Entity Partnerships, Interests in Hybrid Entity Grantor Trusts, and Separate Units Owned Indirectly Through Partnerships and Grantor Trusts*

The proposed regulations provide rules for determining the extent to which: (1) items of income, gain, deduction and loss that are attributable to a hybrid entity that is a partnership are attributable to an interest in such hybrid entity partnership; and (2) items of income, gain, deduction and loss of a separate unit that is owned indirectly through a partnership are taken into account by a partner in such partnership. These items are taken into account to the extent they are includible in the partner's distributive share of the partnership income, gain, deduction or loss, as determined under the rules and principles of subchapter K, chapter 1 of the Code.

The proposed regulations also provide rules for determining the extent to which: (1) items of income, gain, deduction and loss attributable to a hybrid entity that is a grantor trust are attributable to an interest in such hybrid entity grantor trust; and (2) the items of income, gain, deduction and loss of a separate unit owned indirectly through a grantor trust are taken into account by an owner of such grantor trust. These items are taken into account to the extent they are attributable to trust property that the holder of the trust interest is treated as owning under the rules and principles of subpart E, subchapter J, chapter 1 of the Code.

(g) *Allocation of Items Between Certain Indirectly Owned Separate Units*

The proposed regulations provide special rules for allocating items of income, gain, deduction and loss to foreign branch separate units that are owned, directly or indirectly (other than through a hybrid entity separate unit) by hybrid entities. In such a case, only items that are attributable to the hybrid entity that owns such separate unit (and intervening entities, if any, that are not themselves separate units) are taken into account.

This rule is intended to minimize the items taken into account by a foreign branch separate unit that the foreign jurisdiction would not recognize as being so taken into account. This may occur in these cases because the foreign jurisdiction taxes the hybrid entity as a corporation (or otherwise at the entity level) and therefore likely would not take into account items of its owner. For example, if a domestic corporation indirectly owns a Country X foreign branch separate unit through a Country Y hybrid entity, Country X likely would take into account items of the Country Y hybrid entity as being items of the Country X branch. It is unlikely, however, that Country X would take into account items of the domestic corporation as items of the Country X branch because Country X views the owner of the Country X branch (the Country Y hybrid entity) as a corporation. Therefore, only the items of income, gain, deduction and loss of the Country Y hybrid entity (and not items of the domestic corporation) should be taken into account for purposes of determining the dual consolidated loss of the Country X branch.

The proposed regulations also provide that only income and assets of such hybrid entity are taken into account for purposes of applying the principles of section 864(c) and § 1.882-5, as modified, in determining the items taken into account by the foreign branch separate unit; thus, other income and assets of the domestic owner, for example, are not taken into account for these purposes. This rule is also intended to ensure that the principles under these provisions are applied in a way that best approximates the items that the foreign jurisdiction would recognize as being taken into account by a taxable presence in such jurisdiction.

Finally, the proposed regulations provide that items generally attributable to an interest in a hybrid entity are not taken into account to the extent they are taken into account by a foreign branch separate unit owned, directly or indirectly (other than through a hybrid entity separate unit), by the hybrid entity. This rule prevents two or more separate units from taking into account the same item of income, gain, deduction or loss under different rules.

(h) *Combined Separate Units*

As discussed above, the proposed regulations combine separate units owned, directly or indirectly, by a single domestic corporation, provided certain requirements are satisfied. Because different rules may apply for purposes of attributing items to individual separate units that may be combined into a single separate unit, special rules are necessary to attribute items to combined separate units.

The proposed regulations provide that in the case of a combined separate unit, items are first attributable to, or otherwise taken into account by, the individual separate units composing the combined separate unit, without regard to the combination rule. The combined separate unit then takes into account all of the items attributable to, or taken into account by, the individual separate units that compose such combined separate unit.

(i) *Gain or Loss Recognized on Dispositions of Separate Units*

The current regulations do not indicate whether items of income, gain, deduction and loss recognized on the sale or disposition of a separate unit, or of an interest in a partnership or grantor trust through which a separate unit is indirectly owned, is attributable to or taken into account by such separate unit for purposes of calculating. the dual consolidated loss of the separate unit for the year of the sale (or for purposes of reducing the amount of recapture as a result of a triggering event).

The IRS and Treasury believe that it is appropriate to take into account items of income, gain, deduction and loss recognized on these dispositions. Thus, the proposed regulations provide that items of income, gain, deduction and loss recognized on the disposition of a separate unit (or an interest in a partnership or grantor trust that directly or indirectly owns a separate unit), are attributable to or taken into account by the separate unit to the extent of the gain or loss that would have been recognized had such separate unit sold all its assets in a taxable exchange, immediately before the disposition of the separate unit, for an amount equal to their fair market value. The proposed regulations clarify that for this purpose items of income and gain include loss recapture income or gain under section 367(a)(3)(C) or 904(f)(3).

The proposed regulations also address situations where more than one separate unit is disposed of in the same transaction and items of income, gain, deduction and loss recognized on such disposition are attributable to more than one separate unit. In such a case, items of income, gain, deduction and loss are attributable to or taken into account by each such separate unit based on the gain or loss that would have been recognized by each separate unit if it had sold all of its assets in a taxable exchange, immediately before the disposition of the separate unit, for an amount equal to their fair market value.

(j) *Income Inclusion on Stock*

The current regulations do not indicate whether an amount included in income arising from the ownership of stock in a foreign corporation (income inclusion) is attributable to or taken into account by a separate unit that owns the stock that gave rise to the income inclusion. For example, if a domestic corporation has a section 951(a) inclusion attributable to stock of a controlled foreign corporation that is owned by a hybrid entity separate unit, it is not clear under the current regulations whether such income inclusion is taken into account for purposes of calculating the dual consolidated loss of the hybrid entity separate unit.

The IRS and Treasury believe that, solely for purposes of applying the dual consolidated loss rules, it is appropriate to treat income inclusions arising from the ownership of stock in the same manner that dividend income is treated. Accordingly, the proposed regulations provide that income inclusions are taken into account for purposes of calculating the dual consolidated loss of a separate unit if an actual dividend from such foreign corporation would have been so taken into account.

(k) *Section 987 Gain or Loss*

Section 987 provides that if a taxpayer has one or more qualified business units with a functional currency other than the dollar, the taxpayer must make proper adjustments to take into account foreign currency gain or loss on certain transfers of property between such qualified business units.

In 1991, the IRS and Treasury issued proposed regulations under section 987 that included rules for determining the amount of foreign currency gain or loss recognized on certain transfers of property between qualified business units. On April 3,2000, the IRS and Treasury issued Notice 2000-20 (2000-14 I.R.B. 851) announcing that the IRS and Treasury intend to review and possibly replace the proposed regulations issued under section 987. The IRS and Treasury have opened a regulations project under section 987 and expect to issue new section 987 regulations in the future.

The current regulations do not provide specific rules that indicate whether section 987 gains or losses of a domestic owner are attributable to, or taken into account by, a separate unit for purposes of calculating the separate unit's dual consolidated loss. Because the IRS and Treasury have an open regulations project under section 987 and expect to issue new regulations under section 987, the IRS and Treasury do not believe it is appropriate to address this issue in the proposed regulations. The IRS and Treasury request comments on whether section 987 gains and losses of a domestic owner should be attributable to, or taken into account by, a separate unit, particularly with respect to section 987 gains and losses attributable to, or taken into account by, separate units owned indirectly through hybrid entity separate units.

2. *Effect of a dual consolidated loss*

Section 1.1503-2(d)(2) of the current regulations provides that if a dual resident corporation has a dual consolidated loss that is subject to the general rule restricting it from offsetting the income of a domestic affiliate, the consolidated group of which the dual resident corporation is a member must compute its taxable income without taking into account the items of income, gain, deduction or loss taken into account in computing the dual consolidated loss. The current regulations contain a similar rule for separate units.

These rules do not exclude only the dual consolidated loss in computing taxable income, but instead provide that none of the gross tax accounting items that compose the dual consolidated loss are taken into account. While this approach has the same effect on net income as would excluding only the dual consolidated loss, removing all gross items of income, gain, deduction and loss may have a distortive effect on other federal tax calculations.

The IRS and Treasury believe that this distortive effect will be minimized if only the dual consolidated loss itself is not taken into account. Accordingly, the proposed regulations provide that only a pro rata portion of each item of deduction and loss taken into account in computing the dual consolidated loss are excluded in computing taxable income. In addition, to the extent that a dual consolidated loss is carried over or carried back and, subject to § 1.1502-21(c) (as modified in the proposed regulations), is made available to offset income generated by the dual resident corporation or separate unit, the proposed regulations treat items composing the dual consolidated loss as being used on a pro rata basis.

3. *Basis adjustments*

Section 1.1503-2(d)(3) of the current regulations contains special basis adjustment rules that override the normal investment adjustment rules under § 1.1502-32 for stock of affiliated dual resident corporations or affiliated domestic owners owned by other members of the consolidated group. These rules provide that stock basis is reduced by a dual consolidated loss, even though such loss is subject to the general limitation on the use of a dual consolidated loss to offset income of a domestic affiliate. To avoid reducing the stock basis a second time for the same dual consolidated loss, the rules also provide that no negative adjustment shall be made for the amount of dual consolidated loss subject to the general limitation that is subsequently absorbed in a carryover or carryback year. Finally, the rules provide that there is no basis increase for recapture income recognized as a result of a triggering event. Similar rules apply to separate units arising from ownership of an interest in a partnership. These special basis adjustment rules are generally intended to prevent an indirect deduction of a dual consolidated loss.

The proposed regulations retain the special stock basis adjustment rules, as modified, to prevent the indirect use of a dual consolidated loss. In addition, the proposed regulations retain the rules addressing the effect of a dual consolidated loss on a partner's adjusted basis in its partnership interest in cases where the partnership interest is a separate unit, or a separate unit is owned indirectly through a partnership. These rules require the partner to adjust its basis in accordance with the principles of section 705, subject to certain modifications.

The IRS and Treasury recognize that these rules may lead to harsh results, particularly in light of the fact that the indirect use of the dual consolidated loss would only arise through the disposition of the stock of a dual resident corporation (or a partnership interest) that may not occur for many years after the dual consolidated loss is incurred. In addition, upon such subsequent disposition the resulting deduction or loss would generally be capital in nature, and the definition of a dual consolidated loss excludes capital losses incurred by the dual resident corporation or separate unit. As a result, the IRS and Treasury request comments regarding concerns over these types of indirect uses and whether the special basis rules should be retained. These comments should consider whether the policies underlying section 1503(d) require basis adjustment rules that differ from other basis adjustment rules that apply to non-capital, non-deductible expenses (for example, rules under sections 705 and 1367, and § 1.1502-32(b))

E. *Exceptions to the Domestic Use Limitation Rule—§ 1.1503(d)-4*

1. *No possibility of foreign use*

The proposed regulations provide a new exception to the general rule prohibiting the domestic use of a dual consolidated loss. To qualify under this exception, the consolidated group, unaffiliated dual resident corporation, or unaffiliated domestic owner must: (1) demonstrate, to the satisfaction of the Commissioner, that there can be no foreign use of the dual consolidated loss at any time; and (2) prepare a statement and attach it to its tax return for the taxable year in which the dual consolidated loss is incurred. This statement must include an analysis, in reasonable detail and specificity, supported with an official or certified English translation of the relevant provisions of foreign law, of the treatment of the losses and deductions composing the dual consolidated loss, and the reasons supporting the conclusion that there cannot be a foreign use of the dual consolidated loss by any means at any time.

This exception is intended to replace the exception to the definition of a dual consolidated loss contained in § 1.1503-2(c)(5)(ii)(A) of the current regulations. Thus, under the proposed regulations the question of foreign use is not relevant to the definition of a dual consolidated loss; the issue will instead be whether an exception to the domestic use limitation applies. Consistent with the exception to the definition of a dual consolidated loss contained in the current regulations, the IRS and Treasury believe that this new exception to the domestic use limitation rule contained in the proposed regulations will apply only in rare and unusual circumstances due to the definition of foreign use and general principles of foreign law. For example, if the foreign jurisdiction recognizes any item of deduction or loss composing the dual consolidated loss (regardless of whether recognized currently or deferred, for example, by being reflected in the basis of assets), and such item is available for foreign use through a form of consolidation, carryover or carryback, or a transaction (for example, a merger, basis carryover transaction, or entity classification election), then the exception will not apply.

2. *Domestic use election and agreement*

As discussed above, the current regulations provide an exception to the general rule prohibiting the use of a dual consolidated loss to offset the income of a domestic affiliate if a (g)(2)(i) election is made. Under this exception, the consolidated group, unaffiliated dual resident corporation, or unaffiliated domestic owner must enter into an agreement ((g)(2)(i) agreement) certifying, among other things, that no portion of the deductions or losses taken into account in computing the dual consolidated loss have been, or will be, used to offset the income of any other person under the income tax laws of a foreign country.

The proposed regulations retain this elective exception, with modifications, and refer to it as a *domestic use election*. In addition, the proposed regulations refer to the consolidated group, unaffiliated dual resident corporation, or unaffiliated domestic owner, as the case may be, that makes a domestic use election as an *elector*. In order to elect relief under this exception, the proposed regulations require the elector to enter into a domestic use agreement, which is similar to the (g)(2)(i) agreement required by the current regulations.

3. *Certification period*

Under the current regulations, a (g)(2)(i) agreement generally provides that if there is a triggering event during the 15-year period following the year in which the dual consolidated loss was incurred (certification period), the taxpayer must recapture and report as income the amount of the dual consolidated loss, and pay an interest charge. See § 1.1503-2(g)(2)(iii)(A).

Commentators have questioned whether under the current regulations the 15-year certification period applies only to the use triggering event, or whether it applies to all triggering events. These commentators note that, under this interpretation, triggering events other than use could occur after the expiration of the certification period. The IRS and Treasury believe that the certification period applies to all triggering events. Accordingly, the proposed regulations clarify that all triggering events are subject to the certification period and, therefore, a triggering event cannot occur after the expiration of the certification period.

The IRS and Treasury also believe that a 15-year certification period is not required to deter and monitor double-dipping of losses and deductions. Moreover, the IRS and Treasury believe that requiring taxpayers to comply with the dual consolidated loss regulations, including the need to monitor potential triggering events and to comply with the various filing requirements, for a 15-year period is unnecessarily burdensome to both taxpayers and the Commissioner. As a result, the proposed regulations reduce the certification period from 15 years to seven years with respect to a domestic use election.

4. *Consistency rule*

Section 1.1503-2(g)(2)(ii) of the current regulations contains a consistency rule. Under this rule, if any losses, expenses, or deductions taken into account in computing the dual consolidated loss of a dual resident corporation or separate unit are used to offset the income of another person under the laws of a single foreign country while the dual resident corporation or separate unit is owned by the domestic owner or member of the consolidated group, the losses, expenses, or deductions taken into account in computing the dual consolidated losses of other dual resident corporations or separate units owned by the same consolidated group (or other separate units owned by the unaffiliated domestic owner of the first separate unit) in that year are deemed to offset income of another person in the same foreign country. This rule only applies, however, if such losses, expenses, or deductions are recognized in the foreign country in the same taxable year. Moreover, this rule does not apply if, under foreign law, the other dual resident corporation or separate unit cannot use its losses, expenses, or deductions to offset income of another person in such taxable year.

The consistency rule is intended to ensure that a consolidated group or domestic owner treats uniformly all dual consolidated losses of dual resident corporations or separate units that it owns that are available for use in a foreign country in a given year. The rule is also intended to minimize the administrative burden associated with identifying the items of loss or deduction of a particular dual consolidated loss that are used to offset income of another person under the income tax laws of a foreign country.

Commentators have questioned the need for the consistency rule, noting that it can lead to harsh results.

The IRS and Treasury believe that, despite concerns raised by commentators, the consistency rule continues to be necessary to promote the uniform treatment of dual consolidated losses of dual resident corporations and separate units owned by the consolidated group or domestic owner, and to minimize administrative burdens. As a result, the proposed regulations retain the consistency rule, as modified.

In addition, the proposed regulations clarify that the consistency rule only applies to a dual consolidated loss that is subject to a domestic use agreement (other than a new domestic use agreement). In other words, the proposed regulations clarify that the consistency rule does not apply to a foreign use of a dual consolidated loss that occurs subsequent to a triggering event that terminates the domestic use agreement filed with respect to such dual consolidated loss.

5. *Restrictions on domestic use elections*

The current regulations do not explicitly address situations where a triggering event (discussed below) with respect to a dual consolidated loss occurs in the year in which the dual consolidated loss is incurred. The proposed regulations, however, make clear that a domestic use election cannot be made for a dual consolidated loss incurred in the same year in which a triggering event with respect to such loss occurs.

The current regulations also do not explicitly address the application of section 953(d)(3) (limiting losses of foreign insurance companies that elect to be treated as domestic corporations). The proposed regulations, however, provide that a foreign insurance company that has elected to be treated as a domestic corporation pursuant to section 953(d) may not make a domestic use election. This rule is consistent with section 953(d)(3), which broadly prohibits regulatory exceptions to the general prohibition on the domestic use of dual consolidated losses in such cases.

6. *Triggering events*

(a) *In General*

Section 1.1503-2(g)(2)(iii) of the current regulations provides rules relating to certain events which require the recapture of previously allowed dual consolidated losses. Under these rules, if a consolidated group, unaffiliated dual resident corporation, or unaffiliated domestic owner, as the case may be, makes a (g)(2)(i) election, the dual resident corporation or separate unit must recapture, and the consolidated group, unaffiliated dual resident corporation or unaffiliated domestic owner must report as income the amount of the dual consolidated loss (and pay an interest charge) if a triggering event occurs during the certification period. Taxpayers may, however, rebut these triggering events upon making certain showings to the satisfaction of the Commissioner.

The proposed regulations generally retain the triggering event rules contained in the proposed regulations, as modified, if a taxpayer makes a domestic use election.

(b) *Carryover of Losses, Deductions, and Basis*

Under the current regulations, certain asset transfers by a dual resident corporation that result, under the laws of a foreign country, in a carryover of losses, expenses, or deductions are triggering events. The current regulations contain a similar rule for such transfers by separate units. See § 1.1503-2(g)(2)(iii)(A)(*4*), and (*5*).

The proposed regulations retain these triggering events, as modified, and combine them into a single triggering event. The proposed regulations also clarify that certain asset transfers that result in the carryover of basis in assets under the laws of a foreign country also qualify as triggering events. This is the case because asset basis generally will, at some point in the future, be converted into a loss or deduction as a result of the depreciation, amortization or disposition of the asset. Accordingly, under foreign law, a transaction that results in the carryover of asset basis generally has the same effect as a transaction that results in the carryover of losses or deductions and therefore should be treated similarly.

(c) *Disposition by a Separate Unit or Dual Resident Corporation of an Interest in a Separate Unit or Stock of a Dual Resident Corporation*

The current regulations provide that certain sales or other dispositions of 50 percent or more of the assets of a separate unit or dual resident corporation are deemed to be triggering events. See § 1.1503-2(g)(2)(iii)(A)(*4*) and (*5*). For this purpose, an interest in a separate unit and stock of a dual resident corporation are treated as assets of the separate unit or dual resident corporation. One commentator stated that, as a result of this rule, the disposition of an interest in one separate unit by another separate unit may inappropriately result in a triggering event for both separate units. Accordingly, the commentator suggested that the disposition of the interest in the lower-tier separate unit should not result in a triggering event with respect to dual consolidated losses of the separate unit that disposed of such interest.

The IRS and Treasury believe that the disposition of an interest in a lower-tier separate unit (or the shares of a dual resident corporation) by an upper-tier separate unit (or dual resident corporation) typically will not result in the carryover of the dual consolidated loss of the upper-tier separate unit (or dual resident corporation) under the laws of the foreign jurisdiction such that it could be put to a foreign use. Therefore, the proposed regulations provide that for purposes of determining whether 50 percent or more of the separate unit's or dual resident corporation's assets is disposed of, an interest in a separate unit and the stock of a dual resident corporation shall not be treated as assets of the separate unit or dual resident corporation making such disposition. The IRS and Treasury request comments as to other assets the disposition of which should be excluded from the 50 percent test under this triggering event.

(d) *Fifty Percent Threshold for Asset Transfer Triggering Events*

Section 1.1503-2(g)(2)(iii)(A)(*7*) of the current regulations provides that a triggering event occurs if, within a 12-month period, the domestic owner of a separate unit disposes of 50 percent or more (by voting power or value) of the interest in the separate unit that was owned by the domestic owner on the last day of the taxable year in which the dual consolidated loss was incurred. As noted above, the current regulations also provide that a triggering event occurs if a domestic owner of a separate unit transfers assets of the separate unit in a transaction that results, under the laws of a foreign country, in a carryover of the separate unit's losses, expenses, or deductions. Section 1.1503-2(g)(2)(iii)(A)(*5*). Moreover, the current regulations deem such an asset transfer to be a triggering event if 50 percent or more of the separate unit's assets (measured by fair market value at the time of transfer) are disposed of within a 12-month period.

One commentator noted that the two triggering events discussed above operate differently in that any transfer of assets of a separate unit may constitute a triggering event, while the transfer of an interest in a separate unit constitutes a triggering event only if a 50 percent threshold is met.

The IRS and Treasury believe that these two triggering events should operate in a consistent manner. As a result, the proposed regulations provide that both the asset transfer triggering event and the separate unit interest transfer triggering event occur only if a 50 percent threshold is satisfied. It should be noted, however, that transfers of assets of a dual resident corporation or separate unit, and transfers of interests of separate units, in many cases will subsequently result in a foreign use triggering event, even though the 50 percent threshold for the asset transfer triggering event and the separate unit interest transfer triggering event are not satisfied. For example, if a domestic owner of an interest in a hybrid entity separate unit transfers 25 percent of its interest in the hybrid entity separate unit to a foreign corporation, all or a portion of a dual consolidated loss attributable to such separate unit in a prior year may be available to offset subsequent income of the owner of the transferred interest (that is not a separate unit after such transfer because it is held by a foreign corporation) and therefore may result in a foreign use triggering event.

(e) *S Corporation Conversion*

Under the current regulations, if either an affiliated dual resident corporation or an affiliated domestic owner that has filed a (g)(2)(i) agreement with respect to a dual consolidated loss elects to be an S corporation pursuant to section 1362(a), such election results in a triggering event because it terminates the consolidated group and the affiliated dual resident corporation or affiliated domestic owner ceases to be a member of a consolidated group. See § 1.1503-2(g)(2)(iii)(A)(2). The current regulations do not, however, address an election to be an S corporation by either an unaffiliated dual resident corporation or an unaffiliated domestic owner that has made a (g)(2)(i) election.

The IRS and Treasury believe that the election by an unaffiliated dual resident corporation or unaffiliated domestic owner to be an S corporation should be treated in the same manner as an election by an affiliated dual resident corporation or affiliated domestic owner that is a member of a consolidated group. Accordingly, the proposed regulations add as a new triggering event the election of either an unaffiliated dual resident corporation or unaffiliated domestic owner to be an S corporation.

(f) *Consolidated Group Remains in Existence*

As stated above, and subject to exceptions, the current regulations provide that a triggering event occurs with respect to a dual consolidated loss of an affiliated dual resident corporation or affiliated domestic owner if such dual resident corporation or affiliated domestic owner ceases to be a member of the consolidated group of which it was a member when the dual consolidated loss was incurred. The current regulations also provide that an affiliated dual resident corporation or affiliated domestic owner is considered to cease to be a member of a consolidated group if the consolidated group ceases to exist (group termination triggering event) because, for example, the common parent is no longer in existence. Section 1.1503-2(g)(2)(iii)(A)(2).

One commentator stated that language contained in Revenue Procedure 2000-42 (2000-2 C.B. 394) may imply that there is a group termination triggering event if the common parent of a consolidated group that made a (g)(2)(i) election ceases to exist, or is a party to a reverse acquisition, even though the consolidated group remains in existence. This interpretation is contrary to the principles underlying the triggering events. Accordingly, the proposed regulations clarify that such transactions do not constitute group termination triggering events. See § 1.1503(d)-5(c) *Example 47*.

7. *Rebuttal of triggering events*

Under the current regulations, taxpayers may rebut all but two of the triggering events such that there is no dual consolidated loss recapture (or related interest charge) as a result of a putative triggering event. In general, under the current regulations, a triggering event is rebutted if the taxpayer demonstrates to the satisfaction of the Commissioner that, depending on the triggering event, either: (1) the losses, expenses or deductions of the dual resident corporation (or separate unit) cannot be used to offset income of another person under the laws of a foreign country or; (2) the transfer of assets did not result in a carryover under foreign law of the losses, expenses, or deductions of the dual resident corporation (or separate unit) to the transferee of the assets. See § 1.1503-2(g)(2)(iii)(A)(2) through (7). The policies underpinning the dual consolidated loss rules do not require recapture or an interest charge in such cases because there is no opportunity for any portion of the dual consolidated loss to be used to offset income of any other person under the income tax laws of a foreign country.

The rebuttal rules impose a standard of proof on taxpayers that in many cases is difficult and burdensome to meet, even though there may be little likelihood that any portion of the dual consolidated loss could be used to offset the income of any other person under the income tax laws of a foreign country. For example, demonstrating that no portion of the dual consolidated loss can be used by another person as a result of typical loss carryover transactions under foreign law may not satisfy the burden if there is some potential that any portion of losses or deductions composing the dual consolidated loss could be so used as a result of a transaction that is rare, commercially impractical, or not reasonably foreseeable. In addition, because there are often significant differences between U.S. and foreign law, ruling out the various types of transactions that under U.S. law would allow all or a portion of the dual consolidated loss to be used by another person also may not be sufficient to rebut a triggering event.

Commentators have noted that under the current regulations it may not be possible to rebut certain triggering events if the tax basis of a single asset carries over to another person under foreign law, even though as a result of the transaction recognized losses and accrued deductions generally do not carry over to another person under foreign law. This is the case because the person that receives the carryover asset basis may at some point in the future enjoy the benefit of a loss or deduction as a result of the depreciation, amortization or disposition of the asset. As a result, the carryover of a nominal amount of asset tax basis causes the entire dual consolidated loss to be recaptured. Similar issues arise in connection with assumptions of liabilities that, for example, result in deductions for U.S. tax purposes on an accrual basis, but are deductible under the laws of the foreign jurisdiction at a later time when paid. This result is consistent with the *all or nothing* principle, discussed below.

The IRS and Treasury recognize that in some of these cases the use of a portion of a dual consolidated loss may be denied in both the United States and the foreign jurisdiction. Further, commentators have stated that denying a loss or deduction from offsetting income in both the United States and the foreign jurisdiction generally is inconsistent with the principles underlying section 1503(d) because the statute's purpose is to prevent the use of the same loss or deduction to offset income in multiple jurisdictions.

The proposed regulations retain the rebuttal standard contained in the current regulations, with modifications. Taxpayers may rebut a triggering event under the proposed regulations if it can be demonstrated, to the satisfaction of the Commissioner, that there can be no foreign use of the dual consolidated loss. In addition, unlike the current regulations that have different standards for different triggering events, the proposed regulations apply the same standard to all triggering events (other than a foreign use triggering event, which cannot be rebutted).

The IRS and Treasury believe that when the proposed regulations are finalized the number of transactions undertaken by taxpayers that result in triggering events will be significantly reduced, as compared to the current regulations, because of the significant reduction in the term of the certification period. Nevertheless, the IRS and Treasury believe that the current rebuttal standard may exceed that required to address adequately the concern that all or a portion of a dual consolidated loss could be put to a foreign use. Moreover, the IRS and Treasury believe that more definitive and administrable rebuttal rules should be provided to assist taxpayers and the Commissioner in determining whether the triggering event has been rebutted, and to minimize situations where there is recapture of a dual consolidated loss even though it may be unlikely that a significant portion of the dual consolidated loss could be put to a foreign use. Therefore, it is anticipated that, prior to the finalization of these proposed regulations, a revenue procedure will be issued that will provide safe harbors whereby triggering events will be deemed to be rebutted if the taxpayer satisfies various conditions. The revenue procedure may be issued in proposed form and then made final contemporaneously with these regulations.

It is anticipated that the conditions contained in the revenue procedure would include the requirement that taxpayers demonstrate, to the satisfaction of the Commissioner, that there can be no foreign use of any significant portion of the dual consolidated loss as a result of certain enumerated transactions. It is also anticipated that the revenue procedure will address, and in some cases provide relief for, transactions that result in a *de minimis* carry over of asset basis under foreign law and are difficult or impossible to rebut under the current regulations. Finally, the revenue procedure may provide relief for triggering events resulting from the assumption of liabilities in connection with the acquisition of a trade or business as a result of liabilities incurred in the ordinary course of business being deductible at different times under U.S. law and the law of the foreign jurisdiction.

The IRS and Treasury request comments regarding the transactions that should be included in the revenue procedure, approaches to address basis carryover transactions and liabilities assumed in the ordinary course of business, and other ways to minimize the administrative burden associated with rebutting the triggering events, while ensuring that there is little or no likelihood that a significant portion of the dual consolidated loss can be put to a foreign use.

8. *Triggering event exception for acquisition by an unaffiliated domestic corporation or a new consolidated group*

Section 1.1503-2(g)(2)(iv)(B)(*1*) of the current regulations provides that if certain requirements are satisfied, the following events do not constitute triggering events: (1) an affiliated dual resident corporation or affiliated domestic owner becomes an unaffiliated domestic corporation or a member of a new consolidated group (unless such transaction also qualifies under another exception); (2) assets of a dual resident corporation or a separate unit are acquired by an unaffiliated domestic corporation or a member of a new consolidated group; or (3) a domestic owner of a separate unit transfers its interest in the separate unit to an unaffiliated domestic corporation or to a member of a new consolidated group.

The first requirement necessary for this exception to apply is that the consolidated group, unaffiliated dual resident corporation, or unaffiliated domestic owner that made the (g)(2)(i) election, and the unaffiliated domestic corporation or new consolidated group must enter into a closing agreement with the IRS providing that both parties will be jointly and severally liable for the total amount of the recapture of the dual consolidated loss and interest charge upon a subsequent triggering event. Second, the unaffiliated domestic corporation or new consolidated group must agree to treat any potential recapture as unrealized built-in gain for purposes of section 384, subject to any applicable exceptions thereunder. Finally, the unaffiliated domestic corporation or new consolidated group must file with its timely filed income tax return for the year in which the event occurs a (g)(2)(i) agreement (new (g)(2)(i) agreement), whereby it assumes the same obligations with respect to the dual consolidated loss as the corporation or consolidated group that filed the original (g)(2)(i) agreement with respect to that loss.

On July 30, 2003, the IRS and Treasury issued final regulations (2003 regulations), published in the **Federal Register** at 68 FR 44616, that limited the need for closing agreements to avoid triggering events to only those three transactions described above. The preamble to the 2003 regulations explained that in certain cases the requirement for a closing agreement resulted in an unnecessary administrative burden because the several liability imposed by § 1.1502-6, in conjunction with the original (g)(2)(i) agreement and a new (g)(2)(i) agreement, provided for liability sufficiently comparable to that imposed under a closing agreement. Accordingly, the 2003 regulations provided that if a new (g)(2)(i) agreement is filed by the unaffiliated domestic corporation or new consolidated group, a closing agreement is not required in the following two instances: (1) an unaffiliated dual resident corporation or unaffiliated domestic owner that filed a (g)(2)(i) agreement becomes a member of a consolidated group; and (2) a consolidated group that filed a (g)(2)(i) agreement ceases to exist as a result of a transaction described in § 1.1502-13(j)(5)(i) (unless a member of the terminating group, or successor-in-interest of such member, is not a member of the surviving group immediately after the terminating group ceases to exist).

The preamble to the 2003 regulations noted that the IRS and Treasury were continuing to consider other alternatives to further reduce the administrative and compliance burdens under section 1503(d). After further consideration, the IRS and Treasury believe that, as a result of various requirements contained in the proposed regulations, there are sufficient protections, independent of a closing agreement, in all cases in which a closing agreement is otherwise required under the current regulations. As a result, the proposed regulations eliminate the closing agreement requirement contained in the current regulations and provide an exception to triggering events in all such cases (subsequent elector events) if: (1) the unaffiliated domestic corporation or new consolidated group (subsequent elector) enters into a domestic use agreement (new domestic use agreement); and (2) the corporation or consolidated group that filed the original domestic use agreement (original elector) files a statement with its tax return for the year of the event.

Pursuant to the new domestic use agreement, the subsequent elector must: (1) agree to assume the same obligations with respect to the dual consolidated loss as the original elector had pursuant to its domestic use agreement; (2) agree to treat any potential recapture of the dual consolidated loss at issue as unrealized built-in gain pursuant to section 384, subject to any applicable exceptions thereunder; (3) agree to be subject to the successor elector rules, discussed below; and (4) identify the original elector (and subsequent electors, if any). Pursuant to the statement filed by the original elector, the original elector must agree to be subject to the subsequent elector rules and must identify the subsequent elector.

9. *Triggering event exception—private letter ruling and closing agreement option*

Under the current regulations, only specific triggering events can qualify for an exception as a result of the parties entering into a closing agreement. Therefore, the IRS will not consider entering into a closing agreement in other circumstances, even though the government's interests may be adequately protected in such circumstances such that recapture may not be necessary.

Although the proposed regulations eliminate the need for a closing agreement to qualify for an exception to triggering events, discussed above, the IRS and Treasury are considering whether in limited cases it may be appropriate for the Commissioner, in its sole discretion and subject to the taxpayer satisfying conditions specified by the Commissioner, to enter into closing agreements with taxpayers such that certain other events would not be triggering events. Comments are requested as to the specific and limited types of triggering events that may be suitable for this exception, taking into account the policies underlying section 1503(d), administrative burdens, and the general interests of the U.S. government.

10. *Annual certification reporting requirement*

Section 1.1503-2T(g)(2)(vi)(B) of the current regulations provides that if a (g)(2)(i) election is made with respect to a dual consolidated loss of a dual resident corporation or a hybrid entity separate unit, the consolidated group, unaffiliated dual resident corporation, or unaffiliated domestic owner, as the case may be, must file with its tax return an annual certification during the certification period. This filing certifies that the losses or deductions that make up the dual consolidated loss have not been used to offset the income of another person under the tax laws of a foreign country. The filing also warrants that arrangements have been made to ensure that there will be no such use of the dual consolidated loss and that the taxpayer will be informed if any such use were to occur. The current regulations do not, however, require annual certifications for dual consolidated losses of foreign branch separate units.

The IRS and Treasury believe that annual certifications of dual consolidated losses improve taxpayer compliance with the dual consolidated loss rules and are beneficial to the Commissioner in monitoring such compliance. The IRS and Treasury also believe that foreign branch separate units, hybrid entity separate units, and dual resident corporations should, to the extent possible, be treated consistently to reduce complexity. As a result, the proposed regulations expand the annual certification requirement to include dual consolidated losses of foreign branch separate units. However, the reduction in the certification period from 15 years to seven years should substantially reduce the overall compliance burden of this requirement.

11. *Amount of recapture*

As stated above, under the current regulations a triggering event (other than a foreign use) generally can be rebutted only if no portion of the dual consolidated loss can be used by (or carries over to) another person under foreign law. See § 1.503-2(g)(2)(iii)(A)(2) through (7). Thus, if even a *de minimis* portion of the dual consolidated loss can be used by (or carries over to) another person, the triggering event cannot be rebutted. Similarly, § 1.1503-2(g)(2)(vii)(A) of the current regulations provides that if a triggering event occurs, the entire dual consolidated loss subject to the (g)(2)(i) agreement (reduced by income earned subsequently by the dual resident corporation or separate unit) is recaptured and reported as income, regardless of the amount of the dual consolidated loss used by the other person. Thus, even a *de minimis* foreign use will cause the entire amount of the dual consolidated loss to be recaptured and reported as income.

This so-called *all or nothing* principle is included in the current regulations primarily due to administrative concerns. In many cases, the exact amount of the dual consolidated loss that is used by another person cannot be readily determined. This inability is due, in part, to differences between U.S. and foreign law. For example, there may be temporary and permanent differences in the treatment of items of income, gain, deduction and loss. There may also be differences in loss carryover provisions. These concerns are exacerbated by the principle that certain deductions are fungible and, therefore, cannot easily be traced to a particular loss incurred in a particular year.

Commentators have noted that in some cases the *all or nothing* principle results in a disallowance of deductions in both the United States and the foreign jurisdiction. Nevertheless, the IRS and Treasury believe that making a precise determination as to the amount of the dual consolidated loss put to a foreign use would require the Commissioner and taxpayers to analyze foreign law in great detail and, in some cases, compare the treatment of items under foreign law with their treatment under U.S. law. Such an analysis, however, is inconsistent with the principle underlying the regulations that, to the extent possible, the Commissioner and taxpayers should not be required to analyze foreign law. Moreover, departing from the *all or nothing* principle would likely require detailed ordering, stacking, and tracing rules to determine the amount and nature of dual consolidated losses that are recaptured upon a use. Such rules would add considerable complexity to the regulations. As a result, the proposed regulations retain the *all or nothing* rule contained in the current regulations. However, the IRS and Treasury request comments regarding administrable alternatives to the *all or nothing* rule that would not involve substantial analyses of foreign law. For example, comments are requested as to whether a pro rata recapture rule with respect to dispositions of separate units would be consistent with the general framework of the proposed regulations and would be administrable.

12. *Subsequent elector rules*

Neither the current regulations nor Rev. Proc. 2000-42 (2000-2 C.B. 394) explicitly address the consequences resulting from a triggering event (to which no exception applies) with respect to a dual consolidated loss that was not recaptured due to an earlier triggering event as a result of the parties entering into a closing agreement. In such a case, both parties are jointly and severally liable for the total amount of the recapture of the dual consolidated loss and interest charge resulting from such a subsequent triggering event. However, it is unclear which taxpayer must report the recapture income (and related interest charge) on its tax return upon the subsequent triggering event. In addition, there is little or no procedural guidance outlining how, pursuant to a closing agreement, the IRS would collect recapture tax and the related interest charge from the parties to the closing agreement.

Accordingly, the proposed regulations contain rules regarding subsequent electors. These rules apply when, subsequent to an event that is not a triggering event because the unaffiliated domestic corporation or new consolidated group enters into a new domestic use agreement and satisfies other requirements (excepted event), a triggering event occurs, and no exception applies to such event (subsequent triggering event). The proposed regulations also provide rules that apply in the case of multiple subsequent electors (when subsequent to an excepted event, another excepted event occurs).

The proposed regulations first provide that, except to the extent provided under the subsequent elector rules, the original elector (and in the case of multiple excepted events, any prior subsequent elector) is not subject to the general recapture and interest charge rules provided under the regulations. As a result, only the subsequent elector that owns the dual resident corporation or separate unit at the time of the subsequent triggering event is subject to the general recapture and interest charge rules.

The proposed regulations also provide that, upon a subsequent triggering event to which no exception applies, the subsequent elector must calculate the recapture tax amount with respect to the dual consolidated loss subject to the new domestic use agreement and include it, along with an identification of the dual consolidated losses at issue and the original elector, on a statement attached to its tax return. The subsequent elector calculates the recapture tax amount based on a *with and without* calculation. The recapture tax amount equals the excess (if any) of the income tax liability of the subsequent elector for the taxable year of the subsequent triggering event, over the income tax liability of the subsequent elector for such taxable year computed by excluding the amount of recapture and related interest charge with respect to the dual consolidated losses at issue.

In addition, the proposed regulations provide rules regarding tax assessment and collection procedures. The proposed regulations provide that an assessment identifying an income tax liability of the subsequent elector is considered an assessment of the recapture tax amount where such amount is part of the income tax liability being assessed and the recapture tax amount is reflected in the statement attached to the subsequent elector's tax return. The recapture tax amount is considered to be properly assessed as an income tax liability of the original elector, and each prior subsequent elector, if any, on the same date the income tax liability of the subsequent elector was properly assessed. This liability is joint and several.

The proposed regulations also provide procedures pursuant to which any unpaid balance of the recapture tax amount may be collected from the original elector and the prior subsequent elector, if any. Such amounts may be collected from the original elector, and/or any prior subsequent elector, if each of the following conditions is satisfied: (1) the Commissioner has properly assessed the recapture amount; (2) the Commissioner has issued a notice and demand for payment of the recapture tax amount to the subsequent elector; (3) the subsequent elector has failed to pay all of the recapture tax amount by the date specified in such notice and demand; and (4) the Commissioner has issued a notice and demand for payment of the unpaid portion of the recapture tax amount to the original elector and prior subsequent electors, if any. If the subsequent elector's income tax liability for a taxable period includes a recapture amount, and if such income tax liability is satisfied in part by payment, credit, or offset, such amount shall be allocated first to that portion of the income tax liability that is not attributable to the recapture tax amount, and then to that portion of the income tax liability that is attributable to the recapture tax amount.

Finally, the proposed regulations contain rules regarding the refund of an income tax liability that includes a recapture tax amount.

13. *Character and source of recapture income*

Section 1.1503-2(g)(2)(vii)(D) of the current regulations provides that recapture income is treated as ordinary income having the same source and falling within the same separate category under section 904 as the dual consolidated loss being recaptured. The current regulations do not, however, provide an explicit rule to identify the items that compose the dual consolidated loss. As a result, it is unclear under the current regulations how to determine the source and separate category of recapture income. In addition, the current regulations do not explicitly state how the recapture income is treated for purposes of the Code other than section 904.

The proposed regulations clarify that the character (to the extent consistent with the recapture income being ordinary income in all cases) and source of the recapture income is determined based on the character and source of a pro rata portion of the deductions that were taken into account in calculating the dual consolidated loss. As discussed above, the dual consolidated loss is composed of a pro rata portion of all items of deduction and loss that are taken into account in computing such dual consolidated loss. Moreover, the proposed regulations clarify that the determination of the character and source of such income is not limited to section 904, but applies for all purposes of the Code (for example, section 856(c)(2) and (3)).

Under the proposed regulations, the character and source of losses and deductions composing the dual consolidated loss should be identified during the year in which they are incurred, rather than the year in which they are ultimately used to offset income or gain. This approach attempts to simplify the rules and make them more administrable, rather than providing comprehensive stacking, ordering, and tracing rules that track the ultimate use of such items, which would be complex.

14. *Failure to comply with recapture provisions*

Under the current regulations, if the taxpayer fails to comply with the recapture provisions upon the occurrence of a triggering event, the dual resident corporation or separate unit that incurred the dual consolidated loss (or successor-in-interest) is not eligible to enter into a (g)(2)(i) agreement with respect to any dual consolidated losses incurred in the five taxable years beginning with the taxable year in which recapture is required. The current regulations contain two exceptions to this rule that apply unless the triggering event is an actual use of the dual consolidated loss. Under the first exception, the rule does not apply if the failure to comply is due to reasonable cause. Under the second exception, the rule does not apply if the taxpayer unsuccessfully attempted to rebut the triggering event by timely filing a rebuttal statement with its tax return.

This provision is intended to encourage taxpayers to carefully monitor potential triggering events and properly comply with the recapture provisions upon the occurrence of a triggering event.

The IRS and Treasury believe that the failure to comply penalty contained in the current regulations often does not operate in a manner that encourages compliance with the dual consolidated loss regulations. For example, if a taxpayer sells a dual resident corporation to a third party that is treated as a triggering event, but the taxpayer fails to comply with the recapture rules, the rule contained in the current regulations prevents the purchaser of the dual resident corporation from entering into a (g)(2)(i) agreement with respect to dual consolidated losses of the dual resident corporation for five years; it does not adversely affect the taxpayer that failed to properly comply with the recapture provisions. As a result, the proposed regulations do not include this penalty provision.

Although the proposed regulations do not retain this penalty provision, the Commissioner may consider applying other applicable penalty provisions in appropriate circumstances; for example, the Commissioner may consider applying the accuracy-related penalty of section 6662. In addition, the

IRS and Treasury will continue to consider whether a penalty provision, similar to the one contained in the current regulations, is appropriate, especially in cases of repeated non-compliance.

F. *Effective Date—§1.1503(d)-6*

The proposed regulations are proposed to apply to dual consolidated losses incurred in taxable years beginning after the date that these proposed regulations are published as final regulations in the **Federal Register.**

The IRS and Treasury request comments on the application of the regulations, including comments as to whether the proposed regulations, when finalized, should contain an election that would allow taxpayers to apply all or a portion of the regulations retroactively. In addition, comments are requested as to possible transition rules that may apply, including the application of the proposed regulations, when finalized, to existing (g)(2)(i) agreements.

Effect on Other Documents

When these proposed regulations are adopted as final regulations, Rev. Proc. 2000-42 (2000-2 C.B. 394), will be obsolete with respect to dual consolidated losses incurred in taxable years beginning after the date that these proposed regulations are published as final regulations in the **Federal Register.**

Special Analyses

It has been determined that this notice of proposed rule making is not a significant regulatory action as defined in Executive Order 12866. Therefore, a regulatory assessment is not required. It is hereby certified that these regulations will not have a significant economic impact on a substantial number of small entities. This certification is based on the fact that these regulations will primarily affect affiliated groups of corporations that also have a foreign affiliate, which tend to be larger businesses. Moreover, the number of taxpayers affected and the average burden are minimal. Therefore, a Regulatory Flexibility Analysis is not required. Pursuant to section 7805(f) of the Code, these regulations will be submitted to the Chief Counsel for Advocacy of the Small Business Administration for comment on their impact on small business.

Comments and Public Hearing

A public hearing has been scheduled for September 7, 2005, at 10 a.m., in the Auditorium of the Internal Revenue Building, 1111 Constitution Avenue, NW., Washington, DC. Because of access restrictions, visitors must enter at the main entrance, located at 1111 Constitution Avenue, NW. All visitors must present photo identification to enter the building. Because of access restrictions, visitors will not be admitted beyond the immediate entrance more than 30 minutes before the hearing starts. For information about having your name placed on the building access list to attend hearing, see the "FOR FURTHER INFORMATION CONTACT" portion of this preamble.

The rules of 26 CFR 601.601(a)(3) apply to the hearing. Persons who wish to present oral comments must submit written or electronic comments and an outline of the topic to be discussed and time to be devoted to each topic (preferably a signed original and eight (8) copies) by August 22, 2005. A period of 10 minutes will be allotted to each person for making comments. An agenda showing the scheduling of the speakers will be prepared after the deadline for receiving outlines has passed. Copies of the agenda will be available free of charge at the hearing.

Drafting Information

The principal author of these regulations is Kathryn T. Holman of the Office of Associate Chief Counsel (International). However, other personnel from the IRS and Treasury Department participated in their development.

[¶49,242] Proposed Regulations, Proposed Amendments of Regulations and Partial Withdrawal of Proposed Regulations (REG-105346-03), published in the Federal Register on May 23, 2005.

Partners and partnerships: Transfers of partnership equity: Performance of service: Capital interest v. partnership profit: Elections.—Reg. §1.706-3 and amendments of Reg. §§1.83-3, 1.83-6, 1.704-1, 1.707-1, 1.721-1 and 1.761-1, relating to the tax treatment of certain transfers of partnership equity in connection with the performance of services, are proposed. Previously proposed amendments of Reg. §1.721-1 were withdrawn. A public hearing on this proposal is scheduled for October 5, 2005.

AGENCY: Internal Revenue Service (IRS), Treasury.

ACTION: Partial withdrawal of notice of proposed rulemaking, notice of proposed rulemaking, and notice of public hearing.

SUMMARY: This document withdraws the remaining portion of the notice of proposed rulemaking published in the **Federal Register** on June 3, 1971 (36 FR 10787) and contains proposed regulations relating to the tax treatment of certain transfers of partnership equity in connection with the performance of services. The proposed regulations provide that the transfer of a partnership interest in connection with the performance of services is subject to section 83 of the Internal Revenue Code (Code) and provide rules for coordinating section 83 with partnership taxation principles. The proposed regulations also provide that no gain or loss is recognized by a partnership on the transfer or vesting of an interest in the transferring partnership in connection with the performance of services for the transferring partnership. This document also provides a notice of public hearing on these proposed regulations.

DATES: Written or electronic comments must be received by August 22, 2005.

Outlines of topics to be discussed at the public hearing scheduled for October 5, 2005, at 10 a.m. must be received by September 14, 2005.

ADDRESSES: Send submissions to: CC:PA:LPD:PR (REG-105346-03), room 5203, Internal Revenue Service, PO Box 7604, Ben Franklin Station, Washington, DC 20044. Submissions may be hand-delivered Monday through Friday between the hours of 8 a.m. and 4 p.m. to CC:PA:LPD:PR (REG-105346-03), Courier's Desk, Internal Revenue Service, 1111 Constitution Avenue, NW., Washington, DC, or sent electronically, via the IRS Internet site at *www.irs.gov/regs* or via the Federal eRulemaking Portal at *www.regulations.gov* (IRS REG-105346-03).

FOR FURTHER INFORMATION CONTACT: Concerning the section 83 regulations, Stephen Tackney at (202) 622-6030; concerning the subchapter K regulations, Audrey Ellis or Demetri Yatrakis at (202) 622-3060; concerning submissions, the hearing, and/or to be placed on the building access list to attend the hearing, Robin Jones, (202) 622-7180 (not toll free numbers).

SUPPLEMENTARY INFORMATION:

Paperwork Reduction Act

The collection of information contained in this notice of proposed rulemaking has been submitted to the Office of Management and Budget for review in accordance with the Paperwork Reduction Act of 1995 (44 U.S.C. 3507(d)). Comments on the collection of information should be sent to the **Office of Management and Budget,** Attn: Desk Officer for the Department of the Treasury, Office of Information and Regulatory Affairs, Washington, DC 20503, with copies to the **Internal Revenue Service,** Attn: IRS Reports Clearance Officer, SE:W:CAR:MP:T:T:SP, Washington, DC 20224. Comments on the collection of information should be received by July 25, 2005. Comments are specifically requested concerning:

Whether the proposed collection of information is necessary for the proper performance of the functions of the IRS, including whether the information will have practical utility;

The accuracy of the estimated burden associated with the proposed collection of information (see below);

How the quality, utility, and clarity of the information to be collected may be enhanced;

How the burden of complying with the proposed collection of information may be minimized, including through the application of automated collection techniques or other forms of information technology; and

Estimates of capital or start-up costs and costs of operation, maintenance, and purchase of services to provide information.

The following collections of information in this proposed regulation are in § 1.83-3(l):

(1) Requirement that electing partnerships submit an election with the partnership tax return.

(2) Requirement that certain partners submit a document to the partnership;

(3) Requirement that such documents be retained; and

(4) Requirement that partnerships submit a termination document with the partnership tax return as one method of terminating the election.

These collections of information are required by the IRS to determine whether the amount of tax has been calculated correctly. The respondents are partnerships and partners or other service providers.

The estimated total annual reporting and/or recordkeeping burden is 112,500 hours.

The estimated annual burden per respondent/recordkeeper varies from .10 hours to 10 hours, depending on individual circumstances, with an estimated average of 1 hour for partnerships and .25 hour for a partner or service provider. The estimated number of respondents and/or recordkeepers is 100,000 partnerships and 50,000 partners or other service providers.

The estimated annual frequency of responses (used for reporting requirements only) is on occasion.

An agency may not conduct or sponsor, and a person is not required to respond to, a collection of information unless it displays a valid control number assigned by the **Office of Management and Budget.**

Books or records relating to a collection of information must be retained as long as their contents may become material in the administration of any internal revenue law. Generally, tax returns and tax return information are confidential as required by 26 U.S.C. 6103.

Background

Partnerships issue a variety of instruments in connection with the performance of services. These instruments include interests in partnership capital, interests in partnership profits, and options to acquire such interests (collectively, partnership equity). On June 5, 2000, the Treasury Department and the IRS issued Notice 2000-29 (2000-1 C.B. 1241), inviting public comment on the Federal income tax treatment of the exercise of an option to acquire a partnership interest, the exchange of convertible debt for a partnership interest, and the exchange of a preferred interest in a partnership for a common interest in that partnership. On January 22, 2003, the Treasury Department and the IRS published in the **Federal Register** (REG-103580-02) (68 FR 2930), proposed regulations regarding the Federal income tax consequences of noncompensatory partnership options, convertible equity, and convertible debt. In the preamble to those proposed regulations, the Treasury Department and the IRS requested comments on the proposed amendment to § 1.721-1(b)(1) that was published in the **Federal Register** on June 3, 1971 (36 FR 10787), and on the Federal income tax consequences of the issuance of partnership capital interests in connection with the performance of services and options to acquire such interests. In response to the comments received, the Treasury Department and the IRS are withdrawing the proposed amendment to § 1.721-1(b)(1) and issuing these proposed regulations, which prescribe rules on the application of section 83 to partnership interests and the Federal income tax consequences associated with the transfer, vesting, and forfeiture of partnership interests transferred in connection with the performance of services.

Explanation of Provisions

1. Application of Section 83 to Partnership Interests

Section 83 generally applies to a transfer of property by one person to another in connection with the performance of services. The courts have held that a partnership capital interest is property for this purpose. See *Schulman v. Commissioner*, 93 T.C. 623 (1989) (section 83 governs the issuance of an option to acquire a partnership interest as compensation for services provided as an employee); *Kenroy, Inc. v. Commissioner*, T.C. Memo 1984-232. Therefore, the proposed regulations provide that a partnership interest is property within the meaning of section 83, and that the transfer of a partnership interest in connection with the performance of services is subject to section 83.

The proposed regulations apply section 83 to all partnership interests, without distinguishing between partnership capital interests and partnership profits interests. Although the application of section 83 to partnership profits interests has been the subject of controversy, see, e.g., *Campbell v. Commissioner*, T.C. Memo 1990-162, aff'd in part and rev'd in part, 943 F.2d 815 (8th Cir. 1991), n. 7; *St. John v. U.S.*, 84-1 USTC 9158 (C.D. Ill. 1983), the Treasury Department and the IRS do not believe that there is a substantial basis for distinguishing among partnership interests for purposes of section 83. All partnership interests constitute personal property under state law and give the holder the right to share in future earnings from partnership capital and labor. Moreover, some commentators have suggested that the same tax rules should apply to both partnership profits interests and partnership capital interests. These commentators have suggested that taxpayers may exploit any differences in the tax treatment of partnership profits interests and partnership capital interests. The Treasury Department and the IRS agree with these comments. Therefore, all of the rules in these proposed regulations and the accompanying proposed revenue procedure (described below) apply equally to partnership capital interests and partnership profits interests. However, a right to receive allocations and distributions from a partnership that is described in section 707(a)(2)(A) is not a partnership interest. In section 707(a)(2)(A), Congress directed that such an arrangement should be characterized according to its substance, that is, as a disguised payment of compensation to the service provider. See S. Rep. No. 98-169, 98 Cong. 2d Sess., at 226 (1984).

Section 83(b) allows a person who receives substantially nonvested property in connection with the performance of services to elect to include in gross income the difference between: (A) the fair market value of the property at the time of transfer (determined without regard to a restriction other than a restriction which by its terms will never lapse); and (B) the amount paid for such property. Under section 83(b)(2), the election under section 83(b) must be made within 30 days of the date of the transfer of the property to the service provider.

Consistent with the principles of section 83, the proposed regulations provide that, if a partnership interest is transferred in connection with the performance of services, and if an election under section 83(b) is not made, then the holder of the partnership interest is not treated as a partner until the interest becomes substantially vested. If a section 83(b) election is made with respect to such an interest, the service provider will be treated as a partner for purposes of Subtitle A of the Code. These rules are similar to the current rules pertaining to substantially nonvested stock in a subchapter S corporation. See § 1.1361-1(b)(3) (upon an election under section 83(b), the service provider becomes a shareholder for purposes of subchapter S).

These principles differ from Rev. Proc. 2001-43. Under that revenue procedure, if a partnership profits interest is transferred in connection with the performance of services, then the holder of the partnership interest may be treated as a partner even if no section 83(b) election is made, provided that certain conditions are met.

Certain changes to the regulations under both subchapter K and section 83 are needed to coordinate the principles of subchapter K with the principles of section 83. Among the changes that are proposed in these regulations are: (1) conforming the subchapter K rules to the section 83 timing rules; (2) revising the section 704(b) regulations to take into account the fact that allocations with respect to an unvested interest may be forfeited; and (3) providing that a partnership generally recognizes no gain or loss on the transfer of an interest in the partnership in connection with the performance of services for that partnership. In addition, Rev. Procs. 93-27 (1993-2 C.B. 343), and 2001-43 (2001-2 C.B. 191), which generally provide for nonrecognition by both the partnership and the service provider on the transfer of a profits interest in the partnership for services performed for that partnership, must be modified to be consistent with these proposed regulations. Accordingly, in conjunction with these proposed regulations, the IRS is issuing Notice 2005-43 (2005-24 I.R.B.). That Notice contains a proposed revenue procedure that, when finalized, will obsolete Rev. Procs. 93-27 and 2001-43. The Treasury Department and the IRS intend for these proposed regulations and the proposed revenue procedure to become effective at the same time. The proposed amendments to the regulations under section 83 and subchapter K, as well as the Notice, are described in further detail below.

The proposed revenue procedure and certain parts of the proposed regulations (as described below) only apply to a transfer by a partnership of an interest in that partnership in connection with the performance of services for that partnership (compensatory partnership interests). The Treasury Department and the IRS request comments on the income tax consequences of transactions involving related persons, such as, for example, the transfer of an interest in a lower-tier partnership in exchange for services provided to the upper-tier partnership.

2. Timing of Partnership's Deduction

Except as otherwise provided in § 1.83-6(a)(3), if property is transferred in connection with the performance of services, then the service recipient's deduction, if any, is allowed only for the taxable year of that person in which or with which ends the taxable year of the service provider in which the amount is included as compensation. See section 83(h). In contrast, under section 706(a) and § 1.707-1(c), guaranteed payments described in section 707(c) are included in the partner's income in the partner's taxable year within or with which ends the partnership's taxable year in which the partnership deducted the payments. Under § 1.721-1(b)(2) of the current regulations, an interest in partnership capital issued by the partnership as compensation for services rendered to the partnership is treated as a guaranteed payment under section 707(c). Some commentators suggested that the proposed regulations should resolve the potential conflict between the timing rules of section 83 and the timing rules of section 707(c).

Under the proposed regulations, partnership interests issued to partners for services rendered to the partnership are treated as guaranteed payments. Also, the proposed regulations provide that the section 83 timing rules override the timing rules of section 706(a) and § 1.707-1(c) to the extent they are inconsistent. Accordingly, if a partnership transfers property to a partner in connection with the performance of services, the timing and the amount of the related income inclusion and deduction is determined by section 83 and the regulations thereunder.

In drafting these regulations, the Treasury Department and the IRS considered alternative approaches for resolving the timing inconsistency between section 83 and section 707(c). One alternative approach considered was to provide that the transfer of property in connection with the performance of services is not treated as a guaranteed payment within the meaning of section 707(c). This approach was not adopted in the proposed regulations due to, among other things, concern that such a characterization of these transfers could have unintended consequences on the application of provisions of the Code outside of subchapter K that refer to guaranteed payments. The Treasury Department and the IRS request comments on alternative approaches for resolving the timing inconsistency between section 83 and section 707(c).

3. Allocation of Partnership's Deduction

The proposed regulations provide guidance regarding the allocation of the partnership's deduction for the transfer of property in connection with the performance of services. Some commentators suggested that the proposed regulations require that the partnership's deduction be allocated among the partners in accordance with their interests in the partnership prior to the transfer.

Section 706(d)(1) provides generally that, if, during any taxable year of a partnership, there is a change in any partner's interest in the partnership, each partner's distributive share of any item of income, gain, loss, deduction, or credit of the partnership for such taxable year shall be determined by the use of any method prescribed by regulations which takes into account the varying interests of the partners in the partnership during the taxable year. Regulations have not yet been issued describing the rules for taking into account the varying interests of the partners in the partnership during a taxable year. Section 1.706-1(c)(2)(ii) provides that, in the case of a sale, exchange, or liquidation of a partner's entire interest in a partnership, the partner's share of partnership items for the taxable year may be determined by either: (1) closing the partnership's books as of the date of the transfer (closing of the books method); or (2) allocating to the departing partner that partner's pro rata part of partnership items that the partner would have included in the partner's taxable income had the partner remained a partner until the end of the partnership taxable year (proration method). The Treasury Department and the IRS believe that section 706(d)(1) adequately ensures that partnership deductions that are attributable to the portion of the partnership's taxable year prior to a new partner's entry into the partnership are allocated to the historic partners.

Section 706(d)(2), however, places additional limits on how partnerships may allocate these deductions. Under section 706(d)(2)(B), payments for services by a partnership using the cash receipts and disbursements method of accounting are allocable cash basis items. Under section 706(d)(2)(A), if during any taxable year of a partnership there is a change in any partner's interest in the partnership, then (except to the extent provided in regulations) each partner's distributive share of any allocable cash basis item must be determined under the proration method. To allow partnerships to allocate deductions with respect to property transferred in connection with the performance of services under a closing of the books method, the proposed regulations provide that section 706(d)(2)(A) does not apply to such a transfer.

4. Accounting for Compensatory Partnership Interests

A. Transfer of compensatory partnership interest

Under the proposed regulations, the service provider's capital account is increased by the amount the service provider takes into income under section 83 as a result of receiving the interest, plus any amounts paid for the interest. Some commentators suggested that the amount included in the service provider's income under section 83, plus the amount paid for the interest, may differ from the amount of capital that the partnership has agreed to assign to the service provider. These commentators contend that the substantial economic effect safe harbor in the section 704(b) regulations should be amended to allow partnerships to reallocate capital between the historic partners and the service provider to accord with the economic agreement of the parties.

The reallocation of partnership capital in these circumstances is not consistent with the policies underlying the substantial economic effect safe harbor and the capital account maintenance rules. The purpose of the substantial economic effect safe harbor is to ensure that, to the extent that there is an economic benefit or burden associated with a partnership allocation, the partner to whom the allocation is made receives the economic benefit or bears the economic burden. Under section 83, the economic benefit of receiving a partnership interest in connection with the performance of services is the amount that is included in the compensation income of the service provider, plus the amount paid for the interest. This is the amount by which the service partner's capital account should be increased.

As explained in section 6 below, a proposed revenue procedure issued concurrently with these proposed regulations would allow a partnership, its partners, and the service provider to elect to treat the fair market value of a partnership interest as equal to the liquidation value of that interest. If such an election is made, the capital account of a service provider receiving a partnership interest in connection with the performance of services is increased by the liquidation value of the partnership interest received.

B. Forfeiture of certain compensatory partnership interests

If an election under section 83(b) has been made with respect to a substantially nonvested interest, the holder of the nonvested interest may be allocated partnership items that may later be forfeited. For this reason, allocations of partnership items while the interest is substantially nonvested cannot have economic effect. Under the proposed regulations, such allocations will be treated as being in accordance with the partners' interests in the partnership if: (a) the partnership agreement requires that the partnership make forfeiture allocations if the interest for which the section 83(b) election is made is later forfeited; and (b) all material allocations and capital account adjustments under the partnership agreement not pertaining to substantially nonvested partnership interests for which a section 83(b) election has been made are recognized under section 704(b). This safe harbor does not apply if, at the time of the section 83(b) election, there is a plan that a substantially nonvested interest will be forfeited. All of the facts and circumstances (including the tax status of the holder of the substantially nonvested interest) will be considered in determining whether there is a plan that the interest will be forfeited. In such a case, the partners' distributive shares of partnership items shall be determined in accordance with the partners' interests in the partnership under § 1.704-1(b)(3).

Generally, forfeiture allocations are allocations to the service provider of partnership gross income and gain or gross deduction and loss (to the extent such items are available) that offset prior distributions and allocations of partnership items with respect to the forfeited partnership interest. These rules are designed to ensure that any partnership income (or loss) that was allocated to the service provider prior to the forfeiture is offset by allocations on the forfeiture of the interest. Also, to carry out the prohibition under section 83(b)(1) on deductions with respect to amounts included in income under section 83(b), these rules generally cause a forfeiting partner to be allocated partnership income to offset any distributions to the partner that reduced the partner's basis in the partnership below the amount included in income under section 83(b).

Forfeiture allocations may be made out of the partnership's items for the entire taxable year. In determining the gross income of the partnership in the taxable year of the forfeiture, the rules of § 1.83-6(c) apply. As a result, the partnership generally will have gross income in the taxable year of the forfeiture equal to the amount of the allowable deduction to the service recipient partnership upon the transfer of the interest as a result of the making of the section 83(b) election, regardless of the fair market value of the partnership's assets at the time of forfeiture.

In certain circumstances, the partnership will not have enough income and gain to fully offset prior allocations of loss to the forfeiting service provider. The proposed revenue procedure includes a rule that requires the recapture of losses taken by the service provider prior to the forfeiture of the interest to the extent that those losses are not recaptured through forfeiture allocations of income and gain to the service provider. This rule does not provide the other partners in the partnership with the opportunity to increase their shares of partnership loss (or reduce their shares of partnership income) for the year of the forfeiture by the amount of loss that was previously allocated to the forfeiting service provider.

In other circumstances, the partnership will not have enough deductions and loss to fully offset prior allocations of income to the forfeiting service provider. It appears that, in such a case, section 83(b)(1) may prohibit the service provider from claiming a loss with respect to partnership income that was previously allocated to the service provider. However, a forfeiting partner is entitled to a loss for any basis in a partnership that is attributable to contributions of money or property to the partnership (including amounts paid for the interest) remaining after the forfeiture allocations have been made. See § 1.83-2(a).

Comments are requested as to whether the regulations should require or allow partnerships to create notional tax items to make forfeiture allocations where the partnership does not have enough actual tax items to make such allocations. Comments are also requested as to whether section 83(b)(1) should be read to allow a forfeiting service provider to claim a loss with respect to partnership income that was previously allocated to the service provider and not offset by forfeiture allocations of loss and deduction and, if so, whether it is appropriate to require the other partners in the partnership to recognize income in the year of the forfeiture equal to the amount of the loss claimed by the service provider. In particular, comments are requested as to whether section 83 or another section of the Code provides authority for such a rule.

5. Valuation of Compensatory Partnership Interests

Commentators requested guidance regarding the valuation of partnership interests transferred in connection with the performance of services. Section 83 generally provides that the recipient of property transferred in connection with the performance of services recognizes income equal to the fair market value of the property, disregarding lapse restrictions. See *Schulman v. Commissioner*, 93 T.C. 623 (1989). However, some authorities have concluded that, under the particular facts and circumstances of the case, a partnership profits interest had only a speculative value or that the fair market value of a partnership interest should be determined by reference to the liquidation value of that interest. See § 1.704-1(e)(1)(v); *Campbell v. Commissioner*, 943 F.2d 815 (8th Cir. 1991); *St. John v. U.S.*, 1984-1 USTC 9158 (C.D. Ill. 1983). But see *Diamond v. Commissioner*, 492 F.2d 286 (7th Cir. 1974) (holding under pre-section 83 law that the receipt of a profits interest with a determinable value at the time of receipt resulted in immediate taxation); *Campbell v. Commissioner*, T.C. Memo 1990-162, aff'd in part and rev'd in part, 943 F.2d 815 (8th Cir. 1991).

The Treasury Department and the IRS have determined that, provided certain requirements are satisfied, it is appropriate to allow partnerships and service providers to value partnership interests based on liquidation value. This approach ensures consistency in the treatment of partnership profits interests and partnership capital interests, and accords with other regulations issued under subchapter K, such as the regulations under section 704(b).

In accordance with these proposed regulations, the revenue procedure proposed in Notice 2005-43 (2005-24 I.R.B.) will, when finalized, provide additional rules that partnerships, partners, and persons providing services to the partnership in exchange for interests in that partnership would be required to follow when electing under § 1.83-3(l) of these proposed regulations to treat the fair market value of those interests as being equal to the liquidation value of those interests. For this purpose, the liquidation value of a partnership interest is the amount of cash that the holder of that interest would receive with respect to the interest if, immediately after the transfer of the interest, the partnership sold all of its assets (including goodwill, going concern value, and any other intangibles associated with the partnership's operations) for cash equal to the fair market value of those assets, and then liquidated.

6. Application of Section 721 to Partnership on Transfer

There is a dispute among commentators as to whether a partnership should recognize gain or loss on the transfer of a compensatory partnership interest. Some commentators believe that, on the transfer of such an interest, the partnership should be treated as satisfying its compensation obligation with a fractional interest in each asset of the partnership. Under this deemed sale of assets theory, the partnership would recognize gain or loss equal to the excess of the fair market value of each partial asset deemed transferred to the service provider over the partnership's adjusted basis in that partial asset. Other commentators believe that a partnership should not recognize gain or loss on the transfer of a compensatory partnership interest. They argue, among other things, that the transfer of such an interest is not properly treated as a realization event for the partnership because no property owned by the partnership has changed hands. They also argue that taxing a partnership on the transfer of such an interest would result in inappropriate gain acceleration, would be difficult to administer, and would cause economically similar transactions to be taxed differently.

Generally, when appreciated property is used to pay an obligation, gain on the property is recognized. The Treasury Department and the IRS are still analyzing whether an exception to this general rule is appropriate on the transfer of an interest in the capital or profits of a partnership to satisfy certain partnership obligations (such as the obligations to pay interest or rent). However, the Treasury Department and the IRS believe that partnerships should not be required to recognize gain on the transfer of a compensatory partnership interest. Such a rule is more consistent with the policies underlying section 721—to defer recognition of gain and loss when persons join together to conduct a business—than would be a rule requiring the partnership to recognize gain on the transfer of these types of interests. Therefore, the proposed regulations provide that partnerships are not taxed on the transfer or substantial vesting of a compensatory partnership interest. Under § 1.704-1(b)(4)(i) (reverse section 704(c) principles), the historic partners generally will be required to recognize any income or loss attributable to the partnership's assets as those assets are sold, depreciated, or amortized.

The rule providing for nonrecognition of gain or loss does not apply to the transfer or substantial vesting of an interest in an eligible entity, as defined in § 301.7701-3(a) of the Procedure and Administration Regulations, that becomes a partnership under § 301.7701-3(f)(2) as a result of the transfer or substantial vesting of the interest. See *McDougal v. Commissioner*, 62 T.C. 720 (1974) (holding that the service recipient recognized gain on the transfer of a one-half interest in appreciated property to the service provider, immediately prior to the contribution by the service recipient and the service provider of their respective interests in the property to a newly formed partnership).

7. Revaluations of Partnership Property

The proposed regulations concerning noncompensatory partnership options published on January 22, 2003, contained special rules regarding the revaluations of partnership property while noncompensatory partnership options were outstanding. Specifically, the regulations proposed modifications to § 1.704-1(b)(2)(iv)(*f*) and (*h*) to provide that any revaluation during the period in which there are outstanding noncompensatory options generally must take into account the fair market value, if any, of outstanding options. These proposed regulations do not contain similar provisions, because under recently proposed modifications to the regulations under § 1.704-1(b)(2)(iv), the obligation to issue a partnership interest in satisfaction of an option agreement is a liability that is taken into account in determining the fair market value of partnership assets as a result of a revaluation. See REG-106736-00, 68 FR 37434 (June 24, 2003) (relating to the assumption of certain obligations by partnerships from partners).

8. Characterization Rule

The proposed regulations concerning noncompensatory partnership options published on January 22, 2003 contained a rule (§ 1.761-3) providing that the holder of a noncompensatory option is treated as a partner under certain circumstances. However, the Treasury Department and the IRS have concluded that these proposed regulations should not contain a similar rule for partnership options transferred in connection with the performance of services because of the possibility that constructive transfers of property, subject to section 83, may occur under circumstances other than those described in the proposed rules for treating the holder of a noncompensatory option as a partner. The Treasury Department and the IRS request comments on whether anti-abuse rules are necessary to prevent taxpayers from using the rules in these proposed regulations or the rules in Notice 2005-43 to inappropriately shift items of partnership income or loss between the service provider and the other partners.

9. Retroactive Allocations

Section 761(c) generally allows a partnership to modify its agreement at any time on or prior to the due date for the partnership's return for the taxable year (without regard to extensions). Thus, for example, a partnership could, at the end of its taxable year, amend its partnership agreement to provide that a service provider was entitled to a substantially vested or nonvested interest in partnership profits and losses from the beginning of the partnership's taxable year. It is expected that, if a substantially vested compensatory partnership interest is transferred to an employee or independent contractor (or an election under section 83(b) is made with respect to the transfer of a substantially nonvested compensatory partnership interest to an employee or independent contractor), the partnership will report the transfer on Form W-2, "Wage and Tax Statement," or Form 1099-MISC, "Miscellaneous Income," as appropriate. The Form W-2 or Form 1099-MISC would be issued to the service provider by the partnership by January 31 of the year following the calendar year in which the partnership interest is transferred, and the partnership would file such forms with the Social Security Administration or IRS, respectively, by February 28 (March 31 if filed electronically) of the year following the calendar year in which the partnership interest is transferred. The service provider would be required to report any income recognized on the transfer of the partnership interest on the service provider's return for the taxable year (of the service provider) in which the transfer occurs.

It is unclear whether the retroactive commencement date of such an interest should be treated as the date of the transfer of the interest for purposes of section 83 and other provisions of the Code outside of subchapter K. If the retroactive effective date of the interest is treated as the transfer date for all purposes, a number of administrative concerns arise. For example, the partnership may not, by the January 31 deadline, have the information necessary to issue Form W-2 or Form 1099-MISC to the service provider. Also, the service provider may not, by the due date for filing the section 83(b) election, have the information necessary to file the election. The Treasury Department and the IRS request comments on the timing for section 83 purposes of retroactive transfers of partnership interests and on any actions that may be appropriate to address the associated administrative concerns.

10. Information Reporting to Partners

As explained above, the proposed regulations treat the transfer of a partnership interest to a partner in connection with the performance of services as a guaranteed payment. To ensure that the service provider partner has the information necessary to include the transfer in income for the taxable year in which the transfer occurs (rather than the taxable year in which or with which ends the partnership taxable year in which the transfer occurs), the Treasury Department and the IRS are considering the possibility of amending the section 6041 regulations to provide that this type of guaranteed payment must be reported by the partnership on Form 1099-MISC, which is required to be issued to the service provider on or before January 31 of the year following the calendar year of such transfer. The Treasury Department and the IRS request comments on whether such a requirement is appropriate and administrable.

Proposed Effective Date

These regulations are proposed to apply to transfers of property on or after the date final regulations are published in the **Federal Register**.

Special Analyses

It has been determined that this notice of proposed rulemaking is not a significant regulatory action as defined in Executive Order 12866. Therefore, a regulatory assessment is not required. It also has been determined that section 553(b) of the Administrative Procedure Act (5 U.S.C. chapter 5) does not apply to these regulations. It is hereby certified that the collection of information in these regulations will not have a significant economic impact on a substantial number of small entities. This certification is based upon the fact that the reporting burden, as discussed earlier in this preamble, is not expected to be significant. Partnerships with partnership agreements that contain the binding provisions referred to in § 1.83-3(l) only will be required to submit a single election form in order to rely on the safe harbor described in that paragraph. Partnerships that desire to elect to use the safe harbor described in § 1.83-3(l), but which do not have partnership agreements containing these provisions, are required to obtain partner-level consents to the election. However, these partnerships are expected to be rare. Moreover, in most cases the partners in such partnerships are not expected to be small businesses. Therefore, a Regulatory Flexibility Analysis under the Regulatory Flexibility Act (5 U.S.C. chapter 6) is not required. Pursuant to section 7805(f) of the Code, this notice of proposed rulemaking will be submitted to the Chief Counsel for Advocacy of the Small Business Administration for comment on its impact on small business.

Comments and Public Hearing

Before these proposed regulations are adopted as final regulations, consideration will be given to any electronic or written comments (a signed original and eight copies) that are submitted timely to the IRS. The IRS and the Treasury Department request comments on the clarity of the proposed rules and how they can be made easier to understand. All comments will be available for public inspection and copying.

A public hearing has been scheduled for October 5, 2005, beginning at 10 a.m. in the IRS Auditorium, Internal Revenue Building, 1111 Constitution Avenue, NW., Washington, DC. Due to building security procedures, visitors must enter at the Constitution Avenue entrance. In addition, all visitors must present photo identification to enter the building. Because of access restrictions, visitors will not be admitted beyond the immediate entrance area more than 30 minutes before the hearing starts. For information about having your name placed on the building access list to attend the hearing, see the "FOR FURTHER INFORMATION CONTACT" portion of this preamble.

The rules of 26 CFR 601.601(a)(3) apply to the hearing. Persons who wish to present oral comments must submit written comments and an outline of the topics to be discussed and the time to be devoted to each topic (a signed original and eight (8) copies) by September 14, 2005. A period of 10 minutes will be allotted to each person for making comments. An agenda showing the scheduling of the speakers will be prepared after the deadline for reviewing outlines has passed. Copies of the agenda will be available free of charge at the hearing.

Drafting Information

The principal authors of these regulations are Audrey Ellis and Demetri Yatrakis of the Office of Associate Chief Counsel (Passthroughs and Special Industries), and Stephen Tackney of the Office of Associate Chief Counsel (Tax Exempt and Government Entities). However, other personnel from the IRS and Treasury Department participated in their development.

[¶49,247] Proposed Regulations (REG-133578-05), published in the Federal Register on August 24, 2005.

Corporations: Dividends paid deduction: Employee stock ownership plans (ESOPs): Applicable dividends: Payments to reacquire stock.—Reg. § 1.404(k)-2, concerning which corporation is entitled to the deduction for applicable dividends under Code Sec. 404(k) and clarifying that a payment in redemption of employer securities held by an employee stock ownership plan (ESOP) is not deductible, is proposed. Reg. §§ 1.162(k)-1 and 1.404(k)-3 were adopted by T.D. 9282 on August 29, 2006.

AGENCY: Internal Revenue Service (IRS), Treasury.

ACTION: Notice of proposed rulemaking.

SUMMARY: This document contains proposed regulations under sections 162(k) and 404(k) of the Internal Revenue Code (Code) relating to employee stock ownership plans (ESOPs). The regulations provide guidance concerning which corporation is entitled to the deduction for applicable dividends under section 404(k). These regulations also clarify that a payment in redemption of employer securities held by an ESOP is not deductible. These regulations will affect administrators of, employers maintaining, participants in, and beneficiaries of ESOPs. In addition, they will affect corporations that make distributions in redemption of stock held in an ESOP.

DATES: Written or electronic comments and requests for a public hearing must be received by November 23, 2005.

ADDRESSES: Send submissions to: CC:PA:LPD:PR (REG-133578-05), room 5203, Internal Revenue Service, POB 7604, Ben Franklin Station, Washington, DC 20044. Submissions may be hand-delivered Monday through Friday between the hours of 8 a.m. and 4 p.m. to: CC:PA:LPD:PR (REG-133578-05), Courier's Desk, Internal Revenue Service, 1111 Constitution Avenue, NW., Washington D.C. Alternatively, taxpayers may submit comments electronically directly to the IRS Internet site at *www.irs.gov/regs*, or via the Federal eRulemaking Portal at *www.regulations.gov* (IRS-REG-133578-05).

FOR FURTHER INFORMATION CONTACT: Concerning the regulations, John T. Ricotta at (202) 622-6060 with respect to section 404(k) or Martin Huck at (202) 622-7750 with respect to section 162(k); concerning submission of comments or to request a public hearing, Robin Jones at (202) 622-7180 (not toll-free numbers).

SUPPLEMENTARY INFORMATION:

Background and Explanation of Provisions

This document contains proposed regulations under sections 162(k) and 404(k) of the Internal Revenue Code (Code). These regulations address two issues that have arisen in the application of these sections. The first issue arises in a case in which the applicable employer securities held in an employee stock ownership plan (ESOP) are not securities of the corporation or corporations that maintain the plan. The issue is which corporation is entitled to the deduction under section 404(k) for certain dividends paid with respect to the stock held in the ESOP. The second issue is whether payments in redemption of stock held by an ESOP are deductible.

Code and Regulations

Section 404(a) provides that contributions paid by an employer to or under a stock bonus, pension, profit sharing, or annuity plan are deductible under section 404(a), if they would be otherwise deductible, within the limitations of that section. Section 404(k)(1) provides that, in the case of a C corporation, there is allowed as a deduction for a taxable year the amount of any applicable dividend paid in cash by such corporation during the taxable year with respect to applicable employer securities held by an ESOP. The deduction under section 404(k) is in addition to the deductions allowed under section 404(a).

Section 4975(e)(7) provides, in relevant part, that an ESOP is a defined contribution plan that is a stock bonus plan qualified under section 401(a) and designed to invest primarily in qualifying employer securities. Section 4975(e)(8) states that the term *qualifying employer security* means any employer security within the meaning of section 409(l). Section 409(l) generally provides that the term *employer security* means common stock issued by the employer (or a corporation that is a member of the same controlled group) that is readily tradable on an established securities market, if the corporation (or a member of the controlled group) has common stock that is readily tradable on an established securities market. Section 409(l)(4)(A) provides that, for purposes of section 409(l), the term *controlled group of corporations* has the meaning given to that term by section 1563(a) (determined without regard to subsections (a)(4) and (e)(3)(C) of section 1563). Section 409(l)(4)(B) provides that, for purposes of section 409(l)(4)(A), if a common parent owns directly stock possessing at least 50 percent of the voting power of all classes of stock and at least 50 percent of each class of nonvoting stock in a first tier subsidiary, such subsidiary (and all corporations below it in the chain which would meet the 80 percent test of section 1563(a) if the first tier subsidiary were the common parent) are treated as includible corporations.

Section 404(k)(2), for taxable years beginning on or after January 1, 2002, generally provides that the term *applicable dividend* means any dividend which, in accordance with the plan provisions—(i) is paid in cash to the participants in the plan or their beneficiaries, (ii) is paid to the plan and is distributed in cash to participants in the plan or their beneficiaries not later than 90 days after the close of the plan year in which paid, (iii) is, at the election of such participants or their beneficiaries—(I) payable as provided in clause (i) or (ii), or (II) paid to the plan and reinvested in qualifying employer securities, or (iv) is used to make payments on a loan described in section 404(a)(9), the proceeds of which were used to acquire the employer securities (whether or not allocated to participants) with respect to which the dividend is paid. Under section 404(k)(4), the deduction is allowable in the taxable year of the corporation in which the dividend is paid or distributed to a participant or beneficiary.

Prior to 2002, section 404(k)(5)(A) provided that the Secretary may disallow the deduction under section 404(k) for any dividend if the Secretary determines that such dividend constitutes, in substance, an evasion of taxation. Section 662(b) of the Economic Growth and Tax Relief Reconciliation Act of 2001 (115 Stat. 38, 2001) amended section 404(k)(5)(A) to provide that the Secretary may disallow a deduction under section 404(k) for any dividend the Secretary determines constitutes, in substance, an avoidance or evasion of taxation. The amendment is effective for tax years after December 31, 2001.

Section 162(k)(1) generally provides that no deduction otherwise allowable under chapter 1 of the Code is allowed for any amount paid or incurred by a corporation in connection with the reacquisition of its stock or the stock of any related person (as defined in section 465(b)(3)(C)). The legislative history of section 162(k) states that the phrase "in connection with" is "intended to be construed broadly." H.R. Conf. Rep. No. 99-841, at 168 (1986).

Corporation Entitled to Section 404(k) Deduction

An ESOP may benefit employees of more than one corporation. In addition, an ESOP may be maintained by a corporation other than the payor of a dividend. In these cases, the issue arises as to which entity is entitled to the deduction provided under section 404(k). Assume, for example, that a publicly traded corporation owns all of the stock of a subsidiary. The subsidiary operates a trade or business with employees in the U.S. and maintains an ESOP that holds stock of its parent for its employees. If the parent distributes a dividend with respect to its stock held in the ESOP maintained by the subsidiary, questions have arisen as to whether the parent or subsidiary is entitled to the deduction under section 404(k). This question arises in cases in which the parent and subsidiary file a consolidated return as well as in cases in which the parent and subsidiary do not file a consolidated return.

The IRS and Treasury Department believe that the statutory language of section 404(k) clearly provides that only the payor of the applicable dividend is entitled to the deduction under section 404(k), regardless of whether the employees of multiple corporations benefit under the ESOP and regardless of whether another member of the controlled group maintains the ESOP. Therefore, in the example above, the parent, not the subsidiary, is entitled to the deduction under section 404(k).

Treatment of Payments Made to Reacquire Stock

Some corporations have claimed deductions under section 404(k) for payments in redemption of stock held by an ESOP that are used to make benefit distributions to participants or beneficiaries, including distributions of a participant's account balance upon severance from employment. These taxpayers have argued that the payments in redemption qualify as dividends under sections 301 and 316 and, therefore, are deductible under section 404(k).

In Rev. Rul. 2001-6 (2001-1 C.B. 491), the IRS concluded that section 162(k) bars a deduction for payments made in redemption of stock from an ESOP. This conclusion was based on the fact that section 162(k)(1) disallows a deduction for payments paid in connection with the reacquisition of an issuer's stock and that the redemption payments are such payments. The IRS also concluded that such payments were not applicable dividends under section 404(k)(1). The IRS reasoned that allowing a deduction for redemption amounts would vitiate important rights and protections for recipients of ESOP distributions, including the right to reduce taxes by utilizing the return of basis provisions under section 72, the right to make rollovers of ESOP distributions received upon separation from service, and the protection against involuntary cash-outs. Finally, the IRS stated that a deduction under section 404(k)(1) for such amounts would constitute, in substance, an evasion of tax.

In *Boise Cascade Corporation v. United States*, 329 F.3d 751 (9th Cir. 2003), the Court of Appeals for the Ninth Circuit held that payments made by a corporation to redeem its stock held by its ESOP were deductible as dividends paid under section 404(k), and that the deduction was not precluded by section 162(k). The court reasoned that the distribution by the ESOP of the redemption proceeds to the participants was a transaction separate from the redemption transaction. Therefore, the court concluded that the distribution did not constitute a payment *in connection with* the corporation's reacquisition of its stock, and section 162(k) did not bar the deduction of such payments.

For the reasons stated in Rev. Rul. 2001-6, the IRS and Treasury Department continue to believe that allowing a deduction for amounts paid to reacquire stock is inconsistent with the intent of, and policies underlying, section 404. In addition, the IRS and Treasury Department believe that allowing such a deduction would constitute, in substance, an avoidance or evasion of taxation within the meaning of section 404(k)(5)(A) because it would allow a corporation to claim two deductions for the same economic cost: once for the value of the stock originally contributed to the ESOP and again for the amount paid to redeem the same stock. See *Charles Ilfeld Co. v. Hernandez*, 292 U.S. 62 (1934). Moreover, despite the Ninth's Circuit's conclusion in *Boise Cascade*, the IRS and Treasury Department continue to believe that, even if a payment in redemption of stock held by an ESOP were to qualify as an applicable dividend, section 162(k) would disallow a deduction for that amount because such payment would be in connection with the reacquisition of the corporation's stock.

This notice of proposed rulemaking, therefore, includes proposed regulations under section 404(k) that confirm that payments made to reacquire stock held by an ESOP are not deductible under section 404(k) because such payments do not constitute applicable dividends under section 404(k)(2) and a deduction for such payments would constitute, in substance, an avoidance or evasion of taxation within the meaning of section 404(k)(5). It also includes proposed regulations under section 162(k) that provide that section 162(k), subject to certain exceptions, disallows any deduction for amounts paid or incurred by a corporation in connection with the reacquisition of its stock or the stock of any related person (as defined in section 465(b)(3)(C)). The proposed regulations also provide that amounts paid or incurred in connection with the reacquisition of stock include amounts paid by a corporation to reacquire its stock from an ESOP that are then distributed by the ESOP to its participants (or their beneficiaries) or otherwise used in a manner described in section 404(k)(2)(A).

Proposed Effective Date

These regulations are proposed to be effective on the date of issuance of final regulations. However, before these regulations become effective, the IRS will continue to assert in any matter in controversy outside of the Ninth Circuit that sections 162(k) and 404(k) disallow a deduction for payments to reacquire employer securities held by an ESOP. See Chief Counsel Notice 2004-038 (October 1, 2004) available at *www.irs.gov/foia* through the *electronic reading room*.

Special Analyses

It has been determined that this notice of proposed rulemaking is not a significant regulatory action as defined in Executive Order 12866. Therefore, a regulatory assessment is not required. It has also been determined that section 553(b) of the Administrative Procedure Act (5 U.S.C. chapter 5) does not apply to these regulations, and, because the regulations do not impose a collection of information on small entities, the Regulatory Flexibility Act (5 U.S.C. chapter 6) does not apply. Pursuant to section 7805(f) of the Code, this notice of proposed rulemaking will be submitted to the Chief Counsel for Advocacy of the Small Business Administration for comment on its impact on small business.

Comments and Public Hearing

Before these proposed regulations are adopted as final regulations, consideration will be given to any written (a signed original and eight (8) copies) or electronic comments that are submitted timely to the IRS. The IRS and Treasury Department specifically request comments on the clarity of the proposed regulations and how they may be made easier to understand. All comments will be available for public inspection and copying. A public hearing will be scheduled if requested in writing by any person that timely submits written comments. If a public hearing is scheduled, notice of the date, time, and place for the public hearing will be published in the **Federal Register**.

Drafting Information

The principal authors of these regulations are John T. Ricotta, Office of Division Counsel/Associate Chief Counsel (Tax Exempt and Government Entities) and Martin Huck of Office of Associate Chief Counsel (Corporate). However, other personnel from the IRS and Treasury participated in the development of these regulations.

[¶49,277] Proposed Amendments of Regulations (REG-121509-00), published in the Federal Register on August 29, 2006 (corrected 12/8/2006).

[Code Secs. 959, 961 and 1502]

Controlled foreign corporations: Previously taxed income: Basis adjustments: Consolidated returns.—Reg. §§1.961-3 and 1.961-4, and amendments of Reg. §§1.959-1, 1.959-2, 1.959-3, 1.959-4, 1.961-1, 1.961-2, 1.1502-12 and 1.1502-32, relating to the exclusion from gross income of previously taxed earnings and profits under section 959 of the Internal Revenue Code and related basis adjustments under 961 of the Code, are proposed.

AGENCY: Internal Revenue Service (IRS), Treasury.

ACTION: Notice of proposed rulemaking.

SUMMARY: This document contains proposed regulations that provide guidance relating to the exclusion from gross income of previously taxed earnings and profits under section 959 of the Internal Revenue Code (Code) and related basis adjustments under section 961 of the Code. These regulations reflect relevant statutory changes made in years subsequent to 1983. These regulations also address a number of issues that the current section 959 and section 961 regulations do not clearly answer. These regulations, in general, will affect United States shareholders of controlled foreign corporations and their successors in interest.

DATES: Written or electronic comments and requests for a public hearing must be received by November 27, 2006.

ADDRESSES: Send submissions to: CC:PA:LPD:PR (REG-121509-00), Internal Revenue Service, PO Box 7604, Ben Franklin Station, Washington, DC 20044 or send electronically, via the IRS Internet site at *www.irs.gov/regs* or via the Federal eRulemaking Portal at *www.regulations.gov* (IRS REG-121509-00).

FOR FURTHER INFORMATION CONTACT: Concerning the proposed regulations, Ethan Atticks, (202) 622-3840; concerning submissions of comments, Kelly Banks, (202) 622-0392 (not toll-free numbers).

SUPPLEMENTARY INFORMATION:

Background

This document contains proposed amendments to 26 CFR Part 1 under sections 959, 961 and 1502. Section 959(a)(1) generally provides an exclusion from the gross income of a United States shareholder for distributions of earnings and profits of a foreign corporation attributable to amounts which are, or have been, included in a United States shareholder's gross income under section 951(a). Section 959(a)(2) excludes from the gross income of a United States shareholder earnings and profits attributable to amounts which are, or have been, included in the gross income of a United States shareholder under section 951(a) which would, but for section 959(a)(2), be again included in gross income of a United States shareholder under section 951(a)(1)(B) as an amount determined under section 956 (section 956 amounts). Earnings and profits of a foreign corporation included in a United States shareholder's gross income under section 951(a) are referred to as previously taxed earnings and profits or previously taxed income (PTI).

Section 959(b) generally provides that for purposes of section 951(a), PTI shall not, when distributed through a chain of ownership described in section 958(a), be included in the gross income of a controlled foreign corporation (CFC) in such chain for purposes of the application of section 951(a) to such CFC.

Section 959(c) generally provides for the allocation of distributions by a foreign corporation to three different categories of the corporation's earnings and profits: (1) PTI attributable to section 956 amounts that are included in the gross income of a United States shareholder under section 951(a)(1)(B) and section 956 amounts that would have been so included but for section 959(a)(2), (2) PTI attributable to amounts included in gross income under section 951(a)(1)(A), and (3) other earnings and profits (non-PTI). Section 959(f) provides for the allocation of section 956 amounts first to PTI arising from a United States shareholder's income inclusions under section 951(a)(1)(A) and then to non-PTI. In addition, section 959(f) provides a priority rule under which actual distributions of earnings and profits are taken into account before section 956 amounts.

Certain amounts are treated as amounts included in the gross income of a United States shareholder under section 951(a)(1)(A) for purposes of section 959. For example, section 959(e) generally provides that any amount included in the gross income of any person as a dividend by reason of subsection (a) or (f) of section 1248 is treated for purposes of section 959 as an amount included in the gross income of such person under section 951(a)(1)(A).

Section 961 authorizes the Secretary of the Treasury to promulgate regulations adjusting the basis of stock in a foreign corporation, as well as the basis of other property by reason of which a United States person is considered under section 958(a) to own stock in a foreign corporation. Section 961(a) generally provides for an increase in a United States shareholder's basis in its CFC stock, or in the property by reason of which it is considered to own such stock, by the amount required to be included in its gross income under section 951(a) with respect to such stock.

Under section 961(b), and the regulations thereunder, when a United States person receives an amount which is excluded from gross income under section 959(a), the adjusted basis of the foreign corporation stock or the property by reason of which the shareholder is considered to own such stock is reduced by the amount of the exclusion. In addition, section 961(c) generally provides for regulations under which adjustments similar to those provided for under section 961(a) and (b) are made to the basis of stock in a CFC which is owned by another CFC (and certain other CFCs in the chain) for the purpose of determining the amount included under section 951 in the gross income of a United States shareholder.

Section 959 was enacted so that PTI is excluded from gross income and, thus, not taxed again when distributed by the foreign corporation. Moreover, section 959 effects the relevant gross income exclusion at the earliest possible point. Thus, the "allocation of distribution" rules of section 959(c) ensure that distributions from the foreign corporation are to be paid first out of earnings and profits attributable to amounts that have been previously included in income by the United States shareholders. Accordingly, as a result of its section 951(a)(1) inclusion, a United States shareholder is made whole by receiving, without further U.S. tax, PTI attributable to its stock in a foreign corporation before it receives any taxable distributions from the foreign corporation. Section 961, which adjusts basis in the stock in a foreign corporation for PTI attributable to such stock, also ensures that PTI is not taxed twice if the stock in the foreign corporation is sold before the PTI is distributed.

The existing regulations under sections 959 and 961 were published in 1965. See TD 6795 (1965-1 CB 287). Minor amendments were made to the regulations in 1974, 1978, and 1983. See TD 7334 (1975-1 CB 246); TD 7545 (1978-1 CB 245); TD 7893 (1983-1 CB 132). The regulations have not been updated since 1983 to reflect relevant statutory changes in subsequent years. For example, section 959(e) (described above) was added by the Deficit Reduction Act of 1984 (Public Law 98-369). Section 304(b)(6) was enacted by the IRS Restructuring and Reform Act of 1998 (Public Law 105-206) and provides that in the case of a section 304 transaction in which the acquiring corporation or the issuing corporation is a foreign corporation, the Secretary of the Treasury is to prescribe regulations providing rules to prevent the multiple inclusion of any item in income and to provide appropriate basis adjustments, including rules modifying the application of sections 959 and 961. The determination of the amount includible in a United States shareholder's gross income as a result of a CFC's investments in United States property under section 956 was modified by the Omnibus Budget Reconciliation Act of 1993 (Public Law 103-66). Congress enacted section 961(c) (described in this preamble) as part of the Taxpayer Relief Act of 1997 (Public Law 105-34) and further modified the provision in the Gulf Opportunity Zone Act of 2005 (Public Law 109-135). Section 986 was added to the Code by the Tax Reform Act of 1986 (Public Law 99-514) and provides that earnings and profits of foreign corporations are maintained in the foreign corporation's functional currency and translated into United States dollars when taken into account by a United States person at the appropriate exchange rate specified in section 989.

Further, in addition to raising issues about the complexities of section 959 in cross-chain stock sales subject to section 304(a)(1), commentators and taxpayers have raised a number of other issues that the current section 959 regulations do not clearly answer. For example, issues have been raised about distributions of PTI through a chain of CFCs and the status of PTI when a United States shareholder's stock in a foreign corporation is sold to a foreign person. There are numerous other examples where the existing section 959 regulations simply do not provide sufficient guidance. As a result, additional regulatory guidance is needed to address these and other section 959 issues. In addition, the IRS and Treasury Department are currently studying the new section 954(c)(6) rule enacted by the Tax Increase Prevention and Reconciliation Act of 2005 (Public Law 109-222), which generally provides for look-through treatment of payments between related CFCs under the foreign personal holding company rules of section 954(c), to determine whether that rule requires any additional regulatory guidance under section 959. Any such guidance will be included in a subsequent project.

Explanation of Provisions

These proposed regulations provide guidance with respect to a number of issues that are not specifically addressed in the current regulations and also resolve some of the complexities raised regarding the application of sections 959 and 961. The guidance needed to answer open issues under sections 959 and 961 is intended to be consistent with the legislative intent of avoiding double taxation and allowing United States persons to receive the full benefit of their PTI at the earliest possible time.

In order to carry out this legislative intent, these regulations propose new rules that are primarily based on maintaining shareholder accounts for PTI. As described in this preamble, maintaining shareholder accounts for PTI will better ensure that taxpayers are able to receive distributions of PTI before receiving taxable distributions, provide consistency for treatment of PTI by taxpayers and also, provide more rational and clear rules for resolving many of the issues that have been raised by taxpayers since the current section 959 regulations were issued. Under the proposed rules, earnings and profits will still be maintained at the foreign corporation level in the PTI and non-PTI categories described in section 959(c) on an aggregate basis with respect to all of the foreign corporation's outstanding shares.

The proposed rules also would modify the current regulations to reflect amendments to the law since 1965, such as the addition of section 959(e) and section 961(c), and the modification of sections 304 and 956. Minor changes have also been proposed to reflect changes in IRS titles and organizational units used in the current regulations.

A. *Shareholder-level Exclusion Under Section 959(a)*

1. *In general*

Section 959 provides rules for the exclusion from gross income of PTI. Prop. Reg. § 1.959-1 describes the scope and purpose of the proposed regulations under section 959 in paragraph (a), and provides definitions in paragraph (b). Paragraph (c) generally provides for the exclusion from a covered shareholder's gross income of a distribution or section 956 amount based upon the amount of adjustments made to a shareholder's PTI accounts with respect to the relevant stock under Prop. Reg. § 1.959-3 because of that distribution or section 956 amount, as discussed below. A covered shareholder is defined to mean a person who is (1) a United States person who owns stock (within the meaning of section 958(a)) in a foreign corporation and who has had a section 951(a) inclusion with respect to its stock in such corporation, (2) a "successor in interest" (defined in this preamble), or (3) a corporation that is not described in (1) or (2) and that owns stock (within the meaning of section 958(a)) in a foreign corporation in which another corporation is a covered shareholder described in (1) or (2), if both corporations are members of the same consolidated group.

2. *Shareholder PTI accounts*

Prop. Reg. § 1.959-1(d)(1) requires each covered shareholder of a foreign corporation to maintain a PTI account for each share of stock in a foreign corporation that the shareholder owns directly or indirectly under section 958(a). Although the PTI account is share specific, as a matter of administrative convenience, Prop. Reg. § 1.959-1(d)(1) permits a shareholder to maintain the account with respect to an entire block of stock in foreign corporation if the PTI attributable to each share in the block is the same. For a discussion of the rules for maintaining a PTI account, see Part C of this discussion.

3. *Successors in interest*

Section 959(a) extends the exclusion from gross income for PTI to any United States person who acquires from any person any portion of the interest of a United States shareholder (as the term is defined in section 951(b) or section 953(c)(1)(A)) in a foreign corporation, but only to the extent of that portion and subject to such proof of the identity of such interest as the Secretary of the Treasury may by regulations prescribe. Consequently, Prop. Reg. § 1.959-1(d)(2)(i) provides that a transferee of stock in a foreign corporation acquires the PTI account of the transferor for such stock and may exclude PTI from gross income under section 959(a) by reference to the PTI account for the stock acquired, if the transferee is a United States person that can prove the right to the exclusion (successor in interest).

In order to establish a United States person's right to the exclusion, the proposed regulations provide that a person must attach a statement to its return that provides that it is excluding amounts from gross income because it is a successor in interest and that provides the name of the foreign corporation. Further, a person must be prepared to provide, within 30 days upon the request of the Director of Field Operations, certain additional information (e.g., evidence showing that the earnings and profits for which an exclusion is claimed are PTI and that such amounts were not previously excluded from the gross income of a United States person). The information that may be required under these proposed regulations remains substantially unchanged from the information that is currently required to be included in a statement with the United States person's return under § 1.959-1(d).

Moreover, Prop. Reg. § 1.959-1(d)(2)(ii) provides that the amount of the PTI account for stock that is transferred to someone who is not a successor in interest (e.g., a foreign person) is preserved unchanged during the period of such person's ownership of such stock. However, section 959(a) extends the section 959(a) exclusion to a United States person who acquires a United States shareholder's interest in a foreign corporation from any person. Accordingly, Prop. Reg. § 1.959-1(d)(2)(i) provides that if a United States person acquires stock in a foreign corporation from any person, including a person who is not a successor in interest, such as a foreign person, and the United States person qualifies as a successor in interest, the United States person acquires the PTI account attributable to the foreign corporation stock acquired and may exclude PTI from gross income under section 959(a) by reference to the PTI account for such stock.

B. *CFC-level Exclusion Under Section 959(b)*

Section 959(b) provides an exclusion pursuant to which the earnings and profits of a CFC (lower-tier CFC) attributable to amounts which are, or have been, included in the gross income of a United States shareholder under section 951(a) shall not, when distributed through a chain of ownership described in section 958(a), be also included in the gross income of the CFC receiving the distribution (upper-tier CFC) in such chain for purposes of the application of section 951(a) to such upper-tier CFC with respect to such United States shareholder. Prop. Reg. § 1.959-2 contains rules relating to the section 959(b) exclusion. These rules are intended to reflect the holding of Rev. Rul. 82-16 (1982-1 CB 106) as well as to provide guidance regarding cross-chain sales of stock in a foreign corporation by a CFC subject to section 304(a)(1).

In Rev. Rul. 82-16, an upper-tier CFC, 70 percent owned by a United States shareholder (USP) and 30 percent owned by a foreign person, received a distribution of $200x of earnings and profits from a lower-tier CFC wholly-owned by the upper-tier CFC. The lower-tier CFC had earned $100x of subpart F income for the year of the distribution ($70x of which was included in USP's gross income under section 951(a)) and a $100x of non-subpart F income. The ruling held that $100x, rather than $70x, was excluded from the gross income of the upper-tier CFC under section 959(b). If only $70x were excluded, USP would be required to include in gross income $21x of subpart F income with respect to the remaining $30x included in the upper-tier CFC's gross income, resulting in a total inclusion in USP's gross income of $91x ((70% ×$30x) + (70% × $100x)).

Prop. Reg. § 1.959-2(a) addresses the issue raised in Rev. Rul. 82-16, and accordingly, provides that the amount of the exclusion provided under section 959(b) is the entire amount distributed by the lower-tier CFC to the upper-tier CFC that gave rise (in whole or in part) to an adjustment of the United States shareholder's PTI accounts with respect to the stock it owns (within the meaning of section 958(a)) in the lower- and upper-tier CFC under Prop. Reg. § 1.959-3(e)(3) (discussed in this preamble). This amount shall not exceed the earnings and profits of the distributor CFC attributable to amounts described in section 951(a). Such amount is not limited to the amount of the adjustment to the United States shareholder's PTI account.

For example, under the facts of Rev. Rul. 82-16, the amount excluded from the upper-tier CFC's gross income for purposes of applying section 951(a) to USP under Prop. Reg. § 1.959-2(a) is $100x. That is, the entire amount of the earnings and profits distributed by the lower-tier CFC that were attributable to amounts described in section 951(a) and that caused an adjustment to USP's PTI accounts in both the upper-and lower-tier CFCs under Prop. Reg. § 1.959-3(e)(3).

Prop. Reg. § 1.959-2(a) produces results consistent with Rev. Rul. 82-16, while ensuring that section 959(b) does not inappropriately prevent taxation under section 951(a) of a United States shareholder that has acquired stock in a CFC from a person that was not taxed on the subpart F income of a lower-tier CFC in the year such income was earned (e.g., a foreign person). For example, assume the same facts as those of Rev. Rul. 82-16, except that: (1) the subpart F income was earned by the lower-tier CFC in year 1, (2) another United States shareholder (DC) acquired the 30 percent interest in the upper-tier CFC in year 2 from the foreign person with a zero PTI account, and (3) the lower-tier CFC did not distribute any property until year 3. Under Prop. Reg. § 1.959-2(a), the section 959(b) exclusion for the upper-tier CFC for purposes of calculating USP's section 951(a) inclusion is still $100x. In contrast, Prop. Reg. § 1.959-2(a) provides that the section 959(b) exclusion for the upper-tier CFC for purposes of determining DC's section 951(a) inclusion is zero because none of the earnings and profits distributed were attributable to amounts included in income under section 951(a) with respect to DC or the person to whom DC is a successor in interest. Therefore, DC may have an income inclusion under section 951(a).

In addition, Prop. Reg. § 1.959-2(b) provides guidance with respect to the application of section 959(b) in the context of stock sales subject to section 304(a)(1) where the selling corporation is a CFC. The proposed regulations clarify that in the case of a deemed redemption resulting from a transaction described in section 304(a)(1) in which earnings and profits of an acquiring foreign corporation or an acquired foreign corporation or both are deemed distributed to a selling CFC, the selling CFC is deemed for purposes of section 959(b) to receive such distributions through a chain of ownership described under section 958(a).

C. *Maintenance of PTI Accounts*

The proposed regulations contain detailed rules regarding the maintenance of shareholder PTI accounts and the maintenance of pools of PTI and non-PTI earnings and profits with respect to a foreign corporation, including rules for adjusting PTI accounts as a result of certain transactions. In addition, the proposed regulations provide rules for covered shareholders that have more than one share of stock in a foreign corporation and covered shareholders that are members of a consolidated group.

1. *Shareholder-level accounting of PTI*

The proposed regulations provide that a covered shareholder's PTI account with respect to its stock in a foreign corporation shall identify the amounts included in gross income by a United States shareholder under section 951(a)(1)(A) with respect to the stock (PTI described in section 959(c)(2)), and amounts that are included in the gross income of a United States shareholder under section 951(a)(1)(B) and section 956 amounts that would have been so included but for section 959(a)(2) (PTI described in section 959(c)(1)) by such shareholder that owns the stock or by a successor in interest. A shareholder account must also reflect these amounts in the functional currency of the foreign corporation and the annual dollar basis of each category of PTI in the account.

2. *Corporate-level accounting of PTI*

The proposed regulations also provide that separate aggregate categories (with respect to all of the shareholders of a foreign corporation) of PTI described in section 959(c)(1) and section 959(c)(2) and non-PTI shall be maintained with respect to foreign corporations. These categories of earnings and profits of a foreign corporation shall be maintained in the functional currency of the foreign corporation.

The proposed regulations reflect the basic allocation rules under section 959(c) and (e). Those rules provide that distributions are considered to be made on a last-in first-out basis under section 316(a), first from any PTI described in section 959(c)(1), then from PTI described in section 959(c)(2), and finally from non-PTI earnings and profits. In addition, section 956 amounts are allocated first to section 959(c)(2) earnings and profits and then to non-PTI earnings and profits. Consequently, PTI resulting from section 956 amounts in a prior year cannot exclude section 956 amounts in a later year from otherwise being included in a United States shareholder's gross income under section 951(a)(1)(B).

The proposed regulations also provide that these allocations to PTI are made in conjunction with the shareholder-level adjustments to shareholder-level PTI accounts. In addition, any adjustments to earnings and profits required under section 312 or other sections of the Code or Treasury regulations shall generally be made only to non-PTI.

3. *Foreign currency and foreign tax credit rules*

The proposed regulations also contain several rules that reflect the significant changes made to the foreign currency translation rules since the existing section 959 regulations were issued. The proposed regulations also contain rules regarding the foreign tax credit rules relating to PTI.

a. *Dollar basis pooling election*

The proposed regulations provide that a shareholder account must reflect the annual dollar basis of each category of PTI in the account. However, Prop. Reg.§ 1.959-3(b)(2)(ii) allows taxpayers to elect to treat distributions as being made from a single pool of post-1986 PTI for purposes of computing foreign currency gain or loss under section 986(c) and basis adjustments under section 961 with respect to distributions of PTI. Thus, the reduction of the basis of shares in a foreign corporation and the foreign currency gain (or loss) attributable to a PTI distribution may both be determined by assigning a pro rata portion of the shareholder's aggregate dollar basis in its PTI account to a distribution of PTI. The proposed regulations make this pooled approach available to taxpayers for purposes of section 986(c) at the taxpayer's election. The proposed regulations provide that the election is made by using a dollar basis pool to compute foreign currency gain or loss under section 986(c) with respect to distributions of PTI of a foreign corporation, or to compute gain or loss with respect to its stock in the foreign corporation, whichever occurs first. Any subsequent change in the taxpayer's method of assigning dollar basis may only be made with the consent of the Commissioner.

b. *Taxes and other expenses attributable to PTI*

Prop. Reg. § 1.959-3(c) provides that the corporate-level and shareholder-level PTI accounts are reduced by the functional currency amount of any income, war profits, or excess profits taxes imposed by any foreign country or a possession of the United States on or with respect to PTI as it is distributed by a foreign corporation to another foreign corporation through a chain of ownership described in section 958(a). The proposed regulations further provide that such taxes are not added to the foreign corporation's post-1986 foreign income taxes pool, which is maintained with respect to the foreign corporation's post-1986 undistributed earnings. Rather, such taxes are maintained in a separate account and allowed as a credit pursuant to section 960(a)(3) when the associated PTI is distributed to a United States shareholder (or its successor in interest). This rule ensures that amounts previously included in income that are used to pay creditable foreign taxes and so are unavailable for distribution to covered shareholders reduce the amount of PTI available for distribution but may be claimed as a foreign tax credit at the appropriate time. The proposed regulations also provide for corresponding adjustments to the covered shareholder's dollar basis of the PTI account.

Prop. Reg. § 1.959-3(d) provides that no expenses of a foreign corporation, other than creditable foreign income taxes described in Prop. Reg. § 1.959-3(c), shall be allocated and apportioned to reduce PTI. By allocating all such expenses to non-PTI, this rule preserves the amount of PTI that may be distributed to a United States shareholder (or its successor in interest) in a non-taxable manner.

4. *Adjustment of shareholder PTI accounts*

The proposed regulations generally provide rules for the adjustment of a covered shareholder's PTI account upon an inclusion of income by the shareholder under section 951, an actual distribution of earnings and profits to the shareholder, or a determination of a section 956 amount with respect to the shareholder. The proposed regulations provide that the adjustment of PTI accounts occur according to the ordering rules of section 959 to determine the tax consequences of the various events. For purposes of determining the tax consequences to a covered shareholder in a foreign corporation, the proposed regulations provide that with respect to a foreign corporation's taxable year, and for the taxable year of the covered shareholder in which or with which such taxable year of the foreign corporation ends, the following events are taken into account in the following order: (1) the covered shareholder's inclusion of subpart F income or other amounts in gross income under section 951(a)(1)(A) for a taxable year, (2) any actual distributions of current or accumulated earnings and profits by a foreign corporation during the year, including redemptions treated as distributions of property to which section 301 applies pursuant to section 302(d); and (3) any investments in United States property by a CFC during the year resulting in a section 956 amount for one or more United States shareholders for the year. For purposes of the proposed regulations, amounts included in the gross income of any person as a dividend under section 1248(a) or (f) are generally treated as section 951(a)(1)(A) inclusions.

Thus, under Prop. Reg. § 1.959-3(e)(2), at the end of the foreign corporation's taxable year, a shareholder's PTI account is first adjusted upward by the amount of any subpart F income included in gross income by the shareholder under section 951(a) with respect to the shareholder's stock in the foreign corporation. Second, a shareholder's PTI account is adjusted downward by the amount of any distributions of PTI to the shareholder with respect to the stock during the year. However, a PTI account can never be reduced below zero. Third, to the extent that any section 956 amount for the year is equal to (or less than) the amount of PTI described in section 959(c)(2), an amount of such PTI equal to the section 956 amount is reclassified as PTI described in section 959(c)(1), but does not decrease the shareholder's PTI account. Finally, the shareholder's PTI account is adjusted upward by any section 956 amount in excess of the PTI described in section 959(c)(2) for the year. Corresponding adjustments are made to the dollar basis of the PTI account.

This sequence of adjustments may be affected by the PTI sharing rules discussed below. Although the sharing rules are described in greater detail in Prop. Reg. §§1.959-3(f) and (g), the order of the adjustments described in these sections are provided for in the steps described in Prop. Reg. §1.959-3(e)(2).

The amount of a downward adjustment to the covered shareholder's PTI account under the second step described above is excluded from the shareholder's gross income under section 959(a)(1) and Prop. Reg. §1.959-1(c)(1). Similarly, the amount of section 959(c)(2) PTI which is reclassified as section 959(c)(1) PTI under the third step described above is excluded from the covered shareholder's gross income under section 959(a)(2) and Prop. Reg. §1.959-1(c)(2).

5. *Adjustment to PTI accounts upon distributions to intermediary CFCs*

Where stock in a lower-tier CFC is owned indirectly by a United States shareholder (or successor in interest) through one or more upper-tier CFCs in a chain of ownership under section 958(a), the shareholder's PTI accounts with respect to stock in the relevant foreign corporations in the chain must be adjusted when the lower-tier CFC makes a distribution of PTI to an upper-tier CFC in the chain. Prop. Reg. §1.959-3(e)(3) provides that the shareholder's PTI account with respect to stock in the distributing foreign corporation is decreased by the amount of PTI distributed with respect to such stock, and the shareholder's PTI account with respect to stock in the recipient foreign corporation is increased by the same amount (in addition to being increased by any non-PTI portion of the distribution that results in an inclusion in the shareholder's gross income under section 951(a) as subpart F income of the receiving CFC). Prop. Reg. §1.959-3(e)(3) provides a spot rate translation convention for cases in which the distributing and receiving corporations use different functional currencies.

6. *Effect of deficits in earnings and profits*

Prop. Reg. §1.959-3(e)(5) provides that a shareholder's PTI account is not adjusted to take into account any deficit in earnings and profits of the corporation for the taxable year. Deficits will reduce only the non-PTI of the corporation under section 312.

7. *Distribution in excess of the PTI account*

Under Prop. Reg. §1.959-3(e)(5), when a foreign corporation distributes to a shareholder an amount exceeding the PTI account with respect to the relevant stock, the treatment of the excess amount depends on the facts and circumstances. Subject to the PTI sharing rules discussed below, the excess amount of a distribution generally is treated as a dividend under section 316 to the extent of the distributing corporation's non-PTI, and thereafter as a return of capital (reducing the shareholder's basis in its stock in the foreign corporation) under section 301(c)(2). Any portion of the distribution remaining after the shareholder's basis of the stock in the foreign corporation is reduced to zero is treated as capital gain under section 301(c)(3).

8. *PTI sharing rules*

The purpose of section 959 is to prevent double taxation of amounts that have been previously included in gross income by a United States shareholder under section 951(a) and, importantly, to prevent such double taxation at the earliest possible time. Section 951 subjects a United States shareholder to tax on undistributed income of a CFC, so the ordering rule of section 959(c) effectuates this statutory purpose by treating actual distributions to the shareholder as coming first out of PTI. As one of the goals of section 959 is to treat distributions as first coming from PTI, the IRS and Treasury Department believe that a United States shareholder (or successor in interest) should be entitled to exclude from gross income under section 959(a) all of a foreign corporation's distributions of earnings and profits and section 956 amounts to the extent of PTI associated with any of the United States person's stock in the foreign corporation, before that person is required to include additional distributions of earnings and profits or section 956 amounts of the foreign corporation in gross income.

The IRS and Treasury Department believe that similar rules should apply with respect to members of a consolidated group. Although the taxation of a consolidated group represents a hybrid of single and separate entity treatment, consolidated attribute utilization is generally based on single entity treatment. For example, when determining consolidated taxable income for a given year, subject to certain limitations, the group is entitled to offset its income with any consolidated net operating losses that are carried forward to such year (regardless of which member or members recognized the income or incurred the losses). Given the broad regulatory authority of section 1502 and the statutory mandate in section 959 to allow United States shareholders (or successors in interest) to recover PTI at the earliest possible time, the IRS and Treasury Department believe that PTI is an attribute for which single entity treatment of United States consolidated groups is appropriate. As a result, the IRS and Treasury Department have concluded that a shareholder of a foreign corporation that is a member of a consolidated group should be entitled to exclude from gross income under section 959(a) all of a foreign corporation's distributions of earnings and profits, and section 956 amounts, to the extent of PTI associated with any stock in the foreign corporation owned by any member of the consolidated group (with appropriate adjustments). Therefore, the proposed regulations provide for sharing of PTI between accounts of different members of a consolidated group in a manner similar to the sharing of PTI between multiple accounts of a single shareholder, as described below.

a. *Shareholder with multiple PTI accounts*

Prop. Reg. § 1.959-3(f) provides a special rule that applies when a United States shareholder has more than one PTI account with respect to stock in a foreign corporation, and during its taxable year, the foreign corporation distributes earnings and profits in an amount that exceeds one or more of such PTI accounts. In that case, the shareholder's PTI accounts with respect to all of its other stock in the foreign corporation that it owns at the end of the foreign corporation's taxable year shall be reduced, in the aggregate, by the amount of the excess, on a pro rata basis by reference to the level of such PTI accounts (after such PTI accounts have first been adjusted to reflect any distributions of earnings and profits with respect to those blocks of stock).

The aggregate reduction in such PTI accounts produces a corresponding increase in the PTI account that would have been exceeded by the amount distributed but for the operation of this sharing rule. That PTI account is then reduced to zero to reflect the amount of earnings and profits distributed with respect to that block of stock during the year.

Similarly, if the section 959(c)(2) portion of a PTI account for a share in a foreign corporation is exceeded by the section 956 amount attributable to the share, the aggregate amount of the section 959(c)(2) portion of the PTI accounts for all other stock of the foreign corporation owned by the shareholder on the last day of the foreign corporation's taxable year is available for purposes of excluding the section 956 amount from gross income under section 959(a)(2).

b. *Shareholder that is a member of a consolidated group*

Prop. Reg. § 1.959-3(g) provides similar sharing rules where stock in a foreign corporation is owned by two or more members of a consolidated group. For purposes of administrative convenience, however, this rule focuses on whether the shareholders are members of the same consolidated group at the end of the foreign corporation's taxable year and not at the time the PTI in question was generated. Specifically, if the total amount of a United States shareholder's PTI account or accounts for stock in a foreign corporation is exceeded by the amount of earnings and profits distributed by the corporation to the shareholder during the year, the PTI accounts of other members of the shareholder's consolidated group that own stock in the corporation are decreased on a pro rata basis (after adjustment) and the shareholder's PTI accounts or account, as the case may be, will be correspondingly increased and then adjusted downward to zero.

Similarly, if the total amount of the section 959(c)(2) portion of a shareholder's PTI account or accounts for stock in a foreign corporation is exceeded by the shareholder's section 956 amount for the year, the aggregate amount of the section 959(c)(2) portions of the PTI accounts of other member's of the shareholder's consolidated group at the end of the foreign corporation's taxable year that own stock in the foreign corporation will be available to the shareholder for purposes of excluding the section 956 amount from gross income under section 959(a)(2).

9. *Redemptions, including section 304 transactions*

The proposed regulations provide rules for the adjustment of PTI accounts and the effect on the corporation's non-PTI when a foreign corporation redeems its stock. The effect of a distribution in redemption of stock (redemption distribution) depends on whether the redemption distribution is treated as a payment in exchange for the stock under sections 302(a) or 303, or as a distribution of property to which section 301 applies pursuant to section 302(d).

a. *Redemptions treated as sales or exchanges*

If a redemption distribution is treated as a sale or exchange, generally the amount chargeable to the earnings and profits of the redeeming corporation is limited by section 312(n)(7) to a ratable share of the earnings and profits. Where the redeeming corporation is a foreign corporation and there is a PTI account with respect to the redeemed stock, the proposed regulations provide that section 312(n)(7) is applied by limiting the reduction of the redeeming corporation's earnings and profits to an amount which does not exceed the sum of (1) the amount in the PTI account for the redeemed stock and (2) a ratable share of the corporation's non-PTI attributable to the redeemed shares, if any. This sum first reduces the PTI account with respect to the redeemed stock and then reduces the corporation's non-PTI.

The IRS and Treasury Department believe that, in the case where a foreign corporation redeems stock in a transaction treated as a sale or exchange for an amount that is less than the PTI account for that stock, it would be inappropriate to transfer the remainder of the PTI account to any other PTI accounts with respect to stock in the foreign corporation. Under section 961(a) and the regulations thereunder, the basis of stock in a foreign corporation is increased by the amount included in the shareholder's gross income under section 951(a), which is reflected in the PTI account with respect to such stock. The shareholder recovers this increase in basis upon a sale of the stock, preventing the shareholder from suffering double taxation on gain attributable to PTI (or in appropriate cases enabling the shareholder to recognize a loss). Consequently, under the proposed regulations, the remainder of the PTI account in the situation described above is not transferred to any other PTI account because it was already accounted for in the treatment of the redemption as a sale or exchange. Any corporate-level PTI attributable to the redeemed stock that remains after the reduction under section 312(n)(7) loses its character as PTI and is reclassified as non-PTI of the corporation. The IRS and Treasury Department believe that because the redeemed shareholder is able to use the loss resulting from the redemption to offset other income, its excess PTI must become other earnings and profits that remain with the foreign corporation so that those earnings and profits can be subject to tax.

b. *Redemptions treated as section 301 distributions*

If, under section 302(d), a redemption distribution is treated as a distribution of property to which section 301 applies, the proposed regulations provide that the rules of Prop. Reg. §§1.959-1 and -3 shall apply in the same manner as they do to any other distribution to which section 301(c) applies. The PTI account with respect to the redeemed stock is reduced by the amount of the redemption distribution. If the redemption distribution exceeds such PTI account, the sharing rules described above regarding nonredemptive distributions of earnings and profits will be applicable. If, instead, the PTI account with respect to the redeemed shares exceeds the amount of the redemption distribution, the excess PTI is reallocated to the PTI accounts with respect to the remaining stock in the foreign corporation in a manner consistent with, and in proportion to, the proper adjustments of the basis in the remaining shares of the foreign corporation pursuant to §1.302-2(c). Accordingly, the proposed regulations also require proper adjustment of the basis of the shareholder's remaining stock in the redeeming corporation, and of stock in the redeeming corporation held by related persons (not limited to members of the shareholder's consolidated group).

c. *Deemed redemptions under section 304*

With respect to amounts paid to acquire stock in a transaction described in section 304(a)(1) and to which section 301(c) applies, the rules of Prop. Reg. §§1.959-1 and -3 shall apply in the same manner as they do to any other distribution to which section 301(c) applies. As discussed below, the sharing rules described above are applicable to such redemption distributions that are treated as distributions of property to which section 301 applies. In addition, a covered shareholder receiving such a distribution of earnings and profits shall have a PTI account with respect to the stock of each foreign corporation deemed to have distributed its earnings and profits under section 304(b)(2).

The Senate Report on the IRS Restructuring and Reform Act of 1998 states with respect to the Secretary's authority to prescribe regulations resulting from the enactment of section 304(b)(6), "It is expected that such regulations will provide for an exclusion from income for distributions from earnings and profits of the acquiring corporation and the issuing corporation that represent previously taxed income under subpart F. It further is expected that such regulations will provide for appropriate adjustments to the basis of stock held by the corporation treated as receiving the distribution or by the corporation that had the prior inclusion with respect to the previously taxed income." S. Rep. No. 105-174 at 179 (1998). The Conference agreement on the Act follows the Senate amendment. H.R. Conf. Rep. No. 105-599 (1998).

In the case where members of a United States consolidated group own stock in the issuing corporation and the acquiring corporation in a section 304(a)(1) transaction, the PTI accounting and sharing rules are intended to prevent double taxation of PTI, as intended by Congress in enacting sections 304(b)(6) and 959. A lower-tier, cross-chain acquisition of stock is generally subject to section 304(a)(1) and the transferor is treated as having transferred the stock in the issuing corporation to the acquiring corporation in exchange for stock in the acquiring corporation in a transaction to which section 351(a) applies. The acquiring corporation is treated as having redeemed those shares pursuant to a redemption distribution to which section 301 applies. As a result, in accordance with these regulations, a PTI account with respect to the stock in the foreign corporation that is treated as redeemed under section 304(a)(1) would be considered to arise at the time of the transaction. Any PTI accounts with respect to stock in the foreign corporation owned by other members of the shareholder's consolidated group would be reduced, and the PTI account of the redeemed shareholder increased (and then reduced to zero), under the PTI sharing rules described above.

D. *Basis Adjustments*

The proposed regulations contain corresponding amendments to the regulations under section 961. These proposed regulations generally provide for increases and reductions in the basis of foreign corporation stock or other property through which foreign corporation stock is owned which match the increases and reductions in the PTI account with respect to such stock under the section 959 proposed regulations. The proposed regulations provide translation conventions for determining dollar basis adjustments under section 961 as a result of inclusions under section 951(a), distributions, and the foreign income taxes imposed on PTI as it is distributed through tiers of foreign corporations.

The proposed regulations also implement section 961(c) by providing for adjustments to the basis of stock in a CFC that is held by another CFC in a chain of ownership described in section 958(a) for the purpose of determining the amount properly includible in gross income under section 951(a) by a United States shareholder upon a sale of stock in a lower-tier CFC.

The regulations also contain rules describing basis adjustments resulting from cross-chain sales of foreign corporation stock under section 304(a)(1).

E. *Basis Adjustments of Consolidated Group Members*

In the case where there is sharing of PTI among members of a U.S. consolidated group, the proposed regulations also clarify the interaction of the investment adjustment provisions in the consolidated return regulations with the section 961 basis adjustment provisions. Accordingly, the proposed regulations clarify that a consolidated group member who utilizes PTI of another member shall treat the increase in its PTI account as the receipt of tax exempt income under Prop. Reg. § 1.1502-32(b)(3)(ii)(D), and a member whose PTI is utilized shall treat the reduction in its PTI account as a noncapital nondeductible expense under Prop. Reg. § 1.1502-32(b)(3)(iii)(B) for purposes of making the investment adjustments required by § 1.1502-32.

F. *Proposed Effective Date and Transition Rule*

These regulations are proposed to apply to taxable years of foreign corporations beginning on or after the date these regulations are published as final regulations in the **Federal Register**, and taxable years of U.S. shareholders with or within which such taxable years of foreign corporations end. After these regulations become effective, foreign corporations and shareholders who are currently accounting for PTI in a manner other than that which is provided in these regulations may use any reasonable method to conform their current accounting of PTI to the rules provided in these regulations.

Request for Comments

A. *Coordination of Shareholder-level and Corporate-level Accounts*

Prop. Reg. § 1.959-3(e)(4) requires aggregate categories of PTI to be maintained at the corporate level and to be adjusted in accordance with adjustments made to the individual shareholder-level PTI accounts. No explicit rules are provided for how shareholder-level and corporate-level PTI information is to be shared among the shareholders of a foreign corporation. Comments are requested on whether such information sharing rules are necessary and, if so, how they should operate to ensure conformity between shareholder-level and corporate-level PTI accounting.

B. *PTI and Consolidated Groups*

The application of the PTI sharing rules in the proposed regulations result in corresponding adjustments to the basis of stock in the sharing member corporations (and potentially higher tier members) held by other members of the shareholder's consolidated group. As noted above, the IRS and Treasury Department believe that the PTI sharing rules result in the corresponding basis adjustments under the current investment adjustment provisions. There is some tension between single and separate entity treatment of a consolidated group regarding the PTI sharing rules, and the IRS and Treasury Department are continuing to study how to balance the policy in favor of minimizing multiple income inclusions with the policy of preserving the location of attributes within a consolidated group. In particular, the IRS and Treasury Department are concerned about the potential basis shifting that may occur as a result of the PTI sharing rules. The IRS and Treasury Department request comments on the proposed rules and whether there are more appropriate rules for determining the basis of: (1) the stock in a member of the consolidated group that transfers PTI to another member of the consolidated group under the proposed regulations, (2) the stock in the member of the consolidated group that receives the transferred PTI under the proposed regulations and (3) the stock in the higher tier members of the consolidated group that directly or indirectly own the stock in the members of the consolidated group whose PTI accounts are affected by the sharing rules in the proposed regulations.

The proposed regulations do not limit the application of the PTI sharing rules between members of a consolidated group to PTI earned by a foreign corporation while the member with excess PTI was a member of such group. The IRS and Treasury Department did not adopt such a limitation out of concern that it would be overly complex and concern that such a limitation might not be consistent with the successor in interest rule. However, the IRS and Treasury Department recognize that some may believe that such a limitation might be more consistent with other attribute sharing rules in the consolidated group context. Consequently, the IRS and Treasury Department request comments as to whether a limitation on PTI sharing between members of a consolidated group similar to those of § 1.1502-21(c) is appropriate.

The IRS and Treasury Department believe that transactions described in section 304 are generally covered by the PTI sharing rules contained in Prop. Reg. §§ 1.959-3(h)(1) through (3) that are applicable to typical redemptions. However, a specific rule has also been provided in Prop. Reg. § 1.959-3(h)(4) that makes the PTI sharing rules explicitly applicable to transactions described in section 304(a)(1) that are treated as distributions of property to which section 301 applies. The IRS and Treasury Department request comments regarding whether the PTI sharing rules should also be made explicitly applicable to transactions described in section 304(a)(1) that are treated as sales or exchanges or to transactions described in section 304(a)(2). In addition, comments are requested on whether rules should be provided to address the proper allocation of PTI after a transaction described in section 355.

C. *PTI and Section 367(b) Transactions.*

On November 15, 2000, the IRS and Treasury Department issued proposed regulations in the **Federal Register** (65 FR 69138) (REG-116050-99) addressing (1) the carryover of certain tax attributes, such as earnings and profits and foreign income tax accounts, when two corporations combine in a section 367(b) transaction described in section 381, and (2) the allocation of certain tax attributes when a corporation distributes stock in another corporation in a section 367(b) transaction (a foreign divisive transaction). In the preamble to those proposed regulations, the IRS and Treasury Department indicated that further guidance under section 959 would be required prior to addressing PTI issues that arise under section 367(b). At that time the IRS and Treasury Department requested comments with respect to proposed § 1.367(b) regarding whether PTI should be transferable and retain its character as PTI for section 959 purposes, as well as the various implications that result from that determination. Additionally, in the 2000 proposed regulations, the IRS and Treasury Department requested comments with respect to § 1.367(b)-8 of the proposed regulations regarding the proper adjustment of the PTI of a CFC following a foreign divisive transaction.

On August 8, 2006, the IRS and Treasury Department issued final regulations under § § 1.367(b)-3 and -7 with respect to the carryover of non-PTI amounts, among other things, while reserving final regulations under § 1.367(b)-8 with respect to the allocation of tax attributes in foreign divisive transactions.

The IRS and Treasury Department invite comments regarding the proper extension of the principles in these proposed regulations (including shareholder-level accounting of PTI and the PTI sharing rules) to § § 1.367(b)-3 and -7, as well as Prop. Reg. § 1.367(b)—8.

D. *Foreign Currency Gain or Loss and Foreign Tax Credits With Respect to PTI Distributions*

Under section 986(c) of the Code, foreign currency gain or loss with respect to distributions of PTI that is attributable to movements in exchange rates between the date(s) of the income inclusion that created the PTI and the distribution of such PTI shall be recognized and treated as ordinary income or loss from the same source as the associated income inclusion. The IRS and Treasury Department invite comments regarding additional guidance that may be needed under section 986(c) in light of the proposed regulations under section 959. The IRS and Treasury Department also invite comments regarding additional guidance that is needed to ensure that section 960(a)(3) provides appropriate foreign tax credit rules with respect to taxes imposed on PTI that is distributed through tiers of foreign corporations.

E. *Section 962*

The IRS and Treasury Department have not determined how the proposed accounting rules and basis rules should apply to a United States individual shareholder who has elected to be taxed as a corporation under section 962. Therefore, those rules are reserved for future study. The IRS and Treasury Department, however, invite comments about how the PTI rules and basis rules should apply for purposes of section 962.

F. *Section 961(c) Basis Adjustments*

Section 961(c) is only applicable for purposes of determining the amount included under section 951 in gross income of a United States shareholder. Consequently, the IRS and Treasury Department have so limited the application of Prop. Reg. § 1.961-3. In the event of a sale of a lower-tier CFC by an upper-tier CFC for which the rules of section 961(c) are implicated in determining the gain on the sale, the basis created in the lower-tier CFC stock for purposes of applying section 951 would not apply, for example, to determine the earnings and profits of the upper-tier CFC. However, the IRS and Treasury Department are concerned about the potential double taxation that may result in the event of the later distribution of these earnings and profits to a United States person.

G. *Transition Rule*

These regulations are proposed to apply to taxable years of foreign corporations beginning on or after the date these regulations are published as final regulations in the **Federal Register**, and taxable years of U.S. shareholders with or within which such taxable years of foreign corporations end. After these regulations become effective, foreign corporations and shareholders who are currently accounting for PTI in a manner other than that which is provided in these regulations may use any reasonable method to conform their current accounting of PTI to the rules provided in these regulations. Comments are requested on whether more detailed transition rules should be provided, and, if so, how such transition rules should operate to conform existing methods of PTI accounting with the method of PTI accounting required by these regulations.

Special Analyses

It has been determined that this notice of proposed rulemaking is not a significant regulatory action as defined in Executive Order 12866. Therefore, a regulatory assessment is not required. It has also been determined that section 553(b) of the Administrative Procedure Act (5 U.S.C. chapter 5) does not apply to these regulations and because the proposed regulation does not impose a collection of information on small entities, the Regulatory Flexibility Act (5 U.S.C. Ch. 6) does not apply. Pursuant to section 7805(f) of the Code, this notice of proposed rulemaking will be submitted to the Chief Counsel for Advocacy of the Small Business Administration for comment on its impact on small business.

Comments and Requests for Public Hearing

Before these proposed regulations are adopted as final regulations, consideration will be given to any written (a signed original and eight (8) copies) or electronic comments that are submitted timely to the IRS. The IRS and Treasury Department request comments on the clarity of the proposed rules and how they can be made easier to understand. All comments will be available for public inspection and copying. A public hearing will be scheduled if requested in writing by any person that timely submits written comments. If a public hearing is scheduled, notice of the date, time, and place for the public hearing will be published in the **Federal Register**.

Drafting Information

The principal author of these regulations is Ethan Atticks, Office of Associate Chief Counsel (International). However, other personnel from the IRS and Treasury Department participated in their development.

[¶49,280] Proposed Amendments of Regulations (REG-141901-05), published in the Federal Register on October 18, 2006.

[Code Secs. 72 and 1001]

Sales and exchanges: Annuities: Gain or loss recognition.—Amendments of Reg. §§1.72-6 and 1.1001-1, providing guidance on the taxation of the exchange of property for an annuity contract, are proposed.

AGENCY: Internal Revenue Service (IRS), Treasury.

ACTION: Notice of proposed rulemaking and notice of public hearing.

SUMMARY: This document contains proposed regulations that provide guidance on the taxation of the exchange of property for an annuity contract. These regulations are necessary to outline the proper taxation of these exchanges and will affect participants in transactions involving these exchanges. This document also provides notice of public hearing.

DATES: Written or electronic comments must be received by January 16, 2007. Outlines of topics to be discussed at the public hearing scheduled for February 16, 2007, at 10 a.m. must be received by January 16, 2007.

ADDRESSES: Send submissions to: CC:PA:LPD:PR (REG-141901-05), room 5203, Internal Revenue Service, PO Box 7604, Ben Franklin Station, Washington, DC 20044. Submissions may be hand delivered to CC:PA:LPD:PR (REG-141901-05), Courier's Desk, Internal Revenue Service, Crystal Mall 4 Building, 1901 S. Bell St., Arlington, VA, or sent electronically, via the IRS internet site at www.irs.gov/regs or via the Federal eRulemaking Portal at www.regulations.gov (IRS and REG141901-05).

FOR FURTHER INFORMATION CONTACT: Concerning the proposed regulations, James Polfer, at (202) 622-3970; concerning submissions of comments, the hearing, and/or to be placed on the building access list to attend the hearing, Kelly Banks, at (202) 622-0392 (not toll-free numbers).

SUPPLEMENTARY INFORMATION:

Background

This document contains proposed amendments to the Income Tax Regulations.

Section 1001 of the Internal Revenue Code (Code) provides rules for determining the amount of gain or loss recognized. Gain from the sale or other disposition of property equals the excess of the amount realized therefrom over the adjusted basis of the property; loss from the sale or other disposition of property equals the excess of the adjusted basis of the property over the amount realized. Section 1.1001-1(a) of the Income Tax Regulations provides further that the exchange of property for other property differing materially either in kind or in extent is treated as income or as loss sustained. Under section 1001(b), the amount realized from the sale or other disposition of property is the sum of any money received plus the fair market value of any property (other than money) received. Except as otherwise provided in the Code, the entire amount of gain or loss on the sale or exchange of property is recognized.

Under section 72(a), gross income includes any amount received as an annuity (whether for a period certain or for the life or lives of one or more individuals) under an annuity, endowment, or life insurance contract. Section 72(b) provides that gross income does not include that part of any amount received as an annuity which bears the same ratio to such amount as the investment in the contract bears to the expected return under the contract. Under section 72(e), amounts received under an annuity contract before the annuity starting date are included in gross income to the extent allocable to income on the contract, and are excluded from gross income to the extent allocable to the investment in the contract. Investment in the contract is defined in section 72(c) as the aggregate amount of premiums or other consideration paid, reduced by amounts received before the annuity starting date that were excluded from gross income.

In *Lloyd v. Commissioner*, 33 B.T.A. 903 (1936), *nonacq.*, XV-2 CB 39 (1936), *nonacq. withdrawn and acq.*, 1950-2 CB 3, the Board of Tax Appeals considered the taxation of gain from a father's sale of property to his son for an annuity contract. The Board concluded that the annuity contract had no fair market value within the meaning of the predecessor of section 1001(b) because of the uncertainty of payment from the son. Because the annuity contract had no fair market value under that provision, the Board held that the gain from the sale of the property was not required to be recognized immediately but rather would be included in income only when the annuity payments exceeded the property's basis. In reaching its holding, the Board applied the open transaction doctrine articulated by the Supreme Court in *Burnet v. Logan*, 283 U.S. 404 (1931). Under this doctrine, if an amount realized from a sale cannot be determined with certainty, the seller recovers the basis of the property sold before any income is realized on the sale.

In Rev. Rul. 69-74, 1969-1 CB 43, a father transferred a capital asset having an adjusted basis of $20,000 and a fair market value of $60,000 to his son in exchange for the son's legally enforceable promise to pay him a life annuity of $7,200 per year, in equal monthly installments of $600. The present value of the life annuity was $47,713.08. The ruling concluded that: (1) the father realized capital gain based on the difference between the father's basis in the property and the present value of the annuity; (2) the gain was reported ratably over the father's life expectancy; (3) the investment in the contract for purposes of computing the exclusion ratio was the father's basis in the property transferred; (4) the excess of the fair market value of the property transferred over the present value of the annuity was a gift from the father to the son; and (5) the prorated capital gain reported annually was derived from the portion of each annuity payment that was not excludible.

In *Estate of Bell v. Commissioner*, 60 T.C. 469 (1973), *acq. in part and nonacq. in part*, 1974 WL 36039 (Jan. 8, 1974), *acq.*, AOD No. 1979-184 (August 15, 1979), a husband and wife transferred stock in two closely held corporations to their son and daughter and their spouses in exchange for an annuity contract. The fair market value of the stock substantially exceeded the value of the annuity contract. The stock transferred was placed in escrow to secure the promise of the transferees. As further security, the annuity agreement provided for a cognovit judgment against the transferees in the event of default. Because of the secured nature of the annuity, the tax court held that (i) the difference between the value of the stock and the value of the annuity contract constituted a gift; (ii) the difference between the adjusted basis of the stock and the value of the annuity contract constituted gain that was taxable in the year of the transfer (which was not before the court); and (iii) the investment in the annuity contract equaled the present value of the annuity. Similarly, in *212 Corp. v. Commissioner*, 70 T.C. 788 (1978), the tax court held that the entire amount of gain realized from the exchange of appreciated real property for an annuity contract was fully taxable in the year of the exchange because the annuity contract was secured by (i) an agreement that the annuity payments would be considered a charge against the rents from the property, (ii) an agreement not to mortgage or sell the property without written consent of the transferors, and (iii) the authorization of a confession of judgment against the transferee in the event of default.

The Treasury Department and the IRS have learned that some taxpayers are inappropriately avoiding or deferring gain on the exchange of highly appreciated property for the issuance of annuity contracts. Many of these transactions involve private annuity contracts issued by family members or by business entities that are owned, directly or indirectly, by the annuitants themselves or by their family members. Many of these transactions involve a variety of mechanisms to secure the payment of amounts due under the annuity contracts.

The Treasury Department and the IRS believe that neither the open transaction approach of *Lloyd v. Commissioner* nor the ratable recognition approach of Rev. Rul. 69-74 clearly reflects the income of the transferor of property in exchange for an annuity contract. Contrary to the premise underlying these authorities, an annuity contract - whether secured or unsecured - may be valued at the time it is received in exchange for property. See generally section 7520 (requiring the use of tables to value any annuity contract for federal income tax purposes, except for purposes of any provision specified in regulations); §1.1001-1(a) ("The fair market value of property is a question of fact, but only in rare and unusual circumstances will property be considered to have no fair market value."). The Treasury Department and the IRS believe that the transferors should be taxed in a consistent manner regardless of whether they exchange property for an annuity or sell that property and use the proceeds to purchase an annuity.

Explanation of Provisions

These proposed amendments provide that, if an annuity contract is received in exchange for property (other than money), (i) the amount realized attributable to the annuity contract is the fair market value (as determined under section 7520) of the annuity contract at the time of the exchange; (ii) the entire amount of the gain or loss, if any, is recognized at the time of the exchange, regardless of the taxpayer's method of accounting; and (iii) for purposes of determining the initial investment in the annuity contract under section 72(c)(1), the aggregate amount of premiums or other consideration paid for the annuity contract equals the amount realized attributable to the annuity contract (the fair market value of the annuity contract). Thus, in situations where the fair market value of the property exchanged equals the fair market value of the annuity contract received, the investment in the annuity contract equals the fair market value of the property exchanged for the annuity contract.

In order to apply the proposed regulations to an exchange of property for an annuity contract, taxpayers will need to determine the fair market value of the annuity contract as determined under section 7520. In the case of an exchange of property for an annuity contract that is in part a sale and in part a gift, the proposed regulations apply the same rules that apply to any other such exchange under section 1001.

The proposed regulations provide that, for purposes of determining the investment in the annuity contract under section 72(c)(1), the aggregate amount of premiums or other consideration paid for the annuity contract is the portion of the amount realized on the exchange that is attributable to the annuity contract (which is the fair market value of the annuity contract at the time of the exchange). This rule is intended to ensure that no portion of the gain or loss on the exchange is duplicated or omitted by the application of section 72 in the years after the exchange. The annuitant's investment in the contract would be reduced in subsequent years under section 72(c)(1)(B) for amounts already received under the contract subsequent to the exchange and excluded from gross income when received as a return of the annuitant's investment in the contract.

The proposed regulations do not distinguish between secured and unsecured annuity contracts, or between annuity contracts issued by an insurance company subject to tax under subchapter L and those issued by a taxpayer that is not an insurance company. Instead, the proposed regulations provide a single set of rules that leave the transferor and transferee in the same position before tax as if the transferor had sold the property for cash and used the proceeds to purchase an annuity contract. The same rules would apply whether the exchange produces a gain or loss. The regulations do not, however, prevent the application of other provisions, such as section 267, to limit deductible losses in the case of some exchanges. The proposed regulations apply to exchanges of property for an annuity contract, regardless of whether the property is exchanged for a newly issued annuity contract or whether the property is exchanged for an already existing annuity contract.

Existing regulations in §1.1011-2 govern the tax treatment of an exchange of property that constitutes a bargain sale to a charitable organization (including an exchange of property for a charitable gift annuity). Example 8 in section 2(c) of those regulations provides that any gain on such an exchange is reported ratably, rather than entirely in the year of the exchange. This notice of proposed rulemaking does not propose to change the existing regulations in §1.1011-2. However, comments are requested as to whether a change should be made in the future to conform the tax treatment of exchanges governed by §1.1011-2 to the tax treatment prescribed in these proposed regulations.

The Treasury Department and the IRS are aware that property is sometimes exchanged for an annuity contract, including a private annuity contract, for valid, non-tax reasons related to estate planning and succession planning for closely held businesses. The proposed regulations are not intended to frustrate these transactions, but will ensure that income from the transactions is accounted for in the appropriate periods. In section 453, Congress set forth rules permitting the deferral of income from a transaction that qualifies as an installment sale. Taxpayers retain the ability to structure transactions as installment sales within the meaning of section 453(b), provided the other requirements of section 453 are met. The Treasury Department and IRS request comments as to the circumstances, if any, in which an exchange of property for an annuity contract should be treated as an installment sale, and as to any changes to the regulations under section 453 that might be advisable with regard to those circumstances.

Proposed Effective Date

The Treasury Department and the IRS propose §1.1001-1(j) to be effective generally for exchanges of property for an annuity contract after October 18, 2006. Thus, the regulations would not apply to amounts received after October 18, 2006, under annuity contracts that were received in exchange for property before that date. For a limited class of transactions, however, §1.1001-1(j) is proposed to be effective for exchanges of property for an annuity contract after April 18, 2007.

The Treasury Department and the IRS propose §1.72-6(e) to be effective generally for annuity contracts received in such exchanges after October 18, 2006. For a limited class of transactions, however, §1.72-6(e) is proposed to be effective for annuity contracts received in exchange for property after April 18, 2007. The Treasury Department and the IRS also propose to declare Rev. Rul. 69-74 obsolete effective contemporaneously with the effective date of these regulations. Thus, the obsolescence would be effective April 18, 2007, for exchanges described in §1.1001-1(j)(2)(ii) and §1.72-6(e)(2)(ii), and effective October 18, 2006, for all other exchanges of property for an annuity contract.

In both regulations, the effective date is delayed for six months for transactions in which (i) the issuer of the annuity contract is an individual; (ii) the obligations under the annuity contract are not secured, either directly or indirectly; and (iii) the property transferred in the exchange is not subsequently sold or otherwise disposed of by the transferee during the two-year period beginning on the date of the exchange. The Treasury Department and the IRS believe that the later proposed effective date for these transactions provides ample notice of the proposed rules for taxpayers currently planning transactions that present the least opportunity for abuse.

Special Analyses

It has been determined that this notice of proposed rulemaking is not a significant regulatory action as defined in Executive Order 12866. Therefore, a regulatory assessment is not required. It is hereby certified that these regulations will not have a significant economic impact on a substantial number of small entities. Accordingly, a regulation flexibility analysis is not required. This certification is based on the fact that typically only natural persons within the meaning of section 72(u) exchange property for an annuity contract. In addition, these regulations do not impose new reporting, recordkeeping, or other compliance requirements on taxpayers. Pursuant to section 7805(f) of the Code, the notice of proposed rulemaking will be submitted to the Chief Counsel for Advocacy of the Small Business Administration for comment on their impact on small business.

Comments and Public Hearing

Before these proposed regulations are adopted as final regulations, consideration will be given to any written (a signed original and eight (8) copies) or electronic comments that are timely submitted to the IRS. In addition to comments on the proposed regulations more generally, the Treasury Department and the IRS specifically request comments on (i) the clarity of the proposed regulations and how they can be made easier to understand; (ii) what guidance, if any, is needed in addition to Rev. Rul. 55-119, 1955-1 CB 352, see §601.601(d)(2), on the treatment of the issuer of an annuity contract that is not taxed under the provisions of subchapter L of the Code; (iii) whether any changes to §1.1011-2 (concerning a bargain sale to a charitable organization in exchange for an annuity contract), conforming those regulations to the proposed regulations, would be appropriate; (iv) circumstances (and corresponding changes to the regulations under section 453, if any) in which it might be appropriate to treat an exchange of property for an annuity contract as an installment sale; (v) circumstances, if any, in which the fair market value of an annuity contract for purposes of § 1.1001-1(j) should be determined other than by tables promulgated under the authority of section 7520; and (vi) additional transactions, if any, for which the six month delayed effective date would be appropriate. All comments will be available for public inspection and copying.

A public hearing has been scheduled for February 16, 2007, at 10 a.m., in the auditorium, Internal Revenue Service, New Carrollton Building, 5000 Ellin Road, Lanham, MD 20706. All visitors must present photo identification to enter the building. Because of access restrictions, visitors will not be admitted beyond the immediate entrance area lobby more than 30 minutes before the hearing starts. For information about having your name placed on the access list to attend the hearing, see the "FOR FURTHER INFORMATION CONTACT" portion of this preamble.

The rules of 26 CFR 601.601(a)(3) apply to the hearing.

Persons who wish to present oral comments at the hearing must submit written comments by January 16, 2007, and submit an outline of the topics to be discussed and the time to be devoted to each topic (a signed original and eight (8) copies) by that same date.

A period of 10 minutes will be allotted to each person making comments. An agenda showing the scheduling of the speakers will be prepared after the deadline for receiving outlines has passed. Copies of the agenda will be available free of charge at the hearing.

Drafting Information

The principal author of these proposed regulations is James Polfer, Office of the Associate Chief Counsel (Financial Institutions and Products), Internal Revenue Service.

[¶ 49,293] Proposed Amendments of Regulations (REG-156779-06), published in the Federal Register on March 30, 2007 (corrected 5/10/2007).

[Code Sec. 901]

Foreign tax credit: Foreign tax payments: Structured passive investment arrangements: Noncompulsory payments: U.S-owned foreign entities: Loss transfers: Combined settlements.—Amendments of Reg. § 1.901-2, which affect taxpayers that claim direct and indirect foreign tax credits, are proposed. Amendments to Reg. § 1.901-2(e)(5)(iv) adopted as Temporary Reg. § 1.901-2T(e)(5)(iv) by T.D. 9416 on July 15, 2008.

AGENCY: Internal Revenue Service (IRS), Treasury.

ACTION: Notice of proposed rulemaking and notice of public hearing

SUMMARY: These proposed regulations provide guidance relating to the determination of the amount of taxes paid for purposes of section 901.

The proposed regulations affect taxpayers that claim direct and indirect foreign tax credits. This document also provides notice of a public hearing.

DATES: Written or electronic comments must be received by June 28, 2007. Outlines of topics to be discussed at the public hearing scheduled for July 30, 2007, at 10 a.m. must be received by July 9, 2007.

ADDRESSES: Send submissions to CC:PA:LPD:PR (REG-156779-06), Room 5203, Internal Revenue Service, P.O. Box 7604, Ben Franklin Station, Washington, DC 20044. Submissions may be hand delivered Monday through Friday between the hours of 8 a.m. and 4 p.m. to CC:PA:LPD:PR (REG-156779-06), Courier's Desk, Internal Revenue Service, 1111 Constitution Avenue, N.W., Washington, DC, or sent electronically via the Federal eRulemaking Portal at http://www.regulations.gov (IRS REG-156779-06). The public hearing will be held in the Auditorium of the Internal Revenue Building, 1111 Constitution Avenue, NW., Washington, DC.

FOR FURTHER INFORMATION CONTACT: Concerning submission of comments, the hearing, and/or to be placed on the building access list to attend the hearing, Kelly Banks (202) 622-7180; concerning the regulations, Bethany A. Ingwalson, (202) 622-3850 (not toll-free numbers).

SUPPLEMENTARY INFORMATION:

Background

Section 901 of the Internal Revenue Code (Code) permits taxpayers to claim a credit for income, war profits, and excess profits taxes paid or accrued (or deemed paid) during the taxable year to any foreign country or to any possession of the United States.

Section 1.901-2(a) of the regulations defines a tax as a compulsory payment pursuant to the authority of a foreign country to levy taxes, and further provides that a tax is an income, war profits, or excess profits tax if the predominant character of the tax is that of an income tax in the U.S. sense. Section 1.901-2(e) provides rules for determining the amount of tax paid by a taxpayer for purposes of section 901. Section 1.901-2(e)(5) provides that an amount paid is not a compulsory payment, and thus is not an amount of tax paid, to the extent that the amount paid exceeds the amount of liability under foreign law for tax. For purposes of determining whether an amount paid exceeds the amount of liability under foreign law for tax, § 1.901-2(e)(5) provides the following rule:

An amount paid does not exceed the amount of such liability if the amount paid is determined by the taxpayer in a manner that is consistent with a reasonable interpretation and application of the substantive and procedural provisions of foreign law (including applicable tax treaties) in such a way as to reduce, over time, the taxpayer's reasonably expected liability under foreign law for tax, and if the taxpayer exhausts all effective and practical remedies, including invocation of competent authority procedures available under applicable tax treaties, to reduce, over time, the taxpayer's liability for foreign tax (including liability pursuant to a foreign tax audit adjustment).

Section 1.901-2(e)(5) provides further that if foreign tax law includes options or elections whereby a taxpayer's liability may be shifted, in whole or part, to a different year, the taxpayer's use or failure to use such options or elections does not result in a noncompulsory payment, and that a settlement by a taxpayer of two or more issues will be evaluated on an overall basis, not on an issue-by-issue basis, in determining whether an amount is a compulsory amount. In addition, it provides that a taxpayer is not required to alter its form of doing business, its business conduct, or the form of any transaction in order to reduce its liability for tax under foreign law.

A. U.S.-Owned Foreign Entities

Commentators have raised questions regarding the application of § 1.901-2(e)(5) to a U.S. person that owns one or more foreign entities. In particular, commentators have raised questions concerning the application of the regulation when one foreign entity directly or indirectly owned by a U.S. person transfers, pursuant to a group relief type regime, a net loss to another foreign entity, which may or may not also be owned by the U.S. person. Certain commentators have expressed concern that foreign taxes paid by the transferor in a subsequent tax year might not be compulsory payments to the extent the transferor could have reduced its liability for those foreign taxes had it chosen not to transfer the net loss in the prior year. This concern arises because the current final regulations apply on a taxpayer-by-taxpayer basis, obligating each taxpayer to minimize its liability for foreign taxes over time, even though the net effect of the loss surrender may be to minimize the amount of foreign taxes paid in the aggregate by the controlled group over time.

Similar questions and concerns arise when one or more foreign subsidiaries of a U.S. person reach a combined settlement with a foreign taxing authority that results in an increase in the amount of one foreign subsidiary's foreign tax liability and a decrease in the amount of a second foreign subsidiary's foreign tax liability.

B. Certain Structured Passive Investment Arrangements

The IRS and Treasury Department have become aware that certain U.S. taxpayers are engaging in highly structured transactions with foreign counterparties in order to generate foreign tax credits. These transactions are intentionally structured to create a foreign tax liability when, removed from the elaborately engineered structure, the basic underlying business transaction generally would result in significantly less, or even no, foreign taxes. In particular, the transactions purport to convert what would otherwise be an ordinary course financing arrangement between a U.S. person and a foreign counterparty, or a portfolio investment of a U.S. person, into some form of equity ownership in a foreign special purpose vehicle (SPV). The transaction is deliberately structured to create income in the SPV for foreign tax purposes, which income is purportedly subject to foreign tax. The parties exploit differences between U.S. and foreign law in order to permit the U.S. taxpayer to claim a credit for the purported foreign tax payments while also allowing the foreign counterparty to claim a foreign tax benefit. The U.S. taxpayer and the foreign counterparty share the cost of the purported foreign tax payments through the pricing of the arrangement.

Explanation of Provisions

The proposed regulations address the application of § 1.901-2(e)(5) in cases where a U.S. person directly or indirectly owns one or more foreign entities and in cases in which a U.S. person is a party to a highly structured passive investment arrangement described in this preamble. The proposed regulations would treat as a single taxpayer for purposes of § 1.901-2(e)(5) all foreign entities with respect to which a U.S. person has a direct or indirect interest of 80 percent or more. The proposed regulations would treat foreign payments attributable to highly structured passive investment arrangements as noncompulsory payments under § 1.901-2(e)(5) and, thus, would disallow credits for such amounts.

A. U.S.-Owned Foreign Entities

Section 1.901-2(e)(5) requires a taxpayer to interpret and apply foreign law reasonably in such a way as to reduce, over time, the taxpayer's reasonably expected liability under foreign law for tax. This requirement ensures that a taxpayer will make reasonable efforts to minimize its foreign tax liability even though the taxpayer may otherwise be indifferent to the imposition of foreign tax due to the availability of the foreign tax credit. The purpose of this requirement is served if all foreign entities owned by such person, in the aggregate, satisfy the requirements of the regulation. Accordingly, for purposes of determining compliance with § 1.901-2(e)(5), the proposed regulations would treat as a single taxpayer all foreign entities in which the same U.S. person has a direct or indirect interest of 80 percent or more. For this purpose, an interest of 80 percent or more means stock possessing 80 percent or more of the vote and value (in the case of a foreign corporation) or an interest representing 80 percent or more of the income (in the case of non-corporate foreign entities).

The proposed regulations provide that if one 80 percent-owned foreign entity transfers or surrenders a net loss for the taxable year to a second such entity pursuant to a foreign law group relief or similar regime, foreign tax paid by the transferor in a different tax year does not fail to be a compulsory payment solely because such tax would not have been due had the transferor retained the net loss and carried it over to such other year. Similarly, it provides that if one or more 80 percent-owned foreign entities enter into a combined settlement under foreign law of two or more issues, such settlement will be evaluated on an overall basis, not on an issue-by-issue or entity-by-entity basis, in determining whether an amount is a compulsory amount. The proposed regulations include examples to illustrate the proposed rule.

The IRS and Treasury Department intend to monitor structures involving U.S.-owned foreign groups, including those that would be covered by the proposed regulations, to determine whether taxpayers are utilizing such structures to separate foreign taxes from the related income. The IRS and Treasury Department may issue additional regulations in the future in order to address arrangements that result in the inappropriate separation of foreign tax and income.

B. Certain Structured Passive Investment Arrangements

The structured arrangements discovered and identified by the IRS and the Treasury Department can be grouped into three general categories: (1) U.S. borrower transactions, (2) U.S. lender transactions, and (3) asset holding transactions. The transactions, including the claimed U.S. tax results, are described in section B.1 of this preamble. Section B.2 of this preamble discusses the purpose of the foreign tax credit regime and explains why allowing a credit in the transactions is inconsistent with this purpose. Section B.3 of this preamble discusses comments the IRS and the Treasury Department have received on the transactions and describes the proposed regulations. The IRS is continuing to scrutinize the transactions under current law and intends to utilize all tools available to challenge the claimed U.S. tax results in appropriate cases.

1. Categories of structured passive investment arrangements

(a) U.S. borrower transactions. The first category consists of transactions in which a U.S. person indirectly borrows funds from an unrelated foreign counterparty. If a U.S. person were to borrow funds directly from a foreign person, the U.S. person generally would make nondeductible principal payments and deductible interest payments. The U.S. person would not incur foreign tax. The foreign lender generally would owe foreign tax on its interest income. In a structured financing arrangement, the U.S. borrower attempts to convert all or a portion of its deductible interest payments and, in certain cases, its nondeductible principal payments into creditable foreign tax payments. The U.S. borrower's foreign tax credit benefit is shared by the parties through the pricing of the arrangement. See Example 1 of proposed § 1.901-2(e)(5)(iv)(D).

In a typical structured financing arrangement, the loan is made indirectly through an SPV. The foreign lender's interest income (and, in many cases, other income) is effectively isolated in the SPV. The U.S. borrower acquires a direct or indirect interest in the SPV and asserts that it has a direct or indirect equity interest in the SPV for U.S. tax purposes. The U.S. borrower claims a credit for foreign taxes imposed on the income derived by the SPV. The U.S. borrower's purported equity interest may be treated as debt for foreign tax purposes or it may be treated as an equity interest that is owned by the foreign lender for foreign tax purposes. In either case, the foreign lender is treated as owning an equity interest in the SPV for foreign tax purposes, which entitles the foreign lender to receive tax-free distributions from the SPV.

For example, assume that a U.S. person seeks to borrow $1.5 billion from a foreign person. Instead of borrowing the funds directly, the U.S. borrower forms a corporation (SPV) in the same country as the foreign counterparty. The U.S. borrower contributes $1.5 billion to SPV in exchange for 100 percent of the stock of SPV. SPV, in turn, loans the entire $1.5 billion to a corporation wholly owned by the U.S. borrower. The U.S. borrower recovers its $1.5 billion by selling its entire interest in SPV to the foreign counterparty, subject to an obligation to repurchase the interest in five years for $1.5 billion. Each year, SPV earns $120 million of interest income from the U.S. borrower's subsidiary. SPV pays $36 million of foreign tax and distributes the remaining $84 million to the foreign counterparty.

The U.S. borrower takes the position that, for U.S. tax purposes, the sale-repurchase transaction is a borrowing secured by the SPV stock. Accordingly, the U.S. borrower asserts that it owns the stock of SPV for U.S. tax purposes and has an outstanding debt obligation to the foreign counterparty. It reports the distribution from SPV as dividend income and claims indirect credits under section 902 for the $36 million of foreign taxes paid by SPV. It includes in income the cash dividend of $84 million paid to the foreign counterparty, plus a section 78 gross-up amount of $36 million, for a total of $120 million. The U.S. borrower claims a deduction of $84 million as interest on its debt obligation to the foreign counterparty. In addition, the U.S. borrower's subsidiary claims an interest deduction of $120 million. In the aggregate, the U.S. borrower and its subsidiary claim a foreign tax credit of $36 million and an interest expense deduction (net of income inclusions) of $84 million.

For foreign tax purposes, the foreign counterparty owns the equity of SPV and is not subject to additional foreign tax upon receipt of the dividend. Thus, the net result is that the foreign jurisdiction receives foreign tax payments attributable to what is in substance the lender's interest income, which is consistent with the foreign tax results that would be expected from a direct borrowing.

Both parties benefit from the arrangement. The foreign lender obtains an after-foreign tax interest rate that is higher than the after-foreign tax interest rate it would earn on a direct loan. The U.S. borrower's funding costs are lower on an after-U.S. tax basis (though not on a pre-U.S. tax basis) because it has converted interest expense into creditable foreign tax payments.

The benefit to the parties is solely attributable to the reduction in the U.S. borrower's U.S. tax liability resulting from the foreign tax credits claimed by the U.S. borrower. The foreign jurisdiction benefits from the arrangement because the amount of interest received by SPV exceeds the amount of interest that would have been received by the foreign lender if the transaction had been structured as a direct loan. As a result, the amount paid by SPV to the foreign jurisdiction exceeds the amount of foreign tax the foreign jurisdiction would have imposed on the foreign lender's interest income in connection with a direct loan.

(b) U.S. lender transactions. The second category consists of transactions in which a U.S person indirectly loans funds to an unrelated foreign counterparty. If a U.S. person were to loan the funds directly to the foreign person, the U.S. person generally would be subject to U.S. tax on its interest income and the borrower would receive a corresponding deduction for the interest expense. The U.S. person generally would not be subject to foreign tax other than, in certain circumstances, a gross basis withholding tax.

In a typical structured financing arrangement, the U.S. person advances funds to a foreign borrower indirectly through an SPV. The U.S. person asserts that its interest in the SPV is equity for U.S. tax purposes. Income of the foreign borrower (or another foreign counterparty) is effectively shifted into the SPV. The U.S. person receives cash payments from the SPV and claims a credit for foreign taxes imposed on the income recognized by the SPV for foreign tax purposes. The foreign tax credits eliminate all or substantially all of the U.S. tax the U.S. person would otherwise owe on its return and, in many cases, U.S. tax the U.S. person would otherwise owe on unrelated foreign source income. The economic cost of the foreign taxes is shared through the pricing of the arrangement. See Example 4 of proposed § 1.901-2(e)(5)(iv)(D).

For example, assume a U.S. person seeks to loan $1 billion to a foreign person. In lieu of a direct loan, the U.S. lender contributes $1 billion to a newly-formed corporation (SPV). The foreign counterparty contributes $2 billion to SPV, which is organized in the same country as the foreign counterparty. SPV contributes the total $3 billion to a second special purpose entity (RH), receiving a 99 percent equity interest in RH in exchange. The foreign counterparty owns the remaining 1 percent of RH. RH loans the funds to the foreign counterparty in exchange for a note that pays interest currently and a second zero-coupon note. RH is a corporation for U.S. tax purposes and a flow-through entity for foreign tax purposes.

Each year, the foreign counterparty pays $92 million of interest to RH, and RH accrues $113 million of interest on the zero-coupon note. RH distributes the $92 million of cash it receives to SPV. Because RH is a partnership for foreign tax purposes, SPV is required to report for foreign tax purposes 99 percent ($203 million) of the income recognized by RH. Because RH is a corporation for U.S. tax purposes, SPV recognizes only the cash distributions of $92 million for U.S. tax purposes. SPV pays foreign tax of $48 million on its net income (30 percent of $159 million, or $203 interest income less $44 million interest deduction) and distributes its remaining cash of $44 million to the U.S. lender.

The U.S. lender takes the position that it has an equity interest in SPV for U.S. tax purposes. It claims an indirect credit for the $48 million of foreign taxes paid by SPV. It includes in income the cash dividend of $44 million, plus a section 78 gross-up amount of $48 million. For foreign tax purposes, the U.S. lender's interest in SPV is debt, and the foreign borrower owns 100 percent of the equity of SPV. The foreign counterparty and SPV, in the aggregate, have a net deduction of $44 million for foreign tax purposes.

Both parties benefit from the transaction. The foreign borrower obtains "cheap financing" because the $44 million of cash distributed to the U.S. lender is less than the amount of interest it would have to pay on a direct loan with respect to which the U.S. lender would owe U.S. tax. The U.S. lender is better off on an after-U.S. tax basis because of the foreign tax credits, which eliminate the U.S. lender's U.S. tax on the "dividend" income.

The benefit to the parties is solely attributable to the reduction in the U.S. lender's U.S. tax liability resulting from the foreign tax credits claimed by the U.S. lender. The foreign jurisdiction benefits because the aggregate foreign tax result is a deduction for the foreign borrower that is less than the amount of the interest deduction the foreign borrower would have had upon a direct loan.

(c) Asset holding transactions. The third category of transactions ("asset holding transactions") consists of transactions in which a U.S. person that owns an income-producing asset moves the asset into a foreign taxing jurisdiction. For example, assume a U.S. person owns passive-type assets (such as debt obligations) generating an income stream that is subject to U.S. tax. In an asset holding transaction, the U.S. person transfers the assets to an SPV that is subject to tax in a foreign jurisdiction on the income stream. Ordinarily, such a transfer would not affect the U.S. person's after-tax position since the U.S. person could claim a credit for the foreign tax paid and, thereby, obtain a corresponding reduction in the amount of U.S. tax it would otherwise owe. In the structured transactions, however, the cost of the foreign tax is shared by a foreign person who obtains a foreign tax benefit by participating in the arrangement. Thus, the U.S. person is better off paying the foreign tax instead of U.S. tax because it does not bear the full economic burden of the foreign tax.

In a typical structured transaction, a foreign counterparty participates in the arrangement with the SPV. For example, the foreign counterparty may be considered to own a direct or indirect interest in the SPV for foreign tax purposes. The foreign counterparty's participation in the arrangement allows it to obtain a foreign tax benefit that it would not otherwise enjoy. The foreign counterparty compensates the U.S. person for this benefit in some manner. This compensation, which can be viewed as a reimbursement for a portion of the foreign tax liability resulting from the transfer of the assets, puts the U.S. person in a better after-U.S. tax position. See Example 7 of proposed § 1.901-2(e)(5)(iv)(D).

The benefit to the parties is solely attributable to the reduction in the U.S. taxpayer's U.S. tax liability resulting from the foreign tax credits claimed by the U.S. taxpayer. The foreign jurisdiction benefits because the foreign taxes purportedly paid by the SPV exceed the amount by which the foreign counterparty's taxes are reduced.

2. Purpose of the Foreign Tax Credit

The purpose of the foreign tax credit is to mitigate double taxation of foreign source income. Because the foreign tax credit provides a dollar-for-dollar reduction in U.S. tax that a U.S. person would otherwise owe, the U.S. person generally is indifferent, subject to various foreign tax credit limitations, as to whether it pays foreign tax on its foreign source income (if fully offset by the foreign tax credit) or whether it pays U.S. (and no foreign) tax on that income.

The structured arrangements described in section B.1 of this preamble violate this purpose. A common feature of all these arrangements is that the U.S. person and a foreign counterparty share the economic cost of the foreign taxes claimed as credits by the U.S. person. This creates an incentive for the U.S. person to subject itself voluntarily to the foreign tax because there is a U.S. tax motivation to do so. The result is an erosion of the U.S. tax base in a manner that is not consistent with the purpose of the foreign tax credit provisions.

Although the foreign counterparty derives a foreign tax benefit in these arrangements, the foreign jurisdiction generally is made whole because of the payments to the foreign jurisdiction made by the special purpose vehicle. In fact, the aggregate amount of payments to the foreign jurisdictions in connection with these transactions generally exceeds the amount of foreign tax that would have been imposed in the ordinary course. Only the U.S. fisc experiences a reduction in tax payments as a result of the structured arrangements.

The IRS and Treasury Department recognize that often there is a business purpose for the financing or portfolio investment underlying the otherwise elaborately engineered transactions. However, it is inconsistent with the purpose of the foreign tax credit to permit a credit for foreign taxes that result from intentionally structuring a transaction to generate foreign taxes in a manner that allows the parties to obtain duplicate tax benefits and share the cost of the tax payments. The result in these structured arrangements is that both parties as well as the foreign jurisdiction benefit at the expense of the U.S. fisc.

3. Comments and Proposed Regulations

The IRS and Treasury Department have determined that it is not appropriate to allow a credit in connection with these highly engineered transactions where the U.S. taxpayer benefits by intentionally subjecting itself to foreign tax. The proposed regulations would revise § 1.901-2(e)(5) to provide that an amount paid to a foreign country in connection with such an arrangement is not an amount of tax paid. Accordingly, under the proposed regulations, a taxpayer would not be eligible to claim a foreign tax credit for such a payment. For periods prior to the effective date of final regulations, the IRS will continue to utilize all available tools under current law to challenge the U.S. tax results claimed in connection with such arrangements, including the substance over form doctrine, the economic substance doctrine, debt-equity principles, tax ownership principles, existing § 1.901-2(e), section 269, and the partnership anti-abuse rules of § 1.701-2.

Certain commentators recommended that the IRS and Treasury Department adopt a broad anti-abuse rule that would deny a foreign tax credit in any case where allowance of the credit would be inconsistent with the purpose of the foreign tax credit regime. Other commentators recommended a narrower approach that would only deny foreign tax credits attributable to transactions that include particular features. The IRS and Treasury Department are concerned that a broad anti-abuse rule would create uncertainty for both taxpayers and the IRS. The IRS and Treasury Department have concluded that, at this time, a targeted rule denying foreign tax credits in arrangements similar to the arrangements described in section B.1 of this preamble is more appropriate.

For periods after the effective date of final regulations, the IRS and Treasury Department will continue to scrutinize other arrangements that are not covered by the regulations but are inconsistent with the purpose of the foreign tax credit. Such arrangements may include arrangements that are similar to arrangements described in the proposed regulations, but that do not meet all of the conditions included in the proposed regulations. The IRS will utilize all available tools, including those described above, to challenge the claimed U.S. tax results in appropriate cases. In addition, the IRS and Treasury Department may issue additional regulations in the future in order to address such other arrangements.

The proposed regulations would retain the general rule in the existing regulations that a taxpayer need not alter its form of doing business or the form of any transaction in order to reduce its foreign tax liability. However, the proposed regulations would provide that, notwithstanding the general rule, an amount paid to a foreign country (a "foreign payment") is not a compulsory payment, and thus is not an amount of tax paid, if the foreign payment is attributable to a structured passive investment arrangement. For this purpose, the proposed regulations would define a structured passive investment arrangement as an arrangement that satisfies six conditions. The six conditions consist of features that are common to the three types of arrangements identified in section B.1 of this preamble. The IRS and Treasury Department believe it is appropriate to treat foreign payments attributable to these arrangements as voluntary payments because such arrangements are intentionally structured to generate the foreign payment.

The first condition is that the arrangement utilizes an entity that meets two requirements (an "SPV"). The first requirement is that substantially all of the gross income (for United States tax purposes) of the entity is attributable to passive investment income and substantially all of the assets of the entity are assets held to produce such passive investment income. The second requirement is that there is a purported foreign tax payment attributable to income of the entity. The purported foreign tax may be paid by the entity itself, by the owner(s) of the entity (if the entity is treated as a pass-through entity under foreign law) or by a lower-tier entity (if the lower-tier entity is treated as a pass-through entity under U.S. law).

For purposes of this first requirement, passive investment income is defined as income described in section 954(c), with two modifications. The first modification is that if the entity is a holding company that owns a direct equity interest (other than a preferred interest) of 10 percent or more in another entity (a lower-tier entity) that is predominantly engaged in the active conduct of a trade or business (or substantially all the assets of which consist of qualifying equity interests in other entities that are predominantly engaged in the active conduct of a trade or business), passive investment income does not include income attributable to the interest in such lower-tier entity. This exception does not apply if there are arrangements under which substantially all of the opportunity for gain and risk of loss with respect to such interest in the lower-tier entity are borne by either the U.S. party or the counterparty (but not both). Accordingly, a direct equity interest in any such lower-tier entity is not held to produce passive investment income provided there are no arrangements under which substantially all of the entity's opportunity for gain and risk of loss with respect to the lower-tier entity are borne by either the U.S. party or the counterparty (but not both). This modification is based on the notion that an entity is not a passive investment vehicle of the type targeted by these regulations if the entity is a holding company for one or more operating companies. This modification ensures that a joint venture arrangement between a U.S. person and a foreign person is not treated as a passive investment arrangement solely because the joint venture is conducted through a holding company structure.

The second modification is that passive investment income is determined by disregarding sections 954(c)(3) and (c)(6) and by treating income attributable to transactions with the counterparties (described in this preamble) as ineligible for the exclusions under sections 954(h) and (i). Sections 954(c)(3) and (c)(6) provide exclusions for certain related party payments of dividends, interest, rents, and royalties. Those exclusions are not appropriate for these transactions because these transactions can be structured utilizing related party payments. The modifications to the application of sections 954(h) and (i) are intended to ensure that income derived from the counterparty cannot qualify for the exclusion from passive investment income, but will not prevent other income from qualifying for those exclusions. The IRS and Treasury Department intend that the structured financing arrangements described in this preamble do not qualify for the active banking, financing or insurance business exceptions to the definition of passive investment income. Comments are requested on whether further modifications or clarifications to the proposed regulations' definition of passive investment income are appropriate to ensure this result.

The requirement that substantially all of the assets of the entity produce passive investment income is intended to ensure that an entity engaged in an active trade or business is not treated as an SPV solely because, in a particular year, it derives only passive investment income.

The second overall condition is that a person (a "U.S. party") would be eligible to claim a credit under section 901(a) (including a credit for foreign taxes deemed paid under section 902 or 960) for all or a portion of the foreign payment if such payment were an amount of tax paid. Such eligibility to claim the credit could arise because the U.S. party would be treated as having paid or accrued the foreign payment for purposes of section 901 if it were an amount of tax paid. Alternatively, the U.S. party's eligibility to claim the credit could arise because the U.S. party owns an equity interest in the SPV or another entity that would be treated as having paid or accrued the foreign payment for purposes of section 901 if it were an amount of tax paid.

The third overall condition is that the foreign payment or payments are (or are expected to be) substantially greater than the amount of credits, if any, that the U.S. party would reasonably expect to be eligible to claim under section 901(a) if such U.S. party directly owned its proportionate share of the assets owned by the SPV other than through a branch, a permanent establishment or any other arrangement (such as an agency arrangement) that would subject the income generated by its share of the assets to a net basis foreign tax. For example, if the SPV owns a note that generates interest income with respect to which a foreign payment is made, but foreign law (including an applicable treaty) provides for a zero rate of withholding tax on interest paid to non-residents, the U.S. party would not reasonably expect to pay foreign tax for which it could claim foreign tax credits if it directly owned the note and directly earned the interest income.

The fourth condition is that the arrangement is structured in such a manner that it results in a foreign tax benefit (such as a credit, deduction, loss, exemption or a disregarded payment) for a counterparty or for a person that is related to the counterparty, but not related to the U.S. party.

The fifth condition is that the arrangement involves a counterparty. A counterparty is a person (other than the SPV) that is unrelated to the U.S. party and that (i) directly or indirectly owns 10 percent or more of the equity of the SPV under the tax laws of a foreign country in which such person is subject to tax on the basis of place of management, place of incorporation or similar criterion or otherwise subject to a net basis foreign tax or (ii) acquires 20 percent or more of the assets of the SPV under the tax laws of a foreign country in which such person is subject to tax on the basis of place of management, place of incorporation or similar criterion or otherwise subject to a net basis foreign tax.

The sixth condition is that the U.S. and an applicable foreign country treat the arrangement differently under their respective tax systems. For this purpose, an applicable foreign country is any foreign country in which either the counterparty, a person related to the counterparty (but not related to the U.S. party) or the SPV is subject to net basis tax. To provide clarity and limit the scope of this factor, the proposed regulations provide that the arrangement must be subject to one of four specified types of inconsistent treatment. Specifically, the U.S. and the foreign country (or countries) must treat one or more of the following aspects of the arrangement differently, and the U.S. treatment of the inconsistent aspect must materially affect the amount of foreign tax credits claimed, or the amount of income recognized, by the U.S. party to the arrangement: (i) The classification of an entity as a corporation or other entity subject to an entity-level tax, a partnership or other flow-through entity or an entity that is disregarded for tax purposes; (ii) the characterization as debt, equity or an instrument that is disregarded for tax purposes of an instrument issued in the transaction, (iii) the proportion of the equity of the SPV (or an entity that directly or indirectly owns the SPV) that is considered to be owned directly or indirectly by the U.S. party and the counterparty; or (iv) the amount of taxable income of the SPV for one or more tax years during which the arrangement is in effect.

Under the proposed regulations, a foreign payment would not be a compulsory payment if it is attributable to an arrangement that meets the six conditions. The proposed regulations would treat a foreign payment as attributable to such an arrangement if the foreign payment is attributable to income of the SPV. Such foreign payments include a payment by the SPV, a payment by the owner of the SPV (if the SPV is a pass-through entity under foreign law) and a payment by a lower-tier entity that is treated as a pass-through entity under U.S. law. For this purpose, a foreign payment is not treated as attributable to the income of the SPV if the foreign payment is a gross basis withholding tax imposed on a distribution or payment from the SPV to the U.S. party. Such taxes could be considered to be noncompulsory payments because the U.S. party intentionally subjects itself to the taxes as part of the arrangement. However, the IRS and Treasury Department have determined that such taxes should not be treated as attributable to the arrangement because, among other reasons, the foreign counterparty generally does not derive a duplicative foreign tax benefit and, therefore, generally does not share the economic cost of such taxes.

The IRS and Treasury Department considered excluding all foreign payments with respect to which the economic cost is not shared from the definition of foreign payments attributable to the arrangement, but determined that such a rule would be difficult to administer. The IRS and Treasury Department request comments on whether it would be appropriate to exclude certain foreign payments from the definition of foreign taxes attributable to the structured passive investment arrangement. Comments should address the rationale and administrable criteria for identifying any such exclusions.

Certain commentators recommended that the proposed regulations include a requirement that the foreign tax credits attributable to the arrangement be disproportionate to the amount of taxable income attributable to the arrangement. This recommendation has not been adopted for three reasons. First, the IRS and Treasury Department were concerned that such a requirement would create too much uncertainty and would be unduly burdensome for taxpayers and the IRS. Second, the extent to which interest and other expenses, as well as returns on borrowed funds and capital, should be considered attributable to a particular arrangement is not entirely clear. A narrow view could present opportunities for manipulation, especially for financial institutions having numerous alternative placements of leverage for use within the group, while an expansive view could undercut the utility of such a test. Third, the fundamental concern in these transactions is that they create an incentive for taxpayers voluntarily to subject themselves to foreign tax. This concern exists irrespective of whether the particular arrangement generates a disproportionate amount of foreign tax credits.

The IRS and Treasury Department considered whether it would be appropriate to permit a taxpayer to treat a foreign payment attributable to an arrangement that meets the definition of a structured passive investment arrangement as an amount of tax paid, if the taxpayer can show that tax considerations were not a principal purpose for the structure of the arrangement. Alternatively, the IRS and Treasury Department considered whether it would be appropriate to treat a foreign payment as an amount of tax paid if a taxpayer shows that there is a substantial business purpose for utilizing a hybrid instrument or entity, which would not include reducing the taxpayer's after-tax costs or enhancing the taxpayer's after-tax return through duplicative foreign tax benefits. The IRS and Treasury Department determined not to include such a rule in these proposed regulations due to administrability concerns. Comments are requested, however, on whether the final regulations should include such a rule as well as how such a rule could be made to be administrable in practice, including what reasonably ascertainable evidence would be sufficient to establish such a substantial non-tax business purpose, or the lack of a tax-related principal purpose. Comments should also address whether it would be appropriate to adopt a broader anti-abuse rule and permit a taxpayer to demonstrate that it should not apply.

C. Effective Date

The regulations are proposed to be effective for foreign taxes paid or accrued during taxable years of the taxpayer ending on or after the date on which the final regulations are published in the Federal Register. No inference is intended regarding the U.S. tax consequences of structured passive investment arrangements prior to the effective date of the regulations.

Special Analyses

It has been determined that this notice of proposed rulemaking is not a significant regulatory action as defined in Executive Order 12866. Therefore, a regulatory assessment is not required. It also has been determined that section 553(b) of the Administrative Procedure Act (5 U.S.C. chapter 5) does not apply to these regulations, and because the regulations do not impose a collection of information on small entities, the Regulatory Flexibility Act (5 U.S.C. chapter 6), does not apply. Pursuant to section 7805(f) of the Internal Revenue Code, this regulation has been submitted to the Chief Counsel for Advocacy of the Small Business Administration for comment on its impact on small businesses.

Comments and Public Hearing

Before these proposed regulations are adopted as final regulations, consideration will be given to any written (a signed original and eight (8) copies) or electronic comments that are submitted timely to the IRS. The IRS and Treasury Department request comments on the clarity of the proposed regulations and how they can be made easier to understand. All comments will be available for public inspection and copying.

A public hearing has been scheduled for July 30, 2007, at 10 a.m. in the Internal Revenue Building, 1111 Constitution Avenue, NW., Washington, DC. All visitors must present photo identification to enter the building. Because of access restrictions, visitors will not be admitted beyond the immediate entrance area more than 30 minutes before the hearing starts. For information about having your name placed on the building access list to attend the hearing, see the FOR FURTHER INFORMATION CONTACT section of this preamble.

The rules of 26 CFR 601.601(a)(3) apply to the hearing. Persons who wish to present oral comments must submit electronic or written comments and an outline of the topics to be discussed and time to be devoted to each topic (a signed original and eight (8) copies) by July 9, 2007. A period of 10 minutes will be allotted to each person for making comments. An agenda showing the scheduling of the speakers will be prepared after the deadline for receiving outlines has passed. Copies of the agenda will be available free of charge at the hearing.

Drafting Information

The principal author of these regulations is Bethany A. Ingwalson, Office of Associate Chief Counsel (International). However, other personnel from the IRS and the Treasury Department participated in their development.

[¶49,297] Proposed Amendments of Regulations (REG-123365-03), published in the Federal Register on May 8, 2007 (corrected 6/5/2007).

[Code Sec. 355]

Corporate distributions: Section 355 distribution: Active trade or business requirement: Acquisition of trade or business: Affiliated group members: Pre-distribution period: Multi-step acquisitions.—Amendments of Reg. §§1.355-0, 1.355-1 and 1.355-3, providing guidance regarding the active trade or business requirement under section 355(b) of the Internal Revenue Code, are proposed.

AGENCY: Internal Revenue Service (IRS), Treasury.

ACTION: Notice of proposed rulemaking.

SUMMARY: This document contains proposed regulations that provide guidance regarding the active trade or business requirement under section 355(b) of the Internal Revenue Code. These proposed regulations provide guidance on issues involving the active trade or business requirement under section 355(b), including guidance resulting from the enactment of section 355(b)(3). These proposed regulations will affect corporations and their shareholders.

DATES: Written or electronic comments and requests for a public hearing must be received by August 8, 2007.

ADDRESSES: Send submissions to: CC:PA:LPD:PR (REG-123365-03), room 5203, Internal Revenue Service, PO Box 7604, Ben Franklin Station, Washington, DC 20044. Submissions may be hand-delivered Monday through Friday between the hours of 8 a.m. and 4 p.m. to CC:PA:LPD:PR (REG-123365-03), Courier's Desk, Internal Revenue Service, 1111 Constitution Avenue, NW., Washington, DC, or sent electronically via the Federal eRulemaking Portal at *www.regulations.gov* (IRS REG-123365-03).

FOR FURTHER INFORMATION CONTACT: Concerning the proposed regulations, Russell P. Subin, (202) 622-7790; concerning submissions and the hearing, Kelly Banks, (202) 622-7180 (not toll-free numbers).

SUPPLEMENTARY INFORMATION:

Background and Explanation of Provisions

A. *Background and Overview of the Key Aspects of the Proposed Regulations*

1. *Background*

Section 355(a) of the Internal Revenue Code (Code) provides that, under certain circumstances, a corporation may distribute stock and securities of a corporation it controls to its shareholders and security holders without causing either the corporation or its shareholders and security holders to recognize income, gain or loss. Sections 355(a)(1)(C) and 355(b)(1) generally require that the distributing corporation (distributing) and controlled corporation (controlled) each be engaged, immediately after the distribution, in the active conduct of a trade or business. Section 355(b)(2)(A) provides that a corporation shall be treated as engaged in the active conduct of a trade or business if and only if it is engaged in the active conduct of a trade or business, or substantially all of its assets consist of stock and securities of a corporation controlled by it (immediately after the distribution) which is so engaged. For this purpose, control is defined under section 368(c). All references to control in this preamble are references to control as defined in section 368(c).

Section 202 of the Tax Increase Prevention and Reconciliation Act of 2005, Public Law 109-222 (120 Stat. 345, 348) (TIPRA) amended section 355(b) by adding section 355(b)(3). Section 355(b)(3)(A), as amended by Division A, Section 410 of the Tax Relief and Health Care Act of 2006, Public Law 109-432 (120 Stat. 2922, 2963), provides that in the case of any distribution made after May 17, 2006, a corporation shall be treated as meeting the requirement of section 355(b)(2)(A) if and only if such corporation is engaged in the active conduct of a trade or business. Section 355(b)(3)(B) provides that for purposes of section 355(b)(3)(A) (and, consequently, section 355(b)(2)(A)), all members of such corporation's separate affiliated group (SAG) shall be treated as one corporation (SAG rule). For purposes of the preceding sentence, a corporation's SAG is the affiliated group which would be determined under section 1504(a) if such corporation were the common parent and section 1504(b) did not apply.

Thus, the separate affiliated group of distributing (DSAG) is the affiliated group that consists of distributing as the common parent and all corporations affiliated with distributing through stock ownership described in section 1504(a)(1)(B) (regardless of whether the corporations are includible corporations under section 1504(b)). The separate affiliated group of controlled (CSAG) is determined in a similar manner (with controlled as the common parent). Accordingly, unlike prior law, a corporation is not treated as engaged in the active conduct of a trade or business solely as a result of substantially all of its assets consisting of stock, or stock and securities, of one or more corporations that are merely controlled by it (immediately after the distribution) each of which is engaged in the active conduct of a trade or business.

Section 355(b)(2)(B) requires that the trade or business have been actively conducted throughout the five-year period ending on the date of the distribution (pre-distribution period). Section 355(b)(2)(C) provides that the trade or business must not have been acquired in a transaction in which gain or loss was recognized, in whole or in part, within the pre-distribution period. Section 355(b)(2)(D), as amended in 1987 and 1988, provides that control of a corporation which (at the time of acquisition of control) was conducting the trade or business must not have been directly or indirectly acquired by any distributee corporation or by distributing during the pre-distribution period in a transaction in which gain or loss was recognized, in whole or in part. See Public Law 100-203 (101 Stat. 1330, 1330-411 (1987)) and Public Law 100-647 (102 Stat. 3342, 3605 (1988)). For purposes of section 355(b)(2)(D), all distributee corporations which are members of the same affiliated group (as defined in section 1504(a) without regard to section 1504(b)) shall be treated as one distributee corporation. The requirements under section 355(b) are collectively referred to in this preamble as either the active trade or business requirement or the requirements of section 355(b).

Accordingly, the requirements of section 355(b) are generally satisfied if distributing and controlled each have engaged in the active conduct of a trade or business throughout the pre-distribution period, are so engaged immediately after the distribution, and there have been no acquisitions of control of distributing or controlled during such period.

The active trade or business requirement is one of several requirements that must be satisfied in order for a distribution to qualify under section 355. For example, section 355(a)(1)(B) states that a transaction must not be used principally as a device for distributing the earnings and profits of distributing, controlled, or both. In addition, § 1.355-2(b)(1) provides that section 355 will apply to a transaction only if it is carried out for one or more corporate business purposes.

The active trade or business requirement, in tandem with the device prohibition and business purpose requirement, limits a corporation's ability to convert dividend income into capital gain through the use of a section 355 distribution. See S. Rep. No. 83-1622, at 50-51 (1954) and *Coady v. Commissioner*, 33 TC 771, 777 (1960), *acq.*, 1965-2 CB 4, *aff'd*, 289 F.2d 490 (6th Cir. 1961). In *Coady*, the Tax Court stated that one purpose of section 355(b) is "to prevent the tax-free separation of *active* and *inactive* assets into *active* and *inactive* corporate entities." The court also stated that a tax-free separation under section 355 "will involve the separation only of those assets attributable to the carrying on of an active trade or business . . . ." *Coady*, 33 TC at 777.

The IRS and Treasury Department are aware of a number of issues that have arisen regarding the active trade or business requirement, including issues arising as a result of the enactment of section 355(b)(3). The following sections describe the active trade or business requirement and the significant issues that are addressed in these proposed regulations. No inference should be drawn from these proposed regulations regarding the definition of trade or business or active trade or business under any other provision of the Code or Treasury regulations, even if such provision specifically references section 355. Comments are requested as to whether or the extent to which these proposed regulations should apply to other provisions that specifically reference section 355.

2. *Overview of the key aspects of the proposed regulations*

Principally, these proposed regulations provide guidance regarding the application of section 355(b)(3), the application of the acquisition rules in section 355(b)(2)(C) and (D) and the impact thereon of section 355(b)(3), and the determination of whether a corporation is engaged in a trade or business through the attribution of trade or business assets and activities from a partnership.

As discussed in section A. 1. of this preamble, section 355(b)(3) treats all SAG members as one corporation. Accordingly, as discussed in detail in section B. of this preamble, these proposed regulations provide that subsidiary SAG members (SAG members that are not the common parent of such SAG) are treated like divisions of distributing or controlled, as the case may be. These proposed regulations also clarify that controlled may be a DSAG member during the pre-distribution period. Most significantly, these provisions treat a stock acquisition that results in a corporation becoming a subsidiary SAG member as an asset acquisition. As a result, the applicability of section 355(b)(2)(D) is substantially reduced. Further, as discussed in section E. of this preamble, this treatment alters the analysis regarding whether an existing business may be expanded as a result of a stock acquisition.

Notwithstanding that these proposed regulations provide that certain stock acquisitions may be treated as asset acquisitions under section 355(b)(3), purchases of stock of controlled during the pre-distribution period may be subject to section 355(a)(3)(B). See section F. of this preamble.

As discussed in detail in section C. and section D. of this preamble, these proposed regulations interpret section 355(b)(2)(C) and (D) to mean that a corporation generally cannot use its assets to acquire a trade or business to be relied on to facilitate a distribution under section 355. Accordingly, these proposed regulations generally prohibit acquisitions made in exchange for distributing's assets even if no gain or loss is recognized in connection with the acquisition. Further, these proposed regulations provide certain exceptions to the literal application of section 355(b)(2)(C) and (D) for acquisitions in which gain or loss is recognized where the purposes of that section are not violated. However, these proposed regulations do not disregard the recognition of gain or loss in transactions between affiliates unless the affiliates are members of the same SAG. See section G. of this preamble.

Section I. of this preamble explains how these proposed regulations clarify a corporation's ability to be attributed the trade or business assets and activities of a partnership. Most significantly, these partnership provisions yield results similar to the rules regarding the satisfaction of the continuity of business enterprise requirement, and thus allow a partner to be attributed the partnership's trade or business assets and activities where the partner owns a significant interest in the partnership.

B. *TIPRA*

Congress enacted section 355(b)(3) because it was concerned that, prior to a distribution under section 355, corporate groups conducting business in separate corporate entities often had to undergo elaborate restructurings to place active businesses in the proper entities to satisfy the active trade or business requirement. See, for example, H.R. Rep. No. 109-304, at 53, 54 (2005). By treating a SAG as one corporation, Congress believed that it would greatly reduce the need for such restructurings. However, the introduction of the affiliation-based SAG rule into the active trade or business requirement significantly impacts the application of section 355(b)(2) in certain situations.

Accordingly, consistent with congressional intent, these proposed regulations provide several rules interpreting section 355(b)(3) in a manner that diminishes the need for pre-distribution restructurings while fully integrating the various provisions in section 355(b). These rules are intended to more closely reflect the way corporate groups structure their businesses while, at the same time, ensuring that the purposes underlying section 355(b)(2)(C) and (D) are not circumvented.

Specifically, to accomplish these objectives the IRS and Treasury Department believe that it is appropriate to apply the SAG rule by disregarding the separate existence of all subsidiary SAG members for purposes of determining whether distributing and controlled satisfy the requirements of section 355(b).

1. *SAG rule applicable during the pre-distribution period*

The IRS and Treasury Department believe that it is appropriate to apply the SAG rule for purposes of determining whether the trade or business was actively conducted throughout the pre-distribution period and whether the requirements of section 355(b)(2)(C) or (D) have been violated.

The SAG rule applies for purposes of determining whether distributing and controlled are engaged in the active conduct of a trade or business immediately after the distribution. Specifically, the legislative history to section 355(b)(3) describes the corporations included in the DSAG and CSAG by reference to post-distribution affiliation. See H.R. Rep. No. 109-455, at 88 (2006) (Conf. Rep.); H.R. Rep. No. 109-304, at 54 (2005). However, there is nothing in the statute or legislative history that precludes the SAG rule from applying throughout the pre-distribution period.

The IRS and Treasury Department believe that applying the SAG rule throughout the pre-distribution period is consistent with the single-entity approach. If the SAG rule is not applied during the pre-distribution period, there may be unintended consequences. For example, assume that an active trade or business is segmented among the SAG members in a manner that precludes any one member from individually being treated as engaged in an active trade or business. Under the SAG rule the segments are aggregated and may be treated as a single active trade or business immediately after the distribution. However, if the SAG rule is not applied throughout the pre-distribution period, there would be no five-year active trade or business because no one member would be engaged in that trade or business. The IRS and Treasury Department do not believe there is any policy reason to apply the SAG rule in such a disparate manner. Accordingly, these proposed regulations apply the SAG rule throughout the pre-distribution period. This approach is consistent with Congressional intent to view SAGs as an aggregate for purposes of the active trade or business requirement.

Because the SAG rule treats all SAG members as one corporation, the separate existence of subsidiary SAG members is disregarded and all assets (and activities) owned (and performed) by SAG members are treated as owned (and performed) by distributing or controlled, as the case may be, for purposes of determining whether distributing or controlled is engaged in a five-year active trade or business. Therefore, where one DSAG or CSAG member satisfies the active trade or business requirement, distributing or controlled, as the case may be, satisfies the active trade or business requirement.

Consistent with the foregoing, these proposed regulations provide that the SAG rule also applies for purposes of determining whether there has been an impermissible acquisition, as discussed in section C. of this preamble, of a trade or business during the pre-distribution period under section 355(b)(2)(C) or (D). Because the SAG rule disregards the separate existence of subsidiary SAG members, these proposed regulations generally treat stock acquisitions that result in a corporation becoming a subsidiary SAG member as a direct acquisition of any assets (or activities) owned (or performed) by the acquired corporation. Further, these proposed regulations generally disregard transfers of assets (or activities) that are owned (or performed) by the SAG immediately before and immediately after the transfer. Such transfers cannot result in an acquisition. Under the SAG rule, such transfers have the effect of a transfer between divisions of a single corporation.

2. *The DSAG may include CSAG members throughout the pre-distribution period*

The IRS and Treasury Department believe that it is appropriate to include the CSAG members in the DSAG during the pre-distribution period if the applicable affiliation requirements are satisfied. The IRS and Treasury Department believe this approach is consistent with the purposes of section 355(b)(3) and the SAG rule's general single-entity approach, and provides flexibility for the division of SAG members between distributing and controlled.

For example, assume that during the pre-distribution period, segments or portions of the business to be conducted by controlled are held by distributing (or other subsidiaries that are not directly or indirectly owned by controlled) and that distributing intends to transfer those portions of the business to controlled immediately prior to the distribution. If the DSAG does not include the CSAG members throughout the pre-distribution period, it is possible that neither SAG would be engaged in the active conduct of that trade or business throughout the pre-distribution period, because neither SAG would have all the appropriate segments of that business to satisfy the active trade or business requirement. The IRS and Treasury Department believe that such a result is inconsistent with the purposes of section 355(b)(3). Accordingly, by including the CSAG members in the DSAG throughout the pre-distribution period if the ownership requirements are satisfied, these proposed regulations give appropriate credit to five-year active trades or businesses regardless of how the assets and activities may be owned (and performed) by the SAG members throughout the pre-distribution period.

3. *Acquisitions of stock in subsidiary SAG members*

Section 355(b)(3) treats SAG members as one corporation for purposes of satisfying the requirements of section 355(b). As a result, the SAG rule alters the application of section 355(b)(2)(C) and (D) with respect to the acquisition of stock of a corporation that is or becomes a subsidiary SAG member. Further, because section 355(b)(3) supplanted the holding company rule in section 355(b)(2)(A), section 355(b)(2)(D) is now only applicable to certain acquisitions of stock of distributing and certain acquisitions of stock of controlled.

The SAG rule alters the application of section 355(b)(2)(C) and (D) with respect to the acquisition of stock of a corporation that is or becomes a subsidiary SAG member. Section 355(b)(3) treats SAG members as one corporation for purposes of satisfying section 355(b). Consequently, a transaction that results in a corporation — including controlled — becoming a subsidiary SAG member is treated as a direct acquisition of all the assets (and activities) owned (and performed) by the acquired corporation at the time of the acquisition. Thus, such an acquisition is tested under section 355(b)(2)(C) rather than section 355(b)(2)(D). Nevertheless, as discussed in sections B.4. and C.3.a.ii. of this preamble, section 355(b)(2)(D) has continuing limited application.

In addition, an acquisition that results in a corporation becoming a subsidiary SAG member in a transaction in which gain or loss is recognized might satisfy the requirements of section 355(b)(2)(C) as an expansion of one of the acquiring SAG's existing businesses, as discussed in section E. of this preamble. Finally, because the SAG rule treats subsidiary SAG members like divisions, the acquisition of additional stock of a current subsidiary SAG member has no effect for purposes of applying section 355(b)(2)(C).

4. *Acquisitions of control of controlled where it is not a DSAG member*

While section 355(b)(2)(D) is not applicable to acquisitions of stock of subsidiary SAG members, the requirements of section 355(b)(2)(D) must be satisfied where the DSAG acquires control of controlled where controlled is not and does not become a DSAG member prior to the distribution. This rule applies where distributing acquires stock constituting control of controlled but not stock meeting the requirements of section 1504(a)(2).

C. *Acquisitions of a Trade or Business*

Section 355(b)(2)(C) and (D) generally provides that a trade or business acquired, directly or indirectly, during the pre-distribution period will not satisfy the active trade or business requirement unless it was acquired in a transaction in which no gain or loss was recognized. The IRS and Treasury Department believe that these provisions have been and should continue to be interpreted and applied in a manner consistent with the overall purposes of section 355. For example, in certain situations, transactions in which gain or loss is recognized have been found not to violate the purposes of section 355(b)(2)(C) and (D). See, for example, *C.I.R. v. Gordon*, 382 F.2d 499 (2d Cir.1967), *rev'd on other grounds*, 391 US 83 (1968) (discussed in section C.2. of this preamble). Additionally, while the enactment of section 355(b)(3) substantially revised how distributing and controlled may satisfy the active trade or business requirement, TIPRA did not contain conforming amendments to section 355(b)(2)(C) and (D). As such, the IRS and Treasury Department also believe that a purpose-based interpretation of section 355(b)(2) is essential to harmonize these provisions. Accordingly, these proposed regulations interpret and apply section 355(b)(2)(C) and (D), and section 355(b)(3), in a manner consistent with their purpose, even if not always consistent with the literal language of the statute.

1. *Purpose of section 355(b)(2)(C) and (D)*

Section 355 "contemplates that a tax-free separation shall involve only the separation of assets attributable to the carrying on of an active business." S. Rep. No. 83-1622, at 50 (1954). The active trade or business requirement is intended to ensure that only these types of separations qualify under section 355. Further, it operates as an additional safeguard to the device prohibition (a prohibition against disguised dividends) in section 355(a)(1)(B).

As discussed in section A. of this preamble, the active trade or business requirement is designed to limit the potential for the conversion of dividend income into capital gain through a section 355 distribution. Specifically, section 355(b)(2)(C) and (D) is intended to prevent dividend avoidance otherwise available through the purchase of a new business in order to facilitate a tax-free distribution under section 355. See *Gordon*, 382 F.2d at 506-507 (stating that "[t]o safeguard against this possibility, subsections (b)(2)(C) and (D) prohibit acquisition of a trade or business, or of a corporation, in a transaction in which gain or loss was recognized."). Thus, the statute prohibits acquisitions of a trade or business in which gain or loss is recognized. Nevertheless, the recognition of gain or loss, in and of itself, does not violate the purposes of section 355. Rather, recognition of gain or loss is generally indicative of the type of consideration used in the transaction. Typically, a transaction in which gain or loss is recognized consists of an acquisition in exchange for assets. On the other hand, a transaction in which no gain or loss is recognized typically consists of an acquisition in exchange for the corporation's equity.

Accordingly, the IRS and Treasury Department believe that the common purpose of section 355(b)(2)(C) and (D) is to prevent distributing from using assets — instead of its stock or stock of a corporation in control of distributing — to acquire a new trade or business in anticipation of distributing that trade or business (or facilitating the distribution of another trade or business) to its shareholders in a tax-free distribution. A distribution of a corporation holding assets that would have been used to effect a purchase generally would be treated as a dividend and section 355 was not intended to allow a tax-free separation of such assets. Acquiring a new trade or business using these assets and distributing it (or an existing trade or business) would effectively accomplish such a separation, and should not qualify under section 355.

Complementing the principle that the common purpose of section 355(b)(2)(C) and (D) is to prevent distributing from using its assets — instead of its stock, or stock of a corporation in control of distributing — to acquire a new trade or business is the notion that section 355 is intended to apply to separations of active trades or businesses with which the participants have a historic relationship. Section 355, like the reorganization provisions, involves the maintenance by the shareholders of a continuing interest in their business or businesses in modified corporate forms. For section 355 to apply to a divisive transaction, it is essential that distributing and its shareholders have a historic relationship with the active trades or businesses in the two resulting corporations. See, for example, § 1.355-1(b) ("[section 355] applies only to the separation of existing businesses that have been in active operation for at least five years . . . and which, in general, have been owned, directly or indirectly, for at least five years by the distributing corporation"). These requirements ensure that the historic owners of the acquired trade or business are participants in the divisive transaction and minimize the potential for transactions that violate the common purpose of section 355(b)(2)(C) and (D).

Where distributing issues its own equity (or uses the equity of a corporation in control of distributing) to acquire an active trade or business in a transaction in which no gain or loss is recognized, distributing is not acquiring the trade or business in exchange for its assets and the historic owners of the trade or business will be participants in the divisive transaction. In such cases, the common purpose of section 355(b)(2)(C) and (D) is carried out.

Finally, an additional purpose of section 355(b)(2)(D) is to prevent a distributee corporation from acquiring control of distributing in anticipation of a distribution to which section 355 would otherwise apply, enabling the disposition of controlled without the proper recognition of corporate level gain. See H.R. Rep. No. 100-391, at 1080, 1082-1083 (1987).

2. *Current law and the § 1.355-3(b)(4) regulations*

Under current law, several authorities depart from the literal language of section 355(b)(2)(C) and (D) in order to carry out the common purpose underlying section 355(b)(2)(C) and (D). For example, in *Gordon*, gain was recognized when distributing transferred a trade or business to controlled. The Second Circuit concluded that, even though gain was recognized, section 355(b)(2)(C) was not violated because new assets were not brought within the combined corporate shells of distributing and controlled. Therefore, the common purpose of section 355(b)(2)(C) and (D) was not violated. Furthermore, Rev. Rul. 69-461 (1969-2 CB 52) held that a first-tier subsidiary's taxable distribution of stock of a second-tier subsidiary to its parent did not violate section 355(b)(2)(D). The ruling stated that section 355(b)(2)(D) is intended to prevent the acquisition of control of a corporation from a party not within the direct or indirect control of distributing. In addition, Rev. Rul. 78-442 (1978-2 CB 143) held that gain under section 357(c) on the transfer from distributing to controlled does not violate section 355(b)(2)(C). Rev. Rul. 78-442 stated that section 355(b)(2)(C) is intended to prevent the acquisition of a trade or business by distributing or controlled from an outside party in a taxable transaction within five years of a distribution.

Similarly, § 1.355-3(b)(4) (generally applicable to distributions on or before December 15, 1987, but applied in various situations by the IRS administratively to distributions occurring after that date) provides an exception from the literal language of section 355(b)(2)(C) and (D) for the direct or indirect acquisition of a trade or business by one member of an affiliated group from another member of the group, stating that an acquisition from another member of the affiliated group "is not the type of transaction to which section 355(b)(2)(C) and (D) is intended to apply." See § 1.355-3(b)(4)(iii).

Section 1.355-3(b)(4) also departs from the literal language of section 355(b) in providing that a trade or business acquired, directly or indirectly, within the pre-distribution period in a transaction in which the basis of the assets acquired was not determined in whole or in part by reference to the transferor's basis does not qualify under section 355(b)(2), even though no gain or loss was recognized by the transferor. See § 1.355-3(b)(4)(i). The reason for this departure is that in some circumstances a transaction in which no gain or loss is recognized may nevertheless constitute a prohibited acquisition of a trade or business in exchange for assets.

3. *The proposed regulations*

Consistent with current law (and § 1.355-3(b)(4)), these proposed regulations generally prohibit acquisitions in which gain or loss was recognized but apply section 355(b)(2)(C) and (D) in a manner consistent with their purposes. Accordingly, these proposed regulations provide for certain exceptions for acquisitions in which gain or loss is recognized, and prohibit certain transactions in which no gain or loss is recognized. a. Certain Transactions in Which Recognized Gain or Loss is Disregarded

Under these proposed regulations, certain acquisitions are excepted from the general rule under section 355(b)(2)(C) and (D) that a trade or business, or control of a corporation engaged in a trade or business, cannot satisfy the active trade or business requirement if it was acquired during the pre-distribution period in a transaction in which gain or loss was recognized. These transactions are so excepted because they do not violate the purposes of section 355(b)(2)(C) and (D).

i. Certain Acquisitions By the DSAG or CSAG

These proposed regulations provide a number of exceptions to the application of section 355(b)(2)(C) and (D) not contained in the current regulations (or § 1.355-3(b)(4)). One of these exceptions disregards any gain or loss recognized in connection with an acquisition by the CSAG from the DSAG of a trade or business, an interest in a partnership engaged in a trade or business, or stock of a corporation engaged in a trade or business. This exception is appropriate because it is not a use of distributing's assets to acquire the trade or business.

Another exception disregards gain or loss recognized in an acquisition solely as a result of the payment of cash to shareholders for fractional shares where the cash paid represents a mere rounding off of the fractional shares in the exchange and is not separately bargained for consideration. The IRS and Treasury Department believe that this is not the type of transaction to which section 355(b)(2)(C) or (D) is intended to apply. Although such a transaction involves a small use of assets, these proposed regulations except such acquisitions because the small amount of assets are not separately bargained for and are used merely to simplify the exchange. Other authorities reach similar conclusions in the context of reorganizations. See Rev. Rul. 66-365 (1966-2 CB 116), amplified by Rev. Rul. 81-81 (1981-1 CB 122) (concluding that cash in lieu of fractional shares does not violate the solely for voting stock requirement of section 368(a)(1)(B) and (C) because it was merely a mathematical rounding off for simplicity, and the transaction "was for all practical purposes 'solely in exchange for voting stock'").

In addition, as discussed in section G. of this preamble, these proposed regulations provide a limited exception for taxable acquisitions from affiliates that are members of the same SAG. Specifically, acquisitions between SAG members (where the assets (or activities) are owned (or performed) by the SAG immediately before and immediately after the transfer) are disregarded whether they are taxable or not.

Like the current regulations, these proposed regulations provide that acquisitions that expand a pre-existing business are generally exempted from the nonrecognition requirement. See § 1.355-3(b)(3)(ii). While these transactions may involve the use of the DSAG's or CSAG's assets, they are not acquisitions of a new or different trade or business. Because the DSAG or CSAG, as the case may be, is already in the business, such transactions are not considered acquisitions of a trade or business under section 355(b)(2)(C) and (D).

ii. Certain Acquisitions By a Distributee Corporation

Consistent with the principles of Rev. Rul. 74-5 (1974-1 CB 82), obsoleted by Rev. Rul. 89-37 (1989-1 CB 107), these proposed regulations disregard the recognition of gain or loss in applying section 355(b)(2)(D) to certain acquisitions of the stock of distributing by a distributee corporation. Prior to the 1987 and 1988 amendments noted in section A.1. of this preamble, section 355(b)(2)(D) was not violated in a case where distributing distributed the stock of controlled even though a purchaser acquired distributing's stock during the pre-distribution period in a transaction in which gain or loss was recognized. See Rev. Rul. 74-5 (reasoning that the purpose of section 355(b)(2)(D) was to prevent distributing, rather than the shareholder of distributing, from accumulating excess funds to purchase the stock of a corporation engaged in an active trade or business). However, Rev. Rul. 74-5 held that the purchaser could not then further distribute the stock of controlled until five years after such purchase, reasoning that the purchaser, the distributing corporation in the second distribution, indirectly acquired the stock of controlled through another corporation, the distributing corporation in the first distribution.

The 1987 and 1988 amendments to section 355(b)(2)(D) prohibited such transactions because of a concern that such acquisitions were similar to transactions that permitted a corporation to dispose of an appreciated subsidiary without the proper recognition of gain contrary to the repeal of the *General Utilities* doctrine. For example, assume P, a corporation, acquired the stock of D in a transaction in which gain or loss was recognized and D immediately distributed the stock of C to P in a section 355 transaction. P would allocate its basis in the newly acquired D stock between the D stock and the C stock received in the distribution. P could then potentially sell the C stock without the appropriate recognition of gain. See H.R. Rep. No. 100-391, at 1080, 1082-1083 (1987).

However, there are transactions that violate the literal requirements of section 355(b)(2)(D) but do not violate the purpose of the 1987 and 1988 amendments. For example, assume that for more than five years, T, a corporation, owned all of the stock of D, which in turn owned all the stock of C. Throughout this period, D and C have each engaged in the active conduct of a trade or business. In year 6, P acquires the stock of T in a transaction in which gain or loss is recognized, and holds the T stock with a cost basis determined under section 1012. In year 7, P liquidates T in a transaction to which section 332 applies and in which no gain or loss is recognized, thereby eliminating its cost basis in the T stock. Thereafter, P holds the D stock with a basis equal to T's basis in the D stock. In year 8, D distributes the C stock to P. Under these facts, P cannot dispose of the D or C stock without recognizing the same amount of gain or loss that T would have recognized.

Similarly, assume the same facts as the previous example, except that in year 6 P acquires all of T's assets, including the D stock, in exchange for P stock and cash in a reorganization described in section 368(a)(1)(A). Because all of the cash is distributed to the T shareholders, T does not recognize any gain, and P's basis in the D stock is equal to T's basis in the D stock. See section 362(b). In year 7, D distributes the C stock to P. Under these facts, P cannot dispose of the D or C stock without recognizing the same amount of gain or loss that T would have recognized.

The IRS and Treasury Department believe that the distributee corporation language in section 355(b)(2)(D)(i) is intended only to prevent transactions that are contrary to the repeal of the *General Utilities* doctrine. In both of the examples just described, neither the D stock nor C stock can be disposed of in a manner that is contrary to the repeal of the *General Utilities* doctrine. Accordingly, these proposed regulations provide that section 355(b)(2)(D) is not violated where there is a direct or indirect acquisition by a distributee corporation of control of distributing in one or more transactions in which gain or loss is recognized where the basis of the acquired distributing stock in the hands of the distributee corporation is determined in whole by reference to the transferor's basis. However, consistent with the principles of Rev. Rul. 74-5, this rule is only applicable with respect to a distribution by the acquired distributing, and does not apply for purposes of any subsequent distribution by any distributee corporation.

b. Certain Nonrecognition Transactions Treated as Recognition Transactions

Because the IRS and Treasury Department believe that acquisitions made in exchange for assets violate the common purpose of section 355(b)(2)(C) and (D) even if no gain or loss is recognized, these proposed regulations provide that such transactions are treated as transactions in which gain or loss is recognized.

i. Acquisitions in Exchange for Assets

As discussed in section C.1. of this preamble, the common purpose underlying section 355(b)(2)(C) and (D) is that distributing generally should not be able to use its assets to acquire a new trade or business in anticipation of distributing that trade or business (or facilitating the distribution of another trade or business) to its shareholders in a tax-free transaction. Similarly, and also discussed in section C.1. of this preamble, section 355(b), by permitting the use of distributing stock to acquire a trade or business, ensures a historic relationship between the distributing shareholders and the trades or businesses relied upon to satisfy the active trade or business requirement.

The following examples illustrate distributing's use of its assets to acquire a new trade or business.

First, assume that D, a corporation that does not directly conduct a five-year active trade or business, owns all of the stock of C, a corporation with a five-year active trade or business. D wishes to spin-off C to its shareholders, but to do so D must satisfy the active trade or business requirement. Accordingly, D contributes assets to an unrelated partnership that is engaged in a five-year active trade or business in a transaction to which section 721 applies in exchange for an interest in the partnership that otherwise satisfies the requirements for D to be attributed the trade or business assets and activities of the partnership, as discussed in section I. of this preamble. Two years after the transfer, when D's only active trade or business is the business conducted by the partnership, D distributes the C stock pro rata to the D shareholders.

Alternatively, assume that D, a corporation with a five-year active trade or business, transfers assets to unrelated T, a corporation with a five-year active trade or business, in a transaction to which section 351 applies in exchange for an amount of T stock constituting control. Two years after the transfer, when T's only active trade or business is the business T conducted before D's transfer, D distributes the T stock pro rata to the D shareholders.

Similarly, assume that D, a corporation with a five-year active trade or business, owns all of the stock of C, a corporation that does not have a five-year active trade or business but has other assets. To cause C to satisfy the active trade or business requirement, D arranges for C to acquire a five-year active trade or business from T, an unrelated corporation, in a reorganization described in section 368(a)(1)(A). In the reorganization, the shareholders of T receive solely common stock of C representing 20 percent or less of the voting power of all classes of C stock. Two years after the reorganization, D distributes the C stock pro rata to the D shareholders.

In each of these examples, D has directly or indirectly acquired a trade or business in exchange for assets. See and compare Situation 2 of Rev. Rul. 2002-49 (2002-2 CB 288) (corporation's use of appreciated securities to acquire a trade or business of a partnership in a transaction to which section 721 applies is treated as an acquisition in which gain or loss was recognized); section 4.01(29) of Rev. Proc. 2007-3 (2007-1 IRB 108) (the IRS will not ordinarily rule where distributing acquires control of controlled by transferring inactive assets in a transaction meeting the requirements of section 351(a) or section 368(a)(1)(D) and in which no gain or loss is recognized). While these transactions satisfy the literal requirements of section 355(b)(2)(C) or (D), the underlying common purpose of those provisions has been violated. In each case, distributing has acquired in exchange for distributing's assets, either directly or indirectly through the issuance of controlled stock the trade or business to be relied on by distributing or controlled.

Furthermore, in each of these examples, the historic owners have supplied a trade or business for distributing or controlled, but they are not participants in the divisive transaction. Not being shareholders of D, the position of the historic owners of the acquired business is not altered by the distribution of the controlled stock. Accordingly, neither distributing nor the distributing shareholders have a historic relationship with the separated businesses, and the distribution of the controlled stock is not the type of transaction to which section 355 was intended to apply.

By contrast, had D issued its own stock in the reorganization in the last example, the substance of the transaction would be different. D would not have indirectly acquired a trade or business in exchange for assets but rather for its own equity. Because D would not be purchasing a business for its shareholders, the distribution is not a substitute for a taxable distribution of the consideration that would have been used in the purchase. Furthermore, where D stock is used as the consideration the former T shareholders would have joined D's shareholder base, and become participants in the divisive reorganization.

These proposed regulations prohibit the acquisition of a trade or business directly or indirectly in exchange for assets in order to ensure that the common purpose of section 355(b)(2)(C) and (D) is satisfied. Such an acquisition also would include a swap of an interest in an existing five-year active trade or business for an interest in a new active trade or business. This type of an acquisition could occur through the formation of a joint venture structure.

For example, assume D and X form a partnership joint venture in which D contributes a five-year active trade or business (ATBD) and X contributes a different five-year active trade or business (ATBX). D and X each receive a 50-percent interest in the partnership. D's interest is sufficient to satisfy the requirements for D to be attributed the partnership's trade or business assets and activities (as discussed in section I. of this preamble). Prior to a potential section 355 distribution by D, and within five years of the contribution, the partnership sells ATBD.

D cannot rely on ATBX until five years after the acquisition of its interest in the partnership because, in effect, at the time of the contributions D exchanged a 50-percent undivided interest in ATBD for a 50-percent undivided interest in ATBX. Therefore, D acquired its interest in ATBX in exchange for its assets. While this was a transaction in which no gain or loss was recognized, the exchange of assets violates the common purpose of section 355(b)(2)(C) and (D). Further, the historic owner of ATBX would not participate in any distribution of controlled stock by D. Accordingly, such a distribution would not be the type of transaction to which section 355 was intended to apply.

Similarly, a corporation can effectively swap its assets through the issuance of stock of a subsidiary (including controlled). Accordingly, these proposed regulations provide a specific rule to address tax-free acquisitions involving the issuance of subsidiary stock. These proposed regulations provide that if a SAG directly or indirectly owns stock of a subsidiary (including a subsidiary SAG member) and the subsidiary directly or indirectly acquires a trade or business, an interest in a partnership engaged in a trade or business, or stock of a corporation engaged in a trade or business from a person other than such SAG in exchange for stock of such subsidiary in a transaction in which no gain or loss is recognized (the acquisition), solely for purposes of applying section 355(b)(2)(C) or (D) with respect to the trade or business, partnership interest, or stock acquired by the subsidiary in the acquisition, the subsidiary's stock directly or indirectly owned by the SAG immediately after the acquisition is treated as acquired at the time of the acquisition in a transaction in which gain or loss is recognized.

This rule reflects the fact that although the acquiring subsidiary did not make the acquisition in exchange for its assets (it issued its own stock), the SAG that owns stock of the subsidiary has exchanged an indirect interest in the subsidiary's assets for an indirect interest in the trade or business acquired by the subsidiary in the acquisition. Thus, the SAG has indirectly acquired a portion of the subsidiary's newly acquired trade or business (equal to the shareholder's stock interest in the subsidiary immediately after the acquisition) in exchange for assets. Further, the IRS and

Treasury Department believe that it would be inappropriate to allow such acquired trade or business to be relied on to satisfy the active trade or business requirement within five years of its acquisition because the historic owners of that trade or business would not participate in any distribution of controlled stock.

However, because such a transaction does not result in an acquisition of any pre-existing trade or business of the subsidiary, this rule merely treats the SAG's stock in the subsidiary immediately after the acquisition as acquired in a gain or loss transaction for purposes of applying section 355(b)(2)(C) or (D) to the newly acquired trade or business. Further, the impact of such a transaction on the ability to rely on the newly acquired trade or business to satisfy the requirements of section 355(b) depends upon how much subsidiary stock the SAG owns immediately after the transaction.

For example, assume D owns all of the sole class of stock of S, a corporation that does not conduct a five-year active trade or business. T, an unrelated corporation with a five-year active trade or business (ATBT), merges into S in a reorganization described in section 368(a)(1)(A) and (D) solely in exchange for 80 percent of the S stock, and no gain or loss is recognized. Immediately after the merger, D owns only 20 percent of the sole class of S stock. Solely for purposes of determining whether ATBT can be relied on to satisfy the active trade or business requirement, D is treated as having acquired its 20 percent of the S stock at the time of the merger of T into S in a transaction in which gain or loss was recognized. Accordingly, as described in section D.2.a. of this preamble regarding certain multi-step acquisitions of a subsidiary SAG member, if D subsequently acquired the 80 percent of the S stock held by the other shareholders solely in exchange for D voting stock in a reorganization described in section 368(a)(1)(B) in which no gain or loss was recognized, S would become a DSAG member and D could rely on ATBT to satisfy the active trade or business requirement.

Accordingly, in light of all of these concerns, these proposed regulations generally provide that acquisitions paid for in whole or in part, directly or indirectly, with assets of the DSAG will be treated as acquisitions in which gain or loss is recognized. However, if a DSAG member or controlled acquires the trade or business solely in exchange for distributing stock, distributing acquires control of controlled solely in exchange for distributing stock, or controlled acquires the trade or business from distributing solely in exchange for stock of controlled, in a transaction in which no gain or loss is recognized, the requirements of section 355(b)(2)(C) and (D) are satisfied. Such acquisitions are not made in exchange for assets of the DSAG.

An additional question arising under section 355(b)(2)(C) and (D) is whether the assumption of liabilities is treated as a payment of money or other property, and hence the use of assets. See *United States v. Hendler*, 303 US 564, reh'g denied, 304 US 588 (1938) (viewing an assumption of a liability by a transferee as in substance a payment to the transferor). Congress has indicated that the assumption of liabilities is not to be treated as the payment of money or other property in certain transactions in which no gain or loss is recognized. For example, the assumption of liabilities is not treated as the payment of money or other property in certain exchanges to which section 351 or 361 applies. See section 357(a). Further, the assumption of liabilities does not violate the solely for voting stock requirement in a reorganization described in section 368(a)(1)(C) where the acquiring corporation does not otherwise exchange money or other property. See section 368(a)(1)(C) and (a)(2)(B). Because Congress has granted this special treatment for liability assumptions in certain nonrecognition transactions, the IRS and Treasury Department believe that similar treatment is generally appropriate for purposes of section 355(b)(2)(C) and (D). Accordingly, these proposed regulations provide that the assumption by the DSAG or CSAG of liabilities of a transferor shall not, in and of itself, be treated as the payment of assets if such assumption is not treated as the payment of money or other property under any other applicable provision.

Finally, these proposed regulations clarify that an acquisition to which section 304(a)(1) applies does not satisfy the requirements of section 355(b)(2)(C) or (D). The IRS and Treasury Department believe that a stock acquisition to which section 304 applies is a transaction in which gain or loss is recognized for purposes of section 355(b)(2)(C) and (D) even if it merely results in the transferor's receipt of dividend income. These proposed regulations clarify that, regardless of the tax consequences to the transferor, such a transaction is an acquisition made in exchange for assets, and therefore does not satisfy the requirements of section 355(b)(2)(C) and (D).

ii. Partnership Distributions

These proposed regulations provide that an acquisition consisting of a distribution from a partnership is generally treated as a transaction in which gain or loss is recognized because it constitutes an acquisition in exchange for assets. That is, the distributee partner is generally exchanging an indirect interest in all the assets of the partnership for a direct interest in the property distributed. However, these proposed regulations provide that if the corporation is already attributed the trade or business assets and activities of a partnership, the corporation's acquisition of such trade or business assets and activities from the partnership is not, in and of itself, the acquisition of a new trade or business. Further, these proposed regulations provide that an acquisition consisting of a pro rata distribution from a partnership of stock or an interest in a lower-tier partnership is not an acquisition in exchange for assets to the extent the distributee partner did not acquire the interest in the distributing partnership during the pre-distribution period in a transaction in which gain or loss was recognized and to the extent the distributing partnership did not acquire the distributed stock or partnership interest within such period. In such a case, the distributee partner has merely exchanged an indirect interest for a direct interest in the distributed stock or partnership interest, and continues to possess the same indirect interest in the remaining assets of the partnership.

iii. Lack of Transferred Basis

Section 1.355-3(b)(4)(i) provides that a trade or business acquired, directly or indirectly, within the pre-distribution period in a transaction in which the basis of the assets acquired was not determined in whole or in part by reference to the transferor's basis does not qualify under section 355(b)(2), even though no gain or loss was recognized by the transferor. These proposed regulations do not include a similar provision. The IRS and Treasury Department believe that the prohibition against acquisitions in exchange for assets fully addresses such acquisitions.

c. Application of Section 355(b)(2)(C) and (D) to Predecessors

Unlike § 1.355-3(b)(4)(i), which only took "a predecessor in interest" into account for purposes of applying section 355(b)(2)(D), these proposed regulations provide that any reference to a corporation includes a reference to a predecessor of such corporation in applying both section 355(b)(2)(C) and (D). The IRS and Treasury Department believe that predecessors should be taken into account in applying both section 355(b)(2)(C) and (D) because the same policy concerns exist regardless of whether the transaction involves the acquisition of assets or stock. For this purpose, the proposed regulations define a predecessor of a corporation as a corporation that transfers its assets to such corporation in a transaction to which section 381 applies. The IRS and Treasury Department believe that it is appropriate to take predecessors into account in applying these provisions in order to appropriately minimize the significance of which corporation is the acquiror and which corporation is the target.

Further, because the SAG rule effectively treats SAG members as a single-entity for purposes of section 355(b), these proposed regulations also apply section 355(b)(2)(C) and (D) to acquisitions during the pre-distribution period by corporations that later become DSAG or CSAG members. These types of acquisitions are similar to predecessor asset acquisitions.

4. *Requests for comments regarding exceptions to section 355(b)(2)(C) and (D)*

The IRS and Treasury Department request comments regarding whether any additional exceptions to section 355(b)(2)(C) and (D) are appropriate. In particular, the IRS and Treasury Department request comments regarding whether acquisitions in which gain is recognized solely as a result of the application of section 367 should be treated as violating section 355(b)(2)(C) or (D). The IRS and Treasury Department also request comments regarding whether an exception should exist for taxable acquisitions made by distributing solely in exchange for distributing stock because such acquisitions are not made in exchange for distributing's assets and do not appear to violate the common purpose of section 355(b)(2)(C) and (D).

In addition, the IRS and Treasury Department request comments regarding whether a redemption of stock should be a transaction to which section 355(b)(2)(C) or (D) applies. Under current law, no relief is provided for such transactions. See *McLaulin v. Commissioner*, 276 F.3d 1269 (11th Cir. 2001) (concluding that section 355(b)(2)(D) applies when distributing acquires control of a subsidiary through a redemption of subsidiary stock). Compare Rev. Rul. 57-144 (1957-1 CB 123). Specifically, comments are requested on whether all types of redemptions should be subject to the same rule, whether the treatment of redemptions should be determined by the source of payment, whether the redemption constitutes an indirect exchange for assets of distributing or controlled, and the method of making these determinations. Alternatively, the IRS and Treasury Department request comments on whether an exception should be provided for redemptions of shareholders that exercise dissenters' rights. Compare Rev. Rul. 68-285 (1968-1 CB 147) (concluding that cash paid to dissenting target corporation shareholders by the target corporation does not violate the solely for voting stock requirement of section 368(a)(1)(B)) with Rev. Rul. 73-102 (1973-1 CB 186) (concluding that cash paid to dissenting target corporation shareholders by the acquiring corporation is treated as money or other property paid by the acquiring corporation for the properties of the target corporation in a reorganization under section 368(a)(1)(C)). These proposed regulations do not include an exception for redemptions generally or for those in connection with the exercise of dissenters' rights.

Finally, the IRS and Treasury Department request comments regarding whether a transaction in which a distributee corporation acquires in a transaction in which no gain or loss is recognized newly issued stock of distributing in exchange for money or property previously acquired for cash during the pre-distribution period should be treated as a transaction in which gain or loss is recognized. For example, assume D and C have each engaged in the active conduct of a trade or business for more than five years. During the pre-distribution period, P, an unrelated corporation, purchases trucks and transfers them to D in exchange for D stock meeting the requirements of section 368(c) in a transaction to which section 351 applies. No gain or loss is recognized. D subsequently distributes all the C stock to P in a separate transaction within five years of P's acquisition of the D stock. Notwithstanding that this transaction satisfies the literal requirements of section 355(b)(2)(D), it appears to violate the *General Utilities* doctrine because it permits the distributee corporation, P, to receive a fair market value basis (or close to a fair market value basis) in the distributing stock, enabling the potential sale of controlled stock without the appropriate recognition of gain. Additionally, the IRS and Treasury Department are studying whether the principles of the foregoing rule should be extended to any distributee in regulations under section 355(d), and request comments on this point.

D. *Treatment of Certain Multi-step Acquisitions*

These proposed regulations provide specific rules regarding the application of section 355(b)(2)(C) and (D) to certain multi-step acquisitions. Based on the interpretation of section 355(b)(2)(D), and the enactment of section 355(b)(3), the IRS and Treasury Department believe that it is appropriate to apply section 355(b)(2)(C) and (D) to multi-step acquisitions in a consistent manner. Further, the IRS and Treasury Department believe that it is appropriate to treat certain multi-step acquisitions of target corporation stock as satisfying the requirements of section 355(b)(2)(C) or (D) (as applicable) notwithstanding that some portion of the stock may have been acquired in a separate transaction in which gain or loss was recognized.

1. *Multi-step acquisition of control of distributing or controlled*

a. Direct Acquisitions

Section 355(b)(2)(D) provides that control of distributing or controlled may be acquired within the pre-distribution period provided that "in each case in which such control was so acquired, it was so acquired, only by reason of transactions in which gain or loss was not recognized in whole or in part, or only by reason of such transactions combined with acquisitions before the beginning of such period." The IRS and Treasury Department interpret this language to mean that at the time control is first acquired, the acquiring corporation (or its SAG) is required to own stock meeting the requirements of section 368(c) that was acquired in one or more transactions in which no gain or loss was recognized or by reason of such transactions combined with acquisitions before the beginning of the pre-distribution period. Thus, at the time an acquiring corporation (or its SAG) first satisfies the section 368(c) control requirement, the acquiring corporation (or its SAG) must possess section 368(c) control without relying on any stock acquired in a transaction in which gain or loss was recognized during the pre-distribution period.

For example, assume that C has two classes of stock outstanding. X owns all 95 shares of the class A stock of C representing 95 percent of the voting power and 70 percent of the value and Y owns all of the class B stock of C representing five percent of the voting power and 30 percent of the value. In year 1, unrelated D acquires 10 shares of the class A C stock from X in a transaction in which gain or loss is recognized. In year 2, D acquires an additional 80 shares of class A C stock from X in a separate transaction in which no gain or loss is recognized. In year 3, D acquires the remaining five shares of class A C stock from X in a separate transaction in which gain or loss is recognized. In year 4, D distributes the 95 shares of class A C stock to the D shareholders. Assuming all of the other requirements of section 355(b) are satisfied, the requirements of section 355(b)(2)(D)(ii) are satisfied because at the time D first acquired control of C (immediately after the year 2 acquisition), D owned an amount of C stock constituting control that was acquired in a transaction in which no gain or loss was recognized (the 80 shares of class A C stock acquired in year 2). (However, the 10 shares of class A C stock acquired in year 1 and the five shares of class A C stock acquired in year 3 may be treated as boot under section 355(a)(3)(B).)

On the other hand, assume the same facts as the previous example, except that, in year 2, D acquires only 75 shares of class A C stock from X. The requirements of section 355(b)(2)(D)(ii) are not satisfied because at the time D first acquired control of C (immediately after the year 2 acquisition), D did not own an amount of C stock constituting control that was acquired in one or more transactions in which no gain or loss was recognized or acquired prior to the pre-distribution period. D only owns C voting stock representing 75 percent of the total voting power that was acquired in a transaction in which no gain or loss was recognized. The result would be the same if the year 3 acquisition was also a transaction in which no gain or loss was recognized.

b. Indirect Acquisitions

These proposed regulations also provide that the principles of this rule will be applied with respect to an indirect acquisition of distributing or controlled stock. For example, assume T corporation owns stock of C (an unaffiliated subsidiary) constituting control (and no more). Unrelated D acquires 10 percent of the sole outstanding class of stock of T in a transaction in which gain or loss is recognized. In a separate transaction, T merges into D solely in exchange for D stock in a transaction in which no gain or loss is recognized. In applying this multi-step acquisition rule to D's subsequent acquisition of control of C in the merger, the prior acquisition of T stock in the transaction in which gain or loss was recognized is treated as an acquisition of 10 percent of the C stock owned by T (representing 8 percent of the total combined voting power of the C stock) in a transaction in which gain or loss is recognized. Accordingly, the requirements of section 355(b)(2)(D)(ii) are not satisfied because at the time D first acquires control of C, D does not own an amount of C stock constituting control that was acquired in one or more transactions in which no gain or loss is recognized or acquired prior to the pre-distribution period. At that time, D had only acquired C stock representing 72 percent of the total combined voting power of the C stock in a transaction in which no gain or loss is recognized.

2. *Other multiple-step acquisitions*

As discussed in sections A.1., B.1., and B.3. of this preamble, if D acquires section 1504(a)(2) stock of a corporation, the acquired corporation will become a DSAG member and the corporation will be treated like a division of D for purposes of the active trade or business requirement. As such, D is treated as if it acquired the assets and activities of the new subsidiary SAG member, and the acquisition must satisfy the requirements of section 355(b)(2)(C) rather than section 355(b)(2)(D). If D subsequently acquires the remaining stock of the corporation in a separate transaction, such acquisition is disregarded for purposes of satisfying the active trade or business requirement (regardless of whether gain or loss was recognized in the separate transaction) because the subsidiary is already treated as a division of D for this purpose. The IRS and Treasury Department believe that the order of these acquisitions should not be determinative in applying section 355(b)(2)(C), provided that at the time the corporation first becomes a subsidiary SAG member, the SAG owns section 1504(a)(2) stock in the corporation without relying on any stock acquired in a transaction in which gain or loss was recognized during the pre-distribution period.

a. Direct SAG Acquisitions

Consistent with the treatment of multi-step acquisitions of control of a corporation discussed in section D.1. of this preamble, these proposed regulations provide that multi-step acquisitions of stock resulting in a corporation becoming a subsidiary SAG member will satisfy the requirements of section 355(b)(2)(C), provided that at the time the corporation first becomes a subsidiary SAG member, the SAG owns section 1504(a)(2) stock in the corporation without relying on any stock acquired in a transaction in which gain or loss was recognized during the pre-distribution period.

For example, assume that in year 1, D does not conduct an active trade or business and has owned control of C for more than five years. C and T, an unrelated corporation, have each engaged in the active conduct of a trade or business for more than five years. In year 1, D acquires 10 percent of T's sole outstanding class of stock in a transaction in which gain or loss was recognized. In year 2, D acquires an additional 80 percent of T's stock in a separate transaction in which no gain or loss was recognized. T becomes a DSAG member as a result of the year 2 stock acquisition. In year 3, D distributes the C stock to the D shareholders. Assuming all of the other requirements of section 355(b) are satisfied, the requirements of section 355(b)(2)(C) are satisfied because at the time T first became a DSAG member (immediately after the year 2 acquisition), D owned an amount of T stock meeting the requirements of section 1504(a)(2) that was acquired in a transaction in which no gain or loss was recognized (the T stock acquired in year 2).

On the other hand, assume the same facts as the previous example except that, in year 2, D only acquires an additional 75 percent of T's stock. The requirements of section 355(b)(2)(C) are not satisfied because at the time T first became a DSAG member (immediately after the year 2 acquisition), D did not own an amount of T stock meeting the requirements of section 1504(a)(2) that was acquired in one or more transactions in which no gain or loss was recognized or acquired prior to the pre-distribution period. D owns only 75 percent of T's stock that was acquired in a transaction in which no gain or loss was recognized. The result would be the same even if, in year 3 prior to the distribution of the C stock, D acquired the remaining 15 percent of the T stock in a transaction in which no gain or loss is recognized.

b. Indirect SAG Acquisitions

Similar to the rule regarding multi-step acquisitions of control of distributing or controlled, these proposed regulations also provide that the principles of this rule will be applied with respect to an indirect acquisition by the SAG of stock of a corporation that becomes a SAG member. For example, assume a DSAG member acquires 25 percent of the sole outstanding class of stock of T, a corporation that wholly owns S, in a transaction in which gain or loss is recognized. In a separate transaction, another DSAG member acquires all of the stock of S from T solely in exchange for D voting stock in a reorganization described in section 368(a)(1)(B) in which no gain or loss is recognized. As a result, S becomes a DSAG member. In applying this multi-step acquisition rule to the DSAG's subsequent acquisition of S stock, the acquisition of 25 percent of the T stock in the transaction in which gain or loss was recognized will be treated as an acquisition of 25 percent of the S stock in a transaction in which gain or loss is recognized. Accordingly, the requirements of section 355(b)(2)(C) are not satisfied because at the time S first becomes a DSAG member, the DSAG does not own section 1504(a)(2) stock of S that was acquired in one or more transactions in which no gain or loss is recognized or acquired prior to the pre-distribution period.

c. Multi-step Asset Acquisitions

Because stock acquisitions that result in a corporation becoming a subsidiary SAG member are treated as direct acquisitions of the target corporation's assets for purposes of applying section 355(b), these proposed regulations apply a comparable multi-step acquisition rule to acquisitions of stock in non-SAG members where such non-members' assets are subsequently directly acquired by a SAG member. Specifically, these proposed regulations provide that if immediately before a SAG's direct acquisition of a trade or business (or an interest in a partnership engaged in a trade or business) held by a corporation (owner) in a transaction to which section 381 applies and in which no gain or loss is recognized, the SAG owns an amount of stock of the owner that it acquired in one or more transactions during the pre-distribution period in which gain or loss was recognized such that all of the other stock of the owner does not meet the requirements of section 1504(a)(2), such direct acquisition shall be treated as a transaction in which gain or loss was recognized. Thus, these proposed regulations apply section 355(b)(2)(C) to multi-step acquisitions in the same manner regardless of whether the separate steps result in the target corporation becoming a subsidiary SAG member or result in a direct acquisition of the target corporation's assets.

For example, assume that in year 1, D does not conduct an active trade or business, and has owned control of C for more than five years. C and T, an unrelated corporation, have each engaged in the active conduct of a trade or business for more than five years. In year 1, D acquires 10 percent of T's sole outstanding class of stock in a transaction in which gain or loss was recognized. In year 2, in a separate reorganization described in section 368(a)(1)(A), T merges into D and the T shareholders receive solely D stock in exchange for their T stock. No gain or loss is recognized in the merger. In year 3, D distributes the stock of C to the D shareholders. Assuming all of the other requirements of section 355(b) are satisfied, the requirements of section 355(b)(2)(C) are satisfied because, at the time D acquires T's active trade or business, D did not own an amount of T stock that was acquired in one or more transactions during the pre-distribution period in which gain or loss was recognized such that all of the other T stock does not meet the requirements of section 1504(a)(2).

On the other hand, assume the same facts as the previous example except that in year 1 D acquires 21 percent of T's stock. The requirements of section 355(b)(2)(C) are not satisfied because, at the time D acquires T's active trade or business, D owned an amount of T stock that was acquired in one or more transactions during the pre-distribution period in which gain or loss was recognized such that all of the other T stock does not meet the requirements of section 1504(a)(2).

These proposed regulations also provide that the principles of this rule will be applied with respect to an indirect acquisition of the target corporation's stock by the SAG.

E. *Expansion Acquisitions*

The legislative history, the courts, and the current regulations acknowledge that a trade or business can undergo many changes during the pre-distribution period and still satisfy the requirements of section 355(b). See H.R. No. 83-2543, at 37, 38 (1954) (Conf. Rep.); *Estate of Lockwood v. Commissioner*, 350 F.2d 712 (8th Cir. 1965); and § 1.355-3(b)(3)(ii). Furthermore, § 1.355-3(b)(3)(ii) provides "if a corporation engaged in the active conduct of one trade or business during that five-year period purchased, created, or otherwise acquired another trade or business in the same line of business, then the acquisition of that other business is ordinarily treated as an expansion of the original business, all of which is treated as having been actively conducted during that five-year period, unless that purchase, creation, or other acquisition effects a change of such a character as to constitute the acquisition of a new or different business." Therefore, an acquired trade or business that is an expansion of the original trade or business inherits the business history of the expanded business.

None of these authorities, however, addresses whether an existing trade or business can be expanded by acquiring the stock of a corporation engaged in a trade or business in the same line of business as the acquiror. Because the SAG rule causes a stock acquisition in which the acquired corporation becomes a subsidiary SAG member to be treated as an asset acquisition, a corporation engaged in a trade or business should be able to expand its existing trade or business by acquiring stock of a corporation (including controlled) engaged in a trade or business in the same line of business provided the acquisition results in the acquired corporation becoming a subsidiary SAG member.

On the other hand, section 355(b)(3) does not allow a corporation to rely on the trade or business of a non-SAG subsidiary — even if the corporation controls the subsidiary — to satisfy the active trade or business requirement. As such, it effectively precludes stock expansions where the acquired corporation does not become a subsidiary SAG member. The IRS and Treasury Department believe that section 355(b)(3) is the exclusive means by which a corporation is attributed the assets (or activities) owned (or conducted) by another corporation. Accordingly, a stock acquisition that does not result in the acquired corporation becoming a subsidiary SAG member should not be an expansion of the SAG's original business.

In addition, these proposed regulations provide certain facts and circumstances to be considered in determining whether one trade or business is in the same line of business as another trade or business. The inclusion of these facts and circumstances in these proposed regulations is not intended to be a substantive change, but merely to clarify and restate the current law regarding expansions. See Rev. Rul. 2003-18 (2003-1 CB 467) and Rev. Rul. 2003-38 (2003-1 CB 811). Some of the examples from the current regulations have been altered in these proposed regulations to reflect this inclusion (as well as certain stylistic changes).

F. *Rules Related to Hot Stock*

Section 355(a)(3)(B) provides that stock of controlled acquired by distributing during the pre-distribution period in a transaction in which gain or loss is recognized is treated as boot. Section 1.355-2(g) provides guidance regarding the application of section 355(a)(3)(B). The IRS and Treasury Department request comments regarding whether § 1.355-2(g) should be amended to adopt rules under section 355(a)(3)(B) similar to those provided in these proposed regulations for determining whether an acquisition is one in which gain or loss is recognized for purposes of section 355(b)(2)(C) or (D).

In particular, the IRS and Treasury Department request comments concerning the application of section 355(a)(3)(B) to acquisitions of stock of controlled in gain or loss transactions that, under these proposed regulations, are not treated as violating the requirements of section 355(b). For example, where distributing acquires stock of controlled in a gain or loss transaction that is treated as an expansion of distributing's existing trade or business (because controlled is in distributing's line of business and becomes a DSAG member), what portion, if any, of the acquired stock should be subject to section 355(a)(3)(B)?

The current authorities may suggest a linkage between the interpretation of sections 355(a)(3)(B) and 355(b). See § 1.355-2(g)(1) (not applying section 355(a)(3)(B) to a taxable acquisition from an affiliate); Rev. Rul. 78-442 (stating "[l]ikewise, for the same reasons [that section 355(b)(2)(C) does not apply], section 355(a)(3)[(B)]of the Code is not applicable"). However, section 355(b)(3) by its literal terms does not appear to apply for purposes section 355(a)(3)(B).

The IRS and Treasury Department continue to study how to coordinate the application of these provisions and request comments in this regard. Accordingly, these proposed regulations contain no proposal to change § 1.355-2(g) at this time.

G. *Limited Affiliate Exception*

Other than with respect to transfers of assets (or activities) that are owned (or performed) by the SAG immediately before and immediately after the transfer, these proposed regulations do not include the special treatment accorded affiliated group members in § 1.355-3(b)(4)(iii). Thus, these proposed regulations treat non-SAG member affiliates of distributing or controlled in the same manner as unrelated persons for purposes of applying section 355(b)(2)(C) and (D). While distributing is the common parent of its SAG, distributing may be a subsidiary member of a larger affiliated group. Therefore, not all members of distributing's affiliated group are DSAG members.

Section 1.355-3(b)(4)(iii) provides that acquisitions by one member of an affiliated group from another member of the group are disregarded in applying section 355(b)(2)(C) and (D), even if gain or loss is recognized. Section 1.355-3(b)(4)(iii) provides for this treatment for affiliates because although "[t]he requirements of section 355(b)(2)(C) and (D) are intended to prevent the direct or indirect acquisition of a trade or business by a corporation in anticipation of a distribution by the corporation of that trade or business in a distribution to which section 355 would otherwise apply[,]" acquisitions from affiliates are not the type of transaction to which these provisions were intended to apply. Section 1.355-3(b)(4)(iv) defines the term "affiliated group" as an affiliated group as defined in section 1504(a) (without regard to section 1504(b)), except that the term "stock" includes nonvoting stock described in section 1504(a)(4).

The IRS and Treasury Department believe that limiting this special treatment to transfers in which the assets (or activities) remain in the SAG (as opposed to the larger affiliated group) is more consistent with the purposes of section 355(b)(3). As discussed in section A.1. of this preamble, section 355(b)(3) states, in effect, that in determining whether distributing or controlled is engaged in a trade or business all DSAG or CSAG members, as the case may be, are treated as one corporation. Therefore, a transfer of trade or business assets (or activities) from one SAG member to another SAG member is disregarded, and is not an acquisition for purposes of section 355(b)(2)(C) (or section 355(b)(2)(D) in the case of stock of controlled that is not a DSAG member). The SAG rule implies a corollary, which is that if the trade or business assets (or activities) are not owned (or performed) by the SAG, such assets (or activities) should generally not be able to be acquired from outside the SAG in a transaction in which gain or loss is recognized. Thus, these proposed regulations generally do not permit taxable acquisitions of an active trade or business from outside the SAG.

The IRS and Treasury Department recognize that not providing this special treatment for non-SAG member affiliates is a change from how the law has been administered in various situations. Further, the IRS and Treasury Department recognize that this change can represent a relaxing or tightening of the law in this area, depending upon the circumstances. For example, under these proposed regulations the requirements of section 355(b)(2)(C) are satisfied where P, a higher-tier affiliate of distributing, purchases a trade or business for cash and contributes it to distributing solely in exchange for distributing stock in a transaction in which no gain or loss is recognized. On the other hand, under these proposed regulations, the requirements of section 355(b)(2)(C) are not satisfied where P has actively conducted a trade or business for more than five years and sells it to D in exchange for cash.

H. *Activities Performed by Certain Related Parties*

Current § 1.355-3(b)(2)(iii) provides, in part, that to satisfy the active trade or business requirement, the corporation itself generally is required to perform active and substantial management and operational functions. That regulation further provides that activities performed by the corporation itself generally do not include activities performed by independent contractors. In this regard, "a corporation must engage in entrepreneurial endeavors of such a nature and to such an extent as to qualitatively distinguish its operations from mere investments [, and] . . . there should be objective indicia of such corporate operations." *Rafferty v. Commissioner*, 452 F.2d 767, 772 (1st Cir. 1971) *cert. denied* 408 US 922 (1972) (concluding that a corporation that did not pay salaries or rent, did not employ independent contractors, and merely collected rent, paid taxes, and kept separate books, failed to satisfy these requirements). The IRS and Treasury Department believe that a corporation may rely on the activities performed by certain related parties in conducting its "entrepreneurial endeavors," and such activities can constitute "objective indicia" of corporate operations.

While section 355(b)(3) treats all SAG members as one corporation, the IRS and Treasury Department are aware that affiliated groups of corporations that include non-SAG member affiliates might use employees of one member of the group to perform management or operational functions for another member of the group. The IRS and the Treasury Department believe that a corporation can satisfy the active trade or business requirement even if all the management and operational functions are performed by employees of affiliates that are not members of either the DSAG or CSAG. In other words, the DSAG or CSAG can be engaged in "entrepreneurial endeavors" that are distinguishable from mere passive investment even if the management and operational functions are performed for the DSAG or CSAG by employees of non-SAG affiliates. Such individuals bear a close enough relationship to the DSAG or CSAG to be distinguished from mere independent contractors for purposes of the active trade or business requirement. The IRS and Treasury Department believe that this treatment is appropriate and consistent with previously published guidance.

Issued prior to the enactment of section 355(b)(3), Rev. Rul. 79-394 (1979-2 CB 141), amplified by Rev. Rul. 80-181 (1980-2 CB 121), concludes that controlled satisfies the active trade or business requirement even though all of the operational activities of its business are conducted by an affiliate's employees before the distribution. The IRS and Treasury Department believe that extending the principles of Rev. Rul. 79-394 and Rev. Rul. 80-181 to the performance of management (in addition to operational) functions by employees of an affiliate is consistent with the purposes underlying the active trade or business requirement. Accordingly, these proposed regulations provide that, in determining whether a corporation is engaged in the active conduct of a trade or business, activities (including management and operational functions) performed by employees of the corporation's affiliates (including non-SAG members) are taken into account.

Furthermore, the IRS and Treasury Department believe that a corporation can satisfy the active trade or business requirement even if all the management and operational functions are performed by shareholders of the corporation if it is closely held. The shareholders of closely held corporations possess a close relationship with the corporation, similar to employees of affiliates. Accordingly, these proposed regulations provide that, in determining whether a corporation is engaged in the active conduct of a trade or business, activities (including management and operational functions) performed by shareholders of a closely held corporation are taken into account in certain cases.

The IRS and Treasury Department do not believe that the absence of an exception for acquisitions from non-SAG member affiliates is inconsistent with concluding that a corporation can satisfy the active trade or business requirement by relying on the management and operational functions performed by employees of non-SAG member affiliates. Relying on the activities of such employees does not involve the acquisition of a trade or business. As such, it is not the type of transaction or arrangement section 355(b)(2) was intended to address. Accordingly, the IRS and Treasury Department believe it is appropriate to apply a broader standard with respect to relying on employees of non-SAG member affiliates.

While it is appropriate to consider the management and operational activities of employees of all affiliates in determining whether a corporation satisfies the active trade or business requirement, the IRS and Treasury Department believe that a corporation should satisfy the active trade or business requirement only if it (or another SAG member, or a partnership from which the trade or business assets and activities are attributed) is the principal owner of the goodwill and significant assets of the trade or business for Federal income tax purposes. Accordingly, a corporation will be treated as engaged in the active conduct of a trade or business only if, for Federal income tax purposes, it (or its SAG member, or a partnership from which the trade or business assets and activities are attributed) is the principal owner of the goodwill and significant assets of the trade or business. Accordingly, some of the examples from the current regulations have been altered in these proposed regulations to reflect this goodwill and significant asset standard (as well as certain stylistic changes).

I. *Activities Conducted by a Partnership*

Revenue Ruling 92-17 (1992-1 CB 142) and Rev. Rul. 2002-49 (2002-2 CB 288) address in a number of fact situations whether a corporation that is a partner in a partnership can satisfy the active trade or business requirement by reason of its ownership of the partnership interest where the partnership conducts a trade or business. Those rulings illustrate that a corporation owning a 20-percent interest in a state law partnership or limited liability company (LLC) that is classified as a partnership for Federal income tax purposes can be treated as engaged in the active conduct of the trade or business of the partnership if the corporation performs active and substantial management functions for the partnership's business. In addition, Rev. Rul. 2002-49 concludes that such a corporation can be treated as engaged in the active conduct of a partnership's trade or business, even if another partner also performs active and substantial management functions for the partnership's trade or business.

Consistent with the principles set forth in Rev. Rul. 92-17 and Rev. Rul. 2002-49 regarding satisfying the active trade or business requirement through an interest in a partnership, these proposed regulations provide that for purposes of section 355(b) a partner will be attributed the trade or business assets and activities of a partnership if the partner (1) performs active and substantial management functions for the partnership with respect to the trade or business assets or activities (for example, makes decisions regarding significant business issues of the partnership and regularly participates in the overall supervision, direction, and control of the employees performing the operational functions for the partnership), and (2) owns a meaningful interest in the partnership. Further, because a partnership might only conduct a portion of a trade or business, the IRS and Treasury Department believe that a partner that satisfies these requirements can be attributed the portions of a trade or business (or assets and activities) that are conducted by a partnership. Under these circumstances the IRS and Treasury Department believe that it is appropriate to aggregate the partnership's trade or business assets and activities with those of the partner for purposes of determining whether the partner satisfies the active trade or business requirement. However, the stock of a corporation held by the partnership is not attributed to a partner.

The IRS and Treasury Department understand that the facts presented in Rev. Rul. 92-17 and Rev. Rul. 2002-49 do not necessarily reflect the exclusive methods by which corporations engage in a trade or business through a partnership. In particular, the IRS and Treasury Department understand that both the management and operational activities of an LLC are often conducted by the LLC itself, rather than by its members, to protect its members from liability for the LLC's activities. In these cases, Rev. Rul. 92-17 and Rev. Rul. 2002-49 do not explicitly support the conclusion that a corporation may rely on the trade or business assets and activities of an LLC to satisfy the active trade or business requirement, since no activities are performed by the corporate partner.

The IRS and Treasury Department believe that, in certain cases, a partner that owns a significant interest in an entity that is treated as a partnership for Federal income tax purposes should be attributed the trade or business assets and activities of a partnership, even if the partner does not directly conduct any activities relating to the business of the partnership. By comparison, the IRS and Treasury Department have promulgated regulations regarding the treatment of acquired assets held by a partnership for purposes of satisfying the continuity of business enterprise requirement applicable to reorganizations. Those regulations provide that a partner will be treated as owning the acquired target business assets used in the business of a partnership in satisfaction of the continuity of business enterprise requirement if the members of the qualified group, in the aggregate, own an interest in the partnership representing a significant interest in that partnership business. See § 1.368-1(d)(4)(iii)(B)(*1*). Those regulations include an example concluding that the continuity of business enterprise requirement is satisfied where a partner owns a one-third interest in a partnership that continues the business of the target corporation, even though the partner performs no management or operational functions for that business. See § 1.368-1(d)(5) *Example 9*.

These proposed regulations yield results similar to the continuity of business enterprise rule in determining whether the active trade or business requirement is satisfied when a corporation conducts a trade or business or portions of a trade or business through a partnership but does not participate in the partnership's activities. Specifically, these proposed regulations provide that for purposes of section 355(b) a partner will be attributed the trade or business assets and activities of a partnership provided the partner owns a significant interest in the partnership. The IRS and Treasury Department intend that the term "significant interest" requires an ownership interest that is greater than that suggested by the term "meaningful interest," which is the level of ownership required for a partner to be attributed the trade or business assets and activities of a partnership in cases where the partner performs active and substantial management functions for the partnership.

However, a partner will be attributed the trade or business assets and activities of a partnership only during the period it owns a significant interest or alternatively owns a meaningful interest and performs active and substantial management functions.

J. *Additional Requests for Comments*

The IRS and Treasury Department request comments regarding whether the regulations should include a rule that would treat an acquisition in which no gain or loss is recognized as an acquisition in which gain or loss is recognized if that would be the treatment had the transaction been executed in the opposite direction. For example, assume that, in year 1, P, a corporation not engaged in an active trade or business, acquires 50 percent of all of the outstanding stock of D (which is engaged in an active trade or business, and owns control of C, which is also engaged in an active trade or business) in a transaction in which gain or loss is recognized, and then, in a separate transaction in year 3, D merges into P solely in exchange for P stock in a transaction described in section 368(a)(1)(A) in which no gain or loss is recognized. P then distributes the C stock to its shareholders in year 4. Under these proposed regulations, P is treated as having acquired D's trade or business and control of C during the pre-distribution period in a transaction in which gain or loss is recognized because P acquired more than 20 percent of D's stock during the pre-distribution period in a transaction in which gain or loss was recognized (see sections D.1.b. and D.2.c. of this preamble). However, if P merges downstream into D solely in exchange for D stock in a reorganization described in section 368(a)(1)(A) and (D) in which no gain or loss is recognized, there literally is not an acquisition in which gain or loss is recognized under these proposed regulations, because D did not acquire any interest in an active trade or business from P. Comments are requested regarding whether the result should differ depending upon the direction of the merger. See and compare § 1.355-3(b)(4)(ii) (predecessor of distributing acquiring control of distributing).

Further, the IRS and Treasury Department request comments regarding the appropriate methods of measuring indirect acquisitions of stock for purposes of the rules regarding multi-step acquisitions, as discussed in section D. of this preamble. Specifically, comments are requested regarding how the indirect acquisition should be measured where the acquired corporation has multiple classes of stock outstanding, or where the acquired entity is a partnership. For example, assume T is a corporation that owns all of the stock of a subsidiary, S, and T has class A common stock, class B common stock, and preferred stock outstanding. If D acquires 10 percent of the T class A common stock, how should one determine what percentage of S stock D has indirectly acquired? Should it be based on the value of the T stock D acquired relative to the value of all of the T stock or other factors? How should the voting power of the acquired T stock be taken into account in applying these rules to potential indirect acquisitions of control?

In addition, the IRS and Treasury Department request comments regarding whether the parameters of the good faith and inadvertence exceptions in Notice 2004-37 (2004-1 CB 947) regarding the value requirement in section 1504(a)(2)(B) should apply for purposes of determining whether corporations are SAG members even if they are not members of a consolidated group. That is, the IRS and Treasury Department request comments regarding whether the policies underlying the SAG rule and the reference to section 1504(a) in section 355(b)(3)(B) suggest that the good faith and inadvertence exceptions should apply and be interpreted in the same way for SAG membership as for affiliation for purposes of filing consolidated returns.

The IRS and Treasury Department also request comments regarding whether the regulations should clarify the circumstances under which the separation of a segment of an active trade or business should be treated as a separate active trade or business after it is spun off and, if so, what the governing principle should be. See, for example, § 1.355-3(c) *Example 9* (separation of a corporation's research department from the rest of its manufacturing business).

Although these regulations are generally proposed to be applicable to distributions that occur after the date these regulations are published as final regulations in the **Federal Register,** the IRS and Treasury Department invite comments regarding whether it would be appropriate and desirable to allow taxpayers to elect to apply these provisions retroactively (subject to the applicability of section 355(b)(3)).

Proposed Effective Date

These proposed regulations are proposed to apply to distributions that occur after the date these regulations are published as final regulations in the **Federal Register.**

Special Analyses

It has been determined that this notice of proposed rulemaking is not a significant regulatory action as defined in Executive Order 12866. Therefore, a regulatory assessment is not required. It has also been determined that section 553(b) of the Administrative Procedure Act (5 U.S.C. chapter 5) does not apply to these regulations, and, because these regulations do not impose a collection of information on small entities, the Regulatory Flexibility Act (5 U.S.C. chapter 6) does not apply. Pursuant to section 7805(f) of the Code, these regulations have been submitted to the Chief Counsel for Advocacy of the Small Business Administration for comment on its impact on small businesses.

Comments and Requests for Public Hearing

Before these proposed regulations are adopted as final regulations, consideration will be given to any written (a signed original and eight (8) copies) or electronic comments that are submitted timely to the IRS. The IRS and Treasury Department request comments on the clarity of the proposed rules and how they can be made easier to understand. All comments will be available for public inspection and copying. A public hearing will be scheduled if requested in writing by any person that timely submits written comments. If a public hearing is scheduled, notice of the date, time, and place for the public hearing will be published in the **Federal Register.**

Drafting Information

The principal author of these proposed regulations is Russell P. Subin of the Office of Associate Chief Counsel (Corporate). However, other personnel from the IRS and Treasury Department participated in their development.

Availability of IRS Documents

IRS revenue rulings, procedures, and notices cited in this preamble are made available by the Superintendent of Documents, U.S. Government Printing Office, Washington, DC 20402.

[¶ 49,315] Proposed Regulations (REG-142695-05), published with the Federal Register on August 6, 2007 (corrected 9/20/2007).

[Code Sec. 125]

Employers: Compensation and benefits: Cafeteria plans: Proposed regulations.—Reg. §§ 1.125-0, 1.125-1, 1.125-2, 1.125-5, 1.125-6 and 1.125-7, providing guidance on cafeteria plans, are proposed. Proposed Reg. § 1.125-1 and § 1.125-2 are withdrawn.

AGENCY: Internal Revenue Service (IRS), Treasury.

ACTION: Withdrawal of prior notices of proposed rulemaking, notice of proposed rulemaking and notice of public hearing.

SUMMARY: This document contains new proposed regulations providing guidance on cafeteria plans. This document also withdraws the notices of proposed rulemaking relating to cafeteria plans under section 125 that were published on May 7, 1984, December 31, 1984, March 7, 1989, November 7, 1997 and March 23, 2000. In general, these proposed regulations would affect employers that sponsor a cafeteria plan, employees that participate in a cafeteria plan, and third-party cafeteria plan administrators.

DATES: Written or electronic comments must be received by November 5, 2007. Outlines of topics to be discussed at the hearing scheduled for November 15, 2007, at 10 a.m., must be received by October 25, 2007.

ADDRESSES: Send submissions to: CC:PA:LPD:PR (REG-142695-05), room 5203, Internal Revenue Service, P.O. Box 7604, Ben Franklin Station, Washington, DC 20044. Submissions may be hand delivered Monday through Friday between the hours of 8 a.m. and 4 p.m. to CC:PA:LPD:PR (REG-142695-05), Courier's Desk, Internal Revenue Service, 1111 Constitution Avenue, NW., Washington, DC or sent electronically via the Federal eRulemaking Portal at *www.regulations.gov* (IRS REG-142695-05). The public hearing will be held at the IRS Auditorium, Internal Revenue Building, 1111 Constitution Avenue, NW, Washington, DC.

FOR FURTHER INFORMATION CONTACT: Concerning the proposed regulations, Mireille T. Khoury at (202) 622-6080; concerning submissions of comments, the hearing, and/or to be placed on the building access list to attend the hearing, Oluwafunmilayo Taylor of the Publications and Regulations Branch at (202) 622-7180 (not toll-free numbers).

SUPPLEMENTARY INFORMATION

Paperwork Reduction Act

The collections of information contained in this notice of proposed rulemaking have been submitted to the Office of Management and Budget for review in accordance with the Paperwork Reduction Act of 1995 (44 U.S.C. 3507(d)). Comments on the collections of information should be sent to the **Office of Management and Budget**, Attn: Desk Officer for the Department of Treasury, Office of Information and Regulatory Affairs, Washington, DC 20503, with copies to the **Internal Revenue Service**, Attn: IRS Reports Clearance Officer, SE:W:CAR:MP:T:T:SP, Washington, DC 20224. Comments on the collections of information should be received by October 5, 2007. Comments are specifically requested concerning:

Whether the proposed collections of information is necessary for the proper performance of the functions of the Internal Revenue Service, including whether the information will have practical utility;

The accuracy of the estimated burden associated with the proposed collection of information;

How the quality, utility, and clarity of the information to be collected may be enhanced;

How the burden of complying with the proposed collections of information may be minimized, including through the application of automatic collection techniques or other forms of information technology; and

Estimates of the capital or start-up costs and costs of operation, maintenance, and purchase of service to provide information.

The collection of information in this proposed regulation is in §1.125-2 (cafeteria plan elections); §1.125-6(b)-(g) (substantiation of expenses), and §1.125-7 (cafeteria plan nondiscrimination rules). This information is required to file employment tax returns and Forms W-2. The collection of information is voluntary to obtain a benefit. The likely respondents are Federal, state or local governments, business or other for-profit institutions, nonprofit institutions, and small businesses or organizations.

Estimated total annual reporting burden: 34,000,000 hours.

Estimated average annual burden per respondent: 5 hours.

Estimated annual frequency of responses: once.

An agency may not conduct or sponsor, and a person is not required to respond to, a collection of information unless it displays a valid control number assigned by the Office of Management and Budget.

Books or records relating to a collection of information must be retained as long as their contents may become material in the administration of any internal revenue law. Generally, tax returns and tax return information are confidential, as required by 26 U.S.C. 6103.

Background

This document contains proposed Income Tax Regulations (26 CFR Part 1) under section 125 of the Internal Revenue Code (Code). On May 7, 1984, December 31, 1984, March 7, 1989, November 7, 1997, and March 23, 2000, the IRS and Treasury Department published proposed amendments to 26 CFR Part 1 under section 125 in the **Federal Register** (49 FR 19321, 49 FR 50733, 54 FR 9460, 62 FR 60196 and 65 FR 15587). These 1984, 1989, 1997 and 2000 proposed regulations are hereby withdrawn. Also, the temporary regulations under section 125 that were published on February 4, 1986 in the **Federal Register** (51 FR 4318) are being withdrawn in a separate document. The new proposed regulations that are published in this document replace those proposed regulations.

Explanation of Provisions

Overview

The new proposed regulations are organized as follows: general rules on qualified and nonqualified benefits in cafeteria plans (new proposed §1.125-1), general rules on elections (new proposed §1.125-2), general rules on flexible spending arrangements (new proposed §1.125-5), general rules on substantiation of expenses for qualified benefits (new proposed §1.125-6) and nondiscrimination rules (new proposed §1.125-7). The new proposed regulations, new Proposed §§1.125-1, 1.125-2, 1.125-5, 1.125-6 and §1.125-7, consolidate and restate Proposed §1.125-1 (1984, 1997, 2000), §1.125-2 (1989, 1997, 2000) and §1.125-2T (1986). Unless otherwise indicated, references to "new proposed regulations" or "these proposed regulations" mean the proposed section 125 regulations being published in this document.

The new proposed regulations reflect changes in tax law since the prior regulations were proposed, including: the change in the definition of dependent (section 152) and the addition of the following as qualified benefits: adoption assistance (section 137), additional deferred compensation benefits described in section 125(d)(1)(B), (C) and (D), Health Savings Accounts (HSAs) (sections 223, 125(d)(2)(D) and 4980G), and qualified HSA distributions from health FSAs (section 106(e)). Other changes include the prohibition against long-term care insurance and long-term care services (section 125(f)) and the addition of the key employee concentration test in section 125(b)(2).

The prior proposed regulations, §§1.125-1 and 1.125-2, provide the basic framework and requirements for cafeteria plans and elections under cafeteria plans. The prior proposed regulations also outlined the most significant rules for benefits under a health flexible spending arrangement (health FSA) offered by a cafeteria plan - the requirement that the maximum reimbursement be available at all times during the coverage period (the uniform coverage rule), the requirement of a 12-month period of coverage, the requirement that the health FSA only reimburse medical expenses, the requirement that all medical expenses be substantiated by a third party before reimbursement, the requirement that expenses be incurred during the period of coverage, and the prohibition against deferral of compensation (including the use-or-lose rule). The prior proposed regulations also provided guidelines for dependent care FSAs, and the application of section 125 to paid vacation days offered under a cafeteria plan. These remain substantially unchanged in the new proposed regulations, with certain clarifications. Finally, the prior proposed regulations included a number of Q & As addressing transitional issues relating to the enactment of section 125, as well as the application of the now-repealed section 89 (special nondiscrimination rules with respect to certain employee benefit plans). These provisions are omitted from the new proposed regulations.

I. *New Proposed § 1.125-1—Qualified and nonqualified benefits in cafeteria plans Section 125 exclusive noninclusion rule*

Section 125 provides that, except in the case of certain discriminatory benefits, no amount shall be included in the gross income of a participant in a cafeteria plan (as defined in section 125(d)) solely because, under the plan, the participant may choose among the benefits of the plan. The new proposed regulations clarify and amplify the general rule in the prior proposed regulations that section 125 is the exclusive means by which an employer can offer employees a choice between taxable and nontaxable benefits without the choice itself resulting in inclusion in gross income by the employees. When employees may elect between taxable and nontaxable benefits, this election results in gross income to employees, unless a specific Internal Revenue Code (Code) section (such as section 125) intervenes to prevent gross income inclusion. Thus, except for an election made through a cafeteria plan that satisfies section 125 or another specific Code section (such as section 132(f)(4)), any opportunity to elect among taxable and nontaxable benefits results in inclusion of the taxable benefit regardless of what benefit is elected and when the election is made. This interpretation of section 125 is consistent with the legislative history of section 125. The legislative history begins with the interim ERISA rules for cafeteria plans:

> Under . . . ERISA, an employer contribution made before January 1, 1977, to a cafeteria plan in existence on June 27, 1974, is required to be included in an employees' gross income only to the extent that the employee actually elects taxable benefits. In the case of a plan not in existence on June 27, 1974, the employer contribution is required to be included in an employee's gross income to the extent the employee could have elected taxable benefits. S. Rep. No. 1263, 95th Cong., 2d Sess. 74 (1978), reprinted in 1978 U.S.C.C.A.N. 6837; H. R. Rep. No. 1445, 95th Cong., 2d Sess. 63 (1978); H.R. Conf. Rep. No. 1800, 95th Cong., 2d Sess. 206 (1978).

The legislative history also provides:

> [G]enerally, employer contributions under a written cafeteria plan which permits employees to elect between taxable and nontaxable benefits are excluded from the gross income of an employee to the extent that nontaxable benefits are elected.
>
> S. Rep. No. 1263, 95th Cong., 2d Sess. 75 (1978), reprinted in 1978 U.S.C.C.A.N. 6838; H. R. Rep. No. 1445, 95th Cong., 2d Sess. 63 (1978). See also H.R. Conf. Rep. No. 1800, 95th Cong., 2d Sess. 206 (1978).

The legislative history to the 1984 amendments to section 125 continues:

> The cafeteria plan rules of the Code provide that a participant in a nondiscriminatory cafeteria plan will not be treated as having received a taxable benefit offered under the plan solely because the participant has the opportunity, before the benefit becomes available, to choose among the taxable and nontaxable benefits under the plan.
>
> H.R. Conf. Rep. No. 861, 98th Cong., 2d Sess. 1173 (1984), reprinted in 1984 U.S.C.C.A.N. 1861. See also H.R. Conf. Rep. No. 736, 104th Cong., 2d Sess. 295, reprinted in 1996 U.S.C.C.A.N. 2108.

The new proposed regulations provide that unless a plan satisfies the requirements of section 125 and the regulations, the plan is not a cafeteria plan. Reasons that a plan would fail to satisfy the section 125 requirements include: offering nonqualified benefits; not offering an election between at least one permitted taxable benefit and at least one qualified benefit; deferring compensation; failing to comply with the uniform coverage rule or use-or-lose rule; allowing employees to revoke elections or make new elections during a plan year, except as provided in § 1.125-4; failing to comply with substantiation requirements; paying or reimbursing expenses incurred for qualified benefits before the effective date of the cafeteria plan or before a period of coverage; allocating experience gains (forfeitures) other than as expressly allowed in the new proposed regulations; and failing to comply with grace period rules.

Definition of a cafeteria plan

The new proposed regulations provide that a cafeteria plan is a separate written plan that complies with the requirements of section 125 and the regulations, that is maintained by an employer for employees and that is operated in compliance with the requirements of section 125 and the regulations. Participants in a cafeteria plan must be permitted to choose among at least one permitted taxable benefit (for example, cash, including salary reduction) and at least one qualified benefit. A plan offering only elections among nontaxable benefits is not a cafeteria plan. Also, a plan offering only elections among taxable benefits is not a cafeteria plan. See Rev. Rul. 2002-27, Situation 2 (2002-1 CB 925), see § 601.601(d)(2)(ii)(*b*). Finally, a cafeteria plan must not provide for deferral of compensation, except as specifically permitted in section 125(d)(2)(B), (C), or (D).

Written plan

Section 125(d)(1) requires that a cafeteria plan be in writing. The cafeteria plan must be operated in accordance with the written plan terms. The new proposed regulations require that the written plan specifically describe all benefits, set forth the rules for eligibility to participate and the procedure for making elections, provide that all elections are irrevocable (except to the extend that the plan includes the optional change in status rules in § 1.125-4), and state how employer contributions may be made under the plan (for example, salary reduction or nonelective employer contributions), the maximum amount of elective contributions, and the plan year. If the plan includes a flexible spending arrangement (FSA), the written plan must include provisions complying with the uniform coverage rule and the use-or-lose rule. Because section 125(d)(1)(A) states that a cafeteria plan is a written plan under which "all participants are employees," the new proposed regulations require that the written cafeteria plan specify that only employees may participate in the cafeteria plan. The new proposed regulations also require that all provisions of the written plan apply uniformly to all participants.

Individuals who may participate in a cafeteria plan

All participants in a cafeteria plan must be employees. See section 125(d)(1)(A). These proposed regulations provide that employees include common law employees, leased employees described in section 414(n), and full-time life insurance salesmen (as defined in section 7701(a)(20)). These proposed regulations further provide that former employees (including laid-off employees and retired employees) may participate in a plan, but a plan may not be maintained predominantly for former employees. See Rev. Rul. 82-196 (1982-2 CB 53); Rev. Rul. 85-121 (1985-2 CB 57), see § 601.601(d)(2)(ii)(*b*). All employees who are treated as employed by a single employer under section 414(b), (c) or (m) are treated as employed by a single employer for purposes of section 125. See section 125(g)(4). A participant's spouse or dependents may receive benefits through a cafeteria plan although they cannot participate in the cafeteria plan.

Self-employed individuals are not treated as employees for purposes of section 125. Accordingly, the new proposed regulations make clear that sole proprietors, partners, and directors of corporations are not employees and may not participate in a cafeteria plan. In addition, the new proposed regulations clarify that 2-percent shareholders of an S corporation are not employees for purposes of section 125. The new proposed regulations provide rules for dual status individuals and individuals moving between employee and non-employee status. A self-employed individual may, however, sponsor a cafeteria plan for his or her employees.

Election between taxable and nontaxable benefits

The new proposed regulations require that a cafeteria plan offer employees an election among only permitted taxable benefits (including cash) and qualified nontaxable benefits. See section 125(d)(1)(B). For purposes of section 125, cash means cash from current compensation (including salary reduction), payment for annual leave, sick leave, or other paid time off, severance pay, property, and certain after-tax employee contributions. Distributions from qualified retirement plans are not cash or taxable benefits for purposes of section 125. See Rev. Rul. 2003-62 (2003-1 CB 1034) (distributions to former employees from a qualified employees' trust, applied to pay health insurance premiums, are includible in former employees' gross income under section 402), see § 601.601(d)(2)(ii)(*b*).

Qualified benefits

In general, in order for a benefit to be a qualified benefit for purposes of section 125, the benefit must be excludible from employees' gross income under a specific provision of the Code and must not defer compensation, except as specifically allowed in section 125(d)(2)(B), (C) or (D). Examples of qualified benefits include the following: group-term life insurance on the life of an employee (section 79); employer-provided accident and health plans, including health flexible spending arrangements, and accidental death and dismemberment policies (sections 106 and 105(b)); a dependent care assistance program (section 129); an adoption assistance program (section 137); contributions to a section 401(k) plan; contributions to certain plans maintained by educational organizations, and contributions to HSAs. Section 125(f), (d)(2)(B), (C), (D). See Notice 97-9 (1997-2 CB 35) (adoption assistance), see § 601.601(d)(2)(ii)(*b*); Notice 2004-2, Q & A-33 (2004-1 CB 269) (HSAs), see § 601.601(d)(2)(ii)(*b*). A cafeteria plan may also offer long-term and short-term disability coverage as a qualified benefit (see section 106). However, see paragraph (q) in § 1.125-1 for nonqualified benefits.

Group-term life insurance

An employer may provide group-term life insurance through a combination of methods. Generally, under section 79(a), the cost of $50,000 or less of group-term life insurance on the life of an employee provided under a policy (or policies) carried directly or indirectly by an employer is excludible from the employee's gross income. (Special rules apply to key employees if the group-term life insurance plan does not satisfy the nondiscrimination rules in section 79(d)). However, if the group-term life insurance provided to an employee by an employer or employers exceeds $50,000 (taking into account all coverage provided both through a cafeteria plan and outside a cafeteria plan), the cost of coverage exceeding coverage of $50,000 is includible in the employee's gross income. For this purpose, the cost of group-term life insurance is shown in § 1.79-3(d)(2), Table I (Table I). The Table I cost of the excess group-term life insurance (minus all after-tax contributions by the employee for group-term life insurance coverage) is includible in each covered employee's gross income. The new proposed regulations provide that the cost of group-term life insurance on the life of an employee, that either is less than or equal to the amount excludible from gross income under section 79(a) or provides coverage in excess of that amount, but not combined with any permanent benefit, is a qualified benefit that may be offered in a cafeteria plan. The new proposed regulations also provide that the entire amount of salary reduction and employer flex-credits for group-term life insurance coverage on the life of an employee is excludible from an employee's gross income.

The rule in the new proposed regulations differs from Notice 89-110 (1989-2 CB 447), see § 601.601(d)(2)(ii)(*b*). Notice 89-110 provides that an employee includes in gross income the greater of the Table I cost of group-term life insurance coverage exceeding $50,000 or the employee's salary reduction and employer flex-credits for excess group-term life insurance coverage. The new proposed regulations provide instead that the employee includes in gross income the Table I cost of the excess coverage (minus all after-tax contributions by the employee for group-term life insurance coverage) and that the entire amount of salary reduction and employer flex-credits for group-term life insurance coverage on the life of the employee is excludible from the employee's gross income. As noted in this preamble, taxpayers may rely on the new proposed regulations for guidance pending the issuance of final regulations.

Employer-provided accident and health plan

Coverage under an employer-provided accident and health plan that satisfies the requirements of section 105(b) may be provided as a qualified benefit through a cafeteria plan and is excludible from employees' gross income. Section 106; § 1.106-1. The nondiscrimination rules under section 105(h) apply to self-insured medical reimbursement arrangements (including health FSAs).

The new proposed regulations specifically permit a cafeteria plan (but not a health FSA) to pay or reimburse substantiated individual accident and health insurance premiums. See Rev. Rul. 61-146 (1961-2 CB 25), see § 601.601(d)(2)(ii)(*b*). In addition, a cafeteria plan may provide for payment of COBRA premiums for an employee.

For employer-provided accident and health plans and medical reimbursement plans, the definition of dependents is the definition in section 105(b) as amended by the Working Families Tax Relief Act of 2004 (WFTRA), Public Law 108-311, section 207(9) (118 Stat. 1166) (that is, a dependent as defined in section 152, determined without regard to section 152(b)(1), (b)(2), or (d)(1)(B)). See Notice 2004-79 (2004-2 CB 898), see § 601.601(d)(2)(ii)(*b*). For purposes of the exclusion from employees' gross income for accident and health plans and for medical reimbursement under sections 105(b) and 106, the spouse or dependent of a former employee (including a retired employee or a laid-off employee) or of a deceased employee is treated as a spouse or dependent. See Rev. Rul. 82-196 (1982-2 CB 53); Rev. Rul. 85-121 (1985-2 CB 57), see § 601.601(d)(2)(ii)(*b*).

Dependent care assistance programs and adoption assistance programs

If the requirements of section 129 are satisfied, up to $5,000 of employer-provided assistance for amounts paid or incurred by employees for dependent care is excludible from employees' gross income. The new proposed regulations outline the general requirements for providing dependent care assistance programs and adoption assistance programs under section 137 through a cafeteria plan. See Notice 97-9, section II (1997-2 CB 35), see § 601.601(d)(2)(ii)(*b*).

Cafeteria plan year

The new proposed regulations require that a cafeteria plan year must be 12 consecutive months and must be set out in the written cafeteria plan. A short plan year (or a change in plan year resulting in a short plan year) is permitted only for a valid business purpose. A change in plan year resulting in a short plan year, for other than a valid business purpose, is disregarded. If a principal purpose of a change in plan year is to circumvent the rules of section 125, the change in plan year is ineffective.

No deferral of compensation

Qualified benefits must be current benefits. In general, a cafeteria plan may not offer benefits that defer compensation or operate to defer compensation. Section 125(d)(2)(A). In general, benefits may not be carried over to a later plan year or used in one plan year to purchase benefits to be provided in a later plan year. For example, life insurance with a cash value build-up or group-term life insurance with a permanent benefit (within the meaning of § 1.79-0) defers the receipt of compensation and thus is not a qualified benefit.

The new proposed regulations clarify whether certain benefits and plan administration practices defer compensation. For example, the regulations permit an accident and health insurance policy to provide certain benefit features that apply for more than one plan year, such as reasonable lifetime limits on benefits, level premiums, premium waiver during disability, guaranteed renewability of coverage, coverage for specified accidental injury or specific diseases, and the payment of a fixed amount per day for hospitalization. But these insurance policies must not provide an investment fund or cash value to pay premiums, and no part of the premium may be held in a separate account for any beneficiary. The new proposed regulations also provide that the following benefits and practices do not defer compensation: a long-term disability policy paying benefits over more than one plan year; reasonable premium rebates or policy dividends; certain two-year lock-in vision and dental policies; certain advance payments for orthodontia; salary reduction contributions in the last month of a plan year used to pay accident and health insurance premiums for the first month of the following plan year; reimbursement of section 213(d) expenses for durable medical equipment; and allocation of experience gains (forfeitures) among participants.

Paid time off

Under the prior proposed regulations, permitted taxable benefits included various forms of paid leave. Since the prior proposed regulations were issued, many employers have recharacterized and combined vacation days, sick leave and personal days into a single category of "paid time off." The new proposed regulations use the term "paid time off" to refer to vacation days and other types of paid leave. The new proposed regulations contain the same ordering rule for elective and nonelective paid time off as set forth in Prop. § 1.125-1, Q & A-7 (1984). A plan offering an election solely between paid time off and taxable benefits is not a cafeteria plan.

Grace period

The new proposed regulations allow a written cafeteria plan to provide an optional grace period immediately following the end of each plan year, extending the period for incurring expenses for qualified benefits. A grace period may apply to one or more qualified benefits (for example, health FSA or dependent care assistance program) but in no event does it apply to paid time off or contributions to section 401(k) plans. Unused benefits or contributions for one qualified benefit may only be used to reimburse expenses incurred during the grace period for that same qualified benefit. The amount of unused benefits and contributions available during the grace period may be limited by the employer. A grace period may extend to the fifteenth day of the third month after the end of the plan year (but may be for a shorter period). Benefits or contributions not used as of the end of the grace period are forfeited under the use-or-lose rule. The grace period applies to all employees who are participants (including through COBRA), as of the last day of the plan year. Grace period rules must apply uniformly to all participants. The grace period rules in these proposed regulations are based on Notice 2005-42 (2005-1 CB 1204), modified in Notice 2007-22 (2007-10 IRB 670), see § 601.601(d)(2)(ii)(*b*), amplified in Notice 2005-86 (2005-2 CB 1075), amplified in Notice 2007-22 (2007-10 IRB 670), see § 601.601(d)(2)(ii)(*b*). For eligibility to contribute to a Health Savings Account (HSA) during a grace period, see Notice 2005-86 (2005-2 CB 1075), see § 601.601(d)(2)(ii)(*b*). For Form W-2 reporting for unused dependent care assistance used for expenses incurred during a grace period, see Notice 2005-61 (2005-2 CB 607), see § 601.601(d)(2)(ii)(*b*).

Contributions to section 401(k) plans through a cafeteria plan

A cafeteria plan may include contributions to a section 401(k) plan. Section 125(d)(2)(B). The new proposed regulations clarify the interactions between section 125 and section 401(k). Contributions to a section 401(k) plan expressed as a percentage of compensation are permitted. Pursuant to § 1.401(k)-1(a)(3)(ii), elective contributions to a section 401(k) plan may be made through automatic enrollment (that is, when the employee does not affirmatively elect cash, the employee's compensation is reduced by a fixed percentage, which is contributed to a section 401(k) plan).

Nonqualified benefits

A cafeteria plan must not offer any of the following benefits: scholarships (section 117); employer-provided meals and lodging (section 119); educational assistance (section 127); fringe benefits (section 132); long-term care insurance. See section 125(f). Long-term care services are nonqualified benefits, H.R. Conf. Rep. No. 736, 104th Cong., 2d Sess. 296, reprinted in 1996 U.S.C.C.A.N. 2109. (An HSA funded through a cafeteria plan may, however, be used to pay premiums for long-term care insurance or for long-term care services.) The new proposed regulations clarify that contributions to Archer Medical Savings Accounts (sections 220, 106(b)), group term life insurance for an employee's spouse, child or dependent, and elective deferrals to section 403(b) plans are also nonqualified benefits. A plan offering any nonqualified benefit is not a cafeteria plan. A cafeteria plan may not offer a health FSA that provides for the carryover of unused benefits. See Notice 2002-45, Part I (2002-2 CB 93); Rev. Rul. 2002-41 (2002-2 CB 75), see § 601.601(d)(2)(ii)(*b*).

After-tax employee contributions

The new proposed regulations allow a cafeteria plan to offer after-tax employee contributions for qualified benefits or paid time off. A cafeteria plan may only offer the taxable benefits specifically permitted in the new proposed regulations. Nonqualified benefits may not be offered through a cafeteria plan, even if paid with after-tax employee contributions.

Employer contributions through salary reduction

Employees electing a qualified benefit through salary reduction are electing to forego salary and instead to receive a benefit which is excludible from gross income because it is provided by employer contributions. Section 125 provides that the employee is treated as receiving the qualified benefit from the employer in lieu of the taxable benefit. A cafeteria plan may also impose reasonable fees to administer the cafeteria plan which may be paid through salary reduction. A cafeteria plan is not required to allow employees to pay for any qualified benefit with after-tax employee contributions.

II. *New Prop. § 1.125-2 - Elections in cafeteria plans*

Making, revoking and changing elections

Generally, a cafeteria plan must require employees to elect annually between taxable benefits and qualified benefits. Elections must be made before the earlier of the first day of the period of coverage or when benefits are first currently available. The determination of whether a taxable benefit is currently available does not depend on whether it has been constructively received by the employee for purposes of section 451. Annual elections generally must be irrevocable and may not be changed during the plan year. However, § 1.125-4 permits a cafeteria plan to provide for changes in elections based on certain changes in status. An employer that wishes to permit such changes in elections must incorporate the rules in § 1.125-4 in its written cafeteria plan. These proposed regulations omit the rule in Q & A-6(b) in Prop. § 1.125-2 (1989) (cessation of required contributions), because the change in status rules in § 1.125-4 superseded this provision of the 1989 proposed regulations.

If HSA contributions are made through salary reduction under a cafeteria plan, employees may prospectively elect, revoke or change salary reduction elections for HSA contributions at any time during the plan year with respect to salary that has not become currently available at the time of the election.

A cafeteria plan is permitted to include an automatic election for new employees or current employees. Rev. Rul. 2002-27 (2002-1 CB 925), see § 601.601(d)(2)(ii)(*b*). A new rule also permits a cafeteria plan to provide an optional election for new employees between cash and qualified benefits. New employees avoid gross income inclusion if they make an election within 30 days after the date of hire even if benefits provided pursuant to the election relate back to the date of hire. However, salary reduction amounts used to pay for such an election must be from compensation not yet currently available on the date of the election. Also, this special election rule for new employees does not apply to any employee who terminates employment and is rehired within 30 days after terminating employment (or who returns to employment following an unpaid leave of absence of less than 30 days).

New elections and revocations or changes in elections can be made electronically. The safe harbor for electronic elections in § 1.401(a)-21 is available. Only an employee can make an election or revoke or change his or her election. An employee's spouse or dependent may not make an election under a cafeteria plan and may not revoke or change an employee's election.

III. *New Prop. § 1.125-5-Flexible spending arrangements*

Overview

In general, a flexible spending arrangement (FSA) is a benefit designed to reimburse employees for expenses incurred for certain qualified benefits, up to a maximum amount not substantially in excess of the salary reduction and employer flex-credits allocated for the benefit. The maximum amount of reimbursement reasonably available must be less than five times the value of the coverage. Employer flex-credits are non-elective employer contributions that an employer makes available for every employee eligible to participate in the cafeteria plan, to be used at the employee's election only for one or more qualified benefits (but not as cash or other taxable benefits). The three types of FSAs are dependent care assistance, adoption assistance and medical care reimbursements (health FSA).

Uniform coverage rule

The new proposed regulations retain the rule that the maximum amount of reimbursement from a health FSA must be available at all times during the period of coverage (properly reduced as of any particular time for prior reimbursements). The uniform coverage rule does not apply to FSAs for dependent care assistance or adoption assistance.

Use-or-lose rule

An FSA must satisfy all the requirements of section 125, including the prohibition against deferring compensation. In general, as discussed under "No deferral of compensation", in order to satisfy this requirement of section 125, all benefits and contributions must be used by the end of the plan year (or grace period, if applicable), or are forfeited. The new proposed regulations continue the use-or-lose rule.

Period of coverage

The required period of coverage for all FSAs continues to be twelve months, with an exception for short plan years that satisfy the conditions in the new proposed regulations. The period of coverage and the plan year need not be the same. The beginning and end of a period of coverage is clarified. The new proposed regulations also clarify that FSAs for different qualified benefits need not have the same coverage period. See also "Grace period", discussed in this preamble. The new proposed regulations also continue to provide that expenses are incurred when services are provided. Expenses incurred before or after the period of coverage may not be reimbursed.

Health FSA

A health FSA may only reimburse certain substantiated section 213(d) medical care expenses incurred by the employee, or by the employee's spouse or dependents. A health FSA may be limited to a subset of permitted section 213(d) medical expenses (for example, a health FSA is permitted to exclude reimbursement of over-the-counter drugs described in Rev. Rul. 2003-102 (2003-2 CB 559), see § 601.601(d)(2)(ii)(*b*)). Similarly, a health FSA may be an HSA-compatible limited-purpose health FSA or post-deductible health FSA. Rev. Rul. 2004-45 (2004-1 CB 971), see § 601.601(d)(2)(ii)(*b*), amplified, Notice 2005-86 (2005-2 CB 1075). A health FSA may not reimburse premiums for accident and health insurance or long-term care insurance. See section 125(f).

A health FSA must satisfy all requirements of section 105(b), §§ 1.105-1 and 1.105-2. The section 105(h) nondiscrimination rules apply to health FSAs. All medical expenses must be substantiated before expenses are reimbursed. See *Incurring and reimbursing expenses for qualified* benefits, discussed in this preamble. The new proposed regulations also clarify when medical expenses are incurred.[1] A

---

[1] See Rev. Rul. 2005-55 (2005-2 CB 284) and Rev. Rul. 2005-24 (2005-1 CB 892), see § 601.601(d)(2)(ii)(*b*) (section 105(b) exclusion only applicable to reimbursements for medical expenses incurred by employee, or by the employee's spouse or dependents); Rev. Rul. 2002-3 (2002-1 CB 316) (purported reimbursements to employees of health insurance premiums not paid by employees and therefore impermissible); Rev. Rul. 2002-80 (2002-2 CB 925), see § 601.601(d)(2)(ii)(*b*) (so-called advance reimbursements and purported loans are impermissible); Rev. Rul. 2003-43 (2003-1 CB 935), see § 601.601(d)(2)(ii)(*b*); Notice 2006-69 (2006-31 IRB 107) (substantiation requirements for debit

cafeteria plan may limit enrollment in a health FSA to those employees who participate in the employer's accident and health plan.

Qualified HSA distributions

Section 106(e), enacted in section 302 of the Health Opportunity Patient Empowerment Act of 2006, Public Law 109-432 (120 Stat. 2922 (2006)) allows "qualified HSA distributions" from health FSAs to HSAs. Section 106(e) applies to distributions between December 20, 2006 and December 31, 2011. The proposed regulations incorporate the rules on qualified HSA distributions set forth in Notice 2007-22 (2007-10 IRB 670). See § 601.601(d)(2)(ii)(*b*).

Dependent care assistance after termination

A new optional rule permits an employer to reimburse a terminated employee's qualified dependent care expenses incurred after termination through a dependent care FSA, if all section 129 requirements are otherwise satisfied.

Experience gains

If an employee fails to use all contributions and benefits for a plan year before the end of the plan year (and the grace period, if applicable), those unused contributions and benefits are forfeited under the use-or-lose rule. Unused amounts are also known as experience gains. The new proposed regulations retain the forfeiture allocation rules in the 1989 proposed regulations, and clarify that the employer sponsoring the cafeteria plan may retain forfeitures, use forfeitures to defray expenses of administering the plan or allocate forfeitures among employees contributing through salary reduction on a reasonable and uniform basis.

FSA Administrative rules

Salary reduction contributions may be made at whatever interval the employer selects, including ratably over the plan year based on the employer's payroll periods or in equal installments at other regular intervals (for example, quarterly installments). These rules must apply uniformly to all participants.

IV. *New Prop. § 1.125-6-Substantiation of expenses for all cafeteria plans Incurring and reimbursing expenses for qualified benefits*

The new proposed regulations provide that only expenses for qualified benefits incurred after the later of the effective date or the adoption date of the cafeteria plan are permitted to be reimbursed under the cafeteria plan. Similarly, if a plan amendment adds a new qualified benefit, only expenses incurred after the later of the effective date or the adoption date are eligible for reimbursement.[2] This rule applies to all qualified benefits. Similarly, a cafeteria plan may pay or reimburse only expenses for qualified benefits incurred during a participant's period of coverage.

Substantiation and reimbursement of expenses for qualified benefits

The new proposed regulations provide, after an employee incurs an expense for a qualified benefit during the coverage period, the expense must first be substantiated before the expense may be paid or reimbursed. All expenses must be substantiated (substantiating only a limited number of total claims, or not substantiating claims below a certain dollar amount does not satisfy the requirements in the new proposed regulations). See § 1.105-2; Rul. 2003-80; Rev. Rul. 2003-43 (2002-1 CB 935), see § 601.601(d)(2)(ii)(*b*); Notice 2006-69 (2006-31 IRB 107), Notice 2007-2 (2007-2 IRB 254). FSAs for dependent care assistance and adoption assistance must follow the substantiation procedures applicable to health FSAs.

Debit cards

The new proposed regulations incorporate previously issued guidance on substantiating, paying and reimbursing expenses for section 213(d) medical care incurred at a medical care provider when payment is made with a debit card. Rev. Rul. 2003-43 (2003-1 CB 935), amplified, Notice 2006-69 (2006-31 IRB 107), Notice 2007-2 (2007-2 IRB 254); Rev. Proc. 98-25 (1998-1 CB 689), see § 601.601(d)(2)(ii)(*b*). Among the permissible substantiation methods are copayment matches, recurring expenses, and real-time substantiation. The new proposed regulations also allow point-of-sale substantiation through matching inventory information with a list of section 213(d) medical expenses. The employer is responsible for ensuring that the inventory information approval system complies with the new regulations and with the recordkeeping requirements in section 6001. Rev. Rul. 2003-43 (2003-1 CB 935), amplified, Notice 2006-69 (2006-31 IRB 107), Notice 2007-2 (2007-2 IRB 254); Rev. Proc. 98-25 (1998-1 CB 689), see § 601.601(d)(2)(ii)(*b*). The new proposed regulations also provide rules under which an FSA may pay or reimburse dependent care expenses using debit cards.

Pursuant to prior guidance (in Notice 2006-69 (2006-31 IRB 107), amplified, Notice 2007-2 (2007-2 IRB 254)), for plan years beginning after December 31, 2006, the recordkeeping requirements described in paragraph (f) in § 1.125-6 apply (that is, responsibility of employers relying on the inventory information approval system for health FSA debit cards to ensure that the system complies with the new proposed recordkeeping requirements, including Rev. Proc. 98-25 (1998-1 CB 689), Notice 2006-69 (2006-31 IRB 107), amplified, Notice 2007-2 (2007-2 IRB 254). For health FSA debit card

(Footnote Continued)

cards), amplified in Notice 2007-2 (2007-2 IRB 254), see § 601.601(d)(2)(ii)(*b*).

[2] See *American Family Mut. Ins. Co. v. United States*, 815 F. Supp. 1206 (W.D. Wis. 1992); *Wollenberg v. United States*, 75 F. Supp.2d 1032 (D. Neb. 1999); Rev. Rul. 2002-58 (2002-2 CB 541), see § 601.601(d)(2)(ii)(*b*); Notice 97-9, section II (adoption assistance).

transactions occurring on or before December 31, 2007, all supermarkets, grocery stores, discount stores and wholesale clubs that do not have a medical care merchant category code (as described in Rev. Rul. 2003-43 (2003-2 CB 935) are nevertheless deemed to be an "other medical provider" as described in Rev. Rul. 2003-43. (For a list of merchant category codes, see Rev. Proc. 2004-43 (2004-2 CB 124).) During this time period, mail-order vendors and web-based vendors that sell prescription drugs are also deemed to be an "other medical provider" as described in Rev. Rul. 2003-43. After December 31, 2008, health FSA debit cards may not be used at stores with the Drug Stores and Pharmacies merchant category code unless (1) the store participates in the inventory information approval system described in Notice 2006-69, or (2) on a store location by store location basis, 90 percent of the store's gross receipts during the prior taxable year consisted of items which qualify as expenses for medical care under section 213(d) (including nonprescription medications described in Rev. Rul. 2003-102 (2003-2 CB 559)). Notice 2006-69 (2006-31 IRB 107), amplified, Notice 2007-2 (2007-2 IRB 254).

V. *New Prop. § 1.125-7-Nondiscrimination rules*

Discriminatory benefits provided to highly compensated participants and individuals and key employees are included in these employees' gross income. See section 125(b), (c). The new proposed regulations reflect changes in tax law since Prop. § 1.125-1, Q & A-9 through 13 and 19 were proposed in 1984, including the key employee concentration test, statutory nontaxable benefits (enacted in the Deficit Reduction Act of 1984 (DEFRA), Public Law 98-369, section 531(b), (98 Stat. 881(1984)), and the change in definition of dependent in WFTRA.

The new proposed regulations provide additional guidance on the cafeteria plan nondiscrimination rules, including definitions of key terms, guidance on the eligibility test and the contributions and benefits tests, descriptions of employees allowed to be excluded from testing and a safe harbor nondiscrimination test for premium-only-plans.

Specifically, the new proposed regulations define several key terms, including highly compensated individual or participant (consistent with the section 414(q) definition of highly compensated employee), officer, five percent shareholder, key employee and compensation. The new proposed regulations also provide guidance on the nondiscrimination as to eligibility requirement by incorporating some of the rules under section 410(b) (specifically the rules under § 1.410(b)-4(b) and (c) dealing with reasonable classification, the safe harbor percentage test and the unsafe harbor percentage component of the facts and circumstances test).

The new proposed regulations also provide additional guidance on the contributions and benefits test and, unlike the prior proposed regulations, the new proposed regulations provide an objective test to determine when the actual election of benefits is discriminatory. Specifically, the new proposed regulations provide that a cafeteria plan must give each similarly situated participant a uniform opportunity to elect qualified benefits, and that highly compensated participants must not actually disproportionately elect qualified benefits. Finally, the new rules provide guidance on the safe harbor for cafeteria plans providing health benefits and create a safe harbor for premium-only-plans that satisfy certain requirements.

The example in Prop. § 1.125-1, Q & A-11 (1984) is deleted because it concerns a qualified legal services plan, which is no longer a qualified benefit.

Other issues

These proposed regulations provide guidance under section 125 (26 U.S.C. 125). Other statutes may impose additional requirements (for example, the Employee Retirement Income Security Act of 1974 (ERISA) (29 U.S.C. 1000), the Health Insurance Portability and Accountability Act of 1996 (HIPAA), (sections 9801-9803); and the continuation coverage requirements under the Consolidated Omnibus Budget Reconciliation Act of 1985 (COBRA) (section 4980B).

Proposed Effective Date

With the exceptions noted in the "Effect on other documents" section of this preamble and under the "Debit cards" section of the preamble, it is proposed that these regulations apply for plan years beginning on or after January 1, 2009. Taxpayers may rely on these regulations for guidance pending the issuance of final regulations. Prior published guidance on qualified benefits under sections 79, 105, 106, 129, 137 and 223 that is affected by these proposed regulations remains applicable through the effective date of the final regulations (except as modified in "Effect on other documents" section of this preamble).

Effect on Other Documents

Notice 89-110 (1989-2 CB 447), see § 601.601(d)(2)(ii)(*b*), states that where group-term life insurance provided to an employee by an employer exceeds $50,000, the employee includes in gross income the greater of the cost of group-term life insurance shown in § 1.79-3(d)(2), Table I (Table I) on the excess coverage or the employee's salary reduction and employer flex-credits for excess coverage. Notice 89-110 is modified, effective as of the date the proposed regulations are published in the **Federal Register**.

Published guidance under § 105(b) states that if any person has the right to receive cash or any other taxable or nontaxable benefit under a health FSA other than the reimbursement of section 213(d) medical expenses of the employee, employee's spouse or employee's dependents, then all distributions made from the arrangement are included in the employee's gross income, even amounts paid to reimburse medical care. See Rev. Rul. 2006-36 (2006-36 IRB 353); Rev. Rul. 2005-24 (2005-1 CB 892); Rev. Rul. 2003-102 (2003-2 CB 559); Notice 2002-45 (2002-2 CB 93); Rev. Rul. 2002-41 (2002-2 CB

75); Rev. Rul. 69-141 (1969-1 CB 48). New section 106(e) provides that a health FSA will not fail to satisfy the requirements of sections 105 or 106 merely because the plan provides for a qualified HSA distribution. Amounts rolled into an HSA may be used for purposes other than reimbursing the section 213(d) medical expenses of the employee, spouse or dependents. Accordingly, Rev. Rul. 2006-36, Rev. Rul. 2005-24, Rev. Rul. 2003-102, Notice 2002-45, Rev. Rul. 2002-41, and Rev. Rul. 69-141 are modified with respect to qualified HSA distributions described in section 106(e). See Notice 2007-22 (2007-10 IRB 670), see § 601.601(d)(2)(ii)(*b*).

Special Analyses

It has been determined that this notice of proposed rulemaking is not a significant regulatory action as defined in Executive Order 12866. Therefore, a regulatory assessment is not required. It also has been determined that section 553(b) of the Administrative Procedure Act (5 U.S.C. chapter 5) does not apply to this regulation. It is hereby certified that the collection of information in this regulation will not have a significant economic impact on a substantial number of small entities. This certification is based on the fact that the regulations will only minimally increase the burdens on small entities. The requirements under these regulations relating to maintaining a section 125 cafeteria plan are a minimal additional burden independent of the burdens encompassed under existing rules for underlying employee benefit plans, which exist whether or not the benefits are provided through a cafeteria plan. In addition, most small entities that will maintain cafeteria plans already use a third-party plan administrator to administer the cafeteria plan. The collection of information required in these regulations, which is required to comply with the existing substantiation requirements of sections 105, 106, 129 and 125, and the recordkeeping requirements of section 6001, will only minimally increase the third-party administrator's burden with respect to the cafeteria plan. Therefore, an analysis under the Regulatory Flexibility Act (5 U.S.C. chapter 6) is not required. Pursuant to section 7805(f) of the Internal Revenue Code, this proposed regulation has been submitted to the Chief Counsel for Advocacy of the Small Business Administration for comment on its impact on small business.

Comments and Public Hearing

Before these proposed regulations are adopted as final regulations, consideration will be given to any written comments (a signed original and eight (8) copies) or electronic comments that are submitted timely to the IRS. The IRS and Treasury Department specifically request comments on the clarity of the proposed rules and how they can be made easier to understand. In addition, comments are requested on the following issues:

1. Whether, consistent with section 125 of the Internal Revenue Code, multiple employers (other than members of a controlled group described in section 125(g)(4)) may sponsor a single cafeteria plan;

2. Whether salary reduction contributions may be based on employees' tips and how that would work;

3. For cafeteria plans adopting the change in status rules in § 1.125-4, when a participant has a change in status and changes his or her salary reduction amount, how should the participant's uniform coverage amount be computed after the change in status.

All comments will be available for public inspection and copying.

A public hearing has been scheduled for November 15, 2007, beginning at 10 a.m. in the Auditorium, Internal Revenue Service, 1111 Constitution Avenue, NW., Washington, DC. Due to building security procedures, visitors must enter at the Constitution Avenue entrance. In addition, all visitors must present photo identification to enter the building. Because of access restrictions, visitors will not be admitted beyond the immediate entrance area more than 30 minutes before the hearing starts. For information about having your name placed on the building access list to attend the hearing, see the "FOR FURTHER INFORMATION CONTACT" section of this preamble.

The rules of 26 CFR 601.601(a)(3) apply to the hearing. Persons who wish to present oral comments at the hearing must submit written or electronic comments and an outline of the topics to be discussed and the amount of time to be devoted to each topic (a signed original and eight (8) copies) by October 25, 2007. A period of 10 minutes will be allotted to each person for making comments. An agenda showing the scheduling of the speakers will be prepared after the deadline for receiving outlines has passed. Copies of the agenda will be available free of charge at the hearing.

Drafting Information

The principal author of these proposed regulations is Mireille T. Khoury, Office of Division Counsel/Associate Chief Counsel (Tax Exempt and Government Entities), Internal Revenue Service. However, personnel from other offices of the IRS and Treasury Department participated in their development.

[¶ 49,318] Proposed Amendments of Regulations (REG-143397-05), published in the Federal Register on August 22, 2007 (corrected 11/6/2007).

[Code Secs. 704 and 737]

Partnerships: Distributions: Allocation of pre-contribution gain and loss: Assets-over partnership merger.—Amendments of Reg. §§ 1.704-3, 1.704-4, 1.737-1, 1.737-2 and 1.737-5, relating to the applications of Code Secs. 704(c)(1)(B) and 737 to distributions of property after two partnerships engage in an assets-over merger, are proposed.

AGENCY: Internal Revenue Service (IRS), Treasury.

ACTION: Notice of proposed regulations and notice of public hearing.

SUMMARY: This document contains regulations that provide rules concerning the application of sections 704(c)(1)(B) and 737 to distributions of property after two partnerships engage in an assets-over merger. The proposed regulations affect partnerships and their partners. This document also provides a notice of public hearing on these proposed regulations.

DATES: Written or electronic comments must be received by November 20, 2007. Outlines of the topic to be discussed at the public hearing scheduled for December 5, 2007 at 10 a.m. must be received by November 21, 2007.

ADDRESSES: Send submissions to: CC:PA:LPD:PR (REG-143397-05), room 5203, Internal Revenue Service, PO Box 7604, Ben Franklin Station, Washington DC 20044. Submissions may be hand delivered Monday through Friday, between the hours of 8 a.m. and 4 p.m. to CC:PA:LPD:PR (REG-143397-05), Courier's Desk, Internal Revenue Service, 1111 Constitution Avenue, NW., Washington, DC or sent electronically via the Federal eRulemaking Portal at *http://www.regulations.gov* (IRS REG-143397-05). The public hearing will be held in the Auditorium, Internal Revenue Building, 1111 Constitution Avenue NW, Washington, DC.

FOR FURTHER INFORMATION CONTACT: Concerning the proposed regulations, Jason Smyczek or Laura Fields (202) 622-3050, concerning submissions of comments, the hearing, and/or to be placed on the building access list to attend the hearing, Richard Hurst, *Richard.A.Hurst@irscounsel.treas.gov*, (202) 622-7180 (not toll-free numbers).

SUPPLEMENTAL INFORMATION:

Background

Section 704(c)(1)(B) provides that a partner that contributes section 704(c) property to a partnership must recognize gain or loss on the distribution of such property to another partner within seven years of its contribution to the partnership in an amount equal to the gain or loss that would have been allocated to such partner under section 704(c) if the distributed property had been sold by the partnership to the distributee partner for its fair market value at the time of the distribution.

Section 737(a) provides that a partner that contributes section 704(c) property to the partnership and then receives a distribution of property (other than money) within seven years of its contribution must recognize gain in an amount equal to the lesser of (1) the excess (if any) of (A) the fair market value of property (other than money) received in the distribution over (B) the adjusted basis of the partner's interest in the partnership immediately before the distribution reduced (but not below zero) by the amount of money received in the distribution, or (2) the net precontribution gain of the partner.

Section 737(b) provides that for purposes of section 737, the term "net precontribution gain" means the net gain (if any) which would have been recognized by the distributee partner under section 704(c)(1)(B) if all property which (1) had been contributed to the partnership by the distributee partner within seven years of the distribution, and (2) is held by the partnership immediately before the distribution, had been distributed by the partnership to another partner.

Rev. Rul. 2004-43, 2004-1 CB 842, (see § 601.601(d)(2) of this chapter) issued on April 12, 2004, addressed the application of sections 704(c)(1)(B) and 737 in an assets-over partnership merger described in § 1.708-1(c)(3)(i). Rev. Rul. 2004-43 held that section 704(c)(1)(B) applies to newly created section 704(c) gain or loss in property contributed by the transferor partnership to the transferee partnership in an assets-over partnership merger. The revenue ruling also held that for purposes of section 737(b), net precontribution gain includes newly created section 704(c) gain or loss in property contributed by the transferor partnership to the transferee partnership in an assets-over partnership merger. In addition, the revenue ruling held that section 704(c)(1)(B) will not apply to, and, for purposes of section 737, net precontribution gain will not include, reverse section 704(c) gain or loss resulting from a revaluation of property of the transferee partnership.

Some commentators argued that Rev. Rul. 2004-43 was not consistent with the existing regulations under sections 704(c)(1)(B) and 737, and that the conclusions contained in the ruling should not be applied retroactively. In response to these comments, the Treasury Department and the IRS issued Notice 2005-15, 2005-7 IRB 527, (see § 601.601(d)(2) of this chapter) indicating their intent to issue regulations under sections 704(c)(1)(B) and 737 implementing the principles of the ruling, and issued Rev. Rul. 2005-10, 2005-7 IRB 492, (see § 601.601(d)(2) of this chapter) officially revoking Rev. Rul. 2004-43. The Notice provided that any such regulations would be effective for distributions made after January 19, 2005.

Explanation of Provisions

A. Assets-Over Partnership Mergers

These proposed regulations implement the principles articulated in Rev. Rul. 2004-43. The proposed regulations under § 1.704-4(c)(4) and § 1.737-2(b) provide that in an assets-over merger, sections 704(c)(1)(B) and 737 do not apply to the transfer by a partnership (the transferor partnership) of all of its assets and liabilities to another partnership (the transferee partnership), followed by a distribution of the interests in the transferee partnership in liquidation of the transferor partnership as part of the same plan or arrangement.

The proposed regulations, however, provide that section 704(c)(1)(B) applies to a subsequent distribution by the transferee partnership of section 704(c) property contributed in the assets-over merger by the transferor partnership to the transferee partnership. The proposed regulations also provide that section 737 applies when a partner of the transferor partnership receives a subsequent distribution of property (other than money) from the transferee partnership.

The proposed regulations provide that for property contributed to the transferor partnership (original contribution), the amount of original section 704(c) gain or loss is the difference between the property's fair market value and the contributing partner's adjusted basis at the time of contribution to the extent such difference has not been eliminated by section 704(c) allocations, prior revaluations, or in connection with the merger. In the case of property contributed with original section 704(c) loss, section 704(c)(1)(C) which was added by the American Jobs Creation Act of 2004 provides special rules for determining the basis of the property contributed. The Treasury Department and IRS are currently developing guidance that will implement the provisions of section 704(c)(1)(C). Thus, the proposed regulations do not address the impact of section 704(c)(1)(C) in applying these rules. However, when finalized, these regulations will clarify the application of section 704(c)(1)(C) to these rules.

The proposed regulations provide that the seven year period will not restart with respect to the original section 704(c) gain or loss as a result of the merger. Accordingly, a subsequent distribution by the transferee partnership of property with original section 704(c) gain or loss is subject to sections 704(c)(1)(B) and 737 if the distribution occurs within seven years of the contribution of the property to the transferor partnership (original contribution). However, with respect to new section 704(c) gain or loss, the regulations provide that the seven-year period in sections 704(c)(1)(B) and 737 begins on the date of merger. Thus, a subsequent distribution by the transferee partnership of property with new section 704(c) gain or loss is subject to sections 704(c)(1)(B) and 737 if the distribution occurs within seven years of the merger.

The regulations further provide that no original section 704(c) gain or loss will be recognized under section 704(c)(1)(B) or section 737 if property that was originally contributed to the transferor partnership is distributed to the original contributor. If property has new section 704(c) gain or loss, then a subsequent distribution of such property within seven years of the merger to one of the former partners of the transferor partnership (former partner) is subject to section 704(c)(1)(B) only to the extent of the other former partners' shares of such gain or loss.

New section 704(c) gain or loss shall be allocated among the partners of the transferor partnership in a manner consistent with the principles of §§ 1.704-3(a)(7) and newly designated 1.704-3(a)(10) (previously § 1.704-3(a)(9)). In addition, the partners of the transferor partnership are deemed to have contributed an undivided interest in the assets of the partnership. The proposed regulations provide that the determination of the partners' undivided interest for this purpose shall be made by the transferor partnership using any reasonable method. The Treasury Department and the IRS request comments on methods that should be considered reasonable for this purpose.

The proposed regulations also provide that if less than all of a section 704(c) property is distributed, then a proportionate amount of original and new section 704(c) gain or loss must be recognized under section 704(c)(1)(B). Similarly, if gain is required to be recognized under section 737, a proportionate amount of original and new section 704(c) gain must be recognized under section 737. Each partner must recognize its respective proportionate share of gain or loss required to be recognized.

The proposed regulations further provide a subsequent merger rule. This rule provides that if the transferee partnership is subsequently merged (a subsequent merger) the new section 704(c) gain or loss that resulted from the original merger shall be subject to section 704(c)(1)(B) for seven years from the time of the original merger and the new section 704(c) gain or loss that resulted from the subsequent merger will be subject to section 704(c)(1)(B) for seven years from the time of the subsequent merger.

In addition, the proposed regulations provide an identical ownership and a de minimis change in ownership exception to sections 704(c)(1)(B) and 737 with regard to assets-over partnership mergers. Under the identical ownership exception, section 704(c)(1)(B) will not apply to, and section 737 net precontribution gain will not include, new section 704(c) gain or loss in any property contributed in an assets-over partnership merger where the ownership of both partnerships is identical. In order for merging partnerships to qualify for the identical ownership exception, each partner must own identical interests in book capital and in each item of income, gain, loss, deductions and credit, and identical shares of distributions and liabilities in each of the transferor and transferee partnerships. Where ownership of both partnerships is identical, the merger more accurately represents a change in form, and should have no substantive tax consequences. The same principles apply where the change in ownership is de minimis. For purposes of the de minimis exception, a difference in ownership is de minimis if ninety seven percent of the interests in book capital, items of income, gain, loss, deduction and credit and share of distributions and liabilities of the transferor partnership and transferee partnership are owned by the same owners in the same proportions.

Proposed regulations under § 1.704-3(c)(9) provide that taxpayers may distinguish between the original and new portions of section 704(c) gain or loss. The proposed regulations provide that the transferee partnership may continue to use the section 704(c) allocation method adopted by the transferor partnership with respect to original section 704(c) property, or it may adopt another reasonable section 704(c) method. In addition, the transferee partnership may adopt any reasonable section 704(c) method with respect to new section 704(c) gain or loss. With respect to both the original and the new section 704(c) gain or loss, the transferee partnership must use a reasonable method that is consistent with the purpose of sections 704(b) and 704(c).

B. Miscellaneous Provisions

As part of this proposed regulation, the Treasury Department and the IRS are also making certain regulatory changes to reflect statutory changes that occurred as part of the Taxpayer Relief Act of 1997 (Public Law 105-34). Effective June 8, 1997, Congress lengthened the period of time from five years to seven for accounting for section 704(c) gain or loss with respect to distributions. Consistent with the statutory changes, various provisions in § 1.704-4 and § 1.737-1 have been amended.

Effective Dates

Except as otherwise provided, these proposed regulations will be effective for any distributions of property after January 19, 2005, if such property was contributed in an assets-over merger after May 3, 2004. Provisions relating to the change in the regulations in § 1.704-4 and § 1.737-1 from the previous five-year rule to the seven-year rule will be effective August 22, 2007.

Special Analyses

It has been determined that this notice of proposed rulemaking is not a significant regulatory action as defined in Executive Order 12866. Therefore, a regulatory assessment is not required. It has also been determined that section 553(b) of the Administrative Procedure Act (5 U.S.C. chapter 5) does not apply to these regulations, and because the regulation does not impose a collection of information on small entities, the Regulatory Flexibility Act (5 U.S.C. chapter 6) does not apply. Pursuant to section 7805(f) of the Code, this notice of proposed rulemaking will be submitted to the Chief Counsel for Advocacy of the Small Business Administration for comment on its impact on small business.

Comments and Public Hearing

Before these proposed regulations are adopted as final regulations, consideration will be given to any written comments (a signed original and eight (8) copies) or electronic comments that are submitted timely to the IRS. The Treasury Department and IRS request comments on the clarity of the proposed rules and how they may be made easier to understand. All comments will be available for public inspection and copying.

A public hearing has been scheduled for **December 5, 2007**, 10 a.m. in the Auditorium, Internal Revenue Building, 1111 Constitution Avenue, N.W., Washington, DC. Due to building security procedures, visitors must enter at the Constitution Avenue entrance. In addition, all visitors must present photo identification to enter the building. Because of access restrictions, visitors will not be admitted beyond the immediate entrance area more than 15 minutes before the hearing starts. For information about having your name placed on the building access list to attend the hearing, see the "FOR FURTHER INFORMATION CONTACT" section of this preamble.

The rules of 26 CFR 601.601(a)(3) apply to the hearing. Persons who wish to present oral comments at the hearing must submit written or electronic comments by November 20, 2007, and an outline of the topics to be discussed and time to be devoted to each topic (a signed original and eight (8) copies) by November 21, 2007. A period of 10 minutes will be allotted to each person for making comments. An agenda showing the scheduling of the speakers will be prepared after the deadline for receiving outlines has passed. Copies of the agenda will be available free of charge at the hearing.

Drafting Information

The principal authors of these proposed regulations are Jason Smyczek and Laura Fields, Office of the Associate Chief Counsel (Passthroughs and Special Industries), IRS. However, other personnel from the IRS and the Treasury Department participated in their development.

[¶ 49,322] Proposed Amendments of Regulations (REG-129916-07), published in the Federal Register on September 26, 2007.

[Code Secs. 6011 and 6111]

Proposed regulations: Patenting of tax advice or tax strategies: Reportable transactions: Disclosure: List maintenance.—Amendments of Reg. § 1.6011-4 and 301.6111-3, relating to the disclosure of reportable transactions under Code Secs. 6011 and 6111, are proposed.

AGENCY: Internal Revenue Service (IRS), Treasury.

ACTION: Notice of proposed rulemaking.

SUMMARY: This document contains proposed regulations that provide rules relating to the disclosure of reportable transactions under sections 6011 and 6111 of the Internal Revenue Code (Code). These regulations propose to add the patented transactions category of reportable transaction to the regulations under § 1.6011-4 of the Income Tax Regulations. The regulations also include conforming changes to the rules relating to the disclosure of reportable transactions by material advisors under section 6111. The regulations affect taxpayers participating in reportable transactions under section 6011, material advisors responsible for disclosing reportable transactions under section 6111, and material advisors responsible for keeping lists under section 6112.

DATES: Written or electronic comments and requests for a public hearing must be received by December 26, 2007.

ADDRESSES: Send submissions to: CC:PA:LPD:PR (REG-129916-07), room 5203, Internal Revenue Service, PO Box 7604, Ben Franklin Station, Washington, DC 20044. Submissions may be hand-delivered Monday through Friday between the hours of 8 a.m. and 4 p.m. to CC:PA:LPD:PR (REG-129916-07), Courier's Desk, Internal Revenue Service, 1111 Constitution Avenue, NW., Washington, DC, or sent electronically, via the Federal eRulemaking Portal at www.regulations.gov (IRS-REG-129916-07).

FOR FURTHER INFORMATION CONTACT: Concerning the proposed regulations, Michael H. Beker or Charles D. Wien, (202) 622-3070; concerning the submissions of comments and requests for hearing, Richard Hurst at Richard.A.Hurst@irscounsel.treas.gov or (202) 622-7180 (not toll-free numbers).

SUPPLEMENTARY INFORMATION:

Background

This document proposes to amend 26 CFR parts 1 and 301 by adding the patented transactions category of reportable transaction to the rules under section 6011 and by making conforming changes to the rules relating to the disclosure of reportable transactions by material advisors under section 6111.

On November 1, 2006, the IRS and Treasury Department issued a notice of proposed rulemaking and temporary and final regulations under sections 6011, 6111, and 6112 (REG-103038-05, REG-103039-05, REG-103043-05, TD 9295) (the November 2006 regulations). The November 2006 regulations were published in the **Federal Register** (71 FR 64488, 71 FR 64496, 71 FR 64501, 71 FR 64458) on November 2, 2006. In the preamble to those proposed regulations, the IRS and Treasury Department expressed concern, shared by many commentators, regarding the patenting of tax advice or tax strategies that have the potential for tax avoidance. A patent for tax advice or a tax strategy might be interpreted by taxpayers as approval by the IRS and Treasury Department of the transaction, which might impede the efforts of the IRS and Treasury Department to obtain information regarding tax avoidance transactions and have an impact on effective tax administration. Consequently, the IRS and Treasury Department requested comments regarding the creation of a new category of reportable transaction to address these concerns.

The IRS and Treasury Department received written public comments responding to the proposed regulations and held a public hearing regarding the proposed rules on March 20, 2007. After consideration of the comments received, the IRS and Treasury Department are issuing these proposed regulations with respect to patented transactions. Upon publication of final regulations, these regulations will be effective for transactions entered into on or after the date of publication of this notice of proposed rulemaking.

Explanation of Provisions

In response to the request for comments, the IRS and Treasury Department received five comments regarding the creation of a new category of reportable transaction to address the patenting of tax advice or tax strategies. One commentator suggested that the patenting of tax advice or tax strategies should not be addressed through the addition of a new category of reportable transaction. The commentator suggested that the IRS should require a form of notification or have a disclosure requirement informing the IRS when the United States Patent and Trademark Office (USPTO) issues a tax strategy patent. The commentator suggested that this could be accomplished through cooperation between the IRS and the USPTO. To the extent cooperation does not result in the necessary disclosures, the commentator suggested that the current reportable transaction regime or another mechanism could provide the necessary notifications and disclosures.

One commentator suggested that the patenting of tax advice or tax strategies should be addressed through the transaction of interest category of reportable transaction under § 1.6011-4(b)(6). The commentator suggested that each application for, or grant of a patent be automatically included within the scope of a transaction of interest, thereby requiring anyone who "participated" in the transaction to file a disclosure statement. In addition, the commentator suggested that the party who files an application for a patent, or for whom a patent is granted, be considered a material advisor, as defined in § 301.6111-3(b) of the Procedure and Administration Regulations. The commentator noted that treating the patent applicant or holder as a material advisor would obligate that party to file a disclosure statement under § 301.6111-3 and also to maintain an investor list under § 301.6112-1. Further, the commentator proposed that each material advisor should be required to disclose to each taxpayer on that material advisor's list of investors that the transaction is a transaction of interest and that the taxpayer is required to disclose the transaction.

Two commentators suggested the creation of a new category of reportable transaction for taxpayers who participate in a transaction that uses a patented tax strategy for each year in which the taxpayer's return reports items attributable to such transaction. The two commentators both suggested treating the patent holder as a material advisor within the meaning of section 6111. One of the two commentators suggested lowering the gross income threshold amounts for material advisors in § 301.6111-3(b)(3). One of the commentators recommended that a material advisor should only include the owner of the patent and advisors who pay fees directly or indirectly for the patented tax strategy or advice. This commentator also recommended that the disclosure obligations be narrowly construed so as not to apply to those taxpayers and material advisors who implement patented tax strategies and provided advice without any knowledge that the tax strategy or advice has been patented.

Another commentator also recommended limiting the scope of a category of reportable transaction for patents so that the category applies only to those taxpayers and material advisors who have a legal right to use the patented tax strategy or tax advice. Finally, commentators recommended excluding from the category of reportable transaction the use of patented tax methods or processes for complying with return preparation and filing and other administrative requirements.

After careful consideration of the comments received, the IRS and Treasury Department continue to be concerned about the patenting of tax advice or tax strategies and believe that adding a new category of reportable transaction to the section 6011 regulations for patented transactions will assist the IRS and Treasury Department in obtaining disclosures of tax avoidance transactions and in providing effective tax administration. Under the new category of reportable transactions, the "patented transaction" is a transaction for which a taxpayer pays (directly or indirectly) a fee in any amount to a patent holder or the patent holder's agent for the legal right to use a tax planning method that the taxpayer knows or has reason to know is the subject of the patent. A patented transaction also is a transaction for which a taxpayer (the patent holder or the patent holder's agent) has the right to payment for another person's use of a tax planning method that is the subject of the patent.

The proposed regulations exclude mathematical calculations or mechanical assistance in the preparation of tax returns from the patented transaction category of reportable transactions. Thus, a patented transaction does not include patent-protected tax preparation software or other tools used to perform or model mathematical calculations or to provide mechanical assistance in the preparation of tax or information returns.

For purposes of the new patented transaction category, a taxpayer has participated in a patented transaction if the taxpayer's tax return reflects a tax benefit from the transaction (including a deduction for fees paid in any amount to the patent holder or patent holder's agent). A taxpayer also has participated in a patented transaction if the taxpayer is the patent holder or patent holder's agent and the taxpayer's tax return reflects a tax benefit in relation to obtaining a patent for a tax planning method (including any deduction for amounts paid to the United States Patent and Trademark Office as required by title 35 of the United States Code and attorney's fees) or reflects income from a payment received from another person for the use of the tax planning method that is the subject of the patent.

These regulations also describe when a person is a material advisor with respect to a patented transaction under section 6111. Because of the nature of patented transactions and how those transactions are marketed, the threshold amount as described in section 6111(b) is reduced from $50,000 to $250 and from $250,000 to $500. A person who is a material advisor with respect to a patented transaction will have a list maintenance obligation under section 6112.

Special Analyses

It has been determined that these regulations are not a significant regulatory action as defined in Executive Order 12866. Therefore, a regulatory assessment is not required. It has also been determined that section 553(b) of the Administrative Procedure Act (5 U.S.C. chapter 5) does not apply to these regulations. It is hereby certified that the collection of information in these regulations will not have a significant economic impact on a substantial number of small entities. This certification is based on the fact that most information is already required to be reported on the disclosure statement referenced in the regulation and approved under OMB control number 1545-0074; the new information required by these proposed regulations add little or no new burden to the existing requirements. Therefore, a Regulatory Flexibility Analysis under the provisions of the Regulatory Flexibility Act (5 U.S.C. chapter 6) is not required. Pursuant to section 7805(f) of the Code, this notice of proposed rulemaking will be submitted to the Chief Counsel for Advocacy of the Small Business Administration for comment on its impact on small business.

Comments and Requests for a Public Hearing

Before these proposed regulations are adopted as final regulations, consideration will be given to any written comments (a signed original and eight (8) copies) or electronic comments that are submitted timely to the IRS. The IRS and Treasury Department specifically request comments on the clarity of the proposed rules, how they can be made easier to understand, and the administrability of the rules in the proposed regulations. All comments will be available for public inspection and copying. A public hearing will be scheduled if requested in writing by any person that submits timely written or electronic comments. If a public hearing is scheduled, notice of the date, time, and place for the public hearing will be published in the **Federal Register.**

Drafting Information

The principal authors of these regulations are Michael H. Beker and Charles D. Wien, Office of the Associate Chief Counsel (Passthroughs and Special Industries). However, other personnel from the IRS and Treasury Department participated in their development.

[¶49,326] Proposed Amendments of Regulations (REG-140206-06), published in the Federal Register on October 17, 2007 (corrected 11/7/2007).

[Code Sec. 1441]

Withholding of tax: Corporate distributions: Procedures.—Amendments of Reg. §1.1441-3, regarding a withholding agent's obligation to withhold and report tax under Chapter 3 of the Internal Revenue Code when there is a distribution in redemption of stock of a corporation that is actively traded on an established financial market, are proposed.

AGENCY: Internal Revenue Service (IRS), Treasury.

ACTION: Notice of proposed rulemaking and notice of public hearing.

SUMMARY: This document contains proposed regulations regarding a withholding agent's obligation to withhold and report tax under Chapter 3 of the Internal Revenue Code when there is a distribution in redemption of stock of a corporation that is actively traded on an established financial market. Specifically, the proposed regulations provide an escrow procedure that a withholding agent must apply while making the determination under section 302 as to whether the distribution in redemption of the stock held by a foreign shareholder is treated as a dividend subject to withholding, or a distribution in part or full payment in exchange for stock. These regulations would affect corporations that are actively traded on an established financial market and their shareholders. This document also provides a notice of public hearing on these proposed regulations.

DATES: Written or electronic comments must be received by January 16, 2008. Outlines of topics to be discussed at the public hearing scheduled for February 6, 2008 at 10 a.m. must be received by January 16, 2008.

ADDRESSES: Send submissions to CC:PA:LPD:PR (REG-140206-06), room 5203, Internal Revenue Service, PO Box 7604, Ben Franklin Station, Washington, DC 20044. Submissions may be hand delivered Monday through Friday between the hours of 8 a.m. and 4 p.m. to CC:PA:LPD:PR (REG-140206-06), Courier's Desk, Internal Revenue Service, 1111 Constitution Avenue, NW., Washington, DC or sent electronically, via the Federal eRulemaking Portal at www.regulations.gov (IRS REG-140206-06). The public hearing will be held in room 2140, Internal Revenue Building, 1111 Constitution Avenue, NW., Washington, DC.

FOR FURTHER INFORMATION CONTACT: Concerning the proposed regulations, Kathryn Holman, (202) 622-3840 (not a toll-free number); concerning submissions of comments, the hearing, and/or to be placed on the building access list to attend the hearing, e-mail Richard.A.Hurst@irscounsel.treas.gov.

SUPPLEMENTARY INFORMATION:

Paperwork Reduction Act

The collections of information contained in this notice of proposed rulemaking have been submitted to the Office of Management and Budget for review in accordance with the Paperwork Reduction Act of 1995 (44 U.S.C. 3507(d)). Comments on the collections of information should be sent to the Office of Management and Budget, Attn: Desk Office for the Department of the Treasury, Office of Information and Regulatory Affairs, Washington, DC 20503, with copies to the Internal Revenue Service, Attn: IRS Reports Clearance Officer, SE:W:CAR:MP:T:T:SP, Washington, DC 20224. Comments on the collection of information should be received by January 16, 2008. Comments are specifically requested concerning:

Whether the proposed collection of information is necessary for the proper performance of the functions of the Internal Revenue Service, including whether the information will have practical utility;

The accuracy of the estimated burden associated with the proposed collection of information;

How the quality, utility, and clarity of the information to be collected may be enhanced;

How the burden of complying with the proposed collections of information may be minimized, including through the application of automated collection techniques or other forms of information technology; and

Estimates of capital or start-up costs and costs of operation, maintenance and purchase of service to provide information.

The collection of information in these proposed regulations is in § 1.1441-3(c)(5)(iii). This information is required to allow a U.S. financial institution that is applying the escrow procedure to properly comply with its withholding and reporting obligations under sections 1441, 1442 and 1443 in the case of a distribution made by a corporation with respect to its stock that is actively traded on an established financial market and that requires a determination under section 302 as to whether the distribution is treated as a dividend or a distribution in part or full payment in exchange for stock. The collection of information is mandatory and the respondents are nonresident aliens and foreign corporations.

Estimated total annual reporting burden: 1400 hours.

The estimated annual burden per respondent: 2 hours.

Estimated number of respondents: 700.

Estimated annual frequency of responses: 5 times.

An agency may not conduct or sponsor, and a person is not required to respond to, a collection of information unless it displays a valid control number assigned by the Office of Management and Budget.

Books or records relating to a collection of information must be retained as long as their contents may become material in the administration of any internal revenue law. Generally, tax returns and tax return information are confidential as required by 26 U.S.C. 6103.

Background

These proposed regulations, REG-140206-06, provide guidance regarding the withholding and reporting obligations of a withholding agent under Chapter 3 of the Internal Revenue Code (Code) in the case of a distribution in redemption of the stock of a corporation that is actively traded on an established financial market within the meaning of § 1.1092(d)-1 (publicly traded). In general the proposed regulations contemplate a transaction where a publicly traded corporation offers to purchase stock from its shareholders (a self tender), where the amount of stock purchased and the shareholders involved in the transaction (the participating shareholders) depend on a number of factors, including each shareholder's willingness to sell some or all of its stock, and the terms set forth in the offer. The regulations would also apply to transactions described in section 304(a)(2).

In the case of a self-tender, a corporation may purchase stock from some or all of its shareholders and, as a result, each participating shareholder's percentage ownership interest in the corporation may increase, decrease, or remain the same. Although the corporation's self tender offer is denominated as an offer to purchase shares, the tax consequences to the corporation and any participating shareholder of the payment to such a shareholder, as described in this preamble, depend on several factors. Further, where the participating shareholder is a foreign person, withholding under Chapter 3 of the Code may or may not be required.

Sections 1441 and 1442 and § 1.1441-1(b)(1) generally require a person that makes a payment of an "amount subject to withholding" to a beneficial owner that is a foreign person to deduct and withhold 30 percent of the payment unless the payor can reliably associate the payment with documentation upon which the payor can rely to treat the payment as made to a beneficial owner that is a U.S. person or as made to a beneficial owner that is a foreign person entitled to a reduced rate of withholding under the Code, regulations or an income tax treaty.

Section 1.1441-2(a) provides that the term amounts subject to withholding means amounts from sources within the United States that constitute fixed or determinable annual or periodical income (FDAP) described in § 1.1441-2(b) or other amounts subject to withholding described in § 1.1441-2(c).

Section 1.1441-2(b)(1) provides that FDAP includes all income described in section 61 of the Code, unless the item of income is described in § 1.1441-2(b)(2). Section 1.1441-2(b)(2)(i) generally excludes from FDAP gains derived from the sale of property. Thus, a distribution to a shareholder that is treated as gain from the sale of stock is excluded from FDAP. Further, to the extent a distribution is a return of capital, it is not gross income under section 61, and thus also is not FDAP.

Section 302 provides rules for determining when a distribution in redemption of stock is treated as a distribution in part or full payment in exchange for stock. That section generally requires a comparison of a shareholder's overall interest in the corporation before the distribution and its overall interest in such corporation after the distribution. See section 302(b). In conducting the comparison, the constructive ownership rules of section 318 generally apply. If the shareholder's interest in the corporation has been sufficiently reduced, then the distribution is treated as a payment in exchange for the shareholder's stock under section 302(a). If the shareholder's interest in the corporation has not been sufficiently reduced, the tax consequences of the distribution are determined under section 301, and such distribution is a dividend to the shareholder to the extent the distribution is out of the distributing corporation's earnings and profits, then applied against and reduce the adjusted basis of the stock, and finally treated as gain from the sale or exchange of property. See section 301(c).

When a publicly held corporation makes a distribution in redemption of its stock, a determination must be made under section 302 with respect to each shareholder as to whether the redemption is treated as a distribution of property to which section 301 applies (potentially constituting a dividend in whole or in part) or as a distribution in part or full payment in exchange for stock. However, the information necessary for each shareholder to make such a determination generally is not available until after the transaction is completed because the redemption of stock held by other shareholders must be taken into account. Further, because of the application of the constructive ownership rules of section 318, when a distribution is made to a foreign shareholder, a withholding agent will often not be in the best position to make a determination as to whether the distribution to the foreign shareholder should be treated as a payment in exchange for the shareholder's stock or a dividend.

There are two revenue rulings that consider the issue of whether the interest of a shareholder in a publicly held corporation has been sufficiently reduced as a result of a distribution to effect exchange treatment under section 302(a).

In Rev. Rul. 76-385, 1976-2 CB 92, See § 601.601(d)(2)(ii)(b), the IRS ruled that a shareholder who actually and constructively owned 0.0001118% of a publicly traded corporation's stock before a redemption, but only constructively owned 0.0001081% after the redemption, had experienced a "meaningful reduction in proportionate interest" in the corporation under the principles of United States v. Davis, 397 U.S. 301 (1970), rehearing denied, 397 U.S. 107 (1970). The shareholder's interest in the corporation after the redemption therefore was approximately 96.7% of the shareholder's interest before the redemption, taking constructive ownership into account. Nevertheless, the reduction was considered meaningful, and so the distribution to the shareholder was treated as not essentially equivalent to a dividend under section 302(b)(1) and as a payment in exchange for the shareholder's stock under section 302(a).

Consistent with Rev. Rul. 76-385, in Rev. Rul. 81-289, 1981-2 CB 82, See § 601.601(d)(2)(ii)(b), the IRS ruled that a shareholder who owned 0.2% of the common stock of a publicly traded company before a redemption, and 0.2% of the common stock in the company after the redemption, did not satisfy the "meaningful reduction" standard of United States v. Davis, and that the redemption did not qualify for exchange treatment under section 302(a).

Under the analysis adopted in these revenue rulings, each minority shareholder who participates in a self tender must compute its percentage ownership of the total outstanding stock of the corporation before and after the transaction. If after the transaction the shareholder's percentage ownership is less than it was before the transaction, the shareholder generally has experienced a "meaningful reduction" in the shareholder's proportionate interest in the corporation, and the transaction, at least with respect to that shareholder, is considered a distribution in exchange for the stock under section 302(a) and not a distribution of property to which section 301 applies. This result occurs even if another participating shareholder in the same self tender experiences no change or an increase in its percentage ownership of the corporation, and, therefore, is considered to receive a distribution of property to which section 301 applies. See also section 302(b)(2), (3), and (4).

Section 1.1441-3(c) requires a corporation making a distribution with respect to its stock to a foreign shareholder, as well as any intermediary (such as a broker) making a payment of such a distribution, to withhold on the entire amount of the distribution, unless it elects to reduce the amount of withholding under § 1.1441-3(c). Section 1.1441-3(c)(2)(i)(B) provides that a distributing corporation or intermediary may elect to not withhold on a distribution to the extent it represents a distribution in part or full payment in exchange for stock. Section 1.1441-3(c)(2)(i) provides that a corporation or intermediary makes the election by reducing the amount of withholding at the time that the payment is made. However, a withholding agent cannot avail itself of this election unless it knows the extent to which a distribution represents a payment in exchange for stock under section 302(a). As previously noted, in the context of a distribution in redemption of stock held in a publicly traded corporation, the withholding agent generally will not have this information unless, at the time of the redemption, it has obtained information from each participating shareholder regarding actual and constructive ownership of stock for purposes of the foregoing analysis.

The Treasury Department and the IRS are aware that, in the context of transactions involving distributions in redemption of stock held by foreign persons where such stock is actively traded on an established financial market, the means of compliance with sections 1441, 1442, and 1443 is varied. The Treasury Department and the IRS believe that the discretion permitted by the current regulations, and the resulting different treatment of similar transactions is not appropriate. Accordingly, these proposed regulations provide the procedure ("escrow procedure") to be followed by U.S. withholding agents to satisfy the withholding, reporting and deposit requirements of the regulations under sections 1441, 1442, and 1443 with respect to any payment of a corporate distribution in redemption of stock made to a foreign account holder with respect to certain self tenders.

Explanation of Provisions

The proposed regulations set forth an escrow procedure for withholding agents to follow in the case of a payment made after December 31, 2008 of a corporate distribution in redemption of stock that is actively traded on an established financial market within the meaning of § 1.1092(d)-1 (section 302 payment).

In general, the proposed regulations require a U.S. financial institution (withholding agent) to set aside in an escrow account 30 percent (or the applicable dividend rate provided under a treaty) of the amount of the section 302 payment. The withholding agent is then required to provide information to the foreign beneficial owner regarding the distribution, including the total number of the distributing corporation's shares outstanding before and after the distribution. The withholding agent must also provide a written statement explaining the conditions under which the section 302 payment will be treated as a dividend or a payment in exchange for stock (including an explanation of the constructive ownership rules under section 318). In the written explanation provided to the foreign beneficial owner, the withholding agent must request that the beneficial owner provide a written certification to the withholding agent within 60 days as to whether the distribution is either a dividend or a payment in exchange for stock.

The certification to be provided by the foreign beneficial owner must contain, among other requirements, the beneficial owner's name and account number, a certification that the distribution is a payment in exchange for stock or is a dividend, and the number of shares actually and constructively owned by the beneficial owner before and after the distribution. The beneficial owner's certification must be signed under penalties of perjury.

A withholding agent may generally rely on a certification received from a foreign beneficial owner in determining its section 1441 obligations with respect to payments for such beneficial owner's stock. However, if the withholding agent knows or has reason to know that the certification is unreliable or incorrect, or the withholding agent does not receive a certification from a foreign beneficial owner, the withholding agent is required to treat the amount set aside in escrow as tax withheld on the 61st day, and deposit that amount pursuant to the applicable regulations.

Although a qualified intermediary (QI) may, and a withholding foreign partnership and a withholding foreign trust (WP/WT) must, assume primary withholding responsibility under section 1441 and receive payments without any withholding by the U.S. financial institution, under the proposed regulations, in the case of a section 3 02 payment, the QI or WP/WT cannot assume primary withholding responsibility and receive the payment in gross. The QI or WP/WT must apply the procedure described in this preamble and provide the U.S. financial institution with a withholding statement that details the appropriate rate of withholding and information reporting for amounts paid to the QI or WP/WT. In addition, if there is a chain of QIs or WPs/WTs this procedure must be followed at each level in the chain. The U.S. financial institution shall treat beneficial owners that are U.S. non-exempt recipients, and that hold stock in the distributing corporation through QIs, WPs/WTs, NQIs and flow-throughs, in accordance with the section 302 payment certifications obtained from those U.S. non-exempt recipients and shall instruct foreign intermediaries and foreign flow-through entities to do the same.

These proposed regulations would apply for redemptions of stock that are made after December 31, 2008. However, a withholding agent may, at its option, rely on these proposed regulations for a redemption of stock that occurs before January 1, 2009.

The Treasury Department and the IRS are aware that withholding agents serve various customer bases: some may maintain accounts for a small number of account holders, others may maintain accounts for a much greater number of account holders. Comments are requested on alternatives to the escrow procedure described in this proposed regulation for withholding agents that maintain accounts for large numbers of customers.

Special Analyses

It has been determined that this notice of proposed rulemaking is not a significant regulatory action as defined in Executive Order 12866. Therefore, a regulatory assessment is not required.

It has been determined that section 553(b) of the Administrative Procedure Act (5 U.S.C. chapter 5) does not apply to these regulations.

These regulations impose a collection of information on small entities, and the Regulatory Flexibility Act (5 U.S.C. chapter 6) applies. This rule regulates securities brokerages that have foreign customers that respond to a tender offer by a U.S. publicly traded corporation to purchase some of its stock from its shareholders. The Small Business Administration (SBA) has established size standards for types of economic activities which are classified based on the North American Industry Classification Codes (NAICS). The regulations specifying size standards are set forth in Title 13, Code of Federal Regulations, part 121 (13 CFR part 121), Small Business Size Regulations. The NAICS Code for a small securities brokerage is specified at 13 CFR 121.201. Pursuant to subsector 523120 of the NAICS, a small securities brokerage is one with receipts of less than 6.5 million dollars. According to NAICS 523120, U.S. Census Bureau, Statistics of U.S. Business (2002), there are a total of 7,886 securities brokerages of which 7,113 generate revenue less than $5 million and 224 generate revenue between $5 million and $10 million. It is estimated that 7,213 of the securities brokerages are considered small businesses. The IRS requests information regarding the number of transactions these small securities brokerages engage in each year involving self tenders by public corporations. In the case of a tender offer by a publicly held corporation, it is estimated that a brokerage clerk would spend two hours preparing the paperwork and verifying the computations required to accurately withhold with respect to foreign customers. According to the Bureau of Labor Statistics, the mean hourly wage of a brokerage clerk is $18.34, so it is estimated that it will cost a small securities brokerage $36.68 per transaction. This cost is not significant when compared to the annual revenue of the small securities brokerage. Pursuant to section 605(b) of the Regulatory Flexibility Act, 5 U.S.C. 605, the Chief Counsel certifies that this rule will not have a significant economic impact on a substantial number of small entities. The IRS invites specific comments on the economic impact of compliance from members of the public who believe there will be a significant economic impact on small businesses that are regulated by this rule. Pursuant to section 7805(f) of the Internal Revenue Code, this regulation has been submitted to the Chief Counsel for Advocacy of the Small Business Administration for comment on its impact on small businesses.

Comments and Public Hearing

Before these proposed regulations are adopted as final regulations, consideration will be given to any written (a signed original and eight (8) copies) or electronic comments that are submitted timely to the IRS. The IRS and the Treasury Department request comments on the clarity of the proposed rules and how they can be made easier to understand. All comments will be available for public inspection and copying.

A public hearing has been scheduled for February 6, 2008, beginning at 10 a.m. in room 2140 of the Internal Revenue Building, 1111 Constitution Avenue, NW., Washington, DC. Due to building security procedures, visitors must enter at the 12th street entrance. In addition, all visitors must present photo identification to enter the building. Because of access restrictions, visitors will not be admitted beyond the immediate entrance area more than 30 minutes before the hearing starts. For information about having your name placed on the building access list to attend the hearing, see the FOR FURTHER INFORMATION CONTACT section of this preamble.

The rules of 26 CFR 601.601(a)(3) apply to the hearing. Persons who wish to present oral comments at the hearing must submit electronic or written comments, and an outline of the topics to be discussed, and the time to be devoted to each topic (signed original and eight (8) copies) by January 16, 2008. A period of 10 minutes will be allotted to each person for making comments. An agenda showing the scheduling of the speakers will be prepared after the deadline for receiving outlines has passed. Copies of the agenda will be available free of charge at the hearing.

Drafting Information

The principal author of these proposed regulations is Kathryn Holman, Office of Associate Chief Counsel (International). However, other personnel from the IRS and Treasury Department participated in their development.

[¶49,327] Proposed Amendments of Regulations (REG-114125-07), published in the Federal Register on October 17, 2007.

[Code Sec. 861]

International tax: Compensation: Source: United States v. foreign.—Amendments of Reg. §1.861-4, regarding clarification of the determination of source of compensation of a person, including an artist or athlete, who is compensated for labor or personal services performed at specific events, are proposed.

AGENCY: Internal Revenue Service (IRS), Treasury.

ACTION: Notice of proposed rulemaking.

SUMMARY: This document contains proposed changes to existing final regulations regarding the source of compensation for labor or personal services. The proposed changes are needed to clarify the determination of source of compensation of a person, including an artist or athlete, who is compensated for labor or personal services performed at specific events. These proposed regulations affect such an individual.

DATE: Written or electronic comments and requests for a public hearing must be received by January 15, 2008.

ADDRESSES: Send submissions to: CC:PA:LPD:PR (REG-114125-07), room 5203, Internal Revenue Service, PO Box 7604, Ben Franklin Station, Washington, DC 20044. Submissions may be hand-delivered Monday through Friday between the hours of 8 a.m. and 4 p.m. to: CC:PA:LPD:PR (REG-114125-07), Courier's Desk, Internal Revenue Service, 1111 Constitution Avenue, NW, Washington, DC, or sent electronically via the Federal eRulemaking Portal at http://www.regulations.gov (IRS-REG-114125-07).

FOR FURTHER INFORMATION CONTACT: Concerning the proposed regulations, David Bergkuist at (202) 622-3850; concerning the submissions of comments and requests for a hearing, Regina Johnson at (202) 622-7180 (not toll free numbers).

SUPPLEMENTARY INFORMATION

Background

This document contains proposed amendments under 26 CFR part 1 under section 861 of the Internal Revenue Code (Code). On July 14, 2005, final regulations that revised and amended §1.861-4 were published in the Federal Register (70 FR 40663) as TD 9212. In these final regulations, §1.861-4(b)(2)(ii)(C)(3) was reserved with respect to compensation for labor or personal services performed partly within and partly without the United States by an artist or an athlete who is an employee.

Section 861(a)(3) of the Internal Revenue Code provides that, subject to certain exceptions, compensation for labor or personal services performed in the United States is gross income from sources within the United States. See also §1.861-4(a) of the regulations. Section 862(a)(3) of the Code provides that compensation for labor or personal services performed without the United States is gross income from sources without the United States. Section 1.861-4(b) provides rules for determining the source of compensation for labor or personal services performed partly within and partly without the United States. Section 1.861-4(b)(2)(i) provides rules for determining the source of compensation for labor or personal services performed partly within and partly without the United States by an individual other than as an employee. Section 1.861-4(b)(2)(ii) provides rules for determining the source of compensation for labor or personal services performed partly within and partly without the United States by an individual as an employee.

Under §1.861-4(b)(2)(ii), if an individual performs labor or personal services as an employee, the source of the individual's compensation is generally determined on a time basis, with certain fringe benefits sourced on a geographic basis. An individual may determine the source of his or her compensation as an employee for labor or personal services performed partly within and partly without the United States under an alternative basis if the individual establishes to the satisfaction of the Commissioner that, under the facts and circumstances of the particular case, the alternative basis more properly determines the source of the compensation than the general rules of §1.861-4(b)(2)(ii). See §1.861-4(b)(2)(ii)(C)(1)(i). In addition, the Commissioner may, under the facts and circumstances of the particular case, determine the source of compensation that is received by an individual as an employee under an alternative basis if such compensation is not for a specific time period, provided that the Commissioner's alternative basis determines the source of compensation in a more reasonable manner than the basis used by the individual.

The final regulations at §1.861-4(b)(2)(ii)(C)(3) provided a reservation with respect to the source of compensation for labor or personal services performed partly within and partly without the United States by an artist or athlete who is an employee. The preamble of TD 9212 indicated that it was intended that the rule for artists and athletes who are employees, when issued, would require such individuals to determine the proper source of their compensation for labor or personal services on the basis that most correctly reflects the proper source of income under the facts and circumstances of the particular case, consistent with current law.

Explanation of Provisions

The proposed regulations would set forth a new "events basis" rule in §1.861-4(b)(2)(ii)(G) and make certain other clarifying changes to the existing final regulations. The proposed regulations also would remove §1.861-4(b)(2)(ii)(C)(3), which reserved with respect to artists and athletes.

The amount of income received by a person, including an individual who is an artist or an athlete, that is properly treated as compensation from the performance of labor or personal services is determined based on all of the facts and circumstances of the particular case. Proposed § 1.861-4(b)(2)(ii)(G) specifies that the amount of compensation for labor or personal services determined on an event basis is the amount of the person's compensation which, based on the facts and circumstances, is attributable to the labor or personal services performed at the location of a specific event.

The IRS and the Treasury Department have determined that the proper source of compensation received by a person, including an individual who is an artist or athlete, specifically for performing labor or personal services at an event is the location of the event. A basis that purports to determine the source of compensation from the performance of labor or personal services at a specific event, whether on a time basis or otherwise, by taking into account the location of labor or personal services performed in preparation for the performance of labor or personal services at the specific event will generally not be the basis that most correctly determines the source of the compensation. This rule applies to situations covered by § 1.861-4(a) and (b).

Under § 1.861-4(a), the source of compensation for labor or personal services performed wholly within the United States is generally from sources within the United States. Therefore, if a person, including an individual who is an artist or an athlete, is specifically compensated for performing labor or personal services at an event in the United States, the source of such compensation is wholly within the United States because the labor or personal services were performed wholly at an event within the United States. The proposed regulations state that a basis that purports to determine the source of such income on a time basis by taking into account the location of labor or personal services performed in preparation for the performance of labor or personal services at the specific event will generally not be a more reasonable basis for determining source of the compensation. The proposed regulations add an example to § 1.861-4(c) to illustrate the application of this rule.

Section 1.861-4(b) applies to instances in which a person is compensated for performing labor or personal services at multiple events, only some of which are within the United States, and at least a portion of the person's compensation cannot be specifically attributed to the person's performance of labor or personal services at a specific location. If the person is not an individual who is compensated as an employee, the source of compensation for labor or personal services is determined on the basis that most correctly reflects the proper source of that income under the facts and circumstances of the particular case. See § 1.861-4(b)(1) and (2)(i). If a person is compensated specifically for labor or personal services performed at multiple events, the basis that most correctly reflects the proper source of that income under the facts and circumstances of the particular case will generally be the location of the events. In addition, a basis that purports to determine the source of such income on a time basis by taking into account the location of labor or personal services performed in preparation for the performance of labor or personal services at the specific event will generally not be the basis that most correctly reflects the proper source of the compensation under proposed § 1.861-4(b)(2)(ii)(G).

The Commissioner may, under the facts and circumstances of the particular case, determine the source of compensation that is received by an individual as an employee under an alternative basis if such compensation is not for a specific time period, provided that the Commissioner's alternative basis determines the source of compensation in a more reasonable manner than the basis used by the individual. Compensation specifically for labor or personal services performed at a specific event is not compensation for a specific time period. The basis that most correctly reflects the proper source of that income will generally be the location of the event under proposed § 1.861-4(b)(2)(ii)(G). In addition, a basis that purports to determine the source of such income on a facts and circumstances basis by taking into account the location of labor or personal services performed in preparation for the performance of labor or personal services at the specific event will generally not more properly determine the source of the compensation under proposed § 1.861-4(b)(2)(ii)(G).

These proposed regulations provide examples to illustrate the event basis for determining the source of compensation of an individual, including an artist or athlete, who is compensated specifically for performing labor or personal services at an event.

The revisions to § 1.861-4(b)(1), (b)(2)(i), and (b)(ii)(C)(1)(i) and (ii) which refer to the event basis; the revisions in § 1.861-4(b)(2)(ii)(C)(3), (b)(2)(ii)(E), and (b)(2)(ii)(F), (b)(2)(ii)(G), and (c); and new Examples 7 through 11 of § 1.861-4(c) would be effective for taxable years beginning after the date final regulations are published in the Federal Register.

Special Analysis

It has been determined that this notice of proposed rulemaking is not a significant regulatory action as defined in Executive Order 12866. Therefore, a regulatory assessment is not required. It has also been determined that section 553(b) of the Administrative Procedure Act (5 U.S.C. chapter 5) does not apply to these regulations. Because these regulations do not impose a collection of information on small entities, the provisions of the Regulatory Flexibility Act (5 U.S.C. chapter 6) do not apply. Pursuant to section 7805(f) of the Internal Revenue Code, this notice of proposed rulemaking has been submitted to the Chief Counsel for Advocacy of the Small Business Administration for comment on its impact on small business.

Comments and Requests for a Public Hearing

Before these proposed regulations are adopted as final regulations, consideration will be given to any written (a signed original and eight (8) copies) or electronic comment that is submitted timely to the

IRS. The Treasury Department and the IRS request comments on the clarity of the proposed rules and how they can be made easier to understand. All comments will be available for public inspection and copying. A hearing will be scheduled if requested in writing by any person that timely submits written comments. If a public hearing is scheduled, notice of the date, time, and place for a public hearing will be published in the Federal Register.

Drafting Information

The principal author of these proposed regulations is David Bergkuist, Office of the Associate Chief Counsel (International). However, other personnel from the IRS and the Treasury Department participated in their development.

[¶49,329] Proposed Amendments of Regulations (REG-209020-86), published in the Federal Register on November 7, 2007 (corrected 12/18/2007).

[Code Secs. 905 and 6689]

Foreign taxes: Penalties, civil: Foreign tax credit: Redetermination of tax: Notification to IRS.—Reg. §§1.905-3, 1.905-4, 1.905-5 and 301.6689-1, relating to Code Sec. 905(c) and Code Sec. 6689, are proposed. Amendments of Reg. 1.905-3(d)(2)(iii)-(iv) and 1.905-3(d)(4) are withdrawn.

AGENCY: Internal Revenue Service (IRS), Treasury.

ACTION: Partial withdrawal of notice of proposed rulemaking and notice of proposed rulemaking by cross-reference to temporary regulations.

SUMMARY: This document withdraws portions of the notice of proposed rulemaking published on June 23, 1988, relating to sections 905(c) and 6689 (the 1988 proposed regulations). In addition, in the Rules and Regulations section of this issue of the Federal Register, the IRS and the Treasury Department are issuing temporary regulations relating to a taxpayer's obligation under section 905(c) of the Internal Revenue Code to notify the IRS of a foreign tax redetermination. The IRS and the Treasury Department are also issuing temporary regulations on Procedure and Administration under section 6689 relating to the civil penalty for failure to notify the IRS of a foreign tax redetermination as required under section 905(c). These temporary regulations affect taxpayers that have paid foreign taxes which have been redetermined and provide guidance needed to comply with statutory changes made to the applicable law by the Taxpayer Relief Act of 1997 and the American Jobs Creation Act of 2004. The text of those temporary regulations also serves as the text of these proposed regulations.

DATES: Written or electronic comments and requests for a public hearing must be received by February 5, 2008.

ADDRESSES: Send submissions to: CC:PA:LPD:PR (REG-209020-86), room 5203, Internal Revenue Service, PO Box 7604, Ben Franklin Station, Washington, DC 20044. Submissions may be hand-delivered between the hours of 8 a.m. and 4 p.m. to CC:PA:LPD:PR (REG-209020-86), Courier's Desk, Internal Revenue Service, 1111 Constitution Ave., NW., Washington, DC or sent electronically via the Federal eRulemaking Portal at www.regulations.gov (IRS REG-209020-86).

FOR FURTHER INFORMATION CONTACT: Concerning the proposed regulations, Teresa Burridge Hughes, (202) 622-3850 (not a toll-free number); concerning the submission of comments, Kelly Banks, (202) 622-7180 (not a toll-free number).

SUPPLEMENTARY INFORMATION:

Paperwork Reduction Act

The collections of information contained in this notice of proposed rulemaking have been submitted to the Office of Management and Budget for review in accordance with the Paperwork Reduction Act of 1995 (44 U.S.C. 3507(d)). Comments on the collection of information should be sent to the Office of Management and Budget, Attn: Desk Officer for the Department of Treasury, Office of Information and Regulatory-Affairs, Washington, DC 20503, with copies to the Internal Revenue Service, Attn: IRS Reports Clearance Officer, SE:W:CAR:MP:T:T:SP, Washington, DC 20224. Comments on the collection of information should be received by January 7, 2008. Comments are specifically requested concerning:

Whether the proposed collections of information is necessary for the proper performance of the functions of the IRS, including whether the information will have practical utility;

The accuracy of the estimated burden associated with the proposed collections of information;

How the quality, utility, and clarity of the information to be collected may be enhanced;

How the burden of complying with the proposed collections of information may be minimized, including through the application of automated collection techniques or other forms of information technology; and

Estimates of capital or start-up costs and costs of operation, maintenance, and purchase of service to provide information.

The collections of information in this notice of proposed rulemaking are in § 1.905-4. This information is required to enable the IRS to verify the amounts of the foreign tax redeterminations and to determine the amount of the penalty under section 6689, if a taxpayer fails to notify the IRS of a foreign tax redetermination. This information will be used by the IRS for examination purposes. The collections of information are mandatory. The likely respondents are individuals and business or other for-profit institutions.

Estimated total annual reporting: 54,000 hours.

The estimated annual burden per respondent varies from 3 hours to 8 hours, depending on individual circumstances, with an estimated average of 4.2 hours.

Estimated number of respondents: 13,000.

Estimated frequency of responses: Annually.

An agency may not conduct or sponsor, and a person is not required to respond to, a collection of information unless it displays a valid control number assigned by the Office of Management and Budget.

Books or records relating to a collection of information must be retained as long as their contents may become material in the administration of any internal revenue law. Generally, tax returns and tax return information are confidential, as required by 26 U.S.C. 6103.

Background and Explanation of Provisions

On June 23, 1988, the IRS published in the Federal Register a notice of proposed rulemaking (53 FR 23659) (INTL-061-86) (the 1988 proposed regulations) that would have provided rules with respect to the time and manner of reporting a foreign tax redetermination and to the penalty under section 6689. Written comments were received; however, no hearing was requested or held. Subsequently, section 1102(a)(1) and 1102(a)(2) of the Taxpayer Relief Act of 1997, Public Law 105-34 (111 Stat. 788, 963-966 (1997)), amended section 905(c), effective for taxes paid or accrued in taxable years beginning after December 31, 1997. Subsequently, section 408(a) of the American Jobs Creation Act of 2004, Public Law 108-357 (118 Stat. 1418, 1499 (2004)), modified section 986(a), effective for taxable years beginning after December 31, 2004. In light of the comments received on the 1988 proposed regulations and the statutory changes to sections 905(c) and 986(a), sections of the 1988 proposed regulations are revised and other sections are withdrawn. The preamble to the temporary regulations explains the temporary regulations and these proposed regulations.

Special Analyses

It has been determined that this notice of proposed rulemaking is not a significant regulatory action as defined in Executive Order 12866. Therefore, a regulatory assessment is not required. It also has been determined that section 553(b) of the Administrative Procedure Act (5 U.S.C. chapter 5) does not apply to the following regulations, §§1.905-3, 1.905-4, 1.905-5, and 301.6689-1. With respect to §1.905-4, it is hereby certified that this regulation will not have a significant economic impact on a substantial number of small entities. This certification is based on the fact that the collection of information requirement under §1.905-4 that is imposed on small entities flows directly from section 905(c), which states that, "[T]he taxpayer shall notify the Secretary," of a foreign tax redetermination that may result in a redetermination of the taxpayer's United States tax liability. In order for the taxpayer to satisfy this notification requirement, information with respect to all foreign tax redeterminations must be collected. Therefore, a regulatory flexibility analysis is not required. Pursuant to section 7805(f) of the Internal Revenue Code, this regulation has been submitted to the Chief Counsel for Advocacy of the Small Business Administration for comment on their impact on small businesses.

Comments and Requests for a Public Hearing

Before these proposed regulations are adopted as final regulations, consideration will be given to any written (a signed original and eight (8) copies) or electronic comments that are submitted timely to the IRS. All comments will be available for public inspection and copying. A public hearing may be scheduled if requested in writing by any person that timely submits written or electronic comments. If a public hearing is scheduled, notice of the date, time, and place for the public hearing will be published in the Federal Register.

Drafting Information

The principal author of this document is Teresa Burridge Hughes, Office of Associate Chief Counsel (International). However, other personnel from the IRS and the Treasury Department participated in its development.

[¶49,357] **Proposed Regulations (REG-151135-07)**, published in the Federal Register on March 18, 2008 (corrected 4/9/2008).

[Code Sec. 432]

Multiemployer retirement plans: Determination of critical or endangered status: Certification of status: Notice of status.—Reg. §§1.432(a)-1 and 1.432(b)-1, providing additional rules for certain multiemployer defined benefit plans that are in effect on July 16, 2006, are proposed.

AGENCY: Internal Revenue Service (IRS), Treasury

ACTION: Notice of proposed rulemaking.

SUMMARY: This document contains proposed regulations under section 432 of the Internal Revenue Code (Code). These proposed regulations provide additional rules for certain multiemployer defined benefit plans that are in effect on July 16, 2006. These proposed regulations affect sponsors and administrators of, and participants in multiemployer plans that are in either endangered or critical status. These regulations are necessary to implement the new rules set forth in section 432 that are effective for plan years beginning after 2007. The proposed regulations reflect changes made by the Pension Protection Act of 2006.

DATES: Written or electronic comments and requests for public hearing must be received by June 16, 2008.

ADDRESSES: Send submissions to: CC:PA:LPD:PR (REG-151135-07), room 5203, Internal Revenue Service, PO Box 7604, Ben Franklin Station, Washington, DC 20044. Submissions may be hand-delivered Monday through Friday between the hours of 8 a.m. and 4 p.m. to CC:PA:LPD:PR (REG-151135-07), Courier's Desk, Internal Revenue Service, 1111 Constitution Avenue, NW, Washington, DC 20224, or sent electronically via the Federal eRulemaking Portal at *www.regulations.gov* (IRS REG-151135-07).

FOR FURTHER INFORMATION CONTACT: Concerning the regulations, Bruce Perlin, (202) 622-6090; concerning submissions and requests for a public hearing, *Richard.A.Hurst@irscounsel.treas.gov* or at (202) 622-7180 (not toll-free numbers).

SUPPLEMENTARY INFORMATION:

Paperwork Reduction Act

The collection of information contained in this notice of proposed rulemaking have been submitted to the Office of Management and Budget for review in accordance with the Paperwork Reduction Act of 1995 (44 U.S.C. 3507(d). Comments on the collection of information should be sent to the **Office of Management and Budget,** Attn: Desk Officer for the Department of the Treasury, Office of Information and Regulatory Affairs, Washington, DC 20503, with copies to the **Internal Revenue Service,** Attn: IRS Reports Clearance Officer, SE:CAR:MP:T:T:SP, Washington, DC 20224. Comments on the collection of information should be received by May 19, 2008.

Comments are specifically requested concerning:

Whether the proposed collection of information is necessary for the proper performance of the functions of the Internal Revenue Service, including whether the information will have practical utility;

The accuracy of the estimated burden associated with the collection of information;

How the quality, utility, and clarity of the information to be collected may be enhanced;

How the burden of complying with the collection of information may be minimized, including through the application of automated collection techniques or other forms of information technology; and

Estimates of capital or start-up costs and costs of operation, maintenance, and purchase of service to provide information.

The collection of information in this regulation is in §1.432(b)-1(d) and (e). This information is required in order for a qualified multiemployer defined benefit plan's enrolled actuary to provide a timely certification of the plan's funding status. In addition, if it is certified that a plan is or will be in critical or endangered status, the plan sponsor is required to notify the Department of Labor, the Pension Benefit Guaranty Corporation, the bargaining parties, participants, and beneficiaries of the status designation. For plans in critical status, the plan sponsor is required to include in the notice an explanation of the possibility that adjustable benefits may be reduced at a later date and that certain benefits are restricted as of the date the notice is sent. The annual certification by the enrolled actuary for the plan will be used to provide an accurate determination and certification of the plan's funded status and to provide notice to the required parties of the status designation. The collection of information is mandatory. The likely respondents are multiemployer plan sponsors and enrolled actuaries.

Estimated total annual reporting burden: 1,200 hours.

Estimated average annual burden hours per respondent: 0.75 hours.

Estimated number of respondents: 1,600.

Estimated annual frequency of responses: occasional.

An agency may not conduct or sponsor, and a person is not required to respond to, a collection of information unless it displays a valid control number assigned by the Office of Management and Budget.

Books or records relating to a collection of information must be retained as long as their contents may become material in the administration of any internal revenue law. Generally, tax returns and tax return information are confidential, as required by 26 U.S.C. 6103.

Background

This document contains proposed Income Tax Regulations (26 CFR part 1) under section 432, as added to the Internal Revenue Code by the Pension Protection Act of 2006 (PPA '06), Public Law 109-280, 120 Stat 780.

Section 412 contains minimum funding rules that generally apply to pension plans. Section 431 sets forth the funding rules that apply specifically to multiemployer defined benefit plans. Section 432 sets forth additional rules that apply to multiemployer plans in effect on July 16, 2006, that are in endangered or critical status[1].

---

[1] Section 302 and section 304 of the Employee Retirement Income Security Act of 1974, as amended (ERISA) sets forth funding rules that are parallel to those in section 412 and section 431 of the Code. Section 305 of ERISA sets forth additional rules for multiemployer plans that are parallel to those in section 432 of the Code. Under section 101 of Reorganization Plan No. 4 of 1978 (43 FR 47713) and section 302 of ERISA, the Secretary of the Treasury has interpretive jurisdiction over the subject matter addressed in these proposed regulations for purposes of ERISA, as well as the Code. Thus, these Treasury Department regulations issued under section 432 of the Code apply as well for purposes of ERISA section 305.

Section 432 generally provides for a determination by the enrolled actuary for a multiemployer plan as to whether the plan is in endangered status or in critical status for a plan year. In the first year that the actuary certifies that the plan is in endangered status, section 432(a)(1) requires that the plan sponsor adopt a funding improvement plan. The funding improvement plan must meet the requirements of section 432(c) and the plan must apply the rules of section 432(d) during the period that begins when the plan is certified to be in endangered status and ends when the plan is no longer in that status. In the first year that the actuary certifies that the plan is in critical status, section 432 (a)(2) requires that the plan sponsor adopt a rehabilitation plan. The rehabilitation plan must meet the requirements of section 432(e) and the plan must apply the rules of section 432(f) during the period that begins when the plan is certified to be in critical status and ends when the plan is no longer in that status. In addition, section 432(f)(2) requires that the plan suspend certain actions as described more fully in this preamble.

Section 432(b)(3)(A) requires an actuarial certification of whether or not a multiemployer plan is in endangered status, and whether or not a multiemployer plan is or will be in critical status, for each plan year. This certification must be completed by the 90th day of the plan year and must be provided to the Secretary of the Treasury and to the plan sponsor. If the certification is with respect to a plan year that is within the plan's funding improvement period or rehabilitation period arising from a prior certification of endangered or critical status, the actuary must also certify whether or not the plan is making scheduled progress in meeting the requirements of its funding improvement or rehabilitation plan. Failure of the plan's actuary to certify the status of the plan is treated as a failure to file the annual report under section 502(c)(2) of the Employee Retirement Income Security Act of 1974 (ERISA). Thus, a penalty of up to $1,100 per day applies.

Under section 432(b)(1), a multiemployer plan is in endangered status if the plan is not in critical status and, as of the beginning of the plan year, (1) the plan's funded percentage for the plan year is less than 80 percent, or (2) the plan has an accumulated funding deficiency for the plan year or is projected to have an accumulated funding deficiency in any of the six succeeding plan years (taking into account amortization extensions under section 431(d)). Under section 432(i), a plan's funded percentage is the percentage determined by dividing the value of the plan's assets by the accrued liability of the plan.

Under section 432(b)(2), a multiemployer plan is in critical status for a plan year if it meets any of four specified tests. Under section 432(b)(2)(A), a plan is in critical status if, as of the beginning of the plan year: (1) the funded percentage of the plan is less than 65 percent and (2) the sum of (A) the market value of plan assets, plus (B) the present value of reasonably anticipated employer contributions for the current plan year and each of the six succeeding plan years is less than the present value of all nonforfeitable benefits projected to be payable under the plan during the current plan year and each of the six succeeding plan years (plus administrative expenses). For this purpose, employer contributions are determined assuming that the terms of all collective bargaining agreements pursuant to which the plan is maintained for the current plan year continue in effect for succeeding plan years.

Under section 432(b)(2)(B), a plan is in critical status if the plan has an accumulated funding deficiency for the current plan year or is projected to have an accumulated funding deficiency for any of the three succeeding plan years. For purposes of this test, the determination of accumulated funding deficiency is made not taking into account any amortization extension under section 431(d). In addition, if a plan has a funded percentage of 65 percent or less, the three-year period for projecting whether the plan will have an accumulated funding deficiency is extended to four years.

Under section 432(b)(2)(C), a plan is in critical status for the plan year if (1) the plan's normal cost for the current plan year, plus interest for the current plan year on the amount of unfunded benefit liabilities under the plan as of the last day of the preceding year, exceeds the present value of the reasonably anticipated employer and employee contributions for the current plan year, (2) the present value of nonforfeitable benefits of inactive participants is greater than the present value of nonforfeitable benefits of active participants, and (3) the plan has an accumulated funding deficiency for the current plan year, or is projected to have an accumulated funding deficiency for any of the four succeeding plan years (not taking into account amortization period extensions under section 431(d)).

Under section 432(b)(2)(D), a plan is in critical status for a plan year if the sum of (A) the market value of plan assets, and (B) the present value of the reasonably anticipated employer contributions for the current plan year and each of the four succeeding plan years is less than the present value of all benefits projected to be payable under the plan during the current plan year and each of the four succeeding plan years (plus administrative expenses). For this purpose, employer contributions are determined assuming that the terms of all collective bargaining agreements pursuant to which the plan is maintained for the current plan year continue in effect for succeeding plan years.

In making the determinations and projections applicable under the endangered and critical status rules, the plan actuary must make projections for the current and succeeding plan years of the current value of the assets of the plan and the present value of all liabilities to participants and beneficiaries under the plan for the current plan year as of the beginning of such year. The actuary's projections must be based on reasonable actuarial estimates, assumptions, and methods that offer the actuary's best estimate of anticipated experience under the plan. An exception to this rule applies in the case of projected industry activity. Any projection of activity in the industry or industries covered by the plan, including future covered employment and contribution levels, must be based on information provided by the plan sponsor, and the plan sponsor must act reasonably and in good faith. The projected present value of liabilities as of the beginning of the year must be based on either the most recent actuarial statement required with respect to the most recently filed annual report or the actuarial valuation for the preceding plan year.

Under section 432(b)(3)(B)(ii), any actuarial projection of plan assets must assume (1) reasonably anticipated employer contributions for the current and succeeding plan years, assuming that the terms of one or more collective bargaining agreements pursuant to which the plan is maintained for the current plan year continue in effect for the succeeding plan years, or (2) that employer contributions for the most recent plan year will continue indefinitely, but only if the plan actuary determines that there have been no significant demographic changes that would make continued application of such terms unreasonable.

The first year that an actuary certifies that a plan is in endangered or critical status establishes a timetable for a number of actions. Under section 432(b)(3)(D), within 30 days after the date of certification, the plan sponsor must notify the participants and beneficiaries, the bargaining parties, the PBGC and the Secretary of Labor of the plan's endangered or critical status. If it is certified that a plan is or will be in critical status, the plan sponsor must include in the notice an explanation of the possibility that (1) adjustable benefits (as defined in section 432(e)(8)) may be reduced and (2) such reductions may apply to participants and beneficiaries whose benefit commencement date is on or after the date such notice is provided for the first plan year in which the plan is in critical status.

If a plan is certified to be in critical status, the plan must take certain actions after notifying the plan participants of the critical status. Specifically, section 432(f)(2) restricts the payment of benefits that are in excess of a single life annuity (plus any social security supplement) effective on the date the notice is sent. Section 432(f)(2)(B) provides that this restriction does not apply to amounts that may be immediately distributed without the consent of the employee under section 411(a)(11) and to any makeup payment in the case of a retroactive annuity starting date or a similar payment of benefits owed with respect to a prior period. In addition, the plan sponsor must refrain from making any payment for the purchase of an irrevocable commitment from an insurer to pay benefits.

Sections 432(c)(1) and 432(e)(1) provide that in the first year that a plan is certified to be in endangered or critical status, the plan sponsor must adopt a funding improvement plan (in the case of a plan that is in endangered status) or a rehabilitation plan (in the case of a plan that is in critical status). The deadline for adoption of the funding improvement plan or rehabilitation plan is 240 days after the deadline for the certification. Accordingly, if the actuarial certification is made after the 90-day deadline, the amount of time for adopting the funding improvement plan or rehabilitation plan is shortened.

Section 432(c)(3) defines a funding improvement plan as a plan which consists of the actions, including options or a range of options, to be proposed to the bargaining parties, formulated to provide, based on reasonably anticipated experience and reasonable actuarial assumptions, for the attainment by the plan of certain requirements. Those requirements are based on a statutorily specified improvement in the plan's funding percentage from the percentage that applied on the first day of the funding improvement period. The first day of the funding improvement period is defined in section 432(c)(4) as the first day of the first plan year beginning after the earlier of (1) the second anniversary of the date of the adoption of the funding improvement plan or (2) the expiration of the collective bargaining agreements in effect on the due date for the actuarial certification of endangered status for the initial endangered year and covering, as of such due date, at least 75 percent of the active participants in such multiemployer plan.

Section 432(d)(1) sets forth rules that apply after the certification of endangered status and before the first day of the funding improvement period. After the adoption of the funding improvement plan, section 432(d)(2) prohibits any amendments that are inconsistent with the funding improvement plan. In addition, section 432(d)(2) provides special rules for acceptance of collective bargaining agreements and plan amendments that increase benefits.

A rehabilitation plan is a plan which consists of the actions, including options or a range of options, to be proposed to the bargaining parties, formulated to provide, based on reasonably anticipated experience and reasonable actuarial assumptions, for the attainment by the plan of certain requirements. Generally, the rehabilitation plan should enable the plan to emerge from critical status by the end of a 10-year period that begins after the earlier of (1) the second anniversary of the date of the adoption of the rehabilitation plan or (2) the expiration of the collective bargaining agreements in effect on the due date for the actuarial certification of critical status for the initial critical year and covering, as of such due date, at least 75 percent of the active participants in such multiemployer plan. For this purpose a plan emerges from critical status when the plan actuary certifies that the plan is not projected to have an accumulated funding deficiency for the plan year or any of the nine succeeding plan years, without regard to the use of the shortfall method and taking into account amortization period extensions under section 431(d). As an alternative, if the plan sponsor determines that, based on reasonable actuarial assumptions and upon exhaustion of all reasonable measures, the plan cannot reasonably be expected to emerge from critical status by the end of the 10-year period, the requirements for a rehabilitation plan are that the plan include reasonable measures to emerge from critical status at a later time or to forestall possible insolvency (within the meaning of section 4245 of ERISA).

Section 432(e)(8) allows a rehabilitation plan for a plan that is in critical status to provide for a reduction of certain "adjustable" benefits that would otherwise be protected by section 411(d)(6). These adjustable benefits include early retirement benefits and retirement-type subsidies within the meaning of section 411 (d)(6)(B)(i). Under section 432(e)(8)(A)(ii), no reduction will apply to a participant whose benefit commencement date is before the date the notice under section 432(b)(3)(D) for the initial critical year is provided. Under section 432(e)(8)(B), except with respect to certain benefit increases described in 432(e)(8)(A)(iv)(III), a plan is not permitted to reduce the level of a participant's accrued benefit payable at normal retirement age. Furthermore, section 432(e)(8)(C) prohibits any reduction until 30 days after plan participants and beneficiaries, employers and employee organizations are notified of the reduction.

In years after the initial critical year or initial endangered year, sections 432(c)(6) and 432(e)(3)(B) provide that the plan sponsor must annually update the funding improvement or rehabilitation plan. This includes updating the schedule of contribution rates. Updates are required to be filed with the plan's annual report.

Section 432(f)(4) sets forth rules that apply after the certification of critical status and before the first day of the rehabilitation period. After the adoption of the rehabilitation plan, section 432(f)(1) prohibits any amendments that are inconsistent with the rehabilitation plan.

Section 432(h) provides rules for the treatment of employees who participate in the plan even though they are not covered by a collective bargaining agreement.

Section 432(i) provides a number of definitions that apply for purposes of section 432. For example, under section 432(i)(8), the actuary's determination with respect to a plan's normal cost, actuarial accrued liability, and improvements in a plan's funded percentage must be based on the unit credit funding method (whether or not that method is used for the plan's actuarial valuation).

Section 432 is effective for plan years beginning on or after January 1, 2008. Section 212(e)(2) of PPA '06 provides a special rule permitting a plan to provide the notice described in section 432(b)(3)(D) on an early basis. Specifically, if the plan actuary certifies that the plan is reasonably expected to be in critical status for the first plan year beginning after 2007, the plan is permitted to provide the notice described in section 432(b)(3)(D) at any time between the enactment of PPA '06 and the date the notice is otherwise required to be provided.

Explanation of Provisions

Overview

These regulations provide guidance with respect to certain of the provisions of section 432. Specifically, these regulations provide guidance regarding the determination of when a plan is in endangered status or critical status and the associated notices. These regulations do not provide guidance with respect to all issues relating to a multiemployer plan that is in endangered or critical status. For example, no guidance is provided on the parameters for the adoption of a funding improvement plan or rehabilitation plan. Guidance with respect to additional issues will be included in a second set of regulations that are expected to be issued this year.

§1.432(a)-1 General rules relating to section 432

Section 1.432(a)-1 provides general rules relating to section 432, including definitions of certain terms used for purposes of section 432 and the special rules that apply to participants in multiemployer plans who are not participating pursuant to a collective bargaining agreement.

The regulations provide that effective on the date that a notice of critical status for the initial critical year is sent to the plan participants, the plan must not pay any benefit in excess of the monthly amount paid under a single life annuity (plus any social security supplement) and is not permitted to purchase an irrevocable commitment from an insurer to pay benefits. The restriction does not apply to the small-dollar cash-outs allowed under section 411(a)(11) nor to the make-up payments under a retroactive annuity starting date.

The regulations provide that if the notice described in section 432(b)(3)(D) has been sent and the restrictions provided under section 432(f)(2) have been applied, and it is later determined that the restrictions should not have been applied, then the plan must correct any benefit payments that were restricted in error. The regulations provide two examples of situations requiring this correction, each of which involves an actuary certifying that the plan is reasonably expected to be in critical status for the first plan year beginning after 2007, followed by an early notification of critical status that is made to employees under the rules of section 212(e)(2) of PPA '06. In one example of a plan taking actions that require correction, the plan restricts benefits before the first plan year beginning after 2007 (the effective date of section 432). In the second such example, the plan is not in critical status for the first plan year beginning after 2007 (even though the enrolled actuary for the plan had certified that it is reasonably expected that the plan will be in critical status with respect to that year).

The regulations incorporate a number of definitions listed in section 432(i) along with other definitions that are located in sections 432(c) and (e). The regulations do not include the broad provision under section 432(i)(8) to use the unit credit funding method for purposes of the plan's "normal cost, actuarial accrued liability, and improvements in a plan's funded percentage." Instead, consistent with the intended scope of section 432(i)(8), the regulations require the use of this funding method solely for purposes of determining a plan's funded percentage and the section 432(b)(2)(C)(i) comparison of contributions with the sum of the plan's normal cost and interest on the amount of unfunded liability. Thus, the determination of whether a plan is projected to have an accumulated funding deficiency in the determination of a plan's status under section 432 is based on the plan's actual funding method, rather than the unit credit funding method. The regulations substitute the term "initial endangered year" for the statutory term "initial determination year."

In addition, the regulations provide guidance for plans that change their status in subsequent years. For example, a plan that is in critical status may emerge from that status and later reenter critical status. In such a circumstance, the year of reentry into critical status is treated as the initial critical year. Similarly, a plan that is in endangered status may have a status change and at a later date reenter endangered status. In such a circumstance, the year of reentry into endangered status is treated as the initial endangered year.

§1.432(b)-1 Determination of status and adoption of a plan

The regulations provide rules for the determination of whether a plan is in endangered status or critical status within the meaning of section 432(b)(1) and (2). These rules reflect the different ways a plan can be in endangered status under section 432(b)(1)(A) or (B) and in critical status under section 432(b)(2)(A), (B), (C), or (D). The regulations also provide that a plan is in critical status for a plan year if it was in critical status in the immediately preceding year and the plan does not meet the emergence from critical status rule of section 432(e)(4)(B). Thus, a plan that was in critical status for the prior year will remain in critical status if the enrolled actuary for the plan certifies that the plan is projected to have an accumulated funding deficiency for the plan year or any of the 9 succeeding plan years, without regard to the use of the shortfall funding method, but taking into account any extensions of the amortization periods under section 431(d).

The regulations provide limited guidance on the actuarial projections that are used for purposes of the certification of status by the enrolled actuary for the plan. The projections must generally be based on reasonable actuarial assumptions and methods that, as under section 431(c)(3), offer the actuary's best estimate of anticipated experience under the plan. The actuarial projection of future contributions and assets must assume either that the terms of the one or more collective bargaining agreements pursuant to which the plan is maintained for the current plan year continue in effect for succeeding plan years, or that the dollar amount of employer contributions for the most recent plan year will continue indefinitely. If the actuarial projections assume the continued maintenance of the collective bargaining agreements, the plan sponsor must provide a projection of activity in the industry, including future covered employment, to the plan actuary, and the actuary is permitted to rely on those projections. In making these projections, the plan sponsor must act reasonably and in good faith. The alternative assumption that the dollar amount of contributions remains unchanged into the future is only available if the enrolled actuary for the plan determines there have been no significant demographic changes that would make such assumption unreasonable. In addition, the regulations provide that the alternative assumption is not available for purposes of determining whether the plan is in critical status under the tests in section 432(b)(2)(A) and (D).

The projected present value of liabilities as of the beginning of such year is determined based on the most recent information reported on the most recent of either the actuarial statement required under section 103(d) of ERISA that has been filed with respect to the most recent year, or the actuarial valuation for the preceding plan year.

The regulations provide that, for purposes of section 432, if the plan received an extension of any amortization period under section 412(e), the extension is treated the same as an extension under section 431(d). Thus, such an extension is taken into account in determining endangered status under section 432(b)(1)(B) and emergence from critical status under section 432(e)(4)(B). In contrast, such an extension is not taken into account in determining whether a plan has or will have an accumulated funding deficiency for purposes of determining critical status under section 432(b)(2)(B) and (C).

The regulations describe the content of the annual certification required under section 432(b)(3) that must be sent to the plan sponsor and the IRS. The annual certification must be provided regardless of whether the plan is in endangered or critical status. If the plan is certified to be in endangered or critical status, then the certification must identify the plan, the plan sponsor, and the enrolled actuary who signs the certification; provide contact information for the plan sponsor and actuary; state whether or not the plan is in endangered or critical status for the plan year; and, if the certification is for a year other than the initial endangered year or the initial critical year, whether the plan is making the scheduled progress described in the plan's funding improvement plan or rehabilitation plan. The regulations also provide an IRS address to which the certification is to be mailed.

The regulations also provide that the content of the annual certification and the IRS address to which it is mailed may be added to or modified in guidance of general applicability to be published in the Internal Revenue Bulletin. Such additional information may include, for instance, which endangered status or critical status standard(s) applies to the plan; supporting information for the classification; a description of the actuarial assumptions used in making the certification; and a projection of the plan's funded percentage for future years. The guidance may also require additional supporting information for certifications made prior to the issuance of the guidance.

The regulations provide guidance on the notice required under section 432(b)(3)(D).[2] In particular the regulations require that, in the case of a plan that is in critical status and which provides for

[2] Under section 432(b)(3)(D)(ii), the Secretary of Labor is to prescribe a model notice that a multiemployer plan may use to satisfy this notice requirement.

benefits that would be restricted under section 432(f)(2), the notice for the initial critical year must tell participants about the restriction. A plan sponsor that sends the model notice provided by the Secretary of Labor pursuant to section 432(b)(3)(D)(iii) satisfies this requirement.

If a section 432(b)(3)(D) notice for such a plan was sent prior to the deadline in that section and the notice did not contain the disclosure regarding the immediate restriction on benefits under section 432(f)(2), then the regulations provide that the notice does not satisfy the requirements for notice under section 432(b)(3)(D). Accordingly, the restrictions under section 432(f)(2) do not apply as a result of the issuance of such a notice and the plan will not be treated as having issued the notice for purposes of the section 432(e)(8)(A)(ii) restriction on reducing adjustable benefits for participants whose benefit commencement dates are prior to the issuance of that notice. However, if additional notice that includes all of the information required under the regulations is provided prior to the required date for notice for the initial critical year under section 432(b)(3)(D) (that is, 30 days after the certification for the plan year), then the notice requirements of section 432(b)(3)(D) are satisfied as of the date of the later notice. In such a case, if the earlier notice contained the information described in section 432(b)(3)(D)(ii), then the date of that earlier notice will apply for purposes of the section 432(e)(8)(A)(ii) restriction.

The regulations reflect the rules of section 212(e)(2) of PPA under which a plan sponsor is permitted to send an early notice to plan participants. This early notice, which applies solely to the first plan year beginning after 2007, is only available if the plan actuary certifies to the plan sponsor that the plan is reasonably expected to be in critical status for that initial plan year. This preliminary certification that the plan is reasonably expected to be in critical status is different from the annual certification that the plan actuary must make; accordingly, the plan actuary must still certify whether the plan is in critical or endangered status (or in neither critical nor endangered status) for that plan year by the normal 90-day deadline for the certification.

Proposed legislation

As of the date of the issuance of these proposed regulations, bills have been introduced in the House of Representatives and the Senate that would exclude from the section 432(f)(2) limitation on accelerated benefits a distribution with an annuity starting date that is before the date that the notice under section 432(b)(3)(D) is provided.[3] Section 1.432(a)-1(a)(3)(iii)(C) has been reserved in order to accommodate any enacted changes.

Effective/Applicability Dates

These regulations apply to plan years ending after March, 18, 2008, but only with respect to plan years that begin on or after January 1, 2008. These regulations do not address the sunset provision provided by PPA '06 section 221(c).

Special Analyses

It has been determined that this notice of proposed rulemaking is not a significant regulatory action as defined in Executive Order 12866. Therefore, a regulatory assessment is not required. It has also been determined that section 553(b) of the Administrative Procedure Act (5 U.S.C. chapter 5) does not apply to these regulations. It is hereby certified that the collection of information imposed by these proposed regulations will not have a significant economic impact on a substantial number of small entities. Accordingly, a regulatory flexibility analysis is not required. The estimated burden imposed by the collection of information contained in these proposed regulations is 0.75 hours per respondent. Moreover, most of this burden is attributable to the requirement for a qualified multiemployer defined benefit plan's enrolled actuary to provide a timely certification of the plan's funding status. In addition, if a plan is certified that it is or will be in critical or endangered status, the plan sponsor is required to notify the Department of Labor, the Pension Benefit Guaranty Corporation, the bargaining parties, participants, and beneficiaries of the status designation. For plans in critical status, the plan sponsor is required to include an explanation of the possibility that adjustable benefits may be reduced and that certain benefits are restricted as of the date the notice is sent. Pursuant to section 7805(f) of the Internal Revenue Code, this regulations has been submitted to the Chief Counsel for Advocacy of the Small Business Administration for comment on its impact on small business.

Comments and Requests for a Public Hearing

Before these proposed regulations are adopted as final regulations, consideration will be given to any written (one signed and eight (8) copies) or electronic comments that are submitted timely to the IRS. The IRS and the Treasury Department request comments on the clarity of the proposed rules and how they may be made easier to understand. All comments will be available for public inspection and copying. A public hearing will be scheduled if requested in writing by any person who timely submits written comments. If a public hearing is scheduled, notice of the date, time, and place of the public hearing will be published in the **Federal Register.**

Drafting Information

The principal author of this regulation is Bruce Perlin, Office of Division Counsel/Associate Chief Counsel (Tax Exempt and Government Entities). However, other personnel from the IRS and the Treasury Department participated in their development.

---

[3] See H.R. 3361 (August 3, 2007) and S. 1974 (August 2, 2007) at sections 3(b)(1)(E) and 3(b)(2)(E)(ii). However, S. 1974, as amended and passed by the Senate on December 19, 2007, did not include this provision.

[¶49,363] Proposed Amendments of Regulations (REG-147775-06), published in the Federal Register on April 17, 2008.

[Code Sec. 2642]

Generation-skipping transfer tax: Allocation of exemption: Elections: Extension of time.—Amendments of Reg. §301.9100-3, describing the circumstances and procedures under which an extension of time will be granted under Code Sec. 2642(g)(1), are proposed. A hearing for this proposal has been scheduled for August 5, 2008.

AGENCY: Internal Revenue Service (IRS), Treasury.

ACTION: Notice of proposed rulemaking and notice of public hearing.

SUMMARY: This document contains proposed regulations providing guidance under section 2642(g)(1). The proposed regulations describe the circumstances and procedures under which an extension of time will be granted under section 2642(g)(1). The proposed guidance affects individuals (or their estates) who failed to make a timely allocation of generation-skipping transfer (GST) exemption to a transfer, and individuals (or their estates) who failed to make a timely election under section 2632(b)(3) or (c)(5). This document also provides notice of a public hearing.

DATES: Written or electronic comments must be received by July 17, 2008.

Outlines of topics to be discussed at the public hearing scheduled for August 5, 2008, must be received by July 15, 2008.

ADDRESSES: Send submissions to: CC:PA:LPD:PR (REG-147775-06), Internal Revenue Service, Room 5203, PO Box 7604, Ben Franklin Station, Washington, DC 20044. Submissions may be hand delivered Monday through Friday between the hours of 8 a.m. and 4 p.m. to CC:PA:LPD:PR (REG-147775-06), 1111 Constitution Avenue NW., Washington, DC 20224; or sent electronically via the Federal eRulemaking Portal at *www.regulations.gov* (IRS-REG-147775-06). The public hearing will be held in the IRS auditorium.

FOR FURTHER INFORMATION CONTACT: Concerning the proposed regulations, Theresa M. Melchiorre, (202) 622-3090; concerning submissions of comments, the hearing, and/or to be placed on the building access list to attend the hearing, Richard Hurst at *Richard.A.Hurst @irscounsel.treas.gov* or (202) 622-7180 (not toll-free numbers).

SUPPLEMENTARY INFORMATION:

Paperwork Reduction Act

The collections of information contained in this notice of proposed rulemaking have been submitted to the Office of Management and Budget for review in accordance with the Paperwork Reduction Act of 1995 (44 U.S.C. 3507(d)). Comments on the collections of information should be sent to the **Office of Management and Budget**, Attn: Desk Officer for the Department of the Treasury, Office of Information and Regulatory Affairs, Washington, DC 20503, with copies to the **Internal Revenue Service**, Attn: IRS Reports Clearance Officer, SE:W:CAR:MP:T:T:SP, Washington, DC 20224. Comments on the collection of information should be received by June 17, 2008.

Comments are specifically requested concerning:

Whether the proposed collection of information is necessary for the proper performance of the functions of the IRS, including whether the information will have practical utility;

The accuracy of the estimated burden associated with the proposed collection of information;

How the quality, utility, and clarity of the information to be collected may be enhanced;

How the burden of complying with the proposed collection of information may be minimized, including through the application of automated collection techniques or other forms of information technology; and

Estimates of capital or start-up costs and costs of operation, maintenance, and purchase of service to provide information.

The reporting requirement in these proposed regulations is in §26.2642-7(h)(2) and (3). This information must be reported by transferors or the executors of transferors' estates requesting relief under section 2642(g)(1). This information will be used by the IRS to determine whether to grant a transferor or a transferor's estate an extension of time to: (1) allocate GST exemption, as defined in section 2631, to a transfer; (2) elect under section 2632(b)(3) (the election not to have the deemed allocation of GST exemption apply to a direct skip); (3) elect under section 2632(c)(5)(A)(i) (the election not to have the deemed allocation of GST exemption apply to an indirect skip or transfers made to a particular trust); and (4) elect under section 2632(c)(5)(A)(ii) (the election to treat any trust as a GST trust for purposes of section 2632(c)).

The following estimates are an approximation of the average time expected to be necessary for a collection of information. They are based on the information that is available to the IRS. Individual respondents may require greater or less time, depending on their particular circumstances.

Estimated total annual reporting burden: 1800 hours.

Estimated average annual burden: 2 hours.

Estimated number of respondents: 900.

Estimated annual frequency of response: When relief is requested.

An agency may not conduct or sponsor, and a person is not required to respond to, a collection of information unless it displays a valid control number assigned by the Office of Management and Budget.

Books or records relating to a collection of information must be retained as long as their contents may become material in the administration of any internal revenue law. Generally, tax returns and tax return information are confidential, as required by 26 U.S.C. 6103.

Background

The proposed regulations provide guidance on the application of section 2642(g)(1). Congress added section 2642(g)(1) to the Internal Revenue Code (Code) in section 564 of the Economic Growth and Tax Relief Reconciliation Act of 2001 (EGTRRA), (Public Law 107-16, § 564, 115 Stat. 91). This section directs the Secretary to issue regulations describing the circumstances and procedures under which an extension of time will be granted to: (1) allocate GST exemption, as defined in section 2631(a), to a transfer; (2) elect under section 2632(b)(3) (the election not to have the deemed allocation of GST exemption apply to a direct skip); (3) elect under section 2632(c)(5)(A)(i) (the election not to have the deemed allocation of GST exemption apply to an indirect skip or transfers made to a particular trust); and (4) elect under section 2632(c)(5)(A)(ii) (the election to treat any trust as a GST trust for purposes of section 2632(c)). In determining whether to grant relief, section 2642(g)(1) directs that all relevant circumstances be considered including evidence of intent contained in the trust instrument or the instrument of transfer.

The legislative history accompanying section 2642(g)(1) indicates that Congress believed that, in appropriate circumstances, an individual should be granted an extension of time to allocate GST exemption regardless of whether any period of limitations had expired. Those circumstances include situations in which the taxpayer intended to allocate GST exemption and the failure to allocate the exemption was inadvertent. H.R. Conf. Rep. No. 107-84, 202 (2001).

After the enactment of section 2642(g)(1), the IRS issued Notice 2001-50 (2001-2 CB 189), which announced that transferors may seek an extension of time to make an allocation of GST exemption. The Notice provides, generally, that relief will be granted under § 301.9100-3 of the Procedure and Administration Regulations if the taxpayer satisfies the requirements of those regulations and establishes to the satisfaction of the Commissioner that the taxpayer acted reasonably and in good faith and that a grant of the requested relief will not prejudice the interests of the Government. If relief is granted under § 301.9100-3 and the allocation is made, the amount of GST exemption allocated to the transfer is the Federal gift or estate tax value of the property as of the date of the transfer and the allocation is effective as of the date of the transfer. (Notice 2001-50 will be made obsolete upon the publication of the Treasury decision adopting these proposed regulations as final regulations in the **Federal Register**.)

On August 2, 2004, the IRS issued Rev. Proc. 2004-46 (2004-2 CB 142), which provides an alternate simplified method to obtain an extension of time to allocate GST exemption in certain situations. Generally, this method is available only with regard to an inter vivos transfer to a trust from which a GST may be made and only if each of the following requirements is met: (1) the transfer qualified for the gift tax annual exclusion under section 2503(b); (2) the sum of the amount of the transfer and all other gifts by the transferor to the donee in the same year did not exceed the applicable annual exclusion amount for that year; (3) no GST exemption was allocated to the transfer; (4) the taxpayer has unused GST exemption to allocate to the transfer as of the filing of the request for relief; and (5) no taxable distributions or taxable terminations have occurred as of the filing of the request for relief.

To date, the IRS has issued numerous private letter rulings under § 301.9100-3 granting an extension of time to timely allocate GST exemption in situations in which transferors (or their executors) failed to allocate GST exemption to a trust on a timely filed Federal gift or estate tax return. These proposed regulations are intended to replace § 301.9100-3 with regard to relief under section 2642(g)(1).

Accordingly, § 301.9100-3 will be amended to provide that relief under section 2642(g)(1) cannot be obtained through the provisions of §§ 301.9100-1 and 301.9100-3 after the date of publication of the Treasury decision adopting these rules as final regulations in the **Federal Register**. Relief under § 301.9100-2(b) (the automatic 6-month extension) will continue to be available to transferors or transferor's estates qualifying for that relief. In addition, the procedures contained in Revenue Procedure 2004-46 will remain effective for transferors within the scope of that Revenue Procedure.

Explanation of Provisions

The proposed regulations identify the standards that the IRS will apply in determining whether to grant a transferor or a transferor's estate an extension of time to: (1) allocate GST exemption, as defined in section 2631, to a transfer; (2) elect under section 2632(b)(3) (the election not to have the deemed allocation of GST exemption apply to a direct skip); (3) elect under section 2632(c)(5)(A)(i) (the election not to have the deemed allocation of GST exemption apply to an indirect skip or transfers made to a particular trust); and (4) elect under section 2632(c)(5)(A)(ii) (the election to treat any trust as a GST trust for purposes of section 2632(c)). The proposed regulations also identify situations with facts that do not satisfy the standards for granting relief and in which, as a result, an extension of time will not be granted.

If an extension of time to allocate GST exemption is granted under section 2642(g)(1), the allocation of GST exemption will be considered effective as of the date of the transfer, and the value of the property transferred for purposes of chapter 11 or chapter 12 will determine the amount of GST exemption to be allocated. If an extension of time to elect out of the automatic allocation of GST exemption under section 2632(b)(3) or (c)(5)(A)(i) is granted under section 2642(g)(1), the election will be considered effective as of the date of the transfer. If an extension of time to elect to treat any trust as a GST trust under section 2632(c)(5)(A)(ii) is granted under section 2642(g)(1), the election will be considered effective as of the date of the first (or each) transfer covered by that election.

The amount of GST exemption that may be allocated to a transfer pursuant to an extension granted under section 2642(g)(1) is limited to the amount of the transferor's unused GST exemption under section 2631(c) as of the date of the transfer. Thus, if the amount of GST exemption has increased since the date of the transfer, no portion of the increased amount may be applied by reason of the grant of relief under section 2642(g)(1) to a transfer taking place in an earlier year and prior to the effective date of that increase.

Requests for relief under section 2642(g)(1) will be granted when the taxpayer establishes to the satisfaction of the IRS that the taxpayer acted reasonably and in good faith, and that the grant of relief will not prejudice the interests of the Government. For purposes of section 2642(g)(1), the following nonexclusive list of factors will be used to determine whether a transferor or the executor of a transferor's estate acted reasonably and in good faith: (1) the intent of the transferor or the executor of the transferor's estate to timely allocate GST exemption or to timely make an election under section 2632(b)(3) or (c)(5) as evidenced in the trust instrument, instrument of transfer, or contemporaneous documents, such as Federal gift or estate tax returns or correspondence; (2) the occurrence of intervening events beyond the control of the transferor as defined in section 2652(a), or of the executor of the transferor's estate as defined in section 2203, that caused the failure to allocate GST exemption to a transfer or the failure to elect under section 2632(b)(3) or (c)(5); (3) the lack of awareness by the transferor or the executor of the transferor's estate of the need to allocate GST exemption to a transfer after exercising reasonable diligence, taking into account the experience of the transferor or the executor of the transferor's estate and the complexity of the GST issue; (4) evidence of consistency by the transferor in allocating (or not allocating) the transferor's GST exemption, although evidence of consistency may be less relevant if there is evidence of a change of circumstances or change of trust beneficiaries that would otherwise support a deviation from prior GST tax exemption allocation practices; and (5) reasonable reliance by the transferor or the executor of the transferor's estate on the advice of a qualified tax professional retained or employed by either (or both) of them, and the failure of the transferor or executor, in reliance on or consistent with that advice, to allocate GST exemption to the transfer or to make an election described in section 2632(b)(3) or (c)(5). The IRS will consider all relevant facts and circumstances in making this determination.

For purposes of section 2642(g)(1), the following nonexclusive list of factors will be used to determine whether the interests of the Government would be prejudiced: (1) the grant of requested relief would permit the use of hindsight to produce an economic advantage or other benefit that either would not have been available if the allocation or election had been timely made, or that results from the selection of one out of a number of alternatives (other than whether or not to make an allocation or election) that were available at the time the allocation or election could have been made timely; (2) if the transferor or the executor of the transferor's estate delayed the filing of the request for relief with the intent to deprive the IRS of sufficient time (by reason of the expiration or the impending expiration of the applicable statute of limitations or otherwise) to challenge the claimed identity of the transferor, the value of the transferred property that is the subject of the requested relief, or any other aspect of the transfer that is relevant for transfer tax purposes; and (3) a determination by the IRS that, in the event of a grant of relief under section 2642(g)(1), it would be unreasonably disruptive or difficult to adjust the GST tax consequences of a taxable termination or a taxable distribution that occurred between the time for making a timely allocation of GST exemption or a timely election described in section 2632(b)(3) or (c)(5) and the time at which the request for relief under section 2642(g)(1) was filed. The IRS will consider all relevant facts and circumstances in making this determination.

Relief under section 2642(g)(1) will not be granted when the standard of reasonableness, good faith and lack of prejudice to the interests of the Government is not met. This standard is not met in the following situations: (1) the transferor or the executor of the transferor's estate made an allocation of GST exemption as described in § 26.2632-1(b)(4)(ii)(A)(*1*), or an election under section 2632(b)(3) or (c)(5), on a timely filed Federal gift or estate tax return, and the relief requested would decrease or revoke that allocation or election; (2) the transferor or the transferor's executor delayed in requesting relief in order to preclude the IRS, as a practical matter, from challenging the identity of the transferor, the value of the transferred interest on the Federal estate or gift tax return, or any other aspect of the transaction that is relevant for Federal estate or gift tax purposes; (3) the action or inaction that is the subject of the request for relief reflected or implemented the decision with regard to the allocation of GST exemption or an election described in section 2632(b)(3) or (c)(5) that was made by the transferor or executor of the transferor's estate who had been accurately informed in all material respects by a qualified tax professional retained or employed by either (or both) of them; or (4) the IRS determines that the transferor's request is an attempt to benefit from hindsight.

A request for relief under section 2642(g)(1) does not reopen, suspend or extend the period of limitations on assessment of any estate, gift, or GST tax under section 6501. Thus, the IRS may request that the transferor or the transferor's executor consent under section 6501(c)(4) to extend the period of limitations on assessment of any or all gift and GST taxes on the transfer(s) for which relief under section 2642(g)(1) has been requested. The transferor or the transferor's executor has the right to refuse to extend the period of limitations, or to limit such extension to particular issues or to a particular period of time. See section 6501(c)(4)(B).

If the grant of relief under section 2642(g)(1) results in a potential tax refund claim, no refund will be paid or credited to the taxpayer or the taxpayer's estate if, at the time of filing the request for relief, the period of limitations for filing a claim for a credit or refund of Federal gift, estate, or GST tax under section 6511 on the transfer for which relief is granted has expired.

Relief provided under section 2642(g)(1) will be granted through the IRS letter ruling program.

Proposed Effective Date

Section 26.2642-7 applies to requests for relief filed on or after the date of publication of the Treasury decision adopting these rules as final regulations in the **Federal Register**.

Availability of IRS Documents

The IRS notice and revenue procedure cited in this preamble are published in the Cumulative Bulletin and are available at www.irs.gov.

Special Analyses

It has been determined that this notice of proposed rulemaking is not a significant regulatory action as defined in Executive Order 12866. Therefore, a regulatory assessment is not required. Pursuant to the Regulatory Flexibility Act (RFA) (5 U.S.C. chapter 6), it is hereby certified that this regulation will not have a significant economic impact on a substantial number of small entities. The applicability of this rule is limited to individuals (or their estates) and trusts, which are not small entities as defined by the RFA (5 U.S.C. 601). Although it is anticipated that there may be a beneficial economic impact for some small entities, including entities that provide tax and legal services that assist individuals in the private letter ruling program, any benefit to those entities would be indirect. Further, this indirect benefit will not affect a substantial number of these small entities because only a limited number of individuals (or their estates) and trusts would submit a private letter ruling request under this rule. Therefore, only a small fraction of tax and legal services entities would generate business or benefit from this rule. Accordingly, a regulatory flexibility analysis is not required. Pursuant to section 7805(f) of the Code, this regulation has been submitted to the Chief Counsel for Advocacy of the Small Business Administration for comment on its impact on small entities.

Comments and Public Hearing

Before these proposed regulations are adopted as final regulations, consideration will be given to any written (a signed original and eight (8) copies) or electronic comments that are submitted timely to the IRS. The IRS and Treasury Department request comments on the clarity of the proposed rules and also on how they can be made easier to understand. All comments will be available for public inspection and copying.

A public hearing has been scheduled for August 5, 2008 in the IRS auditorium. Due to building security procedures, visitors must enter at the Constitution Avenue entrance. In addition, all visitors must present photo identification to enter the building. Because of access restrictions, visitors will not be admitted beyond the immediate entrance area more than 30 minutes before the hearing starts. For more information about having your name placed on the list to attend the hearing, see the "FOR FURTHER INFORMATION CONTACT" section of this preamble.

The rules of 26 CFR 601.601(a)(3) apply to the hearing. Persons who wish to present oral comments at the hearing must submit written (a signed original and eight (8) copies) or electronic comments by July 17, 2008 and an outline of the topics to be discussed and the time to be devoted to each topic by July 15, 2008. A period of 10 minutes will be allotted to each person for making comments. An agenda showing the scheduling of the speakers will be prepared after the deadline for receiving outlines has passed. Copies of the agenda will be available free of charge at the hearing.

Drafting Information

The principal author of these regulations is Theresa M. Melchiorre, Office of Chief Counsel, IRS.

[¶49,374] Proposed Regulations (REG-100464-08), published with the Federal Register on June 18, 2008.

[Code Sec. 411]

Retirement plans: Defined benefit plans: Accrued benefits testing: Greatest of two or more separate formulas.—Amendments of Reg. §1.411(b)-1, providing guidance on the application of the accrual rule for defined benefit plans under Code Sec. 411(b)(1)(B) in cases where plan benefits are determined on the basis of the greatest of two or more separate formulas, are proposed.

AGENCY: Internal Revenue Service (IRS), Treasury.

ACTION: Notice of proposed rulemaking and notice of public hearing.

SUMMARY: This document contains proposed regulations providing guidance on the application of the accrual rule for defined benefit plans under section 411(b)(1)(B) of the Internal Revenue Code (Code) in cases where plan benefits are determined on the basis of the greatest of two or more separate formulas. These regulations would affect sponsors, administrators, participants, and beneficiaries of defined benefit plans. This document also provides a notice of a public hearing on these proposed regulations.

DATES: Written or electronic comments must be received by September 18, 2008. Outlines of topics to be discussed at the public hearing scheduled for October 15, 2008, at 10 a.m. must be received by September 24, 2008. ADDRESSES: Send submissions to: CC:PA:LPD:PR (REG 100464-08), room 5203,

Internal Revenue Service, PO Box 7604, Ben Franklin Station, Washington, DC 20044. Submissions may be hand-delivered Monday through Friday between the hours of 8 a.m. and 4 p.m. to CC:PA:LPD:PR (REG 100464-08), Courier's Desk, Internal Revenue Service, 1111 Constitution Avenue NW., Washington, DC., or sent electronically via the Federal eRulemaking Portal at www.regulations.gov (IRS REG-100464-08). The public hearing will be held in the IRS Auditorium, Internal Revenue Building, 1111 Constitution Avenue NW., Washington, DC.

FOR FURTHER INFORMATION CONTACT: Concerning the regulations, Lauson C. Green or Linda S. F. Marshall at (202) 622-6090; concerning submissions of comments, the hearing, and/or being placed on the building access list to attend the hearing, Richard A. Hurst at Richard.A.Hurst@irscounsel.treas.gov or at (202) 622-7180 (not toll-free numbers).

SUPPLEMENTARY INFORMATION:

Background

This document contains proposed Income Tax Regulations (26 CFR part 1) under section 411(b) of the Code.[1]

Section 401(a)(7) provides that a trust is not a qualified trust under section 401 unless the plan of which such trust is a part satisfies the requirements of section 411 (relating to minimum vesting standards).

Section 411(a) requires a qualified plan to provide that an employee's right to the normal retirement benefit is nonforfeitable upon attainment of normal retirement age and that an employee's right to his or her accrued benefit is nonforfeitable upon completion of the specified number of years of service under one of the vesting schedules set forth in section 411(a)(2). Section 411(a)(7)(A)(i) defines a participant's accrued benefit under a defined benefit plan as the employee's accrued benefit determined under the plan, expressed in the form of an annual benefit commencing at normal retirement age, subject to an exception in section 411(c)(3) under which the accrued benefit is the actuarial equivalent of the annual benefit commencing at normal retirement age in the case of a plan that does not express the accrued benefit as an annual benefit commencing at normal retirement age.

Section 411(a) also requires that a defined benefit plan satisfy the requirements of section 411(b)(1). Section 411(b)(1) provides that a defined benefit plan must satisfy one of the three accrual rules of section 411(b)(1)(A), (B), and (C) with respect to benefits accruing under the plan. The three accrual rules are the 3 percent method of section 411(b)(1)(A), the 133$^1/_3$ percent rule of section 411(b)(1)(B), and the fractional rule of section 411(b)(1)(C).

Section 411(b)(1)(A) provides that a defined benefit plan satisfies the requirements of the 3 percent method if, under the plan, the accrued benefit payable upon the participant's separation from service is not less than (A) 3 percent of the normal retirement benefit to which the participant would be entitled if the participant commenced participation at the earliest possible entry age under the plan and served continuously until the earlier of age 65 or the normal retirement age under the plan, multiplied by (B) the number of years (not in excess of 33 $^1/_3$ years) of his or her participation in the plan. Section 411(b)(1)(A) provides that, in the case of a plan providing retirement benefits based on compensation during any period, the normal retirement benefit to which a participant would be entitled is determined as if the participant continued to earn annually the average rate of compensation during consecutive years of service, not in excess of 10, for which his or her compensation was highest. Section 411(b)(1)(A) also provides that Social Security benefits and all other relevant factors used to compute benefits are treated as remaining constant as of the current plan year for all years after the current year.

Section 411(b)(1)(B) provides that a defined benefit plan satisfies the requirements of the 133 $^1/_3$ percent rule for a particular plan year if, under the plan, the accrued benefit payable at the normal retirement age is equal to the normal retirement benefit, and the annual rate at which any individual who is or could be a participant can accrue the retirement benefits payable at normal retirement age under the plan for any later plan year is not more than 133 $^1/_3$ percent of the annual rate at which the individual can accrue benefits for any plan year beginning on or after such particular plan year and before such later plan year.

For purposes of applying the 133 $^1/_3$ percent rule, section 411(b)(1)(B)(i) provides that any amendment to the plan which is in effect for the current year is treated as in effect for all other plan years. Section 411(b)(1)(B)(ii) provides that any change in an accrual rate which does not apply to any individual who is or could be a participant in the current plan year is disregarded. Section 411(b)(1)(B)(iii) provides that the fact that benefits under the plan may be payable to certain participants before normal retirement age is disregarded. Section 411(b)(1)(B)(iv) provides that Social Security benefits and all other relevant factors used to compute benefits are treated as remaining constant as of the current plan year for all years after the current year.

---

[1] Section 204(b) of the Employee Retirement Income Security Act of 1974, Public Law 93-406 (88 Stat. 829), as amended (ERISA), sets forth rules that are parallel to those in section 411(b) of the Code. Under section 101 of Reorganization Plan No. 4 of 1978 (43 FR 47713), the Secretary of the Treasury has interpretive jurisdiction over the subject matter addressed in these proposed regulations for purposes of ERISA, as well as the Code. Thus, these proposed Treasury regulations issued under section 411(b)(1)(B) of the Code would apply as well for purposes of section 204(b)(1)(B) of ERISA.

Section 411(b)(1)(C) provides that a defined benefit plan satisfies the fractional rule if the accrued benefit to which any participant is entitled upon his or her separation from service is not less than a fraction of the annual benefit commencing at normal retirement age to which the participant would be entitled under the plan as in effect on the date of separation if the participant continued to earn annually until normal retirement age the same rate of compensation upon which the normal retirement benefit would be computed under the plan, determined as if the participant had attained normal retirement age on the date on which any such determination is made (but taking into account no more than 10 years of service immediately preceding separation from service). This fraction, which cannot exceed 1, has a numerator that is the total number of the participant's years of participation in the plan (as of the date of separation from service) and a denominator that is the total number of years the participant would have participated in the plan if the participant separated from service at normal retirement age. Section 411(b)(1)(C) also provides that Social Security benefits and all other relevant factors used to compute benefits are treated as remaining constant as of the current plan year for all years after the current year.

Section 1.411(a)-7(a)(1) of the Income Tax Regulations provides that, for purposes of section 411 and the regulations under section 411, the accrued benefit of a participant under a defined benefit plan is either (A) the accrued benefit determined under the plan if the plan provides for an accrued benefit in the form of an annual benefit commencing at normal retirement age, or (B) an annual benefit commencing at normal retirement age which is the actuarial equivalent (determined under section 411(c)(3) and § 1.411(c)-1)) of the accrued benefit under the plan if the plan does not provide for an accrued benefit in the form of an annual benefit commencing at normal retirement age.

Section 1.411(b)-1(a)(1) provides that a defined benefit plan is not a qualified plan unless the method provided by the plan for determining accrued benefits satisfies at least one of the alternative methods in § 1.411(b)-1(b) for determining accrued benefits with respect to all active participants under the plan. The three alternative methods are the 3 percent method, the 133 1/3 percent rule, and the fractional rule. A defined benefit plan may provide that accrued benefits for participants are determined under more than one plan formula. Section 1.411(b)-1(a)(1) provides that, in such a case, the accrued benefits under all such formulas must be aggregated in order to determine whether or not the accrued benefits under the plan for participants satisfy one of these methods. Under § 1.411(b)-1(a)(1), a plan may satisfy different methods with respect to different classifications of employees, or separately satisfy one method with respect to the accrued benefits for each such classification, provided that such classifications are not so structured as to evade the accrued benefit requirements of section 411(b) and § 1.411(b)-1.

Section 1.411(b)-1(b)(2)(i) provides that a defined benefit plan satisfies the 133 1/3 percent rule for a particular plan year if (A) under the plan the accrued benefit payable at the normal retirement age (determined under the plan) is equal to the normal retirement benefit (determined under the plan), and (B) the annual rate at which any individual who is or could be a participant can accrue the retirement benefits payable at normal retirement age under the plan for any later plan year cannot be more than 133 1/3 percent of the annual rate at which the participant can accrue benefits for any plan year beginning on or after such particular plan year and before such later plan year.

Section 1.411(b)-1(b)(2)(ii)(A) through (D) sets forth a series of rules that correspond to the rules of section 411(b)(1)(B)(i) through (iv). For example, § 1.411(b)-1(b)(2)(ii)(A) sets forth a special plan amendment rule for purposes of satisfying the 133 1/3 percent rule that corresponds to section 411(b)(1)(B)(i). Under that rule, any amendment to a plan that is in effect for the current year is treated as if it were in effect for all other plan years.

Section 1.411(b)-1(b)(2)(ii)(E) provides that a plan is not treated as failing to satisfy the requirements of § 1.411(b)-1(b)(2) for a plan year merely because no benefits under the plan accrue to a participant who continues service with the employer after the participant has attained normal retirement age.[2] Section 1.411(b)-1(b)(2)(ii)(F) provides that a plan does not satisfy the requirements of § 1.411(b)-1(b)(2) if the base for the computation of retirement benefits changes solely by reason of an increase in the number of years of participation.

Rev. Rul. 2008-7 (2008-7 IRB 419), see § 601.601(d)(2)(ii)(b), describes the application of the accrual rules of section 411(b)(1)(A) through (C) and the regulations under section 411(b)(1)(A) through (C) to a defined benefit plan that was amended to change the plan's benefit formula from a traditional formula based on highest average compensation to a new lump sum-based benefit formula. Under the terms of the plan described in the revenue ruling, for an employee who was employed on the day before the change, a hypothetical account was established equal to the actuarial present value of the employee's accrued benefit as of that date, and that account was also to be credited with subsequent pay credits and interest credits. Under transition rules set forth in the plan, the accrued benefit of certain participants is the greater of the accrued benefit provided by the hypothetical account balance at the age 65 normal retirement age and the accrued benefit determined under the traditional formula as in effect on the day before the change, but taking into account post-amendment compensation and service for a limited number of years.

Revenue Ruling 2008-7 describes how the accrued benefits of different participant groups satisfy, or fail to satisfy, the accrual rules under section 411(b)(1)(A) through (C), taking into account the

[2] However, section 411(b)(1)(H), which was added to the Code after the issuance of § 1.411(b)-1, generally requires the continued accrual of benefits after attainment of normal retirement age.

requirement in § 1.411(b)-1(a)(1) that a plan that determines a participant's accrued benefits under more than one formula must aggregate the accrued benefits under all of those formulas in order to determine whether or not the accrued benefits under the plan satisfy one of the alternative methods under section 411(b)(1)(A) through (C). However, Revenue Ruling 2008-7 explains that, in the case of a plan amendment that replaces the benefit formula under the plan for all periods after the amendment, pursuant to section 411(b)(1)(B)(i) and § 1.411(b)-1(b)(2)(ii)(A), the rule that would otherwise require aggregation of the multiple formulas does not apply. Under section 411(b)(1)(B)(i) and § 1.411(b)-1(b)(2)(ii)(A), any amendment to the plan which is in effect for the current plan year is treated as if it were in effect for all other plan years (including past and future plan years).

Revenue Ruling 2008-7 illustrates the application of this rule with respect to participants who only accrue benefits under the new formula (who in the ruling are referred to as participants who are not "grandfathered"). For these participants, the plan amendment completely ceases accruals under a traditional pension benefit formula that provides an annuity at normal retirement age based on service and average pay and, for all periods after the amendment, provides for the greater of the section 411(d)(6) protected benefit under the pre-amendment formula and the benefit under a new post-amendment lump sum-based benefit formula. In such a case, as stated in Revenue Ruling 2008-7, the section 411(d)(6) protected benefit under the pre-amendment formula is not aggregated with the post-amendment formula, but rather is entirely disregarded, for purposes of applying the 133 1/3 percent rule because the new formula is treated under section 411(b)(1)(B)(i) and § 1.411(b)-1(b)(2)(ii)(A) as having been in effect for all plan years. This analysis was reflected in *Register v. PNC Fin. Servs. Group, Inc.*, 477 F.3d 56 (3d Cir. 2007).

In addition to satisfying the requirements of section 411(b)(1)(B), a defined benefit plan must also satisfy the age discrimination rules of section 411(b)(1)(H), taking into account section 411(b)(5), as added to the Code by the Pension Protection Act of 2006, Public Law 109-280 (120 Stat. 780) (PPA '06). In the case of a conversion of a plan to a statutory hybrid plan pursuant to an amendment that is adopted after June 29, 2005 (a "post-PPA conversion plan"), the conversion amendment must satisfy the rule of section 411(b)(5)(B)(iii) that prohibits wearaway of benefits upon conversion. In the case of a plan converted to a statutory hybrid plan pursuant to an amendment that is adopted on or before June 29, 2005 (a "pre-PPA conversion plan"), as provided in Notice 2007-6, the IRS will not consider and will not issue determination letters with respect to whether such a pre-PPA conversion plan satisfies the requirements of section 411(b)(1)(H) (as in effect prior to the addition of section 411(b)(5) by PPA '06), including the effect of any wearaway. Thus, although wearaway upon conversion is expressly prohibited with respect to post-PPA conversion plans pursuant to section 411(b)(5), the IRS will not address and will not issue determination letters with respect to whether a conversion that results in wearaway with respect to a pre-PPA conversion plan violates the age discrimination rules of section 411(b)(1)(H). See § 601.601(d)(2)(ii)(*b*).

Revenue Ruling 2008-7 provides a different analysis as to whether a plan with wearaway fails to satisfy the accrual rules of section 411(b)(1)(B) when the preamendment formula continues in place after the amendment for a group of participants. In such a case, where an amendment has gone into effect but continues the prior formula for some period of time with respect to one or more participants, the application of the rule in section 411(b)(1)(B)(i) and § 1.411(b)-1(b)(2)(ii)(A) does not result in a disregard of the prior plan formula (which remains in effect after the amendment). Instead, the 133 1/3 percent rule must be applied with respect to those participants based on the combined effect of the two ongoing formulas.[3]

Revenue Ruling 2008-7 provides relief from disqualification under the Internal Revenue Code (under the authority of section 7805(b)) for a limited class of plans under which a group of employees specified under the plan receives a benefit equal to the greatest of the benefits provided under two or more formulas (an applicable "greater-of" benefit), provided that each such formula standing alone would satisfy an accrual rule of section 411(b)(1)(A), (B), or (C) for the years involved. Under the relief set forth in Rev. Rul. 2008-7, for plan years beginning before January 1, 2009, the IRS will not treat a plan eligible for the relief as failing to satisfy the accrual rules of section 411(b)(1)(A), (B), and (C) solely because the plan provides an applicable "greater-of" benefit, where the separate formulas, standing alone, would satisfy an accrual rule of section 411(b)(1)(A), (B), and (C).

Explanation of Provisions

The fact pattern described in Revenue Ruling 2008-7 has occurred in a number of situations over the past few years. Employers sponsoring these plans have suggested that their plans should satisfy the accrual rules of section 411(b)(1)(A), (B), and (C), contending that any technical violation of the accrual rules is directly because the participant has higher frontloaded accruals under one formula when compared to the other formula that will ultimately provide the larger benefit under the plan. While the relief under section 7805(b) that is provided under Revenue Ruling 2008-7 addresses the situation for past years, the relief does not apply for the parallel accrual rules of section 204(b)(1)(A), (B) and (C) of ERISA and only applies to plan years beginning before January 1, 2009.

---

[3] Two federal courts have taken a position contrary to this interpretation of section 411(b)(1)(B)(i) and § 1.411(b)-1(b)(2)(ii)(A) as set forth in Revenue Ruling 2008-7. See *Tomlinson v. El Paso Corp.*, 2008 WL 762456 (D. Colo. Mar. 19, 2008); *Wheeler v. Pension Value Plan for Employees of Boeing Corp.*, 2007 WL 2608875 (S.D. Ill. Sept. 6, 2007).

The proposed regulations would provide a limited exception to the existing requirement under § 1.411(b)-1(a)(1) to aggregate the accrued benefits under all formulas in order to determine whether or not the accrued benefits under the plan for participants satisfy one of the alternative methods under section 411(b)(1)(A) through (C). Under this limited exception, certain plans that determine a participant's benefits as the greatest of the benefits determined under two or more separate formulas would be permitted to demonstrate satisfaction of the 133 1/3 percent rule of section 411(b)(1)(B) by demonstrating that each separate formula satisfies the 133 1/3 percent rule of section 411(b)(1)(B).[4]

A plan would be eligible for this exception only if each of the separate formulas uses a different basis for determining benefits. For example, a plan would be eligible for this special rule if it provides a benefit equal to the greater of the benefits under two formulas, one of which determines benefits on the basis of highest average compensation and the other of which determines benefits on the basis of career average compensation. As another example, a traditional defined benefit plan which determined benefits based on highest average compensation that is amended to add a cash balance formula (as in the facts of Rev. Rul. 2008-7) would be eligible for this exception where, in order to provide a better transition for longer service active participants, the plan provides that a group of participants is entitled to the greater of the benefit provided by the hypothetical account balance and the benefit determined under the continuing traditional formula. In each of the above two examples, each separate formula under the plan uses a different basis for determining benefits and, therefore, both of those plans would be eligible to utilize this exception. Accordingly, both plans would be permitted to demonstrate satisfaction of the 133 1/3 percent rule of section 411(b)(1)(B) by demonstrating that each separate formula under the plan satisfies the 133 1/3 percent rule of section 411(b)(1)(B).

The utility of this exception can be seen from the following example of a plan that provides a benefit equal to the greater of two formulas. One formula provides a benefit of 1 percent of average compensation for the 3 consecutive years of service with the highest such average multiplied by the number of years of service at normal retirement age (not in excess of 25 years of service), and the other formula provides a benefit that is the accumulation of 1.5 percent of compensation for each year of service. Under the existing final regulations, the 133 1/3 percent rule of section 411(b)(1)(B) is applied by reference to the annual rate of accrual for each year from the year of the test through normal retirement age. If the participant's accrued benefit currently is determined using the 1 percent formula (because the high-3 average compensation is significantly higher than the effective career average compensation that is used under the 1.5 percent formula), but the participant's normal retirement benefit will ultimately be determined using the 1.5 percent formula if service continues to normal retirement age (because the 25-year service cap will apply to the 1 percent formula, but not the 1.5 percent formula), then the annual rate of accrual will have to be determined for testing purposes on a consistent basis for each year, either using each year's compensation or high-3 average compensation. Thus, in order to test the plan under the 133 1/3 percent rule, the existing final regulations would require that either the accruals under the 1 percent formula be expressed in terms of a single year's pay or the accruals under the 1.5 percent formula be expressed in terms of high-3 average compensation. In either case, the annual rates of accrual would differ from the stated rates under the plan formulas. In addition, the annual rates of accrual for the accumulation formula when those rates are expressed in terms of high-3 average compensation could be negative in some cases. In contrast, using the exception set forth in the proposed regulation would enable the plan to be tested using the annual rates of accrual expressed in the plan formulas.

The proposed regulations would also provide an extension of this exception in the case of a plan that provides benefits based on the greatest of three or more benefit formulas. In such a case, the plan would be eligible for a modified version of the formula-by-formula testing under the proposed regulations. Under this modification, the accrued benefits determined under all benefit formulas that have the same basis are first aggregated and then those aggregated formulas are treated as a single formula for purposes of applying the separate testing rule under the proposed regulations.

Eligibility for separate testing under the proposed regulations would be constrained by an anti-abuse rule. The proposed regulations would provide that a plan is not eligible for separate testing if the Commissioner determines that the plan's use of separate formulas with different bases is structured to evade the general requirement to aggregate formulas under § 1.411(b)-1(a)(1) (for example, if the differences between the bases of the separate formulas are minor).

Proposed Effective/Applicability Date

These regulations are proposed to be effective for plan years beginning on or after January 1, 2009.

Special Analyses

It has been determined that this notice of proposed rulemaking is not a significant regulatory action as defined in Executive Order 12866. Therefore, a regulatory assessment is not required. It also has been determined that section 553(b) of the Administrative Procedure Act (5 U.S.C. chapter 5) does not apply to these regulations, and because the regulations do not impose a collection of information on small entities, the Regulatory Flexibility Act (5 U.S.C. chapter 6) does not apply. Pursuant to section

[4] These proposed regulations would only apply for purposes of the 133 1/3 percent rule of section 411(b)(1)(B) (and the parallel rule of section 204(b)(1)(B) of ERISA). Neither Rev. Rul. 2008-7 nor these proposed regulations are relevant to (and thus they do not affect) the application of the age discrimination rules of section 411(b)(1)(H) (or the parallel age discrimination rules of section 204(b)(1)(H) of ERISA).

7805(f) of the Code, this regulation has been submitted to the Chief Counsel for Advocacy of the Small Business Administration for comment on its impact on small business.

Comments and Public Hearing

Before these proposed regulations are adopted as final regulations, consideration will be given to any written (a signed original and eight (8) copies) or electronic comments that are submitted timely to the IRS. The IRS and the Treasury Department specifically request comments on the clarity of the proposed regulations and how they may be made easier to understand. All comments will be available for public inspection and copying.

Under these proposed regulations, a plan eligible for the separate testing option would not violate the accrual rules merely because the plan provides higher frontloaded accruals under one formula when compared to the other formula that will ultimately provide the larger benefit under the plan. Some commentators have suggested a broader rule that would modify the regulations to provide that a plan does not violate the accrual rules where the plan provides a pattern of accruals that affords higher benefits in earlier years (that is, benefit accruals are frontloaded) relative to a pattern of accruals that satisfies the accrual rules. The 3 percent method of section 411(b)(1)(A) and the fractional rule of section 411(b)(1)(C) automatically achieve this result because they are cumulative tests that test on the basis of the total accrued benefit compared to the projected normal retirement benefit. By contrast, the 133 1/3 percent rule is based on a comparison of the "annual rate at which any individual who is or could be a participant can accrue the retirement benefits payable at normal retirement age" for a later plan year with the annual rate for an earlier plan year. The existing final regulations include an example (§ 1.411(b)-1(b)(2)(iii), Example (3)) that demonstrates how a plan fails the 133 1/3 percent rule where it provides accruals in earlier years that are frontloaded relative to accruals that apply in later years. The proposed regulations do not include a provision under the 133 1/3 percent rule that recognizes prior frontloading of benefits. However, commentators who would suggest such a provision under the 133 1/3 percent rule should describe how that provision would fit within the statutory language of section 411(b)(1)(B), including the application of section 411(b)(1)(B)(i) (which requires that an amendment to the plan that is in effect for the current year be treated as in effect for all other plan years).

A public hearing has been scheduled for October 15, 2008, beginning at 10 a.m. in the Auditorium, Internal Revenue Service, 1111 Constitution Avenue, NW., Washington, DC. Due to building security procedures, visitors must enter at the Constitution Avenue entrance. In addition, all visitors must present photo identification to enter the building. Because of access restrictions, visitors will not be admitted beyond the immediate entrance area more than 30 minutes before the hearing starts. For information about having your name placed on the building access list to attend the hearing, see the **FOR FURTHER INFORMATION CONTACT** section of this preamble.

The rules of 26 CFR 601.601(a)(3) apply to the hearing. Persons who wish to present oral comments at the hearing must submit written or electronic comments by September 18, 2008, and an outline of topics to be discussed and the amount of time to be devoted to each topic (a signed original and eight (8) copies) by September 24, 2008. A period of 10 minutes will be allotted to each person for making comments. An agenda showing the scheduling of the speakers will be prepared after the deadline for receiving outlines has passed. Copies of the agenda will be available free of charge at the hearing.

Drafting Information

The principal authors of these regulations are Lauson C. Green and Linda S. F. Marshall, Office of Division Counsel/Associate Chief Counsel (Tax Exempt and Government Entities). However, other personnel from the IRS and the Treasury Department participated in the development of these regulations.

[¶ 49,376] Proposed Amendments of Regulations (REG-143453-05), published in the Federal Register on June 26, 2008.

[Code Sec. 179B]

Qualified capital costs: Diesel fuel: Sulfur control: Deduction.—Reg. § 1.179B-1, relating to the deduction for qualified capital costs paid or incurred by a small business refiner to comply with the highway diesel fuel sulfur control requirements of the Environmental Protection Agency, is proposed.

AGENCY: Internal Revenue Service (IRS), Treasury.

ACTION: Notice of proposed rulemaking by cross-reference to temporary regulations and notice of public hearing.

SUMMARY: In the Rules and Regulations section of this issue of the **Federal Register** , the IRS is issuing temporary regulations under section 179B of the Internal Revenue Code (Code) relating to the deduction for qualified capital costs paid or incurred by a small business refiner to comply with the highway diesel fuel sulfur control requirements of the Environmental Protection Agency (EPA). The temporary regulations implement changes to the law made by the American Jobs Creation Act of 2004, the Energy Policy Act of 2005, and the Tax Technical Corrections Act of 2007. The text of those temporary regulations also serves as the text of these proposed regulations. This document also provides notice of a public hearing on these proposed regulations.

DATES: Written or electronic comments must be received by September 25, 2008. Outlines of topics to be discussed at the public hearing scheduled for October 28, 2008, at 10 a.m. must be received by September 22, 2008.

ADDRESSES: Send submissions to: CC:PA:LPD:PR (REG-143453-05), room 5203, Internal Revenue Service, PO Box 7604, Ben Franklin Station, Washington, DC 20044. Submissions may be hand-delivered Monday through Friday between the hours of 8 a.m. and 4 p.m. to CC:PA:LPD:PR (REG-143453-05), Courier's Desk, Internal Revenue Service, 1111 Constitution Avenue NW., Washington, DC, or sent electronically via the Federal eRulemaking Portal at http://www.regulations.gov (IRS REG-143453-05). The public hearing will be held in the IRS Auditorium, Internal Revenue Building, 1111 Constitution Avenue, NW, Washington, DC.

FOR FURTHER INFORMATION CONTACT: Concerning the proposed regulations, Nicole Cimino, (202) 622-3110; concerning submissions of comments, the hearing, and/or to be placed on the building access list to attend the hearing, Oulwafunmilayo Taylor, (202) 622-7180 (not toll-free numbers).

SUPPLEMENTARY INFORMATION:

Paperwork Reduction Act

The collection of information contained in this notice of proposed rulemaking has been submitted to the Office of Management and Budget for review in accordance with the Paperwork Reduction Act of 1995 (44 U.S.C. 3507(d)). Comments on the collection of information should be sent to the **Office of Management and Budget** , Attn: Desk Officer for the Department of the Treasury, Office of Information and Regulatory Affairs, Washington, DC 20503, with copies to the **Internal Revenue Service** , Attn: IRS Reports Clearance Officer, SE:W:CAR: MP:T:T:SP, Washington, DC 20224. Comments on the collection of information should be received by August 26, 2008. Comments are specifically requested concerning:

Whether the proposed collection of information is necessary for the proper performance of the functions of the IRS, including whether the information will have practical utility;

The accuracy of the estimated burden associated with the proposed collection of information;

How the quality, utility, and clarity of the information to be collected may be enhanced;

How the burden of complying with the proposed collection of information may be minimized, including through the application of automated collection techniques or other forms of information technology; and

Estimates of capital or start-up costs and costs of operation, maintenance, and purchase of service to provide information.

The collection of information in this proposed regulation is in section 1.179B-1T(d) and section 1.179B-1T(e). This information collected under section 1.179B-1T(d) relates to the election under section 179B(a) by a small business refiner to deduct a portion of the qualified capital costs paid or incurred. The information collected under section 1.179B-1T(e) relates to the election under section 179B(e) by a cooperative small business refiner to allocate all or some of its section 179B(a) deduction to its cooperative owners and to notify those cooperative owners of the allocated amount. This information will be used by the IRS for examination purposes. The collection of information is required to obtain a benefit. The likely respondents are small business refiners.

Estimated total annual reporting burden: 50 hours.

The estimated annual burden per respondent varies from .75 to 1.5 hours, depending on individual circumstances, with an estimated average of 1 hour.

Estimated number of respondents: 50.

Estimated frequency of responses: Annually.

An agency may not conduct or sponsor, and a person is not required to respond to, a collection of information unless it displays a valid control number assigned by the Office of Management and Budget.

Books or records relating to a collection of information must be retained as long as their contents may become material in the administration of any internal revenue law. Generally, tax returns and tax return information are confidential, as required by 26 U.S.C. 6103.

Background

Temporary regulations in the Rules and Regulations section of this issue of the **Federal Register** amend 26 CFR part 1 by adding regulations under section 179B of the Code. The temporary regulations contain rules relating to the deduction provided under section 179B for qualified costs paid or incurred by a small business refiner to comply with the highway diesel fuel sulfur control requirements of the EPA. The text of those temporary regulations also serves as the text of these proposed regulations. The preamble to the temporary regulations explains the temporary regulations and these proposed regulations.

Special Analyses

It has been determined that this notice of proposed rulemaking is not a significant regulatory action as defined in Executive Order 12866. Therefore, a regulatory assessment is not required. It also has been determined that section 553(b) of the Administrative Procedure Act (5 U.S.C. chapter 5) does not apply to these regulations. It is hereby certified that the collection of information in these regulations will not have a significant economic impact on a substantial number of small entities. This certification is based upon the fact, as discussed earlier in this preamble, that the amount of time necessary to record and retain the required information is estimated to average one hour for those taxpayers electing to deduct qualified capital costs and electing to allocate all or some of that deduction to certain owners. Therefore, a Regulatory Flexibility Analysis under the Regulatory Flexibility Act (5 U.S.C. chapter 6) is not required. Pursuant to section 7805(f) of the Code, this notice of proposed rulemaking has been submitted to the Chief Counsel for Advocacy of the Small Business Administration for comment on its impact on small business.

Comments and Public Hearing

Before these proposed regulations are adopted as final regulations, consideration will be given to any written comments (a signed original and eight (8) copies) or electronic comments that are submitted timely to the IRS. The IRS and the Treasury Department specifically request comments on the clarity of the proposed rules and how they may be made easier to understand. All comments will be available for public inspection and copying.

A public hearing has been scheduled for October 28, 2008, beginning at 10:00 a.m. in the IRS Auditorium, Internal Revenue Building, 1111 Constitution Avenue, NW., Washington, DC. Due to building security procedures, all visitors must enter at the Constitution Avenue entrance. In addition, all visitors must present photo identification to enter the building. Because of access restrictions, visitors will not be admitted beyond the immediate entrance area more than 30 minutes before the hearing starts. For information about having your name placed on the building access list to attend the hearing, see the **FOR FURTHER INFORMATION CONTACT** section of this preamble.

The rules of 26 CFR 601.601(a)(3) apply to the hearing. Persons who wish to present oral comments at the hearing must submit written or electronic comments by September 25, 2008 and an outline of the topics to be discussed and the time to be devoted to each topic (signed original and eight (8) copies) by September 22, 2008. A period of 10 minutes will be allotted to each person for making comments. An agenda showing the scheduling of the speakers will be prepared after the deadline for receiving outlines has passed. Copies of the agenda will be available free of charge at the hearing.

Drafting Information

The principal author of these regulations is Nicole R. Cimino, Office of Associate Chief Counsel (Passthroughs and Special Industries). However, other personnel from the IRS and the Treasury Department participated in their development.

[¶49,389] Proposed Amendments of Regulations (REG-155087-05), published in the Federal Register on July 29, 2008.

[Code Secs. 40 and 40A]

Excise tax: Fuel credits: Alcohol mixtures: Biodiesel mixtures: Renewable diesel mixtures: Alternative fuel mixtures: Alternative fuel.—Amendments of Reg. §§1.40-1, 1.40-2 and 1.40A-1 relating to credits and payments for alcohol mixtures, biodiesel mixtures, renewable diesel mixtures, alternative fuel mixtures, and alternative fuel sold of use or used as a fuel, are proposed.

AGENCY: Internal Revenue Service (IRS), Treasury.

ACTION: Notice of proposed rulemaking.

SUMMARY: This document contains proposed regulations relating to credits and payments for alcohol mixtures, biodiesel mixtures, renewable diesel mixtures, alternative fuel mixtures, and alternative fuel sold for use or used as a fuel, as well as proposed regulations relating to the definition of gasoline and diesel fuel. These regulations reflect changes made by the American Jobs Creation Act of 2004, the Energy Policy Act of 2005, the Safe, Accountable, Flexible, Efficient Transportation Equity Act: A Legacy for Users, and the Tax Technical Corrections Act of 2007. These regulations affect producers of alcohol, biodiesel, and renewable diesel; producers of alcohol, biodiesel, renewable diesel, and alternative fuel mixtures; sellers and users of alternative fuel; and certain persons liable for the tax on removals, entries, or sales of gasoline or diesel fuel.

DATES: Written or electronic comments and requests for a public hearing must be received by October 28, 2008.

ADDRESSES: Send submissions to CC:PA:LPD:PR (REG-155087-05), room 5203, Internal Revenue Service, PO Box 7604, Ben Franklin Station, Washington, DC 20044. Submissions may be hand delivered Monday through Friday between the hours of 8 a.m. and 4 p.m. to CC:PA:LPD:PR (REG-155087-05), Courier's Desk, Internal Revenue Service, 1111 Constitution Avenue, NW, Washington, DC, or sent electronically, via the Federal eRulemaking Portal at *http:/www.regulations.gov* (IRS REG-155087-05).

FOR FURTHER INFORMATION CONTACT: Concerning the proposed regulations, Stephanie Bland, Taylor Cortright, or DeAnn Malone, all of whom can be reached at (202) 622-3130 (not a toll-free call); concerning the submission of comments or requests for a public hearing, Oluwafunmilayo Taylor at (202) 622-7180 (not a toll-free call).

SUPPLEMENTARY INFORMATION:

Paperwork Reduction Act

The collections of information contained in this notice of proposed rulemaking have been submitted to the Office of Management and Budget for review in accordance with the Paperwork Reduction Act of 1995 (44 U.S.C. 3507(d)). Comments on the collection of information should be sent to the **Office of Management and Budget**, Attn: Desk Officer for the Department of the Treasury, Office of Information and Regulatory Affairs, Washington, DC 20503, with copies to the Internal Revenue

Service, Attn: IRS Reports Clearance Officer, SE:W:CAR:MP:T:T:SP, Washington, DC 20224. Comments on the collection of information should be received by September 28, 2008. Comments are specifically requested concerning:

Whether the proposed collection of information is necessary for the proper performance of the functions of the Internal Revenue Service, including whether the information will have practical utility;

The accuracy of the estimated burden associated with the proposed collection of information;

How the quality, utility, and clarity of the information to be collected may be enhanced;

How the burden of complying with the proposed collection of information may be minimized, including through the application of automated collection techniques or other forms of information technology; and

Estimates of capital or start-up costs and costs of operation, maintenance, and purchase of service to provide information.

The collection of information in this proposed regulation is in §48.6426-3(e), describing the certificate the biodiesel producer must give to the claimant of a biodiesel mixture credit or biodiesel credit; §48.6426-3(f), describing the statement a biodiesel reseller must give to the claimant of a biodiesel mixture credit or biodiesel credit; §48.6426-4(e), describing the certificate the renewable diesel producer must give to the claimant of a renewable diesel mixture credit or renewable diesel credit; §48.6426-4(f), describing the statement a renewable diesel reseller must give to the claimant of a renewable diesel mixture credit or renewable diesel credit; and §48.6426-6(c), describing the statement given to a seller of liquefied natural gas. This information is required to obtain a tax benefit. This information will be used by the IRS to substantiate claims for the tax benefits. The likely recordkeepers are business or other for-profit institutions and small businesses or organizations.

Estimated total annual reporting burden: 17,710 hours.

Estimated average annual burden hours per respondent varies from 2.5 hours to 25 hours, depending on individual circumstances, with an estimated average of 22 hours.

Estimated number of respondents: 756.

Estimated annual frequency of responses: On occasion.

An agency may not conduct or sponsor, and a person is not required to respond to, a collection of information unless it displays a valid control number assigned by the Office of Management and Budget.

Books or records relating to a collection of information must be retained as long as their contents may become material in the administration of any internal revenue law. Generally, tax returns and tax return information are confidential, as required by 26 U.S.C. 6103.

Background

The Internal Revenue Code (Code) provides incentives for certain renewable and alternative fuels. Before January 1, 2005, a reduced rate of tax applied to most alcohol-blended fuels. The American Jobs Creation Act of 2004 (Public Law 108-357) replaced the reduced rate of tax for alcohol-blended fuels with credits or payments for alcohol and alcohol mixtures that are sold for use or used as a fuel. The Act also added credits and payments for biodiesel and biodiesel mixtures sold for use or used as a fuel. Credit and payment provisions for renewable diesel, renewable diesel mixtures, alternative fuel, alternative fuel mixtures, and diesel-water fuel emulsions were added to the Code by the Energy Policy Act of 2005 (Public Law 109-58) and the Safe, Accountable, Flexible, Efficient Transportation Equity Act: A Legacy for Users (Public Law 109-59) (SAFETEA). Technical corrections to SAFETEA were made by the Tax Technical Corrections Act of 2007 (Public Law 110-172).

The incentives include a credit under section 6426 for alcohol fuel mixtures, biodiesel mixtures, renewable diesel mixtures (incorporated into section 6426 by section 40A(f)), and alternative fuel mixtures sold for use or used as a fuel and alternative fuel sold for use or used as a fuel in a motor vehicle or motorboat. The credit under section 6426 is allowed against the claimant's fuel tax liability. The incentives for these fuels also include a payment under section 6427(e) and a refundable income tax credit under section 34. The amount allowed as a payment or credit under these provisions is reduced by the claimant's excise tax liability against which a credit is allowed under section 6426. Section 40 provides a nonrefundable income tax credit for alcohol fuel mixtures, alcohol that is sold for use or used as a fuel, and for the production of alcohol by certain small ethanol producers; section 40A provides similar rules relating to biodiesel and renewable diesel. The Code includes coordination rules that limit the maximum incentive that may be claimed for any particular gallon of alcohol, biodiesel, renewable diesel, and alternative fuel. Generally, for alcohol that is ethanol, the benefit is $0.51 per gallon; for biodiesel, the incentive is $0.50 per gallon ($1.00 per gallon in the case of agri-biodiesel); for renewable diesel, the incentive is $1.00 per gallon; and, for alternative fuel, the incentive is $0.50 per gallon. In the case of small ethanol producers and small agri-biodiesel producers, however, the Code allows an additional income tax credit of $0.10 per gallon.

Notice 2005-4 (2005-1 CB 289) describes the alcohol and biodiesel credits and payments and provides general guidance for these incentives. Comments received after the publication of Notice 2005-4 requested additional guidance with regard to the biodiesel producer certificates in the case of resale, commingled biodiesel, the definition of agri-biodiesel, and the definition of a biodiesel mixture. Guidance on these issues was provided in Notice 2005-62 (2005-2 CB 443). Notice 2005-80 (2005-2 CB 953) describes the registration requirements related to diesel-water fuel emulsions. Notice 2006-92, (2006-43 IRB. 774) describes the alternative fuel credits and payments. Notice 2007-37

(2007-17 IRB 1002) provides guidance on renewable diesel. Notice 2007-97 (2007-49 IRB 1092) provides guidance on liquid hydrocarbons for purposes of the definition of alternative fuel. Comments were received in response to these notices and have been considered in the development of this notice of proposed rulemaking.

Renewable and alternative fuels; currently applicable rules.

The IRS has received numerous inquiries about the proper steps that must be taken to comply with the tax laws and to take full advantage of the tax incentives for certain renewable and alternative fuels. The following are general rules that are currently applicable and would not be changed by these proposed regulations.

Registration.

Registration by the IRS is required for each person that produces alcohol, biodiesel, renewable diesel, or blended taxable fuel or claims credits or payments with respect to alternative fuel.

Application for registration is made on Form 637, "Application for Registration (For Certain Excise Tax Activities)." A person generally may not engage in an activity for which registration is required until the IRS has approved the person's registration with respect to the activity.

Imposition of tax.

Tax is imposed on the removal of a biodiesel mixture that is diesel fuel from the terminal at the terminal rack. In the case of blended taxable fuel, tax is imposed on a blender's sale or removal of the fuel and the blender is liable for the tax. Blended taxable fuel includes diesel fuel or gasoline produced outside of the bulk transfer/terminal system by mixing an untaxed liquid, such as biodiesel or alcohol, with a taxable fuel, such as diesel fuel or gasoline, that has been previously taxed (even if only at the Leaking Underground Storage Tank Trust Fund financing rate). Thus, for example, if a person produces, outside the bulk transfer/terminal system, a biodiesel mixture that is diesel fuel, that person is liable for tax on its removal or sale of the mixture. Further, tax generally is imposed on the delivery of fuel that has not been taxed into the fuel supply tank of a motor vehicle or diesel-powered train and on the delivery of alternative fuel (liquid fuel other than gas oil, fuel oil, or taxable fuel) into the fuel supply tank of a motorboat unless the delivery of the fuel or alternative fuel is for a nontaxable purpose.

Liability for these excise taxes is reported on Form 720, "Quarterly Federal Excise Tax Return." Persons that are liable for excise taxes may also be required to make semi-monthly deposits. See Form 720 for more information on deposits.

Tax incentives for mixtures.

The excise tax credits for mixtures containing alcohol, biodiesel, renewable diesel, or alternative fuel must be claimed on Form 720, Schedule C. These credits are allowed to the extent of certain fuel tax liability. The credits are claimed by the person producing the mixture.

The mixture producer may also claim payments (or refundable income tax credits) for incentives that exceed tax liability; that is, for the amount by which the maximum incentive allowable for the mixture exceeds the credit allowed on the Form 720. Notice 2005-62 contains guidance on the computation of payment limitations. Claims for payment are made either on Form 8849, "Claim for Refund of Excise Taxes," or Schedule C, Form 720, "Quarterly Federal Excise Tax Return." (Thus, claims on Form 720 may be for both an excise tax credit and a payment.) Claims for the refundable income tax credit are made on Form 4136, "Credit for Federal Tax Paid on Fuel," which is attached to the claimant's income tax return.

Tax incentives for neat fuels.

A nonrefundable general business tax credit may be claimed for alcohol, biodiesel, and renewable diesel fuels that are not in a mixture and are used as a fuel. This is the only credit or payment allowed with respect to the use of these neat fuels as a fuel. Claims for the credit are made by the person using the renewable fuel in a trade or business or by the person that sold the fuel at retail and delivered it into a vehicle. The small ethanol producer credit and the small agri-biodiesel producer credit are also nonrefundable general business credits. Claims for nonrefundable general business credits are made on Form 6478, "Credit for Alcohol Used as Fuel," and Form 8864, "Biodiesel and Renewable Diesel Fuels Credit," attached to the claimant's income tax return.

An excise tax credit may be claimed for alternative fuel that is not in a mixture and is used as a fuel. The excise tax credit is claimed on Form 720, Schedule C. The credit is allowed to the extent of certain fuel excise tax liability. The credit is claimed by the alternative fueler (unmixed fuel). If the incentive for unmixed alternative fuel exceeds the applicable excise tax liability the excess may be claimed as a payment on Form 8849 or as a refundable income tax credit on Form 4136.

Explanation of Provisions

The proposed regulations add provisions relating to registration requirements and excise tax credits or payments for alcohol, biodiesel, renewable diesel and alternative fuel mixtures and for alternative fuel and dieselwater fuel emulsions. The regulations provide definitions and prescribe rules for claiming a credit or payment. Specifically, the regulations prescribe the conditions to allowance of a credit or payment, the content of claims for credit or payment, and the form of applicable certificates. The proposed regulations also remove obsolete regulations relating to gasohol and other alcohol fuels.

The proposed regulations generally adopt the rules of Notices 2005-4, 2005-62, 2005-80, 2006-92, 2007-37, and 2007-97. Differences between the notices and the proposed regulations are described in this preamble.

Biodiesel mixtures and liability for tax.

Notice 2005-62 provides that *biodiesel mixture* means a mixture of biodiesel and diesel fuel that contains at least 0.1 percent (by volume) of diesel fuel. That rule is unchanged by these proposed regulations.

Under existing regulations, diesel fuel does not include "excluded liquid"; biodiesel mixtures with a high concentration of biodiesel typically are classified as an excluded liquid. The definition of "excluded liquid" predates the biodiesel incentives and was intended to ensure that the diesel fuel tax was not imposed on certain liquids typically not used as fuel. The proposed regulations revise the definition of "excluded liquid" so that all biodiesel mixtures, which are generally used as a substitute for diesel fuel, will be classified as diesel fuel for tax purposes. As a result, under the proposed regulations, tax is imposed on a biodiesel mixture when it is removed from the bulk transfer/terminal system. If a biodiesel mixture is produced outside the bulk transfer/terminal system, tax is imposed on the sale or removal of the mixture by the mixture producer. The mixture producer is liable for the tax and must be registered as a blender of taxable fuel. The tax incentive for the biodiesel mixture generally must be taken as a credit against the producer's fuel tax liability and any excess over the fuel tax liability is allowable as either a payment or an income tax credit.

Also, the de minimis exception to the definition of "blended taxable fuel" is removed. Under this exception, a mixture is not blended fuel if the person creating the mixture adds less than 400 gallons of untaxed liquid to previously taxed fuel during the quarter and the operator of the vehicle using the mixture is liable for the tax on the untaxed liquid. Thus, in cases in which the untaxed liquid is alcohol, biodiesel, or alternative fuel, the exception prevents the credit for which the mixture producer is eligible from being used to offset the tax. With the removal of this exception, the same person (the producer of the mixture) will be liable for the tax and eligible for the credit that can be used to offset the tax.

Biodiesel and EPA registration requirements.

The Code defines *biodiesel* as monoalkyl esters of long chain fatty acids derived from plant or animal matter that meet (1) the registration requirements of the Environmental Protection Agency (EPA) for fuel and fuel additives and, (2) ASTM D6751. Under the proposed regulations, a product meets the EPA registration requirements if the EPA does not require the product to be registered. Thus, for example, if a biodiesel mixture is to be sold only at a marina for use in boats, the biodiesel in the mixture meets the EPA registration requirement because EPA registration requirements do not apply to fuels or fuel additives sold for use in boats.

Biodiesel certificates.

The Code provides that a claim relating to a biodiesel mixture is not allowed unless, among other conditions, the claimant obtains the prescribed certificate from the biodiesel producer. Under existing rules, as well as the proposed regulations, this certificate must be attached to the claim that is filed with the IRS. However, the proposed regulations do not require a separate certificate to accompany the claim filed by a mixture producer that is also the producer of the biodiesel in the mixture. Further, the proposed regulations require, as a condition to allowance of an excise tax credit or a payment, that the claimant obtain the certificate from a registered biodiesel producer. If the claim is for a nonrefundable general business credit, the certificate may be from the registered producer or importer.

Erroneous biodiesel certificates.

Under the Code, a claim relating to a biodiesel mixture is not allowed if the mixture does not actually contain biodiesel. Guidance was requested on whether a claim would be allowed if the claimant attached a certificate for biodiesel and the information on the certificate proved to be incorrect. The proposed regulations make clear that such a claim is not allowed even if the claim is based on a biodiesel certificate that the claimant accepted in good faith. In such a case, however, the proposed regulations generally provide that reliance on the certificate will be treated as reasonable cause for purposes of the penalties imposed by sections 6651 (relating to failure to pay) and 6675 (relating to excessive claims).

Alternative fuel.

The Code allows a credit or payment for alternative fuel that is not in a mixture if the alternative fuel is sold for use or used as a fuel in a motor vehicle or motorboat. If the claim is based on a sale, the claimant must deliver the fuel into the fuel supply tank of the motor vehicle or motorboat or, in the case of a bulk sale, obtain the statement described in §48.4041-5(a)(2), §48.4041-21(b), or proposed §48.6426-6(c).

Registration of alternative fuelers.

A person must be registered by the IRS before claiming the alternative fuel or alternative fuel mixture credit or payment. Section 34 allows a refundable income tax credit with respect to alternative fuel or an alternative fuel mixture. This credit is claimed on Form 4136 filed with the claimant's Federal income tax return. Because partnerships do not file federal income tax returns, the refundable income tax credit allowable with respect to a partnership's sale or use of alternative fuel is made by its partners. The partners may file Form 4136 with their income tax returns to claim a credit based on the information provided them on the partnership's Schedule K-1.

The proposed regulations provide that a partner in a partnership is treated as a registered alternative fueler for purposes of claims on Form 4136 if the partnership is registered for purposes of claims for an excise tax credit or payment. A partner that is treated as registered under this rule is to provide the partnership's registration number on Form 4136. These rules also apply for purposes of ultimate vendor claims by partners in partnerships that are ultimate vendors of diesel fuel or kerosene.

Small ethanol producer credit.

Section 40(a)(3) provides an income tax credit for ethanol produced by eligible small ethanol producers. The amount of ethanol that is eligible for the credit during any taxable year cannot exceed 15,000,000 gallons for any producer. A small ethanol producer generally means a person whose productive capacity for all alcohol, including alcohol for which a credit is not allowable under section 40, does not exceed 60,000,000 gallons at any time during the taxable year. Section 40(g)(5) authorizes the Secretary to prescribe regulations to prevent the credit from benefiting a person that directly or indirectly has a productive capacity for alcohol in excess of 60,000,000 gallons and to prevent any person from directly or indirectly benefiting with respect to more than 15,000,000 gallons during the taxable year. Section 40A provides similar rules with respect to the small agri-biodiesel producer credit.

The proposed regulations provide that *producer* means the person that has title to the ethanol immediately after the ethanol is created. Also, the producer must use a feedstock other than ethanol to produce the ethanol. The proposed regulations do not allow the credit for ethanol produced at the facilities of a contract manufacturer if the contract manufacturer has a direct or indirect productive capacity of more than 60,000,000 gallons of alcohol during the taxable year. Similarly, if the manufacturer does not have a productive capacity of more than 60,000,000 gallons but more than 15,000,000 gallons of ethanol is produced at the manufacturer's facilities during the taxable year, the proposed regulations allow the credit with respect to only the first 15,000,000 gallons of ethanol produced at the facilities during the taxable year. These rules apply to small agribiodiesel producers also.

Gasoline and gasoline blends.

The Code defines gasoline as including gasoline blends. The proposed regulations generally define a gasoline blend as any liquid that contains at least 0.1 percent (by volume) of finished gasoline and that is suitable for use as a fuel in a motor vehicle or motorboat. Thus, for example, E-85 (a mixture of 85 percent ethanol made from corn or other agricultural products and 15 percent gasoline) is treated as a gasoline blend. Tax is imposed on the gasoline blend when it is removed from the bulk transfer/terminal system or, if it is blended taxable fuel, when it is sold or removed by the blender. The proposed regulations also classify leaded gasoline as gasoline. Thus, for example, gasoline products that are sold as "racing gasoline" generally are treated as gasoline even though their lead content make them unsuitable for highway use.

Excise tax returns.

The privilege to file consolidated returns under section 1501 applies only to income tax returns and not to excise tax returns. The proposed regulations note this rule and also reflect the rules of §301.7701-2(c)(2)(v), which was added by TD 9356 (72 FR 45891, August 16, 2007), relating to the excise tax treatment of certain business entities that are treated as separate from their owner for income tax purposes.

Proposed effective/applicability date.

The amendments to the regulations generally are proposed to be effective on the date they are published as final regulations in the **Federal Register**.

Future regulations projects.

Future proposed regulations will address other fuel-related provisions in the American Jobs Creation Act, the Energy Policy Act, and SAFETEA. These include provisions related to kerosene used in aviation, the Leaking Underground Storage Tank Trust Fund tax, the tax on alternative fuel, and two-party exchanges.

Availability of IRS documents

IRS notices cited in this preamble are published in the Internal Revenue Bulletin or Cumulative Bulletin and are available at IRS.gov.

Special Analyses

It has been determined that this notice of proposed rulemaking is not a significant regulatory action as defined in Executive Order 12866. Therefore, a regulatory assessment is not required. It also has been determined that section 553(b) of the Administrative Procedure Act (5 U.S.C. chapter 5) does not apply to these proposed regulations. It is hereby certified that this regulation will not have a significant economic impact on a substantial number of small entities. This certification is based on IRS estimates that less than 700 small entities will be required to provide certificates each year, such certificates will be provided only on occasion, and the average annual burden per respondent will be 22 hours. The economic impact of the collection of information is limited to completing a certificate in the form prescribed by the regulations. The certificate can be completed by filling in a small number of fields with information that is readily available to the taxpayer, and completion of a certificate should generally take less than 15 minutes. Accordingly, the time and resources required to prepare and provide these certificates is minimal and will not have a significant effect on those entities providing them. Therefore, an analysis under the Regulatory Flexibility Act (5 U.S.C. chapter 6) is not required. Pursuant to section 7805(f) of the Internal Revenue Code, this notice of proposed rulemaking has been submitted to the Chief Counsel for Advocacy of the Small Business Administration for comment on its impact on small business.

Comments and Requests for a Public Hearing

Before these proposed regulations are adopted as final regulations, consideration will be given to any written (a signed original and eight (8) copies) or electronic comments that are submitted timely to the IRS. The IRS and the Treasury Department request comments on the clarity of the proposed regulations and how they may be made easier to understand. All comments will be available for public inspection and copying. A public hearing will be scheduled if requested in writing by any person that timely submits written comments. If a public hearing is scheduled, notice of the date, time, and place for the hearing will be published in the **Federal Register**.

Drafting Information

The principal authors of these regulations are Taylor Cortright and Frank Boland, Office of Associate Chief Counsel (Passthroughs and Special Industries). However, other personnel from the IRS and the Treasury Department participated in their development.

[¶ 49,390] **Proposed Amendments of Regulations (REG-120844-07)**, published in the Federal Register on August 4, 2008.

[Code Sec. 460]

Long-term contracts: Construction contracts: Home construction contracts.—Amendments of Reg. §§1.460-3, 1.460-4, 1.460-5 and 1.460-6, providing guidance to taxpayers in the home construction industry regarding accounting for certain long-term construction contracts that qualify as home construction contracts, are proposed..

AGENCY: Internal Revenue Service (IRS), Treasury.

ACTION: Notice of proposed rulemaking and Notice of Public Hearing.

SUMMARY: This document contains proposed regulations amending the regulations under § 1.460 to provide guidance to taxpayers in the home construction industry regarding accounting for certain long-term construction contracts that qualify as home construction contracts under section 460(e)(6) of the Internal Revenue Code (Code) and to provide guidance to taxpayers with long-term contracts under section 460(f) regarding certain changes in method of accounting for long-term contracts. This document also provides a notice of a public hearing on these proposed regulations.

DATES: Written comments must be received by November 3, 2008. Outlines of topics to be discussed at the public hearing scheduled for December 5, 2008, at 10:00 a.m. must be received by November 13, 2008.

ADDRESSES: Send submissions to CC:PA:LPD:PR (REG-120844-07), room 5203, Internal Revenue Service, POB 7604 Ben Franklin Station, Washington, DC 20224. Submissions may be hand delivered Monday through Friday between the hours of 8 a.m. and 4 p.m. to CC:PA:LPD:PR (REG-120844-07), Courier's Desk, Internal Revenue Service, 1111 Constitution Avenue, NW., Washington, DC. Alternatively, taxpayers may submit comments electronically via the Federal eRulemaking Portal at www.regulations.gov (IRS REG-120844-07). The public hearing will be held in the auditorium, Internal Revenue Service Building, 1111 Constitution Avenue, NW., Washington, DC.

FOR FURTHER INFORMATION CONTACT: Concerning the proposed regulations, Brendan P. O'Hara, (202) 622-4920; concerning submission of comments, the hearing, or to be placed on the building access list to attend the hearing, Richard Hurst, (202) 622-7180 (not toll-free numbers).

SUPPLEMENTARY INFORMATION:

Background and Explanation of Provisions

This document contains a proposed amendment to the Income Tax Regulations, 26 CFR Part 1, under section 460 and §§1.460-3, 1.460-4, 1.460-5 and 1.460-6 of the Income Tax Regulations. In general, section 460(a) requires taxpayers to use the percentage of completion method (PCM) to account for taxable income from any long-term contract. Section 460(e) exempts home construction contracts from the general requirement to use the percentage of completion method of accounting. Section 460(e)(6) defines a home construction contract to be any construction contract if 80 percent or more of the total estimated contract costs are reasonably expected to be attributable to the construction of (i) dwelling units contained in buildings containing 4 or fewer dwelling units, and (ii) improvements to real property directly related to such dwelling units and located on the site of such dwelling units. Section 460(e)(4) defines a construction contract to be any contract for the building, construction, reconstruction, or rehabilitation of, or the installation of any integral component to, or improvement of, real property.

These proposed regulations expand the types of contracts eligible for the home construction contract exemption and amend the rules for how taxpayer-initiated changes in methods of accounting to comply with the regulations under section 460 may be implemented.

Definition of a Home Construction Contract

Improvements to real property

The definition of a *construction contract* under section 460(e) includes many transactions involving land developers and construction service providers in the home construction industry. For example, a construction contract under section 460(e) includes a contract for the provision of land by the taxpayer if the estimated total allocable contract costs attributable to the taxpayer's construction activities (not including the cost of the land provided to the customer) are 10 percent or more of the contract's total contract price.

As noted, section 460(a) requires that the income from any long-term contract be recognized using the percentage of completion method. However, taxpayers with contracts that meet the definition of a "home construction contract" are not required to use the percentage of completion method for those contracts and may use an exempt method. Exempt methods commonly used to account for home construction contracts include the completed contract method (CCM) and the accrual method.

Under section 460, a home construction contract includes any construction contract if 80 percent of the total estimated contract costs are reasonably expected to be attributable to the construction of improvements to real property directly related to qualifying dwelling units and located on the site of such dwelling units. Commentators have suggested that many contracts entered into by land developers in the home construction industry should fall within the definition of a home construction contract.

The proposed regulations expand the scope of the home construction contract exemption by providing that a contract for the construction of common improvements is considered a contract for the construction of improvements to real property directly related to the dwelling unit(s) and located on the site of such dwelling unit(s), even if the contract is not for the construction of any dwelling unit. Therefore, under the proposed regulations, a land developer that is selling individual lots (and its contractors and subcontractors) may have long-term construction contracts that qualify for the home construction contract exemption.

Townhouses, rowhouses, and condominiums

Under section 460, a home construction contract also includes any construction contract if 80 percent of the total contract costs are reasonably expected to be attributable to the construction of dwelling units contained in buildings containing four or fewer dwelling units. Section 460(e)(6) states that each townhouse or rowhouse shall be treated as a separate building, regardless of the number of townhouses or rowhouses physically attached to each other. In certain circumstances, the terms condominium and townhouse are used interchangeably to describe similar structures. Individual condominium units possess many of the characteristics generally associated with townhouses and rowhouses such as private ownership, shared portions of their structures, residential housing, and the economics of the underlying purchase transactions.

The proposed regulations expand what is considered a townhouse or rowhouse, for purposes of the home construction contract exemption, to include an individual condominium unit. This will have the effect of allowing each condominium unit to be treated as a separate building for purposes of determining whether the underlying contract qualifies as a home construction contract.

Completed contract method

Under the current regulations under section 460, the appropriate severing of a home construction contract requires a facts and circumstances analysis based upon certain factors that are neither specific nor always relevant to home construction contracts. Likewise, the date a home construction contract is considered completed and accepted is determined using a facts and circumstances analysis.

The IRS and Treasury Department are aware of controversies related to the application of the existing facts and circumstances analyses for determining the appropriate severance and final completion and acceptance of home construction contracts accounted for using the completed contract method. Expanding the definition of a home construction contract as provided in these proposed regulations may heighten the significance of these issues. As a result, the IRS and Treasury Department expect to propose specific severing and completion rules for home construction contracts accounted for using the completed contract method. Taxpayers are encouraged to submit comments on the types of severing and completion rules that would result in the clear reflection of income for home construction contracts accounted for using the completed contract method. Specifically, the IRS and the Treasury Department request comments on the circumstances (if any) in which it would not be appropriate to require severing and completion of a home construction contract to be determined on a dwelling unit by dwelling unit or lot by lot basis or, when a contract is not for the sale of a dwelling unit or lot, on the basis of when the taxpayer receives payment(s) under the contract.

Method of accounting

Currently, the regulations under section 460 provide that a taxpayer that uses the percentage-of-completion method (PCM), the exempt-contract percentage-of-completion method (EPCM), or elects the 10-percent method or special alternative minimum taxable income (AMTI) method, or that adopts or elects a cost allocation method of accounting (or changes to another method of accounting with the Commissioner's consent) must apply the method(s) consistently for all similarly classified contracts until the taxpayer obtains the Commissioner's consent under section 446 to change to another method of accounting. The regulations further provide that a taxpayer-initiated change in method of accounting will be permitted only on a cut-off basis (that is, for contracts entered into on or after the year of change), and thus, a section 481(a) adjustment will not be permitted nor required. The proposed regulations continue this cut-off method of implementation but only for taxpayer-initiated changes from a permissible PCM method to another permissible PCM method for long-term contracts for which PCM is required and for taxpayer-initiated changes from a cost allocation method of accounting that complies with the cost allocation rules of § 1.460-5 to another cost allocation method of accounting that complies with the cost allocation rules of § 1.460-5. Under the proposed regulations all other taxpayer-initiated changes in method of accounting under section 460 will be made with a section 481(a) adjustment.

The proposed regulations provide that in determining the hypothetical underpayment or overpayment of tax for any year as part of the look-back computation, amounts reported as section 481(a) adjustments shall generally be taken into account in the tax year or years they are reported. For purposes of determining whether there is a hypothetical underpayment or overpayment of tax under the look-back computation, a taxpayer would use amounts reported under its old method for the years the old method was used and would use amounts reported under its new method for the years the new method was used, netted against the amount of any section 481(a) adjustments required to be taken into account. Thus, a look-back computation would not be required upon contract completion simply because the taxpayer has changed its method of accounting. However, a look-back computation would be required upon contract completion if actual costs or the contract price differ from the estimated amounts notwithstanding the fact a change in method of accounting occurred. For example, if a taxpayer using PCM changed its method of accounting for construction costs incurred in a contract reported under PCM, the section 460 look-back would be computed using the costs recognized prior to the year of change (reported under the taxpayer's old method of accounting) and the costs recognized in subsequent years using the new method of accounting, netted against any applicable section 481(a) adjustment. Similarly, for changes in methods of accounting where no costs were recognized under the old method of accounting (for example, a change in method of accounting from CCM to PCM), look-back would effectively only apply to years in which the taxpayer's new method of accounting was used to the extent that no costs were recognized prior to the year of change under the old method of accounting. This approach to the look-back computation is consistent with the underlying purpose of look-back as well as the general accounting method change procedures. Comments are specifically requested with respect to issues that taxpayers may foresee with respect to the rules provided in these proposed regulations for taking into account section 481(a) adjustments in the year reported for purposes of the look-back computation.

Proposed Effective/Applicability Date

These regulations are proposed to apply to taxable years beginning on or after the date the final regulations are published in the **Federal Register**. The final regulations will provide rules applicable to taxpayers that seek to change a method of accounting to comply with the rules contained in the final regulations. Taxpayers may not change or otherwise use a method of accounting in reliance upon the rules contained in these new proposed regulations until the rules are published as final regulations in the **Federal Register**.

Special Analyses

It has been determined that this proposed regulation is not a significant regulatory action as defined in Executive Order 12866. Therefore, a regulatory assessment is not required. It has also been determined that section 553(b) of the Administrative Procedure Act (5 U.S.C. chapter 5) does not apply, and because the regulations do not impose a collection of information on small entities, the Regulatory Flexibility Act (5 U.S.C. chapter 6) does not apply. Pursuant to section 7805(f) of the Code, this notice of proposed rulemaking will be submitted to the Chief Counsel for Advocacy of the Small Business Administration for comment on its impact on small businesses.

Comments and Public Hearing

Before these proposed regulations are adopted as final regulations, consideration will be given to any written comments (a signed original with eight (8) copies) or electronic comments that are submitted timely to the IRS. The IRS and Treasury Department request comments on the clarity of the proposed regulations and how they may be made easier to understand. All comments will be available for public inspection and copying.

A public hearing has been scheduled for December 5, 2008, beginning at 10:00 a.m., in the auditorium of the Internal Revenue Building, 1111 Constitution Avenue, NW., Washington, DC. Due to building security procedures, visitors must enter at the Constitution Avenue entrance. In addition, all visitors must present photo identification to enter the building. Because of access restrictions, visitors will not be admitted beyond the immediate entrance area more than 30 minutes before the hearing starts. For information about having your name placed on the building access list to attend the hearing, see the "FOR FURTHER INFORMATION CONTACT" section of this preamble.

The rules of 26 CFR 601.601(a)(3) apply to the hearing. Persons who wish to present oral comments at the hearing must submit electronic or written comments and an outline of the topics to be discussed and the time to be devoted to each topic (signed original and eight (8) copies) by November 13, 2008. A period of 10 minutes will be allotted to each person for making comments. An agenda showing the scheduling of the speakers will be prepared after the deadline for receiving outlines has passed. Copies of the agenda will be available free of charge at the hearing.

Drafting Information

The principal author of these regulations is Brendan P. O'Hara, Office of Associate Chief Counsel (Income Tax and Accounting). However, other personnel from the IRS and Treasury Department participated in their development.

[¶49,393] Proposed Amendments of Regulations (REG-149404-07), published in the Federal Register on August 11, 2008.

[Code Sec. 45D]

Credits: Business related credits: New markets tax credit.—Amendments of Reg. §1.45D-1, relating to the new markets tax credit under section 45D of the Internal Revenue Code, are proposed.

AGENCY: Internal Revenue Service (IRS), Treasury.

ACTION: Notice of proposed rulemaking and notice of public hearing.

SUMMARY: This document contains proposed regulations relating to the new markets tax credit under section 45D of the Internal Revenue Code (Code). The proposed regulations revise and clarify certain rules relating to recapture of the new markets tax credit and will affect certain taxpayers claiming the new markets tax credit. This document also provides a notice of a public hearing on these proposed regulations.

DATES: Written or electronic comments must be received by November 10, 2008. Outlines of topics to be discussed at the public hearing scheduled for December 12, 2008, at 10:00 a.m. must be received by November 3, 2008.

ADDRESSES: Send submissions to: CC:PA:LPD:PR (REG-149404-07), room 5203, Internal Revenue Service, PO Box 7604, Ben Franklin Station, Washington, DC 20044. Submissions may be hand delivered Monday through Friday between the hours of 8 a.m. and 4 p.m. to: CC:PA:LPD:PR (REG-149404-07), Courier's Desk, Internal Revenue Service, 1111 Constitution Avenue, NW, Washington, DC, or sent electronically, via the Federal eRulemaking Portal at http://www.regulations.gov (IRS REG-149404-07). The public hearing will be held in the IRS Auditorium, Internal Revenue Building, 1111 Constitution Avenue, NW, Washington, DC.

FOR FURTHER INFORMATION CONTACT: Concerning the proposed regulations, Julie Hanlon-Bolton, (202) 622-7028; concerning submission of comments, the hearing, and/or to be placed on the building access list to attend the hearing, Regina Johnson, (202) 622-7180 (not toll-free numbers).

SUPPLEMENTARY INFORMATION:

Background

This document amends 26 CFR part 1 to provide and clarify rules relating to the new markets tax credit under section 45D of the Code. Section 45D was added to the Code by section 121 of the Community Renewal Tax Relief Act of 2000, Public Law 106-554 (114 Stat. 2763 (2000)) and amended by section 221 of the American Jobs Creation Act of 2004, Public Law 108-357 (118 Stat. 1418 (2004)), section 101 of the Gulf Opportunity Zone Act of 2005, Public Law 109-135 (119 Stat. 25 (2005)), and Division A, section 102 of the Tax Relief and Health Care Act of 2006, Public Law 109-432 (120 Stat. 2922 (2006)). On December 28, 2004, the IRS and the Treasury Department published final regulations under section 45D (69 FR 77625), with corrections on January 28, 2005 (70 FR 4012).

Groups and organizations representing investors, qualified community development entities, businesses, and other entities involved with the new markets tax credit program have since submitted comments requesting further guidance on the recapture of the credit. The commentators suggested that revising the final regulations to reduce recapture uncertainty would encourage investors to bring increased amounts of capital to low-income communities.

General Overview

Section 45D(a)(1) provides a new markets tax credit on a taxpayer's qualified equity investment (QEI) in a qualified community development entity (CDE). To qualify for the credit, among other requirements, substantially all of the taxpayer's cash must be used by the CDE to make qualified low-income community investments (QLICIs) pursuant to section 45D(b)(1)(B).

A CDE is any domestic corporation or partnership if, among other requirements, the primary mission of the entity is serving, or providing investment capital for, lowincome communities or low-income persons pursuant to section 45D(c)(1). Section 45D(d)(1) provides that a QLICI is: (A) any capital or equity investment in, or loan to, any qualified active low-income community business (QALICB); (B) the purchase from another CDE of any loan made by the entity that is a QLICI; (C) financial counseling and other services to businesses located in, and residents of, low-income communities; and (D) any equity investment in, or loan to, any CDE. A QALICB is any corporation or partnership in which at least 50 percent of the total gross income of the entity is derived from the active conduct of a qualified business within any low-income community, provided certain other requirements are met pursuant to section 45D(d)(2).

Section 45D(g)(1) provides that, if there is a recapture event at any time during the 7-year period beginning on the date of the original issue of a QEI in a CDE, then the tax imposed by this chapter for the taxable year in which the event occurs must be increased by the credit recapture amount. Section 45D(g)(3) provides that a recapture event occurs with respect to an equity investment in a CDE if (A) such entity ceases to be a CDE, (B) the proceeds of the investment cease to be used to make QLICIs as required by section 45D(b)(1)(B), or (C) the QEI is redeemed by the CDE.

Explanation of Provisions

Redemption Safe Harbor for Partnership CDEs

Section 1.45D-1(e)(3)(iii) provides that, in the case of an equity investment that is a capital interest in a CDE that is a partnership for Federal tax purposes, a pro rata cash distribution by the CDE to its partners based on each partner's capital interest in the CDE during the taxable year will not be treated as a redemption for purposes of §1.45D-1(e)(2)(iii) if the distribution does not exceed the CDE's operating income for the taxable year. In addition, a non-pro rata *de minimis* cash distribution by a CDE to a partner or partners during the taxable year will not be treated as a redemption provided the distribution does not exceed the lesser of 5 percent of the CDE's operating income for that taxable year or 10 percent of the partner's capital interest in the CDE.

Commentators expressed the concern that a CDE may not be able to calculate its operating income in time to make a distribution during the taxable year. Because most CDEs will make a low estimate of operating income in order to lessen the risk of not satisfying the requirements of the redemption safe harbor, many CDEs may not distribute the entire amount of operating income during the taxable year. In response to this concern, the proposed regulations provide that, in the case of an equity investment that is a capital interest in a CDE that is a partnership for Federal tax purposes, a pro rata cash distribution by the CDE to its partners based on each partner's capital interest in the CDE during the taxable year will not be treated as a redemption for purposes of §1.45D-1(e)(2)(iii) if the distribution does not exceed the sum of the CDE's operating income for the taxable year and the CDE's undistributed operating income (if any) for the prior taxable year.

Additionally, for purposes of the redemption safe harbor for partnership CDEs, §1.45D-1(e)(3)(iii) defines *operating income* as the sum of (A) the CDE's taxable income as determined under section 703 (except that (*1*) the items described in section 703(a)(1) shall be aggregated with the non-separately stated tax items of the partnership; and (*2*) any gain resulting from the sale of a capital asset under section 1221(a) or section 1231 property shall not be included in taxable income); (B) deductions under section 165 (but only to the extent the losses were realized from QLICIs under §1.45D-1(d)(1)); (C) deductions under sections 167 and 168 (including the additional first-year depreciation under section 168(k)); (D) start-up expenditures amortized under section 195; and (E) organizational expenses amortized under section 709. The proposed regulations add tax-exempt income under section 103 and any other depreciation and amortization deductions under the Code to the list of Code sections that determine the amount of operating income.

Commentators have indicated that some CDEs are adding their distributive share of the deductions listed in §1.45D-1(e)(3)(iii) from another partnership to the CDE's calculation of operating income. For example, some CDEs are adding their distributive share of the amortization and depreciation deductions under sections 167 and 168 from another partnership to the CDE's calculation of operating income. The proposed regulations clarify that a CDE may rely on §1.704-1(b)(1)(vii) to determine its allocable share of the deductions listed in §1.45D-1(e)(3)(iii) from another partnership to the CDE's calculation of its operating income. Therefore, §1.704-1(b)(1)(vii) applies to treat an allocation to a partner of its share of partnership net or "bottom line" taxable income or loss as an allocation to such partner of the same share of each item of income, gain, loss, and deduction that is taken into account in computing the partner's net or "bottom line" taxable income or loss.

Termination of a Partnership CDE under Section 708(b)(1)(B)

Under section 708(b)(1)(B), a partnership is considered as terminated if within a twelve-month period there is a sale or exchange of 50 percent or more of the total interest in partnership capital and profits. Section 1.708-1(b)(4) provides, in part, that if a partnership is terminated by a sale or exchange of an interest, the following is deemed to occur: the partnership contributes all of its assets and liabilities to a new partnership in exchange for an interest in the new partnership; and, immediately thereafter, the terminated partnership distributes interests in the new partnership to the purchasing partner and the other remaining partners in proportion to their respective interests in the terminated partnership in liquidation of the terminated partnership, either for the continuation of the business by the new partnership or for its dissolution and winding up.

If the terminating partnership is a CDE, because of the deemed distribution of interests in that new partnership to the purchasing partner and the other remaining partners, a recapture event may be triggered under section 45D(g)(3)(C) and §1.45D-1(e)(2)(iii). However, because the sale of a QEI is not a recapture event under section 45D(g)(3) and because the remaining partner or partners are not being cashed out, the IRS and the Treasury Department do not believe that the sale of a QEI that causes the termination of a CDE partnership under section 708(b)(1)(B) should trigger recapture. Accordingly, the proposed regulations provide that a termination under section 708(b)(1)(B) of a CDE partnership is not a recapture event.

Reasonable Expectations

Section 1.45D-1(d)(6)(i) provides that an entity is generally treated as a QALICB for the duration of the CDE's investment in the entity if the CDE reasonably expects, at the time the CDE makes the capital or equity investment in, or loan to, the entity, that the entity will satisfy the requirements to be a QALICB under §1.45D-1(d)(4)(i) throughout the entire period of the investment or loan. The proposed regulations clarify how the reasonable expectations rule of §1.45D-1(d)(6)(i) applies when a CDE makes an investment in or loan to another CDE.

The proposed regulations provide that a CDE may rely on §1.45D-1(d)(6)(i) to treat an entity as a QALICB even if the CDE's investment in or loan to the entity is made through other CDEs under §1.45D-1(d)(1)(iv)(A).

Commentators indicated that some CDEs are unsure whether they may rely on §1.45D-1(d)(6)(i) if their investments involve the portions of business rule under section 45D(d)(2)(C), the rental to others of real property under sections 45D(d)(3)(A), and the exclusions from the definition of a qualified business under §1.45D-1(d)(5)(iii). Section 1.45D-1(d)(6)(i) already applies to all of these rules in determining whether an entity meets the requirements to be a QALICB under § 1.45D-1(d)(4)(i). Nevertheless, the proposed regulations clarify that CDEs may rely on these rules when applying § 1.45D-1(d)(6)(i).

Proposed Effective Date

The rules contained in these regulations are proposed to apply to taxable years ending on or after the date of publication of the Treasury decision adopting these rules as final regulations in the **Federal Register**.

Request for Comments

The IRS and the Treasury Department invite taxpayers to submit comments on issues relating to this notice of proposed rulemaking. In particular, the IRS and the Treasury Department encourage taxpayers to submit comments on how to define, under § 1.45D-1(d)(2)(i), the dollar amounts received by a CDE "in payment of, or for, capital, equity, or principal" that are set aside either for financial counseling and other services, for an equity investment, or as principal received on a loan. Section 1.45D-1(d)(2)(i) provides that such amounts must be reinvested by the CDE in a QLICI no later than twelve months from the date of receipt to be treated as continuously invested in a QLICI. Commentators suggested defining amounts received "in payment of, or for, capital, equity, or principal" by using the same rules and redemption safe harbor in § 1.45D-1(e)(3), which defines when an investment is redeemed or otherwise cashed out by a CDE. The proposed regulations do not adopt this suggestion. The IRS and the Treasury Department believe this approach may be inappropriate because redeeming one dollar of an equity investment is a recapture event under section 45D(g)(3)(C), while failing to reinvest one dollar in a QLICI under § 1.45D-1(d)(2)(i) lowers the dollar amount treated as meeting the substantially-all requirement by one dollar.

Special Analyses

It has been determined that this notice of proposed rulemaking is not a significant regulatory action as defined in Executive Order 12866. Therefore, a regulatory assessment is not required. It also has been determined that section 553(b) of the Administrative Procedure Act (5 U.S.C. chapter 5) does not apply to these regulations, and because the regulations do not impose a collection of information on small entities, the Regulatory Flexibility Act (5 U.S.C. chapter 6) does not apply. Pursuant to section 7805(f) of the Code, this notice of proposed rulemaking has been submitted to the Chief Counsel for Advocacy of the Small Business Administration for comment on its impact on small business.

Comments and Public Hearing

Before these proposed regulations are adopted as final regulations, consideration will be given to any written comments (a signed original and eight (8) copies) or electronic comments that are submitted timely to the IRS. Comments are requested on all aspects of the proposed regulations. All comments will be available for public inspection and copying.

A public hearing has been scheduled for December 12, 2008, beginning at 10:00 a.m. in the IRS Auditorium, Internal Revenue Building, 1111 Constitution Avenue, NW, Washington, DC. Due to building security procedures, visitors must enter at the Constitution Avenue entrance. In addition, all visitors must present photo identification to enter the building. Because of access restrictions, visitors will not be admitted beyond the immediate entrance area more than 30 minutes before the hearing starts. For information about having your name placed on the building access list to attend the hearing, see the FOR FURTHER INFORMATION CONTACT section of this preamble.

The rules of 26 CFR 601.601(a)(3) apply to the hearing. Persons who wish to present oral comments at the hearing must submit electronic or written comments by November 10, 2008. Outline of the topics to be discussed and the time to be devoted to each topic (a signed original and eight (8) copies) by November 3, 2008. A period of 10 minutes will be allotted to each person for making comments. An agenda showing the scheduling of the speakers will be prepared after the deadline for receiving outlines has passed. Copies of the agenda will be available free of charge at the hearing.

Drafting Information

The principal author of these regulations is Julie Hanlon-Bolton with the Office of the Associate Chief Counsel (Passthroughs and Special Industries). However, other personnel from the IRS and the Treasury Department participated in their development.

[¶ 49,401] Proposed Amendments of Regulations (REG-107318-08), published in the Federal Register on October 9, 2008.

[Code Secs. 401, 402, 411 and 417]

Retirement plans: Notice: Deferral: Immediately distributable benefit: Election period: Waiver of joint and survivor annuity: Notice timing.—Amendments of Reg. §§ 1.401(a)-13, 1.401(a)-20, 1.402(f)-1, 1.411(a)-11 and 1.417(e)-1, providing that the notice required under section 411(a)(11) to be provided to a participant of his or her right, if any, to defer receipt of an immediately distributable benefit must also describe the consequences of failing to defer receipt of the distribution, are proposed.

AGENCY: Internal Revenue Service (IRS), Treasury.

ACTION: Notice of Proposed Rulemaking and notice of public hearing.

SUMMARY: This document contains proposed regulations under sections 402(f), 411(a)(11), and 417 of the Internal Revenue Code (Code). The proposed regulations would provide that the notice required under section 411(a)(11) to be provided to a participant of his or her right, if any, to defer receipt of an immediately distributable benefit must also describe the consequences of failing to defer receipt of the distribution. The proposed regulations would also provide that the applicable election period for waiving the qualified joint and survivor annuity form of benefit under section 417 is the 180-day period ending on the annuity starting date, and that a notice required to be provided under section 402(f), section 411(a)(11), or section 417 may be provided to a participant as much as 180 days before the annuity starting date (or, for a notice under section 402(f), the distribution date). These regulations would affect administrators of, employers maintaining, participants in, and beneficiaries of tax-favored retirement plans.

DATES: Written or electronic comments and requests to speak at the public hearing must be received by January 7, 2009.

ADDRESSES: Send submissions to: CC:PA:LPD:PR (REG-107318-08), room 5203, Internal Revenue Service, PO Box 7604, Ben Franklin Station, Washington D.C. 20044. Submissions may be hand-delivered Monday through Friday between the hours of 8 a.m. and 4 p.m. to: CC:PA:LPD:PR (REG-107318-08), Courier's Desk, Internal Revenue Service, 1111 Constitution Avenue, N.W., Washington, D.C., or sent electronically via the Federal eRulemaking Portal at *http://www.regulations.gov* (IRS REG-107318-08).

FOR FURTHER INFORMATION CONTACT: Concerning the regulations, Michael P. Brewer at (202) 622-6090; concerning submission of comments or to request to speak at the public hearing, Funmi Taylor at (202) 622-7180 (not toll-free numbers).

SUPPLEMENTARY INFORMATION:

Paperwork Reduction Act

The collection of information contained in this notice of proposed rulemaking has been submitted to the Office of Management and Budget for review in accordance with the Paperwork Reduction Act of 1995 (44 U.S.C. 3507(d)). Comments on the collection of information should be sent to the **Office of Management and Budget**, Attn: Desk Officer for the Department of the Treasury, Office of Information and Regulatory Affairs, Washington, DC 20503, with copies to the **Internal Revenue Service**, Attn: IRS Reports Clearance Officer, SE:W:CAR:MP:T:T:SP; Washington, DC 20224. Comments on the collection of information should be received by December 8, 2008. Comments are specifically requested concerning:

Whether the proposed collection of information is necessary for the proper performance of the functions of the Internal Revenue Service, including whether the information will have practical utility;

The accuracy of the estimated burden associated with the proposed collection of information;

How the quality, utility, and clarity of the information to be collected may be enhanced;

How the burden of complying with the proposed collections of information may be minimized, including through the application of automated collection techniques or other forms of information technology; and

Estimates of capital or start-up costs and costs of operation, maintenance, and purchase of service to provide information.

The collection of information in these proposed regulations is in § 1.411(a)-11(c)(2) of the Income Tax Regulations. This collection of information is required to comply with the statutory notice requirements of section 411(a), and is expected to be included in the notices currently provided to employees that inform them of their rights and benefits under the plan. The likely recordkeepers are businesses or other forprofit institutions and nonprofit institutions and organizations.

Estimated total annual recordkeeping burden: 100,000 hours.

Estimated average annual burden hours per recordkeeper: 1 hour.

Estimated number of recordkeepers: 100,000.

An agency may not conduct or sponsor, and a person is not required to respond to, a collection of information unless it displays a valid control number assigned by the Office of Management and Budget.

Books or records relating to a collection of information must be retained as long as their contents may become material in the administration of any internal revenue law. Generally, tax returns and tax return information are confidential, as required by 26 U.S.C. 6103.

Background

A. Notice of Consequences of Failing to Defer

Section 411(a)(11)(A) provides that, if the present value of any nonforfeitable accrued benefit exceeds $5,000, a qualified plan must provide that such benefit may not be immediately distributed without the consent of the participant. Similarly, section 203(e) of the Employee Retirement Income Security Act of 1974, as amended (ERISA), provides that if the present value of any nonforfeitable accrued benefit with respect to a participant in a plan exceeds $5,000, the benefit may not be immediately distributed without the consent of the participant.

Section 1102(b)(1) of the Pension Protection Act of 2006 (PPA '06), 109 Public Law 280, 120 Stat. 780, instructs the Secretary of the Treasury to modify the regulations under section 411(a)(11) of the Code "to provide that the description of a participant's right, if any, to defer receipt of a distribution shall also describe the consequences of failing to defer such receipt." Section 1102(b)(2)(A) of PPA '06 provides that the modifications required by section 1102(b)(1) of PPA '06 shall apply to years beginning after December 31, 2006. Section 1102(b)(2)(B) of PPA '06, however, states that a plan shall not be treated as failing to meet the requirements of section 411(a)(11) with respect to any description of the consequences of failing to defer provided "within 90 days after the Secretary of the Treasury issues the modifications required by [section 1102(b)(1) of PPA '06]if the plan administrator makes a reasonable attempt to comply with such requirements."

Section 1.411(a)-11(c)(2)(i) states that, in order for a plan to obtain valid consent under section 411(a)(11), "so long as a benefit is immediately distributable, a participant must be informed of the right, if any, to defer receipt of the distribution." Section 1.411(a)-11(c)(4) states that a distribution is immediately distributable prior to the later of the time a participant has attained normal retirement age or age 62.

Q&A-32 of Notice 2007-7, 2007-5 I.R.B. 395, provides that a plan administrator is required to revise the notice required under section 411 to reflect the modifications made by section 1102(b) of PPA '06 for notices provided in plan years beginning after December 31, 2006. Notice 2007-7 further provides that, pursuant to section 1102(b)(2)(B) of PPA '06, a plan will not be treated as failing to meet the new requirements of section 1102(b) of PPA '06 if the plan administrator makes a reasonable attempt to comply with the new requirements with respect to a notice that is provided prior to the 90th day after the issuance of regulations reflecting the modifications required by such section 1102(b) of PPA '06. See § 601.601 (b) (2) (ii) (*b*).

Q&A-33 of Notice 2007-7 includes a safe harbor that would be considered a reasonable attempt to comply with the requirement in section 1102(b)(1) of PPA '06 that a description of a participant's right to defer receipt of a distribution include a description of the consequences of failing to defer. In particular, Q&A-33 provides that a description that is written in a manner reasonably calculated to be understood by the average participant and that includes the following information is a reasonable attempt to comply with the requirements of section 1102(b)(2)(B) of PPA '06: (a) in the case of a defined benefit plan, a description of how much larger benefits will be if the commencement of distributions is deferred; (b) in the case of a defined contribution plan, a description indicating the investment options available under the plan (including fees) that will be available if distributions are deferred; and (c) the portion of the summary plan description that contains any special rules that might materially affect a participant's decision to defer. For purposes of clause (a), a plan administrator can use a description that includes the financial effect of deferring distributions, as described in §1.417(a)(3)-1(d)(2)(i), based solely on the normal form of benefit.

Q&A-31 of Notice 2007-7 provides that the provisions of section 1102 apply to plan years that begin after December 31, 2006. Q&A-31 explains that this means that the new rules relating to the content of the notices apply only to notices issued in those plan years, without regard to the annuity starting date for the distributions.

B. Expansion of Applicable Election Period

Section 401(a)(11)(A)(i) provides that, except as provided in section 417, a plan that is qualified under section 401(a) must provide the accrued benefit payable to a vested participant who does not die before the annuity starting date in the form of a qualified joint and survivor annuity.

Section 417(a)(1)(A) provides that, in general, a plan satisfies section 401(a)(11) only if each participant may elect at any time during the "applicable election period" to waive the qualified joint and survivor annuity form of benefit (and to revoke the waiver), and certain other requirements are satisfied. Before PPA '06, section 417(a)(6)(A) provided that the "applicable election period" for a participant to waive the qualified joint and survivor annuity form of distribution was the 90-day period ending on the annuity starting date.

Section 1102(a)(1)(A) of PPA '06 amended section 417(a)(6)(A) by changing the 90-day "applicable election period" for electing a distribution subject to the qualified joint and survivor annuity (QJSA) rules of sections 401(a)(11) and 417 in a form other than a QJSA to a 180-day applicable election period. Section 1102(a)(2)(A) of PPA '06 made a parallel amendment to section 205(c)(7)(A) of ERISA by striking "90-day" and inserting "180-day".

Sections 1102(a)(1)(B) and 1102(a)(2)(B) of PPA '06 provide that the Secretary of the Treasury shall modify the regulations relating to section 417 of the Code and section 205 of ERISA by substituting "180 days" for "90 days" each place it appears.

Section 1102(a)(3) of PPA '06 provides that the amendments to the applicable election period apply to years beginning after December 31, 2006.

C. Expansion of Period for Notices

Section 417(a)(3)(A) of the Code and section 205(c)(3)(A) of ERISA provide that a plan must provide to each participant, "within a reasonable period of time before the annuity starting date" and consistent with such regulations as the Secretary of the Treasury may prescribe, a written explanation that describes the terms and conditions of the qualified joint and survivor annuity and certain other information. Similarly, section 402(f)(1) provides that a plan administrator must, "within a reasonable period of time" before making an eligible rollover distribution, provide to recipients an explanation of certain tax consequences of the distribution.

Section 1102(a)(1)(B) of PPA '06 provides that the Secretary of the Treasury shall modify the regulations under sections 402(f), 411(a)(11), and 417 by substituting "180 days" for "90 days" each place it appears in §§1.402(f)-1, 1.411(a)-11(c), and 1.417(e)-1(b). Similarly, section 1102(a)(2)(B) of PPA '06 provides that the Secretary of the Treasury shall modify the regulations relating to sections 203(e) and 205 of ERISA by substituting "180 days" for "90 days" each place it appears.

Section 1102(a)(3) provides that the amendments to the notice periods apply to years beginning after December 31, 2006. Q&A-31 of Notice 2007-7 explains that the 180-day period for distributing notices applies to notices distributed in a plan year that begins after December 31, 2006.

D. Requirements under ERISA

ERISA section 203(e) is the parallel provision to section 411(a)(11) of the Code and ERISA section 205 is the ERISA parallel to section 417 of the Code. Pursuant to section 101 of Reorganization Plan No. 4 of 1978, 29 U.S.C. 1001nt (the Reorganization Plan), the Secretary of the Treasury generally has authority to issue regulations under parts 2 and 3 of subtitle B of title I of ERISA, including sections 203(e) and 205 of ERISA. Thus, the changes required by section 1102 of PPA '06 would apply as well for purposes of ERISA sections 203(e) and 205.

Explanation of Provisions

A. Notice of Consequences of Failing to Defer

These proposed regulations would provide that the notice required by section 411(a)(11) advising a participant of the right, if any, to defer receipt of a distribution must also inform the participant of the consequences of failing to defer such receipt. The proposed regulations would also provide guidance on the relevant information that must be provided to a participant in order to satisfy the requirement that the participant be notified of the consequences of failing to defer.

Specifically, these proposed regulations would require that the participant be provided a description of specified federal tax implications of failing to defer and, in the case of a defined benefit plan, a statement of the amount payable to the participant under the normal form of benefit both upon immediate commencement and when the benefit is no longer immediately distributable (that is, the later of age 62 or attainment of normal retirement age). Section 1.417(a)(3)-1(c)(2)(ii) permits a plan to provide participants with a QJSA explanation, which does not vary based on the participant's marital status, of the relative value of optional forms of benefit compared to the value of a QJSA. These proposed regulations would permit the statement of the amount payable to not be based on the participant's marital status, to the extent the plan is permitted under § 1.417(a)(3)-1(c)(2)(ii) to use a QJSA explanation that does not vary based on whether the participant is married or unmarried.

The proposed regulations would also require the information in the notice to include, in the case of a defined contribution plan, a statement that some currently available investment options in the plan may not be generally available on similar terms outside the plan and contact information for obtaining additional information on the general availability outside the plan of currently available investment options in the plan. In addition, the proposed regulations would require the notice to include, in the case of a defined contribution plan, a statement that fees and expenses (including administrative or investment-related fees) outside the plan may be different from fees and expenses that apply to the participant's account and contact information for obtaining information on such fees.

The proposed regulations also include an additional category of information that must be provided relating to any provisions of the plan (and provisions of any accident or health plan maintained by the employer) that could reasonably be expected to materially affect a participant's decision whether to defer receipt of the distribution. Thus, for example, the proposed regulations would require a description of the eligibility requirements for retiree health benefits if such benefits are limited to participants who have an undistributed benefit under the employer's retirement plan.

In general, the proposed regulations would also provide that the required information regarding the consequences of a participant's failing to defer receipt of a distribution must appear together. However, the proposed regulations would permit a cross-reference to where the required information may be found in notices or other information provided or made available to the participant, as long as the notice of consequences of failing to defer includes a statement of how the referenced information may be obtained without charge and explains why the referenced information is relevant to a decision whether to defer.

B. Expansion of Applicable Election Period and Period for Notices

Consistent with sections 1102(a)(1)(A) and (1)(B) and 1102(a)(2)(A) and (2)(B) of PPA '06, the proposed regulations would both (1) expand the definition of applicable election period to up to 180 days, and (2) expand the time period for notices issued under sections 402(f), 411(a)(11), and 417 to allow the notices to be issued up to 180 days prior to the annuity starting date (or, in the case of a notice under section 402(f), the date of distribution). Specifically, the proposed regulations would substitute "180 days" for "90 days" and "180-day" for "90-day" each place those terms appear in § 1.401(a)-13(g)(4)(ii), § 1.401(a)-20, A-3(b)(1), A-4, A-10(a), A-16, and A-24(a)(1), § 1.402(f)-1, § 1.411(a)-11(c), and § 1.417(e)-1(b).

Pursuant to section 101 of the Reorganization Plan, the Secretary of Treasury has the authority to issue regulations under ERISA sections 203(e) and 205. Thus, these proposed regulations that apply to sections 402(f), 411(a)(11), and 417 of the Code would apply as well for purposes of sections 203(e) and 205 of ERISA.

Proposed Effective/Applicability Date

These regulations are proposed to become effective for notices provided (and election periods beginning) on or after the first day of the first plan year beginning on or after January 1, 2010. However, in no event will the regulations become effective for notices provided (and election periods beginning) earlier than the first day of the first plan year beginning 90 days after publication of final regulations in the **Federal Register**.

With respect to the regulations relating to the notice of consequences of failing to defer the receipt of distributions, until these regulations become effective, a plan will be treated as complying if: (1) the plan complies either with these proposed regulations or with Q&A-32 and Q&A-33 in Notice 2007-7; or (2) if the plan administrator makes a reasonable attempt to comply with the requirement that the description of a participant's right, if any, to defer receipt of a distribution shall also describe the consequences of failing to defer such receipt.

With respect to the proposed regulations relating to the expanded applicable election period and the expanded period for notices, plans may rely on these proposed regulations for notices provided (and election periods beginning) during the period beginning on the first day of the first plan year beginning on or after January 1, 2007 and ending on the effective date of final regulations.

Special Analyses

It has been determined that this notice of proposed rulemaking is not a significant regulatory action as defined in Executive Order 12866. Therefore, a regulatory assessment is not required. It also has been determined that section 553(b) of the Administrative Procedure Act (5 U.S.C. chapter 5) does not apply to these regulations.

It is hereby certified that the collection of information contained in this regulation will not have a significant economic impact on a substantial number of small entities. This certification is based on several factors, including that the regulation merely provides guidance to implement a statutorily-required notice, and that the incremental burden in the regulation would be minimal because it only requires including additional information in notices already provided by all of the affected entities. Accordingly, a Regulatory Flexibility Analysis under the Regulatory Flexibility Act (5 U.S.C. chapter 6) is not required. Pursuant to section 7805(f) of the Code, this notice of proposed rulemaking will be submitted to the Chief Counsel for Advocacy of the Small Business Administration for comment on its impact on small business.

Comments and Public Hearing

Before these proposed regulations are adopted as final regulations, consideration will be given to any written (one signed and eight (8) copies) or electronic comments that are submitted timely to the IRS. All comments will be available for public inspection and copying.

A public hearing has been scheduled for Friday, February 20, 2009, at 10 a.m. in the IRS Auditorium, Internal Revenue Building, 1111 Constitution Avenue, N.W., Washington, DC. Due to building security procedures, visitors must enter at the Constitution Avenue entrance. In addition, all visitors must present photo identification to enter the building. Because of access restrictions, visitors will not be admitted beyond the immediate entrance area more than 30 minutes before the hearing starts. For information about having your name placed on the building access list to attend the hearing, see the FOR FURTHER INFORMATION CONTACT section of this preamble.

Persons who wish to present oral comments at the hearing must submit written or electronic comments by January 7, 2008 and submit an outline of the topics to be discussed and the amount of time to be devoted to each topic (a signed original and eight (8) copies) by January 16, 2009. A period of 10 minutes will be allotted to each person for making comments.

An agenda showing the scheduling of the speakers will be prepared after the deadline for receiving outlines has passed. Copies of the agenda will be available free of charge at the hearing.

Drafting Information

The principal author of these regulations is Michael P. Brewer, Office of Division Counsel/Associate Chief Counsel (Tax Exempt and Government Entities). However, other personnel from the Office of Chief Counsel, IRS, and the Department of Treasury participated in the development of these regulations.

[¶49,406] Proposed Regulations, NPRM REG-148326-05, published in the Federal Register on December 8, 2008 (corrected 2/18/2009).

[Code Sec. 409A]

Retirement plans: Nonqualified deferred compensation: Plan compliance failure: Calculating income to include in year of failure: Calculating additional income tax.—Reg. §1.409A-4 and amendments of Reg. §1.409A-0, relating to the calculation of amounts includible in income under Code Sec. 409A and the additional taxes imposed by such section with respect to service providers participating in certain nonqualified deferred compensation plants, are proposed.

AGENCY: Internal Revenue Service (IRS), Treasury.

ACTION: Notice of proposed rulemaking and notice of public hearing.

SUMMARY: This document contains proposed regulations on the calculation of amounts includible in income under section 409A(a) and the additional taxes imposed by such section with respect to service providers participating in certain nonqualified deferred compensation plans. The regulations would affect such service providers and the service recipients for whom the service providers provide services. This document also provides a notice of public hearing on these proposed regulations.

DATES: Written or electronic comments must be received by March 7, 2009.

Outlines of topics to be discussed at the public hearing scheduled for April 2, 2009, must be received by March 9, 2009.

ADDRESSES: Send submissions to: CC:PA:LPD:PR (REG-148326-05), room 5203, Internal Revenue Service, PO Box 7604, Ben Franklin Station, Washington, DC 20044. Submissions may be hand-delivered Monday through Friday between the hours of 8 a.m. and 4 p.m. to CC:PA:LPD:PR (REG-148326-05), Courier's Desk, Internal Revenue Service, 1111 Constitution Avenue, NW., Washington, DC or sent electronically, via the Federal eRulemaking Portal at *www. Regulations.gov* (IRS REG-148326-05). The public hearing will be held in the auditorium, Internal Revenue Building, 1111 Constitution Avenue, NW., Washington, DC.
FOR FURTHER INFORMATION CONTACT: Concerning the proposed regulations, Stephen Tackney, at (202) 927-9639; concerning submissions of comments, the hearing, and/or to be placed on the building access list to attend the hearing, Funmi Taylor at (202) 622-3628 (not toll-free numbers).
SUPPLEMENTARY INFORMATION:

Background

Section 409A was added to the Internal Revenue Code (Code) by section 885 of the American Jobs Creation Act of 2004, Public Law 108-357 (118 Stat. 1418). Section 409A generally provides that if certain requirements are not met at any time during a taxable year, amounts deferred under a nonqualified deferred compensation plan for that year and all previous taxable years are currently includible in gross income to the extent not subject to a substantial risk of forfeiture and not previously included in gross income. Section 409A also includes rules applicable to certain trusts or similar arrangements associated with nonqualified deferred compensation.

On December 20, 2004, the IRS issued Notice 2005-1 (2005-2 CB 274), setting forth initial guidance on the application of section 409A, and providing transition guidance in accordance with the terms of the statute. On April 10, 2007, the Treasury Department and the IRS issued final regulations under section 409A. (72 FR 19234, April 17, 2007). The final regulations are applicable for taxable years beginning after December 31, 2008. See Notice 2007-86 (2007-46 IRB 990). Notice 2005-1 and the final regulations do not address the calculation of the amount includible in income under section 409A if a plan fails to meet the requirements of section 409A and the calculation of the additional taxes applicable to such income. On November 30, 2006, the Treasury Department and the IRS issued Notice 2006-100 (2006-51 IRB 1109) providing interim guidance for taxable years beginning in 2005 and 2006 on the calculation of the amount includible in income if the requirements of section 409A were not met, and requesting comments on these issues for use in formulating future guidance. On October 23, 2007, the Treasury Department and the IRS issued Notice 2007-89 (2007-46 IRB 998) providing similar interim guidance for taxable years beginning in 2007. See § 601.601(d)(2)(ii)(*b*).

Commentators submitted a number of comments addressing the topics covered by these proposed regulations in response to Notice 2005-1, Notice 2006-100, Notice 2007-89, and the regulations, all of which were considered by the Treasury Department and the IRS in formulating these proposed regulations.

Explanation of Provisions

I. *Scope of Proposed Regulations*

These proposed regulations address the calculation of amounts includible in income under section 409A(a), and related issues including the calculation of the additional taxes applicable to such income. Section 409A(a) generally provides that amounts deferred under a nonqualified deferred compensation plan in all years are includible in income unless certain requirements are met. The requirements under section 409A(a) generally relate to the time and form of payment of amounts deferred under the plan, including the establishment of the time and form of payment through initial deferral elections and restrictions on the ability to change the time and form of payment through subsequent deferral elections or the acceleration of payment schedules. As provided in the regulations previously issued under section 409A, a nonqualified deferred compensation plan must comply with the requirements of section 409A(a) both in form and in operation.

Taxpayers may also be required to include amounts in income under section 409A(b). Section 409A(b) generally applies to a transfer of assets to a trust or similar arrangement, or to a restriction of assets, for purposes of paying nonqualified deferred compensation, if such trust or assets are located outside the United States, if such assets are transferred during a restricted period with respect to a single-employer defined benefit plan sponsored by the service recipient, or if such assets are restricted to the provision of benefits under a nonqualified deferred compensation plan in connection with a change in the service recipient's financial health. These proposed regulations do not address the application of section 409A(b), including the calculation of amounts includible in income if the requirements of section 409A(b) are not met. For guidance on the calculation of such amounts for taxable years beginning on or before January 1, 2007, including the application of the Federal income tax withholding requirements, see Notice 2007-89. The Treasury Department and the IRS anticipate issuing further interim guidance for later taxable years on the calculation of the amount includible in income under section 409A(b) and the application of the Federal income tax withholding requirements to such an amount.

II. *Effect of a Failure to Comply with Section 409A(a) on Amounts Deferred in Subsequent Years*

Commentators asked how section 409A(a) applies if a plan fails to comply with section 409A(a) during a taxable year and the service provider continues to have amounts deferred under the plan in subsequent years during which the plan otherwise complies with section 409A(a) both in form and in operation. The statutory language may be construed to provide that a failure is treated as continuing during taxable years beyond the year in which the initial failure occurred, if the failure continues to affect amounts deferred under the plan. For example, if an amount has been improperly deferred under the plan, the statutory language could be construed to provide that the plan fails to comply with section 409A(a) during all taxable years during which the improperly deferred amounts remain deferred. However, this position could cause harsh results and would add administrative complexity. For example, a service provider could be required to include in income, and pay additional taxes on, amounts deferred over a number of taxable years even if the sole failure to comply with section 409A(a) occurred many years earlier. In addition, even if there were no failure in the current year, to determine a taxpayer's liability for income taxes with respect to nonqualified deferred compensation for a particular year, the taxpayer and the IRS would need to examine the plan's form and operation for every year in which the service provider had an amount deferred under the plan to determine if there was a failure to comply with section 409A(a) during any of those years.

For these reasons, the proposed regulations do not adopt this interpretation and instead generally would apply the adverse tax consequences that result from a failure to comply with section 409A(a) only with respect to amounts deferred under a plan in the year in which such noncompliance occurs and all previous taxable years, to the extent such amounts are not subject to a substantial risk of forfeiture and have not previously been included in income. Therefore, under the proposed regulations, a failure to meet the requirements of section 409A(a) during a service provider's taxable year generally would not affect the taxation of amounts deferred under the plan for a subsequent taxable year during which the plan complies with section 409A(a) in form and in operation with respect to all amounts deferred under the plan. This would apply even though the amount deferred under the plan as of the end of such subsequent taxable year includes amounts deferred in earlier years during which the plan failed to comply with section 409A(a) (including, for example, amounts deferred pursuant to an untimely deferral election in the earlier year), as long as there was no failure under the plan in a later year. Because there would be no continuing or permanent failure with respect to a plan that fails to comply with section 409A(a) during an earlier year, each taxable year would be analyzed independently to determine if there was a failure. As a result, assessment of tax liabilities due to a plan's failure to comply with the requirements of section 409A(a) in a closed year would be time-barred. But, if a service provider fails to properly include amounts in income under section 409A(a) for a taxable year during which there was a failure to comply with section 409A(a), and assessment of taxes with respect to such year becomes barred by the statute of limitations, then the taxpayer's duty of consistency would prevent the service provider from claiming a tax benefit in a later year with respect to such amount (such as, for example, by claiming any type of "basis" or "investment in the contract" in the year the service recipient paid such amount to the service provider pursuant to the plan's terms).

Under the general rule in the proposed regulations, if all of a taxpayer's deferred amounts under a plan are nonvested and the taxpayer makes an impermissible deferral election or accelerates the time of payment with respect to some or all of the nonvested deferred amount, the nonvested deferred amount generally would not be includible in income under section 409A(a) in the year of the impermissible change in time and form of payment (although if there were vested amounts deferred under the plan, such amounts would be includible in income under section 409A(a)). In the subsequent taxable year in which the service provider becomes vested in the deferred amount, the plan might comply with section 409A(a) in form and in operation, so that under the general rule no income inclusion would be required and no additional taxes would be due for that year as a result of the late deferral election or acceleration of payment. In proposing to adopt this interpretation of the statute, the Treasury Department and the IRS do not intend to create an opportunity for taxpayers who ignore the requirements of section 409A(a) with respect to nonvested amounts to avoid the payment of taxes that would otherwise be due as a result of such a failure to comply. To ensure that this rule does not become a means for taxpayers to disregard the requirements of the statute, the proposed regulations would disregard a substantial risk of forfeiture for purposes of determining the amount includible in income under section 409A[1] with respect to certain nonvested deferred amounts, if the facts and circumstances indicate that the service recipient has a pattern or practice of permitting such impermissible changes in the time and form of payment with respect to nonvested deferred amounts (regardless of whether such changes also apply to vested deferred amounts). If such a pattern or practice exists, an amount deferred under a plan that is otherwise subject to a substantial risk of forfeiture is not treated as subject to a substantial risk of forfeiture if an impermissible change in the time and form of payment (including an impermissible initial deferral election) applies to the amount deferred or if the facts and circumstances indicate that the amount deferred would be affected by such pattern or practice.

III. *Calculation of the Amount Deferred under a Plan for the Taxable Year in which the Plan Fails to Meet the Requirements of Section 409A(a) and all Preceding Taxable Years*

A. *In general*

Section 409A(a)(1)(A) generally provides that if at any time during a taxable year a nonqualified deferred compensation plan fails to meet the requirements of section 409A(a)(2) (payments), section 409A(a)(3) (the acceleration of payments), or section 409A(a)(4) (deferral elections), or is not operated in accordance with such requirements, all compensation deferred under the plan for the taxable year

---

[1] Under section 409A(e)(5), the Treasury Department and the IRS have the authority to disregard a substantial risk of forfeiture where necessary to carry out the purposes of section 409A.

and all preceding taxable years is includible in gross income for the taxable year to the extent not subject to a substantial risk of forfeiture and not previously included in gross income. Accordingly, to calculate the amount includible in income upon a failure to meet the requirements of section 409A(a), the first step is to determine the total amount deferred under the plan for the service provider's taxable year and all preceding taxable years. The second step is to calculate the portion of the total amount deferred for the taxable year, if any, that is either subject to a substantial risk of forfeiture (nonvested) or has been included in income in a previous taxable year. The last step is to subtract the amount determined in step two from the amount determined in step one. The excess of the amount determined in step one over the amount determined in step two is the amount includible in income and subject to additional income taxes for the year as a result of the plan's failure to comply with section 409A(a). Sections III.B through III.D of this preamble explain how the proposed regulations would address the first step in the process of determining the amount includible in income under section 409A, calculating the total amount deferred for the taxable year.

B. *Total amount deferred*

1. In General

In general, under the proposed regulations, the amount deferred under a plan[2] for a taxable year and all preceding taxable years would be referred to as the total amount deferred for a taxable year and would be determined as of the last day of the taxable year. Therefore, for calendar year taxpayers, such as most individuals, the relevant calculation date would be December 31. Determining the total amount deferred for the taxable year as of the last day of the taxable year during which a plan fails to comply with section 409A(a) would allow taxpayers to avoid the administrative burden of tracking amounts deferred under a plan on a daily basis, because adjustments would not be made to reflect notional earnings or losses or other fluctuations in the amount payable under the plan as they occur during the taxable year, but would be applied only on a net basis as of the last day of the taxable year. For example, if a service provider has a calendar year taxable year, and if the service provider's account balance under a plan is $105,000 as of July 1, but is only $100,000 as of December 31 of the same year, due solely to deemed investment losses (with no payments made under the plan during the year), the total amount deferred under the plan for that taxable year would be $100,000.

Similarly, the total amount deferred for a taxable year would not necessarily be the greatest total amount deferred for any previous year, even if no amount has been paid under the plan. For example, if a service provider has a calendar year taxable year, and if the service provider's account balance under a plan as of December 31, 2010 is $105,000, as of December 31, 2011 is $100,000, and as of December 31, 2012 is $95,000, and if those decreases are due solely to deemed investment losses (and no payments were made under the plan in 2011 or 2012), then the total amount deferred for 2011 would be $100,000 and the total amount deferred for 2012 would be $95,000.

2. Treatment of Payments

If a service recipient pays an amount deferred under a plan during a taxable year, the amount remaining to be paid to (or on behalf of) the service provider under the plan as of the last day of the taxable year will have been reduced as a result of such payment. To reasonably reflect the effect of payments made during a taxable year, the proposed regulations provide that the sum of all payments of amounts deferred under a plan during a taxable year, including all payments that are substitutes for an amount deferred, would be added to the amounts deferred outstanding as of the last day of the taxable year (determined in accordance with the regulations) to calculate the total amount deferred for such taxable year. To lower the administrative burden of the calculation, the proposed regulations provide that the addition of such payments to the total amount deferred for the taxable year would not be increased by any interest or other amount to reflect the time value of money. The total amount deferred for a taxable year would include all payments, regardless of whether the service recipient made some or all of the payments in accordance with the requirements of section 409A(a). For example, if during a taxable year an employee receives a single sum payment of the entire amount deferred under a plan, the employee would have a total amount deferred under the plan for the taxable year equal to the amount paid.

3. Treatment of Deemed Losses

Because the total amount deferred would be determined as of the last day of the taxable year, losses that occur during a taxable year (due to losses on deemed investments, actuarial losses, and other similar reductions in the amount payable under a plan) generally would be netted with any gains that occur during the same taxable year (due to deemed investment or actuarial gains, additional deferrals, or other additions to the amount payable under the plan). To that extent, deemed investment losses, actuarial losses, or other similar reductions could offset deemed investment or actuarial gains, additional deferrals, or other increases in the amount deferred under the plan for purposes of determining the total amount deferred for the taxable year. This would apply regardless of whether a deemed loss occurs before or after the date of any specific failure to comply with section 409A(a). For example, assume a service provider begins a taxable year with a $10,000 balance under an account balance plan. During the year, the service provider has an additional

---

[2] For this purpose, the term plan refers to a plan as defined under § 1.409A-1(c), including any applicable plan aggregation rules.

deferral to the plan of $5,000 and incurs net deemed investment losses of $2,000. No payments are made pursuant to the plan during the year, the employee has no vested legally binding right to further deferrals to the plan, and there are no other changes to the account balance. The total amount deferred for the taxable year would equal the $13,000 account balance ($10,000 + $5,000 - $2,000) as of the last day of the taxable year.

4. Treatment of Rights to Deemed Earnings on Amounts Deferred

Under section 409A(d)(5), income (whether actual or notional) attributable to deferred compensation constitutes deferred compensation for purposes of section 409A. See § 1.409A-1(b)(2). For example, if a service provider must include a deferred amount in income because an account balance plan in which the service provider participates fails to satisfy the requirements of section 409A(a), notional earnings credited with respect to such amount constitute deferred compensation and are subject to section 409A. If the plan also fails to comply with the requirements of section 409A(a) during a subsequent taxable year, the notional earnings must be included in income and are subject to the additional taxes under section 409A(a), notwithstanding that the "principal" amount of deferred compensation has already been included in income under section 409A(a) for a previous year.

In this respect, the treatment of earnings on nonqualified deferred compensation for purposes of section 409A is significantly different from the treatment of such earnings for purposes of section 3121(v)(2) (application of Federal Insurance Contributions Act (FICA) tax to nonqualified deferred compensation). As a result, notional earnings ordinarily are deferred compensation that is subject to section 409A even if such earnings would not constitute wages for purposes of the FICA tax when paid to the service provider because of the special timing rule under section 3121(v)(2) and § 31.3121(v)(2)-1(a)(2). Accordingly, the proposed regulations provide that earnings that are credited with respect to deferred compensation during a taxable year or that were credited in previous taxable years, and earnings with respect to deferred compensation that are paid during such taxable year, must be included in determining the total amount deferred for the taxable year.

5. Total Amount Deferred for a Taxable Year Relates to the Entire Taxable Year, Regardless of Date or Period of Failure

Section 409A(a)(1)(A)(i) states that if at any time during a taxable year a nonqualified deferred compensation plan fails to meet the requirements of section 409A(a), all compensation deferred under the plan for the taxable year and all preceding years shall be includible in gross income for the taxable year to the extent not subject to a substantial risk of forfeiture (vested) and not previously included in gross income. The statutory reference to the deferred compensation required to be included in income under section 409A(a) does not distinguish between amounts deferred in a taxable year before a failure to meet the requirements of section 409A(a), and amounts deferred in the same taxable year after such failure. Accordingly, under the proposed regulations the total amount deferred under a plan for a taxable year would refer to the total amount deferred as of the last day of the taxable year, regardless of the date upon which a failure occurs. For example, if a plan is amended during a service provider's taxable year to add a provision that fails to meet the requirements of section 409A(a), the total amount deferred as of the last day of the taxable year would be includible in income under section 409A(a). This would include all payments under the plan during the taxable year, including payments made before the amendment (regardless of whether such payments are made in accordance with the requirements of section 409A(a)). Similarly, if the plan in operation fails to meet the requirements of section 409A(a) during the taxable year, the total amount deferred for the taxable year would include all payments under the plan during the taxable year, including payments made before and after the date the failure occurred.

The proposed regulations provide that amounts deferred under a plan during a taxable year in which a failure occurs must be included in income under section 409A(a) even if such deferrals occur after the failure and are otherwise made in compliance with section 409A(a). For example, salary deferrals for periods during a taxable year after an impermissible accelerated payment under the same plan during the same taxable year would be required to be included in the total amount deferred for the taxable year and included in income under section 409A(a), regardless of whether the salary deferrals are made in accordance with an otherwise compliant deferral election.

6. Treatment of Short-Term Deferrals

Under § 1.409A-1(b)(4), an arrangement may not provide for deferred compensation if the amount is payable, and is paid, during a limited period of time following the later of the date the service provider obtains a legally binding right to the payment or the date such right is no longer subject to a substantial risk of forfeiture (generally referred to as the applicable 2 1/2 month period). Whether an amount will be treated as a short-term deferral or as deferred compensation may not be determinable as of the last day of the service provider's taxable year, because it may depend upon whether the amount is paid on or before the end of the applicable 2 1/2 month period. For purposes of calculating the total amount deferred for a taxable year, the proposed regulations provide that the right to a payment that, under the terms of the arrangement and the facts and circumstances as of the last day of the taxable year, may or may not be a short-term deferral, is not included in the total amount deferred. In addition, even if such amount is not paid by the end of the applicable 2 1/2 month period so that the amount would be deferred compensation, the amount would not be includible in the total amount deferred until the service provider's taxable year in which the applicable 2 1/2 month period expired. For example, assume that as of December 31, 2010, an employee whose taxable year is the calendar year is entitled to an annual bonus that is scheduled to be paid on March 15, 2011, and that the bonus would qualify as a shortterm deferral if paid on or before the end of the applicable 2 1/2 month period, which ends on March 15, 2011. The bonus would not be included in the total amount deferred for 2010. This would be true regardless of whether the bonus is paid on or before March 15, 2011. However, the bonus would be includible in the total amount deferred for 2011 if the bonus is not paid on or before March 15, 2011.

C. *Calculation of total amount deferred - general principles*

1. General Rule

Generally, the proposed regulations provide that the total amount deferred under a plan for a taxable year is the present value as of the close of the last day of a service provider's taxable year of all amounts payable to the service provider under the plan, plus amounts paid to the service provider during the taxable year. For this purpose, present value generally would mean the value as of the close of the last day of the service provider's relevant taxable year of the amount or series of amounts due thereafter, where each such amount is multiplied by the probability that the condition or conditions on which payment of the amount is contingent would be satisfied (subject to special treatment for certain contingencies), discounted according to an assumed rate of interest to reflect the time value of money. A discount for the probability that the service provider will die before commencement of payments under the plan would be permitted to the extent that the payments would be forfeited upon the service provider's death. The proposed regulations provide that the present value cannot be discounted for the probability that payments will not be made (or will be reduced) because of the unfunded status of the plan, the risk associated with any deemed investment of amounts deferred under the plan, the risk that the service recipient or another party will be unwilling or unable to pay amounts deferred under the plan when due, the possibility of future plan amendments, the possibility of a future change in the law, or similar risks or contingencies. The proposed regulations further provide that restrictions on payment that will or may lapse with the passage of time, such as a temporary risk of forfeiture that is not a substantial risk of forfeiture, are not taken into account in determining present value. However, any potential additional deferrals contingent upon a bona fide requirement that the service provider perform services after the taxable year, such as potential salary deferrals, service credits or additions due to increases in compensation, would not be taken into account in determining the total amount deferred for the taxable year.

For purposes of calculating the present value of the benefit, the proposed regulations require the use of reasonable actuarial assumptions and methods. Whether assumptions and methods are reasonable for this purpose would be determined as of each date the benefit is valued for purposes of determining the total amount deferred.

The proposed regulations also provide certain rules relating to the crediting of earnings, generally providing that the schedule for crediting earnings will be respected if the earnings are credited at least once a year. In general, if the rules with respect to the crediting of earnings are met, any additional earnings that would be credited after the end of the taxable year only if the service provider continued performing services after the end of the year would not be includible in the total amount deferred for the year. If the right to earnings is based on an unreasonably high interest rate, the proposed regulations generally would characterize the unreasonable portion of earnings as a current right to additional deferred compensation. In addition, if earnings are based on a rate of return that does not qualify as a predetermined actual investment or a reasonable interest rate, the proposed regulations provide that the general calculation rules as applied to formula amounts would apply.

The proposed regulations provide other general rules that address issues such as plan terms under which amounts may be payable when a triggering event occurs, rather than on a fixed date, or plan terms under which the amount payable is determined in accordance with a formula, rather than being set at a fixed amount. In addition, the proposed regulations provide specific rules under which the total amounts deferred under certain types of nonqualified deferred compensation plans would be determined. The rules applicable to specific types of plans would apply in conjunction with the general rules. As a result, under the proposed regulations, an amount of deferred compensation may be includible in income under section 409A(a) even if the same amount would not yet be includible in wages under section 3121(v)(2).

2. Rules Regarding Alternative Times and Forms of Payment

To calculate the total amount deferred under a nonqualified deferred compensation plan, it is necessary to determine the time and form of payment pursuant to which the amount will be paid. Under the proposed regulations, if an amount deferred under a plan could be payable pursuant to more than one time and form of payment under the plan, the amount would be treated as payable in the available time and form of payment that has the highest present value. For this purpose, a time and form of payment generally would be an available time and form of payment to the extent a deferred amount under the plan could be payable pursuant to such time and form of payment under the plan's terms; provided that if there is a bona fide requirement that the service provider continue to perform services after the end of the taxable year to be eligible for the time and form of payment, the time and form of payment would not be treated as available. If an alternative time and form of payment is available only at the service recipient's discretion, the time and form of payment would not be treated as available unless the service provider has a legally binding right under the principles of § 1.409A-1(b)(1) to any additional value that would be generated by the service recipient's exercise of such discretion. If a service provider has begun receiving payments of an amount deferred under a plan and neither the service provider nor the service recipient can change the time and form of payment of such deferred amount without the other party's approval, then no other time and form of payment under the plan would be treated as available if such approval requirement has substantive significance.

In certain instances, a service provider will be eligible for an alternative time and form of payment only if the service provider has a certain status as of a future date. For example, a time and form of payment may be available only if the service provider is married at the time the payment commences. The proposed regulations generally provide that for purposes of determining whether the service provider will meet the eligibility requirements so that an alternative time and form of payment is available, the service provider is assumed to continue in the service provider's status as of the last day of the taxable year. However, if the eligibility requirement is not bona fide and does not serve a bona fide business purpose, the eligibility requirement would be disregarded and the service provider would be treated as eligible for the alternative time and form of payment. For this purpose, an eligibility condition based upon the service provider's marital status, parental status, or status as a U.S. citizen or lawful permanent resident would be presumed to be bona fide and to serve a bona fide business purpose.

If the calculation of the present value of the amount payable to a service provider under a plan requires assumptions relating to the timing of the payment because the payment date is, or could be, a triggering event rather than a specified date, the proposed regulations specify certain assumptions that must be applied to make such calculation. First, the possibility that a particular payment trigger would occur generally would not be taken into account if the right to the payment would be subject to a substantial risk of forfeiture if that payment trigger were the only specified payment trigger. For example, if an amount is payable upon the earlier of the attainment of a specified age or an involuntary separation from service (as defined in the § 1.409A-1(n)), the present value of the amount payable upon involuntary separation from service would not be taken into account if the payment would be subject to a substantial risk of forfeiture if that were the only payment trigger. However, if multiple triggers with respect to the same payment would, applied individually, constitute substantial risks of forfeiture, such triggers would not be disregarded under this rule unless all such triggers, applied in the aggregate, would also constitute a substantial risk of forfeiture. Second, the possibility that an unforeseeable emergency, as defined in § 1.409A-3(i)(3), would occur and result in a payment also would not be taken into account for purposes of calculating the amount deferred.

If an amount is payable upon a service provider's death, it generally would not be necessary to make assumptions concerning when the service provider would die because any additional value due to the amount becoming payable upon the service provider's death generally would be treated as an amount payable under a death benefit plan, and amounts payable under a death benefit plan are not deferred compensation for purposes of section 409A(a). Similarly, such assumptions generally would not be necessary for an amount payable upon a service provider's disability, because any additional value due to the amount becoming payable upon the service provider's disability generally would be payable under a disability plan, and amounts payable under a disability plan are not deferred compensation for purposes of section 409A. See § 1.409A-1(a)(5).

In other cases where it is necessary to make assumptions concerning when a payment trigger would occur to determine the amount deferred under a plan, taxpayers generally would be required to assume that the payment trigger would occur at the earliest possible time that the conditions under which the amount would become payable reasonably could occur, based on the facts and circumstances as of the last day of the taxable year. However, the proposed regulations provide a special rule for amounts payable due to the service provider's separation from service, termination of employment, or other event requiring the service provider's reduction or cessation of services for the service recipient. In such a case, the total amount deferred would be calculated as if the service provider had met the required reduction or cessation of services as of the close of the last day of the service provider's taxable year for which such calculation was being made. These rules would apply regardless of whether the payment trigger has or has not occurred as of any future date upon which the amount deferred for a prior taxable year was being determined.

The Treasury Department and the IRS recognize that for some service providers, the earliest possible time that a payment trigger reasonably could occur will not be the most likely time the trigger will occur. Similarly, the Treasury Department and the IRS recognize that for many service providers, the assumption that the service provider ceases providing services as of the end of the taxable year may not be realistic. The Treasury Department and the IRS request comments on alternative standards that could be utilized for these payment triggers.

An alternative approach might presume a date upon which the service provider will separate from service such as, for example, 100 months after the last day of the service provider's taxable year for which the amount deferred is being calculated. Cf. § 1.280G-1 Q&A 24(c)(4). Such a standard, however, would not reflect the value of additional deferred compensation that would be paid only if the service provider separates from service before the end of the 100-month period, such as an early retirement subsidy or a window benefit, unless special rules were developed to address such situations. Another issue that arises is whether such a standard should apply if the service provider is likely to retire during the next 100 months, such as if a service provider has attained a certain age, number of years of service, or level of financial independence. However, the Treasury Department and the IRS are concerned whether an approach involving the application of individualized standards to determine the probability that a particular service provider will separate from service will be administrable in practice.

3. Treatment of Rights to Formula Amounts

Once the date that a payment will occur has been fixed (either as a specified date under the plan's terms or through application of the rules in the proposed regulations), it is necessary to quantify the amount of the payment to which the service provider will be entitled to calculate the total amount deferred under a nonqualified deferred compensation plan. However, certain plans may define the amount payable by a formula or other method that is based on factors that may vary in future years. In general, if, at the end of the service provider's taxable year, the amount to be paid in a future year is a formula amount, the proposed regulations provide that the amount payable in the future year for purposes of calculating the total amount deferred must be determined using reasonable assumptions.

A deferred amount generally would be a formula amount subject to the reasonable assumptions standard if calculating the payment amount is dependent upon factors that are not determinable after taking into consideration all of the assumptions and other calculation rules provided in the proposed regulations. For example, a future payment equal to one percent of a corporation's net profits over five calendar years generally would be a formula amount until the last day of the fifth year, because the corporation's net profits over the five calendar years could not be determined by applying the assumptions and rules set out in the proposed regulations until the end of the fifth calendar year.

A deferred amount would not be a formula amount at the end of the taxable year merely because the information necessary to determine the amount is not readily available, if such information exists at the end of such taxable year. For example, if a deferred amount is based upon the service recipient's profits for its taxable year that coincides with the service provider's taxable year, the amount would be considered a non-formula amount at the end of the taxable year because the information necessary to determine the service recipient's profits exists, although such information may not be immediately accessible.

The right to have a deferred amount credited with reasonable earnings that may vary, for example because the earnings are based on the value of a deemed investment, would not affect whether the right to the underlying deferred amount is a formula amount. In addition, the amount of earnings to which the service provider has become entitled at the end of a particular taxable year would not be treated as a formula amount, regardless of whether such earnings could subsequently be reduced by future losses. For example, assume a service provider has a $10,000 account under an account balance plan, to be paid out in three years subject to earnings based on a mutual fund designed to replicate the performance of the S&P 500 index. At the end of Year 1, the account balance is $10,500. For Year 1, the service provider would have a total amount deferred equal to $10,500, notwithstanding that the amount could be reduced by future losses based on losses in the mutual fund.

D. *Calculation of total amounts deferred - specific types of plans*

1. Account Balance Plans

Under the proposed regulations, the amount deferred under an account balance plan for a taxable year generally equals the aggregate balance of all accounts under the plan as of the close of the last day of the taxable year, plus any amounts paid from such plan during the taxable year, so long as the aggregate account balance is determined using not more than a reasonable interest rate or the return on a predetermined actual investment. This rule would apply regardless of whether the applicable interest rate used to determine the earnings was higher or lower than the applicable Federal rate (AFR) under section 1274(d), provided that the interest rate was no more than a reasonable rate of interest. For a description of the proposed rules on how to calculate the total amount deferred if the right to earnings is based on an unreasonably high interest rate, see section III.C.1 of this preamble.

2. Nonaccount Balance Plans

Under the proposed regulations, the total amount deferred for a taxable year under a nonaccount balance plan generally is calculated under the general calculation rule. See section III.C of this preamble. For example, if a service provider has the right to be paid on a specified future date a fixed amount that is not credited with earnings, the total amount deferred for a year generally would be the present value as of the last day of the service provider's taxable year of the amount to which the service provider has a right to be paid in the future year (assuming no payments were made under the plan during the year). Increases in the present value of the payment in subsequent years due to the passage of time would be treated as earnings in the years in which such increases occur. For example, a right to a payment of $10,000 in Year 3 may have a present value in Year 1 equal to $8,900, and a present value in Year 2 equal to $9,434, so that the total amount deferred in Year 1 would be $8,900, the total amount deferred in Year 2 would be $9,434, and the total amount deferred in Year 3 would be $10,000 (assuming no payments were made during any year except Year 3). Any potential additional service credits or increases in compensation after the end of the taxable year for which the calculation is being made would not be taken into account in determining the total amount deferred for the taxable year.

3. Stock Rights

In general, the proposed regulations provide that the total amount deferred under an outstanding stock right is the amount of money and the fair market value of the property that the service provider would receive by exercising the right on the last day of the taxable year, reduced by the amount (if any) the service provider must pay to exercise the right and any amount the service provider paid for the right, which is commonly referred to as the spread. Accordingly, for an outstanding stock option, the total amount deferred generally would equal the underlying stock's fair market value on the last day of the taxable year, less the sum of the exercise price and any amount paid for the stock option. For an outstanding stock appreciation right, the total amount deferred generally would equal the underlying stock's fair market value on the last day of the taxable year, less the sum of the exercise price and any amount paid for the stock appreciation right. For this purpose, the stock's fair market value would be determined applying the principles set forth in § 1.409A-1(b)(5).

The Treasury Department and the IRS recognize that the spread generally is less than the fair market value of the stock right, which is used for purposes of determining the amount taxable under other Code provisions such as section 83 (if a stock option has a readily ascertainable fair market value), section 4999, and section 457(f). However, because these types of stock rights typically will fail to comply with section 409A(a) in multiple years, a taxpayer who holds such a stock right generally will be required to include amounts in income under section 409A in more than one taxable year. Therefore, the Treasury Department and the IRS believe that it is more appropriate to use the spread for purposes of applying section 409A(a) to stock rights.

4. Separation Pay Arrangements

A deferred amount that is payable only upon an involuntary separation from service generally will be treated as subject to a substantial risk of forfeiture until the service provider involuntarily separates from service. Accordingly, under the proposed regulations the amount of deferred compensation generally would not be required to be calculated until the service provider has involuntarily separated from service. In addition, if the amount were payable upon either an involuntary separation from service or some other trigger, such as a fixed date, the possibility of payment upon an involuntary separation from service generally would be ignored for purposes of determining the total amount deferred under the arrangement. See section III.C.2 of this preamble. Once an involuntary separation from service has occurred, the amount deferred under the plan would be determined using the rules that would apply to the schedule of payments if the right to payment were not contingent upon an involuntary separation from service. For example, if the amounts payable are installment payments and the remaining installment payments include interest credited at a reasonable rate, the total amount deferred under the plan would be determined under the rules governing account balance plans. If more than one type of deferred compensation arrangement were provided under the separation pay agreement, the amount deferred under each arrangement would be determined using the rules applicable to that type of arrangement. The total amount deferred for the taxable year would be the sum of all of the amounts deferred under the various arrangements constituting the plan.

5. Reimbursement Arrangements

The proposed regulations provide a method of calculating the amount deferred under a reimbursement arrangement, including an arrangement where the benefit is provided as an in-kind benefit from the service recipient or the service recipient will pay directly the third-party provider of the goods or services to the service provider. For example, the amount deferred under an arrangement providing a specified number of hours of financial planning services after a service provider's separation from service would be determined using the rules applicable to reimbursement arrangements, regardless of whether the service recipient reimburses the service provider for the service provider's expenses in purchasing such services, provides the financial planning services directly to the service provider, or pays a third-party financial planner to provide such services. The rules for reimbursement arrangements would apply to all such types of arrangements, including arrangements that would not be disaggregated from a nonaccount balance plan under § 1.409A-1(c)(2)(i)(E) because the amounts subject to reimbursement exceed the applicable limits.

The proposed calculation rules provide that if a service provider has a right to reimbursements but only up to a specified maximum amount, it is presumed that the taxpayer will incur the maximum amount of expenses eligible for reimbursement, at the earliest possible time such expenses may be incurred and payable at the earliest possible time the amount may be reimbursed under the plan's terms. The service provider could rebut the presumption if the service provider demonstrates by clear and convincing evidence that it is unreasonable to assume that the service provider would expend (or would have expended) the maximum amount of expenses eligible for reimbursement. For example, if a service provider is entitled to the reimbursement of country club dues the service provider incurs in the next taxable year, not to exceed $30,000, if the service provider can demonstrate that the most expensive country club within reasonable geographic proximity of the service provider's residence and work location will cost $20,000 per year, and that the service provider's level of compensation and financial resources make it unreasonable to assume that the service provider would travel periodically to the locales of other, more expensive country clubs, the service provider can calculate the amount deferred based upon the $20,000 being eligible for reimbursement. The presumption of maximum utilization of expenses eligible for reimbursement generally would not apply if the expenses subject to reimbursement are medical expenses.

If a right to reimbursement is not subject to a maximum amount, the taxpayer would be treated as having deferred a formula amount, provided that the taxpayer would be required to calculate the amount based on the maximum amount that reasonably could be expended and reimbursed. The amount would be considered a nonformula amount as soon as the taxpayer incurs the expense that is subject to reimbursement, in an amount equal to the reimbursement to which the taxpayer is entitled.

For example, a right to the reimbursement of half of the expenses the service provider incurs to purchase a boat without any limitation with respect to the cost would be treated as a deferral of a formula amount, until such time as the service provider purchases the boat.

6. Split-Dollar Life Insurance Arrangements

The amount deferred under a split-dollar life insurance arrangement would be determined based upon the amount that would be required to be included in income in a future year under the applicable split-dollar life insurance rules. Determination of the amount includible in income would depend upon the Federal tax regime and guidance applicable to such arrangement. If the split-dollar life insurance arrangement is not subject to § 1.61-22 or § 1.7872-15 due to application of the effective date provisions under § 1.61-22(j), the amount payable would be determined by reference to Notice 2002-8 (2002-1 CB 398) and any other applicable guidance. If the split-dollar life insurance arrangement is subject to § 1.61-22 or § 1.7872-15, the amount payable would be determined by reference to such regulations, based upon the type of arrangement. For this purpose, the amount includible in income generally would be determined by applying the split-dollar life insurance rules to the arrangement in conjunction with the general rules providing assumptions on payment dates of deferred amounts. However, in the case of an arrangement subject to § 1.7872-15, to the extent the rules regarding time and form of payment and other payment assumptions under these proposed regulations conflict with the provisions of § 1.7872-15, the provisions of § 1.7872-15 would apply instead of the conflicting rules under these proposed regulations. As provided in Notice 2007-34 (2007-17 IRB 996), the portion of the benefit provided under the split-dollar life insurance arrangement consisting of the cost of current life insurance protection is not treated as deferred compensation for this purpose. See § 601.601(d)(2)(ii)(*b*).

7. Foreign Arrangements

Although certain foreign arrangements are a separate category under the plan aggregation rules (§ 1.409A-1(c)(2)(i)(G)), the amounts deferred under such arrangements would be determined using the same rules that would apply if the arrangements were not foreign arrangements. For example, the total amount deferred by a United States citizen participating in a salary deferral arrangement in France that meets the requirements of § 1.409A-1(c)(2)(i)(G), but that otherwise would constitute an elective account balance plan under § 1.409A-1(c)(2)(i)(A), would be determined using the rules applicable to account balance plans.

8. Other Plans

The calculation of the total amount deferred under a plan that does not fall into any of the enunciated categories (and accordingly is treated as a separate plan under § 1.409A-1(c)(2)(i)(I)), would be determined by applying the general calculation rules.

E. *Calculation of amounts includible in income.*

This section III.E of the preamble addresses the second step in determining the amount includible in income under section 409A for a taxable year - the determination of the portion of the total amount deferred for a taxable year that was either subject to a substantial risk of forfeiture or had previously been included in income. That portion of the total amount deferred for the taxable year would not be includible in income under section 409A.

1. Determination of the Portion of the Total Amount Deferred for a Taxable Year that is Subject to a Substantial Risk of Forfeiture

In general, the proposed regulations provide that the portion of the total amount deferred for a taxable year that is subject to a substantial risk of forfeiture (nonvested) is determined as of the last day of the service provider's taxable year. Accordingly, all amounts that vest during the taxable year in which a failure occurs would be treated as vested for purposes of section 409A(a), regardless of whether the vesting event occurs before or after the failure to meet the requirements of section 409A(a). For example, if a plan fails to comply with section 409A(a) due to an operational failure on July 1 of a taxable year, and the substantial risk of forfeiture applicable to an amount deferred under the plan lapses as of October 1 of the same taxable year, that amount would be treated as a vested amount for purposes of determining the amount includible in income for the taxable year.

2. Determination of the Portion of the Total Amount Deferred for a Taxable Year that has been Previously Included in Income

For a deferred amount to be treated as previously included in income, the proposed regulations would require that the service provider actually and properly have included the amount in income in accordance with a provision of the Internal Revenue Code. This would include amounts reflected on an original or amended return filed before expiration of the applicable statute of limitations on assessment and amounts included in income as part of an audit or closing agreement process. In addition, a deferred amount would be treated as an amount previously included in income only until the amount is paid. Accordingly, if a deferred amount is paid in the same taxable year in which an amount is included in income under section 409A, or all or a portion of an amount previously included in income is allocable to a payment made under the plan (see section VI.A of this preamble), in subsequent taxable years that amount would not be treated as an amount previously included in income. For example, if an employee includes $100,000 in income under section 409A(a), and $10,000 of the amount includible in income consists of a payment under the plan during the taxable year, only $90,000 would remain to be treated as a deferred amount previously included in income. Similarly, if in the next year the employee receives a payment, to the extent any or all of that $90,000 amount previously included in income is allocated to that payment so that all or a portion of the payment is not includible in gross income, the amount allocated would no longer be treated as an amount previously included in income.

F. *Treatment of failures continuing during more than one taxable year*

A plan term that fails to meet the requirements of section 409A(a) may be retained in the plan over multiple taxable years. In addition, operational failures may occur in multiple years. This section III.F of the preamble discusses how section 409A(a) applies in such cases.

Each of the service provider's taxable years would be analyzed independently to determine if amounts were includible in income under section 409A(a). See section II of this preamble. Thus, for any taxable year during which a failure occurs, all amounts deferred under the plan would be includible in income unless the amount has previously been included in income or is subject to a substantial risk of forfeiture. Generally, this means that a service provider who includes in income under section 409A(a) all amounts deferred under a plan for a taxable year would not be relieved of the requirement to include amounts in income for an earlier taxable year in which a failure also occurred. It would undermine the statutory purpose to allow a service provider to include an amount in income under section 409A(a) (or otherwise) on a current basis with respect to a failure that occurred in a prior taxable year and thereby eliminate the taxes owed for the earlier year, especially if intervening payments of deferred amounts have reduced the total amount deferred as of the end of such current year. In addition, this rule generally would prohibit a service provider from selecting from among several previous taxable years the most favorable year in which to include income. However, if an amount was actually and properly included in income under section 409A(a) in a previous year, the amount would be treated as an amount previously in income for purposes of all subsequent years. Accordingly, this rule would never make the same amount includible in income twice under section 409A(a).

For example, assume an employee participates in a nonqualified deferred compensation plan and defers $10,000 each year, credited annually with interest at 5 percent (assumed to be reasonable for purposes of this example), and receives no payments under the plan. The employee's total amount deferred would be $10,500 for Year 1, $21,525 for Year 2, and $33,101 for Year 3. If the nonqualified deferred compensation plan fails to meet the requirements of section 409A(a) in each year, the employee would be required to include $10,500 in income under section 409A(a) for Year 1, $11,025 in income for Year 2, and $11,576 in income for Year 3. If the employee includes $33,101 in income under section 409A(a) for Year 3, the employee would not have properly reported income for Year 1 and Year 2. However, an amount included in income for Year 3 would be treated as previously included in income for purposes of any further failures in subsequent years. In addition, if the employee subsequently properly includes amounts in income for Year 1 and Year 2 on amended returns, the employee could claim a refund of the tax paid on the excess amounts included in income for Year 3. Similar consequences apply to the employer. If the employer fails to report and withhold on amounts includible in income under section 409A(a) in Year 1 and Year 2, the employer could not avoid liability for the failure to withhold in Year 1 and Year 2 by reporting the full amount and withholding in Year 3.

Because each taxable year would be analyzed independently, the IRS could elect to audit and assess with respect to a single taxable year, and require inclusion of all amounts deferred under the plan through that taxable year (even if failures also occurred in prior taxable years). Under those circumstances, the taxpayer could simply include amounts in income under section 409A(a) for that taxable year. However, before expiration of the applicable statute of limitations, the taxpayer could amend returns for previous taxable years and include in income amounts required to be included under section 409A(a), lowering the amount includible in income under section 409A(a) for the audited taxable year because, for purposes of that taxable year, those amounts would have been included in income in previous years. For example, an audit of Year 3 in the example above could result in an adjustment requiring $33,101 to be included in income under section 409A(a). However, before expiration of the applicable statute of limitations, the employee could amend the employee's Year 1 and Year 2 Federal tax returns to include $10,500 in income under section 409A(a) for Year 1, and $11,025 in income under section 409A(a) for Year 2, and accordingly include only $11,576 in income under section 409A(a) for Year 3. However, the employee would be required to pay the additional section 409A(a) taxes for Year 1 and Year 2, including the premium interest tax. In addition, if amounts deferred under the plan had been paid in Year 1 or Year 2, the employee would be required to include those additional amounts in income under section 409A(a) for the year paid (meaning, if the payment had been included in income for the year in which it was paid, the employee would be required to amend the previously filed tax returns to pay the additional section 409A(a) taxes on such income).

IV. *Application of Additional 20 Percent Tax*

Section 409A(a)(1)(B)(i)(II) provides that if compensation is required to be included in gross income under section 409A(a)(1)(A) for a taxable year, the income tax imposed is increased by an amount equal to 20 percent of the compensation that is required to be included in gross income. This amount is an additional income tax, subject to the rules governing the assessment, collection, and payment of income tax, and is not an excise tax.

V. *Application of Premium Interest Tax*

A. *In general*

Section 409A(a)(1)(B)(i)(I) provides that if compensation is required to be included in gross income under section 409A(a)(1)(A) for a taxable year, the income tax imposed is increased by an amount equal to the amount of interest determined under section 409A(a)(1)(B)(ii). This amount is an additional income tax, subject to the rules governing assessment, collection, and payment of income tax, and is not an excise tax or interest on an underpayment. Section 409A(a)(1)(B)(ii) provides that this premium interest tax is determined as the amount of interest at the underpayment rate (established under section 6621) plus one percentage point on the underpayments that would have occurred had the deferred compensation been includible in gross income for the taxable year in which first deferred or, if later, the first taxable year in which such deferred compensation is not subject to a substantial risk of forfeiture (vested). Thus, section 409A(a)(1)(B) requires that the premium interest tax be applied to hypothetical underpayments where the hypothetical underpayments are determined by first allocating the amounts deferred under the plan required to be included in income under section 409A(a) to the initial year (or years) the amount was deferred or vested, then determining the hypothetical underpayment that would have resulted had such amounts been includible in income at that time, and then determining the interest that would be due upon that hypothetical underpayment based upon a premium interest rate equal to the underpayment rate plus one percentage point.

B. *Amounts to which the premium interest tax applies*

Section 409A(a)(1)(B)(ii) provides for an additional tax based upon the interest that would be applied to the resulting underpayments of tax if the deferred compensation includible in income under section 409A(a) had been includible in income in previous years. Because the total amount deferred for the taxable year in which a failure occurs (the current year) may be less than the amounts deferred under the same plan in a previous year due to payments or deemed investment or other losses in the previous year, so that a portion of the amount deferred in the previous year would not be includible in income under section 409A(a) for the current year, commentators have asked what amounts deferred under the plan must be taken into account in determining the premium interest tax. Section 409A(a)(1)(B)(i) refers first to the compensation required to be included in gross income under section 409A(a)(1)(A). Accordingly, under the proposed regulations the amount required to be included in income under section 409A(a) for the taxable year is the only deferred amount required to be allocated to previous taxable years for purposes of determining the premium interest tax under section 409A(a)(1)(B)(i)(I).

For example, assume an employee who participates in a plan has a total amount deferred in Year 1 of $100,000 and a total amount deferred in Year 2 of $80,000 due to deemed investment losses in Year 2. If the plan fails to meet the requirements of section 409A(a) in Year 2 (and not Year 1), the employee is required to include $80,000 in income under section 409A(a). In calculating the premium interest tax, the employee must allocate only the $80,000 required to be included in income under section 409A(a) to the year or years the amount was first deferred or vested, even though additional amounts were deferred under the plan in previous taxable years.

C. *Identification of initial years of deferral for includible amounts*

1. Identification of Amounts Deferred in a Particular Taxable Year - General Principles

To calculate the premium underpayment interest tax, the taxable year or years during which the amount required to be included in income was first deferred or first vested must be determined. The proposed regulations provide that the amount deferred during a particular taxable year generally is the excess (if any) of the vested total amount deferred for that taxable year over the vested total amount deferred for the immediately preceding taxable year. For example, if a service provider first participated in a plan in the taxable year 2010 and has a vested total amount deferred under the plan for 2010 of $10,000, a vested total amount deferred for 2011 of $15,000, and a vested total amount deferred for 2012 of $25,000, then the service provider would be treated as having first deferred $10,000 during 2010, $5,000 during 2011, and $10,000 during 2012.

2. Identification of Initial Years of Deferral -Treatment of Amounts Previously Included in Income, Payments, and Investment Losses

The general rule would apply in cases where during previous taxable years there have been no payments under the plan, no net deemed investment or other losses, and no amounts otherwise included in income. If a service provider has received a payment, incurred net deemed losses, or included an amount in income, the general rule would need to be modified. For example, assume that the vested total amount deferred for Year 1 is $100,000, for Year 2 is $200,000 (including a $50,000 payment), and for Year 3 is $250,000. If there is a failure to meet the requirements of section 409A(a) in Year 3, the service provider would be required to include $250,000 in income. The service provider would also need to determine the year or years during which the $250,000 was first deferred and vested for purposes of calculating the premium interest tax. The issue then arises whether the $50,000 payment in Year 2 was a payment of an amount first deferred and vested in Year 1 or Year 2. If the $50,000 payment is treated as a payment of an amount first deferred and vested in Year 1, then only $50,000 of the $100,000 deferred in Year 1 would remain to be treated as part of the $250,000 includible in income in Year 3. In contrast, if the $50,000 payment is treated as a payment of an amount first deferred in Year 2, then the entire $100,000 deferred in Year 1 would remain to be treated as part of the $250,000. Similar issues arise with respect to the treatment of deemed investment losses and amounts previously included in income.

Under the calculation method set forth in the proposed regulations, payments, deemed investment or other losses, and amounts included in income during taxable years before the year in which the failure occurs, generally are attributed to amounts deferred and vested in the earliest year or years in which there are amounts deferred. The proposed calculation method generally achieves this result by reducing the amount deferred for each year preceding the payment or deemed investment or other loss, and treating only the remaining deferred amounts as the source of the outstanding deferrals and payments includible in income under section 409A for the year in which the failure occurs. This proposed rule generally should result in the lowest possible amount of premium interest tax, because deferred amounts includible in income under section 409A would be treated as first deferred and vested in the latest possible years, resulting in less premium interest on the hypothetical underpayments.

D. *Calculation of the hypothetical underpayment*

The hypothetical underpayment would be calculated as if the amount were paid to the service provider as a cash payment of compensation during the taxable year. Further, the hypothetical underpayment would be calculated based on the taxpayer's taxable income, credits, filing status, and other tax information for the year, based on the original return the taxpayer filed for such year, as adjusted as a result of any examination for such year or any amended return the taxpayer filed for such year that was accepted by the IRS. The hypothetical underpayment would reflect the effect that such additional compensation would have had on the amount of Federal income tax owed by the taxpayer for such year, including the continued availability of any deductions taken, and the use of any carryovers such as carryover losses. For purposes of calculating a hypothetical underpayment in a subsequent year (whether or not a portion of the deferred amount was first deferred and vested in the subsequent year), any changes to the taxpayer's Federal income tax liability for the subsequent year that would have occurred if the portion of the deferred amount that was first deferred and vested during the previous taxable year had been included in the taxpayer's income for the previous year would be taken into account. For example, if in calculating the hypothetical underpayment for one year, an additional amount of unused charitable contribution deductions is absorbed, the use of the additional charitable contributions would be reflected in determining the hypothetical underpayment for a subsequent year (meaning that the same portion of the charitable contribution could not be deducted twice in determining the hypothetical underpayments for more than one year).

Calculation of the premium interest tax would take into account only the consequences the additional income would have had on the Federal income tax due based on items of income and deduction, credits, filing status and similar information existing as of the end of the taxable year at issue. Other potential effects of the additional compensation payment on service provider or service recipient actions or elections would not be taken into account, including how such additional compensation could have affected participation in an employee benefit plan or other arrangement. For example, the impact such additional compensation would have had on contributions to a qualified plan, even if the additional compensation would have affected the amount the service provider would have been permitted or required to contribute, would be disregarded.

E. *Potential safe harbor calculation methods*

The Treasury Department and the IRS recognize that calculation of the premium underpayment interest tax may be cumbersome, potentially involving the recalculation of several years' tax returns. In response, the Treasury Department and the IRS are considering whether safe harbor calculation methods could be devised that would reduce the calculation burden but still result in an appropriate amount of tax applicable to the amount includible in income under section 409A(a). Specifically, the Treasury Department and the IRS request comments on calculation methods that would more easily identify the taxable year or years during which an amount includible in income under section 409A(a) was first deferred and vested, and that would more easily determine the hypothetical underpayments applicable to such year or years. Comments should consider both how the safe harbor method would be applied by taxpayers, and the extent to which such methods could be applied by the IRS in the examination context.

VI. *Treatment of Payments, Forfeitures, or Permanent Losses of Deferred Amounts in Taxable Years after the Amount is Included in Income under Section 409A(a)*

A. *Payments of deferred compensation in taxable years after the inclusion of such amounts in income under section 409A(a)*

Section 409A(c) provides that any amount included in gross income under section 409A is not required to be included in gross income under any other provision of the Code or any other rule of law later than the time provided in section 409A. Accordingly, if a service provider includes an amount in income under section 409A, the proposed regulations provide for a type of deemed "basis" or "investment in the contract" such that the amount would not be required to be included in income again (for example, when the amount was actually paid). For this purpose, the amount previously included in income would be treated as the inclusion in income of an amount deferred under the plan, but would not be allocated to any specific amount deferred under the plan. Accordingly, if an amount under the plan would be includible in income if section 409A were disregarded (for example, because an amount is paid under the plan), the amount previously included in income would be immediately applied to the amount paid under the plan such that the amount paid would not be required to be included in gross income a second time.

For example, assume that in Year 1 an employee defers $10,000 under a salary deferral elective account balance plan and is required to include that amount in income under section 409A. Assume that in Year 2 the employee defers $15,000 under the same salary deferral elective account balance plan, and an additional $5,000 under a bonus deferral elective account balance plan, both of which are compliant with section 409A. Assume that in Year 3 the employee receives a payment of $5,000 under the bonus deferral elective account balance plan. Because the payment would be treated for purposes of section 409A as made from a single elective account balance plan in which the employee participated, and because the employee has already included $10,000 in income under section 409A due to participation in the plan, the employee would apply $5,000 of the $10,000 that was previously included in income to the $5,000 payment and not include the $5,000 payment in gross income in Year 3 (or any subsequent year). The remaining amount previously included in income would be $5,000.

The employee could not elect the extent to which the amount previously included in income would be applied in this context. Rather, the amount previously included in income would be required to be applied immediately to the extent an amount deferred under the same plan would otherwise become includible in income under a Code section other than section 409A. The inclusion of any amount in income and the resulting amount previously included in income for subsequent years would not affect the potential for earnings related to such amounts to be subject to section 409A or to be required to be included in income under section 409A.

B. *Permanent forfeiture or loss of a deferred amount previously included in income under section 409A(a)*

The application of section 409A(a) may require inclusion in income of amounts that the service provider ultimately never receives. This result may occur under four different circumstances. First, because a nonqualified deferred compensation plan generally involves an unfunded, unsecured promise of a service recipient to pay compensation in a future year, the funds to pay the deferred amount may not be available in the future year. For example, the service recipient may be insolvent, bankrupt or have ceased to exist at the time the payment is due.

Second, some amounts of deferred compensation may be included in income under section 409A(a) if the amounts are subject to a risk of forfeiture, but the risk of forfeiture does not qualify as a substantial risk of forfeiture. For example, a deferred amount payable only if the service provider does not compete with the service recipient for a defined period is not subject to a substantial risk of forfeiture. However, if the service provider actually competes with the service recipient, the service provider may forfeit the right to the amount.

Third, the deferred amount may be subject to deemed investment losses. If losses occur after the deferred amount has been included in income under section 409A(a), the amount paid to the service provider may be less than the amount included in income.

Fourth, in the case of a formula amount, the calculation of the deferred amount may result in the inclusion in income under section 409A(a) of an amount that is greater than the amount ultimately paid. For example, if a service provider receives a right to a certain percentage of the service recipient's profits payable at separation from service, and determines that the total amount deferred under the plan is $100,000, once the profits are calculated the service provider may be entitled to a lesser amount.

1. Effect on Service Provider

The proposed regulations provide that a service provider who is required to include an amount in income under section 409A(a) with respect to a deferred amount under a nonqualified deferred compensation plan is entitled to a deduction at the time the service provider's legally binding right to all deferred compensation under the plan (including all arrangements treated as a single plan under the aggregation rules) is permanently forfeited under the plan's terms, or the right to such compensation is otherwise permanently lost. The available deduction would equal the excess of the amount included in income under section 409A(a) in a previous year over any amount actually or constructively received by the service provider. A right to an amount would not be treated as permanently lost merely because the deferred amount had decreased, for example due to deemed investment losses, if the service provider retains a right to an amount deferred under the plan. In addition, a right to an amount would not be treated as permanently forfeited or otherwise lost if the obligation to make such payment is substituted for another deferred amount or obligation to make a payment in a future year. However, the right to an amount would be treated as permanently lost if the right to the payment of the amount becomes wholly worthless. A service provider would not be entitled to a deduction with respect to an amount previously included in income under section 409A(a) if the service provider retains a right to any amount deferred under all arrangements treated as a single plan under § 1.409A-1(c)(2). However, if the entire deferred amount payable under the plan has been paid out and the service recipient has no remaining liability to the service provider under the plan, any remaining unpaid deferred amount that had previously been included in income would be treated as permanently lost.

For example, if at the end of Year 1 an employee has an account balance of $100,000 which is required to be included in income under section 409A, and at the end of Year 2 an employee has an account balance of $90,000 due to notional investment losses, the employee would not be entitled to a deduction for Year 2. However, if in Year 3 the entire account balance of $95,000 is paid to the employee, so there no longer are any amounts deferred under the plan (determined after applying applicable aggregation rules) and nothing remains to be paid to the employee, the employee would be entitled to a $5,000 deduction for Year 3.

In the case of a service provider that is an employee, the available deduction generally would be treated as a miscellaneous itemized deduction, subject to the deduction limitations applicable to such expenses. Section 1341 would not be applicable to such deduction because inclusion of an amount in income as a result of noncompliance with section 409A(a) would not constitute receipt of an amount to which it appeared that the taxpayer had an unrestricted right in the taxable year of inclusion. In the first circumstance listed above, a service provider that does not receive payment of deferred compensation because of the bankruptcy or insolvency of the service recipient retains the legal right to the income even though the income is not collectible. In each of the three other circumstances in which such a deduction becomes available, the deferred compensation is not paid because of an event that occurred after the taxable year in which the amount deferred was included in income under section 409A, rather than from the absence of a right to the deferred compensation in the year in which it was includible in gross income. Finally, certain of such circumstances, such as the actual amount received differing from the amount included in income because the amount deferred was a formula amount, result from the inherent uncertainties in valuing rights to such amounts, rather than from a lack of a claim of right to income.

2. Effect on Service Recipient

If a service provider is entitled to a deduction with respect to a deferred amount included in income under section 409A(a) that is subsequently permanently forfeited or otherwise lost, to the extent the service recipient has benefited from a deduction or increased the basis of an asset because the deferred amount was included in the service provider's gross income, or such inclusion by the service provider has otherwise reduced or could otherwise reduce the service recipient's gross income, the service recipient may be required to recognize income under the tax benefit rule and section 111, or make other appropriate adjustments to reflect that the deferred amount included in income by the service provider under section 409A(a) has been permanently forfeited or otherwise lost, and thus will not be paid by the service recipient.

VII. *Service Provider Income Inclusion and Additional Taxes and Service Recipient Reporting and Withholding Obligations*

A. *Service provider income inclusion*

The Treasury Department and the IRS anticipate issuing interim guidance during 2008 addressing the extent to which taxpayers may rely on the proposed regulations with respect to the calculation of the amounts includible in income under section 409A(a) and the calculation of the additional taxes under section 409A(a). The interim guidance is also expected to address the calculation of the amounts includible in income and additional taxes under section 409A(b) and service recipient reporting and withholding obligations with respect to amounts includible in income under section 409A(a) or (b) for taxable years beginning before the final regulations become applicable. The Treasury Department and the IRS anticipate that such interim guidance will provide that taxpayers may rely upon the proposed regulations in their entirety (but that taxpayers may not rely on part, but not all, of the proposed regulations).

B. *Annual deferral reporting*

Section 885(b) of the Act amended sections 6041 and 6051 to require that an employer or payer report all deferrals for the year under a nonqualified deferred compensation plan on a Form W-2, "Wage and Tax Statement" or a Form 1099-MISC, "Miscellaneous Income", regardless of whether such deferred compensation is includible in gross income under section 409A(a) (annual deferral reporting). Notice 2007-89 permanently waives this requirement for 2007 Forms W-2 and Forms 1099. Notice 2006-100 permanently waives this requirement for 2005 and 2006 Forms W-2 and Forms 1099. The Treasury Department and the IRS anticipate that this reporting will be implemented beginning with the first taxable year for which these proposed regulations are finalized and effective. The Treasury Department and the IRS further anticipate that the annual deferral reporting rules will be based upon the principles set forth in these regulations as finalized, except that taxpayers will not be required to report deferred amounts that are not reasonably ascertainable (as defined in §31.3121(v)(2)-1(e)(4)(i)(B)) until such amounts become reasonably ascertainable. The Treasury Department and the IRS anticipate that the deferred amounts required to be reported will reflect earnings on the amounts deferred in previous years, if the amount of such earnings is reasonably ascertainable, because section 409A specifically treats earnings on deferred amounts as additional deferred amounts. The Treasury Department and the IRS request comments on the potential application of the standards set forth in these regulations to this reporting requirement, including suggestions for possible adaptations or modifications that may decrease the administrative burden of compliance while maintaining the integrity of the information reported.

C. *Income inclusion reporting and income tax withholding*

Section 885(b) of the Act also amended section 3401(a) to provide that the term "wages" includes any amount includible in the gross income of an employee under section 409A, and amended section 6041 to require that a payer report amounts includible in gross income under section 409A that are not treated as wages under section 3401(a) (income inclusion reporting). Notice 2005-1 provides that an employer should report amounts includible in gross income under section 409A and in wages under section 3401(a) in box 1 of Form W-2 as wages paid to the employee during the year and subject to income tax withholding, and that the employer should also report such amounts in box 12 of Form W-2 using code Z. Notice 2005-1 also provides that a payer should report amounts includible in gross income under section 409A and not treated as wages under section 3401(a) as nonemployee compensation in box 7 of Form 1099-MISC, and should also report such amounts in box 15b of Form 1099-MISC. Notice 2006-100 provided guidance on income inclusion reporting for the 2005 and 2006 Forms W-2 and Forms 1099. Notice 2007-89 provided guidance on income inclusion reporting for the 2007 Forms W-2 and Forms 1099. The Treasury Department and the IRS anticipate issuing further interim guidance during 2008 on income inclusion reporting for 2008 Forms W-2 and Forms 1099 for taxable years beginning before the final regulations become applicable. The Treasury Department and the IRS anticipate that such interim guidance will provide that taxpayers may rely upon the proposed regulations in their entirety (but that taxpayers may not rely on part, but not all, of the proposed regulations).

Amounts includible in an employee's income under section 409A also are treated as wages for purposes of section 3401. Notice 2007-89 provides guidance on a service recipient's income tax withholding obligations for 2007. The Treasury Department and the IRS anticipate issuing further interim guidance during 2008 on a service recipient's income tax withholding obligations for calendar years beginning before the final regulations become applicable. The Treasury Department and the IRS anticipate that such interim guidance will provide that taxpayers may rely upon the proposed regulations in their entirety (but that taxpayers may not rely on part, but not all, of the proposed regulations).

Proposed Effective Date

These regulations are proposed to be generally applicable for taxable years beginning on or after the issuance of final regulations. Before the applicability date of the final regulations, taxpayers may rely on these proposed regulations only to the extent provided in further guidance.

Special Analyses

It has been determined that this notice of proposed rulemaking is not a significant regulatory action as defined in Executive Order 12866. Therefore, a regulatory assessment is not required. It has also been determined that section 553(b) of the Administrative Procedure Act (5 U.S.C. chapter 5) does not apply to these regulations, and because the regulation does not impose a collection of information on small entities, the Regulatory Flexibility Act (5 U.S.C. chapter 6) does not apply. Pursuant to section 7805(f) of the Code, this notice of proposed rulemaking will be submitted to the Chief Counsel for Advocacy of the Small Business Administration for comment on its impact on small business.

Comments and Public Hearing

Before these proposed regulations are adopted as final regulations, consideration will be given to any written (a signed original and eight (8) copies) or electronic comments that are submitted timely to the IRS. The IRS and Treasury Department request comments on the clarity of the proposed rules and how they can be made easier to understand. All comments will be available for public inspection and copying.

A public hearing has been scheduled for April 2, 2009 at 10:00 a.m., in the auditorium. Due to building security procedures, visitors must enter at the Constitution Avenue entrance. In addition, all visitors must present photo identification to enter the building. Because of access restrictions, visitors will not be admitted beyond the immediate entrance area more than 30 minutes before the hearing starts. For information about having your name placed on the building access list to attend the hearing, see the "FOR FURTHER INFORMATION CONTACT" section of this preamble.

The rules of 26 CFR 601.601(a)(3) apply to the hearing. Persons who wish to present oral comments at the hearing must submit written or electronic comments and an outline of the topics to be discussed and the time to be devoted to each topic (a signed original and eight (8) copies) by March 9, 2009. A period of 10 minutes will be allotted to each person for making comments. An agenda showing the scheduling of the speakers will be prepared after the deadline for receiving outlines has passed. Copies of the agenda will be available free of charge at the hearing.

Drafting Information

The principal author of these regulations is Stephen Tackney of the Office of Division Counsel/Associate Chief Counsel (Tax Exempt and Government Entities). However, other personnel from the IRS and the Treasury Department participated in their development.

[¶49,413] Proposed Amendments of Regulations (REG-143686-07), published in the Federal Register on January 21, 2009 (corrected 3/5/2009).

[Code Secs. 301, 302, 304, 351, 354, 355, 356, 358, 368, 861, 1002, 1016 and 1374]

Corporate distributions: Redemptions: Dividends: Corporate reorganizations: Receipt of additional consideration: Gain or loss: Basis of property received.—Reg. §§1.301-2, 1.302-5 and 1.861-12 and amendments of Reg. §§1.302-2, 1.304-1, 1.304-2, 1.304-3, 1.304-5, 1.351-2, 1.354-1, 1.355-1, 1.356-1, 1.358-1, 1.358-2, 1.358-6, 1.368-1, 1.1002-1, 1.1016-2 and 1.1374-10, regarding the recovery of stock basis in distributions under section 301 and transactions that are treated as dividends to which section 301 applies, as well as guidance regarding the determination of gain and the basis of stock or securities received in exchange for, or with respect to, stock or securities in certain transactions, are withdrawn.

[¶49,415] **Proposed Amendments of Regulations (REG-147636-08)**, published in the Federal Register on February 11, 2009.

[Code Secs. 367 and 1248]

Foreign corporation: Distribution of property: Stock: Sale or exchange: Gain.—Reg. §1.367(a)-9, concerning transfers of stock to a foreign corporation that are described in Code Sec. 351 by reason of Code Sec. 304(a)(1) and recognized by a shareholder under Code Sec. 301(c)(3) in connection with the receipt of a distribution of property from a foreign corporation with respect to its stock shall be treated as gain from the sale or exchange of the stock of such foreign corporation, is proposed. Amendments of Reg. §1.1248-1 were adopted on 4/23/2012 by T.D. 9585. Amendments of Reg. §1.367(b)-4 were withdrawn and then re-proposed by REG-135734-14 on April 8, 2016 (see ¶49,693).

AGENCY: Internal Revenue Service (IRS), Treasury.

ACTION: Notice of proposed rulemaking by cross-reference to temporary regulations.

SUMMARY: In the Rules and Regulations section of this issue of the **Federal Register**, the IRS and Treasury Department are issuing temporary regulations under sections 304 and 1248 of the Internal Revenue Code (Code). The temporary regulations provide rules under section 367(a) and (b) that apply to certain transfers of stock by a United States person to a foreign corporation described in section 304(a)(1). The temporary regulations under section 1248(a) provide that, for purposes of section 1248(a), gain recognized by a shareholder under section 301(c)(3) in connection with the receipt of a distribution of property from a foreign corporation with respect to its stock shall be treated as gain from the sale or exchange of the stock of such foreign corporation. The temporary regulations affect certain shareholders that transfer stock in a corporation to a foreign corporation in a transaction to which section 304(a)(1) applies, or that receive a distribution from a foreign corporation described in section 301(c)(3). The text of the temporary regulations also serves as the text of these proposed regulations. The preamble to the temporary regulations explains the temporary regulations and these proposed regulations.

DATES: Written or electronic comments and requests for a public hearing must be received by May 12, 2009.

ADDRESSES: Send submissions to: CC:PA:LPD:PR (REG-147636-08), room 5205, Internal Revenue Service, PO Box 7604, Ben Franklin Station, Washington, DC 20044. Submissions may be hand-delivered Monday through Friday between the hours of 8 a.m. and 4 p.m. to CC:PA:LPD:PR (REG-147636-08), Courier's Desk, Internal Revenue Service, 1111 Constitution Avenue NW., Washington, DC, or sent electronically via the Federal eRulemaking Portal at *www.regulations.gov* (IRS REG-147636-08).

FOR FURTHER INFORMATION CONTACT: Concerning the proposed regulations, Sean W. Mullaney, (202) 622-3860; concerning submissions of comments or requests for a public hearing, Richard.A.Hurst@irscounsel.treas.gov; at (202) 622-7180 (not tollfree numbers).

SUPPLEMENTARY INFORMATION:

Background and Explanation of Provisions

Temporary regulations in the Rules and Regulations section of this issue of the **Federal Register** amend the Income Tax Regulations (26 CFR part 1) relating to sections 304 and 1248 of the Code. The text of those regulations also serves as the text of these proposed regulations. The preamble to the temporary regulations explains the temporary regulations and these proposed regulations.

Special Analyses

It has been determined that this notice of proposed rulemaking is not a significant regulatory action as defined in Executive Order 12866. Therefore, a regulatory assessment is not required. These regulations are necessary to ensure that the appropriate amount of income (dividend income, capital gain or both) is recognized currently in the transactions described in the explanation of provisions section in this preamble. Accordingly, good cause is found for dispensing with notice and public comment pursuant to 5 U.S.C. 553(b) and (c) and with a delayed effective date pursuant to 5 U.S.C. 553(d). For applicability of the Regulatory Flexibility Act, see the cross-referenced notice of proposed rulemaking published elsewhere in this **Federal Register**. Pursuant to section 7805(f) of the Code, these regulations have been submitted to the Chief Counsel for Advocacy of the Small Business Administration for comment on its impact on small business.

Comments and Requests for a Public Hearing

Comments are also requested regarding whether IRS and Treasury Department should exercise the regulatory authority under section 304(b)(6) to permit an increase to the basis of the transferred stock in a section 304(a)(1) transaction to the extent the distribution in redemption of the shares deemed issued by the acquiring corporation is treated as a dividend from the earnings and profits of the issuing corporation.

Before these proposed regulations are adopted as final regulations, consideration will be given to any written comments (a signed original and eight (8) copies) or electronic comments that are submitted timely to the IRS. The IRS and Treasury Department specifically request comments on the clarity of the proposed rules and how they can be made easier to understand. All comments will be available for public inspection and copying. A public hearing will be scheduled if requested in writing by any person that timely submits written comments. If a public hearing is scheduled, notice of the date, time, and place for the public hearing will be published in the **Federal Register**.

Drafting Information

The principal author of these proposed regulations is Sean W. Mullaney of the Office of Associate Chief Counsel (International). However, other personnel from the IRS and the Treasury Department participated in their development.

[¶49,426] Proposed Amendments of Regulations (REG-112756-09), published in the Federal Register on August 5, 2009.

[Code Sec. 7611]

Exempt organizations: Church tax inquiries: IRS restructuring.—Amendments of Reg. §301.7611-1, amending the questions and answers relating to church tax inquiries and examinations, are proposed.

AGENCY: Internal Revenue Service ("IRS"), Treasury.

ACTION: Notice of proposed rulemaking.

SUMMARY: This document contains proposed regulations amending the questions and answers relating to church tax inquiries and examinations. These proposed regulations replace references to positions that were abolished by the Internal Revenue Service Restructuring and Reform Act of 1998 with references that are consistent both with the statute and the IRS's current organizational structure.

DATES: Written or electronic comments and requests for a public hearing must be received by November 3, 2009.

ADDRESSES: Send submissions to: CC:PA:LPD:PR (REG-112756-09), room 5205, Internal Revenue Service, PO Box 7604, Ben Franklin Station, Washington, DC 20044. Submissions may be hand-delivered Monday through Friday between the hours of 8 a.m. and 4 p.m. to CC:PA:LPD:PR (REG-112756-09), Courier's Desk, Internal Revenue Service, 1111 Constitution Avenue, NW, Washington, DC, or sent electronically, via the Federal eRulemaking Portal at *www.regulations.gov* (IRS-REG-112756-09).

FOR FURTHER INFORMATION CONTACT: Concerning these proposed regulations, Benjamin Akins at (202) 622-1124 or Monice Rosenbaum at (202) 622-6070; concerning submission of comments and requests for a public hearing, Richard Hurst, *Richard.A.Hurst@irscounsel.treas.gov*, (202) 622-7180 (not a toll-free numbers).

SUPPLEMENTARY INFORMATION:

Background

Restrictions on Church Tax Inquiries and Examinations

This document contains amendments to the regulations on Procedure and Administration (26 CFR part 301) under section 7611 of the Internal Revenue Code. Section 7611 was enacted by section 1033 of the Deficit Reduction Act of 1984 (Public Law 98-369, 98 Stat. 1034-1039) ("DRA 1984").

Prior to the enactment of section 7611, section 7605(c) imposed special requirements that the IRS had to meet before it could examine church books of account, but there were no special requirements imposed before the IRS could commence an investigation or inquiry into a church's tax liabilities. As explained in the Conference Report accompanying DRA 1984, H.R. Rep. No. 98-861, 98th Cong., 2d Sess. 1101 (1984), 1984-3 CB Vol. 2 355, Congress sought to address certain problems that arise when the IRS examines the records of a church. Thus, Congress expanded the requirements relating to IRS interactions with churches. Although prior law imposed limitations on the examination of church records, those limitations were somewhat vague and relied on internal IRS procedures to protect the rights of a church in the examination process. Additionally, there was some uncertainty regarding the scope of the investigations to which prior law applied and the nature of the records protected by the law. The enactment of section 7611 attempted to resolve these competing considerations by providing detailed rules for the IRS to follow in making tax inquiries to churches, both as to tax-exempt status and as to the existence of unrelated business income.

Section 7611(a)(2) permits the IRS to begin an inquiry into whether a church qualifies for exemption from income tax as an organization described in section 501(c)(3) or whether a church has a liability for unrelated business income tax only if an appropriate high-level Treasury official first reasonably believes on the basis of facts and circumstances, recorded in writing, that the church may not be exempt under section 501(a), or that the church may be carrying on an unrelated trade or business, or may be otherwise engaged in activities subject to tax. Section 7611(h)(7) provides that the term "appropriate high-level Treasury official" means the Secretary of the Treasury or any delegate of the Secretary whose rank is no lower than that of a principal Internal Revenue officer for an internal revenue region. The legislative history of section 7611 interprets the term "appropriate high-level Treasury official" to mean an IRS Regional Commissioner (or higher official). H.R. Rep. No. 98-861, 98th Cong. 2d Sess. 1101 (1984), 1984-3 CB Vol. 2 355. Final regulations under section 7611, which were published on February 21, 1986, 50 Fed. Reg. 6219, also interpret the term to mean an IRS Regional Commissioner. See Treas. Reg. §301.7611 Q1-A1.

Section 7611(b)(2)(A) provides that at least 15 days before the beginning of a church tax examination, the IRS must provide notice of the examination to both the church and the appropriate regional counsel. Section 7611(b)(3)(C) provides that any regional counsel who receives notice under section 7611(b)(2)(A) may submit to a regional commissioner an advisory objection to the examination within 15 days after the notice of examination is provided.

Section 7611(c)(1)(A) provides that the IRS must make a final determination as to any church tax inquiry or examination within two years of the date the notice of examination is provided to the church under section 7611(b). In instances where no examination follows a church tax inquiry, section 7611(c)(1)(B) requires the IRS to make a final determination as to the inquiry no later than 90 days after the date the notice of inquiry is provided to the church under section 7611(a). Section 7611(c)(2) suspends the periods described in section 7611(c)(1) (that is, 2 year period and 90 day period) while certain judicial proceedings are pending or being appealed, including proceedings brought by the IRS against a church seeking to compel compliance with a reasonable request to examine church records or religious activities.

Section 7611(d)(1) prohibits the IRS from making certain final determinations (that is, revocation of tax-exempt status, notice of deficiency, or assessment) regarding a church until after the appropriate regional counsel determines in writing that there has been substantial compliance with the requirements of section 7611. Section 7611(d)(1) further requires the appropriate regional counsel's written approval of such final determination before the IRS can make the determination.

Section 7611(e)(1) provides that if the IRS has not substantially complied with the requirements of section 7611, any proceeding to compel compliance with a summons shall be stayed until the court finds that the IRS has taken all practicable steps to correct the noncompliance. Section 7611(e)(2) states that the remedy provided in subsection (e)(1) shall be the exclusive remedy for a church in regard to any noncompliance by the IRS with the requirements of section 7611.

Under section 7611(f), the IRS may not commence an inquiry or examination of a church if, within the previous five years, the IRS completed an inquiry or examination regarding the church that did not result in a revocation, notice of deficiency, assessment, or a request for a significant change in the church's operating practices. An exception exists where the Secretary or his delegate approves the second inquiry or examination in writing. There is also an exception where the issues involved in the subsequent inquiry or examination are not the same or similar to issues involved in the preceding inquiry or examination. Prior to the Internal Revenue Service Restructuring and Reform Act of 1998, Public Law 105-206 ("RRA 1998"), discussed below, section 7611(f) required the Assistant Commissioner (Employee Plans and Exempt Organizations), instead of the Secretary or his delegate, to approve subsequent inquiries and examinations for the exception to apply.

Reorganization of the IRS

Section 1001 of RRA 1998 requires the Commissioner of Internal Revenue to develop and implement a plan to reorganize the IRS. The congressional mandate provides that the plan shall "eliminate or substantially modify the existing organization of the IRS which is based on a national, regional, and district structure; [and] establish organizational units serving particular groups of taxpayers with similar needs ...." Under the reorganized IRS, four nationwide operating divisions were established to serve different types of taxpayers. One of these operating divisions serves tax exempt and government entities, including churches.

Section 1102(e)(3) of RRA 1998 amended section 7611(f)(1), relating to second inquiries and examinations within five years of a previous inquiry or examination, by replacing Assistant Commissioner (Employee Plans and Exempt Organizations) with Secretary. Under section 7701(a)(11)(B), Secretary is defined to refer to the Secretary of the Treasury or his delegate. RRA 1998 did not amend other portions of section 7611, such as references to "appropriate high-level Treasury official" and "appropriate regional counsel."

In mandating the restructuring of the IRS under RRA 1998, Congress realized that certain positions within the IRS would be eliminated as a result of transitioning from a geographic structure to a structure based on nationwide jurisdiction of similar types of taxpayers. Accordingly, Congress included a savings provision in RRA 1998. Section 1001(b) provides, "All orders, determinations, rules, regulations ... and other administrative actions ... which are in effect at the time this section takes effect ... shall continue in effect according to their terms until modified, terminated, superseded, set aside or revoked in accordance with law by ... the Secretary of the Treasury [or] the Commissioner of Internal Revenue ...." This provision keeps in effect regulations that make reference to officers whose positions no longer exist. The legislative history of RRA 1998 at H.R. Conf. Rep. No. 105-599, 105th Cong., 2d Sess. 195 (1998) explains that "[t]he legality of IRS actions will not be affected pending further appropriate statutory changes relating to such a reorganization (e.g., eliminating statutory references to obsolete positions)." Accordingly, the Treasury Regulations under section 7611 have remained in effect notwithstanding their references to the positions of Regional Commissioner, Regional Counsel, and Assistant Commissioner (Employee Plans and Exempt Organizations), positions that were eliminated by the reorganization. Delegation Order 193 (Rev. 6) (11/08/2000) provides in part that actions previously delegated to Regional Commissioners by Treasury Regulations (par. 7) are now delegated to "Assistant Deputy Commissioners, Division Commissioners; Chiefs; and Directors, Submission Processing Field, Compliance Services Field, and Accounts Management Field." In the Internal Revenue Manual ("IRM"), the IRS designated the Director, Exempt Organizations Examinations as the appropriate high-level Treasury official for purposes of section 7611. See IRM § 4.76.7.

Recent litigation has challenged the IRS's interpretation of the term "appropriate high-level Treasury official" following the reorganization. See *United States v. Living Word Christian Center*, Civil No. 08-mc-37, D.C. Minn. (Jan. 30, 2009) ("*LWCC*"). In particular, concern has been expressed about the need for an update to the regulations in light of the statutorily mandated reorganization and the elimination of internal revenue regions.

In *LWCC*, the District Court for the District of Minnesota ruled that the Director, Exempt Organizations Examinations is not an appropriate high-level Treasury official to make the "reasonable belief" determination required before the IRS may commence a church tax inquiry under section 7611. *LWCC* at 2. The district court concluded that the Director, Exempt Organizations Examinations is not an appropriate high-level Treasury official within the meaning of section 7611(h) because that official does not have a comparable breadth of responsibility to a regional commissioner nor as high a position within the IRS. Although the IRS disagrees with the district court's reasoning and conclusion in *LWCC*, the IRS acknowledges that it would be beneficial to revise the regulations in light of the changes in IRS organization made in the wake of RRA 1998 to clarify who is an appropriate high-level Treasury official for purposes of section 7611. Further, the IRS recognizes the significance of the special procedural requirements for church tax inquiries and examinations. These proposed regulations assign responsibility for making the determinations required under section 7611(a) to the Director, Exempt Organizations.

Explanation of Provisions

These proposed regulations eliminate references to the positions of Regional Commissioner and Regional Counsel under the existing regulations and give responsibilities formerly assigned to these now defunct positions to the Director, Exempt Organizations and the Division Counsel / Associate Chief Counsel, Tax Exempt and Government Entities, respectively. In addition, these proposed regulations eliminate references to the position of Assistant Commissioner (Employee Plans and Exempt Organizations) under the existing regulations and give responsibilities formerly assigned to that position to the Commissioner, Tax Exempt and Government Entities or the Deputy Commissioner, Tax Exempt and Government Entities.

Reasonable Belief and Inquiry Notice Requirement

With respect to the initiation of the church tax inquiry process, Treas. Reg. § 301.7611-1 Q1-A1 provides that a "Regional Commissioner (or higher Treasury official)" is the appropriate high-level Treasury official for purposes of this reasonable belief requirement. Similarly, Treas. Reg. § 301.7611-1 Q7-A7 states, "Repeated (two or more) failures by a church or its agents to reply to routine requests . . . will be considered by the appropriate Internal Revenue Service Regional Commissioner to be a reasonable basis for commencement of a church tax inquiry under the church tax inquiry and examination procedures of section 7611." In addition, Treas. Reg. § 301.7611 Q9-A9 requires a Regional Commissioner to provide written notice to the church of the beginning of an inquiry.

These proposed regulations eliminate references to the Regional Commissioner and instead provide that the Director, Exempt Organizations is the "appropriate high-level Treasury official" for purposes of the reasonable belief and inquiry notice requirements of Treas. Reg. § 301.7611-1 Q1-A1, Q7-A7, and Q9-A9. The Director, Exempt Organizations is a senior executive who reports to the Commissioner / Deputy Commissioner, Tax Exempt and Government Entities Division, and who is responsible for planning, managing, directing and executing nationwide activities for Exempt Organizations. See IRM § 1.1.23.5 for a comprehensive description of these activities.

Examination Notice Requirement

Under section 7611(b)(2) and Treas. Reg. § 301.7611-1 Q10-A10, a church tax examination cannot be commenced without first providing written notice of such examination to the church and to the "appropriate Regional Counsel" at least 15 days before the IRS begins the church tax examination. The regulation allows the Regional Counsel to file an advisory objection to the examination within this same 15-day period.

These proposed regulations amend Treas. Reg. § 301.7611-1 Q10-A10 by substituting Division Counsel / Associate Chief Counsel, Tax Exempt and Government Entities, for each occurrence of Regional Counsel. These proposed regulations further specify that before the notice of examination is provided to the church, a copy of the notice must be provided to the Division Counsel / Associate Chief Counsel, Tax Exempt and Government Entities.

Revocation of Exemption or of Church Status

Section 7611(d)(1) and Treas. Reg. § 301.7611-1 Q11-A11 require the Regional Counsel to approve, in writing, certain final determinations that are within the scope of section 7611 and adversely affect the tax-exempt status or increase any tax liability of a church. Further, prior to such adverse action, section 7611(d) requires Regional Counsel to determine, in writing, that there has been substantial compliance with the requirements of section 7611, when applicable.

These proposed regulations amend Treas. Reg. § 301.7611-1 Q11-A11 by providing that the Division Counsel / Associate Chief Counsel, Tax Exempt and Government Entities, is the official responsible for complying with the written determination and approval requirements of section 7611(d)(1).

Limitations on Period of Assessment

Section 7611(d)(2) and Treas. Reg. § 301.7611-1 Q15-A15 provide special limitation periods for church tax liabilities. These special rules are not to be construed to increase an otherwise applicable limitation period. Treas. Reg. § 301.7611-1 Q15-A15 states that, for purposes of section 7611(d)(2)(A), that is, the statute of limitations applicable to liabilities arising from church tax examinations, a church is determined not to be a church exempt from tax when the appropriate Regional Commissioner approves, in writing, the completed findings of the examining agent that the organization is not a church exempt from tax for one or more of the three most recently completed taxable years ending before the examination notice date. The regulation also states that the Regional Commissioner cannot delegate this approval to a subordinate official. Further, the completed findings of the examining agent, which are approved by the appropriate Regional Commissioner, are not considered a final revenue agent's report (defined in section 7611(g)).

These proposed regulations substitute the Director, Exempt Organizations for the appropriate Regional Commissioner for purposes of Treas. Reg. § 301.7611-1 Q15-A15.

Multiple Examinations

Consistent with the language of section 7611(f)(1) prior to enactment of RRA 1998, Treas. Reg. § 301-7611-1 Q16-A16 provides that the Assistant Commissioner (Employee Plans and Exempt Organizations) is responsible for providing the written approval necessary to begin a second inquiry or examination of a church. These proposed regulations provide that the Commissioner, Tax Exempt and Government Entities or the Deputy Commissioner, Tax Exempt and Government Entities is responsible for approving second inquiries and examinations under section 7611(f).

Remedies for Violation of Section 7611

Section 7611(e) and Treas. Reg. § 301.7611-1 Q17-A17 provide that, if there has not been substantial compliance with certain requirements in section 7611, including the notice requirements of section 7611(a) and (b), the exclusive remedy for such noncompliance is a stay in an enforcement proceeding to compel compliance with a summons with respect to the inquiry or examination. The stay continues until the court finds that all practicable steps to correct the noncompliance have been taken. Treas. Reg. § 301.7611-1 Q17-A17 further states that failure of the Regional Commissioner to approve an inquiry may not be raised as a defense or as an affirmative ground for relief in a summons proceeding or any other judicial proceeding other than as specifically set forth in the regulation.

These proposed regulations amend Treas. Reg. § 301.7611-1 Q17-A17 to replace each reference to Regional Commissioner with Director, Exempt Organizations.

Special Analyses

It has been determined that this notice of proposed rulemaking is not a significant regulatory action as defined in Executive Order 12866. Therefore, a regulatory assessment is not required. It has also been determined that section 553(b) of the Administrative Procedure Act (5 U.S.C. chapter 5) does not apply to these proposed regulations and because the regulation does not impose a collection of information on small entities, the Regulatory Flexibility Act (5 U.S.C. 601) does not apply.

Pursuant to section 7805(f) of the Code, these proposed regulations have been submitted to the Chief Counsel for Advocacy of the Small Business Administration for comment on its impact on small business.

Comments and Requests for a Public Hearing

Before these proposed regulations are adopted as final regulations, consideration will be given to any written comments (a signed original and eight (8) copies) or electronic comments that are submitted timely to the IRS. Comments are requested on all aspects of the proposed regulations. All comments will be available for public inspection and copying. A public hearing will be scheduled if requested in writing by any person that timely submits written or electronic comments. If a public hearing is scheduled, notice of the date, time, and place for the public hearing will be published in the **Federal Register**.

Drafting Information

The principal authors of these proposed regulations are Benjamin Akins and Monice Rosenbaum of the Office of Division Counsel / Associate Chief Counsel (Tax Exempt and Government Entities). However, other personnel from the IRS and the Treasury Department participated in their development.

[¶ 49,435] Proposed Regulations (REG-123829-08), published in the Federal Register on October 7, 2009.

[Code Sec. 9802]

Group health plans: Genetic information nondiscrimination regulations: Proposed regulations.—Reg. § 54.9802-3, providing guidance to employers and group health plans relating to the group health plan genetic nondiscrimination requirements, is proposed.

AGENCY: Internal Revenue Service (IRS), Treasury.

ACTION: Notice of proposed rulemaking by cross-reference to temporary regulations.

SUMMARY: Elsewhere in this issue of the **Federal Register**, the IRS is issuing temporary and final regulations governing the provisions of the Genetic Information Nondiscrimination Act (GINA) prohibiting discrimination based on genetic information for group health plans. The IRS is issuing the temporary and final regulations at the same time that the Employee Benefits Security Administration of the U.S. Department of Labor and the Centers for Medicare & Medicaid Services of the U.S. Department of Health and Human Services are issuing substantially similar interim final regulations with respect to GINA for group health plans and issuers of health insurance coverage offered in connection with a group health plan under the Employee Retirement Income Security Act of 1974 and the Public Health Service Act. The temporary regulations provide guidance to employers and group health plans relating to the group health plan genetic nondiscrimination requirements. The text of those temporary regulations also serves as the text of these proposed regulations.

DATES: Written or electronic comments and requests for a public hearing must be received by January 5, 2010.

ADDRESSES: Send submissions to: CC:PA:LPD:PR (REG-123829-08), room 5205, Internal Revenue Service, P.O. Box 7604, Ben Franklin Station, Washington, DC 20044. Submissions may be hand-delivered to: CC:PA:LPD:PR (REG-123829-08), Courier's Desk, Internal Revenue Service, 1111 Constitution Avenue, NW, Washington DC 20224. Alternatively, taxpayers may submit comments electronically via the Federal eRulemaking Portal at *http://www.regulations.gov* (IRS REG-123829-08).

FOR FURTHER INFORMATION CONTACT: Concerning the regulations, Russ Weinheimer at 202-622-6080; concerning submissions of comments, Oluwafumilayo Taylor at (202) 622-7180 (not toll-free numbers).

SUPPLEMENTARY INFORMATION:

Paperwork Reduction Act

The collection of information referenced in this notice of proposed rulemaking has been submitted to the Office of Management and Budget for review in accordance with the Paperwork Reduction Act of 1995 (44 U.S.C. 3507(d)). Comments on the collection of information should be sent to the **Office of Management and Budget**, Attn: Desk Officer for the Department of the Treasury, Office of Information and Regulatory Affairs, Washington, DC 20503, with copies to the **Internal Revenue Service**, Attn: IRS Reports Clearance Officer, SE:W:CAR:MP:T:T:SP, Washington, DC 20224. Comments on the collection of information should be received by December 7, 2009. Comments are specifically requested concerning:

- Whether the proposed collection of information is necessary for the proper performance of the functions of the Internal Revenue Service, including whether the information will have practical utility;
- The accuracy of the estimated burden associated with the proposed collection of information (see the preamble to the temporary regulations published elsewhere in this issue of the **Federal Register**);
- How to enhance the quality, utility, and clarity of the information to be collected;
- How to minimize the burden of complying with the proposed collection of information, including the application of automated collection techniques or other forms of information technology; and
- Estimates of capital or start-up costs and costs of operation, maintenance, and purchase of services to provide information.

The collection of information is in §54.9802-3 (see the temporary regulations published elsewhere in this issue of the **Federal Register**). The collection of information is required so that the IRS can be apprised when a group health plan is conducting research with respect to genetic information of plan participants or beneficiaries to ensure that all the requirements of the research exception to GINA are being complied with. The likely respondents are business or other for-profit institutions, and nonprofit institutions. Responses to this collection of information are required if a plan wishes to conduct genetic research with respect to participants or beneficiaries of the plan.

An agency may not conduct or sponsor, and a person is not required to respond to, a collection of information unless it displays a valid control number assigned by the Office of Management and Budget.

Books or records relating to a collection of information must be retained as long as their contents may become material in the administration of any internal revenue law. Generally tax returns and tax return information are confidential, as required by 26 U.S.C. 6103.

Background

The temporary regulations published elsewhere in this issue of the **Federal Register** add a new §54.9802-3T to the Miscellaneous Excise Tax Regulations. In the same document, certain conforming changes are also being made to the final regulations under §§54.9801-1, 54.9801-2, 54.9802-1, and 54.9831-1. The proposed, temporary, and final regulations are being published as part of a joint rulemaking with the Department of Labor and the Department of Health and Human Services (the joint rulemaking). The text of those temporary regulations also serves as the text of these proposed regulations. The preamble to the temporary regulations explains the temporary regulations.

Special Analyses

It has been determined that this notice of proposed rulemaking is not a significant regulatory action as defined in Executive Order 12866. Therefore, a regulatory assessment is not required. It has also been determined that section 553(b) of the Administrative Procedure Act (5 U.S.C. chapter 5) does not apply to this proposed regulation. It is hereby certified that the collection of information contained in this notice of proposed rulemaking will not have a significant impact on a substantial number of small entities. Accordingly, a regulatory flexibility analysis is not required. GINA requires group health plans claiming the research exception to GINA to notify the Secretary of the Treasury when the exception is being claimed. This notice of proposed rulemaking does not add to the reporting requirement imposed by the statute. Moreover, it is anticipated that very few and only the largest group health plans are likely to claim the research exception to GINA and thus be subject to the reporting requirement. For this reason, the burden imposed by the reporting requirement of the statute and this notice of proposed rulemaking on small entities is expected to be near zero. For further information and for analyses relating to the joint rulemaking, see the preamble to the joint rulemaking. Pursuant to section 7805(f) of the Internal Revenue Code, this notice of proposed rulemaking will be submitted to the Chief Counsel for Advocacy of the Small Business Administration for comment on its impact on small business.

Comments and Requests for a Public Hearing

Before these proposed regulations are adopted as final regulations, consideration will be given to any written comments (a signed original and eight (8) copies) or electronic comments that are submitted timely to the IRS. Comments are specifically requested on the clarity of the proposed regulations and how they may be made easier to understand. All comments will be available for public inspection and copying. A public hearing may be scheduled if requested in writing by a person that timely submits written comments. If a public hearing is scheduled, notice of the date, time, and place for the hearing will be published in the **Federal Register**.

Drafting Information

The principal author of these proposed regulations is Russ Weinheimer, Office of the Division Counsel/Associate Chief Counsel (Tax Exempt and Government Entities), IRS. The proposed regulations, as well as the temporary and final regulations, have been developed in coordination with personnel from the U.S. Department of Labor and the U.S. Department of Health and Human Services.

[¶49,439] Proposed Amendments of Regulations, NPRM REG-101896-09, published in the Federal Register on December 17, 2009 (corrected 1/21/2010).

[Code Secs. 408, 1012, 3406, 6039, 6042, 6044, 6045, 6045A, 6045B, 6049, 6051, 6721 and 6722]

Information reporting: Return of brokers: Basis and other reporting obligations: Proposed regulations.—Amendments of Reg. §31.3406(b)(3)-2, relating to reporting sales of securities by brokers and determining the basis of securities, are proposed. Reg. §§1.6045A-1 and 1.6045B-1, and amendments of Reg. §§1.408-7, 1.1012-1, 1.6039-2, 1.6042-4, 1.6044-5, 1.6045-1, 1.6045-2, 1.6045-3, 1.6045-4, 1.6045-5, 1.6049-6, 31.6051-4, 301.6721-1 and 301.6722-1 were adopted by T.D. 9504 on October 12, 2010..

AGENCY: Internal Revenue Service (IRS), Treasury.

ACTION: Notice of proposed rulemaking and notice of public hearing.

SUMMARY: This document contains proposed regulations relating to reporting sales of securities by brokers and determining the basis of securities. The proposed regulations reflect changes in the law made by the Energy Improvement and Extension Act of 2008 that require brokers when reporting the sale of securities to the IRS to include the customer's adjusted basis in the sold securities and to classify any gain or loss as longterm or short-term. This document also contains proposed regulations reflecting changes in the law that alter how taxpayers compute basis when averaging the basis of shares acquired at different prices and that expand the ability of taxpayers to compute basis by averaging. The document also proposes regulations that provide brokers and others until February 15 to furnish certain information statements to customers. This document also contains proposed regulations that implement new reporting requirements imposed upon persons that transfer custody of stock and upon issuers of stock regarding organizational actions that affect the basis of the issued stock. This document also contains proposed regulations reflecting changes in the law that alter how brokers report short sales of securities. Finally, this document provides for a notice of a public hearing on these proposed regulations.

DATES: Written or electronic comments must be received by February 8, 2010. Outlines of topics to be discussed at the public hearing scheduled for February 17, 2010 must be received by February 8, 2010.

ADDRESSES: Send submissions to: CC:PA:LPD:PR (REG-101896-09), room 5203, Internal Revenue Service, PO Box 7604, Ben Franklin Station, Washington, DC 20044. Submissions may be hand-delivered Monday through Friday between the hours of 8 a.m. and 4 p.m. to CC:PA:LPD:PR (REG-101896-09), Courier's Desk, Internal Revenue Service, 1111 Constitution Avenue, NW., Washington, DC, or sent electronically via the Federal eRulemaking Portal at *www.regulations.gov* (IRS REG-101896-09). The public hearing will be held in the auditorium of the IRS New Carrollton Federal Building, 5000 Ellin Road, Lanham, Maryland 20706.

FOR FURTHER INFORMATION CONTACT: Concerning the proposed regulations under section 1012, Edward C. Schwartz of the Office of Associate Chief Counsel (Income Tax and Accounting) at (202) 622-4960; concerning the proposed regulations under sections 3406, 6045, 6045A, 6045B, 6721, and 6722, Stephen Schaeffer of the Office of Associate Chief Counsel (Procedure and Administration) at (202) 622-4910; concerning submissions of comments, the public hearing, and/or to be placed on the building access list to attend the public hearing, Funmi Taylor of the Office of Associate Chief Counsel (Procedure and Administration) at (202) 622-7180 (not toll-free numbers).

SUPPLEMENTARY INFORMATION:

Paperwork Reduction Act

The collection of information contained in this notice of proposed rulemaking related to the furnishing of information in connection with the transfer of securities has been submitted to the Office of Management and Budget in accordance with the Paperwork Reduction Act of 1995 (44 U.S.C. 3507(d)). Comments on the collection of information should be sent to the **Office of Management and Budget**, Attn: Desk Officer for the Department of the Treasury, Office of Information and Regulatory Affairs, Washington, DC 20503, with copies to the **Internal Revenue Service**, Attn: IRS

Reports Clearance Officer, SE:W:CAR:MP:T:T:SP, Washington, DC 20224. Comments on the collection of information should be received by February 16, 2010. Comments are specifically requested concerning:

Whether the proposed collection of information is necessary for the proper performance of the functions of the IRS, including whether the information will have practical utility;

The accuracy of the estimated burden associated with the proposed collection of information;

How the quality, utility, and clarity of the information to be collected may be enhanced;

How the burden of complying with the proposed collection of information may be minimized, including through the application of automated collection techniques or other forms of information technology; and

Estimates of capital or start-up costs and costs of operation, maintenance, and purchase of services to provide information.

The collection of information in these proposed regulations in §§1.6045-1(c)(3)(xi)(C) and 1.6045A-1 concerning furnishing information in connection with a transfer of securities is necessary to allow brokers that effect sales of transferred covered securities to determine and report the adjusted basis of the securities and whether any gain or loss with respect to the securities is long-term or short-term in compliance with section 6045(g) of the Internal Revenue Code (Code). The collection of information is required to comply with the provisions of section 403 of the Energy Improvement and Extension Act of 2008, Division B of Public Law 110-343 (122 Stat. 3765, 3854 (2008)). The likely respondents are brokers of securities and issuers, transfer agents, and professional custodians of securities that do not effect sales.

Estimated total annual reporting burden: 240,000 hours.

Estimated average annual burden per respondent: 8 hours.

Estimated average burden per response: 4 minutes.

Estimated number of respondents: 30,000.

Estimated frequency of responses: 4,000,000.

The burden for the collection of information contained in proposed regulation §1.6045-1 except for §1.6045-1(c)(3)(xi)(C) will be reflected in the burden on Form 1099-B, "Proceeds from Broker and Barter Exchange Transactions," when revised to request the additional information in that proposed regulation. The burden for the collection of information contained in proposed regulation §1.6045B-1 will be reflected in the burden on the form that the IRS will create to request the information in that proposed regulation.

An agency may not conduct or sponsor, and a person is not required to respond to, a collection of information unless it displays a valid control number assigned by the Office of Management and Budget.

Background

This document contains proposed amendments to the Income Tax Regulations (26 CFR part 1), the Regulations on Employment Tax and Collection of Income Tax at the Source (26 CFR part 31), and the Regulations on Procedure and Administration (26 CFR part 301) relating to information reporting by brokers and others as required by section 6045. The document also contains proposed amendments relating to the scope and computation of basis by the average basis method under section 1012 and to new information reporting requirements by brokers, custodians, and issuers of securities under sections 6045A and 6045B. These sections were amended or added by section 403 of the Energy Improvement and Extension Act of 2008, Division B of Public Law 110-343 (122 Stat. 3765, 3854 (2008)) (the Act). These proposed regulations are proposed to be issued under the authority contained in sections 1012, 3406, 6045, 6045A, 6045B, and 7805.

1. *Returns of Brokers*

Section 6045(g) provides that every broker that is required to file a return with the IRS under section 6045(a) showing the gross proceeds from the sale of a covered security must include in the return the customer's adjusted basis in the security and whether any gain or loss with respect to the security is long-term or short-term. Thus, a broker that is currently subject to gross proceeds reporting under section 6045(a) with respect to the sale of a covered security is also subject to the reporting of adjusted basis of that security and whether any gain or loss with respect to that security is longterm or short-term under section 6045(g).

Section 1.6045-1(a)(1) provides that the term *broker* generally means any U.S. or foreign person that, in the ordinary course of a trade or business, stands ready to effect sales to be made by others. However, with respect to a sale (including a redemption or retirement) effected at an office outside the United States, a broker includes only a person described as a U.S. payor or U.S. middleman in §1.6049-5(c)(5). Additionally, under §1.6045-1(g)(1), reporting is not required with respect to certain holders of securities that are exempt foreign persons. U.S. and foreign brokers that are subject to gross proceeds reporting under the existing rules will also be subject to reporting under the rules of section 6045(g).

a. *Covered security*

For purposes of reporting under section 6045(g), section 6045(g)(3)(A) provides that a covered security is any specified security acquired on or after the applicable date if the security: (1) was acquired through a transaction in the account in which the security was held; or (2) was transferred to that account from an account in which the security was a covered security, but only if the broker receiving custody of the security receives a statement under section 6045A (described later in this preamble) with respect to the transfer.

b. *Specified security*

Section 6045(g)(3)(B) provides that a specified security is any: (1) share of stock in a corporation; (2) note, bond, debenture, or other evidence of indebtedness; (3) commodity, or a contract or a derivative with respect to the commodity, if the Secretary determines that adjusted basis reporting is appropriate; and (4) other financial instrument with respect to which the Secretary determines that adjusted basis reporting is appropriate.

c. *Applicable date*

The applicable date of the reporting requirements under section 6045(g) depends on the type of specified security that is sold. For stock in or of a corporation (other than stock in a regulated investment company (RIC) or stock acquired in connection with a dividend reinvestment plan (DRP)), section 6045(g)(3)(C)(i) provides that the applicable date is January 1, 2011. For stock in a RIC (RIC stock) or stock acquired in connection with a DRP (DRP stock) (for which additional rules are described later in this preamble), section 6045(g)(3)(C)(ii) provides that the applicable date is January 1, 2012. For any other specified security, section 6045(g)(3)(C)(iii) provides that the applicable date is January 1, 2013, or a later date determined by the Secretary. The reporting rules related to options transactions apply only to options granted or acquired on or after January 1, 2013, as provided in section 6045(h)(3).

d. *Reporting method*

A broker must report a customer's adjusted basis under the following statutory rules. Under section 6045(g)(2)(B)(i)(I), a broker must report the adjusted basis of any security (other than RIC stock or DRP stock) using the first-in, first-out (FIFO) basis determination method unless the customer notifies the broker of the specific stock to be sold or transferred by means of making an adequate identification of the stock sold or transferred at the time of sale or transfer. Under section 6045(g)(2)(B)(i)(II), a broker must report the adjusted basis of RIC stock or DRP stock in accordance with the broker's default method under section 1012 unless the customer notifies the broker that the customer elects another permitted method.

2. *Determination of Basis*

a. *In general*

For any sale, exchange, or other disposition of a specified security on or after the applicable date, section 1012(c) provides that the conventions prescribed by regulations under section 1012 for determining adjusted basis apply on an account by account basis.

b. *RIC stock*

Section 1012(c)(2) provides that RIC stock acquired before January 1, 2012, is treated as held in a separate account from RIC stock acquired on or after that date. However, a RIC may elect (at the time and in the form and manner prescribed by the Secretary), on a stockholder by stockholder basis, to treat all stock in the RIC held by the stockholder as one account without regard to when the stock was acquired (singleaccount election). When this election applies, the average basis of a customer's stock is computed by averaging the basis of shares of identical stock acquired before, on, and after January 1, 2012, and all the shares are treated as covered securities. If a broker holds RIC stock as a nominee of the beneficial owner of the shares, the broker makes the election.

c. *DRP stock*

If stock is acquired on or after January 1, 2011, in connection with a DRP, section 1012(d)(1) provides that the basis of that stock is determined under one of the basis computation methods permissible for RIC stock. Accordingly, the average basis method may be used for determining the basis of DRP stock. This special rule for DRP stock, however, applies only while the stock is held as part of the DRP. If the stock is transferred to another account, under section 1012(d)(2), each share of stock has a cost basis in that other account equal to its basis in the DRP immediately before the transfer (with adjustment for charges connected with the transfer).

Section 1012(d)(4)(A) provides that a DRP is any arrangement under which dividends on stock are reinvested in stock identical to the stock on which the dividends are paid. Stock is treated as acquired in connection with a DRP if the stock is acquired pursuant to the DRP or if the dividends paid on the stock are subject to the DRP. Under section 1012(d)(3), in determining basis under this rule, the account by account rules of section 1012(c), including the single-account election available to RICs, apply.

3. *Other Broker Reporting Provisions*

a. *Wash sales*

Section 6045(g)(2)(B)(ii) provides that, unless the Secretary provides otherwise, a customer's adjusted basis in a covered security generally is determined for reporting purposes without taking into account the effect on basis of the wash sale rules of section 1091 unless the purchase and sale transactions resulting in a wash sale occur in the same account and are in identical securities (rather than substantially identical securities as required by section 1091).

b. *S corporations*

Section 6045(g)(4) provides that, for purposes of section 6045, an S corporation (other than a financial institution) is treated in the same manner as a partnership. This rule applies to any sale of a covered security acquired by an S corporation (other than a financial institution) after December 31,

2011. When this rule takes effect, brokers generally will be required to report gross proceeds and basis information to customers that are S corporations for securities purchased on or after January 1, 2012.

c. *Short sales*

In the case of a short sale, section 6045(g)(5) provides that gross proceeds and basis reporting under section 6045 generally is required for the year in which the short sale is closed (rather than, as under the present rule for gross proceeds reporting, the year in which the short sale is entered into).

d. *Options*

Section 6045(h)(1) provides that if a covered security is acquired or disposed of pursuant to the exercise of an option that was granted or acquired in the same account as the covered security, the amount received with respect to the grant or paid with respect to the acquisition of such option must be treated for reporting purposes as an adjustment to gross proceeds or as an adjustment to basis, as the case may be. Section 6045(h)(2) provides that gross proceeds and basis reporting is required when there is a lapse of, or a closing transaction with respect to, an option on a specified security or an exercise of a cash-settled option on a specified security. Section 6045(h)(3) provides that section 6045(h)(1) and (h)(2) do not apply to any option granted or acquired before January 1, 2013.

e. *Time for furnishing statements*

The Act amended section 6045(b) to extend the due date from January 31 to February 15 for furnishing certain information statements to customers, effective for statements required to be furnished after December 31, 2008. Section 6045(b) provides that the statements to which the new February 15 due date applies are statements required under section 6045 and statements with respect to other reportable items that are furnished with these statements in a consolidated reporting statement (as defined in regulations under section 6045). See Notice 2009-11 (2009-5 IRB 420), providing that, with respect to reportable items from calendar year 2008, brokers had until February 17, 2009, to report all items that they customarily reported on their annual composite form recipient statements. See § 601.601(d)(2).

4. *Transfer Statements*

The Act added section 6045A, which provides that a broker and any other person specified in Treasury regulations (applicable person) that transfers to a broker a security that is a covered security in the hands of the transferring person must furnish to the broker receiving custody of the security (receiving broker) a written statement that allows the receiving broker to satisfy the basis reporting requirements of section 6045(g). Section 6045A(c) provides that, unless the Secretary provides otherwise, the statement required by this rule must be furnished to the receiving broker not later than fifteen days after the transfer of the covered security.

5. *Issuer Reporting*

The Act added section 6045B, which provides that an issuer of specified securities must file a return according to forms or regulations prescribed by the Secretary describing any organizational action (such as a stock split, merger, or acquisition) that affects the basis of the specified security, the quantitative effect on the basis of that specified security, and any other information the Secretary requires. Section 6045B(b) provides that this return must be filed within forty-five days after the date of the organizational action, unless the action occurs in December, in which case the return must be filed by January 15th of the following year.

Section 6045B(c) provides that an issuer must furnish, according to forms or regulations prescribed by the Secretary, to each nominee with respect to that security (or to each certificate holder if there is no nominee) a written statement showing: (1) the name, address, and telephone number of the information contact of the person required to file the return; (2) the information required to be included on the return with respect to the security; and (3) any other information required by the Secretary. This statement must be furnished to the nominee or certificate holder on or before January 15th of the year following the calendar year in which the organizational action took place.

Section 6045B(e) provides that the Secretary may waive the return filing and information statement requirements if the person to which the requirements apply makes publicly available, in the form and manner determined by the Secretary, the name, address, telephone number, and e-mail address of the information contact of that person, and the information about the organizational action and its effect on basis otherwise required to be included in the return.

6. *Penalties*

The Act amended the list of returns and statements in section 6724(d) for which sections 6721 and 6722 impose penalties for any failure to file or furnish complete and correct returns and statements. This section imposes a penalty on brokers for a failure to file returns or furnish complete and correct statements after a sale of securities as required by section 6045. Section 6724(d) now also imposes penalties with respect to the returns and statements required by sections 6045A and 6045B.

7. *Request for Comments*

Notice 2009-17 (2009-8 IRB 575), published by the IRS on February 23, 2009, invited public comments regarding guidance under the new reporting requirements in sections 6045, 6045A, and 6045B and for determining the basis of certain securities under section 1012. In particular, Notice 2009-17 requested comments on the applicability of the reporting requirements, basis method elections, DRPs, reconciliation with customer reporting, special rules and mechanical issues, transfer reporting, issuer reporting, and broker practices and procedures. Many comments were received in response to Notice 2009-17. The comments were considered in developing the proposed regulations. See § 601.601(d)(2).

Explanation of the Provisions and Summary of Comments

The proposed regulations provide rules for determining basis and for reporting adjusted basis and whether any gain or loss on a sale is long-term or short-term. The proposed regulations also address the new reporting requirements imposed upon persons transferring custody of stock and upon issuers of stock.

The proposed regulations do not address rules regarding reporting for options, compensatory options, or other equity-based compensation arrangements, or reporting of adjusted basis for indebtedness, because indebtedness is only subject to the requirements of section 6045(g) if acquired on or after January 1, 2013, and options are only subject to the requirements of section 6045(g) and (h) if granted or acquired on or after January 1, 2013. These rules are expected to be addressed in future guidance.

The proposed regulations generally are limited to the amendments to the Internal Revenue Code (Code) under the Act in sections 1012, 6045, 6045A, 6045B, and 6724 and do not address requests from commentators regarding changes to substantive rules in other areas such as the rules regarding allocation of a return of capital. The proposed regulations also do not address technical issues related to information reporting such as electronic delivery of returns by brokers to customers. These comments are outside the scope of the proposed regulations.

1. *Returns of Brokers*

Section 1.6045-1(c) requires brokers to make a return of information with respect to each sale by a customer of the broker effected by the broker in the ordinary course of a trade or business in which the broker stands ready to effect sales to be made by others. Section 1.6045-1(d) sets forth the information that the broker must include on the return.

The proposed regulations amend the definition of *broker* in § 1.6045-1(a)(1) to modify the exception for non-U.S. payors and non-U.S. middlemen. Under the revised rule, a non-U.S. payor or non-U.S. middleman would be a broker to the extent provided in a withholding agreement described in § 1.1441-1(e)(5)(iii) between a qualified intermediary and the IRS or similar agreement with the IRS. The Treasury Department and IRS expect that such agreements generally will provide that the broker that is party to such agreement will be subject to the broker reporting requirements under section 6045 to the same extent as U.S. payors and U.S. middlemen. The Treasury Department and IRS request comments regarding the usefulness of information received from non-U.S. payors and non-U.S. middlemen, the costs to non-U.S. payors and non-U.S. middlemen of complying with such a requirement, and other potential effects of such a requirement in a withholding or reporting agreement with the IRS.

a. *Form and manner of new broker reporting requirements*

The proposed regulations provide that brokers must report adjusted basis and whether any gain or loss with respect to the security is long-term or short-term on Form 1099-B, "Proceeds from Broker and Barter Exchange Transactions," or any successor form under section 6045(a) when reporting the sale of a covered security. They clarify that the basis reported by a broker is the total amount paid by a customer or credited against a customer's account as a result of the acquisition of securities adjusted for commissions and the effects of other transactions occurring within the account. The proposed regulations also require brokers to adjust the basis they report to take into account the information received on a transfer statement in connection with the transfer of a covered security (including transfers from a decedent and gift transfers) as well as information received from issuers of stock about the quantitative effect on basis from corporate actions. The proposed regulations generally do not require a broker to adjust the reported basis for transactions, elections, or events occurring outside the account. For example, with respect to wash sales (discussed in more detail later in this preamble), the proposed regulations require that a broker adjust the reported basis in accordance with section 1091 if both the purchase and sale transactions occur with respect to identical securities in the same account.

Commentators suggested that brokers be required to report certain warnings or indicators to a customer about potential discrepancies between the broker-reported basis and the basis the customer must report on the customer's income tax return. For example, commentators suggested that a flag be added to the information return that would alert a customer that a foreign issuer may not have reported to the broker all issuer actions affecting basis. The proposed regulations do not adopt these suggestions but, as discussed with respect to wash sales later in this preamble, require a broker to report to customers engaging in wash sales the amount of any disallowed loss. Brokers may communicate additional information on other statements furnished to customers if desired. The Treasury Department and IRS request further comments regarding whether additional information items should be required on the information return. A draft of the 2011 Form 1099-B is available for viewing and comment on the IRS web site at *http://www.irs.gov/pub/irs-dft/f1099b--dft.pdf*.

For a sale of securities that were acquired on different dates or at different prices, some commentators requested that brokers be permitted to report the sale on a single information return. Other commentators asked that the proposed regulations require separate reporting of the sale of securities acquired on different dates or at different prices. The proposed regulations generally maintain the current requirement that brokers report a sale of securities within an account on one return, even if the sale involves multiple acquisitions, to limit the number of separate returns filed with the IRS and statements furnished to customers. However, because brokers must report whether any gain or loss on the sale of a covered security is short-term or long-term, and because noncovered securities must be reported separately from covered securities to avoid treatment as covered securities, a single sale in an account could necessitate as many as three returns if the sale included covered securities held more than a year, covered securities held one year or less, and noncovered securities.

b. *Scope of covered securities and treatment of noncovered securities*

The proposed regulations clarify that a broker is not required to report adjusted basis and whether any gain or loss on a sale is long-term or short-term for securities that are excepted from all reporting under section 6045 at the time of their acquisition. For example, the new basis reporting requirements do not apply to a security purchased by an organization that is tax-exempt even if the organization later loses its tax-exempt status and becomes subject to gross proceeds reporting on the sale of securities under section 6045(a).

With respect to a security transferred into an account in a non-sale transaction, the security is a covered security under the proposed regulations if it was a covered security prior to transfer and the broker receives the statement required under section 6045A for the transfer (the transfer statement, discussed in more detail later in this preamble) indicating that the security is a covered security. Conversely, a security is a noncovered security if the broker receives a transfer statement indicating that the security is a noncovered security. A transferred security will be presumed to be a covered security unless the transfer statement expressly states that the security is a noncovered security.

If the receiving broker does not receive a transfer statement or receives a transfer statement that does not contain all of the required information, the proposed regulations permit the broker to treat the security as a noncovered security if, as suggested by commentators, the broker notifies the person that effected the transfer and requests a complete statement, and no complete statement is provided in response to this request before the broker reports the sale or subsequent transfer of the security. The proposed regulations do not require brokers to make this request more than once.

If a broker receives the information required on the transfer statement after reporting the sale of the security, the proposed regulations require the broker to file a corrected Form 1099-B if the reporting was incorrect or incomplete. Similarly, if an issuer furnishes the return required by section 6045B concerning corporate organizational actions (the issuer statement, discussed in more detail later in this preamble) after the broker has reported the sale of the security, the proposed regulations require the broker to file a corrected Form 1099-B to report any adjustments to basis not reflected previously. Commentators requested that corrected reporting not be required for de minimis adjustments or for statements furnished beyond a specific period after the close of the calendar year. The proposed regulations do not adopt either suggestion. The Treasury Department and IRS request further comments regarding corrected reporting.

Commentators expressed concern regarding the difficulty, in some cases, of determining whether a security is stock (for which basis must be reported for acquisitions beginning in January 2011 or January 2012) or indebtedness or another financial instrument (for which basis does not need to be reported for acquisitions in 2011 or 2012). Some commentators suggested that the proposed regulations classify each security or require issuers to file a classification report with the IRS to permit the IRS to publish a report identifying each security. The proposed regulations do not adopt this approach. Instead, the proposed regulations provide that, solely for purposes of determining the applicable date for basis reporting, any security an issuer classifies as stock is treated as stock. If no issuer classification has been made, the security is not treated as stock unless the broker knows, or has reason to know, that the security is reasonably classified as stock under general tax principles.

Some commentators expressed a desire to report adjusted basis and whether any gain or loss on a sale is long-term or short-term for noncovered securities. Other commentators requested that the regulations prohibit such reporting on Form 1099-B and permit reporting only of adjusted basis and whether any gain or loss on a sale is long-term or short-term to the customer on statements not filed with the IRS. In order to encourage more reporting of information and simplify reporting by taxpayers on their income tax returns, the proposed regulations allow brokers the option of reporting adjusted basis and whether any gain or loss on a sale is long-term or short-term for noncovered securities on a security by security basis. Therefore, a broker may choose to report this information for any given noncovered security. The proposed regulations also provide that a broker that chooses to report this information with respect to a noncovered security is not subject to penalties under section 6721 or 6722 for any failure to report such information correctly, provided that the broker indicates on Form 1099-B that the sale reported is a sale of a noncovered security. The instructions to the tax return will inform taxpayers of their duty to verify the information reported by brokers and to adjust the reported information when necessary to reflect the taxpayer's correct information. This duty applies equally to covered and noncovered securities.

c. *Determination of basis required to be reported*

Section 6045(g)(2)(B)(i)(I) provides that, except for RIC stock or DRP stock, a broker must report using the FIFO basis determination method unless the customer notifies the broker of the specific security to be sold or transferred by means of making an adequate identification of the security sold or transferred at the time of sale or transfer. With respect to RIC stock or DRP stock, section 6045(g)(2)(B)(i)(II) provides that a broker must report adjusted basis in accordance with the broker's default method under section 1012 unless the customer notifies the broker that the customer elects another permitted method.

The proposed regulations clarify that, when a customer sells less than the entire position of a security in an account, the selling broker must follow the customer's instruction, if any, adequately identifying the security sold or, when applicable, requesting that average basis be used to compute the basis of eligible stock. Thus, under the proposed regulations, a broker must report basis using any permitted lot identification and basis determination method the customer chooses when the customer provides a valid instruction (discussed in more detail later in this preamble). Absent a valid instruction from the customer, the proposed regulations clarify that a broker must report basis of a security (other than stock eligible for averaging) using the FIFO basis determination method when reporting the sale. The proposed regulations also clarify that, absent a valid instruction to use another method, a broker must report basis for stock eligible for averaging using the broker's default basis determination method.

Commentators requested that brokers and customers be permitted to report basis by different methods and that brokers be permitted to report basis for all sales using only one of the permitted basis determination methods, for example, the average basis method. The proposed regulations do not adopt these requests because section 1012 permits customers to report basis by a different permissible method than the default method selected by the broker and section 6045 requires brokers to follow instructions from customers regarding this selection. The requested rules are inconsistent with the goal of conforming broker reporting with taxpayer basis determination method elections to facilitate and promote compliance in taxpayer reporting of income.

2. *Average Basis Method*

Section 1.1012-1(e) provides rules for computing the basis of RIC stock by averaging the cost of all shares in the account (the average basis method). Taxpayers may elect to use the average basis method for RIC stock acquired at different prices and maintained by a custodian or agent in an account for the periodic acquisition, redemption, sale, or other disposition of the stock.

Consistent with section 1012(d)(1), the proposed regulations extend the average basis method to shares of stock acquired after December 31, 2010, in connection with a DRP, and clarify that shares are eligible for averaging only if they are identical.

Commentators suggested that stock should be eligible for averaging together if it has the same Committee on Uniform Security Identification Procedures (CUSIP) number. The proposed regulations adopt this suggestion and define *identical shares of stock* as stock with the same CUSIP number (or other security identifier number as permitted in additional guidance of general applicability, see § 601.601(d)(2)). However, for purposes of defining a DRP, the proposed regulations provide that the stock of a successor entity or entities that result from certain corporate actions such as mergers, consolidations, split-offs, or spinoffs, is identical to the stock of the predecessor entity. Thus, corporate actions will not cause stock acquired in connection with a DRP to become ineligible for averaging because, for example, a dividend declared before the action and paid after the action is completed is not reinvested in stock with the same CUSIP number. The proposed regulations further provide, however, that shares of stock acquired in connection with a DRP are not identical to shares of stock with the same CUSIP number that are not acquired in connection with a DRP.

3. *Broker's Default Basis Determination Method*

Consistent with section 6045(g)(2)(B)(i)(II), the proposed regulations provide that the basis of RIC stock and DRP stock is determined in accordance with a broker's default method, unless a taxpayer elects another permitted method.

a. *Consistency in use of average basis method*

Commentators suggested that the proposed regulations should not require brokers to compute basis for a DRP using the average basis method for taxpayers electing this method. The proposed regulations do not adopt this recommendation because it is inconsistent with the statutory requirement that the average basis method be available to any taxpayer that desires to use it for a DRP, as well as with the goal of conforming broker reporting with taxpayer basis determination method elections to facilitate and promote compliance in taxpayer reporting of income. The proposed regulations specify that a broker must compute basis using the basis determination method the taxpayer elects. The proposed regulations also provide that the taxpayer must report gain or loss on its return using the method the taxpayer elects or, if the taxpayer fails to make an election, the broker's default method.

b. *Default method*

Commentators suggested that a broker should be allowed to determine a default basis determination method when a taxpayer fails to elect a method for determining the basis of RIC stock or DRP stock. Consistent with section 6045(g)(2)(B)(i)(II), the proposed regulations do not prescribe a broker default method, which each broker may determine.

c. *Communicating default method to taxpayers*

A commentator suggested that the proposed regulations should require that a broker notify a taxpayer of the broker's default method by the earlier of opening a new account or January 1 of the year the average basis method election is effective. Other commentators suggested, however, that the proposed regulations should not specify how brokers communicate their default basis determination method to taxpayers. The proposed regulations do not require a specific method or time for this communication.

4. *Definition of Dividend Reinvestment Plan*

a. *Issuer and non-issuer plans*

A commentator requested that the proposed regulations broadly define *dividend reinvestment plan* to include both broker administered plans and issuer, or corporate, administered plans. Other commentators suggested, however, that if brokers are required to use the average basis method, the definition should include only issueradministered plans. The proposed regulations define dividend reinvestment plan to include a written arrangement, plan, or program administered by an issuer or non-issuer of stock. Neither the statute nor the legislative history indicates any Congressional intent to limit the average basis method to issuer-administered plans.

b. *Reinvestment of dividends*

A commentator suggested that a plan requiring reinvestment of only a portion of the dividends paid should qualify as a DRP under the proposed regulations. The proposed regulations provide that a plan qualifies as a DRP if the plan documents require that at least 10 percent of any dividend paid be reinvested in identical stock. Assuming this 10 percent requirement is met, a plan may reinvest different percentages of dividends in different stocks.

A commentator opined that a plan should not be considered a DRP if the stock is not paying dividends when the issuer offers the plan. Another commentator verbally stated that the proposed regulations should provide that a plan may qualify as a DRP even if the stock has never issued dividends or ceases to pay dividends. This commentator noted that the stock of a start-up company may be included in a DRP in the expectation of paying dividends in the future, and that a company that traditionally pays dividends may be required to temporarily suspend dividends, for example in the case of bankruptcy reorganization. The proposed regulations provide that a stock may be held in a DRP even if no dividends have ever been declared or paid or the issuer has ceased paying dividends.

A commentator suggested that the term *dividends* should include all income from stock for purposes of a DRP. The proposed regulations do not define dividends. Specific comments are requested on whether and how the regulations should define dividends, such as whether the regulations should define the term by reference to section 316, or more broadly to include any payment or distribution from stock, including ordinary dividends, capital gains dividends or distributions, non-taxable returns of capital, and cash dividends in lieu of fractional shares. Comments may address industry practices that relate to this definition.

c. *Acquired in connection with a DRP*

Commentators suggested that subsequent additions to a DRP, such as purchases or transfers of stock, be eligible for the average basis method. A commentator recommended that subsequent additions be separated into separate averaging pools. Another commentator suggested that a single averaging pool should be allowed for all post-effective date identical stock. One commentator stated that brokers have difficulty distinguishing non-DRP purchases of stock from purchases of stock with the same CUSIP number in a DRP, and therefore brokers should be allowed to apply the same basis determination method to all stock with the same CUSIP number in an account.

Consistent with section 1012(d)(4), the proposed regulations provide that stock is acquired in connection with a DRP if the stock is acquired under the DRP or the dividends paid are subject to the DRP. Stock acquired in connection with a DRP includes the initial purchase of stock in the DRP, subsequent transfers of identical stock into the DRP, additional periodic purchases of identical stock through the DRP, and all identical stock acquired through reinvestment of dividends paid under the DRP.

d. *Withdrawal from or termination of a DRP*

A commentator asked about the consequences if a DRP is terminated or a taxpayer transfers shares from a DRP at one broker to a broker that does not offer a DRP. The proposed regulations provide that, if a taxpayer withdraws from a DRP or the plan administrator terminates the DRP, shares of identical stock acquired after the withdrawal or termination are not acquired in connection with a DRP. After the withdrawal or termination, the taxpayer may no longer use the average basis method for the stock, but the basis of each share of stock immediately after the change is the same as the basis immediately before the change.

5. *Computing Average Basis*

a. *Elimination of double-category method*

Under § 1.1012-1(e)(3) and (4), taxpayers compute average basis using either a double-category method, which divides stock by holding period and averages long-term shares separately from short-term shares, or a single-category method, which averages all shares together regardless of holding period.

Commentators suggested that the proposed regulations eliminate the doublecategory method and noted that it is not widely used. One commentator stated that problems may occur when shares are transferred between accounts that use different methods. The proposed regulations adopt this suggestion and eliminate the doublecategory method. The proposed regulations provide that average basis is computed by averaging the basis of all identical stock in an account regardless of holding period and include a transition rule that requires taxpayers using the double-category method to average the basis of all identical stock in an account on the date of publication of final regulations. Specific comments are requested on whether the double-category method should be retained.

Section 1.1012-1(e)(4)(iii) provides that the single-category method may not be used if it appears that the taxpayer's purpose is to convert long-term gain or loss into short-term gain or loss, or vice versa. Consistent with the elimination of the doublecategory method, the proposed regulations remove this provision. The proposed regulations include ordering rules that specify that the holding period of stock to which the average basis method applies is determined on a FIFO basis.

b. *Wash sales*

Section 1.1012-1(e)(4)(iv) provides that section 1091(d) and the associated regulations apply to wash sales of stock from an account using the single-category method of computing average basis. Commentators suggested that brokers should not be required to apply these rules to stock held in separate accounts.

Section 6045(g)(2)(B)(ii) provides that, for purposes of reporting, brokers must apply the wash sale rules only to acquisition and sale transactions in the same account and for identical securities. The rules for brokers are discussed later in this preamble.

For a taxpayer using the average basis method, the proposed regulations provide that the taxpayer must apply section 1091 and the associated regulations (dealing with wash sales of substantially identical securities) in computing average basis regardless of whether the stock or security sold or otherwise disposed of and the stock acquired are in the same account or in different accounts.

c. *Basis after change from average basis method*

The proposed regulations provide that, except for a revocation of the average basis method election (discussed later in this preamble), if a taxpayer changes from the average basis method to another basis determination method for any reason, the basis of each share of stock immediately after the change is the same as the basis immediately before the change.

6. *Time and Manner of Making the Average Basis Method Election*

Section 1.1012-1(e)(6) provides that a taxpayer elects to use the average basis method on an income tax return for the first taxable year the taxpayer wants the election to apply.

a. *Manner of making the average basis method election*

Under the proposed regulations, a taxpayer elects the average basis method for covered securities by notifying the custodian or other agent for the taxpayer's account in writing. The taxpayer makes a separate election for each account holding stock for which the average basis method is permissible. A taxpayer uses the procedures under the current regulations to elect the average basis method for noncovered securities.

Commentators requested that the proposed regulations provide guidance on how taxpayers must inform brokers of their basis determination method. Commentators suggested that brokers may obtain this information through documents provided to a taxpayer opening an account and urged that the rules be flexible and allow electronic communication. The proposed regulations require that a taxpayer must notify a custodian or agent in writing of an average basis method election, but otherwise do not specify how a taxpayer must communicate a basis determination method.

b. *Time for making the average basis method election*

Some commentators suggested that taxpayers should be allowed or required to choose a basis determination method when opening an account or when acquiring stock for which the average basis method is permitted. Other commentators stated that taxpayers should choose a method by the date of a sale. The proposed regulations provide that taxpayers may elect the average basis method at any time, effective for sales after the date of the election.

c. *Revocation of average basis method election*

A commentator asked for clarification on how long brokers must retain basis information. Another commentator suggested that any revocation period should end by the earlier of the date of first sale, the end of the calendar year, or one year from the first purchase of stock.

In order to minimize broker recordkeeping requirements, the proposed regulations provide that a taxpayer may revoke the average basis method election by the earlier of one year from the date of making the election or the first sale or other disposition of the stock following the election. A broker may extend the one-year period but no longer than the first sale. A revocation applies to all identical stock in an account and is effective when the taxpayer notifies the broker or other custodian of the revocation. If a taxpayer revokes the election, the basis of each share of stock in the account is determined using another permissible method.

d. *Change from average basis method*

Section 1.1012-1(e)(6)(ii) provides that a taxpayer that elects to use the average basis method may not revoke the election without the consent of the Commissioner. Under Rev. Proc. 2008-52 (2008-36 IRB 587), Section 30 of the Appendix, a taxpayer within the scope of Rev. Proc. 2008-52 uses the automatic consent procedures to change to the basis determination method described in §1.1012-1(c)(1) (FIFO or specific identification, discussed later in this preamble). The revenue procedure provides that the automatic consent procedures do not apply to RIC stock or to a change from FIFO to specific identification or vice versa, which is not a change in method of accounting. See §601.601(d)(2).

A commentator recommended that taxpayers should not be able to change from the average basis method except by opening a new account. Other commentators opined that taxpayers should have broad discretion to change from the average basis method. Several commentators suggested that brokers should not be required to recreate a stock's original basis if a taxpayer changes from the average basis method.

The proposed regulations provide that a taxpayer may change from the average basis method to another permissible method at any time. A taxpayer's change in basis determination method applies to stock acquired on or after January 1, 2012, in a different manner than to stock acquired before January 1, 2012. Consistent with the account by account rules, discussed later in this preamble, a change in basis determination method applies to identical stock a taxpayer acquires on or after January 1, 2012, that the taxpayer holds in the same account. By contrast, a taxpayer's change in basis determination method applies to all identical stock the taxpayer acquires before January 1, 2012, that the taxpayer holds in any account. Unless the taxpayer revokes the average basis method election, discussed earlier in this preamble, the taxpayer must change from the average basis method prospectively. Thus, the basis of each share of stock to which the change applies is the basis immediately before the change.

A commentator requested clarification on how often a taxpayer may change a basis method election. Commentators suggested that changes should be limited, for example to once per year. The proposed regulations do not limit the number of times or frequency a taxpayer may change basis determination methods.

A commentator suggested that the proposed regulations should require taxpayers to obtain the Commissioner's permission to change basis determination methods. Another commentator recommended that taxpayers be allowed to change from the average basis method without the Commissioner's permission. The proposed regulations clarify that a change in basis determination method is a change in method of accounting to which the provisions of sections 446 and 481 and the associated regulations apply. A taxpayer may change its basis determination method by obtaining the consent of the Commissioner under applicable administrative procedures. The IRS may publish additional guidance of general applicability, see §601.601(d)(2), that provides broad consent for taxpayers to change basis determination methods.

7. *Applying Average Basis Method Account by Account*

Section 1.1012-1(e)(2) provides that a taxpayer must use the same basis determination method for all of the taxpayer's accounts in the same RIC. Section 1.1012-1(e)(6)(ii) provides that a taxpayer must apply an average basis method election to all shares (except certain gift shares) of a particular RIC that the taxpayer holds in any account.

a. *Definition of account*

Commentators requested that the proposed regulations define the term "account." Commentators noted that each fund of a RIC is treated as a single account, while a broker may hold other securities with different CUSIP numbers in a single account. Commentators suggested that accounts should be treated as separate accounts if they have different account numbers, and that subaccounts such as cash and margin accounts should not be treated as separate accounts.

The proposed regulations do not define the term account. Instead, the proposed regulations provide rules prescribing when stock must be treated as held in separate accounts and the result of that treatment.

b. *Basis determination methods applied account by account*

Commentators suggested that the proposed regulations allow a taxpayer to make separate basis calculations for the same stock held in two separate accounts, even if held by the same broker. The proposed regulations adopt this suggestion. Consistent with section 1012(c), the proposed regulations provide that the average basis method election applies to all identical RIC stock or DRP stock in an account. For sales or other dispositions of stock after 2011, a taxpayer may use different basis determination methods for identical stock held in two separate accounts, even if held by the same broker. A taxpayer also may use different basis determination methods for shares of stock held in the same account that are not identical.

For sales or other dispositions before 2012 of RIC stock or DRP stock for which a taxpayer has used the average basis method, the proposed regulations retain the rules requiring that the taxpayer use the average basis method for identical stock held in separate accounts. However, a taxpayer may use different basis determination methods for shares of stock held in the same account that are not identical.

c. *Separate accounts*

Consistent with section 1012(c)(2)(A), the proposed regulations provide that, absent a single-account election (explained later in this preamble), RIC stock or DRP stock that a taxpayer acquires before January 1, 2012, is treated as held in a separate account from any stock acquired on or after that date. The proposed regulations further provide that any stock that is a covered security (within the meaning of section 6045(g)(3)) is treated as held in a separate account from any stock that is a noncovered security regardless of when acquired, as is consistent with Congressional intent. The proposed regulations include an example in which a security acquired on or after January 1, 2012, is a noncovered security.

8. *Single-account Election*

Section 1012(c)(2) provides that, with respect to RIC stock, a RIC may elect (at the time and in the form and manner prescribed by the Secretary), on a stockholder by stockholder basis, to treat all stock in the RIC held by the stockholder as one account without regard to when the stock was acquired (single-account election). Section 1012(d)(3) provides that the account by account rules of section 1012(c), including the single-account election available to RICs, also apply to DRP stock.

a. *Application and scope of election*

The proposed regulations provide that a RIC or DRP may make a single-account election to treat identical RIC stock or identical DRP stock held in separate accounts for which the taxpayer has elected to use the average basis method as held in a single account. If a broker holds the stock as a nominee, the broker, and not the RIC or DRP, makes the election. The single-account election is irrevocable. Commentators opined that a single-account election should not encompass stock a taxpayer acquires before January 1, 2012, if the basis information is unreliable. A commentator requested that the proposed regulations include a standard of reliability or, alternatively, allow brokers to exclude stock for which reliable basis information is not available from the singleaccount election. Another commentator requested penalty relief if reliable basis information is not available for pre-effective date shares.

The proposed regulations provide that a RIC, DRP, or broker may make a singleaccount election only for stock for which it has accurate basis information. A RIC, DRP, or broker has accurate basis information if the RIC, DRP, or broker neither knows nor has reason to know that the basis information is inaccurate. See also section 6724 and the regulations thereunder regarding standards for relief from information reporting penalties. Stock for which accurate basis information is unavailable may not be included in the single-account election and must be treated as held in a separate account.

The proposed regulations provide that, once the single-account election is made, it applies to all identical stock that is a covered security a taxpayer later acquires in an account. If a taxpayer acquires identical stock that is a noncovered security in an account, a RIC, DRP, or broker may make another single-account election if the RIC, DRP, or broker has accurate basis information. In addition to allowing a RIC, DRP, or broker to make a single-account election for some taxpayers and not others, consistent with section 1012(c)(2)(B), the proposed regulations allow a RIC, DRP, or broker to make the election for some identical stocks held for a taxpayer and not for other stocks.

b. *Time and manner for making the single-account election*

The proposed regulations provide that a RIC, DRP, or broker makes the singleaccount election by clearly noting it on its books and records. The books and records must reflect the date of the election; the taxpayer's name, account number, and taxpayer identification number; the stock subject to the election; and the taxpayer's basis in the stock. The books and records reflecting the election must be provided to the taxpayer upon request. The proposed regulations provide that the single-account election may be made at any time and more than once for a specific stock.

The proposed regulations require a RIC, DRP, or broker to use reasonable means to notify a taxpayer of a single-account election. Reasonable means include mailings, circulars, and electronic mail. The notification may be sent separately to the taxpayer or included with the taxpayer's account statement, or by other means calculated to provide actual notice. The notice must identify the securities subject to the election and advise the taxpayer that the stock will be treated as covered securities without regard to the date acquired.

9. *FIFO and Specific Identification Methods*

Section 1.1012-1(c)(1) provides that if a taxpayer acquires shares of stock on different dates or at different prices and sells or transfers some of those shares, and does not adequately identify the lot from which the shares are sold or transferred, the shares deemed sold or transferred are the earliest acquired shares (the FIFO rule). If a taxpayer makes an adequate identification of the shares sold under § 1.1012-1(c)(2), (3), or (4), the shares treated as sold are the shares the taxpayer identified.

a. *FIFO rule*

A commentator verbally requested that the proposed regulations clarify how the FIFO rule of § 1.1012-1(c)(1) applies to stock splits. The commentator asked whether shares acquired from the split are treated as acquired on the date of the purchase of the original shares or on the date of the split. In general, the shares that are first acquired are the shares with the longest holding period. Therefore, this question is addressed by rules under sections 307 and 1223 and the associated regulations and is outside the scope of these regulations.

A commentator requested clarification on whether the FIFO rule applies to stock that is part of a stock certificate that includes multiple lots. In response to this comment, the proposed regulations clarify that the FIFO rule also applies to multiple lots represented by a single stock certificate.

b. *Timing of lot selection*

Commentators suggested that taxpayers that wish to identify a specific lot of stock to be sold should be required to do so at the time of trade. Some commentators recommended that taxpayers should be allowed to wait to identify stock until the settlement date or until the end of the year. Other commentators opined that post-sale changes to specific identification of stock should not be allowed.

Rev. Rul. 67-436 (1967-2 CB 266) holds that an identification of stock by the time of delivery, which was within four days of the sale date, complied with the requirement to identify stock at the time of the sale or transfer. Consistent with Rev. Rul. 67-436, the proposed regulations provide that a taxpayer makes an adequate identification of stock at the time of sale, transfer, delivery, or distribution if the taxpayer identifies the stock no later than the earlier of the settlement date or the time for settlement under Securities and Exchange Commission regulations. Rev. Rul. 67-436 will be obsoleted when these regulations are published as final regulations. See § 601.601(d)(2).

c. *Standing lot selection orders*

Several commentators recommended that the proposed regulations allow taxpayers to specify a lot selection method to their brokers through standing orders such as last-in-first-out or highest-in-first-out. In response to these comments, the proposed regulations clarify that taxpayers may establish a lot selection method by standing order.

d. *Method of communicating lot selection*

To provide maximum flexibility, the proposed regulations do not designate how taxpayers must communicate lot selection to brokers. Any reasonable method of communication, including electronic and oral communication, is permissible.

e. *Confirmation of sales*

Section 1.1012-1(c)(3)(i)(b) and (ii)(b) requires a broker or agent to provide written confirmation of the sale of stock a taxpayer has specifically identified within a reasonable time after sale. Commentators suggested that the broker or agent should determine whether to provide a confirmation and its form, and that current technology renders the confirmation requirement obsolete. Another commentator suggested that the proposed regulations allow brokers to provide lot information to taxpayers either by trade confirmation, monthly statements, or year-end reports. The proposed regulations do not amend the current confirmation requirement, which ensures that taxpayers receive necessary information in a timely manner. What is reasonable depends on the facts and circumstances.

f. *Writing in electronic format*

Commentators suggested that the proposed regulations specifically authorize electronic written confirmation or recordkeeping. In response to these comments, the proposed regulations clarify that a written confirmation, record, document, instruction, or advice includes a writing in electronic format.

g. *Identification by trustee or executor*

Section 1.1012-1(c)(4) provides that a trustee of a trust or executor or administrator of an estate makes an adequate identification if the trustee, executor, or administrator specifies the stock in writing in the books and records of the trust or estate. If the stock is distributed, the trustee, executor, or administrator must identify the stock in writing to the distributee.

A commentator verbally noted that this rule does not require a trustee, executor, or administrator to identify stock to a broker or other agent selling the stock. The proposed regulations add the requirement that the trustee, executor, or administrator identify the stock to the broker or agent.

10. *Reporting of Wash Sales*

Section 6045(g)(2)(B)(ii) provides that, unless the Secretary instructs otherwise, a broker is required to report the adjusted basis of a covered security without taking into account the effect on basis of the wash sale rules of section 1091 unless the purchase and sale transactions resulting in a wash sale occur in the same account and are for identical securities (rather than substantially identical securities).

The proposed regulations provide that a broker is required to report adjusted basis in accordance with section 1091 only if both the purchase and sale transactions occur with respect to covered securities in the same account with the same CUSIP number (or other security identifier number that the Secretary may designate by publication in the **Federal Register** or in the Internal Revenue Bulletin). If a broker is required to apply section 1091 for reporting purposes, the broker must report the amount of the disallowed loss in addition to adjusted basis and gross proceeds for the sold security. The proposed regulations further provide that the broker must adjust the basis of the purchased security by the amount of the disallowed loss when reporting the eventual sale of the purchased security.

Commentators requested exceptions from reporting wash sales resulting in de minimis adjustments and wash sales triggered by scheduled periodic investments such as in an employee stock purchase plan or by automatic dividend reinvestment. Because the underlying substantive rules disallow losses in these situations, the proposed regulations do not adopt these recommendations. In addition, commentators requested an exception from reporting for wash sales for high frequency traders such as day traders based on the belief that high frequency traders generally make timely and valid elections to use the mark-to-market method of accounting under section 475(e) or (f) and that section 475(d)(1) therefore exempts them from the wash sale rules. Commentators also requested that the regulations provide a general exception from basis reporting for high frequency traders based on the belief that section 475 makes basis reporting superfluous for most high frequency traders. The proposed regulations do not adopt these recommendations, in part because the proposed regulations provide generally that reporting should occur without regard to the mark-to-market method of accounting. The Treasury Department and IRS request further comments on the treatment of high frequency traders, including specifics about the burden that basis reporting may impose, and how brokers can identify customers that have made valid and timely mark-to-market accounting method elections under section 475(e) or (f) and which transactions by these persons are subject to the provisions of section 475.

Commentators asserted that identical securities could have separate CUSIP numbers, potentially after a change to the name of the issuer. To facilitate administration of wash sale reporting, the proposed regulations interpret identical securities to mean securities with the same CUSIP number (or other security identifier number that the Secretary may designate by publication in the **Federal Register** or in the Internal Revenue Bulletin).

11. *Reporting of Short Sales*

In the case of a short sale, section 6045(g)(5) provides that gross proceeds and basis reporting under section 6045 is generally required for the year in which the short sale is closed rather than, as under the present law rule for gross proceeds reporting, the year in which the short sale is entered into.

The proposed regulations implement this change to reporting of short sales by requiring brokers to report all short sales opened on or after January 1, 2010, for the year in which the short sale is closed. For sales that are opened and closed in 2010, the proposed regulations require brokers to report only gross proceeds information with respect to the securities sold to open the short sale, which is consistent with how brokers currently report short sale transactions. For sales closed on or after January 1, 2011, using covered securities, however, the proposed regulations require brokers to report both the information concerning the securities sold to open the short sale and the information concerning the securities acquired to close the short sale on a single return of information. For sales closed on or after January 1, 2011, using noncovered securities, the proposed regulations require brokers to report only the information concerning the securities sold to open the short sale and permit, but do not require, brokers to report adjusted basis for the securities acquired to close the short sale and whether any gain or loss on the short sale is long-term or short-term. The proposed regulations provide that reporting adjusted basis and whether any gain or loss on the short sale is long-term or short-term is not subject to penalty under section 6721 or 6722 if the Form 1099-B indicates that the sale reported is a sale of a noncovered security. These requirements are in line with the reporting beginning with calendar year 2011 of both adjusted basis and gross proceeds on Form 1099-B.

Under section 1233, satisfaction of a short sale obligation through other borrowed property does not close a short sale. The proposed regulations address this situation and provide that, if an obligation arising from a short sale is satisfied by the receipt of transferred securities that themselves are borrowed from or through the person effecting the transfer, the receiving broker should not file a Form 1099-B but should instead provide the information regarding the short sale of the borrowed securities to the person effecting the transfer. Under the proposed regulations, the person effecting the transfer must file Form 1099-B when the obligation is finally satisfied and the short sale is closed.

The proposed regulations modify the backup withholding rules for short sales to provide that backup withholding can occur only at the time the short sale is closed and becomes subject to reporting under section 6045(g)(5).

Commentators requested that brokers not be responsible for the additional reporting requirements related to short sales that are opened before January 2011 but also requested clear guidance on how to implement reporting for short sales opened prior to January 2011 to prevent duplicate reporting. The proposed regulations prevent duplicate reporting by requiring brokers to report short sales opened prior to January 2011 under current rules except for short sales opened in 2010 that remain open into 2011. Instead of reporting the sale for calendar year 2010, the proposed regulations require that brokers report these sales for the year in which the sale is closed.

Finally, commentators requested that the reporting of short sales not require brokers to apply the constructive sale rules of section 1259, which can trigger the recognition of gain if the investor also holds or acquires an appreciated position in the same securities, or the rules under section 1233(h) concerning limitations imposed on investors that own property substantially identical to the short sale property. The proposed regulations provide for these exclusions from reporting.

12. *Reporting of Sales by S Corporations*

Under § 1.6045-1(c)(3)(i)(B)(*1*), a broker currently is not required to report sales of securities by corporations. Section 1.6045-1(c)(3)(i)(C) currently permits a broker to treat a customer as a corporation if the broker has actual knowledge that the customer is a corporation, if the customer files a Form W-9, "Request for Taxpayer Identification Number and Certification," exemption certificate claiming an exemption as a corporation, or, absent knowledge to the contrary, if the name of the customer contains an unambiguous expression of corporate status such as "Corporation" or "Incorporated."

To comply with the new requirement under section 6045(g)(4) that brokers report sales by customers that are S corporations of covered securities acquired on or after January 1, 2012, the proposed regulations exclude S corporations from the list of exempt Form 1099-B recipients, but only for sales of covered securities acquired on or after January 1, 2012. The proposed regulations also curtail the ability of brokers to rely solely on the name of the customer to determine whether the customer is a corporation exempt from reporting, but only for sales of covered securities acquired on or after January 1, 2012. Commentators requested that the proposed regulations retain this rule because its removal potentially requires brokers to seek a certification from all corporate customers. The proposed regulations do not adopt this recommendation, however, because brokers cannot infer from a customer's name whether the customer is taxed as an S corporation or C corporation. Commentators also requested that accounts opened by corporations before January 2012 be excepted from reporting. The proposed regulations do not adopt this request as contrary to the statute.

Commentators requested that Form W-9 be updated to facilitate a customer's statement to its broker of its current election to be taxed as an S corporation and that the proposed regulations require brokers to solicit or re-solicit Form W-9 from each existing corporate customer. The IRS is currently considering the requested modification to Form W-9. The proposed regulations do not impose a requirement to solicit or re-solicit Form W-9 from all existing corporate customers because, under § 1.6045-1(c)(3)(i)(C), Form W-9 is only one method by which brokers may determine whether a corporate customer is exempt from all reporting beginning in 2012. However, if a broker does not have actual knowledge that a corporate customer is taxed as a C corporation or is otherwise exempt (for example, because it is a bank or organization exempt from tax under section 501(a)), a broker must request a Form W-9 exemption certificate or else must make a return of information for any sales by the corporation of covered securities acquired on or after January 1, 2012. A broker also may be required to backup withhold on gross proceeds paid to the customer.

Commentators requested that brokers be permitted to report other Form 1099 information such as interest and dividends for S corporations because reporting of the sales of securities is done on composite statements containing all such information. The proposed regulations do not address this topic directly because no penalty is imposed for the act of filing a nonrequired return.

13. *Reporting to Trust Interest Holders in a WHFIT*

Commentators requested that the proposed regulations except trustees and middlemen from any requirement to report information under sections 6045(g) to trust interest holders in a widely held fixed investment trust (WHFIT) with respect to both the securities held by a WHFIT and trust interests in a WHFIT because the WHFIT rules in § 1.671-5 already provide a framework for communicating similar information to trust interest holders. These proposed regulations clarify that the sale of a trust interest in a WHFIT by a trust interest holder is required to be reported under section 6045(a). However, to the extent that a trustee or middleman has a requirement to provide information under section 6045(g), the trustee or middleman is deemed to meet those requirements by complying with the WHFIT rules in § 1.671-5. The Treasury Department and IRS request additional comments on whether any basis reporting rules are needed in addition to those provided under § 1.671-5 to accommodate trust interest holders in a WHFIT.

14. *Due date for Payee Statements Furnished in a Consolidated Reporting Statement*

Section 6045(b) extends the due date to furnish all of the payee statements required under section 6045 to customers from January 31 to February 15, effective for statements required to be furnished after December 31, 2008. Thus, in addition to Form 1099-B, "Proceeds from Broker and Barter Exchange Transactions," the February 15 due date applies to Form 1099-S, "Proceeds from Real Estate Transactions," and, when reporting payments to attorneys or substitute payments by brokers in lieu of dividends or interest, Form 1099-MISC, "Miscellaneous Income." This February 15 due date also applies to any other statement required to be furnished on or before January 31 of a calendar year if furnished with a statement required under section 6045 in a consolidated reporting statement. The Act did not define consolidated reporting statement but provided that the term would be defined in regulations. See Notice 2009-11 (2009-5 IRB 420), providing that, with respect to reportable items from calendar year 2008, brokers had until February 17, 2009, to report all items that they customarily reported on their annual composite form recipient statements. See § 601.601(d)(2).

The proposed regulations define *consolidated reporting statement* as a grouping of statements furnished to the same customer or same group of customers on the same date whether or not the statements are furnished with respect to the same or different accounts or transactions. Importantly, the proposed regulations require that the grouping of statements be limited to those furnished to the customer based on the same relationship as the statement furnished under section 6045 (for example, broker, payor, or real estate settlement agent), and not as a result of any other relationship between the parties such as debtor to creditor or employer to employee. Based on this limitation, the following forms may be furnished in a consolidated reporting statement with a statement required under section 6045: Form 1099-DIV, "Dividends and Distributions"; Form 1099-INT, "Interest Income"; Form 1099-MISC, "Miscellaneous Income"; Form 1099-OID, "Original Issue Discount"; Form 1099-PATR, "Taxable Distributions Received From Cooperatives"; Form 1099-Q, "Payments From Qualified Education Programs (Under Sections 529 and 530)"; Form 1099-R, "Distributions From Pensions, Annuities, Retirement or Profit-Sharing Plans, IRAs, Insurance Contracts, etc."; Form 3921, "Exercise of an Incentive Stock Option Under Section 422(b)" (in development); Form 3922, "Transfer of Stock Acquired Through an Employee Stock Purchase Plan Under Section 423(c)" (in development); and Form 5498, "IRA Contribution Information." The Treasury Department and IRS request further comments regarding whether any other forms should be included in the definition of consolidated reporting statement.

For statements filed by brokers with respect to sales, the proposed regulations acknowledge that a customer may not sell securities in an account in every year and, thus, may not receive Form 1099-B every year. The proposed regulations provide that a broker may treat any customer as receiving a required statement under section 6045 if the customer has an account for which a statement would be required to be furnished under section 6045 had a sale occurred during the year.

15. *Reporting Required in Connection with Transfers of Securities*

Under new section 6045A, a broker and any other person specified in Treasury regulations (applicable person) that transfers to a broker a security that is a covered security in the hands of the applicable person must furnish to the receiving broker a written statement for purposes of enabling the receiving broker to satisfy the reporting requirements of section 6045(g). Section 6045A(c) provides that, unless the Secretary provides otherwise, the statement required by this rule must be furnished to the receiving broker not later than fifteen days after the transfer of the covered security.

a. *Transfer reporting generally*

The proposed regulations create a presumption that every transfer of custody effected by an applicable person to a broker or other professional custodian of any share of stock in a corporation on or after January 1, 2011, that is not a sale is a transfer of a covered security subject to reporting. Thus, the proposed regulations provide that a transfer statement must be furnished for every such transfer. This duty applies even if the security transferred is a noncovered security or is treated as a noncovered security because it was excepted from all reporting under section 6045 (for example, because the customer was an exempt recipient) at the time of its acquisition. In either situation, the transfer statement is not required to include any other required information provided that the transfer statement indicates that the security transferred is a noncovered security. This presumption that all transferred securities are covered securities and the requirement to provide a transfer statement for noncovered or excepted securities solely for the purpose of establishing that the security is a noncovered or excepted security will reduce uncertainty for receiving brokers and custodians. The person initiating the transfer of custody is permitted, but not required, to provide other information about the noncovered or excepted security.

The proposed regulations place the duty to furnish the transfer statement on the person effecting the transfer of custody if the person is an applicable person. Under the proposed regulations, an *applicable person* is a broker within the meaning of § 1.6045-1(a)(1), any person that acts as a custodian of securities in the ordinary course of a trade or business, any issuer of securities, and any agent of these persons. An applicable person does not include the beneficial owner of the securities, any governmental unit or agency or instrumentality of a governmental unit with respect to escheated securities, or any person that acts solely as a clearing house for the transfer.

Under the proposed regulations, an applicable person has a duty to furnish a transfer statement if that person effects the transfer of custody of the securities. For securities held by direct registration with the issuer, including certificated shares, the person effecting the transfer is the issuer or its transfer agent. For securities held in street name, the person effecting the transfer is the broker or other firm carrying the securities.

Although the person responsible for providing a transfer statement will often be a broker or other applicable person that effects sales, the proposed regulations also impose this duty on issuers, transfer agents, professional custodians, and other applicable persons that may not effect sales. For these applicable persons, this duty is limited to a duty to receive the statement when receiving custody of transferred securities and then to retransmit the information on the statement when transferring custody of those securities to a broker (or, if no statement is received, to furnish a statement that the securities are noncovered securities). The proposed regulations regarding transfer statements do not impose a duty on those that do not effect sales to update basis in response to adjustments announced by issuers under section 6045B or to compute basis by average cost under section 1012. These computations apply only to basis reporting at the time of sale under section 6045 and, thus, apply only to brokers effecting sales. The Treasury Department and IRS request further comments regarding the scope of the transfer statement requirement.

Because the transfer statement is not filed with the IRS, no official form or format will be required. Instead, the proposed regulations specify the information required on the statement. At the request of commentators, the proposed regulations permit flexibility in the format and method by which the information is furnished pursuant to agreement of the parties. The Treasury Department and IRS request further comments about the form and format for the transfer statement and any substitutes thereto.

Under the proposed regulations, the transfer statement must identify the applicable person furnishing the statement, the broker receiving the statement, the owner or owners transferring the securities, and, if different, the owner or owners of the securities after any transfer other than a sale, such as a transfer of gifted or inherited securities. The transfer statement must also identify the securities being transferred and information about the transfer such as the date the transfer was initiated and the settlement date of the transfer (if known when reporting).

Under the proposed regulations, a transfer statement must include the total adjusted basis of the securities, the original date of acquisition, and the date for determining whether any gain or loss with respect to the security would be long-term or short-term at the time of sale. The transfer statement must also indicate the extent to which the reported basis amount has been adjusted to reflect any corporate actions that affect the basis of the security by reporting the number from the issuer statement required under section 6045B (discussed later in this preamble) of the most recent corporate action that is reflected on the transfer statement. Additionally, if the average basis method is used to determine basis, the proposed regulations permit reporting an original acquisition date of "VARIOUS" for securities owned at least five years.

Commentators suggested that additional information items be required on the statement such as the original purchase amount, the reason why the securities are (or are treated as) noncovered securities (if applicable), and the basis method used by the taxpayer immediately prior to the transfer. The proposed regulations do not require this additional information on the statement because the proposed regulations do not require this information to be reported on Form 1099-B. Additional information may be communicated with the statement, even if not required.

If an applicable person furnishing a transfer statement later receives a statement for an earlier transfer that reports that the transferred securities are covered securities and includes information inconsistent with the subsequent transfer statement, the proposed regulations require that a corrected statement be furnished to correct the inconsistent information within fifteen days following the receipt of the prior transfer statement.

b. *Reporting required in connection with transfers of gifted and inherited securities*

Under section 6045(g)(3)(A)(ii), a covered security includes stock or indebtedness acquired on or after the applicable date if the security is transferred from an account in which the security was a covered security (but only if the receiving broker or other professional custodian receives a transfer statement). Therefore, under the proposed regulations, gifted and inherited securities that were covered securities in the account of the donor or decedent remain covered securities when transferred to the recipient's account and accompanied by a transfer statement.

Under the proposed regulations, when covered securities are transferred from a decedent, the transfer statement must indicate that the securities are inherited. The transfer statement must also report the date of death as the acquisition date and must report adjusted basis in accordance with the instructions and valuations provided by an authorized representative of the estate. The proposed regulations require that the selling broker take these basis adjustments into account in reporting adjusted basis upon the subsequent sale or other disposition of these securities.

When covered securities are transferred to a different owner as a gift, the proposed regulations require the statement to indicate that the transfer consists of gifted securities and to state the adjusted basis of the securities in the hands of the donor and the donor's original acquisition date of the securities. The transfer statement must also report the date of the gift (if known when furnishing the statement) and the fair market value of the gift on that date (if known or readily ascertainable). Upon the subsequent sale or other disposition of these securities, the selling broker must apply the relevant basis rules for gifts when reporting adjusted basis.

Commentators opposed subjecting transfers of gifted and inherited securities to the requirements of transfer reporting because the substantive rules governing basis computation for these securities are complex. The proposed rules do not exclude transfers of gifted and inherited securities, however, because these transfers fall within the plain language of the statute. The proposed regulations provide workable rules to minimize complexity.

Issuers and transfer agents commented that they often do not know the reason for the transfer of shares from one owner to another. The proposed regulations provide that, if the request to transfer ownership between different people is silent as to the reason for the transfer, the transfer should generally be treated as a gift.

Commentators expressed concern regarding gifted and inherited securities about the potential burden to value privately traded securities or other securities for which fair market value is not easily determined. For inherited securities, the proposed regulations allow the applicable person effecting the transfer to rely on the authorized estate representative to provide the instructions and valuations necessary to report correct basis for any transferred securities. If the applicable person effecting the transfer does not receive instructions and valuations from the authorized estate representative, the applicable person must request this information from the authorized estate representative before preparing the transfer statement. If this information is not provided before the transfer statement is prepared, then the transfer statement must indicate that the transfer consists of an inherited security but must report the security as a noncovered security. If this information is provided after the transfer statement is sent, the applicable person effecting the transfer must send a corrected transfer statement.

For gifted securities, the proposed regulations only require the applicable person effecting the gift transfer to report the date of the gift if known at the time the transfer statement is prepared and the fair market value of the securities on the date of the gift if known or readily ascertainable at that time. However, the proposed regulations provide that, if the gifted securities are subsequently transferred to a different account of the same owner, the applicable person must include the date of the gift on the subsequent transfer statement and, if known or readily ascertainable at the time the subsequent transfer statement is prepared, the fair market value of the securities as of the date of the gift. The proposed regulations provide a special reporting rule for brokers that applies on the sale of a gifted security when the security's adjusted basis depends upon its fair market value as of the date of the gift but the transfer statement received by the selling broker does not report this amount and this amount is not readily ascertainable by the broker. Under these circumstances, the proposed regulations provide that the broker must report adjusted basis equal to the gross proceeds from the sale.

c. *Reporting required in connection with transfers of borrowed securities*

To facilitate the correct reporting of short sales involving transfers of borrowed securities, the proposed regulations require the transfer statement to indicate that the transferred securities are borrowed and provide instructions on how the receiving broker can provide information to the applicable person effecting the transfer about any short position potentially being closed by the transfer or other sale of the securities. This information is required to alert the receiving broker that, if the transferred securities are used to satisfy a short sale obligation, the short sale remains open and should not be reported as closed to the IRS or to the customer.

16. *Reporting by Issuers of Actions Affecting Basis of Securities*

If an organizational action (such as a stock split or a merger or acquisition) by an issuer affects the basis of a specified security, new section 6045B requires the issuer to file a return with the IRS and furnish to each nominee (or to each certificate holder if there is no nominee) a written statement regarding the action. The return filing and information statement requirements may be waived under section 6045B(e) if the issuer makes the information about the action publicly available, in the form and manner determined by the Secretary.

The proposed regulations require a reporting issuer to identify itself and the security on the return and provide information about the organizational action and the quantitative effect on the basis resulting from the action. The proposed regulations also require the issuer to assign and report a sequential number determined separately by security for each information report the issuer files.

The proposed regulations require a domestic or foreign issuer to furnish a written statement to each holder of record that is not an exempt recipient as defined in § 1.6045B-1(b)(5) as of the record date of the corporate action and all subsequent holders of record through the date the issuer furnishes the statement. The Treasury Department and IRS request comments as to the extent to which foreign issuers will be able to comply with such a reporting requirement, and whether it may be appropriate to limit foreign issuers' reporting requirements (such as, for example, limiting foreign issuers' reporting requirements to securities that are traded on a securities exchange in the United States).

If the security is held in the name of someone other than the holder of record on the books of the issuer, the proposed regulations require the issuer to furnish the statement to the nominee listed on its books unless such nominee is the issuer or the issuer's agent. For example, an issuer must furnish statements to the participants of the issuer's direct stock purchase plan even if the plan is listed as a nominee for the participants. The proposed regulations permit an issuer to furnish to its holders and nominees a copy of the return that it files with the IRS.

The proposed regulations provide that both the return filing and information statement requirements under section 6045B are waived if an issuer posts a statement with the required information in a readily accessible format in an area of its primary public website dedicated to this purpose by the same due date for reporting the organizational action to the IRS and keeps the form accessible to the public. Under the proposed regulations, this public reporting relieves the issuer of its duty both to file the return with the IRS and to furnish the statement to its nominees and certificate holders.

Commentators have questioned how issuers could report the effect on basis within 45 days of a corporate action when the effect may not be determinable until the conclusion of other events such as the end of the issuer's fiscal year. Any request to extend the due date was not adopted as inconsistent with the 45-day statutory due date. The proposed regulations provide that an issuer may make reasonable assumptions about facts that cannot be determined prior to this due date and must file a corrected return once the facts are determined if necessary to report the correct quantitative effect on basis. Under the proposed regulations, it is expected that an issuer will treat a payment that may be a dividend consistently with its treatment of the payment under section 6042(b)(3) and § 1.6042-3(c).

Some commentators suggested that the IRS establish a central repository on its website for posting information statements from issuers that wish to report publicly in lieu of filing returns. This suggestion was not adopted in the proposed regulations due to IRS resource and system constraints. The Treasury Department and IRS request comments on the definition of public reporting including rules about retaining the returns on the website and alternatives other than the use of a central repository.

Commentators requested that the proposed regulations except actions by S corporations from reporting under section 6045B because adjustments are specific to the shareholder and are reported on Schedule K-1 (Form 1120S), "Shareholder's Share of Income, Deductions, Credits, etc." The proposed regulations do not except reporting by S corporations, but deem an S corporation to satisfy the requirements under section 6045B if it reports the effect of the organizational action on the proper Schedule K-1 for each shareholder, timely files the schedules with the IRS, and timely furnishes the schedules to all proper parties.

17. *Penalty Provisions*

The current regulations impose penalties on brokers for failing to file or furnish complete and correct returns and statements after the sale of a security. The proposed regulations expand the list of required statements and returns filed with the IRS in § 301.6721-1 and the list of required statements furnished to payees in § 301.6722-1 to include the new penalties associated with the new transfer statements and issuer statements. The proposed regulations also update the full list of returns and statements included in section 6724(d).

Commentators expressed concern that the IRS would assert penalties against a broker for reporting an incorrect adjusted basis or incorrectly reporting whether any gain or loss on a sale is long-term or short-term after relying on incorrect information provided by others. Under the proposed regulations, brokers generally must adjust basis reported for covered securities to reflect: (1) information received on any transfer statement under section 6045A; and (2) information reported by the issuer under section 6045B regarding the effect on basis of any organizational actions. The proposed regulations provide that any failure to report correct information that arises solely from this reliance is deemed to be due to reasonable cause with respect to the penalties under sections 6721 and 6722.

The proposed regulations permit, but do not require, a broker to adjust the reported basis in accordance with information that is not reflected on a transfer statement or issuer statement, including any information the broker has about securities held by the same customer in other accounts with the broker. The proposed regulations deem that a broker that takes into account information received from a customer or third party other than information reflected on a transfer statement or issuer statement relies upon such information in good faith in accordance with existing rules found in § 301.6724-1(c)(6) if the broker neither knows nor has reason to know that the information is incorrect.

Proposed Effective and Applicability Dates

These regulations are proposed to take effect when published in the **Federal Register** as final regulations except as follows. The regulations regarding reporting basis and whether any gain or loss on a sale is long-term or short-term under section 6045(g) are proposed to apply to: (1) any share of stock other than RIC stock or DRP stock acquired on or after January 1, 2011; and (2) any share of RIC stock or DRP stock acquired on or after January 1, 2012. The regulations regarding the determination of basis under section 1012 are proposed to apply for taxable years beginning after the date the regulations are published as final regulations in the **Federal Register**. However, the rules in § 1.1012-1(e)(1)(i), in part, apply to stock acquired on or after January 1, 2011, the rules in § 1.1012-1(e)(2) and (e)(9), in part, apply to stock acquired on or after January 1, 2012, and the rules in § 1.1012-1(e)(7)(i), in part, and in § 1.1012-1(e)(10), in part, apply to sales, exchanges, or other dispositions of stock on or after January 1, 2012.

The regulations regarding transfer statement reporting under section 6045A are proposed to apply to: (1) transfers of stock other than RIC stock or DRP stock that occur on or after January 1, 2011; and (2) transfers of RIC stock or DRP stock that occur on or after January 1, 2012. The regulations regarding issuer reporting under section 6045B are proposed to apply to: (1) organizational actions affecting basis of stock other than RIC stock that occur on or after January 1, 2011; and (2) organizational actions affecting basis of RIC stock that occur on or after January 1, 2012. The regulations regarding the timing for reporting short sales of securities under section 6045 and for collecting backup withholding in connection with short sales under section 3406 are proposed to apply to short sales opened on or after the date the final regulations are published in the **Federal Register** but no earlier than January 1, 2010.

Effect on Other Documents

Rev. Rul. 67-436 will be obsoleted as of the date these regulations are published as final regulations in the **Federal Register**.

Special Analyses

It has been determined that this notice of proposed rulemaking is not a significant regulatory action as defined in Executive Order 12866. Therefore, a regulatory assessment is not required. It also has been determined that section 553(b) of the Administrative Procedure Act (5 U.S.C. chapter 5) does not apply to this regulation.

Pursuant to the Regulatory Flexibility Act (5 U.S.C. chapter 6), it is hereby certified that this regulation will not have a significant economic impact on a substantial number of small entities, because any effect on small entities by the rules proposed in this document flows directly from section 403 of the Energy Improvement and Extension Act of 2008, Division B of Public Law 110-343 (122 Stat. 3765, 3854 (2008)).

Section 403(a) of the Act modifies section 6045 to require that brokers report the adjusted basis of the securities and whether any gain or loss with respect to the securities is long-term or short-term when reporting the sale of a covered security. It is anticipated that this statutory requirement will fall only on financial services firms with annual receipts greater than $7 million and, therefore, on no small entities. Further, in implementing the statutory requirement, the regulation proposes to limit reporting to the information described in the Act: adjusted basis and whether any gain or loss with respect to the securities is long-term or short-term.

Section 403(c) of the Act adds new section 6045A, which requires applicable persons to furnish a transfer statement in connection with the transfer of custody of a covered security. In implementing this statutory requirement, the regulation proposes to define applicable person to include brokers, professional custodians of securities, and issuers of securities. This definition effectuates the Act by giving the broker who receives the transfer statement the information necessary to determine and report adjusted basis and whether any gain or loss with respect to the security is long-term or short-term as required by section 6045 when the security is subsequently sold. Consequently, the regulation does not add to the impact on small entities imposed by the statutory scheme. Instead, it limits reporting to only these necessary entities. It also limits the information to be reported to only those items necessary to effectuate the statutory scheme.

Section 403(d) of the Act adds new section 6045B, which requires issuer reporting by all issuers of specified securities regardless of size and even when the securities are not publicly traded. In implementing this statutory requirement, the regulation proposes to limit reporting to those items necessary to meet the Act's requirements. Additionally, the regulation proposes to mitigate the burden imposed by the Act by providing rules to permit issuers to report each action publicly as permitted by the Act instead of filing a return and furnishing each nominee or holder a statement about the action. The regulation therefore does not add to the statutory impact on small entities but instead eases this impact to the extent the statute permits.

Therefore, because this regulation will not have a significant economic impact on a substantial number of small entities, a regulatory flexibility analysis is not required. The Treasury Department and IRS request comments on the accuracy of this statement. Pursuant to section 7805(f) of the Code, this regulation has been submitted to the Chief Counsel for Advocacy of the Small Business Administration for comment on its impact on small business.

Comments and Public Hearing

Before these proposed regulations are adopted as final regulations, consideration will be given to any written (a signed original and eight (8) copies) or electronic comments that are timely submitted to the IRS. The Treasury Department and IRS request comments on the clarity of the proposed regulations and how they can be made easier to understand. All comments will be available for public inspection and copying.

A public hearing has been scheduled for February 17, 2010, beginning at 10 a.m., in the auditorium of the IRS New Carrollton Federal Building, 5000Ellin Road, Lanham, Maryland 20706. All visitors must present photo identification to enter the building. Because of access restrictions, visitors will not be admitted beyond the immediate entrance area more than 30 minutes before the hearing starts. For information about having your name placed on the building access list to attend the hearing, see the "FOR FURTHER INFORMATION CONTACT" section of this preamble.

The rules of 26 CFR 601.601(a)(3) apply to the hearing. Persons who wish to present oral comments at the hearing must submit written or electronic comments by February 8, 2010 and an outline of the topics to be discussed and the time to be devoted to each topic (a signed original and eight (8) copies) by February 8, 2010. A period of ten minutes will be allotted to each person for making comments. An agenda showing the scheduling of speakers will be prepared after the deadline for receiving outlines has passed. Copies of the agenda will be available free of charge at the hearing.

Drafting Information

The principal authors of these proposed regulations are Edward C. Schwartz, Amy J. Pfalzgraf, and William L. Candler, Office of Associate Chief Counsel (Income Tax and Accounting), and Stephen Schaeffer, Office of Associate Chief Counsel (Procedure and Administration). However, other personnel from the IRS and the Treasury Department participated in their development.

[¶49,450] Proposed Amendments of Regulations (REG-151605-09), published in the Federal Register on June 23, 2010.

[Code Sec. 1502]

Consolidated returns: Net operating loss: Extended carryback period.—Amendments of Reg. §1.1502-21, providing guidance to consolidated groups that implements the revisions to section 172(b)(1)(H), are proposed.

AGENCY: Internal Revenue Service (IRS), Treasury.

ACTION: Notice of proposed rulemaking by cross-reference to temporary regulations.

SUMMARY: In the Rules and Regulations section of this issue of the **Federal Register**, the IRS is issuing temporary regulations that provides guidance to consolidated groups that implements the revisions to section 172(b)(1)(H). The text of those regulations also serves as the text of these proposed regulations.

DATES: Written or electronic comments and a request for a public hearing must be received by September 21, 2010.

ADDRESSES: Send submissions to: CC:PA:LPD:PR (REG-151605-09), Room 5203, Internal Revenue Service, P.O. Box 7604, Ben Franklin Station, Washington, DC 20044. Submissions may be hand-delivered Monday through Friday between the hours of 8 a.m. and 4 p.m. to CC:PA:LPD:PR (REG-151605- 09), Courier's Desk, Internal Revenue Service, 1111 Constitution Avenue NW, Washington, DC, or sent electronically via the Federal eRulemaking Portal at *http://www.regulations.gov* (IRS REG-151605-09).

FOR FURTHER INFORMATION CONTACT: Concerning the proposed regulations, Grid Glyer, (202) 622-7930, concerning submissions of comments, Regina Johnson (202) 622-7180 (not toll-free numbers).

SUPPLEMENTARY INFORMATION:

Paperwork Reduction Act

The collection of information contained in this notice of proposed rulemaking has been submitted to the Office of Management and Budget for review in accordance with the Paperwork Reduction Act of 1995 (44 U.S.C. 3507(d) under control number 1545-2171). Comments on the collection of information should be sent to the **Office of Management and Budget**, Attn: Desk Officer for the Department of the Treasury, Office of Information and Regulatory Affairs, Washington, D.C. 20503, with copies to the **Internal Revenue Service**, Attn: IRS Reports Clearance Officer, SE:W:CAR:MP:T:T:SP, Washington, D.C. 20224. Comments on the collection of information should be received by August 23, 2010. Comments are specifically requested concerning:

Whether the proposed collection of information is necessary for the proper performance of the functions of the **Internal Revenue Service**, including whether the information will have practical utility;

The accuracy of the estimated burden associated with the proposed collection of information;

How the quality, utility and clarity of the information to be collected may be enhanced;

How the burden of complying with the proposed collection of information may be minimized, including through the application of automated collection techniques or other forms of information technology; and

Estimates of capital or start-up costs and costs of operation, maintenance and purchase of service to provide information.

The collection of information in these proposed regulations is in §§1.1502-21(b)(3)(ii)(C)(2) and 1.1502-21(b)(3)(ii)(C)(*3*).

The proposed regulations provide guidance to consolidated groups that implements the revisions to section 172(b)(1)(H).

The collection of information is required in order to obtain a benefit. The likely respondents are corporations that are members of consolidated groups.

Estimated total annual reporting burden: 1,000 hours.

Estimated average annual burden hours per respondent: 0.25 hours.

Estimated number of respondents: 4,000.

Estimated frequency of responses: Once.

An agency may not conduct or sponsor, and a person is not required to respond to, a collection of information unless it displays a valid control number assigned by the Office of Management and Budget.

Books or records relating to a collection of information must be retained as long as their contents may become material in the administration of any internal revenue law. Generally, tax returns and tax return information are confidential, as required by 26 U.S.C. 6103.

Background and Explanation of Provisions

Temporary regulations in the Rules and Regulations section of this issue of the **Federal Register** amend 26 CFR Part 1 to revise §1.1502-21T. The text of those temporary regulations also serves as the text of these proposed regulations. The preamble to the temporary regulations explains the amendments.

Special Analyses

It has been determined that this notice of proposed rulemaking is not a significant regulatory action as defined in Executive Order 12866. Therefore, a regulatory assessment is not required. With respect to the proposed regulation, §1.1502-21, it is hereby certified that this provision will not have a significant economic impact on a substantial number of small entities. This certification is based on the fact that these regulations primarily affect large corporations that are members of consolidated groups and will provide a benefit if the election is made. Therefore, a regulatory flexibility analysis is not required. Pursuant to section 7805(f) of the Internal Revenue Code, these regulations have been submitted to the Chief Counsel for Advocacy of the Small Business Administration for comment on their impact on small business.

Comments and Requests for a Public Hearing

Before these proposed regulations are adopted as final regulations, consideration will be given to any written comments (a signed original and eight (8) copies) or electronic comments that are submitted timely to the IRS. All comments will be available for public inspection and copying. A public hearing may be scheduled if requested in writing by any person that timely submits written comments. If a public hearing is scheduled, notice of the date, time, and place for the public hearing will be published in the **Federal Register**.

Drafting Information

The principal author of these regulations is Grid Glyer of the Office of Associate Chief Counsel (Corporate). Other personnel from the Treasury Department and the IRS participated in their development.

[¶49,462] Proposed Amendments of Regulations (REG-119921-09), published in the Federal Register on September 14, 2010.

[Code Secs. 6011, 6071 and 7701]

Series limited liability companies: Cell companies: Entity classification.—Reg. §§301.6011-6 and 301.6071-2, and amendments of Reg. §301.7701-1, regarding the classification for Federal tax purposes of a series of a domestic series limited liability company (LLC), a cell of a domestic cell company, or a foreign series or cell that conducts an insurance business, are proposed.

AGENCY: Internal Revenue Service (IRS), Treasury.

ACTION: Notice of proposed rulemaking.

SUMMARY: This document contains proposed regulations regarding the classification for Federal tax purposes of a series of a domestic series limited liability company (LLC), a cell of a domestic cell company, or a foreign series or cell that conducts an insurance business. The proposed regulations provide that, whether or not a series of a domestic series LLC, a cell of a domestic cell company, or a foreign series or cell that conducts an insurance business is a juridical person for local law purposes, for Federal tax purposes it is treated as an entity formed under local law. Classification of a series or cell that is treated as a separate entity for Federal tax purposes generally is determined under the same rules that govern the classification of other types of separate entities. The proposed regulations provide examples illustrating the application of the rule. The proposed regulations will affect domestic series LLCs; domestic cell companies; foreign series, or cells that conduct insurance businesses; and their owners.

DATES: Written or electronic comments and requests for a public hearing must be received by December 13, 2010.

ADDRESSES: Send submissions to: CC:PA:LPD:PR (REG-119921-09), Room 5203, Internal Revenue Service, PO Box 7604, Ben Franklin Station, Washington, DC 20044. Submissions may be hand-delivered Monday through Friday between the hours of 8 a.m. and 4 p.m. to CC:PA:LPD:PR (REG-119921-09), Courier's Desk, Internal Revenue Service, 1111 Constitution Avenue, NW, Washington, DC, or sent electronically, via the Federal eRulemaking portal at *www.regulations.gov* (IRS REG-119921-09).

FOR FURTHER INFORMATION CONTACT: Concerning the proposed regulations, Joy Spies, (202) 622-3050; concerning submissions of comments, Oluwafunmilayo (Funmi) Taylor, (202) 622-7180 (not toll-free numbers).

SUPPLEMENTARY INFORMATION:

Background

1. *Introduction*

A number of states have enacted statutes providing for the creation of entities that may establish series, including limited liability companies (series LLCs). In general, series LLC statutes provide that a limited liability company may establish separate series. Although series of a series LLC generally are not treated as separate entities for state law purposes and, thus, cannot have members, each series has "associated" with it specified members, assets, rights, obligations, and investment objectives or business purposes. Members' association with one or more particular series is comparable to direct ownership by the members in such series, in that their rights, duties, and powers with respect to the series are direct and specifically identified. If the conditions enumerated in the relevant statute are satisfied, the debts, liabilities, and obligations of one series generally are enforceable only against the assets of that series and not against assets of other series or of the series LLC.

Certain jurisdictions have enacted statutes providing for entities similar to the series LLC. For example, certain statutes provide for the chartering of a legal entity (or the establishment of cells) under a structure commonly known as a protected cell company, segregated account company or segregated portfolio company (cell company). A cell company may establish multiple accounts, or cells, each of which has its own name and is identified with a specific participant, but generally is not treated under local law as a legal entity distinct from the cell company. The assets of each cell are statutorily protected from the creditors of any other cell and from the creditors of the cell company.

Under current law, there is little specific guidance regarding whether for Federal tax purposes a series (or cell) is treated as an entity separate from other series or the series LLC (or other cells or the cell company, as the case may be), or whether the company and all of its series (or cells) should be treated as a single entity.

Notice 2008-19 (2008-5 IRB 366) requested comments on proposed guidance concerning issues that arise if arrangements entered into by a cell constitute insurance for Federal income tax purposes. The notice also requested comments on the need for guidance concerning similar segregated arrangements that do not involve insurance. The IRS received a number of comments requesting guidance for similar arrangements not involving insurance, including series LLCs and cell companies. These comments generally recommended that series and cells should be treated as separate entities for Federal tax purposes if they are established under a statute with provisions similar to the series LLC statutes currently in effect in several states. The IRS and Treasury Department generally agree with these comments. See § 601.601(d)(2)(ii)(*b*).

2. *Entity Classification for Federal Tax Purposes*

A. *Regulatory framework*

Sections 301.7701-1 through 301.7701-4 of the Procedure and Administration Regulations provide the framework for determining an organization's entity classification for Federal tax purposes. Classification of an organization depends on whether the organization is treated as: (i) a separate entity under § 301.7701-1, (ii) a "business entity" within the meaning of § 301.7701-2(a) or a trust under § 301.7701-4, and (iii) an "eligible entity" under § 301.7701-3.

Section 301.7701-1(a)(1) provides that the determination of whether an entity is separate from its owners for Federal tax purposes is a matter of Federal tax law and does not depend on whether the organization is recognized as an entity under local law. Section 301.7701-1(a)(2) provides that a joint venture or other contractual arrangement may create a separate entity for Federal tax purposes if the participants carry on a trade, business, financial operation, or venture and divide the profits therefrom. However, a joint undertaking merely to share expenses does not create a separate entity for Federal tax purposes, nor does mere co-ownership of property where activities are limited to keeping property maintained, in repair, and rented or leased. *Id.*

Section 301.7701-1(b) provides that the tax classification of an organization recognized as a separate entity for tax purposes generally is determined under § § 301.7701-2, 301.7701-3, and 301.7701-4. Thus, for example, an organization recognized as an entity that does not have associates or an objective to carry on a business may be classified as a trust under § 301.7701-4.

Section 301.7701-2(a) provides that a business entity is any entity recognized for Federal tax purposes (including an entity with a single owner that may be disregarded as an entity separate from its owner under § 301.7701-3) that is not properly classified as a trust or otherwise subject to special treatment under the Internal Revenue Code (Code). A business entity with two or more members is classified for Federal tax purposes as a corporation or a partnership. See § 301.7701-2(a). A business entity with one owner is classified as a corporation or is disregarded. See § 301.7701-2(a). If the entity is disregarded, its activities are treated in the same manner as a sole proprietorship, branch, or division of the owner. However, § 301.7701-2(c)(2)(iv) and (v) provides for an otherwise disregarded entity to be treated as a corporation for certain Federal employment tax and excise tax purposes.

Section 301.7701-3(a) generally provides that an eligible entity, which is a business entity that is not a corporation under § 301.7701-2(b), may elect its classification for Federal tax purposes.

B. *Separate entity classification*

The threshold question for determining the tax classification of a series of a series LLC or a cell of a cell company is whether an individual series or cell should be considered an entity for Federal tax purposes. The determination of whether an organization is an entity separate from its owners for Federal tax purposes is a matter of Federal tax law and does not depend on whether the organization is recognized as an entity under local law. Section 301.7701-1(a)(1). In *Moline Properties, Inc. v. Commissioner*, 319 U.S. 436 (1943), the Supreme Court noted that, so long as a corporation was formed for a purpose that is the equivalent of business activity or the corporation actually carries on a business, the corporation remains a taxable entity separate from its shareholders. Although entities that are recognized under local law generally are also recognized for Federal tax purposes, a state law entity may be disregarded if it lacks business purpose or any business activity other than tax avoidance. See *Bertoli v. Commissioner*, 103 T.C. 501 (1994); *Aldon Homes, Inc. v. Commissioner*, 33 T.C. 582 (1959).

The Supreme Court in *Commissioner v. Culbertson*, 337 U.S. 733 (1949), and *Commissioner v. Tower*, 327 U.S. 280 (1946), set forth the basic standard for determining whether a partnership will be respected for Federal tax purposes. In general, a partnership will be respected if, considering all the facts, the parties in good faith and acting with a business purpose intended to join together to conduct an enterprise and share in its profits and losses. This determination is made considering not only the stated intent of the parties, but also the terms of their agreement and their conduct. *Madison Gas & Elec. Co. v. Commissioner*, 633 F.2d 512, 514 (7th Cir. 1980); *Luna v. Commissioner*, 42 T.C. 1067, 1077-78 (1964).

Conversely, under certain circumstances, arrangements that are not recognized as entities under state law may be treated as separate entities for Federal tax purposes. Section 301.7701-1(a)(2). For example, courts have found entities for tax purposes in some co-ownership situations where the co-owners agree to restrict their ability to sell, lease or encumber their interests, waive their rights to partition property, or allow certain management decisions to be made other than by unanimous agreement among co-owners. *Bergford v. Commissioner*, 12 F.3d 166 (9th Cir. 1993); *Bussing v. Commissioner*, 89 T.C. 1050 (1987); *Alhouse v. Commissioner*, T.C. Memo. 1991-652. However, the Internal Revenue Service (IRS) has ruled that a co-ownership does not rise to the level of an entity for Federal tax purposes if the owner employs an agent whose activities are limited to collecting rents, paying property taxes, insurance premiums, repair and maintenance expenses, and providing tenants with customary services. Rev. Rul. 75-374 (1975-2 CB 261). See also Rev. Rul. 79-77 (1979-1 CB 448), (see § 601.601(d)(2)(ii)(*b*)).

Rev. Proc. 2002-22 (2002-1 CB 733), (see § 601.601(d)(2)(ii)(*b*)), specifies the conditions under which the IRS will consider a request for a private letter ruling that an undivided fractional interest in rental real property is not an interest in a business entity under § 301.7701-2(a). A number of factors must be present to obtain a ruling under the revenue procedure, including a limit on the number of co-owners, a requirement that the co-owners not treat the co-ownership as an entity (that is, that the co-ownership may not file a partnership or corporate tax return, conduct business under a common name, execute an agreement identifying any or all of the co-owners as partners, shareholders, or members of a business entity, or otherwise hold itself out as a partnership or other form of business entity), and a requirement that certain rights with respect to the property (including the power to make certain management decisions) must be retained by co-owners. The revenue procedure provides that an organization that is an entity for state law purposes may not be characterized as a co-ownership under the guidance in the revenue procedure.

The courts and the IRS have addressed the Federal tax classification of investment trusts with assets divided among a number of series. In *National Securities Series-Industrial Stocks Series v. Commissioner*, 13 T.C. 884 (1949), *acq.*, 1950-1 CB 4, several series that differed only in the nature of their assets were created within a statutory open-end investment trust. Each series regularly issued certificates representing shares in the property held in trust and regularly redeemed the certificates solely from the assets and earnings of the individual series. The Tax Court stated that each series of the trust was taxable as a separate regulated investment company. See also Rev. Rul. 55-416 (1955-1 CB 416), (see § 601.601(d)(2)(ii)(*b*)). But see *Union Trusteed Funds v. Commissioner*, 8 T.C. 1133 (1947), (series funds organized by a state law corporation could not be treated as if each fund were a separate corporation).

In 1986, Congress added section 851(g) to the Code. Section 851(g) contains a special rule for series funds and provides that, in the case of a regulated investment company (within the meaning of section 851(a)) with more than one fund, each fund generally is treated as a separate corporation. For these purposes, a fund is a segregated portfolio of assets the beneficial interests in which are owned by holders of interests in the regulated investment company that are preferred over other classes or series with respect to these assets.

C. *Insurance company classification*

Section 7701(a)(3) and § 301.7701-2(b)(4) provide that an arrangement that qualifies as an insurance company is a corporation for Federal income tax purposes. Sections 816(a) and 831(c) define an insurance company as any company more than half the business of which during the taxable year is the issuing of insurance or annuity contracts or the reinsuring of risks underwritten by insurance companies. See also § 1.801-3(a)(1), ("[T]hough its name, charter powers, and subjection to State insurance laws are significant in determining the business which a company is authorized and intends to carry on, it is the character of the business actually done in the taxable year which determines whether a company is taxable as an insurance company under the Internal Revenue Code."). Thus, an insurance company includes an arrangement that conducts insurance business, whether or not the arrangement is a state law entity.

3. *Overview of Series LLC Statutes and Cell Company Statutes*

A. *Domestic statutes*

Although § 301.7701-1(a)(1) provides that state classification of an entity is not controlling for Federal tax purposes, the characteristics of series LLCs and cell companies under their governing statutes are an important factor in analyzing whether series and cells generally should be treated as separate entities for Federal tax purposes.

Series LLC statutes have been enacted in Delaware, Illinois, Iowa, Nevada, Oklahoma, Tennessee, Texas, Utah and Puerto Rico. Delaware enacted the first series LLC statute in 1996. Del. Code Ann. Tit. 6, section 18-215 (the Delaware statute). Statutes enacted subsequently by other states are similar, but not identical, to the Delaware statute. All of the statutes provide a significant degree of separateness for individual series within a series LLC, but none provides series with all of the attributes of a typical state law entity, such as an ordinary limited liability company. Individual series generally are not treated as separate entities for state law purposes. However, in certain states (currently Illinois and Iowa), a series is treated as a separate entity to the extent provided in the series LLC's articles of organization.

The Delaware statute provides that a limited liability company may establish, or provide for the establishment of, one or more designated series of members, managers, LLC interests or assets. Under the Delaware statute, any such series may have separate rights, powers, or duties with respect to specified property or obligations of the LLC or profits and losses associated with specified property or obligations, and any such series may have a separate business purpose or investment objective. Additionally, the Delaware statute provides that the debts, liabilities, obligations, and expenses of a particular series are enforceable against the assets of that series only, and not against the assets of the series LLC generally or any other series of the LLC, and, unless the LLC agreement provides otherwise, none of the debts, liabilities, obligations, and expenses of the series LLC generally or of any other series of the series LLC are enforceable against the assets of the series, provided that the following requirements are met: (1) the LLC agreement establishes or provides for the establishment of one or more series; (2) records maintained for any such series account for the assets of the series separately from the other assets of the series LLC, or of any other series of the series LLC; (3) the LLC agreement so provides; and (4) notice of the limitation on liabilities of a series is set forth in the series LLC's certificate of formation.

Unless otherwise provided in the LLC agreement, a series established under Delaware law has the power and capacity to, in its own name, contract, hold title to assets, grant liens and security interests, and sue and be sued. A series may be managed by the members of the series or by a manager. Any event that causes a manager to cease to be a manager with respect to a series will not, in itself, cause the manager to cease to be a manager of the LLC or of any other series of the LLC.

Under the Delaware statute, unless the LLC agreement provides otherwise, any event that causes a member to cease to be associated with a series will not, in itself, cause the member to cease to be associated with any other series or with the LLC, or cause termination of the series, even if there are no remaining members of the series. Additionally, the Delaware statute allows a series to be terminated and its affairs wound up without causing the dissolution of the LLC. However, all series of the LLC terminate when the LLC dissolves. Finally, under the Delaware statute, a series generally may not make a distribution to the extent that the distribution will cause the liabilities of the series to exceed the fair market value of the series' assets.

The series LLC statutes of Illinois, 805 ILCS 180/37-40 (the Illinois statute), and Iowa, I.C.A. § 489.1201 (the Iowa statute) provide that a series with limited liability will be treated as a separate entity to the extent set forth in the articles of organization. The Illinois statute provides that the LLC and any of its series may elect to consolidate their operations as a single taxpayer to the extent permitted under applicable law, elect to work cooperatively, elect to contract jointly, or elect to be treated as a single business for purposes of qualification to do business in Illinois or any other state.

In addition, under the Illinois statute, a series' existence begins upon filing of a certificate of designation with the Illinois secretary of state. A certificate of designation must be filed for each series that is to have limited liability. The name of a series with limited liability must contain the entire name of the LLC and be distinguishable from the names of the other series of the LLC. If different from the LLC, the certificate of designation for each series must list the names of the members if the series is member-managed or the names of the managers if the series is manager-managed. The Iowa and Illinois statutes both provide that, unless modified by the series LLC provisions, the provisions generally applicable to LLCs and their managers, members, and transferees are applicable to each series.

Some states have enacted series provisions outside of LLC statutes. For example, Delaware has enacted series limited partnership provisions (6 Del. C. § 17-218). In addition, Delaware's statutory trust statute permits a statutory trust to establish series (12 Del. C. § 3804). Both of these statutes contain provisions that are nearly identical to the corresponding provisions of the Delaware series LLC statute with respect to the ability of the limited partnership or trust to create or establish separate series with the same liability protection enjoyed by series of a Delaware series LLC.

All of the series LLC statutes contain provisions that grant series certain attributes of separate entities. For example, individual series may have separate business purposes, investment objectives, members, and managers. Assets of a particular series are not subject to the claims of creditors of other series of the series LLC or of the series LLC itself, provided that certain record-keeping and notice requirements are observed. Finally, most series LLC statutes provide that an event that causes a member to cease to be associated with a series does not cause the member to cease to be associated with the series LLC or any other series of the series LLC.

However, all of the state statutes limit the powers of series of series LLCs. For example, a series of a series LLC may not convert into another type of entity, merge with another entity, or domesticate in another state independent from the series LLC. Several of the series LLC statutes do not expressly address a series' ability to sue or be sued, hold title to property, or contract in its own name. Ordinary LLCs and series LLCs generally may exercise these rights. Additionally, most of the series LLC statutes provide that the dissolution of a series LLC will cause the termination of each of its series.

B. *Statutes with respect to insurance*

The insurance codes of a number of states include statutes that provide for the chartering of a legal entity commonly known as a protected cell company, segregated account company, or segregated portfolio company. See, for example, Vt. Stat. Ann. tit. 8, chap.141, § § 6031-6038 (sponsored captive insurance companies and protected cells of such companies); S.C. Code Ann. tit. 38, chap. 10, § § 38-10-10 through 39-10-80 (protected cell insurance companies). Under those statutes, as under the series LLC statutes described above, the assets of each cell are segregated from the assets of any other cell. The cell may issue insurance or annuity contracts, reinsure such contracts, or facilitate the securitization of obligations of a sponsoring insurance company. Rev. Rul. 2008-8 (2008-1 CB 340), (see § 601.601(d)(2)(ii)(*b*)), analyzes whether an arrangement entered into between a protected cell and its owner possesses the requisite risk shifting and risk distribution to qualify as insurance for Federal income tax purposes. Under certain domestic insurance codes, the sponsor may be organized under a corporate or unincorporated entity statute.

Series or cell company statutes in a number of foreign jurisdictions allow series or cells to engage in insurance businesses. See, for example, The Companies (Guernsey) Law, 2008 Part XXVII (Protected Cell Companies), Part XXVIII (Incorporated Cell Companies); The Companies (Jersey) law, 1991, Part 18D; Companies Law, Part XIV (2009 Revision) (Cayman Isl.) (Segregated Portfolio Companies); and Segregated Accounts Companies Act (2000) (Bermuda).

Explanation of Provisions

1. *In General*

The proposed regulations provide that, for Federal tax purposes, a domestic series, whether or not a juridical person for local law purposes, is treated as an entity formed under local law.

With one exception, the proposed regulations do not apply to series or cells organized or established under the laws of a foreign jurisdiction. The one exception is that the proposed regulations apply to a foreign series that engages in an insurance business.

Whether a series that is treated as a local law entity under the proposed regulations is recognized as a separate entity for Federal tax purposes is determined under § 301.7701-1 and general tax principles. The proposed regulations further provide that the classification of a series that is recognized as a separate entity for Federal tax purposes is determined under § 301.7701-1(b), which provides the rules for classifying organizations that are recognized as entities for Federal tax purposes.

The proposed regulations define a *series organization* as a juridical entity that establishes and maintains, or under which is established and maintained, a series. A series organization includes a series limited liability company, series partnership, series trust, protected cell company, segregated cell company, segregated portfolio company, or segregated account company.

The proposed regulations define a *series statute* as a statute of a State or foreign jurisdiction that explicitly provides for the organization or establishment of a series of a juridical person and explicitly permits (1) members or participants of a series organization to have rights, powers, or duties with respect to the series; (2) a series to have separate rights, powers, or duties with respect to specified property or obligations; and (3) the segregation of assets and liabilities such that none of the debts and liabilities of the series organization (other than liabilities to the State or foreign jurisdiction related to the organization or operation of the series organization, such as franchise fees or administrative costs) or of any other series of the series organization are enforceable against the assets of a particular series of the series organization. For purposes of this definition, a "participant" of a series organization includes an officer or director of the series organization who has no ownership interest in the series or series organization, but has rights, powers, or duties with respect to the series.

The proposed regulations define a series as a segregated group of assets and liabilities that is established pursuant to a series statute by agreement of a series organization. A series includes a cell, segregated account, or segregated portfolio, including a cell, segregated account, or segregated portfolio that is formed under the insurance code of a jurisdiction or is engaged in an insurance business. However, the term "series" does not include a segregated asset account of a life insurance company, which consists of all assets the investment return and market value of which must be allocated in an identical manner to any variable life insurance or annuity contract invested in any of the assets. See § 1.817-5(e). Such an account is accorded special treatment under subchapter L. See generally section 817(a) through (c).

Certain series statutes provide that the series liability limitation provisions do not apply if the series organization or series does not maintain records adequately accounting for the assets associated with each series separately from the assets of the series organization or any other series of the series organization. The IRS and the Treasury Department considered whether a failure to elect or qualify for the liability limitations under the series statute should affect whether a series is a separate entity for Federal tax purposes. However, limitations on liability of owners of an entity for debts and obligations of the entity and the rights of creditors to hold owners liable for debts and obligations of the entity generally do not alter the characterization of the entity for Federal tax purposes. Therefore, the proposed regulations provide that an election, agreement, or other arrangement that permits debts and liabilities of other series or the series organization to be enforceable against the assets of a particular series, or a failure to comply with the record keeping requirements for the limitation on liability available under the relevant series statute, will not prevent a series from meeting the definition of "series" in the proposed regulations. For example, a series generally will not cease to be an entity under the proposed regulations simply because it guarantees the debt of another series within the series organization.

The proposed regulations treat a series as created or organized under the laws of the same jurisdiction in which the series is established. Because a series may not be a separate juridical entity for local law purposes, this rule provides the means for establishing the jurisdiction of the series for Federal tax purposes.

Under § 301.7701-1(b), § 301.7701-2(b) applies to a series that is recognized as a separate entity for Federal tax purposes. Therefore, a series that is itself described in § 301.7701-2(b)(1) through (8) would be classified as a corporation regardless of the classification of the series organization.

The proposed regulations also provide that, for Federal tax purposes, ownership of interests in a series and of the assets associated with a series is determined under general tax principles. A series organization is not treated as the owner of a series or of the assets associated with a series merely because the series organization holds legal title to the assets associated with the series. For example, if a series organization holds legal title to assets associated with a series because the statute under which the series organization was organized does not expressly permit a series to hold assets in its own name, the series will be treated as the owner of the assets for Federal tax purposes if it bears the economic benefits and burdens of the assets under general Federal tax principles. Similarly, for Federal tax purposes, the obligor for the liability of a series is determined under general tax principles.

In general, the same legal principles that apply to determine who owns interests in other types of entities apply to determine the ownership of interests in series and series organizations. These principles generally look to who bears the economic benefits and burdens of ownership. See, for example, Rev. Rul. 55-39 (1955-1 CB 403), (see § 601.601(d)(2)(ii)(*b*)). Furthermore, common law principles apply to the determination of whether a person is a partner in a series that is classified as a partnership for Federal tax purposes under § 301.7701-3. See, for example, *Commissioner v. Culbertson*, 337 U.S. 733 (1949); *Commissioner v. Tower*, 327 U.S. 280 (1946).

The IRS and the Treasury Department considered other approaches to the classification of series for Federal tax purposes. In particular, the IRS and the Treasury Department considered whether series should be disregarded as entities separate from the series organization for Federal tax purposes. This approach would be supported by the fact that series are not generally considered entities for local law purposes (except, for example, potentially under the statutes of Illinois and Iowa, where a series may be treated as a separate entity to the extent set forth in the articles of organization). Additionally, while the statutes enabling series organizations grant series significant autonomy, under no current statute do series possess all of the attributes of independence that entities recognized under local law generally possess. For example, series generally cannot convert into another type of entity, merge with another entity, or domesticate in another jurisdiction independent of the series organization. In addition, the dissolution of a series organization generally will terminate all of its series.

The IRS and the Treasury Department believe that, notwithstanding that series differ in some respects from more traditional local law entities, domestic series generally should be treated for Federal tax purposes as entities formed under local law. Because Federal tax law, and not local law, governs the question of whether an organization is an entity for Federal tax purposes, it is not dispositive that domestic series generally are not considered entities for local law purposes. Additionally, the IRS and the Treasury Department believe that, overall, the factors supporting separate entity status for series outweigh the factors in favor of disregarding series as entities separate from the series organization and other series of the series organization. Specifically, managers and equity holders are "associated with" a series, and their rights, duties, and powers with respect to the series are direct and specifically identified. Also, individual series may (but generally are not required to) have separate business purposes and investment objectives. The IRS and the Treasury Department believe these factors are sufficient to treat domestic series as entities formed under local law.

Although some statutes creating series organizations permit an individual series to enter into contracts, sue, be sued, and/or hold property in its own name, the IRS and the Treasury Department do not believe that the failure of a statute to explicitly provide these rights should alter the treatment of a domestic series as an entity formed under local law. These attributes primarily involve procedural formalities and do not appear to affect the substantive economic rights of series or their creditors with respect to their property and liabilities. Even in jurisdictions where series may not possess these attributes, the statutory liability shields would still apply to the assets of a particular series, provided the statutory requirements are satisfied.

Furthermore, the rule provided in the proposed regulations would provide greater certainty to both taxpayers and the IRS regarding the tax status of domestic series and foreign series that conduct insurance businesses. In effect, taxpayers that establish domestic series are placed in the same position as persons that file a certificate of organization for a state law entity. The IRS and the Treasury Department believe that the approach of the proposed regulations is straightforward and administrable, and is preferable to engaging in a case by case determination of the status of each series that would require a detailed examination of the terms of the relevant statute. Finally, the IRS and the Treasury Department believe that a rule generally treating domestic series as local law entities would be consistent with taxpayers' current ability to create similar structures using multiple local law entities that can elect their Federal tax classification pursuant to § 301.7701-3.

The IRS and the Treasury Department believe that domestic series should be classified as separate local law entities based on the characteristics granted to them under the various series statutes. However, except as specifically stated in the proposed regulations, a particular series need not actually possess all of the attributes that its enabling statute permits it to possess. The IRS and the Treasury Department believe that a domestic series should be treated as a separate local law entity even if its business purpose, investment objective, or ownership overlaps with that of other series or the series organization itself. Separate state law entities may have common or overlapping business purposes, investment objectives and ownership, but generally are still treated as separate local law entities for Federal tax purposes.

The proposed regulations do not address the entity status for Federal tax purposes of a series organization. Specifically, the proposed regulations do not address whether a series organization is recognized as a separate entity for Federal tax purposes if it has no assets and engages in no activities independent of its series.

Until further guidance is issued, the entity status of a foreign series that does not conduct an insurance business will be determined under applicable law. Foreign series raise novel Federal income tax issues that continue to be considered and addressed by the IRS and the Treasury Department.

2. *Classification of a Series that is Treated as a Separate Entity for Federal Tax Purposes*

If a domestic series or a foreign series engaged in an insurance business is treated as a separate entity for Federal tax purposes, then § 301.7701-1(b) applies to determine the proper tax classification of the series. However, the proposed regulations do not provide how a series should be treated for Federal employment tax purposes. If a domestic series is treated as a separate entity for Federal tax purposes, then the series generally is subject to the same treatment as any other entity for Federal tax purposes. For example, a series that is treated as a separate entity for Federal tax purposes may make any Federal tax elections it is otherwise eligible to make independently of other series or the series organization itself, and regardless of whether other series (or the series organization) do not make certain elections or make different elections.

3. *Entity Status of Series Organizations*

The proposed regulations do not address the entity status or filing requirements of series organizations for Federal tax purposes. A series organization generally is an entity for local law purposes. An organization that is an entity for local law purposes generally is treated as an entity for Federal tax purposes. However, an organization characterized as an entity for Federal income tax purposes may not have an income or information tax filing obligation. For example, § 301.6031(a)-(1)(a)(3)(i) provides that a partnership with no income, deductions, or credits for Federal income tax purposes for a taxable year is not required to file a partnership return for that year. Generally, filing fees of a series organization paid by series of the series organization would be treated as expenses of the series and not as expenses of the series organization. Thus, a series organization characterized as a partnership for Federal tax purposes that does not have income, deductions, or credits for a taxable year need not file a partnership return for the year.

4. *Continuing Applicability of Tax Law Authority to Series*

Notwithstanding that a domestic series or a foreign series engaged in an insurance business is treated as an entity formed under local law under the proposed regulations, the Commissioner may under applicable law, including common law tax principles, characterize a series or a portion of a series other than as a separate entity for Federal tax purposes. Series covered by the proposed regulations are subject to applicable law to the same extent as other entities. Thus, a series may be disregarded under applicable law even if it satisfies the requirements of the proposed regulations to be treated as an entity formed under local law. For example, if a series has no business purpose or business activity other than tax avoidance, it may be disregarded under appropriate circumstances. See *Bertoli v. Commissioner*, 103 T.C. 501 (1994); *Aldon Homes, Inc. v. Commissioner*, 33 T.C. 582 (1959). Furthermore, the anti-abuse rule of § 1.701-2 is applicable to a series or series organization that is classified as a partnership for Federal tax purposes.

5. *Applicability to Organizations that Qualify as Insurance Companies*

Notice 2008-19 requested comments on proposed guidance setting forth conditions under which a cell of a protected cell company would be treated as an insurance company separate from any other entity for Federal income tax purposes. Those who commented on the notice generally supported the proposed guidance, and further commented that it should extend to non-insurance arrangements as well, including series LLCs. Rather than provide independent guidance for insurance company status setting forth what is essentially the same standard, the proposed regulations define the term *series* to include a cell, segregated account, or segregated portfolio that is formed under the insurance code of a jurisdiction or is engaged in an insurance business (other than a segregated asset account of a life insurance company).

Although the proposed regulations do not apply to a series organized or established under the laws of a foreign jurisdiction, an exception is provided for certain series conducting an insurance business. Under this exception, a series that is organized or established under the laws of a foreign jurisdiction is treated as an entity if the arrangements and other activities of the series, if conducted by a domestic company, would result in its being classified as an insurance company. Thus, a foreign series would be treated as an entity if more than half of the series' business is the issuing or reinsuring of insurance or annuity contracts. The IRS and the Treasury Department believe it is appropriate to provide this rule even though the proposed regulations otherwise do not apply to a foreign series because an insurance company is classified as a per se corporation under section 7701(a)(3) regardless of how it otherwise would be treated under §§ 301.7701-1, 301.7701-2, or 301.7701-3.

The IRS and the Treasury Department are aware that insurance-specific guidance may still be needed to address the issues identified in § 3.02 of Notice 2008-19 and insurance-specific transition issues that may arise for protected cell companies that previously reported in a manner inconsistent with the regulations. See § 601.601(d)(2)(ii)(*b*).

6. *Effect of Local Law Classification on Tax Collection*

The IRS and Treasury Department understand that there are differences in local law governing series (for example, rights to hold title to property and to sue and be sued are expressly addressed in some statutes but not in others) that may affect how creditors of series, including state taxing authorities, may enforce obligations of a series. Thus, the proposed regulations provide that, to the extent Federal or local law permits a creditor to collect a liability attributable to a series from the series organization or other series of the series organization, the series organization and other series of the series organization may also be considered the taxpayer from whom the tax assessed against the series may be collected pursuant to administrative or judicial means. Further, when a creditor is permitted to collect a liability attributable to a series organization from any series of the series organization, a tax liability assessed against the series organization may be collected directly from a series of the series organization by administrative or judicial means.

7. *Employment Tax and Employee Benefits Issues*

A. *In general*

The domestic statutes authorizing the creation of series contemplate that a series may operate a business. If the operating business has workers, it will be necessary to determine how the business satisfies any employment tax obligations, whether it has the ability to maintain any employee benefit plans and, if so, whether it complies with the rules applicable to those plans. Application of the employment tax requirements will depend principally on whether the workers are employees, and, if so, who is considered the employer for Federal income and employment tax purposes. In general, an employment relationship exists when the person for whom services are performed has the right to control and direct the individual who performs the services, not only as to the result to be accomplished by the work but also as to the details and means by which that result is accomplished. See §§ 31.3121(d)-1(c)(2), 31.3306(i)-1(b), and 31.3401(c)-1(b).

B. *Employment tax*

An entity must be a person in order to be an employer for Federal employment tax purposes. See sections 3121(b), 3306(a)(1), 3306(c), and 3401(d) and § 31.3121(d)-2(a). However, status as a person, by itself, is not enough to make an entity an employer for Federal employment tax purposes. The entity must also satisfy the criteria to be an employer under Federal employment tax statutes and regulations for purposes of the determination of the proper amount of employment taxes and the party liable for reporting and paying the taxes. Treatment of a series as a separate person for Federal employment tax purposes would create the possibility that the series could be an "employer" for Federal employment tax purposes, which would raise both substantive and administrative issues.

The series structure would make it difficult to determine whether the series or the series organization is the employer under the relevant criteria with respect to the services provided. For example, if workers perform all of their services under the direction and control of individuals who own the interests in a series, but the series has no legal authority to enter into contracts or to sue or be sued, could the series nonetheless be the employer of the workers? If workers perform services under the direction and control of the series, but they are paid by the series organization, would the series organization, as the nominal owner of all the series assets, have control over the payment of wages such that it would be liable as the employer under section 3401(d)?

The structure of a series organization could also affect the type of employment tax liability. For example, if a series were recognized as a distinct person for Federal employment tax purposes, a worker providing services as an employee of one series and as a member of another series or the series organization would be subject to FICA tax on the wages paid for services as an employee and self-employment tax on the member income. Note further that, if a domestic series were classified as a separate entity that is a business entity, then, under § 301.7701-3, the series would be classified as either a partnership or a corporation. While a business entity with one owner is generally classified as a corporation or is disregarded for Federal tax purposes, such an entity cannot be disregarded for Federal employment tax purposes. See § 301.7701-2(c)(2)(iv).

Once the employer is identified, additional issues arise, including but not limited to the following: How would the wage base be determined for employees, particularly if they work for more than one series in a common line of business? How would the common paymaster rules apply? Who would be authorized to designate an agent under section 3504 for reporting and payment of employment taxes, and how would the authorization be accomplished? How would the statutory exceptions from the definitions of employment and wages apply given that they may be based on the identity of the employer? Which entity would be eligible for tax credits that go to the employer such as the Work Opportunity Tax Credit under section 51 or the tip credit under section 45B? If a series organization handles payroll for a series and is also the nominal owner of the series assets, would the owners or the managers of the series organization be responsible persons for the Trust Fund Recovery Penalty under section 6672?

Special administrative issues might arise if the series were to be treated as the employer for Federal employment tax purposes but not for state law purposes. For example, if the series were the employer for Federal employment tax purposes and filed a Form W-2, "Wage and Tax Statement," reporting wages and employment taxes withheld, but the series were not recognized as a juridical person for state law purposes, then administrative problems might ensue unless separate Forms W-2 were prepared for state and local tax purposes. Similarly, the IRS and the states might encounter challenges in awarding the FUTA credit under section 3302 to the appropriate entity and certifying the amount of state unemployment tax paid.

In light of these issues, the proposed regulations do not currently provide how a series should be treated for Federal employment tax purposes.

C. *Employee benefits*

Various issues arise with respect to the ability of a series to maintain an employee benefit plan, including issues related to those described above with respect to whether a series may be an employer. The proposed regulations do not address these issues. However, to the extent that a series can maintain an employee benefit plan, the aggregation rules under section 414(b), (c), (m), (o) and (t), as well as the leased employee rules under section 414(n), would apply. In this connection, the IRS and Treasury Department expect to issue regulations under section 414(o) that would prevent the avoidance of any employee benefit plan requirement through the use of the separate entity status of a series.

8. *Statement Containing Identifying Information about Series*

As the series organization or a series of the series organization may be treated as a separate entity for Federal tax and related reporting purposes but may not be a separate entity under local law, the IRS and Treasury Department believe that a new statement may need to be created and required to be filed annually by the series organization and each series of the series organization to provide the IRS with certain identifying information to ensure the proper assessment and collection of tax. Accordingly, these regulations propose to amend the Procedure and Administration Regulations under section 6011 to include this requirement and a cross-reference to those regulations is included under § 301.7701-1. The IRS and Treasury Department are considering what information should be required by these statements. Information tentatively being considered includes (1) the name, address, and taxpayer identification number of the series organization and each of its series and status of each as a series of a series organization or as the series organization; (2) the jurisdiction in which the series organization was formed; and (3) an indication of whether the series holds title to its assets or whether title is held by another series or the series organization and, if held by another series or the series organization, the name, address, and taxpayer identification number of the series organization and each series holding title to any of its assets. The IRS and Treasury Department are also considering the best time to require taxpayers to file the statement. For example, the IRS and Treasury Department are considering whether the statement should be filed when returns, such as income tax returns and excise tax returns, are required to be filed or whether it should be a stand-alone statement filed separately by a set date each year, as with information returns such as Forms 1099. A cross-reference to these regulations was added to the Procedure and Administration regulations under section 6071 for the time to file returns and statements. The proposed regulations under section 6071 provide that the statement will be a stand-alone statement due March 15th of each year. In addition, the IRS and Treasury Department are considering revising Form SS-4, "Application for Employer Identification Number," to include questions regarding series organizations.

Proposed Effective Date

These regulations generally apply on the date final regulations are published in the **Federal Register**. Generally, when final regulations become effective, taxpayers that are treating series differently for Federal tax purposes than series are treated under the final regulations will be required to change their treatment of series. In this situation, a series organization that previously was treated as one entity with all of its series may be required to begin treating each series as a separate entity for Federal tax purposes. General tax principles will apply to determine the consequences of the conversion from one entity to multiple entities for Federal tax purposes. See, for example, section 708 for rules relating to partnership divisions in the case of a series organization previously treated as a partnership for Federal tax purposes converting into multiple partnerships upon recognition of the series organization's series as separate entities. While a division of a partnership may be tax-free, gain may be recognized in certain situations under section 704(c)(1)(B) or section 737. Sections 355 and 368(a)(1)(D) provide rules that govern certain divisions of a corporation. The division of a series organization into multiple corporations may be tax-free to the corporation and to its shareholders; however, if the corporate division does not satisfy one or more of the requirements in section 355, the division may result in taxable events to the corporation, its shareholders, or both.

The regulations include an exception for series established prior to publication of the proposed regulations that treat all series and the series organization as one entity. If the requirements for this exception are satisfied, after issuance of the final regulations the series may continue to be treated together with the series organization as one entity for Federal tax purposes. Specifically, these requirements are satisfied if (1) The series was established prior to September 14, 2010; (2) The series (independent of the series organization or other series of the series organization) conducted business or investment activity or, in the case of a foreign series, more than half the business of the series was the issuing of insurance or annuity contracts or the reinsuring of risks underwritten by insurance companies, on and prior to September 14, 2010; (3) If the series was established pursuant to a foreign statute, the series' classification was relevant (as defined in § 301.7701-3(d)), and more than half the business of the series was the issuing of insurance or annuity contracts or the reinsuring of risks underwritten by insurance companies for all taxable years beginning with the taxable year that includes September 14, 2010; (4) No owner of the series treats the series as an entity separate from any other series of the series organization or from the series organization for purposes of filing any Federal income tax returns, information returns, or withholding documents for any taxable year; (5) The series and series organization had a reasonable basis (within the meaning of section 6662) for their claimed classification; and (6) Neither the series nor any owner of the series nor the series organization was notified in writing on or before the date final regulations are published in the **Federal Register** that classification of the series was under examination (in which case the series' classification will be determined in the examination).

This exception will cease to apply on the date any person or persons who were not owners of the series organization (or series) prior to September 14, 2010 own, in the aggregate, a 50 percent or greater interest in the series organization (or series). For this purpose, the term *interest* means (i) in the case of a partnership, a capital or profits interest and (ii) in the case of a corporation, an equity interest measured by vote or value. This transition rule does not apply to any determination other than the entity status of a series, for example, tax ownership of a series or series organization or qualification of a series or series organization conducting an insurance business as a controlled foreign corporation.

Special Analyses

It has been determined that this notice of proposed rulemaking is not a significant regulatory action as defined in Executive Order 12866. Therefore, a regulatory assessment is not required. It also has been determined that section 553(b) of the Administrative Procedure Act (5 U.S.C. chapter 5) does not apply to these regulations.

Pursuant to the Regulatory Flexibility Act (5.U.S.C. chapter 6), it is hereby certified that the regulations will not have a significant economic impact on a substantial number of small entities. The regulations require that series and series organizations file a statement to provide the IRS with certain identifying information to ensure the proper assessment and collection of tax. The regulations affect domestic series LLCs, domestic cell companies, and foreign series and cells that conduct insurance businesses, and their owners. Based on information available at this time, the IRS and the Treasury Department believe that many series and series organizations are large insurance companies or investment firms and, thus, are not small entities. Although a number of small entities may be subject to the information reporting requirement of the new statement, any economic impact will be minimal. The information that the IRS and the Treasury Department are considering requiring on the proposed statement should be known by or readily available to the series or the series organization. Therefore, it should take minimal time and expense to collect and report this information. For example, the IRS and the Treasury Department are considering requiring the following information: (1) The name, address, and taxpayer identification number of the series organization and each of its series and status of each as a series of a series organization or as the series organization; (2) The jurisdiction in which the series organization was formed; and (3) An indication of whether the series holds title to its assets or whether title is held by another series or the series organization and, if held by another series or the series organization, the name, address, and taxpayer identification number of the series organization and each series holding title to any of its assets. The IRS and the Treasury Department request comments on the accuracy of the statement that the regulations in this document will not have a significant economic impact on a substantial number of small entities. Pursuant to section 7805(f) of the Code, this notice of proposed rulemaking has been submitted to the Chief Counsel for Advocacy of the Small Business Administration for comment on its impact on small businesses.

Comments and Requests for a Public Hearing

Before these proposed regulations are adopted as final regulations, consideration will be given to any written comments (a signed original and eight (8) copies) that are submitted timely to the IRS. Alternatively, taxpayers may submit comments electronically directly to the Federal eRulemaking portal at *www.regulations.gov*.

The IRS and the Treasury Department request comments on the proposed regulations. In addition, the IRS and the Treasury Department request comments on the following issues:

(1) Whether a series organization should be recognized as a separate entity for Federal tax purposes if it has no assets and engages in no activities independent of its series;

(2) The appropriate treatment of a series that does not terminate for local law purposes when it has no members associated with it;

(3) The entity status for Federal tax purposes of foreign cells that do not conduct insurance businesses and other tax consequences of establishing, operating, and terminating all foreign cells;

(4) How the Federal employment tax issues discussed and similar technical issues should be resolved;

(5) How series and series organizations will be treated for state employment tax purposes and other state employment-related purposes and how that treatment should affect the Federal employment tax treatment of series and series organizations (comments from the states would be particularly helpful);

(6) What issues could arise with respect to the provision of employee benefits by a series organization or series; and

(7) The requirement for the series organization and each series of the series organization to file a statement and what information should be included on the statement.

All comments will be available for public inspection and copying. A public hearing may be scheduled if requested in writing by a person who timely submits comments. If a public hearing is scheduled, notice of the date, time and place for the hearing will be published in the **Federal Register**.

Drafting Information

The principal author of these proposed regulations is Joy Spies, IRS Office of the Associate Chief Counsel (Passthroughs and Special Industries). However, other personnel from the IRS and the Treasury Department participated in their development.

[¶ 49,475] Proposed Amendments of Regulations (REG-140108-08), published in the Federal Register on March 15, 2011.

[Code Sec. 6104]

Disclosure of information to state officials: Tax-exempt organizations: Obtaining and inspecting returns and return information.—Amendments of Reg. §301.6104(c)-1, amending existing regulations to reflect changes to Code Sec. 6104(c) made by the Pension Protection Act of 2006 (PPA) (P.L. 109-280), are proposed.

AGENCY: Internal Revenue Service (IRS), Treasury.

ACTION: Notice of proposed rulemaking.

SUMMARY: This document contains proposed regulations that amend existing regulations to reflect changes to section 6104(c) of the Internal Revenue Code (Code) made by the Pension Protection Act of 2006 (PPA). These rules provide guidance to states regarding the process by which they may obtain or inspect certain returns and return information (including information about final and proposed denials and revocations of tax-exempt status) for the purpose of administering state laws governing certain tax-exempt organizations and their activities. These regulations will affect such exempt organizations, as well as those state agencies choosing to obtain information from the Internal Revenue Service (IRS) under section 6104(c).

DATES: Written or electronic comments and requests for a public hearing must be received by June 13, 2011.

ADDRESSES: Send submissions to: CC:PA:LPD:PR (REG-140108-08), Room 5203, Internal Revenue Service, P.O. Box 7604, Ben Franklin Station, Washington, DC 20044. Submissions may be hand-delivered Monday through Friday between the hours of 8 a.m. and 4 p.m. to CC:PA:LPD:PR (REG-140108-08), Courier's Desk, Internal Revenue Service, 1111 Constitution Avenue, NW, Washington, DC, or sent electronically via the Federal eRulemaking Portal at *www.regulations.gov* (IRS REG-140108-08).

FOR FURTHER INFORMATION CONTACT: Concerning submission of comments, Oluwafunmilayo Taylor, (202) 622-7180 (not a toll-free number); concerning the proposed regulations, Casey Lothamer, (202) 622-6070 (not a toll-free number).

SUPPLEMENTARY INFORMATION:

Background

I. In general

This document contains proposed amendments to 26 CFR part 301 under section 6104(c), which will replace current § 301.6104(c)-1 in its entirety. Section 6104(c) governs when the IRS may disclose to state officials certain information about organizations described in section 501(c)(3) ("charitable organizations"), organizations that have applied for recognition as organizations described in section 501(c)(3) ("applicants"), and certain other exempt organizations. Section 6104(c) was added to the Code by section 101(e) of the Tax Reform Act of 1969 (Public Law 91-172, 83 Stat. 523) and significantly amended by section 1224(a) of the PPA (Public Law 109-280, 120 Stat. 1091).

Section 501(c)(3) organizations may be affected by the expanded disclosures to state officials authorized under the statute and proposed regulations. First, the IRS is now authorized (under new section 6104(c)(2), as added by the PPA) to disclose information about certain proposed revocations and proposed denials before an administrative appeal has been made and a final revocation or denial has been issued. For those organizations that have received a determination letter stating that they are described in section 501(c)(3), the IRS may disclose a proposed revocation (before any administrative appeal) to an appropriate state officer (ASO). This broader authority applies both where the organization was required under section 508 to apply for the determination letter and where the organization elected to apply for a determination letter even though it was not required to do so. The IRS continues to be authorized to disclose final revocations and final denials issued after any administrative appeal has been concluded for any section 501(c)(3) organization.

Second, under the authority of new section 6104(c)(2)(D), as added by the PPA, the IRS may disclose returns or return information of any section 501(c)(3) organization to ASOs on its own initiative, regardless of whether it has initiated an examination, if it determines that the information may be evidence of noncompliance with state laws under the jurisdiction of the ASO. Thus, if the IRS believes these conditions are met, it may, for example, disclose to ASOs a proposed revocation of exemption for a section 501(c)(3) organization that does not have a determination letter. All disclosures authorized under section 6104(c) may be made only if the state receiving the information is following applicable disclosure, recordkeeping and safeguard procedures.

The statute and proposed regulations also permit disclosure of information to state officials about all applicants for section 501(c)(3) status.

Exempt organizations other than section 501(c)(3) organizations also may be affected by the disclosures to state officials authorized under the statute and proposed regulations. The IRS is authorized to disclose returns and return information of these organizations to ASOs upon written request, but only to the extent necessary to administer state laws regulating the solicitation or administration of charitable funds or charitable assets. Again, all such disclosures may be made only if the state receiving the information is following applicable disclosure, recordkeeping and safeguard procedures.

Section 6104(c)(1), which is unchanged by the PPA, directs the IRS to share certain information with ASOs regarding charitable organizations and applicants. Specifically, section 6104(c)(1) provides that the IRS is to notify the ASO of the following final determinations: (1) a refusal to recognize an entity as an organization described in section 501(c)(3); (2) the operation of a section 501(c)(3) organization in a manner not meeting, or no longer meeting, the requirements of its exemption; and (3) the mailing of a notice of deficiency for any tax imposed under section 507, chapter 41, or chapter 42. See section 6104(c)(1)(A) and (c)(1)(B). The directive under section 6104(c)(1)(A) to notify ASOs of an organization no longer meeting the requirements for exemption under section 501(c)(3) includes not only notice of a revocation of exemption, but also notice (when the IRS is so informed) that a charitable organization is terminating or has dissolved in accordance with its governing documents. Upon request, an ASO may inspect and copy the returns, filed statements, records, reports, and other information relating to a final determination as described in this paragraph, as are relevant to any determination under state law. See section 6104(c)(1)(C).

II. PPA changes to section 6104(c)

The PPA amended section 6104(c) by striking paragraph (2) and inserting new paragraphs (2) through (6) as follows.

(1) The IRS may disclose to an ASO proposed refusals to recognize organizations as charitable organizations, and proposed revocations of such recognition. The PPA also allows disclosure of notices of proposed deficiencies of excise taxes imposed by section 507 and chapters 41 and 42 relating to charitable organizations. See section 6104(c)(2)(A)(i) and (c)(2)(A)(ii). Previously, only final determinations of this kind (denials of recognition, revocations, and notices of deficiency) could be disclosed under section 6104(c).

(2) The IRS may disclose to an ASO the names, addresses, and taxpayer identification numbers of applicants. See section 6104(c)(2)(A)(iii). Previously, information on applicants, other than information relating to a denial of recognition, could not be disclosed under section 6104(c).

(3) The IRS may disclose to an ASO the returns and return information of organizations with respect to which information is disclosed as described in paragraphs (1) and (2) of this section II (proposed determinations and applicant identifying information). See section 6104(c)(2)(B). Prior law allowed for disclosure under section 6104(c) only of returns and return information related to final determinations.

(4) Proposed determinations, identifying information, and the related returns and return information with respect to charitable organizations and applicants may be disclosed to an ASO only upon the ASO's written request and only as necessary to administer state laws regulating charitable organizations, such as laws governing tax-exempt status, charitable trusts, charitable solicitation, and fraud. See section 6104(c)(2)(C). Prior law provided for automatic disclosure (without a request), but only of final determinations and their related returns and return information.

(5) The IRS may disclose to an ASO on its own initiative (without a written request) returns and return information with respect to charitable organizations and applicants if the IRS determines that this information might constitute evidence of noncompliance with the laws under the jurisdiction of the ASO. See section 6104(c)(2)(D). There was no such provision under section 6104(c) previously.

(6) The IRS may disclose returns and return information of section 501(c) organizations other than those described in section 501(c)(1) or (c)(3) to an ASO upon the ASO's written request, but only to the extent necessary in administering state laws relating to the solicitation or administration of charitable funds or charitable assets of such organizations. See section 6104(c)(3). Previously, only information relating to charitable organizations or applicants was disclosed under section 6104(c).

(7) Returns and return information of organizations and taxable persons disclosed under section 6104(c) may be disclosed in civil administrative and civil judicial proceedings pertaining to the enforcement of state laws regulating such organizations, under procedures prescribed by the IRS similar to those under section 6103(h)(4). See section 6104(c)(4). There was no such provision under section 6104(c) previously.

(8) No return or return information may be disclosed under section 6104(c) to the extent the IRS determines that such disclosure would seriously impair federal tax administration. See section 6104(c)(5). This disclosure prohibition, though new in the PPA, was provided previously by regulation. See current § 301.6104(c)-1(b)(3)(ii).

(9) The IRS may disclose returns and return information under section 6104(c) to a state officer or employee designated by the ASO to receive such information on the ASO's behalf. See section 6104(c)(2)(C) (flush language) and (c)(3). Prior law did not provide for IRS disclosures to persons other than ASOs.

(10) An ASO is defined as the state attorney general, state tax officer, any state official charged with overseeing charitable organizations (in the case of charitable organizations and applicants), and the head of the state agency charged with the primary responsibility for overseeing the solicitation of funds for charitable purposes (in the case of section 501(c) organizations other than those described in section 501(c)(1) or (c)(3)). See section 6104(c)(6)(B). Before its amendment by the PPA, section 6104(c)(2) defined ASO as the state attorney general, state tax officer, or any state official charged with overseeing organizations of the type described in section 501(c)(3).

III. Related PPA provisions

The PPA amended section 6103(p) to make the disclosure of returns and return information under section 6104(c) subject to the disclosure, recordkeeping, and safeguard provisions of section 6103. These provisions include—

(1) section 6103(a), which is the general prohibition on the disclosure of returns and return information, except as authorized by Title 26 of the United States Code;

(2) section 6103(p)(3), which requires the IRS to maintain permanent standardized records of all requests for inspection or disclosure of returns or return information under section 6104(c) and of all such information inspected or disclosed pursuant to those requests; and

(3) section 6103(p)(4), which requires an ASO, as a condition for receiving returns or return information under section 6104(c), to establish and maintain certain safeguards, such as keeping permanent standardized records of all requests and disclosures, maintaining a secure information storage area, restricting access to the information, and providing whatever other safeguards the IRS deems necessary to protect the confidentiality of the information. See § 301.6103(p)(4)-1 and IRS Publication 1075, Tax Information Security Guidelines for Federal, State and Local Agencies and Entities. Publication 1075 can be found at www.irs.gov/formspubs.

The PPA also included amendments to sections 7213, 7213A, and 7431 to impose civil and criminal penalties for the unauthorized disclosure or inspection of section 6104(c) information.

IV. IRS disclosure procedures

In general, before any federal or state agency may receive returns and return information from the IRS under a particular Code provision, it must file with the IRS a report detailing the physical, administrative, and technical safeguards implemented by the agency to protect this information from unauthorized inspection or disclosure. Only upon approval of these safeguards by the IRS, as well as satisfaction of any other statutory requirements (such as submission of a written request), may an agency receive the information to which it is entitled under the Code, and then only for the use specified by the relevant statute. See section 6103(p)(4).

Under various disclosure programs, the IRS and other federal and state agencies often execute agreements detailing the responsibilities of the parties and the terms and parameters of the disclosure arrangement. For example, under section 6103(d), the IRS executes a disclosure agreement (the "Basic Agreement") with each state tax agency to which it discloses information. The Basic Agreement, which serves as the written request required by section 6103(d), has been the foundation of the state tax disclosure program under this provision of the Code for over 30 years. See Internal Revenue Manual Exhibit 11.3.32-1 (sample Basic Agreement).

After the PPA, the IRS revised its disclosure procedures under section 6104(c) to model them after the highly successful section 6103(d) program. The section 6104(c) program uses a disclosure agreement patterned after the Basic Agreement but tailored to the specific requirements and restrictions of section 6104(c).

Explanation of Provisions

These proposed regulations provide guidance regarding disclosures under section 6104(c), as amended by the PPA. The PPA amendments to sections 6104(c) and 6103 expand the scope of information the IRS may disclose to an ASO, but make such disclosures contingent on the ASO adopting the safeguard standards and procedures of section 6103 that apply to federal and state agencies that receive returns and return information under other provisions of the Code. Accordingly, these proposed regulations provide that, without prior safeguard approval, the IRS will not give automatic notification of any determinations or other information that may be disclosed under section 6104(c).

Under these proposed regulations, the IRS may (and currently does) require an ASO to enter into a disclosure agreement with the IRS, which will stipulate the procedures for disclosure under section 6104(c), as well as the restrictions on use and redisclosure. These proposed regulations provide that this agreement, or any similar document, satisfies the requirement under section 6104(c) for a written request for disclosure.

An ASO who meets the safeguard and other procedural requirements of section 6103(p)(4) may receive information from the IRS to be used in the administration of state laws governing charitable organizations, as well as laws governing the solicitation or administration of charitable funds or charitable assets of certain noncharitable exempt organizations. The information available to ASOs under these proposed regulations not only is greater in scope than what was available under section 6104(c) before its amendment by the PPA, but comes at an earlier stage in the IRS administrative and enforcement processes. Thus, the IRS may disclose such information as whether an organization has applied for recognition as a charitable organization and, if so, whether the IRS proposes to deny such recognition, or the organization has withdrawn its application; whether an organization's charitable status has terminated; whether the IRS proposes to assess any chapter 42 excise taxes (for example, the tax on excess benefit transactions under section 4958); and whether the IRS has revoked an organization's exemption, or proposes to revoke the recognition of its exemption.

Without a written request, but still subject to the safeguard requirements of section 6103(p)(4), the IRS has the authority under section 6104(c)(2)(D) to disclose returns and return information of charitable organizations and applicants if it determines that such information may constitute evidence of noncompliance with the laws under the ASO's jurisdiction. The IRS may make these disclosures on its own initiative. These proposed regulations clarify that the IRS' authority under section 6104(c)(2)(D) is in addition to its disclosure authority under other provisions of section 6104(c)(1) and (c)(2), to the effect that discretionary disclosures may be made before the IRS issues a proposed determination or takes other action. The proposed regulations also make clear that the determination required by the statute concerns possible noncompliance with state laws regulating charitable organizations and not just any state law violation.

The disclosure provisions of section 6104(c), as amended by the PPA, offer significant advantages to states in their enforcement efforts. The ability of the IRS to disclose returns and return information early in its own administrative and enforcement processes, as well as the IRS' authority under section 6104(c)(2)(D) to disclose information on its own initiative, greatly enhance the administration and enforcement of state laws, both tax and nontax, governing charitable activities, funds, and assets.

These proposed regulations define certain key terms for purposes of section 6104(c), including "appropriate state officer", "return", "return information", and "taxable person."

Special Analyses

It has been determined that this notice of proposed rulemaking is not a significant regulatory action as defined in Executive Order 12866; therefore, a regulatory assessment is not required. It also has been determined that section 553(b) of the Administrative Procedure Act (5 U.S.C. chapter 5) and the Regulatory Flexibility Act (5 U.S.C. chapter 6) do not apply to the proposed regulations; therefore, a regulatory flexibility analysis is not required. Pursuant to section 7805(f) of the Internal Revenue Code, the proposed regulations have been submitted to the Chief Counsel for Advocacy of the Small Business Administration for comments regarding their impact on small businesses.

Comments and Requests for a Public Hearing

Before these proposed regulations are adopted as final, any written (signed original and 8 copies) or electronic comments timely submitted to the IRS will be considered. The IRS and Treasury Department request comments on the clarity of these proposed regulations and how they might be made easier to understand. Of particular interest are comments on whether paragraph (e) of these proposed regulations, describing the organizations to which disclosure applies, lists all the organizations with respect to which ASOs might legitimately need information. All comments will be available for public inspection and copying. A public hearing will be scheduled if requested in writing by any person who timely submits written comments. If a public hearing is scheduled, notice of the date, time, and place for the public hearing will be published in the **Federal Register**.

Drafting Information

The principal author of these regulations is Casey Lothamer of the Office of Division Counsel/ Associate Chief Counsel (Tax Exempt and Government Entities), though other persons in the IRS and Treasury Department participated in their development.

[¶49,493] Proposed Amendments of Regulations (REG-111283-11), published in the Federal Register on September 16, 2011.

[Code Secs. 446, 512, 863, 954, 988 and 1256]

Swap contracts: Notional principal contracts: Section 1256 contracts: Qualified board or exchange.—Reg. §§1.1256(b)-1 and 1.1256(g)-1, and amendments of Reg. §§1.446-3, 1.512(b)-1, 1.863-7, 1.954-2 and 1.988-1, describing swaps and similar agreements that fall within the meaning of Code Sec. 1256(b)(2)(B), are proposed.

AGENCY: Internal Revenue Service (IRS), Treasury.

ACTION: Notice of proposed rulemaking and notice of public hearing.

SUMMARY: This document contains proposed regulations that describe swaps and similar agreements that fall within the meaning of section 1256(b)(2)(B) of the Internal Revenue Code (Code). This document also contains proposed regulations that revise the definition of a notional principal contract under §1.446-3 of the Income Tax Regulations. This document provides a notice of public hearing on these proposed regulations.

DATES: Written or electronic comments must be received by December 15, 2011. Outlines of topics to be discussed at the public hearing scheduled for January 19, 2012, must be received by December 14, 2011.

ADDRESSES: Send submissions to: CC:PA:LPD:PR (REG-111283-11), room 5203, Internal Revenue Service, POB 7604, Ben Franklin Station, Washington DC 20044. Submissions may be hand delivered Monday through Friday, between the hours of 8 a.m. and 4 p.m. to CC:PA:LPD:PR (REG-111283-11), Courier's Desk, Internal Revenue Service, 1111 Constitution Avenue, N.W., Washington, DC. Alternatively, taxpayers may submit comments electronically via the Federal eRulemaking Portal at *www.regulations.gov/* (IRS-REG-111283-11). The public hearing will be held in the Auditorium, Internal Revenue Building, 1111 Constitution Avenue, N.W., Washington, DC.

FOR FURTHER INFORMATION CONTACT: Concerning the proposed regulations, K. Scott Brown (202) 622-7454; concerning submissions of comments, the hearing, and/or to be placed on the building access list to attend the hearing, Richard Hurst, (202) 622-7180 (not toll-free numbers).

SUPPLEMENTARY INFORMATION:

Background

This document contains proposed amendments to the Income Tax Regulations (26 CFR 1) under sections 1256 and 446 of the Code. Section 1256(b)(2)(B) was added to the Code by section 1601 of the Dodd-Frank Wall Street Reform and Consumer Protection Act (Public Law No. 111-203, §1601, 124 Stat. 1376, 2223 (2010)) (the Dodd-Frank Act). Section 1256(b)(2)(B) provides that certain swaps and similar agreements are not subject to section 1256 of the Code. These proposed regulations provide guidance on the category of swaps and similar agreements that are within the scope of section 1256(b)(2)(B). These proposed regulations also revise the definition and scope of a notional principal contract under §1.446-3 of the Income Tax Regulations.

Explanation of Provisions

A. *Section 1256(b)(2)(B) Language and Legislative History*

Section 1256 provides that contracts classified as section 1256 contracts are marked to market and any gain or loss is generally treated as 60 percent long-term capital gain or loss and 40 percent short-term capital gain or loss. Section 1256(b)(1) defines the term "section 1256 contract" as a regulated futures contract, foreign currency contract, nonequity option, dealer equity option, and dealer securities futures contract. With the exception of a foreign currency contract, a section 1256 contract must be traded on or subject to the rules of a "qualified board or exchange" as defined in section 1256(g)(7).

Section 1601 of the Dodd-Frank Act added section 1256(b)(2)(B), which excludes swaps and similar agreements from the definition of a section 1256 contract. Section 1256(b)(2)(B) provides that the term "section 1256 contract" shall not include—

> any interest rate swap, currency swap, basis swap, interest rate cap, interest rate floor, commodity swap, equity swap, equity index swap, credit default swap, or similar agreement.

Congress enacted section 1256(b)(2)(B) to resolve uncertainty under section 1256 for swap contracts that are traded on regulated exchanges. The specific uncertainty addressed by the enactment of section 1256(b)(2)(B) was described in the Conference Report:

> The title contains a provision to address the recharacterization of income as a result of increased exchange-trading of derivatives contracts by clarifying that section 1256 of the Internal Revenue Code does not apply to certain derivatives contracts transacted on exchanges.

H.R. Conf. Rep. No. 111-517, at 879 (2010).

Section 1256(b)(2)(B) contemplates that a swap contract, even if traded on or subject to the rules of a qualified board or exchange, will not be a section 1256 contract.

B. *Scope of Swaps Excluded by Section 1256(b)(2)(B)*

1. *Notional principal contracts and credit default swaps*

Congress incorporated into section 1256(b)(2)(B) a list of swaps that parallels the list of swaps included under the definition of a notional principal contract in § 1.446-3(c) with the addition of credit default swaps. The parallel language suggests that Congress was attempting to harmonize the category of swaps excluded under section 1256(b)(2)(B) with swaps that qualify as notional principal contracts under § 1.446-3(c), rather than with the contracts defined as "swaps" under section 721 of the Dodd-Frank Act. Accordingly, § 1.1256(b)-1(a) of the proposed regulations provides that a section 1256 contract does not include a contract that qualifies as a notional principal contract as defined in proposed § 1.446-3(c). As discussed herein, the proposed regulations under § 1.446-3 also expressly provide that a credit default swap is a notional principal contract.

2. *Option on a notional principal contract*

Section 1256(b)(2)(B) raises questions as to whether an option on a notional principal contract that is traded on a qualified board or exchange would constitute a "similar agreement" or would instead be treated as a nonequity option under section 1256(g)(3). Since an option on a notional principal contract is closely connected with the underlying contract, the Treasury Department and the IRS believe that such an option should be treated as a similar agreement within the meaning of section 1256(b)(2)(B). Accordingly, § 1.1256(b)-1(a) of the proposed regulations also provides that a section 1256 contract does not include an option on any contract that is a notional principal contract defined in § 1.446-3(c) of the proposed regulations.

3. *Ordering rule*

The proposed regulations provide an ordering rule for a contract that trades as a futures contract regulated by the Commodity Futures Trading Commission (CFTC), but that also meets the definition of a notional principal contract. The Treasury Department and the IRS believe that such a contract is not a commodity futures contract of the kind envisioned by Congress when it enacted section 1256. Accordingly, § 1.1256(b)-1(a) of the proposed regulations provides that section 1256 does not include any contract, or option on such contract, that is both a section 1256 contract and a notional principal contract as defined in § 1.446-3(c) of the proposed regulations.

C. *Definition of Regulated Futures Contract*

Section 1256(g)(1) defines a regulated futures contract as "a contract (A) with respect to which the amount required to be deposited and the amount which may be withdrawn depends on a system of marking to market, and (B) which is traded on or subject to the rules of a qualified board or exchange." The apparent breadth of section 1256(g)(1) has raised questions in the past as to whether a contract other than a futures contract can be a regulated futures contract. The Treasury Department and the IRS have historically limited the scope of a regulated futures contract to those futures contracts that have the characteristics of traditional futures contracts. Under the Dodd-Frank Act, a "designated contract market" may trade both futures contracts and swap contracts, although there will be specific reporting rules for swap contracts. In order to properly limit section 1256 to futures contracts that trade on designated contract markets, § 1.1256(b)-1(b) of the proposed regulations provides that a regulated futures contract is a section 1256 contract only if the contract is a futures contract that is not required to be reported as a swap under the Commodity Exchange Act (7 U.S.C. 1) (the CEA). The reporting provisions for swaps under the CEA will not be effective until the CFTC has published final rules implementing such provisions. It is anticipated that swap reporting rules will be in effect before these regulations are finalized. If, however, these proposed income tax regulations are finalized before the swap reporting provisions become effective, the Treasury Department and the IRS will evaluate whether the provisions of § 1.1256(b)-1(b) need to be adjusted.

Questions have also been raised as to whether the requirement that a regulated futures contract be "traded on or subject to the rules of" a qualified board or exchange includes off-exchange transactions such as an exchange of a futures contract for a cash commodity, or an exchange of a futures contract for a swap, that are carried out subject to the rules of a CFTC designated contract market. The phrase "traded on or subject to the rules of" appears to have originated under the CEA. Section 4(a) of the CEA provides, in part, that it is unlawful to engage in any transaction in, or in connection with, a commodity futures contract unless such transaction is conducted on or subject to the rules of a board of trade which has been designated as a contract market and such contract is executed or consummated by or through a contract market. Section 5(d) of the CEA, as amended by section 735 of the Dodd-Frank Act, provides that the rules of a designated contract market may authorize, for bona fide business purposes, transfer trades or office trades, or an exchange of (i) futures in connection with a cash commodity transaction, (ii) futures for cash commodities, or (iii) futures for swaps. As such, the Treasury Department and the IRS believe that a futures contract that results from one of these transactions is a regulated futures contract under section 1256(g)(1) because the contract is traded subject to the rules of a designated contract market.

D. *Qualified Board or Exchange*

Section 1256(g)(7)(C) provides that a qualified board or exchange includes any other exchange, board of trade, or other market which the Secretary determines has rules adequate to carry out the purposes of section 1256. Section 1.1256(g)-1(a) of the proposed regulations specifies that such determinations are only made through published guidance in the **Federal Register** or in the Internal Revenue Bulletin.

Since section 1256(g)(7) was adopted, the Treasury Department and the IRS have issued determinations for six entities, all of them foreign futures exchanges. See Rev. Rul. 2010-3 (2010-1 CB 272 (London International Financial Futures and Options Exchange)), Rev. Rul. 2009-24 (2009-2 CB 306 (ICE Futures Canada)), Rev. Rul. 2009-4 (2009-1 CB 408 (Dubai Mercantile Exchange)), Rev. Rul. 2007-26 (2007-1 CB 970 (ICE Futures)), Rev. Rul. 86-7 (1986-1 CB 295 (The Mercantile Division of the Montreal Exchange)), and Rev. Rul. 85-72 (1985-1 CB 286 (International Futures Exchange (Bermuda))). The IRS has followed a two step process for making each of the six qualified board or exchange determinations under section 1256(g)(7). See § 601.601(d)(2)(ii)(b).

In the first step, the exchange submitted a private letter ruling to the IRS requesting a determination that the exchange is a qualified board or exchange within the meaning of section 1256(g)(7)(C). Once the IRS determined that the exchange had rules sufficient to carry out the purposes of section 1256, the Treasury Department and the IRS published a revenue ruling announcing that the named exchange was a qualified board or exchange. The revenue rulings apply to commodity futures contracts and futures contract options of the type described under the CEA that are entered into on the named exchange. The revenue ruling does not apply to contracts that are entered into on another exchange that is affiliated with the named exchange.

In determining whether a foreign exchange is a qualified board or exchange under section 1256(g)(7)(C), the Treasury Department and the IRS have looked to whether the exchange received a CFTC "direct access" no-action relief letter permitting the exchange to make its electronic trading and matching system available in the United States, notwithstanding that the exchange was not designated as a contract market pursuant to section 5 of the CEA. Section 738 of the Dodd-Frank Act, however, provides the CFTC with authority to adopt rules and regulations that require registration of a foreign board of trade that provides United States participants direct access to the foreign board of trade's electronic trading system. In formulating these rules and regulations, the CFTC is directed to consider whether comparable supervision and regulation exists in the foreign board of trade's home country. Pursuant to section 738, the CFTC has proposed a registration system to replace the direct access no-action letter process. Under the proposed registration system, a foreign board of trade operating pursuant to an existing direct access no-action relief letter must apply through a limited application process for an "Order of Registration" which will replace the foreign board of trade's existing direct access no-action letter. Many of the proposed requirements for and conditions applied to a foreign board of trade's registration will be based upon those applicable to the foreign board of trade's currently granted direct access no-action relief letter.

The IRS has conditioned a foreign exchange's qualified board or exchange status under section 1256(g)(7)(C) on the exchange continuing to satisfy all CFTC conditions necessary to retain its direct access no-action relief letter. Consequently, if the CFTC adopts the proposed registration system, an exchange that has previously received a qualified board or exchange determination under section 1256(g)(7)(C) must obtain a CFTC Order of Registration in order to maintain its qualified board or exchange status. The IRS will continue to evaluate the CFTC's rules in this regard to determine if any changes to the IRS's section 1256(g)(7)(C) guidance process are warranted.

E. *Definition and Scope of a Notional Principal Contract*

1. *Payments under a notional principal contract*

In 1993, the IRS promulgated § 1.446-3(c) which defines a notional principal contract as a financial instrument that provides for the payment of amounts by one party to another at specified intervals calculated by reference to a specified index upon a notional principal amount in exchange for specified consideration or a promise to pay similar amounts. Questions have arisen as to the proper interpretation of this requirement. Sections 1.446-3(c)(1)(i) and (ii) of the proposed regulations expressly provide that a notional principal contract requires one party to make two or more payments to a counterparty. For this purpose, the fixing of an amount is treated as a payment, even if the actual payment reflecting that amount is to be made at a later date. Thus, for example, a contract that provides for a settlement payment referenced to the appreciation or depreciation on a specified number of shares of common stock, adjusted for actual dividends paid during the term of the contract, is treated as a contract with more than one payment with respect to that leg of the contract.

2. *Credit default swaps*

In Notice 2004-52 (2004-2 CB 168), the Treasury Department and the IRS described four possible characterizations of a credit default swap. See § 601.601(d)(2)(ii)(b). These proposed regulations resolve this uncertainty by adding credit default swaps to the list of swaps categorized as notional principal contracts governed by the rules of § 1.446-3.

3. *Weather-related and other non-financial index based swaps*

Since the time that the § 1.446-3 regulations were promulgated, markets have developed for contracts based on non-financial indices. Many of these contracts are structured as swaps, and payments are calculated based on indices such as temperature, precipitation, snowfall, or frost. For example, payments made under a weather derivative may be based on heating degree days and cooling degree days. As a technical matter, a weather-related swap currently is not a notional principal contract because a weather index does not qualify as a "specified index" under § 1.446-3(c)(2) of the current regulations, which generally require that such index be a financial index.

The Treasury Department and the IRS believe that swaps on non-financial indices should be treated as notional principal contracts. Accordingly, § 1.446-3(c)(2)(ii) of the proposed regulations expands a specified index to include non-financial indices that are comprised of any objectively determinable information that is not within the control of any of the parties to the contract and is not unique to one of the parties' circumstances, and that cannot be reasonably expected to front-load or back-load payments accruing under the contract.

4. *Excluded contracts*

Section 1.446-3(c)(1)(ii) currently provides that a contract described in section 1256(b) and a futures contract are not notional principal contracts. In order to remove the circularity that would otherwise exist between excluded contracts under § 1.446-3(c)(1)(ii) and proposed § 1.1256(b)-1, a contract described in section 1256(b) and a futures contract have been deleted from excluded contracts under proposed § 1.446-3(c)(1)(iv).

5. *Conforming Amendments*

The definition of a notional principal contract in § 1.446-3(c) of the proposed regulations is intended to be the operative definition for all Federal income tax purposes, except where a different or more limited definition is specifically prescribed. Thus, the regulations under sections 512, 863, 954, and 988 have been amended to reference the definition of a notional principal contract in § 1.446-3(c).

Proposed Effective/Applicability Date

These regulations are proposed to apply to contracts entered into on or after the date the final regulations are published in the **Federal Register**.

Special Analyses

It has been determined that this notice of proposed rulemaking is not a significant regulatory action as defined in Executive Order 12866. Therefore, a regulatory assessment is not required. It has also been determined that section 553(b) of the Administrative Procedure Act (5 U.S.C. chapter 5) does not apply to these regulations, and because the regulation does not impose a collection of information on small entities, the Regulatory Flexibility Act (5 U.S.C. chapter 6) does not apply. Pursuant to section 7805(f) of the Code, this notice of proposed rulemaking will be submitted to the Chief Counsel for Advocacy of the Small Business Administration for comment on its impact on small business.

Comments and Public Hearing

Before these proposed regulations are adopted as final regulations, consideration will be given to any written comments (a signed original and eight (8) copies) or electronic comments that are submitted timely to the IRS. The Treasury Department and IRS invite comments on the clarity of the proposed rules and how they can be made easier to understand. All comments will be available at *www.regulations.gov* or upon request.

A public hearing has been scheduled for January 19, 2012, beginning at 10 a.m. in the Auditorium, Internal Revenue Building, 1111 Constitution Avenue, N.W., Washington, DC. Due to building security procedures, visitors must enter at the Constitution Avenue entrance. In addition, all visitors must present photo identification to enter the building. Because of access restrictions, visitors will not be admitted beyond the immediate entrance area more than 30 minutes before the hearing starts. For information about having your name placed on the building access list to attend the hearing, see the "FOR FURTHER INFORMATION CONTACT" section of this preamble.

The rules of 26 CFR 601.601(a)(3) apply to the hearing. Persons who wish to present oral comments at the hearing must submit written or electronic comments by December 15, 2011 and an outline of the topics to be discussed and the time to be devoted to each topic (a signed original and eight (8) copies) by December 14, 2011. A period of 10 minutes will be allotted to each person for making comments. An agenda showing the scheduling of the speakers will be prepared after the deadline for receiving outlines has passed. Copies of the agenda will be available free of charge at the hearing.

Drafting Information

The principal author of these proposed regulations is K. Scott Brown, Office of the Associate Chief Counsel (Financial Institutions and Products). However, other personnel from the IRS and Treasury Department participated in their development.

[¶49,499] Proposed Amendments of Regulations (REG-133002-10), published in the Federal Register on October 24, 2011.

[Code Sec. 1502]

Corporations: Consolidated returns: Net unrealized built-in gains: Net unrealized built-in losses.—Amendments of Reg. § 1.1502-91, relating to corporations filing consolidated returns, are proposed.

AGENCY: Internal Revenue Service (IRS), Treasury.

ACTION: Notice of proposed rulemaking.

SUMMARY: This document contains proposed regulations under section 1502 of the Internal Revenue Code. The regulations will apply to corporations filing consolidated returns. The regulations will require a loss group or loss subgroup to redetermine its consolidated net unrealized built-in gain and loss in certain circumstances. This document also invites comments from the public regarding these proposed regulations.

DATES: Written or electronic comments and requests for a public hearing must be received by January 23, 2012.

ADDRESSES: Send submissions to: CC:PA:LPD:PR (REG-133002-10), room 5205, Internal Revenue Service, PO Box 7604, Ben Franklin Station, Washington, DC 20044. Submissions may be hand-delivered Monday through Friday between the hours of 8 a.m. and 4 p.m. to CC:PA:LPD:PR

(REG-133002-10), Courier's Desk, Internal Revenue Service, 1111 Constitution Avenue, NW, Washington, DC, or sent electronically, via the Federal eRulemaking Portal at *http://www.regulations.gov* (IRS REG-133002-10).

FOR FURTHER INFORMATION CONTACT: Concerning the proposed regulations, Grid Glyer (202) 622-7930; concerning submissions of comments and requests for a public hearing, Oluwafunmilayo Taylor (202) 622-7180 (not toll-free numbers).

SUPPLEMENTARY INFORMATION:

Background

To prevent loss trafficking, section 382 imposes a limitation (the section 382 limitation) on a loss corporation's ability to use net operating losses that arose prior to an ownership change. Section 382(b)(1). In addition, if a loss corporation has a net unrealized built-in loss (NUBIL) at the time of an ownership change, built-in losses will be subject to the section 382 limitation as if they were pre-change losses of the loss corporation if they are recognized during the five-year period following the ownership change (the recognition period). Section 382(h)(1)(B). If a corporation has a net unrealized built-in gain (NUBIG) at the time of its ownership change, recognized built-in gains will increase the section 382 limitation if they are recognized during the recognition period. Section 382(h)(1)(A). Rules for determining whether a loss corporation has a NUBIG or NUBIL are found in section 382(h)(3).

Sections 1.1502-90 through 1.1502-99 provide guidance for applying section 382 with respect to a consolidated loss group or loss subgroup. In this preamble, the term loss group refers to both loss groups and loss subgroups. See § § 1.1502-91(c)(1) and 1.1502-91(d).

Section 1.1502-91(g) provides rules for determining whether a loss group has a NUBIG or NUBIL. Section 1.1502-91(g)(1) provides that the determination of whether a loss group has a consolidated NUBIG or NUBIL is based on the aggregate amount of the separately determined NUBIGs and NUBILs of each member included in the loss group. Under this rule, unrealized gain or loss with respect to the stock of a member of the loss group (an included subsidiary) is disregarded in determining the separately determined NUBIG or NUBIL.

Explanation of Provisions

The current regulations under § 1.1502-91(g) are premised upon the observation that unrecognized gain or loss on included subsidiary stock generally reflects the same economic gain or loss reflected in the subsidiary's assets and that the consolidated return regulations generally prevent the group from taking that duplicative gain or loss into account more than once. This is the case because, if the subsidiary first recognizes the duplicated gain or loss on its assets, § 1.1502-32 eliminates the duplicative gain or loss reflected in stock basis. Conversely, if a member first recognizes duplicated loss on the subsidiary stock, § 1.1502-36 eliminates the duplicative asset loss. Although the regulations do not specifically address the recognition of duplicated gain on subsidiary stock, taxpayers generally avoid duplicative gain recognition, for example, through actual and section 338 deemed asset sales and through stock elimination transactions, such as section 332 liquidations. Because duplicative gain and loss is expected to be taken into account only once, the determination of NUBIG and NUBIL would be distorted if it included such amounts more than once.

To illustrate, assume P, the common parent of a consolidated group, contributes $100 to S in exchange for S's sole share of stock. S uses the $100 to purchase a truck. The value of the truck then declines to $70. At this point, the stock has a basis of $100 and a value of $70, reflecting a $30 loss. In addition, the truck has a basis of $100 and value of $70, also reflecting a $30 loss. Thus, it would appear the group has $60 of loss available. However, if S sells the truck and the group absorbs the $30 loss, P will reduce its basis in the S stock by $30 under § 1.1502-32, and the duplicative stock loss will be eliminated. On the other hand, if P sells its S share before the loss on the truck is recognized and absorbed, the duplicated loss (on either the truck or the stock, as P chooses) will be eliminated by § 1.1502-36. As a result, the group takes into account a single $30 economic loss, and the inclusion of both the unrecognized stock loss and the unrecognized asset loss in the NUBIL determination would overstate the amount of loss actually available to the group.

However, if an unrecognized gain or loss on subsidiary stock exceeds the included subsidiary's gain or loss on its assets, disregarding this unduplicated gain or loss on the stock understates the amount that the group may take into account.

To illustrate, assume the same facts as in the previous example except that P originally purchased the S stock for $150 (S's basis in the truck is still $100). In this case, there is $80 of loss available to the group, the $30 loss that is duplicated (reflected in the bases of both the stock and the truck), as well as the $50 unduplicated stock loss. Disregarding P's loss in its S stock causes the group's NUBIL to be understated by $50. These proposed regulations are intended to prevent such understatement.

The current rule is administratively less burdensome to taxpayers and the government than a rule that would require taxpayers to identify and take into account all unduplicated gain and loss on stock of included subsidiaries when determining NUBIG and NUBIL. Nevertheless, the IRS and the Treasury Department believe that the purpose of section 382(h) would be better served by a rule that does not wholly disregard such gain and loss. A rule that takes into account unduplicated gain or loss on stock would avoid both the understating of loss available to the group (when there is unduplicated stock loss) and the overstating of loss trafficking potential (when there is unduplicated stock gain).

The IRS and the Treasury Department are concerned, however, that requiring all consolidated NUBIG and NUBIL determinations to include all unduplicated stock gains and losses would significantly increase the administrative burden on both taxpayers and the government.

Accordingly, the IRS and the Treasury Department propose to modify the current regulations to take into account the unduplicated gain or loss on stock of included subsidiaries, but only to the extent that such gain or loss is taken into account by the group during the recognition period. This will generally be the case only if, within the recognition period, such stock is sold to a nonmember or becomes worthless, or a member takes an intercompany item into account with respect to such stock.

More specifically, the proposed regulations would revise § 1.1502-91(g) by adding a rule that would apply when any member of the consolidated group directly or indirectly (for example, through a partnership) takes any amount of gain or loss into account with respect to a share of stock of an included subsidiary (S), whether or not such amount is absorbed. When the rule applies, the loss group would be required to redetermine NUBIG or NUBIL to include any unduplicated built-in gain or loss with respect to the share. As used in these proposed regulations, the term unduplicated built-in stock gain or loss refers to the portion of the built-in stock gain or loss that was not originally reflected in the loss group's NUBIG or NUBIL as unrealized gain or loss on the assets of a lower-tier included subsidiary. The proposed regulations identify unduplicated built-in stock gain or loss by treating the separate NUBIG or NUBIL of each included subsidiary that is lower-tier to S as having been taken into account and absorbed immediately before the change date. These amounts are then deemed to tier-up to tentatively adjust the basis in the S shares under the principles of § 1.1502-32. The difference between the tentatively adjusted change-date basis in a share of S stock and the fair market value of the share (as of the change date) is the unduplicated gain or loss in the S share. However, if, immediately before the change date, a member of the loss group has a deferred gain or loss on S stock and that gain or loss is taken into account during the recognition period, the unduplicated portion of such gain or loss is determined as of the date of the transaction in which the deferred gain or loss was recognized, notwithstanding that such date would be prior to the change date.

The loss group then redetermines its NUBIG or NUBIL by including its unduplicated gain or loss on the S share (or shares) with respect to which an amount is taken into account. Under the proposed regulations, the redetermined NUBIG or NUBIL is given effect only immediately before the gain or loss on the stock is taken into account. It has no effect on the treatment of built-in gain or loss that is recognized and taken into account prior to the time that built-in stock gain or loss is taken into account. Thus, for example, the fact that a NUBIL group was redetermined to be a NUBIG group, or that a NUBIL that exceeded the 15 percent threshold amount in section 382(h)(3)(B) no longer exceeds such amount, has no effect on the tax treatment of amounts taken into account prior to the redetermination of NUBIG or NUBIL.

The proposed regulations also reorganize § 1.1502-91(g) and revise § 1.1502-91(h)(2) and (h)(4) without substantive change.

Effective/Applicability Date

These proposed regulations will apply to amounts taken into account with respect to a share of stock of an included subsidiary on or after the date that final regulations are published in the **FEDERAL REGISTER**, but only with respect to ownership changes occurring on or after October 24, 2011.

Special Analyses

It has been determined that this notice of proposed rulemaking is not a significant regulatory action as defined in Executive Order 12866, as supplemented by Executive Order 13565. Therefore, a regulatory assessment is not required. Pursuant to the Regulatory Flexibility Act (5 U.S.C. chapter 6), it is hereby certified that these proposed regulations would not have a significant economic impact on a substantial number of small entities. This certification is based on the fact that these proposed regulations would primarily affect members of consolidated groups which tend to be large corporations. Accordingly, a regulatory flexibility analysis is not required. Pursuant to section 7805(f) of the Internal Revenue Code, these regulations have been submitted to the Chief Counsel for Advocacy of the Small Business Administration for comment on their impact on small business.

Comments and Requests for a Public Hearing

Before these proposed regulations are adopted as final regulations, consideration will be given to any written (a signed original and eight (8) copies) or electronic comments that are submitted timely to the IRS. All comments will be available for public inspection and copying. A public hearing may be scheduled if requested in writing by any person that timely submits written or electronic comments. If a public hearing is scheduled, notice of the date, time, and place for the public hearing will be published in the **Federal Register**.

Drafting Information

The principal author of these regulations is Grid Glyer of the Office of Associate Chief Counsel (Corporate). However, other personnel from the IRS and the Treasury Department participated in its development.

[¶49,503] **Proposed Amendments of Regulations (REG-146537-06)**, published in the Federal Register on November 3, 2011 (corrected 11/23/2011).

[Code Sec. 892]

International taxation: Foreign governments: International organizations: Income from U.S. sources.—Reg. §1.892-4 and amendments of Reg. §1.892-5, relating to the taxation of the income of foreign governments from investments in the United States under Code Sec. 892, are proposed.

AGENCY: Internal Revenue Service (IRS), Treasury.

ACTION: Notice of proposed rulemaking.

SUMMARY: This document contains proposed Income Tax Regulations that provide guidance relating to the taxation of the income of foreign governments from investments in the United States under section 892 of the Internal Revenue Code of 1986 (Code). The regulations will affect foreign governments that derive income from sources within the United States.

DATES: Written or electronic comments and requests for a public hearing must be received by February 1, 2012.

ADDRESSES: Send submissions to: CC:PA:LPD:PR (REG-146537-06), Room 5205, Internal Revenue Service, PO Box 7604, Ben Franklin Station, Washington, DC 20044. Submissions may be hand-delivered Monday through Friday between the hours of 8 a.m. and 4 p.m. to CC:PA:LPD:PR (REG-146537-06), Courier's Desk, Internal Revenue Service, 1111 Constitution Avenue, NW, Washington, DC, or sent electronically, via the Federal eRulemaking Portal at *www.regulations.gov* (IRS REG-146537-06).

FOR FURTHER INFORMATION CONTACT: Concerning the proposed regulations, David A. Juster, (202) 622-3850 (not a toll-free number); concerning submission of comments, contact Richard A. Hurst at *Richard.A.Hurst@irscounsel.treas.gov*.

SUPPLEMENTARY INFORMATION:

Paperwork Reduction Act

The collections of information contained in this notice of proposed rulemaking have been submitted to the Office of Management and Budget (OMB) for review and approval under OMB approval number 1545-1053 in accordance with the Paperwork Reduction Act of 1995 (44 U.S.C. 3507(d)). Comments on the collections of information should be sent to the **Office of Management and Budget**, Attn: Desk Officer for the Department of the Treasury, Office of Information and Regulatory Affairs, Washington, DC 20503, with copies to the **Internal Revenue Service**, Attn: IRS Reports Clearance Officer, SE:CAR:MP:T:T:SP, Washington, DC 20224. Comments on the collections of information should be received by January 3, 2012. Comments are specifically requested concerning:

Whether the proposed collections of information are necessary for the proper performance of the functions of the Internal Revenue Service, including whether the information will have practical utility;

The accuracy of the estimated burden associate with the proposed collections of information;

How the quality, utility, and clarity of the information to be collected may be enhanced;

How the burden of complying with the proposed collections of information may be minimized, including through the application of automated collection techniques or other forms of information technology; and

Estimates of capital or start-up costs and costs of operation, maintenance, and purchase of services to provide information.

The collections of information in this proposed regulations are in §§1.892-5(a)(2)(ii)(B) and 1.892-5(a)(2)(iv). This information is required to determine if taxpayers qualify for exemption from tax under section 892. The collections of information are voluntary to obtain a benefit. The likely respondents are foreign governments.

Estimated total annual reporting burden: 975 hours.

Estimated average annual burden hours per respondent: 5 hours.

Estimated number of respondents: 195.

Estimated annual frequency of responses: 1.

An agency may not conduct or sponsor, and a person is not required to respond to, a collection of information unless it displays a valid control number assigned by the Office of Management and Budget.

Books or records relating to a collection of information must be retained as long as their contents may become material in the administration of any internal revenue law. Generally, tax returns and tax return information are confidential, as required by 26 U.S.C. 6103.

Background

This document contains proposed amendments to 26 CFR part 1 and to 26 CFR part 602. On June 27, 1988, temporary regulations under section 892 (TD 8211, 53 FR 24060) (1988 temporary regulations) with a cross-reference notice of proposed rulemaking (53 FR 24100) were published in the **Federal Register** to provide guidance concerning the taxation of income of foreign governments and international organizations from investments in the United States. The proposed regulations contained herein supplement the cross-reference notice of proposed rulemaking to provide additional guidance for determining when a foreign government's investment income is exempt from U.S. taxation.

Explanation of Provisions

The Treasury Department and the IRS have recently received numerous written comments on the 1988 temporary regulations. The proposed regulations are issued in response to those comments.

Treatment of Controlled Entities

Section 892 exempts from U.S. income taxation certain qualified investment income derived by a foreign government. Section 1.892-2T defines the term foreign government to mean only the integral parts or controlled entities of a foreign sovereign. The exemption from U.S. income tax under section 892 does not apply to income (1) derived from the conduct of any commercial activity, (2) received by a controlled commercial entity or received (directly or indirectly) from a controlled commercial entity, or (3) derived from the disposition of any interest in a controlled commercial entity. Section 892(a)(2)(B) defines a controlled commercial entity as an entity owned by the foreign government that meets certain ownership or control thresholds and that is engaged in commercial activities anywhere in the world. Accordingly, an integral part of a foreign sovereign that derives income from both qualified investments and from the conduct of commercial activity is eligible to claim the section 892 exemption with respect to the income from qualified investments, but not with respect to the income derived from the conduct of commercial activity. In contrast, if a controlled entity (as defined in § 1.892-2T(a)(3)) engages in commercial activities anywhere in the world, it is treated as a controlled commercial entity, and none of its income (including income from otherwise qualified investments) qualifies for exemption from tax under section 892. In addition, none of the income derived from the controlled entity (e.g., dividends), including the portion attributable to qualified investments of the controlled entity, will be eligible for the section 892 exemption. Several comments raised concerns that this so-called "all or nothing" rule represents an unnecessary administrative and operational burden for foreign governments and a trap for unwary foreign governments that inadvertently conduct a small level of commercial activity. These comments have requested that the Treasury Department and the IRS revise § 1.892-5T(a) to provide for a de minimis exception under which an entity would not be treated as a controlled commercial entity as a result of certain inadvertent commercial activity.

In response to these comments, the proposed regulations at § 1.892-5(a)(2) provide that an entity will not be considered to engage in commercial activities if it conducts only inadvertent commercial activity. Commercial activity will be treated as inadvertent commercial activity only if: (1) the failure to avoid conducting the commercial activity is reasonable; (2) the commercial activity is promptly cured; and (3) certain record maintenance requirements are met. However, none of the income derived from such inadvertent commercial activity will qualify for exemption from tax under section 892.

In determining whether an entity's failure to avoid conducting a particular commercial activity is reasonable, due regard will be given to the number of commercial activities conducted during the taxable year, as well as the amount of income earned from, and assets used in, the conduct of the commercial activity in relationship to the entity's total income and assets. However, a failure to avoid conducting commercial activity will not be considered reasonable unless adequate written policies and operational procedures are in place to monitor the entity's worldwide activities. The proposed regulations include a safe harbor at § 1.892-5(a)(2)(ii)(C) under which, provided that there are adequate written policies and operational procedures in place to monitor the entity's worldwide activities, the controlled entity's failure to avoid the conduct of commercial activity during a taxable year will be considered reasonable if: (1) the value of the assets used in, or held for use in, the activity does not exceed five percent of the total value of the assets reflected on the entity's balance sheet for the taxable year as prepared for financial accounting purposes; and (2) the income earned by the entity from the commercial activity does not exceed five percent of the entity's gross income as reflected on its income statement for the taxable year as prepared for financial accounting purposes.

Comments also requested further guidance on the duration of a determination that an entity is a controlled commercial entity. In response to these comments, the proposed regulations at § 1.892-5(a)(3) provide that the determination of whether an entity is a controlled commercial entity within the meaning of section 892(a)(2)(B) will be made on an annual basis. Accordingly, an entity will not be considered a controlled commercial entity for a taxable year solely because the entity engaged in commercial activities in a prior taxable year.

Definition of Commercial Activity

Section 1.892-4T of the 1988 temporary regulations provides rules for determining whether income is derived from the conduct of a commercial activity, and specifically identifies certain activities that are not commercial, including certain investments, trading activities, cultural events, non-profit activities, and governmental functions. Several comments have expressed uncertainty about the applicable U.S. standard for determining when an activity will be considered a commercial activity, a non-profit activity, or governmental function for purposes of section 892 and § 1.892-4T.

Section 1.892-4(d) of the proposed regulations restates the general rule adopted in the 1988 temporary regulations that, subject to certain enumerated exceptions, all activities ordinarily conducted for the current or future production of income or gain are commercial activities. Section 1.892-4(d) of the proposed regulations further provides that only the nature of an activity, not the purpose or motivation for conducting the activity, is determinative of whether the activity is a commercial activity. This standard also applies for purposes of determining whether an activity is characterized as a non-profit activity or governmental function under § 1.892-4T(c)(3) and (c)(4). In addition, § 1.892-4(d) of the proposed regulations clarifies the rule in the 1988 temporary regulations by providing that an activity may be considered a commercial activity even if the activity does not constitute a trade or business for purposes of section 162 or does not constitute (or would not constitute if undertaken in the United States) the conduct of a trade or business in the United States for purposes of section 864(b).

Section 1.892-4T(c) lists certain activities that will not be considered commercial activities. One such activity is investments in financial instruments, as defined in § 1.892-3T(a)(4), which, if held in the execution of governmental financial or monetary policy, are not commercial activities for purposes of section 892. Several comments have requested that the condition that financial instruments be "held in the execution of governmental financial or monetary policy" be eliminated to more closely conform the treatment of investments in financial instruments, including derivatives, with investments in physical stocks and securities, which under the 1988 temporary regulations generally are not commercial activities regardless of whether they are held in the execution of governmental financial or monetary policy. Section 1.892-4(e)(1)(i) of the proposed regulations modifies the rules in § 1.892-4T(c)(1)(i) by providing that investments in financial instruments will not be treated as commercial activities for purposes of section 892, irrespective of whether such financial instruments are held in the execution of governmental financial or monetary policy. In addition, § 1.892-4(e)(1)(ii) of the proposed regulations expands the existing exception in § 1.892-4T(c)(1)(ii) from commercial activity for trading of stocks, securities, and commodities to include financial instruments, without regard to whether such financial instruments are held in the execution of governmental financial or monetary policy. These revisions address only the definition of commercial activity for purposes of determining whether a government will be considered to derive income from the conduct of a commercial activity, or whether an entity will be considered to be engaged in commercial activities. They do not address whether income from activities that are not commercial activities will be exempt from tax under section 892. Pursuant to § 1.892-3T(a), only income derived from investments in financial instruments held in the execution of governmental financial or monetary policy will qualify for exemption from tax under section 892.

Comments have requested clarification as to whether an entity that disposes of a United States real property interest (USRPI) as defined in section 897(c) will be deemed to be engaged in commercial activities solely by reason of this disposition. Section 897(a)(1) requires that a nonresident alien or foreign corporation take into account gain or loss from the disposition of a USRPI as if the taxpayer were engaged in a trade or business within the United States during the taxable year and as if such gain or loss were effectively connected with that trade or business. The Treasury Department and the IRS believe that an entity that only holds passive investments and is not otherwise engaged in commercial activities should not be deemed to be engaged in commercial activities solely by reason of the operation of section 897(a)(1). Accordingly, § 1.892-4(e)(1)(iv) of the proposed regulations provides that a disposition, including a deemed disposition under section 897(h)(1), of a USRPI, by itself, does not constitute the conduct of a commercial activity. However, as provided in § 1.892-3T(a), the income derived from the disposition of the USRPI described in section 897(c)(1)(A)(i) shall in no event qualify for the exemption from tax under section 892.

After the 1988 temporary regulations were published, section 892(a)(2)(A) was amended by the Technical and Miscellaneous Revenue Act of 1988 (TAMRA), Public Law No. 100-647, 102 Stat. 3342 to provide that income derived from the disposition of any interest in a controlled commercial entity does not qualify for the exemption under section 892. The proposed regulations revise § 1.892-5(a) to reflect the amendment of section 892 by TAMRA.

Treatment of Partnerships

Section 1.892-5T(d)(3) provides a general rule that commercial activities of a partnership are attributable to its general and limited partners ("partnership attribution rule") and provides a limited exception to this rule for partners of publicly traded partnerships (PTPs). Several comments have requested that the Treasury Department and the IRS modify the partnership attribution rule to provide that the activities of a partnership will not be attributed to a foreign government partner if that government: (i) holds a minority interest, as a limited partner, in the partnership; and (ii) has no greater rights to participate in the management and conduct of the partnership's business than would a minority shareholder in a corporation conducting the same activities as the partnership. The comments assert that the partnership attribution rule causes many controlled entities of foreign sovereigns to forego making investments in foreign partnerships or other foreign entities that do not invest in the United States out of concern that such investments might cause those controlled entities to be treated as controlled commercial entities.

In response to these comments, § 1.892-5(d)(5)(iii) of the proposed regulations modifies the existing exception to the partnership attribution rule for PTP interests by providing a more general exception for limited partnership interests. Under this revised exception, an entity that is not otherwise engaged in commercial activities will not be treated as engaged in commercial activities solely because it holds an interest as a limited partner in a limited partnership, including a publicly traded partnership that qualifies as a limited partnership.

For this purpose, an interest as a limited partner in a limited partnership is defined as an interest in an entity classified as a partnership for federal tax purposes if the holder of the interest does not have rights to participate in the management and conduct of the partnership's business at any time during the partnership's taxable year under the law of the jurisdiction in which the partnership is organized or under the governing agreement. This definition of an interest as a limited partner in a limited partnership applies solely for purposes of this exception, and no inference is intended that the same definition would apply for any other provision of the Code making or requiring a distinction between a general partner and a limited partner.

Although the commercial activity of a limited partnership will not cause a controlled entity of a foreign sovereign limited partner meeting the requirements of the exception for limited partnerships to be engaged in commercial activities, the controlled entity partner's distributive share of partnership income attributable to such commercial activity will be considered to be derived from the conduct of commercial activity, and therefore will not be exempt from taxation under section 892. Additionally, in the case of a partnership that is a controlled commercial entity, no part of the foreign government partner's distributive share of partnership income will qualify for exemption from tax under section 892.

Comments also assert that disparity in tax treatment exists under the temporary regulations regarding foreign government trading activity described in § 1.892-4T(c)(1)(ii) because trading for a foreign government's own account does not constitute a commercial activity but no similar rule applies in the case of trading done by a partnership of which a foreign government is a partner. The comments note that this disparity is not generally present in determining whether an activity is a trade or business within the United States under section 864(b). See § 1.864-2(c)(2)(i) and (d)(2)(i). In response to these comments, § 1.892-5(d)(5)(ii) of the proposed regulations provides that an entity that is not otherwise engaged in commercial activities will not be considered to be engaged in commercial activities solely because it is a member of a partnership that effects transactions in stocks, bonds, other securities, commodities, or financial instruments for the partnership's own account. However, this exception does not apply in the case of a partnership that is a dealer in stocks, bonds, other securities, commodities, or financial instruments. For this purpose, whether a partnership is a dealer is determined under the principles of § 1.864-2(c)(2)(iv)(a).

Proposed Effective/Applicability Date

These regulations are proposed to apply on the date of publication of the Treasury decision adopting these rules as final regulations in the **Federal Register**. For rules applicable to periods prior to the publication date, see the corresponding provisions in §§ 1.892-4T and 1.892-5T in the 1988 temporary regulations and in § 1.892-5(a) as issued under TD 9012 (August 1, 2002).

Reliance on Proposed Regulations

Taxpayers may rely on the proposed regulations until final regulations are issued.

Special Analyses

It has been determined that this notice of proposed rulemaking is not a significant regulatory action as defined in Executive Order 12866. Therefore, a regulatory assessment is not required. It has also been determined that section 553(b) of the Administrative Procedure Act (5 U.S.C. chapter 5) does not apply to these regulations and because the proposed regulations do not impose a collection of information on small entities, the Regulatory Flexibility Act (5 U.S.C. chapter 6) does not apply. Pursuant to section 7805(f) of the Code, this notice of proposed rulemaking has been submitted to the Chief Counsel for Advocacy of the Small Business Administration for comment on its impact on small business.

Comments and Requests for Public Hearing

Before the proposed regulations are adopted as final regulations, consideration will be given to any written (a signed original and eight (8) copies) or electronic comments, that are submitted timely to the IRS. The Treasury Department and the IRS request comments on the clarity of the proposed regulations and how they can be made easier to understand. All comments will be available for public inspection and copying. A public hearing will be scheduled if requested in writing by any person that timely submits written comments. If a public hearing is scheduled, notice of the date, time, and place for the public hearing will be published in the **Federal Register**.

Drafting Information

The principal author of these regulations is David A. Juster of the Office of Associate Chief Counsel (International), within the Office of Chief Counsel, IRS. Other personnel from the Treasury Department and the IRS participated in developing the regulations.

[¶ 49,504] Proposed Amendments of Regulations (REG-114749-09) and Withdrawal of Notice of Proposed Rulemaking (INTL-0018-92/REG-209545-92), published in the Federal Register on November 4, 2011.

[Code Sec. 964]

Foreign income: Controlled foreign corporations: Domestic shareholders: Elections: Method of accounting: Tax year.—Amendments of Reg. § 1.964-1, relating to clarify the rules for controlling domestic shareholders to adopt or change a method of accounting or tax year on behalf of a foreign corporation, are proposed. The notice of proposed rulemaking published on July 1, 1992, is withdrawn.

AGENCY: Internal Revenue Service (IRS), Treasury.

ACTION: Withdrawal of notice of proposed rulemaking and notice of proposed rulemaking.

SUMMARY: These proposed regulations would clarify the rules for controlling domestic shareholders to adopt or change a method of accounting or taxable year on behalf of a foreign corporation. The regulations affect United States persons that own stock in certain foreign corporations.

DATES: Written or electronic comments and requests for a public hearing must be received by February 2, 2012.

ADDRESSES: Send submissions to CC:PA:LPD:PR (REG-114749-09), Room 5203, Internal Revenue Service, PO Box 7604, Ben Franklin Station, Washington, DC 20044. Submissions may be hand-delivered between the hours of 8 a.m. and 4 p.m. to CC:PA:LPD:PR (REG-114749-09), Courier's Desk, Internal Revenue Service, 1111 Constitution Avenue NW; Washington DC, 20224 or sent electronically via the Federal Rulemaking Portal at *www.regulations.gov* (IRS REG-114749-09).

FOR FURTHER INFORMATION CONTACT: Concerning submission of comments, Oluwafunmilayo (Funmi) Taylor (202) 622-7180; concerning the regulations, Joseph W. Vetting (202) 622-3402 (not toll-free numbers).

SUPPLEMENTARY INFORMATION:

Background

On April 17, 1991, a notice of proposed rulemaking (INTL-939-86) under sections 953, 954, 964, 1248, and 6046 of the Internal Revenue Code (Code) was published in the **Federal Register** (56 FR 15540) (the 1991 proposed regulations). No comments were received with respect to the proposed amendments under section 964, which would provide a special definition of controlling domestic shareholders for certain controlled foreign corporations with insurance income. Comments were received on other provisions of the 1991 proposed regulations, but no public hearing was requested and none was held.

On July 1, 1992, a notice of proposed rulemaking (INTL-0018-92) under sections 952 and 964 of the Code was published in the **Federal Register** (57 FR 29246). A correction to the notice of proposed rulemaking was published on October 8, 1992, in the **Federal Register** (57 FR 46355). The proposed regulations would modify the regulations relating to required book-to-tax adjustments in respect of depreciation and inventory accounting. Comments were received. A public hearing was not requested and none was held.

Final regulations published on June 10, 2009 (TD 9452) provided guidance for shareholders of certain foreign corporations to elect or change a method of accounting or a taxable year on behalf of the foreign corporation under section 964 of the Code.

Explanation of Provisions

These proposed regulations provide clarification of the required book-to-tax adjustments, including those in respect of depreciation and amortization, and additional examples illustrating the application of §1.964-1(a) and (c). The proposed regulations also would delete §1.964-1(b)(3), *Example* 2. The example refers to section 963, which was repealed for taxable years beginning after December 31, 1975. Additionally, the proposed regulations provide rules regarding IRS-initiated method changes.

The Treasury Department and the IRS again request comments on whether the special control group definition contained in the 1991 proposed regulations should be adopted.

Special Analyses

It has been determined that this notice of proposed rulemaking is not a significant regulatory action as defined in Executive Order 12866. Therefore, a regulatory assessment is not required. It also has been determined that section 553(b) of the Administrative Procedure Act (5 U.S.C. chapter 5) does not apply to these regulations, and because the regulations do not impose a collection of information on small entities, the Regulatory Flexibility Act (5 U.S.C. chapter 6) does not apply. Pursuant to section 7805(f) of the Internal Revenue Code, these regulations will be submitted to the Chief Counsel for Advocacy of the Small Business Administration for comment on their impact on small businesses.

Comments and Request for a Public Hearing

Before these proposed regulations are adopted as final regulations, consideration will be given to any written (a signed original and eight (8) copies) or electronic comments that are submitted timely to the IRS. The IRS and Treasury Department request comments on the clarity of the proposed regulations and how they can be made easier to understand. All comments will be available for public inspection and copying at *www.regulations.gov* or upon request. A public hearing may be scheduled if requested in writing by a person who timely submits comments. If a public hearing is scheduled, notice of the date, time, and place for the hearing will be published in the **Federal Register**.

Drafting Information

The principal author of these regulations is Joseph W. Vetting, Office of Associate Chief Counsel (International). However, other personnel from the IRS and Treasury Department participated in their development.

[¶49,509] Proposed Amendments of Regulations (REG-109369-10), published in the Federal Register on November 28, 2011.

[Code Sec. 469]

Partners and partnerships: Limited partners: Limited partnerships: Definition of limited partner: Material participation: Business activity: Passive activity losses.—Amendments of Reg. §§1.469-0, 1.469-5, 1.469-9 and Temporary Reg. §1.469-5T, regarding the definition of an "interest

in a limited partnership as a limited partner" for purposes of determining whether a taxpayer materially participates in an activity under Code Sec. 469, are proposed.

AGENCY: Internal Revenue Service (IRS), Treasury.

ACTION: Notice of proposed rulemaking.

SUMMARY: This document contains proposed regulations regarding the definition of an "interest in a limited partnership as a limited partner" for purposes of determining whether a taxpayer materially participates in an activity under section 469 of the Internal Revenue Code (Code). These proposed regulations affect individuals who are partners in partnerships.

DATES: Written or electronic comments and requests for a public hearing must be received by February 27, 2012.

ADDRESSES: Send submissions to: CC:PA:LPD:PR (REG-109369-10), Room 5203, Internal Revenue Service, P.O. Box 7604, Ben Franklin Station, Washington, DC 20044. Submissions may be hand-delivered Monday through Friday between the hours of 8 a.m. and 4 p.m. to: CC:PA:LPD:PR (REG-109369-10), Courier's Desk, Internal Revenue Service, 1111 Constitution Avenue NW., Washington, DC, or sent electronically, via the Federal eRulemaking Portal at *http://www.regulations.gov/(IRS REG-109369-10)*.

FOR FURTHER INFORMATION CONTACT: Concerning the proposed regulations, Michala Irons, (202) 622-3050; concerning submissions of comments and requests for public hearing, Oluwafunmilayo Taylor, (202) 622-7180 (not toll free numbers).

SUPPLEMENTARY INFORMATION:

Background

Section 469(a)(1) limits the ability of certain taxpayers to deduct losses from passive activities. Section 469(b) permits passive losses disallowed in one year to be carried over to the next year. Section 469(c)(1) provides that a passive activity means any activity which involves the conduct of any trade or business, and in which the taxpayer does not materially participate. Section 469(h)(1) provides that a taxpayer shall be treated as materially participating in an activity only if the taxpayer is involved in the operations of the activity on a basis which is regular, continuous, and substantial. The Treasury Department and the IRS promulgated temporary regulations under section 469 in 1988. See TD 8175, 53 FR 5686 (February 25, 1988). Section 1.469-5T(a) provides that an individual taxpayer shall be treated as materially participating in an activity for the taxable year if and only if:

(1) The individual participates in the activity for more than 500 hours during such year;

(2) The individual's participation in the activity for the taxable year constitutes substantially all of the participation in such activity of all individuals (including individuals who are not owners of interests in the activity) for such year;

(3) The individual participates in the activity for more than 100 hours during the taxable year, and such individual's participation in the activity for the taxable year is not less than the participation in the activity of any other individual (including individuals who are not owners of interests in the activity) for such year;

(4) The activity is a significant participation activity (within the meaning of § 1.469-5T(c)) for the taxable year, and the individual's aggregate participation in all significant participation activities during such year exceeds 500 hours;

(5) The individual materially participated in the activity (determined without regard to § 1.469-5T(a)(5)) for any five taxable years (whether or not consecutive) during the ten taxable years that immediately precede the taxable year;

(6) The activity is a personal service activity (within the meaning of § 1.469-5T(d)), and the individual materially participated in the activity for any three taxable years (whether or not consecutive) preceding the taxable year; or

(7) Based on all of the facts and circumstances (taking into account the rules in § 1.469-5T(b)), the individual participates in the activity on a regular, continuous, and substantial basis during such year.

Section 469(h)(2) presumptively treats losses from interests in limited partnerships as passive. Section 469(h)(2) provides that, except as provided in regulations, no interest in a limited partnership as a limited partner shall be treated as an interest with respect to which a taxpayer materially participates. Section 1.469-5T(e)(2) permits an individual taxpayer to establish material participation in a limited partnership but constrains the individual taxpayer to only three of the seven regulatory tests in § 1.469-5T(a), (§ 1.469-5T(a)(1), (a)(5), or (a)(6)).

Section 1.469-5T(e)(3)(i) generally provides that a partnership interest shall be treated as a limited partnership interest if (A) such interest is either designated as a limited partnership interest in the limited partnership agreement or the certificate of limited partnership, without regard to whether the liability of the holder of such interest for obligations of the partnership is limited under applicable State law; or (B) the liability of the holder of such interest for obligations of the partnership is limited, under the law of the State in which the partnership is organized, to a determinable fixed amount (for example, the sum of the holder's capital contributions to the partnership and contractual obligations to make additional capital contributions to the partnership). However, even if the interest is characterized as a limited partnership interest under § 1.469-5T(e)(3)(i), an exception under § 1.469-5T(e)(3)(ii) applies if the individual is a general partner in the partnership at all times during the partnership's taxable year ending with or within the individual's taxable year (or portion of the partnership's taxable year during which the individual (directly or indirectly) owns such limited partnership interest) (the "general partner exception"). If the general partner exception applies, the limited partnership interest will not be treated as such for the year in which the individual taxpayer is a general partner in the partnership. This allows the individual taxpayer to demonstrate material participation through any of the seven regulatory tests in § 1.469-5T(a).

Courts have concluded, in certain instances, that the holder of a limited liability company (LLC) interest is not treated as holding an interest in a limited partnership as a limited partner for purposes of applying the section 469 material participation tests. In *Gregg v. U.S.*, 186 F.Supp.2d 1123 (D. Or. 2000), an Oregon district court concluded that, in the absence of regulations to the effect that an LLC member should be treated as a limited partner, the limited partner exception in section 469(h)(2) was not applicable to LLC members. In *Garnett v. Comm'r*, 132 T.C. 368 (2009), the Tax Court found that the taxpayers' ownership interests in limited liability partnerships and LLCs were not interests in limited partnerships because their interests fit within the general partner exception in § 1.469-5T(e)(3)(ii). Shortly thereafter, in *Thompson v. U.S.*, 87 Fed. Cl. 728 (2009), the Court of Federal Claims concluded that the regulations under section 469(h)(2) require the taxpayer's ownership interest to be in a partnership under State law rather than a partnership under Federal income tax law. Accordingly, because an LLC member is not a limited partner under State law, the court concluded that section 469(h)(2) did not apply to an LLC member. Most recently, the Tax Court in *Newell v. Comm'r*, T.C. Memo. 2010-23, concluded that section 469(h)(2) did not apply to the managing member of an LLC and that the member fell within the general partner exception in § 1.469-5T(e)(3)(ii). On April 5, 2010, the IRS issued an Action on Decision acquiescing in the result only in *Thompson v. U.S.*, AOD 2010-02, 2010-14 I.R.B. 515.

Explanation of Provisions

The proposed regulations provide that an interest in an entity will be treated as an interest in a limited partnership under section 469(h)(2) if (A) the entity in which such interest is held is classified as a partnership for Federal income tax purposes under § 301.7701-3; and (B) the holder of such interest does not have rights to manage the entity at all times during the entity's taxable year under the law of the jurisdiction in which the entity was organized and under the governing agreement. Rights to manage include the power to bind the entity. The proposed regulations provide rules concerning an interest in a limited partnership based on the purposes for which section 469 was enacted, and the manner in which the provision is structured and operates within the Code. Accordingly, the rules concerning an interest in a limited partnership in the proposed regulations are provided solely for purposes of section 469 and no inference is intended that the same rules would apply for any other provisions of the Code requiring a distinction between a general partner and a limited partner.

In *Garnett v. Comm'r, supra,* the Tax Court noted that Congress enacted section 469(h)(2) to address the limitations on a limited partner's ability to participate in the control of the partnership's business. Under the Uniform Limited Partnership Act of 1916, limited partners could lose their limited liability protection if they participated in the control of the partnership. The regulations under section 469(h)(2) were drafted with these constraints in mind. Today, many states have adopted a variation of the Revised Uniform Limited Partnership Act of 1985 (RULPA). Under RULPA, limited partners may participate in the management and control of the partnership without losing their limited liability. As a consequence, limited partners under RULPA are now more akin to general partners and LLC members with respect to their rights in the management of the entity. Under the Uniform Limited Liability Company Act of 1996, LLC members of member-managed LLCs do not lose their limited liability by participating in the management and conduct of the company's business. In *Newell v. Comm'r, supra,* the Tax Court noted that the managing member of the LLC at issue managed the day-to-day operations of the LLC and was the "substantial equivalent" of a general partner. Recognizing that the original presumptions regarding the limitations on a limited partner's participation in the activities of the entity are no longer valid today, and also recognizing the emergence of LLCs, the proposed regulations eliminate the current regulations' reliance on limited liability for purposes of determining whether an interest is an interest in a limited partnership as a limited partner under section 469(h)(2) and instead adopt an approach that relies on the individual partner's right to participate in the management of the entity.

The regulations are proposed to apply to taxable years beginning on or after the date of publication of the Treasury decision adopting these regulations as final regulations in the **Federal Register.**

Special Analyses

It has been determined that this notice of proposed rulemaking is not a significant regulatory action as defined in Executive Order 12866, as supplemented by Executive Order 13563. Therefore, a regulatory assessment is not required. It has also been determined that section 553(b) of the Administrative Procedure Act (5 U.S.C. chapter 5) does not apply to this regulation, and because the regulation does not impose a collection of information on small entities, the Regulatory Flexibility Act (5 U.S.C. chapter 6) does not apply. Pursuant to section 7805(f) of the Code, these regulations will be submitted to the Chief Counsel for Advocacy of the Small Business Administration for comment on its impact on small business.

Comments and Requests Public Hearing

Before these proposed regulations are adopted as final regulations, consideration will be given to any written (a signed original and eight (8) copies) or electronic comments that are submitted timely to the IRS. All comments will be available for public inspection and copying. A public hearing will be scheduled if requested in writing by any person that timely submits written comments. If a public hearing is scheduled, notice of the date, time, and place for the public hearing will be published in the **Federal Register.**

Drafting Information

The principal author of these proposed regulations is Michala Irons, Office of the Associate Chief Counsel (Passthroughs and Special Industries). However, other personnel from the Treasury Department and the IRS participated in their development.

[¶ 49,524] Proposed Amendments of Regulations (REG-124791-11), published in the Federal Register on February 15, 2012.

[Code Sec. 6109]

Identifying numbers: Obtaining identifying numbers: Tax return preparers: Preparers tax identification number (PTIN).—Amendments of Reg. § 1.6109-2, providing guidance on the eligibility of tax return preparers to obtain a preparer tax identification number (PTIN), are proposed.

AGENCY: Internal Revenue Service (IRS), Treasury.

ACTION: Notice of proposed rulemaking.

SUMMARY: This document contains proposed regulations that provide guidance on the eligibility of tax return preparers to obtain a preparer tax identification number (PTIN). These proposed regulations expand the list of tax return preparers who may obtain and renew a PTIN. The proposed regulations additionally provide guidance concerning those tax forms submitted to the Internal Revenue Service that are considered returns of tax or claims for refund of tax for purposes of the requirement to obtain a PTIN and related provisions. This document also invites comments from the public regarding these proposed regulations.

DATES: Written or electronic comments and requests for a public hearing must be received by May 15, 2012.

ADDRESSES: Send submissions to: CC:PA:LPD:PR (REG-124791-11), room 5205, Internal Revenue Service, P.O. Box 7604, Ben Franklin Station, Washington, DC 20044. Submissions may be hand-delivered Monday through Friday between the hours of 8 a.m. and 4 p.m. to CC:PA:LPD:PR (REG-124791-11), Courier's Desk, Internal Revenue Service, 1111 Constitution Avenue, NW., Washington, DC 20224, or sent electronically via the Federal eRulemaking Portal at *www.regulations.gov* (IRS REG-124791-11).

FOR FURTHER INFORMATION CONTACT: Concerning the proposed regulations, Stuart Murray at (202) 622-4940; concerning submissions of comments and requests for a hearing, Oluwafunmilayo (Funmi) Taylor at (202) 622-7180 (not a toll-free numbers).

SUPPLEMENTARY INFORMATION:

Background

This document contains proposed amendments to regulations under section 6109 of the Internal Revenue Code (Code) relating to the identifying number of a tax return preparer and furnishing a tax return preparer's identifying number on tax returns and claims for refund of tax. The Department of Treasury and the Internal Revenue Service published in the **Federal Register** on September 30, 2010 (75 FR 60309) final regulations under section 6109 that prescribe certain requirements relating to the identifying number of tax return preparers.

In particular, the final regulations provided that for tax returns or claims for refund of tax filed after December 31, 2010, the identifying number of a tax return preparer is a PTIN or other identifying number that the IRS prescribes in forms, instructions, or other guidance. The final regulations also provided that after December 31, 2010, a tax return preparer must have a PTIN that is applied for and renewed in the manner the IRS prescribes. The final regulations added § 1.6109-2(d) to the regulations under title 26, providing that to obtain a PTIN or other prescribed identifying number, a tax return preparer must be an attorney, certified public accountant, enrolled agent, or registered tax return preparer authorized to practice before the IRS under Treasury Department Circular No. 230, 31 CFR Part 10 (which Treasury and the IRS amended in final regulations published in the **Federal Register** on June 3, 2011 (76 FR 32286)). For purposes of these requirements, a *tax return preparer* means any individual who is compensated for preparing, or assisting in the preparation of, all or substantially all of a tax return or claim for refund of tax. The final regulations under section 6109 additionally added § 1.6109-2(f), which provides that the IRS may conduct a Federal tax compliance check on a tax return preparer who applies for or renews a PTIN or other prescribed identifying number.

Although the rules in the final regulations under section 6109 went into effect on January 1, 2011, § 1.6109-2(h) allows Treasury and the IRS to prescribe, through forms, instructions, or other appropriate guidance, exceptions to the rules in § 1.6109-2, as necessary, in the interest of effective tax administration. Section 1.6109-2(h) also provides that the IRS may specify through other appropriate guidance "specific returns, schedules, and other forms that qualify as tax returns or claims for refund for purposes of these regulations."

After § 1.6109-2 was amended, Treasury and the IRS issued Notice 2011-6 (2011 IRB 315 January 17, 2011) (see § 601.601(d)(2)(ii)(*b*) of this chapter), which provides additional guidance on the implementation of § 1.6109-2. Specifically, Notice 2011-6, in part, provides further guidance as to tax return preparers who may obtain a PTIN. As explained in Notice 2011-6, the IRS "decided to allow certain individuals who are not attorneys, certified public accountants, enrolled agents, or registered tax return preparers to obtain a PTIN and prepare, or assist in the preparation of, all or substantially all of a tax return in certain discrete circumstances." Pursuant to the authority in § 1.6109-2(h), Notice 2011-6 established two additional categories of tax return preparers who may obtain a PTIN: (1) tax return preparers supervised by attorneys, certified public accountants, enrolled agents, enrolled retirement plan agents, and enrolled actuaries (see § 1.02a of Notice 2011-6); and (2) tax return preparers who prepare tax returns not covered by a competency examination applicable to registered tax return preparers (see § 1.02b of Notice 2011-6). Notice 2011-6 prescribes the requirements an individual must satisfy under each of these two categories, including passing a Federal tax compliance check and a suitability check (when available). Individuals who obtain or renew a PTIN under either of these categories are not registered tax return preparers. Registered tax return preparers are subject to separate, more extensive requirements in Circular 230, including continuing education.

Also pursuant to the authority in § 1.6109-2(h), the IRS in Notice 2011-6 specified that all tax returns, claims for refund, and other tax forms submitted to the IRS are considered tax returns or claims for refund of tax for purposes of § 1.6109-2 unless the IRS provides otherwise. Section 1.03 of Notice 2011-6 explains that the IRS interprets the term "tax forms" broadly for this purpose, and a tax return preparer must obtain a PTIN to prepare for compensation, or to assist in preparing for compensation, all or substantially all of "any form" except those forms that the IRS explicitly excludes. Notice 2011-6 lists the forms by number and title that are currently excluded.

Explanation of Provisions

Treasury and the IRS propose to incorporate the relevant provisions of Notice 2011-6 discussed earlier in this preamble in § 1.6109-2. The proposed regulations provide for two additional categories of tax return preparers to obtain a PTIN (or other identifying number the IRS prescribes), namely, certain supervised tax return preparers and tax return preparers who prepare tax returns and claims for refund that are not covered by a competency examination. As to the first category, the proposed regulations provide that any individual 18 years of age or older is eligible for a PTIN if the individual is supervised as a tax return preparer by an attorney, certified public accountant, enrolled agent, enrolled retirement plan agent, or enrolled actuary authorized to practice before the IRS under Circular 230. The proposed regulations provide that the supervision must be in accordance with any requirements the IRS may prescribe; these requirements are currently set forth in § 1.02a of Notice 2011-6.

As to the second category, the proposed regulations provide that any individual 18 years of age or older is eligible for a PTIN if the individual exclusively prepares tax returns and claims for refund that are not covered by any minimum competency test or tests that the IRS prescribes for registered tax return preparers. To be eligible for a PTIN, an individual must certify, at the time and in whatever manner the IRS may prescribe, that the individual only prepares tax returns and claims for refund that are not covered by a minimum competency test. Under the proposed regulations, the individual must also comply with any other eligibility requirements that the IRS may prescribe; these requirements are currently set forth in § 1.02b of Notice 2011-6.

The proposed regulations provide that for purposes of § 1.6109-2, the terms *tax return* and *claim for refund of tax* include all tax forms submitted to the IRS except forms that the IRS specifically excludes in other appropriate guidance. Notice 2011-6 (§ 1.03) is the current guidance specifying the excluded tax forms. The proposed regulations also amend § 1.6109-2(f) to clarify that the IRS may conduct a suitability check, in addition to a Federal tax compliance check, on certain tax return preparers who apply for or renew a PTIN or other prescribed identifying number. This clarification is consistent with the provisions in both the final Circular 230 regulations and Notice 2011-6 stating that certain individuals who apply to obtain or renew a PTIN or to become a registered tax return preparer will be subject to a suitability check, as well as a tax compliance check.

Proposed Effective/Applicability Date

These regulations are effective on the date that final regulations are published in the **Federal Register**. For proposed dates of applicability, see § 1.6109-2(i).

Special Analyses

It has been determined that this notice of proposed rulemaking is not a significant regulatory action as defined in Executive Order 12866, as supplemented by Executive Order 13563. Therefore, a regulatory assessment is not required. It has also been determined that section 553(b) of the Administrative Procedure Act (5 U.S.C. chapter 5) does not apply to these regulations, and because the regulation does not impose a collection of information on small entities, the Regulatory Flexibility Act (5 U.S.C. chapter 6) does not apply. Pursuant to section 7805(f) of the Code, this notice of proposed rulemaking has been submitted to the Chief Counsel for Advocacy of the Small Business Administration for comment on its impact on small business.

Comments and Requests for Public Hearing

Before these proposed regulations are adopted as final regulations, consideration will be given to any written comments (a signed original and eight (8) copies) or electronic comments that are submitted timely to the IRS. Treasury and the IRS request comments on all aspects of the proposed rules. All comments that are submitted by the public will be available for public inspection and copying. A public hearing will be scheduled if requested in writing by any person who timely submits comments. If a public hearing is scheduled, notice of the date, time, and place for the public hearing will be published in the **Federal Register**.

Drafting Information

The principal author of these proposed regulations is Stuart Murray of the Office of the Associate Chief Counsel, Procedure and Administration.

[¶49,539] Proposed Amendments of Regulations (REG-153627-08), published in the Federal Register on June 21, 2012 (corrected 7/19/2012).

[Code Secs. 6057 and 6081]

Pension plans: Annual registration: Information returns: When to file: Automatic extension to file.—Amendments of Reg. §§301.6057-1, 301.6057-2 and 1.6081-11, providing guidance relating to automatic extensions of time for filing certain employee plan returns by adding the Form 8955-SSA, "Annual Registration Statement Identifying Separated Participants With Deferred Vested Benefits," to the list of forms that are covered by the Income Tax Regulations on automatic extensions, are proposed.

AGENCY: Internal Revenue Service (IRS), Treasury

ACTION: Notice of proposed rulemaking.

SUMMARY: This document contains proposed regulations that would provide guidance relating to automatic extensions of time for filing certain employee plan returns by adding the Form 8955-SSA, "Annual Registration Statement Identifying Separated Participants With Deferred Vested Benefits," to the list of forms that are covered by the Income Tax Regulations on automatic extensions. The proposed regulations would also provide guidance on applicable reporting and participant notice rules that require certain plan administrators to file registration statements and provide notices that set forth information for deferred vested participants. These regulations would affect administrators of, employers maintaining, participants in, and beneficiaries of plans that are subject to the reporting and participant notice requirements.

DATES: Comments and requests for a public hearing must be received by September 19, 2012.

ADDRESSES: Send submissions to CC:PA:LPD:PR (REG-153627-08), room 5205, Internal Revenue Service, PO Box 7604, Ben Franklin Station, Washington D.C. 20044. Submissions may be hand-delivered Monday through Friday between the hours of 8 a.m. and 4 p.m. to CC:PA:LPD:PR (REG-153627-08), Courier's Desk, Internal Revenue Service, 1111 Constitution Avenue, N.W., Washington, DC, 20224, or sent electronically via the Federal eRulemaking Portal at *www.regulations.gov* (IRS REG-153627-08).

FOR FURTHER INFORMATION CONTACT: Concerning the proposed regulations, William Gibbs, Sarah Bolen, or Pamela Kinard at (202) 622-6060; concerning the submission of comments or to request a public hearing, Oluwafunmilayo Taylor, (202) 622-7180 (not toll-free numbers).

SUPPLEMENTARY INFORMATION:

Paperwork Reduction Act

The collection of information contained in this notice of proposed rulemaking has been approved by the Office of Management and Budget for review in accordance with the Paperwork Reduction Act of 1995 (44 U.S.C. 3507(d)) under 1545-2187 and 1545-0212. Comments on the collection of information should be sent to the **Office of Management and Budget,** Attn: Desk Officer for the Department of the Treasury, Office of Information and Regulatory Affairs, Washington D.C. 20503, with copies to the **Internal Revenue Service**, Attn: IRS Reports Clearance Officer, SE:CAR:MP:T:T:SP; Washington DC 20224. Comments on the collection of information should be received by August 20, 2012. Comments are specifically requested concerning:

Whether the proposed collection of information is necessary for the proper performance of the functions of the Internal Revenue Service, including whether the information will have practical utility;

The accuracy of the estimated burden associated with the proposed collection of information;

How the quality, utility, and clarity of the information to be collected may be enhanced;

How the burden of complying with the proposed collection of information may be minimized, including through the application of automated collection techniques or other forms of information technology; and

Estimates of capital or start-up costs and costs of operation, maintenance, and purchase of service to provide information.

The collection of information in these proposed regulations is in §§301.6057-1 and 1.6081-11. This information is required in order to comply with the reporting and notice requirements of section 6057 and to provide automatic extensions of time for filing certain employee plan returns under section 6081. Information relating to these proposed regulations will be collected through Form 8955-SSA and Form 5558. This information relates to plan participants who separate from service covered under the plan and who are entitled to deferred vested retirement benefits under the plan. Any burden relating to these proposed regulations will be included and reported in the next revisions of Form 8955-SSA and Form 5558, after these proposed regulations are accepted as final.

An agency may not conduct or sponsor, and a person is not required to respond to, a collection of information, unless it displays a valid control number assigned by the Office of Management and Budget.

Books or records relating to a collection of information must be retained as long as their contents may become material in the administration of any internal revenue law. Generally, tax returns and tax return information are confidential, as required by 26 U.S.C. 6103.

Background

Section 6057(a) of the Internal Revenue Code (Code) requires the administrator of a plan that is subject to the vesting standards of section 203 of the Employee Retirement Income Security Act of 1974 (ERISA) to file, within the time prescribed by regulations, a registration statement with the Secretary of the Treasury. The registration statement sets forth certain information relating to the plan, plan participants who separate from service covered by the plan and are entitled to deferred vested retirement benefits, and the nature, amount, and form of deferred vested retirement benefits to which the plan participants are entitled.

Section 6057(b) provides that any plan administrator required to register under section 6057(a) shall, within the time prescribed by regulations, also notify the Secretary of any change in the name of the plan or the name and address of the plan administrator, the termination of the plan, or the merger or consolidation of the plan with any other plan or its division into two or more plans.

Section 6057(c) provides that, to the extent provided in regulations prescribed by the Secretary, the administrator of a plan not subject to the reporting requirements of section 6057(a) (including a governmental plan within the meaning of section 414(d) or a church plan within the meaning of section 414(e)) may at its option file such information as the plan administrator may wish to file with respect to the deferred retirement vested benefit rights of any plan participant separated from service covered by the plan.

Section 6057(d) requires the Secretary to transmit copies of any statements, notifications, reports, or other information obtained by the Secretary under section 6057 to the Commissioner of Social Security.

Section 6057(e) of the Code and section 105(c) of ERISA require each plan administrator that is subject to the reporting requirements of section 6057 to furnish to each deferred vested participant an individual statement setting forth the information required by section 6057(a)(2). The individual statement required by section 6057(e) must also notify each participant of any benefits that are forfeitable if the participant dies before a certain date. The individual statement must be furnished no later than the date for filing the registration statement required under section 6057(a).

Section 6057(f)(1) provides that the Secretary, after consultation with the Commissioner of Social Security, may issue such regulations as may be necessary to carry out the provisions of this section.

Since the enactment of ERISA, the Schedule SSA, a schedule to the Form 5500, "Annual Return/ Report of Employee Benefit Plan," has been the form used by plan administrators to comply with the reporting requirements of section 6057. On July 21, 2006, the Department of Labor (DOL) published a final rule in the **Federal Register** (71 FR 41359) requiring electronic filing of the Form 5500 series for plan years beginning after January 1, 2008. On November 16, 2007, the DOL published a final rule in the **Federal Register** (72 FR 64710) postponing the effective date of the electronic filing mandate to apply to plan years beginning on or after January 1, 2009. See 29 CFR § 2520.104a-2.

In order to implement the DOL's mandate for electronic filing of the Form 5500, the IRS-only schedules to the Form 5500, including the Schedule SSA, were eliminated from the Form 5500. One result of the elimination of the Schedule SSA is that Form 5500 filings that include Schedule SSA information regarding participants are now subject to rejection (even for late or amended filings for plan years before 2009). The Schedule SSA was replaced by Form 8955-SSA, "Annual Registration Statement Identifying Separated Participants With Deferred Vested Benefits," an IRS-only stand-alone form. Announcement 2011-21 (2011-12 IRB 567), see § 601.601(d)(2), designates Form 8955-SSA as the form to be used to satisfy the reporting requirements of section 6057 for plan years beginning on or after January 1, 2009. Announcement 2011-21 also established an annual due date for the filing of the Form 8955-SSA. In general, if a Form 8955-SSA must be filed for a plan year, it must be filed by the last day of the 7th month following the last day of that plan year (plus extensions).

Section 6081(a) provides that the Secretary may grant a reasonable extension of time for filing any required return, declaration, statement, or other document. Except for certain taxpayers, the extension of time shall not exceed 6 months.

Section 1.6081-1(a) of the Income Tax Regulations provides that the Commissioner is authorized to grant a reasonable extension of time for filing any return, declaration, statement, or other document that relates to any tax imposed under subtitle A of the Code. Under § 1.6081-1(b), the application must be in writing, be signed by the taxpayer or his representative, and set forth the reason for requesting an extension.

Section 1.6081-11 of the regulations provides that a plan administrator or sponsor of an employee benefit plan required to file a Form 5500 will be allowed an automatic extension of the time to file the Form 5500. To receive an automatic extension of time to file, the plan administrator or sponsor must complete a Form 5558, "Application for Extension of Time to File Certain Employee Plan Returns,"and file the application with the Internal Revenue Service on or before the date that the Form 5500 series return must be filed.

Form 5558 is used to request an automatic extension of time to file a Form 5500 return or Form 8955-SSA. In accordance with § 1.6081-11 and Form 5558 (including instructions), an application for an extension of time to file a Form 5500 series return need not be signed. However, in accordance with § 1.6081-1, Form 5558 provides that an application for an extension of time to file Form 8955-SSA must be signed.

Explanation of Provisions

After the current version of the Form 5558 was issued, several comments were received that questioned the need for a signature to extend the time for filing Form 8955-SSA, particularly since a signature is not required to extend the time to file a Form 5500 series return. The commentators noted that, like its predecessor, the Schedule SSA, the Form 8955-SSA is generally prepared in conjunction with the preparation of a plan's Form 5500. They also stated that a signature requirement for the Form 8955-SSA is likely to cause confusion and missed deadlines because of the different rule for the Form 5500. Finally, the commentators contended that the signature requirement is burdensome for both filers and the IRS because the requirement complicates the extension request process.

The proposed regulations would amend § 1.6081-11, relating to automatic extensions of time for filing certain employee plan returns, by adding the Form 8955-SSA to the list of forms that are covered by the automatic 2$^1/_2$ month extension that applies by filing Form 5558. This will permit a plan administrator to receive an automatic extension of 2$^1/_2$ months by submitting, on or before the general due date of the Form 8955-SSA, a Form 5558 indicating that an extension is being requested for filing the Form 8955-SSA. Thus, under the proposed regulations, the same rules that apply to request an extension of time to file the Form 5500 series would also apply to request an extension of time to file Form 8955-SSA. In addition, the proposed regulations would amend § 1.6081-11 to provide that a signature would not be required to request an extension of time to file Form 5500 and Form 8955-SSA. It is anticipated that the Form 5558 and instructions will be revised to reflect this change for the Form 8955-SSA.

In addition, pursuant to section 6011(a), these proposed regulations would formally designate the Form 8955-SSA as the form used to satisfy the reporting requirements of section 6057. These proposed regulations would retain the general reporting requirements that applied to the Schedule SSA with certain minor modifications.

As discussed in the background section of this preamble, section 6057(a) requires the plan administrator (within the meaning of section 414(g)) of a plan that is subject to the vesting standards of section 203 of ERISA to file, within the time prescribed by regulations, a registration statement that sets forth certain information on deferred vested participants. Under existing § 301.6057-1(c)(1) of the Procedure and Administration regulations, the plan administrator of an employee benefit plan described in § 301.6057-1(a)(3), or any other employee retirement benefit plan (including a governmental or church plan), may at its option file on the Schedule SSA information relating to the deferred vested retirement benefit of any plan participant who separates at any time from service covered under the plan. These proposed regulations would retain the ability of such plans to report deferred vested information on a voluntary basis but require that the information be submitted to the IRS on Form 8955-SSA. The proposed regulations would also delegate authority to the Commissioner of the Internal Revenue Service to provide special rules under section 6057 (including designating the form used to comply with section 6057) in revenue rulings, notices, or other guidance published in the Internal Revenue Bulletin (see § 601.601(d)(2)(ii)(*b*) of this chapter). Finally, the proposed regulations would delete certain obsolete transition rules and update cross-references in § § 1.6057-1 and 1.6057-2.

Proposed Effective Date

These regulations are generally proposed to be effective on or after June 21, 2012. Taxpayers may rely on these proposed regulations for guidance pending the issuance of final regulations. If, and to the extent, the final regulations are more restrictive than the guidance in these proposed regulations, those provisions of the final regulations will be applied without retroactive effect.

Special Analyses

It has been determined that this notice of proposed rulemaking is not a significant regulatory action as defined in Executive Order 12866. Therefore, a regulatory assessment is not required. It has been determined that 5 U.S.C. 533(b) of the Administrative Procedure Act (5 U.S.C. chapter 5) does not apply to these regulations. It is hereby certified that the collection of information in these proposed regulations will not have a significant economic impact on a substantial number of small entities. This certification is based on the fact that most small entities that maintain employee retirement income benefit plans use third party administrators to perform their recordkeeping function. Therefore, an analysis under the Regulatory Flexibility Act (5 U.S.C. chapter 6) is not required. Pursuant to section 7805(f) of the Internal Revenue Code, these regulations have been submitted to the Office of Chief Counsel for Advocacy of the Small Business Administration for comments on its impact on small business.

Comments and Requests for Public Hearing

Before these proposed regulations are adopted as final regulations, consideration will be given to any comments that are submitted timely to the IRS as prescribed in this preamble under the "Addresses" heading. The IRS and Treasury Department request comments on all aspects of the proposed rules. All comments are available at *www.regulations.gov* or upon request. A public hearing will be scheduled if requested in writing by any person who timely submits written comments. If a public hearing is scheduled, notice of the date, time, and place of the public hearing will be published in the **Federal Register**.

Drafting Information

The principal authors of these regulations are Sarah R. Bolen and Pamela R. Kinard, Office of Division Counsel/Associate Chief Counsel (Tax Exempt and Government Entities). However, other personnel from the IRS and the Treasury Department participated in the development of these regulations.

[¶49,542] Proposed Amendments of Regulations (REG-134935-11), published in the Federal Register on June 25, 2012.

[Code Sec. 904]

Foreign tax credit: Limitations on credit: Categories of income: Recapture: Foreign losses: Property dispositions: Ordering rules.—Amendments of Reg. §§1.904-4 and 1.904(g)-3, providing guidance regarding the coordination of the rules for determining high-taxed income with capital gains adjustments and the allocation and recapture of overall foreign losses and overall domestic losses, as well as the coordination of the recapture of overall foreign losses on certain dispositions of property and other rules concerning overall foreign losses and overall domestic losses, are proposed.

AGENCY: Internal Revenue Service (IRS), Treasury.

ACTION: Notice of proposed rulemaking.

SUMMARY: These proposed regulations provide guidance regarding the coordination of the rules for determining high-taxed income with capital gains adjustments and the allocation and recapture of overall foreign losses and overall domestic losses, as well as the coordination of the recapture of overall foreign losses on certain dispositions of property and other rules concerning overall foreign losses and overall domestic losses. These regulations affect individuals and corporations claiming foreign tax credits.

DATES: Written or electronic comments and requests for a public hearing must be received by August 24, 2012.

ADDRESSES: Send submissions to CC:PA:LPD:PR (REG-134935-11), room 5203, Internal Revenue Service, PO Box 7604, Ben Franklin Station, Washington, DC 20044. Submissions may be hand delivered Monday through Friday between the hours of 8 a.m. and 4 p.m. to CC:PA:LPD:PR (REG-134935-11), Courier's desk, Internal Revenue Service, 1111 Constitution Avenue, NW., Washington, DC 20044, or sent electronically, via the Federal eRulemaking Portal at *www.regulations.gov* (IRS REG-134935-11).

FOR FURTHER INFORMATION CONTACT: Concerning the regulations, Jeffrey L. Parry, (202) 622-3850; concerning submissions of comments, Oluwafunmilayo (Funmi) Taylor, (202) 622-7180 (not toll-free numbers).

SUPPLEMENTARY INFORMATION:

Background and Explanation of Provisions

1. High-taxed income

Section 904(d)(2)(F) of the Internal Revenue Code (Code) provides that certain high-taxed income that would otherwise be passive income will be treated as general category income if the foreign taxes paid or accrued, and deemed paid or accrued, with respect to such income exceeds the highest rate of tax specified in section 1 or section 11, whichever applies, multiplied by the amount of such income. Section 1.904-4(c) provides detailed rules for determining whether income is high-taxed, including rules for testing income based on subgroups within passive income and allocating expenses, losses and other deductions to that income.

Questions have arisen regarding the coordination of these rules with the capital gains adjustments under section 904(b) and loss allocations and loss account recapture under section 904(f) and (g). The proposed regulations at §1.904-4(c) clarify that the determination as to whether income is high-taxed is made before taking into account any adjustments under section 904(b) or any allocation of losses or recapture of loss accounts under section 904(f) and (g). The Treasury Department and the IRS believe these ordering rules are consistent with the use in section 904(d)(2)(F) of the highest statutory U.S. tax rate, rather than the taxpayer's pre-credit effective U.S. tax rate, to determine whether income is high-taxed.

2. Dispositions of Property under Section 904(f)(3)

Section 904(f)(3) provides that if a taxpayer disposes of certain property used or held for use predominantly without the United States in a trade or business, gain is recognized on that disposition and treated as foreign source income, regardless of whether the gain would otherwise be recognized, to the extent of any overall foreign loss account in the separate category of foreign source taxable income generated by the property. Section 1.904(f)-2(d) provides separate rules for dispositions in which gain is recognized irrespective of section 904(f)(3) and dispositions in which the gain would not otherwise be recognized.

Questions have arisen regarding the coordination of overall foreign loss recapture under section 904(f)(3) with other provisions of section 904(f) and (g). Accordingly, these proposed regulations revise the ordering rules under §1.904(g)-3 that generally provide for the coordination of section 904(f) and (g) to include specific references for taking into account overall foreign loss recapture under section 904(f)(3).

In the case of dispositions in which gain is recognized irrespective of section 904(f)(3), the overall foreign loss recapture is included in Step Five along with other general overall foreign loss recapture.

Dispositions in which the gain would not otherwise be recognized are addressed separately. Section 1.904(f)-2(d)(4)(i) provides, in part, that where gain would not otherwise be recognized on a disposition, the amount of gain that will be recognized under section 904(f)(3) is equal to the balance in the applicable foreign loss account after taking into account any amounts recaptured from the account from other recognized income for the year (as well as certain other adjustments). In other words, the additional amount of income to be recognized can only be determined after the first seven steps of the ordering rules in § 1.904(g)-3 have been completed. Accordingly, a new Step Eight is added to those ordering rules to address the recognition of the additional income under section 904(f)(3) and the corresponding recapture of the applicable overall foreign loss account. New Step Eight also provides that if the additional recognition of gain increases the allowable amount of the net operating loss deduction, then the recapture of the overall foreign loss account occurs first before the additional net operating loss carryover is taken into account to offset all or a portion of that gain. The Treasury Department and the IRS believe priority should be given to the additional recapture of the overall foreign loss account pursuant to section 904(f)(3) before any net operating loss carryover reduces that gain. This is because the primary reason for recognizing the otherwise unrecognized gain is to recapture the overall foreign loss account.

Proposed Effective Date

The regulations, as proposed, will apply to any taxable year ending on or after the date of publication of a Treasury decision adopting these rules as final regulations in the **Federal Register**.

Special Analyses

It has been determined that this notice of proposed rulemaking is not a significant regulatory action as defined in Executive Order 12866. Therefore, a regulatory assessment is not required. It has also been determined that section 553(b) of the Administrative Procedure Act (5 U.S.C. chapter 5) does not apply to these regulations, and because the regulations do not impose a collection of information on small entities, the Regulatory Flexibility Act (5 U.S.C. chapter 6) does not apply. Pursuant to section 7805(f) of the Code, these regulations have been submitted to the Chief Counsel for Advocacy of the Small Business Administration for comment on its impact on small business.

Comments and Requests for Public Hearing

Before these proposed regulations are adopted as final regulations, consideration will be given to any electronic or written comments (a signed original and eight (8) copies) that are submitted timely to the IRS. The Treasury Department and the IRS request comments on all aspects of the proposed rules. All comments will be available for public inspection and copying. A public hearing will be scheduled if requested in writing by any person that timely submits comments. If a public hearing is scheduled, notice of the date, time, and place for the public hearing will be published in the **Federal Register**.

Drafting Information

The principal author of these regulations is Jeffrey L. Parry of the Office of Chief Counsel (International). However, other personnel from the IRS and the Treasury Department participated in their development.

[¶ 49,548] Proposed Amendments of Regulations (REG-140668-07), published in the Federal Register on September 17, 2012 (corrected 10/23/2012).

[Code Secs. 172 and 1502]

Corporations: Consolidated returns: Corporate equity reduction transactions (CERTs): Consolidated net operating losses (CNOLs): Election to carry back CNOLs.—Reg. §§ 1.172(h)-0—1.172(h)-5 and 1.1502-72 and amendments of Reg. § 1.1502-21, regarding the treatment of corporate equity reduction transactions (CERTs), including the treatment of multiple-step plans for the acquisition of stock and CERTs involving members of a consolidated group, are proposed.

AGENCY: Internal Revenue Service (IRS), Treasury.

ACTION: Notice of proposed rulemaking.

SUMMARY: This document contains proposed regulations under section 172(h) and section 1502 of the Internal Revenue Code. These proposed regulations provide guidance regarding the treatment of corporate equity reduction transactions (CERTs), including the treatment of multiple step plans for the acquisition of stock and CERTs involving members of a consolidated group. These proposed regulations also provide guidance regarding certain elections relating to the carryback of consolidated net operating losses (CNOLs) to separate return years. These proposed regulations will affect C corporations and corporations filing consolidated returns.

DATES: Written or electronic comments and requests for a public hearing must be received by December 17, 2012.

ADDRESSES: Send submissions to: CC:PA:LPD:PR (REG-140668-07), Room 5203, Internal Revenue Service, P.O. Box 7604, Ben Franklin Station, Washington, DC 20044. Submissions may be hand-delivered Monday through Friday between the hours of 8 a.m. and 4 p.m. to CC:PA:LPD:PR (REG-140668-07), Courier's Desk, Internal Revenue Service, 1111 Constitution Avenue, NW, Washington, DC, or sent electronically, via the Federal eRulemaking Portal at *www.regulations.gov* (IRS REG-140668-07).

FOR FURTHER INFORMATION CONTACT: Concerning the proposed regulations, Amie Colwell Breslow or Marie C. Milnes-Vasquez at (202) 622-7530; concerning submissions of comments and request for public hearing, Oluwafunmilayo Taylor at Oluwafunmilayo.P.Taylor@irscounsel.treas.gov or (202) 622-7180 (not toll-free numbers).

SUPPLEMENTARY INFORMATION:

Paperwork Reduction Act

The collection of information contained in this notice of proposed rulemaking has been submitted to the Office of Management and Budget for review in accordance with the Paperwork Reduction Act of 1995 (44 U.S.C. 3507(d)) under control number 1545-2171. Comments on the collection of information should be sent to the **Office of Management and Budget**, Attn: Desk Officer for the Department of the Treasury, Office of Information and Regulatory Affairs, Washington, D.C. 20503, with copies to the **Internal Revenue Service**, Attn: IRS Reports Clearance Officer, SE:W:CAR:MP:T:T:SP, Washington, D.C. 20224. Comments on the collection of information should be received by November 16, 2012. Comments are specifically requested concerning:

Whether the proposed collection of information is necessary for the proper performance of the functions of the **Internal Revenue Service**, including whether the information will have practical utility;

The accuracy of the estimated burden associated with the proposed collection of information;

How the quality, utility and clarity of the information to be collected may be enhanced;

How the burden of complying with the proposed collection of information may be minimized, including through the application of automated collection techniques or other forms of information technology; and

Estimates of capital or start-up costs and costs of operation, maintenance, and purchase of service to provide information.

The collection of information in these proposed regulations is in §§1.1502-21(b)(3)(ii)(B) and 1.1502-72(e).

The proposed regulations provide guidance regarding application of section 172(b)(1)(E) and (h) and section 1502.

The collection of information is required in order to obtain a benefit. The likely respondents are corporations that are members of consolidated groups.

Estimated total annual reporting burden: 120,000 hours.

Estimated average annual burden hours per respondent: 15 hours.

Estimated number of respondents: 8,000.

Estimated frequency of responses: Once.

An agency may not conduct or sponsor, and a person is not required to respond to, a collection of information unless it displays a valid control number assigned by the Office of Management and Budget.

Books or records relating to a collection of information must be retained as long as their contents may become material in the administration of any internal revenue law. Generally, tax returns and tax return information are confidential, as required by 26 U.S.C. 6103.

Background

Section 172 provides rules relating to net operating loss (NOL) carrybacks and carryovers. Section 172(b)(1)(A) states that the NOL for any taxable year generally is carried back to each of the 2 years preceding the taxable year of the loss and carried over to each of the 20 years following the taxable year of the loss.

The corporate equity reduction transaction rules of section 172(b)(1)(E) and (h) were enacted in 1989 in response to the use of NOL carrybacks to finance leveraged buyout transactions. Congress enacted these rules to limit a corporation's ability to obtain tax refunds as the result of the carryback of NOLs that were attributable to interest deductions allocable to such transactions. See Explanation of Corporate Tax Refund Restriction Bill, 135 Cong. Rec. S9936-01, at S9944 (1989); 1989 WL 193512.

Section 172(h)(3)(A) defines a *corporate equity reduction transaction* (CERT) as a "major stock acquisition" (MSA) or an "excess distribution" (ED). Section 172(h)(3)(B) defines *major stock acquisition* as the acquisition by a corporation, pursuant to a plan of such corporation (or any group of persons acting in concert with such corporation), of stock in another corporation representing 50 percent or more (by vote or value) of the stock in such other corporation. Section 172(h)(3)(C) defines *excess distribution* as the excess (if any) of the aggregate distributions (including redemptions) made during a taxable year by a corporation with respect to its stock over the greater of: 150 percent of the average of such distributions during the 3 taxable years immediately preceding such taxable year, or 10 percent of the fair market value of the stock of the corporation at the beginning of such taxable year. Thus, the total of distributions that may be treated as an ED is limited to the amount that exceeds the greater of two baselines: one tied to a historical, three-year average and the other based on the fair market value of the distributor.

If an MSA or ED occurs, section 172(b)(1)(E) and (h) limit the carryback of the portion of an NOL that constitutes a "corporate equity reduction interest loss" (CERIL) of an "applicable corporation" in any "loss limitation year." See section 172(b)(1)(E)(i). Section 172(b)(1)(E)(iii) defines an *applicable corporation* as a C corporation that acquires stock, or the stock of which is acquired, in an MSA; a C corporation making distributions with respect to, or redeeming, its stock in connection with an ED; or a C corporation that is a successor to one of the other types of applicable corporations. Section 172(b)(1)(E)(ii) defines *loss limitation year* as the taxable year in which a CERT occurs and each of the two succeeding taxable years. Section 172(h)(1) defines *corporate equity reduction interest loss* as the excess of (1) the total NOL for a loss limitation year, over (2) the NOL for the loss limitation year computed without regard to the allocable interest deductions that are otherwise taken into account in computing the NOL. Section 172(h)(2)(A) defines *allocable interest deductions* as deductions allowed on the portion of any indebtedness allocable to a CERT.

Under section 172(h)(2)(B), except as provided in regulations or section 172(h)(2)(E), indebtedness is allocable to a CERT in the manner prescribed under section 263A(f)(2)(A) without regard to paragraph (i) thereof (relating to traced debt). Thus, a portion of the taxpayer's total interest expense is allocable to the CERT. See H.R. Rep. No. 101-247, at 1251 (Conf. Rep.). However, section 172(h)(2)(C) limits the amount of allocable interest deductions for any loss limitation year to (1) the amount allowable as a deduction for interest paid or accrued by the taxpayer during the loss limitation year, less (2) the average of deductions allowed for interest paid or accrued by the taxpayer for the three taxable years preceding the taxable year in which the CERT occurred. Therefore, the allocable interest deductions are limited to the increase in interest deductions over a historical, three-year baseline.

Section 172(h)(3)(C) and (E) sets forth specific rules for determining whether an ED has occurred. For purposes of determining a corporation's aggregate distributions for a taxable year under section 172(h)(3)(C)(i) and the average of such distributions during the three taxable years preceding the relevant taxable year under section 172(h)(3)(C)(ii)(I), section 172(h)(3)(E)(ii) provides that the distributions taken into account are reduced by the aggregate amount of stock issued by the corporation during the applicable period in exchange for money or property other than stock in the corporation. However, section 172(h)(3)(E)(i) provides that stock described in section 1504(a)(4) (certain preferred stock) and distributions (including redemptions) with respect to such stock are disregarded.

For purposes of applying section 172(b)(1)(E) and (h), an applicable corporation and all members of its consolidated group are treated as a single taxpayer. See section 172(h)(4)(C).

Currently, there are no regulations under section 172(b)(1)(E) and (h). Section 172(h)(5) grants the Secretary the authority to prescribe such regulations as may be necessary to carry out the purposes of section 172(h), including regulations: (A) for applying section 172(h) to successor corporations and to cases in which a taxpayer becomes (or ceases to be) a member of a consolidated group; (B) to prevent the avoidance of section 172(h) through the use of related parties, pass-through entities, and intermediaries; and (C) for applying section 172(h) when more than one corporation is involved in a CERT. In addition, section 172(h)(2)(B) grants the Secretary authority to issue regulations prescribing a method for allocating indebtedness to a CERT other than the method contained in section 263A(f)(2)(A). Section 1502 provides the Secretary with broad authority to prescribe rules applicable to corporations that file consolidated returns that are different from the income tax provisions that would apply if those corporations filed separate returns.

These proposed regulations provide general rules addressing whether a CERT has occurred, the computation of a CERIL, and the treatment of successors. The proposed regulations also address issues specific to the application of section 172(b)(1)(E) and (h) to consolidated groups, including: (1) treatment of the consolidated group as a single taxpayer; (2) determination of the group's three-year average that is relevant to a particular consolidated return loss limitation year; (3) application of these rules if the corporation participating in a CERT becomes a member of a consolidated group; (4) application of these rules if a group member deconsolidates after the group has participated in (or is treated as having participated in) a CERT; (5) apportionment of a CERIL (and other special status CNOLs) to members of a consolidated group for carryback or carryover to separate return years; and (6) application of section 172(b)(1)(E) and (h) to a life-nonlife group. The proposed regulations also provide rules that would amend the loss carryback waivers available to deconsolidating group members.

At this time, the Department of Treasury and the IRS are not providing rules addressing the application of section 172(h) to related parties, pass-through entities, or intermediaries. However, the Department of Treasury and the IRS continue to study the circumstances under which these persons should be subject to section 172(b)(1)(E) and (h). For example, the purposes of the statute may be furthered if section 172(b)(1)(E) and (h) apply to the acquisition of 100 percent of the stock of a target by a partnership in which a corporation (or consolidated group) holds a controlling interest. On the other hand, the purposes of the statute may not be advanced if 100 percent of the stock of a target is acquired in a single transaction, but the percentage of target stock indirectly attributable to corporate acquirers is relatively small. The Department of Treasury and the IRS request comments regarding the parameters for applying section 172(b)(1)(E) and (h) to indirect corporate acquirers, and what special computational rules, if any, would be needed to implement its application.

The Department of Treasury and the IRS considered inclusion of an anti-avoidance rule to prevent taxpayers from engaging in section 381 transactions to shorten loss limitation years. However, the Department of Treasury and the IRS believe that the detrimental effects of shortening tax years make it unlikely that taxpayers will attempt to undertake such transactions as a planning technique. For example, shortening a loss limitation year will reduce the income in that year, and, accordingly, will limit the ability to carry back any losses to that year. The Department of Treasury and the IRS continue to study whether an anti-abuse rule is needed and request comments on this issue.

In addition, the Department of Treasury and the IRS are not providing rules addressing the application of section 172(b)(1)(E) and (h) to transactions occurring before these rules are adopted as final regulations (transitional issues). However, the Department of Treasury and the IRS continue to study, and request comments on, transitional issues. For example, the Department of Treasury and the IRS request comments regarding the application of section 172(b)(1)(E) and (h) if a taxable year constitutes a loss limitation year with regard to more than one CERT, one occurring before and the other occurring after the adoption of these proposed regulations as final regulations.

Explanation of Provisions

1. *General CERT Rules*

A. *Determination of existence of a CERT*

As discussed, a CERT is either an MSA or an ED. The statute does not exclude tax-free transactions from treatment as an MSA or an ED. In addition, the concerns targeted by Congress in enacting section 172(b)(1)(E) and (h) can exist in the context of both taxable and tax-free transactions. Accordingly, the proposed regulations provide that a tax-free transaction that meets the statutory definition of an MSA or an ED must be tested as a CERT under section 172(b)(1)(E) and (h) and these proposed regulations (collectively, the "CERT rules"). For example, a section 355 transaction, a corporate organization under section 351, or a stock acquisition that qualifies for reorganization treatment under section 368(a)(1)(A) and (a)(2)(E) must be tested under the CERT rules.

These proposed regulations also provide that an integrated plan of stock acquisition including multiple steps will be tested as a single potential MSA for purposes of determining the consequences of the transaction under the CERT rules. This treatment applies even if a step in the plan might separately constitute an ED, or might so qualify in conjunction with other distributions in the same taxable year.

Section 172(h)(3)(C)(ii) limits the amount of distributions in a taxable year that may be treated as an ED. Under one prong of this limitation, the taxpayer's distributions are treated as an ED only to the extent that they exceed 150 percent of the taxpayer's average of distributions (three-year distribution average) made in the three taxable years preceding the taxable year in which a potential ED occurs (the distribution lookback period). These proposed regulations provide that, to the extent that a distribution is part of an integrated plan that is treated as an MSA, the distribution is excluded from the computation of the taxpayer's three-year distribution average that is relevant to any other potential ED. These proposed regulations provide additional rules for calculating the taxpayer's three-year distribution average under section 172(h)(3)(C)(ii)(I) relevant to potential EDs that occur in taxable years that are not full 12-month years.

B. *Loss limitation years*

The proposed regulations generally provide that the taxable year in which a CERT occurs and each of the two succeeding taxable years constitute loss limitation years with regard to the CERT. The proposed regulations also provide special rules addressing loss limitation years of successors, consolidated groups, and former members of consolidated groups.

C. *Computation of a CERIL*

Under section 172(h)(1), the term *CERIL* means, with respect to any loss limitation year, the excess (if any) of (1) the NOL for such taxable year, over (2) the NOL for such taxable year determined without regard to any allocable interest deductions otherwise taken into account in computing such loss. Section 172(h)(2)(A) defines *allocable interest deductions* as deductions allowed for interest on any indebtedness allocable to a CERT. Section 172(h)(2)(B) states that, except as provided in regulations and section 172(h)(2)(E), the indebtedness allocable to a CERT is determined under the avoided cost methodology of section 263A(f)(2)(A), with certain adjustments.

Under section 263A(f)(2)(A) and the regulations thereunder, allocable interest deductions are computed by multiplying the "weighted average interest rate" by "average excess expenditures" as those terms are defined in § 1.263A-9(c)(5)(ii) and (iii). Because section 263A contemplates transactions that are very different in nature from CERTs, it is often difficult to identify the costs associated with a CERT that are analogous to average excess expenditures. To ameliorate this difficulty, these proposed regulations provide MSA- and ED-specific rules for computing costs associated with a CERT (CERT costs). Further, these proposed regulations identify additional CERT costs by looking to the capitalization rules under section 263(a). Specifically, the proposed regulations treat as CERT costs amounts paid or incurred to facilitate an MSA or ED to the extent that those amounts are required to be capitalized under section 263(a) (with certain modifications), and any amounts disallowed under section 162(k). Because most CERTs occur under circumstances that already require application of section 263(a), invoking those rules should result in greater administrability. Once the CERT costs are identified, the interest allocable to those costs is computed under the principles of section 263A(f)(2)(A) and the regulations thereunder (with adjustments). The avoided cost methodology of section 263A(f)(2)(A) effectively allocates interest to a CERT to the extent that the taxpayer's interest costs could have been reduced if the taxpayer had not engaged in the CERT. For purposes of applying the avoided cost rules of section 263A(f)(2)(A), all CERT costs are treated as if they were cash expenditures.

Under the proposed regulations, *CERT costs* with regard to an MSA include the fair market value of the stock acquired, whether that stock is acquired in exchange for cash, stock of the acquirer, or other property. The inclusion of the fair market value of stock acquired in stock-for-stock exchanges ensures that such transactions are treated similarly to an issuance of acquirer's stock for cash followed by an MSA funded with the cash proceeds. Further, inclusion of the fair market value of stock acquired is consistent with the avoided cost methodology applied under section 172(h)(2) because the CERT statute rejects tracing and assumes that debt is used to fund all CERT costs.

In addition, CERT costs of an MSA include the fair market value of any distribution that is part of an integrated transaction constituting the MSA. CERT costs also include amounts paid or incurred to facilitate any step of the MSA to the extent that those amounts are required to be capitalized under section 263(a), and any amounts disallowed under section 162(k).

Under the proposed regulations, CERT costs associated with an ED include the fair market value of distributions to shareholders that are determined to be EDs during the year in which the CERT occurs. CERT costs also include a portion of amounts paid or incurred to facilitate the distributions to the extent that those amounts are required to be capitalized under section 263(a), and any amounts disallowed under section 162(k). However, if neither section 263(a) nor section 162(k) applies or if only section 162(k) applies to a distribution included in an ED, additional CERT costs associated with the distribution are determined under the principles of § 1.263(a)-4(e) (relating to the capitalization of costs that facilitate the acquisition or creation of intangibles), applied as if the ED were a transaction within the scope of § 1.263(a)-4.

As discussed, the rules of section 263(a) are applied in the CERT context with certain modifications. For the purpose of identifying CERT costs under these proposed regulations, modifications to the operation of § 1.263(a)-4 and -5 include treating certain borrowing costs as facilitative of an MSA or ED. Therefore, CERT costs will include these borrowing costs. Congress objected to the carryback of NOLs resulting from leveraging that directly or indirectly enables CERTs; therefore, the Department of Treasury and the IRS believe that it is appropriate to include borrowing costs in total CERT costs. However, the Department of Treasury and the IRS request comments regarding the extent to which borrowing costs should be included in CERT costs.

The computation of interest allocable to CERTs under the rules of section 263A(f)(2)(A) involves the time-weighted average of costs incurred as of various dates in the taxable year. Therefore, these proposed regulations set forth rules for determining when CERT costs should be taken into account. Under these proposed regulations, accumulated CERT costs as of a particular date are the total CERT costs that have been taken into account as of that date under the applicable corporation's method of accounting. A special proration rule is provided to determine accumulated CERT costs related to an ED. Finally, CERT costs incurred in any year prior to the year in which the CERT occurs are included in accumulated CERT costs beginning on the first day of the year in which the CERT occurs.

Section 172(h)(2)(E) requires that the allocation of interest to a CERT be reduced if an unforeseeable extraordinary adverse event occurs during a loss limitation year but after the CERT. The proposed regulations do not provide guidance with regard to unforeseeable extraordinary adverse events. However, the Department of Treasury and the IRS request comments regarding whether rules are necessary and, if so, what type of events should constitute unforeseeable extraordinary adverse events.

D. *Limitation on interest deductions*

The CERT rules generally provide that the portion of an NOL for any loss limitation year that is attributable to the interest deductions allocable to a CERT (that is, a CERIL) may not be carried back to any year prior to the year in which the CERT occurred. As discussed, section 172(h)(2)(C) limits the amount of interest treated as an allocable interest deduction to the excess of the amount allowable as a deduction for interest paid or accrued by the taxpayer during the loss limitation year, over the average of amounts allowable as a deduction for interest paid or accrued (the three-year average) during the three taxable years preceding the taxable year in which the CERT occurred (the lookback period). These proposed regulations provide special rules for computing the three-year average in special situations, such as if an applicable corporation is not in existence for the entire lookback period. Further, the proposed regulations adjust the three-year average if the relevant loss limitation year is not a full 12-month taxable period. These proposed regulations also set forth special rules for any taxable year that constitutes a loss limitation year with regard to multiple CERTs.

The legislative history indicates that Congress expected the Department of Treasury and the IRS to write rules that provide that increases attributable solely to fluctuations in interest rates would not be taken into account for purposes of applying the three-year average. Out of concern that the additional complexities of such rules would outweigh the benefit, these proposed regulations do not include rules that factor out increases in interest deductions attributable solely to fluctuations in interest rates. However, the Department of Treasury and the IRS are studying a rule that, for purposes of applying the three-year average, would factor out interest deductions that are attributable to increases in a taxpayer's interest rate that occur after the date of a CERT. Under the rule being considered, the measurement of a baseline interest rate after the CERT occurs would take into account the fact that CERT activity will often decrease a taxpayer's creditworthiness and increase its average cost of borrowing, and accordingly that the existence of the CERT, in and of itself, will increase a taxpayer's borrowing expenses. The Department of Treasury and the IRS request comments on whether such a baseline would effectively account for fluctuations in interest rates or whether an alternative measure would be more appropriate.

E. *Predecessor and successor*

As discussed, the CERT rules apply only to applicable corporations. Under section 172(b)(1)(E)(iii)(III), an applicable corporation includes any corporation that is a successor of: a corporation that acquires stock in an MSA; a corporation the stock of which is acquired in an MSA; or a corporation making a distribution with respect to, or redeeming, its stock in connection with an ED. For purposes of applying the CERT rules, these proposed regulations define *successor* as a transferee or distributee in a transaction to which section 381(a) applies. Further, if a successor to a previous applicable corporation with regard to a CERT itself transfers assets to a further successor, the further successor corporation is treated as an applicable corporation with regard to that CERT. In addition, these proposed regulations set forth special rules for computing a successor's CERIL.

F. *Operating rules*

The proposed regulations include special rules regarding the prohibition on carryback of a CERIL. These rules provide that no CERIL may be carried back to any taxable year that includes solely dates that precede the date on which the CERT at issue occurred. In applying this rule to multi-step MSAs and to EDs that include multiple distributions, the date on which the CERT occurs is the earliest date on which the requirements for CERT status have been satisfied. These proposed regulations also provide that, for purposes of determining whether an ED has occurred, the computation of any three-year distribution average under section 172(h)(3)(C)(ii)(I) will be reduced by the average of the stock issuances made by the applicable corporation during the three years of the distribution lookback period.

The principles of the proposed regulations apply to the computation of the alternative minimum tax net operating loss under section 56(d).

2. *Special CERT Rules Applicable to Consolidated Groups*

A. *Single entity treatment*

Section 172(h)(4)(C) states that, except as provided by regulation, all members of a consolidated group are treated as a single taxpayer for purposes of section 172(b)(1)(E) and (h). These proposed regulations provide further guidance regarding the application of single entity principles. These proposed regulations affirm that transactions and expenditures undertaken by a particular member are not separately tracked; rather, the entire group is treated as a single applicable corporation. For example, if multiple members of a group acquire in total 50 percent or more (by vote or value) of the stock of another corporation, the group has engaged in an MSA. Likewise, the computation of a group's CERIL under section 172(h)(1) for any loss limitation year that is a consolidated return year includes the debt of all members and all interest deductions that are allowed on the group's consolidated return.

Intercompany transactions (including interest accruals and payments on intercompany obligations) are generally disregarded under the proposed regulations. However, these proposed regulations provide that a transaction will not be disregarded if a party to the transaction becomes a non-member as a part of the same plan or arrangement.

The most difficult issues in the CERT area arise from the application of single entity concepts if different corporations join and deconsolidate from a group within the same three-year period. The fungibility of money and the ease of moving cash and debt within a consolidated group may provide a consolidated group with an unwarranted ability to manipulate the application of the CERT rules, further complicating the analysis. After considering different approaches, the Department of Treasury and the IRS have determined that application of single entity principles, under which corporations cease to be separately tracked for CERT purposes after their inclusion in a group, will limit complexity and promote administrability. Furthermore, single entity treatment is consistent with the statutory default of treating the consolidated group as a single taxpayer.

Consistent with single entity treatment, these proposed regulations provide that, if an applicable corporation with regard to a CERT occurring in a separate return year (pre-existing CERT member) joins a consolidated group, the group is treated as a single applicable corporation with regard to that CERT in the consolidated return year of the acquisition and any relevant succeeding year. The pre-existing CERT member will no longer have separate status as an applicable corporation. Beginning on the day the pre-existing CERT member is first included in the group, the only CERIL computation will be that of the group.

These proposed regulations also provide that, in the consolidated return context, both the debt of a new member acquired in a CERT and the corresponding interest expenses are included in the group's CERIL computation, even if the group would not have been in a position to pay off the debt of the acquired corporation if the CERT had not occurred. For example, if a target corporation acquired by a consolidated group has debt outstanding prior to the acquisition, the group takes into account interest incurred by the group that is attributable to the target's pre-existing debt, despite the fact that the group would have had no reason to satisfy the target's debt if the acquisition had not occurred. If the acquisition had not occurred, the debt of the target would not have become a liability of the applicable corporation (the group), and the associated interest expense would not have been deducted by the group. As will be discussed, the historical interest expense of the target is also included in the group's computation of the three-year average applied to limit the interest allocated to the CERT.

B. *Applicable corporation status and allocation of CERT costs following deconsolidation from a group*

These proposed regulations provide that, if a member deconsolidates from a group on or after (1) the date on which the group engages in a CERT, or (2) the date on which the group acquires a pre-existing CERT member, then, following the deconsolidation, both the deconsolidating member and the group generally will be treated as applicable corporations with regard to the CERT. The deconsolidating member will be apportioned a pro rata share of the group's CERT costs incurred through the date of the deconsolidation. The proration is based on the relative fair market values of the deconsolidating corporation (immediately after its deconsolidation) and the entire group (immediately before the deconsolidation). This rule applies regardless of whether any particular corporation would have constituted an applicable corporation with regard to the CERT without the application of the single entity treatment. The Department of Treasury and the IRS request comments regarding alternatives for allocating CERT costs following deconsolidation from a group.

The CERT costs that are allocated and apportioned to the deconsolidating member are subtracted from the group's CERT costs and will not attract allocable interest in any loss limitation year of the group (or any separate return loss limitation year of another group member) after the year of deconsolidation. Therefore, the group may have less CERIL in the years following the deconsolidation. Apportionment of CERT costs to the deconsolidating member may result in that corporation having a CERIL in the period following its deconsolidation.

Under these proposed regulations, the deconsolidating member (or the common parent of any group that the deconsolidating member joins immediately after deconsolidation) may elect out of the general rule of apportionment. In making this election, the member or common parent permanently waives all carrybacks of losses allocable to the deconsolidating member to years of the former group and any preceding taxable years. If this election is made, the deconsolidating member will not be treated as an applicable corporation with regard to the CERT, and it will not be allocated any CERT costs. Applicable corporation status and CERT costs will remain with the former group. This is true even if the deconsolidating member directly engaged in the CERT. Further, none of the interest history of the group will be allocated to the deconsolidating member for CERT purposes, including determining the CERIL related to any future CERT. The resulting lack of interest history may increase the amount of a CERIL in future taxable years associated with other CERTs of the deconsolidating corporation. This election is available to any deconsolidating member, even if the former group is not an applicable corporation with regard to any CERT at the time of the deconsolidation.

C. *Loss limitation years*

Because all members of a consolidated group are treated as a single taxpayer under section 172(h)(4)(C), a consolidated group is treated as the "applicable corporation" with regard to a CERT. These proposed regulations provide special rules for determining loss limitation years of consolidated groups and former members of consolidated groups. Under these proposed regulations, the taxable year in which a CERT actually occurs is a loss limitation year. Any other taxable year (potential loss limitation year) of any applicable corporation (including a consolidated group) will constitute a loss limitation year with regard to the CERT only if, under the carryover rules of sections 172(b)(1)(A)(ii) and 381(c)(1), the potential loss limitation year would constitute the first or second taxable year following the taxable year of the corporation or consolidated group that actually engaged in the CERT, which includes the date of the CERT. For purposes of tracking taxable years, sections 172 and 381 are applied as if the inclusion of any corporation in a consolidated group or the deconsolidation of any member from a group were a transaction described in section 381(a).

The proposed regulations provide that the separate return years of a corporation that deconsolidates from a consolidated group may be loss limitation years with regard to a CERT of the former group. This may occur only if the consolidated return year of the deconsolidation is a first or second loss limitation year with regard to that CERT. The taxable years of more than one applicable corporation (including a consolidated group) may be loss limitation years with regard to the same CERT, even if those taxable years include the same dates.

The special rules for determining loss limitation years can be illustrated as follows: T corporation maintains a calendar taxable year and does not join in the filing of a consolidated return. The X group holds 60 percent of the only class of T stock. On July 1, Year 5, T engages in a CERT. The X group, which includes member S, maintains a calendar taxable year. On December 31, Year 5, the X group acquires all of the remaining T stock. T is first included in the X group on January 1, Year 6. On June 30, Year 6, S deconsolidates from the X group, and thereafter S maintains a calendar taxable year. The first loss limitation year with respect to the T CERT is T's calendar Year 5. Pursuant to these proposed regulations, as a result of acquiring T, the X group is treated as an applicable corporation with respect to the T CERT. The X group's loss limitation years with respect to the T CERT are its calendar Years 6 and 7. Because no election is made with respect to the deconsolidation of S, following the deconsolidation, S is also treated as an applicable corporation with regard to the T CERT. Because consolidated return Year 6 (the year of the deconsolidation) is a second loss limitation year with regard to the CERT, S's short year ending December 31, Year 6 will be S's only loss limitation year with regard to the T CERT.

D. *Determining the three-year average of a group*

As discussed in section 1.D. of this preamble, under section 172(h)(2)(C), the interest deductions treated as allocable to a CERT are limited to the difference between the interest paid or accrued in the loss limitation year at issue and the average of the interest paid or accrued in the three years preceding the year of the CERT (three-year average). These proposed regulations adopt single entity concepts intended, in part, to decrease the complexity of the computation of the three-year average resulting from the entry of corporations into, and the deconsolidation of corporations from, a consolidated group. Under these proposed regulations, with regard to a corporation joining a group, the interest history of that corporation is combined with that of the acquiring group. For purposes of the CERT rules, this interest is thereafter generally treated as having been paid or accrued by the group and is no longer separately traced to the acquired corporation. Similarly, with regard to the deconsolidation of a member from a group, a portion of the group's entire interest history is generally apportioned to the deconsolidating member for purposes of the CERT rules. The apportionment is based on the relative fair market values of the deconsolidating corporation (immediately after its deconsolidation) and the entire group (immediately before the deconsolidation). Under these proposed regulations, the allocated and apportioned history is subtracted from the group's interest history solely for purposes of the CERT rules and is unavailable to the group with regard to any loss limitation year of the group (or any separate return loss limitation year of another group member) after the year of deconsolidation. Consistent with single entity treatment and rejection of a tracing regime, the interest allocated to a particular deconsolidating member is not tied to that member's actual interest history.

These proposed regulations also provide special rules relevant to any loss limitation year during which a corporation (partial-year member) becomes a member of, or ceases to be a member of, a group (transitional year). For purposes of computing any three-year average of a group that is relevant to a transitional year, these rules require proration of the interest history that is attributable to the partial-year member so that a group that includes a particular member for only a portion of a loss limitation year includes only a pro rata portion of that member's three-year interest history. These proposed regulations also provide special rules for computing the three-year average if a group is not in existence for three taxable years prior to the consolidated return year in which the CERT occurs (the lookback period) and for determining the lookback period if a group acquires a corporation that previously engaged in a CERT.

E. *Excess distributions in groups*

These proposed regulations contain rules pertaining to the computation of EDs of consolidated groups and of corporations that have been consolidated group members. Consistent with single entity treatment under section 172(h)(4)(C), the proposed regulations provide that the distributions relevant for purposes of computing an ED of a consolidated group generally include only non-intercompany distributions. However, this general rule does not apply if a party to the transaction deconsolidates as part of the same plan or arrangement. Under those circumstances, the distribution will be tested on a separate entity basis as a potential CERT.

As discussed in section 1.A. of this preamble, section 172(h)(3)(C)(ii) places a limitation on the amount of distributions in a taxable year that may be treated as ED, and the limitation is based in part on 150 percent of the taxpayer's average of distributions (three-year distribution average) made in the three taxable years preceding the taxable year of the potential ED. These proposed regulations provide that single entity principles generally apply to the computation of the three-year distribution average of a consolidated group or a corporation that has been a consolidated group member. That is, the only distributions taken into account are those made to non-member shareholders. However, in computing the three-year distribution average of a consolidated group that includes a member for less than the entire consolidated return year of a potential ED, the group takes into account only a pro rata portion of the actual distribution history of that member. Further, a corporation that deconsolidates from a group takes into account its actual history of non-intercompany distributions for purposes of applying the CERT rules in future separate return years. The corporation is not apportioned a pro rata share of the total distribution history of the group.

Additional rules apply with regard to computation of stock issuances and valuation of the group, which are intended to ensure that the rules in those areas are applied on a single entity basis. Specifically, the proposed regulations provide that, in applying section 172(h)(3)(E)(ii) to determine the offset of stock issuances against distributions, only stock that is issued to non-members is taken into account. Further, the proposed regulations provide that the value of the group, computed pursuant to section 172(h)(3)(C)(ii)(II), equals the value of the stock of all members other than stock that is owned directly or indirectly by another member.

F. *Reverse acquisitions*

These proposed regulations address the application of the MSA rules to reverse acquisitions, as defined in § 1.1502-75(d)(3). The proposed regulations provide that, if a reverse acquisition occurs, the CERT rules will be applied by treating the acquirer in form as the target corporation, and treating the target in form as the acquiring corporation. They also provide special rules regarding the computation of the CERT costs in a reverse acquisition.

G. *Life-nonlife groups*

These proposed regulations provide rules for applying the CERT rules to a group that elects under section 1504(c)(2) to file a consolidated return (life-nonlife group). As with consolidated groups generally, the fungibility of money and the ease of moving cash and debt within a life-nonlife group may provide an unwarranted ability to manipulate the application of the CERT rules. Accordingly, these proposed regulations generally apply the CERT rules and the consolidated return CERT rules to a life-nonlife group on a single entity basis, and not on a subgroup basis. Under the proposed regulations, a single CERIL is computed with regard to any loss limitation year of a life-nonlife group, which includes all life-nonlife group members' CERT costs, debt, and interest paid or accrued for that year. However, for purposes of determining the CERIL of a life-nonlife group under section 172(h)(1) for any loss limitation year, the sum of the nonlife consolidated net operating loss (nonlife CNOL) (if any) and the life consolidated loss from operations (LO) (if any) for that year is treated as a notional "NOL" of the group. For this purpose, nonlife consolidated taxable income does not offset any LO, and consolidated partial life insurance company taxable income (as used in § 1.1502-47(g)) does not offset any nonlife CNOL.

If a CERIL exists for a loss limitation year of a life-nonlife group, that CERIL is allocated on a pro rata basis between the nonlife CNOL and the LO of the group, based on the relative sizes of the two attributes.

3. *Specialized CNOL Carryback Rules*

These proposed regulations provide rules regarding the apportionment of CNOLs that contain a component portion of special status loss, such as a CERIL or a specified liability loss. See section 172(h)(1) and (f)(1). Under these rules, a special status loss is apportioned to each group member, separately from the remainder of the CNOL, under the method provided in § 1.1502-21(b)(2)(iv). This apportionment occurs without separate entity inquiry into whether a particular member incurred the specific expenses or engaged in the particular activities required by the provisions governing the special status loss.

The proposed regulations also amend and expand the current election under § 1.1502-21(b)(3)(ii)(B), informally referred to as the "split-waiver" election. That election is currently available to any group that acquires one or more members from another group. By making the election, the acquiring group relinquishes, with respect to all CNOLs attributable to the newly-acquired corporation, the portion of the carryback period during which that corporation was a member of another group. The current rule does not allow a group to waive the portion of the carryback period for which a newly-acquired corporation was not a member of a consolidated group. The current election is a one-time election and must be made with the acquiring group's timely-filed original return for the year of the acquisition.

The proposed regulations amend the split waiver election to make the election available to any group that acquires a corporation, regardless of whether such corporation was acquired from another group. An election results in the waiver of the entire carryback period with regard to CNOLs allocable to the acquired corporation, not only the period during which the corporation was a member of another group. Further, any election that is made with regard to a newly-acquired member that had been a member of another group at the time of its acquisition must include all members acquired from the same group during the taxable year of the acquiring group.

In addition, the proposed regulations give the electing group a choice of making the one-time election or making the split-waiver election on an annual basis with regard to the CNOL of a particular consolidated return year. Any annual split-waiver election must be filed with the group's timely filed original return for the year of the CNOL. The one-time election and the annual split-waiver election that are available under proposed § 1.1502-21(b)(3)(ii)(B) apply generally with respect to losses attributable to the acquired corporation. These split-waiver elections are in addition to the one-time election available under the CERT rules to elect out of the general rule of apportionment for CERT costs and interest history to a deconsolidating member, which also results in the waiver of all carrybacks of losses allocable to the deconsolidating member to any prior taxable years. As a result, under these proposed regulations, corporations may have three, mutually exclusive, irrevocable elections to waive carryback of CNOLs to separate return years: an annual election, a one-time election, and a special CERT election.

Proposed Effective Date

Sections 1.172(h)-1 through 1.172(h)-5 and § 1.1502-72 (except § 1.1502-72(e)) are effective for CERTs occurring on or after the date of publication of the Treasury decision adopting these rules as final regulations in the **Federal Register**, except that they do not apply to any CERTs occurring pursuant to a written agreement that is binding prior to the date of publication of the Treasury decision adopting these rules as final regulations in the **Federal Register**. The amendments to § 1.1502-21(b)(2) are effective for taxable years for which the due date of the original return (without extensions) is on or after the date of publication of the Treasury decision adopting these rules as final regulations in the **Federal Register**. Section 1.1502-72(e) and the amendments to § 1.1502-21(b)(3) are effective for acquisitions or deconsolidations, as appropriate, occurring on or after the date of publication of the Treasury decision adopting these rules as final regulations in the **Federal Register**, except that they do not apply to any acquisition or deconsolidations, as appropriate, occurring pursuant to a written agreement that is binding before the date of publication of the Treasury decision adopting these rules as final regulations in the **Federal Register**.

Special Analyses

It has been determined that this notice of proposed rulemaking is not a significant regulatory action as defined in Executive Order 12866, as supplemented by Executive Order 13563. Therefore, a regulatory assessment is not required. Pursuant to the Regulatory Flexibility Act (5 U.S.C. chapter 6), it is hereby certified that these proposed regulations will not have a significant economic impact on a substantial number of small entities. This certification is based on the fact that these proposed regulations will primarily affect C corporations and members of consolidated groups, which tend to be large corporations. Accordingly, a regulatory flexibility analysis is not required. Pursuant to section 7805(f) of the Internal Revenue Code, these regulations have been submitted to the Chief Counsel for Advocacy of the Small Business Administration for comment on their impact on small business.

Comments and Requests for Public Hearing

Before these proposed regulations are adopted as final regulations, consideration will be given to any written (a signed original and eight (8) copies) or electronic comments that are submitted timely to the IRS. The Department of Treasury and the IRS request comments on all aspects of the proposed regulations. All comments will be available for public inspection and copying. A public hearing will be scheduled if requested in writing by any person that timely submits written comments. If a public hearing is scheduled, notice of the date, time, and place for the public hearing will be published in the **Federal Register.**

Drafting Information

The principal authors of these proposed regulations are Rebecca J. Holtje and Marie C. Milnes-Vasquez of the Office of Associate Chief Counsel (Corporate). However, other personnel from the Department of Treasury and the IRS participated in their development.

[¶49,564] Proposed Amendments of Regulations (REG-106918-08), published in the Federal Register on February 5, 2013.

[Code Secs. 761 and 1234]

Partnerships: Options: Recognition of gain or loss: Noncompensatory partnership options: Characterization rule measurement event.—Amendments of Reg. §§1.761-3 and 1.1234-3, relating to the tax treatment of noncompensatory options and convertible instruments issued by a partnership, are proposed.

AGENCY: Internal Revenue Service (IRS), Treasury.

ACTION: Notice of proposed rulemaking.

SUMMARY: This document contains proposed regulations relating to the tax treatment of noncompensatory options and convertible instruments issued by a partnership. Specifically, the proposed regulations expand the characterization rule measurement events to include certain transfers of interests in the issuing partnership and other lookthrough entities, and provide additional guidance in determining the character of the grantor's gain or loss as a result of a closing transaction with respect to, or a lapse of, an option on a partnership interest. The proposed regulations will affect partnerships that issue noncompensatory options, the partners of such partnerships, and the holders of such options.

DATES: Written or electronic comments and requests for a public hearing must be received by May 6, 2013.

ADDRESSES: Send submissions to: CC:PA:LPD:PR (REG-106918-08), room 5203, Internal Revenue Service, PO Box 7604, Ben Franklin Station, Washington, DC 20044. Submissions may be hand-delivered Monday through Friday between the hours of 8 a.m. and 4 p.m. to CC:PA:LPD:PR (REG-106918-08), Courier's Desk, Internal Revenue Service, 1111 Constitution Avenue, NW., Washington, DC, or sent electronically via the Federal eRulemaking Portal at *www.regulations.gov* (IRS REG-106918-08).

FOR FURTHER INFORMATION CONTACT: Concerning the proposed regulations under §1.761-3, Benjamin Weaver at (202) 622-3050; concerning the proposed regulations under §*1.1234-3*, Shawn Tetelman at (202) 622-3930; concerning submissions of comments and requests for a public hearing, Oluwafunmilayo (Funmi) Taylor, (202) 622-7180 (not toll free numbers).

SUPPLEMENTARY INFORMATION:

Background

This document contains proposed amendments to 26 CFR part 1 under sections 761 and 1234 of the Internal Revenue Code (Code). On January 22, 2003, proposed regulations (REG-103580-02) relating to the tax treatment of noncompensatory options and convertible instruments issued by a partnership (noncompensatory partnership option regulations) were published in the **Federal Register** (68 FR 2930). Final regulations in the Rules and Regulations section of this issue of the **Federal Register** contain amendments to the Income Tax Regulations (26 CFR Part 1), which finalize the proposed regulations. However, the Treasury Department and the IRS have decided to propose amendments to the regulations expanding the characterization rule measurement events to include certain transfers of interests in the issuing partnership and other look-through entities.

Additionally, the Treasury Department and the IRS received comments on the proposed regulations expressing uncertainty as to whether section 1234(b) applies to the grantor of an option on a partnership interest on the lapse or repurchase of the option. The comments indicated that it was unclear whether the term "securities," as used in section 1234(b)(2)(B), includes partnership interests. After consideration of all comments received, the IRS and Treasury Department believe that it is appropriate to propose an amendment to the regulations under section 1234(b) to expressly treat partnership interests as securities for purposes of section 1234(b).

Explanation of Provisions

1. *Proposed Additions to the Noncompensatory Partnership Option Characterization Rule Measurement Events*

The final regulations being published elsewhere in this issue of the **Federal Register**, relating to the tax treatment of noncompensatory partnership options, contain a characterization rule providing that the holder of a noncompensatory option is treated as a partner under certain circumstances. Under the characterization rule, a noncompensatory option is treated as a partnership interest if, on the date of a measurement event (1) the noncompensatory option provides the option holder with rights that are substantially similar to the rights afforded a partner, and (2) there is a strong likelihood that the failure to treat the holder of the noncompensatory option as a partner would result in a substantial reduction in the present value of the partners' and noncompensatory option holder's aggregate Federal tax liabilities. The final regulations define a measurement event as: (1) issuance of the noncompensatory option; (2) an adjustment of the terms (modification) of the noncompensatory option or of the underlying partnership interest (including an adjustment pursuant to the terms of the noncompensatory option or the underlying partnership interest); or (3) transfer of the noncompensatory option if either (A) the option may be exercised (or settled) more than 12 months after its issuance, or (B) the transfer is pursuant to a plan in existence at the time of the issuance or modification of the noncompensatory option that has as a principal purpose the substantial reduction of the present value of the aggregate Federal tax liabilities of the partners and the noncompensatory option holder.

The Treasury Department and the IRS believe it is appropriate to expand the list of measurement events to include certain transfers of interests in the issuing partnership and look-through entities. The proposed regulations add three measurement events to the list above, but apply only if those measurement events are pursuant to a plan in existence at the time of the issuance or modification of the noncompensatory option that has as a principal purpose the substantial reduction of the present value of the aggregate Federal tax liabilities of the partners and the noncompensatory option holder. The three additional measurement events are: (1) issuance, transfer, or modification of an interest in, or liquidation of, the issuing partnership; (2) issuance, transfer, or modification of an interest in any look-through entity that directly, or indirectly through one or more look-through entities, owns the noncompensatory option; and (3) issuance, transfer, or modification of an interest in any look-through entity that directly, or indirectly through one or more look-through entities, owns an interest in the issuing partnership. The Treasury Department and the IRS believe that the first of these measurement events is necessary because it is inconsistent to test a noncompensatory option under the characterization rule upon transfer of the noncompensatory option, but not upon transfer of an interest in the issuing partnership, because either type of transfer may change the analysis of whether there is a strong likelihood that the failure to treat the option holder as a partner would result in a substantial reduction in the present value of the partners' and option holder's aggregate tax liabilities. The Treasury Department and the IRS believe that the second and third measurement events are necessary to prevent avoidance of the characterization rule through the use of look-through entities.

Like the measurement events in the final regulations, the three measurement events in the proposed regulations are subject to exceptions in § 1.761-3(c)(2). The Treasury Department and the IRS believe that the limitations on these measurement events will reduce the administrative burden associated with testing under the characterization rule upon these events.

The Treasury Department and the IRS request comments on the appropriate procedures for notifying the partners and the partnership upon the occurrence of a measurement event.

2. *Character of Gain or Loss on Lapse, Sale, or Exchange of Partnership Options*

A. *Character of gain or loss to the grantor of the option*

In response to comments, the proposed regulations address the application of section 1234(b) to the grantor of an option on a partnership interest on the lapse or repurchase of the option. Section 1234(b) provides that, in the case of the grantor of an option, gain or loss from any closing transaction with respect to, and gain on lapse of, an option in property shall be treated as gain or loss from the sale or exchange of a capital asset held not more than one year. Section 1234(b)(2)(B) defines the term property to mean stock and securities (including stocks and securities dealt with on a when issued basis), commodities, and commodity futures. Accordingly, for section 1234(b) to apply to a closing transaction with respect to, or lapse of, an option on a partnership interest, a partnership interest would have to be a security and, thus, property within the meaning of section 1234(b)(2)(B). The proposed regulations provide that the term "securities" as used in section 1234(b)(2)(B) includes partnership interests. As a result, in the case of the grantor of an option on a partnership interest, gain or loss from any closing transaction with respect to, and gain on lapse of, the option is generally treated under the proposed regulations as gain or loss from the sale or exchange of a capital asset held not more than 1 year.

B. *Character of gain or loss to the option holder*

With respect to an option holder, under section 1234(a), gain or loss on the sale or exchange of, or loss on failure to exercise, an option is considered gain or loss from the sale or exchange of property that has the same character as the property to which the option relates would have in the hands of the taxpayer. Although a partnership interest is generally considered a capital asset, section 751(a) may apply to recharacterize a portion of a partner's gain on the sale or exchange of a partnership interest as ordinary. A number of commenters on the noncompensatory partnership option proposed regulations questioned whether section 751 applies to the lapse, repurchase, sale, exchange, or other termination of a noncompensatory option.

The Treasury Department and the IRS continue to study this issue and request comments on (1) if section 751(a) applies to the lapse, repurchase, sale, or exchange of a noncompensatory option, (a) how the option holder's share of income or loss from section 751 property would be determined under § 1.751-1(a)(2), and (b) how a partner in the issuing partnership that transfers its partnership interest while the option is outstanding would determine its share of income or loss from section 751 property under § 1.751-1(a)(2) (that is, should it be reduced by the amount of income or loss from section 751 property attributable to the option holder); and (2) if section 751(a) does not apply to the lapse, repurchase, sale, or exchange of a noncompensatory option, what measures, if any, should be taken to ensure that ordinary income is not permanently eliminated.

Effective/Applicability Date

To coordinate the proposed regulations with the final noncompensatory partnership option regulations, the proposed regulations are proposed to have the same effective date as the final noncompensatory partnership option regulations. Therefore, the proposed regulations are proposed to apply to options issued on or after February 5, 2013.

Special Analyses

It has been determined that this notice of proposed rulemaking is not a significant regulatory action as defined in Executive Order 12866, as supplemented by Executive Order 13563. Therefore, a regulatory assessment is not required. It also has been determined that section 553(b) of the Administrative Procedure Act (5 U.S.C. chapter 5) does not apply to this regulation, and because the regulation does not impose a collection of information requirement on small entities, the Regulatory Flexibility Act (5 U.S.C. chapter 6) does not apply. Pursuant to section 7805(f) of the Code, this regulation has been submitted to the Chief Counsel for Advocacy of the Small Business Administration for comment on its impact on small business.

Comments and Requests for Public Hearing

Before these proposed regulations are adopted as final regulations, consideration will be given to any written (a signed original and eight (8) copies) or electronic comments that are submitted timely to the IRS. The Treasury Department and the IRS request comments on all aspects of the proposed rules. All comments are available at *www.regulations.gov* or upon request. A public hearing may be scheduled if requested in writing by any person that timely submits written comments. If a public hearing is scheduled, notice of the date, time, and place for the public hearing will be published in the **Federal Register**.

Drafting Information

The principal authors of these proposed regulations are Benjamin Weaver of the Office of Associate Chief Counsel (Passthroughs and Special Industries) and Shawn Tetelman of the Office of Associate Chief Counsel (Financial Institutions and Products). However, other personnel from the IRS and Treasury Department participated in their development.

[¶ 49,574] Proposed Amendments of Regulations (REG-125398-12), published in the Federal Register on May 3, 2013.

[Code Secs. 36B and 6011]

Credits: Health insurance premium tax credit: Qualified health plan.—Amendments of Reg. §§ 1.36B-0, 1.36B-1, 1.36B-2, 1.36B-3, 1.36B-6 and 1.6011-8, relating to the health insurance premium tax credit enacted by the Patient Protection and Affordable Care Act (P.L. 111-148) and the Health Care and Education Reconciliation Act of 2010 (P.L. 111-152), as amended by the Medicare and Medicaid Extenders Act of 2010 (P.L. 111-309), the Comprehensive 1099 Taxpayer Protection and Repayment of Exchange Subsidy Overpayments Act of 2011 (P.L. 112-9), and the Department of Defense and Full-Year Continuing Appropriations Act, 2011 (P.L. 112-10) and providing guidance on determining whether health coverage under an eligible employer-sponsored plan provides minimum value and affect employers that offer health coverage and their employees, are adopted. NOTE: Only some of the amendments to proposed Reg. § 1.36B-6 were adopted by T.D. 9745.

AGENCY: Internal Revenue Service (IRS), Treasury.

ACTION: Notice of proposed rulemaking.

SUMMARY: This document contains proposed regulations relating to the health insurance premium tax credit enacted by the Patient Protection and Affordable Care Act and the Health Care and Education Reconciliation Act of 2010, as amended by the Medicare and Medicaid Extenders Act of 2010, the Comprehensive 1099 Taxpayer Protection and Repayment of Exchange Subsidy Overpayments Act of 2011, and the Department of Defense and Full-Year Continuing Appropriations Act, 2011. These proposed regulations affect individuals who enroll in qualified health plans through Affordable Insurance Exchanges (Exchanges) and claim the premium tax credit, and Exchanges that make qualified health plans available to individuals and employers. These proposed regulations also provide guidance on determining whether health coverage under an eligible employer-sponsored plan provides minimum value and affect employers that offer health coverage and their employees.

DATES: Written (including electronic) comments and requests for a public hearing must be received by July 2, 2013.

ADDRESSES: Send submissions to: CC:PA:LPD:PR (REG-125398-12), Room 5203, Internal Revenue Service, PO Box 7604, Ben Franklin Station, Washington, DC 20044. Submissions may be hand-delivered Monday through Friday between the hours of 8 a.m. and 4 p.m. to CC:PA:LPD:PR (REG-125398-12), Courier's Desk, Internal Revenue Service, 1111 Constitution Avenue, NW., Washington, DC, or sent electronically via the Federal eRulemaking Portal at *www.regulations.gov* (IRS REG-125398-12).

FOR FURTHER INFORMATION CONTACT: Concerning the proposed regulations, Andrew S. Braden, (202) 622-4960; concerning the submission of comments and/or requests for a public hearing, Oluwafunmilayo Taylor, (202) 622-7180 (not toll-free calls).

SUPPLEMENTARY INFORMATION:

Background

Beginning in 2014, under the Patient Protection and Affordable Care Act, Public Law 111-148 (124 Stat. 119 (2010)), and the Health Care and Education Reconciliation Act of 2010, Public Law 111-152 (124 Stat. 1029 (2010)) (collectively, the Affordable Care Act), eligible individuals who purchase coverage under a qualified health plan through an Affordable Insurance Exchange may receive a premium tax credit under section 36B of the Internal Revenue Code (Code). Section 36B was subsequently amended by the Medicare and Medicaid Extenders Act of 2010, Public Law 111-309 (124 Stat. 3285 (2010)); the Comprehensive 1099 Taxpayer Protection and Repayment of Exchange Subsidy Overpayments Act of 2011, Public Law 112-9 (125 Stat. 36 (2011)); and the Department of Defense and Full-Year Continuing Appropriations Act, 2011, Public Law 112-10 (125 Stat. 38 (2011)).

Notice 2012-31 (2012-20 IRB 910) requested comments on methods for determining whether health coverage under an eligible employer-sponsored plan provides minimum value (MV). Final regulations under section 36B (TD 9590) were published on May 23, 2012 (77 FR 30377). The final regulations requested comments on issues to be addressed in further guidance. The comments have been considered in developing these proposed regulations.

Minimum Value

Individuals generally may not receive a premium tax credit if they are eligible for affordable coverage under an eligible employer-sponsored plan that provides MV. An applicable large employer (as defined in section 4980H(c)(2)) may be liable for an assessable payment under section 4980H if a full-time employee receives a premium tax credit.

Under section 36B(c)(2)(C)(ii), a plan fails to provide MV if the plan's share of the total allowed costs of benefits provided under the plan is less than 60 percent of the costs. Section 1302(d)(2)(C) of the Affordable Care Act provides that, in determining the percentage of the total allowed costs of benefits provided under a group health plan, the regulations promulgated by the Secretary of Health and Human Services (HHS) under section 1302(d)(2) apply.

HHS published final regulations under section 1302(d)(2) on February 25, 2013 (78 FR 12834). The HHS regulations at 45 CFR 156.20 define the percentage of the total allowed costs of benefits provided under a group health plan as (1) the anticipated covered medical spending for essential health benefits (EHB) coverage (as defined in 45 CFR 156.110(a)) paid by a health plan for a standard population, (2) computed in accordance with the plan's cost-sharing, and (3) divided by the total anticipated allowed charges for EHB coverage provided to a standard population. In addition, 45 CFR 156.145(c) provides that the standard population used to compute this percentage for MV (as developed by HHS for this purpose) reflects the population covered by typical self-insured group health plans.

The HHS regulations describe several options for determining MV. Under 45 CFR 156.145(a)(1), plans may use the MV Calculator (available at *http://cciio.cms.gov/resources/regulations/index.html*). Alternatively, 45 CFR 156.145(a)(2) provides that a plan may determine MV through a safe harbor established by HHS and IRS. For plans with nonstandard features that are incompatible with the MV Calculator or a safe harbor, 45 CFR 156.145(a)(3) provides that the plan may determine MV through an actuarial certification from a member of the American Academy of Actuaries after performing an analysis in accordance with generally accepted actuarial principles and methodologies. Finally, 45 CFR 156.145(a)(4) provides that a plan in the small group market satisfies MV if it meets the requirements for any of the levels of metal coverage defined at 45 CFR 156.140(b) (bronze, silver, gold, or platinum).

Miscellaneous Provisions Under Section 36B

To be eligible for a premium tax credit, an individual must be an applicable taxpayer. Under section 36B(c)(1), an applicable taxpayer is a taxpayer whose household income for the taxable year is between 100 percent and 400 percent of the federal poverty line (FPL) for the taxpayer's family size.

Section 36B(b)(1) provides that the premium assistance credit amount is the sum of the premium assistance amounts for all coverage months in the taxable year for individuals in the taxpayer's family. The premium assistance amount for a coverage month is the lesser of (1) the premiums for the month for one or more qualified health plans that cover a taxpayer or family member, or (2) the excess of the adjusted monthly premium for the second lowest cost silver plan (as described in section 1302(d)(1)(B) of the Affordable Care Act (42 U.S.C. 18022(d)(1)(B)) (the benchmark plan) that applies to the taxpayer over 1/12 of the product of the taxpayer's household income and the applicable percentage for the taxable year. The adjusted monthly premium, in general, is the premium an insurer would charge for the plan adjusted only for the ages of the covered individuals.

Under section 36B(c)(2)(A), a coverage month is any month for which the taxpayer or a family member is covered by a qualified health plan enrolled in through an Exchange and the premium is paid by the taxpayer or through an advance credit payment. Section 36B(c)(2) provides that a month is not a coverage month for an individual who is eligible for other minimum essential coverage. If the other coverage is eligible employer-sponsored coverage, however, it is treated as minimum essential coverage only if it is affordable and provides MV. Eligible employer-sponsored coverage is affordable for an employee and related individuals if the portion of the annual premium the employee must pay for self-only coverage does not exceed the required contribution percentage (9.5 percent for taxable years beginning before January 1, 2015) of the taxpayer's household income. The MV requirement is discussed in the Explanation of Provisions.

Any arrangement under which employees are required, as a condition of employment or otherwise, to be enrolled in an employer-sponsored plan that does not provide minimum value or is unaffordable, and that does not give the employees an effective opportunity to terminate or decline the coverage, raises a variety of issues. Proposed regulations under section 4980H indicate that if an employer maintains such an arrangement it would not be treated as having made an offer of coverage. As a result, an applicable large employer could be subject to an assessable payment under that section. See Proposed § 54.4980H-4(b), 78 FR 250 (January 2, 2013). Such an arrangement would also raise additional concerns. For example, it is questionable whether the law permits interference with an individual's ability to apply for a section 36B premium tax credit by seeking to involuntarily impose coverage that does not provide minimum value. (See, for example, the Fair Labor Standards Act, as amended by section 1558 of the Affordable Care Act, 29 U.S.C. 218c(a).) If an employer sought to involuntarily impose on its employees coverage that did not provide minimum value or was unaffordable, the IRS and Treasury, as well as other relevant departments, may treat such arrangements as impermissible interference with an employee's ability to access premium tax credits, as contemplated by the Affordable Care Act.

Explanation of Provisions and Summary of Comments

1. *Minimum Value*

a. *In general*

The proposed regulations refer to the proportion of the total allowed costs of benefits provided to an employee that are paid by the plan as the plan's MV percentage. The MV percentage is determined by dividing the cost of certain benefits (described in paragraph b.) the plan would pay for a standard population by the total cost of certain benefits for the standard population, including amounts the plan pays and amounts the employee pays through cost-sharing, and then converting the result to a percentage.

b. *Health benefits measured in determining MV*

Commentators sought clarification of the health benefits considered in determining the share of benefit costs paid by a plan. Some commentators maintained that MV should be based on the plan's share of the cost of coverage for all EHBs, including those a plan does not offer. Other commentators suggested that the MV percentage should be based on the plan's share of the costs of only those categories of EHBs the plan covers.

The proposed regulations do not require employer-sponsored self-insured and insured large group plans to cover every EHB category or conform their plans to an EHB benchmark that applies to qualified health plans. The preamble to the HHS regulations (see 78 FR 12833) notes that employer-sponsored group health plans are not required to offer EHBs unless they are health plans offered in the small group market subject to section 2707(a) of the Public Health Service Act. The preamble also states that, under section 1302(d)(2) of the Affordable Care Act, MV is measured based on the provision of EHBs to a standard population and plans may account for any benefits covered by the employer that also are covered in any one of the EHB-benchmark plans. See 45 CFR 156.145(b)(2).

Consistent with 45 CFR 156.145(a)-(c) and the assumptions described in Notice 2012-31, these proposed regulations provide that MV is based on the anticipated spending for a standard population. The plan's anticipated spending for benefits provided under any particular EHB-benchmark plan for any State counts towards MV.

c. *Health reimbursement arrangements, health savings accounts, and wellness program incentives*

i. Arrangements that Reduce Cost-Sharing

Some commentators suggested that current year health savings account (HSA) contributions and amounts newly made available under a health reimbursement arrangement (HRA) should be fully counted toward the plan's share of costs included in calculating MV. Some commentators suggested that only HRA contributions that may be used to pay for cost sharing and not HRAs restricted to other uses should be counted in the MV calculation.

Consistent with 45 CFR 156.135(c), the proposed regulations provide that all amounts contributed by an employer for the current plan year to an HSA are taken into account in determining the plan's share of costs for purposes of MV and are treated as amounts available for first dollar coverage. Amounts newly made available under an HRA that is integrated with an eligible employer-sponsored plan for the current plan year count for purposes of MV in the same manner if the amounts may be used only for cost-sharing and may not be used to pay insurance premiums. It is anticipated that regulations will provide that whether an HRA is integrated with an eligible employer-sponsored plan is determined under rules that apply for purposes of section 2711 of the Public Health Service Act (42 U.S.C. 300gg-11). Commentators offered differing opinions about how nondiscriminatory wellness program incentives that may affect an employee's cost sharing should be taken into account for purposes of the MV calculation. Some commentators noted that the rules governing wellness incentives require that they be available to all similarly situated individuals. These commentators suggested that because eligible individuals have the opportunity to reduce their cost-sharing if they choose, a plan's share of costs should be based on the costs paid by individuals who satisfy the terms of the wellness program. Other commentators expressed concern that, despite the safeguards of the regulations governing wellness incentives, certain individuals inevitably will face barriers to participation and fail to qualify for rewards. These commentators suggested that a plan's share of costs should be determined without assuming that individuals would qualify for the reduced cost-sharing available under a wellness program.

The proposed regulations provide that a plan's share of costs for MV purposes is determined without regard to reduced cost-sharing available under a nondiscriminatory wellness program. However, for nondiscriminatory wellness programs designed to prevent or reduce tobacco use, MV may be calculated assuming that every eligible individual satisfies the terms of the program relating to prevention or reduction of tobacco use. This exception is consistent with other Affordable Care Act provisions (such as the ability to charge higher premiums based on tobacco use) reflecting a policy about individual responsibility regarding tobacco use.

ii. Arrangements that Reduce Premiums

Section 36B(c)(2)(C)(i)(II) and the final regulations provide that eligible employer-sponsored coverage is affordable only if an employee's required contribution for self-only coverage does not exceed 9.5 percent of household income. The preamble to the final regulations indicated that rules for determining how HRAs and wellness program incentives are counted in determining the affordability of eligible employer-sponsored coverage would be provided in later guidance.

Some commentators asserted that an employer's entire annual contribution to an HRA plus prior year contributions should be taken into account in determining affordability. The proposed regulations provide that amounts newly made available under an HRA that is integrated with an eligible employer-sponsored plan for the current plan year are taken into account only in determining affordability if the employee may use the amounts only for premiums or may choose to use the amounts for either premiums or cost-sharing. Treating amounts that may be used either for premiums or cost-sharing only towards affordability prevents double counting the HRA amounts when assessing MV and affordability of eligible employer-sponsored coverage.

It is anticipated that regulations under section 5000A will provide that amounts newly made available under an HRA that is integrated with an eligible employer-sponsored plan for the current plan year are also taken into account for purposes of the affordability exemption under section 5000A(e)(1) if the employee may use the amounts only for premiums or for either premiums or cost-sharing.

The final regulations requested specific comments on the nature of wellness incentives and how they should be treated for determining affordability. Commentators expressed similar views about the treatment of wellness incentives that affect the cost of premiums as about the treatment of wellness incentives that affect cost-sharing.

Like the rule for determining MV, the proposed regulations provide that the affordability of an employer-sponsored plan is determined by assuming that each employee fails to satisfy the requirements of a wellness program, except the requirements of a nondiscriminatory wellness program related to tobacco use. Thus, the affordability of a plan that charges a higher initial premium for tobacco users will be determined based on the premium that is charged to non-tobacco users, or tobacco users who complete the related wellness program, such as attending smoking cessation classes.

In many circumstances these rules relating to the effect of premium-related wellness program rewards on affordability will have no practical consequences. They matter only when the employer sets the level of the employee's required contribution to self-only premium, and establishes a wellness program that provides for a level of premium discount, in such a manner that the employee's required contribution to premium would exceed 9.5 percent of household income (or wages, under an affordability safe harbor under the section 4980H proposed regulations) but for the potential premium discount under the wellness program. If, for example, the employee's household income was at least $25,000, and the employee's required contribution for self-only coverage did not exceed $2,375 (9.5 percent of $25,000), the coverage would be affordable whether or not a wellness premium discount was taken into account to reduce the $2,375 required contribution.

It is anticipated that regulations under section 5000A will provide that nondiscriminatory wellness programs that affect premiums will be treated for purposes of the affordability exemption under section 5000A(e)(1) in the same manner as they are treated for purposes of determining affordability under section 36B.

Solely for purposes of applying section 4980H and solely for plan years of an employer's group health plan beginning before January 1, 2015, with respect to an employee described in the next sentence, an employer will not be subject to an assessable payment under section 4980H(b) with respect to an employee who received a premium tax credit because the offer of coverage was not affordable or did not satisfy MV, if the offer of coverage to the employee under the employer's group health plan would have been affordable or would have satisfied MV based on the total required employee premium and cost-sharing for that group health plan that would have applied to the employee if the employee satisfied the requirements of any wellness program described in the next sentence, including a wellness program with requirements unrelated to tobacco use. The rule in the preceding sentence applies only (1) to the extent of the reward as of May 3, 2013, expressed as either a dollar amount or a fraction of the total required employee contribution to the premium (or the employee cost-sharing, as applicable), (2) under the terms of a wellness program as in effect on May 3, 2013, and (3) with respect to an employee who is in a category of employees eligible under the terms of the wellness program as in effect on May 3, 2013 (regardless of whether the employee was hired before or after that date). Any required employee contribution to premium determined based upon assumed satisfaction of the requirements of a wellness program available under this transition relief may be applied to the use of an affordability safe harbor provided in the proposed regulations under section 4980H.

d. *Standard population and utilization*

Consistent with 45 CFR 156.145(c), the proposed regulations provide that the standard population used to determine MV reflects the population covered by self-insured group health plans. HHS has developed the MV standard population and described it through summary statistics (for example, continuance tables). MV continuance tables and an explanation of the MV Calculator methodology and the health claims data HHS has used to develop the continuance tables are available at *http://cciio.cms.gov/resources/regulations/index.html.*

e. *Methods for determining minimum value*

Notice 2012-31 and 45 CFR 156.145(a) describe several methods for determining MV: the MV Calculator, a safe harbor, actuarial certification, and, for small group market plans, a metal level. Some commentators requested that plans be allowed to choose one of the four methods in determining MV. Other commentators favored requiring employers to use the most precise method for plans that may be close to the 60 percent threshold.

The proposed regulations provide that taxpayers may determine whether a plan provides MV by using the MV Calculator made available by HHS and the IRS. Taxpayers must use the MV Calculator to measure standard plan features (unless a safe harbor applies), but the percentage may be adjusted based on an actuarial analysis of plan features that are outside the parameters of the calculator.

Certain safe harbor plan designs that satisfy MV will be specified in additional guidance under section 36B or 4980H, see § 601.601(d). It is anticipated that the guidance will provide that the safe harbors are examples of plan designs that clearly would satisfy the 60 percent threshold if measured using the MV Calculator. The safe harbors are intended to provide an easy way for sponsors of typical employer-sponsored group health plans to determine whether a plan meets the MV threshold without having to use the MV Calculator.

Plan designs meeting the following specifications are proposed as safe harbors for determining MV if the plans cover all of the benefits included in the MV Calculator: (1) a plan with a $3,500 integrated medical and drug deductible, 80 percent plan cost-sharing, and a $6,000 maximum out-of-pocket limit for employee cost-sharing; (2) a plan with a $4,500 integrated medical and drug deductible, 70 percent plan cost-sharing, a $6,400 maximum out-of-pocket limit, and a $500 employer contribution to an HSA; and (3) a plan with a $3,500 medical deductible, $0 drug deductible, 60 percent plan medical expense cost-sharing, 75 percent plan drug cost-sharing, a $6,400 maximum out-of-pocket limit, and drug co-pays of $10/$20/$50 for the first, second and third prescription drug tiers, with 75 percent coinsurance for specialty drugs. Comments are requested on these and other common plan designs that would satisfy MV and should be designated as safe harbors.

Consistent with 45 CFR 156.145(a), the proposed regulations require plans with nonstandard features that cannot determine MV using the MV Calculator or a safe harbor to use the actuarial certification method. The actuary must be a member of the American Academy of Actuaries and must perform the analysis in accordance with generally accepted actuarial principles and methodologies and any additional standards that subsequent guidance requires.

f. *Other issues*

Commentators suggested a de minimis exception to the MV 60 percent level of coverage, noting that similar de minimis variations are permitted in determining actuarial value for qualified health plans. However, as other commentators noted, permitting a de minimis exception would have the effect of lowering the minimum level of coverage to a percentage below 60 percent. Under section 36B(c)(2)(C)(ii), coverage below 60 percent does not provide MV. Accordingly, the proposed regulations do not provide for a de minimis exception.

2. *Miscellaneous Issues Under Section 36B*

a. *Definition of modified adjusted gross income*

Section 36B(d)(2) provides that the term *household income* means the modified adjusted gross income of the taxpayer plus the modified adjusted gross income of all members of the taxpayer's family required to file a tax return under section 1 for the taxable year. The final regulations provide that the determination of whether a family member is required to file a return is made without regard to section 1(g)(7). Under section 1(g)(7), a parent may, if certain requirements are met, elect to include in the parent's gross income, the gross income of his or her child. If the parent makes the election, the child is treated as having no gross income for the taxable year.

The proposed regulations remove "without regard to section 1(g)(7)" from the final regulations because that language implies that the child's gross income is included in both the parent's adjusted gross income and the child's adjusted gross income in determining household income. Thus, the proposed regulations clarify that if a parent makes an election under section 1(g)(7), household income includes the child's gross income included on the parent's return and the child is treated as having no gross income.

b. *Rating area*

Section 36B(b)(3)(B) determines the applicable benchmark plan by reference to the rating area where a taxpayer resides. The final regulations reserved the definition of *rating area*. The proposed regulations provide that the term *rating area* has the same meaning as used in section 2701(a)(2) of the Public Health Service Act (42 U.S.C. 300gg) and 45 CFR 156.255.

c. *Retiree coverage*

The section 36B final regulations provide that an individual who may enroll in continuation coverage required under Federal law or a State law that provides comparable continuation coverage is eligible for minimum essential coverage only for months that the individual is enrolled in the coverage. These proposed regulations apply this rule to former employees only. Active employees eligible for continuation coverage as a result of reduced hours should be subject to the same rules for eligibility of affordable employer-sponsored coverage offering MV as other active employees. The proposed regulations add a comparable rule for health coverage offered to retired employees (retiree coverage). Accordingly, an individual who may enroll in retiree coverage is eligible for minimum essential coverage under the coverage only for the months the individual is enrolled in the coverage.

d *Coverage month for newborns and new adoptees*

Under section 36B(c)(2)(A)(i) and the final regulations, a month is a coverage month for an individual only if, as of the first day of the month, the individual is enrolled in a qualified health plan through an Exchange. A child born or adopted during the month is not enrolled in coverage on the first day and therefore would not be eligible for the premium tax credit or cost-sharing reductions for that month. Accordingly, the proposed regulations provide that a child enrolled in a qualified health plan in the month of the child's birth, adoption, or placement with the taxpayer for adoption or in foster care, is treated as enrolled as of the first day of the month.

e. *Adjusted monthly premium for family members enrolled for less than a full month*

Under section 36B(c), the premium assistance amount for a coverage month is computed by reference to the adjusted monthly premium for an applicable benchmark plan. The final regulations provide that the applicable benchmark plan is the plan that applies to a taxpayer's coverage family. The final regulations do not address whether changes to a coverage family, for example as the result of the birth and enrollment of a child or the disenrollment of another family member, that occur during the month affect the premium assistance amount. The proposed regulations provide that the adjusted monthly premium is determined as if all members of the coverage family for that month were enrolled in a qualified health plan for the entire month.

f. *Premium assistance amount for partial months of coverage*

The final regulations do not address the computation of the premium assistance amount if coverage under a qualified health plan is terminated during the month. The proposed regulations provide that when coverage under a qualified health plan is terminated before the last day of a month and, as a result, the issuer reduces or refunds a portion of the monthly premium the premium assistance amount for the month is prorated based on the number of days of coverage in the month.

g. *Family members residing at different locations.*

The final regulations reserved rules on determining the premium for the applicable benchmark plan if family members are geographically separated and enroll in separate qualified health plans. The proposed regulations provide that the premium for the applicable benchmark plan in this situation is the sum of the premiums for the applicable benchmark plans for each group of family members residing in a different State.

h. *Correction to applicable percentage table*

The applicable percentage table in the final regulations erroneously states that the 9.5 percentage applies only to taxpayers whose household income is less than 400 percent of the FPL. The proposed regulations clarify that the 9.5 percentage applies to taxpayers whose household income is not more than 400 percent of the FPL.

i. *Additional benefits and applicable benchmark plan*

Under section 36B(b)(3)(D) and the final regulations, only the portion of the premium for a qualified health plan properly allocable to EHBs determines a taxpayer's premium assistance amount. Premiums allocable to benefits other than EHBs (additional benefits) are disregarded. The final regulations do not address, however, whether a taxpayer's benchmark plan is determined before or after premiums have been allocated to additional benefits. The proposed regulations provide that premiums are allocated to additional benefits before determining the applicable benchmark plan. Thus, only essential health benefits are considered in determining the applicable benchmark plan, consistent with the requirement in section 36B(b)(3)(D) that only essential health benefits are considered in determining the premium assistance amount. In addition, allocating premium to benefits that exceed EHBs before determining the applicable benchmark plan results in a more accurate determination of the premium assistance amount.

j. *Requirement to file a return to reconcile advance credit payments*

The final regulations provided that a taxpayer who receives advance credit payments must file an income tax return for that taxable year on or before the fifteenth day of the fourth month following the close of the taxable year. Under the proposed regulations, a taxpayer who receives advance credit payments must file an income tax return on or before the due date for the return (including extensions).

Effective/Applicability Date

These regulations are proposed to apply for taxable years ending after December 31, 2013. Taxpayers may apply the proposed regulations for taxable years ending before January 1, 2015.

Special Analyses

It has been determined that this notice of proposed rulemaking is not a significant regulatory action as defined in Executive Order 12866, as supplemented by Executive Order 13563. Therefore, a regulatory assessment is not required. It has also been determined that section 553(b) of the Administrative Procedure Act (5 U.S.C. chapter 5) does not apply to these regulations and, because the regulations do not impose a collection of information on small entities, the Regulatory Flexibility Act (5 U.S.C. chapter 6) does not apply. Pursuant to section 7805(f) of the Code, this notice of proposed rulemaking has been submitted to the Chief Counsel for Advocacy of the Small Business Administration for comment on its impact on small business.

Comments and Requests for Public Hearing

Before these proposed regulations are adopted as final regulations, consideration will be given to any comments that are submitted timely to the IRS as prescribed in this preamble under the "Addresses" heading. Treasury and the IRS request comments on all aspects of the proposed rules. All comments will be available at *www.regulations.gov* or upon request. A public hearing will be scheduled if requested in writing by any person who timely submits written comments. If a public hearing is scheduled, notice of the date, time and place for the hearing will be published in the **Federal Register**.

Drafting Information

The principal authors of these proposed regulations are Andrew S. Braden, Frank W. Dunham III, and Stephen J. Toomey of the Office of Associate Chief Counsel (Income Tax and Accounting). However, other personnel from the IRS and the Treasury Department participated in the development of the regulations.

[¶49,580] Proposed Amendments of Regulations (REG-132251-11), published in the Federal Register on August 13, 2013.

[Code Secs. 66 and 6015]

Joint and several liability: Community property laws: Innocent spouse relief: When to request relief: How to request relief.—Amendments of Reg. §§1.66-4, 1.66-5, 1.6015-0, 1.6015-5 and 1.6015-9, relating to relief from joint and several tax liability under Code Sec. 6015 and relief from the federal income tax liability resulting from the operation of state community property laws under Code Sec. 66, are proposed.

AGENCY: Internal Revenue Service (IRS), Treasury.

ACTION: Notice of proposed rulemaking.

SUMMARY: This document contains proposed regulations relating to relief from joint and several tax liability under section 6015 of the Internal Revenue Code (Code) and relief from the Federal income tax liability resulting from the operation of state community property laws under section 66. The proposed regulations provide guidance to taxpayers on when and how to request relief under sections 66 and 6015. This document also invites comments from the public regarding these proposed regulations.

DATES: Written or electronic comments and requests for a public hearing must be received by November 12, 2013.

ADDRESSES: Send submissions to: CC:PA:LPD:PR (REG-132251-11), room 5205, Internal Revenue Service, P.O. Box 7604, Ben Franklin Station, Washington, DC 20044. Submissions may be hand-delivered Monday through Friday between the hours of 8 a.m. and 4 p.m. to CC:PA:LPD:PR (REG-132251-11), Courier's Desk, Internal Revenue Service, 1111 Constitution Avenue, N.W., Washington, DC; or sent electronically via the Federal eRulemaking Portal at *www.regulations.gov* (IRS REG-132251-11).

FOR FURTHER INFORMATION CONTACT: Concerning the proposed regulations, Mark Shurtliff at (202) 622-4910; concerning submissions of comments and requests for a hearing, Oluwafunmilayo (Funmi) Taylor at (202) 622-7180 (not toll-free numbers).

SUPPLEMENTARY INFORMATION:

Background

Section 6013(a) of the Code permits taxpayers who are husband and wife to file a joint Federal income tax return. Married individuals who choose to file a joint income tax return are each jointly and severally liable under section 6013(d)(3) for the tax arising from that return, which, pursuant to sections 6601(e)(1) and 6665(a)(2), includes any additions to tax, additional amounts, penalties, and interest. Because the liability is joint and several, the IRS is authorized to collect the entire amount from either spouse, without regard to which spouse the items of income, deduction, credit, or basis that gave rise to the liability are attributable.

Section 6015 was enacted in 1998 to provide relief from joint and several liability in certain circumstances. Section 6015 sets forth three bases for relief from joint and several liability. First, section 6015(b) allows a taxpayer to elect relief from understatements of tax attributable to erroneous items of the other spouse if the taxpayer had no reason to know of the understatement and, taking into account all the facts and circumstances, it is inequitable to hold the taxpayer liable. Second, section 6015(c) allows a taxpayer who is divorced or legally separated from, or no longer living with, the spouse or former spouse with whom the joint return was filed to elect to allocate a deficiency (or a portion of a deficiency) to the other spouse, as if the spouses had filed separate tax returns. Third, section 6015(f) provides that a taxpayer may request, under "procedures prescribed by the Secretary," relief from a tax understatement or underpayment when the taxpayer does not qualify for relief under the other two subsections and it would be inequitable to hold the taxpayer liable considering all the facts and circumstances.

Section 6015(h) directs the Treasury Department and the IRS to prescribe such regulations as are necessary to carry out the provisions of section 6015. The Treasury Department and the IRS exercised that authority by promulgating regulations under section 6015 on July 18, 2002 (TD 9003, 67 FR 47278). Sections 1.6015-2, 1.6015-3, and 1.6015-4 of the final regulations provide guidance on the bases for relief in section 6015(b), (c), and (f), respectively. Section 1.6015-5 provides rules on the time and manner to request section 6015 relief.

By their terms, paragraphs (b) and (c) of section 6015 impose a two-year deadline for a taxpayer to elect the application of either subsection. Under the deadline, a taxpayer must make the election no later than two years after the date of the IRS's first collection activity with respect to the taxpayer. See section 6015(b)(1)(E) and (c)(3)(B). In contrast, paragraph (f) of section 6015 does not contain an explicit deadline to request relief. In accordance with the authority in section 6015(f) to prescribe procedures for the administration of equitable relief, the Treasury Department and the IRS, beginning in 1998, prescribed in published guidance a two-year deadline to request equitable relief under section 6015(f) to be consistent with the statutory time limit to claim relief under section 6015(b) and (c). The two-year deadline to request equitable relief was first prescribed in Notice 98-61 (1998-2 CB 758 (December 21, 1998)) (see § 601.601(d)(2)(ii)(b) of this chapter). The two-year deadline was reiterated in Rev. Proc. 2000-15 (2000-1 CB 447), which was superseded by Rev. Proc. 2003-61 (2003-2 CB 296), and ultimately adopted in the regulations under section 6015, which were issued on July 18, 2002, as § 1.6015-5(b)(1).

Besides establishing when and how to request relief from joint and several liability, § 1.6015-5 also defines key terms, such as "collection activity," sets forth examples illustrating the time and manner provisions, and explains the effect of a final administrative determination.

In *Lantz v. Commissioner*, 132 T.C. 131 (2009), the Tax Court considered for the first time whether the two-year deadline to request equitable relief was valid. After analyzing the issue under the standard for judicial review of an agency regulation, the Tax Court held the two-year deadline for equitable relief in § 1.6015-5(b)(1) invalid. The *Lantz* decision was reversed on appeal by the United States Court of Appeals for the Seventh Circuit in an opinion upholding the validity of the deadline to request equitable relief. *Lantz v. Commissioner*, 607 F.3d 479 (7th Cir. 2010). After *Lantz*, the Tax Court continued to find the two-year deadline invalid in cases not appealable to the Seventh Circuit but the deadline was upheld again in *Mannella v. Commissioner*, 631 F.3d 115 (3d Cir. 2011), and *Jones v. Commissioner*, 642 F.3d 459 (4th Cir. 2011).

Notwithstanding the validity of the regulation setting the two-year deadline, the Treasury Department and the IRS considered whether to retain the deadline and determined, in the interest of tax administration, that the time period to request equitable relief under section 6015(f) should be extended. As announced in Notice 2011-70 (2011-32 IRB 135 (Aug. 8, 2011)), the two-year deadline no longer applies to requests for equitable relief under section 6015(f). In place of the prior two-year deadline, Notice 2011-70 provides that, to be considered for equitable relief, a request must be filed with the IRS within the period of limitation for collection of tax in section 6502 or, for any credit or refund of tax, within the period of limitation in section 6511. Notice 2011-70 explains that the regulations under section 6015 will be revised to reflect the change. These proposed regulations reflect the changes made by Notice 2011-70. Notice 2011-70 has no effect on the two-year deadline to elect relief under section 6015(b) (and § 1.6015-2) or section 6015(c) (and § 1.6015-3).

Notice 2011-70 specifies transitional rules that apply until the Treasury Department and the IRS amend the regulations under section 6015. Under the transitional rules, the two-year deadline does not apply to any request for equitable relief filed on or after July 25, 2011 (the date Notice 2011-70 was issued) or any request already filed and pending with the IRS as of that date. The transitional rules provide that the IRS will consider these current and future requests for equitable relief if they were filed within the applicable limitation period under section 6502 or 6511. As for past requests for equitable relief—requests that the IRS denied as untimely under the two-year deadline—the notice allows the individuals who filed those requests to reapply for equitable relief, unless the individual litigated the denial or the denial included a determination that the individual was not entitled to equitable relief on the merits. In addition, Notice 2011-70 provides separate rules for claiming equitable relief with respect to litigated cases.

A similar rule is added to § 1.66-4 for claims for equitable relief under section 66(c). Section 66(c) provides two avenues for married taxpayers who do not file a joint Federal income tax return in a community property state to request relief from the operation of the state community property laws. Under state law, each spouse generally is responsible for the tax on one-half of all the community income for the year. Traditional relief under section 66(c) allows the requesting spouse to avoid liability for tax on community income of which the requesting spouse did not know and had no reason to know. If a requesting spouse does not satisfy the requirements for traditional relief, the Secretary may grant equitable relief. The IRS uses the same procedures for determining eligibility for equitable relief under section 66(c) as it does for equitable relief under section 6015(f). As a result, it is appropriate for the IRS to use the same timing rules for consideration of requests for equitable relief, whether under section 66(c) or section 6015(f).

Explanation of Provisions

The Treasury Department and the IRS propose to amend the provisions of § 1.6015-5 on the time and manner for requesting relief from joint and several liability under section 6015. A similar rule is added to § 1.66-4(j)(2)(ii) for claims for equitable relief from the Federal income tax liability resulting from the operation of state community property law.

1. *Requesting Relief as Part of Collection Due Process*

The proposed regulations revise § 1.6015-5(a) to reflect that a requesting spouse (defined in § 1.6015-1(h)(1)) may elect the application of section 6015(b) [§ 1.6015-2] or section 6015(c) [§ 1.6015-3] or request equitable relief under section 6015(f) [§ 1.6015-4] as part of the collection due process (CDP) hearing procedures under sections 6320 and 6330. A corresponding change is made to § 1.6015-5(c)(1) to clarify that, although section 6015 relief may be raised in a CDP proceeding, a requesting spouse may not request section 6015 relief in the course of a CDP hearing if the requesting spouse previously requested section 6015 relief and the IRS ruled on that request by issuing a final administrative determination. These proposed regulations do not change existing CDP hearing procedures. See § 301.6330-1(e)(2). Rather, these changes make the regulations under section 6015 consistent with the regulations under section 6330.

2. *Time to Request Relief*

Section 1.6015-5(b) of the proposed regulations retains the two-year deadline, measured from the date of the first collection activity, to elect the application of § 1.6015-2 (describing the circumstances in which a taxpayer may be eligible for relief under section 6015(b)) or 1.6015-3 (describing the circumstances in which a taxpayer may be eligible for relief under section 6015(c)). In accordance with Notice 2011-70, the deadline is removed for a request for equitable relief under § 1.6015-4 (describing the circumstances in which a taxpayer may be eligible for relief under section 6015(f)) and replaced with a requirement that a request for equitable relief must be filed with the IRS within the period of limitation in section 6502 for collection of tax or the period of limitation in section 6511 for credit or refund of tax, as applicable to the specific request. A similar rule is added to § 1.66-4(j)(2)(ii) for claims for equitable relief from the Federal income tax liability resulting from the operation of state community property law.

Under section 6502(a)(1), the period of limitation on collection of tax is normally ten years after the date of assessment of the tax, although it may be extended by other provisions of the Code. Under section 6511(a), the period of limitation to claim a credit or refund of tax is generally the later of three years after the date a tax return for the taxable period was filed or two years after the date the tax was paid. If no return was filed, the two-year period applies.

Section 1.6015-5(b)(2) of the proposed regulations explains that if a requesting spouse files a request for equitable relief under § 1.6015-4 within the limitation period on collection of tax, the IRS will consider the request, but any relief in the form of a tax credit or refund depends on whether the limitation period for credit or refund was also open as of the date the claim for relief was filed and the other requirements relating to credits or refunds are satisfied. In cases in which the limitation period for credit or refund happens to be the longer of the two periods and is open when a request for equitable relief is filed, the request can be considered for a potential refund or credit of any amounts collected or otherwise paid by the requesting spouse during the applicable look-back period of section 6511(b)(2), even if the collection period is closed.

If a request for equitable relief is filed after the expiration of the limitation period for collection of a joint tax liability, the IRS is barred from collecting any remaining unpaid tax from the requesting spouse. Similarly, if a request for equitable relief under § 1.6015-4 is filed after the expiration of the limitation period for a credit or refund of tax, section 6511(b)(1) bars the IRS from allowing, and a taxpayer from receiving, a credit or refund. The proposed regulations provide, therefore, that the IRS will not consider an individual's request to be equitably relieved from a tax that is no longer legally collectible.

3. *Collection Activity*

The proposed regulations clarify what constitutes collection activity for purposes of starting the two-year deadline that continues to apply to § § 1.6015-2 and 1.6015-3.

A notice of intent to levy and right to request a CDP hearing (section 6330 notice) is a type of collection activity that starts the two-year period applicable to applications to elect relief under § § 1.6015-2 and 1.6015-3. The proposed regulations at § 1.6015-5(b)(3)(ii) clarify that the two-year period will start irrespective of a requesting spouse's actual receipt of the section 6330 notice, if the notice was sent by certified or registered mail to the requesting spouse's last known address. This clarification is consistent with the holding in *Mannella v. Commissioner*, 132 T.C. 196 (2009), *rev'd on other grounds*, 631 F.3d 115 (3d Cir. 2011).

4. *Examples*

Section 1.6015-5 in its current form contains several examples intended to illustrate how the timing rules for requesting relief under section 6015 operate. The proposed regulations update these examples to reflect the proposed changes to the timing rules. Thus, *Example 1* is revised to explicitly limit it to elections under § 1.6015-2 or 1.6015-3. *Example 2* illustrates the operation of both the two-year deadline for purposes of §§1.6015-2 and 1.6015-3 and the periods of limitation that apply to equitable relief requests under §1.6015-4, including a situation in which the requesting spouse will still be considered for relief for unpaid amounts even though the limitation period for credit or refund had expired when the request was filed as discussed in §1.6015-5(b)(2). *Example 3* is principally intended to illustrate that collection activity against a nonrequesting spouse (defined in §1.6015-1(h)(2)) does not begin the time in which a requesting spouse must elect the application of §1.6015-2 or 1.6015-3. *Example 4* illustrates the rule of §1.6015-5(c)(3)(i) that a section 6330 notice sent to a requesting spouse's last known address, even if not actually received by the requesting spouse, is a collection activity for purposes of the timing rules, but the issuance of the notice, or the time between the mailing of the notice and the filing of a request for relief, does not affect the IRS's consideration of equitable relief under §1.6015-4 as no two-year deadline applies. *Example 5* illustrates the timing rules in §1.6015-5(b)(2) under which if a requesting spouse has paid some or all of a joint tax liability, or if the IRS has collected all or a part of the liability from a requesting spouse, the requesting spouse will be considered for equitable relief under §1.6015-4 if the requesting spouse filed for relief within the limitation period for a credit or refund of tax, even though the limitation period for collection of tax was expired when the request was filed. The example further illustrates that in a case of payments or collection activity over time, a requesting spouse is eligible for a credit or refund only for amounts of tax for which the period of limitation allows a credit or refund as of when the request for relief was filed. The last example, *Example 6*, builds off of *Example 5* and illustrates a situation in which the IRS will not consider a request for equitable relief under §1.6015-4 because both the limitation period for a credit or refund of tax and the limitation period for collection of tax had expired as of the date the claim for relief was filed.

5. *Reconsideration and Effect of a Final Administrative Determination*

The proposed regulations also revise §1.6015-5(c), which prescribes the effect of a final administrative determination. Under §1.6015-5(c)(1), a requesting spouse generally is entitled to submit only one request for relief under section 6015 from a joint tax liability (except as provided in §1.6015-1(h)(5)), and the IRS will issue only one final administrative determination. The proposed regulations clarify in §1.6015-5(c)(1) that after a final administrative determination, a requesting spouse may not, even under the procedures for a CDP hearing, again request relief under section 6015 with respect to the same joint tax liability.

Consistent with the general restriction, but to provide flexibility within that framework, the IRS has developed procedures in the Internal Revenue Manual (Chapter 25.15.17 (Rev. 03/08/2013)) to reconsider a final administrative determination if a requesting spouse submits additional information not previously submitted and considered and the requesting spouse did not petition the Tax Court from the prior final administrative determination. If the requesting spouse did petition the Tax Court, then the requesting spouse is not eligible for reconsideration unless the Tax Court case was dismissed for lack of jurisdiction. A reconsideration process allows for relief in situations where a requesting spouse was unable to initially provide the information, such as the requesting spouse not fully understanding how to file a complete request for relief under section 6015. The reconsideration process, however, does not replace the IRS's final administrative determination for purposes of determining whether Tax Court review is available or whether a Tax Court petition was timely filed. A request for reconsideration is not a qualifying election ("the first timely claim for relief from joint and several liability for the tax year for which relief is sought") under §1.6015-2 or 1.6015-3, or request under §1.6015-4, for purposes of §1.6015-1(h)(5), and does not trigger the restrictions on collection pursuant to section 6015(e)(1)(B) or the suspension of the collection period of limitation under section 6015(e)(2). A reconsideration letter (formerly Letter 4277C and currently either Letter 5186C, Letter 5187C, or Letter 5188C)) is not a final determination letter for purposes of section 6015(e) and §1.6015-7. Accordingly, a requesting spouse who receives a reconsideration letter may not petition the Tax Court to challenge a denial of relief following the IRS's reconsideration even if the requesting spouse provided new information not previously considered. The proposed regulations add a new provision to §1.6015-5(c) acknowledging the reconsideration process but also providing that the reconsideration letter is not the IRS's final determination and is not subject to review by the Tax Court.

The general restriction in the regulations to one request for relief under section 6015 per tax liability and one final administrative determination of that request does not prohibit a requesting spouse from reapplying for equitable relief under §1.6015-4 pursuant to the terms of Notice 2011-70 if the requesting spouse's request for relief under §1.6015-4 was denied solely for being untimely and that denial was not litigated. The notice allows individuals who filed requests for equitable relief that were denied by the IRS solely on the basis of the two-year deadline and were not litigated to reapply to the IRS for equitable relief. A Form 8857, "Request for Innocent Spouse Relief," or substitute written statement, signed under the penalties of perjury, filed as a reapplication for equitable relief under Notice 2011-70 is not considered a second request, and the resulting determination will be the final administrative determination for purposes of the regulations. A reapplication under Notice 2011-70 is not a reconsideration under the IRS's reconsideration process, and a denial of equitable relief on reapplication may be timely petitioned to the Tax Court for review.

Proposed Effective/Applicability Date

Except as provided below, these proposed regulations are effective as of the date that final regulations are published in the **Federal Register**. For proposed dates of applicability, see §1.6015-9.

Notice 2011-70 announced that the Treasury Department and the IRS intended to amend the regulations under section 6015 to remove the requirement that taxpayers request equitable relief under section 6015(f) and § 1.6015-4 within two years of the first collection activity. Under section 7805(b)(1)(C), the proposed regulations provide that § 1.6015-5(b)(1) and (b)(2) will be effective as of July 25, 2011, the date that Notice 2011-70 was issued to the public.

Statement of Availability for IRS Documents

For copies of recently issued Revenue Procedures, Revenue Rulings, Notices and other guidance published in the Internal Revenue Bulletin or Cumulative Bulletin, please visit the IRS website at *http://www.irs.gov*.

Special Analyses

It has been determined that this notice of proposed rulemaking is not a significant regulatory action as defined in Executive Order 12866, as supplemented by Executive Order 13563. Therefore, a regulatory assessment is not required. It has also been determined that section 553(b) of the Administrative Procedure Act (5 U.S.C. chapter 5) does not apply to these regulations. In addition, because the regulation does not impose a collection of information on small entities, the Regulatory Flexibility Act (5 U.S.C. chapter 6) does not apply. Accordingly, a regulatory flexibility analysis is not required under the Regulatory Flexibility Act (5 U.S.C. chapter 6). Pursuant to section 7805(f) of the Code, this notice of proposed rulemaking has been submitted to the Chief Counsel for Advocacy of the Small Business Administration for comment on its impact on small business.

Comments and Requests for Public Hearing

Before these proposed regulations are adopted as final regulations, consideration will be given to any written comments (a signed original and eight (8) copies) or electronic comments that are submitted timely to the IRS. The Treasury Department and the IRS request comments on all aspects of the proposed rules. All comments submitted by the public will be made available for public inspection and copying at *http://www.regulations.gov* or upon request. A public hearing may be scheduled if requested in writing by any person who timely submits comments. If a public hearing is scheduled, notice of the date, time, and place for the public hearing will be published in the **Federal Register**.

Drafting Information

The principal authors of these proposed regulations are Stuart Murray and Mark Shurtliff of the Office of the Associate Chief Counsel, Procedure and Administration.

[¶ 49,587] Proposed Amendments of Regulations (REG-132455-11), published in the Federal Register on September 9, 2013.

[Code Secs. 6011, 6055, 6081, 6721 and 6722]

Patient Protection and Affordable Care Act (PPACA): Minimum essential health coverage: Information reporting: Employers: Insurers: Coverage providers.—Reg. § 301.6011-8, providing guidance to providers of minimum essential health coverage that are subject to the information reporting requirements of section 6055 of the Internal Revenue Code (Code), enacted by the Affordable Care Act, is proposed. Reg. §§ 1.6055-1, 1.6055-2 and amendments of Reg. §§ 1.6081-8, 301.6721-1 and 301.6722-1 were adopted by T.D. 9660 on March 5, 2014.

AGENCY: Internal Revenue Service (IRS), Treasury.

ACTION: Notice of proposed rulemaking and notice of public hearing.

SUMMARY: This document contains proposed regulations providing guidance to providers of minimum essential health coverage that are subject to the information reporting requirements of section 6055 of the Internal Revenue Code (Code), enacted by the Affordable Care Act. Health insurance issuers, certain employers, and others that provide minimum essential coverage to individuals must report to the IRS information about the type and period of coverage and furnish related statements to covered individuals. These proposed regulations affect health insurance issuers, employers, governments, and other persons that provide minimum essential coverage to individuals.

DATES: Written or electronic comments must be received by November 8, 2013. Requests to speak and outlines of topics to be discussed at the public hearing scheduled for November 19, 2013, at 10 a.m., must be received by November 8, 2013.

ADDRESSES: Send submissions to: CC:PA:LPD:PR (REG-132455-11), Room 5203, Internal Revenue Service, PO Box 7604, Ben Franklin Station, Washington, DC 20044. Submissions may be hand-delivered Monday through Friday between the hours of 8 a.m. and 4 p.m. to CC:PA:LPD:PR (REG-132455-11), Courier's Desk, Internal Revenue Service, 1111 Constitution Avenue, NW, Washington, DC, or sent electronically via the Federal eRulemaking Portal at *http://www.regulations.gov* (IRS REG-132455-11).

FOR FURTHER INFORMATION CONTACT: Concerning the proposed regulations, Andrew Braden, (202) 622-4960; concerning the submission of comments and/or to be placed on the building access list to attend the public hearing, Oluwafunmilayo (Funmi) Taylor, (202) 622-7180 (not toll-free calls).

SUPPLEMENTARY INFORMATION:

Paperwork Reduction Act

The collection of information contained in this notice of proposed rulemaking has been submitted to the Office of Management and Budget in accordance with the Paperwork Reduction Act of 1995 (44 U.S.C. 3507(d)). Comments on the collection of information should be sent to the **Office of Manage-**

ment and Budget, Attn: Desk Officer for the Department of the Treasury, Office of Information and Regulatory Affairs, Washington, DC 20503, with copies to the **Internal Revenue Service**, Attn: IRS Reports Clearance Officer, SE:W:CAR:MP:T:T:SP, Washington, DC 20224. Comments on the collection of information should be received by November 8, 2013. Comments are specifically requested concerning:

Whether the proposed collection of information is necessary for the proper performance of the functions of the IRS, including whether the information will have practical utility;

How the quality, utility, and clarity of the information to be collected may be enhanced;

How the burden of complying with the proposed collection of information may be minimized, including through the application of automated collection techniques or other forms of information technology; and

Estimates of capital or start-up costs and costs of operation, maintenance, and purchase of services to provide information.

The collection of information in these proposed regulations is in §§1.6055-1 and 1.6055-2. The collection of information will be used to determine whether an individual has minimum essential coverage under section 1501(b) of the Patient Protection and Affordable Care Act (26 U.S.C. 5000A(f)). The collection of information is required to comply with the provisions of section 6055 of the Code. The likely respondents are health insurers, self-insured employers or other sponsors of self-insured health plans, and governments that provide minimum essential coverage.

The burden for the collection of information contained in these proposed regulations will be reflected in the burden on Form 1095-B or another form that the IRS designates, which will request the information in the proposed regulation.

An agency may not conduct or sponsor, and a person is not required to respond to, a collection of information unless it displays a valid control number assigned by the Office of Management and Budget.

Background

Beginning in 2014, under the Patient Protection and Affordable Care Act, Public Law 111-148 (124 Stat. 119 (2010)), and the Health Care and Education Reconciliation Act of 2010, Public Law 111-152 (124 Stat. 1029 (2010)) (collectively, the Affordable Care Act), nonexempt individuals have the choice of maintaining minimum essential coverage (as defined in section 5000A(f)) or paying an individual shared responsibility payment with their income tax returns. Minimum essential coverage may be health insurance coverage offered in the individual market (such as a qualified health plan offered through an Affordable Insurance Exchange (Exchange, also known as a Marketplace)), an employer-sponsored plan, or a government-sponsored program. Section 5000A(f)(1)(A) specifies that Medicare Part A, Medicaid, the Children's Health Insurance Program established under title XXI of the Social Security Act (42 U.S.C. 1397aa et seq.) (CHIP), TRICARE, certain health care programs for veterans and other individuals under chapter 17 or 18 of Title 38 U.S.C., coverage for Peace Corps volunteers under 22 USC 2504(e), and coverage under the Nonappropriated Fund Health Benefits Program under section 349 of Public Law 103-337, are government-sponsored programs that qualify as minimum essential coverage.

Section 1401 of the Affordable Care Act enacted section 36B, allowing certain taxpayers a refundable premium tax credit that will make minimum essential coverage in qualified health plans offered in the individual market through an Exchange more affordable.

Section 1502 of the Affordable Care Act enacted section 6055 regarding information reporting by any person that provides minimum essential coverage to an individual. Section 6055(b)(1)(B) requires providers of minimum essential coverage to report (1) the name, address, and taxpayer identification number (TIN) of the primary insured, (2) the name, dates of coverage, and TIN of each individual covered under a policy, (3) whether health insurance coverage is a qualified health plan offered through an Exchange, (4) for a qualified health plan, the amount of any advance payments of the premium tax credit under section 1412 of the Affordable Care Act and cost-sharing reductions under section 1402 of the Affordable Care Act, and (5) other information the Secretary requires.

Section 6055(b)(2) requires, for coverage through an employer's group health plan, reporting (1) the name, address, and employer identification number (EIN) of the employer maintaining the plan, (2) the portion of the premium (if any) paid by the employer, and (3) any other information that the Secretary requires for administering the credit under section 45R (the tax credit for employee health insurance expenses of small employers).

Section 6055(c) directs a person filing an information return under section 6055 to provide a written statement to each individual listed on the return that shows the name, address, and contact phone number of the reporting entity and information reported to the IRS for that individual. The statement must be furnished to the individual by January 31 of the year following the coverage year.

The information reported under section 6055 will allow taxpayers to establish and the IRS to verify that the taxpayers were covered by minimum essential coverage and their months of enrollment during a calendar year.

Under section 6724(d), as amended by the Affordable Care Act, a reporting entity that fails to comply with the filing and statement furnishing requirements of section 6055 may be subject to penalties for failure to file a correct information return (section 6721) and failure to furnish correct payee statements (section 6722). However, these penalties may be waived if the failure was due to reasonable cause and not to willful neglect (section 6724(a)).

Section 1514 of the Affordable Care Act enacted section 6056, which requires applicable large employers (generally employers with 50 or more full-time employees) to report to the IRS information about the coverage that they offer to their full-time employees and requires them to furnish related statements to employees.

Notice 2012-32 (2012-20 IRB 910) requested public comments on issues to be addressed in regulations under section 6055. In addition, Notice 2012-33 (2012-20 IRB 912) requested public comments on issues to be addressed in regulations under section 6056. As described later in this preamble, the written comments in response to Notice 2012-32 and other written comments have been considered in connection with the development of these proposed regulations.

As discussed in Notice 2013-45 (2013-31 IRB 116), Treasury and the IRS have engaged in dialogue with stakeholders in an effort to simplify section 6055 (and section 6056) reporting consistent with effective implementation of the law. This process has included discussions with stakeholders representing a wide range of interests to assist in the consideration of effective information reporting rules that will be as streamlined, simple, and workable as possible. The effort to develop these proposed information reporting rules has reflected a considered balancing of the importance of (1) providing individuals the information to complete their tax returns accurately, including with respect to the individual responsibility provisions and eligibility for the premium tax credit, (2) minimizing cost and administrative tasks for the reporting entities and individuals, and (3) providing the IRS with information needed for effective and efficient tax administration. As noted elsewhere in this preamble, the proposed regulations will be the subject of public comments, including comments that are specifically invited regarding particular issues identified in the preamble.

Notice 2013-45 provides as transition relief that section 6055 information reporting will be optional for 2014. The IRS will not impose penalties for failure to timely and accurately report under section 6055 for coverage in 2014. As stated in Notice 2013-45, the IRS encourages voluntary section 6055 reporting for coverage in 2014.

Explanation of Provisions and Summary of Comments

1. *Persons Subject to Information Reporting Requirement*

a. *Plans in the individual market*

Under section 36B(f)(3) and § 1.36B-5, an Exchange must report information relating to enrollment in qualified health plans in the individual market to the IRS and taxpayers. This information includes the period coverage was in effect, the names and TINs of each individual covered, the amount of advance credit payments relating to the coverage, and the amount of premiums for the coverage. This reporting facilitates compliance with and administration of the premium tax credit under section 36B. A commenter suggested that issuers of qualified health plans should not be required to report under section 6055 regarding minimum essential coverage that they provide in the individual market through the Exchange because the Exchange reporting provides the IRS and taxpayers with the necessary information about this coverage.

In response to this comment and to reduce the burden associated with reporting under section 6055, the proposed regulations provide that issuers are not required to submit section 6055 information returns for coverage under a qualified health plan in the individual market enrolled in through an Exchange. For individuals enrolled in this coverage, the IRS and individuals will receive information necessary to administer or comply with the individual shared responsibility provision through information reporting by Exchanges under section 36B(f)(3). Issuers must report, however, on qualified health plans in the small group market enrolled in through the Small Business Health Options Program (SHOP), because annual information reporting by Exchanges under section 36B(f)(3) does not include these plans.

b. *Employer-sponsored insured group health plans*

Commenters recommended that the proposed regulations require employers rather than health insurance issuers to report under section 6055 for insured coverage under an employer-sponsored group health plan. The commenters suggested that employers have more direct access to information required to be reported for an employee enrolled in a group health plan.

Because section 6055(a) requires reporting by the entities providing the coverage, which for insured coverage is the issuer, the proposed regulations provide that health insurance issuers are responsible for reporting under section 6055 for all insured coverage, except coverage under certain government-sponsored programs (such as Medicaid and Medicare) that provide coverage through a health insurance issuer and coverage under qualified health plans in the individual market enrolled in through an Exchange.

Reporting entities are permitted to use third parties to facilitate filing returns and furnishing statements to comply with reporting requirements, including those under section 6055. These arrangements do not, however, transfer the potential liability for failure of the reporting entity to report and furnish under the regulations.

A party preparing returns or statements required under section 6055 that is a tax return preparer will be subject to the requirements that generally apply to return preparers.

c. *Self-insured group health plans*

The proposed regulations provide that sponsors of self-insured health coverage are responsible for reporting under section 6055. The proposed regulations identify the employer as the plan sponsor and reporting entity for a self-insured group health plan established or maintained by a single employer. This rule is consistent with section 3(16)(B)(i) of the Employee Retirement Income Security Act of 1974 (ERISA), which states that the term "plan sponsor" means the employer in the case of an employee benefit plan established or maintained by a single employer.

Commenters noted that individuals may be covered under a self-insured arrangement that is a multiemployer plan and offered suggestions for identifying the entity responsible for reporting. Some commenters stated that employers that participate in a multiemployer plan do not have access to the information required to be reported under section 6055 and that the multiemployer plan or its administrator, for example, the joint board of trustees, should report for the participating employers. Another commenter suggested that labor unions report for multiemployer plans. Other commenters asserted that a plan's administrator or trustees generally are in the best position to report minimum essential coverage funded under a collective bargaining agreement unless the plan is funded by a single employer. A commenter asserted that each participating employer should be responsible for reporting under section 6055 for a multiple employer welfare arrangement (MEWA) under section 3(40) of ERISA (29 U.S.C. 1002(40)).

In response to these comments, the proposed regulations identify the sponsor and reporting entity for various types of self-insured arrangements (for example, the joint board of trustees for a multiemployer plan). For these purposes, the section 414 employer aggregation rules do not apply. Accordingly, a self-insured group health plan or arrangement covering employees of related corporations is treated as sponsored by more than one employer and each employer must report for its employees. However, one member of the group may assist the other members by filing returns and furnishing statements on behalf of all members.

Section 6055(d) provides that an appropriately designated person may report under section 6055 on behalf of a government employer. Accordingly, the proposed regulations allow a government employer providing self-insured coverage for its employees to report under section 6055 on its own behalf or to designate as the reporting entity another governmental unit or agency or instrumentality of a governmental unit that is part of or related to the same governmental unit as the government employer. If the designation is made before the filing deadline and the designee accepts it, the designated governmental unit, agency, or instrumentality is the sponsor responsible for section 6055 reporting. Comments are requested on issues specific to government employer plans and arrangements.

As noted, section 6056 requires applicable large employers to report information about the coverage that they offer to their full-time employees and to furnish related statements to employees. Commenters suggested that applicable large employers with self-insured health plans that must report under both sections 6055 and 6056 should be allowed to combine that reporting.

The general rules described in the proposed regulations assume separate reporting, but include other rules that reduce duplicative reporting and otherwise simplify reporting. For example, the proposed regulations allow the use of substitute forms and statements to individuals, which may permit self-insured health plans to furnish a single substitute statement to covered individuals for both sections 6055 and 6056.

In addition, the preamble to proposed regulations under section 6056 advises that the IRS and the Treasury Department are considering permitting applicable large employers with self-insured plans that provide mandatory, minimum value coverage to employees, and offer that coverage to spouses and dependents, all with no employee contribution, to forgo providing section 6056 statements to those covered employees. Because the section 6055 return would provide the individual taxpayers information to accurately file the taxpayers' income tax returns, and would provide the IRS the information concerning those employees to administer the premium tax credit and employer shared responsibility provisions, Treasury and the IRS are considering whether for those employees the employer could file and furnish only the return required under section 6055 and include a code on the employees' Forms W-2.

Comments are requested on other ways to simplify and combine reporting.

d. *Foreign employers that provide minimum essential coverage*

Section 6055(b)(2)(A) requires that reporting for coverage under a group health plan include the employer's EIN. A commenter noted that a foreign employer may provide minimum essential coverage but may not have an EIN. Comments are requested on rules for reporting by foreign employers without EINs that sponsor self-insured plans and on any other issues specific to reporting coverage provided by foreign employers.

e. *Government-sponsored programs*

The proposed regulations provide that the executive department or agency of a governmental unit that provides coverage under a government-sponsored program (within the meaning of section 5000A(f)(1)(A)) is responsible for reporting under section 6055. For example, the Department of Defense is responsible for reporting coverage under the TRICARE program. The proposed regulations identify the State agency that administers the Medicaid or CHIP program, rather than the Department of Health and Human Services, as the reporting entity for these programs. Additionally, under the proposed regulations, the responsible government department or agency, and not the issuer, is the reporting entity for coverage under a government-sponsored program provided through a health insurance issuer (such as some Medicaid, CHIP, and Medicare programs). Comments are requested on issues specific to reporting coverage under government-sponsored programs.

f. *Other arrangements designated as minimum essential coverage*

Section 5000A(f)(1)(E) provides that the Secretary of Health and Human Services (HHS), in coordination with the Secretary of the Treasury, may recognize other health benefits coverage as minimum essential coverage. On July 1, 2013, HHS published final regulations designating certain coverage as minimum essential coverage and outlining substantive and procedural requirements that other types of coverage must fulfill to be recognized as minimum essential coverage. Patient Protection and Affordable Care Act: Exchange Functions: Eligibility for Exemptions; Miscellaneous Minimum Essential Coverage Provisions, 78 FR 39494 (HHS MEC regulations). These regulations designate as minimum essential coverage (1) self-funded student health coverage for plan or policy years beginning on or before December 31, 2014, (2) Refugee Medical Assistance supported by the Administration for Children and Families, (3) Medicare Advantage plans, and (4) State high risk pools for plan or policy years beginning on or before December 31, 2014.

The proposed rule that designates the government department or agency as the reporting entity for coverage under a government-sponsored program provided through a health insurance issuer applies to Medicare Advantage plans. Comments are requested on appropriate rules for identifying the reporting entity for other arrangements recognized as minimum essential coverage under section 5000A(f)(1)(E).

2. *Information Required to Be Reported*

a. *In general*

The proposed regulations provide that the section 6055 information return must include the name of each individual enrolled in minimum essential coverage and the name and address of the primary insured or other related person (for example, a parent or spouse) who submits the application for coverage (the responsible individual). The proposed regulations use the term *responsible individual* rather than the term *primary insured* because minimum essential coverage may not be insured coverage (for example, health coverage provided by the Department of Veterans Affairs). The return also must report the TIN and months of coverage for each individual who is covered under the policy or program and other information specified in forms, instructions, or published guidance, see §§601.601(d) and 601.602. For employer-provided coverage, the proposed regulations require reporting the name, address, and EIN of the employer maintaining the plan and whether coverage was enrolled in through the SHOP.

As part of the effort to minimize the cost and administrative steps associated with the reporting requirements, the proposed regulations do not require reporting information that would not be needed by individual taxpayers or the IRS for purposes of administering the individual shared responsibility provisions or the credit for small employers. Accordingly, the proposed regulations do not require reporting the portion of the premium paid by an employer, which the IRS does not need to determine if an individual is covered by minimum essential coverage. The proposed regulations require reporting the months of coverage rather than the specific dates of coverage, because minimum essential coverage applies month by month. The proposed regulations do not require reporting the amount of any cost-sharing reductions, which are not administered by the IRS. Finally, the proposed regulations do not require reporting the amount of advance payments or on coverage in a qualified health plan in the individual market enrolled in through an Exchange, since in both cases this information is reported to the IRS and provided to individuals by the Exchanges under section 36B(f)(3).

b. *Identifying information*

Health insurance issuers and employers with self-funded plans expressed concern that they do not typically collect TINs from dependents covered under their policies and that they may have difficulty obtaining TINs for some covered individuals. Other commenters suggested allowing alternative means of identifying individuals, such as unique enrollee identification numbers similar to the method used by the Massachusetts Health Connector (the State-based exchange), or allowing reporting without TINs for individuals who enroll in coverage but decline to provide a TIN. Some commenters suggested simplifying reporting requirements for dependents or providing alternatives in reporting TINs for new beneficiaries and others who may not provide TINs at the time of enrollment.

The proposed regulations adopt TIN reporting, consistent with the statute. Section 6055 reporting allows individuals to confirm their coverage and the IRS to verify that coverage without the need to contact the individuals. The use of TINs to cross-check individuals against coverage months is the most efficient way for individuals and the IRS to avoid the need for follow-up. Accordingly, covered individuals have an interest in providing TINs to reporting entities.

Federal tax records for individuals for all purposes are maintained by TIN and individual taxpayers identify themselves on their returns by TIN. Establishing another method of identifying individuals for sections 5000A and 6055 purposes would require the IRS to create, and taxpayers to adapt to, an entire parallel identification system solely for this purpose.

While section 6055 and the proposed regulations require TINs for administering section 5000A, reporting entities that make reasonable efforts to collect TINs but do not receive them will not be subject to penalties under sections 6721 and 6722 for failure to timely and accurately report. In particular, section 6055 reporting is governed by the same procedures, limitations, and protections as other information reporting that requires obtaining and reporting TINs. Section 6724 and the regulations under that section waive penalties on reporting entities for a reasonable failure to include correct TIN information on a return or statement, including those required under section 6055. Penalties are waived if the reporting entity demonstrates that it acted in a responsible manner both before and after the failure occurred, and that the failure was due to significant mitigating factors or events beyond the reporting entity's control. In general, a reporting entity acts responsibly in attempting to solicit a TIN if after an initial, unsuccessful request for a TIN (for example, at the time of enrollment), the reporting entity makes two consecutive annual TIN solicitations. No section 6724 penalty is imposed unless the reporting entity fails to make the two additional solicitations. Accordingly, section 6055 reporting entities will not be unduly penalized for failing to report a TIN.

As a backstop to reporting a TIN, the proposed regulations allow reporting entities to report date of birth if a TIN is not available. This alternative should not be used, however, unless the reporting entity has made reasonable efforts to obtain the information by requesting that a covered individual provide the TIN.

A commenter requested that the proposed regulations provide rules authorizing reporting entities to request TINs. This authority exists under section 6109(a)(2) and § 301.6109-1(b)(1) of the Procedure and Administration Regulations, which require individuals to furnish TINs to persons that must file information returns.

A commenter noted that issuers and employers may have difficulty obtaining overseas addresses for individuals living abroad. The proposed regulations provide that only the last known address for the responsible individual must be reported.

c. *Coverage dates*

For purposes of section 5000A, an individual who has coverage on any day in a month is treated as having minimum essential coverage for the entire month. See proposed § 1.5000A-1(b) (78 FR 7314). As a result, the specific coverage dates are not necessary for administering and complying with rules relating to minimum essential coverage. Accordingly, the proposed regulations do not require reporting of the specific dates of coverage. Instead, the proposed regulations generally require reporting of the months during which an individual is treated as having minimum essential coverage.

A commenter noted that coverage dates may be inaccurate because coverage may be terminated or reinstated after the reporting date for periods occurring before the reporting date. Under section 6724 and the regulations under that section, the IRS may waive penalties if there is reasonable cause for the failure to correct an information return for retroactive terminations or reinstatements that are determined after the calendar year in which coverage was terminated or reinstated.

A commenter recommended permitting separate returns or creating special forms to report coverage for individuals who change their coverage during the year to a different health plan with the same issuer. Although the proposed regulations do not adopt a rule addressing this situation, additional procedures that are responsive to this comment may be provided in IRS forms and instructions, see § 601.602.

A commenter noted that employers face challenges in determining coverage dates for employees and dependents, including seasonal and temporary workers whose term of employment changes during the year. The commenter recommended that the rules allow reporting an individual's enrollment in minimum essential coverage as of a fixed date each year to accommodate an employer's administrative, payroll, and recordkeeping procedures. The individual responsibility payment under section 5000A applies to individuals on a monthly basis, so reporting based on one day during the year would not be sufficient. Additionally, varying reporting dates would be difficult to administer and would produce information less useful to taxpayers, who generally file their tax returns and must determine their coverage based on a calendar year. Accordingly, the proposed regulations do not adopt this suggestion. Comments are welcome on potential alternative ways to address the challenges associated with determining coverage dates when employment changes.

d. *Supplemental coverage arrangements*

A commenter asked whether an employer and an issuer must coordinate section 6055 reporting for an employer-sponsored group health plan that consists of an insured high-deductible health plan (HDHP) and additional health benefits provided through a contribution to a health savings account. Health savings accounts are not minimum essential coverage, and therefore section 6055 reporting is not required for them. Additionally, the proposed regulations provide that reporting is not required for arrangements such as health reimbursement arrangements that supplement minimum essential coverage.

3. *Time and Manner of Filing*

a. *Form of return*

The proposed regulations provide that the return under section 6055 may be made on Form 1095-B or another form the IRS designates, or on a substitute form. A substitute form must comply with revenue procedures or other published guidance, see § 601.601(d)(2), that apply to substitute forms. The proposed regulations require that information returns be submitted to the IRS with a transmittal form, Form 1094-B. In accordance with usual procedure, these forms will be made available in draft form at a later date.

b. *Time for filing returns*

The proposed regulations provide for reporting entities to file the return and transmittal form on or before February 28 (or March 31 if filed electronically) of the year following the calendar year in which they provided minimum essential coverage. Commenters suggested that the proposed regulations provide different reporting deadlines for fiscal year health plans to avoid calendar year reporting of data from multiple plan years. Since most individuals file calendar year returns, permitting fiscal year reporting would interfere with return preparation and processing for individuals potentially subject to the section 5000A individual shared responsibility payment. Therefore, the proposed regulations do not adopt this comment.

c. *Electronic reporting*

Commenters recommended permitting electronic reporting under section 6055. Section 6011(e) and § 301.6011-2 require high-volume filers (those who file 250 or more returns during the calendar year) to file electronically. The proposed regulations provide that these electronic filing requirements apply to information returns under section 6055, but do not limit electronic filing to high-volume filers. Accordingly, any reporting entity may file electronically under section 6055.

4. *Combined Reporting*

As discussed earlier in this preamble, applicable large employers that provide minimum essential coverage on a self-insured basis are subject to the reporting requirements of sections 6055 and 6056, as well as the requirement under section 6051 to file Form W-2, Wage and Tax Statement, showing wages paid to employees and taxes withheld. Notices 2012-32 and 2012-33 requested comments on how to minimize duplication in reporting under these provisions.

Several commenters recommended that the regulations allow combined information reporting under sections 6055 and 6056 for applicable large employers that sponsor self-insured group health plans and must report under both sections. Other commenters recommended that employers be permitted to use a single information return to report under sections 6051 and 6055, for example by adding the information required under section 6055 to Form W-2.

As discussed elsewhere in this preamble, these proposed regulations seek to simplify reporting and reduce duplication through a number of approaches. In particular, the proposed regulations provide that issuers need not report under section 6055 for individual market qualified health plans enrolled in through an Exchange. The proposed regulations also provide relief from the requirement to report several items of information that are unnecessary for tax administration or are available from other reporting, and they allow the use of substitute forms and statements to individuals, which, under future guidance, may include furnishing a single substitute statement to covered individuals for both sections 6055 and 6056.

Accordingly, while the rules for section 6055 reporting in the proposed regulations do not assume full combined reporting under sections 6055, 6056 and 6051, they reflect other means of avoiding duplication and simplifying reporting. We continue to seek comments on other ways to streamline the reporting methods that would be permissible under the statute.

5. *Statements Furnished to Individuals*

The proposed regulations provide that a reporting entity must furnish a statement to the covered individual providing the policy number and the name, address, and a contact number for the reporting entity, and the information required to be reported to the IRS. The proposed regulations permit substitute statements that include the information required to be shown on the return filed with the IRS and comply with applicable requirements in published guidance relating to substitute statements. See § 601.601(d)(2) of this chapter. A substitute statement that includes the information required by both sections 6055 and 6056 in a single statement may be permitted by future guidance.

Commenters recommended permitting electronic delivery of statements to individuals. A commenter suggested that the regulations provide rules for electronic delivery of statements to individuals that are similar to the rules under section 2715 of the Public Health Service Act for providing a summary of benefits and coverage. The commenter suggested that these reporting regulations permit the furnishing of one electronic statement per home address rather than multiple statements per household. Another commenter requested guidance on procedures when an email notice is returned due to an incorrect address.

The proposed regulations permit electronic delivery of statements to individuals if the recipient consents. In response to concerns about the need to furnish a statement to each individual, the proposed regulations also permit furnishing only one statement per address. Comments are requested on whether and under what circumstances the regulations should direct reporting entities to provide a statement to another individual (who may, for example, need the statement to determine his or her tax liability).

Commenters expressed concern about protecting the privacy of individuals who provide TINs and about disclosure of the TINs to other parties. The regulations provide that section 6055 information reporting will be included in the IRS truncated TIN program. Accordingly, to protect the privacy of covered individuals, statements furnished to individuals under section 6055 are not required to disclose their complete TINs.

A commenter recommended that the statement to individuals should explain minimum essential coverage and advise taxpayers that they may be subject to a penalty for months in which they do not have minimum essential coverage. The proposed regulations do not include rules addressing educational content in the statement. However, information on the section 5000A individual shared responsibility payment may be included in IRS forms, instructions, and publications.

6. *Penalties*

Commenters recommended providing procedures for correcting errors in reporting and a safe harbor from penalties for an issuer that fails to report information that another entity fails to provide to the issuer. The proposed regulations provide that the provisions of section 6724(a) providing relief for a failure due to reasonable cause apply to reporting under section 6055. Because the procedures described in §301.6721-1(b), which provide for reduced penalties for reporting errors that are timely corrected, will apply to corrections of errors in reporting under section 6055 that are not due to reasonable cause, the proposed regulations do not prescribe separate rules for correcting errors.

Proposed Effective/Applicability Date

These regulations are proposed to apply for calendar years beginning after December 31, 2014. Consistent with Notice 2013-45, reporting entities will not be subject to penalties for failure to comply with the section 6055 reporting requirements for coverage in 2014, which would have resulted in reporting in 2015 and furnishing statements to covered individuals in 2015. Accordingly, a reporting entity will not be subject to penalties if it first reports beginning in 2016 for 2015, including the furnishing of statements to covered individuals in 2016 with respect to 2015. Taxpayers are encouraged, however, to voluntarily comply with section 6055 information reporting for minimum essential coverage provided in 2014 by applying these regulations once finalized.

Special Analyses

It has been determined that this notice of proposed rulemaking is not a significant regulatory action as defined in Executive Order 12866, as supplemented by Executive Order 13563. Therefore, a regulatory assessment is not required. It has also been determined that section 553(b) of the Administrative Procedure Act (5 U.S.C. chapter 5) does not apply to these regulations.

It is hereby certified that these regulations will not have a significant economic impact on a substantial number of small entities. This certification is based on the fact that the information collection required under these regulations is imposed under section 6055. Consistent with the statute, the proposed regulations require a person that provides minimum essential coverage to an individual to file a return with the IRS reporting certain information and to furnish a statement to the responsible individual who enrolled an individual or family in the coverage. These regulations primarily provide the method of filing and furnishing returns and statements under section 6055. Moreover, the proposed regulations attempt to minimize the burden associated with this collection of information by limiting reporting to the information that the IRS will use to verify minimum essential coverage and administer tax credits.

Based on these facts, a Regulatory Flexibility Analysis under the Regulatory Flexibility Act (5 U.S.C. chapter 6) is not required.

Pursuant to section 7805(f) of the Code, this notice of proposed rulemaking has been submitted to the Chief Counsel for Advocacy of the Small Business Administration for comment on its impact on small business.

Comments and Public Hearing

Before these proposed regulations are adopted as final regulations, consideration will be given to any comments that are submitted timely to the IRS as prescribed in this preamble under the "Addresses" heading. The IRS and Treasury Department request comments on all aspects of the proposed rules. All comments will be available at www.regulations.gov or upon request.

A public hearing has been scheduled for November 19, 2013, at 10 a.m., in the auditorium, Internal Revenue Building, 1111 Constitution Avenue NW., Washington, DC. Due to building security procedures, visitors must enter at the Constitution Avenue entrance. All visitors must present photo identification to enter the building. Because of access restrictions, visitors will not be admitted beyond the immediate entrance more than 30 minutes before the hearing starts. For information about having your name placed on the building access list to attend the hearing, see the "**FOR FURTHER INFORMATION CONTACT**" section of this preamble.

The rules of 26 CFR 601.601(a)(3) apply to the hearing. Persons who wish to present oral comments at the hearing must submit written or electronic comments by November 8, 2013, an outline of topics to be discussed and the time to be devoted to each topic by (signed original and eight (8) copies by November 8, 2013. A period of 10 minutes will be allotted to each person for making comments.

An agenda showing the scheduling of the speakers will be prepared after the deadline for receiving outlines has passed. Copies of the agenda will be available free of charge at the hearing.

Drafting Information

The principal authors of these proposed regulations are Andrew Braden and Frank W. Dunham III of the Office of Associate Chief Counsel (Income Tax and Accounting). However, other personnel from the IRS and the Treasury Department participated in the development of the regulations.

[¶49,588] Proposed Amendments of Regulations (REG-136630-12), published in the Federal Register on September 9, 2013.

[Code Secs. 6011 and 6056]

Patient Protection and Affordable Care Act (PPACA): Minimum essential health coverage: Information reporting: Employers: Insurers: Coverage providers.—Reg. §301.6011-9, providing guidance to employers that are subject to the information reporting requirements under section

6056 of the Internal Revenue Code (Code), enacted by the Affordable Care Act, is proposed. Reg. §§301.6056-1 and 301.6056-2 were adopted by T.D. 9661 on March 5, 2014.

AGENCY: Internal Revenue Service (IRS), Treasury.

ACTION: Notice of proposed rulemaking and notice of public hearing.

SUMMARY: This document contains proposed regulations providing guidance to employers that are subject to the information reporting requirements under section 6056 of the Internal Revenue Code (Code), enacted by the Affordable Care Act. Section 6056 requires those employers to report to the IRS information about their compliance with the employer shared responsibility provisions of section 4980H of the Code and about the health care coverage they have offered employees. Section 6056 also requires those employers to furnish related statements to employees so that employees may use the statements to help determine whether, for each month of the calendar year, they can claim on their tax returns a premium tax credit under section 36B of the Code (premium tax credit). In addition, that information will be used to administer and ensure compliance with the eligibility requirements for the employer shared responsibility provisions and the premium tax credit. The proposed regulations affect applicable large employers (generally meaning employers with 50 or more full-time employees, including full-time equivalent employees, in the prior year), employees and other individuals.

This document also provides notice of a public hearing on these proposed rules. DATES: Written or electronic comments must be received by November 8, 2013. Requests to speak and outlines of topics to be discussed at the public hearing scheduled for November 18, 2013, at 10 a.m., must be received by November 8, 2013.

ADDRESSES: Send submissions to: CC:PA:LPD:PR (REG-136630-12), room 5205, Internal Revenue Service, PO Box 7604, Ben Franklin Station, Washington, DC 20044. Submissions may be hand-delivered Monday through Friday between the hours of 8 a.m. and 4 p.m. to CC:PA:LPD:PR (REG-136630-12), Courier's Desk, Internal Revenue Service, 1111 Constitution Avenue, NW, Washington, DC, or sent electronically, via the Federal eRulemaking Portal at www.regulations.gov (IRS REG-136630-12). The public hearing will be held in the Auditorium, Internal Revenue Building, 1111 Constitution Avenue, NW, Washington, DC.

FOR FURTHER INFORMATION CONTACT: Concerning the proposed regulations, Ligeia Donis (202) 927-9639; concerning submission of comments, the hearing, and/or to be placed on the building access list to attend the hearing, please contact Oluwafunmilayo (Funmi) Taylor at (202) 622-7180 (not toll-free numbers).

SUPPLEMENTARY INFORMATION

Paperwork Reduction Act

The collection of information contained in this notice of proposed rulemaking has been submitted to the Office of Management and Budget for review in accordance with the Paperwork Reduction Act of 1995 (44 U.S.C. 3507(d)). Comments on the collection of information should be sent to the **Office of Management and Budget,** Attn: Desk Officer for the Department of the Treasury, Office of Information and Regulatory Affairs, Washington, DC 20503, with copies to the **Internal Revenue Service**, Attn: IRS Reports Clearance Officer, SE:W:CAR:MP:T:T:SP, Washington, DC 20224. Comments on the collection of information should be received by November 8, 2013. Comments are specifically requested concerning:

Whether the proposed collection of information is necessary for the proper performance of the functions of the IRS, including whether the information will have practical utility;

How the quality, utility, and clarity of the information to be collected may be enhanced;

How the burden of complying with the proposed collection of information may be minimized, including through the application of automated collection techniques or other forms of information technology; and

Estimates of capital or start-up costs and costs of operation, maintenance, and purchase of services to provide information.

The collection of information in these proposed regulations is in proposed regulation §§301.6011-9, 301.6056-1, and 301.6056-2. This information will be used by the IRS to verify compliance with the return and employee statement requirements under section 6056 for purposes of section 4980H, and with the eligibility requirements for the premium tax credit. This information will be used to determine whether the information has been reported and calculated correctly for purposes of section 4980H and section 6056, and whether claims for the premium tax credit are correct. The likely respondents are employers that are applicable large employers, as defined under section 4980H(c)(2).

An agency may not conduct or sponsor, and a person is not required to respond to, a collection of information unless it displays a valid control number assigned by the Office of Management and Budget.

Books or records relating to a collection of information must be retained as long as their contents may become material in the administration of any internal revenue law. Generally, tax returns and tax return information are confidential, as required by 26 U.S.C. 6103.

Background

Sections I through V of the preamble ("Background") describe the statutory provisions governing the information reporting requirements, as well as related statutory provisions. Sections VI through XIII of the preamble ("Explanation of Provisions and Summary of Comments") describe and explain how these regulations propose to implement the statutory provisions of section 6056 and include a discussion of a variety of potential simplified reporting methods that are under consideration. As is typical with regulations on information reporting, these proposed regulations refer generally to additional information that may be required under the applicable forms and instructions. Sections IX.B and C of this preamble set forth the specific data elements that Treasury and the IRS anticipate will be included with the reporting, including the data elements that Treasury and the IRS anticipate will be provided through the use of an indicator code.

Section 6056[1] requires applicable large employers, as defined in section 4980H(c)(2), to file returns at the time prescribed by the Secretary with respect to each full-time employee and furnish a statement to each full-time employee by January 31 of the calendar year following the calendar year for which the return must be filed. Section 6056 specifies certain information that must be reported on the section 6056 return and related statement, and authorizes the Secretary to require additional information and determine the form of the return. Section 6056 is effective for periods beginning after December 31, 2013; however, Notice 2013-45 (2013-31 IRB 116) provides transition relief for 2014 from the section 6056 information reporting requirements (as well as the section 6055 information reporting requirements relating to the section 5000A individual shared responsibility provisions and the section 4980H employer shared responsibility provisions).

I. *Shared Responsibility for Employers (Section 4980H)*

One of the purposes of section 6056 reporting is to assist with the administration of the employer shared responsibility provisions added by the Affordable Care Act as section 4980H of the Code. Section 4980H imposes an assessable payment on applicable large employers if certain requirements relating to the provision of health care coverage to full-time employees are not met and one or more full-time employees claim a premium tax credit. On December 28, 2012, Treasury and the IRS released proposed regulations under section 4980H. The proposed regulations under section 4980H were published in the **Federal Register** on January 2, 2013 (REG-138006-12 [78 FR 218]). Section 4980H is effective for months after December 31, 2013; however, Notice 2013-45, issued on July 9, 2013, provides transition relief for 2014 from the section 4980H employer shared responsibility provisions.

The reporting requirements under section 6056 apply only to employers that are subject to section 4980H (which the statute refers to as "applicable large employers"). Section 4980H(c)(2) defines the term "applicable large employer" as, with respect to a calendar year, an employer that employed an average of at least 50 full-time employees on business days during the preceding calendar year. Generally, for purposes of determining applicable large employer status, a full-time employee includes any employee who was employed on average at least 30 hours of service per week and any full-time equivalents determined pursuant to section 4980H(c)(2)(E). All employers treated as a single employer under section 414(b), (c), (m), or (o) are treated as one employer for purposes of determining applicable large employer status. Section 4980H contains rules for determining whether an employer qualifies as an applicable large employer, including special rules addressing an employer's first year of existence and predecessor and successor employers. See section 4980H(c)(2)(C) and proposed § 54.4980H-2. Proposed regulations under section 4980H provide guidance on determining applicable large employer status and determining full-time employee status, including defining and providing rules for calculating hours of service. See proposed § § 54.4980H-1(a)(21) (definition of hours of service), 54.4980H-2 (determination of applicable large employer status), and 54.4980H-3 (determination of full-time employee status).

II. *Premium Tax Credit (Section 36B)*

Section 6056 reporting will also be used for the administration of the premium tax credit, which was added by the Affordable Care Act as section 36B of the Code. Section 36B allows an advanceable and refundable premium tax credit to help individuals and families afford health insurance coverage purchased through an Affordable Insurance Exchange (Exchange). An employee is not eligible for a premium tax credit to subsidize the cost of Exchange coverage if the employee is offered affordable coverage under an employer-sponsored plan that provides minimum value, or if the employee enrolls in an employer-sponsored plan. For this purpose, an employer-sponsored plan is affordable if the employee's required contribution for the lowest-cost self-only minimum value coverage offered does not exceed 9.5% of the employee's household income. Thus, an employee (and in the case of an employer-sponsored plan that offers coverage to an employee's spouse or dependents, the employee's spouse and dependents) who does not accept an offer of affordable minimum value coverage under an employer-sponsored plan and who purchase coverage on an Exchange may not be eligible for a premium tax credit. Individuals and the IRS will use the information on the cost of the lowest-cost employer-sponsored self-only coverage that provides minimum value to verify the individual's eligibility for the premium tax credit.[2]

---

[1] Section 6056 was enacted by section 1514(a) of the Patient Protection and Affordable Care Act, Public Law 111-148 (124 Stat. 119 (2010)), amended by the Health Care and Education Reconciliation Act of 2010, Public Law 111-152 (124 Stat. 1029 (2010)), and further amended by the Department of Defense and Full-Year Continuing Appropriations Act of 2011, Public Law 112-10 (125 Stat. 38 (2011)) (collectively, the Affordable Care Act).

[2] In connection with providing advance payment of the premium tax credit, the Exchanges will employ a verification process. Because the information concerning household income and other relevant factors that are known to the individual and the Exchanges at that time may differ from the information used to file the tax return after the close of the coverage year, an individual who receives an advance payment of the premium tax credit will also need to calculate the appropriate amount of the credit when filing his or

III. *Individual Shared Responsibility (Section 5000A)*

In addition, the Affordable Care Act added section 5000A to the Code. Section 5000A provides nonexempt individuals with a choice: maintain minimum essential coverage for themselves and any nonexempt family members, or include an additional payment with their Federal income tax return. Section 5000A(f)(1)(B) provides that minimum essential coverage includes coverage under an eligible employer-sponsored plan. Under section 5000A(f)(2), an eligible employer-sponsored plan is, with respect to an employee, a group health plan or group health insurance coverage offered by an employer to the employee that is (1) a governmental plan, within the meaning of section 2791(d)(8) of the Public Health Service Act (42 U.S.C. 300gg-91(d)(8)), or (2) any other plan or coverage offered in the small or large group market within a State. An eligible employer-sponsored plan also includes a grandfathered health plan, as defined in section 5000A(f)(1)(D), offered in a group market. Group health plans within the meaning of section 1301(b)(3) of the Affordable Care Act (42 U.S.C. 18021(b)(3)) include both insured health plans and self-insured health plans. Accordingly, a self-insured group health plan is an eligible employer-sponsored plan. See the Questions and Answers on the Individual Shared Responsibility Provision available on the IRS website at www.irs.gov.

IV. *Information Reporting By Providers of Coverage (Issuers, Self-Insuring Employers, and Sponsors of Certain Government-Sponsored Programs) (Section 6055)*

The Affordable Care Act also added section 6055 to the Code, providing for information reporting for the administration of section 5000A. The section 6055 reporting requirements are effective for years beginning after December 31, 2013; however, Notice 2013-45 provides transition relief for 2014 from the section 6055 reporting requirements. Section 6055 requires information reporting by any person that provides minimum essential coverage to an individual during a calendar year, including coverage provided under an eligible employer-sponsored plan, and the furnishing to taxpayers of a related statement covering each individual listed on the section 6055 return. The information reported under section 6055 can be used by individuals and the IRS to verify the months (if any) in which they were covered by minimum essential coverage. Treasury and the IRS are issuing proposed regulations under section 6055 (REG-132455-11) concurrently with these proposed regulations.

V. *Reporting Requirements for Applicable Large Employers (Section 6056)*

Section 6056 directs an applicable large employer (within the meaning of section 4980H(c)(2)) to file a return with the IRS that reports for each employee who was a full-time employee for one or more months during the calendar year certain information described in section 6056(b) about the health care coverage the employer offered to that employee (or, if applicable, that the employer did not offer health care coverage to that employee). Section 6056 also requires such employers to furnish by January 31 of the calendar year following the calendar year for which the return must be filed a related statement described in section 6056(c) to each full-time employee for whom information is required to be included on the return.

Section 6056(b) describes the return required to be filed with the IRS under section 6056. It states that a return meets the requirements of section 6056 if the return is in such form as the Secretary may prescribe and contains (1) the name, date, and employer's employer identification number (EIN), (2) a certification as to whether the employer offers to its full-time employees (and their dependents) the opportunity to enroll in minimum essential coverage under an eligible employer-sponsored plan (as defined in section 5000A(f)(2)), (3) the number of full-time employees for each month during the calendar year, and (4) the name, address, and taxpayer identification number of each full-time employee during the calendar year and the months, if any, during which that employee (and any dependents) were covered under any such health benefits plans.

If the applicable large employer certifies that it offered to its full-time employees (and their dependents) the opportunity to enroll in minimum essential coverage under an eligible employer-sponsored plan (as defined in section 5000A(f)(2)), section 6056 specifies that the return must also include (1) the length of any waiting period (as defined in section 2701(b)(4) of the Public Health Service Act (42 USC 300gg(b)(4)) with respect to that coverage,[3] (2) the months during the calendar year for which coverage under the plan was available, (3) the monthly premium for the lowest cost option in each of the enrollment categories under the plan, and (4) the employer's share of the total allowed costs of benefits provided under the plan. Section 6056(b)(2)(F) provides that the return must include such other information as the Secretary may require. See section IX of this preamble for a discussion of the information proposed to be included in these proposed regulations as part of the reporting requirements, as well as additional information that may be required under the applicable forms and instructions, as is typical with regulations on information reporting.

(Footnote Continued)

her tax return, and the credit may be more or less than the advance payment.

[3] While section 6056(b)(2)(C)(i) refers to the term "waiting period" as defined in section 2701(b)(4) of the PHS Act, amendments made by section 1201 of the Affordable Care Act moved this definition from section 2701(b)(4) of the PHS Act to section 2704(b)(4). Separately, section 2708 of the PHS Act prohibits a group health plan and a health insurance issuer offering group health insurance coverage from applying any waiting period that exceeds 90 days. The Affordable Care Act adds section 715(a)(1) to the Employee Retirement Income Security Act (ERISA) and section 9815(a)(1) to the Code to incorporate the provisions of part A of title XXVII of the PHS Act (specifically, PHS Act sections 2701 through 2728) into ERISA and the Code, and to make them applicable to group health plans and health insurance issuers providing health insurance coverage in connection with group health plans.

Section 6056(c) requires that every person required to make a return under section 6056(a) furnish to each full-time employee whose name is required to be set forth in the return a written statement showing (1) the name and address of the person required to make that return and the phone number of the information contact for that person, and (2) the information required to be shown on the return with respect to that individual. The written statement must be furnished on or before January 31 of the year following the calendar year for which the return under section 6056(a) was required to be made.

As discussed in section IX.B of this preamble, the approach contemplated by these proposed regulations would give effect to these statutory provisions by limiting the information elements listed and other information that would be provided annually to those that are needed by individual taxpayers to accurately complete their tax returns or by the IRS to effectively administer other provisions of the Affordable Care Act. Treasury and the IRS seek comments on ways to achieve these goals efficiently and effectively.

Section 6056(d) provides that to the maximum extent feasible, the Secretary may permit combined reporting under section 6056, section 6051 (employers filing and furnishing Forms W-2, Wage and Tax Statement, with respect to employees) or section 6055, and in the case of an applicable large employer offering health insurance coverage of a health insurance issuer, the employer may enter into an agreement with the issuer to include information required under section 6056 with the return and statement required to be provided by the issuer under section 6055.

Section 6056(e) generally permits governmental units, or any agency or instrumentality thereof, to designate a person to comply with the section 6056 requirements on behalf of the governmental unit, agency or instrumentality.

Under section 6724(d), as amended by the Affordable Care Act, an applicable large employer that fails to comply with the filing and statement furnishing requirements of section 6056 may be subject to penalties for failure to file a correct information return (section 6721) and failure to furnish correct payee statements (section 6722). However, these penalties may be waived if the failure is due to reasonable cause and not to willful neglect (section 6724).

Notice 2012-32 (2012-20 IRB 910) requested public comments on issues to be addressed in regulations under section 6055. Notice 2012-33 (2012-20 IRB 912) requested public comments on issues to be addressed in regulations under section 6056. In developing these proposed regulations and the proposed regulations under section 6055, including the potential further simplified reporting methods described in section XI of this preamble, Treasury and the IRS have considered the written comments submitted in response to these notices and other written comments received.

In addition, consistent with Notice 2013-45, Treasury and the IRS have engaged in further dialogue with stakeholders in an effort to simplify section 6056 and section 6055 reporting consistent with effective implementation of the law. This process has included discussions with stakeholders representing a wide range of interests to assist in the consideration of effective information reporting rules that will be as streamlined, simple, and workable as possible. The effort to develop these proposed information reporting rules has reflected a considered balancing of the importance of (1) providing individuals the information to complete their tax returns accurately, including with respect to the individual responsibility provisions and eligibility for the premium tax credit, (2) minimizing cost and administrative tasks for the reporting entities and individuals, and (3) providing the IRS with information to use for effective and efficient tax administration. As noted elsewhere in this preamble, the proposed regulations will be the subject of public comments, including comments that are specifically invited regarding particular issues identified in the preamble.

Explanation of Provisions and Summary of Comments

VI. *Introduction*

The Explanation of Provisions that follows (Sections VII through XIII of the preamble) describes the regulatory provisions proposed to implement the statutory reporting provisions described in the Background portion of the preamble. Specifically, this section includes the following:

Section VII . . . . Key Terms

Section VIII . . . . ALE Member Subject to Section 6056 Requirements With Respect to Full-Time Employees

Section IX . . . . General Method -Content, Manner, and Timing of Information Required to be Reported to the IRS and Furnished to Full-Time Employees

Section X . . . . Combined Reporting Under Section 6056 and Section 6051 or 6055

Section XI . . . . Potential Simplified Methods for Section 6056 Information Reporting

Section XII . . . . Person Responsible for Section 6056 Reporting

Section XIII . . . . Applicability of Information Return Requirements

VII. *Key Terms*

These proposed regulations under section 6056 use a number of terms that are defined in other Code provisions or regulations. For example, section 6056(f) provides that any term used in section 6056 that is also used in section 4980H shall have the same meaning given to the term by section 4980H. Relevant terms include the following:

A. *Applicable Large Employer*

The proposed regulations provide that the term applicable large employer has the same meaning as in section 4980H(c)(2) and any applicable guidance. See proposed § 54.4980H-1(a)(4).

B. *ALE Member*

All persons treated as a single employer under section 414(b), (c), (m), or (o) are treated as one employer for purposes of determining applicable large employer status.[4] Under the proposed regulations, the section 6056 filing and furnishing requirements are applied separately to each person comprising the applicable large employer consistent with the approach taken in the section 4980H proposed regulations (REG-138006-12 [78 FR 218]) with respect to the determination of any assessable payment under section 4980H. The person or persons that comprise the applicable large employer are referred to as ALE members. The proposed regulations define the term *ALE member* as a person that, together with one or more other persons, is treated as a single employer that is an applicable large employer. For this purpose, if a person, together with one or more other persons, is treated as a single employer that is an applicable large employer on any day of a calendar month, that person is an ALE member for that calendar month. This definition is the same as the definition provided in the proposed regulations under section 4980H. See § 54.4980H-1(a)(5).

C. *Dependent*

The proposed regulations provide that the term *dependent* has the same meaning as in section 4980H(a) and (b) and any applicable guidance. See proposed § 54.4980H-1(a)(11).

D. *Eligible Employer-Sponsored Plan*

The proposed regulations provide that the term eligible *employer-sponsored plan* has the same meaning as in section 5000A(f)(2) and any applicable guidance.

E. *Full-time Employee*

The proposed regulations provide that the term *full-time employee* has the same meaning as in section 4980H(c)(4) and any applicable guidance as applied to the determination and calculation of liability under section 4980H(a) and (b) with respect to any individual employee. See proposed § 54.4980H-1(a)(18).

F. *Governmental Unit and Agency or Instrumentality of a Governmental Unit*

The proposed regulations define the term *governmental* unit as the government of the United States, any State or political subdivision thereof, or any Indian tribal government (as defined in section 7701(a)(40)) or subdivision of an Indian tribal government (as defined in section 7871(d)). The proposed regulations do not define the term *agency or instrumentality of a governmental unit*, but rather reserve on the issue.

G. *Minimum Essential Coverage*

The proposed regulations provide that the term *minimum essential coverage* has the same meaning as in section 5000A(f)(1) and any applicable guidance.

H. *Minimum Value*

The proposed regulations provide that the term minimum value has the same meaning as in section 36B and any applicable guidance. See proposed § 1.36B-6.

I. *Person*

The proposed regulations provide that the term *person* has the same meaning as provided in section 7701(a)(1) and the regulations thereunder.

VIII. *ALE Member Subject to Section 6056 Requirements with Respect to Full-Time Employees*

As discussed earlier in section VII.B of this preamble, an ALE member is any person that is an applicable large employer or a member of an aggregated group (determined under section 414(b), 414(c), 414(m) or 414(o)) that is determined to be an applicable large employer. Under the proposed regulations, the section 6056 filing and statement furnishing requirements apply on a member-by-member basis to each ALE member, even though the determination of whether an entity is an applicable large employer is made at the aggregated group level. For example, if an applicable large employer is comprised of a parent corporation and 10 wholly-owned subsidiary corporations, there are 11 ALE members (the parent corporation and each of the 10 subsidiary corporations). Under the proposed regulations, each ALE member with full-time employees, rather than the group of entities that comprise the applicable large employer, is the entity responsible for filing and furnishing statements with respect to its full-time employees under section 6056. This is consistent with the manner in which any potential assessable payments under section 4980H will be calculated and administered.

Treasury and the IRS understand that ALE members may benefit from the assistance of a third party in preparing these returns, for example a third-party plan administrator or a related ALE member tasked with preparing the returns for all the members of that applicable large employer. For a discussion of how these third parties may help an ALE member fulfill its reporting obligations, see section XII.C of this preamble.

Whether an employee is a full-time employee is determined under section 4980H(c)(4) and any applicable guidance. See proposed § § 54.4980H-1(a)(18) and 54.4980H-3. This includes any full-time

---

[4] As explained in section 1.A.2 of the preamble to the proposed regulations under section 4980H (REG-138006-12 [78 FR 218]), until further guidance is issued, government entities, churches, and a convention or association of churches may apply a reasonable, good faith interpretation of section 414(b), (c), (m), and (o) in determining whether a person or group of persons is an applicable large employer and whether a particular entity is an applicable large employer member. See proposed § 54.4980H-1(a)(5).

employees who may perform services for multiple ALE members within the applicable large employer.[5] Under the proposed regulations, only ALE members with full-time employees are subject to the filing and statement furnishing requirements of section 6056 (and only with respect to their full-time employees).

Generally, the ALE member providing the section 6056 reporting is the common law employer. Disregarded entities are treated for section 4980H purposes, and therefore for section 6056 purposes, similarly to the way they are treated for employment tax purposes, so that the reporting requirements under section 6056 are imposed on a disregarded entity that is an applicable large employer, and not on its owner.[6]

IX. *General Method - Content, Manner, and Timing of Information Required to be Reported to the IRS and Furnished to Full-Time Employees*

This section describes the general method for reporting to the IRS and furnishing statements to employees pursuant to section 6056 that is set forth in the proposed regulations. This general method would be available for all employers and with respect to reporting for all employees. Treasury and the IRS are also considering certain simplified reporting methods, such as using codes on Form W-2 to report whether full-time employees, spouses, and their dependents have been offered coverage, which in some cases may be available only with respect to certain groups of employees. In those cases, with respect to those employees for whom the simplified reporting method was not available, the employer would use the general method. In any case, however, the simplified reporting methods under consideration would be optional so that an employer could choose to report for all of its full-time employees using the general method described in these proposed regulations even if a simplified reporting method is available. For a further description of the simplified reporting methods under consideration, see section XI of this preamble.

A. *Information Reporting to the IRS*

In accordance with section 6056, the proposed regulations provide for every ALE member to file a section 6056 return with respect to its full-time employees. Similar to the separate Form W-2, Wage and Tax Statement, filed by an employer for each employee and the Form W-3, Transmittal of Wage and Tax Statements, filed as a transmittal form for the Forms W-2, the proposed regulations provide that a separate return is required for each full-time employee, accompanied by a single transmittal form for all of the returns filed for a given calendar year.

As a general method, the proposed regulations further provide that the section 6056 return may be made by filing Form 1094-C (a transmittal) and Form 1095-C (an employee statement), or other forms the IRS designates. Alternatively, the section 6056 return may be made by filing other form(s) designated by the IRS or a substitute form. Under the proposed regulations, a substitute form must include all of the information required to be reported on Forms 1094-C and 1095-C or other forms the IRS designates and comply with applicable revenue procedures or other published guidance relating to substitute returns. See § 601.601(d)(2). In accordance with usual procedures, these forms will be made available in draft form at a later date.

B. *Information Required to Be Reported and Furnished*

The proposed regulations provide that every ALE member will report on the section 6056 information return the following information: (1) the name, address, and employer identification number of the ALE member, the name and telephone number of the applicable large employer's contact person, and the calendar year for which the information is reported; (2) a certification as to whether the ALE member offered to its full-time employees (and their dependents) the opportunity to enroll in minimum essential coverage under an eligible employer-sponsored plan (as defined in section 5000A(f)(2)), by calendar month; (3) the number of full-time employees for each month during the calendar year; (4) for each full-time employee, the months during the calendar year for which coverage under the plan was available; (5) for each full-time employee, the employee's share of the lowest cost monthly premium (self-only) for coverage providing minimum value offered to that full-time employee under an eligible employer-sponsored plan, by calendar month; and (6) the name, address, and taxpayer identification number of each full-time employee during the calendar year and the months, if any, during which the employee was covered under an eligible employer-sponsored plan. In addition, the proposed regulations provide, as with other information reporting, that the section 6056 information return may request such other information as the Secretary may prescribe or as may be required by the form or instructions.

As part of the effort to minimize the cost and administrative steps associated with the reporting requirements, Treasury and the IRS have sought to identify any information that would not be relevant to individual taxpayers or the IRS for purposes of administering the premium tax credit and

---

[5] For example, if an employee performs services for two applicable large employer members within an applicable large employer and the combined hours of service for the two applicable large employer members are sufficient to trigger a reporting obligation under section 6056, each applicable large employer member is required to file and furnish a section 6056 return with respect to services performed by the employee for that applicable large employer member. See proposed § 54.4980H-5(d).

[6] Specifically, the proposed regulations under section 7701 (REG-138006-12 [78 FR 218]) treat the disregarded entity (as defined in § 301.7701-2) as a corporation with respect to the reporting requirements under section 6056. See proposed § 301.7701-2(c)(2)(v)(A)(5). These rules would also apply to a qualified subchapter S subsidiary. See proposed § 1.1361-4(a)(8)(i)(E).

employer shared responsibility provisions or that is already provided at the same time through other means. Specifically, the proposed regulations do not require the reporting of the following four data elements (a more detailed description of the data elements that Treasury and the IRS anticipate will be included is provided later in this section of the preamble).

First, the proposed regulations do not require the reporting of the length of any waiting period, because the length of the waiting period is not relevant for administration of the premium tax credit or employer shared responsibility provisions or for an individual in preparing his or her tax return. However, Treasury and the IRS anticipate that information will be requested, using an indicator code, regarding whether an employee's coverage was not effective during certain months because of a waiting period since this information is relevant to the administration of the employer shared responsibility provisions.

Second, the proposed regulations do not require reporting of the employer's share of the total allowed costs of benefits provided under the plan because this information also is not relevant to the administration of the premium tax credit and the employer shared responsibility provisions. In contrast, whether the employer-sponsored plan provides minimum value coverage is relevant information; accordingly, Treasury and the IRS anticipate that information will be requested, also using an indicator code.

Third, the proposed regulations do not require the reporting of the monthly premium for the lowest-cost option in each of the enrollment categories (such as self-only coverage or family coverage) under the plan. Rather, because only the lowest-cost option of self-only coverage offered under any of the enrollment categories for which the employee is eligible is relevant to the determination of whether coverage is affordable (and thus to the administration of the premium tax credit and employer shared responsibility provisions), that is the only cost information proposed to be requested.

Fourth, the proposed regulations do not require the reporting of the months, if any, during which any of the employee's dependents were covered under the plan. Instead, the proposed regulations require reporting only regarding whether the employee was covered under a plan. This is because information relating to the months during which any of the employee's dependents were covered under the plan will be reported on the section 6055 information return associated with that employee's coverage.

Under the proposed regulations, each ALE member must file and furnish the section 6056 return and employee statement using its EIN. Any ALE member that does not have an EIN may easily apply for one online, by telephone, fax, or mail. See Publication 1635, Employer Identification Number, for further information at *www.irs.gov*.

Having considered the information required by section 6056 and the information needed to verify employer-sponsored coverage and to administer the employer shared responsibility provisions under section 4980H and the premium tax credit, Treasury and the IRS anticipate that as part of the general method for section 6056 reporting, the IRS will need certain information not specifically set forth under section 6056 but authorized under section 6056(b)(2)(F). Accordingly, the proposed regulations provide, in a manner similar to other information reporting guidance, that additional information may be prescribed by guidance, forms, or instructions. Treasury and the IRS are also considering potential simplified reporting methods that in certain situations may permit an employer to provide less information than all data elements required under the general method for reporting. See section XI of this preamble.

Under the general method of section 6056 reporting, the following information is expected to be requested, through the use of indicator codes for some information, as part of the section 6056 return (as well as an indication of how many individual employee statements are being submitted):

(1) information as to whether the coverage offered to employees and their dependents under an employer-sponsored plan meets minimum value and whether the employee had the opportunity to enroll his or her spouse in the coverage;

(2) the total number of employees, by calendar month;

(3) whether an employee's effective date of coverage was affected by a waiting period;

(4) if the ALE member was not conducting business during any particular month, by month;

(5) if the ALE member expects that it will not be an ALE member the following year;

(6) information regarding whether the ALE member is a person that is a member of an aggregated group, determined under section 414(b), 414(c), 414(m), or 414(o), and, if applicable, the name and EIN of each employer member of the aggregated group constituting the applicable large employer on any day of the calendar year for which the information is reported;

(7) if an appropriately designated entity is reporting on behalf of an ALE member that is a governmental unit or any agency or instrumentality thereof for purposes of section 6056, the name, address, and identification number of the appropriately designated person;

(8) if an ALE member is a contributing employer to a multiemployer plan, whether a full-time employee is treated as eligible to participate in a multiemployer plan due to the employer's contributions to the multiemployer plan; and

(9) if the administrator of a multiemployer plan is reporting on behalf of the ALE member with respect to the ALE member's full-time employees who are eligible for coverage under the multiemployer plan, the name, address, and identification number of the administrator of the multiemployer

plan (in addition to the name, address, and EIN of the ALE member already required under the proposed regulations).

C. *Use of Indicator Codes to Provide Information With Respect to a Particular Full-Time Employee*

In an effort to simplify and streamline the section 6056 reporting process even under the general section 6056 reporting rules, Treasury and the IRS anticipate that certain of the information described above as applied to a particular full-time employee will be reported to the IRS, and furnished to the full-time employee, through the use of a code rather than by providing specific or detailed information. Specifically, it is contemplated that the following information will be reported with respect to each full-time employee for each calendar month using a code:[7]

(1) minimum essential coverage meeting minimum value was offered to:
 a. the employee only;
 b. the employee and the employee's dependents only;
 c. the employee and the employee's spouse only; or
 d. the employee, the employee's spouse and dependents;

(2) coverage was not offered to the employee and:
 a. the employee was in a waiting period that complies with the requirements of PHS Act section 2708 and its implementing regulations;
 b. the employee was not a full-time employee;
 c. the employee was not employed by the ALE member during that month; or
 d. no other code or exception applies;

(3) coverage was offered to the employee for the month although the employee was not a full-time employee during that month; and

(4) the ALE member met one of the affordability safe harbors under proposed § 54.4980H-5(e)(2) with respect to the employee.

It is anticipated that if multiple codes apply with respect to a full-time employee for a particular calendar month, the reporting format will accommodate the necessary codes.

D. *Section 6056 Statements to Full-time Employees*

Under the general section 6056 reporting rules set forth in the proposed regulations, every ALE member required to file a section 6056 return must furnish a section 6056 employee statement to each of its full-time employees that includes the name, address and EIN of the ALE member and the information required to be shown on the section 6056 return with respect to the full-time employee. The section 6056 employee statement is not required to include a copy of the transmittal form that accompanies the returns. As part of the potential simplified reporting methods Treasury and the IRS are also considering whether, in certain circumstances, other methods of furnishing information to an employee may be sufficient (for example, through the use of a code on the Form W-2). For a detailed description of these potential simplified reporting methods, see section XI of this preamble.

Some employers may wish to have the flexibility to use a substitute type of statement to provide the necessary information to full-time employees. The proposed regulations provide that the section 6056 employee statement may be made by furnishing a copy of the section 6056 return on Form 1095-C (or another form the IRS designates) or a substitute employee statement for that full-time employee. Under the proposed regulations, a substitute statement must include the information required to be shown on the section 6056 return filed with the IRS with respect to that employee and must comply with applicable revenue procedures or other published guidance relating to substitute statements. See § 601.601(d)(2). These proposed regulations provide that section 6056 employee statements filed using Form 1095-C or another form the IRS designates will be included in the proposed IRS truncated TIN program. Under this proposed program, an IRS truncated taxpayer identifying number may be used as the identifying number for an individual in lieu of the identifying number appearing on the corresponding information return filed with the IRS. See the proposed regulations on IRS Truncated Taxpayer Identification Numbers (REG-148873-09 [78 FR 913]).

E. *Time for Filing Section 6056 Returns and Furnishing Employee Statements*

The proposed regulations provide that section 6056 returns must be filed with the IRS annually, no later than February 28 (March 31 if filed electronically) of the year immediately following the calendar year to which the return relates. This is the same filing schedule applicable to other information returns with which employers are familiar such as Forms W-2 and 1099. Because Notice 2013-45 provided transition relief for section 6056 reporting for 2014, the first section 6056 returns required to be filed are for the 2015 calendar year and must be filed no later than March 1, 2016 (February 28, 2016, being a Sunday), or March 31, 2016, if filed electronically. In addition, the regulations propose that the section 6056 employee statements be furnished annually to full-time employees on or before January 31 of the year immediately following the calendar year to which the employee statements relate. This means that the first section 6056 employee statements (meaning the

---

[7] Treasury and the IRS have received comments regarding whether transition relief previously provided in the section 4980H proposed regulations (REG-138006-12 [78 FR 218]) with respect to the transition from 2013 to 2014 will be extended to the transition from 2014 to 2015. The issue is currently under consideration and will be addressed in future guidance under section 4980H. If further transition relief is provided under section 4980H, it is expected that additional indicator codes will be available on the section 6056 return to indicate that an employer is using the transition relief.

statements for 2015) must be furnished no later than February 1, 2016 (January 31, 2016, being a Sunday).

In preparation for the application of the section 4980H provisions beginning in 2015, employers are encouraged to voluntarily comply for 2014 (that is, for section 6056 returns and statements filed and furnished in 2015) with the information reporting provisions (once the information reporting rules have been issued) and to maintain or expand health coverage in 2014. Real-world testing of reporting systems and plan designs through voluntary compliance for 2014 will contribute to a smoother transition to full implementation for 2015.

Some commenters asked for use of an alternate filing date for employers whose health plan is not a calendar year plan. While Treasury and the IRS understand that employers may collect information on a plan year basis, employees generally will need to receive their section 6056 employee statements early in the calendar year in order to have the requisite information to correctly and completely file their income tax returns reflecting any available premium tax credit. For this reason, the proposed regulations do not adopt this suggestion. However, Treasury and the IRS are considering a simplified reporting method, described in section XI of this preamble, that in certain circumstances could permit the employer to report the required information on the Form W-2 which is already being furnished to an employee on the same schedule.

These proposed regulations do not include rules regarding extensions of the time to file section 6056 returns but this topic is addressed elsewhere. Specifically, the notice of proposed rulemaking under section 6055 (REG-132455-11) includes proposed amendments to the regulations under section 6081 relating to general rules on extensions of time to file to include returns under both sections 6055 and 6056. The final section 6056 regulations are expected to cross-reference the amendments to the regulations under section 6081. These proposed regulations reserve a paragraph for this cross-reference.

F. *Manner of Filing of Section 6056 Information Returns and Furnishing of Section 6056 Employee Statements.*

Treasury and the IRS understand that electronic filing is often easier and more efficient for taxpayers, and several commenters requested that employers be permitted to file section 6056 returns electronically. The proposed regulations require electronic filing of section 6056 information returns except for an ALE member filing fewer than 250 returns during the calendar year. Each section 6056 return for a full-time employee is a separate return. Although an ALE member filing fewer than 250 returns during the calendar year may always choose to make the section 6056 returns on the prescribed paper form, that member is permitted (and encouraged) to file section 6056 returns electronically. This proposed requirement for electronic filing is the same as the current requirements for other information returns.

The proposed regulations provide that all returns are aggregated for the purpose of applying the 250-return threshold so that, for example, an ALE member required to file 150 section 6056 returns and 200 Forms W-2 will be required to electronically file section 6056 returns. A reporting entity must submit the prescribed form(s) to request authorization and obtain a Transmitter Control Code from the IRS to be able to file an information return electronically.

In addition to electronic filing, Treasury and the IRS understand that electronic methods are often a simpler and more efficient method to supply employees with the required information, and several commenters requested that employers be permitted to electronically furnish section 6056 employee statements to full-time employees. In response, the proposed regulations permit electronic furnishing of section 6056 employee statements if certain notice, consent, and hardware or software requirements are met. To provide rules for electronic furnishing with which employers are already familiar, the proposed regulations adopt by analogy the process currently in place for the electronic furnishing of employee statements (that is, Forms W-2) pursuant to section 6051 and applicable regulations.

X. *Combined Reporting Under Section 6056 and Section 6051 or 6055*

In addition to the reporting under section 6056, two other reporting provisions provide for annual reporting with respect to certain individuals and the furnishing of statements to those individuals. Specifically, section 6051 requires employers to provide Forms W-2 reporting wages paid and taxes withheld. Section 6055 requires information reporting by any person that provides minimum essential coverage to an individual. ALE members that provide minimum essential coverage on a self-insured basis are subject to the reporting requirements of all three sections (6051, 6055 and 6056). Notices 2012-32 and 2012-33 requested comments on how to minimize duplication in reporting under these provisions.

Several commenters recommended that the regulations allow combined information reporting under sections 6055 and 6056 for applicable large employers that sponsor self-insured plans and must report under both sections. Other commenters recommended that employers be permitted to use a single information return to report under sections 6051 (Form W-2) and 6055. Some commenters suggested adding section 6055 or section 6056 reporting to Form W-2.

Because not all employers are subject to each of these three reporting requirements, independent reporting methods under each section need to be available; otherwise, employers subject to only one reporting requirement may have to expend additional effort to use a combined reporting method. Optional combined reporting therefore would require development of multiple forms for each reporting requirement (some forms for combined reporting, other forms for separate reporting), which could create administrative complexity and create confusion for employees.

In addition, any consideration of combined reporting must take into account that sections 6051, 6055 and 6056 apply to different types of entities (subject to the various reporting requirements, which differ among the Code provisions), and require reporting of different types of information. Section 6051 requires reporting of certain wage and wage-related information on an annual basis by all employers for all employees (and only employees). Section 6055 requires reporting of certain health coverage information by various entities (issuers, employers sponsoring self-insured group health plans, and governmental units) only for individuals who are actually covered (and not for individuals who are offered coverage but do not enroll), and multiple covered individuals may be included on one return. Section 6056 requires reporting of information by applicable large employers on offers of coverage that have or have not been made only to full-time employees (whether or not the offer has been accepted). Further, unlike Form W-2 reporting under section 6051, which provides annual information, both sections 6055 and 6056 require reporting some information on a monthly basis. Accordingly, the general section 6056 reporting method under the proposed regulations does not assume overall combined reporting under sections 6051, 6055, and 6056.

However, as described more fully below in section XI of this preamble, Treasury and the IRS are considering whether it may be possible to permit a type of combined reporting under sections 6051 and 6056 by providing an option to use a code on the Form W-2 in certain circumstances to provide information needed by both the employee and the IRS rather than through the use of the section 6056 employee statement (with employer-level information being provided separately). In addition, in other limited circumstances involving no-cost or very low-cost coverage provided under a self-insured group health plan, Treasury and the IRS are considering whether the employee and the IRS could rely solely on the information provided by the employer on a section 6055 return and the Form W-2 without any further information reporting under section 6056. For further discussion of these potential approaches, see section XI of this preamble.

In response to comments, Treasury and the IRS also have considered suggestions to use, for section 6055 and 6056 reporting purposes, information that employers communicate to employees about employer-sponsored coverage prior to employees' potential enrollment in Exchange coverage. These comments have observed that, under the Affordable Care Act, employers are required to provide pre-enrollment information to employees by various means, including information in the Notice of Coverage Options provided to employees pursuant to the requirements under section 18B of the Fair Labor Standards Act[8] in the Exchanges and potentially via the Employer Coverage Tool developed by the Department of Health and Human Services (HHS) that supports the application for enrollment in a qualified health plan and insurance affordability programs.[9]

Treasury and the IRS have considered and coordinated with the Departments of HHS and Labor regarding the various reporting provisions with a view to identifying ways to make the entire process as effective and efficient as possible for all parties. That said, the various reports are designed for different purposes, and pre-enrollment reporting regarding anticipated employer coverage in an upcoming coverage year is unlikely to be helpful to individual taxpayers in accurately completing their tax returns more than a year later, after the coverage year. Among other issues, the pre-enrollment information may not be readily available to individuals at the time they are filing their tax returns, could be confused with the more recently received pre-enrollment information that applies to the subsequent year (not the year for which the tax return is being filed), and is in a format that does not facilitate easy transfer to the appropriate location on the Federal income tax return. Notwithstanding these challenges, Treasury and the IRS continue to work with the other Departments and stakeholders to consider approaches that might help minimize cost and administrative complexity and realize efficiencies in the reporting process.

Both sections 6055 and 6056 require employers to furnish to employees information about health care coverage. Solely for the purpose of furnishing information to employees (as opposed to filing with the IRS), Treasury and the IRS are considering whether employers sponsoring self-insured group health plans could fulfill their obligation to furnish an employee statement under both sections 6055 and 6056 through the use of a single substitute statement, within the parameters of the rules provided in revenue procedures or other published guidance relating to substitute returns. See § 601.601(d)(2) of this chapter.

XI. *Potential Simplified Methods for Section 6056 Information Reporting*

In developing these regulations, Treasury and the IRS have sought to develop simplified reporting methods that will minimize the cost and administrative tasks for employers, consistent with the statutory requirements to file an information return and furnish an employee statement to each full-time employee. Comments have suggested that, at least for some employers, the collection, assembling and processing of the necessary data into an appropriate format for filing may not be necessary if the employer offers sufficient coverage to make it unlikely that the employer will be subject to an assessable payment under section 4980H because the employee will be ineligible for a premium tax credit. Treasury and the IRS have considered these comments in formulating the potential simplified

---

[8] On May 8, 2013, the Department of Labor issued Technical Release 2013-02 providing temporary guidance under Fair Labor Standards Act section 18B, as well as model notices. *See* Technical Release 2013-02, model notice for employers who offer a health plan to some or all employees, and model notice for employers who do not offer a health plan, available at *http://www.dol.gov/ebsa/healthreform/*. Guidance on the Notice to Employees of Coverage

[9] Available at *https://www.healthcare.gov/downloads/ECT_Application_508_130615.pdf*

reporting methods described in this section. If Treasury and the IRS adopt one or more of these simplified reporting methods, they would be optional alternatives to the general reporting method set forth in the proposed regulations, which could substantially reduce the data elements reported using the general method. It is anticipated that, if an employer uses one or more of the simplified reporting methods, the employer would indicate on its section 6056 transmittal which simplified reporting method(s) was used and the number of employees for which the particular method was used. Comments are invited on these potential simplified reporting methods and on other possible simplified approaches that would benefit employers while providing sufficient and timely information to individual taxpayers and the IRS.

The information provided to the IRS and the employee pursuant to section 6056 is important for administering the section 4980H shared employer responsibility provisions and the premium tax credit. However, in looking at the potential flow of information, Treasury and the IRS have determined that in some circumstances only some of the information required under the general method is necessary. Treasury and the IRS have attempted to identify the specific groups of employees for whom simplified reporting would provide sufficient information, and simplified reporting approaches for these groups are outlined below. In many situations, not every full-time employee of an employer would fit into the groups of employees for which simplified reporting would be available. In that case, the employer would continue to use the general reporting method in the proposed regulations for those full-time employees for whom the employers could not use a simplified method. However, it is anticipated that a significant number of employers will have a sufficient number of employees that fit into one or more of the categories described below to make use of the simplified reporting method preferable to the general reporting method.

Subsections A through F of this section XI of the preamble describe, and comments are invited on, possible simplified methods of reporting under section 6056. Each of these possible methods would be optional for the reporting employer, and, except where specifically noted, would not affect any reporting obligations under section 6055.

Subsection A . . . . Eliminating Section 6056 Employee Statements in Favor of Form W-2 Reporting for Certain Groups of Employees Offered Coverage

Subsection B . . . . No Need to Determine Full-Time Employees If Minimum Value Coverage Is Offered to All Potentially Full-Time Employees

Subsection C . . . . Self-Insured Employers Offering Employees, Their Spouses and Dependents Mandatory No-Cost Minimum Value Coverage

Subsection D . . . . Voluntarily Reporting Section 6056 Elements During or Prior to the Year of Coverage

Subsection E . . . . Reporting for Employees Potentially Ineligible for the Premium Tax Credit

Subsection F . . . . Combinations of Simplified Reporting Methods

A. *Eliminating Section 6056 Employee Statements in Favor of Form W-2 Reporting for Certain Groups of Employees Offered Coverage*

In response to stakeholder comments, Treasury and the IRS are considering allowing employers in certain circumstances to report offers of minimum value coverage on an employee's Form W-2, instead of reporting the offers to the IRS on a section 6056 employee statement or furnishing a section 6056 employee statement to the employee. The reporting is envisioned as using an existing box on the Form W-2 to provide the monthly dollar amount of the required employee contribution for the lowest cost minimum value self-only coverage offered to the employee and using a letter code to describe the offer of coverage. Specifically, Treasury and the IRS anticipate that this approach could be used for any employee employed by the employer for the entire calendar year when the offer, the individuals to whom the offer is made, and the employee contribution for the lowest-cost option for self-only coverage all remained the same for all twelve months of the calendar year. The letter code could be used to indicate that minimum value coverage was offered to: (1) the employee, the employee's spouse and the employee's dependents, (2) the employee and the employee's dependents but not the employee's spouse; (3) the employee and the employee's spouse but not the employee's dependents; (4) the employee, but not the employee's spouse or the employee's dependents; or that the employee was (5) only offered coverage that was not minimum value coverage; or (6) not offered coverage. For this purpose, an employer is treated as offering coverage to the employee's spouse or dependents even if the employee does not have a spouse or dependent, if the employee could elect such coverage if the employee did have a spouse or dependent. If an employee was not offered coverage, it is anticipated that the dollar amount of the employee share of the lowest-cost employee-only coverage option would be shown as zero.

Example: Employer has 100 full-time employees, all of whom are employed for the entire year. Employer offers all of its full-time employees, spouses and dependents the opportunity to enroll in health care coverage that provides minimum value. Under the potential simplified reporting method, it is contemplated that, for all employees, Employer would be permitted to avoid filing or furnishing section 6056 employee statements if it used a letter code on the Form W-2 to report that an offer of coverage had been made to the employee, the employee's spouse (if any), and the employee's dependents (if any), and a dollar amount indicating the required monthly employee contribution to purchase the lowest cost option offered to the employee for self-only coverage.

Treasury and the IRS are also considering whether this or a similar simplified reporting method could be extended to cases in which the required monthly employee contribution is below a specified threshold. For example, if the annual employee cost of self-only coverage is $800 or less, the employer would be permitted to report zero as the employee cost. The $800 amount is less than 9.5 percent of the federal poverty line for a single individual. Thus, regardless of the size of the employee's household or the level of other income or loss of any member of the employee's household, either the employer's coverage will be affordable for purposes of section 36B(c)(2)(C)(i) or the employee's household income will be less than 100 percent of the federal poverty line and the employee will not be an applicable taxpayer under section 36B(c)(2) who is eligible for the credit. In addition, even if other income increases the employee's household income, the employee would not be entitled to the affordability exemption to the shared responsibility payment under section 5000A(e)(1) because the $800 amount would not exceed 8 percent of the employee's household income. Alternatively, if other losses reduce the employee's household income below the income tax filing threshold, the employee will qualify for the exemption under section 5000A(e)(2), and the information otherwise reported under section 6056 would not be required to determine whether the employee satisfied section 5000A. Comments are also requested on the extent to which this approach could reasonably be combined with the other simplified reporting methods described in this section XI of the preamble.

An employer that decides to use this simplified reporting method would not be required to file or furnish a section 6056 employee statement with respect to the employees for whom this method was used. Instead, the employer would simply indicate on a section 6056 transmittal that it had chosen to use this method. If the Form W-2 for an employee used an EIN other than the employer's EIN (for example, a thirdparty payor treated as an employer under section 3401(d)(1) of the Code filed the Form W-2), the employer (that is, the ALE member) may be required as part of the 6056 transmittal to identify those employees for whom a third party reported on Form W-2 without the employer's EIN and to list the employees' social security numbers.

Stakeholders have inquired whether a similar optional Form W-2 reporting method could be used for employees offered coverage under their employer's plan for less than a full calendar year (for example for a new employee hired during the year), but offered no coverage for the remainder of the year. Treasury and the IRS note that this type of reporting would leave gaps in information that would otherwise be used for tax administration purposes. For example, the reporting would not provide any information regarding the particular calendar months during which coverage was offered (or not offered). Even if the employer represented that the coverage was offered during all periods of employment, the reporting would not be able to be reconciled, for example, with another Form W-2 received by the employee from another employer using the same reporting method. That is because while both employers would report the number of months coverage was offered, that information would not be sufficient to determine whether offers of coverage were overlapping (because the employee was employed simultaneously at both employers).

Additionally, for months for which coverage was not offered, information as to whether the employee was employed and also the reason coverage was not offered during certain months of the calendar year would not be captured (for example, the employee was in a waiting period or employed but not as a full-time employee). The specific reason coverage was not offered is relevant to the administration of the employer shared responsibility provisions since the failure to offer coverage for certain reasons does not result in an assessable payment under the employer shared responsibility provisions for a calendar month, even if the full-time employee receives a premium tax credit for that month. Comments are requested on whether this approach to reporting would be useful for employers and, if so, on possible ways to address issues concerning the information gaps that would exist in reporting on employees offered coverage for less than a full calendar year.

B. *No Need to Determine Full-Time Employees If Minimum Value Coverage Is Offered to All Potentially Full-Time Employees*

Treasury and the IRS understand that some employers offer coverage to all or nearly all of their employees, and are able to accurately represent that the only employees not offered coverage are not full-time employees. In that case, the employer will have determined that it would not owe an assessable payment under section 4980H(a) because it would have made an offer of coverage to all of its full-time employees. However, the employer might not have determined whether every employee to whom coverage is offered is or is not a full-time employee. Treasury and the IRS are considering whether these employers may provide section 6056 reporting that does not identify the number of full-time employees and that does not specify whether a particular employee offered coverage is a full-time employee, provided that the employer certifies that all of its employees to whom it did not offer coverage during the calendar year were not full-time employees (or were otherwise ineligible for coverage, for example because they were in the initial permitted waiting period following the date of hire). This method would permit the employer to forgo identifying the full-time status of its employees prior to filing a section 6056 return. However, if an employee who was offered coverage claimed a premium tax credit, the employer could be asked to confirm at a later date (after the filing of the section 6056 return and the relevant Form 1040 return) whether that employee was a full-time employee during that calendar year (in the same manner that an employer reporting only on behalf of full-time employees might later be asked about the status of an employee claiming the premium tax credit if the employee was not listed on that employer's section 6056 return). Treasury and the IRS recognize that this method often would result in over-reporting of certain elements in the sense that reporting would occur with respect to one or more employees who may not be full-time employees during the calendar year. But some employers have indicated that they anticipate relatively few of their employees will claim the premium tax credit, and that determining those few employees' status as full-time employees later would be administratively easier than determining the full-time employee status of all employees at the time of the initial filing.

Example: Employer has 100 employees. Employer makes an offer of minimum value coverage to 90 of the employees. Employer has determined that the ten employees to whom coverage is not offered are not full-time employees for any calendar month during the year. Employer has not determined which of the remaining 90 employees were full-time employees for one or more calendar months during the year. Employer certifies as part of its section 6056 transmittal return that the only employees to whom it did not offer coverage were not full-time employees or were otherwise not required to be offered coverage for all months of employment (for example, a full-time employee was hired in November and, under the terms of the plan, which comply with the Affordable Care Act, would not be initially offered coverage until the following calendar year).

Employer would file a section 6056 return and furnish an employee statement for each of the 90 employees, but would not be required to report either the total number of full-time employees for the year or whether any particular employee was a full-time employee for any calendar month during the year. If one of the employees included as part of the return declined the offer of coverage and properly claimed a premium tax credit with respect to coverage provided through an Exchange, and the employer were contacted by the IRS to determine whether the employer did or did not owe an assessable payment under section 4980H(b), the employer could determine at that point whether the employee was a full-time employee for one or more months during that calendar year and supply that information to the IRS.

C. *Self-Insured Employers Offering Employees, Their Spouses, and Dependents Mandatory No-Cost Minimum Value Coverage*

Some employers may provide mandatory minimum value coverage under a selfinsured group health plan to an employee, an employee's spouse, and an employee's dependents, with no employee contribution. In that case, none of those individuals would be eligible for a premium tax credit for any month during which the coverage was provided, and the employer would indicate on the return required under section 6055 for the employee all months for which that coverage was provided with respect to each individual in the employee's family. Because the section 6055 return would provide the individual taxpayers the necessary information to accurately file the taxpayers' income tax returns, and would provide the IRS the information concerning those employees to administer the premium tax credit and employer shared responsibility provisions, Treasury and the IRS are considering whether for those employees the employer could file and furnish only the return required under section 6055, a code on the Form W-2, the summary information provided in the section 6056 transmittal form, and no further information reporting under section 6056.

D. *Voluntarily Reporting Section 6056 Elements During or Prior to the Year of Coverage*

Some employers have expressed an interest in voluntarily reporting information about the coverage they offer their employees prior to the end of a coverage year, for example at their open enrollment or before the open enrollment at the Exchanges, on the theory that earlier section 6056 reporting to the IRS could lead to greater efficiency in the employer verification system employed by Exchanges to determine eligibility for premium tax credits. Under such an arrangement, they believe that if some employers chose to provide part of their section 6056 reporting to the IRS earlier in the process, the IRS, in turn, would be able to transmit any pertinent data to the Exchanges.

A proposal of this kind would need to address a number of issues. First, the regulations under section 6103 do not authorize the IRS to share taxpayer information in this manner. Even if this information sharing were permitted, information reporting plays a role in enabling individuals to file complete and accurate tax returns. Under the proposal, individuals would not receive the information for their tax return preparation proximate to when they are completing their tax returns. Employees may bear less burden and prepare more accurate tax returns when their employer furnishes a statement at the start of the relevant tax season reflecting all the information the employee needs to file a correct tax return for the prior year. Gaps in complete and timely information increase the need for additional follow-up communication among employers, employees, and the IRS.

Also, offering two sets of reporting alternatives with filing occurring at different time periods would present challenges. Because the reporting options would be voluntary, different reporting protocols and regimes would need to be established and would need to accommodate employer choices to change the method of reporting from year to year. The multiple forms, procedures, and protocols could create complexity and be difficult to administer.

In addition, the information about the offer of coverage made before the year starts may change during the calendar year. For example, during the year, an employee may be hired or may terminate employment, a part-time employee may become full-time and be eligible for different coverage options, or an employee may change positions during the year and no longer be offered coverage. Accordingly, disclosure before the coverage year does not adequately substitute for disclosure to employees and reporting to the IRS after the coverage year.

Employers, employees, and the IRS share the goal of aligning eligibility for advance payments of premium tax credits as closely as possible with eligibility for the premium tax credit on the employee's annual tax return filed after the coverage year. This would reduce confusion and minimize the risk of employees owing advance payments back as liabilities on their tax returns. Regardless of the final rules on section 6056 information reporting, employers are encouraged to make their pre-enrollment disclosures to employees and Exchanges as effective and helpful to individuals as possible.

Comments are invited on whether there could be a way to design such a voluntary partial early reporting arrangement that would reduce complexity and avoid confusion for employers and employees, be administrable for the IRS, and provide timely information to individuals so that they can meet their income tax filing obligation without undue burden or undue risk of inaccuracy.

E. *Reporting for Employees Potentially Ineligible for the Premium Tax Credit*

Some employers have indicated that, because many of their employees are relatively highly paid, they are unlikely to be eligible for a premium tax credit. The assumption is that the employee's household income is likely to exceed 400 percent of the Federal poverty line, and therefore the employee would not benefit from receiving the information otherwise included with a section 6056 employee statement. Further, because the employee is unlikely to qualify for a premium tax credit, employers have stated that the information will not be useful to the IRS in administering the employer shared responsibility provisions because the precondition of a section 4980H(b) assessable payment—that the employee receive a premium tax credit—is unlikely to be satisfied.

Treasury and the IRS have considered this request and welcome comments both on its potential usefulness to employers and its administrability. Employers would still need to report to the IRS the months during which the employee was a full-time employee, at least to the extent the employee being was included in a full-time employee count. Additionally, employers will not be in a position to know the correlation between an employee's Form W-2 wages and household income with sufficient accuracy to determine whether an employee may be eligible for the premium tax credit. The only pertinent information the employer retains is the employee's annual wages, yet the poverty level from which the premium tax credit income threshold is determined varies considerably based on family size (which employers will not necessarily know). In addition, employees for whom an employer may use an affordability safe harbor based on wages for purposes of compliance with the employer shared responsibility provisions under section 4980H might still be eligible for a premium tax credit based on their household income. Employers generally do not know employees' household income, and will not have information as to whether the employee (or another member of the employee's household) has incurred losses or expenses (such as alimony, casualty losses, Schedule C business deductions, and the like) that reduce the employee's household modified adjusted gross income below 400 percent of the Federal poverty line. Accordingly, it is unclear whether Form W-2 wages alone would provide sufficient information to determine eligibility for the premium tax credit because the employee's household income may be well below the employee's Form W-2 wages. Comments are requested as to whether there is a level of Form W-2 wages at which such a determination might be made with sufficient confidence, and whether that level of wages is so high as not to be of practical use to employers.

F. *Combinations of Simplified Reporting Methods*

The potential simplified reporting methods described above would apply to particular groups of employees that in many cases would not overlap. In such cases, two different potential simplified reporting methods could not be applied to the same employee. Treasury and the IRS anticipate that, to the extent any of these potential reporting methods are adopted in final regulations or other administrative guidance, including forms and instructions, an employer would be permitted to use different simplified methods for different employees at the employer's election.

XII. *Person Responsible For Section 6056 Reporting*

Under the proposed regulations, in general, each ALE member must file a section 6056 return with respect to its full-time employees for a calendar year.

A. *Special Rules for Governmental Units: Designation*

In accordance with section 6056(e), the proposed regulations provide that in the case of any ALE member that is a governmental unit or any agency or instrumentality thereof (together referred to in this preamble as a governmental unit), that governmental unit may report under section 6056 on its own behalf or may appropriately designate another person or persons to report on its behalf.[10] For purposes of designation, another person is appropriately designated for purposes of the filing and furnishing requirements of section 6056 if that other person is part of or related to the same governmental unit as the ALE member. For example, a political subdivision of a state may designate the state, another political subdivision of the state, or an agency or instrumentality of the foregoing as the designated person for purposes of section 6056 reporting. The person designated might be the governmental unit that operates the relevant health plan or the governmental unit that does other information reporting on behalf of the designating governmental unit. Further, the governmental unit may designate more than one governmental unit to file and furnish under section 6056 on its behalf, such as, for example, if different categories of employees are offered coverage under different health plans operated by different governmental units. In addition, a governmental unit may designate another person to file and furnish with respect to all or some of its full-time employees. If the

[10] Until further guidance is issued, government entities, churches, and a convention or association of churches may apply a reasonable, good faith interpretation of section 414(b), (c), (m), and (o) in determining whether a person or group of persons is an applicable large employer.

designation is accepted by the designee and is made before the filing deadline, the designated governmental unit is the designated entity responsible for section 6056 reporting.

The person (or persons) appropriately designated for this purpose would report under section 6056 on behalf of the ALE member. Accordingly, the person (or persons) appropriately designated is (are) the person(s) responsible for section 6056 reporting on behalf of the ALE member and subject to the penalties for failure to comply with information return requirements under sections 6721 and 6722. However, the ALE member remains subject to the requirements of section 4980H.

Under the proposed regulations, a separate section 6056 return and transmittal must be filed for each ALE member for which the appropriately designated person is reporting. The designated entity must report its name, address, and EIN on the section 6056 return to indicate it is the appropriately designated person.

The proposed regulations further provide that the designation under section 6056(e) must be in writing and must contain certain language. Specifically, under the proposed regulations, the designation must be signed by both the ALE member and the designated person, and must be effective under all applicable laws. The proposed regulations also require that the designation set forth the name and EIN of the designated person, and appoint that person as the person responsible for reporting under section 6056 on behalf of the ALE member. The designation must contain information identifying the category of full-time employees (which may be full-time employees eligible for a specified health plan, or in a particular job category, provided that the specific employees covered by the designation can be identified) for which the designated person is responsible for reporting under section 6056 on behalf of the ALE member. If the designated person is responsible for reporting under section 6056 for all full-time employees of an ALE member, the designation should so indicate.

The designation must also contain language that the designated person agrees that it is the appropriately designated person under section 6056(e), and an acknowledgement that the designated person is responsible for reporting under section 6056 on behalf of the ALE member and subject to the requirements of section 6056, and the information reporting penalty provisions of sections 6721 and 6722. The designation must also set forth the name and EIN of the ALE member, identifying the ALE member as the person subject to the requirements of section 4980H. The proposed regulations provide that an equivalent applicable statutory or regulatory designation containing similar language will be treated as a written designation for purposes of section 6056(e).

B. *ALE Members Participating in Multiemployer Plans*

Several commenters suggested that administrators of multiemployer plans may be willing to file section 6056 returns reporting information for coverage offered to full-time employees under the multiemployer plan and recommended in such cases that an ALE member not be required to report coverage information for those employees.

Treasury and the IRS understand that the plan administrator of a multiemployer plan may have better access than a participating employer to certain information on participating employees required to be included as part of section 6056 reporting. For this reason, Treasury and the IRS anticipate that the section 6056 reporting with respect to full-time employees eligible to participate in a multiemployer plan will be permitted to be provided in a bifurcated manner. Under the bifurcated approach, one return would pertain to the full-time employees eligible to participate in the multiemployer plan (or, if the employer participates in more than one multiemployer plan, one return for each relevant multiemployer plan in which full-time employees are eligible to participate), and another return would pertain to the remaining full-time employees (those who are not eligible to participate in a multiemployer plan). As in the case of other third parties, as discussed in section XII.C of this preamble, the administrator (or administrators, in the case of an employer contributing to two or more multiemployer plans) of a multiemployer plan is permitted to report on behalf of an ALE member that is a contributing employer, and is permitted to report with respect to the ALE member's full-time employees who are eligible for coverage under the multiemployer plan (but not with respect to any other full-time employees of the ALE member). The administrator of the multiemployer plan would file a separate section 6056 return for any ALE member that is a contributing employer on behalf of whom it files using the ALE member's EIN. The administrator of the multiemployer plan would also provide its own name, address, and identification number (in addition to the name, address, and EIN of the ALE member already required). The ALE member would remain the responsible person under section 6056 with respect to all of its full-time employees and accordingly would be required to sign the section 6056 return filed on its behalf and be subject to any potential liability for failure to properly file returns or furnish statements. To the extent the plan administrator that prepares returns or statements required under section 6056 is a tax return preparer, it will be subject to the requirements generally applicable to return preparers.

C. *Section 6056 Reporting Facilitated by Third Parties*

Treasury and the IRS understand that third party administrators or other third party service providers are integral to the operation of many employers' health plans, including with respect to compliance with any reporting requirements. As requested by several commenters, ALE members are permitted to contract with and use third parties to facilitate filing returns and furnishing employee statements to comply with section 6056. The proposed regulations make clear, however, that ALE members are responsible for reporting under section 6056, with the exception of certain governmental unit applicable large employers that properly designate under section 6056(e). While the proposed regulations do not provide guidance on contractual or other reporting arrangements between private

ALE members and other parties, they do not prohibit these arrangements. Such contractual arrangements would not transfer the potential liability of the ALE member for failure to report and furnish under section 6056 and the regulations, or the ALE member's potential liability under section 4980H.

As one example, an applicable large employer that is a member of an aggregated group of related entities (determined under section 414(b), 414(c), 414(m) or 414(o)), may file returns and furnish employee statements on behalf of one or more of the other ALE members of the aggregated group. Each other ALE member of the group, for example, could have the ALE member that operates the employer-sponsored plan file section 6056 returns and furnish section 6056 employee statements on its behalf. However, a separate section 6056 return must be filed for each ALE member, providing that ALE member's EIN. Each ALE member in the aggregated group would continue to be the responsible person under section 6056, would be required to sign the return filed on its behalf, and would be subject to any potential liability for failure to properly file returns or furnish statements. To the extent the other party that prepares returns or statements required under section 6056 is a tax return preparer, it will be subject to the requirements generally applicable to return preparers.

XIII. *Applicability of Information Return Requirements*

The proposed regulations provide that an ALE member that fails to comply with the section 6056 information return and employee statement requirements may be subject to the general reporting penalty provisions under sections 6721 (failure to file correct information returns), and 6722 (failure to furnish correct payee statement). The proposed regulations also provide, however, that the waiver of penalty and special rules under section 6724 and the applicable regulations, including abatement of information return penalties for reasonable cause, apply. The proposed regulations under section 6055 (REG-132455-11) include proposed amendments to the regulations under sections 6721 and 6722 to include returns under both sections 6055 and 6056 in the definitions of information return and payee statement. Treasury and the IRS anticipate that the final regulations under section 6056 will cross-reference those amendments to the regulations under sections 6721 and 6722.

Proposed Effective/Applicability Dates

These regulations are proposed to be effective the date the final regulations are published in the **Federal Register**. These regulations are proposed to apply for calendar years beginning after December 31, 2014. Consistent with Notice 2013-45, reporting entities will not be subject to penalties for failure to comply with the section 6506 information reporting provisions for 2014 (including the furnishing of employee statements in 2015). Accordingly, a reporting entity will not be subject to penalties if it first reports beginning in 2016 for 2015 (including the furnishing of employee statements). Taxpayers are encouraged, however, to voluntarily comply with section 6056 information reporting for 2014 by using the general reporting method set forth in these regulations once finalized.

Special Analyses

It has been determined that this notice of proposed rulemaking is not a significant regulatory action as defined in Executive Order 12866, as supplemented by Executive Order 13563. Therefore, a regulatory assessment is not required. It has also been determined that section 553(b) of the Administrative Procedure Act (5 U.S.C. chapter 5) does not apply to these regulations.

It is hereby certified that these regulations will not have a significant economic impact on a substantial number of small entities. This certification is based on the fact that the regulations are consistent with the requirements imposed by section 6056. Consistent with the statute, the regulations require applicable large employers, as defined in section 4980H(c)(2), to file a return with the IRS, using either the prescribed form or a substitute form, for each full-time employee reporting certain information regarding the health care coverage offered and provided to the employee for the year. Consistent with the statute, the proposed regulations further require applicable large employers to furnish to each full-time employee a copy of the return, or a substitute statement, required to be filed by the applicable large employer with respect to the employee. Accordingly, these regulations merely prescribe the method of filing and furnishing returns and employee statements as required under section 6056. Moreover, the proposed regulations attempt to minimize the burden associated with this collection of information by requiring that applicable large employers file and furnish only information that the IRS will utilize to administer the shared employer responsibility provisions under section 4980H and administer the premium tax credit under section 36B, and information employees will need in order to complete their tax returns.

Based on these facts, a Regulatory Flexibility Analysis under the Regulatory Flexibility Act (5 U.S.C. chapter 6) is not required.

Pursuant to section 7805(f) of the Code, this notice of proposed rulemaking has been submitted to the Chief Counsel for Advocacy of the Small Business Administration for comment on its impact on small business.

Comments and a Public Hearing

Before these proposed regulations are adopted as final regulations, consideration will be given to any written comments (a signed original and eight (8) copies) or electronic comments that are submitted timely to the IRS as prescribed in this preamble under the "Addresses" heading. Treasury and the IRS specifically request comments on the clarity of the proposed rules and how they can be made easier to understand. All comments will be available for public inspection at www.regulations.gov or upon request. A public hearing has been scheduled for November 18, 2013, in the Auditorium, Internal Revenue Building, 1111 Constitution Avenue, NW, Washington, DC. Due to building security procedures, visitors must enter at the Constitution Avenue entrance. In addition, all visitors must present photo identification to enter the building. Because of access restrictions, visitors will not be admitted beyond the immediate entrance area more than 30 minutes before the hearing starts. For information about having your name placed on the building access list to attend the hearing, see the "FOR FURTHER INFORMATION CONTACT" section of this preamble.

The rules of 26 CFR 601.601(a)(3) apply to the hearing. Persons who wish to present oral comments at the hearing must submit written or electronic comments by November 8, 2013 and an outline of the topics to be discussed and the time to be devoted to each topic (signed original and eight (8) copies) by November 8, 2013.

A period of 10 minutes will be allotted to each person for making comments. An agenda showing the scheduling of the speakers will be prepared after the deadline for receiving outlines has passed. Copies of the agenda will be available free of charge at the hearing.

Drafting Information

The principal author of these proposed regulations is Ligeia M. Donis of the Office of the Division Counsel/Associate Chief Counsel (Tax Exempt and Government Entities). However, other personnel from the IRS and Treasury participated in their development.

[¶49,593] Proposed Amendments of Regulations (REG-120927-13), published in the Federal Register on November 15, 2013.

[Code Sec. 415]

Retirement plans: Indian tribal governments: Exempt income: Safe harbors: Compensation.—Amendments of Reg. §1.415(c)-2, clarifying that amounts paid to an Indian tribe member as remuneration for services performed in a fishing rights-related activity may be treated as compensation for purposes of applying the limits on qualified plan benefits and contributions, are proposed.

AGENCY: Internal Revenue Service (IRS), Treasury

ACTION: Notice of proposed rulemaking.

SUMMARY: This document contains proposed regulations that would clarify that amounts paid to an Indian tribe member as remuneration for services performed in a fishing rights-related activity may be treated as compensation for purposes of applying the limits on qualified plan benefits and contributions. These regulations would affect sponsors of, and participants in, employee benefit plans of Indian tribal governments.

DATES: Comments and requests for a public hearing must be received by February 13, 2014.

ADDRESSES: Send submissions to CC:PA:LPD:PR (REG-120927-13), room 5205, Internal Revenue Service, PO Box 7604, Ben Franklin Station, Washington D.C. 20044. Submissions may be hand-delivered Monday through Friday between the hours of 8 a.m. and 4 p.m. to CC:PA:LPD:PR (REG-120927-13), Courier's Desk, Internal Revenue Service, 1111 Constitution Avenue, N.W., Washington, DC, 20224, or sent electronically via the Federal eRulemaking Portal at *www.regulations.gov* (IRS REG-120927-13).

FOR FURTHER INFORMATION CONTACT: Concerning the proposed regulations, Sarah Bolen or Pamela Kinard at (202) 622-6060 or (202) 317-6700; concerning the submission of comments or to request a public hearing, Oluwafunmilayo Taylor, (202) 622-7180 or (202) 317-6901 (not toll-free numbers).

SUPPLEMENTARY INFORMATION:

Background

Indian tribal governments (ITGs) and individual tribe members conduct fishing activities to generate revenue, protect critical habitats, and preserve tribal customs and traditions. Various treaties, federal statutes, and Presidential executive orders reserve to Indian tribe members the right to fish for subsistence and commercial purposes both on and off reservations. Because many of the treaties, statutes, and executive orders were adopted before passage of the Federal income tax, they often do not expressly address the question of whether income derived by Indians and ITGs from protected fishing activities is exempt from taxation. *See* H.R. Rep. 100-1104, at p. 77 (1988).

Congress added section 7873 to the Internal Revenue Code as part of the Technical and Miscellaneous Revenue Act of 1988 (Public Law 100-647). Section 7873(a)(1) provides that no income tax shall be imposed on income derived from a fishing rights-related activity of an Indian tribe by (A) a member of the tribe directly or through a qualified Indian entity, or (B) a qualified Indian entity. Section 7873(a)(2) provides that no employment tax shall be imposed on remuneration paid for services performed in a fishing rights-related activity of an Indian tribe by a member of such tribe for another member of such tribe or for a qualified Indian entity. Thus, section 7873(a) exempts income derived from a fishing rights-related activity ("fishing rights-related income") from both income and employment taxes.

Section 7873(b)(1) defines fishing rights-related activity with respect to an Indian tribe as any activity directly related to harvesting, processing, or transporting fish harvested in the exercise of a recognized fishing right of the tribe or to selling such fish but only if substantially all of such harvesting was performed by members of such tribe.

Section 415(a)(1) provides that a trust that is part of a pension, profit-sharing, or stock bonus plan shall not constitute a qualified trust under section 401(a) if (A) in the case of a defined benefit plan, the plan provides for the payment of benefits with respect to a participant which exceed the limitation of section 415(b), or (B) in the case of a defined contribution plan, contributions and other additions under the plan with respect to any participant for any taxable year exceed the limitation of section 415(c).

Section 415(b)(1) provides that benefits with respect to a participant exceed the annual limitation for defined benefit plans if, when expressed as an annual benefit (within the meaning of section 415(b)(2)), the participant's annual benefit is greater than the lesser of $160,000 (as adjusted in accordance with section 415(d)(1)) or 100 percent of the participant's average compensation for the participant's high 3 years.

Section 415(b)(3) provides that, for purposes of section 415(b)(1), a participant's high 3 years will be the period of consecutive calendar years (not more than 3) during which the participant had the greatest aggregate compensation from the employer. In the case of an employee within the meaning of section 401(c)(1) (that is, a self-employed individual treated as an employee), the preceding sentence is applied by substituting for "compensation from the employer" the following: "the participant's earned income (within the meaning of section 401(c)(2) but determined without regard to any exclusion under section 911)."

Section 415(c)(1) provides that contributions and other additions with respect to a participant exceed the annual limitation for defined contribution plans if, when expressed as an annual addition (within the meaning of section 415(c)(2)) to the participant's account, the participant's annual addition is greater than the lesser of $40,000 (as adjusted in accordance with section 415(d)(1)) or 100 percent of the participant's compensation. Section 415(c)(3) provides that the term "participant's compensation" means the compensation of the participant from the employer for the year. Section 1.415(c)-2(a) of the Income Tax Regulations generally provides that compensation from the employer within the meaning of section 415(c)(3) includes all items of remuneration described in § 1.415(c)-2(b), but excludes the items of remuneration described in § 1.415(c)-2(c).

Section 1.415(c)-2(b) generally provides that, for purposes of applying the limitations of section 415, the term compensation means remuneration for services. Specifically, under § 1.415(c)-2(b)(1), compensation includes employee wages, salaries, fees for professional services, and other amounts received (without regard to whether or not an amount is paid in cash) for personal services actually rendered in the course of employment with the employer maintaining the plan, to the extent that the amounts are includible in gross income. In addition, § 1.415(c)-2(b)(2) provides that in the case of an employee within the meaning of section 401(c)(1) (a self-employed employee), compensation includes the employee's earned income (as described in section 401(c)(2)) plus amounts deferred at the election of the employee that would be includible in gross income but for the rules of section 402(e)(3), 402(h)(1)(B), 402(k), or 457(b).

Section 1.415(c)-2(c) excludes certain items from the definition of compensation under section 415(c)(3). Specifically, § 1.415(c)-2(c)(1) excludes contributions (other than certain elective contributions) made by the employer to a plan of deferred compensation to the extent that the contributions are not includible in the gross income of the employee for the taxable year in which contributed. Likewise, distributions from plans (whether qualified or not) are generally not considered to be compensation for section 415 purposes. Section 1.415(c)-2(c)(2) excludes from compensation amounts realized from the exercise of nonstatutory options and amounts realized when restricted stock or other property held by an employee becomes freely transferable or is no longer subject to a substantial risk of forfeiture. Section 1.415(c)-2(c)(3) excludes from compensation amounts realized from the sale, exchange, or other disposition of stock acquired under a statutory stock option (as defined in § 1.421-1(b)). Finally, § 1.415(c)-2(c)(4) excludes from compensation other amounts that receive special tax benefits, such as certain premiums for group-term life insurance.

Section 1.415(c)-2(d) provides safe harbor definitions that a plan is permitted to use to define compensation in a manner that satisfies section 415(c)(3). Section 1.415(c)-2(d)(2) provides a safe harbor definition of compensation that includes only those items listed in § 1.415(c)-2(b)(1) or (b)(2) and excludes all the items listed in § 1.415(c)-2(c). Section 415(c)-2(d)(3) provides a separate safe harbor definition of compensation that includes wages within the meaning of section 3401(a), plus amounts that would be included in wages but for an election under section 125(a), 132(f)(4), 402(e)(3), 402(h)(1)(b), 402(k), or 457(b).

Explanation of Provisions

Because fishing rights-related income is not subject to income tax, an issue has been raised as to whether such income is included as compensation for purposes of section 415(c)(3) and § 1.415(c)-2(b). The proposed regulations would clarify that certain fishing rights-related income is included in the definition of compensation. Specifically, these regulations would provide that amounts paid to a member of an Indian tribe as remuneration for services performed in a fishing rights-related activity (as defined in section 7873(b)(1)) do not fail to be treated as compensation under § 1.415(c)-2(b)(1) and (b)(2) (and are not excluded from the definition of compensation pursuant to § 1.415(c)-2(c)(4)) merely because those amounts are not subject to income tax as a result of section 7873(a)(1). Thus, the determination of whether an amount constitutes wages, salaries, or earned income for purposes of § 1.415(c)-2(b)(1) or (b)(2) is made without regard to the exemption from taxation under section 7873(b)(1) and (b)(2). In addition, by permitting fishing rights-related income to be treated as wages, salaries, or earned income under § 1.415(c)-2(b)(1) and (b)(2), plans that accept contributions of fishing rights-related income would not be precluded from utilizing the safe harbor definitions of compensation under § 1.415(c)-2(d)(2) and (d)(3) of the regulations.

Proposed Applicability Date

These regulations are proposed to apply for taxable years ending on or after the date of publication of the Treasury decision adopting these rules as final regulations in the **Federal Register**. Taxpayers, however, may rely on these proposed regulations for periods preceding the effective date, pending the issuance of final regulations. If, and to the extent, the final regulations are more restrictive than the rules in these proposed regulations, those provisions of the final regulations will be applied without retroactive effect.

Special Analyses

It has been determined that this notice of proposed rulemaking is not a significant regulatory action as defined in Executive Order 12866, as supplemented by Executive Order 13563. Therefore, a regulatory assessment is not required. It has also been determined that 5 U.S.C. 533(b) of the Administrative Procedure Act (5 U.S.C. chapter 5) does not apply to these regulations. Because these regulations do not impose a collection of information on small entities, the provisions of the Regulatory Flexibility Act (5 U.S.C. chapter 6) do not apply and a Regulatory Flexibility Analysis is not required. Pursuant to section 7805(f) of the Internal Revenue Code, these regulations have been submitted to the Office of Chief Counsel for Advocacy of the Small Business Administration for comments on its impact on small business.

Comments and Requests for Public Hearing

Before these proposed regulations are adopted as final regulations, consideration will be given to any comments that are submitted timely to the IRS as prescribed in this preamble under the "Addresses" heading. In addition to general comments on the proposed regulations, the IRS and the Treasury Department request comments on the taxation of qualified plan distributions that are attributable to fishing rights-related income, and the application of section 72(f)(2) (which treats certain amounts as basis for purposes of computing employee contributions if those amounts would have not been includible in income had they been paid directly to the employee). All comments are available at *www.regulations.gov* or upon request. A public hearing will be scheduled if requested in writing by any person who timely submits written comments. If a public hearing is scheduled, notice of the date, time, and place of the public hearing will be published in the **Federal Register**.

Consultation and Coordination with Indian Tribal Governments

These proposed regulations take into account comments provided through a number of general consultation sessions held with the Indian tribal community in recent years. Consistent with Executive Order 13175, the Treasury Department and the IRS expect to hold a telephone consultation on a date between November 15, 2013 and February 13, 2014. This telephone consultation session will focus principally on the contribution of section 7873 income to qualified retirement plans and the taxation of qualified plan distributions that are attributable to this income. Information relating to the consultation, including the date, time, registration requirements, and procedures for submitting written and oral comments, will be available on the IRS website relating to Indian tribal governments at: http://www.irs.gov/Government-Entities/Indian-Tribal-Governments.

Drafting Information

The principal author of these regulations is Sarah R. Bolen, Office of Division Counsel/Associate Chief Counsel (Tax Exempt and Government Entities). However, other personnel from the IRS and the Treasury Department participated in the development of these regulations.

[¶49,594] Proposed Amendments of Regulations and Withdrawal of Proposed Regulations (REG-130843-13), published in the Federal Register on December 2, 2013 (corrected 2/24/2014).

[Code Sec. 1411]

Patient Protection and Affordable Care Act: Net investment income tax: Net investment income: Computation.—Reg. §1.1411-7 and amendments of Reg. §§1.1411-0, 1.1411-3 and 1.1411-4, providing guidance on the computation of net investment income, are proposed. Reg. §1.1411-7, proposed on December 5, 2012 (REG-130507-11), is withdrawn.

AGENCY: Internal Revenue Service (IRS), Treasury.

ACTION: Withdrawal of notice of proposed rulemaking and notice of proposed rulemaking.

SUMMARY: This document contains proposed regulations under section 1411 of the Internal Revenue Code (Code). These regulations provide guidance on the computation of net investment income. The regulations affect individuals, estates, and trusts whose incomes meet certain income thresholds.

DATES: The proposed rule published December 5, 2012 (77 FR 72612), is withdrawn as of December 2, 2013. Comments on this proposed rule must be received by March 3, 2014. Comments on the collection of information for this proposed rule should be received by January 31, 2014.

ADDRESSES: Send submissions to: CC:PA:LPD:PR (REG-130843-13), room 5205, Internal Revenue Service, PO Box 7604, Ben Franklin Station, Washington, DC 20044. Submissions may be hand-delivered Monday through Friday between the hours of 8 a.m. and 4 p.m. to CC:PA:LPD:PR (REG-130843-13), Courier's Desk, Internal Revenue Service, 1111 Constitution Avenue, NW., Washington, DC, or sent electronically, via the Federal eRulemaking portal at *www.regulations.gov* (IRS REG-130843-13).

FOR FURTHER INFORMATION CONTACT: Concerning the proposed regulations, David H. Kirk or Adrienne M. Mikolashek at (202) 317-6852; concerning submissions of comments or to request a hearing, Oluwafunmilayo Taylor, (202) 317-6901 (not toll-free numbers).

SUPPLEMENTARY INFORMATION:

Paperwork Reduction Act

The collection of information contained in this notice of proposed rulemaking has been submitted to the Office of Management and Budget for review in accordance with the Paperwork Reduction Act of 1995 (44 U.S.C. 3507(d)) under control number 1545-2227. Comments on the collection of information should be sent to the **Office of Management and Budget**, Attn: Desk Officer for the Department of the Treasury, Office of Information and Regulatory Affairs, Washington, DC 20503, with copies to the **Internal Revenue Service**, Attn: IRS Reports Clearance Officer, SE:W:CAR:MP:T:T:SP, Washington, DC 20224. Comments on the collection of information should be received by January 31, 2014. Comments are specifically requested concerning:

Whether the proposed collection of information is necessary for the proper performance of the functions of the IRS, including whether the information will have practical utility;

The accuracy of the estimated burden associated with the proposed collection of information; and

Estimates of capital or start-up costs and costs of operation, maintenance, and purchase of services to provide information.

The collection of information in these proposed regulations is in § 1.1411-7(g).

The information collected in proposed § 1.1411-7(g) is required by the IRS to verify the taxpayer's reported adjustment under section 1411(c)(4). This information will be used to determine whether the amount of tax has been reported and calculated correctly. The likely respondents are owners of interests in partnerships and S corporations.

The burden for the collection of information contained in these proposed regulations will be reflected in the burden on Form 8960 or another form that the IRS designates, which will request the information in the proposed regulations.

An agency may not conduct or sponsor, and a person is not required to respond to, a collection of information unless it displays a valid control number assigned by the Office of Management and Budget.

Books or records relating to a collection of information must be retained as long as their contents may become material in the administration of any internal revenue law. Generally, tax returns and tax return information are confidential, as required by section 6103.

Background

I. *Statutory Background*

Section 1402(a)(1) of the Health Care and Education Reconciliation Act of 2010 (Public Law 111-152, 124 Stat. 1029) added section 1411 to a new chapter 2A of subtitle A (Income Taxes) of the Code effective for taxable years beginning after December 31, 2012. Section 1411 imposes a 3.8 percent tax on certain individuals, estates, and trusts.

In the case of an individual, section 1411(a)(1) imposes a tax (in addition to any other tax imposed by subtitle A) for each taxable year equal to 3.8 percent of the lesser of: (A) the individual's net investment income for such taxable year, or (B) the excess (if any) of: (i) the individual's modified adjusted gross income for such taxable year, over (ii) the threshold amount. Section 1411(b) provides that the threshold amount is: (1) in the case of a taxpayer making a joint return under section 6013 or a surviving spouse (as defined in section 2(a)), $250,000; (2) in the case of a married taxpayer (as defined in section 7703) filing a separate return, $125,000; and (3) in the case of any other individual, $200,000. Section 1411(d) defines modified adjusted gross income as adjusted gross income increased by the excess of: (1) the amount excluded from gross income under section 911(a)(1), over (2) the amount of any deductions (taken into account in computing adjusted gross income) or exclusions disallowed under section 911(d)(6) with respect to the amount excluded from gross income under section 911(a)(1).

In the case of an estate or trust, section 1411(a)(2) imposes a tax (in addition to any other tax imposed by subtitle A) for each taxable year equal to 3.8 percent of the lesser of: (A) the estate's or trust's undistributed net investment income, or (B) the excess (if any) of (i) the estate's or trust's adjusted gross income (as defined in section 67(e)) for such taxable year, over (ii) the dollar amount at which the highest tax bracket in section 1(e) begins for such taxable year.

Section 1411(c)(1) provides that net investment income means the excess (if any) of: (A) the sum of (i) gross income from interest, dividends, annuities, royalties, and rents, other than such income derived in the ordinary course of a trade or business to which the tax does not apply, (ii) other gross income derived from a trade or business to which the tax applies, and (iii) net gain (to the extent taken into account in computing taxable income) attributable to the disposition of property other than property held in a trade or business to which the tax does not apply; over (B) the deductions allowed by subtitle A that are properly allocable to such gross income or net gain.

II. *Regulatory Background*

This document contains proposed amendments to 26 CFR part 1 under section 1411 of the Code. On December 5, 2012, the Treasury Department and the IRS published a notice of proposed rulemaking in the **Federal Register** (REG-130507-11; 77 FR 72612) relating to the Net Investment Income Tax. On January 31, 2013, corrections to the proposed regulations were published in the **Federal Register** (78 FR 6781) (collectively, the "2012 Proposed Regulations"). Final regulations, issued contemporaneously with these proposed regulations in the Rules and Regulations section of this issue of the **Federal Register**, contain amendments to the Income Tax Regulations (26 CFR Part

1), which finalize the 2012 Proposed Regulations (the "2013 Final Regulations"). However, the Treasury Department and the IRS also are proposing amendments to the 2013 Final Regulations to provide additional clarification and guidance with respect to the application of section 1411 to certain specific types of property. Furthermore, the Treasury Department and the IRS are also interested in receiving comments about other aspects of section 1411 that are not addressed in the 2013 Final Regulations or these proposed regulations. If such comments are received, the Treasury Department and the IRS will consider them for inclusion on future Guidance Priority Lists.

The Treasury Department and the IRS received comments on the 2012 Proposed Regulations requesting that they address the treatment of section 707(c) guaranteed payments for capital, section 736 payments to retiring or deceased partners for section 1411 purposes, and certain capital loss carryovers. After consideration of all comments received, the Treasury Department and the IRS believe that it is appropriate to address the treatment of these items in regulations. Because such guidance had not been proposed in the 2012 Proposed Regulations, it is being issued for notice and comment in these new proposed regulations.

The Treasury Department and the IRS also received comments on the simplified method for applying section 1411 to income recipients of charitable remainder trusts (CRTs) that was proposed in the 2012 Proposed Regulations. The comments recommended that the section 1411 classification incorporate the existing category and class system under section 664. These proposed regulations provide special rules for the application of the section 664 system to CRTs that derive income from controlled foreign corporations (CFCs) or passive foreign investment companies (PFICs) with respect to which an election under § 1.1411-10(g) is not in place. Specifically, these proposed regulations coordinate the application of the rules applicable to shareholders of CFCs and PFICs in § 1.1411-10 with the section 664 category and class system adopted in § 1.1411-3(d)(2) of the 2013 Final Regulations.

Furthermore, these proposed regulations allow CRTs to elect to apply the section 664 system adopted in the 2013 Final Regulations or the simplified method set forth in the 2012 Proposed Regulations. Some comments responding to the 2012 Proposed Regulations requested that we provide an election. The Treasury Department and the IRS request comments with regard to whether or not taxpayers believe this election is preferable to the section 664 system adopted in the 2013 Final Regulations. If it appears that there is no significant interest in having the election, the Treasury Department and the IRS may omit it from the regulations when finalized, and the simplified method contained in the 2012 Proposed Regulations would no longer be an option.

These proposed regulations also address the net investment income tax characterization of income and deductions attributable to common trust funds (CTFs), residual interests in real estate mortgage investment conduits (REMICs), and certain notional principal contracts.

The Treasury Department and the IRS also received comments on the 2012 Proposed Regulations questioning the proposed regulation's methodology for adjusting a transferor's gain or loss on the disposition of its partnership interest or S corporation stock. In view of these comments, the 2013 Final Regulations removed § 1.1411-7 of the 2012 Proposed Regulations and reserved § 1.1411-7 in the 2013 Final Regulations. This notice of proposed rulemaking proposes revised rules regarding the calculation of net gain from the disposition of a partnership interest or S corporation stock (each a "Passthrough Entity") to which section 1411(c)(4) may apply.

Explanation of Provisions

1. *Overview of Proposed Regulations*

These proposed regulations propose additions and modifications to the 2013 Final Regulations, including guidance with respect to certain paragraphs that were reserved in the 2013 Final Regulations.

To coordinate these proposed regulations with the 2013 Final Regulations, the proposed regulations are proposed to have the same effective date as the 2013 Final Regulations. However, any provisions adopted when these proposed regulations are finalized that are more restrictive than these proposed regulations would apply prospectively only. Taxpayers may rely on these proposed regulations for purposes of compliance with section 1411 until the issuance of these regulations as final regulations. See § 1.1411-1(f).

2. *Special Rules for Certain Partnership Payments*

Section 731(a) treats gain from distributions as gain from the sale or exchange of a partnership interest. In general, the section 1411 treatment of gain to a partner under section 731 is governed by the rules of section 1411(c)(1)(A)(iii). Such gain is thus generally treated as net investment income for purposes of section 1411 (other than as determined under section 1411(c)(4)). However, certain partnership payments to partners are treated as not from the sale or exchange of a partnership interest. These payments include section 707(c) guaranteed payments for services or the use of capital and certain section 736 distributions to a partner in liquidation of that partner's partnership interest. Because these payments are not treated as from the sale or exchange of a partnership interest, their treatment under section 1411 may differ from the general rule of section 1411(c)(1)(A)(iii). The proposed regulations therefore provide rules for the section 1411 treatment of these payments.

A. *Section 707(c) payments*

Section 707(c) provides that a partnership payment to a partner is a "guaranteed payment" if the payment is made for services or the use of the capital, and the payment amount does not depend on partnership income. Section 1.707-1(c) provides that guaranteed payments to a partner for services are considered as made to a person who is not a partner, but only for the purposes of section 61(a) (relating to gross income) and, subject to section 263, section 162(a) (relating to trade or business expenses). Section 1.704-1(b)(2)(iv)(o) provides that guaranteed payments are not part of a partner's distributive share for purposes of section 704(b).

The proposed regulations' treatment of section 707(c) guaranteed payments under section 1411 depends on whether the partner receives the payment for services or the use of capital. The proposed regulations exclude all section 707(c) payments received for services from net investment income, regardless of whether these payments are subject to self-employment tax, because payments for services are not included in net investment income.

The Treasury Department and the IRS believe that guaranteed payments for the use of capital share many of the characteristics of substitute interest, and therefore should be included as net investment income. This treatment is consistent with existing guidance under section 707(c) and other sections of the Code in which guaranteed payments for the use of capital are treated as interest. See, for example, §§ 1.263A-9(c)(2)(iii) and 1.469-2(e)(2)(ii).

B. *Treatment of section 736 payments*

i. In General

Section 736 applies to payments made by a partnership to a retiring partner or to a deceased partner's successor in interest in liquidation of the partner's entire interest in the partnership. Section 736 does not apply to distributions made to a continuing partner, distributions made in the course of liquidating a partnership entirely, or to payments received from persons other than the partnership in exchange for the partner's interest. Section 736 categorizes liquidating distributions based on the nature of the payment as in consideration for either the partner's share of partnership property or the partner's share of partnership income. Section 736(b) generally treats a payment in exchange for the retiring partner's share of partnership property as a distribution governed by section 731. Section 736(a) treats payments in exchange for past services or use of capital as either distributive share or a guaranteed payment. Section 736(a) payments also include payments to retiring general partners of service partnerships in exchange for unrealized receivables (other than receivables described in the flush language of section 751(c)) or for goodwill (other than payments for goodwill provided for in the partnership agreement) (collectively, "Section 736(a) Property").

Because the application of section 1411 depends on the underlying nature of the payment received, the section 736 categorization controls whether a liquidating distribution is treated as net investment income for purposes of section 1411. Thus, the treatment of the payment for purposes of section 1411 differs depending on whether the distribution is a section 736(b) distribution in exchange for partnership property or a section 736(a) distribution in exchange for past services, use of capital, or Section 736(a) Property. Among section 736(a) payments, the proposed regulations further differentiate the treatment of payments depending on: (i) whether or not the payment amounts are determined with regard to the income of the partnership and (ii) whether the payment relates to Section 736(a) Property or relates to services or use of capital.

Section 1.469-2(e)(2)(iii) contains rules pertaining to whether section 736 liquidating distributions paid to a partner will be treated as income or loss from a passive activity. Where payments to a retiring partner are made over a period of years, the composition of the assets and the status of the partner as passive or nonpassive may change. Section 1.469-2(e)(2)(iii) contains rules on the extent to which those payments are classified as passive or nonpassive for purposes of section 469. The proposed regulations generally align the section 1411 characterization of section 736 payments with the treatment of the payments as passive or nonpassive under § 1.469-2(e)(2)(iii).

ii. Treatment of Section 736(b) Payments

Section 736(b) payments to retiring partners in exchange for partnership property (other than payments to retiring general partners of service partnerships in exchange for Section 736(a) Property) are governed by the rules generally applicable to partnership distributions. Thus, gain or loss recognized on these distributions is treated as gain or loss from the sale or exchange of the distributee partner's partnership interest under section 731(a).

The proposed regulations provide that section 736(b) payments will be taken into account as net investment income for section 1411 purposes under section 1411(c)(1)(A)(iii) as net gain or loss from the disposition of property. If the retiring partner materially participates in a partnership trade or business, then the retiring partner must also apply § 1.1411-7 of these proposed regulations to reduce appropriately the net investment income under section 1411(c)(4). Gain or loss relating to section 736(b) payments is included in net investment income under section 1411(c)(1)(A)(iii) regardless of whether the payments are classified as capital gain or ordinary income (for example, by reason of section 751).

In the case of section 736(b) payments that are paid over multiple years, the proposed regulations provide that the characterization of gain or loss as passive or nonpassive is determined for all payments as though all payments were made at the time that the liquidation of the exiting partner's interest commenced and is not retested annually. The proposed regulations thus adopt for section 1411 purposes the section 469 treatment of section 736(b) payments paid over multiple years as set forth in § 1.469-2(e)(2)(iii)(A).

iii. Treatment of Section 736(a) Payments

As described in part 2.B.i., section 736 provides for several different categories of liquidating distributions under section 736(a). Payments received under section 736(a) may be an amount determined with regard to the income of the partnership taxable as distributive share under section 736(a)(1) or a fixed amount taxable as a guaranteed payment under section 736(a)(2). The categorization of the payment as distributive share or guaranteed payment will govern the treatment of the payment for purposes of section 1411.

The determination of whether section 736(a) payments received over multiple years are characterized as passive or nonpassive depends on whether the payments are received in exchange for Section 736(a) Property. With respect to section 736(a)(1) payments in exchange for Section 736(a) Property, § 1.469-2(e)(2)(iii)(B) provides a special rule that computes a percentage of passive income that would result if the partnership sold the retiring partner's entire share of Section 736(a) Property at the time that the liquidation of the partner's interest commenced. The percentage of passive income is then applied to each payment received. See § 1.469-2(e)(2)(iii)(B)(1). These rules apply to section 736(a)(1) and section 736(a)(2) payments for Section 736(a) Property. The proposed regulations adopt this treatment as set forth in section 469 for purposes of section 1411.

a. Section 736(a)(1) payments taxable as distributive share

Section 736(a)(1) provides that if the amount of a liquidating distribution (other than a payment for partnership property described in section 736(b)) is determined with regard to the partnership's income, then the payment is treated as a distributive share of income to the retiring partner. For purposes of section 1411, the items of income, gain, loss, and deduction attributable to the distributive share are taken into account in computing net investment income under section 1411(c)(1) in a manner consistent with the item's chapter 1 character and treatment. For example, if the partner's distributive share includes income from a trade or business not described in section 1411(c)(2), that income will be excluded from net investment income. However, if the distributive share includes, for example, interest income from working capital, then that income is net investment income.

The proposed regulations treat section 736(a)(1) payments unrelated to Section 736(a) Property as characterized annually as passive or nonpassive by applying the general rules of section 469 to each payment in the year received. To the extent that any payment under section 736(a)(1) is characterized as passive income under the principles of section 469, that payment also will be characterized as passive income for purposes of section 1411.

b. Section 736(a)(2) payments taxable as guaranteed payments

Section 736(a)(2) provides that if the amount of a liquidating distribution (other than a payment for partnership property described in section 736(b)) is determined without regard to the partnership's income, then the payment is treated as a guaranteed payment as described in section 707(c). Payments under section 736(a)(2) might be in exchange for services, use of capital, or Section 736(a) Property. The section 1411 treatment of guaranteed payments for services or the use of capital follows the general rules for guaranteed payments set forth in part 2.A of this preamble. Thus, section 736(a)(2) payments for services are not included as net investment income, and section 736(a)(2) payments for the use of capital are included as net investment income.

Section 736(a)(2) payments in exchange for Section 736 Property are treated as gain or loss from the disposition of a partnership interest, which is generally included in net investment income under section 1411(c)(1)(A)(iii). If the retiring partner materially participates in a partnership trade or business, then the retiring partner must also apply § 1.1411-7 of these proposed regulations to reduce appropriately the net investment income under section 1411(c)(4). To the extent that section 736(a)(2) payments exceed the fair market value of Section 736(a) Property, the proposed regulations provide that the excess will be treated as either interest income or as income in exchange for services, in a manner consistent with the treatment under § 1.469-2(e)(2)(iii). iv. Application of Section 1411(c)(4) to Section 736 Payments

The proposed regulations provide that section 1411(c)(4) applies to section 736(a)(2) and section 736(b) payments. Thus, the inclusion of these payments as net investment income may be limited if the retiring partner materially participated in all or a portion of the partnership's trade or business. The extent of any limitation is determined under the rules of § 1.1411-7.

The proposed regulations provide that, when section 736 payments are made over multiple years, the characterization of gain or loss as passive or nonpassive and the values of the partnership assets are computed for all payments as though all payments were made at the time that the liquidation of the exiting partner's interest commenced, similar to the treatment in § 1.469-2(e)(2)(iii)(A).

If a partner's net investment income is reduced pursuant to section 1411(c)(4), then the difference between the amount of gain recognized for chapter 1 and the amount includable in net investment income after the application of section 1411(c)(4) is treated as an addition to basis, in a manner similar to an installment sale for purposes of calculating the partner's net investment income attributable to these payments.

v. Additional Public Comments

Commentators to the 2012 Proposed Regulations requested that the Treasury Department and the IRS issue guidance under section 1411 regarding the treatment of section 736 payments to retiring and deceased partners. Some commentators sought clarification regarding the interaction between section 736 payments and the net investment income exclusions in sections 1411(c)(5) and 1411(c)(6).

Section 1411(c)(5) provides that net investment income shall not include certain items of income attributable to distributions from specifically enumerated qualified plans. One commentator suggested that section 736 payments should be excluded from net investment income under section 1411(c)(5) as analogous to qualified plan distributions. The Treasury Department and the IRS believe that section 1411(c)(5) does not apply to section 736 payments because these payments do not originate from a qualified plan described in section 1411(c)(5). Therefore, section 736 payments are not excluded by reason of section 1411(c)(5).

Section 1411(c)(6) provides that net investment income does not include any item taken into account in determining self-employment income for a taxable year on which a tax is imposed by section 1401(b). In the context of section 1411(c)(6), § 1.1411-9(a) of the 2013 Final Regulations provides that the term "taken into account" for self-employment tax purposes does not include amounts excluded from net earnings from self-employment under sections 1402(a)(1)-(17). Commentators suggested that certain section 736 payments are excluded from net earnings from self-employment by reason of section 1402(a)(10) and § 1.1402(a)-17, and therefore should be excluded from net investment income under section 1411(c)(6) for similar policy reasons. The Treasury Department and the IRS believe that section 1411(c)(6) does not apply to section 736 payments, except to the extent that such payments are taken into account, within the meaning of § 1.1411-9(a), in determining net earnings from self-employment. In such a case, the section 736 payment would be subject to self-employment tax and therefore is not included in net investment income by reason of section 1411(c)(6) and § 1.1411-9(a).

Commentators also recommended special rules for the interaction between section 736 payments and the section 469 material participation rules solely for purposes of section 1411. As discussed in this part of the preamble, the proposed section 1411 rules rely heavily on the chacterization of the section 736 payments under section 469. Therefore, the Treasury Department and the IRS do not believe that special section 469 rules are necessary solely for purposes of section 1411.

3. *Treatment of Certain Capital Loss Carryforwards*

In general, under chapter 1, capital losses that exceed capital gains are allowed as a deduction against ordinary income only to the extent allowed by section 1211(b). In the case of capital losses in excess of the amounts allowed by section 1211(b), section 1212(b)(1) treats these losses as incurred in the following year. Section 1.1411-4(d) adopts these principles when computing net gain under section 1411(c)(1)(A)(iii). Therefore, capital losses incurred in a year prior to the effective date of section 1411 may be taken into account in the computation of section 1411(c)(1)(A)(iii) net gain by reason of the mechanics of section 1212(b)(1). However, certain capital losses may not be taken into account in determining net investment income within the meaning of section 1411(c)(1)(A)(iii) or by reason of the exception in section 1411(c)(4)(B) (generally, an "excluded capital loss"). In the case of section 1411(c)(1)(A)(iii), § 1.1411-4(d)(4)(i) provides that capital losses attributable to the disposition of property used in a trade or business not described in section 1411(c)(2) and § 1.1411-5 are excluded from the computation of net gain. In the case of section 1411(c)(4)(B), some or all of a capital loss resulting from the disposition of certain partnerships or S corporations is excluded from the determination of net gain. Although these capital losses are excluded from the calculation of net gain in the year of recognition by reason of § 1.1411-4(d)(4), such losses may not be fully offset by capital gains for chapter 1 purposes in the same year. In that case, some (or all) of the capital loss carryforward will constitute excluded capital losses in the subsequent year(s) by reason of the mechanics of section 1212(b)(1). Several commentators identified this issue and requested that the Treasury Department and the IRS provide guidance on the identification, tracking, and use of embedded, excluded capital losses within a capital loss carryforward.

In response to these comments, proposed § 1.1411-4(d)(4)(iii) creates an annual adjustment to capital loss carryforwards to prevent capital losses excluded from the net investment income calculation in the year of recognition from becoming deductible losses in future years. The annual adjustment in § 1.1411-4(d)(4)(iii) provides a method of identification and an ordering rule that eliminate the need for taxpayers to maintain a separate set of books and records for this item to comply with section 1411. However, the rule requires that taxpayers perform the calculation annually, regardless of whether they have a section 1411 tax liability in a particular year, to maintain the integrity of the rule's carryforward adjustment amounts for a subsequent year in which they are subject to liability under section 1411.

The rule provides that, for purposes of computing net gain in § 1.1411-4(d) and any properly allocable deduction for excess losses in § 1.1411-4(f)(4) (if any), the taxpayer's capital loss carryforward from the previous year is reduced by the lesser of: (A) the amount of capital loss taken into account in the current year by reason of section 1212(b)(1), or (B) the amount of net capital loss excluded from net investment income in the immediately preceding year. For purposes of (B), the amount of net capital loss excluded from net investment income in the previous year includes amounts excluded by reason of § 1.1411-4(d)(4) (amount of capital losses recognized in the preceding year) plus the amount of the previous year's adjustment required by this rule. Section 1.1411-4(d)(4)(iii) provides a multi-year example to illustrate the application of the rule.

The mechanics of the capital loss adjustment accomplishes several objectives. First, the rule causes all capital losses incurred prior to 2013 to be allowable losses for the computation of net gain under § 1.1411-4(d) and any properly allocable deduction for excess losses in § 1.1411-4(f)(4) (if any). This result is accomplished by the application of part (B) of the rule described in the preceding paragraph. Since the adjustment is based on the lesser of (A) or (B), the amount of excluded capital losses in the year immediately before the effective date of section 1411 is zero, so the loss adjustment in the year following the effective date of section 1411 will also be zero. Second, the rule only requires an adjustment when a taxpayer has excluded losses embedded within a capital loss carryforward.

Therefore, taxpayers with no excluded capital losses do not have to make any adjustment. Third, the rule also provides a mechanism for ordering the use of capital losses to offset gains. The rule causes excluded capital gains recognized in the current year to be offset by excluded capital losses that are embedded in the capital loss carryforward from the previous year. This matching is accomplished by the use of the term "net capital loss" in § 1.1411-4(d)(4)(iii)(B). If the excluded gain exceeds the amount of excluded capital loss included in the carryforward amount and any excluded capital loss amounts recognized in the current year, the amount of adjustment will be zero in the subsequent year because there was no "net capital loss" in the preceding year. In this situation, no adjustment is required because the previous year's excluded gains were fully absorbed by the excluded losses. Finally, the rule allows taxpayers to use capital non-excluded losses for purposes of the excess loss deduction in § 1.1411-4(f)(4) before subjecting excluded losses to the limitation.

4. *Treatment of Income and Deductions from Common Trust Funds (CTFs)*

Section 584(c) provides that each participant in a CTF shall include in its taxable income, whether or not distributed and whether or not distributable, its proportionate share of: (1) short-term capital gain or loss, (2) long-term capital gain or loss, and (3) ordinary taxable income or the ordinary net loss of the CTF. The flush language of section 584(c) further provides that "the proportionate share of each participant in the amount of dividends received by the CTF and to which section 1(h)(11) applies shall be considered for purposes of such paragraph as having been received by such participant."

Section 584(d) provides, in relevant part, that "[t]he taxable income of a common trust fund shall be computed in the same manner and on the same basis as in the case of an individual, except . . . after excluding all items of gain and loss from sales or exchanges of capital assets, there shall be computed (A) an ordinary taxable income which shall consist of the excess of the gross income over deductions; or (B) an ordinary net loss which shall consist of the excess of the deductions over the gross income."

The Treasury Department and the IRS have become aware that taxpayers may be considering the use of CTFs to recharacterize income items that otherwise would be includable in net investment income under section 1411. Because section 584(c)(3) simply requires the participant to include in its income its share of "net ordinary income or loss," taxpayers may attempt to claim that section 584(c)(3) ordinary income or loss inclusions are not explicitly section 1411(c)(1)(A)(i) net investment income, and therefore escape taxation under section 1411.

Using a CTF to recharacterize the underlying character of CTF income for section 1411 purposes is closely analogous to the past use of CTFs to cleanse unrelated business taxable income (UBTI) for tax-exempt participants. In 1984, the Treasury Department and the IRS promulgated § 1.584-2(c)(3), which created a special look-through rule to prevent taxpayers from using CTFs to recharacterize UBTI. Section 1.584-2(c)(3) provides, in relevant part, that "any amount of income or loss of the common trust fund which is included in the computation of a participant's taxable income for the taxable year shall be treated as income or loss from an unrelated trade or business to the extent that such amount would have been income or loss from an unrelated trade or business if such participant had made directly the investments of the common trust fund."

Similarly, proposed § 1.1411-4(e)(3) includes a rule that provides income or loss from a CTF is net investment income or deduction to the extent that such amount would have been net investment income or deduction if the participant had made directly the investments of the CTF.

5. *Treatment of Income and Deductions Related to Residual Interests in REMICs*

The 2012 Proposed Regulations did not explicitly address income and deductions related to residual interests in REMICs. A REMIC residual interest represents an equity-like interest in a REMIC. A REMIC is not treated as carrying on a trade or business for purposes of section 162, and a REMIC's taxable income or net loss generally is derived from dispositions of qualified mortgages or permitted investments, interest income from the mortgages, and interest expense from the regular interests (treated as debt) issued by the REMIC. Section 860C(a)(1) generally requires the holder of a REMIC residual interest to take into account the daily portion of the REMIC's taxable income or net loss. One commentator suggested that the regulations expressly include income from a REMIC residual interest in determining net investment income. The Treasury Department and the IRS agree with this comment because, if a taxpayer directly held the underlying assets of the REMIC, the items of income, gain, loss, and deductions attributable to those assets would be taken into account in computing net investment income. Therefore, the proposed regulations provide that a holder of a residual interest in a REMIC takes into account the daily portion of taxable income (or net loss) under section 860C in determining net investment income.

6. *Treatment of Income and Deductions from Certain Notional Principal Contracts (NPCs)*

Under the 2012 Proposed Regulations (and the 2013 Final Regulations), gain on the disposition of an NPC is included in net investment income, and any other gross income from an NPC (including net income attributable to periodic payments on an NPC) is included in net investment income if it is derived from a trade or business described in § 1.1411-5. Several commentators on the 2012 Proposed Regulations suggested that the proper treatment of periodic payments on an NPC should not turn solely upon whether the NPC was entered into as part of a trading business and recommended that NPC periodic payments should be included in net investment income. One commentator indicated that the omission of NPC periodic income seems unusual and inconsistent with the portions of the 2012 Proposed Regulations (and 2013 Final Regulations) that provide for the inclusion in net investment income of substitute interest and substitute dividends.

After consideration of the comments, the Treasury Department and the IRS agree that periodic payments on an NPC should be included in net investment income even if the net income from such payments is not derived in a trade or business described in § 1.1411-5. As a result, the proposed regulations provide that net income (or net deduction) attributable to periodic and nonperiodic payments on an NPC under § 1.446-3(d) is taken into account in determining net investment income. However, the proposed regulations only apply to the net income (or net deduction) on an NPC described in § 1.446-3(c)(1) that is referenced to property (including an index) that produces (or would produce if the property were to produce income) interest, dividends, royalties, or rents if the property were held directly by the taxpayer. The proposed regulations would not affect the treatment of net income attributable to periodic and nonperiodic payments on any NPC derived in a trade or business described in § 1.1411-5, that is net investment income under section 1411(c)(1)(A)(ii).

7. *Charitable Remainder Trusts (CRTs) with Income from Controlled Foreign Corporations (CFCs) or Passive Foreign Investment Companies (PFICs)*

Section 1.1411-3(d)(2) of the 2013 Final Regulations provides rules on the categorization and distribution of net investment income from a CRT based on the existing section 664 category and class system. In general, § 1.1411-3(d)(2) provides that, if a CRT has both excluded income and accumulated net investment income (ANII) in an income category, such excluded income and ANII constitute separate classes of income for purposes of § 1.664-1(d)(1)(i)(b). Section 1.1411-10 of the 2013 Final Regulations provides rules for calculating net investment income when a taxpayer owns a direct or indirect interest in a CFC or PFIC.

The 2013 Final Regulations reserve paragraph § 1.1411-3(d)(2)(ii) for special rules that the Treasury Department and the IRS believe are necessary to apply the section 664 category and class system contained in § 1.664-1(d), and adopted by § 1.1411-3(d)(2), to CRTs that own interests in certain CFCs or PFICs. The special rules generally apply to taxpayers that: (i) own CFCs or qualified electing funds (QEFs) with respect to which an election under § 1.1411-10(g) is not in place; or (ii) are subject to the rules of section 1291 with respect to a PFIC. These proposed regulations provide those special rules and are proposed to apply to taxable years beginning after December 31, 2013. There are no special rules necessary for a United States person that has elected to mark to market its PFIC stock under section 1296. See § 1.1411-10(c)(2)(ii).

A. *CFCs and QEFs*

For purposes of chapter 1, a United States shareholder (as defined in section 951(b)) of a CFC is required to include certain amounts in income currently under section 951(a) (section 951 inclusions). Similarly, a U.S. person that owns shares of a PFIC also is required to include amounts in income currently under section 1293(a) (section 1293 inclusions) if the person makes a QEF election under section 1295 with respect to the PFIC.

For purposes of chapter 1, a CRT's section 951 inclusions and section 1293 inclusions are included in the appropriate section 664 category and class for the year in which those amounts are includable in the CRT's income for purposes of chapter 1. The application of the ordering rules in § 1.664-1(d)(1) determines the tax character of the annuity or unitrust distributions to the CRT's income beneficiary. These ordering rules are equally applicable for purposes of section 1411 under the 2013 Final Regulations. In the case of a CRT that directly or indirectly owns an interest in a CFC or QEF, some portion of the annual distribution(s) may consist of current or previous years' section 951 inclusions or section 1293 inclusions.

As discussed in the preamble to the 2013 Final Regulations, § 1.1411-10 generally provides that distributions of previously taxed earnings and profits attributable to section 951 inclusions and section 1293 inclusions that are not treated as dividends for purposes of chapter 1 under section 959(d) or section 1293(c) are dividends for purposes of section 1411, absent an election under § 1.1411-10(g). Without that election, taxpayers generally do not include section 951 inclusions or section 1293 inclusions in net investment income for purposes of section 1411. As a result, the timing of income derived from an investment in a CFC or QEF may be different for purposes of chapter 1 and section 1411. Thus, § 1.1411-10(e) provides adjustments to a taxpayer's modified adjusted gross income (MAGI), or to the adjusted gross income (AGI) of an estate or trust, when the taxpayer owns a CFC or QEF with respect to which an election is not in place to coordinate the rules in § 1.1411-10 with calculation of the section 1411 tax, the applicability of which is based, in part, on MAGI or AGI.

B. *Section 1291 funds*

The 2013 Final Regulations also provide special rules that apply to a United States shareholder of a PFIC who is subject to the tax and interest charge applicable to excess distributions under section 1291. Accordingly, § 1.1411-10(e) also provides adjustments to a taxpayer's MAGI, or to the AGI of an estate or trust, when the taxpayer owns a PFIC and is subject to these special rules. In particular, MAGI (or AGI for an estate or trust) is increased by: (i) the amount of any excess distribution to the extent the distribution is a dividend under section 316(a) and is not otherwise included in income for purposes of chapter 1 under section 1291(a)(1)(B), and (ii) any gain treated as an excess distribution under section 1291(a)(2) to the extent not otherwise included in income for purposes of chapter 1 under section 1291(a)(1)(B).

C. *Rules in proposed regulation § 1.1411-3(d)(2)(ii)*

The rules in proposed § 1.1411-3(d)(2)(ii) coordinate the rules of § 1.1411-10 with the section 664 category and class system. These proposed regulations contain three rules that generally apply when a CRT directly or indirectly owns an interest in a CFC or QEF and a § 1.1411-10(g) election is not in effect with respect to the CFC or QEF. First, § 1.1411-3(d)(2)(ii)(A) provides that section 951 inclusions and section 1293 inclusions that are included in gross income for purposes of chapter 1 for a calendar year and in one or more categories described in § 1.664-1(d)(1) are considered excluded income (within the meaning of § 1.1411-1(d)) in the year the amount is included in income for purposes of chapter 1.

Second, proposed § 1.1411-3(d)(2)(ii)(B) provides that, when a CRT receives a distribution of previously taxed earnings and profits that is not treated as a dividend for purposes of chapter 1 under sections 953(d) and 1293(c) but that is taken into account as net investment income for purposes of section 1411 (referred to as an *NII Inclusion Amount*), the CRT must allocate such amounts among the categories described in section 664(b)(1)-(3). For this purpose, the NII Inclusion Amount includes net investment income described in § 1.1411-10(c)(1)(i) (certain distributions from a CFC or QEF), § 1.1411-10(c)(1)(ii) (certain distributions from a section 1291 fund), § 1.1411-10(c)(2)(i) (gain derived from the disposition of a section 1291 fund), and § 1.1411-10(c)(4) (distributions from an estate or trust attributable to income or gain derived from a CFC or QEF with respect to which an election under § 1.1411-10(g) is not in effect). Specifically, proposed § 1.1411-3(d)(2)(ii)(B) provides that, to the extent the CRT has amounts of excluded income in the Ordinary Income Category and the Capital Gain Category under § 1.664-1(d)(1), the NII Inclusion Amount is allocated to the CRT's classes of excluded income in the Ordinary Income Category, and then to the classes of excluded income in the Capital Gain Category, in turn, until exhaustion of each such class, beginning with the class of excluded income within a category with the highest Federal income tax rate. Any remaining NII Inclusion Amount not so allocated to classes within the Ordinary Income and Capital Gain Categories shall be placed in the category described in section 664(b)(3) (the Other Income Category). To the extent the CRT distributes amounts from this Other Income Category, that distribution shall constitute a distribution described in § 1.1411-10(c)(4) and thus § 1.1411-10(e)(1) causes the beneficiary to increase its MAGI (or AGI for an estate or trust) by the same amount.

The third rule in proposed § 1.1411-3(d)(2)(ii) addresses the differential in gain or loss associated with tax basis disparities between chapter 1 and section 1411 that are caused by the recognition of income under chapter 1 and of the corresponding net investment income in different taxable years. See § 1.1411-10(d) for special basis calculation rules for CFCs, QEFs, and partnerships and S corporations that own interests in CFCs or QEFs. The proposed rules for the allocation of such gain or loss within the section 664 categories and classes generally are consistent with the allocation rules for NII Inclusions Amounts, except that the Capital Gain Category is the first category to which the gain or loss is to be allocated, and then the Ordinary Income Category. The order of the categories is changed for gains and losses to more closely match the adjustments to the income that produced the net investment income, and to minimize the need for adjustments to MAGI or AGI.

Proposed § 1.1411-3(d)(2)(ii)(C)(*1*) provides rules similar to proposed § 1.1411-3(d)(2)(ii)(B) for gains that are higher for section 1411 purposes than they are for chapter 1 purposes. The difference between the rule for gains in proposed §§ 1.1411-3(d)(2)(ii)(C)(*1*) and 1.1411-3(d)(2)(ii)(B) is that proposed § 1.1411-3(d)(2)(ii)(C)(*1*) requires this additional gain to be allocated within the Capital Gain Category before any allocation within the Ordinary Income Category. The Treasury Department and the IRS believe this difference more accurately reflects the nature of the net investment income within the section 664 category and class system because this NII Inclusion Amount is attributable to a transaction that generated capital gain or loss (rather than ordinary income inclusions and dividends attributable to proposed § 1.1411-3(d)(2)(ii)(B) items).

Proposed § 1.1411-3(d)(2)(ii)(C)(2) provides rules similar to proposed § 1.1411-3(d)(2)(ii)(C)(*1*) for losses (and gains that are lower for section 1411 purposes than they are for chapter 1), but with a different ordering rule. In these cases, the tax basis is higher for section 1411 (generating a smaller gain or larger loss for 1411 purposes). However, unlike dividends and gains addressed in proposed §§ 1.1411-3(d)(2)(ii)(B) and 1.1411-3(d)(2)(ii)(C)(*1*), respectively, which can require an increase in MAGI (or AGI for an estate or trust), losses are accompanied by a reduction in MAGI (or AGI for an estate or trust) under § 1.1411-10(e). Therefore, proposed § 1.1411-3(d)(2)(ii)(C)(2) generally follows the ordering rule for gains with one exception. The loss ordering rule in proposed § 1.1411-3(d)(2)(ii)(C)(2) begins with allocating the decrease to the Other Income Category that was created or increased in the current or previous year, presumably due to an allocation under § 1.1411-3(d)(2)(ii)(B). The purpose of the different ordering rule is to eliminate the ANII within Other Income Category first in an effort to reduce the incidence of required MAGI (or AGI for an estate or trust) adjustments by the beneficiary. Once this income is eliminated, the CRT or beneficiary will not have to separately account for a MAGI (or AGI for an estate or trust) increase because the timing differences caused by § 1.1411-10 may have been corrected within the 664 class and category system before such income is distributed to the beneficiary.

8. *Simplified Method for Charitable Remainder Trusts*

The 2012 Proposed Regulations provided a method for the CRT to track net investment income received after December 31, 2012, and later distributed to the beneficiary. Section 1.1411-3(c)(2)(i) of the 2012 Proposed Regulations provided that distributions from a CRT to a beneficiary for a taxable year consist of net investment income in an amount equal to the lesser of the total amount of the distributions for that year, or the current and accumulated net investment income of the CRT.

As discussed in part 4.C of the preamble to the 2013 Final Regulations, multiple commentators asked that the final regulations follow the existing rules under section 664 that create subclasses in each category of income as the tax rates on certain types of income are changed from time to time. However, some of the commentators suggested that the final regulations allow the trustee to elect between the method described in the 2012 Proposed Regulations and the existing rules under section 664.

These proposed regulations provide CRTs with a choice of methods. Section 1.1411-3(d)(2) of the 2013 Final Regulations, along with the proposed additions in these proposed regulations, provide guidance on the application of the section 664 method of tracking net investment income. Proposed § 1.1411-3(d)(3) allows the CRT to elect to use the simplified method included in the 2012 Proposed Regulations, with one modification. Proposed § 1.1411-3(d)(3)(ii) provides that a CRT that elects to use the simplified method is not limited by the general excess deduction rule in § 1.1411-4(f)(1)(ii). Section 1.1411-4(f)(1)(ii) provides that section 1411(c)(1)(B) deductions in excess of gross income and net gain described in section 1411(c)(1)(A) are not taken into account in determining net investment income in any other taxable year, except as allowed under chapter 1. In the case of CRTs, for chapter 1 purposes, the section 664(d) regulations allow for losses within each income class to be carried forward to offset income earned by the CRT within the same class in a future year. Therefore, this provision of the simplified method retains the chapter 1 principle that a CRT's losses are carried forward and offset income in future years. For example, if a CRT has a longterm capital loss of $10,000 in year 1 and a $11,000 long-term capital gain in year 2, the section 664(d) regulations provide that the CRT will have $1,000 of long-term gain available for distribution in year 2. Proposed § 1.1411-3(d)(3)(ii) is intended to provide the same result such that the CRT would have $1,000 of accumulated net investment income available for distribution in year 2.

In the case of a CRT established after December 31, 2012, the CRT's election must be made on its income tax return for the taxable year in which the CRT is established. In the case of a CRT established before January 1, 2013, the CRT's election must be made on its income tax return for its first taxable year beginning on or after January 1, 2013. Additionally, the CRT may make the election on an amended return for that year only if neither the taxable year for which the election is made, nor any taxable year that is affected by the election, for both the CRT and its beneficiaries, is closed by the period of limitations on assessments under section 6501. Once made, the election is irrevocable.

If, after consideration of all comments received in response to these proposed regulations, it appears that there is no significant interest among taxpayers in having the option of using the simplified method, the Treasury Department and the IRS may omit this election from the regulations when finalized.

9. *Calculation of Gain or Loss Attributable to the Disposition of Certain Interests in Partnerships and S Corporations*

Section 1411(c)(4)(A) provides that, in the case of a disposition of an interest in a partnership or of stock in an S corporation (either, a "*Passthrough Entity*"), gain from the disposition shall be taken into account under section 1411(c)(1)(A)(iii) only to the extent of the net gain which would be taken into account by the transferor if the Passthrough Entity sold all of its property for fair market value immediately before the disposition of the interest. Section 1411(c)(4)(B) provides a similar rule for losses from dispositions.

The 2012 Proposed Regulations required that a transferor of a partnership interest or S corporation stock first compute its gain (or loss) from the disposition of the interest in the Passthrough Entity to which section 1411(c)(4) may apply, and then reduce that gain (or loss) by the amount of non-passive gain (or loss) that would have been allocated to the transferor upon a hypothetical sale of all of the Passthrough Entity's assets for fair market value immediately before the transfer. The Treasury Department and the IRS received several comments questioning this approach based on the commentators' reading of section 1411(c)(4) to include gain/loss from the disposition of a partnership interest or S corporation stock *only to the extent of* the transferor's share of gain/loss from the Passthrough Entity's passive assets.

The 2013 Final Regulations do not provide rules regarding the calculation of net gain from the disposition of an interest in a Passthrough Entity to which section 1411(c)(4) may apply. After considering the comments received, the Treasury Department and the IRS have withdrawn the 2012 Proposed Regulations implementing section 1411(c)(4) and are issuing this notice of proposed rulemaking to propose revised rules for the implementation of section 1411(c)(4) adopting the commentators' suggestion. Accordingly, the 2013 Final Regulations reserve on this issue.

Proposed § 1.1411-7(b) provides a calculation to determine how much of the gain or loss that is recognized for chapter 1 purposes is attributable to property owned, directly or indirectly, by the Passthrough Entity that, if sold, would give rise to net gain within the meaning of section 1411(c)(1)(A)(iii) ("*Section 1411 Property*"). Section 1411 Property is any property owned by, or held through, the Passthrough Entity that, if sold, would result in net gain or loss allocable to the partner or shareholder that is includable in determining the partner or shareholder's net investment income under § 1.1411-4(a)(1)(iii). This definition recognizes that the items of property inside the Passthrough Entity that constitute Section 1411 Property might vary among transferors because a transferor may or may not be "passive" with respect to the property.

Proposed § 1.1411-7(c) provides an optional simplified reporting method that qualified transferors may use in lieu of the calculation described in proposed § 1.1411-7(b). Proposed § 1.1411-7(d) contains additional rules that apply when a transferor disposes of its interest in the Passthrough Entity in a deferred recognition transaction to which section 1411 applies. Proposed § 1.1411-7(f) provides rules for adjusting the amount of gain or loss computed under this paragraph for transferors subject to basis adjustments required by § 1.1411-10(d). Proposed § 1.1411-7(g) provides rules for information disclosures by a Passthrough Entity to transferors and for information reporting by individuals, trusts, and estates.

A. *Applicability of section 1411(c)(4)*

In the case of an individual, trust, or estate, the proposed regulations provide that section 1411(c)(4) applies to "*Section 1411(c)(4) Dispositions.*" A Section 1411(c)(4) Disposition is the disposition of an interest in a Passthrough Entity by an individual, estate, or trust if: (i) the Passthrough Entity is engaged in one or more trades or businesses, or owns an interest (directly or indirectly) in another Passthrough Entity that is engaged in one or more trades or businesses, other than the business of trading in financial instruments or commodities (within the meaning of § 1.1411-5(a)(2)); and (ii) one or more of the trades or businesses of the Passthrough Entity is not a passive activity (within the meaning of § 1.1411-5(a)(1)) of the transferor. Thus, if the transferor materially participates in one or more of the Passthrough Entity's trades or businesses (other than a trade or business of trading in financial instruments or commodities), then the transferor must use section 1411(c)(4) to calculate how much of the chapter 1 gain or loss from the disposition to include under section 1411(c)(1)(A)(iii). Section 1411(c)(4) only applies to dispositions of equity interests in partnerships and stock in S corporations, and does not apply to gain or loss recognized on, for example, indebtedness owed to the taxpayer by a partnership or S corporation.

Proposed § 1.1411-7(a)(3) also addresses dispositions by Passthrough Entities of interests in lower-tier Passthrough Entities (a "*Subsidiary Passthrough Entity*"). Proposed § 1.1411-7(a)(3)(ii) provides a "look through rule" that treats a partner or shareholder as owning a proportionate share of any Subsidiary Passthrough Entity, as if the partner or shareholder owned the interest directly. Thus, each partner of the uppertier Passthrough Entity must determine whether the disposition of the Subsidiary Passthrough Entity is a Section 1411(c)(4) Disposition based on whether the disposition would qualify as a Section 1411(c)(4) Disposition if that owner owned its interest in the Subsidiary Passthrough Entity directly.

The Treasury Department and the IRS anticipate that taxpayers who dispose of an interest in a partial recognition transaction or partial disposition transaction will apply the principles of this section by including a pro rata amount of gain or loss from the Passthrough Entity's Section 1411 Property. In addition, the Treasury Department and the IRS believe that the application of section 1411(c)(4) to gain or loss on distributions from a Passthrough Entity is adequately addressed in section 469, which is incorporated into section 1411(c)(4) through the general definition of passive activity contained in section 1411(c)(2)(A). Thus, the proposed regulations do not include special rules on partial recognition, partial disposition, and distribution transactions. However, the Treasury Department and the IRS request comments on whether additional rules on these topics are required.

B. *Definitions and special rules*

Proposed § 1.1411-7(a)(2) contains certain definitions and special rules that are unique to determining gain or loss under section 1411(c)(4) and apply only for purposes of proposed § 1.1411-7.

i. Definitions

Proposed § 1.1411-7 refers to partnerships or S corporations collectively as "Passthrough Entities" and the disposition of an interest in one of these entities is referred to as a "Section 1411(c)(4) Disposition." The purpose of section 1411(c)(4) is to allow gain attributable to non-passive activities to be excluded from the calculation of section 1411 tax upon the disposition of an interest in a Passthrough Entity. To accomplish this, section 1411(c)(4)(A) provides that gain from the disposition of an interest in a Passthrough Entity shall be taken into account in computing net investment income only to the extent of the amount of gain the transferor would have included under section 1411(c)(1)(A)(iii) if the Passthrough Entity sold all of its assets immediately before the Section 1411(c)(4) Disposition. The proposed regulations refer to the property that would generate gain for inclusion in section 1411(c)(1)(A)(iii) as "Section 1411 Property."

ii. Rules for Certain Liquidations

Proposed § 1.1411-7(a)(4)(i) provides that if a fully taxable disposition of the Passthrough Entity's assets is followed by the liquidation of the Passthrough Entity as part of a single plan, then the disposition will be treated as an asset sale for purposes of section 1411. Thus, no additional gain or loss is included in net investment income under § 1.1411-4(a)(1)(iii) on the subsequent liquidation of the Passthrough Entity by any transferor provided that the transferor would have satisfied proposed § 1.1411-7(a)(3) prior to the sale. The proposed regulations also state that, when an S corporation makes a section 336(e) or section 338(h)(10) election on the sale of its stock, the transaction will be treated under section 1411 as a fully taxable asset sale by the Passthrough Entity followed by a liquidation of the entity. Thus, no additional gain or loss is included in net investment income on the subsequent liquidation of the S corporation stock, provided a section 336(e) or section 338(h)(10) election is in effect.

iii. Rules for S Corporation Shareholders

Proposed § 1.1411-7(a)(4) provides two special rules for S corporation shareholders. First, proposed § 1.1411-7(a)(4)(ii) provides that the Passthrough Entity will be considered an S corporation for purposes of section 1411 and proposed § 1.1411-7 even though § 1.1362-3(a) treats the day of the transfer as the first date of the Passthrough Entity's C corporation short year (as defined therein). Second, proposed § 1.1411-7(a)(4)(iii) provides that the calculation under proposed § 1.1411-7(b) does not take into account any adjustment resulting from the hypothetical imposition of tax under section 1374 as a result of the proposed § 1.1411-7(b) deemed sale. This provision was also included in the 2012 Proposed Regulations. See also part 9.H of this preamble for a discussion of the application of section 1411(c)(4) to Qualified Subchapter S Trusts.

C. *Calculation of gain or loss includable in net investment income*

i. Primary Method - Proposed § 1.1411-7(b)

Proposed § 1.1411-7(b) provides the calculation for determining the amount of the transferor's gain or loss under section 1411(c)(1)(A)(iii) from the disposition of an interest in a Passthrough Entity. For dispositions resulting in chapter 1 gain, the transferor's gain equals the lesser of: (i) the amount of gain the transferor recognizes for chapter 1 purposes, or (ii) the transferor's allocable share of net gain from a deemed sale of the Passthrough Entity's Section 1411 Property (in other words, property which, if sold, would give rise to gain or loss that is includable in determining the transferor's net investment income under § 1.1411-4(a)(1)(iii)). The proposed regulations contain a similar rule when a transferor recognizes a loss for chapter 1 purposes.

The 2012 Proposed Regulations required that a transferor of an interest in a Passthrough Entity in which the transferor materially participated value each asset held by the Passthrough Entity to determine the total amount of gain or loss to include under section 1411(c)(4). Commentators indicated that this valuation requirement imposed undue administrative burdens on the transferor. The Treasury Department and the IRS acknowledge that for transferors of certain active interests in Passthrough Entities this property-by-property valuation requirement could be burdensome. Accordingly, these proposed regulations instead direct the transferor to rely on the valuation requirements under § 1.469-2T(e)(3), which the materially participating transferor should already be applying for purposes of chapter 1. These valuation requirements allow the transferor to compute gain or loss activity by activity.

Section 1.469-2T(e)(3) addresses dispositions of partnership interests and S corporation stock in the context of the passive activity loss rules for purposes of chapter 1. Section 1.469-2T(e)(3) provides guidance on allocating disposition gains or losses among the activities of the entity. These rules require the taxpayer to determine the overall gain or loss from each activity (regardless of whether or not the taxpayer materially participates in the activity). For this purpose, § 1.469-2T(e)(3)(ii)(B)(*1*)(*i*) to compute for each activity "the amount of net gain . . . that would have been allocated to the holder of such interest with respect thereto if the passthrough entity had sold its entire interest in such activity for its fair market value on the applicable valuation date." Section 1.469-2T(e)(3)(ii)(B)(*2*)(*i*) contains a corollary rule for dispositions at a loss.

Thus, the proposed regulations require a materially participating transferor to calculate its section 1411(c)(4) gain or loss by reference to the activity gain and loss amounts computed for chapter 1 purposes under §§ 1.469-2T(e)(3)(ii)(B)(*1*)(*i*) and (e)(3)(ii)(B)(*2*)(*i*). Specifically for purposes of section 1411, the transferor's allocable share of gain or loss from a deemed sale of the Passthrough Entity's Section 1411 Property equals the sum of the transferor's allocable shares of net gains and net losses (as determined under the section 469 principles described above) from a hypothetical deemed sale of the activities in which the transferor does not materially participate.

Because section 1411(c)(4) applies to all activities in which a transferor in a Section 1411(c)(4) Disposition does not materially participate (whether held at a gain or a loss), certain provisions under section 469 do not apply for purposes of these rules. Proposed § 1.1411-7(b)(1)(i)(B) and (b)(1)(ii)(B) both apply § 1.469-2T(e)(3) without the recharacterization rule of § 1.469-2T(e)(3)(iii) because the recharacterization rule in § 1.469-2T(e)(3)(iii) is intended to recharacterize gains in certain circumstances as not being from a passive activity, and is thus not relevant in the context of section 1411.

The Treasury Department and the IRS request comments on other possible methods that would implement section 1411(c)(4) for dispositions described in proposed § 1.1411-7(a)(3)(i) (individuals, estates, and trusts) and proposed § 1.1411-7(a)(3)(ii) (tiered Passthrough Entity structures) in a manner consistent with the statute while reducing the administrative burden to the transferor and the Passthrough Entity.

ii. Optional Simplified Reporting Method - Proposed § 1.1411-7(c)

The proposed regulations also allow certain transferors to apply an optional simplified method in proposed § 1.1411-7(c) for calculating gain or loss for purposes of § 1.1411-4(a)(1)(iii). The Treasury Department and the IRS believe a simplified method is warranted when the amount of gain associated with passive assets owned by the Passthrough Entity is likely to be relatively small. To use the optional simplified reporting method, the transferor must meet certain qualifications under proposed § 1.1411-7(c)(2) and not be otherwise excluded under proposed § 1.1411-7(c)(3). Use of this simplified method is not mandatory for qualifying transferors. However, as discussed in part 10.G of this preamble, the Passthrough Entity may not be required under proposed § 1.1411-7(g) to provide (but is not precluded from providing) a transferor who qualifies to use the simplified method with information that the transferor would need to report under the primary method described in proposed § 1.1411-7(g).

The simplified reporting method is intended to limit the information sharing burden on Passthrough Entities by allowing transferors to rely on readily available information to calculate the amount of gain or loss included in net investment income under section 1411(c)(4). For this purpose, the optional simplified method relies on historic distributive share amounts received by the transferor from the Passthrough Entity to extrapolate a percentage of the assets within the Passthrough Entity that are passive with respect to the transferor for purposes of section 1411(c)(4). For example, if ten percent of the income reported on the applicable Schedules K-1 is of a type that would be included in net investment income, then the simplified reporting method presumes that ten percent of the chapter 1 gain on the disposition of the transferor's interest relates to Section 1411 Property of the Passthrough Entity for purposes of section 1411(c)(4).

a. Qualifications

To qualify for the optional simplified reporting method, a transferor in a Section 1411(c)(4) Disposition must meet at least one of two requirements. A transferor satisfies the first requirement if: (i) the sum of the transferor's allocable share during the "*Section 1411 Holding Period*" (as defined in the following paragraph, but generally the year of the disposition and the preceding two years) of separately stated items of income, gain, loss, and deduction (with any separately stated loss and deduction items included as positive numbers) of a type that the transferor would take into account in calculating net investment income is five percent or less of the sum of all separately stated items of income, gain, loss, and deduction (with any separately stated loss and deduction items included as positive numbers) allocated to the transferor during the Section 1411 Holding Period, and (ii) the gain recognized under chapter 1 by the transferor from the disposition of the Passthrough Entity is $5 million or less (including gains from multiple dispositions as part of a plan). A transferor satisfies the second alternative requirement if the gain recognized under chapter 1 by the transferor from the disposition of the Passthrough Entity is $250,000 or less (including gains from multiple dispositions as part of a plan). All dispositions of interests in the Passthrough Entity that occur during the transferor's taxable year will be presumed to be part of a plan.

Section 1411 Holding Period is defined to mean the year of disposition and the transferor's two taxable years preceding the disposition or the time period the transferor held the interest, whichever is less. Where the transferor acquires its interest from another Passthrough Entity in a nonrecognition transaction during the year of disposition or the prior two taxable years, the transferor must include in its Section 1411 Holding Period the period that the previous owner or owners held the interest. Also, where the transferor transferred an interest in a Subsidiary Passthrough Entity to a Passthrough Entity in a nonrecognition transaction during the year of the disposition or the prior two taxable years, the transferor must include in its Section 1411 Holding Period that period that it held the interest in the Subsidiary Passthrough Entity.

b. Nonavailability of optional simplified reporting method

Proposed § 1.1411-7(c)(4) provides certain exceptions for situations in which a transferor is ineligible to use the optional simplified reporting method. These exceptions include situations in which the transferor's historical distributive share amounts are less likely to reflect the gain in the Passthrough Entity's Section 1411 Property on the date of the transferor's disposition. The proposed regulations provide five exceptions for this purpose: (i) transferors that have held the interest for less than 12 months, (ii) certain contributions and distributions during the Section 1411 Holding Period, (iii) Passthrough Entities that have significantly modified the composition of their assets, (iv) S corporations that have recently converted from C corporations, and (v) partial dispositions.

The first exception requires that the transferor has held directly the interest in the Passthrough Entity (or held the interest indirectly in the case of a Subsidiary Passthrough Entity) for the twelve-month period preceding the Section 1411(c)(4) Disposition.

The second exception provides that a transferor is ineligible to use the optional simplified reporting method if the transferor transferred Section 1411 Property (other than cash or cash equivalents) to the Passthrough Entity, or received a distribution of property (other than Section 1411 property) from the Passthrough Entity, as part of a plan that includes the transfer of the interest in the Passthrough Entity. A transferor who contributes, directly or indirectly, Section 1411 Property (other than cash or cash equivalents) within 120 days of the disposition of the interest in the Passthrough Entity is presumed to have made the contribution as part of a plan that includes the transfer of the interest in the Passthrough Entity.

The third exception focuses on changes to the composition of the Passthrough Entity's assets during the Section 1411 Holding Period. Under this exception, the transferor is ineligible to use the optional simplified reporting method if the transferor knows or has reason to know that the percentage of the Passthrough Entity's gross assets that consists of Section 1411 Property (other than cash or cash equivalents) has increased or decreased by 25 percentage points or more during the transferor's Section 1411 Holding Period due to contributions, distributions, or asset acquisitions or dispositions in taxable or nonrecognition transactions.

The fourth exception provides that the optional simplified reporting method is not available if the Passthrough Entity was a C corporation during the Section 1411 Holding Period, and elected under section 1361 during that period to be taxed as an S corporation.

The final exception provides that a transferor partner cannot use the optional simplified reporting method if the transferor transfers only a partial interest that does not represent a proportionate share of all of the partner's economic rights in the partnership. For example, a partner who transfers a preferred interest in a partnership while retaining a common interest in that partnership cannot use the optional simplified reporting method.

iii. Request for Comments

The Treasury Department and the IRS request comments on the proposed section 1411(c)(4) calculation and on the optional simplified reporting method, including recommendations for other simplified means of calculating the gain or loss under section 1411(c)(4). The Treasury Department and the IRS also request comments regarding all aspects of the provisions relating to eligibility for the simplified method, including whether the 25 percentage point threshold for changes in the asset composition of a Passthrough Entity is appropriate.

D. *Tiered passthrough dispositions*

The Treasury Department and the IRS have reserved proposed § 1.1411-7(e) to further consider a simplified method for determining the section 1411(c)(4) gain resulting from the disposition by a Passthrough Entity of an interest in a Subsidiary Passthrough Entity as illustrated by the following example: A holds an interest in UTP, a Passthrough Entity that owns a 50-percent interest in LTP, a Subsidiary Passthrough Entity that is a real estate development company. A is a real estate developer and elected to group his real estate activities under § 1.469-9. When UTP sells its interest in LTP, any gain from the sale of that interest allocable to A through UTP may qualify under proposed § 1.1411-7(a)(2). However, A lacks access to the books of LTP that would allow A to compute its section 1411(c)(4) inclusion under the general rule of proposed § 1.1411-7(b). Additionally, A receives insufficient information from UTP to allow A to determine whether A qualifies to apply the Optional Simplified Reporting Method of proposed § 1.1411-7(c) or to undertake that computation. The Treasury Department and the IRS request comments regarding a simplified method for determining the section 1411(c)(4) gain resulting in such cases, including a detailed technical analysis with examples.

E. *Deferred recognition transactions*

To address the application of proposed § 1.1411-7 to deferred recognition transactions, such as installment sales and certain private annuities, the proposed regulations provide that the calculations under proposed § § 1.1411-7(b)(1), 1.1411-7(c)(2) and 1.1411-7(c)(4) (as applicable) are performed in the year of disposition as though the entire gain was recognized and taken into account in that year. For this purpose, it is assumed that any contingencies potentially affecting consideration to the transferor that are reasonably expected to occur will occur, and in the case of annuities based on the life expectancy of one or more individuals, the present value of the annuity (using existing Federal tax valuation methods) is used to determine the estimated gain. This approach allows the transferor to determine its section 1411 inclusion for each future installment. If under this approach no gain or loss from the disposition would be included in net investment income, then the transferor excludes each payment received from the deferred recognition transaction from net investment income. If under this approach only a portion of the chapter 1 gain on the disposition would be included in net investment income, then the difference between the gain recognized for chapter 1 purposes and the gain recognized for section 1411 purposes is considered an addition to basis, and after taking those basis adjustments into account, gain amounts are included in net investment income under § 1.1411-4(a)(1)(iii) as payments are received in accordance with the existing rules for installment sales or private annuities.

F. *Adjustment to gain or loss due to section 1411 basis differences*

In addition to the calculation of gain or loss included in net investment income by reason of section 1411(c)(4) and proposed § 1.1411-7, proposed § 1.1411-7(f)(2) adjusts the gain or loss to take into account any disparities in the transferor's interest in the Passthrough Entity as a result of § 1.1411-10(d) (relating to certain income from controlled foreign corporations and passive foreign investment companies where no § 1.1411-10(g) election is made). These adjustments apply after applying the calculations set forth in paragraphs (b) through (e) of proposed § 1.1411-7. Because the proposed § 1.1411-7(f)(2) adjustments operate independently of the rules in paragraphs (b) through (e) of proposed § 1.1411-7, they may result in gain for section 1411 purposes that exceeds chapter 1 gain (or a loss that exceeds the chapter 1 loss), or may result in a section 1411 loss when the transferor recognizes a chapter 1 gain (or vice versa).

G. *Information reporting*

Several commentators to the 2012 Proposed Regulations requested revisions to the proposed information reporting requirements. Other commentators expressed concern that the 2012 Proposed Regulations lacked provisions to compel a Passthrough Entity to provide the transferor with information required to comply with the 2012 Proposed Regulations § 1.1411-7. In response, these proposed regulations simplify the information reporting requirements for transferors of interests in Passthrough Entities and impose information reporting requirements on certain Passthrough Entities to ensure that the transferor has sufficient information to comply with the computational requirements of proposed § 1.1411-7.

i. Information Reporting by the Passthrough Entity

To compute the amount of gain or loss under proposed § 1.1411-7(b), the transferors that compute section 1411(c)(4) gain or loss under the primary computation method of proposed § 1.1411-7(b) must generally obtain from the Passthrough Entity the transferor's allocable share of the net gain or loss from the deemed sale of the Passthrough Entity's Section 1411 Property. However, the proposed regulations only require the Passthrough Entity to provide this information to transferors that are ineligible for the optional simplified reporting method in proposed § 1.1411-7(c).

If a transferor qualifies to use the optional simplified reporting method in proposed § 1.1411-7(c), but prefers to determine net gain or loss under proposed § 1.1411-7(b), then the transferor must negotiate with the Passthrough Entity the terms under which the information will be supplied.

ii. Information Reporting by the Seller

Any transferor applying proposed § 1.1411-7, including in reliance on the proposed regulations, must attach a statement to the transferor's income tax return for the year of disposition. That statement must include: (1) the taxpayer's name and taxpayer identification number; (2) the name and taxpayer identification number of the Passthrough Entity in which the interest was transferred; (3) the amount of the transferor's gain or loss on the disposition of the interest under chapter 1; and (4) the amount of adjustment to gain or loss by reason of basis differences for chapter 1 and section 1411 purposes. The transferor must also attach a copy of any information provided by the Passthrough Entity to the transferor relating to the transferor's allocable share of gain or loss from the deemed sale of the Passthrough Entity's Section 1411 Property.

H. *Qualified subchapter S trusts (QSSTs)*

The preamble to the 2012 Proposed Regulations requested comments on whether special coordination rules are necessary to address dispositions of stock in an S corporation held by a QSST. Specifically, the request for comments deals with the application of section 1411(c)(4) to the existing QSST stock disposition mechanics in § 1.1361-1(j)(8).

In general, if an income beneficiary of a trust that meets the QSST requirements under section 1361(d)(3) makes a QSST election, the income beneficiary is treated as the section 678 owner with respect to the S corporation stock held by the trust. Section 1.1361-1(j)(8), however, provides that the trust, rather than the income beneficiary, is treated as the owner of the S corporation stock in determining the income tax consequences of the disposition of the stock by the QSST. Section 1361(d)(1)(C) and the last sentence of § 1.1361-1(j)(8) provide that, solely for purposes of applying sections 465 and 469 to the income beneficiary, a disposition of S corporation stock by a QSST is treated as a disposition by the income beneficiary. However, in this special case, the QSST beneficiary, for chapter 1 purposes, does not have any passive activity gain from the disposition. Therefore, the entire suspended loss (to the extent not allowed by reason of the beneficiary's other passive net income in the disposition year) is a section 469(g)(1) loss, and is considered a loss from a nonpassive activity.

For purposes of section 1411, the inclusion of the operating income or loss of an S corporation in the beneficiary's net investment income is determined in a manner consistent with the treatment of a QSST beneficiary in chapter 1 (as explained in the preceding paragraph), which includes the determination of whether the S corporation is a passive activity of the beneficiary under section 469. However, because gain or loss resulting from the sale of S corporation stock by the QSST will be reported by the QSST and taxed to the trust by reason of § 1.1361-1(j)(8), it is not clear whether the beneficiary's section 469 status with respect to the S corporation is attributed to the trust.

One commentator recommended that the disposition of S corporation stock by a QSST should be treated as a disposition of the stock by the income beneficiary for purposes of determining material participation for purposes of section 1411. In addition, the commentator recommended that the final regulations confirm that the special rule stated in the last sentence of § 1.1361-1(j)(8) applies for purposes of section 1411 as it does for section 469 and 465.

After consideration of the comments, these proposed regulations provide that, in the case of a QSST, the application of section 1411(c)(4) is made at the trust level. This treatment is consistent with the chapter 1 treatment of the QSST by reason of § 1.1361-1(j)(8). However, these proposed regulations do not provide any special computational rules for QSSTs within the context of section 1411(c)(4) for two reasons. First, the treatment of the stock sale as passive or nonpassive income is determined under section 469, which involves the issue of whether there is material participation by the trust. As discussed in part 4.F of the preamble to the 2013 Final Regulations, the Treasury Department and the IRS believe that the issue of material participation by estates and trusts, including QSSTs, is more appropriately addressed under section 469.

Additionally, one commentator noted that the IRS has addressed the treatment of certain asset sales as the functional equivalent of stock sales for purposes of § 1.1361-1(j)(8) in a limited number of private letter rulings. In these cases, the private letter rulings held that gain from the sale of assets, which was followed by a liquidation, would be taxed at the trust level under § 1.1361-1(j)(8) rather than being taxed at the beneficiary level. The commentator recommended that an asset sale followed by a liquidation, within the context of § 1.1361-1(j)(8), should have a similar result under section 1411(c)(4). Similar to the issue of material participation by QSSTs discussed in the preceding paragraph, the Treasury Department and the IRS believe that the issue of whether an asset sale (deemed or actual) is the equivalent of a stock sale for purpose of the QSST rules should be addressed under the § 1.1361-1(j) QSST regulations, rather than in § 1.1411-7. However, the Treasury Department and the IRS believe that proposed § 1.1411-7(a)(4)(i), which provides that asset sales followed by a liquidation is a disposition of S corporation stock for purposes of section 1411(c)(4), address the commentator's QSST issue.

Second, with respect to the section 1411 treatment of the disposition by the beneficiary by reason of section 1361(d)(1)(C) and the last sentence of § 1.1361-1(j)(8), the Treasury Department and the IRS believe that the general administrative principles enumerated in § 1.1411-1(a), when combined with the general treatment of section 469(g) losses within § 1.1411-4, provide an adequate framework for the treatment of QSSTs beneficiaries without the need for a special computational rule within § 1.1411-7.

Proposed Applicability Date

These regulations are proposed to apply for taxable years beginning after December 31, 2013, except that § 1.1411-3(d)(3) is proposed to apply to taxable years beginning after December 31, 2012.

Special Analyses

It has been determined that this notice of proposed rulemaking is not a significant regulatory action as defined in Executive Order 12866, as supplemented by Executive Order 13563. Therefore, a regulatory assessment is not required. It also has been determined that section 553(b) of the Administrative Procedure Act (5 U.S.C. chapter 5) does not apply to the proposed regulations. Pursuant to the Regulatory Flexibility Act (RFA) (5 U.S.C. chapter 6), it is hereby certified that the proposed regulations will not have a significant economic impact on a substantial number of small entities. The applicability of the proposed regulations are limited to individuals, estates, and trusts, that are not small entities as defined by the RFA (5 U.S.C. 601). Accordingly, the RFA does not apply. Therefore, a regulatory flexibility analysis is not required. Pursuant to section 7805(f) of the Code, the proposed regulations have been submitted to the Chief Counsel for Advocacy of the Small Business Administration for comment on its impact on small business.

Comments and Requests for a Public Hearing

Before these proposed regulations are adopted as final regulations, consideration will be given to any comments that are submitted timely to the IRS as prescribed in this preamble under the "Addresses" heading. The Treasury Department and the IRS specifically request comments on all aspects of the proposed rules. All comments will be available at *www.regulations.gov* or upon request. A public hearing will be scheduled if requested in writing by any person that timely submits written comments. If a public hearing is scheduled, notice of the date, time, and place for the public hearing will be published in the **Federal Register**.

Drafting Information

The principal authors of the proposed regulations are David H. Kirk and Adrienne M. Mikolashek, IRS Office of the Associate Chief Counsel (Passthroughs and Special Industries). However, other personnel from the Treasury Department and the IRS participated in their development.

[¶ 49,595] Proposed Amendments of Regulations (REG-134417-13), published in the Federal Register on November 29, 2013.

[Code Sec. 501]

Tax-exempt organizations: Social welfare organizations: Qualifications: Candidate-related political activity.—Amendments of Reg. § 1.501(c)(4)-1, providing guidance to tax-exempt social welfare organizations on political activities related to candidates that will not be considered to promote social welfare, are proposed.

AGENCY: Internal Revenue Service (IRS), Treasury.

ACTION: Notice of proposed rulemaking.

SUMMARY: This document contains proposed regulations that provide guidance to tax-exempt social welfare organizations on political activities related to candidates that will not be considered to promote social welfare. These regulations will affect tax-exempt social welfare organizations and organizations seeking such status. This document requests comments from the public regarding these proposed regulations. This document also requests comments from the public regarding the standard under current regulations that considers a tax-exempt social welfare organization to be operated exclusively for the promotion of social welfare if it is "primarily" engaged in activities that promote the common good and general welfare of the people of the community, including how this standard should be measured and whether this standard should be changed.

DATES: Written or electronic comments and requests for a public hearing must be received by February 27, 2014.

ADDRESSES: Send submissions to: CC:PA:LPD:PR (REG-134417-13), Room 5205, Internal Revenue Service, P.O. Box 7604, Ben Franklin Station, Washington, DC 20044. Submissions may be hand-delivered Monday through Friday between the hours of 8 a.m. and 4 p.m. to CC:PA:LPD:PR (REG-134417-13), Courier's Desk, Internal Revenue Service, 1111 Constitution Avenue NW, Washington, DC, or sent electronically via the Federal eRulemaking Portal at *http://www.regulations.gov* (IRS REG-134417-13).

FOR FURTHER INFORMATION CONTACT: Concerning the proposed regulations, Amy F. Giuliano at (202) 317-5800; concerning submission of comments and requests for a public hearing, Oluwafunmilayo Taylor at (202) 317-6901 (not toll-free numbers).

SUPPLEMENTARY INFORMATION:

Paperwork Reduction Act

The collection of information contained in this notice of proposed rulemaking has been submitted to the Office of Management and Budget for review in accordance with the Paperwork Reduction Act of 1995 (44 U.S.C. 3507(d)). Comments on the collection of information should be sent to the **Office of Management and Budget**, Attn: Desk Officer for the Department of the Treasury, Office of Information and Regulatory Affairs, Washington, DC 20503, with copies to the **Internal Revenue Service**, Attn: IRS Reports Clearance Officer, SE:W:CAR:MP:T:T:SP, Washington, DC 20224. Comments on the collection of information should be received by January 28, 2014.

Comments are specifically requested concerning:

Whether the proposed collection of information is necessary for the proper performance of the functions of the IRS, including whether the information will have practical utility;

The accuracy of the estimated burden associated with the proposed collection of information;

How the quality, utility, and clarity of the information to be collected may be enhanced; and

How the burden of complying with the proposed collection of information may be minimized, including through forms of information technology.

The collection of information in these proposed regulations is in § 1.501(c)(4)-1(a)(2)(iii)(D), which provides a special rule for contributions by an organization described in section 501(c)(4) of the Internal Revenue Code (Code) to an organization described in section 501(c). Generally, a contribution by a section 501(c)(4) organization to a section 501(c) organization that engages in candidate-related political activity will be considered candidate-related political activity by the section 501(c)(4) organization. The special rule in § 1.501(c)(4)-1(a)(2)(iii)(D) provides that a contribution to a section 501(c) organization will not be treated as a contribution to an organization engaged in candidate-related political activity if the contributor organization obtains a written representation from an authorized officer of the recipient organization stating that the recipient organization does not engage in any such activity and the contribution is subject to a written restriction that it not be used for candidate-related political activity. This special provision would not apply if the contributor organization knows or has reason to know that the representation is inaccurate or unreliable. The expected recordkeepers are section 501(c)(4) organizations that choose to contribute to, and to seek a written representation from, a section 501(c) organization.

Estimated number of recordkeepers: 2,000.

Estimated average annual burden hours per recordkeeper: 2 hours.

Estimated total annual recordkeeping burden: 4,000 hours.

A particular section 501(c)(4) organization may require more or less time, depending on the number of contributions for which a representation is sought.

An agency may not conduct or sponsor, and a person is not required to respond to, a collection of information unless it displays a valid control number assigned by the Office of Management and Budget.

Books or records relating to a collection of information must be retained as long as their contents may become material in the administration of any internal revenue law. Generally, tax returns and return information are confidential, as required by section 6103.

Background

Section 501(c)(4) of the Code provides a Federal income tax exemption, in part, for "[c]ivic leagues or organizations not organized for profit but operated exclusively for the promotion of social welfare." This exemption dates back to the enactment of the federal income tax in 1913. See Tariff Act of 1913, 38 Stat. 114 (1913). The statutory provision was largely unchanged until 1996, when section 501(c)(4) was amended to prohibit inurement of an organization's net earnings to private shareholders or individuals.

Prior to 1924, the accompanying Treasury regulations did not elaborate on the meaning of "promotion of social welfare." See Regulations 33 (Rev.), art. 67 (1918). Treasury regulations promulgated in 1924 explained that civic leagues qualifying for exemption under section 231(8) of the Revenue Act of 1924, the predecessor to section 501(c)(4) of the 1986 Code, are "those not organized for profit but operated exclusively for purposes beneficial to the community as a whole," and generally include "organizations engaged in promoting the welfare of mankind, other than organizations comprehended within [section 231(6) of the Revenue Act of 1924, the predecessor to section 501(c)(3) of the 1986 Code]." See Regulations 65, art. 519 (1924). The regulations remained substantially the same until 1959.

The current regulations under section 501(c)(4) were proposed and finalized in 1959. They provide that "[a]n organization is operated exclusively for the promotion of social welfare if it is primarily engaged in promoting in some way the common good and general welfare of the people of the community." Treas. Reg. § 1.501(c)(4)-1(a)(2)(i). An organization "embraced" within section 501(c)(4) is one that is "operated primarily for the purpose of bringing about civic betterments and social improvements." Id. The regulations further provide that "[t]he promotion of social welfare does not include direct or indirect participation or intervention in political campaigns on behalf of or in opposition to any candidate for public office." Treas. Reg. § 1.501(c)(4)-1(a)(2)(ii). This language is similar to language that appears in section 501(c)(3) requiring section 501(c)(3) organizations not to "participate in, or intervene in (including the publishing or distributing of statements), any political campaign on behalf of (or in opposition to) any candidate for public office" ("political campaign intervention"). However, unlike the absolute prohibition that applies to charitable organizations described in section 501(c)(3), an organization that primarily engages in activities that promote social welfare will be considered under the current regulations to be operating exclusively for the promotion of social welfare, and may qualify for taxexempt status under section 501(c)(4), even though it engages in some political campaign intervention.

The section 501(c)(4) regulations have not been amended since 1959, although Congress took steps in the intervening years to address further the relationship of political campaign activities to tax-exempt status. In particular, section 527, which governs the tax treatment of political organizations, was enacted in 1975 and provides generally that amounts received as contributions and other funds raised for political purposes (section 527 exempt function income) are not subject to tax. Section

527(e)(1) defines a "political organization" as "a party, committee, association, fund, or other organization (whether or not incorporated) organized and operated primarily for the purpose of directly or indirectly accepting contributions or making expenditures, or both, for an exempt function." Section 527(f) also imposes a tax on exempt organizations described in section 501(c), including section 501(c)(4) social welfare organizations, that make an expenditure furthering a section 527 exempt function. The tax is imposed on the lesser of the organization's net investment income or section 527 exempt function expenditures. Section 527(e)(2) defines "exempt function" as "the function of influencing or attempting to influence the selection, nomination, election, or appointment of any individual to any federal, state, or local public office or office in a political organization, or the election of Presidential or Vice-Presidential electors" (referred to in this document as "section 527 exempt function").[1]

Unlike the section 501(c)(3) standard of political campaign intervention, and the similar standard currently applied under section 501(c)(4), both of which focus solely on candidates for elective public office, a section 527 exempt function encompasses activities related to a broader range of officials, including those who are appointed or nominated, such as executive branch officials and certain judges. Thus, while there is currently significant overlap in the activities that constitute political campaign intervention under sections 501(c)(3) and 501(c)(4) and those that further a section 527 exempt function, the concepts are not synonymous.

Over the years, the IRS has stated that whether an organization is engaged in political campaign intervention depends upon all of the facts and circumstances of each case. See Rev. Rul. 78-248 (1978-1 CB 154) (illustrating application of the facts and circumstances analysis to voter education activities conducted by section 501(c)(3) organizations); Rev. Rul. 80-282 (1980-2 CB 178) (amplifying Rev. Rul. 78-248 regarding the timing and distribution of voter education materials); Rev. Rul. 86-95 (1986-2 CB 73) (holding a public forum for the purpose of educating and informing the voters, which provides fair and impartial treatment of candidates, and which does not promote or advance one candidate over another, does not constitute political campaign intervention under section 501(c)(3)). More recently, the IRS released Rev. Rul. 2007-41 (2007-1 CB 1421), providing 21 examples illustrating facts and circumstances to be considered in determining whether a section 501(c)(3) organization's activities (including voter education, voter registration, and get-out-the-vote drives; individual activity by organization leaders; candidate appearances; business activities; and Web sites) result in political campaign intervention. The IRS generally applies the same facts and circumstances analysis under section 501(c)(4). See Rev. Rul. 81-95 (1981-1 CB 332) (citing revenue rulings under section 501(c)(3) for examples of what constitutes participation or intervention in political campaigns for purposes of section 501(c)(4)).

Similarly, Rev. Rul. 2004-6 (2004-1 CB 328) provides six examples illustrating facts and circumstances to be considered in determining whether a section 501(c) organization (such as a section 501(c)(4) social welfare organization) that engages in public policy advocacy has expended funds for a section 527 exempt function. The analysis reflected in these revenue rulings for determining whether an organization has engaged in political campaign intervention, or has expended funds for a section 527 exempt function, is fact-intensive.

Recently, increased attention has been focused on potential political campaign intervention by section 501(c)(4) organizations. A recent IRS report relating to IRS review of applications for tax-exempt status states that "[o]ne of the significant challenges with the 501(c)(4) [application] review process has been the lack of a clear and concise definition of 'political campaign intervention.'" Internal Revenue Service, "Charting a Path Forward at the IRS: Initial Assessment and Plan of Action" at 20 (June 24, 2013). In addition, "[t]he distinction between campaign intervention and social welfare activity, and the measurement of the organization's social welfare activities relative to its total activities, have created considerable confusion for both the public and the IRS in making appropriate section 501(c)(4) determinations." *Id.* at 28. The Treasury Department and the IRS recognize that both the public and the IRS would benefit from clearer definitions of these concepts.

Explanation of Provisions

1. *Overview*

The Treasury Department and the IRS recognize that more definitive rules with respect to political activities related to candidates -rather than the existing, fact-intensive analysis - would be helpful in applying the rules regarding qualification for tax-exempt status under section 501(c)(4). Although more definitive rules might fail to capture (or might sweep in) activities that would (or would not) be captured under the IRS' traditional facts and circumstances approach, adopting rules with sharper distinctions in this area would provide greater certainty and reduce the need for detailed factual analysis in determining whether an organization is described in section 501(c)(4). Accordingly, the Treasury Department and the IRS propose to amend Treas. Reg. §1.501(c)(4)-1(a)(2) to identify specific political activities that would be considered candidate-related political activities that do not promote social welfare.

---

[1] In 2000 and 2002, section 527 was amended to require political organizations (with some exceptions) to file a notice with the IRS when first organized and to periodically disclose publicly certain information regarding their expenditures and contributions. See sections 527(i) and 527(j).

To distinguish the proposed rules under section 501(c)(4) from the section 501(c)(3) standard and the similar standard currently applied under section 501(c)(4), the proposed regulations would amend Treas. Reg. § 1.501(c)(4)-1(a)(2)(ii) to delete the current reference to "direct or indirect participation or intervention in political campaigns on behalf of or in opposition to any candidate for public office," which is similar to language in the section 501(c)(3) statute and regulations. Instead the proposed regulations would revise Treas. Reg. § 1.501(c)(4)-1(a)(2)(ii) to state that "[t]he promotion of social welfare does not include direct or indirect candidate-related political activity." As explained in more detail in section 2 of this preamble, the proposed rules draw upon existing definitions of political campaign activity, both in the Code and in federal election law, to define candidate-related political activity that would not be considered to promote social welfare. The proposed rules draw in particular from certain statutory provisions of section 527, which specifically deals with political organizations and taxes section 501(c) organizations, including section 501(c)(4) organizations, on certain types of political campaign activities. Recognizing that it may be beneficial to have a more uniform set of rules relating to political campaign activity for tax-exempt organizations, the Treasury Department and the IRS request comments in subparagraphs a through c of this section of the preamble regarding whether the same or a similar approach should be adopted in addressing political campaign activities of other section 501(c) organizations, as well as whether the regulations under section 527 should be revised to adopt the same or a similar approach in defining section 527 exempt function activity.

a. *Interaction with section 501(c)(3)*

These proposed regulations do not address the definition of political campaign intervention under section 501(c)(3). The Treasury Department and the IRS recognize that, because such intervention is absolutely prohibited under section 501(c)(3), a more nuanced consideration of the totality of facts and circumstances may be appropriate in that context. The Treasury Department and the IRS request comments on the advisability of adopting an approach to defining political campaign intervention under section 501(c)(3) similar to the approach set forth in these regulations, either in lieu of the facts and circumstances approach reflected in Rev. Rul. 2007-41 or in addition to that approach (for example, by creating a clearly defined presumption or safe harbor). The Treasury Department and the IRS also request comments on whether any modifications or exceptions would be needed in the section 501(c)(3) context and, if so, how to ensure that any such modifications or exceptions are clearly defined and administrable. Any such change would be introduced in the form of proposed regulations to allow an additional opportunity for public comment.

b. *Interaction with section 527*

As noted in the "Background" section of this preamble, a section 501(c)(4) organization is subject to tax under section 527(f) if it makes expenditures for a section 527 exempt function. Consistent with section 527, the proposed regulations provide that "candidate-related political activity" for purposes of section 501(c)(4) includes activities relating to selection, nomination, election, or appointment of individuals to serve as public officials, officers in a political organization, or Presidential or Vice Presidential electors. These proposed regulations do not, however, address the definition of "exempt function" activity under section 527 or the application of section 527(f). The Treasury Department and the IRS request comments on the advisability of adopting rules that are the same as or similar to these proposed regulations for purposes of defining section 527 exempt function activity in lieu of the facts and circumstances approach reflected in Rev. Rul. 2004-6. Any such change would be introduced in the form of proposed regulations to allow an additional opportunity for public comment.

c. *Interaction with sections 501(c)(5) and 501(c)(6)*

The proposed regulations define candidate-related political activity for social welfare organizations described in section 501(c)(4). The Treasury Department and the IRS are considering whether to amend the current regulations under sections 501(c)(5) and 501(c)(6) to provide that exempt purposes under those regulations (which include "the betterment of the conditions of those engaged in [labor, agricultural, or horticultural] pursuits" in the case of a section 501(c)(5) organization and promoting a "common business interest" in the case of a section 501(c)(6) organization) do not include candidaterelated political activity as defined in these proposed regulations. The Treasury Department and the IRS request comments on the advisability of adopting this approach in defining activities that do not further exempt purposes under sections 501(c)(5) and 501(c)(6). Any such change would be introduced in the form of proposed regulations to allow an additional opportunity for public comment.

d. *Additional guidance on the meaning of "operated exclusively for the promotion of social welfare"*

The Treasury Department and the IRS have received requests for guidance on the meaning of "primarily" as used in the current regulations under section 501(c)(4). The current regulations provide, in part, that an organization is operated exclusively for the promotion of social welfare within the meaning of section 501(c)(4) if it is "primarily engaged" in promoting in some way the common good and general welfare of the people of the community. Treas. Reg. § 1.501(c)(4)-1(a)(2)(i). As part of the same 1959 Treasury decision promulgating the current section 501(c)(4) regulations, regulations under section 501(c)(3) were adopted containing similar language: "[a]n organization will be regarded as 'operated exclusively' for one or more exempt purposes only if it engages primarily in activities which accomplish one or more of such exempt purposes specified in section 501(c)(3)." Treas. Reg. § 1.501(c)(3)-1(c)(1). Unlike the section 501(c)(4) regulations, however, the section 501(c)(3) regulations also provide that "[a]n organization will not be so regarded if more than an insubstantial part of its activities is not in furtherance of an exempt purpose." *Id.*

Some have questioned the use of the "primarily" standard in the section 501(c)(4) regulations and suggested that this standard should be changed. The Treasury Department and the IRS are considering whether the current section 501(c)(4) regulations should be modified in this regard and, if the "primarily" standard is retained, whether the standard should be defined with more precision or revised to mirror the standard under the section 501(c)(3) regulations. Given the potential impact on organizations currently recognized as described in section 501(c)(4) of any change in the "primarily" standard, the Treasury Department and the IRS wish to receive comments from a broad range of organizations before deciding how to proceed. Accordingly, the Treasury Department and the IRS invite comments from the public on what proportion of an organization's activities must promote social welfare for an organization to qualify under section 501(c)(4) and whether additional limits should be imposed on any or all activities that do not further social welfare. The Treasury Department and the IRS also request comments on how to measure the activities of organizations seeking to qualify as section 501(c)(4) social welfare organizations for these purposes.

2. *Definition of Candidate-Related Political Activity*

These proposed regulations provide guidance on which activities will be considered candidate-related political activity for purposes of the regulations under section 501(c)(4). These proposed regulations would replace the language in the existing final regulation under section 501(c)(4) – "participation or intervention in political campaigns on behalf of or in opposition to any candidate for public office" – with a new term – "candidate-related political activity" – to differentiate the proposed section 501(c)(4) rule from the standard employed under section 501(c)(3) (and currently employed under section 501(c)(4)). The proposed rule is intended to help organizations and the IRS more readily identify activities that constitute candidate-related political activity and, therefore, do not promote social welfare within the meaning of section 501(c)(4). These proposed regulations do not otherwise define the promotion of social welfare under section 501(c)(4). The Treasury Department and the IRS note that the fact that an activity is not candidate-related political activity under these proposed regulations does not mean that the activity promotes social welfare. Whether such an activity promotes social welfare is an independent determination.

In defining candidate-related political activity for purposes of section 501(c)(4), these proposed regulations draw key concepts from the federal election campaign laws, with appropriate modifications reflecting the purpose of these regulations to define which organizations may receive the benefits of section 501(c)(4) tax-exempt status and to promote tax compliance (as opposed to campaign finance regulation). In addition, the concepts drawn from the federal election campaign laws have been modified to reflect that section 501(c)(4) organizations may be involved in activities related to local or state elections (in addition to federal elections), as well as the broader scope of the proposed definition of candidate (which is not limited to candidates for federal elective office).

The proposed regulations provide that candidate-related political activity includes activities that the IRS has traditionally considered to be political campaign activity per se, such as contributions to candidates and communications that expressly advocate for the election or defeat of a candidate. The proposed regulations also would treat as candidate-related political activity certain activities that, because they occur close in time to an election or are election-related, have a greater potential to affect the outcome of an election. Currently, such activities are subject to a facts and circumstances analysis before a determination can be made as to whether the activity furthers social welfare within the meaning of section 501(c)(4). Under the approach in these proposed regulations, such activities instead would be subject to a more definitive rule. In addition, consistent with the goal of providing greater clarity, the proposed regulations would identify certain specific activities as candidate-related political activity. The Treasury Department and the IRS acknowledge that the approach taken in these proposed regulations, while clearer, may be both more restrictive and more permissive than the current approach, but believe the proposed approach is justified by the need to provide greater certainty to section 501(c)(4) organizations regarding their activities and reduce the need for fact-intensive determinations.

The Treasury Department and the IRS note that a particular activity may fit within one or more categories of candidate-related political activity described in subsections b through e of this section 2 of the preamble; the categories are not mutually exclusive. For example, the category of express advocacy communications may overlap with the category of certain communications close in time to an election.

a. *Definition of "candidate"*

These proposed regulations provide that, consistent with the scope of section 527, "candidate" means an individual who identifies himself or is proposed by another for selection, nomination, election, or appointment to any public office or office in a political organization, or to be a Presidential or Vice-Presidential elector, whether or not the individual is ultimately selected, nominated, elected, or appointed. In addition, the proposed regulations clarify that for these purposes the term "candidate" also includes any officeholder who is the subject of a recall election. The Treasury Department and the IRS note that defining "candidate-related political activity" in these proposed regulations to include activities related to candidates for a broader range of offices (such as activities relating to the appointment or confirmation of executive branch officials and judicial nominees) is a change from the historical application in the section 501(c)(4) context of the section 501(c)(3) standard of political campaign intervention, which focuses on candidates for elective public office only. See Treas. Reg. § 1.501(c)(3)-1(c)(3)(iii). These proposed regulations instead would apply a definition that reflects the broader scope of section 527 and that is already applied to a section 501(c)(4) organization engaged in section 527 exempt function activity through section 527(f).

b. *Express advocacy communications*

These proposed regulations provide that candidate-related political activity includes communications that expressly advocate for or against a candidate. These proposed regulations draw from Federal Election Commission rules in defining "expressly advocate," but expand the concept to include communications expressing a view on the selection, nomination, or appointment of individuals, or on the election or defeat of one or more candidates or of candidates of a political party. These proposed regulations make clear that all communications – including written, printed, electronic (including Internet), video, and oral communications – that express a view, whether for or against, on a clearly identified candidate (or on candidates of a political party) would constitute candidate-related political activity. A candidate can be "clearly identified" in a communication by name, photograph, or reference (such as "the incumbent" or a reference to a particular issue or characteristic distinguishing the candidate from others). The proposed regulations also provide that candidate-related political activity includes any express advocacy communication the expenditures for which an organization reports to the Federal Election Commission under the Federal Election Campaign Act as an independent expenditure.

c. *Public communications close in time to an election*

Under current guidance, the timing of a communication about a candidate that is made shortly before an election is a factor tending to indicate a greater risk of political campaign intervention or section 527 exempt function activity. In the interest of greater clarity, these proposed regulations would move away from the facts and circumstances approach that the IRS has traditionally applied in analyzing certain activities conducted close in time to an election. These proposed regulations draw from provisions of federal election campaign laws that treat certain communications that are close in time to an election and that refer to a clearly identified candidate as electioneering communications, but make certain modifications. The proposed regulations expand the types of candidates and communications that are covered to reflect the types of activities an organization might conduct related to local and state, as well as federal, contests, including any election or ballot measure to recall an individual who holds state or local elective public office. In addition, the expansion of the types of communications covered in the proposed regulations reflects the fact that an organization's tax exempt status is determined based on all of its activities, even low cost and volunteer activities, not just its large expenditures.

Under the proposed definition, any public communication that is made within 60 days before a general election or 30 days before a primary election and that clearly identifies a candidate for public office (or, in the case of a general election, refers to a political party represented in that election) would be considered candidate-related political activity. These timeframes are the same as those appearing in the Federal Election Campaign Act definition of electioneering communications. The definition of "election," including what would be treated as a primary or a general election, is consistent with section 527(j) and the federal election campaign laws.

A communication is "public" if it is made using certain mass media (specifically, by broadcast, in a newspaper, or on the Internet), constitutes paid advertising, or reaches or is intended to reach at least 500 people (including mass mailings or telephone banks). The Treasury Department and the IRS intend that content previously posted by an organization on its Web site that clearly identifies a candidate and remains on the Web site during the specified pre-election period would be treated as candidate-related political activity.

The proposed regulations also provide that candidate-related political activity includes any communication the expenditures for which an organization reports to the Federal Election Commission under the Federal Election Campaign Act, including electioneering communications.

The approach taken in the proposed definition of candidate-related political activity would avoid the need to consider potential mitigating or aggravating circumstances in particular cases (such as whether an issue-oriented communication is "neutral" or "biased" with respect to a candidate). Thus, this definition would apply without regard to whether a public communication is intended to influence the election or some other, non-electoral action (such as a vote on pending legislation) and without regard to whether such communication was part of a series of similar communications. Moreover, a public communication made outside the 60-day or 30-day period would not be candidate-related political activity if it does not fall within the ambit of express advocacy communications or another specific provision of the definition. The Treasury Department and the IRS request comments on whether the length of the period should be longer (or shorter) and whether there are particular communications that (regardless of timing) should be excluded from the definition because they can be presumed to neither influence nor constitute an attempt to influence the outcome of an election. Any comments should specifically address how the proposed exclusion is consistent with the goal of providing clear rules that avoid fact-intensive determinations.

The Treasury Department and the IRS also note that this rule regarding public communications close in time to an election would not apply to public communications identifying a candidate for a state or federal appointive office that are made within a specified number of days before a scheduled appointment, confirmation hearing or vote, or other selection event. The Treasury Department and the IRS request comments on whether a similar rule should apply with respect to communications within a specified period of time before such a scheduled appointment, confirmation hearing or vote, or other selection event.

d. *Contributions to a candidate, political organization, or any section 501(c) entity engaged in candidate-related political activity*

The proposed definition of candidate-related political activity would include contributions of money or anything of value to or the solicitation of contributions on behalf of (1) any person if such contribution is recognized under applicable federal, state, or local campaign finance law as a reportable contribution; (2) any political party, political committee, or other section 527 organization; or (3) any organization described in section 501(c) that engages in candidate-related political activity within the meaning of this proposed rule. This definition of contribution is similar to the definition of contribution that applies for purposes of section 527. The Treasury Department and the IRS intend that the term "anything of value" would include both in-kind donations and other support (for example, volunteer hours and free or discounted rentals of facilities or mailing lists). The Treasury Department and the IRS request comments on whether other transfers, such as indirect contributions described in section 276 to political parties or political candidates, should be treated as candidate-related political activity.

The Treasury Department and the IRS recognize that a section 501(c)(4) organization making a contribution may not know whether a recipient section 501(c) organization engages in candidate-related political activity. The proposed regulations provide that, for purposes of this definition, a recipient organization would not be treated as a section 501(c) organization engaged in candidate-related political activity if the contributor organization obtains a written representation from an authorized officer of the recipient organization stating that the recipient organization does not engage in any such activity and the contribution is subject to a written restriction that it not be used for candidate-related political activity. This special provision would apply only if the contributor organization does not know or have reason to know that the representation is inaccurate or unreliable.

e. *Election-related activities*

The proposed definition of candidate-related political activity would include certain specified election-related activities, including the conduct of voter registration and get-out-the-vote drives, distribution of material prepared by or on behalf of a candidate or section 527 organization, and preparation or distribution of a voter guide and accompanying material that refers to a candidate or a political party. In addition, an organization that hosts an event on its premises or conducts an event off-site within 30 days of a primary election or 60 days of a general election at which one or more candidates in such election appear as part of the program (whether or not such appearance was previously scheduled) would be engaged in candidate-related political activity under the proposed definition.

The Treasury Department and the IRS acknowledge that under the facts and circumstances analysis currently used for section 501(c)(4) organizations as well as for section 501(c)(3) organizations, these election-related activities may not be considered political campaign intervention if conducted in a non-partisan and unbiased manner. However, these determinations are highly fact-intensive. The Treasury Department and the IRS request comments on whether any particular activities conducted by section 501(c)(4) organizations should be excepted from the definition of candidate-related political activity as voter education activity and, if so, a description of how the proposed exception will both ensure that excepted activities are conducted in a non-partisan and unbiased manner and avoid a fact-intensive analysis.

f. *Attribution to a section 501(c)(4) organization of certain activities and communications*

These proposed regulations provide that activities conducted by an organization include, but are not limited to, (1) activities paid for by the organization or conducted by the organization's officers, directors, or employees acting in that capacity, or by volunteers acting under the organization's direction or supervision; (2) communications made (whether or not such communications were previously scheduled) as part of the program at an official function of the organization or in an official publication of the organization; and (3) other communications (such as television advertisements) the creation or distribution of which is paid for by the organization. These proposed regulations also provide that an organization's Web site is an official publication of the organization, so that material posted by the organization on its Web site may constitute candidate-related political activity. The proposed regulations do not specifically address material posted by third parties on an organization's Web site. The Treasury Department and the IRS request comments on whether, and under what circumstances, material posted by a third party on an interactive part of the organization's Web site should be attributed to the organization for purposes of this rule. In addition, the Treasury Department and the IRS have stated in guidance under section 501(c)(3) regarding political campaign intervention that when a charitable organization chooses to establish a link to another Web site, the organization is responsible for the consequences of establishing and maintaining that link, even if it does not have control over the content of the linked site. See Rev. Rul. 2007-41. The Treasury Department and the IRS request comments on whether the consequences of establishing and maintaining a link to another Web site should be the same or different for purposes of the proposed definition of candidate-related political activity.

Proposed Effective/Applicability Date

These regulations are proposed to be effective the date of publication of the Treasury decision adopting these rules as final regulations in the **Federal Register**. For proposed date of applicability, see § 1.501(c)(4)-1(c).

Statement of Availability for IRS Documents

For copies of recently issued Revenue Procedures, Revenue Rulings, Notices, and other guidance published in the Internal Revenue Bulletin or Cumulative Bulletin, please visit the IRS Web site at *http://www.irs.gov* or the Superintendent of Documents, U.S. Government Printing Office, Washington, DC 20402.

Special Analyses

It has been determined that this notice of proposed rulemaking is not a significant regulatory action as defined in Executive Order 12866, as supplemented by Executive Order 13563. Therefore, a regulatory assessment is not required. It also has been determined that section 553(b) of the Administrative Procedure Act (5 U.S.C. chapter 5) does not apply to these regulations. It is hereby certified that this rule will not have a significant economic impact on a substantial number of small entities. This certification is based on the fact that only a minimal burden would be imposed by the rule, if adopted. Under the proposal, if a section 501(c)(4) organization chooses to contribute to a section 501(c) organization and wants assurance that the contribution will not be treated as candidate-related political activity, it may seek a written representation that the recipient does not engage in candidate-related political activity within the meaning of these regulations. Therefore, a regulatory flexibility analysis under the Regulatory Flexibility Act (5 U.S.C. chapter 6) is not required. Pursuant to section 7805(f) of the Code, this notice of proposed rulemaking has been submitted to the Chief Counsel for Advocacy of the Small Business Administration for comment on its impact on small business.

Comments and Requests for Public Hearing

Before these proposed regulations are adopted as final regulations, consideration will be given to any written comments (a signed original and eight (8) copies) or electronic comments that are submitted timely to the IRS. The Treasury Department and the IRS generally request comments on all aspects of the proposed rules. In particular, the Treasury Department and the IRS request comments on whether there are other specific activities that should be included in, or excepted from, the definition of candidate-related political activity for purposes of section 501(c)(4). Such comments should address how the proposed addition or exception is consistent with the goals of providing more definitive rules and reducing the need for fact-intensive analysis of the activity. All comments submitted by the public will be made available for public inspection and copying at *www.regulations.gov* or upon request.

A public hearing will be scheduled if requested in writing by any person who timely submits written comments. If a public hearing is scheduled, notice of the date, time, and place for the public hearing will be published in the **Federal Register**.

Drafting Information

The principal author of these regulations is Amy F. Giuliano, Office of Associate Chief Counsel (Tax Exempt and Government Entities). However, other personnel from the IRS and Treasury Department participated in their development.

[¶ 49,599] Proposed Amendments of Regulations (REG-159420-04), published in the Federal Register on December 13, 2013.

[Code Sec. 41]

Research credit: Qualified research expenditures: Intra-group gross receipts: Controlled groups of corporations.—Amendments of Reg. §§ 1.41-0 and 1.41-6, relating to the treatment of qualified research expenditures (QREs) and gross receipts resulting from transactions between members of a controlled group of corporations or a group of trades or businesses under common control (intra-group transactions) for purposes of determining the credit under Code Sec. 41 for increasing research activities, are proposed.

AGENCY: Internal Revenue Service (IRS), Treasury.

ACTION: Notice of proposed rulemaking and notice of public hearing.

SUMMARY: This document contains proposed regulations under section 41 of the Internal Revenue Code (Code) relating to the treatment of qualified research expenditures (QREs) and gross receipts resulting from transactions between members of a controlled group of corporations or a group of trades or businesses under common control (intra-group transactions) for purposes of determining the credit under section 41 for increasing research activities (research credit). These proposed regulations will affect controlled groups of corporations or groups of trades or businesses under common control (controlled groups) that are engaged in research activities. This document also provides notice of a public hearing on these proposed regulations.

DATES: Written or electronic comments must be received by March 13, 2014. Outlines of topics to be discussed at the public hearing scheduled for April 23, 2014, at 10:00 a.m. must be received by March 13, 2014.

ADDRESSES: Send submissions to: CC:PA:LPD:PR (REG-159420-04), Room 5205, Internal Revenue Service, PO Box 7604, Ben Franklin Station, Washington, DC 20044. Submissions also may be hand delivered Monday through Friday between the hours of 8 a.m. and 4 p.m. to: CC:PA:LPD:PR (REG-159420-04), Courier's Desk, Internal Revenue Service, 1111 Constitution Avenue, NW, Washington, DC, or sent electronically via the Federal eRulemaking Portal at http://www.regulations.gov (IRS REG-159420-04). The public hearing will be held in the IRS Auditorium, Internal Revenue Building, 1111 Constitution Avenue, NW, Washington, DC.

FOR FURTHER INFORMATION CONTACT: Concerning these proposed regulations, David Selig, (202) 317-4137; concerning submission of comments, the hearing, and/or to be placed on the building access list to attend the hearing, Oluwafunmilayo (Funmi) Taylor, (202) 317-6901 (not toll-free numbers).

SUPPLEMENTARY INFORMATION:

Background

These proposed regulations address how the interaction of section 41(f)(1) (relating to the treatment of controlled groups as a single taxpayer) and section 41(c)(7) (relating to the exclusion from gross receipts of amounts received by a foreign corporation that are not effectively connected to a United States trade or business) affects the computation of gross receipts resulting from intra-group transactions between domestic controlled group members (domestic members) and foreign corporate members of the controlled group (foreign corporate members). These proposed regulations apply to an intra-group transaction that is followed by a transaction between a foreign corporate member and a party outside of the controlled group involving the same or a modified version of tangible or intangible property or services that was the subject of the intra-group transaction, and the transaction with the party outside of the controlled group does not give rise to gross receipts that are effectively connected with a trade or business within the United States, the Commonwealth of Puerto Rico, or any possession of the United States.

Section 41(f)(1) provides that in determining the amount of the research credit, all members of the same controlled group of corporations and all commonly controlled trades or businesses (whether or not incorporated) shall be treated as a single taxpayer. For this purpose, controlled group is defined by reference to section 1563(a), except that "more than 50 percent" is substituted for "at least 80 percent," and the determination is made without regard to subsections (a)(4) (regarding certain insurance companies) and (e)(3)(C) (regarding stock owned by an employees' trust). The statute provides no rules, however, regarding how the single taxpayer treatment is to be implemented. Commentators have noted the ambiguity associated with similar provisions of the Code. See, e.g., Prop. Reg. § 1.199-1, 70 FR 67220, 67236 (November 4, 2005) ("the single corporation language in section 199(d)(4)(A) has created confusion among commentators and the proposed regulations clarify the meaning of this language").

The IRS and the Treasury Department believe that the single taxpayer concept should be interpreted consistently with the purpose the statute is intended to advance. The single taxpayer concept as it relates to the computation of the research credit first appeared in 1981 when Congress initially enacted the research credit. As originally enacted, the research credit was determined solely by reference to a taxpayer's QREs. Specifically, to ensure that the research credit was available only for actual increases in research expenditures, former section 44F(f)(1) provided that the QREs of a controlled group of corporations and all commonly controlled trades or businesses (whether or not incorporated) were aggregated and treated as those of a single taxpayer. H. Rept. No. 97-201, 1981-2 CB 364-365 (demonstrating that controlled groups are prevented from increasing research expenditures by shifting these expenditures from an entity that has a high baseline of research expenditures to one that does not).

In 1989, Congress modified the computation of the research credit (now section 41 of the Code) by adding the base amount concept embodied in section 41(a)(1)(B), which included gross receipts in the calculation of the research credit for the first time. See the Omnibus Budget Reconciliation Act of 1989 (Public Law 101-239, § 7110) (the "1989 Act"). The legislative history of the 1989 Act explains that gross receipts were included in the computation of the research credit to address concerns with the existing rules and incentivize spending on research activities. In particular, Congress wished to modify the pre-existing incremental credit structure in order to maximize the research credit's efficiency by not allowing (to the extent possible) credits for research that would have been undertaken in any event. Congress believed that businesses often determine their research budgets as a fixed percentage of gross receipts and determined that it was appropriate to compute the research credit, in part, based on the increase in a taxpayer's gross receipts. This approach also had the advantage of effectively indexing the research credit for inflation and preventing taxpayers from being rewarded for increases in research spending that are attributable solely to inflation. See H.R. Rep. No. 101-247, 101st Cong., 1st Sess. 1199-1200 (1989).

The 1989 Act also amended section 41 to provide certain parameters for measuring gross receipts. Specifically, section 41(c)(7) provides that gross receipts are reduced by returns and allowances made during the taxable year. Section 41(c)(7) also provides that in the case of a foreign corporation, only gross receipts effectively connected with the conduct of a trade or business within the United States, the Commonwealth of Puerto Rico, or any possession of the United States are taken into account in the computation of the research credit. See section 41(c)(7), as amended. The legislative history of the 1989 Act does not expressly address the purpose of the gross receipts provision relating to foreign corporations. The enactment of the controlled group aggregation rules in section 41(f)(1) (treating all members of a controlled group as a single taxpayer) preceded the enactment of the foreign corporation gross receipts rule in section 41(c)(7). Congress, however, did not make clear how the two provisions should interact and did not provide any additional indication regarding the consequences of being treated as a single taxpayer, including when the deemed single taxpayer is comprised of both domestic and foreign controlled group members.

Current Regulatory Scheme

Section 1.41-3(c) defines gross receipts generally as the total amount, determined under the taxpayer's method of accounting, derived from all its activities and from all sources. Section 1.41-6(i) interprets the single taxpayer concept of section 41(f)(1) to provide that transfers between members of a controlled group of corporations are generally disregarded for purposes of determining the research credit under section 41 for both gross receipts and QREs. The IRS and the Treasury Department believe that, in most cases, the general rule that disregards intra-group transactions for both gross receipts and QREs furthers the statutory purpose of ensuring that the computation of the research credit is based upon an economic measure of gross receipts relative to QREs and not artificially increased by multiple intra-group transactions.

The IRS and the Treasury Department believe, however, that an interpretation of section 41(f)(1) that completely excludes gross receipts associated with certain transactions is inconsistent with Congressional intent. For example, assume that a domestic corporation incurs research expenditures and sells a product that it produced to a foreign corporate member, and the foreign corporate member then sells the product to a customer in a transaction that does not give rise to gross receipts effectively connected with a trade or business within the United States, the Commonwealth of Puerto Rico, or any possession of the United States. If gross receipts from the sales transactions are excluded because the intra-group transaction is disregarded under §1.41-6 and the foreign corporate member's gross receipts are excluded under section 41(c)(7) for the second transaction, the aggregate amount of gross receipts for purposes of determining the research credit is distorted. The distortion results because the QREs of the domestic member are included, but its gross receipts from the sale to the foreign corporate member are not. Accordingly, the IRS and the Treasury Department propose to revise the regulations to include gross receipts in this situation, including in cases where the property is modified prior to being transferred by the foreign corporate member, the gross receipts are in the form of royalties, interest, or other cash or non-cash remuneration, or the gross receipts relate to services ultimately provided by the foreign corporate member to a third-party customer.

However, the IRS and the Treasury Department believe that multiple inclusions of gross receipts associated with intra-group transactions involving the same or a modified version of tangible or intangible property or services would be inconsistent with Congressional intent. Thus, for example, it would not be appropriate to overstate gross receipts, and thereby reduce the research credit available to a controlled group, by taking into account the transfer of a single piece of property (including a modified form of the same property) more than one time (that is, first as a transfer between controlled group members and then as a transfer with a third party).

Explanation of Provisions

The proposed regulations retain the current rule that generally disregards transactions among members of a controlled group for purposes of computing the research credit, but provide a narrow exception to this rule. Under the exception, gross receipts (within the meaning of §1.41-3(c)) from an intra-group transaction are taken into account if (1) a foreign corporate member engages in a transaction with a party outside of the group (external transaction) involving the same or a modified version of tangible or intangible property or a service that was previously the subject of one or more intra-group transactions (an internal transaction); and (2) the external transaction does not give rise to gross receipts that are effectively connected with a trade or business within the United States, the Commonwealth of Puerto Rico, or any possession of the United States. The exception harmonizes the application of sections 41(f)(1) and 41(c)(7) and is consistent with the purposes of these provisions as well as the broader statutory changes that made gross receipts a central feature of the research credit computation.

For example, if a domestic member transfers property to a foreign corporate member, and the foreign corporate member then transfers the property outside of the controlled group in a transaction that does not give rise to gross receipts that are effectively connected with a trade or business within the United States, the Commonwealth of Puerto Rico, or any possession of the United States, the proposed regulations provide that the domestic member includes in its gross receipts amounts received from the foreign corporate member for that transaction. The amounts are taken into account in computing gross receipts in the taxable year in which the foreign corporate member engages in the external transaction. The fact that the foreign corporate member that ultimately engages in a transaction involving the property outside of the controlled group is not the same foreign corporate member to which the domestic member directly transferred the property (for example, one foreign corporate member re-transfers the property to another foreign corporate member) is not material to the determination of the domestic member's gross receipts.

To prevent multiple inclusions of gross receipts in cases in which transactions involving the same or a modified version of tangible or intangible property or services occur successively between domestic and foreign corporate members, the proposed regulations provide that only the last internal transaction giving rise to gross receipts (within the meaning of section 1.41-3(c)) is taken into account in the research credit computation.

These proposed regulations embody the statutory requirement of consistency in determining a taxpayer's base amount (generally, the product of the fixed-base percentage and 4-year average annual gross receipts preceding the credit year). *See* section 41(c)(6). Accordingly, in computing the research credit for taxable years beginning on or after the date of publication of these proposed regulations as final regulations, QREs and gross receipts taken into account in computing a taxpayer's fixed-base percentage and a taxpayer's base amount must be determined on a basis consistent with the definition of QREs and gross receipts for the credit year, without regard to the law in effect for the earlier taxable years that are taken into account in computing the fixed-base percentage or the base amount. However, the proposed regulations do not specify the manner in which a taxpayer must make the base amount adjustments. The IRS and the Treasury Department recognize that accounting for intra-group transactions in prior years presents a unique burden because taxpayers may not have records for the base years with sufficient information to satisfy the proposed regulations' requirement of consistency. These proposed regulations are intended to capture some measure of intra-group gross receipts for purposes of satisfying the requirement of consistency, but are not intended to preclude research credit claims for taxpayers that do not have adequate information in their books and records for the base years. Accordingly, the IRS and Treasury Department request comments regarding the need for a rule or safe harbor in applying the consistency rule for purposes of determining the base amount in accordance with these proposed regulations.

QREs

These proposed regulations remove the rules in §1.41-6(i)(4) (relating to the treatment of lease payments as QREs) to reflect changes to section 41 by the Tax Reform Act of 1986, Public Law 99-514.

These proposed regulations generally would not change the rules concerning whether payments between members of a controlled group constitute QREs. The IRS and the Treasury Department request comments concerning whether any revisions are necessary.

Proposed Effective Date

The amendments to §1.41-6(i) are proposed to apply to taxable years beginning on or after the date that these regulations are published as final regulations in the **Federal Register**.

Special Analysis

It has been determined that this notice of proposed rulemaking is not a significant regulatory action as defined in Executive Order 12866, as supplemented by Executive Order 13563. It also has been determined that section 553(b) of the Administrative Procedures Act (5 U.S.C. chapter 5) does not apply to these regulations, and because these regulations do not impose a collection of information on small entities, the Regulatory Flexibility Act (5 U.S.C. chapter 6) does not apply. Therefore, a Regulatory Flexibility Analysis is not required. Pursuant to section 7805(f) of the Code, this notice of proposed rulemaking has been submitted to the Chief Counsel for Advocacy of the Small Business Administration for comment on its impact on small business.

Comments and Public Hearing

Before these proposed regulations are adopted as final regulations, consideration will be given to any electronic or written comments (a signed original and eight (8) copies) that are submitted timely to the IRS. The IRS and the Treasury Department request comments on all aspects of the proposed rules.

All comments will be available for public inspection and copying.

A public hearing has been scheduled for April 23, 2014, beginning at 10:00 a.m. in the IRS Auditorium, Internal Revenue Building, 1111 Constitution Avenue, N.W., Washington, DC. Due to building security procedures, visitors must enter at the Constitution Avenue entrance. In addition, all visitors must present photo identification to enter the building. Because of access restrictions, visitors will not be admitted beyond the immediate entrance area more than 30 minutes before the hearing starts. For information about having your name placed on the building access list to attend the hearing, see the "FOR FURTHER INFORMATION CONTACT" section of this preamble.

The rules of 26 CFR 601.601(a)(3) apply to the hearing. Persons who wish to present oral comments at the hearing must submit electronic or written comments by March 13, 2014, and submit an outline of the topics to be discussed and the amount of time to be devoted to each topic (a signed original and eight (8) copies) by March 13, 2014. A period of 10 minutes will be allotted to each person for making comments. An agenda showing the scheduling of the speakers will be prepared after the deadline for receiving outlines has passed. Copies of the agenda will be available free of charge at the hearing.

Drafting Information

The principal author of these proposed regulations is David Selig, Office of the Associate Chief Counsel (Passthroughs and Special Industries). However, other personnel from the IRS and the Treasury Department participated in their development.

[¶49,600] Proposed Amendments of Regulations (REG-136984-12), published in the Federal Register on December 16, 2013 (corrected 5/23/2014).

[Code Sec. 752]

Partnerships: Partners: Overlapping economic risk of loss: Nonrecourse loan to partnership.—Amendments of Reg. §§1.752-0, 1.752-2, 1.752-4 and 1.752-5, relating to recourse liabilities of a partnership and the special rules for related persons, are proposed.

AGENCY: Internal Revenue Service (IRS), Treasury.
ACTION: Notice of proposed rulemaking.
SUMMARY: This document contains proposed regulations under section 752 of the Internal Revenue Code (Code) relating to recourse liabilities of a partnership and the special rules for related persons. The proposed regulations affect partnerships and their partners.
DATES: Written or electronic comments and request for a public hearing must be received by March 17, 2014.
ADDRESSES: Send submissions to: CC:PA:LPD:PR (REG-136984-12), room 5203, Internal Revenue Service, PO Box 7604, Ben Franklin Station, Washington, DC 20044. Submissions may be hand-delivered Monday through Friday between the hours of 8 a.m. and 4 p.m. to CC:PA:LPD:PR (REG-136984-12), Courier's Desk, Internal Revenue Service, 1111 Constitution Avenue, NW, Washington, DC, or sent electronically, via the Federal eRulemaking Portal at *www.regulations.gov* (IRS REG-136984-12).
FOR FURTHER INFORMATION CONTACT: Concerning the proposed regulations, Caroline E. Hay or Deane M. Burke, at (202) 317-5279; concerning the submissions of comments and requests for a public hearing, Oluwafunmilayo (Funmi) Taylor at (202) 317-5179 (not toll-free numbers).
SUPPLEMENTARY INFORMATION:

Background

This document contains proposed amendments to the Income Tax Regulations (26 CFR part 1) under section 752 regarding a partner's share of recourse partnership liabilities.

Section 752(a) provides, in general, that any increase in a partner's share of partnership liabilities (or an increase in a partner's individual liabilities by reason of the assumption by the partner of partnership liabilities) will be considered a contribution of money by such partner to the partnership. Conversely, section 752(b) provides that any decrease in a partner's share of partnership liabilities (or a decrease in a partner's individual liabilities by reason of the assumption by the partnership of such individual liabilities) will be considered a distribution of money to the partner by the partnership.

When determining a partner's share of partnership liabilities, the regulations under section 752 distinguish between two categories of liabilities—recourse and nonrecourse. In general, a partnership liability is recourse to the extent that a partner or related person bears the economic risk of loss as provided in §1.752-2 and nonrecourse to the extent that no partner or related person bears the economic risk of loss. See §1.752-1(a)(1) and (2).

These proposed regulations provide guidance as to when and to what extent a partner is treated as bearing the economic risk of loss for a partnership liability when multiple partners bear the economic risk of loss for the same partnership liability (overlapping economic risk of loss). In addition, these proposed regulations provide guidance when a partner has a payment obligation with respect to a liability or makes a nonrecourse loan to the partnership (and no other partner bears the economic risk of loss for that liability) and such partner is related to another partner in the partnership.

Explanation of Provisions

1. *Overlapping Risk of Loss*

Under §1.752-2(a), a partner's share of a recourse partnership liability equals the portion of that liability, if any, for which the partner or related person bears the economic risk of loss. Section 1.752-2(b)(1) provides that a partner bears the economic risk of loss for a partnership liability to the extent that, if the partnership constructively liquidated, the partner or related person would be obligated to make a payment on the partnership obligation to any person or a contribution to the partnership (payment obligation) because the liability becomes due and payable and the partner or related person would not be entitled to reimbursement from another partner or a person that is related to another partner. Moreover, under §1.752-2(c)(1), a partner bears the economic risk of loss for a partnership liability to the extent that the partner or a related person makes (or acquires an interest in) a nonrecourse loan to the partnership and the economic risk of loss for the liability is not borne by another partner. Section 1.752-4(c) provides that the amount of an indebtedness is taken into account only once.

The IRS and the Treasury Department are aware that there is uncertainty as to how partners should share a partnership liability if multiple partners bear the economic risk of loss with respect to the same liability. The temporary regulations under §1.752- 1T(d)(3)(i) that preceded the existing final regulations under section 752 addressed the issue of overlapping economic risk of loss by providing that "if the aggregate amount of the economic risk of loss that all partners are determined to bear with respect to a partnership liability (or portion thereof) . . . exceeds the amount of such liability (or portion thereof), then the economic risk of loss borne by each partner with respect to such liability shall equal the amount determined by multiplying the amount of such liability (or portion thereof) by the fraction obtained by dividing the amount of the economic risk of loss that such partner is determined to bear with respect to that liability (or portion thereof) by the sum of such amounts for all partners." The rule in the temporary regulations, however, was not included in the final regulations in part in response to comments that the proposed regulations addressed too many topics generally and should be simplified to focus on more basic concepts. See 56 FR 36704- 02 (1991-2 CB 1125).

The IRS and the Treasury Department have received comments requesting guidance in this area. The IRS and the Treasury Department continue to balance the importance of simplicity in regulations under section 752 against the utility of providing additional guidance on identified issues. In light of comments received, the IRS and the Treasury Department believe that a rule is needed to address overlapping economic risk of loss due to uncertainty under the current regulations and believe that the concepts from the temporary regulations regarding the overlapping risk of loss rule provide a reasonable approach in addressing how a partnership liability should be shared among partners bearing the economic risk of loss for the same liability. Accordingly, these proposed regulations adopt the rule from the temporary regulations.

2. *Tiered Partnerships*

The rules under section 752 regarding the allocation of liabilities in a tiered partnership structure also may result in overlapping economic risk of loss. Section 1.752-2(i) provides that if a partnership (the "upper-tier partnership") owns (directly or indirectly through one or more partnerships) an interest in another partnership (the "lower-tier partnership"), the liabilities of the lower-tier partnership are allocated to the upper-tier partnership in an amount equal to the sum of the following: (1) the amount of the economic risk of loss that the upper-tier partnership bears with respect to the liabilities; and (2) the amount of any other liabilities with respect to which partners of the upper-tier partnership bear the economic risk of loss. Section 1.752-4(a) further provides that an upper-tier partnership's share of the liabilities of a lower-tier partnership (other than any liability of the lower-tier partnership that is owed to the upper-tier partnership) is treated as a liability of the upper-tier partnership for purposes of applying section 752 and the regulations thereunder to the partners of the upper-tier partnership.

The regulations therefore allocate a recourse liability of a lower-tier partnership to an upper-tier partnership if either that upper-tier partnership, or one of its partners, bears the economic risk of loss for the liability. When a partner of the upper-tier partnership is also a partner in the lower-tier partnership, and that partner bears the economic risk of loss with respect to a liability of the lower-tier partnership, the current regulations do not provide guidance as to how the lower-tier partnership should allocate the liability between the upper-tier partnership and the partner. The IRS and the Treasury Department believe that the lower-tier partnership should allocate the liability directly to the partner. The IRS and the Treasury Department believe that this approach is more administrable and ensures that the additional basis resulting from the liability is only for the benefit of the partner that bears the economic risk of loss for the liability. Thus, the proposed regulations modify the tiered-partnership rule in § 1.752-2(i)(2) to prevent a liability of a lower-tier partnership from being allocated to an upper-tier partnership when a partner of the lower-tier partnership and the upper-tier partnership bears the economic risk of loss for such liability.

3. *Related Party Rules*

A. *Constructive Owner of Stock*

Under § 1.752-4(b)(1), a person is related to a partner if the partner and the person bear a relationship to each other that is specified in sections 267(b) or 707(b)(1), except that 80 percent or more is substituted for 50 percent or more in each of those sections, a person's family is determined by excluding siblings, and sections 267(e)(1) and 267(f)(1)(A) are disregarded.

In determining whether a partner and a person bear a relationship to each other that is specified in section 267(b), the constructive stock ownership rules in section 267(c) are applicable. Specific to partnerships, section 267(c)(1) provides, in part, that stock owned directly or indirectly by or for a partnership is considered as being owned proportionately by or for its partners. Therefore, if a partnership owns all of the stock in a corporation, a partner that owns 80 percent or more of the interests in the partnership is considered to be related to the corporation under § 1.752-4(b)(1). If the corporation has a payment obligation with respect to a liability of its partnership owner, or the corporation lends to the partnership and the economic risk of loss for the liability is not borne by another partner, any partner that is treated as related to the corporation bears the economic risk of loss for the partnership liability under § 1.752-2. The IRS and the Treasury Department believe that partners in a partnership, where that partnership owns stock in a corporation that is a lender to the partnership or has a payment obligation with respect to a liability of its partnership owner, should not be treated as related, through ownership of the partnership, to the corporation. A partner's economic risk of loss that is limited to the partner's equity investment in the partnership should be treated differently than the risk of loss beyond that investment. Thus, for purposes of § 1.752-4(b)(1), the proposed regulations disregard section 267(c)(1) in determining whether a partner in a partnership is considered as owning stock in a corporation to the extent the corporation is a lender or has a payment obligation with respect to a liability of its partnership owner.

B. *Person Related to Multiple Partners*

Section 1.752-4(b)(2)(i) provides that if a person is related to more than one partner in a partnership under § 1.752-4(b)(1), the related party rules in § 1.752-4(b)(1) are applied by treating the person as related only to the partner with whom there is the highest percentage of related ownership (greatest percentage rule). If, however, two or more partners have the same percentage of related ownership and no other partner has a greater percentage, the liability is allocated equally among the partners having the equal percentages of related ownership.

The IRS and the Treasury Department have recently received comments requesting that the greatest percentage rule be removed. The commenter explains that if a person is related to more than one partner under § 1.752-4(b)(1), the ultimate determination of a person's relatedness to a partner should not be based on which partner has the highest percentage of related ownership because differences in ownership percentages within a 20-percent range do not justify treating a person as related to one partner over another. After considering the comments, the IRS and the Treasury Department agree with the comments, especially given the administrative burden associated with determining precise ownership percentages above the 80- percent threshold in § 1.752-4(b)(1)(i). Therefore, the proposed regulations remove the greatest percentage rule and provide that if a person is a lender or has a payment obligation for a partnership liability and is related to more than one partner, those partners share the liability equally.

C. *Related Partner Exception to Related Party Rules*

Section 1.752-4(b)(2)(iii) provides that persons owning interests directly or indirectly in the same partnership are not treated as related persons for purposes of determining the economic risk of loss borne by each of them for the liabilities of the partnership (the related partner exception). The IRS and the Treasury Department are aware that taxpayers are uncertain of the application of the related partner exception following the decision in *IPO II v. Commissioner*, 122 T.C. 295 (2004). *IPO II* involved an individual, Mr. Forsythe, who owned 100 percent of an S corporation, Indeck Overseas, and 70 percent of a second S corporation, Indeck Energy. Mr. Forsythe's children owned the remaining 30 percent of Indeck Energy. Mr. Forsythe and Indeck Overseas formed a partnership, IPO II, which received a loan from a bank. To secure that loan, Mr. Forsythe, Indeck Energy, and Indeck Power (a C corporation of which Mr. Forsythe owned 63 percent) entered into guarantees with the bank. IPO II allocated 99 percent of the increase in basis attributable to this liability to Indeck Overseas. *Id.* at 296-97. The Tax Court held that this allocation was incorrect because Indeck Overseas was not directly or indirectly liable for the debt. The court, while stressing that it interprets "the policy behind the related partner exception as preventing the shifting of basis from a party who bears actual economic risk of loss to one who does not," did not end its analysis by stating that Mr. Forsythe guaranteed the debt, and thus his economic risk of loss could not be shifted to Indeck Overseas which did not guarantee the debt. *Id.* at 303. The court instead examined whether Indeck Overseas indirectly bore the economic risk of loss due to its relationship with a related party, Indeck Energy. The Tax Court held that the relationship between Indeck Overseas and Indeck Energy arose through Mr. Forsythe. Because the related partner exception shuts off the relationship between Mr. Forsythe and Indeck Overseas, it should be turned off for all purposes; therefore, Indeck Energy was not related to Indeck Overseas. *Id.* at 304.

The IRS and Treasury Department believe the related partner exception should only apply where a partner has a payment obligation or is the lender with respect to a partnership liability. *IPO II* may be read to expand the related partner exception to turn off relationships between related partners in a partnership without limitation. Under this broad interpretation, the related partner exception could be improperly applied to turn off attribution of economic risk of loss between related partners even when none of the related partners directly bears the economic risk of loss for a partnership liability. The IRS and the Treasury Department believe that such an interpretation could have unintended results, including causing intercompany debts to be treated as nonrecourse because no partner alone owns 80 percent or more of the lending company and the partners are not treated as related to each other. The proposed regulations provide that the related partner exception only applies when a partner bears the economic risk of loss for a liability of the partnership because the partner is a lender under § 1.752-2(c)(1) or has a payment obligation for the partnership liability. The proposed regulations also clarify that an indirect interest in a partnership is an indirect interest through one or more partnerships.

D. *Special Rule Where Entity Structured To Avoid Related Person Status*

Section 1.752-4(b)(2)(iv) provides special rules for when an entity is structured to avoid related person status. The proposed regulations do not propose any changes to these rules. However, as a result of other changes made to simplify the organization of § 1.752-4, the rules in § 1.752-4(b)(2)(iv) are now in § 1.752-4(b)(4) of the proposed regulations. In addition, the example in § 1.752-4(b)(2)(iv)(C) is now *Example 5* under § 1.752-4(b)(5) of the proposed regulations.

4. *Request for Comments: Liquidating Distributions of Tiered Partnership Interests*

The IRS and the Treasury Department are considering the proper treatment of liabilities when an upper-tier partnership (transferor) bears the economic risk of loss for a lower-tier partnership liability and distributes, in a liquidating distribution, its interest in the lower-tier partnership to one of its partners (transferee) but the partner does not bear the economic risk of loss for the lower-tier partnership's liability. The IRS and the Treasury Department request comments on the timing of the liability reallocation relative to the transaction that causes the liability to change from recourse to nonrecourse.

Proposed Applicability Date

The regulations are proposed to apply to liabilities incurred or assumed by a partnership on or after the date these regulations are published as final regulations in the **Federal Register**, other than liabilities incurred or assumed by a partnership pursuant to a written binding contract in effect prior to that date.

Special Analyses

It has been determined that this notice of proposed rulemaking is not a significant regulatory action as defined in Executive Order 12866, as supplemented by Executive Order 13563. Therefore, a regulatory assessment is not required. It also has been determined that section 553(b) of the Administrative Procedure Act (5 U.S.C. chapter 5) does not apply to these proposed regulations.

Because these proposed regulations do not impose a collection of information on small entities, the Regulatory Flexibility Act (5 U.S.C. chapter 6) does not apply. Pursuant to section 7805(f) of the Code, this notice of proposed rulemaking will be submitted to the Chief Counsel for Advocacy of the Small Business Administration for comment on its impact on small business.

Comments and Requests for a Public Hearing

Before these proposed regulations are adopted as final regulations, consideration will be given to any comments that are submitted timely to the IRS as prescribed in this preamble under the "Addresses" heading. The IRS and the Treasury Department request comments on all aspects of the proposed rules. All comments will be available at www.regulations.gov or upon request. A public hearing will be scheduled if requested in writing by any person that timely submits written comments. If a public hearing is scheduled, notice of the date, time, and place for the public hearing will be published in the **Federal Register**.

Drafting Information

The principal authors of these proposed regulations are Caroline E. Hay and Deane M. Burke, Office of the Associate Chief Counsel (Passthroughs and Special Industries). However, other personnel from the IRS and Treasury Department participated in their development.

[¶49,604] Proposed Amendments of Regulations (REG-144468-05), published in the Federal Register on January 16, 2014 (corrected 4/15/2014).

[Code Secs. 704, 732, 734, 737, 743, 755 and 1502]

Partnerships: Built-in gains and losses: Partnership allocations.—Amendments of Reg. §§1.704-3, 1.704-4, 1.732-2, 1.734-1, 1.734-2, 1.737-1, 1.743-1, 1.755-1 and 1.1502-13, providing guidance on certain provisions of the American Jobs Creation Act of 2004 and conforming the regulations to statutory changes in the Taxpayer Relief Act of 1997, are proposed.

AGENCY: Internal Revenue Service (IRS), Treasury.

ACTION: Notice of proposed rulemaking and notice of public hearing.

SUMMARY: The proposed regulations provide guidance on certain provisions of the American Jobs Creation Act of 2004 and conform the regulations to statutory changes in the Taxpayer Relief Act of 1997. The proposed regulations also modify the basis allocation rules to prevent certain unintended consequences of the current basis allocation rules for substituted basis transactions. Finally, the proposed regulations provide additional guidance on allocations resulting from revaluations of partnership property. The proposed regulations affect partnerships and their partners. This document also contains a notice of a public hearing on these proposed regulations. DATES: Comments must be received by April 16, 2014. Requests to speak and outlines of the topics to be discussed at the public hearing scheduled for April 30, 2014, at 10 a.m., must be received by April 16, 2014.

ADDRESSES: Send submissions to: CC:PA:LPD:PR (REG-144468-05), room 5203, Internal Revenue Service, P.O. Box 7604, Ben Franklin Station, Washington, DC 20044. Submissions may be hand-delivered Monday through Friday between the hours of 8 a.m. and 4 p.m. to: CC:PA:LPD:PR (REG-144468-05), Courier's Desk, Internal Revenue Service, 1111 Constitution Avenue NW, Washington, DC. Alternatively, taxpayers may submit comments electronically via the Federal eRulemaking Portal at *www.regulations.gov* (IRS REG-144468-05).

FOR FURTHER INFORMATION CONTACT: Concerning the proposed regulations, Wendy Kribell or Benjamin Weaver at (202) 317-6850; concerning submissions of comments, the hearing, and/or to be placed on the building access list to attend the hearing, Oluwafunmilayo (Funmi) Taylor, (202) 317-6901 (not toll-free numbers).

SUPPLEMENTARY INFORMATION:

Paperwork Reduction Act

The collection of information contained in this notice of proposed rulemaking has been submitted to the Office of Management and Budget for review in accordance with the Paperwork Reduction Act of 1995 (44 U.S.C. 3507(d)). Comments on the collection of information should be sent to the **Office of Management and Budget**, Attn: Desk Officer for the Department of the Treasury, Office of Information and Regulatory Affairs, Washington, DC 20503, with copies to the **Internal Revenue Service**, Attn: IRS Reports Clearance Officer, SE:W:CAR:MP:T:T:SP, Washington, DC 20224. Comments on the collection of information should be received by March 17, 2014. Comments are specifically requested concerning:

Whether the proposed collection of information is necessary for the proper performance of the functions of the IRS, including whether the information will have practical utility;

The accuracy of the estimated burden associated with the proposed collection of information; and

Estimates of capital or start-up costs and costs of operation, maintenance, and purchase of services to provide information.

The collections of information in the proposed regulations are in proposed §§1.704-3(f), 1.734-1(d), 1.743-1(k), and 1.743-1(n). This information will be used by the IRS to assure compliance with certain provisions of the American Jobs Creation Act of 2004. The collections of information are either required to obtain a benefit or are mandatory. The likely respondents are individuals and partnerships.

The burden for the collection of information in §1.704-3(f) is as follows:

Estimated total annual reporting burden: 324,850 hours.

Estimated average annual burden per respondent: 2 hours.
Estimated number of respondents: 162,425.
Estimated annual frequency of responses: On occasion.

The burden for the collection of information in § 1.734-1(d) is as follows:
Estimated total annual reporting burden: 1,650 hours.
Estimated average annual burden per respondent: 3 hours.
Estimated number of respondents: 550.
Estimated annual frequency of responses: On occasion.

The burden for the collection of information in § 1.743-1(k)(1) is as follows:
Estimated total annual reporting burden: 1,650 hours.
Estimated average annual burden per respondent: 3 hours.
Estimated number of respondents: 550.
Estimated annual frequency of responses: On occasion.

The burden for the collection of information in § 1.743-1(k)(2) is as follows:
Estimated total annual reporting burden: 550 hours.
Estimated average annual burden per respondent: 1 hour.
Estimated number of respondents: 550.
Estimated annual frequency of responses: On occasion.

The burden for the collection of information in § 1.743-1(n)(10) is as follows:
Estimated total annual reporting burden: 3,600.
Estimated average annual burden per respondent: 1 hour.
Estimated number of respondents: 3,600 hours.
Estimated annual frequency of responses: Various.

The burden for the collection of information in § 1.743-1(n)(11) is as follows:
Estimated total annual reporting burden: 2,700 hours.
Estimated average annual burden per respondent: 1.5 hours.
Estimated number of respondents: 1,800.
Estimated annual frequency of responses: On occasion

An agency may not conduct or sponsor, and a person is not required to respond to, a collection of information unless it displays a valid control number assigned by the Office of Management and Budget.

Books or records relating to a collection of information must be retained as long as their contents may become material in the administration of any internal revenue law. Generally, tax returns and tax return information are confidential, as required by section 6103.

Background

1. *Contributions of Built-in Loss Property*

Under section 721(a) of the Internal Revenue Code (the Code), if a partner contributes property in exchange for a partnership interest, neither the partners nor the partnership recognize gain or loss. Section 722 provides that when a partner contributes property to a partnership, the basis in the partnership interest received equals the adjusted basis of the contributed property. Similarly, under section 723, the partnership's adjusted basis in the contributed property equals the contributing partner's adjusted basis in the property. Section 704(c)(1)(A) requires the partnership to allocate items of partnership income, gain, loss, and deduction with respect to contributed property among the partners so as to take into account any built-in gain or built-in loss in the contributed property. This rule is intended to prevent the transfer of built-in gain or built-in loss from the contributing partner to other partners. If a partner contributes built-in gain or built-in loss property to a partnership and later transfers the interest in the partnership, § 1.704-3(a)(7) provides that the built-in gain or built-in loss must be allocated to the transferee as it would have been allocated to the transferor.

Section 833(a) of the American Jobs Creation Act of 2004, Public Law 108-357, 118 Stat. 1418 (the AJCA) added section 704(c)(1)(C) to the Code for contributions of built-in loss property to partnerships after October 22, 2004. In general, section 704(c)(1)(C) provides that a partner's built-in loss may only be taken into account in determining the contributing partner's share of partnership items. Prior to the AJCA, a contributing partner could transfer losses to a transferee partner or other partners when the contributing partner was no longer a partner in the partnership. *See* H. R. Rep. 108-548 at 282 (2004) (House Committee Report) and H.R. Rep. 108-755 at 622 (2004) (Conference Report). Thus, Congress enacted section 704(c)(1)(C) to prevent the inappropriate transfer of built-in losses to partners other than the contributing partner. *See* House Committee Report, at 283. More specifically, Congress enacted section 704(c)(1)(C) to prevent a transferee partner from receiving an allocation of the transferor partner's share of losses relating to the transferor's contribution of built-in loss property and to prevent remaining partners from receiving an allocation of a distributee partner's share of losses relating to the distributee's contribution of built-in loss property when the distributee receives a liquidating distribution. *See* House Committee Report, at 282 and Conference Report, at 621-622. To that end, section 704(c)(1)(C) provides that if property contributed to a partnership has a built-in loss, (i) such built-in loss shall be taken into account only in determining the amount of items allocated to the contributing partner; and (ii) except as provided by regulations, in determining the amount of items allocated to other partners, the basis of the contributed property in the hands of the partnership is equal to its fair market value at the time of the contribution. For purposes of section 704(c)(1)(C), the term *built-in loss* means the excess of the adjusted basis of the property (determined without regard to section 704(c)(1)(C)(ii)) over its fair market value at the time of contribution.

2. *Mandatory Basis Adjustment Provisions*

a. *Overview*

The mandatory basis adjustment provisions in section 833(b) and (c) of the AJCA reflect Congress' belief that the "electivity of partnership basis adjustments upon transfers and distributions leads to anomalous tax results, causes inaccurate income measurement, and gives rise to opportunities for tax sheltering." *See* S. Rep. 108-192 at 189 (2003) (Grassley Report). Specifically, Congress was concerned that the optional basis adjustment regime permitted partners to duplicate losses and inappropriately transfer losses among partners. *Id.* According to the legislative history, Congress intended these amendments to prevent the inappropriate transfer of losses among partners, while preserving the simplification aspects of the existing partnership rules for transactions involving smaller amounts (as described in this preamble, a $250,000 threshold). *See* House Committee Report, at 283. Thus, section 743 and section 734 were amended as described in sections 2.b. and 2.c. of the background section of this preamble.

b. *Section 743 substantial built-in loss provisions*

i. *In general*

Before the enactment of the AJCA, under section 743(a), upon the transfer of a partnership interest by sale or exchange or upon the death of a partner, a partnership was not required to adjust the basis of partnership property unless the partnership had a section 754 election in effect. If the partnership had a section 754 election in effect at the time of a transfer, section 743(b) required the partnership to increase or decrease the adjusted basis of the partnership property to take into account the difference between the transferee's proportionate share of the adjusted basis of the partnership property and the transferee's basis in its partnership interest.

As amended by the AJCA, section 743(a) and (b) require a partnership to adjust the basis of partnership property upon a sale or exchange of an interest in the partnership or upon the death of a partner if there is a section 754 election in effect, or, for transfers after October 22, 2004, if the partnership has a substantial built-in loss immediately after the transfer (regardless of whether the partnership has a section 754 election in effect). Section 743(d)(1) provides that, for purposes of section 743, a partnership has a substantial built-in loss if the partnership's adjusted basis in the partnership property exceeds the fair market value of the property by more than $250,000. Section 743(d)(2) provides that the Secretary shall prescribe such regulations as may be appropriate to carry out the purposes of section 743(d)(1), including regulations aggregating related partnerships and disregarding property acquired by the partnership in an attempt to avoid such purposes.

ii. *Electing investment partnerships*

Section 833(b) of the AJCA also added section 743(e) to the Code, which provides alternative rules for electing investment partnerships (EIPs). According to the legislative history, Congress was aware that mandating section 743(b) adjustments would impose administrative difficulties on certain types of investment partnerships that are engaged in investment activities and that typically did not make section 754 elections prior to the AJCA, even when the adjustments to the bases of partnership property would be upward adjustments. *See* House Committee Report, at 283. Accordingly, for partnerships that meet the requirements of an EIP in section 743(e)(6) and that elect to apply the provisions of section 743(e), section 743(e)(1) provides that for purposes of section 743, an EIP shall not be treated as having a substantial built-in loss with respect to any transfer occurring while the EIP election is in effect. Instead, section 743(e)(2) provides that, in the case of a transfer of an interest in an EIP, the transferee's distributive share of losses (without regard to gains) from the sale or exchange of partnership property shall not be allowed except to the extent that it is established that such losses exceed the loss (if any) recognized by the transferor (or any prior transferor to the extent not fully offset by a prior disallowance under section 743(e)(2)) on the transfer of the partnership interest. Section 743(e)(3) further provides that losses disallowed under section 743(e)(2) shall not decrease the transferee's basis in the partnership interest. In the case of partnership property that has a built-in loss at the time of the transfer, the loss disallowance rules in section 743(e)(2) and (e)(3) approximate the effect of a basis adjustment and prevent the transferee from taking into account an allocation of the preexisting built-in loss (and the corresponding basis reduction) without requiring the partnership to adjust the bases of all partnership property. In addition, section 743(e)(5) provides that in the case of a transferee whose basis in distributed partnership property is reduced under section 732(a)(2), the amount of the loss recognized by the transferor on the transfer that is taken into account under section 743(e)(2) shall be reduced by the amount of such basis reduction.

Section 743(e)(6) defines an *electing investment partnership* as any partnership if (A) the partnership makes an election to have section 743(e) apply; (B) the partnership would be an investment company under section 3(a)(1)(A) of the Investment Company Act of 1940 but for an exemption under paragraph (1) or (7) of section 3(c) of the Act; (C) the partnership has never been engaged in a trade or business; (D) substantially all of the assets of the partnership are held for investment; (E) at least 95 percent of the assets contributed to the partnership consist of money; (F) no assets contributed to the partnership had an adjusted basis in excess of fair market value at the time of contribution; (G) all partnership interests are issued pursuant to a private offering before the date that is 24 months after the date of the first capital contribution to the partnership; (H) the partnership agreement has substantive restrictions on each partner's ability to cause a redemption of the partner's interest; and (I) the partnership agreement provides for a term that is not in excess of 15 years. The flush language of section 743(e)(6) provides that the EIP election, once made, shall be irrevocable except with the consent of the Secretary. Section 833(d) of the AJCA provides a transition rule with respect to section 743(e)(6)(H) and (I) for partnerships eligible to make an election to be an EIP that were in existence on June 4, 2004. For those partnerships, section 743(e)(6)(H) does not apply and the term in section 743(e)(6)(I) is 20 years.

According to the legislative history, Congress expected EIPs to include venture capital funds, buyout funds, and funds of funds. *See* Conference Report, at 626. The legislative history further indicates that, with respect to the requirement in section 743(e)(6)(G), Congress intended that "dry" closings in which partnership interests are issued without the contribution of capital not start the running of the 24-month period. *Id.* Furthermore, with respect to the requirement in section 743(e)(6)(H), Congress provided illustrative examples of substantive restrictions: a violation of Federal or State law (such as ERISA or the Bank Holding Company Act) or an imposition of the Federal excise tax on, or a change in the Federal tax-exempt status of, a tax-exempt partner. *Id.*

Section 743(e)(4) also provides that section 743(e) shall be applied without regard to any termination of a partnership under section 708(b)(1)(B). Finally, section 743(e)(7) provides that the Secretary shall prescribe such regulations as may be appropriate to carry out the purposes of section 743(e), including regulations for applying section 743(e) to tiered partnerships.

Section 833(b) of the AJCA prescribed certain reporting requirements for EIPs by adding section 6031(f) to the Code. Section 6031(f) provides that in the case of an EIP, the information required under section 6031(b) (relating to furnishing copies of returns of partnership income to partners) to be furnished to a partner to whom section 743(e)(2) applies shall include information as is necessary to enable the partner to compute the amount of losses disallowed under section 743(e).

On April 1, 2005, the Treasury Department and the IRS issued Notice 2005-32 (2005-1 CB 895), which provides, in part, interim procedures and reporting requirements for EIPs; interim procedures for transferors of EIP interests; and guidance regarding whether a partnership is engaged in a trade or business for purposes of section 743(e)(6)(C). Public comments on Notice 2005-32 are discussed in Parts 2.a.i and 2.a.ii of the Explanation of Provisions section of this preamble. *See* § 601.601(d)(2)(ii)(b).

iii. *Securitization partnerships*

Finally, section 833 of the AJCA added section 743(f) to the Code, which provides an exception from the mandatory basis adjustment provisions in section 743(a) and (b) for securitization partnerships. Section 743(f)(1) states that for purposes of section 743, a securitization partnership shall not be treated as having a substantial built-in loss with respect to any transfer. Section 743(f)(2) provides that the term *securitization partnership* means a partnership the sole business activity of which is to issue securities that provide for a fixed principal (or similar) amount and that are primarily serviced by the cash flows of a discrete pool (either fixed or revolving) of receivables or other financial assets that by their terms convert into cash in a finite period, but only if the sponsor of the pool reasonably believes that the receivables and other financial assets comprising the pool are not acquired so as to be disposed of. For purposes of the "reasonable belief" standard, the legislative history indicates that Congress intended rules similar to the rules in § 1.860G-2(a)(3) (relating to a reasonable belief safe harbor for obligations principally secured by an interest in real property) to apply. *See* Conference Report, at 627. Furthermore, Congress did not intend for the mandatory basis adjustment rules to be avoided by securitization partnerships through dispositions of pool assets. *Id.* Finally, the legislative history states that if a partnership ceases to meet the qualifications of a securitization partnership, the mandatory basis adjustment provisions apply to the first transfer thereafter and to each subsequent transfer. *Id.*

c. *Section 734 substantial basis reduction provisions*

Section 734(b) requires a partnership to increase or decrease the adjusted basis of partnership property to take into account any gain or loss recognized to the distributee and the difference between the partnership's and the distributee's bases in distributed property. Similar to section 743, prior to the AJCA, section 734(a) did not require a partnership to adjust the basis of partnership property upon a distribution of partnership property to a partner unless the partnership had a section 754 election in effect.

Consistent with the amendments to section 743, section 833(c) of the AJCA amended section 734(a) and (b) to require a partnership to adjust the basis of partnership property upon a distribution of partnership property to a partner if there is a section 754 election in effect or, for distributions occurring after October 22, 2004, if there is a substantial basis reduction with respect to the distribution. Section 734(d)(1) provides that for purposes of section 734, there is a substantial basis reduction with respect to a distribution if the sum of the amounts described in section 734(b)(2)(A) and 734(b)(2)(B) exceeds $250,000. The amount described in section 734(b)(2)(A) is the amount of loss recognized to the distributee partner with respect to the distribution under section 731(a)(2). The amount described in section 734(b)(2)(B) is, in the case of distributed property to which section 732(b) applies, the excess of the basis of the distributed property to the distributee, as determined under section 732, over the adjusted basis of the distributed property to the partnership immediately before the distribution (as adjusted by section 732(d)). Section 734(d)(2) provides regulatory authority for the Secretary to carry out the purposes of section 734(d) by crossreference to section 743(d)(2). Section 743(d)(2) is discussed in Part 2.b.i of the Background section of this preamble.

As with section 743(b) adjustments, section 734(e) provides an exception to the mandatory basis adjustment provisions in section 734 for securitization partnerships. A securitization partnership (which is defined by reference to section 743(f)) is not treated as having a substantial basis reduction with respect to any distribution of property to a partner. *See* Part 2.b.iii of the Background section of this preamble for the definition of securitization partnership in section 743(f). Like the rules under section 743, the mandatory basis adjustment provisions under section 734 will apply with respect to the first distribution that occurs after the partnership ceases to meet the definition of a securitization partnership and to each subsequent distribution.

d. *Interim reporting requirements for mandatory basis adjustments*

The Treasury Department and the IRS issued general interim procedures for mandatory basis adjustments under sections 734 and 743. These interim procedures, which are described in Notice 2005-32, state that until further guidance is provided, partnerships required to reduce the bases of partnership properties under the substantial basis reduction provisions in section 734 must comply with § 1.734-1(d) as if an election under section 754 were in effect at the time of the relevant distribution. Similarly, partnerships that are required to reduce the bases of partnership properties under the substantial built-in loss provisions in section 743 must comply with § 1.743-1(k)(1), (3), (4), and (5) as if an election under section 754 were in effect at the time of the relevant transfer. Furthermore, a transferee of an interest in a partnership that is required to reduce the bases of partnership properties under the substantial built-in loss provisions must comply with § 1.743-1(k)(2) as if an election under section 754 were in effect at the time of the relevant transfer.

3. *Section 755 Rules for Allocation of Basis*

a. *Section 755(c)*

If section 734(a) requires a basis adjustment (either because the partnership has a section 754 election in effect or because there is a substantial basis reduction with respect to the distribution), section 734(b) provides that the partnership increases or decreases the basis of partnership property by any gain or loss recognized by the distributee and the difference (if any) between the partnership's and the distributee's adjusted bases in the distributed property. Section 755(a) generally provides that any increase or decrease in the adjusted basis of partnership property under section 734(b) shall be allocated in a manner that: (1) reduces the difference between the fair market value and the adjusted basis of partnership properties, or (2) in any other manner permitted by regulations. Generally, section 755(b) requires a partnership to allocate increases or decreases in the adjusted basis of partnership property arising from the distribution of property to property of a like character to the property distributed (either to (1) capital assets and property described in section 1231(b), or (2) any other property).

According to the Joint Committee on Taxation's (the JCT's) investigative report of Enron Corporation (*See* Joint Committee on Taxation, Report of Investigation of Enron Corporation and Related Entities Regarding Federal Tax and Compensation Issues, and Policy Recommendations, JCS-3-03 (February 2003) (JCT Enron Report)), taxpayers were engaging in transactions to achieve unintended tax results through the interaction of these partnership basis adjustment rules and the rules in section 1032 protecting a corporation from recognizing gain on its stock. Section 1032(a) provides that no gain or loss is recognized to a corporation on the receipt of money or other property in exchange for stock of the corporation. In particular, the JCT Enron Report describes Enron Corporation's Project Condor as structured to take advantage of the interaction between sections 754 and 1032 by increasing the basis of depreciable assets under section 732 while decreasing the basis under section 734(b) of preferred stock of a corporate partner held by the partnership. The step down in the basis of the corporate partner's preferred stock had no ultimate tax effect because the corporate partner could avoid recognizing the gain in the stock through section 1032, which prevents a corporation from recognizing gain on the sale of its stock. The transaction thus duplicated tax deductions at no economic cost. *See* Grassley Report, at 127 and House Committee Report, at 287. The JCT expressed specific concern about the exclusion of gain under section 1032 following a negative basis adjustment under section 734(b) to stock of a corporate partner. JCT Enron Report, at 220-21. Therefore, the JCT recommended that the partnership basis rules preclude an increase in basis to an asset if the offsetting basis reduction would be allocated to stock of a partner (or related party). *Id.* at 221.

In response to these recommendations, section 834(a) of the AJCA enacted section 755(c), which provides that in making an allocation under section 755(a) of any decrease in the adjusted basis of partnership property under section 734(b)—(1) no allocation may be made to stock in a corporation (or any person related (within the meaning of sections 267(b) and 707(b)(1)) to such corporation) that is a partner in the partnership, and (2) any amount not allocable to stock by reason of section 755(c)(1) shall be allocated under section 755(a) to other partnership property. The flush language of section 755(c) further provides that a partnership recognizes gain to the extent that the amount required to be allocated under section 755(c)(2) to other partnership property exceeds the aggregate adjusted basis of such other property immediately before the required allocation.

b. *Basis adjustment allocation rules for substituted basis transactions*

A basis adjustment under section 743(a) is determined in accordance with section 743(b). The partnership must allocate any increase or decrease in the adjusted basis of partnership property required under section 743(b) under the rules of section 755. Section 1.755-1(b)(5) provides additional guidance on how to allocate basis adjustments under section 743(b) that result from substituted basis transactions, which are defined as exchanges in which the transferee's basis in the partnership interest is determined in whole or in part by reference to the transferor's basis in that interest. For exchanges on or after June 9, 2003, § 1.755-1(b)(5) also applies to basis adjustments that result from exchanges in which the transferee's basis in the partnership interest is determined by reference to other property held at any time by the transferee.

Generally, § 1.755-1(b)(5)(ii) provides that if there is an increase in basis to be allocated to partnership assets, the increase must be allocated to capital gain property or ordinary income property, respectively, only if the total amount of gain or loss (including any remedial allocations under § 1.704-3(d)) that would be allocated to the transferee (to the extent attributable to the acquired partnership interest) from the hypothetical sale of all such property would result in a net gain or net income, as the case may be, to the transferee. Similarly, if there is a decrease in basis to be allocated to partnership assets, § 1.755-1(b)(5)(ii) generally provides that the decrease must be allocated to capital gain property or ordinary income property, respectively, only if the total amount of gain or loss (including any remedial allocations under § 1.704-3(d)) that would be allocated to the transferee (to the extent attributable to the acquired partnership interest) from the hypothetical sale of all such property would result in a net loss to the transferee. Thus, whether or not a basis adjustment resulting from a substituted basis transaction can be allocated to partnership property depends on whether the transferee partner would be allocated a net gain or net income, in the case of a positive basis adjustment, or net loss, in the case of a negative basis adjustment.

Section 1.755-1(b)(5)(iii) provides rules for allocating increases or decreases in basis within the classes of property. Of note, in the case of a decrease, § 1.755-1(b)(5)(iii)(B) states that the decrease must be allocated first to properties with unrealized depreciation in proportion to the transferee's shares of the respective amounts of unrealized depreciation before the decrease (but only to the extent of the transferee's share of each property's unrealized depreciation). Any remaining decrease must be allocated among the properties within the class in proportion to the transferee's shares of their adjusted bases (as adjusted under the preceding sentence) (subject to a limitation in decrease of basis in § 1.755-1(b)(5)(iii)(C) and a carryover rule in § 1.755-1(b)(5)(iii)(D)).

In addition, § 1.743-1(f) provides that, when there has been more than one transfer of a partnership interest, a partnership determines a transferee's basis adjustment without regard to any prior transferee's basis adjustment. Accordingly, if a partner acquires its partnership interest in a transaction other than a substituted basis transaction and then subsequently transfers its interest in a substituted basis transaction, the transferee's basis adjustment may shift among partnership assets.

4. *Miscellaneous Provisions*

a. *Section 704(c) allocations*

Property contributed to a partnership by a partner is section 704(c) property if, at the time of contribution, the property has a built-in gain or built-in loss ("forward section 704(c) gain or loss"). Section 704(c)(1)(A) requires a partnership to allocate income, gain, loss, and deduction so as to take into account the built-in gain or built-in loss. For this purpose, § 1.704-3(a)(3)(ii) provides that a built-in gain or built-in loss is generally the difference between the property's book value and the contributing partner's adjusted tax basis upon contribution (reduced by decreases in the difference between the property's book value and adjusted tax basis). Section 1.704-3(a)(6)(i) provides that the principles of section 704(c) also apply to allocations with respect to property for which differences between book value and adjusted tax basis are created when a partnership revalues property pursuant to § 1.704-1(b)(2)(iv)(*f*) or § 1.704-1(b)(2)(iv)(*s*) ("reverse section 704(c) allocations"). Partnerships are not required to use the same allocation method for forward and reverse section 704(c) allocations, but the allocation method (or combination of methods) must be reasonable. *See* §§ 1.704-3(a)(6)(i) and 1.704-3(a)(10)(i). Section 1.704-3(a)(10)(i) provides that an allocation method is not reasonable if the contribution or revaluation event and the corresponding allocation are made with a view to shifting the tax consequences of built-in gain or built-in loss among the partners in a manner that substantially reduces the present value of the partners' aggregate tax liability.

On August 12, 2009, the Treasury Department and the IRS published Notice 2009-70, 2009-2 CB 255, which requested comments on the proper application of the rules relating to the creation and maintenance of forward and multiple reverse section 704(c) allocations (referred to as "section 704(c) layers" in this preamble). Specifically, Notice 2009-70 requested comments on, among other things, whether taxpayers should net reverse section 704(c) allocations against existing section 704(c) layers or maintain separate section 704(c) layers if the section 704(c) layers offset one another; how partnerships should allocate tax depreciation, depletion, amortization, and gain or loss between multiple section 704(c) layers (including any offsetting section 704(c) layers); and whether there are other issues relating to section 704(c) layers. Public comments on Notice 2009-70 are discussed in Part 4.a of the Explanation of Provisions section of this preamble. *See* § 601.601(d)(2)(ii)(b).

b. *Extension of time period for taxing precontribution gain*

The Taxpayer Relief Act of 1997 (Pub. Law 105-34, 111 Stat. 788) extended the time period in sections 704(c)(1)(B) and 737(b)(1) for taxing precontribution gain for property contributed to a partnership after June 8, 1997, from five years to seven years (the rule does not, however, apply to any property contributed pursuant to a written binding contract in effect on June 8, 1997, and at all times thereafter before such contribution if such contract provides for the contribution of a fixed amount of property). The regulations under sections 704, 737, and 1502 have not been revised to reflect this statutory change.

Explanation of Provisions

1. *Contributions of Built-in Loss Property*

a. *Overview*

Section 704(c)(1)(C)(i) provides that if property contributed to a partnership has a built-in loss ("section 704(c)(1)(C) property"), such built-in loss shall be taken into account only in determining the amount of items allocated to the contributing partner ("section 704(c)(1)(C) partner"). Section 704(c)(1)(C)(ii) further provides that, except as provided by regulations, in determining the amount of items allocated to other partners, the basis of the contributed property in the hands of the partnership is equal to its fair market value at the time of the contribution. For purposes of section 704(c)(1)(C), the term *built-in loss* means the excess of the adjusted basis of the section 704(c)(1)(C) property (determined without regard to section 704(c)(1)(C)(ii)) over its fair market value at the time of contribution.

The Treasury Department and the IRS believe additional guidance is needed with respect to the application of section 704(c)(1)(C). Accordingly, the proposed regulations provide rules regarding: (1) the scope of section 704(c)(1)(C); (2) the effect of the built-in loss; (3) distributions by partnerships holding section 704(c)(1)(C) property; (4) transfers of a section 704(c)(1)(C) partner's partnership interest; (5) transfers of section 704(c)(1)(C) property; and (6) reporting requirements.

b. *Scope of section 704(c)(1)(C)*

The proposed regulations define section 704(c)(1)(C) property as section 704(c) property with a built-in loss at the time of contribution. Thus, in addition to the rules in the proposed regulations, section 704(c)(1)(C) property is subject to the existing rules and regulations applicable to section 704(c) property generally (see, for example, § 1.704-3(a)(9), which provides special rules for tiered partnerships), except as provided in the proposed regulations.

The Treasury Department and the IRS considered whether the principles of section 704(c)(1)(C) should apply to reverse section 704(c) allocations (within the meaning of § 1.704-3(a)(6)(i)). The Treasury Department and the IRS concluded that applying the proposed regulations to reverse section 704(c) allocations would be difficult for taxpayers to comply with and for the IRS to administer. Therefore, the proposed regulations do not apply to reverse section 704(c) allocations.

The Treasury Department and the IRS also considered whether section 704(c)(1)(C) should apply to § 1.752-7 liabilities. Under § 1.752-7(b)(3)(i), a § 1.752-7 liability is an obligation described in § 1.752-1(a)(4)(ii) (generally any fixed or contingent obligation to make payment without regard to whether the obligation is otherwise taken into account for purposes of Code) to the extent that the obligation either is not described in § 1.752-1(a)(4)(i) or the amount of the obligation exceeds the amount taken into account under § 1.752-1(a)(4)(i). The preamble to the final regulations under § 1.752-7, published on May 26, 2005, acknowledges that the rules in section 704(c)(1)(C) and the rules under § 1.752-7 are similar. *See* TD 9207, 70 FR 30334. The preamble explains that it is possible to view the contribution of property with an adjusted tax basis equal to the fair market value of the property, determined without regard to any § 1.752-7 liabilities, as built-in loss property after the § 1.752-7 liability is taken into account (when the § 1.752-7 liability is related to the contributed property). However, the preamble further provides that § 1.752-7 shall be applied without regard to the amendments made by the AJCA, unless future guidance provides to the contrary. The Treasury Department and the IRS believe the rules regarding § 1.752-7 liabilities adequately address the issues posed by § 1.752-7 liabilities and, thus, the proposed regulations provide that section 704(c)(1)(C) property does not include a § 1.752-7 liability.

c. *Effect of section 704(c)(1)(C) basis adjustment*

The legislative history indicates that Congress intended the built-in loss attributable to section 704(c)(1)(C) property to be for the benefit of the contributing partner only. Conceptually, the built-in loss is similar to a section 743(b) adjustment, which is an adjustment to the basis of partnership property solely with respect to the transferee partner. The current regulations under section 743 provide detailed rules regarding accounting for, maintenance of, recovery of, and transfers of assets with, section 743(b) adjustments. The Treasury Department and the IRS believe it is appropriate that the proposed regulations provide rules similar to those applicable to positive basis adjustments under section 743(b). The Treasury Department and the IRS believe that this approach simplifies the application and administration of section 704(c)(1)(C) and provides a framework of rules familiar to partners, partnerships, and the IRS. Even though the proposed regulations generally adopt the approach taken with respect to section 743(b) adjustments, the Treasury Department and the IRS believe that some of the rules governing section 743(b) adjustments should not apply with respect to a built-in loss and that additional rules are necessary for section 704(c)(1)(C). Thus, the proposed regulations import and specifically apply certain concepts contained in the section 743 regulations to section 704(c)(1)(C), as opposed to simply providing that principles similar to those contained in the regulations under section 743 apply to section 704(c)(1)(C) by cross-reference. The following discussion describes both the substantive rules applied under section 704(c)(1)(C) and, where applicable, how those rules differ from their counterparts under section 743(b).

The proposed regulations create the concept of a section 704(c)(1)(C) basis adjustment. The section 704(c)(1)(C) basis adjustment is initially equal to the built-in loss associated with the section 704(c)(1)(C) property at the contribution and then is adjusted in accordance with the proposed regulations. For example, if A contributes, in a section 721 transaction, property with a fair market value of $6,000 and an adjusted basis of $11,000 to a partnership, the partnership's basis in the property is $6,000, A's basis in its partnership interest is $11,000, and A has a section 704(c)(1)(C) basis adjustment of $5,000. Similar to basis adjustments under section 743(b), a section 704(c)(1)(C) basis adjustment is unique to the section 704(c)(1)(C) partner and does not affect the basis of partnership property or the partnership's computation of any item under section 703. The rules regarding the effect of the section 704(c)(1)(C) basis adjustment are similar to the rules for section 743(b) adjustments in §§1.743-1(j)(1) through (j)(3), including: (1) the effect of the section 704(c)(1)(C) basis adjustment on the basis of partnership property; (2) the computation and allocation of the partnership's items of income, deduction, gain, or loss; (3) adjustments to the partners' capital accounts; (4) adjustments to the section 704(c)(1)(C) partner's distributive share; and (5) the determination of a section 704(c)(1)(C) partner's income, gain, or loss from the sale or exchange of section 704(c)(1)(C) property. The Treasury Department and the IRS believe the rule regarding recovery of the section 704(c)(1)(C) basis adjustment should be consistent with the rule regarding recovery of the adjusted tax basis in the property that is not subject to section 704(c)(1)(C). Thus, for property eligible for cost recovery, the proposed regulations provide that, regarding the effect of the basis adjustment in determining items of deduction, if section 704(c)(1)(C) property is subject to amortization under section 197, depreciation under section 168, or other cost recovery in the hands of the section 704(c)(1)(C) partner, the section 704(c)(1)(C) basis adjustment associated with the property is recovered in accordance with section 197(f)(2), section 168(i)(7), or other applicable Code sections. Similar to section 743, the proposed regulations further provide that the amount of any section 704(c)(1)(C) basis adjustment that is recovered by the section 704(c)(1)(C) partner in any year is added to the section 704(c)(1)(C) partner's distributive share of the partnership's depreciation or amortization deductions for the year. The section 704(c)(1)(C) basis adjustment is adjusted under section 1016(a)(2) to reflect the recovery of the section 704(c)(1)(C) basis adjustment.

d. *Distribution by partnership holding section 704(c)(1)(C) property*

The proposed regulations provide guidance on current distributions of section 704(c)(1)(C) property to the section 704(c)(1)(C) partner; distributions of section 704(c)(1)(C) property to another partner; and liquidating distributions to a section 704(c)(1)(C) partner. The Treasury Department and the IRS believe it is appropriate to apply principles similar to section 743 to simplify the administration of section 704(c)(1)(C) for partners, partnerships, and the IRS. Thus, the proposed regulations generally provide rules similar to those for section 743(b) adjustments.

i. *Current distribution of section 704(c)(1)(C) property to section 704(c)(1)(C) partner*

Under the proposed regulations, the adjusted partnership basis of section 704(c)(1)(C) property distributed to the section 704(c)(1)(C) partner includes the section 704(c)(1)(C) basis adjustment for purposes of determining the amount of any adjustment under section 734. However, the proposed regulations provide that section 704(c)(1)(C) basis adjustments are not taken into account in making allocations under §1.755-1(c).

ii. *Distribution of section 704(c)(1)(C) property to another partner*

Under the proposed regulations, if a partner receives a distribution of property in which another partner has a section 704(c)(1)(C) basis adjustment, the distributee partner does not take the section 704(c)(1)(C) basis adjustment into account under section 732. However, the Treasury Department and the IRS request comments on whether a section 704(c)(1)(C) adjustment to distributed stock should be taken into account for purposes of section 732(f) notwithstanding the general rule that section 704(c)(1)(C) adjustments are not taken into account under section 732.

Upon the distribution of section 704(c)(1)(C) property to another partner, the section 704(c)(1)(C) partner reallocates its section 704(c)(1)(C) basis adjustment relating to the distributed property among the remaining items of partnership property under §1.755-1(c), which is similar to the rule in §1.743-1(g)(2)(ii) for reallocating section 743(b) adjustments. This rule allocates the basis adjustment to partnership property without regard to the section 704(c)(1)(C) partner's allocable share of income, gain, or loss in each partnership asset. The Treasury Department and the IRS request comments on whether the reallocations of section 704(c)(1)(C) basis adjustments and section 743(b) basis adjustments should instead be made under the principles of §1.755-1(b)(5)(iii) to take into account the partner's allocable share of income, gain, or loss from each partnership asset.

The proposed regulations further provide that if section 704(c)(1)(B) applies to treat the section 704(c)(1)(C) partner as recognizing loss on the sale of the distributed property, the section 704(c)(1)(C) basis adjustment is taken into account in determining the amount of loss. Accordingly, when the section 704(c)(1)(C) property is distributed to a partner other than the contributing partner within seven years of its contribution to the partnership, the loss will be taken into account by the contributing partner. The Treasury Department and the IRS considered extending the seven-year period so that the loss will be taken into account by the contributing partner on any distribution of section 704(c)(1)(C) property to a partner other than the contributing partner. The Treasury Department and the IRS do not adopt this approach in the proposed regulations because it would be inconsistent with section 704(c)(1)(B) generally and would be more difficult to administer.

iii. *Distribution in complete liquidation of a section 704(c)(1)(C) partner's interest*

The proposed regulations provide that if a section 704(c)(1)(C) partner receives a distribution of property (whether or not the property is section 704(c)(1)(C) property) in liquidation of its interest in the partnership, the adjusted basis to the partnership of the distributed property immediately before the distribution includes the section 704(c)(1)(C) partner's section 704(c)(1)(C) basis adjustment for the property in which the section 704(c)(1)(C) partner relinquished an interest (if any) by reason of the liquidation. For purposes of determining the redeemed section 704(c)(1)(C) partner's basis in distributed property under section 732, the partnership reallocates any section 704(c)(1)(C) basis adjustment from section 704(c)(1)(C) property retained by the partnership to distributed properties of like character under the principles of § 1.755-1(c)(i), after applying sections 704(c)(1)(B) and 737. If section 704(c)(1)(C) property is retained by the partnership, and no property of like character is distributed, then that property's section 704(c)(1)(C) basis adjustment is not reallocated to the distributed property for purposes of applying section 732.

If any section 704(c)(1)(C) basis adjustment is not reallocated to the distributed property in connection with the distribution, then that remaining section 704(c)(1)(C) basis adjustment shall be treated as a positive section 734(b) adjustment. If the distribution also gives rise to a negative section 734(b) adjustment, then the negative section 734(b) adjustment and the section 704(c)(1)(C) basis adjustment reallocation are netted together, and the net amount is allocated under § 1.755-1(c). If the partnership does not have a section 754 election in effect at the time of the liquidating distribution, the partnership shall be treated as having made a section 754 election solely for purposes of computing any negative section 734(b) adjustment that would arise from the distribution.

e. *Transfer of section 704(c)(1)(C) partner's partnership interest*

i. *In general*

Under section 722, a section 704(c)(1)(C) partner's basis in its partnership interest fully reflects the built-in loss portion of the basis of the contributed property and the built-in loss generally is taken into account by the section 704(c)(1)(C) partner upon disposition of the partnership interest. Therefore, in accordance with section 704(c)(1)(C)'s overall policy objective of preventing the inappropriate transfer of built-in losses through partnerships, the proposed regulations provide that the transferee of a section 704(c)(1)(C) partner's partnership interest generally does not succeed to the section 704(c)(1)(C) partner's section 704(c)(1)(C) basis adjustment. Instead, the share of the section 704(c)(1)(C) basis adjustment attributable to the interest transferred is eliminated. For example, if a section 704(c)(1)(C) partner sells 20 percent of its interest in a partnership, the partner recognizes its outside loss with respect to that 20 percent but 20 percent of the partner's section 704(c)(1)(C) basis adjustment for each section 704(c)(1)(C) property contributed by the partner is eliminated. The transferor remains a section 704(c)(1)(C) partner with respect to any remaining section 704(c)(1)(C) basis adjustments. The proposed regulations provide exceptions to this general rule for nonrecognition transactions, which are discussed in Part 1.e.ii of the Explanation of Provisions section of this preamble.

ii. *Nonrecognition transactions*

Under the proposed regulations, the general rule that a section 704(c)(1)(C) basis adjustment is not transferred with the related partnership interest does not apply to the extent a section 704(c)(1)(C) partner transfers its partnership interest in a nonrecognition transaction, with certain exceptions. The legislative history notes that Congress intended to treat a corporation succeeding to the attributes of a contributing corporate partner under section 381 in the same manner as the contributing partner. *See* Conference Report, at 623 n. 546. The Treasury Department and the IRS considered whether similar successor rules should apply in other nonrecognition transactions. Some of the considerations included: (1) providing consistent results regardless of the order in which a transaction occurs; (2) ensuring that built-in losses are not duplicated; (3) preventing the shifting of basis to other assets; (4) recognizing that other provisions in subchapter K (for example, section 743(b)) already apply to prevent many of the potential abuses; and (5) providing administrable rules for partners, partnerships, and the IRS. The Treasury Department and the IRS concluded that these considerations and the policy rationale underlying the successor rule for section 381 transactions in the legislative history weigh in favor of applying similar successor rules to other nonrecognition transactions, including section 721 transactions, section 351 transactions, and distributions governed by section 731. Thus, when the partnership interest is transferred in one of these nonrecognition transactions, the transferee generally succeeds to the transferor's section 704(c)(1)(C) basis adjustments attributable to the interest transferred and is treated as the section 704(c)(1)(C) partner with respect to such interest. If the nonrecognition transaction is described in section 168(i)(7)(B), then the rules in section 168(i)(7)(A) apply with respect to the transferor's cost recovery deductions under section 168 with respect to the section 704(c)(1)(C) basis adjustment. The proposed regulations further provide that if gain or loss is recognized in the transaction, appropriate adjustments must be made to the section 704(c)(1)(C) basis adjustment.

The Treasury Department and the IRS believe that a section 743(b) adjustment generally will prevent inappropriate duplication of loss when a partnership has a section 754 election in effect or a substantial built-in loss with respect to the transfer. (*See* Part 2.a.i. of the Explanation of Provisions section of this preamble for rules regarding substantial built-in loss transactions). To the extent that the transferee partner's basis in the transferred partnership interest does not reflect a built-in loss, a section 743(b) adjustment should require the partnership to reduce the basis of its properties to reflect the elimination of the built-in loss. The Treasury Department and the IRS believe that the amount of the section 704(c)(1)(C) adjustment and any negative 743(b) adjustment should be netted for this purpose. The Treasury Department and the IRS believe that similar treatment is appropriate when a partnership does not have a section 754 election in effect at the time of transfer to prevent duplication of the built-in loss. Therefore, regardless of whether a section 754 election is in effect or a substantial builtin loss exists with respect to a transfer, the proposed regulations provide that the transferee partner succeeds to the transferor's section 704(c)(1)(C) basis adjustment, as reduced by the amount of any negative section 743(b) adjustment that would be allocated to the section 704(c)(1)(C) property if the partnership had a section 754 election in effect at the time of the transfer.

The proposed regulations also provide that the general rule regarding nonrecognition transactions does not apply to the transfer of all or a portion of a section 704(c)(1)(C) partner's partnership interest by gift because the gift recipient does not fit within Congress's notion of a successor as described in the legislative history. *See* Conference Report, at 623 n. 546. Thus, the general transfer rule applies instead, and the section 704(c)(1)(C) basis adjustment is eliminated.

f. *Transfers of section 704(c)(1)(C) property*

The proposed regulations also provide guidance on the treatment of the section 704(c)(1)(C) partner and the section 704(c)(1)(C) basis adjustment when the partnership transfers section 704(c)(1)(C) property. Consistent with the rules under section 743, a section 704(c)(1)(C) partner's section 704(c)(1)(C) basis adjustment is generally taken into account in determining the section 704(c)(1)(C) partner's income, gain, loss, or deduction from the sale or exchange of section 704(c)(1)(C) property.

With certain exceptions, if section 704(c)(1)(C) property is transferred in a nonrecognition transaction, the proposed regulations provide that the section 704(c)(1)(C) partner retains the section 704(c)(1)(C) basis adjustment in the replacement property (in the case of a section 1031 transaction), in stock (in the case of a section 351 transaction), in a lower-tier partnership interest (in the case of a section 721 transaction), or in the same property held by a new partnership (in the case of a section 708(b)(1)(B) technical termination). The proposed regulations also provide additional rules for section 721 and section 351 transactions, which are described in the following sections.

i. *Contribution of section 704(c)(1)(C) property under section 721*

The proposed regulations provide rules for when, after a section 704(c)(1)(C) partner contributes section 704(c)(1)(C) property to an upper-tier partnership, the uppertier partnership contributes the property to a lower-tier partnership in a transaction described in section 721(a). The proposed regulations ensure that the section 704(c)(1)(C) adjustment amount is ultimately tracked back to the initial contributing partner, similar to the rules for section 721 contributions of property in which a partner has a section 743(b) adjustment.

In particular, the proposed regulations provide that the interest in the lower-tier partnership received by the upper-tier partnership is treated as the section 704(c)(1)(C) property with the same section 704(c)(1)(C) basis adjustment as the contributed property. The lower-tier partnership determines its basis in the contributed property by excluding the existing section 704(c)(1)(C) basis adjustment. However, the lower-tier partnership also succeeds to the upper-tier partnership's section 704(c)(1)(C) basis adjustment. The portion of the upper-tier partnership's basis in its interest in the lowertier partnership attributable to the section 704(c)(1)(C) basis adjustment must be segregated and allocated solely to the section 704(c)(1)(C) partner for whom the initial section 704(c)(1)(C) basis adjustment was made. Similarly, the section 704(c)(1)(C) basis adjustment to which the lower-tier partnership succeeds must be segregated and allocated solely to the upper-tier partnership, and the section 704(c)(1)(C) partner for whom the initial section 704(c)(1)(C) basis adjustment was made. If gain or loss is recognized on the transaction, appropriate adjustments must be made to the section 704(c)(1)(C) basis adjustment.

The proposed regulations provide that to the extent that any section 704(c)(1)(C) basis adjustment in a tiered partnership is recovered (for example, by sale or depreciation of the property), or is otherwise reduced, upper or lower partnerships in the tiered structure must make conforming reductions to related section 704(c)(1)(C) basis adjustments to prevent duplication of loss.

The proposed regulations recognize that the contribution from the upper-tier partnership to the lower-tier partnership will give rise to an additional section 704(c)(1)(C) basis adjustment if the value of the property has fallen below its common basis to the upper-tier partnership; this additional section 704(c)(1)(C) adjustment will be allocated among the partners of the upper-tier partnership in a manner that reflects their relative shares of that loss.

ii. *Transfer of section 704(c)(1)(C) property in a section 351 transaction*

The transfer of the section 704(c)(1)(C) property by a partnership to a corporation in a section 351 transaction severs the contributing partner's connection with the section 704(c)(1)(C) property at the partnership level. The section 704(c)(1)(C) partner, now an indirect shareholder of the corporation, no longer has a section 704(c)(1)(C) basis adjustment with respect to the property. The proposed regulations provide that if, in an exchange described in section 351, a partnership transfers section 704(c)(1)(C) property to a corporation, the stock the partnership receives in the exchange is treated, solely with respect to the section 704(c)(1)(C) partner, as section 704(c)(1)(C) property that generally has the same section 704(c)(1)(C) basis adjustment as the section 704(c)(1)(C) property transferred to the corporation (reduced by any portion of the section 704(c)(1)(C) basis adjustment that reduced the partner's share of any gain on the transaction). The transferee corporation's adjusted basis in the transferred property is determined under section 362 (including by applying section 362(e)), taking into account any section 704(c)(1)(C) basis adjustments in the transferred property. However, the proposed regulations provide that, if a partnership recognizes gain on the transfer, the partnership's gain is determined without regard to any section 704(c)(1)(C) basis adjustment, but the section 704(c)(1)(C) partner's gain does take into account the section 704(c)(1)(C) basis adjustment. *See* § 1.362-4(e)(1) for additional rules regarding the application of section 362(e) to transfers by partnerships.

iii. *Partnership technical terminations*

The proposed regulations provide that a partner with a section 704(c)(1)(C) basis adjustment in section 704(c)(1)(C) property held by a partnership that terminates under section 708(b)(1)(B) will continue to have the same section 704(c)(1)(C) basis adjustment with respect to section 704(c)(1)(C) property deemed contributed by the terminated partnership to the new partnership under §1.708-1(b)(4). In addition, the deemed contribution of property by a terminated partnership to a new partnership is not subject to the proposed regulations and does not create a section 704(c)(1)(C) basis adjustment.

iv. *Miscellaneous provisions*

The proposed regulations also provide additional rules for like-kind exchanges of section 704(c)(1)(C) property, dispositions of section 704(c)(1)(C) property in installment sales, and contributed contracts.

g. *Reporting requirements under section 704(c)(1)(C)*

The proposed regulations prescribe certain reporting requirements for section 704(c)(1)(C) basis adjustments that are similar to the requirements for section 743(b) adjustments. Specifically, the proposed regulations provide that a partnership that owns property for which there is a section 704(c)(1)(C) basis adjustment must attach a statement to the partnership return for the year of the contribution of the section 704(c)(1)(C) property setting forth the name and taxpayer identification number of the section 704(c)(1)(C) partner as well as the section 704(c)(1)(C) basis adjustment and the section 704(c)(1)(C) property to which the adjustment relates.

2. *Mandatory Basis Adjustment Provisions*

a. *Section 743 substantial built-in loss provisions*

i. *General provisions*

The proposed regulations generally restate the statutory language in section 743(a) and (b) regarding substantial built-in losses, but provide additional guidance in several areas. The proposed regulations clarify that, if a partnership has a substantial built-in loss immediately after the transfer of a partnership interest, the partnership is treated as having a section 754 election in effect for the taxable year in which the transfer occurs, but only with respect to that transfer (unless another transaction is also subject to the mandatory basis adjustment provisions of sections 734 or 743).

The proposed regulations also provide that in determining whether there is a substantial built-in loss, section 743(b) adjustments and section 704(c)(1)(C) basis adjustments (except the transferee's section 743(b) adjustments and section 704(c)(1)(C) basis adjustments, if any) are disregarded.

The proposed regulations also provide special rules for determining fair market value in the case of a tiered partnership. The Treasury Department and the IRS are aware that there is some uncertainty as to how to determine the fair market value of a lower-tier partnership interest for purposes of determining whether the partnership has a substantial built-in loss in its assets when the upper-tier partnership is allocated a share of the lower-tier partnership's liabilities under section 752. The Treasury Department and the IRS believe it is appropriate for this purpose to gross up the fair market value of the lower-tier partnership interest by the upper-tier partnership's allocated share of liabilities; otherwise, the regulations could inappropriately treat a lower-tier partnership interest as a loss asset. Thus, under the proposed regulations, the fair market value of a lower-tier partnership interest (solely for purposes of computing the upper-tier partnership's basis adjustment under section 743(b)) is equal to the sum of: (i) the amount of cash that the upper-tier partnership would receive if the lower-tier partnership sold all of its property for cash to an unrelated person for an amount equal to the fair market value of such property, satisfied all of its liabilities, and liquidated; and (ii) the upper-tier partnership's share of the lower-tier partnership's liabilities (as determined under section 752 and the regulations).

In addition, the proposed regulations provide special rules for basis adjustments with respect to tiered partnerships. Under the authority granted by section 743(d)(2), the proposed regulations provide that if a partner transfers an interest in an upper-tier partnership that holds a direct or indirect interest in a lower-tier partnership, and the upper-tier partnership has a substantial built-in loss with respect to the transfer, each lower-tier partnership is treated, solely with respect to the transfer, as if it had made a section 754 election for the taxable year of the transfer. The Treasury Department and the IRS are aware of the practical and administrative difficulties associated with requiring a lower-tier partnership that has not elected under section 754 to adjust the basis of its assets in connection with the transfer of an interest in an upper-tier partnership. Comments are requested on the scope of this rule and on measures to ease administrative burdens while still accomplishing the objective of the statute.

These proposed regulations also provide guidance on the application of section 743(b) adjustments in tiered partnership situations generally. Consistent with Rev. Rul. 87-115, 1987-2 CB 163, the proposed regulations provide that if an interest in an uppertier partnership that holds an interest in a lower-tier partnership is transferred by sale or exchange or upon the death of a partner, and the upper-tier partnership and the lowertier partnership both have elections in effect under section 754, then an interest in the lower-tier partnership will be deemed to have been transferred by sale or exchange or upon the death of a partner, as the case may be. The amount of the interest in the lower-tier partnership deemed to have been transferred is the portion of the upper-tier partnership's interest in the lower-tier partnership that is attributable to the interest in the upper-tier partnership being transferred. Accordingly, to the extent the adjusted basis of the upper-tier partnership's interest in a lower-tier partnership is adjusted, the lower-tier partnership must adjust the basis of its properties.

Section 743(e)(7) provides that the Secretary may prescribe regulations for applying the EIP rules to tiered partnerships, and the legislative history makes clear that Congress did not intend for EIPs to avoid the mandatory basis adjustment provisions through the use of tiered partnerships. *See* Conference Report, at 627. The Treasury Department and the IRS believe that the same concerns exist for tiered EIPs as exist for all other partnerships subject to the mandatory basis adjustment provisions. Accordingly, the proposed regulations do not include specific rules for tiered EIPs beyond the rules governing all tiered partnerships.

The proposed regulations provide anti-abuse rules. The purpose of the amendments to section 743 is to prevent a partner that purchases an interest in a partnership with an existing built-in loss and no election under section 754 in effect from being allocated a share of the loss when the partnership disposes of the property or takes cost recovery deductions with respect to the property. Accordingly, consistent with the purpose of the amendments and the specific grant of regulatory authority in section 743(d)(2), the proposed regulations provide that the provisions of section 743 and the regulations thereunder regarding substantial built-in loss transactions must be applied in a manner consistent with the purpose of such provisions and the substance of the transaction. Thus, if a principal purpose of a transaction is to avoid the application of the substantial built-in loss rules with respect to a transfer, the Commissioner can recast the transaction for Federal income tax purposes as appropriate to achieve tax results that are consistent with the purpose of the provisions. Whether a tax result is inconsistent with the purpose of the substantial built-in loss provisions is determined based on all the facts and circumstances. For example, under the proposed regulations, property held by related partnerships may be aggregated and a contribution of property to a partnership may be disregarded in applying the substantial built-in loss provisions in section 743 and the regulations thereunder if the property was transferred with a principal purpose of avoiding the application of such provisions.

Finally, the proposed regulations clarify that a partnership that has a substantial built-in loss immediately following the transfer of a partnership interest must comply with certain provisions of §1.743-1(k). In this case, the partnership must attach a statement of adjustments to its partnership return as if an election under section 754 were in effect at the time of the transfer solely with respect to the transfer for which there is a substantial built-in loss.

One commenter on the Notice requested that the Treasury Department and the IRS provide a de minimis exception for the substantial built-in loss provisions for transfers of small interests (subject to an annual limit on aggregate transfers during a taxable year). The substantial built-in loss provisions are intended to prevent the inappropriate shifting of losses among partners, and neither the legislative history nor the statute suggests that Congress intended to limit the scope of the rule to the transfer of large interests. Accordingly, the Treasury Department and the IRS decline to provide an exception to the substantial built-in loss rules based on the size of the interest transferred. The Treasury Department and the IRS will continue to study, and request comments on, whether a rule is warranted that excludes de minimis basis adjustments from the mandatory adjustment provisions.

ii. *EIPs*

The proposed regulations generally adopt the statutory language in section 743(e) and the provisions in the Notice. The Notice requested comments on certain aspects of the interim procedures for EIPs, and the Treasury Department and the IRS received comments in response to that request, which are described in this section.

The Notice detailed reporting requirements for transferors of EIP interests so that transferees could comply with the loss limitation rule in section 743(e)(2). The proposed regulations clarify that the reporting requirements with respect to transferors of an interest in an EIP described in the Notice do not apply if the transferor recognizes gain on the transfer and no prior transferor recognized a loss on any transfer. The Treasury Department and the IRS do not believe reporting is necessary in this limited circumstance because the transferee should not be subject to the loss limitation rule of section 743(e)(2).

In regard to the requirement in section 743(e)(6)(I) that the partnership agreement provide for a term that is not in excess of 15 years, one commenter requested that regulations provide that a partnership may still qualify as an EIP even if the partnership's initial term is greater than 15 years, particularly in cases in which the amount of the partnership's equity investment in the remaining assets is small (for example, 25 percent of the total committed capital). However, Congress considered the circumstances in which it would be appropriate to provide an extension of the term and specifically provided an exception to the 15-year requirement for EIPs in existence on June 4, 2004. Accordingly, the Treasury Department and the IRS decline to adopt this comment in the proposed regulations.

The Notice also provides guidance on whether a partnership has ever been engaged in a trade or business for purposes of section 743(e)(6)(C). The Notice provides that until further guidance is issued, an upper-tier partnership will not be treated as engaged in the trade or business of a lower-tier partnership if, at all times during the period in which the upper-tier partnership owns an interest in the lower-tier partnership, the adjusted basis of its interest in the lower-tier partnership is less than 25 percent of the total capital that is required to be contributed to the upper-tier partnership by its partners during the entire term of the upper-tier partnership (the "25% Rule"). The Notice specifically requests comments on rules that would be appropriate for future guidance in determining whether an upper-tier partnership is treated as engaged in a trade or business that is conducted by a lower-tier partnership. One commenter requested that the Treasury Department and the IRS confirm whether the 25% Rule is a safe harbor or whether a violation of the 25% Rule disqualifies a partnership from being an EIP. This commenter also requested that the Treasury Department and the IRS clarify the 25% Rule in the case of borrowing. The commenter noted that lower-tier partnership interests are often acquired with capital contributions and the proceeds of borrowing. Therefore, the commenter requested that any safe harbor take into account leverage. This commenter further suggested that rules similar to the rules in § 1.731-2(e)(3) (providing circumstances in which a partnership would not be treated as engaged in a trade or business for purposes of section 731(c)(3)(C)) should apply for purposes of section 743(e)(6)(C). Finally, the commenter requested that the Treasury Department and the IRS provide additional safe harbors (for example, where the uppertier partnership is organized for investment services and the partners and managers of the upper-tier partnership do not engage in the day-to-day operations of the lower-tier partnership's trade or business activity, but partners and/or managers are on the board of directors of the lower-tier partnership).

The Treasury Department and the IRS view the 25% Rule as a bright-line rule. Therefore, a failure to meet the 25% Rule will mean that the partnership fails to qualify as an EIP. The Treasury Department and the IRS agree that the rules in § 1.731-2(e)(3) should apply for purposes of section 743(e)(6)(C). Therefore, the proposed regulations provide a safe harbor by cross-referencing those rules. Under the proposed regulations, if a partnership would not be treated as engaged in a trade or business under § 1.731-2(e)(3) for purposes of section 731(c)(3)(C), the partnership also will not be treated as engaged in a trade or business for purposes of section 743(e)(6)(C). The Treasury Department and the IRS believe the 25% Rule and the cross-reference to § 1.731-2(e)(3) provide appropriate guidance under section 743(e)(6)(C) and therefore the proposed regulations do not provide any additional safe harbors. The Treasury Department and the IRS are continuing to study the extent to which borrowing should be taken into account in applying the 25% Rule and therefore request comments on appropriate rules.

A commenter also requested additional guidance regarding section 743(e)(6)(H), which provides that one of the eligibility requirements for an EIP is that the partnership agreement have substantive restrictions on each partner's ability to cause a redemption of the partner's interest. The proposed regulations follow the examples in the legislative history and provide that substantive restrictions for purposes of section 743(e)(7)(H) include cases in which a redemption is permitted under a partnership agreement only if the redemption is necessary to avoid a violation of state, federal, or local laws (such as ERISA or the Bank Holding Company Act) or the imposition of a federal excise tax on, or a change in the federal tax-exempt status of, a tax-exempt partner. *See* Conference Report at 626. The Treasury Department and the IRS request comments on other restrictions that could be considered substantive restrictions on a partner's ability to cause a redemption of the partner's interest for purposes of section 743(e)(6)(H).

The proposed regulations provide that the EIP election must be made on a timely filed original return, including extensions. One commenter requested relief for certain instances in which the partnership fails to make a valid EIP election. The commenter requested relief when: (1) a partnership makes an EIP election, but did not qualify to make the election; (2) the partnership attempts to make an EIP election, but it is defective; or (3) the partnership makes an EIP election, but fails to continue to qualify. In each case, the commenter believes that the Treasury Department and the IRS should treat the partnership as an EIP if: (a) its failure to qualify or the defect was inadvertent; (b) the partners and the partnership consistently treated the partnership as an EIP; (c) steps were taken to cure the defect in a reasonable period of time; and (d) the partners and the EIP agree to make any necessary adjustments. The Treasury Department and the IRS do not adopt this comment in the proposed regulations because there are existing procedures for situations in which a regulatory election is defective.

The Treasury Department and the IRS request comments on appropriate rules for situations in which a partnership that has elected to be an EIP fails to qualify in a particular year, but then qualifies again in a future year. The Treasury Department and the IRS also request comments on the circumstances in which a qualifying partnership that has revoked an EIP election should be permitted to reelect and the rules and procedures that should apply to the reelection.

iii. *Securitization partnerships*

The proposed regulations generally restate the statutory provisions relating to the exception from the substantial built-in loss provisions for securitization partnerships.

b. *Section 734 substantial basis reduction provisions*

i. *General provisions*

The proposed regulations generally follow the statutory provisions regarding substantial basis reductions. Questions have been raised regarding whether the $250,000 threshold in section 734(d)(1) applies to a partnership's aggregate distributions for a taxable year. The Treasury Department and the IRS believe that the better interpretation of section 734(a), (b), and (d) is that the threshold applies separately with respect to each distributee because: (1) both section 734(a) and (b) refer to a distribution of property to "a partner;" and (2) section 734(b)(2)(A) and (B), referenced in section 734(d), refer to the "distributee partner" or the "distributee." These references indicate that the substantial built-in loss provisions apply to each partner-distributee separately, but with respect to the entire distribution made to the distributee. That is, where multiple properties are distributed to a partner-distributee, the $250,000 threshold is determined by reference to all properties distributed to the partner-distributee as part of the same distribution.

The proposed regulations also provide additional guidance in several areas. The proposed regulations provide that if there is a substantial basis reduction, the partnership is treated as having an election under section 754 in effect for the taxable year in which the distribution occurs, but solely for the distribution to which the substantial basis reduction relates (unless another transaction is subject to the mandatory basis adjustment provisions of sections 734 or 743). For example, if a partnership without a section 754 election in effect has a substantial basis reduction with respect to a distribution, and a partner in the partnership in that same year transfers a partnership interest (and the partnership does not have a substantial built-in loss immediately after the transfer), the partnership will be treated as having a section 754 election in effect for the distribution but not the transfer.

The same issues exist in the context of section 734(b) adjustments and tiered partnerships as exist with respect to section 743(b) adjustments and tiered partnerships. Thus, the proposed regulations also provide guidance for substantial basis reductions in tiered partnership arrangements. Under the proposed regulations, if there is a substantial basis reduction with respect to a distribution by an upper-tier partnership that (either directly or indirectly through one or more partnerships) holds an interest in a lower-tier partnership, each lower-tier partnership is treated, solely with respect to the distribution, as if it had made an election under section 754 for the taxable year in which the distribution occurs.

These proposed regulations also provide guidance on the application of section 734(b) adjustments in tiered partnership situations generally. Consistent with Rev. Rul. 92-15, 1992-1 CB 215, if an upper-tier partnership makes an adjustment under section 734(b) to the basis of an interest it holds in a lower-tier partnership that has an election under section 754 in effect, the lower-tier partnership must make adjustments to the upper-tier partnership's share of the lower-tier partnership's assets. The amount of the lower-tier partnership's adjustment is equal to the adjustment made by the upper-tier partnership to the basis of its interest in the lower-tier partnership. The lower-tier partnership's adjustment to the upper-tier partnership's share of its assets is for the upper-tier partnership only and does not affect the basis in the lower-tier partnership's property for the other partners of the lower-tier partnership.

The Treasury Department and the IRS are aware of the practical and administrative difficulties associated with the requirement that a lower-tier partnership adjust the basis of its assets with respect to adjustments under both section 734 and section 743 and request comments on the scope of this rule and measures to ease the administrative burden while still accomplishing the objective of the statute.

The proposed regulations also update § 1.734-1(d) to clarify that its reporting requirements apply if there is a substantial basis reduction with respect to a distribution. In this case, the provisions of § 1.734-1(d) apply solely with respect to the distribution to which the substantial basis reduction relates as if an election under section 754 were in effect at the time of the transfer.

ii. *Securitization partnerships*

The proposed regulations generally restate the statutory provisions relating to the exception from the substantial basis reduction provisions for securitization partnerships.

3. *Section 755 Basis Allocation Rules*

a. *Section 755(c)*

The proposed regulations generally restate the statutory provisions of section 755(c) and provide rules applicable to an allocation of a downward adjustment in the basis of partnership property under sections 734(b) and 755(a). As discussed in Part 3 of the Background section of this preamble, Congress enacted section 755(c) in response to the JCT's investigation of Enron Corporation. In addressing transactions among related parties, the JCT Enron Report specifically provides that:

> Partnership allocations between members of the same affiliated group (and, in general, related parties) may not have the same economic consequences as allocations between unrelated partners. As a result, related partners can use the partnership allocation rules inappropriately to shift basis among assets . . . The Joint Committee staff recommends that . . . the partnership basis rules should be altered to preclude an increase in basis to an asset if the offsetting basis reduction would be allocated to stock of a partner (or related party).

JCT Enron Report, at 29-30. The proposed regulations provide that in making an allocation under section 755(a) of any decrease in the adjusted basis of partnership property under section 734(b), no allocation may be made to stock in a corporation (or any person related (within the meaning of sections 267(b) or 707(b)(1)) to such corporation) that is a partner in the partnership. Given Congress's intent to prevent taxpayers from shifting tax gain to stock of a corporate partner or corporation related to a corporate partner, the Treasury Department and the IRS believe it is appropriate to interpret section 755(c) to apply broadly to related persons under either section 267(b) or section 707(b)(1). *See* Grassley Report, at 127 and House Committee Report, at 287. If section 755(c) only applied to persons treated as related within the meaning of both section 267(b) and section 707(b)(1), then the provision would apply in very limited circumstances, significantly restricting the scope of section 755(c).

b. *Modification of basis allocation rules for substituted basis transactions*

The Treasury Department and the IRS are aware that the current basis allocation rules for substituted basis transactions can result in unintended consequences, particularly with regard to the "net gain" and "net loss" requirement in § 1.755-1(b)(5)(ii). The net gain or net loss requirement in § 1.755-1(b)(5)(ii) may, in certain situations, cause a partnership to be unable to properly adjust the basis of partnership property with respect to a transferee partner. For example, when there is an increase in basis to be allocated to partnership assets and the property of the partnership does not have overall unrealized net gain or net income, the basis increase cannot be allocated under § 1.755-1(b)(5). Conversely, if there is a decrease in basis to be allocated to partnership assets and the property of the partnership does not have overall unrealized net loss, the basis decrease cannot be allocated under § 1.755-1(b)(5). The Treasury Department and the IRS believe this result is inappropriate. Accordingly, the Treasury Department and the IRS propose to amend the current regulations as described in this preamble.

i. *Allocations between classes of property*

The proposed regulations provide that if there is an increase in basis to be allocated to partnership assets under § 1.755-1(b)(5), the increase must be allocated between capital gain property and ordinary income property in proportion to, and to the extent of, gross gain or gross income (including any remedial allocations under § 1.704-3(d)) that would be allocated to the transferee (to the extent attributable to the acquired partnership interest) from the hypothetical sale of all property in each class. The proposed regulations further provide that any remaining increase must be allocated between the classes in proportion to the fair market value of all property in each class.

If there is a decrease in basis to be allocated to partnership assets under § 1.755-1(b)(5), the proposed regulations provide that the decrease must be allocated between capital gain property and ordinary income property in proportion to, and to the extent of, the gross loss (including any remedial allocations under § 1.704-3(d)) that would be allocated to the transferee (to the extent attributable to the acquired partnership interest) from the hypothetical sale of all property in each class. Any remaining decrease must be allocated between the classes in proportion to the transferee's shares of the adjusted bases of all property in each class (as adjusted under the preceding sentence). Thus, the proposed regulations remove the requirements that (1) there be an overall net gain or net income in partnership property for an increase in basis to be allocated to a particular class of property; and (2) there be an overall net loss in partnership property for a decrease in basis to be allocated to a particular class of property.

ii. *Allocations within classes of property*

The Treasury Department and the IRS are aware that there is uncertainty regarding whether the transferee's shares of unrealized appreciation and depreciation described in § 1.755-1(b)(5)(iii)(A) and (B) include only amounts attributable to the acquired partnership interest. The proposed regulations clarify that the transferee's shares of the items are limited to the amounts attributable to the acquired partnership interest.

In addition, § 1.755-1(b)(5)(iii)(C) has a limitation that provides that a transferee's negative basis adjustment is limited to the transferee's share of the partnership's adjusted basis in all depreciated assets in that class. By focusing on the transferee's share of adjusted basis with respect to only depreciated assets in the class, as opposed to all assets in the class, this rule subjects more of the negative basis adjustment to the carryover rules in § 1.755-1(b)(5)(iii)(D). The Treasury Department and the IRS believe this result is inappropriate. Accordingly, the proposed regulations provide that if a decrease in basis must be allocated to partnership property and the amount of the decrease otherwise allocable to a particular class exceeds the transferee's share of the adjusted basis to the partnership of all assets in that class, the basis of the property is reduced to zero (but not below zero). Therefore, under the proposed regulations, the negative basis adjustment is no longer limited to the transferee's share of the partnership's adjusted basis in all depreciated assets in a class.

c. *Succeeding to transferor's basis adjustment*

The proposed regulations amend the regulations under section 743 to provide an exception to the rule that a transferee's basis adjustment is determined without regard to any prior transferee's basis adjustment. The Treasury Department and the IRS believe that this rule can lead to inappropriate results when the transferor transfers its partnership interest in a substituted basis transaction (within the meaning of § 1.755-1(b)(5)) and the transferor had a basis adjustment under section 743(b) attributable to the transferred interest that was allocated pursuant to § 1.755-1(b)(2) through (b)(4). Under the current regulations, the transferee does not succeed to the transferor's section 743(b) adjustment but, rather, is entitled to a new section 743(b) adjustment that is allocated under a different set of rules, which may result in the inappropriate shifting of basis among the partnership's assets. The proposed regulations provide that the transferee in a substituted basis transaction succeeds to that portion of the transferor's basis adjustment attributable to the transferred partnership interest and that the adjustment is taken into account in determining the transferee's share of the adjusted basis to the partnership for purposes of § § 1.743-1(b) and 1.755-1(b)(5).

4. *Miscellaneous Provisions*

a. *Special rules for forward and reverse section 704(c) allocations*

One commenter on Notice 2009-70 noted that the definitions of the terms "built-in gain" and "built-in loss" in § 1.704-3(a)(3)(ii) imply that section 704(c) layers with "different signs" should be netted against each other because the regulations provide that built-in gain or built-in loss is reduced by decreases in the difference between the property's adjusted tax basis and book value.

In response to this comment, the proposed regulations provide that built-in gain and built-in loss do not take into account any decreases or increases, as the case may be, to the property's book value pursuant to a revaluation of partnership property under § 1.704-1(b)(2)(iv)(*f*) or § 1.704-1(b)(2)(iv)(*s*). Thus, for example, under the proposed regulations, reverse section 704(c) allocations do not reduce forward section 704(c) gain or loss.

The Treasury Department and the IRS also received several comments regarding the proper treatment of section 704(c) layers, suggesting one of two approaches. Under the layering approach, a partnership would create and maintain multiple section 704(c) layers for the property. Under the netting approach, a partnership would net multiple section 704(c) layers for the property and therefore each section 704(c) property would have one section 704(c) layer. One commenter recommended that the layering approach be the default rule, but that certain partnerships should be permitted to adopt a netting approach depending on the value of the partnership's assets. This commenter believed that the layering approach is more appropriate because the netting approach can result in distortions when partnerships use the traditional method of allocating section 704(c) amounts and the ceiling rule is implicated. The commenter also argued that the layering approach better maintains the economic expectations of the partners and is generally more consistent with the policy underlying section 704(c). However, this commenter also acknowledged that the netting approach is simpler to apply, and that in many cases both approaches will reach the same result. Another commenter suggested that partnerships be given the option of using either the layering approach or the netting approach. According to the commenter, this would allow partnerships to avoid the burden and expense of maintaining section 704(c) layers, particularly when maintaining section 704(c) layers is unnecessary.

The proposed regulations do not permit taxpayers to use a netting approach because a netting approach could lead to distortions. The Treasury Department and the IRS understand, however, that maintaining section 704(c) layers may result in additional administrative burdens and, therefore, request comments on when it is appropriate for partnerships to use a netting approach (for example, small partnerships).

One commenter noted that guidance was necessary with respect to how to allocate tax items among multiple section 704(c) layers. This commenter suggested three methods for allocating tax items: (1) allocate tax items to the oldest layer first; (2) allocate tax items to the newest section 704(c) layers first; and (3) allocate tax items among the section 704(c) layers pro rata based on the amount of each layer. The commenter suggested that the Treasury Department and the IRS provide a default rule that would allocate to the oldest section 704(c) layers first, but permit partnerships to elect any reasonable method (such as the three methods described).

The Treasury Department and the IRS agree that partnerships should be permitted to use any reasonable method in allocating tax items. The Treasury Department and the IRS decline to adopt a default rule for allocating tax items because no single method is more appropriate than other methods. Therefore, the proposed regulations provide that a partnership may use any reasonable method to allocate items of income, gain, loss, and deduction associated with an item of property among the property's forward and reverse section 704(c) layers subject to the anti-abuse rule in § 1.704-3(a)(10). The partnership's choice of method is also subject to § 1.704-3(a)(2), which provides that a partnership may use different methods with respect to different items of contributed property, provided that the partnership and the partners consistently apply a single reasonable method for each item of contributed property and that the overall method or combination of methods is reasonable based on the facts and circumstances and consistent with the purpose of section 704(c). The Treasury Department and the IRS are considering providing examples of reasonable methods in future guidance and therefore request comments on these and other methods for allocating tax items.

b. *Extension of time period for taxing precontribution gain*

The proposed regulations amend various provisions in §§ 1.704-4, 1.737-1, and 1.1502-13 to reflect the amendments to sections 704(c)(1)(B) and 737(b)(1) that lengthen the period of time for taxing precontribution gain from five years to seven years. The proposed regulations also clarify how partners determine the seven-year period. Specifically, the proposed regulations provide that the seven-year period begins on, and includes, the date of contribution, and ends on, and includes, the last date that is within seven years of the contribution.

Proposed Effective Date

These regulations are generally proposed to apply to partnership contributions and transactions occurring on or after the date final regulations are published in the **Federal Register**. The proposed regulations under § 1.755-1(b)(5) will apply to transfers of partnership interests occurring on or after January 16, 2014. No inference is intended as to the tax consequences of transactions occurring before the effective date of these regulations.

Special Analyses

It has been determined that this notice of proposed rulemaking is not a significant regulatory action as defined in Executive Order 12866, as supplemented by Executive Order 13563. Therefore, a regulatory assessment is not required. It has also been determined that section 553(b) of the Administrative Procedure Act (5 U.S.C. chapter 5) does not apply to these regulations. It is hereby certified that the collection of information in this notice of proposed rulemaking will not have a significant economic impact on a substantial number of small entities within the meaning of section 601(6) of the Regulatory Flexibility Act (5 U.S.C. chapter 6). The Treasury Department and the IRS believe that the economic impact on small entities as a result of the collection of information in this notice of proposed rulemaking will not be significant. The small entities subject to the collection are business entities formed as partnerships that: (1) receive a contribution of built-in loss property; (2) are required to make a mandatory basis adjustment under section 734 or section 743; and/or (3) are eligible for, and elect to apply, the electing investment partnership provisions in section 743(e). In the case of the contribution of built-in loss property, the partnership is required to provide a statement in the year of contribution setting forth basic information that the partnership will need in order to properly apply the rules. Similarly, in the case of the mandatory basis adjustment provisions, the partnership will already have the information subject to the collection in order to comply with the rules. In the case of EIPs, the collections are either one-time (election) or annual (annual statement). The collection only applies if the partnership elects to be an EIP. Furthermore, the proposed regulations provide the specific language for the annual statement. Finally, the collection regarding the mandatory basis adjustment provisions and the EIP rules have been in effect since 2005, as required by Notice 2005-32, and the Treasury Department and the IRS have not received comments that the collections have a significant economic impact. For these reasons, the Treasury Department and the IRS do not believe that the collection of information in this notice of proposed rulemaking has a significant economic impact. Pursuant to section 7805(f) of the Code, this notice of proposed rulemaking will be submitted to the Chief Counsel for Advocacy of the Small Business Administration for comment on its impact on small business.

Comments and Public Hearing

Before the proposed regulations are adopted as final regulations, consideration will be given to any written (a signed original and eight (8) copies) or electronic comments that are submitted timely to the IRS. The Treasury Department and the IRS request comments on all aspects of the proposed rules. All comments will be available for public inspection and copying.

A public hearing has been scheduled for April 30, 2014 beginning at 10:00 a.m. in the Auditorium, Internal Revenue Building, 1111 Constitution Avenue NW, Washington, DC. Due to building security procedures, visitors must enter at the Constitution Avenue entrance. In addition, all visitors must present photo identification to enter the building. Because of access restrictions, visitors will not be admitted beyond the immediate entrance area more than 30 minutes before the hearing starts. For information about having your name placed on the building access list to attend the hearing, see the "FOR FURTHER INFORMATION CONTACT" section of this preamble.

The rules of 26 CFR 601.601(a)(3) apply to the hearing. Persons who wish to present oral comments at the hearing must submit electronic or written comments by April 16, 2014, and an outline of the topics to be discussed and the time to be devoted to each topic (signed original and eight (8) copies) by April 16, 2014. A period of 10 minutes will be allotted to each person for making comments. An agenda showing the scheduling of the speakers will be prepared after the deadline for receiving outlines has passed. Copies of the agenda will be available free of charge at the hearing.

Drafting Information

The principal authors of these regulations are Wendy L. Kribell and Benjamin H. Weaver, Office of the Associate Chief Counsel (Passthroughs & Special Industries). However, other personnel from the Treasury Department and the IRS participated in their development.

[¶49,609] Proposed Regulations (REG-143874-10) and Withdrawal of Notice of Proposed Rulemaking (EE-96-85), published in the Federal Register on February 6, 2014.

[Code Sec. 512]

Exempt organizations: Unrelated business income: Covered entities.—Reg. §1.512(a)-5, providing guidance on how certain organizations that provide employee benefits must calculate unrelated business taxable income (UBTI), is proposed. Reg. §1.512(a)-5 that was proposed on February 4, 1986, is withdrawn.

AGENCY: Internal Revenue Service (IRS), Treasury.

ACTION: Withdrawal of notice of proposed rulemaking and notice of proposed rulemaking.

SUMMARY: This document contains a new proposed regulation providing guidance on how certain organizations that provide employee benefits must calculate unrelated business taxable income (UBTI). This document also withdraws the notice of proposed rulemaking relating to UBTI that was published on February 4, 1986.

DATES: The notice of proposed rulemaking that was published on February 4, 1986, at 51 FR 4391 is withdrawn as of February 6, 2014. Written or electronic comments and request for a public hearing must be received by May 7, 2014.

ADDRESSES: Send Submissions to: CC:PA:LPD:PR (REG-143874-10), room 5203, Internal Revenue Service, P.O. Box 7604, Ben Franklin Station, Washington, DC 20224. Submissions may be hand delivered Monday through Friday between the hours of 8 a.m. and 4 p.m. to CC:PA:LPD:PR (REG-143874-10), Courier's Desk, Internal Revenue Service, 1111 Constitution Avenue NW, Washington, DC, or sent electronically via the Federal eRulemaking Portal at *www.regulations.gov* (IRS REG-143874-10).

FOR FURTHER INFORMATION CONTACT: Concerning the proposed regulation, Dara Alderman or Janet Laufer at (202) 317-5500 (not a toll-free number); concerning submissions of comments and/or to request a hearing, Oluwafunmilayo (Fumni) Taylor at (202) 317-6901 (not a toll-free number).

SUPPLEMENTARY INFORMATION:

Background

This document contains proposed Income Tax Regulations (26 CFR part 1) under section 512(a) of the Code. Organizations that are otherwise exempt from tax under section 501(a) are subject to tax on their unrelated business taxable income (UBTI) under section 511(a). Section 512(a) of the Code generally defines UBTI of exempt organizations and provides special rules for calculating UBTI for organizations described in section 501(c)(7) (social and recreational clubs), voluntary employees' beneficiary associations described in section 501(c)(9) (VEBAs), supplemental unemployment benefit trusts described in section 501(c)(17) (SUBs), and group legal services organizations described in section 501(c)(20) (GLSOs).

Section 512(a)(1) provides a general rule that UBTI is the gross income from any unrelated trade or business regularly carried on by the organization, less certain deductions. Under section 512(a)(3)(A), in the case of social and recreational clubs, VEBAs, SUBs, and GLSOs, UBTI is defined as gross income, less directly connected expenses, but excluding "exempt function income."

Exempt function income is defined in section 512(a)(3)(B) as gross income from two sources. The first type of exempt function income is amounts paid by members as consideration for providing the members or their dependents or guests with goods, facilities, or services in furtherance of the organization's exempt purposes. The second type of exempt function income is all income (other than an amount equal to the gross income derived from any unrelated trade or business regularly carried on by the organization computed as if the organization were subject to section 512(a)(1)) that is set aside: (1) for a charitable purpose specified in section 170(c)(4); (2) in the case of a VEBA, SUB, or GLSO, to provide for the payment of life, sick, accident, or other benefits; or (3) for reasonable costs of administration directly connected with a purpose described in (1) or (2).

Section 512(a)(3)(E) generally limits the amount that a VEBA, SUB, or GLSO may set aside as exempt function income to an amount that does not result in an amount of total assets in the VEBA, SUB, or GLSO at the end of the taxable year that exceeds the section 419A account limit for the taxable year. For this purpose, however, the account limit does not take into account any reserve under section 419A(c)(2)(A) for post-retirement medical benefits.

Section 512(a)(3)(E) was added to the Code under the Tax Reform Act of 1984, Public Law 98-369 (98 Stat. 598 (1984)). Congress enacted section 512(a)(3)(E) to limit the extent to which a VEBA, SUB, or GLSO's income is exempt from tax, noting that "[p]resent law does not specifically limit the amount of income that can be set aside" by a VEBA, SUB, or GLSO on a tax-free basis. H.R. Rep. No. 98-432, pt. 2, at 1275.

To implement section 512(a)(3)(E), § 1.512(a)-5T was published in the **Federal Register** as TD 8073 on February 4,1986 (51 FR 4312), with an immediate effective date. A cross-referencing Notice of Proposed Rulemaking (the 1986 Proposed Regulation) was issued contemporaneously with the temporary regulation. Written comments were received on the 1986 Proposed Regulation, and a public hearing was held on June 26, 1986. The 1986 Proposed Regulation is hereby withdrawn and replaced by the new proposed regulation that is published in this document. Section 1.512(a)-5T will continue to apply until it is removed by a final rule published in the **Federal Register**. This new proposed regulation contains some changes to improve clarity and respond to comments received on the 1986 Proposed Regulation, but otherwise generally has the same effect as the 1986 Proposed Regulation and § 1.512(a)-5T.

Explanation of Provisions

Covered Entity

This new proposed regulation uses the uniform term "Covered Entity" to describe VEBAs and SUBs subject to the UBTI computation rules of section 512(a)(3).[1] For taxable years beginning after June 30, 1992, GLSOs are no longer exempt as section 501(c)(20) organizations. *See* section 120(e). Therefore, a GLSO is no longer a Covered Entity. Effective July 1, 1992, a GLSO could, if it otherwise qualified, request a ruling or determination modifying the basis for its exemption from section 501(c)(20) to section 501(c)(9).

Limitation on Amounts Set Aside for Exempt Purposes

The 1986 Proposed Regulation and § 1.512(a)-5T provide that under section 512(a)(3)(E)(i), a Covered Entity's UBTI is generally the lesser of two amounts: (1) the investment income of the Covered Entity for the taxable year (excluding member contributions), or (2) the excess of the total amount set aside as of the close of the taxable year (including member contributions and excluding certain long-term assets) over the qualified asset account limit (calculated without regard to the otherwise permitted reserve for post-retirement medical benefits) for the taxable year. In the view of the Treasury Department and the IRS, this means that UBTI is calculated based on the extent to which the assets of a Covered Entity at the end of the year exceed the section 512 limitation, regardless of whether income was allocated to payment of benefits during the course of the year.

---

[1] While section 501(c)(7) organizations are also subject to the UBTI computation rules of section 512(a)(3), this proposed regulation addresses only computations for VEBAs and SUBs.

In *CNG Transmission Mgmt. VEBA v. U.S.*, 588 F.3d 1376 (Fed. Cir. 2009), *aff'g*, 84 Fed. Cl. 327 (2008), the Federal Circuit Court of Appeals decided in favor of the IRS on this issue. The Court said that the "language of section 512(a)(3)(E) is clear and unambiguous," and that a VEBA "may not avoid the limitation on exempt function income in [section] 512(a)(3)(E)(i) merely by allocating investment income toward the payment of welfare benefits during the course of the tax year." *CNG*, 558 F.3d at 1379, 1377-78; *accord Northrop Corp. Employee Insurance Benefit Plans Master Trust v. U.S.*, 99 Fed. Cl. 1 (2011), *aff'd*, 467 Fed. Appx. 886 (Fed. Cir. April 10, 2012), *cert. denied*, (Dec. 3, 2012).

Notwithstanding the view of the Treasury Department and the IRS and support for that view in the foregoing cases, one court has applied a different interpretation. In *Sherwin-Williams Co. Employee Health Plan Trust v. Comm'r*, 330 F.3d 449 (6th Cir. 2003), *rev'g*, 115 T.C. 440 (2000), the Sixth Circuit Court of Appeals held that investment income that the taxpayer VEBA earmarked and claimed was spent before year-end on reasonable costs of administration was not subject to the section 512(a)(3)(E) limit on exempt function income.[2] The Treasury Department and the IRS believe that the decision in *Sherwin-Williams* is contrary to the statute, the legislative history of section 512(a)(3)(E), § 1.512(a)-5T, and the 1986 Proposed Regulation, and have determined that it is appropriate to issue this proposed regulation clarifying the proper way to make the calculation.[3] If the final regulation follows the approach taken in this proposed regulation, the IRS will no longer recognize the precedential effect of *Sherwin-Williams* in the Sixth Circuit.

This new proposed regulation retains the formula set forth in the 1986 Proposed Regulation and § 1.512(a)-5T but modifies and clarifies the description and adds examples. This new proposed regulation specifically states that any investment income a Covered Entity earns during the taxable year is subject to unrelated business income tax (UBIT) to the extent the Covered Entity's year-end assets exceed the account limit, and clarifies that this rule applies regardless of how that income is used.

To further improve clarity, this new proposed regulation slightly modifies language from the prior version of Q&A-3, separates it into a new Q&A-2 and -3, and adds examples.

This new proposed regulation also reflects the rule under section 512(a)(3)(B) that the UBTI of a Covered Entity includes UBTI derived by the Covered Entity from any unrelated trade or business (as defined in section 513) regularly carried on by it, computed as if the organization were subject to section 512(a)(1).

In addition, this new proposed regulation reflects the special rule under section 512(a)(3)(E)(iii). Accordingly, a Covered Entity is not subject to the limitation under section 512(a)(3)(E) if substantially all of the contributions to the Covered Entity are made by employers who were tax exempt throughout the five-year taxable period ending with the taxable year in which the contributions are made.

Special Rules Relating to Sections 419A(f)(5) and 419A(f)(6)

Some commenters on the 1986 Proposed Regulation requested that the regulations explicitly provide that the special account limits under section 419A(f)(5) for collectively bargained plans be used in determining the set aside limits under section 512. The 1986 Proposed Regulation contained a rule that references § 1.419A-2T for special rules relating to collectively bargained welfare benefit funds. The Treasury Department and the IRS are actively working on regulations under section 419A(f)(5) relating to collectively-bargained welfare benefit funds and believe it is appropriate to address issues related to collectively bargained welfare benefit funds in that project.

A number of commenters suggested that a VEBA that is part of a 10 or more employer plan described in section 419A(f)(6) should be exempted from the UBTI rules under section 512. However, after the 1986 Proposed Regulation and § 1.512(a)-5T were published, the Technical Corrections to the Tax Reform Act of 1984, which was part of the Tax Reform Act of 1986, Public Law 99-514, added language to section 512(a)(3)(E)(i) that specifically subjects 10 or more employer plans to the set aside limit described in that section. *See* section 1851(a)(10)(A) of Public Law 99-514. Consistent with this change in the law, this new proposed regulation provides that a Covered Entity that is part of a 10 or more employer plan is subject to the set aside limit, and that the account limit is determined as if the plan is not subject to the exception under section 419A(f)(6).

Treatment of Existing Reserves

A number of concerns were raised by commenters relating to the rules in the 1986 Proposed Regulation regarding existing reserves. For example, one commentator stated that the requirement that an employer must charge all post-retirement claims paid on or after July 18, 1984 against any

---

[2] As noted by the Federal Circuit in *CNG*, *Sherwin-Williams* can be viewed as distinguishable on its facts because the government there agreed to a stipulation that the investment income at issue had been spent on administrative costs, and in *CNG* there was not an equivalent stipulation. The Treasury Department and the IRS believe that the stipulation in *Sherwin-Williams* is not a distinction that should have affected the outcome. Specifically, the Treasury Department and the IRS believe that regardless of whether investment income is earmarked for (or otherwise traceable to) the payment of program benefits and administrative expenses during the year, the formula set forth in the 1986 Proposed Regulation and § 1.512(a)-5T, as well as the new proposed regulation, operates the same way.

[3] The IRS's interpretation is set forth in its non-acquiescence to the *Sherwin-Williams* decision (AOD 2005-02, 2005-35 I.R.B. 422). In AOD 2005-02, the IRS recognized the precedential effect of the decision to cases appealable to the Sixth Circuit and indicated that it would follow *Sherwin-Williams* with respect to cases within that circuit if the opinion cannot be meaningfully distinguished.

existing reserve as of July 18, 1984 (and earnings on existing reserves) is burdensome. However, this treatment of existing reserves is required under section 512(a)(3)(E)(ii)(III). Thus, this new proposed regulation retains the rules regarding existing reserves in the 1986 Proposed Regulation and adds a clarification to the example.

Proposed Effective Date

This regulation is proposed to apply to taxable years ending on or after the date of publication of the final regulation.

Special Analyses

It has been determined that this notice of proposed rulemaking is not a significant regulatory action as defined in Executive Order 12866. Therefore, a regulatory assessment is not required. It has also been determined that section 553(b) of the Administrative Procedure Act (5 U.S.C. chapter 5) does not apply to this regulation, and because the regulation does not impose a collection of information on small entities, the Regulatory Flexibility Act (5 U.S.C. chapter 6) does not apply. Pursuant to section 7805(f) of the Code, this regulation has been submitted to the Chief Counsel for Advocacy of the Small Business Administration for comment on its impact on small business.

Comments and Requests for Public Hearing

Before this proposed regulation is adopted as a final regulation, consideration will be given to any written (a signed original and eight (8) copies) or electronic comments that are timely submitted to the IRS. The Treasury Department and the IRS request comments on all aspects of the proposed rules. All comments will be available for public inspection and copying. A public hearing will be scheduled if requested in writing by any person that timely submits written or electronic comments. If a public hearing is scheduled, notice of the date, time, and place for the hearing will be published in the **Federal Register**.

Drafting Information

The principal authors of this regulation are Dara Alderman and Janet Laufer, Office of Division Counsel/Associate Chief Counsel (Tax Exempt and Government Entities). However, other personnel from the Treasury Department and the IRS participated in the development of this regulation.

[¶49,619] Proposed Amendments of Regulations (REG-110948-14), published in the Federal Register on July 2, 2014.

[Code Secs. 501 and 508]

Tax-exempt status: Application for exemption: Streamlined process.—Amendments of Reg. §§1.501(a)-1, 1.501(c)(3)-1 and 1.508-1, providing guidance to organizations that seek recognition of tax-exempt status under Code Sec. 501(c)(3), are proposed.

AGENCY: Internal Revenue Service (IRS), Treasury.

ACTION: Notice of proposed rulemaking by cross-reference to temporary regulations.

SUMMARY: In the Rules and Regulations section of this issue of the **Federal Register**, the IRS is issuing regulations that provide guidance to organizations that seek recognition of tax-exempt status under section 501(c)(3) of the Internal Revenue Code. The final and temporary regulations amend current regulations to allow the Commissioner of Internal Revenue to adopt a streamlined application process that certain organizations may use to apply for recognition of tax-exempt status under section 501(c)(3). The text of those temporary regulations also serves as the text of these proposed regulations.

DATES: Comments and requests for a public hearing must be received by September 30, 2014.

ADDRESSES: Send submissions to: CC:PA:LPD:PR (REG-110948-14), room 5205, Internal Revenue Service, PO Box 7604, Ben Franklin Station, Washington, DC 20044. Submissions may be hand-delivered Monday through Friday between the hours of 8 a.m. and 4 p.m. to CC:PA:LPD:PR (REG-110948-14), Courier's Desk, Internal Revenue Service, 1111 Constitution Avenue NW, Washington, DC, or sent electronically via the Federal eRulemaking Portal at *http://www.regulations.gov* (IRS REG-110948-14).

FOR FURTHER INFORMATION CONTACT: Concerning the proposed regulations, James R. Martin or Robin Ehrenberg at (202) 317-5800; concerning submission of comments and request for hearing, Oluwafunmilayo Taylor at (202) 317-6901 (not toll-free numbers).

SUPPLEMENTARY INFORMATION:

Background and Explanation of Provisions

Temporary regulations in the Rules and Regulations section of this issue of the **Federal Register** amend the existing regulations under sections 501 and 508 to allow for an additional form of application to be used to satisfy the notice requirement under section 508(a). The text of those temporary regulations also serves as the text of these proposed regulations. The preamble to the temporary regulations explains the amendments.

Special Analyses

It has been determined that this notice of proposed rulemaking is not a significant regulatory action as defined in Executive Order 12866, as supplemented by Executive Order 13563. Therefore, a regulatory assessment is not required. It also has been determined that section 553(b) of the Administrative Procedure Act (5 U.S.C. chapter 5) does not apply to these regulations. It is hereby certified that this rule will not have a significant economic impact on a substantial number of small entities. Although this rule may affect a substantial number of small entities that choose to use the new form that streamlines the application process that eligible organizations may use to apply for recognition of tax-exempt status under section 501(c)(3), we intend for this rule to reduce the economic impact on small entities. This rule merely provides guidance about the streamlined form of application available to satisfy the notice requirement under Section 508(a). Therefore, a Regulatory Flexibility Analysis under the Regulatory Flexibility Act (5 U.S.C. Chapter 6) is not required.

Comments and Requests for Public Hearing

Before these proposed regulations are adopted as final regulations, consideration will be given to any comments that are submitted timely to the IRS as prescribed in this preamble under the "Addresses" heading. The Treasury Department and the IRS request comments on all aspects of the proposed rules. All comments will be available at *www.regulations.gov* or upon request.

A public hearing will be scheduled if requested in writing by any person that timely submits written comments. If a public hearing is scheduled, notice of the date, time, and place for the public hearing will be published in the **Federal Register**.

Drafting Information

The principal authors of these regulations are James R. Martin and Robin Ehrenberg, Office of Associate Chief Counsel (Tax Exempt and Government Entities). However, other personnel from the IRS and the Treasury Department participated in their development.

[¶49,624] Proposed Amendments of Regulations (REG-104579-13), published in the Federal Register on July 28, 2014.

[Code Secs. 36B and 162]

Qualified health plan: Affordable insurance exchanges: Premium tax credit: Guidance.—Reg. §1.162(l)-1 and amendments of Reg. §§1.36B-2, 1.36B-3 and 1.36B-4, providing guidance to individuals who enroll in qualified health plans through Affordable Insurance Exchanges and claim the premium tax credit, and Exchanges that make qualified health plans available to individuals and employers, are proposed.

AGENCY: Internal Revenue Service (IRS), Treasury.

ACTION: Notice of proposed rulemaking by cross-reference to temporary regulations.

SUMMARY: In the Rules and Regulations section of this issue of the **Federal Register**, the IRS is issuing final and temporary regulations under section 36B of the Internal Revenue Code (Code) relating to the health insurance premium tax credit. The regulations provide guidance to individuals who enroll in qualified health plans through Affordable Insurance Exchanges (Exchanges) and claim the premium tax credit, and Exchanges that make qualified health plans available to individuals and employers. The text of those temporary regulations also serves as the text of these proposed regulations.

DATES: Comments and requests for a public hearing must be received by October 27, 2014.

ADDRESSES: Send submissions to: CC:PA:LPD:PR (REG-104579-13), Internal Revenue Service, POB 7604, Ben Franklin Station, Washington, DC 20044. Taxpayers also may submit comments electronically via the Federal eRulemaking Portal at *www.regulations.gov* (IRS REG-104579-13).

FOR FURTHER INFORMATION CONTACT: Concerning the proposed regulations, Arvind Ravichandran, (202) 317-4718; concerning submission of comments or to request a hearing, Oluwafunmilayo Taylor, (202) 317-6901 (not toll-free numbers).

SUPPLEMENTARY INFORMATION:

Background and Explanation of Provisions

Final and temporary regulations in the Rules and Regulations section of this issue of the **Federal Register** amend the Income Tax Regulations (26 CFR Part 1) relating to section 36B and section 162(l) of the Code. The final and temporary regulations provide guidance for individuals who enroll in qualified health plans through Affordable Insurance Exchanges (Exchanges) and claim the premium tax credit, and Exchanges that make qualified health plans available to individuals and employers. The text of those temporary regulations also serves as the text of these proposed regulations. The preamble to the final and temporary regulations explains the amendments.

Proposed Effective Date

These regulations are proposed to apply for taxable years ending after December 31, 2013. *See* §1.36B-1(o). Taxpayers must apply the final and temporary regulations until publication of final regulations.

Special Analyses

It has been determined that this notice of proposed rulemaking is not a significant regulatory action as defined in Executive Order 12866. Therefore, a regulatory assessment is not required. It also has been determined that section 553(b) of the Administrative Procedure Act (5 U.S.C. chapter 5) does not apply to these regulations, and because the regulations do not impose a collection of information on small entities, the Regulatory Flexibility Act (5 U.S.C. chapter 6) does not apply. Pursuant to section 7805(f) of the Code, this regulation has been submitted to the Chief Counsel for Advocacy of the Small Business Administration for comment on its impact on small business.

Comments and Requests for a Public Hearing

Before these proposed regulations are adopted as final regulations, consideration will be given to any comments that are submitted timely to the IRS as prescribed in this preamble under "Addresses" heading. The IRS and the Treasury Department request comments on all aspects of the proposed rules. All comments will be available at www.regulations.gov or upon request. A public hearing will be scheduled if requested in writing by any person that timely submits written comments. If a public hearing is scheduled, notice of the date, time, and place for the public hearing will be published in the **Federal Register**.

Drafting Information

The principal authors of these regulations are Arvind Ravichandran, Shareen Pflanz and Steve Toomey of the Office of Associate Chief Counsel (Income Tax & Accounting). However, other personnel from the IRS and the Treasury Department participated in their development.

[¶49,625] Proposed Amendments of Regulations (REG-123286-14), published in the Federal Register on July 28, 2014 (corrected 9/26/2014).

[Code Sec. 275]

Branded prescription drug fee: Prescription drugs: Fee calculation: Dispute resolution: Deadline: Covered entities: Error reports: Refund claims.—Amendments of Reg. §§51.2 and 51.11, relating to the branded prescription drug fee, are proposed.

AGENCY: Internal Revenue Service (IRS), Treasury.

ACTION: Notice of proposed rulemaking by cross-reference to temporary regulations.

SUMMARY: In the Rules and Regulations section of this issue of the **Federal Register**, the IRS is issuing temporary regulations relating to the branded prescription drug fee. This fee was enacted by section 9008 of the Patient Protection and Affordable Care Act, as amended by section 1404 of the Health Care and Education Reconciliation Act of 2010, and the Health Care and Reconciliation Act of 2010 (collectively the ACA). The proposed regulations modify the definition of controlled group for purposes of the branded prescription drug fee. The proposed regulations affect persons engaged in the business of manufacturing or importing certain branded prescription drugs. The text of the temporary regulations also serves as the text of the proposed regulations.

DATES: Comments and requests for a public hearing must be received by October 27, 2014.

ADDRESSES: Send submissions to: CC:PA:LPD:PR (REG-123286-14), room 5205, Internal Revenue Service, PO Box 7604, Ben Franklin Station, Washington, DC 20044. Submissions may be hand-delivered Monday through Friday between the hours of 8 a.m. and 4 p.m. to: CC:PA:LPD:PR (REG-123286-14), Courier's Desk, Internal Revenue Service, 1111 Constitution Avenue, NW, Washington, DC, or sent electronically via the Federal eRulemaking Portal at *www.regulations.gov* (IRS REG-123286-14).

FOR FURTHER INFORMATION CONTACT: Concerning the proposed regulations, Celia Gabrysh, (202) 317-6855; concerning submissions of comments and request for a hearing, Oluwafunmilayo Taylor, (202) 317-6901 (not toll-free calls).

SUPPLEMENTARY INFORMATION:

Background

Temporary regulations in the Rules and Regulations section of this issue of the **Federal Register** amend §§51.2(e)(3) and 51.11(c) of the Branded Prescription Drug Fee Regulations, 26 CFR Part 51. The text of those regulations also serves as the text of these proposed regulations. The preamble to the temporary regulations explains the amendment.

Special Analyses

It has been determined that this notice of proposed rulemaking is not a significant regulatory action as defined in Executive Order 12866, as supplemented by Executive Order 13563. Therefore, a regulatory flexibility assessment is not required. It also has been determined that section 553(b) of the Administrative Procedure Act (5 U.S.C. chapter 5) does not apply to these regulations. Because these regulations do not impose a collection of information on small entities, a Regulatory Flexibility Analysis under the Regulatory Flexibility Act (5 U.S.C. chapter 6) is not required. Pursuant to section 7805(f) of the Internal Revenue Code, this notice of proposed rulemaking has been submitted to the Chief Counsel for Advocacy of the Small Business Administration for comment on its impact on small business.

Comments and Requests for a Public Hearing

Before these proposed regulations are adopted as final regulations, consideration will be given to any comments that are submitted timely to the IRS as prescribed in this preamble under the "Addresses" heading. Comments are requested on all aspects of the proposed regulations. All comments will be available at www.regulations.gov or upon request. A public hearing may be scheduled if requested in writing by any person that timely submits written comments. If a public hearing is scheduled, notice of the date, time, and place for the hearing will be published in the **Federal Register**.

Drafting Information

The principal author of these regulations is Celia Gabrysh, Office of Associate Chief Counsel (Passthroughs and Special Industries). However, other personnel from the IRS and the Treasury Department participated in their development.

[¶49,633] Proposed Amendments of Regulations (REG-151416-06), published in the Federal Register on November 3, 2014 (corrected 1/26/2015).

[Code Secs. 617, 704, 732, 736, 751, 755, 995, 1231, 1245, 1248, 1250, 1252, 1254 and 6050K]

Partners and partnerships: Inventories, appreciation in value.—Amendments of Reg. §§1.617-4, 1.704-1, 1.704-3, 1.732-1, 1.736-1, 1.751-1, 1.755-1, 1.995-4, 1.1231-1, 1.1245-1, 1.1245-2, 1.1245-4, 1.1248-1, 1.1250-1, 1.1252-2, 1.1254-5 and 1.6050K-1, prescribing how a partner should measure its interest in a partnership's unrealized receivables and inventory items and providing guidance regarding the tax consequences of a distribution that causes a reduction in that interest, are proposed.

AGENCY: Internal Revenue Service (IRS), Treasury.

ACTION: Notice of proposed rulemaking.

SUMMARY: This document contains proposed regulations that prescribe how a partner should measure its interest in a partnership's unrealized receivables and inventory items, and that provide guidance regarding the tax consequences of a distribution that causes a reduction in that interest. The proposed regulations take into account statutory changes that have occurred subsequent to the issuance of the existing regulations. The proposed regulations affect partners in partnerships that own unrealized receivables and inventory items and that make a distribution to one or more partners.

DATES: Comments and requests for a public hearing must be received by February 2, 2015.

ADDRESSES: Send submissions to CC:PA:LPD:PR (REG-151416-06), room 5203, Internal Revenue Service, P.O. Box 7604, Ben Franklin Station, Washington, D.C., 20044. Submissions may be hand-delivered Monday through Friday between the hours of 8 a.m. and 4 p.m. to CC:PA:LPD:PR (REG-151416-06), Courier's Desk, Internal Revenue Service, 1111 Constitution Avenue, N.W., Washington, D.C., 20224, or via the Federal eRulemaking Portal at *www.regulations.gov* (IRS REG-151416-06).

FOR FURTHER INFORMATION CONTACT: Concerning the proposed regulations, Allison R. Carmody at (202) 317-5279 or Frank J. Fisher at (202) 317-6850; concerning submissions of comments and requests for hearing, Oluwafunmilayo Taylor at (202) 317-6901 (not toll-free numbers).

SUPPLEMENTARY INFORMATION:

Paperwork Reduction Act

The collection of information contained in this notice of proposed rulemaking has been submitted to the Office of Management and Budget for review in accordance with the Paperwork Reduction Act of 1995 (44 U.S.C. 3507(d)). Comments on the collection of information should be sent to the Office of Management and Budget, Attn: Desk Officer for the Department of the Treasury, Office of Information and Regulatory Affairs, Washington, DC 20503, with copies to the Internal Revenue Service, Attn: IRS Reports Clearance Officer, SE-:CAR:MP:T:T:SP, Washington, DC 20224. Comments on the collection of information should be received by January 2, 2015.

Comments are specifically requested concerning:

Whether the proposed collection of information is necessary for the proper performance of the Internal Revenue Service, including whether the information will have practical utility;

The accuracy of the estimated burden associated with the proposed collection of information;

How the quality, utility, and clarity of the information to be collected may be enhanced;

How the burden of complying with the proposed collection of information may be minimized, including through the application of automated collection techniques or other forms of information technology; and

Estimates of capital or start-up costs and costs of operation, maintenance, and purchase of service to provide information.

The collection of information required by this proposed regulation is in §1.751-1(b)(3) and (b)(6), and in §1.755-1(c)(2)(vi). This information is required for a partnership and certain partners to report the information to the IRS necessary to ensure that the partners of the partnership properly report in accordance with the rules of the proposed regulations the correct amount of ordinary income and/or capital gain upon a distribution of property from the partnership to its partners. The collection of information is necessary to ensure tax compliance.

The likely respondents are business or other for-profit institutions.

Estimated total annual reporting burden: 22,500 hours.

Estimated average annual burden hours per respondent vary from 30 minutes to 2 hours, depending on individual circumstances, with an estimated average of 1 hour.

Estimated number of respondents: 22,500.

Estimated annual frequency of responses: annually.

An agency may not conduct or sponsor, and a person is not required to respond to, a collection of information unless it displays a valid control number assigned by the Office of Management and Budget.

Books or records relating to a collection of information must be retained as long as their contents may become material in the administration of any internal revenue law. Generally, tax returns and tax return information are confidential, as required by section 6103.

Background

This document contains proposed amendments to the Income Tax Regulations (26 CFR part 1) under section 751(b) of the Internal Revenue Code (the Code). In 1954, Congress enacted section 751 to prevent the use of a partnership to convert potential ordinary income into capital gain. *See* H.R. Rep. No. 1337 at 70 (1954), reprinted in 1954 U.S.C.C.A.N. 4017, 4097. To that end, section 751(a) provides that the amount of any money, or the fair market value of any property, received by a transferor partner in exchange for all or part of that partner's interest in the partnership's unrealized receivables and inventory items is considered as an amount realized from the sale or exchange of property other than a capital asset. Further, section 751(b) overrides the nonrecognition provisions of section 731 to the extent a partner receives a distribution from the partnership that causes a shift between the partner's interest in the partnership's unrealized receivables or substantially appreciated inventory items (collectively, the partnership's "section 751 property") and the partner's interest in the partnership's other property.

Whether section 751(b) applies depends on the partner's interest in the partnership's section 751 property before and after a distribution. The statute does not define a partner's interest in a partnership's section 751 property, but the legislative history indicates that Congress believed a partner's interest in a partnership's section 751 property equals the partner's rights to income from the partnership's section 751 property:

> The provisions relating to unrealized receivables and appreciated inventory items are necessary to prevent the use of the partnership as a device for obtaining capital-gain treatment on fees or other rights to income and on appreciated inventory. Amounts attributable to such rights would be treated as ordinary income if realized in normal course by the partnership. The sale of a partnership interest or distributions to partners should not be permitted to change the character of this income. *The statutory treatment proposed, in general, regards the income rights as severable from the partnership interest and as subject to the same tax consequences which would be accorded an individual entrepreneur.*

S. Rep. No. 1622 at 99 (1954), reprinted in 1954 U.S.C.C.A.N. 4621, 4732. (Emphasis added.)

In 1984, Congress amended section 704(c), making mandatory its application to property contributed to a partnership. While Congress did not specifically address the overlap of section 704(c) and section 751, the Conference Report indicates that the 1984 Congress understood that the section 704(c) amendment would impact other provisions in subchapter K and provides regulatory authority to the Secretary of the Treasury to address those repercussions. *See* H.R. Conf. Rep. No. 861, 98th Cong., 2d Sess., June 23, 1984, reprinted in 1984 U.S.C.C.A.N. 1445, 1545.

The IRS and the Treasury Department first issued regulations implementing section 751 in 1956. Following the changes to section 704(c) making its application mandatory, the IRS and the Treasury Department amended the regulations under section 751(a) to provide generally that a partner's interest in section 751 property is the amount of income or loss from section 751 property that would be allocated to the partner if the partnership had sold all of its property in a fully taxable transaction for cash in an amount equal to the fair market value of such property. (*See* TD 8847, 64 FR 69903, Dec. 15, 1999.) However, the 1956 regulations with respect to section 751(b) remained unchanged.

The examples in the current regulations under section 751(b) determine a partner's interest in section 751 property by reference to the partner's share of the gross value of the partnership's assets (the "gross value" approach), not by reference to the partner's share of the unrealized gain or loss in the property. *See*, for example, § 1.751-1(g), *Example 2*. Because the gross value approach focuses on a partner's share of the asset's value rather than the partner's share of the unrealized gain, the examples in the current regulations may be too narrow in some respects, and too broad in others, to carry out the intended purpose of section 751(b). That is, the gross value approach may allow a distribution that reduces a partner's share of the unrealized gain in the partnership's section 751 property without triggering section 751(b), and, conversely, may trigger section 751(b) even if the partner's share of the unrealized gain in the partnership's section 751 property is not reduced. For example, Rev. Rul. 84-102 (1984-2 CB 119) provides that deemed distributions under section 752 resulting from shifting allocations of indebtedness may result in the partners' shares of asset gross value changing, even though the partners' shares of unrealized gain associated with section 751 property would not necessarily have changed.

If the distribution results in a shift between the partner's interest in the partnership's section 751 property and the partnership's other property, the current regulations require a deemed asset exchange of both section 751 property and other property between the partner and the partnership to determine the tax consequences of the distribution (the "asset exchange" approach). *See*, for example, § 1.751-1(g), *Example 6*, of the current regulations. The asset exchange approach is complex, requiring the partnership and partner to determine the tax consequences of both a deemed distribution of relinquished property and a deemed taxable exchange of that property back to the partnership. The asset exchange approach also often accelerates capital gain unnecessarily by requiring certain partners to recognize capital gain even when their shares of partnership capital gain have not been reduced.

In 2006, the IRS and the Treasury Department published Notice 2006-14 (2006-1 CB 498), which suggested, and requested comments on, alternative approaches to section 751(b) that were intended to better achieve the purpose of the statute while providing greater simplicity. *See* § 601.601(d)(2)(ii)(*b*). Specifically, Notice 2006-14 asked for comments on: (1) replacing the gross value approach with a "hypothetical sale" approach for purposes of determining a partner's interest in the partnership's section 751 property, and (2) replacing the asset exchange approach with a "hot asset sale" approach to determine the tax consequences when section 751(b) applies. The hypothetical sale approach and the hot asset sale approach are described in Parts 1.A and 3, respectively, of the Summary of Comments and Explanation of Provisions section of this preamble. Notice 2006-14 also requested comments on other possible approaches to simplifying compliance with section 751(b).

As described in Notice 2006-14, the hypothetical sale approach for section 751(b) is similar to the approach taken in the 1999 regulations issued under section 751(a), shifting the focus to tax gain and away from gross value. Under the hypothetical sale approach, a partner's interest in section 751 property is determined by reference to the amount of ordinary income that would be allocated to the partner if the partnership disposed of all of its property for fair market value immediately before the distribution. More specifically, the hypothetical sale approach applies section 704(c) principles in comparing: (1) the amount of ordinary income that each partner would recognize if the partnership sold all of its property for fair market value immediately before the distribution, with (2) the amount of ordinary income each partner would recognize if the partnership sold all of its property (and the distributee partners sold the distributed assets) for fair market value immediately after the distribution. If the distribution reduces the amount of ordinary income (or increases the amount of ordinary loss) from section 751 property that would be allocated to, or recognized by, a partner (thus reducing that partner's interest in the partnership's section 751 property), the distribution triggers section 751(b).

Notice 2006-14 indicated that changes to the framework of subchapter K since the promulgation of the existing regulations would work in tandem with the hypothetical sale approach to achieve the statute's objective of ensuring that a partner recognizes its proper share of the partnership's income from section 751 property without unnecessarily accelerating the recognition of that income. For example, regulations under section 704(b) allow a partnership to revalue its assets upon a distribution in consideration of a partnership interest. Any revaluation gain or loss is subject to the rules of section 704(c), which generally preserve each partner's share of the unrealized gain and loss in the partnership's assets.

Notice 2006-14 also requested comments on using the hot asset sale approach, rather than the asset exchange approach, to determine the tax consequences of the distribution that is subject to section 751(b). The hot asset sale approach deems the partnership to distribute the relinquished section 751 property to the partner whose interest in the partnership's section 751 property is reduced, and then deems the partner to sell the relinquished section 751 property back to the partnership immediately before the actual distribution.

Summary of Comments and Explanation of Provisions

The IRS and the Treasury Department received both formal and informal responses to Notice 2006-14. In addition, a number of commentators published articles analyzing the proposals outlined in Notice 2006-14. Commentators' responses to Notice 2006-14 were predominantly favorable.

These proposed regulations adopt many of the principles described in Notice 2006-14. Part 1 of this section describes the rules included in the proposed regulations for determining partners' interests in section 751 property. Part 2 of this section sets forth the proposed regulations' test to determine whether section 751(b) applies to a partnership distribution, including anti-abuse principles that may apply in certain situations in which the test would not otherwise be satisfied. Part 3 of this section explains the tax consequences of a section 751(b) distribution under the proposed regulations. Finally, Part 4 of this section describes certain ancillary issues relating to the proposed regulations, including a clarification to the scope of § 1.751-1(a).

1. *Determination of a Partner's Interest in Section 751 Property*

Section 751(b) applies to a partnership distribution to the extent the distribution reduces a partner's interest in section 751 property. As discussed further in this Part 1, the proposed regulations establish an approach for measuring partners' interests in section 751 property, provide new rules under section 704(c) to help partnerships compute partner gain in section 751 property more precisely, and describe how basis adjustments under sections 734(b) and 743(b) affect the computation of partners' interests in section 751 property.

A. *Adoption of Hypothetical Sale Approach*

The first step in computing the effect of section 751(b) is to measure the partners' interests in section 751 property. Commentators generally agreed that the hypothetical sale approach is a substantial improvement over the gross value approach in the existing regulations. As described in this preamble, the hypothetical sale approach requires a partnership to compare: (1) the amount of ordinary income (or ordinary loss) that each partner would recognize if the partnership sold its property for fair market value immediately before the distribution with (2) the amount of ordinary income (or ordinary loss) each partner would recognize if the partnership sold its property, and the distributee partner sold the distributed assets, for fair market value immediately after the distribution. The commentators agreed that, when compared against the gross value approach, the hypothetical sale approach is more consistent with Congress's intent in enacting section 751(b), is easier to apply, and reduces the likelihood that section 751(b) would unnecessarily accelerate ordinary income. Accordingly, these proposed regulations adopt the hypothetical sale approach as the method by which the partners must measure their respective interests in section 751 property for the purpose of determining whether a distribution reduces a partner's interest in the partnership's section 751 property. (A distribution that reduces a partner's interest in the partnership's section 751 property is referred to as a "section 751(b) distribution.")

B. *Revaluations*

Because the hypothetical sale approach relies on the principles of section 704(c) to preserve a partner's share of the unrealized gain and loss in the partnership's section 751 property, these proposed regulations make several changes to the regulations relating to section 704(c). Specifically, the proposed regulations revise § 1.704-1(b)(2)(iv)(*f*), regarding revaluations of partnership property, to make its provisions mandatory if a partnership distributes money or other property to a partner as consideration for an interest in the partnership, and the partnership owns section 751 property immediately after the distribution. (A partnership that does not own section 751 property immediately after the distribution may still revalue its property under the existing regulation, but is not required to do so under these proposed regulations.) If a partnership does not maintain capital accounts in accordance with § 1.704-1(b)(2)(iv), the partnership must comply with this requirement by computing each partner's share of gain or loss in each partnership asset prior to a distribution, and making future allocations of partnership items in a manner that takes these amounts into account (making subsequent adjustments for cost recovery and other events that affect the property basis of each such asset).

In addition, the proposed regulations contain a special revaluation rule for distributing partnerships that own an interest in a lower-tier partnership. Because a partnership's section 751 property includes, under section 751(f), the partnership's proportionate share of section 751 property owned by any other partnership in which the distributing partnership is a partner, these proposed regulations also require a partnership in which the distributing partnership owns a controlling interest (which is defined as a greater than 50 percent interest) to revalue its property if the lower-tier partnership owns section 751 property immediately after the distribution. If the distributing partnership owns a non-controlling (that is, less than or equal to 50 percent) interest in a lower-tier partnership, these proposed regulations require the distributing partnership to allocate its distributive share of the lower-tier partnership's items among its partners in a manner that reflects the allocations that would have been made had the lower-tier partnership revalued its partnership property. The IRS and the Treasury Department are aware that in some instances a distributing partnership may be unable to obtain sufficient information to comply with this requirement from a lower-tier partnership in which the distributing partnership holds a non-controlling interest. We request comments on reasonable approaches to address this issue.

Upon the revaluation of partnership property in connection with a partnership distribution, the regulations under section 704(c) permit a partnership to choose any reasonable method to account for the built-in gain or built-in loss that is consistent with the purpose of section 704(c). If property with built-in gain decreases in value (or property with built-in loss increases in value), then the partnership may be unable to allocate tax losses (or gains) to a non-contributing partner in an amount equal to the partner's economic loss (or gain). If the property with built-in gain (or loss) is section 751 property, then the inability to allocate those tax losses (or gains) may cause ordinary income to shift among the partners. The regulations under section 704(c) provide two reasonable methods for a partnership to allocate items to cure or remediate that shift. However, the regulations under section 704(c) also provide a third reasonable method, the traditional method, under which the shift of ordinary income is not cured. The IRS and the Treasury Department are aware that distortions created under the section 704(c) traditional method may cause ordinary income to shift among partners. However, the regulations under section 704(c) contain an anti-abuse rule that provides that a method is not reasonable if, for example, the event that results in a reverse section 704(c) allocation and the corresponding allocation of tax items with respect to the property are made with a view to shifting the tax consequences of built-in gain or built-in loss among the partners in a manner that substantially reduces the present value of the partners' aggregate tax liability. The IRS and the Treasury Department believe that this anti-abuse provision under section 704(c) properly addresses the possibility that taxpayers would use the traditional method to shift ordinary income.

Some commentators suggested changing the regulations under section 704(c) to minimize the situations in which section 751(b) applies. Generally, when a partnership revalues its assets, the partnership allocates a reverse section 704(c) amount with respect to each partnership asset, as opposed to an aggregate section 704(c) amount with respect to all assets (subject to certain exceptions). As a result, any distribution of appreciated section 751 property in which another partner has a share of income would trigger section 751(b) under the hypothetical sale approach. The commentators recommended that the IRS and the Treasury Department narrow the application of section 751(b) by allowing partners (subject to the substantiality requirements of § 1.704-1(b)(2)(iii)) to "exchange" reverse section 704(c) amounts resulting from a section 751 distribution. These proposed regulations do not adopt this comment because it is beyond the scope of these regulations and would impact other provisions of subchapter K. However, the IRS and the Treasury Department believe that the issue merits further study and request comments on how such permissible exchanges of reverse section 704(c) amounts might be addressed in future regulations.

C. *Effect of Basis Adjustments on Section 751(b) Computations*

While section 704(c) revaluations generally preserve partners' interests in section 751 property upon a partnership distribution, certain basis adjustments under sections 732(c) or 734(b) may alter partners' interests in section 751 property following the distribution. Accordingly, these proposed regulations provide rules on the effect of these basis adjustments on the computation of partners' interests in section 751 property.

If a distribution of capital gain property results in a basis adjustment under section 734(b), that basis adjustment is allocated to capital gain property of the partnership under § 1.755-1(c)(1). However, some property that is characterized as capital gain property for purposes of section 755 can also result in ordinary income when sold. For example, section 1231 property is characterized as a capital asset for purposes of section 755, but selling the property can also result in ordinary income from recapture under section 1245(a)(1). The regulations under section 755 do not differentiate between the capital gain aspect of the property and the ordinary income aspect of the property for this purpose. Accordingly, allocating a section 734(b) positive basis adjustment to such property as capital gain property may reduce the amount of ordinary income that would result on a sale of the property. Under these proposed regulations, that reduction in ordinary income would constitute a reduction in the partners' shares of unrealized gain in the partnership's section 751 property, which could trigger section 751(b) in situations in which section 751(b) would not have otherwise applied. A similar reduction in section 751 property could occur if the basis of the distributed property increases under section 732.

One commentator recommended allowing partnerships to avoid this result by eliminating a positive section 734(b) adjustment to the extent the section 734(b) adjustment would reduce the partnership's ordinary income. Another commentator recommended allocating the section 734(b) adjustment to other partnership capital gain property. The same commentator alternatively recommended treating a positive section 734(b) adjustment that reduced the partnership's ordinary income as a separate asset.

Although these proposed regulations do not treat the section 734(b) adjustment as a separate asset, the proposed regulations reach a similar result to this last recommendation. They provide that a basis adjustment under section 732(c) or section 734(b) (as adjusted for recovery of the basis adjustment) that is allocated to capital gain property and that reduces the ordinary income (attributable, for example, to recapture under section 1245(a)(1)) that the partner or partnership would recognize on a taxable disposition of the property is not taken into account in determining (1) the partnership's basis for purposes of sections 617(d)(1), 1245(a)(1), 1250(a)(1), 1252(a)(1), and 1254(a)(1), and (2) the partner or partnership's respective gain or loss for purposes of sections 995(c), 1231(a), and 1248(a). The IRS and the Treasury Department intend for these amendments to apply for purposes of other provisions that cross-reference those sections (for example, the reference in § 1.367(b)-2(c) to section 1248). The IRS and the Treasury Department are aware that these rules may result in additional administrative burden and, therefore, permit a partnership and its partners to elect to recognize ordinary income currently under section 751(b) in lieu of applying these rules.

In addition, one commentator raised questions about the application of section 751(b) upon the distribution to a partner of section 751 property for which another partner has a basis adjustment under section 743(b) (the transferee partner). The commentator questioned whether the distributee partner's share of section 751 property could be increased inappropriately if the special basis adjustment is not taken into account in determining the distributee's basis in the section 751 property under section 732. The IRS and the Treasury Department believe that although the distributee partner does not take the section 743(b) basis adjustment into account in determining its basis in the distributed property, the reallocation of the section 743(b) basis adjustment pursuant to § 1.743-1(g)(2)(ii) should generally reduce the transferee partner's share of section 751 property, triggering an income inclusion to that partner under section 751(b) which is offset by the basis adjustment. The IRS and the Treasury Department acknowledge that, in situations in which the partnership holds no other section 751 property (and the section 743(b) basis adjustment is temporarily suspended under §§ 1.743-1(g)(2)(ii) and 1.755-1(c)(4) until the partnership acquires additional ordinary income property), the application of section 751(b) may be unclear. Accordingly, the proposed regulations require that partners include the effect of carryover basis adjustments when determining their shares of section 751 property, as though those basis adjustments were immediately allocable to ordinary income property. *See Example 4* in § 1.751-1(g) of the proposed regulations.

2. *Distributions to which Section 751(b) Applies*

A. *General Principle*

The purpose of section 751 is to prevent a partner from converting its share of potential ordinary income into capital gain. A distribution of partnership property (including money) is a section 751(b) distribution if the distribution reduces any partner's share of net section 751 unrealized gain or increases any partner's share of net section 751 unrealized loss (as determined under the hypothetical sale approach described in Part 1.A of the Summary of Comments and Explanation of Provisions section of this preamble). For this purpose, a partner's net section 751 unrealized gain or loss immediately before a distribution equals the amount of net gain or loss, as the case may be, from section 751 property that would be allocated to the partner if the partnership disposed of all of the partnership's assets for cash in an amount equal to the fair market value of such property (taking into account section 7701(g)). A partner's net section 751 unrealized gain or loss includes any remedial allocations under § 1.704-3(d).

A partner's net section 751 unrealized gain or loss also takes into account any section 743 basis adjustment pursuant to § 1.743-1(j)(3), including any carryover basis adjustment that results under any of § 1.743-1(g)(2)(ii), § 1.755-1(b)(5)(iii)(D), or § 1.755-1(c)(4) when the partnership must adjust the basis of a specific class of assets, but that adjustment is suspended because the partnership does not own assets in that class. The regulations take such suspended basis adjustments into account as though the basis adjustment is applied to the basis of notional partnership section 751 property with a fair market value of zero. For example, if A and B are partners in the AB partnership, which owns capital assets and a single ordinary income asset that is the subject of a section 743(b) adjustment with respect to B, and that asset is distributed to partner A, B's basis adjustment is suspended because the partnership lacks other ordinary income property. However, the basis adjustment will eventually benefit B when the partnership acquires new ordinary income property. For this reason, the proposed regulations require B to take the suspended adjustment into account when determining whether section 751(b) applies to B with respect to the distribution.

A partner's share of net section 751 unrealized gain or loss from section 751 property immediately following a distribution is computed using the same formula. However, the distributee partner also includes in its post-distribution amount its share of net income or loss from a hypothetical sale of the distributed section 751 property.

If section 751(b) applies to a distribution, each partner must generally recognize or take into account currently ordinary income equal to its "section 751(b) amount." If a partner has net section 751 unrealized gain both before and after the distribution, then the partner's section 751(b) amount equals the partner's net section 751 unrealized gain immediately before the distribution less the partner's net section 751 unrealized gain immediately after the distribution. If a partner has net section 751 unrealized loss both before and after the distribution, then the partner's section 751(b) amount equals the partner's net section 751 unrealized loss immediately after the distribution less the partner's net section 751 unrealized loss immediately before the distribution. If a partner has net section 751 unrealized gain before the distribution and net section 751 unrealized loss after the distribution, then the partner's section 751(b) amount equals the sum of the partner's net section 751 unrealized gain immediately before the distribution and the partner's net section 751 unrealized loss immediately after the distribution.

Commentators requested a de minimis exception to section 751(b). The IRS and the Treasury Department continue to study the issue and request comments describing the parameters of a de minimis rule that would be helpful.

B. *Section 751 Anti-Abuse Rule*

The IRS and the Treasury Department believe that, despite the general principle that section 751(b) should apply only at the time that a partner's share of net section 751 unrealized gain is reduced (or net section 751 loss is increased), the deferral of ordinary income upon the receipt of a distribution is inappropriate in certain circumstances. Specifically, deferral is inappropriate if a partner engages in a transaction that relies on the rules of section 704(c) to defer or eliminate ordinary income while monetizing most of the value of the partnership interest. Accordingly, these proposed regulations provide an anti-abuse rule that requires taxpayers to apply the rules set forth in the proposed regulations in a manner consistent with the purpose of section 751, and that allows the Commissioner to recast transactions for federal tax purposes as appropriate to achieve tax results that are consistent with the purpose of section 751.

The proposed regulations provide a list of situations that are presumed inconsistent with the purpose of section 751. Under this list, a distribution is presumed inconsistent with the purpose of section 751 if section 751(b) would apply but for the application of section 704(c) principles, and one or more of the following conditions exists: (1) a partner's interest in net section 751 unrealized gain is at least four times greater than the partner's capital account immediately after the distribution, (2) a distribution reduces a partner's interest to such an extent that the partner has little or no exposure to partnership losses and does not meaningfully participate in partnership profits aside from a preferred return for the use of capital, (3) the net value of the partner (or its successor) becomes less than its potential tax liability from section 751 property as a result of a transaction, (4) a partner transfers a portion of its partnership interest within five years after the distribution to a tax-indifferent party in a manner that would not trigger ordinary income recognition in the absence of this anti-abuse rule, or (5) a partnership transfers to a corporation in a nonrecognition transaction section 751 property other than pursuant to a transfer of all property used in a trade or business (excluding assets that are not material to a continuation of the trade or business). In addition, the proposed regulations provide that an amendment to the partnership agreement that results in a reduction in a partner's interest in section 751 property is also presumed inconsistent with the purpose of section 751. A partnership or a partner taking a position on its return that section 751 does not apply to a transaction that meets one or more of these situations must disclose its position on Form 8275-R, Regulation Disclosure Statement.

3. *Tax Consequences of a Section 751(b) Distribution*

If section 751(b) applies to a distribution under the principles set forth in Part 2 of the Summary of Comments and Explanation of Provisions section of this preamble, then the partners must determine the consequences of its application to the partnership and its partners. As described in the Background section of this preamble, Notice 2006-14 discussed replacing the asset exchange approach with a hot asset sale approach to determine these consequences. While most commentators agreed that the hot asset sale approach is an improvement over the existing regulations' asset exchange approach, commentators were able to identify situations in which the hot asset sale approach fails to achieve the correct result or causes undesirable results under other Code provisions. Two commentators advocated adopting, in lieu of the hot asset sale approach, an approach similar to that taken in section 704(c)(1)(B) (referred to in this preamble as a "deemed gain" approach), in which a section

751(b) distribution results in: (1) the partnership recognizing ordinary income in the aggregate amount of each partner's reduction in the partner's interest in section 751 property, (2) the partnership allocating ordinary income to the partner or partners whose interest in section 751(b) property was reduced by the distribution, and (3) the partnership making appropriate basis adjustments to its assets to reflect its ordinary income recognition. One variation of the deemed gain approach would require capital gain recognition in certain cases.

The IRS and the Treasury Department determined that a deemed gain approach produces an appropriate outcome in the greatest number of circumstances out of the approaches under consideration, and that the hot asset sale approach also produced an appropriate outcome in most circumstances. However, no one approach produced an appropriate outcome in all circumstances. Therefore, these proposed regulations withdraw the asset exchange approach of the current regulations, but do not require the use of a particular approach for determining the tax consequences of a section 751(b) distribution. Instead, these proposed regulations provide that if, under the hypothetical sale approach, a distribution reduces a partner's interest in the partnership's section 751 property, giving rise to a section 751(b) amount, then the partnership must use a reasonable approach that is consistent with the purpose of section 751(b) to determine the tax consequences of the reduction. Except in limited situations, a partnership must continue to use the same approach, once chosen, including after a termination of the partnership under section 708(b)(1)(B). These proposed regulations include examples in which the approach adopted is generally reasonable based on the facts of the examples, and one example in which it is determined that the adopted approach is not reasonable based on the facts of the example.

Finally, some commentators recommended allowing taxpayers to elect to recognize capital gain in certain situations (for example, in the situation described in *Example 2* in Notice 2006-14 involving distributions of section 751(b) property to a partner that has insufficient basis in its partnership interest to absorb fully the partnership's basis in the distributed property). Recognition of gain may be appropriate where failing to recognize gain would cause an adjustment to the basis of distributed property (under section 732) or to the basis of partnership property (under section 734(b)) if those basis adjustments would change the partners' shares of ordinary income already determined under the principles described in Part 1 of the Summary of Comments and Explanation of Provisions section of this preamble. Such changes in ordinary income amounts could (in the case of certain adjustments under section 734(b)) decrease partners' shares of partnership ordinary income, requiring the recognition of additional income under section 751(b), or could (in the case of certain adjustments under section 732) convert a distributee partner's share of capital gain into ordinary income. Thus, these proposed regulations require that distributee partners recognize capital gain in certain situations, and permit distributee partners to elect to recognize capital gain in certain other situations.

The proposed regulations require a distributee partner to recognize capital gain to the extent necessary to prevent the distribution from triggering a basis adjustment under section 734(b) that would reduce other partners' shares of net unrealized section 751 gain or loss. Capital gain recognition is necessary in this situation because the section 734(b) basis adjustment was not taken into account in determining the partners' net section 751 unrealized gain or loss immediately after the section 751 distribution, and the IRS and the Treasury Department believe that an approach under which a partnership redetermines a partner's net section 751 unrealized gain or loss to account for section 734(b) basis adjustments would be both administratively burdensome and would accelerate ordinary income unnecessarily. *See Examples 5* and *6* in § 1.751-1(g) of the proposed regulations. Gain recognized in this event is generally capital; however, if the partnership makes an election under § 1.755-1(c)(2)(vi), then the partner must characterize all or a portion of the gain recognized under this rule as ordinary income or a dividend, as appropriate, to preserve the character of the gain in the adjusted asset. *See Example 9* in § 1.751-1(g) of the proposed regulations.

These proposed regulations also allow distributee partners to elect to recognize capital gain in certain circumstances to avoid decreases to the basis of distributed section 751 property. Elective capital gain recognition is appropriate to eliminate a negative section 732(a)(2) or (b) basis adjustment to the asset or assets received in distribution if, and to the extent that, the distributee partner's net section 751 unrealized gain would otherwise be greater immediately after the distribution than it was immediately before the distribution (or would cause the distributee partner's net section 751 unrealized loss to be less immediately after the distribution than it was immediately before the distribution). For example, elective capital gain recognition is appropriate if a partner with zero basis in its partnership interest receives a distribution of partnership section 751 property with basis in the hands of the partnership equal to its value, and the distribution otherwise increases the distributee partner's net section 751 unrealized gain.

4. *Miscellaneous*

A. *Section 751(a)*

As described in Parts 2.A and 2.B of this preamble, these proposed regulations generally defer the recognition of ordinary income upon a distribution when the partner's unrealized gain and loss in the partnership's section 751 property is preserved through the application of the principles of section 704(c). This approach is consistent with the 1984 amendment to section 704(c). By mandating the application of section 704(c) principles, that amendment partially severed the relationship that had generally existed between a partner's distributive share (that is, the right to share in the economic gain or loss) associated with a partnership item and the partner's share of tax gain or loss from the sale of that item. The IRS and the Treasury Department believe that, by mandating the application of section 704(c) principles in 1984, Congress intended that impacted provisions be interpreted consistent with this new emphasis on tax gain or loss. Congress provided a broad delegation of authority to the Treasury Department to address these repercussions of amending section 704(c) on other provisions in subchapter K.

Some commentators interpret section 751(a) as limiting the amount of ordinary income that a transferor partner may recognize upon a transfer of a partnership interest to the amount of any money or property received by the transferor partner, without taking into account the total amount of ordinary income attributable to the partnership interest transferred that relates to section 751 property. However, interpreting section 751(a) as limiting ordinary income in this way would contravene Congress's intent to tax partners on their shares of partnership ordinary income as determined by applying section 704(c) principles. The IRS and the Treasury Department believe that section 751(a) should be interpreted in a manner that accounts for the impact of section 704(c). Thus, these proposed regulations provide that the amount of money or the fair market value of property received for purposes of section 751(a) takes into account the transferor partner's share of income or gain from section 751 property.

The IRS and the Treasury Department alternatively considered addressing this issue by deeming a partner that sells or exchanges its partnership interest to receive a distribution of the partner's share of the section 751 property, followed by a sale of the property back to the partnership for its fair market value, recognizing the deferred ordinary income inherent in the section 751 property. The partner would then be deemed to contribute the cash proceeds to the partnership thereby increasing the partner's basis in the partner's partnership interest. Finally, upon the sale or exchange of the partnership interest, the partner would recognize the appropriate amount of capital loss. This potential multi-step deemed approach would result in additional complexity and would reach the same result that the current regulations under § 1.751-1(a) reach as clarified by these proposed regulations. Therefore, the IRS and the Treasury Department are not proposing this alternative approach.

B. *Previously Contributed Property Exception*

Section 751(b)(2)(A) provides that section 751(b) does not apply to a distribution of property that the distributee contributed to the partnership ("previously contributed property exception"). Unlike other provisions in subchapter K that include similar previously contributed property exceptions, the current regulations under section 751(b) do not contain successor rules for purposes of applying the section 751(b) previously contributed property exception. These proposed regulations add successor rules to section 751(b) similar to the successor rules contained in other previously contributed property exceptions within subchapter K.

C. *Mergers and Divisions*

A commentator requested guidance confirming how the rules of section 751(b) apply in the case of an incorporation, merger, or division of a partnership. The proposed regulations do not adopt this comment because the IRS and the Treasury Department believe such guidance is beyond the scope of these proposed regulations.

D. *Substantial Appreciation Test*

These proposed regulations also make a number of technical corrections to account for changes in the law since the issuance of existing regulations under section 751. For example, these proposed regulations remove the language "substantially appreciated" from the first sentence of § 1.751-1(a)(1), which applies with respect to sales or exchanges of an interest in a partnership. In addition to conforming the language of the regulations to that of the Code, this change is intended to clarify that, upon a sale or exchange of a partnership interest, unrealized receivables and inventory items are treated in the same manner. Thus, a transferor partner may recognize an ordinary loss with respect to inventory items pursuant to section 751(a) to the extent the transferor would be allocated a net ordinary loss pursuant to § 1.751-1(a)(2). These proposed regulations also update the definition of "inventory items which have appreciated substantially in value" with respect to section 751(b) to reflect the 1993 amendment to the statute that eliminated the 10-percent test from the definition of "*substantial appreciation*." *See* Public Law 103-66, Sec. 13206(e)(1). These proposed regulations also clarify that unrealized receivables are not included in the term "inventory items which have appreciated substantially in value."

E. *Other Changes Relating to Revaluations*

Finally, these proposed regulations address some of the comments received in response to Notice 2009-70 (2009-2 CB 255), in which the IRS and the Treasury Department requested comments on, among other things, whether additional events should be added to the list of events permitting a revaluation of partnership property pursuant to § 1.704-1(b)(2)(iv)(*f*) and whether, in a tiered partnership structure, a revaluation at one partnership in the tier should permit another partnership in the tier to revalue that partnership's property. Commentators recommended that partnership recapitalizations (changes to the way partners agree to share partnership profits and losses) be added as a permissible revaluation event. The IRS and the Treasury Department agree that partnership recapitalizations should be added as a permissible event because, absent providing for a special allocation of any unrealized gain or loss in partnership assets that arose prior to the recapitalization, a revaluation is necessary to preserve each partner's share of such unrealized amounts. In addition, commentators recommended that a partnership in a tiered partnership structure be able to revalue its partnership property if another partnership in the tiered structure was permitted to revalue its partnership property. The IRS and the Treasury Department agree and believe that permitting successive revaluations in a tiered partnership structure is necessary to properly allocate items with respect to a reverse section 704(c) allocation to the appropriate partner.

Availability of IRS Documents

IRS notices cited in this preamble are made available by the Superintendent of Documents, U.S. Government Printing Office, Washington, DC 20402.

Effect on Other Documents

The following publication will be obsolete as of the date of publication of a Treasury decision adopting these rules as final regulations in the **Federal Register**:

Rev. Rul. 84-102 (1984-2 CB 119).

Proposed Effective/Applicability Date

The regulations, as proposed, apply to distributions occurring in any taxable period ending on or after the date of publication of a Treasury decision adopting these rules as final regulations in the **Federal Register**. The rules contained in § 1.751-1(a)(2) would apply to transfers of partnership interests that occur on or after November 3, 2014. However, the rules contained in § 1.751-1(a)(2) are a clarification of existing rules, and no inference is intended from the change to § 1.751-1(a)(2) with respect to sales or exchanges of partnership interests prior to the effective date for § 1.751-1(a)(2). The rules contained in § 1.751-1(a)(3) continue to apply to transfers of partnership interests that occur on or after December 15, 1999. A partnership and its partners would be able to rely on § 1.751-1(b)(2) of these proposed regulations for purposes of determining a partner's interest in the partnership's section 751 property on or after November 3, 2014 provided the partnership and its partners apply each of § 1.751-1(a)(2), § 1.751-1(b)(2), and § 1.751-1(b)(4) of these proposed regulations consistently for all partnership distributions and sales or exchanges, including for any distributions and sales or exchanges the partnership makes after a termination of the partnership under section 708(b)(1)(B).

Special Analyses

It has been determined that this notice of proposed rulemaking is not a significant regulatory action as defined in Executive Order 12866, as supplemented by Executive Order 13653. Therefore, a regulatory assessment is not required. It has also been determined that section 553(b) of the Administrative Procedure Act (5 U.S.C. chapter 5) does not apply to these regulations. It is hereby certified that the collection of information in these regulations will not have a significant economic impact on a substantial number of small entities. This certification is based on the fact that the amount of time necessary to prepare the required disclosure is not lengthy and few small businesses are likely to be partners or partnerships required to make the disclosures required by the rule. Accordingly, a Regulatory Flexibility Analysis under the Regulatory Flexibility Act (5 U.S.C. chapter 6) does not apply. Pursuant to section 7805(f) of the Code, this notice of proposed rulemaking has been submitted to the Chief Counsel for Advocacy of the Small Business Administration for comment on its impact on small business.

Comments and Requests for Public Hearing

The IRS and the Treasury Department request comments on all aspects of the proposed rules. In particular, the IRS and the Treasury Department request comments, in addition to those previously requested in this preamble, on: (1) whether and how carryover adjustments to ordinary income property under sections 734(b) and 743(b) should be taken into account under the hypothetical sale approach, (2) whether the final regulations should exclude certain types of transactions from the previously contributed property successor rules provided in these proposed regulations, (3) whether the regulations should specifically describe approaches as generally reasonable approaches for determining the tax consequences of a section 751(b) distribution, and which approaches should be specified as generally reasonable, (4) whether the final regulations should provide rules similar to those proposed in new § 1.755-1(c)(2)(iii) through (vi) in § 1.755-1(b)(5) with respect to section 743(b) adjustments in substituted basis transactions, and (5) what disclosures the IRS and the Treasury Department should require from partners and partnerships that either recognize gain under section 751(a) or (b), or rely on reverse section 704(c) allocations to defer the gain recognition required by section 751(a) or (b).

The IRS and the Treasury Department also request comments on a topic that, although not specific to section 751, may impact the rules under section 751. The IRS and the Treasury Department are aware that the regulations under § 1.1245-1(e)(3) (concerning the interaction of section 1245 and section 743), and § 1.1250-1(f), by reference to § 1.1245-1(e)(3), are out of date. The intent of the regulations under § 1.1245-1(e)(3) is, in part, to ensure that a transferee partner does not recognize ordinary income with respect to section 1245 property to the extent a section 743 adjustment has displaced that ordinary income. For example, if a partner sells in a fully taxable exchange its interest in a partnership that has elected under section 754, and the selling partner recognizes ordinary income under section 751(a) with respect to partnership section 1245 property, then the rules under sections 1245 and 743 are intended to ensure that the transferee partner recognizes no ordinary income on an immediately subsequent disposition of the section 1245 property in a fully taxable transaction. However, the regulations under § 1.1245-1(e)(3) have not been amended to take into account changes to subchapter K, including the regulations under section 751, resulting in issues and uncertainties. The IRS and the Treasury Department are studying these issues and request comments in this area.

Finally, the IRS and the Treasury Department request comments as to how section 751(b) should interact with rules for withholding and reporting with respect to nonresident aliens and foreign corporations. For example, the IRS and the Treasury Department are considering whether regulations should provide that for purposes of withholding under chapter 3 of Subtitle A (for example, under section 1446), income recognized as a result of a section 751(b) distribution is treated as recognized by the partnership regardless of the approach chosen to determine the U.S. tax consequences of the section 751(b) distribution. The IRS and the Treasury Department are also considering whether additional guidance with respect to tax or information returns (for example, pursuant to section 6031(b) or section 6050K) is necessary for gain recognized on section 751(b) distributions affecting these taxpayers.

Before these proposed regulations are adopted as final regulations, consideration will be given to any comments that are submitted timely to the IRS as prescribed in this preamble under the "Addresses" heading. All comments will be available at *www.regulations.gov* or upon request. A public hearing will be scheduled if requested in writing by any person who submits timely written or electronic comments. If a public hearing is scheduled, notice of the date, time, and place for the public hearing will be published in the **Federal Register**.

Drafting Information

The principal authors of these regulations are Allison R. Carmody and Frank J. Fisher, Office of the Associate Chief Counsel (Passthroughs and Special Industries). However, other personnel from the IRS and the Treasury Department participated in their development.

[¶49,635] Proposed Regulations (REG-109187-11), published in the Federal Register on December 23, 2014.

[Code Secs. 351, Code Sec. 361, Code Sec. 453B and Code Sec. 721]

Accounting methods: Installment method: Gain or loss on disposition of installment obligations.—Reg. § 1.453B-1 and amendments of Reg. §§ 1.351-1(a)(1), 1.361-1 and 1.721-1(a), relating to the nonrecognition of gain or loss on certain dispositions of an installment obligation, are proposed.

AGENCY: Internal Revenue Service (IRS), Treasury.

ACTION: Notice of proposed rulemaking.

SUMMARY: This document contains proposed regulations relating to the nonrecognition of gain or loss on certain dispositions of an installment obligation. In general, under the proposed regulations a transferor does not recognize gain or loss on certain dispositions of an installment obligation if gain or loss is not recognized on the disposition under another provision of the Internal Revenue Code. The proposed regulations also provide that this general rule does not apply to the satisfaction of an installment obligation. For example, an installment obligation of an issuer, such as a corporation or partnership, is satisfied when the holder transfers the obligation to the issuer for an equity interest in the issuer.

DATES: Comments or a request for a public hearing must be received by March 23, 2015. ADDRESSES: Send submissions to CC:PA:LPD:PR (REG-109187-11), room 5203, Internal Revenue Service, PO Box 7604, Ben Franklin Station, Washington, DC 20044. Submissions may be hand delivered Monday through Friday between the hours of 8 a.m. and 4 p.m. to CC:PA:LPD:PR (REG-109187-11), Courier's Desk, Internal Revenue Service, 1111 Constitution Avenue, NW., Washington, DC, or sent electronically via the Federal eRulemaking Portal at *www.regulations.gov* (IRS REG-109187-11).

FOR FURTHER INFORMATION CONTACT: Concerning the proposed regulations, Arvind Ravichandran, (202) 317-4718; concerning the submission of comments and/or requests for a public hearing, Olawafunmilayo (Funmi) Taylor at (202) 317-6901 (not toll-free numbers).

SUPPLEMENTARY INFORMATION:

Background

This document contains proposed amendments to the regulations in 26 CFR part 1 under section 453B of the Internal Revenue Code (Code) relating to gain or loss on the disposition of installment obligations. Section 453B was added to the Code by the Installment Sales Revision Act of 1980, Public Law 96-471 (94 Stat. 2252 (1980)).

Section 453B replaces and provides generally the same rules as former section 453(d). In general, under section 453B(a) gain or loss is recognized upon the satisfaction of an installment obligation at other than its face value, or upon the distribution, transmission, sale, or other disposition of the installment obligation. Section 1.453-9(c)(2) of the Income Tax Regulations, issued under former section 453(d), provides an exception to the general rule. Under § 1.453-9(c)(2), if the Code provides an exception to the recognition of gain or loss for certain dispositions, then gain or loss is not recognized under former section 453(d) on the disposition of an installment obligation within that exception. The exceptions identified in § 1.453-9(c)(2) include certain transfers to corporations under sections 351 and 361, contributions to partnerships under section 721, and distributions by partnerships to partners under section 731 (except as provided by section 736 and section 751).

Under Rev. Rul. 73-423, 1973-2 CB 161, the exceptions in § 1.453-9(c)(2) to recognition of gain or loss under the installment sale rules do not apply to the transfer of an installment obligation that results in a satisfaction of the obligation. Thus, the revenue ruling holds that the transfer of a corporation's installment obligation to the issuing corporation in exchange for stock of the issuing corporation results in a satisfaction of the obligation. In that case, the transferor must recognize gain or loss on the satisfaction of the obligation to the extent of the difference between the transferor's basis in the obligation and the fair market value of the stock received, even though gain or loss generally is not recognized on section 351 transfers.

Explanation of Provisions

These proposed regulations republish in § 1.453B-1(c) the general rule in § 1.4539(c)(2) under which gain or loss is not recognized upon certain dispositions. In addition, the proposed regulations incorporate and expand the holding of Rev. Rul. 73-423 to provide that a transferor recognizes gain or loss under section 453B(a) when the transferor disposes of an installment obligation in a transaction that results in the satisfaction of the installment obligation, including, for example, when an installment obligation of a corporation or partnership is contributed to the corporation or partnership in exchange for an equity interest in the corporation or partnership. Finally, the proposed regulations amend the regulations under sections 351, 361, and 721 to include a cross-reference to the regulations under section 453B regarding recognition of any gain or loss upon the satisfaction of an installment obligation. The IRS and the Treasury Department anticipate publishing regulations addressing the general rule under section 453B(a) and the basis of an obligation under section 453B(b) in the future. Therefore, regulations under § 1.453B-1(a) and (b) are reserved.

Proposed Effective/Applicability Date

These regulations are proposed to apply to satisfactions, distributions, transmissions, sales, or other dispositions of installment obligations after the date these regulations are published as final regulations in the **Federal Register**.

Special Analyses

This notice of proposed rulemaking is not a significant regulatory action as defined in Executive Order 12866, as supplemented by Executive Order 13563. Therefore, a regulatory assessment is not required. It also has been determined that section 553(b) of the Administrative Procedure Act (5 U.S.C. chapter 5) does not apply to these regulations, and because the regulation does not impose a collection of information on small entities, the Regulatory Flexibility Act (5 U.S.C. chapter 6) does not apply. Pursuant to section 7805(f) of the Code, this notice of proposed rulemaking has been submitted to the Chief Counsel for Advocacy of the Small Business Administration for comment on its impact on small business.

Comments and Requests for a Public Hearing

Before these proposed regulations are adopted as final regulations, consideration will be given to any written comments that are submitted timely to the IRS as prescribed in this preamble under the "Addresses" heading. The Treasury Department and the IRS invite comments on all aspects of the proposed rules. In particular, the Treasury Department and the IRS request comments on how a partnership's distribution of a partner's installment obligation to the obligor partnershould be treated under section 453B, and whether there are circumstances in which such a distribution should not result in gain or loss recognition by the partnership. All comments will be available for public inspection and copying at www.regulations.gov or upon request. A public hearing will be scheduled if requested in writing by any person who timely submits written comments. If a public hearing is scheduled, notice of the date, time and place for the hearing will be published in the **Federal Register**.

Drafting Information

The principal author of these regulations is Arvind Ravichandran, Office of the Associate Chief Counsel (Income Tax and Accounting). However, other personnel from the IRS and the Treasury Department participated in their development.

[¶ 49,640] Proposed Amendments of Regulations (REG-100400-14), published in the Federal Register on March 6, 2015.

[Code Secs. 1361, 1362 and 1502]

Proposed regulations: Consolidated returns: Corporations becoming members: Corporations ceasing to be members: Reporting periods: Short period returns: Change in status: End of the day rule: Next day rule: Previous day rule: S corporation exception: Anti-avoidance rule.—Amendments of Reg. §§ 1.1361-5, 1.1362-3, 1.1502-13, 1.1502-21, 1.1502-22, 1.1502-28 and 1.1502-76, containing proposed amendments to the consolidated return regulations, are proposed.

AGENCY: Internal Revenue Service (IRS), Treasury.

ACTION: Notice of proposed rulemaking.

SUMMARY: This document contains proposed amendments to the consolidated return regulations. These proposed regulations would revise the rules for reporting certain items of income and deduction that are reportable on the day a corporation joins or leaves a consolidated group. The proposed regulations would affect such corporations and the consolidated groups that they join or leave.

DATES: Written or electronic comments and requests for a public hearing must be received by June 4, 2015.

ADDRESSES: Send submissions to: CC:PA:LPD:PR (REG-100400-14), Room 5203, Internal Revenue Service, P.O. Box 7604, Ben Franklin Station, Washington, DC 20044. Submissions may be hand-delivered Monday through Friday between the hours of 8 a.m. and 4 p.m. to CC:PA:LPD:PR

(REG-100400-14), Courier's Desk, Internal Revenue Service, 1111 Constitution Avenue NW., Washington, DC, or sent electronically via the Federal eRulemaking Portal at *http://www.regulations.gov/* (IRS REG-100400-14).

FOR FURTHER INFORMATION CONTACT: Concerning the proposed regulations, Russell G. Jones, (202) 317-6847; concerning the submission of comments or to request a public hearing, Oluwafunmilayo (Funmi) P. Taylor, (202) 317-6901 (not toll-free numbers).

SUPPLEMENTARY INFORMATION:

Background and Explanation of Provisions

1. Introduction

This notice of proposed rulemaking contains proposed regulations that amend 26 CFR part 1 under section 1502 of the Internal Revenue Code (Code). Section 1502 authorizes the Secretary to prescribe regulations for corporations that join in filing a consolidated return, and it expressly provides that those rules may be different from the provisions of chapter 1 of subtitle A of the Code that would apply if those corporations filed separate returns. Terms used in the consolidated return regulations generally are defined in §1.1502-1.

These proposed regulations provide guidance under §1.1502-76, which prescribes rules for determining the taxable period in which items of income, gain, deduction, loss, and credit (tax items) of a corporation that joins in filing a consolidated return are included. Section 1.1502-76(b) provides, in part, that if a corporation (S) becomes or ceases to be a member of a consolidated group during a consolidated return year, S must include in the consolidated return its tax items for the period during which it is a member. S also must file a separate return (including a consolidated return of another group) that includes its items for the period during which it is not a member.

2. Prior and Current Regulations

On September 8, 1966, the IRS and the Treasury Department promulgated regulations under §1.1502-76 in TD 6894, 31 FR 11794 (1966 regulations). Section 1.1502-76(b) of the 1966 regulations was silent regarding the treatment of S's tax items that accrued on the day S became or ceased to be a member of a consolidated group (S's change in status). Thus, whether S's tax items for the day of S's change in status should have been reflected on S's tax return for the short period ending with S's change in status, or whether these tax items should have been reflected instead on S's tax return for the short period beginning after S's change in status, was unclear under the 1966 regulations.

On August 15, 1994, the IRS and the Treasury Department published final regulations (TD 8560; 59 FR 41666) under §1.1502-76(b) (current regulations) that revised the 1966 regulations to eliminate uncertainty regarding the treatment of tax items recognized by S on the day of S's change in status. Under the general rule of §1.1502-76(b)(1)(ii)(A)(*1*) of the current regulations (current end of the day rule), S is treated for all federal income tax purposes as becoming or ceasing to be a member of a consolidated group at the end of the day of S's change in status, and S's tax items that are reportable on that day generally are included in the tax return for the taxable year that ends as a result of S's change in status.

The notice of proposed rulemaking that proposed the current end of the day rule (57 FR 53634, Nov. 12, 1992) (1992 NPRM) indicated that the current end of the day rule was intended to provide certainty and prevent inconsistent reporting of S's items between the consolidated and separate returns. Prior to the 1992 NPRM, some taxpayers had inferred (based upon the administrative practice of the IRS) that the inclusion in a particular return of a tax item of S incurred on the day of S's change in status depended on a factual determination of whether the transaction occurred before or after noon on the day of S's change in status (the so-called "lunch rule").

There are two exceptions to the current end of the day rule. The first exception (in §1.1502-76(b)(1)(ii)(A)(2)) provides that if a corporation is an S corporation (within the meaning of section 1361(a)(1)) immediately before becoming a member of a consolidated group, the corporation becomes a member of the group at the beginning of the day the termination of its S corporation election is effective (termination date), and its taxable year ends for all federal income tax purposes at the end of the preceding day (S corporation exception). The S corporation exception was added by TD 8842 (64 FR 61205; Nov. 10, 1999) to eliminate the need to file a one-day C corporation return for the day an S corporation is acquired by a consolidated group. No additional rule was necessary with respect to a qualified S corporation subsidiary (QSub) of an S corporation that joins a consolidated group. See §1.1361-5(a)(3).

Added at the same time as the current end of the day rule, the second exception (in §1.1502-76(b)(1)(ii)(B)) provides that if a transaction occurs on the day of S's change in status that is properly allocable to the portion of S's day after the event resulting in S's change in status, S and certain related persons must treat the transaction as occurring at the beginning of the following day for all federal income tax purposes (current next day rule). The current next day rule was added in response to comments to the 1992 NPRM suggesting that the current end of the day rule created a "seller beware" problem with respect to S's tax items arising on the day of S's change in status but after the event causing S's change in status. Commenters suggested that, for example, if consolidated group A sold the stock of S to consolidated group B, and group B caused S to sell one of its divisions on the same day it was acquired by group B, the gain from the sale of the division would be inappropriately allocable to group A's consolidated return. Commenters recommended that final regulations adopt rules substantially similar to the current next day rule to protect the reasonable expectations of sellers and buyers of S's stock. Commenters suggested that a rule providing this type of protection was most appropriate with respect to extraordinary items, and some commenters suggested that a rule similar to the current next day rule should operate unless the seller and buyer of S agreed otherwise.

3. Proposed Regulations

A. Overview

The IRS and the Treasury Department have determined that changes should be made to the regulations under § 1.1502-76(b) due to uncertainty regarding the appropriate application of the current next day rule. These proposed regulations address this concern as well as additional concerns with the current regulations, as summarized in this section 3.A. and discussed in greater detail in sections 3.B. through 3.K. of this preamble.

To provide certainty, the proposed regulations generally clarify the period in which S must report certain tax items by replacing the current next day rule with a new exception to the end of the day rule (proposed next day rule) that is more narrowly tailored to clearly reflect taxable income and prevent certain post-closing actions from adversely impacting S's tax return for the period ending on the day of S's change in status. The proposed next day rule applies only to "extraordinary items" (as defined in § 1.1502-76(b)(2)(ii)(C) of the proposed regulations) that result from transactions that occur on the day of S's change in status, but after the event causing the change, and that would be taken into account by S on that day. This rule requires those extraordinary items to be allocated to S's tax return for the period beginning the next day. The proposed next day rule is expressly inapplicable to any extraordinary item that arises simultaneously with the event that causes S's change in status.

The proposed regulations further clarify that fees for services rendered in connection with S's change in status constitute a "compensation-related deduction" for purposes of § 1.1502-76(b)(2)(ii)(C)(*9*) (if payment of the fees would give rise to a deduction), and therefore an extraordinary item. The proposed regulations also clarify that the anti-avoidance rule in § 1.1502-76(b)(3) may apply to situations in which a person modifies an existing contract or other agreement in anticipation of S's change in status.

The proposed regulations also add a rule (previous day rule, described in section 3.C. of this preamble) to clarify the application of the S corporation exception. In addition, the proposed regulations limit the scope of the end of the day rule, the next day rule, the S corporation exception, and the previous day rule to determining the period in which S must report certain tax items and determining the treatment of an asset or a tax item for purposes of sections 382(h) and 1374 (as opposed to applying for all federal income tax purposes).

Additionally, the proposed regulations provide that short taxable years resulting from intercompany transactions to which section 381(a) applies (intercompany section 381 transactions) are not taken into account in determining the carryover period for a tax item of the distributor or transferor member in the intercompany section 381 transaction or for purposes of section 481(a). Furthermore, the proposed regulations provide that the due date for filing S's separate return for the taxable year that ends as a result of S becoming a member is not accelerated if S ceases to exist in the same consolidated return year.

The proposed regulations make several other conforming and non-substantive changes to the current regulations as well. Finally, the proposed regulations add several examples to illustrate the proposed rules.

The IRS and the Treasury Department note that neither the current regulations nor the proposed regulations are intended to supersede general rules in the Code and regulations concerning whether an item is otherwise includible or deductible.

B. Proposed Next Day Rule

The current next day rule provides that S and certain related persons must treat a transaction as occurring at the beginning of the day following S's change in status if the transaction occurs on the day of S's change in status and is "properly allocable" to the portion of that day following S's change in status. The IRS and the Treasury Department believe, however, that the standards provided in the current next day rule for determining whether a transaction is "properly allocable" to the portion of S's day after the event resulting in S's change in status have been inappropriately interpreted by taxpayers. The current next day rule provides that a determination of whether a transaction is "properly allocable" to the portion of S's day after the event resulting in S's change in status is respected if it is "reasonable and consistently applied by all affected persons." In determining whether an allocation is "reasonable," certain factors enumerated in the current regulations are to be considered, including whether tax items arising from the same transaction are allocated inconsistently. Some taxpayers have interpreted these rules as providing flexibility in reporting tax items that result from transactions occurring on the day of S's change in status so that those items can be allocated by agreement to the day of, or to the day following, S's change in status. The IRS and the Treasury Department view this interpretation of the current next day rule as inappropriate because it effectively would permit taxpayers to elect the income tax return on which these tax items are reported and therefore may not result in an allocation that clearly reflects taxable income. This electivity is inconsistent with the purpose of § 1.1502-76(b) to clearly reflect the income of S and the consolidated group. Further, the IRS and the Treasury Department have observed that the current regulations create controversy between taxpayers and the IRS as to whether certain of S's tax items that become reportable on the day of S's change in status are properly allocated to S's tax return for the period ending that day rather than to S's tax return for the period beginning the next day.

The proposed next day rule is intended to eliminate the perceived electivity and the source of these controversies. Under the proposed regulations, the application of the proposed next day rule is mandatory rather than elective—if an extraordinary item results from a transaction that occurs on the day of S's change in status, but after the event resulting in the change, and if the item would be taken into account by S on that day, the transaction resulting in the extraordinary item is treated as occurring at the beginning of the following day for purposes of determining the period in which S must report the item.

The proposed regulations also provide that the proposed next day rule is inapplicable to items that arise simultaneously with the event that causes S's change in status. Under the end of the day rule (as revised by these proposed regulations), those items are reported on S's tax return for the short period ending on the day of S's change in status. The proposed regulations are expected to afford taxpayers and the IRS greater certainty regarding the period to which S's tax items resulting from such a transaction are allocated.

C. Previous Day Rule

As noted in section 2 of this preamble, the special rule for S corporations provides an exception to the end of the day rule if an S corporation joins a consolidated group. To avoid creating a one-day C corporation tax return for the termination date, the S corporation exception provides that S becomes a member of the group at the beginning of the termination date, and that S's taxable year ends for all federal income tax purposes at the end of the preceding day.

Although these proposed regulations retain the S corporation exception, the proposed regulations add a previous day rule that mirrors the principles of the proposed next day rule. Whereas the proposed next day rule requires extraordinary items resulting from transactions that occur on the day of S's change in status (but after the event causing the change) to be allocated to S's tax return for the short period that begins the following day, the previous day rule requires extraordinary items resulting from transactions that occur on the termination date (but before or simultaneously with the event causing S's status as an S corporation to terminate) to be allocated to S's tax return for the short period that ends on the previous day (that is, the day preceding the termination date).

D. Revised Scope of the End of the Day Rule and Related Rules

Under the current end of the day rule, S becomes or ceases to be a member at the end of the day on which its status as a member changes, and its tax year ends "for all federal income tax purposes" at the end of that day. However, applying the end of the day rule for purposes other than the reporting of S's tax items could yield results inconsistent with other consolidated return rules. For example, under §§1.1502-13 and 1.1502-80(d)(1), if a member contributes property subject to a liability in excess of the property's basis to a nonmember in exchange for the nonmember's stock, and if the transferee becomes a member of the transferor's consolidated group as a result of the exchange, the transaction is treated as an intercompany transaction and section 357(c) does not apply. However, if the end of the day rule applies "for all federal income tax purposes," it may be unclear whether the transferee becomes a member "immediately after the transaction," whether the transaction is an intercompany transaction, and whether section 357(c) could apply to the transaction.

To eliminate possible confusion arising from application of the current end of the day rule and related rules, these proposed regulations provide that the end of the day rule, the proposed next day rule, the S corporation exception, and the previous day rule apply for purposes of determining the period in which S must report its tax items, as well as for purposes of sections 382(h) and 1374 (discussed in section 3.I. of this preamble).

E. Extraordinary Items

The proposed next day rule mandatorily applies to extraordinary items that result from a transaction that occurs on the day of S's change in status but after the event that causes the change. In contrast, the previous day rule mandatorily applies to extraordinary items that result from a transaction that occurs on the day of S's change in status but before or simultaneously with the event that causes S's status as an S corporation to terminate.

One category of extraordinary items, set forth in §1.1502-76(b)(2)(ii)(C)(*9*) of the current regulations, applies to any "compensation-related deduction in connection with S's change in status." The proposed regulations clarify that this category of extraordinary items includes (among other items) a deduction for fees for services rendered in connection with S's change in status. For example, if payment of a fee for the services of a financial adviser is contingent upon a successful acquisition of S's stock, to the extent the fee gives rise to a deduction, the deduction for the accrual of that expense is an extraordinary item, and the deduction is allowable only in S's taxable year that ends at the close of the day of the change.

The IRS and the Treasury Department request comments as to whether the list of extraordinary items set forth in §1.1502-76(b)(2)(ii)(C) should be modified to include any item not currently listed or whether any item currently included should be deleted or modified. Specifically, the IRS and the Treasury Department are considering whether the item in §1.1502-76(b)(2)(ii)(C)(*5*) ("[a]ny item carried to or from any portion of the original year (*e.g.*, a net operating loss carried under section 172), and any section 481(a) adjustment") should be modified to include "any section 481(a) adjustment or the acceleration thereof," and whether the item in §1.1502-76(b)(2)(ii)(C)(*6*) ("[t]he effects of any change in accounting method initiated by the filing of the appropriate form after S's change in status") should continue to be included in the list of extraordinary items.

The IRS and the Treasury Department also request comments as to whether any extraordinary item should be excluded, in whole or in part, from application of the next day rule and the previous day rule. In particular, the IRS and the Treasury Department request comments as to whether the extraordinary items set forth in § 1.1502-76(b)(2)(ii)(C)(*5*) and (*6*) of the current regulations should be excluded, in whole or in part, from application of these rules.

F. Ratable Allocation

Rather than require S to perform a closing of the books on the day of its change in status, the current regulations under § 1.1502-76(b)(2)(ii) permit S's tax items, other than the extraordinary items, to be ratably allocated between S's two short taxable years if certain conditions are met. The IRS and the Treasury Department request comments as to whether S no longer should be permitted to elect to ratably allocate its tax items between the periods ending and beginning with S's change in status.

G. Certain Foreign Entities

Solely for purposes of determining the short taxable year of S to which the items of a passthrough entity in which S owns an interest are allocated, § 1.1502-76(b)(2)(vi)(A) of the current regulations generally provides that S is treated as selling or exchanging its entire interest in the entity immediately before S's change in status. This rule does not apply to certain foreign corporations the ownership of which may give rise to deemed income inclusions under the Code. In addition, a deemed income inclusion from a foreign corporation and a deferred tax amount from a passive foreign investment company under section 1291 are treated as extraordinary items under § 1.1502-76(b)(2)(ii)(C)(*11*). The IRS and the Treasury Department request comments as to whether such deemed income inclusions or deferred tax amounts should continue to be treated as extraordinary items, whether rules having similar effects to the rule in § 1.1502-76(b)(2)(vi)(A) relating to passthrough entities should be adopted for controlled foreign corporations and passive foreign investment companies in which S owns an interest, and whether any other changes should be made to § 1.1502-76(b)(2)(vi) of the current regulations.

H. Anti-Avoidance Rule

Under § 1.1502-76(b)(3) of the current regulations, if any person acts with a principal purpose contrary to the purposes of § 1.1502-76(b) to substantially reduce the federal income tax liability of any person (prohibited purpose), adjustments must be made as necessary to carry out the purposes of § 1.1502-76 of the current regulations (anti-avoidance rule). The proposed regulations clarify that the anti-avoidance rule may apply to situations in which a person modifies an existing contract or other agreement in anticipation of S's change in status in order to shift an item between the taxable years that end and begin as a result of S's change in status if such actions are undertaken with a prohibited purpose. The IRS and the Treasury Department request comments regarding this proposed amendment to the anti-avoidance rule.

I. Coordination With Sections 382(h) and 1374

1. Section 382

For purposes of section 382, the term *recognized built-in loss* (RBIL) means any loss recognized during the recognition period on the disposition of any asset held by the loss corporation immediately before the date of the section 382 ownership change (change date), to the extent the loss reflects a built-in loss on the change date. Section 382(h)(2)(B). The term *recognition period* means the five-year period beginning on the change date. Section 382(h)(7)(A).

Section 382(h)(1)(B) generally provides that if a loss corporation has a net unrealized built-in loss (NUBIL), then any RBIL taken into account in a taxable year any portion of which falls in the recognition period (recognition period taxable year) is treated as a deduction subject to the loss corporation's section 382 limitation as if the RBIL were a pre-change loss. The amount of RBILs subject to the section 382 limitation in any recognition period taxable year is limited, however, to the excess of the NUBIL over total RBILs in prior taxable years ending in the recognition period. (The amount of such excess is referred to in this preamble as the outstanding NUBIL balance.) In other words, the amount of the NUBIL limits the amount of RBILs that are treated as pre-change losses, and any built-in loss treated as an RBIL further reduces the outstanding NUBIL balance.

In many cases, the event that causes S's change in status for purposes of § 1.1502-76(b)(1)(ii) also causes S to undergo an ownership change for purposes of section 382. Thus, an item of deduction or loss that becomes reportable on the day of S's change in status falls within the recognition period beginning that day, even if the item is allocated to S's short period ending that day under the end of the day rule. As a consequence, an item that should be a pre-change loss is treated as an RBIL that reduces the outstanding NUBIL balance. For example, assume consolidated group A sells all of S's stock to consolidated group B. If on the day of S's change in status (but before the event causing the change), S recognizes a loss on the sale of an asset, under the end of the day rule the loss is reported on group A's consolidated return. However, notwithstanding that the loss may not be claimed by group B, the loss may be treated as an RBIL and reduce the outstanding NUBIL balance.

To prevent such an outcome, these proposed regulations provide that, for purposes of section 382(h), items includible in the short taxable year that ends as a result of S's change in status (including items allocated to that taxable year under the end of the day rule) are not treated as occurring in the recognition period. Rather, only items includible in S's short taxable year that begins as a result of S's change in status (including items allocated to that taxable year under the proposed next day rule) are treated as occurring in the recognition period. Therefore, the beginning of the recognition period for purposes of section 382(h) would correspond with the beginning of S's short taxable year that begins on the day after S's change in status.

2. Section 1374

Section 1374 generally imposes a corporate-level tax (section 1374 tax) on the recognition of gain by an S corporation that formerly was a C corporation (or that acquired assets from a C corporation in a transferred basis transaction) during a recognition period specified in section 1374(d)(7) (section 1374 recognition period), but only to the extent of the corporation's net recognized built-in gain (as defined in section 1374(d)(2)) for a given taxable year. The section 1374 tax also applies to certain tax items attributable to the corporation's C corporation taxable years. In addition, regulations under section 337(d) extend section 1374 treatment to (1) a C corporation's conversion to a real estate investment trust (REIT), regulated investment company (RIC), and certain tax-exempt entities, or (2) certain cases in which a REIT, RIC, or tax-exempt entity acquires assets in a transferred basis transaction from a C corporation.

As with the application of section 382(h), the event that causes S's change in status for purposes of § 1.1502-76(b)(1)(ii) may be the event that results in S being a corporation that is subject to the section 1374 tax. Therefore, it is necessary to determine in which return (the group's consolidated return or S's separate return beginning the day after S's change in status) S's tax items for the day of S's change in status are included. Similarly, if the event that causes S's change in status for purposes of § 1.1502-76(b)(1)(ii) is the event that results in S ceasing to be a corporation subject to the section 1374 tax, it is necessary to determine in which return (the group's consolidated return or S's separate return for the period ending the day before S's change in status) S's tax items for the day of S's change in status are included. The proposed regulations thus provide that if S ceases to be a corporation subject to the section 1374 tax upon becoming a member, or if S elects to be a corporation that is subject to the section 1374 tax for its first separate return year after ceasing to be a member, S's items of recognized built-in gain or loss for purposes of section 1374 will include only the amounts reported on S's separate return (including items reported on that return under the previous day rule or the next day rule).

J. Intercompany Section 381 Transactions

Under the current consolidated return regulations, if a member distributes or transfers its assets to another corporation that is a member immediately after the distribution or transfer in an intercompany section 381 transaction, and if the distributor or transferor member has a net operating loss carryover or a net capital loss carryover, the distributor or transferor member will not be treated as having a short taxable year for purposes of determining the years to which the loss may be carried. Sections 1.1502-21(b)(3)(iii) and 1.1502-22(b)(4).

These proposed regulations would amend current law by moving these rules to § 1.1502-76(b)(2)(i) and making conforming changes to §§ 1.1502-21(b)(3)(iii) and 1.1502-22(b)(4). In addition, these proposed regulations would expand these rules by providing that a short taxable year of the distributor or transferor member by reason of an intercompany section 381 transaction is not counted as a separate taxable year for purposes of determining either the taxable years to which any tax attribute of the distributor or transferor member may be carried or the taxable years in which an adjustment under section 481(a) is taken into account. No inference should be drawn from the proposed changes to these rules as to whether a short taxable year of a member resulting from an intercompany section 381 transaction is counted under current law for purposes of determining the years to which a tax credit may be carried or in which a section 481 adjustment is taken into account.

K. Due Date for Filing Tax Returns

The proposed regulations also eliminate a provision that could cause taxpayers to inadvertently miss a return filing deadline. Under § 1.1502-76(b)(4) of the current regulations, if S joins a consolidated group, the due date for filing S's separate return is the earlier of the due date (with extensions) of the group's return or the due date (with extensions) of S's return if S had not joined the group. If S goes out of existence during the consolidated return year in which S joins a group, its taxable year would end. Under section 6072, the due date for S's short period return would be the 15th day of the third month (ninth month, with extensions) following the date on which S ceases to exist. Accordingly, if S ceases to exist during the same consolidated return year in which it becomes a member, the due date for S's tax return for the short period that ended as a result of S becoming a member could be accelerated. To prevent a taxpayer from inadvertently missing a filing date and being subject to potential penalties for filing a late return, the proposed regulations provide that if S goes out of existence in the same consolidated return year in which it becomes a member, the due date for filing S's separate return is determined without regard to S's ceasing to exist.

L. Non-Substantive Changes

In addition to the changes described in this preamble, the proposed regulations make several non-substantive changes to the current regulations, including moving an example concerning § 1.1502-80(d) from the text of § 1.1502-76(b)(1)(ii)(B)(2) of the current regulations to § 1.1502-13(c)(7)(ii), Example 3(e).

Effective/Applicability Date

The amendments to §§ 1.1502-21(b)(3)(iii), 1.1502-22(b)(4)(i), 1.1502-76(b)(2)(i), and 1.1502-76(b)(4) will apply to consolidated return years beginning on or after the date these regulations are published as final regulations in the March 5, 2015. The other amendments to § 1.1502-76(b) will apply to corporations becoming or ceasing to be members of consolidated groups on or after the date these regulations are published as final regulations in the March 5, 2015.

Special Analyses

It has been determined that this notice of proposed rulemaking is not a significant regulatory action as defined in Executive Order 12866, as supplemented by Executive Order 13563. Therefore, a regulatory assessment is not required. It is hereby certified that these regulations will not have a significant impact on a substantial number of small entities. This certification is based on the fact that the regulations apply only to transactions involving corporations that file consolidated federal income tax returns, and that such corporations tend to be larger businesses. Accordingly, a Regulatory Flexibility Analysis under the Regulatory Flexibility Act (5 U.S.C. chapter 6) is not required. Pursuant to section 7805(f) of the Code, these regulations will be submitted to the Chief Counsel for Advocacy of the Small Business Administration for comment on their impact on small business.

Comments and Public Hearing

Before these proposed regulations are adopted as final regulations, consideration will be given to any comments that are submitted timely to the IRS as prescribed in this preamble under the "Addresses" heading. The IRS and the Treasury Department request comments on all aspects of the proposed rules. All comments will be available for public inspection and copying. A public hearing may be scheduled if requested in writing by any person who timely submits written comments. If a public hearing is scheduled, notice of the date, time, and place of the hearing will be published in the March 5, 2015.

Drafting Information

The principal author of these proposed regulations is Russell G. Jones of the Office of Associate Chief Counsel (Corporate). However, other personnel from the IRS and the Treasury Department participated in their development.

[¶49,645] Proposed Regulations (REG-108214-15), published in the Federal Register on April 24, 2015.

[Code Sec. 1297]

Passive foreign investment company (PFIC): Passive income: Foreign insurance company income.—Reg. §1.1297-4, regarding when a foreign insurance company's income is excluded from the definition of passive income under section 1297(b)(2)(B), is proposed.

AGENCY: Internal Revenue Service (IRS), Treasury.

ACTION: Notice of proposed rulemaking.

SUMMARY: This document contains proposed regulations that provide guidance regarding when a foreign insurance company's income is excluded from the definition of passive income under section 1297(b)(2)(B). The proposed regulations affect the U.S. shareholders of foreign corporations. This document also invites comments from the public on all aspects of the proposed rules and provides the opportunity for the public to request a public hearing.

DATES: Written or electronic comments and requests for a public hearing must be received by July 23, 2015.

ADDRESSES: Send submissions to: CC:PA:LPD:PR (REG-108214-15), room 5203, Internal Revenue Service, P.O. Box 7604, Ben Franklin Station, Washington, DC 20044. Submissions may be hand-delivered Monday through Friday between the hours of 8 a.m. and 4 p.m. to CC:PA:LPD:PR (REG-108214-15), Courier's Desk, Internal Revenue Service, 1111 Constitution Avenue NW., Washington, DC, or sent electronically via the Federal eRulemaking Portal at *http://www.regulations.gov* (IRS REG-108214-15).

FOR FURTHER INFORMATION CONTACT: Concerning the proposed regulations, Josephine Firehock, (202) 317-4932; concerning submissions of comments or requests for a public hearing, Oluwafunmilayo (Funmi) Taylor at (202) 317-6901 (not toll-free numbers).

SUPPLEMENTARY INFORMATION:

Background and Explanation of Provisions

The Department of Treasury (Treasury) and the IRS are aware of situations in which a hedge fund establishes a purported foreign reinsurance company in order to defer and reduce the tax that otherwise would be due with respect to investment income. Such foreign corporations may be Passive Foreign Investment Companies (PFICs). For a description of the recent trends and legislative proposals to address the issue, see "Background and Data with Respect to Hedge Fund Reinsurance Arrangements," JCT (July 31, 2014) (2014 JCT Report); see also Notice 2003-34, 2003-23 IRB 990 (May 9, 2003).

Under section 1297 of the Internal Revenue Code (Code), a foreign corporation is a PFIC if either 75 percent or more of its gross income for the taxable year is passive income ("passive income test"), or on average 50 percent or more of its assets produce passive income or are held for the production of passive income ("passive asset test"). Section 1297(b)(1) generally defines the term "passive income" to mean any income of a kind that would be "foreign personal holding company income" as defined in section 954(c). In general, an asset is characterized as passive if it generates (or is reasonably expected to generate in the reasonably foreseeable future) passive income as defined in section 1297(b). Assets that generate both passive and non-passive income in a taxable year are treated as partly passive and partly non-passive assets in proportion to the relative amounts of income generated by those assets in that year. See Notice 88-22, 1988-1 CB 489 (February 26, 1988).

For purposes of applying the passive income test, section 1297(b)(2)(B) provides that, except as provided in regulations, the term "passive income" does not include any income that is derived in the active conduct of an insurance business by a corporation which is predominantly engaged in an insurance business and which would be subject to tax under subchapter L as an insurance company if the corporation were a domestic corporation. As the terms "active conduct" and "insurance business" are not defined in section 1297, Treasury and the IRS are proposing regulations to clarify the circumstances under which investment income earned by a foreign insurance company is derived in the active conduct of an insurance business for purposes of determining whether the income is passive income, and thus the extent to which the company's assets are treated as passive assets for purposes of determining whether the company is a PFIC.

The proposed regulations provide that the term "active conduct" has the same meaning as in § 1.367(a)-2T(b)(3), except that officers and employees are not considered to include the officers and employees of related entities. The proposed regulations define the term "insurance business" to mean the business activity of issuing insurance and annuity contracts and the reinsuring of risks underwritten by insurance companies, together with investment activities and administrative services that are required to support or are substantially related to insurance contracts issued or reinsured by the foreign insurance company.[1] The regulations also provide that an investment activity is any activity engaged in to produce income of a kind that would be foreign personal holding company income as defined in section 954(c). The proposed regulations further provide that investment activities will be treated as required to support or as substantially related to insurance or annuity contracts issued or reinsured by the foreign corporation to the extent that income from the activities is earned from assets held by the foreign corporation to meet obligations under the contracts.

The proposed regulations do not set forth a method to determine the portion of assets held to meet obligations under insurance and annuity contracts. Comments are requested on appropriate methodologies for determining the extent to which assets are held to meet obligations under insurance and annuity contracts.

The proposed regulations also do not define what it means to be "predominantly engaged" in an insurance business. Prior to 1984, the Code did not define an insurance company. Section 1.801-3(a) of the regulations, however, provides in relevant part that an insurance company is a company whose primary and predominant business activity during the taxable year is the issuing of insurance or annuity contracts or the reinsuring of risks underwritten by insurance companies.

In 1984, Congress enacted a definition of an "insurance company" that applied only to life insurance companies, and in 2004, a conforming amendment was made to apply the same definition to non-life insurance companies. See sections 816(a) and 831(c). Under this definition, in order for a corporation to be subject to tax as an insurance company under subchapter L, more than half of its business during the taxable year is required to be the issuing of insurance or annuity contracts or the reinsuring of risks underwritten by insurance companies. By requiring that more than half of the company's business activity, rather than its predominant business activity, be insurance activity, the current subchapter L statutory rules adopt a stricter and more precise standard than the "primary and predominant" regulatory standard under prior law.[2] Thus, any company taxable under subchapter L as an insurance company is necessarily predominantly engaged in an insurance business for purposes of section 1297(a)(2)(B).

Proposed Effective/Applicability Date

These regulations are proposed to apply on the date of publication of the Treasury decision adopting these rules as final regulations in the **Federal Register**.

Special Analyses

It has been determined that this notice of proposed rulemaking is not a significant regulatory action as defined in Executive Order 12866, as supplemented by Executive Order 13563. Therefore, a regulatory assessment is not required. It also has been determined that section 553(b) of the Administrative Procedure Act (5 U.S.C. Chapter 5) does not apply to these regulations, and because the regulations do not impose a collection of information on small entities, the Regulatory Flexibility Act (5 U.S.C. chapter 6) does not apply. Pursuant to section 7805(f) of the Code, this notice of proposed rulemaking has been submitted to the Chief Counsel of Advocacy of the Small Business Administration for comment on its impact on small business.

---

[1] Cf. Committee on Ways and Means U.S. House of Representatives, Supplemental Report, The Deficit Reduction Act of 1984, 98th Cong. 2d Sess., H.R. Rept. 98-432, part 2, at 531 (Mar. 5, 1984); Committee on Finance United States Senate, The Deficit Reduction Act of 1984, S. Rept. 98-169, vol. 1, at 1407-08 (April 2, 1984); H.R. Rept. 98-861, 98th Cong. 2d Sess. at 1045 (June 23, 1984) (Conference Report).

[2] Committee on Ways and Means U.S. House of Representatives, Supplemental Report, The Deficit Reduction Act of 1984, 98th Cong. 2d Sess., H.R. Rept. 98-432, part 2, at 1402-3 (March 5, 1984); Committee on Finance United States Senate, The Deficit Reduction Act of 1984, 98th Cong. 2d Sess., S. Rpt. 98-169, vol. 1, at 525-6 (April 2, 1984); Committee on Ways and Means U.S. House of Representatives, Supplemental Report, The Deficit Reduction Act of 1984, 98th Cong. 2d Sess., H.R. Rept. 98-432, part 2, at 1042-2 (March 5, 1984) (Conference Report); H.R. Rept. 108-457, Pension Funding Equity Act of 2004, 108th Cong. 2d Sess.at 52-53 (April 1, 2004).

Comments and Requests for Public Hearing

Before these proposed regulations are adopted as final regulations, consideration will be given to any comments that are submitted timely to the IRS as prescribed in this preamble under "Addresses." Treasury and the IRS request comments on all aspects of the proposed rules. Comments specifically are requested with regard to how to determine the portion of a foreign insurance company's assets that are held to meet obligations under insurance contracts issued or reinsured by the company. For example, assets could be considered as held to meet obligations under insurance or annuity contracts issued or reinsured by the corporation to the extent the corporation's assets in the calendar year do not exceed a specified percentage of the corporation's total insurance liabilities for the year (for example, the sum of the corporation's "total reserves" (as defined in section 816(c)) plus (to the extent not included in total reserves) the items referred to in paragraphs (3), (4), (5), and (6) of section 807(c)). Comments are requested with regard to what percentage would be appropriate. Also, comments are requested with regard to whether other methods would be more appropriate to determine the portion of assets that are held to meet obligations under insurance and annuity contracts.

All comments will be available at *www.regulations.gov* or upon request. A public hearing will be scheduled if requested in writing by any person that timely submits comments. If a public hearing is scheduled, notice of the date, time, and place for the public hearing will be published in the **Federal Register**.

Drafting Information

The principal author of these proposed regulations is Josephine Firehock of the Office of Associate Chief Counsel (International). However, other personnel from the IRS and the Treasury Department participated in their development.

[¶49,647] Proposed Amendments of Regulations and Withdrawal of Notice of Proposed Regulations (REG-102656-15; REG-107548-11), published in the Federal Register on May 8, 2015.

[Code Secs. 446 and 956]

Notional principal contracts: Swaps with nonperiodic payments: United States property.—Amendments of Reg. §§1.446-3 and 1.956-2, amending the treatment of nonperiodic payments made or received pursuant to certain notional principal contracts, are proposed. Amendments of Reg. §1.956-2, proposed on May 11, 2012 (REG-107548-11), are withdrawn.

AGENCY: Internal Revenue Service (IRS), Treasury.

ACTION: Withdrawal of notice of proposed rulemaking; notice of proposed rulemaking by cross-reference to temporary regulations.

SUMMARY: In the Rules and Regulations section of this issue of the **Federal Register**, the IRS is issuing final and temporary regulations that amend the treatment of nonperiodic payments made or received pursuant to certain notional principal contracts. These regulations provide that, subject to certain exceptions, a notional principal contract with a nonperiodic payment, regardless of whether it is significant, must be treated as two separate transactions consisting of one or more loans and an on-market, level payment swap. The regulations provide an exception from the definition of United States property. These regulations affect parties making and receiving payments under notional principal contracts, including United States shareholders of controlled foreign corporations and tax-exempt organizations. The text of the temporary regulations also serves as the text of these proposed regulations. This document withdraws the notice of proposed rulemaking (REG-107548-11; RIN 1545-BK10) published in the **Federal Register** on May 11, 2012 (77 FR 27669).

DATES: Comments and requests for a public hearing must be received by August 6, 2015.

ADDRESSES: Send submissions to CC:PA:LPD:PR (REG-102656-15), room 5203, Internal Revenue Service, P.O. Box 7604, Ben Franklin Station, Washington, DC 20044. Submissions may be hand-delivered Monday through Friday between the hours of 8 a.m. and 4 p.m. to CC:PA:LPD:PR (REG-102656-15), Courier's Desk, Internal Revenue Service, 1111 Constitution Avenue NW., Washington, DC 20224, or sent electronically via the Federal eRulemaking Portal at *www.regulations.gov* (IRS REG-102656-15).

FOR FURTHER INFORMATION CONTACT: Concerning the proposed regulations under section 446, Alexa T. Dubert or Anna H. Kim at (202) 317-6895; concerning the proposed regulations under section 956, Kristine A. Crabtree at (202) 317-6934; concerning submissions of comments or to request a public hearing, Oluwafunmilayo Taylor, (202) 317-6901 (not toll-free numbers).

SUPPLEMENTARY INFORMATION:

Background and Explanation of Provisions

On May 11, 2012, the Treasury Department and the IRS published temporary regulations under section 956 (TD 9589) in the **Federal Register** (77 FR 27612). On the same date, a notice of proposed rulemaking (REG-107548-11) by cross-reference to the temporary regulations was published in the **Federal Register** (77 FR 27669). This document withdraws those proposed regulations (REG-107548-11; RIN 1545-BK10) and provides new proposed regulations (REG-102656-15).

Final and temporary regulations in the Rules and Regulations section of this issue of the **Federal Register** amend the Income Tax Regulations (26 CFR Part 1). The final and temporary regulations amend the regulations under section 446 of the Internal Revenue Code (Code) relating to the treatment of nonperiodic payments made or received pursuant to certain notional principal contracts for U.S. federal income tax purposes. The final and temporary regulations also amend the regulations under section 956 of the Code regarding an exception from the definition of United States property. The text of the final and temporary regulations also serves as the text of these proposed regulations. The preamble to the final and temporary regulations explains those regulations and these proposed regulations.

Special Analyses

It has been determined that this notice of proposed rulemaking is not a significant regulatory action as defined in Executive Order 12866, as supplemented by Executive Order 13653. Therefore, a regulatory assessment is not required. It also has been determined that section 553(b) of the Administrative Procedure Act (5 U.S.C. chapter 5) does not apply to these regulations, and because these regulations do not impose a collection of information on small entities, the Regulatory Flexibility Act (5 U.S.C. chapter 6) does not apply. Pursuant to section 7805(f) of the Code, this notice of proposed rulemaking has been submitted to the Chief Counsel for Advocacy of the Small Business Administration for comment on its impact on small entities.

Comments and Requests for Public Hearing

Before these proposed regulations are adopted as final regulations, consideration will be given to any comments that are submitted timely to the IRS as prescribed in this preamble under the "Addresses" heading. The Treasury Department and the IRS request comments on all aspects of the proposed rules. All comments will be available at *www.regulations.gov* or upon request. A public hearing will be scheduled if requested in writing by any person that timely submits written comments. If a public hearing is scheduled, notice of the date, time, and place for the hearing will be published in the **Federal Register**.

Drafting information

The principal authors of these regulations are Alexa T. Dubert and Anna H. Kim of the Office of Associate Chief Counsel (Financial Institutions and Products). However, other personnel from the Treasury Department and the IRS participated in their development.

[¶49,650] Proposed Amendments of Regulations (REG-101652-10), published in the Federal Register on June 11, 2015.

[Code Secs. 1502 and 6402]

Consolidated returns: Consolidated net operating loss: Disposition of subsidiary's stock: Apportionment of consolidated net operating loss: Absorption of member's losses: Circular basis adjustments.—Amendments of Reg. §§1.1502-11, 1.1502-12, 1.1502-21, 1.1502-21A, 1.1502-22, 1.1502-22A, 1.1502-23A, 1.1502-24 and 301.6402-7, containing proposed amendments to the consolidated return regulations, are proposed.

AGENCY: Internal Revenue Service (IRS), Treasury.

ACTION: Notice of proposed rulemaking.

SUMMARY: This document contains proposed amendments to the consolidated return regulations. These amendments would revise the rules concerning the use of a consolidated group's losses in a consolidated return year in which stock of a subsidiary is disposed of. The regulations would affect corporations filing consolidated returns.

DATES: Written or electronic comments, and a request for a public hearing, must be received by September 9, 2015.

ADDRESSES: Send submissions to: CC:PA:LPD:PR (REG-101652-10), room 5205, Internal Revenue Service, PO Box 7604, Ben Franklin Station, Washington, DC 20044. Submissions may be hand-delivered Monday through Friday between the hours of 8 a.m. and 4 p.m. to CC:PA:LPD:PR (REG-101652-10), Courier's Desk, Internal Revenue Service, 1111 Constitution Avenue, N.W., Washington, DC, or sent electronically via the Federal eRulemaking Portal at *http://www.regulations.gov* (IRS REG-101652-10). FOR FURTHER INFORMATION CONTACT: Concerning the proposed regulations, Robert M. Rhyne, (202) 317-6848; concerning submissions of comments or to request a public hearing, Oluwafunmilayo (Funmi) Taylor, (202) 317-6901 (not toll-free numbers).

SUPPLEMENTARY INFORMATION:

Background and Explanation of Provisions

1. Introduction

This document contains proposed amendments to 26 CFR part 1 under section 1502 of the Internal Revenue Code (Code). Section 1502 authorizes the Secretary to prescribe regulations for corporations that join in filing consolidated returns to reflect clearly the income tax liability of the group and to prevent avoidance of such tax liability, and provides that these rules may be different from the provisions of chapter 1 of subtitle A of the Code that would apply if the corporations filed separate returns. Terms used in the consolidated return regulations generally are defined in §1.1502-1.

These proposed regulations would provide guidance regarding the absorption of members' losses in a consolidated return year, and provide guidance to eliminate the "circular basis problem" in a broader class of transactions than under current law.

This document also contains proposed conforming amendments to 26 CFR part 301 under section 6402. Section 6402 authorizes the Secretary to make credits and refunds. The proposed regulations would amend §301.6402-7(g) (relating to claims for refunds and application for tentative carryback adjustments involving consolidated groups that include financial institutions) by revising the definition of separate net operating loss of a member in light of the proposed amendments to § 1.1502-21 (relating to the determination and treatment of consolidated and separate net operating losses, carrybacks, and carryovers).

2. Allocation and Absorption of Members' Losses

In general, the consolidated taxable income (CTI) or consolidated net operating loss (CNOL) of a consolidated group is the sum of each member's separately computed taxable income or loss (computed pursuant to § 1.1502-12) and certain items of income and deduction that are computed on a consolidated basis pursuant to § 1.1502-11.

Section 1.1502-21(b)(2)(i) (relating to carryovers and carrybacks of CNOLs to separate return years) provides generally that if a group has a CNOL and a portion of the CNOL would be carried to a member's separate return year, the CNOL must be apportioned between the group and the member (or members) with the separate return year(s) in accordance with the amount of the CNOL attributable to those member(s). For this purpose, § 1.1502-21(b)(2)(iv) employs a fraction to determine the percentage amount of the CNOL attributable to a member. The numerator of the fraction is the separate net operating loss of the member for the consolidated return year, and the denominator is the sum of the separate net operating losses of all members for that year. For this purpose, the separate net operating loss of a member is determined by computing the CNOL, taking into account only the member's items of income, gain, deduction, and loss. Although the current consolidated return regulations provide rules for apportioning a CNOL among members when a member's loss may be carried to a separate return year, the regulations do not expressly adopt the fraction-based methodology of § 1.1502-21(b)(2)(iv) for computing the amount of each member's absorbed loss that is used to offset the income of members with positive separate taxable income or net capital gain for the consolidated return year in which the loss is recognized.

Furthermore, although the method provided for apportioning a CNOL under current law generally yields appropriate results, the apportionment may produce anomalies if capital gains are present. For example, assume a stand-alone corporation, P, acquires the stock of corporation S, and P and S file a consolidated return for the first taxable year of P ending after the acquisition. For the consolidated return year, P generates $100 of capital gain and incurs $100 of deductible expenses. S incurs a $100 capital loss. Thus, the group has a $100 CNOL. Under current law, the percentage of the CNOL attributable to each member is determined by its relative separate net operating loss, taking into account only its items. The CNOL that the group would have if only P's items were taken into account is zero ($100 of capital gain offset by $100 of deductible expenses). If only S's items were taken into account the group would have a consolidated net capital loss, but the CNOL would also be zero. Accordingly, because neither P nor S has a separate net operating loss, the allocation of the group's $100 CNOL is not clear.

Both to provide an absorption rule for apportioning ordinary and capital losses incurred in the same consolidated return year, and to address the CNOL apportionment issue, the proposed regulations would amend the current regulations in the following two ways. First, the proposed regulations add a new paragraph (e) to § 1.1502-11 to clarify that the absorption of members' losses to offset income of other members in the consolidated return year is made on a pro rata basis, consistent with the pro rata absorption of losses from taxable years ending on the same date that are carried back or forward under the rules of § § 1.1502-21(b) and 1.1502-22(b) (relating to net capital loss carrybacks and carryovers). Second, to address apportionment anomalies that may arise if capital gains are present, the proposed regulations would provide that the separate net operating loss of a member, solely for apportionment purposes, is its loss determined without regard to capital gains (or losses) or amounts treated as capital gains. Thus, in the example in the preceding paragraph, P would be allocated the entire $100 CNOL. Excluding capital gains and losses from the computation is consistent with excluding capital gains and losses in determining a member's separate taxable income under § 1.1502-12, and taking capital gains and losses into account on a group, rather than a separate member, basis. A conforming amendment is made to § 301.6402-7(g)(2)(ii) (relating to refunds to certain statutory or court-appointed fiduciaries of an insolvent financial institution), which contains a similar allocation rule.

3. Circular Adjustments to Basis

A. The circular basis problem and current regulations

To prevent the income, gain, deduction, or loss of a subsidiary from being reflected more than once in a consolidated group's income, the consolidated return regulations adjust an owning member's basis in a subsidiary's stock to reflect those items. As a group takes into account a subsidiary's items of income or gain, an owning member's basis in the subsidiary's stock increases. Likewise, as a group absorbs a subsidiary's deductions or losses, an owning member's basis in the subsidiary's stock decreases. These adjustments take place under what is generally referred to as the investment adjustment system. See § 1.1502-32.

If a group absorbs a portion of a subsidiary's loss in the same consolidated return year in which an owning member disposes of that subsidiary's stock, the owning member's basis in the subsidiary's stock is reduced immediately before the disposition. Consequently, the amount of the owning member's gain or loss on the disposition may be affected. Any change in the amount of gain or loss resulting from the disposition may in turn affect the amount of the subsidiary's loss that the group absorbs. Any further absorption of the subsidiary's loss triggers further adjustments to the basis in the subsidiary's stock. These iterative computations, which may completely eliminate the benefit of the disposed of member's losses, are referred to as the circular basis problem.

For example, assume P owns all the stock of S, and the group has a $100 consolidated net capital loss carryover, all of which is attributable to S. On December 31, P sells all of S's stock to a nonmember at a $10 gain. Absent the current rules in § 1.1502-11(b), P's $10 capital gain on the sale of S's stock would be offset by $10 of the consolidated net capital loss carryover (all of which is attributable to S). The use of the loss would cause P's basis in S's stock to be reduced by $10 (immediately before the sale), causing P to recognize $20 of gain on the sale of S's stock. Similarly, that $20 gain would be offset by $20 of S's consolidated net capital loss carryover, and so on, until the entire consolidated net capital loss carryover was depleted. At the end of these iterative calculations, the group would still report $10 of consolidated net capital gain. The current regulations prevent this result.

The Treasury Department and the IRS have considered a variety of approaches to the circular basis problem since the introduction of the investment adjustment system in 1966. The options considered, and either rejected or adopted in regulations to date, appear to have been motivated by differing views concerning the scope and severity of the circular basis problem. The circumstances in which the consolidated return regulations have provided relief to date have been limited to preventing the disposed of subsidiary's loss absorption from affecting the gain or loss recognized on the sale of that subsidiary. This is the case notwithstanding that many commentators have criticized the scope of relief as being too narrow, and have maintained that relief should be extended to, for example, the sales of brother-sister subsidiaries within the same consolidated return year.

Regulations promulgated in 1966 provided no relief from the circular basis problem, even though some relief was initially proposed. Section 1.1502-11(b), published in 1972, provided some relief from the circular basis problem, and those regulations were revised in 1994 into their current form (the circular basis rules).

To resolve the circular basis problem, the circular basis rules require that a tentative computation of CTI be made without taking into account any gain or loss on the disposition of a subsidiary's stock. The amount of the subsidiary's losses that would be absorbed under the tentative computation becomes a limitation on that subsidiary's losses that may be absorbed in the consolidated return year of disposition or as a carryback to a prior year. The limitation is intended to eliminate the circular basis adjustments to the subsidiary's stock and thus prevent iterative computations.

For example, assume a consolidated group consists of P, the common parent, and S, its wholly owned subsidiary, and neither P nor S had income or gain in a prior year. At the beginning of the consolidated return year, P has a $500 basis in S's stock. P sells S's stock for $520 at the end of the year. For the year, P has $30 of ordinary income (determined without taking into account P's gain or loss on the disposition of S's stock) and S has $80 of ordinary loss. To determine the limitation on the amount of S's loss that the group may use during the consolidated return year or as a carryback to a prior year, CTI is tentatively determined without taking into account P's gain or loss on the disposition of S's stock. Accordingly, the use of S's loss in the consolidated return year of disposition is limited to $30. The group is tentatively treated as having a CNOL of $50 (P's $30 of income minus S's $80 loss). The absorption of $30 of S's loss reduces P's basis in S's stock to $470, and results in $50 [$520 – ($500 - $30)] of gain to P on the disposition. Thus, iterative computations are avoided.

Nevertheless, the circular basis rules do not prevent iterative computations in all cases — not even all cases in which the stock of a single subsidiary with a loss is disposed of. For example, if a member other than the disposed of subsidiary also has a loss, and the sum of the losses of the disposed subsidiary and the other member exceeds the income of the group (without regard to gain on the disposed subsidiary's stock) a tentative computation applying a pro rata rule for absorption establishes a limitation on the use of the disposed of subsidiary's loss. That amount will be used to reduce the owning member's basis in the subsidiary's stock and determine the gain or loss on the stock disposition. If the stock disposition results in gain, that gain will be taken into account in an actual computation of CTI. If the sum of the other member's loss and the disposed of subsidiary's limited loss still exceeds the income and gain of other members, the pro rata absorption rule will be applied again. That computation will result in a lower amount for the absorption of the disposed of subsidiary's loss, which will be different than the amount by which the owning member's stock basis was reduced. Accordingly, iterative computations would be required.

To illustrate, assume a consolidated group consists of P, the common parent, and its wholly owned subsidiaries, S1 and S2. At the beginning of the consolidated return year, P has a $500 basis in S1's stock. P sells all of its S1 stock for $500 at the end of the year. For the year, P has a $60 capital gain (determined without taking into account P's gain or loss on the disposition of S1's stock), S1 has a $40 net capital loss and S2 has an $80 net capital loss. To determine the limitation on the amount of S1's capital loss that the group may use during the consolidated return year, CTI is tentatively determined without taking into account gain or loss on the disposition of S1's stock, but with regard to S2's net capital loss. Because S2 has an $80 net capital loss in addition to S1's $40 net capital loss, $40 of S2's loss [$60 × ($80/$120)] and $20 of S1's loss [$60 × ($40/$120)] will be used (assuming pro rata absorption of losses as described in section 2 of the Explanation of Provisions of this preamble). Accordingly, the group's use of S1's loss is limited to $20. Thus, P's basis in S1's stock is reduced by $20 before P disposes of the stock. Therefore, P is assumed to recognize $20 [$500 - ($500 - $20)] of gain on the disposition of its S1 stock, which leaves P with a total capital gain for the year of $80.

Again, because S2 has an $80 loss in addition to S1's $20 usable loss, a pro rata portion of each subsidiary's losses will be absorbed in computing the P group's CTI. Assuming pro rata absorption of losses, P's $80 capital gain is offset with $16 of S1's capital loss [$80 × ($20/$100)]. This amount, however, is less than the $20 amount determined in the tentative computation by which P's basis in S1's stock was reduced. Thus, iterative computations would be required.

In considering the circular basis problem, the Treasury Department and the IRS have become aware that taxpayers have taken a broad range of approaches in cases in which the circular basis problem persists. Some taxpayers may undertake many iterative computations while, under similar facts, others will undertake few. Some commentators have suggested using simultaneous equations. That method can produce appropriate results in the simplest fact patterns, but becomes highly complex if both ordinary income and capital gains are present, or if the stock of more than one subsidiary is sold.

One approach that the Treasury Department and IRS considered but did not adopt in these proposed regulations was to disallow the absorption of any losses of a subsidiary in the year of disposition. Such a rule would have an adverse impact on any consolidated group with ordinary income that otherwise would be offset by the subsidiary's losses. Furthermore, a blanket prohibition on the use of a subsidiary's losses would be inappropriately harsh if a subsidiary's stock was sold at a loss and the unified loss rules required a stock basis reduction that was greater than the amount of S's loss. In such a case, the use of S's loss to offset income of other members allowed under current law reduces CTI, but the basis reduction that results from the absorption of the loss has no net effect on the owning member's basis in the subsidiary's stock. Prohibiting the use of the disposed of subsidiary's losses would simply increase the group's CTI.

The Treasury Department and IRS also considered but did not adopt an approach similar to the current rules that would compute a tentative amount of S's losses, and then require a reduction to P's basis in S's stock, regardless of whether S's losses were actually absorbed. This approach could lead to non-economic consequences when another subsidiary's losses are actually absorbed instead of S's according to the general rules of the Code and regulations, but S's losses are nonetheless treated as absorbed for purposes of reducing P's basis in S's stock.

A third approach that the Treasury Department and IRS considered but did not adopt was to turn-off the investment adjustment rules for losses of a subsidiary used in the year of disposition. Such an approach would allow a double deduction and undermine a bedrock principle of consolidated returns as articulated by the Supreme Court in *Charles Ilfeld Co. v. Hernandez*, 292 U.S. 62 (1934).

B. Proposed circular basis rules

i. In general.

The proposed regulations would provide relief and certainty to cases in which the circular basis problem persists, yet adhere to underlying consolidated return concepts without undue complexity. To prevent iterative computations for a consolidated return year in which the stock of one or more subsidiaries is disposed of, these proposed regulations require a group to first determine the amount of each disposed subsidiary's loss that will be absorbed by computing CTI without regard to gain or loss on the disposition of the stock of any subsidiary (the absorbed amount). Once the amount of a subsidiary's absorbed loss is determined under that computation, the absorbed amount for each disposed of subsidiary is not redetermined. Determining each disposed of subsidiary's absorbed amount establishes an immutable number that will also be the amount of reduction to the basis of S's stock taken into account in computing the owning member's gain or loss on the disposition of S's stock. After the absorbed amount is determined, the owning member's basis of the S stock is adjusted under § 1.1502-32 (and § 1.1502-36 as relevant). The actual computation of CTI can then be made, taking into account losses of each disposed of subsidiary equal to that amount. In some cases, however, applying the generally applicable rules of the Code and regulations would result in less than all of a disposed of subsidiary's absorbed amount being used.

For example, assume S has an ordinary loss of $100 and P has capital gain net income of $100 (unrelated to its disposition of S stock), then S's absorbed amount would be determined to be $100. If after taking into account S's $100 absorbed amount P would have a $100 capital loss on a sale of S's stock, P's capital loss on its S stock would offset P's $100 capital gain, and S's ordinary loss would not be used in that year and would become a CNOL carryover (assuming no ability to carry back the loss). If an amount of S's losses equal to its absorbed amount were not used, P's basis in its S stock would not be reduced by the absorbed amount, and the amount of P's loss on S's stock would be changed.

The proposed regulations prevent such a result by providing for an alternative four-step computation of CTI if, applying the general ordering rules of the Code and regulations, less than all of a disposed of subsidiary's absorbed amount would be used. See *Examples 5, 6, 7, 8* and *9* of § 1.1502-11(b)(2)(vi) as proposed herein.

Under the first step, any income, gain, or loss on any share of subsidiary stock is excluded from the computation of CTI and the group uses losses of each disposed of subsidiary equal in both amount and character and from the same taxable years as those used in the computation of its absorbed amount. Thus, by excluding any income, gain, or loss on a stock disposition, and by giving priority to the losses of all disposed of subsidiaries, the proposed regulations would solve the circularity problem.

Under the second step, a disposing member offsets its gain on subsidiary stock with its losses on subsidiary stock (determined after applying § 1.1502-36(b) and (c), and so much of § 1.1502-36(d) as is necessary to give effect to an election actually made under § 1.1502-36(d)(6)). If the disposing member has net income or gain on the subsidiary stock, and if the disposing member also has a loss of the same character (determined without regard to the stock net income or gain), the disposing member's loss is used to offset the net income or gain on the subsidiary stock to the extent of such income or gain. Any remaining net income or gain is added to the group's remaining income or gain as determined under the first step. Giving priority to S's losses ahead of other members' losses and excluding gain or loss on subsidiary stock are departures from the general rules that require a member to net its income and gain with its own losses before those amounts are combined in a consolidated computation. These departures may distort the amount of absorbed losses of a disposing member relative to the absorbed losses of other members. Thus, in order to put losses of a disposing member (unrelated to its loss on a stock disposition) on a par with losses of other members, the proposed regulations allow P's losses to offset the group's income before other members, but only to the extent of the gain (or income) on the disposed of subsidiary's stock.

Under the third step if, after the application of the second step of the alternative computation, the group has remaining income or gain and a disposing member has a net loss on subsidiary stock (determined after applying § 1.1502-36(b) and (c), and so much of § 1.1502-36(d) as is necessary to give effect to an election actually made under § 1.1502-36(d)(6)), that income or gain is then offset by the loss on the disposition of subsidiary stock, subject to generally applicable rules of the Code and regulations. The amount of the offset, however, is limited to the lesser of the total remaining ordinary income or capital gain of the group (determined after the application of the second step) or the amount of the disposing member's ordinary income or capital gain (determined without regard to the stock loss).

Finally, under the fourth step, if the group has remaining income or gain, the unused losses of all members are applied on a pro rata basis.

The Treasury Department and the IRS recognize that the special rules in these proposed regulations may in certain cases alter the general rule under section 1211(a) that allows the deduction of losses from the sale or exchange of capital assets to the extent of capital gains. However, giving priority to the absorption of a disposed subsidiary's losses will prevent the need for iterative computations.

The Treasury Department and the IRS also recognize that the proposed regulations may increase the number of cases in which the general ordering rules for the absorption of members' losses will be altered and may in certain cases result in more gain (or less loss) on the sale of a subsidiary's stock than under current law. However, the Treasury Department and the IRS believe that the benefits derived from the certainty that the proposed rules achieve generally outweigh the potential detriments of these deviations from the general rules. Comments are requested on whether there are alternative approaches that would both eliminate the circular basis problem and preserve the general rule for the absorption of capital and ordinary losses.

ii. Higher-tier subsidiaries.

Under § 1.1502-11(b)(4)(ii) of the current regulations, if S is a higher-tier subsidiary of another subsidiary (T), the use of T's losses is subject to the circular basis rules upon a disposition of S's stock, but only if 100 percent of T's items of income, gain, deduction, and loss would be reflected in the basis of S's stock in the hands of the owning member (100-percent requirement). If another member of S's consolidated group or a nonmember owns any stock of either S or T, the circular basis rules do not apply.

These proposed regulations would remove the 100-percent requirement. Thus, if any stock of a higher-tier subsidiary is disposed of, the absorption of losses of a lower-tier subsidiary is subject to the proposed circular basis rules by treating the lower-tier subsidiary as if its stock had been disposed of. The Treasury Department and the IRS request comments regarding whether, and under what circumstances, the 100-percent requirement should be retained.

C. Other Provisions

Ordinary income and deductions are generally taken into account on a separate company basis before the computation of CTI occurs. A member's separate taxable income under § 1.1502-12 is computed in accordance with the provisions of the Code subject to certain modifications. These modifications generally relate to items that are determined on a consolidated basis (for example, the use of capital losses and the limitation on charitable contribution deductions). Although gain or loss on the disposition of a subsidiary's stock is usually capital, a worthless stock deduction could be ordinary if the conditions of section 165(g)(3) are satisfied. In addition, a gain on the disposition of such stock can be ordinary if the recapture rules of section 1017(d) apply. Under these proposed regulations, gain and loss on the disposition of subsidiary stock are disregarded in determining the subsidiary's absorbed amount, and in an alternative computation of CTI. Consequently, if stock of a subsidiary is disposed of, these proposed regulations may require a departure from the general rules for the computation of an owning member's separate taxable income. The Treasury Department and the IRS believe that this departure from the general rules is necessary to avoid iterative computations and request comments as to whether an alternative methodology would be preferable.

These proposed regulations clarify the interaction of the Unified Loss Rule of § 1.1502-36 with the circular basis rules. Adjustments under § 1.1502-36(b), (c), and (d)(6) (if an election is made to reattribute losses or reduce stock basis) will affect the computation of CTI. Therefore, these proposed regulations contain guidance as to the point in the computation that those adjustments are made.

The proposed regulations also contain a rule to prevent iterative computations in determining the amount of deductions that are determined by reference to or are limited by the group's CTI, for example, the consolidated charitable contributions deduction under § 1.1502-24 and a member's percentage depletion deduction with respect to oil or gas property for independent producers and royalty owners under § 1.1502-44. The amount of those deductions is taken into account in determining the group's CTI and may affect the computation of a disposed of subsidiary's absorbed amount. The absorbed amount will reduce the stock basis and affect the amount of gain or loss on the disposition of the subsidiary's stock, which will change the amount of CTI, and thus the amount of the group's deduction. To prevent these iterative computations, the proposed regulations provide that the amount of those deductions is determined without regard to gain or loss on the disposition of a subsidiary's stock.

As a result of the later addition of § 1.1502-11(c), current § 1.1502-11(b) does not apply if a member realizes discharge of indebtedness income that is excluded from gross income under section 108(a). The rules applicable in that case, contained in paragraph (c) of § 1.1502-11, are generally not addressed by these proposed regulations, but to the extent that paragraph (c) uses the absorbed amount described in § 1.1502-11(b)(2) as a starting point, the computation will be affected. Comments are requested regarding appropriate additional changes to § 1.1502-11(c).

Finally, the proposed regulations include modifications to § § 1.1502-11(a), 1.1502-12, 1.1502-22(a), and 1.1502-24 of the current regulations and removal of § § 1.1502-21A, 1.1502-22A and 1.1502-23A. These modifications are not changes to current substantive law; they are intended solely to update the regulations to reflect certain statutory changes and remove cross-references to outdated regulatory provisions.

Proposed Effective Date

These regulations are proposed to be effective for consolidated return years beginning on or after the date these regulations are published as final regulations in the **Federal Register**.

Special Analyses

It has been determined that this notice of proposed rulemaking is not a significant regulatory action as defined in Executive Order 12866, as supplemented by Executive Order 13563. Therefore, a regulatory assessment is not required. These proposed regulations would not impose a collection of information on small entities. Further, under the Regulatory Flexibility Act (5 U.S.C. chapter 6), it is hereby certified that these proposed regulations would not have a significant economic impact on a substantial number of small entities. This certification is based on the fact that these proposed regulations would primarily affect members of consolidated groups that tend to be large corporations. Accordingly, a regulatory flexibility analysis is not required. Pursuant to section 7805(f) of the Code, this notice of proposed rulemaking has been submitted to the Chief Counsel for Advocacy of the Small Business Administration for comment on its impact on small business.

Comments and Requests for a Public Hearing

Before these proposed regulations are adopted as final regulations, consideration will be given to any written (a signed original with eight (8) copies) or electronic comments that are submitted timely to the IRS. The Treasury Department and the IRS request comments on all aspects of the proposed regulations.

All comments will be available for public inspection and copying at *www.regulations.gov* or upon request. A public hearing may be scheduled if requested by any person that timely submits comments. If a public hearing is scheduled, notice of the date, time, and place for the public hearing will be published in the **Federal Register**.

Drafting Information

The principal author of these regulations is Robert M. Rhyne, Office of Associate Chief Counsel (Corporate). However, other personnel from the IRS and the Treasury Department participated in their development.

[¶ 49,654] Proposed Amendments of Regulations (REG-102837-15), published in the Federal Register on June 22, 2015 (corrected 8/7/2015).

[Code Secs. 511, 513, 529A and 6011]

ABLE account: Program requirements: Proposed regulations.—Reg. § § 1.529A-0, 1.529A-1, 1.529A-2, 1.529A-3, 1.529A-4, 1.529A-5, 1.529A-6 and 1.529A-7 and amendments of Reg. § § 1.511-2, 1.513-1 and 301.6011-2, regarding programs under The Stephen Beck, Jr., Achieving a Better Life Experience Act of 2014, are proposed.

AGENCY: Internal Revenue Service (IRS), Treasury.

ACTION: Notice of proposed rulemaking and notice of public hearing.

SUMMARY: This document contains proposed regulations under section 529A of the Internal Revenue Code that provide guidance regarding programs under The Stephen Beck, Jr., Achieving a Better Life Experience Act of 2014. Section 529A provides rules under which States or State agencies or instrumentalities may establish and maintain a new type of tax-favored savings program through which contributions may be made to the account of an eligible disabled individual to meet qualified disability expenses. These accounts also receive favorable treatment for purposes of certain means-tested Federal programs. In addition, these proposed regulations provide corresponding amendments to regulations under sections 511 and 513, with respect to unrelated business taxable income, sections 2501, 2503, 2511, 2642 and 2652, with respect to gift and generation-skipping transfer taxes, and section 6011, with respect to reporting requirements. This document also provides notice of a public hearing on these proposed regulations.

DATES: Comments must be received by September 21, 2015. Outlines of topics to be discussed at the public hearing scheduled for October 14, 2015, at 10 am, must be received by September 21, 2015.

ADDRESSES: Send submissions to: CC:PA:LPD:PR (REG-102837-15), room 5203, Internal Revenue Service, PO Box 7604, Ben Franklin Station, Washington DC 20044. Submissions may be hand delivered Monday through Friday between the hours of 8 a.m. and 4 p.m. to CC:PA:LPD:PR (REG-102837-15), Courier's Desk, Internal Revenue Service, 1111 Constitution Avenue NW, Washington, DC, or sent electronically via the Federal eRulemaking Portal at *http://www.regulations.gov* (IRS REG-102837-15). The public hearing will be held in the Auditorium, Internal Revenue Building, 1111 Constitution Avenue, NW, Washington, DC.

FOR FURTHER INFORMATION CONTACT: Concerning the proposed regulations under section 529A, Taina Edlund or Terri Harris, (202) 317-4541, or Sean Barnett, (202) 317-5800; concerning the proposed estate and gift tax regulations, Theresa Melchiorre, (202) 317-4643; concerning the reporting provisions under section 529A, Mark Bond, (202) 317-6844; concerning submissions of comments, the hearing, and/or to be placed on the building access list to attend the hearing, call Regina Johnson, (202) 317-6901 (not toll-free numbers).

SUPPLEMENTARY INFORMATION:

Paperwork Reduction Act

The collection of information contained in this notice of proposed rulemaking has been submitted to the Office of Management and Budget for review and approval in accordance with the Paperwork Reduction Act of 1995 (44 U.S.C. 3507(d)). Comments on the collection of information should be sent to the **Office of Management and Budget**, Attn: Desk Officer for the Department of the Treasury, Office of Information and Regulatory Affairs, Washington, DC 20503, with copies to the **Internal Revenue Service**, Attn: IRS Reports Clearance Officer, SE:W:CAR:MP:T:T:SP, Washington, DC 20224. Comments on the collection of information should be received by August 21, 2015.

Comments are specifically requested concerning:

Whether the proposed collection of information is necessary for the proper performance of the functions of the Internal Revenue Service, including whether the information will have practical utility;

The accuracy of the estimated burden associated with the proposed collection of information;

How the quality, utility, and clarity of the information to be collected may be enhanced;

How the burden of complying with the proposed collection of information may be minimized, including through forms of information technology; and

Estimates of capital or start-up costs and costs of operation, maintenance, and purchase of services to provide information.

The collection of information in the proposed regulations is in §§1.529A-2, 1.529A-5, 1.529A-6 and 1.529A-7. The collection of information flows from sections 529A(d)(1), (d)(2), (d)(3), (e)(1) and (e)(2) of the Internal Revenue Code (Code). Section 529A(d)(1) requires qualified ABLE programs to provide reports to the Secretary and to designated beneficiaries with respect to contributions, distributions, the return of excess contributions, and such other matters as the Secretary may require. Section 529A(d)(2) provides that the Secretary shall make available to the public reports containing aggregate information, by diagnosis and other relevant characteristics, on contributions and distributions from the qualified ABLE program. Section 529(d)(3) requires qualified ABLE. Programs to provide notice to the Secretary upon the establishment of an ABLE account, containing the name and State of residence of the designated beneficiary and such other information as the Secretary may require. Section 529A(e)(1) requires that a disability certification with respect to certain individuals be filed with the Secretary. Section 529A(e)(2) provides that the disability certification include a certification to the satisfaction of the Secretary that the individual has a medically determinable physical or mental impairment that occurred before the date on which the individual attained age 26 and also include a copy of a physician's diagnosis. The burden under §§1.529A-5 and 1.529A-6 is reflected in the burden under the new Form 5498-QA, "ABLE Account Contribution Information," and the new Form 1099-QA, "Distributions from ABLE Accounts," respectively.

The expected recordkeepers are programs described in section 529A, established and maintained by a State or a State agency or instrumentality and individuals with ABLE accounts.

Estimated number of recordkeepers: 10,050.

Estimated average annual burden hours per recordkeeper: 1.6 hours.

Estimated total annual recordkeeping burden: 16,080.

An agency may not conduct or sponsor, and a person is not required to respond to, a collection of information unless it displays a valid control number assigned by the Office of Management and Budget.

Books or records relating to a collection of information must be retained as long as their contents may become material in the administration of any internal revenue law. Generally, tax returns and return information are confidential, as required by 26 U.S.C. 6103.

Background

The Stephen Beck, Jr., Achieving a Better Life Experience (ABLE) Act of 2014, enacted on December 19, 2014, as part of The Tax Increase Prevention Act of 2014 (Public Law 113-295), added section 529A to the Internal Revenue Code. Congress recognized the special financial burdens borne by families raising children with disabilities and the fact that increased financial needs generally continue throughout the disabled person's lifetime. Section 101 of the ABLE Act confirms that one of the purposes of the Act is to "provide secure funding for disability-related expenses on behalf of designated beneficiaries with disabilities that will supplement, but not supplant, benefits" otherwise available to those individuals, whether through private sources, employment, public programs, or otherwise. Prior to the enactment of the ABLE Act, various types of tax-advantaged savings arrangements existed, but none adequately served the goal of promoting saving for these financial needs. Section 529A allows the creation of a qualified ABLE program by a State (or agency or instrumentality thereof) under which a separate ABLE account may be established for a disabled individual who is the designated beneficiary and owner of that account. Generally, contributions to that account are subject to both an annual and a cumulative limit, and, when made by a person other than the designated beneficiary, are treated as non-taxable gifts to the designated beneficiary. Distributions made from an ABLE account for qualified disability expenses of the designated beneficiary are not included in the designated beneficiary's gross income. The earnings portion of distributions from the ABLE account in excess of the qualified disability expenses is includible in the gross income of the designated beneficiary. An ABLE account may be used for the long-term benefit and/or short-term needs of the designated beneficiary.

Section 103 of the ABLE Act, while not a tax provision, is critical to achieving the goal of the ABLE Act of providing financial resources for the benefit of disabled individuals. Because so many of the programs that provide essential financial, occupational, and other resources and services to disabled individuals are available only to persons whose resources and income do not exceed relatively low dollar limits, section 103 generally provides that a designated beneficiary's ABLE account (specifically, its account balance, contributions to the account, and distributions from the account) is disregarded for purposes of determining the designated beneficiary's eligibility for and the amount of any assistance or benefit provided under certain means-tested Federal programs. However, in the case of the Supplemental Security Income program under title XVI of the Social Security Act, distributions for certain housing expenses are not disregarded, and the balance (including earnings) in an ABLE account is considered a resource of the designated beneficiary to the extent that balance exceeds $100,000. Section 103 also addresses the impact of an excess balance in an ABLE account on the designated beneficiary's eligibility under the Supplemental Security Income program and Medicaid.

Finally, section 104 of the ABLE Act addresses the treatment of ABLE accounts in bankruptcy proceedings.

Notice 2015-18, 2015-12 IRB 765 (March 23, 2015), provides that the section 529A guidance will confirm that the owner of the ABLE account is the designated beneficiary of the account, and that the person with signature authority over (if not the designated beneficiary of) the account may neither have nor acquire any beneficial interest in the ABLE account and must administer that account for the benefit of the designated beneficiary of that account. The Notice further provides that, in the event that state legislation creating ABLE programs enacted in accordance with section 529A prior to issuance of guidance does not fully comport with the guidance when issued, the Treasury Department and the IRS intend to provide transition relief to provide sufficient time to allow States to implement the changes necessary to avoid the disqualification of the program and of the ABLE accounts already established under the program.

The Treasury Department and the IRS reiterate that States that enact legislation creating an ABLE program in accordance with section 529A, and those individuals establishing ABLE accounts in accordance with such legislation, will not fail to receive the benefits of section 529A merely because the legislation or the account documents do not fully comport with the final regulations when they are issued. The Treasury Department and the IRS intend to provide transition relief to enable those State programs and accounts to be brought into compliance with the requirements in the final regulations, including providing sufficient time after issuance of the final regulations in order for changes to be implemented.

Explanation of Provisions

Qualification as an ABLE program

The proposed regulations provide guidance on the requirements a program must satisfy in order to be a qualified ABLE program described in section 529A. Specifically, in addition to other requirements, the program must: be established and maintained by a State or a State's agency or instrumentality; permit the establishment of an ABLE account only for a designated beneficiary who is a resident of that State, or a State contracting with that State for purposes of the ABLE program; permit the establishment of an ABLE account only for a designated beneficiary who is an eligible individual; limit a designated beneficiary to only one ABLE account, wherever located; permit contributions to an ABLE account established to meet the qualified disability expenses of the account's designated beneficiary; limit the nature and amount of contributions that can be made to an ABLE account; require a separate accounting for the ABLE account of each designated beneficiary with an ABLE account in the program; limit the designated beneficiary to no more than two opportunities in any calendar year to provide investment direction, whether directly or indirectly, for the ABLE account; and prohibit the pledging of an interest in an ABLE account as security for a loan.

Because each qualified ABLE program will have significant administrative obligations beyond what is required for the administration of qualified tuition programs under section 529 (on which section 529A was loosely modeled), and because the frequency of distributions from the ABLE accounts is likely to be far greater than those made from qualified tuition accounts, the proposed regulations expressly allow a qualified ABLE program or any of its contractors to contract with one or more Community Development Financial Institutions (CDFIs) that commonly serve disabled individuals and their families to provide one or more required services. For example, a CDFI could provide screening and verification of disabilities, certification of the qualified purpose of distributions, debit card services to facilitate distributions, and social data collection and reporting. A CDFI also may be able to obtain grants to defray the cost of administering the program. In general, if certified by the Treasury Department, a CDFI may receive a financial assistance award from the CDFI Fund that was established within the Treasury Department in 1994 to promote community development in economically distressed communities through investments in CDFIs across the country.

Established and maintained

The proposed regulations provide that a program is established by a State, or its agency or instrumentality, if the program is initiated by State statute or regulation, or by an act of a State official or agency with the authority to act on behalf of the State. A program is maintained by a State or its agency or instrumentality if: all the terms and conditions of the program are set by the State or its agency or instrumentality, and the State or its agency or instrumentality is actively involved on an ongoing basis in the administration of the program, including supervising all decisions relating to the investment of assets contributed to the program. The proposed regulations set forth factors that are relevant in determining whether a State, or its agency or instrumentality, is actively involved in the administration of the program. Included in the factors is the manner and extent to which it is permissible for the program to contract out for professional and financial services.

Establishment of an ABLE account

The proposed regulations provide that, consistent with the definition of a designated beneficiary in section 529A(e)(3), the designated beneficiary of an ABLE account is the eligible individual who establishes the account or an eligible individual who succeeded the original designated beneficiary. The proposed regulations also provide that the designated beneficiary is the owner of that account.

The Treasury Department and the IRS recognize, however, that certain eligible individuals may be unable to establish an account themselves. Therefore, the proposed regulations clarify that, if the eligible individual cannot establish the account, the eligible individual's agent under a power of attorney or, if none, his or her parent or legal guardian may establish the ABLE account for that eligible individual. For purposes of these proposed regulations, because each of these individuals would be acting on behalf of the designated beneficiary, references to actions of the designated beneficiary, such as opening or managing the ABLE account, are deemed to include the actions of any other such individual with signature authority over the ABLE account. The proposed regulations also provide that, consistent with Notice 2015-18, a person other than the designated beneficiary with signature authority over the account of the designated beneficiary may neither have, nor acquire, any beneficial interest in the account during the designated beneficiary's lifetime and must administer the account for the benefit of the designated beneficiary.

At the time an ABLE account is created for a designated beneficiary, the designated beneficiary must provide evidence that the designated beneficiary is an eligible individual as defined in section 529A(e)(1). Section 529A(e)(1) provides that an individual is an eligible individual for a taxable year if, during that year, either the individual is entitled to benefits based on blindness or disability under title II or XVI of the Social Security Act and the blindness or disability occurred before the date on which the individual attained age 26, or a disability certification meeting specified requirements is filed with the Secretary. If an individual is asserting he or she is entitled to benefits based on blindness or disability under title II or XVI of the Social Security Act and the blindness or disability occurred before the date on which the individual attained age 26, the proposed regulations provide that each qualified ABLE program may determine the evidence required to establish the individual's eligibility. For example, a qualified ABLE program could require the individual to provide a copy of a benefit verification letter from the Social Security Administration and allow the individual to certify, under penalties of perjury, that the blindness or disability occurred before the date on which the individual attained age 26.

Alternatively, the designated beneficiary must submit the disability certification when opening the ABLE account. Consistent with section 529A(e)(2), the proposed regulations provide that a disability certification is a certification by the designated beneficiary that he or she: (1) has a medically determinable physical or mental impairment, which results in marked or severe functional limitations, and which (i) can be expected to result in death or (ii) has lasted or can be expected to last for a continuous period of not less than 12 months; or (2) is blind (within the meaning of section 1614(a)(2) of the Social Security Act) and that such blindness or disability occurred before the date on which the individual attained age 26. The certification must include a copy of the individual's diagnosis relating to the individual's relevant impairment or impairments, signed by a licensed physician (as defined in section 1861(r) of the Social Security Act, 42 U.S.C. 1395x(r)). Consistent with other IRS filing requirements, the proposed regulations also provide that the certification must be signed under penalties of perjury.

While evidence of an individual's eligibility based on entitlement to Social Security benefits should be objectively verifiable, the sufficiency of a disability certification that an individual is an eligible individual for purposes of section 529A might not be as easy to establish. Nevertheless, the Treasury Department and the IRS wish to facilitate an eligible individual's ability to establish an ABLE account without undue delay. Therefore, the proposed regulations provide that an eligible individual must present the disability certification, accompanied by the diagnosis, to the qualified ABLE program to demonstrate eligibility to establish an ABLE account. The proposed regulations further provide that the disability certification will be deemed to be filed with the Secretary once the qualified ABLE program has received the disability certification or a disability certification has been deemed to have been received under the rules of the qualified ABLE program, which information the qualified ABLE program, as discussed further below, will file with the IRS in accordance with the filing requirements under § 1.529A-5(c)(2)(iv).

Disability determination

Consistent with section 529A(g)(4), the Treasury Department and the IRS have consulted with the Commissioner of Social Security regarding disability certifications and determinations of disability. For purposes of the disability certification, the proposed regulations provide that the phrase "marked and severe functional limitations" means the standard of disability in the Social Security Act for children claiming benefits under the Supplemental Security Income for the Aged, Blind, and Disabled (SSI) program based on disability, but without regard to the age of the individual. This phrase refers to a level of severity of an impairment that meets, medically equals, or functionally equals the listings in the Listing of Impairments (the listings) in appendix 1 of subpart P of 20 CFR part 404. (*See* 20 CFR 416.906, 416.924 and 416.926a). This listing developed and used by the Social Security Administration describes for each of the major body systems impairments that cause marked and severe functional limitations. Most body system sections are in two parts: an introduction, followed by the specific listings. The introduction contains information relevant to the use of the listings with respect to that body system, such as examples of common impairments in the body system and definitions used in the listings for that body system. The introduction may also include specific criteria for establishing a diagnosis, confirming the existence of an impairment, or establishing that an impairment satisfies the criteria of a particular listing with respect to the body system. The specific listings that follow the introduction for each body system specify the objective medical and other findings needed to satisfy the criteria of that listing. Most of the listed impairments are permanent or expected to result in death, although some listings state a specific period of time for which an impairment will meet the listing.

An impairment is medically equivalent to a listing if it is at least equal in severity and duration to the severity and duration of any listing. An impairment that does not meet or medically equal any listing may result in limitations that functionally equal the listings if it results in marked limitations in two domains of functioning or an extreme limitation in one domain of functioning, as explained in 20 CFR 416.926a. In addition, the proposed regulations provide that certain conditions, specifically those listed in the Compassionate Allowances Conditions list maintained by the Social Security Administration, are deemed to meet the requirements of an impairment sufficient for a disability certification without a physician's diagnosis, provided that the condition was present before the date on which the individual attained age 26. The proposed regulations also provide the flexibility from time to time to identify additional impairments that will be deemed to meet these requirements. The Treasury Department and the IRS request comments on what other conditions should be deemed to meet the requirements of section 529A(e)(2)(A)(i).

Change in eligible individual status

The Treasury Department and the IRS recognize that there may be circumstances in which a designated beneficiary ceases to be an eligible individual but subsequently regains that status. Consequently, the Treasury Department and the IRS believe that it is appropriate to permit continuation of the ABLE account (albeit with some changes in the applicable rules) during the period in which a designated beneficiary is not an eligible individual as long as the designated beneficiary was an eligible individual when the account was established. Therefore, if at any time a designated beneficiary no longer meets the definition of an eligible individual, his or her ABLE account remains an ABLE account to which all of the provisions of the ABLE Act continue to apply, and no (taxable) distribution of the account balance is deemed to occur. However, the proposed regulations provide that, beginning on the first day of the taxable year following the taxable year in which the designated beneficiary ceased to be an eligible individual, no contributions to the ABLE account may be accepted. If the designated beneficiary subsequently again becomes an eligible individual, then additional contributions may be accepted subject to the applicable annual and cumulative limits. In this way, the Treasury Department and the IRS intend to prevent a deemed distribution of the ABLE account (and preserve the account's qualification as an ABLE account for all purposes) if, for example, the disease that caused the impairment goes into a temporary remission, and to preserve the ABLE account with its tax-free distributions for qualified disability expenses if the impairment resumes and once again qualifies the designated beneficiary as an eligible individual. Note that expenses will not be qualified disability expenses if they are incurred at a time when a designated beneficiary is neither disabled nor blind within the meaning of § 1.529A-1(b)(9)(A) or § 1.529A-2(e)(1)(i).

The proposed regulations provide flexibility regarding annual recertifications. A qualified ABLE program generally must require annual recertifications that the designated beneficiary continues to satisfy the definition of an eligible individual. However, a qualified ABLE program may deem an annual recertification to have been provided in appropriate circumstances. For example, a qualified ABLE program may permit certification by an individual that he or she has a permanent disability to be considered to meet the annual requirement to present a certification to the qualified ABLE program. In other cases, a program may require all of the same evidence needed for the initial disability certification when the account was established, may require a statement under penalties of perjury that nothing has changed that would change the original disability certification, or may incorporate some other method of ensuring that the designated beneficiary continuously qualifies as an eligible individual. Alternatively, a qualified ABLE program may identify certain impairments or categories of impairments for which recertifications will be deemed to have been made annually to the qualified ABLE program unless and until the qualified ABLE program provides otherwise (for example, if a cure is discovered for a disease that causes an impairment). An initial certification or recertification that meets the requirements of the qualified ABLE program will be deemed to have met the requirement of section 529A(e)(1)(B). The Treasury Department and the IRS request comments regarding how a qualified ABLE program will be able to demonstrate eligibility in subsequent years if it allows deemed recertifications.

Contributions to an ABLE account

The proposed regulations provide that, as a general rule, all contributions to an ABLE account must be made in cash. The proposed regulations provide that a qualified ABLE program may accept cash contributions in the form of cash or a check, money order, credit card payment, or other similar method of payment. In addition, the proposed regulations provide that the total contributions to an ABLE account in the designated beneficiary's taxable year, other than amounts received in rollovers and program-to-program transfers, must not exceed the amount of the annual per-donee gift tax exclusion under section 2503(b) in effect for that calendar year (currently $14,000) in which the designated beneficiary's taxable year begins. Finally, a qualified ABLE program must provide adequate safeguards to ensure that total contributions to an ABLE account (including the proceeds from a preexisting ABLE account) do not exceed that State's limit for aggregate contributions under its qualified tuition program.

To implement these requirements, the proposed regulations provide that a qualified ABLE program must return contributions in excess of the annual gift tax exclusion (excess contributions) to the contributor(s), along with all net income attributable to those excess contributions. Similarly, the proposed regulations also require the return of all contributions, along with all net income attributable to those contributions, that caused an ABLE account to exceed the limit established by the State for its qualified tuition program (excess aggregate contributions). If an excess contribution or excess aggregate contribution is returned to a contributor other than the designated beneficiary, the qualified ABLE program must notify the designated beneficiary of such return at the time of the return. The proposed regulations further provide that such returns of excess contributions and excess aggregate contributions must be received by the contributor(s) on or before the due date (including extensions) of the designated beneficiary's income tax return for the year in which the excess contributions were made or in the year the excess aggregate contributions caused amounts in the ABLE account to exceed the limit in effect under section 529A(b)(6), respectively. The proposed regulations provide rules for determining the net income attributable to a contribution made to an ABLE account, and also provide that these excess contributions and excess aggregate contributions must be returned to contributors on a last-in, first-out basis. In the case of contributions that exceed the annual gift tax exclusion, a failure to return such excess contributions within the time period discussed in this paragraph will result in the imposition on the designated beneficiary of a 6 percent excise tax under section 4973(a)(6) on the amount of excess contributions. As part of a planned revision of IRA regulations, the Treasury Department and the IRS intend to propose regulations under section 4973 to reflect that ABLE accounts are subject to section 4973.

Application of gift tax to contributions to an ABLE account

Gift tax consequences may arise from contributions to an ABLE account even though the aggregate amount of such contributions to an ABLE account from all contributors may not exceed the annual exclusion amount under section 2503(b) applicable to any single contributor. Specifically, if a contributor makes other gifts to a designated beneficiary in addition to the gift to the designated beneficiary's ABLE account, the contributor's total gifts made to the designated beneficiary in that year could give rise to a gift tax liability.

Contributions may be made by any person. The term *person* is defined in section 7701(a)(1) to include an individual, trust, estate, partnership, association, company, or corporation. Therefore, for purposes of section 529A(b)(1)(A), a person would include an individual and each of the entities described in section 7701(a)(1). Under section 2501(a)(1), the gift tax applies only to gifts by individuals, but it also applies to gifts made directly or indirectly. As a result, a gift made by a trust, estate, association, company, corporation, or partnership is treated as having been made by the owner(s) of that entity. For example, a gift from a corporation to a designated beneficiary is treated as a gift from the shareholders of the corporation to the designated beneficiary. *See Example (1)* of

§ 25.2511-1(h). Accordingly, the proposed regulations provide that, for purposes of sections 529A(b)(1)(A) and 529A(c)(1)(C), a contribution by a corporation is treated as a gift by its shareholders and a contribution by a partnership is treated as a gift by its partners. This rule also applies to trusts, estates, associations, and companies. *See* section 2511 and § 25.2511-1(c).

The legislative history of section 529A suggests that a "person" described in section 529A(b)(1)(A) includes the designated beneficiary of an ABLE account. *See* 160 CONG. REC. H7051, H8317, H8318, H8321, H8322 (2014). A person may transfer his or her property into an account, such as a bank account or a trust, for his or her benefit and retain dominion and control over the property transferred. Because an individual cannot make a transfer of property to himself or herself and a transfer of property is a fundamental requirement for a completed gift, this type of transfer from a person's own property cannot be treated as a completed gift for tax purposes. *See* § 25.2511-2(b) and (c). Therefore, the proposed regulations provide that any contribution by a designated beneficiary to a qualified ABLE program benefitting the designated beneficiary is not treated as a completed gift. Because the designated beneficiary remains the owner of the account for purposes of chapter 12, if the designated beneficiary transfers the funds in the account to another person as permitted under these proposed regulations, the designated beneficiary making the transfer is the donor for purposes of chapter 12 and the transferor for generation-skipping transfer tax purposes of chapter 13.

Distributions

If distributions from an ABLE account do not exceed the designated beneficiary's qualified disability expenses, no amount is includible in the designated beneficiary's gross income. Otherwise, the earnings portion of the distributions from the ABLE account as determined in the manner provided under section 72, reduced by the product of such earnings portion and the ratio of the amount of the distributions for qualified disability expenses to total distributions, is includible in the gross income of the designated beneficiary to the extent not otherwise excluded from gross income. As required by section 529A(c)(1)(D), the proposed regulations provide that, for purposes of applying section 72 to amounts distributed from an ABLE account: (1) all distributions during a taxable year are treated as one distribution; and (2) the value of the contract, income on the contract, and investment in the contract are computed as of the close of the calendar year in which the designated beneficiary's taxable year begins.

The proposed regulations also provide that, in addition to the income tax on the portion of a distribution included in gross income, an additional tax of 10 percent of the amount includible in gross income is imposed. This additional tax does not apply, however, to distributions on or after the designated beneficiary's death or to returns of excess contributions, excess aggregate contributions, or contributions to additional purported ABLE accounts made by the due date (including extensions) of the designated beneficiary's tax return for the year in which the relevant contributions were made.

Section 529A(c)(1)(C) addresses the tax consequences of the rollover of an ABLE account to an ABLE account for the same designated beneficiary maintained under a different State's qualified ABLE program, as well as a change of designated beneficiary. The proposed regulations describe with respect to these two situations the circumstances in which amounts will not be includible in income. The first is any change of designated beneficiary if the new designated beneficiary is both (1) an eligible individual for his or her taxable year in which the change is made and (2) a sibling of the former designated beneficiary. For purposes of these proposed regulations, a sibling also includes step-siblings and half-siblings, whether by blood or by adoption. The proposed regulations provide that a qualified ABLE program must permit a change of designated beneficiary, as long as the change is made prior to the death of the former designated beneficiary and as long as the successor designated beneficiary is an eligible individual. Because the designated beneficiary will be subject to gift and/or generation-skipping transfer tax if the successor designated beneficiary is not a sibling of the designated beneficiary, the Treasury Department and the IRS request comments regarding whether the final regulations should permit States to require that a successor designated beneficiary also must be a sibling of the designated beneficiary.

The second situation in which a distribution is not included in gross income arises if a distribution to the designated beneficiary of the ABLE account is paid, not later than the 60th day after the date of the distribution, to another (or the same) ABLE account for the benefit of the designated beneficiary or for the benefit of an eligible individual who is a sibling of the designated beneficiary. However, the preceding sentence does not apply to such a distribution that occurs within 12 months of a previous rollover to another ABLE account for the same designated beneficiary.

The Treasury Department and the IRS have been asked whether a qualified tuition account under section 529 may be rolled into an ABLE account for the same designated beneficiary free of tax. Because such a distribution to the ABLE account would not constitute a qualified higher education expense under section 529, the Treasury Department and the IRS do not believe they have the authority to allow such a transfer on a tax-free basis.

In addition, the proposed regulations authorize a qualified ABLE program to allow program-to-program transfers to effectuate a change of qualified ABLE program or a change of designated beneficiary to another eligible individual. Such a direct transfer is neither a distribution taxed in accordance with section 72 nor an excess contribution. A program-to-program transfer also could be accomplished, if permitted by the qualified ABLE program, through a check delivered to the designated beneficiary but negotiable only by the qualified State program under which the new ABLE account is being established.

The Treasury Department and the IRS recognize that moving funds by use of a program-to-program transfer may be preferable to moving them by a rollover because a rollover, even if made within the permissible 60-day period, may jeopardize the designated beneficiary's eligibility for certain benefits under various means-tested programs. Moreover, a direct program-to-program transfer could facilitate the efficient transfer of all relevant information regarding the application of contribution limits and the total amount of accumulated earnings that will also apply to the new account. The Treasury Department and the IRS request comments as to whether and to what extent a qualified ABLE program should be permitted to require that funds from another State's ABLE program be accepted only through program-to-program transfers.

Qualified disability expenses

Section 529A(e)(5) defines a *qualified disability expense.* Consistent with that subsection, the proposed regulations provide that qualified disability expenses are expenses that relate to the designated beneficiary's blindness or disability and are for the benefit of that designated beneficiary in maintaining or improving his or her health, independence, or quality of life. Such expenses include, but are not limited to, expenses for education, housing, transportation, employment training and support, assistive technology and personal support services, health, prevention and wellness, financial management and administrative services, legal fees, expenses for oversight and monitoring, funeral and burial expenses, and other expenses that may be identified from time to time in future guidance published in the Internal Revenue Bulletin. As previously stated, expenses incurred at a time when a designated beneficiary is neither disabled nor blind within the meaning of the proposed regulations are not qualified disability expenses.

In order to implement the legislative purpose of assisting eligible individuals in maintaining or improving their health, independence, or quality of life, the Treasury Department and the IRS conclude that the term "qualified disability expenses" should be broadly construed to permit the inclusion of basic living expenses and should not be limited to expenses for items for which there is a medical necessity or which provide no benefits to others in addition to the benefit to the eligible individual. For example, expenses for common items such as smart phones could be considered qualified disability expenses if they are an effective and safe communication or navigation aid for a child with autism. The Treasury Department and the IRS request comments regarding what types of expenses should be considered qualified disability expenses and under what circumstances. The proposed regulations authorize the identification of additional types of qualified disability expenses in guidance published in the Internal Revenue Bulletin. *See* § 601.601(d)(2). A qualified ABLE program must establish safeguards to distinguish between distributions used for the payment of qualified disability expenses and other distributions, and to permit the identification of the amounts distributed for housing expenses as that term is defined for purposes of the Supplemental Security Income program of the Social Security Administration.

Limitation on number of ABLE accounts of a designated beneficiary

Section 529A(c)(4) generally provides that, except with respect to certain rollovers, once an ABLE account has been established for a designated beneficiary, no account subsequently established for that same designated beneficiary may qualify as an ABLE account. The proposed regulations provide that, except with respect to rollovers and program-to-program transfers, no designated beneficiary may have more than one ABLE account in existence at the same time, but provides that a prior ABLE account that has been closed does not prohibit the subsequent creation of another ABLE account for the same designated beneficiary. A qualified ABLE program must obtain a verification from the eligible individual, signed under penalties of perjury, that he or she has no other ABLE account (except in the case of a rollover or program-to-program transfer). The proposed regulations provide that, in the event that any additional ABLE account is opened for a designated beneficiary with an ABLE account already in existence, only the first such account created for that designated beneficiary qualifies as an ABLE account, and each other account is treated for all purposes as being an account of the designated beneficiary that is not an ABLE account under a qualified ABLE program. The proposed regulations also provide, however, that a return, in accordance with the rules that apply to returns of excess contributions and excess aggregate contributions under § 1.529A-2(g)(4), of the entire balance of a second or other subsequent account received by the contributor(s) on or before the due date (including extensions) for filing the designated beneficiary's income tax return for the year in which the account was opened and contributions to the second or subsequent account were made will not be treated as a gift or distribution to the designated beneficiary for purposes of section 529A.

The prohibition of multiple ABLE accounts, however, does not apply to prevent a timely rollover or program-to-program transfer of the designated beneficiary's account to an ABLE account under a different qualified ABLE program.

Residency requirements

Consistent with section 529A(b)(1)(C), the proposed regulations require that an ABLE account for a designated beneficiary may be established only under the qualified ABLE program of the State in which that designated beneficiary is a resident or with which the State of the designated beneficiary's residence has contracted for the provision of ABLE accounts. If a State does not establish and maintain a qualified ABLE program, it may contract with another State to provide an ABLE program for its residents. The statute is silent as to whether a designated beneficiary must move his or her existing ABLE account when the designated beneficiary changes his or her residence. The Treasury Department and the IRS are concerned about imposing undue administrative burdens and costs on designated beneficiaries who frequently change State residency, such as members of military families. Therefore, the proposed regulations provide that a qualified ABLE program may permit a designated beneficiary to continue to maintain his or her ABLE account that was created in that State, even after the designated beneficiary is no longer a resident of that State. However, in order to enforce the one ABLE account limitation and in accordance with section 529A(g)(1), the proposed regulations provide that, other than in the case of a rollover or a program-to-program transfer of a designated beneficiary's ABLE account, a qualified ABLE program must require the designated beneficiary to verify, under penalties of perjury, when creating an ABLE account that the account being established is the designated beneficiary's only ABLE account. For example, the eligible individual could be required to check a box providing such verification on a form used to establish the account. The Treasury Department and the IRS are concerned that without such safeguards individuals could inadvertently establish two accounts with adverse tax consequences due to the loss of ABLE account status for the second account and expect qualified ABLE programs to establish safeguards to ensure that the required limit of one ABLE account per designated beneficiary is not violated.

Investment direction

Section 529A(b)(4) states that a program shall not be treated as a qualified ABLE program unless it provides that the designated beneficiary may directly or indirectly direct the investment of any contributions to the program or any earnings thereon no more than two times in any calendar year. A program will not violate this requirement merely because it permits a designated beneficiary or a person with signature authority over a designated beneficiary's account to serve as one of the program's board members or employees, or as a board member or employee of a contractor that the program hires to perform administrative services.

Cap on contributions

Section 529A(b)(6) provides that a qualified ABLE program must provide adequate safeguards to prevent aggregate contributions on behalf of a designated beneficiary in excess of the limit established by the State under section 529(b)(6) relating to Qualified State Tuition Programs. The proposed regulations provide a safe harbor that permits a qualified ABLE program to satisfy this requirement regarding total cumulative contributions if the program prohibits any additional contributions to an account as soon as the account balance reaches the specified contribution limit under such State's program established under section 529. Once the account balance falls below the prescribed limit, contributions may resume, subject to the same limitation. The Treasury Department and the IRS believe that recommencement of contributions is appropriate based on the nature and purposes of the ABLE program.

Gift and generation-skipping transfer (GST) taxes

The proposed regulations provide that contributions to an ABLE account by a person other than the designated beneficiary are treated as completed gifts to the designated beneficiary of the account, and that such gifts are neither gifts of a future interest nor a qualified transfer under section 2503(e). Accordingly, no distribution from an ABLE account to the designated beneficiary of that account is treated as a taxable gift. Finally, neither gift nor GST taxes apply to the change of designated beneficiary of an ABLE account, as long as the new designated beneficiary is an eligible individual who is a sibling of the former designated beneficiary.

Distribution on death

The proposed regulations provide that, upon the death of the designated beneficiary, all amounts remaining in the ABLE account are includible in the designated beneficiary's gross estate for purposes of the estate tax. *See* section 2031. Further, the proposed regulations cross-reference section 2053 for purposes of determining the deductibility by the designated beneficiary's estate of amounts payable from the ABLE account to satisfy claims by creditors such as a State and also cross-reference section 2652(a)(1) for treatment of the deceased designated beneficiary as the transferor of any property remaining in the ABLE account that may pass to a beneficiary.

Pursuant to section 529A(f), a qualified ABLE program must provide that, upon the designated beneficiary's death, any State may file a claim (either with the person with signature authority over the ABLE account or the executor of the designated beneficiary's estate as defined in section 2203) for the amount of the total medical assistance paid for the designated beneficiary under the State's Medicaid plan after the establishment of the ABLE account. The amount paid in satisfaction of such a claim is not a taxable distribution from the ABLE account. Further, the amount is to be paid only after the payment of all outstanding payments due for the qualified disability expenses of the designated beneficiary and is to be reduced by the amount of all premiums paid by or on behalf of the designated beneficiary to a Medicaid Buy-In program under that State's Medicaid plan.

Unrelated business taxable income and filing requirements

A qualified ABLE program generally is exempt from income taxation. A qualified ABLE program, however, is subject to the taxes imposed by section 511 relating to the imposition of tax on unrelated business taxable income ("UBTI"). For purposes of this tax, certain administrative and other fees do not constitute unrelated business income to the ABLE program. A qualified ABLE program is not required to file Form 990, "Return of Organization Exempt From Income Tax," but will be required to file Form 990-T, "Exempt Organization Business Income Tax Return," if a filing would be required under the rules of §§1.6012-2(e) and 1.6012-3(a)(5) if the ABLE program were an organization described in those sections.

Reporting requirements

The proposed regulations set forth recordkeeping and reporting requirements. A qualified ABLE program must maintain records that enable the program to account to the Secretary with respect to all contributions, distributions, returns of excess contributions or additional accounts, income earned, and account balances for any designated beneficiary's ABLE account. In addition, a qualified ABLE program must report to the Secretary the establishment of each ABLE account, including the name and residence of the designated beneficiary, and other relevant information regarding the account that is included on the new Form 5498-QA, "ABLE Account Contribution Information." It is anticipated that the qualified ABLE program will report if the eligible individual has presented an adequate disability certification, accompanied by a diagnosis, to demonstrate eligibility to establish an account. Information regarding distributions will be reported on the new Form 1099-QA, "Distributions from ABLE Accounts." The proposed regulations contain more detail on how the information must be reported.

In addition, section 529A(b)(3) requires that a qualified ABLE program provide separate accounting for each designated beneficiary. Separate accounting requires that contributions for the benefit of a designated beneficiary, as well as earnings attributable to those contributions, are allocated to that designated beneficiary's account. Whether or not a program ordinarily provides each designated beneficiary an annual account statement showing the income and transactions related to the account, the program must give this information to the designated beneficiary upon request.

Section 529A(d)(4) provides that States are required to submit electronically to the Commissioner of Social Security, on a monthly basis and in the manner specified by the Commissioner of Social Security, statements on relevant distributions and account balances from all ABLE accounts. The report of the Committee on Ways and Means (H.R. Rep. No. 113-614, pt. 1, at 15 (2014)) indicates that States should work with the Commissioner of Social Security to identify data elements for the monthly reports, including the type of qualified disability expenses.

Effective Date/Applicability Date

These regulations are proposed to be effective as of the date of publication of the Treasury decision adopting these rules as final regulations in the **Federal Register**. These rules, when adopted as final regulations, will apply to taxable years beginning after December 31, 2014. The reporting requirements of §§1.529A-5 through 1.529A-7 will apply to information returns required to be filed, and payee statements required to be furnished, after December 31, 2015. Until the issuance of final regulations, taxpayers and qualified ABLE programs may rely on these proposed regulations.

Special Analyses

It has been determined that this notice of proposed rulemaking is not a significant regulatory action as defined in Executive Order 12866, as supplemented by Executive Order 13563. It has also been determined that section 553(b) of the Administrative Procedure Act (5 U.S.C. chapter 5) does not apply to this regulation and, because the regulation does not impose a collection of information on small entities, the Regulatory Flexibility Act (5 U.S.C. chapter 6) does not apply. This regulation, if adopted, would primarily affect states and individuals and therefore would not have a significant economic impact on a substantial number of small entities. Therefore, a regulatory flexibility analysis is not required. Pursuant to section 7805(f) of the Internal Revenue Code, this notice of proposed rulemaking will be submitted to the Chief Counsel for Advocacy of the Small Business Administration for comment on its impact on small businesses.

Comments and Public Hearing

Before these proposed regulations are adopted as final regulations, consideration will be given to any comments that are timely submitted to the IRS as prescribed in this preamble under the "Addresses" heading. The Treasury Department and the IRS request comments on all aspects of the proposed rules. All comments will be available at *www.regulations.gov* or upon request. A public hearing will be scheduled if requested in writing by any person that timely submits written or electronic comments. If a public hearing is scheduled, notice of the date, time, and place for the hearing will be published in the **Federal Register**.

A public hearing has been scheduled for **October 14, 2015**, beginning at **10:00 am** in the Auditorium, Internal Revenue Building, 1111 Constitution Avenue, NW, Washington, DC. Due to building security procedures, visitors must enter at the Constitution Avenue entrance. In addition, all visitors must present photo identification to enter the building. Because of access restrictions, visitors will not be admitted beyond the immediate entrance area more than 30 minutes before the hearing starts. For information about having your name placed on the building access list to attend the hearing, see the "FOR FURTHER INFORMATION CONTACT" section of this preamble.

The rules of 26 CFR 601.601(a)(3) apply to the hearing. Persons who wish to present oral comments at the hearing must submit written comments by September 21, 2015, and an outline of the topics to be discussed and the time to be devoted to each topic (signed original and eight (8) copies) by September 21, 2015. Submit a signed paper original and eight (8) copies or an electronic copy. A period of 10 minutes will be allotted to each person for making comments. An agenda showing the scheduling of the speakers will be prepared after the deadline for receiving outlines has passed. Copies of the agenda will be available free of charge at the hearing.

Drafting Information

The principal authors of these regulations are Terri Harris and Sean Barnett, Office of Associate Chief Counsel (Tax Exempt and Government Entities). However, other personnel from the Treasury Department and the IRS participated in the development of these regulations.

[¶49,657] Proposed Amendments of Regulations (REG-115452-14), published in the Federal Register on July 23, 2015 (corrected 8/19/2015).

[Code Sec. 707]

Partnerships: Partners: Transactions between partner and partnership: Transfers of property: Disguised payment for services.—Reg. §1.707-2 and amendments of Reg. §§1.707-0, 1.707-1, 1.707-9 and 1.736-1, relating to disguised payments for services under section 707(a)(2)(A) of the Internal Revenue Code, are proposed.

AGENCY: Internal Revenue Service (IRS), Treasury

ACTION: Notice of proposed rulemaking.

SUMMARY: This document contains proposed regulations relating to disguised payments for services under section 707(a)(2)(A) of the Internal Revenue Code. The proposed regulations provide guidance to partnerships and their partners regarding when an arrangement will be treated as a disguised payment for services. This document also proposes conforming modifications to the regulations governing guaranteed payments under section 707(c). Additionally, this document provides notice of proposed modifications to Rev. Procs. 93-27 and 2001-43 relating to the issuance of interests in partnership profits to service providers.

DATES: Written and electronic comments and requests for a public hearing must be received by October 21, 2015.

ADDRESSES: Send submissions to CC:PA:LPD:PR (REG-115452-14), room 5203, Internal Revenue Service, PO Box 7604, Ben Franklin Station, Washington, DC 20044. Submissions may be hand-delivered Monday through Friday between the hours of 8 a.m. and 4 p.m. to CC:PA:LPD:PR (REG-115452-14), Courier's Desk, Internal Revenue Service, 1111 Constitution Avenue, N.W., Washington, DC, 20224 or sent electronically, via the Federal eRulemaking Portal at *http://www.regulations.gov* (indicate IRS and REG-115452-14).

FOR FURTHER INFORMATION CONTACT: Concerning submissions of comments, Oluwafunmilayo (Funmi) Taylor (202) 517-6901; concerning the proposed regulations, Jaclyn M. Goldberg (202) 317-6850 (not toll-free numbers).

SUPPLEMENTARY INFORMATION:

Background

Generally, under the statutory framework of Subchapter K of the Code, an allocation or distribution between a partnership and a partner for the provision of services can be treated in one of three ways: (1) a distributive share under section 704(b); (2) a guaranteed payment under section 707(c); or (3) as a transaction in which a partner has rendered services to the partnership in its capacity as other than a partner under section 707(a).

Distributive Share Treatment

Partnership allocations that are determined with regard to partnership income and that are made to a partner for services rendered by the partner in its capacity as a partner are generally treated as distributive shares of partnership income, taxable under the general rules of sections 702, 703, and 704. In some cases, the right to a distributive share may qualify as a profits interest defined in Rev. Proc. 93-27, 1993-2 C.B. 343. Rev. Proc. 93-27, clarified by Rev. Proc. 2001-43, 2001-2 C.B. 191, provides guidance on the treatment of the receipt of a profits interest for services provided to or for the benefit of the partnership.

Arrangements subject to sections 707(c) or 707(a)(1).

In 1954, Congress added section 707 to the Code to clarify transactions between a partner and a partnership. Section 707(a) addresses arrangements in which a partner engages with the partnership other than in its capacity as a partner. The legislative history to section 707(a) provides the general rule that a partner who engages in a transaction with the partnership, other than in its capacity as a partner is treated as though it were not a partner. The provision was intended to apply to the sale of property by the partner to the partnership, the purchase of property by the partner from the partnership, and the rendering of services by the partner to the partnership or by the partnership to the partner. H.R. Rep. No. 1337, 83d Cong., 2d Sess. 227 (1954) (House Report); S. Rep. No. 1622, 83d Cong., 2d Sess. 387 (1954) (Senate Report).

Congress simultaneously added section 707(c) to address payments to partners of the partnership acting in their partner capacity. Section 707(c) provides that to the extent determined without regard to the income of the partnership, payment to a partner for services shall be considered as made to a person who is not a partner, but only for purposes of sections 61(a) and 162(a). The Senate Report and the House Report provide that a fixed salary, payable without regard to partnership income, to a partner who renders services to the partnership is a guaranteed payment. The amount of the payment shall be included in the partner's gross income, and shall not be considered a distributive share of income or gain. A partner who is guaranteed a minimum annual amount for its services shall be treated as receiving a fixed payment in that amount. House Report at 227; Senate Report at 387.

In 1956, the Treasury Department and the IRS issued additional guidance under § 1.707-1 relating to a partner not acting in its capacity as a partner under section 707(a) and to guaranteed payments under section 707(c). See TD 6175. However, it remained unclear when a partner's services to the partnership were rendered in a non-partner capacity under section 707(a) rather than in a partner capacity under section 707(c).

In 1975, the Tax Court distinguished sections 707(a) and 707(c) payments in *Pratt v. Commissioner*, 64 T.C. 204 (1975), *aff'd* in part, *rev'd* in part, 550 F.2d 1023 (5th Cir. 1977). In *Pratt*, the general partners in two limited partnerships formed to purchase, develop, and operate two shopping centers received a fixed percentage of gross rentals in exchange for the performance of managerial services. The Tax Court held that these payments were not guaranteed payments under section 707(c) because they were computed based on a percentage of gross rental income and therefore were not paid without regard to partnership income. The Tax Court further held that section 707(a) did not apply because the general partners performed managerial duties in their partner capacities in accordance with their basic duties under the partnership agreement. On appeal, the Fifth Circuit affirmed the Tax Court's decision. The Fifth Circuit reasoned that Congress enacted section 707(a) to apply to partners who perform services for the partnership that are outside the scope of the partnership's activities. The Court indicated that if the partner performs services that the partnership itself provides, then the compensation to the service provider is merely a rearrangement among the partners of their distributive shares in the partnership income.

In response to the decision in *Pratt*, the Treasury Department and the IRS issued Rev. Rul. 81-300, 1981-2 C.B. 143 and Rev. Rul. 81-301, 1981-2 C.B. 144 to clarify the treatment of transactions under sections 707(a) and 707(c). As in the *Pratt* case, Rev. Rul. 81-300 considers a partnership formed to purchase, develop, and operate a shopping center. The partnership agreement required the general partners to contribute their time, managerial abilities, and best efforts to the partnership. In return for these services, the general partners received a fee equal to five percent of the partnership's gross rental income. The ruling concluded that the taxpayers performed managerial services in their capacities as general partners, and characterized the management fees as guaranteed payments under section 707(c). The ruling provides that, although guaranteed payments under section 707(c) frequently involve a fixed amount, they are not limited to fixed amounts. Thus, the ruling concluded that a payment for services determined by reference to an item of gross income will be a guaranteed payment if, on the basis of all facts and circumstances, the payment is compensation rather than a share of profits.

Rev. Rul. 81-301 describes a limited partnership which has two classes of general partners. The first class of general partner (director general partners) had complete control over the management, conduct, and operation of partnership activities. The second class of general partner (adviser general partner) rendered to the partnership services that were substantially the same as those that the adviser general partner rendered to other persons as an independent contractor. The adviser general partner received 10 percent of daily gross income in exchange for the management services it provided to the partnership. Rev. Rul. 81-301 held that the adviser general partner received its gross income allocation in a non-partner capacity under section 707(a) because the adviser general partner provided similar services to other parties, was subject to removal by the director general partners, was not personally liable to the other partners for any losses, and its management was supervised by the director general partners.

Enactment of Section 707(a)(2)(A)

Congress revisited the scope of section 707(a) in 1984, in part to prevent partners from circumventing the capitalization requirements of sections 263 and 709 by structuring payments for services as allocations of partnership income under section 704. H.R. Rep. No. 432 (Pt. 2), 98th Cong., 2d Sess. 1216-21 (1984) (H.R. Rep.); S. Prt. No. 169 (Vol. 1), 98th Cong., 2d Sess. 223-32 (1984) (S. Prt.). Congress specifically addressed the holdings in Rev. Rul. 81-300 and Rev. Rul. 81-301, affirming Rev. Rul. 81-301 and concluding that the payment in Rev. Rul. 81-300 should be recharacterized as a section 707(a) payment. S. Prt. at 230. Accordingly, the Treasury Department and the IRS are obsoleting Rev. Rul. 81-300 and request comments on whether it should be reissued with modified facts.

Congress also added an anti-abuse rule to section 707(a) relating to payments to partner service providers. Section 707(a)(2)(A) provides that if a partner performs services for a partnership and receives a related direct or indirect allocation and distribution, and the performance of services and allocation and distribution, when viewed together, are properly characterized as a transaction occurring between the partnership and a partner acting other than in its capacity as a partner, the transaction will be treated as occurring between the partnership and one who is not a partner under section 707(a)(1). See section 73 of the Tax Reform Act of 1984 (the 1984 Act). The Treasury Department and the IRS have concluded that section 707(a)(2) applies to arrangements in which distributions to the service provider depend on an allocation of an item of income, and section 707(c) applies to amounts whose payments are unrelated to partnership income.

Section 707(a)(2) grants the Secretary broad regulatory authority to identify transactions involving disguised payments for services under section 707(a)(2)(A). This grant of regulatory authority stems from Congress's concern that partnerships and service providers were inappropriately treating payments as allocations and distributions to a partner even when the service provider acted in a capacity other than as a partner. S. Prt. at 225. Congress determined that allocations and distributions that were, in substance, direct payments for services should be treated as a payment of fees rather than as an arrangement for the allocation and distribution of partnership income. H.R. Rep. at 1218; S. Prt. at 225. Congress differentiated these arrangements from situations in which a partner receives an allocation (or increased allocation) for an extended period to reflect its contribution of property or services to the partnership, such that the partner receives the allocation in its capacity as a partner. In balancing these potentially conflicting concerns, Congress anticipated that the regulations would take five factors into account in determining whether a service provider would receive its putative allocation and distribution in its capacity as a partner. H.R. Rep. at 1219-20; S. Prt. at 227.

Congress identified as its first and most important factor whether the payment is subject to significant entrepreneurial risk as to both the amount and fact of payment. In explaining why entrepreneurial risk is the most important factor, Congress provides that "[p]artners extract the profits of the partnership with reference to the business success of the venture, while third parties generally receive payments which are not subject to this risk." S. Prt. at 227. An arrangement for an allocation and distribution to a service provider which involves limited risk as to amount and payment is treated as a fee under section 707(a)(2)(A). Congress specified examples of allocations that presumptively limit a partner's risk, including (i) capped allocations of income, (ii) allocations for a fixed number of years under which the income that will go to the partner is reasonably certain, (iii) continuing arrangements in which purported allocations and distributions are fixed in amount or reasonably determinable under all facts and circumstances, and (iv) allocations of gross income items.

An arrangement in which an allocation and distribution to a service provider are subject to significant entrepreneurial risk as to amount will generally be recognized as a distributive share, although other factors are also relevant. The legislative history to section 707(a)(2)(A) includes the following examples of factors that could bear on this determination: (i) whether the partner status of the recipient is transitory; (ii) whether the allocation and distribution that are made to the partner are close in time to the partner's performance of services; (iii) whether the facts and circumstances indicate that the recipient became a partner primarily to obtain tax benefits for itself or the partnership that would not otherwise have been available; and (iv) whether the value of the recipient's interest in general and in continuing partnership profits is small in relation to the allocation in question.

Explanation of Provisions

Section 1.707-1 sets forth general rules on the operation of section 707. Section 1.707-2 is titled "Disguised payments for services" and is currently reserved. Sections 1.707-3 through 1.707-7 provide guidance regarding transactions involving disguised sales under section 707(a)(2)(B). These proposed regulations are issued under § 1.707-2 and provide guidance regarding transactions involving disguised payments for services under section 707(a)(2)(A). The effective date of the proposed regulations is provided under § 1.707-9.

I. *General Rules Regarding Disguised Payments for Services*

A. *Scope*

Consistent with the language of section 707(a)(2)(A), § 1.707-2(b) of the proposed regulations provides that an arrangement will be treated as a disguised payment for services if (i) a person (service provider), either in a partner capacity or in anticipation of being a partner, performs services (directly or through its delegate) to or for the benefit of the partnership; (ii) there is a related direct or indirect allocation and distribution to the service provider; and (iii) the performance of the services and the allocation and distribution when viewed together, are properly characterized as a transaction occurring between the partnership and a person acting other than in that person's capacity as a partner.

The proposed regulations provide a mechanism for determining whether or not an arrangement is treated as a disguised payment for services under section 707(a)(2)(A). An arrangement that is treated as a disguised payment for services under these proposed regulations will be treated as a payment for services for all purposes of the Code. Thus, the partnership must treat the payments as payments to a non-partner in determining the remaining partners' shares of taxable income or loss. Where appropriate, the partnership must capitalize the payments or otherwise treat them in a manner consistent with the recharacterization.

The consequence of characterizing an arrangement as a payment for services is otherwise beyond the scope of these regulations. For example, the proposed regulations do not address the timing of inclusion by the service provider or the timing of a deduction by the partnership other than to provide that each is taken into account as provided for under applicable law by applying all relevant sections of the Code and all relevant judicial doctrines. Further, if an arrangement is subject to section 707(a), taxpayers should look to relevant authorities to determine the status of the service provider as an independent contractor or employee. See, generally, Rev. Rul. 69-184, 1969-1 C.B. 256. The Treasury Department and the IRS believe that section 707(a)(2)(A) generally should not apply to arrangements that the partnership has reasonably characterized as a guaranteed payment under section 707(c).

Allocations pursuant to an arrangement between a partnership and a service provider to which sections 707(a) and 707(c) do not apply will be treated as a distributive share under section 704(b). Rev. Proc. 93-27 and Rev. Proc. 2001-43 may apply to such an arrangement if the specific requirements of those Revenue Procedures are also satisfied. The Treasury Department and the IRS intend to modify the exceptions set forth in those revenue procedures to include an additional exception for profits interests issued in conjunction with a partner forgoing payment of a substantially fixed amount. This exception is discussed in part IV of the Explanation of Provisions section of this preamble.

B. *Application and Timing*

These proposed regulations apply to a service provider who purports to be a partner even if applying the regulations causes the service provider to be treated as a person who is not a partner. S. Prt. at 227. Further, the proposed regulations may apply even if their application results in a determination that no partnership exists. The regulations also apply to a special allocation and distribution received in exchange for services by a service provider who receives other allocations and distributions in a partner capacity under section 704(b).

The proposed regulations characterize the nature of an arrangement at the time at which the parties enter into or modify the arrangement. Although section 707(a)(2)(A)(ii) requires both an allocation and a distribution to the service provider, the Treasury Department and the IRS believe that a premise of section 704(b) is that an income allocation correlates with an increased distribution right, justifying the assumption that an arrangement that provides for an income allocation should be treated as also providing for an associated distribution for purposes of applying section 707(a)(2)(A). The Treasury Department and the IRS considered that some arrangements provide for distributions in a later year, and that those later distributions may be subject to independent risk. However, the Treasury Department and the IRS believe that recharacterizing an arrangement retroactively is administratively difficult. Thus, the proposed regulations characterize the nature of an arrangement when the arrangement is entered into (or modified) regardless of when income is allocated and when money or property is distributed. The proposed regulations apply to both onetime transactions and continuing arrangements. S. Prt. at 226.

II. *Factors Considered*

Whether an arrangement constitutes a payment for services (in whole or in part) depends on all of the facts and circumstances. The proposed regulations include six non-exclusive factors that may indicate that an arrangement constitutes a disguised payment for services. Of these factors, the first five factors generally track the facts and circumstances identified as relevant in the legislative history for purposes of applying section 707(a)(2)(A). The proposed regulations also add a sixth factor not specifically identified by Congress. The first of these six factors, the existence of significant entrepreneurial risk, is accorded more weight than the other factors, and arrangements that lack significant entrepreneurial risk are treated as disguised payments for services. The weight given to each of the other five factors depends on the particular case, and the absence of a particular factor (other than significant entrepreneurial risk) is not necessarily determinative of whether an arrangement is treated as a payment for services.

A. *Significant Entrepreneurial Risk*

As described in the Background section of this preamble, Congress indicated that the most important factor in determining whether or not an arrangement constitutes a payment for services is that the allocation and distribution is subject to significant entrepreneurial risk. S. Prt. at 227. Congress noted that partners extract the profits of the partnership based on the business success of the venture, while third parties generally receive payments that are not subject to this risk. Id.

The proposed regulations reflect Congress's view that this factor is most important. Under the proposed regulations, an arrangement that lacks significant entrepreneurial risk constitutes a disguised payment for services. An arrangement in which allocations and distributions to the service provider are subject to significant entrepreneurial risk will generally be recognized as a distributive share but the ultimate determination depends on the totality of the facts and circumstances. The Treasury Department and the IRS request comments on whether allocations to service providers that lack significant entrepreneurial risk could be characterized as distributive shares under section 704(b) in any circumstances.

Whether an arrangement lacks significant entrepreneurial risk is based on the service provider's entrepreneurial risk relative to the overall entrepreneurial risk of the partnership. For example, a service provider who receives a percentage of net profits in each of a partnership that invests in high-quality debt instruments and a partnership that invests in volatile or unproven businesses may have significant entrepreneurial risk with respect to both interests.

Section 1.707-2(c)(1)(i) through (v) of the proposed regulations set forth arrangements that presumptively lack significant entrepreneurial risk. These arrangements are presumed to result in an absence of significant entrepreneurial risk (and therefore, a disguised payment for services) unless other facts and circumstances can establish the presence of significant entrepreneurial risk by clear and convincing evidence. These examples generally describe facts and circumstances in which there is a high likelihood that the service provider will receive an allocation regardless of the overall success of the business operation, including (i) capped allocations of partnership income if the cap would reasonably be expected to apply in most years, (ii) allocations for a fixed number of years under which the service provider's distributive share of income is reasonably certain, (iii) allocations of gross income items, (iv) an allocation (under a formula or otherwise) that is predominantly fixed in amount, is reasonably determinable under all the facts and circumstances, or is designed to assure that sufficient net profits are highly likely to be available to make the allocation to the service provider (for example, if the partnership agreement provides for an allocation of net profits from specific transactions or accounting periods and this allocation does not depend on the overall success of the enterprise), and (v) arrangements in which a service provider either waives its right to receive payment for the future performance of services in a manner that is non-binding or fails to timely notify the partnership and its partners of the waiver and its terms.

With respect to the fourth example, the presence of certain facts, when coupled with a priority allocation to the service provider that is measured over any accounting period of the partnership of 12 months or less, may create opportunities that will lead to a higher likelihood that sufficient net profits will be available to make the allocation. One fact is that the value of partnership assets is not easily ascertainable and the partnership agreement allows the service provider or a related party in connection with a revaluation to control the determination of asset values, including by controlling events that may affect those values (such as timing of announcements that affect the value of the assets). (See Example 3(iv).) Another fact is that the service provider or a related party controls the entities in which the partnership invests, including controlling the timing and amount of distributions by those controlled entities. (These two facts by themselves do not, however, necessarily establish the absence of significant entrepreneurial risk.) By contrast, certain priority allocations that are intended to equalize a service provider's return with priority allocations already allocated to investing partners over the life of the partnership (commonly known as "catch-up allocations") typically will not fall within the types of allocations covered by the fourth example and will not lack significant entrepreneurial risk, although all of the facts and circumstances are considered in making that determination.

With respect to the fifth example, the Treasury Department and the IRS request suggestions regarding fee waiver requirements that sufficiently bind the waiving service provider and that are administrable by the partnership and its partners.

Congress's emphasis on entrepreneurial risk requires changes to existing regulations under section 707(c). Specifically, Example 2 of § 1.707-1(c) provides that if a partner is entitled to an allocation of the greater of 30 percent of partnership income or a minimum guaranteed amount, and the income allocation exceeds the minimum guaranteed amount, then the entire income allocation is treated as a distributive share under section 704(b). Example 2 also provides that if the income allocation is less than the guaranteed amount, then the partner is treated as receiving a distributive share to the extent of the income allocation and a guaranteed payment to the extent that the minimum guaranteed payment exceeds the income allocation. The treatment of the arrangements in Example 2 is inconsistent with the concept that an allocation must be subject to significant entrepreneurial risk to be treated as a distributive share under section 704(b). Accordingly, the proposed regulations modify Example 2 to provide that the entire minimum amount is treated as a guaranteed payment under section 707(c) regardless of the amount of the income allocation. Rev. Rul. 66-95, 1966-1 C.B. 169, and Rev. Rul. 69-180, 1969-1 C.B. 183, are also inconsistent with these proposed regulations. The Treasury Department and the IRS intend to obsolete Rev. Rul. 66-95 and Rev. Rul. 69-180, when these regulations are published in final form.

B. *Secondary factors*

Section 1.707-2(c)(2) through (6) describes additional factors of secondary importance in determining whether or not an arrangement that gives the appearance of significant entrepreneurial risk constitutes a payment for services. The weight given to each of the other factors depends on the particular case, and the absence of a particular factor is not necessarily determinative of whether an arrangement is treated as a payment for services. Four of these factors, described by Congress in the legislative history to section 707(a)(2)(A), are (i) that the service provider holds, or is expected to hold, a transitory partnership interest or a partnership interest for only a short duration, (ii) that the service provider receives an allocation and distribution in a time frame comparable to the time frame that a non-partner service provider would typically receive payment, (iii) that the service provider became a partner primarily to obtain tax benefits which would not have been available if the services were rendered to the partnership in a third party capacity, and (iv) that the value of the service provider's interest in general and continuing partnership profits is small in relation to the allocation and distribution.

To these four factors, the proposed regulations add a fifth factor. The fifth factor is present if the arrangement provides for different allocations or distributions with respect to different services received, where the services are provided either by a single person or by persons that are related under sections 707(b) or 267(b), and the terms of the differing allocations or distributions are subject to levels of entrepreneurial risk that vary significantly. For example, assume that a partnership receives services from both its general partner and from a management company that is related to the general partner under section 707(b). Both the general partner and the management company receive a share in future partnership net profits in exchange for their services. The general partner is entitled to an allocation of 20 percent of net profits and undertakes an enforceable obligation to repay any amounts distributed pursuant to its interest (reduced by reasonable allowance for tax payments made on the general partner's allocable shares of partnership income and gain) that exceed 20 percent of the overall net amount of partnership profits computed over the partnership's life and it is reasonable to anticipate that the general partner can and will comply fully with this obligation. The proposed regulations refer to this type of obligation and similar obligations, as a "clawback obligation." In contrast, the management company is entitled to a preferred amount of net income that, once paid, is not subject to a clawback obligation. Because the general partner and the management company are service providers that are related parties under section 707(b), and because the terms of the allocations and distributions to the management company create a significantly lower level of economic risk than the terms for the general partner, the management company's arrangement might properly be treated as a disguised payment for services (depending on all other facts and circumstances, including amount of entrepreneurial risk).

III. *Examples*

Section 1.707-2(d) of the proposed regulations contains a number of examples illustrating the application of the factors described in § 1.707-2(c). The examples illustrate the application of these regulations to arrangements that contain certain facts and circumstances that the Treasury Department and the IRS believe demonstrate the existence or absence of significant entrepreneurial risk.

Several of the examples consider arrangements in which a partner agrees to forgo fees for services and also receives a share of future partnership income and gains. The examples consider the application of section 707(a)(2)(A) based on the manner in which the service provider (i) forgoes its right to receive fees, and (ii) is entitled to share in future partnership income and gains. In Examples 5 and 6, the service provider forgoes the right to receive fees in a manner that supports the existence of significant entrepreneurial risk by forgoing its right to receive fees before the period begins and by executing a waiver that is binding, irrevocable, and clearly communicated to the other partners. Similarly, the service provider's arrangement in these examples include the following facts and circumstances that taken together support the existence of significant entrepreneurial risk: the allocation to the service provider is determined out of net profits and is neither highly likely to be available nor reasonably determinable based on all facts and circumstances available at the time of the arrangement, and the service provider undertakes a clawback obligation and is reasonably expected to be able to comply with that obligation. The presence of each fact described in these examples is not necessarily required to determine that section 707(a)(2)(A) does not apply to an arrangement. However, the absence of certain facts, such as a failure to measure future profits over at least a 12-month period, may suggest that an arrangement constitutes a fee for services.

The proposed regulations also contain examples that consider arrangements to which section 707(a)(2)(A) applies. Example 1 concludes that an arrangement in which a service provider receives a capped amount of partnership allocations and distributions and the cap is likely to apply provides for a disguised payment for services under section 707(a)(2)(A). In Example 3(iii), a service provider is entitled to a share of future partnership net profits, the partnership can allocate net profits from specific transactions or accounting periods, those allocations do not depend on the long-term future success of the enterprise, and a party that is related to the service provider controls the timing of purchases, sales, and distributions. The example concludes that under these facts, the arrangement lacks significant entrepreneurial risk and provides for a disguised payment for services. Example 4 considers similar facts, but assumes that the partnership's assets are publicly traded and are marked-to-market under section 475(f)(1). Under these facts, the example concludes that the arrangement has significant entrepreneurial risk, and thus that section 707(a)(2)(A) does not apply.

IV. *Safe Harbor Revenue Procedures*

Rev. Proc. 93-27 provides that in certain circumstances if a person receives a profits interest for the provision of services to or for the benefit of a partnership in a partner capacity or in anticipation of becoming a partner, the IRS will not treat the receipt of such interest as a taxable event for the partner or the partnership. The revenue procedure does not apply if (1) the profits interest relates to a substantially certain and predictable stream of income from partnership assets, such as income from high-quality debt securities or a high-quality net lease; (2) within two years of receipt, the partner disposes of the profits interest; or (3) the profits interest is a limited partnership interest in a "publicly traded partnership" within the meaning of section 7704(b).

Rev. Proc. 2001-43 provides that, for purposes of Rev. Proc. 93-27, if a partnership grants a substantially nonvested profits interest in the partnership to a service provider, the service provider will be treated as receiving the interest on the date of its grant, provided that: (i) the partnership and the service provider treat the service provider as the owner of the partnership interest from the date of its grant, and the service provider takes into account the distributive share of partnership income, gain, loss, deduction and credit associated with that interest in computing the service provider's income tax liability for the entire period during which the service provider has the interest; (ii) upon the grant of the interest or at the time that the interest becomes substantially vested, neither the partnership nor any of the partners deducts any amount (as wages, compensation, or otherwise) for the fair market value of the interest; and (iii) all other conditions of Rev. Proc. 93-27 are satisfied.

The Treasury Department and the IRS are aware of transactions in which one party provides services and another party receives a seemingly associated allocation and distribution of partnership income or gain. For example, a management company that provides services to a fund in exchange for a fee may waive that fee, while a party related to the management company receives an interest in future partnership profits the value of which approximates the amount of the waived fee. The Treasury Department and the IRS have determined that Rev. Proc. 93-27 does not apply to such transactions because they would not satisfy the requirement that receipt of an interest in partnership profits be for the provision of services to or for the benefit of the partnership in a partner capacity or in anticipation of being a partner, and because the service provider would effectively have disposed of the partnership interest (through a constructive transfer to the related party) within two years of receipt.

Further, the Treasury Department and the IRS plan to issue a revenue procedure providing an additional exception to the safe harbor in Rev. Proc. 93-27 in conjunction with the publication of these regulations in final form. The additional exception will apply to a profits interest issued in conjunction with a partner forgoing payment of an amount that is substantially fixed (including a substantially fixed amount determined by formula, such as a fee based on a percentage of partner capital commitments) for the performance of services, including a guaranteed payment under section 707(c) or a payment in a non-partner capacity under section 707(a).

In conjunction with the issuance of proposed regulations (REG-105346-03; 70 FR 29675-01; 2005-1 C.B. 1244) relating to the tax treatment of certain transfers of partnership equity in connection with the performance of services, the Treasury Department and the IRS issued Notice 2005-43, 2005-24 I.R.B. 1221. Notice 2005-43 includes a proposed revenue procedure regarding partnership interests transferred in connection with the performance of services. In the event that the proposed revenue procedure provided for in Notice 2005-43 is finalized, it will include the additional exception referenced.

Effective Dates

The proposed regulations would be effective on the date the final regulations are published in the **Federal Register** and would apply to any arrangement entered into or modified on or after the date of publication of the final regulations. In the case of any arrangement entered into or modified before the final regulations are published in the **Federal Register**, the determination of whether an arrangement is a disguised payment for services under section 707(a)(2)(A) is made on the basis of the statute and the guidance provided regarding that provision in the legislative history of section 707(a)(2)(A). Pending the publication of final regulations, the position of the Treasury Department and the IRS is that the proposed regulations generally reflect Congressional intent as to which arrangements are appropriately treated as disguised payments for services.

Effect on Other Documents

The following publication is obsolete as of July 23, 2015:

Rev. Rul. 81-300 (1981-2 C.B. 143).

The following publications will be obsolete as of the date of a Treasury decision adopting these rules as final regulations in the **Federal Register**:

Rev. Rul. 66-95 (1966-1 C.B. 169); and

Rev. Rul. 69-180 (1969-1 C.B. 183).

Special Analyses

It has been determined that this notice of proposed rulemaking is not a significant regulatory action as defined in Executive Order 12866, as supplemented by Executive Order 13563. Therefore, a regulatory assessment is not required. It has also been determined that section 553(b) of the Administrative Procedure Act (5 U.S.C. chapter 5) does not apply to these regulations, and because the regulation does not impose a collection of information on small entities, the Regulatory Flexibility Act (5 U.S.C. chapter 6) does not apply. Pursuant to section 7805(f) of the Code, this notice of proposed rulemaking will be submitted to the Chief Counsel for Advocacy of the Small Business Administration for comment on its impact on small business.

Comments and Requests for Public Hearing

The Treasury Department and the IRS invite public comment on these proposed regulations. The legislative history supporting section 707(a)(2)(A) indicates that an arrangement that lacks significant entrepreneurial risk is generally treated as a disguised payment for services. The Treasury Department and the IRS have concluded that the presence of significant entrepreneurial risk in an arrangement is necessary for the arrangement to be treated as occurring between a partnership and a partner acting in a partner capacity. Nonetheless, the Treasury Department and the IRS request comments on, and examples of, whether arrangements could exist that should be treated as a distributive share under section 704(b) despite the absence of significant entrepreneurial risk. In addition, the Treasury Department and the IRS request comments on sufficient notification requirements to effectively render a fee waiver binding upon the service provider and the partnership.

The Treasury Department and the IRS have become aware that some partnerships that assert reliance on § 1.704-1(b)(2)(ii)(i) (the economic effect equivalence rule) have expressed uncertainty on the proper treatment of partners who receive an increased right to share in partnership property upon a partnership liquidation without respect to the partnership's net income. These partnerships typically set forth each partner's distribution rights upon a liquidation of the partnership and require the partnership to allocate net income annually in a manner that causes partners' capital accounts to match partnership distribution rights to the extent possible. Such agreements are commonly referred to as "targeted capital account agreements." Some taxpayers have expressed uncertainty whether a partnership with a targeted capital account agreement must allocate income or a guaranteed payment to a partner who has an increased right to partnership assets determined as if the partnership liquidated at the end of the year even in the event that the partnership recognizes no, or insufficient, net income. The Treasury Department and the IRS generally believe that existing rules under §§ 1.704-1(b)(2)(ii) and 1.707-1(c) address this circumstance by requiring partner capital accounts to reflect the partner's distribution rights as if the partnership liquidated at the end of the taxable year, but request comments on specific issues and examples with respect to which further guidance would be helpful. No inference is intended as to whether and when targeted capital account agreements could satisfy the economic effect equivalence rule.

Before these proposed regulations are adopted as final regulations, consideration will be given to any written (a signed original and eight (8) copies) or electronic comments that are submitted timely to the IRS. The Treasury Department and the IRS request comments on all aspects of the proposed regulations. All comments will be available for public inspection and copying upon request. A public hearing will be scheduled if requested in writing by any person that timely submits written or electronic comments. If a public hearing is scheduled, notice of the date, time, and place for the public hearing will be published in the **Federal Register**.

Drafting Information

The principal author of these proposed regulations is Jaclyn M. Goldberg of the Office Associate Chief Counsel (Passthroughs and Special Industries). However, other personnel from the Internal Revenue Service and the Treasury Department participated in their development.

[¶49,658] Proposed Amendments of Regulations and Partial Withdrawal of Notice of Proposed Regulations (REG-109370-10), published in the Federal Register on August 3, 2015 (corrected 10/29/2015).

[Code Sec. 706]

Tiered partnerships: Partnership income: Distributive share: Allocable cash basis: Partnership's tax year: Partners: Partner's tax year: Change of interest.—Reg. §§1.706-2 and 1.706-3 and amendments of 1.706-0, 1.706-2T, 1.706-3 and 1.706-4, during a partnership taxable year in which a partner's interest changes, are proposed. Amendments of Reg. §1.706-3(a), proposed on May 24, 2005, are withdrawn.

AGENCY: Internal Revenue Service (IRS), Treasury.

ACTION: Partial withdrawal of notice of proposed rulemaking and notice of proposed rulemaking.

SUMMARY: This document contains proposed regulations regarding the determination of a partner's distributive share of certain allocable cash basis items and items attributable to an interest in a lower-tier partnership during a partnership taxable year in which a partner's interest changes. These proposed regulations affect partnerships and their partners.

DATES: Written or electronic comments and requests for a public hearing must be received by November 2, 2015. As of August 3, 2015, the notice of proposed rulemaking that was published in the **Federal Register** on May 24, 2005 (70 FR 29675), is partially withdrawn.

ADDRESSES: Send submissions to: CC:PA:LPD:PR (REG-109370-10), room 5203, Internal Revenue Service, PO Box 7604, Ben Franklin Station, Washington, DC 20044. Submissions may be hand-delivered Monday through Friday between the hours of 8 a.m. and 4 p.m. to:. CC:PA:LPD:PR (REG-109370-10), Courier's Desk, Internal Revenue Service, 1111 Constitution Avenue, NW, Washington, DC, or sent electronically, via the Federal eRulemaking Portal at http://www.regulations.gov/ (IRS REG-109370-10).

FOR FURTHER INFORMATION CONTACT: Concerning the proposed regulations, Benjamin H. Weaver, (202) 317-6850; concerning submissions of comments and requests for public hearing, Regina Johnson, (202) 317-6901 (not toll free numbers).

SUPPLEMENTARY INFORMATION:

Background

Section 706 of the Internal Revenue Code (the Code) generally provides rules for the taxable years of partners and partnerships. Section 72 of the Deficit Reduction Act of 1984, Public Law 98-369 (98 Stat. 494 (1984)) added section 706(d) to the Code to prevent a partner who acquires an interest in the partnership late in the taxable year from deducting partnership expenses incurred prior to the partner's entry into the partnership (retroactive allocations). Section 706(d)(1) provides that, except as provided in section 706(d)(2) and (d)(3), if during any taxable year of the partnership there is a change in any partner's interest in the partnership, each partner's distributive share of any item of income, gain, loss, deduction, or credit of the partnership for such taxable year shall be determined by the use of any method prescribed by regulations which takes into account the varying interests of the partners in the partnership during such taxable year.

On April 14, 2009, the Treasury Department and the IRS published a notice of proposed rulemaking (REG-144689-04) (the 2009 proposed regulations) in the **Federal Register** to provide guidance under section 706(d)(1) and to conform the Income Tax Regulations for certain provisions of section 1246 of the Taxpayer Relief Act of 1997, Public Law 105-34 (111 Stat. 788 (1997)) and section 72 of the Deficit Reduction Act of 1984, Public Law 98-369 (98 Stat. 494 (1984)). The Treasury Department and the IRS are publishing final regulations under section 706(d)(1) (the final regulations) contemporaneously with these proposed regulations. However, the Treasury Department and the IRS have decided to propose an amendment to the final regulations expanding the list of extraordinary items to include two new items: (1) for publicly traded partnerships, any item of income that is an amount subject to withholding as defined in §1.1441-2(a) (excluding amounts effectively connected with the conduct of a trade or business within the United States) or a withholdable payment under §1.1473-1(a) occurring during a taxable year if, for that taxable year, the partners agree to treat all such items as extraordinary items, and (2) for any partnership, deductions for the transfer of partnership equity in connection with the performance of services. In addition, these proposed regulations provide guidance under sections 706(d)(2) and (3).

1. *Allocable cash basis items*

Section 706(d)(2) provides rules for certain allocable cash basis items. Section 706(d)(2)(A) provides that if during any taxable year of the partnership there is a change in any partner's interest in the partnership, then (except to the extent provided in regulations) each partner's distributive share of any allocable cash basis item shall be determined (i) by assigning the appropriate portion of such item to each day in the period to which it is attributable, and (ii) by allocating the portion assigned to any such day among the partners in proportion to their interests in the partnership at the close of such day. Section 706(d)(2)(B) defines "allocable cash basis item" as any of the following items with respect to which the partnership uses the cash receipts and disbursements method of accounting (cash method): (i) interest, (ii) taxes, (iii) payments for services or for the use of property, or (iv) any other item of a kind specified in regulations prescribed by the Secretary as being an item with respect to which the application of section 706(d)(2) is appropriate to avoid significant misstatements of the income of the partners. Section 706(d)(2)(C) further provides that if any portion of any allocable cash basis item is attributable to (i) any period before the beginning of the taxable year, such portion shall be assigned under section 706(d)(2)(A)(i) to the first day of the taxable year, or (ii) any period after the close of the taxable year, such portion shall be assigned under section 706(d)(2)(A)(i) to the last day of the taxable year. Finally, section 706(d)(2)(D) provides that if any portion of a deductible cash basis item is assigned under section 706(d)(2)(C)(i) to the first day of any taxable year, (i) such portion shall be allocated among persons who are partners in the partnership during the period to which such portion is attributable in accordance with their varying interests in the partnership during such period, and (ii) any amount allocated under section 706(d)(2)(D)(i) to a person who is not a partner in the partnership on such first day shall be capitalized by the partnership and treated in the manner provided for in section 755.

The legislative history explains that section 706(d)(2) was enacted to prevent cash method partnerships from avoiding the retroactive allocation rules:

> [P]artnerships may attempt to avoid the retroactive allocation rules by using the cash method of accounting and deferring actual payment of deductible items until near the close of the partnership's taxable year. For example, if a partnership defers the payment of an expense (e.g., interest) until December 31, and the partnership uses the interim closing method of allocations, a partner admitted on December 31 may be allowed a deduction for a full portion of the expense. This may be the case although the expense has economically accrued at an equal rate throughout the taxable year . . . In adding these rules, Congress rejected the argument that the retroactive allocations were proper because the funds invested by the new partners served to reimburse the original partners for their expenditures so that, as an economic matter, the new partners had incurred the costs for which they were claiming deductions.

H.R. Rep. No. 98-432, at 1212-1213 (1984).

On November 30, 1984, the Treasury Department and the IRS issued temporary regulations under section 706(d)(2) (§1.706-2T (TD 7991)) to address the interaction of sections 706(d)(2) and 267(a)(2). The temporary regulations provide that a deduction for any expense that is deferred under section 267 constitutes an allocable cash basis item under section 706(d)(2)(B)(iv). Specifically, the temporary regulations provide:

> Question 1: For purposes of section 706(d), how is an otherwise deductible amount that is deferred under section 267(a)(2) treated?
>
> Answer 1: In the year the deduction is allowed, the deduction will constitute an allocable cash basis item under section 706(d)(2)(B)(iv).

Neither the 2009 proposed regulations nor the final regulations provide guidance under section 706(d)(2). However, the 2009 proposed regulations specifically requested comments on issues that arise concerning allocable cash basis items, in particular whether the list of items in section 706(d)(2)(B) should be expanded (to include, for example, items such as property insurance), as well as any other issues with regard to allocating cash basis items. The Treasury Department and the IRS received comments relating to allocable cash basis items in response to the 2009 proposed regulations. The comments are discussed in this preamble.

2. *Tiered Partnerships*

Section 706(a) provides that, in computing the taxable income of a partner for a taxable year, the inclusions required by section 702 and section 707(c) with respect to a partnership shall be based on the income, gain, loss, deduction, or credit of the partnership for any taxable year of the partnership ending within or with the taxable year of the partner. Prior to the issuance of Rev. Rul. 77-311, 1977-2 CB 218, in 1977 and the enactment of section 706(d)(3) in 1984, some taxpayers took the position that, in the case of tiered partnerships, the language of section 706(a) means that an upper-tier partnership's distributive share of items from a lower-tier partnership is sustained by the upper-tier partnership on the last day of the lower-tier partnership's taxable year. These taxpayers therefore allocated the upper-tier partnership's share of the lower-tier partnership's items based solely upon the upper-tier partnership's partners' interests as of the last day of the lower-tier partnerships' taxable year. Rev. Rul. 77-311 rejected that position, and explains through an example that an upper-tier partnership's distributive share of any items of income, gain, loss, deduction, or credit from a lower-tier partnership is considered to be realized or sustained by the upper-tier partnership at the same time and in the same manner as such items were realized or sustained by the lower-tier partnership. Therefore, in allocating items from a lower-tier partnership, the upper-tier partnership must take into account variations among its partners' interests throughout the year, rather than merely looking to its partners' interests as of the last day of the lower-tier partnership's taxable year.

Section 706(d)(3) was enacted in 1984 and confirms the analysis of Rev. Rul. 77-311. Section 706(d)(3) provides that if during any taxable year of the partnership there is a change in any partner's interest in the partnership (the "upper-tier partnership"), and such partnership is a partner in another partnership (the "lower-tier partnership"), then (except to the extent provided in regulations) each partner's distributive share of any item of the upper-tier partnership attributable to the lower-tier partnership shall be determined by assigning the appropriate portion (determined by applying principles similar to the principles of section 706(d)(2)(C) and (D)) of each such item to the appropriate days during which the upper-tier partnership is a partner in the lower-tier partnership and by allocating the portion assigned to any such day among the partners in proportion to their interests in the upper-tier partnership at the close of such day.

Neither the 2009 proposed regulations nor the final regulations provide guidance under section 706(d)(3). However, the 2009 proposed regulations specifically requested comments on issues that arise concerning tiered partnerships, and stated that the daily allocation method, used for cash basis items, applies to all items of the lower-tier partnership if there is a change in the partnership interests in the upper-tier partnership. The Treasury Department and the IRS received comments relating to tiered partnerships in response to the 2009 proposed regulations. The comments are discussed in this preamble.

Explanation of Provisions and Summary of Comments

1. *Allocable cash basis items*

With respect to allocable cash basis items, the proposed regulations generally restate the statutory provisions. Commenters requested that regulations clarify whether section 706(d)(2) applies only to items of deduction and loss or whether it also applies to items of income and gain. Generally, under the Code, the word "item" includes items of income, gain, deduction, and loss. Other than the item "taxes," the items listed in section 706(d)(2)(B) can be either items of income (and gain) or deduction (and loss), depending on a taxpayer's particular circumstances. Section 706(d)(2)(B)(iv) also provides broad regulatory authority for the Secretary to add "any other item . . . with respect to which the application of this paragraph is appropriate to avoid significant misstatements of the income of the partners." A significant misstatement of the income of partners can occur equally through an item of deduction or loss or an item of income or gain. Partnerships using the cash method that also use the interim closing method for accounting for partners' varying interests can use this distortion to affect the allocation of income to an incoming or outgoing partner. For these reasons, the proposed regulations provide that the allocable cash basis item rules apply to items of deduction, loss, income, and gain.

The proposed regulations provide that the term "allocable cash basis item" generally includes items of deduction, loss, income, or gain specifically listed in the statute: (i) interest, (ii) taxes, and (iii) payments for services or for the use of property. However, as discussed in part 4 of this preamble, the proposed regulations contain an exception for deductions for the transfer of an interest in the partnership in connection with the performance of services; such deductions generally must be allocated under the rules for extraordinary items in § 1.706-4(d).

Section 706(d)(2)(B)(iv) specifically grants the Secretary regulatory authority to include additional items in the list of allocable cash basis items to avoid significant misstatements of the income of the partners. Pursuant to the regulatory authority granted in section 706(d)(2)(B)(iv), the proposed regulations provide that the term "allocable cash basis item" includes any allowable deduction that had been previously deferred under section 267(a)(2). This provision incorporates the concept of § 1.706-2T and includes within the meaning of "allocable cash basis item" amounts deferred under section 267(a)(2) in the year in which the deduction is allowed. Accordingly, § 1.706-2T is proposed to be withdrawn by final regulations issued under section 706(d)(2).

Finally, pursuant to the regulatory authority granted in section 706(d)(2)(B)(iv), the proposed regulations provide that the term "allocable cash basis item" also includes any item of income, gain, loss, or deduction that accrues over time and that would, if not allocated as an allocable cash basis item, result in the significant misstatement of a partner's income. To provide additional clarification on the scope of the rule in proposed § 1.706-2(a)(2)(v), the Treasury Department and the IRS believe that items such as rebate payments, refund payments, insurance premiums, prepayments, and cash advances are examples of items which, if not allocated in the manner described in section 706(d)(2), could result in the significant misstatement of a partner's income. The Treasury Department and the IRS request comments on the inclusion of these items and other items within the meaning of "allocable cash basis items."

One commenter noted that section 706(d)(2) imposes the same administrative burden on partnerships regardless of the percentage of the partner's total expenses that are allocable cash basis items and therefore recommended that regulations under section 706(d)(2) include a de minimis rule. The Treasury Department and the IRS agree that a de minimis rule is appropriate given the scope of the proposed regulations. Accordingly, the proposed regulations provide that an allocable cash basis item will not be subject to the rules in section 706(d)(2) if, for the partnership's taxable year: (1) the total of the particular class of allocable cash basis items (for example, all interest income) is less than five percent of the partnership's (a) gross income, including tax-exempt income described in section 705(a)(1)(B), in the case of income or gain items, or (b) gross expenses and losses, including section

705(a)(2)(B) expenditures, in the case of losses and expense items; and (2) the total amount of allocable cash basis items from all classes of allocable cash basis items amounting to less than five percent of the partnership's (a) gross income, including tax-exempt income described in section 705(a)(1)(B), in the case of income or gain items, or (b) gross expenses and losses, including section 705(a)(2)(B) expenditures, in the case of losses and expense items, does not exceed $10 million in the taxable year, determined by treating all such allocable cash basis items as positive amounts.

Additionally, the Treasury Department and the IRS request comments on whether the final regulations should provide an exception for certain items of income or deduction arising from payments for services or for the use of property. For example, comments are requested on whether payments for services or for the use of property should be excluded from the rules in section 706(d)(2) if they arise and are, as applicable, paid or received in the ordinary course of the partnership's business (such as the regular payment of wages to employees), and whether deferred compensation or contingency or success-based fees and other payments for services based on performance conditions (which are not calculated based on an hourly rate) should be subject to the rules of section 706(d)(2) (and, if so, on the proper method for assigning the appropriate portion of such item to each day in the period).

The proposed regulations contain two examples illustrating the operation of section 706(d)(2)(D)(ii), which requires certain portions of deductible cash basis items to be capitalized in the manner provided in section 755 in the event that the deduction is otherwise partially allocable to a former partner who is no longer a partner as of the first day of the partnership's taxable year. The Treasury Department and the IRS request comments on the appropriate interaction between the principles and rules of section 755 and section 706(d), including whether the final regulations should provide an exception to the capitalization rules of section 706(d)(2)(D)(ii) in cases where the former partner ceased to be a partner in the partnership as a result of the partner's contribution of its partnership interest to another entity in a non-recognition transaction.

2. *Tiered Partnerships*

With respect to tiered partnerships, the proposed regulations provide that the daily allocation method used for cash basis items applies to all items of the lower-tier partnership if there is a change in any partner's interest in the upper-tier partnership.

Commenters noted the administrative burden of the daily allocation method on tiered partnerships. Commenters stated that obtaining information from a lower-tier partnership to track changes in the ownership interest in an upper-tier partnership is burdensome, and often impractical, unless the upper-tier partnership owns a controlling interest in the lower-tier partnership. One commenter suggested that the Treasury Department and the IRS issue interim guidance to provide that section 706(d)(3) should not apply to a change in a partner's interest in an upper-tier partnership unless the upper-tier partnership owns an interest in more than 50 percent of the profits and capital of the lower-tier partnership. Another commenter recommended an exception when the upper-tier partnership owns a relatively small portion (such as 10 percent or less) of the lower-tier partnership. The Treasury Department and the IRS acknowledge that a lack of information sharing among tiered partnerships may make it difficult to comply with a daily allocation requirement. Thus, the proposed regulations provide an exception from section 706(d)(3) if the upper-tier partnership directly owns an interest in less than 10 percent of the profits and capital of the lower-tier partnership ("a de minimis upper-tier partnership"), all de minimis upper-tier partnerships in aggregate own an interest in less than 30 percent of the profits and capital of the lower-tier partnership, and if no partnership is created with a purpose of avoiding the application of the tiered partnership rules of section 706(d)(3). The application of this exception is determined at each tier, depending on the interests held by the direct partners at each tier. Thus, in the case of an upper-tier partnership owning an interest in a middle tier partnership, which in turn owns an interest in a lower-tier partnership, it may be the case that the exception applies to the upper-tier partnership's interest in the middle tier partnership, but not to the middle tier partnership's interest in the lower-tier partnership (or vice-versa).

If the de minimis upper-tier partnership exception applies, the upper-tier partnership may, but is not required to, apply the general rules of § 1.706-4 in allocating items attributable to the lower-tier partnership. However, as explained in Rev. Rul. 77-311, an upper-tier partnership's distributive share of any items of income, gain, loss, deduction, or credit from a lower-tier partnership is considered to be realized or sustained by the upper-tier partnership at the same time and in the same manner as such items were realized or sustained by the lower-tier partnership. Thus, if the de minimis upper-tier partnership exception applies to an upper-tier partnership using the interim closing method, the upper-tier partnership's allocations of the lower-tier partnership items under the general rules of § 1.706-4 will generally reach the same result as applying the rules of section 706(d)(3). On the other hand, if the de minimis upper-tier partnership exception applies to an upper-tier partnership using the proration method, the upper-tier partnership may prorate the items from the lower-tier partnership across the upper-tier partnership's segments (or, if the upper-tier partnership has only one segment for its entire taxable year, it may prorate the items across its entire taxable year). Even if the de minimis upper-tier partnership exception applies, the upper-tier partnership may choose to allocate the items attributable to the lower-tier partnership according the tiered partnership rules instead. However, the proposed regulations do not impose on lower-tier partnerships an obligation to disclose to upper-tier partnerships the timing of the lower-tier partnership's items. The proposed regulations contain three examples illustrating these principles.

Commenters also requested additional guidance on the application of section 706(d)(3) in certain circumstances. One commenter requested that the final regulations provide guidance on tiered partnerships that would allow an upper-tier partnership to determine the items from the lower-tier partnership that are allocable to the upper-tier partnership segments based on an interim closing method (as of any upper-tier partnership segment end) applied to the lower-tier partnership if the upper-tier partnership: (i) has the same taxable year as its lower-tier partnership; (ii) holds a fixed percentage interest in the lower-tier partnership during a taxable year; and (iii) uses the interim closing method. This commenter also recommended that guidance provide that an upper-tier partnership that has the same taxable year as its lower-tier partnership and holds a fixed percentage interest in that lower-tier partnership during the upper-tier partnership's taxable year may prorate the non-extraordinary items of the lower-tier partnership to each day of the upper-tier partnership's taxable year, without regard to whether the upper-tier partnership uses the proration method or the interim closing method.

However, as explained in this preamble, the Treasury Department and the IRS believe that because an upper-tier partnership's distributive share of any items of income, gain, loss, deduction, or credit from a lower-tier partnership is considered to be realized or sustained by the upper-tier partnership at the same time and in the same manner as such items were realized or sustained by the lower-tier partnership, application of the interim closing method will generally reach the same result as applying the rules of section 706(d)(3). The Treasury Department and the IRS also believe that allowing an upper-tier partnership that uses the interim closing method to prorate items from a lower-tier partnership across the upper-tier partnership's entire taxable year would be inconsistent with the principles explained in Rev. Rul. 77-311. Therefore, the proposed regulations do not adopt these comments. However, the Treasury Department and the IRS request comments on safe harbors that might be appropriate in these circumstances as well as comments on the treatment of an upper-tier partnership and a lower-tier partnership that have different taxable years.

One commenter also recommended that guidance provide that the default method for tiered partnerships is the proration method unless the upper-tier partnership agrees to use the interim closing method and receives sufficient information from the lower-tier partnership to use that method. Under section 706(d)(1) as implemented by § 1.706-4, the interim closing method is the default method unless the partners agree in writing to use the proration method. Because the recommended rule would be inconsistent with section 706(d)(1) as implemented by § 1.706-4, the Treasury Department and the IRS did not adopt this rule in the proposed regulations.

A commenter further recommended that any conventions applicable to the upper-tier partnership should apply to income from the lower-tier partnership. In general, the Treasury Department and the IRS believe that any conventions applicable to the upper-tier partnership should apply to items from the lower-tier partnership, but are continuing to consider this recommendation in the context of section 706(d)(3) and request comments on safe harbors when the upper-tier partnership and the lower-tier partnership use the same method, but different conventions.

Another commenter recommended that the final regulations permit partnerships to voluntarily apply the rules of section 706(d)(3) if the upper-tier partnership and the lower-tier partnership have an advance agreement establishing the allocation method for items derived from the upper-tier partnership's interest in the lower-tier partnership. As described in this preamble, the Treasury Department and the IRS are requesting comments on appropriate safe harbors and will continue to consider this recommendation.

The Treasury Department and the IRS also request comments on appropriate rules, if any, when there is a variance at both the upper-tier partnership and lower-tier partnership.

More generally, the Treasury Department and the IRS request comments on the appropriate coordination between the rules of sections 706(d)(2) and (3) and the rules of § 1.706-4. In particular, the Treasury Department and the IRS request comments on whether certain items such as contingency or success-based fees and other payments for services based on performance conditions are more appropriately addressed under the rules of section 706(d)(2) and (3), which require allocation of items across the period to which they are attributable, or under the rules for the allocation of extraordinary items under § 1.706-4(e), which requires allocation of items according to the partners' interests at the time of day on which the extraordinary item occurs. Additionally, the Treasury Department and the IRS request comments on whether certain items subject to section 706(d)(2) and (3) may instead be simply allocated under the proration method of § 1.706-4(d) without impinging on the Congressional intent behind sections 706(d)(2) and (3) or resulting in a substantial distortion of income.

3. *Additional Extraordinary Item for Publicly Traded Partnerships (PTPs)*

Section 1.706-4(e) of the final regulations provides rules for the allocation of certain "extraordinary items." In general, extraordinary items must be allocated among the partners in proportion to their interests in the partnership item at the time of day on which the extraordinary item occurs. Section 1.706-4(e)(2) contains a list of extraordinary items. These proposed regulations add two additional extraordinary items to that list.

The first proposed additional extraordinary item responds to comments received on the 2009 proposed regulations regarding the administrative difficulty PTPs face in satisfying withholding obligations under section 1441 if PTPs are not permitted to use a quarterly convention. As explained in Part 1.C.iii of the preamble to the final regulations, the final regulations do not permit PTPs to use a quarterly convention. One commenter on the 2009 proposed regulations suggested other options of addressing this issue if the Treasury Department and the IRS are concerned that allowing a quarterly convention would be too broad. One option suggested was to permit PTPs that have income subject to withholding under section 1441 to treat that income as an extraordinary item allocated to PTP unit holders who are the record holders on the date the distribution is declared. The Treasury Department and the IRS agree that a special rule is desirable to link each partner's distributive share to the related cash distributions, thereby enabling PTPs and their transfer agents to satisfy their withholding obligations under chapter 4 of the Code and sections 1441 through 1443 from distributions. Therefore, these proposed regulations generally adopt this suggested alternative to a quarterly convention.

Specifically, these proposed regulations provide that for PTPs, all items of income that are amounts subject to withholding as defined in § 1.1441-2(a) (excluding income effectively connected with the conduct of a trade or business within the United States) or withholdable payments under § 1.1473-1(a) occurring during a taxable year may be treated as extraordinary items if the partners agree (within the meaning of § 1.706-4(f)) to consistently treat all such items as extraordinary items for that taxable year. If the partners so agree, then for purposes of section 706 such items shall be treated as occurring at the next time as of which the recipients of a distribution by the PTP are determined, or, to the extent such income items arise between the final time during the taxable year as of which the recipients of a distribution are determined and the end of the taxable year, such items shall be treated as occurring at the final time during the taxable year as of which the recipients of a distribution by the PTP are determined. However, this rule does not apply unless the PTP has a regular practice of making at least four distributions (other than de minimis distributions) to its partners each taxable year. The proposed regulations contain an example illustrating this rule.

The final regulations generally require extraordinary items to be allocated without regard to the partnership's method or convention. However, § 1.706-4(e)(1) of the final regulations provides that PTPs may, but are not required to, respect the applicable conventions in determining who held their publicly traded units at the time of the occurrence of an extraordinary item. The Treasury Department and the IRS believe that this exception should be turned off for all items subject to the new proposed extraordinary item rule for PTPs to ensure that each partner's distributive share of such items is linked to the related cash distributions. Accordingly, the proposed regulations modify the rule in § 1.706-4(e)(1) to provide that PTPs that choose to treat items subject to withholding under section 1441 as extraordinary items must allocate those items among the partners in proportion to their interests in those items at the time as of which the recipients of the relevant distribution are determined, regardless of the method and convention otherwise used by the PTP.

Taxpayers may rely on this proposed additional extraordinary item until final regulations are published. The proposed regulations do not use the phrase "record holders on the date the distribution is declared," because the Treasury Department and the IRS understand that the recipients of a distribution by a PTP may be determined as of a time other than on the date the distribution is declared. The Treasury Department and the IRS request comments on the operation of this special rule, and on the interaction between the rules under section 706 and PTP allocations generally.

4. *Coordination with proposed Partnership Equity for Services regulations*

On May 24, 2005, the Treasury Department and the IRS published a notice of proposed rulemaking (REG-105346-03, 70 FR 29675) in the **Federal Register,** the proposed Partnership Equity for Services regulations, relating to the tax treatment of certain transfers of partnership interests in connection with the performance of services. The proposed Partnership Equity for Services regulations provide rules for coordinating section 83 with partnership taxation principles. On June 13, 2005, the Treasury Department and the IRS published Notice 2005-43, I.R.B. 2005-24, setting forth a proposed revenue procedure providing additional related guidance. The proposed Partnership Equity for Services regulations and the proposed revenue procedure are not effective until finalized. Notice 2005-43 provides that, until then, taxpayers may continue to rely on Rev. Proc. 93-27, 1993-2 C.B. 343, and Rev. Proc. 2001-43, 2001-2 C.B. 191. The Treasury Department and the IRS continue to consider the interaction of section 83 with partnership taxation principles. No inferences should be drawn from these proposed regulations as to the resolution of the issues addressed in the proposed Partnership Equity for Services regulations or any other related issues.

The proposed Partnership Equity for Services regulations contain two provisions relating to the varying interest rule under section 706. First, proposed § 1.706-3(a) of the proposed Partnership Equity for Services regulations is intended to provide an exception to the allocable cash basis item rules of section 706(d)(2) for deductions for the transfer of partnership interests and other property subject to section 83. The preamble to the proposed Partnership Equity for Services regulations indicates that the exception was intended to allow partnerships to allocate such deductions under a closing of the books method. The preamble indicates that the Treasury Department and the IRS had concluded that, absent treatment under the allocable cash basis item rules of section 706(d)(2), the application of section 706(d)(1) would adequately ensure that partnership deductions that are attributable to the portion of the partnership's taxable year prior to a new partner's entry into the partnership are allocated to the historic partners.

The Treasury Department and the IRS have concluded that, in the case of a transfer of a partnership interest in connection with the performance of services, no portion of the partnership's deduction should be allocated to the person who performs the services. However, the Treasury Department and the IRS have also concluded that the scope of the exception to allocable cash basis treatment in proposed § 1.706-3(a) may have been too broad because it applies to all transfers of property subject to section 83, for which the Treasury Department and the IRS request comments under these proposed regulations. Therefore, the Treasury Department and the IRS withdraw proposed § 1.706-3(a). Instead, these proposed regulations provide an exception to allocable cash basis treatment for deductions for transfers of partnership interests in connection with the performance of services. Additionally, to ensure that such deductions are allocated solely to partners other than the person who performed the services, the proposed regulations add to the list of extraordinary items in § 1.706-4(e)(2) any deduction for the transfer of an interest in the partnership in connection with the performance of services, and clarify that such extraordinary item is treated as occurring immediately before the transfer or vesting of the partnership interest that results in compensation income for the person who performs the services.

As explained in the final § 1.706-4 in the Rules and Regulations section of this issue of the Federal Register, extraordinary items generally must be allocated among the partners in proportion to their interests in the partnership item at the time of day on which the extraordinary item occurs. However, there are exceptions to the extraordinary item rules for certain small items in § 1.704-4(e)(3) and for partnerships for which capital is not a material income-producing factor in § 1.706-4(b)(2)). To ensure that partnership deductions attributable to the transfer of interests in the partnership in connection with the performance of services are always allocated solely to the historic partners, the proposed regulations turn off these exceptions to extraordinary item treatment for such deductions. Thus, treatment as an extraordinary item subject to the special timing rule will ensure that, for both accrual and cash-method partnerships, no portion of the deduction for the transfer of a partnership interest in connection with the performance of services will be allocated to the person who performs the services.

Second, proposed § 1.706-3(b) of the proposed Partnership Equity for Services regulations provides that a partnership must make certain forfeiture allocations upon forfeiture of a partnership interest for which a section 83(b) election was made. In particular, proposed § 1.706-3(b) provides that although the person forfeiting the interest may not have been a partner for the entire taxable year, forfeiture allocations may be made out of the partnership's items for the entire taxable year. The Treasury Department and the IRS anticipate that if the rules for forfeiture allocations in proposed § 1.706-3(b) are adopted when the proposed Partnership Equity for Services regulations are finalized, those rules will include in § 1.706-3(b) an additional exception to the general application of the varying interest rule. In the meantime, these proposed regulations move § 1.706-3(b) of the proposed Partnership Equity for Services regulations to new proposed § 1.706-6(a) to accommodate the new proposed regulations in § 1.706-3.

Proposed Effective Date

The regulations are proposed to apply to partnership taxable years beginning on or after the date of publication of the Treasury decision adopting these regulations as final regulations in the **Federal Register**.

Reliance on Proposed Regulations

Taxpayers may rely on § § 1.706-4(e)(1) and 1.706-4(e)(2)(ix) of the proposed regulations (relating to a publicly traded partnership's treatment of all amounts subject to withholding as defined in § 1.1441-2(a) that are not effectively connected with the conduct of a trade or business within the United States or withholdable payments under § 1.1473-1(a) as extraordinary items) until final regulations are issued.

Special Analyses

It has been determined that this notice of proposed rulemaking is not a significant regulatory action as defined in Executive Order 12866, as supplemented by Executive Order 13563. Therefore, a regulatory assessment is not required. It has also been determined that section 553(b) of the Administrative Procedure Act (5 U.S.C. chapter 5) does not apply to this proposed regulation, and because this proposed regulation does not impose a collection of information on small entities, the Regulatory Flexibility Act (5 U.S.C. chapter 6) does not apply. Pursuant to section 7805(f) of the Code, these regulations have been submitted to the Chief Counsel for Advocacy of the Small Business Administration for comment on its impact on small business.

Comments and Requests for a Public Hearing

Before these proposed regulations are adopted as final regulations, consideration will be given to any written comments (a signed original and eight (8) copies) or electronic comments that are submitted timely to the IRS. The Treasury Department and the IRS specifically request comments on the clarity of the proposed rules and how they can be made easier to understand. All comments will be available for public inspection and copying. A public hearing will be scheduled if requested in writing by any person that timely submits written comments. If a public hearing is scheduled, notice of the date, time, and place for the public hearing will be published in the **Federal Register**.

Drafting Information

The principal author of these proposed regulations is Benjamin H. Weaver, Office of the Associate Chief Counsel (Passthroughs and Special Industries). However, other personnel from the Treasury Department and the IRS participated in their development.

[¶49,661] Proposed Amendments of Regulations (REG-136459-09), published in the Federal Register on August 27, 2015.

[Code Sec. 199]

Business expenses: Deductions: Domestic production activities (DPA): Claiming the DPA deduction.—Amendments of Reg. §§1.199-0, 1.199-1, 1.199-2, 1.199-3, 1.199-4, 1.199-6 and 1.199-8, involving the domestic production activities deduction under section 199 of the Internal Revenue Code (Code), are proposed.

AGENCY: Internal Revenue Service (IRS), Treasury.

ACTION: Notice of proposed rulemaking, notice of proposed rulemaking by cross reference to temporary regulations and notice of public hearing.

SUMMARY: This document contains proposed regulations involving the domestic production activities deduction under section 199 of the Internal Revenue Code (Code). The proposed regulations provide guidance to taxpayers on the amendments made to section 199 by the Energy Improvement and Extension Act of 2008 and the Tax Extenders and Alternative Minimum Tax Relief Act of 2008, involving oil related qualified production activities income and qualified films, and the American Taxpayer Relief Act of 2012, involving activities in Puerto Rico. The proposed regulations also provide guidance on: determining domestic production gross receipts; the terms manufactured, produced, grown, or extracted; contract manufacturing; hedging transactions; construction activities; allocating cost of goods sold; and agricultural and horticultural cooperatives. In the Rules and Regulations of this issue of the **Federal Register**, the Treasury Department and the IRS also are issuing temporary regulations (TD 9731) clarifying how taxpayers calculate W-2 wages for purposes of the W-2 wage limitation in the case of a short taxable year or an acquisition or disposition of a trade or business (including the major portion of a trade or business, or the major portion of a separate unit of a trade or business) during the taxable year. This document also contains a notice of a public hearing on the proposed regulations.

DATES: Written or electronic comments must be received by November 27, 2015. Outlines of topics to be discussed at the public hearing scheduled for December 16, 2015, at 10:00 am, must be received by November 27, 2015.

ADDRESSES: Send submissions to: CC:PA:LPD:PR (REG-136459-09), room 5203, Internal Revenue Service, P.O. Box 7604, Ben Franklin Station, Washington, DC 20044. Submissions may be hand-delivered Monday through Friday between the hours of 8 a.m. and 4 p.m. to CC:PA:LPD:PR (REG-136459-09), Courier's Desk, Internal Revenue Service, 1111 Constitution Avenue, NW., Washington, DC, or sent electronically, via the Federal eRulemaking Portal at *http://www.regulations.gov* (IRS REG-136459-09). The public hearing will be held in the Auditorium of the Internal Revenue Building, 1111 Constitution Avenue, NW., Washington, DC.

FOR FURTHER INFORMATION CONTACT: Concerning §§1.199-1(f), 1.199-2(c), 1.199-2(e), 1.199-2(f), 1.199-3(b), 1.199-3(e), 1.199-3(h), 1.199-3(k), 1.199-3(m), 1.199-6(m), and 1.199-8(i) of the proposed regulations, James Holmes, (202) 317-4137; concerning §1.199-4(b) of the proposed regulations, Natasha Mulleneaux (202) 317-7007; concerning submissions of comments, the hearing, or to be placed on the building access list to attend the hearing, Regina Johnson, at (202) 317-6901 (not toll-free numbers).

SUPPLEMENTARY INFORMATION:

Background

This document contains proposed amendments to §§1.199-0, 1.199-1, 1.199-2, 1.199-3, 1.199-4(b), 1.199-6, and 1.199-8(i) of the Income Tax Regulations (26 CFR part 1). Section 1.199-1 relates to income that is attributable to domestic production activities. Section 1.199-2 relates to W-2 wages as defined in section 199(b). Section 1.199-3 relates to determining domestic production gross receipts (DPGR). Section 1.199-4(b) describes the costs of goods sold allocable to DPGR. Section 1.199-6 applies to agricultural and horticultural cooperatives. Section 1.199-8(i) provides the effective/applicability dates.

Section 199 was added to the Code by section 102 of the American Jobs Creation Act of 2004 (Public Law 108-357, 118 Stat. 1418 (2004)), and amended by section 403(a) of the Gulf Opportunity Zone Act of 2005 (Public Law 109-135, 119 Stat. 25 (2005)), section 514 of the Tax Increase Prevention and Reconciliation Act of 2005 (Public Law 109-222, 120 Stat. 345 (2005)), section 401 of the Tax Relief and Health Care Act of 2006 (Public Law 109-432, 120 Stat. 2922 (2006)), section 401(a), Division B of the Energy Improvement and Extension Act of 2008 (Public Law 110-343, 122 Stat. 3765 (2008)) (Energy Extension Act of 2008), sections 312(a) and 502(c), Division C of the Tax Extenders and Alternative Minimum Tax Relief Act of 2008 (Public Law 110-343, 122 Stat. 3765 (2008)) (Tax Extenders Act of 2008), section 746(a) of the Tax Relief, Unemployment Insurance Reauthorization, and Job Creation Act of 2010 (Public Law 111-312, 124 Stat. 3296 (2010)), section 318 of the American Taxpayer Relief Act of 2012 (Public Law 112-240, 126 Stat. 2313 (2013)), and sections 130 and 219(b) of the Tax Increase Prevention Act of 2014 (Public Law 113-295, 128 Stat. 4010 (2014)).

General Overview

Section 199(a)(1) allows a deduction equal to nine percent (three percent in the case of taxable years beginning in 2005 or 2006, and six percent in the case of taxable years beginning in 2007, 2008, or 2009) of the lesser of: (A) the qualified production activities income (QPAI) of the taxpayer for the taxable year, or (B) taxable income (determined without regard to section 199) for the taxable year (or, in the case of an individual, adjusted gross income).

Section 199(b)(1) provides that the amount of the deduction allowable under section 199(a) for any taxable year shall not exceed 50 percent of the W-2 wages of the taxpayer for the taxable year. Section 199(b)(2)(A) generally defines *W-2 wages*, with respect to any person for any taxable year of such person, as the sum of amounts described in section 6051(a)(3) and (8) paid by such person with respect to employment of employees by such person during the calendar year ending during such taxable year. Section 199(b)(3), after its amendment by section 219(b) of the Tax Increase Prevention Act of 2014, provides that the Secretary shall provide for the application of section 199(b) in cases of a short taxable year or where the taxpayer acquires, or disposes of, the major portion of a trade or business, or the major portion of a separate unit of a trade or business during the taxable year. Section 199(b)(2)(B) limits the W-2 wages to those properly allocable to DPGR for taxable years beginning after May 17, 2006.

Section 199(c)(1) defines QPAI for any taxable year as an amount equal to the excess (if any) of: (A) the taxpayer's DPGR for such taxable year, over (B) the sum of: (i) the cost of goods sold (CGS) that are allocable to such receipts; and (ii) other expenses, losses, or deductions (other than the deduction under section 199) that are properly allocable to such receipts.

Section 199(c)(4)(A)(i) provides that the term DPGR means the taxpayer's gross receipts that are derived from any lease, rental, license, sale, exchange, or other disposition of: (I) qualifying production property (QPP) that was manufactured, produced, grown, or extracted (MPGE) by the taxpayer in whole or in significant part within the United States; (II) any qualified film produced by the taxpayer; or (III) electricity, natural gas, or potable water (utilities) produced by the taxpayer in the United States.

Section 199(d)(10), as renumbered by section 401(a), Division B of the Energy Extension Act of 2008, authorizes the Secretary to prescribe such regulations as are necessary to carry out the purposes of section 199, including regulations that prevent more than one taxpayer from being allowed a deduction under section 199 with respect to any activity described in section 199(c)(4)(A)(i).

Explanation of Provisions

1. Allocation of W-2 Wages in a Short Taxable Year and in an Acquisition or Disposition of a Trade or Business (or Major Portion)

Temporary regulations in the Rules and Regulations section of this issue of the **Federal Register** contain amendments to the Income Tax Regulations that provide rules clarifying how taxpayers calculate W-2 wages for purposes of the W-2 wage limitation under section 199(b)(1) in the case of a short taxable year or where a taxpayer acquires, or disposes of, the major portion of a trade or business, or the major portion of a separate unit of a trade or business during the taxable year under section 199(b)(3). The text of those regulations serves as the text of these proposed regulations. The preamble to the temporary regulations explains the temporary regulations.

2. Oil Related Qualified Production Activities Income

Section 401(a), Division B of the Energy Extension Act of 2008 added new section 199(d)(9), which applies to taxable years beginning after December 31, 2008. Section 199(d)(9) reduces the otherwise allowable section 199 deduction when a taxpayer has oil related qualified production activities income (oil related QPAI), and defines oil related QPAI. Section 199(d)(9)(A) provides that if a taxpayer has oil related QPAI for any taxable year beginning after 2009, the amount otherwise allowable as a deduction under section 199(a) must be reduced by three percent of the least of: (i) the oil related QPAI of the taxpayer for the taxable year, (ii) the QPAI of the taxpayer for the taxable year, or (iii) taxable income (determined without regard to section 199).

Section 1.199-1(f) of the proposed regulations provides guidance on oil related QPAI. In defining oil related QPAI, the Treasury Department and the IRS considered the relationship between QPAI and oil related QPAI. Section 199(c)(1) defines QPAI as the amount equal to the excess (if any) of the taxpayer's DPGR for the taxable year over the sum of CGS allocable to such receipts and other costs, expenses, losses, and deductions allocable to such receipts. So, for example, if gross receipts are not included within DPGR, those gross receipts are not included when calculating QPAI. Section 199(d)(9)(B) defines oil related QPAI as QPAI attributable to the production, refining, processing, transportation, or distribution of oil, gas, or any primary product thereof. In general, gross receipts from the transportation and distribution of QPP are not includable in DPGR because those activities are not considered part of the MPGE of QPP. See §1.199-3(e)(1), which defines MPGE. Section 199(c)(4)(B)(ii) specifically excludes gross receipts attributable to the transmission or distribution of natural gas from the definition of DPGR.

Based on these considerations, the proposed regulations define *oil related QPAI* as an amount equal to the excess (if any) of the taxpayer's DPGR from the production, refining, or processing of oil, gas, or any primary product thereof (oil related DPGR) over the sum of the CGS that is allocable to such receipts and other expenses, losses, or deductions that are properly allocable to such receipts. The proposed regulations specifically provide that oil related DPGR does not include gross receipts derived from the transportation or distribution of oil, gas, or any primary product thereof, except if the de minimis rule under §1.199-1(d)(3)(i) or an exception for embedded services applies under §1.199-3(i)(4)(i)(B). The proposed regulations further provide that, to the extent a taxpayer treats gross receipts derived from the transportation or distribution of oil, gas, or any primary product thereof as DPGR under §1.199-1(d)(3)(i) or §1.199-3(i)(4)(i)(B), the taxpayer must include those gross receipts in oil related DPGR.

The proposed regulations define *oil* as including oil recovered from both conventional and nonconventional recovery methods, including crude oil, shale oil, and oil recovered from tar/oil sands. Section 199(d)(9)(C) defines *primary product* as having the same meaning as when used in section 927(a)(2)(C) (relating to property excluded from the term *export property* under the former foreign sales corporations rules), as in effect before its repeal. The proposed regulations incorporate the rules in §1.927(a)-1T(g)(2)(i) regarding the definition of a primary product with modifications that are consistent with the definition of oil for purposes of section 199(d)(9).

Section 1.199-1(f)(2) of the proposed regulations provides guidance on how a taxpayer should allocate and apportion costs under the section 861 method, the simplified deduction method, and the small business simplified overall method when determining oil related QPAI. The proposed regulations require taxpayers to use the same cost allocation method to allocate and apportion costs to oil related DPGR as the taxpayer uses to allocate and apportion costs to DPGR.

3. Qualified Films

a. Statutory amendments

Section 502(c), Division C of the Tax Extenders Act of 2008 amended the rules relating to qualified films. Section 502(c)(1) added section 199(b)(2)(D) to broaden the definition of the term *W-2 wages* as applied to a qualified film to include compensation for services performed in the United States by actors, production personnel, directors, and producers.

Section 502(c)(2), Division C of the Tax Extenders Act of 2008 amended the definition of qualified film in section 199(c)(6) to mean any property described in section 168(f)(3) if not less than 50 percent of the total compensation relating to production of the property is compensation for services performed in the United States by actors, production personnel, directors, and producers. The term does not include property with respect to which records are required to be maintained under 18 U.S.C. section 2257 (generally, films, videotapes, or other matter that depict actual sexually explicit conduct and are produced in whole or in part with materials that have been mailed or shipped in interstate or foreign commerce, or are shipped or transported or are intended for shipment or transportation in interstate or foreign commerce). Section 502(c)(2), Division C of the Tax Extenders Act of 2008 also amended the definition of a qualified film under section 199(c)(6) to include any copyrights, trademarks, or other intangibles with respect to such film. The method and means of distributing a qualified film does not affect the availability of the deduction.

Section 502(c)(3), Division C of the Tax Extenders Act of 2008 added an attribution rule for a qualified film for taxpayers who are partnerships or S corporations, or partners or shareholders of such entities under section 199(d)(1)(A)(iv). Section 199(d)(1)(A)(iv) provides that in the case of each partner of a partnership, or shareholder of an S corporation, who owns (directly or indirectly) at least 20 percent of the capital interests in such partnership or the stock of such S corporation, such partner or shareholder is treated as having engaged directly in any film produced by such partnership or S corporation, and that such partnership or S Corporation is treated as having engaged directly in any film produced by such partner or shareholder.

The amendments made by section 502(c), Division C of the Tax Extenders Act of 2008 apply to taxable years beginning after December 31, 2007.

b. W-2 wages

Section 1.199-2(e)(1) of the proposed regulations modifies the definition of W-2 wages to include compensation for services (as defined in §1.199-3(k)(4)) performed in the United States by actors, production personnel, directors, and producers (as defined in §1.199-3(k)(1)).

c. Definition of qualified films

To address the amendments to the definition of qualified film in section 199(c)(6) for taxable years beginning after 2007, the proposed regulations amend the definition of qualified film in §1.199-3(k)(1) to include copyrights, trademarks, or other intangibles with respect to such film. The proposed regulations define other intangibles with a nonexclusive list of intangibles that fall within the definition.

Section 1.199-3(k)(10) provides a special rule for disposition of promotional films to address concerns of the Treasury Department and the IRS that the inclusion of intangibles in the definition of qualified film could be interpreted too broadly. This rule clarifies that, when a taxpayer produces a qualified film that is promoting a product or service, the gross receipts a taxpayer later derives from the disposition of the product or service promoted in the qualified film are derived from the disposition of the product or service and not from a disposition of the qualified film (including any intangible with respect to such qualified film). The rule is intended to prevent taxpayers from claiming that gross receipts are derived from the disposition of a qualified film (rather than the product or service itself) when a taxpayer sells a product or service with a logo, trademark, or other intangible that appears in a promotional film produced by the taxpayer. The Treasury Department and the IRS recognize that a taxpayer can, in certain cases, derive gross receipts from a disposition of a promotional film or the intangibles in a promotional film. The proposed regulations add *Example 9* in §1.199-3(k)(11) relating to a license to reproduce a character used in a promotional film to illustrate a situation where gross receipts can qualify as DPGR because the gross receipts are distinct (separate and apart) from the disposition of the product or service. The Treasury Department and the IRS request comments on how to determine when gross receipts are distinct.

The proposed regulations add four examples in redesignated § 1.199-3(k)(11), formerly § 1.199-3(k)(10), to illustrate application of the amended definition of qualified film that includes copyrights, trademarks, or other intangibles.

The proposed regulations remove the last sentence of § 1.199-3(k)(3)(ii) (which states that gross receipts derived from a license of the right to use or exploit film characters are not gross receipts derived from a qualified film) because gross receipts derived from a license of the right to use or exploit film characters are now considered gross receipts derived from a qualified film.

Section 1.199-3(k)(2)(ii), which allows a taxpayer to treat certain tangible personal property as a qualified film (for example, a DVD), is amended to exclude film intangibles because tangible personal property affixed with a film intangible (such as a trademark) should not be treated as a qualified film. For example, the total revenue from the sale of an imported t-shirt affixed with a film intangible should not be treated as gross receipts derived from the sale of a qualified film. The portion of the gross receipts attributable to the qualified film intangible separate from receipts attributable to the t-shirt may qualify as DPGR, however. The proposed regulations also add *Example 10* and *Example 11* in redesignated § 1.199-3(k)(11) to address situations in which tangible personal property is offered for sale in combination with a qualified film affixed to a DVD.

Section 1.199-3(k)(3)(i) and (k)(3)(ii) of the proposed regulations address the amendment to section 199(c)(6) (effective for taxable years beginning after 2007) that provides the methods and means of distributing a qualified film will not affect the availability of the deduction under section 199. The exception that describes the receipts from showing a qualified film in a movie theater or by broadcast on a television station as not derived from a qualified film is removed from § 1.199-3(k)(3)(ii) because, if a taxpayer produces a qualified film, then the receipts the taxpayer derives from these showings qualify as DPGR in taxable years beginning after 2007. In addition, *Example 4* in § 1.199-3(i)(5)(iii) and *Example 3* in § 1.199-3(k)(11) (formerly § 1.199-3(k)(10)) have been revised to illustrate that, for taxable years beginning after 2007, product placement and advertising income derived from the distribution of a qualified film qualifies as DPGR if the qualified film containing the product placements and advertising is broadcast over the air or watched over the Internet.

The proposed regulations also add a sentence to § 1.199-3(k)(6) to clarify that production activities do not include activities related to the transmission or distribution of films. The Treasury Department and the IRS are aware that some taxpayers have taken the inappropriate position that these activities are part of the production of a film. The Treasury Department and the IRS consider film production as distinct from the transmission and distribution of films. This clarification is also consistent with the amendment to the definition of qualified film, which provides that the methods and means of distribution do not affect the availability of the deduction under section 199.

d. Partnerships and S corporations

Section 1.199-3(i)(9) of the proposed regulations describes the application of section 199(d)(1)(A)(iv) to partners and partnerships and shareholders and S corporations for taxable years beginning after 2007. The Treasury Department and the IRS have determined that for a partnership to apply the provisions of section 199(d)(1)(A)(iv) to treat itself as having engaged directly in a film produced by a partner, the partnership must treat itself as a partnership for all purposes of the Code. Further, a partner of a partnership can apply the provisions of section 199(d)(1)(A)(iv) to treat itself as having engaged directly in a film produced by the partnership only if the partnership treats itself as a partnership for all purposes of the Code. Section 1.199-3(i)(9)(i) describes generally that a partner of a partnership or shareholder of an S corporation who owns (directly or indirectly) at least 20 percent of the capital interests in such partnership or the stock of such S corporation is treated as having engaged directly in any film produced by such partnership or S corporation. Further, such partnership or S corporation is treated as having engaged directly in any film produced by such partner or shareholder.

Section 1.199-3(i)(9)(ii) of the proposed regulations generally prohibits attribution between partners of a partnership or shareholders of an S corporation, partnerships with a partner in common, or S corporations with a shareholder in common. Thus, when a partnership or S corporation is treated as having engaged directly in any film produced by a partner or shareholder, any other partners or shareholders who did not participate directly in the production of the film are treated as not having engaged directly in the production of the film at the partner or shareholder level. Similarly, when a partner or shareholder is treated as having engaged directly in any film produced by a partnership or S corporation, any other partnerships or S corporations in which that partner or shareholder owns an interest (excluding the partnership or S corporation that produced the film) are treated as not having engaged directly in the production of the film at the partnership or S corporation level.

Section 1.199-3(i)(9)(iii) of the proposed regulations describes the attribution period for a partner or partnership or shareholder or S corporation under section 199(d)(1)(A)(iv). A partner or shareholder is treated as having engaged directly in any qualified film produced by the partnership or S corporation, and a partnership or S corporation is treated as having engaged directly in any qualified film produced by the partner or shareholder, regardless of when the qualified film was produced, during the period in which the partner or shareholder owns (directly or indirectly) at least 20 percent of the capital interests in the partnership or the stock of the S corporation. During any period that a partner or shareholder owns less than 20 percent of the capital interests in such partnership or the stock of such S corporation that partner or shareholder is not treated as having engaged directly in the qualified film produced by the partnership or S corporation for purposes of § 1.199-3(i)(9)(iii), and that partnership or S corporation is not treated as having engaged directly in any qualified film produced by the partner or shareholder.

Section 1.199-3(i)(9)(iv) of the proposed regulations provides examples that illustrate section 199(d)(1)(A)(iv).

e. Qualified film safe harbor

Existing § 1.199-3(k)(7)(i) provides a safe harbor that treats a film as a qualified film produced by the taxpayer if not less than 50 percent of the total compensation for services paid by the taxpayer is compensation for services performed in the United States and the taxpayer satisfies the safe harbor in § 1.199-3(g)(3) for treating a taxpayer as MPGE QPP in whole or significant part in the United States. The Treasury Department and the IRS are aware that it may be unclear how the safe harbor in § 1.199-3(k)(7)(i) applies to costs of live or delayed television programs that may be expensed (specifically, whether such expensed costs are part of the CGS or unadjusted depreciable basis of the qualified film for purposes of § 1.199-3(g)(3)). Further, it may be unclear whether license fees paid for third-party produced programs are included in direct labor and overhead when applying the safe harbor in § 1.199-3(g)(3). The proposed regulations clarify how a taxpayer producing live or delayed television programs should apply the safe harbor in § 1.199-3(k)(7)(i); in particular, how a taxpayer should calculate its unadjusted depreciable basis under § 1.199-3(g)(3)(ii). Specifically, proposed § 1.199-3(k)(7)(i) requires a taxpayer to include all costs paid or incurred in the production of a live or delayed television program in the taxpayer's unadjusted depreciable basis of such program under § 1.199-3(g)(3)(ii), including the licensing fees paid to a third party under § 1.199-3(g)(3)(ii). The proposed regulations further clarify that license fees for third-party produced programs are not included in the direct labor and overhead to produce the film for purposes of applying § 1.199-3(g)(3).

4. Treatment of Activities in Puerto Rico

Section 199(d)(8)(A) provides that in the case of any taxpayer with gross receipts for any taxable year from sources within the Commonwealth of Puerto Rico, if all of such receipts are taxable under section 1 or 11 for such taxable year, then for purposes of determining the DPGR of such taxpayer for such taxable year under section 199(c)(4), the term *United States* includes the Commonwealth of Puerto Rico. Section 199(d)(8)(B) provides that in the case of a taxpayer described in section 199(d)(8)(A), for purposes of applying the wage limitation under section 199(b) for any taxable year, the determination of W-2 wages of such taxpayer is made without regard to any exclusion under section 3401(a)(8) for remuneration paid for services performed in Puerto Rico. Section 130 of the Tax Increase Prevention Act of 2014 amended section 199(d)(8)(C) for taxable years beginning after December 31, 2013. As amended, section 199(d)(8)(C) provides that section 199(d)(8) applies only with respect to the first nine taxable years of the taxpayer beginning after December 31, 2005, and before January 1, 2015.

Section 1.199-2(f) of the proposed regulations modifies the W-2 wage limitation under section 199(b) to the extent provided by section 199(d)(8). Section 1.199-3(h)(2) of the proposed regulations modifies the term *United States* to include the Commonwealth of Puerto Rico to the extent provided by section 199(d)(8).

5. Determining DPGR on Item-By-Item Basis

Section 1.199-3(d)(1) provides that a taxpayer determines, using any reasonable method that is satisfactory to the Secretary based on all of the facts and circumstances, whether gross receipts qualify as DPGR on an item-by-item basis. Section 1.199-3(d)(1)(i) provides that item means the property offered by the taxpayer in the normal course of the taxpayer's business for lease, rental, license, sale, exchange, or other disposition (for purposes of § 1.199-3(d), collectively referred to as disposition) to customers, if the gross receipts from the disposition of such property qualify as DPGR. Section 1.199-3(d)(2)(iii) provides that, in the case of construction activities and services or engineering and architectural services, a taxpayer may use any reasonable method that is satisfactory to the Secretary based on all of the facts and circumstances to determine what construction activities and services or engineering or architectural services constitute an item.

The Treasury Department and the IRS are aware that the item rule in § 1.199-3(d)(2)(iii) has been interpreted to mean that the gross receipts derived from the sale of a multiple-building project may be treated as DPGR when only one building in the project is substantially renovated. The Treasury Department and the IRS have concluded that treating gross receipts from the sale of a multiple-building project as DPGR, and the multiple-building project as one item, is not a reasonable method satisfactory to the Secretary for purposes of § 1.199-3(d)(2)(iii) if a taxpayer did not substantially renovate each building in the multiple-building project. Section 1.199-3(d)(4) of the proposed regulations includes an example (*Example 14*) illustrating the appropriate application of § 1.199-3(d)(2)(iii) to a multiple building project.

In addition, the Treasury Department and the IRS are aware that taxpayers may be unsure how to apply the item rule in § 1.199-3(d)(2)(i) when the property offered for disposition to customers includes embedded services as described in § 1.199-3(i)(4)(i). The proposed regulations add *Example 6* to § 1.199-3(d)(4) to clarify that the item rule applies after excluding the gross receipts attributable to services.

6. MPGE

Section 1.199-3(e)(1) provides that the term *MPGE* includes manufacturing, producing, growing, extracting, installing, developing, improving, and creating QPP; making QPP out of scrap, salvage, or junk material as well as from new or raw material by processing, manipulating, refining, or changing the form of an article, or by combining or assembling two or more articles; cultivating soil, raising livestock, fishing, and mining minerals. The Treasury Department and the IRS are aware that *Example 5* in § 1.199-3(e)(5) has been interpreted to mean that testing activities qualify as an MPGE activity even if the taxpayer engages in no other MPGE activity. The Treasury Department and the IRS disagree that testing activities, alone, qualify as an MPGE activity. The proposed regulations add a sentence to *Example 5* in § 1.199-3(e)(5) to further illustrate that certain activities will not be treated as MPGE activities if they are not performed as part of the MPGE of QPP. Taxpayers are not required to allocate gross receipts to certain activities that are not MPGE activities when those activities are performed in connection with the MPGE of QPP. However, if the taxpayer in *Example 5* in § 1.199-3(e)(5) did not MPGE QPP, then the activities described in the example, including testing, are not MPGE activities.

Section 1.199-3(e)(2) provides that if a taxpayer packages, repackages, labels, or performs minor assembly of QPP and the taxpayer engages in no other MPGE activities with respect to that QPP, the taxpayer's packaging, repackaging, labeling, or minor assembly does not qualify as MPGE with respect to that QPP. This rule has been the subject of recent litigation. See *United States v. Dean*, 945 F. Supp. 2d 1110 (C.D. Cal. 2013) (concluding that the taxpayer's activity of preparing gift baskets was a manufacturing activity and not solely packaging or repackaging for purposes of section 199). The Treasury Department and the IRS disagree with the interpretation of § 1.199-3(e)(2) adopted by the court in *United States v. Dean*, and the proposed regulations add an example (*Example 9*) that illustrates the appropriate application of this rule in a situation in which the taxpayer is engaged in no other MPGE activities with respect to the QPP other than those described in § 1.199-3(e)(2).

7. Definition of "by the taxpayer"

Section 1.199-3(f)(1) provides that if one taxpayer performs a qualifying activity under § 1.199-3(e)(1), § 1.199-3(k)(1), or § 1.199-3(l)(1) pursuant to a contract with another party, then only the taxpayer that has the benefits and burdens of ownership of the QPP, qualified film, or utilities under Federal income tax principles during the period in which the qualifying activity occurs is treated as engaging in the qualifying activity.

Taxpayers and the IRS have had difficulty determining which party to a contract manufacturing arrangement has the benefits and burdens of ownership of the property while the qualifying activity occurs. Cases analyzing the benefits and burdens of ownership have considered the following factors relevant: (1) whether legal title passes; (2) how the parties treat the transaction; (3) whether an equity interest was acquired; (4) whether the contract creates a present obligation on the seller to execute and deliver a deed and a present obligation on the purchaser to make payments; (5) whether the right of possession is vested in the purchaser and which party has control of the property or process; (6) which party pays the property taxes; (7) which party bears the risk of loss or damage to the property; (8) which party receives the profits from the operation and sale of the property; and (9) whether a taxpayer actively and extensively participated in the management and operations of the activity. See *ADVO, Inc. & Subsidiaries v. Commissioner*, 141 T.C. 298, 324-25 (2013); see also *Grodt & McKay Realty, Inc. v. Commissioner*, 77 T.C. 1221 (1981). The *ADVO* court noted that the factors it used in its analysis are not exclusive or controlling, but that they were in the particular case sufficient to determine which party had the benefits and burdens of ownership. *ADVO, Inc.*, 141 T.C. at 325 n. 21. Determining which party has the benefits and burdens of ownership under Federal income tax principles for purposes of section 199 requires an analysis and weighing of many factors, which in some contexts could result in more than one taxpayer claiming the benefits of section 199 with respect to a particular activity. Resolving the benefits and burdens of ownership issue often requires significant IRS and taxpayer resources.

Section 199(d)(10) directs the Treasury Department to provide regulations that prevent more than one taxpayer from being allowed a deduction under section 199 with respect to any qualifying activity (as described in section 199(c)(4)(A)(i)). The Treasury Department and the IRS have interpreted the statute to mean that only one taxpayer may claim the section 199 deduction with respect to the same activity performed with respect to the same property. See § 1.199-3(f)(1). *Example 1* and *Example 2* in § 1.199-3(f)(4) currently illustrate this one-taxpayer rule using factors that are relevant to the determination of who has the benefits and burdens of ownership.

The Large Business and International (LB&I) Division issued an Industry Director Directive on February 1, 2012 (LB&I Control No. LB&I-4-0112-01) (Directive) addressing the benefits and burdens factors. The Directive provides a three-step analysis of facts and circumstances relating to contract terms, production activities, and economic risks to determine whether a taxpayer has the benefits and burdens of ownership for purposes of § 1.199-3(f)(1). LB&I issued a superseding second directive on July 24, 2013 (LB&I Control No. LB&I-04-0713-006), and a third directive updating the second directive on October 29, 2013 (LB&I Control No. LB&I-04-1013-008). The third directive allows a taxpayer to provide a statement explaining the taxpayer's determination that it had the benefits and burdens of ownership, along with certification statements signed under penalties of perjury by the taxpayer and the counterparty verifying that only the taxpayer is claiming the section 199 deduction.

To provide administrable rules that are consistent with section 199, reduce the burden on taxpayers and the IRS in evaluating factors related to the benefits and burdens of ownership, and prevent more than one taxpayer from being allowed a deduction under section 199 with respect to any qualifying activity, the proposed regulations remove the rule in § 1.199-3(f)(1) that treats a taxpayer in a contract manufacturing arrangement as engaging in the qualifying activity only if the taxpayer has the benefits and burdens of ownership during the period in which the qualifying activity occurs. In place of the benefits and burdens of ownership rule, these proposed regulations provide that if a qualifying activity is performed under a contract, then the party that performs the activity is the taxpayer for purposes of section 199(c)(4)(A)(i). This rule, which applies solely for purposes of section 199, reflects the conclusion that the party actually producing the property should be treated as engaging in the qualifying activity for purposes of section 199, and is therefore consistent with the statute's goal of incentivizing domestic manufacturers and producers. The proposed rule would also provide a readily administrable approach that would prevent more than one taxpayer from being allowed a deduction under section 199 with respect to any qualifying activity.

Example 1 has been revised, and current *Example 2* has been removed, to reflect the new rule. In addition, the benefits and burdens language has been removed from: (1) the definition of MPGE in § 1.199-3(e)(1) and (3), including *Example 1*, *Example 4*, and *Example 5* in § 1.199-3(e)(5); (2) the definition of in whole or in significant part in § 1.199-3(g)(1); (3) *Example 5* in the qualified film rules in existing § 1.199-3(k)(7); and (4) the production pursuant to a contract in the qualified film rules in § 1.199-3(k)(8).

The Treasury Department and the IRS request comments on whether there are narrow circumstances that could justify an exception to the proposed rule. In particular, the Treasury Department and the IRS request comments on whether there should be a limited exception to the proposed rule for certain fully cost-plus or cost-reimbursable contracts. Under such an exception, the party that is not performing the qualifying activity would be treated as the taxpayer engaged in the qualifying activity if the party performing the qualifying activity is (i) reimbursed for, or provided with, all materials, labor, and overhead costs related to fulfilling the contract, and (ii) provided with an additional payment to allow for a profit. The Treasury Department and the IRS are uncertain regarding the extent to which such fully cost-plus or cost-reimbursable contracts are in fact used in practice. Comments suggesting circumstances that could justify an exception to the proposed rule should address the rationale for the proposed exception, the ability of the IRS to administer the exception, and how the suggested exception will prevent two taxpayers from claiming the deduction for the qualifying activity.

8. Hedging Transactions

The proposed regulations make several revisions to the hedging rules in § 1.199-3(i)(3). Section 1.199-3(i) of the proposed regulations defines a hedging transaction to include transactions in which the risk being hedged relates to property described in section 1221(a)(1) giving rise to DPGR, whereas the existing regulations require the risk being hedged relate to QPP described in section 1221(a)(1). A taxpayer commented in a letter to the Treasury Department and the IRS that there is no reason to limit the hedging rules to QPP giving rise to DPGR, and the proposed regulations accept the comment.

The other changes to the hedging rules are administrative. Section 1.199-3(i)(3)(ii) of the existing regulations on currency fluctuations was eliminated because the regulations under sections 988(d) and 1221 adequately cover the treatment of currency hedges. Similarly, the rules in § 1.199-3(i)(3)(iii) that address the effect of identification and non-identification were duplicative of the rules in the section 1221 regulations. Accordingly, § 1.199-3(i)(3)(ii) has been revised to cross-reference the appropriate rules in § 1.1221-2(g), and to clarify that the consequence of an abusive identification or non-identification is that deduction or loss, but not income or gain, is taken into account in calculating DPGR.

9. Construction Activities

Section 199(c)(4)(A)(ii) includes in DPGR, in the case of a taxpayer engaged in the active conduct of a construction trade or business, gross receipts derived from construction of real property performed in the United States by the taxpayer in the ordinary course of such trade or business. Under § 1.199-3(m)(2)(i), activities constituting construction include activities performed by a general contractor or activities typically performed by a general contractor, for example, activities relating to management and oversight of the construction process such as approvals, periodic inspection of progress of the construction project, and required job modifications. The Treasury Department and the IRS are aware that some taxpayers have interpreted this language to mean that a taxpayer who only approves or authorizes payments is engaged in activities typically performed by a general contractor under § 1.199-3(m)(2)(i). The Treasury Department and the IRS disagree that a taxpayer who only approves or authorizes payments is engaged in construction for purposes of § 1.199-3(m)(2)(i). Accordingly, § 1.199-3(m)(2)(i) of the proposed regulations clarifies that a taxpayer must engage in construction activities that include more than the approval or authorization of payments or invoices for that taxpayer's activities to be considered as activities typically performed by a general contractor.

Section 1.199-3(m)(2)(i) provides that activities constituting construction are activities performed in connection with a project to erect or substantially renovate real property. Section 1.199-3(m)(5) currently defines substantial renovation to mean the renovation of a major component or substantial structural part of real property that materially increases the value of the property, substantially prolongs the useful life of the property, or adapts the property to a new or different use. This standard reflects regulations under § 1.263(a)-3 related to amounts paid to improve tangible property that existed at the time of publication of the final § 1.199-3(m)(5) regulations (TD 9263 [71 FR 31268] June 19, 2006) but which have since been revised. See (TD 9636 [78 FR 57686] September 19, 2013).

The proposed regulations under § 1.199-3(m)(5) revise the definition of substantial renovation to conform to the final regulations under § 1.263(a)-3, which provide rules requiring capitalization of amounts paid for improvements to a unit of property owned by a taxpayer. Improvements under § 1.263(a)-3 are amounts paid for a betterment to a unit of property, amounts paid to restore a unit of property, and amounts paid to adapt a unit of property to a new or different use. See § 1.263(a)-3(j), (k), and (l). Under the proposed regulations, a substantial renovation of real property is a renovation the costs of which are required to be capitalized as an improvement under § 1.263(a)-3, other than an amount described in § 1.263(a)-3(k)(1)(i) through (iii) (relating to amounts for which a loss deduction or basis adjustment requires capitalization as an improvement). The improvement rules under § 1.263(a)-3 provide specific rules of application for buildings (see § 1.263(a)-3(j)(2)(ii), (k)(2), and (l)(2)), which apply for purposes of § 1.199-3(m)(5).

10. Allocating Cost of Goods Sold

Section 1.199-4(b)(1) describes how a taxpayer determines its CGS allocable to DPGR. The Treasury Department and the IRS are aware that in the case of transactions accounted for under a long-term contract method of accounting (either the percentage-of-completion method (PCM) or the completed-contract method (CCM)), a taxpayer incurs allocable contract costs. The Treasury Department and the IRS recognize that allocable contract costs under PCM or CCM are analogous to CGS and should be treated in the same manner. Section 1.199-4(b)(1) of the proposed regulations provides that in the case of a long-term contract accounted for under PCM or CCM, CGS for purposes of § 1.199-4(b)(1) includes allocable contract costs described in § 1.460-5(b) or § 1.460-5(d), as applicable.

Existing § 1.199-4(b)(2)(i) provides that a taxpayer must use a reasonable method that is satisfactory to the Secretary based on all of the facts and circumstances to allocate CGS between DPGR and non-DPGR. This allocation must be determined based on the rules provided in § 1.199-4(b)(2)(i) and (ii). Taxpayers have asserted that under § 1.199-4(b)(2)(ii) the portion of current year CGS associated with activities in earlier tax years (including pre-section 199 tax years) may be allocated to non-DPGR even if the related gross receipts are treated by the taxpayer as DPGR. Section 1.199-4(b)(2)(iii)(A) of the proposed regulations clarifies that the CGS must be allocated between DPGR and non-DPGR, regardless of whether any component of the costs included in CGS can be associated with activities undertaken in an earlier taxable year. Section 1.199-4(b)(2)(iii)(B) of the proposed regulations provides an example illustrating this rule.

11. Agricultural and Horticultural Cooperatives

Section 199(d)(3)(A) provides that any person who receives a qualified payment from a specified agricultural or horticultural cooperative must be allowed for the taxable year in which such payment is received a deduction under section 199(a) equal to the portion of the deduction allowed under section 199(a) to such cooperative that is (i) allowed with respect to the portion of the QPAI to which such payment is attributable, and (ii) identified by such cooperative in a written notice mailed to such person during the payment period described in section 1382(d).

Under § 1.199-6(c), the cooperative's QPAI is computed without taking into account any deduction allowable under section 1382(b) or section 1382(c) (relating to patronage dividends, per-unit retain allocations, and nonpatronage distributions).

Section 1.199-6(e) provides that the term *qualified payment* means any amount of a patronage dividend or per-unit retain allocation, as described in section 1385(a)(1) or section 1385(a)(3), received by a patron from a cooperative that is attributable to the portion of the cooperative's QPAI for which the cooperative is allowed a section 199 deduction. For this purpose, patronage dividends and per-unit retain allocations include any advances on patronage and per-unit retains paid in money during the taxable year.

Section 1388(f) defines the term *per-unit retain allocation* to mean any allocation by an organization to which part I of subchapter T applies to a patron with respect to products marketed for him, the amount of which is fixed without reference to net earnings of the organization pursuant to an agreement between the organization and the patron. Per-unit retain allocations may be made in money, property, or certificates.

The Treasury Department and the IRS are aware that *Example 1* in § 1.199-6(m) has been interpreted as describing that the cooperative's payment for its members' corn is a per-unit retain allocation paid in money as defined in sections 1382(b)(3) and 1388(f). *Example 1* in § 1.199-6(m) does not identify the cooperative's payment for its members' corn as a per-unit retain allocation and is not intended to illustrate how QPAI is computed when a cooperative's payments to its patrons are per-unit retain allocations. The proposed regulations provide an example (*Example 4*) in § 1.199-6(m) illustrating how QPAI is computed when the cooperative's payments to members for corn qualify as per-unit retain allocations paid in money under section 1388(f). The new example has the same facts as *Example 1* in § 1.199-6(m), except that the cooperative's payments for its members' corn qualify as per-unit retain allocations paid in money under section 1388(f) and the cooperative reports per-unit retain allocations paid in money on Form 1099-PATR, "Taxable Distributions Received From Cooperatives."

Request for Comments

Existing § 1.199-3(e)(2) provides that if a taxpayer packages, repackages, labels, or performs minor assembly of QPP and the taxpayer engages in no other MPGE activity with respect to that QPP, the taxpayer's packaging, repackaging, labeling, or minor assembly does not qualify as MPGE with respect to that QPP.

The term *minor assembly* for purposes of section 199 was first introduced in Notice 2005-14 (2005-1 CB 498 (February 14, 2005)) (see § 601.601(d)(2)(ii)(b)) (Notice 2005-14), and was used (by exclusion) in determining whether a taxpayer met the in-whole-or-in-significant-part requirement. Specifically, section 3.04(5)(d) of Notice 2005-14 states that in connection with the MPGE of QPP, packaging, repackaging, and minor assembly operations should not be considered in applying the general "substantial in nature" test, and the costs should not be considered in applying the safe harbor. The section further states that this rule is similar to the rule in § 1.954-3(a)(4)(iii). The rule in § 1.954-3(a)(4)(iii) applies when deciding whether a taxpayer selling property will be treated as selling a manufactured product rather than components of that sold property.

Section 1.199-3(g) of the current regulations, which superseded Notice 2005-14, does not provide a specific definition of minor assembly, but it does allow taxpayers to consider minor assembly activities to determine whether the taxpayer has met the in-whole-or-in-significant-part requirement (either by showing their activities were substantial in nature under § 1.199-3(g)(2) or by meeting the safe harbor in § 1.199-3(g)(3)). However, the current regulations also contain § 1.199-3(e)(2), which excludes certain activities from the definition of MPGE. Section 1.199-3(e)(2) provides that if a taxpayer packages, repackages, labels, or performs minor assembly of QPP and the taxpayer engages in no other MPGE activity with respect to that QPP, the taxpayer's packaging, repackaging, labeling, or minor assembly does not qualify as MPGE with respect to that QPP. Therefore, a taxpayer with only minor assembly activities would not meet the definition of MPGE and a determination of whether a taxpayer met the in-whole-or-in-significant-part requirement is not made.

In considering whether to provide a specific definition of minor assembly, the Treasury Department and the IRS have found it difficult to identify an objective test that would be widely applicable.

The definition of minor assembly could focus on whether a taxpayer's activity is only a single process that does not transform an article into a materially different QPP. Such process may include, but would not be limited to, blending or mixing two materials together, painting an article, cutting, chopping, crushing (non-agricultural products), or other similar activities. An example of blending or mixing two materials is using a paint mixing machine to combine paint with a pigment to match a customer's color selection when a taxpayer did not MPGE the paint or the pigment. An example of cutting is a taxpayer using an industrial key cutting machine to custom cut keys for customers using blank keys that taxpayer purchased from unrelated third parties. Examples of other similar activities include adding an additive to extend the shelf life of a product and time ripening produce that was purchased from unrelated third parties.

Another possible definition could be based on whether an end user could reasonably engage in the same assembly activity of the taxpayer. For example, assume QPP made up of component parts purchased by taxpayer is sold by a taxpayer to end users in either assembled or disassembled form. To the extent an end user can reasonably assemble the QPP sold in disassembled form, the taxpayer's assembly activity would be considered minor assembly.

The Treasury Department and the IRS request comments on how the term *minor assembly* in § 1.199-3(e)(2) should be defined and encourage the submission of examples illustrating the term.

Special Analyses

Certain IRS regulations, including this one, are exempt from the requirements of Executive Order 12866 of, as supplemented and reaffirmed by Executive Order 13563. Therefore, a regulatory assessment is not required. It also has been determined that section 553(b) of the Administrative Procedure Act (5 U.S.C. chapter 5) does not apply to these regulations, and because the regulations do not impose a collection of information on small entities, the Regulatory Flexibility Act (5 U.S.C. chapter 6) does not apply. Pursuant to section 7805(f) of the Code, this notice of proposed rulemaking has been submitted to the Chief Counsel for Advocacy of the Small Business Administration for comment on their impact on small business.

Comments and Public Hearing

Before these proposed regulations are adopted as final regulations, consideration will be given to any written comments (a signed original and eight (8) copies) or electronic comments that are submitted timely to the IRS. Comments are requested on all aspects of the proposed regulations. All comments will be available for public inspection and copying at *http://www.regulations.gov* or upon request.

A public hearing has been scheduled for December 16, 2015, beginning at 10 a.m. in the Auditorium of the Internal Revenue Building, 1111 Constitution Avenue, NW., Washington, DC. Due to building security procedures, visitors must enter at the Constitution Avenue entrance. Because of access restrictions, visitors will not be admitted beyond the immediate entrance area more than 30 minutes before the hearing starts. In addition, all visitors must present photo identification to enter the building. For information about having your name placed on the building access list to attend the hearing, see the "**FOR FURTHER INFORMATION CONTACT**" section of this preamble.

The rules of 26 CFR 601.601(a)(3) apply to the hearing. Persons who wish to present oral comments at the hearing must submit electronic or written comments by November 27, 2015 and an outline of the topics to be discussed and the time to be devoted to each topic by November 27, 2015. A period of 10 minutes will be allotted to each person for making comments. An agenda showing the scheduling of the speakers will be prepared after the deadline for receiving outlines has passed. Copies of the agenda will be available free of charge at the hearing.

Drafting Information

The principal author of these regulations is James Holmes, Office of the Associate Chief Counsel (Passthroughs and Special Industries). However, other personnel from the Treasury Department and the IRS participated in their development.

[¶49,662] Proposed Amendments of Regulations (REG-109813-11), published in the Federal Register on August 27, 2015.

[Code Sec. 937]

U.S. possessions: Bona fide residence: Presence test.—Amendments of Reg. §1.937-1, determining whether an individual is a bona fide resident of a U.S. territory, is proposed.

AGENCY: Internal Revenue Service (IRS), Treasury.

ACTION: Notice of proposed rulemaking.

SUMMARY: This document contains proposed amendments to the regulations for determining whether an individual is a bona fide resident of a U.S. territory. These proposed amendments affect individuals establishing bona fide residency in a U.S. territory by allowing additional days of constructive presence in a U.S. territory.

DATES: Written or electronic comments and requests for a public hearing must be received by November 27, 2015.

ADDRESSES: Send submissions to: CC:PA:LPD:PR (REG-109813-11), room 5203, Internal Revenue Service, PO Box 7604, Ben Franklin Station, Washington, DC 20044. Submissions may be hand-delivered Monday through Friday between the hours of 8 a.m. and 4 p.m. to CC:PA:LPD:PR (REG-109813-11), Courier's Desk, Internal Revenue Service, 1111 Constitution Avenue, NW, Washington, DC, or sent electronically, via the Federal eRulemaking Portal at *www.regulations.gov* (IRS REG-109813-11).

FOR FURTHER INFORMATION CONTACT: Concerning the proposed regulations, Stephen Huggs, (202) 317-6941; concerning submission of comments and/or requests for a hearing, Oluwafunmilayo (Funmi) Taylor, (202) 317-6901 (not toll-free numbers). SUPPLEMENTARY INFORMATION:

Background

This document contains proposed amendments to the Income Tax Regulations (26 CFR part 1) under section 937 of the Internal Revenue Code (Code). Section 937 was added to the Code by the American Jobs Creation Act of 2004 (Public Law 108-357, 118 Stat. 1418 (2004)). Section 937(a) provides rules for determining if an individual is a bona fide resident of a U.S. possession (generally referred to in this preamble as a "U.S. territory").

On April 11, 2005, the **Federal Register** published temporary regulations (TD 9194, 70 FR 18920) and proposed regulations (REG-159243-03, 70 FR 18949) under section 937, providing rules to implement section 937 and conforming existing regulations to other legislative changes with respect to the U.S. territories. On January 31, 2006, the **Federal Register** published final regulations (TD 9248, 71 FR 4996) under section 937(a) concerning whether an individual is a bona fide resident of a U.S. territory. Section 1.937-1 was amended on November 14, 2006, and on April 9, 2008, to provide additional guidance concerning bona fide residency in the U.S. territories. See TD 9297 (71 FR 66232) and TD 9391 (73 FR 19350).

Section 937(a) provides that an individual is a bona fide resident of a U.S. territory if the individual meets a presence test, a tax home test, and a closer connection test. In order to satisfy the presence test, an individual must be present in the U.S. territory for at least 183 days during the taxable year (183-day rule), unless otherwise provided in regulations.

Section 1.937-1 provides several alternatives to the 183-day rule. An individual who does not satisfy the 183-day rule nevertheless meets the presence test if the individual satisfies one of four alternative tests: (1) the individual is present in the relevant U.S. territory for at least 549 days during the three-year period consisting of the current taxable year and the two immediately preceding taxable years, provided the individual is present in the U.S. territory for at least 60 days during each taxable year of the period; (2) the individual is present no more than 90 days in the United States during the taxable year; (3) the individual has no more than $3,000 of earned income from U.S. sources and is present for more days in the U.S. territory than in the United States during the taxable year; or (4) the individual has no significant connection to the United States during the taxable year. The term "significant connection" is generally defined as a permanent home, voter registration, spouse, or minor child in the United States. See §1.937-1(c)(5). Section 1.937-1 also provides that certain days count as days of presence in the relevant U.S. territory for purposes of the presence test, even if the individual is not physically present in the U.S. territory (constructive presence).

Explanation of Provisions

Following the original issuance of §1.937-1, the Department of the Treasury (Treasury Department) and the Internal Revenue Service (IRS) received comments requesting that the presence test be revisited to make it more flexible. These comments included a proposal to allow days of constructive presence for business or personal travel outside of the relevant U.S. territory. The Treasury Department and the IRS have concluded that it would be appropriate to allow additional days of constructive presence subject to certain limitations. Accordingly, these proposed regulations provide an additional rule for calculating days of presence in the relevant U.S. territory for purposes of the presence test in §1.937-1(c)(1).

Under the proposed amendment, an individual would be considered to be present in the relevant U.S. territory for up to 30 days during which the individual is outside of both the United States and the relevant U.S. territory. The proposed amendment would not apply, however, if the number of days that the individual is considered to be present in the United States during the taxable year equals or exceeds the number of days that the individual is considered to be present in the relevant U.S. territory during the taxable year, determined without taking into account any days for which the individual would be treated as present in the U.S. territory under this proposed amendment. Furthermore, the 30-day constructive presence rule would not apply for purposes of calculating the minimum 60 days of presence in the relevant U.S. territory that is required for the 549-day test under § 1.937-1(c)(1)(ii). Therefore, an individual invoking § 1.937-1(c)(1)(ii) must otherwise be considered to have been present at least 60 days in the relevant U.S. territory in each of the three years in order to benefit from the 30-day constructive presence rule.

Proposed Effective/Applicability Date

These amendments to the regulations are proposed to apply to taxable years beginning after the date these regulations are published as final regulations in the **Federal Register**.

Reliance on Proposed Regulations

Until these regulations are published as final regulations in the **Federal Register**, taxpayers may rely on these proposed regulations with respect to taxable years beginning on or after the date these proposed regulations are published in the **Federal Register**.

Special Analyses

Certain IRS regulations, including this one, are exempt from the requirements of Executive Order 12866, as supplemented and reaffirmed by Executive Order 13563. Therefore, a regulatory impact assessment is not required. It has also been determined that section 553(b) of the Administrative Procedure Act (5 U.S.C. chapter 5) does not apply to these regulations, and because the regulations do not impose a collection of information on small entities, the Regulatory Flexibility Act (5 U.S.C. chapter 6) does not apply. Pursuant to section 7805(f) of the Code, this regulation has been submitted to the Chief Counsel for Advocacy of the Small Business Administration for comment on its impact on small business.

Comments and Requests for Public Hearing

Before these proposed regulations are adopted as final regulations, consideration will be given to any comments that are submitted timely to the IRS as prescribed in this preamble under the "Addresses" heading. The Treasury Department and the IRS request comments on all aspects of the proposed rules. All comments will be available at *www.regulations.gov* or upon request. A public hearing will be scheduled if requested in writing by any person that timely submits written comments. If a public hearing is scheduled, notice of the date, time, and place for the public hearing will be published in the **Federal Register**.

Drafting Information

The principal author of these proposed regulations is Cleve Lisecki, formerly of the Office of Associate Chief Counsel (International). However, other personnel from the Treasury Department and the IRS participated in their development.

[¶49,664] Proposed Amendments of Regulations and Partial Withdrawal of Notice of Proposed Regulations (REG-143800-14), published in the Federal Register on September 1, 2015.

[Code Sec. 36B]

Health coverage: Employer-sponsored plan: Minimum value.—Amendments of Reg. § 1.36B-6, determining whether health coverage under an eligible employer-sponsored plan provides minimum value, are proposed. Previously proposed amendments to Reg. § 1.36B-6(a) and (g) were withdrawn (see ¶49,574). Portions of the 2015 proposed amendments to Reg. § 1.36B-6 were adopted by T.D. 9745.

AGENCY: Internal Revenue Service (IRS), Treasury.

ACTION: Supplemental notice of proposed rulemaking.

SUMMARY: This document withdraws, in part, a notice of proposed rulemaking published on May 3, 2013, relating to the health insurance premium tax credit enacted by the Affordable Care Act (including guidance on determining whether health coverage under an eligible employer-sponsored plan provides minimum value) and replaces the withdrawn portion with new proposed regulations providing guidance on determining whether health coverage under an eligible employer-sponsored plan provides minimum value. The proposed regulations affect participants in eligible employer-sponsored health plans and employers that sponsor these plans.

DATES: Written (including electronic) comments and requests for a public hearing must be received by November 1, 2015.

ADDRESSES: Send submissions to: CC:PA:LPD:PR (REG-143800-14), Room 5203, Internal Revenue Service, PO Box 7604, Ben Franklin Station, Washington, DC 20044. Submissions may be hand-delivered Monday through Friday between the hours of 8 a.m. and 4 p.m. to CC:PA:LPD:PR (REG-143800-14), Courier's Desk, Internal Revenue Service, 1111 Constitution Avenue, NW., Washington, DC, or sent electronically via the Federal eRulemaking Portal at *www.regulations.gov* (IRS REG-143800-14).

FOR FURTHER INFORMATION CONTACT: Concerning the proposed regulations, Andrew S. Braden, (202) 317-4725; concerning the submission of comments and/or requests for a public hearing, Oluwafunmilayo Taylor, (202) 317-5179 (not toll-free calls).

SUPPLEMENTARY INFORMATION:

Background

This document withdraws, in part, a notice of proposed rulemaking (REG-125398-12), which was published in the **Federal Register** on May 3, 2013 (78 FR 25909) and replaces the portion withdrawn with new proposed regulations. The 2013 proposed regulations added §1.36B-6 of the Income Tax Regulations, providing rules for determining the minimum value of eligible employer-sponsored plans for purposes of the premium tax credit under section 36B of the Internal Revenue Code (Code). Notice 2014-69 (2014-48 IRB 903) advised taxpayers that the Department of Health and Human Service (HHS) and the Treasury Department and the IRS intended to propose regulations providing that plans that fail to provide substantial coverage for inpatient hospitalization or physician services do not provide minimum value. Accordingly, the proposed regulations under §1.36B-6(a) and (g) are withdrawn.

Beginning in 2014, under the Patient Protection and Affordable Care Act, Public Law 111-148 (124 Stat. 119 (2010)), and the Health Care and Education Reconciliation Act of 2010, Public Law 111-152 (124 Stat. 1029 (2010)) (collectively, the Affordable Care Act), eligible individuals who enroll in, or whose family member enrolls in, coverage under a qualified health plan through an Affordable Insurance Exchange (Exchange), also known as a Health Insurance Marketplace, may receive a premium tax credit under section 36B of the Code.

Premium Tax Credit

Section 36B allows a refundable premium tax credit, which subsidizes the cost of health insurance coverage enrolled in through an Exchange. A taxpayer may claim the premium tax credit on the taxpayer's tax return only if the taxpayer or a member of the taxpayer's tax family (the persons for whom the taxpayer claims a personal exemption deduction on the taxpayer's tax return, generally the taxpayer, spouse, and dependents) has a coverage month. An individual has a coverage month only if the individual enrolls in a qualified health plan through an Exchange, is not eligible for minimum essential coverage other than coverage in the individual market, and premiums for the qualified health plan are paid. Section 36B(b) and (c)(2)(B). Minimum essential coverage includes coverage under an eligible employer-sponsored plan. See section 5000A(f)(1)(B). However, for purposes of the premium tax credit, an individual is not eligible for coverage under an eligible employer-sponsored plan unless the coverage is affordable and provides minimum value or unless the individual enrolls in the plan. Section 36B(c)(2)(C). Final regulations under section 36B (TD 9590) were published on May 23, 2012 (77 FR 30377).

Employer Shared Responsibility Provision

Section 4980H(b) imposes an assessable payment on applicable large employers (as defined in section 4980H(c)(2)) that offer minimum essential coverage under an eligible employer-sponsored plan that is not affordable or does not provide minimum value for one or more full-time employees who receive a premium tax credit subsidy. Final regulations under section 4980H (TD 9655) were published on February 12, 2014 (79 FR 8544).

Minimum Value

Under section 36B(c)(2)(C)(ii), an eligible employer-sponsored plan provides minimum value only if the plan's share of the total allowed costs of benefits provided under the plan is at least 60 percent. Section 1302(d)(2)(C) of the Affordable Care Act provides that, in determining the percentage of the total allowed costs of benefits provided under a group health plan, the regulations promulgated by HHS under section 1302(d)(2), dealing with actuarial value, apply.

HHS published final regulations under section 1302(d)(2) on February 25, 2013 (78 FR 12834). HHS regulations at 45 CFR 156.20, which apply to the actuarial value of plans required to provide coverage of all essential health benefits, define the percentage of the total allowed costs of benefits provided under a group health plan as (1) the anticipated covered medical spending for essential health benefits coverage (as defined in 45 CFR 156.110(a)) paid by a health plan for a standard population, computed in accordance with the plan's cost-sharing, divided by (2) the total anticipated allowed charges for essential health benefit coverage provided to a standard population.

Under section 1302(b) of the Affordable Care Act, only individual market and insured small group market health plans are required to cover the essential health benefits. Minimum value, however, applies to all eligible employer-sponsored plans, including self-insured plans and insured plans in the large group market. Accordingly, HHS regulations at 45 CFR 156.145(b)(2) and (c) apply the actuarial value definition in the context of minimum value by (1) defining the standard population as the population covered by typical self-insured group health plans, and (2) taking into account the benefits a plan provides that are included in any one benchmark plan a state uses to specify the benefits included in essential health benefits.

Notice 2014-69, advising taxpayers of the intent to propose regulations providing that plans that fail to provide substantial coverage for inpatient hospitalization or physician services do not provide minimum value, was released on November 4, 2014. Notice 2014-69 also advised that it was anticipated that, for purposes of section 4980H liability, the final regulations would not apply to certain plans (as described later in this preamble) before the end of a plan year beginning no later than March 1, 2015. However, an offer of coverage under these plans to an employee does not preclude the employee from obtaining a premium tax credit, if otherwise eligible.

As announced by Notice 2014-69, HHS published proposed regulations on November 26, 2014 (79 FR 70674, 70757), and final regulations on February 27, 2015 (80 FR 10872), amending 45 CFR 156.145(a). The HHS regulations provide that an eligible employer-sponsored plan provides minimum value only if, in addition to covering at least 60 percent of the total allowed costs of benefits provided under the plan, the plan benefits include substantial coverage of inpatient hospitalization and physician services. Consistent with Notice 2014-69, the HHS regulations indicate that the changes to the minimum value regulations do not apply before the end of the plan year beginning no later than March 1, 2015 to a plan that fails to provide substantial coverage for inpatient hospitalization services or for physician services (or both), provided that the employer had entered into a binding written commitment to adopt, or had begun enrolling employees in, the plan before November 4, 2014. For this purpose, the plan year is the plan year in effect under the terms of the plan on November 3, 2014. Also for this purpose, a binding written commitment exists when an employer is contractually required to pay for an arrangement, and a plan begins enrolling employees when it begins accepting employee elections to participate in the plan. See 80 FR 10828.

Explanation of Provisions

The preamble to the HHS regulations acknowledges that self-insured and large group market group health plans are not required to cover the essential health benefits, but notes that a health plan that does not provide substantial coverage for inpatient hospitalization and physician services does not meet a universally accepted minimum standard of value expected from and inherent in any arrangement that can reasonably be called a health plan and that is intended to provide the primary health coverage for employees. The preamble concludes that it is evident in the structure of and policy underlying the Affordable Care Act that the minimum value standard may be interpreted to require that employer-sponsored plans cover critical benefits. See 80 FR 10827-10828.

As the preamble notes, allowing plans that fail to provide substantial coverage of inpatient hospital or physician services to be treated as providing minimum value would adversely affect employees (particularly those with significant health risks) who may find this coverage insufficient, by denying them access to a premium tax credit for individual coverage purchased through an Exchange, while at the same time avoiding the employer shared responsibility payment under section 4980H. Plans that omit critical benefits used disproportionately by individuals in poor health would likely enroll far fewer of these individuals, effectively driving down employer costs at the expense of those who, because of their individual health status, are discouraged from enrolling. See 80 FR 10827-10829.

Accordingly, these proposed regulations incorporate the substance of the rule in the HHS regulations. They provide that an eligible employer-sponsored plan provides minimum value only if the plan's share of the total allowed costs of benefits provided to an employee is at least 60 percent and the plan provides substantial coverage of inpatient hospital and physician services. Comments are requested on rules for determining whether a plan provides "substantial coverage" of inpatient hospital and physician services.

Effective/Applicability Date and Transition Relief

These regulations are proposed to apply for plan years beginning after November 3, 2014. However, for purposes of section 4980H(b), the changes to the minimum value regulations (in §1.36B-6(a)(2) of these proposed regulations) do not apply before the end of the plan year beginning no later than March 1, 2015 to a plan that fails to provide substantial coverage for in-patient hospitalization services or for physician services (or both), provided that the employer had entered into a binding written commitment to adopt the noncompliant plan terms, or had begun enrolling employees in the plan with noncompliant plan terms, before November 4, 2014. For this purpose, the plan year is the plan year in effect under the terms of the plan on November 3, 2014. Also for this purpose, a binding written commitment exists when an employer is contractually required to pay for an arrangement, and a plan begins enrolling employees when it begins accepting employee elections to participate in the plan. The relief provided in this section does not apply to an applicable large employer that would have been liable for a payment under section 4980H without regard to §1.36B-6(a)(2) of these proposed regulations.

An offer of coverage under an eligible employer-sponsored plan that does not comply with §1.36B-6(a)(2) of these proposed regulations does not preclude an employee from obtaining a premium tax credit under section 36B, if otherwise eligible.

Special Analyses

Certain IRS regulations, including this one, are exempt from the requirements of Executive Order 12866, as supplemented and reaffirmed by Executive Order 13563. Therefore, a regulatory impact assessment is not required. It has been determined that section 553(b) of the Administrative Procedure Act (5 U.S.C. chapter 5) does not apply to these regulations and, because the regulations do not impose a collection of information on small entities, the Regulatory Flexibility Act (5 U.S.C. chapter 6) does not apply. Pursuant to section 7805(f) of the Code, this notice of proposed rulemaking has been submitted to the Chief Counsel for Advocacy of the Small Business Administration for comment on its impact on small business.

Comments and Requests for Public Hearing

Before these proposed regulations are adopted as final regulations, consideration will be given to any comments that are submitted timely to the IRS as prescribed in this preamble under the

"Addresses" heading. The Treasury Department and the IRS request comments on all aspects of the proposed rules. All comments will be available at *www.regulations.gov* or upon request. A public hearing will be scheduled if requested in writing by any person who timely submits written comments. If a public hearing is scheduled, notice of the date, time, and place for the hearing will be published in the **Federal Register**.

Drafting Information

The principal author of these regulations is Andrew Braden of the Office of the Associate Chief Counsel (Income Tax and Accounting). However, other personnel from the Treasury Department and the IRS participated in their development.

[¶49,667] Proposed Amendments of Regulations (REG-139483-13), published in the Federal Register on September 16, 2015 (corrected 11/4/2015).

[Code Secs. 367, 482, 884, 1248 and 6038]

Property transfers: U.S. to foreign corporation: Nonrecognition transaction: Foreign goodwill: Going concern value: Transfer pricing .—Reg. §1.482-1, relating to certain transfers of property by United States persons to foreign corporations, are proposed. Reg. §§1.367(a)-0, 1.367(a)-6 and 1.367(d)-1 and amendments of Reg. §§1.367(a)-1, 1.367(a)-2, 1.367(a)-3, 1.367(a)-4, 1.367(a)-5, 1.367(a)-7, 1.367(a)-8, 1.367(e)-2, 1.884-5, 1.1248-8, 1.1248(f)-2 and 1.6038B-1 were adopted by T.D. 9803 on December 14, 2016.

AGENCY: Internal Revenue Service (IRS), Treasury.

ACTION: Notice of proposed rulemaking; notice of proposed rulemaking by cross-reference to temporary regulation.

SUMMARY: This document contains proposed regulations relating to certain transfers of property by United States persons to foreign corporations. The proposed regulations affect United States persons that transfer certain property, including foreign goodwill and going concern value, to foreign corporations in nonrecognition transactions described in section 367 of the Internal Revenue Code (Code). The proposed regulations also combine portions of the existing regulations under section 367(a) into a single regulation. In addition, in the Rules and Regulations section of this issue of the **Federal Register**, temporary regulations are being issued under section 482 to clarify the coordination of the transfer pricing rules with other Code provisions. The text of those temporary regulations serves as the text of a portion of these proposed regulations.

DATES: Written or electronic comments and requests for a public hearing must be received by December 15, 2015.

ADDRESSES: Send submissions to: CC:PA:LPD:PR (REG-139483-13), Internal Revenue Service, Room 5203, P.O. Box 7604, Ben Franklin Station, Washington, DC 20044. Submissions may be hand-delivered Monday through Friday between the hours of 8 a.m. and 4 p.m. to CC:PA:LPD:PR (REG-139483-13), Courier's Desk, Internal Revenue Service, 1111 Constitution Avenue, NW, Washington, DC 20224; or sent electronically via the Federal eRulemaking Portal at http://www.regulations.gov (IRS REG-139483-13).

FOR FURTHER INFORMATION CONTACT: Concerning the proposed regulations, Ryan A. Bowen, (202) 317-6937; concerning submissions of comments or requests for a public hearing, Regina Johnson, (202) 317-6901 (not toll-free numbers). SUPPLEMENTARY INFORMATION:

Paperwork Reduction Act

The collections of information contained in the regulations have been submitted for review and approved by the Office of Management and Budget in accordance with the Paperwork Reduction Act of 1995 (44 U.S.C. 3507 (d)) under control number 1545-0026.

The collections of information are in §1.6038B-1(c)(4) and (d)(1). The collections of information are mandatory. The likely respondents are domestic corporations. Burdens associated with these requirements will be reflected in the burden for Form 926. Estimates for completing the Form 926 can be located in the form instructions.

An agency may not conduct or sponsor, and a person is not required to respond to, a collection of information unless it displays a valid control number.

Books and records relating to a collection of information must be retained as long as their contents might become material in the administration of any internal revenue law. Generally, tax returns and tax return information are confidential, as required by 26 U.S.C. 6103.

Background

I. *Current Law*

A. *Section 367(a)*

Section 367(a)(1) provides that if, in connection with any exchange described in section 332, 351, 354, 356, or 361, a United States person (U.S. transferor) transfers property to a foreign corporation (outbound transfer), the transferee foreign corporation will not, for purposes of determining the extent to which gain shall be recognized on such transfer, be considered to be a corporation. As a result, under section 367(a)(1), the U.S. transferor recognizes any gain (but not loss) on the outbound transfer of the property. Section 367(a)(2) provides an exception to the application of section 367(a)(1) for certain transfers of stock or securities, and section 367(a)(3) provides an exception for transfers of certain property used in a trade or business.

Specifically, section 367(a)(3)(A) provides that, except as provided in regulations prescribed by the Secretary, the general rule of section 367(a)(1) will not apply to any property transferred to a foreign corporation for use by such foreign corporation in the active conduct of a trade or business outside of the United States (ATB exception). Section 367(a)(3)(B) provides that, except as provided in regulations prescribed by the Secretary, certain property is not eligible for the ATB exception. The statute describes five categories of property that are not eligible for the ATB exception: (i) property described in paragraph (1) or (3) of section 1221(a) (relating to inventory and copyrights, etc.); (ii) installment obligations, accounts receivable, or similar property; (iii) foreign currency or other property denominated in foreign currency; (iv) intangible property within the meaning of section 936(h)(3)(B); and (v) property with respect to which the U.S. transferor is a lessor at the time of the transfer, unless the foreign corporation was the lessee.

Section 367(a)(3)(C) provides that, except as provided in regulations prescribed by the Secretary, the ATB exception will not apply to gain realized on an outbound transfer of the assets of a foreign branch to the extent that previously deducted losses of the branch exceed the taxable income earned by the branch after the losses were incurred (branch loss recapture rule). However, any realized gain in the property transferred that exceeds the branch losses that must be recaptured under this rule may qualify for the ATB exception.

Section 367(a)(6) provides that section 367(a)(1) will not apply to an outbound transfer of any property that the Secretary, in order to carry out the purposes of section 367(a), designates by regulation.

Sections 1.367(a)-2 and 1.367(a)-2T provide general rules for determining whether property is transferred for use by a transferee foreign corporation in the active conduct of a trade or business outside of the United States for purposes of the ATB exception.

Sections 1.367(a)-4 and 1.367(a)-4T provide special rules for determining whether certain property satisfies the ATB exception, including rules that apply to (i) property to be leased by the transferee foreign corporation, (ii) oil and gas working interests, (iii) compulsory transfers of property, and (iv) property to be sold by the foreign corporation. Section 1.367(a)-4T also provides special rules requiring the recapture of depreciation upon an outbound transfer of U.S. depreciated property and exempting outbound transfers of property to a FSC (within the meaning of section 922(a)) from the application of paragraphs (a) and (d) of section 367.

Sections 1.367(a)-5 and 1.367(a)-5T address the five categories of property ineligible for the ATB exception that are described in section 367(a)(3)(B) and provide narrow exceptions to certain of those categories. Section 1.367(a)-5T(d) (which addresses foreign currency and other property denominated in a foreign currency) allows certain property denominated in the foreign currency of the country in which the foreign corporation is organized to qualify under the ATB exception if that property was acquired in the ordinary course of the business of the U.S. transferor that will be carried on by the foreign corporation. Section 1.367(a)-5T(e) (which addresses intangible property) contains a deadwood reference to the application of section 367(a)(1) to a transfer of intangible property pursuant to section 332. In this regard, see § 1.367(e)-2(a)(2), providing that section 367(a) does not apply to a liquidation described in section 332 of a U.S. subsidiary into a foreign parent corporation. Section 1.367(a)-5T(e) also provides a cross reference to section 367(d) for transfers of intangible property described in section 351 or 361.

Sections 1.367(a)-6 and 1.367(a)-6T provide rules for applying the branch loss recapture rule of section 367(a)(3)(C).

B. *Section 367(d)*

Section 367(d) provides rules for certain outbound transfers of intangible property. Section 367(d)(1) provides that, except as provided in regulations, if a U.S. transferor transfers any intangible property, within the meaning of section 936(h)(3)(B), to a foreign corporation in an exchange described in section 351 or 361, section 367(d) (and not section 367(a)) applies to such transfer.

Section 936(h)(3)(B) defines intangible property broadly to mean any:

(i) patent, invention, formula, process, design, pattern, or know-how;

(ii) copyright, literary, musical, or artistic composition;

(iii) trademark, trade name, or brand name;

(iv) franchise, license, or contract;

(v) method, program, system, procedure, campaign, survey, study, forecast, estimate, customer list, or technical data; or

(vi) any similar item,

which has substantial value independent of the services of any individual (section 936(h)(3)(B) intangible property).

Section 367(d)(2)(A) provides that a U.S. transferor that transfers intangible property subject to section 367(d) is treated as having sold the property in exchange for payments that are contingent upon the productivity, use, or disposition of the property. Specifically, the U.S. transferor is treated as receiving amounts that reasonably reflect the amounts that would have been received annually in the form of such payments over the useful life of such property (section 367(d)(2)(A)(ii)(I)), or in the case of a disposition of the intangible property following such transfer (whether direct or indirect), at the time of the disposition (section 367(d)(2)(A)(ii)(II)). The amounts taken into account under section

367(d)(2)(A)(ii) must be commensurate with the income attributable to the intangible. Section 367(d)(2)(A) (flush language).

Section 1.367(d)-1T(b) generally provides that section 367(d) and § 1.367(d)-1T apply to the transfer of any intangible property, but not to the transfer of foreign goodwill or going concern value, as defined in § 1.367(a)-1T(d)(5)(iii) (foreign goodwill exception). Section 1.367(a)-1T(d)(5)(i) generally defines "intangible property," for purposes of section 367, as knowledge, rights, documents, and any other intangible item within the meaning of section 936(h)(3)(B) that constitutes property for purposes of section 332, 351, 354, 355, 356, or 361, as applicable. The regulation further provides that a working interest in oil and gas property will not be considered to be intangible property for purposes of section 367 and the regulations thereunder.

Section 1.367(a)-1T(d)(5)(iii) defines "foreign goodwill or going concern value" as the residual value of a business operation conducted outside of the United States after all other tangible and intangible assets have been identified and valued. Section 1.367(a)-1T(d)(5)(iii) also provides that, for purposes of section 367 and the regulations thereunder, the value of a right to use a corporate name in a foreign country is treated as foreign goodwill or going concern value.

In addition to providing the foreign goodwill exception, § 1.367(d)-1T(b) also excepts from section 367(d) property that is described in § 1.367(a)-5T(b)(2), which, in general, consists of copyrights and other items described in section 1221(a)(3). Those items, however, are not eligible for the ATB exception by reason of § 1.367(a)-5T.

For purposes of § 1.367(d)-1T, the useful life of intangible property is limited to 20 years under § 1.367(d)-1T(c)(3).

C. *Legislative History of Section 367(d)*

Congress amended section 367 in 1984 to create objective statutory rules because, among other reasons, the IRS was experiencing challenges administering the prior version of the statute. The prior version provided that certain outbound transfers of property qualified for tax-free treatment only if the U.S. transferor established that the outbound transfer was "not in pursuance of a plan having as one its principal purposes the avoidance of Federal income taxes."

In amending section 367, Congress also noted that "specific and unique problems exist" with respect to outbound transfers of intangible property and enacted section 367(d) in substantially its present form to address these transfers. S. REP. NO. 169, 98th Cong., 2d Sess., at 360 (1984); H.R. REP. NO. 432, 98th Cong., 2d Sess., at 1315 (1984). Congress identified problems as arising when "transferor U.S. companies hope to reduce their U.S. taxable income by deducting substantial research and experimentation expenses associated with the development of the transferred intangible and, by transferring the intangible to a foreign corporation at the point of profitability, to ensure deferral of U.S. tax on the profits generated by the intangible." *Id.*

The favorable treatment of foreign goodwill and going concern value available under existing law is premised on statements in the legislative history of section 367(d). "The committee contemplates that, ordinarily, no gain will be recognized on the transfer of goodwill or going concern value for use in an active trade or business." S. REP. NO. 169, 98th Cong., 2d Sess., at 364; H.R. REP. NO. 432, 98th Cong., 2d Sess., at 1319. The Senate Finance Committee and the House Committee on Ways and Means each noted, without explanation, that it "does not anticipate that the transfer of goodwill or going concern value developed by a foreign branch to a newly organized foreign corporation will result in abuse of the U.S. tax system." S. REP. NO. 169, 98th Cong., 2d Sess., at 362; H.R. REP. NO. 432, 98th Cong., 2d Sess., at 1317. However, neither section 367 nor its legislative history defines goodwill or going concern value of a foreign branch or discusses how goodwill or going concern value is attributed to a foreign branch.

D. *Taxpayer Interpretations Regarding Foreign Goodwill and Going Concern Value Under Section 367*

In general, taxpayers interpret section 367 and the regulations under section 367(a) and (d) in one of two alternative ways when claiming favorable treatment for foreign goodwill and going concern value.

Under one interpretation, taxpayers take the position that goodwill and going concern value are not section 936(h)(3)(B) intangible property and therefore are not subject to section 367(d) because section 367(d) applies only to section 936(h)(3)(B) intangible property. Under this interpretation, taxpayers assert that the foreign goodwill exception has no application. Furthermore, these taxpayers assert that gain realized with respect to the outbound transfer of goodwill or going concern value is not recognized under the general rule of section 367(a)(1) because the goodwill or going concern value is eligible for, and satisfies, the ATB exception under section 367(a)(3)(A).

Under a second interpretation, taxpayers take the position that, although goodwill and going concern value are section 936(h)(3)(B) intangible property, the foreign goodwill exception applies. These taxpayers also assert that section 367(a)(1) does not apply to foreign goodwill or going concern value, either because of section 367(d)(1)(A) (providing that, except as provided in regulations, section 367(d) and not section 367(a) applies to section 936(h)(3)(B) intangible property) or because of the ATB exception.

II. *Reasons for Change*

The Treasury Department and the IRS are aware that, in the context of outbound transfers, certain taxpayers attempt to avoid recognizing gain or income attributable to high-value intangible property by asserting that an inappropriately large share (in many cases, the majority) of the value of the property transferred is foreign goodwill or going concern value that is eligible for favorable treatment under section 367.

Specifically, the Treasury Department and the IRS are aware that some taxpayers value the property transferred in a manner contrary to section 482 in order to minimize the value of the property transferred that they identify as section 936(h)(3)(B) intangible property for which a deemed income inclusion is required under section 367(d) and to maximize the value of the property transferred that they identify as exempt from current tax. For example, some taxpayers (i) use valuation methods that value items of intangible property on an item-by-item basis, when valuing the items on an aggregate basis would achieve a more reliable result under the arm's length standard of the section 482 regulations, or (ii) do not properly perform a full factual and functional analysis of the business in which the intangible property is employed.

The Treasury Department and the IRS also are aware that some taxpayers broadly interpret the meaning of foreign goodwill and going concern value for purposes of section 367. Specifically, although the existing regulations under section 367 define foreign goodwill or going concern value by reference to a business operation conducted outside of the United States, some taxpayers have asserted that they have transferred significant foreign goodwill or going concern value when a large share of that value was associated with a business operated primarily by employees in the United States, where the business simply earned income remotely from foreign customers. In addition, some taxpayers take the position that value created through customer-facing activities occurring within the United States is foreign goodwill or going concern value.

The Treasury Department and the IRS have concluded that the taxpayer positions and interpretations described in this section of the preamble raise significant policy concerns and are inconsistent with the expectation, expressed in legislative history, that the transfer of foreign goodwill or going concern value developed by a foreign branch to a foreign corporation was unlikely to result in abuse of the U.S. tax system. *See* S. REP. NO. 169, 98th Cong., 2d Sess., at 362; H.R. REP. NO. 432, 98th Cong., 2d Sess., at 1317. The Treasury Department and the IRS considered whether the favorable treatment for foreign goodwill and going concern value under current law could be preserved while protecting the U.S. tax base through regulations expressly prescribing parameters for the portion of the value of a business that qualifies for the favorable treatment. For example, regulations could require that, to be eligible for the favorable treatment, the value must have been created by activities conducted outside of the United States through an actual foreign branch that had been in operation for a minimum number of years and be attributable to unrelated foreign customers. The Treasury Department and the IRS ultimately determined, however, that such an approach would be impractical to administer. In particular, while the temporary regulations under section 482 that are published in the Rules and Regulations section of this issue of the **Federal Register** clarify the proper application of section 482 in important respects, there will continue to be challenges in administering the transfer pricing rules whenever the transfer of different types of intangible property gives rise to significantly different tax consequences. Given the amounts at stake, as long as foreign goodwill and going concern value are afforded favorable treatment, taxpayers will continue to have strong incentives to take aggressive transfer pricing positions to inappropriately exploit the favorable treatment of foreign goodwill and going concern value, however defined, and thereby erode the U.S. tax base.

For the reasons discussed in this section of the preamble, the Treasury Department and the IRS have determined that allowing intangible property to be transferred outbound in a tax-free manner is inconsistent with the policies of section 367 and sound tax administration and therefore will amend the regulations under section 367 as described in the Explanation of Provisions section of this preamble.

III. *Coordination with Section 482*

The temporary regulations under section 482 published in the Rules and Regulations section of this issue of the **Federal Register** clarify the coordination of the application of the arm's length standard and the best method rule in the regulations under section 482 in conjunction with other Code provisions, including section 367, in determining the proper tax treatment of controlled transactions. The text of the temporary regulations under section 482 also serves as the text of a portion of these proposed regulations. The preamble to the temporary regulations explains the temporary regulations and the corresponding proposed regulations.

Explanation of Provisions

I. *Eliminating the Foreign Goodwill Exception and Limiting the Scope of the ATB Exception*

A. *In General*

The proposed regulations eliminate the foreign goodwill exception under § 1.367(d)-1T and limit the scope of property that is eligible for the ATB exception generally to certain tangible property and financial assets. Accordingly, under the proposed regulations, upon an outbound transfer of foreign goodwill or going concern value, a U.S. transferor will be subject to either current gain recognition under section 367(a)(1) or the tax treatment provided under section 367(d).

B. *Modifications to § 1.367(d)-1T*

Proposed § 1.367(d)-1(b) provides that section 367(d) and § 1.367(d)-1 apply to an outbound transfer of intangible property, as defined in proposed § 1.367(a)-1(d)(5). Proposed § 1.367(d)-1(b) does not provide an exception for any intangible property. Rather, as described in part II. of the Explanation of Provisions section of this preamble, proposed § 1.367(a)-1(d)(5) modifies the definition of intangible property that applies for purposes of section 367(a) and (d). The modified definition facilitates both the elimination of the foreign goodwill exception as well as the addition of a rule under which U.S. transferors may apply section 367(d) with respect to certain outbound transfers of property that otherwise would be subject to section 367(a) under the U.S. transferor's interpretation of section 936(h)(3)(B). The proposed regulations make certain coordinating changes to § 1.367(d)-1T to take into account the elimination of the foreign goodwill exception and the revised definition of intangible property. The specific provisions of the temporary regulations that will be replaced by the proposed regulations will be removed upon finalization. The proposed regulations also eliminate the definition of foreign goodwill and going concern value under existing § 1.367(a)-1T(d)(5)(iii) because it is no longer needed.

In addition, the proposed regulations eliminate the existing rule under § 1.367(d)-1T(c)(3) that limits the useful life of intangible property to 20 years. When the useful life of the intangible property transferred exceeds 20 years, the limitation might result in less than all of the income attributable to the property being taken into account by the U.S. transferor. Accordingly, proposed § 1.367(d)-1(c)(3) provides that the useful life of intangible property is the entire period during which the exploitation of the intangible property is reasonably anticipated to occur, as of the time of transfer. For this purpose, exploitation includes use of the intangible property in research and development. Consistent with the guidance for cost sharing arrangements in § 1.482-7(g)(2)(ii)(A), if the intangible property is reasonably anticipated to contribute to its own further development or to developing other intangibles, then the period includes the period, reasonably anticipated at the time of the transfer, of exploiting (including use in research and development) such further development. Consequently, depending on the facts, the cessation of exploitation activity after a specific period of time may or may not be reasonably anticipated. *See, e.g.*, § 1.482-7(g)(4)(viii), *Examples 1* (cessation anticipated after 15 years) and 7 (cessation not anticipated at any determinable date).

C. *Modifications Relating to the ATB Exception*

The rules for determining whether property is eligible for the ATB exception and whether the property satisfies the ATB exception currently are found in numerous regulations, namely § § 1.367(a)-2, 1.367(a)-2T, 1.367(a)-4, 1.367(a)-4T, 1.367(a)-5, and 1.367(a)-5T (collectively, the ATB regulations). To make the regulations more accessible, the proposed regulations combine the ATB regulations, other than the depreciation recapture rule, into a single regulation under proposed § 1.367(a)-2. Accordingly, upon finalization of the proposed regulations, current § § 1.367(a)-2T, 4T, and 5T will be removed. The proposed regulations retain a coordination rule pursuant to which a transfer of stock or securities in an exchange subject to § 1.367(a)-3 is not subject to § 1.367(a)-2. *See* § 1.367(a)-2(a)(1). The proposed regulations make conforming changes to the depreciation recapture rule, which is moved from § 1.367(a)-4T to § 1.367(a)-4, and the branch loss recapture rule, which remains under § § 1.367(a)-6 and 1.367(a)-6T. Although minor wording changes have been made to certain aspects of the ATB regulations as part of consolidating them into a single regulation, the proposed regulations are not intended to be interpreted as making substantive changes to the ATB regulations except as otherwise described in this section of the preamble.

Under existing regulations, all property is eligible for the ATB exception, unless the property is specifically excluded. Under this structure, taxpayers have an incentive to take the position that certain intangible property is not described in section 936(h)(3)(B) and therefore not subject to section 367(d) and is instead subject to section 367(a) but eligible for the ATB exception because the intangible property is not specifically excluded from the ATB exception. The Treasury Department and the IRS have concluded that providing an exclusive list of property eligible for the ATB exception will reduce the incentives for taxpayers to undervalue intangible property subject to section 367(d).

Thus, the proposed regulations provide that only certain types of property (as described in the next paragraph) are eligible for the ATB exception. However, in order for eligible property to satisfy the ATB exception, that property must also be considered transferred for use in the active conduct of a trade or business outside of the United States. Specifically, proposed § 1.367(a)-2(a)(2) provides the general rule that an outbound transfer of property satisfies the ATB exception if (i) the property constitutes eligible property, (ii) the property is transferred for use by the foreign corporation in the active conduct of a trade or business outside of the United States, and (iii) certain reporting requirements under section 6038B are satisfied.

Under proposed § 1.367(a)-2(b), eligible property is tangible property, working interests in oil and gas property, and certain financial assets, unless the property is also described in one of four categories of ineligible property. Proposed § 1.367(a)-2(c) lists four categories of property not eligible for the ATB exception, which, in general, are (i) inventory or similar property; (ii) installment obligations, accounts receivable, or similar property; (iii) foreign currency or certain other property denominated in foreign currency; and (iv) certain leased tangible property. These four categories of property not eligible for the ATB exception include four of the five categories described in existing regulations under § § 1.367(a)-5 and 1.367-5T. The category for intangible property is not retained because it is not relevant: Intangible property transferred to a foreign corporation pursuant to section 351 or 361 is not eligible property under proposed § 1.367(a)-2(b) without regard to the application of proposed § 1.367(a)-2(c).

The proposed regulations also eliminate the exception in existing § 1.367(a)-5T(d)(2) that allows certain property denominated in the foreign currency of the country in which the foreign corporation is organized to qualify under the ATB exception if that property was acquired in the ordinary course of the business of the U.S. transferor that will be carried on by the foreign corporation. The Treasury Department and the IRS have determined that removing the exception is consistent with the general policy of section 367(a)(3)(B)(iii) to require gain to be recognized on an outbound transfer of foreign currency denominated property. Removing the exception will preserve the character, source, and amount of gain attributable to section 988 transactions that otherwise could be lost or changed if such gain were not immediately recognized but instead were reflected only in the U.S. transferor's basis in the stock of the foreign corporation.

The general rules for determining whether eligible property is transferred for use in the active conduct of a trade or business outside of the United States are described in proposed § 1.367(a)-2(d). Also, paragraphs (e) through (h) of proposed § 1.367(a)-2 provide special rules for certain property to be leased after the transfer, a working interest in oil and gas property, property that is re-transferred by the transferee foreign corporation to another person, and certain compulsory transfers of property, respectively. The proposed regulations also combine existing § 1.367(a)-2T(c) (relating to property that is re-transferred by the foreign corporation) and a portion of § 1.367(a)-4T(d) (relating to property to be sold by the foreign corporation) into proposed § 1.367(a)-2(g), because both of these existing provisions relate to subsequent transfers of property by the foreign corporation. *See* proposed § 1.367(a)-2(g)(1) and (2), respectively. Proposed § 1.367(a)-2(g)(2) does not retain the portion of existing § 1.367(a)-4T(d) that applies to certain transfers of stock or securities. The Treasury Department and the IRS have determined that §§ 1.367(a)-3 and 1.367(a)-8 (generally requiring U.S. transferors that own five-percent or more of the stock of the foreign corporation to enter into a gain recognition agreement to avoid recognizing gain under section 367(a)(1) upon the outbound transfer of stock or securities) adequately carry out the policy of section 367(a) with respect to the transfer of stock or securities.

The proposed regulations modify the scope of the term U.S. depreciated property for purposes of the depreciation recapture rule to include section 126 property (as defined in section 1255(a)(2)).

The proposed regulations eliminate the special rules for outbound transfers of property to a FSC, because the FSC provisions have been repealed. Tax Increase Prevention and Reconciliation Act of 2005, Pub L. No. 109-222, § 513, 120 Stat. 366 (2006); FSC Repeal and Extraterritorial Income Exclusion Act of 2000, Pub. L. No. 106-519, § 2, 114 Stat. 2423 (2000).

Finally, the proposed regulations make conforming changes to the reporting requirements under § 1.6038B-1(c)(4) to take into account the proposed regulations under § 1.367(a)-2. The proposed regulations retain a rule providing relief for certain failures to comply with the reporting requirements of section 6038B and the regulations thereunder for qualification under the ATB exception, but that rule is moved to proposed § 1.367(a)-2(j).

II. *Treatment of Certain Property as Subject to Section 367(d)*

Taxpayers take different positions as to whether goodwill and going concern value are section 936(h)(3)(B) intangible property, as discussed in part I.D. of the Background section of this preamble. The proposed regulations do not address this issue. However, the proposed regulations under § 1.367(a)-1(b)(5) provide that a U.S. transferor may apply section 367(d) to a transfer of property, other than certain property described below, that otherwise would be subject to section 367(a) under the U.S. transferor's interpretation of section 936(h)(3)(B). Under this rule, a U.S. transferor that takes the position that goodwill and going concern value are not section 936(h)(3)(B) intangible property may nonetheless apply section 367(d) to goodwill and going concern value. This rule furthers sound tax administration by reducing the consequences of uncertainty as to whether value is attributable to property subject to section 367(a) or property subject to section 367(d). The application of section 367(d) in lieu of section 367(a) is available only for property that is not eligible property, as defined in proposed § 1.367(a)-2(b) but, for this purpose, determined without regard to § 1.367(a)-2(c) (which describes four categories of property explicitly excluded from the ATB exception). A U.S. transferor must disclose whether it is applying section 367(a) or (d) to a transfer of such property. *See* proposed §§ 1.6038B-1(c)(4)(vii) and -1(d)(1)(iv).

To implement this new rule under proposed § 1.367(a)-1(b)(5) and the removal of the foreign goodwill exception, the proposed regulations revise the definition of "intangible property" that applies for purposes of sections 367(a) and (d). As revised, the term means either property described in section 936(h)(3)(B) or property to which a U.S. transferor applies section 367(d) (in lieu of applying section 367(a)). However, for this purpose and consistent with existing regulations, intangible property does not include property described in section 1221(a)(3) (generally relating to certain copyrights) or a working interest in oil and gas property.

The regulations under § 1.367(a)-7 (concerning outbound transfers of property subject to section 367(a) in certain asset reorganizations) use the term "section 367(d) property" to describe property that is not subject to section 367(a) and is therefore not subject to § 1.367(a)-7. The proposed regulations modify the definition of section 367(d) property in § 1.367(a)-7(f)(11) (which currently defines section 367(d) property as property described in section 936(h)(3)(B)) by reference to the new definition of "intangible property" under the proposed regulations. When the Treasury Department and the IRS issue regulations to implement the guidance described in Notice 2012-39 (IRB 2012-31) (announcing regulations to be issued addressing outbound transfers of intangible property subject to section 367(d) in certain asset reorganizations), the definition of "section 367(d) property" provided in section 4.05(3) of the notice will be similarly modified.

III. *Modifications to § 1.367(a)-1T*

Section 1.482-1T(f)(2)(i) of the temporary regulations published elsewhere in the Rules and Regulations section of this issue of the **Federal Register** clarify the coordination of the application of the arm's length standard and the best method rule in the regulations under section 482 in conjunction with other Code provisions, including section 367, in determining the proper tax treatment of controlled transactions. Proposed § 1.367(a)-1(b)(3) provides that, in cases where an outbound transfer of property subject to section 367(a) constitutes a controlled transaction, as defined in § 1.482-1(i)(8), the value of the property transferred is determined in accordance with section 482 and the regulations thereunder. This rule replaces existing § 1.367(a)-1T(b)(3), which includes three rules.

First, § 1.367(a)-1T(b)(3)(i) provides that "the gain required to be recognized . . . shall in no event exceed the gain that would have been recognized on a taxable sale of those items of property *if sold individually and without offsetting individual losses against individual gains*" (emphasis added). The Treasury Department and the IRS are concerned that in controlled transactions, taxpayers might have interpreted the wording "if sold individually" as inconsistent with § 1.482-1T(f)(2)(i)(B) (as clarified in temporary regulations published elsewhere in the Rules and Regulations section in this issue of the **Federal Register**), which provides that an aggregate analysis of transactions may provide the most reliable measure of an arm's length result in certain circumstances.

Second, § 1.367(a)-1T(b)(3)(ii) provides that no loss may be recognized by reason of section 367. That rule duplicates a loss disallowance rule in § 1.367(a)-1T(b)(1), which provides that section 367(a)(1) denies nonrecognition only to transfers of items of property on which gain is realized and that losses do not affect the amount of the gain recognized because of section 367(a)(1).

Third, § 1.367(a)-1T(b)(3)(iii) provides a rule to address a scenario in which ordinary income and capital gain could exceed the amount described in § 1.367(a)-1T(b)(3)(i). Because these regulations replace § 1.367(a)-1T(b)(3)(i), § 1.367(a)-1T(b)(3)(iii) is no longer necessary.

IV. *Proposed Effective/Applicability Dates*

The proposed regulations are proposed to apply to transfers occurring on or after September 14, 2015 and to transfers occurring before September 14, 2015 resulting from entity classification elections made under § 301.7701-3 that are filed on or after September 14, 2015. However, the removal of the exception currently provided in § 1.367(a)-5T(d)(2) will apply to transfers occurring on or after the date that the rules proposed in this section are adopted as final regulations in a Treasury decision published in the **Federal Register** and to transfers occurring before that date resulting from entity classification elections made under § 301.7701-3 that are filed on or after that date. For proposed dates of applicability, see § 1.367(a)-1(g)(5), -2(k), -4(b), -6(k), -7(j)(2), 1.367(d)-1(j), and 1.6038B-1(g)(7). No inference is intended as to the application of the provisions proposed to be amended by these proposed regulations under current law. The IRS may, where appropriate, challenge transactions under applicable provisions or judicial doctrines.

Special Analyses

Certain IRS regulations, including this one, are exempt from the requirements of Executive Order 12866, as supplemented and reaffirmed by Executive Order 13563. Therefore, a regulatory impact assessment is not required. It has been determined that section 553(b) and (d) of the Administrative Procedure Act (5 U.S.C. chapter 5) does not apply to these regulations. It is hereby certified that the collection of information contained in this regulation will not have a significant economic impact on a substantial number of small entities. Accordingly, a regulatory flexibility analysis is not required. This certification is based on the fact that the proposed regulations under section 367(a) and (d) simplify existing regulations, and the regulations under section 6038B make relatively minor changes to existing information reporting requirements. Moreover, these regulations primarily will affect large domestic corporations filing consolidated returns. In addition, the Regulatory Flexibility Act (5 U.S.C. chapter 6) does not apply to the regulations under section 482 that are proposed herein, and published as temporary regulations in the Rules and Regulations section of this issue of the **Federal Register**, because those regulations do not impose a collection of information requirement on small entities. Pursuant to section 7805(f) of the Code, these regulations have been submitted to the Chief Counsel for Advocacy of the Small Business Administration for comment on their impact on small business.

Comments and Requests for Public Hearing

Before these proposed regulations are adopted as final regulations, consideration will be given to any comments that are submitted timely to the IRS as prescribed in this preamble under the "Addresses" heading. The Treasury Department and the IRS request comments on all aspects of the proposed rules. In particular, comments are requested on whether, with respect to the proposed elimination of the foreign goodwill exception and narrowing of the scope of the ATB exception, a limited exception should be provided for certain narrow cases where there is limited potential for abuse. One such case, for example, might be a financial services business that operates in true branch form and for which there is regulatory pressure or compulsion to incorporate the assets of the branch in a foreign corporation. Comments should discuss how the IRS would administer any such exception. With respect to the ATB exception, comments are requested as to whether the definition of "financial asset" under proposed § 1.367(a)-2(b)(3) should be expanded to include other items. With respect to the proposed elimination of the 20-year limitation on the useful life of intangible property under § 1.367(d)-1T(c)(3), comments are requested on ways to simplify the administration of inclusions that section 367(d) requires for property with a very long useful life. All comments will be available at www.regulations.gov or upon request. A public hearing will be scheduled if requested in writing by any person that timely submits written comments. If a public hearing is scheduled, notice of the date, time, and place for the public hearing will be published in the **Federal Register**.

Drafting information

The principal author of these proposed regulations is Ryan Bowen, Office of Associate Chief Counsel (International). However, other personnel from the Treasury Department and the IRS participated in their development.

[¶49,674] Proposed Amendments of Regulations (REG-134219-08), published in the Federal Register on November 20, 2015 (corrected 1/13/2016).

[Code Secs. 66 and 6015]

Equitable relief: Joint and several liability: Innocent spouse relief: Suspension of collection: Statute of limitations: Res judicata: Underpayment, definition: Meaningful participation in prior hearing.—Amendments of Reg. §§1.66-1, 1.66-2, 1.66-3, 1.66-4, 1.66-5, 1.6015-0, 1.6015-1, 1.6015-2, 1.6015-3, 1.6015-4, 1.6015-5, 1.6015-6, 1.6015-7, 1.6015-8 and 1.6015-9 relating to relief from joint and several liability under section 6015 of the Internal Revenue Code (Code), are proposed.

AGENCY: Internal Revenue Service (IRS), Treasury.

ACTION: Notice of proposed rulemaking.

SUMMARY: This document contains proposed regulations relating to relief from joint and several liability under section 6015 of the Internal Revenue Code (Code). The regulations reflect changes in the law made by the Tax Relief and Health Care Act of 2006 as well as changes in the law arising from litigation. The regulations provide guidance to married individuals who filed joint returns and later seek relief from joint and several liability.

DATES: Written or electronic comments and requests for a public hearing must be received by February 18, 2016.

ADDRESSES: Send submissions to: CC:PA:LPD:PR (REG-134219-08), room 5203, Internal Revenue Service, PO Box 7604, Ben Franklin Station, Washington, DC 20044. Submissions may be hand-delivered Monday through Friday between the hours of 8 a.m. and 4 p.m. to CC:PA:LPD:PR (REG-134219-08), Courier's Desk, Internal Revenue Service, 1111 Constitution Avenue, N.W., Washington, DC; or sent electronically via the Federal eRulemaking Portal at www.regulations.gov (IRS REG-134219-08).

FOR FURTHER INFORMATION CONTACT: Concerning the proposed regulations, Nancy Rose at (202) 317-6844; concerning submissions of comments contact Oluwafunmilayo Taylor, (202) 317-6901 (not toll-free numbers).

SUPPLEMENTARY INFORMATION:

Background

This document contains proposed amendments to the Income Tax Regulations (26 CFR part 1) for relief from joint and several liability under section 6015 of the Code and relief from the operation of state community property law under section 66.

Section 6013(a) permits a husband and wife to file a joint income tax return. Section 6013(d)(3) provides that spouses filing a joint income tax return are jointly and severally liable for liabilities for tax arising from that return. The term "tax" includes additions to tax, additional amounts, penalties, and interest. See sections 6665(a)(2) and 6601(e)(1). Joint and several liability allows the IRS to collect the entire liability from either spouse who signed the joint return, without regard to whom the items of income, deduction, credit, or basis that gave rise to the liability are attributable. Prior to 1998, section 6013(e) provided limited relief from joint and several liability. In 1998, Congress enacted the Internal Revenue Service Restructuring and Reform Act of 1998, Public Law No. 105-206, 112 Stat. 685 (1998), which repealed section 6013(e) and replaced it with section 6015. Section 6015 applies to liabilities arising after July 22, 1998, and liabilities that arose on or before July 22, 1998, but remained unpaid as of that date.

Section 6015 provides three avenues for relief from joint and several liability-sections 6015(b), (c) and (f). To be eligible for relief from joint and several liability, a spouse must request relief. Under section 6015(b), a requesting spouse may be entitled to relief from joint and several liability for an understatement of tax attributable to erroneous items of the nonrequesting spouse. Section 6015(c) permits a taxpayer who is divorced, separated, widowed, or who had been living apart from the other spouse for 12 months to allocate his or her tax deficiency between the spouses as if separate returns had been filed. Claims for relief under section 6015(b) and (c) must be made within two years of the IRS's first collection activity against the requesting spouse. Finally, section 6015(f) confers discretion upon the Commissioner to grant equitable relief from joint and several liability for understatements and underpayments, based on all the facts and circumstances. Regulations under section 6015 were first prescribed in TD 9003, **Federal Register** (67 FR 47278) on July 18, 2002.

These proposed amendments are necessary to carry out the provisions of section 6015 and to reflect changes in the law since the publication of TD 9003. On December 20, 2006, Congress enacted the Tax Relief and Health Care Act of 2006, Public Law No. 109-432, div. C, title IV, section 408, 120 Stat. 2922, 3061-62 (2006) (the 2006 Act). The 2006 Act amended section 6015 to provide the United States Tax Court with jurisdiction to review the Commissioner's determination to deny equitable relief under section 6015(f) when the Commissioner has not determined a deficiency and to suspend the period of limitation for collection under section 6502 when relief is requested only under section 6015(f). The proposed regulations also provide clarification and additional guidance on procedural and substantive issues related to the three types of relief from joint and several liability under section 6015.

Section 66 provides relief for a spouse who did not file a joint return in a community property state and did not include in gross income an item of community income that would be attributable solely to the nonrequesting spouse but for the operation of state community property law. Regulations under section 66 were first prescribed in TD 9074, **Federal Register** (68 FR 41067) on July 10, 2003. The proposed regulations under section 66 contain only non-substantive changes.

Recently, other amendments to the regulations under section 6015 were proposed in a notice of proposed rulemaking (REG-132251-11) published in the **Federal Register** (78 FR 49242) on August 13, 2013. Those regulations proposed changes to § 1.6015-5 to remove the two-year deadline for taxpayers to file requests for equitable relief under section 6015(f), and other changes related to the time and manner for requesting relief. Additionally, on September 16, 2013, the IRS issued Rev. Proc. 2013-34 (2013-2 CB 397). Rev. Proc. 2013-34 revised the factors used in determining if a requesting spouse is eligible for equitable relief under sections 66(c) and 6015(f).

Explanation of Provisions

These regulations propose to make a number of significant changes to the existing regulations. These changes include providing additional guidance on the judicial doctrine of res judicata and the section 6015(g)(2) exception to res judicata when a requesting spouse did not meaningfully participate in a prior court proceeding. The regulations propose to add a list of acts to be considered in making the determination as to whether the requesting spouse meaningfully participated in a prior proceeding and provide examples of the operation of these rules. The regulations also (1) propose a definition of underpayment or unpaid tax for purposes of section 6015(f); (2) provide detailed rules regarding credits and refunds in innocent spouse cases; (3) expand the rule that penalties and interest are not separate items from which relief can be obtained to cases involving underpayments; (4) incorporate an administratively developed rule that attribution of an erroneous item follows the attribution of the underlying item that caused the increase to adjusted gross income (AGI); (5) update the discussion of the allocation rules under section 6015(c) and (d); and (6) revise the rules regarding prohibition on collection and suspension of the collection statute.

1. Section 1.6015-1

The procedures for requesting relief on Form 8857, "Request for Innocent Spouse Relief," under section 6015 have changed since 2006 because of the amendments to section 6015(e) made by Section 408 of Title IV of Division C of the 2006 Act. The amendments to section 6015(e) conferred jurisdiction on the Tax Court to review the Commissioner's denial of relief under section 6015(f) in cases in which a deficiency had not been asserted. The amendments also provided for a prohibition on collection and a corresponding tolling of the collection statute under section 6502 upon the filing of a request for relief under section 6015(f). The amendments apply to any liability for taxes arising on or after December 20, 2006, and to any liability for taxes arising before December 20, 2006, and remaining unpaid as of that date. As a result of the amendments, any request for relief under section 6015 will toll the collection statute, making it unnecessary for a spouse to elect or request a particular type of relief as required under § 1.6015-1(a)(2) of the current regulations. Accordingly, § 1.6015-1 and all sections referencing an election under § § 1.6015-2 and 1.6015-3 or a request for relief under § 1.6015-4 are proposed to be revised to reflect that a requesting spouse is no longer required to elect or request relief under a specific provision of section 6015. Thus, beginning with the June 2007 revision to the Form 8857, a requesting spouse makes a single request for relief on Form 8857. Section 1.6015-1 is also being revised to provide that the IRS will consider in all cases whether the requesting spouse is eligible for relief under § 1.6015-2 or § 1.6015-3, and if relief is not available under either of those sections, under § 1.6015-4.

Section 6015(g)(2) provides an exception to the common law doctrine of res judicata except in a case in which relief under section 6015 was at issue in a prior court proceeding or if a requesting spouse meaningfully participated in a prior proceeding in which relief under section 6015 could have been raised. Current § 1.6015-(e) is being revised in these proposed regulations to provide more detailed guidance on how the exception to res judicata and the meaningful participation rule work, and to reflect developments in the case law since 2002 (described below). Proposed § 1.6015-1(e)(1) restates the general rule from the current regulations.

Proposed § 1.6015-1(e)(2) incorporates the holding in *Deihl v. Commissioner*, 134 T.C. 156 (2010) (When a requesting spouse generally raises relief under section 6015 in a proceeding but does not specifically plead relief under any subsection of section 6015, relief under section 6015(c) will not be treated as being at issue in that proceeding if the requesting spouse was not eligible to elect relief under section 6015(c) because the requesting spouse was not divorced, widowed, legally separated, or living apart for 12 months at any time during the prior proceeding.).

Proposed § 1.6015-1(e)(3) provides guidance on the meaningful participation exception to res judicata provided by section 6015(g)(2). A requesting spouse meaningfully participated in the prior proceeding if the requesting spouse was involved in the proceeding so that the requesting spouse could have raised the issue of relief under section 6015 in that proceeding. Meaningful participation is a facts and circumstances determination. A nonexclusive list of acts was added in proposed § 1.6015-1(e)(3) to provide indicators of "meaningful participation" within the context of a bar against relief based on the judicial doctrine of res judicata. Whether a requesting spouse meaningfully participated in a prior proceeding is based on all the facts and circumstances. No one act necessarily determines the outcome. The degree of importance of each act varies depending on the requesting spouse's facts and circumstances. The following acts, derived from case law and experience since 2002, are among the acts the IRS and courts consider in making the determination regarding meaningful participation: whether the requesting spouse participated in the IRS Appeals process while the prior case was docketed; whether the requesting spouse participated in discovery; whether the requesting spouse participated in pretrial meetings, settlement negotiations, or trial; whether the requesting spouse signed court documents; and whether the requesting spouse was represented by counsel in the prior proceedings.

Proposed § 1.6015-1(e)(3)(i) provides a new rule under which the requesting spouse will not be considered to have meaningfully participated in the prior proceeding if the requesting spouse establishes that the requesting spouse performed any of the acts listed in proposed § 1.6015-1(e)(3) because the nonrequesting spouse abused or maintained control over the requesting spouse, and the requesting spouse did not challenge the nonrequesting spouse for fear of the nonrequesting spouse's retaliation. Proposed § 1.6015-1(e)(3)(ii) restates the rule from the current regulations that a requesting spouse did not meaningfully participate in a prior proceeding if, due to the effective date of section 6015, relief under section 6015 was not available in that proceeding.

Proposed § 1.6015-1(e)(3)(iii) provides that in a case petitioned from a statutory notice of deficiency under section 6213, the fact that the requesting spouse did not have the ability to effectively contest the underlying deficiency is irrelevant for purposes of determining whether the requesting spouse meaningfully participated in the prior proceeding. Treasury and the IRS disagree with the holding in *Harbin v. Commissioner*, 137 T.C. 93 (2011), in which the Tax Court concluded that Mr. Harbin did not meaningfully participate in the deficiency case in part because he could not effectively contest the part of the deficiency related to his ex-wife's gambling losses without her. The Tax Court found that Mr. Harbin could not effectively contest this part of the deficiency without his ex-wife because she "was the one with personal knowledge of the winnings and losses from the gambling activities" and was the one "who maintained and provided all of the documentation relating to the gambling activities." The Tax Court concluded that this knowledge and control of the documentation resulted in Mr. Harbin's ex-wife effectively exercising "exclusive control" of the case. *Harbin v. Commissioner*, 137 T.C. at 98.

Treasury and the IRS believe that the Tax Court applied the incorrect standard to determine whether a taxpayer meaningfully participated in a proceeding for purposes of section 6015(g)(2). The purpose of the meaningful participation exception to res judicata is not to ensure that a taxpayer had the opportunity to contest the deficiency but rather to ensure that the taxpayer could have raised relief under section 6015. *Moore v. Commissioner*, T.C. Memo. 2007-156. This is evident because, if section 6015 relief was at issue in the prior case, the taxpayer is not permitted to raise section 6015 relief in a subsequent proceeding regardless of the degree to which the taxpayer participated or whether the taxpayer's ability to contest the deficiency was impaired. *See Deihl v. Commissioner*, 134 T.C. 156, 161 (2010).

Proposed § 1.6015-1(e)(4) provides examples of how the rules in paragraphs (e)(1), (e)(2), and (e)(3) work. Proposed § 1.6015-1(e)(5) restates the collateral estoppel rule from current § 1.6015-1(e) without change.

Proposed § 1.6015-1(h)(1) and (h)(5) are being revised to remove the distinction between electing and requesting relief as discussed earlier in this preamble.

Proposed § 1.6015-1(h)(6) defines "unpaid tax" for purposes of § 1.6015-4. For purposes of § 1.6015-4, the regulations propose that the terms "unpaid tax" and "underpayment" have the same meaning. The unpaid tax or underpayment on a joint return is the balance shown as due on the return reduced by the tax paid with the return or paid on or before the due date for payment (without considering any extension of time to pay). The balance due is determined after applying withholding credits, estimated tax payments, payments with an extension, and other credits applied against the total tax reported on the return. Payments made with the return include payments made by check in the same envelope with the return or remitted at a later date (but before the due date for payment) with Form 1040-V, "Payment Voucher." Payments made with the return also include remittances made by direct debit, credit card, or other commercially acceptable means under section 6311 on or before the due date for payment. The determination of the existence and amount of unpaid tax is made as of the date the joint return is filed, or as of the due date for payment if payments are made after the return is filed but on or before the due date.

If the payments made with the joint return, including any payments made on or before the due date for payment (without considering any extension of time for payment), completely satisfy the balance due shown on the return, then there is no unpaid tax for purposes of § 1.6015-4. A requesting spouse is not entitled to be considered for relief (credit or refund) under § 1.6015-4 for any tax paid with the joint return (including a joint amended return). Payments made after the later of the date the joint return is filed or the due date for payment (without considering any extension of time for payment), including offsets of overpayments from other tax years, do not change the amount of unpaid tax reported on the joint return. Under § 1.6015-4, a requesting spouse can only get relief from the unpaid tax on the return, and if refunds are available, from any payments made on the liability after the later of the date the joint return was filed or the due date for payment (without considering any extension of time for payment).

Proposed § 1.6015-1(h)(7) and (h)(8) define understatement and deficiency, respectively. Section 6015(b)(3) provides that an "understatement" for purposes of section 6015 has the same meaning given to that term by section 6662(d)(2)(A). The definition of understatement is in current § 1.6015-2(b) and therefore only applies to requests under that section. The term "understatement," however, is a term that is relevant to relief under sections 6015(b), (c), and (f). These regulations propose to move the definition of "understatement" to proposed § 1.6015-1(h)(7) to allow a consistent definition to apply throughout the regulations. Likewise, proposed § 1.6015-1(h)(8) adds a definition of deficiency, by reference to section 6211 and the regulations under section 6211, to clarify that the term deficiency has the same meaning throughout the regulations.

Section 6015(g)(1) provides that requesting spouses generally can receive a credit or refund of payments made on the joint liability if the requesting spouse is entitled to relief under section 6015. This general rule is set forth in proposed § 1.6015-1(k)(1). Section 6015(g) also provides some limitations on the availability of credit or refund. New § 1.6015-1(k)(2) through (5) discuss these and other limitations on credit or refund when a requesting spouse is eligible for relief.

Proposed § 1.6015-1(k)(2) sets forth the limitation on refunds from section 6015(g)(3) when a requesting spouse is entitled to relief under § 1.6015-3. Proposed § 1.6015-1(k)(3) sets forth the rule from current § 1.6015-4(b) that relief under § 1.6015-4 is not available when the requesting spouse is entitled to full relief under § 1.6015-3 but is not entitled to a refund because of the limitation in section 6015(g)(3) and proposed § 1.6015-1(k)(2). Proposed § 1.6015-1(k)(4) incorporates, consistent with section 6015(g)(1), the limitations on credit or refund provided by sections 6511 (general limitations on credits or refunds) and 6512(b) (limitations on credits or refunds where the Tax Court determines that a taxpayer made an overpayment). This section also clarifies that, in general, Form 8857 will be treated as the requesting spouse's claim for credit or refund.

Proposed § 1.6015-1(k)(5) sets forth the general rule that a requesting spouse who is entitled to relief is generally not eligible for a credit or refund of joint payments made with the nonrequesting spouse. Under the proposed rule, a requesting spouse, however, may be eligible for a credit or refund of the requesting spouse's portion of the requesting and nonrequesting spouse's joint overpayment from another tax year that was applied to the joint income tax liability to the extent that the requesting spouse can establish his or her contribution to the overpayment. Both spouses have an interest in a joint overpayment relative to each spouse's contribution to the overpayment. See, for example, *Gordon v. United States*, 757 F.2d 1157, 1160 (11th Cir. 1985) ("Where spouses claim a refund under a joint return, the refund is divided between the spouses, with each receiving a percentage of the refund equivalent to his or her proportion of the withheld tax payments."). If the requesting spouse contributed to the joint overpayment through withholding, estimated tax, or other payments, then the requesting spouse may be entitled to a refund of that portion of the overpayment that was applied to the joint liability. Under the proposed rule, a requesting spouse in a state that is not a community property state may establish his or her portion of a joint overpayment using the allocation rules of Rev. Rul. 80-7 (1980-1 CB 296), or successor guidance. A requesting spouse in a community property state may establish his or her portion of a joint overpayment using the allocation rules of Rev. Rul. 2004-71 (2004-2 CB 74), Rev. Rul. 2004-72 (2004-2 CB 77), Rev. Rul. 2004-73 (2004-2 CB 80), or Rev. Rul. 2004-74 (2004-2 CB 84), or successor guidance, whichever is applicable to the state in which the requesting spouse is domiciled. For copies of Revenue Procedures, Revenue Rulings, notices, and other guidance published in the Internal Revenue Bulletin, please visit the IRS website at http://www.irs.gov.

These proposed regulations reflect the elimination of the more restrictive rule regarding credit or refund when relief is granted under § 1.6015-4 in cases involving a deficiency, as provided by Rev. Proc. 2013-34. A credit or refund, subject to the limitations in § 1.6015-1(k), is available to a requesting spouse who is entitled to relief under § 1.6015-4 in both underpayment and deficiency cases.

Current § 1.6015-1(h)(4) provides, in part, that penalties and interest are not separate erroneous items from which a requesting spouse can be relieved separate from the tax. Rather, relief from penalties and interest related to an understatement or deficiency will generally be determined based on the proportion of the total erroneous items from which the requesting spouse is relieved.

Thus, under the existing regulations, a requesting spouse who is determined not to be eligible for relief from the understatement or deficiency stemming from an erroneous item cannot be separately relieved from a penalty, such as the accuracy-related penalty, related to the item under section 6015. If a requesting spouse is entitled to partial relief (such as relief from two of three erroneous items giving rise to the understatement or deficiency), then the requesting spouse will be entitled to relief from the accuracy-related penalty applicable to those two items.

These regulations propose to move the discussion in current § 1.6015-1(h)(4) to proposed § 1.6015-1(m). Proposed § 1.6015-1(m) additionally clarifies, consistent with the statutory interpretation in current § 1.6015-1(h)(4), that penalties and interest on an underpayment also are not separate items from which a requesting spouse may obtain relief under § 1.6015-4. Rather, relief from penalties and interest on the underpayment will be determined based on the amount of relief from the underpayment to which the requesting spouse is entitled. If a requesting spouse remains liable for a portion of the underpayment after application of § 1.6015-4, the requesting spouse is not eligible for relief under section 6015 for the penalties and interest related to that portion of the underpayment. *Cf. Weiler v. Commissioner*, T.C. Memo. 2003-255 (a requesting spouse is not relieved from liabilities for penalties and interest resulting from items attributable to the requesting spouse). This position is consistent with how the IRS currently treats relief from penalties and interest after determining the relief from the underlying tax. See IRM 25.15.3.4.1.1(2) (Revised 03/08/2013).

If an assessed deficiency is paid in full, or the unpaid tax reported on the joint return is later paid in full, but penalties and interest remain unpaid, under the proposed rule, a requesting spouse may be considered for relief from the penalties and interest under section 6015. The determination of relief from the penalties and interest is made by considering whether the requesting spouse would be entitled to relief from the underlying tax and not considering the penalties and interest as if they were separate items. A requesting spouse may be relieved from the penalties and interest even if relief in the form of a refund of the payments made on the underlying tax is barred (for example, § 1.6015-1(k)(2) (no refunds allowed under § 1.6015-3) or § 1.6015-1(k)(4) (refund barred by the limitations of sections 6511 or 6512(b)).

Proposed § 1.6015-1(n) provides attribution rules for a portion of an understatement or deficiency relating to the disallowance of certain items. Specifically, § 1.6015-1(n) addresses items that are otherwise not erroneous items, but are disallowed solely due to the increase of adjusted gross income (or modified adjusted gross income) over a phase-out threshold as a result of an erroneous item attributable to the nonrequesting spouse. One common example of this is when the nonrequesting spouse's omitted income increases adjusted gross income so that the Earned Income Tax Credit (EITC) is phased out and the understatement or deficiency partially represents the recapture of the refunded EITC.

Under proposed § 1.6015-1(n), the understatement or deficiency related to the item disallowed due to the increase to adjusted gross income will be attributable to the spouse whose erroneous item caused the increase to adjusted gross income, unless the evidence shows that a different result is appropriate. If the increase to adjusted gross income is the result of erroneous items of both spouses, the item disallowed due to the increase to adjusted gross income will be attributable to the requesting spouse in the same ratio as the amount of the item or items attributable to the requesting spouse over the total amount of the items that resulted in the increase to adjusted gross income. Corresponding rules are proposed to be added to § § 1.6015-2(b) and 1.6015-3(c)(2)(i) to provide that a requesting spouse knows or has reason to know of the item disallowed due to the increase in adjusted gross income if the requesting spouse knows or has reason to know of the erroneous item or items that resulted in the increase to adjusted gross income. Likewise, for purposes of proposed § 1.6015-4 and Rev. Proc. 2013-34, a requesting spouse knows or has reason to know of the portion of an understatement or deficiency related to an item attributable to the nonrequesting spouse under § 1.6015-1(n) if the requesting spouse knows or has reason to know of the nonrequesting spouse's erroneous item or items that resulted in the increase to adjusted gross income.

Examples are provided to illustrate how this rule applies in situations involving the EITC, the phase-out of itemized deductions, and the application of the alternative minimum tax. This rule, however, can be implicated in other situations. It should be noted that this proposed rule would not apply if there is another reason for disallowing the item, such as no qualifying child for the EITC, no substantiation for a claimed deduction, or the lack of any basis in law or fact for the deduction. In this situation, the normal attribution rules applicable to § § 1.6015-2, 1.6015-3, and 1.6015-4 apply.

Proposed § 1.6015-1(o) provides a definition of abuse for purposes of proposed § § 1.6015-2(b) and 1.6015-3(c)(vi). The definition of abuse is taken directly from Rev. Proc. 2013-34, section 4.03(2)(c)(iv).

2. Section 1.6015-2

Only minor substantive changes are proposed to current § 1.6015-2. The proposed amendments reorganize the section, update references, and provide clarification where needed. Proposed § 1.6015-2(a) changes the language in the existing regulations, "the requesting spouse elects the application of this section," to "the requesting spouse requests relief" consistent with the discussion earlier in this preamble. The definition of "understatement" in current § 1.6015-2(b) is removed as the definition will now be located in proposed § 1.6015-1(h)(7). Current § 1.6015-2(c) is redesignated as proposed § 1.6015-2(b), adds additional facts and circumstances from Rev. Proc. 2013-34 to consider in determining whether a requesting spouse had reason to know, adds a knowledge rule to correspond to proposed § 1.6015-1(n) as discussed earlier in this preamble, and clarifies, consistent with the changes made in Rev. Proc. 2013-34, that abuse or financial control by the nonrequesting spouse will result in the requesting spouse being treated as not having knowledge or reason to know of the items giving rise to the understatement. Current § 1.6015-2(d) is redesignated as proposed § 1.6015-2(c) and provides an updated cross-reference to the most recent revenue procedure providing the criteria to be used in determining equitable relief, Rev. Proc. 2013-34. Current § 1.6015-2(e)(1) is redesignated as proposed § 1.6015-2(d)(1) and the word "only" is removed to clarify the rule. Current § 1.6015-2(e)(2) is redesignated as proposed § 1.6015-2(d)(2) and the example is updated to use more current years and dates, but otherwise no substantive changes were made.

3. Section 1.6015-3

Among other clarifying changes, these regulations propose to clarify the difference between full and partial relief under section 6015(c) and to reflect case law regarding the tax benefit rule of section 6015(d)(3)(B), including new examples.

Proposed § 1.6015-3(a) provides a revised heading and a cross-reference to the definition of deficiency in proposed § 1.6015-1(h)(8).

Section 6015(g)(3) provides that no credit or refund is allowed as a result of an allocation of a deficiency under section 6015(c). Proposed § 1.6015-3(c)(1) clarifies the existing regulations and provides that whether relief is available to a requesting spouse under section 6015(c) is not dependent on the availability of credit or refund. Thus, if a requesting spouse is eligible to allocate the entire deficiency to the nonrequesting spouse, the requesting spouse has received full relief even if the requesting spouse made payments on the deficiency and is not entitled to a refund of those payments because of section 6015(g)(3). Further, the requesting spouse is not eligible to be considered for relief (and a refund) under section 6015(f) for the amount of any paid liability because a prerequisite to relief under section 6015(f) is the unavailability of relief under section 6015(b) or (c) and the spouse received full relief under section 6015(c). A requesting spouse may still be considered for relief (and a refund) under section 6015(b) for the amount of any paid liability. If a requesting spouse only receives partial relief (for example, some part of the deficiency is still allocated to the requesting spouse), then the requesting spouse may be considered for relief under section 6015(f) for the portion of the deficiency allocable to the requesting spouse. A new sentence is added to § 1.6015-3(c)(2)(i) to add a knowledge rule to correspond to proposed § 1.6015-1(n), which, as discussed earlier in this preamble, provides an attribution rule for the portion of a deficiency relating to the disallowance or reduction of an otherwise valid item solely due to the increase in AGI as a result of the disallowance of an erroneous item.

Proposed § 1.6015-3(d)(2)(i) illustrates that, under the tax benefit rule of section 6015(d)(3)(B), the amount of an erroneous item allocated to a requesting spouse may increase or decrease depending upon the tax benefit to the requesting and nonrequesting spouses. Thus, these proposed regulations adopt the holding of *Hopkins v. Commissioner*, 121 T.C. 73 (2003) (a requesting spouse was entitled to relief from her own item under the tax benefit rule of section 6015(d)(3)(B) because the nonrequesting spouse was the only person who reported income on the returns, and therefore, the only one who received any tax benefit from the item). In addition, five new examples have been added to § 1.6015-3(d)(5) to provide additional guidance on the application of the tax benefit rule of § 1.6015-3(d)(2)(i). *Example 7* demonstrates the application of § 1.6015-3(d)(2)(i)(B), which provides that each spouse's hypothetical separate taxable income may need to be determined to properly apply the tax benefit rule. *Example 8* demonstrates the holding in *Hopkins* by showing that a requesting spouse's allocated portion of a deficiency will be decreased when the nonrequesting spouse receives a tax benefit from the item. *Example 9* demonstrates the allocation of a liability when the erroneous item is a loss from a jointly-owned investment. *Example 10* demonstrates how the tax benefit rule works when the erroneous item is a loss from a jointly-owned investment. In addition, *Example 11* is added to demonstrate how the rule in § 1.6015-3(d)(2)(ii) regarding fraud works.

Section 1.6015-3(c)(2)(iv) currently provides that the requesting spouse's joint ownership (with the nonrequesting spouse) of the property that resulted in the erroneous item is a factor that may be relied upon in demonstrating that the requesting spouse had actual knowledge of the item. Under the tax benefit rule of § 1.6015-3(d)(2)(i), as stated earlier in this preamble, a requesting spouse can be relieved of liability for the requesting spouse's own erroneous item if the item is otherwise allocable in full or in part to the nonrequesting spouse under section 6015(d). Therefore, proposed § 1.6015-3(c)(2)(iv) revises the current regulations to clarify that the requesting spouse's separate ownership of the erroneous item is also a factor that may be relied upon in demonstrating that the requesting spouse had actual knowledge of the item. Current § 1.6015-3(c)(2)(v) is redesignated as proposed § 1.6015-3(c)(2)(vi) and the discussion of community property in current § 1.6015-3(c)(iv) is removed and is now located in proposed § 1.6015-3(c)(2)(v). Proposed § 1.6015-3(c)(vi) is revised to clarify, consistent with the changes made in Rev. Proc. 2013-34, that abuse or financial control by the nonrequesting spouse will result in the requesting spouse being treated as not having actual knowledge of the items giving rise to the understatement.

4. Section 1.6015-4

No substantive changes are proposed to current § 1.6015-4. The proposed amendments update references and provide a clarifying change consistent with proposed § 1.6015-3(c)(1), which provides the rule that refunds are not allowed under section 6015(c).

Proposed § 1.6015-4(a) was revised to provide a cross-reference to the definitions of unpaid tax, understatement, and deficiency in proposed § § 1.6015-1(h)(6), (h)(7), and (h)(8).

Proposed § 1.6015-4(b) was revised to provide a cross-reference to proposed § 1.6015-1(k)(3). The paragraph also clarifies that if only partial relief is available under § 1.6015-3, then relief may be considered under § 1.6015-4 for the portion of the deficiency for which the requesting spouse remains liable.

Proposed § 1.6015-4(c) replaces the citation to Rev. Proc. 2000-15 (2000-1 CB 447) with Rev. Proc. 2013-34, which revised the factors used in determining if the requesting spouse is eligible for equitable relief under section 6015(f).

5. Section 1.6015-5

A notice of proposed rulemaking (REG-132251-11) was published in the **Federal Register** (78 FR 49242) on August 13, 2013. Those regulations proposed changes to § 1.6015-5 to remove the two-year deadline for taxpayers to file requests for equitable relief under section 6015(f), and other changes related to the time and manner for requesting relief. These proposed regulations revise the notice of proposed rulemaking published on August 13, 2013 to add an effective date provision.

6. Section 1.6015-6

The changes in proposed § 1.6015-6 are intended to update the current regulations to reflect existing practice and guidance. Proposed § 1.6015-6(a)(1) replaces the term "election" under § 1.6015-2 or

§1.6015-3 with "request for relief." Proposed §1.6015-6(a)(2) includes a reference to Rev. Proc. 2003-19 (2003-1 CB 371), which provides guidance on a nonrequesting spouse's right to appeal a preliminary determination to IRS Appeals.

7. Section 1.6015-7

Section 1.6015-7 was revised to reflect the amendments to section 6015(e) in the 2006 Act that, as noted earlier in this preamble, conferred jurisdiction on the United States Tax Court to review the IRS's denial of relief in cases in which taxpayers requested equitable relief under section 6015(f), without regard to whether the IRS has determined a deficiency. Prior to these amendments, the United States Tax Court lacked jurisdiction to review section 6015(f) determinations if no deficiency had been determined. The amendments apply to any liability for tax that arose on or after December 20, 2006, and any liability for tax that arose before December 20, 2006, but remained unpaid as of that date. Proposed §1.6015-7(c) revises the current regulations to reflect the changes to the restrictions on collection and corresponding tolling of the collection statute under section 6502. On versions of the Form 8857 dated before June 2007 a requesting spouse could request relief under just one subsection of section 6015. For claims for relief that were made under sections 6015(b) and (c) (and the corresponding §§1.6015-2 and 1.6015-3), the IRS is prohibited from collecting against the requesting spouse (and the collection statute is tolled) beginning on the date the claim is filed. For requests for relief made solely under section 6015(f) (and the corresponding §1.6015-4), the IRS is prohibited from collecting against the requesting spouse (and the collection statute is tolled) only for liabilities arising on or after December 20, 2006, or liabilities arising before December 20, 2006, but remaining unpaid as of that date. For requests for relief made solely under §1.6015-4, the restrictions on collection and tolling of the collection statute do not start until December 20, 2006, for any requests filed before that date, assuming the tax remained unpaid as of that date. The restrictions on collection and tolling of the collection statute start as of the date the request is filed for requests filed on or after December 20, 2006.

8. Section 1.66-4

The only changes to the existing regulations under section 66 are non-substantive changes. Proposed §1.66-4(a)(3) and (b) replace the citation to Rev. Proc. 2000-15 with Rev. Proc. 2013-34, which revised the factors used in determining whether a requesting spouse is eligible for equitable relief under section 66(c).

9. Effective and Applicability Dates

Additionally, the effective and applicability date sections in the regulations under section 66 and section 6015 are reorganized to move the effective and applicability date sections within the specific regulation to which the dates apply. The separate effective date sections under §§1.66-5 and 1.6015-9 are removed.

Special Analyses

Certain IRS regulations, including this one, are exempt from the requirements of Executive Order 12866, as supplemented and reaffirmed by Executive Order 13563. Therefore, a regulatory impact assessment is not required. It has also been determined that section 553(b) of the Administrative Procedure Act (5 U.S.C. chapter 5) does not apply to these regulations. In addition, because the regulations do not impose a collection of information on small entities, the Regulatory Flexibility Act (5 U.S.C. chapter 6) does not apply. Accordingly, a regulatory flexibility analysis is not required under the Regulatory Flexibility Act (5 U.S.C. chapter 6). Pursuant to section 7805(f) of the Code, this notice of proposed rulemaking has been submitted to the Chief Counsel for Advocacy of the Small Business Administration for comment on its impact on small business.

Comments and Requests for Public Hearing

Before these proposed regulations are adopted as final regulations, consideration will be given to any comments that are submitted timely to the IRS as prescribed in the preamble under the "Addresses" heading. Treasury and the IRS request comments on all aspects of the proposed regulations. All comments will be available at www.regulations.gov or upon request. A public hearing will be scheduled if requested in writing by any person that timely submits written comments. If a public hearing is scheduled, notice of the date, time, and place for the public hearing will be published in the **Federal Register**.

Drafting Information

The principal author of these regulations is Nancy Rose of the Office of the Associate Chief Counsel (Procedure and Administration).

[¶49,678] Proposed Amendments of Regulations (REG-147310-12), published in the Federal Register on January 27, 2016.

[Code Sec. 401]

Retirement defined benefit plans: Governmental plans: Normal Retirement age.—Amendments of Reg. §1.401(a)-1, containing regulations under section 401(a) of the Internal Revenue Code (Code), are proposed.

AGENCY: Internal Revenue Service (IRS), Treasury

ACTION: Notice of proposed rulemaking.

SUMMARY: This document contains proposed regulations under section 401(a) of the Internal Revenue Code (Code). These regulations would provide rules relating to the determination of whether the normal retirement age under a governmental plan (within the meaning of section 414(d) of the Code) that is a pension plan satisfies the requirements of section 401(a) and whether the payment of definitely determinable benefits that commence at the plan's normal retirement age satisfies these requirements. These regulations would affect sponsors and administrators of governmental pension plans, as well as participants in such plans.

DATES: Comments and requests for a public hearing must be received by April 26, 2016.

ADDRESSES: Send submissions to CC:PA:LPD:PR (REG-147310-12), room 5205, Internal Revenue Service, PO Box 7604, Ben Franklin Station, Washington D.C. 20044. Submissions may be hand-delivered Monday through Friday between the hours of 8 a.m. and 4 p.m. to CC:PA:LPD:PR (REG-147310-12), Courier's Desk, Internal Revenue Service, 1111 Constitution Avenue, N.W., Washington, DC, 20224, or sent electronically via the Federal eRulemaking Portal at *www.regulations.gov* (IRS REG-147310-12).

FOR FURTHER INFORMATION CONTACT: Concerning the proposed regulations, Pamela Kinard at (202) 317-4148 or Robert Walsh at (202) 317-4102; concerning the submission of comments or to request a public hearing, Oluwafunmilayo (Funmi) Taylor, (202) 317-7180 or (202) 317-6901 (not toll-free numbers).

SUPPLEMENTARY INFORMATION:

Background

I. *Normal Retirement Age Generally*

This document contains proposed regulations under section 401(a) of the Internal Revenue Code (Code). Section 401(a) sets forth the qualification requirements for a trust forming part of a stock bonus, pension, or profit-sharing plan of an employer. Several of these qualification requirements are based on a plan's normal retirement age, including the regulatory interpretation of the requirement that the plan provide for definitely determinable benefits (generally after retirement). Final regulations defining normal retirement age for the definitely determinable requirement were published in the **Federal Register** as TD 9325 on May 22, 2007 (72 FR 28604) (2007 NRA regulations).

Section 1.401(a)-1(b)(1) of the 2007 NRA regulations generally requires that a pension plan be established and maintained primarily to provide systematically for the payment of definitely determinable benefits over a period of years, usually for life, after retirement. The 2007 NRA regulations include two exceptions to the general rule that payments commence after retirement: (1) payments can commence after attainment of normal retirement age; and (2) in accordance with section 401(a)(36), payments can commence after an employee reaches age 62.

Section 1.401(a)-1(b)(2)(i) of the 2007 NRA regulations provides that, as a general rule, a normal retirement age under a pension plan must be an age that is not earlier than the earliest age that is reasonably representative of the typical retirement age for the industry in which the covered workforce is employed (reasonably representative requirement). Section 1.401(a)-1(b)(2)(ii) of the 2007 NRA regulations provides that a normal retirement age of age 62 or later is deemed to satisfy the reasonably representative requirement. Under section 1.401(a)-1(b)(2)(iii) of the 2007 NRA regulations, whether a normal retirement age that is not earlier than age 55 but is below age 62 satisfies the reasonably representative requirement is based on a facts and circumstances analysis. Section 1.401(a)-1(b)(2)(iv) of the 2007 NRA regulations provides that a normal retirement age that is lower than age 55 is presumed not to satisfy the reasonably representative requirement unless the Commissioner determines otherwise on the basis of facts and circumstances. Under § 1.401(a)-1(b)(2)(v) of the 2007 NRA regulations, in the case of a pension plan in which substantially all of the participants are qualified public safety employees (within the meaning of section 72(t)(10)(B)), a normal retirement age of age 50 or later is deemed to satisfy the reasonably representative requirement.

As previously explained, normal retirement age is used by a pension plan in a variety of circumstances relating to plan qualification. Generally, in the case of a pension plan that is not a governmental plan under section 414(d) and is subject to the rules of section 411(a) through (d), normal retirement age is used in applying the rules under section 411(b) that are designed to preclude avoidance of the minimum vesting standards through the backloading of benefits (such as a benefit formula under which the rate of benefit accrual is increased disproportionately for employees with longer service). Normal retirement age is also relevant for such a plan for other purposes, including the application of the rules relating to suspension of benefits under section 411(a)(3)(B), plan offset rules under section 411(b)(1)(H)(iii), and the minimum benefit rules applicable to non-key employee participants in the case of a top-heavy defined benefit plan under section 416. In addition, for such a plan, section 411(a)(8) defines the term *normal retirement age* as the earlier of (a) the time a participant attains normal retirement age under the plan or (b) the later of the time a plan participant attains age 65 or the 5th anniversary of the time a plan participant commenced participation in the plan.[1]

---

[1] Section 411(f) provides a special normal retirement age rule that applies only to certain defined benefit plans that are subject to section 411(a) through (d). Section 411(f) was added to the Code on December 16, 2014 by Section 2 of Division P of the Consolidated and Further Continuing Appropriations Act, 2015, Public Law No. 113-235 (128 Stat. 2130 (2014)), which also made a corresponding change to section 204 of the Employee Retirement Income Security Act of 1974, Public Law 93-406 (88 Stat. 829 (1974)), as amended (ERISA). Under section 101 of Reorganization Plan No. 4 of 1978 (92 Stat. 3790), the Secretary of the Treasury has interpretive jurisdiction over the subject matter addressed in section 411(f) for purposes of ERISA, as well as the Code.

II. *Normal Retirement Age under a Governmental Plan*

A. *Application of section 411 to governmental plans*

Section 414(d) of the Code provides that the term *governmental plan* generally means a plan established and maintained for its employees by the Government of the United States, by the government of any State or political subdivision thereof, or by any agency or instrumentality of any of the foregoing.[2] See sections 3(32) and 4021(b)(2) of ERISA for definitions of the term *governmental plan* for purposes of title I and title IV of ERISA, respectively.

Section 411(e)(1) of the Code provides that the provisions of section 411, other than section 411(e)(2), do not apply to a governmental plan. Under section 411(e)(2), a governmental plan is treated as meeting the requirements of section 411, for purposes of section 401(a), if the plan meets the vesting requirements resulting from the application of sections 401(a)(4) and 401(a)(7) as in effect on September 1, 1974 (pre-ERISA vesting rules). The only requirements under section 411 that apply to a governmental plan are the pre-ERISA vesting rules under section 411(e)(2). Thus, the definition of normal retirement age under section 411(a)(8) does not apply to a governmental plan. In addition, other rules of section 411, including section 411(a)(3)(B) (related to suspension of benefits), section 411(b)(1) (related to backloading of benefits in a defined benefit plan), and section 411(b)(1)(H)(iii) (related to offsets after normal retirement age) do not apply to a governmental plan. Therefore, except for specific circumstances in which in-service benefit payments are permitted under § 1.401(a)-1(b)(1), the definition of normal retirement age need not be used by a governmental plan for the same purposes that apply to a plan subject to section 411(a) through (d).[3]

B. *Pre-ERISA vesting requirements for governmental plans*

Under section 411(e)(2), a normal retirement age under a governmental plan must satisfy the pre-ERISA vesting rules. The pre-ERISA vesting rules applicable to governmental plans contain two basic components: (a) rules relating to vesting and (b) rules relating to the right to commence benefits without reduction for early commencement. Rev. Rul. 66-11, 1966-1 C.B. 71, and Rev. Rul. 68-302, 1968-1 C.B. 163, illustrate the interplay between normal retirement age under the pre-ERISA vesting rules and section 401(a). As described in these rulings, to satisfy the requirements of section 401(a), a plan that is subject to the pre-ERISA vesting rules must provide for full vesting of the contributions made to or benefits payable under the plan for any employee who has attained normal retirement age under the plan and satisfied any reasonable and uniformly applicable requirements as to length of service or participation described in the plan. For more information about these rules, see Part 5(c) of Publication 778, *Guides for Qualification of Pension, Profit-Sharing, and Stock Bonus Plans (Pub. 778).*

Rev. Rul. 71-24, 1971-1 C.B. 114, illustrates the application of the pre-ERISA vesting rules to benefits provided under a pension plan for employees who continue employment after normal retirement age. Rev. Rul. 71-24 includes an example under which benefits are permitted to commence during employment after normal retirement age.

As described in Rev. Rul. 71-147,[4] 1971-1 C.B. 116, the normal retirement age in a pension or annuity plan under the pre-ERISA vesting rules is generally the lowest age specified in the plan at which the employee has the right to retire without the consent of the employer and receive retirement benefits based on the amount of the employee's service to the date of retirement at the full rate set forth in the plan (that is, without actuarial or similar reduction because of retirement before some later specified age). Rev. Rul. 71-147 does not explicitly require a plan to include a provision defining normal retirement age. Instead, a plan's normal retirement age may be deduced from other plan provisions. As described in Rev. Rul. 71-147, although normal retirement age under a pension or annuity plan is ordinarily age 65, a plan may specify a lower age at which the employee has the right to retire without the consent of the employer and to receive retirement benefits based on the amount of the employee's service at the full rate set forth in the plan if this lower age would be an age at which employees customarily retire in the particular company or industry, and if the provision permitting receipt of unreduced benefits at this age is not a device to accelerate funding. For more information about these rules, see also Part 5(e) of Pub. 778.

---

[2] The term *governmental plan* also includes a plan that is established and maintained by an Indian tribal government (as defined in section 7701(a)(40)), a subdivision of an Indian tribal government (determined in accordance with section 7871(d)), or an agency or instrumentality of either, and all the participants of which are employees of such entity substantially all of whose services as such an employee are in the performance of essential governmental functions but not in the performance of commercial activities (whether or not an essential government function). In addition, the term *governmental plan* includes any plan to which the Railroad Retirement Act of 1935 or 1937 (49 Stat. 967, as amended by 50 Stat. 307) applies and which is financed by contributions required under that Act and any plan of an international organization that is exempt from taxation by reason of the International Organizations Immunities Act, Public Law 79-291 (59 Stat. 669).

[3] Normal retirement age may also be relevant to participant eligibility for certain favorable tax treatment, including section 402(l) (providing an income exclusion of up to $3,000 annually for certain distributions for health insurance and long-term care insurance premiums to eligible retired public safety officers who separate from service by reason of disability or attainment of normal retirement age) and the special catch-up provisions under § 1.457-4(c)(3)(v)(A).

[4] Even though Rev. Rul. 71-147 was superseded by Rev. Rul. 80-276, 1980-1 C.B. 131, for plans subject to section 411(a)(8), Rev. Rul. 71-147 remains valid guidance for purposes of the pre-ERISA vesting rules.

III. *Application of the 2007 NRA Regulations to Governmental Plans*

Notice 2007-69, 2007-2 C.B. 468, asked for comments "on whether and how a pension plan with a normal retirement age conditioned on the completion of a stated number of years of service satisfies the requirement in § 1.401(a)-1(b)(1)(i) that a pension plan be maintained primarily to provide for the payment of definitely determinable benefits after retirement or attainment of normal retirement age and how such a plan satisfies the pre-ERISA vesting rules." Comments were received on a variety of issues, including comments that guidance should be issued to (1) clarify that governmental plans are not required to define normal retirement age, (2) provide safe harbor rules that would permit a governmental plan to define normal retirement age that includes a service component, and (3) provide that the age-50 safe harbor rule in § 1.401(a)-1(b)(2)(v) for qualified public safety employees can apply to these employees even if less than substantially all of a plan's participants are qualified public safety employees.

The 2007 NRA regulations provided that, in the case of governmental plans, the regulations would be effective for plan years beginning on or after January 1, 2009. Notices 2008-98, 2008-44 I.R.B 1080, and 2009-86, 2009-6 I.R.B. 629, provided that the Department of the Treasury and the IRS intended to amend the 2007 NRA regulations to change the effective date of the 2007 NRA regulations for governmental plans to January 1, 2013.

Notice 2012-29, 2012-18 I.R.B. 872, announced that the Department of the Treasury and the IRS intend to modify provisions of the 2007 NRA regulations as applied to governmental plans in two ways. First, Notice 2012-29 announced the intent to modify the regulations to clarify that a governmental plan that is not subject to section 411(a) through (d) and does not provide for the payment of in-service distributions before age 62 will not fail to satisfy the requirement that the plan provide definitely determinable benefits to employees after retirement or attainment of normal retirement age merely because the pension plan does not have a definition of normal retirement age or does not have a definition of normal retirement age that satisfies the requirements of the 2007 NRA regulations.

Second, Notice 2012-29 announced the intent to modify the 2007 NRA regulations to provide that the rule deeming age 50 or later to be a normal retirement age that satisfies the 2007 NRA regulations will apply to a group of employees substantially all of whom are qualified public safety employees, whether or not the group of qualified public safety employees are covered by a separate plan. Thus, under the intended modification, a governmental plan would be permitted to satisfy the reasonably representative requirement using a normal retirement age as low as 50 for a group substantially all of whom are qualified public safety employees and a later normal retirement age that otherwise satisfies the 2007 NRA requirements for all other participants.

Notice 2012-29 requested comments from governmental stakeholders on the guidance under consideration. Specific comments were requested on whether a new rule should be provided under which retirement after 20 to 30 years of service may be a normal retirement age that is reasonably representative of the typical retirement age for the industry in which qualified public safety employees are employed because these employees tend to have career spans that commence at a young age and continue over a limited number of years. Many commenters wrote that such a rule would be helpful and appropriate. Several commenters requested a rule that would permit a governmental plan to use the completion of 20 or more years of service as a normal retirement age for public safety employees.

Comments were also requested on whether there are other categories of governmental employees who have career spans similar to qualified public safety employees for whom a rule should be provided that is similar to the safe harbor for qualified public safety employees. Many commenters recommended a rule that would permit governmental plans to use the completion of a number of years of service as a normal retirement age for all employees, not just qualified public safety employees.

Notice 2012-29 also requested information on the overall retirement patterns of employees in government service to assist the Department of the Treasury and the IRS in determining the earliest age that is reasonably representative of the typical retirement ages for the industry in which these employees are employed. One commenter provided data on the retirement patterns and median normal retirement ages for participants in a state retirement system.

Notice 2012-29 also provided that the Department of the Treasury and the IRS intend to amend the 2007 NRA regulations to modify the effective date of the 2007 NRA regulations for governmental plans to annuity starting dates that occur in plan years beginning on or after the later of (1) January 1, 2015 or (2) the close of the first regular legislative session of the legislative body with the authority to amend the plan that begins on or after the date that is 3 months after the final regulations are published in the **Federal Register**.

Explanation of Provisions

I. *Overview*

These proposed regulations would provide guidance with respect to the applicability of the 2007 NRA regulations to governmental plans. These proposed regulations, when finalized, would provide guidance relating to the determination of whether the normal retirement age under a governmental plan satisfies the requirements of section 401(a) by amending the 2007 NRA regulations to provide additional rules for governmental plans. In addition, these proposed regulations would also include a minor change to the 2007 NRA regulations to reflect the addition of section 411(f), which provides a special rule for determining a permissible normal retirement age that applies only to certain defined benefit plans that are not governmental plans.

II. *Use of Years of Service as a Component of the Pre-ERISA Vesting Rules*

In response to Notice 2012-29, the Department of the Treasury and the IRS received a range of comments regarding the pre-ERISA vesting rules that apply to a governmental plan's normal retirement age. In particular, the Department of the Treasury and the IRS received many comments requesting rules that would permit governmental plans to define normal retirement age by reference to a period of service. Comments also focused on whether a governmental plan is required to include an explicit definition of normal retirement age.

As previously stated, a normal retirement age under a governmental plan must satisfy the pre-ERISA vesting rules. The Department of the Treasury and the IRS generally agree with those commenters who indicated that the pre-ERISA vesting rules applicable to normal retirement age may be read to permit a governmental plan to use a normal retirement age that reflects a period of service. Under pre-ERISA vesting rules, use of a period of service to determine normal retirement age under a governmental plan would be permissible if the period of service used is reasonable and uniformly applicable and the other pre-ERISA rules related to normal retirement age are satisfied. One of the pre-ERISA rules permits a governmental plan to specify a normal retirement age that is lower than age 65 if that age represents the age at which employees customarily retire in the industry.

Under the pre-ERISA rules related to normal retirement age, the terms of a governmental plan are not required to include an explicit definition of the term normal retirement age in order to satisfy section 401(a). However, in the absence of an explicit definition of normal retirement age, the terms of the plan must specify the earliest age at which a participant has the right to retire without the consent of the employer and to receive retirement benefits based upon the amount of the participant's service on the date of retirement at the full rate set forth in the plan (that is, without actuarial or similar reduction because of retirement before some later specified age). That age (the earliest age described in the preceding sentence) will be considered the plan's normal retirement age for purposes of any statutory or regulatory requirements based on a normal retirement age.

Consistent with Notice 2012-29, the proposed regulations would provide that a governmental plan that does not provide for the payment of in-service distributions before age 62 would not fail to satisfy § 1.401(a)-1(b)(1) under these proposed regulations merely because the pension plan has a normal retirement age that is earlier than otherwise permitted under the requirements of § 1.401(a)-1(b)(2) of the 2007 NRA regulations (as proposed to be amended by these proposed regulations). Instead, because section 411(a) through (d) does not apply, the earlier normal retirement age under such a plan is treated as the age as of which an unreduced early retirement benefit is payable for purposes of these regulations.

III. *Normal Retirement Age Must Satisfy the Reasonably Representative Requirement*

A. *In general*

These proposed regulations would apply the reasonably representative requirement in the 2007 NRA regulations to governmental plans. Thus, the normal retirement age under a governmental plan must be an age that is not earlier than the earliest age that is reasonably representative of the typical retirement age for the industry in which the covered workforce is employed.

B. *General safe harbor*

These proposed regulations would apply to governmental plans the safe harbor in the 2007 NRA regulations that a normal retirement age of at least age 62 is deemed to satisfy the reasonably representative requirement. Thus, a governmental plan satisfies this safe harbor if the normal retirement age under the plan is age 62 or if the normal retirement age is the later of age 62 or another specified date, such as the fifth anniversary of plan participation.

C. *Safe harbors for governmental plans*

To address comments regarding the need for additional safe harbors for governmental plans, including safe harbors that reflect permissible periods of service, these proposed regulations would provide several additional alternative safe harbors that a governmental plan could satisfy. The safe harbors included in these proposed regulations were developed based upon feedback provided in comments received in response to Notices 2007-69 and 2012-29.

1. *Age 60 and 5 years of service*

Under these proposed regulations, a normal retirement age under a governmental plan that is the later of age 60 or the age at which the participant has been credited with at least 5 years of service would be deemed to satisfy the reasonably representative requirement.

2. *Age 55 and 10 years of service*

Similarly, a normal retirement age under a governmental plan that is the later of 55 or the age at which the participant has been credited with at least 10 years of service would be deemed to satisfy the reasonably representative requirement. Thus, for example, a normal retirement age under a governmental plan that is the later of age 55 or the age at which the participant has been credited with 12 years of service would satisfy this safe harbor.

3. *Combined age and years of service of 80 or more*

A normal retirement age under a governmental plan that is the participant's age if the sum of the participant's age plus the number of years of service that have been credited to the participant under the plan equals 80 or more would also be deemed to satisfy the reasonably representative requirement. For example, a participant in a governmental plan who is age 55 and who has been credited with 25 years of service under the plan would satisfy this safe harbor.

4. *Any age with 25 years of service (in combination with a safe harbor that includes an age)*

A governmental plan would also be permitted to combine any of the other safe harbors (except for the qualified public safety employee safe harbors) provided under the proposed regulations with 25 years of service, so that a participant's normal retirement age would be the participant's age when the number of years of service that have been credited to the participant under the plan equals 25 if that age is earlier than what the participant's normal retirement age would be under the other safe harbor(s). For example, a normal retirement age under a governmental plan would satisfy the reasonably representative requirement if the normal retirement age is the earlier of (1) the participant's age when the participant has been credited with 25 years of service under the plan and (2) the later of age 60 or the age when the participant has been credited with 5 years of service under the plan. Use of 25 years of service by a governmental plan for normal retirement age generally would not satisfy the pre-ERISA vesting requirement relating to normal retirement age, unless it is used in conjunction with an alternative normal retirement age that includes an age component and that otherwise satisfies the pre-ERISA rules. This is because the pre-ERISA vesting requirements allow for a service component only if that component does not unreasonably delay full vesting. For example, applying a 25 years of service requirement (without an alternative normal retirement age) to a newly-hired 63-year-old employee would not be reasonable because it would result in a normal retirement age of 88. See generally, Rev. Rul. 66-11.

D. *Qualified public safety employees*

The proposed regulations include three safe harbors specifically for qualified public safety employees. The safe harbors were developed based upon feedback provided in comments received in response to Notices 2007-69 and 2012-29. Consistent with Notice 2012-29 and in response to comments, the proposed regulations would make clear that a governmental plan is permitted to use one or more of the safe harbors for qualified public safety employees to satisfy the reasonably representative requirement for those employees even if a different normal retirement age or ages is used under the plan for one or more other categories of participants who are not qualified public safety employees. The safe harbors for qualified public safety employees are not permitted to be used for these other categories of participants; a different normal retirement age (or ages) must be used for participants in a plan who are not qualified public safety employees.

As under the 2007 NRA regulations, the term *qualified public safety employee* would be defined by reference to section 72(t)(10)(B), under which a qualified public safety employee means any employee of a State or political subdivision of a State who provides police protection, firefighting services, or emergency medical services for any area within the jurisdiction of such State or political subdivision.[5] Defining qualified public safety employee by reference to section 72(t)(10)(B) has been retained because it is closely aligned with the categories of employees described in the Age Discrimination in Employment Act that an employer may refrain from hiring after a certain age.[6] Because qualified public safety employees typically commence plan participation at younger ages, the period of service required for full vesting at normal retirement age under each of the safe harbors for qualified public safety employees should be reasonable.

1. *Age 50*

The proposed regulations would modify the safe harbor for qualified public safety employees that was provided in the 2007 NRA regulations under which a normal retirement age of age 50 or later is deemed to satisfy the reasonably representative requirement and would expand on the guidance under consideration described in Notice 2012-29. The proposed regulations would make clear that a governmental plan is permitted to use the safe harbor (alone or together with one or both of the other safe harbors for qualified public safety employees described in this preamble) for one or more qualified public safety employees in a governmental plan without regard to any "substantially all" requirement (that is, without regard to whether substantially all of the participants in the plan or substantially all of the participants within a group of participants are qualified public safety employees).

---

[5] Section 72(t)(10)(B) was amended by section 2(a) of Defending Public Safety Employees' Retirement Act, Public Law 114-26 (129 Stat. 319) (2015)) and section 308 of Protecting Americans From Tax Hikes Act of 2015 (PATH Act), enacted as part of the Consolidated Appropriations Act, 2016, Public Law 114-113 (129 Stat. 2422), to include federal public safety employees as qualified public safety employees for purposes of the rules under section 72(t)(10). Thus, for distributions made after December 31, 2015, the term *qualified public safety employee* means any employee of a State or political subdivision of a State who provides police protection, firefighting services, or emergency medical services for any area within the jurisdiction of such State or political subdivision, or any Federal law enforcement officer described in section 8331(20) or 8401(17) of title 5, United States Code, any Federal customs and border protection officer described in section 8331(31) or 8401(36) of such title, any Federal firefighter described in section 8331(21) or 8401(14) of such title, or any air traffic controller described in 8331(30) or 8401(35) of such title, any nuclear materials courier described in section 8331(27) or 8401(33) of such title, any member of the United States Capitol Police, any member of the Supreme Court Police, and any diplomatic security special agent of the Department of State.

[6] See section 4(j) of the Age Discrimination in Employment Act, 29 U.S.C. 623(j).

2. *Combined age and years of service of 70 or more*

The proposed regulations would add a safe harbor under which a normal retirement age for qualified public safety employees under a governmental plan that is the participant's age when the sum of the participant's age plus the number of years of service that have been credited to the participant under the plan equals 70 or more would be deemed to satisfy the reasonably representative requirement.

3. *Any age with 20 years of service*

The proposed regulations would also add a safe harbor under which a normal retirement age for qualified public safety employees under a governmental plan that is the participant's age when the number of years of service that have been credited to the participant under the plan equals 20 or more would be deemed to satisfy the reasonably representative requirement. For example, a normal retirement age for qualified public safety employees under a plan that is 25 years of service would satisfy this safe harbor. The Department of the Treasury and the IRS agree with the comments received in response to Notice 2012-29 that indicated that a safe harbor based solely on a period of service would be appropriate for qualified public safety employees because these employees typically have career spans that commence at a young age and continue over a limited period of years.

E. *Multiple normal retirement ages in a governmental plan*

Commenters on Notice 2012-29 stated that it is a common practice for governmental plans to have a normal retirement age that is a combination of age and years of service. In light of these comments, some of the safe harbors proposed in these regulations contemplate a combination of age and years of service, such as, for example, the use of a normal retirement age that is the earlier of (1) the participant's age when the participant has been credited with 30 years of service under the plan or (2) the later of age 60 or the age when the participant has been credited with 5 years of service under the plan. A normal retirement age under a governmental plan that is consistent with the safe harbors in these proposed regulations would not fail to satisfy the pre-ERISA requirements, including the requirement that any period of service required for vesting at normal retirement age be uniformly applicable to all employees in a plan, merely because the plan uses such a normal retirement age.

Commenters to Notice 2012-29 also stated that governmental plans typically provide multiple normal retirement ages, often based on different benefit structures or classifications of employees in a single plan. These comments expressed concern that certain language in Notice 2012-29[7] could be read to indicate that a governmental plan could only have two normal retirement ages if one of the normal retirement ages covered qualified public safety employees and the other normal retirement age covered all of the other participants in the plan.

Use of one normal retirement age for one classification of employees (such as qualified public safety employees) and one or more other normal retirement ages for one or more different classifications of employees would not be inconsistent with these proposed regulations and generally would not be inconsistent with the applicable pre-ERISA requirements, including the requirement that any period of service required for full vesting at normal retirement age be uniformly applicable. Similarly, the use of one normal retirement age under a governmental plan for employees hired before a certain date and another normal retirement age under the plan for employees hired on or after that date generally would not fail to satisfy the applicable pre-ERISA requirements.

F. *Other normal retirement ages*

The proposed regulations would provide that in the case of a normal retirement age under a governmental plan that fails to satisfy any of the governmental plan safe harbors, whether the normal retirement age satisfies the reasonably representative requirement would be based on all of the relevant facts and circumstances. Similar to the treatment of normal retirement ages between ages 55 and 62 under the 2007 NRA regulations, it is generally expected that a good faith determination of the typical retirement age for the industry in which the covered workforce is employed that is made by the employer will be given deference, assuming that the determination is reasonable under the facts and circumstances and that the normal retirement age is otherwise consistent with the pre-ERISA vesting requirements.

Proposed Effective Date

These regulations are proposed to be effective for employees hired during plan years beginning on or after the later of (1) January 1, 2017 or (2) the close of the first regular legislative session of the legislative body with the authority to amend the plan that begins on or after the date that is 3 months after the final regulations are published in the **Federal Register**. Governmental plan sponsors may rely on these proposed regulations for periods preceding the effective date, pending the issuance of final regulations. If and to the extent the final regulations are more restrictive than the rules in these proposed regulations, those provisions of the final regulations will be applied without retroactive effect.

---

[7] Notice 2012-29 provided that, under an anticipated amendment to the 2007 NRA regulations, a governmental plan would be permitted to satisfy the reasonably representative requirement using a normal retirement age as low as 50 for a group substantially all of whom are qualified public safety employees and a later normal retirement age that otherwise satisfies the 2007 NRA requirements for all other participants.

Statement of Availability for IRS Documents

For copies of recently issued Revenue Procedures, Revenue Rulings, Notices, and other guidance published in the Internal Revenue Bulletin or Cumulative Bulletin, please visit the IRS Web site at http://www.irs.gov or the Superintendent of Documents, U.S. Government Printing Office, Washington, DC 20402.

Special Analyses

Certain IRS regulations, including this one, are exempt from the requirements of Executive Order 12866, as supplemented and reaffirmed by Executive Order 13563. Therefore, a regulatory assessment is not required. It has also been determined that 5 U.S.C. 533(b) of the Administrative Procedure Act (5 U.S.C. chapter 5) does not apply to these regulations. In addition, because no collection of information is imposed on small entities, the provisions of the Regulatory Flexibility Act (5 U.S.C. chapter 6) do not apply and a Regulatory Flexibility Analysis is not required. Pursuant to section 7805(f) of the Internal Revenue Code, these regulations have been submitted to the Office of Chief Counsel for Advocacy of the Small Business Administration for comments on its impact on small business.

Comments and Requests for Public Hearing

Before these proposed regulations are adopted as final regulations, consideration will be given to any comments that are submitted timely to the IRS as prescribed in this preamble under the "Addresses" heading. All comments are available at www.regulations.gov or upon request. A public hearing will be scheduled if requested in writing by any person who timely submits written comments. If a public hearing is scheduled, notice of the date, time, and place of the public hearing will be published in the **Federal Register**.

Drafting Information

The principal authors of these regulations are Sarah R. Bolen and Pamela R. Kinard, Office of Associate Chief Counsel (Tax Exempt and Government Entities). However, other personnel from the Department of the Treasury and the IRS participated in the development of these regulations.

[¶49,679] Proposed Amendments of Regulations (REG-125761-14), published in the Federal Register on January 29, 2016.

[Code Sec. 401]

Retirement plans: Nondiscrimination testing: Closed plans.—Amendments of Reg. §§1.401(a)(4)-0, §1.401(a)(4)-2, §1.401(a)(4)-3, §1.401(a)(4)-4, §1.401(a)(4)-8, §1.401(a)(4)-9, §1.401(a)(4)-12 and §1.401(a)(4)-13 following certain changes in the coverage of a defined benefit plan or a defined benefit plan formula, are proposed.

AGENCY: Internal Revenue Service (IRS), Treasury.

ACTION: Notice of proposed rulemaking and notice of public hearing.

SUMMARY: This document contains proposed regulations that modify the nondiscrimination requirements applicable to certain retirement plans that provide additional benefits to a grandfathered group of employees following certain changes in the coverage of a defined benefit plan or a defined benefit plan formula. The proposed regulations also make certain other changes to the nondiscrimination rules that are not limited to these plans. These regulations would affect participants in, beneficiaries of, employers maintaining, and administrators of tax-qualified retirement plans.

DATES: Written or electronic comments and must be received by April 28, 2016. Outlines of topics to be discussed at the public hearing scheduled for May 19, 2016 at 10 a.m., must be received by April 28, 2016.

ADDRESSES: Send submissions to: CC:PA:LPD:PR (REG-125761-14), room 5203, Internal Revenue Service, PO Box 7604, Ben Franklin Station, Washington D.C. 20044. Submissions may be hand-delivered Monday through Friday between the hours of 8 a.m. and 4 p.m. to: CC:PA:LPD:PR (REG-125761-14), Courier's Desk, Internal Revenue Service, 1111 Constitution Avenue, N.W., Washington, D.C., or sent electronically via the Federal eRulemaking Portal at *http://www.regulations.gov* (IRS REG-125761-14).

FOR FURTHER INFORMATION CONTACT: Concerning the regulations, Kelly C. Scanlon and Linda S. F. Marshall at (202) 317-6700; concerning submissions of comments, the hearing, and/or being placed on the building access list to attend the hearing, Oluwafunmilayo (Funmi) Taylor at (202) 317-6901 (not toll-free numbers).

SUPPLEMENTARY INFORMATION:

Background

Section 401(a)(4) provides generally that a plan is a qualified plan only if the contributions or benefits provided under the plan do not discriminate in favor of highly compensated employees. In 1991, the Treasury Department and the IRS issued comprehensive regulations under section 401(a)(4) (TD 8360, 56 FR 47524) setting forth several alternative methods for testing compliance with this statutory requirement. In 1993, the Treasury Department and the IRS made significant amendments to those regulations (TD 8485, 58 FR 46773).

Under the section 401(a)(4) regulations, a plan is permitted to demonstrate that either the contributions or the benefits provided under the plan are nondiscriminatory in amount, regardless of whether the plan is a defined benefit or defined contribution plan. See §1.401(a)(4)-1(b)(2). In order to test a defined contribution plan on the basis of benefits, the amounts allocated to employees under the plan must be converted to equivalent benefits. This conversion is done using an interest rate between 7.5% and 8.5%.[1] In addition, for purposes of section 401(a)(4), a defined benefit plan and a defined contribution plan are permitted to be aggregated and treated as a single plan pursuant to § 1.401(a)(4)-9, which refers to such an aggregated plan as a DB/DC plan.

After issuance of the final regulations, a new type of plan design developed. This type of plan is often referred to as a "new comparability" plan and is typically a defined contribution plan that provides higher allocation rates to an older and more highly compensated group of employees. This type of plan nonetheless satisfies the nondiscrimination requirements by testing the contributions on the basis of equivalent benefits because the conversion to equivalent benefits reflects assumed growth to normal retirement age and therefore results in relatively lower equivalent benefits for the highly compensated employees who are closer to normal retirement age. The Treasury Department and the IRS concluded that this type of plan was inconsistent with the intent behind the nondiscrimination regulations. Consequently, the Treasury Department and the IRS amended the section 401(a)(4) regulations in 2001 to require that a new comparability plan provide a higher minimum contribution to nonhighly compensated employees[2] in order for the plan to be eligible to demonstrate compliance with the nondiscrimination requirements of section 401(a)(4) on the basis of equivalent benefits (TD 8954, 66 FR 34535) (the "2001 amendments").

This higher minimum contribution requirement was directed at the new comparability plans. Other defined contribution plans that provide "broadly available allocation rates" or allocation rates that are "based on a gradual age or service schedule" are not subject to the higher minimum contribution requirement even if they demonstrate compliance with the nondiscrimination requirements of section 401(a)(4) on the basis of equivalent benefits.[3] In addition, under the 2001 amendments, defined benefit replacement allocations ("DBRAs") may be disregarded when determining whether a defined contribution plan has broadly available allocation rates. The 2001 amendments also prescribe rules regarding DB/DC plans that provide for benefits in a manner similar to new comparability plans. Under these rules (contained in § 1.401(a)(4)-9(b)(2)(v)), in order for a DB/DC plan to be eligible to demonstrate compliance with the section 401(a)(4) nondiscrimination requirements on the basis of equivalent benefits, it must satisfy a minimum aggregate allocation gateway unless the DB/DC plan either fits within the definition of "primarily defined benefit in character" or consists of "broadly available separate plans." This minimum aggregate allocation gateway requires a minimum allocation rate (or equivalent allocation rate) for each nonhighly compensated employee.

Since 2001, a number of employers have moved away from providing retirement benefits through traditional defined benefit plans. In many of these cases, employers have either significantly changed the type of benefit formula provided under the plan (such as in the case of a conversion to a cash balance plan), or have prohibited new employees from entering the plan entirely. The employers may then have allowed employees who had already begun participation in the defined benefit plan (or who are older or have been credited with longer service under the plan) to continue to earn pension benefits under the defined benefit plan while closing the plan or formula to all other employees. These defined benefit plans are sometimes referred to as "closed plans," and the employees who continue to earn pension benefits under the closed plan are often known as a "grandfathered group of employees." In situations in which new employees continue to earn benefits under the defined benefit plan, but are under a new formula, any formula that continues to apply to a grandfathered group of employees is sometimes referred to as a "closed formula."

Closed plans are required to meet the coverage rules under section 410(b) and the nondiscrimination rules under section 401(a)(4) (including a nondiscrimination requirement regarding the availability of benefits, rights, and features). Many closed plans, however, may eventually find it difficult to meet these requirements because the proportion of the grandfathered group of employees who are highly compensated employees compared to the employer's total workforce increases over time. This occurs because members of the grandfathered group of employees usually continue to receive pay raises (and so may become highly compensated employees), and new employees (who are generally nonhighly compensated employees) are not covered by the closed plan.

When a closed defined benefit plan can no longer meet the nondiscrimination requirements on a stand-alone basis because of the demographic changes previously described, it can demonstrate compliance with section 401(a)(4) by aggregating with the employer's defined contribution plan. In general, it is easier to meet the nondiscrimination requirements if the resulting DB/DC plan demonstrates compliance with section 401(a)(4) based on the benefits or equivalent benefits provided to the employees (rather than based on contributions).

On January 6, 2014, the Treasury Department and the IRS published Notice 2014-5, 2014-2 I.R.B. 276. Notice 2014-5 provided temporary nondiscrimination relief for certain closed plans. Specifically, under Notice 2014-5, if certain criteria are satisfied,[4] a plan sponsor is permitted to test a DB/DC plan

---

[1] See § 1.401(a)(4)-8(c)(2)(ii) and § 1.401(a)(4)-12 (definition of standard interest rate). This standard interest rate is used to determine assumed growth of a defined contribution plan account and to convert the projected account balance to an annuity at normal retirement age.

[2] This higher minimum contribution rate is required under § 1.401(a)(4)-8(b)(1)(i)(B)(3) and (b)(1)(vi)..

[3] See § 1.401(a)(4)-8(b)(1)(i)(B)(*1*) and (*2*), (b)(1)(iii), and (b)(1)(iv).

[4] Generally, in order to be eligible for the relief provided by Notice 2014-5, each defined benefit plan that is part of an aggregated DB/DC plan must have satisfied the requirements of section 401(a)(4) without using the minimum aggregate allocation gateway under § 1.401(a)(4)-9(b)(2)(v)(D).

that includes a closed plan that was closed before December 13, 2013, on a benefits basis for plan years beginning before January 1, 2016, without complying with the minimum aggregate allocation gateway, even if that would otherwise be required under the current regulations. Notice 2015-28, 2015-14 I.R.B. 848, extended that relief for an additional year by applying it to plan years beginning before 2017 provided that the conditions of Notice 2014-5 are satisfied.

Notice 2014-5 also requested comments on whether the section 401(a)(4) regulations should be amended to provide additional alternatives that would allow a DB/DC plan to satisfy the nondiscrimination in amount requirements on the basis of equivalent benefits, and whether certain other permanent changes should be made to the nondiscrimination regulations, such as modifications to the rules regarding nondiscriminatory benefits, rights, and features.[5] The comments received in response to Notice 2014-5 generally supported these types of changes. In addition, all of the commenters requested permanent changes to the nondiscrimination requirements in order to make it easier for closed plans to continue to satisfy the nondiscrimination requirements.

The Treasury Department and the IRS agree that permanent changes to the nondiscrimination rules should be made in order to help employers and plan sponsors preserve the retirement expectations of certain grandfathered groups of employees. These changes are meant to apply to situations in which the proportion of the grandfathered group of employees who are highly compensated employees compared to the employer's total workforce has increased due to ordinary demographic changes, as previously described in this preamble.

Explanation of Provisions

I. Overview

The proposed regulations modify a number of provisions in the existing regulations under section 401(a)(4) to address situations and plan designs, including closed plans and formulas, that were not contemplated in the development of the regulations and the 2001 amendments. While many of the changes in the proposed regulations provide nondiscrimination relief for certain closed plans and formulas, the proposed regulations also include other changes that are not limited to closed plans and formulas.

II. Rules related to closed plans and similar arrangements

The proposed regulations set forth special rules that allow closed plans and similar arrangements to satisfy the nondiscrimination rules in additional situations. These special rules are based on the existing rules for DBRAs, as modified to respond to concerns raised by stakeholders with respect to those existing rules.

Under the proposed regulations, the eligibility conditions set forth in the modified DBRA rules (described in section II.A of this portion of the preamble) provide a framework for the eligibility conditions for the snapshot rule related to closed plans in a DB/DC plan (described in section II.B of this portion of the preamble). The modified DBRA rules are also used as a basis for the special testing rule for benefits, rights, and features provided to a grandfathered group of employees (described in section II.C of this portion of the preamble). For example, the special testing rule for a benefit, right, or feature provided to a grandfathered group of employees under a defined contribution plan establishes nondiscrimination relief for matching contributions provided to a grandfathered group of employees who formerly participated in a defined benefit plan that is intended to be consistent with the nondiscrimination relief provided by the modified DBRA rules for nonelective contributions provided to such a grandfathered group of employees.

A. Modifications to the DBRA rules under § 1.401(a)(4)-8

The proposed regulations modify the rules applicable to DBRAs under § 1.401(a)(4)-8, which allow certain defined contribution plan allocations to be disregarded when determining whether a defined contribution plan has broadly available allocation rates. The rules applicable to DBRAs allow employers to provide, in a nondiscriminatory manner, certain allocations to replace defined benefit plan retirement benefits without having to satisfy the minimum aggregate allocation gateway. The modifications in the proposed regulations are intended to allow more allocations to fit within the DBRA rules. For example, under the existing regulations a DBRA must be reasonably designed to replace the benefits that would have been provided under the closed defined benefit plan. The proposed regulations provide greater flexibility in this respect and allow the allocations to be reasonably designed to replace some or all of the benefits that would have been provided under the closed plan, subject to a requirement that the allocations be provided in a consistent manner to all similarly situated employees.

(Footnote Continued)

Thus, the defined benefit plan must have either been primarily defined benefit in character (within the meaning of § 1.401(a)(4)-9(b)(2)(v)(B)), consisted of broadly available separate plans (within the meaning of § 1.401(a)(4)-9(b)(2)(v)(C)), or satisfied the applicable nondiscrimination rules without being aggregated with a DC plan.

[5] Section 1.401(a)(4)-4 provides rules for determining whether the benefits, right, and features provided under a plan are made available in a nondiscriminatory manner. Under these rules, each benefit, right, or feature must satisfy the current availability requirement of § 1.401(a)(4)-4(b) (which requires testing of the group to which the benefit, right, or feature is currently available) and the effective availability requirement of § 1.401(a)(4)-4(c) (which requires that the group of employees to whom the benefit, right, or feature is effectively available must not substantially favor highly compensated employees).

The proposed regulations incorporate a modified version of the conditions for an allocation to be a DBRA that were reflected in Rev. Rul. 2001-30, 2001-2 C.B. 46. For example, under one of the conditions set forth in Rev. Rul. 2001-30, in order for an allocation to be a DBRA, the defined benefit plan's benefit formula for the group of employees who formerly benefitted under that plan must have generated equivalent normal allocation rates that increased from year to year as employees attained higher ages. The proposed regulations ease this restriction on the types of defined benefit plans with respect to which a DBRA can be provided by allowing a DBRA also to replace the benefit provided under a defined benefit plan with a benefit formula that generated equivalent normal allocation rates that increased from year to year as employees were credited with additional years of service (rather than only as the employees attained higher ages).

The existing regulation also requires that the group of employees who receive a DBRA must be a nondiscriminatory group of employees, and Rev. Rul. 2001-30 interprets this rule as requiring that the group of employees satisfy the minimum coverage requirements of section 410(b) (determined without regard to the average benefit percentage test). The proposed regulations incorporate this interpretation, but limit its application so that the rule only applies for the first 5 years after the closure date. In addition, the proposed regulations incorporate the interpretation in Rev. Rul. 2001-30 regarding whether the defined benefit plan was an established nondiscriminatory defined benefit plan by requiring that the closed plan be in effect for 5 years before the closure date (with one year substituted for 5 years, as provided by Rev. Rul. 2001-30, in the case of a defined benefit plan maintained by a former employer) with no substantial change to the closed plan during that time (except for certain permitted amendments allowed by the proposed regulations).

In addition, the proposed regulations expand the list of permitted amendments to a closed plan that do not prevent allocations under a plan from being DBRAs. For example, the proposed regulations permit an amendment to a closed plan during the 5-year period before it was closed, provided that the amendment does not increase the accrued benefit or future accruals for any employee, does not expand coverage, and does not reduce the ratio-percentage under any applicable nondiscrimination test. In addition, under the proposed regulations, an amendment during this period could extend coverage to an acquired group of employees provided that all similarly situated employees within that group are treated in a consistent manner.

As under the existing regulations, the proposed regulations contain a general restriction on plan amendments relating to a DBRA; however, the proposed regulations expand the list of plan amendments that are excepted from this rule. The proposed regulations retain the exception from this restriction on plan amendments for an amendment that makes *de minimis* changes in the calculation of a DBRA and for an amendment that adds or removes a "greater-of" plan provision (under which a participant receives the greater of the otherwise applicable allocation and the DBRA). In addition, the proposed regulations provide an exception from this restriction for any plan amendment modifying a DBRA that does not reduce the ratio percentage under any applicable nondiscrimination test.

B. Closed plan rule added to the plan aggregation and restructuring rules under §1.401(a)(4)-9

The proposed regulations add a new exception to the requirement that a DB/DC plan must satisfy the minimum aggregate allocation gateway once the other conditions under §1.401(a)(4)-9 are not met (the "closed plan rule"). This closed plan rule, which applies to a DB/DC plan that includes a closed plan, provides an exception to the minimum aggregate allocation gateway that would otherwise apply, but only if the closed plan was in effect for 5 years before the closure date and no significant change was made to the closed plan during or since that time (except for certain permitted amendments).

The DB/DC plan may use this closed plan rule for a plan year that begins on or after the fifth anniversary of the closure date. To be eligible for the closed plan rule, during the 5-year period following the closure date, either the DB/DC plan must satisfy the nondiscrimination in amount requirement of section 401(a)(4) without using the minimum aggregate allocation gateway, or the closed plan must satisfy that requirement without aggregation with any defined contribution plan. This requirement is comparable to the requirement that the group of employees who receive DBRAs must be a group of employees who satisfy the minimum coverage requirements of section 410(b).

Under the proposed regulations, certain amendments to a closed defined benefit plan do not prevent the plan from using the closed plan rule. These plan amendments are intended to allow a plan sponsor of a closed plan to address changed circumstances. For example, under the proposed regulations, a plan amendment during the 5-year period ending on the closure date does not prevent the plan from later using the closed plan rule, provided that the plan amendment does not increase the accrued benefit or future accruals for any employee, does not expand coverage, and does not reduce the ratio percentage under any applicable nondiscrimination test. Similarly, an amendment to the closed plan is permitted after the closure date, provided that the amendment does not reduce the ratio percentage under any applicable nondiscrimination test. Thus, for example, under the proposed regulations, a plan sponsor may add nonhighly compensated employees to a coverage group after it is closed in order to satisfy the nondiscrimination rules. *De minimis* changes to the closed plan's benefit formula are also permitted under the proposed regulations.

C. Special testing rule for the nondiscriminatory availability of a benefit, right, or feature provided to a grandfathered group of employees under §1.401(a)(4)-4

The proposed regulations establish a special nondiscrimination testing rule under §1.401(a)(4)-4 that applies if a benefit, right, or feature is made available only to a grandfathered group of employees with respect to a closed plan. This special rule provides relief in certain circumstances from certain nondiscrimination testing for a benefit, right, or feature provided under the closed plan, or for a rate of matching contributions provided to a grandfathered group under a defined contribution plan.

If the eligibility conditions are satisfied, the special testing rule treats a benefit, right, or feature that is provided only to a grandfathered group of employees as satisfying the current and effective availability tests of § 1.401(a)(4)-4(b) and (c). The special testing rule applies to plan years beginning on or after the fifth anniversary of the closure date and applies on a plan-year by plan-year basis. To be eligible for the special testing rule, the benefit, right or feature must be currently available to a group of employees that satisfies the minimum coverage requirements of section 410(b) for the plan years that begin within 5 years after the closure date. Once the special testing rule applies to a benefit, right, or feature, the special testing rule continues to apply for purposes of that benefit, right, or feature indefinitely (unless a later amendment changes the eligibility for the benefit, right, or feature). If a plan amendment changes the eligibility for the benefit, right, or feature after the closure date, then the special testing rule will cease to apply (subject to certain specified exceptions).

If the benefit, right, or feature that is available solely to a grandfathered group of employees is provided under a defined benefit plan, then it must be provided under the closed plan (rather than a different defined benefit plan). This is because the purpose of the special rule is to accommodate a plan amendment under which the benefit formula has been changed, but the prior benefit formula has been preserved for a grandfathered group of employees and the benefit, right, or feature is made available only to the grandfathered group of employees who continue to accrue benefits under the prior benefit formula.[6] Accordingly, the special testing rule is available only if the amendment restricting the availability of the benefit, right, or feature also resulted in a significant change in the type of the defined benefit plan's formula. For example, a conversion to a cash balance plan would be a significant change in the type of benefit formula, so that the special testing rule would apply to facilitate preservation of any subsidized early retirement factors for the employees who continue to benefit under the prior benefit formula. By contrast, in the case of a benefit formula that determines benefits as a percentage of compensation, a change in that formula to reduce that percentage would not be considered a significant change in the type of benefit formula, even if the reduction is large.

The special testing rule for a benefit, right, or feature provided under the closed plan also requires that the benefit, right, or feature has been in effect without being amended for a 5-year period before the closure date (subject to a limited exception for acquired employees). This rule is designed to ensure that the special treatment is available only for a long-standing provision and cannot be used for a benefit, right, or feature that has not been provided long enough for participants to have established a reasonable expectation that it will continue. In addition, this rule prevents a plan sponsor from obtaining special treatment for a benefit, right, or feature added shortly before and in anticipation of the closure of the plan. The proposed regulations set forth a list of permitted plan amendments that do not result in the loss of this special testing rule that are generally comparable to the list of permitted amendments for other closed plan arrangements.

The special testing rule also applies to a rate of matching contributions under a defined contribution plan that meets certain requirements. In order to be eligible for this testing rule, the rate of matching contributions must be reasonably designed so that the matching contributions will replace some or all of the value of the benefit accruals that each employee in the grandfathered group of employees would have been provided under the closed plan in the absence of a closure amendment. In addition, the rate of matching contributions for the grandfathered group of employees must be provided in a consistent manner to all similarly situated employees.

III. Modification of testing options under § 1.401(a)(4)-9 for DB/DC plans, including DB/DC plans that do not include a closed plan

In addition to providing a special rule for closed plans and similar arrangements, the proposed regulations generally ease the rules under which any DB/DC plan can satisfy the nondiscrimination in amount requirement on the basis of benefits. These changes are intended to facilitate the ongoing maintenance of a defined benefit plan that provides coverage to a group of employees that is determined using a reasonable business classification.

The proposed regulations expand the ability to use the average of the equivalent allocation rates under the defined benefit plan for purposes of satisfying the minimum aggregate allocation gateway by permitting the averaging of allocation rates for nonhighly compensated employees under the defined contribution plan for this purpose. This modification is intended to better accommodate plan sponsors that have a defined contribution plan with service-or age-based allocation formulas. The Treasury Department and the IRS have determined that it is appropriate, in this context, to allow shorter-service nonhighly compensated employees to be provided less than the minimum aggregate allocation gateway rate, as long as longer-service nonhighly compensated employees are provided allocation rates that are sufficiently higher than the minimum aggregate allocation gateway rate. The Treasury Department and the IRS are considering whether any restrictions on this rule are appropriate so that the rule serves its intended purpose of facilitating formulas that provide higher allocation

---

[6] The existing regulations provide a special rule for current availability testing for a benefit, right, or feature that applies solely to benefits accrued before the amendment date. *See* § 1.401(a)(4)-4(d)(2).

rates to longer-service nonhighly compensated employees, and invite comments on ways to permit appropriate flexibility while ensuring the provision is not used to circumvent the purpose of the nondiscrimination rules.

The proposed regulations also include a limitation on the averaging of rates that applies to both defined contribution and defined benefit plans in order to minimize the impact of outliers. In general, this special rule applies a cap under which any equivalent normal allocation rate or allocation rate in excess of 15% is treated as equal to 15%. However, this cap is raised to 25% for any allocation rate or equivalent normal allocation rate that results solely from a plan design providing allocation rates or generating equivalent normal allocation rates that are a function of age or service under which higher rates are provided to older or longer-service employees.

In addition, under the proposed regulations, the average of the matching contributions actually made for nonhighly compensated employees may be used to a limited extent (up to 3 percent of compensation) for purposes of determining whether each nonhighly compensated employee satisfies the minimum aggregate allocation gateway test. Thus, for example, if the minimum aggregate allocation gateway is 7% and the average of the matching contributions actually made for nonhighly compensated employees is 3%, then a non-elective contribution of 4% for each individual would be needed in order to satisfy the minimum aggregate allocation gateway under the proposed regulations. The regulations use the average matching contributions, rather than matching contributions allocated for each employee, in order to avoid diluting the incentive effect of an employer match.

The proposed regulations also provide a new alternative to the minimum aggregate allocation gateway. Under this alternative, a DB/DC plan is not required to satisfy the minimum aggregate allocation gateway if it can satisfy the nondiscrimination in amount requirement on the basis of equivalent benefits using an interest rate of 6%, rather than the current standard interest rate of between 7.5% and 8.5%.

IV. Benefit formulas for individual employees or groups without a reasonable business purpose; modifications to the amounts testing rules under § 1.401(a)(4)-2 and § 1.401(a)(4)-3

The proposed regulations also include changes to address certain arrangements that take advantage of the flexibility in the existing nondiscrimination rules[7] to provide a special benefit formula for selected employees without extending that formula to a classification of employees that is reasonable and is established under objective business criteria. A plan satisfies the minimum coverage requirements of section 410(b) if the plan's ratio percentage is 70% or higher or the plan satisfies the average benefit test. To satisfy the average benefit test, pursuant to § 1.410(b)-4, the group of employees must be determined using a classification that is reasonable and that is established under objective business criteria pursuant to § 1.410(b)-4(b) and must have a ratio percentage that is described in § 1.410(b)-4(c) (which includes safe harbor and unsafe harbor percentages). A classification of employees that is reasonable and is established under objective business criteria is referred to in this preamble as a "reasonable business classification." To the extent that a plan provides a special benefit formula and can still pass the nondiscrimination requirements, the plan sponsor can use a qualified retirement plan to provide benefits that would otherwise be provided under a nonqualified plan. These arrangements are sometimes referred to as qualified supplemental executive retirement plans (or QSERPs).

Under the general test in the existing regulations, if a plan satisfies the minimum coverage requirements of section 410(b) using the average benefit percentage test, then the rate group for each highly compensated employee is treated as satisfying the minimum coverage requirements if the ratio percentage for the rate group is equal to the midpoint between the safe harbor and the unsafe harbor percentages (or the ratio percentage for the plan as a whole, if less). This rule recognizes that the composition of a rate group may be unpredictable and so the rate group should not be subject to a reasonable business classification standard. However, that same consideration is not relevant if the group of employees to whom the allocation formula under a defined contribution plan (or benefit formula under a defined benefit plan) applies is not a reasonable business classification.

Accordingly, the proposed regulations limit the existing rule under which a rate group with respect to a highly compensated employee is treated as satisfying the average benefit percentage test to those situations in which the allocation formula (or benefit formula) that applies to the highly compensated employee also applies to a reasonable business classification. For example, if a benefit formula applies solely to a highly compensated employee who is identified by name, it does not apply to a reasonable business classification. See § 1.410(b)-4(b). In such a case, the proposed regulations would require that the rate group with respect to that individual satisfy the ratio percentage test.

Proposed Applicability Date

Except as described below, these regulations are proposed to be applicable to plan years beginning on or after the date of publication of the Treasury decision adopting these rules as final regulations in the **Federal Register**. Taxpayers are permitted to apply the provisions of these proposed regulations except for those described in section III of the Explanation of Provisions portion of the preamble for

---

[7] Under the existing regulations, the nondiscrimination requirements of section 401(a)(4) and the coverage rules of section 410(b) are coordinated. The general test under the section 401(a)(4) regulations is applied by determining whether each rate group under the plan (that is, for each highly compensated employee, the group of employees with a benefit or contribution rate that is greater than or equal to the benefit or contribution rate for the highly compensated employee) satisfies section 410(b) as if it were a plan.

plan years beginning before this proposed applicability date, but not for plan years earlier than those beginning on or after January 1, 2014. Accordingly, the ability to rely on a provision of these proposed regulations for periods prior to the proposed applicability date for these regulations applies to the disregard of certain defined benefit replacement allocations in cross-testing; the exception from the minimum aggregate allocation gateway with respect to certain closed plans; the special testing rule for benefits, rights, and features with respect to certain closed plans; and the rule applying the ratio percentage test to a rate group in the case of a benefit formula that does not apply to a reasonable business classification. Taxpayers may rely on these provisions (that is, the provisions that the proposed regulations would permit a taxpayer to apply before the proposed applicability date for these regulations) in order to satisfy the nondiscrimination requirements of section 401(a)(4) for plan years beginning on or after January 1, 2014, and until the corresponding final regulations become applicable.

Special Analyses

Certain IRS regulations, including this one, are exempt from the requirements of Executive Order 12866, as supplemented and reaffirmed by Executive Order 13563. Therefore, a regulatory impact assessment is not required. It also has been determined that section 553(b) of the Administrative Procedure Act (5 U.S.C. chapter 5) does not apply to these regulations, and because the regulation does not impose a collection of information on small entities, the Regulatory Flexibility Act (5 U.S.C. chapter 6) does not apply. Pursuant to section 7805(f) of the Internal Revenue Code, these regulations have been submitted to the Chief Counsel for Advocacy of the Small Business Administration for comment on their impact on small business.

Comments and Public Hearing

Before these proposed regulations are adopted as final regulations, consideration will be given to any comments that are submitted timely to the IRS as prescribed in this preamble under the "ADDRESSES" heading. Treasury and the IRS request comments on all aspects of the proposed rules, including the proposed applicability date. Treasury and the IRS also request comments on the following issues:

- Whether guidance needs to be developed for a plan that has more than one closure or closure amendment?
- Whether the rules regarding transition allocations and successor employers are still needed in light of the modifications to the DBRA rules?

All comments will be available for public inspection and copying at www.regulations.gov or upon request.

A public hearing has been scheduled for May 19, 2016, beginning at 10 a.m. in the Auditorium, Internal Revenue Service, 1111 Constitution Avenue, N.W., Washington D.C. Because of building security procedures, visitors must enter at the Constitution Avenue entrance. In addition, all visitors must present photo identification to enter the building. Due to access restrictions, visitors will not be admitted beyond the immediate entrance area more than 30 minutes before the hearing starts. For information about having your name placed on the building access list to attend the hearing, see the "FOR FURTHER INFORMATION CONTACT" section of this preamble.

The rules of 26 CFR 601.601(a)(3) apply to the hearing. Persons who wish to present oral comments at the hearing must submit written or electronic comments by April 28, 2016 and an outline of the topics to be discussed and the time to be devoted to each topic by April 28, 2016. A signed paper or electronic copy of the outline should be submitted as prescribed in this preamble under the "ADDRESSES" heading. A period of 10 minutes will be allotted to each person for making comments. An agenda showing the scheduling of the speakers will be prepared after the deadline for receiving outlines has passed. Copies of the agenda will be available free of charge at the hearing.

Statement of Availability for IRS Documents

For copies of recently issued Revenue Procedures, Revenue Rulings, notices, and other guidance published in the Internal Revenue Bulletin, please visit the IRS website at http://irs.gov.

Drafting Information

The principal authors of these proposed regulations are Kelly C. Scanlon and Linda S. F. Marshall, IRS Office of Associate Chief Counsel (Tax Exempt and Government Entities). However, other personnel from the IRS and the Department of Treasury participated in the development of the proposed regulations.

[¶49,680] Proposed Amendments of Regulations (REG-100861-15), published in the Federal Register on February 4, 2016.

[Code Sec. 704]

Partnerships: Creditable foreign tax expenditures.—Amendments of Reg. §1.704-1, issuing temporary regulations that provide guidance relating to the allocation by a partnership of foreign income taxes, are proposed.

AGENCY: Internal Revenue Service (IRS), Treasury.

ACTION: Notice of proposed rulemaking by cross-reference to temporary regulations.

SUMMARY: In the Rules and Regulations section in this issue of the **Federal Register**, the IRS is issuing temporary regulations that provide guidance relating to the allocation by a partnership of foreign income taxes. Those temporary regulations are necessary to improve the operation of an existing safe harbor rule that is used for determining whether allocations of creditable foreign tax expenditures are deemed to be in accordance with the partners' interests in the partnership. The text of those temporary regulations published in this issue of the **Federal Register** also serves as the text of these proposed regulations.

DATES: Comments and requests for a public hearing must be received by May 4, 2016.

ADDRESSES: Send submissions to CC:PA:LPD:PR (REG-100861-15), room 5205, Internal Revenue Service, PO Box 7604, Ben Franklin Station, Washington, DC 20044. Submissions may be hand delivered Monday through Friday between the hours of 8 a.m. and 4 p.m. to CC:PA:LPD:PR (REG-100861-15), Courier's desk, Internal Revenue Service, 1111 Constitution Avenue, NW., Washington, DC 20224, or sent electronically, via the Federal eRulemaking Portal at www.regulations.gov (IRS REG-100861-15). FOR FURTHER INFORMATION CONTACT: Concerning the regulations, Suzanne M. Walsh, (202) 317-4908; concerning submissions of comments, Oluwafunmilayo Taylor, (202) 317-5179 (not toll-free numbers).

SUPPLEMENTARY INFORMATION:

Background and Explanation of Provisions

Temporary regulations in the Rules and Regulations section of this issue of the **Federal Register** contain amendments to the Income Tax Regulations (26 CFR part 1) which provide guidance relating to the allocation by a partnership of foreign income taxes. The text of those regulations also serves as the text of these proposed regulations. The preamble to the temporary regulations explains the temporary regulations and these proposed regulations. The regulations affect partnerships and their partners.

Special Analyses

Certain IRS regulations, including this one, are exempt from the requirements of Executive Order 12866, as supplemented and reaffirmed by Executive Order 13563. Therefore, a regulatory assessment is not required. It has also been determined that section 553(b) of the Administrative Procedure Act (5 U.S.C. chapter 5) does not apply to these regulations, and because the regulations do not impose a collection of information on small entities, the Regulatory Flexibility Act (5 U.S.C. chapter 6) does not apply. Pursuant to section 7805(f), these regulations have been submitted to the Chief Counsel for Advocacy of the Small Business Administration for comment on its impact on small business.

Comments and Requests for Public Hearing

Before these proposed regulations are adopted as final regulations, consideration will be given to any comments that are submitted timely to the IRS as prescribed in this preamble under "ADDRESSES." The Treasury Department and the IRS request comments on all aspects of the proposed rules. All comments will be available at www.regulations.gov or upon request. A public hearing will be scheduled if requested in writing by any person that timely submits comments. If a public hearing is scheduled, notice of the date, time, and place for the public hearing will be published in the **Federal Register**.

Drafting Information

The principal author of these regulations is Suzanne M. Walsh of the Office of Associate Chief Counsel (International). However, other personnel from the IRS and the Treasury Department participated in their development.

[¶49,682] Proposed Amendments of Regulations (REG-118867-10), published in the Federal Register on February 19, 2016.

[Code Sec. 509]

Private foundations: Supporting organizations: Integral part test.—Amendments of Reg. §1.509(a)-4, regarding the prohibition on certain contributions to Type I and Type III supporting organizations and the requirements for Type III supporting organizations, are proposed.

AGENCY: Internal Revenue Service (IRS), Treasury.

ACTION: Notice of proposed rulemaking.

SUMMARY: This document contains proposed regulations regarding the prohibition on certain contributions to Type I and Type III supporting organizations and the requirements for Type III supporting organizations. The regulations reflect changes to the law made by the Pension Protection Act of 2006. The regulations will affect Type I and Type III supporting organizations and their supported organizations.

DATES: Written or electronic comments and requests for a public hearing must be received by May 19, 2016.

ADDRESSES: Send submissions to: CC:PA:LPD:PR (REG-118867-10), Room 5203, Internal Revenue Service, P.O. Box 7604, Ben Franklin Station, Washington, DC 20044. Submissions may be hand-delivered Monday through Friday between the hours of 8:00 a.m. and 4 p.m. to CC:PA:LPD:PR (REG-118867-10), Courier's Desk, Internal Revenue Service, 1111 Constitution Avenue, NW, Washington, DC, 20224 or sent electronically via the Federal eRulemaking Portal at http://www.regulations.gov/ (IRS REG-118867-10). FOR FURTHER INFORMATION CONTACT: concerning the proposed regulations, Jonathan Carter at (202) 317-5800 or Mike Repass at (202) 317-4086; concerning submissions of comments and requests for a public hearing, Regina Johnson at (202) 317-6901 (not toll-free numbers).

SUPPLEMENTARY INFORMATION:

Paperwork Reduction Act

The collection of information contained in this notice of proposed rulemaking has been submitted to the Office of Management and Budget for review and approval in accordance with the Paperwork Reduction Act of 1995 (44 U.S.C. 3507(d)). Comments on the collection of information should be sent to the Office of Management and Budget, Attn: Desk Officer for the Department of the Treasury, Office of Information and Regulatory Affairs, Washington, DC 20503, with copies to the Internal Revenue Service, Attn: IRS Reports Clearance Officer, SE:W:CAR:MP:T:T:SP, Washington, DC 20224. Comments on the collection of information should be received by May 19, 2016.

Comments are specifically requested concerning:

- Whether the proposed collection of information is necessary for the proper performance of the functions of the IRS, including whether the information will have practical utility;
- The accuracy of the estimated burden associated with the proposed collection of information;
- How the quality, utility, and clarity of the information to be collected may be enhanced;
- How the burden of complying with the proposed collection of information may be minimized, including through forms of information technology; and
- Estimates of capital or start-up costs and costs of operation, maintenance, and purchase of services to provide information.

The collection of information in these proposed regulations is in §1.509(a)-4(i)(4)(iv)(D) (written record of close cooperation and coordination by the governmental supported organizations) and §1.509(a)-4(i)(6)(iii)(B) (written record of contributions received by the supported organization). Requiring the supporting organization to collect written records of its governmental supported organizations' close cooperation and coordination with each other and written records of the contributions its supported organizations directly received in response to solicitations by the supporting organization permits the IRS to determine whether the supporting organization satisfies the requirements to be a functionally integrated or non-functionally integrated Type III supporting organization. The record keepers are Type III supporting organizations.

Estimated number of recordkeepers: 7,872.

Estimated average annual burden hours per recordkeeper: 2 hours.

Estimated total annual recordkeeping burden: 15,744.

Estimated frequency of collection of such information: Annual.

An agency may not conduct or sponsor, and a person is not required to respond to, a collection of information unless it displays a valid control number assigned by the Office of Management and Budget.

Books or records relating to a collection of information must be retained as long as their contents may become material in the administration of any internal revenue law. Generally, tax returns and return information are confidential, as required by 26 U.S.C. 6103.

Background

1. *Overview*

This document contains proposed amendments to the Income Tax Regulations (26 CFR part 1) regarding organizations described in section 509(a)(3) of the Internal Revenue Code (Code). An organization described in section 501(c)(3) is classified as either a private foundation or a public charity. To be classified as a public charity, an organization must be described in section 509(a)(1), (2), or (3). Organizations described in section 509(a)(3) are known as "supporting organizations." Supporting organizations achieve their public charity status by providing support to one or more organizations described in section 509(a)(1) or (2), which in this context are referred to as "supported organizations."

To be described in section 509(a)(3), an organization must satisfy (1) an organizational test, (2) an operational test, (3) a relationship test, and (4) a disqualified person control test. The organizational and operational tests require that a supporting organization be organized and at all times thereafter operated exclusively for the benefit of, to perform the functions of, or to carry out the purposes of one or more supported organizations. The relationship test requires a supporting organization to establish one of three types of relationships with one or more supported organizations. A supporting organization that is operated, supervised or controlled by one or more supported organizations is known as a "Type I" supporting organization. The relationship of a Type I supporting organization with its supported organization(s) is comparable to that of a corporate parent-subsidiary relationship. A supporting organization that is supervised or controlled in connection with one or more supported organizations is known as a "Type II" supporting organization. The relationship of a Type II supporting organization with its supported organization(s) involves common supervision or control by the persons supervising or controlling both the supporting organization and the supported organization(s). A supporting organization that is operated in connection with one or more supported organizations is known as a "Type III" supporting organization and is discussed further in the remainder of this preamble. Finally, the disqualified person control test requires that a supporting organization not be controlled directly or indirectly by certain disqualified persons.

These proposed regulations focus primarily on the relationship test for Type III supporting organizations. Specifically, the proposed regulations reflect statutory changes enacted by sections 1241 through 1243 of the Pension Protection Act of 2006, Public Law 109-280 (120 Stat. 780) (2006)

(PPA)), which made the following five changes to the requirements an organization must satisfy to qualify as a Type III supporting organization:

(1) Removed the ability of a charitable trust to rely on the special rule under § 1.509(a)-4(i)(2)(iii) of the regulations then in effect;

(2) Directed the Secretary of the Treasury to promulgate regulations under section 509 that establish a new distribution requirement for Type III supporting organizations that are not "functionally integrated" (a non-functionally integrated (NFI) Type III supporting organization) to ensure that a "significant amount" is paid to supported organizations (for this purpose the term "functionally integrated" means a Type III supporting organization that is not required under Treasury regulations to make payments to supported organizations, because the supporting organization engages in activities that relate to performing the functions of, or carrying out the purposes of, its supported organization(s));

(3) Required a Type III supporting organization to provide annually to each of its supported organizations the information required by the Treasury Department and the IRS to ensure that the supporting organization is responsive to the needs or demands of its supported organization(s);

(4) Prohibited a Type III supporting organization from supporting any supported organization not organized in the United States; and

(5) Prohibited a Type I or Type III supporting organization from accepting a gift or contribution from a person who, alone or together with certain related persons, directly or indirectly controls the governing body of a supported organization of the Type I or Type III supporting organization.

These proposed regulations set forth additional rules on the requirements for Type III supporting organizations, including additional requirements to meet the responsiveness test for all Type III supporting organizations; additional rules regarding the qualification of an organization as a functionally integrated Type III supporting organization under § 1.509(a)-4(i)(4), including provisions for supporting organizations that support governmental entities; and additional rules regarding the required annual distributions under § 1.509(a)-4(i)(5) by a NFI Type III supporting organization. The proposed regulations also define the term "control" for purposes of section 509(f)(2), which prohibits a Type I supporting organization or a Type III supporting organization from accepting contributions from persons who control the governing body of its supported organization(s).

2. *Prior Rulemaking*

On August 2, 2007, the Treasury Department and the IRS published in the **Federal Register** (72 FR 42335) an advanced notice of proposed rulemaking (ANPRM) (REG-155929-06) in response to the PPA. The ANPRM described proposed rules to implement the changes made by the PPA to the Type III supporting organization requirements and solicited comments regarding those proposed rules.

On September 24, 2009, the Treasury Department and the IRS published in the **Federal Register** (74 FR 48672) a notice of proposed rulemaking (the 2009 NPRM) (REG-155929-06). The 2009 NPRM contained proposed regulations (the 2009 proposed regulations) setting forth the requirements to qualify as a Type III supporting organization under the PPA.

On December 28, 2012, the Treasury Department and the IRS published in the **Federal Register** (77 FR 76382) a Treasury decision (TD 9605) containing final and temporary regulations (the 2012 TD) regarding the requirements to qualify as a Type III supporting organization. Based on the comments received, the 2012 TD made certain changes to the rules proposed in the 2009 NPRM, included in the temporary regulations significant changes to the distribution requirement, and reserved certain topics for further consideration. Also on December 28, 2012, the Treasury Department and the IRS published in the **Federal Register** (77 FR 76426) a notice of proposed rulemaking (the 2012 NPRM) (REG-155929-06) that incorporated the text of the temporary regulations in the 2012 TD by cross-reference. The 2012 TD provided transition relief for Type III supporting organizations in existence on December 28, 2012, that met and continued to meet the test under former § 1.509(a)-4(i)(3)(ii), as in effect prior to December 28, 2012, treating them as functionally integrated until the first day of their second taxable years beginning after December 28, 2012. The preamble to the 2012 TD also identified issues for possible future rulemaking and requested comments. The IRS received three comments on these issues. The comments were considered in developing these proposed regulations and are available for public inspection at *www.regulations.gov* or upon request. No public hearing was requested.

The Treasury Department and the IRS published Notice 2014-4, 2014-2 I.R.B. 274, to provide additional transition relief for any Type III supporting organization that (1) supports at least one governmental supported organization to which the supporting organization is responsive within the meaning of § 1.509(a)-4(i)(3) and (2) engages in activities for or on behalf of the governmental supported organization that perform the functions of, or carry out the purposes of, the governmental supported organization and that, but for the involvement of the supporting organization, would normally be engaged in by the governmental supported organization itself. Notice 2014-4 provides that such an organization will be treated as a functionally integrated Type III supporting organization until the earlier of the date final regulations are published under § 1.509(a)-4(i)(4)(iv) in the **Federal Register** or the first day of the organization's third taxable year beginning after December 31, 2013.

On December 23, 2015, the Treasury Department and the IRS published in the **Federal Register** (80 FR 79684) a Treasury Decision (TD 9746) containing final regulations (the 2015 TD) regarding the distribution requirement for NFI Type III supporting organizations. The preamble of those regulations provided that supporting organizations supporting a governmental supported organization could continue to rely on Notice 2014-4 until the date of publication of the notice of proposed rulemaking prescribing the new proposed regulations under § 1.509(a)-4(i)(4)(iv). The IRS received three comments in response to Notice 2014-4, which the Treasury Department and the IRS considered in developing these proposed regulations.

Explanation of Provisions and Summary of Comments

This section describes the proposed provisions and addresses comments that the Treasury Department and the IRS received in response to the 2012 TD and Notice 2014-4.

1. *Gifts from Controlling Donor - Meaning of Control*

Type I and Type III supporting organizations are prohibited from accepting a gift or contribution from a person who, alone or together with certain related persons, directly or indirectly controls the governing body of a supported organization of the Type I or Type III supporting organization, or from persons related to a person possessing such control. Section 509(f)(2) and § 1.509(a)-4(f)(5). For this purpose, related persons include family members and 35-percent controlled entities within the meaning of section 4958(f). Although the 2012 TD reserved § 1.509(a)-4(f)(5)(ii), "Meaning of control," the preamble to the 2012 TD indicated that the Treasury Department and the IRS intended to issue proposed regulations that would provide such a definition.

These proposed regulations define "control" for this purpose consistently with § 1.509(a)-4(j), which relates to control by disqualified persons for purposes of the disqualified person control test. In general, under the proposed regulations, the governing body of a supported organization is considered "controlled" by a person if that person, alone or by aggregating his or her votes or positions of authority with certain related persons, as described in section 509(f)(2)(B)(ii) and (iii), may require the governing body of the supported organization to perform any act that significantly affects its operations or may prevent the governing body of the supported organization from performing any such act.

2. *Type III Supporting Organization Relationship Test*

Section 1.509(a)-4(i)(1) provides that for each taxable year, a Type III supporting organization must satisfy (i) a notification requirement, (ii) a responsiveness test, and (iii) an integral part test provided in the regulations. These proposed regulations provide additional rules regarding each of these requirements.

A. *Notification Requirement*

Section 509(f)(1)(A) provides that an organization shall not be considered a Type III supporting organization unless the organization provides to each supported organization, for each taxable year, such information as the Secretary may require to ensure that the organization is responsive to the needs or demands of the supported organizations.

To satisfy this notification requirement, § 1.509(a)-4(i)(2) requires a Type III supporting organization to provide to each of its supported organizations for each taxable year: (1) A written notice addressed to a principal officer of the supported organization describing the type and amount of all of the support it provided to the supported organization during the supporting organization's preceding taxable year; (2) a copy of the supporting organization's most recently filed Form 990, "Return of Organization Exempt from Income Tax," or other annual information return required to be filed under section 6033; and (3) a copy of the supporting organization's governing documents, including any amendments (unless previously provided and not subsequently amended). For NFI Type III supporting organizations, the description of support in the written notice includes all of the distributions described in § 1.509(a)-4(i)(6) to the supported organization.

The proposed regulations amend § 1.509(a)-4(i)(2) to clarify that a supporting organization must deliver the required documents to each of its supported organizations by the last day of the fifth month of the taxable year after the taxable year in which the supporting organization provided the support it is reporting. This proposed change is intended to reduce confusion, but does not substantively change the due date or the content of the required notification. Date of delivery is determined applying the general principles of section 7502. B.

B. *Responsiveness Test*

Section 1.509(a)-4(i)(3)(i) provides that a supporting organization meets the responsiveness test if it is "responsive to the needs or demands of a supported organization." To meet this responsiveness test, an organization must satisfy: (1) A relationship test described in § 1.509(a)-4(i)(3)(ii) under which the officers, directors, or trustees of the organization have a specified relationship with the officers, directors, or trustees (and in some cases the members) of the supported organization; and (2) a significant voice test described in § 1.509(a)-4(i)(3)(iii) under which the officers, directors, or trustees of the supported organization, by reason of this relationship, have a significant voice in the investment policies of the supporting organization, the timing of grants, the manner of making grants, and the selection of grant recipients by the supporting organization, and in otherwise directing the use of the income or assets of the supporting organization. The preamble to the 2012 TD stated that, in determining the appropriate distribution amount for NFI Type III supporting organizations, the Treasury Department and the IRS considered the required relationship between a supporting organization and its supported organizations, and that the Treasury Department and the IRS intended to issue proposed regulations in the future that would amend the responsiveness test by requiring a Type III supporting organization to be responsive to all of its supported organizations.

In response to this proposal in the preamble to the 2012 TD, one commenter stated that a supporting organization should not be required to be responsive to all of its supported organizations because the resulting administrative burden would effectively limit the total number of organizations a supporting organization could support. The commenter suggested alternatives under which a supporting organization would be responsive to only a subset of its supported organizations that would vary from year to year.

The Treasury Department and the IRS note that the distinguishing characteristic of Type III supporting organizations, and the basis for their public charity classification, is that they are responsive to and significantly involved in the operations of their publicly supported organizations. *See* § 1.509(a)-4(f)(4). The Treasury Department and the IRS believe that, unless a Type III supporting organization is responsive to each of its supported organizations, the supported organizations cannot exercise the requisite level of oversight of and engagement with the supporting organization. Limiting the responsiveness requirement to fewer than all of the supported organizations may result in the necessary oversight and accountability being present for less than all of a supporting organization's operations. Therefore, the proposed regulations revise § 1.509(a)-4(i)(3)(i) to require a supporting organization to be responsive to the needs and demands of each of its supported organizations in order to meet the responsiveness test.

To illustrate how concerns about potential administrative burdens may be addressed consistent with the responsiveness test, the proposed regulations include a new example. The proposed example is intended to demonstrate one way in which a Type III supporting organization that supports multiple organizations may satisfy the responsiveness test in a manner that can be cost-effective. The example shows that a supporting organization can, with respect to each of its supported organizations, meet a different subset of the required relationships with the supporting organization's officers, directors, or trustees listed in § 1.509(a)-4(i)(3)(ii). It also shows how a supporting organization can organize and hold regular meetings, provide information, and encourage communication to help ensure that the supported organizations have a significant voice in the operations of the supporting organization.

Another commenter requested additional guidance regarding the ability of trusts to satisfy the significant voice requirement of the responsiveness test. The new Example 3 provides further illustration of how Type III supporting organizations, including charitable trusts, might satisfy the significant voice requirement of the responsiveness test. The Treasury Department and the IRS note that although the examples in the regulations relating to the responsiveness test may involve a Type III supporting organization that is organized as either a corporation or a trust, the applicable law and relevant regulatory provisions, as modified by the proposed regulations, are applicable to all Type III supporting organizations in the same manner, whether organized as a corporation or a trust. The Treasury Department and the IRS anticipate that Type III supporting organizations may be able to demonstrate they satisfy the responsiveness test in a variety of ways, and that the determination will be based on all the facts and circumstances.

As a result of the proposed changes to the responsiveness test, the proposed regulations also include conforming changes to examples and other regulatory provisions.

C. *Integral Part Test - Functionally Integrated Type III Supporting Organizations*

Section 1.509(a)-4(i)(1) provides that, for each taxable year, a Type III supporting organization must satisfy the integral part test. The integral part test is satisfied under § 1.509(a)-4(i)(1)(iii) by maintaining significant involvement in the operations of one or more supported organizations and providing support on which the supported organizations are dependent. To satisfy this test, a Type III supporting organization must meet the requirements either for a functionally integrated Type III supporting organization or for an NFI Type III supporting organization, as set forth in § 1.509(a)-4(i)(4) or (5), respectively.

A Type III organization is functionally integrated under § 1.509(a)-4(i)(4) if (1) it engages in activities substantially all of which directly further the exempt purposes of one or more supported organizations and otherwise meets the requirements described in paragraph (i)(4)(ii) of that section, (2) it is the parent of each of its supported organizations as described in paragraph (i)(4)(iii) of that section, or (3) it supports a governmental supported organization and otherwise meets the requirements of paragraph (i)(4)(iv) of that section. The direct furtherance test is not addressed by these regulations.

i. Parent of Each Supported Organization

Under the current regulations, a supporting organization is the parent of a supported organization if the supporting organization exercises a substantial degree of direction over the policies, programs, and activities of the supported organization and a majority of the officers, directors, or trustees of the supported organization is appointed or elected, directly or indirectly, by the governing body, members of the governing body, or officers (acting in their official capacities) of the supporting organization. *See* § 1.509(a)-4(i)(4)(iii). This definition was adopted by the 2012 TD; however, the preamble to the 2012 TD stated that the Treasury Department and the IRS had determined that the definition of parent was insufficiently specific. It further stated that the Treasury Department and the IRS intended to issue proposed regulations that would provide a new definition of parent.

As noted in the preamble to the 2009 NPRM, the classification of a parent organization as functionally integrated was intended to "apply to supporting organizations that oversee or facilitate the operation of an integrated system, such as hospital systems." To more fully accomplish this purpose, the proposed regulations amend § 1.509(a)-4(i)(4)(iii) to clarify that in order for a supporting organization to qualify as the parent of each of its supported organizations, the supporting organization and its supported organizations must be part of an integrated system (such as a hospital system), and the supporting organization must engage in activities typical of the parent of an integrated system. Examples of these activities include (but are not limited to) coordinating the activities of the supported organizations and engaging in overall planning, policy development, budgeting, and resource allocation for the supported organizations. The Treasury Department and the IRS request comments on what activities are typical of the parent of an integrated system, and whether additional activities should be explicitly listed as examples.

The proposed regulations retain the requirement that the governing body, members of the governing body, or officers of the supporting organization must appoint or elect a majority of the officers, directors, or trustees of the supported organization. The Treasury Department and the IRS intend, as stated in the 2009 NPRM, the use of the phrase "appointed or elected, directly or indirectly" to mean the supporting organization could qualify as a parent of a second-tier (or lower) subsidiary. Thus, for example, if the directors of supporting organization A appoint a majority of the directors of supported organization B, which in turn appoints a majority of the directors of supported organization C, the directors of supporting organization A will be treated as appointing the majority of the directors of both supported organization B and supported organization C.

The preamble to the 2012 TD stated that the Treasury Department and the IRS intended that the new definition of parent would specifically address the power to remove and replace officers, directors, or trustees of the supported organization. The Treasury Department and the IRS interpret the existing requirement under § 1.509(a)-4(i)(4)(iii) that the parent organization have the power to appoint or elect a majority of the officers, directors, or trustees of each supported organization to include the requirement that the parent organization also have the power to remove and replace such officers, directors, or trustees, or otherwise have an ongoing power to appoint or elect with reasonable frequency. The Treasury Department and the IRS request comments on whether § 1.509(a)-4(i)(4)(iii) should be amended to provide further clarification on this issue.

ii. Supporting a Governmental Supported Organization

The 2009 NPRM proposed an exception to the general rules for qualifying as a functionally integrated Type III supporting organization if the supporting organization supported only one governmental entity, which was defined as an entity the assets of which are subject to the appropriations process of a federal, state, local, or Indian tribal government. The 2009 NPRM also provided that in order to be considered functionally integrated, a substantial part of the supporting organization's total activities had to directly further the exempt purpose(s) of its supported organization, and that exempt purposes are not directly furthered by fundraising, grantmaking, or investing and managing non-exempt-use assets. The Treasury Department and IRS received multiple comments regarding this proposal. The 2012 TD stated the Treasury Department and the IRS were continuing to consider the public comments on the 2009 NPRM regarding this governmental entity exception and reserved § 1.509(a)-4(i)(4)(iv) for future guidance on how a Type III supporting organization can qualify as functionally integrated by supporting a governmental entity.

These proposed regulations take the prior comments into consideration and provide rules to qualify as functionally integrated both for new and existing Type III supporting organizations that support governmental supported organizations. These proposed rules also define the term "governmental supported organization."

One commenter stated that the definition of a governmental supported organization in the 2009 NPRM was too complicated and difficult to understand and administer. This commenter proposed using the existing definition of a governmental unit in section 170(b)(1)(A)(v) and (c)(1).

The Treasury Department and the IRS agree with the commenter that for simplicity and administrability the term "governmental supported organization" should be defined by using an existing Code definition of a governmental unit. The proposed regulations define a governmental supported organization as a governmental unit described in section 170(c)(1), or an organization described in section 170(c)(2) and (b)(1)(A) (other than in clauses (vii) and (viii)) that is an instrumentality of one or more governmental units described in section 170(c)(1). The Treasury Department and the IRS further note that a governmental unit described in section 170(c)(1) includes all of the agencies, departments, and divisions of the governmental unit, and all such agencies, departments, and divisions will be treated as one governmental supported organization for purposes of § 1.509(a)-4(i)(4)(iv). The Treasury Department and the IRS specifically request comments on the proposed definition of governmental supported organization.

Two commenters said that the 2009 NPRM's limit of only one governmental supported organization was too strict and instead recommended allowing a supporting organization to qualify for this exception if it supports at least one governmental supported organization, as Notice 2014-4 provides. One commenter noted that the 2009 NPRM's limit of only one governmental supported organization would adversely affect existing supporting organizations that support an additional supported organization that is not itself a governmental entity, but that has a substantial operational connection with the governmental supported organization. Another commenter said that the test in Notice 2014-4 was not sufficient because it did not cover activities, such as fundraising and grant making, that the governmental supported organization could not otherwise perform.

In response to these comments, the Treasury Department and the IRS propose a new test for Type III supporting organizations that support only governmental supported organizations to qualify as functionally integrated. The Treasury Department and the IRS agree it would be appropriate to treat a Type III supporting organization that supports two or more governmental supported organizations as functionally integrated, provided that the governmental supported organizations are themselves connected geographically or operationally, which will help ensure that the supported organizations provide sufficient input to and oversight of the supporting organization. Thus, the proposed regulations provide that a supporting organization that supports more than one governmental supported organization may be considered functionally integrated if all of its governmental supported organizations either: (1) Operate within the same geographic region (defined as a city, county, or metropolitan area); or (2) work in close coordination or collaboration with one another to conduct a service, program, or activity that the supporting organization supports. To satisfy the close cooperation or coordination requirement, the proposed regulations require a supporting organization to maintain on file a letter from each of the governmental supported organizations (or a joint letter from all of them) describing their collaborative or cooperative efforts with respect to the particular service, program, or activity. In addition, the proposed regulations incorporate the 2009 NPRM proposed requirement that a substantial part of the supporting organization's total activities must directly further the exempt purposes of its governmental supported organization(s). The Treasury Department and the IRS believe that using a substantial part requirement, instead of the substantially all requirement in §1.509(a)-4(i)(4)(iv)(A), is appropriate when supporting organizations support only governmental supported organizations operating in the same geographic region or working in close collaboration because the input from and oversight by the governmental supported organizations minimize the potential for abuse.

Two commenters stated that activities such as fundraising, grant-making, and managing non-exempt-use assets should be considered activities that directly further the exempt purposes of a governmental supported organization. The Treasury Department and the IRS note that the integral part test's definition of "directly further" in §1.509(a)-4(i)(4)(ii)(C) generally excludes fundraising, making grants, and investing and managing non-exempt-use assets. The Treasury Department and the IRS excluded these items because they determined that a Type III supporting organization should qualify as functionally integrated only if the supporting organization itself conducts activities that perform the functions of or carry out the purposes of the supported organization (as distinguished from providing financial support for the activities carried out by the supported organization). The Treasury Department and the IRS do not believe a different definition of "directly further" should apply to supporting organizations that support governmental supported organizations. Accordingly, the proposed regulations do not adopt this comment. However, under the proposed rules, these types of organizations would be considered functionally integrated if a substantial part, but not substantially all, of their total activities directly further the exempt purposes of their governmental supported organization(s). Accordingly, these proposed regulations allow these organizations to conduct more fundraising and other financial activities, if certain requirements are met, than is permitted under the substantially all test of §1.509(a)-4(i)(4)(ii).

In response to comments, the proposed regulations also provide a special rule for existing Type III supporting organizations, provided that they support no more than one additional supported organization that is not a governmental supported organization. A Type III supporting organization in existence on or before February 19, 2016 is treated as functionally integrated if: (1) It supports one or more governmental supported organizations and no more than one supported organization that is not a governmental supported organization; (2) it designated each of its supported organizations as provided in §1.509(a)-4(d)(4) on or before February 19, 2016; and (3) a substantial part of its total activities directly furthers the exempt purposes of its governmental supported organization(s).

The proposed regulations also further extend the transition relief provided in Notice 2014-4 and extended by the 2015 TD. Under the proposed regulations, a Type III supporting organization in existence on or before February 19, 2016 that continues to meet the requirements of Notice 2014-4 is treated as functionally integrated until the earlier of the first day of the organization's first taxable year beginning after the date final regulations under §1.509(a)-4(i)(4)(iv) are published or the first day of the organization's second taxable year beginning after February 19, 2016.

D. *Integral Part Test - Non-Functionally Integrated Type III Supporting Organizations*

Section 1.509(a)-4(i)(5) generally provides that an NFI Type III supporting organization meets the integral part test if it satisfies the distribution requirement of paragraph (i)(5)(ii) of that section and the attentiveness requirement of paragraph (i)(5)(iii) of that section. Section 1.509(a)-4(i)(5)(ii) provides that, with respect to each taxable year, a supporting organization must distribute to or for the use of one or more supported organizations an amount equaling or exceeding its "distributable amount". Section 1.509(a)-4(i)(6) provides the amount of a distribution made to a supported organization is the amount of cash or the fair market value of the property distributed.

For clarity and consistency, the proposed regulations revise §1.509(a)-4(i)(5)(ii) to state that a supporting organization must make distributions as described in §1.509(a)-4(i)(6) to satisfy the distribution requirement, and revise section 1.509(a)-4(i)(6) to describe in detail what distributions count towards the distribution requirement.

i. Reduction of Distributable Amount for Taxes Subtitle A Imposes

Section 1.509(a)-4(i)(5)(ii)(B) provides that the distributable amount is equal to the greater of 85 percent of an organization's adjusted net income for the immediately preceding taxable year (as determined by applying the principles of section 4942(f) and § 53.4942(a)-2(d)) or its minimum asset amount for the immediately preceding taxable year, reduced by the amount of taxes imposed on the supporting organization under subtitle A of the Code during the immediately preceding taxable year. *See* § 1.509(a)-4(i)(5)(ii)(B).

The Treasury Department and the IRS believe that, because the taxes under subtitle A of the Code are imposed on a supporting organization's unrelated business taxable income (pursuant to section 511) and the activity that produces the unrelated business taxable income does not further the supported organization's exempt purposes, these taxes should not be treated as an amount distributed to a supported organization. Therefore, the proposed regulations remove the provision in § 1.509(a)-4(i)(5)(ii)(B) that reduces the distributable amount by the amount of taxes subtitle A of the Code imposed on a supporting organization during the immediately preceding taxable year.

ii. Distributions that Count toward Distribution Requirement

As noted above, § 1.509(a)-4(i)(6) provides details on the distributions by a supporting organization that count toward satisfying the distribution requirement imposed in § 1.509(a)-4(i)(5)(ii). The current regulations provide that distributions include but are not limited to: (1) Any amount paid to a supported organization to accomplish the supported organization's exempt purposes; (2) any amount paid by the supporting organization to perform an activity that directly furthers the exempt purposes of the supported organization within the meaning of § 1.509(a)-4(i)(4)(ii), but only to the extent such amount exceeds any income derived by the supporting organization from the activity; (3) any reasonable and necessary administrative expenses paid to accomplish the exempt purposes of the supported organization(s), which do not include expenses incurred in the production of investment income; (4) any amount paid to acquire an exempt-use asset described in § 1.509(a)-4(i)(8)(ii); and (5) any amount set aside for a specific project that accomplishes the exempt purposes of a supported organization to which the supporting organization is responsive.

The preamble to the 2012 TD stated that the list in § 1.509(a)-4(i)(6) is not exhaustive and other distributions may count toward the distribution requirement. The preamble further stated the Treasury Department and the IRS intended to propose regulations that more fully describe the expenditures (including expenditures for administrative and additional charitable activities) that do and do not count toward the distribution requirement.

The Treasury Department and the IRS believe that the non-exclusive list in the current regulations creates uncertainty for supporting organizations and the IRS about what counts toward the distribution requirement. Therefore, the proposed regulations revise and clarify the list in § 1.509(a)-4(i)(6) of what counts toward the distribution requirement and make it an exclusive list.

The 2012 TD clarified that reasonable and necessary administrative expenses paid to accomplish the exempt purposes of supported organizations, and not expenses incurred in the production of investment income, count toward the distribution requirement. For example, if a supporting organization conducts exempt activities that are for the benefit of, perform the functions of, or carry out the purposes of its supported organization(s) and also conducts nonexempt activities (such as investment activities or unrelated business activities), then the supporting organization's administrative expenses (such as salaries, rent, utilities and other overhead expenses) must be allocated between the exempt and nonexempt activities on a reasonable and consistently-applied basis. The administrative expenses attributable to the exempt activities are treated as distributions to its supported organization(s) if such expenses are reasonable and necessary. The administrative expenses and operating costs attributable to the nonexempt activities are not treated as distributions to the supported organization(s). The proposed regulations retain this provision, but also provide additional guidance on fundraising expenses.

The 2012 TD did not specifically address whether fundraising expenses count toward the distribution requirement. The proposed regulations specify that reasonable and necessary administrative expenses paid to accomplish the exempt purposes of a supported organization generally do not include fundraising expenses the supporting organization incurs. However, under the proposed regulations, reasonable and necessary expenses incurred by the supporting organization to solicit contributions that a supported organization receives directly from donors count toward the distribution requirement, but only to the extent that the amount of such expenses does not exceed the amount of contributions actually received by the supported organization as a result of the solicitation activities of the supporting organization. The Treasury Department and the IRS believe this rule would provide greater consistency with the treatment of contributions that supporting organizations receive directly and then distribute to their supported organizations (net of the supporting organizations' solicitation expenses). To ensure that a supporting organization has the information it needs to calculate the allowable expenses, the proposed regulations require the supporting organization to obtain written substantiation from the supported organization of the amount of contributions the supported organization actually received as a result of the supporting organization's solicitations.

One commenter requested that program related investments (PRIs) count toward the distribution requirement. The preamble to the 2012 TD stated the 2012 final and temporary regulations did not specifically address whether or not PRIs may count toward the distribution requirement or are excluded in calculating a supporting organization's distributable amount for a taxable year. The

Treasury Department and the IRS recognize that private foundations may use PRIs in a variety of ways to accomplish their exempt purposes and that PRIs thus are treated as qualifying distributions under section 4942. However, because supporting organizations must be operated exclusively for the benefit of, to perform the functions of, or to carry out the purposes of their supported organizations, they differ from private foundations. For purposes of meeting the integral part test, the Treasury Department and the IRS do not believe that PRIs should be treated as distributions to supported organizations. The Treasury Department and the IRS believe that other provisions relating to the distribution requirement, such as the availability of set asides and the potential for carry-forwards of excess distributions, provide significant flexibility for supporting organizations to meet the current and future needs of their supported organizations. For these reasons, the proposed regulations do not adopt this comment.

Effective Date and Reliance

These regulations are proposed to be effective on the date the Treasury decision adopting these rules as final or temporary regulations is published in the **Federal Register**. However, taxpayers may rely on the provisions of the proposed regulations until final or temporary regulations are issued.

Statement of Availability of IRS Documents

The IRS Notice 2014-4 cited in this preamble is published in the Internal Revenue Bulletin and is available from the Superintendent of Documents, U.S. Government Printing Office, Washington, DC 20402, or by visiting the IRS Web site at http://www.irs.gov.

Special Analyses

Certain IRS regulations, including this one, are exempt from the requirements of Executive Order 12866, as supplemented and reaffirmed by Executive Order 13563. Therefore, a regulatory impact assessment is not required. It has also been determined that section 553(b) of the Administrative Procedure Act (5 U.S.C. chapter 5) does not apply to these regulations.

In connection with the requirements of the Regulatory Flexibility Act (5 U.S.C. chapter 6), it is hereby certified that the collection of information contained in the proposed regulations will not have a significant economic impact on a substantial number of small entities. This certification is based on the fact that the proposed regulations will not impact a substantial number of small entities.

Based on IRS Statistics of Income data for 2013, there are 1,052,495 active nonprofit charitable organizations recognized by the IRS under section 501(c)(3), of which only 7,872 organizations self-identified as Type III supporting organizations. The universe of organizations that would be affected by the collection of information under proposed § 1.509(a)-4(i)(4)(iii) and § 1.509(a)-4(i)(6)(iii) is a subset of all Type III supporting organizations. Thus, the number of organizations that would be affected by the collection of information under proposed § 1.509(a)-4(i)(4)(iii) and (i)(6)(iii), which is expected to be significantly less than 7,872, would not be substantial. Moreover, the time to complete the recordkeeping requirements is expected to be no more than 2 hours for each organization, which would not have a significant economic impact. Therefore, the collection of information under proposed § 1.509(a)-4(i)(4)(iii) and (i)(6)(iii) would not have a significant economic impact.

Pursuant to section 7805(f) of the Code, this regulation has been submitted to the Chief Counsel for Advocacy of the Small Business Administration for comment on its impact on small business.

Comments and Requests for a Public Hearing

Before these proposed regulations are adopted as final regulations, consideration will be given to any electronic comments or written comments (a signed original and eight (8) copies) that are submitted timely to the IRS. The Treasury Department and the IRS request comments on all aspects of the proposed rules. All comments that are submitted by the public will be available for public inspection and copying at www.regulations.gov or upon request. A public hearing may be scheduled if requested in writing by any person that timely submits written comments. If a public hearing is scheduled, notice of the date, time, and place for the public hearing will be published in the **Federal Register**.

Drafting Information

The principal authors of these regulations are Jonathan Carter and Mike Repass, Office of Associate Chief Counsel (Tax-Exempt and Government Entities). However, other personnel from the Treasury Department and the IRS participated in their development.

[¶ 49,687] Proposed Amendments of Regulations (REG-150349-12), published in the Federal Register on February 25, 2016.

[Code Sec. 42]

Low-income housing credit: Physical inspection: Certification review.—Amendments of Reg. § 1.42-5, concerning the compliance-monitoring duties of a State or local housing credit agency for purposes of the low-income housing credit, are proposed.

AGENCY: Internal Revenue Service (IRS), Treasury.

ACTION: Notice of proposed rulemaking by cross-reference to temporary regulations.

SUMMARY: In the Rules and Regulations section of this issue of the **Federal Register**, the IRS is issuing final and temporary regulations concerning the compliance-monitoring duties of a State or local housing credit agency (Agency) for purposes of the low-income housing credit. The final and temporary regulations revise and clarify certain rules relating to the requirements to conduct physical inspections and review low-income certifications and other documentation. The text of the temporary regulations also serves as the text of these proposed regulations.

DATES: Comments and requests for a public hearing must be received by May 25, 2016. ADDRESSES: Send submissions to: CC:PA:LPD:PR (REG-150349-12), room 5203, Internal Revenue Service, P.O. Box 7604, Ben Franklin Station, Washington, DC 20044. Submissions may be hand delivered Monday through Friday between the hours of 8 a.m. and 4 p.m. to: CC:PA:LPD:PR (REG-150349-12), Courier's Desk, Internal Revenue Service, 1111 Constitution Avenue, NW., Washington, DC. Submissions may also be sent electronically via the Federal eRulemaking Portal at www.regulations.gov (IRS REG-150349-12).

FOR FURTHER INFORMATION CONTACT: Concerning the regulations, Jian H. Grant, (202) 317-4137, and Martha M. Garcia, (202) 317-6853 (not toll-free numbers); concerning submission of comments, the hearing, and/or to be placed on the building access list to attend the hearing, Oluwafunmilayo Taylor at (202) 317-6901 (not a toll-free number).

SUPPLEMENTARY INFORMATION:

Background

Final and temporary regulations in the Rules and Regulations section of this issue of the **Federal Register** amend the Income Tax Regulations (26 CFR Part 1) relating to section 42 and serve as the text for these proposed regulations.

Special Analyses

Certain IRS regulations, including this one, are exempt from the requirements of Executive Order 12866, as supplemented and reaffirmed by Executive Order 13563. Therefore, a regulatory assessment is not required. It also has been determined that section 553(b) of the Administrative Procedure Act (5 U.S.C. chapter 5) does not apply to these regulations, and because the regulations do not impose a collection of information on small entities, the Regulatory Flexibility Act (5 U.S.C. chapter 6) does not apply. Pursuant to section 7805(f) of the Internal Revenue Code, this notice of proposed rulemaking will be submitted to the Chief Counsel for Advocacy of the Small Business Administration for comment on their impact on small business.

Comments and Requests for Public Hearing

Before these proposed regulations are adopted as final regulations, consideration will be given to any comments that are submitted timely to the IRS as prescribed in this preamble under the "Addresses" heading. The Treasury Department and the IRS request comments on all aspects of the proposed rules. All comments will be available at www.regulations.gov or upon request. A public hearing will be scheduled if requested in writing by any person that timely submits written comments. If a public hearing is scheduled, notice of the date, time, and place for the public hearing will be published in the **Federal Register**.

Drafting Information

The principal authors of these regulations are Jian H. Grant and Martha M. Garcia, Office of the Associate Chief Counsel (Passthroughs and Special Industries). However, other personnel from the IRS and the Treasury Department participated in their development.

[¶49,689] Proposed Amendments of Regulations (REG-123867-14), published in the Federal Register on March 3, 2016.

[Code Sec. 42]

Low-income housing credit: Utility allowance: Submetering rules.—Amendment of Reg. §1.42-10, containing proposed regulations that amend the utility allowance regulations concerning the low-income housing credit, is proposed.

AGENCY: Internal Revenue Service (IRS), Treasury.

ACTION: Notice of proposed rulemaking by cross-reference to temporary regulations.

SUMMARY: This document contains proposed regulations that amend the utility allowance regulations concerning the low-income housing credit. The proposed regulations relate to the circumstances in which utility costs paid by a tenant based on actual consumption in a submetered rent-restricted unit are treated as paid by the tenant directly to the utility company. The proposed regulations extend those rules to situations in which a building owner sells to tenants energy that is produced from a renewable source and that is not delivered by a local utility company. The proposed regulations affect owners of low-income housing projects that claim the credit, the tenants in those low-income housing projects, and the State and local housing credit agencies that administer the credit. In the Rules and Regulations section of this issue of the **Federal Register**, the IRS is issuing temporary regulations concerning utility allowance regulations when the utility is generated from renewable sources and is not delivered by the local utility company. The text of those regulations also serves as the text of these proposed regulations. This document also contains a notice of a public hearing on these proposed regulations.

DATES: Comments and requests for a public hearing must be received by May 2, 2016.

ADRESSES: Send submissions to: CC:PA:LPD:PR (REG-123867-14), room 5203, Internal Revenue Service, P.O. Box 7604, Ben Franklin Station, Washington, DC 20044. Submissions may be hand-delivered Monday through Friday between the hours of 8 a.m. and 4 p.m. to CC:PA:LPD:PR (REG-123867-14), Courier's Desk, Internal Revenue Service, 1111 Constitution Avenue, NW., Washington, DC, or sent electronically, via the Federal eRulemaking Portal at http:// www.regulations.gov/ (IRS REG-123867-14).

FOR FURTHER INFORMATION CONTACT: Concerning the proposed regulations, James Rider at (202) 317-4137; concerning submissions of comments and requests for a public hearing, Oluwafunmilayo Taylor at (202) 317-6901 (not toll-free numbers).

SUPPLEMENTARY INFORMATION:

Background

Temporary regulations in the Rules and Regulations section of this issue of the **Federal Register** amend 26 CFR part 1. The temporary regulations provide a special rule for a renewable-source utility arrangement in which the building owner does not pay a local utility company for the utility consumed by the tenant. The text of those regulations also serves as the text of these regulations. The preamble to the temporary regulations explains the temporary regulations and these proposed regulations.

Special Analyses

Certain IRS regulations, including this one, are exempt from the requirements of Executive Order 12866, as supplemented and reaffirmed by Executive Order 13563. Therefore, a regulatory assessment is not required. It also has been determined that section 553(b) of the Administrative Procedure Act (5 U.S.C. chapter 5) does not apply to this regulation, and because the regulation does not impose a collection of information on small entities, the Regulatory Flexibility Act (5 U.S.C. chapter 6) does not apply. Pursuant to section 7805(f) of the Internal Revenue Code, this notice of proposed rulemaking has been submitted to the Chief Counsel for Advocacy of the Small Business Administration for comment on its impact on small business.

Comments and Requests for Public Hearing

Before these proposed regulations are adopted as final regulations, consideration will be given to any written comments (a signed original and eight (8) copies) or electronic comments that are submitted timely to the IRS as prescribed in this preamble under the "**ADDRESSES**" heading. The IRS and the Treasury Department request comments on all aspects of the proposed regulations. All comments that are submitted by the public will be available for public inspection and copying at www.regulations.gov or upon request. A public hearing will be scheduled if requested in writing by any person that timely submits comments. If a public hearing is scheduled, notice of the date, time, and place for the public hearing will be published in the **Federal Register**.

Drafting Information

The principal author of these regulations is David Selig, Office of the Associate Chief Counsel (Passthroughs and Special Industries), IRS. However, other personnel from the IRS and the Treasury Department participated in their development.

[¶49,690] Proposed Amendments of Regulations (REG-127923-15), published in the Federal Register on March 4, 2016.

[Code Secs. 1014, 6035, 6662, 6721 and 6722]

Estates: Estate tax: Property: Basis: Reporting.—Reg. §§1.1014-10, 1.6035-2 and 1.6662-8, and amendments of Reg. §§1.6035-1, 301.6721-1 and 301.6722-1, regarding the requirement that a recipient's basis in certain property acquired from a decedent be consistent with the value of the property as finally determined for Federal estate tax purposes, are proposed.

AGENCY: Internal Revenue Service (IRS), Treasury.

ACTION: Notice of proposed rulemaking, and notice of proposed rulemaking by cross-reference to temporary regulations.

SUMMARY: This document contains proposed regulations that provide guidance regarding the requirement that a recipient's basis in certain property acquired from a decedent be consistent with the value of the property as finally determined for Federal estate tax purposes. In addition, these proposed regulations provide guidance on the reporting requirements for executors or other persons required to file Federal estate tax returns. Temporary regulations in the Rules and Regulations section of this issue of the **Federal Register** provide transition relief to executors and other persons required to file or furnish certain statements. The text of those temporary regulations (TD 9757) published in the Rules and Regulations section of this issue of the **Federal Register** also serves as the text of the proposed regulations regarding the transition relief. These proposed regulations as well as TD 9757 published elsewhere in the Rules and Regulations section of this issue of this **Federal Register** affect executors or other persons who file estate tax returns after July 31, 2015. The proposed regulations also affect beneficiaries who acquire certain property from these estates, and subsequent transferees to whom beneficiaries transfer the property in transactions that do not result in the recognition of gain or loss for Federal income tax purposes.

DATES: Written or electronic comments and requests for a public hearing must be received by June 2, 2016.

ADDRESSES: Send submissions to: CC:PA:LPD:PR (REG-127923-15), Internal Revenue Service, Room 5203, PO Box 7604, Ben Franklin Station, Washington, DC 20044. Submissions may be hand delivered Monday through Friday between the hours of 8 a.m. and 4 p.m. to CC:PA:LPD:PR (REG-127923-15), Courier's Desk, Internal Revenue Service, 1111 Constitution Avenue NW, Washington, DC 20224; or sent electronically via the Federal eRulemaking Portal at *http://www.regulations.gov* (IRS-REG-127923-15).

FOR FURTHER INFORMATION CONTACT: Concerning the proposed regulations, Theresa M. Melchiorre, at (202) 317-6859; concerning submissions of comments or, to request a hearing, Regina Johnson, at (202) 317-6901 (not toll-free numbers). SUPPLEMENTARY INFORMATION:

Paperwork Reduction Act

The collection of information contained in this notice of proposed rulemaking has been submitted to the Office of Management and Budget for review in accordance with the Paperwork Reduction Act of 1995 (44 U.S.C. 3507(d). Comments on the collection of information should be sent to the Office of Management and Budget, Attn: Desk Officer for the Department of the Treasury, Office of Information and Regulatory Affairs, Washington, DC 20503, with copies to the Internal Revenue Service, Attn: IRS Reports Clearance Officer, SE:W:CAR:MP:T:T:SP, Washington, DC 20224. Comments on the collection of information should be received by May 3, 2016.

Comments are specifically requested concerning:

Whether the proposed collection of information is necessary for the proper performance of the functions of the Internal Revenue Service (IRS), including whether the information will have practical utility;

The accuracy of the estimated burden associated with the proposed collection of information;

How the quality, utility, and clarity of the information to be collected may be enhanced;

How the burden of complying with the proposed collection of information may be minimized, including through the application of automated collection techniques or other forms of information technology; and

Estimates of capital or start-up costs and costs of operation, maintenance, and purchase of service to provide information.

The reporting requirements in these proposed regulations are in § 1.6035-1(a) and (d) and require executors and other persons required to file a return under section 6018 to furnish a statement to the IRS and to each beneficiary providing information regarding the value of the property the beneficiary acquires from the decedent. The IRS will use this information to determine whether the beneficiary (or transferee) reports a basis for that property that is consistent with the value of that property as finally determined for Federal estate tax purposes when the beneficiary (or transferee) depreciates the property, or sells, exchanges, or otherwise disposes of some or all of that property in transactions that result in the recognition of gain or loss for Federal income tax purposes.

The collection of information may vary depending on the property includible in the gross estate and the number of beneficiaries receiving the property. The following estimates are based on the information that is available to the IRS. A respondent may require more or less time, depending on the circumstances.

Estimated total annual reporting burden. The estimated total annual reporting burden per respondent is 5.31 hours.

Estimated annual number of respondents. The estimated annual number of respondents is 10,000.

An agency may not conduct or sponsor, and a person is not required to respond to, a collection of information unless it displays a valid control number assigned by the Office of Management and Budget.

Books or records relating to a collection of information must be retained as long as their contents may become material in the administration of any internal revenue law. Generally, tax returns and tax return information are confidential, as required by 26 U.S.C. 6103.

Background

1. *Overview.*

On July 31, 2015, the President of the United States signed into law H.R. 3236, the *Surface Transportation and Veterans Health Care Choice Improvement Act of 2015*, Public Law 114-41, 129 Stat. 443 (Act). Section 2004 of the Act enacted sections 1014(f), 6035, 6662(b)(8), 6662(k), 6724(d)(1)(D), and 6724(d)(2)(II) of the Internal Revenue Code (Code). This document contains proposed regulations that amend 26 CFR parts 1 and 301 under those Code provisions to achieve consistency between a recipient's basis in certain property acquired from a decedent and the value of the property as finally determined for Federal estate tax purposes. This notice of proposed rulemaking also cross-references to temporary regulations (TD 9757) published in the Rules and Regulations section of this issue of the **Federal Register**, which provide transition relief to certain persons required to file or furnish statements under section 6035. This document also proposes to remove from 26 CFR part 1 regulations under former section 6035 as a result of the repeal of that Code provision in 2004.

2. *Summary of new statutory framework.*

A. *Section 1014(f).*

Section 1014(f) imposes an obligation of consistency between the basis of certain inherited property and the value of that property for Federal estate tax purposes. Section 1014(f)(1) provides that the basis of property acquired from a decedent cannot exceed that property's final value for purposes of the Federal estate tax imposed on the estate of the decedent, or, if the final value has not been determined, the value reported on a statement required by section 6035(a).

Section 1014(f)(2) provides that section 1014(f)(1) only applies to property the inclusion of which in the decedent's gross estate increased the estate's liability for the Federal estate tax (reduced by credits allowable against the tax).

Section 1014(f)(3) provides that, for purposes of section 1014(f)(1), the basis of property has been determined for Federal estate tax purposes if (A) the value of the property is shown on a return under section 6018 and that value is not contested by the Secretary before the expiration of the time for assessing the estate tax; (B) in a case not described in (A), the value is specified by the Secretary and that value is not timely contested by the executor of the estate; or (C) the value is determined by a court or pursuant to a settlement agreement with the Secretary.

B. *Section 6035.*

Section 6035 requires the reporting, both to the IRS and the beneficiary, of the value of property included on a required Federal estate tax return.

Section 6035(a)(1) provides that the executor of any estate required to file a return under section 6018(a) must furnish, both to the Secretary and to the person acquiring any interest in property included in the estate, a statement identifying the value of each interest in the property as reported on the return and any other information as the Secretary may prescribe.

Section 6035(a)(2) provides that each person required to file a return under section 6018(b) must furnish to the Secretary and to each other person who holds a legal or beneficial interest in the property to which the return relates a statement identifying the information described in section 6035(a)(1).

Section 6035(a)(3)(A) provides that this statement is due no later than the earlier of (i) 30 days after the due date of the return under section 6018 (including extensions, if any) or (ii) 30 days after the date the return is filed. If there is an adjustment to the information required to be included on this statement, section 6035(a)(3)(B) requires the executor (or other person required to file the statement) to provide a supplemental statement to the Secretary and to each affected beneficiary no later than 30 days after the adjustment is made.

Section 6035(b) authorizes the Secretary to prescribe regulations to carry out section 6035, including regulations relating to (1) the application of this section to property to which no Federal estate tax return is required to be filed, and (2) situations in which the surviving joint tenant or other recipient may have better information than the executor regarding the basis or fair market value of the property.

C. *Penalties under sections 6662, 6721, and 6722.*

Section 2004(c) of the Act added a new accuracy-related penalty for underpayments attributable to an inconsistent estate basis. See section 6662(b)(8). Section 6662(k) provides that there is an inconsistent estate basis if the basis of property claimed on a return exceeds the basis as determined under section 1014(f).

Section 2004(c) of the Act adds statements under section 6035 to the list of information returns and payee statements subject to the penalties under section 6721 and section 6722, respectively. Specifically, the Act adds new paragraph (D) to section 6724(d)(1) to provide that the term *information return* means any statement required to be filed with the Secretary under section 6035. The Act also adds new paragraph (II) to section 6724(d)(2) to provide that the term *payee statement* means any statement required to be furnished under section 6035 (other than a statement described in section 6724(d)(1)(D)).

3. *Notice 2015-57.*

On August 21, 2015, the Treasury Department and the IRS issued Notice 2015-57, 2015-36 IRB 294. That notice delayed until February 29, 2016, the due date for any statements required under section 6035(a)(3)(A) to be provided before February 29, 2016. The notice also stated that the Treasury Department and the IRS expect to issue additional guidance to assist taxpayers in complying with sections 1014(f) and 6035 and invited comments. The Treasury Department and the IRS received numerous comments in response to the notice and considered all comments in the drafting of the proposed regulations. The comments are discussed in more detail in this preamble.

4. *Notice 2016-19.*

On February 11, 2016, the Treasury Department and the IRS issued Notice 2016-19, 2016-09 IRB 362. That notice provides that executors or other persons required to file or furnish a statement under section 6035(a)(1) or (a)(2) before March 31, 2016, need not do so until March 31, 2016.

Summary of Comments on Notice 2015-57 and Explanation of Provisions

1. *Section 1014(f)(1) – Consistency of basis with estate tax return.*

The general rule of section 1014 is that the basis of property received from a decedent (or as a result of a decedent's death) is that property's fair market value on the decedent's date of death (or the alternate valuation date, if elected). Newly enacted section 1014(f)(1) provides that the basis of certain property acquired from a decedent cannot exceed that property's final value as determined for Federal estate tax purposes. If no final value has been determined when the taxpayer's basis in the property becomes relevant for Federal tax purposes, for example, to calculate depreciation or amortization, or to calculate gain or loss on the sale, exchange or disposition of the property, the taxpayer uses the value reported on the statement required by section 6035(a) (the fair market value reported on the Federal estate tax return) to determine the taxpayer's basis for Federal tax purposes.

Proposed § 1.1014-10(a)(1) provides that a taxpayer's initial basis in certain property acquired from a decedent may not exceed the *final value* of the property as that term is defined in § 1.1014-10(c). This limitation applies to the property whenever the taxpayer reports to the IRS a taxable event with respect to the property (for example, depreciation or amortization) and continues to apply until the property is sold, exchanged, or otherwise disposed of in one or more transactions that result in the recognition of gain or loss for Federal income tax purposes. The property for this purpose includes any other property the basis of which is determined in whole or in part by reference to the basis of the property acquired from the estate or as a result of the death of the decedent (for example as the result of a like-kind exchange or involuntary conversion).

2. *Effect of other provisions of the Code that govern basis.*

Section 6662(b)(8) imposes an accuracy-related penalty on the portion of any underpayment of tax required to be shown on a return that is attributable to an *inconsistent estate basis.* Under newly enacted section 6662(k), an inconsistent estate basis arises if the basis of property claimed on a return exceeds its final value as determined under section 1014(f).

Commenters have expressed concern that section 1014(f) and section 6662(k) appear to prohibit otherwise permissible adjustments to the basis of property as a result of post-death events. In response, proposed §§ 1.1014-10(a)(2) and 1.6662-8(b) clarify that sections 1014(f) and 6662(k) do not prohibit adjustments to the basis of property as a result of post-death events that are allowed under other sections of the Code, and provide that such basis adjustments will not cause a taxpayer to violate the provisions of section 1014(f) or section 6662(k) on the date of sale, exchange, or disposition. The proposed regulations interpret sections 1014(f) and 6662(k) to require only that the beneficiary's initial basis of the inherited property cannot exceed the final value of the property for Federal estate tax purposes. Adjustments to the basis of the inherited property permitted by other sections of the Code as a result of post-death events (for example, depreciation or amortization, or a sale, exchange, or disposition of the property) will not cause the taxpayer's basis in the property on the date of a taxable event with respect to the property to be treated as exceeding the final value of the property. As a result, there cannot be an underpayment attributable to an inconsistent estate basis arising from these basis adjustments, and the accuracy-related penalty under section 6662(b)(8) cannot apply solely as a result of these basis adjustments.

3. *Section 1014(f)(2) – Property that increases estate tax liability.*

The consistent basis requirement of section 1014(f)(1) applies only to property the inclusion of which in the decedent's gross estate for Federal estate tax purposes increases the Federal estate tax liability payable by the decedent's estate. Proposed § 1.1014-10(b) defines this property as property includible in the gross estate under section 2031, as well as property subject to tax under section 2106, that generates a Federal estate tax liability in excess of allowable credits. The proposed regulations specifically exclude all property reported on a Federal estate tax return required to be filed by section 6018 if no Federal estate tax is imposed upon the estate due to allowable credits (other than a credit for a prepayment of that tax). In cases where Federal estate tax is imposed on the estate, the proposed regulations exclude property that qualifies for a charitable or marital deduction under section 2055, 2056, or 2056A because this property does not increase the Federal estate tax liability. In addition, the proposed regulations exclude any tangible personal property for which an appraisal is not required under § 20.2031-6(b) (relating to the valuation of certain household and personal effects) because of its value. Thus, if any Federal estate tax liability is incurred, all of the property in the gross estate (other than that described in the preceding two sentences) is deemed to increase the Federal estate tax liability and is subject to the consistency requirement of section 1014(f).

4. *Section 1014(f)(3) – Final value of property acquired from a decedent.*

Section 1014(f)(3) provides that, for purposes of section 1014(f)(1), the *final value* of property has been determined for Federal estate tax purposes if: (A) the value is reported on a Federal estate tax return filed with the IRS and is not contested by the IRS before the period of limitation on assessment expires; (B) the value is specified by the IRS and is not timely contested by the executor of the estate; or (C) the value is determined by a court or pursuant to a settlement agreement with the IRS.

Proposed § 1.1014-10(c)(1) defines the *final value* of property that is reported on a Federal estate tax return filed with the IRS. That value is the value reported on the Federal estate tax return once the period of limitations on assessment for adjusting or contesting that value has expired. The IRS may specify a value for the property by determining a value in the course of carrying out its responsibilities under section 7803(a)(2). If the IRS determines a value different from the value reported, the final value is the value determined by the IRS once that value can no longer be contested by the estate. If the value determined or specified by the IRS is timely contested by the estate, the final value is the value determined in an agreement that is binding on all parties, or the value determined by a court once the court's determination is final.

Proposed § 1.1014-10(c)(2) provides that the recipient of property to which the consistency requirement applies may not claim a basis in excess of the value reported on the statement required to be furnished under section 6035(a) (the value shown on the Federal estate tax return) if the taxpayer's basis in the property is relevant for any purpose under the Internal Revenue Code before the final value of that property has been determined under proposed § 1.1014-10(c)(1). However, under section 1014(f)(1), basis cannot exceed the property's final value. Therefore, proposed § 1.1014-10(c)(2) provides that, if the final value is determined before the period of limitation on assessment expires for any Federal income tax return of the recipient on which the taxpayer's basis is relevant and the final value differs from the initial basis claimed with respect to that return, a deficiency and an underpayment may result.

5. *After-discovered or omitted property.*

Commenters requested that the regulations clarify how the consistent basis requirement applies to property that is discovered after the filing of the Federal estate tax return or is otherwise omitted from that return. If this property would have generated a Federal estate tax liability if it had been reported on the Federal estate tax return that was filed with IRS, proposed § 1.1014-10(c)(3)(i) provides two different results based upon whether the period of limitation on assessment has expired for the Federal estate tax imposed on the estate. Proposed § 1.1014-10(c)(3)(i)(A) provides that, if the executor reports the after-discovered or omitted property on an estate tax return filed before the expiration of the period of limitation on assessment of the estate tax, the final value of the property is determined under proposed § 1.1014-10(c)(1) or (2). Alternatively, proposed § 1.1014-10(c)(3)(i)(B) provides that, if the after-discovered or omitted property is not reported before the period of limitation on assessment expires, the final value of the after-discovered or omitted property is zero.

Finally, to address situations in which no Federal estate tax return was filed, proposed § 1.1014-10(c)(3)(ii) provides that the final value of all property includible in the gross estate subject to the consistent basis requirement is zero until the final value is determined under proposed § 1.1014-10(c)(1) or (2).

6. *Definition of executor for purposes of sections 1014(f) and 6035.*

The proposed regulations adopt the definition of the term *executor* found in section 2203 applicable for Federal estate tax purposes and expand it to include a person required to file a return under section 6018(b).

7. *Requirement to provide Information Return and Statement(s) under section 6035.*

The proposed regulations define the term *Information Return* as the Form 8971, Information Regarding Beneficiaries Acquiring Property from a Decedent, which includes a copy of a Schedule A (Statement) for each person who has received or will receive property from the estate or by reason of the decedent's death.

Proposed § 1.6035-1(a)(1) provides that an executor who is required to file a Federal estate tax return also is required to file an Information Return with the IRS to report the final value of certain property, the recipient of that property, and other information prescribed by the Information Return and the related instructions. The executor also is required to furnish a Statement to each beneficiary who has acquired (or will acquire) property from the decedent or by reason of the death of the decedent to report the property the beneficiary has acquired (or will acquire) and the final value of that property.

8. *Circumstances under which no Information Return or Statement(s) is required under section 6035.*

Commenters expressed concern that the section 6035 filing requirements might extend to a return filed by an estate solely to make the portability election under section 2010(c)(5), or a generation-skipping transfer tax election or exemption allocation. The proposed regulations provide that the filing requirements of section 6035 do not apply to such returns because these returns are not required by section 6018.

9. *Property to be reported on an Information Return and Statement(s).*

Commenters requested that the regulations clarify the types of property to be reported on the Information Return and one or more Statements. In response, proposed § 1.6035-1(b) defines the property to be reported on an Information Return and Statement(s) as all property included in the gross estate for Federal estate tax purposes with four exceptions: cash (other than coins or paper bills with numismatic value); income in respect of a decedent; those items of tangible personal property for which an appraisal is not required under § 20.2031-6(b); and property that is sold or otherwise disposed of by the estate (and therefore not distributed to a beneficiary) in a transaction in which capital gain or loss is recognized.

10. *Beneficiaries.*

Proposed § 1.6035-1(c)(1) provides that each beneficiary (including a beneficiary who is also the executor of the estate) who receives property to be reported on the estate's Information Return must receive a copy of the Statement reporting the property distributable to that beneficiary. Proposed § 1.6035-1(c)(2) provides that, if the beneficiary is a trust, estate, or business entity instead of an individual, the executor is to furnish the entity's Statement to the trustee, executor, or to the business entity itself, and not to the beneficiaries of the trust or estate or to the owners of the business entity.

Commenters requested guidance on how to comply with the section 6035 reporting requirements when the executor cannot determine the exact distribution of the estate's property and thus the beneficiary of each property by the due date of the Information Return and the related Statements. This situation can arise, for example, when tangible personal property defined in § 20.2031-6 is to be distributed among a group of beneficiaries as that group determines, the residuary estate is distributable to multiple beneficiaries, or when multiple residuary trusts are to be funded. In response, proposed § 1.6035-1(c)(3) provides that, if by the due date the executor does not yet know what property will be used to satisfy the interest of each beneficiary, the executor is required to report on the Statement for each beneficiary all of the property that could be used to satisfy that beneficiary's interest. This results in the duplicate reporting of those assets on multiple Statements, but each beneficiary will have been advised of the final value of each property that may be received by that beneficiary and therefore will be able to comply with the basis consistency requirement, if applicable.

Proposed § 1.6035-1(c)(4) provides that, if the executor is unable to locate a beneficiary by the due date of the Information Return, the executor is required to report that on that Information Return and explain the efforts taken to locate the beneficiary. If the executor subsequently locates the beneficiary, the executor is required to furnish the beneficiary with a Statement and file a supplemental Information Return with the IRS within 30 days of locating the beneficiary. If the executor is unable to locate a beneficiary and distributes the property to a different beneficiary who was not identified in the Information Return as the recipient of that property, the executor is required to file a supplemental Information Return with the IRS and furnish the successor beneficiary with a Statement within 30 days after distributing the property.

11. *Due date for Information Return and Statements.*

Proposed § 1.6035-1(d)(1) provides that the executor is required to file the Information Return with the IRS, and is required to furnish each beneficiary with that beneficiary's Statement, on or before the earlier of the date that is 30 days after the due date of the Federal estate tax return (including extensions actually granted, if any), or the date that is 30 days after the date on which that return is filed with the IRS. In response to comments, proposed § 1.6035-1(d)(2) provides a transition rule for any Federal estate tax return that was due on or before July 31, 2015, but that is filed after July 31, 2015. In this case, the due date of the Information Return and all Statements is 30 days after the date on which the return is filed. Otherwise, as commenters noted, the due date for the Information Return and Statement(s) may be prior to the effective date of section 6035.

12. *Supplemental Information Return and Statement(s).*

Proposed § 1.6035-1(e)(1) and (2) generally requires a supplemental Information Return and corresponding supplemental Statement(s) upon a change to the information required to be reported on the Information Return or a Statement that causes the information as reported to be incorrect or incomplete. Such changes include, for example, the discovery of property that should have been, but was not, reported on the Federal estate tax return, a change in the value of property pursuant to an examination or litigation, or (except as provided by proposed § 1.6035-1(e)(3)(B)) a change in the identity of the beneficiary to whom the property is to be distributed (for example, pursuant to a death, disclaimer, bankruptcy, or otherwise). Proposed § 1.6035-1(e)(3) provides that a supplemental Information Return and Statement(s) may be filed, but they are not required, to correct an inconsequential error or omission within the meaning of § 301.6722-1(b) or to specify the actual distribution of assets previously reported as being available to satisfy the interests of multiple beneficiaries in the situation described in proposed § 1.6035-1(c)(3).

Proposed § 1.6035-1(e)(4) provides that the due date for the supplemental Information Return and each supplemental Statement is 30 days after: (i) the final value (within the meaning of proposed § 1.1014-10(c)(1)) of property is determined; (ii) the executor discovers that the information reported on the Information Return or Statement is otherwise incorrect or incomplete; or (iii) a supplemental Federal estate tax return is filed. However, at the suggestion of a commenter, if these events occur prior to the distribution to the beneficiary of probate property or of the property of a revocable trust, a supplemental Information Return or Statement is not due until 30 days after the property is distributed. This is likely to be approximately the same time when the executor would provide the beneficiary with information as to changes, if any, to the basis of the property that have occurred since the decedent's death and prior to the distribution. Because that basis adjustment information is not part of what is required to be reported under section 6035, however, if the executor chooses to provide that basis adjustment information on the Schedule A provided to the beneficiary, the basis adjustment information must be shown separately from the final value required to be reported on the beneficiary's Statement.

13. *Subsequent transfers.*

As discussed earlier in this preamble, section 6035(a)(2) imposes a reporting requirement on the executor of the decedent's estate and on any other person required to file a return under section 6018. The purpose of this reporting is to enable the IRS to monitor whether the basis claimed by an owner of the property is properly based on the final value of that property for estate tax purposes. The Treasury Department and the IRS are concerned, however, that opportunities may exist in some circumstances for the recipient of such reporting to circumvent the purpose of the statute (for example, by making a gift of the property to a complex trust for the benefit of the transferor's family).

Accordingly, pursuant to the regulatory authority granted in section 6035(b)(2), the proposed regulations require additional information reporting by certain subsequent transferors in limited circumstances. Specifically, proposed § 1.6035-1(f) provides that, with regard to property that previously was reported or is required to be reported on a Statement furnished to a recipient, when the recipient distributes or transfers (by gift or otherwise) all or any portion of that property to a related transferee, whether directly or indirectly, in a transaction in which the transferee's basis for Federal income tax purposes is determined in whole or in part with reference to the transferor's basis, the transferor is required to file and furnish with the IRS and the transferee, respectively, a supplemental Statement documenting the new ownership of this property. This proposed reporting requirement is imposed on each such recipient of the property. For purposes of this provision, a related transferee means any member of the transferor's family as defined in section 2704(c)(2), any controlled entity (a corporation or any other entity in which the transferor and members of the transferor's family, whether directly or indirectly, have control within the meaning of section 2701(b)(2)(A) or (B)), and any trust of which the transferor is a deemed owner for income tax purposes.

In the event such transfer occurs before a final value is determined within the meaning of proposed § 1.1014-10(c), the transferor must provide the executor with a copy of the supplemental Statement filed with the IRS and furnished to the transferee reporting the new ownership of the property. When a final value is determined, the executor will then provide a supplemental Statement to the new transferee instead of to the transferor. The supplemental Statements are due no later than 30 days after the transferor distributes or transfers all or a portion of the property to the transferee.

14. *Surviving joint tenants or other recipients under section 6035(b)(2).*

Section 6035(b)(2) authorizes the IRS to prescribe regulations relating to situations in which the surviving joint tenant or other recipient may have better information than the executor regarding the basis or fair market value of the property received by reason of the decedent's death. Section 6018(b) addresses these situations. Section 6018(b) generally requires that, if the executor is unable to make a complete return as to any part of the gross estate of the decedent, the executor must include on the return a description of that part of the gross estate and the name of every person holding a legal or beneficial interest in it. Upon notice from the Secretary, any such person must in like manner make a return as to this part of the gross estate. Section 6035(a)(2) and these proposed regulations require a person required to file a return under section 6018(b) to file an Information Return with the IRS and to furnish the Statement(s) to each beneficiary of that property. Therefore, the Treasury Department and the IRS have determined that no additional regulations applicable only to surviving joint tenants or other recipients are necessary for this purpose.

15. *Removal of regulations under former Section 6035*

The *American Jobs Creation Act of 2004* (Public Law 108-357, 118 Stat. 1418) (Jobs Act) repealed former section 6035, effective for taxable years of foreign corporations beginning after December 31, 2004, and for taxable years of United States shareholders with or within which the tax years of foreign corporations end. Prior to repeal, former section 6035 set forth information reporting requirements for certain United States persons that were officers, directors, or 10-percent shareholders of a foreign personal holding company. Section 1.6035-1 (TD 8573), § 301.6035-1 (TD 6498), § 1.6035-2 (TD 8028), and § 1.6035-3 (TD 8028) (collectively, the FPHC regulations) provide guidance on the information reporting required under former section 6035, as in effect prior to amendment by the *Tax Equity and Fiscal Responsibility Act of 1982* (Public Law 97-248, 96 Stat. 328), and prior to its repeal by the Jobs Act.

This document proposes to withdraw the FPHC regulations. However, the FPHC regulations referenced above contained in 26 CFR parts 1 and 301, revised as of April 1, 2015, continue to apply for taxable years of foreign corporations beginning on or before December 31, 2004, and for taxable years of United States shareholders in which former section 6035 applies with or within which the tax years of foreign corporations end.

16. *Request for new process.*

One commenter requested the creation of a process to allow an estate beneficiary to challenge the value reported by the executor. There is no such process under the Federal law regarding returns described in section 6018. The beneficiary's rights with regard to the estate tax valuation of property are governed by applicable state law. Accordingly, the proposed regulations do not create a new Federal process for challenging the value reported by the executor.

Proposed Effective/Applicability Date

Upon the publication of the Treasury Decision adopting these rules as final in the **Federal Register**, these proposed regulations will apply to property acquired from a decedent or by reason of the death of a decedent whose return required by section 6018 is filed after July 31, 2015. Persons may rely upon these rules before the date of publication of the Treasury Decision adopting these rules as final in the **Federal Register**.

Statement of Availability of IRS Documents

IRS Revenue Procedures, Revenue Rulings notices, notices and other guidance cited in this preamble are published in the Internal Revenue Bulletin (or Cumulative Bulletin) and are available from the Superintendent of Documents, U.S. Government Printing Office, Washington, DC 20402, or by visiting the IRS website at *http://www.irs.gov*.

Special Analyses

Certain IRS regulations, including this one, are exempt from the requirements of Executive Order 12866, as supplemented and reaffirmed by Executive Order 13563. Therefore, a regulatory impact assessment is not required. It is hereby certified that the collection of information in these regulations will not have a significant economic impact on a substantial number of small entities. This certification is based on the fact that this rule primarily affects individuals (or their estates) and trusts, which are not small entities as defined by the Regulatory Flexibility Act (5 U.S.C. 601). Although it is anticipated that there may be an incremental economic impact on executors that are small entities, including entities that provide tax and legal services that assist individuals in preparing tax returns, any impact would not be significant and would not affect a substantial number of small entities. Therefore, a Regulatory Flexibility Analysis under the Regulatory Flexibility Act (5 U.S.C. chapter 6) is not required. Pursuant to section 7805(f) of the Code, the notice of proposed rulemaking will be submitted to the Chief Counsel for Advocacy of the Small Business Administration for comment on its impact on small business.

Comments and Requests for a Public Hearing

Before these proposed regulations are adopted as final regulations, consideration will be given to any written (a signed original and eight (8) copies) or electronic comments that are submitted timely to the IRS. Comments are requested on all aspects of the proposed rules. All comments will be available for public inspection and copying. A public hearing may be scheduled if requested in writing by any person that timely submits written comments. If a public hearing is scheduled, notice of the date, time, and place for the hearing will be published in the **Federal Register. Drafting Information**

The principal author of these proposed regulations is Theresa M. Melchiorre, Office of Associate Chief Counsel (Passthroughs and Special Industries). Other personnel from the Treasury Department and the IRS participated in their development.

[¶49,695] Proposed Amendments of Regulations (REG-133673-15), published in the Federal Register on April 13, 2016 (corrected 7/5/2016).

[Code Secs. 305, 860G, 861, 1441, 1461, 1471, 1473 and 6045B]

Corporations: Stock rights: Deemed distributions.—Amendments of Reg. §§1.305-1, 1.305-3, 1.305-7, 1.860G-3, 1.861-3, 1.1441-2, 1.1441-3, 1.1441-7, 1.1461-2, 1.1471-2, 1.1473-1 and 1.6045B-1, containing proposed regulations regarding deemed distributions of stock and rights to acquire stock, are proposed.

AGENCY: Internal Revenue Service (IRS), Treasury.

ACTION: Notice of proposed rulemaking.

SUMMARY: This document contains proposed regulations regarding deemed distributions of stock and rights to acquire stock. The proposed regulations would resolve ambiguities concerning the amount and timing of deemed distributions that are or result from adjustments to rights to acquire stock. The proposed regulations also would provide additional guidance to withholding agents regarding their current withholding and information reporting obligations under chapters 3 and 4 with respect to these deemed distributions. The proposed regulations would affect corporations issuing rights to acquire stock, their shareholders and holders of these rights, and withholding agents with respect to these deemed distributions.

DATES: Written or electronic comments and requests for a public hearing must be received by July 12, 2016.

ADDRESSES: Send submissions to: CC:PA:LPD:PR (REG-133673-15), Room 5203, Internal Revenue Service, PO Box 7604, Ben Franklin Station, Washington, DC, 20044. Submissions may be hand-delivered Monday through Friday between the hours of 8 a.m. and 4 p.m. to CC:PA:LPD:PR (REG-133673-15), Courier's Desk, Internal Revenue Service, 1111 Constitution Avenue, NW, Washington, DC, 20224 or sent electronically, via the Federal eRulemaking Portal at www.regulations.gov (indicate IRS and REG-133673-15).

FOR FURTHER INFORMATION CONTACT: Concerning the proposed regulations under section 305, Maurice M. LaBrie, (202) 317-5322; concerning the proposed regulations under sections 860G, 861, 1441, 1461, 1471, and 1473, Subin Seth, (202) 317-6942; concerning the proposed regulations under section 6045B, Pamela Lew, (202) 317-7053; concerning submission of comments, contact Regina Johnson, (202) 317-6901 (not toll-free numbers).

SUPPLEMENTARY INFORMATION:

Background and Explanation of Provisions

1. Overview

This document contains proposed regulations that amend 26 CFR part 1 under sections 305, 860G, 861, 1441, 1461, 1471, 1473, and 6045B of the Internal Revenue Code of 1986 (Code) concerning deemed distributions that are or result from adjustments to rights to acquire stock.

Final regulations under section 305 were published in the **Federal Register** on July 12, 1973 (TD 7281, 38 FR 18531), and amendments to those final regulations were published in the **Federal Register** on October 15, 1974 (TD 7329, 39 FR 36860), and in the **Federal Register** on December 21, 1995 (TD 8643, 60 FR 66134).

Final regulations under sections 1441 and 1461 were published in the **Federal Register** on October 14, 1997 (TD 8734, 62 FR 53387), and the following amendments to those final regulations were published in the **Federal Register** on: December 31, 1998 (TD 8804, 63 FR 72187); December 30, 1999 (TD 8856, 64 FR 73412); May 22, 2000 (TD 8881, 65 FR 32186); August 1, 2006 (TD 9272, 71 FR 43366); July 14, 2008 (TD 9415, 73 FR 40172) (corrected on August 6, 2008 (73 FR 45612)); January 23, 2012 (TD 9572, 77 FR 3109); December 5, 2013 (TD 9648, 78 FR 73081); March 6, 2014 (TD 9658, 79 FR 12726) (corrected on July 1, 2014 (79 FR 37175)); and, September 18, 2015 (TD 9734, 80 FR 56866). Final regulations under sections 1471 and 1473 were published in the **Federal Register** on January 28, 2013 (TD 9610, 78 FR 5874) (corrected on September 10, 2013 (78 FR 55202)), and the amendments to those final regulations were published as temporary regulations in the **Federal Register** on March 6, 2014 (TD 9657, 79 FR 12812) (corrected on July 1, 2014 (79 FR 37175)).

Final regulations under section 6045B were published in the **Federal Register** on October 18, 2010 (TD 9504, 75 FR 64072), and amendments to those final regulations were published in the **Federal Register** on April 18, 2013 (TD 9616, 78 FR 23116).

2. Amount and Timing of Deemed Distributions Under Section 305(c)

A. Application of section 305(b) and (c) generally

Section 305 and the regulations thereunder apply to actual and deemed distributions by a corporation of its own stock and rights to acquire its own stock. Section 305(a) provides the general rule that the receipt of these distributions is not included in the gross income of the recipient; however, under section 305(b)(1) through (b)(5) certain actual and deemed distributions of stock and stock rights are treated as distributions of property to which section 301 applies. For example, under section 305(b)(2), if a distribution (or series of distributions) by a corporation has the result of a receipt of property by some shareholders and an increase in the proportionate interests of other shareholders in the assets or earnings and profits of the corporation, all the distributions are treated as distributions of property to which section 301 applies.

Section 305(c) authorizes the Secretary to prescribe regulations to treat changes in the conversion ratio of instruments convertible into stock and other events having similar effects as distributions to shareholders whose proportionate interests in the assets or earnings and profits of the corporation are increased by such events.

Under section 305(d)(1) and current § 1.305-1(d), for purposes of section 305 and the regulations thereunder, the term *stock* includes rights to acquire stock, and under section 305(d)(2), for purposes of section 305(b) and (c) and the regulations thereunder, the term *shareholder* includes a holder of rights to acquire stock. For purposes of this preamble:

The term *actual shareholder* means a holder of stock (not including rights to acquire stock).

The term *deemed shareholder* means a holder of a right to acquire stock.

The term *deemed distribution* means a transaction or event, other than an actual distribution of stock, money, or other property, that is a distribution under section 305(b) and (c).

The term *applicable adjustment* means an adjustment to a right to acquire stock, including an increase or reduction in conversion ratio, conversion price, option price, or number of shares the holder would receive upon conversion or exercise.

The term *right to acquire stock* means any right to acquire stock, whether pursuant to a convertible instrument (such as a debt instrument that is convertible into shares of stock), a warrant, subscription right, or stock right issued by the corporation that issued or will issue the underlying stock, or any other right to acquire stock of the corporation issuing such right (whether settled in stock or in cash).

Under current § 1.305-1(b)(1), when a distribution of stock (including a right to acquire stock) is a distribution of property to which sections 305(b) and 301 apply, the amount of the distribution is the fair market value, on the date of the distribution, of the stock or right to acquire stock that is distributed.

B. Application of section 305(b) and (c) to adjustments to rights to acquire stock

A corporation may issue rights to acquire its stock in a number of forms, including warrants, subscription rights, options, convertible instruments that give the holder a right to convert the instruments into shares of stock in the issuing corporation, and similar instruments. In any of these forms, rights to acquire stock may provide for applicable adjustments that grant deemed shareholders economic benefits that correspond to distributions of stock, cash, or other property made to actual shareholders. Similarly, rights to acquire stock may provide for adjustments to prevent actual shareholders' interests from being diluted as a result of distributions of stock, cash, or other property to deemed shareholders (that is, holders of rights to acquire stock).

An applicable adjustment to a convertible instrument may consist of an increase in the number of shares of stock a holder would receive upon conversion. Similarly, an applicable adjustment to a warrant, subscription right, stock right, option, or similar right to acquire stock may consist of an increase in the number of shares the holder would receive upon exercise. In either situation, the applicable adjustment may have the effect of increasing the deemed shareholders' proportionate interests in the assets or earnings and profits of the corporation. If this increase has a result described in section 305(b), then under section 305(c) the applicable adjustment is a deemed distribution to the deemed shareholder, and section 301 applies to the deemed distribution.

Under current § 1.305-7(b)(1), an applicable adjustment made pursuant to a bona fide, reasonable adjustment formula that has the effect of preventing dilution of a shareholder's interest is not a deemed distribution of stock to which sections 305(b) and 301 apply. However, also under current § 1.305-7(b)(1), an applicable adjustment to compensate for a distribution of cash or property to actual shareholders that is taxable under section 301, 356(a)(2), 871(a)(1)(A), 881(a)(1), 852(b), or 857(b) is not considered as made pursuant to such a bona fide, reasonable adjustment formula, and therefore may be a distribution to which sections 305(b) and 301 apply.

The Treasury Department and the IRS have concluded that, under section 305(b) and (c) and the regulations thereunder, it is clear that an applicable adjustment is a deemed distribution to which section 301 applies, if: (i) the applicable adjustment increases the proportionate interest of an actual shareholder or a deemed shareholder in the corporation's assets or earnings and profits; (ii) such increase in proportionate interest has a result described in section 305(b); and (iii) the anti-dilution exception of § 1.305-7(b)(1) does not apply. For example, it has been the position of the Treasury Department and the IRS for over forty years that, under section 305(b) and (c) and the regulations thereunder, an increase in the conversion ratio of a convertible debt instrument may be treated as a deemed distribution to the deemed shareholder that holds the instrument, and, if so treated, section 301 applies to the deemed distribution. *See* Rev. Rul. 75-513 (1975-2 CB 114) (section 301 applied to deemed distribution where conversion ratio of convertible debentures increased due to payment of cash dividend to common shareholders); and Rev. Rul. 76-186 (1976-1 CB 86) (same; basis of the convertible debentures was increased by the value of the deemed distribution); *cf.* Rev. Rul. 77-37 (1977-1 CB 85) (no deemed distribution because anti-dilution exception of § 1.305-7(b) applied where distribution to actual shareholders was tax-free under section 355).

The current regulations are unclear, however, as to the amount of a deemed distribution to a deemed shareholder. The current regulations may reasonably be interpreted as providing either that such a deemed distribution is treated as a distribution of a right to acquire stock (the amount of which is the fair market value of the right), or that such a distribution is treated as a distribution of the actual stock to which the right relates (the amount of which is the fair market value of the stock). Accordingly, for deemed distributions to deemed shareholders occurring before final regulations are published, the IRS will not challenge either position.

The current regulations are also unclear as to the timing of such a distribution. Under the proposed regulations, such a distribution generally would be deemed to occur at the time the applicable adjustment occurs, in accordance with the instrument setting forth the terms of the right to acquire stock, but in no event later than the date of the distribution of cash or property that results in the deemed distribution (taking into account § 1.305-3(b)).

These proposed regulations would amend the current regulations under section 305(b) and (c) only to clarify the amount and timing of such deemed distributions, not the fact of their occurrence, which is clear under current law.

C. Summary of proposed regulations

i. Amount of deemed distributions

After studying this area, the Treasury Department and the IRS have concluded that a deemed distribution of a right to acquire stock is more accurately viewed as a distribution of additional rights to acquire stock, the amount of which is the fair market value of the right.

Under the terms of a convertible instrument, a distribution of cash or property to actual shareholders may increase the number of shares the holder of the convertible instrument would receive upon conversion. Similarly, a distribution of cash or property to actual shareholders may increase the number of shares the holder of other rights to acquire stock, such as warrants or options, would receive upon exercise. In either case, the increase is an applicable adjustment and a deemed distribution of additional rights to acquire stock to the holders of the rights to acquire stock. Under the proposed regulations, the amount of the deemed distribution would be the excess of (i) the fair market value of the right to acquire stock immediately after the applicable adjustment over (ii) the fair market value of the right to acquire stock without the applicable adjustment. In determining the fair market value of a right to acquire stock, any particular facts pertaining to the deemed shareholder's rights, including the number of actual shares of stock or rights to acquire stock held by such deemed shareholder, would be disregarded.

Also, under the terms of a convertible debt instrument or other right to acquire stock, a payment of cash or property to the holder may cause a reduction in the number of shares the holder would receive upon conversion or exercise. Such a reduction is an applicable adjustment that increases the actual shareholders' proportionate interests in the assets or earnings and profits of the corporation. Thus, the applicable adjustment results in a deemed distribution of stock to the actual shareholders, and section 301 applies to the deemed distribution. Under the proposed regulations, the amount of this deemed distribution would be the fair market value of the stock deemed distributed, determined in accordance with § 1.305-3(e), *Examples 8* and *9* (relating to deemed distributions to shareholders resulting from certain redemptions of stock from other shareholders). *See also* Tax Revenue Act of 1969: Hearings on H.R. 13270 Before the House Ways and Means Comm., 91st Cong. 1st Sess., pt. 14, 5196-98 (1969).

ii. Timing of deemed distributions

When an applicable adjustment is or results in a deemed distribution under proposed § 1.305-7(c)(1) or (2), the deemed distribution occurs at the time such applicable adjustment occurs, in accordance with the instrument setting forth the terms of the right to acquire stock, but in no event later than the date of the distribution of cash or property that results in the deemed distribution (taking into account § 1.305-3(b)). For such an applicable adjustment relating to a right to acquire publicly-traded stock, if the instrument setting forth the terms of such right does not set forth the date and time the applicable adjustment occurs, the deemed distribution would occur immediately prior to the opening of business on the ex-dividend date for the distribution of cash or property that results in the deemed distribution. For such an applicable adjustment relating to a right to acquire non-publicly traded stock, if the instrument setting forth the terms of such right does not set forth the date and time the applicable adjustment occurs, the deemed distribution occurs on the date that a holder is legally entitled to the distribution of cash or property that results in the deemed distribution.

3. Withholding under Chapters 3 and 4 on Deemed Distributions under Section 305(c)

This section provides a discussion of the proposed rules regarding deemed distributions under section 305(c). Section 4 of the preamble provides a discussion of the proposed rules regarding substitute dividend payments that are deemed payments determined with respect to a deemed distribution under section 305(c). The proposed rules that would apply for deemed payments are analogous to the proposed rules that would apply to deemed distributions.

A. Background

Sections 1441 and 1442 (referred to herein as "chapter 3") require all persons having the control, receipt, custody, disposal, or payment of items of income subject to withholding of any nonresident alien, foreign partnership, or foreign corporation to withhold tax at a 30-percent rate unless a reduced rate of withholding applies. Amounts subject to withholding include amounts from sources within the United States that are fixed or determinable annual or periodical income, which generally includes, among other things, interest, dividends, and similar types of investment income. § 1.1441-2(b)(1)(i). Under § 1.1441-2(e)(1), "a payment" is considered made to a person "if that person realizes income whether or not such income results from an actual transfer of cash or other property." For this purpose, a payment is considered made when the amount would be includible in the income of the beneficial owner under the U.S. tax principles governing the cash basis method of accounting. § 1.1441-2(e)(1).

On March 18, 2010, the Hiring Incentives to Restore Employment Act of 2010, Pub. L. 111-147 (H.R. 2847), added chapter 4 to the Code (sections 1471 through 1474, commonly known as "FATCA"). Chapter 4 generally requires a withholding agent to withhold tax at a 30-percent rate on a "withholdable payment" (as defined in § 1.1473-1(a)) made to a foreign financial institution (FFI) unless the FFI has entered into an agreement described in section 1471(b) to obtain status as a participating FFI or the FFI is deemed to have satisfied the requirements of section 1471(b). Chapter 4 also generally requires a withholding agent to withhold tax at a 30-percent rate on a withholdable payment made to a nonfinancial foreign entity (NFFE) unless the NFFE has provided information to the withholding agent with respect to the NFFE's substantial U.S. owners or has certified that it has no such owners. *See* section 1472.

These proposed regulations would provide guidance to withholding agents regarding their obligations to withhold under chapters 3 and 4 on deemed distributions under section 305(c). Withholding agents have commented that ambiguities in the current law have made it difficult for them to satisfy their withholding obligations. In particular, withholding agents have commented that these deemed distributions often occur when there is no cash payment that corresponds to the deemed distribution, which makes it difficult for them to satisfy their withholding obligation on the date of the deemed distribution. In addition, withholding agents commented that they often lack knowledge of the fact that a deemed distribution on a security has been made and are therefore unable to withhold on the date of the deemed distribution.

B. Amendments to Chapter 3

i. Withholding on deemed distributions, and new exception for deemed distributions on specified securities

Proposed § 1.1441-2(d)(4)(i) would clarify that a withholding agent has an obligation to withhold on a deemed distribution (as defined in § 1.305-1(d)(7)) that is made on a security. Proposed § 1.1441-7(a)(4) would clarify that an issuer of a security upon which a deemed distribution is made and any person that holds directly or indirectly (for example, through an account maintained for an intermediary) a security on behalf of the beneficial owner of the security, or a flow-through entity that owns directly or indirectly (through another flow-through entity) a security, is considered to have custody of or control over the deemed distribution made on the security and, therefore, is a withholding agent with respect to the distribution.

Under current § 1.1441-2(d)(1), a withholding agent does not have an obligation to withhold on a payment when it lacks control over, or custody of, money or property of the recipient, or knowledge of the facts giving rise to the payment (the general exception). This general exception does not apply when, in relevant part, the payment is a distribution with respect to stock. The proposed regulations, however, would allow a withholding agent (other than the issuer of the specified security) to benefit from a new exception to withholding in proposed § 1.1441-2(d)(4) for deemed distributions (as defined in § 1.305-1(d)(7)) of stock or a right to acquire stock on a specified security (as defined in § 1.6045-1(a)(14)). Under this new exception, a withholding agent (other than the issuer of the specified security) would have an obligation to withhold on such a deemed distribution only if, before the due date (not including extensions) for filing Form 1042, Annual Withholding Tax Return for U.S. Source Income of Foreign Persons, with respect to the calendar year in which the deemed distribution occurred, either (i) the issuer meets its reporting requirements under § 1.6045B-1 (by furnishing an issuer statement or publicly reporting the information required under that section) or (ii) the withholding agent has actual knowledge that a deemed distribution has occurred, in which case the obligation to withhold would not arise until January 15 of the year following the calendar year of the deemed distribution.

ii. When and how to withhold

Once the requirements of proposed § 1.1441-2(d)(4)(i) have been satisfied, a withholding agent would have an obligation to withhold on a deemed distribution. Except as provided in § 1.1441-5 regarding the time to withhold for partnerships and trusts, under proposed § 1.1441-2(d)(4)(ii), a withholding agent would be required to satisfy its withholding obligation by withholding on the earliest of (i) the date on which a future cash payment is made with respect to the security; (ii) the date on which the security is sold, exchanged, or otherwise disposed of (including a transfer of the security to another account not maintained by the withholding agent or a termination of the account relationship); or (iii) the due date (not including extensions) for filing Form 1042 with respect to the calendar year in which the deemed distribution occurred. Under this approach, a withholding agent that continues to directly or indirectly hold or own the security when the requirements of proposed

§ 1.1441-2(d)(4)(i) are satisfied generally would be able to satisfy its withholding obligation by withholding on future cash payments on the security (for example, an interest payment on a convertible bond). If, however, the security is disposed of before sufficient future cash payments have been made on the security, the withholding agent would be required to withhold at the time of disposition and generally would be expected to do so by, for example, withholding on the proceeds from the disposal, liquidating other property held in custody for the beneficial owner, or obtaining other funds directly or indirectly from the beneficial owner to satisfy the withholding.

If there are not sufficient future cash payments on the security and the security has not been disposed of or transferred before the due date (not including extensions) for filing Form 1042 with respect to the calendar year in which the deemed distribution occurred, then, to avoid having to pay the tax out of the withholding agent's own funds, the withholding agent may apply current § 1.1461-2(b) in order to collect the underwithheld amount. Under these rules, the withholding agent can satisfy the tax by withholding on other cash payments made to the same beneficial owner or by liquidating other property held in custody for the beneficial owner or over which it has control. The proposed regulations would amend current § 1.1461-2(b) to clarify that a withholding agent may obtain the property from which to withhold under these rules through additional contributions obtained directly or indirectly from the beneficial owner. The proposed regulations also would add a sentence to current § 1.1461-2(b) to clarify that a withholding agent that satisfies its obligation to withhold under § 1.1461-2(b) will not be subject to any penalties for failure to deposit or failure to pay under sections 6656, 6672, and 7202 when it deposits the amounts obtained in this manner by the due date (not including extensions) for filing Form 1042 with respect to the calendar year in which the deemed distribution occurred. These clarifications reflect the IRS interpretation of current § 1.1461-2(b) in applying these penalties, and thus no penalties will be imposed for withholding agents that apply these rules to satisfy their obligations to withhold before the effective date of these regulations.

When the requirements of proposed § 1.1441-2(d)(4)(i) are satisfied after a withholding agent has terminated its relationship with the beneficial owner of the security, the withholding agent would remain liable for any underwithheld amount with respect to the deemed distribution. In order to avoid having to pay the tax due out of the withholding agent's own funds, before terminating an account relationship, a withholding agent should make arrangements with the beneficial owner to ensure that the withholding agent can satisfy any tax due, such as by retaining funds or other property of the owner.

iii. Foreign entities assuming withholding responsibilities

Proposed § 1.1441-2(d)(4)(iii) would provide that a withholding agent may treat certain foreign entities (qualified intermediaries, withholding foreign partnerships, withholding foreign trusts, and U.S. branches treated as U.S. persons) as assuming primary chapter 3 withholding responsibilities for a deemed distribution on a specified security only if (i) the withholding agent provides the foreign entity with a copy of the issuer statement described in § 1.6045B-1(b)(1) within 10 days of the issuer furnishing the statement to the holder of record or its nominee, or (ii) the issuer has met the public reporting requirements under § 1.6045B-1(a)(3). The foreign entity would have an obligation to withhold on the deemed distribution only if it receives a copy of the issuer statement or if the issuer has met the public reporting requirements by the due date (not including extensions) for filing Form 1042 with respect to the calendar year in which the deemed distribution occurred. A withholding agent that fails to provide a copy of the issuer statement to a foreign entity (in the absence of public reporting) would not be permitted to treat the foreign entity as having assumed primary withholding responsibilities for the deemed distribution and would therefore have to withhold and report based on the information that it has regarding the recipient of the deemed distribution. The purpose of this proposed rule is to ensure that foreign entities that assume primary withholding responsibilities for deemed distributions will possess the information described in § 1.6045B-1 to meet their withholding and information reporting obligations, as these entities (or their nominees) may not be holders of record that otherwise would receive the issuer statement described in § 1.6045B-1(b)(1).

iv. Reliance on issuer information reporting

Under proposed § 1.1441-3(c)(5), a withholding agent (other than the issuer of the specified security) would be permitted to rely on the information that an issuer provides on an issuer statement described in § 1.6045B-1(b)(1) or on a public website described in § 1.6045B-1(a)(3) to determine the proper amount of withholding on a deemed distribution on a specified security unless it knows that the information is incorrect or unreliable. Additionally, a foreign entity that has assumed primary withholding responsibilities would be permitted to rely on the copy of the issuer statement described in § 1.6045B-1(b)(1) that it receives from another withholding agent under the circumstances described in proposed § 1.1441-2(d)(4)(iii) unless it knows that the information is incorrect or unreliable.

v. Other changes to current § 1.1441-2(d)(1)

The proposed regulations would add language to § 1.1441-2(d)(1) to clarify that a withholding agent does not lack control over money or property if it directs another person to make a payment, and that a withholding agent does not lack knowledge of the facts that give rise to a payment merely because the withholding agent does not know the character or source of the payment for U.S. tax purposes. The proposed regulations also would add an example to § 1.1441-2(d)(1) of when a withholding agent lacks knowledge of the facts that give rise to a payment. These clarifications and the example are consistent with similar rules in current § 1.1471-2(a)(4)(i) that apply for chapter 4 purposes.

The proposed regulations also would make nonsubstantive changes to reorganize the structure of current § 1.1441-2(d)(1).

C. Amendments to Chapter 4

The proposed regulations would modify the regulations under chapter 4 to provide guidance similar to the rules described in proposed §§ 1.1441-2(d)(1), 1.1441-2(d)(4), 1.1441-3(c)(5), and 1.1441-7(a)(4) for withholding on a deemed distribution (as defined in § 1.305-1(d)(7)) that is a withholdable payment under chapter 4. The amendment to proposed § 1.1461-2(b) that clarifies that a withholding agent may obtain additional contributions of property directly or indirectly from a beneficial owner and the new sentence added to proposed § 1.1461-2(b) regarding penalties also would apply to withholding agents adjusting underwithholding under chapter 4 through cross-reference in § 1.1474-2(b). The proposed regulations also would make nonsubstantive changes to reorganize the structure of current § 1.1471-2(a)(4)(i), which are consistent with the organizational changes proposed for current § 1.1441-2(d)(1).

4. A Substitute Dividend May Include Deemed Payments

Section 1.861-3(a)(6) provides that a substitute dividend payment made to a transferor in a securities lending transaction or sale-repurchase transaction is sourced in the same manner as a dividend on the transferred securities. The regulations define a substitute dividend payment as "a payment, made to the transferor of a security in a securities lending transaction or a sale-repurchase transaction, of an amount equivalent to a dividend distribution which the owner of the transferred security is entitled to receive during the term of the transaction." These proposed regulations would modify § 1.861-3(a)(6) to clarify that a substitute dividend payment includes a deemed payment made in the amount (as determined under § 1.305-7(c)(4)) of a deemed distribution (as defined in § 1.305-1(d)(7)).

These proposed regulations would provide that the general exception to withholding in § 1.1441-2(d)(1)(i) does not apply for deemed payments (as defined in § 1.861-3(a)(6)). However, proposed § 1.1441-2(d)(4) would allow a withholding agent to benefit from the same exception to withholding that would apply to deemed distributions (as defined in § 1.305-1(d)(7)) on a specified security for deemed payments (as defined in § 1.861-3(a)(6)) that are determined with respect to a deemed distribution on a specified security. Thus, a withholding agent would have an obligation to withhold on such a deemed payment only if, before the due date (not including extensions) for filing Form 1042, Annual Withholding Tax Return for U.S. Source Income of Foreign Persons, with respect to the calendar year in which the deemed distribution on a specified security occurred, either (i) the issuer meets its reporting requirements under § 1.6045B-1 (by furnishing an issuer statement or publicly reporting the information required under that section) or (ii) the withholding agent has actual knowledge that a deemed distribution has occurred, in which case the obligation to withhold would not arise until January 15 of the year following the calendar year of the deemed distribution or the deemed payment. If a withholding agent has an obligation to withhold on a deemed payment (as defined in § 1.861-3(a)(6)) under § 1.1441-2(d)(4)(i), it would be required to withhold subject to the rules regarding when and how to withhold in proposed § 1.1441-2(d)(4)(ii) and the rules regarding foreign entities that assume withholding responsibilities in § 1.1441-2(d)(4)(iii). These proposed regulations also would modify the regulations under chapter 4 to provide similar guidance with respect to deemed payments that are withholdable payments.

5. Issuer Reporting Under Section 6045B

To facilitate broker reporting of a security's adjusted basis to the holder of the security under section 6045, section 6045B provides that, according to the forms or regulations prescribed by the Secretary, an issuer of a specified security (for example, stock, a convertible debt instrument, or a warrant) must report certain information relating to an organizational action that affects the basis of the security to both the IRS and the holders of the security. Under section 6045B and current § 1.6045B-1, an issuer must file an issuer return (Form 8937, Report of Organizational Actions Affecting Basis of Securities) with the IRS by the earlier of 45 days after the organizational action or January 15 of the calendar year following the organizational action. In addition, the issuer must send a written statement (for example, a copy of the issuer return) to holders by January 15 of the calendar year following the organizational action. In lieu of filing the issuer return with the IRS and furnishing the written statement to holders, current § 1.6045B-1(a)(3) permits an issuer to post the required information on its public website by the due date for reporting the issuer return to the IRS. Under current § 1.6045B-1, however, an issuer is not required to send a statement to exempt recipients, such as C corporations and foreign persons, nor is an issuer required to file an issuer return if the issuer reasonably determines that all of the holders of the security are exempt recipients. An issuer must comply with current § 1.6045B-1 for an organizational action that occurs on or after the applicability date prescribed in current § 1.6045B-1(j). For example, an issuer of a convertible debt instrument must comply with current § 1.6045B-1 for an organizational action that occurs after December 31, 2015.

An applicable adjustment, including a conversion ratio adjustment, is an organizational action that often will affect the holder's basis in a specified security. For example, the instructions to Form 8937 provide that if a conversion ratio adjustment on a convertible debt instrument occurring after December 31, 2015, results in a distribution under section 305(c) (for example, because it is made in conjunction with a cash distribution to shareholders), the issuer of the debt instrument must file Form 8937.

Brokers and withholding agents have expressed concerns about the difficulty of complying with their reporting and withholding obligations in the absence of information about the fact and amount of a deemed distribution under section 305(c), including a deemed distribution under section 305(c) resulting from an applicable adjustment. Even after December 31, 2015, when issuers are generally required to report an applicable adjustment on a convertible debt instrument, brokers and withholding agents may not have the necessary information to comply with their reporting and withholding obligations because of the exempt recipient exception for providing a written statement (and assuming that the issuer does not choose the public reporting alternative). In response to these concerns, § 1.6045B-1(i)(2) of the proposed regulations would require that an issuer provide an issuer return to the IRS and a written statement to each holder of record of a specified security (or to the holder's nominee) relating to a deemed distribution under section 305(c) on the security, without regard to any of the general exceptions in the current regulations under section 6045B or in the instructions to Form 8937. The proposed regulations, like the current regulations, permit an issuer to not provide an issuer return to the IRS or a written statement to the holders regarding the deemed distribution if the issuer satisfies the public reporting requirements in current § 1.6045B-1(a)(3).

6. Reporting for U.S. Persons

Section 1.6045B-1 generally applies when a deemed distribution affects the basis of a specified security. It is expected that similar principles would apply under section 6042 with respect to reporting of deemed distributions made to U.S. persons on Form 1099-DIV. Comments are requested on the implementation of Form 1099-DIV reporting on these amounts.

Proposed Effective/Applicability Date

The proposed regulations under section 305 would apply to deemed distributions occurring on or after the date of publication of the Treasury decision adopting these rules as final regulations in the **Federal Register**. A taxpayer, however, may rely on these proposed regulations for deemed distributions under section 305(c) that occur prior to such date. For purposes of determining the amount of a deemed distribution to a deemed shareholder occurring prior to the date of publication, a taxpayer may determine the amount of the deemed distribution by treating such distribution either as a distribution of a right to acquire stock or as a distribution of the actual stock to which the right relates.

The proposed regulations under sections 860G, 861, 1441, 1461, 1471, and 1473 would apply to payments made on or after the date of publication. A withholding agent, however, may rely on the proposed regulations under sections 861, 1441, 1471, and 1473 for all deemed distributions under section 305(c) or, to the extent applicable, deemed payments (as defined in § 1.861-3(a)(6)) occurring on or after January 1, 2016 until the date of publication. No inference as to the application of these provisions under current law is intended by permitting reliance on these proposed regulations. A withholding agent also may rely on the proposed regulations under section 1461 for any payments occurring on or after January 1, 2016 until the date of publication, including for any deemed distribution under section 305(c) or deemed payment (as defined in § 1.861-3(a)(6)) for which the withholding agent failed to withhold.

Section 1.6045B-1(i)(2) would apply to a deemed distribution under section 305(c) occurring on or after the date of publication. In addition, an issuer would report the amount and timing of a deemed distribution in accordance with the proposed regulations under section 305 for a deemed distribution occurring on or after the date of publication. For purposes of reporting the amount of a deemed distribution occurring prior to the date of publication, an issuer may determine the amount of the deemed distribution by treating such distribution either as a distribution of a right to acquire stock, or as a distribution of the shares of stock that would be received upon exercise of the right. In addition, an issuer may rely on § 1.305-7(c)(5) of the proposed regulations to determine the date of a deemed distribution occurring prior to the date of publication.

Statement of Availability of IRS Documents

IRS Revenue Rulings cited in this preamble are published in the Internal Revenue Bulletin (or Cumulative Bulletin) and are available from the Superintendent of Documents, U.S. Government Printing Office, Washington, DC 20402, or by visiting the IRS website at *http://www.irs.gov*.

Effect on Other Documents

The IRS will modify, clarify, or obsolete publications as necessary to conform to these proposed regulations as of the date of publication of the Treasury decision adopting these rules as final regulations in the **Federal Register**. *See, e.g.*, Rev. Rul. 75-513 (1975-2 CB 114) and Rev. Rul. 76-186 (1976-1 CB 186). The IRS solicits comments as to whether other publications should be modified, clarified, or obsoleted.

Special Analyses

Certain IRS regulations, including this one, are exempt from the requirements of Executive Order 12866, as supplemented and reaffirmed by Executive Order 13563. Therefore, a regulatory impact assessment is not required. It also has been determined that section 553(b) of the Administrative Procedure Act (5 U.S.C. chapter 5) does not apply to these regulations.

Pursuant to the Regulatory Flexibility Act (5 U.S.C. chapter 6), it is hereby certified that the proposed regulations under section 6045B in this document will not have a significant economic impact on a substantial number of small entities. Any effect on small entities by the rules in the proposed regulations flows directly from section 403 of the Energy Improvement and Extension Act of 2008, Division B of Public Law 110-343 (122 Stat. 3765, 3854 (2008)) (the Act).

Section 403(d) of the Act added section 6045B, which requires an issuer, including an issuer that is a small entity, to report certain information relating to any organizational action by the issuer that affects the basis of a specified security. In general, an issuer reports the information required under section 6045B to the IRS and to holders or nominees on Form 8937. The proposed regulations limit reporting to the information necessary to meet the Act's requirements. In addition, the proposed regulations retain the rule in the current regulations under section 6045B that permits an issuer to report each action publicly on its website instead of filing a return and furnishing each holder or nominee a statement about the action. The proposed regulations therefore do not add to the statutory impact on small entities but instead eases this impact to the extent the statute permits. Moreover, any economic impact on small entities is expected to be minimal.

Therefore, because the proposed regulations in this document will not have a significant economic impact on a substantial number of small entities, a regulatory flexibility analysis is not required.

Pursuant to section 7805(f) of the Code, this notice of proposed rulemaking has been submitted to the Chief Counsel for Advocacy of the Small Business Administration for comment on its impact on small business.

Comments and Requests for Public Hearing

Before the proposed regulations are adopted as final regulations, consideration will be given to any comments that are submitted timely to the IRS as prescribed in this preamble under the "Addresses" heading. The Treasury Department and the IRS request comments on all aspects of the proposed regulations. All comments will be available for public inspection and copying upon request, or at *www.regulations.gov*. A public hearing will be scheduled if requested in writing by any person that timely submits written comments. If a public hearing is scheduled, notice of the date, time, and place for the public hearing will be published in the **Federal Register**.

Drafting Information

The principal authors of these regulations are: with respect to the regulations under section 305, Maurice M. LaBrie of the Office of Associate Chief Counsel (Corporate); with respect to the regulations under sections 860G, 861, 1441, 1461, 1471, and 1473, Subin Seth of the Office of Associate Chief Counsel (International); and with respect to the regulations under section 6045B, Pamela Lew of the Office of Associate Chief Counsel (Financial Institutions and Products), all within the Office of Chief Counsel, IRS. Other personnel from the Treasury Department and the IRS participated in developing the regulations.

[¶49,696] Proposed Amendments of Regulations (NPRM REG-114307-15), published in the Federal Register on May 4, 2016.

[Code Sec. 7701]

Definitions: Disregarded entities: Partnerships: Self-employment tax.—Amendments of Reg. §301.7701-2, clarifying the employment tax treatment of partners in a partnership that owns a disregarded entity, are proposed.

AGENCY: Internal Revenue Service (IRS), Treasury.

ACTION: Notice of proposed rulemaking by cross-reference to temporary regulations.

SUMMARY: In the Rules and Regulations section of this issue of the **Federal Register**, the IRS is issuing temporary regulations that clarify the employment tax treatment of partners in a partnership that owns a disregarded entity. These regulations affect partners in a partnership that owns a disregarded entity. The text of those temporary regulations serves as the text of these proposed regulations.

DATES: Comments and requests for a public hearing must be received by August 2, 2016.

ADDRESSES: Send submissions to: CC:PA:LPD:PR (REG-114307-15), room 5203, Internal Revenue Service, PO Box 7604, Ben Franklin Station, Washington, DC 20044. Submissions may be hand-delivered Monday through Friday between the hours of 8 a.m. and 4 p.m. to CC:PA:LPD:PR (REG-114307-15), Courier's Desk, Internal Revenue Service, 1111 Constitution Avenue, N.W., Washington, DC, 20224 or sent electronically, via the Federal eRulemaking Portal at http://www.regulations.gov/ (IRS REG-114307-15).

FOR FUTHER INFORMATION CONTACT: Concerning the proposed regulations, Andrew K. Holubeck at (202) 317-4774; concerning submission of comments, or a request for a public hearing please contact Regina Johnson at (202) 317-6901 (not toll-free numbers).

SUPPLEMENTARY INFORMATION

Background and Explanation of Provisions

Temporary regulations in the Rules and Regulations section of this issue of the **Federal Register** amend the Procedure and Administration Regulations (26 CFR part 301) relating to section 7701. The temporary regulations clarify that an entity disregarded as separate from its owner (a disregarded entity), that is treated as a corporation for purposes of employment taxes imposed under subtitle C, is not treated as a corporation for purposes of employing its individual owner (who is treated as a sole proprietor) or for purposes of employing an individual that is a partner in a partnership that owns the disregarded entity. Rather, the entity is disregarded as an entity separate from its owner for this purpose. The partners are subject to the same self-employment tax rules as partners in a partnership that does not own an entity that is disregarded as separate from its owner. The text of those regulations also serves as the text of these proposed regulations. The preamble to the temporary regulations explains the amendments.

Special Analysis

Certain IRS regulations, including this one, are exempt from the requirements of Executive Order 12866, as supplemented and reaffirmed by Executive Order 13563. Therefore, a regulatory impact assessment is not required. It has also been determined that section 553(b) of the Administrative Procedure Act (5 U.S.C. chapter 5) does not apply to these regulations, and because the regulations do not impose a collection of information on small entities, the Regulatory Flexibility Act (5 U.S.C. chapter 6) does not apply. Pursuant to section 7805(f) of the Internal Revenue Code, this notice of proposed rulemaking will be submitted to the Chief Counsel for Advocacy of the Small Business Administration for comment on their impact on small business.

Comments and Requests for Public Hearing

Before these proposed regulations are adopted as final regulations, consideration will be given to any comments that are submitted timely to the IRS as prescribed in this preamble under the "Addresses" heading. The Treasury Department and the IRS request comments on all aspects of the proposed rules. All comments will be available at www.regulations.gov or upon request. A public hearing will be scheduled if requested in writing by any person that timely submits written comments. If a public hearing is scheduled, notice of the date, time, and place for the hearing will be published in the **Federal Register**.

Drafting Information

The principal author of these regulations is Andrew Holubeck of the Office of the Division Counsel/Associate Chief Counsel (Tax Exempt and Government Entities). However, other personnel from the IRS and the Treasury Department participated in their development.

[¶49,697] Proposed Amendments of Regulations (REG-127561-15), published in the Federal Register on May 6, 2016.

[Code Secs. 3511 and 7705]

Professional employer organizations : Employee-leasing organizations: Certification: Certification requirements.—Reg. §§31.3511-1, 301.7705-1 and 301.7705-2, setting forth the Federal employment tax liabilities and other obligations of persons certified by the IRS as certified professional employer organizations (CPEOs) in accordance with provisions enacted as part of The Stephen Beck, Jr., Achieving a Better Life Experience Act of 2014, are proposed.

AGENCY: Internal Revenue Service (IRS), Treasury.

ACTION: Notice of proposed rulemaking and notice of proposed rulemaking by cross-reference to temporary regulations.

SUMMARY: This document contains proposed regulations that set forth the Federal employment tax liabilities and other obligations of persons certified by the IRS as certified professional employer organizations (CPEOs) in accordance with provisions enacted as part of The Stephen Beck, Jr., Achieving a Better Life Experience Act of 2014. The proposed regulations also propose to adopt, by cross-reference, the text of temporary regulations in the Rules and Regulations section of this issue of the **Federal Register**, which relate to the requirements for applying for, receiving, and maintaining certification as a CPEO. These proposed regulations will affect persons who apply to be treated as CPEOs and who are certified by the IRS as meeting the applicable requirements. In certain instances, the proposed regulations will also affect the federal employment tax liabilities and other obligations of customers of the CPEO.

DATES: Comments and requests for a public hearing must be received by August 4, 2016.

ADDRESSES: Send submissions to: CC:PA:LPD:PR (REG-127561-15), room 5203, Internal Revenue Service, P.O. Box 7604, Ben Franklin Station, Washington, D.C. 20044. Submissions may be hand-delivered Monday through Friday between the hours of 8 a.m. and 4 p.m. to CC:PA:LPD:PR (REG-127561-15), Courier's Desk, Internal Revenue Service, 1111 Constitution Avenue, N.W., Washington, D.C. 20224 or sent electronically, via the Federal eRulemaking Portal at *www.regulations.gov* (REG-127561-15).

FOR FURTHER INFORMATION CONTACT: Concerning these proposed regulations, Melissa L. Duce at (202) 317-6798; concerning submissions of comments or to request a public hearing, Oluwafunmilayo Taylor at (202) 317-6901 (not toll-free numbers). SUPPLEMENTARY INFORMATION:

Paperwork Reduction Act

The collection of information contained in this notice of proposed rulemaking has been submitted to the Office of Management and Budget for review and approval in accordance with the Paperwork Reduction Act of 1995 (44 U.S.C. 3507(d)). Comments on the collection of information should be sent to the Office of Management and Budget, Attn: Desk Officer for the Department of the Treasury, Office of Information and Regulatory Affairs, Washington, D.C. 20503, with copies to the Internal Revenue Service, Attn: IRS Reports Clearance Officer, SE:W:CAR:MP:T:T:SP, Washington, D.C. 20224. Comments on the collection of information should be received by July 5, 2016.

Comments are specifically requested concerning:

Whether the proposed collection of information is necessary for the proper performance of the functions of the Internal Revenue Service, including whether the information will have practical utility;

The accuracy of the estimated burden associated with the proposed collection of information;

How the quality, utility, and clarity of the information to be collected may be enhanced;

How the burden of complying with the proposed collection of information may be minimized, including through forms of information technology; and

Estimates of capital or start-up costs and costs of operation, maintenance, and purchase of services to provide information.

The collection of information in the proposed regulations is in § 31.3511-1(g) and flows from section 3511(g) of the Internal Revenue Code (Code), which provides that the Secretary shall develop such reporting and recordkeeping rules, regulations, and procedures as the Secretary determines necessary or appropriate to ensure compliance by CPEOs with subtitle C of the Code. Section 31.3511-1(g)(1) clarifies that the reporting and recordkeeping requirements described in subtitle F of the Code that are currently applicable to employers apply to CPEOs that are treated as employers under § 31.3511-1(a), and § 31.3511-1(g)(3)(ii) specifically requires a CPEO to file on magnetic media Form 940, "Employer's Annual Federal Unemployment (FUTA) Tax Return," and Form 941, "Employer's QUARTERLY Federal Tax Return," along with all required schedules. The collection of information associated with complying with such reporting and recordkeeping requirements is reflected in the burden estimates for the relevant requirements under subtitle F. The collection of information associated with § § 31.3511-1(g)(3)(i) and (ii), relating to information that CPEOs must report to the IRS regarding their customers, will be reflected in the burden estimates for new Form 8973, "Certified Professional Employer Organization/Customer Reporting Agreement," and in the amendments made to the applicable Schedules R of Forms 940 and 941. The collection of information associated with § § 31.3511-1(g)(3)(iii) through (vi) relates to requirements imposed by § 301.7705-2T and are reflected in the burden estimates for that section. The collections of information associated with § 31.3511-1(g)(3)(vii) and (viii), relating to any information the IRS determines is necessary to promote compliance with respect to credits described in section 3511(d) and any other information the Commissioner may prescribe in further guidance, will be reflected in the future guidance requesting such information from CPEOs.

The collection of information in § 31.3511-1(g)(4) of the proposed regulations, regarding information a CPEO must provide to its customers, relates to: (1) an annual requirement to provide customers with the information necessary to claim specified credits for which the amount of the credit is determined by reference to the amount of employment tax wages or federal employment taxes; (2) a requirement to notify a customer of any transfers by the CPEO of the customer's contract meeting the requirements of section 7705(e)(2) (CPEO contract) or of any suspension or revocation of the CPEO's certification; and (3) if any covered employees are not or cease to be work site employees because they perform services at a location where the 85 percent threshold described in the definition of "work site employee" in § 301.7705-1(b)(17) is not met, a requirement to notify the customer that it may also be liable for federal employment taxes imposed on remuneration remitted by the CPEO to such covered employees. Similarly, § 31.3511-1(g)(5)(i) requires that any CPEO contract between a CPEO and a customer must: (1) contain the name and Employer Identification Number (EIN) of the CPEO fulfilling the federal employment tax obligations covered by the contract; (2) require the CPEO to provide the notices outlined in § 31.3511-1(g)(4); (3) describe the information that the CPEO will provide that is necessary for the customer to claim specified credits; and (4) specify that the CPEO must notify the customer that it may also be liable for federal employment taxes on remuneration remitted by the CPEO to any employees who are not work site employees. Further, any service agreement described in § 31.3504-2(b)(2) that is not a CPEO contract, must notify (or be accompanied by notification to) the client that the agreement does not alter the client's liability for federal employment taxes on remuneration remitted by the CPEO to the employees covered by the agreement. While a CPEO must provide customers with the information necessary to claim the specified credits annually and agree to provide customers and clients with the described notifications in each new CPEO contract or service agreement entered into during a particular taxable year, the remaining notification obligations outlined in § § 31.3511-1(g)(4) and (5) relate to other events that are less predictable and may be infrequent -such as transfers of existing CPEO contracts, suspension or revocation of the CPEO's certification, or the reclassification of employees at a particular work site as non-work site employees. Moreover, the Department of the Treasury (Treasury Department) and the IRS expect that CPEOs participating in this voluntary program will be able to build upon pre-existing systems and processes through which they communicate with their clients. With regard to the collections of information required in § § 31.3511-1(g)(4) and (5), the Treasury Department and the IRS have reached the following reporting burden estimates for the expected recordkeepers (which are CPEOs):

Estimated number of recordkeepers: 275.

Estimated average annual burden hours per recordkeeper: 6 hours.

Estimated total annual recordkeeping burden: 1650 hours.

Estimated frequency of collections of such information: Periodic.

The collection of information in the temporary regulations is in § 301.7705-2T and flows from sections 7705(b) and (c), which relate to the requirements that a person must satisfy to become and remain certified as a CPEO. The collection of information required to apply for and receive certification and to meet the requirements under § 301.7705-2T related to posting a security bond will be reflected in the burden estimates for Form 14737, "Request for Voluntary IRS Certification of a Professional Employer Organization"; Form 14737-A, "Responsible Individual Personal Attestation"; and Form 14751, "Certified Professional Employer Organization Surety Bond." The collection of information required by §§ 301.7705-2T(j) and (k), relating to periodic verification that the CPEO continues to meet the requirements of § 301.7705-2T and a CPEO's obligation to report any change that materially affects the continuing accuracy of any agreement or information that was previously made or provided to the IRS, will be published in a future revenue procedure that will prescribe the procedures related to these requirements.

Section 301.7705-2T(e) of the temporary regulations requires a CPEO to provide annually a copy of its annual audited financial statements and an opinion of a certified public accountant (CPA) regarding such financial statements. The collection of information required by § 301.7705-2T(f)(1)(i) relates to quarterly assertions that the CPEO has withheld and made deposits of all required federal employment taxes for the calendar quarter and examination level attestations from a CPA stating that such assertion is fairly stated in all material respects. In addition, § 301.7705-2T(f)(1)(ii) requires a quarterly statement signed by a responsible individual verifying that the CPEO has positive working capital with respect to the most recently completed fiscal quarter. While it is expected that CPEOs will generally maintain annual audited financial statements during the normal course of their business, rather than solely as a result of § 301.7705-2T(e), the Treasury Department and the IRS recognize that § 301.7705-2T(e) may impose new reporting requirements relating to underlying elements of those financial statements that will require additional time on the part of the CPEO and additional review by a CPA. In addition, § 301.7705-2T(f) requires CPEOs to submit statements regarding their working capital and assertions and exam level attestations related to their tax compliance on a quarterly basis. With respect to the collections of information required in §§ 301.7705-2T(e) and (f), the Treasury Department and the IRS have reached the following reporting burden estimates for CPEOs:

Estimated number of recordkeepers: 275.

Estimated average annual burden hours per recordkeeper: 60 hours.

Estimated total annual recordkeeping burden: 16,500 hours.

Estimated frequency of collections of such information: Quarterly.

An agency may not conduct or sponsor, and a person is not required to respond to, a collection of information unless it displays a valid control number assigned by the Office of Management and Budget.

Books or records relating to a collection of information must be retained as long as their contents may become material in the administration of any internal revenue law. Generally, tax returns and return information are confidential, as required by 26 U.S.C. 6103.

Background

The Stephen Beck, Jr., Achieving a Better Life Experience Act of 2014 (the ABLE Act), enacted on December 19, 2014, as part of the Tax Increase Prevention Act of 2014 (Pub. L. 113-295), added new sections 3511 and 7705 to the Code relating to the federal employment tax obligations and certification requirements of a "certified professional employer organization" (CPEO). Additionally, the ABLE Act made conforming amendments to sections 3302, 3303(a), 6053(c), 6652, and 7528 relating to obligations, requirements, and penalties applicable to a CPEO. This notice of proposed rulemaking contains proposed regulations under sections 3511 and 7705 regarding federal employment tax obligations of a CPEO and related definitions. This document also proposes to adopt, by cross-reference, temporary regulations under section 7705 published in the Rules and Regulations portion of this issue of the **Federal Register**, which relate to the requirements for applying for, receiving, and maintaining certification as a CPEO. The preamble to the temporary regulations explains those regulations and the statutory provisions they are designed to implement.

Federal Employment Taxes

When an individual performs services for another person, an employer-employee relationship may exist. Generally, the Code provides that the existence of an employer-employee relationship is determined by applying the usual common law rules to the particular facts and circumstances of each case. *See* section 3121(d)(2). Under the common law rules, an employment relationship exists when the person for whom the services are performed has the right to control and direct the individual who performs the services, not only as to the result to be accomplished by the work but also as to the details and means by which that result is accomplished. *See* §§ 31.3121(d)-1(c), 31.3231(b)-1(a)(2), 31.3306(i)-1(b), and 31.3401(c)-1(b).

Employers generally are required to deduct and withhold federal income tax and Federal Insurance Contributions Act (FICA) taxes from wages paid to their employees under sections 3402(a) and 3102(a) and are separately liable for the employer's share of FICA taxes under section 3111. FICA taxes consist of the Old-Age, Survivors, and Disability Insurance (OASDI) tax and the Hospital Insurance (HI) tax (which includes the additional tax under section 3101(b)(2), known commonly as the Additional Medicare Tax (AdMT)). The amount of wages for OASDI purposes is limited to wages paid by an employer to an employee during a calendar year not exceeding the contribution and benefit base (as determined under section 230 of the Social Security Act), which is an annually adjusted amount. Thus, there is a ceiling on the wages subject to OASDI. Accordingly, once an employee's wages from an employer reach this annually adjusted amount, the OASDI portion of the FICA tax does not apply for the remainder of the calendar year.

In contrast, there is no ceiling on wages subject to the HI tax. *See* sections 3101, 3111, and 3121(a). However, under section 3102(f)(1), employers are only required to withhold AdMT from an employee's wages to the extent that those wages exceed $200,000 in a calendar year. Thus, there is a withholding threshold of $200,000 annually on wages subject to AdMT withholding.

Instead of FICA taxes, railroad employers are required to deduct and withhold Railroad Retirement Tax Act (RRTA) taxes from their employees' compensation and are separately liable for the employer's share of RRTA taxes. RRTA taxes consist of tier 1 taxes and tier 2 taxes. Tier 1 taxes parallel the OASDI and HI taxes applicable to other employers and employees. Tier 2 taxes consist of employer and employee taxes on railroad compensation up to the tier 2 contribution base for the calendar year. *See* sections 3201(a), 3211(a), and 3221(a).

Under the Federal Unemployment Tax Act (FUTA), taxes are imposed on the first $7,000 of wages paid to a covered employee by an employer during the calendar year. *See* section 3301(2). An employer may take a credit against its FUTA tax liability for its contributions to a state unemployment fund and, in certain cases, an additional credit for contributions that would have been required if the employer had been subject to a higher contribution rate under state law. *See* section 3301 *et seq.*

All taxes imposed under subtitle C of the Code, including income tax withholding, FICA, RRTA, and FUTA taxes, are collectively referred to in this preamble as "federal employment taxes." The applicable contribution bases for FICA, RRTA, and FUTA taxes, collectively, are referred to in this preamble as the "annual wage base." Sections 31.3102-1(d), 31.3202-1(e), and 31.3403-1 establish that the employer is the person liable for the withholding and payment of federal employment taxes, whether or not amounts are actually withheld.

An employer must file an employment tax return reporting federal employment taxes for each employment tax return period. Generally, an employer files Form 941, "Employer's QUARTERLY Federal Tax Return," to report wages the employer paid during a quarter of a calendar year that are subject to federal income tax withholding and FICA taxes. Wages an employer pays that are subject to FUTA tax are reported annually on Form 940, "Employer's Annual Federal Unemployment Tax (FUTA) Return." Employers that pay compensation subject to the RRTA tax file Form CT-1, "Employer's Annual Railroad Retirement Tax Return," as well as Form 941, to report federal income tax withholding. All employers that pay wages or compensation subject to federal income tax withholding, FICA tax, or RRTA tax must file Forms W-2, "Wage and Tax Statement," and Form W-3, "Transmittal of Wage and Tax Statements," with the Social Security Administration (SSA) and furnish a Form W-2 to each employee.

Federal employment taxes generally apply to all remuneration for services performed by an employee for an employer. However, specific exceptions apply to particular types of remuneration and particular types of services, which may depend on the type of employer for whom services are performed or the nature of those services. For example, remuneration paid by an organization exempt from federal income tax under section 501(a) to an employee who is paid less than $100 in a calendar year is excluded from the definition of "wages" for FICA purposes, and services performed in the employ of certain tax-exempt organizations are excluded from the definition of "employment" for FUTA purposes. In addition, various definitions and special rules, relevant for purposes of computing the applicable annual wage base, apply to certain types of employers, employees, and employment relationships.

Furthermore, as noted earlier in this preamble, remuneration paid by an employer to an employee within any calendar year is excepted from the OASDI portion of FICA, the equivalent portion of tier 1 RRTA, and FUTA taxes to the extent it exceeds the applicable annual wage base. However, the annual wage base applies on an employer-by-employer basis, and, thus, only remuneration received during any calendar year by an employee from the same employer is considered in applying the annual wage bases for purposes of the remuneration paid by that employer. *See* §§31.3121(a)(1)-1(a)(3) and 31.3306(b)(1)-1(a)(3) for FICA and FUTA taxes, respectively. Similarly, the AdMT withholding threshold applies only with regard to remuneration received during any calendar year by an employee from the same employer.

Accordingly, if during a calendar year the employee receives remuneration from more than one employer, generally, both the annual wage base and withholding threshold apply separately to the remuneration that the employee received during that calendar year from each employer.[1] Consequently, if an employee works for multiple employers during a year, a separate annual wage base and withholding threshold generally apply in determining each employer's tax liability with respect to remuneration paid to the employee. However, if during any calendar year an employer (the "successor employer") acquires substantially all of the property used in a trade or business of another employer (the "predecessor employer") then, for purposes of the annual wage base, any remunera-

[1] In such case, remuneration received in any calendar year from each employer up to the amount of the applicable annual wage base constitutes wages and is subject to the OASDI portion of FICA tax and the equivalent portion of tier 1 RRTA tax. However, under section 6413(c), the employee may be entitled to a special credit or refund of a portion of the employee tax deducted from wages received during the calendar year. Thus, an employee is subject to OASDI or RRTA tax only with respect to remuneration up to the applicable wage base for a year, regardless of whether the employee works for only one employer or for more than one employer during the year. *See* §31.6413(c)-1.

tion with respect to employment paid to such individual by the predecessor employer during such calendar year and prior to the acquisition is considered as having been paid by the successor employer. *See* sections 3121(a)(1), 3231(e)(2)(C), and 3306(b)(1).

If a person (payor) pays wages or compensation to employees who are employed by one or more employers, the Secretary is authorized, in accordance with regulations prescribed by the Secretary under section 3504, to designate such payor to perform acts required of employers under the Code. Section 3504 further provides that, except as otherwise prescribed by the Secretary, all provisions of law (including penalties) applicable with respect to an employer are applicable to the payor so designated, but each employer for whom the payor acts remains subject to the provisions of the law (including penalties) applicable to the employer. Consequently, both an employer and the payor designated in accordance with regulations under section 3504 are liable for the federal employment taxes on wages or compensation paid by the payor. Section 31.3504-2 of the regulations provides circumstances under which a payor is designated to perform the acts required of an employer and is liable for federal employment taxes with respect to wages or compensation paid by the payor to individuals performing services for the payor's client pursuant to a service agreement between the payor and the client, as defined therein. Consistent with section 3504, §31.3504-2 provides that the client remains liable for the federal employment taxes on wages paid by the payor to employees of the client.

In addition to an employer's federal employment tax obligations, various tax credits are available to employers based on the amount of wages and federal employment taxes paid by the employer. For example, the amount of an employer's work opportunity credit is based on a portion of FUTA wages paid by the employer to employees who are members of certain specified groups. *See* section 51(c).

Certain reporting requirements relating to tips apply to large food or beverage establishments. In the case of such an establishment, an employer is generally required to report certain information relating to receipts and tips to the IRS each calendar year. Additionally, the employer must also provide employees with written statements showing certain information for each calendar year, including the amount of tips allocated to the employee for the year. *See* section 6053(c).

Professional Employer Organizations

A professional employer organization (PEO), sometimes referred to as an employee leasing company, is an entity that enters into an agreement with a client to perform some or all of the federal employment tax withholding, reporting, and payment functions related to workers performing services for the client. A PEO also may manage human resources, employee benefits, workers compensation claims, and unemployment insurance claims for the client. The terms of a PEO arrangement typically provide that the PEO is the employer or "co-employer" of the workers and is responsible for paying the workers and for the related federal employment tax compliance. Under this arrangement, the PEO remits the wages to the workers and typically files, under its name and EIN, Forms 940 and 941 and, where applicable, Form CT-1 to report the wages or compensation and employment taxes it paid. Additionally, the PEO files Forms W-2 and Form W-3 with the SSA and furnishes a Form W-2 to each worker.

The client typically pays the PEO a fee based on payroll costs plus an additional amount. In most cases, however, the workers working in the client's business are the employees of the client under the common law rules, and the client is legally responsible for federal employment tax compliance, even though the PEO may also be legally responsible for federal employment tax compliance under §31.3504-2.

The ABLE Act of 2014

The ABLE Act requires the IRS to establish a voluntary certification program for PEOs. Section 7705(a) defines a CPEO as a person that applies to the Secretary of the Treasury (Secretary) to be treated as a CPEO for purposes of section 3511 and has been certified by the Secretary as meeting certain requirements. Those requirements are described in the temporary regulations under section 7705 published in the Rules and Regulations portion of this issue of the **Federal Register**.

Under sections 3511(a)(1) and (c)(1), for purposes of federal employment taxes and other obligations under the federal employment tax rules, a CPEO is generally treated as the employer of any individual performing services for a customer of the CPEO and covered by a contract described in section 7705(e)(2) between the CPEO and the customer (CPEO contract), but only with respect to remuneration remitted to the individual by the CPEO. A contract meets the requirements of section 7705(e)(2) with respect to an individual performing services for the customer and, therefore, is a CPEO contract if the contract is in writing and provides that the CPEO will assume responsibility, without regard to the receipt or adequacy of payment from the customer, for: (1) payment of wages to the individual; (2) reporting, withholding, and payment of any federal employment taxes with respect to the individual's wages; and (3) any employee benefits that the contract may require the CPEO to provide to the individual. The CPEO must also assume responsibility in a CPEO contract for recruiting, hiring, and firing the individual (in addition to the customer's responsibility in that regard) and for maintaining employee records relating to the individual. Finally, the CPEO must agree in a CPEO contract to be treated as a CPEO for federal employment tax purposes with respect to the individual.

With respect to an individual covered by a CPEO contract who performs services for a customer at a work site meeting the requirements of section 7705(e)(3) (a work site employee), section 3511(a)(1) specifies that no person other than the CPEO is treated as the employer for federal employment tax purposes with respect to remuneration remitted by the CPEO to such individual. A work site meets the requirements of section 7705(e)(3) with respect to an individual if at least 85 percent of the individuals performing services for the customer at the work site where the individual performs services are subject to one or more CPEO contracts with the CPEO. For this purpose, individuals who are excluded employees within the meaning of section 414(q)(5) (such as newly hired or part-time employees) are not taken into account.

Sections 3511(a)(2) and (c)(2) provide that the exceptions, exclusions, definitions, and other rules that are based on type of employer and that would apply if the CPEO were not treated as the employer under sections 3511(a)(1) or (c)(1) of the provision continue to apply. Thus, for example, if services performed in the employ of a customer that is a tax-exempt organization would be excluded from employment for FUTA purposes, the fact that a CPEO is treated as the employer for federal employment tax purposes does not affect the application of the exclusion.

On entering into a CPEO contract with a customer with respect to a work site employee, section 3511(b) provides that a CPEO is treated as a successor employer and the customer is treated as a predecessor employer during the term of the CPEO contract. On termination of a CPEO contract with respect to a work site employee, the customer is treated as a successor employer and the CPEO is treated as a predecessor employer.

For purposes of various tax credits enumerated in section 3511(d) under which the amount of the credit is determined by reference to the amount of federal employment taxes or the amount of wages subject to federal employment taxes, the credit with respect to a work site employee performing services for a customer applies to the customer, not to the CPEO. Consequently, in determining the amount of the credit, the customer, and not the CPEO, is to take into account federal employment taxes and wages paid by the CPEO with respect to the work site employee and for which the CPEO receives payment from the customer. The CPEO is required to furnish the customer and the Secretary with any information necessary for the customer to claim the credit.

The CPEO provisions do not apply in the case of a customer which bears a relationship to a CPEO described in section 267(b) (relating to transactions between related taxpayers) or section 707(b) (relating to transactions between a partner and partnership). In the application of such sections, rules based on more than 50 percent ownership are applied by substituting 10 percent for 50 percent. *See* section 3511(e).

A CPEO has no federal employment tax liability under section 3511(a) or (c) with respect to remuneration paid by the CPEO to an individual that constitutes net earnings from self-employment to the individual. Specifically, section 3511(f) provides that an individual with net earnings from self-employment derived from a CPEO customer's trade or business, including a partner of a customer that is a partnership, is not a work site employee for federal employment tax purposes with respect to remuneration paid by a CPEO. In addition, section 3511(c) provides that, for purposes of its federal employment tax liability, a CPEO is not treated as the employer of any individual covered by a CPEO contract and described in section 3511(f) with respect to remuneration paid by the CPEO to the individual. Together, these two provisions relieve the CPEO of any federal employment tax liability under section 3511(a) or (c) with respect to such self-employed individuals.

Under section 3511(g), the Secretary is directed to develop such reporting and recordkeeping rules, regulations, and procedures as the Secretary determines necessary or appropriate to ensure compliance with the applicable federal employment tax provisions by CPEOs. Such rules are to address: (1) notification of the Secretary in the case of the commencement or termination of a service contract with a customer and the EIN of the customer; (2) information the Secretary determines is necessary for the customer to claim specified credits and the manner in which the information is to be provided; and (3) other information the Secretary determines is essential to promote compliance with respect to specified credits and FUTA credits under section 3302. Such rules are to be designed in a manner that streamlines, to the extent possible, the application of the requirements of sections 3511 and 7705, the exchange of information between a CPEO and its customers, and the reporting and recordkeeping obligations of the CPEO. Similarly, under section 3511(h), the Secretary is directed to prescribe such regulations as may be necessary or appropriate to carry out the purposes of section 3511.

In addition to adding new sections 3511 and 7705 to the Code, the ABLE Act made conforming amendments to sections 3302, 3303(a), 6053(c), 6652, and 7528 relating to obligations, requirements, and penalties applicable to a CPEO. If a CPEO, or a customer of a CPEO, makes a contribution to a state's unemployment fund with respect to wages paid to a work site employee, the CPEO is eligible for the credits available under section 3302 with respect to such contribution. See section 3302(h). Similarly, under section 3303(a)(4), a CPEO is allowed an additional credit under section 3302(b) with respect to any reduced rate of contributions permitted by a state law if the Secretary of Labor finds that under such law the CPEO is permitted to collect and remit contributions during the taxable year to the state unemployment fund with respect to a work site employee. The Treasury Department and the IRS recognize that section 3302(h) and section 3303(a)(4) apply exclusively with respect to wages paid to work site employees and request comments on the application of the respective credits with respect to wages paid to individuals covered by a CPEO contract who are not work site employees.

For purposes of reporting requirements relating to large food or beverage establishments, section 6053(c)(8) provides that, if a CPEO is treated as the employer of a work site employee under section 3511, the customer for whom the work site employee performs services is the employer for purposes of the applicable reporting requirements. However, the CPEO is required to furnish the customer and the Secretary with any information the Secretary prescribes as necessary to complete the required reporting.

Section 6652 provides for certain penalties for failure to file certain information returns, registration statements, and similar reports. The ABLE Act provided a new penalty in section 6652(n) specifically for failures to timely make a complete report required under sections 3511, 6053(c)(8), or 7705. In the case of such a failure, section 6652(n) imposes a penalty to be paid (on notice and demand by the Secretary and in the same manner as tax) by the CPEO in an amount equal to $50 for each report with respect to which there was such a failure. In the case of any failure due to negligence or intentional disregard, an amount equal to $100 for each report shall be paid.

Finally, section 7528(b)(4) provides that the fee charged in connection with the CPEO program shall be an annual fee not to exceed $1,000 per year per applicant.

Explanation of Provisions

1. *Applicable Definitions*

Section 7705 provides numerous statutory definitions related to the operation of section 3511. The proposed regulations incorporate these statutory definitions and clarify the following terms: customer, covered employee, work site employee, work site, and self-employed individual.

The proposed regulations define a "customer" as any person who enters into a CPEO contract (that is, a contract that meets the requirements of section 7705(e)(2), as described in the Background section of this preamble) with a CPEO. A provider of employment-related services that uses its own EIN for filing federal employment tax returns on behalf of its clients (or who used its own EIN immediately prior to entering into a CPEO contract with the CPEO) is specifically excluded from being a customer of a CPEO for purposes of section 3511, even if such provider has entered into a CPEO contract with the CPEO and would, but for this exclusion, be a customer of the CPEO.[2]

With respect to a customer, a "covered employee" is any individual (other than a self-employed individual, as described subsequently in this section of the preamble) who is covered by a CPEO contract with that customer. Consistent with section 7705(e), the proposed regulations define the term "work site employee" as a covered employee who performs services for a customer of a CPEO at a "work site" where at least 85 percent of the individuals performing services are subject to one or more CPEO contracts between the CPEO and the customer.

The proposed regulations generally define "work site" as a physical location at which an individual regularly performs services for a customer of a CPEO. If there is no such location, the work site is the location from which the customer assigns work to the individual. Thus, for example, the "work site" for a technician who performs assignments at various or changing locations is the location from which the technician is dispatched on each particular assignment. The work site may not be the individual's residence or a telework site unless the customer requires the individual to work at that site. In applying the term "work site," contiguous locations are treated as a single physical location and thus a single work site, and noncontiguous locations that are not reasonably proximate are treated as separate physical locations and thus separate work sites. However, the CPEO may treat noncontiguous locations that are reasonably proximate as a single physical location and thus a single work site. Any two work sites that are separated by 35 or more miles or that operate in a different industry or industries will not be treated as reasonably proximate. The Treasury Department and the IRS recognize that, under certain circumstances, the physical location at which an individual regularly performs services for a customer may be difficult to ascertain. Accordingly, comments are requested on the definition of work site as set forth in § 301.7705-1(b)(16) and any additional clarifications that would facilitate a determination of an individual's work site.

The proposed regulations also provide that a covered employee will be considered a work site employee for the entirety of a calendar quarter if he or she qualifies as a work site employee at any time during that quarter. Consequently, for any calendar quarter, a covered employee is either a work site employee or not a work site employee for the entire quarter and cannot be a work site employee for part of the quarter and a non-work site employee for the other part. On the other hand, a covered employee can be a work site employee for one or more calendar quarters of the year and a non-work site employee for other calendar quarters during the same year.

The proposed regulations provide that the determination of whether a covered employee is a work site employee is made separately with regard to each work site at which the covered employee regularly provides services and for each customer for which the covered employee is providing services. If, during the same calendar quarter, a covered employee regularly provides services at more than one work site for a single customer or more than one customer of a particular CPEO, that employee may be counted among the covered employees at each of those sites. In accordance with section 7705(e)(3), the proposed regulations provide that, in determining whether the 85 percent threshold is met, individuals who are excluded employees within the meaning of section 414(q)(5) (such as newly hired or part-time employees) are not taken into account as either covered employees

[2] References in this preamble and the proposed regulations to "customers" are limited to those persons who have entered into a CPEO contract and any rules applicable to a customer apply only with respect to that contract. In contrast, the term "client" is used more broadly to include persons receiving services from a provider of employment-related services (that may or may not be a CPEO) in instances when those services are not covered by a CPEO contract.

or individuals performing services, although such individuals may otherwise be covered employees and work site employees under the proposed regulations.

Finally, the proposed regulations also clarify that, in determining whether at least 85 percent of the individuals performing services are subject to one or more CPEO contracts between the CPEO and the customer, a self-employed individual who would be a covered employee but for the exclusion of self-employed individuals from the definition of covered employee (as described in this section of the preamble) is taken into account. For this and other purposes, the proposed regulations define a "self-employed individual" as an individual with net earnings from self-employment (as defined in section 1402(a) and without regard to the exceptions thereunder) derived from providing services covered by a CPEO contract, whether such net earnings are derived from providing services as a non-employee to a customer of a CPEO, from the individual's own trade or business as a sole proprietor customer of the CPEO, or as a partner in a partnership that is a customer of the CPEO, but only with regard to such net earnings. Accordingly, a self-employed individual, whether an independent contractor to the customer, a sole proprietor customer of the CPEO, or a partner in a partnership customer of the CPEO, is not considered to be a work site employee under section 3511(f) with regard to such earnings. However, in the limited case in which such an individual also is paid wages by a CPEO under a CPEO contract with the customer, the individual may nevertheless be a work site employee with respect to such wages. In all cases, the self-employed individual covered by a CPEO contract is appropriately counted in determining whether the 85 percent threshold is met.

2. *CPEO as Employer of Covered Employees*

Consistent with sections 3511(a)(1) and (c)(1), the proposed regulations provide that, for purposes of federal employment taxes and other obligations under the federal employment tax rules, a CPEO is treated as the employer of any covered employee (whether or not a work site employee), but only with respect to remuneration remitted to the individual by the CPEO. Consistent with section 3511(a)(1), the proposed regulations also provide that, with respect to a covered employee who is a work site employee, no person other than the CPEO will be treated as the employer of the work site employee for federal employment tax purposes with respect to remuneration remitted by the CPEO to such work site employee. In contrast, in the case of a covered employee who is not a work site employee, the proposed regulations provide that a person other than the CPEO is also treated as an employer of the employee for purposes of federal employment taxes imposed on remuneration remitted by the CPEO to the employee if such person is determined to be an employer of the employee without regard to the application of section 3511.

3. *Application of Federal Employment Tax Exemptions, Exclusions, Definitions, and Other Rules*

Under sections 3511(a)(2) and (c)(2), the exceptions, exclusions, definitions, and other rules that are based on the type of employer and that would apply if the CPEO were not treated as the employer under section 3511 continue to apply with respect to remuneration remitted by the CPEO. Thus, sections 3511(a)(2) and (c)(2) necessitate a determination of whether the CPEO, the customer, or a third party is the employer of a covered employee without regard to section 3511 for purposes of applying federal employment tax exemptions, exclusions, definitions, and other rules. Under the Code, the existence of an employer-employee relationship is generally determined by applying the common law rules to the particular facts and circumstances of each case. While the terms of a PEO arrangement typically provide that the PEO is the employer (or "co-employer") of the employees and is responsible for paying the employees and for the related federal employment tax compliance, in most instances the customer is actually the common law employer of such employees.

To avoid the need to make a common law employment determination for purposes of sections 3511(a)(2) and (c)(2), the proposed regulations provide that, for purposes of federal employment taxes, the exemptions, exclusions, definitions, and other rules that are based on type of employer and that apply to remuneration remitted by a CPEO to a covered employee are presumed to be based on the customer for whom the covered employee provides services. Additionally, if a covered employee provides services for more than one customer of the CPEO during the calendar year, the presumption applies separately to remuneration remitted by the CPEO to the covered employee with respect to each such customer. This presumption in the proposed regulations generally eliminates the need to make a determination as to which person is the employer (in the absence of section 3511) for purposes of the exceptions, exclusions, definitions, and other rules that are based on type of employer.

The proposed regulations also provide, however, that the presumption may be rebutted if the Commissioner determines, or the CPEO demonstrates by clear and convincing evidence, that the relationship between the customer and the covered employee is not the legal relationship of employer and employee. If the presumption is rebutted, the exemptions, exclusions, definitions, and other rules that are based on type of employer and which apply to remuneration remitted by a CPEO to a covered employee will be based on the person determined to be the employer of the covered employee without regard to the application of section 3511. The presumption can be rebutted by a demonstration that either the CPEO or a third party other than the customer is actually the employer for federal employment tax purposes and, therefore, the proper party on which to base the exceptions, exclusions, definitions, and other rules. In any event, the presumption does not create any inference with respect to who is an employer or employee or whether an employment relationship exists for other federal tax purposes or any other provision of law.

4. *Annual Wage Base and Withholding Threshold*

Under sections 3511(a) and (c), a CPEO is treated as the employer of any covered employee with respect to remuneration remitted to the individual by the CPEO. Thus, pursuant to section 3511, a CPEO has an employment relationship with the covered employee of a customer during the term of the CPEO contract with the customer that is separate from and independent of any employment relationship the customer may have with the employee. Consequently, during the calendar year in which a CPEO enters into a CPEO contract with a customer with respect to a covered employee, the covered employee may receive remuneration from more than one employer.

The proposed regulations provide that, except as provided with respect to successor and predecessor employers described in section 5 of this preamble, remuneration received by a covered employee from a CPEO for performing services for a customer of the CPEO within any calendar year is subject to a separate annual wage base and withholding threshold that are each computed with respect to such remuneration, without regard to any remuneration received by the covered employee during the calendar year from any other employer (including, if applicable, remuneration received directly from the customer receiving services from the employee). Thus, upon entering into a CPEO contract with a customer with respect to a covered employee, the CPEO starts a new annual wage base and withholding threshold with respect to the covered employee (unless the CPEO is treated as a successor or predecessor employer, as described in section 5 of this preamble). Additionally, any remuneration paid by the customer directly to a covered employee during the term of a CPEO contract is not paid by the CPEO and, consequently, is not included in the CPEO's annual wage base and withholding threshold with respect to the covered employee.

The proposed regulations also provide that if, during a calendar year, a covered employee receives remuneration from a CPEO for services performed by the covered employee for more than one customer of the CPEO, the annual wage base and withholding threshold do not apply to the aggregate remuneration received by the covered employee from the CPEO for services performed for all such customers. Rather, the annual wage base and withholding threshold apply separately to the remuneration received by the covered employee from the CPEO with respect to services performed for each customer. The maintenance of a separate annual wage base and withholding threshold with respect to each customer for which a covered employee performs services during a calendar year recognizes both the CPEO's status as an employer of the covered employee under section 3511 and the CPEO's responsibilities under a CPEO contract with respect to services performed by a covered employee for each individual customer. Additionally, a separate annual wage base and withholding threshold with respect to each customer for which a covered employee performs services is needed for purposes of applying some of the exemptions, exclusions, definitions, and other rules discussed in section 3 of this preamble and the treatment of some of the credits discussed in section 6 of this preamble. Thus, if a single employee receives remuneration under CPEO contracts with more than one customer, the CPEO must maintain a separate annual wage base and withholding threshold for the employee with respect to each customer.

5. *Successor Employer Status*

Consistent with section 3511(b), the proposed regulations also provide that, for purposes of computing the annual wage base, a CPEO and its customer are treated as: (1) a successor and predecessor employer, respectively, upon entering into a CPEO contract with respect to a work site employee who is performing services for the customer; and (2) a predecessor and successor employer, respectively, upon termination of the CPEO contract between the CPEO and the customer with respect to the work site employee. Consistent with the quarterly work site employee determination discussed in section 1 of this preamble, the determination of whether an employee is a work site employee for this purpose is made during the quarter in which the CPEO enters into (or terminates) the CPEO contract with respect to the employee. That is, an employee will be considered a work site employee for the entirety of a calendar quarter if he or she qualifies as a work site employee at any time during that quarter. Accordingly, a CPEO is a successor employer (or predecessor employer) with regard to any covered employee who is a work site employee at any point during the quarter in which the CPEO entered into (or terminated) the CPEO contract with respect to the employee. On the other hand, as also noted in section 1 of this preamble, a covered employee can be a work site employee for one or more calendar quarters of the year and a non-work site employee for other calendar quarters during the same year. Accordingly, the proposed regulations provide that a CPEO entering into a CPEO contract with a customer with respect to a covered employee who is not a work site employee at any time during that calendar quarter will not be treated as a successor employer regardless of whether, during the term of the CPEO contract, the covered employee subsequently becomes a work site employee. Similarly, a CPEO terminating a CPEO contract with a customer with respect to a covered employee who is not a work site employee at any time during that calendar quarter will not be treated as a predecessor employer regardless of whether, during the term of the CPEO contract, the covered employee had previously been a work site employee. The quarterly determination of work site employee status is utilized for purposes of the successor employer and predecessor employer determinations (as well as for other purposes under the proposed regulations) in order to have a consistent quarterly work site employee determination for all purposes and therefore assist with administrability.

6. *Treatment of Credits*

Section 3511(d) governs the treatment of various tax credits under which the amount of the credit is determined by reference to the amount of wages or federal employment taxes. Section 3511(d)(2) specifies these credits as the credits under section 41 (credit for increasing research activity), section 45A (Indian employment credit), section 45B (credit for portion of employer social security taxes paid with respect to employee cash tips), section 45C (clinical testing expenses for certain drugs for rare diseases or conditions), section 45R (employee health insurance expenses of small employers), section 51 (work opportunity credit), section 1396 (empowerment zone employment credit), and any other section as provided by the Secretary. Consistent with section 3511(d), the proposed regulations provide that any specified credit with respect to a work site employee performing services for a customer applies to the customer, not to the CPEO. Consequently, in determining the amount of the credit, the customer, and not the CPEO, takes into account wages and federal employment taxes paid by the CPEO with respect to the work site employee and for which the CPEO receives payment from the customer. As noted in the discussion of the annual wage base and withholding threshold in section 4 of this preamble, a CPEO must maintain a separate annual wage base and withholding threshold with respect to each customer for which a covered employee performs services during a calendar year. Consequently, with respect to a work site employee performing services for more than one customer of a CPEO during a calendar year, each customer for which the employee performs services takes into account wages and federal employment taxes paid by the CPEO only with respect to services performed by the work site employee for that customer in determining the treatment of credits by that customer. The proposed regulations also provide that, consistent with section 3511(d)(2)(H), the Commissioner may specify other credits subject to the treatment provided for under section 3511(d).

The proposed regulations do not specify any other credits, but the Treasury Department and the IRS request comments on whether other credits should be specified in these regulations or in other guidance. Additionally, the Treasury Department and the IRS recognize that the application of the specified tax credits to the customer under section 3511(d) applies exclusively with respect to work site employees. Accordingly, comments are also requested on the treatment of tax credits with respect to covered employees who are not work site employees.

7. *Special Rules Applicable to Related Customers, Self-Employed Individuals, and Other Circumstances*

Consistent with section 3511(e), the proposed regulations do not apply in the case of a customer that is related to the CPEO. For these purposes, the proposed regulations provide that a customer is related to a CPEO if that customer bears a relationship to a CPEO described in section 267(b) or section 707(b), except that "10 percent" will be substituted for "50 percent" wherever the latter term appears in those sections. For administrative purposes such as verifying correct CPEO employment tax reporting and determining whether successor employer rules apply, the IRS must know when a CPEO has entered into a CPEO contract with a customer. For this reason, the proposed regulations also exclude from section 3511 any customer that has commenced a service contract with a CPEO if the commencement of such service contract has not been reported to the IRS in accordance with the requirements described in § 31.3511-1(g)(3)(i) of the proposed regulations (discussed in section 8 of this preamble).

Consistent with section 3511(f), which provides that a self-employed individual is not a work site employee with respect to remuneration paid by a CPEO, and with section 3511(c), which provides that a CPEO is not treated as an employer of a self-employed individual, the proposed regulations provide that section 3511 does not apply to any self-employed individual. Nevertheless, as discussed in section 1 of this preamble, a self-employed individual may be counted as an employee covered by a CPEO contract for purposes of determining whether the 85 percent threshold for qualification of other covered employees as work site employees is met, as described in section 1 of this preamble.

Finally, the proposed regulations provide that section 3511 does not apply to any CPEO contract in which a CPEO enters while its certification has been suspended by the IRS or to a CPEO whose certification has been revoked or voluntarily terminated.

8. *Reporting and Recordkeeping Requirements*

Consistent with section 3511(g), the proposed regulations describe various recordkeeping and reporting requirements applicable to CPEOs that are designed to ensure compliance with the applicable federal employment tax provisions. Significantly, the proposed regulations provide that a CPEO that is treated as an employer of a covered employee pursuant to section 3511 must meet all reporting and recordkeeping requirements described in subtitle F of the Code that are applicable to employers in a manner consistent with such treatment. Additionally, a CPEO must file the returns required of all employers by subtitle F.

Moreover, a CPEO must file Forms 940 and 941, and all required accompanying schedules, on magnetic media unless the CPEO is provided a waiver by the Commissioner. The proposed regulations define magnetic media as electronic filing, as well as other media specifically permitted under the applicable regulations, revenue procedures, publications, forms, instructions, or other guidance.

a. *Reporting to the IRS by CPEOs*

Consistent with section 3511(g)(1), the proposed regulations provide that a CPEO must report information relating to the commencement or termination of any CPEO contract with a customer and the name and EIN of such customer.

The proposed regulations also provide that, with any Form 940 or Form 941 that a CPEO files, the CPEO must attach the applicable Schedule R (or any successor form) containing such information as the Commissioner may require about each of its customers under a CPEO contract and any clients under a service agreement described in § 31.3504-2(b)(2). As noted previously, a CPEO is also required to file Forms 940 and 941, including all required schedules, on magnetic media as a condition of certification.

So that the IRS can better reconcile the total amounts of wages and taxes reported on Forms 940 and 941 with the amounts of wages and taxes reported on the attached Schedule R, the proposed regulations provide that, in addition to providing information about each customer under a CPEO contract, a CPEO must also include such information as the Commissioner may require about each of its clients under a service agreement described in § 31.3504-2(b)(2) that is not a CPEO contract. To assist the IRS in verifying which entities reported on the Schedule R are customers under a CPEO contract, and which are clients under a service agreement described in § 31.3504-2(b)(2) that is not a CPEO contract, the proposed regulations require that a CPEO must also report information relating to the commencement or termination of a service agreement described in § 31.3504-2(b)(2) with a client, and the name and EIN of each such client.

In addition, the proposed regulations specify that a CPEO must provide periodic verification to the IRS that it continues to meet the CPEO certification requirements of the temporary regulations, as described in § 301.7705-2T(j), and report any change that materially affects the continuing accuracy of any agreement or information that was previously made or provided by the CPEO to the IRS, as described in § 301.7705-2T(k). The time and manner of this ongoing periodic verification will be specified in further guidance. Finally, the proposed regulations require that a CPEO provide: (1) a copy of its audited financial statements and an opinion of a certified public accountant regarding such financial statements, as described in § 301.7705-2T(e)(1); (2) the quarterly statements, assertions, and attestations regarding those assertions described in § 301.7705-2T(f); (3) any information that the IRS specifies in further guidance is necessary to promote compliance with respect to the credits described in § 31.3511-1(e)(2) of the proposed regulations and section 3302; and (4) any other information the Commissioner may prescribe in further guidance.

b. Reporting to customers by CPEOs

The proposed regulations require a CPEO to report certain information to its customers. Consistent with sections 3511(g)(2) and (3), a CPEO must provide each of its customers with the information necessary for the customer to claim the specified credits for which the amount of the credit is determined by reference to the amount of wages or federal employment taxes. The proposed regulations provide that a CPEO must also notify the customer if its CPEO contract has been transferred to another person (or if another person will report, withhold, or pay, under such other person's EIN, any applicable federal employment taxes with respect to the wages of any individuals covered by its CPEO contract), and provide the customer with the name and EIN of such other person. In addition, a CPEO must also notify each of its current customers of any suspension or revocation of the CPEO's certification. Finally, if any covered employees are not or cease to be work site employees with respect to a calendar quarter because they perform services at a location at which the 85 percent threshold described in section 1 of this preamble is no longer met, the proposed regulations provide that the CPEO must notify the customer that it may be liable for federal employment taxes imposed on remuneration remitted by the CPEO to such covered employees.

c. Information and agreements in any contract or agreement between a CPEO and client

The proposed regulations provide that any CPEO contract with a customer must: (1) contain the name and EIN of the CPEO reporting, withholding, and paying any applicable federal employment taxes with respect to any remuneration paid to individuals covered by the CPEO contract or service agreement; (2) require the CPEO to provide the customer with all of the notices and information described in section 8.b of this preamble; (3) describe the information that the CPEO will provide which is necessary for the customer to claim credits; and (4) specify that the CPEO must notify the customer that the customer may also be liable for federal employment taxes on remuneration remitted by the CPEO to covered employees if the sites at which they perform services do not (or ever cease to) meet the 85 percent threshold described in § 301.7705-1(b)(18). The proposed regulations also provide that if a service agreement described in § 31.3504-2(b)(2) is not a CPEO contract (and thus the employees covered by that service agreement are not covered employees), or if section 3511 does not otherwise apply to a contract as described in section 7 of this preamble, the service agreement or contract should be accompanied by a notification to the client explaining that the service agreement or contract is not covered by section 3511 and does not alter the client's liability for federal employment taxes on remuneration remitted by the CPEO to the individuals covered by the service agreement or contract.

9. *Penalties Applicable to CPEOs*

Although the ABLE Act provided the new penalty under section 6652(n) for failures to timely make required reports under sections 3511, 6053(c)(8), and 7705, the Treasury Department and the IRS note that many of the reports required under sections 3511 and 7705 are also subject to existing penalties and additions to tax. For example, because CPEOs are treated as employers of covered employees, CPEOs must meet the reporting requirements applicable to employers, including the filing of quarterly Forms 941. A CPEO that fails to file a Form 941 is subject to the addition to tax under section 6651(a)(1). Accordingly, the proposed regulations provide that a CPEO that is treated as an employer of a covered employee under section 3511 and that is required to meet the reporting requirements of an employer is subject to the same penalties and additions to tax as an employer with respect to such reporting requirements, including but not limited to penalties and additions to tax under sections 6651, 6656, 6672, 6721, 6722, and 6723.

The proposed regulations further clarify that the section 6652(n) penalty will apply to reports required under section 3511. The proposed regulations provide that a CPEO is subject to penalty under section 6652(n) for any failure to attach the applicable Schedule R (or any successor form) to Forms 940 or 941. The proposed regulations also provide that the CPEO is subject to penalty under section 6723 for any failure (including multiple failures within a single document) to include the EIN of each customer on Schedule R.

Finally, the proposed regulations clarify that, because the requirement to file Forms 940 and 941 on magnetic media is a condition of certification, any failure to file those forms, along with all required schedules, on magnetic media does not constitute a failure to file for the purposes of the section 6651(a)(1) addition to tax or failure to make a report for the purposes of the penalty under section 6652(n). The consequence of any failure to file these forms and associated schedules on magnetic media is the potential suspension or revocation of certification as a CPEO.

Proposed Effective/Applicability Dates

These regulations are proposed to be effective on and after the date these rules are published in the **Federal Register** as final or temporary regulations. Taxpayers may rely on these proposed regulations beginning July 1, 2016, and until final or temporary regulations are published.

Availability of IRS Documents

IRS revenue procedures, revenue rulings, notices, and other guidance cited in this document are published in the Internal Revenue Bulletin (or Cumulative Bulletin) and are available from the Superintendent of Documents, U.S. Government Printing Office, Washington, DC 20402, or by visiting the IRS Web site at *http://www.irs.gov*.

Special Analyses

Certain IRS regulations, including this one, are exempt from the requirements of Executive Order 12866, as supplemented and reaffirmed by Executive Order 13563. Therefore, a regulatory impact assessment is not required. It also has been determined that section 553(b) of the Administrative Procedure Act (5 U.S.C. chapter 5) does not apply to these regulations. It is hereby certified that the regulations will not have a significant economic impact on a substantial number of small entities. The collection of information is in §§31.3511-1(g) and 301.7705-2T. The certification is based on the following:

The Treasury Department and the IRS anticipate that the organizations that choose to apply for this voluntary certification program are likely to be entities that already have many of the systems and processes in place that are needed to comply with these regulations. For example, it is expected that CPEOs will generally maintain annual audited financial statements during the normal course of their business, rather than solely as a result of §301.7705-2T(e). Moreover, the requirements in §§301.7705-2T(e) and (f) for demonstrating positive working capital on an annual basis and for the quarterly assertions regarding employment tax compliance build upon requirements already reflected in many state PEO certification and registration laws, thereby minimizing the economic impact on those CPEO applicants already subject to the similar state law requirements.

In addition, many of the requirements in §§31.3511-1(g) and 301.7705-2T that impose a collection of information on CPEOs constitute one-time notifications to the IRS, customers, or clients or notifications that relate to events in the life cycle of a CPEO that are less predictable and may be infrequent - such as transfers of existing CPEO contracts, making material changes to agreements previously provided to the IRS, suspension or revocation of the CPEO's certification, or the reclassification of employees at a particular work site as non-work site employees - and thus will have a minimal economic impact on the CPEO. Moreover, the Treasury Department and the IRS expect that CPEOs participating in this voluntary program will be able to build upon pre-existing systems and processes through which they already communicate with their clients.

For these reasons, a Regulatory Flexibility Analysis under the Regulatory Flexibility Act (5 U.S.C. chapter 6) is not required. Pursuant to section 7805(f) of the Code, these regulations have been submitted to the Chief Counsel for Advocacy of the Small Business Administration for comment on their impact on small business.

Comments and Requests for Public Hearing

Before these proposed regulations are adopted as final regulations, consideration will be given to any comments that are submitted timely to the IRS as prescribed in this preamble under the "Addresses" heading. The Treasury Department and the IRS request comments on all aspects of the proposed rules. All comments will be available at www.regulations.gov or upon request. A public hearing will be scheduled if requested in writing by any person that timely submits written comments. If a public hearing is scheduled, notice of the date, time, and place for the hearing will be published in the **Federal Register**.

Drafting Information

The principal authors of these regulations are Melissa Duce, Andrew Holubeck, and Neil Shepherd of the Office of Associate Chief Counsel (Tax Exempt and Government Entities). However, other personnel from the Treasury Department and the IRS participated in the development of these regulations.

[¶49,700] **Proposed Amendments of Regulations (REG-126452-15)**, published in the Federal Register on June 8, 2016.

[Code Sec. 337]

Transfer of C corporation property to RIC or REIT: Corporate level tax on property transfers: Conversion property: Conversion transaction: Related Code Sec. 355 transaction.—Amendments of Reg. §1.337(d)-7, imposing corporate level tax on certain transactions in which property of a C corporation becomes the property of a REIT, are proposed. Proposed amendments of Reg. §1.337(d)-7(b)(2)(iii) and (g)(2)(iii) adopted by T.D. 9810 on January 17, 2017. Proposed amendments of Reg. §1.337(d)-7(c)(6), (f) and (g)(2)(ii) and (iv) withdrawn by REG-113943-17 on March 27, 2019.

AGENCY: Internal Revenue Service (IRS), Treasury.

ACTION: Notice of proposed rulemaking and notice of proposed rulemaking by cross-reference to temporary regulations.

SUMMARY: In the Rules and Regulations section of this issue of the **Federal Register**, the IRS is issuing temporary regulations effecting the repeal of the *General Utilities* doctrine by the Tax Reform Act of 1986. The text of those regulations also serves as part of the text of these proposed regulations. These proposed regulations would impose corporate level tax on certain transactions in which property of a C corporation becomes the property of a REIT. The proposed regulations also make an amendment not addressed in the temporary regulations. The proposed regulations affect RICs, REITs, C corporations the property of which becomes the property of a RIC or a REIT, and their shareholders.

DATES: Comments and requests for a public hearing must be received by August 8, 2016. ADDRESSES: Send submissions to: CC:PA:LPD:PR (REG-126452-15), room 5203, Internal Revenue Service, PO Box 7604, Ben Franklin Station, Washington, DC 20044. Submissions may be hand-delivered Monday through Friday between the hours of 8 a.m. and 4 p.m. to CC:PA:LPD:PR (REG-126452-15), Courier's Desk, Internal Revenue Service, 1111 Constitution Avenue, N.W., Washington, DC, 20224 or sent electronically via the Federal eRulemaking Portal at http://www.regulations.gov/ (IRS REG-126452-15).

FOR FURTHER INFORMATION CONTACT: Concerning the proposed regulations, Austin M. Diamond-Jones, (202) 317-5085; concerning the submission of comments or to request a public hearing, Regina Johnson, (202) 317-6901 (not toll-free numbers).

SUPPLEMENTARY INFORMATION:

Background and Explanation of Provisions

Temporary regulations in the Rules and Regulations section of this issue of the **Federal Register** amend the Income Tax Regulations (26 CFR part 1) relating to section 337(d). The temporary regulations impose corporate level tax on certain transactions in which property of a C corporation becomes the property of a REIT. The text of those regulations also serves as the text of these proposed regulations. The preamble to the temporary regulations explains the amendments.

The proposed regulations also include a modification to the definition of converted property that is not addressed in the temporary regulations. This modification treats as converted property any property the basis of which is determined, directly or indirectly, in whole or in part, by reference to the basis of property owned by a C corporation that becomes the property of a RIC or a REIT. The Treasury Department and the IRS believe that such property presents similar concerns with regard to the purposes of *General Utilities* repeal as other property of a C corporation that becomes the property of a RIC or REIT.

Special Analyses

Certain IRS regulations, including this one, are exempt from the requirements of Executive Order 12866, as supplemented and reaffirmed by Executive Order 13653. Therefore, a regulatory impact assessment is not required. Pursuant to the Regulatory Flexibility Act (5 U.S.C. chapter 6), it is hereby certified that these proposed regulations would not have a significant economic impact on a substantial number of small entities. This certification is based on the fact that these proposed regulations would primarily affect large corporations with a substantial number of shareholders. Therefore, a regulatory flexibility analysis is not required. Pursuant to section 7805(f) of the Code, this regulation has been submitted to the Chief Counsel for Advocacy of the Small Business Administration for comment on its impact on small business.

Comments and Requests for Public Hearing

Before these proposed regulations are adopted as final regulations, consideration will be given to any comments that are submitted timely to the IRS as prescribed in this preamble under the "Addresses" heading. The Treasury Department and the IRS request comments on all aspects of the proposed regulations. In particular, comments are requested regarding the scope of the terms predecessors and successors. In addition, although related section 355 distributions occurring before or after conversion transactions involving RICs do not present the same degree of concern regarding the purposes of *General Utilities* repeal, comments are requested as to whether the proposed regulations regarding related section 355 distributions should, like the rules of §1.337(d)-7 generally, apply to both conversion transactions involving RICs and conversion transactions involving REITs. All comments will be available at www.regulations.gov or upon request. A public hearing will be scheduled if requested in writing by any person that timely submits written comments. If a public hearing is scheduled, notice of the date, time, and place of the public hearing will be published in the **Federal Register**.

Drafting Information

The principal author of these regulations is Austin M. Diamond-Jones of the Office of Associate Chief Counsel (Corporate). Other personnel from the Treasury Department and the IRS participated in their development.

[¶49,701] Proposed Amendments of Regulations (REG-135702-15), published in the Federal Register on June 10, 2016.

[Code Secs. 162, 5000A, 6055, 6056, 9801, 9815, 9831 and 9833]

International tax: Health care coverage: Expatriates: Expatriate health coverage: Expatriate health plan issuers: Expatriate health plans.—Amendments of Reg. §§1.162-31, 1.5000A-2, 1.6055-2, 54.9801-2, 54.9831-1, and 301.6056-2 relating to the rules for expatriate health plans, expatriate health plan issuers, and qualified expatriates under the Expatriate Health Coverage Clarification Act of 2014 (EHCCA), are proposed. Amendments of Reg. §§54.9815-2711 and 54.9833-1 and portions of amendments of Reg. §§54.9801-2 and 54.9831-1 adopted by T.D. 9791 on October 28, 2016.

AGENCIES: Internal Revenue Service, Department of the Treasury; Employee Benefits Security Administration, Department of Labor; Centers for Medicare & Medicaid Services, Department of Health and Human Services.

ACTION: Proposed rule.

SUMMARY: This document contains proposed regulations on the rules for expatriate health plans, expatriate health plan issuers, and qualified expatriates under the Expatriate Health Coverage Clarification Act of 2014 (EHCCA). This document also includes proposed conforming amendments to certain regulations to implement the provisions of the EHCCA. Further, this document proposes standards for travel insurance and supplemental health insurance coverage to be considered excepted benefits and revisions to the definition of short-term, limited-duration insurance for purposes of the exclusion from the definition of individual health insurance coverage. These proposed regulations affect expatriates with health coverage under expatriate health plans and sponsors, issuers and administrators of expatriate health plans, individuals with and plan sponsors of travel insurance and supplemental health insurance coverage, and individuals with short-term, limited-duration insurance. In addition, this document proposes to amend a reference in the final regulations relating to prohibitions on lifetime and annual dollar limits and proposes to require that a notice be provided in connection with hospital indemnity and other fixed indemnity insurance in the group health insurance market for it to be considered excepted benefits.

DATES: Comments are due on or before August 9, 2016.

ADDRESSES: Comments, identified by "Expatriate Health Plans and other issues," may be submitted by one of the following methods:

Hand delivery or mail: Written comment submissions may be submitted to CC:PA:LPD:PR (REG-135702-15), Internal Revenue Service, PO Box 7604, Ben Franklin Station, Washington DC 20044. Comment submissions may be hand-delivered Monday through Friday between the hours of 8 a.m. and 4 p.m. to CC:PA:LPD:PR (REG-135702-15).

Federal eRulemaking Portal: http://www.regulations.gov. Follow the instructions for submitting comments.

Comments received will be posted without change to www.regulations.gov and available for public inspection. Any comment that is submitted will be shared with the Department of Labor (DOL) and Department of Health and Human Services (HHS). Warning: Do not include any personally identifiable information (such as name, address, or other contact information) or confidential business information that you do not want publicly disclosed. All comments may be posted on the Internet and can be retrieved by most Internet search engines. No deletions, modifications, or redactions will be made to the comments received, as they are public records. **FOR FURTHER INFORMATION CONTACT:** Concerning the proposed regulations, with respect to the treatment of expatriate health plan coverage as minimum essential coverage under section 5000A of the Internal Revenue Code, John Lovelace, at 202-317-7006; with respect to the provisions relating to the health insurance providers fee imposed by section 9010 of the Affordable Care Act, Rachel Smith, at 202-317-6855; with respect to the definition of expatriate health plans, expatriate health insurance issuers, and qualified expatriates, and the provisions relating to the market reforms (such as excepted benefits, and short-term, limited-duration coverage), R. Lisa Mojiri-Azad of the IRS Office of Chief Counsel, at 202-317-5500, Elizabeth Schumacher or Matthew Litton of the Department of Labor, at 202-693-8335, Jacob Ackerman of the Centers for Medicare & Medicaid Services, Department of Health and Human Services, at 301-492-4179. Concerning the submission of comments or to request a public hearing, Regina Johnson. (202) 317-6901 (not toll-free numbers).

Customer Service Information: Individuals interested in obtaining information from the Department of Labor concerning employment-based health coverage laws may call the EBSA Toll-Free Hotline, at

1-866-444-EBSA (3272) or visit the Department of Labor's website (http://www.dol.gov/ebsa). In addition, information from HHS on private health insurance for consumers can be found on the Centers for Medicare & Medicaid Services (CMS) website (www.cms.gov/cciio) and information on health reform can be found at www.HealthCare.gov.

SUPPLEMENTARY INFORMATION:

I. Background

This document contains proposed amendments to Department of the Treasury (Treasury Department) regulations at 26 CFR part 1 (Income taxes), 26 CFR part 46 (Excise taxes, Health care, Health insurance, Pensions, Reporting and recordkeeping requirements), 26 CFR part 54 (Pension and excise taxes), 26 CFR part 57 (Health insurance providers fee), and 26 CFR part 301 (relating to procedure and administration) to implement the rules for expatriate health plans, expatriate health plan issuers, and qualified expatriates under the Expatriate Health Coverage Clarification Act of 2014 (EHCCA), which was enacted as Division M of the Consolidated and Further Continuing Appropriations Act, 2015, Public Law 113-235 (128 Stat. 2130). This document also contains proposed amendments to DOL regulations at 29 CFR part 2590 and HHS regulations at 45 CFR part 147, which are substantively identical to the amendments to 26 CFR part 54.

The EHCCA generally provides that the requirements of the Affordable Care Act[1] (ACA) do not apply with respect to expatriate health plans, expatriate health insurance issuers for coverage under expatriate health plans, and employers in their capacity as plan sponsors of expatriate health plans, except that: (1) an expatriate health plan shall be treated as minimum essential coverage under section 5000A(f) of the Internal Revenue Code of 1986, as amended (the Code) and any other section of the Code that incorporates the definition of minimum essential coverage; (2) the employer shared responsibility provisions of section 4980H of the Code continue to apply; (3) the health care reporting provisions of sections 6055 and 6056 of the Code continue to apply but with certain modifications relating to the use of electronic media for required statements to enrollees; (4) the excise tax provisions of section 4980I of the Code continue to apply with respect to coverage of certain qualified expatriates who are assigned (rather than transferred) to work in the United States; and (5) the annual health insurance providers fee imposed by section 9010 of the ACA takes into account expatriate health insurance issuers for certain purposes for calendar years 2014 and 2015 only.

This document also contains proposed amendments to 26 CFR part 54, 29 CFR part 2590, and 45 CFR parts 146 and 148, which would specify conditions for travel insurance, supplemental health insurance coverage, and hospital indemnity and other fixed indemnity insurance to be considered excepted benefits. Excepted benefits are exempt from the requirements that generally apply under title XXVII of the Public Health Service Act (PHS Act), part 7 of the Employee Retirement Income Security Act of 1974, as amended (ERISA), and Chapter 100 of the Code. In addition, this document contains proposed amendments to (1) the definition of "short-term, limited-duration insurance," for purposes of the exclusion from the definition of "individual health insurance coverage" and (2) the definition of "essential health benefits," for purposes of the prohibition on annual and lifetime dollar limits in 26 CFR part 54, 29 CFR 2590, and 45 CFR parts 144 and 147.

This document clarifies an exemption set forth in 45 CFR 153.400(a)(1)(iii) related to the transitional reinsurance program. Section 1341 of the Affordable Care Act provides for the establishment of a transitional reinsurance program in each State to help pay the cost of treating high-cost enrollees in the individual market in the 2014 through 2016 benefit years. Section 1341(b)(3)(B) of the ACA and 45 CFR 153.400(a)(1) require contributing entities to make reinsurance contributions for major medical coverage that is considered to be part of a commercial book of business.

This document also contains proposed conforming amendments to 45 CFR part 158 that address the separate medical loss ratio (MLR) reporting requirements for expatriate policies that are not expatriate health plans under the EHCCA.

General Statutory Background and Enactment of ACA

The Health Insurance Portability and Accountability Act of 1996 (HIPAA), Public Law 104-191 (110 Stat. 1936), added title XXVII of the PHS Act, part 7 of ERISA, and Chapter 100 of the Code, which impose portability and nondiscrimination rules with respect to health coverage. These provisions of the PHS Act, ERISA, and the Code were later augmented by other consumer protection laws, including the Mental Health Parity Act of 1996, the Paul Wellstone and Pete Domenici Mental Health Parity and Addiction Equity Act of 2008, the Newborns' and Mothers' Health Protection Act, the Women's Health and Cancer Rights Act, the Genetic Information Nondiscrimination Act of 2008, the Children's Health Insurance Program Reauthorization Act of 2009, Michelle's Law, and the ACA.

The ACA reorganizes, amends, and adds to the provisions of part A of title XXVII of the PHS Act relating to group health plans and health insurance issuers in the group and individual markets. For this purpose, the term "group health plan" includes both insured and self-insured group health plans.[2] The ACA added section 715(a)(1) of ERISA and section 9815(a)(1) of the Code to incorporate

---

[1] The Patient Protection and Affordable Care Act, Pub. L. 111-148, was enacted on March 23, 2010, and the Health Care and Education Reconciliation Act, Pub. L. 111-152, was enacted on March 30, 2010. They are collectively known as the "Affordable Care Act."

[2] The term "group health plan" is used in title XXVII of the PHS Act, part 7 of ERISA, and Chapter 100 of the Code, and is distinct from the term "health plan," as used in other provisions of title I of the ACA. The term "health plan" does not include self-insured group health plans.

the provisions of part A of title XXVII of the PHS Act (generally, sections 2701 through 2728 of the PHS Act) into ERISA and the Code to make them applicable to group health plans and health insurance issuers providing health insurance coverage in connection with group health plans.

Expatriate Health Plans, Expatriate Health Plan Issuers and Qualified Expatriates

Prior to the enactment of the EHCCA, employers, issuers and covered individuals had expressed concerns about the application of the ACA market reform rules to expatriate health plans and whether coverage under expatriate health plans was minimum essential coverage for purposes of section 5000A of the Code. To address these concerns on an interim basis, on March 8, 2013, the Departments of Labor, HHS, and the Treasury (collectively, the Departments[3]) issued Affordable Care Act Implementation Frequently Asked Questions (FAQs) Part XIII, Q&A-1, providing relief from the ACA market reform requirements for certain expatriate group health insurance coverage.[4] For plan years ending on or before December 31, 2015, the FAQ provides that, with respect to expatriate health plans, the Departments will consider the requirements of subtitles A and C of title I of the ACA to be satisfied if the plan and issuer comply with the pre-ACA version of title XXVII of the PHS Act. For purposes of the relief, an expatriate health plan is an insured group health plan with respect to which enrollment is limited to primary insureds who reside outside of their home country for at least six months of the plan year and any covered dependents, and its associated group health insurance coverage. The FAQ also states that coverage provided under an expatriate group health plan is a form of minimum essential coverage under section 5000A of the Code. On January 9, 2014, the Departments issued Affordable Care Act Implementation FAQs Part XVIII, Q&A-6 and Q&A-7, which extended the relief of Affordable Care Act Implementation FAQs Part XIII, Q&A-1 for insured expatriate health plans to subtitle D of title I of the ACA and also provided that the relief from the requirements of subtitles A, C, and D of title I of the ACA would apply for plan years ending on or before December 31, 2016.[5]

Subsequently, the EHCCA was enacted on December 16, 2014. Section 3(a) of the EHCCA provides that the ACA generally does not apply to expatriate health plans, employers with respect to expatriate health plans but solely in their capacity as plan sponsors of these plans, and expatriate health insurance issuers with respect to coverage offered by such issuers under expatriate health plans. Under section 3(b) of the EHCCA, however, the ACA continues to apply to expatriate health plans with respect to the employer shared responsibility provisions of section 4980H of the Code, the reporting requirements of sections 6055 and 6056 of the Code, and the excise tax provisions of section 4980I of the Code. Section 3(b) of the EHCCA further provides that an expatriate health plan offered to primary enrollees described in sections 3(d)(3)(A) and (B) of the EHCCA shall be treated as an eligible employer sponsored plan under section 5000A(f)(2) of the Code, and that an expatriate health plan offered to primary enrollees described in section 3(d)(3)(C) of the EHCCA shall be treated as a plan in the individual market under section 5000A(f)(1)(C) of the Code. Section 3(c) of the EHCCA sets forth rules for expatriate health plans with respect to the annual health insurance providers fee imposed by section 9010 of the ACA.

Sections 4375 and 4376 of the Code impose the Patient-Centered Outcomes Research Trust Fund (PCORTF) fee only with respect to individuals residing in the United States. Final regulations regarding the PCORTF fee exempt any specified health insurance policy or applicable self-insured group health plan designed and issued specifically to cover employees who are working and residing outside the United States from the fee. The exclusion from the ACA for expatriate health plans, employers with respect to expatriate health plans but solely in their capacity as plan sponsors of these plans, and expatriate health insurance issuers with respect to coverage offered by such issuers under expatriate health plans would apply to the PCORTF fee to the extent an expatriate health plan was not already excluded from the fee.

Section 1341 of the ACA establishes a transitional reinsurance program to help stabilize premiums for non-grandfathered health insurance coverage in the individual health insurance market from 2014 through 2016. Section 1341(b)(3)(B) of the ACA and the implementing regulations at 45 CFR 153.400(a)(1) require health insurance issuers and certain self-insured group health plans ("contributing entities") to make reinsurance contributions for major medical coverage that is considered to be part of a commercial book of business. This language has been interpreted to exclude "expatriate health coverage."[6] As such, HHS regulation at 45 CFR 153.400(a)(1)(iii) provides that a contributing entity must make reinsurance contributions for lives covered by its self-insured group health plans and health insurance coverage, except to the extent that such plan or coverage is expatriate health coverage, as defined by the Secretary of HHS, or for the 2015 and 2016 benefit years only, is a self-insured group health plan with respect to which enrollment is limited to participants who reside

---

[3] Note, however, that in sections under headings listing only two of the three Departments, the term "Departments" generally refers only to the two Departments listed in the heading.

[4] Frequently Asked Questions about Affordable Care Act Implementation (Part XIII), available at http://www.dol.gov/ebsa/pdf/faq-aca13.pdf and http://www.cms.gov/CCIIO/Resources/Fact-Sheets-andFAQs/ACA_implementation_faq13.html.

[5] Frequently Asked Questions about Affordable Care Act Implementation (Part XVIII), available at https://www.dol.gov/ebsa/faqs/faq-aca18.html and https://www.cms.gov/CCIIO/Resources/Fact-Sheets-and-FAQs/aca_implementation_faqs18.html.

[6] See HHS Notice of Benefit and Payment Parameters for 2014 (78 FR 15410) (March 11, 2013) and HHS Notice of Benefit and Payment Parameters for 2016 (80 FR 10750) (February 27, 2015).

outside of their home country for at least six months of the plan year and any covered dependents of such participants. As noted in the March 8, 2013 Affordable Care Act Implementation FAQs Part XIII, Q&A-1, the FAQ definition of "expatriate health plan" was extended to the definition of "expatriate health coverage" under 45 CFR 153.400(a)(1)(iii).

Section 3(a) of the EHCCA provides that the ACA generally does not apply to expatriate health plans, employers with respect to expatriate health plans but solely in their capacity as plan sponsors of expatriate health plans, and expatriate health insurance issuers with respect to coverage offered by such issuers under expatriate health plans. Accordingly, under the EHCCA, the transitional reinsurance program contribution obligation under section 1341 of the ACA does not apply to expatriate health plans.

Section 5000A of the Code, as added by section 1501 of the ACA, provides that, for each month, taxpayers must have minimum essential coverage, qualify for a health coverage exemption, or make an individual shared responsibility payment when filing a federal income tax return. Section 5000A(f)(1)(B) of the Code provides that minimum essential coverage includes coverage under an eligible employer-sponsored plan. Section 5000A(f)(2) of the Code and 26 CFR 1.5000A-2(c) provide that an eligible employer-sponsored plan means, with respect to an employee, group health insurance coverage that is a governmental plan or any other plan or coverage offered in the small or large group market within a State, or a self-insured group health plan. Under section 5000A(f)(1)(C) of the Code, minimum essential coverage includes coverage under a health plan offered in the individual market within a State.

Section 3(b)(1)(A) of the EHCCA provides that an expatriate health plan that is offered to primary enrollees who are qualified expatriates described in sections 3(d)(3)(A) and 3(d)(3)(B) of the EHCCA is treated as an eligible employer-sponsored plan within the meaning of section 5000A(f)(2) of the Code. Section 3(b)(1)(B) of the EHCCA provides that, in the case of an expatriate health plan that is offered to primary enrollees who are qualified expatriates described in section 3(d)(3)(C) of the EHCCA, the coverage is treated as a plan in the individual market within the meaning of section 5000A(f)(1)(C) of the Code, for purposes of sections 36B, 5000A and 6055 of the Code.

Under section 6055 of the Code, as added by section 1502 of the ACA, providers of minimum essential coverage must file an information return with the Internal Revenue Service (IRS) and furnish a written statement to covered individuals reporting the months that an individual had minimum essential coverage. Under section 6056 of the Code, as added by section 1514 of the ACA, an applicable large employer (as defined in section 4980H(c)(2) of the Code and 26 CFR 54.4980H-1(a)(4) and 54.4980H-2) must file an information return with the IRS and furnish a written statement to its full-time employees reporting details regarding the minimum essential coverage, if any, offered by the employer. Under both sections 6055 and 6056 of the Code, reporting entities may satisfy the requirement to furnish statements to covered individuals and employees, respectively, by electronic means only if the individual or employee affirmatively consents to receiving the statements electronically.[7]

Under section 4980H of the Code, as added by section 1513 of the ACA, an applicable large employer that does not offer minimum essential coverage to its full-time employees (and their dependents) or offers minimum essential coverage that does not meet the standards for affordability and minimum value will owe an assessable payment if a full-time employee is certified as having enrolled in a qualified health plan on an Exchange with respect to which a premium tax credit is allowed with respect to the employee.

Section 3(b)(2) of the EHCCA provides that the reporting requirements of sections 6055 and 6056 of the Code and the provisions of section 4980H of the Code relating to the employer shared responsibility provisions for applicable large employers continue to apply with respect to expatriate health plans and qualified expatriates. Section 3(b)(2) of the EHCCA provides a special rule for the use of electronic media for statements required under sections 6055 and 6056 of the Code. Specifically, the required statements may be provided to a primary insured for coverage under an expatriate health plan using electronic media unless the primary insured has explicitly refused to consent to receive the statement electronically.

Section 4980I of the Code, as added by section 9001 of the ACA, imposes an excise tax if the aggregate cost of applicable employer-sponsored coverage provided to an employee exceeds a statutory dollar limit. Section 3(b)(2) of the EHCCA provides that section 4980I of the Code continues to apply to applicable employer-sponsored coverage (as defined in section 4980I(d)(1) of the Code) of a qualified expatriate (as described in section 3(d)(3)(A)(i) of the EHCCA) who is assigned (rather than transferred) to work in the United States.

Section 9010 of the ACA imposes a fee on covered entities engaged in the business of providing health insurance for United States health risks. Section 3(c)(1) of the EHCCA excludes expatriate health plans from the health insurance providers fee imposed by section 9010 of the ACA by providing that, for calendar years after 2015, a qualified expatriate (and any spouse, dependent, or any other individual enrolled in the plan) enrolled in an expatriate health plan is not considered a United States health risk. Section 3(c)(2) of the EHCCA provides a special rule solely for purposes of

---

[7] See 26 CFR 1.6055-2(a)(2)(i) and 301.6056-2(a)(2)(i).

determining the health insurance providers fee imposed by section 9010 of the ACA for the 2014 and 2015 fee years.

Section 162(m)(6) of the Code, as added by section 9014 of the ACA, in general, limits to $500,000 the allowable deduction for remuneration attributable to services performed by certain individuals for a covered health insurance provider. For taxable years beginning after December 31, 2012, section 162(m)(6)(C)(i) of the Code and 26 CFR 1.162-31(b)(4)(A) provide that a health insurance issuer is a covered health insurance provider if not less than 25 percent of the gross premiums that it receives from providing health insurance coverage during the taxable year are from minimum essential coverage. Section 3(a)(3) of the EHCCA provides that the provisions of the ACA (including section 162(m)(6) of the Code) do not apply to expatriate health insurance issuers with respect to coverage offered by such issuers under expatriate health plans.

Section 3(d)(2) of the EHCCA provides that an expatriate health plan means a group health plan, health insurance coverage offered in connection with a group health plan, or health insurance coverage offered to certain groups of similarly situated individuals, provided that the plan or coverage meets a number of specific requirements. Section 3(d)(2)(A) of the EHCCA provides that substantially all of the primary enrollees of an expatriate health plan must be qualified expatriates. For this purpose, primary enrollees do not include individuals who are not nationals of the United States and reside in the country of their citizenship. Section 3(d)(2)(B) of the EHCCA provides that substantially all of the benefits provided under a plan or coverage must be benefits that are not excepted benefits. Section 3(d)(2)(C) of the EHCCA provides that the plan or coverage must provide coverage for inpatient hospital services, outpatient facility services, physician services, and emergency services that are comparable to the emergency services coverage that was described in or offered under 5 U.S.C. 8903(1) for the 2009 plan year.[8] Also, coverage for these services must be provided in certain countries. For qualified expatriates described in section 3(d)(3)(A) of the EHCCA (category A) and qualified expatriates described in section 3(d)(3)(B) of the EHCCA (category B), coverage for these services must be provided in the country or countries where the individual is working, and such other country or countries as the Secretary of HHS, in consultation with the Secretary of the Treasury and the Secretary of Labor, may designate. For qualified expatriates who are members of a group of similarly situated individuals described in section 3(d)(3)(C) of the EHCCA (category C), the coverage must be provided in the country or countries that the Secretary of HHS, in consultation with the Secretary of the Treasury and the Secretary of Labor, may designate.

Section 3(d)(2)(D) of the EHCCA provides that a plan qualifies as an expatriate health plan under the EHCCA only if the plan sponsor reasonably believes that benefits under the plan satisfy a standard at least actuarially equivalent to the level provided for in section 36B(c)(2)(C)(ii) of the Code (that is, "minimum value"). Section 3(d)(2)(E) of the EHCCA provides that dependent coverage of children, if offered under the expatriate health plan, must continue to be available until the individual attains age 26 (unless the individual is the child of a child receiving dependent coverage). Section 3(d)(2)(G) of the EHCCA provides that an expatriate health plan must satisfy the provisions of title XXVII of the PHS Act, Chapter 100 of the Code, and part 7 of subtitle B of title I of ERISA, that would otherwise apply if the ACA had not been enacted. These provisions are sometimes referred to as the HIPAA portability and nondiscrimination requirements.

Section 3(d)(1) of the EHCCA provides that an expatriate health insurance issuer means a health insurance issuer that issues expatriate health plans. Section 3(d)(2)(F)(i) of the EHCCA provides that an expatriate health plan or coverage must be issued by an expatriate health plan issuer, or administered by an administrator, that together with any person in the issuer's or administrator's controlled group: (1) maintains network provider agreements that provide for direct claims payments (directly or through third-party contracts), with health care providers in eight or more countries; (2) maintains call centers (directly or through third-party contracts) in three or more countries and accepts calls in eight or more languages; (3) processes at least $ 1 million in claims in foreign currency equivalents each year; (4) makes global evacuation/repatriation coverage available; (5) maintains legal and compliance resources in three or more countries; and (6) has licenses to sell insurance in more than two countries. In addition, section 3(d)(2)(F)(ii) of the EHCCA provides that the plan or coverage must offer reimbursement for items or services under such plan or coverage in the local currency in eight or more countries.

Section 3(d)(3) of the EHCCA describes three categories of qualified expatriates. A category A qualified expatriate, under section 3(d)(3)(A) of the EHCCA, is an individual whose skills, qualifications, job duties, or expertise has caused the individual's employer to transfer or assign the individual to the United States for a specific and temporary purpose or assignment tied to the individual's employment and who the plan sponsor has reasonably determined requires access to health insurance and other related services and support in multiple countries, and is offered other multinational benefits on a periodic basis (such as tax equalization, compensation for cross-border moving expenses, or compensation to enable the expatriate to return to the expatriate's home country). A category B qualified expatriate, under section 3(d)(3)(B) of the EHCCA, is a primary insured who is working outside the United States for at least 180 days during a consecutive 12-month period that overlaps with the plan year. A category C qualified expatriate, under section 3(d)(3)(C) of the

---

[8] These are emergency services comparable to emergency services offered under a government-wide comprehensive health plan under the Federal Employees Health Benefits (FEHB) program prior to the enactment of the ACA.

EHCCA, is an individual who is a member of a group of similarly situated individuals that is formed for the purpose of traveling or relocating internationally in service of one or more of the purposes listed in section 501(c)(3) or (4) of the Code, or similarly situated organizations or groups, provided the group is not formed primarily for the sale of health insurance coverage and the Secretary of HHS, in consultation with the Secretary of the Treasury and the Secretary of Labor, determines the group requires access to health insurance and other related services and support in multiple countries.

Section 3(d)(4) of the EHCCA defines the United States as the 50 States, the District of Columbia, and Puerto Rico.

Section 3(f) of the EHCCA provides that, unless otherwise specified, the requirements of the EHCCA apply to expatriate health plans issued or renewed on or after July 1, 2015.

IRS Notice 2015-43

On July 20, 2015, the Treasury Department and the IRS issued Notice 2015-43 (2015-29 IRB 73) to provide interim guidance on the implementation of the EHCCA and the application of certain provisions of the ACA to expatriate health insurance issuers, expatriate health plans, and employers in their capacity as plan sponsors of expatriate health plans. The Departments of Labor and HHS reviewed and concurred with the interim guidance of Notice 2015-43. Comments were received in response to Notice 2015-43, and these comments have been considered in drafting these proposed regulations. The relevant portions of Notice 2015-43 and the related comments are discussed in the Overview of Proposed Regulations section of this preamble.[9]

IRS Notices 2015-29 and 2016-14

On March 30, 2015, the Treasury Department and the IRS issued Notice 2015-29 (2015-15 IRB 873) to provide guidance implementing the special rule of section 3(c)(2) of the EHCCA for fee years 2014 and 2015 with respect to the health insurance providers fee imposed by section 9010 of the ACA. Notice 2015-29 defines expatriate health plan by reference to the definition of expatriate policies in the MLR final rule issued by HHS[10] (MLR final rule definition) solely for the purpose of applying the special rule for fee years 2014 and 2015. The Treasury Department and the IRS determined that the MLR final rule definition of expatriate policies was sufficiently broad to cover potential expatriate health plans described in section 3(d)(2) of the EHCCA. The MLR final rule defines expatriate policies as predominantly group health insurance policies that provide coverage to employees, substantially all of whom are: (1) working outside their country of citizenship; (2) working outside their country of citizenship and outside the employer's country of domicile; or (3) non-U.S. citizens working in their home country.

On January 29, 2016, the Treasury Department and the IRS issued Notice 2016-14 (2016-7 IRB 315) to provide guidance implementing the definition of expatriate health plan for fee year 2016 with respect to the health insurance providers fee imposed by section 9010 of the ACA. Like Notice 2015-29, Notice 2016-14 provides that the definition of expatriate health plan will be the same as provided in the MLR final rule definition, solely for the purpose of the health insurance providers fee imposed by section 9010 of the ACA for fee year 2016.[11]

The Consolidated Appropriations Act, 2016, Public Law 114-113, Division P, Title II, § 201, Moratorium on Annual Fee on Health Insurance Providers (the Consolidated Appropriations Act), suspends collection of the health insurance providers fee for the 2017 calendar year. Thus, health insurance issuers are not required to pay the fee for 2017.

Excepted Benefits

Sections 2722 and 2763 of the PHS Act, section 732 of ERISA, and section 9831 of the Code provide that the respective requirements of title XXVII of the PHS Act, part 7 of ERISA, and Chapter 100 of the Code generally do not apply to the provision of certain types of benefits, known as "excepted benefits." These excepted benefits are described in section 2791(c) of the PHS Act, section 733(c) of ERISA, and section 9832(c) of the Code.

There are four statutorily enumerated categories of excepted benefits. One category, under section 2791(c)(1) of the PHS Act, section 733(c)(1) of ERISA, and section 9832(c)(1) of the Code, identifies benefits that are excepted in all circumstances, including automobile insurance, liability insurance, workers compensation, and accidental death and dismemberment coverage. Under section 2791(c)(1)(H) of the PHS Act (and the parallel provisions of ERISA and the Code), this category of excepted benefits also includes "[o]ther similar insurance coverage, specified in regulations, under which benefits for medical care are secondary or incidental to other insurance benefits."

The second category of excepted benefits is limited excepted benefits, which may include limited scope vision or dental benefits, and benefits for long-term care, nursing home care, home health care, or community-based care. Section 2791(c)(2)(C) of the PHS Act, section 733(c)(2)(C) of ERISA, and section 9832(c)(2)(C) of the Code authorize the Secretaries of HHS, Labor, and the Treasury (collectively, the Secretaries) to issue regulations establishing other, similar limited benefits as excepted benefits. The Secretaries exercised this authority previously with respect to certain health flexible spending arrangements.[12] To be an excepted benefit under this second category, the statute provides that these limited benefits must either: (1) be provided under a separate policy, certificate, or contract

---

[9] See 26 CFR 601.601(d)(2)(ii)(B).

[10] 45 CFR 158.120(d)(4).

[11] See 26 CFR 601.601(d)(2)(ii)(B).

[12] 26 CFR 54.9831-1(c)(3)(v), 29 CFR 2590.732(c)(3)(v), 45 CFR 146.145(b)(3)(v).

of insurance; or (2) otherwise not be an integral part of a group health plan, whether insured or self-insured.[13]

The third category of excepted benefits, referred to as "noncoordinated excepted benefits," includes both coverage for only a specified disease or illness (such as cancer-only policies), and hospital indemnity or other fixed indemnity insurance. These benefits are excepted under section 2722(c)(2) of the PHS Act, section 732(c)(2) of ERISA, and section 9831(c)(2) of the Code only if all of the following conditions are met: (1) the benefits are provided under a separate policy, certificate, or contract of insurance; (2) there is no coordination between the provision of such benefits and any exclusion of benefits under any group health plan maintained by the same plan sponsor; and (3) the benefits are paid with respect to any event without regard to whether benefits are provided under any group health plan maintained by the same plan sponsor. In the group market, the regulations further provide that to be hospital indemnity or other fixed indemnity insurance, the insurance must pay a fixed dollar amount per day (or per other time period) of hospitalization or illness (for example, $100/day) regardless of the amount of expenses incurred.[14]

Since the issuance of these regulations, the Departments have released FAQs to address various requests for clarification as to what types of coverage meet the conditions necessary to be hospital indemnity or other fixed indemnity insurance that are excepted benefits. Affordable Care Act Implementation FAQs Part XI, Q&A-7 clarified that group health insurance coverage in which benefits are provided in varying amounts based on the type of procedure or item, such as the type of surgery actually performed or prescription drug provided is not a hospital indemnity or other fixed indemnity insurance excepted benefit because it does not meet the condition that benefits be provided on a per day (or per other time period, such as per week) basis, regardless of the amount of expenses incurred.[15]

The fourth category, under section 2791(c)(4) of the PHS Act, section 733(c)(4) of ERISA, and section 9832(c)(4) of the Code, is supplemental excepted benefits. Benefits are supplemental excepted benefits only if they are provided under a separate policy, certificate, or contract of insurance and are Medicare supplemental health insurance (also known as Medigap), TRICARE supplemental programs, or "similar supplemental coverage provided to coverage under a group health plan." The phrase "similar supplemental coverage provided to coverage under a group health plan" is not defined in the statute or regulations. However, the Departments' regulations clarify that one requirement to be similar supplemental coverage is that the coverage "must be specifically designed to fill gaps in primary coverage, such as coinsurance or deductibles."[16]

In 2007 and 2008, the Departments issued guidance on the circumstances under which supplemental health insurance would be considered excepted benefits under section 2791(c)(4) of the PHS Act (and the parallel provisions of ERISA, and the Code).[17] The guidance identifies several factors the Departments will apply when evaluating whether supplemental health insurance will be considered to be "similar supplemental coverage provided to coverage under a group health plan." Specifically the Departments' guidance provides that supplemental health insurance will be considered an excepted benefit if it is provided through a policy, certificate, or contract of insurance separate from the primary coverage under the plan and meets all of the following requirements: (1) the supplemental policy, certificate, or contract of insurance is issued by an entity that does not provide the primary coverage under the plan; (2) the supplemental policy, certificate, or contract of insurance is specifically designed to fill gaps in primary coverage, such as coinsurance or deductibles, but does not include a policy, certificate, or contract of insurance that becomes secondary or supplemental only under a coordination of benefits provision; (3) the cost of the supplemental coverage is 15 percent or less of the cost of primary coverage (determined in the same manner as the applicable premium is calculated under a COBRA continuation provision); and (4) the supplemental coverage sold in the group health insurance market does not differentiate among individuals in eligibility, benefits, or premiums based upon any health factor of the individual (or any dependents of the individual).

On February 13, 2015, the Departments issued Affordable Care Act Implementation FAQs Part XXIII, providing additional guidance on the circumstances under which health insurance coverage that supplements group health plan coverage may be considered supplemental excepted benefits.[18] The FAQ states that the Departments intend to propose regulations clarifying the circumstances under which supplemental insurance products that do not fill in cost-sharing under the primary plan are considered to be specifically designed to fill gaps in primary coverage. Specifically, the FAQ provides that health insurance coverage that supplements group health coverage by providing

---

[13] PHS Act section 2722(c)(1), ERISA section 732(c)(1), Code section 9831(c)(1).

[14] 26 CFR 54.9831-1(c)(4)(i), 29 CFR 2590.732(c)(4)(i), 45 CFR 146.145(b)(4)(i).

[15] Frequently Asked Questions about Affordable Care Act Implementation (Part XI), available at http://www.dol.gov/ebsa/faqs/faq-aca11.html and http://www.cms.gov/CCIIO/Resources/Fact-Sheets-and-FAQs/aca_implementation_faqs11.html.

[16] 26 CFR 54.9831-1(c)(5)(i)(C), 29 CFR 2590.732(c)(5)(i)(C), and 45 CFR 146.145(b)(5)(i)(C)

[17] See EBSA Field Assistance Bulletin No. 2007-04 (available at http://www.dol.gov/ebsa/regs/fab2007-4.html); CMS Insurance Standards Bulletin 08-01 (available at http://www.cms.gov/CCIIO/Resources/Files/Downloads/hipaa_08_01_508.pdf); and IRS Notice 2008-23 (available at http://www.irs.gov/irb/2008-07_IRB/ar09.html).

[18] Frequently Asked Questions about Affordable Care Act Implementation (Part XXIII), available at http://www.dol.gov/ebsa/pdf/faq-aca23.pdf and https://www.cms.gov/CCIIO/Resources/Fact-Sheets-and-FAQs/Downloads/Supplmental-FAQ_2-13-15-final.pdf.

coverage of additional categories of benefits (as opposed to filling in cost-sharing gaps under the primary plan) would be considered to be designed to "fill in the gaps" of the primary coverage only if the benefits covered by the supplemental insurance product are not essential health benefits (EHB) in the State in which the product is being marketed. The FAQ further states that, until regulations are issued and effective, the Departments will not take enforcement action under certain conditions for failure to comply with the applicable insurance market reforms with respect to group or individual health insurance coverage that provides coverage of additional categories of benefits that are not EHBs in the applicable State. States were encouraged to exercise similar enforcement discretion.

Short-Term, Limited-Duration Insurance Coverage

Short-term limited duration insurance is a type of health insurance coverage that is designed to fill in temporary gaps in coverage when an individual is transitioning from one plan or coverage to another plan or coverage. Although short-term, limited-duration insurance is not an excepted benefit, it is similarly exempt from PHS Act requirements because it is not individual health insurance coverage. Section 2791(b)(5) of the PHS Act provides that the term "individual health insurance coverage" means health insurance coverage offered to individuals in the individual market, but does not include short-term, limited-duration insurance. The PHS Act does not define short-term, limited-duration insurance. Under existing regulations, short-term, limited-duration insurance means "health insurance coverage provided pursuant to a contract with an issuer that has an expiration date specified in the contract (taking into account any extensions that may be elected by the policyholder without the issuer's consent) that is less than 12 months after the original effective date of the contract."[19]

Prohibition on Lifetime and Annual Limits

Section 2711 of the PHS Act, as added by the ACA, generally prohibits group health plans and health insurance issuers offering group or individual health insurance coverage from imposing lifetime and annual dollar limits on EHB, as defined in section 1302(b) of the ACA. These prohibitions apply to both grandfathered and non-grandfathered health plans, except the annual limits prohibition does not apply to grandfathered individual health insurance coverage.

Under the ACA, self-insured group health plans, large group market health plans, and grandfathered health plans are not required to offer EHB, but they generally cannot place lifetime or annual dollar limits on covered services that are considered EHB. The Departments' regulations provide that, for plan years (in the individual market, policy years) beginning on or after January 1, 2017, a plan or issuer that is not required to provide EHB may select from among any of the 51 base-benchmark plans selected by a State or applied by default pursuant to 45 CFR 156.100, or one of the three FEHBP options specified at 45 CFR 156.100(a)(3), for purposes of complying with the lifetime and annual limits prohibition in section 2711 of the PHS Act.[20]

II. Overview of the Proposed Regulations

A. *Expatriate Health Plans*

In General

Section 3(a) of the EHCCA provides that the ACA generally does not apply to expatriate health plans, employers with respect to expatriate health plans but solely in their capacity as plan sponsors of expatriate health plans, and expatriate health insurance issuers with respect to coverage offered by such issuers under expatriate health plans. Consistent with this provision, the proposed regulations provide that the market reform provisions enacted or amended as part of the ACA, included in sections 2701 through 2728 of the PHS Act and incorporated into section 9815 of the Code and section 715 of ERISA, do not apply to an expatriate health plan, an employer, solely in its capacity as plan sponsor of an expatriate health plan, and an expatriate health insurance issuer with respect to coverage under an expatriate health plan. Similarly, section 162(m)(6) of the Code does not apply to an expatriate health insurance issuer with respect to premiums received for coverage under an expatriate health plan. In addition, under the EHCCA, the PCORTF fee under sections 4375 and 4376 of the Code and the transitional reinsurance program fee under section 1341 of the ACA do not apply to expatriate health plans. The EHCCA excludes expatriate health plans from the health insurance providers fee imposed by section 9010 except that the EHCCA provides a special rule solely for purposes of determining the fee for the 2014 and 2015 fee years. The EHCCA also designates certain coverage by an expatriate health plan as minimum essential coverage under section 5000A(f) of the Code, and provides special rules for the application of the reporting rules under sections 6055 and 6056 of the Code to expatriate health plans.

Definition of Expatriate Health Insurance Issuer

Consistent with sections 3(d)(1) and (d)(2)(F) of the EHCCA, the proposed regulations define "expatriate health insurance issuer" as a health insurance issuer (as defined under 26 CFR 54.9801-2, 29 CFR 2590.701-2 and 45 CFR 144.103) that issues expatriate health plans and satisfies certain requirements.[21] The requirements for the issuer to be an expatriate health insurance issuer include

---

[19] 26 CFR 54.9801-2, 29 CFR 2590.701-2, 45 CFR 144.103.

[20] 26 CFR 54.9815-2711(c), 29 CFR 2590.715-2711(c), 45 CFR 147.126(c).

[21] Section 3(d)(1) of the EHCCA provides that the term "expatriate health insurance issuer" means a health insurance issuer that issues expatriate health plans; section 3(d)(5)(A) of the EHCCA provides that the term "health insurance issuer" has the meaning given in section 2791 of the PHS Act. The definition of health insurance issuer in section 9832(b)(2) of the Code and section 733(b)(2) of ER-

that, in the course of its normal business operations, the issuer: (1) maintains network provider agreements that provide for direct claims payments with health care providers in eight or more countries; (2) maintains call centers in three or more countries, and accepts calls from customers in eight or more languages; (3) processed at least $1 million in claims in foreign currency equivalents during the preceding calendar year; (4) makes global evacuation/repatriation coverage available; (5) maintains legal and compliance resources in three or more countries; and (6) has licenses or other authority to sell insurance in more than two countries, including the United States. For purposes of meeting the $1 million threshold for claims processed in foreign currency equivalents, the proposed regulations provide that the dollar value of claims processed is determined using the Treasury Department's currency exchange rate in effect on the last day of the preceding calendar year.[22] Comments are requested regarding whether use of the calendar year as the basis for measuring the dollar amount of claims processed presents administrative challenges, and how the resulting challenges, if any, may be addressed. The proposed regulations provide that each of the applicable requirements may be satisfied by two or more entities (including one entity that is the health insurance issuer) that are members of the health insurance issuer's controlled group or through contracts between the expatriate health insurance issuer and third parties.

Definition of Expatriate Health Plan

Consistent with section 3(d)(2) of the EHCCA, the proposed regulations define "expatriate health plan" as a plan offered to qualified expatriates and that satisfies certain requirements. With respect to qualified expatriates in categories A or B, the plan must be a group health plan (whether or not insured). In contrast, with respect to qualified expatriates in category C, the plan must be health insurance coverage that is not a group health plan. In addition, consistent with section 3(d)(2)(A) of the EHCCA, the proposed regulations require that substantially all primary enrollees in the expatriate health plan must be qualified expatriates. The proposed regulations define a primary enrollee as the individual covered by the plan or policy whose eligibility for coverage is not due to that individual's status as the spouse, dependent, or other beneficiary of another covered individual. However, notwithstanding this definition, an individual is not a primary enrollee if the individual is not a national of the United States and the individual resides in his or her country of citizenship. Further, the proposed regulations provide that, for this purpose, a "national of the United States" has the meaning used in the Immigration and Nationality Act (8 U.S.C. 1101 et. seq.) and 8 CFR parts 301 to 392, including U.S. citizens. Thus, for example, an individual born in American Samoa is a national of the United States at birth for purposes of the EHCCA and the proposed regulations.

Comments in response to Notice 2015-43 requested clarification of the "substantially all" enrollment requirement, with one comment suggesting that 93 percent of the enrollees would be an appropriate threshold. In response to the request for clarification, the proposed regulations provide that a plan satisfies the "substantially all" enrollment requirement if, on the first day of the plan year, less than 5 percent of the primary enrollees (or less than 5 primary enrollees if greater) are not qualified expatriates (effectively a 95 percent threshold). Consistent with section 3(d)(2)(B) of the EHCCA, the proposed regulations further provide that substantially all of the benefits provided under an expatriate health plan must be benefits that are not excepted benefits as described in 26 CFR 54.9831-1(c), 29 CFR 2590.732(c), 45 CFR 146.145(b) and 148.220, as applicable. The Departments intend that the first day of the plan year approach, which has been used in other contexts, will be simple to administer.[23] Moreover, the 95% threshold has been used in certain other circumstances in applying a "substantially all" standard.[24] The Departments solicit comment on this regulatory approach and whether the current regulatory language is sufficient to protect against potential abuses, or whether any further anti-abuse provision is necessary.

Consistent with section 3(d)(2)(C) of the EHCCA, the proposed regulations also require that an expatriate health plan cover certain types of services. Specifically, an expatriate health plan must provide coverage for inpatient hospital services, outpatient facility services, physician services, and emergency services (comparable to emergency services coverage that was described in and offered under section 8903(1) of title 5, United States Code for plan year 2009). Coverage for such services must be available in certain countries depending on the type of qualified expatriates covered by the plan. The statute authorizes the Secretary of HHS, in consultation with the Secretary of the Treasury and Secretary of Labor, to designate other countries where coverage for such services must be made available to the qualified expatriate.

Consistent with section 3(d)(2)(D) of the EHCCA, the proposed regulations provide that in the case of an expatriate health plan, the plan sponsor must reasonably believe that benefits provided by the

(Footnote Continued)

ISA and underlying regulations are substantively identical to the definition under section 2791 of the PHS Act and its underlying regulations. As discussed in the section of this preamble entitled "Definition of Expatriate Health Plan" a health insurance issuer as defined in section 2791 of the PHS Act is limited to an entity licensed to engage in the business of insurance in a State and subject to State law that regulates insurance.

[22] The most recent Treasury Department currency exchange rate can be found at https://www.fiscal.treasury.gov/fsreports/rpt/treasRptRateExch/currentRates.htm.

[23] 26 CFR 54.9831-1(b), 29 CFR 2590.732(b), 45 CFR 146.145(b).

[24] See e.g., 26 CFR 1.460-6(d)(4)(i)(D)(1).

plan satisfy the minimum value requirements of section 36B(c)(2)(C)(ii) of the Code.[25] For this purpose, the proposed regulations provide that the plan sponsor is permitted to rely on the reasonable representations of the issuer or administrator regarding whether benefits offered by the group health plan or issuer satisfy the minimum value requirements unless the plan sponsor knows or has reason to know that the benefits fail to satisfy the minimum value requirements. Consistent with section 3(d)(2)(D) of the EHCCA, in the case of an expatriate health plan that provides dependent coverage of children, the proposed regulations provide that such coverage must be available until the individual attains age 26, unless the individual is the child of a child receiving dependent coverage. Additionally, consistent with section 3(d)(2)(F)(ii) of the EHCCA, the plan or coverage must offer reimbursements for items or services in the local currency in eight or more countries.

Consistent with section 3(d)(2)(F) of the EHCCA, the proposed regulations also provide that the policy or coverage under an expatriate health plan must be issued by an expatriate health insurance issuer or administered by an expatriate health plan administrator. With respect to qualified expatriates in categories A or B (generally, individuals whose travel or relocation is related to their employment with an employer), the coverage must be under a group health plan (whether insured or self-insured). With respect to qualified expatriates in category C (generally, groups of similarly situated individuals travelling for certain tax-exempt purposes), the coverage must be under a policy issued by an expatriate health insurance issuer.

Finally, consistent with section 3(d)(2)(G) of the EHCCA, the proposed regulations provide that an expatriate health plan must satisfy the provisions of Chapter 100 of the Code, part 7 of subtitle B of title I of ERISA and title XXVII of the PHS Act that would otherwise apply if the ACA had not been enacted. Among other requirements, those provisions limited the ability of a group health plan or group health insurance issuer to impose preexisting condition exclusions (which are now prohibited for grandfathered and non-grandfathered group health plans and health insurance coverage offered in connection with such plans, and non-grandfathered individual health insurance coverage under the ACA), including a requirement that the period of any preexisting condition exclusion be reduced by the length of any period of creditable coverage the individual had without a 63-day break in coverage.

Prior to the enactment of the ACA, HIPAA and underlying regulations also generally required that plans and issuers provide certificates of creditable coverage when an individual ceased to be covered by a plan or policy and upon request. Following the enactment of the ACA, the regulations under these provisions have eliminated the requirement for providing certificates of creditable coverage beginning December 31, 2014, because the requirement is generally no longer relevant to plans and participants as a result of the prohibition on preexisting condition exclusions. The Departments recognize that reimposing the requirement to provide certificates of creditable coverage on expatriate health plans would only be useful in situations in which an individual transferred from one expatriate health plan to another and that reimposing the requirement on all health plans would require certificates that would be unnecessary except in limited cases, such as for an individual who ceased coverage with a health plan or policy and began coverage under an expatriate health plan that imposed a preexisting condition exclusion. Because reimposing the requirement to provide certificates of creditable coverage would be inefficient and overly broad, and relevant in only limited circumstances, the proposed regulations do not require expatriate health plans to provide certificates of creditable coverage. However, expatriate health plans imposing a preexisting condition exclusion must still comply with certain limitations on preexisting condition exclusions that would otherwise apply if the ACA had not been enacted. Therefore, the proposed regulations require expatriate health plans to ensure that individuals who enroll in the expatriate health plan are provided an opportunity to demonstrate creditable coverage to offset any preexisting condition exclusion. For example, an email from the prior issuer (or former plan administrator or plan sponsor) providing information about past coverage could be sufficient confirmation of prior creditable coverage.

Comments in response to Notice 2015-43 requested clarification of the treatment of health coverage provided by a foreign government. Specifically, comments requested that health coverage provided by a foreign government be treated as minimum essential coverage under section 5000A of the Code, and that, for purposes of the employer shared responsibility provision of section 4980H of the Code, an offer of such coverage be treated as an offer of minimum essential coverage for certain foreign employees working in the United States. These issues are generally beyond the scope of these proposed regulations. Under the existing regulations under section 5000A(f)(1)(E) of the Code, there are procedures for health benefits coverage not otherwise designated under section 5000A(f)(1) of the Code as minimum essential coverage to be recognized by the Secretary of HHS, in coordination with the Secretary of the Treasury, as minimum essential coverage. The Secretary of HHS has provided that coverage under a group health plan provided through insurance regulated by a foreign government is minimum essential coverage for expatriates who meet specified conditions.[26] Further-

[25] For this purpose, generally "minimum value" takes into account the provision of "essential health benefits" as defined in section 1302(b)(1) of the Affordable Care Act.

[26] See CMS Insurance Standards Bulletin Series. CCIIO Sub-Regulatory Guidance: Process for Obtaining Recognition as Minimum Essential Coverage (Oct. 31, 2013), available at https://www.cms.gov/CCIIO/Resources/Regulations-and-Guidance/Downloads/mec-guidance-10-31-2013.pdf.

more, plan sponsors of health coverage that is not recognized as minimum essential coverage through statute, regulation, or guidance may submit an application to CMS for minimum essential coverage recognition pursuant to 45 CFR 156.604.[27] For a complete list of coverage recognized by CMS as minimum essential coverage under section 5000A(f)(1)(E) of the Code, see https://www.cms.gov/CCIIO/Programs-and-Initiatives/Health-Insurance-Market-Reforms/minimum-essential-coverage.html.

Comments also requested that policies sold by non-United States health insurance issuers be treated as minimum essential coverage under section 5000A of the Code, or as expatriate health plans. Section 3(d)(5)(A) of the EHCCA specifies that the terms "health insurance issuer" and "health insurance coverage" have the meanings given those terms by section 2791 of the PHS Act. Section 2791 of the PHS Act (and parallel provisions in section 9832(b) of the Code and section 733(b) of ERISA) define those terms by reference to an entity licensed to engage in the business of insurance in a State and subject to State law that regulates insurance. Under section 2791 of the PHS Act, the term "State" means each of the several States, the District of Columbia, Puerto Rico, the Virgin Islands, Guam, American Samoa, and the Northern Mariana Islands. Consistent with those provisions, these proposed regulations limit an expatriate health insurance issuer to a health insurance issuer within the meaning of those sections (and that meets the other requirements set forth in the proposed regulations). As such, a non-United States health insurance issuer does not qualify as an expatriate health insurance issuer within the meaning of the EHCCA, and coverage issued by a non-United States issuer that is not otherwise minimum essential coverage is not minimum essential coverage pursuant to the EHCCA.

Definition of Expatriate Health Plan Administrator

The proposed regulations define "expatriate health plan administrator," with respect to self-insured coverage, as an administrator of self-insured coverage that generally satisfies the same requirements as an "expatriate health insurance issuer."

Definition of Qualified Expatriate

Consistent with section 3(d)(3) of the EHCCA, the proposed regulations define "qualified expatriate" as one of three types of individuals. The first type of qualified expatriate, a category A expatriate, is an individual who has the skills, qualifications, job duties, or expertise that has caused the individual's employer to transfer or assign the individual to the United States for a specific and temporary purpose or assignment that is tied to the individual's employment with the employer. A category A expatriate may only be an individual who: (1) the plan sponsor has reasonably determined requires access to health coverage and other related services and support in multiple countries, (2) is offered other multinational benefits on a periodic basis (such as tax equalization, compensation for cross-border moving expenses, or compensation to enable the individual to return to the individual's home country), and (3) is not a national of the United States. The proposed regulations provide that an individual who is not expected to travel outside the United States at least one time per year during the coverage period would not reasonably "require access" to health coverage and other related services and support in multiple countries. Furthermore, under the proposed regulations, the offer of a one-time *de minimis* benefit would not meet the standard for the "periodic" offer of "other multinational benefits."

Section 3(d)(3)(B) of the EHCCA provides that a second type of qualified expatriate, a category B expatriate, is an individual who works outside the United States for a period of at least 180 days in a consecutive 12-month period that overlaps with the plan year. A comment requested that the regulations clarify that the 12-month period could either be within a single plan year, or across two consecutive plan years. Consistent with the statutory language, the proposed regulations provide that a category B expatriate is an individual who is a national of the United States and who works outside the United States for at least 180 days in a consecutive 12-month period that is within a single plan year, or across two consecutive plan years. Section 3(d)(2)(C)(ii) of the EHCCA requires an expatriate health plan provided to category B expatriates to cover certain specified services, such as inpatient and outpatient services, in the country in which the individual is "present in connection" with his employment. The Departments request comments on whether it would be helpful to provide further administrative clarification of this statutory language regarding the country or countries in which the services must be provided, and, if so, whether there are facts or circumstances that will present particular challenges in applying this rule.

Finally, consistent with section 3(d)(3)(C) of the EHCCA, the proposed regulations provide that a third type of qualified expatriate, a category C expatriate, is an individual who is a member of a group of similarly situated individuals that is formed for the purpose of traveling or relocating internationally in service of one or more of the purposes listed in section 501(c)(3) or (4) of the Code, or similarly situated organizations or groups, and meets certain other conditions.[28] A category C

---

[27] See CMS Insurance Standards Bulletin Series. CCIIO Sub-Regulatory Guidance: Process for Obtaining Recognition as Minimum Essential Coverage (Oct. 31, 2013), available at https://www.cms.gov/CCIIO/Resources/Regulations-and-Guidance/Downloads/mec-guidance-10-31-2013.pdf. See also CMS Insurance Standards Bulletin Series. CCIIO Sub-Regulatory Guidance: Minimum Essential Coverage

[28] Code section 501(c)(3) describes an organization formed for religious, charitable, scientific, public safety, literary, or educational purposes, or to foster national or international amateur sports competition, or for the prevention of cruelty to children or animals, and not for political candi-

expatriate does not include an individual in a group that is formed primarily for the sale or purchase of health insurance coverage. To qualify as this type of qualified expatriate, the Secretary of HHS, in consultation with the Secretary of the Treasury and the Secretary of Labor, must determine that the group requires access to health coverage and other related services and support in multiple countries. The proposed regulations clarify that a category C expatriate does not include an individual whose international travel or relocation is related to employment. Thus, an individual whose travel is employment-related may be a qualified expatriate only in category A or B. The proposed regulations also provide that, in the case of a group organized to travel or relocate outside the United States, the individual must be expected to travel or reside outside the United States for at least 180 days in a consecutive 12-month period that overlaps with the policy year (or in the case of a policy year that is less than 12 months, at least half of the policy year), and in the case of a group organized to travel or relocate within the United States, the individual must be expected to travel or reside in the United States for not more than 12 months. The proposed regulations provide that a group of category C expatriates must also meet the test for having associational ties under section 2791(d)(3)(B) through (F) of the PHS Act (42 U.S.C. 300gg-91(d)(3)(B) through (F)).

For purposes of section 3(d)(3)(C)(iii) of the EHCCA, the proposed regulations provide that the Secretary of HHS, in consultation with the Secretary of the Treasury and the Secretary of Labor, has determined that, in the case of a group of similarly situated individuals that meets all of the criteria in the proposed regulations, the group requires access to health coverage and other related services and support in multiple countries.

Comments in response to Notice 2015-43 requested that category C expatriates not be limited to individuals expected to travel or reside in the United States for 12 or fewer months. While the EHCCA does not include a time limit for category C expatriates, section 3(e) of the EHCCA provides that the Departments "may promulgate regulations necessary to carry out this Act, including such rules as may be necessary to prevent inappropriate expansion of the exclusions under the Act from applicable laws and regulations." In the group market, the EHCCA and the proposed regulations define a category A expatriate with respect to a "specific and temporary purpose or assignment" tied to the individual's employment in the United States. It is the view of HHS, in consultation with the Departments of Labor and the Treasury, that similar safeguards are necessary in the individual market to prevent inappropriate expansion of the exception for category C expatriates.

Comments are requested on all aspects of the proposed definition of a category C expatriate. Comments are also requested on the time limit for category C expatriates being expected to travel or reside in the United States, and what standards, if any, may be adopted in lieu of the 12-month maximum that would ensure that the definition does not permit inappropriate expansion of the exception. For example, comments are requested on whether a "specific and temporary purpose" standard should be adopted for category C expatriates, consistent with the standard for category A expatriates, or whether category C expatriates should be expected to seek medical care outside the United States at least one time per year in order to be considered to reasonably require access to health coverage and other related services and support in multiple countries. Comments are also requested on the proposed standard with respect to category C expatriates being expected to travel or reside outside the United States for at least 180 days in a consecutive 12-month period that overlaps with the policy year, and whether there are fact patterns in which the 12-month period could either be within a single policy year, or across two consecutive policy years.

Definitions of Group Health Plan and United States

Consistent with section 3(d)(5)(A) of the EHCCA, for purposes of applying the definition of expatriate health plan, "group health plan" means a group health plan as defined under 26 CFR 54.9831-1(a)(1), 29 CFR 2590.732(a)(1) or 45 CFR 146.145(a)(1), as applicable. Consistent with section 3(d)(4) of the EHCCA, the proposed regulations define "United States" to mean the 50 States, the District of Columbia and Puerto Rico.

Section 9010 of the ACA

Section 3(c)(1) of the EHCCA provides that, for purposes of the health insurance providers fee imposed by section 9010 of the ACA, a qualified expatriate enrolled in an expatriate health plan is not a United States health risk for calendar years after 2015. Section 3(c)(2) of the EHCCA provides a special rule applicable to calendar years 2014 and 2015. The Treasury Department and the IRS issued Notices 2015-29 and 2016-14 to address the definition of expatriate health plan for purposes of the health insurance providers fee imposed by section 9010 for the 2014, 2015, and 2016 fee years. No fee is due in the 2017 fee year because the Consolidated Appropriations Act suspends collection of the health insurance providers fee imposed by section 9010 of ACA for 2017.

These proposed regulations provide that, for any fee that is due on or after the date final regulations are published in the Federal Register, a qualified expatriate enrolled in an expatriate health plan as defined in these proposed regulations is not a United States health risk. These proposed regulations also authorize the IRS to specify in guidance in the Internal Revenue Bulletin the manner of determining excluded premiums for qualified expatriates in expatriate health plans.

(Footnote Continued)

date campaign or legislative purposes or propaganda. Code section 501(c)(4) describes an organization operated exclusively for the promotion of social welfare.

Until the date the final regulations are published in the Federal Register, taxpayers may rely on these proposed regulations with respect to any fee that is due beginning with the 2018 fee year.

Federal Tax Provision: Section 162(m)(6) of the Code

Section 162(m)(6) of the Code, as added by section 9014 of the ACA, in general, limits to $500,000 the allowable deduction for remuneration attributable to services performed by certain individuals for a covered health insurance provider. For taxable years beginning after December 31, 2012, section 162(m)(6)(C)(i) of the Code and 26 CFR 1.162-31(b)(4)(A) provide that a health insurance issuer is a covered health insurance provider if not less than 25 percent of the gross premiums that it receives from providing health insurance coverage during the taxable year are from minimum essential coverage. Section 3(a)(3) of the EHCCA provides that the provisions of the ACA (which include section 162(m)(6) of the Code) do not apply to expatriate health insurance issuers with respect to coverage offered by such issuers under expatriate health plans. Consistent with this rule, the proposed regulations exclude from the definition of the term "premium" for purposes of section 162(m)(6) of the Code amounts received in payment for coverage under an expatriate health plan. As a result, those amounts received are included in neither the numerator nor the denominator for purposes of determining whether the 25 percent standard under section 162(m)(6)(C)(i) of the Code and 26 CFR 1.162-31(b)(4)(A) is met, and they have no impact on whether a particular issuer is a covered health insurance provider.

Federal Tax Provision: Section 4980I of the Code

Section 3(b)(2) of the EHCCA provides that section 4980I of the Code applies to employer-sponsored coverage of a qualified expatriate who is assigned, rather than transferred, to work in the United States. As amended by section 101 of Division P of the Consolidated Appropriations Act, section 4980I of the Code first applies to coverage provided in taxable years beginning after December 31, 2019. Comments in response to Notice 2015-43 requested additional guidance on what it means for an employer to assign rather than transfer an employee. These proposed regulations do not address the interaction of the EHCCA and section 4980I of the Code because the Treasury Department and the IRS anticipate that this issue will be addressed in future guidance promulgated under section 4980I of the Code.

Federal Tax Provision: Section 5000A of the Code and Minimum Essential Coverage

The proposed regulations provide that, beginning January 1, 2017, coverage under an expatriate health plan that provides coverage for a qualified expatriate qualifies as minimum essential coverage for all participants in the plan. If the expatriate health plan provides coverage to category A or category B expatriates, the coverage of any participant in the plan is treated as an eligible employer-sponsored plan under section 5000A(f)(2) of the Code. If the expatriate health plan provides coverage to category C expatriates, the coverage of any enrollee in the plan is treated as a plan in the individual market under section 5000A(f)(1)(C) of the Code.

Federal Tax Provision: Sections 6055 and 6056 of the Code

Section 3(b)(2) of the EHCCA permits the use of electronic media to provide the statements required under sections 6055 and 6056 of the Code to individuals for coverage under an expatriate health plan unless the primary insured has explicitly refused to receive the statement electronically. The proposed regulations provide that, for an expatriate health plan, the recipient is treated as having consented to receive the required statement electronically unless the recipient has explicitly refused to receive the statement in an electronic format. In addition, the proposed regulations provide that the recipient may explicitly refuse either electronically or in a paper document. For a recipient to be treated as having consented under this special rule, the furnisher must provide a notice in compliance with the general disclosure requirements under sections 6055 and 6056 that informs the recipient that the statement will be furnished electronically unless the recipient explicitly refuses to consent to receive the statement in electronic form. The notice must be provided to the recipient at least 30 days prior to the due date for furnishing of the first statement the furnisher intends to furnish electronically to the recipient. Absent receipt of this notice, a recipient will not be treated as having consented to electronic furnishing of statements. Treasury and IRS request comments on further guidance that will assist issuers and plan sponsors in providing this notice in the least burdensome manner while still ensuring that the recipient has sufficient information and opportunity to opt out of the electronic reporting if the recipient desires. For example, Treasury and the IRS specifically request comments on whether the ability to provide this notice as part of the enrollment materials for the coverage would meet these goals.

Federal Tax Provision: PCORTF Fee

The proposed regulations provide that the excise tax under sections 4375 and 4376 of the Code (the PCORTF fee) does not apply to an expatriate health plan as defined at 26 CFR 54.9831-1(f)(3). Section 4375 of the Code limits the application of the fee to policies issued to individuals residing in the United States. Existing regulations under sections 4375, 4376, and 4377 of the Code exclude coverage under a plan from the fee if the plan is designed specifically to cover primarily employees who are working and residing outside the United States. A comment requested clarification about the existing PCORTF fee exemption for plans that primarily cover employees working and residing outside the United States. Consistent with the provisions of the EHCCA, the proposed regulations expand the exclusion from the PCORTF fee to also exclude an expatriate health plan regardless of whether the plan provides coverage for qualified expatriates residing or working in or outside the United States if the plan is an expatriate health plan.

Section 1341 of the ACA: Transitional Reinsurance Program

A comment also requested that the current exclusion under the PCORTF fee regulations for individuals working and residing outside the United States be applied to the transitional reinsurance fee under section 1341 of the ACA. Existing regulations relating to section 1341 of the ACA include an exception for certain expatriate health plans,[29] including expatriate group health coverage as defined by the Secretary of HHS and, for the 2015 and 2016 benefit years, self-insured group health plans with respect to which enrollment is limited to participants who reside outside their home country for at least six months of the plan year, and any covered dependents. HHS solicits comment on whether amendments are needed to 45 CFR 153.400(a)(1)(iii) to clarify the alignment with the EHCCA and exempt all expatriate plans from the requirement to make reinsurance contributions.

Section 2718 of the PHS Act: MLR Program

Section 2718 of the PHS Act, as added by sections 1001 and 10101 of the ACA, generally requires health insurance issuers to provide rebates to consumers if issuers do not achieve specified MLRs, as well as to submit an annual MLR report to HHS. The proposed regulations provide that expatriate policies described in 45 CFR 158.120(d)(4) continue to be subject to the reporting and rebate requirements of 45 CFR Part 158, but update the description of expatriate policies in 45 CFR 158.120(d)(4) to exclude policies that are expatriate health plans under the EHCCA. Given this modification, issuers may find that the number of expatriate policies that remain subject to MLR requirements is low, and that it is administratively burdensome and there is no longer a qualitative justification for continuing separate reporting of such policies. Therefore, comments are requested on whether the treatment of expatriate policies for purposes of the MLR regulations should be amended so that expatriate policies that do not meet the definition of expatriate health plan under the EHCCA would not be required to be reported separately from other health insurance policies.

Section 833(c)(5) of the Code, as added by section 9016 of the ACA, and amended by section 102 of Division N of the Consolidated and Further Continuing Appropriations Act, 2015 (Public Law 113-235, 128 Stat. 2130), provides that section 833(a)(2) and (3) do not apply to any organization unless the organization's MLR for the taxable year was at least 85 percent. In describing the MLR computation under section 833(c)(5), the statute and implementing regulations provide that the elements in the MLR computation are to be "as reported under section 2718 of the Public Service Health Act." Accordingly, the proposed regulations under section 2718 of the PHS Act would effectively apply the EHCCA exemption to section 833(c)(5) of the Code by carving out expatriate health plans under the EHCCA from the section 833(c)(5) requirements as well.

Excepted Benefits

Supplemental Health Insurance Coverage

The proposed regulations incorporate the guidance from the Affordable Care Act Implementation FAQs Part XXIII addressing supplemental health insurance products that provide categories of benefits in addition to those in the primary coverage. Under the proposed regulations, if group or individual supplemental health insurance coverage provides benefits for items and services not covered by the primary coverage (referred to as providing "additional categories of benefits"), the coverage would be considered to be designed "to fill gaps in primary coverage," for purposes of being supplemental excepted benefits if none of the benefits provided by the supplemental policy are an EHB, as defined for purposes of section 1302(b) of the ACA, in the State in which the coverage is issued. Conversely, if any benefit provided by the supplemental policy is an EHB in the State where the coverage is issued, the insurance coverage would not be supplemental excepted benefits under the proposed regulations. This standard is proposed to apply only to the extent that the supplemental health insurance provides coverage of additional categories of benefits. Supplemental health insurance products that both fill in cost sharing in the primary coverage, such as coinsurance or deductibles, and cover additional categories of benefits that are not EHB, also would be considered supplemental excepted benefits under these proposed regulations provided all other criteria are met.

Travel Insurance

The Departments are aware that certain travel insurance products may include limited health benefits. However, these products typically are not designed as major medical coverage. Instead, the risks being insured relate primarily to: (1) the interruption or cancellation of a trip (2) the loss of baggage or personal effects; (3) damages to accommodations or rental vehicles; or (4) sickness, accident, disability, or death occurring during travel, with any health benefits usually incidental to other coverage.

Section 2791(c)(1)(H) of the PHS Act, section 733(c)(1)(H) of ERISA, and section 9832(c)(1)(H) of the Code provide that the Departments may, in regulations, designate as excepted benefits "benefits for medical care that are secondary or incidental to other insurance benefits." Pursuant to this authority, and to clarify which types of travel-related insurance products are excepted benefits under the PHS Act, ERISA, and the Code, the proposed regulations provide that certain travel-related products that provide only incidental health benefits are excepted benefits. The proposed regulations define the term "travel insurance" as insurance coverage for personal risks incident to planned travel, which may include, but is not limited to, interruption or cancellation of a trip or event, loss of baggage or personal effects, damages to accommodations or rental vehicles, and sickness, accident, disability, or

---

[29] 45 CFR 153.400(a)(1)(iii).

death occurring during travel, provided that the health benefits are not offered on a stand-alone basis and are incidental to other coverage. For this purpose, travel insurance does not include major medical plans that provide comprehensive medical protection for travelers with trips lasting 6 months or longer, including, for example, those working overseas as an expatriate or military personnel being deployed. This definition is consistent with the definition of travel insurance under final regulations for the health insurance providers fee imposed by section 9010 of the ACA issued by the Treasury Department and the IRS,[30] which uses a modified version of the National Association of Insurance Commissioners (NAIC) definition of travel insurance.

Hospital Indemnity and Other Fixed Indemnity Insurance

These proposed regulations also include an amendment to the "noncoordinated excepted benefits" category as it relates to hospital indemnity and other fixed indemnity insurance in the group market. Since the issuance of final regulations defining excepted benefits, the Departments have become aware of some hospital indemnity and other fixed indemnity insurance policies that provide comprehensive benefits related to health care costs. In addition, although hospital indemnity and other fixed indemnity insurance under section 2791 of the PHS Act, section 733 of ERISA, and section 9832 of the Code is not intended to be major medical coverage, the Departments are aware that some group health plans that provide coverage through hospital indemnity or other fixed indemnity insurance policies that meet the conditions necessary to be an excepted benefit have made representations to participants that the coverage is minimum essential coverage under section 5000A of the Code. The Departments are concerned that some individuals may incorrectly understand these policies to be comprehensive major medical coverage that would be considered minimum essential coverage.

To avoid confusion among group health plan enrollees and potential enrollees, the proposed regulations revise the conditions necessary for hospital indemnity and other fixed indemnity insurance in the group market to be excepted benefits so that any application or enrollment materials provided to enrollees and potential enrollees at or before the time enrollees and potential enrollees are given the opportunity to enroll in the coverage must include a statement that the coverage is a supplement to, rather than a substitute for, major medical coverage and that a lack of minimum essential coverage may result in an additional tax payment. The proposed regulations include specific language that must be used by group health plans and issuers of group health insurance coverage to satisfy this notice requirement, which is consistent with the notice requirement for individual market fixed indemnity coverage under regulations issued by HHS.[31] The Departments request comments on this proposed notice requirement as well as whether any additional requirements should be added to prevent confusion among enrollees and potential enrollees regarding the limited coverage provided by hospital indemnity and other fixed indemnity insurance. The Departments anticipate that conforming changes will be made in the final regulations to ensure the notice language in the individual market is consistent with the notice language in the group market, and solicit comments on this approach.

Additionally, the Departments have become aware of hospital indemnity or other fixed indemnity insurance policies that provide benefits for doctors' visits at a fixed amount per visit, for prescription drugs at a fixed amount per drug, or for certain services at a fixed amount per day but in amounts that vary by the type of service. These types of policies do not meet the condition that benefits be provided on a per day (or per other time period, such as per week) basis. Accordingly, the proposed regulations clarify this standard by stating that the amount of benefits provided must be determined without regard to the type of items or services received. The proposed regulations add two examples demonstrating that group health plans and issuers of group health insurance coverage that provide coverage through hospital indemnity or fixed indemnity insurance policies that provide benefits based on the type of item or services received do not meet the conditions necessary to be an excepted benefit. The first example would incorporate into regulations guidance previously provided by the Departments in Affordable Care Act Implementation FAQs Part XI, which clarified that if a policy provides benefits in varying amounts based on the type of procedure or item received, the policy does not satisfy the condition that benefits be provided on a per day (or per other time period, such as per week) basis. The second example demonstrates that a hospital indemnity or other fixed indemnity insurance policy that provides benefits for certain services at a fixed amount per day, but in varying amounts depending on the type of service, does not meet the condition that benefits be provided on a per day (or per other time period, such as per week) basis. The Departments request comments on these examples specifically, as well as on the requirement that hospital indemnity and other fixed indemnity insurance in the group market that are excepted benefits must provide benefits on a per day (or per other time period, such as per week) basis in an amount that does not vary based on the type of items or services received. The Departments also request comments on whether the conditions for hospital indemnity or other fixed indemnity insurance to be considered excepted benefits should be more substantively aligned between the group and individual markets. For example, the requirements for hospital indemnity or other fixed indemnity insurance in the individual market could be modified to be consistent with the group market provisions of these proposed regulations by limiting payment strictly on a per-period basis and not on a per-service basis.

---

[30] 26 CFR 57.2(h)(4).

[31] 45 CFR 148.220(b)(4)(iv).

Specified Disease Coverage

The Departments have been asked whether a policy covering multiple specified diseases or illnesses may be considered to be excepted benefits. The statute provides that the noncoordinated excepted benefits category includes "coverage of a specified disease or illness" if the coverage meets the conditions for being offered as independent, noncoordinated benefits, and the Departments' implementing regulations identify cancer-only policies as one example of specified disease coverage.[32] The Departments are concerned that individuals who purchase a specified disease policy covering multiple diseases or illnesses (including policies that cover one overarching medical condition such as "mental illness" as opposed to a specific condition such as depression) may incorrectly believe they are purchasing comprehensive medical coverage when, in fact, these polices may not include many of the important consumer protections under the PHS Act, ERISA, and the Code. The Departments solicit comments on this issue and on whether, if such policies are permitted to be considered excepted benefits, protections are needed to ensure such policies are not mistaken for comprehensive medical coverage. For example, the Departments solicit comments on whether to limit the number of diseases or illnesses that may be covered in a specified disease policy that is considered to be excepted benefits or whether issuers should be required to disclose that such policies are not minimum essential coverage under section 5000A(f) of the Code.

Short-Term, Limited-Duration Insurance

Under existing regulations, short-term, limited-duration insurance means "health insurance coverage provided pursuant to a contract with an issuer that has an expiration date specified in the contract (taking into account any extensions that may be elected by the policyholder without the issuer's consent) that is less than 12 months after the original effective date of the contract."[33] Before enactment of the ACA, short-term, limited-duration insurance was an important means for individuals to obtain health coverage when transitioning from one job to another (and from one group health plan to another) or in a similar situation. But with the guaranteed availability of coverage and special enrollment period requirements in the individual health insurance market under the ACA, short-term, limited-duration insurance is no longer the only means to obtain transitional coverage.

The Departments recently have become aware that short-term, limited-duration insurance is being sold to address situations other than the situations that the exception was initially intended to address.[34] In some instances individuals are purchasing this coverage as their primary form of health coverage and, contrary to the intent of the 12-month coverage limitation in the current definition of short-term, limited-duration insurance, some issuers are providing renewals of the coverage that extend the duration beyond 12 months. The Departments are concerned that these policies, because they are exempt from market reforms, may have significant limitations, such as lifetime and annual dollar limits on EHBs and pre-existing condition exclusions, and therefore may not provide meaningful health coverage. Further, because these policies can be medically underwritten based on health status, healthier individuals may be targeted for this type of coverage, thus adversely impacting the risk pool for ACA-compliant coverage.

To address the issue of short-term, limited-duration insurance being sold as a type of primary coverage, the proposed regulations revise the definition of short-term, limited-duration insurance so that the coverage must be less than three months in duration, including any period for which the policyholder renews or has an option to renew with or without the issuer's consent. The proposed regulations also provide that a notice must be prominently displayed in the contract and in any application materials provided in connection with enrollment in such coverage with the following language: THIS IS NOT QUALIFYING HEALTH COVERAGE ("MINIMUM ESSENTIAL COVERAGE") THAT SATISFIES THE HEALTH COVERAGE REQUIREMENT OF THE AFFORDABLE CARE ACT. IF YOU DON'T HAVE MINIMUM ESSENTIAL COVERAGE, YOU MAY OWE AN ADDITIONAL PAYMENT WITH YOUR TAXES.

This change would align the definition more closely with the initial intent of the regulation: to refer to coverage intended to fill temporary coverage gaps when an individual transitions between primary coverage. Further, limiting the coverage to less than three months improves coordination with the exemption from the individual shared responsibility provision of section 5000A of the Code for gaps in coverage of less than three months (the short coverage gap exemption), 26 CFR 1.5000A-3. Under current law, individuals who are enrolled in short-term, limited-duration coverage instead of minimum essential coverage for three months or more are generally not eligible for the short coverage gap exemption. The proposed regulations help ensure that individuals who purchase short-term, limited-duration coverage will still be eligible for the short coverage gap exemption (assuming other requirements are met) during the temporary coverage period.

In addition to proposing to reduce the length of short-term, limited-duration insurance to less than three months, the proposed regulations add the words "with or" in front of "without the issuer's consent" to address the Departments' concern that some issuers are taking liberty with the current definition of short-term, limited-duration insurance either by automatically renewing such policies or having a simplified reapplication process with the result being that such coverage lasts much longer

[32] 26 CFR 54.9831-1(c)(4), 29 CFR 2590.732(c)(4), 45 CFR 146.145(b)(4) and 148.220(b)(3).

[33] 26 CFR 54.9801-2, 29 CFR 2590.702-2, 45 CFR 144.103.

[34] See e.g., Mathews, Anna W. "Sales of Short-Term Health Policies Surge," *The Wall Street Journal* April 10, 2016, available at http://www.wsj.com/articles/sales-of-short-term-health-policies-surge-1460328539.

than 12 months and serves as an individual's primary coverage but does not contain the important protections of the ACA. As indicated above, this type of coverage should only be sold for the purpose of providing coverage on a short-term basis such as filling in coverage gaps as a result of transitioning from one group health plan to another. The addition of the words "with or" clarifies that short-term, limited-duration insurance must be less than 3 months in total taking into account any option to renew or to reapply for the same or similar coverage.

The Departments seek comment on this proposal, including information and data on the number of short-term, limited-duration insurance policies offered for sale in the market, the types of individuals who typically purchase this coverage, and the reasons for which they purchase it.

Definition of EHB for Purposes of the Prohibition on Lifetime and Annual Limits.

On November 18, 2015, the Departments issued final regulations implementing section 2711 of the PHS Act.[35] The final regulations provide that, for plan years beginning on or after January 1, 2017, a plan or issuer that is not required to provide EHBs must define EHB, for purposes of the prohibition on lifetime and annual dollar limits, in a manner consistent with any of the 51 EHB base-benchmark plans applicable in a State or the District of Columbia, or one of the three FEHBP base-benchmarks, as specified under 45 CFR 156.100.

The final regulations under section 2711 of the PHS Act include a reference to selecting a "base-benchmark" plan, as specified under 45 CFR 156.100, for purposes of determining which benefits cannot be subject to lifetime or annual dollar limits. The base-benchmark plan selected by a State or applied by default under 45 CFR 156.100, however, may not reflect the complete definition of EHB in the applicable State. For that reason, the Departments propose to amend the regulations at 26 CFR 54.9815-2711(c), 29 CFR 2590.715-2711(c), and 45 CFR 147.126(c) to refer to the provisions that capture the complete definition of EHB in a State. Specifically, the Departments propose to replace the phrase "in a manner consistent with one of the three Federal Employees Health Benefit Program (FEHBP) options as defined by 45 CFR 156.100(a)(3) or one of the base-benchmark plans selected by a State or applied by default pursuant to 45 CFR 156.100" in each of the regulations with the following: "in a manner that is consistent with (1) one of the EHB-benchmark plans applicable in a State under 45 CFR 156.110, and includes coverage of any additional required benefits that are considered essential health benefits consistent with 45 CFR 155.170(a)(2); or (2) one of the three Federal Employees Health Benefit Program (FEHBP) options as defined by 45 CFR 156.100(a)(3), supplemented, as necessary, to meet the standards in 45 CFR 156.110." This change reflects the possibility that base-benchmark plans, including the FEHBP plan options, could require supplementation under 45 CFR 156.110, and ensures the inclusion of State-required benefit mandates enacted on or before December 31, 2011 in accordance with 45 CFR 155.170, which when coupled with a State's EHB-benchmark plan, establish the definition of EHB in that State under regulations implementing section 1302(b) of the ACA.[36] The Departments seek comment on the requirement that, when one of the FEHBP plan options is selected as the benchmark, it would be supplemented, as needed, to ensure coverage in all ten statutory EHB categories, and the benchmark plan options that should be available for this purpose.

Proposed Applicability Date and Reliance

Except as otherwise provided herein, these proposed regulations are proposed to be applicable for plan years (or, in the individual market, policy years) beginning on or after January 1, 2017. Issuers, employers, administrators, and individuals are permitted to rely on these proposed regulations pending the applicability date of final regulations in the **Federal Register**. To the extent final regulations or other guidance is more restrictive on issuers, employers, administrators, and individuals than these proposed regulations, the final regulations or other guidance will be applied without retroactive effect and issuers, employers, administrators, and individuals will be provided sufficient time to come into compliance with the final regulations.

III. Economic Impact and Paperwork Burden

A. *Summary — Department of Labor and Department of Health and Human Services*

As stated above, the proposed regulations would provide guidance on the rules for expatriate health plans, expatriate health plan issuers, and qualified expatriates under the EHCCA. The EHCCA generally provides that the requirements of the ACA do not apply with respect to expatriate health plans, expatriate health insurance issuers for coverage under expatriate health plans, and employers in their capacity as plan sponsors of expatriate health plans.

The proposed regulations address how certain requirements relating to minimum essential coverage under section 5000A of the Code, the health care reporting provisions of sections 6055 and 6056 of the Code, and the health insurance providers fee imposed by section 9010 of the ACA continue to

---

[35] 80 FR 72192.

[36] In the HHS Notice of Benefit and Payment Parameters for 2016 published February 27, 2015 (80 FR 10750), HHS instructed States to select a new base-benchmark plan to take effect beginning with plan or policy years beginning in 2017. The new final EHB base-benchmark plans selected as a result of this process are publicly available at downloads.cms.gov/cciio/Final%20List%20of%20BMPs_15_10_21.pdf. Additional information about the new base-benchmark plans, including plan documents and summaries of benefits, is available at www.cms.gov/CCIIO/Resources/Data-Resources/ehb.html. The definition of EHB in each of the 50 states and the District of Columbia is based on the base-benchmark plan, and takes into account any additions to the base-benchmark plan, such as supplementation under 45 CFR 156.110, and State-required benefit mandates in accordance with 45 CFR 155.170.

apply subject to certain provisions while providing that the excise tax under sections 4375 and 4376 of the Code do not apply to expatriate health plans.

The proposed regulations also propose amendments to the Departments' regulations concerning excepted benefits, which would specify the conditions for supplemental health insurance products that are designed "to fill gaps in primary coverage" by providing additional categories of benefits (as opposed to filling in gaps in cost sharing) to constitute supplemental excepted benefits, and clarify that certain travel-related insurance products that provide only incidental health benefits constitute excepted benefits. The proposed regulations also require that, to be considered hospital indemnity or other fixed indemnity insurance in the group market, any application or enrollment materials provided to participants at or before the time participants are given the opportunity to enroll in the coverage must include a statement that the coverage is a supplement to, rather than a substitute for, major medical coverage and that a lack of minimum essential coverage may result in an additional tax payment. Further, the regulations clarify that hospital indemnity and other fixed indemnity insurance must pay a fixed dollar amount per day (or per other time period, such as per week) regardless of the type of items or services received.

The regulations also propose revisions to the definition of short-term, limited-duration insurance so that the coverage has to be less than 3 months in duration (as opposed to the current definition of less than 12 months in duration), and that a notice must be prominently displayed in the contract and in any application materials provided in connection with the coverage that provides that such coverage is not minimum essential coverage.

The proposed regulations also include amendments to 45 CFR part 158 to clarify that the MLR reporting requirements do not apply to expatriate health plans under the EHCCA.

Finally, the proposed regulations propose to amend the definition of "essential health benefits" for purposes of the prohibition of annual and lifetime dollar limits for group health plans and health insurance issuers that are not required to provide essential health benefits.

The Departments are publishing these proposed regulations to implement the protections intended by the Congress in the most economically efficient manner possible. The Departments have examined the effects of this rule as required by Executive Order 13563 (76 FR 3821, January 21, 2011), Executive Order 12866 (58 FR 51735, September 1993, Regulatory Planning and Review), the Regulatory Flexibility Act (RFA) (September 19, 1980, Pub. L. 96-354), the Unfunded Mandates Reform Act of 1995 (Pub. L. 104-4), Executive Order 13132 on Federalism, and the Congressional Review Act (5 U.S.C. 804(2)).

B. *Executive Orders 12866 and 13563 — Department of Labor and Department of Health and Human Services*

Executive Order 12866 (58 FR 51735) directs agencies to assess all costs and benefits of available regulatory alternatives and, if regulation is necessary, to select regulatory approaches that maximize net benefits (including potential economic, environmental, public health and safety effects; distributive impacts; and equity). Executive Order 13563 (76 FR 3821, January 21, 2011) is supplemental to and reaffirms the principles, structures, and definitions governing regulatory review as established in Executive Order 12866.

Section 3(f) of Executive Order 12866 defines a "significant regulatory action" as an action that is likely to result in a final rule — (1) having an annual effect on the economy of $100 million or more in any one year, or adversely and materially affecting a sector of the economy, productivity, competition, jobs, the environment, public health or safety, or state, local or tribal governments or communities (also referred to as "economically significant"); (2) creating a serious inconsistency or otherwise interfering with an action taken or planned by another agency; (3) materially altering the budgetary impacts of entitlement grants, user fees, or loan programs or the rights and obligations of recipients thereof; or (4) raising novel legal or policy issues arising out of legal mandates, the President's priorities, or the principles set forth in the Executive Order.

A regulatory impact analysis (RIA) must be prepared for rules with economically significant effects (for example, $100 million or more in any 1 year), and a "significant" regulatory action is subject to review by the OMB. The Departments have determined that this regulatory action is not likely to have economic impacts of $100 million or more in any one year, and therefore is not significant within the meaning of Executive Order 12866. The Departments expect the impact of these proposed regulations to be limited because they do not require any additional action or impose any requirements on issuers, employers and plan sponsors.

1. *Need for Regulatory Action*

Consistent with the EHCCA, enacted as Division M of the Consolidated Clarification Continuing Appropriations Act, 2015 Public Law 113-235 (128 Stat. 2130), these proposed regulations provide that the market reform provisions enacted as part of the ACA generally do not apply to expatriate health plans, any employer solely in its capacity as a plan sponsor of an expatriate health plan, and any expatriate health insurance issuer with respect to coverage under an expatriate health plan. Further, the proposed regulations define the benefit and administrative requirements for expatriate health issuers, expatriate health plans, and qualified expatriates and provide clarification regarding the applicability of certain fee and reporting requirements under the Code.

Consistent with section 2 of the EHCCA, these proposed regulations are necessary to carry out the intent of Congress that (1) American expatriate health insurance issuers should be permitted to compete on a level playing field in the global marketplace; (2) the global competitiveness of American companies should be encouraged; and (3) in implementing the health insurance providers fee imposed by section 9010 of the ACA and other provisions of the ACA, the unique and multinational features of expatriate health plans and the United States companies that operate such plans and the competitive pressures of such plans and companies should continue to be recognized.

In response to feedback the Departments have received from stakeholders, the proposed regulations would also clarify the conditions for supplemental health insurance and travel insurance to be considered excepted benefits. These clarifications will provide health insurance issuers offering supplemental insurance coverage and travel insurance products with a clearer understanding of whether these types of coverage are subject to the market reforms under title XXVII of the PHS Act, part 7 of ERISA, and Chapter 100 of the Code. The proposed regulations also would amend the definition of short-term, limited-duration insurance and impose a new notice requirement in response to recent reports that this type of coverage is being sold for purposes other than for which the exclusion for short-term, limited-duration insurance was initially intended to cover.

2. *Summary of Impacts*

These proposed regulations would implement the rules for expatriate health plans, expatriate health insurance issuers, and qualified expatriates under the EHCCA. The proposed regulations also outline the conditions for travel insurance and supplemental insurance coverage to be considered excepted benefits, and revise the definition of short-term, limited-duration insurance.

Based on the NAIC 2014 Supplemental Health Care Exhibit Report,[37] which generally uses the definition of expatriate coverage in the MLR final rule at 45 CFR 158.120(d)(4),[38] there are an estimated eight issuers (one issuer in the small group market and seven issuers in the large group market) domiciled in the United States that provide expatriate health plans for approximately 270,349 enrollees. While the Departments acknowledge that some expatriate health insurance issuers and employers in their capacity as plan sponsor of an expatriate health plan may incur costs in order to comply with certain provisions of the EHCCA and these proposed regulations, as discussed below, the Departments believe that these costs will be relatively insignificant and limited.

The vast majority of expatriate health plans described in the EHCCA would qualify as expatriate health plans under the transitional relief provided in the Departments' Affordable Care Act Implementation FAQs Part XVIII, Q&A-6 and Q&A-7. The FAQs provide that expatriate health plans with plan years ending on or before December 31, 2016 are exempt from the ACA market reforms and provide that coverage provided under an expatriate group health plan is a form of minimum essential coverage under section 5000A of the Code. The EHCCA permanently exempts expatriate health plans with plan or policy years beginning on or after July 1, 2015 from the ACA market reform requirements and provides that coverage provided under an expatriate health plan is a form of minimum essential coverage under section 5000A of the Code.

Because the Departments believe that most, if not all, expatriate health plans described in the EHCCA would qualify as expatriate health plans under the Departments' previous guidance, and the proposed regulations codify the provisions of the EHCCA by making the temporary relief in the Departments' Affordable Care Act Implementation FAQs Part XVIII, Q&A-6 and Q&A-7 permanent for specified expatriate health plans, the Departments believe that the proposed regulations will result in only marginal, if any, impact on these plans. Furthermore, the Departments believe the proposed regulations outlining the conditions for travel insurance and supplemental insurance coverage to be considered excepted benefits are consistent with prevailing industry practice and will not result in significant cost to health insurance issuers of these products.

The Departments believe that any costs incurred by issuers of short-term, limited-duration insurance and hospital indemnity and other fixed indemnity insurance to include the required notice in application or enrollment materials will be negligible since the Departments have provided the exact text for the notice. Further, the Departments note that issuers of hospital indemnity and other fixed indemnity insurance in the individual market already provide a similar notice.

As a result, the Departments have concluded that the impacts of these proposed regulations are not economically significant. The Departments request comments on the assumptions used to evaluate the economic impact of these proposed regulations, including specific data and information on the number of expatriate health plans.

C. *Paperwork Reduction Act*

1. *Department of the Treasury.*

The collection of information in these proposed regulations are in 26 CFR 1.6055-2(a)(8) and 301.6056-2(a)(8). The collection of information in these proposed regulations relates to statements required to be furnished to a responsible individual under section 6055 of the Code and statements required to be furnished to an employee under section 6056 of the Code. The collection of information in these proposed regulations would, in accordance with the EHCCA, permit a furnisher to furnish the required statements electronically unless the recipient has explicitly refused to consent to receive the statement in an electronic format. The collection of information contained in this notice of

---

[37] NAIC, 2014 Supplemental Health Care Exhibit Report, Volume 1 (2015), available at http://www.naic.org/documents/prod_serv_statistical_hcs_zb.pdf.

[38] Section 45 CFR 158.120(d)(4) defines expatriate policies as predominantly group health insurance policies that provide coverage to employees, substantially all of whom are: (1) working outside their country of citizenship; (2) working outside their country of citizenship and outside the employer's country of domicile; or (3) non-U.S. citizens working in their home country.

proposed rulemaking will be taken into account and submitted to the Office of Management and Budget in accordance with the Paperwork Reduction Act of 1995 (44 U.S.C. 3507(d)) in connection with the next review of the collection of information for IRS Form 1095-B (OMB # 1545-2252) and IRS Form 1095-C (OMB # 1545-2251).

Comments on the collection of information should be sent to the Office of Management and Budget, Attn: Desk Officer for the Department of the Treasury, Office of Information and Regulatory Affairs, Washington, DC 20503, with copies to the Internal Revenue Service, Attn: IRS Reports Clearance Officer, SE:CAR:MP:T:T:SP, Washington DC 20224. Comments on the collection of information should be received by August 9, 2016. Comments are sought on whether the proposed collection of information is necessary for the proper performance of the IRS, including whether the information will have practical utility; the accuracy of the estimated burden associated with the proposed collection of information; how the quality, utility, and clarity of the information to be collected may be enhanced; how the burden of complying with the proposed collection of information may be minimized, including through the application of automated collection techniques and other forms of information technology; and estimates of capital or start-up costs and costs of operation, maintenance, and purchase of service to provide information. Comments on the collection of information should be received by August 9, 2016.

An agency may not conduct or sponsor, and a person is not required to respond to, a collection of information unless it displays a valid control number assigned by the Office of Management and Budget.

Books or records relating to a collection of information must be retained as long as their contents may become material in the administration of any internal revenue law. Generally, tax returns and tax return information are confidential, as required by 26 U.S.C. 6103.

2. *Department of the Treasury, Department of Labor, and Department of Health and Human Services.*

The proposed regulations provide that to be considered hospital or other fixed indemnity excepted benefits in the group market for plan years beginning on or after January 1, 2017, a notice must be included in any application or enrollment materials provided to participants at or before the time participants are given the opportunity to enroll in the coverage, indicating that the coverage is a supplement to, rather than a substitute for major medical coverage and that a lack of minimum essential coverage may result in an additional tax payment. The proposed regulations also provide that to be considered short-term, limited-duration insurance for policy years beginning on or after January 1, 2017, a notice must be prominently displayed in the contract and in any application materials, stating that the coverage is not minimum essential coverage and that failure to have minimum essential coverage may result in an additional tax payment. The Departments have provided the exact text for these notice requirements and the language will not need to be customized. The burden associated with these notices is not subject to the Paperwork Reduction Act of 1995 in accordance with 5 CFR 1320.3(c)(2) because they do not contain a "collection of information" as defined in 44 U.S.C. 3502(11).

D. *Regulatory Flexibility Act*

The Regulatory Flexibility Act (5 U.S.C. 601 *et seq.)* (RFA) imposes certain requirements with respect to Federal rules that are subject to the notice and comment requirements of section 553(b) of the Administrative Procedure Act (5 U.S.C. 551 *et seq.)* and that are likely to have a significant economic impact on a substantial number of small entities. Unless an agency certifies that a proposed rule is not likely to have a significant economic impact on a substantial number of small entities, section 603 of RFA requires that the agency present an initial regulatory flexibility analysis at the time of the publication of the notice of proposed rulemaking describing the impact of the rule on small entities and seeking public comment on such impact. Small entities include small businesses, organizations and governmental jurisdictions.

The RFA generally defines a "small entity" as (1) a proprietary firm meeting the size standards of the Small Business Administration (SBA) (13 CFR 121.201); (2) a nonprofit organization that is not dominant in its field; or (3) a small government jurisdiction with a population of less than 50,000. (States and individuals are not included in the definition of "small entity.") The Departments use as their measure of significant economic impact on a substantial number of small entities a change in revenues of more than 3 to 5 percent.

These proposed regulations are not likely to impose additional costs on small entities. According to SBA size standards, entities with average annual receipts of $38.5 million or less would be considered small entities for these North American Industry Classification System codes. The Departments believe that, since the majority of small issuers belong to larger holding groups, many if not all are likely to have non-health lines of business that would result in their revenues exceeding $38.5 million. Therefore, the Departments certify that the proposed regulations will not have a significant impact on a substantial number of small entities. In addition, section 1102(b) of the Social Security Act requires agencies to prepare a regulatory impact analysis if a rule may have a significant economic impact on the operations of a substantial number of small rural hospitals. This analysis must conform to the provisions of section 604 of the RFA. These proposed regulations would not affect small rural hospitals. Therefore, the Departments have determined that these proposed regulations would not have a significant impact on the operations of a substantial number of small rural hospitals.

E. Special Analysis - Department of the Treasury

Certain IRS regulations, including this one, are exempt from the requirements of Executive Order 12866, as supplemented and reaffirmed by Executive Order 13563. Therefore, a regulatory impact assessment is not required. It also has been determined that section 553(b) of the Administrative Procedure Act (5 U.S.C. Chapter 5) does not apply to these regulations. For applicability of RFA, see paragraph D of this section III. Pursuant to section 7805(f) of the Code, these regulations have been submitted to the Chief Counsel for Advocacy of the Small Business Administration for comment on their impact on small business.

F. Unfunded Mandates Reform Act

For purposes of the Unfunded Mandates Reform Act of 1995 (2 U.S.C. 1501 *et seq.)*, as well as Executive Order 12875, these proposed rules do not include any Federal mandate that may result in expenditures by State, local, or tribal governments, or the private sector, which may impose an annual burden of $146 million adjusted for inflation since 1995.

G. *Federalism — Department of Labor and Department of Health and Human Services*

Executive Order 13132 outlines fundamental principles of federalism. It requires adherence to specific criteria by Federal agencies in formulating and implementing policies that have "substantial direct effects" on the States, the relationship between the national government and States, or on the distribution of power and responsibilities among the various levels of government. Federal agencies promulgating regulations that have these federalism implications must consult with State and local officials, and describe the extent of their consultation and the nature of the concerns of State and local officials in the preamble to the final regulation.

In the Departments' view, these proposed regulations do not have federalism implications, because they do not have direct effects on the States, the relationship between the national government and States, or on the distribution of power and responsibilities among various levels of government.

H. Congressional Review Act

These proposed regulations are subject to the Congressional Review Act provisions of the Small Business Regulatory Enforcement Fairness Act of 1996 (5 U.S.C. 801 et seq.), and, if finalized, will be transmitted to the Congress and to the **Comptroller General** for review in accordance with such provisions.

I. Statement of Availability of IRS Documents

IRS Revenue Procedures, Revenue Rulings notices, and other guidance cited in this document are published in the Internal Revenue Bulletin (or Cumulative Bulletin) and are available from the Superintendent of Documents, U.S. Government Printing Office, Washington, DC 20402, or by visiting the IRS website at *http://www.irs.gov.*

IV. Statutory Authority

The Department of the Treasury regulations are proposed to be adopted pursuant to the authority contained in sections 7805 and 9833 of the Code.

The Department of Labor regulations are proposed pursuant to the authority contained in 29 U.S.C. 1135,and 1191c; Secretary of Labor's Order 1-2011, 77 FR 1088 (Jan. 9, 2012).

The Department of Health and Human Services regulations are proposed to be adopted pursuant to the authority contained in sections 2701 through 2763, 2791, and 2792 of the PHS Act (42 U.S.C. 300gg through 300gg-63, 300gg-91, and 300gg-92), as amended.

[¶49,702] Proposed Amendments of Regulations (REG-123854-12) Proposed Regulations, NPRM REG-123854-12, published in the Federal Register on June 22, 2016 (corrected 8/4/2016).

[Code Sec. 409A]

Nonqualified deferred compensation plans: Code Sec. 409A: Proposed regulations.—Amendments of Reg. §§1.409A-0, 1.409A-1, 1.409A-2,1.409A-3, 1.409A-4 and 1.409A-6, regarding the calculation of amounts includible in income under section 409A(a)(1), are proposed.

AGENCY: Internal Revenue Service (IRS), Treasury.

ACTION: Partial withdrawal of notice of proposed rulemaking; notice of proposed rulemaking.

SUMMARY: This document contains proposed regulations that would clarify or modify certain specific provisions of the final regulations under section 409A (TD 9321, 72 FR 19234). This document also withdraws a specific provision of the notice of proposed rulemaking (REG-148326-05) published in the *Federal Register* on December 8, 2008 (73 FR 74380) regarding the calculation of amounts includible in income under section 409A(a)(1) and replaces that provision with revised proposed regulations. These proposed regulations would affect participants, beneficiaries, sponsors, and administrators of nonqualified deferred compensation plans.

DATES: Comments and requests for a public hearing must be received by September 20, 2016.

ADDRESSES: Send submissions to: CC:PA:LPD:PR (REG-123854-12), Room 5203, Internal Revenue Service, PO Box 7604, Ben Franklin Station, Washington DC, 20044. Submissions may be hand delivered Monday through Friday, between the hours of 8 a.m. and 4 p.m. to CC:PA:LPD:PR (REG-123854-12), Courier's Desk, Internal Revenue Service, 1111 Constitution Avenue, NW., Washington, DC, 20224 or sent electronically, via the Federal Rulemaking Portal at www.regulations.gov (IRS REG-123854-12).

FOR FURTHER INFORMATION CONTACT: Concerning these proposed regulations under section 409A, Gregory Burns at (202) 927-9639, concerning submission of comments and/or requests for a hearing, Regina Johnson at (202) 317-6901 (not toll-free numbers).

SUPPLEMENTARY INFORMATION:

Background

Section 885 of the American Jobs Creation Act of 2004, Public Law 108-357 (118 Stat. 1418) (AJCA '04) added section 409A to the Internal Revenue Code (Code). Section 409A(a)(1)(A) generally provides that, if certain requirements are not met at any time during a taxable year, amounts deferred under a nonqualified deferred compensation plan for that year and all previous taxable years are currently includible in gross income to the extent not subject to a substantial risk of forfeiture and not previously included in gross income.

On April 17, 2007 (72 FR 19234), the Treasury Department and the IRS issued final regulations under section 409A (TD 9321), which include §§1.409A-1, 1.409A-2, 1.409A-3, and 1.409A-6 (the final regulations). The final regulations define certain terms used in section 409A and in the final regulations, set forth the requirements for deferral elections and for the time and form of payments under nonqualified deferred compensation plans, and address certain other issues under section 409A.

On December 8, 2008 (73 FR 74380), the Treasury Department and the IRS issued additional proposed regulations under section 409A (REG-148326-05), which include proposed §1.409A-4 (the proposed income inclusion regulations). The proposed income inclusion regulations provide guidance regarding the calculation of amounts includible in income under section 409A(a)(1) and the additional taxes imposed by section 409A with respect to service providers participating in certain nonqualified deferred compensation plans and other arrangements that do not comply with the requirements of section 409A(a).

Explanation of Provisions

I. Overview

The Treasury Department and the IRS have concluded that certain clarifications and modifications to the final regulations and the proposed income inclusion regulations will help taxpayers comply with the requirements of section 409A. These proposed regulations address certain specific provisions of the final regulations and the proposed income inclusion regulations and are not intended to propose a general revision of, or broad changes to, the final regulations or the proposed income inclusion regulations. The narrow and specific purpose of these proposed regulations should be taken into account when submitting comments on these proposed regulations. As provided in the section of this preamble titled "Proposed Effective Dates," taxpayers may rely upon these proposed regulations immediately.

These proposed regulations:

(1) Clarify that the rules under section 409A apply to nonqualified deferred compensation plans separately and in addition to the rules under section 457A.

(2) Modify the short-term deferral rule to permit a delay in payments to avoid violating Federal securities laws or other applicable law.

(3) Clarify that a stock right that does not otherwise provide for a deferral of compensation will not be treated as providing for a deferral of compensation solely because the amount payable under the stock right upon an involuntary separation from service for cause, or the occurrence of a condition within the service provider's control, is based on a measure that is less than fair market value.

(4) Modify the definition of the term "eligible issuer of service recipient stock" to provide that it includes a corporation (or other entity) for which a person is reasonably expected to begin, and actually begins, providing services within 12 months after the grant date of a stock right.

(5) Clarify that certain separation pay plans that do not provide for a deferral of compensation may apply to a service provider who had no compensation from the service recipient during the year preceding the year in which a separation from service occurs.

(6) Provide that a plan under which a service provider has a right to payment or reimbursement of reasonable attorneys' fees and other expenses incurred to pursue a bona fide legal claim against the service recipient with respect to the service relationship does not provide for a deferral of compensation.

(7) Modify the rules regarding recurring part-year compensation.

(8) Clarify that a stock purchase treated as a deemed asset sale under section 338 is not a sale or other disposition of assets for purposes of determining whether a service provider has a separation from service.

(9) Clarify that a service provider who ceases providing services as an employee and begins providing services as an independent contractor is treated as having a separation from service if, at the time of the change in employment status, the level of services reasonably anticipated to be provided after the change would result in a separation from service under the rules applicable to employees.

(10) Provide a rule that is generally applicable to determine when a "payment" has been made for purposes of section 409A.

(11) Modify the rules applicable to amounts payable following death.

(12) Clarify that the rules for transaction-based compensation apply to stock rights that do not provide for a deferral of compensation and statutory stock options.

(13) Provide that the addition of the death, disability, or unforeseeable emergency of a beneficiary who has become entitled to a payment due to a service provider's death as a potentially earlier or intervening payment event will not violate the prohibition on the acceleration of payments.

(14) Modify the conflict of interest exception to the prohibition on the acceleration of payments to permit the payment of all types of deferred compensation (and not only certain types of foreign earned income) to comply with bona fide foreign ethics or conflicts of interest laws.

(15) Clarify the provision permitting payments upon the termination and liquidation of a plan in connection with bankruptcy.

(16) Clarify other rules permitting payments in connection with the termination and liquidation of a plan.

(17) Provide that a plan may accelerate the time of payment to comply with Federal debt collection laws.

(18) Clarify and modify § 1.409A-4(a)(1)(ii)(B) of the proposed income inclusion regulations regarding the treatment of deferred amounts subject to a substantial risk of forfeiture for purposes of calculating the amount includible in income under section 409A(a)(1).

(19) Clarify various provisions of the final regulations to recognize that a service provider can be an entity as well as an individual.

II. Deferral of Compensation

A. Section 457(f) and Section 457A Plans

Section 457(f) generally provides that compensation deferred under a plan of an eligible employer (as that term is defined under section 457) is included in gross income in the first taxable year in which there is no substantial risk of forfeiture of the rights to the compensation. The final regulations provide that a deferred compensation plan subject to section 457(f) may be a nonqualified deferred compensation plan for purposes of section 409A and that the rules of section 409A apply to deferred compensation plans separately and in addition to any requirements applicable to such plans under section 457(f).

Similarly, section 457A, which was enacted more than a year after publication of the final regulations, generally provides that any compensation deferred under a nonqualified deferred compensation plan of a nonqualified entity (as these terms are defined under section 457A) is includible in gross income when there is no substantial risk of forfeiture of the rights to the compensation. These proposed regulations clarify that a nonqualified deferred compensation plan under section 457A, like a deferred compensation plan under section 457(f), may be a nonqualified deferred compensation plan for purposes of section 409A and that the rules of section 409A apply to such a plan separately and in addition to any requirements applicable to the plan under section 457A.

B. Short-term Deferral Rule

The final regulations provide that a deferral of compensation does not occur for purposes of section 409A under a plan with respect to any payment that is not a deferred payment[1] provided that the service provider actually or constructively receives the payment on or before the later of: (1) The 15th day of the third month following the end of the service provider's first taxable year in which the right to the payment is no longer subject to a substantial risk of forfeiture, or (2) the 15th day of the third month following the end of the service recipient's first taxable year in which the right to the payment is no longer subject to a substantial risk of forfeiture (the applicable 2½ month period). A payment that meets these requirements of the short-term deferral rule (described more fully in § 1.409A-1(b)(4)) is referred to as a short-term deferral and is generally exempt from the requirements applicable to plans that provide for a deferral of compensation.

The final regulations provide that a payment that otherwise qualifies as a short-term deferral, but is made after the applicable 2½ month period, may continue to qualify as a short-term deferral if the payment is delayed for one of three reasons: (1) The taxpayer establishes that it was administratively impracticable for the service recipient to make the payment by the end of the applicable 2½ month period; (2) making the payment by the end of the applicable 2½ month period would have jeopardized the service recipient's ability to continue as a going concern; or (3) the service recipient reasonably anticipates that a deduction for the payment would not be permitted under section 162(m).

Similar exceptions apply under the general time and form of payment rules of section 409A. Under § 1.409A-3(d), a payment is treated as made on the date specified under the plan if the payment is delayed due to administrative impracticability or because making the payment would jeopardize the ability of the service recipient to continue as a going concern. Under § 1.409A-2(b)(7), a payment may be delayed to a date after the payment date designated in a plan without failing to meet the requirements of section 409A(a) if the service recipient reasonably anticipates that a deduction for the payment would not be permitted under section 162(m) or if making the payment would violate Federal securities laws or other applicable law. Together, these rules generally permit payments

[1] Under § 1.409A-1(b)(4)(i)(D), a payment is a deferred payment if it is made pursuant to a provision of a plan that provides for the payment to be made or completed on or after any date, or upon the occurrence of any event, that will or may occur later than the end of the applicable 2½ month period.

under section 409A to be delayed due to administrative impracticability or because making the payment would jeopardize the ability of the service recipient to continue as a going concern, the payment would not be deductible under section 162(m), or making the payment would violate Federal securities laws or other applicable law.

Some commenters have suggested that the exception for payments that would violate Federal securities laws or other applicable law should also apply to payments that are intended to be short-term deferrals. These commenters have noted that the policy reasons for excusing a timely payment when the payment would violate Federal securities laws or other applicable law apply equally to the general time and form of payment rules under section 409A and the short-term deferral rule. In response to these comments, the Treasury Department and the IRS have determined that it is appropriate to extend this exception to the short-term deferral rule. Accordingly, these proposed regulations provide that a payment that otherwise qualifies as a short-term deferral, but is made after the end of the applicable $2^1/_2$ month period, may still qualify as a short-term deferral if the service recipient reasonably anticipates that making the payment during the applicable $2^1/_2$ month period will violate Federal securities laws or other applicable law and the payment is made as soon as reasonably practicable following the first date on which the service recipient anticipates or reasonably should anticipate that making the payment would not cause a violation. For this purpose, making a payment that would cause inclusion in gross income or the application of any penalty provision or other provision of the Code is not treated as a violation of applicable law.

C. Stock rights

1. Service Recipient Stock

The final regulations provide that certain stock options and stock appreciation rights (collectively, stock rights) granted with respect to service recipient stock do not provide for the deferral of compensation. The term "service recipient stock" means a class of stock that, as of the date of grant, is common stock for purposes of section 305 and the regulations thereunder of a corporation that is an eligible issuer of service recipient stock. For this purpose, service recipient stock does not include any stock that is subject to a mandatory repurchase obligation (other than a right of first refusal), or a permanent put or call right, if the stock price under such right or obligation is based on a measure other than the fair market value (disregarding lapse restrictions) of the equity interest in the corporation represented by the stock.

Commenters have noted that employers often want to deter employees from engaging in behavior that could be detrimental to the employer and have customarily reduced the amount that an employee receives under a stock rights arrangement if the employee is dismissed for cause or violates a noncompetition or nondisclosure agreement. These commenters have observed that this type of reduction is generally prohibited under the definition of service recipient stock in the final regulations but have argued that neither the statutory language nor the underlying policies of section 409A should prohibit a reduction under these circumstances. The Treasury Department and the IRS agree with these conclusions. Accordingly, these proposed regulations provide that a stock price will not be treated as based on a measure other than fair market value if the amount payable upon a service provider's involuntary separation from service for cause, or the occurrence of a condition that is within the control of the service provider, such as the violation of a covenant not to compete or a covenant not to disclose certain information, is based on a measure that is less than fair market value.

2. Eligible Issuer of Service Recipient Stock

Under the final regulations, the term "eligible issuer of service recipient stock" means the corporation or other entity for which the service provider provides direct services on the date of grant of the stock right and certain affiliated corporations or entities. Some commenters have asserted that this definition of "eligible issuer of service recipient stock" hinders employment negotiations because it prevents service recipients from granting stock rights to service providers before they are employed by the service recipient. In response to these comments, these proposed regulations provide that, if it is reasonably anticipated that a person will begin providing services to a corporation or other entity within 12 months after the date of grant of a stock right, and the person actually begins providing services to the corporation or other entity within 12 months after the date of grant (or, if services do not begin within that period, the stock right is forfeited), the corporation or other entity will be an eligible issuer of service recipient stock.

D. Separation pay plans

Under the final regulations, separation pay plans that provide for payment only upon an involuntary separation from service or pursuant to a window program do not provide for a deferral of compensation to the extent that they meet certain requirements. One of these requirements is that the separation pay generally not exceed two times the lesser of (1) the service provider's annualized compensation based upon the annual rate of pay for the service provider's taxable year preceding the service provider's taxable year in which the separation from service occurs, or (2) the limit under section 401(a)(17) for the year in which the service provider separates from service.

Some commenters have questioned whether this exception for separation pay plans is available for a service provider whose employment begins and ends during the same taxable year because the service provider was not employed by, and did not receive any compensation from, the service recipient for the taxable year preceding the taxable year in which the separation from service occurs. These proposed regulations clarify that the separation pay plan exception is available for service providers whose employment begins and ends in the same taxable year. In that circumstance, these proposed regulations provide that the service provider's annualized compensation for the taxable year in which the service provider separates from service may be used for purposes of this separation pay plan exception if the service provider had no compensation from the service recipient in the taxable year preceding the year in which the service provider separates from service.

E. Employment-related legal fees and expenses

Under the final regulations, an arrangement does not provide for a deferral of compensation to the extent that it provides for amounts to be paid as settlements or awards resolving *bona fide* legal claims based on wrongful termination, employment discrimination, the Fair Labor Standards Act, or workers' compensation statutes, including claims under applicable Federal, state, local, or foreign laws, or for reimbursements or payments of reasonable attorneys' fees or other reasonable expenses incurred by the service provider related to such *bona fide* legal claims.

Commenters have requested guidance on the application of section 409A(a) to provisions commonly included in employment agreements that provide for the reimbursement of attorneys' fees in connection with employment-related disputes and have asserted that there is no reason to distinguish between arrangements that provide for payment of reasonable attorneys' fees and expenses for the types of legal claims currently specified in the final regulations and any other *bona fide* legal claim with respect to the service relationship between a service provider and a service recipient. In response to these comments, these proposed regulations provide that an arrangement does not provide for a deferral of compensation to the extent that it provides for the payment or reimbursement of a service provider's reasonable attorneys' fees and other expenses incurred to enforce a claim by the service provider against the service recipient with respect to the service relationship.

F. Recurring Part-year Compensation

After publication of the final regulations, commenters have expressed concerns about the application of section 409A to recurring part-year compensation. The final regulations define recurring part-year compensation as compensation paid for services rendered in a position that the service recipient and service provider reasonably anticipate will continue on similar terms and conditions in subsequent years, and will require services to be provided during successive service periods each of which comprises less than 12 months and each of which begins in one taxable year of the service provider and ends in the next taxable year. For example, a teacher providing services during school years comprised of 10 consecutive months would have recurring part-year compensation. See §1.409A-2(a)(14). In general, commenters have asserted that section 409A should not apply to this situation because the amount being deferred from one taxable year to a subsequent taxable year is typically only a small amount and because most service providers who receive recurring part-year compensation (typically teachers and other educational workers) view an election to annualize this compensation as a cash flow decision, rather than a tax-deferral opportunity.

In response, the Treasury Department and the IRS issued Notice 2008-62 (2008-29 IRB 130), which provides that arrangements involving recurring part-year compensation do not provide for a deferral of compensation for purposes of section 409A or section 457(f) if: (1) The arrangement does not defer payment of any of the recurring part-year compensation beyond the last day of the 13th month following the beginning of the service period, and (2) the arrangement does not defer from one taxable year to the next taxable year the payment of more than the applicable dollar amount under section 402(g)(1)(B) in effect for the calendar year in which the service period begins ($18,000 for 2016). Notice 2008-62 also states that a conforming change is intended be made to the final regulations to reflect these rules.

Commenters have expressed concerns that Notice 2008-62 would not adequately address some teaching positions, such as college and university faculty members. They have noted that, depending on several variables (such as the calendar month in which a service provider commences service or the length of the service period), the dollar limitation in the notice may result in adverse tax consequences to service providers with annual compensation as low as $80,000. Commenters have further observed that some of these arrangements are nonelective, and therefore some service providers cannot opt out of a recurring part-year compensation arrangement. In recognition that service recipients in the field of education frequently structure their pay plans to include recurring part-year compensation and that the main purpose of this design is to provide uninterrupted cash flow for service providers who do not work for a portion of the year, these proposed regulations modify the recurring part-year compensation rule. These proposed regulations provide that a plan or arrangement under which a service provider receives recurring part-year compensation that is earned over a period of service does not provide for the deferral of compensation if the plan does not defer payment of any of the recurring part-year compensation to a date beyond the last day of the 13th month following the first day of the service period for which the recurring part-year compensation is paid, and the amount of the service provider's recurring part-year compensation (not merely the amount deferred) does not exceed the annual compensation limit under section 401(a)(17) ($265,000 for 2016) for the calendar year in which the service period commences. A conforming change is being made for purposes of section 457(f) under proposed section 457(f) regulations (REG-147196-07) that are also published in the Proposed Rules section of this issue of the *Federal Register*.

III. Separation from Service Definition

A. *Asset Purchase Transactions*

The final regulations permit the seller and an unrelated buyer in an asset purchase transaction to specify whether a person who is a service provider of the seller immediately before the transaction is treated as separating from service if the service provider provides services to the buyer after and as a result of the transaction. Commenters have asked whether this rule may be used with respect to a transaction that is treated as a deemed asset sale under section 338.

The provision of the final regulations giving buyers and sellers in asset transactions the discretion to treat employees as separating from service is based on the recognition that, while employees formally terminate employment with the seller and immediately recommence employment with the buyer in a typical asset transaction, the employees often experience no change in the type or level of services they provide. In a deemed asset sale under section 338, however, employees do not experience a termination of employment, formal or otherwise. Accordingly, the Treasury Department and the IRS have determined that it would be inconsistent with section 409A to permit the parties to a deemed asset sale to treat service providers as having separated from service upon the occurrence of the transaction. These proposed regulations affirm and make explicit that a stock purchase transaction that is treated as a deemed asset sale under section 338 is not a sale or other disposition of assets for purposes of this rule under section 409A.

B. *Dual Status As Employee and Independent Contractor and Changes in Status from Employee to Independent Contractor (or Vice Versa)*

The final regulations provide that an employee separates from service with an employer if the employee dies, retires, or otherwise has a termination of employment with the employer. Under the final regulations, a termination of employment generally occurs if the facts and circumstances indicate that the employer and employee reasonably anticipate that no further services would be performed after a certain date or that the level of *bona fide* services the employee would perform after that date (whether as an employee or as an independent contractor) would permanently decrease to no more than 20 percent of the average level of *bona fide* services performed (whether as an employee or an independent contractor) over the immediately preceding 36-month period (or if the employee has been providing services to the employer for less than 36 months, the full period of services). The final regulations provide that an independent contractor separates from service with a service recipient upon the expiration of the contract (or, if applicable, all contracts) under which services are performed for the service recipient if the expiration is a good-faith and complete termination of the contractual relationship.

The final regulations also provide that if a service provider provides services both as an employee and an independent contractor of a service recipient, the service provider must separate from service both as an employee and as an independent contractor to be treated as having separated from service. The final regulations further provide that "[i]f a service provider ceases providing services as an independent contractor and begins providing services as an employee, or ceases providing services as an employee and begins providing services as an independent contractor, the service provider will not be considered to have a separation from service until the service provider has ceased providing services in both capacities."

Some commenters have observed that the quoted sentence could be read to provide that a service provider who performs services for a service recipient as an employee, but who becomes an independent contractor for the same service recipient and whose anticipated level of services upon becoming an independent contractor are 20 percent or less than the average level of services performed during the immediately preceding 36-month period, would not have a separation from service because a complete termination of the contractual relationship with the service recipient has not occurred and, therefore, there is no separation from service as an independent contractor. Such a reading, however, would be inconsistent with the more specific rule that a service provider who is an employee separates from service if the employer and employee reasonably anticipate that the level of services to be performed after a certain date (whether as an employee or as an independent contractor) would permanently decrease to no more than 20 percent of the average level of services performed (whether as an employee or an independent contractor) over the immediately preceding 36-month period. To avoid potential confusion, these proposed regulations delete the quoted sentence from the regulations.

However, if a service provider, who performs services for a service recipient as an employee, becomes an independent contractor for the same service recipient but does not have a separation from service when he or she becomes an independent contractor (because at that time it is not reasonably anticipated that the level of services that would be provided by the service provider in the future would decrease to no more than 20 percent of the average level of services performed over the immediately preceding 36-month period), the service provider will have a separation from service in the future when the service provider has a separation from service based on the rules that apply to independent contractors.

IV. References to a Payment Being Made

As discussed in section II.B of this preamble entitled "Short-term Deferral Rule," the final regulations provide that a deferral of compensation does not occur under a plan if the service provider actually or constructively receives a payment that is not a deferred payment on or before the last day of the applicable $2^1/_2$ month period. The final regulations further provide that, for this purpose, a payment is treated as actually or constructively received if the payment is includible in income, including if the payment is includible under the economic benefit doctrine, section 83, section 402(b), or section 457(f). Further, § 1.409A-2(b)(2) of the final regulations provides that, for purposes of subsequent changes in the time or form of payment, the term "payment" generally refers to each separately identified amount to which a service provider is entitled to payment under a plan on a determinable date. This section of the final regulations provides that a payment includes the provision of any taxable benefit, including cash or property. It also provides that a payment includes, but is not limited to, the transfer, cancellation, or reduction of an amount of deferred compensation in exchange for benefits under a welfare plan, a fringe benefit excludible from income, or any other benefit excludible from income. The final regulations, however, do not include a rule that is generally applicable for all purposes under section 409A to determine when a payment is made.

These proposed regulations add a generally applicable rule to determine when a payment has been made for all provisions of the regulations under section 409A. Under these proposed regulations, a payment is made, or the payment of an amount occurs, when any taxable benefit is actually or constructively received. Consistent with the final regulations, these proposed regulations provide that a payment includes a transfer of cash, any event that results in the inclusion of an amount in income under the economic benefit doctrine, a transfer of property includible in income under section 83, a contribution to a trust described in section 402(b) at the time includible in income under section 402(b), and the transfer or creation of a beneficial interest in a section 402(b) trust at the time includible in income under section 402(b). In addition, a payment is made upon the transfer, cancellation, or reduction of an amount of deferred compensation in exchange for benefits under a welfare plan, a non-taxable fringe benefit, or any other nontaxable benefit.

The final regulations generally provide that the inclusion of an amount in income under section 457(f)(1)(A) is treated as a payment under section 409A for purposes of the short-term deferral rule under § 1.409A-1(b)(4), but is generally not treated as a payment for other purposes under section 409A. Commenters, however, have observed that this treatment of income inclusion under section 457(f)(1)(A) is inconsistent with the rules under section 409A that generally treat the inclusion of any amount in income as a payment for all purposes under section 409A. These commenters have also noted that a primary purpose of section 409A is to limit the ability of a service provider or service recipient to change the time at which deferred compensation is included in income after the time of payment is established and that the failure to treat income inclusion under section 457(f)(1)(A) as a payment would be inconsistent with this purpose. In response to these observations, these proposed regulations provide that the inclusion of an amount in income under section 457(f)(1)(A) is treated a payment for all purposes under section 409A.

Under this rule, if the plan provides for a deferral of compensation under section 409A: (1) Plan terms that specify the conditions to which the payment is subject and thus when a substantial risk of forfeiture lapses for purposes of section 457(f)(1)(A) (and, consequently, determine when an amount is includible in income) would be treated as plan terms providing for the payment of the amount includible in income, and (2) all rules under section 409A applicable to the payment of an amount would apply to the inclusion of an amount under section 457(f)(1)(A). A plan would not be a deferred compensation plan within the meaning of section 409A to the extent that the amounts payable under the plan are short-term deferrals under § 1.409A-1(b)(4). However, in certain limited circumstances, amounts includible in income under section 457(f)(1)(A) may not be short-term deferrals under § 1.409A-1(b)(4). For example, under the proposed section 457(f) regulations (REG-147196-07), which are also published in the Proposed Rules section of this issue of the *Federal Register*, in certain circumstances conditioning a payment upon compliance with a noncompetition agreement will result in the payment being subject to a substantial risk of forfeiture for purposes of section 457(f)(1)(A), but that payment would not be treated as subject to a substantial risk of forfeiture for purposes of section 409A. In such cases, the amount payable at the end of the term of the noncompetition agreement upon compliance with the noncompete will be includible in income under section 457(f)(1)(A) only at the end of the term of the agreement under the section 457(f) regulations as proposed, but for purposes of section 409A will be deferred compensation (and not a short-term deferral), the payment of which is subject to the rules of section 409A.[2] See proposed § 1.457-12(e) (REG-147196-07); see also proposed § 1.457-12(a)(4) (REG-147196-07).

The Treasury Department and the IRS request comments on whether rules similar to those applicable to amounts included in income under section 457(f) should be adopted for amounts included in income under section 457A.

These proposed regulations also clarify that a transfer of property that is substantially nonvested (as defined under § 1.83-3(b)) to satisfy an obligation under a nonqualified deferred compensation plan is not a payment for purposes of section 409A unless the recipient makes an election under section 83(b) to include in income the fair market value of the property (disregarding lapse restrictions), less any amount paid for the property. These proposed regulations also make conforming

---

[2] There may also be instances in which a portion of an amount payable under an arrangement that is subject to section 457(f) is a short-term deferral for purposes of both section 409A and section 457(f)(1)(A), while another portion of the amount is a deferral of compensation for purposes of section 409A. For example, assume an arrangement subject to section 457(f) provides for payment of a specified dollar amount plus earnings upon separation from service, with vesting to occur when the service provider has completed three years of service. The specified dollar amount plus earnings to date is includible in income under section 457(f)(1)(A) when the service provider completes three years of service, and that amount will be a short-term deferral under section 409A if the service provider includes it in income at that time. The service provider's right to receive a payment of additional earnings accruing after the vesting date is a deferred compensation plan under section 409A.

clarifications to rules under § 1.409A-1(a)(4) regarding nonqualified deferred compensation plans subject to sections 457(f) and 457A, § 1.409A-1(b)(4) regarding the short-term deferral rule, and § 1.409A-2(b)(2) regarding the separate payment rule.

V. Permissible Payments

A. Death

The final regulations provide that an amount deferred under a nonqualified deferred compensation plan may be paid only at a specified time or upon an event set forth under the regulations. One of the permissible events upon which an amount may be paid is the service provider's death. The final regulations also provide that a payment is treated as made upon a date specified under the plan (including at the time a specified event occurs) if the payment is made on that date or on a later date within the same taxable year of the service provider or, if later, by the 15th day of the third calendar month following the date specified under the plan, provided that the service provider is not permitted, directly or indirectly, to designate the taxable year of the payment.

Some commenters have questioned whether these and other rules in the final regulations applicable to amounts payable upon the death of a service provider also apply in the case of the death of a beneficiary who has become entitled to the payment of an amount due to a service provider's death. These proposed regulations clarify that the rules applicable to amounts payable upon the death of a service provider also apply to amounts payable upon the death of a beneficiary.

Also, some commenters have indicated that the time periods for the payment of amounts following death often are not long enough to resolve certain issues related to the death (for example, confirming the death and completing probate). In view of the practical issues that often arise following a death, these proposed regulations provide that an amount payable following the death of a service provider, or following the death of a beneficiary who has become entitled to payment due to the service provider's death, that is to be paid at any time during the period beginning on the date of death and ending on December 31 of the first calendar year following the calendar year during which the death occurs is treated as timely paid if it is paid at any time during this period. A plan is not required to specify any particular date within this period as the payment date and may rely on this rule if the plan provides that an amount will be paid at some time during this period, including if the plan provides that payment will be made upon death without defining the period for payment following death in any other manner, and including if the plan provides that payment will be made on a date within this period determined in the discretion of the beneficiary. These proposed regulations further provide that a plan providing for the payment of an amount at any time during this specified period may be amended to provide for the payment of that amount (or the payment of that amount may be made without amending the plan) at any other time during this period (including a time determined in the discretion of a beneficiary) without failing to meet the requirements of the deferral election provisions of § 1.409A-2 or the permissible payment provisions of § 1.409A-3, including the prohibition on the acceleration of payments under § 1.409A-3(j). For example, a plan that provides for a payment to be made during the first calendar year beginning after the death of a service provider may be amended to provide for the payment of the amount (or the payment may be made under the plan without such amendment) at any time during the period beginning on the date of death and ending on December 31 of the first calendar year following the calendar year during which the death occurs. For additional rules concerning payments due upon a beneficiary's death, see section VI.A of this preamble.

B. *Certain Transaction-based Compensation*

The final regulations provide special rules for payments of transaction-based compensation. Transaction-based compensation payments are payments related to certain types of changes in control that (1) occur because a service recipient purchases its stock held by a service provider or because the service recipient or a third party purchases a stock right held by a service provider, or (2) are calculated by reference to the value of service recipient stock. Under the final regulations, transaction-based compensation may be treated as paid at a designated date or pursuant to a payment schedule that complies with the requirements of section 409A(a) if it is paid on the same schedule and under the same terms and conditions as apply to payments to shareholders generally with respect to stock of the service recipient pursuant to the change in control. Likewise, transaction-based compensation meeting these requirements will not fail to meet the requirements of the initial or subsequent deferral election rules under section 409A if it is paid not later than five years after the change in control event. These proposed regulations clarify that the special payment rules for transaction-based compensation apply to a statutory stock option or a stock right that did not otherwise provide for deferred compensation before the purchase or agreement to purchase the stock right. Accordingly, the purchase (or agreement to purchase) such a statutory stock option or stock right in a manner consistent with these rules does not result in the statutory stock option or stock right being treated as having provided for the deferral of compensation from the original grant date.

VI. Prohibition on Acceleration of Payments

A. Payments to Beneficiaries Upon Death, Disability, or Unforeseeable Emergency

Under the final regulations, a prohibited acceleration of a payment does not result from the addition of death, disability, or unforeseeable emergency as a potentially earlier alternative payment event for an amount previously deferred. However, under the final regulations, this exception applies only with respect to a service provider's death, disability, or unforeseeable emergency and does not apply with respect to the death, disability, or unforeseeable emergency of a beneficiary who has become entitled to a payment due to the service provider's death. These proposed regulations provide that this exception also applies to the payment of deferred amounts upon the death, disability, or unforeseeable emergency of a beneficiary who has become entitled to payment due to a service provider's death. These proposed regulations also clarify that a schedule of payments (including payments treated as a single payment) that has already commenced prior to a service provider's or a beneficiary's death, disability, or unforeseeable emergency may be accelerated upon the death, disability, or unforeseeable emergency.

B. Compliance With Bona Fide Foreign Ethics Laws or Conflicts of Interest Laws

Under the final regulations, a plan may provide for acceleration of the time or schedule of a payment, or a payment may be made under a plan, to the extent reasonably necessary to avoid the violation of a Federal, state, local, or foreign ethics or conflicts of interest law. However, with respect to a foreign ethics or conflicts of interest law, this exception applies only to foreign earned income from sources within the foreign country that promulgated the law. Commenters have suggested that this provision should not be limited to foreign earned income because the requirements of foreign ethics or conflicts of interest laws may affect both the payment of foreign and United States earned income. These proposed regulations expand the scope of this provision to permit the acceleration of any nonqualified deferred compensation if the acceleration is reasonably necessary to comply with a *bona fide* foreign ethics or conflicts of interest law.

C. Plan Terminations and Liquidations

Under the final regulations, a plan may provide for the acceleration of a payment made pursuant to the termination and liquidation of a plan under certain circumstances. Specifically, a plan may provide for the acceleration of a payment if the plan is terminated and liquidated within 12 months of a corporate dissolution taxed under section 331, or with the approval of a bankruptcy court pursuant to 11 U.S.C. section 503(b)(1)(A) if certain other conditions are satisfied. The citation to 11 U.S.C. section 503(b)(1)(A) is erroneous. These proposed regulations correct this provision by retaining the operative rule but deleting the section reference.

The final regulations also provide that a payment may be accelerated pursuant to a change in control event as described under § 1.409A-3(j)(4)(ix)(B) or in other circumstances provided certain requirements are satisfied, as described under § 1.409A-3(j)(4)(ix)(C). To terminate a plan pursuant to § 1.409A-3(j)(4)(ix)(C), the final regulations provide that the service recipient must terminate and liquidate all plans sponsored by the service recipient that would be aggregated with the terminated plan under the plan aggregation rules under § 1.409A-1(c) of the final regulations if the same service provider had deferrals of compensation under all such plans. The final regulations also provide that for three years following the date on which the service recipient took all necessary action to irrevocably terminate and liquidate the plan the service recipient cannot adopt a new plan that would be aggregated with the terminated and liquidated plan if the same service provider participated in both plans. Some commenters have asked whether these rules mean that only the plans of a particular category in which a particular service provider actually participates must be terminated if a plan in which that service provider participates is terminated.

The plan aggregation rules under § 1.409A-1(c)(2) of the final regulations identify nine different types of nonqualified deferred compensation plans - account balance plans providing for elective deferrals, account balance plans that do not provide for elective deferrals, nonaccount balance plans, separation pay plans, plans providing for in-kind benefits or reimbursements, split-dollar plans, foreign earned income plans, stock right plans, and plans that are not any of the foregoing. All plans of the same type in which the same service provider participates are treated as a single plan. The rule set forth under § 1.409A-3(j)(4)(ix)(C) that requires the termination and liquidation of all plans sponsored by the service recipient that would be aggregated with the terminated plan "if the same service provider had deferrals of compensation" under all of those plans is intended to require the termination of all plans in the same plan category sponsored by the service recipient. The reference to the "same service provider" having deferrals of compensation under all of those plans refers to participation of a hypothetical service provider in all such plans, which would be required to aggregate all of the plans under the section 409A plan aggregation rules.

The Treasury Department and the IRS have concluded that the meaning of the plan termination rule under § 1.409A-3(j)(4)(ix)(C) is not ambiguous. However, to address the questions raised by commenters, these proposed regulations further clarify that the acceleration of a payment pursuant to this rule is permitted only if the service recipient terminates and liquidates all plans of the same category that the service recipient sponsors, and not merely all plans of the same category in which a particular service provider actually participates. These proposed regulations also clarify that under this rule, for a period of three years following the termination and liquidation of a plan, the service recipient cannot adopt a new plan of the same category as the terminated and liquidated plan, regardless of which service providers participate in the plan.

D. Offset Provisions

The final regulations provide that the payment of an amount as a substitute for a payment of deferred compensation is generally treated as a payment of the deferred compensation. They also provide that when the payment of an amount results in an actual or potential reduction of, or current or future offset to, an amount of deferred compensation, the payment is a substitute for the deferred compensation. Further, the final regulations provide that if a service provider's right to deferred compensation is made subject to anticipation, alienation, sale, transfer, assignment, pledge, encumbrance, attachment, or garnishment by the service provider's creditors, the deferred compensation is treated as having been paid. Under certain circumstances, these provisions may result in an amount being paid (or treated as paid) before the payment date or event specified in the plan in violation of the prohibition on the acceleration of payments under section 409A. The final regulations, however, include a de minimis exception to these rules pursuant to which a plan may provide for the acceleration of the time or schedule of a payment, or a payment may be made under a plan, in satisfaction of a debt of the service provider if the debt is incurred in the ordinary course of the service relationship, the entire offset in any taxable year does not exceed $5,000, and the offset is taken at the same time and in the same amount as the debt otherwise would have been due from the service provider.

Stakeholders have observed that the prohibition on offsets may conflict with certain laws regarding debt collection by the Federal government (for example, 31 U.S.C. sections 3711, *et. seq.*), and that the exception for small debts is insufficient to permit the enforcement of these laws. Because these laws would effectively prevent certain government entities from providing nonqualified deferred compensation in a manner that complies with the requirements of section 409A(a) and because of the limited applicability of Federal debt collection laws, the Treasury Department and the IRS have determined that it is appropriate to expand the current exception to the prohibition on accelerated payments for certain offsets to permit a plan to provide for the acceleration of the time or schedule of a payment, or to make a payment, to the extent reasonably necessary to comply with Federal laws regarding debt collection.

VII. Amount Includible in Income under Section 409A

The proposed income inclusion regulations provide that the amount includible in income for a taxable year if a nonqualified deferred compensation plan fails to meet the requirements of section 409A(a) at any time during that taxable year equals the excess of (1) the total amount deferred under the plan for that taxable year, including any payments under the plan during that taxable year, over (2) the portion of that amount, if any, that is either subject to a substantial risk of forfeiture or has been previously included in income. The proposed income inclusion regulations, however, include an anti-abuse provision under § 1.409A-4(a)(1)(ii)(B), which provides that an amount otherwise subject to a substantial risk of forfeiture for purposes of determining the amount includible in income under a plan will be treated as not subject to a substantial risk of forfeiture for these purposes if the facts and circumstances indicate that a service recipient has a pattern or practice of permitting impermissible changes in the time or form of payment with respect to nonvested deferred amounts under one or more nonqualified deferred compensation plans and either (i) an impermissible change in the time or form of payment applies to the amount or (ii) the facts and circumstances indicate that the amount would be affected by the pattern or practice.

Although these rules permit the correction of certain plan provisions that fail to comply with the requirements of section 409A(a) while amounts are nonvested without including the amounts in income or incurring an additional tax, they were not intended to allow service recipients to change time or form of payment provisions that otherwise meet the requirements of section 409A(a) in a manner that fails to comply with section 409A(a), and they were not intended to permit service recipients to create errors in nonqualified deferred compensation plans with respect to nonvested amounts with the intention of using those errors as a pretext for establishing or changing a time or form of payment in a manner that fails to comply with section 409A(a). Accordingly, these proposed regulations clarify and modify the anti-abuse rule under § 1.409A-4(a)(1)(ii)(B) of the proposed income inclusion regulations to preclude changes of this nature.

First, these proposed regulations clarify that a deferred amount that is otherwise subject to a substantial risk of forfeiture is treated as not subject to a substantial risk of forfeiture for a service provider's taxable year during which there is a change in a plan provision (including an initial deferral election provision) that is not otherwise permitted under section 409A and the final regulations and that affects the time or form of payment of the amount if there is no reasonable, good faith basis for concluding that the original provision failed to meet the requirements of section 409A(a) and that the change is necessary to bring the plan into compliance with the requirements of section 409A(a).

Second, these proposed regulations provide examples of the types of facts and circumstances that indicate whether a service recipient has a pattern or practice of permitting impermissible changes in the time or form of payment with respect to nonvested deferred amounts under one or more plans. If the service recipient has such a pattern or practice that would affect a nonvested deferred amount, that amount is treated as not subject to a substantial risk of forfeiture. The facts and circumstances include: Whether a service recipient has taken commercially reasonable measures to identify and correct substantially similar failures promptly upon discovery; whether substantially similar failures have occurred with respect to nonvested deferred amounts to a greater extent than with respect to vested deferred amounts; whether substantially similar failures occur more frequently with respect to newly adopted plans; and whether substantially similar failures appear intentional, are numerous, or repeat common past failures that have since been corrected.

Third, these proposed regulations provide that, to the extent generally applicable guidance regarding the correction of section 409A failures prescribes a particular correction method (or methods) for a type of plan failure, that correction method (or one of the permissible correction methods) must be used if a service recipient chooses to correct that type of a failure with respect to a nonvested deferred amount. In addition, these proposed regulations provide that substantially similar failures affecting nonvested deferred amounts must be corrected in substantially the same manner.

A service recipient correcting a plan failure affecting a nonvested deferred amount is not required, solely with respect to the nonvested deferred amount, to comply with any requirement under generally applicable guidance regarding the correction of section 409A failures that is unrelated to the method for correcting the failure, such as general eligibility requirements, income inclusion, additional taxes, premium interest, or information reporting by the service recipient or service provider. Accordingly, a service recipient may amend a noncompliant plan term in a manner permitted under applicable correction guidance even though the failure may not have been eligible for correction under that guidance (for example, due to applicable timing requirements). In addition, the portion of the nonvested deferred amount that is affected by the correction is not subject to income inclusion, additional taxes, or applicable premium interest under section 409A(a)(1), and neither the service recipient nor the service provider is required to notify the IRS of the correction. For a description of the currently available corrections methods, see Notice 2008-113 (2008-51 IRB 1305), Notice 2010-6 (2010-3 IRB 275), and Notice 2010-80 (2010-51 IRB 853).

VIII. Individual and Entity Service Providers

Under the final regulations, the term service provider includes an individual, corporation, subchapter S corporation, partnership, personal service corporation, noncorporate entity that would be a personal service corporation if it were a corporation, qualified personal service corporation, and noncorporate entity that would be a qualified personal service corporation if it were a corporation. These proposed regulations clarify §§1.409A-1(b)(5)(vi)(A), 1.409A-1(b)(5)(vi)(E), 1.409A-1(b)(5)(vi)(F), and 1.409A-3(i)(5)(iii) of the final regulations to reflect that a service provider can be an entity as well as an individual. These proposed regulations also clarify §1.409A-1(b)(3) of the final regulations to correct an erroneous reference to "service provider" that should be "service recipient."

Proposed Effective Dates

General Applicability Date for Amendments to Final Regulations

The provisions of these proposed regulations amending the final regulations are proposed to be applicable on or after the date on which they are published as final regulations in the *Federal Register*. For periods before this date, the existing final regulations and other applicable guidance apply (without regard to these proposed regulations). The applicability date for the existing final regulations in §1.409A-6(b) is accordingly amended to reflect extension of certain transition relief through 2008 under Notice 2007-86, 2007-46 IRB 990. Taxpayers may, however, rely on these proposed regulations before they are published as final regulations, and until final regulations are published the IRS will not assert positions that are contrary to the positions set forth in these proposed regulations.

Certain provisions of these proposed amendments to the final regulations are not intended as substantive changes to the current requirements under section 409A. Accordingly, the Treasury Department and the IRS have concluded that the following positions may not properly be taken under the existing final regulations: (1) That the transfer of restricted stock for which no section 83(b) election is made or the transfer of a stock option that does not have a readily ascertainable fair market value would result in a payment under a plan; (2) that a contribution to a section 402(b) trust includible in income under section 402(b) to fund an obligation under a plan would not result in a payment under a plan; (3) that a stock purchase treated as a deemed asset sale under section 338 is a sale or other disposition of assets for purposes of determining when a service provider separates from service as a result of an asset purchase transaction; or (4) that the exception to the prohibition on acceleration of a payment upon a termination and liquidation of a plan pursuant to §1.409A-3(j)(4)(ix)(C) applies if the service recipient terminates and liquidates only the plans of the same category in which a particular service provider participates, rather than all plans of the same category that the service recipient sponsors.

General Applicability Date for Amendments to Proposed Income Inclusion Regulations

The proposed income inclusion regulations are proposed to be applicable on or after the date on which they are published as final regulations in the *Federal Register*. Notice 2008-115 provides that, until the Treasury Department and the IRS issue further guidance, compliance with the provisions of the proposed income inclusion regulations with respect to the calculation of the amount includible in income under section 409A(a)(1) and the calculation of the additional taxes under section 409A(a)(1) will be treated as compliance with the requirements of section 409A(a), provided that the taxpayer complies with all of the provisions of the proposed regulations. Until the Treasury Department and the IRS issue further guidance, taxpayers may rely on the proposed income inclusion regulations, as modified by the amendment of §1.409A-4(a)(1)(ii)(B) in these proposed regulations, for purposes of calculating the amount includible in income under section 409A(a)(1) (including the identification and treatment of deferred amounts subject to a substantial risk of forfeiture) and the calculation of the additional taxes under section 409A(a)(1), and the IRS will not assert positions with respect to periods before the date final regulations are published in the *Federal Register* that are contrary to the positions set forth in the proposed income inclusion regulations as amended by these proposed regulations.

Special Applicability Dates for Amendments to Recurring Part-Year Compensation Rules

The rules set forth in these proposed regulations regarding recurring part-year compensation are proposed to be applicable on and after the date on which these proposed regulations are published as final regulations in the *Federal Register*. However, taxpayers may rely on either the rules in these proposed regulations or the rules in Notice 2008-62 relating to recurring part-year compensation for the taxable year in which these proposed regulations are published as final regulations and all prior taxable years.

Effect on Other Documents

These proposed regulations do not affect the applicability of other guidance issued with respect to section 409A, including Notice 2008-115, except that, for the permitted reliance on the proposed income inclusion regulations, these proposed regulations withdraw §1.409A-4(a)(1)(ii)(B) of the proposed income inclusion regulations and replace it with a new §1.409A-4(a)(1)(ii)(B).

Statement of Availability of IRS Documents

IRS Revenue Procedures, Revenue Rulings notices, and other guidance cited in this document are published in the Internal Revenue Bulletin (or Cumulative Bulletin) and are available from the Superintendent of Documents, U.S. Government Printing Office, Washington, DC 20402, or by visiting the IRS website at *http://www.irs.gov*. (See §601.601(d)(2)(ii)(*b*) of this chapter.)

Special Analyses

Certain IRS regulations, including this one, are exempt from the requirements of Executive Order 12866, as supplemented and reaffirmed by Executive Order 13563. Therefore, a regulatory impact assessment is not required. It also has been determined that section 553(b) of the Administrative Procedure Act (5 U.S.C. chapter 5) does not apply to these proposed regulations. It is hereby certified that the collection of information in these proposed regulations would not have a significant impact on a substantial number of small entities. This certification is based on the fact that these proposed regulations only provide guidance on how to satisfy existing collection of information requirements. Accordingly, a Regulatory Flexibility Analysis is not required. Pursuant to section 7805(f) of the Code, these proposed regulations have been submitted to the Chief Counsel for Advocacy of the Small Business Administration for comment on its impact on small business.

Comments and Requests for Public Hearing

Before these proposed regulations are adopted as final regulations, consideration will be given to any comments that are submitted timely to the IRS as prescribed in this preamble under the "ADDRESSES" heading. The Treasury Department and the IRS request comments on all aspects of the rules proposed by these proposed regulations. All comments will be available at www.regulations.gov or upon request. A public hearing may be scheduled if requested by any person who timely submits comments. If a public hearing is scheduled, notice of the date, time and place for the hearing will be published in the *Federal Register*.

Drafting Information

The principal author of these proposed regulations is Gregory Burns, Office of Division Counsel/ Associate Chief Counsel (Tax Exempt and Government Entities). However, other personnel from the Treasury Department and the IRS participated in their development.

[¶49,703] Proposed Amendments of Regulations (REG-147196-07) Proposed Regulations, NPRM REG-147196-07, published in the Federal Register on June 22, 2016.

[Code Sec. 457]

Deferred compensation plans: Government and Tax-Exempt: Proposed regulations.—Amendments of Reg. §§1.457-1, 1.457-2, 1.457-4, 1.457-6, 1.457-7, 1.457-9, 1.457-10, 1.457-11, 1.457-12 and 1.457-13, prescribing rules under section 457 of the Internal Revenue Code for the taxation of compensation deferred under plans established and maintained by State or local governments or other tax exempt organizations, are proposed.

AGENCY: Internal Revenue Service (IRS), Treasury.

ACTION: Notice of proposed rulemaking and notice of public hearing.

SUMMARY: This document contains proposed regulations prescribing rules under section 457 of the Internal Revenue Code for the taxation of compensation deferred under plans established and maintained by State or local governments or other tax exempt organizations. These proposed regulations include rules for determining when amounts deferred under these plans are includible in income, the amounts that are includible in income, and the types of plans that are not subject to these rules. The proposed regulations would affect participants, beneficiaries, sponsors, and administrators of certain plans sponsored by State or local governments or tax-exempt organizations that provide for a deferral of compensation. This document also provides a notice of a public hearing on the proposed regulations.

DATES: Written or electronic comments on these proposed regulations must be received by September 20, 2016. Outline of topics to be discussed at the public hearing scheduled for October 18, 2016 at 10 a.m. must be received by September 20, 2016.

ADDRESSES: Send submissions to: CC:PA:LPD:PR (REG-147196-07), room 5203, Internal Revenue Service, P.O. Box 7604, Ben Franklin Station, Washington DC, 20044. Submissions may be hand delivered Monday through Friday, between the hours of 8 a.m. and 4 p.m. to CC:PA:LPD:PR (REG-147196-07), Courier's Desk, Internal Revenue Service, 1111 Constitution Avenue, N.W., Washington DC, 20224 or sent electronically, via the Federal eRulemaking Portal at www.regulations.gov (IRS REG-147196-07). The public hearing will be held in the IRS Auditorium, Internal Revenue Building, 1111 Constitution Avenue, N.W., Washington DC, 20224.

FOR FURTHER INFORMATION CONTACT: Concerning the proposed regulations under section 457, Keith Kost at (202) 317-6799 or Cheryl Press at (202) 317-4148, concerning submission of comments, the hearing, and/or to be placed on the building access list to attend the hearing, Regina Johnson at (202) 317-6901 (not toll-free numbers).

SUPPLEMENTARY INFORMATION:

Background

This document contains proposed amendments to the Income Tax Regulations (26 CFR part 1) under section 457(a), (b), and (f) of the Internal Revenue Code (Code), as well as proposed regulations under section 457(e)(11), (e)(12), and (g)(4). Generally, if a deferred compensation plan of a State or local government or tax-exempt entity does not satisfy the requirements of section 457(b), (c), (d), and, in the case of a plan that is maintained by a State or local government, (g), compensation deferred under the plan will be included in income in accordance with section 457(f) unless the plan is not subject to section 457 or is treated as not providing for a deferral of compensation for purposes of section 457. Section 457(e) includes certain definitions and special rules for purposes of section 457 and describes certain plans that either are not subject to section 457 or are treated as not providing for a deferral of compensation under section 457.[1]

Section 457(a)(1) provides that any amount of compensation deferred under an eligible deferred compensation plan as defined in section 457(b) (an eligible plan), and any income attributable to the amounts so deferred, is includible in gross income only for the taxable year in which the compensation or other income is paid to the participant or beneficiary in the case of an eligible employer described in section 457(e)(1)(A) or is paid or otherwise made available to the participant or beneficiary in the case of an eligible employer described in section 457(e)(1)(B). An eligible employer described in section 457(e)(1)(A) means a State, a political subdivision of a State, or any agency or instrumentality of a State or political subdivision of a State (a governmental entity). An eligible employer described in section 457(e)(1)(B) means any organization other than a governmental entity that is exempt from tax under subtitle A (a tax-exempt entity).

Section 457(f)(1)(A) provides that, in the case of a plan of an eligible employer providing for a deferral of compensation, if the plan is not an eligible plan, the compensation is included in gross income when the rights to payment of the compensation are not subject to a substantial risk of forfeiture, as defined in section 457(f)(3)(B).[2] Section 457(f)(1)(B) provides that the tax treatment of any amount made available under the plan will be determined under section 72. Section 457(f)(2) provides that section 457(f)(1) does not apply to a plan that is described in section 401(a) or an annuity plan or contract described in section 403, the portion of any plan that consists of a transfer of property described in section 83, the portion of a plan that consists of a trust described in section 402(b), a qualified governmental excess benefit arrangement described in section 415(m), or the portion of any applicable employment retention plan described in section 457(f)(4).

Section 457(e)(11) provides that certain plans are treated as not providing for a deferral of compensation. These plans include any bona fide vacation leave, sick leave, compensatory time, severance pay, disability pay, or death benefit plan, as well as any plan paying solely length of service awards to certain bona fide volunteers (or their beneficiaries) and certain voluntary early retirement incentive plans.[3] Section 457(e)(12) provides that section 457 does not apply to certain nonelective deferred compensation of nonemployees.

On July 11, 2003, the Treasury Department and the IRS issued final regulations under section 457 (TD 9075) (68 FR 41230) (2003 final regulations). The 2003 final regulations provide guidance on deferred compensation plans of eligible employers, including eligible plans under section 457(b). The 2003 final regulations also reflect the changes made to section 457 by the Tax Reform Act of 1986, Public Law 99-514 (100 Stat. 2494), the Small Business Job Protection Act of 1996, Public Law 104-188 (110 Stat. 1755), the Taxpayer Relief Act of 1997, Public Law 105-34 (111 Stat. 788), the Economic Growth and Tax Relief Reconciliation Act of 2001, Public Law 107-16 (115 Stat. 38), and the Job Creation and Worker Assistance Act of 2002, Public Law 107-147 (116 Stat. 21). The proposed amendments to the 2003 final regulations under section 457(a), (b), and (g) contained in this

---

[1] Plans described in certain statutes that are not incorporated into the Code are not subject to section 457. See sections 1107(c)(3)(B), 1107(c)(4), and 1107(c)(5) of the Tax Reform Act of 1986, Public Law 99-514 (100 Stat. 2494 (1986)), as amended, and sections 1101(e)(6), 6064(d)(2), and 6064(d)(3) of the Technical and Miscellaneous Revenue Act of 1988, Public Law 100-647 (102 Stat. 3342 (1988)).

[2] In Notice 2007-62 (2007-2 CB 331 (August 6, 2007)), the Treasury Department and the IRS announced the intent to issue guidance under section 457, including providing definitions of a bona fide severance pay plan under section 457(e)(11) and substantial risk of forfeiture under section 457(f)(3)(B). In response to comments received in response to a request in Notice 2007-62 (on subjects including but not limited to severance pay, covenants not to compete, and the definition of substantial risk of forfeiture), the rules in these proposed regulations have been modified from the proposals announced in that notice.

[3] Announcement 2000-1 (2000-1 CB 294 (January 1, 2000)), provides transitional guidance on the reporting requirements for certain broad-based, nonelective deferred compensation plans maintained by State or local governments. The announcement states that, pending the issuance of further guidance, a State or local government should not report amounts for any year before the year in which a participant or beneficiary is in actual or constructive receipt of those amounts if the amounts are provided under a plan that the State or local government has been treating as a bona fide severance pay plan under section 457(e)(11) for years before calendar year 1999. To be eligible for this transitional relief, the plan must satisfy certain requirements described in the announcement.

document include amendments to reflect subsequent statutory changes made to section 457. The following sections of this preamble provide a chronological description of the relevant changes made after the 2003 final regulations were issued. (For a summary of the proposed changes to the 2003 final regulations, see the Explanation of Provisions section of this preamble.)

I. *American Jobs Creation Act of 2004*

Section 885 of the American Jobs Creation Act of 2004, Public Law 108-357 (118 Stat. 1418), added section 409A to the Code. Section 409A generally provides that, if at any time during a taxable year a nonqualified deferred compensation plan fails to meet the requirements of section 409A or is not operated in accordance with those requirements, all amounts deferred under the plan for the taxable year and all preceding taxable years are includible in gross income to the extent the amounts are not subject to a substantial risk of forfeiture and were not previously included in gross income.

On April 17, 2007, the Treasury Department and the IRS issued final regulations under section 409A (TD 9312) at 72 FR 19234 (final section 409A regulations). The final section 409A regulations provide guidance on the definition of certain terms and the types of plans covered under section 409A, permissible deferral elections under section 409A, and permissible payments under section 409A. The final section 409A regulations provide that a deferred compensation plan of a governmental entity or a tax-exempt entity that is subject to section 457(f) may constitute a nonqualified deferred compensation plan for purposes of section 409A and that the rules of section 409A apply separately and in addition to any requirements applicable to these plans under section 457(f).

On December 8, 2008, proposed regulations under section 409A were published in the **Federal Register** (73 FR 74380) (proposed section 409A regulations) that provide guidance on the calculation of amounts includible in income under section 409A(a) and the additional taxes imposed by that section with respect to arrangements that do not comply with the requirements of section 409A(a).

In Notice 2008-62 (2008-29 IRB 130 (July 21, 2008)), the Treasury Department and the IRS provided guidance under sections 409A and 457(f) regarding recurring part-year compensation. For this purpose, recurring part-year compensation is compensation paid for services rendered in a position that the employer and employee reasonably anticipate will continue under similar terms and conditions in subsequent years, and under which the employee will be required to provide services during successive service periods each of which comprises less than 12 months (for example, a teacher providing services during a school year comprised of 10 consecutive months) and each of which begins in one taxable year of the employee and ends in the next taxable year. Notice 2008-62 provides that an arrangement under which an employee or independent contractor receives recurring part-year compensation does not provide for the deferral of compensation for purposes of section 409A or for purposes of section 457(f) if (A) the arrangement does not defer payment of any of the recurring part-year compensation beyond the last day of the 13th month following the beginning of the service period, and (B) the arrangement does not defer from one taxable year to the next taxable year the payment of more than the applicable dollar amount under section 402(g)(1)(B) ($18,000 for 2016). The notice provides that taxpayers may rely on this rule beginning in the first taxable year that includes July 1, 2008.

II. *Pension Protection Act of 2006*

The Pension Protection Act of 2006, Public Law 109-280 (120 Stat. 780) (PPA '06), permits a participant's designated beneficiary who is not a surviving spouse to roll over, in a direct trustee-to-trustee transfer, distributions from an eligible plan maintained by a governmental entity (an eligible governmental plan) to an individual retirement account or annuity (IRA). Section 829 of PPA '06 added section 402(c)(11) to the Code, which provides that this type of transfer is treated as an eligible rollover distribution for purposes of section 402(c).

Section 845(b)(3) of PPA '06 added section 457(a)(3) to the Code, which provides an exclusion from gross income for amounts that are distributed from an eligible governmental plan to the extent provided in section 402(l). Section 402(l) provides that distributions from certain governmental retirement plans are excluded from the gross income of an eligible retired public safety officer to the extent the distributions do not exceed the amount paid by the retired officer for qualified health insurance premiums for the year, up to a maximum of $3,000. See Notice 2007-7, part IV (2007-1 CB 395 (January 29, 2007)), as well as Notice 2007-99 (2007-2 CB 1243 (December 26, 2007)), for guidance on the application of section 402(l).

Section 1104(a)(1) of PPA '06 added section 457(e)(11)(D) to the Code, which treats applicable voluntary early retirement incentive plans as bona fide severance pay plans that do not provide for a deferral of compensation under section 457 with respect to payments or supplements that are an early retirement benefit, a retirement-type subsidy, or a social security supplement in coordination with a defined benefit pension plan. This treatment applies only to the extent the payments otherwise could have been provided under the defined benefit plan (determined as if section 411 applied to the defined benefit plan). Under section 457(e)(11)(D)(ii), an applicable voluntary early retirement incentive plan may be maintained only by a local educational agency or a tax-exempt education association.[4]

---

[4] A local education agency is defined in section 9101 of the Elementary and Secondary Education Act of 1965, Public Law 89-10 (79 Stat. 27), as a public board of education or other public authority legally constituted within a State for either administrative control or direction of, or to perform a service function for, public elementary schools or secondary

Section 1104(b)(1) of PPA '06 added section 457(f)(2)(F) to the Code, which provides that section 457(f)(1) does not apply to an applicable employment retention plan. Under section 457(f)(4), an applicable employment retention plan is a plan maintained by a local educational agency or a tax-exempt education association to pay additional compensation upon severance from employment for purposes of employee retention or rewarding employees to the extent that the benefits payable under the plan do not exceed twice the applicable annual dollar limit on deferrals in section 457(e)(15).[5]

III. *Heroes Earnings Assistance and Relief Tax Act of 2008*

Section 104(c) of the Heroes Earnings Assistance and Relief Tax Act of 2008, Public Law 110-245 (122 Stat. 1624) (HEART Act), amended section 457 to add section 457(g)(4) regarding benefits payable upon death during qualified active military service under the Uniformed Services Employment and Reemployment Rights Act of 1994, Public Law 103-353 (108 Stat. 3149). Section 457(g)(4) provides that an eligible governmental plan must meet the requirements of section 401(a)(37). Under section 401(a)(37), a plan is not treated as a qualified retirement plan unless the plan provides that, in the case of a participant who dies while performing qualified military service, the survivors of the participant are generally entitled to any additional benefits that would have been provided under the plan if the participant had resumed and then terminated employment on account of death. Section 105(b) of the HEART Act added section 414(u)(12) to the Code, which provides rules regarding (A) the treatment of differential wage payments as compensation and (B) the treatment of service in the uniformed services (as described in section 3401(h)(2)(A)) as a severance from employment for purposes of plan distribution requirements, including the distribution requirements of section 457(d)(1)(A)(ii).

IV. *Small Business Jobs Act of 2010 and American Taxpayer Relief Act of 2012*

Section 2111 of the Small Business Jobs Act of 2010, Public Law 111-240 (124 Stat. 2504) (SBJA), amended section 402A of the Code to allow an eligible governmental plan to include a qualified Roth contribution program, effective for taxable years beginning after December 31, 2010. SBJA also amended section 402A to permit taxable in-plan rollovers to qualified Roth accounts under eligible governmental plans. Section 902 of the American Taxpayer Relief Act of 2012, Public Law 112-240 (126 Stat. 2313), expanded the types of amounts eligible for an in-plan Roth rollover. For guidance relating to in-plan rollovers to qualified Roth accounts, see Notice 2013-74 (2013-52 IRB 819 (December 23, 2013)) and Notice 2010-84 (2010-51 IRB 872 (July 19, 2010)).

Explanation of Provisions

I. *Overview*

These proposed regulations make certain changes to the 2003 final regulations under sections 457(a), 457(b), and 457(g) to reflect statutory changes to section 457 since the publication of those regulations. In addition, these proposed regulations provide guidance on certain issues under sections 457(e)(11) and 457(e)(12) that are not addressed in the 2003 final regulations and provide additional guidance under section 457(f). Consistent with the 2003 final regulations, although the rules under section 457 apply to plan participants and beneficiaries without regard to whether the related services are provided by an employee or independent contractor, these proposed regulations often use the terms employee and employer to describe a service provider and a service recipient, respectively, without regard to whether the service provider is an independent contractor.[6]

II. *Regulatory Amendments to Reflect Statutory Changes to Section 457*

A. *Qualified Roth contribution program*

Section 1.457-4 of the 2003 final regulations provides that annual deferrals to an eligible plan that satisfy certain requirements are excluded from the gross income of the participant in the year deferred or contributed and are not includable in gross income until paid to the participant, in the case of an eligible governmental plan, or until paid or otherwise made available to the participant, in the case of an eligible plan of a tax-exempt entity. These proposed regulations amend § 1.457-4(a) and (b) to reflect the change made by SBJA to allow an eligible governmental plan to include a qualified Roth contribution program, as defined in section 402A(c)(1), under which designated Roth contributions are included in income in the year of deferral. Consistent with section 402A(b)(2), these proposed regulations provide that contributions and withdrawals of a participant's designated Roth contributions must be credited and debited to a designated Roth account maintained for the participant, and that the plan must maintain a record of each participant's investment in the contract with respect to the account. In addition, the proposed regulations provide that no forfeitures may be

(Footnote Continued)

schools in a city, county, township, school district, or other political subdivision of a State, or of or for a combination of school districts or counties that is recognized in a State as an administrative agency for its public elementary schools or secondary schools. A tax-exempt education association is an association that principally represents employees of one or more local education agencies and is an entity described in section 501(c)(5) or (6) that is exempt from tax under section 501(a).

[5] See also section 1104(c) of PPA '06, which amended section 3(2) of the Employee Retirement Income Security Act of 1974, Public Law 93-406 (88 Stat. 829) (ERISA), to provide that applicable voluntary early retirement incentive plans and applicable employment retention plans are treated as welfare plans (and not pension plans) for purposes of ERISA.

[6] Section 457(e)(2) provides that the performance of services for purposes of section 457 includes the performance of services as an independent contractor and that the person (or governmental entity) for whom these services are performed is treated as an employer.

allocated to a designated Roth account and that no contributions other than designated Roth contributions and rollover contributions described in section 402A(c)(3)(A) may be made to the account.

These proposed regulations also amend § 1.457-7(b)(1), which provides guidance regarding the circumstances under which amounts are included in income under an eligible governmental plan, to specify that qualified distributions from a designated Roth account are excluded from gross income.

B. *Certain distributions for qualified accident and health insurance premiums*

The proposed regulations amend the rules for the taxation of eligible governmental plan distributions under § 1.457-7(b) to reflect the change made by PPA '06 with respect to certain amounts distributed to an eligible public safety officer. The proposed regulations provide that distributions from an eligible governmental plan meeting the requirements of section 402(l) are excluded from gross income and are not subject to the general rule providing that amounts deferred under an eligible governmental plan are includable in the gross income of a participant or beneficiary for the taxable year in which they are paid. For this purpose, see section 402(l) for rules regarding the extent to which this income exclusion applies to a distribution (including the dollar limitation on the exclusion) and section 402(l)(4)(C) for the meaning of the term public safety officer.

C. *Rules related to qualified military service*

The proposed regulations amend § 1.457-2(f) to implement the requirements of section 457(g)(4), which was added by the HEART Act and which provides that an eligible governmental plan must meet the requirements of section 401(a)(37) (providing that, in the case of a participant who dies while performing qualified military service, the survivors of the participant generally are entitled to any additional benefits that would have been provided under the plan if the participant had resumed and then terminated employment on account of death). In addition the proposed regulations amend § 1.457-6(b)(1) to provide a cross reference to the rules under section 414(u)(12)(B) (providing that leave for certain military service is treated as a severance from employment for purposes of the plan distribution restrictions that apply to eligible plans).

III. *Certain Plans That Are Not Subject to Section 457 or Are Not Treated as Providing for a Deferral of Compensation Under Section 457*

A. *In general*

Section 1.457-2(k) of the 2003 final regulations defines the term plan for purposes of section 457 to include any plan, agreement, method, program, or other arrangement, including an individual employment agreement, of an eligible employer under which the payment of compensation is deferred. Section 1.457-2(k) of the 2003 regulations also identifies certain plans that are not subject to section 457 (pursuant to section 457(e)(12) and (f)(2) and statutes not incorporated into the Code) and certain plans that are treated as not providing for a deferral of compensation for purposes of section 457 (pursuant to section 457(e)(11)). These proposed regulations amend the definition of plan for purposes of section 457 to remove from § 1.457-2(k) the provisions identifying plans that are not subject to section 457 and plans that are treated as not providing for a deferral of compensation for purposes of section 457, and move the provisions regarding most of these plans to § 1.457-11 of the proposed regulations. In addition, § 1.457-11 provides additional guidance on:

- bona fide vacation leave, sick leave, compensatory time, severance pay, disability pay, and death benefit plans, as described in section 457(e)(11)(A)(i), which are treated as not providing for a deferral of compensation for purposes of section 457; and
- plans paying solely length of service awards to bona fide volunteers (or their beneficiaries), as described in section 457(e)(11)(A)(ii), that also are treated as not providing for a deferral of compensation for purposes of section 457.[7]

The proposed regulations also provide guidance in a new § 1.457-12 on plans described in section 457(f)(2), to which section 457(f)(1) does not apply.

B. *Bona fide severance pay plans*

1. General Requirements

The proposed regulations provide that a plan must meet certain requirements to be a bona fide severance pay plan that is treated under section 457(e)(11)(A)(i) as not providing for the deferral of compensation (and therefore not subject to section 457). First, the benefits provided under the plan must be payable only upon a participant's involuntary severance from employment or pursuant to a window program or voluntary early retirement incentive plan. Second, the amount payable under the plan with respect to a participant must not exceed two times the participant's annualized compensation based upon the annual rate of pay for services provided to the eligible employer for the calendar year preceding the calendar year in which the participant has a severance from employment (or the current calendar year if the participant had no compensation from the eligible employer in the preceding calendar year), adjusted for any increase in compensation during the year used to measure the rate of pay that was expected to continue indefinitely if the participant had not had a severance from employment. Third, pursuant to the written terms of the plan, the severance benefits must be paid no later than the last day of the second calendar year following the calendar year in which the severance from employment occurs. The rules in these proposed regulations for severance pay plans

[7] See section 457(e)(11)(B) for special rules relating to length of service award plans.

are similar to the rules for separation pay plans in §1.409A-1(b)(9) of the final section 409A regulations.

2. Involuntary Severance from Employment

a. In general

The proposed regulations require that benefits under a bona fide severance pay plan be payable only upon an involuntary severance from employment or pursuant to a window or voluntary early retirement incentive program. For this purpose, an involuntary severance from employment is a severance from employment due to the eligible employer's independent exercise of its authority to terminate the participant's services, other than due to the participant's implicit or explicit request, if the participant is willing and able to continue to perform services. The determination of whether a severance from employment is involuntary is based on the relevant facts and circumstances. If a severance from employment is designated as an involuntary severance from employment, but the facts and circumstances indicate otherwise, the severance from employment will not be treated as involuntary for purposes of section 457.

b. Severance from employment for good reason

The proposed regulations provide that an employee's voluntary severance from employment may be treated as an involuntary severance from employment for purposes of section 457 if the severance from employment is for good reason. A severance from employment is for good reason if it occurs under certain bona fide conditions that are pre-specified in writing under circumstances in which the avoidance of section 457 is not the primary purpose of the inclusion of these conditions in the plan or of the actions by the employer in connection with the satisfaction of those conditions. Notwithstanding the previous sentence, once the bona fide conditions have been established, the elimination of one or more of the conditions may result in the extension of a substantial risk of forfeiture, the recognition of which would be subject to the rules discussed in section III.E of this preamble.

To be treated as an involuntary severance from employment, a severance from employment for good reason must result from unilateral action taken by the eligible employer resulting in a material adverse change to the working relationship (such as a material reduction in the employee's duties, working conditions, or pay). Other factors that may be taken into account in determining whether a termination for good reason effectively constitutes an involuntary severance from employment include the following:

- whether the payments upon severance from employment for good reason are in the same amount and paid at the same time as payments conditioned upon an employer-initiated severance from employment without cause; and
- whether the employee is required to give notice to the employer of the material adverse change in conditions and provide the employer with an opportunity to remedy the adverse change.

The proposed regulations also provide a safe harbor under which a plan providing for the payment of amounts upon a voluntary severance from employment under certain conditions, that are specified in writing by the time the legally binding right to the payment arises, will be treated as providing for a payment upon a severance from employment for good reason.

c. Window programs

The proposed regulations provide that the involuntary severance from employment requirement does not apply to window programs. The proposed regulations define the term window program to mean a program established by an employer to provide separation pay in connection with an impending severance from employment. To be a window program, the program must be offered for a limited period of time (typically no longer than 12 months), and the eligible employer must make the program available to employees who have a severance from employment during that period or who have a severance from employment during that period under specified circumstances. A program is not offered for a limited period of time (and, therefore, is not a window program) if there is a pattern of repeatedly providing similar programs. Whether the recurrence of programs constitutes a pattern of repeatedly providing similar programs is based on all of the relevant facts and circumstances, including whether the benefits are on account of a specific reduction in workforce (or other operational conditions), whether there is a relationship between the separation pay and an event or condition, and whether the event or condition is temporary and discrete or is a permanent aspect of the employer's operations.

d. Voluntary early retirement incentive plans

The proposed regulations also provide that the involuntary severance from employment requirement does not apply to an applicable voluntary early retirement incentive plan described in section 457(e)(11)(D)(ii). That section describes an applicable voluntary early retirement incentive plan as a bona fide severance pay plan for purposes of section 457 with respect to payments or supplements that are made as an early retirement benefit, a retirement-type subsidy, or an early retirement benefit that is greater than a normal retirement benefit, as described in section 411(a)(9), and that are paid in coordination with a defined benefit pension plan that is qualified under section 401(a) and maintained by an eligible employer that is a governmental entity or a tax-exempt education association as described in section 457(e)(11)(D)(ii)(II). Section 457(e)(11)(D) provides that these payments or supplements are treated as provided under a bona fide severance pay plan only to the extent that they otherwise could have been provided under the defined benefit plan with which the applicable voluntary early retirement incentive plan is coordinated (determined as if the rules in section 411 applied to the defined benefit plan).

e. Transitional relief in Announcement 2000-1

Announcement 2000-1 provides transitional guidance on certain broad-based nonelective plans of State or local governments that were in existence before December 22, 1999, and were treated as bona fide severance pay plans for years before 1999. Under the announcement, an eligible employer that is a governmental entity is not required to report, including on Form W-2, "Wage and Tax Statement," or Form 1099-R "Distributions From Pensions, Annuities, Retirement or Profit-Sharing Plans, IRAs, Insurance Contracts, etc.," amounts payable under plans that meet certain requirements until the amounts are actually or constructively received. The rules described in these proposed regulations regarding bona fide severance pay plans, as modified when these proposed regulations are finalized and become applicable, will supersede the transitional guidance in Announcement 2000-1. See section V.B of this preamble for special applicability dates for governmental plans.

C. *Bona fide death benefit plan*

The proposed regulations provide that a bona fide death benefit plan, which is treated as not providing for the deferral of compensation pursuant to section 457(e)(11)(A)(i), is a plan providing for death benefits as defined in § 31.3121(v)(2)-1(b)(4)(iv)(C) (relating to the application of the Federal Insurance Contributions Act to nonqualified deferred compensation). The proposed regulations further provide that benefits under a bona fide death benefit plan may be provided through insurance and that any lifetime benefits payable under the plan that may be includible in gross income will not be treated as including the value of any term life insurance coverage provided under the plan.

D. *Bona fide disability pay plan*

The proposed regulations provide that a bona fide disability pay plan, which is treated as not providing for the deferral of compensation pursuant to section 457(e)(11)(A)(i), is a plan that pays benefits only in the event of a participant's disability. For this purpose, the value of any taxable disability insurance coverage under the plan that is included in gross income is disregarded. These proposed regulations provide that a participant is disabled for this purpose if the participant meets any of the following three conditions:

- the participant is unable to engage in substantial gainful activity by reason of a medically determinable physical or mental impairment that can be expected to result in death or last for a continuous period of not less than 12 months;
- the participant is, by reason of any medically determinable physical or mental impairment that can be expected to result in death or last for a continuous period of not less than 12 months, receiving income replacement benefits for a continuous period of not less than three months under an accident or health plan covering employees of the eligible employer; or
- the participant is determined to be totally disabled by the Social Security Administration or the Railroad Retirement Board.

E. *Bona fide sick leave and vacation leave plans*

1. General Requirements

Under the proposed regulations, whether a sick or vacation leave plan is a bona fide sick or vacation leave plan, and therefore treated as not providing for the deferral of compensation under section 457(e)(11)(A)(i), is determined based on the facts and circumstances. A sick or vacation leave plan is generally treated as bona fide, and not as a plan providing for the deferral of compensation, if the facts and circumstances demonstrate that the primary purpose of the plan is to provide employees with paid time off from work because of sickness, vacation, or other personal reasons. Factors used in determining whether a plan is a bona fide sick or vacation leave plan include the following:

- whether the amount of leave provided could reasonably be expected to be used by the employee in the normal course (and before the cessation of services);
- limits, if any, on the ability to exchange unused accumulated leave for cash or other benefits and any applicable accrual restrictions (for example, where permissible under applicable law, the use of forfeiture provisions often referred to as use-or-lose rules);
- the amount and frequency of any in-service distributions of cash or other benefits offered in exchange for accumulated and unused leave;
- whether the payment of unused sick or vacation leave is made promptly upon severance from employment (or, instead, is paid over a period of time after severance from employment); and
- whether the sick leave, vacation leave, or combined sick and vacation leave offered under the plan is broadly applicable or is available only to certain employees.

2. Delegation of Authority to Commissioner

The Treasury Department and the IRS recognize that eligible employers sponsor a wide variety of sick and vacation leave plans and that additional rules on more specific arrangements or features of these plans may be beneficial. Accordingly, the proposed regulations provide that the Commissioner may issue additional rules regarding bona fide sick or vacation leave plans in revenue rulings, notices, or other guidance published in the Internal Revenue Bulletin, as the Commissioner determines to be necessary or appropriate.

F. *Constructive receipt*

Bona fide sick or vacation leave plans (and certain other plans) are treated as not providing for the deferral of compensation for purposes of section 457, and the general federal tax principles for determining the timing and amount of income inclusion, including the constructive receipt rules of section 451, apply to these plans. See § § 1.451-1 and 1.451-2 for rules regarding constructive receipt of income.

IV. *Ineligible Plans Under Section 457(f)*

A. *Tax treatment of amounts deferred under section 457(f)*

Consistent with section 457(f)(1)(A), the proposed regulations provide that if a plan of an eligible employer provides for a deferral of compensation for the benefit of a participant or beneficiary and the plan is not an eligible plan (an ineligible plan), the compensation deferred under the plan is includible in the gross income of the participant or beneficiary under section 457(f)(1)(A) on the date (referred to in this preamble and the proposed regulations as the applicable date) that is the later of the date the participant or beneficiary obtains a legally binding right to the compensation or, if the compensation is subject to a substantial risk of forfeiture at that time, the date the substantial risk of forfeiture lapses. Generally, the amount of the compensation deferred under the plan that is includible in gross income on the applicable date is the present value, as of that date, of the amount of compensation deferred. For this purpose, the amount of compensation deferred under a plan as of an applicable date includes any earnings as of that date on amounts deferred under the plan.

Consistent with section 457(f)(1)(B), the proposed regulations provide that any earnings credited thereafter on compensation that was included in gross income under section 457(f)(1)(A) are includible in the gross income of a participant or beneficiary when paid or made available to the participant or beneficiary and are taxable under section 72. For purposes of section 72, the participant (or beneficiary) is treated as having an investment in the contract equal to the amount actually included in gross income on the applicable date.

Consistent with section 457(f)(2), the proposed regulations provide that section 457(f)(1) does not apply to a qualified plan described in section 401(a), an annuity plan or contract described in section 403, the portion of a plan that consists of a trust to which section 402(b) applies, a qualified governmental excess benefit arrangement described in section 415(m), the portion of a plan that consists of a transfer of property to which section 83 applies, or the portion of an applicable employment retention plan described in section 457(f)(4) with respect to any participant.

B. *Calculation of the present value of compensation deferred under an ineligible plan*

1. Overview

The proposed regulations provide general rules for determining the present value of compensation deferred under an ineligible plan. The proposed regulations also include specific rules for determining the present value of compensation deferred under ineligible plans that are account balance plans. The rules for determining present value in the proposed regulations are similar to the rules for determining present value in the proposed section 409A regulations.[8]

The Treasury Department and the IRS expect that these regulations will be finalized after the proposed section 409A regulations are finalized and that these proposed regulations, when finalized, will adopt many provisions of § 1.409A-4 for ease of administration. Accordingly, these proposed regulations include cross references to certain provisions of § 1.409A-4 as currently proposed, including rules for determining present value under certain specific types of plans, such as reimbursement and in-kind benefit arrangements[9] and split-dollar life insurance arrangements,[10] and rules regarding the treatment of payment restrictions and alternative times and forms of a future payment. The Treasury Department and the IRS request comments on whether it is appropriate to provide any additional exceptions from the application of the rules currently described in the proposed section 409A regulations to amounts includible in income under section 457(f), to account for the different manners in which the two provisions apply to an amount deferred.

2. Present Value of Compensation Deferred Under an Account Balance Plan

The proposed regulations provide specific rules for calculating the present value of compensation deferred under an ineligible plan that is an account balance plan (as defined in § 31.3121(v)(2)-1(c)(1)(ii) and (iii)).[11] Provided that the account balance is determined using a predetermined actual investment or a reasonable rate of interest, the present value of an amount payable under an account balance plan as of an applicable date is generally the amount credited to the account, which includes both the principal and any earnings or losses through the applicable date. If the account balance is not determined using a predetermined actual investment or a reasonable rate of interest, the present value of compensation deferred under the plan as of an applicable date is equal to the amount credited to the participant's account as of that date, plus the present value of the excess (if any) of the earnings to be credited under the plan after the applicable date and through the

---

[8] One difference between these proposed regulations and the proposed section 409A regulations is that income inclusion under section 457(f) and § 1.457-12(a)(2), and the present value calculation under these proposed regulations, is determined as of the applicable date, whereas income inclusion under section 409A, and the present value calculation under the proposed § 1.409A-4, is determined as of the end of the service provider's taxable year.

[9] A reimbursement or in-kind benefit arrangement is an arrangement in which benefits for a participant are provided under a nonqualified deferred compensation arrangement described in § 1.409A-1(c)(2)(i)(E).

[10] A split-dollar insurance arrangement is an arrangement in which benefits for a participant are provided under a nonqualified deferred compensation plan described in § 1.409A-1(c)(2)(i)(F).

[11] The rules in these regulations, however, do not apply with respect to Federal Insurance Contributions Act and Federal Unemployment Tax Act taxation liability under sections 3121(v)(2) and 3306(r)(2), respectively, and the regulations thereunder.

projected payment date over the earnings that would be credited during that period using a reasonable rate of interest. If the present value of compensation deferred under the plan is not determined and is not taken into account by the taxpayer in this manner, the present value of the compensation deferred under the plan as of the applicable date will be treated as equal to the amount credited to the participant's account as of that date, plus the present value of the excess (if any) of the earnings to be credited under the plan through the projected payment date over the earnings that would be credited using the applicable Federal rate. The proposed regulations also provide that if the amount of earnings or losses credited under an account balance plan is based on the greater of the earnings on two or more investments or interest rates, then the amount included in income on the applicable date is the sum of the amount credited to the participant's account as of the applicable date and the present value (determined as described in section IV.B.3 of this preamble) of the right to future earnings.

3. Present Value of Compensation Deferred Under a Plan That Is Not an Account Balance Plan

a. Reasonable actuarial assumptions

The proposed regulations also set forth rules for calculating the present value of compensation deferred under an ineligible plan that is not an account balance plan. Under the proposed regulations, the present value of an amount deferred under such a plan as of an applicable date is the value, as of that date, of the right to receive payment of the compensation in the future, taking into account the time value of money and the probability that the payment will be made. Any actuarial assumptions used to calculate the present value of the compensation deferred must be reasonable as of the applicable date, determined based on all of the relevant facts and circumstances. For this purpose, taking into account the probability that a participant might die before receiving certain benefits is a reasonable actuarial assumption only if the plan provides that the benefits will be forfeited upon death. Discounts based on the probability that payments will not be made due to the unfunded status of the plan, the risk that the eligible employer or another party may be unwilling or unable to pay, the possibility of future plan amendments or changes in law, and other similar contingencies are not permitted for purposes of determining present value under the proposed regulations.

b. Treatment of severance from employment

If the present value of an amount depends on the time when a severance from employment occurs and the severance from employment has not occurred by the applicable date, then, for purposes of determining the present value of the amount, the severance from employment generally may be treated as occurring on any date on or before the fifth anniversary of the applicable date, unless, as of the applicable date, it would be unreasonable to use such an assumption. For example, if the applicable date occurs in 2017 and the employer knows on the applicable date that the severance from employment will occur in 2018, it would be unreasonable to use a date after the expected severance from employment date to determine the present value of the compensation.

c. Treatment of payments based on formula amounts

Some ineligible plans may provide that all or part of the amount payable under the plan is determined by reference to one or more factors that are indeterminable on the applicable date. For example, an amount payable may be dependent on a participant's final average compensation and total years of service. These proposed regulations refer to such an amount as a formula amount. The proposed regulations provide that the determination of the present value of a formula amount under an ineligible plan must be based on reasonable, good faith assumptions with respect to any contingencies as to the amount of the payment, with the assumptions based on all the facts and circumstances existing on the applicable date. The proposed regulations also provide that, if only a portion of the compensation deferred under the plan consists of a formula amount, the amount payable with respect to that portion is determined under the rules applicable to formula amounts, and the remaining balance is determined under the rules applicable to amounts that are not formula amounts.

d. Unreasonable actuarial assumptions

If the Commissioner determines that the actuarial assumptions used by an employer in determining present value are not reasonable, the proposed regulations provide that the Commissioner will determine the present value of the compensation deferred using actuarial assumptions and methods that the Commissioner determines to be reasonable based on all of the facts and circumstances.

4. Loss Deduction Rules

The proposed regulations contain rules similar to the loss deduction rules in the proposed section 409A regulations. Under the rules in these proposed regulations, if a participant includes an amount of deferred compensation in income under section 457(f)(1)(A), but the compensation that is subsequently paid or made available is less than the amount included in income because the participant has forfeited or lost some or all of the compensation due to death or some other reason (for example, due to investment performance), the participant is entitled to a deduction for the taxable year in which any remaining right to the amount is permanently forfeited under the plan's terms or otherwise permanently lost. The deduction allowed for the taxable year in which the permanent forfeiture or loss occurs is equal to the amount previously included in income under section 457(f)(1)(A), less the total amount of compensation that is actually paid or made available under the plan that constitutes a return of investment in the contract. In the case of an employee, the available deduction generally would be treated as a miscellaneous itemized deduction, subject to the deduction limitations applicable to such expenses under sections 67 and 68.[12]

5. Examples Illustrating the Present Value Rules

The proposed regulations include several examples illustrating the application of the present value rules to the more common types of plans providing for the deferral of compensation under section 457(f). The regulations do not illustrate the application of these valuation rules to plans that are more unusual for employees of governmental and tax-exempt entities, such as compensatory options to acquire stock or other property. The amount includible in income on the applicable date under these less common types of plans would be determined under the general rules for plans that are not account balance plans.

C. *Definition of deferral of compensation*

1. In General

The proposed regulations define the term deferral of compensation for purposes of determining whether section 457(f) applies to an arrangement because it provides for a deferral of compensation. In general, a plan provides for a deferral of compensation if a participant has a legally binding right during a taxable year to compensation that, pursuant to the terms of the plan, is or may be payable in a later taxable year. However, the proposed regulations generally provide that a participant does not have a legally binding right to compensation to the extent that it may be unilaterally reduced or eliminated by the employer after the services creating the right have been performed.

Whether a plan provides for a deferral of compensation is generally based on the terms of the plan and the relevant facts and circumstances at the time that the participant obtains a legally binding right to the compensation, or, if later, when a plan is amended to convert a right that does not provide for a deferral of compensation into a right that does provide for a deferral of compensation. For example, if a plan providing retiree health care does not initially provide for a deferral of compensation but is later amended to provide the ability to receive future cash payments instead of health benefits, it may become a plan that provides for the deferral of compensation at the time of the amendment.

Under the proposed regulations, an amount of compensation deferred under a plan that provides for the deferral of compensation does not cease to be an amount subject to section 457(f) by reason of any change to the plan that would recharacterize the right to the amount as a right that does not provide for the deferral of compensation. In addition, any change under the plan that results in an exchange of an amount deferred under the plan for some other right or benefit that would otherwise be excluded from the participants' gross income does not affect the characterization of the plan as one that provides for a deferral of compensation. Thus, for example, if a plan that provides for a deferral of compensation is amended to provide health benefits instead of cash, it will retain its character as a plan that provides for a deferral of compensation.

2. Short-term Deferrals

The proposed regulations provide that a deferral of compensation does not occur with respect to any amount that would be a short-term deferral under § 1.409A-1(b)(4), substituting the definition of a substantial risk of forfeiture provided under these proposed regulations for the definition under § 1.409A-1(d). Accordingly, a deferral of compensation does not occur with respect to any payment that is not a deferred payment, provided that the participant actually or constructively receives the payment on or before the last day of the applicable 2 1/2 month period. For this purpose, the applicable 2 1/2 month period is the period ending on the later of the 15th day of the third month following the end of the first calendar year in which the right to the payment is no longer subject to a substantial risk of forfeiture or the 15th day of the third month following the end of the eligible employer's first taxable year in which the right to the payment is no longer subject to a substantial risk of forfeiture.

Because there is considerable overlap between the definition of substantial risk of forfeiture for purposes of section 457(f) and the definition of substantial risk of forfeiture for purposes of section 409A, in many cases amounts that, under this rule, are not deferred compensation subject to section 457(f) are also not deferred compensation subject to section 409A. For example, if an arrangement provides for the payment of a bonus on or before March 15 of the year following the calendar year in which the right to the bonus is no longer subject to a substantial risk of forfeiture (within the meaning of both these proposed regulations and § 1.409A-1(d)) and the bonus is paid on or before that March 15, the arrangement would not be a plan providing for a deferral of compensation to which section 457(f) (or section 409A) applies. For circumstances in which a payment under a plan made after that March 15 may still qualify as a short-term deferral for purposes of sections 409A and 457(f) (due to incorporation of the section 409A regulatory provisions into these proposed regulations under section 457(f)), see § 1.409A-1(b)(4)(ii).

3. Recurring Part-Year Compensation

After issuance of the final section 409A regulations, commenters expressed concerns about the application of section 409A to situations involving certain recurring part-year compensation. For this

---

[12] Section 1341 would not be applicable to this type of loss because inclusion of an amount in income as a result of section 457(f) would not constitute receipt of an amount to which it appeared that the taxpayer had an unrestricted right in the taxable year of inclusion.

purpose, recurring part-year compensation is compensation paid for services rendered in a position that the employer and employee reasonably anticipate will continue under similar terms and conditions in subsequent years, and under which the employee will be required to provide services during successive service periods each of which comprises less than 12 months (for example, a teacher providing services during a school year comprised of 10 consecutive months) and each of which begins in one taxable year of the employee and ends in the next taxable year. In general, commenters asserted that section 409A should not apply to situations involving recurring part-year compensation because the amount being deferred from one taxable year to the next taxable year is typically small and because most taxpayers view that type of arrangement as a method of managing cash flow, rather than a tax-deferral opportunity.

In response to these comments, Notice 2008-62 provided that an arrangement under which an employee or independent contractor receives recurring part-year compensation does not provide for the deferral of compensation for purposes of section 409A or for purposes of section 457(f) if (i) the arrangement does not defer payment of any of the recurring part-year compensation beyond the last day of the 13th month following the beginning of the service period, and (ii) the arrangement does not defer from one taxable year to the next taxable year the payment of more than the applicable dollar amount under section 402(g)(1)(B) ($18,000 for 2016).

Some commenters, however, subsequently expressed concerns that Notice 2008-62 does not adequately address some teaching positions, such as those of college and university faculty members. They asserted that, depending on several variables (such as the month in which the service period begins), the dollar limitation in the notice could result in adverse tax consequences to teachers with academic year compensation as low as $80,000. Commenters further observed that some of these arrangements are nonelective and, therefore, some employees cannot opt out of a recurring part-year compensation arrangement. Some commenters also contended that the rules set forth in the notice were difficult to apply.

To simplify the rule set forth in Notice 2008-62, and recognizing that educational employers frequently structure their pay plans to include recurring part-year compensation and that the main purpose of this design is to achieve an even cash flow for employees who do not work for a portion of the year, these proposed regulations modify the recurring part-year compensation rule for purposes of section 457(f). The proposed regulations provide that a plan or arrangement under which an employee receives recurring part-year compensation that is earned over a period of service does not provide for the deferral of compensation if the plan or arrangement does not defer payment of any of the recurring part-year compensation to a date beyond the last day of the 13th month following the first day of the service period for which the recurring part-year compensation is paid, and the amount of the recurring part-year compensation (not merely the amount deferred) does not exceed the annual compensation limit under section 401(a)(17) ($265,000 for 2016) for the calendar year in which the service period commences. A conforming change is included in proposed regulations under section 409A that are also published in the Proposed Rules section of this issue of the **Federal Register**.

D. *Interaction of section 457 with section 409A*

The proposed regulations also address the interaction of the rules under section 457(f) and section 409A. Section 409A(c) provides that nothing in section 409A is to be construed to prevent the inclusion of amounts in gross income under any other provision of chapter 1 of subtitle A of the Code (Normal taxes and surtaxes) or any other rule of law earlier than the time provided in section 409A. In addition, it provides that any amount included in gross income under section 409A is not required to be included in gross income under any other provision of chapter 1 of subtitle A or any other rule of law later than the time provided in section 409A. The proposed regulations provide that the rules under section 457(f) apply to plans separately and in addition to the requirements under section 409A.[13] Thus, a deferred compensation plan of an eligible employer that is subject to section 457(f) may also be a nonqualified deferred compensation plan that is subject to section 409A. Section 1.457-12(d)(5)(iii) of the proposed regulations provides an example of the interaction of sections 409A and 457(f), and it is intended that this example will also be included in § 1.409A-4 when those currently proposed regulations are finalized.

E. *Rules relating to substantial risk of forfeiture*

The proposed regulations provide rules regarding the conditions that constitute a substantial risk of forfeiture for purposes of section 457(f). As discussed in section IV.A of this preamble, an amount to which an employee has a legally binding right under an ineligible plan is generally includible in gross income on the later of the date the employee obtains the legally binding right to the compensation or, if the compensation is subject to a substantial risk of forfeiture, the date the substantial risk of forfeiture lapses. The proposed regulations provide that an amount is generally subject to a substantial risk of forfeiture for this purpose only if entitlement to that amount is conditioned on the future performance of substantial services, or upon the occurrence of a condition that is related to a purpose of the compensation if the possibility of forfeiture is substantial. A special rule applies to determine whether initial deferrals of current compensation may be treated as subject to a substantial risk of forfeiture and whether a substantial risk of forfeiture can be extended. For this purpose, current

[13] See also § 1.409A-1(a)(4).

compensation refers to compensation that is payable on a current basis such as salary, commissions, and certain bonuses, and does not include compensation that is deferred compensation.

Whether an amount is conditioned on the future performance of substantial services is based on all of the relevant facts and circumstances, such as whether the hours required to be performed during the relevant period are substantial in relation to the amount of compensation. A condition is related to a purpose of the compensation only if the condition relates to the employee's performance of services for the employer or to the employer's tax exempt or governmental activities, as applicable, or organizational goals. A substantial risk of forfeiture exists based on a condition related to the purpose of the compensation only if the likelihood that the forfeiture event will occur is substantial. Also, an amount is not subject to a substantial risk of forfeiture if the facts and circumstances indicate that the forfeiture condition is unlikely to be enforced. Factors considered for purposes of determining the likelihood that the forfeiture will be enforced include, but are not limited to, the past practices of the employer, the level of control or influence of the employee with respect to the organization and the individual(s) who would be responsible for enforcing the forfeiture, and the enforceability of the provisions under applicable law.

Under these proposed regulations, if a plan provides that entitlement to an amount is conditioned on an involuntary severance from employment without cause, the right is subject to a substantial risk of forfeiture if the possibility of forfeiture is substantial. For this purpose, a voluntary severance from employment that would be treated as an involuntary severance from employment under a bona fide severance pay plan for purposes of section 457(e)(11)(A)(i) (that is, a severance from employment for good reason) is also treated as an involuntary severance from employment without cause. See section III.B.2 of this preamble for a discussion of circumstances under which a severance from employment for good reason may be treated as an involuntary severance from employment for purposes of section 457(e)(11)(A)(i).

The proposed regulations provide that compensation is not considered to be subject to a substantial risk of forfeiture merely because it would be forfeited if the employee accepts a position with a competing employer unless certain conditions are satisfied. First, the right to the compensation must be expressly conditioned on the employee refraining from the performance of future services pursuant to a written agreement that is enforceable under applicable law. Second, the employer must consistently make reasonable efforts to verify compliance with all of the noncompetition agreements to which it is a party (including the noncompetition agreement at issue). Third, at the time the noncompetition agreement becomes binding, the facts and circumstances must show that the employer has a substantial and bona fide interest in preventing the employee from performing the prohibited services and that the employee has a bona fide interest in engaging, and an ability to engage, in the prohibited services. The proposed regulations identify several factors that are relevant for this purpose.

Additional conditions apply with respect to the ability to treat initial deferrals of current compensation as being subject to a substantial risk of forfeiture. Similarly, an attempt to extend the period covered by a risk of forfeiture, often referred to as a rolling risk of forfeiture, is generally disregarded under the proposed regulations unless certain conditions are met.

Specifically, the proposed regulations permit initial deferrals of current compensation to be subject to a substantial risk of forfeiture and also allow an existing risk of forfeiture to be extended only if all of the following requirements are met. First, the present value of the amount to be paid upon the lapse of the substantial risk of forfeiture (as extended, if applicable) must be materially greater than the amount the employee otherwise would be paid in the absence of the substantial risk of forfeiture (or absence of the extension). The proposed regulations provide that an amount is materially greater for this purpose only if the present value of the amount to be paid upon the lapse of the substantial risk of forfeiture, measured as of the date the amount would have otherwise been paid (or in the case of an extension of the risk of forfeiture, the date that the substantial risk of forfeiture would have lapsed without regard to the extension), is more than 125 percent of the amount the participant otherwise would have received on that date in the absence of the new or extended substantial risk of forfeiture. (No implication is intended that this standard would also apply for purposes of § 1.409A-1(d)(1).)

Second, the initial or extended substantial risk of forfeiture must be based upon the future performance of substantial services or adherence to an agreement not to compete. It may not be based solely on the occurrence of a condition related to the purpose of the transfer (for example, a performance goal for the organization), though that type of condition may be combined with a sufficient service condition.

Third, the period for which substantial future services must be performed may not be less than two years (absent an intervening event such as death, disability, or involuntary severance from employment).

Fourth, the agreement subjecting the amount to a substantial risk of forfeiture must be made in writing before the beginning of the calendar year in which any services giving rise to the compensation are performed in the case of initial deferrals of current compensation or at least 90 days before the date on which an existing substantial risk of forfeiture would have lapsed in the absence of an extension. Special rules apply to new employees. The proposed regulations do not extend these special rules for new employees to employees who are newly eligible to participate in a plan. The Treasury Department and the IRS request comments on whether special provisions for newly eligible employees are needed in the context of arrangements subject to section 457(f), and if so whether the rules under §§1.409A-1(c)(2) and 1.409A-2(a)(7) would be a useful basis for similar rules under section 457(f) and how an aggregated single plan (versus multiple plans) should be defined for this purpose to ensure that the rules are not subject to manipulation.

V. *Proposed Applicability Dates*

A. *General applicability date*

Generally, these regulations are proposed to apply to compensation deferred under a plan for calendar years beginning after the date of publication of the Treasury decision adopting these rules as final regulations in the **Federal Register**, including deferred amounts to which the legally binding right arose during prior calendar years that were not previously included in income during one or more prior calendar years. No implication is intended regarding application of the law before these proposed regulations become applicable. Taxpayers may rely on these proposed regulations until the applicability date.

B. *Special applicability dates*

These regulations are proposed to include three special applicability dates for specific provisions. First, in the case of a plan that is maintained pursuant to one or more collective bargaining agreements that have been ratified and are in effect on the date of publication of the Treasury decision adopting these rules as final regulations in the **Federal Register,** these regulations would not apply to compensation deferred under the plan before the earlier of (1) the date on which the last of the collective bargaining agreements terminates (determined without regard to any extension thereof after the date of publication of the Treasury decision adopting these rules as final regulations in the **Federal Register**, or (2) the date that is three years after the date of publication of the Treasury decision adopting these rules as final regulations in the **Federal Register**.

Second, for all plans, with respect to the rules regarding recurring part-year compensation for periods before the applicability date of these regulations, taxpayers may rely on either the rules set forth in these proposed regulations or the rules set forth in Notice 2008-62.

Third, to the extent that legislation is required to amend a governmental plan, the proposed regulations would apply only to compensation deferred under the plan in calendar years beginning on or after the close of the second regular legislative session of the legislative body with the authority to amend the plan that begins after the date of publication of the Treasury decision adopting these rules as final regulations in the **Federal Register**.

Special Analyses

Certain IRS regulations, including this one, are exempt from the requirements of Executive Order 12866, as supplemented and reaffirmed by Executive Order 13563. Therefore, a regulatory impact assessment is not required. It also has been determined that section 553(b) of the Administrative Procedure Act (5 U.S.C. chapter 5) does not apply to these regulations, and because the regulations do not impose a collection of information on small entities, the Regulatory Flexibility Act (5 U.S.C. chapter 6) does not apply. Pursuant to section 7805(f) of the Code, this notice of proposed rulemaking has been submitted to the Chief Counsel for Advocacy of the Small Business Administration for comment on its impact on small business.

Comments and Public Hearing

Before the proposed regulations are adopted as final regulations, consideration will be given to any written (a signed original and eight (8) copies) or electronic comments that are submitted timely to the IRS as prescribed in this preamble under the "ADDRESSES" heading. The Treasury Department and the IRS request comments on all aspects of the proposed rules, including whether special transition rules are needed for plans established before the proposed applicability dates of these regulations (including sick and vacation leave or severance pay plans that may be treated as providing deferred compensation subject to section 457, but that, under the proposed regulations, may be treated as providing deferred compensation subject to section 457(f), whether additional exceptions are appropriate to the general application of the rules currently described in the proposed section 409A regulations to determine the amounts includible in income under section 457(f), and whether special provisions for newly eligible employees are needed in the context of arrangements subject to section 457(f) (and if so whether the rules under §§1.409A-1(c)(2) and 1.409A-2(a)(7) would be a useful basis for similar rules under section 457(f)). All comments submitted by the public will be available at www.regulations.gov or upon request.

A public hearing has been scheduled for October 18, 2016, beginning at 10 a.m. in the Auditorium, Internal Revenue Service, 1111 Constitution Avenue, N.W., Washington, DC. Due to building security procedures, visitors must enter at the Constitution Avenue entrance. In addition, all visitors must present photo identification to enter the building. Because of access restrictions, visitors will not be admitted beyond the immediate entrance area more than 30 minutes before the hearing starts. For information about having your name placed on the building access list to attend the hearing, see the "FOR FURTHER INFORMATION CONTACT" section of this preamble.

The rules of 26 CFR 601.601(a)(3) apply to the hearing. Persons who wish to present oral comments at the hearing must submit written or electronic comments by September 20, 2016 and an outline of the topics to be discussed and the amount of time to be devoted to each topic (a signed original and eight (8) copies) by September 20, 2016. A period of 10 minutes will be allotted to each person for making comments. An agenda showing the scheduling of the speakers will be prepared after the deadline for receiving outlines has passed. Copies of the agenda will be available free of charge at the hearing.

Statement of Availability of IRS Documents

For copies of recently issued revenue procedures, revenue rulings, notices, and other guidance published in the Internal Revenue Bulletin, please visit the IRS website at http://www.irs.gov or contact the Superintendent of Documents, U.S. Government Printing Office, Washington, DC 20402.

Drafting Information

The principal author of the proposed regulations is Keith R. Kost, Office of Associate Chief Counsel (Tax Exempt and Government Entities). However, other personnel from the Treasury Department and the IRS participated in their development.

[¶49,704] Proposed Amendments of Regulations (REG-109086-15), published in the Federal Register on July 8, 2016 (corrected 9/14/2016).

[Code Secs. 36B and 5000A]

Affordable Care Act: Premium tax credit: Individual shared responsibility.—Amendments of Reg. §§1.36B-2 and 1.5000A-3, relating to the health insurance premium tax credit (premium tax credit) and the individual shared responsibility provision, are proposed. Amendments of Reg. SS1.36B-0, 1.36B-1, 1.36B-2, 1.36B-3, 1.36B-5, 1.6011-8 and 301.6011-2 were adopted by T.D. 9804 on December 14, 2016.

AGENCY: Internal Revenue Service (IRS), Treasury.

ACTION: Notice of proposed rulemaking.

SUMMARY: This document contains proposed regulations relating to the health insurance premium tax credit (premium tax credit) and the individual shared responsibility provision. These proposed regulations affect individuals who enroll in qualified health plans through Health Insurance Exchanges (Exchanges, also called Marketplaces) and claim the premium tax credit, and Exchanges that make qualified health plans available to individuals and employers. These proposed regulations also affect individuals who are eligible for employer-sponsored health coverage and individuals who seek to claim an exemption from the individual shared responsibility provision because of unaffordable coverage. Although employers are not directly affected by rules governing the premium tax credit, these proposed regulations may indirectly affect employers through the employer shared responsibility provisions and the related information reporting provisions.

DATES: Written (including electronic) comments and requests for a public hearing must be received by September 6, 2016.

ADDRESSES: Send submissions to: CC:PA:LPD:PR (REG-109086-15), Room 5203, Internal Revenue Service, PO Box 7604, Ben Franklin Station, Washington, DC 20044. Submissions may be hand-delivered Monday through Friday between the hours of 8 a.m. and 4 p.m. to CC:PA:LPD:PR (REG-109086-15), Courier's Desk, Internal Revenue Service, 1111 Constitution Avenue, NW, Washington, DC, or sent electronically via the Federal eRulemaking Portal at *http://www.regulations.gov* (REG-109086-15).

FOR FURTHER INFORMATION CONTACT: Concerning the proposed regulations, Shareen Pflanz, (202) 317-4727; concerning the submission of comments and/or requests for a public hearing, Oluwafunmilayo Taylor, (202) 317-6901 (not toll-free calls).

SUPPLEMENTARY INFORMATION:

Paperwork Reduction Act

The collection of information contained in this notice of proposed rulemaking has been submitted to the Office of Management and Budget in accordance with the Paperwork Reduction Act of 1995 (44 U.S.C. 3507(d)). Comments on the collection of information should be sent to the **Office of Management and Budget**, Attn: Desk Officer for the Department of the Treasury, Office of Information and Regulatory Affairs, Washington, DC 20503, with copies to the **Internal Revenue Service**, Attn: IRS Reports Clearance Officer, SE:W:CAR:MP:T:T:SP, Washington, DC 20224. Comments on the collection of information should be received by September 6, 2016. Comments are specifically requested concerning:

Whether the proposed collection of information is necessary for the proper performance of the functions of the IRS, including whether the information will have practical utility;

How the quality, utility, and clarity of the information to be collected may be enhanced;

How the burden of complying with the proposed collection of information may be minimized, including through the application of automated collection techniques or other forms of information technology; and

Estimates of capital or start-up costs and costs of operation, maintenance, and purchase of services to provide information.

The collection of information in these proposed regulations is in §1.36B-5. The collection of information is necessary to reconcile advance payments of the premium tax credit and determine the allowable premium tax credit. The collection of information is required to comply with the provisions of section 36B of the Internal Revenue Code (Code). The likely respondents are Marketplaces that enroll individuals in qualified health plans.

The burden for the collection of information contained in these proposed regulations will be reflected in the burden on Form 1095-A, *Health Insurance Marketplace Statement*, which is the form that will request the information from the Marketplaces in the proposed regulations.

An agency may not conduct or sponsor, and a person is not required to respond to, a collection of information unless it displays a valid control number assigned by the Office of Management and Budget.

Background

Beginning in 2014, under the Patient Protection and Affordable Care Act, Public Law 111-148 (124 Stat. 119 (2010)), and the Health Care and Education Reconciliation Act of 2010, Public Law 111-152 (124 Stat. 1029 (2010)) (collectively, the Affordable Care Act), eligible individuals who purchase coverage under a qualified health plan through an Exchange may claim a premium tax credit under section 36B of the Code. Section 36B was subsequently amended by the Medicare and Medicaid Extenders Act of 2010, Public Law 111-309 (124 Stat. 3285 (2010)); the Comprehensive 1099 Taxpayer Protection and Repayment of Exchange Subsidy Overpayments Act of 2011, Public Law 112-9 (125 Stat. 36 (2011)); and the Department of Defense and Full-Year Continuing Appropriations Act, 2011, Public Law 112-10 (125 Stat. 38 (2011)).

The Affordable Care Act also added section 5000A to the Code. Section 5000A was subsequently amended by the TRICARE Affirmation Act of 2010, Public Law 111-159 (124 Stat. 1123 (2010)) and Public Law 111-173 (124 Stat. 1215 (2010)). Section 5000A provides that, for months beginning after December 31, 2013, a nonexempt individual must have qualifying healthcare coverage (called minimum essential coverage) or make an individual shared responsibility payment.

Applicable Taxpayers

To be eligible for a premium tax credit, an individual must be an applicable taxpayer. Among other requirements, under section 36B(c)(1) an applicable taxpayer is a taxpayer whose household income for the taxable year is between 100 percent and 400 percent of the Federal poverty line (FPL) for the taxpayer's family size (or is a lawfully present non-citizen who has income below 100 percent of the FPL and is ineligible for Medicaid). A taxpayer's family size is equal to the number of individuals in the taxpayer's family. Under section 36B(d)(1), a taxpayer's family consists of the individuals for whom the taxpayer claims a personal exemption deduction under section 151 for the taxable year. Taxpayers may claim a personal exemption deduction for themselves, a spouse, and each of their dependents.

Under section 1412 of the Affordable Care Act, advance payments of the premium tax credit (advance credit payments) may be made directly to insurers on behalf of eligible individuals. The amount of advance credit payments made on behalf of a taxpayer in a taxable year is determined by a number of factors including projections of the taxpayer's household income and family size for the taxable year. Taxpayers who receive the benefit of advance credit payments are required to file an income tax return to reconcile the amount of advance credit payments made during the year with the amount of the credit allowable for the taxable year.

Under § 1.36B-2(b)(6), in general, a taxpayer whose household income for a taxable year is less than 100 percent of the applicable FPL is nonetheless treated as an applicable taxpayer if (1) the taxpayer or a family member enrolls in a qualified health plan, (2) an Exchange estimates at the time of enrollment that the taxpayer's household income for the taxable year will be between 100 and 400 percent of the applicable FPL, (3) advance credit payments are authorized and paid for one or more months during the taxable year, and (4) the taxpayer would be an applicable taxpayer but for the fact that the taxpayer's household income for the taxable year is below 100 percent of the applicable FPL.

Premium Assistance Credit Amount

Under section 36B(a), a taxpayer's premium tax credit is equal to the premium assistance credit amount for the taxable year. Section 36B(b)(1) and § 1.36B-3(d) generally provide that the premium assistance credit amount is the sum of the premium assistance amounts for all coverage months in the taxable year for individuals in the taxpayer's family. The premium assistance amount for a coverage month is the lesser of (1) the premiums for the month for one or more qualified health plans that cover a taxpayer or family member (enrollment premium), or (2) the excess of the adjusted monthly premium for the second lowest cost silver plan (as described in section 1302(d)(1)(B) of the Affordable Care Act (42 U.S.C. 18022(d)(1)(B)) offered through the Exchange for the rating area where the taxpayer resides that would provide coverage to the taxpayer's coverage family (the benchmark plan), over 1/12 of the product of the taxpayer's household income and the applicable percentage for the taxable year (the contribution amount). In general, the benchmark plan's adjusted monthly premium is the premium an insurer would charge for the plan adjusted only for the ages of the covered individuals. The applicable percentage is provided in a table that is updated annually and represents the portion of a taxpayer's household income that the taxpayer is expected to pay if the taxpayer's coverage family enrolls in the benchmark plan. See, for example, Rev. Proc. 2014-62, 2014-2 C.B. 948 (providing the applicable percentage table for taxable years beginning in 2016) and Rev. Proc. 2014-37, 2014-2 C.B. 363 (providing the applicable percentage table for taxable years beginning in 2015). A taxpayer's coverage family refers to all members of the taxpayer's family who enroll in a qualified health plan in a month and are not eligible for minimum essential coverage as defined in section 5000A(f) (other than coverage in the individual market) for that month.

Under section 1301(a)(1)(B) of the Affordable Care Act, a qualified health plan must offer the essential health benefits package described in section 1302(a). Under section 1302(b)(1)(J) of the

Affordable Care Act, the essential health benefits package includes pediatric services, including oral and vision care. Section 1302(b)(4)(F) of the Affordable Care Act provides that, if an Exchange offers a plan described in section 1311(d)(2)(B)(ii)(I) of the Affordable Care Act (42 U.S.C. 13031(d)(2)(B)(ii)(I)) (a stand-alone dental plan), other health plans offered through the Exchange will not fail to be qualified health plans solely because the plans do not offer pediatric dental benefits.

For purposes of calculating the premium assistance amount for a taxpayer who enrolls in both a qualified health plan and a stand-alone dental plan, section 36B(b)(3)(E) provides that the enrollment premium includes the portion of the premium for the stand-alone dental plan properly allocable to pediatric dental benefits that are included in the essential health benefits required to be provided by a qualified health plan.

Section 36B(b)(3)(B) provides that the benchmark plan with respect to an applicable taxpayer is the second lowest cost silver plan offered by the Marketplace through which the applicable taxpayer (or a family member) enrolled and which provides (1) self-only coverage, in the case of unmarried individuals (other than a surviving spouse or head of household) who do not claim any dependents, or any other individual who enrolls in self-only coverage, and (2) family coverage, in the case of any other applicable taxpayer. Section 1.36B-1(l) provides that self-only coverage means health insurance that covers one individual. Section 1.36B-1(m) provides that family coverage means health insurance that covers more than one individual.

Under § 1.36B-3(f)(3), if there are one or more silver-level plans offered through the Exchange for the rating area where the taxpayer resides that do not cover all members of a taxpayer's coverage family under one policy (for example, because of the relationships within the family), the benchmark plan premium is the second lowest-cost option for covering all members of the taxpayer's family, which may be either a single silver-level policy or more than one silver-level policy.

Section 1.36B-3(d)(2) provides that, if a qualified health plan is terminated before the last day of a month or an individual is enrolled in coverage effective on the date of the individual's birth, adoption, or placement for adoption or in foster care, or on the effective date of a court order, the premium assistance amount for the month is the lesser of the enrollment premiums for the month (reduced by any amounts that were refunded) or the excess of the benchmark plan premium for a full month of coverage over the full contribution amount for the month.

Coverage Month

Under section 36B(c)(2)(A) and § 1.36B-3(c)(1), a coverage month is generally any month for which the taxpayer or a family member is covered by a qualified health plan enrolled in through an Exchange on the first day of the month and the premium is paid by the taxpayer or through an advance credit payment. However, section 36B(c)(2) provides that a month is not a coverage month for an individual who is eligible for minimum essential coverage other than coverage in the individual market. Under section 36B(c)(2)(B)(ii), minimum essential coverage is defined by reference to section 5000A(f). Minimum essential coverage includes government-sponsored programs such as most Medicaid coverage, Medicare part A, the Children's Health Insurance Program (CHIP), most TRICARE programs, most coverage provided to veterans under title 38 of the United States Code, and the Nonappropriated Fund Health Benefits Program of the Department of Defense. See section 5000A(f)(1) and § 1.5000A-2(b). Section 1.36B-2(c)(3)(i) provides that, for purposes of section 36B, the government-sponsored programs described in section 5000A(f)(1)(A) are not considered eligible employer-sponsored plans.

Under § 1.36B-2(c)(2)(i), an individual generally is treated as eligible for government-sponsored minimum essential coverage as of the first day of the first full month that the individual meets the criteria for coverage and is eligible to receive benefits under the government program. However, under § 1.36B-2(c)(2)(v) an individual is treated as not eligible for Medicaid, CHIP, or a similar program for a period of coverage under a qualified health plan if, when the individual enrolls in the qualified health plan, an Exchange determines or considers (within the meaning of 45 CFR 155.302(b)) the individual to be ineligible for such program. In addition, § 1.36B-2(c)(2)(iv) provides that if an individual receiving the benefit of advance credit payments is determined to be eligible for a government-sponsored program, and that eligibility is effective retroactively, then, for purposes of the premium tax credit, the individual is treated as eligible for the program no earlier than the first day of the first calendar month beginning after the approval.

Coverage under an eligible employer-sponsored plan is minimum essential coverage. In general, an eligible employer-sponsored plan is coverage provided by an employer to its employees (and their dependents) under a group health plan maintained by the employer. *See* section 5000A(f)(2) and § 1.5000A-2(c). Under section 5000A(f)(3) and § 1.5000A-2(g), minimum essential coverage does not include any coverage that consists solely of excepted benefits described in section 2791(c)(1), (c)(2), (c)(3), or (c)(4) of the Public Health Service Act (PHS Act) (42 U.S.C. 300gg-91(c)), or regulations issued under those provisions (45 CFR 148.220). In general, excepted benefits are benefits that are limited in scope or are conditional.

Under section 36B(c)(2)(C) and § 1.36B-2(c)(3)(i), except as provided in the next paragraph of this preamble, an individual is treated as eligible for coverage under an eligible employer-sponsored plan only if the employee's share of the premium is affordable and the coverage provides minimum value. Under section 36B(c)(2)(C), an eligible employer-sponsored plan is treated as affordable for an employee if the amount of the employee's required contribution (within the meaning of section 5000A(e)(1)(B)) for self-only coverage does not exceed a specified percentage of the employee's household income. The affordability of coverage for individuals related to an employee is determined in the same manner. Thus, under section 36B(c)(2)(C)(i) and § 1.36B-2(c)(3)(v)(A)(2), an eligible employer-sponsored plan is treated as affordable for an individual eligible for the plan because of a relationship to an employee if the amount of the employee's required contribution for self-only coverage does not exceed a specified percentage of the employee's household income.

Under § 1.36B-2(c)(3)(v)(A)(3), an eligible employer-sponsored plan is not considered affordable if, when an individual enrolls in a qualified health plan, the Marketplace determines that the eligible employer-sponsored plan is not affordable. However, that rule does not apply for an individual who, with reckless disregard for the facts, provides incorrect information to a Marketplace concerning the employee's portion of the annual premium for coverage under the eligible employer-sponsored plan. In addition, under section 36B(c)(2)(C)(iii) and § 1.36B-2(c)(3)(vii)(A), an individual is treated as eligible for employer-sponsored coverage if the individual actually enrolls in an eligible employer-sponsored plan, even if the coverage is not affordable or does not provide minimum value.

Section 1.36B-2(c)(3)(iii)(A) provides that, subject to the rules described above, an employee or related individual may be considered eligible for coverage under an eligible employer-sponsored plan for a month during a plan year if the employee or related individual could have enrolled in the plan for that month during an open or special enrollment period. Under § 1.36B-2(c)(3)(ii), plan year means an eligible employer-sponsored plan's regular 12-month coverage period (or the remainder of a 12-month coverage period for a new employee or an individual who enrolls during a special enrollment period).

Although coverage in the individual market is minimum essential coverage under section 5000A(f)(1)(C), under section 36B(c)(2)(B)(i), an individual who is eligible for or enrolled in coverage in the individual market (whether or not obtained through the Marketplace) nevertheless may have a coverage month for purposes of the premium tax credit.

Required Contribution for Employer-Sponsored Coverage

Under section 36B(c)(2)(C) and § 1.36B-2(c)(3)(v)(A)(1) and (2), an eligible employer-sponsored plan is treated as affordable for an employee or a related individual if the amount the employee must pay for self-only coverage whether by salary reduction or otherwise (the employee's required contribution) does not exceed a specified percentage of the employee's household income. Under section 36B(c)(2)(C)(i)(II), an employee's required contribution has the same meaning for purposes of the premium tax credit as in section 5000A(e)(1)(B).

Section 5000A provides that, for each month, taxpayers must have minimum essential coverage, qualify for a health coverage exemption, or make an individual shared responsibility payment when they file a Federal income tax return. Section 5000A(e)(1) and § 1.5000A-3(e)(1) provide that an individual is exempt for a month when the individual cannot afford minimum essential coverage. For this purpose, an individual cannot afford coverage if the individual's required contribution (determined on an annual basis) for minimum essential coverage exceeds a specified percentage of the individual's household income. Under section 5000A(e)(1)(B)(i) and § 1.5000A-3(e)(3)(ii)(A), for employees eligible for coverage under an eligible employer-sponsored plan, the employee's required contribution is the amount an employee would have to pay for self-only coverage (whether paid through salary reduction or otherwise) under the plan. For individuals eligible to enroll in employer-sponsored coverage because of a relationship to an employee (related individual), under section 5000A(e)(1)(C) and § 1.5000A-3(e)(3)(ii)(B), the required contribution is the portion of the annual premium that the employee would pay (whether through salary reduction or otherwise) for the lowest cost family coverage that would cover the employee and all related individuals who are included in the employee's family and are not otherwise exempt under § 1.5000A-3.

Notice 2015-87, 2015-52 I.R.B. 889, provides guidance on determining the affordability of an employer's offer of eligible employer-sponsored coverage for purposes of sections 36B, 5000A, and 4980H (and the related information reporting under section 6056).[1] In relevant part, Notice 2015-87 addresses how to determine the affordability of an employer's offer of eligible employer-sponsored coverage if an employer also makes available an opt-out payment, which is a payment that (1) is available only if the employee declines coverage (which includes waiving coverage in which the employee would otherwise be enrolled) under the employer-sponsored plan, and (2) cannot be used to pay for coverage under the employer-sponsored plan. The arrangement under which the opt-out payment is made available is an opt-out arrangement.

---

[1] An assessable payment under section 4980H(b) may arise if at least one full-time employee (as defined in § 54.4980H-1(a)(21)) of the applicable large employer (as defined in § 54.4980H-1(a)(4)) receives the premium tax credit. A full-time employee generally is ineligible for the premium tax credit if the employee is offered minimum essential coverage under an eligible employer-sponsored plan that is affordable and provides minimum value. The determination of whether an applicable large employer has made an offer of affordable coverage under an eligible employer-sponsored plan for purposes of section 4980H(b) generally is based on the standard set forth in section 36B, which provides that an offer is affordable if the employee's required contribution is at or below 9.5 percent (as indexed) of the employee's household income. However, because an employer generally will not know the taxpayer employee's household income, § 54.4980H-5(e)(2) sets forth three safe harbors under which an employer may determine affordability (solely for purposes of section 4980H) based on information that is readily available to the employer (that is, Form W-2 wages, the rate of pay, or the Federal poverty line).

As Notice 2015-87 explains, the Treasury Department and the IRS have determined that it is generally appropriate to treat an opt-out payment that is made available under an unconditional opt-out arrangement in the same manner as a salary reduction contribution for purposes of determining an employee's required contribution under sections 36B and 5000A and any related consequences under sections 4980H(b) and 6056. Accordingly, Notice 2015-87 provides that the Treasury Department and the IRS intend to propose regulations reflecting this rule and to request comments on those regulations. For this purpose, an unconditional opt-out arrangement refers to an arrangement providing payments conditioned solely on an employee declining coverage under employer-sponsored coverage and not on an employee satisfying any other meaningful requirement related to the provision of health care to employees, such as a requirement to provide proof of coverage through a plan of a spouse's employer.

Notice 2015-87 also provides that the Treasury Department and the IRS anticipate requesting comments on the treatment of conditional opt-out arrangements, meaning opt-out arrangements under which payments are conditioned not only on the employee declining employer-sponsored coverage but also on satisfaction of one or more additional meaningful conditions (such as the employee providing proof of enrollment in coverage provided by a spouse's employer or other coverage).

Notice 2015-87 provides that, until the applicability date of any final regulations (and in any event for plan years beginning before 2017), individuals may treat opt-out payments made available under unconditional opt-out arrangements as increasing the employee's required contribution for purposes of sections 36B and 5000A.[2] In addition, for the same period, an individual who can demonstrate that he or she meets the condition(s) (in addition to declining the employer's health coverage) that must be satisfied to receive an opt-out payment (such as demonstrating that the employee has coverage under a spouse's group health plan) may treat the amount of the conditional opt-out payment as increasing the employee's required contribution for purposes of sections 36B and 5000A. See the section of this preamble entitled *"Effective/Applicability Date"* for additional related discussion.

Notice 2015-87 included a request for comments on opt-out arrangements. The Treasury Department and the IRS received a number of comments, and the comments are discussed in section 2.f. of this preamble entitled *"Opt-out arrangements and an employee's required contribution."*

Information Reporting

Section 36B(f)(3) provides that Exchanges must report to the IRS and to taxpayers certain information required to administer the premium tax credit. Section 1.36B-5(c)(1) provides that the information required to be reported annually includes (1) identifying information for each enrollee, (2) identifying information for the coverage, (3) the amount of enrollment premiums and advance credit payments for the coverage, (4) the premium for the benchmark plan used to calculate the amount of the advance credit payments made on behalf of the taxpayer or other enrollee, if advance credit payments were made, and the benchmark plan premium that would apply to all individuals enrolled in the coverage if advance credit payments were not made, and (5) the dates the coverage started and ended. Section 1.36B-5(c)(3)(i) provides that an Exchange must report this information for each family enrolled in the coverage.

Explanation of Provisions

1. Effective/Applicability Date

Except as otherwise provided in this section, these regulations are proposed to apply for taxable years beginning after December 31, 2016. As indicated in this section, taxpayers may rely on certain provisions of the proposed regulations for taxable years ending after December 31, 2013. In addition, several rules are proposed to apply for taxable years beginning after December 31, 2018. See the later section of this preamble entitled *"Effective/Applicability Date"* for information on the applicability date for the regulations on opt-out arrangements.

2. Eligibility

a. Applicable taxpayers

To avoid repayments of advance credit payments for taxpayers who experience an unforeseen decline in income, the existing regulations provide that if an Exchange determines at enrollment that the taxpayer's household income will be at least 100 percent but will not exceed 400 percent of the applicable FPL, the taxpayer will not lose his or her status as an applicable taxpayer solely because household income for the year turns out to be below 100 percent of the applicable FPL. To reduce the likelihood that individuals who recklessly or intentionally provide inaccurate information to an Exchange will benefit from an Exchange determination, the proposed regulations provide that a

[2] Notice 2015-87 also provides that the Treasury Department and the IRS anticipate that the regulations generally will apply only for periods after the issuance of final regulations and that for the period prior to the applicability date of the final regulations, employers are not required to increase the amount of an employee's required contribution by the amount of an opt-out payment made available under an opt-out arrangement (other than a payment made available under a non-relief-eligible opt-out arrangement) for purposes of section 6056 (Form 1095-C), and an opt-out payment made available under an opt-out arrangement (other than a payment made available under a non-relief-eligible opt-out arrangement) will not be treated as increasing an employee's required contribution for purposes of any potential consequences under section 4980H(b). For a discussion of non-relief-eligible opt-out arrangements see Notice 2015-87, Q&A-9.

taxpayer whose household income is below 100 percent of the FPL for the taxpayer's family size is not treated as an applicable taxpayer if, with intentional or reckless disregard for the facts, the taxpayer provided incorrect information to an Exchange for the year of coverage.

b. Exchange determination of ineligibility for Medicaid or CHIP

Similar to the rule for taxpayers who received the benefit of advance credit payments but ended the taxable year with household income below 100 percent of the applicable FPL, the existing regulations do not require a repayment of advance credit payments for taxpayers with household income within the range for eligibility for certain government-sponsored programs if an Exchange determined or considered (within the meaning of 45 CFR 155.302(b)) the taxpayer or a member of the taxpayer's family to be ineligible for the program. To reduce the likelihood that individuals who recklessly or intentionally provide inaccurate information to an Exchange will benefit from an Exchange determination, the proposed regulations provide that an individual who was determined or considered by an Exchange to be ineligible for Medicaid, CHIP, or a similar program (such as a Basic Health Program) may be treated as eligible for coverage under the program if, with intentional or reckless disregard for the facts, the individual (or a person claiming a personal exemption for the individual) provided incorrect information to the Exchange.

c. Nonappropriated Fund Health Benefits Program

The existing regulations under section 36B provide that government-sponsored programs described in section 5000A(f)(1)(A), which include the Nonappropriated Fund Health Benefits Program of the Department of Defense, established under section 349 of the National Defense Authorization Act for Fiscal Year 1995 (Public Law 103-337; 10 U.S.C. 1587 note), are not eligible employer-sponsored plans. However, § 1.5000A-2(c)(2) provides that, because the Nonappropriated Fund Health Benefits Program (Program) is offered by an instrumentality of the Department of Defense to its employees, the Program is an eligible employer-sponsored plan. The proposed regulations conform the section 36B regulations to the section 5000A regulations and provide that the Program is treated as an eligible employer-sponsored plan for purposes of determining if an individual is eligible for minimum essential coverage under section 36B. Thus, if coverage under the Program does not provide minimum value (under § 1.36B-2(c)(3)(vi)) or is not affordable (under § 36B-2(c)(3)(v)) for an individual who does not enroll in the coverage, he or she is not treated as eligible for minimum essential coverage under the Program for purposes of premium tax credit eligibility.

d. Eligibility for employer-sponsored coverage for months during a plan year

The existing regulations under section 36B provide that an individual is eligible for minimum essential coverage through an eligible employer-sponsored plan if the individual had the opportunity to enroll in the plan and the plan is affordable and provides minimum value. The Treasury Department and the IRS are aware that in some instances individuals may not be allowed an annual opportunity to decide whether to enroll in eligible employer-sponsored coverage. This lack of an annual opportunity to enroll in employer-sponsored coverage should not limit an individual's annual choice from available coverage options through the Marketplace with the possibility of benefitting from the premium tax credit. Thus, the proposed regulations clarify that if an individual declines to enroll in employer-sponsored coverage for a plan year and does not have the opportunity to enroll in that coverage for one or more succeeding plan years, for purposes of section 36B, the individual is treated as ineligible for that coverage for the succeeding plan year or years for which there is no enrollment opportunity.[3]

e. Excepted benefits

Under section 36B and § 1.36B-2(c)(3)(vii)(A), an individual is treated as eligible for minimum essential coverage through an eligible employer-sponsored plan if the individual actually enrolls in the coverage, even if the coverage is not affordable or does not provide minimum value. Although health coverage that consists solely of excepted benefits may be a group health plan and, therefore, is an eligible employer-sponsored plan under section 5000A(f)(2) and § 1.5000A-2(c)(1), section 5000A(f)(3) provides that health coverage that consists solely of excepted benefits is not minimum essential coverage. Therefore, individuals enrolled in a plan consisting solely of excepted benefits still must obtain minimum essential coverage to satisfy the individual shared responsibility provision. The proposed regulations clarify that for purposes of section 36B an individual is considered eligible for coverage under an eligible employer-sponsored plan only if that plan is minimum essential coverage. Accordingly, an individual enrolled in or offered a plan consisting solely of excepted benefits is not denied the premium tax credit by virtue of that excepted benefits offer or coverage. Taxpayers may rely on this rule for all taxable years beginning after December 31, 2013.

f. Opt-out arrangements and an employee's required contribution

Sections 1.36B-2(c)(3)(v) and 1.5000A-3(e)(3)(ii)(A) provide that, in determining whether employer-sponsored coverage is affordable to an employee, an employee's required contribution for the

---

[3] Note that for purposes of section 4980H, in general, an applicable large employer will not be treated as having made an offer of coverage to a full-time employee for a plan year if the employee does not have an effective opportunity to elect to enroll in the coverage at least once with respect to the plan year. For this purpose, a plan year must be twelve consecutive months, unless a short plan year of less than twelve consecutive months is permitted for a valid business purpose. For additional rules on the definition of "offer" and "plan year" under section 4980H, see §§ 54.4980H-1(a)(35), 54.4980H-4(b), and 54.4980H-5(b).

coverage includes the amount by which the employee's salary would be reduced to enroll in the coverage.[4] If an employer makes an opt-out payment available to an employee, the choice between cash and health coverage presented by the opt-out arrangement is analogous to the cash-or-coverage choice presented by the option to pay for coverage by salary reduction. In both cases, the employee may purchase the employer-sponsored coverage only at the price of forgoing a specified amount of cash compensation that the employee would otherwise receive - salary, in the case of a salary reduction, or an equal amount of other compensation, in the case of an opt-out payment. Therefore, the economic cost to the employee of the employer-sponsored coverage is the same under both arrangements. Accordingly, the employee's required contribution generally should be determined similarly regardless of the type of payment that an employee must forgo.

Notice 2015-87 requested comments on the proposed treatment of opt-out arrangements outlined in Q&A-9 of that notice. Several commenters objected to the proposal that the amount of an available unconditional opt-out payment increases the employee's required contribution on the basis that forgoing opt-out payments as part of enrolling in coverage has not traditionally been viewed by employers or employees as economically equivalent to making a salary reduction election and that such a rule would discourage employers from making opt-out payments available. None of the commenters, however, offered a persuasive economic basis for distinguishing unconditional opt-out payments from other compensation that an employee must forgo to enroll in employer-sponsored coverage, such as a salary reduction. Because forgoing an unconditional opt-out payment is economically equivalent to forgoing salary pursuant to a salary reduction election, and because §§1.36B-2(c)(3)(v) and 1.5000A-3(e)(3)(ii)(A) provide that the employee's required contribution includes the amount of any salary reduction, the proposed regulations adopt the approach described in Notice 2015-87 for opt-out payments made available under unconditional opt-out arrangements and provide that the amount of an opt-out payment made available to the employee under an unconditional opt-out arrangement increases the employee's required contribution.[5]

Notice 2015-87 provides that, for periods prior to the applicability date of any final regulations, employers are not required to increase the amount of an employee's required contribution by amounts made available under an opt-out arrangement for purposes of section 4980H(b) or section 6056 (in particular Form 1095-C, *Employer-Provided Health Insurance Offer and Coverage*), except that, for periods after December 16, 2015, the employee's required contribution must include amounts made available under an unconditional opt-out arrangement that is adopted after December 16, 2015. However, Notice 2015-87 provided that, for this purpose, an opt-out arrangement will not be treated as adopted after December 16, 2015, under limited circumstances, including in cases in which a board, committee, or similar body or an authorized officer of the employer specifically adopted the opt-out arrangement before December 16, 2015.

Some commenters requested clarification that an unconditional opt-out arrangement that is required under the terms of a collective bargaining agreement in effect before December 16, 2015, should be treated as having been adopted prior to December 16, 2015, and that amounts made available under such an opt-out arrangement should not be included in an employee's required contribution for purposes of sections 4980H(b) or 6056 through the expiration of the collective bargaining agreement that provides for the opt-out arrangement. The Treasury Department and the IRS now clarify that, under Notice 2015-87, for purposes of sections 4980H(b) and 6056, an unconditional opt-out arrangement that is required under the terms of a collective bargaining agreement in effect before December 16, 2015, will be treated as having been adopted prior to December 16, 2015. In addition, until the later of (1) the beginning of the first plan year that begins following the expiration of the collective bargaining agreement in effect before December 16, 2015 (disregarding any extensions on or after December 16, 2015), or (2) the applicability date of these regulations with respect to sections 4980H and 6056, employers participating in the collective bargaining agreement are not required to increase the amount of an employee's required contribution by amounts made available under such an opt-out arrangement for purposes of sections 4980H(b) or 6056 (Form 1095-C). The Treasury Department and the IRS further adopt these commenters' request that this treatment apply to any successor employer adopting the opt-out arrangement before the expiration of the collective bargaining agreement in effect before December 16, 2015 (disregarding any extensions on or after December 16, 2015). Commenters raised the issue of whether other types of agreements covering employees may need a similar extension of the relief through the end of the agreement's term. The Treasury Department and the IRS request comments identifying the types of agreements raising this

---

[4] Section 5000A(e)(1)(C) and §1.5000A-3(e)(3)(ii)(B) provide that, for purposes of the individual shared responsibility provision, the required contribution for individuals eligible to enroll in employer coverage because of a relationship to an employee (related individual) is the portion of the annual premium that the employee would pay (whether through salary reduction or otherwise) for the lowest cost family coverage that would cover the employee and all related individuals who are included in the employee's family and are not otherwise exempt under §1.5000A-3.

[5] To distinguish between opt-out payments and employer contributions to a section 125 cafeteria plan (which in some cases could be paid in cash to an employee who declines coverage in the health plan or other available benefits), the proposed regulations further clarify that an amount provided as an employer contribution to a cafeteria plan and that may be used by the employee to purchase minimum essential coverage is not an opt-out payment, whether or not the employee may receive the amount as a taxable benefit. This provision clarifies that the effect on an employee's required contribution of employer contributions to a cafeteria plan is determined under §1.36B-2(c)(3)(v)(A)(6) rather than §1.36B-2(c)(3)(v)(A)(7).

issue due to their similarity to collective bargaining agreements because, for example, the agreement is similar in scope to a collective bargaining agreement, binding on the parties involved for a multi-year period, and subject to a statutory or regulatory regime.

Several commenters suggested that, notwithstanding the proposal on unconditional opt-out arrangements, the amount of an opt-out payment made available should not increase an employee's required contribution if the opt-out payment is conditioned on the employee having minimum essential coverage through another source, such as a spouse's employer-sponsored plan. These commenters argued that the amount of such a conditional opt-out payment should not affect the affordability of an employer's offer of employer-sponsored coverage for an employee who does not satisfy the applicable condition because that employee is ineligible to receive the opt-out payment. Moreover, commenters argued that an employee who satisfies the condition (that is, who has alternative minimum essential coverage) is ineligible for the premium tax credit and does not need to determine the affordability of the employer's coverage offer. Thus, the commenters asserted, an amount made available under such an arrangement should be excluded from the required contribution.

While it is clear that the availability of an unconditional opt-out payment increases an individual's required contribution, the effect of the availability of a conditional opt-out payment is less obvious. In particular, under an unconditional opt-out arrangement, an individual who enrolls in the employer coverage loses the opt-out payment as a direct result of enrolling in the employer coverage. By contrast, in the case of a conditional opt-out arrangement, the availability of the opt-out payment may depend on information that is not generally available to the employer (who, if it is an applicable large employer, must report the required contribution under section 6056 and whose potential liability under section 4980H may be affected). Because of this difficulty of ascertaining which individuals could have met the condition and, therefore, would actually forgo the opt-out payment when enrolling in employer-sponsored coverage, it generally is not feasible to have a rule under which the required contribution perfectly captures the cost of coverage for each specific individual offered a conditional opt-out payment.

Similarly, another way to view opt-out payments that are conditioned on alternative coverage is that, rather than raising the cost to the employee of the employer's coverage, they reduce the cost to the employee of the alternative coverage. However, because employers generally do not have information about the existence and cost of other options available to the individual, it is not practical to take into account any offer of coverage other than the offer made by the employer in determining the required contribution with respect to the employer coverage (that is, the coverage that the employee must decline to receive the opt-out payment).

While commenters indicated that the required contribution with respect to the employer coverage does not matter for an individual enrolled in any other minimum essential coverage because the individual would be ineligible for the premium tax credit, this statement is not true if the other coverage is individual market coverage. In particular, while enrollment in most types of minimum essential coverage results in an individual being ineligible for a premium tax credit, that is not the case for coverage in the individual market. Moreover, for individual market coverage offered through a Marketplace, the required contribution with respect to the employer coverage frequently will be relevant in determining whether the individual is eligible for a premium tax credit. In such cases, as in the case of an unconditional opt-out payment, the availability of a conditional opt-out payment effectively increases the cost to the individual of enrolling in the employer coverage (at least relative to Marketplace coverage).

Further, an opt-out arrangement that is conditioned on an employee's ability to obtain other coverage (if that coverage can be coverage in the individual market, whether inside or outside the Marketplace) does not generally raise the issues described earlier in this section of the preamble regarding the difficulty of ascertaining which individuals could meet the condition under a conditional opt-out arrangement. This is because generally all individuals are able to obtain coverage in the individual market, pursuant to the guaranteed issue requirements in section 2702 of the PHS Act. Thus, in the sense that all individuals can satisfy the applicable condition, such an opt-out arrangement is similar to an unconditional opt-out arrangement.

In an effort to provide a workable rule that balances these competing concerns, the proposed regulations provide that amounts made available under conditional opt-out arrangements are disregarded in determining the required contribution if the arrangement satisfies certain conditions (an "eligible opt-out arrangement"), but otherwise the amounts are taken into account. The proposed regulations define an "eligible opt-out arrangement" as an arrangement under which the employee's right to receive the opt-out payment is conditioned on (1) the employee declining to enroll in the employer-sponsored coverage and (2) the employee providing reasonable evidence that the employee and all other individuals for whom the employee reasonably expects to claim a personal exemption deduction for the taxable year or years that begin or end in or with the employer's plan year to which the opt-out arrangement applies (employee's expected tax family) have or will have minimum essential coverage (other than coverage in the individual market, whether or not obtained through the Marketplace) during the period of coverage to which the opt-out arrangement applies. For example, if an employee's expected tax family consists of the employee, the employee's spouse, and two children, the employee would meet this requirement by providing reasonable evidence that the employee, the employee's spouse, and the two children, will have coverage under the group health plan of the spouse' s employer for the period to which the opt-out arrangement applies.[6]

The Treasury Department and the IRS invite comments on this proposed rule, including suggestions for other workable rules that result in the required contribution more accurately reflecting the individual's cost of coverage while minimizing undesirable consequences and incentives.

For purposes of the proposed eligible opt-out arrangement rule, reasonable evidence of alternative coverage includes the employee's attestation that the employee and all other members of the employee's expected tax family, if any, have or will have minimum essential coverage (other than coverage in the individual market, whether or not obtained through the Marketplace) or other reasonable evidence. Notwithstanding the evidence of alternative coverage required under the arrangement, to qualify as an eligible opt-out arrangement, the arrangement must also provide that any opt-out payment will not be made (and the payment must not in fact be made) if the employer knows or has reason to know that the employee or any other member of the employee's expected tax family does not have (or will not have) the required alternative coverage. An eligible opt-out arrangement must also require that the evidence of coverage be provided no less frequently than every plan year to which the eligible opt-out arrangement applies, and that the evidence be provided no earlier than a reasonable period before the commencement of the period of coverage to which the eligible opt-out arrangement applies. Obtaining the reasonable evidence (such as an attestation) as part of the regular annual open enrollment period that occurs within a few months before the commencement of the next plan year of employer-sponsored coverage meets this reasonable period requirement. Alternatively, the eligible opt-out arrangement would be permitted to require evidence of alternative coverage to be provided later, such as after the plan year starts, which would enable the employer to require evidence that the employee and other members of the employee's expected tax family have already obtained the alternative coverage.

Commenters on Notice 2015-87 generally stated that typical conditions under an opt-out arrangement include a requirement that the employee have alternative coverage through employer-sponsored coverage of a spouse or another relative, such as a parent. Provided that, as required under the opt-out arrangement, the employee provided reasonable evidence of this alternative coverage for the employee and the other members of the employee's expected tax family, and met the related conditions described in this preamble, these types of opt-out arrangements would be eligible opt-out arrangements, and opt-out payments made available under such arrangements would not increase the employee's required contribution.

The Treasury Department and the IRS did not receive comments on opt-out arrangements indicating that the meaningful conditions imposed include any requirement other than one relating to alternative coverage. Therefore, the proposed rules do not address other opt-out conditions and would not treat an opt-out arrangement based on other conditions as an eligible opt-out arrangement. However, the Treasury Department and the IRS invite comments on whether opt-out payments are made subject to additional types of conditions in some cases, whether those types of conditions should be addressed in further guidance, and, if so, how.

One commenter suggested that, if opt-out payments conditioned on alternative coverage are not included in an employee's required contribution, rules will be needed for cases in which an employee receives an opt-out payment and that employee's alternative coverage subsequently terminates. The commenter suggested that, in that case, the termination of the alternative coverage should have no impact on the determination of the employee's required contribution for the employer-sponsored coverage from which the employee opted out. In response, under the proposed regulations, provided that the reasonable evidence requirement is met, the amount of an opt-out payment made available under an eligible opt-out arrangement may continue to be excluded from the employee's required contribution for the remainder of the period of coverage to which the opt-out payment originally applied. The opt-out payment may be excluded for this period even if the alternative coverage subsequently terminates for the employee or any other member of the employee's expected tax family, regardless of whether the opt-out payment is required to be adjusted or terminated due to the loss of alternative coverage, and regardless of whether the employee is required to provide notice of the loss of alternative coverage to the employer.

The Treasury Department and the IRS are aware that the way in which opt-out arrangements affect the calculation of affordability is important not only to an employee and the other members of the employee's expected tax family in determining whether they may be eligible for a premium tax credit or whether an individual may be exempt under the individual shared responsibility provisions, but also to an employer subject to the employer shared responsibility provisions under section 4980H in determining whether the employer may be subject to an assessable payment under section 4980H(b). An employer subject to the employer shared responsibility provisions will be subject to a payment under section 4980H(b) only with respect to a full-time employee who receives a premium tax credit,

---

[6] The Treasury Department and the IRS note that if an opt-out payment is conditioned on an employee obtaining individual market coverage, that opt-out arrangement could act as a reimbursement arrangement for some or all of the employee's premium for that individual market coverage; therefore, the opt-out arrangement could operate as an employer payment plan as discussed in Notice 2015-87, Notice 2015-17, 2015-14 I.R.B. 845, and Notice 2013-54, 2013-40 I.R.B. 287. Nothing in these proposed regulations is intended to affect the prior guidance on employer payment plans.

and an employee will not be eligible for the premium tax credit if the employer's offer of coverage was affordable and provided minimum value.[7] Commenters expressed concern that if the rule adopted for conditional opt-outs required an employee to provide reasonable evidence that the employee has or will have minimum essential coverage, the employer may not know whether the employee is being truthful and has obtained (or will obtain) such coverage, or how long such coverage will continue. Under these proposed regulations, however, the employee's required contribution will not be increased by an opt-out payment made available under an eligible opt-out arrangement, provided that the arrangement provides that the employer makes the payment only if the employee provides reasonable evidence of alternative coverage and the employer does not know or have reason to know that the employee or any other member of the employee's expected tax family fails or will fail to meet the requirement to have alternative coverage (other than individual market coverage, whether or not obtained through the Marketplace).

Some commenters requested exceptions for special circumstances from the general rule that the employee's required contribution is increased by the amount of an opt-out payment made available. These circumstances include (1) conditional opt-out payments that are required under the terms of a collective bargaining agreement and (2) opt-out payments that are below a de minimis amount. Regarding opt-out arrangements contained in collective bargaining agreements, the Treasury Department and the IRS anticipate that the proposed treatment of eligible opt-out arrangements, generally, will address the concerns raised in the comments. Accordingly, the Treasury Department and the IRS do not propose to provide a permanent exception for opt-out arrangements provided under collective bargaining agreements. Earlier in this section of the preamble, however, the Treasury Department and the IRS clarify and expand the transition relief provided under Notice 2015-87 for opt-out arrangements provided under collective bargaining agreements in effect before December 16, 2015. As for an exception for de minimis amounts, the Treasury Department and the IRS decline to adopt such an exception because there is neither a statutory nor an economic basis for establishing a de minimis threshold under which an unconditional opt-out payment would be excluded from the employee's required contribution.

g. Effective date of eligibility for minimum essential coverage when advance credit payments discontinuance is delayed

Section 36B and the regulations under section 36B provide that an individual who may enroll in minimum essential coverage outside the Marketplace (other than individual market coverage) for a month is generally not allowed a premium tax credit for that month. Consequently, individuals enrolled in a qualified health plan with advance credit payments must return to the Exchange to report eligibility for other minimum essential coverage so the Exchange can discontinue the advance credit payments for Marketplace coverage. Similarly, individuals enrolled in a qualified health plan with advance credit payments may be determined eligible for coverage under a government-sponsored program, such as Medicaid. In some cases, individuals may inform the Exchange of their opportunity to enroll in other minimum essential coverage or receive approval for coverage under a government-sponsored program after the time for which the Exchange can discontinue advance credit payments for the next month. Because taxpayers should generally not have to repay the advance credit payments for that next month in these circumstances, the proposed regulations provide a rule for situations in which an Exchange's discontinuance of advance credit payments is delayed. Under the proposed regulations, if an individual who is enrolled in a qualified health plan for which advance credit payments are made informs the Exchange that the individual is or will soon be eligible for other minimum essential coverage and that advance credit payments should be discontinued, but the Exchange does not discontinue advance credit payments for the first calendar month beginning after the month the individual notifies the Exchange, the individual is treated as eligible for the other minimum essential coverage no earlier than the first day of the second calendar month beginning after the first month the individual may enroll in the other minimum essential coverage. Similarly, if a determination is made that an individual is eligible for Medicaid or CHIP but advance credit payments are not discontinued for the first calendar month beginning after the eligibility determination, the individual is treated as eligible for Medicaid or CHIP no earlier than the first day of the second calendar month beginning after the determination. Taxpayers may rely on this rule for all taxable years beginning after December 31, 2013.

3. Premium Assistance Amount

a. Payment of taxpayer's share of premiums for advance credit payments following appeal determinations

Under § 1.36B-3(c)(1)(ii), a month in which an individual who is enrolled in a qualified health plan is a coverage month for the individual only if the taxpayer's share of the premium for the individual's coverage for the month is paid by the unextended due date of the taxpayer's income tax return for the year of coverage, or the premium is fully paid by advance credit payments.

One of the functions of an Exchange is to make determinations as to whether an individual who enrolls in a qualified health plan is eligible for advance credit payments for the coverage. If an Exchange determines that the individual is not eligible for advance credit payments, the individual

---

[7] The affordability rules under section 36B, including rules regarding opt-out payments, may also affect the application of section 4980H(a) because one element that is required for an applicable large employer to be subject to an assessable payment under section 4980H(a) is that at least one full-time employee must receive the premium tax credit.

may appeal that decision. An individual who is initially determined ineligible for advance credit payments, does not enroll in a qualified health plan under the contested determination, and is later determined to be eligible for advance credit payments through the appeals process, may elect to be retroactively enrolled in a health plan through the Exchange. In that case, the individual is treated as having been enrolled in the qualified health plan from the date on which the individual would have enrolled had he or she initially been determined eligible for advance credit payments. If retroactively enrolled, the deadline for paying premiums for the retroactive coverage may be after the unextended due date for filing an income tax return for the year of coverage. Consequently, the proposed regulations provide that a taxpayer who is eligible for advance credit payments pursuant to an eligibility appeal for a member of the taxpayer's coverage family who, based on the appeals decision, retroactively enrolls in a qualified health plan, is considered to have met the requirement in § 1.36B-3(c)(1)(ii) for a month if the taxpayer pays the taxpayer's share of the premium for coverage under the plan for the month on or before the 120th day following the date of the appeals decision. Taxpayers may rely on this rule for all taxable years beginning after December 31, 2013.

b. Month that coverage is terminated

Section 1.36B-3(d)(2) provides that if a qualified health plan is terminated before the last day of a month, the premium assistance amount for the month is the lesser of the enrollment premiums for the month (reduced by any amounts that were refunded), or the excess of the benchmark plan premium for a full month of coverage over the full contribution amount for the month. Section 1.36B-3(c)(2) provides that an individual whose enrollment in a qualified health plan is effective on the date of the individual's birth or adoption, or placement for foster care, or upon the effective date of a court order, is treated as enrolled as of the first day of the month and, therefore, the month of enrollment may be a coverage month. The regulations, however, do not expressly address how the premium assistance amount is computed when a covered individual disenrolls before the last day of a month but the plan is not terminated because other individuals remain enrolled. For purposes of the premium tax credit, the premium assistance amount for an individual who is not enrolled for an entire month should be the same regardless of the circumstances causing the partial-month coverage, provided that the individual was enrolled, or is treated as enrolled, as of the first day of the month (that is, so long as the month is a coverage month). Accordingly, to provide consistency for all individuals who have a coverage month that is less than a full calendar month, the proposed regulations provide that the premium assistance amount for a month is the lesser of the enrollment premiums for the month (reduced by any amounts that were refunded), or the excess of the benchmark plan premium over the contribution amount for the month. Taxpayers may rely on this rule for all taxable years beginning after December 31, 2013.

4. Benchmark Plan Premium

a. Effective/applicability date of benchmark plan rules

The rules relating to the benchmark plan in this section are proposed to apply for taxable years beginning after December 31, 2018.

b. Pediatric dental benefits

Under section 1311(d)(2)(B) of the Affordable Care Act, only qualified health plans, including stand-alone dental plans offering pediatric dental benefits, may be offered through a Marketplace. In general, a qualified health plan is required to provide coverage for all ten essential health benefits described in section 1302(b) of the Affordable Care Act, including pediatric dental coverage. However, under section 1302(b)(4)(F), a plan that does not provide pediatric dental benefits may nonetheless be a qualified health plan if it covers each essential health benefit described in section 1302(b) other than pediatric dental benefits and if it is offered through a Marketplace in which a stand-alone dental plan offering pediatric dental benefits is offered as well.

Section 36B(b)(3)(E) and § 1.36B-3(k) provide that if an individual enrolls in both a qualified health plan and a stand-alone dental plan, the portion of the premium for the stand-alone dental plan properly allocable to pediatric dental benefits is treated as a premium payable for the individual's qualified health plan. Thus, in determining a taxpayer's premium assistance amount for a month in which a member of the taxpayer's coverage family is enrolled in a stand-alone dental plan, the taxpayer's enrollment premium includes the portion of the premium for the stand-alone dental plan allocable to pediatric dental benefits. The existing regulations do not provide a similar adjustment for the taxpayer's applicable benchmark plan premium to reflect the cost of pediatric dental benefits in cases where the second-lowest cost silver plan does not provide pediatric dental benefits.

Section 36B(b)(3)(B) provides that the applicable benchmark plan with respect to a taxpayer is the second lowest cost silver plan available through the applicable Marketplace that provides "self-only coverage" or "family coverage," depending generally on whether the coverage family includes one or more individuals. Neither the Code nor the Affordable Care Act defines the terms "self-only coverage" or "family coverage" for this purpose.

Under the existing regulations, the references in section 36B(b)(3)(B) to plans that provide self-only coverage and family coverage are interpreted to refer to all qualified health plans offered through the applicable Marketplace, regardless of whether the coverage offered by those plans includes all ten essential health benefits. Because qualified health plans that do not offer pediatric dental benefits tend to be cheaper than qualified health plans that cover all ten essential health benefits, the second lowest-cost silver plan (and therefore the premium tax credit) for taxpayers purchasing coverage through a Marketplace in which stand-alone dental plans are offered is likely to not account for the cost of obtaining pediatric dental coverage.

The Treasury Department and the IRS believe that the current rule frustrates the statute's goal of making coverage that provides the essential health benefits affordable to individuals eligible for the premium tax credit. Accordingly, the proposed regulations reflect a modification in the interpretation of the terms "self-only coverage" and "family coverage" in section 36B(b)(3)(B) to refer to coverage that provides each of the essential health benefits described in section 1302(b) of the Affordable Care Act. This coverage may be obtained from either a qualified health plan alone or from a qualified health plan in combination with a stand-alone dental plan. In particular, self-only coverage refers to coverage obtained from such plans where the coverage family is a single individual. Similarly, family coverage refers to coverage obtained from such plans where the coverage family includes more than one individual.

Consistent with this interpretation, the proposed regulations provide that for taxable years beginning after December 31, 2018, if an Exchange offers one or more silver-level qualified health plans that do not cover pediatric dental benefits, the applicable benchmark plan is determined by ranking (1) the premiums for the silver-level qualified health plans that include pediatric dental benefits offered by the Exchange and (2) the aggregate of the premiums for the silver-level qualified health plans offered by the Exchange that do not include pediatric dental benefits plus the portion of the premium allocable to pediatric dental benefits for stand-alone dental plans offered by the Exchange. In constructing this ranking, the premium for the lowest-cost silver plan that does not include pediatric dental benefits is added to the lowest-cost portion of the premium for a stand-alone dental plan that is allocable to pediatric dental benefits, and similarly, the premium for the second lowest-cost silver plan that does not include pediatric dental benefits is added to the secondlowest- cost portion of the premium for a stand-alone dental plan that is allocable to pediatric dental benefits. The second lowest-cost amount from this combined ranking is the taxpayer's applicable benchmark plan premium.

c. Coverage family members residing in different locations

Under § 1.36B-3(f), a taxpayer's applicable benchmark plan is the second lowest cost silver plan offered at the time a taxpayer or family member enrolls in a qualified health plan through the Exchange for the rating area where the taxpayer resides. Under § 1.36B-3(f)(4), if members of a taxpayer's family reside in different states and enroll in separate qualified health plans, the premium for the taxpayer's applicable benchmark plan is the sum of the premiums for the applicable benchmark plans for each group of family members living in the same state.

Referring to the residence of the taxpayer to establish the cost for a benchmark health plan is appropriate when the taxpayer and all members of the taxpayer's coverage family live in the same location because it reflects the cost of available coverage for the taxpayer's coverage family. However, because premiums and plan availability may vary based on location, the existing rule for a taxpayer whose family members reside in different locations in the same state may not accurately reflect the cost of available coverage. In addition, the rules for calculating the premium tax credit should operate the same for families residing in multiple locations within a state and families residing in multiple states. Accordingly, § 1.36B-3(f)(4) of the proposed regulations provides that if a taxpayer's coverage family members reside in multiple locations, whether within the same state or in different states, the taxpayer's benchmark plan is determined based on the cost of available coverage in the locations where members of the taxpayer's coverage family reside. In particular, if members of a taxpayer's coverage family reside in different locations, the taxpayer's benchmark plan premium is the sum of the premiums for the applicable benchmark plans for each group of coverage family members residing in different locations, based on the plans offered to the group through the Exchange for the rating area where the group resides. If all members of a taxpayer's coverage family reside in a single location that is different from where the taxpayer resides, the taxpayer's benchmark plan premium is the premium for the applicable benchmark plan for the coverage family, based on the plans offered to the taxpayer's coverage family through the Exchange for the rating area where the coverage family resides.

d. Aggregation of silver-level policies

Section 1.36B-3(f)(3) provides that if one or more silver-level plans offered through an Exchange do not cover all members of a taxpayer's coverage family under one policy (for example, because an issuer will not cover a taxpayer's dependent parent on the same policy the taxpayer enrolls in), the premium for the applicable benchmark plan may be the premium for a single policy or for more than one policy, whichever is the second lowest-cost silver option. This rule does not specify which combinations of policies must be taken into account for this purpose, suggesting that all such combinations must be considered, which is unduly complex for taxpayers, difficult for Exchanges to implement, and difficult for the IRS to administer. Accordingly, to clarify and simplify the benchmark premium determination for situations in which a silver-level plan does not cover all the members of a taxpayer's coverage family under one policy, the proposed regulations delete the existing rule and provide a new rule in its place.

Under the proposed regulations, if a silver-level plan offers coverage to all members of a taxpayer's coverage family who reside in the same location under a single policy, the plan premium taken into account for purposes of determining the applicable benchmark plan is the premium for that policy. In contrast, if a silver-level plan would require multiple policies to cover all members of a taxpayer's coverage family who reside in the same location, the plan premium taken into account for purposes of determining the applicable benchmark plan is the sum of the premiums for self-only policies under the plan for each member of the coverage family who resides in the same location. Under the proposed regulations, similar rules would apply to the portion of premiums for stand-alone dental plans allocable to pediatric dental coverage taken into account for purposes of determining the premium for a taxpayer's applicable benchmark plan.

Comments are requested on the rule contained in the proposed regulations, as well as on an alternative rule under which the plan premium taken into account for purposes of determining a taxpayer's applicable benchmark plan would be equal to the sum of the self-only policies under a plan for each member of the taxpayer's coverage family, regardless of whether all members of the taxpayer's coverage family could be covered under a single policy under the plan.

e. Silver-level plan not available for enrollment

Section 1.36B-3(f)(5) provides that if a qualified health plan is closed to enrollment for a taxpayer or a member of the taxpayer's coverage family, that plan is disregarded in determining the taxpayer's applicable benchmark plan. Similarly, § 1.36B-3(f)(6) provides that a plan that is the applicable benchmark plan for a taxpayer does not cease to be the applicable benchmark plan solely because the plan or a lower cost plan terminates or closes to enrollment during the taxable year. Because standalone dental plans are considered in determining a taxpayer's applicable benchmark plan under the proposed regulations, the proposed regulations provide consistency in the treatment of qualified health plans and stand-alone dental plans that are closed to enrollment or that terminate during the taxable year.

f. Only one silver-level plan offered to the coverage family

In general, § 1.36B-3(f)(1) provides that a taxpayer's applicable benchmark plan is the second lowest-cost silver-level plan available to the taxpayer for self-only or family coverage. However, for taxpayers who reside in certain locations, only one silver-level plan providing such coverage may be available. Section § 1.36B-3(f)(8) of the proposed regulations clarifies that if there is only one silver-level qualified health plan offered through the Exchange that would cover all members of the taxpayer's coverage family (whether under one policy or multiple policies), that silver-level plan is used for purposes of the taxpayer's applicable benchmark plan. Similarly, if there is only one stand-alone dental plan offered through the Exchange that would cover all members of the taxpayer's coverage family (whether under one policy or multiple policies), the portion of the premium of that plan that is allocable to pediatric dental benefits is used for purposes of determining the taxpayer's applicable benchmark plan.

5. Reconciliation of Advance Credit Payments

Section 301.6011-8 provides that a taxpayer who receives the benefit of advance credit payments must file an income tax return for that taxable year on or before the due date for the return (including extensions of time for filing) and reconcile the advance credit payments. In addition, the regulations under section 36B provide that if advance credit payments are made for coverage of an individual for whom no taxpayer claims a personal exemption deduction, the taxpayer who attests to the Exchange to the intention to claim a personal exemption deduction for the individual as part of the determination that the taxpayer is eligible for advance credit payments for coverage of the individual must reconcile the advance credit payments.

Questions have been raised concerning how these two rules apply, and consequently which individual must reconcile advance credit payments, when a taxpayer (a parent, for example) attests that he or she will claim a personal exemption deduction for an individual, the advance payments are made with respect to coverage for the individual, the taxpayer does not claim a personal exemption deduction for the individual, and the individual does not file a tax return for the year. The intent of the existing regulation is that the taxpayer, not the individual for whose coverage advance credit payments were made, must reconcile the advance credit payments in situations in which a taxpayer attests to the intention to claim a personal exemption for the individual and no one claims a personal exemption deduction for the individual. Consequently, the proposed regulations clarify that if advance credit payments are made for coverage of an individual for whom no taxpayer claims a personal exemption deduction, the taxpayer who attests to the Exchange to the intention to claim a personal exemption deduction for the individual, not the individual for whose coverage the advance credit payments were made, must file a tax return and reconcile the advance credit payments.

6. Information Reporting

a. Two or more families enrolled in single qualified health plan

Section 1.36B-3(h) provides that if a qualified health plan covers more than one family under a single policy (for example, a plan covers a taxpayer and the taxpayer's child who is 25 and not a dependent of the taxpayer), the premium tax credit is computed for each applicable taxpayer covered by the plan. In addition, in computing the tax credit for each taxpayer, premiums for the qualified health plan the taxpayers purchase (the enrollment premiums) are allocated to each taxpayer in proportion to the premiums for each taxpayer's applicable benchmark plan.

The existing regulations provide that the Exchange must report the enrollment premiums for each family, but do not specify the manner in which the Exchange must divide the enrollment premiums among the families enrolled in the policy. Consequently, the proposed regulations clarify that when multiple families enroll in a single qualified health plan and advance credit payments are made for the coverage, the enrollment premiums reported by the Exchange for each family is the family's allocable share of the enrollment premiums, which is based on the proportion of each family's applicable benchmark plan premium.

b. Partial months of enrollment

The existing regulations do not specify how the enrollment premiums and benchmark plan premiums are reported in cases in which one or more individuals is enrolled or disenrolled in coverage mid-month. To ensure that this reporting is consistent with the rules for calculating the premium assistance amounts for partial months of coverage, the proposed regulations provide that, if an individual is enrolled in a qualified health plan after the first day of a month, generally no value should be reported for the individual's enrollment premium or benchmark plan premium for that month. However, if an individual's coverage in a qualified health plan is terminated before the last day of a month, or an individual is enrolled in coverage after the first day of a month and the coverage is effective on the date of the individual's birth, adoption, or placement for adoption or in foster care, or on the effective date of a court order, an Exchange must report the premium for the applicable benchmark plan for a full month of coverage (excluding the premium allocated to benefits in excess of essential health benefits). In addition, the proposed regulations provide that the Exchange must report the enrollment premiums for the month (excluding the premium allocated to benefits in excess of essential health benefits), reduced by any amount that was refunded due to the plan's termination.

c. Use of electronic media

Section 301.6011-2(b) provides that if the use of certain forms, including the Form 1095 series, is required by the applicable regulations or revenue procedures for the purpose of making an information return, the information required by the form must be submitted on magnetic media. Form 1095-A should not have been included in § 301.6011-2 because Form 1095-A is not an information return. Consequently, the proposed regulations replace the general reference in § 301.6011-2(b) to the forms in the 1095 series with specific references to Forms 1095-B and 1095-C, but not Form 1095-A.

Effective/Applicability Date

Except as otherwise provided, these regulations are proposed to apply for taxable years beginning after December 31, 2016. In addition, taxpayers may rely on certain provisions of the proposed regulations for taxable years ending after December 31, 2013, as indicated earlier in this preamble. In addition, rules relating to the benchmark plan described in section 4 of this preamble are proposed to apply for taxable years beginning after December 31, 2018.

Notwithstanding the proposed applicability date, nothing in the proposed regulations is intended to limit any relief for opt-out arrangements provided in Notice 2015-87, Q&A 9, or in section 2.f of the preamble to these proposed regulations (regarding opt-out arrangements provided for in collective bargaining agreements). For purposes of sections 36B and 5000A, although under the proposed regulations amounts made available under an eligible opt-out arrangement are not added to an employee's required contribution, for periods before the final regulations are applicable and, if later, through the end of the most recent plan year beginning before January 1, 2017, an individual who can demonstrate that he or she meets the condition for an opt-out payment under an eligible opt-out arrangement is permitted to treat the opt-out payment as increasing the employee's required contribution.[8]

For purposes of the consequences of these regulations under sections 4980H and 6056 (and in particular Form 1095-C), the regulations regarding opt-out arrangements are proposed to be first applicable for plan years beginning on or after January 1, 2017,[9] and for the period prior to this applicability date employers are not required to increase the amount of an employee's required contribution by the amount of an opt-out payment made available under an opt-out arrangement (other than a payment made available under a non-relief-eligible opt-out arrangement[10]). See also section 2.f of this preamble for transition relief provided under Notice 2015-87 as clarified and expanded for opt-out arrangements contained in collective bargaining agreements in effect before December 16, 2015. See § 601.601(d)(2)(ii)(b).

Special Analyses

Certain IRS regulations, including this one, are exempt from the requirements of Executive Order 12866, as supplemented and reaffirmed by Executive Order 13563. Therefore, a regulatory assessment is not required. It has also been determined that section 553(b) of the Administrative Procedure Act (5 U.S.C. chapter 5) does not apply to these regulations.

It is hereby certified that these regulations will not have a significant economic impact on a substantial number of small entities. This certification is based on the fact that the information collection required under these regulations is imposed under section 36B. Consistent with the statute, the proposed regulations require a person that provides minimum essential coverage to an individual

---

8 For periods prior to the applicability date, an individual who cannot demonstrate that he or she meets the condition for an opt-out payment under an eligible opt-out arrangement is not permitted to treat the opt-out payment as increasing the employee's required contribution.

9 Notice 2015-87, Q&A 9 provides that the Treasury Department and the IRS anticipate that the regulations on opt-out arrangements generally will apply only for periods after the issuance of final regulations. The Treasury Department and the IRS anticipate finalizing these regulations prior to the end of 2016.

10 For a discussion of non-relief-eligible opt-out arrangements see Notice 2015-87, Q&A-9.

to file a return with the IRS reporting certain information and to furnish a statement to the responsible individual who enrolled an individual or family in the coverage. These regulations merely provide the method of filing and furnishing returns and statements under section 36B. Moreover, the proposed regulations attempt to minimize the burden associated with this collection of information by limiting reporting to the information that the IRS requires to verify minimum essential coverage and administer tax credits.

Based on these facts, a Regulatory Flexibility Analysis under the Regulatory Flexibility Act (5 U.S.C. chapter 6) is not required.

Pursuant to section 7805(f) of the Code, this notice of proposed rulemaking has been submitted to the Chief Counsel for Advocacy of the Small Business Administration for comment on its impact on small business.

Comments and Requests for Public Hearing

Before these proposed regulations are adopted as final regulations, consideration will be given to any comments that are submitted timely to the IRS as prescribed in this preamble under the "Addresses" heading. Treasury and the IRS request comments on all aspects of the proposed rules. All comments will be available at *www.regulations.gov* or upon request. A public hearing will be scheduled if requested in writing by any person who timely submits written comments. If a public hearing is scheduled, notice of the date, time, and place for the hearing will be published in the **Federal Register**.

Drafting Information

The principal authors of these proposed regulations are Shareen S. Pflanz and Stephen J. Toomey of the Office of Associate Chief Counsel (Income Tax and Accounting). However, other personnel from the IRS and the Treasury Department participated in the development of the regulations.

[¶49,705] Proposed Amendments of Regulations (REG-101689-16), published in the Federal Register on July 12, 2016.

[Code Sec. 506]

Tax-exempt organizations: Notification requirement: Intent to operate under 501(c)(4).—Reg. §1.506-1 relating to the requirement, added by the Protecting Americans from Tax Hikes Act of 2015, that organizations must notify the IRS of their intent to operate under section 501(c)(4) of the Internal Revenue Code (Code), is proposed.

AGENCY: Internal Revenue Service (IRS), Treasury.

ACTION: Notice of proposed rulemaking by cross-reference to temporary regulations.

SUMMARY: In the Rules and Regulations section of this issue of the **Federal Register**, the IRS is issuing temporary regulations relating to the requirement, added by the Protecting Americans from Tax Hikes Act of 2015, that organizations must notify the IRS of their intent to operate under section 501(c)(4) of the Internal Revenue Code (Code). The text of those temporary regulations also serves as the text of these proposed regulations.

DATES: Comments and requests for a public hearing must be received by October 8, 2016.

ADDRESSES: Send submissions to: CC:PA:LPD:PR (REG-101689-16), room 5205, Internal Revenue Service, PO Box 7604, Ben Franklin Station, Washington, DC 20044. Submissions may be hand-delivered Monday through Friday between the hours of 8 a.m. and 4 p.m. to CC:PA:LPD:PR (REG-101689-16), Courier's Desk, Internal Revenue Service, 1111 Constitution Avenue N.W., Washington, DC, or sent electronically via the Federal eRulemaking Portal at *http://www.regulations.gov* (IRS REG-101689-16).

FOR FURTHER INFORMATION CONTACT: Concerning the proposed regulations, Chelsea Rubin at (202) 317-5800; concerning submission of comments and request for hearing, Regina Johnson at (202) 317-6901 (not toll-free numbers).

SUPPLEMENTARY INFORMATION:

Paperwork Reduction Act

The collection of information contained in this notice of proposed rulemaking will be reviewed and, pending receipt and evaluation of public comments, approved by the Office of Management and Budget under control number 1545-2268 in accordance with the Paperwork Reduction Act of 1995 (44 U.S.C. 3507(d)). Comments on the collection of information should be sent to the Office of Management and Budget, Attn: Desk Officer for the Department of the Treasury, Office of Information and Regulatory Affairs, Washington, DC 20503, with copies to the Internal Revenue Service, Attn: IRS Reports Clearance Officer, SE:W:CAR:MP:T:T:SP, Washington, DC 20224. Comments on the collection of information should be received by September 8, 2016.

The collection of information is in §1.506-1T(a)(2). The likely respondents are organizations described in section 501(c)(4) of the Code (section 501(c)(4) organizations). The collection of information in §1.506-1T(a)(2) flows from section 506(b) of the Code, which requires a section 501(c)(4) organization to submit a notification including the following items of information: (1) the name, address, and taxpayer identification number of the organization; (2) the date on which, and the state under the laws of which, the organization was organized; and (3) a statement of the purpose of the organization. The temporary regulations provide that the notification must be submitted on Form 8976, "Notice of Intent to Operate Under Section 501(c)(4)," or its successor. In addition to the specific information required by statute, the temporary regulations require that an organization provide any additional information that may be specified in published guidance in the Internal Revenue Bulletin or in other guidance, such as forms or instructions, issued with respect to the notification. Form 8976 requires an organization to provide its annual accounting period to ensure that the statutorily-required items of information in the notification are correlated accurately within existing IRS systems. The burden for the collection of information in § 1.506-1T(a)(2)(i) through (iv) associated with the one-time submission of the notification will be reflected in the burden estimate for Form 8976.

An agency may not conduct or sponsor, and a person is not required to respond to, a collection of information unless it displays a valid control number assigned by the Office of Management and Budget.

Books or records relating to a collection of information must be retained as long as their contents may become material in the administration of any internal revenue law. Generally, tax returns and return information are confidential, as required by 26 U.S.C. 6103.

Background and Explanation of Provisions

Temporary regulations in the Rules and Regulations section of this issue of the **Federal Register** contain amendments to the Income Tax Regulations (26 CFR part 1) that provide guidance relating to section 405 of the Protecting Americans from Tax Hikes Act of 2015 (Pub. L. No. 114-113, div. Q), regarding the new requirement that organizations must notify the IRS of their intent to operate under section 501(c)(4) of the Code. The text of those temporary regulations also serves as the text of these proposed regulations and the preamble to the temporary regulations explains the relevant provisions.

Statement of Availability of IRS Documents

For copies of recently issued revenue procedures, revenue rulings, notices, and other guidance published in the Internal Revenue Bulletin, please visit the IRS website at *http://www.irs.gov.*

Special Analyses

Certain IRS regulations, including this one, are exempt from the requirements of Executive Order 12866, as supplemented and reaffirmed by Executive Order 13563. Therefore, a regulatory assessment is not required. It also has been determined that section 553(b) of the Administrative Procedure Act (5 U.S.C. chapter 5) does not apply to these regulations. It is hereby certified that the collection of information in these regulations will not have a significant impact on a substantial number of small entities. The collection of information is in § 1.506-1T(a)(2). The certification is based on the following:

Section 1.506-1T(a)(2) requires the notification to include only a few pieces of basic information: (1) the name, address, and taxpayer identification number of the organization; (2) the date on which, and the state or other jurisdiction under the laws of which, the organization was organized; (3) a statement of the purpose of the organization; and (4) such additional information as may be prescribed by published guidance in the Internal Revenue Bulletin or in other guidance, such as forms or instructions, issued with respect to the notification.

These requirements will have a minimal burden on section 501(c)(4) organizations submitting the notification, including small section 501(c)(4) organizations. The notification requires only basic information regarding the organization and, as such, will require little time to submit. Moreover, the burden on small organizations is further minimized because the information is only required to be submitted once.

For these reasons, a Regulatory Flexibility Analysis under the Regulatory Flexibility Act (5 U.S.C. chapter 6) is not required. Pursuant to section 7805(f) of the Code, these regulations have been submitted to the Chief Counsel for Advocacy of the Small Business Administration for comment on its impact on small business.

Comments and Requests for Public Hearing

Before these proposed regulations are adopted as final regulations, consideration will be given to any comments that are submitted timely to the IRS as prescribed in this preamble under the "Addresses" heading. The Treasury Department and the IRS request comments on all aspects of the proposed rules. All comments will be available at *www.regulations.gov* or upon request.

A public hearing will be scheduled if requested in writing by any person that timely submits written comments. If a public hearing is scheduled, notice of the date, time, and place for the public hearing will be published in the **Federal Register**.

Drafting Information

The principal author of these regulations is Chelsea R. Rubin, Office of Associate Chief Counsel (Tax Exempt and Government Entities). However, other personnel from the Treasury Department and the IRS participated in their development.

[¶49,706] Proposed Amendments of Regulations (REG-134016-15), published in the Federal Register on July 15, 2016.

[Code Sec. 355]

Divisive transactions: Code Sec. 355 distributions: Active business requirement: Device and nondevice factors: Per se device test: Five-year active business asset percentage.—Reg. §§ 1.355-8 and 1.355-9 and amendments of Reg. §§ 1.355-0 and 1.355-2, clarifying the application of the device prohibition and the active business requirement of section 355, are proposed.

AGENCY: Internal Revenue Service (IRS), Treasury.

ACTION: Notice of proposed rulemaking.

SUMMARY: This document contains proposed regulations under section 355 of the Internal Revenue Code (Code). The proposed regulations would clarify the application of the device prohibition and the active business requirement of section 355. The proposed regulations would affect corporations that distribute the stock of controlled corporations, their shareholders, and their security holders.

DATES: Written or electronic comments and requests for a public hearing must be received by October 13, 2016.

ADDRESSES: Send submissions to: CC:PA:LPD:PR (REG-134016-15), Room 5203, Internal Revenue Service, P.O. Box 7604, Ben Franklin Station, Washington, DC 20224. Submissions may be hand-delivered Monday through Friday between the hours of 8 a.m. and 4 p.m. to: CC:PA:LPD:PR (REG-134016-15), Courier's Desk, Internal Revenue Service, 1111 Constitution Avenue, NW, Washington, DC 20224. Submissions may also be sent electronically via the Federal eRulemaking Portal at *http://www.regulations.gov* (IRS REG-134016-15).

FOR FURTHER INFORMATION CONTACT: Concerning the proposed regulations, Stephanie D. Floyd or Russell P. Subin at (202) 317-6848; concerning submissions of comments and/or requests for a public hearing, Regina Johnson at (202) 317-6901 (not toll-free numbers).

SUPPLEMENTARY INFORMATION:

Background

A. *Introduction*

This document contains proposed regulations that would amend 26 CFR part 1 under section 355 of the Code. The proposed regulations would provide additional guidance regarding the device prohibition of section 355(a)(1)(B) and provide a minimum threshold for the assets of one or more active trades or businesses, within the meaning of section 355(a)(1)(C) and (b), of the distributing corporation and each controlled corporation (in each case, within the meaning of section 355(a)(1)(A)).

This Background section of the preamble (1) summarizes the requirements of section 355, (2) discusses the development of current law and IRS practice under section 355 and the regulations thereunder, and (3) explains the reasons for the proposed regulations.

B. *Section 355 Requirements*

Generally, if a corporation distributes property with respect to its stock to a shareholder, section 301(b) provides that the amount of the distribution is equal to the amount of money and the fair market value of other property received. Under section 301(c), this amount is treated as (1) the receipt by the shareholder of a dividend to the extent of the corporation's earnings and profits, (2) the recovery of the shareholder's basis in the stock, and/or (3) gain from the sale or exchange of property. The corporation recognizes gain under section 311(b) to the extent the fair market value of the property distributed exceeds the corporation's adjusted basis in the property. However, section 355 provides that, under certain circumstances, a corporation (Distributing) may distribute stock and securities in a corporation it controls within the meaning of section 368(c) (Controlled) to its shareholders and security holders without causing either Distributing or its shareholders or security holders to recognize income, gain, or loss on the distribution.

Section 355 has numerous requirements for a distribution to be tax-free to Distributing and its shareholders. Some of these requirements are intended to prevent a distribution from being used inappropriately to avoid shareholder-level tax on dividend income. As examples, section 355(a)(1)(B) provides that the transaction must not be used principally as a device for the distribution of the earnings and profits of Distributing or Controlled or both (a device), and section 355(a)(1)(C) and (b) require Distributing and Controlled each to be engaged, immediately after the distribution, in the active conduct of a trade or business (an active business). To qualify for this purpose, an active business must have been actively conducted throughout the five-year period ending on the date of the distribution and must not have been acquired, directly or indirectly, within this period in a transaction in which gain or loss was recognized. Section 355(b)(2)(B), (C), and (D).

Distributions of the stock of Controlled generally take three different forms: (1) a pro rata distribution to Distributing's shareholders of the stock of Controlled (a spin-off), (2) a distribution of the stock of Controlled in redemption of Distributing stock (a split-off), or (3) a liquidating distribution in which Distributing distributes the stock of more than one Controlled, either pro rata or non-pro rata (in either case, a split-up).

C. *Development of Current Law and IRS Practice*

1. *Early legislation*

The earliest predecessor of section 355 was section 202(b) of the Revenue Act of 1918, ch. 18 (40 Stat. 1057, 1060), which permitted a tax-free exchange by a shareholder of stock in a corporation for stock in another corporation in connection with a reorganization. This section did not allow tax-free spin-offs. In section 203(c) of the Revenue Act of 1924, ch. 234 (43 Stat. 253, 256), Congress amended this provision to allow tax-free spin-offs pursuant to plans of reorganization.

Taxpayers tried to use this provision to avoid the dividend provisions of the Code by having Distributing contribute surplus cash or liquid assets to a newly formed Controlled and distribute the Controlled stock to its shareholders. *See, e.g., Gregory v. Helvering*, 293 U.S. 465 (1935). Congress reacted to this abuse by eliminating the spin-off provision in the Revenue Act of 1934, ch. 277 (48 Stat.

680). The legislative history states that the provision had provided a method for corporations "to pay what would otherwise be taxable dividends, without any taxes upon their shareholders" and that "this means of avoidance should be ended." H.R. Rep. No. 73-704, at 14 (1934).

In section 317(a) of the Revenue Act of 1951, ch. 521 (65 Stat. 452, 493), Congress re-authorized spin-offs pursuant to plans of reorganization:

> . . . unless it appears that (A) any corporation which is a party to such reorganization was not intended to continue the active conduct of a trade or business after such reorganization, or (B) the corporation whose stock is distributed was used principally as a device for the distribution of earnings and profits to the shareholders of any corporation a party to the reorganization.

During debate on this legislation, Senator Hubert Humphrey expressed concerns about spin-offs and argued that these restrictions were necessary. *See, e.g.*, 97 Cong. Rec. 11812 (1951) ("Unless strictly safeguarded, [a spin-off provision] can result in a loophole that will enable a corporation to distribute earnings and profits to stockholders without payment of the usual income taxes."); *Id.* ("Clauses (A) and (B) of section 317 provide very important safeguards against the tax avoidance which would be possible if section 317 were adopted without clauses (A) and (B)."). *See also* 96 Cong. Rec. 13686 (1950) ("It was the viewpoint of the committee that [a spin-off] must be strictly a bona fide transaction, not colorable, not for the purpose of evading the tax.").

Until 1954, a spin-off, split-off, or split-up was eligible for tax-free treatment only if Distributing transferred property to Controlled as part of a reorganization. In 1954, Congress adopted section 355 as part of the 1954 Code. As a significant innovation, section 355 allowed spin-offs, split-offs, and split-ups to be tax-free without a reorganization, and this innovation remains in effect.

2. *Case law*

Courts applying section 355 (or a predecessor provision) have generally placed greater emphasis on the substance of the transaction than on compliance with the technical requirements of the statute. Thus, some courts have determined that a transaction does not qualify under section 355 (or a predecessor provision), notwithstanding strict statutory compliance, on the basis that the substance of the transaction was inconsistent with congressional intent. For example, in *Gregory*, the Supreme Court held that compliance with the letter of the spin-off statute was insufficient if the transaction was otherwise indistinguishable from a dividend. The Supreme Court observed that the transaction in *Gregory* was "an operation having no business or corporate purpose-a mere device which put on the form of a corporate reorganization as a disguise for concealing its real character." *Gregory*, 293 U.S. at 469.

Other courts have found that a transaction does qualify under section 355 despite its failure to comply with all of the statutory requirements. For example, in *Commissioner v. Gordon*, 382 F.2d 499 (2d Cir.1967), *rev'd on other grounds*, 391 U.S. 83 (1968), the court addressed section 355(b)(2)(C). Pursuant to that section, a corporation is treated as engaged in the active conduct of a trade or business only if the trade or business was not acquired in a transaction in which gain or loss was recognized in whole or in part within the five-year period ending on the date of the distribution. The court concluded that, despite the fact that gain was recognized when Distributing transferred a trade or business to Controlled, section 355(b)(2)(C) was not violated because new assets were not brought within the combined corporate shells of Distributing and Controlled. The court stated:

> We think that the draftsmen of Section 355 intended these subsections to apply only to the bringing of new assets within the combined corporate shells of the distributing and the controlled corporations. Therefore, it is irrelevant in this case whether gain was recognized on the intercorporate transfer.

Id. at 507.

3. *Device regulations*

a. 1955 Regulations

Regulations under section 355 of the 1954 Code were issued in 1955 (the 1955 regulations). TD 6152 (20 FR 8875). These regulations included § 1.355-2(b)(3), which provided the following:

> In determining whether a transaction was used principally as a device for the distribution of the earnings and profits of the distributing corporation or of the controlled corporation or both, consideration will be given to all of the facts and circumstances of the transaction. In particular, consideration will be given to the nature, kind and amount of the assets of both corporations (and corporations controlled by them) immediately after the transaction. The fact that at the time of the transaction substantially all of the assets of each of the corporations involved are and have been used in the active conduct of trades or businesses which meet the requirements of section 355(b) will be considered evidence that the transaction was not used principally as such a device.

b. 1989 Regulations

Additional regulations under section 355 were issued in 1989 (the 1989 regulations). TD 8238 (54 FR 283). These regulations provide substantially more guidance than the 1955 regulations to determine whether a distribution was a device. Section 1.355-2(d)(1) provides that "a tax-free distribution of the stock of a controlled corporation presents a potential for tax avoidance by facilitating the avoidance of the dividend provisions of the Code through the subsequent sale or exchange of stock of one corporation and the retention of the stock of another corporation. A device can include a transaction that effects a recovery of basis."

This provision clarifies that, although the device prohibition primarily targets the conversion of dividend income to capital gain, a device can still exist if there would be a recovery of stock basis in lieu of receipt of dividend income and even if the shareholder's federal income tax rates on dividend income and capital gain are the same.

The 1989 regulations also expand on the statement in the 1955 regulations that the device analysis takes into account all of the facts and circumstances by specifying three factors that are evidence of device and three factors that are evidence of nondevice. One of the device factors, described in § 1.355-2(d)(2)(iv)(B), expands the statement in the 1955 regulations that consideration will be given to the nature, kind, and amount of the assets of Distributing and Controlled immediately after the transaction (the nature and use of assets device factor). First, this provision provides that "[t]he existence of assets that are not used in a trade or business that satisfies the requirements of section 355(b) is evidence of device. For this purpose, assets that are not used in a trade or business that satisfies the requirements of section 355(b) include, but are not limited to, cash and other liquid assets that are not related to the reasonable needs of a business satisfying such section." This provision continues to provide that "[t]he strength of the evidence of device depends on all the facts and circumstances, including, but not limited to, the ratio for each corporation of the value of assets not used in a trade or business that satisfies the requirements of section 355(b) to the value of its business that satisfies such requirements." Finally, the provision provides that "[a] difference in the ratio described in the preceding sentence for the distributing and controlled corporation is ordinarily not evidence of device if the distribution is not pro rata among the shareholders of the distributing corporation and such difference is attributable to a need to equalize the value of the stock distributed and the value of the stock or securities exchanged by the distributees."

Although this provision describes the factor, it provides little guidance relating to the quality or quantity of the relevant assets and no guidance on how the factor relates to other device factors or nondevice factors.

The nondevice factors in § 1.355-2(d)(3) are the presence of a corporate business purpose, the fact that the stock of Distributing is publicly traded and widely held, and the fact that the distribution is made to certain domestic corporate shareholders.

Section 1.355-2(d)(5) specifies certain distributions that ordinarily are not considered a device, notwithstanding the presence of device factors, because they ordinarily do not present the potential for federal income tax avoidance in converting dividend income to capital gain or using stock basis to reduce shareholder-level tax. These transactions include a distribution that, in the absence of section 355, with respect to each distributee, would be a redemption to which sale-or-exchange treatment applies.

4. *Active business requirement regulations*

Section 1.355-3 provides rules for determining whether Distributing and Controlled satisfy the active business requirement. Proposed regulations issued in 2007 would amend § 1.355-3. REG-123365-03 (72 FR 26012). The Treasury Department and the IRS continue to study the active business requirement issues considered in those proposed regulations.

5. *Administration of the active business requirement*

The fact that Distributing's or Controlled's qualifying active business is small in relation to all the assets of Distributing or Controlled is generally recognized as a device factor. A separate issue is whether a relatively small active business satisfies the active business requirement. In Rev. Rul. 73-44 (1973-1 CB 182), Controlled's active business represented a "substantial portion" but less than half of the value of its total assets. The revenue ruling states:

> There is no requirement in section 355(b) that a specific percentage of the corporation's assets be devoted to the active conduct of a trade or business. In the instant case, therefore, it is not controlling for purposes of the active business requirement that the active business assets of the controlled corporation, Y, represent less than half of the value of the controlled corporation immediately after the distribution.

The IRS has taken the position, in letter rulings and internal memoranda, that an active business can satisfy the active business requirement regardless of its absolute or relative size. However, no published guidance issued by the Treasury Department or the IRS takes this position.

In 1996, the Treasury Department and the IRS issued Rev. Proc. 96-43 (1996-2 CB 330), which provided that (1) the IRS ordinarily would not issue a letter ruling or determination letter on whether a distribution was described in section 355(a)(1) if the gross assets of the active business would have a fair market value that was less than five percent of the total fair market value of the gross assets of the corporation directly conducting the active business, but (2) a ruling might be issued "if it can be established that, based upon all relevant facts and circumstances, the trades or businesses are not de minimis compared with the other assets or activities of the corporation and its subsidiaries." This no-rule provision was eliminated in Rev. Proc. 2003-48 (2003-2 CB 86). Since that time, until the publication of Rev. Proc. 2015-43 (2015-40 IRB 467) and Notice 2015-59 (2015-40 IRB 459), discussed in Part D.1 of this Background section of the preamble, the IRS maintained its position that the relative size of an active business is a device factor rather than a section 355(b) requirement. The IRS issued numerous letter rulings on section 355 distributions involving active businesses that were de minimis in value compared to the other assets of Distributing or Controlled.

The IRS interpreted section 355(b) in this manner in part as a result of the mechanical difficulties of satisfying the active business requirement. These mechanical difficulties are discussed further in Part D.3.c of this Background section of the preamble.

As an example, until section 355(b) was amended by section 202 of the Tax Increase Prevention and Reconciliation Act of 2005, Public Law 109-222 (120 Stat. 345, 348); Division A, section 410 of the Tax Relief and Health Care Act of 2006, Public Law 109-432 (120 Stat. 2922, 2963); and section 4(b) of the Tax Technical Corrections Act of 2007, Public Law 110-172 (121 Stat. 2473, 2476) (the Separate Affiliated Group, or SAG, Amendments), if, immediately after the distribution, a corporation did not directly engage in an active business, it could satisfy the active business requirement only if substantially all of its assets consisted of stock and securities of corporations it controlled that were engaged in an active business (the holding company rule). *See* section 355(b) prior to the SAG Amendments. Because of the limited application of the holding company rule, corporations often had to undergo burdensome restructurings prior to section 355 distributions merely to satisfy the active business requirement. *See, e.g.*, H.R. Rep. No. 109-304, at 54 (2005).

As another example, until 1992, no guidance provided that Distributing or Controlled could rely on activities conducted by a partnership to satisfy the active business requirement, even if Distributing or Controlled held a substantial interest in the partnership and participated in its management. This situation changed after the Treasury Department and the IRS published revenue rulings permitting this reliance. *See* Rev. Rul. 92-17 (1992-1 CB 142) *amplified by* Rev. Rul. 2002-49 (2002-2 CB 288) *and modified by* Rev. Rul. 2007-42 (2007-2 CB 44).

6. *Administration of the device prohibition*

The device prohibition continues to be important even though the federal income tax rates for dividend income and capital gain may be identical for many taxpayers. In Rev. Proc. 2003-48, the Treasury Department and the IRS announced that the IRS would no longer rule on whether a transaction is a device or has a business purpose. As a result, since the publication of Rev. Proc. 2003-48, the IRS has made only limited inquiries as to device and business purpose issues raised in requests for private letter rulings under section 355.

D. *Reasons for Proposed Regulations*

1. *Rev. Proc. 2015-43 and Notice 2015-59*

As explained in Part C of this Background section of the preamble, section 355 and its predecessors have had a long and contentious history. Despite the safeguards in the Code and regulations, and the courts' interpretations in accordance with congressionally-articulated statutory purposes, taxpayers have attempted to use section 355 distributions in ways that the Treasury Department and the IRS have determined to be inconsistent with the purpose of section 355.

On September 14, 2015, the Treasury Department and the IRS issued Rev. Proc. 2015-43 and Notice 2015-59 in response to concerns relating to distributions involving relatively small active businesses, substantial amounts of investment assets, and regulated investment companies (RICs) or real estate investment trusts (REITs). The notice states that the Treasury Department and the IRS are studying issues under sections 337(d) and 355 relating to these transactions and that these transactions may present evidence of device, lack an adequate business purpose or a qualifying active business, or circumvent the purposes of Code provisions intended to implement repeal of the *General Utilities* doctrine, a doctrine under which a corporation generally could distribute appreciated property to its shareholders without recognizing gain (*General Utilities* repeal). The notice invited comments with respect to these issues and one commenter (the commenter) submitted a comment letter.

The proposed regulations in this notice of proposed rulemaking would address the device prohibition (including the business purpose requirement as it pertains to device) and the active business requirement. Congress has addressed certain other issues discussed in Notice 2015-59. *See* section 311 of the Protecting Americans from Tax Hikes Act of 2015, Public Law 114-113 (129 Stat. 3040, 3090), in which Congress added section 355(h), which generally denies section 355 treatment if either Distributing or Controlled is a REIT unless both are REITs immediately after the distribution, and section 856(c)(8), which generally provides that Distributing or Controlled will not be eligible to make a REIT election within the ten-year period after a section 355 distribution. Separate temporary and proposed regulations address transactions that avoid the application of sections 355(h) and 856(c)(8). *See* REG-126452-15 (Certain Transfers of Property to RICs and REITs) (81 FR 36816), cross-referencing TD 9770 (81 FR 36793). The Treasury Department and the IRS continue to study issues relating to *General Utilities* repeal presented by other transactions involving the separation of nonbusiness assets from business assets, and are considering issuing guidance under section 337(d) to address these issues. *See* Part D.4 of this Background section of the preamble.

2. *Comments regarding device*

The commenter believes that new rules are not needed for transactions that raise the purely shareholder-level concerns that are the subject of the device prohibition. According to the commenter, those transactions likely do not qualify under section 355 under current law and are infrequent. Although largely agreeing with this statement, the Treasury Department and the IRS have determined that certain clarifying changes should be made to the device rules. As discussed in Part C.3.b of this Background section of the preamble, the current regulations relating to device are not specific as to the quality or quantity of assets relevant in the nature and use of assets device factor or the appropriate weighing of the device and nondevice factors. The Treasury Department and the IRS have determined that, in some situations, insufficient weight has been given to the nature and use of assets device factor and that device factors have not been balanced correctly against nondevice factors.

For example, if, after a distribution, Distributing or Controlled holds mostly liquid nonbusiness assets, the shareholders of that corporation can sell their stock at a price that reflects the value of the nonbusiness assets, and such a sale is economically similar to a distribution of the liquid nonbusiness assets to the shareholders that would have been treated as a dividend to the extent of earnings and profits of the corporation. *See, e.g., Gregory*. If Distributing's ratio of nonbusiness assets to total assets differs substantially from Controlled's ratio, the distribution could facilitate a separation of the nonbusiness assets from the business assets by means of the sale of the stock in the corporation with a large percentage of nonbusiness assets. No corporate-level gain, and possibly little or no shareholder-level gain, would be recognized.

Taxpayers have taken the position that nondevice factors in the regulations can outweigh the substantial evidence of device presented in such distributions. For example, certain taxpayers have viewed even a weak business purpose, combined with the fact that the stock of Distributing is publicly traded, as offsetting evidence of device presented by distributions effecting a separation of nonbusiness assets from business assets, even if pressure from public shareholders was a significant motivation for the distribution. The Treasury Department and the IRS do not agree that these types of nondevice factors should outweigh the substantial evidence of device presented by a distribution that separates nonbusiness assets from business assets.

Accordingly, the Treasury Department and the IRS have determined that the regulations should provide clearer, more objective guidance regarding the nature and use of assets device factor and the appropriate weighing of device factors and nondevice factors. The Treasury Department and the IRS also have determined that if a high enough proportion of assets of Distributing or Controlled consists of nonbusiness assets, and if the assets of the other corporation include a much lower proportion of nonbusiness assets, the evidence of device is so strong that nondevice factors generally should not be allowed to overcome the evidence of device.

The commenter also noted that the importance of device, traditionally understood as reflecting shareholder-level policies, has diminished in the context of a unified rate regime for long-term capital gains and qualified dividend income for some taxpayers. However, because of continuing differences in the federal income tax treatment of capital gains and dividends, including the potential for basis recovery (*see* § 1.355-2(d)(1)) and the availability of capital gains to absorb capital losses, the device prohibition continues to be important.

3. *Comments regarding active business*

a. Section 355(b) Requires Minimum Size Active Business

The commenter stated that section 355 is meant to apply to genuine separations of businesses, and that section 355(b) should not function as a formality. Nevertheless, the commenter does not believe that the active business requirement needs to be strengthened through the adoption of a requirement of a minimum amount of active business assets.

After studying this issue, the Treasury Department and the IRS have determined that Distributing or Controlled should not satisfy the active business requirement by holding a relatively de minimis active business. As described in the remainder of this Part D.3, the Treasury Department and the IRS have determined that interpreting section 355(b) as having meaning and substance and therefore requiring an active business that is economically significant is consistent with congressional intent, case law, and the reorganization provisions. In addition, given the developments in the tax law described in Part D.3.c of this Background section of the preamble, the Treasury Department and the IRS have determined that allowing a de minimis active business to satisfy the active business requirement is not necessary to reduce the burden of compliance with the active business requirement. Furthermore, requiring a minimum relative size for an active business is not inconsistent with the facts of Rev. Rul. 73-44 or with its conclusion. *See* Part D.3.d of this Background section of the preamble.

b. Consistent with Congressional Intent, Case Law, and the Reorganization Provisions

Allowing section 355(b) to be satisfied with an active business that is economically insignificant in relation to other assets of Distributing or Controlled is not consistent with the congressional purpose for adopting the active business requirement. It is generally understood that Congress intended section 355 to be used to separate businesses, not to separate inactive assets from a business. *See* S. Rep. No. 83-1622, at 50-51 (section 355 "contemplates that a tax-free separation shall involve only the separation of assets attributable to the carrying on of an active business" and does not permit "the tax free separation of an existing corporation into active and inactive entities"); *see also Coady v. Commissioner*, 33 T.C. 771, 777 (1960), *aff'd*, 289 F.2d 490 (6th Cir. 1961) (stating that a function of section 355(b) is "to prevent the tax-free separation of *active* and *inactive* assets into *active* and *inactive* corporate entities") (emphasis in original); § 1.355-1(b) ("[s]ection 355 provides for the separation . . . of one or more existing businesses"). Additionally, when the active business of Distributing or Controlled is economically insignificant in relation to its other assets, it is unlikely that any non-federal tax purpose for separating that business from other businesses is a significant purpose for the distribution. *See* § 1.355-2(b)(1) ("Section 355 applies to a transaction only if it is carried out for one or more corporate business purposes . . . The potential for the avoidance of Federal taxes by the distributing or controlled corporations . . . is relevant in determining the extent to which an existing corporate business purpose motivated the distribution.").

Further, as the Supreme Court held in *Gregory*, transactions are to be taxed in accordance with their substance. The reorganization regulations adopt the same principle. For example, § 1.368-1(b) provides that "[b]oth the terms of the specifications [of the reorganization provisions] and their underlying assumptions and purposes must be satisfied in order to entitle the taxpayer to the benefit of the exception from the general rule." Additionally, § 1.368-1(c) provides that "[a] scheme, which involves an abrupt departure from normal reorganization procedure in connection with a transaction on which the imposition of tax is imminent, such as a mere device that puts on the form of a corporate reorganization as a disguise for concealing its real character, and the object and accomplishment of which is the consummation of a preconceived plan having no business or corporate purpose, is not a plan of reorganization."

Accordingly, when a corporation that owns only nonbusiness assets and a relatively de minimis active business is separated from a corporation with another active business, the substance of the transaction is not a separation of businesses as contemplated by section 355.

c. Developments in the Tax Law Reduce the Burden of Complying with Section 355

In the past, the active business requirement was more difficult to satisfy than it is today, in part because of the limited application of the holding company rule, discussed in Part C.5 of this Background section of the preamble. However, several developments in the tax law have occurred that make the active business requirement easier to satisfy and negate the historical need to reduce the administrative burden of complying with section 355(b).

In the SAG Amendments, Congress amended section 355(b) to adopt the separate affiliated group rules of section 355(b)(3). Section 355(b)(3)(A) provides that, for purposes of determining whether a corporation meets the requirements of section 355(b)(2)(A), all members of the corporation's separate affiliated group (SAG) are treated as one corporation. Section 355(b)(3)(B) provides that a corporation's SAG is the affiliated group which would be determined under section 1504(a) if the corporation were the common parent and section 1504(b) did not apply.

Additionally, as discussed in Part C.5 of this Background section of the preamble, section 355(b) now can be satisfied through the ownership of certain interests in a partnership that is engaged in an active business. *See* Rev. Rul. 2007-42 and Rev. Rul. 92-17. Similarly, § 301.7701-3 now allows an eligible entity to elect to be disregarded as an entity separate from its owner and permits a corporation to satisfy the active business requirement through a tax-free acquisition without having to assume liabilities relating to an active business. Finally, the expansion rules of § 1.355-3(b)(3)(ii) have been developed so that it is easier to acquire the assets of an active business in a taxable transaction while complying with section 355(b). *See, e.g.*, Rev. Rul. 2003-18 (2003-1 CB 467) and Rev. Rul. 2003-38 (2003-1 CB 811) (both describing facts and circumstances to be considered in determining whether one trade or business is in the same line of business as another).

d. Rev. Rul. 73-44

Rev. Rul. 73-44 is sometimes cited in support of the proposition that a de minimis active business satisfies the section 355(b) requirement. However, Rev. Rul. 73-44 states only that there is no requirement in section 355(b) that a specific percentage of a corporation's assets be devoted to the active conduct of a trade or business, not that any size active business can satisfy section 355(b). In fact, the size of the active business in that ruling represented a substantial portion of Controlled's assets, although less than half of Controlled's value. Accordingly, Rev. Rul. 73-44 does not validate a section 355 distribution involving a de minimis active business, and the proposed regulations in this notice of proposed rulemaking addressing the minimum relative size of active businesses would not change the conclusion set forth in that revenue ruling. Nevertheless, the Treasury Department and the IRS intend to modify Rev. Rul. 73-44 with regard to the statement in the revenue ruling that there is no requirement that a specific percentage of a corporation's assets be devoted to the active conduct of a trade or business.

4. *General Utilities repeal*

The Treasury Department and the IRS have observed, as noted in Notice 2015-59, that taxpayers may attempt to use section 355 distributions in ways that are inconsistent with the purpose of *General Utilities* repeal. Specifically, the Treasury Department and the IRS are concerned that certain taxpayers may be interpreting the current regulations under sections 337(d) and 355 in a manner allowing tax-free distributions motivated in whole or substantial part by a purpose of avoiding corporate-level taxation of built-in gain in investment or nonbusiness assets. *See* § 1.355-1(b) ("Section 355 provides for the separation . . . of one or more existing businesses formerly operated, directly or indirectly, by a single corporation . . . ."). The Treasury Department and the IRS continue to study whether permitting tax-free separations of large amounts of nonbusiness assets from business assets, especially when the gain in the nonbusiness assets is expected to be eliminated, is consistent with *General Utilities* repeal in all circumstances. Comments are welcome on potential additional guidance under section 337(d) addressing such transactions.

Explanation of Provisions

A. *Modification of Device Regulations*

The proposed regulations would modify § 1.355-2(d), which addresses transactions that are or are not a device. The proposed regulations would modify the nature and use of assets device factor in § 1.355-2(d)(2)(iv), modify the corporate business purpose nondevice factor in § 1.355-2(d)(3)(ii), and add a per se device test.

1. *Nature and use of assets*

The Treasury Department and the IRS have determined that device potential generally exists either if Distributing or Controlled owns a large percentage of assets not used in business operations compared to total assets or if Distributing's and Controlled's percentages of these assets differs substantially. A proposed change to the nature and use of assets device factor in § 1.355-2(d)(2)(iv) would focus on assets used in a Business (Business Assets) (each as defined in proposed § 1.355-2(d)(2)(iv)(B)) rather than assets used in an active business meeting the requirements of section 355(b) (a Five-Year-Active Business, as defined in proposed § 1.355-9(a)(2)). In general, Business would have the same meaning as a Five-Year-Active Business, but without regard to whether the business has been operated or owned for at least five years prior to the date of the distribution or whether the collection of income requirement in § 1.355-3(b)(2)(ii) is satisfied. Business Assets would be gross assets used in a Business, including reasonable amounts of cash and cash equivalents held for working capital and assets required to be held to provide for exigencies related to a Business or for regulatory purposes with respect to a Business. The Treasury Department and the IRS have determined that the presence of Business Assets generally does not raise any more device concerns than the presence of assets used in a Five-Year-Active Business (Five-Year-Active-Business Assets). Thus, the proposed regulations would modify § 1.355-2(d)(2)(iv)(B) to take into account Business Assets, not just Five-Year-Active-Business Assets.

Rev. Proc. 2015-43 (now incorporated into Rev. Proc. 2016-3 (2016-1 IRB 126)) and Notice 2015-59 focus on investment assets (using a modified section 355(g) definition) of a corporation as assets that may raise device concerns. However, after further study, the Treasury Department and the IRS have determined that investment assets as defined therein may include certain assets that do not raise device concerns, such as cash needed by a corporation for working capital, and may not include other assets that do raise device concerns, such as real estate not related to the taxpayer's Business. The Treasury Department and the IRS have determined that focusing on Nonbusiness Assets, as defined in the proposed regulations, is a better method of evaluating device or nondevice as compared to using investment assets as described in Rev. Proc. 2016-3 and Notice 2015-59. Thus, the proposed regulations would focus on Nonbusiness Assets rather than investment assets.

The proposed regulations would provide thresholds for determining whether the ownership of Nonbusiness Assets (gross assets that are not Business Assets) and/or differences in the Nonbusiness Asset Percentages (the percentage of a corporation's Total Assets (its Business Assets and Nonbusiness Assets) that are Nonbusiness Assets) for Distributing and Controlled are evidence of device. If neither Distributing nor Controlled has Nonbusiness Assets that comprise 20 percent or more of its Total Assets, the ownership of Nonbusiness Assets ordinarily would not be evidence of device. Additionally, a difference in the Nonbusiness Asset Percentages for Distributing and Controlled ordinarily would not be evidence of device if such difference is less than 10 percentage points or, in the case of a non-pro rata distribution, if the difference is attributable to a need to equalize the value of the Controlled stock and securities distributed and the consideration exchanged therefor by the distributees. Accordingly, the Treasury Department and the IRS propose to treat such circumstances as ordinarily not constituting evidence of device.

2. *Corporate business purpose*

The Treasury Department and the IRS also propose to revise the nondevice factor in § 1.355-2(d)(3)(ii), which relates to corporate business purpose for a transaction as evidence of nondevice. Under the proposed revision, a corporate business purpose that relates to a separation of Nonbusiness Assets from one or more Businesses or from Business Assets would not be evidence of nondevice, unless the business purpose involves an exigency that requires an investment or other use of the Nonbusiness Assets in a Business. The Treasury Department and the IRS have determined that, absent such an exigency, such separations are not consistent with the intent of Congress to prevent section 355 from applying to a distribution that is used principally as a device.

3. *Per se device test*

The Treasury Department and the IRS also propose to add a per se device test to the device determination in proposed § 1.355-2(d)(5). Under proposed § 1.355-2(d)(5), if designated percentages of Distributing's and/or Controlled's Total Assets are Nonbusiness Assets, the transaction would be considered a device, notwithstanding the presence of any other nondevice factors, for example, a corporate business purpose or stock being publicly traded and widely held. By their nature, these transactions present such clear evidence of device that the Treasury Department and the IRS have determined that the nondevice factors can never overcome the device potential. The only exceptions to this per se device rule would apply if the distribution is also described in § 1.355-2(d)(3)(iv) (distributions in which the corporate distributee would be entitled to a dividends received deduction under section 243(a) or 245(b)) or in redesignated § 1.355-2(d)(6) (§ 1.355-2(d)(5) of the current regulations, relating to transactions ordinarily not considered as a device).

The per se device test would have two prongs, both of which must be met for the distribution to be treated as a per se device.

The first prong would be if Distributing or Controlled has a Nonbusiness Asset Percentage of 66 2/3 percent or more. If 66 2/3 percent or more of the Total Assets of either corporation consist of Nonbusiness Assets, a strong device potential exists.

The second prong of the test would compare the Nonbusiness Asset Percentage of Distributing with that of Controlled. The comparison would be similar to the comparison, in § 1.355-2(d)(2)(iv)(B) of the current regulations, between Distributing's ratio of assets not used in a Five-Year-Active Business to assets used in a Five-Year-Active Business and Controlled's ratio of such assets. However, the Treasury Department and the IRS recognize that valuation of assets may be difficult and that determining whether certain assets are Business Assets also may be difficult. Accordingly, rather than requiring Distributing and Controlled to make exact determinations of their Nonbusiness Asset Percentages, which would then be compared to the other corporation's Nonbusiness Asset Percentage, the second prong of the per se device test would provide for three bands in making this comparison. These bands generally would provide for the comparison of the Nonbusiness Asset Percentages of Distributing and Controlled but require less precision in asset valuation.

In the first band, if one corporation's Nonbusiness Asset Percentage is 66 2/3 percent or more, but less than 80 percent, the distribution would fall within the band if the other corporation's Nonbusiness Asset Percentage is less than 30 percent. In the second band, if one corporation's Nonbusiness Asset Percentage is 80 percent or more, but less than 90 percent, the distribution would fall within the band if the other corporation's Nonbusiness Asset Percentage is less than 40 percent. In the third band, if one corporation's Nonbusiness Asset Percentage is 90 percent or more, the distribution would fall within the band if the other corporation's Nonbusiness Asset Percentage is less than 50 percent. All of these bands represent cases in which the Nonbusiness Asset Percentages of Distributing and Controlled are significantly different.

If both prongs of the per se device test are met, that is, if the Nonbusiness Asset Percentage for either Distributing or Controlled is 66 2/3 percent or more and the Nonbusiness Asset Percentages of Distributing and Controlled fall within one of the three bands, the distribution would be a per se device. Otherwise, the general facts-and-circumstances test of § 1.355-2(d), as modified by these proposed regulations, would apply to determine if the transaction was a device.

4. *Certain operating rules*

In making the determination of which assets of a corporation are Business Assets and which are Nonbusiness Assets, if Distributing or Controlled owns a partnership interest or stock in another corporation, the proposed regulations would provide four operating rules.

First, all members of a SAG with respect to which Controlled is the common parent (CSAG) and all members of a SAG with respect to which Distributing is the common parent excluding Controlled and its SAG (DSAG) would be treated as a single corporation. Thus, any stock owned by one member of a SAG in another member of the same SAG and any intercompany obligations between the same SAG members would be disregarded.

Second, a partnership interest would generally be considered a Nonbusiness Asset. However, if, by reason of a corporation's ownership interest or its ownership interest and participation in management of the partnership, the corporation is considered to be engaged in the Business conducted by such partnership (based on the criteria that would be used to determine whether such corporation is considered to be engaged in the Five-Year-Active Business of such partnership under Rev. Ruls. 92-17, 2002-49, and 2007-42), the fair market value of the partnership interest would be allocated between Business Assets and Nonbusiness Assets in the same proportion as the proportion of the fair market values of the Business Assets and the Nonbusiness Assets of the partnership.

Third, a rule similar to the partnership interest rule would apply for corporate stock owned by Distributing or Controlled. That is, stock in a corporation, other than a member of the DSAG or the CSAG, would generally be a Nonbusiness Asset. However, there would be an exception for stock in a Member of a 50-Percent-Owned Group. For this purpose, a 50-Percent-Owned Group would have the same meaning as SAG, except substituting "50-percent" for "80-percent," and a Member of a 50-Percent-Owned Group would be a corporation that would be a member of a DSAG or CSAG, with such substitution. If a Member of a 50-Percent-Owned Group with respect to Distributing or Controlled owns stock in another Member of such 50-Percent-Owned Group (other than a member of the DSAG or the CSAG, respectively), the fair market value of such stock would be allocated between Business Assets and Nonbusiness Assets in the same proportion as the proportion of the fair market values of the Business Assets and the Nonbusiness Assets of the issuing corporation.

Fourth, the proposed regulations would provide for adjustments to prevent distortion if Distributing or Controlled owes money to or is owed money by a partnership or Member of a 50-Percent-Owned Group.

The partnership rules and the 50-Percent-Owned Group rules are designed to recognize that ownership of a partnership interest or stock in a Member of a 50-Percent-Owned Group may reflect an investment in Business Assets, Nonbusiness Assets, or both, while minimizing the significance of changes in the form of ownership of Business Assets and Nonbusiness Assets.

5. *Multiple Controlleds*

If a transaction involves distributions by Distributing of the stock of more than one Controlled, proposed § § 1.355-2(d)(2)(iv) and 1.355-2(d)(5) would apply to all such Controlleds. To the extent any rule would require a comparison between characteristics of Distributing and Controlled, there would have to be a comparison between Distributing and each Controlled and between each Controlled and each other Controlled. If any comparison under proposed § 1.355-2(d)(2)(iv) or § 1.355-2(d)(5) would result in a determination that a distribution is a device, then all distributions involved in the transaction would be considered a device.

B. *Minimum Size for Active Business*

Section 355(b) does not literally provide a minimum absolute or relative size requirement for an active business to qualify under section 355(b). Nevertheless, as discussed in Part D.3 of the Background section of the preamble, the Treasury Department and the IRS have determined that Congress intended that section 355(b) would require that distributions have substance and that a distribution involving only a relatively de minimis active business should not qualify under section 355 because such a distribution is not a separation of businesses as contemplated by section 355.

To ensure that congressional intent is satisfied and to reduce uncertainty, the Treasury Department and the IRS propose to add new § 1.355-9. This section would provide that, for the requirements of section 355(a)(1)(C) and (b) to be satisfied with respect to a distribution, the Five-Year-Active-Business Asset Percentage (the percentage determined by dividing the fair market value of a corporation's Five-Year-Active-Business Assets by the fair market value of its Total Assets) of each of Controlled (or the CSAG) and Distributing (or the DSAG excluding Controlled and other CSAG members) must be at least five percent. Similar to the proposed definition of Business Assets, Five-Year-Active-Business Assets would include reasonable amounts of cash and cash equivalents held for working capital and assets required to be held to provide for exigencies related to a Five-Year-Active Business or for regulatory purposes with respect to a Five-Year-Active Business.

In making the determination of the percentage of a corporation's assets that are Five-Year-Active-Business Assets, if a corporation is considered to be engaged in a Five-Year-Active Business of a partnership, the fair market value of the partnership interest would be allocated between Five-Year-Active-Business Assets and Non-Five-Year-Active-Business Assets (assets other than Five-Year-Active-Business Assets) in the same proportion as the proportion of the fair market values of Five-Year-Active-Business Assets and Non-Five-Year-Active-Business Assets of the partnership.

Except in the case of a member of its SAG, neither Distributing nor Controlled would be considered to be engaged in the Five-Year-Active Business of a corporation in which it owns stock. Accordingly, such stock in a corporation would be considered a Non-Five-Year-Active-Business Asset. Although the proposed regulations relating to the device prohibition would provide an allocation rule for assets held by a Member of a 50-Percent-Owned Group, discussed in Part A.4 of this Explanation of Provisions section of the preamble, the Treasury Department and the IRS believe the SAG Amendments, discussed in Parts C.5 and D.3.c of the Background section of the preamble, limit the ability to take into account assets held by subsidiaries for purposes of the active business requirement. Accordingly, proposed § 1.355-9 would not provide a similar allocation rule for stock owned by Distributing or Controlled.

The commenter stated that the regulations should not provide a minimum size requirement for an active business in any distribution and that such a requirement could be especially problematic in intra-group distributions in preparation for a distribution outside of a group. Internal distributions often are necessary to align the proper assets within Distributing and Controlled prior to a distribution of the stock of Controlled outside the group. If a minimum size requirement is imposed on each of these internal distributions, taxpayers may have to undertake movements of active businesses within groups to meet the minimum size requirement for each internal distribution.

In enacting the SAG Amendments, Congress did not provide an exception to the requirements of section 355(b) for internal distributions that are preparatory to external distributions, although Congress permitted Distributing and Controlled to rely on active businesses held by members of their respective SAGs, even if such assets were distributed or sold within the SAG in a taxable transaction. Under the commenter's rationale, the regulations should not only permit an internal distribution with a de minimis active business, but could also permit tax-free treatment for taxable distributions or sales of assets within the SAG if such assets need to be moved in preparation of the external distribution. The Treasury Department and the IRS have determined that each distribution must meet all the requirements of section 355, including the requirement that Distributing and each Controlled conduct an active business immediately after the distribution. Accordingly, the proposed regulations would provide a five-percent minimum Five-Year-Active-Business Asset Percentage requirement for all distributions.

C. *Timing of Asset Identification, Characterization, and Valuation*

For purposes of determining whether a transaction would be considered a device and whether one or more Five-Year-Active Businesses would meet the five-percent minimum Five-Year-Active-Business Asset Percentage requirement of proposed § 1.355-9, the assets held by Distributing and by Controlled must be identified, and their character and fair market value must be determined. The assets under consideration would be the assets held by Distributing and by Controlled immediately after the distribution. Thus, for example, the stock of Controlled that is distributed would not be an asset of Distributing for this purpose. The character of the assets held by Distributing and by Controlled, as Business Assets or Nonbusiness Assets or as Five-Year-Active-Business Assets or Non-Five-Year-Active-Business Assets, also would be the character as determined immediately after the distribution.

The proposed regulations would provide, however, that the fair market value of assets would be determined, at the election of the parties on a consistent basis, either (a) immediately before the distribution, (b) on any date within the 60-day period before the distribution, (c) on the date of an agreement with respect to the distribution that was binding on Distributing on such date and at all times thereafter, or (d) on the date of a public announcement or filing with the Securities and

Exchange Commission with respect to the distribution. The parties would be required to make consistent determinations between themselves, and use the same date, for purposes of applying the device rules of proposed § 1.355-2(d) and the five-percent minimum Five-Year-Active-Business Asset Percentage requirement of proposed § 1.355-9. If the parties do not meet these consistency requirements, the valuation would be determined as of immediately before the distribution unless the Commissioner determines that the use of such date is inconsistent with the purposes of section 355 and the regulations thereunder.

D. *Anti-abuse Rules*

The proposed regulations would also provide anti-abuse rules. Under the anti-abuse rules, a transaction or series of transactions (such as a change in the form of ownership of an asset; an issuance, assumption or repayment of indebtedness; or an issuance or redemption of stock) would not be given effect if undertaken with a principal purpose of affecting the Nonbusiness Asset Percentage of any corporation in order to avoid a determination that a distribution was a device or affecting the Five-Year-Active-Business Asset Percentage of any corporation in order to avoid a determination that a distribution does not meet the requirements of § 1.355-9. The transactions covered by the anti-abuse rules generally would not include an acquisition or disposition of assets, other than an acquisition from or disposition to a person the ownership of whose stock would, under section 318(a) (other than paragraph (4) thereof), be attributed to Distributing or Controlled, or a transfer of assets between Distributing and Controlled. However, such transactions would not be given effect if they are transitory, for example, if Distributing contributes cash to Controlled and retains some of the stock of Controlled or Controlled debt instruments, and there is a plan or intention for Controlled to return the cash to Distributing in redemption of the stock or repayment of the debt.

Statement of Availability of IRS Documents

IRS revenue procedures, revenue rulings, notices, and other guidance cited in this document are published in the Internal Revenue Bulletin (or Cumulative Bulletin) and are available from the Superintendent of Documents, U.S. Government Printing Office, Washington, D.C. 20402, or by visiting the IRS website at http://www.irs.gov.

Effect on Other Documents

Section 3 of Notice 2015-59 is obsolete as of July 15, 2016. The IRS will modify Rev. Rul. 73-44, as of the date the Treasury decision adopting these regulations as final regulations is published in the **Federal Register**, as necessary to conform to § 1.355-9 of these proposed regulations. The IRS solicits comments as to whether other publications should be modified, clarified, or obsoleted.

Special Analyses

Certain IRS regulations, including this one, are exempt from the requirements of Executive Order 12866, as supplemented and reaffirmed by Executive Order 13563. Therefore, a regulatory impact assessment is not required. It has also been determined that section 553(b) of the Administrative Procedure Act (5 U.S.C. chapter 5) does not apply to these proposed regulations. Pursuant to the Regulatory Flexibility Act (5 U.S.C. chapter 6), it is hereby certified that this regulation will not have a significant economic impact on a substantial number of small entities. This certification is based on the fact that these regulations primarily affect larger corporations operating more than one business and with a substantial number of shareholders. Thus, these regulations are not expected to affect a substantial number of small entities. Accordingly, a regulatory flexibility analysis is not required. Pursuant to section 7805(f) of the Code, these regulations will be submitted to the Chief Counsel for Advocacy of the Small Business Administration for comment on their impact on small business.

Comments and Requests for Public Hearing

Before these proposed regulations are adopted as final regulations, consideration will be given to any written or electronic comments that are submitted timely to the IRS as prescribed in this preamble under the **ADDRESSES** heading. The Treasury Department and the IRS request comments on all aspects of the proposed regulations, including—

1. Whether there should be any exceptions to the application of proposed § 1.355-9.

2. Whether additional exceptions should be incorporated into the per se device rule in proposed § 1.355-2(d)(5).

3. The scope of the safe harbors relating to presence of Nonbusiness Assets as evidence of device under proposed § 1.355-2(d)(2)(iv)(C)(*1*) and (*2*) and whether additional safe harbors should be added to proposed § 1.355-2(d).

4. Whether the definition of Business Assets in proposed § 1.355-2(d)(2)(iv)(B)(*2*) should be revised, for example, to include additional categories of assets or to include cash or cash equivalents expected to be used for other categories of expenditures.

5. Whether the operating rules applicable to proposed § 1.355-2(d)(2)(iv)(D)(*6*) through (*8*) concerning the allocation of the value of a partnership interest between Business Assets and Nonbusiness Assets to its partners, the allocation of the value of the stock of a Member of a 50-Percent-Owned Group between Business Assets and Nonbusiness Assets to its shareholders, and certain borrowings should be modified, including whether the partnership rule should allocate an allocable share of the partnership's gross assets to its partners, whether different allocation rules should be used for partnership interests with different characteristics(for example, limited liability vs. non-limited liabil-

ity), and whether the rules relating to borrowing between a partnership and a partner or between a Member of a 50-Percent-Owned Group and a shareholder should be made more specific.

6. Whether the anti-abuse rules in the proposed regulations pertaining to device and the five-percent minimum Five-Year-Active-Business Assets requirement should be revised, for example, to include or exclude additional transactions or to include a reference to acquisitions of assets by Distributing or Controlled on behalf of shareholders.

7. Whether the absence of any device factor, for example, a small difference in Nonbusiness Asset Percentages for Distributing and Controlled, should be considered a nondevice factor.

All comments will be available at www.regulations.gov or upon request.

A public hearing will be scheduled if requested in writing by any person that timely submits written or electronic comments. If a public hearing is scheduled, notice of the date, time, and place for the public hearing will be published in the **Federal Register**.

Drafting Information

The principal authors of these proposed regulations are Stephanie D. Floyd and Russell P. Subin of the Office of Associate Chief Counsel (Corporate). Other personnel from the Treasury Department and the IRS participated in their development.

[¶49,707] Proposed Amendments of Regulations and Withdrawal of Notice of Proposed Regulations (REG-102516-15), published in the Federal Register on July 22, 2016.

[Code Sec. 50]

Investment tax credit: Lessor election to treat lessee as acquiring property: Income inclusion recapture.—Reg. §1.50-1, relating to the income inclusion rules under section 50(d)(5) of the Internal Revenue Code (Code) that are applicable to a lessee of investment credit property when a lessor of such property elects to treat the lessee as having acquired the property, is proposed. Reg. §1.196-1 and amendments of Reg. §§1.46-3, 1.47-1, 1.48-4, 1.48-9, 1.167(a)-11, 1.312-15 and 1.705-1 proposed on December 20, 1985, and September 21, 1987, are withdrawn.

AGENCY: Internal Revenue Service (IRS), Treasury.

ACTION: Withdrawal of notice of proposed rulemaking; and notice of proposed rulemaking by cross-reference to temporary regulations.

SUMMARY: This document withdraws the notice of proposed rulemaking published in the **Federal Register** on December 20, 1985, and the notice of proposed rulemaking published in the **Federal Register** on September 21, 1987. In the Rules and Regulations section of this issue of the **Federal Register**, the Treasury Department and the IRS are issuing temporary regulations relating to the income inclusion rules under section 50(d)(5) of the Internal Revenue Code (Code) that are applicable to a lessee of investment credit property when a lessor of such property elects to treat the lessee as having acquired the property. The text of those regulations also serves as the text of these proposed regulations. DATES: Written or electronic comments and requests for a public hearing must be received by October 20, 2016.

ADDRESSES: Send submissions to: CC:PA:LPD:PR (REG-102516-15), room 5203, Internal Revenue Service, P.O. Box 7604, Ben Franklin Station, Washington, DC 20044. Submissions may be hand-delivered Monday through Friday between the hours of 8 a.m. and 4 p.m. to: CC:PA:LPD:PR (REG-102516-15), Courier's Desk, Internal Revenue Service, 1111 Constitution Avenue, NW., Washington, DC, or sent electronically via the Federal eRulemaking Portal at www.regulations.gov (IRS REG-102516-15).

FOR FURTHER INFORMATION CONTACT: Concerning the regulations, Jennifer A. Records at (202) 317-6853; concerning submissions of comments and requests for a public hearing, Regina Johnson of the Publications and Regulations Branch at (202) 317-6901 (not toll-free numbers).

SUPPLEMENTARY INFORMATION:

Background and Explanation of Provisions

On December 20, 1985, the Treasury Department and the IRS published in the **Federal Register** (50 FR 51874-01) a notice of proposed rulemaking (LR-92-73) under sections 46, 47, 48, and 167 providing proposed rules related to the determination of the amount of taxpayer's qualified investment and recapture of the investment credit with respect to mass assets. On September 21, 1987, the Treasury Department and the IRS published in the **Federal Register** (52 FR 35438-01) a notice of proposed rulemaking (LR-183-82) under sections 48, 196, 312, and 705 providing proposed rules related to the adjustment in the basis of property with respect to which a taxpayer claimed the investment credit. On April 27, 1993, the Treasury Department and the IRS withdrew (58 FR 25587-01) the proposed amendments to §1.48-7 of the Income Tax Regulations that were published as part of the notice of proposed rulemaking (LR-183-82) published in the **Federal Register** (52 FR 35438-01) on September 21, 1987. Because of numerous statutory changes since the publication of those proposed regulations, the remainder of the proposed regulations (50 FR 51874-01 and 52 FR 35438-01) are withdrawn.

Temporary regulations in the Rules and Regulations section of this issue of the **Federal Register** amend the Income Tax Regulations (26 CFR part 1) relating to section 50(d)(5). The temporary regulations provide rules regarding the income inclusion required under section 50(d)(5) of the Code by a lessee of investment credit property when a lessor of such property elects to treat the lessee as having acquired the property. The temporary regulations also provide rules to coordinate the section 50(a) recapture rules with the section 50(d)(5) income inclusion rules and rules regarding income inclusion upon a disposition or lease termination outside of the recapture period. The text of those regulations also serves as the text of these proposed regulations. The preamble to the temporary regulations explains the amendments.

Special Analyses

Certain IRS regulations, including this one, are exempt from the requirements of Executive Order 12866, as supplemented and reaffirmed by Executive Order 13563. Therefore, a regulatory impact assessment is not required. It also has been determined that section 553(b) of the Administrative Procedure Act (5 U.S.C. chapter 5) does not apply to these regulations, and, because these regulations do not impose a collection of information on small entities, the Regulatory Flexibility Act (5 U.S.C. chapter 6) does not apply. Therefore, a regulatory flexibility analysis is not required. Pursuant to section 7805(f) of the Code, these proposed regulations have been submitted to the Chief Counsel for Advocacy of the Small Business Administration for comment on their impact on small business.

Comments and Requests for a Public Hearing

Before these proposed regulations are adopted as final regulations, consideration will be given to any written (a signed original and eight (8) copies) or electronic comments that are submitted timely to the IRS. The Treasury Department and the IRS request comments on all aspects of these proposed regulations. Specifically, the Treasury Department and the IRS request comments regarding whether guidance is needed to address the applicability of the income inclusion rules under section 50(d)(5) to trusts, estates, and/or electing large partnerships. All comments will be available for public inspection and copying. A public hearing will be scheduled if requested in writing by any person that timely submits written comments. If a public hearing is scheduled, notice of the date, time, and place for the public hearing will be published in the **Federal Register**.

Drafting Information

The principal author of these regulations is Jennifer A. Records, Office of the Associate Chief Counsel (Passthroughs and Special Industries), IRS. However, other personnel from the Treasury Department and the IRS participated in their development.

[¶49,708] Proposed Amendments of Regulations (REG-103058-16), published in the Federal Register on August 2, 2016.

[Code Secs. 6055 and 6724]

Affordable Care Act: Information Reporting: Health insurance issuers.—Amendments of Reg. §1.6055-1 and Reg. §301.6724-1, relating to information reporting of minimum essential coverage under section 6055 of the Internal Revenue Code, are proposed.

AGENCY: Internal Revenue Service (IRS), Treasury.

ACTION: Notice of proposed rulemaking.

SUMMARY: This document contains proposed regulations relating to information reporting of minimum essential coverage under section 6055 of the Internal Revenue Code (Code). Health insurance issuers, certain employers, and others that provide minimum essential coverage to individuals must report to the IRS information about the type and period of coverage and furnish related statements to covered individuals. These proposed regulations affect health insurance issuers, employers, governments, and other persons that provide minimum essential coverage to individuals.

DATES: Written or electronic comments and requests for a public hearing must be received by October 1, 2016.

ADDRESSES: Send submissions to: CC:PA:LPD:PR (REG-103058-16), Room 5203, Internal Revenue Service, PO Box 7604, Ben Franklin Station, Washington, DC 20044. Submissions may be hand-delivered Monday through Friday between the hours of 8 a.m. and 4 p.m. to CC:PA:LPD:PR (REG-103058-16), Courier's Desk, Internal Revenue Service, 1111 Constitution Avenue, NW, Washington, DC 20224, or sent electronically via the Federal eRulemaking Portal at *http://www.regulations.gov* (IRS REG-103058-16).

FOR FURTHER INFORMATION CONTACT: Concerning the proposed regulations under section 6055, John B. Lovelace, (202) 317-7006; concerning the proposed regulations under section 6724, Hollie Marx, (202) 317-6844; concerning the submission of comments, Regina Johnson, (202) 317-6901 (not toll-free calls). SUPPLEMENTARY INFORMATION:

Paperwork Reduction Act

The collection of information contained in this notice of proposed rulemaking has been submitted to the Office of Management and Budget in accordance with the Paperwork Reduction Act of 1995 (44 U.S.C. 3507(d)). Comments on the collection of information should be sent to the **Office of Management and Budget**, Attn: Desk Officer for the Department of the Treasury, Office of Information and Regulatory Affairs, Washington, DC 20503, with copies to the **Internal Revenue Service**, Attn: IRS Reports Clearance Officer, SE:W:CAR:MP:T:T:SP, Washington, DC 20224. Comments on the collection of information should be received by October 1, 2016. Comments are specifically requested concerning:

Whether the proposed collection of information is necessary for the proper performance of the functions of the IRS, including whether the information will have practical utility;

How the quality, utility, and clarity of the information to be collected may be enhanced;

How the burden of complying with the proposed collection of information may be minimized, including through the application of automated collection techniques or other forms of information technology; and

Estimates of capital or start-up costs and costs of operation, maintenance, and purchase of services to provide information.

The collection of information in these proposed regulations is in § 1.6055-1. The collection of information will be used to determine whether an individual has minimum essential coverage under section 1501(b) of the Patient Protection and Affordable Care Act (26 U.S.C. 5000A(f)). The collection of information is required to comply with the provisions of section 6055. The likely respondents are health insurers, self-insured employers or other sponsors of self-insured health plans, and governments that provide minimum essential coverage.

The burden for the collection of information contained in these proposed regulations will be reflected in the burden on Form 1095-B, Health Coverage, or another form that the IRS designates, which will request the information in the proposed regulation.

An agency may not conduct or sponsor, and a person is not required to respond to, a collection of information unless it displays a valid control number assigned by the Office of Management and Budget.

Background

Under section 5000A, individuals must for each month have minimum essential coverage, qualify for a health coverage exemption, or make an individual shared responsibility payment with their income tax returns. Section 6055 provides that all persons who provide minimum essential coverage to an individual must report certain information to the IRS that identifies covered individuals and the period of coverage, and must furnish a statement to the covered individuals containing the same information. The information reported under section 6055 allows individuals to establish, and the IRS to verify, that the individuals were covered by minimum essential coverage for months during the year.

Information returns under section 6055 generally are filed using Form 1095-B. A separate and distinct health coverage-related reporting requirement under section 6056 requires that certain large employers report information on Form 1095-C, Employer-Provided Health Insurance Offer and Coverage. Self-insured employers required to file Form 1095-C use Part III of that form, rather than Form 1095-B, to report information required under section 6055 for individuals enrolled in the self-insured employer-sponsored coverage. These proposed regulations provide guidance under section 6055 only, which relates to Form 1095-B and Form 1095-C, Part III. These proposed regulations do not affect information reporting under section 6056 on Form 1095-C, Parts I and II.

Under section 5000A(f)(1), various types of health plans and programs are minimum essential coverage, including: (1) specified government-sponsored programs such as Medicare Part A, the Medicaid program under Title XIX of the Social Security Act (42 U.S.C. 1936 and following sections), the Children's Health Insurance Program under Title XXI of the Social Security Act (42 U.S.C. 1397aa and following sections) (CHIP), the TRICARE program under chapter 55 of Title 10, U.S.C., health care programs for veterans and other individuals under chapter 17 or 18 of Title 38 U.S.C., coverage for Peace Corps volunteers under 22 U.S.C. 2504(e), and coverage under the Nonappropriated Fund Health Benefits Program under section 349 of Public Law 103-337, (2) coverage under an eligible employer-sponsored plan, (3) coverage under a plan in the individual market (such as a qualified health plan offered through an Affordable Insurance Exchange (Exchange, also known as a Marketplace)), (4) coverage under a grandfathered health plan, and (5) other coverage recognized as minimum essential coverage by the Secretary of Health and Human Services, in coordination with the Secretary of the Treasury.

Under section 5000A(f)(3) and § 1.5000A-2(g) of the Income Tax Regulations, coverage that consists solely of excepted benefits described in section 2791(c)(1), (c)(2), (c)(3), or (c)(4) of the Public Health Service Act (42 U.S.C. 300gg-91(c)), and the regulations under that section, is not minimum essential coverage. Section 1.5000A-2(b)(2) lists government-sponsored programs that provide limited benefits and which are not minimum essential coverage.

Under section 5000A(f)(4), an individual who is a bona fide resident of a United States possession for a month is treated as having minimum essential coverage for that month.

Notice 2015-68, 2015-41 I.R.B. 547, provides guidance on various issues under section 6055. In Notice 2015-68, the Treasury Department and the IRS stated that they intend to propose regulations under section 6055 addressing certain of these issues and requested comments. Comments were requested about the application of the reasonable cause rules under section 6724 to section 6055 reporting, in particular as applied to taxpayer identification number (TIN) solicitation and reporting.

Persons Required To Report

Under § 1.6055-1(c)(1)(iii), the executive department or agency of the governmental unit that provides coverage under a government-sponsored program is the reporting entity for government-sponsored minimum essential coverage. Section 1.6055-1(c)(3)(i) specifically provides that the State agency that administers the Medicaid or CHIP program, respectively, must report government-sponsored coverage under section 6055. Notice 2015-68 provides that Medicaid and CHIP agencies in U.S. possessions or territories are not required to report Medicaid and CHIP coverage because an individual eligible for that coverage is generally a bona fide resident of the possession or territory who is deemed to have minimum essential coverage under section 5000A(f)(4) and, therefore, does not require reporting under section 6055 to verify compliance with section 5000A.

In general, under § 1.6055-1(c)(1)(ii) the reporting entity for coverage under a self-insured group health plan is the plan sponsor. Section 1.6055-1(c)(2) provides rules for identifying which entity is the plan sponsor of a self-insured group health plan for purposes of section 6055. For this purpose, the employer is the plan sponsor of a self-insured group health plan established by a single employer (determined without aggregating related entities under section 414). If the plan or arrangement is established or maintained by more than one employer (including a Multiple Employer Welfare Arrangement (as defined in section 3(40) of the Employee Retirement Income Security Act of 1974 (ERISA)), and the plan is not a multiemployer plan (as defined in section 3(37) of ERISA), each participating employer is a plan sponsor with respect to that employer's employees. For a self-insured group health plan or arrangement that is a multiemployer plan, the plan sponsor is the association, committee, joint board of trustees, or other similar group of representatives of the parties who establish or maintain the plan. For a self-insured group health plan or arrangement maintained solely by an employee organization, the plan sponsor is the employee organization.

The existing regulations at § 1.6055-1(d)(2) provide that no reporting is required for minimum essential coverage that provides benefits in addition or as a supplement to other coverage that is minimum essential coverage if the primary and supplemental coverage have the same plan sponsor or the coverage supplements government-sponsored minimum essential coverage. Notice 2015-68 explained that this rule had proven to be confusing, and, accordingly, the Treasury Department and the IRS intended to propose regulations providing that (1) if an individual is covered by multiple minimum essential coverage plans or programs provided by the same provider, reporting is only required for one of the plans or programs; and (2) reporting generally is not required for an individual's minimum essential coverage to the extent that the individual is eligible for that coverage only if the individual is also covered by other minimum essential coverage for which section 6055 reporting is required.

Information Required To Be Reported

Under section 6055(b) and § 1.6055-1(e)(1), providers of minimum essential coverage must report to the IRS (1) the name, address, and employer identification number (EIN) of the reporting entity required to file the return; (2) the name, address, and TIN, or date of birth if a TIN is not available, of the responsible individual (except that a reporting entity may, but is not required to, report the TIN of a responsible individual not enrolled in the coverage); (3) the name and TIN, or date of birth if a TIN is not available, of each individual who is covered under the policy or program; and (4) the months of coverage for each covered individual.[1] Section 1.6055-1(b)(11) provides that the responsible individual includes a primary insured, employee, former employee, uniformed services sponsor, parent, or other related person named on an application who enrolls one or more individuals, including him or herself, in minimum essential coverage.

In addition, under § 1.6055-1(e)(2), for coverage provided by a health insurance issuer through a group health plan, information returns must report (1) the name, address, and EIN of the employer maintaining the plan, and (2) any other information that the Secretary requires for administering the credit under section 45R (relating to the tax credit for employee health insurance expenses of small employers).

A reporting entity that fails to comply with the filing and statement furnishing requirements of section 6055 may be subject to penalties for failure to file timely a correct information return (section 6721) or failure to furnish timely a correct statement (section 6722). See section 6724(d); see also § 1.6055-1(h)(1). These penalties may be waived if the failure is due to reasonable cause and is not due to willful neglect. See section 6724(a). In particular, under § 301.6724-1(a)(2) of the Procedure and Administration Regulations penalties are waived if a reporting entity demonstrates that it acted in a responsible manner and that the failure is due to significant mitigating factors or events beyond the reporting entity's control. For purposes of section 6055 reporting, if the information reported on a return is incomplete or incorrect as a result of a change in circumstances (such as a retroactive change in coverage), a failure to timely file or furnish a corrected document is a failure to file a correct return or furnish a correct statement under sections 6721 and 6722. See § 1.6055-1(h)(2).

In general, under § 301.6724-1(e) a person will be treated as acting in a responsible manner if the person properly solicits a TIN but does not receive it. For this purpose, proper solicitation of a TIN involves an initial solicitation and two subsequent annual solicitations. In general, an initial solicitation is made when the relationship between the reporting entity and the taxpayer is established. If the reporting entity does not receive the TIN, the first annual solicitation is generally required by December 31 of the year in which the relationship with the taxpayer begins (January 31 of the

---

[1] The Affordable Care Act also added section 6056, which requires that applicable large employers file and furnish statements containing information related to offers of coverage, if any, made to each full-time employee. To complete these statements properly, employers must have each employee's TIN. In accordance with the requirements of a different Code section (section 3402(f)(2)(A)), employers should have already sought each employee's TIN in advance of the deadline for filing and furnishing statements required under section 6056. Therefore, the TIN solicitation rules in these proposed regulations *only apply* to information reporting under section 6055 (which in the case of an applicable large employer providing coverage under a self-insured plan, includes information reporting on Form 1095-C, Part III).

following year if the relationship begins in December). Generally, if the TIN is still not provided, a second annual solicitation is required by December 31 of the following year. Similar rules applying to filers who file or furnish information reports with incorrect TINs are in § 301.6724-1(f).

The preamble to the section 6055 regulations (T.D. 9660, 79 FR 13220) provides short-term relief from reporting penalties for 2015 coverage. Specifically, the IRS will not impose penalties under sections 6721 and 6722 on reporting entities that can show that they have made good faith efforts to comply with the information reporting requirements. This relief applies to incorrect or incomplete information, including TINs or dates of birth, reported on a return or statement.

Explanation of Provisions and Summary of Comments

1. *Reporting of Catastrophic Plans*

Under § 1.36B-5(a), Exchanges must report to the IRS information relating to qualified health plans in which individuals enroll through the Exchange. Under section 36B(c)(3)(A), the term qualified health plan has the same meaning as defined in section 1301 of the Affordable Care Act except that it does not include a catastrophic plan described in section 1302 of the Affordable Care Act. Thus, Exchanges are not required to report on catastrophic coverage. Section 1.6055-1(d) provides that health insurance issuers need not report on coverage in a qualified health plan in the individual market enrolled in through an Exchange, because that information is generally reported by Exchanges pursuant to § 1.36B-5. Thus, currently neither the Exchanges nor health insurance issuers are responsible for reporting coverage under a catastrophic plan.

Effective administration of section 5000A generally requires reporting of all minimum essential coverage, including catastrophic plans in which individuals enroll through an Exchange. Accordingly, Notice 2015-68 indicated that the Treasury Department and the IRS intended to propose regulations under section 6055 to narrow the relief provided to issuers in § 1.6055-1(d) by requiring issuers of catastrophic plans to report catastrophic plan coverage on Form 1095-B, effective for coverage in 2016 and returns and statements filed and furnished in 2017. Consistent with Notice 2015-68, the proposed regulations include this requirement but, to allow reporting entities sufficient time to implement these reporting requirements, are proposed to be effective for coverage in 2017 and returns and statements filed and furnished in 2018.

Notice 2015-68 indicated that health insurance issuers could voluntarily report on 2015 catastrophic coverage (on returns and statements filed and furnished in 2016) and were encouraged to do so. Notice 2015-68 further provided that an issuer that reports on 2015 catastrophic coverage will not be subject to penalties for these returns. Given the 2017 effective date for reporting of catastrophic coverage provided in these proposed regulations, health insurance issuers similarly may voluntarily report on 2016 catastrophic coverage (on returns and statements filed and furnished in 2017) and are encouraged to do so. An issuer that reports on 2016 catastrophic coverage will not be subject to penalties for these returns.

2. *Reporting of Coverage under Basic Health Programs*

Section 1331 of the Affordable Care Act allows states to establish a Basic Health Program to provide an additional healthcare coverage option to certain individuals not eligible for Medicaid. See 42 CFR Part 600. The Basic Health Program is designated as minimum essential coverage under 42 CFR 600.5.

Section 5000A(f) does not identify the Basic Health Program as a government-sponsored program, but it closely resembles government-sponsored coverage such as Medicaid and CHIP. Accordingly, Notice 2015-68 indicated that the state agency that administers the Basic Health Program is the entity that must report that coverage under section 6055. Consistent with Notice 2015-68, these proposed regulations provide that the State agency administering coverage under the Basic Health Program is required to report that coverage under section 6055.

3. *Truncated TINs*

Section 6055(b) and § 1.6055-1(e) require that health insurance issuers and carriers reporting coverage under insured group health plans report information about the employer sponsoring the plan, including the employer's EIN, to the IRS. Section 6055(c) and § 1.6055-1(g) require that health insurance issuers and carriers reporting information to the IRS furnish a statement to a taxpayer providing information about the filer and the covered individuals. Section 301.6109-4(b)(1) provides that the TIN of a person other than the filer, including an EIN, may be truncated on statements furnished to recipients unless, among other reasons, such truncation is otherwise prohibited by statute or regulations. Thus, under § 1.6055-1(g)(3) of the existing regulations, a recipient's TIN may appear in the form of an IRS truncated taxpayer identification number (TTIN) on a statement furnished to the recipient. These proposed regulations amend the existing regulations to clarify that a TTIN is not an alternative identifying number; rather, it is one of the ways that a TIN may appear, subject to the rules in § 301.6109-4(b)(1).

Existing regulations do not address whether health insurance issuers and carriers are permitted to truncate a sponsoring employer's EIN on statements furnished to taxpayers. Notice 2015-68 advised that the Treasury Department and the IRS intended to propose regulations to clarify that the EIN of the employer sponsoring the plan may be truncated to appear as an IRS TTIN on statements health insurance issuers and carriers furnish to taxpayers. Consistent with Notice 2015-68, the proposed regulations clarify that the EIN of the employer sponsoring the plan may be truncated to appear as an IRS TTIN on statements health insurance issuers and carriers furnish to taxpayers. Section 301.6109-4(b)(2)(ii) prohibits using TTINs if, among other things, a statute specifically requires the use of an EIN. While section 6055(b)(2)(A) requires that the information return filed with the IRS includes the employer's EIN, and section 6055(c)(1)(B) requires that the statement furnished to a taxpayer includes the information required to be shown on the information return with respect to such individual, the statute does not require that the full EIN appear on the statement furnished to taxpayers and the employer's EIN may be truncated to appear in the form of an IRS TTIN.

4. *Plans for Which Reporting is Not Required*

Information reporting under section 6055(a) is generally required of every person who provides minimum essential coverage to an individual during the year. In certain instances where the reporting would be duplicative, the existing regulations allow the person who provides supplemental coverage to forgo information reporting. This supplemental coverage rule in §1.6055–1(d)(2) was intended to eliminate duplicate reporting of an individual's minimum essential coverage under circumstances when there is reasonable certainty that the provider of the "primary" coverage will report. This rule has proven to be confusing.

The Treasury Department and the IRS indicated in Notice 2015-68 that regulations would be proposed to replace the existing rules. Accordingly, the proposed regulations provide that (1) if an individual is covered by more than one minimum essential coverage plan or program provided by the same reporting entity, reporting is required for only one of the plans or programs; and (2) reporting is not required for an individual's minimum essential coverage to the extent that the individual is eligible for that coverage only if the individual is also covered by other minimum essential coverage for which section 6055 reporting is required. As in Notice 2015-68, the proposed regulations provide that the second rule applies to eligible employer-sponsored coverage only if the supplemental coverage is offered by the same employer that offered the eligible employer-sponsored coverage for which section 6055 reporting is required. These rules apply month by month and individual by individual.

Thus, under the proposed regulations, applying the first rule, if for a month an individual is enrolled in a self-insured group health plan provided by an employer and also is enrolled in a self-insured health reimbursement arrangement (HRA) provided by the same employer, the reporting entity (the employer) is required to report only one type of coverage for that individual. If an employee is covered under both self-insured arrangements for some months of the year but retires or otherwise drops coverage under the non-HRA group health plan and is covered only under the HRA for other months, the employer must report coverage under the HRA for the months after the employee retires or drops the non-HRA coverage.

Applying the second rule, reporting is not required for minimum essential coverage for a month if that coverage is offered only to individuals who are also covered by other minimum essential coverage, including Medicare, TRICARE, Medicaid, or certain employer-sponsored coverage, for which reporting is required. In these arrangements, the program for which reporting is required represents the primary coverage while the other minimum essential coverage is supplemental to the primary plan.

Under the application of the second rule to eligible employer-sponsored coverage, if an employer offers both an insured group health plan and an HRA for which an employee is eligible if enrolled in the insured group health plan, and an employee enrolls in both, the employer is not required to report the employee's coverage under the HRA. However, if an employee is enrolled in his or her employer's HRA and in a spouse's non-HRA group health plan, the employee's employer is required to report for the HRA, and the employee's spouse's employer (or the health insurance issuer or carrier, if the plan is insured) is required to report for the non-HRA group health plan coverage. The proposed regulations clarify that, for purposes of this rule, an employer is treated as offering minimum essential coverage that is offered by another employer with whom the employer is treated as a single employer under section 414(b), (c), (m), or (o).

Separately, Notice 2015-68 also stated that, because Medicaid and CHIP coverage provided by the governments of American Samoa, the Commonwealth of the Northern Mariana Islands, Guam, Puerto Rico, and the U.S. Virgin Islands is generally made available only to individuals who are treated as having minimum essential coverage under section 5000A(f)(4) (and, therefore, do not need section 6055 reporting to verify minimum essential coverage), the Medicaid and CHIP agencies in those U.S. possessions or territories are not required to report that coverage under section 6055. Consistent with that rule, the proposed regulations provide that reporting under section 6055 is not required with respect to Medicaid and CHIP agencies in U.S. possessions or territories.

5. *TIN Solicitation*

Information reporting under section 6055 is subject to the penalty provisions of sections 6721 and 6722 for failure to file timely a correct information return or failure to furnish timely a correct statement to the individual. See §1.6055-1(h). The penalties may be waived under section 6724(a) if the failure is due to reasonable cause and not due to willful neglect; that is, if a reporting entity demonstrates that it acted in a responsible manner and that the failure is due to significant mitigating factors or events beyond the reporting entity's control. See §301.6724-1(a)(2). Under §301.6724-1(e), in cases of a missing TIN, the reporting entity is treated as acting in a responsible manner in soliciting a TIN if the reporting entity makes (1) an initial solicitation when an account is opened or a relationship is established, (2) a first annual solicitation by December 31 of the year the account is opened (or January 31 of the following year if the account is opened in December), and (3) a second annual solicitation by December 31 of the year following the year in which the account is opened.

Similar rules apply regarding incorrect TINs under § 301.6724-1(f). The rules in § 301.6724-1(e) and (f) were issued prior to the enactment of section 6055 and apply to most forms of information reporting.

Comments received in response to the first notice of proposed rulemaking (REG-132455-11) under section 6055, published in the **Federal Register** (78 FR 54986) on September 9, 2013, raised concerns about the application of the TIN solicitation rules to section 6055 reporting. Accordingly, Notice 2015-68 provided that, pending the issuance of additional guidance, reporting entities will not be subject to penalties for failure to report a TIN if they comply with the requirements of § 301.6724-1(e) with the following modifications: (1) the initial solicitation is made at an individual's first enrollment or, if already enrolled on September 17, 2015, the next open season, (2) the second solicitation (the first annual solicitation) is made at a reasonable time thereafter, and (3) the third solicitation (the second annual solicitation) is made by December 31 of the year following the initial solicitation. Notice 2015-68 also requested comments on the application of the reasonable cause rules under section 6724 to section 6055 reporting.

In response to the request for comments in Notice 2015-68, one commenter requested that the proposed regulations include detailed rules tailored to TIN solicitation for information returns required by section 6055. This commenter expressed concern that, because the current rules were designed primarily to apply to financial relationships, they are difficult to apply to section 6055 reporting, particularly the rules for demonstrating that the filer acted in a responsible manner as described in § 301.6724-1(e) and (f). The Treasury Department and the IRS agree with the commenter that some modification to the rules in § 301.6724-1(e) is warranted to account for the differences between information reporting under section 6055 and information reporting under other provisions of the Code. Accordingly, the Treasury Department and the IRS propose regulations to provide specific TIN solicitation rules for section 6055 reporting. Until final regulations are released, reporting entities may rely on these proposed rules and Notice 2015-68. The preamble below also includes some additional transition rules that apply to reporting entities in certain situations.

Section 301.6724-1(e)(1)(i) provides that an initial TIN solicitation must occur when an account (which includes accounts, relationships, and other transactions) is opened. Section 301.6724-1(e) does not define the term "opened" for this purpose. Commenters requested clarification as to how the term "opened" should be interpreted for purposes of reporting under section 6055. In the context of financial accounts, an account is generally considered opened on the first day it is available for use by its owner. In most cases, this would be shortly after the application to open that account is received, and this day would be no earlier than the day the application was received. Health coverage does not work in the same way. In some cases, the first effective date of health coverage is before the day the application was received, making it impractical to solicit TINs before the coverage takes effect. In other cases, the effective date of coverage may be months after the day the application was received. To account for this different timing, the proposed regulations provide that, for purposes of section 6055 reporting, an account is considered "opened" on the date the filer receives a substantially complete application for new coverage or to add an individual to existing coverage. Accordingly, health coverage providers may generally satisfy the requirement for the initial solicitation by requesting enrollees' TINs as part of the application for coverage.

To address differences in the way financial accounts and health coverage are opened, the proposed regulations also change the timing of the first annual solicitation (the second solicitation overall) with respect to missing TINs. Under § 301.6724-1(e)(1)(ii), a first annual solicitation must be made by December 31 of the year the account is opened (or by January 31 of the following calendar year if the account is opened in December). The timing of the first annual solicitation is dictated by the need to have accurate reporting of information to taxpayers and the IRS in preparation for the filing of an income tax return. Accounts, relationships, and other transactions may be opened or begun throughout the year, and may remain active indefinitely. It is beneficial to the IRS, filers, and taxpayers in the context of accounts, relationships, and other transactions to have a single deadline for the first annual solicitation at the end of the calendar year (or January if the account is opened in December).

By contrast, health coverage is generally offered on an annual basis. While individuals may, depending on their circumstances, enroll in coverage at any point during the year, many covered individuals enroll in coverage during the open enrollment period, which is in advance of the beginning of the coverage year. The most common coverage year is the calendar year and many individuals enroll late each year for coverage the following year. For such individuals, requiring the first annual solicitation (the second solicitation overall) by December 31 of the year in which the application is received is earlier than is necessary (because reporting is not due until more than a year later) and coincides with the end of a plan year, which is already the busiest time of year for coverage providers. To address these considerations, the proposed regulations require that the first annual solicitation be made no later than seventy-five days after the date on which the account was "opened" (i.e., the day the filer received the substantially complete application for coverage), or, if the coverage is retroactive, no later than the seventy-fifth day after the determination of retroactive coverage is made. The deadline for the second annual solicitation (third solicitation overall) remains December 31 of the year following the year the account is opened as required by § 301.6724-1(e)(1)(iii).

As noted above, taxpayers may rely on these proposed regulations and on Notice 2015-68 until final regulations are published. To provide additional relief and ensure that the requirements for the first annual and second annual solicitations may be satisfied with respect to individuals already enrolled in coverage, an additional rule is provided. Under this rule, if an individual was enrolled in coverage on any day before **July 29, 2016**, the account is considered opened on **July 29, 2016**. Accordingly, reporting entities have satisfied the requirement for the initial solicitation with respect to already enrolled individuals so long as they requested enrollee TINs either as part of the application for coverage or at any other point before **July 29, 2016**. The deadlines for the first and second annual solicitations are set by reference to the date the account is opened. Thus, the rule above that treats all accounts for individuals currently enrolled in coverage for which a TIN has not been provided as opened on **July 29, 2016,** provides additional time for the annual solicitations as well. Specifically, consistent with Notice 2015-68, the first annual solicitation should be made at a reasonable time after **July 29, 2016**. For this purpose, a reporting entity that makes the first annual solicitation within 75 days of the initial solicitation will be treated as having made the second solicitation within a reasonable time. Reporting entities that have not made the initial solicitation before **July 29, 2016** should comply with the first annual solicitation requirement by making a solicitation within a reasonable time of **July 29, 2016**. Notice 2015-68 also provided that a reporting entity is deemed to have satisfied the initial, first annual, and second annual solicitations for an individual whose coverage was terminated prior to September 17, 2015, and taxpayers may continue to rely on this rule as well.

Section 301.6724-1(e)(1)(v) provides that the initial and first annual solicitations relate to failures on returns filed for the year in which the account is opened (meaning that showing reasonable cause with respect to the year the account is opened generally requires making the initial and first annual solicitations in the year the account is opened). Because these proposed regulations provide that an account is considered opened for section 6055 purposes when a substantially complete application for that account is received, an account would, in some cases, be considered open in a year prior to the year for which coverage is actually effective and for which reporting is required. This would occur, for example, when a reporting entity receives an application during open enrollment for coverage effective as of the first day of the next coverage year. To ensure that reporting entities that make the initial solicitation and first annual solicitation are eligible for relief for the first year for which reporting is required, the proposed regulations provide that, for purposes of reporting under section 6055, the initial and first annual solicitations relate to failures on returns required to be filed for the year that includes the day that is the first effective date of coverage for a covered individual. Similarly, § 301.6724-1(e)(1)(v) provides that the second annual solicitation relates to failures on returns filed for the year immediately following the year in which the account is opened and succeeding calendar years (meaning that showing reasonable cause with respect to years after the account is opened generally requires making the second annual solicitation during the year following the year the account is opened). As with the initial and first annual solicitations, the existing rule under § 301.6724-1(e)(1)(v) could provide relief for the wrong year when combined with the proposed definition of account opening under section 6055. Accordingly, the proposed regulations provide that the second annual solicitation relates to failures on returns filed for the year immediately following the year to which the first annual solicitation relates, and succeeding calendar years.

In contrast to missing TINs, the Treasury Department and the IRS do not recognize a similar need to modify the existing first annual solicitation rules for incorrect TINs in § 301.6724-1(f)(1)(ii). As with many other types of information reports, information reports of health coverage are generally filed after the end of the tax year, and thus, it is only after the tax year that a filer would generally receive notice of an incorrect TIN. Because the end of the tax year typically corresponds with the end of the coverage year, there is no reason to distinguish the timing of the correction of incorrect TINs for health coverage from all other types of accounts for which information reporting is required. Consequently, the proposed regulations do not alter the rules for incorrect TINs in § 301.6724-1(f)(1)(ii) and (iii) as applied to information reporting under section 6055. However, as with the rules regarding missing TINs under § 301.6724-1(e)(1)(ii), the rules regarding incorrect TINs in § 301.6724-1(f)(1)(i) make reference to the time an account is "opened." Accordingly, the proposed regulations, which provides that for purposes of section 6055 reporting an account is considered "opened" at the time the filer receives an application for new coverage or to add an individual to existing coverage, also applies for purposes of the initial solicitation for incorrect TINs in § 301.6724-1(f)(1)(i).[2]

a. *Application of the TIN Solicitation Rules to "Responsible Individuals" and "Covered Individuals"*

A commenter requested clarification that the initial and annual solicitations of § 301.6724-1(e)(1)(i) and (ii) need be made only to the responsible individual for all individuals covered under a single policy. The commenter further suggested that TIN solicitations made to a responsible individual be treated as TIN solicitations made to all individuals named on the responsible individual's policy.

Under § 1.6055-1(e)(1)(ii) and (iii), filers must report the TIN of each covered individual (who, under § 301.6721-1(g)(5), are also "payees"), and § 1.6055-1(g)(1) requires that the TIN of each covered individual be shown on statements furnished to the responsible individual. Current § 1.6055-1(g)(1) provides that, for purposes of the penalties under section 6722, the furnishing of a statement to the

---

[2] A filer of the information return required under § 1.6055-1 may receive an error message from the IRS indicating that a TIN and name provided on the return do not match IRS records. An error message is neither a Notice 972CG, Notice of Proposed Civil Penalty, nor a requirement that the filer must solicit a TIN in response to the error message.

responsible individual is treated as the furnishing of a statement to a covered individual. This rule is intended to allow reporting entities to satisfy the section 6722 requirements for all covered individuals by furnishing the required statement only to the responsible individual. The Treasury Department and the IRS also intend for a similar rule to apply to the TIN solicitation rules under the section 6724 regulations. To clarify that this is how these rules apply, the proposed regulations expressly provide that TIN solicitations (both initial and annual) made to the responsible individual for a policy or plan are treated as TIN solicitations of every covered individual on the policy or plan for purposes of § 301.6724-1(e)(1) and (f)(1). The filer does not need to make separate solicitations from the responsible individual for each covered individual nor does it need to separately solicit the TINs of each covered individual by contacting each covered individual directly. However, we decline to adopt the commenter's suggestion that a TIN solicitation made to a responsible individual be treated as a TIN solicitation made to all individuals named on that responsible individual's policy at any time, including those individuals added to a policy after the TIN solicitations. When a new individual is added to a policy, the coverage provider establishes a relationship with that individual. The individual is new to the filer, and it is the filer's responsibility to solicit that individual's TIN. Accordingly, to qualify for the penalty waiver, filers must solicit TINs for each individual added to a policy under the procedures outlined in § 301.6724-1(e)(1)(i) and (f)(1)(i); however, any other individual for whom the filer already has a TIN or already has solicited a TIN the prescribed amount of times need not be solicited again regardless of what changes take place during the filer's coverage of that individual.

b. *Different Forms of TIN Solicitations*

A commenter to Notice 2015-68 requested that the provision of renewal applications to enrollees be permitted to satisfy the annual solicitation requirement for purposes of § 301.6724-1(e)(1)(ii) and (iii) and (f)(1)(ii) and (iii) if those renewal applications request TINs from covered individuals. Under current law, TIN requests may be made in a number of different formats. The provision of a renewal application that requests TINs for all covered individuals satisfies the annual solicitation provisions of § 301.6724-1(e)(1)(ii) and (iii) and (f)(1)(ii) and (iii) if it is sent by the deadline for those annual solicitations. Thus, no changes to the regulations are necessary for renewal applications to satisfy the annual solicitation requirement.

The same commenter requested that the requirement in § 301.6724-1(e)(2)(i)(B) to provide the responsible individual with a Form W-9 should be eliminated. The commenter was concerned that this requirement imposes burdens on responsible individuals that make it less likely that they will respond to a TIN solicitation. Section 301.6724-1(e)(2)(i)(B) requires that an annual solicitation include a "Form W-9 or an acceptable substitute . . ." Thus, the existing regulations do not require that Form W-9 be sent. Filers are allowed to request TINs on an acceptable substitute for Form W-9, which includes a renewal application or other request for a TIN. Thus, this comment is not adopted.

This commenter also requested that the requirement in § 301.6724-1(e)(2)(i)(C) that annual solicitations include a return envelope be eliminated, and, if not eliminated, that clarification be provided as to how this requirement applies to multiple TINs. Existing regulations include this requirement because individuals are more likely to comply with a TIN solicitation if that solicitation includes a return envelope. We see no reason that the requirement to include a return envelope, which exists for other information reporting provisions, should be removed for reporting under section 6055. Thus, the proposed regulations do not adopt this comment. However, filers may request more than one TIN at the same time and do not need to send separate envelopes with each request. For example, on a renewal application requesting the TINs for all covered individuals, filers need only provide one return envelope for that application or request.

c. *Solicitations by Employers*

A commenter requested that employers be permitted to make TIN solicitations on behalf of filers. The commenter offered that employers are frequently in a better position than coverage providers to request TINs from the employers' employees and the employees' dependents, and, for practical reasons, it would make sense to allow employers to step in the shoes of the coverage provider for purposes of making the solicitations under § 301.6724-1(e)(1) and (f)(1).

Under existing regulations, actions taken by employers may satisfy the requirement for making an initial or annual TIN solicitation. Employers may, for example, provide their employees with applications for health coverage. If these applications request that the applicants provide TINs for all individuals to be covered, the coverage provider has made an initial solicitation for these individuals' TINs.

The commenter further requested that a filer that arranges to have an employer take on responsibility for the TIN solicitations be treated as having met the penalty waiver requirements of § 301.6724-1(e)(1) and (f)(1). Under existing regulations, qualifying for a penalty waiver requires that the solicitations actually be made. To avoid creating a less stringent standard in cases where an employer is acting on the filer's behalf, the proposed regulations do not adopt the commenter's proposal.

d. *Electronic TIN Solicitations*

A commenter requested that filers be permitted to make annual TIN solicitations by electronic means if the responsible individual has consented to the receipt of information concerning his or her coverage in the same electronic format in which the annual solicitation is made. IRS Publication 1586, Reasonable Cause Regulations and Requirements for Missing and Incorrect Name/TINs (including instructions for reading CD/DVDs), provides that filers may establish an electronic system for payees (including covered individuals) to receive and respond to TIN solicitations, provided certain listed requirements are met. IRS Publication 1586 can be found at *www.irs.gov/forms-pubs*. Because filers are already able to solicit TINs electronically, it is unnecessary to address the commenter's recommendation for electronic TIN solicitations with these proposed regulations.

Proposed Effective/Applicability Date

These regulations are generally proposed to apply for taxable years ending after December 31, 2015, and may be relied on for calendar years ending after December 31, 2013.

The only exception is the rules in section 1 of this preamble relating to reporting of coverage under catastrophic plans. Those rules are proposed to apply for calendar years beginning after December 31, 2016. Health insurance issuers may voluntarily report on 2015 and 2016 catastrophic coverage (on returns and statements filed and furnished in 2016 and 2017 respectively). An issuer that reports on 2015 and/or 2016 catastrophic coverage will not be subject to penalties for these returns.

In addition, until these the proposed regulations are finalized, taxpayers may continue to rely on the rules provided in Notice 2015-68.

Special Analyses

Certain IRS regulations, including this one, are exempt from the requirements of Executive Order 12866, as supplemented and reaffirmed by Executive Order 13563. Therefore, a regulatory impact assessment is not required.

It has also been determined that section 553(b) of the Administrative Procedure Act (5 U.S.C. chapter 5) does not apply to these regulations.

It is hereby certified that these regulations will not have a significant economic impact on a substantial number of small entities. This certification is based on the fact that the information collection required under these regulations is imposed under section 6055. Consistent with the statute, the proposed regulations require a person that provides minimum essential coverage to an individual to file a return with the IRS reporting certain information and to furnish a statement to the responsible individual who enrolled an individual or family in the coverage. These regulations primarily provide the method of filing and furnishing returns and statements under section 6055. Moreover, the proposed regulations attempt to minimize the burden associated with this collection of information by limiting reporting to the information that the IRS will use to verify minimum essential coverage and administer tax credits.

Based on these facts, a Regulatory Flexibility Analysis under the Regulatory Flexibility Act (5 U.S.C. chapter 6) is not required.

Pursuant to section 7805(f), this notice of proposed rulemaking will be submitted to the Chief Counsel for Advocacy of the Small Business Administration for comment on its impact on small business.

Statement of Availability of IRS Documents

IRS Revenue Procedures, Revenue Rulings notices, notices and other guidance cited in this preamble are published in the Internal Revenue Bulletin (or Cumulative Bulletin) and are available from the Superintendent of Documents, U.S. Government Printing Office, Washington, DC 20402, or by visiting the IRS website at *http://www.irs.gov*.

Comments and Requests for Public Hearing

Before these proposed regulations are adopted as final regulations, consideration will be given to any comments that are submitted timely to the IRS as prescribed in this preamble under the "Addresses" heading. The Treasury Department and the IRS request comments on all aspects of the proposed rules. All comments will be available for public inspection at *www.regulations.gov* or upon request. A public hearing will be scheduled if requested in writing by any person that timely submits written comments. If a public hearing is scheduled, notice of the date, time, and place for the public hearing will be published in the **Federal Register**.

Drafting Information

The principal author of these proposed regulations is John B. Lovelace of the Office of Associate Chief Counsel (Income Tax and Accounting). However, other personnel from the IRS and the Treasury Department participated in the development of the regulations.

[¶49,709] Proposed Amendments of Regulations (REG-131418-14), published in the Federal Register on August 2, 2016 (corrected 9/26/2016).

[Code Secs. 25A, 66050S and 6724]

Education tax credits: Qualified tuition expenses: Related expenses: Form 1098-T: Reporting requirements: Protecting Americans from Tax Hikes Act of 2015.—Amendments of Reg. §§1.25A-0, Reg. §1.25A-1, Reg. §1.25A-2, Reg. §1.25A-5, Reg. §1.6050S-0, Reg. §1.6050S-1 and Reg. §301.6724-1, reporting qualified tuition and related expenses under section 6050S on a Form 1098-T, "Tuition Statement," and conforming the regulations to the changes made to section 6050S by the Protecting Americans from Tax Hikes Act of 2015, are proposed.

AGENCY: Internal Revenue Service (IRS), Treasury.

ACTION: Notice of proposed rulemaking and notice of public hearing.

SUMMARY: This document contains proposed regulations that revise the rules for reporting qualified tuition and related expenses under section 6050S on a Form 1098-T, "Tuition Statement," and conforms the regulations to the changes made to section 6050S by the Protecting Americans from Tax Hikes Act of 2015. This document also seeks to amend the regulations on the education tax credits under section 25A generally as well as to conform the regulations to changes made to section 25A by the Trade Preferences Extension Act of 2015 and the Protecting Americans from Tax Hikes Act of 2015. The proposed regulations affect certain higher educational institutions required to file Form 1098-T and taxpayers eligible to claim an education tax credit. This document also provides notice of a public hearing on these proposed regulations. DATES: Written or electronic comments must be received by November 1, 2016. Outlines of topics to be discussed at the public hearing scheduled for November 30, 2016 must be received by November 1, 2016. ADDRESSES: Send submissions to: CC:PA:LPD:PR (REG-131418-14), room 5203, Internal Revenue Service, P.O. Box 7604, Ben Franklin Station, Washington, DC 20044. Submissions may be hand-delivered Monday through Friday between the hours of 8:00 a.m. and 4:00 p.m. to CC:PA:LPD:PR (REG-131418-14), Courier's Desk, Internal Revenue Service, 1111 Constitution Avenue, NW., Washington, DC 20224. Alternatively, taxpayers may submit comments electronically via the Federal eRulemaking Portal at www.regulations.gov (IRS REG-131418-14).

FOR FURTHER INFORMATION CONTACT: Concerning the proposed regulations, Gerald Semasek of the Office of Associate Chief Counsel (Procedure and Administration) for the proposed regulations under sections 6050S and 6724, (202) 317-6845, and Sheldon Iskow of the Office of Associate Chief Counsel (Income Tax and Accounting) for the proposed regulations under section 25A, (202) 317-4718; concerning the submission of comments and requests for a public hearing, Regina Johnson, (202) 317-6901 (not toll-free calls).

SUPPLEMENTARY INFORMATION:

Paperwork Reduction Act

The collection of information contained in this notice of proposed rulemaking has been approved by the Office of Management and Budget through Form 1040 (OMB No. 1545-0074), Form 8863 (OMB No. 1545-0074) and Form 1098-T (OMB No. 1545-1574) in accordance with the Paperwork Reduction Act of 1995 (44 U.S.C. 3507(d)). Notice and an opportunity to comment on the proposed changes to burden hours for the forms related to this proposed rule will be published in a separate notice in the **Federal Register**.

Background

This document contains proposed regulations to amend the Income Tax Regulations (26 CFR part 1) under section 25A of the Internal Revenue Code (Code) and the Procedure and Administration Regulations (26 CFR Part 301) under section 6050S, to reflect the amendments to sections 25A and 6724 under the Trade Preferences Extension Act of 2015 (Public Law 114-27 (129 Stat. 362 (2015)) (TPEA) and the amendments to sections 25A and 6050S under the Protecting Americans from Tax Hikes Act of 2015 (Public Law 114-113 (129 Stat. 2242 (2015)) (PATH). Furthermore, the document contains proposed regulations to amend the Income Tax Regulations under section 25A to update the definition of qualified tuition and related expenses in §1.25A-2(d) to reflect the changes made by the American Recovery and Reinvestment Act of 2009 (Public Law 111-5 (123 Stat. 115) (ARRA)), to clarify the prepayment rule in §1.25A-5(e), and to clarify the rule for refunds in §1.25A-5(f).

1. Section 25A-Education Tax Credits

The Taxpayer Relief Act of 1997 (Public Law 105-34 (111 Stat. 788) (TRA '97)) added section 25A to provide students and their families with two new nonrefundable tax credits to help pay for college (education tax credits). Pursuant to TRA '97, section 25A allowed eligible taxpayers to claim either the Hope Scholarship Credit or the Lifetime Learning Credit (LLC) for qualified tuition and related expenses paid during the taxable year for an academic period beginning during the taxable year. In general, either the student or the parent who claims a dependency exemption for the student may claim a credit for the student's qualified tuition and related expenses. Section 25A(f)(1) defines "qualified tuition and related expenses" as tuition and fees required for enrollment or attendance at an eligible educational institution (institution). Section 25A(f)(2) generally defines an "eligible educational institution" as an institution described in the Higher Education Act of 1965 that is eligible to participate in federal college financial aid programs. Section 25A(g)(4) provides that amounts paid during the taxable year for enrollment during an academic period beginning within the first three months of the following taxable year are treated as amounts paid for an academic period beginning during the taxable year. Section 25A(g)(5) provides that no credit is allowed for any expenses for which a deduction is allowed under another provision of the Code.

Final regulations under section 25A were published in the **Federal Register** (67 FR 78687) on December 26, 2002. Section 1.25A-2(d)(1) of these regulations defines "qualified tuition and related expenses" to mean tuition and fees required for the enrollment or attendance of a student for courses of instruction at an institution. Section 1.25A-2(d)(2)(i) provides that only fees required to be paid to the institution as a condition of the student's enrollment or attendance at the institution are treated as qualified tuition and related expenses for purposes of section 25A. Under this rule, fees for books, supplies, and equipment used in a course of study are required fees only if the fees must be paid to the institution for the enrollment or attendance of the student at the institution. See §1.25A-2(d)(2)(ii). In addition, §1.25A-5(e)(1) provides that an education tax credit is allowed only for payments of qualified tuition and related expenses for an academic period beginning in the same taxable year as the year the payment is made. Section 1.25A-5(e)(2) provides that qualified tuition and related expenses paid during one taxable year for an academic period beginning in the first three months of the taxable year following the taxable year in which the payment is made will be treated as paid for an academic period beginning in the same taxable year as the year the payment is made (prepayment rule).

Section 1.25A-5(f) provides rules for refunds of qualified tuition and related expenses. If qualified tuition and related expenses are paid and a refund of these expenses is received in the same taxable year, qualified tuition and related expenses for the taxable year are reduced by the amount of the refund. Section 1.25A-5(f)(1). If a taxpayer receives a refund of qualified tuition and related expenses in the current taxable year (current year) that were paid in the prior taxable year (prior year) before the taxpayer files his/her federal income tax return for the prior year, the taxpayer reduces the qualified tuition and related expenses for the prior year by the refund amount. Section 1.25A-5(f)(2). However, if the taxpayer receives the refund after filing his/her federal income tax return for the prior year, the taxpayer must increase the tax imposed for the current year by the recapture amount. Section 1.25A-5(f)(3)(i). The recapture amount is calculated in the manner provided in §1.25A-5(f)(3)(ii). Sections 1.25A-5(f)(4) and (f)(5) provide that refunds of loan proceeds and receipt of excludable educational assistance are treated as refunds for purposes of §1.25A-5(f)(1), (2), and (3), as appropriate.

In 2009, ARRA enacted section 25A(i), which expanded the Hope Scholarship Credit with the American Opportunity Tax Credit (AOTC) for taxable years beginning after 2008. The definition of "qualified tuition and related expenses" for purposes of the AOTC is broader than the definition of qualified tuition and related expenses for the Hope Scholarship Credit and the LLC because it includes expenses paid for course materials. See section 25A(i)(3).

2. Section 222-Deduction for Qualified Expenses

Section 431(a) of the Economic Growth and Tax Relief Reconciliation Act of 2001, Public Law 107-16 (115 Stat. 38) added section 222, which generally allows a deduction for qualified tuition and related expenses paid by a taxpayer during the taxable year subject to certain dollar and income limitations. Section 222(b) provides that no deduction is allowed if the taxpayer claims an education tax credit for the student.

3. Section 6050S-Information Reporting for Eligible Educational Institutions

TRA '97 also added section 6050S to require eligible educational institutions to file information returns and to furnish written statements to assist taxpayers and the IRS in determining whether a taxpayer is eligible for an education tax credit under section 25A, as well as other education tax benefits. These returns and statements are made on Form 1098-T, "Tuition Statement." Prior to the enactment of PATH, section 6050S(b)(2)(B)(i) permitted institutions to report either the aggregate amount of payments received or the aggregate amount billed for qualified tuition and related expenses during the calendar year for individuals enrolled for any academic period. Institutions also must report the aggregate amount of scholarships or grants received for an individual's costs of attendance that the institution administered and processed during the calendar year. See section 6050S(b)(2)(B)(ii). Section 6050S(b)(2)(B)(iii) requires that institutions must separately report adjustments (that is, refunds of payments or reductions in charges) made during the calendar year to qualified tuition and related expenses that were reported in a prior calendar year and that institutions also must separately report adjustments (that is, refunds or reductions) made during the calendar year to scholarships that were reported in a prior calendar year. Section 6050S(b)(2)(D) requires that the information return include other information as the Secretary may prescribe.

In addition, sections 6050S(a)(2) and (a)(3) require any person engaged in a trade or business of making payments to any individual under an insurance agreement as reimbursements or refunds of qualified expenses (an insurer) or who receives from any individual $600 or more of interest during the calendar year on qualified education loans to file information returns and to furnish written information statements. Section 6050S(b)(2) provides that these information returns must contain the name, address, and TIN of any individual with respect to whom these payments were made or received, the aggregate amount of reimbursements or refunds (or similar amounts paid to such individuals during the calendar year by an insurer), the aggregate amount of interest received for the calendar year from the individual, and such other information as the Secretary may prescribe.

Section 6050S(d) provides that every person required to make a return under section 6050S(a) must furnish a written statement to each individual whose name is set forth on the return showing the name, address, and phone number of the person required to make the return and the amounts described in section 6050S(b)(2)(B). For taxable years beginning after June 29, 2015, all of the information required by section 6050S(b)(2), not just the amounts, must be included on the written statement. The written statement must be furnished by January 31 of the year following the year for which the return is required to be made.

Final regulations under section 6050S were published in the **Federal Register** (67 FR 77678) in the same Treasury Decision as the final regulations for section 25A on December 19, 2002. The section 6050S regulations provide exceptions to the reporting requirements for educational institutions for students who are nonresident aliens, for noncredit courses, for certain billing arrangements, and in cases where qualified tuition and related expenses are paid entirely with scholarships or grants. These regulations also set forth the specific information that institutions must report to the IRS, as well as information that the institution must include with the statement furnished to the student. These regulations also include requirements regarding the time and manner for soliciting the student's TIN.

4. Sections 6721, 6722 and 6724-Information Reporting Penalties and Penalty Relief

Section 6721 imposes a penalty on an eligible educational institution that fails to timely file correct information returns with the IRS. Section 6722 imposes a penalty on an educational institution that fails to timely furnish correct written statements to the student. Generally, the penalty under section 6721 and section 6722 is $100 per failure, with an annual maximum penalty of $1.5 million. The penalty is increased to $250 per failure and the annual maximum penalty is increased to $3 million for returns required to be filed and statements required to be made after December 31, 2015. However, section 6724(a) provides that the penalty under section 6721 or 6722 may be waived if it is shown that the failure was due to reasonable cause and not due to willful neglect.

Section 301.6724-1(a)(2) provides that the penalty is waived for reasonable cause only if the filer establishes that: (1) either there are significant mitigating factors with respect to the failure or that the failure arose from events beyond the filer's control and (2) the filer acted in a responsible manner both before and after the failure. In the case of a missing or incorrect TIN, § 301.6724-1(d)(2) provides that the filer acted in a responsible manner if the filer satisfies the solicitation requirements in § 301.6724-1(e) (regarding a missing TIN) or (f) (regarding an incorrect TIN).

Section 1.6050S-1(e)(3) provides that the rules regarding reasonable cause under § 301.6724-1 do not apply in the case of failure to include a correct TIN on a Form 1098-T. Instead, § 1.6050S-1(e)(3) provides special rules for institutions to establish reasonable cause for a failure to include a correct TIN on Form 1098-T.

Section 1.6050S-1(e)(3)(i) provides that reasonable cause for a failure to include a correct TIN on the Form 1098-T may be established if (1) the failure arose from events beyond the institution's control, such as a failure of the individual to furnish a correct TIN, and (2) the institution acted in a responsible manner before and after the failure. Section 1.6050S-1(e)(3)(ii) provides that if the institution does not have the student's correct TIN in its records, acting in a responsible manner means making a single solicitation for the TIN by December 31 of the calendar year for which the payment is made, the amount is billed, or a reimbursement is made. Section 1.6050S-1(e)(3)(iii) also provides for the manner by which an educational institution should request the individual's TIN. The solicitation must be done in writing and must clearly notify the individual that the law requires the individual to furnish a TIN so that it may be included on an information return filed by the institution. The solicitation may be made on Form W-9S, "Request for Student's or Borrower's Taxpayer Identification Number and Certification," or the institution may develop its own form and incorporate it into other forms customarily used by the institution, such as financial aid forms. In the instance that an institution does not have a student's TIN in its records and the student does not provide the TIN in response to a solicitation described in § 1.6050S-1(e), the institution must file and furnish the Form 1098-T, leaving the space for the TIN blank.

5. TPEA Amendments to Sections 25A, 222 and 6724

Section 804(a) of TPEA amended section 25A by adding a new subparagraph (g)(8), which provides that, for taxable years beginning after June 29, 2015, except as provided by the Secretary, a taxpayer may not claim an education tax credit under section 25A unless the taxpayer receives a statement furnished by an eligible educational institution that contains all of the information required in section 6050S(d)(2) (that is, the recipient's copy of the Form 1098-T). Section 804(b) similarly amends section 222(d) to provide that, for taxable years beginning after June 29, 2015, except as provided by the Secretary, a taxpayer may not claim a deduction for qualified tuition and related expenses unless the taxpayer receives the recipient's copy of the Form 1098-T. For purposes of both the education tax credit and the deduction, a taxpayer who claims a student as a dependent will be treated as receiving the statement if the student receives the statement.

Section 805 of TPEA amends section 6724 by adding a new subsection (f), which provides that no penalty will be imposed under section 6721 or 6722 against an eligible educational institution solely by reason of failing to include the individual's TIN on a Form 1098-T or related statement if the institution contemporaneously certifies under penalties of perjury in the form and manner prescribed by the Secretary that it has complied with the standards promulgated by the Secretary for obtaining the individual's TIN. The provision applies to returns required to be made and statements required to be furnished after December 31, 2015.

6. PATH Amendments to Sections 25A, 222 and 6050S

a. AOTC permanent and section 222 extended

Section 102(a) of PATH amends section 25A(i) to make the AOTC permanent. Section 153(a) of PATH amends section 222(e) to retroactively extend the deduction for qualified tuition and related expenses for taxable years beginning after December 31, 2014, and ending on or before December 31, 2016.

b. Amendments to section 25A

Section 206(a)(2) of PATH amends section 25A(i) to provide that the AOTC is not allowed if the student's TIN and the TIN of the taxpayer claiming the credit is issued after the due date for filing the return for the taxable year. Pursuant to section 206(b)(1), this amendment is effective for returns (including an amended return) filed after December 18, 2015. Section 206(b)(2) of PATH provides, however, that this amendment does not apply to any return (other than an amendment to any return) for a taxable year that includes the date of enactment of PATH (December 18, 2015) if the return is filed on or before the due date for such return.

Section 211(a) of PATH amends section 25A(i) to provide that the AOTC is not allowed if the return does not include the employer identification number (EIN) of any institution to which the qualified tuition and related expenses were paid with respect to the student. This amendment is effective for taxable years beginning after December 31, 2015.

c. Amendments to section 6050S

Section 211(b) of PATH amends section 6050S(b)(2) to require eligible educational institutions and insurers to report their EIN on the return and statement. This amendment is effective for expenses paid after December 31, 2015, for education furnished in academic periods beginning after such date.

Section 212 of PATH amends section 6050S(b)(2)(B)(i) to eliminate the option for eligible educational institutions to report aggregate qualified tuition and related expenses billed for the calendar year. Accordingly, for expenses paid after December 31, 2015, for education furnished in academic periods beginning after such date, eligible educational institutions are required to report aggregate payments of qualified tuition and related expenses received during the calendar year.

Explanation of Provisions

1. Changes to Implement TPEA and PATH

a. Changes to section 25A and section 222

Both TPEA and PATH add new requirements for claiming education tax benefits. Under TPEA, the student is required to receive a Form 1098-T in order to claim the LLC or the AOTC or claim the deduction under section 222. Under PATH, the ability to claim the AOTC is further limited. First, the taxpayer can claim the AOTC only if the taxpayer includes, on his/her return for which the credit is claimed, the EIN of any educational institution to which qualified tuition and related expenses are paid. Second, the taxpayer can claim the AOTC only if the TIN of the student and the TIN of the taxpayer, on the return for which the credit is claimed, are issued on or before the due date of the original return.

i. Form 1098-T requirement under TPEA

Form 1098-T assists taxpayers in determining whether they are eligible to claim education tax credits under section 25A or the deduction for qualified tuition and related expenses under section 222. However, before TPEA, there was no requirement that the taxpayer (or the taxpayer's dependent if the taxpayer's dependent is the student) receive a Form 1098-T to claim these tax benefits.

Section 804 of TPEA changes the requirements for a taxpayer to claim education tax benefits under section 25A or section 222. For qualified tuition and related expenses paid during taxable years beginning after June 29, 2015, TPEA provides that, unless the Secretary provides otherwise, a taxpayer must receive a Form 1098-T to claim either a credit under section 25A or a deduction under section 222.

The proposed regulations reflect these changes. Specifically, the proposed regulations add a new paragraph (f) to § 1.25A-1 to require that for taxable years beginning after June 29, 2015, unless an exception applies, no education tax credit is allowed unless the taxpayer (or the taxpayer's dependent) receives a Form 1098-T. However, the proposed regulations explain that the amount reported on the Form 1098-T may not reflect the total amount of qualified tuition and related expenses that the taxpayer has paid during the taxable year because certain expenses are not required to be reported on the Form 1098-T. For example, under § 1.25A-2(d)(3), expenses for course materials paid to a vendor other than an eligible educational institution are eligible for the AOTC. However, because these expenses are not paid to an eligible educational institution, these expenses are not required to be reported on a Form 1098-T. Accordingly, a taxpayer who meets the requirements in § 1.25A-1(f) regarding the Form 1098-T requirement to claim the credit and who can substantiate payment of qualified tuition and related expenses may include these unreported expenses in the computation of the amount of the education tax credit allowable for the taxable year even though the expenses are not reported on a Form 1098-T.

Proposed § 1.25A-1(f)(2)(i) provides an exception to the Form 1098-T requirement in § 1.25A-1(f)(1) if the student has not received a Form 1098-T by the later of (a) January 31 of the taxable year following the taxable year to which the education credit relates or (b) the date the federal income tax return claiming the education tax credit is filed. This exception only applies if the taxpayer or taxpayer's dependent (i) has requested, in the manner prescribed in publications, forms and instructions, or published guidance, the eligible educational institution to furnish the Form 1098-T after January 31 of the year following the taxable year to which the education tax credit relates but on or before the date the return is filed claiming the education tax credit, and (ii) has cooperated fully with the eligible educational institution's efforts to obtain information necessary to furnish the statement. Proposed § 1.25A-1(f)(2)(ii) provides that the receipt of a Form 1098-T is not required if the reporting rules under section 6050S and related regulations provide that the eligible educational institution is exempt from providing a Form 1098-T to the student (for example, non-credit courses). Proposed § 1.25A-1(f)(2)(iii) also provides that the IRS may provide additional exceptions in published guidance of general applicability, see § 601.601(d)(2). The proposed regulations under § 1.25A-1(f) apply to education tax credits claimed for taxable years beginning after June 29, 2015.

Until the proposed regulations under § § 1.25A-1(f) and 1.6050S-1(a) are published in the **Federal Register** as final regulations, a taxpayer (or the taxpayer's dependent) (other than a non-resident alien) who does not receive a Form 1098-T because its institution is exempt from furnishing a Form 1098-T under current § 1.6050S-1(a)(2) may claim an education tax credit under section 25A(a) if the taxpayer (1) is otherwise qualified, (2) can demonstrate that the taxpayer (or the taxpayer's dependent) was enrolled at an eligible educational institution, and (3) can substantiate the payment of qualified tuition and related expenses. Section 804(b) of TPEA also amends section 222 to require a Form 1098-T to claim a deduction for qualified tuition and related expenses for taxable years beginning after June 29, 2015. Rules similar to those in proposed § 1.25A-1(f), including the exceptions, apply for purposes of section 222.

ii. Identification requirements for AOTC under PATH

Section 206(a)(2) of PATH amends section 25A(i) to provide that the AOTC is not allowed if the student's TIN or the TIN of the taxpayer claiming the credit is issued after the due date for filing the return for the taxable year. This amendment is generally effective for any return or amended return filed after December 18, 2015. The proposed regulations reflect this change. Specifically, the proposed regulations add new § 1.25A-1(e)(2)(i), which provides that, for any federal income tax return (including an amended return) filed after December 18, 2015, no AOTC is allowed unless the student's TIN and the taxpayer's TIN are issued on or before the due date (including an extension, if timely requested) for filing the return for that taxable year.

Section 211 of PATH amends section 25A(i) to provide that the AOTC is not allowed unless the taxpayer's return includes the EIN of any institution to which the qualified tuition and related expenses were paid with respect to the student. The proposed regulations reflect this change by adding new § 1.25A-1(e)(2)(ii).

b. Changes to section 6050S reporting to conform with TPEA 1098-T requirement

i. Exceptions to reporting requirement and clarifying changes

Currently, the regulations under section 6050S include exceptions to reporting. For instance, under § 1.6050S-1(a)(2)(i), institutions are not required to file a Form 1098-T with the IRS or provide a Form 1098-T to a nonresident alien, unless the individual requests a Form 1098-T. Under § 1.6050S-1(a)(2)(ii), institutions are not required to report information with respect to courses for which no academic credit is awarded. In addition, reporting is not required with respect to individuals whose qualified tuition and related expenses are paid entirely with scholarships under § 1.6050S-1(a)(2)(iii) or individuals whose qualified tuition and related expenses are paid under a formal billing arrangement under § 1.6050S-1(a)(2)(iv).

The exceptions in § § 1.6050S-1(a)(2)(i), (iii), and (iv) to reporting on Form 1098-T are inconsistent with the TPEA, which generally requires a student to receive a Form 1098-T from the educational institution to claim a section 25A education credit. With these exceptions, a significant number of taxpayers claiming the credit will not have a Form 1098-T, which would frustrate the explicit purpose of TPEA. Therefore, the proposed regulations remove these exceptions.

Removal of the exceptions in § § 1.6050S-1(a)(2)(i), (iii), and (iv) also assists students. Students to whom these exceptions apply are deprived of important information that they need to determine their eligibility for education tax credits. The Form 1098-T provides students with the amount of tuition paid (or billed for calendar year 2016 only), the amount of scholarships and grants that the institution administered and processed, and an indication of whether the student was enrolled at least a half time for an academic period. Students who do not receive a Form 1098-T cannot use the information that would be provided on the form to assist them in determining the proper amount of education credits they may claim. Further, removal of these exceptions will improve the IRS's ability to use the Form 1098-T to verify whether taxpayers should be allowed the education tax benefits that are claimed. In addition, removal of these exceptions would improve the IRS's ability to determine whether the institutions are complying with their reporting obligations.

The proposed regulations would not remove the exception to reporting under § 1.6050S-1(a)(2)(ii) for courses for which no academic credit is awarded. Treasury and the IRS understand that in many cases fees for these courses are charged outside of the financial systems used for students who are taking courses for credit. In addition, given that non-credit courses would not be eligible for the AOTC (or Hope Credit) and would only be eligible for the LLC if the student is taking the course to acquire or improve job skills, reporting expenses paid for non-credit courses could cause confusion and unintended non-compliance.

Treasury and the IRS believe that students benefit from receipt of the Form 1098-T because the information on the form assists the student in determining eligibility for education tax benefits that make higher education more affordable. Reporting that does not provide useful information to students and the IRS, however, unduly burdens institutions and the IRS and could confuse students about whether they are eligible to claim education tax benefits. Therefore, Treasury and the IRS are asking for comments regarding exceptions to the reporting under section 6050S. Specifically, comments are requested regarding the exception to reporting for students who are nonresident aliens, including how an institution determines that a student is a nonresident alien and experience administering the existing exception. Comments are also requested regarding whether the exception for noncredit courses should be retained, and if so, whether there should be any changes to the exception.

The proposed regulations also revise the information that institutions are required to report on the Form 1098-T in an effort to provide more precise information for students to use when determining eligibility for and the amount of an education tax credit and for the IRS to use to verify compliance with the requirements for claiming the education tax credits. For instance, the current regulations under § 1.6050S-1(b)(2)(ii)(D) require that the Form 1098-T include an indication of whether amounts reported relate to an academic period that begins in the first three months of the next calendar year pursuant to the prepayment rule in § 1.25A-5(e)(2). The proposed regulations revise this section to include a requirement that the amount paid that relates to an academic period that begins in the first three months of the next calendar year be specifically stated on the Form 1098-T. This will assist the IRS in identifying credits claimed in two years for the same qualified tuition and related expenses.

In addition, the proposed regulations add a new paragraph (I) to § 1.6050S-1(b)(2)(ii) to require the institution to indicate the number of months that a student was a full-time student during the calendar year. The proposed regulations also add to that paragraph a definition of what constitutes a month. This information will assist the IRS in determining whether a parent properly claimed the student as a dependent and, therefore, properly claimed the credit for the student's qualified tuition and related expenses. See § 1.25A-1(f) for rules relating to claiming the credit in the case of a dependent.

The proposed regulations clarify § 1.6050S-1(b)(2)(v) regarding the rules for determining the amount of payments received for qualified tuition and related expenses. This clarification is intended to provide a uniform rule for all institutions to determine whether a payment received by an institution should be reported on a Form 1098-T as qualified tuition and related expenses in the current year. Under the proposed rule, payments received during a calendar year are treated first as payments of qualified tuition and related expenses up to the total amount billed by the institution for qualified tuition and related expenses for enrollment during the calendar year and then as payments of expenses other than qualified tuition and related expenses for enrollment during the calendar year. A similar rule applies in the case of payments received during the calendar year with respect to enrollment in an academic period beginning during the first three months of the next calendar year. In that case, the payments received by the institution with respect to the amount billed for enrollment in an academic period beginning during the first three months of the next calendar year are treated as payments of qualified tuition and related expenses for the calendar year in which the payments are received. Examples have been added to § 1.6050S-1(b)(2)(vii) to illustrate these rules. Treasury and the IRS request comments regarding these rules, including alternative approaches and recommendations for addressing other issues that should be covered by these rules.

The proposed regulations also revise § 1.6050S-1(c)(1)(iii) regarding the instructions accompanying the Form 1098-T that the institution must furnish to students. The proposed regulations add a new paragraph (D) to § 1.6050S-1(c)(1)(iii) to require institutions to include a paragraph in the instructions informing students that they may be able to optimize their federal tax benefits by taking a portion of a scholarship or grant into income. This new paragraph will alert students about their ability to optimize their federal education tax benefits by allocating all or a portion of their scholarship or grant to pay the student's actual living expenses (if permitted by the terms of the scholarship or grant) by including such amounts in income on the student's tax return if the student is required to file a return. By including such amounts in income, the scholarship or grant is no longer tax free, and the student is not required to reduce qualified tuition and related expenses by the amount paid with the now taxable scholarship or grant. See section 25A(g)(2) and § 1.25A-5(c)(3) for rules regarding allocation of scholarships and grants between qualified tuition and related expenses and other expenses. Minor revisions have also been made to the other paragraphs required to be included in instructions, including addition of the name of the form (Form 1098-T) on which reporting occurs and specific identification of Publication 970, "Tax Benefits for Education," as a resource for taxpayers.

The proposed regulations also provide a definition of "administered and processed" for purposes of determining which scholarships and grants an institution is required to report on the Form 1098-T. The current regulations do not have a definition of this term, and the lack of a definition has resulted in uncertainty and inconsistent reporting. The proposed regulations resolve this by adding a definition of "administered and processed" to § 1.6050S-1(e)(1)(i). Under this definition, a scholarship or grant is administered and processed by an institution if the institution receives payment of an amount (whether by cash, check, or other means of payment) that the institution knows or reasonably should know, is a scholarship or grant, regardless of whether the institution is named as the payee or a co-payee of the amount and regardless of whether, in the case of a payment other than in cash, the student endorses the check or other means of payment for the benefit of the institution. Pell Grants are provided as an example of a scholarship or grant that is treated as administered and processed by an institution.

ii. PATH eliminates option to report amount billed

These proposed regulations also implement the amendment to section 6050S(b)(2)(B)(i) under PATH, which eliminates the option for eligible educational institutions to report the aggregate amount billed for qualified tuition and related expenses for expenses paid after December 31, 2015, for education furnished in academic periods beginning after such date. Eligible educational institutions have informed the IRS that they cannot implement the necessary changes in technology to enable reporting of aggregate payments of qualified tuition and expenses for the first year in which the statutory amendment applies, calendar year 2016. Therefore, in Announcement 2016-17, I.R.B. 2016-20, the IRS stated that it will not impose penalties under section 6721 or 6722 against an eligible educational institution required to file 2016 Forms 1098-T solely because the institution reports the aggregate amount billed for qualified tuition and expenses rather than the aggregate payments of qualified tuition and related expenses received. Thus, for calendar year 2016, no penalties will be imposed if an educational institution fails to implement the PATH's amendment to section 6050S(b)(2)(B)(i) and continues to report the amount billed.

The proposed regulations reflect the PATH amendment by eliminating the option to report the amount billed. These regulations are proposed to be effective on publication of final regulations in the **Federal Register**. In the interim, the limited penalty relief in Announcement 2016-17 will apply to allow educational institutions to report the amount billed for calendar year 2016.

iii. No change required to implement EIN reporting requirement

Current regulations under § 1.6050S-1(b)(2)(ii)(A) require that the eligible educational institution report its name, address, and TIN on the Form 1098-T. Accordingly, the amendment to section 6050S(b)(2) by section 211(b) of PATH requiring eligible educational institutions and insurers to report their EIN does not require a change to the regulations.

c. Changes to implement new section 6724(f)

Section 1.6050S-1(f)(4) of the proposed regulations reflects the enactment of section 6724(f) by section 805 of TPEA. Under section 6724(f), the IRS may not impose information reporting penalties under section 6721 and section 6722 against an eligible educational institution for failure to include a correct TIN on the Form 1098-T if the institution certifies compliance with IRS standards for soliciting TINs. Relief under section 6724(f) applies only to eligible educational institutions and does not apply to insurers required to file Forms 1098-T under section 6050S(a)(2).

The IRS generally sends penalty notices to taxpayers who fail to file information returns when required or who file incorrect information returns. Filers seeking penalty relief based on reasonable cause must respond to the penalty notice with a statement explaining how the filer qualifies for relief. Under section 6724(f), however, no penalty under section 6721 or 6722 is imposed in the first instance if the educational institution contemporaneously makes a true and accurate certification under penalties of perjury in such form and manner as may be prescribed by the Secretary that it complied with the standards promulgated by the Secretary to obtain the student's TIN. Section 6724(f) is effective for returns required to be filed and statements required to be furnished after December 31, 2015.

Standards for obtaining the student's TIN are set forth in § 1.6050S-1(e)(3)(ii) and (iii) of the existing regulations. These regulations are proposed to be redesignated as § 1.6050S-1(f)(3)(ii) and (iii). Under these standards, the institution does not have to solicit a student's TIN, but may use the TIN that it has in its records. If the institution does not have the student's correct TIN in its records, then it must solicit the TIN in the time and manner described in redesignated § 1.6050S-1(f). To implement section 6724(f), § 1.6050S-1(f)(4) of the proposed regulations has been added to provide that for returns required to be filed and statements required to be furnished after December 31, 2015, the IRS will not impose a penalty against an institution under section 6721 or 6722 for failure to include the student's correct TIN on the return or statement if the institution certifies to the IRS under penalties of perjury in the form and manner prescribed by the Secretary in publications, forms and instructions, or other published guidance at the time of filing of the return that the institution complied with the requirements in § 1.6050S-1(f)(3)(ii) and (iii). However, the proposed regulations make clear that the certification will not protect the institution from penalty if the IRS determines subsequently that the requirements of § 1.6050S-1(f)(3)(ii) and (iii) were not satisfied or if the failure to file correct information returns relates to something other than a failure to provide the correct TIN for the student. In addition, a cross-reference is proposed to be added to the regulations under section 6724 to alert taxpayers that the rules for penalty relief for eligible educational institutions with respect to reporting obligations under section 6050S are contained in § 1.6050S-1(f).

d. *Penalty relief under section 6724(f) for calendar year 2015 Forms 1098-T*

Section 6724(f) requires the IRS to develop procedures enabling an eligible educational institution to avoid imposition of the section 6721 and section 6722 penalty for failure to include a student's correct TIN on the Form 1098-T by certifying under penalties of perjury at the time of filing or furnishing the form that the institution complied with the IRS standards for obtaining a student's TIN. In Announcement 2016-03, I.R.B. 2016-4, the IRS stated that it will not impose penalties under section 6721 or 6722 against an eligible educational institution required to file Forms 1098-T for calendar year 2015 solely because the student's TIN is missing or incorrect.

2. *Other Changes to Regulations Under Section 25A and Section 6050S*

The proposed regulations also update and clarify the regulations under section 25A. The proposed regulations update § 1.25A-2(d) to reflect the changes made by ARRA allowing students to claim the AOTC for expenses paid for course materials (such as books, supplies, and equipment) required for enrollment or attendance, whether or not the course materials are purchased from the institution. Prior to ARRA, the term "qualified tuition and related expenses" included tuition and fees, but did not include course materials, such as books, unless the cost of these materials was a fee that was required to be paid to the institution as a condition of attendance or enrollment. See section 25A(f)(1) and § 1.25A-2(d)(2)(ii).

When Congress enacted the AOTC in 2009, it expanded the definition of qualified tuition and related expenses for purposes of the AOTC to include expenses paid for course materials. See H.R. Conf. Rep. 111-16, 111th Cong., 1st Sess. p. 525 (February 29, 2009). Course materials are qualified expenses only for the AOTC and not for the LLC. See Tax Increase Prevention Act of 2014 (Public Law 113-295, 128 Stat. 4010). The proposed regulations update § 1.25A-2(d) to provide that, for purposes of claiming the AOTC for tax years beginning after December 31, 2008, the definition of qualified tuition and related expenses includes not only tuition and fees required for enrollment or attendance at an eligible educational institution, but also expenses paid for course materials needed for enrollment or attendance at an eligible educational institution. Accordingly, after ARRA, for purposes of claiming the Hope Scholarship Credit and LLC, qualified tuition and related expenses continue to exclude the cost of books, supplies, and equipment if they can be purchased from any vendor. However, for purposes of claiming the AOTC, qualified tuition and related expenses includes the cost of course materials such as books, supplies and equipment that is needed for meaningful attendance or enrollment in a course of study, whether or not the materials are purchased from the institution. The proposed regulations provide an example that illustrates that for purposes of the AOTC qualified tuition and related expenses includes the cost of course material, including books, even if a taxpayer purchases these materials from a vendor other than the institution.

In addition, the proposed regulations add a new section under section 6050S to eliminate uncertainty in the reporting requirements that may result from these proposed amendments to § 1.25A-2(d). Under proposed § 1.6050S-1(a)(2)(i), an institution is not required to report the amount paid or billed for books, supplies, and equipment unless the amount is a fee that must be paid to the eligible educational institution as a condition of enrollment or attendance under § 1.25A-2(d)(2)(ii).

The proposed regulations also clarify the example in § 1.25A-5(e)(2)(ii) regarding the prepayment rule. Under § 1.25A-5(e)(2)(i), if qualified tuition and related expenses are paid during one taxable year for an academic period that begins during the first three months of the taxpayer's next taxable year (that is, in January, February, or March of the next taxable year for calendar year taxpayers), an education tax credit is allowed for the qualified tuition and related expenses only in the taxable year in which the taxpayer pays the expenses. The Treasury Department and the IRS are aware that there is some uncertainty regarding the application of the prepayment rule to amounts paid in the prior year and the current year for an academic period beginning during the current year. The proposed regulations clarify the proper treatment in this situation by expanding the Example in § 1.25A-5(e)(2)(ii) to illustrate that a student who pays part of a semester's tuition in Year 1, and the remainder in Year 2, may claim a credit for Year 1, for the portion of the tuition paid in December Year 1 and a separate credit for Year 2 for the portion of the tuition paid in February Year 2.

The proposed regulations also clarify the rules under § 1.25A-5(f) regarding a refund of qualified tuition and related expenses received from an eligible educational institution. The current regulations do not address the situation where the taxpayer receives a refund in the current taxable year of qualified tuition and related expenses for an academic period beginning in the current taxable year for which payments were made during the prior taxable year under the prepayment rule and payments were made during the current taxable year. To address this situation, the proposed regulations provide that the taxpayer may allocate the refund in any proportion to reduce qualified tuition and related expenses paid in either taxable year, except that the amount of the refund allocated to a taxable year may not exceed the qualified tuition and related expenses paid in the taxable year for the academic period to which the refund relates. The sum of the amounts allocated to each taxable year cannot exceed the amount of the refund. The proposed regulations add an example to illustrate this rule.

Proposed Effective and Applicability Dates

These regulations are proposed to take effect when published in the **Federal Register** as final regulations.

Statement of Availability of IRS Documents

IRS published guidance cited in this preamble is published in the Internal Revenue Bulletin and is available from the Superintendent of Documents, U.S. Government Publishing Office, Washington, DC 20402, or by visiting the IRS website at *http://www.irs.gov*.

Special Analyses

Certain IRS regulations, including this one, are exempt from the requirements of Executive Order 12866, as supplemented and reaffirmed by Executive Order 13563. Therefore, a regulatory impact assessment is not required. It has also been determined that section 553(b) of the Administrative Procedure Act (5 U.S.C. chapter 5) does not apply to these regulations.

It is hereby certified that the collection of information in this notice of proposed rulemaking will not have a significant economic impact on a substantial number of small entities within the meaning of section 601(6) of the Regulatory Flexibility Act (5 U.S.C. chapter 6). The type of small entities to which the regulations may apply are small eligible educational institutions (generally colleges and universities eligible to receive federal financial aid for education under the Higher Education Act of 1965). This certification is based on the fact that few, if any, new eligible educational institutions will be subject to reporting and the changes made by this notice of proposed rulemaking require little, if any, additional time for compliance by institutions currently subject to reporting requirements. The collection of information in this regulation implements the statute and should not require eligible educational institutions to collect information that is not already maintained by the institution. Eligible educational institutions have been subject to information reporting under section 6050S since 1998, and the obligations under the existing final regulations that are the foundation for these proposed regulations are already in place. Any additional information returns required to be filed under this notice of proposed rulemaking should result in few, if any, new eligible educational institutions being subject to reporting that were not already required to file Forms 1098-T. Only eligible educational institutions, not all educational institutions, are subject to these reporting rules. For this purpose, an eligible educational institution means an institution described in section 481 of the Higher Education Act of 1965 (20 U.S.C. 1088) as in effect on the date of enactment (August 5,

1997), and which is eligible to participate in a program under title IV of such act (generally colleges and universities whose students are eligible to receive federal financial aid for higher education). See sections 25A(f)(2) and 6050S(e). Further, this notice of proposed rulemaking contains modifications that should simplify compliance and thereby reduce the time needed to comply with the information reporting obligations under section 6050S. Therefore, a Regulatory Flexibility Analysis under the Regulatory Flexibility Act is not required. Pursuant to section 7805(f) of the Code, this proposed regulation has been submitted to the Chief Counsel for Advocacy of the Small Business Administration for comment on its impact on small businesses. The Internal Revenue Service invites the public to comment on this certification.

Comments and Requests for a Public Hearing

Before these proposed regulations are adopted as final regulations, consideration will be given to any comments that are submitted timely to the IRS as prescribed in this preamble under the "DATES" and "ADDRESSES" headings. The Treasury Department and the IRS request comments on all aspects of the proposed rules. All comments will be available at www.regulations.gov or upon request.

A public hearing has been scheduled for November 30, 2016 at 10:00 a.m. in the IRS Auditorium, Internal Revenue Service Building, 1111 Constitution Avenue, NW, Washington, DC 20224. Due to building security procedures, visitors must enter at the Constitution Avenue entrance. In addition, all visitors must present photo identification to enter the building. Because of access restrictions, visitors will not be admitted beyond the immediate entrance area more than 30 minutes before the hearing starts. For information about having your name placed onto the building access list to attend the hearing, see the "FOR FURTHER INFORMATION CONTACT" section of this preamble.

The rules of 26 CFR 601.601(a)(3) apply to the hearing. Persons who wish to present oral comments at the hearing must submit written or electronic comments by November 1, 2016 and an outline of the topics to be discussed and the time to be devoted to each topic (a signed original and eight (8) copies) by November 1, 2016. A period of 10 minutes will be allotted to each person for making comments. An agenda showing the scheduling of speakers will be prepared after the deadline for receiving outlines has passed. Copies of the agenda will be available free of charge at the hearing.

Drafting Information

The principal author of these proposed regulations is Gerald Semasek of the Office of Associate Chief Counsel (Procedure and Administration) for the proposed regulations under section 6050S and section 6724 and Sheldon Iskow of the Office of Associate Chief Counsel (Income Tax and Accounting) for the proposed regulations under section 25A.

[¶ 49,713] Proposed Amendments of Regulations (REG-123600-16), published in the Federal Register on September 28, 2016.

[Code Sec. 851]

Regulated investment company: Income test: Asset diversification requirements.—Amendments of Reg. § 1.851-2, relating to the income test and the asset diversification requirements that are used to determine whether a corporation may qualify as a regulated investment company (RIC) for federal income tax purposes, is proposed.

AGENCY: Internal Revenue Service (IRS), Treasury.

ACTION: Notice of proposed rulemaking.

SUMMARY: This document provides guidance relating to the income test and the asset diversification requirements that are used to determine whether a corporation may qualify as a regulated investment company (RIC) for federal income tax purposes. These proposed regulations provide guidance to corporations that intend to qualify as RICs.

DATES: Written or electronic comments and requests for a public hearing must be received by December 27, 2016.

ADDRESSES: Send submissions to: CC:PA:LPD:PR (REG-123600-16), room 5203, Internal Revenue Service, PO Box 7604, Ben Franklin Station, Washington, DC 20044. Submissions may be hand delivered Monday through Friday between the hours of 8 am and 4 pm to: CC:PA:LPD:PR (REG-123600-16), Courier's Desk, Internal Revenue Service, 1111 Constitution Avenue, NW, Washington, DC 20224, or sent electronically via the Federal eRulemaking Portal at *www.regulations.gov* (IRS REG-123600-16).

FOR FURTHER INFORMATION CONTACT: Concerning the proposed regulations, Matthew Howard of the Office of Associate Chief Counsel (Financial Institutions and Products) at (202) 317-7053; concerning submissions of comments and requests for a public hearing, Regina Johnson (202) 317-6901 (not toll-free numbers).

SUPPLEMENTARY INFORMATION:

Background and Explanation of Provisions

This document contains amendments to the Income Tax Regulations (26 CFR part 1) relating to RICs. Section 851 of the Internal Revenue Code (Code) sets forth requirements for qualifying as a RIC.

Section 851(a) provides that a RIC is any domestic corporation that (1) at all times during the taxable year is registered under the Investment Company Act of 1940, Pub. L. No. 76-768, 54 Stat. 789 (codified as amended at 15 U.S.C. 80a-1 – 80a-64 (2016)) (the 1940 Act), as a management company or unit investment trust or has in effect an election under the 1940 Act to be treated as a business development company; or (2) is a common trust fund or other similar fund excluded by section

3(c)(3) of the 1940 Act from the definition of "investment company" and is not included in the definition of "common trust fund" by section 584(a).

To be treated as a RIC for a taxable year, a corporation must satisfy the income test set forth in section 851(b). The income test under section 851(b)(2) requires that at least 90 percent of the corporation's gross income for the taxable year be derived from:

(A) dividends, interest, payments with respect to securities loans (as defined in section 512(a)(5)), and gains from the sale or other disposition of stock or securities (as defined in section 2(a)(36) of the [1940 Act]) or foreign currencies, or other income (including but not limited to gains from options, futures or forward contracts) derived with respect to its business of investing in such stock, securities, or currencies, and

(B) net income derived from an interest in a qualified publicly traded partnership (as defined in [section 851(h)]).

Section 851(b)(3) provides that to be treated as a RIC a corporation also must satisfy the following asset diversification requirements at the close of each quarter of the corporation's taxable year:

(A) at least 50 percent of the value of its total assets is represented by—

(i) cash and cash items (including receivables), Government securities and securities of other [RICs], and

(ii) other securities for purposes of this calculation limited, except and to the extent provided in [section 851(e)], in respect of any one issuer to an amount not greater in value than 5 percent of the value of the total assets of the taxpayer and to not more than 10 percent of the outstanding voting securities of such issuer, and

(B) not more than 25 percent of the value of its total assets is invested in—

(i) the securities (other than Government securities or the securities of other [RICs]) of any one issuer,

(ii) the securities (other than the securities of other [RICs]) of two or more issuers which the taxpayer controls and which are determined, under regulations prescribed by the Secretary, to be engaged in the same or similar trades or businesses or related trades or businesses, or

(iii) the securities of one or more qualified publicly traded partnerships (as defined in [section 851(h)]).

These proposed regulations relate to the RIC income test and asset diversification requirements. Section A. of this preamble concerns the meaning of security. Section B. of this preamble addresses inclusions under sections 951(a)(1)(A)(i) and 1293(a). These proposed regulations also revise § 1.851-2(b)(1) of the existing final regulations to merely incorporate changes to section 851(b)(2) since the existing final regulations were published in the **Federal Register** on November 26, 1960, in TD 6500 (25 FR 11910).

A. *Defining Securities*

The income test and asset diversification requirements both use the term "securities." For purposes of the income test, a security is defined by reference to section 2(a)(36) of the 1940 Act, while section 851(c) provides rules and definitions that apply for purposes of the asset diversification requirements of section 851(b)(3) but does not specifically define "security." Section 851(c)(6), however, provides that the terms used in section 851(b)(3) and (c) have the same meaning as when used in the 1940 Act. An asset is therefore a security for purposes of the income test and the asset diversification requirements if it is a security under the 1940 Act.

The Treasury Department and the IRS have in the past addressed whether certain instruments or positions are securities for purposes of section 851. In particular, Rev. Rul. 2006-1 (2006-1 CB 261) concludes that a derivative contract with respect to a commodity index is not a security for purposes of section 851(b)(2). The ruling also holds that income from such a contract is not qualifying other income for purposes of section 851(b)(2) because that income is not derived with respect to the RIC's business of investing in stocks, securities, or currencies. Rev. Rul. 2006-1 was modified and clarified by Rev. Rul. 2006-31 (2006-1 CB 1133), which states that Rev. Rul. 2006-1 was not intended to preclude a conclusion that income from certain instruments (such as certain structured notes) that create commodity exposure for the holder is qualifying income under section 851(b)(2).

After the issuance of Rev. Rul. 2006-31, the IRS received a number of private letter ruling requests concerning whether certain instruments that provide RICs with commodity exposure were securities for purposes of the income test and the asset diversification requirements. By 2010, the IRS was devoting substantial resources to these private letter ruling requests. Moreover, it is not clear whether Congress intended to allow RICs to invest in securities that provided commodity exposure. Consequently, in July 2011, the IRS notified taxpayers that the IRS would not issue further private letter rulings addressing specific proposed RIC commodity-related investments while the IRS reviewed the issues and considered guidance of broader applicability.

Finally, determining whether certain investments that provide RICs with commodity exposure are securities for purposes of the income test and the asset diversification requirements requires the IRS implicitly to determine what is a security within the meaning of section 2(a)(36) of the 1940 Act. Section 38 of the 1940 Act, however, grants exclusive rulemaking authority under the 1940 Act to the Securities and Exchange Commission (SEC), including "defining accounting, technical, and trade terms" used in the 1940 Act. Any future guidance regarding whether particular financial instruments, including investments that provide RICs with commodity exposure, are securities for purposes of the 1940 Act is therefore within the jurisdiction of the SEC.

Section 2.01 of Rev. Proc. 2016-3 (2016-1 IRB 126) provides that the IRS may decline to issue a letter ruling or a determination letter when appropriate in the interest of sound tax administration (including due to resource constraints) or on other grounds whenever warranted by the facts or circumstances of a particular case. If the IRS determines that it is not in the interest of sound tax administration to issue a letter ruling or determination letter due to resource constraints, the IRS will adopt a consistent approach with respect to taxpayers that request a ruling on the same issue. The IRS will also consider adding the issue to the no rule list at the first opportunity.

The Treasury Department and the IRS have reviewed the issues, considered the concerns expressed, considered resource constraints, and determined that the IRS should no longer issue letter rulings on questions relating to the treatment of a corporation as a RIC that require a determination of whether a financial instrument or position is a security under the 1940 Act. Contemporaneously with the publication of these proposed regulations, the Treasury Department and the IRS are issuing Rev. Proc. 2016-50 (2016-43 IRB __), which provides that the IRS ordinarily will not issue rulings or determination letters on any issue relating to the treatment of a corporation as a RIC that requires a determination of whether a financial instrument or position is a security under the 1940 Act. Thus, for example, the IRS ordinarily will not issue a ruling on whether income is of a type described in the income test of section 851(b)(2) if that ruling depends on whether an instrument is a security under the 1940 Act.

The Treasury Department and the IRS request comments as to whether Rev. Rul. 2006-1, Rev. Rul. 2006-31, and other previously issued guidance that involves determinations of whether a financial instrument or position held by a RIC is a security under the 1940 Act should be withdrawn effective as of the date of publication in the **Federal Register** of a Treasury decision adopting these proposed regulations as final regulations.

B. *Inclusions Under Section 951(a)(1)(A)(i) or 1293(a)*

In certain circumstances, a U.S. person may be required under section 951(a)(1)(A)(i) or 1293(a) to include in taxable income certain earnings of a foreign corporation in which the U.S. person holds an interest, without regard to whether the foreign corporation makes a corresponding distribution of cash or property to the U.S. person. Section 851(b) was amended by the Tax Reduction Act of 1975, Pub. L. No. 94-12, section 602, 89 Stat. 26, 58 (the "1975 Act") (for inclusions under section 951(a)(1)(A)(i)), and by the Tax Reform Act of 1986, Pub. L. No. 99-514, section 1235, 100 Stat. 2085, 2575 (the "1986 Act") (for inclusions under section 1293(a)), to specify how a RIC treats amounts included in income under section 951(a)(1)(A)(i) or 1293(a) for purposes of the income test of section 851(b)(2). The language added in those amendments provides:

> For purposes of [section 851(b)(2)], there shall be treated as dividends amounts included in gross income under section 951(a)(1)(A)(i) or 1293(a) for the taxable year to the extent that, under section 959(a)(1) or 1293(c) (as the case may be), there is a distribution out of the earnings and profits of the taxable year which are attributable to the amounts so included.

The significance of treating an inclusion as a dividend under section 851 is that a dividend is qualifying income under section 851(b)(2). The amendments to section 851(b) made by the 1975 Act and the 1986 Act unambiguously condition dividend treatment of an inclusion under section 951(a)(1)(A)(i) or 1293(a) on a distribution from the foreign corporation's earnings and profits attributable to the amount included. Absent a distribution, there is no support in the Code for treating an inclusion under section 951(a)(1)(A)(i) or 1293(a) as a dividend under section 851.

Notwithstanding the distribution required by section 851(b), in certain circumstances the IRS has previously issued letter rulings under section 851(b)(2) that permit an inclusion under section 951(a)(1)(A)(i) or 1293(a) to qualify as "other income" derived with respect to a RIC's business of investing in currencies or 1940 Act stock or securities even in the absence of a distribution. Reading section 851(b)(2) in this manner ignores the requirement in section 851(b) that amounts be distributed in order to treat these inclusions as dividends. This distribution requirement is a more specific provision than the other income clause. In addition, it cannot be suggested that the distribution requirement was superseded by the other income clause because the other income clause and the distribution requirement for inclusions under section 1293(a) were both added by the 1986 Act. Therefore, these proposed regulations specify that an inclusion under section 951(a)(1)(A)(i) or 1293(a) is treated as a dividend for purposes of section 851(b)(2) only to the extent that the distribution requirement in section 851(b) is met. These proposed regulations further provide that, for purposes of section 851(b)(2), an inclusion under section 951(a)(1) or 1293(a) does not qualify as other income derived with respect to a RIC's business of investing in stock, securities, or currencies.

Proposed Effective/Applicability Date

The rule in § 1.851-2(b)(2)(iii) of the proposed regulations applies to taxable years that begin on or after the date that is 90 days after the date of publication in the **Federal Register** of a Treasury decision adopting these proposed regulations as final regulations.

Special Analyses

Certain IRS regulations, including this one, are exempt from the requirements of Executive Order 12866, as supplemented and reaffirmed by Executive Order 13563. Therefore, a regulatory impact assessment is not required. It also has been determined that section 553(b) of the Administrative Procedure Act (5 U.S.C. chapter 5) does not apply to these regulations, and because the regulations do not impose a collection of information on small entities, the Regulatory Flexibility Act (5 U.S.C. chapter 6) does not apply. Pursuant to section 7805(f) of the Internal Revenue Code, this notice of proposed rulemaking will be submitted to the Chief Counsel for Advocacy of the Small Business Administration for comment on its impact on small business.

Comments and Requests for a Public Hearing

Before these proposed regulations are adopted as final regulations, consideration will be given to any comments that are submitted timely to the IRS as prescribed in this preamble under the "Addresses" heading. The Treasury Department and the IRS specifically request comments on the clarity of the proposed regulations and how they can be made easier to understand. All comments will be made available for public inspection at www.regulations.gov or upon request. A public hearing will be scheduled if requested in writing by any person that timely submits written comments. If a public hearing is scheduled, notice of the date, time, and place for the public hearing will be published in the **Federal Register**.

Drafting Information

The principal author of these proposed regulations is Matthew Howard, Office of Associate Chief Council (Financial Institutions and Products). However, other personnel from the Treasury Department and the IRS participated in their development.

[¶49,714] Proposed Amendments of Regulations and Partial Withdrawal of Notice of Proposed Regulations (REG-122855-15), published in the Federal Register on October 5, 2016.

[Code Secs. 704, 707 and 752]

Partners and partnerships: Transactions between: Disguised sales of property: Liabilities: Allocation of: Recourse liabilities: Partner's share of recourse liabilities.—Amendments of Reg. §§1.704-1, 1.707-0, 1.707-5, 1.707-9, 1.752-0 and 1.752-2, addressing when certain obligations to restore a deficit balance in a partner's capital account are disregarded under section 704 of the Internal Revenue Code (Code) and when partnership liabilities are treated as recourse liabilities under section 752, are proposed. Amendments of Reg. §1.752-2, proposed on January 30, 2014, are withdrawn.

AGENCY: Internal Revenue Service (IRS), Treasury.

ACTION: Partial withdrawal of notice of proposed rulemaking and notice of proposed rulemaking, including by cross reference to temporary regulations.

SUMMARY: This document contains proposed regulations that incorporate the text of related temporary regulations and withdraws a portion of a notice of proposed rulemaking (REG-119305-11) to the extent not adopted by final regulations. This document also contains new proposed regulations addressing when certain obligations to restore a deficit balance in a partner's capital account are disregarded under section 704 of the Internal Revenue Code (Code) and when partnership liabilities are treated as recourse liabilities under section 752. These regulations would affect partnerships and their partners.

DATES: The notice of proposed rulemaking under sections 707 and 752 that was published in the **Federal Register** on January 30, 2014 (REG-119305-11, 79 FR 4826), is partially withdrawn as of October 5, 2016. Written or electronic comments and requests for a public hearing must be received by January 3, 2017.

ADDRESSES: Send submissions to: CC:PA:LPD:PR (REG-122855-15), room 5203, Internal Revenue Service, PO Box 7604, Ben Franklin Station, Washington, DC 20044. Submissions may be hand-delivered Monday through Friday between the hours of 8 a.m. and 4 p.m. to: CC:PA:LPD:PR (REG-122855-15), Courier's Desk, Internal Revenue Service, 1111 Constitution Avenue, N.W., Washington, DC, or sent electronically, via the Federal eRulemaking Portal site at http://www.regulations.gov (indicate IRS and REG-122855-15).

FOR FURTHER INFORMATION CONTACT: Concerning the proposed regulations, Caroline E. Hay or Deane M. Burke, (202) 317-5279; concerning submissions of comments and requests for a public hearing, Regina L. Johnson, (202) 317-6901 (not toll-free numbers).

SUPPLEMENTARY INFORMATION: In addition to these proposed regulations, the Treasury Department and the IRS are publishing in the Rules and Regulations section in this issue of the **Federal Register**: (1) final regulations under section 707 concerning disguised sales and under section 752 regarding the allocation of excess nonrecourse liabilities and (2) temporary regulations concerning a partner's share of partnership liabilities for purposes of section 707 and the treatment of certain payment obligations under section 752.

Paperwork Reduction Act

The collection of information related to these proposed regulations under section 752 is reported on Form 8275, Disclosure Statement, and has been reviewed in accordance with the Paperwork Reduction Act (44 U.S.C. 3507) and approved by the Office of Management and Budget under control number 1545-0889. Comments concerning the collection of information and the accuracy of estimated average annual burden and suggestions for reducing this burden should be sent to the Office of Management and Budget, Attn: Desk Officer for the Department of the Treasury, Office of Information and Regulatory Affairs, Washington, DC 20503, with copies to the Internal Revenue Service, IRS Reports Clearance Officer, SE:W:CAR:MP:T:T:SP, Washington, DC 20224. Comments on the burden associated with this collection of information should be received by December 5, 2016.

The collection of information in these proposed regulations is in proposed § 1.752-2(b)(3)(ii)(D) (which cross references the requirement in § 1.752-2T(b)(3)(ii)(D)). This information is required by the IRS to ensure that section 752 of the Code and applicable regulations are properly applied for allocations of partnership liabilities. The respondents will be partners and partnerships.

An agency may not conduct or sponsor, and a person is not required to respond to, a collection of information unless it displays a valid control number assigned by the Office of Management and Budget.

Books or records relating to a collection of information must be retained as long as their contents may become material in the administration of any internal revenue law. Generally, tax returns and tax return information are confidential, as required by section 6103.

Background

1. *Overview*

This document contains proposed amendments to the Income Tax Regulations (26 CFR part 1) under sections 704, 707, and 752 of the Code. On January 30, 2014, the Treasury Department and the IRS published a notice of proposed rulemaking in the **Federal Register** (REG-119305-11, 79 FR 4826) to amend the then existing regulations under section 707 relating to disguised sales of property to or by a partnership and under section 752 concerning the treatment of partnership liabilities (the 2014 Proposed Regulations). The 2014 Proposed Regulations provided certain technical rules intended to clarify the application of the disguised sale rules under section 707. The 2014 Proposed Regulations also contained rules regarding the sharing of partnership recourse and nonrecourse liabilities under section 752.

A public hearing on the 2014 Proposed Regulations was not requested or held, but the Treasury Department and the IRS received written comments. After consideration of, and in response to, the comments on the 2014 Proposed Regulations, the Treasury Department and the IRS are withdrawing the 2014 Proposed Regulations under § 1.752-2 and publishing new proposed regulations under § 1.752-2, as well as proposed regulations under section 704. Concurrently in this issue of the **Federal Register**, the Treasury Department and the IRS are also publishing final regulations that adopt, as modified, the 2014 Proposed Regulations under section 707 and § 1.752-3, and temporary regulations under sections 707 and 752.

2. *Summary of Applicable Law*

Section 752 separates partnership liabilities into two categories: recourse liabilities and nonrecourse liabilities. Section 1.752-1(a)(1) provides that a partnership liability is a recourse liability to the extent that any partner or related person bears the economic risk of loss (EROL) for that liability under § 1.752-2. Section 1.752-1(a)(2) provides that a partnership liability is a nonrecourse liability to the extent that no partner or related person bears the EROL for that liability under § 1.752-2.

A partner generally bears the EROL for a partnership liability if the partner or related person has an obligation to make a payment to any person within the meaning of § 1.752-2(b). For purposes of determining the extent to which a partner or related person has an obligation to make a payment, an obligation to restore a deficit capital account upon liquidation of the partnership under the section 704(b) regulations is taken into account. Further, for this purpose, § 1.752-2(b)(6) of the existing regulations presumes that partners and related persons who have payment obligations actually perform those obligations, irrespective of their net worth, unless the facts and circumstances indicate a plan to circumvent or avoid the obligation (the satisfaction presumption). However, the satisfaction presumption is subject to an anti-abuse rule in § 1.752-2(j) pursuant to which a payment obligation of a partner or related person may be disregarded or treated as an obligation of another person if facts and circumstances indicate that a principal purpose of the arrangement is to eliminate the partner's EROL with respect to that obligation or create the appearance of the partner or related person bearing the EROL when the substance is otherwise. Under the existing rules, the satisfaction presumption is also subject to a disregarded entity net value requirement under § 1.752-2(k) pursuant to which, for purposes of determining the extent to which a partner bears the EROL for a partnership liability, a payment obligation of a disregarded entity is taken into account only to the extent of the net value of the disregarded entity as of the allocation date that is allocated to the partnership liability.

3. *2014 Proposed Regulations*

As discussed in greater detail in the Summary of Comments and Explanation of Provisions section of this preamble, § 1.752-2 of the 2014 Proposed Regulations generally, among other things, (1) provided that a partner's or related person's obligation to make a payment with respect to a partnership liability (excluding those imposed by state law) would not be recognized for purposes of section 752 unless each recognition factor was satisfied; (2) applied the list of recognition factors to all payment obligations under § 1.752-2(b), including a partner's obligation to restore a deficit capital account upon liquidation of a partnership (deficit restoration obligations, or DROs) as provided under the section 704(b) regulations; and (3) provided generally that a payment obligation would be recognized to the extent of the net value of a partner or related person as of the allocation date.

After consideration of the comments received on the 2014 Proposed Regulations, the Treasury Department and the IRS are reconsidering the rules under section 752 regarding payment obligations that are recognized under § 1.752-2(b)(3), the satisfaction presumption under § 1.752-2(b)(6), the anti-abuse rule provided in § 1.752-2(j), and the net value requirement as provided in § 1.752-2(k). Accordingly, the Treasury Department and the IRS are withdrawing § 1.752-2 of the 2014 Proposed Regulations and publishing these new proposed regulations that would amend existing regulations under sections 704 and 752. These new provisions, and comments received on the 2014 Proposed Regulations that are pertinent to these new provisions, are discussed in the Summary of Comments and Explanation of Provisions section of the preamble that follows.

4. *Final and Temporary Regulations Under Section 707 and Requests for Comments*

As previously mentioned, the Treasury Department and the IRS are concurrently publishing temporary regulations under section 707 (concerning disguised sales) (the 707 Temporary Regulations) and section 752 (concerning recourse liabilities, in particular bottom dollar payment obligations) (the 752 Temporary Regulations), and final regulations under section 707 and § 1.752-3. The temporary regulations are incorporated by cross reference in these proposed regulations. Notably, the 707 Temporary Regulations provide that, for disguised sale purposes, partners determine their share of any partnership liability in the manner in which excess nonrecourse liabilities are allocated under § 1.752-3(a)(3) (with certain limitations). Generally, a partner's share of the excess nonrecourse liability is determined in accordance with the partner's share of partnership profits taking into account all the facts and circumstances relating to the economic arrangement of the partners. The Treasury Department and the IRS recognize that taxpayers may require further guidance regarding reasonable methods for determining a partner's share of partnership profits under § 1.752-3(a)(3) for disguised sale purposes, especially given that a partner's share may change from year to year or differ with respect to different partnership assets and believe it may be appropriate to issue administrative guidance for this purpose. Accordingly, comments are requested regarding possible safe harbors and reasonable methods for determining a partner's share of profits, taking into account all of the relevant facts and circumstances relating to the economic arrangement of the partners. The preamble to the temporary regulations describes the provisions in greater detail. In addition, the final regulations under section 707 also include a request for comments concerning the exception for reimbursements of preformation capital expenditures under § 1.707-4(d), which is described in greater detail in the preamble to the final regulations.

Summary of Comments and Explanation of Provisions

1. *Rights of Reimbursement*

Section 1.752-2(b)(1) provides that, except as otherwise provided in § 1.752-2, a partner bears the EROL for a partnership liability to the extent that, if the partnership constructively liquidated, the partner or related person would be obligated to make a payment to any person (or a contribution to the partnership) because that liability becomes due and payable and the partner or related person would not be entitled to reimbursement from another partner or a person that is a related person to another partner. Section 1.752-2(b)(1) presumes that, in the constructive liquidation, the partnership has a value of zero with which to pay its liabilities. Under the 2014 Proposed Regulations, a partner would not bear the EROL under § 1.752-2(b)(1) if the partner or related person is entitled to a reimbursement from "any person." Commenters noted that a reimbursement from "any person" would include a reimbursement from the partnership, which is contrary to the intent of the regulations under section 752. A right to be reimbursed by the partnership should be disregarded, as § 1.752-2(b)(1) presumes that the partnership would not be able to pay the liability or reimburse the partner. The Treasury Department and the IRS agree with the concerns expressed in the comments; therefore, these proposed regulations do not include the changes to § 1.752-2(b)(1) that were in the 2014 Proposed Regulations.

2. *Arrangements Part of a Plan to Circumvent or Avoid an Obligation*

The 2014 Proposed Regulations provided that a partner's or related person's obligation to make a payment with respect to a partnership liability (excluding those imposed by state law) will not be recognized for purposes of section 752 unless: (1) the partner or related person is (A) required to maintain a commercially reasonable net worth throughout the term of the payment obligation or (B) subject to commercially reasonable contractual restrictions on transfers of assets for inadequate consideration; (2) the partner or related person is required periodically to provide commercially reasonable documentation regarding the partner's or related person's financial condition; (3) the term of the payment obligation does not end prior to the term of the partnership liability; (4) the payment obligation does not require that the primary obligor or any other obligor with respect to the partnership liability directly or indirectly hold money or other liquid assets in an amount that exceeds the reasonable needs of such obligor; (5) the partner or related person received arm's length consideration for assuming the payment obligation; and (6) the obligation is not a bottom dollar guarantee or indemnity (recognition factors).

Commenters expressed concerns with the all-or-nothing approach in the 2014 Proposed Regulations. One commenter noted that a partner could cause an obligation to deliberately fail one of the recognition factors so as to cause a liability to be treated as nonrecourse if such characterization potentially would be beneficial to such partner, even if that partner did, in fact, bear the EROL. This commenter also noted that commercial arrangements rarely satisfy each and every one of the recognition factors and commercial practices tend to change over time, thereby rendering the recognition factors out of date. This commenter recommended that regulations instead provide a nonexclusive list of facts and circumstances containing as factors many of the items identified in the 2014 Proposed Regulations.

The Treasury Department and the IRS believe that the concerns expressed by the commenters are valid and thus propose to move the list of factors to an anti-abuse rule in § 1.752-2(j), other than the recognition factors concerning bottom dollar guarantees and indemnities, which are addressed in the

752 Temporary Regulations. Under the anti-abuse rule, factors are weighed to determine whether a payment obligation should be respected. The list of factors in the anti-abuse rule in these proposed regulations is nonexclusive, and the weight to be given to any particular factor depends on the particular case. Furthermore, the presence or absence of any particular factor, in itself, is not necessarily indicative of whether or not a payment obligation is recognized under § 1.752-2(b).

In addition to comments addressing the recognition factor approach in the 2014 Proposed Regulations, the Treasury Department and the IRS received specific comments regarding the individual recognition factors. With respect to the first recognition factor regarding commercially reasonable net worth or restrictions on transfers, one commenter agreed that an obligor should have the wherewithal to make a payment to the extent required for the entire duration of its obligation, but believed that this concern is alleviated by the anti-abuse rule in the current regulations under § 1.752-2(j). This commenter suggested that the anti-abuse rule in § 1.752-2(j) contain additional examples to illustrate abusive or problematic situations. Another commenter noted that the 2014 Proposed Regulations did not address the consequences if a partner or related person breaches its payment obligation under an agreement regarding net worth or restrictions on transfers and suggested that the regulations address such consequences in an anti-abuse rule (for example, a partner's or related person's payment obligation may be disregarded if it is determined that the creditor lacked the intent to enforce its rights under the agreement).

With respect to the first two recognition factors, commenters expressed concerns with the use of the terms "commercially reasonable" and "commercially reasonable documentation." One commenter believed that these terms are vague and subjective and would require partnerships to make difficult judgments as to whether these recognition factors have been met prior to allocating any partnership liability. Another commenter noted that the "commercially reasonable documentation" recognition factor did not specify who should receive the documentation and that such documentation should be provided to the lender.

Moving the list of factors to an anti-abuse rule should alleviate some of the concerns expressed regarding both whether a payment obligor has the wherewithal to pay and the use of the term "commercially reasonable." The proposed regulations also revise the first two factors to provide clarity by limiting the first factor to examine solely whether the partner or related person is subject to commercially reasonable contractual restrictions that protect the likelihood of payment, such as restrictions on transfers for inadequate consideration or equity distributions. In addition, the proposed regulations do not retain the subjective commercially reasonable net worth factor, but instead include a new factor that examines whether the payment obligation restricts the creditor from promptly pursuing payment following a default on the partnership liability or whether there are other arrangements that indicate a plan to delay collection.

The proposed regulations retain the use of the "commercially reasonable" standard, however, because different facts may require a different standard of whether contractual restrictions and documentation are "commercially reasonable" with respect to a particular industry, and the flexible nature of the term is helpful in informing partnerships and their partners that obligations should be consistent with what is customary in the marketplace. With respect to the second recognition factor regarding documentation, these proposed regulations also clarify that the factor examines whether commercially reasonable documentation was provided to the party that benefits from the payment obligation (for example, the creditor in the case of a guarantee or the indemnified party in the case of an indemnification arrangement).

Commenters also noted that certain recognition factors do not take into account industry specific practices. One commenter pointed out that the requirement that a payment obligation last throughout the full term of the partnership's loan is contrary to commercial practice in some cases. In particular, the commenter noted that, in the real estate industry context, it is common for a construction loan to be guaranteed until the property reaches a required level of stabilization. This commenter did believe, however, that a payment obligation should be disregarded if the guarantor or other obligor has an unrestricted unilateral right to terminate the obligation at will, including immediately before the obligation becomes due and payable. Commenters also noted that the recognition factor that would require arm's length consideration is not commercial, as a partner is often willing to enter into a guarantee or other payment obligation with respect to a partnership liability because the partner will benefit from the liability in the obligor's capacity as a partner. The Treasury Department and the IRS agree with these recommendations; thus, these proposed regulations take into account industry practice with respect to terminations of payment obligations and do not include the arm's length consideration factor.

A commenter also expressed concerns regarding the recognition factor that examines whether a primary obligor or any other obligor with respect to the partnership liability is required to hold assets in an amount that exceeds the reasonable needs of the obligor. The commenter noted that partnership agreements often include restrictions on distributions before certain hurdles are satisfied for a variety of reasons, such as to protect the interests of preferred partners or for prudent business management. Another commenter agreed with the legal theory underpinning the recognition factor (to address fact patterns in which the taxpayer intended and acted to ensure the partnership maintained sufficient collateral to repay the creditor without exposing the obligor to meaningful liability) but suggested that commercially required or prudent reserves not be considered. Both commenters suggested that an example illustrating the restrictions that violate this factor would be helpful.

The commenters' concerns should be largely addressed by making this recognition factor one of many examined under the anti-abuse rule that looks to whether there is a plan to circumvent or avoid the obligation. Under the anti-abuse rule, an obligor's retention of assets for its reasonable foreseeable needs (such as for commercial or prudent business reasons) generally would not, on its own, indicate that there is a plan to circumvent or avoid the obligation.

Finally, the proposed regulations provide two additional factors that indicate when a plan to circumvent or avoid an obligation exists. The first provides that, in the case of a guarantee or similar arrangement, the terms of the liability would be substantially the same had the partner or related person not agreed to provide the guarantee. This factor indicates that the guarantee was not required by the lender, presumably because the partnership had sufficient assets to satisfy its obligation. The second additional factor examines whether the creditor or other party benefiting from the obligation received executed documents with respect to the payment obligation from the partner or related person before, or within a commercially reasonable time after, the creation of the obligation.

3. *Deficit Restoration Obligations*

The 2014 Proposed Regulations applied the list of recognition factors discussed in Section 2 of this Summary of Comments and Explanation of Provisions to all payment obligations under § 1.752-2(b), including a DRO, as provided under the section 704(b) regulations. Commenters explained that not all of the recognition factors could be satisfied with respect to a DRO. In addition, commenters suggested that the regulations under section 704(b) be amended to clarify that if a DRO is not given effect under section 752, it should not be given effect under section 704(b).

A DRO is an obligation to the partnership that is imposed by the partnership agreement. In contrast, a guarantee or indemnity is a contractual obligation outside the partnership agreement. As a result of this difference and based on the comments on the 2014 Proposed Regulations, the proposed regulations refine the list of factors applicable to DROs and clarify the interaction of section 752 with section 704 regarding DROs. Under § 1.704-1(b)(2)(ii)(*c*)(*2*) of the existing regulations, a partner's DRO is not respected if the facts and circumstances indicate a plan to circumvent or avoid the partner's DRO. These proposed regulations add a list of factors to § 1.704-1(b)(2)(ii)(*c*) that are similar to the factors in the proposed anti-abuse rule under § 1.752-2(j), but specific to DROs, to indicate when a plan to circumvent or avoid an obligation exists. Under the proposed regulations, the following factors indicate a plan to circumvent or avoid an obligation: (1) the partner is not subject to commercially reasonable provisions for enforcement and collection of the obligation; (2) the partner is not required to provide (either at the time the obligation is made or periodically) commercially reasonable documentation regarding the partner's financial condition to the partnership; (3) the obligation ends or could, by its terms, be terminated before the liquidation of the partner's interest in the partnership or when the partner's capital account as provided in § 1.704-1(b)(2)(iv) is negative; and (4) the terms of the obligation are not provided to all the partners in the partnership in a timely manner.

Notwithstanding the proposed factors, the Treasury Department and the IRS have concerns with whether and to what extent it is appropriate to recognize DROs (and certain partner notes treated as DROs) as meaningful payment obligations. Many DROs are triggered only on the liquidation of a partnership. However, some partnerships are intended to have perpetual life and other partnerships can effectively cease operations but not actually liquidate; therefore, a partner's DRO may never be required to be satisfied. In addition, some DROs can be terminated or significantly reduced in a manner that may not be appropriate, and therefore, the DRO similarly may never be triggered. The Treasury Department and the IRS request comments on the extent to which such DROs should be recognized. In addition, certain partner notes are treated as DROs under § 1.704-1(b)(2)(ii)(*c*)(*1*) and (*3*) of these proposed regulations. The Treasury Department and the IRS also request comments concerning whether these obligations should continue to be treated as DROs.

4. *Exculpatory Liabilities*

One commenter suggested that the 2014 Proposed Regulations would result in more liabilities being characterized as nonrecourse liabilities, in particular, so-called, "exculpatory liabilities," and urged the Treasury Department and the IRS to provide guidance with respect to such liabilities. An exculpatory liability is a liability that is recourse to an entity under state law and section 1001, but no partner bears the EROL within the meaning of section 752. Thus, the liability is treated as nonrecourse for section 752 purposes. The Treasury Department and the IRS are studying the treatment of exculpatory liabilities under sections 704 and 752 and agree that guidance is warranted in this area. However, the treatment of exculpatory liabilities is beyond the scope of these proposed regulations. The Treasury Department and the IRS seek additional comments regarding the proper treatment of an exculpatory liability under regulations under section 704(b) and the effect of such a liability's classification under section 1001. Further, the Treasury Department and the IRS request additional comments addressing the allocation of an exculpatory liability among multiple assets and possible methods for calculating minimum gain with respect to such liability, such as the so-called "floating lien" approach (whereby all the assets in the entity, including cash, are considered to be subject to the exculpatory liability) or a specific allocation approach.

5. *Net Value*

Section 1.752-2(b)(6) of the existing regulations provides that, for purposes of determining the extent to which a partner or related person has a payment obligation and the EROL, it is assumed that all partners and related persons who have obligations to make payments actually perform those obligations, irrespective of their actual net worth, unless the facts and circumstances indicate a plan to circumvent or avoid the obligation. See § 1.752-2(b)(6), cross referencing § 1.752-2(j) and (k). Under the anti-abuse rule in § 1.752-2(j), a payment obligation is disregarded if there is a plan to circumvent or avoid such obligation. Section 1.752-2(k)(1) provides that, when determining the extent to which a partner bears the EROL for a partnership liability, a payment obligation of a business entity that is disregarded as an entity separate from its owner under section 856(i), section 1361(b)(3), or § § 301.7701-1 through 301.7701-3 of the Procedure and Administration Regulations (a disregarded entity) is taken into account only to the extent of the net value of the disregarded entity as of the allocation date that is allocated to the partnership liability. Section 1.752-2(k)(2)(i) provides, in part, that net value is the fair market value of all assets owned by the disregarded entity that may be subject to creditors' claims under local law less all obligations of the disregarded entity that do not constitute § 1.752-2(b)(1) payment obligations of the disregarded entity.

The 2014 Proposed Regulations provided that, in determining the extent to which a partner or related person other than an individual or a decedent's estate bears the EROL for a partnership liability other than a trade payable, a payment obligation is recognized only to the extent of the net value of the partner or related person that, as of the allocation date, is allocated to the liability, as determined under § 1.752-2(k). The 2014 Proposed Regulations also provided that the partner must provide a statement concerning the net value of the payment obligor to the partnership. The preamble to the 2014 Proposed Regulations requested comments concerning whether the net value rule should also apply to individuals and estates and whether the regulations should consolidate these rules under § 1.752-2(k).

Commenters expressed concerns that an expansion of the net value rule would add considerable burden and expense to taxpayers and would likely lead to time consuming and costly disputes regarding valuations. Another commenter explained that taxpayers have often avoided the net value regulations (by not using disregarded entities) or have applied the regulations only when the disregarded entity has minimal or no assets.

Commenters suggested that if the net value rule is retained, § 1.752-2(k) should be extended to all partners and related persons other than individuals. One commenter expressed concerns that a partner who may be treated as bearing the EROL with respect to a partnership liability would have to provide information regarding the net value of the payment obligor, which is unnecessarily intrusive. Another commenter believed that if the rules requiring net value were extended to all partners in partnerships, the attempt to achieve more realistic substance would be accompanied by a corresponding increase in the potential for manipulation.

The Treasury Department and the IRS remain concerned with ensuring that a partner or related person only be presumed to satisfy its payment obligation to the extent that such partner or related person would be able to pay on the obligation. After consideration of the comments, however, the Treasury Department and the IRS agree that expanding the application of the net value rules under § 1.752-2(k) may lead to more litigation and may unduly burden taxpayers. Furthermore, net value as provided in § 1.752-2(k) may not accurately take into account the future earnings of a business entity, which normally factor into lending decisions. Therefore, the Treasury Department and the IRS propose to remove § 1.752-2(k) and instead create a new presumption under the anti-abuse rule in § 1.752-2(j). Under the presumption in the proposed regulations, evidence of a plan to circumvent or avoid an obligation is deemed to exist if the facts and circumstances indicate that there is not a reasonable expectation that the payment obligor will have the ability to make the required payments if the payment obligation becomes due and payable. A payment obligor includes disregarded entities (including grantor trusts). These proposed regulations also add an example to illustrate the application of the anti-abuse rule when the payment obligor is an underfunded entity. Under these proposed regulations, § 1.752-2(b)(6) continues to presume that payment obligations with respect to a partnership liability will be satisfied unless evidence of a plan to circumvent or avoid the obligation exists as determined under § 1.752-2(j). If evidence of a plan to circumvent or avoid the obligation exists or is deemed to exist, the obligation is not recognized under § 1.752-2(b) and therefore the partnership liability is treated as a nonrecourse liability under § 1.752-1(a)(2).

Proposed Applicability Dates

The amendments to § 1.704-1 are proposed to apply on or after the date these regulations are published as final regulations in the **Federal Register**. The amendments to § 1.752-2 are proposed to apply to liabilities incurred or assumed by a partnership and to payment obligations imposed or undertaken with respect to a partnership liability on or after the date these regulations are published as final regulations in the **Federal Register**. Partnerships and their partners may rely on these proposed regulations prior to the date they are published as final regulations in the **Federal Register**. However, the rules in § 1.752-2(k) still apply to disregarded entities until the proposed regulations are published as final regulations in the **Federal Register**.

Some commenters were concerned that the 2014 Proposed Regulations "delinked" the regulations under sections 704 and 752 concerning DROs, that is, that a DRO may somehow still be recognized under section 704 despite not meeting the requirements to be recognized as a payment obligation under section 752. DROs are subject to the bottom dollar payment obligation rules in the 752 Temporary Regulations, but the rules in these proposed regulations concerning DROs will not be effective prior to the date they are published as final regulations in the **Federal Register**. However, these proposed regulations allow partnerships and their partners to rely on the proposed regulations, which should address this concern.

Special Analyses

Certain IRS regulations, including this one, are exempt from the requirements of Executive Order 12866, as supplemented and reaffirmed by Executive Order 13563. Therefore, a regulatory impact assessment is not required. It also has been determined that section 553(b) of the Administrative Procedure Act (5 U.S.C. chapter 5) does not apply to these regulations. It is hereby certified that the collection of information in these regulations will not have a significant economic impact on a substantial number of small entities. This certification is based on the fact that the amount of time necessary to report the required information will be minimal in that it requires partnerships (including partnerships that may be small entities) to provide information they already maintain or can easily obtain to the IRS. Moreover, it should take a partnership no more than 2 hours to satisfy the information requirement in these regulations. Accordingly, a Regulatory Flexibility Analysis under the Regulatory Flexibility Act (5 U.S.C. chapter 6) does not apply. Pursuant to section 7805(f) of the Code, this notice of proposed rulemaking has been submitted to the Chief Counsel for Advocacy of the Small Business Administration for comment on its impact on small business.

Comments and Requests for a Public Hearing

Before these proposed regulations are adopted as final regulations, consideration will be given to any written comments (a signed original and eight (8) copies) or electronic comments that are submitted timely to the IRS. The Treasury Department and the IRS request comments on all aspects of the proposed regulations. All comments will be available for public inspection and copying at www.regulations.gov or upon request. A public hearing will be scheduled if requested in writing by a person who timely submits written comments. If a public hearing is scheduled, notice of the date, time, and place of the hearing will be published in the **Federal Register**.

Drafting Information

The principal authors of these regulations are Caroline E. Hay and Deane M. Burke of the Office of the Associate Chief Counsel (Passthroughs & Special Industries), IRS. However, other personnel from the Treasury Department and the IRS participated in their development.

[¶49,715] Proposed Amendments of Regulations (REG-108934-16), published in the Federal Register on October 13, 2016.

[Code Sec. 7122]

Offers in compromise: User fee: Fee increase.—Amendments of Reg. §300.3, affecting taxpayers who wish to pay their liabilities through offers in compromise, is proposed.

AGENCY: Internal Revenue Service (IRS), Treasury.

ACTION: Notice of proposed rulemaking and notice of public hearing.

SUMMARY: This document contains proposed amendments to the regulations that provide user fees for offers in compromise. The proposed amendments affect taxpayers who wish to pay their liabilities through offers in compromise. The proposed effective date for these proposed amendments to the regulations is for offers in compromise submitted on or after February 27, 2017. This document also provides a notice of public hearing on these proposed amendments to the regulations.

DATES: Written or electronic comments must be received by November 28, 2016. Outlines of topics to be discussed at the public hearing scheduled for December 16, 2016 at 10:00 a.m. must be received by November 28, 2016.

ADDRESSES: Send submissions to: Internal Revenue Service, CC:PA:LPD:PR (REG-108934-16), Room 5203, Post Office Box 7604, Ben Franklin Station, Washington, DC 20044. Submissions may be hand-delivered Monday through Friday between the hours of 8 a.m. and 4 p.m. to CC:PA:LPD:PR (REG-108934-16), Courier's Desk, Internal Revenue Service, 1111 Constitution Avenue, NW., Washington, DC 20224 or sent electronically via the Federal eRulemaking Portal at *http://www.regulations.gov* (indicate IRS and REG-108934-16). The public hearing will be held in the Main IR Auditorium beginning at 10:00 am in the Internal Revenue Service Building, 1111 Constitution Avenue, NW., Washington, DC 20224.

FOR FURTHER INFORMATION CONTACT: Concerning the proposed amendments to the regulations, Maria Del Pilar Austin at (202) 317-5437; concerning submissions of comments, the hearing, or to be placed on the building access list to attend the hearing, Regina Johnson, at (202) 317-6901; concerning cost methodology, Eva Williams, at (202) 803-9728 (not toll-free numbers).

SUPPLEMENTARY INFORMATION:

Background

This document contains proposed regulations that would amend §300.3 of the User Fee Regulations (26 CFR part 300), which provides for a user fee applicable to offers in compromise under section 7122 of the Internal Revenue Code (Code).

Section 7122(a) provides the Secretary the authority to compromise any civil or criminal case arising under the internal revenue laws, prior to the referral of that case to the Department of Justice. Section 7122(d)(1) requires the IRS to prescribe guidelines for officers and employees of the IRS to determine whether an offer in compromise is adequate and should be accepted to resolve a dispute. Those guidelines can generally be found in §301.7122-1. Under those guidelines, an offer in compromise may be accepted if there is doubt as to liability, if there is doubt as to collectability, or if acceptance will promote effective tax administration. See § 301.7122-1(b).

When the IRS receives an offer in compromise, it initially determines whether the taxpayer submitting the offer is eligible for the offer in compromise program and, if the taxpayer is eligible, whether the offer submitted is otherwise processable. Currently, a taxpayer may be ineligible for the offer in compromise program for a number of reasons, including if the taxpayer is in bankruptcy or has not filed all required tax returns. The IRS will return an offer as nonprocessable if the taxpayer is ineligible or if the offer has not been properly submitted.

If the IRS determines the offer in compromise is processable, then except where the offer is made under section 7122(d)(3)(B) relating only to issues of liability and the case is processed without a financial investigation, the IRS investigates and verifies the taxpayer's financial information submitted with the offer to determine whether such a compromise is appropriate before accepting the terms of the offer in compromise. If the IRS initially rejects a processable offer in compromise based on an investigation of the taxpayer's financial position, section 7122(e)(1) provides that the IRS must conduct an independent administrative review of that decision before communicating the rejection to the taxpayer. If the independent administrative review upholds the IRS's initial decision to reject a processable offer in compromise, section 7122(e)(2) provides that the taxpayer is notified of the rejection and has the right to appeal the rejection to the IRS's Appeals Office. When the IRS accepts an offer in compromise, the IRS processes the payments and monitors the taxpayer's compliance with the terms of the offer.

Under § 300.3, the IRS currently charges $186 for processing an offer in compromise, which includes reviewing and monitoring the offer. Under § 300.3(b)(2)(i) and (ii), if a fee is charged and the offer is accepted to promote effective tax administration or accepted based on doubt as to collectability where the IRS has determined that collection of an amount greater than the amount offered would create economic hardship, then the user fee is applied against the amount to be paid under the offer unless the taxpayer requests that it be refunded. Section 300.3(b)(1)(i) and (ii) provide that no fee is charged if an offer is based solely on doubt as to liability, or made by a low-income taxpayer.

Explanation of Provisions

A. *Overview*

To bring the user fee rate for offers in compromise closer to the full cost to the IRS of providing this taxpayer specific service, the proposed regulations under § 300.3 would increase the user fee for an offer in compromise to $300. The proposed regulations do not modify other portions of the User Fee Regulations regarding offers in compromise, such as § 300.3(b)(1)(i) and (ii) which waive the user fee for offers in compromise submitted by low-income taxpayers and offers in compromise based solely on doubt as to liability. The increased user fee for offers in compromise is proposed to be effective for offers submitted on or after February 27, 2017.

B. *User Fee Authority*

The Independent Offices Appropriations Act (IOAA) (31 U.S.C. 9701) authorizes each agency to promulgate regulations establishing the charge for services provided by the agency (user fees). The IOAA provides that these user fee regulations are subject to policies prescribed by the President and shall be as uniform as practicable. Those policies are currently set forth in the Office of Management and Budget (OMB) Circular A-25, 58 FR 38142 (July 15, 1993; OMB Circular).

The IOAA states that the services provided by an agency should be self-sustaining to the extent possible. 31 U.S.C. 9701(a). The OMB Circular states that agencies that provide services that confer special benefits on identifiable recipients beyond those accruing to the general public are to establish user fees that recover the full cost of providing those services. The OMB Circular requires that agencies identify all services that confer special benefits and determine whether user fees should be assessed for those services.

Agencies are to review user fees biennially and update them as necessary to reflect changes in the cost of providing the underlying services. During this biennial review, an agency must calculate the full cost of providing each service, taking into account all direct and indirect costs to any part of the U.S. government. The full cost of providing a service includes, but is not limited to, salaries, retirement benefits, rents, utilities, travel, and management costs, as well as an appropriate allocation of overhead and other support costs associated with providing the service.

An agency should set the user fee at an amount that recovers the full cost of providing the service unless the agency requests, and the OMB grants, an exception to the full cost requirement. The OMB may grant exceptions only where the cost of collecting the fees would represent an unduly large part of the fee for the activity or any other condition exists that, in the opinion of the agency head, justifies an exception. When the OMB grants an exception, the agency does not collect the full cost of providing the service and therefore must fund the remaining cost of providing the service from other available funding sources. By doing so, the agency subsidizes the cost of the service to the recipients of reduced-fee services even though the service confers a special benefit on those recipients who should otherwise be required to pay the full costs of receiving that benefit as provided for by the IOAA and the OMB Circular.

C. *Offer in Compromise Program User Fee*

The offer in compromise program confers a special benefit on identifiable recipients beyond those accruing to the general public. A taxpayer with an accepted offer in compromise receives the special benefit of resolving his or her tax liabilities for a compromised amount, provided the taxpayer complies with the terms of the offer, and the benefit of paying the compromised amount over a period not to exceed 24 months. Further, section 6331(k)(1) of the Code generally prohibits the IRS from levying to collect taxes while a request to enter into an offer in compromise is pending, for 30 days after a rejection, and, if a timely appeal of a rejection is filed, for the duration of the appeal. Because of these special benefits, the IOAA and the OMB Circular authorize the IRS to charge a user fee for the offer in compromise that reflects the full cost of providing the service of the offer in compromise program to the taxpayer.

The amount of the offer in compromise user fee was last changed in 2014. As required by the IOAA and the OMB Circular, the IRS completed its 2015 biennial review of the offer in compromise program and determined that the full cost of an offer in compromise is $2,450.

In accordance with the OMB Circular, this proposed amendment to the regulations increases the offer in compromise fee to recover more of the costs associated with such offers. These proposed regulations propose to charge less than full cost. While agencies are generally required to charge full cost, the OMB Circular permits certain limited exceptions to this requirement. The IRS requested and the OMB approved an exception to the full cost requirement. The proposed fee for processing an offer in compromise is $300. In light of constraints on IRS resources for tax administration, the Treasury Department and the IRS have determined that it is necessary to recoup more of the costs of the offer in compromise program. The IRS will continue its practice of providing services subject to user fees at costs less than otherwise charged where there is a compelling tax administration reason to do so. Therefore, these proposed regulations do not modify the portions of the current regulations that except low-income taxpayers and offers based on doubt as to liability from the user fee. The proposed fee balances the need to recover more of the costs with the goal of encouraging offers in compromise.

As required under the OMB Circular, the IRS will review the user fee for offers in compromise during its 2017 biennial review. The IRS also plans to evaluate the impact of the current proposed fee increase on the offer in compromise program, and the IRS will take this impact into consideration when revising the offer in compromise user fee in the future.

D. *Calculation of User Fees Generally*

User fee calculations begin by first determining the full cost for the service. The IRS follows the guidance provided by the OMB Circular to compute the full cost of the service, which includes all indirect and direct costs to any part of the U.S. government including but not limited to direct and indirect personnel costs, physical overhead, rents, utilities, travel, and management costs. The IRS's cost methodology is described below.

Once the total amount of direct and indirect costs associated with a service is determined, the IRS follows the guidance in the OMB Circular to determine the costs associated with providing the service to each recipient, which represents the average per unit cost of that service. This average per unit cost is the amount of the user fee that will recover the full cost of the service.

The IRS follows generally accepted accounting principles (GAAP), as established by the Federal Accounting Standards Advisory Board (FASAB) in calculating the full cost of providing services. The FASAB Handbook of Accounting Standards and Other Pronouncements, as amended, which is available at *http://files.fasab.gov/pdffiles/2015_fasab_handbook.pdf,* includes the Statement of Federal Financial Accounting Standards SFFAS No. 4: Managerial Cost Accounting Concepts and Standards for the Federal Government (SFFAS No. 4). SFFAS No. 4 establishes internal costing standards under GAAP to accurately measure and manage the full cost of federal programs. The methodology described below is in accordance with SFFAS No. 4.

1. *Cost center allocation*

The IRS determines the cost of its services and the activities involved in producing them through a cost accounting system that tracks costs to organizational units. The lowest organizational unit in the IRS's cost accounting system is called a cost center. Cost centers are usually separate offices that are distinguished by subject-matter area of responsibility or geographic region. All costs of operating a cost center are recorded in the IRS's cost accounting system and allocated to that cost center. The costs allocated to a cost center are the direct costs for the cost center's activities as well as all indirect costs, including overhead, associated with that cost center. Each cost is recorded in only one cost center.

2. *Determining the per unit cost*

To establish the per unit cost, the total cost of providing the service is divided by the volume of services provided. The volume of services provided includes both services for which a fee is charged as well as subsidized services. The subsidized services are those where OMB has approved an exception to the full cost requirement, for example, to charge a reduced fee to low-income taxpayers. The volume of subsidized services is included in the total volume of services provided to ensure that the IRS, and not those who are paying full cost, subsidizes the cost of the reduced-cost services.

3. *Cost estimation of direct labor and benefits*

Not all cost centers are fully devoted to only one service for which the IRS charges a user fee. Some cost centers work on a number of different services. In these cases, the IRS estimates the cost incurred in those cost centers attributable to the service for which a user fee is being calculated by measuring the time required to accomplish activities related to the service, and estimating the average time required to accomplish these activities. The average time required to accomplish these activities is multiplied by the relevant organizational unit's average labor and benefits cost per unit of time to determine the labor and benefits cost incurred to provide the service. To determine the full cost, the IRS then adds an appropriate overhead charge as discussed below.

4. *Calculating Overhead*

Overhead is an indirect cost of operating an organization that cannot be immediately associated with an activity that the organization performs. Overhead includes costs of resources that are jointly or commonly consumed by one or more organizational unit's activities but are not specifically identifiable to a single activity. These costs can include:

- General management and administrative services of sustaining and support organizations.
- Facilities management and ground maintenance services (security, rent, utilities, and building maintenance).
- Procurement and contracting services.
- Financial management and accounting services.
- Information technology services.
- Services to acquire and operate property, plants and equipment.
- Publication, reproduction, and graphics and video services.
- Research, analytical, and statistical services.
- Human resources/personnel services.
- Library and legal services.

To calculate the overhead allocable to a service, the IRS first calculates the Corporate Overhead rate and then multiplies the Corporate Overhead rate by the direct labor and benefits costs determined as discussed above. The IRS calculates the Corporate Overhead rate annually based on cost elements underlying the Statement of Net Cost included in the IRS Annual Financial Statements, which are audited by the Government Accountability Office. The Corporate Overhead rate is the ratio of the sum of the IRS's indirect labor and benefits costs from the supporting and sustaining organizational units—those that do not interact directly with taxpayers—and all non-labor costs to the IRS's labor and benefits costs of its organizational units that interact directly with taxpayers.

The Corporate Overhead rate of 65.85 percent for costs reviewed during FY 2015 was calculated based on FY 2014 costs as follows:

Indirect Labor and Benefits Costs	$1,693,339,843
Non-Labor Costs	+ *$2,832,262,970*
Total Indirect Costs	$4,525,602,813
Direct Labor and Benefits Costs	÷ *$6,872,934,473*
Corporate Overhead Rate	*65.85%*

E. *Calculation of Offer in Compromise User Fee*

The IRS used data from cost centers dedicated to the offer in compromise program and cost centers that work on the offer in compromise program, as well as other IRS programs, to determine the full cost of the offer in compromise program. The IRS used the most recent two years of data, in this case FY 2013 and FY 2014, and averaged those costs in order to assure anomalies, such as short term increases or decreases in costs or numbers of offers in compromise, would not artificially impact the measured costs.

The offer in compromise program work is primarily performed by dedicated offices; therefore, the cost of most of the program can be determined through the costs recorded in the cost centers underlying the offices dedicated to the offer in compromise program. The IRS identified the offices that provide 100 percent of their time to this program (Offer in Compromise Offices), determined the full costs of the Offer in Compromise Offices for FY 2013 and 2014, and averaged the costs for those two years to determine the annual average costs of those offices. The average costs for the Offer in Compromise Offices were as follows:

Offer in Compromise Offices	**Average Costs**
Labor and Benefits	$61,125,895
Non-Labor and Support Costs	$90,730,487
Offer in Compromise Offices Full Cost	$151,856,382

Because overhead and support costs are already included in the "Non-Labor and Support Costs" allocated to these cost centers, a Corporate Overhead factor has not been added to determine the full cost of the Offer in Compromise Offices.

There are three IRS organizations that perform work for the offer in compromise program, but that are not exclusively dedicated to the offer in compromise program (Non-OIC Dedicated Offices). Those organizations are:

- Office of Chief Counsel
- Small Business/Self-Employed (Examination)
- Office of Appeals

To calculate the average offer in compromise program costs attributable to these Non-OIC Dedicated Offices, the IRS obtained the time spent by each organization on the offer in compromise program for FY 2013 and 2014, calculated an annual average of that time for each office, and multiplied that annual average time by the average hourly rates for that organization. After determining the total labor and benefits costs for the Non-OIC Dedicated Offices, the IRS added the Corporate Overhead costs allocable to these organizations to determine the full cost of the services provided by the Non-OIC Dedicated Offices. The costs are calculated as follows:

Non-OIC Dedicated Offices	
Office of Chief Counsel	
Average Hours	13,688
Average Salary and Benefits Rate	$57.00
Chief Counsel Labor Cost	$780,216
Examination	
Average Hours	3,723
Average Salary and Benefits Rate	$52.72
Examination Labor Cost	$196,277
Office of Appeals	
Average Hours	128,610
Average Salary and Benefits Rate	$55.10
Examination Labor Cost	$7,086,411
Total Cost for Chief Counsel, Examination and Appeals	
Total Labor and Benefits Cost	$8,062,904
Corporate Overhead at 65.85%	$5,309,422
Total Non-OIC Dedicated Offices Cost	$13,372,326

To determine the full cost of the offer in compromise program, the IRS combined the Offer in Compromise Offices' full cost and the Non-OIC Dedicated Offices' full cost. The IRS calculated the unit cost by dividing the total offer in compromise program cost by the average of offer in compromise cases that were closed in FY 2013 and in FY 2014. Closed offers are offers that have been issued an acceptance letter, closed as rejected or withdrawn/terminated, or returned. An offer may be returned either because the offer was not processable when received, or after the offer was initially determined to be processable circumstances occur that cause the offer to no longer be processable or the Service is unable to proceed with the offer investigation. The IRS closed 70,622 offer in compromise cases in FY 2013 and 64,332 offer in compromise cases in FY 2014, for an average of offer in compromise cases closed in FY 2013 and FY 2014 of 67,477.

Unit Cost for Offer in Compromise	
Total Offer in Compromise Offices	$151,856,382
Total Non-OIC Dedicated Offices	$13,372,326
Offer in Compromise Program Full Cost	$165,228,708
Average FY 2013 and 2014 Annual Volume of Closed Offers in Compromise	67,477
Unit Cost	**$2,450**

Special Analyses

Certain IRS regulations, including this one, are exempt from the requirements of Executive Order 12866, as supplemented and reaffirmed by Executive Order 13563. Therefore, a regulatory impact assessment is not required. It is hereby certified that these regulations will not have a significant economic impact on a substantial number of small entities. This certification is based on the information that follows. The economic impact of these regulations on any small entity would result from the entity being required to pay a fee prescribed by these regulations in order to obtain a particular service. The dollar amount of the fee is not, however, substantial enough to have a significant economic impact on any entity subject to the fee because generally the fee is applied to offset an existing tax obligation that the entity owes the IRS. As such, the fee does not represent a payment of any amount greater than what a substantial number of entities owe the IRS. Low-income taxpayers and taxpayers making offers in compromise based on doubt as to liability will continue not to be charged a fee and therefore will not be impacted economically by these proposed regulations. Accordingly, a regulatory flexibility analysis is not required. Pursuant to section 7805(f) of the Internal Revenue Code, this notice of proposed rulemaking will be submitted to the Chief Counsel for Advocacy of the Small Business Administration for comment on its impact on small business.

Comments and Public Hearing

Before these proposed amendments to the regulations are adopted as final regulations, consideration will be given to any comments that are submitted timely to the IRS as prescribed in this preamble under the "ADDRESSES" heading. The Treasury Department and the IRS request comments on all aspects of the proposed regulations. All comments will be available at *www.regulations.gov* or upon request.

A public hearing has been scheduled for December 16, 2016, beginning at 10:00 am in the Main IR Auditorium of the Internal Revenue Service Building, 1111 Constitution Avenue NW., Washington, DC. 20224. Due to building security procedures, visitors must enter at the Constitution Avenue entrance. In addition, all visitors must present photo identification to enter the building. Because of access restrictions, visitors will not be admitted beyond the immediate entrance area more than 30 minutes before the hearing starts. For information about having your name placed on the building access list to attend the hearing, see the "FOR FURTHER INFORMATION CONTACT" section of this preamble.

The rules of 26 CFR §601.601(a)(3) apply to the hearing. Persons who wish to present oral comments at the hearing must submit written comments or electronic comments by November 28, 2016 and submit an outline of the topics to be discussed and the amount of time to be devoted to each topic (a signed original and 8 copies) by November 28, 2016. A period of 10 minutes will be allotted to each person for making comments. An agenda showing the scheduling of the speakers will be prepared after the deadline for receiving outlines has passed. Copies of the agenda will be available free of charge at the hearing.

Drafting Information

The principal author of these regulations is Maria Del Pilar Austin of the Office of the Associate Chief Counsel (Procedure and Administration). Other personnel from the Treasury Department and the IRS participated in their development.

[¶49,716] Proposed Amendments of Regulations (REG-150992-13), published in the Federal Register on October 14, 2016.

[Code Sec. 165]

Disaster loss: Disaster loss election: Prior year election: Federally declared disaster area.—Amendments of Reg. §1.165-11, relating to the election to take a disaster loss in the preceding year, are proposed.

AGENCY: Internal Revenue Service (IRS), Treasury.

ACTION: Notice of Proposed Rulemaking by cross-reference to temporary regulations.

SUMMARY: In the Rules and Regulations section of this issue of the **Federal Register**, the IRS is issuing temporary regulations under section 165(i) of the Internal Revenue Code (Code) relating to the election to take a disaster loss in the preceding year. The text of those temporary regulations also serves as the text of these proposed regulations. This document also invites comments from the public regarding these proposed regulations.

DATES: Written or electronic comments and requests for a public hearing must be received by January 12, 2017.

ADDRESSES: Send submissions to CC:PA:LPD:PR (REG-150992-13), room 5203, Internal Revenue Service, POB 7604, Ben Franklin Station, Washington, DC 20044. Submissions may be hand-delivered Monday through Friday between the hours of 8 a.m. and 4 p.m. to: CC:PA:LPD:PR (REG-150992-13), Courier's Desk, Internal Revenue Service, 1111 Constitution Avenue, NW, Washington, DC, or sent electronically via the Federal eRulemaking Portal at www.regulations.gov (IRS REG-150992-13).

FOR FURTHER INFORMATION CONTACT: Concerning the proposed regulations, Daniel Cassano at (202) 317-7011; concerning comments or a request for a public hearing, Oluwafunmilayo Taylor (202) 317-6901 (not toll-free numbers).

SUPPLEMENTARY INFORMATION:

Background and Explanation of Provisions

Final and temporary regulations in the Rules and Regulations section of this issue of the **Federal Register** amend the Income Tax Regulations (26 CFR part 1) relating to section 165(i) of the Code. The temporary regulations extend the due date by which a taxpayer may elect to treat an allowable loss occurring in a disaster area and attributable to a Federally declared disaster as sustained in the taxable year immediately prior to the taxable year in which the disaster occurred, as provided in section 165(i). The temporary regulations provide rules governing the time and manner of making a section 165(i) election, as well as the time and manner of revoking a section 165(i) election. The text of those temporary regulations also serves as the text of these proposed regulations. The preamble to the temporary regulations explains the amendments.

Special Analyses

Certain IRS regulations, including these, are exempt from the requirements of Executive Order 12866, as supplemented and reaffirmed by Executive Order 13563. Therefore, a regulatory assessment is not required. It also has been determined that section 553(b) of the Administrative Procedure Act (5 U.S.C. chapter 5) does not apply to these regulations, and because the regulation does not impose a collection of information on small entities, the Regulatory Flexibility Act (5 U.S.C. chapter 6) does not apply. Pursuant to section 7805(f) of the Internal Revenue Code, this notice of proposed rulemaking will be submitted to the Chief Counsel for Advocacy of the Small Business Administration for comment on its impact on small business.

Comments and Requests for a Public Hearing

Before these proposed regulations are adopted as final regulations, consideration will be given to any written comments (a signed original and eight (8) copies) or electronic comments that are submitted timely to the IRS. The Department of the Treasury and the IRS request comments concerning the extension of the due date by which a taxpayer may make a section 165(i) election, as well as the time and manner in which a taxpayer may revoke a section 165(i) election. All comments will be available for public inspection and copying.

A public hearing will be scheduled if requested in writing by any person who timely submits comments. If a public hearing is scheduled, notice of the date, time, and place for the public hearing will be published in the **Federal Register**.

Drafting Information

The principal authors of these regulations are Daniel Cassano and Christopher Wrobel of the Office of the Associate Chief Counsel (Income Tax & Accounting). However, other personnel from the Department of the Treasury and the IRS participated in their development.

[¶ 49,717] Proposed Amendments of Regulations (REG-130314-16), published in the Federal Register on October 21, 2016.

[Code Secs. 385 and 752]

Corporations: Multinational corporations: Related-party transactions: Indebtedness: Equity.—Reg. §1.385-4 and amendments of Reg. §§1.385-3, and 1.752-2 affecting corporations and partnerships that issue purported indebtedness to related corporations or partnerships in the Rules and Regulations section of this issue of the Federal Register, are proposed.

AGENCY: Internal Revenue Service (IRS), Treasury.

ACTION: Notice of proposed rulemaking by cross-reference to temporary regulation.

SUMMARY: The Department of the Treasury (Treasury Department) and the IRS are issuing temporary regulations that affect corporations and partnerships that issue purported indebtedness to related corporations or partnerships in the Rules and Regulations section of this issue of the **Federal Register**. The temporary regulations provide rules addressing the treatment of instruments issued by partnerships, consolidated groups, and certain transactions involving qualified cash-management arrangements. The text of the temporary regulations also serves as the text of these proposed regulations.

DATES: Written or electronic comments and requests for a public hearing must be received by January 19, 2017.

ADDRESSES: Send submissions to: CC:PA:LPD:PR (REG-130314-16), room 5203, Internal Revenue Service, P.O. Box 7604, Ben Franklin Station, Washington, DC 20224. Submissions may be hand-delivered Monday through Friday between the hours of 8 a.m. and 4 p.m. to CC:PA:LPD:PR (REG-130314-16), Courier's Desk, Internal Revenue Service, 1111 Constitution Avenue NW, Washington, DC 20224, or sent electronically via the Federal eRulemaking Portal at *http://www.regulations.gov* (IRS REG-130314-16).

FOR FURTHER INFORMATION CONTACT: Concerning the proposed regulations, Austin M. Diamond-Jones, (202) 317-5363, or Joshua G. Rabon, (202) 317-6937; concerning submissions of comments or requests for a public hearing, Regina Johnson, (202) 317-5177 (not toll-free numbers).

SUPPLEMENTARY INFORMATION:

Background

The temporary regulations in the Rules and Regulations section of this issue of the **Federal Register** contain rules under sections 385 and 752 of the Internal Revenue Code (Code) that establish requirements that ordinarily must be satisfied in order for certain related-party interests in a corporation to be treated as indebtedness for federal tax purposes. The text of the temporary regulations also serves as the text of the proposed regulations herein. The preamble to the temporary regulations explains the temporary regulations and the corresponding proposed regulations.

Special Analyses

I. *Regulatory Planning and Review*

Executive Orders 13563 and 12866 direct agencies to assess costs and benefits of available regulatory alternatives and, if regulation is necessary, to select regulatory approaches that maximize net benefits (including potential economic, environmental, public health and safety effects, distributive impacts, and equity). Executive Order 13563 emphasizes the importance of quantifying both costs and benefits, of reducing costs, of harmonizing rules, and of promoting flexibility. Related rules in the final and temporary regulations under section 385 in TD 9790, published in the Rules and Regulations section of this issue of the **Federal Register**, have been designated a "significant regulatory action" under section 3(f) of Executive Order 12866. For a discussion of the economic impact of those final and temporary regulations, as well as these proposed regulations, please see the Regulatory Assessment accompanying TD 9790, published in the Rules and Regulations section of this issue of the **Federal Register**.

II. *Regulatory Flexibility Act*

Pursuant to the Regulatory Flexibility Act (5 U.S.C. Chapter 6), it is hereby certified that the final and temporary regulations in TD 9790, published in the Rules and Regulations section of this issue of the **Federal Register**, and accordingly, these proposed regulations proposed by cross-reference to the temporary regulations, will not have a significant economic impact on a substantial number of small entities. Accordingly, a regulatory flexibility analysis is not required.

To facilitate the federal tax analysis of an interest in a corporation, taxpayers are required under existing law to substantiate their classification of an interest as stock or indebtedness for federal tax purposes. Section 1.385-3 provides that certain interests in a corporation that are held by a member of the corporation's expanded group and that otherwise would be treated as indebtedness for federal tax purposes are treated as stock. Section 1.385-3T provides that for certain debt instruments issued by a controlled partnership, the holder is deemed to transfer all or a portion of the debt instrument to the partner or partners in the partnership in exchange for stock in the partner or partners. Section 1.385-4T provides rules regarding the application of §§1.385-3 and 1.385-3T to members of a consolidated group. Sections 1.385-3 and 1.385-3T include multiple exceptions that limit their application. In particular, the threshold exception provides that the first $50 million of expanded group debt instruments that otherwise would be reclassified as stock or deemed to be transferred to a partner in a controlled partnership under §1.385-3 or §1.385-3T will not be reclassified or deemed transferred under §1.385-3 or §1.385-3T. Although it is possible that the classification rules in §§1.385-3, 1.385-3T, and 1.385-4T could have an effect on small entities, the threshold exception of the first $50 million of debt instruments otherwise subject to recharacterization or deemed transfer under §§1.385-3, 1.385-3T, and 1.385-4T makes it unlikely that a substantial number of small entities will be affected by §§1.385-3T or 1.385-4T.

Pursuant to section 7805(f) of the Code, the final regulations in TD 9790, published in the Rules and Regulations section of this issue of the **Federal Register**, have been submitted to the Chief Counsel for Advocacy of the Small Business Administration for comment on their impact on small business. Comments were received requesting that the monetary thresholds contained in proposed §§1.385-2, 1.385-3, and 1.385-4 be increased in order to mitigate the impact on small businesses. These comments are addressed in Parts IV.B.1.d and V.E.4 of the Summary of Comments and Explanation of Revisions in the preamble of TD 9790, published in the Rules and Regulations section of this issue of the **Federal Register**. No comments were received concerning the economic impact on small entities from the Small Business Administration.

Comments and Requests for Public Hearing

Before these proposed regulations are adopted as final regulations, consideration will be given to any comments that are submitted timely to the IRS as prescribed in this preamble under the "Addresses" heading. Treasury and the IRS request comments on all aspects of the proposed rules. All comments will be available at *www.regulations.gov* or upon request. A public hearing will be scheduled if requested in writing by any person that timely submits electronic or written comments. If a public hearing is scheduled, notice of the date, time, and place for the public hearing will be published in the **Federal Register**.

Drafting Information

The principal authors of these regulations are Austin M. Diamond-Jones of the Office of Associate Chief Counsel (Corporate) and Joshua G. Rabon of the Office of Associate Chief Counsel (International). However, other personnel from the Treasury Department and the IRS participated in their development.

[¶49,720] Proposed Amendments of Regulations (REG-114734-16), published in the Federal Register on November 3, 2016 (corrected 12/28/2016).

[Code Sec. 956]

Controlled foreign corporation: U.S. property: CFC property held through partnership: Earnings invested in U.S. property.—Amendments of Reg. §1.956-4, regarding the determination of the amount of United States property treated as held by a controlled foreign corporation (CFC) through a partnership, are proposed.

AGENCY: Internal Revenue Service (IRS), Treasury.

ACTION: Notice of proposed rulemaking.

SUMMARY: This document contains proposed regulations that provide rules regarding the determination of the amount of United States property treated as held by a controlled foreign corporation (CFC) through a partnership. The proposed regulations affect United States shareholders of CFCs.

DATES: Written or electronic comments and requests for a public hearing must be received by February 1, 2017.

ADDRESSES: Send submissions to: CC:PA:LPD:PR (REG-114734-16), room 5203, Internal Revenue Service, P.O. Box 7604, Ben Franklin Station, Washington, DC 20044. Submissions may be hand-delivered Monday through Friday between the hours of 8 a.m. and 4 p.m. to CC:PA:LPD:PR (REG-114734-16), Courier's Desk, Internal Revenue Service, 1111 Constitution Avenue NW, Washington, DC, or sent electronically via the Federal eRulemaking Portal at *http://www.regulations.gov* (IRS REG-114734-16).

FOR FURTHER INFORMATION CONTACT: Concerning the proposed regulations, Rose E. Jenkins, (202) 317-6934; concerning submissions of comments or requests for a public hearing, Regina Johnson, (202) 317-6901 (not toll-free numbers). SUPPLEMENTARY INFORMATION:

Background

In the Rules and Regulations section of this issue of the **Federal Register**, the Department of Treasury (Treasury Department) and the IRS are issuing final regulations that amend the Income Tax Regulations (26 CFR part 1) relating to sections 954 and 956. Under §1.956-4(b), a CFC that is a partner in a partnership determines its share of United States property held by the partnership in accordance with the CFC's liquidation value percentage in the partnership, or, when relevant, based on a special allocation of income (or, where appropriate, gain) from the property. This document proposes to amend §1.956-4(b) so that a CFC that is a partner in a controlled partnership determines its share of United States property held by the partnership under the liquidation value percentage method, regardless of the existence of any special allocation of income or gain from the property.

Explanation of Provisions

Section 956 determines the amount that a United States shareholder (as defined in section 951(b)) of a CFC must include in gross income with respect to the CFC under section 951(a)(1)(B). This amount is determined, in part, based on the average of the amounts of United States property held, directly or indirectly, by the CFC at the close of each quarter during its taxable year. For this purpose, in general, the amount taken into account with respect to any United States property is the adjusted basis of the property, reduced by any liability to which the property is subject. See section 956(a) and § 1.956-1(e). Section 956(e) grants the Secretary authority to prescribe such regulations as may be necessary to carry out the purposes of section 956, including regulations to prevent the avoidance of section 956 through reorganizations or otherwise.

Under § 1.956-4(b), a CFC that is a partner in a partnership generally is treated as holding its share of United States property held by the partnership in accordance with the CFC partner's liquidation value percentage in the partnership. However, if there is a special allocation of income (or, where appropriate, gain) from United States property that is respected for Federal income tax purposes under section 704(b) and the regulations thereunder and does not have a principal purpose of avoiding the purposes of section 956, the partner's attributable share of that property is determined solely by reference to the special allocation. See § 1.956-4(b)(2)(ii). The Treasury Department and the IRS have concluded that, in general, these rules provide a reasonable means of determining a partner's interest in property held by a partnership for purposes of section 956 because they generally result in an allocation of specific items of property that corresponds with each partner's economic interest in that property, including any income or gain that may be subject to special allocations.

The Treasury Department and the IRS are concerned, however, that special allocations with respect to a partnership that is controlled by a single multinational group are unlikely to have economic significance for the group as a whole and can facilitate tax planning that is inconsistent with the purposes of section 956. Accordingly, these proposed regulations propose to revise § 1.956-4(b) such that a partner's attributable share of each item of property of a partnership controlled by the partner would be determined solely in accordance with the partner's liquidation value percentage, even if income or gain from the property is subject to a special allocation. Specifically, under proposed § 1.956-4(b)(2)(iii), the rule in § 1.956-4(b)(2)(ii) requiring a partner's attributable share of partnership property to be determined by reference to special allocations with respect to the property would not apply in the case of a partnership controlled by the partner. For this purpose, a partner is treated as controlling a partnership if the partner and the partnership are related within the meaning of section 267(b) or section 707(b), substituting "at least 80 percent" for "more than 50 percent". The examples in § 1.956-4(b)(3) are proposed to be modified in accordance with the proposed rule.

These proposed regulations are proposed to be effective for taxable years of CFCs ending on or after the date of publication in the **Federal Register** of the Treasury decision adopting them as final regulations, and taxable years of United States shareholders in which or with which such taxable years end, with respect to property acquired on or after the date of publication in the **Federal Register** of the Treasury decision adopting them as final regulations. The IRS may, where appropriate, challenge transactions under currently applicable Code or regulatory provisions or judicial doctrines.

Special Analyses

Certain IRS regulations, including these regulations, are exempt from the requirements of Executive Order 12866, as supplemented and reaffirmed by Executive Order 13563. Therefore, a regulatory assessment is not required. It has also been determined that section 553(b) of the Administrative Procedure Act (5 U.S.C. Chapter 5) does not apply to these regulations, and because the regulations do not impose a collection of information on small entities, the Regulatory Flexibility Act (5 U.S.C. chapter 6) does not apply. Pursuant to section 7805(f), this notice of proposed rulemaking has been submitted to the Chief Counsel of Advocacy of the Small Business Administration for comment on its impact on small business.

Comments and Requests for Public Hearing

Before these proposed regulations are adopted as final regulations, consideration will be given to any comments that are submitted timely to the IRS as prescribed in this preamble under the "Addresses" heading. The Treasury Department and the IRS request comments on all aspects of the proposed rules. All comments will be available at *www.regulations.gov* or upon request. A public hearing will be scheduled if requested in writing by any person that timely submits electronic or written comments. If a public hearing is scheduled, notice of the date, time, and place for the public hearing will be published in the **Federal Register**.

Drafting Information

The principal author of these proposed regulations is Rose E. Jenkins of the Office of Associate Chief Counsel (International). However, other personnel from the Treasury Department and the IRS participated in their development.

[¶49,721] Proposed Amendments of Regulations (REG-136978-12), published in the Federal Register on November 23, 2016.

[Code Sec. 514]

Debt financed income, unrelated: Real estate investments: Qualified organizations.—Amendments of Reg. §1.514(c)-2, relating to the application of section 514(c)(9)(E) of the Internal Revenue Code (Code) to partnerships that hold debt-financed real property and have one or more (but not all) qualified tax-exempt organization partners within the meaning of section 514(c)(9)(C), are proposed.

AGENCY: Internal Revenue Service (IRS), Treasury.

ACTION: Notice of proposed rulemaking.

SUMMARY: This document contains proposed regulations relating to the application of section 514(c)(9)(E) of the Internal Revenue Code (Code) to partnerships that hold debt-financed real property and have one or more (but not all) qualified tax-exempt organization partners within the meaning of section 514(c)(9)(C). The proposed regulations amend the current regulations under section 514(c)(9)(E) to allow certain allocations resulting from specified common business practices to comply with the rules under section 514(c)(9)(E). These regulations affect partnerships with qualified tax-exempt organization partners and their partners.

DATES: Written and electronic comments and requests for a public hearing must be received by February 21, 2017.

ADDRESSES: Send submissions to: CC:PA:LPD:PR (REG-136978-12), room 5203, Internal Revenue Service, PO Box 7604, Ben Franklin Station, Washington, DC 20044. Submissions may be hand-delivered Monday through Friday between the hours of 8 a.m. and 4 p.m. to: CC:PA:LPD:PR (REG-136978-12), Courier's Desk, Internal Revenue Service, 1111 Constitution Avenue, N.W., Washington, DC, or sent electronically, via the Federal eRulemaking Portal site at *http://www.regulations.gov* (indicate IRS and REG-136978-12).

FOR FURTHER INFORMATION CONTACT: Concerning the proposed regulations, Caroline E. Hay at (202) 317-5279; concerning the submissions of comments and requests for a public hearing, Regina L. Johnson at (202) 317-6901 (not toll-free numbers).

SUPPLEMENTARY INFORMATION:

Background

This document proposes amendments to the Income Tax Regulations (26 CFR part 1) under section 514(c)(9)(E) regarding the application of the fractions rule (as defined in the Background section of this preamble) to partnerships that hold debt-financed real property and have one or more (but not all) qualified tax-exempt organization partners.

In general, section 511 imposes a tax on the unrelated business taxable income (UBTI) of tax-exempt organizations. Section 514(a) defines UBTI to include a specified percentage of the gross income derived from debt-financed property described in section 514(b). Section 514(c)(9)(A) generally excepts from UBTI income derived from debt-financed real property acquired or improved by certain qualified organizations (QOs) described in section 514(c)(9)(C). Under section 514(c)(9)(C), a QO includes an educational organization described in section 170(b)(1)(A)(ii) and its affiliated support organizations described in section 509(a)(3), any trust which constitutes a qualified trust under section 401, an organization described in section 501(c)(25), and a retirement income account described in section 403(b)(9).

Section 514(c)(9)(B)(vi) provides that the exception from UBTI in section 514(c)(9)(A) does not apply if a QO owns an interest in a partnership that holds debt-financed real property (the partnership limitation), unless the partnership meets one of the following requirements: (1) all of the partners of the partnership are QOs, (2) each allocation to a QO is a qualified allocation (within the meaning of section 168(h)(6)), or (3) each partnership allocation has substantial economic effect under section 704(b)(2) and satisfies section 514(c)(9)(E)(i)(I) (the fractions rule).

A partnership allocation satisfies the fractions rule if the allocation of items to any partner that is a QO does not result in that partner having a share of overall partnership income for any taxable year greater than that partner's fractions rule percentage (the partner's share of overall partnership loss for the taxable year for which the partner's loss share is the smallest). Section 1.514(c)-2(c)(1) describes overall partnership income as the amount by which the aggregate items of partnership income and gain for the taxable year exceed the aggregate items of partnership loss and deduction for the year. Overall partnership loss is the amount by which the aggregate items of partnership loss and deduction for the taxable year exceed the aggregate items of partnership income and gain for the year.

Generally, under §1.514(c)-2(b)(2)(i), a partnership must satisfy the fractions rule both on a prospective basis and on an actual basis for each taxable year of the partnership, beginning with the first taxable year of the partnership in which the partnership holds debt-financed real property and has a QO partner. However, certain allocations are taken into account for purposes of determining overall partnership income or loss only when actually made, and do not create an immediate violation of the fractions rule. See §1.514(c)-2(b)(2)(i). Certain other allocations are disregarded for purposes of making fractions rule calculations. See, for example, §1.514(c)-2(d) (reasonable preferred returns and reasonable guaranteed payments), §1.514(c)-2(e) (certain chargebacks and offsets), §1.514(c)-2(f) (reasonable partner-specific items of deduction and loss), §1.514(c)-2(g) (unlikely losses and deductions), and §1.514(c)-2(k)(3) (certain de minimis allocations of losses and deductions). In addition, § 1.514(c)-2(k)(1) provides that changes in partnership allocations that result from transfers or shifts of partnership interests (other than transfers from a QO to another QO) will be closely scrutinized, but generally will be taken into account only in determining whether the partnership satisfies the fractions rule in the taxable year of the change and subsequent taxable years. Section 1.514(c)-2(m) provides special rules for applying the fractions rule to tiered partnerships.

The Treasury Department and the IRS have received comments requesting targeted changes to the existing regulations under section 514(c)(9)(E) to allow certain allocations resulting from specified common business practices to comply with the rules under section 514(c)(9)(E). Section 514(c)(9)(E)(iii) grants the Secretary authority to prescribe regulations as may be necessary to carry out the purposes of section 514(c)(9)(E), including regulations that may provide for the exclusion or segregation of items. In response to comments and under the regulatory authority in section 514(c)(9)(E), these proposed regulations provide guidance in determining a partner's share of overall partnership income or loss for purposes of the fractions rule, including allowing allocations consistent with common arrangements involving preferred returns, partner-specific expenditures, unlikely losses, and chargebacks of partner-specific expenditures and unlikely losses. The proposed regulations also simplify one of the examples involving tiered partnerships and provide rules regarding changes to partnership allocations as a result of capital commitment defaults and later acquisitions of partnership interests. These proposed regulations except from applying the fractions rule certain partnerships in which all partners other than QOs own five percent or less of the capital or profits interests in the partnership. Finally, these proposed regulations increase the threshold for de minimis allocations away from QO partners.

Explanation of Provisions

1. *Preferred Returns*

Section 1.514(c)-2(d)(1) and (2) of the existing regulations disregard in computing overall partnership income for purposes of the fractions rule items of income (including gross income) and gain that may be allocated to a partner with respect to a current or cumulative reasonable preferred return for capital (including allocations of minimum gain attributable to nonrecourse liability (or partner nonrecourse debt) proceeds distributed to the partner as a reasonable preferred return) if that preferred return is set forth in a binding, written partnership agreement. Section 1.514(c)-2(d)(2) of the existing regulations also provides that if a partnership agreement provides for a reasonable preferred return with an allocation of what would otherwise be overall partnership income, items comprising that allocation are disregarded in computing overall partnership income for purposes of the fractions rule.

Section 1.514(c)-2(d)(6)(i) of the existing regulations limits the amount of income and gain allocated with respect to a preferred return that can be disregarded for purposes of the fractions rule to: (A) the aggregate of the amount that has been distributed to the partner as a reasonable preferred return for the taxable year of the allocation and prior taxable years, on or before the due date (not including extensions) for filing the partnership's return for the taxable year of the allocation; minus (B) the aggregate amount of corresponding income and gain (and what would otherwise be overall partnership income) allocated to the partner in all prior years. Thus, this rule requires a current distribution of preferred returns for the allocations of income with respect to those preferred returns to be disregarded.

The Treasury Department and the IRS have received comments requesting that the current distribution requirement be eliminated from the regulations because it interferes with normal market practice, creates unnecessary complication, and, in some cases, causes economic distortions for partnerships with QO partners. The preamble to the existing final regulations under section 514(c)(9)(E) responded to objections regarding the current distribution requirement by explaining that if the requirement were eliminated, partnerships might attempt to optimize their overall economics by allocating significant amounts of partnership income and gain to QOs in the form of preferred returns. The preamble explained that these allocations "would be a departure from the normal commercial practice followed by partnerships in which the money partners are generally subject to income tax." TD 8539, 59 FR 24924. A recent commenter explained that the vast majority of partnerships holding debt-financed real property (real estate partnerships) with preferred returns to investing partners (either the QO or the taxable partner) make allocations that match the preferred return as it accrues, without regard to whether cash has been distributed with respect to the preferred return. Instead of requiring distributions equal to the full amount of their preferred returns, taxable partners generally negotiate for tax distributions to pay any tax liabilities associated with their partnership interest.

The Treasury Department and the IRS have reconsidered the necessity of the current distribution requirement to prevent abuses of the fractions rule. So long as the preferred return is required to be distributed prior to other distributions (with an exception for certain distributions intended to facilitate the payment of taxes) and any undistributed amount compounds, the likelihood of abuse is minimized. Therefore, the proposed regulations remove the current distribution requirement and instead disregard allocations of items of income and gain with respect to a preferred return for purposes of the fractions rule, but only if the partnership agreement requires that the partnership make distributions first to pay any accrued, cumulative, and compounding unpaid preferred return to the extent such accrued but unpaid preferred return has not otherwise been reversed by an allocation of loss prior to such distribution (preferred return distribution requirement). The preferred return distribution requirement, however, is subject to an exception under the proposed regulations that allows distributions intended to facilitate partner payment of taxes imposed on the partner's allocable share of partnership income or gain, if the distributions are made pursuant to a provision in the partnership agreement, are treated as an advance against distributions to which the distributee partner would otherwise be entitled under the partnership agreement, and do not exceed the distributee partner's allocable share of net partnership income and gain multiplied by the sum of the highest statutory federal, state, and local tax rates applicable to that partner.

2. *Partner-Specific Expenditures and Management Fees*

Section 1.514(c)-2(f) of the existing regulations provides a list of certain partner-specific expenditures that are disregarded in computing overall partnership income or loss for purposes of the fractions rule. These expenditures include expenditures attributable to a partner for additional record-keeping and accounting costs including in connection with the transfer of a partnership interest, additional administrative costs from having a foreign partner, and state and local taxes. The Treasury Department and the IRS are aware that some real estate partnerships allow investing partners to negotiate for management and similar fees paid to the general partner that differ from fees paid with respect to investments by other partners. These fees include the general partner's fees for managing the partnership and may include fees paid in connection with the acquisition, disposition, or refinancing of an investment. Compliance with the fractions rule may preclude a real estate partnership with QO partners from allocating deductions attributable to these management expenses in a manner that follows the economic fee arrangement because the fractions rule limits the ability of the partnership to make disproportionate allocations.

The Treasury Department and the IRS have determined that real estate partnerships with QO partners should be permitted to allocate management and similar fees among partners to reflect the manner in which the partners agreed to bear the expense without causing a fractions rule violation. Accordingly, the proposed regulations add management (and similar) fees to the current list of excluded partner-specific expenditures in §1.514(c)-2(f) of the existing regulations to the extent such fees do not, in the aggregate, exceed two percent of the partner's aggregate committed capital.

It has been suggested to the Treasury Department and the IRS that similar partner-specific expenditure issues may arise under the new partnership audit rules in section 1101 of the Bipartisan Budget Act of 2015, Public Law No. 114-74 (the BBA), which was enacted into law on November 2, 2015. Section 1101 of the BBA repeals the current rules governing partnership audits and replaces them with a new centralized partnership audit regime that, in general, assesses and collects tax at the partnership level as an imputed underpayment. Some have suggested that the manner in which an imputed underpayment is borne by partners potentially could implicate similar concerns as special allocations of partner-specific items. As the Treasury Department and the IRS continue to consider how to implement the BBA, the Treasury Department and the IRS request comments regarding whether an imputed underpayment should be included among the list of partner-specific expenditures.

3. *Unlikely Losses*

Similar to §1.514(c)-2(f), §1.514(c)-2(g) of the existing regulations generally disregards specially allocated unlikely losses or deductions (other than items of nonrecourse deduction) in computing overall partnership income or loss for purposes of the fractions rule. To be disregarded under §1.514(c)-2(g), a loss or deduction must have a low likelihood of occurring, taking into account all relevant facts, circumstances, and information available to the partners (including bona fide financial projections). Section 1.514(c)-2(g) describes types of events that give rise to unlikely losses or deductions.

The Treasury Department and the IRS have received comments suggesting that a "more likely than not" standard is appropriate for determining when a loss or deduction is unlikely to occur. Notice 90-41 (1990-1 CB 350) (see §601.601(d)(2)(ii)(b)), which preceded the initial proposed regulations under section 514(c)(9)(E), outlined this standard. The commenter explained that the "low likelihood of occurring" standard in the existing regulations is vague and gives little comfort to QOs and their taxable partners when drafting allocations to reflect legitimate business arrangements (such as, drafting allocations to account for cost overruns). The Treasury Department and the IRS are considering changing the standard in §1.514(c)-2(g) and request further comments explaining why "more likely than not" is a more appropriate standard than the standard contained in the existing regulations, or whether another standard turning upon a level of risk that is between "more likely than not" and "low likelihood of occurring" might be more appropriate and what such other standard could be.

4. *Chargebacks of Partner-Specific Expenditures and Unlikely Losses*

Because allocations of partner-specific expenditures in §1.514(c)-2(f) and unlikely losses in §1.514(c)-2(g) are disregarded in computing overall partnership income or loss, allocations of items of income or gain or net income to reverse the prior partner-specific expenditure or unlikely loss could cause a violation of the fractions rule. For example, a QO may contribute capital to a partnership to pay a specific expenditure with the understanding that it will receive a special allocation of income to reverse the prior expenditure once the partnership earns certain profits. If the allocation of income is greater than the QO's fractions rule percentage, the allocation will cause a fractions rule violation.

Section 1.514(c)-2(e)(1) of the existing regulations generally disregards certain allocations of income or loss made to chargeback previous allocations of income or loss in computing overall partnership income or loss for purposes of the fractions rule. Specifically, §1.514(c)-2(e)(1)(i) disregards allocations of what would otherwise be overall partnership income that chargeback (that is, reverse) prior disproportionately large allocations of overall partnership loss (or part of the overall partnership loss) to a QO (the chargeback exception). The chargeback exception applies to a chargeback of an allocation of part of the overall partnership income or loss only if that part consists of a pro rata portion of each item of partnership income, gain, loss, and deduction (other than nonrecourse deductions, as well as partner nonrecourse deductions and compensating allocations) that is included in computing overall partnership income or loss.

The Treasury Department and the IRS understand that often a real estate partnership with QO partners may seek to reverse a special allocation of unlikely losses or partner-specific items with net profits of the partnership, which could result in allocations that would violate the fractions rule. Such allocations of net income to reverse special allocations of unlikely losses or partner-specific items that were disregarded in computing overall partnership income or loss for purposes of the fractions rule under § 1.514(c)-2(f) or (g), respectively, do not violate the purpose of the fractions rule. Accordingly, the proposed regulations modify the chargeback exception to disregard in computing overall partnership income or loss for purposes of the fractions rule an allocation of what would otherwise have been an allocation of overall partnership income to chargeback (that is, reverse) a special allocation of a partner-specific expenditure under § 1.514(c)-2(f) or a special allocation of an unlikely loss under § 1.514(c)-2(g). Notwithstanding the rule in the proposed regulations, an allocation of an unlikely loss or a partner-specific expenditure that is disregarded when allocated, but is taken into account for purposes of determining the partners' economic entitlement to a chargeback of such loss or expense may, in certain circumstances, give rise to complexities in determining applicable percentages for purposes of fractions rule compliance. Accordingly, the Treasury Department and the IRS request comments regarding the interaction of disregarded partner-specific expenditures and unlikely losses with chargebacks of such items with overall partnership income.

5. *Acquisition of Partnership Interests after Initial Formation of Partnership*

Section 1.514(c)-2(k)(1) of the existing regulations provides special rules regarding changes in partnership allocations arising from a change in partners' interests. Specifically, § 1.514(c)-2(k)(1) provides that changes in partnership allocations that result from transfers or shifts of partnership interests (other than transfers from a QO to another QO) will be closely scrutinized (to determine whether the transfer or shift stems from a prior agreement, understanding, or plan or could otherwise be expected given the structure of the transaction), but generally will be taken into account only in determining whether the partnership satisfies the fractions rule in the taxable year of the change and subsequent taxable years. Section 1.514(c)-2(k)(4) of the existing regulations provides that § 1.514(c)-2 may not be applied in a manner inconsistent with the purpose of the fractions rule, which is to prevent tax avoidance by limiting the permanent or temporary transfer of tax benefits from tax-exempt partners to taxable partners.

The Treasury Department and the IRS have received comments requesting guidance in applying the fractions rule when additional partners are admitted to a partnership after the initial formation of the partnership. The commenter explained that many real estate partnerships with QO partners admit new partners in a number of rounds of closings, but treat the partners as having entered at the same time for purposes of sharing in profits and losses (staged closings). A number of commercial arrangements are used to effect staged closings. For example, the initial operations of the partnership may be funded entirely through debt financing, with all partners contributing their committed capital at a later date. Alternatively, later entering partners may contribute capital and an interest factor, some or both of which is then distributed to the earlier admitted partners to compensate them for the time value of their earlier contributions.

Under existing regulations, staged closings could cause violations of the fractions rule in two ways. First, when new partners are admitted to a partnership, shifts of partnership interests occur. Changes in allocations that result from shifts of partnership interests are closely scrutinized under § 1.514(c)-2(k)(1) of the existing regulations if pursuant to a prior agreement and could be determined to violate the fractions rule. Second, after admitting new partners, partnerships may disproportionately allocate income or loss to the partners to adjust the partners' capital accounts as a result of the staged closings. These disproportionate allocations could cause fractions rule violations if one of the partners is a QO.

The Treasury Department and the IRS have determined that changes in allocations and disproportionate allocations resulting from common commercial staged closings should not violate the fractions rule if they are not inconsistent with the purpose of the fractions rule under § 1.514(c)-2(k)(4) and certain conditions are satisfied. The conditions include the following: (A) the new partner acquires the partnership interest no later than 18 months following the formation of the partnership (applicable period); (B) the partnership agreement and other relevant documents anticipate the new partners acquiring the partnership interests during the applicable period, set forth the time frame in which the new partners will acquire the partnership interests, and provide for the amount of capital the partnership intends to raise; (C) the partnership agreement and any other relevant documents specifically set forth the method of determining any applicable interest factor and for allocating income, loss, or deduction to the partners to adjust partners' capital accounts after the new partner acquires the partnership interest; and (D) the interest rate for any applicable interest factor is not greater than 150 percent of the highest applicable Federal rate, at the appropriate compounding period or periods, at the time the partnership was formed.

Under the proposed regulations, if those conditions are satisfied, the IRS will not closely scrutinize changes in allocations resulting from staged closings under § 1.514(c)-2(k)(1) and will disregard in computing overall partnership income or loss for purposes of the fractions rule disproportionate allocations of income, loss, or deduction made to adjust the capital accounts when a new partner acquires its partnership interest after the partnership's formation.

6. *Capital Commitment Defaults or Reductions*

The Treasury Department and the IRS received comments requesting guidance with respect to calculations of overall partnership income and loss when allocations change as a result of capital commitment defaults or reductions. The commenter indicated that, in the typical real estate partnership, a limited partner generally will not contribute its entire investment upon being admitted as a partner. Rather, that limited partner will commit to contribute a certain dollar amount over a fixed period of time, and the general partner will then "call" on that committed, but uncontributed, capital as needed. These calls will be made in proportion to the partners' commitments to the partnership.

The commenter identified certain remedies that partnership agreements provide if a partner fails to contribute a portion (or all) of its committed capital. These remedies commonly include: (i) allowing the non-defaulting partner(s) to contribute additional capital in return for a preferred return on that additional capital; (ii) causing the defaulting partner to forfeit all or a portion of its interest in the partnership; (iii) forcing the defaulting partner to sell its interest in the partnership, or (iv) excluding the defaulting partner from making future capital contributions. Alternatively, the agreement may allow partners to reduce their commitment amounts, reducing allocations of income and loss as well. The commenter noted that, depending on the facts, any of these partnership agreement provisions could raise fractions rule concerns.

There is little guidance in the existing regulations regarding changes to allocations of a partner's share of income and losses from defaulted capital calls and reductions in capital commitments. Section 1.514(c)-2(k)(1) applies to changes in allocations resulting from a default if there is a "transfer or shift" of partnership interests. The Treasury Department and the IRS have determined that changes in allocations resulting from unanticipated defaults or reductions do not run afoul of the purpose of the fractions rule if such changes are provided for in the partnership agreement. Therefore, the proposed regulations provide that, if the partnership agreement provides for changes to allocations due to an unanticipated partner default on a capital contribution commitment or an unanticipated reduction in a partner's capital contribution commitment, and those changes in allocations are not inconsistent with the purpose of the fractions rule under § 1.514(c)-2(k)(4), then: (A) changes to partnership allocations provided in the agreement will not be closely scrutinized under § 1.514(c)-2(k)(1) and (B) partnership allocations of income, loss, or deduction (including allocations to adjust partners' capital accounts to be consistent with the partners' adjusted capital commitments) to partners to adjust the partners' capital accounts as a result of unanticipated capital contribution defaults or reductions will be disregarded in computing overall partnership income or loss for purposes of the fractions rule.

7. *Applying the Fractions Rule to Tiered Partnerships*

Section 1.514(c)-2(m)(1) of the existing regulations provides that if a QO holds an indirect interest in real property through one or more tiers of partnerships (a chain), the fractions rule is satisfied if: (i) the avoidance of tax is not a principal purpose for using the tiered-ownership structure; and (ii) the relevant partnerships can demonstrate under "any reasonable method" that the relevant chains satisfy the requirements of § 1.514(c)-2(b)(2) through (k). Section 1.514(c)-2(m)(2) of the existing regulations provides examples that illustrate three different "reasonable methods:" the collapsing approach, the entity-by-entity approach, and the independent chain approach.

The Treasury Department and the IRS have received comments requesting guidance with respect to tiered partnerships and the application of the independent chain approach. Under the independent chain approach in § 1.514(c)-2(m)(2) *Example 3* of the existing regulations, different lower-tiered partnership chains (one or more tiers of partnerships) are examined independently of each other, even if these lower-tiered partnerships are owned by a common upper-tier partnership. The example provides, however, that chains are examined independently only if the upper-tier partnership allocates the items of each lower-tier partnership separately from the items of another lower-tier partnership.

The comment noted that in practice, a real estate partnership generally invests in a significant number of properties, often through joint ventures with other partners. A typical real estate partnership will not make separate allocations to its partners of lower-tier partnership items. Accordingly, the proposed regulations amend § 1.514(c)-2(m)(2) *Example 3* to remove the requirement that a partnership allocate items from lower-tier partnerships separately from one another. Partnership provisions require that partnership items such as items that would give rise to UBTI be separately stated. *See* § 1.702-1(a)(8)(ii). That requirement suffices to separate the tiers of partnerships, and, thus, the proposed regulations do not require the upper-tier partnership to separately allocate partnership items from separate lower-tier partnerships. The proposed regulations also revise § 1.514(c)-2(m)(1)(ii) to remove the discussion of minimum gain chargebacks that refers to language that has been deleted from the example.

8. *De Minimis Exceptions from Application of the Fractions Rule*

Section 1.514(c)-2(k)(2) of the existing regulations provides that the partnership limitation in section 514(c)(9)(B)(vi) does not apply to a partnership if all QOs hold a de minimis interest in the partnership, defined as no more than five percent in the capital or profits of the partnership, and taxable partners own substantial interests in the partnership through which they participate in the partnership on substantially the same terms as the QO partners. If the partnership limitation in section 514(c)(9)(B)(vi) does not apply to the partnership, the fractions rule does not apply to the partnership. Because the fractions rule does not apply to a partnership if all QOs are de minimis interest holders in the partnership, the Treasury Department and the IRS considered whether the inverse fact pattern, in which all non-QO partners are de minimis partners, implicates the purpose of the fractions rule. *See* § 1.514(c)-2(k)(4) (providing that the purpose of the fractions rule is to "prevent tax avoidance by limiting the permanent or temporary transfer of tax benefits from tax-exempt partners to taxable partners, whether by directing income or gain to tax-exempt partners, by directing losses, deductions or credits to taxable partners, or by some similar manner.").

The Treasury Department and the IRS have determined that the purpose of the fractions rule is similarly not violated if all non-QO partners hold a de minimis interest. Therefore, the proposed regulations provide that the fractions rule does not apply to a partnership in which non-QO partners do not hold (directly or indirectly through a partnership), in the aggregate, interests of greater than five percent in the capital or profits of the partnership, so long as the partnership's allocations have substantial economic effect. For purposes of the proposed rule, the determination of whether an allocation has substantial economic effect is made without application of the special rules in § 1.704-1(b)(2)(iii)(*c*)(2) (regarding the presumption that there is a reasonable possibility that allocations will affect substantially the dollar amounts to be received by the partners from the partnership if there is a strong likelihood that offsetting allocations will not be made in five years, and the presumption that the adjusted tax basis (or book value) of partnership property is equal to the fair market value of such property).

The existing regulations also provide for a de minimis exception for allocations away from QO partners. Section 1.514(c)-2(k)(3) of the existing regulations provides that a QO's fractions rule percentage of the partnership's items of loss and deduction, other than nonrecourse and partner nonrecourse deductions, that are allocated away from the QO and to other partners in any taxable year, are treated as having been allocated to the QO for purposes of the fractions rule if: (i) the allocation was neither planned nor motivated by tax avoidance; and (ii) the total amount of those items of partnership loss or deduction is less than both one percent of the partnership's aggregate items of gross loss and deduction for the taxable year and $50,000. The preamble to the existing final regulations under section 514(c)(9)(E) explained that the de minimis allocation exception was "to provide relief for what would otherwise be minor inadvertent violations of the fractions rule." TD 8539, 59 FR 24924. The exception was "not intended . . . [to] be used routinely by partnerships to allocate some of the partnership's losses and deductions." *Id.* To that end, the final regulations limited the exception to $50,000. As an example of a de minimis allocation intended to meet this exception, the preamble described a scenario in which a plumber's bill is paid by the partnership but overlooked until after the partner's allocations have been computed and then is allocated entirely to the taxable partner. *Id.*

In current business practices, a $50,000 threshold does not provide sufficient relief for de minimis allocations away from the QO partner. The proposed regulations still require that allocations not exceed one percent of the partnership's aggregate items of gross loss and deduction for the taxable year, but raise the threshold from $50,000 to $1,000,000.

Proposed Applicability Date

The regulations under section 514(c)(9)(E) are proposed to apply to taxable years ending on or after the date these regulations are published as final regulations in the **Federal Register**. However, a partnership and its partners may apply all the rules in these proposed regulations for taxable years ending on or after November 23, 2016.

Special Analyses

Certain IRS regulations, including this one, are exempt from the requirements of Executive Order 12866, as supplemented and reaffirmed by Executive Order 13563. Therefore, a regulatory impact assessment is not required. It also has been determined that section 553(b) of the Administrative Procedure Act (5 U.S.C. chapter 5) does not apply to these regulations. Because these proposed regulations do not impose a collection of information on small entities, the Regulatory Flexibility Act (5 U.S.C. chapter 6) does not apply. Pursuant to section 7805(f) of the Code, this notice of proposed rulemaking has been submitted to the Chief Counsel for Advocacy of the Small Business Administration for comment on its impact on small business.

Comments and Requests for a Public Hearing

Before these proposed regulations are adopted as final regulations, consideration will be given to any comments that are submitted timely to the IRS as prescribed in this preamble under the "Addresses" heading. The Treasury Department and the IRS request comments on all aspects of the proposed rules. All comments will be available at *www.regulations.gov* or upon request. A public hearing will be scheduled if requested in writing by any person that timely submits written comments. If a public hearing is scheduled, notice of the date, time, and place for the public hearing will be published in the **Federal Register**.

Drafting Information

The principal author of these proposed regulations is Caroline E. Hay, Office of the Associate Chief Counsel (Passthroughs and Special Industries). However, other personnel from the Treasury Department and the IRS participated in their development.

[¶49,722] Proposed Amendments of Regulations (REG-107424-12), published in the Federal Register on November 25, 2016.

[Code Sec. 417]

Pension plans: Cash-outs of accrued benefits: Minimum present value requirements.—Amendments of Reg. §1.417(e)-1, relating to the minimum present value requirements applicable to certain defined benefit pension plans, are proposed.

AGENCY: Internal Revenue Service (IRS), Treasury.

ACTION: Notice of proposed rulemaking and notice of public hearing.

SUMMARY: This document contains proposed regulations providing guidance relating to the minimum present value requirements applicable to certain defined benefit pension plans. These proposed regulations would provide guidance on changes made by the Pension Protection Act of 2006 and would provide other modifications to these rules as well. These regulations would affect participants, beneficiaries, sponsors, and administrators of defined benefit pension plans. This document also provides a notice of a public hearing on these proposed regulations.

DATES: Written or electronic comments must be received by February 23, 2017. Outlines of topics to be discussed at the public hearing scheduled for March 7, 2017, must be received by February 23, 2017.

ADDRESSES: Send submissions to: CC:PA:LPD:PR (REG-107424-12), Room 5203, Internal Revenue Service, PO Box 7604, Ben Franklin Station, Washington, DC 20044. Submissions may be hand-delivered Monday through Friday between the hours of 8 a.m. and 4 p.m. to: CC:PA:LPD:PR (REG-107424-12), Courier's Desk, Internal Revenue Service, 1111 Constitution Avenue, NW, Washington, DC, or sent electronically, via the Federal eRulemaking Portal at *http://www.regulations.gov* (IRS REG-107424-12). The public hearing will be held in the IRS Auditorium, Internal Revenue Building, 1111 Constitution Avenue, NW., Washington, DC.

FOR FURTHER INFORMATION CONTACT: Concerning the regulations, Neil S. Sandhu or Linda S. F. Marshall at (202) 317-6700; concerning submissions of comments, the hearing, and/or being placed on the building access list to attend the hearing, Oluwafunmilayo (Funmi) Taylor at (202) 317-6901 (not toll-free numbers).

SUPPLEMENTARY INFORMATION:

Background

Section 401(a)(11) of the Internal Revenue Code (Code) provides that, in order for a defined benefit plan to qualify under section 401(a), except as provided under section 417, in the case of a vested participant who does not die before the annuity starting date, the accrued benefit payable to such participant must be provided in the form of a qualified joint and survivor annuity. In the case of a vested participant who dies before the annuity starting date and who has a surviving spouse, a defined benefit plan must provide a qualified preretirement survivor annuity to the surviving spouse of such participant, except as provided under section 417.

Section 411(d)(6)(B) provides that a plan amendment that has the effect of eliminating or reducing an early retirement benefit or a retirement-type subsidy, or eliminating an optional form of benefit, with respect to benefits attributable to service before the amendment is treated as impermissibly reducing accrued benefits. However, the last sentence of section 411(d)(6)(B) provides that the Secretary may by regulations provide that section 411(d)(6)(B) does not apply to a plan amendment that eliminates an optional form of benefit (other than a plan amendment that has the effect of eliminating or reducing an early retirement benefit or a retirement-type subsidy).

Section 417(e)(1) provides that a plan may provide that the present value of a qualified joint and survivor annuity or a qualified preretirement survivor annuity will be immediately distributed if that present value does not exceed the amount that can be distributed without the participant's consent under section 411(a)(11). Section 417(e)(2) provides that, if the present value of the qualified joint and survivor annuity or the qualified preretirement survivor annuity exceeds the amount that can be distributed without the participant's consent under section 411(a)(11), then a plan may immediately distribute the present value of a qualified joint and survivor annuity or the qualified preretirement survivor annuity only if the participant and the spouse of the participant (or where the participant has died, the surviving spouse) consent in writing to the distribution.

Section 417(e)(3)(A) provides that the present value shall not be less than the present value calculated by using the applicable mortality table and the applicable interest rate.[1]

Section 417(e)(3)(B) of the Code, as amended by section 302 of the Pension Protection Act of 2006 (PPA '06), Public Law 109-280, 120 Stat. 780 (2006), provides that the term "applicable mortality table" means a mortality table, modified as appropriate by the Secretary, based on the mortality table

---

[1] Under section 411(a)(11)(B), the same applicable mortality table and applicable interest rate are used for purposes of determining whether the present value of a participant's nonforfeitable accrued benefit exceeds the maximum amount that can be immediately distributed without the participant's consent.

specified for the plan year under section 430(h)(3)(A) (without regard to section 430(h)(3)(C) or (3)(D)).

Section 417(e)(3)(C) of the Code, as amended by section 302 of PPA '06, provides that the term "applicable interest rate" means the adjusted first, second, and third segment rates applied under rules similar to the rules of section 430(h)(2)(C) of the Code for the month before the date of the distribution or such other time as the Secretary may prescribe by regulations. However, for purposes of section 417(e)(3), these rates are to be determined without regard to the segment rate stabilization rules of section 430(h)(2)(C)(iv). In addition, under section 417(e)(3)(D), these rates are to be determined using the average yields for a month, rather than the 24-month average used under section 430(h)(2)(D).

Section 411(a)(13) of the Code, as added by section 701(b) of PPA '06, provides that an "applicable defined benefit plan," as defined by section 411(a)(13)(C), is not treated as failing to meet the requirements of section 417(e) with respect to accrued benefits derived from employer contributions solely because the present value of a participant's accrued benefit (or any portion thereof) may be, under the terms of the plan, equal to the amount expressed as the hypothetical account balance or as an accumulated percentage of such participant's final average compensation.

Section 1107(a)(2) of PPA '06 provides that a pension plan does not fail to meet the requirements of section 411(d)(6) by reason of a plan amendment to which section 1107 applies, except as provided by the Secretary of the Treasury. Section 1107 of PPA '06 applies to plan amendments made pursuant to the provisions of PPA '06 or regulations issued thereunder that are adopted no later than a specified date, generally the last day of the first plan year beginning on or after January 1, 2009.

Final regulations under section 417 relating to the qualified joint and survivor and qualified preretirement survivor annuity requirements have not been amended to reflect PPA '06. The regulations, which were issued on August 22, 1988, were amended on April 3, 1998, to reflect changes enacted by the Uruguay Round Agreements Act, Public Law 103-465 (GATT).

Section 1.417(e)-1(d)(1) provides that a defined benefit plan generally must provide that the present value of any accrued benefit and the amount of any distribution, including a single sum, must not be less than the amount calculated using the specified applicable interest rate and the specified applicable mortality table. The present value of any optional form of benefit cannot be less than the present value of the accrued benefit determined in accordance with the preceding sentence.

Section 1.417(e)-1(d)(6) provides an exception from the minimum present value requirements of section 417(e) and § 1.417(e)-1(d). This exception applies to the amount of a distribution paid in the form of an annual benefit that either does not decrease during the life of the participant (or, in the case of a qualified preretirement survivor annuity, the life of the participant's spouse), or that decreases during the life of the participant merely because of the death of the survivor annuitant (but only if the reduction is to a level not below 50 percent of the annual benefit payable before the death of such survivor annuitant) or the cessation or reduction of Social Security supplements or qualified disability benefits.

Notice 2007-81, 2007-2 CB 899 (see 26 CFR 601.601(d)(2)(ii)(*b*)), provides guidance on the applicable interest rate. Rev. Rul. 2007-67, 2007-2 CB 1047 (see 26 CFR 601.601(d)(2)(ii)(*b*)), provides guidance on the applicable mortality table[2] and the timing rules that apply to the determination of the applicable interest rate and the applicable mortality table.

The Worker, Retiree, and Employer Recovery Act of 2008, Public Law 109-280 (120 Stat. 780), amended section 415(b)(2)(E)(v) to provide that the applicable mortality table under section 417(e)(3)(B) applies for purposes of adjusting a benefit or limitation pursuant to section 415(b)(2)(B), (C), or (D).

Sections 205(g), 203(e), and 204(g) of the Employee Retirement Income Security Act of 1974 (ERISA) contain rules that are parallel to Code sections 417(e), 411(a)(11), and 411(d)(6), respectively. Under section 101 of Reorganization Plan No. 4 of 1978 (43 FR 47713), the Secretary of the Treasury has interpretive jurisdiction over the subject matter addressed in these regulations for purposes of ERISA, as well as the Code. Thus, these regulations apply for purposes of the Code and the corresponding provisions of ERISA.

In *West v. AK Steel Corporation Retirement Accumulation Pension Plan*, 484 F.3d 395 (6th Cir. 2007), the court held that a preretirement mortality discount could not be used in the computation of the present value of a participant's single-sum distribution under a cash balance plan if the death benefit under the plan was equal in value to the participant's accrued benefit under the plan. The court found that, if a participant's beneficiary is entitled to the participant's entire accrued benefit upon the participant's death before attainment of normal retirement age, the use of a mortality discount for the period before normal retirement age would result in a partial forfeiture of benefits in violation of the ERISA vesting rules that correspond to the rules of section 411(a). See also *Berger v. Xerox Corporation Retirement Income Guarantee Plan*, 338 F.3d 755 (7th Cir. 2003); *Crosby v. Bowater, Inc. Ret. Plan*, 212 F.R.D. 350 (W.D. Mich. 2002), rev'd on other grounds, 382 F.3d 587 (6th Cir. 2004) (accrued benefits include not only retirement benefits themselves, but also death benefits which are directly related to the value of the retirement benefits). In *Stewart v. AT&T Inc.*, 354 Fed. Appx. 111 (5th Cir. 2009),

[2] Notice 2008-85, 2008-2 CB 905, Notice 2013-49, 2013-32 IRB 127, Notice 2015-53, 2015-33 IRB 190, and Notice 2016-50, 2016-38 IRB 371, set forth the section 417(e)(3) applicable mortality tables for 2009 through 2017.

however, the court held that a preretirement mortality discount was appropriately applied to determine a single-sum distribution under a traditional defined benefit plan. The court distinguished *AK Steel* and *Berger* on the basis that the plans at issue in those cases did not provide for a forfeiture of the accrued benefit on the death of the participant before retirement, whereas the plan at issue in *Stewart* provided for such a forfeiture.

Final regulations (TD 9783) under section 417(e) that permit defined benefit plans to simplify the treatment of certain optional forms of benefit that are paid partly in the form of an annuity and partly in a more accelerated form were published by the Treasury Department and the IRS in the **Federal Register** on September 9, 2016 (81 FR 62359).

Explanation of Provisions

Overview

These proposed regulations would amend the current final regulations under section 417(e) regarding the minimum present value requirements of section 417(e)(3) in several areas. Specifically, the proposed regulations would update the regulations for changes made by PPA '06 and to eliminate certain obsolete provisions. The proposed regulations also contain a few other clarifying changes.

Updates to reflect statutory and regulatory changes

The proposed regulations would update the existing regulatory provisions to reflect the statutory changes made by PPA '06, including the new interest rates and mortality tables set forth in section 417(e)(3) and the exception from the valuation rules for certain applicable defined benefit plans set forth in section 411(a)(13). The proposed regulations clarify that the interest rates that are published by the Commissioner pursuant to the provisions as modified by PPA '06 are to be used without further adjustment. In addition, the proposed regulations would eliminate obsolete provisions of the regulations relating to the transition from pre-1995 law to the interest rates and mortality assumptions provided by GATT. Furthermore, the proposed regulations make conforming changes to reflect the final regulations under section 417(e) that permit defined benefit plans to simplify the treatment of certain optional forms of benefit that are paid partly in the form of an annuity and partly in a more accelerated form.

Other clarifying changes

A. *Treatment of preretirement mortality*

The proposed regulations would include rules relating to the treatment of preretirement mortality discounts in determining the minimum present value of accrued benefits under the regulations to address the issue raised by *AK Steel* and *Berger* of whether a plan that provides a death benefit equal in value to the accrued benefit may apply a preretirement mortality discount for the probability of death when determining the amount of a single-sum distribution.

Section 411(a) generally prohibits forfeitures of accrued benefits. Under section 411(a)(1), an employee's rights in his accrued benefit derived from employee contributions must be nonforfeitable, and under section 411(a)(2), an employee's rights in his accrued benefit derived from employer contributions must become nonforfeitable in accordance with a vesting schedule that is specified in the statute. Section 411(a)(3)(A) provides that a right to an accrued benefit derived from employer contributions is not treated as forfeitable solely because the plan provides that it is not payable if the participant dies (except in the case of a survivor annuity which is payable as provided in section 401(a)(11)).

Section 411(a)(7)(A)(i) defines a participant's accrued benefit under a defined benefit plan as the employee's accrued benefit determined under the plan and, except as provided in section 411(c)(3), expressed in the form of an annual benefit commencing at normal retirement age. Section 1.411(a)-7(a)(1) defines a participant's accrued benefit under a defined benefit plan as the annual benefit commencing at normal retirement age if the plan provides an accrued benefit in that form. If a defined benefit plan does not provide an accrued benefit in the form of an annual benefit commencing at normal retirement age, § 1.411(a)-7(a)(1)(ii) defines the accrued benefit as an annual benefit commencing at normal retirement age which is the actuarial equivalent of the accrued benefit determined under the plan. The regulation further clarifies that the term "accrued benefits" refers only to pension or retirement benefits. Consequently, accrued benefits do not include ancillary benefits not directly related to retirement benefits, such as incidental death benefits.

Section 411(d)(6)(A) prohibits a plan amendment that decreases a participant's accrued benefit. Section 411(d)(6)(B) provides that a plan amendment that has the effect of eliminating or reducing an early retirement benefit or retirement-type subsidy or eliminating an optional form of benefit with respect to benefits attributable to service before the amendment is treated as reducing accrued benefits for this purpose. Section 1.411(d)-3(g)(2)(v) provides that a death benefit under a defined benefit plan other than a death benefit that is part of an optional form of benefit is an ancillary benefit. Section 1.411(d)-3(g)(6)(ii)(B) describes death benefits payable after the annuity starting date that are considered part of an optional form of benefit. Pursuant to § 1.411(d)-3(g)(14) and (15), section 411(d)(6) protected benefits do not include a death benefit under a defined benefit plan that is an ancillary benefit and not part of an optional form of benefit.

A death benefit under a defined benefit plan that is payable when the participant dies before attaining normal retirement age and before benefits commence is not part of the participant's accrued benefit within the meaning of section 411(a)(7). Accordingly, the anti-forfeiture rules of section 411(a) do not apply to such a death benefit. This is the case even if the amount of the death benefit is the same as the amount the participant would have received had the participant separated from service and elected to receive a distribution immediately before death. Moreover, such a death benefit is an ancillary benefit within the meaning of § 1.411(d)-3(g)(2)(v) — rather than a section 411(d)(6) protected benefit — and therefore can be eliminated by plan amendment (provided that a qualified preretirement survivor annuity for a surviving spouse is preserved, pursuant to section 401(a)(11)).

The minimum present value requirements of section 417(e)(3) do not take into account the value of ancillary benefits that are not part of the participant's accrued benefit under the plan. Consistent with this, § 1.417(e)-1(d)(1)(i) does not require ancillary death benefits to be taken into account in the required minimum present value calculation. Because questions have arisen regarding this rule, the proposed regulations would clarify that the probability of death under the applicable mortality table is generally taken into account for purposes of determining the present value under section 417(e)(3), without regard to the death benefits provided under the plan other than a death benefit that is part of the normal form of benefit or part of another optional form of benefit (as described in § 1.411(d)-3(g)(6)(ii)(B)) for which present value is determined.

However, a different rule applies with respect to whether the probability of death under the applicable mortality table is taken into account for purposes of determining the present value with respect to the accrued benefit derived from contributions made by an employee. This is because an employee's rights in the accrued benefit derived from the employee's own contributions are nonforfeitable under section 411(a)(1), and the exception for death under section 411(a)(3)(A) to the nonforfeitability of accrued benefits does not apply to the accrued benefit derived from employee contributions. As a result, for purposes of determining the present value under section 417(e)(3) with respect to the accrued benefit derived from contributions made by an employee (that is computed in accordance with the requirements of section 411(c)(3)), the probability of death during the assumed deferral period, if any, is not taken into account. For purposes of the preceding sentence, the assumed deferral period is the period between the date of the present value determination and the assumed commencement date for the annuity attributable to contributions made by an employee.

The proposed regulations include an example to illustrate the application of the minimum present value requirements of section 417(e)(3) in the case of a single-sum distribution of a participant's entire accrued benefit that consists both of an accrued benefit derived from employee contributions and an employer-provided accrued benefit. Consistent with the rules in these proposed regulations, the example illustrates that a single-sum distribution of the participant's entire accrued benefit in such a case must equal the sum of the minimum present value of the accrued benefit derived from employee contributions, determined under section 417(e)(3) (applying the special rules set forth in the preceding paragraph), and the minimum present value of the employer-provided accrued benefit, determined under section 417(e)(3). Note that Rev. Rul. 89-60, 1989-1 CB 113 (1989) suggests that it is sufficient for a single-sum distribution in such a case to merely equal the greater of the minimum present value of the accrued benefit derived from employee contributions and the minimum present value of the participant's entire accrued benefit. To the extent the guidance under Rev. Rul. 89-60 is inconsistent with the final regulations that adopt these proposed regulations, the regulations would supersede the guidance in Rev. Rul. 89-60.

B. *Social security level income options*

Questions have arisen regarding whether the minimum present value requirements of section 417(e)(3) apply to a social security level income option. As noted above, § 1.417(e)-1(d)(6) provides that the minimum present value requirements of section 417(e)(3) do not apply to the amount of a distribution paid in the form of an annual benefit that does not decrease during the life of the participant, or that decreases during the life of the participant merely because of the death of the survivor annuitant or the cessation or reduction of social security supplements or qualified disability benefits.

A social security supplement is defined in § 1.411(a)-7(c)(4) as a benefit for plan participants that commences before and terminates before the age when participants are entitled to old-age insurance benefits, unreduced on account of age, under title II of the Social Security Act, and does not exceed such old-age insurance benefit. A social security supplement (other than a QSUPP as defined in § 1.401(a)(4)-12) is an ancillary benefit that is not a section 411(d)(6) protected benefit.

A social security level income option is an optional form of benefit (protected under section 411(d)(6)) under which a participant's accrued benefit is paid in the form of an annuity with larger payments in earlier years, before an assumed social security commencement age, to provide the participant with approximately level retirement income when the assumed social security payments are taken into account. It is appropriate to subject a social security level income option to the rules of section 417(e)(3) because, when a participant's accrued benefit is paid as a social security level income option, a portion of the participant's accrued benefit (which may be substantial) is accelerated and paid over a short period of time until social security retirement age. Because the periodic payments under a social security level income option decrease during the lifetime of the participant and the decrease is not the result of the cessation of an ancillary social security supplement, § 1.417(e)-1(d)(6) does not provide an exception from the minimum present value requirements of section 417(e)(3) for such a distribution. These proposed regulations contain an example that illustrates this point.

C. *Application of required assumptions to the accrued benefit*

The proposed regulations would clarify the scope of the rule of § 1.417(e)-1(d)(1) under which the present value of any optional form of benefit cannot be less than the present value of the normal retirement benefit (with both values determined using the applicable interest rate and the applicable mortality table). The proposed regulations would require that the present value of any optional form of benefit cannot be less than the present value of the accrued benefit payable at normal retirement age, and would provide an exception for an optional form of benefit payable after normal retirement age to the extent that a suspension of benefits applies pursuant to section 411(a)(3)(B).

Effective/Applicability Dates

The changes under the proposed regulations are proposed to apply to distributions with annuity starting dates in plan years beginning on or after the date regulations that finalize these proposed regulations are published in the **Federal Register**. Prior to this applicability date, taxpayers must continue to apply existing regulations relating to section 417(e), modified to reflect the relevant statutory provisions during the applicable period (and guidance of general applicability relating to those statutory provisions, such as Rev. Rul. 2007-67).

Special Analyses

Certain IRS regulations, including this one, are exempt from the requirements of Executive Order 12866, as supplemented and reaffirmed by Executive Order 13563. Therefore, a regulatory assessment is not required. It also has been determined that section 553(b) of the Administrative Procedure Act (5 U.S.C. chapter 5) does not apply to these regulations, and because the proposed regulation does not impose a collection of information on small entities, the Regulatory Flexibility Act (5 U.S.C. chapter 6) does not apply. Pursuant to section 7805(f) of the Code, this notice of proposed rulemaking has been submitted to the Chief Counsel for Advocacy of the Small Business Administration for comment on its impact on small business.

Comments and Public Hearing

Before these proposed regulations are adopted as final regulations, consideration will be given to any written (a signed original and eight (8) copies) or electronic comments that are submitted timely to the IRS. The Treasury Department and the IRS request comments on all aspects of these proposed regulations. In addition, the Treasury Department and the IRS specifically request comments on whether, in the case of a plan that provides a subsidized annuity payable upon early retirement and determines a single-sum distribution as the present value of the early retirement annuity, the present-value determination should be required to be calculated using the applicable interest rate and the applicable mortality table applied to the early retirement annuity (or whether the requirement to have a minimum present value that is equal to the present value of the annuity payable at normal retirement age determined in accordance with section 417(e)(3) provides the level of protection for the participant that is required by section 417(e)(3)). See *Rybarczyk v. TRW*, 235 F.3d 975 (6th Cir. 2000).

All comments will be available at www.regulations.gov or upon request. A public hearing has been scheduled for March 7, 2017, beginning at 10 a.m. in the Auditorium, Internal Revenue Service, 1111 Constitution Avenue, NW., Washington, DC. Due to building security procedures, visitors must enter at the Constitution Avenue entrance. In addition, all visitors must present photo identification to enter the building. Because of access restrictions, visitors will not be admitted beyond the immediate entrance area more than 30 minutes before the hearing starts. For information about having your name placed on the building access list to attend the hearing, see the **FOR FURTHER INFORMATION CONTACT** section of this preamble.

The rules of 26 CFR 601.601(a)(3) apply to the hearing. Persons who wish to present oral comments at the hearing must submit written or electronic comments by February 23, 2017, and an outline of topics to be discussed and the amount of time to be devoted to each topic (a signed original and eight (8) copies) by February 23, 2017. A period of 10 minutes will be allotted to each person for making comments. An agenda showing the scheduling of the speakers will be prepared after the deadline for receiving outlines has passed. Copies of the agenda will be available free of charge at the hearing.

Drafting Information

The principal authors of these regulations are Neil S. Sandhu and Linda S. F. Marshall, Office of Division Counsel/Associate Chief Counsel (Tax Exempt and Government Entities). However, other personnel from the IRS and the Treasury Department participated in the development of these regulations.

[¶49,723] Proposed Amendments of Regulations (REG-125946-10), published in the Federal Register on November 28, 2016.

[Code Sec. 472]

Tax Accounting: Inventory: Dollar-Value LIFO Method: IPIC Pools.—Amendments of Reg. §1.472-8, relating to the establishment of dollar-value last-in, first-out (LIFO) inventory pools by certain taxpayers that use the inventory price index computation (IPIC) pooling method, are proposed.

AGENCY: Internal Revenue Service (IRS), Treasury.

ACTION: Notice of proposed rulemaking.

SUMMARY: This document contains proposed regulations that relate to the establishment of dollar-value last-in, first-out (LIFO) inventory pools by certain taxpayers that use the inventory price index computation (IPIC) pooling method. The proposed regulations provide rules regarding the proper pooling of manufactured or processed goods and wholesale or retail (resale) goods. The proposed regulations would affect taxpayers who use the IPIC pooling method and whose inventory for a trade or business consists of manufactured or processed goods and resale goods.

DATES: Comments and requests for a public hearing must be received by February 27, 2017.

ADDRESSES: Send submissions to: CC:PA:LPD:PR (REG-125946-10), Room 5205, Internal Revenue Service, PO Box 7604, Ben Franklin Station, Washington, DC 20044. Submissions may be hand delivered Monday through Friday between the hours of 8 a.m. and 4 p.m. to: CC:PA:LPD:PR (REG-125946-10), Courier's Desk, Internal Revenue Service, 1111 Constitution Avenue NW., Washington, DC, or sent electronically via the Federal eRulemaking Portal at *http://www.regulations.gov/* (IRS REG-125946-10).

FOR FURTHER INFORMATION CONTACT: Concerning the proposed regulations, Natasha M. Mulleneaux, (202) 317-7007; concerning submission of comments and requests for a public hearing, Regina Johnson, (202) 317-6901 (not toll-free numbers).

SUPPLEMENTARY INFORMATION:

Background

Section 472 of the Internal Revenue Code permits a taxpayer to account for inventories using the LIFO method of accounting. The LIFO method of accounting for goods treats inventories on hand at the end of the year as consisting first of inventory on hand at the beginning of the year and then of inventories acquired during the year.

Section 1.472-8(a) of the Income Tax Regulations (26 CFR part 1) provides that any taxpayer may elect to determine the cost of its LIFO inventories using the dollar-value method, provided such method is used consistently and clearly reflects income. The dollar-value method of valuing LIFO inventories is a method of determining cost by using "base-year" cost expressed in terms of total dollars rather than the quantity and price of specific goods as the unit of measurement. The "base-year" cost is the aggregate of the cost (determined as of the beginning of the tax year for which the LIFO method is first adopted) of all items in a pool.

Pooling is central to the operation of the dollar-value LIFO method. Pooling requires costs related to different inventory products to be grouped into one or more inventory pools. To determine whether there is an increment or liquidation in a pool for a particular taxable year, the end of the year inventory of the pool expressed in terms of base-year cost is compared with the beginning of the year inventory of the pool expressed in terms of base-year cost. The regulations prescribe rules for determining whether the number and composition of the pools used by the taxpayer are appropriate. The rules vary depending upon whether the taxpayer is engaged in the activity of manufacturing or processing or the activity of wholesaling or retailing.

The general pooling rules applicable to dollar-value LIFO taxpayers are in § 1.472-8(b) and (c). These paragraphs provide separate pooling principles for taxpayers engaged in the manufacturing or processing of goods (§ 1.472-8(b)), and for taxpayers engaged in the wholesaling or retailing of goods purchased from others (§ 1.472-8(c)).

Section 1.472-8(b)(1) requires a manufacturer or processor to establish one pool for each natural business unit (natural business unit pooling method) unless the manufacturer or processor elects under § 1.472-8(b)(3) to establish multiple pools. Further, § 1.472-8(b)(2) provides that where a manufacturer or processor is also engaged in the wholesaling or retailing of goods purchased from others, the wholesaling or retailing operations with respect to such purchased goods shall not be considered a part of any manufacturing or processing unit. Additionally, § 1.472-8(b)(1) requires that where the manufacturer or processor is also engaged in the wholesaling or retailing of goods purchased from others, any pooling of the LIFO inventory of such purchased goods for wholesaling and retailing operations shall be determined in accordance with § 1.472-8(c).

In *Amity Leather Products Co.* v. *Commissioner*, 82 T.C. 726 (1984), the Tax Court considered whether a taxpayer that used the natural business unit pooling method was subject to the separate pooling requirements by virtue of being both a manufacturer and a wholesaler or retailer of merchandise. The court concluded that requiring separate inventory accounting for the two functions was reasonable and held that, where the taxpayer manufactured goods and regularly purchased identical goods from a subsidiary for resale, it was required to maintain separate pools for manufactured and purchased inventory.

A manufacturer or processor using the natural business unit pooling method may elect to use the multiple pooling method described in § 1.472-8(b)(3) for inventory items that are not within a natural business unit. Alternatively, a manufacturer or processor that does not use the natural business unit pooling method may elect to use the multiple pooling method. Under the multiple pooling method, generally each pool should consist of a group of inventory items that are substantially similar. Thus, raw materials that are substantially similar should be pooled together. Similarly, finished goods and goods-in-process should be placed in pools classified by major classes or types of goods.

Section 1.472-8(c)(1) requires wholesalers, retailer, jobbers, and distributors to establish inventory pools by major lines, types, or classes of goods. Mirroring § 1.472-8(b)(1), § 1.472-8(c)(1) requires that where a wholesaler or retailer is also engaged in the manufacturing or processing of goods, the pooling of the LIFO inventory for the manufacturing or processing operations must be determined in accordance with § 1.472-8(b).

In general, any taxpayer that elects to use the dollar-value LIFO method to value LIFO inventories may elect to use the IPIC method to compute the base-year cost and determine the LIFO value of a dollar-value pool for a trade or business. A taxpayer that elects to use the IPIC method of determining the value of a dollar-value LIFO pool for a trade or business may also elect to establish dollar-value pools, for those items accounted for using the IPIC method, using the IPIC pooling method provided in § 1.472-8(b)(4) and (c)(2). Section 1.472-8(b)(4) governs the application of the IPIC pooling method to manufacturers and processors that elect to use the IPIC method for a trade or business. Section 1.472-8(c)(2) governs the application of the IPIC pooling method to wholesalers, retailers, jobbers, and distributors that elect to use the IPIC method for a trade or business.

For manufacturers and processors using the IPIC pooling method under § 1.472-8(b)(4), pools may be established for those items accounted for using the IPIC method based on the 2-digit commodity codes (that is, major commodity groups) in Table 9 (formerly Table 6) of the Producer Price Index Detailed Report (PPI Detailed Report), which is published monthly by the United States Bureau of Labor Statistics (BLS). A taxpayer establishing IPIC pools under § 1.472-8(b)(4) may combine IPIC pools that comprise less than 5 percent of the total inventory value of all dollar-value pools to form a single miscellaneous IPIC pool. If the resulting miscellaneous IPIC pool is less than 5 percent of the total inventory value of all dollar-value pools, the taxpayer may combine the miscellaneous IPIC pool with its largest IPIC pool.

For retailers using the IPIC pooling method under § 1.472-8(c)(2), pools may be established for those purchased items accounted for using the IPIC method based on either the general expenditure categories (that is, major groups) in Table 3 of the Consumer Price Index Detailed Report (CPI Detailed Report), published monthly by BLS, or the 2-digit commodity codes (that is, major commodity groups) in Table 9 of the PPI Detailed Report. For wholesalers, jobbers, or distributors using the IPIC pooling method under § 1.472-8(c)(2), pools may be established for those items accounted for using the IPIC method based on the 2-digit commodity codes in Table 9 of the PPI Detailed Report. A taxpayer establishing IPIC pools under § 1.472-8(c)(2) may combine pools that comprise less than 5 percent of the total inventory value of all dollar-value pools to form a single miscellaneous IPIC pool. If the resulting miscellaneous IPIC pool is less than 5 percent of the total inventory value of all dollar-value pools, the taxpayer may combine the miscellaneous IPIC pool with its largest IPIC pool.

Each of the 5-percent rules provided in § 1.472-8(b)(4) or (c)(2) is a method of accounting. Thus, a taxpayer may not change to, or cease using either 5-percent rule without obtaining the prior consent of the Commissioner. Whether a specific IPIC pool or the miscellaneous IPIC pool satisfies the applicable 5-percent rule must be determined in the year of adoption or year of change (whichever is applicable) and redetermined every third taxable year. Any change in pooling required or permitted under a 5-percent rule is also a change in method of accounting. A taxpayer must secure the consent of the Commissioner before combining or separating pools. The general procedures under section 446(e) and § 1.446-1(e) that a taxpayer must follow to obtain the consent of the Commissioner to change a method of accounting for federal income tax purposes are contained in Rev. Proc. 2015-13, 2015-5 I.R.B. 419 (or its successors), as modified by Rev. Proc. 2015-33, 2015-24 I.R.B. 1067. See § 601.601(d)(2)(ii)(b).

The general pooling rules of § 1.472-8(b) and (c) provide that where a taxpayer is engaged in both a manufacturing or processing activity and a wholesaling or retailing activity, separate pooling rules apply to the separate activities, and goods purchased for resale may not be included in the same pool as manufactured or purchased goods. On the other hand, the IPIC pooling rules address circumstances where a trade or business consists entirely of a manufacturing, processing, retailing, or wholesaling activity. The Treasury Department and the IRS have become aware of confusion concerning how the IPIC pooling rules apply where a taxpayer is engaged in both a manufacturing or processing activity and a wholesaling or retailing activity. Accordingly, these proposed regulations address this issue.

Explanation of Provisions

Changes to IPIC Pooling Rules

The proposed regulations amend the IPIC pooling rules to clarify that those rules are applied consistently with the general LIFO pooling rule that manufactured or processed goods and resale goods may not be included in the same dollar-value LIFO pool. This general rule is intended to limit cost transference, an inherent problem with pooling. Cost transference may occur, among other circumstances, when inventory items from separate economic activities (for example, manufacturing and resale activities) are placed in the same pool and may cause misallocation of cost or distortion of income.

Accordingly, the proposed regulations clarify that an IPIC-method taxpayer who elects the IPIC pooling method described in § 1.472-8(b)(4) or (c)(2) and whose trade or business consists of both manufacturing or processing activity and resale activity may not commingle the manufactured or processed goods and the resale goods within the same IPIC pool.

Specifically, the proposed regulations provide that a manufacturer or processor using the IPIC pooling method under § 1.472-8(b)(4) that is also engaged, within the same trade or business, in wholesaling or retailing goods purchased from others may elect to establish dollar-value pools for the manufactured or processed items accounted for using the IPIC method based on the 2-digit commodity codes in Table 9 of the PPI Detailed Report. If the manufacturer or processor makes this election, the manufacturer or processor must also establish pools for its resale goods in accordance with § 1.472-8(c)(2) (that is, based on the general expenditure categories in Table 3 of the CPI Detailed Report in the case of a retailer or the 2-digit commodity codes in Table 9 of the PPI Detailed Report in the case of a retailer, wholesaler, jobber, or distributor).

If the manufacturer or processor chooses to use the 5-percent method of pooling, manufactured or processed IPIC pools (IPIC pools consisting of manufactured or processed goods) of less than 5 percent of the total current year cost of all dollar-value pools may be combined to form a single miscellaneous IPIC pool of manufactured or processed goods. The manufacturer or processor may also combine resale IPIC pools (IPIC pools consisting of resale goods) of less than 5 percent of the total value of inventory to form a single miscellaneous IPIC pool of resale goods. If the miscellaneous IPIC pool of manufactured or processed goods is less than 5 percent of the total value of inventory, the manufacturer or processor may combine the miscellaneous IPIC pool of manufactured or processed goods with its largest manufactured or processed IPIC pool. The miscellaneous IPIC pool of resale goods may not be combined with any other IPIC pool.

The proposed regulations also provide that a wholesaler, retailer, jobber, or distributor using the IPIC pooling method under § 1.472-8(c)(2) that is also engaged, within the same trade or business, in manufacturing or processing activities may elect to establish dollar-value pools for the resale goods accounted for using the IPIC method in accordance with § 1.472-8(c)(2) (that is, based on the general expenditure categories in Table 3 of the CPI Detailed Report in the case of retailer or the 2-digit commodity codes in Table 9 of the PPI Detailed Report in the case of a wholesaler, retailer, jobber, or distributor). If the wholesaler, retailer, jobber, or distributor makes this election, it must also establish pools for its manufactured or processed goods based on the 2-digit commodity codes in Table 9 of the PPI Detailed Report.

If the wholesaler, retailer, jobber, or distributor chooses to use the 5-percent method of pooling, resale IPIC pools of less than 5 percent of the total value of inventory may be combined to form a single miscellaneous IPIC pool of resale goods. The wholesaler, retailer, jobber, or distributor may also combine the IPIC pools of manufactured or processed goods of less than 5 percent of the total value of inventory to form a single miscellaneous IPIC pool of manufactured or processed goods. If the resale miscellaneous IPIC pool is less than 5 percent of the total value of inventory, the wholesaler, retailer, jobber, or distributor may combine the resale miscellaneous IPIC pool with the largest resale IPIC pool. The miscellaneous IPIC pool of manufactured or processed goods may not be combined with any other IPIC pool.

The Treasury Department and the IRS specifically request comments on the requirement that a taxpayer engaged in both manufacturing and resale activities within the same trade or business is required to use IPIC pooling for both activities.

Changes To Conform With Current BLS Publications

These proposed regulations modify § 1.472-8(b), (c), and (e)(3) to update references from Table 6 (Producer price indexes and percent changes for commodity groupings and individual items, not seasonally adjusted) to Table 9 (Producer price indexes and percent changes for commodity and service groupings and individual items, not seasonally adjusted) because of BLS changes in the PPI Detailed Report.

These proposed regulations also modify § 1.472-8(e)(3)(ii) to remove the exception to the trade or business requirement for taxpayers using the Department Store Inventory Price Indexes because BLS discontinued publishing these indexes after December 2013.

Effective/Applicability Date

These regulations are proposed to apply for taxable years ending on or after the date the regulations are published as final regulations in the **Federal Register**.

Special Analyses

Certain IRS regulations, including these, are exempt from the requirements of Executive Order 12866, as supplemented and reaffirmed by Executive Order 13563. Therefore, a regulatory impact assessment is not required. It also has been determined that section 553(b) of the Administrative Procedure Act (5 U.S.C. chapter 5) does not apply to these regulations, and, because these regulations do not impose a collection of information on small entities, the Regulatory Flexibility Act (5 U.S.C. chapter 6) does not apply. Pursuant to section 7805(f) of the Internal Revenue Code, these proposed regulations will be submitted to the Chief Counsel for Advocacy of the Small Business Administration for comment on their impact on small business.

Comments and Request for a Public Hearing

Before these proposed regulations are adopted as final regulations, consideration will be given to any written (a signed original and eight (8) copies) or electronic comments that are submitted timely to the IRS. The Treasury Department and the IRS request comments on all aspects of the proposed rules. All comments will be available at *www.regulations.gov* or upon request.

A public hearing will be scheduled if requested in writing by any person that timely submits written comments. If a public hearing is scheduled, notice of the date, time, and place for the public hearing will be published in the **Federal Register**.

Drafting Information

The principal author of these regulations is Natasha M. Mulleneaux of the Office of the Associate Chief Counsel (Income Tax & Accounting). However, other personnel from the IRS and the Treasury Department participated in their development.

[¶ 49,725] Proposed Amendments of Regulations (REG-129128-14), published in the Federal Register on December 7, 2016.

[Code Secs. 704 and 901]

Foreign taxes: Foreign tax credit: Covered asset acquisitions.—Reg. §§1.901(m)-1, 1.901(m)-2, 1.901(m)-3, 1.901(m)-4, 1.901(m)-5, 1.901(m)-6, 1.901(m)-7, 1.901(m)-8 and amendments of Reg. §§1.704-1, respecting to transactions that generally are treated as asset acquisitions for U.S. income tax purposes and either are treated as stock acquisitions or are disregarded for foreign income tax purposes, are proposed.

AGENCY: Internal Revenue Service (IRS), Treasury.

ACTION: Notice of proposed rulemaking by cross-reference in part to temporary regulations.

SUMMARY: This document contains proposed Income Tax Regulations under section 901(m) of the Internal Revenue Code (Code) with respect to transactions that generally are treated as asset acquisitions for U.S. income tax purposes and either are treated as stock acquisitions or are disregarded for foreign income tax purposes. In the Rules and Regulations section of this issue of the **Federal Register**, temporary regulations are being issued under section 901(m) (the temporary regulations), the text of which serves as the text of a portion of these proposed regulations. These regulations are necessary to provide guidance on applying section 901(m). These regulations affect taxpayers claiming foreign tax credits.

DATES: Comments and requests for a public hearing must be received by March 7, 2017.

ADDRESSES: Send submissions to CC:PA:LPD:PR (REG-129128-14), room 5205, Internal Revenue Service, PO Box 7604, Ben Franklin Station, Washington, DC 20044. Submissions may be hand delivered Monday through Friday between the hours of 8 a.m. and 4 p.m. to CC:PA:LPD:PR (REG-129128-14), Courier's desk, Internal Revenue Service, 1111 Constitution Avenue, NW., Washington, DC 20044, or sent electronically, via the Federal eRulemaking Portal at *www.regulations.gov* (IRS REG-129128-14). FOR FURTHER INFORMATION CONTACT: Concerning the regulations, Jeffrey L. Parry, (202) 317-6936; concerning submissions of comments, Regina Johnson, (202) 317-6901 (not toll-free numbers).

SUPPLEMENTARY INFORMATION:

Background

I. *Section 901(m)*

Section 212 of the Education Jobs and Medicaid Assistance Act (EJMAA), enacted on August 10, 2010 (Public Law 111-226), added section 901(m) to the Code. Section 901(m)(1) provides that, in the case of a covered asset acquisition (CAA), the disqualified portion of any foreign income tax determined with respect to the income or gain attributable to relevant foreign assets (RFAs) will not be taken into account in determining the foreign tax credit allowed under section 901(a), and, in the case of foreign income tax paid by a section 902 corporation (as defined in section 909(d)(5)), will not be taken into account for purposes of section 902 or 960. Instead, the disqualified portion of any foreign income tax (the disqualified tax amount) is permitted as a deduction. See section 901(m)(6).

Under section 901(m)(2), a CAA is (i) a qualified stock purchase (as defined in section 338(d)(3)) to which section 338(a) applies; (ii) any transaction that is treated as an acquisition of assets for U.S. income tax purposes and as the acquisition of stock of a corporation (or is disregarded) for purposes of a foreign income tax; (iii) any acquisition of an interest in a partnership that has an election in effect under section 754; and (iv) to the extent provided by the Secretary, any other similar transaction. The Joint Committee on Taxation's technical explanation of EJMAA states that it is anticipated that the Secretary will issue regulations identifying other similar transactions that result in an increase to the basis of assets for U.S. income tax purposes without a corresponding increase for foreign income tax purposes. Staff of the Joint Committee on Taxation, Technical Explanation of the Revenue Provisions of the Senate Amendment to the House Amendment to the Senate Amendment to H.R. 1586, Scheduled for Consideration by the House of Representatives on August 10, 2010, at 14 (Aug. 10, 2010) (JCT Explanation).

Section 901(m)(3)(A) provides that the term "disqualified portion" means, with respect to any CAA, for any taxable year, the ratio (expressed as a percentage) of (i) the aggregate basis differences (but not below zero) allocable to such taxable year with respect to all RFAs; divided by (ii) the income on which the foreign income tax referenced in section 901(m)(1) is determined. If the taxpayer fails to substantiate the income on which the foreign income tax is determined to the satisfaction of the Secretary, such income will be determined by dividing the amount of such foreign income tax by the highest marginal tax rate applicable to the taxpayer's income in the relevant jurisdiction. The JCT Explanation states that for this purpose the income on which the foreign income tax is determined is the income as determined under the law of the relevant jurisdiction. See JCT Explanation at 14.

Section 901(m)(3)(B)(i) provides the general rule that the basis difference with respect to any RFA will be allocated to taxable years using the applicable cost recovery method for U.S. income tax purposes. Section 901(m)(3)(B)(ii) provides that, except as otherwise provided by the Secretary, if there is a disposition of an RFA, the basis difference allocated to the taxable year of the disposition will be the excess of the basis difference of such asset over the aggregate basis difference of such asset that has been allocated to all prior taxable years. The statute further provides that no basis difference with respect to such asset will be allocated to any taxable year thereafter.

Section 901(m)(3)(C)(i) provides that basis difference means, with respect to any RFA, the excess of: (i) the adjusted basis of such asset immediately after the CAA, over (ii) the adjusted basis of such asset immediately before the CAA. If the adjusted basis of an RFA immediately before the CAA exceeds the adjusted basis of the RFA immediately after the CAA (that is, where the adjusted basis of an asset with a built-in loss is reduced in a CAA), such excess is taken into account as a basis difference of a negative amount. See section 901(m)(3)(C)(ii).

The JCT Explanation states that, for purposes of determining basis difference, it is the tax basis for U.S. income tax purposes that is relevant and not the tax basis as determined under the law of the relevant jurisdiction. See JCT Explanation at 14. However, the JCT Explanation further states that it is anticipated that the Secretary will issue regulations identifying those circumstances in which, for purposes of determining the adjusted basis of such assets immediately before the CAA, it may be acceptable to use foreign basis or another reasonable method. Id.

Section 901(m)(4) provides that an RFA means, with respect to a CAA, any asset (including goodwill, going concern value, or other intangible) with respect to such acquisition if income, deduction, gain, or loss attributable to such asset is taken into account in determining the foreign income tax referenced in section 901(m)(1).

Section 901(m)(7) provides that the Secretary may issue regulations or other guidance as is necessary or appropriate to carry out the purposes of section 901(m), including to exempt from its application certain CAAs and RFAs with respect to which the basis difference is de minimis. The JCT Explanation states that regulations may also exclude from the application of section 901(m) CAAs that are not taxable for U.S. income tax purposes, or in which the basis of the RFAs is also increased for purposes of the law of the relevant foreign jurisdiction. See JCT Explanation at 16.

Section 901(m) generally applies to CAAs occurring after December 31, 2010. Section 901(m), however, does not apply to any CAA with respect to which the transferor and transferee are not related if the acquisition is made pursuant to a written agreement that was binding on January 1, 2011, and at all times thereafter; described in a ruling request submitted to the IRS on or before July 29, 2010; or described on or before January 1, 2011, in a public announcement or in a filing with the Securities and Exchange Commission. See EJMAA, section 212(b).

II. *Notices 2014-44 and 2014-45*

The Department of the Treasury (Treasury Department) and the IRS issued Notice 2014-44 (2014-32 I.R.B. 270 (July 21, 2014)) and Notice 2014-45 (2014-34 I.R.B. 388 (July 29, 2014)), announcing the intent to issue regulations addressing the application of section 901(m) to dispositions of RFAs following CAAs and to CAAs described in section 901(m)(2)(C) (regarding section 754 elections). In addition, the notices announced the intent to issue regulations providing successor rules for the continued application of section 901(m) after subsequent transfers of RFAs with remaining basis difference. The temporary regulations issued in the Rules and Regulations section of this issue of the **Federal Register** provide the rules described in those Notices.

Explanation of Provisions

I. *Overview*

These proposed regulations provide rules for computing the disqualified portion of foreign income taxes under section 901(m). Proposed § 1.901(m)-1 provides definitions that apply for purposes of the proposed regulations. Proposed § 1.901(m)-2 identifies the transactions that are CAAs, including additional categories of transactions that are identified as CAAs pursuant to the authority granted in section 901(m)(2)(D), and provides rules for identifying assets that are RFAs with respect to a CAA. Proposed § 1.901(m)-3 provides rules for computing the disqualified portion of foreign income taxes, describes the treatment under section 901(m)(1) of the disqualified portion, and provides rules for determining whether and to what extent basis difference that is assigned to a given taxable year is carried over to subsequent taxable years. Proposed § 1.901(m)-4 provides rules for determining the basis difference with respect to an RFA, including an election to use foreign basis for purposes of this determination. Proposed § 1.901(m)-5 provides rules for taking into account basis difference under an applicable cost recovery method or as a result of a disposition of an RFA, rules for allocating that basis difference, when necessary, to one or more persons subject to section 901(m), and rules for assigning that basis difference to a U.S. taxable year. Proposed § 1.901(m)-6 provides successor rules for applying section 901(m) to subsequent transfers of RFAs that have basis difference that has not yet been fully taken into account, as well as for transferring an aggregate basis difference carryover of a person subject to section 901(m) either to another aggregate basis difference carryover account of such person or to another person subject to section 901(m). Proposed § 1.901(m)-7 provides de minimis rules under which certain basis differences are not taken into account under section 901(m). Proposed § 1.901(m)-8 provides guidance on the application of section 901(m) to pre-1987 foreign income taxes and anti-abuse rules relating to built-in loss assets.

II. *Relevance of the Terms Section 901(m) Payor, Foreign Payor, RFA Owner (U.S.), and RFA Owner (foreign)*

As provided under proposed § 1.901(m)-1, a section 901(m) payor is a person that is eligible to claim the foreign tax credit allowed under section 901(a), regardless of whether the person chooses to claim the foreign tax credit, as well as a section 902 corporation. Therefore, a section 901(m) payor is the person required to compute a disqualified tax amount when section 901(m) applies. The foreign payor is the individual or entity (including a disregarded entity) subject to a foreign income tax. The RFA owner (U.S.) is the person that owns one or more RFAs for U.S. income tax purposes and therefore is required to report, or otherwise track, items of income, deduction, gain, or loss attributable to the RFAs for purposes of computing the U.S. taxable income of the RFA owner (U.S.). Similarly, the RFA owner (foreign) is the individual or entity (including a disregarded entity) that owns one or more RFAs for purposes of a foreign income tax and that therefore generally would report, or otherwise track, items of income, deduction, gain, or loss attributable to the RFAs for purposes of determining income reported on a foreign income tax return.

The section 901(m) payor may also be the foreign payor, the RFA owner (U.S.), or the RFA owner (foreign), or any combination thereof; alternatively, the section 901(m) payor may not be any of them depending upon the application of the entity classification rules for U.S. income tax purposes. Further, the foreign payor and the RFA owner (foreign) may or may not be the same person for purposes of a foreign income tax depending upon whether the RFA owner (foreign) is a fiscally transparent entity for purposes of the foreign income tax. For example, if a foreign corporation, which is a section 902 corporation, owns RFAs and is the entity that is subject to a foreign income tax under the relevant foreign law, the foreign corporation is the section 901(m) payor, foreign payor, RFA owner (U.S.), and RFA owner (foreign). As another example, if two U.S. corporations each own a 50 percent interest in a partnership and the partnership owns a disregarded entity that is subject to a foreign income tax and that, for purposes of the foreign income tax, owns one or more RFAs, the corporate partners are each a section 901(m) payor, the disregarded entity is the foreign payor and the RFA owner (foreign), and the partnership is the RFA owner (U.S.).

Finally, because the computation of a section 901(m) payor's disqualified tax amount is based on items determined at the level of the foreign payor, the RFA owner (U.S.), and the RFA owner (foreign), the regulations provide rules for allocating those items when the section 901(m) payor is not the foreign payor, the RFA owner (U.S.), or the RFA owner (foreign), or any combination thereof.

III. *CAAs and RFAs*

A. *CAAs*

Proposed § 1.901(m)-2(b) identifies six categories of transactions that constitute CAAs, three of which are specified in the statute (incorporated by cross reference to the temporary regulations) and three of which are additional categories of transactions that are identified as CAAs pursuant to the authority granted under section 901(m)(2)(D). In addition, for transactions that occurred on or after January 1, 2011, and before the general applicability date of the temporary regulations (referred to as the "transition period" in the preamble to the temporary regulations and in this preamble), proposed § 1.901(m)-2(d) (incorporated by cross reference to the temporary regulations) defines CAAs by reference to the statutory definition under section 901(m)(2). Transactions are CAAs regardless of whether any gain, income, loss, or deduction realized in connection with the transaction is taken into account for U.S. income tax purposes. However, basis difference resulting from a CAA may not be taken into account under section 901(m) pursuant to de minimis rules in proposed § 1.901(m)-7.

Proposed § 1.901(m)-2(b)(1) through (4) describes four specific types of transactions that are generally expected to result in an increase in the basis of assets for U.S. income tax purposes without a corresponding increase in basis for foreign income tax purposes. This is because these transactions generally are treated as an acquisition of assets for U.S. income tax purposes and either are treated as an acquisition of stock or of a partnership interest or are disregarded for foreign income tax purposes. The other two categories of transactions described in proposed § 1.901(m)-2(b)(5) and (6), which involve an acquisition of assets for both U.S. and foreign income tax purposes, are CAAs only if the transaction results in an increase in the basis of an asset for U.S. income tax purposes but not for foreign income tax purposes. Such transactions may include, for example, an acquisition of assets that is structured to avoid the application of the Code's corporate nonrecognition provisions, such as section 332, 351, or 361, while still qualifying for nonrecognition treatment for foreign income tax purposes.

B. *RFAs*

Proposed § 1.901(m)-2(c)(1) incorporates by cross reference to the temporary regulations the general definition of an RFA, which provides that an RFA means, with respect to a foreign income tax and a CAA, any asset (including goodwill, going concern value, or other intangible) subject to the CAA that is relevant in determining foreign income for purposes of the foreign income tax. In addition, for CAAs that occurred during the transition period, proposed § 1.901(m)-2(d) (incorporated by cross reference to the temporary regulations) defines RFAs by reference to the statutory definition under section 901(m)(4).

Proposed § 1.901(m)-2(c)(2) generally provides that an asset is relevant in determining foreign income if income, deduction, gain, or loss attributable to such asset is or would be taken into account in determining foreign income immediately after the CAA. Proposed § 1.901(m)-2(c)(3) provides, however, that, after a CAA, an asset will become an RFA with respect to another foreign income tax if, pursuant to a plan or series of related transactions that have a principal purpose of avoiding the application of section 901(m), an asset that is not relevant in determining foreign income for purposes of that foreign income tax immediately after the CAA later becomes relevant in determining such foreign income. A principal purpose of avoiding section 901(m) will be deemed to exist if income, deduction, gain, or loss attributable to the asset is taken into account in determining such foreign income within the one-year period following the CAA.

IV. *Disqualified Tax Amount and Aggregate Basis Difference Carryover*

A. *Disqualified tax amount*

Proposed § 1.901(m)-3 sets forth the rules for computing the disqualified portion of foreign income taxes (referred to in the regulations as the "disqualified tax amount"). Proposed § 1.901(m)-3 also sets forth the treatment under section 901(m)(1) of the disqualified tax amount and provides rules for determining whether and to what extent basis difference that is assigned to a given U.S. taxable year is carried over to subsequent U.S. taxable years (referred to in the regulations as "aggregate basis difference carryover").

In general, a disqualified tax amount is computed separately for each foreign tax return that takes into account income, gain, deduction, or loss from one or more RFAs in computing the foreign taxable income and for each section 901(m) payor that pays or accrues, or that is considered to pay or accrue, a portion of the foreign income taxes reflected on the foreign tax return. Furthermore, if the foreign income taxes relate to more than one separate category described in § 1.904-4(m) (including section 904(d) categories), a separate disqualified tax amount computation is done for each such separate category. Members of a U.S. affiliated group of corporations (as defined in section 1504) that file a consolidated return are each treated as a separate section 901(m) payor; therefore, disqualified tax amounts are computed at the member-level.

The proposed regulations refer to the total taxable income (or loss) that is computed under foreign law for a foreign taxable year and reflected on a foreign tax return as "foreign income" and the total amount of tax reflected on a foreign tax return as a "foreign income tax amount." Thus, foreign income does not include income that is exempt from the foreign income tax. The proposed regulations use the term "foreign country creditable taxes" (or "FCCTs") to refer to any foreign income taxes imposed by another foreign country or possession of the United States that were allowed under the relevant foreign law as a credit to reduce the foreign income tax amount and for which a credit is allowed under section 901 or 903. In addition, the proposed regulations define "foreign income tax" (by cross reference to the temporary regulations) to mean any income, war profits, or excess profits tax for which a credit is allowable under section 901 or 903, other than any withholding tax determined on a gross basis as described in section 901(k)(1)(B).

The foreign income, foreign income tax amount, and any FCCTs are determined at the foreign-payor level. If the foreign payor is not a section 901(m) payor, current law provides rules for determining the person that is considered to pay or accrue a foreign income tax amount for purposes of the foreign tax credit (see, for example, § § 1.702-1(a)(6) and 1.901-2(f)). Those rules are not changed by these proposed regulations and therefore apply for purposes of determining the extent to which a foreign income tax amount is paid or accrued by, or considered paid or accrued by, a section 901(m) payor for purposes of section 901(m).

Proposed § 1.901(m)-3(b) sets forth the treatment of the disqualified tax amount and the computation of the disqualified tax amount. Pursuant to section 901(m)(1) and proposed § 1.901(m)-3(b)(1), the disqualified tax amount is not taken into account for purposes of determining foreign tax credits under section 901, 902, or 960. A section 901(m) payor must compute a disqualified tax amount for any U.S. taxable year for which it is assigned a portion of the basis difference with respect to one or more RFAs.

The disqualified tax amount is the lesser of the tentative disqualified tax amount and the foreign income tax amount paid or accrued by, or considered paid or accrued by, a section 901(m) payor. The tentative disqualified tax amount is determined using a modified version of the formula provided in section 901(m)(3). To determine the tentative disqualified tax amount, the foreign income tax amount paid or accrued by, or considered paid or accrued by, the section 901(m) payor for its U.S. taxable year (multiplicand) is multiplied by a ratio (disqualified ratio), the numerator of which is the sum of the portion of the basis difference for all RFAs that is taken into account and assigned to the U.S. taxable year of the section 901(m) payor, and the denominator of which is the portion of the foreign income reflected on the foreign tax return that relates to the foreign income tax amount included in the multiplicand. The numerator and the denominator of the disqualified ratio are referred to in the proposed regulations as the "aggregate basis difference" and "allocable foreign income," respectively.

Allocable foreign income (the denominator of the disqualified ratio) and the foreign income tax amount (the multiplicand) are determined using the total amount of foreign income and foreign income tax amount reflected on the foreign income tax return that are allocable to the section 901(m) payor, instead of by reference only to the amounts determined with respect to the RFAs. The Treasury Department and the IRS have determined that this approach appropriately carries out the purposes of section 901(m) while avoiding the administrative and compliance burdens that would result from a requirement to trace amounts of income to RFAs and identify the portion of foreign income taxes imposed on that income.

If a foreign income tax amount is computed taking into account an FCCT, the multiplicand of the tentative disqualified tax amount computation is the sum of the foreign income tax amount and any FCCTs paid or accrued by, or considered paid or accrued by, the section 901(m) payor. The Treasury Department and the IRS have determined that it is appropriate to include any FCCTs in the multiplicand to better reflect the effective tax rate imposed on the aggregate basis difference. However, the tentative disqualified tax amount is reduced (but not below zero) to the extent any portion of the FCCTs is itself treated as a disqualified tax amount of the section 901(m) payor with respect to a different foreign income tax.

The aggregate basis difference in the numerator includes cost recovery amounts and disposition amounts taken into account with respect to RFAs and assigned to the U.S. taxable year of the section 901(m) payor under proposed § 1.901(m)-5, as discussed in section VI. of this the Explanation of Provisions of this preamble. When the numerator and denominator are both positive amounts, the amount of aggregate basis difference included in the numerator is limited to the amount of foreign income in the denominator of the disqualified ratio (in other words, the allocable foreign income).

This limitation ensures that multiplying the foreign income tax amount included in the multiplicand by the disqualified ratio would not produce a disqualified tax amount greater than 100 percent of the foreign income tax amount. See section IV.B. of the Explanation of Provisions section of this preamble for the treatment of any excess of the aggregate basis difference over the allocable foreign income as an aggregate basis difference carryover.

The denominator of the disqualified ratio is the allocable foreign income. When the entire foreign income tax amount reflected on a foreign tax return is paid or accrued by, or considered paid or accrued by, a single section 901(m) payor for U.S. income tax purposes, the allocable foreign income is simply the total foreign income reflected on the foreign tax return. In general, this will be the case when the section 901(m) payor is the foreign payor or owns a disregarded entity that is the foreign payor, unless there is a change in ownership or a change in entity classification in the foreign payor requiring an allocation of the foreign income tax amount of the foreign payor (a mid-year transaction).

If, however, the foreign income tax amount reflected on a foreign tax return is allocated to more than one person for U.S. income tax purposes, the allocable foreign income in the denominator of the disqualified ratio for a particular section 901(m) payor is equal to the portion of the foreign income reflected on the foreign tax return that relates to the foreign income tax amount allocated to, and considered paid or accrued by, that section 901(m) payor (and therefore that is included in the multiplicand of the tentative disqualified tax amount computation). Proposed § 1.901(m)-3(b)(2)(iii)(C) provides guidance on how to determine the allocable foreign income in three types of cases: (i) the foreign income tax amount is allocated to a section 901(m) payor because the foreign payor is involved in a mid-year transaction, such as the transfer of a disregarded entity during the disregarded entity's foreign taxable year or acquisitions involving elections under section 338 or 336(e); (ii) the foreign income tax amount is allocated to a section 901(m) payor that is a partner because the foreign payor is a partnership for U.S. income tax purposes that is legally liable for the foreign income tax amount under § 1.901-2(f)(4)(i) (or the foreign payor is a disregarded entity and its assets are owned for U.S. income tax purposes by an entity that is treated as a partnership for U.S. income tax purposes and that is legally liable for the foreign income tax amount under § 1.901-2(f)(4)(ii)); and (iii) the foreign income tax amount is allocated to a section 901(m) payor under § 1.901-2(f)(3)(i) because the section 901(m) payor is a member of a group whose income is taxed on a combined basis for foreign income tax purposes.

Notwithstanding the rules described in the two preceding paragraphs for determining allocable foreign income, if a section 901(m) payor fails to substantiate its allocable foreign income to the satisfaction of the Secretary, then proposed § 1.901(m)-3(b)(2)(iii)(D) provides that allocable foreign income will equal the amount determined by dividing the sum of the foreign income tax amount and the FCCTs that are paid or accrued by, or considered paid or accrued by, the section 901(m) payor, by the highest marginal tax rate applicable to income of the foreign payor under the relevant foreign income tax. See section 901(m)(3)(A).

If the numerator is less than zero, the denominator is less than or equal to zero, or the multiplicand is zero, the tentative disqualified tax amount (and therefore the disqualified tax amount) is zero. If the disqualified tax amount for a year either is zero or is limited by the foreign income tax amount paid or accrued by, or considered paid or accrued by, a section 901(m) payor, there will be an aggregate basis difference carryover as described in the next section.

B. *Aggregate basis difference carryover*

Proposed § 1.901(m)-3(c) provides rules for determining the amount of aggregate basis difference carryover for a given U.S. taxable year of a section 901(m) payor that will be included in the section 901(m) payor's aggregate basis difference for the next U.S. taxable year (and therefore included in the numerator of the disqualified ratio for purposes of the next year's disqualified tax amount computation). The carryover reflects the extent to which the aggregate basis difference for a U.S. taxable year has not yet given rise to a disqualified tax amount.

If the disqualified tax amount is zero, none of the aggregate basis difference gives rise to a disqualified tax amount and therefore the full amount of the section 901(m) payor's aggregate basis difference for that year will be reflected in an aggregate basis difference carryover (positive or negative).

If the disqualified tax amount is not zero, an aggregate basis difference carryover may still arise in two situations. First, if the aggregate basis difference exceeds the section 901(m) payor's allocable foreign income (the denominator of the disqualified ratio) and therefore the amount of the aggregate basis difference included in the numerator is limited, the excess is reflected in an aggregate basis difference carryover. Second, if the tentative disqualified tax amount (which takes into account FCCTs) exceeds the foreign income tax amount paid or accrued by the section 901(m) payor (which does not include FCCTs), that excess tax amount is converted into an equivalent amount of aggregate basis difference that is reflected in an aggregate basis difference carryover. See Prop. § 1.901(m)-3(c)(2)(ii)(B).

V. *Determination of Basis Difference*

Proposed § 1.901(m)-4 incorporates by cross reference the general rules in the temporary regulations for determining basis difference. Under these rules, basis difference is determined separately with respect to each foreign income tax for which an asset is an RFA.

Proposed § 1.901(m)-4(c)(1) provides for a foreign basis election, pursuant to which basis difference is equal to the U.S. basis in the RFA immediately after the CAA less the foreign basis in the RFA immediately after the CAA (including any adjustments to the foreign basis resulting from the CAA). Proposed § 1.901(m)-4(c)(2) through (4) provide rules for making a foreign basis election. A foreign basis election generally is made by the RFA owner (U.S.). For example, in a section 338 CAA, the foreign basis election is made by the corporation that is the subject of the qualified stock purchase (new target as defined in § 1.338-2(c)(17)). If the RFA owner (U.S.) is a partnership, however, each partner in the partnership (and not the partnership) may independently make a foreign basis election. A foreign basis election is made separately for each CAA and with respect to each foreign income tax and each foreign payor. For this purpose, a series of CAAs occurring as part of a plan (referred to in the regulations as an "aggregated CAA transaction") are treated as a single CAA. The proposed regulations contain examples illustrating the scope of the foreign basis election.

The election is made by using foreign basis to determine the basis differences for purposes of computing a disqualified tax amount and an aggregate basis difference carryover. The election generally must be reflected on a timely filed original federal income tax return for the first U.S. taxable year that the foreign basis election is relevant. Proposed § 1.901(m)-4(c)(5) provides an exception for certain cases in which the RFA owner (U.S.) is a partnership. This exception generally provides relief when one or more partners and the partnership have agreed that the partnership would determine whether to provide the partners with information to apply section 901(m) based on foreign basis and, in fact, the partnership provided the information to the partner using foreign basis, but when the partner timely filed its tax return it failed to report the application of section 901(m). The purpose of the relief is to address situations in which a partner must file an amended return in order to properly reflect the application of section 901(m) but does not have access to the necessary information to apply section 901(m) using U.S. basis. The criteria for qualifying for this relief should prevent partners from using hindsight in determining whether to make the foreign basis election.

Proposed § 1.901(m)-4(c)(6) provides another exception to the requirement to make the election in a timely filed original federal income tax return that applies if a taxpayer chooses to consistently apply these proposed regulations retroactively to all CAAs occurring before the regulations are issued in final form, including CAAs for which the taxpayer chooses not to make a foreign basis election. In this case, a foreign basis election may be reflected on a timely filed amended federal income tax return (or tax returns, as appropriate), provided that all amended returns are filed no later than one year following the date of publication of the Treasury decision adopting these rules as final regulations in the **Federal Register**.

VI. *Basis Difference Taken into Account*

Section 1.901(m)-5 provides rules for determining the amount of basis difference with respect to an RFA that is taken into account in a given U.S. taxable year (referred to in the regulations as "allocated basis difference"). This allocated basis difference is used to compute a disqualified tax amount for a U.S. taxable year. Basis difference is taken into account in two ways: under an applicable cost recovery method or as a result of a disposition of the RFA.

For purposes of the discussion under this section VI of the Explanation of Provisions section of the preamble, unless otherwise indicated, a reference to direct ownership of an interest in an entity refers to direct ownership for U.S. income tax purposes, which includes ownership through one or more disregarded entities. A reference to indirect ownership of an interest in an entity refers to ownership through one or more entities that are treated as fiscally transparent for U.S. income tax purposes, at least one of which is not a disregarded entity. Finally, a reference to indirect ownership of an interest in an entity for foreign income tax purposes means ownership through one or more entities that are treated as fiscally transparent for foreign income tax purposes.

A. *Cost recovery rules*

1. Determining a cost recovery amount

Proposed § 1.901(m)-5(b)(2)(i) incorporates by cross reference the general rule in the temporary regulations that a cost recovery amount for an RFA is determined by applying an applicable cost recovery method to the basis difference rather than to the U.S. basis of the RFA.

Proposed § 1.901(m)-5(b)(2)(ii) provides that if the entire U.S. basis of the RFA is not subject to the same cost recovery method, the applicable cost recovery method for determining the cost recovery amount is the cost recovery method that applies to the portion of the U.S. basis that corresponds to the basis difference.

Proposed § 1.901(m)-5(b)(3) provides that, for purposes of section 901(m), an applicable cost recovery method includes any method for recovering the cost of property over time for U.S. income tax purposes (each application of a method giving rise to a "U.S. basis deduction"). Such methods include depreciation, amortization, or depletion, as well as a method that allows the cost (or a portion of the cost) of property to be expensed in the year of acquisition or in the placed-in-service year, such as under section 179. Applicable cost recovery methods do not include any provision allowing for the recovery of U.S. basis upon a disposition of an RFA.

2. Attributing or allocating a cost recovery amount to a section 901(m) payor

Under proposed § 1.901(m)-5(b)(1), when an RFA owner (U.S.) is a section 901(m) payor, all of the cost recovery amount is attributed to the section 901(m) payor and assigned to the U.S. taxable year of the section 901(m) payor in which the corresponding U.S. basis deduction with respect to the RFA is taken into account under the applicable cost recovery method. This is the case regardless of whether the deduction is deferred or disallowed under other Code provisions (for example, see section 263A, which requires the capitalization of certain costs and expenses).

If instead the RFA owner (U.S.) is not a section 901(m) payor but a fiscally transparent entity for U.S. income tax purposes in which a section 901(m) payor directly or indirectly owns an interest, proposed § 1.901(m)-5(d)(2) allocates all or a portion of the cost recovery amount to the section 901(m) payor. Under those rules, a cost recovery amount is allocated to the section 901(m) payor to the extent the U.S. basis deduction that corresponds to the cost recovery amount (both of which are determined at the level of the RFA owner (U.S.)) is (or will be) included in the section 901(m) payor's distributive share of the income of the RFA owner (U.S.) for U.S. income tax purposes. Proposed § 1.901(m)-5(d)(6) assigns an allocated cost recovery amount to the U.S. taxable year of the section 901(m) payor that includes the last day of the U.S. taxable year of the RFA owner (U.S.) in which the RFA owner (U.S.) takes into account the corresponding U.S. basis deduction (without regard to whether the deduction is deferred or disallowed under other Code provisions).

Special rules under proposed § 1.901(m)-5(e), discussed in section VI.D of the Explanation of Provisions section of this preamble, allocate a cost recovery amount that arises from an RFA with respect to certain section 743(b) CAAs. In addition, special rules under proposed § 1.901(m)-5(g), discussed in section VI.F of the Explanation of Provisions section of this preamble, allocate a cost recovery amount to a section 901(m) payor in certain cases in which the RFA owner (U.S.) either is a reverse hybrid or is a fiscally transparent entity for both U.S. and foreign income tax purposes that is directly or indirectly owned by a reverse hybrid. A reverse hybrid is an entity that is treated as a corporation for U.S. income tax purposes but as a fiscally transparent entity for foreign income tax purposes.

B. *General disposition rules*

1. Definition of disposition and determining a disposition amount

Proposed § 1.901(m)-1(a)(10) defines (by cross reference to the temporary regulations) a disposition for purposes of section 901(m) as an event that results in gain or loss being recognized with respect to an RFA for purposes of U.S. income tax, a foreign income tax, or both. Proposed § 1.901(m)-5(c)(2) incorporates by cross reference the rules provided in the temporary regulations for determining the amount of basis difference taken into account upon a disposition of an RFA (the disposition amount). Section 1.901(m)-5T(c)(2) provides that, if a disposition of an RFA is fully taxable for U.S. and foreign income tax purposes, the disposition amount will be any remaining unallocated basis difference (positive or negative). Section 1.901(m)-5T(c)(2) further provides that, if a disposition of an RFA is not fully taxable for both U.S. and foreign income tax purposes and the RFA has a *positive* basis difference, the disposition amount is based solely on the amount, if any, of foreign disposition gain and U.S. disposition loss. If, on the other hand, a disposition of an RFA is not fully taxable for both U.S. and foreign income tax purposes and the RFA has a *negative* basis difference, the temporary regulations provide that the disposition amount is based solely on the amount, if any, of foreign disposition loss and U.S. disposition gain. See section V.B of the preamble to the temporary regulations for a further discussion of these provisions.

2. Attributing or allocating a disposition amount to a section 901(m) payor

Under proposed § 1.901(m)-5(c)(1), when the RFA owner (U.S.) is a section 901(m) payor, all of the disposition amount is attributed to the section 901(m) payor and assigned to the U.S. taxable year of the section 901(m) payor in which the disposition occurs.

If instead the RFA owner (U.S.) is not a section 901(m) payor but a fiscally transparent entity for U.S. income tax purposes in which a section 901(m) payor directly or indirectly owns an interest, proposed § 1.901(m)-5(d), discussed in section VI.C of the Explanation of Provisions section of this preamble, allocates all or a portion of a disposition amount to the section 901(m) payor and assigns it to a U.S. taxable year of the section 901(m) payor.

Special rules under proposed § 1.901(m)-5(e), discussed in section VI.D of the Explanation of Provisions section of this preamble, allocate a disposition amount to a section 901(m) payor and assign it to a U.S. taxable year of the section 901(m) payor when the disposition amount arises from an RFA with respect to certain section 743(b) CAAs. Special rules under proposed § 1.901(m)-5(f), discussed in section VI.E of the Explanation of Provisions section of this preamble, allocate a disposition amount attributable to foreign disposition gain or foreign disposition loss to a section 901(m) payor and assign it to a U.S. taxable year of the section 901(m) payor when there is a mid-year transaction. Special rules under proposed § 1.901(m)-5(g), discussed in section VI.F of the Explanation of Provisions section of this preamble, allocate a disposition amount to a section 901(m) payor and assign it to a U.S. taxable year of the section 901(m) payor in certain cases in which the RFA owner (U.S.) either is a reverse hybrid or is a fiscally transparent entity for both U.S. and foreign income tax purposes that is directly or indirectly owned by a reverse hybrid.

C. *Rules for allocating and assigning a disposition amount when the RFA owner (U.S.) is a fiscally transparent entity*

This section describes the rules for allocating a disposition amount to a section 901(m) payor when the RFA owner (U.S.) is a fiscally transparent entity for U.S. income tax purposes in which a section 901(m) payor directly or indirectly owns an interest, as well as rules for assigning the allocated amount to a U.S. taxable year of the section 901(m) payor.

The allocation rules (discussed in sections VI.C.1 and 2 of the Explanation of Provisions section of this preamble) vary depending on whether the disposition amount is attributable to foreign disposition gain or loss or U.S. disposition gain or loss. The rules for determining the extent to which a disposition amount is attributable to foreign or U.S. disposition gain or loss are discussed in section VI.C.3 of the Explanation of Provisions section of this preamble. The rules for assigning allocated disposition amounts to a U.S. taxable year of a section 901(m) payor are discussed in section VI.C.4 of the Explanation of Provisions section of this preamble.

1. Allocation of a disposition amount attributable to foreign disposition gain or foreign disposition loss

Proposed § 1.901(m)-5(d)(3) addresses the allocation of a disposition amount attributable to foreign disposition gain or foreign disposition loss of an RFA. These rules should be interpreted and applied in a manner consistent with the principle that a disposition amount attributable to foreign disposition gain or foreign disposition loss should be allocated to a section 901(m) payor in the same proportion that the gain or loss is taken into account in computing a foreign income tax amount that is paid or accrued by, or considered paid or accrued by, the section 901(m) payor. This is because, for example, if an RFA has a positive basis difference, a disposition amount attributable to foreign disposition gain represents an amount of gain in years following the CAA that is included in foreign income but never included in U.S. taxable income or earnings and profits because of the step-up in the U.S. basis of the RFA that occurred as a result of the CAA. Accordingly, to the extent a foreign disposition gain is taken into account in computing a foreign income tax amount, a portion of that foreign income tax amount should be disallowed as a foreign tax credit under section 901(m). Similarly, if an RFA has a negative basis difference and a foreign disposition loss is taken into account in computing a foreign income tax amount, this should result in an offset to the amount of the foreign income tax that otherwise would be disallowed as a foreign tax credit under section 901(m) as a result of a positive basis difference with respect to one or more other RFAs.

There are two separate rules for identifying the extent to which a foreign disposition gain or foreign disposition loss is taken into account in computing a foreign income tax amount that is paid or accrued by, or considered paid or accrued by, a section 901(m) payor that directly or indirectly owns an interest in an RFA owner (U.S.) that is a fiscally transparent entity for U.S. income tax purposes. The first rule, which is described in proposed § 1.901(m)-5(d)(3)(ii), applies when the foreign income tax amount is not allocated, for example, when the foreign payor is the section 901(m) payor. The second rule, which is described in proposed § 1.901(m)-5(d)(3)(iii), applies when the foreign income tax amount is allocated, for example, under § 1.704-1(b)(4)(viii) when the foreign payor is a partnership for U.S. income tax purposes in which the section 901(m) payor is a partner.

a. First allocation rule

The first allocation rule applies when a section 901(m) payor, or a disregarded entity directly owned by a section 901(m) payor, is a foreign payor whose foreign income includes a distributive share of the foreign income (that includes the foreign disposition gain or foreign disposition loss) of the RFA owner (foreign). In this structure, the entire foreign income tax amount reflected on the foreign income tax return of the foreign payor is paid or accrued by, or considered paid or accrued by, the section 901(m) payor. This will be the case when the RFA owner (U.S.) is treated as a fiscally transparent entity not just for U.S. income tax purposes, but also for foreign income tax purposes, and the section 901(m) payor directly or indirectly owns an interest in the RFA owner (U.S.), provided that, in the case of indirect ownership, any entities in the ownership chain between the section 901(m) payor and the RFA owner (U.S), or, when one or more disregarded entities are directly owned by the section 901(m) payor, between the lowest-tier disregarded entity and the RFA owner (U.S.), are fiscally transparent for both U.S. and foreign income tax purposes. In these cases, the RFA owner (U.S.) and the RFA owner (foreign) are the same entity, except in the unusual case where the RFA owner (U.S.) is an entity that is disregarded as separate from its owner for foreign income tax purposes.

The first allocation rule allocates a portion of a disposition amount attributable to foreign disposition gain or foreign disposition loss, as applicable, to the section 901(m) payor proportionally to the amount of the foreign disposition gain or foreign disposition loss that is included in the foreign payor's (in other words, the section 901(m) payor or the disregarded entity, as the case may be) distributive share of the foreign income of the RFA owner (foreign) for foreign income tax purposes.

The following example illustrates the first allocation rule. A domestic entity that is a corporation for both U.S. and foreign income tax purposes (corporate partner) directly owns, for both U.S. and foreign income tax purposes, an interest in a foreign entity that is a partnership for both U.S. and foreign income tax purposes and that is the RFA owner (U.S.) and the RFA owner (foreign). In this case, when the partnership recognizes foreign disposition gain with respect to an RFA, the foreign income tax amount with respect to such gain is paid by the partners on their distributive shares of the foreign income of the partnership that includes the foreign disposition gain. The corporate partner, and not the partnership, is therefore a foreign payor and a section 901(m) payor. Accordingly, under the first allocation rule, a disposition amount attributable to foreign disposition gain is allocated to the corporate partner proportionally to the amount of the foreign disposition gain that is included in the corporate partner's distributive share of the foreign income of the partnership. Thus, for example, if the partnership recognizes $100 of foreign disposition gain and 50 percent of that gain is included in the corporate partner's distributive share of the foreign income of the partnership, and the disposition amount attributable to the foreign disposition gain is $40, the corporate partner would be allocated $20 of that amount (50 percent of $40). The same result would apply if the corporate partner directly owned the partnership interest through a disregarded entity that is the foreign payor.

b. Second allocation rule

The second allocation rule applies when, instead of a section 901(m) payor or a disregarded entity directly owned by a section 901(m) being a foreign payor, a section 901(m) payor directly or indirectly owns an interest in a fiscally transparent entity for U.S. income tax purposes (other than a disregarded entity directly owned by the section 901(m) payor) that is a foreign payor whose foreign income includes all or a portion of the foreign income (that includes the foreign disposition gain or foreign disposition loss) of the RFA owner (foreign). Therefore, the section 901(m) payor is considered to pay or accrue only an allocated portion of the foreign income tax amount reflected on the foreign income tax return of the foreign payor. This will be the case when a section 901(m) payor directly or indirectly owns an interest in the foreign payor, and the foreign payor is (i) the RFA owner (U.S.), (ii) another fiscally transparent entity for U.S. income tax purposes (other than a disregarded entity directly owned by a section 901(m) payor) that directly or indirectly owns an interest in the RFA owner (U.S.) for both U.S. and foreign income tax purposes, or (iii) a disregarded entity directly owned by the RFA owner (U.S.). In each of these cases, the entity subject to tax for purposes of the foreign income tax (that is, the foreign payor) is treated as a fiscally transparent entity for U.S. income tax purposes.

The mechanics of the second allocation rule are different than those of the first allocation rule. This is because the second allocation rule applies when neither the section 901(m) payor, nor a disregarded entity directly owned by a section 901(m) payor, is a foreign payor that takes into account a foreign disposition gain or foreign disposition loss for purposes of calculating a foreign income tax amount, but instead, for U.S. income tax purposes, a foreign income tax amount of the foreign payor is allocated to, and considered paid or accrued by, the section 901(m) payor. Accordingly, the second allocation rule allocates a portion of a disposition amount attributable to foreign disposition gain or foreign disposition loss, as applicable, to the section 901(m) payor proportionally to the amount of the foreign disposition gain or foreign disposition loss that is included in the allocable foreign income of the section 901(m) payor. As described in section IV.A of the Explanation of Provisions section of this preamble, allocable foreign income is generally the portion of foreign income of a foreign payor that relates to the portion of the foreign income tax amount of that foreign payor that is allocated to and considered paid or accrued by a section 901(m) payor.

The following example illustrates the second allocation rule. A domestic entity that is a corporation for both U.S. and foreign income tax purposes (corporate partner) directly owns an interest in a foreign entity, the RFA owner (U.S.) and RFA owner (foreign), that is a partnership for U.S. income tax purposes but a corporation for purposes of a foreign income tax (a hybrid partnership). In this case, when the hybrid partnership recognizes foreign disposition gain with respect to an RFA, it is the hybrid partnership, rather than the partners, that takes the gain into account for purposes of calculating a foreign income tax amount. The hybrid partnership is therefore the foreign payor. For U.S. income tax purposes, a foreign income tax amount of the hybrid partnership is allocated to, and considered paid or accrued by, its partners, including the corporate partner that is a section 901(m) payor (see §§1.702-1(a)(6), 1.704-1(b)(4)(viii), and 1.901-2(f)(4)(i)). Under the second allocation rule, a disposition amount attributable to foreign disposition gain is allocated to the corporate partner proportionally to the amount of the foreign disposition gain that is included in the corporate partner's allocable foreign income. Thus, for example, if the hybrid partnership pays a foreign income tax amount of $30 on $200 of foreign income that includes $100 of foreign disposition gain and $15 of the foreign income tax amount (50 percent of $30) is allocated to and considered paid by the corporate partner, the corporate partner's allocable foreign income would be $100 (50 percent of the $200 foreign income to which the foreign income tax amount relates), which would include $50 of foreign disposition gain (50 percent of $100). If the disposition amount attributable to the foreign disposition gain is $60, the corporate partner would be allocated $30 of that amount ($60 multiplied by 50 percent, the portion of the total foreign disposition gain that is included in the corporate partner's allocable foreign income).

In this example, the analysis would be similar if the corporate partner instead indirectly owned the partnership interest (for example through an upper-tier partnership), because the corporate partner would continue to be the section 901(m) payor and the hybrid partnership would continue to be the RFA owner (U.S.), the RFA owner (foreign), and the foreign payor.

2. Allocation of a disposition amount attributable to U.S. disposition gain or U.S. disposition loss

Proposed §1.901(m)-5(d)(4) addresses the allocation of a disposition amount attributable to U.S. disposition gain or U.S. disposition loss. Such disposition amounts are allocated to a section 901(m) payor based on the portion of the U.S. disposition gain or U.S. disposition loss (which are determined at the level of the RFA owner (U.S.)) that is (or will be) included in the section 901(m) payor's distributive share of the income of the RFA owner (U.S.) for U.S. income tax purposes.

3. Determining the extent to which a disposition amount is attributable to foreign or U.S. disposition gain or loss

a. Positive basis difference

When an RFA has a positive basis difference, a disposition amount arises from a disposition of the RFA only if the disposition results in a foreign disposition gain or a U.S. disposition loss (or both). To allocate such a disposition amount to a section 901(m) payor, it is necessary to determine the extent to which the disposition amount is attributable to foreign disposition gain or U.S. disposition loss.

Proposed § 1.901(m)-5(d)(5)(i) provides that if the disposition results in either a foreign disposition gain or a U.S. disposition loss, but not both, the entire disposition amount is attributable to foreign disposition gain or U.S. disposition loss, as applicable, even if the disposition amount exceeds the foreign disposition gain or the absolute value of the U.S. disposition loss. If the disposition results in both a foreign disposition gain and a U.S. disposition loss, the disposition amount is attributable first to foreign disposition gain to the extent thereof, and the excess disposition amount, if any, is attributable to the U.S. disposition loss, even if the excess disposition amount exceeds the absolute value of the U.S. disposition loss. In the case of a disposition that is fully taxable for both U.S. and foreign income tax purposes, a disposition amount may exceed the sum of the foreign disposition gain and the absolute value of the U.S. disposition loss if, immediately before the CAA, the foreign basis in the RFA was greater than the U.S basis, and a foreign basis election was not made.

b. Negative basis difference

When an RFA has a negative basis difference, a disposition amount arises from a disposition of the RFA only if the disposition results in a foreign disposition loss or a U.S. disposition gain (or both). To allocate such a disposition amount to a section 901(m) payor, it is necessary to determine the extent to which the disposition amount is attributable to foreign disposition loss or U.S. disposition gain.

Proposed § 1.901(m)-5(d)(5)(ii) provides rules for making this determination when there is a negative basis difference that are similar to those provided in proposed § 1.901(m)-5(d)(5)(i) for a positive basis difference.

4. Assigning a disposition amount to a U.S. taxable year of a section 901(m) payor

When a disposition amount is allocated to a section 901(m) payor under proposed § 1.901(m)-5(d), proposed § 1.901(m)-5(d)(6) provides that the disposition amount is assigned to the U.S. taxable year of the section 901(m) payor that includes the last day of the U.S. taxable year of the RFA owner (U.S.) in which the disposition occurs.

D. *Special allocation rules for certain section 743(b) CAAs*

Proposed § 1.901(m)-5(e) provides that when a section 901(m) payor acquires a partnership interest in a section 743(b) CAA, including a section 743(b) CAA with respect to a lower-tier partnership that results from a direct acquisition by the section 901(m) payor of an interest in an upper-tier partnership, a cost recovery amount or a disposition amount that arises from an RFA with respect to that CAA is allocated to the acquiring section 901(m) payor. These amounts are assigned to the U.S. taxable year of the section 901(m) payor that includes the last day of the U.S. taxable year of the partnership in which, in the case of a cost recovery amount, the partnership takes into account the corresponding U.S. basis deduction, or, in the case of a disposition amount, the disposition occurs.

This special rule does not apply if it is another partnership, and not a section 901(m) payor, that acquires a partnership interest in a section 743(b) CAA. In that case, the general rules for allocating a cost recovery amount or disposition amount when the RFA owner (U.S.) is a fiscally transparent entity apply.

E. *Special allocation rules for certain mid-year transactions*

Proposed § 1.901(m)-5(f) provides rules for allocating a disposition amount when there is a disposition of an RFA during a foreign taxable year in which the foreign payor is involved in a mid-year transaction, and the disposition results in foreign disposition gain or foreign disposition loss that is allocated under the principles of § 1.1502-76(b) to the persons involved in the mid-year transaction for purposes of allocating the foreign income tax amount of the foreign payor. A typical example is when a section 901(m) payor owns a disregarded entity that is both an RFA owner (foreign) and the foreign payor, and the disregarded entity sells the RFA in the same year that the section 901(m) payor sells the disregarded entity to another section 901(m) payor. If the RFA has positive unallocated basis difference and there is foreign disposition gain on the sale of the RFA, the sale will give rise to a disposition amount that will be used by the section 901(m) payors to calculate a disqualified portion of the foreign income tax amount reflected on the foreign income tax return of the disregarded entity. Pursuant to § 1.901-2(f)(4)(ii), that foreign income tax amount must be allocated between the buyer and seller of the disregarded entity based on the respective portions of foreign income that are attributable under the principles of § 1.1502-76(b) to the buyer's and seller's respective periods of ownership of the disregarded entity during its foreign taxable year. Under proposed § 1.901(m)-5(f)(2), the disposition amount attributable to foreign disposition gain is similarly allocated between the buyer and the seller based on the principles in proposed § 1.901(m)-5(d), discussed in section VI.C of the Explanation of Provisions section of this preamble, that apply to allocate a disposition amount when the RFA owner (U.S.) is a fiscally transparent entity for U.S. income tax purposes.

F. *Special allocation rules for certain reverse hybrids*

Proposed § 1.901(m)-5(g) addresses the allocation of cost recovery amounts and disposition amounts when the RFA owner (U.S.) is either a reverse hybrid or a fiscally transparent entity for both U.S. and foreign income tax purposes that is directly or indirectly owned by a reverse hybrid for U.S. and foreign income tax purposes, and in either case, a foreign payor directly or indirectly owns an interest in the reverse hybrid for foreign income tax purposes and therefore includes in its foreign income a distributive share of the foreign income (that includes the foreign disposition gain or foreign disposition loss) of the RFA owner (foreign). These allocation rules are similar to the allocation rules discussed in section VI.C.1 of the Explanation of Provisions section of this preamble that apply to allocate a disposition amount attributable to foreign disposition gain or foreign disposition loss when the RFA owner (U.S.) is a fiscally transparent entity for U.S. income tax purposes. These rules are broader in scope, however, because they apply to allocate not just foreign disposition gain or foreign disposition loss, but rather, both cost recovery amounts and entire disposition amounts (which may be attributable, in whole or in part, to U.S. disposition gain or U.S. disposition loss). This is because the basis difference giving rise to such amounts may not be taken into account in computing U.S. taxable income or earnings and profits of the owners of the reverse hybrid until one or more subsequent U.S. taxable years (for example, upon the receipt of a distribution of property from the reverse hybrid).

These rules should be interpreted and applied in a manner consistent with the principle that a cost recovery amount or a disposition amount (or both) should be allocated to a section 901(m) payor proportionally to the amount of the foreign income of the RFA owner (foreign) that is taken into account in computing a foreign income tax amount of a foreign payor that is paid or accrued by, or considered paid or accrued by, the section 901(m) payor.

There are two separate rules for allocating a cost recovery amount or disposition amount to a section 901(m) payor when the RFA owner (U.S.) either is a reverse hybrid or a fiscally transparent entity for both U.S. and foreign income tax purposes that is directly or indirectly owned by a reverse hybrid for U.S. and foreign income tax purposes. The first rule, which is described in § 1.901(m)-5(g)(2), applies when the foreign income tax amount is not allocated, for example, when the foreign payor is the section 901(m) payor. The second rule, which is described in § 1.901(m)-5(g)(3), applies when the foreign income tax amount is allocated, for example, under § 1.704-1(b)(4)(viii) when the foreign payor is a partnership for U.S. income tax purposes in which the section 901(m) payor is a partner.

1. First allocation rule

The first allocation rule applies when a section 901(m) payor, or a disregarded entity directly owned by a section 901(m) payor, is the foreign payor whose foreign income includes a distributive share of the foreign income of the RFA owner (foreign). In this structure, the entire foreign income tax amount reflected on the foreign income tax return of the foreign payor is paid or accrued by, or considered paid or accrued by, the section 901(m) payor. This will be the case when a section 901(m) payor directly or indirectly owns an interest in the reverse hybrid, provided that in the case of indirect ownership, any entities in the ownership chain between the section 901(m) payor and the reverse hybrid, or, when one or more disregarded entities are directly owned by the section 901(m) payor, between the lowest-tier disregarded entity and the reverse hybird, are fiscally transparent for both U.S. and foreign income tax purposes. In these cases, the RFA owner (U.S.) and the RFA owner (foreign) are the same entity, except in the unusual case where the RFA owner (U.S.) is an entity that is disregarded as separate from its owner for foreign income tax purposes.

The first allocation rule allocates a portion of a cost recovery amount or a disposition amount to the section 901(m) payor proportionally to the amount of the foreign income of the RFA owner (foreign) that is included in the foreign income of the foreign payor (in other words, the section 901(m) payor or the disregarded entity, as the case may be).

The following example illustrates the first allocation rule. A domestic entity that is a corporation for both U.S. and foreign income tax purposes (corporate owner) owns an interest in a reverse hybrid that is the RFA owner (U.S.) and the RFA owner (foreign). A foreign income tax amount with respect to the foreign income of the reverse hybrid is paid by the owners of the reverse hybrid on their distributive shares of such foreign income. The corporate owner, and not the reverse hybrid, is therefore a foreign payor and a section 901(m) payor. Under the first allocation rule, a cost recovery amount or a disposition amount is allocated to the corporate owner proportionally to the amount of the foreign income of the reverse hybrid that is included in the foreign income of the corporate owner. Thus, for example, if 50 percent of the foreign income of the reverse hybrid is included in the foreign income of the corporate owner, the corporate owner would be allocated 50 percent of a cost recovery amount or a disposition amount with respect to an RFA owned by the reverse hybrid. The same result would apply if the corporate owner directly owned the interest in the reverse hybrid through a disregarded entity that is the foreign payor.

Alternatively, if the reverse hybrid was not the RFA owner (foreign) but instead the reverse hybrid owned an interest in the RFA owner (U.S.) and RFA owner (foreign), which is a partnership for both U.S. and foreign income tax purposes, and 60 percent of the foreign income of the partnership is included in the foreign income of the reverse hybrid (and therefore 30 percent (50 percent of 60 percent) of the foreign income of the partnership is included in the foreign income of the corporate owner), the corporate owner would be allocated 30 percent of a cost recovery amount or a disposition amount with respect to an RFA owned by the partnership.

2. Second allocation rule

The second allocation rule applies when instead of a section 901(m) payor, or a disregarded entity directly owned by a section 901(m) payor, being a foreign payor, a section 901(m) payor directly or indirectly owns an interest in the foreign payor whose foreign income includes a distributive share of the foreign income of the RFA owner (foreign). Therefore, the section 901(m) payor is considered to pay or accrue only an allocated portion of the foreign income tax amount reflected on the foreign income tax return of the foreign payor. This will be the case when the foreign payor is a fiscally transparent entity for U.S. income tax purposes (other than a disregarded entity directly owned by the section 901(m) payor) that either directly or indirectly owns an interest in the RFA owner (foreign) for foreign income tax purposes. In these cases, the RFA owner (U.S.) and the RFA owner (foreign) are the same entity, except in the unusual case where the RFA owner (U.S.) is an entity that is disregarded as separate from its owner for foreign income tax purposes.

The mechanics of the second allocation rule are different than those of the first allocation rule. This is because the second allocation rule applies when neither a section 901(m) payor, nor a disregarded entity directly owned by a section 901(m) payor, is a foreign payor that takes into account the foreign income of the RFA owner (foreign) for purposes of calculating a foreign income tax amount, but instead, for U.S. income tax purposes, a foreign income tax amount of the entity that is the foreign payor is allocated to, and considered paid or accrued by, the section 901(m) payor. Accordingly, the second allocation rule allocates a portion of cost recovery amounts and disposition amounts proportionally to the amount of the foreign income of the RFA owner (foreign) that is included in the foreign income of the foreign payor that is then included in the allocable foreign income of the section 901(m) payor. As described in section IV.A of the Explanation of Provisions section of this preamble, allocable foreign income is generally the portion of foreign income of a foreign payor that relates to the portion of the foreign income tax amount of that foreign payor that is allocated to and considered paid or accrued by a section 901(m) payor.

The following example illustrates the second allocation rule. A domestic entity that is a corporation for both U.S. and foreign income tax purposes (corporate partner) owns an interest in an entity that is a partnership for U.S. income tax purposes but a corporation for foreign income tax purposes (hybrid partnership), which, in turn, owns an interest in a reverse hybrid that is the RFA owner (U.S.) and the RFA owner (foreign). A foreign income tax amount with respect to the foreign income of the reverse hybrid is paid by the owners of the reverse hybrid on their distributive shares of such foreign income. Therefore, the hybrid partnership, rather than its partners, is the foreign payor. For U.S. income tax purposes, the foreign income tax amount paid or accrued by the hybrid partnership is allocated to, and considered paid or accrued by, the corporate partner that is the section 901(m) payor (see §§1.702-1(a)(6), 1.704-1(b)(4)(viii), and 1.901-2(f)(4)(i)). Under the second allocation rule, a cost recovery amount or a disposition amount with respect to an RFA owned by the reverse hybrid is allocated to the corporate partner proportionally to the amount of foreign income of the reverse hybrid that is taken into account in determining the foreign income of the hybrid partnership and then the allocable foreign income of the corporate partner. Thus, for example, if the reverse hybrid has $500 of foreign income and the hybrid partnership pays a foreign income tax amount of $30 on $200 of foreign income that includes a $100 distributive share of the foreign income of the reverse hybrid (20 percent of $500) and $15 of the foreign income tax amount (50 percent of $30) is allocated to and considered paid by the corporate partner, then the corporate partner's allocable foreign income would be $100 (50 percent of the $200 foreign income to which the foreign income tax amount relates). A cost recovery amount or disposition amount with respect to the RFAs owned by the reverse hybrid would be allocated 10 percent to the corporate partner (the corporate partner's 50 percent share of the hybrid partnership's 20 percent share of the reverse hybrid's foreign income).

VII. *Successor Rules*

Proposed §1.901(m)-6 provides successor rules for applying section 901(m) following a transfer of RFAs that have basis difference that has not yet been fully taken into account (referred to in the regulations as "unallocated basis difference") as well as for determining when an aggregate basis difference carryover of a section 901(m) payor either becomes an aggregate basis difference carryover of the section 901(m) payor with respect to another foreign payor or is transferred to another section 901(m) payor.

A. *Unallocated basis difference*

Proposed §1.901(m)-6(b)(1) and (2) incorporate by cross reference the successor rules set forth in the temporary regulations, which provide generally that section 901(m) continues to apply to an RFA after it has been transferred for U.S. income tax purposes if the RFA continues to have unallocated basis difference following the transfer (a successor transaction).

Proposed §1.901(m)-6(b)(3) sets forth two clarifications for applying the successor rules. First, if an asset is an RFA with respect to more than one foreign income tax, the successor rules apply separately with respect to each foreign income tax. Second, any subsequent cost recovery amount for an RFA transferred in a successor transaction will be determined based on the applicable cost recovery method that applies to the U.S. basis (or portion thereof) that corresponds to the unallocated basis difference. Thus, if a successor transaction restarts the depreciation schedule for an RFA, the transaction may result in unallocated basis difference being taken into account at a different recovery rate than otherwise would have applied.

Proposed §1.901(m)-6(b)(4)(iii) also incorporates by cross reference the rule set forth in the temporary regulations that provides an exception to the general rule when an RFA is subject to multiple section 743(b) CAAs. See section VI.B. of the Explanation of Provisions section of the preamble to the temporary regulations for a discussion of those provisions.

Proposed §1.901(m)-6(b)(4)(ii), which is not included in the temporary regulations, provides an exception to the general successor rule if a foreign basis election is made under proposed §1.901(m)-4(c) with respect to a subsequent CAA that otherwise would trigger the rules for successor transactions. If a foreign basis election is made with respect to a foreign income tax, the only basis difference that will be taken into account after the subsequent CAA with respect to that foreign income tax is the basis difference determined for the subsequent CAA.

B. *Aggregate basis difference carryover*

Proposed § 1.901(m)-6 provides successor rules for aggregate basis difference carryovers, the computation of which is described in section IV.B of the Explanation of Provisions section of this preamble. An aggregate basis difference carryover is treated as a tax attribute of the section 901(m) payor that retains its character as an aggregate basis difference carryover with respect to a foreign income tax and a foreign payor and with respect to a separate category, as described in § 1.904-4(m) (including the section 904(d) categories). When a section 901(m) payor transfers its assets in a transaction to which section 381 applies, proposed § 1.901(m)-6(c)(1) provides that any aggregate basis difference carryovers of the section 901(m) payor are transferred to the corporation that succeeds to the earnings and profits, if any. When substantially all of the assets of one foreign payor are transferred to another foreign payor, both of which are directly or indirectly owned by the same section 901(m) payor, proposed § 1.901(m)-6(c)(2) provides that an aggregate basis difference carryover of the section 901(m) payor with respect to the transferor foreign payor becomes an aggregate basis difference carryover of the section 901(m) payor with respect to the transferee foreign payor.

Proposed § 1.901(m)-6(c)(3) provides an anti-abuse rule that would transfer an aggregate basis difference carryover when, with a principal purpose of avoiding the application of section 901(m), there is a transfer of assets or a change in either the allocation of foreign income for foreign income tax purposes or the allocation of foreign income tax amounts for U.S. income tax purposes that is intended to separate foreign income tax amounts from the related aggregate basis difference carryover. This anti-abuse rule would apply, for example, if, with the principal purpose of avoiding the application of section 901(m), a partnership agreement is amended in order to reduce the allocation of foreign income to a partner that is a section 901(m) payor with an aggregate basis difference carryover.

VIII. *De Minimis Rules*

Proposed § 1.901(m)-7 describes de minimis rules under which certain basis differences are not taken into account for purposes of section 901(m). This determination is made when an asset subject to a CAA first becomes an RFA. If that same asset is also an RFA by reason of being subject to a subsequent CAA, the de minimis tests are applied only to the additional basis difference, if any, that results from the subsequent CAA. Accordingly, any unallocated basis difference that arose from the prior CAA that did not qualify for the de minimis exemption at the time of the prior CAA will not be retested at the time of the subsequent CAA.

In general, a basis difference with respect to an RFA is not taken into account for purposes of section 901(m) if either (i) the sum of the basis differences for all RFAs with respect to the CAA is less than the greater of $10 million or 10 percent of the total U.S. basis of all RFAs immediately after the CAA; or (ii) the RFA is part of a class of RFAs for which the sum of the basis differences of all RFAs in the class is less than the greater of $2 million or 10 percent of the total U.S. basis of all RFAs in the class. For this purpose, the classes of RFAs are the seven asset classes defined in § 1.338-6(b).

The Treasury Department and the IRS decided that transactions between related parties should be more tightly regulated, and therefore, the threshold dollar amounts and percentages to meet the de minimis exemptions for related party CAAs are lower than those for unrelated party CAAs, replacing the terms "$10 million," "10 percent," and "$2 million" wherever they occur with the terms "$5 million," "5 percent," and "$1 million," respectively. In addition, an anti-abuse provision at proposed § 1.901(m)-7(e) denies application of the de minimis exemptions to CAAs between related parties that are entered into or structured with a principal purpose of avoiding the application of section 901(m).

IX. *Miscellaneous*

Proposed § 1.901(m)-8(b) provides that, when a foreign corporation becomes a section 902 corporation for the first time, as part of the required reconstruction of the U.S. tax history of the pre-1987 foreign income taxes of the foreign corporation, section 901(m) and these regulations must be applied to determine any disqualified tax amounts or aggregate basis difference carryovers that apply to the foreign corporation.

Proposed § 1.901(m)-8(c) provides an anti-abuse rule that applies to disregard an RFA with a built-in loss to the extent it relates to any asset acquisition structured with a principal purpose to use that RFA to avoid the application of section 901(m). This rule may apply, for example, if, with a principal purpose of avoiding the application of section 901(m), an asset is acquired in a transaction that preserves a built-in loss in the asset for U.S. income tax purposes but not for foreign income tax purposes.

X. *Modifications to the Section 704(b) Regulations Related to Section 901(m)*

Section 1.704-1(b)(4)(viii) provides a safe harbor under which allocations of creditable foreign tax expenditures (CFTEs) (as defined in § 1.704-1(b)(4)(viii)(b)) by a partnership to its partners are deemed to be in accordance with the partners' interests in the partnership. In general, the purpose of the safe harbor is to match allocations of CFTEs with the income to which the CFTEs relate. In order to apply the safe harbor, a partnership must (1) determine the partnership's "CFTE categories," (2) determine the partnership's net income in each CFTE category, and (3) allocate the partnership's CFTEs to each category. In order to satisfy the safe harbor, partnership allocations of CFTEs in a CFTE category must be proportionate to the allocations of the partnership's net income in the CFTE category.

A CFTE may be subject to section 901(m) because it is a foreign income tax amount that is paid or accrued by a partnership. Specifically, if a partnership owns an RFA with respect to a foreign income tax and that RFA has a basis difference subject to section 901(m), a portion of a foreign income tax amount paid or accrued by the partnership that relates to that foreign income tax may be disallowed as a foreign tax credit under section 901(m) in the hands of section 901(m) payors to whom the foreign income tax amount is allocated. The disqualified tax amount is determined by taking into account cost recovery amounts and disposition amounts with respect to the RFA that are allocated to those section 901(m) payors pursuant to the rules provided in proposed § 1.901(m)-5. In order to ensure that the proper portion of a foreign income tax amount paid or accrued by a partnership is disallowed under section 901(m), adjustments to the net income (and the allocations of that income) in a CFTE category that includes items attributable to the RFA are necessary in certain cases.

To illustrate such a case, assume a domestic entity that is a partnership for U.S. income tax purposes but a corporation for purposes of a foreign income tax (a hybrid partnership) is owned by partner A and partner B, each of which is a domestic entity that is a corporation for both U.S. and foreign income tax purposes. In this case, the hybrid partnership is the foreign payor and partners A and B are section 901(m) payors. The hybrid partnership is the RFA owner (U.S.) and the RFA owner (foreign) with respect to a single asset that is an RFA. Assume that in a given year the hybrid partnership has 110u of gross income for both U.S. and foreign tax purposes and a 10u depreciation deduction solely for U.S. income tax purposes, which gives rise to a cost recovery amount with respect to the RFA (as determined under proposed § 1.901(m)-5(b)(2)). All partnership items are allocated equally to partners A and B, except that the entire 10u U.S. depreciation deduction is allocated to partner A. Thus, partner A's distributive share of income is 45u (110u x 50%, less 10u) and partner B's distributive share of income is 55u (110u x 50%). Because the entire U.S. depreciation deduction is (or will be included) in partner A's distributive share of income for U.S. income tax purposes, the entire cost recovery amount that corresponds to the U.S. depreciation deduction of 10u is allocated to partner A. See proposed § 1.901(m)-5(d)(2). As a result, Partner A will take into account the 10u cost recovery amount in calculating a disqualified tax amount with respect to the portion of the relevant foreign income tax amount paid or accrued by the hybrid partnership and allocated to partner A under the CFTE allocation rules. In order to ensure that the portion of the foreign income tax amount paid or accrued by the hybrid partnership that is attributable to the 10u basis difference is properly subject to section 901(m), the U.S. depreciation deduction should not be taken into account under the CFTE allocation rules so that the portion of the foreign income tax amount attributable to the 10u basis difference is allocated to partner A. Accordingly, the net income of the CFTE category that includes the U.S. basis deduction should be increased by 10u (from 100u to 110u) to back out the portion of the U.S. depreciation deduction that corresponds to the cost recovery amount, and partner A's share of that net income should be increased by 10u (from 45u to 55u). In this example, as a result of the adjustment, the foreign income tax amount paid or accrued by the hybrid partnership will be allocated equally between partner A and partner B, because they each will have a 50-percent share of the net income in the CFTE category, as adjusted. Absent the adjustment, a portion of the foreign income tax amount attributable to the 10u basis difference would be allocated to partner B, a person that is not subject to section 901(m) (because no cost recovery amount is allocated to partner B).

No modification to the safe harbor is necessary to address cost recovery amounts and disposition amounts attributable to section 743(b) adjustments that are allocated to partners under proposed § 1.901(m)-5(e) (which applies when a section 901(m) payor acquires a partnership interest in a section 743(b) CAA), because, in these cases, § 1.704-1T(b)(4)(viii)(c)(3)(i) already provides that the partnership determines net income in a CFTE category without regard to section 743(b) adjustments that its partners may have to the basis of property of the partnership. However, as discussed in section VI.D of the Explanation of Provisions section of this preamble, proposed § 1.901(m)-5(e) does not apply when another partnership (which by definition cannot be a section 901(m) payor) acquires a partnership interest in a section 743(b) CAA. Thus, modification to the safe harbor is necessary for all CAAs other than those section 743(b) CAAs described in proposed § 1.901(m)-5(e).

Accordingly, these proposed regulations add special rules under proposed § 1.704-1(b)(4)(viii)(c)(4)(*v*), (*vi*), and (*vii*) to address partnership items that give rise to cost recovery amounts and disposition amounts attributable to CAAs (other than section 743(b) CAAs described in proposed § 1.901(m)-5(e)). Specifically, these rules provide that, if an RFA has a positive basis difference, net income in a CFTE category that takes into account partnership items of income, deduction, gain, or loss attributable to the RFA (applicable CFTE category) is increased by the sum of the cost recovery amounts and disposition amounts attributable to U.S. disposition loss that correspond to those partnership items. Furthermore, to the extent a partner is allocated those cost recovery amounts or disposition amounts attributable to U.S. disposition loss, that partner's share of the net income in the CFTE category is increased by the same amount. Alternatively, if an RFA has a negative basis difference, the net income in the applicable CFTE category is decreased by the sum of the cost recovery amounts and disposition amounts attributable to U.S. disposition gain that correspond to partnership items in that CFTE category. Furthermore, to the extent a partner is allocated those cost recovery amounts or disposition amounts attributable to U.S. disposition gain, that partner's share of the net income in the CFTE category is decreased by the same amount.

XI. *Effective/Applicability Dates*

These proposed regulations will apply to CAAs occurring on or after the date of publication of the Treasury decision adopting these rules as final regulations in the **Federal Register**. Taxpayers may, however, rely on the proposed regulations prior to the date the regulations are applicable provided that they both consistently apply proposed § 1.901(m)-2 (excluding § 1.901(m)-2(d)) to all CAAs occurring on or after December 7, 2016 and consistently apply proposed § 1.901(m)-1 and §§ 1.901(m)-3 through 1.901(m)-8 (excluding § 1.901(m)-4(e)) to all CAAs occurring on or after January 1, 2011. For this purpose, persons that are related (within the meaning of section 267(b) or 707(b)) will be treated as a single taxpayer.

Special Analyses

Certain IRS regulations, including these, are exempt from the requirements of Executive Order 12866, as supplemented and reaffirmed by Executive Order 13563. Therefore, a regulatory impact assessment is not required. It has also been determined that the Regulatory Flexibility Act (5 U.S.C. chapter 6) does not apply because the regulations do not impose a collection of information on small entities. Pursuant to section 7805(f), these regulations will be submitted to the Chief Counsel for Advocacy of the Small Business Administration for comment on its impact on small business.

Comments and Requests for Public Hearing

Before these proposed regulations are adopted as final regulations, consideration will be given to any comments that are submitted timely to the IRS as prescribed in this preamble under "Addresses." The Treasury Department and the IRS request comments on all aspects of the proposed rules. All comments will be available at *www.regulations.gov* or upon request. A public hearing will be scheduled if requested in writing by any person that timely submits comments. If a public hearing is scheduled, notice of the date, time, and place for the public hearing will be published in the **Federal Register**.

Drafting Information

The principal author of these regulations is Jeffrey L. Parry of the Office of Associate Chief Counsel (International). However, other personnel from the Treasury Department and the IRS participated in their development.

[¶ 49,726] Proposed Amendments of Regulations (REG-128276-12), published in the Federal Register on December 8, 2016.

[Code Secs. 987 and 988]

Branch transactions: Qualified business units: Income from U.S. sources: Functional currency: Foreign currency transactions: Character of gain or loss: Exchange gain or loss: Special rules.—Amendments of Reg. § 1.987-1, 1.987-2, 1.987-3, 1.987-4, 1.987-6, 1.987-7, 1.987-8, 1.987-12, 1.988-1 and 1.988-2, relating to the recognition and deferral of foreign currency gain or loss under section 987 with respect to a qualified business unit (QBU) in connection with certain QBU terminations and certain other transactions involving partnerships, are proposed.

AGENCY: Internal Revenue Service (IRS), Treasury.

ACTION: Notice of proposed rulemaking by cross-reference to temporary regulations.

SUMMARY: Published elsewhere in this issue of the **Federal Register**, the Treasury Department and the IRS are issuing temporary regulations under section 987 of the Code relating to the recognition and deferral of foreign currency gain or loss under section 987 with respect to a qualified business unit (QBU) in connection with certain QBU terminations and certain other transactions involving partnerships. The temporary regulations also contain rules providing: an annual deemed termination election for a section 987 QBU; an elective method, available to taxpayers that make the annual deemed termination election, for translating all items of income or loss with respect to a section 987 QBU at the yearly average exchange rate; rules regarding the treatment of section 988 transactions of a section 987 QBU; rules regarding QBUs with the U.S. dollar as their functional currency; rules regarding combinations and separations of section 987 QBUs; rules regarding the translation of income used to pay creditable foreign income taxes; and rules regarding the allocation of assets and liabilities of certain partnerships for purposes of section 987. Finally, the temporary regulations contain rules under section 988 requiring the deferral of certain section 988 loss that arises with respect to related-party loans. The text of the temporary regulations serves as the text of these proposed regulations.

DATES: Written or electronic comments and requests for a public hearing must be received by March 8, 2016.

ADDRESSES: Send submissions to: CC:PA:LPD:PR (REG-128276-12), room 5203, Internal Revenue Service, P.O. Box 7604, Ben Franklin Station, Washington, DC 20044. Submissions may be hand-delivered Monday through Friday between the hours of 8 a.m. and 4 p.m. to CC:PA:LPD:PR (REG-128276-12), Courier's Desk, Internal Revenue Service, 1111 Constitution Avenue NW, Washington, DC, or sent electronically via the Federal eRulemaking Portal at *http://www.regulations.gov* (IRS REG-128276-12).

FOR FURTHER INFORMATION CONTACT: Concerning the proposed regulations, Steven D. Jensen at (202) 317-6938; concerning submissions of comments or requests for a public hearing, Regina Johnson, (202) 317-6901 (not toll-free numbers).

SUPPLEMENTARY INFORMATION:

Paperwork Reduction Act

The collection of information contained in this notice of proposed rulemaking has been submitted to the Office of Management and Budget for review in accordance with the Paperwork Reduction Act of 1995 (44 U.S.C. 3507(d)). Comments on the collection of information should be sent to the **Office of Management and Budget**, Attn: Desk Officer for the Department of the Treasury, Office of Information and Regulatory Affairs, Washington, DC 20503, with copies to the **Internal Revenue Service**, Attn: IRS Reports Clearance Officer, SE:CAR:MP:T:T:SP, Washington, DC 20224. Comments on the collection of information should be received by February 8, 2017. Comments are specifically requested concerning:

Whether the proposed collection of information is necessary for the proper performance of the Internal Revenue Service, including whether the information will have practical utility;

The accuracy of the estimated burden associated with the proposed collection of information (see below);

How the quality, utility, and clarity of the information to be collected may be enhanced;

How the burden of complying with the proposed collection of information may be minimized, including through the application of automated collection techniques or other forms of information technology; and

Estimates of capital or start-up costs and costs of operation, maintenance, and purchase of service to provide information.

The collection of information in this proposed regulation is in: (1) §§1.987-1(b)(6)(iii)(A) and 1.987-1(g)(3)(i)(E); (2) §§1.987-3(b)(4)(iii)(C) and 1.987-1(g)(3)(i)(F); (3) §§1.987-3(d) and 1.987-1(g)(3)(i)(G); and (4) §§1.987-8(d) and 1.987-1(g)(3)(i)(H). Sections 1.987-1(b)(6)(iii)(A) and 1.987-1(g)(3)(i)(E) allow a controlled foreign corporation to elect to apply section 987 and the regulations thereunder (with certain exceptions) to a dollar QBU. Sections 1.987-3(b)(4)(iii)(C) and 1.987-1(g)(3)(i)(F) allow a taxpayer to elect to apply a foreign currency mark-to-market method of accounting for qualified short-term section 988 transactions. Sections 1.987-3(d) and 1.987-1(g)(3)(i)(G) allow a taxpayer to elect to translate all items of income, gain, deduction, and loss of the section 987 QBU at the yearly average exchange rate. Sections 1.987-8(d) and 1.987-1(g)(3)(i)(H) allow a taxpayer to elect to deem all of its section 987 QBUs to terminate on the last day of each taxable year. The preceding elections are to be made pursuant to §1.987-1(g). The collection of information is voluntary to obtain a benefit. The likely respondents are business or other for-profit institutions.

Estimated total annual reporting burden: 1,000 hours.

Estimated average annual burden hours per respondent: 1 hour.

Estimated number of respondents: 1,000.

Estimated annual frequency of responses: on occasion.

An agency may not conduct or sponsor, and a person is not required to respond to, a collection of information unless it displays a valid control number assigned by the Office of Management and Budget.

Books or records relating to a collection of information must be retained as long as their contents may become material in the administration of any internal revenue law. Generally, tax returns and tax return information are confidential, as required by 26 U.S.C. 6103.

Background and Explanation of Provisions

The temporary regulations (published in the Rules and Regulations section of this issue of the **Federal Register)** contain rules relating to the recognition and deferral of section 987 gain or loss with respect to a QBU. The temporary regulations also contain rules regarding an annual deemed termination election, an elective method for translating taxable income or loss with respect to a QBU, section 988 transactions of a section 987 QBU, QBUs with the U.S. dollar as their functional currency, combinations and separations of section 987 QBUs, translation of income used to pay creditable foreign income taxes, the allocation of assets and liabilities of certain partnerships for purposes of section 987, and the deferral of section 988 loss with respect to certain related-party loans. The text of the temporary regulations also serves as the text of these proposed regulations. The preamble to the temporary regulations explains those regulations and these proposed regulations.

Special Analyses

Certain IRS regulations, including these, are exempt from the requirements of Executive Order 12866, as supplemented and reaffirmed by Executive Order 13563. Therefore, a regulatory impact assessment is not required. It is hereby certified that these regulations will not have a significant economic impact on a substantial number of small entities within the meaning of section 601(6) of the Regulatory Flexibility Act (5 U.S.C. chapter 6). Accordingly, a regulatory flexibility analysis is not required. This certification is based on the fact that these regulations will primarily affect U.S. corporations that have foreign operations, which tend to be larger businesses. Pursuant to section 7805(f) of the Code, these regulations have been submitted to the Chief Counsel for Advocacy of the Small Business Administration for comment on their impact on small business.

Comments and Public Hearing

Before these proposed regulations are adopted as final regulations, consideration will be given to any comments that are submitted timely to the IRS as prescribed in this preamble under the "Addresses" heading. The Treasury Department and the IRS request comments on all aspects of the proposed rules. In addition, the Treasury Department and the IRS request comments on the application of section 987 to entities and QBUs described in § 1.987-1(b)(1)(ii) to which the final regulations are not applicable (excluded entities and QBUs). Comments are requested on whether the Treasury Department and the IRS should issue regulations applying the foreign exchange exposure pool methodology described in §§ 1.987-3 and -4 to excluded entities and QBUs. Comments are also requested on the modifications, if any, that should be made to the foreign exchange exposure pool methodology adopted in the final regulations with respect to excluded entities and QBUs. All comments will be available at *www.regulations.gov* or upon request. A public hearing will be scheduled if requested in writing by any person that timely submits written comments. If a public hearing is scheduled, notice of the date, time, and place for the hearing will be published in the **Federal Register**.

Drafting Information

The principal author of these regulations is Mark E. Erwin of the Office of Associate Chief Counsel (International). However, other personnel from the IRS and the Treasury Department participated in their development.

[¶ 49,727] **Proposed Amendments of Regulations (REG-133353-16)**, published in the Federal Register on December 9, 2016.

[Code Sec. 6103]

Return information: Authorized disclosure.—Amendments to Reg. § 301.6103(j)(1)-1, authorizing the disclosure of specified return information to the Bureau of the Census (Bureau) for purposes of structuring the censuses and national economic accounts and conducting related statistical activities authorized by title 13, are proposed.

AGENCY: Internal Revenue Service (IRS), Treasury.

ACTION: Notice of proposed rulemaking by cross-reference to temporary regulation. SUMMARY: In the Rules and Regulations section of this issue of the **Federal Register** the IRS is issuing temporary regulations authorizing the disclosure of specified return information to the Bureau of the Census (Bureau) for purposes of structuring the censuses and national economic accounts and conducting related statistical activities authorized by title 13. The temporary regulations are made pursuant to a request from the Secretary of Commerce. The temporary regulations also provide clarifying language for an item of return information and remove duplicative paragraphs contained in the existing final regulations. These regulations require no action by taxpayers and have no effect on their tax liabilities. Thus, no taxpayers are likely to be affected by the disclosures authorized by this guidance. The text of the temporary regulations published in the Rules and Regulations section of the **Federal Register** serves as the text of these proposed regulations.

DATES: Written and electronic comments and requests for a public hearing must be received by March 9, 2016.

Applicability Date: For dates of applicability, see § 301.6103(j)(1)-1(e). ADDRESSES: Send submissions to CC:PA:LPD:PR (REG-133353-16), room 5203, Internal Revenue Service, Post Office Box 7604, Ben Franklin Station, Washington, DC 20044. Submissions may be hand-delivered Monday through Friday between the hours of 8 a.m. and 4 p.m. to CC:PA:LPD:PR (REG-133353-16), Courier's Desk, Internal Revenue Service, 1111 Constitution Avenue, N.W., Washington, DC 20224, or sent electronically, via the Federal eRulemaking Portal at *www.regulations.gov* (IRS REG-133353-16).

FOR FURTHER INFORMATION CONTACT: Concerning the proposed regulations, William Rowe, (202) 317-6834; concerning submissions of comments, Regina Johnson, (202) 317-5177 (not toll-free numbers).

SUPPLEMENTARY INFORMATION:

Background and Explanation of Provisions

This document contains proposed amendments to 26 CFR part 301 relating to section 6103(j)(1)(A) of the Internal Revenue Code (Code). Section 6103(j)(1)(A) authorizes the Secretary of the Treasury to furnish, upon written request by the Secretary of Commerce, such returns or return information as the Secretary of Treasury may prescribe by regulation to officers and employees of the Bureau for the purpose of, but only to the extent necessary in, the structuring of censuses and national economic accounts and conducting related statistical activities authorized by law. Section 301.6103(j)(1)-1 of the regulations further defines such purposes by reference to 13 U.S.C. chapter 5 and provides an itemized description of the return information authorized to be disclosed for such purposes. This document contains proposed regulations authorizing the disclosure of additional items of return information requested by the Secretary of Commerce. These proposed regulations also provide clarifying language for an item of return information and remove duplicative paragraphs contained in the existing regulations. Temporary regulations in the Rules and Regulations section of this issue of the **Federal Register** amend 26 CFR part 301. The text of those temporary regulations serves as the text of these proposed regulations. The preamble to the temporary regulations explains the temporary regulations and these proposed regulations.

Special Analyses

Certain IRS regulations, including this one, are exempt from the requirements of Executive Order 12866, as supplemented and reaffirmed by Executive Order 13563. Therefore, a regulatory assessment is not required. It is hereby certified that these regulations will not have a significant economic impact on a substantial number of small entities because the regulations do not impose a collection of information on small entities. Accordingly, a regulatory flexibility analysis is not required under the Regulatory Flexibility Act (5 U.S.C. chapter 6). Pursuant to section 7805(f) of the Internal Revenue Code, this regulation has been submitted to the Chief Counsel for Advocacy of the Small Business Administration for comment on its impact on small businesses.

Comments and Requests for Public Hearing

Before these proposed regulations are adopted as final regulations, consideration will be given to any comments that are submitted timely to the IRS as prescribed in this preamble under the "Addresses" heading. The IRS and Treasury Department request comments on all aspects of the proposed regulations. All comments that are submitted will be available for public inspection and copying at *www.regulations.gov* or upon request. A public hearing may be scheduled if requested in writing by any person that timely submits written or electronic comments. If a public hearing is scheduled, notice of the date, time, and place for the public hearing will be published in the **Federal Register**.

Drafting Information

The principal author of these proposed regulations is William Rowe, Office of the Associate Chief Counsel (Procedure & Administration).

[¶49,728] **Proposed Amendments of Regulations and Withdrawal of Notice of Proposed Regulations (REG-140328-15)**, published in the Federal Register on December 19, 2016.

[Code Sec. 355]

Corporate divisions: Section 355 distribution: Prohibited stock acquisitions: Predecessor of distributing corporation: Predecessor of controlled corporation: Distributions of stock between affiliated group members.—Amendments of Reg. §§1.355-0 and 1.355-8, regarding the distribution by a distributing corporation of stock or securities of a controlled corporation without the recognition of income, gain, or loss, are proposed. Amendments of Reg. §1.355-8 proposed on November 22, 2004, are withdrawn.

AGENCY: Internal Revenue Service (IRS), Treasury.

ACTION: Withdrawal of notice of proposed rulemaking, notice of proposed rulemaking by cross-reference to temporary regulations.

SUMMARY: In the Rules and Regulations section of this issue of the **Federal Register**, the IRS is issuing temporary regulations that provide guidance regarding the distribution by a distributing corporation of stock or securities of a controlled corporation without the recognition of income, gain, or loss. The temporary regulations provide guidance in determining whether a corporation is a predecessor or successor of a distributing or controlled corporation for purposes of the exception under section 355(e) of the Internal Revenue Code to the nonrecognition treatment afforded qualifying distributions, and they provide certain limitations on the recognition of gain in certain cases involving a predecessor of a distributing corporation. The temporary regulations also provide rules regarding the extent to which section 355(f) causes a distributing corporation (and in certain cases its shareholders) to recognize income or gain on the distribution of stock or securities of a controlled corporation. Those temporary regulations affect corporations that distribute the stock or securities of controlled corporations and their shareholders or security holders of those distributing corporations. The text of those temporary regulations serves as the text of these proposed regulations.

DATES: Comments and requests for a public hearing must be received by March 20, 2017. **ADDRESSES:** Send submissions to: CC:PA:LPD:PR (REG-140328-15), room 5203, Internal Revenue Service, PO Box 7604, Ben Franklin Station, Washington, DC 20044. Submissions may be hand-delivered Monday through Friday between the hours of 8 a.m. and 4 p.m. to CC:PA:LPD:PR (REG-140328-15), Courier's Desk, Internal Revenue Service, 1111 Constitution Avenue, N.W., Washington, DC, 20224, or sent electronically, via the Federal eRulemaking Portal at http://www.regulations.gov/ (REG-140328-15).

FOR FURTHER INFORMATION CONTACT: Concerning the proposed regulations, Richard K. Passales at (202) 317-5024 or Marie C. Milnes-Vasquez, (202) 317-7700; concerning submission of comments, and/or requests for public hearing, Regina Johnson at (202) 317-6901 (not toll-free numbers).

SUPPLEMENTARY INFORMATION:

Background and Explanation of Provisions

On November 22, 2004, the Treasury Department and the IRS published in the **Federal Register** (69 FR 67873) a notice of proposed rulemaking (REG-145535-02) containing proposed regulations under section 355(e)(4)(D) (the 2004 proposed regulations). Those proposed regulations are withdrawn. This notice of proposed rulemaking cross-references to temporary regulations contained in a Treasury decision published in the Rules and Regulations section of this issue of the **Federal Register** which amend the Income Tax Regulations (26 CFR part 1) relating to section 355(e) by adopting the 2004 proposed regulations with certain significant modifications. The Background and Explanation of Provisions contained in the preamble of the temporary regulations also serves as part of this preamble.

Special Analyses

Certain IRS regulations, including this one, are exempt from the requirements of Executive Order 12866, as supplemented and reaffirmed by Executive Order 13653. Therefore, a regulatory impact assessment is not required. Pursuant to the Regulatory Flexibility Act (5 U.S.C. chapter 6), it is hereby certified that these proposed regulations would not have a significant economic impact on a substantial number of small entities. This certification is based on the fact that these proposed regulations would primarily affect large corporations with a substantial number of shareholders, as well as corporations that are members of large corporate groups. Therefore, a regulatory flexibility analysis is not required. Pursuant to section 7805(f) of the Code, this regulation has been submitted to the Chief Counsel for Advocacy of the Small Business Administration for comment on its impact on small business.

Comments and Requests for Public Hearing

Before these proposed regulations are adopted as final regulations, consideration will be given to any comments that are submitted timely to the IRS as prescribed in this preamble under the "ADDRESSES" heading. The Treasury Department and the IRS request comments on all aspects of the proposed rules. All comments will be available at www.regulations.gov or upon request. A public hearing will be scheduled if requested in writing by any person that timely submits written comments. If a public hearing is scheduled, notice of the date, time, and place for the hearing will be published in the **Federal Register**.

Drafting Information

The principal author of these regulations is Lynlee C. Baker, formerly of the Office of Associate Chief Counsel (Corporate). However, other personnel from the Treasury Department and the IRS participated in their development.

[¶49,730] Proposed Amendments of Regulations (REG-112800-16), published in the Federal Register on December 29, 2016.

[Code Sec. 468A]

Deductions: Nuclear Power Plants: Decommissioning Costs.—Amendments of Reg. §§1.468A-1 and 1.468A-5, relating to deductions for contributions to trusts maintained for decommissioning nuclear power plants and the use of the amounts in those trusts to decommission nuclear plants, are proposed.

AGENCY: Internal Revenue Service (IRS), Treasury.

ACTION: Notice of proposed rulemaking.

SUMMARY: This document provides proposed changes to the regulations under section 468A of the Internal Revenue Code of 1986 (Code) relating to deductions for contributions to trusts maintained for decommissioning nuclear power plants and the use of the amounts in those trusts to decommission nuclear plants. The proposed regulations revise certain provisions to: address issues that have arisen as more nuclear plants have begun the decommissioning process; and clarify provisions in the current regulations regarding self-dealing and the definition of substantial completion of decommissioning.

DATES: Written or electronic comments and requests for a public hearing must be received by March 29, 2017.

ADDRESSES: Send submissions to: CC:PA:LPD:PR (REG-112800-16), room 5203, Internal Revenue Service, PO Box 7604, Ben Franklin Station, Washington, DC 20044. Submissions may be hand delivered Monday through Friday between the hours of 8 a.m. and 4 p.m. to: CC:PA:LPD:PR (REG-112800-16), Courier's Desk, Internal Revenue Service, 1111 Constitution Avenue N.W., Washington, DC, or sent electronically, via the Federal eRulemaking Portal at http://www.regulations.gov/ (IRS REG-112800-16).

FOR FURTHER INFORMATION CONTACT: Concerning the regulations, Jennifer C. Bernardini, (202) 317-6853; concerning submissions and to request a hearing, Regina Johnson, (202) 317-6901 (not toll-free numbers).

SUPPLEMENTARY INFORMATION:

Paperwork Reduction Act

There is no new collection of information contained in this notice of proposed rulemaking. The collection of information contained in the regulations under section 468A has been reviewed and approved by the Office of Management and Budget in accordance with the Paperwork Reduction Act of 1995 (44 U.S.C. 3507(d)) under control number 1545-2091. Responses to these collections of information are required to obtain a tax benefit.

An agency may not conduct or sponsor, and a person is not required to respond to, a collection of information unless it displays a valid control number assigned by the Office of Management and Budget.

Books or records relating to a collection of information must be retained as long as their contents may become material in the administration of any internal revenue law. Generally, tax returns and tax return information are confidential, as required by section 6103 of the Code.

Background

This proposed rulemaking consists of several amendments to the existing regulations under section 468A. Section 468A was originally enacted by section 91(c)(1) of the Deficit Reduction Act of 1984,

Public Law 98-369, (98 Stat 604) and has been amended, most recently by section 1310 of the Energy Policy Act of 2005, Public Law 109-58 (119 Stat 594). Temporary regulations (TD 9374) under section 468A were published in the **Federal Register** for December 31, 2007 (72 FR 74175). Regulations finalizing and removing the temporary regulations (TD 9512) were published in the **Federal Register** on December 23, 2010 (75 FR 80697).

Explanation of Provisions

1. *Definition of Nuclear Decommissioning Costs*

A. *Inclusion of amounts related to the storage of spent fuel within definition of nuclear decommissioning costs*

Section 468A is intended to allow taxpayers to currently deduct amounts set aside in a qualified fund (Fund) for the purpose of decommissioning a nuclear power plant. The taxpayer must include the amount of any actual or deemed distribution from the Fund in gross income in the year of the distribution, as provided in §1.468A-2(d)(1). Taxpayers may then claim an offsetting deduction for amounts spent on decommissioning costs as determined under section 461(h) and other sections. See §1.468A-2(e).

Taxpayers that operate nuclear power plants, whether such plants are currently operating or have ceased operations, must safely store spent fuel. Nuclear fuel assemblies are removed from the reactor and those assemblies are stored in a spent fuel pool for cooling. Subsequently, the spent fuel may be inserted into storage casks and the casks transferred to an on-site Independent Spent Fuel Storage Installation (ISFSI). An ISFSI consists of a concrete storage pad on which the storage casks are placed. Although the Nuclear Waste Policy Act of 1982, 42 U.S.C. 10101, et seq, requires the Department of Energy (DOE) to take and dispose of spent nuclear fuel in a permanent geologic repository, no such repository has been established and the government has not yet begun accepting spent fuel. Thus, operators of nuclear power plants must safely store spent fuel in an on-site ISFSI.

Existing §1.468A-1(b)(6) defines nuclear decommissioning costs as including "all otherwise deductible expenses to be incurred in connection with" the disposal of certain nuclear assets. Section 1.468A-1(b)(6) continues that "such term also includes costs incurred in connection with the construction, operation, and ultimate decommissioning of a facility used solely to store, pending acceptance by the government for permanent storage or disposal, spent nuclear fuel generated by the nuclear power plant or plants located on the same site as the storage facility." The Treasury Department and the IRS have become aware that there are questions regarding whether ISFSI-related costs for the construction or purchase of assets that would not necessarily qualify as "otherwise deductible" expenses under the current regulation are included as nuclear decommissioning costs. The proposed regulations clarify the definition of nuclear decommissioning costs to specifically provide for ISFSI-related costs.

B. *Inclusion of amounts for purchase or construction of a depreciable asset as part of decommissioning process within definition of nuclear decommissioning costs*

Under the existing regulations, questions have arisen as to whether a cost must be currently deductible for that amount to be payable currently from the Fund under the "otherwise deductible" language of §1.468A-1(b)(6). For example, where a depreciable asset is purchased or constructed as part of the decommissioning process (and the asset is not considered abandoned) questions have arisen regarding whether the "otherwise deductible" language is satisfied solely by the fact that the property is depreciable or whether the expense is treated as a deductible decommissioning expense only to the extent that depreciation is currently allowed. This raises a timing issue regarding whether a fund may pay for the purchase or construction of a depreciable asset to be used in decommissioning that is not considered abandoned when completed. Under the present regulations, because the asset would be fully depreciable but the cost of the asset is not otherwise deductible, a fund may only pay for the portion of the depreciation allowable in the tax year in which such property is placed in service. The intent of section 468A is to allow owners of nuclear power plants to put amounts in a Fund on a tax-free basis and then to use those amounts and the earnings on those amounts to pay for decommissioning. In order to effectuate that intent, the proposed regulations broaden the definition of nuclear decommissioning costs to include the total cost of depreciable assets by adding the words "or recoverable through depreciation" following "otherwise deductible" in §1.468A-1(b)(6).

2. *Clarification of the Applicability of the Self-Dealing Rules to Transactions Between the Fund and Related Parties*

Section 4951 imposes an excise tax on acts of self-dealing between a "disqualified person" and a trust described in section 501(c)(21). Section 468A(e)(5) provides that, under regulations prescribed by the Secretary, for purposes of section 4951, the Fund shall be treated in the same manner as a trust described in section 501(c)(21). Section 1.468A-5(b)(1) states that the excise taxes imposed by section 4951 apply to each act of self-dealing between the Fund and a disqualified person. Section 1.468A-5(b)(2) defines "self-dealing," for purposes of §1.468A-5(b), as any act described in section 4951(d), but provides for some exclusions, including a payment by a Fund for the purpose of satisfying, in whole or in part, the liability of the taxpayer who has elected section 468A and established a Fund (electing taxpayer) for decommissioning costs of the nuclear power plant to which the Fund relates. Section 1.468A-5(b)(3), by reference to section 4951(e)(4) and §53.4951-1(d), provides that the term "disqualified person" includes, with respect to a trust, a contributor to the trust and a trustee of the trust.

The IRS has issued several private letter rulings holding that a reimbursement to an electing taxpayer or an unrelated party by a Fund of decommissioning costs, such as severance payments and pre-dismantlement decommissioning costs, is made for the purpose of satisfying the liability of the electing taxpayer for decommissioning costs of the nuclear power plant to which the Fund relates and therefore is not self-dealing. Thus, under these rulings, the reimbursement by a Fund of these costs represents a permissible use of the Funds. To remove any lingering uncertainty, as well as to avoid the burden on taxpayers of filing additional ruling requests on these issues, the proposed regulations clarify that reimbursements of decommissioning costs by the Fund to related parties (including the electing taxpayer) that paid such costs are not an act of self-dealing. However, no amount beyond what is actually paid by the related party, including amounts such as direct or indirect overhead or a reasonable profit element, may be included in the reimbursement by the Fund.

3. *Definition of "Substantial Completion" in §1.468A-5(d)(3)(i)*

Existing §1.468A-5(d)(3)(i) defines the substantial completion date as "the date that the maximum acceptable radioactivity levels mandated by the Nuclear Regulatory Commission [NRC] with respect to a decommissioned nuclear power plant are satisfied." However, §1.468A-5(d)(3)(ii) provides that, if a significant portion of the total estimated decommissioning costs are not incurred on or before the substantial completion date, the electing taxpayer may request a ruling that designates a date subsequent to the substantial completion date as the termination date; such later date may be no later than the last day of the third taxable year after the taxable year that includes the substantial completion date. Under certain state and local requirements, the plant operator must return the site of the plant to conditions requiring time beyond that needed to reach the maximum radioactivity level mandated by the NRC. To accommodate these situations without requiring that the taxpayer request a ruling, the proposed regulations amend the definition of "substantial completion" to the date on which all Federal, state, local, and contractual decommissioning liabilities are fully satisfied.

Proposed Effective/Applicability Date

The rules contained in these regulations are proposed to apply to taxable years ending on or after the date of publication of the Treasury decision adopting these rules as final regulations in the **Federal Register**. Notwithstanding the prospective effective date, the IRS will not challenge return positions consistent with these proposed regulations for taxable years ending on or after the date these proposed regulations are published.

Special Analyses

Certain IRS regulations, including these, are exempt from the requirements of Executive Order 12866, as supplemented and affirmed by Executive Order 13563. Therefore, a regulatory assessment is not required. It is hereby certified that these regulations will not have a significant economic impact on a substantial number of small entities. This certification is based on (1) the fact that the rules in these proposed regulations primarily affect owners of nuclear power plants which are not small entities as defined by the Regulatory Flexibility Act (5 U.S.C. 601) and (2) the proposed regulations do not impose a collection of information on small entities. Accordingly, a Regulatory Flexibility Analysis under the Regulatory Flexibility Act (5 U.S.C. 601) is not required. We request comment on the accuracy of this certification. Pursuant to section 7805(f) of the Code, these regulations have been submitted to the Chief Counsel for Advocacy of the Small Business Administration for comment on their impact on small business.

Comments and Requests for a Public Hearing

Before these proposed regulations are adopted as final regulations, consideration will be given to any written comments (a signed original and eight (8) copies) or electronically generated comments that are submitted timely to the IRS. The Treasury Department and the IRS generally request comments on the clarity of the proposed rule and how it may be made easier to understand. All comments will be available for public inspection and copying. A public hearing may be scheduled if requested in writing by a person who timely submits comments. If a public hearing is scheduled, notice of the date, time, and place for the hearing will be published in the **Federal Register**.

Drafting Information

The principal author of these regulations is Jennifer C. Bernardini, Office of Associate Chief Counsel (Passthroughs and Special Industries). However, other personnel from the IRS and Treasury Department participated in their development.

[¶49,732] Proposed Amendments of Regulations (REG-103477-14), published in the Federal Register on January 6, 2017 (corrected September 15, 2017).

[Code Secs. 1471, 1472 and 1474]

Foreign Account Tax Compliance Act (FATCA): Foreign financial institution (FFI): FFI agreement: Chapter 4 due diligence.—Amendments of Reg. §§1.1471-1, 1.1471-3, 1.1471-4 and 1.1474-1, regarding reporting requirements on behalf of certain foreign financial institutions (FFIs) and the chapter 4 due diligence and reporting obligations on behalf of certain nonfinancial foreign entities, are proposed. Proposed amendments to Reg. §§1.1471-5 and 1.1472-1 and portions of proposed amendments to Reg. §§1.1471-1 and 1.1471-4 adopted by T.D. 9852 on March 21, 2019.

AGENCY: Internal Revenue Service (IRS), Treasury.

ACTION: Notice of proposed rulemaking; notice of proposed rulemaking by cross-reference to temporary regulation.

SUMMARY: This document contains proposed regulations under chapter 4 of Subtitle A (sections 1471 through 1474) of the Internal Revenue Code of 1986 (Code) describing the verification requirements (including certifications of compliance) and events of default for entities that agree to perform the chapter 4 due diligence, withholding, and reporting requirements on behalf of certain foreign financial institutions (FFIs) or the chapter 4 due diligence and reporting obligations on behalf of certain nonfinancial foreign entities. These proposed regulations also describe the certification requirements and procedures for IRS's review of certain trustees of trustee-documented trusts and the procedures for IRS's review of periodic certifications provided by registered deemed-compliant FFIs. In addition, these proposed regulations describe the procedures for future modifications to the requirements for certifications of compliance for participating FFIs. These proposed regulations also describe the requirements for certifications of compliance for participating FFIs that are members of consolidated compliance groups. In addition, in the Rules and Regulations section of this issue of the **Federal Register**, the Department of the Treasury (Treasury Department) and IRS are issuing temporary regulations that provide additional guidance under chapter 4 (temporary chapter 4 regulations). The text of the temporary chapter 4 regulations also serves as the text of the regulations contained in this document that are proposed by cross-reference to the temporary chapter 4 regulations. The preamble to the temporary chapter 4 regulations explains the temporary chapter 4 regulations and these proposed regulations that cross-reference to the temporary chapter 4 regulations. DATES: Written or electronic comments and requests for a public hearing must be received by April 6, 2017.

ADDRESSES: Send submissions to: CC:PA:LPD:PR (REG-103477-14), Internal Revenue Service, Room 5203, PO Box 7604, Ben Franklin Station, Washington, DC 20044. Submissions may be hand-delivered Monday through Friday between the hours of 8 a.m. and 4 p.m. to CC:PA:LPD:PR (REG-103477-14), Courier's Desk, Internal Revenue Service, 1111 Constitution Avenue, NW, Washington, DC 20224; or sent electronically via the Federal eRulemaking Portal at *http://www.regulations.gov* (IRS-REG-103477-14).

FOR FURTHER INFORMATION CONTACT: Concerning the proposed regulations, Kamela Nelan, (202) 317-6942; concerning submissions of comments and/or requests for a public hearing, Regina Johnson, (202) 317-6901 (not toll free numbers). SUPPLEMENTARY INFORMATION:

Background

I. *In General*

A. *Chapter 4*

Sections 1471 through 1474 under chapter 4 of Subtitle A (chapter 4) were added to the Code on March 18, 2010, as part of the Hiring Incentives to Restore Employment Act of 2010, Public Law 111-147. Chapter 4 (commonly known as the Foreign Account Tax Compliance Act, or FATCA) generally requires withholding agents to withhold tax on certain payments to foreign financial institutions (FFIs) that do not agree to report certain information to the IRS regarding their U.S. accounts under section 1471(b)(1). Chapter 4 also generally requires withholding agents to withhold tax on certain payments to certain non-financial foreign entities (NFFEs) that do not provide to the withholding agent information on their substantial United States owners (substantial U.S. owners) or a certification that they have no such owners. On January 28, 2013, final regulations (TD 9610) under chapter 4 were published in the **Federal Register** (78 FR 5874), and on September 10, 2013, corrections to the final regulations were published in the **Federal Register** (78 FR 55202). TD 9610 and the September 2013 corrections are referred to collectively in this preamble as the 2013 final regulations. On March 6, 2014, temporary regulations (TD 9657) under chapter 4 were published in the **Federal Register** (79 FR 12812) and corrections to the temporary regulations were published in the **Federal Register** on July 1, 2014, and November 18, 2014 (79 FR 37175 and 78 FR 68619, respectively). In this preamble, TD 9657 and the corrections thereto are referred to collectively as the 2014 temporary regulations, and together with the 2013 final regulations, as the chapter 4 regulations. A notice of proposed rulemaking cross-referencing the 2014 temporary regulations was published in the **Federal Register** on March 6, 2014 (79 FR 12868).

To address situations where foreign law would prevent an FFI from reporting directly to the IRS the information required by chapter 4, the Treasury Department, in collaboration with certain foreign governments, developed two alternative model intergovernmental agreements, known as the Model 1 IGA and the Model 2 IGA. Under the Model 1 IGA, an FFI that is treated as a reporting Model 1 FFI is treated as complying with and not subject to withholding under section 1471 provided that the FFI complies with the requirements specified in the Model 1 IGA and reports information about its U.S. accounts to the Model 1 IGA jurisdiction, which is followed by the automatic exchange of that information on a government-to-government basis with the United States. Under the Model 2 IGA, an FFI that is treated as a reporting Model 2 FFI follows the terms of the FFI agreement and reports information about U.S. accounts directly to the IRS. See Revenue Procedure 2014-38, 2014-29 I.R.B. 131, as may be amended, for the FFI agreement. An FFI identified as a nonreporting financial institution pursuant to a Model 1 or Model 2 IGA is not required to report information on U.S. accounts unless specifically required as a condition of its applicable chapter 4 status.

II. *Background on Sponsored Entities*

A. *In general*

The chapter 4 regulations permit certain FFIs and NFFEs to be sponsored by other entities for purposes of satisfying their chapter 4 requirements. Under the 2013 final regulations, an FFI treated as complying with the requirements of section 1471(b)(1) (a deemed-compliant FFI) includes a sponsored FFI. In addition, the 2014 temporary regulations provide that a NFFE excepted from providing information regarding its substantial U.S. owners to a withholding agent (an excepted NFFE) includes a NFFE that is a direct reporting NFFE or a sponsored direct reporting NFFE. In the preamble to the 2014 temporary regulations, the Treasury Department and IRS announced that regulations describing the verification requirements of a sponsoring entity of a sponsored FFI or sponsored direct reporting NFFE (sponsored entities) would be proposed and issued separately from the 2014 temporary regulations.

B. *Background on sponsored FFIs and trustee-documented trusts*

The chapter 4 regulations provide two general categories of deemed-compliant FFIs: registered deemed-compliant FFIs and certified deemed-compliant FFIs. A registered deemed-compliant FFI includes an FFI that satisfies the requirements of § 1.1471-5(f)(1)(i)(F)(1) or (2) to qualify as either a sponsored investment entity or a sponsored controlled foreign corporation. A certified deemed-compliant FFI includes an FFI that satisfies the requirements of § 1.1471-5(f)(2)(iii) to qualify as a sponsored, closely-held investment vehicle. The chapter 4 regulations provide that a sponsored FFI under any of the foregoing sections must have an agreement with a sponsoring entity under which the sponsoring entity performs, on behalf of the sponsored FFI, all of the due diligence, withholding, reporting, and other requirements that the FFI would have been required to perform if it were a participating FFI. A sponsoring entity of a sponsored FFI must register with the IRS as a sponsoring entity on Form 8957, FATCA Registration, via the FATCA registration website available at http://www.irs.gov/fatca, and must also register any sponsored investment entity or sponsored controlled foreign corporation within the time specified in § 1.1471-5(f)(1)(i)(F)(3)(iii). The 2014 temporary regulations reserve on the rules for verification of compliance and the events of default for a sponsoring entity of a sponsored FFI.

The Model 1 and Model 2 IGAs treat certain financial institutions as nonreporting financial institutions. Under Annex II of the Model 1 IGA, a nonreporting financial institution that is a sponsored investment entity, sponsored controlled foreign corporation, or sponsored, closely held investment vehicle is treated as a deemed-compliant FFI for purposes of section 1471. A sponsoring entity of a sponsored entity subject to a Model 1 IGA agrees to perform, on behalf of the sponsored entity, all of the due diligence, withholding, reporting, and other requirements that the sponsored entity would have been required to perform if it were a reporting Model 1 financial institution. As a result, a sponsoring entity of a sponsored entity subject to a Model 1 IGA reports to the applicable Model 1 IGA jurisdiction with respect to the financial accounts maintained by the sponsored entity.

Under the Model 1 and Model 2 IGAs, a nonreporting financial institution includes a financial institution that "otherwise qualifies as a deemed-compliant FFI . . . under relevant U.S. Treasury Regulations." Thus, a financial institution covered by a Model 1 or Model 2 IGA may choose to qualify as a sponsored investment entity, controlled foreign corporation, or closely held investment vehicle pursuant to § 1.1471-5(f) instead of Annex II of the Model 1 or Model 2 IGA. In such a case, the financial institution must satisfy all of the requirements applicable to such an entity in the regulations, including the requirement for the sponsoring entity to report information directly to the IRS, even in the case of a financial institution covered by a Model 1 IGA.

Under Annex II of the Model 2 IGA, a financial institution that is a sponsored investment entity or sponsored controlled foreign corporation is treated as a registered deemed-compliant FFI, and a financial institution that is a sponsored, closely held investment vehicle is treated as a certified deemed-compliant FFI. A sponsoring entity of a sponsored entity subject to a Model 2 IGA agrees to perform, on behalf of the sponsored entity, all of the due diligence, withholding, reporting, and other requirements that the sponsored entity would have been required to perform if it were a reporting Model 2 FFI. As a result, the sponsoring entity of a sponsored entity subject to a Model 2 IGA registers with the IRS and reports to the IRS with respect to financial accounts of the sponsored entity. Annex II of the Model 2 IGA also provides that a registered deemed-compliant FFI must register with the IRS on the FATCA registration website and have its responsible officer certify every three years to the IRS that all of the requirements for the deemed-compliant category claimed by the financial institution have been satisfied since July 1, 2014.

The Model 1 and Model 2 IGAs treat certain FFIs that are trusts as nonreporting financial institutions. Under Annex II of the Model 1 IGA, a financial institution that is a trustee-documented trust is treated as a deemed-compliant FFI. Under Annex II of the Model 2 IGA, a financial institution that is a trustee-documented trust is treated as a certified deemed-compliant FFI. Under both the Model 1 IGA and the Model 2 IGA, a trust qualifies as a trustee-documented trust provided that the trustee of the trust is a U.S. financial institution, reporting Model 1 FFI, or participating FFI that reports all of the information required to be reported pursuant to the IGA with respect to U.S. accounts or U.S. reportable accounts (as applicable) of the trust. A trustee of a trustee-documented trust subject to a Model 1 or Model 2 IGA should register with the IRS. A trustee of a trustee-documented trust subject to a Model 2 IGA reports to the IRS with respect to the trust, whereas a trustee of a trustee-documented trust subject to a Model 1 IGA reports to the applicable Model 1 IGA jurisdiction.

C. *Background on sponsored direct reporting NFFEs*

Section 1472(c)(1)(G) permits the Treasury Department and IRS to issue regulations exempting withholding agents from withholding or reporting under section 1472(a) with respect to payments beneficially owned by certain persons identified by the Treasury Department and IRS, which are referred to in the chapter 4 regulations as excepted NFFEs. As noted in Part II.A of this Background, the 2014 temporary regulations include direct reporting NFFEs as a class of excepted NFFEs.

A direct reporting NFFE is a NFFE that elects to report information about its substantial U.S. owners directly to the IRS (rather than to the withholding agent) and that meets the requirements of § 1.1472-1(c)(3). A direct reporting NFFE may elect to be treated as a sponsored direct reporting NFFE if another entity, other than a nonparticipating FFI, agrees to act as its sponsoring entity for performing all of the due diligence, reporting, and other requirements that the NFFE would have been required to perform as a direct reporting NFFE. The sponsoring entity of a sponsored direct reporting NFFE must register with the IRS as a sponsoring entity and must also register the NFFE with the IRS as a sponsored direct reporting NFFE as required in the chapter 4 regulations. The sponsoring entity must also comply with the verification procedures and other compliance-related requirements provided in the regulations. The 2014 temporary regulations reserve on the verification procedures and the events of default for a sponsoring entity of a sponsored direct reporting NFFE.

Under section VI(b) of Annex I of the Model 1 and Model 2 IGAs, an active NFFE includes a NFFE that is treated as an excepted NFFE under the chapter 4 regulations. An active NFFE (including a direct reporting NFFE) does not need to be reported as a U.S. account by a reporting Model 1 FFI or reporting Model 2 FFI with which the NFFE holds an account.

III. *Background on Verification Requirements for Participating FFIs and Compliance FIs*

Under the chapter 4 regulations, a participating FFI is required to establish and implement a compliance program for satisfying its requirements under § 1.1471-4. The responsible officer of the FFI must periodically certify to the IRS that the FFI maintains effective internal controls or, if the responsible officer cannot make this certification, he or she must make a qualified certification. If there is an event of default, the IRS will notify the FFI and request remediation. The FFI must respond to the notice of default and provide information to the IRS. If the FFI does not provide a response, the IRS may deliver a notice of termination that terminates the FFI's participating FFI status.

The chapter 4 regulations permit a participating FFI that is a member of an expanded affiliated group to elect to be part of a consolidated compliance program under the authority of a participating FFI, reporting Model 1 FFI, or U.S. financial institution that is a member of the same expanded affiliated group (compliance FI). The compliance FI must establish and maintain the consolidated compliance program and perform a consolidated periodic review on behalf of each member FFI that elects to be part of the consolidated compliance program (electing FFI).

IV. *Background on Certification Requirements for Registered Deemed-Compliant FFIs*

An FFI may be a registered deemed-compliant FFI if it meets the requirements of a class of FFIs specified in § 1.1471-5(f)(1). Certain classes of registered deemed-compliant FFIs have compliance obligations as a condition of their status under this section. For example, a registered deemed-compliant FFI that is a nonreporting member of a participating FFI group under § 1.1471-5(f)(1)(i)(B) must monitor its accounts to ensure that it identifies any account that becomes a U.S. account or an account held by a recalcitrant account holder or nonparticipating FFI and meets its requirement to transfer or close such accounts (or become a participating FFI). In order for the IRS to verify that a registered deemed-compliant FFI meets the requirements of its applicable deemed-compliant status and is satisfying any such compliance obligations, the chapter 4 regulations require a registered deemed-compliant FFI to have its responsible officer certify every three years to the IRS that the FFI meets the requirements for its applicable deemed-compliant status.

Explanation of Provisions

I. *Sponsoring Entities of Sponsored FFIs*

These proposed regulations provide verification requirements for a sponsoring entity of a sponsored FFI that are generally similar to the verification requirements for a compliance FI. See Part IV of this Explanation of Provisions for the verification requirements for consolidated compliance programs. Under these proposed regulations, a sponsoring entity must maintain a compliance program to oversee its compliance with respect to each sponsored FFI for purposes of satisfying the deemed-compliant status requirements of § 1.1471-5(f)(1)(i)(F) or (f)(2)(iii) or an applicable Model 2 IGA. The deemed-compliant status requirements include: (i) the assumption by the sponsoring entity of due diligence, withholding, and reporting obligations on behalf of each sponsored FFI, and (ii) compliance with the additional requirements for status as a sponsoring entity, such as registering with the IRS.

These proposed regulations consolidate all of the verification requirements for a sponsoring entity. The 2014 temporary regulations, in § 1.1471-5T(f)(1)(i)(F)(*3*)(*vi*), (f)(1)(i)(F)(*3*)(*vii*), (f)(2)(iii)(D)(*4*), and (f)(2)(iii)(D)(*5*), require a sponsoring entity to perform the verification procedures described in § 1.1471-4(f) on behalf of a sponsored FFI and also perform the verification procedures described in § 1.1471-5(j) and (k) on behalf of itself. The 2014 temporary regulations, in § 1.1471-5T(j) and (k), reserved such verification procedures. These proposed regulations include all of the sponsoring entity's verification requirements in proposed § 1.1471-5(j).

These proposed regulations also require that a sponsoring entity appoint a responsible officer (as defined in § 1.1471-1(b)(116) of these proposed regulations) to oversee the compliance of the sponsoring entity with respect to each sponsored FFI for purposes of satisfying the requirements of § 1.1471-5(f)(1)(i)(F) or (f)(2)(iii) or of an applicable Model 2 IGA. The responsible officer must certify to the IRS by July 1 of the calendar year following the end of each certification period that the sponsoring entity is compliant with the requirements to be a sponsoring entity and maintains effective internal controls with respect to all sponsored FFIs for which it acts (or provides a qualified certification) on the form and in the manner prescribed by the IRS. A sponsored FFI is not required to appoint its own responsible officer. Although the preamble to the 2014 temporary regulations states that under proposed regulations a sponsoring entity would be required to make two separate compliance certifications (one on behalf of its sponsored FFI(s) and another on the sponsoring entity's own behalf), the Treasury Department and IRS have determined that a single certification is sufficient for this purpose.

Under these proposed regulations, in general, a sponsoring entity must make a certification regarding its compliance with respect to all sponsored FFIs for which it acts during the certification period. However, with respect to a certification period, a sponsoring entity is generally not required to certify for a sponsored FFI that first agrees to be sponsored by the sponsoring entity during the six month period prior to the end of the certification period, provided that the sponsoring entity makes certifications for such sponsored FFI for subsequent certification periods and the first such certification covers both the subsequent certification period and the portion of the prior certification period during which such FFI was sponsored by the sponsoring entity. However, the preceding sentence does not apply with respect to a sponsored FFI that, immediately before the FFI agrees to be sponsored by the sponsoring entity, was a participating FFI, registered deemed-compliant FFI, or sponsored, closely held investment vehicle. The sponsoring entity may certify for a sponsored FFI described in the preceding sentence for the portion of the certification period prior to the date that the FFI first agrees to be sponsored by the sponsoring entity if the sponsoring entity obtains from the FFI (or the FFI's sponsoring entity, if applicable) a written certification that the FFI has complied with its applicable chapter 4 requirements during such portion of the certification period, provided that: (1) the sponsoring entity does not know that such certification is unreliable or incorrect; and (2) the certification for the sponsored FFI for the subsequent certification period covers both the subsequent certification period and the portion of the prior certification period during which such FFI was sponsored by the sponsoring entity. The first certification period begins on the later of the date the sponsoring entity is issued a GIIN to act as a sponsoring entity or June 30, 2014.

The requirements for the certification of compliance may be modified to include additional certifications or information (such as quantitative or factual information related to the sponsoring entity's compliance), provided that such additional information or certifications are published at least 90 days before being made effective in order to allow for public comment. The Treasury Department and IRS intend to coordinate any such modification to the requirements for the certification of compliance for sponsoring entities with any modification to the requirements for the certification of compliance for participating FFIs. See Part IV of this Explanation of Provisions for certifications required by participating FFIs.

These proposed regulations provide that the responsible officer of a sponsoring entity must make the certification described in § 1.1471-4(c)(7) (preexisting account certification of a participating FFI) with respect to each sponsored FFI that enters into the sponsorship agreement with the sponsoring entity during the certification period. However, with respect to a certification period, the preexisting account certification is not required for a sponsored FFI if, immediately before it first agrees to be sponsored by the sponsoring entity, the FFI was a participating FFI, a sponsored FFI, or a registered deemed-compliant FFI that is a local FFI or a restricted fund, and the FFI (or the FFI's former sponsoring entity, if applicable) provides a written certification to the sponsoring entity that the FFI has made the preexisting account certification required of 13 it, provided that the sponsoring entity does not know that such certification is unreliable or incorrect. Furthermore, since a participating FFI could have up to two years to complete the required due diligence on its preexisting accounts under § 1.1471-4(c)(3)(ii) and (c)(5)(i), the preexisting account certification is not required for a sponsored FFI that first agrees to be sponsored by the sponsoring entity during the two year period prior to the end of such certification period, provided that the sponsoring entity makes the preexisting account certification for such FFI for the subsequent certification period. The preexisting account certification for the certification period must be submitted by the due date of the sponsoring entity's certification of compliance for the certification period and on the form and in the manner prescribed by the IRS. With respect to a sponsored FFI for which the sponsoring entity is required to make a preexisting account certification, a preexisting obligation means any account, instrument, or contract (including any debt or equity interest) maintained, executed, or issued by the sponsored FFI that is outstanding on the earlier of the date the FFI is issued a GIIN as a sponsored FFI of the sponsoring entity or the date the FFI or the sponsoring entity first represents to a withholding agent or financial institution that the FFI is a sponsored FFI of the sponsoring entity.

These proposed regulations permit the IRS to make general inquiries to a sponsoring entity regarding its compliance with its applicable requirements, similar to the general inquiries the IRS may make to a participating FFI with respect to its compliance (as provided in final regulations under chapter 4 published together with the temporary chapter 4 regulations). These proposed regulations provide that the IRS may request any additional information from the sponsoring entity (including a copy of the sponsorship agreement that the sponsoring entity has entered into with each sponsored FFI) necessary to determine its compliance with the due diligence, withholding, and reporting requirements of § 1.1471-4 or an applicable Model 2 IGA with respect to each sponsored FFI and to assist the IRS with its review of account holder compliance with tax reporting requirements. These proposed regulations also provide that if the IRS determines that the sponsoring entity may not have substantially complied with the requirements of a sponsoring entity with respect to any sponsored FFI for which it acts, the IRS may make inquiries to the sponsoring entity regarding its compliance with the requirements of a sponsoring entity and may request the performance of specified review procedures. Inquiries regarding the compliance of a sponsoring entity with respect to a sponsored FFI subject to the requirements of an applicable Model 2 IGA will be made using the procedures described in these proposed regulations, except as otherwise provided in an applicable Model 2 IGA.

These proposed regulations describe the events of default for a sponsoring entity and the termination procedures following an event of default. The Treasury Department and IRS recognize that some events of default may relate only to a particular sponsored FFI (or several such FFIs) for which the sponsoring entity acts and thus should not affect the statuses of other sponsored FFIs for which the sponsoring entity acts or the status of the sponsoring entity. In other cases, an event of default may relate to a sponsoring entity's failure to comply with its own requirements, such as when it fails to establish and maintain a compliance program or perform a periodic review.

Accordingly, these proposed regulations provide IRS the discretion to determine whether, based on facts and circumstances, an event of default should result in the termination of the sponsoring entity's status as a sponsoring entity, the deemed-compliant statuses of one or more sponsored FFIs, or both the status of the sponsoring entity and the statuses of one or more sponsored FFIs. If a sponsoring entity's status is terminated, the sponsoring entity may not reregister as a sponsoring entity for any sponsored FFI or any sponsored entity subject to a Model 1 IGA without prior written approval from the IRS. A sponsored FFI whose sponsoring entity's status is terminated may register on the FATCA registration website as a participating FFI or registered deemed-compliant FFI or may be registered on the FATCA registration website as a sponsored FFI of a new sponsoring entity (other than an entity that has a relationship to the terminated sponsoring entity described in section 267(b)), as applicable. However, if the sponsored FFI's status is terminated (independent of a termination of the sponsoring entity), the sponsored FFI must obtain prior written approval from the IRS in order to register as a participating FFI or registered deemed-compliant FFI or be registered as a sponsored FFI of a new sponsoring entity.

The definition of sponsored FFI in the 2013 final regulations is limited to an entity that is a sponsored investment entity, sponsored controlled foreign corporation, or sponsored, closely held investment vehicle under § 1.1471-5(f)(1)(i)(F) or § 1.1471-5(f)(2)(iii). These proposed regulations expand the definition of sponsored FFI to also include a sponsored investment entity, sponsored controlled foreign corporation, or sponsored, closely held investment vehicle treated as a deemed-compliant FFI under an applicable Model 2 IGA. These proposed regulations do not impose verification requirements or specify events of default for a sponsoring entity of a sponsored entity subject to an applicable Model 1 IGA. The obligations of such a sponsoring entity are governed by the laws and requirements of the applicable Model 1 IGA jurisdiction. However, the IRS may treat a sponsored entity covered by a Model 1 IGA as a nonparticipating FFI pursuant to Article 5(2)(b) of an applicable Model 1 IGA if the IRS determines that there is significant non-compliance with the obligations of the IGA by the sponsored entity that has not been resolved within 18 months. In addition, pursuant to the termination procedures described in the previous paragraph, the IRS may revoke the status of a sponsoring entity based on an event of default relating to one or more sponsored FFIs. Consistent with Annex II of the Model 1 IGA, such revocation would prevent the sponsoring entity from sponsoring an FFI subject to a Model 1 IGA. The IRS may also notify such Model 1 IGA jurisdiction of the revocation. A sponsored entity subject to a Model 1 IGA whose sponsor's status is terminated would need to become a reporting Model 1 FFI, obtain a new sponsor, or meet the requirements of another deemed-compliant status.

As described in Part II.B of the Background of this preamble, the Model 2 IGA allows certain sponsored FFIs to be treated as deemed-compliant FFIs and provides that the IRS may revoke a sponsoring entity's status if there is a material failure by the sponsoring entity to comply with the obligations described in Annex II of the IGA. Accordingly, the verification requirements and events of default in these proposed regulations apply to a sponsoring entity of a sponsored FFI subject to an applicable Model 2 IGA. In addition, the procedures for IRS inquiries specified in these proposed regulations apply to a sponsoring entity of a sponsored FFI subject to an applicable Model 2 IGA except to the extent otherwise provided in the applicable Model 2 IGA. Although Annex II of the Model 2 IGA permits the IRS to revoke a sponsoring entity's status upon a material failure (as described above), because the Treasury Department and IRS believe that a consistent standard for when to terminate a sponsoring entity's status should apply, these proposed regulations provide that the IRS will not revoke the status of a sponsoring entity of a sponsored FFI subject to a Model 2 IGA unless there is an event of default and the procedures for termination described in these proposed regulations have been applied.

II. *Trustees of Trustee-Documented Trusts*

These proposed regulations provide that a trustee of a trustee-documented trust subject to a Model 2 IGA shall appoint a responsible officer who will maintain a compliance program and oversee the trustee's compliance with respect to each trustee-documented trust for purposes of satisfying the requirements of an applicable Model 2 IGA. The responsible officer must perform a periodic review of the sufficiency of the trustee's compliance program for each certification period. The responsible officer must also certify to the IRS that the trustee has established a compliance program, performed a periodic review, and reported to the IRS all of the information required to be reported with respect to each trustee-documented trust for each certification period. Certain late-joining trustee-documented trusts may be excluded from a certification under rules similar to those provided in these proposed regulations for sponsored FFIs. The IRS will not unilaterally revoke the status of, or issue a notice of default to, a trustee of such a trust. Instead, subject to the requirements of an applicable Model 2 IGA, these proposed regulations permit the IRS to make inquiries to the trustee regarding its compliance with its applicable requirements and notify the Model 2 IGA jurisdiction if the trustee has not complied with its requirements with respect to one or more trustee-documented trusts established in that jurisdiction. The IRS may also notify an applicable Model 1 IGA jurisdiction of the trustee's non-compliance with respect to its requirements as a trustee of a trustee-documented trust subject to a Model 2 IGA if the trustee also acts on behalf of trustee-documented trusts in the Model 1 IGA jurisdiction or if the trustee is located in the Model 1 IGA jurisdiction.

III. *Sponsoring Entities of Sponsored Direct Reporting NFFEs*

These proposed regulations include verification requirements and the events of default for a sponsoring entity of a sponsored direct reporting NFFE. These proposed regulations also specify the requirements for a sponsorship agreement between a sponsoring entity and each sponsored direct reporting NFFE for which it acts.

Under these proposed regulations, a sponsoring entity must appoint a responsible officer to oversee the compliance of the sponsoring entity with respect to each sponsored direct reporting NFFE. The responsible officer of the sponsoring entity must make a periodic certification to the IRS on the form and in the manner prescribed by the IRS. The certification requirements of a sponsoring entity of a sponsored direct reporting NFFE are more limited than the certification requirements of a sponsoring entity of a sponsored FFI because the obligations of a sponsoring entity of a sponsored direct reporting NFFE are more limited than those of a sponsoring entity of a sponsored FFI. A sponsoring entity of a sponsored direct reporting NFFE must certify that it meets the requirements of a sponsoring entity, that it has a written sponsorship agreement that meets the requirements in these proposed regulations in effect with each sponsored direct reporting NFFE, that there have been no events of default (or that such events have been remediated), and that the sponsoring entity has corrected any failures to 19 report on Form 8966, "FATCA Report," with respect to any sponsored direct reporting NFFE.

In general, a sponsoring entity must make the periodic certification with respect to all sponsored direct reporting NFFEs for which it acts during the certification period. However, with respect to a certification period, a sponsoring entity is not required to certify for a sponsored direct reporting NFFE that first agrees to be sponsored by the sponsoring entity during the six month period prior to the end of the certification period, provided that the sponsoring entity makes certifications for such sponsored direct reporting NFFE for subsequent certification periods and the first such certification covers both the subsequent certification period and the portion of the prior certification period during which the sponsored direct reporting NFFE was sponsored by the sponsoring entity. However, the preceding sentence does not apply to a sponsored direct reporting NFFE that, immediately before the NFFE agrees to be sponsored by the sponsoring entity, was a direct reporting NFFE or sponsored direct reporting NFFE of another sponsoring entity. The sponsoring entity may certify for a sponsored direct reporting NFFE described in the preceding sentence for the portion of the certification period prior to the date that the NFFE first agrees to be sponsored by the sponsoring entity if the sponsoring entity obtains from the NFFE (or the NFFE's sponsoring entity, if applicable) a written certification that the NFFE has complied with its applicable chapter 4 requirements during such portion of the certification period, provided that: (1) the sponsoring entity does not know that such certification is unreliable or incorrect; and (2) the certification for the sponsored direct reporting NFFE for the subsequent certification period covers both the subsequent certification period and the portion of the prior certification period during which such NFFE was sponsored by the sponsoring entity. The first certification period will begin on the later of the date the sponsoring entity is issued a GIIN to act as a sponsoring entity or June 30, 2014.

Under these proposed regulations, the IRS may make inquiries to a sponsoring entity to determine the sponsoring entity's compliance with its requirements. The IRS may also request any additional information from the sponsoring entity (including a copy of the sponsorship agreement that the sponsoring entity has entered into with each sponsored direct reporting NFFE). If the IRS determines that the sponsoring entity may not have substantially complied with the requirements of a sponsoring entity with respect to any sponsored direct reporting NFFE for which it acts, the IRS may request additional information to verify the sponsoring entity's compliance with such requirements and may request the performance of specified review procedures.

These proposed regulations also specify the events of default and termination procedures applicable to a sponsoring entity of a sponsored direct reporting NFFE. Consistent with the verification requirements for direct reporting NFFEs in the chapter 4 regulations, a notice of default is triggered by an event of default. An event of default may result in the termination of the sponsoring entity's status as a sponsoring entity, the statuses of one or more sponsored direct reporting NFFEs as such, or both the status of a sponsoring entity and the statuses of one or more sponsored direct reporting NFFEs. A sponsored direct reporting NFFE whose sponsoring entity's status is terminated may register on the FATCA registration website as a direct reporting NFFE or sponsored direct reporting NFFE, unless the sponsored direct reporting NFFE's status is also terminated, in which case the sponsored direct reporting NFFE must obtain prior written approval from the IRS in order to register.

IV. *Modifications to the Verification Requirements for Participating FFIs and Compliance FIs*

These proposed regulations provide that the requirements for a participating FFI's certification of compliance (described in § 1.1471-4(f)(3)) may be modified through an amendment to the FFI agreement to include additional certifications or information (such as quantitative or factual information related to the FFI's compliance with the FFI agreement), provided that any additional information or certifications required are published at least 90 days before being added to the FFI agreement to allow for public comment. See also section 12.02 of the FFI agreement (covering modifications to the FFI agreement imposing additional requirements on participating FFIs). Additionally, any such amendment to the FFI agreement will be published only after these proposed regulations are published as final regulations.

These proposed regulations modify the procedures and timeframes for notices of default and terminations applicable to participating FFIs in the chapter 4 regulations to conform to the procedures and timeframes for sponsoring entities in these proposed regulations. These proposed regulations include a minimum period of 45 days for a participating FFI to respond to a notice of default. Within 30 days of a termination of an FFI's participating FFI status, the FFI must send a notice of termination to each withholding agent from which the FFI receives payments and each financial institution with which it holds an account to which a withholding certificate or other documentation was provided. Requests for reconsideration of a notice of default or a notice of termination must be made within 90 days of the notice of default or notice of termination (as applicable). An FFI that has had its participating FFI status terminated may not reregister on the FATCA registration website as a participating FFI or a registered deemed-compliant FFI unless it receives written approval from the IRS.

The chapter 4 regulations provide that when an FFI elects to be part of a consolidated compliance program (electing FFI), each branch that it maintains (including a limited branch or a branch described in § 1.1471-5(f)(1)) must be subject to periodic review as part of such program. These proposed regulations clarify that a branch of an electing FFI located in a Model 1 IGA jurisdiction is excluded from the periodic review. In addition, these proposed regulations clarify that the responsible officer of the compliance FI must make the periodic certification described in § 1.1471-4(f)(3) (or a qualified certification) on the form and in the manner prescribed by the IRS. In general, the certification must be made on behalf of all electing FFIs in the compliance group during the certification period. However, with respect to a certification period, a compliance FI is not required to make a certification for an electing FFI that first elects to be part of the consolidated compliance program of the compliance FI during the six month period prior to the end of the certification period, provided that the compliance FI makes certifications for such electing FFI for subsequent certification periods, and the first such certification covers both the subsequent certification period and the portion of the prior certification period during which such FFI was an electing FFI in the consolidated compliance program of the compliance FI. However, the preceding sentence does not apply to an electing FFI that, immediately before the electing FFI elects to be part of the consolidated compliance program, was a participating FFI or registered deemed-compliant FFI. The compliance FI may certify for an electing FFI described in the preceding sentence for the portion of the certification period prior to the date that the electing FFI elects to be part of the consolidated compliance program if the compliance FI obtains from the FFI (or the FFI's former compliance FI, if applicable) a written certification that the FFI has complied with its applicable chapter 4 requirements during such portion of the certification period, provided that: (1) the compliance FI does not know that such certification is unreliable or incorrect; and (2) the certification for the electing FFI for the subsequent certification period covers both the subsequent certification period and the portion of the prior certification period during which such FFI was an electing FFI in the consolidated compliance program of the compliance FI. The first certification period for a compliance group begins on the later of the date the compliance FI is issued a GIIN or June 30, 2014, and ends at the close of the third full calendar year following such date. Each subsequent certification period is the three calendar year period following the previous certification period.

These proposed regulations provide that the responsible officer of a compliance FI must make the certification described in § 1.1471-4(c)(7) (preexisting account certification of a participating FFI) with respect to each electing FFI that elects to be part of the consolidated compliance program under the compliance FI during the certification period (as defined in § 1.1471-4(f)(3)(i)). Notwithstanding the preceding sentence, a preexisting account certification is not required for an electing FFI if, immediately before electing to be part of the consolidated compliance program under the compliance FI, the FFI was a participating FFI or a registered deemed-compliant FFI that is a local FFI or restricted fund, and the FFI (or the FFI's former compliance FI, if applicable) provides a written certification to the compliance FI that the FFI has made the preexisting account certification required of it, unless the compliance FI knows that such certification is unreliable or incorrect. In addition, a preexisting account certification is not required for a certification period for an electing FFI that elects to be part of the consolidated compliance program under the compliance FI during the two year period prior to the end of such certification period, provided that the compliance FI makes the preexisting account certification for such FFI by the due date of the certification of compliance for the subsequent certification period. The preexisting account certification, if required for a certification period, must be submitted by the due date of the FFI's periodic certification of compliance for the certification period, on the form and in the manner prescribed by the IRS.

V. *Certification and Verification Requirements for Registered Deemed-Compliant FFIs*

The chapter 4 regulations do not explicitly provide that the IRS may apply verification procedures and make inquiries regarding the certifications provided by registered deemed-compliant FFIs. These proposed regulations provide that the IRS may make inquiries of, and request additional information from and the performance of specified review procedures by, a registered deemed-compliant FFI to verify the FFI's compliance with the requirements of its applicable deemed-compliant status. These requirements are similar to the provisions for the IRS's verification of a participating FFI's compliance with the FFI agreement. If the IRS determines that a registered deemed-compliant FFI has not complied with the requirements of the deemed-compliant status claimed by the FFI, the IRS may terminate the FFI's deemed-compliant status. A registered deemed-compliant FFI that has had its status terminated may request reconsideration of the termination by submitting a written request to the IRS within 90 days of the notice of termination.

Proposed Effective/Applicability Dates

These proposed regulations apply on the date of publication of a Treasury decision adopting these rules as final regulations in the **Federal Register**.

Special Analyses

Certain IRS regulations, including these, are exempt from the requirements of Executive Order 12866, as supplemented and reaffirmed by Executive Order 13563. Therefore, a regulatory impact assessment is not required.

The IRS intends that the information collection requirements in these proposed regulations will be satisfied by submitting certifications to the IRS electronically. For purposes of the Paperwork Reduction Act, the reporting burden associated with the collection of information in these proposed regulations will be reflected in the OMB Form 83-1, Paperwork Reduction Act Submission, associated with the certification.

It is hereby certified that the collection of information requirement in these proposed regulations will not have a significant economic impact on a substantial number of small entities because these proposed regulations affect foreign persons, not domestic entities. Therefore, a Regulatory Flexibility Analysis under the Regulatory Flexibility Act is not required. Pursuant to section 7805(f) of the Code, this notice of proposed rulemaking has been submitted to the Chief Counsel for Advocacy of the Small Business Administration for comment on its impact on small business.

Comments and Requests for Public Hearing

Before these proposed regulations are adopted as final regulations, consideration will be given to any comments that are submitted timely to the IRS as prescribed in this preamble under the "Addresses" heading. The Treasury Department and IRS request comments on all aspects of the proposed rules, including comments on the clarity of the proposed rules and how they could be made easier with which to comply. All comments will be available for public inspection and copying. A public hearing will be scheduled if requested in writing by any person that timely submits written comments. If a public hearing is scheduled, notice of the date, time, and place for the public hearing will be published in the **Federal Register.**

Drafting Information

The principal author of these proposed regulations is Kamela Nelan, Office of Associate Chief Counsel (International). However, other personnel from the IRS and the Treasury Department participated in their development.

[¶49,733] Proposed Amendments of Regulations (REG-134247-16), published in the Federal Register on January 6, 2017 (corrected September 15, 2017).

[Code Sec. 1441]

Foreign Account Tax Compliance Act (FATCA): Foreign financial institution (FFI): FFI agreement: Withholding.—Amendments of Reg. §§1.1441-1, 1.1441-2, 1.1441-6 and 1.1441-7, regarding withholding of tax on certain U.S. source income paid to foreign persons and requirements for certain claims for refund or credit of income tax made by foreign persons, are proposed.

AGENCY: Internal Revenue Service (IRS), Treasury.

ACTION: Notice of proposed rulemaking by cross-reference to temporary regulations. SUMMARY: In the Rules and Regulations section of this issue of the **Federal Register,** the Department of the Treasury (Treasury Department) and the IRS are issuing temporary regulations (TD 9808) that revise certain provisions of the final regulations regarding withholding of tax on certain U.S. source income paid to foreign persons and requirements for certain claims for refund or credit of income tax made by foreign persons. The text of the temporary regulations also serves as the text of these proposed regulations.

DATES: Written or electronic comments and requests for a public hearing must be received by April 6, 2017.

ADDRESSES: Send submissions to: CC:PA:LPD:PR (REG-134247-16), room 5203, Internal Revenue Service, PO Box 7604, Ben Franklin Station, Washington, DC 20044. Submissions may be hand-delivered Monday through Friday between the hours of 8 a.m. and 4 p.m. to CC:PA:LPD:PR (REG-134247-16), Courier's Desk, Internal Revenue Service, 1111 Constitution Avenue, NW, Washington, DC 20224, or sent electronically, via the Federal eRulemaking Portal at *www.regulations.gov* (IRS REG-134247-16). FOR FURTHER INFORMATION CONTACT: Concerning the proposed regulations,

Leni Perkins, (202) 317-6942; concerning submissions of comments and/or requests for a public hearing, Regina Johnson, (202) 317-6901 (not toll-free numbers).

SUPPLEMENTARY INFORMATION:

Background

The temporary regulations in the Rules and Regulations section of this issue of the **Federal Register** amend the Income Tax Regulations (26 CFR part 1) relating to section 1441 of the Internal Revenue Code (Code). The temporary regulations set forth rules relating to withholding and reporting requirements under chapter 3 of the Code, including rules relating to claims for a reduced rate of withholding under an income tax treaty. The preamble to the temporary regulations explains the temporary regulations and these proposed regulations.

Special Analyses

Certain IRS regulations, including these, are exempt from the requirements of Executive Order 12866, as supplemented and reaffirmed by Executive Order 13653. Therefore, a regulatory assessment is not required.

It is hereby certified that the collection of information in this notice of proposed rulemaking will not have a significant economic impact on a substantial number of small entities within the meaning of section 601(6) of the Regulatory Flexibility Act (5 U.S.C. chapter 6).

The domestic small business entities that are subject to the collections of information in this notice of proposed rulemaking are those domestic business entities that are payors of certain U.S. source income to foreign persons. These domestic small business entities are subject to comprehensive rules under chapter 3 to identify the proper treatment of payees for purposes of that chapter's information reporting and tax withholding purposes. The domestic small business entities subject to the collections of information in this notice of proposed rulemaking are also subject to comprehensive information reporting and tax withholding rules under chapters 4 and 61 with respect to payments of certain U.S. source income subject to information reporting and tax reporting under chapter 3. These payors are also subject to information and reporting rules under section 3406.

Payors of payments that are subject to the information reporting and withholding regimes under chapter 3 play an important role in U.S. tax compliance by providing information about payments made to, and income earned by, U.S. and foreign taxpayers.

Although the Treasury Department and the IRS anticipate that a substantial number of domestic small entities will be affected by the collection of information in this notice of proposed rulemaking, the Treasury Department and the IRS believe that the economic impact to these entities resulting from the information collection requirements will not be significant. The reporting obligations under these proposed regulations flow from the obligations that domestic small entities may have as withholding agents for payments of amounts subject to withholding under sections 1441 or 1442. As withholding agents, these entities have already been subject to the overall framework of these regulations, and the economic burden of complying with any additional requirements will be minimal. Therefore, a Regulatory Flexibility Analysis under the Regulatory Flexibility Act is not required. Pursuant to section 7805(f) of the Code, this regulation has been submitted to the Chief Counsel for Advocacy of the Small Business Administration for comment on its impact on small businesses.

Comments and Public Hearing

Before these proposed regulations are adopted as final regulations, consideration will be given to any written comments that are submitted timely to the IRS as prescribed in this preamble under the "ADDRESSES" heading. The Treasury Department and the IRS request comments on all aspects of the proposed rules, including comments on the clarity of the proposed rules and how compliance therewith could be made easier. All comments will be available for public inspection and copying. A public hearing will be scheduled if requested in writing by any person that timely submits written comments. If a public hearing is scheduled, notice of the date, time, and place for the public hearing will be published in the **Federal Register**.

Drafting Information

The principal author of these proposed regulations is Leni C. Perkins, Office of Associate Chief Counsel (International). However, other personnel from the Treasury Department and the IRS participated in their development.

[¶49,737] Proposed Amendments of Regulation and Withdrawal of Notice of Proposed Rulemaking (REG-137604-07), published in the Federal Register on January 19, 2017.

[Code Secs. 2, 3, 21, 32, 63, 151, 152, 6013 and 6109]

Dependency exemptions: Filing status: Tax tables: Earned income credit: Standard deduction: Taxpayer identification number.—Reg. §§1.63-3, 1.152-0, and 1.152-4, and amendments of Reg. §§1.2-1, 1.2-2, 1.3-1, 1.21-1, 1.32-2, 1.63-1, 1.63-2, 1.151-1, 1.151-2, 1.151-3, 1.151-4, 1.152-1, 1.152-2, 1.152-3, 1.152-4, 1.152-5, 1.6013-1, and 301.6109-3, relating to the definition of an authorized placement agency for purposes of a dependency exemption for a child placed for adoption that were issued prior to the changes made to the law by the Working Families Tax Relief Act of 2004 (WFTRA), are proposed. Amendments of Reg. §1.152-2, proposed by REG-107279-00 on November 30, 2000, are withdrawn.

AGENCY: Internal Revenue Service (IRS), Treasury.

ACTION: Withdrawal of notice of proposed rulemaking and notice of proposed rulemaking.

SUMMARY: This document withdraws proposed regulations relating to the definition of an authorized placement agency for purposes of a dependency exemption for a child placed for adoption that were issued prior to the changes made to the law by the Working Families Tax Relief Act of 2004 (WFTRA). This document contains proposed regulations that reflect changes made by WFTRA and by the Fostering Connections to Success and Increasing Adoptions Act of 2008 (FCSIAA) relating to the dependency exemption. This document also contains proposed regulations that, to reflect current law, amend the regulations relating to the surviving spouse and head of household filing statuses, the tax tables for individuals, the child and dependent care credit, the earned income credit, the standard deduction, joint tax returns, and taxpayer identification numbers for children placed for adoption. These proposed regulations change the IRS's position regarding the category of taxpayers permitted to claim the childless earned income credit. In determining a taxpayer's eligibility to claim a dependency exemption, these proposed regulations change the IRS's position regarding the adjusted gross income of a taxpayer filing a joint return for purposes of the tiebreaker rules and the source of support of certain payments that originated as governmental payments. These regulations provide guidance to individuals who may claim certain child-related tax benefits.

DATES: Written or electronic comments and requests for a public hearing must be received by April 19, 2017.

ADDRESSES: Send submissions to: CC:PA:LPD:PR (REG-137604-07), Room 5203, Internal Revenue Service, PO Box 7604, Ben Franklin Station, Washington, DC 20044. Submissions may be hand-delivered Monday through Friday between the hours of 8 a.m. and 4 p.m. to CC:PA:LPD:PR (REG-137604-07), Courier's Desk, Internal Revenue Service, 1111 Constitution Avenue, NW., Washington, DC 20224, or sent electronically via the Federal eRulemaking Portal at *www.regulations.gov* (IRS REG-137604-07). FOR FURTHER INFORMATION CONTACT: Concerning the proposed regulations, Victoria J. Driscoll, (202) 317-4718; concerning the submission of comments and requests for a public hearing, Regina Johnson, (202) 317-6901 (not toll-free calls). SUPPLEMENTARY INFORMATION:

Background

This document withdraws a notice of proposed rulemaking (REG-107279-00) amending § 1.152-2(c)(2) of the Income Tax Regulations that was published in the **Federal Register** (65 FR 71277) on November 30, 2000 (2000 proposed regulations) relating to the definition of an authorized placement agency for purposes of a dependency exemption for a child placed for adoption under prior law. Prior law required that a child be placed with the taxpayer for adoption by an authorized placement agency. Section 152 of the Internal Revenue Code was amended by section 201 of WFTRA (Public Law 108-311, 118 Stat. 1166, 1169) to provide that a qualifying child eligible to be the dependent of a taxpayer may include a child lawfully placed with the taxpayer for adoption. Accordingly, the proposed regulations in § 1.152-2(c)(2) under prior law are withdrawn.

This document also contains proposed amendments to 26 CFR Part 1 under sections 2, 3, 21, 32, 63, 151, 152, 6013, and to Part 301 under section 6109 to reflect the changes made by WFTRA and FCSIAA (Public Law 110-351, 122 Stat. 3949) relating to the dependency exemption, as well as changes to these sections by other acts. WFTRA amended section 152, in part, to provide a uniform definition of a qualifying child; FCSIAA added to the definition of a qualifying child the requirements that the child must be younger than the taxpayer and that the child must not file a joint return (other than as a claim for refund). FCSIAA also amended the rules that apply if two or more taxpayers are eligible to claim an individual as a qualifying child.

1. *Dependency Rules*

Under section 151, a taxpayer may deduct an exemption amount for a dependent as defined in section 152. Prior to WFTRA, section 151 contained many of the rules related to the definition of a dependent. WFTRA moved those rules to section 152. As amended, section 152(a) defines a *dependent* as a qualifying child or a qualifying relative. Taxpayers should note that a taxpayer's treatment of the dependency exemption under section 151 for a particular qualifying child or qualifying relative might have tax consequences under other Code provisions, such as the education tax credits under section 25A, the premium tax credit under section 36B, and the penalty for failure to maintain minimum essential coverage under section 5000A.

a. *Individual not a dependent*

Section 152(b) provides that an individual who is a qualifying child or a qualifying relative of a taxpayer is not a taxpayer's dependent in certain circumstances. Section 152(b)(2) provides that, to be a dependent of a taxpayer, an individual must not have filed a joint return with his or her spouse. However, the WFTRA conference report provides that the "restriction does not apply if the return was filed solely to obtain a refund and no tax liability would exist for either spouse if they filed separate returns." See H.R. Rep. No. 108-696, at 55 n.38 (2004) (Conf. Rep.).

b. *Qualifying child*

WFTRA established under section 152(c) a uniform definition of a qualifying child. The legislative history identifies five child-related benefits to which the uniform definition applies: the filing status of head of household under section 2(b), the child and dependent care credit under section 21, the child tax credit under section 24, the earned income credit under section 32, and the dependency exemption under section 151. See H.R. Rep. No. 108-696, at 55-65.

Section 152(c) defines a qualifying child as an individual who bears a certain relationship to the taxpayer (qualifying child relationship test), has the same principal place of abode as the taxpayer for more than one-half of the taxable year (residency test), is younger than the taxpayer and is under the age of 19 (or age 24 if a full-time student or any age if permanently and totally disabled) (age test), does not provide more than one-half of his or her own support (qualifying child support test), and does not file a joint return with a spouse except to claim a refund of estimated or withheld taxes (joint return test).

c. *Temporary absence*

A child is considered to reside in the same principal place of abode as a taxpayer during a temporary absence. Under the existing section 152 regulations, a nonpermanent failure to occupy a common abode by reason of illness, education, business, vacation, military service, or a custody agreement may be a temporary absence due to special circumstances. The existing regulations under section 2 defining surviving spouse and head of household include a similar rule relating to the effect of a temporary absence on the requirement to maintain a household, but add the requirement that it is reasonable to assume that the absent person will return to the household. Under case law, a factor to consider in determining whether an absence is temporary is whether the individual intends to establish a new principal place of abode. In *Rowe v. Commissioner*, 128 T.C. 13 (2007), the court concluded that it was reasonable to assume that a taxpayer would return to her home after pretrial confinement and that the taxpayer's absence was temporary. See also *Hein v. Commissioner*, 28 T.C. 826 (1957) (*acq*., 1958-2 CB 6), and Rev. Rul. 66-28 (1966-1 CB 31).

d. *Two or more taxpayers eligible to claim individual as qualifying child*

Section 152(c)(4) provides tiebreaker rules that apply if an individual meets the definition of a qualifying child for two or more taxpayers (eligible taxpayers). In general, the eligible taxpayer who is a parent (eligible parent) of the individual may claim the individual as a qualifying child or, if there is no eligible parent, then the individual may be claimed by the eligible taxpayer with the highest adjusted gross income.

If more than one of the eligible taxpayers is a parent of the individual, more than one eligible parent claims the individual as a qualifying child, and the eligible parents claiming the individual do not file a joint return with each other, the individual is treated as the qualifying child of the eligible parent claiming the individual with whom the individual resided for the longest period of time during the taxable year. If the individual resided with each eligible parent claiming the individual for the same amount of time during the taxable year, the individual is treated as the qualifying child of the eligible parent claiming the individual with the highest adjusted gross income.

If at least one, but not all, of two or more eligible taxpayers is a parent of the individual, but no eligible parent claims the individual as a qualifying child, another eligible taxpayer may claim the individual, but only if the eligible taxpayer's adjusted gross income is higher than the adjusted gross income of each eligible parent. Since 2009, IRS Publication 501, *Exemptions, Standard Deduction, and Filing Information*, has stated that "[i]f a child's parents file a joint return with each other, this rule may be applied by dividing the parents' combined AGI equally between the parents."

Notice 2006-86 (2006-2 CB 680) provides interim guidance on these rules prior to the amendments by FCSIAA. The notice provides that, except to the extent that a noncustodial parent may claim the child as a qualifying child under the special rule for divorced or separated parents in section 152(e), discussed in the next paragraph, if more than one taxpayer claims a child as a qualifying child, the child is treated as the qualifying child of only one taxpayer (as determined under the tiebreaker rules of section 152(c)(4)) for purposes of the five provisions subject to the uniform definition of a qualifying child (the filing status of head of household under section 2(b), the child and dependent care credit under section 21, the child tax credit under section 24, the earned income credit under section 32, and the dependency exemption under section 151, as well as for purposes of the exclusion for dependent care assistance under section 129 (which may apply to the care of a dependent qualifying child under age 13)). Thus, in general, the tiebreaker rules for determining which taxpayer may claim a child as a qualifying child apply to these provisions as a group, rather than on a section-by-section basis.

Notice 2006-86 contains an exception to the rule that only one taxpayer may claim a child as a qualifying child for all purposes. Section 152(e) has a special rule for divorced or separated parents that determines who, as between the custodial and noncustodial parent, may claim a child as a qualifying child or qualifying relative if certain tests (different from the general tests under sections 152(c) and (d)) regarding residency and support are met and the custodial parent releases a claim to exemption for the child. The notice provides that, if this special rule applies, a noncustodial parent may claim a child as a qualifying child for purposes of the dependency exemption and the child tax credit (the only two of the provisions addressed in the notice to which section 152(e) applies in determining who is a qualifying child), and another taxpayer may claim the child for one or more of the other benefits to which section 152(e) does not apply.

Although FCSIAA affects other aspects of section 152(c)(4) and Notice 2006-86, there is nothing in FCSIAA that would compel a change in the rule described in Notice 2006-86 that an individual is treated as the qualifying child of only one taxpayer for the listed child-related tax benefits, except if the special rule in section 152(e) applies.

e. *Qualifying relative*

Under section 152(d), a qualifying relative is an individual who bears a certain relationship to the taxpayer, including an individual who has the same principal place of abode as the taxpayer and is a member of the taxpayer's household for the taxable year (qualifying relative relationship test), has gross income less than the exemption amount for the taxable year (gross income test), receives more than one-half of his or her support from the taxpayer (qualifying relative support test), and is not a qualifying child of any taxpayer (not a qualifying child test).

Notice 2008-5 (2008-1 CB 256) addresses whether a taxpayer meets the test under section 152(d)(1)(D) to claim an individual as a qualifying relative. That provision requires that the individual not be a qualifying child of either the taxpayer or any other taxpayer during a taxable year beginning in the calendar year in which the taxpayer's taxable year begins. The notice provides that, for purposes of section 152(d)(1)(D), an individual is not a qualifying child of "any other taxpayer" if the individual's parent (or other person for whom the individual is defined as a qualifying child) is not required by section 6012 to file an income tax return and (1) does not file an income tax return, or (2) files an income tax return solely to obtain a refund of withheld income taxes.

f. *Support tests*

Under section 152(c)(1)(D), to be a taxpayer's qualifying child, an individual must not have provided over one-half of the individual's own support for the calendar year. Under section 152(d)(1)(C), to be a taxpayer's qualifying relative, a taxpayer must have provided over one-half of an individual's support for the calendar year.

Regarding governmental payments to a person with a qualifying need, the WFTRA conference report, H.R. Rep. No. 108-696, at 57, states that "[g]overnmental payments and subsidies (e.g., Temporary Assistance [for] Needy Families, food stamps, and housing) generally are treated as support provided by a third party." The IRS has successfully asserted in litigation that governmental payments provided to a parent to aid a family with dependent children and used by the parent for support of her children was support of the children provided by the government, and not support provided by the parent. See *Lutter v. Commissioner*, 61 T.C. 685 (1974), *affd. per curiam*, 514 F.2d 1095 (7th Cir. 1975).

2. *Surviving Spouse and Head of Household, and Conforming Changes*

Prior to amendment by section 803(b) of the Tax Reform Act of 1969 (Public Law 91-172, 83 Stat. 487), section 2(a) provided that the return of a surviving spouse is treated as a joint return for purposes of the tax rates, the tax tables for individuals, and the standard deduction. Following the 1969 amendments, section 2(a) defines the term *surviving spouse* for purposes of section 1. The return of a taxpayer filing as a surviving spouse is no longer treated as a joint return under sections 2, 3, or 63. Section 3 provides tax tables for certain individuals in lieu of the tax imposed by section 1. Section 63(c) provides the same basic standard deduction for a taxpayer filing as a surviving spouse as a taxpayer filing a joint return. Accordingly, a taxpayer filing as a surviving spouse is no longer treated as filing a joint return for any tax purpose, but rather, a taxpayer filing as a surviving spouse simply uses the same tax rates under section 1, the same amounts in the tax tables under section 3, and the same standard deduction under section 63 as a taxpayer filing a joint return.

Generally, under section 2(b), to qualify as a head of household, a taxpayer must maintain a household that is the principal place of abode of a qualifying child or other dependent for more than one-half of the taxable year. If the dependent is a parent of the taxpayer and the parent does not share a principal place of abode with the taxpayer, the household maintained by the taxpayer must be the parent's principal place of abode for the entire taxable year.

Prior to WFTRA, section 21 required that a taxpayer maintain a household to claim the credit for dependent care expenses, and regulations on maintaining a household were published under that section. WFTRA removed that requirement from the dependent care credit.

3. *Earned Income Credit*

Section 32 provides a tax credit to eligible taxpayers who work and have earned income below a certain dollar amount. Before the amendment of section 32 by the Omnibus Reconciliation Act of 1993 (Public Law 103-66, 107 Stat. 312), the earned income credit (EIC) was allowable only to a taxpayer with one or more qualifying children. If an individual met the definition of a qualifying child for more than one taxpayer, a tiebreaker rule in section 32 determined which taxpayer was allowed to claim the individual as a qualifying child for the EIC. For taxable years beginning after 1993, section 32(c)(1)(A)(ii) allows a taxpayer without a qualifying child to claim the EIC (childless EIC) if certain requirements are met. Although there is no regulatory guidance on this issue, since 1995, the IRS has taken the position in IRS Publication 596, *Earned Income Credit*, that if an individual meets the definition of a qualifying child for more than one taxpayer and the individual is not treated as the qualifying child of a taxpayer under the tiebreaker rules, then that taxpayer is precluded from claiming the childless EIC. WFTRA moved the tiebreaker rules from section 32 to section 152(c)(4).

Before repeal in 2010, section 3507 allowed advance payment of the EIC. Section 3507 was repealed by the FAA Air Transportation Modernization and Safety Improvement Act (Public Law 111-226, 124 Stat. 2389).

4. *Additional Standard Deduction for the Aged and Blind*

Before the amendments to sections 63 and 151 made by the Tax Reform Act of 1986 (Public Law 99-514, 100 Stat. 2085), a taxpayer was entitled to an additional personal exemption under section 151 for the taxpayer or the taxpayer's spouse (or both), if either was age 65 or older or was blind at the close of the taxable year. As amended, section 63 provides an additional standard deduction for age or blindness instead of an additional personal exemption under section 151.

Explanation of Provisions

The proposed regulations reflect statutory amendments to sections 2, 3, 21, 32, 63, 151, 152, 6013, and 6109. In addition, the regulations address certain significant issues arising under these sections and modify certain IRS positions, as explained below.

1. *Dependency Exemption*

Consistent with the amendments made to sections 151 and 152 by WFTRA, the proposed regulations move rules related to the definition of a dependent from the regulations under section 151 to the regulations under section 152.

a. *Relationship test*

i. General Rules

Section 152(c)(2) provides that a qualifying child must be a child or a descendant of a child of the taxpayer, or a brother, sister, stepbrother, or stepsister of the taxpayer, or a descendant of any of these relatives. Section 152(d)(2) provides that a qualifying relative must bear a certain relationship to the taxpayer, which includes a child or a descendant of a child, a brother, sister, stepbrother, stepsister, parent or ancestor of a parent, or an aunt or uncle of the taxpayer. An individual (other than the taxpayer's spouse) who is not related to the taxpayer in one of the named relationships nevertheless may satisfy the relationship test for a qualifying relative if the individual has the same principal place of abode as the taxpayer and is a member of the taxpayer's household for the taxpayer's taxable year.

The proposed regulations adopt the rule in Notice 2008-5 regarding whether an individual is a qualifying child of a taxpayer for purposes of determining whether that individual may be a qualifying relative. That is, the proposed regulations provide that an individual is not a qualifying child of a person if that person is not required to file an income tax return under section 6012, and either does not file an income tax return or files an income tax return solely to claim a refund of estimated or withheld taxes.

ii. Adopted Child—Adoption by Individual Other than the Taxpayer

Prior to 2005, for purposes of the relationship test, a person's legally adopted child was treated as that person's child by blood. Specifically, section 152(b)(2) provided that "a legally adopted child of an individual (and a child who is a member of an individual's household, if placed with such individual by an authorized placement agency for legal adoption by such individual), . . . shall be treated as a child of such individual by blood." Therefore, a taxpayer other than the adopting "individual" could be eligible to claim an exemption for an adopted child. For example, the parent of the adopting parent could claim a dependency exemption for the legally adopted child of the taxpayer's son or daughter (just as biological grandparents may claim an exemption for a grandchild) if all other requirements were met.

WFTRA amended section 152 to change the reference from a child placed by an authorized placement agency for adoption to a child who is "lawfully placed" for legal adoption. In making that change, however, WFTRA also changed the reference to the adopting person from "an individual" to "the taxpayer," so that section 152(f)(1)(B) currently provides that a legally adopted individual of the taxpayer is treated as a child by blood of the taxpayer. The use of the word "taxpayer" rather than "individual" arguably limits the recognition of a relationship through adoption only to those situations in which the taxpayer claiming a dependency exemption for the child is the person who adopts the child. This interpretation of the amended statutory language would diverge from the results of a legal adoption under property, inheritance, and other nontax law, and from the prior tax treatment of adoptions - a significant change in the applicable law. However, there is nothing in the legislative history indicating that Congress intended to limit the treatment of an adopted child as a child by blood in this manner or that otherwise suggests this change in language was intended to effect a change in existing law.

To fill this apparent gap in the statute, the proposed regulations provide that any child legally adopted by a "person," or any child who is placed with a "person" for legal adoption by that "person," is treated as a child by blood of that person for purposes of the relationship tests under sections 152(c)(2) and 152(d)(2). Similarly, the proposed regulations provide that an eligible foster child is a child who is placed with a "person" rather than with a taxpayer.

iii. Adopted Child and Foster Child—Child Placement

Although WFTRA removed the reference to an authorized placement agency from the provisions relating to an adopted child in section 152(f)(1)(B), the reference to an authorized placement agency continues to appear in section 152(f)(1)(C), relating to an eligible foster child. Prior to amendment by WFTRA, section 152 treated a child who was a member of an individual's household pending adoption as a child by blood of the individual for purposes of the relationship test only if the child was a foster child living with the individual or if the child was placed with the individual by an authorized placement agency for adoption by the individual. Similarly, § 301.6109-3(a) currently provides that a taxpayer may obtain an adoption taxpayer identification number (ATIN) only for a child who was placed for adoption by an authorized placement agency.

As amended by WFTRA, section 152 treats a child placed for adoption as a child by blood of the taxpayer if the child "is lawfully placed with the taxpayer for legal adoption by the taxpayer." A child may be lawfully placed for legal adoption by an authorized placement agency, the child's parents, or other persons authorized by State law to place children for legal adoption. These proposed regulations reflect the changes made by WFTRA and amend the regulations under section 6109 to provide that the IRS will assign an ATIN to a child who has been lawfully placed with a person for legal adoption.

Under section 152(f)(1)(A)(ii) and § 1.152-1(b)(1)(iii) of these proposed regulations, the term *child* also includes an eligible foster child of the taxpayer as defined in 152(f)(1)(C), that is, a child who is placed with the taxpayer by an authorized placement agency or by the judgment, decree, or other order of a court of competent jurisdiction.

iv. Definition of Authorized Placement Agency

The 2000 proposed regulations under § 1.152-2(c)(2) defined an authorized placement agency for purposes of the prior law regarding a child placed for legal adoption. These proposed regulations define an authorized placement agency for purposes of the definition of an eligible foster child and withdraw the 2000 proposed regulations, which defined that term without reference to an Indian Tribal Government (ITG).

These proposed regulations provide that an *authorized placement agency* may be a State, the District of Columbia, a possession of the United States, a foreign country, an agency or organization authorized by, or a political subdivision of, any of these entities to place children in foster care or for adoption. Under the Indian Child Welfare Act of 1978 (25 U.S.C. chapter 21), ITGs and states perform similar functions for foster care and adoption programs. Thus, the proposed regulations provide that an authorized placement agency also may be an ITG (as defined in section 7701(a)(40)), or an agency or organization authorized by, or a political subdivision of, an ITG that places children in foster care or for adoption.

b. *Residency test—principal place of abode*

For purposes of determining whether an individual has the same principal place of abode as the taxpayer in applying the residency test for a qualifying child and the relationship test for a qualifying relative who does not have one of the listed relationships to the taxpayer, the proposed regulations provide that the term *principal place of abode* means a person's main home or dwelling where the person resides. A person's principal place of abode need not be the same physical location throughout the taxable year and may be temporary lodging such as a homeless shelter or relief housing resulting from displacement caused by a natural disaster.

The proposed regulations further provide that a taxpayer and an individual have the same principal place of abode despite a temporary absence by either person. A person is temporarily absent if, based on the facts and circumstances, the person would have resided with the taxpayer but for the temporary absence and it is reasonable to assume the person will return to reside at the place of abode. Thus, the proposed regulations adopt the "reasonable to assume" language from the existing regulations under section 2. The proposed regulations indicate that a nonpermanent failure to occupy the abode by reason of illness, education, business, vacation, military service, institutionalized care for a child who is permanently and totally disabled (as defined in section 22(e)(3)), or incarceration may be treated as a temporary absence due to special circumstances. This definition of temporary absence applies to the residency test for a qualifying child, to the relationship test for a qualifying relative who does not have a listed relationship to the taxpayer, and to the requirements to maintain a household for surviving spouse and head of household.

For purposes of the residency test for a qualifying child, the proposed regulations provide that an individual is treated as having the same principal place of abode as the taxpayer for more than one-half of the taxable year if the individual resides with the taxpayer for at least 183 nights during the taxpayer's taxable year or for at least 184 nights during the taxpayer's taxable year that includes a leap day (residing for more than one-half of the taxable year). The proposed regulations further provide that an individual resides with the taxpayer for a night if the individual sleeps (1) at the taxpayer's residence, or (2) in the company of the taxpayer when the individual does not sleep at the taxpayer's residence (for example, when the parent and the child are on vacation). The regulations provide additional rules for counting nights if a night extends over two taxable years and for taxpayers who work at night.

The proposed regulations provide special rules for determining whether an individual satisfies a residency test if the individual is born or dies during the taxable year, is adopted or placed for adoption, is an eligible foster child, or is a missing child.

c. *Age test*

The age test for a qualifying child requires that an individual be younger than the taxpayer claiming the individual as a qualifying child, and the individual must not have attained the age of 19 (or age 24 if the individual is a student). The age requirement is treated as satisfied if the individual is permanently and totally disabled.

For purposes of this age test, the proposed regulations substantially adopt the existing definition of a student. Accordingly, the proposed regulations provide that the term *student* means an individual who, during some part of each of 5 calendar months during the calendar year in which the taxable year of the taxpayer begins, is a full-time student at an educational organization described in section 170(b)(1)(A)(ii) or is pursuing a full-time course of institutional on-farm training under the supervision of an accredited agent of an educational institution or of a State or political subdivision of a State. An *educational organization*, as defined in section 170(b)(1)(A)(ii), is a school normally maintaining a regular faculty and curriculum and having a regularly enrolled body of students in attendance at the place where its educational activities are regularly carried on.

d. *Support tests*

In determining whether an individual provided more than one-half of the individual's own support (qualifying child support test), or whether a taxpayer provided more than one-half of an individual's support (qualifying relative support test), the proposed regulations compare the amount of support provided by the individual or the taxpayer to the total amount of the individual's support from all sources. In general, the amount of an individual's support from all sources includes support the individual provides and income that is excludable from gross income. The proposed regulations further provide that the amount of an item of support is the amount of expenses paid or incurred to furnish the item of support. If support is furnished in the form of property or a benefit (such as lodging), the amount of that support is the fair market value of the item furnished (Rev. Rul. 58-302 (1958-1 CB 62)).

The proposed regulations provide that the term *support* includes food, shelter, clothing, medical and dental care, education, and similar items for the benefit of the supported individual. Support does not include Federal, State, and local income taxes, or Social Security and Medicare taxes, of an individual paid from the individual's own income (Rev. Rul. 58-67 (1958-1 CB 62)), funeral expenses (Rev. Rul. 65-307 (1965-2 CB 40)), life insurance premiums, or scholarships received by a taxpayer's child who is a student as defined in section 152(f)(2).

The proposed regulations provide that medical insurance premiums are treated as support. These premiums include Part A Basic Medicare premiums, if any, under Title XVIII of the Social Security Act (42 U.S.C. 1395c to 1395i-5), Part B Supplemental Medicare premiums under Title XVIII of the Social Security Act (42 U.S.C. 1395j to 1395w-6), Part C Medicare + Choice Program premiums under Title XVIII of the Social Security Act (42 U.S.C. 1395w-21 to 1395w-29), and Part D Voluntary Prescription Drug Benefit Medicare premiums under Title XVIII of the Social Security Act (42 U.S.C. 1395w-101 to 1395w-154). However, medical insurance proceeds, including benefits received under Medicare Part A, Part B, Part C, and Part D, are not treated as support and are disregarded in determining the amount of the individual's support. Thus, only the premiums paid and the unreimbursed portion of the expenses for the individual's medical care are support. See Rev. Rul. 64-223 (1964-2 CB 50); and Rev. Rul. 70-341 (1970-2 CB 31), revoked in part by Rev. Rul. 79-173 (1979-1 CB 86) to the extent that it held that Part A Medicare benefits are included as a recipient's contribution to support. In addition, services provided to individuals under the medical and dental care provisions of the Armed Forces Act (10 U.S.C. chapter 55) are not treated as support and are disregarded in determining the amount of the individual's support. Finally, payments from a third party (including a third party's insurance company) for the medical care of an injured individual in satisfaction of a legal claim for the personal injury of the individual are not items of support and are disregarded in determining the amount of the individual's support. See Rev. Rul. 64-223.

The proposed regulations provide that, in general, governmental payments and subsidies are treated as support provided by a third party. Consistent with previously issued rulings and case law, these payments and subsidies include, for example, Temporary Assistance for Needy Families (TANF) (42 U.S.C. 601-619), low-income housing assistance (42 U.S.C. 1437f), benefits under the Supplemental Nutrition Assistance Program (7 U.S.C. chapter 51), Supplemental Security Income payments (42 U.S.C. 1381-1383f), foster care maintenance payments, and adoption assistance payments. See H.R. Rep. No. 108-696, at 57 (2004) (Conf. Rep.); *Gulvin v. Commissioner*, 644 F.2d 2 (5th Cir. 1981); and Rev. Rul. 74-153 (1974-1 CB 20).

However, unlike the subsidies described in the previous paragraph that generally are based solely on need, old age benefits under section 202(b) of Title II of the Social Security Act (SSA) (42 U.S.C. 402) are based on an individual's earnings and contributions into the Social Security system and thus are treated as support provided by the recipient to the extent the recipient uses the payments for support. See Rev. Rul. 58-419 (1958-2 CB 57), as modified by Rev. Rul. 64-222 (1964-2 CB 47). Similarly, Social Security survivor and disability insurance benefit payments made under section 202(d) of the SSA to the child of a deceased or disabled parent are treated as support provided by the child to the extent those payments are used for the child's support. See Rev. Rul. 57-344 (1957-2 CB 112) and Rev. Rul. 74-543 (1974-2 CB 39).

The proposed regulations provide a special rule for governmental payments used by the recipient or other intended beneficiary to support another individual. The proposed regulations draw a distinction between: (1) governmental payments (such as Social Security old age benefits, or survivor and disability insurance benefits for a child) made to a recipient that are intended to benefit a particular named individual (whether the recipient, or another intended beneficiary for whom the recipient merely acts as the payee on behalf of that other intended beneficiary); and (2) governmental payments made to a recipient that are intended to support the recipient and other individuals (such as TANF). Although the governmental payments of the former variety are intended to benefit a particular named individual, because money is fungible, the intended beneficiary might use the governmental payments to support another individual. In this situation, the proposed regulations provide that, if the intended beneficiary (whether the recipient or another individual) uses the governmental payments to support another individual, that amount would constitute support of that other individual provided by the intended beneficiary. Similarly, the proposed regulations provide that the use of governmental payments of the latter variety by the recipient to support another individual would constitute support of that other individual provided by the recipient, whereas any part of such a payment used for the support of the recipient would constitute support of the recipient by a third party. For example, if a mother receives TANF and uses the TANF payments to support her children, the proposed regulations treat the mother as having provided that support. Thus, the IRS will no longer assert the position that it took in *Lutter,* which concerned payments received by a mother under a program that was the predecessor of TANF. The Treasury Department and the IRS are proposing this rule for the administrative convenience of both the IRS and taxpayers to avoid the need to trace the use of such governmental payments, as opposed to the use of other funds of the recipient, for the support of another individual.

The Treasury Department and IRS request comments on whether various payments made pursuant to the Patient Protection And Affordable Care Act (Public Law 111-148, 124 Stat. 119) in the form of a cost-sharing reduction, an advanced payment of the premium tax credit, or as a reimbursement of health insurance premiums in the form of a premium tax credit, when used for the benefit of another individual, are support provided by the recipient of those benefits or support provided by a third party.

e. *Citizenship*

Under section 152(b)(3)(A), an individual who is not a citizen or national of the United States is not a dependent unless the individual is a resident of the United States, Canada, or Mexico. Nevertheless, consistent with the exception for certain adopted children in section 152(b)(3)(B), the proposed regulations provide that an adopted child of a taxpayer who is a U.S. citizen or national may qualify as a dependent if, for the taxpayer's taxable year, the child has the same principal place of abode as the taxpayer and is a member of the taxpayer's household, and otherwise qualifies as the taxpayer's dependent.

f. *Tiebreaker rules*

The proposed regulations change the interpretation in Publication 501 regarding a taxpayer's adjusted gross income on a joint return and provide that, in applying the tiebreaker rules that treat an individual as the qualifying child of the eligible taxpayer with the higher or highest adjusted gross income, the adjusted gross income of a taxpayer who files a joint tax return is the total adjusted gross income shown on the return. The prior interpretation is changed to be consistent with other Code sections that require the filing of a joint return to claim a benefit and therefore calculate income based on the entire amount shown on the joint return. For example, the earned income credit under section 32 calculates the earned income amount based on the entire amount shown on the joint return. This joint return rule also is relevant for determining whether section 152(c)(4)(C) applies. Under that provision, if an eligible parent does not claim an individual as a qualifying child, another eligible taxpayer may claim the individual as a qualifying child only if that taxpayer's adjusted gross income is higher than the adjusted gross income of any eligible parent.

The proposed regulations also expand the tiebreaker rule in section 152(c)(4)(C) to address the situation in which an eligible parent does not claim an individual as a qualifying child and two or more taxpayers, none of whom is a parent, are eligible to claim the individual as a qualifying child and each has adjusted gross income higher than any eligible parent. In this situation, the proposed regulations provide that the individual is treated as the qualifying child of the eligible taxpayer with the highest adjusted gross income.

g. *Child of parents who are divorced, separated, or living apart*

Section 152(e) provides, in general, that a child is treated as the qualifying child or qualifying relative of a noncustodial parent for a calendar year if, among other things, the custodial parent provides to the noncustodial parent a written declaration that the custodial parent will not claim the child as a dependent for any taxable year beginning in that calendar year. Under section 152(e)(2)(B), the noncustodial parent must attach the written declaration to his or her return.

The proposed regulations provide that the noncustodial parent must attach a copy of the written declaration to an original or amended return. A taxpayer may submit a copy of the written declaration to the IRS during an examination of that parent's return. However, to provide certainty for both taxpayers and the IRS, the proposed regulations provide that a copy of a written declaration attached to an amended return or provided during an examination will not meet the requirements of section 152(e) and § 1.152-5(e) if the custodial parent signed the written declaration after the custodial parent filed a return claiming a dependency exemption for the child for the year at issue, and the custodial parent has not filed an amended return to remove that claim to a dependency exemption. The proposed regulations provide similar rules for a parent revoking a written declaration.

h. *Filing a return solely to obtain a refund of taxes*

Individuals who file an income tax return solely to obtain a refund of estimated or withheld taxes are subject to special rules under various provisions of section 152. Section 152(c)(1)(E) provides that, for an individual to be a qualifying child of a taxpayer, the individual cannot have filed a joint return "other than only for a claim of refund." Section 152(b)(2) provides that, for an individual to be a dependent of a taxpayer, the individual cannot have filed a joint return with the individual's spouse. However, the WFTRA conference report states that "[t]his restriction does not apply if the return was filed solely to obtain a refund and no tax liability would exist for either spouse if they filed separate returns." Section 152(d)(1)(D) provides that, to be a qualifying relative, an individual may not be the qualifying child of the taxpayer or of any other taxpayer. Notice 2008-5 concludes that an individual is not the qualifying child of "any other taxpayer," within the meaning of section 152(d)(1)(D), if the person who could have claimed the individual as a qualifying child does not have a filing obligation and either does not file a return or files a return solely to obtain a refund of withheld taxes.

The proposed regulations provide a similar exception to the rule in section 152(b)(1) that a taxpayer cannot have a dependent if the taxpayer himself or herself is a dependent of another taxpayer. Specifically, the proposed regulations provide that an individual is not a dependent of a person if that person is not required to file an income tax return under section 6012 and either does not file an income tax return or files an income tax return solely to claim a refund of estimated or withheld taxes.

2. *Surviving Spouse, Head of Household, and Conforming Changes*

The proposed regulations amend the regulations under section 2 regarding the definition of surviving spouse and the definition of head of household to conform to the amendments made by WFTRA. To reflect the amendments made by the Tax Reform Act of 1969, the proposed regulations remove from the regulations under sections 2, 3, and 6013 references to the return of a surviving spouse being treated as a joint return. The proposed regulations also revise and move from the regulations under section 21 to the regulations under section 2 the definition of maintaining a household, in part, to conform to the amendments to section 21 made by WFTRA, which removed the requirement that a taxpayer maintain a household to claim the credit under section 21.

a. *Surviving spouse*

From the time of the 1969 amendment until the enactment of WFTRA, section 2(a)(1)(B) provided that a taxpayer who is a surviving spouse described in section 2(a)(1)(A) may file as a surviving spouse (and thus may use the tax rates of joint filers) only if the taxpayer "maintains as his home a household which constitutes for the taxable year the principal place of abode (as a member of such household) of a dependent (i) who (within the meaning of section 152) is a son, stepson, daughter, or stepdaughter of the taxpayer, and (ii) with respect to whom the taxpayer is entitled to a deduction for the taxable year under section 151." Thus, the member of the taxpayer's household had to be a son or daughter or stepson or stepdaughter for whom the taxpayer was entitled to a dependency deduction.

WFTRA amended section 2(a), as well as certain other sections such as section 42 relating to the low-income housing credit and section 125 relating to cafeteria plans, to provide that the reference to section 152 applies "without regard to subsections (b)(1), (b)(2), and (d)(1)(B)." These three subsections, respectively: (1) deny a dependency exemption to a dependent, (2) deny a dependency exemption for a person filing a joint return with his or her spouse, and (3) require the gross income of a qualifying relative to be less than the amount of the dependency exemption. Thus, the language inserted by the WFTRA technical amendment to section 2(a) was intended to broaden the class of individuals whose members could qualify a taxpayer as a surviving spouse for purposes of section 2. See also Staff of Joint Comm. on Taxation, 108th Cong., *General Explanation of Tax Legislation Enacted in the 108 th Congress* 130 (Comm. Print 2005) ("technical and conforming amendments . . . provide that an individual may qualify as a dependent for certain purposes . . . without regard to whether the individual has gross income . . . or is married and files a joint return.")

However, in amending section 2(a) for this purpose, WFTRA inserted the direction to exclude the three referenced provisions after the reference to section 152 in section 2(a)(1)(B)(i). Thus, this section currently provides, "(i) who (within the meaning of section 152, determined without regard to subsections (b)(1), (b)(2), and (d)(1)(B) thereof) is a son, stepson, daughter, or stepdaughter of the taxpayer." Because section 2(a)(1)(B)(ii) continues to require that the taxpayer be entitled to a deduction under section 151 for the dependent (a requirement that could not be met if any of these three sections applied), read literally, section 2(a)(1)(B)(ii) would override the intent of the statutory change in section 2(a)(1)(B)(i), thus preventing the WFTRA amendment from effecting any change in the statute. Therefore, to give effect to the statutory amendment, the proposed regulations construe the language added by WFTRA instead to modify the section 152 requirements that apply in determining whether the taxpayer is entitled to the dependency exemption under section 151 for purposes of section 2(a)(1)(B)(ii). Accordingly, the proposed regulations provide that an individual is a dependent for purposes of section 2(a) if the taxpayer may claim a deduction under section 151 for the individual without applying sections 152(b)(1), (b)(2), and (d)(1)(B).

b. *Head of household*

The proposed regulations under section 2(b) update and simplify the existing regulations defining head of household. Consistent with the statutory amendments to the definition of a dependent, the proposed regulations provide rules on qualifying as a head of household by maintaining a household that is the principal place of abode of a qualifying child or a dependent. The proposed regulations on head of household apply the rules in the proposed regulations under section 152 for determining principal place of abode, including whether an absence is temporary.

c. *Maintaining a household*

The proposed regulations provide that a taxpayer maintains a household only if the taxpayer pays more than one-half of the cost related to operating the household for the relevant period. Expenses related to operating the household include property taxes, mortgage interest, rent, utility charges, upkeep and repairs, property insurance, and food consumed on the premises. A taxpayer may treat a home's fair market rental value as a cost of maintaining a household (instead of the sum of payments for mortgage interest, property taxes, and insurance). The proposed regulations provide rules that, in certain circumstances, prorate on a monthly basis the annual cost of maintaining a household when a qualifying child or dependent resides in the household for less than the entire taxable year. The proposed regulations also, in certain circumstances, recognize the creation of a new household during a year and treat shared living quarters as separate households.

3. *Tax Tables for Individuals*

The proposed regulations remove from the regulations under section 3 references to the return of a surviving spouse being treated as a joint return to conform to the amendments made by the Tax Reform Act of 1969. The proposed regulations also update the regulations under section 3 to reflect current law.

4. *Earned Income Credit*

The proposed regulations conform the regulations under section 32 to amendments made to section 32 by WFTRA. Consistent with the 2010 repeal of section 3507 by the FAA Air Transportation Modernization and Safety Improvement Act, the proposed regulations delete the paragraphs of the regulations under section 32 discussing advance payment of the earned income credit.

In addition, the proposed regulations reflect a change in the IRS's position on the interaction of sections 152(c)(4) and 32. Specifically, the proposed regulations provide that, if an individual meets the definition of a qualifying child under section 152(c)(1) for more than one taxpayer and the individual is not treated as the qualifying child of one such taxpayer under the tiebreaker rules of section 152(c)(4), then the individual also is not treated as a qualifying child of that taxpayer for purposes of section 32(c)(1)(A). Thus, that taxpayer may be an eligible individual under section 32(c)(1)(A)(ii) and may claim the childless EIC if he or she meets the other requirements of that section. The Treasury Department and the IRS have concluded that this change in position is consistent with the language and purpose of section 32 and will be less confusing to taxpayers and easier for the IRS to administer.

The problems with the current rule may be illustrated by the following example. Two sisters (B and C) live together and each of them is a low-income taxpayer. Neither has a child and each may claim the childless EIC under section 32(c)(1)(A)(ii). Later, B has a child, and B's child meets the definition of a qualifying child under section 152(c)(1) for both B and C. The child is treated as the qualifying child of B under the tiebreaker rules of section 152(c)(4), and B may claim the EIC as an eligible individual with a qualifying child under section 32(c)(1)(A)(i). Under the current rule, C would not be allowed to claim the childless EIC under section 32(c)(1)(A)(ii). The Treasury Department and the IRS have determined that allowing C to continue to claim the childless EIC after the child is born is equitable and consistent with the purpose of section 32 to assist working, low-income taxpayers. Accordingly, the proposed regulations provide that, if an individual is not treated as a qualifying child of a taxpayer after applying the tiebreaker rules of section 152(c)(4), then the individual will not prevent that taxpayer from qualifying for the childless EIC.

5. *Additional Standard Deduction for the Aged and Blind*

The proposed regulations remove the provisions on additional exemptions for age and blindness from the regulations under section 151 and add regulations under section 63 on the additional standard deduction for the aged and the blind to reflect the changes made by the Tax Reform Act of 1986. The proposed regulations amend the regulations under section 63 to remove a cross reference to now-repealed statutory provisions relating to a charitable deduction for taxpayers who do not itemize. To limit impediments to electronic filing, the proposed regulations also delete the requirement that a taxpayer claiming a tax benefit for blindness must attach a certificate or statement to the taxpayer's tax return. Instead, a taxpayer must maintain the certificate or statement in the taxpayer's records.

Applicability Date

These regulations are proposed to apply to taxable years beginning after the date the regulations are published as final regulations in the **Federal Register**. Pending the issuance of the final regulations, taxpayers may choose to apply these proposed regulations in any open taxable years.

Effect on Other Documents

When finalized, the proposed regulations will obsolete Rev. Rul. 57-344, Rev. Rul. 58-67, Rev. Rul. 58-302, Rev. Rul. 64-223, Rev. Rul. 65-307, Rev. Rul. 70-341, Rev. Rul. 74-153, Rev. Rul. 74-543, Rev. Rul. 79-173, Rev. Rul. 84-89, Notice 2006-86, and Notice 2008-5.

Special Analyses

Certain IRS regulations, including these, are exempt from the requirements of Executive Order 12866, as supplemented and reaffirmed by Executive Order 13563. Therefore, a regulatory impact assessment is not required. The regulations affect individuals and do not impose a collection of information on small entities, therefore the Regulatory Flexibility Act (5 U.S.C. chapter 6) does not apply. Pursuant to section 7805(f) of the Code, this notice of proposed rulemaking will be submitted to the Chief Counsel for Advocacy of the Small Business Administration for comment on its impact on small business.

Statement of Availability of IRS Documents

IRS revenue procedures, revenue rulings, notices and other guidance cited in this preamble are published in the Internal Revenue Bulletin (or Cumulative Bulletin) and are available from the Superintendent of Documents, U.S. Government Publishing Office, Washington, DC 20402, or by visiting the IRS website at http://www.irs.gov.

Comments and Requests for a Public Hearing

Before these proposed regulations are adopted as final regulations, consideration will be given to any comments that are submitted timely to the IRS, as prescribed in this preamble under the "Addresses" heading. The IRS and Treasury Department request comments on all aspects of the proposed rules. All comments will be available at www.regulations.gov or upon request. A public hearing will be scheduled if requested in writing by any person that timely submits written comments. If a public hearing is scheduled, notice of the date, time, and place for the hearing will be published in the **Federal Register**.

Drafting Information

The principal authors of these proposed regulations are Christina M. Glendening and Victoria J. Driscoll of the Office of Associate Chief Counsel (Income Tax and Accounting). However, other personnel from the Treasury Department and the IRS participated in the development of the regulations.

[¶49,738] **Proposed Amendments of Regulations (REG-127203-15)**, published in the Federal Register on January 19, 2017.

[Code Sec. 197, 704, 721 and 6038B]

International tax: Partnerships: Partnership with foreign partners: Transfers of appreciated property: Related parties.—Reg. §§1.721(c)-1, 1.721(c)-2, 1.721(c)-3, 1.721(c)-4, 1.721(c)-5, 1.721(c)-6, 1.721(c)-7 and amendments of Reg. §§1.197-2, 1.704-1, 1.704-3 and 1.6038B-2, addressing transfers of appreciated property by U.S. persons to partnerships with foreign partners related to the transferor, are proposed.

AGENCY: Internal Revenue Service (IRS), Treasury.

ACTION: Notice of proposed rulemaking by cross-reference to temporary regulation.

SUMMARY: In the Rules and Regulations section of this issue of the **Federal Register**, temporary regulations are being issued under sections 197, 704, 721(c), and 6038B of the Internal Revenue Code (Code) that address transfers of appreciated property by U.S. persons to partnerships with foreign partners related to the transferor. The temporary regulations affect U.S. partners in domestic or foreign partnerships. The text of the temporary regulations also serves as the text of these proposed regulations.

DATES: Written or electronic comments and requests for a public hearing must be received by ***April 19, 2017***.

ADDRESSES: Send submissions to: CC:PA:LPD:PR (REG-127203-15), Internal Revenue Service, Room 5203, P.O. Box 7604, Ben Franklin Station, Washington, DC 20044. Submissions may be hand-delivered Monday through Friday between the hours of 8 a.m. and 4 p.m. to CC:PA:LPD:PR (REG-127203-15), Courier's Desk, Internal Revenue Service, 1111 Constitution Avenue, NW, Washington, DC 20224, or sent electronically via the Federal eRulemaking Portal at *http://www.regulations.gov* (IRS REG-127203-15).

FOR FURTHER INFORMATION CONTACT: Concerning the proposed regulations, Ryan A. Bowen, (202) 317-6937; concerning submissions of comments or requests for a public hearing, Regina Johnson, (202) 317-6901 (not toll-free numbers).

SUPPLEMENTARY INFORMATION:

Background

The temporary regulations in the Rules and Regulations section of this issue of the **Federal Register** contain regulations under sections 197, 704, 721(c), and 6038B of the Code. The temporary regulations contain rules described in Notice 2015-54, 2015-34 I.R.B. 210, and override nonrecognition of gain under section 721(a) for transfers of property to a partnership with related foreign partners and with substantial related-party ownership unless certain requirements are satisfied. The text of the temporary regulations also serves as the text of these proposed regulations. The preamble to the temporary regulations explains the temporary regulations and the corresponding proposed regulations.

Special Analyses

Certain IRS regulations, including this one, are exempt from the requirements of Executive Order 12866, as supplemented and reaffirmed by Executive Order 13563. Therefore, a regulatory impact assessment is not required. It is hereby certified that the collection of information contained in this regulation will not have a significant economic impact on a substantial number of small entities. Accordingly, a regulatory flexibility analysis is not required. This conclusion is based on the fact that the proposed regulations include a $1,000,000 de minimis exception for certain transfers, and tangible property with built-in gain that does not exceed $20,000 is excluded from the application of the regulations. In addition, the regulations only apply when a U.S. transferor contributes property to a partnership with a related foreign partner, and persons related to the U.S. transferor own 80 percent or more of the interests in the partnership. Accordingly, the Treasury Department and the IRS expect that these regulations primarily will affect large domestic corporations. Pursuant to section 7805(f), this notice of proposed rulemaking has been submitted to the Chief Counsel for Advocacy of the Small Business Administration for comment on its impact on small business.

Comments and Requests for Public Hearing

Before these proposed regulations are adopted as final regulations, consideration will be given to any comments that are submitted timely to the IRS as prescribed in this preamble under the "Addresses" heading. The Treasury Department and the IRS request comments on all aspects of the proposed rules. All comments will be available at *www.regulations.gov* or upon request. A public hearing will be scheduled if requested in writing by any person that timely submits written comments. If a public hearing is scheduled, notice of the date, time, and place for the public hearing will be published in the **Federal Register**.

Drafting information

The principal author of these proposed regulations is Ryan A. Bowen, Office of Associate Chief Counsel (International). However, other personnel from the Treasury Department and the IRS participated in their development.

[¶49,740] Proposed Amendments of Regulations (NPRM REG-135122-16), published in the Federal Register on January 24, 2017.

[Code Sec. 871]

International tax: Nonresident aliens: Financial products: Dividend equivalents: U.S. source dividend payments.—Amendments of Reg. §1.871-15, relating to certain financial products providing for payments that are contingent upon or determined by reference to U.S. source dividend payments, are proposed.

AGENCY: Internal Revenue Service (IRS), Treasury.

ACTION: Notice of proposed rulemaking by cross-reference to temporary regulations.

SUMMARY: This document contains proposed regulations relating to certain financial products providing for payments that are contingent upon or determined by reference to U.S. source dividend payments.

DATES: Written or electronic comments must be received by April 24, 2017.

ADDRESSES: Send submissions to CC:PA:LPD:PR (REG-135122-16), room 5203, Internal Revenue Service, PO Box 7604, Ben Franklin Station, Washington, DC 20044. Submissions may be hand delivered Monday through Friday between the hours of 8 a.m. and 4 p.m. to CC:PA:LPD:PR (REG-135122-16), Courier's desk, Internal Revenue Service, 1111 Constitution Avenue, NW., Washington, DC 20044, or sent electronically, via the Federal eRulemaking Portal at www.regulations.gov (IRS REG-135122-16). The public hearing will be held in the IRS Auditorium, Internal Revenue Building, 1111 Constitution Avenue, N.W., Washington, DC.

FOR FURTHER INFORMATION CONTACT: Concerning the regulations, D. Peter Merkel or Karen Walny at (202) 317-6938; concerning submissions of comments, the hearing, and/or to be placed on the building access list to attend the hearing Regina Johnson at (202) 317-6901 (not toll-free numbers).

SUPPLEMENTARY INFORMATION:

Background and Explanation of Provisions

Final and temporary regulations in the Rules and Regulations section of this issue of the **Federal Register** contain amendments to the Income Tax Regulations (26 CFR Part 1), which provide rules relating to dividend equivalents for purposes of section 871(m). The temporary regulations provide guidance relating to when the delta of an option that is listed on a foreign regulated exchange may be calculated based on the delta of that option at the close of business on the business day prior to the date of issuance. The temporary regulations also provide guidance identifying which party to a potential section 871(m) transaction is responsible for determining whether a transaction is a section 871(m) transaction when multiple brokers or dealers are involved in the transaction. The text of those temporary regulations also serves as the text of these proposed regulations. The preamble to the final and temporary regulations explains the temporary regulations and these proposed regulations. The regulations affect nonresident alien individuals, foreign corporations, and withholding agents, as well as certain other parties to section 871(m) transactions and their agents.

Special Analyses

Certain IRS regulations, including this one, are exempt from the requirements of Executive Order 12866, as supplemented and reaffirmed by Executive Order 13563. Therefore, a regulatory impact assessment is not required. Because the regulations do not impose a collection of information on small entities, the Regulatory Flexibility Act (5 U.S.C. chapter 6) does not apply. Pursuant to section 7805(f), these regulations have been submitted to the Chief Counsel for Advocacy of the Small Business Administration for comment on its impact on small business.

Comments and Request for Public Hearing

Before these proposed regulations are adopted as final regulations, consideration will be given to any comments that are submitted timely to the IRS as prescribed in this preamble under the "Addresses" heading. The Treasury Department and the IRS request comments on all aspects of the proposed rules. All comments will be available at www.regulations.gov or upon request. A public hearing will be scheduled if requested in writing by any person that timely submits written comments. If a public hearing is scheduled, notice of the date, time, and place for the public hearing will be published in the **Federal Register**.

Drafting Information

The principal authors of these regulations are D. Peter Merkel and Karen Walny of the Office of Chief Counsel (International). However, other personnel from the Treasury Department and the IRS participated in their development.

[¶49,743] Proposed Amendments of Regulations (REG-128483-15), published in the Federal Register on July 20, 2017.

[Code Secs. 1446, 6012, 6031, 6032, 6033, 6041, 6071, 6072 and 6081]

Information returns: Due dates: Extensions of time to file: Income tax returns.—Amendments of Reg. §§1.1446-3, 1.6012-6, 1.6031(a)-1, 1.6032-1, 1.6033-2, 1.6041-2, 1.6041-6, 1.6072-2, 1.6081-1, 1.6081-2, 1.6081-3, 1.6081-5, 1.6081-6, 1.6081-9, 31.6071(a)-1, issuing temporary regulations that update the due dates and extensions of time to file certain tax returns and information returns, are proposed.

26 CFR Parts 1 and 31

[REG-128483-15]

RIN 1545-BN12

Return Due Date and Extended Due Date Changes

AGENCY: Internal Revenue Service (IRS), Treasury.

ACTION: Notice of proposed rulemaking by cross-reference to temporary regulations.

SUMMARY: In the Rules and Regulations section of this issue of the **Federal Register**, the IRS is issuing temporary regulations that update the due dates and extensions of time to file certain tax returns and information returns. The text of those regulations also serves as the text of these proposed regulations.

DATES: Written or electronic comments and requests for a public hearing must be received by October 18, 2017.

ADDRESSES: Send submissions to: CC:PA:LPD:PR (REG-128483-15), Room 5203, Internal Revenue Service, P.O. Box 7604, Ben Franklin Station, Washington, DC 20044. Submissions may be hand-delivered between the hours of 8 a.m. and 4 p.m. to CC:PA:LPD:PR (REG-128483-15), Courier's Desk, Internal Revenue Service, 1111 Constitution Avenue, NW., Washington, DC, or sent via the Federal eRulemaking Portal at www.regulations.gov (IRS REG-128483-15).

FOR FURTHER INFORMATION CONTACT: Concerning these proposed regulations, Jonathan R. Black, (202) 317-6845; concerning submissions of comments and/or requests for a hearing, Regina Johnson (202) 317-6901 (not toll-free numbers). SUPPLEMENTARY INFORMATION:

Background and Explanation of Provisions

Temporary regulations in the Rules and Regulations section of this issue of the **Federal Register** amend 26 CFR parts 1 and 31. The temporary regulations update the due dates for the income tax returns of corporations and partnerships to reflect section 2006(a) of the Surface Transportation and Veterans Health Care Choice Improvement Act of 2015 (the Surface Transportation Act), Public Law No. 114-41, 129 Stat. 443 (2015), which amended section 6072 of the Internal Revenue Code. Additionally, the temporary regulations change the duration of automatic extensions of time to file certain tax returns and information returns. The temporary regulations also update the information return due dates to reflect section 201 of the Protecting Americans from Tax Hikes Act of 2015 (PATH Act), Public Law No. 114-113, Div. Q, 129 Stat. 2242 (2015). The text of those temporary regulations also serves as the text of these proposed regulations, except that the proposed regulations are proposed to be applicable for returns filed on or after the date a Treasury Decision incorporating them as final regulations is published in the **Federal Register**. The preamble to the temporary regulations explains the temporary regulations and these proposed regulations.

Special Analysis

Certain IRS regulations, including these, are exempt from the requirements of Executive Order 12866, as supplemented and reaffirmed by Executive Order 13563. Therefore, a regulatory assessment is not required. These regulations do not impose a collection of information on small entities, therefore the Regulatory Flexibility Act (5 U.S.C. chapter 6) does not apply. These regulations only update the due dates and extensions of time to file certain collections of information and include some existing regulatory language concerning collections of information that affect small entities for the convenience of the reader. Pursuant to section 7805(f) of the Internal Revenue Code, these proposed regulations have been submitted to the Chief Counsel for Advocacy of the Small Business Administration for comment on the impact on small businesses.

Comments and Requests for Public Hearing

Before these proposed regulations are adopted as final regulations, consideration will be given to any comments that are submitted timely to the IRS as prescribed in the preamble under the "ADDRESSES" heading. Treasury and the IRS request comments on all aspects of the proposed regulations. All comments submitted will be made available at www.regulations.gov or upon request. A public hearing will be scheduled if requested in writing by any person that timely submits written comments. If a public hearing is scheduled, notice of the date, time, and place for the public hearing will be published in the **Federal Register**.

Drafting Information

The principal author of these regulations is Jonathan R. Black of the Office of the Associate Chief Counsel (Procedure and Administration).

[¶49,744] Proposed Amendments of Regulations (REG-125374-16), published in the Federal Register on September 19, 2017(corrected 9/25/2017).

[Code Secs. 63, 103, 163, 165, 860D, 871, 881, 1287, 4701, 6045, 6049]

Registration-required obligations; Registered form: Passthrough certificates.—Reg. §§1.149(a)-1 and amendments of 1.163-5, 1.163-5T, 1.165-12, 1.860D-1, 1.871-14, 1.881-3, 1.1287-1, 1.6045-1, 1.6049-5, 5f.103-1, 5f.163-1 and 46.4701-1, including guidance on the issuance of pass-through certificates and participation interests in registered form, are proposed. Amendments of Reg. §5f.163-1, proposed on January 21, 1993, are withdrawn.

AGENCY: Internal Revenue Service (IRS), Treasury.

ACTION: Partial withdrawal of notice of proposed rulemaking and notice of proposed rulemaking.

SUMMARY: This document contains proposed regulations that provide guidance on the definitions of registration-required obligation and registered form, including guidance on the issuance of pass-through certificates and participation interests in registered form. This document also withdraws a portion of previously proposed regulations regarding the definition of a registration-required obligation. The proposed regulations generally are necessary to address changes in market practices as well as issues raised by the statutory repeal of the foreign-targeted bearer obligation exception to the registered form requirement. The proposed regulations will affect issuers and holders of obligations in registered form as well as issuers and holders of registration-required obligations that are not issued in registered form.

DATES: Comments and requests for a public hearing must be received by December 18, 2017.

ADDRESSES: Send submissions to CC:PA:LPD:PR (REG-125374-16), room 5203, Internal Revenue Service, P.O. Box 7604, Ben Franklin Station, Washington, DC 20044. Submissions may be hand-delivered Monday through Friday between the hours of 8 a.m. and 4 p.m. to CC:PA:LPD:PR (REG-125374-16), Courier's Desk, Internal Revenue Service, 1111 Constitution Avenue NW, Washington, DC 20224, or sent electronically via the Federal eRulemaking Portal at *www.regulations.gov* (IRS REG-125374-16).

FOR FURTHER INFORMATION CONTACT: Concerning the proposed regulations, Spence Hanemann at (202) 317-6980; concerning submissions of comments and requesting a hearing, Regina Johnson at (202) 317-6901 (not toll-free numbers). SUPPLEMENTARY INFORMATION:

Paperwork Reduction Act

The collection of information contained in this notice of proposed rulemaking has been submitted to the Office of Management and Budget for review under control number 1545-0945 in accordance with the Paperwork Reduction Act of 1995 (44 U.S.C. 3507(d)). The collection of information in this proposed regulation is in §1.163-5(b), which permits issuers of registration-required obligations to satisfy the requirement for those obligations to be in registered form by maintaining a book entry system. Sections 163(f) and 149(a) require that certain obligations be in registered form and expressly permit issuers to satisfy that requirement through a book entry system. Accordingly, the proposed regulations permit issuers to satisfy the registration requirement through a book entry system and detail certain arrangements that qualify as book entry systems. The collection of information in proposed §1.163-5(b) is an increase in the total annual burden under control number 1545-0945. The respondents are businesses and other for-profit organizations, non-profit organizations, and state, local and tribal governments.

Estimated total annual recordkeeping burden: 95,105 hours.

Estimated average annual burden hours per respondent: 0.5 hours.

Estimated number of respondents: 190,210.

Estimated annual frequency of responses: 190,210.

Comments on the collection of information should be sent to the Office of Management and Budget, Attn: Desk Officer for the Department of the Treasury, Office of Information and Regulatory Affairs, Washington, DC 20503, with copies to the Internal Revenue Service, Attn: IRS Reports Clearance Officer, SE:CAR:MP:T:T:SP, Washington DC 20224. Comments on the collection of information should be received by November 18, 2017.

Comments are specifically requested concerning:

Whether the proposed collection of information is necessary for the proper performance of the Internal Revenue Service, including whether the information will have practical utility;

The accuracy of the estimated burden associated with the proposed collection of information;

How the quality, utility, and clarity of the information to be collected may be enhanced;

How the burden of complying with the proposed collection of information may be minimized, including through the application of automated collection techniques or other forms of information technology; and

Estimates of capital or start-up costs and costs of operation, maintenance, and purchase of service to provide information.

An agency may not conduct or sponsor, and a person is not required to respond to, a collection of information unless it displays a valid control number assigned by the Office of Management and Budget.

Books or records relating to a collection of information must be retained as long as their contents may become material in the administration of any internal revenue law. Generally tax returns and tax return information are confidential, as required by section 26 U.S.C. 6103.

Background

This document contains proposed amendments to 26 CFR parts 1, 5f, and 46 under sections 103, 149, 163, 165, 860D, 871, 881, 1287, 4701, 6045, and 6049 of the Internal Revenue Code (Code).

1. *In General*

The classification of an obligation as in bearer or registered form has significant tax implications because a number of Code provisions impose sanctions on issuers and holders of registration-required obligations that are not issued in registered form. An obligation not issued in registered form is a bearer form obligation. Most of the Code provisions that pertain to registration-required obligations were enacted as part of the Tax Equity and Fiscal Responsibility Act of 1982 (TEFRA), Public Law 97-248, 96 Stat. 324, § 310. Among these provisions, section 163(f) denies an issuer an interest deduction for interest on a registration-required obligation that is not in registered form. Section 4701 imposes an excise tax on the issuer of a registration-required obligation that is not in registered form. The excise tax is equal to 1 percent of the principal amount of the obligation multiplied by the number of calendar years (or portions thereof) between the issue date of the obligation and the date of maturity. Section 149(a) provides that interest on a registration-required bond is not exempt from tax under section 103(a) unless the bond is in registered form. In addition, section 871(h) and section 881(c) exempt from federal income tax portfolio interest from sources within the U.S. received by a nonresident alien or foreign corporation (portfolio interest exception) only if the obligation with respect to which the interest was paid is in registered form. Similar restrictions are found in sections 165(j) (generally denying the holder a deduction for a loss sustained on a registration-required obligation not in registered form), 312(m) (generally providing that the issuer's earnings and profits cannot be decreased by interest paid on a registration-required obligation not in registered form), and 1287 (generally treating the holder's gain on sale of a registration-required obligation not in registered form as ordinary income).

Historically, the Code provisions referenced in the preceding paragraph generally did not apply to obligations that complied with the foreign-targeting rules of prior section 163(f)(2)(B) and § 1.163-5(c) (foreign-targeted bearer obligations). Under the foreign-targeting rules, an issuer could issue foreign-targeted bearer obligations without penalty provided the obligations were issued under arrangements reasonably designed to ensure that the obligations were sold only to non-U.S. persons. The portfolio interest exception also applied to interest paid on foreign-targeted bearer obligations issued under such reasonably designed arrangements.

The Hiring Incentives to Restore Employment Act (the HIRE Act), Public Law 111-147, 124 Stat. 71, section 502, repealed section 163(f)(2)(B) and generally eliminated the special treatment of foreign-targeted bearer obligations. Foreign-targeted bearer obligations issued after March 18, 2012, are subject to the sanctions on bearer form obligations under sections 149(a), 163(f), 165(j), 312(m), and 1287. The HIRE Act also revoked the portfolio interest exception for foreign-targeted bearer obligations, thus requiring that obligations issued after March 18, 2012, be in registered form to qualify for that exception. The HIRE Act did not, however, repeal the foreign-targeted bearer obligation exception to the excise tax under section 4701. See section 4701(b)(1)(B)(i).

2. *Registration-Required Obligations*

A. *In general*

Under section 163(f)(2)(A), as amended by the HIRE Act, the term *registration-required obligation* means any obligation other than an obligation that: (1) is issued by a natural person; (2) is not of a type offered to the public; or (3) has a maturity at issue of not more than 1 year. For purposes of sections 165(j), 312(m), and 1287, registration-required obligation has the same meaning as when used in section 163(f). See also section 149(a) (providing a similar definition except for the exclusion for instruments issued by a natural person). For purposes of section 4701, that term also has the same meaning as when used in section 163(f), except that tax-exempt bonds and foreign-targeted bearer obligations are excluded.

Section 5f.163-1(b)(2) provides that the determination as to whether an obligation is of a type offered to the public is based on whether similar obligations are in fact publicly offered or traded. On January 21, 1993, the Department of the Treasury (Treasury) and the IRS published in the **Federal Register** (58 FR 5316) a notice of proposed rulemaking (INTL-0115-90) containing proposed regulations that elaborated upon the meaning of "of a type offered to the public" for purposes of section 163(f)(2)(A) (the 1993 proposed regulations). See Prop. Treas. Reg. § 5f.163-1(b)(2). The preamble to the 1993 proposed regulations cited the report of the Senate Finance Committee on TEFRA for the conclusion that an obligation that represents a "readily negotiable substitute for cash" should be a registration-required obligation. 58 FR 5316 (citing S. Rep. No. 97-494, at 242 (1982)). Treasury and the IRS reasoned in the preamble to the 1993 proposed regulations that, because the standards for determining if an obligation is "readily tradable in an established securities market" under section 453(f)(4)(B) and § 15a.453-1(e)(4) address an analogous concern with negotiability, similar standards should apply for determining whether an obligation is "of a type offered to the public" under section 163(f)(2)(A).

B. *Pass-through certificates*

Section 1.163-5T provides rules to address whether pass-through certificates are registration-required obligations. In their most common form, pass-through certificates are issued by an investment entity (typically a trust) that holds a pool of obligations, such as mortgage loans. Each pass-through certificate represents an interest in the investment entity.

To accommodate these securitization transactions, § 1.163-5T(d)(1) generally provides that a pass-through certificate evidencing an interest in a pool of mortgage loans that is treated as a trust of which the grantor is the owner is considered to be a registration-required obligation if, standing alone, the pass-through certificate meets the definition of a registration-required obligation. Section 1.163-5T(d)(1) also applies to "similar evidence of interest in a similar pooled fund or pooled trust treated as a grantor trust," although commenters have noted the ambiguity of the reference. Similarly, § 1.871-14(d)(1) provides that interest received on a pass-through certificate qualifies for the portfolio interest exception if, standing alone, the pass-through certificate is in registered form.

Commenters have asked that Treasury and the IRS describe the types of arrangements that qualify as pass-through certificates. Specifically, commenters have requested that Treasury and the IRS amend the definition of a pass-through certificate to clarify that the issuer of a pass-through certificate may be either a grantor trust or another type of entity, such as a partnership or a disregarded entity, so long as the obligations in the pool are held through an arrangement that meets the requirements to be in registered form. Commenters have also requested that Treasury and the IRS amend § 1.871-14(d)(1) so that the definition of pass-through certificate for purposes of the portfolio interest exception is identical to the definition of pass-through certificate under § 1.163-5T(d)(1).

3. *Definition of Registered Form*

A. *In general*

For purposes of determining whether an obligation is in registered form under section 163(f)[1], the principles of section 149(a)(3) apply. See section 163(f)(3). Section 149(a)(3)(A) provides that a bond is treated as being in registered form if the right to the principal of, and stated interest on, the bond may be transferred only through a book entry consistent with regulations prescribed by the Secretary. Section 149(a)(3)(B) authorizes the Secretary to prescribe regulations to carry out the requirement that a bond be issued in registered form when there is one or more nominee. For purposes of section 149(a), the conditions for an obligation to be considered in registered form are described in § 5f.103-1(c).[2] The regulations under both section 163(f) and section 871(h), specifically § § 5f.163-1(a) and 1.871-14(c), refer to § 5f.103-1(c) for a definition of registered form. Obligations that do not meet the conditions described in § 5f.103-1(c) are treated as issued in bearer form.

Generally, under § 5f.103-1(c), an obligation is in registered form if: (1) the obligation is registered as to both principal and any stated interest with the issuer (or its agent) and any transfer of the obligation may be effected only by surrender of the old obligation and reissuance to the new holder; (2) the right to principal and stated interest with respect to the obligation may be transferred only through a book entry system maintained by the issuer or its agent; or (3) the obligation is registered as to both principal and stated interest with the issuer or its agent and may be transferred both by surrender and reissuance and through a book entry system. An obligation is considered transferable through a book entry system if ownership of an interest in the obligation is required to be reflected in a book entry, whether or not physical securities are issued. An obligation that would otherwise be considered to be in registered form is not considered to be in registered form if the obligation may be converted at any time in the future into an obligation that is not in registered form. See § 5f.103-1(e).

B. *Dematerialized book entry systems*

Since the publication of § 5f.103-1, market practices have changed with respect to how interests in obligations are recorded and transferred. For example, many obligations trade in fully dematerialized form. An obligation that is fully dematerialized is not represented by a physical (paper) certificate, and a clearing organization that is the registered holder of the obligation operates an electronic book entry system that identifies the clearing organization's member or members holding the obligation (or interests in the obligation). The clearing organization facilitates and records transfers of the obligation (or interests in the obligation) among the clearing organization's members. The members (typically, banks or broker-dealers), in turn, record their clients' ownership of the obligation (or interests in the obligation) in their book entry systems. Alternatively, an obligation may be represented by a physical global certificate that is nominally in bearer form but that is immobilized in a clearing organization, which handles the obligation thereafter exactly as it does an obligation that was fully dematerialized when issued. Commenters have requested additional guidance on how the registered form rules in § 5f.103-1 apply to these arrangements.

---

[1] For purposes of sections 165(j), 312(m), 871(h)(7), 881(c)(7), 1287, and 4701, the term *registered form* has the same meaning as when used in section 163(f).

[2] Section 5f.103-1 was originally published under section 103(j) of the Internal Revenue Code of 1954, which was enacted as part of TEFRA and provided that obligations must be in registered form to be tax-exempt. Section 103(j) was recodified as section 149(a) by section 1301 of the Tax Reform Act of 1986, Public Law 99-514, 100 Stat. 2085.

Treasury and the IRS provided guidance on how to apply the registered form rules to certain of these arrangements in Notice 2006-99, 2006-2 CB 907. Notice 2006-99 addresses an arrangement in which no physical certificates are issued and under which ownership interests in bonds are required to be represented only by book entries in a dematerialized book entry system maintained by a clearing organization. Notice 2006-99 provides that an obligation issued under such an arrangement is treated as in registered form notwithstanding the ability of holders to obtain physical certificates in bearer form upon the termination of the business of the clearing organization without a successor.

The HIRE Act also addressed dematerialized book entry systems. For obligations issued after March 18, 2012, section 163(f)(3), as amended by the HIRE Act, provides that, for purposes of section 163(f), a dematerialized book entry system or other book entry system specified by the Secretary will be treated as a book entry system described in section 149(a)(3). The Joint Committee on Taxation's technical explanation of the HIRE Act further explained that an obligation "that is formally in bearer form is treated, for the purposes of section 163(f), as held in a book entry system as long as the debt obligation may be transferred only through a dematerialized book entry system or other book entry system specified by the Secretary." J. Comm. on Tax'n, *Technical Explanation of the Revenue Provisions Contained in Senate Amendment 3310, the "Hiring Incentives to Restore Employment Act," Under Consideration by the Senate* (JCX-4-10), Feb. 23, 2010, at 53.

C. *Notice 2012-20*

Commenters expressed concern that the explicit reference to a "dematerialized book entry system" in section 163(f)(3), as amended by the HIRE Act, would create uncertainty about obligations issued in a manner not specifically described in Notice 2006-99. In particular, commenters requested guidance to address the treatment of obligations represented by a physical global certificate that is nominally in bearer form, but that is immobilized in a clearing system. In addition, commenters requested guidance regarding whether an obligation will be considered to be in registered form if holders may obtain physical certificates in bearer form under circumstances not described in Notice 2006-99.

In response to these comments, Treasury and the IRS published Notice 2012-20, 2012-13 IRB 574, on March 26, 2012. Notice 2012-20 provides additional guidance on the definition of registered form and further states that Treasury and the IRS intend to publish regulations consistent with the guidance described in the notice. Under Notice 2012-20, an obligation is considered to be in registered form if it is issued either through a dematerialized book entry system in which beneficial interests are transferable only through a book entry system maintained by a clearing organization (or by an agent of the clearing organization) or through a clearing system in which the obligation is effectively immobilized. Notice 2012-20 provides that an obligation is considered to be effectively immobilized if: (1) the obligation is represented by one or more global securities in physical form that are issued to and held by a clearing organization (or by a custodian or depository acting as an agent of the clearing organization) for the benefit of purchasers of interests in the obligation under arrangements that prohibit the transfer of the global securities except to a successor clearing organization subject to the same terms; and (2) beneficial interests in the underlying obligation are transferable only through a book entry system maintained by the clearing organization (or an agent of the clearing organization). Notice 2012-20 further states that an interest in an obligation is considered to be transferable only through a book entry system if the interest would be considered transferable through a book entry system under § 5f.103-1(c)(2), except that holders may obtain physical certificates in bearer form in certain limited circumstances stated in the notice. Finally, Notice 2012-20 states that, for purposes of determining when an obligation is a registration-required obligation under section 4701, rules identical to the foreign-targeting rules under section 163(f)(2)(B), prior to its amendment by the HIRE Act, and § 1.163-5(c) will apply to obligations issued after March 18, 2012.

Explanation of Provisions

1. *In General*

Consistent with Notice 2012-20, these proposed regulations amend the definition of registered form to take into account current market practices and changes made by the HIRE Act, including the repeal of the foreign-targeting rules in section 163(f)(2)(B). In addition, these proposed regulations amend the definition of a registration-required obligation in two ways. First, the proposed regulations specify the types of obligations that are treated as "of a type offered to the public" and withdraw the 1993 proposed regulations. Second, the proposed regulations take into account comments requesting clarification on the types of arrangements that qualify as pass-through certificates.

Though the definitions of the terms *registered form* and *registration-required obligation* are generally consistent across the various provisions in which they are used, the rules are set forth in a number of existing regulations, including several promulgated under section 163(f). To the extent possible, these proposed regulations simplify the definitions of registered form and registration-required obligation by centralizing the rules in § 1.163-5. Thus, the applicable rules have been relocated from § § 5f.103-1 (definition of registered form), 1.163-5T (pass-through certificates and regular interests in REMICs), and 5f.163-1 (definition of registration-required obligation) to paragraphs (a) and (b) of proposed § 1.163-5. Appropriate cross-references to § 1.163-5 are proposed to be added to regulations that rely on one or both definitions, including § § 1.149(a)-1, 1.165-12, 1.860D-1(b)(5)(i)(A), 1.871-14, 1.1287-1, and 46.4701-1.

2. *Registration-Required Obligations*

A. *Obligation of a type offered to the public*

Consistent with the 1993 proposed regulations, Treasury and the IRS continue to believe that it is appropriate to determine whether an obligation is of a type offered to the public by reference to whether the obligation is "traded on an established market." Although a number of Code and regulation sections refer to and define that phrase (for example, sections 453, 1092, 1273, and 7704, as well as the regulations promulgated under those Code sections), Treasury and the IRS have concluded that the definition provided in § 1.1273-2(f) is most appropriate for purposes of defining a registration-required obligation. Thus, the proposed regulations generally treat an obligation as of a type offered to the public if the obligation is traded on an established market as determined under § 1.1273-2(f). For this purpose, however, the proposed regulations do not take into account the exception for small debt issues in § 1.1273-2(f)(6).

B. *Pass-through certificates and participation interests*

Commenters indicated that an entity that issues pass-through certificates may hold a pool of debt instruments that is either fixed or that changes over time. For example, the issuing entity may have the right to acquire additional assets after formation, or the right to dispose of assets at any time. In those situations, the entity generally will not be classified as a grantor trust for federal tax purposes, but that does not preclude it from issuing pass-through certificates. To address these situations, the proposed regulations amend the definition of a pass-through certificate to provide that a pass-through certificate may be issued by a grantor trust or a similar fund, and specify that a similar fund includes entities that are partnerships or disregarded for federal tax purposes and funds that have the power to vary the assets they hold or the sequence of payments to holders. A similar fund, however, does not include a business entity classified as a corporation.

In addition, Treasury and the IRS have concluded that an arrangement that satisfies the definition of a registration-required obligation and the registered form rules should be treated the same as a pass-through certificate even if the arrangement is with respect to only one underlying obligation or if the arrangement is treated as co-ownership of one or more obligations (rather than, for purposes of TEFRA or otherwise, ownership of an entity that holds the underlying obligations). The proposed regulations eliminate the requirement that the fund hold a pool of loans and replace it with a requirement that the fund primarily hold debt instruments. Thus, a fund can hold one or more debt instruments, so long as the fund primarily holds debt instruments.

In addition, the proposed regulations treat an interest that evidences co-ownership of one or more obligations (including a participation interest) as a registration-required obligation if, standing alone, the interest satisfies the definition of a registration-required obligation. The proposed regulations also propose to amend § 1.871-14(d)(1) to include a cross-reference to the rules for pass-through certificates and participation interests in proposed § 1.163-5(a)(3)(i) and (ii) such that similar rules apply for purposes of the portfolio interest exception.

3. *Definition of Registered Form*

The proposed regulations amend the definition of registered form in a number of ways. First, the proposed regulations provide that an obligation is considered to be in registered form if it is transferable through a book entry system, including a dematerialized book entry system, maintained by the issuer of the obligation, an agent of the issuer, or a clearing organization. A clearing organization includes an entity that holds obligations for its members or maintains a system that reflects the ownership interests of members and transfers of obligations among members' accounts without the necessity of physical delivery of the obligation.

Second, the proposed regulations provide that an obligation represented by a physical certificate in bearer form will be considered to be in registered form if the physical certificate is effectively immobilized. To be effectively immobilized, the physical certificate evidencing an obligation must be issued to and held by a clearing organization for the benefit of purchasers of interests in the obligation under arrangements that prohibit the transfer of the physical certificate except to a successor clearing organization and permit transfers of ownership interests in the underlying obligation only through a book entry system maintained by the clearing organization (or a successor clearing organization). As suggested in comments, the proposed regulations change the requirement in Notice 2012-20 that a successor clearing organization hold the physical certificate subject to the same terms as the predecessor; Treasury and the IRS concluded that it is sufficient if the successor clearing organization has rules that effectively immobilize the physical certificate.

Third, the proposed regulations permit holders of obligations (or interests in obligations) to have a right to obtain physical certificates evidencing the obligation (or interests in the obligation) in bearer form without causing the obligation to be treated as not in registered form in two circumstances: (1) a termination of the clearing organization's business without a successor; or (2) the issuance of physical securities at the issuer's request upon a change in tax law that would be adverse to the issuer but for the issuance of physical securities in bearer form. This exception from bearer form treatment is consistent with the guidance provided in Notice 2012-20, except that the proposed regulations do not permit a holder to have a right to obtain a physical bearer certificate if there is an issuer event of default (default exception). Treasury and the IRS understand that in certain situations holders may be required to obtain physical certificates to pursue claims against the issuer, but in such instances it would be appropriate to expect those physical certificates to be issued in registered form. Taxpayers may rely on the default exception in Notice 2012-20 for obligations issued prior to publication of a Treasury decision adopting these rules as final regulations in the **Federal Register**.

After the occurrence of one of the two events described in the first sentence of the preceding paragraph, an obligation will no longer be in registered form if a holder, or a group of holders acting collectively, has a right to obtain a physical certificate in bearer form, regardless of whether any option to obtain a physical certificate in bearer form has actually been exercised.

4. *Section 881*

Commenters requested that examples 10 and 19 set forth in § 1.881-3(e) be removed or revised to take into account the repeal of the foreign-targeted bearer obligation exception. Consistent with these comments, the proposed regulations propose to remove those examples.

5. *Section 4701*

Commenters requested clarification on whether the foreign-targeting rules under § 1.163-5(c) would apply to obligations issued after March 18, 2012, for purposes of section 4701. Consistent with Notice 2012-20, proposed § 46.4701-1 provides that, for purposes of determining whether an obligation is a foreign-targeted bearer obligation, the rules of § 1.163-5(c) apply.

6. *Applicability Dates*

Notice 2012-20 stated that regulations incorporating the guidance described in that notice will be effective for obligations issued after March 18, 2012. Accordingly, the proposed regulations will generally apply to obligations issued after March 18, 2012. However, taxpayers may apply the rules in section 3 of Notice 2012-20, including the default exception, for obligations issued prior to publication of a Treasury decision adopting these rules as final regulations in the **Federal Register**. The rules related to pass-through certificates, participation interests, and regular interests in REMICs and the rules related to obligations not of a type offered to the public are not described in Notice 2012-20 and, therefore, will apply only to obligations issued after the publication of a Treasury decision adopting these rules as final regulations in the **Federal Register**, except as otherwise provided in the next sentence. The existing regulations under § 5f.103-1 will continue to apply to tax-exempt bonds issued prior to the date 90 days after publication of a Treasury decision adopting these rules as final regulations in the **Federal Register**.

Special Analyses

Certain IRS regulations, including these, are exempt from the requirements of Executive Order 12866, as supplemented and reaffirmed by Executive Order 13563. Therefore, a regulatory impact assessment is not required. It is hereby certified that these regulations will not have a significant economic impact on a substantial number of small entities. Sections 163(f) and 149(a) require that certain obligations be in registered form which is satisfied if the obligations are transferable only through a book entry system. The existing regulations under these sections therefore permit issuers to satisfy the registration requirement through a book entry system and describe the arrangements that are necessary for a system to qualify as a book entry system. Certain systems that are now common, however, may not qualify as book entry systems under the existing regulations. Because the proposed regulations merely clarify that these systems are book entry systems, the proposed regulations would not impose a significant economic impact. Accordingly, a regulatory flexibility analysis is not required. Pursuant to section 7805(f) of the Code, this notice of proposed rulemaking will be submitted to the Chief Counsel for Advocacy of the Small Business Administration for comment on its impact on small entities.

Comments and Requests for Public Hearing

Before these proposed regulations are adopted as final regulations, consideration will be given to any comments that are submitted timely to the IRS as prescribed in this preamble under the "ADDRESSES" heading. Treasury and the IRS request comments on all aspects of the proposed rules. All comments will be available at *www.regulations.gov* or upon request. A public hearing will be scheduled if requested in writing by any person that timely submits written comments. If a public hearing is scheduled, notice of the date, time, and place for the hearing will be published in the **Federal Register**.

Drafting Information

The principal authors of these regulations are Spence Hanemann and Diana Imholtz, Office of Associate Chief Counsel (Financial Institutions and Products), IRS. However, other personnel from Treasury and the IRS participated in their development.

[¶ 49,745] Proposed Amendments of Regulations (REG-105004-16), published in the Federal Register on September 20, 2017.

[Code Secs. 6051, 6052 and 6109]

Information returns: Wage and income statements: Forms W-2: Taxpayer identification numbers: Truncated.—Amendments of Reg. §§ 1.6052-2, 31.6051-1, 31.6051-2, 31.6051-3 and 301.6109-4, to permit employers to voluntarily truncate employees' social security numbers (SSNs) on copies of Forms W-2, Wage and Tax Statement, that are furnished to employees so that the truncated SSNs appear in the form of IRS truncated taxpayer identification numbers (TTINs), are proposed.

AGENCY: Internal Revenue Service (IRS), Treasury.

ACTION: Notice of proposed rulemaking.

SUMMARY: This document contains proposed amendments to the regulations under sections 6051 and 6052 of the Internal Revenue Code (Code). To aid employers' efforts to protect employees from identity theft, these proposed regulations would amend existing regulations to permit employers to voluntarily truncate employees' social security numbers (SSNs) on copies of Forms W-2, Wage and Tax Statement, that are furnished to employees so that the truncated SSNs appear in the form of IRS truncated taxpayer identification numbers (TTINs). These proposed regulations also would amend the regulations under section 6109 to clarify the application of the truncation rules to Forms W-2 and to add an example illustrating the application of these rules. Additionally, these proposed amendments would delete obsolete provisions and update cross references in the regulations under sections 6051 and 6052. These proposed regulations affect employers who are required to furnish Forms W-2 and employees who receive Forms W-2.

DATES: Written or electronic comments and requests for a public hearing must be received by **December 18, 2017**.

ADDRESSES: Send submissions to: CC:PA:LPD:PR (REG-105004-16), room 5203, Internal Revenue Service, P.O. Box 7604, Ben Franklin Station, Washington, DC 20044. Submissions may be hand-delivered between the hours of 8 a.m. and 4 p.m. to CC:PA:LPD:PR (REG-105004-16), Courier's Desk, Internal Revenue Service, 1111 Constitution Avenue, N.W., Washington, DC, or sent via the Federal eRulemaking Portal at *www.regulations.gov* (REG-105004-16).

FOR FURTHER INFORMATION CONTACT: Concerning these proposed regulations, Eliezer Mishory, (202) 317-6844; concerning submissions of comments and/or requests for a hearing, Regina Johnson (202) 317-6901 (not toll-free numbers).

SUPPLEMENTARY INFORMATION:

Background:

This document contains proposed amendments to the Income Tax Regulations (26 CFR part 1), the Employment Taxes and Collection of Income Tax at Source Regulations (26 CFR part 31), and the Procedure and Administration Regulations (26 CFR part 301) regarding statements that are required to be furnished to employees by employers or other persons under sections 6051 and 6052 of the Code. Section 6051(a) generally requires that an employer provide to each employee on or before January 31st of the succeeding year a written statement that shows the employee's total amount of wages and the total amount deducted and withheld as tax from those wages, along with other information, for each calendar year. Employers must use Form W-2 (or a substitute statement that complies with applicable revenue procedures relating to such statements) to provide the information required by section 6051(a) to employees. See §31.6051-1(a)(1)(i); Rev. Proc. 2016-54, 2016-45 I.R.B. 685, also published as Publication 1141, "General Rules and Specifications for Substitute Forms W-2 and W-3," or any successor guidance. Section 6051(d) provides that, when required to do so by regulations, employers must file with the Secretary duplicates of the forms required to be furnished to employees under section 6051. Section 31.6051-2(a) generally requires employers to file Social Security Administration copies of Forms W-2 with the Social Security Administration. A person making a payment of third-party sick pay to an employee of another employer (payee) is required under section 6051(f)(1) to furnish a written statement to the employer for whom services are normally rendered containing certain information, including the payee's SSN. Under certain conditions, the employer for whom services are normally rendered is required under section 6051(f)(2) to furnish a Form W-2 to the payee. This situation may arise, for example, when an insurance company is making payments to an employee of another employer because the employee is temporarily absent from work due to injury, sickness or disability, and the insurance company has satisfied the necessary requirements under §32.1(e) of the Temporary Employment Tax Regulations under the Act of December 29, 1981 (Pub. L. 97-123) to transfer the obligation to do Form W-2 reporting to the employer. Employers also must use Form W-2 to file and furnish information regarding payment of wages in the form of group-term life insurance under section 6052.

Section 6109(a) authorizes the Secretary to prescribe regulations with respect to the inclusion in returns, statements, or other documents of an identifying number as may be prescribed for securing proper identification of a person. On July 15, 2014, the Treasury Department and the IRS published in the **Federal Register** (79 FR 41127-02) final regulations (TD 9675) authorizing the use of TTINs on certain payee statements and certain other documents. These final regulations were in response to concerns about the risks of identity theft, including its effect on tax administration.

Section 301.6109-4(b) generally provides that a TTIN may be used to identify any person on any statement or other document that the internal revenue laws require to be furnished to another person. Under §301.6109-4(a), a TTIN is an individual's SSN, IRS individual taxpayer identification number (ITIN), IRS adoption taxpayer identification number (ATIN), or IRS employer identification number (EIN) in which the first five digits of the nine-digit number are replaced with Xs or asterisks. For example, a TTIN replacing an SSN appears in the form XXX-XX-1234 or ***-**-1234. Section 301.6109-4(b)(2)(ii) prohibits using TTINs if, among other things, a statute, regulation, other guidance published in the Internal Revenue Bulletin, form, or instructions specifically requires the use of an SSN. Additionally, §301.6109-4(b)(2)(iii) prohibits the use of TTINs on any return, statement, or other document that is required to be filed with or furnished to the IRS.

Prior to being amended by the Protecting Americans from Tax Hikes (PATH) Act of 2015, Public Law No. 114-113, div. Q, title IV, 129 Stat. 2242, section 6051(a)(2) specifically required employers to include their employees' SSNs on copies of Forms W-2 that are furnished to employees. In addition, current regulations under § 31.6051-1, as well as forms and instructions, require employers to include their employees' SSNs on copies of Forms W-2 that are furnished to employees. Section 409 of the PATH Act amended section 6051(a)(2) by striking "his social security account number" from the list of information required on Form W-2 and inserting "an identifying number for the employee" instead. This statutory amendment is effective for statements issued after December 18, 2015, the date that the PATH Act was signed into law. Because an SSN is no longer required by section 6051, the Treasury Department and the IRS propose amending the regulations to permit employers to truncate employees' SSNs to appear in the form of TTINs on copies of Forms W-2 that are furnished to employees. If the proposed regulations are finalized without change, the IRS intends to incorporate the revised regulations into forms and instructions, permitting employers to use a TTIN on the employee copy of the Form W-2. See § 301.6109-4(b)(2)(i) and (ii).

Explanation of Provisions

Truncated SSN permitted on employee's copies of Form W-2

These proposed regulations amend § 31.6051-1 to permit employers to truncate employees' SSNs to appear in the form of a TTIN on copies of Forms W-2 that are furnished to employees under section 6051. Consistent with the rule in § 301.6109-4(b)(2)(iii), prohibiting the use of TTINs on any return, statement, or other document that is required to be filed with or furnished to the IRS, these proposed regulations amend § 31.6051-2 to clarify that employers may not truncate an employee's SSN to appear in the form of a TTIN on a copy of a Form W-2 that is filed with the Social Security Administration. This result is appropriate because both the IRS and the SSA need to utilize Forms W-2 to properly identify individuals to be able to carry out their respective duties.

Consistent with the rule in § 301.6109-4(b)(2)(ii) that prohibits using TTINs if, among other things, a statute specifically requires the use of an SSN, the proposed regulations also amend § 31.6051-3 to clarify that a payee's SSN may not be truncated to appear in the form of a TTIN on a statement furnished to the employer of the payee who received sick pay from a third party because section 6051(f)(1)(A)(i) specifically requires such a statement to contain the employee's SSN. Nonetheless, these proposed regulations permit employers to truncate payees' SSNs to appear in the form of TTINs on copies of Forms W-2 that are furnished under section 6051(f)(2) to payees that report such third-party sick pay, in accordance with the general rule governing the reporting of wages to employees on Forms W-2 under section 6051(a), because section 6051(f)(2) does not specifically require the use of an SSN.

Further, these proposed regulations amend § 1.6052-2 to permit employers to truncate employees' SSNs to appear in the form of TTINs on copies of Forms W-2 that are furnished to employees under section 6052(b) regarding payment of wages in the form of group-term life insurance.

These proposed regulations amend § 301.6109-4 to clarify that truncation is not allowed on any return, statement, or other document that is required to be filed with or furnished to the Social Security Administration under the internal revenue laws. These proposed regulations also clarify the rule prohibiting truncation if a statute, regulation, other guidance published in the Internal Revenue Bulletin, form, or instructions, specifically requires use of a SSN, ITIN, ATIN, or EIN. The proposed regulations provide that truncation is allowed if a statute or IRS guidance (e.g., regulations, forms, instructions), that specifically requires use of a SSN, ITIN, ATIN, or EIN, also specifically states that the taxpayer identifying number may be truncated. These proposed regulations also add an example illustrating the application of these rules to Forms W-2. These proposed regulations also amend the existing example for clarity.

Miscellaneous updates to regulations under sections 6051 and 6052

In addition to the amendments relating to the truncation of employees' SSNs to appear in the form of TTINs in specific circumstances, these proposed regulations eliminate obsolete provisions and update cross references in the regulations under sections 6051 and 6052, as explained below.

First, these proposed regulations amend § 31.6051-1 to remove obsolete provisions regarding compensation, as defined in the Railroad Retirement Tax Act, paid during 1968, 1969, 1970, and 1971 and reported on the now obsolete Form W-2 (RR); the special rule for statements with respect to the refundable earned income credit for Form W-2 for 1987 and 1988; and references to the annual contribution base (repealed in 1993) for wages subject to the Hospital Insurance tax (commonly known as Medicare tax).

Second, these proposed regulations amend § 31.6051-1 to remove obsolete cross references, including a cross reference to former § 301.6676-1 relating to the penalty for failure to report an identification number or an account number, and a cross reference to section 6723 (prior to its amendment in 1989) that was relevant for Forms W-2 that were due from the beginning of 1987 through the end of 1989.

Third, these proposed regulations amend § 31.6051-2 to update now inaccurate cross references resulting from statutory and regulatory changes regarding penalties for failures to file, and to remove a cross reference to section 6723 (prior to its amendment in 1989) that was relevant for Forms W-2 that were due from the beginning of 1987 through the end of 1989. These proposed regulations also change the title of § 31.6051-2 from "Information returns on Form W-3 and Internal Revenue Service copies of Forms W-2" to "Information returns on Form W-3 and Social Security Administration copies of Forms W-2," to conform with the text of the regulation that refers to the Social Security Administration copies of Form W-2. In addition, these proposed regulations remove obsolete references in § 31.6051-2 to the requirements to submit information on magnetic tape and insert a reference to the requirements to submit information on magnetic media.

Fourth, these proposed regulations amend § 31.6051-3 to remove the obsolete transition rule for third-party sick pay that was paid to a payee after December 31, 1980, and before May 1, 1981.

Fifth, these proposed regulations amend § 1.6052-2 to remove an obsolete rule that allowed employers to use a statement other than a Form W-2 to satisfy the requirement to furnish a statement to an employee with respect to wages paid in the form of group-term life insurance. This rule was relevant for years prior to 1973, before § 1.6052-1 was amended to require employers to report wages in the form of group-term life insurance on Form W-2. At the same time, to conform to this new requirement, § 1.6052-2 was amended to provide that the requirement to furnish a statement to an employee with respect to wages paid in the form of group-term life insurance may be satisfied by furnishing to the employee the employee's copy of Form W-2 that was filed pursuant to § 1.6052-1. Because the transition period to require employers to file Form W-2 has long since passed and because the Treasury Department and the IRS understand that copies of Forms W-2 are used to satisfy the requirement to furnish statements to employees under § 1.6052-2, these proposed regulations require employers to furnish to employees the employees' copies of Forms W-2 that were filed pursuant to § 1.6052-1, and these proposed regulations make conforming changes throughout that section.

Finally, these proposed regulations update the now inaccurate cross reference resulting from statutory changes regarding penalties for failures to furnish statements under section 6052 and remove the deemed compliance rule, which applied only to years before 1972.

Proposed effective/applicability date

These proposed regulations will be effective on the date of the publication of the Treasury Decision adopting these rules as final in the **Federal Register**. These proposed regulations amend the effective/applicability date provisions in § 31.6051-1, § 31.6051-3, and § 301.6109-4, and add applicability date provisions to § 1.6052-2 and § 31.6051-2. Several state tax administrators have requested additional time to develop systems to process the copies of Forms W-2 filed with state income tax returns that may contain truncated SSNs. In light of this request, these proposed regulations will not apply to Forms W-2 required to be furnished before January 1, 2019. Accordingly, these proposed regulations provide that these regulations, as amended, will be applicable for statements required to be filed and furnished under sections 6051 and 6052 after December 31, 2018.

Statement of Availability of IRS Documents

IRS Revenue Procedures, Revenue Rulings notices, and other guidance cited in this preamble are published in the Internal Revenue Bulletin (or Cumulative Bulletin) and are available from the Superintendent of Documents, U.S. Government Printing Office, Washington, DC 20402, or by visiting the IRS website at www.irs.gov.

Special Analyses

Certain IRS regulations, including this one, are exempt from the requirements of Executive Order 12866, as supplemented and reaffirmed by Executive Order 13563. Therefore, a regulatory assessment is not required. Because these proposed regulations do not impose a collection of information on small entities, the Regulatory Flexibility Act (5 U.S.C. chapter 6) does not apply. Pursuant to section 7805(f) of the Code, this notice of proposed rulemaking has been submitted to the Chief Counsel for Advocacy of the Small Business Administration for comment on its impact on small business.

Comments and Requests for Public Hearing

Before these proposed regulations are adopted as final regulations, consideration will be given to any comments that are submitted timely to the IRS as prescribed in the preamble under the ADDRESSES section. The Treasury Department and the IRS request comments on all aspects of these proposed regulations. All comments submitted will be made available at *www.regulations.gov* or upon request. A public hearing may be scheduled if requested in writing by any person that timely submits written comments. If a public hearing is scheduled, notice of the date, time, and place for the hearing will be published in the **Federal Register**.

Drafting Information

The principal author of these proposed regulations is Eliezer Mishory of the Office of the Associate Chief Counsel (Procedure and Administration).

[¶ 49,746] Proposed Amendments of Regulations and Withdrawal of Notice of Proposed Regulations (REG-128841-07), published in the Federal Register on September 28, 2017.

[Code Secs. 142 and 147]

Tax-exempt bonds: Private facility bonds: Approval: Public notice.—Reg. § 1.147(f)-1 and amendments of Reg. § 5f.103-2, updating and streamlining the public approval requirement provided in section 147(f) of the Internal Revenue Code applicable to tax-exempt private activity bonds issued by State and local governments, are adopted. Reg. §§ 1.147(f)-1 and 5f.103-2 proposed on September 9, 2008, and May 11, 1983, respectively, are withdrawn.

[¶49,749] **Proposed Amendments of Regulations (REG-116256-17)**, published in the Federal Register on October 12, 2017.

[Code Sec. 754]

Partnerships and their partners: Partnership property: Basis: Election to adjust basis.—Amendments of Reg. §1.754-1, relating to the requirements for making a valid election under section 754of the Internal Revenue Code of 1986 (Code), as amended, are proposed.

AGENCY: Internal Revenue Service (IRS), Treasury.

ACTION: Notice of proposed rulemaking.

SUMMARY: This document contains proposed amendments to the regulation relating to the requirements for making a valid election under section 754 of the Internal Revenue Code of 1986 (Code), as amended. The proposed regulation affects partnerships and their partners by removing a regulatory burden in making an election to adjust the basis of partnership property.

DATES: Electronic or written comments and requests for a public hearing must be received by November 13, 2017.

ADDRESSES: Send submissions to Internal Revenue Service, CC:PA:LPD:PR (REG-116256-17), Room 5203, PO Box 7604, Ben Franklin Station, Washington, DC 20044. Submissions may be hand-delivered Monday through Friday between the hours of 8 a.m. and 4 p.m. to CC:PA:LPD:PR (REG-116256-17), Courier's Desk, 1111 Constitution Avenue, N.W., Washington, DC, 20224, or sent electronically, via the Federal eRulemaking Portal at www.regulations.gov (indicate IRS and REG-116256-17).

FOR FURTHER INFORMATION CONTACT: Concerning the proposed regulation, Meghan Howard, at (202) 317-5055; concerning submissions of comments and requests for a public hearing, Regina Johnson, at (202) 317-6901 (not toll-free numbers).

SUPPLEMENTARY INFORMATION:

Background and Explanation of Provision

This document contains proposed amendments to 26 CFR part 1 under section 754 of the Code. Specifically, these proposed amendments would remove the signature requirement contained in §1.754-1(b) (current regulation) in order to eliminate a regulatory burden.

Section 754 provides that if a partnership files an election (section 754 election), in accordance with regulations prescribed by the Secretary, the basis of partnership property shall be adjusted, in the case of a distribution of property, in the manner provided in section 734 and, in the case of a transfer of a partnership interest, in the manner provided in section 743. Such an election applies with respect to all distributions of property by the partnership and to all transfers of interests in the partnership during the taxable year with respect to which such election was filed and all subsequent taxable years. Such election may be revoked by the partnership, subject to such limitations as may be provided by regulations prescribed by the Secretary.

The current regulation provides the method to make the section 754 election and states in relevant part that a section 754 election shall be made in a written statement (section 754 election statement) filed with the partnership return for the taxable year during which the distribution or transfer occurs. For the section 754 election to be valid, the return must be filed not later than the time prescribed for filing the return for such taxable year, including extensions. The current regulation requires that the section 754 election statement (i) set forth the name and address of the partnership making the election, (ii) be signed by any one of the partners, and (iii) contain a declaration that the partnership elects under section 754 to apply the provisions of section 734(b) and section 743(b). Accordingly, under the current regulation, a partnership that files an unsigned section 754 election statement with its partnership return (whether filed electronically or in paper) has not made a valid section 754 election.

Currently the only remedy for failing to make a proper section 754 election is to request "9100 relief" to make a late section 754 election either: (1) through automatic relief, if the error is discovered within 12 months pursuant to §301.9100-2 of the Procedure and Administration Regulations; or (2) through a private letter ruling request pursuant to §301.9100-3. The IRS has received numerous requests for 9100 relief with respect to unsigned section 754 election statements, especially where returns have been filed electronically. In order to ease the burden on partnerships seeking to make a valid section 754 election and to eliminate the need to seek 9100 relief, the Treasury Department and the IRS are proposing to amend the current regulation to remove the signature requirement in §1.754-1(b)(1). The amended regulation will provide that a taxpayer making a section 754 election must file a statement with its return that: (i) sets forth the name and address of the partnership making the section 754 election, and (ii) contains a declaration that the partnership elects under section 754 to apply the provisions of section 734(b) and section 743(b).

Proposed Applicability Date

The amendments to this regulation are proposed to apply to taxable years ending on or after the date of publication of the Treasury decision adopting these rules as a final regulation in the **Federal Register**. Taxpayers, however, may rely on this proposed regulation for periods preceding the proposed applicability date. Accordingly, partnerships that filed a timely partnership return containing an otherwise valid section 754 election statement, but for the missing signature of a partner on the statement, will not need to seek 9100 relief in such cases.

Special Analyses

Certain IRS regulations, including this one, are exempt from the requirements of Executive Order 12866, as supplemented and reaffirmed by Executive Order 13563. Therefore, a regulatory impact assessment is not required. It is hereby certified that this regulation, if adopted, would not have a significant economic impact on a substantial number of small entities under the Regulatory Flexibility Act (5 U.S.C. chapter 6). This certification is based on the fact that this regulation reduces the information currently required to be collected in making an election to adjust the basis of partnership property and thereby reduces burden on small entities. Pursuant to section 7805(f) of the Code, this regulation has been submitted to the Chief Counsel for Advocacy of the Small Business Administration for comment on its impact on small businesses.

Comments and Requests for a Public Hearing

Before this proposed regulation is adopted as a final regulation, consideration will be given to any comments that are submitted timely to the IRS as prescribed in this preamble under the "Addresses" heading. The Treasury Department and the IRS request comments on all aspects of the proposed regulation. All comments will be available at www.regulations.gov or upon request. A public hearing will be scheduled if requested in writing by any person that timely submits written comments. If a public hearing is scheduled, notice of the date, time, and place for the public hearing will be published in the **Federal Register**.

Drafting Information

The principal author of this regulation is Meghan M. Howard of the Office of the Associate Chief Counsel (Passthroughs and Special Industries). However, other personnel from the Treasury Department and the IRS participated in their development.

[¶49,753] Proposed Amendments of Regulations (REG-119514-15), published in the Federal Register on December 19, 2017 (corrected 12/27/2016).

[Code Secs. 446, 954 and 988]

Controlled foreign corporation (CFC): Foreign currency gain or loss: Foreign personal holding company income (FPHCI): Mark-to-market method: Exclusions.—Reg. §1.988-7 and amendments of Reg. §§1.446-4, 1.954-0 and 1.954-2, providing guidance on the treatment of foreign currency gain or loss of a controlled foreign corporation (CFC) under the business needs exclusion from foreign personal holding company income (FPHCI), are proposed.

AGENCY: Internal Revenue Service (IRS), Treasury.

ACTION: Notice of proposed rulemaking.

SUMMARY: This document contains proposed regulations that provide guidance on the treatment of foreign currency gain or loss of a controlled foreign corporation (CFC) under the business needs exclusion from foreign personal holding company income (FPHCI). The proposed regulations also provide an election for a taxpayer to use a mark-to-market method of accounting for foreign currency gain or loss attributable to section 988 transactions. In addition, the proposed regulations permit the controlling United States shareholders of a CFC to automatically revoke certain elections concerning the treatment of foreign currency gain or loss. The proposed regulations affect taxpayers and United States shareholders of CFCs that engage in transactions giving rise to foreign currency gain or loss under section 988 of the Internal Revenue Code (Code).

DATES: Written or electronic comments and requests for a public hearing must be received by March 19, 2018.

ADDRESSES: Send submissions to CC:PA:LPD:PR (REG-119514-15), room 5203, Internal Revenue Service, P.O. Box 7604, Ben Franklin Station, Washington, DC 20044. Submissions may be hand-delivered Monday through Friday between the hours of 8 a.m. and 4 p.m. to CC:PA:LPD:PR (REG-119514-15), Courier's Desk, Internal Revenue Service, 1111 Constitution Avenue NW, Washington, DC, or sent electronically via the Federal eRulemaking Portal at http://www.regulations.gov (IRS REG-119514-15).

FOR FURTHER INFORMATION CONTACT: Concerning the proposed regulations, Jeffery G. Mitchell, (202) 317-6934; concerning submissions of comments or requests for a public hearing, Regina Johnson, (202) 317-6901 (not toll-free numbers).

SUPPLEMENTARY INFORMATION:

Paperwork Reduction Act

The collections of information contained in this notice of proposed rulemaking have been submitted to the Office of Management and Budget for review in accordance with the Paperwork Reduction Act of 1995 (44 U.S.C. 3507(d)). Comments on the collections of information should be sent to the **Office of Management and Budget**, Attn: Desk Officer for the Department of the Treasury, Office of Information and Regulatory Affairs, Washington, DC 20503, with copies to the **Internal Revenue Service**, Attn: IRS Reports Clearance Officer, SE:W:CAR:MP:T:T:SP, Washington, DC 20224. Comments on the collection of information should be received by February 20, 2018. Comments are specifically requested concerning:

Whether the proposed collection of information is necessary for the proper performance of the duties of the IRS, including whether the information will have practical utility;

The accuracy of the estimated burden associated with the proposed collection of information;

How the quality, utility, and clarity of the information to be collected may be enhanced;

How the burden of complying with the proposed collection of information may be minimized, including through the application of automated collection techniques or other forms of information technology; and

Estimates of capital or start-up costs and costs of operation, maintenance, and purchases of services to provide information.

The collection of information in these proposed regulations is in proposed §§1.954-2(g)(3)(iii) and (4)(iii) and 1.988-7. The information is required to be provided by taxpayers and United States shareholders of CFCs that make an election or revoke an election with respect to the treatment of foreign currency gains and losses. The information provided will be used by the IRS for tax compliance purposes.

Estimated total annual reporting burden: 5,000 hours.

Estimated average annual burden hours per respondent: one hour.

Estimated number of respondents: 5,000.

Estimated annual frequency of responses: one.

An agency may not conduct or sponsor, and a person is not required to respond to, a collection of information unless it displays a valid control number assigned by the Office of Management and Budget.

Books or records relating to a collection of information must be retained as long as their contents may become material in the administration of any internal revenue law. Generally, tax returns and tax return information are confidential, as required by 26 U.S.C. 6103.

Background

This document contains proposed amendments to 26 CFR part 1 under sections 446, 954(c)(1)(D), and 988 of the Code. Section 446 requires taxpayers to compute taxable income using accounting methods that clearly reflect income. Section 954(c)(1)(D) provides that FPHCI includes the excess of foreign currency gains over foreign currency losses (as defined in section 988(b)) attributable to section 988 transactions, other than transactions directly related to the business needs of the CFC. Section 988 provides rules for determining the source and character of gain or loss from certain foreign currency transactions.

A. Business Needs Exclusion

1. In general

Section 954 defines foreign base company income (FBCI), which generally is income earned by a CFC that is taken into account in computing the amount that a United States shareholder of the CFC must include in income under section 951(a)(1)(A). Under section 954(a)(1), FBCI includes FPHCI, which is defined in section 954(c). The excess of foreign currency gains over foreign currency losses from section 988 transactions is generally included in FPHCI pursuant to section 954(c)(1)(D).

Section 988 transactions generally include the following: the accrual of any item of income or expense that is to be paid or received in a nonfunctional currency after the date of accrual; lending or borrowing in a nonfunctional currency; entering into or acquiring a forward, future, option, or similar contract denominated in a nonfunctional currency; and the disposition of nonfunctional currency. *See* section 988(c). Thus, accruals in connection with ordinary business transactions, such as purchases and sales of inventory or the provision of services, are section 988 transactions if the receivable or payable is denominated in, or determined by reference to, a currency other than the taxpayer's functional currency, as determined under §1.985-1.

Notwithstanding the general rule that includes the excess of foreign currency gains over foreign currency losses from section 988 transactions in FPHCI, section 954(c)(1)(D) excludes from FPHCI any foreign currency gain or loss attributable to a transaction directly related to the business needs of the CFC (business needs exclusion). To qualify for the business needs exclusion, a foreign currency gain or loss must, in addition to satisfying other requirements, arise from a transaction entered into, or property used, in the normal course of the CFC's business that does not itself (and could not reasonably be expected to) give rise to subpart F income (as defined in section 952) other than foreign currency gain or loss. *See* §1.954-2(g)(2)(ii)(B)(*1*).

Foreign currency gain or loss attributable to a bona fide hedging transaction (as defined in §1.954-2(a)(4)(ii)) with respect to a transaction or property that qualifies for the business needs exclusion also qualifies for the business needs exclusion, provided that any gain or loss with respect to such transaction or property that is attributable to changes in exchange rates is clearly determinable from the records of the CFC as being derived from such property or transaction. *See* §1.954-2(g)(2)(ii)(B)(*2*). Generally, bona fide hedging transactions are transactions that meet the requirements for a hedging transaction under §1.1221-2(a) through (d), except that a bona fide hedging transaction also includes a transaction entered into in the normal course of business primarily to manage risk with respect to section 1231 property or a section 988 transaction. Under §1.1221-2(b), a hedging transaction is defined as a transaction that a taxpayer enters into in the normal course of its trade or business primarily to manage the risk of price changes or currency fluctuations with respect to ordinary property that is held or to be held by the taxpayer, or to manage the risk of interest rate or price changes or currency fluctuations with respect to borrowings made or to be made, or ordinary obligations incurred or to be incurred, by the taxpayer. Transactions that manage risks related to assets that would produce capital gain or loss on disposition (capital assets), or assets owned or liabilities owed by a related party, do not qualify as hedging transactions under

§ 1.1221-2(b). To qualify as a bona fide hedging transaction, the transaction must be clearly identified as a hedging transaction before the end of the day on which the CFC acquired, originated, or entered into the transaction. *See* § § 1.1221-2(f) and 1.954-2(a)(4)(ii)(A) and (B).

Section 1.954-2(g)(2)(ii)(C) provides special rules for applying the business needs exclusion to CFCs that are regular dealers as defined in § 1.954-2(a)(4)(iv). Transactions in dealer property (as defined in § 1.954-2(a)(4)(v)) that are entered into by a CFC that is a regular dealer in such property in its capacity as a dealer are treated as directly related to the business needs of the CFC. *See* § 1.954-2(g)(2)(ii)(C)(*1*). In addition, an interest-bearing liability denominated in a nonfunctional currency and incurred by a regular dealer is treated as dealer property if it reduces the CFC's currency risk with respect to dealer property and is identified on the CFC's records as a liability treated as dealer property. *See* § 1.954-2(g)(2)(ii)(C)(*2*). A regular dealer is a CFC that regularly and actively offers to, and in fact does, purchase property from and sell property to unrelated customers in the ordinary course of business, or that regularly and actively offers to, and in fact does, enter into, assume, offset, assign or otherwise terminate positions in property with unrelated customers in the ordinary course of business. *See* § 1.954-2(a)(4)(iv).

2. Use of net foreign currency losses

Under section 954(c)(1)(D), although a foreign currency loss that does not qualify for the business needs exclusion reduces the amount of foreign currency gain that is included in FPHCI, an excess of foreign currency losses over foreign currency gains from section 988 transactions generally does not reduce FPHCI. Such a net foreign currency loss does, however, reduce earnings and profits for purposes of the current earnings and profits limitation on subpart F income in section 952(c)(1). Additionally, as described in Part D of this Background section, when an election under § 1.954-2(g)(3) or (4) is in effect, a foreign currency loss can reduce FPHCI or, in the case of an election under § 1.954-2(g)(3), another category of subpart F income.

3. Inapplicability of business needs exclusion to transactions and property that give rise to both subpart F income and non-subpart F income

In order for the business needs exclusion to apply to exclude foreign currency gain and loss from the computation of FPHCI, the foreign currency gain or loss must arise from a transaction or property that does not itself (and could not reasonably be expected to) give rise to any subpart F income other than foreign currency gain or loss. For example, foreign currency gains and losses related to the purchase and sale of inventory are excluded from the computation of FPHCI if none of the income from the purchase and sale is subpart F income under section 952. However, if the transaction or property gives rise to, or could reasonably be expected to give rise to, any amount of subpart F income (other than foreign currency gain or loss), none of the foreign currency gain or loss attributable to the transaction or property would qualify for the business needs exclusion. Thus, there is a cliff effect: if even a de minimis amount of income or gain from the transaction or property is subpart F income, the entire amount of the foreign currency gain or loss from the transaction or property, or from a bona fide hedging transaction with respect to the transaction or property, is included in the FPHCI computation.

4. Transactions that manage the risk of currency fluctuation in a qualified business unit

A CFC may conduct business through a qualified business unit (as defined in § 1.989(a)-1) (QBU) that is not treated as a separate entity for federal income tax purposes, either because it is a branch or division of the CFC or because it is a business entity that is disregarded as separate from its owner. Although the QBU is not treated as a separate entity, it may have a functional currency under § 1.985-1 that is different from that of the CFC owner, with consequences for the determination of foreign currency gain and loss under sections 987 and 988. The QBU's transactions in its own functional currency are not section 988 transactions of the CFC, and accordingly the CFC does not realize foreign currency gain or loss on such transactions. The CFC generally must, however, take into account under section 987 foreign currency gain or loss with respect to the QBU upon remittances from the QBU.

For business and financial accounting reasons, a CFC may enter into transactions to manage the exchange rate risk associated with its net investment in its QBU. Under generally accepted accounting principles in the United States (U.S. GAAP), a majority owner of a business entity (parent corporation) must consolidate the accounts of the majority-owned entity, including a foreign entity, with its own accounts for purposes of financial reporting. Under U.S. GAAP, the income, assets, liabilities, and other financial results of foreign operations that are conducted in a functional currency that differs from the consolidated parent's functional currency must be translated into the functional currency of the consolidated parent. Foreign currency gains or losses arising from the translation are recorded in a "cumulative translation adjustment" account and reported as a component of shareholders' equity on the balance sheet. *See generally* Accounting Standards Codification (ASC) 830-30-45. Foreign currency gain or loss from transactions that effectively hedge the risk of currency fluctuations in the net equity investment in foreign operations also are recorded in the cumulative translation adjustment account. *See* ASC 815-35-35. A cumulative translation adjustment is not taken into account in computing the income of the consolidated group until the relevant operations are disposed of or liquidated.

The transactions that a CFC uses to manage its exchange rate risk with respect to its net investment in a QBU are typically section 988 transactions. Thus, foreign currency gains or losses attributable to those transactions are taken into account in computing FPHCI, unless the transactions qualify as bona fide hedging transactions that satisfy the requirements of the business needs exclusion. *See* § 1.954-2(g)(2)(ii)(B)(2). Neither the Code nor the section 954 regulations provide specific guidance on whether a transaction entered into to manage exchange rate risk arising from a CFC's net investment in a QBU can qualify as a bona fide hedging transaction eligible for the business needs exclusion. This issue can be consequential because foreign currency gain, but not loss, from a transaction erroneously identified as a bona fide hedging transaction is included in the computation of FPHCI, unless the CFC qualifies for the inadvertent identification exception. *See* § 1.954-2(a)(4)(ii)(C) and (g)(2)(ii)(B)(2). Additionally, even if a transaction entered into to manage exchange rate risk arising from a CFC's net investment in a QBU is eligible for treatment as a bona fide hedging transaction, the transaction would not qualify for the business needs exclusion unless the hedged property did not, and could not reasonably be expected to, give rise to any subpart F income.

Also for business and financial accounting reasons, a CFC may enter into transactions to manage the exchange rate risk with respect to its net investment in a subsidiary CFC. A transaction that manages the risk of price or currency fluctuation with respect to a CFC's net investment in a subsidiary CFC is not considered a hedging transaction for federal income tax purposes. In *Hoover Co. v. Commissioner*, 72 T.C. 706 (1979), the Tax Court held that transactions entered into to manage the risk of a decline in value of a taxpayer's net investment in a foreign subsidiary that might occur if the value of the subsidiary's functional currency declined relative to the U.S. dollar were not hedging transactions for federal income tax purposes. *See also* § 1.1221-2(b) (providing that a hedging transaction must manage risk with respect to "ordinary property . . . that is held or to be held by the taxpayer"). Thus, foreign currency gains and losses on transactions that manage the risk of currency fluctuation on a CFC's net investment in a subsidiary CFC are taken into account in computing FPHCI. B. Timing of Foreign Currency Gains and Losses

1. Hedge timing rules of § 1.446-4

Section 1.446-4 generally requires gain or loss from a hedging transaction, as defined in § 1.1221-2(b), to be taken into account at the same time as the gain or loss from the item being hedged. As noted in Part A.1 of this Background section, bona fide hedging transactions under § 1.954-2(a)(4)(ii) include both hedging transactions as defined in § 1.1221-2(b) and transactions that manage the risk of price or currency fluctuation with respect to section 1231 property and section 988 transactions. Thus, § 1.446-4 does not explicitly apply to all bona fide hedging transactions, which has led to some uncertainty about whether gain or loss from a bona fide hedging transaction that is not described in § 1.1221-2(b) is properly taken into account in the same taxable year as gain or loss on the hedged item. The Department of the Treasury (Treasury Department) and the IRS understand that some taxpayers have applied the hedge timing rules of § 1.446-4 to all bona fide hedging transactions, irrespective of whether those transactions are hedging transactions as defined in § 1.1221-2(b).

2. Treasury center CFCs

It is common for a U.S.-parented multinational group to own one or more CFCs that serve as financing entities for other group members. Such CFCs (treasury center CFCs) may borrow in various currencies from third party lenders or from other members of the group and lend the proceeds to other members of the group. Treasury center CFCs also may be used to centralize the management of currency and other risks of other CFCs within the multinational group. Treasury center CFCs typically qualify as securities dealers under section 475, but if a treasury center CFC transacts primarily or exclusively with related persons, as is often the case, it would not qualify as a regular dealer under § 1.954-2(a)(4)(iv) and thus would not be eligible for the special rules applying the business needs exclusion to certain transactions of regular dealers under § 1.954-2(g)(2)(ii)(C).

When a treasury center CFC borrows nonfunctional currency from related or unrelated parties and makes loans denominated in that nonfunctional currency to a related CFC, the foreign currency gain or loss attributable to the principal amount borrowed by the treasury center CFC will economically offset all or a portion of the foreign currency loss or gain, respectively, attributable to the lending activity. Similarly, the foreign currency gain or loss attributable to the treasury center CFC's accrual of interest income and expense with respect to its lending and borrowing activities, respectively, will offset each other, in whole or in part. Thus, by borrowing and lending in the same nonfunctional currency, a treasury center CFC is said to be "naturally hedged."

Although the borrowing and lending in the same nonfunctional currency are economically offsetting, section 475 creates the potential for a mismatch of gains and losses for a treasury center CFC. If the treasury center CFC qualifies as a dealer under section 475, for example because it regularly purchases debt from related CFCs in the ordinary course of a trade or business, the treasury center CFC generally must use a mark-to-market method of accounting for its securities. *See* section 475 and § 1.475(c)- 1(a)(3)(i). However, § 1.475(c)-2(a)(2) provides that a dealer's own issued debt liabilities are not securities for purposes of section 475. Consequently, a treasury center CFC that marks to market its assets but not its liabilities may recognize any offsetting foreign currency gains and losses in different taxable years. To avoid this mismatch, taxpayers have taken positions that match a treasury center CFC's foreign currency gains and losses under a variety of theories. No inference is intended in these proposed regulations as to whether these positions are permissible in the years prior to the application of these proposed regulations.

C. Foreign Currency Gain or Loss on Interest-Bearing Liabilities and Related Hedging Transactions

As explained in Part A.3 of this Background section, the business needs exclusion does not apply to foreign currency gain or loss with respect to a transaction or property if any subpart F income arises, or could reasonably be expected to arise, from the transaction or property. § 1.954-2(g)(2)(ii)(B)(2). However, § 1.954-2(g)(2)(iii) provides a special rule for foreign currency gain or loss arising from an interest-bearing liability. Under § 1.954-2(g)(2)(iii), such foreign currency gain or loss generally is characterized as subpart F income and non-subpart F income in the same manner that interest expense associated with the liability would be allocated and apportioned between subpart F income and non-subpart F income under § § 1.861-9T and 1.861-12T. Section 1.954-2(g) does not provide a corresponding rule for a bona fide hedging transaction with respect to an interest-bearing liability. However, § 1.861-9T(b)(2) and (b)(6) provide rules that allocate foreign currency gain or loss on certain hedging transactions in the same manner as interest expense. A foreign currency gain or loss arising from a transaction that hedges an interest-bearing liability and that is not governed by § 1.861-9T is subject to the general rule of § 1.954-2(g)(2)(ii)(B)(2) and its "cliff effect." Consequently, although the foreign currency gain or loss on the hedge of an interest-bearing liability economically offsets the foreign currency loss or gain on that liability, the interaction of the regulations under sections 861 and 954 could result in different allocations of foreign currency gains and losses between subpart F income and non-subpart F income.

D. Elections to Treat Foreign Currency Gain or Loss as a Specific Category of Subpart F Income or FBCI or FPHCI

Section 1.954-2 provides two elections with respect to foreign currency gains or losses. Under the first election, the controlling United States shareholders of a CFC may elect to include foreign currency gain or loss that relates to a specific category of subpart F income or, in the case of FBCI, a specific subcategory of FBCI described in § 1.954-1(c)(1)(iii)(A)(*1*) or (*2*), in that category of subpart F income or FBCI, rather than in FPHCI. *See* § 1.954-2(g)(3). Thus, for example, under this election, foreign currency gain or loss on a transaction that hedges currency risk with respect to transactions that result in foreign base company sales income would be included in the foreign base company sales income category for purposes of determining subpart F income. This election associates foreign currency gain or loss that otherwise would be included in the computation of FPHCI with the categories of subpart F income and foreign base company income to which it relates and allows net foreign currency losses with respect to a category to reduce the income in that category. For this treatment to apply, however, the relationship between the foreign currency gain or loss and the category of income must be clearly determinable from the CFC's records. *See* § 1.954-2(g)(3)(i)(A).

Under the second election, the controlling United States shareholders of a CFC may elect to include in the computation of FPHCI all foreign currency gain or loss attributable to any section 988 transaction (except a transaction in which gain or loss is treated as capital gain or loss under section 988(a)(1)(B)) and to certain section 1256 contracts. *See* § 1.954-2(g)(4). When this election is in effect, net foreign currency loss reduces gross income in other categories of FPHCI. Controlling United States shareholders typically make the § 1.954-2(g)(4) election if a CFC has relatively little net foreign currency gain or loss. In those circumstances, the administrative burden of tracing foreign currency gain and loss to specific transactions or property, as is required under the business needs exclusion and the § 1.954-2(g)(3) election, may outweigh the benefit of those provisions. As the CFC's foreign currency gain or loss becomes more significant, the net benefit of the business needs exclusion or the § 1.954-2(g)(3) election may increase and the relative benefit of the § 1.954-2(g)(4) election may decrease.

Explanation of Provisions

A. *Business Needs Exclusion*

1. Transactions and property that give rise to both subpart F income and non-subpart F income

The Treasury Department and the IRS believe that foreign currency gain or loss arising from a transaction or property, or from a bona hedging transaction with respect to such a transaction or property, should be eligible for the business needs exclusion to the extent the transaction or property generates non-subpart F income. Accordingly, proposed § 1.954-2(g)(2)(ii)(C)(1) provides that foreign currency gain or loss attributable to a transaction or property that gives rise to both subpart F income and non-subpart F income, and that otherwise satisfies the requirements of the business needs exclusion, is allocated between subpart F income and non-subpart F income in the same proportion as the income from the underlying transaction or property. As a result, the amount of foreign currency gain or loss allocable to non-subpart F income qualifies for the business needs exclusion, and the amount allocable to subpart F income is taken into account in computing FPHCI. Under proposed § 1.954-2(g)(2)(ii)(C)(1), the entire foreign currency gain or loss arising from property that does not give rise to income (as defined in § 1.954-2(e)(3)), or from a bona fide hedging transaction with respect to such property, is attributable to subpart F income because any gain upon a disposition of such property would be subpart F income.

2. Hedges of net investment in a QBU

The Treasury Department and the IRS believe that a transaction that manages exchange rate risk with respect to a CFC's net investment in a QBU that is not treated as a separate entity for federal income tax purposes should qualify for the business needs exclusion to the extent the underlying property of the QBU does not give rise to subpart F income. Accordingly, proposed § 1.954-2(g)(2)(ii)(C)(2) provides that the qualifying portion of any foreign currency gain or loss that arises from a "financial statement hedging transaction" with respect to a QBU and that is allocable to non-subpart F income is directly related to the business needs of a CFC. A financial statement hedging transaction is defined as a transaction that is entered into by a CFC for the purpose of managing exchange rate risk with respect to part or all of that CFC's net investment in a QBU that is included in the consolidated financial statements of a United States shareholder of the CFC or a corporation that directly or indirectly owns such United States shareholder. The qualifying portion is defined as the amount of foreign currency gain or loss arising from a financial statement hedging transaction that is properly accounted for under U.S. GAAP as a cumulative foreign currency translation adjustment to shareholders' equity. The qualifying portion of any foreign currency gain or loss arising from a financial statement hedging transaction must be allocated between subpart F income and non-subpart F income using the principles of § 1.987-6(b). The amount of the qualifying portion allocated to non-subpart F income qualifies for the business needs exclusion.

The proposed amendment to § 1.446-4(a), discussed in Part B.1 of this Explanation of Provisions section, provides that a bona fide hedging transaction (as defined in § 1.954-2(a)(4)(ii)) is subject to the hedge timing rules of § 1.446-4. Additionally, as noted earlier, proposed § 1.954-2(g)(2)(ii)(C)(2) provides that part or all of the qualifying portion of any foreign currency gain or loss arising from a financial statement hedging transaction is eligible for the business needs exclusion. However, financial statement hedging transactions are not included in the definition of bona fide hedging transaction under § 1.954-2(a)(4)(ii), as proposed to be amended pursuant to these proposed regulations. Thus, foreign currency gain or loss arising from a financial statement hedging transaction is not subject to the hedge timing rules of § 1.446-4 and is taken into account in accordance with the taxpayer's method of accounting. Generally, a taxpayer's financial statement hedging transaction is a section 988 transaction with respect to the taxpayer. Accordingly, to the extent that the taxpayer elects to use a mark-to-market method of accounting for section 988 gain or loss under proposed § 1.988-7, and also makes the annual deemed termination election described in § 1.987-8T(d), the taxpayer generally would recognize annually foreign currency gain or loss from both the financial statement hedging transaction and the QBU with respect to which exchange rate risk is managed. The Treasury Department and the IRS request comments regarding whether the hedge timing rules of § 1.446-4 should apply to a financial statement hedging transaction (as defined in proposed § 1.954-2(g)(2)(ii)(C)(2)) with respect to section 987 QBUs with respect to which no annual deemed termination election is in effect, and, if so, how the appropriate matching should be achieved.

The Treasury Department and the IRS also request comments regarding whether the business needs exclusion should apply to a transaction that is entered into for the purpose of managing the risk of foreign currency fluctuation with respect to a CFC's net investment in a subsidiary CFC. Comments are requested regarding how the gain or loss on such a transaction could or should be allocated between subpart F and non-subpart F income and whether and how the gain or loss could or should be matched with the foreign currency gain or loss on the "hedged" item.

The Treasury Department and the IRS are aware that a CFC may enter into a transaction that manages exchange rate risk arising from a disregarded loan to a QBU. The Treasury Department and the IRS understand that, for U.S. GAAP purposes, exchange gain or loss with respect to a transaction that manages exchange rate risk with respect to the disregarded loan generally would not be reflected as a cumulative foreign currency translation adjustment. For federal income tax purposes, the loan would be disregarded, and exchange gain or loss on the hedging transaction potentially could be subpart F income. The Treasury Department and the IRS request comments regarding whether, taking into account the amendments in the proposed regulations, additional amendments to the business needs exclusion are appropriate to account for foreign currency gain or loss arising from a transaction that is entered into for the purpose of managing the risk of foreign currency fluctuation with respect to disregarded transactions, including disregarded loans, between a CFC and its QBU. Specifically, comments are requested regarding how the foreign currency gain or loss on such a hedging transaction could or should be allocated between subpart F and non-subpart F income and when such foreign currency gain or should be recognized.

B. *Timing of Foreign Currency Gains and Losses*

1. Extension of § 1.446-4 hedge timing rules to bona fide hedging transactions

The proposed amendment to § 1.446-4(a) extends the hedge timing rules of § 1.446-4 to all bona fide hedging transactions as defined in § 1.954-2(a)(4)(ii). Although this amendment will be particularly useful in connection with foreign currency gains and losses from bona fide hedging transactions of treasury center CFCs, the amendment will eliminate timing mismatches for gains and losses arising from all bona fide hedging transactions and from the hedged property or transaction.

In addition, proposed § 1.954-2(a)(4)(ii) revises the definition of a bona fide hedging transaction to permit the acquisition of a debt instrument by a CFC to be treated as a bona fide hedging transaction with respect to an interest-bearing liability of the CFC, provided that the acquisition of the debt instrument has the effect of managing the CFC's exchange rate risk with respect to the liability within the meaning of § 1.1221-2(c)(4) and (d), determined without regard to § 1.1221-2(d)(5), and otherwise meets the requirements of a bona fide hedging transaction. If a CFC, including a treasury center CFC, identifies a debt instrument that manages exchange rate risk as a hedge of an interest-bearing liability, the foreign currency gain or loss arising from that debt instrument will be taken into account under § 1.446-4 at the same time as the foreign currency gain or loss arising from the hedged interest-bearing liability.

Treating a debt instrument as a hedge of an interest-bearing liability, rather than treating the interest-bearing liability as a hedge of the debt instrument, is consistent with the principles underlying § 1.861-9T(b)(2), which allocates and apportions foreign currency gain or losses on a transaction that hedges an interest-bearing liability in the same manner as interest expense with respect to the liability is allocated and apportioned. See part C of this Explanation of Provisions section for further discussion of the impact of this rule on the allocation of foreign currency gain or loss on a debt instrument between subpart F income and non-subpart F income.

2. Elective mark-to-market method of accounting for foreign currency gain and loss

Proposed § 1.988-7 permits a taxpayer, including a CFC, to elect to use a mark-to-market method of accounting for section 988 gain or loss with respect to section 988 transactions, including becoming an obligor under an interest-bearing liability. This elective mark-to-market method of accounting takes into account only changes in the value of the section 988 transaction attributable to exchange rate fluctuations and does not take into account changes in value due to other factors, such as changes in market interest rates or the creditworthiness of the borrower. The proposed regulations require appropriate adjustments to be made to prevent section 988 gain or loss taken into account under the mark-to-market method of accounting from being taken into account again under section 988 or another provision of the Code.

This election is available to any taxpayer but is expected to be particularly relevant in the case of a treasury center CFC. A treasury center CFC that uses a mark-to-market method for securities under section 475 and that makes the election under proposed § 1.988-7 will be able to match the timing of foreign currency gain or loss with respect to an interest-bearing liability (such as a loan from a related or unrelated party) with economically offsetting foreign currency loss or gain arising from its nonfunctional currency-denominated assets (such as a receivable from a related party). Whether the corresponding foreign currency gains and losses qualify for the business needs exclusion is determined under the rules of § 1.954-2(g)(2), as proposed to be amended pursuant to these proposed regulations. Thus, if the foreign currency gains or losses do not fully offset each other, the difference may increase or decrease the CFC's FPHCI. However, the election under proposed § 1.988-7 does not apply to the following: (1) any securities that are marked to market under any other provision; (2) any securities that, pursuant to an election or an identification made by the taxpayer, are excepted from mark-to-market treatment under any other provision; (3) any transactions of a QBU that is subject to section 987; or (4) any section 988 transactions denominated in, or determined by reference to, a hyperinflationary currency.

The election applies for the year in which the election is made and all subsequent taxable years unless it is revoked by the Commissioner or the taxpayer or, in the case of a CFC, the controlling domestic shareholders of the CFC. Proposed § 1.988-7(d) permits a taxpayer or CFC to revoke the election to use a mark-to-market method of accounting for foreign currency gains or losses on section 988 transactions at any time. A subsequent election cannot be made until the sixth taxable year following the year of revocation and cannot be revoked until the sixth taxable year following the year of such subsequent election.

C. *Hedges of Exchange Rate Risk Arising from an Interest-Bearing Liability*

The Treasury Department and the IRS believe that it is appropriate to require foreign currency gain or loss from transactions that have the effect of managing exchange rate risk arising from an interest-bearing liability to be allocated between subpart F income and non-subpart F income in the same manner as the foreign currency gain or loss on the hedged liability. Accordingly, the proposed amendments to § 1.954-2(g)(2)(iii) require foreign currency gains and losses arising from a transaction or property (including debt instruments) that manages exchange rate risk with respect to an interest-bearing liability to be allocated and apportioned between subpart F income and non-subpart F income in the same manner that foreign currency gain or loss from the interest-bearing liability would be allocated and apportioned. As noted in Part B.1 of this Explanation of Provisions, the proposed amendment to § 1.954-2(a)(4)(ii) revises the definition of a bona fide hedging transaction to permit the acquisition of a debt instrument by a CFC to be treated as a bona fide hedging transaction with respect to an interest-bearing liability of the CFC under certain circumstances. As a result of that proposed amendment and the amendment described in this Part C, if a CFC identifies a debt instrument that manages exchange rate risk as a hedge of an interest-bearing liability, the foreign currency gain or loss arising from that debt instrument will be allocated between subpart F income and non-subpart F income in the same manner as the foreign currency gain or loss arising from the hedged interest-bearing liability. Thus, the proposed amendments to the regulations permit a CFC that timely and properly identifies a debt instrument as a hedge of an interest-bearing liability to alleviate the character mismatch that may occur under the existing regulations, as described in Part C of the Background section of this preamble. The proposed amendments to § 1.954-2(g)(2)(iii) also clarify that the special rules in that paragraph apply to foreign currency gain or loss arising from an interest-bearing liability, or from a bona fide hedging transaction with respect to the liability, in lieu of the general rule of the business needs exclusion in § 1.954-2(g)(2)(ii).

D. *Revocation of Election to Treat Foreign Currency Gain or Loss as a Specific Category of Subpart F Income or as FPHCI*

Proposed § 1.954-2(g)(3)(iii) permits a CFC to revoke its election under § 1.954-2(g)(3) (to characterize foreign currency gain or loss that arises from a specific category of subpart F income as gain or loss in that category) at any time without securing the prior consent of the Commissioner. Similarly, proposed § 1.954-2(g)(4)(iii) permits a CFC to revoke its election under § 1.954-2(g)(4) (to treat all foreign currency gain or loss as FPHCI) at any time without securing the prior consent of the Commissioner. The Treasury Department and the IRS remain concerned about CFCs frequently changing these elections without a substantial business reason but also believe that the ability of a taxpayer to automatically revoke these elections would promote sound tax administration. Therefore, the proposed regulations provide that, if an election has been revoked under proposed § 1.954-2(g)(3)(iii) or proposed § 1.954-2(g)(4)(iii), a subsequent election cannot be made until the sixth taxable year following the year of revocation and any subsequent election cannot be revoked until the sixth year following the year of such subsequent election.

E. *Applicability Dates*

The proposed amendments generally are proposed to apply to taxable years ending on or after the date the proposed regulations are published as final regulations in the *Federal Register*. However, the proposed amendments to § § 1.446-4(a), 1.954-2(a)(4)(ii)(A), 1.954-2(g)(2)(ii)(C)(1), and 1.954-2(g)(2)(iii) are proposed to apply to bona fide hedging transactions entered into on or after the date the proposed regulations are published as final regulations in the *Federal Register*. A taxpayer may rely on any of the proposed amendments, other than the amendments to § § 1.446-4(a), 1.954-2(a)(4)(ii)(A), 1.954-2(g)(2)(ii)(C)(1), and 1.954-2(g)(2)(iii), insofar as each applies to a bona fide hedging transaction, for taxable years ending on or after December 19, 2017, provided the taxpayer consistently applies the proposed amendment for all such taxable years that end before the first taxable year ending on or after the date the proposed regulations are published as final regulations in the *Federal Register*. A taxpayer may rely on any of the proposed amendments to § § 1.446-4(a), 1.954-2(a)(4)(ii)(A), 1.954-2(g)(2)(ii)(C)(1), and 1.954-2(g)(2)(iii) with respect to a bona fide hedging transaction entered into on or after December 19, 2017 and prior to the applicability date, provided the taxpayer consistently applies the proposed amendment to all bona fide hedging transactions entered into on or after December 19, 2017 and prior to the date that these regulations are published as final regulations in the *Federal Register*.

Special Analyses

Certain IRS regulations, including these, are exempt from the requirements of Executive Order 12866, as supplemented and reaffirmed by Executive Order 13563. Therefore, a regulatory impact assessment is not required. It is hereby certified that the collection of information requirement will not have a significant economic impact on a substantial number of small entities. This certification is based on the fact that these regulations primarily will affect domestic corporations that have foreign operations, which tend to be larger businesses, and that the average burden is minimal. Accordingly, the Regulatory Flexibility Act (5 U.S.C. chapter 6) does not apply. Pursuant to section 7805(f), this notice of proposed rulemaking has been submitted to the Chief Counsel for Advocacy of the Small Business Administration for comment on its impact on small business.

Comments and Requests for Public Hearing

Before these proposed regulations are adopted as final regulations, consideration will be given to any comments that are submitted timely to the IRS as prescribed in this preamble under "ADDRESSES." The Treasury Department and the IRS request comments on all aspects of the proposed rules. All comments will be available at *www.regulations.gov* or upon request. A public hearing will be scheduled if requested in writing by any person that timely submits comments. If a public hearing is scheduled, notice of the date, time, and place for the public hearing will be published in the *Federal Register*.

Drafting Information

The principal author of these regulations is Jeffery G. Mitchell of the Office of Associate Chief Counsel (International). However, other personnel from the IRS and the Treasury Department participated in their development.

[¶ 49,755] Proposed Amendments of Regulations (REG-132197-17), published in the Federal Register on February 15, 2018.

[Code Secs. 42, 46, 56, 56A, 61, 72, 78, 101, 103, 105, 148, 149, 150, 162, 165, 166, 168, 178, 244, 274, 381, 401, 402, 403, 404, 410, 411, 412, 414, 416, 453, 453A, 475, 501, 503, 593, 643, 665, 667, 704, 802, 803, 806, 809, 810, 815, 822, 831, 832, 856, 861, 871, 902, 921, 922, 923, 924, 925, 926, 927, 951, 962, 964, 1038, 1223, 1232, 1402, 3501, 4972, 4981, 6012, 6035, 6048, 6050H, 6071, 6072, 6091, 6096, 6501, 6511, 6723 and Statement of Procedural Rules Sec. 601.201]

Internal Revenue Service: Regulation repeal: Obsolete regulations: Unnecessary regulations.—Amendments of §§1.921-1T and 1.921-2, removing 298 regulations that are no longer necessary because they do not have any current or future applicability under the Internal Revenue Code (Code) and amending 79 regulations to reflect the proposed removal of the 298 regulations, are proposed. Proposed amendments to Reg. §§1.42-2, 1.46-11, 1.56-1, 1.56A-1, 1.56A-2, 1.56A-3, 1.56A-4, 1.56A-5, 1.56(g)-1, 1.61-2T, 1.61-21, 1.72-15, 1.72-17A, 1.72-18, 1.78-1, 1.101-5, 1.101-6(a), 1.132-1, 1.148-1A, 1.148-2A, 1.148-3A, 1.148-4A, 1.148-5A, 1.148-6A, 1.148-9A, 1.148-10A, 1.149(d)-1A, 1.150-1A, 1.162-25T, 1.165-13T, 1.166-4, 1.168(f)(8)-1T, 1.178-2, 1.178-3, 1.244-1, 1.244-2, 1.274-6T, 1.381(c)(11)-1, 1.401-1, 1.401-4, 1.401-10, 1.401-11, 1.401-12, 1.401-13, Reg. §1.401(e)-1—1.401(e)-6, 1.401(f)-1, 1.402(a)-1, 1.402(e)-1, 1.403(a)-1, 1.404(a)-1, 1.404(a)-2, 1.404(a)-2A, 1.404(a)-3, 1.404(a)-4, 1.404(a)-5, 1.404(a)-6, 1.404(a)-7, 1.404(a)-8, 1.404(a)-9, 1.404(a)-10, 1.404(a)(8)-1T, 1.404(e)-1A, 1.410(a)-1, 1.410(b)-0, 1.410(b)-1, 1.411(a)-1, 1.411(a)-5, 1.411(a)-9, 1.411(d)-2, 1.411(d)-5, 1.412(b)-5, 1.412(c)(1)-3T, 1.412(l)(7)-1, 1.414(r)-8, 1.416-1, 1.453-4, 1.453-5, 1.453-6, 1.453-10, 1.453A-0, 1.453A-1, 1.453A-2, 1.475-0, 1.475(b)-4, 1.501(c)(17)-1, 1.501(c)(18)-1, 1.501(k)-1, 1.503(c)-1, 1.503(e)-4, 1.593-1,

1.593-2, 1.593-3, 1.593-4, 1.593-5, 1.593-6, 1.593-7, 1.593-8, 1.593-10, 1.593-11, 1.643(d)-1, 1.665(f)-1A, 1.665(g)-1A, 1.667(a)-1A, 1.802-2, 1.802-3, 1.802-4, 1.802-5, 1.802(b)-1, 1.803-1—1.803-7, 1.806-1, 1.806-2, 1.809-1, 1.809-2, 1.809-3, 1.809-5, 1.809-7, 1.809-8, 1.810-1, 1.810-2, 1.810-4, 1.815-5, Reg. §1.822-1—1.822-3, 1.822-4, 1.822-8, 1.822-12, 1.831-2, 1.831-4, 1.832-7T, 1.861-9T, 1.871-1, 1.902-3, 1.921-3T, 1.922-1, 1.923-1T, 1.924(a)-1T, 1.924(c)-1, 1.924(d)-1, 1.924(e)-1, 1.925(a)-1, 1.925(a)-1T, 1.925(b)-1T, 1.926(a)-1, 1.926(a)-1T, 1.927(b)-1T, 1.927(d)-1, 1.927(e)-1, 1.927(e)-2T, 1.927(f)-1, 1.951-2, 1.962-1, 1.962-2, 1.962-4, 1.964-4, 1.1038-1, 1.1223-1, 1.1232-1, 1.1232-2, 1.1232-4, 1.1402(g)-1, 1.6012-2, 1.6012-4, 1.6035-1, 1.6035-3, 1.6050H-1, 1.6050H-1T, 1.6050H-2, 1.6071-1, 1.6072-4, 1.6091-1, 5.856-1, 5c.103-1, 5c.103-2, 5c.103-3, 5c.168(f)(8)-1, 5c.168(f)(8)-2, 5c.168(f)(8)-3, 5c.168(f)(8)-4, 5c.168(f)(8)-5, 5c.168(f)(8)-6, 5c.168(f)(8)-7, 5c.168(f)(8)-8, 5c.168(f)(8)-9, 5c.168(f)(8)-10, 5c.168(f)(8)-11, 5f.103-3, 5f.168(f)(8)-1, 7.105-1, 7.105-2, 7.704-1, 11.402(e)(4)(A)-1, 11.402(e)(4)(B)-1, 16.3-1, 31.3501(a)-1T, 54.4972-1, 55.4981-1, 55.4981-2, 301.6048-1, 301.6096-2, 301.6501(o)-1, 301.6501(o)-2, 301.6501(o)-3, 301.6511(d)-7, 301.6511(g)-1, 301.6723-1A, 404.6048-1 and 601.201 adopted by T.D. 9849 on March 11, 2019.

AGENCY: Internal Revenue Service (IRS), Treasury.

ACTION: Notice of proposed rulemaking.

SUMMARY: Pursuant to the policies stated in Executive Orders 13777 and 13789 (the executive orders), the Treasury Department and the IRS conducted a review of existing regulations, with the goal of reducing regulatory burden for taxpayers by revoking or revising existing tax regulations that meet the criteria set forth in the executive orders. This notice of proposed rulemaking proposes to streamline IRS regulations by removing 298 regulations that are no longer necessary because they do not have any current or future applicability under the Internal Revenue Code (Code) and by amending 79 regulations to reflect the proposed removal of the 298 regulations. The proposed removal and amendment of these regulations may affect various categories of taxpayers.

DATES: Written or electronic comments and requests for a public hearing must be received by May 14, 2018.

ADDRESSES: Send submissions to: CC:PA:LPD:PR (REG-132197-17), room 5203, Internal Revenue Service, P.O. Box 7604, Ben Franklin Station, Washington, DC 20044. Submissions may be hand-delivered between the hours of 8 a.m. and 4 p.m. to CC:PA:LPD:PR (REG-132197-17), Courier's Desk, Internal Revenue Service, 1111 Constitution Avenue, NW, Washington, DC, or sent via the Federal eRulemaking Portal at *www.regulations.gov* (REG-132197-17).

FOR FURTHER INFORMATION CONTACT: Concerning the proposed regulations Mark A. Bond of the Office of Associate Chief Counsel (Procedure and Administration), (202) 317-6844; concerning the submission of comments and a request for a public hearing, Regina Johnson, (202) 317-6901 (not toll-free numbers).

SUPPLEMENTARY INFORMATION:

Background

On February 24, 2017, the President issued Executive Order 13777, Enforcing the Regulatory Reform Agenda (82 FR 12285). E.O. 13777 directed each agency to establish a Regulatory Reform Task Force. Each Regulatory Reform Task Force was directed to review existing regulations for regulations that: (i) Eliminate jobs, or inhibit job creation; (ii) are outdated, unnecessary, or ineffective; (iii) impose costs that exceed benefits; (iv) create a serious inconsistency or otherwise interfere with regulatory reform initiatives and policies; (v) are inconsistent with the requirements of the Information Quality Act (section 515 of the Treasury and General Government Appropriations Act of 2001) or OMB Information Quality Guidance issued pursuant to that provision; or (vi) derive from or implement Executive Orders or other Presidential directives that have been subsequently rescinded or substantially modified.

On April 21, 2017, the President issued Executive Order 13789, Presidential Executive Order on Identifying and Reducing Tax Regulatory Burdens (82 FR 19317). This executive order stated a policy that the "Federal tax system should be simple, fair, efficient, and pro-growth" and that "[t]he purposes of tax regulations should be to bring clarity to the already complex Internal Revenue Code . . . and to provide useful guidance to taxpayers." E.O. 13789 also directs that immediate action be taken to "reduce the burden existing tax regulations impose on American taxpayers and thereby to provide tax relief and useful, simplified tax guidance." To further this goal, the executive order directs the Secretary of the Treasury to review all significant tax regulations issued on or after January 1, 2016.

As required by E.O. 13789, on June 22, 2017, the Treasury Department issued an interim report (June report) identifying eight regulations to be revised or withdrawn. On October 2, 2017, the Treasury Department issued a second report (October report) recommending specific actions with respect to the regulations identified in the June report. In addition, in the October report the Treasury Department explained that "in furtherance of the policies stated in Executive Order 13789, Executive Order 13771, and Executive Order 13777, Treasury and the IRS have initiated a comprehensive review, coordinated by the Treasury Regulatory Reform Task Force, of all tax regulations, regardless of when they were issued . . . . This review will identify tax regulations that are unnecessary, create undue complexity, impose excessive burdens, or fail to provide clarity and useful guidance . . . ." In the October report, the Treasury Department noted that the IRS Office of Chief Counsel had already identified over 200 regulations for potential revocation. These regulations are in the Code of Federal Regulations (CFR) "but are, to varying degrees, unnecessary, duplicative, or obsolete, and force taxpayers to navigate unnecessarily complex or confusing rules." The October report also stated that the Treasury Department and the IRS expected to begin the rulemaking process of revoking these regulations in the fourth quarter of 2017.

This notice of proposed rulemaking proposes to remove 298 regulations that have no current or future applicability and, therefore, no longer provide useful guidance. Removing these regulations from the CFR will streamline title 26, Federal Tax Regulations; reduce the volume of regulations taxpayers need to review; and increase clarity of the tax law. The removal of these regulations is unrelated to the substance of rules in the regulations, and no negative inference regarding the stated rules should be made. These regulations are proposed to be removed from the CFR solely because the regulations have no current or future applicability. Removal of these regulations is not intended to alter any non-regulatory guidance that cites to or relies upon these regulations.

This notice of proposed rulemaking also proposes to amend 79 regulations to remove cross-references to the 298 regulations described above. These amendments will further streamline title 26 of the CFR, reduce the volume of regulations taxpayers need to review, and increase clarity of the tax law.

Explanation of Provisions

The tax regulations proposed to be removed fall into one of three categories. The first category includes regulations interpreting provisions of the Code that have been repealed. All of these regulations apply to provisions of the Code that no longer appear in title 26 of the United States Code. The second category includes regulations interpreting Code provisions that, while not repealed, have been significantly revised, and the existing regulations do not account for these statutory changes. To fall in this category, these statutory changes must have rendered the entire regulation inapplicable. The third category includes regulations that, by the terms of the relevant Code provisions or the regulations themselves, are no longer applicable. This category would include, for example, expired temporary regulations; a Code provision that only applies to returns filed before January 1, 1996; or regulations providing for a transition rule that applies only to transactions entered into between January 1, 2000, and March 1, 2001. The specific regulations that fall within each of these three categories are detailed below.

The 79 tax regulations proposed to be amended are regulations that make reference to the 298 tax regulations proposed to be removed. Each amendment removes one or more references to a regulation that is proposed to be removed. For example, §31.3121(b)(10)-1 is proposed to be amended to remove a reference to §31.3121(b)(8)-2, which is proposed to be removed. The proposed amendments also include proposed amendments to remove references to regulations in the authority citation for part 602 of title 26 of the CFR, OMB Control Numbers Under the Paperwork Reduction Act, in cases where regulations are proposed to be removed from the CFR and, in the case of §§1.103-15AT and 1.103-18 because these regulations were previously removed from the CFR without corresponding amendment to Part 602.

I. Regulations Interpreting Repealed Code Provisions

26 CFR Part 1

Treasury Regulations §§1.23-1 through 1.23-6. These regulations provide guidance under former section 23. Former section 23 was repealed by section 11801(a) of the Omnibus Budget Reconciliation Act of 1990, effective November 5, 1990. Public Law No. 101-508.

Treasury Regulations §1.46-11. These regulations provide guidance under former section 46. Former section 46 was repealed by section 11813 of the Omnibus Budget Reconciliation Act of 1990, effective generally with respect to property placed in service after December 31, 1990. Public Law No. 101-508.

Treasury Regulations §§1.56A-1 through 1.56A-5, 1.58-1, and 1.58-9. These regulations provide guidance relating to the alternative minimum tax under section 56A and former section 58. These regulations implement a version of the alternative minimum tax that was repealed by section 701(a) of the Tax Reform Act of 1986, effective for taxable years beginning after December 31, 1986. Public Law No. 99-514.

Treasury Regulations §1.101-5. These regulations provide guidance under section 101(e). Section 101(e) was repealed by section 421(b)(2) of the Deficit Reduction Act of 1984, generally effective for transfers after July 18, 1984, in taxable years ending after July 18, 1984. Public Law No. 98-369.

Treasury Regulations §1.103-2. These regulations provide guidance regarding the tax exemption for dividends from shares and stock of federal agencies or instrumentalities under former section 103. Former section 103 was repealed by section 6 of the Public Debt Act of 1942, effective for securities issued after March 28, 1942. Public Law No. 77-510.

Treasury Regulations §§1.103-3 through 1.103-6. These regulations provide guidance regarding the tax exemption for interest on United States obligations under former section 103. Former section 103 was repealed in part by section 4 of the Public Debt Act of 1941, effective for obligations issued on or after February 28, 1941. Public Law No. 77-7.

Treasury Regulations §1.168(f)(8)-1T. These regulations provide guidance under section 168(f)(8). Section 168(f)(8) was repealed by section 201(a) of the Tax Reform Act of 1986, effective with respect to property placed in service after December 31, 1986, in taxable years ending after December 31, 1986. Public Law No. 99-514.

Treasury Regulations § 1.177-1. These regulations provide guidance under section 177. Section 177 was repealed by section 241(a) of the Tax Reform Act of 1986, generally effective with respect to expenditures paid or incurred after December 31, 1986. Public Law No. 99-514.

Treasury Regulations § 1.179A-1. These regulations provide guidance under section 179A. Section 179A was repealed by section 221(a)(34)(A) of the Tax Increase Prevention Act of 2014, effective December 19, 2014. Public Law No. 113-295.

Treasury Regulations § § 1.244-1 and 1.244-2. These regulations provide guidance under section 244. Section 244 was repealed by section 221(a)(41)(A) of the Tax Increase Prevention Act of 2014, effective December 19, 2014. Public Law No. 113-295.

Treasury Regulations § § 1.341-1 through 1.341-7. These regulations provide guidance under section 341. Section 341 was temporarily repealed until December 31, 2010, by section 302(e)(4) of the Jobs and Growth Tax Relief and Reconciliation Act of 2003, effective for taxable years beginning after December 31, 2002. Public Law No. 108-27. Section 102 of the Tax Relief, Unemployment Insurance Reauthorization, and Job Creation Act of 2010, extended the repeal until December 31, 2012. Public Law No. 111-312. Section 102(a) of the American Taxpayer Relief Act of 2012 made the repeal of section 341 permanent. Public Law No. 112-240.

Treasury Regulations § § 1.405-1 through 1.405-3. These regulations provide guidance under section 405 relating to qualified bond purchase plans. Section 405 was repealed by section 491(a) of the Deficit Reduction Act of 1984, effective for obligations issued after December 31, 1983. Public Law No. 98-369.

Treasury Regulations § 1.501(k)-1. These regulations provide guidance under section 501(s) relating to nonexemption of Communist-controlled organizations. Section 501(s) was repealed by section 221(a)(62) of the Tax Increase Prevention Act of 2014, effective December 19, 2014. Public Law No. 113-295.

Treasury Regulations § § 1.551-3 through 1.551-5. These regulations provide guidance under section 551. Section 551 was repealed by section 413(a)(1) of the American Jobs Creation Act of 2004, effective for taxable years of foreign corporations beginning after December 31, 2004, and for taxable years of United States shareholders with or within which such taxable years of foreign corporations end. Public Law No. 108-357.

Treasury Regulations § § 1.552-1 through 1.552-5. These regulations provide guidance under section 552. Section 552 was repealed by section 413(a)(1) of the American Jobs Creation Act of 2004, effective for taxable years of foreign corporations beginning after December 31, 2004, and for taxable years of United States shareholders with or within which such taxable years of foreign corporations end. Public Law No. 108-357.

Treasury Regulations § 1.553-1. These regulations provide guidance under section 553. Section 553 was repealed by section 413(a)(1) of the American Jobs Creation Act of 2004, effective for taxable years of foreign corporations beginning after December 31, 2004, and for taxable years of United States shareholders with or within which such taxable years of foreign corporations end. Public Law No. 108-357.

Treasury Regulations § 1.554-1. These regulations provide guidance under section 554. Section 554 was repealed by section 413(a)(1) of the American Jobs Creation Act of 2004, effective for taxable years of foreign corporations beginning after December 31, 2004, and for taxable years of United States shareholders with or within which such taxable years of foreign corporations end. Public Law No. 108-357.

Treasury Regulations § § 1.555-1 and 1.555-2. These regulations provide guidance under section 555. Section 555 was repealed by section 413(a)(1) of the American Jobs Creation Act of 2004, effective for taxable years of foreign corporations beginning after December 31, 2004, and for taxable years of United States shareholders with or within which such taxable years of foreign corporations end. Public Law No. 108-357.

Treasury Regulations § § 1.556-1 through 1.556-3. These regulations implement section 556. Section 556 was repealed by section 413(a)(1) of the American Jobs Creation Act of 2004, effective for taxable years of foreign corporations beginning after December 31, 2004, and for taxable years of United States shareholders with or within which such taxable years of foreign corporations end. Public Law No. 108-357.

Treasury Regulations § § 1.586-1 and 1.586-2. These regulations provide guidance under section 586. Section 586 was repealed by section 901(c) of the Tax Reform Act of 1986, effective for taxable years beginning after December 31, 1986. Public Law No. 99-514.

Treasury Regulations § 1.595-1. These regulations provide guidance under section 595. Section 595 was repealed by section 1616(b)(8) of the Small Business Job Protection Act of 1996, effective for property acquired (by foreclosure or otherwise) in taxable years beginning after December 31, 1995. Public Law No. 104-188.

Treasury Regulations § 1.621-1. These regulations provide guidance under section 621. Section 621 was repealed by section 11801(a)(28) of the Omnibus Budget Reconciliation Act of 1990, effective November 5, 1990. Public Law No. 101-508.

Treasury Regulations § § 1.669(a)-1A, 1.669(b)-1A, 1.669(c)-1A through 1.669(c)-3A, 1.669(d)-1A, 1.669(e)-1A, 1.669(e)-2A, 1.669(f)-1A, and 1.669(f)-2A. These regulations provide guidance under section 669. Section 669 was repealed by section 701(d) of the Tax Reform Act of 1976, effective with respect to distributions made in taxable years beginning after December 31, 1975. Public Law No. 94-455.

Treasury Regulations §§1.802(b)-1, 1.802-2, and 1.802-4. These regulations provide guidance under section 802. Section 802 was repealed by section 211(a) of the Deficit Reduction Act of 1984, effective for taxable years beginning after December 31, 1983. Public Law No. 98-369.

Treasury Regulations §§1.806-1 and 1.806-2. These regulations provide guidance under former section 806. Former section 806 was repealed by section 211(a) of the Deficit Reduction Act of 1984, effective for taxable years beginning after December 31, 1983. Public Law No. 98-369.

Treasury Regulations §§1.809-1, 1.809-3, 1.809-7, and 1.809-8. These regulations provide guidance under former section 809 (as enacted by section 2(a) of the Life Insurance Company Income Tax Act of 1959, Pub. L. 86-69). Former section 809 was repealed and replaced with a new section 809 by section 211(a) of the Deficit Reduction Act of 1984, effective for taxable years beginning after December 31, 1983. Public Law No. 98-369.

Treasury Regulations §§1.809-9 and 1.809-10. These regulations provide guidance under section 809 (as enacted by section 211(a) of the Deficit Reduction Act of 1984, Pub. L. 98-369). Section 809 was repealed by section 205(a) of the Pension Funding Equity Act of 2004, effective for taxable years beginning after December 31, 2004. Public Law No. 108-218.

Treasury Regulations §§1.810-1 and 1.810-4. These regulations provide guidance under former section 810. Former section 810 was repealed by section 211(a) of the Deficit Reduction Act of 1984, effective for taxable years beginning after December 31, 1983. Public Law No. 98-369.

Treasury Regulations §§1.821-1 through 1.821-5. These regulations provide guidance under section 821. Section 821 was repealed by section 1024(a)(1) of the Tax Reform Act of 1986, effective for taxable years beginning after December 31, 1986. Public Law No. 99-514.

Treasury Regulations §§1.823-1 through 1.823-8. These regulations provide guidance under section 823. Section 823 was repealed by section 1024(a)(1) of the Tax Reform Act of 1986, effective for taxable years beginning after December 31, 1986. Public Law No. 99-514.

Treasury Regulations §§1.825-1 through 1.825-3. These regulations provide guidance under section 825. Section 825 was repealed by section 1024(a)(1) of the Tax Reform Act of 1986, effective for taxable years beginning after December 31, 1986. Public Law No. 99-514.

Treasury Regulations §§1.921-1T through 1.921-3T. These regulations provide guidance under section 921. Section 921 was repealed by section 2 of the FSC Repeal and Extraterritorial Income Exclusion Act of 2000, effective for transactions after September 30, 2000. Public Law No. 106-519.

Treasury Regulations §1.922-1. These regulations provide guidance under section 922. Section 922 was repealed by section 2 of the FSC Repeal and Extraterritorial Income Exclusion Act of 2000, effective for transactions after September 30, 2000. Public Law No. 106-519.

Treasury Regulations §1.923-1T. These regulations provide guidance under section 923. Section 923 was repealed by section 2 of the FSC Repeal and Extraterritorial Income Exclusion Act of 2000, effective for transactions after September 30, 2000. Public Law No. 106-519.

Treasury Regulations §§1.924(a)-1T, 1.924(c)-1, 1.924(d)-1, and 1.924(e)-1. These regulations provide guidance under section 924. Section 924 was repealed by section 2 of the FSC Repeal and Extraterritorial Income Exclusion Act of 2000, effective for transactions after September 30, 2000. Public Law No. 106-519.

Treasury Regulations §§1.925(a)-1, 1.925(a)-1T, and 1.925(b)-1T. These regulations provide guidance under section 925. Section 925 was repealed by section 2 of the FSC Repeal and Extraterritorial Income Exclusion Act of 2000, effective for transactions after September 30, 2000. Public Law No. 106-519.

Treasury Regulations §§1.926(a)-1 and 1.926(a)-1T. These regulations provide guidance under section 926. Section 926 was repealed by section 2 of the FSC Repeal and Extraterritorial Income Exclusion Act of 2000, effective for transactions after September 30, 2000. Public Law No. 106-519.

Treasury Regulations §§1.927(b)-1T, 1.927(d)-1, 1.927(e)-1, 1.927(e)-2T, and 1.927(f)-1. These regulations provide guidance under section 927. Section 927 was repealed by section 2 of the FSC Repeal and Extraterritorial Income Exclusion Act of 2000, effective for transactions after September 30, 2000. Public Law No. 106-519.

Treasury Regulations §§1.941-1 through 1.941-3. These regulations provide guidance under former section 941. Former section 941 was repealed by section 1053(c) of the Tax Reform Act of 1976, effective for taxable years beginning after December 31, 1975. Public Law No. 94-455.

Treasury Regulations §1.943-1. These regulations provide guidance under former section 943. Former section 943 was repealed by section 1053(c) of the Tax Reform Act of 1976, effective for taxable years beginning after December 31, 1975. Public Law No. 94-455.

Treasury Regulations §1.951-2. These regulations coordinate section 951 with section 1247(a). Section 1247 was repealed by section 413(a)(3) of the American Jobs Creation Act of 2004, effective for taxable years of foreign corporations beginning after December 31, 2004, and for taxable years of United States shareholders with or within which such taxable years of foreign corporations end. Public Law No. 108-357.

Treasury Regulations §§1.963-1, 1.963-4, 1.963-5, 1.963-7, and 1.963-8. These regulations provide guidance under section 963. Section 963 was repealed by section 602(a)(1) of the Tax Reduction Act of 1975, effective for taxable years of foreign corporations beginning after December 31, 1975, and for taxable years of United States shareholders with or within which such taxable years of foreign corporations end. Public Law No. 94-12.

Treasury Regulations § 1.1034-1. These regulations provide guidance under section 1034. Section 1034 was repealed by section 312(b) of the Taxpayer Relief Act of 1997, effective generally for sales and exchanges after May 6, 1997. Public Law No. 105-34.

Treasury Regulations § § 1.1232-2 and 1.1232-4. These regulations provide guidance under sections 1232 and 1232B. Sections 1232 and 1232B were repealed by section 42(a)(1) of the Deficit Reduction Act of 1984, effective for taxable years ending after July 18, 1984. Public Law No. 98-369.

Treasury Regulations § § 1.1247-1 through 1.1247-5. These regulations provide guidance under section 1247. Section 1247 was repealed by section 413(a)(3) of the American Jobs Creation Act of 2004, effective for taxable years of foreign corporations beginning after December 31, 2004, and for taxable years of United States shareholders with or within which such taxable years of foreign corporations end. Public Law No. 108-357.

Treasury Regulations § 1.1491-1. These regulations provide guidance under section 1491. Section 1491 was repealed by section 1131(a) of the Taxpayer Relief Act of 1997, effective August 5, 1997. Public Law No. 105-34.

Treasury Regulations § 1.1492-1. These regulations provide guidance under section 1492. Section 1492 was repealed by section 1131(a) of the Taxpayer Relief Act of 1997, effective August 5, 1997. Public Law No. 105-34.

Treasury Regulations § 1.1493-1. These regulations provide guidance under section 1493. Section 1493 was repealed by section 103 of the Foreign Investors Tax Act of 1966, effective for taxable years beginning after December 31, 1966. Public Law No. 89-809.

Treasury Regulations § § 1.1494-1 and 1.1494-2. These regulations provide guidance under section 1494. Section 1494 was repealed by section 1131(a) of the Taxpayer Relief Act of 1997, effective August 5, 1997. Public Law No. 105-34.

Treasury Regulations § § 1.6035-1 and 1.6035-3. These regulations provide guidance under former section 6035. Former section 6035 was repealed by section 413(c)(26) of the American Jobs Creation Act of 2004, effective for taxable years of foreign corporations beginning after December 31, 2004, and for taxable years of United States shareholders with or within which such taxable years of foreign corporations end. Public Law No. 108-357.

26 CFR Part 5c

Treasury Regulations § § 5c.103-1 through 5c.103-3. These regulations provide guidance relating to section 168(f)(8). Section 168(f)(8) was repealed by section 201(a) of the Tax Reform Act of 1986, effective with respect to property placed in service after December 31, 1986, in taxable years ending after December 31, 1986. Public Law No. 99-514.

Treasury Regulations § § 5c.168(f)(8)-1 through 5c.168(f)(8)-11. These regulations provide guidance under section 168(f)(8). Section 168(f)(8) was repealed by section 201(a) of the Tax Reform Act of 1986, effective with respect to property placed in service after December 31, 1986, in taxable years ending after December 31, 1986. Public Law No. 99-514.

26 CFR Part 5f

Treasury Regulations § 5f.168(f)(8)-1. These regulations implement the transitional rules provided by section 208(d)(2) and (3) of the Tax Equity and Fiscal Responsibility Act of 1982, Public Law No. 97-248, for certain safe harbor leases under section 168(f)(8). Section 168(f)(8) was repealed by section 201(a) of the Tax Reform Act of 1986, effective with respect to property placed in service after December 31, 1986, in taxable years ending after December 31, 1986. Public Law No. 99-514.

26 CFR Part 7

Treasury Regulations § § 7.105-1 and 7.105-2. These regulations provide guidance under section 105(d) relating to the taxation of disability payments. Section 105(d) was repealed by section 122(b) of the Social Security Amendments of 1983, effective for taxable years beginning after December 31, 1983. Public Law No. 98-21.

26 CFR Part 31

Treasury Regulations § 31.3121(a)(9)-1. These regulations provide guidance under section 3121(a)(9) relating to payments to employees for nonwork periods. Section 3121(a)(9) was repealed by section 324(a)(3)(B) of the Social Security Amendments of 1983, effective with respect to remuneration paid after December 31, 1983. Public Law No. 98-21.

Treasury Regulations § § 31.3121(k)-1 through 31.3121(k)-4. These regulations implement section 3121(k) and provide guidance on the constructive filing of waivers of exemption from social security taxes by certain tax-exempt organizations. Section 3121(k) was repealed by section 102(b)(2) of the Social Security Amendments of 1983, effective April 20, 1983. Public Law No. 98-21.

26 CFR Part 48

Treasury Regulations § 48.4041-18. These regulations provide guidance under section 4041(k). Section 4041(k) was repealed by section 301(c)(6) of the American Jobs Creation Act of 2004, effective for fuel sold or used after December 31, 2004. Public Law No. 108-357.

Treasury Regulations § 48.4091-3. These regulations provide guidance under section 4091. Section 4091 was repealed by section 853(d)(1) of the American Jobs Creation Act of 2004, effective with respect to aviation-grade kerosene removed, entered, or sold after December 31, 2004. Public Law No. 108-357.

26 CFR Part 49

Treasury Regulations §§49.4263-1 through 49.4263-4. These regulations provide rules relating to commutation tickets, transportation payments not exceeding $0.60, air transportation provided to certain organizations, and services provided to members of the armed forces under former section 4263. Former section 4263 was repealed by section 205(c)(1) of the Airport and Airway Development Act of 1970, effective July 1, 1970. Public Law No. 91-258.

26 CFR Part 54

Treasury Regulations §54.4972-1. These regulations provide guidance under former section 4972 relating to the tax on excess contributions for self-employed individuals. Former section 4972 was repealed by section 237(c)(1) of the Tax Equity and Fiscal Responsibility Act of 1982, effective for taxable years beginning after December 31, 1983. Public Law No. 97-248.

Treasury Regulations §54.4981A-1T. These regulations provide guidance under section 4981A relating to the tax on excess distributions and excess accumulations, which section was redesignated as section 4980A by section 1011A(g) of the Technical and Miscellaneous Revenue Act of 1988. Public Law No. 100-647. Section 4980A in turn was repealed by section 1073(c) of the Taxpayer Relief Act of 1997. Public Law No. 105-34. The excess distribution repeal was effective for distributions received after December 31, 1996. The excess retirement accumulation repeal was effective for estates of decedents dying after December 31, 1996.

26 CFR Part 301

Treasury Regulations §301.6035-1. These regulations provide guidance under former section 6035. Former section 6035 was repealed by section 413(c)(26) of the American Jobs Creation Act of 2004, effective for taxable years of foreign corporations beginning after December 31, 2004, and for taxable years of United States shareholders with or within which such taxable years of foreign corporations end. Public Law No. 108-357.

Treasury Regulations §301.6241-1T. These regulations provide guidance under former section 6241. Former section 6241 was repealed by section 1307(c)(1) of the Small Business Job Protection Act of 1996, effective for taxable years beginning after December 31, 1996. Public Law No. 104-188.

Treasury Regulations §301.6245-1T. These regulations provide guidance under former section 6245. Former section 6245 was repealed by section 1307(c)(1) of the Small Business Job Protection Act of 1996, effective for taxable years beginning after December 31, 1996. Public Law No. 104-188.

Treasury Regulations §301.6501(o)-1. These regulations provide guidance under section 6501 for the work incentive program credit carryback. The work incentive program credit under sections 40, 50A, and 50B was repealed by section 474(m) of the Deficit Reduction Act of 1984, effective for taxable years beginning after December 31, 1983. Public Law No. 98-369.

II. Regulations Interpreting Code Provisions That Have Been Significantly Revised

26 CFR Part 1

Treasury Regulations §1.42-2. These regulations provide guidance under section 42. Section 3003(f) of the Housing and Economic Recovery Act of 2008 revised section 42(d)(6), removing the requirement of a waiver upon application by the taxpayer and provided that the 10-year rule did not apply to any Federal- or State-assisted building, effective generally for buildings placed in service after July 30, 2008, rendering these regulations no longer applicable. Public Law No. 110-289.

Treasury Regulations §§1.103(n)-1T through 1.103(n)-7T. These regulations provide guidance under section 103(n). Section 103 was revised by section 1301 of the Tax Reform Act of 1986 by the removal of section 103(n), effective generally for bonds issued after August 15, 1986, rendering these regulations no longer applicable. Public Law No. 99-514.

Treasury Regulations §§1.178-2 and 1.178-3. These regulations provide guidance under former section 178(b) and section 178(c). Revisions to section 178 in section 201(d)(2) of the Tax Reform Act of 1986, effective for property placed in service after December 31, 1986, in taxable years ending after December 31, 1986, rendered these regulations no longer applicable. Public Law No. 99-514.

Treasury Regulations §§1.401-11 through 1.401-13. These regulations provide rules relating to special requirements for plans benefitting owner-employees under section 401. Section 401 was revised by section 237 of the Tax Equity and Fiscal Responsibility Act of 1982, effective for taxable years beginning after December 31, 1983, rendering these regulations no longer applicable. Public Law No. 97-248.

Treasury Regulations §§1.401(e)-1 through 1.401(e)-6. These regulations provide rules relating to special requirements for plans benefitting owner-employees under section 401. Section 401 was revised by section 237 of the Tax Equity and Fiscal Responsibility Act of 1982, effective for taxable years beginning after December 31, 1983, rendering these regulations no longer applicable. Public Law No. 97-248.

Treasury Regulations §§1.404(a)-4 through 1.404(a)-7 and §1.404(a)-9. These regulations set forth rules relating to the deductible limit for certain retirement plan contributions under section 404. Revisions to section 404(a)(1) by section 1013(c)(1) of the Employee Retirement Income Security Act of 1974, effective for plan years beginning after September 2, 1974, rendered these regulations no longer applicable. Public Law No. 93-406.

Treasury Regulations §1.410(b)-1. These regulations provide minimum coverage requirements under section 410(b). Revisions to section 410(b) by section 1112(a) of the Tax Reform Act of 1986, effective generally for plan years beginning after December 31, 1988, rendered these regulations no longer applicable. Public Law No. 99-514.

Treasury Regulations § 1.412(l)(7)-1. These regulations provide mortality tables used to determine current liability pursuant to section 412(l)(7)(C)(ii)(II). Section 412 was revised by section 111(a) of the Pension Protection Act of 2006 by the removal of section 412(I)(7), effective for plan years beginning after December 31, 2007, rendering these regulations no longer applicable. Public Law No. 109-280.

Treasury Regulations § 1.665(f)-1A. These regulations provide for the treatment of undistributed capital gains under section 665(f). Section 665 was revised by section 701(d)(3) of the Tax Reform Act of 1976 by the removal of section 665(f), effective for distributions made in taxable years beginning after December 31, 1975, rendering these regulations no longer applicable. Public Law No. 94-455.

Treasury Regulations § 1.665(g)-1A. These regulations provide the applicable definition of capital gain distribution under section 665(g). Section 665 was revised by section 701(d)(3) of the Tax Reform Act of 1976 by the removal of section 665(g), effective for distributions made in taxable years beginning after December 31, 1975, rendering these regulations no longer applicable. Public Law No. 94-455.

Treasury Regulations § 1.667(a)-1A. These regulations provide guidance under section 667. Section 701(a)(1) of the Tax Reform Act of 1976 revised section 667, effective for taxable years beginning after December 31, 1975, rendering these regulations no longer applicable. Public Law No. 94-455.

Treasury Regulations § 1.831-4. These regulations provide guidance relating to the election under former section 831(b) for a multiple line company to be taxed on total income. Section 1024(a)(4) of the Tax Reform Act of 1986 revised section 831(b), effective for taxable years beginning after December 31, 1986, rendering these regulations no longer applicable. Public Law No. 99-514.

26 CFR Part 5f

Treasury Regulations § 5f.103-3. These regulations provide guidance under section 103(l). Section 103 was revised by section 1301 of the Tax Reform Act of 1986 by the removal of section 103(l), effective generally for bonds issued after August 15, 1986, rendering these regulations no longer applicable. Public Law No. 99-514.

26 CFR Part 7

Treasury Regulations § 7.704-1. These regulations provide guidance under section 704(d). Section 201(b)(1) of the Revenue Act of 1978 revised section 704(d), effective for taxable years beginning after December 31, 1978, rendering these regulations no longer applicable. Public Law No. 95-600.

26 CFR Part 11

Treasury Regulations § 11.401(d)(1)-1. These regulations provide rules relating to special requirements for plans benefitting owner-employees under section 401. Section 401 was revised by section 237 of the Tax Equity and Fiscal Responsibility Act of 1982, effective for taxable years beginning after December 31, 1983, rendering these regulations no longer applicable. Public Law No. 97-248.

Treasury Regulations § 11.402(e)(4)(A)-1. These regulations provide rules on lump sum distributions in the case of an employee who has separated from service. Section 402 was revised by section 104 of the Tax Reform Act of 1986, effective for taxable years beginning after December 31, 1986, rendering these regulations no longer applicable. Public Law No. 99-514.

Treasury Regulations § 11.402(e)(4)(B)-1. These regulations provide rules on an election to treat an amount as a lump sum distribution under section 402(e)(4)(A). Section 402 was revised by section 104 of the Tax Reform Act of 1986, effective for taxable years beginning after December 31, 1986, rendering these regulations no longer applicable. Public Law No. 99-514.

26 CFR Part 16

Treasury Regulations § 16.3-1. These regulations provide guidance under section 6048. Section 1901(a) of the Small Business Job Protection Act of 1996 revised section 6048, effective generally August 20, 1996, rendering these regulations no longer applicable. Public Law No. 104-188. Because these regulations are the only regulations in part 16 of the CFR, part 16 of the CFR is proposed to be removed.

26 CFR Part 20

Treasury Regulations § 20.2201-1. These regulations provide guidance under section 2201. Section 103(a) of the Victims of Terrorism Tax Relief Act of 2001 revised section 2201, effective for estates of certain decedents dying on or after September 11, 2001, rendering these regulations no longer applicable. Public Law No. 107-134.

26 CFR Part 31

Treasury Regulations § 31.3121(b)(8)-2. These regulations provide guidance under section 3121(b)(8)(B). Section 102 of the Social Security Amendments of 1983 revised section 3121(b)(8)(B), effective generally with respect to services performed after December 31, 1983, by removing the Federal Insurance Contributions Act (FICA) tax exemption for organizations described in section 501(c)(3) which are exempt from income tax under section 501(a), rendering these regulations no longer applicable. Public Law No. 98-21.

26 CFR Part 49

Treasury Regulations § § 49.4252-1, 49.4252-3, 49.4252-6, and 49.4252-7. These regulations provide rules relating to general telephone services (as defined under former section 4252(a)), telegraph services (as defined under former section 4252(c)), wire mileage services (as defined under section 4252(e)), and wire and equipment services (as defined under section 4252(f)). Section 302 of the Excise

Tax Reduction Act of 1965 revised section 4252 to remove these subsections and, accordingly, the tax on the described services, effective generally January 1, 1966, rendering these regulations no longer applicable. Public Law No. 89-44.

Treasury Regulations §§49.4253-8 and 49.4253-9. These regulations provide rules under former section 4053(h) and former section 4053(i) relating to wire mileage services. Section 302 of the Excise Tax Reduction Act of 1965 revised section 4253 to remove these subsections, effective generally January 1, 1966, rendering these regulations no longer applicable. Public Law No. 89-44.

26 CFR Part 301

Treasury Regulations §301.6048-1. These regulations provide guidance under section 6048. Section 1901(a) of the Small Business Job Protection Act of 1996 revised section 6048, effective generally August 20, 1996, rendering these regulations no longer applicable. Public Law No. 104-188.

Treasury Regulations §301.6511(d)-7. These regulations provide guidance under former section 6511(d)(7). Section 6511 was revised by section 8(b)(2) of an act to revise miscellaneous timing requirements of the revenue laws, and for other purposes, by the removal of former section 6511(d)(7), effective for carrybacks arising in taxable years beginning after November 10, 1978, rendering these regulations no longer applicable. Public Law No. 95-628.

26 CFR Part 404

Treasury Regulations §404.6048-1. These regulations provide guidance under section 6048. Section 1901(a) of the Small Business Job Protection Act of 1996 revised section 6048, effective generally August 20, 1996, rendering these regulations no longer applicable. Public Law No. 104-188.

III. Regulations Having No Future Applicability Under the Code or Regulations

26 CFR Part 1

Treasury Regulations §1.56-1. These regulations provide guidance under section 56. The alternative minimum tax book income adjustment described in these regulations was only in effect for taxable years beginning in 1987 through 1989.

Treasury Regulations §1.61-2T. These regulations provide guidance under section 61. These regulations apply only to fringe benefits for taxable years 1985 through 1988.

Treasury Regulations §§1.132-1T, 1.132-2T, 1.132-3T, 1.132-4T, 1.132-5T, 1.132-6T, 1.132-7T, and 1.132-8T. These regulations provide guidance under section 132. These regulations apply only to fringe benefits for taxable years 1985 through 1988.

Treasury Regulations §§1.148-1A through 1.148-6A, 1.148-9A, 1.148-10A, 1.149(d)-1A, and 1.150-1A. These regulations provide guidance under sections 148A, 149A, and 150A. These regulations apply only to bonds sold prior to July 8, 1997.

Treasury Regulations §1.165-13T. These regulations provide guidance under section 165. These regulations apply only to losses attributable to straddles (in general, offsetting positions in personal property as described in section 1092) entered into before January 1, 1982.

Treasury Regulations §1.401-4. These regulations provide nondiscrimination rules under section 401(a)(4). These regulations generally apply only to plan years beginning before January 1, 1994.

Treasury Regulations §1.401-5. These regulations provide guidance under section 401. These regulations provide rules for correcting provisions for a plan put into effect before September 2, 1974, and to which the provisions of section 401(b) (which became effective September 2, 1974) do not apply.

Treasury Regulations §1.401-8. These regulations provide guidance under section 401. These regulations apply only to custodial accounts prior to January 1, 1974.

Treasury Regulations §1.402(e)-1. These regulations provide guidance under section 402. These regulations provide rules on distributions made after December 31, 1953, and before January 1, 1955, as a result of certain plan terminations.

Treasury Regulations §1.404(a)-2A. These regulations provide guidance under section 404. These regulations specify information that must be furnished for an employer to claim a retirement plan deduction for a taxable year ending on or after December 31, 1971, and before December 31, 1975.

Treasury Regulations §1.404(a)(8)-1T. These regulations provide guidance under section 404. These regulations apply the provisions of a technical correction in anticipation of enactment of that correction and are no longer applicable pursuant to subsequent legislation.

Treasury Regulations §1.404(e)-1. These regulations provide guidance under section 404. These regulations provide rules regarding deductions for retirement plan contributions on behalf of self-employed individuals for years before January 1, 1974.

Treasury Regulations §1.411(a)-9. These regulations provide guidance under section 411. These regulations provide break-in-service rules that are no longer applicable.

Treasury Regulations §1.411(d)-5. These regulations provide guidance under section 411. They provide rules on a special class-year vesting rule, which generally does not apply for plan years beginning after December 31, 1988.

Treasury Regulations §1.412(b)-5. These regulations provide guidance under section 412. These regulations relate to an amortization election that was available to a multiemployer plan for a plan year beginning before January 1, 1982.

Treasury Regulations §1.412(c)(1)-3T. These regulations provide guidance under section 412. These regulations provide rules on applying the minimum funding requirements to restored plans. These regulations were issued as temporary regulations on October 22, 1990, and expired in 1993, pursuant to section 7805(e)(2).

Treasury Regulations § § 1.453-4 through 1.453-6 and 1.453-10. These regulations provide guidance under section 453 relating to installment sales. These regulations do not apply to installment sales occurring in taxable years ending after October 19, 1980.

Treasury Regulations § 1.453A-2. These regulations provide guidance under section 453A. These regulations do not apply to any taxable year beginning after December 31, 1986.

Treasury Regulations § 1.475(b)-4. These regulations provide guidance under section 475. These regulations provide transitional rules for section 475 identification purposes for periods before February 1, 1994.

Treasury Regulations § 1.503(e)-4. These regulations provide guidance under section 503. These regulations provide rules relating to the denial of deductions with respect to gifts or contributions made before January 1, 1970.

Treasury Regulations § § 1.593-1 through 1.593-11. These regulations implement section 593(a) through (d). Section 593(a) through (d) does not apply to taxable years beginning after December 31, 1995.

Treasury Regulations § 1.802-5. These regulations provide guidance under section 802(a)(3). Section 802(a)(3) applies only for taxable years beginning in 1959 or 1960.

Treasury Regulations § § 1.803-1 through 1.803-7. These regulations provide guidance under section 803. These regulations apply only to taxable years beginning after December 31, 1953, and before January 1, 1955.

Treasury Regulations § § 1.822-1 and 1.822-2. These regulations provide guidance under section 822. These regulations apply only to taxable years beginning after December 31, 1953, but before January 1, 1955, and ending after August 16, 1954.

Treasury Regulations § 1.832-7T. These regulations provide guidance under section 832. These regulations apply only to taxable years ending before January 1, 1990.

Treasury Regulations § 1.962-4. These regulations provide guidance under section 962. These regulations apply only to taxable years beginning before January 1, 1966.

Treasury Regulations § 1.6049-7T. These regulations provide guidance under section 6049. The guidance in these temporary regulations was incorporated into § 1.6049-7(f)(2)(i)(G)(2) in T.D. 8431, which was published in the **Federal Register** on September 3, 1992.

Treasury Regulations § 1.6050H-1T. These regulations provide guidance under section 6050H. These regulations apply only to information reporting of mortgage interest received after December 31, 1984, and before January 1, 1988.

Treasury Regulations § 1.6654-4. These regulations provide guidance under section 6654. These regulations apply only to underpayment of estimated tax for taxable years beginning after December 31, 1970, and ending before January 1, 1972.

26 CFR Part 5

Treasury Regulations § 5.856-1. These regulations provide transition rules for extensions of a grace period for treating certain property as foreclosure property under section 856(e), as revised by section 363(c) of the Revenue Act of 1978, effective for extensions granted after November 6, 1978, for periods beginning after December 31, 1977. Public Law No. 95-600. These regulations do not apply to extensions filed on or after March 29, 1980.

26 CFR Part 11

Treasury Regulations § 11.404(a)(6)-1. These regulations provide guidance under section 404. These regulations provide rules regarding an election pursuant to section 402 of the Tax Reduction Act of 1975, Public Law No. 94-12, to apply the provisions of section 404(a)(6) before the generally applicable effective date (plan years beginning on or after January 1, 1976) for existing plans.

26 CFR Part 13

Treasury Regulations § 13.4. These regulations provide rules relating to arbitrage bonds under section 103. These regulations were published in the **Federal Register** in 1970 (T.D. 7072) and were superseded by a document published in the **Federal Register** on May 3, 1973 (T.D. 7273). Current regulations relating to arbitrage bonds are found in § § 1.148-1 through 1.148-11.

26 CFR Part 19

Treasury Regulations § 19.3-1. These regulations provide guidance to determine the appropriate interest rate for purposes of section 483. These regulations were published in the **Federal Register** on April 7, 1964, and were superseded by § § 1.483-1 and 1.483-2, which were published in the **Federal Register** on January 25, 1966. T.D. 6873. Because these regulations are the only regulations in part 19 of the CFR, part 19 of the CFR is proposed to be removed.

26 CFR Part 25

Treasury Regulations § 25.2522(a)-2. These regulations provide guidance under section 2522. These regulations pertain only to transfers made before August 1, 1969.

26 CFR Part 49

Treasury Regulations § 49.4251-3. These regulations provide guidance under section 4251. These regulations provide transition rules for 1959 returns with respect to the applicability of § § 49.4251-1, 49.4251-2, and 49.4251-4 (telephone excise tax regulations). These regulations are no longer applicable because the transition period has ended.

Treasury Regulations §49.4263-6. These regulations provide guidance under section 4263. These regulations apply only to services provided prior to November 16, 1962.

26 CFR Part 55

Treasury Regulations §55.4981-1. These regulations provide guidance under section 4981. These regulations apply only to taxable years ending on or before January 1, 1987.

26 CFR Part 148

Treasury Regulations §148.1-5. These regulations provide guidance under section 4216(b). These regulations were superseded by §§48.4216(b)-1 through 48.4216(b)-4, effective April 23, 1979. Because these regulations are the only regulations in part 148 of the CFR, part 148 of the CFR is proposed to be removed.

26 CFR Part 301

Treasury Regulations §301.6096-2. These regulations provide guidance under section 6096. These regulations apply only to taxable years ending on or after December 31, 1972, and beginning before January 1, 1973.

Treasury Regulations §§301.6501(o)-2 and 301.6501(o)-3. These regulations provide guidance under section 6501. These regulations do not apply to taxable years beginning on or after September 4, 1982.

Treasury Regulations §301.6511(g)-1. These regulations provide guidance under section 6511. These regulations do not apply to taxable years beginning on or after September 4, 1982.

Treasury Regulation §301.6723-1A. These regulations provide guidance under section 6723. These regulations apply only to information returns and payee statements due after December 31, 1986, and before January 1, 1990.

IV. Proposed Applicability Date

The removal of these regulations is proposed to be applicable as of the date the Treasury decision adopting this notice of proposed rulemaking is published in the **Federal Register**.

Special Analyses

These regulations propose to remove regulations that have no current or future applicability. Therefore, the regulations will have no economic effect and do not impose a collection of information on small entities. An economic analysis under E.O. 12866 and an analysis under the Regulatory Flexibility Act (5 U.S.C. chapter 6) are not required. Pursuant to section 7805(f) of the Code, this notice of proposed rulemaking has been submitted to the Chief Counsel for Advocacy of the Small Business Administration for comment on its impact on small business.

Comments and Requests for Public Hearing

Before these proposed regulations are adopted as final regulations, consideration will be given to any comments that are timely submitted to the IRS as prescribed in the preamble under the "ADDRESSES" section. The Treasury Department and the IRS request comments on all aspects of these proposed regulations, including whether any of the regulations proposed to be removed continue to serve any useful purpose and should not be removed and whether there are other regulations that no longer serve a useful purpose and should be removed. All comments submitted will be made available at *www.regulations.gov* or upon request. A public hearing may be scheduled if requested in writing by any person that timely submits written comments. If a public hearing is scheduled, notice of the date, time, and place for the hearing will be published in the **Federal Register**.

Drafting Information

The principal author of these proposed regulations is Mark A. Bond of the Office of the Associate Chief Counsel (Procedure and Administration).

[¶49,758] **Proposed Amendments of Regulations (REG-129260-16)**, published in the Federal Register on March 13, 2018.

[Code Sec. 6103]

Disclosure of information: Seriously delinquent tax debt: State department: Fixing America's Surface Transportation (FAST) Act.—Amendments of Reg. §§301.6103(n)-1, authorizing the Department of State to disclose returns and return information to contractors who assist the Department of State in carrying out its responsibilities under section 32101 of the Fixing America's Surface Transportation (FAST) Act, are proposed.

AGENCY: Internal Revenue Service (IRS), Treasury.

ACTION: Notice of proposed rulemaking.

SUMMARY: This document contains proposed regulations under section 6103(n) of the Internal Revenue Code (Code) to authorize the Department of State to disclose returns and return information to its contractors who assist the Department of State in carrying out its responsibilities under section 32101 of the Fixing America's Surface Transportation (FAST) Act. The FAST Act requires the IRS to notify the Department of State of certified seriously delinquent tax debts, and the Department of State procures services from outside contractors in connection with carrying out its responsibilities under the FAST Act.

DATES: Written and electronic comments and requests for a public hearing must be received by April 12, 2018.

ADDRESSES: Send submissions to: CC:PA:LPD:PR (REG-129260-16), Room 5207, Internal Revenue Service, P.O. Box 7604, Ben Franklin Station, Washington, DC 20044. Submissions may be hand delivered Monday through Friday between the hours of 8:00 a.m. and 4:00 p.m. to CC:PA:LPD:PR (REG-129260-16), Courier's Desk, Internal Revenue Service, 1111 Constitution Avenue, NW, Washington, DC 20224. Alternatively, taxpayers may submit comments electronically via the Federal eRulemaking Portal at *www.regulations.gov* (IRS REG-129260-16).

FOR FURTHER INFORMATION CONTACT: Concerning the proposed regulations, Brittany Harrison of the Office of Associate Chief Counsel (Procedure and Administration), (202) 317-6833; concerning the submission of comments and requests for a public hearing, Regina Johnson, (202) 317-6901 (not toll-free numbers).

SUPPLEMENTARY INFORMATION:

Background and Explanation of Provisions

This document contains proposed amendments to the Procedure and Administration Regulations (26 CFR part 301) under section 6103(n) of the Code. On December 4, 2015, the FAST Act, Public Law 114-94, 129 Stat. 1312, was enacted into law. Section 32101 of the FAST Act adds section 7345 to the Internal Revenue Code. Section 7345 requires the IRS to notify the Department of State of tax debts that the IRS certifies as seriously delinquent. Section 7345(b) generally defines a seriously delinquent tax debt as an unpaid, legally enforceable Federal tax liability of an individual that has been assessed, is greater than $50,000 (as indexed for inflation), and with respect to which a notice of lien has been filed pursuant to section 6323 and the administrative rights under section 6320 with respect to such filing have been exhausted or have lapsed, or a levy has been made pursuant to section 6331. Section 32101 of the FAST Act generally requires the Department of State to deny a passport (or the renewal of a passport) in the case of an individual if notified by the IRS that the individual has been certified as having a seriously delinquent tax debt and permits the Department of State to revoke a passport previously issued to such person.

Under section 6103(a) of the Code, returns and return information are confidential unless the Code otherwise authorizes disclosure. The FAST Act added section 6103(k)(11), which provides that, upon certification under section 7345, the IRS is authorized to disclose return information to the Department of State with respect to a taxpayer who has a seriously delinquent tax debt. Specifically, upon certification under section 7345, section 6103(k)(11)(A) authorizes the IRS to disclose to officers and employees of the Department of State (i) the taxpayer identity information with respect to the certified taxpayer and (ii) the amount of such seriously delinquent tax debt. Section 6103(k)(11)(A). Section 6103(k)(11)(B) limits the use of return information disclosed under subparagraph (A) for the purposes of, and to the extent necessary in, carrying out the requirements of section 32101 of the FAST Act.

The Department of State engages contractors to assist in carrying out its responsibilities with respect to passports, including responsibilities related to implementation of section 32101 of the FAST Act. Because such contractors are not "officers and employees" of the Department of State, section 6103(k)(11) of the Code does not authorize the disclosure of return information to such contractors.

Section 6103(n) of the Code authorizes, pursuant to regulations prescribed by the Secretary, the disclosure of returns and return information to any person for purposes of tax administration to the extent necessary in connection with, among other things, a written contract for services. The definition of the term "tax administration" includes "the administration, management, conduct, direction, and supervision of the execution and application of the internal revenue laws or related statutes . . . ." Section 6103(b)(4). Because implementation of the FAST Act relates to the administration, management, conduct, direction, and supervision of the execution and application of the internal revenue laws and related statutes, disclosure of return information for the purpose of carrying out responsibilities under the FAST Act is a tax administration purpose.

The Treasury regulations provide that, pursuant to the provisions of section 6103(n) of the Code and subject to certain conditions, officers and employees of the Treasury Department, a State tax agency, the Social Security Administration, or the Department of Justice are authorized to disclose returns and return information to any person or to an officer or employee of the person, for purposes of tax administration (as defined in section 6103(b)(4)), to the extent necessary in connection with a written contract or an agreement for the acquisition of the providing of services. Section 301.6103(n)-1(a)(1). Any person, or officer or employee of the person, who receives such disclosed returns or return information may further disclose the returns or return information to its own officers or employees whose duties or responsibilities require such information in order to provide the services. Section 301.6103(n)-1(a)(2)(i). When authorized in writing by the IRS, such person, or officer or employee of the person, may further disclose such information to the extent necessary to provide services, including to its agents or subcontractors (or such agents' or subcontractors' officers or employees). Section 301.6103(n)-1(a)(2)(ii). Agents or subcontractors (or their officers or employees) who receive such returns or return information may further disclose the returns or return information to their officers or employees whose duties or responsibilities require the returns or return information for a purpose described in § 301.6103(n)-1(a). Section 301.6103(n)-1(a)(3). The regulations under section 6103(n) of the Code provide a number of rules related to limitations on such disclosures, penalties potentially applicable to recipients of returns and return information, notification requirements applicable to recipients of returns and return information, and safeguards requirements. See section 301.6103(n)-1(b), -1(c), -1(d), -1(e).

These proposed regulations add the Department of State to the list of agencies in current §301.6103(n)-1(a)(1) whose officers and employees may disclose returns and return information to any person or to an officer or employee of such person for tax administration purposes to the extent necessary in connection with a written contract for the acquisition of property or services. These proposed regulations authorize the Department of State to disclose returns and return information to its contractors providing services in connection with the revocation or denial of passports pursuant to the requirements of section 7345 and the FAST Act.

Special Analyses

Certain IRS regulations, including this one, are exempt from the requirements of Executive Order 12866, as supplemented and reaffirmed by Executive Order 13563. Therefore, a regulatory impact assessment is not required.

The purpose of these regulations is to allow the Department of State to share tax return information with its contractors for tax administration purposes. As a recipient of tax return information, the Department of State is required to comply with the reporting and other requirements under section 6103(p)(4). The Department of State is also responsible for the training and inspection of its contractors and ensuring that all safeguarding standards are met. These proposed regulations do not impose a reporting burden on the Department of State's contractors and will not require the contractors to file information with the IRS. Because the proposed regulations do not impose a collection of information on entities other than the Department of State, they do not impose a collection of information on small entities. Accordingly, it is hereby certified that these regulations will not have a significant economic impact on a substantial number of small entities. Accordingly, a regulatory flexibility analysis is not required under the Regulatory Flexibility Act (5 U.S.C. chapter 6).

Pursuant to section 7805(f) of the Code, these proposed regulations have been submitted to the Chief Counsel for Advocacy of the Small Business Administration for comment on their impact on small business.

Comments and Requests for Public Hearing

Before the regulations proposed herein are adopted as final regulations, consideration will be given to any electronic and written comments that are submitted timely to the IRS as prescribed in this preamble under the **ADDRESSES** heading. The Treasury Department and the IRS request comments on all aspects of the proposed regulations. All comments submitted will be made available at *www.regulations.gov* or upon request. A public hearing may be scheduled if requested in writing by a person that timely submits written comments. If a public hearing is scheduled, notice of the date, time, and place of the hearing will be published in the *Federal Register*.

Drafting Information

The principal author of these proposed regulations is Brittany Harrison of the Office of the Associate Chief Counsel (Procedure and Administration).

[¶49,759] Proposed Amendments of Regulations (REG-132434-17), published in the Federal Register on March 28, 2018.

[Code Sec. 7602]

Nongovernment attorneys: Examinations of books, papers and other data: Summons interview witness: Contractors.—Amendments of Reg. §301.7602-1, relating to administrative proceedings by generally excluding nongovernment attorneys from receiving summoned books, paper, records, or other data or from participating in the interview of a witness summoned by the IRS to provide testimony under oath, are proposed.

AGENCY: Internal Revenue Service (IRS), Treasury.

ACTION: Notice of proposed rulemaking.

SUMMARY: This document contains proposed regulations to amend regulations under section 7602(a) of the Internal Revenue Code relating to administrative proceedings. Current regulations permit any person authorized to receive returns and return information under section 6103(n) and the regulations thereunder to receive and review summoned books, papers, and other data, and, in the presence and under the guidance of an IRS officer or employee, participate fully in the interview of a witness in a summons interview. These proposed regulations significantly narrow the scope of the current regulations by excluding non-government attorneys from receiving summoned books, papers, records, or other data or from participating in the interview of a witness summoned by the IRS to provide testimony under oath, with a limited exception. These proposed regulations affect taxpayers involved in a federal tax examination and other persons whose books and records or testimony are sought to be examined by the IRS under section 7602(a).

DATES: Written or electronic comments and requests for a public hearing must be received by June 26, 2018.

ADDRESSES: Send submissions to: CC:PA:LPD:PR (REG-132434-17), room 5203, Internal Revenue Service, P.O. Box 7604, Ben Franklin Station, Washington, D.C. 20044. Submissions may be hand-delivered Monday through Friday between the hours of 8 a.m. and 4 p.m. to CC:PA:LPD:PR (REG-132434-17), Courier's Desk, Internal Revenue Service, 1111 Constitution Avenue, NW, Washington D.C., or sent electronically via the Federal eRulemaking Portal at www.regulations.gov (IRS-REG-132434-17).

FOR FURTHER INFORMATION CONTACT: Concerning submission of comments, Regina Johnson, (202) 317-6901; concerning the proposed regulations, William V. Spatz at (202) 317-5461 (not toll-free numbers).

SUPPLEMENTARY INFORMATION:

Background

These proposed regulations amend Procedure and Administration Regulations (26 CFR part 301) under section 7602(a) of the Internal Revenue Code relating to participation by persons described in section 6103(n) and Treas. Reg. §301.6103(n)-1(a) in receiving and reviewing summoned books, papers, records, or other data and in interviewing a summoned witness under oath. These proposed regulations narrow the scope of the current regulations by providing that certain non-government attorneys hired by the IRS are not authorized to participate in an examination.

On June 18, 2014, temporary regulations (TD 9669) regarding participation in a summons interview of a person described in section 6103(n) were published in the **Federal Register** (79 FR 34625). A notice of proposed rulemaking (REG-121542-14) cross-referencing the temporary regulations was published in the **Federal Register** (79 FR 34668) the same day. No public hearing was requested or held. The Internal Revenue Service received two comments on the proposed regulations. One comment recommended that the regulations be revised to remove the provision permitting a contractor to question a witness under oath or to ask a witness's representative to clarify an objection or assertion of privilege. The other comment recommended that the proposed and temporary regulations be withdrawn. After consideration of these comments, the proposed regulations were adopted in final regulations (TD 9778) published in the **Federal Register** (81 FR 45409) on July 14, 2016 ("Summons Interview Regulations"). The only change from the temporary regulations in the final regulations was to replace the word "examine" with "review" in the phrase describing what contractors may do with books, papers, records, or other data received by the IRS under a summons. The preamble to the final regulations explains that this was intended to clarify that the regulations do not authorize contractors to direct audits of a taxpayer's return. See 81 FR 45410.

Description of Summons Interview Regulations

The United States tax system relies upon taxpayers' self-assessment and reporting of their tax liability. The expansive information-gathering authority that Congress granted to the IRS under the Code includes the IRS's broad examination and summons authority, which allows the IRS to determine the accuracy of that self-assessment. See United States v. Arthur Young & Co., 65 U.S. 805, 816 (1984). Section 7602(a) provides that, for the purpose of ascertaining the correctness of any return, making a return where none has been made, or determining the liability of any person for any internal revenue tax, the IRS is authorized to examine books and records, issue summonses seeking documents and testimony, and take testimony from witnesses under oath. These provisions have been part of the revenue laws since 1864.

Use of outside specialists is appropriate to assist the IRS in determining the correctness of the taxpayer's self-assessed tax liability. The assistance of persons from outside the IRS, such as economists, engineers, appraisers, industry specialists, and actuaries, promotes fair and efficient administration and enforcement of the laws administered by the IRS by providing specialized knowledge, skills, or abilities that the IRS officers or employees assigned to the examination may not possess. Section 6103(n) and Treas. Reg. §301.6103(n)-1(a) authorize the IRS to disclose returns and return information to these contractors. The regulations under §301.7602-1(b)(3) were issued to clarify that persons described in section 6103(n) and Treas. Reg. §301.6103(n)-1(a) may receive and review books, papers, records, or other data summoned by the IRS and, in the presence and under the guidance of an IRS officer or employee, participate fully in the interview of a person who the IRS has summoned as a witness to provide testimony under oath. See 81 FR 45410.

Executive Order 13789, Notice 2017-38, and the Reports to the President

Executive Order 13789, issued on April 21, 2017 (E.O. 13789, 82 FR 19317), instructs the Secretary of the Treasury (the Secretary) to review all significant tax regulations issued on or after January 1, 2016, and to take appropriate action to alleviate the burdens of regulations that (i) impose an undue financial burden on U.S. taxpayers; (ii) add undue complexity to the Federal tax laws; or (iii) exceed the statutory authority of the IRS.

E.O. 13789 further instructs the Secretary to submit to the President within 60 days a report (First Report) that identifies regulations that meet these criteria. Notice 2017-38 (2017-30 I.R.B. 147 (July 24, 2017)) included the Summons Interview Regulations in a list of eight regulations identified by the Secretary in the First Report as meeting at least one of the first two criteria specified in E.O. 13789. E.O. 13789 further instructs the Secretary to submit to the President a second report (Second Report) that recommends specific actions to mitigate the burden imposed by regulations identified in the First Report.

In response to Notice 2017-38, the Treasury Department and the IRS received seven comments from professional and business associations addressing the Summons Interview Regulations. All but one of these comments recommended removal of the regulations based primarily on the commentators' perception that the regulations create longer and less efficient examinations by improperly delegating authority to outside law firms to conduct examinations. The one commenter that did not recommend removal of the regulations in their entirety requested removal of the provisions permitting a contractor to directly question a witness during a summons interview.

As explained in the preamble to the final Summons Interview Regulations, the regulations do not delegate authority to conduct examinations or summons interviews. Rather, the regulations permit contractors authorized under section 6103(n) to review books and records and be present and ask questions during summons interviews, all under the supervision of IRS officers and employees. See 81 FR 45410-45412.

Comments in response to Notice 2017-38 also raised concerns that the regulations permit the IRS to hire law firms to receive and review summoned information and fully participate in a summons interview on behalf of the government.

On October 16, 2017, the Secretary published the Second Report in the **Federal Register** (82 FR 48013) stating that the Treasury Department and the IRS are considering proposing a prospectively effective amendment to the Summons Interview Regulations to narrow their scope to prohibit non-government attorneys from questioning witnesses on behalf of the IRS, reviewing summoned records, or playing a behind-the-scenes role in an examination, such as consulting on IRS legal strategy, with a limited exception.

The Code provides IRS officers and employees with significant and broad powers under its summons authority to question witnesses under oath and to require the production of books and records. The Summons Interview Regulations require the IRS to retain authority over important decisions when section 6103(n) contractors question witnesses, but there is a perceived risk that the IRS may not be able to maintain full control over the actions of a non-government attorney hired by the IRS when such an attorney, with the limited exception described below, questions witnesses. The actions of the non-governmental attorney while questioning witnesses could foreclose IRS officials from independently exercising their judgment. Managing an examination or summons interview is therefore best exercised solely by government employees, including government attorneys, whose only duty is to serve the public interest. These concerns outweigh the countervailing need for the IRS to use non-government attorneys, except in the limited circumstances set forth in proposed paragraph (b)(3)(ii). Treasury and the IRS remain confident that the core functions of questioning witnesses and conducting examinations are well within the expertise and ability of government attorneys and examination agents.

Explanation of Provisions

Proposed § 301.7602-1(b)(3)(i) retains the rule from the Summons Interview Regulations authorizing section 6103(n) contractors to receive and review summoned information and fully participate in the summons interview, including questioning witnesses. However, proposed § 301.7602-1(b)(3)(ii) is added to prohibit contractors who are attorneys, with the limited exception described below, from participating in the administrative process contemplated by section 7602(a). Under this prohibition, a non-government attorney, with the limited exception described below, may not review summoned books, papers, records or other data or question summoned witnesses on behalf of the IRS unless the attorney is hired by the IRS for a permitted purpose.

As a limited exception to that prohibition, proposed § 301.7602-1(b)(3)(ii) permits the IRS to hire a non-government attorney if the attorney is being hired for specialized substantive subject matter expertise in an area other than federal tax law. Specifically, proposed § 301.7602-1(b)(3)(ii) permits the IRS to hire an attorney who has specialized knowledge of foreign, state, or local law, including tax law, or who is a specialist in non-tax substantive law such as patent law, property law, or environmental law. It would not permit IRS to hire an attorney for non-substantive specialized knowledge, such as civil litigation skills. Proposed § 301.7602-1(b)(3)(ii) also permits the IRS to hire a contractor who may happen to be an attorney, but who is hired for knowledge, skills, or abilities other than providing legal services as an attorney. Further, proposed § 301.7602-1(b)(3)(ii) permits the IRS to hire an entity that employs or is owned by attorneys so long as the expertise they are providing is not prohibited by proposed § 301.7602-1(b)(3)(ii).

These changes are proposed to be effective for examinations begun and summonses served by the IRS on or after the date that these proposed regulations are published in the **Federal Register**.

Special Analyses

Certain IRS regulations, including these, are exempt from the requirements of Executive Order 12866, as supplemented and affirmed by Executive Order 13563. Therefore, a regulatory assessment is not required. Because the proposed regulations would not impose a collection of information on small entities, the Regulatory Flexibility Act (5 U.S.C. chapter 6) does not apply. Therefore, a regulatory flexibility analysis is not required. Pursuant to section 7805(f) of the Internal Revenue Code, the IRS will submit the proposed regulations to the Chief Counsel for Advocacy of the Small Business Administration for comments about the regulations' impact on small businesses.

Comments and Request for a Public Hearing

Before these proposed regulations are adopted as final, the IRS will consider any written (signed original and 8 copies) or electronic comments timely submitted. The IRS requests comments on all aspects of these proposed regulations. All comments will be available for public inspection and copying. The IRS will schedule a public meeting if one is requested, in writing, by a person who submits written comments. If the IRS does schedule a public hearing, the IRS will publish notice of the date, time, and place for the public hearing in the **Federal Register**.

Drafting Information

The principal author of these regulations is William V. Spatz of the Office of Associate Chief Counsel (Procedure and Administration).

[¶49,760] Proposed Amendments of Regulations (REG-102951-16), published in the Federal Register on May 31, 2018.

[Code Secs. 6011 and 6721]

Filing requirements: Information returns: Magnetic media.—Amendments of Reg. §§301.6011-2 and 301.6721-1, amending the rules for determining whether information returns must be filed using magnetic media (electronically), are proposed.

AGENCY: Internal Revenue Service (IRS), Treasury.

ACTION: Notice of proposed rulemaking.

SUMMARY: This document contains proposed regulations amending the rules for determining whether information returns must be filed using magnetic media (electronically). The proposed regulations would require that all information returns, regardless of type, be taken into account to determine whether a person meets the 250-return threshold and, therefore, must file the information returns electronically. The proposed regulations also would require any person required to file information returns electronically to file corrected information returns electronically, regardless of the number of corrected information returns being filed. The proposed regulations will affect persons required to file information returns.

DATES: Written or electronic comments and requests for a public hearing must be received by July 30, 2018.

ADDRESSES: Send submissions to: CC:PA:LPD:PR (REG-102951-16), room 5205, Internal Revenue Service, P.O. Box 7604, Ben Franklin Station, Washington, DC 20044. Submissions may be hand-delivered Monday through Friday between the hours of 8:00 a.m. and 4:00 p.m. to CC:PA:LPD:PR (REG-102951-16), Courier's Desk, Internal Revenue Service, 1111 Constitution Avenue, NW., Washington, DC 20224. Alternatively, persons may submit comments electronically via the Federal eRulemaking Portal at *http://www.regulations.gov* (IRS REG-102951-16).

FOR FURTHER INFORMATION CONTACT: Concerning the proposed regulations, Michael Hara, (202) 317-6845; concerning the submission of comments and requests for a public hearing, Regina L. Johnson, (202) 317-5177 (not toll-free calls).

SUPPLEMENTARY INFORMATION:

Background

This document contains proposed amendments to the Regulations on Procedure and Administration (26 CFR part 301) under section 6011(e) relating to the filing of information returns on magnetic media. Section 6011(e) authorizes the Secretary to prescribe regulations regarding the filing of returns on magnetic media. Section 6011(e)(2)(A) prohibits the Secretary from requiring persons to file returns on magnetic media unless the person is required to file at least 250 returns during the calendar year. Section 6011(e)(2)(B) provides that, in prescribing regulations, the Secretary shall consider the taxpayer's ability to comply at reasonable cost with the regulations' requirements. Section 301.6011-2(a)(1) provides that magnetic media includes any magnetic media permitted under the applicable regulations, revenue procedures, or publications, or, in the case of returns filed with the Social Security Administration, any magnetic media permitted under Social Security Administration publications, including electronic filing.

Section 301.6011-2 provides rules for when information returns described in §301.6011-2(b), such as Form 1042-S, "Foreign Person's U.S. Source Income Subject to Withholding;" forms in the 1099 series; and Form W-2, "Wage and Tax Statement," must be filed electronically. Under §301.6011-2(c), a person is not required to file a type of information return covered by §301.6011-2(b) electronically unless the person is required to file 250 or more such returns during the calendar year. Sections 301.6011-2(c)(1)(i) and (iii) and the Examples in §301.6011-2(c)(1)(iv) describe that the 250-return threshold applies separately to each type of information return and each type of corrected information return filed, and, therefore, the forms are not aggregated for purposes of determining whether the 250-return threshold is satisfied. Section 301.6011-2(c)(2) allows the Commissioner to waive the requirement to file electronically if the request for waiver demonstrates hardship and provides that the principal factor in determining hardship will be the extent, if any, to which the cost of electronic filing exceeds the cost of filing on other media.

When the rules for determining the 250-return threshold, including the rule providing that each type of information return is counted separately and not aggregated, were originally published, electronic filing was in the early stages of development and was not as commonly used as it is today. The non-aggregation rule helped to reduce cost and ease burden on taxpayers, given the existing limits on technology and accessibility to such technology. Since then, significant advances in technology have made electronic filing more prevalent and accessible. As a result, electronic filing is less costly and most often easier than paper filing. In fact, most information returns are filed electronically. In tax year 2015, approximately 98 percent of information returns were filed electronically. In tax year 2016, the percentage of information returns filed electronically rose to 98.5 percent. Advances in tax return preparation software, as well as the prevalence of tax return preparers and third-party service providers who offer information return preparation and electronic filing, have also contributed to the increase in electronic filing.

The concerns regarding taxpayer burden and cost associated with electronic filing have been significantly mitigated since the non-aggregation rule in § 301.6011-2(c)(1)(i) and (iii) of the regulations was first published. Therefore, determining the 250-return threshold on a form-by-form basis without aggregation is no longer necessary to relieve taxpayer burden and cost. Accordingly, these regulations simplify the rules for determining the 250-return threshold by requiring aggregation of all information returns covered by § 301.6011-2(b) for purposes of determining the 250-return threshold. In addition, these regulations provide that corrected information returns must be filed electronically if the original information returns were filed electronically. These rule changes will help facilitate efficient and effective tax administration.

Explanation of Provisions

These proposed regulations remove the non-aggregation rule in § 301.6011-2(c)(1)(iii) that counts the number of information returns required to be filed on a form-by-form basis. The proposed regulations add a new paragraph (4) to § 301.6011-2(b) to provide that if during a calendar year a person is required to file a total of 250 or more information returns of any type covered by § 301.6011-2(b), the person is required to file those information returns electronically. For example, under these proposed regulations, if a person is required to file 200 Forms 1099-INT, "Interest Income," and 200 Forms 1099-DIV, that person must file all Forms 1099-INT and Forms 1099-DIV electronically because that person is required to file, in the aggregate, at least 250 information returns covered by § 301.6011-2(b). Corrected information returns are not taken into account in determining whether the 250-return threshold is met under proposed § 301.6011-2(b)(4) for purposes of determining whether information returns covered by § 301.6011-2(b) must be filed electronically. Examples in proposed § 301.6011-2(c)(1)(iv) illustrate this rule.

The proposed regulations also provide that corrected information returns covered by § 301.6011-2(b) must be filed electronically if the information returns originally filed for the calendar year are required to be filed electronically. If fewer than 250 returns covered by § 301.6011-2(b) are required to be filed for the calendar year, the original returns for the calendar year, as well as the corrected returns for the calendar year, are not required to be filed electronically. See proposed § 301.6011-2 (b)(4).

The proposed regulations also amend § 301.6721-1(a)(2)(ii) regarding the penalty for failure to file correct information returns to remove references to the prior rule for determining the number of returns on a form-by-form basis and the prior corrected return rule.

The proposed regulations do not amend the existing regulations allowing persons who are required to file returns electronically to request a waiver of the electronic-filing requirement. *See* § 301.6011-2(c)(2). This waiver authority will be exercised so as not to unduly burden taxpayers lacking the necessary data-processing capabilities or access to return preparers and third-party service providers at a reasonable cost.

Proposed Effective/Applicability Date

These proposed regulations will be effective on the date of the publication of the Treasury Decision adopting these rules as final in the **Federal Register**. However, to give information-return filers sufficient time to comply with these regulations, these proposed regulations will not apply to information returns required to be filed before January 1, 2019. Accordingly, these proposed regulations provide that §§ 301.6011-2(b)(4) and 301.6721-1(a)(2)(ii), as amended, will be effective for information returns required to be filed after December 31, 2018. Section 301.6011-2(b)(5), as amended, will be effective for corrected information returns filed after December 31, 2018.

Special Analyses

This regulation is not subject to review under section 6(b) of Executive Order 12866 pursuant to the Memorandum of Agreement (April 11, 2018) between the Department of the Treasury and the Office of Management and Budget regarding review of tax regulations.

When the Internal Revenue Service issues a proposed rulemaking imposing a collection of information requirement on small entities, the Regulatory Flexibility Act (RFA) requires the agency to "prepare and make available for public comment an initial regulatory flexibility analysis," which will "describe the impact of the proposed rule on small entities." 5 U.S.C. 603(a). Section 605(b) of the RFA allows an agency to certify a rule, in lieu of preparing an analysis, if the proposed rulemaking is not expected to have a significant economic impact on a substantial number of small entities.

This proposed rule directly affects information-return filers that file more than 250 returns of any type covered by § 301.6011-2(b), which includes a substantial number of small entities. However, the IRS has determined that the economic impact on small entities affected by the proposed rule would not be significant. Under sections 6011(e) and § 301.6011-2(c)(1), information-return filers already must file information returns electronically if during a calendar year a person is required to file a total of 250 or more information returns of any type covered by § 301.6011-2(b). The proposed rule merely amends the method of counting those 250 returns to determine if the 250-return threshold is met. Information filers may request a waiver of the electronic-filing requirement if they lack the necessary data-processing capabilities or access to return preparers and third-party service providers at a reasonable cost, and the IRS routinely grants meritorious hardship waiver requests. Accordingly, the burden on the limited number of small entities that are not currently filing electronically will be slight, and small entities that would experience a hardship because of this proposed rule may seek a waiver. The Commissioner of the IRS hereby certifies that this rule will not have a significant economic impact on a substantial number of small entities. The IRS invites comment from members of the public who believe there will be a significant impact on small information return filers. Pursuant to section 7805(f) of the Code, this notice of proposed rulemaking has been submitted to the Chief Counsel for Advocacy of the Small Business Administration for comment on its impact on small business.

Comments and Requests for Public Hearing

Before these proposed regulations are adopted as final regulations, consideration will be given to any electronic and written comments that are submitted timely to the IRS as prescribed in this preamble under the ADDRESSES heading. The Treasury Department and the IRS request comments on all aspects of the proposed rules. All comments will be available at *www.regulations.gov* or upon request. A public hearing will be scheduled if requested in writing by any person that timely submits written comments. If a public hearing is scheduled, then notice of the date, time, and place for the public hearing will be published in the **Federal Register**.

Drafting Information

The principal author of these proposed regulations is Michael Hara of the Office of the Associate Chief Counsel (Procedure and Administration).

[¶49,762] Proposed Amendments of Regulations (REG-131186-17), published in the Federal Register on June 19, 2018.

[Code Sec. 707]

Proposed amendments: Partnerships: Liabilities: Disguised sales.—Amendments of Reg. §§1.707-5, 1.707-5T, 1.707-9 and 1.707-9T, concerning how partnership liabilities are allocated for disguised sale purposes, are proposed.

AGENCY: Internal Revenue Service (IRS), Treasury.

ACTION: Notice of proposed rulemaking; public hearing; partial withdrawal of notice of proposed rulemaking.

SUMMARY: This document contains proposed regulations concerning how partnership liabilities are allocated for disguised sale purposes. The proposed regulations, if finalized, would replace existing temporary regulations with final regulations that were in effect prior to the temporary regulations. This document also partially withdraws proposed regulations cross-referencing the temporary regulations. These regulations affect partnerships and their partners. Finally, this document provides notice of a public hearing on these proposed regulations.

DATES: Written or electronic comments must be received by July 19, 2018.

A public hearing will be held at 10:00 am on August 21, 2018. Outlines of topics to be discussed at the public hearing must be received by August 3, 2018.

ADDRESSES: Send submissions to: CC:PA:LPD:PR (REG-131186-17), Room 5203, Internal Revenue Service, PO Box 7604, Ben Franklin Station, Washington, DC 20044. Submissions may be hand-delivered Monday through Friday between the hours of 8 a.m. and 4 p.m. to: CC:PA:LPD:PR (REG-131186-17), Courier's Desk, Internal Revenue Service, 1111 Constitution Avenue, NW., Washington, DC, or sent electronically, via the Federal eRulemaking Portal site at http://www.regulations.gov (indicate IRS and REG-131186-17). The public hearing will be held in the IRS Auditorium, Internal Revenue Service Building, 1111 Constitution Ave, NW., Washington, DC 20224.

FOR FURTHER INFORMATION CONTACT: Concerning the proposed regulations, Caroline E. Hay or Deane M. Burke at (202) 317-5279; concerning the submission of comments, the hearing, or to be placed on the building access list to attend the hearing, Regina L. Johnson at (202) 317-6901 (not toll-free numbers).

SUPPLEMENTARY INFORMATION:

Background

This document proposes amendments to the Income Tax Regulations (26 CFR part 1) under section 707 of the Internal Revenue Code (Code) regarding allocations of partnership liabilities for disguised sale purposes. Section 707(a)(2)(B) generally provides that, under regulations prescribed by the Secretary of the Treasury (Secretary), related transfers to and by a partnership that, when viewed together, are more properly characterized as a sale or exchange of property, will be treated either as a transaction between the partnership and one who is not a partner or between two or more partners acting other than in their capacity as partners (generally referred to as "disguised sales").

The Department of the Treasury (Treasury Department) and the IRS published a notice of proposed rulemaking (REG-119305-11) in the *Federal Register* (79 FR 4826) on January 30, 2014, to amend the then-existing regulations under section 707 relating to disguised sales of property to or by a partnership and under section 752 concerning the treatment of partnership liabilities (2014 Proposed Regulations). The 2014 Proposed Regulations provided certain technical rules intended to clarify the application of the disguised sale rules under section 707 and also contained rules regarding the sharing of partnership recourse and nonrecourse liabilities under section 752. A public hearing on the 2014 Proposed Regulations was not requested or held, but the Treasury Department and the IRS received written comments. Based on a comment received on the 2014 Proposed Regulations requesting that guidance under section 752 regarding a partner's share of partnership liabilities apply for disguised sale purposes, the Treasury Department and the IRS reconsidered the rules under

§1.707-5(a)(2) of the 2014 Proposed Regulations for determining a partner's share of partnership liabilities for purposes of section 707.

On October 5, 2016, the Treasury Department and the IRS published in the *Federal Register* (81 FR 69282) final and temporary regulations (T.D. 9788) implementing a new rule concerning the allocation of liabilities for section 707 purposes. On November 17, 2016, the Treasury Department and the IRS published in the *Federal Register* (81 FR 80993 and 81 FR 80994) two correcting amendments to T.D. 9788 (the temporary regulations as so corrected, 707 Temporary Regulations). T.D. 9788 also contained rules concerning the treatment of "bottom dollar payment obligations" (752 Temporary Regulations). The 707 Temporary Regulations were incorporated by cross reference in a notice of proposed rulemaking (REG-122855-15) published on October 5, 2016, in the *Federal Register* (81 FR 69301) (707 Proposed Regulations). That notice of proposed rulemaking also incorporated by cross reference the 752 Temporary Regulations and included new proposed regulations under sections 704 and 752 (752 Proposed Regulations). Also on October 5, 2016, the Treasury Department and the IRS published final regulations under section 707 and §1.752-3 (T.D. 9787) in the *Federal Register* (81 FR 6929). T.D. 9787 was the subject of a correction notice published in the *Federal Register* (81 FR 80587) on November 16, 2016 (the final regulations as so corrected, 707 Final Regulations).

The 707 Temporary Regulations, in response to the comment received on the 2014 Proposed Regulations, adopted an approach that requires a partner to apply the same percentage used to determine the partner's share of excess nonrecourse liabilities under §1.752-3(a)(3) (with certain limitations) in determining the partner's share of all partnership liabilities for disguised sale purposes. Also in response to the comment, the 707 Temporary Regulations provide that a partner's share of a partnership liability for section 707 purposes shall not exceed the partner's share of the partnership liability under section 752 and applicable regulations. The 707 Temporary Regulations reserve on the treatment, for disguised sale purposes, of an obligation that would be treated as a recourse liability under §1.752-1(a)(1) or a nonrecourse liability under §1.752-1(a)(2) if the liability was treated as a partnership liability for purposes of section 752. The Treasury Department and the IRS received comments supporting the approach taken in the 707 Temporary Regulations, but also received comments expressing concern that a new approach was adopted by temporary regulations rather than in proposed regulations, which denied taxpayers the ability to provide comment prior to the 707 Temporary Regulations being effective.

On April 21, 2017, the President issued Executive Order 13789 (E.O. 13789), "Executive Order on Identifying and Reducing Tax Regulatory Burdens" (82 FR 19317, April 26, 2017), which directed the Secretary to review all significant tax regulations issued on or after January 1, 2016, and to take concrete action to alleviate the burdens of regulations that (i) impose an undue financial burden on U.S. taxpayers; (ii) add undue complexity to the Federal tax laws; or (iii) exceed the statutory authority of the IRS. E.O. 13789 further directed the Secretary to submit to the President within 60 days an interim report identifying regulations that meet these criteria. Notice 2017-38 (2017-30 IRB 147 (July 24, 2017)) included the 707 Temporary Regulations in a list of eight regulations identified by the Secretary in the interim report as meeting at least one of the first two criteria specified in E.O. 13789.

E.O. 13789 further directed the Secretary to submit to the President and publish in the *Federal Register* a report recommending specific actions to mitigate the burden imposed by regulations identified in the interim report. On October 16, 2017, the Secretary published this second report in the *Federal Register* (82 FR 48013), "Second Report to the President on Identifying and Reducing Tax Regulatory Burdens" (Second Report). The Second Report stated that, while the Treasury Department and the IRS believe that the 707 Temporary Regulations' novel approach to addressing disguised sale treatment merits further study, the Treasury Department and the IRS agree with commenters that such a change should be studied systematically. The second report further stated that the Treasury Department and the IRS therefore would consider whether the 707 Temporary Regulations and the 707 Proposed Regulations should be removed and withdrawn, respectively, and the prior regulations reinstated. After further consideration, the Treasury Department and the IRS are withdrawing the 707 Proposed Regulations and proposing to remove the 707 Temporary Regulations and reinstate the regulations under §1.707-5(a)(2) as in effect prior to the 707 Temporary Regulations and as contained in 26 CFR part 1 revised as of April 1, 2016 (Prior 707 Regulations).

The Second Report also stated that the Treasury Department and the IRS believe that the 752 Temporary Regulations concerning bottom dollar payment obligations should be retained because, consistent with the view of a number of commenters, the 752 Temporary Regulations are needed to prevent abuses and do not meaningfully increase regulatory burdens for the taxpayers affected. The Treasury Department and the IRS will continue to consider these issues and continue to request comments concerning the 752 Proposed Regulations. The Second Report did not identify the 707 Final Regulations, which are not affected by this notice of proposed rulemaking.

Explanation of Provisions

In addition to withdrawing the 707 Proposed Regulations, this notice of proposed rulemaking proposes to remove the 707 Temporary Regulations and reinstate the Prior 707 Regulations concerning the allocation of liabilities for disguised sale purposes. In determining a partners' share of a partnership liability for disguised sale purposes, §1.707-5(a)(2) of the Prior 707 Regulations prescribed separate rules for a partnership's recourse liability and a partnership's nonrecourse liability. This notice of proposed rulemaking adopts those same rules.

Under § 1.707-5(a)(2)(i) of the Prior 707 Regulations and, if finalized, these proposed regulations, a partner's share of a partnership's recourse liability equals the partner's share of the liability under section 752 and the regulations thereunder. A partnership liability is a recourse liability to the extent that the obligation is a recourse liability under § 1.752-1(a)(1).

Under § 1.707-5(a)(2)(ii) of the Prior 707 Regulations and, if finalized, these proposed regulations, a partner's share of a partnership's nonrecourse liability is determined by applying the same percentage used to determine the partner's share of the excess nonrecourse liability under § 1.752-3(a)(3). A partnership liability is a nonrecourse liability of the partnership to the extent that the obligation is a nonrecourse liability under § 1.752-1(a)(2).

The 707 Final Regulations limited the available methods for determining a partner's share of an excess nonrecourse liability under § 1.752-3(a)(3) for disguised sale purposes. Under the 707 Final Regulations, a partner's share of an excess nonrecourse liability for disguised sale purposes is determined only in accordance with the partner's share of partnership profits and by taking into account all facts and circumstances relating to the economic arrangement of the partners. Thus, the significant item method, the alternative method, and the additional method as defined in § 1.752-3(a)(3) do not apply for purposes of determining a partner's share of a partnership's nonrecourse liability for disguised sale purposes.

In addition, § 1.707-5(a)(2)(i) and (ii) of the Prior 707 Regulations provided that a partnership liability is a recourse or nonrecourse liability to the extent that the obligation would be a recourse liability under § 1.752-1(a)(1) or a nonrecourse liability under § 1.752-1(a)(2), respectively, if the liability was treated as a partnership liability for purposes of section 752 (§ 1.752-7 contingent liabilities). This notice of proposed rulemaking reinstates these rules concerning § 1.752-7 contingent liabilities. However, as noted in the preamble to T.D. 9788, the Treasury Department and the IRS continue to believe additional guidance would be helpful in this area. The preamble to T.D. 9788 explained that, in many cases, § 1.752-7 contingent liabilities may constitute qualified liabilities that would not be taken into account for purposes of determining a disguised sale. Some commenters on the 2014 Proposed Regulations noted that there may be circumstances in which certain transfers of § 1.752-7 contingent liabilities to a partnership may be abusive. The Treasury Department and the IRS continue to study the issue of the effect of contingent liabilities with respect to section 707, as well as other sections of the Code.

Finally, this notice of proposed rulemaking reinstates *Examples 2*, *3*, *7*, and *8* under § 1.707-5(f) of the Prior 707 Regulations. However, language is added to *Example 3* to reflect an amendment to § 1.707-5(a)(3) in the 707 Final Regulations regarding an anticipated reduction in a partner's share of a liability that is not subject to the entrepreneurial risks of partnership operations.

Proposed Applicability Date

The 707 Temporary Regulations are proposed to be removed thirty days following the date these regulations are published as final regulations in the *Federal Register*. The amendments to § 1.707-5 are proposed to apply to any transaction with respect to which all transfers occur on or after thirty days following the date these regulations are published as final regulations in the *Federal Register*. However, a partnership and its partners may apply all the rules in these proposed regulations in lieu of the 707 Temporary Regulations to any transaction with respect to which all transfers occur on or after January 3, 2017.

Special Analyses

These proposed regulations are not subject to review under section 6(b) of Executive Order 12866 pursuant to the Memorandum of Agreement (April 11, 2018) between the Department of the Treasury and the Office of Management and Budget regarding review of tax regulations. These proposed regulations are expected to be an Executive Order 13771 deregulatory action. Details on the estimated cost savings of these proposed regulations will be provided in the final regulations.

Because these proposed regulations do not impose a collection of information on small entities, the Regulatory Flexibility Act (5 U.S.C. chapter 6) does not apply. Pursuant to section 7805(f) of the Code, this notice of proposed rulemaking has been submitted to the Chief Counsel for Advocacy of the Small Business Administration for comment on its impact on small business.

Comments and Public Hearing

Comments Concerning These Proposed Regulations

Before these proposed regulations are adopted as final regulations, consideration will be given to any comments that are submitted timely to the IRS as prescribed in this preamble under the "ADDRESSES" heading. The Treasury Department and the IRS request comments on all aspects of the proposed rules. All comments will be available at *http://www.regulations.gov* or upon request.

A public hearing has been scheduled for August 21, 2018, beginning at 10:00 am in the IRS Auditorium of the Internal Revenue Service Building, 1111 Constitution Avenue, NW., Washington, DC 20224. Due to building security procedures, visitors must enter at the Constitution Avenue entrance. In addition, all visitors must present photo identification to enter the building. Because of access restrictions, visitors will not be admitted beyond the immediate entrance area more than 15 minutes before the hearing starts. For information about having your name placed on the building access list to attend the hearing, see the "FOR FURTHER INFORMATION CONTACT" section of this preamble.

The rules of 26 CFR 601.601(a)(3) apply to the hearing. Persons who wish to present oral comments at the hearing must submit a signed original and eight (8) copies of written or electronic comments by July 19, 2018 and an outline of the topics to be discussed and the time to be devoted to each topic by August 3, 2018. A period of 10 minutes will be allotted to each person for making comments. An agenda showing the scheduling of the speakers will be prepared after the deadline for receiving outlines has passed. Copies of the agenda will be available free of charge at the hearing.

Comments Concerning Approach in the 707 Temporary Regulations

As discussed in the Second Report, the Treasury Department and the IRS believe that the 707 Temporary Regulations' novel approach (treating all liabilities as nonrecourse and allocating in accordance with § 1.752-3(a)(3) for disguised sale purposes) merits further study. The 707 Temporary Regulations explained that this approach reflects the overall economic arrangements of the partners as, in most cases, a partnership will satisfy its liabilities with partnership profits, the partnership's assets do not become worthless, and the payment obligations of partners or related persons are not called upon. The Treasury Department and the IRS continue to study this issue and request comments on the approach adopted in the 707 Temporary Regulations. The request for comments in this paragraph on the approach of the 707 Temporary Regulations is not the subject of the scheduled public hearing.

Drafting Information

The principal authors of these proposed regulations are Caroline E. Hay and Deane M. Burke, Office of the Associate Chief Counsel (Passthroughs and Special Industries). However, other personnel from the Treasury Department and the IRS participated in their development.

[¶ 49,765] Proposed Amendments of Regulations (REG-104397-18), published in the Federal Register on August 8, 2018.

[Code Secs. 48, 167, 168, 169, 179, 312, 704 and 743]

Deduction: Additional first year depreciation: Tax Cuts and Jobs Act (TCJA).—Reg. § 1.168(k)-2 and amendments of Reg. §§ 1.48-12, 1.167(a)-14, 1.168(b)-1, 1.168(d)-1, 1.168(i)-4, 1.168(i)-6, 1.168(k)-0, 1.169-3, 1.179-4, 1.179-6, 1.312-15, 1.704-1, 1.704-3 and 1.743-1, providing guidance regarding the additional first year depreciation deduction under section 168(k) of the Internal Revenue Code (Code), are proposed.

AGENCY: Internal Revenue Service (IRS), Treasury.

ACTION: Notice of proposed rulemaking.

SUMMARY: This document contains proposed regulations that provide guidance regarding the additional first year depreciation deduction under section 168(k) of the Internal Revenue Code (Code). These proposed regulations reflect changes made by the Tax Cuts and Jobs Act. These proposed regulations affect taxpayers who deduct depreciation for qualified property acquired and placed in service after September 27, 2017.

DATES: Written or electronic comments and requests for a public hearing must be received by October 7, 2018.

ADDRESSES: Send submissions to: CC:PA:LPD:PR (REG-104397-18), Room 5203, Internal Revenue Service, P.O. Box 7604, Ben Franklin Station, Washington, DC 20044. Submissions may be hand-delivered Monday through Friday between the hours of 8 a.m. and 4 p.m. to CC:PA:LPD:PR (REG-104397-18), Courier's Desk, Internal Revenue Service, 1111 Constitution Avenue, NW., Washington, DC 20224, or sent electronically via the Federal eRulemaking Portal at *http://www.regulations.gov* (IRS REG-104397-18).

FOR FURTHER INFORMATION CONTACT: Concerning the proposed regulations, Elizabeth R. Binder, (202) 317-7005; concerning submissions of comments or requests for a public hearing, Regina L. Johnson, (202) 317-6901 (not toll-free numbers).

SUPPLEMENTARY INFORMATION:

Background

This document contains proposed amendments to 26 CFR part 1 under section 168(k). Section 168(k) was added to the Code by section 101 of the Job Creation and Worker Assistance Act of 2002, Public Law 107-147 (116 Stat. 21). Section 168(k) allows an additional first year depreciation deduction in the placed-in-service year of qualified property. Subsequent amendments to section 168(k) increased the percentage of the additional first year depreciation deduction from 30 percent to 50 percent (to 100 percent for property acquired and placed in service after September 8, 2010, and generally before January 1, 2012), extended the placed-in-service date generally through December 31, 2019, and made other changes. See section 201 of the Jobs and Growth Tax Relief Reconciliation Act of 2003, Public Law 108-27 (117 Stat. 752), sections 403 and 408 of the Working Families Tax Relief Act of 2004, Public Law 108-311 (118 Stat. 1166), sections 336 and 337 of the American Jobs Creation Act of 2004, Public Law 108-357 (118 Stat. 1418), sections 403 and 405 of the Gulf Opportunity Zone Act of 2005, Public Law 109-135 (119 Stat. 2577), section 103 of the Economic Stimulus Act of 2008, Public Law 110-185 (122 Stat. 613), section 3081 of the Housing Assistance Tax Act of 2008, Public Law 110-289 (122 Stat. 2654), section 1201 of the American Recovery and Reinvestment Tax Act of 2009, Public Law 111-5 (123 Stat. 115), section 2022 of the Small Business Jobs Act of 2010, Public Law 111-240 (124 Stat. 2504), section 401 of the Tax Relief, Unemployment Insurance Reauthorization, and Job Creation Act of 2010, Public Law 111-312 (124 Stat. 3296), section 331 of the American Taxpayer

Relief Act of 2012, Public Law 112-240 (126 Stat. 2313), sections 125, 202, 210, 212, and 214 of the Tax Increase Prevention Act of 2014, Public Law 113-295 (128 Stat. 4010), and section 143 of the Protecting Americans from Tax Hikes Act of 2015, enacted as Division Q of the Consolidated Appropriations Act, 2016, Public Law 114-113 (129 Stat. 2242).

On December 22, 2017, section 168(k) and related provisions were amended by sections 12001(b)(13), 13201, and 13204 of the Tax Cuts and Jobs Act, Public Law 115-97 (131 Stat. 2054) (the "Act") to provide further changes to the additional first year depreciation deduction. Unless otherwise indicated, all references to section 168(k) hereinafter are references to section 168(k) as amended.

Section 167(a) allows as a depreciation deduction a reasonable allowance for the exhaustion, wear and tear, and obsolescence of property used in a trade or business or of property held for the production of income. The depreciation deduction allowable for tangible depreciable property placed in service after 1986 generally is determined under the Modified Accelerated Cost Recovery System provided by section 168 (MACRS property). The depreciation deduction allowable for computer software that is placed in service after August 10, 1993, and is not an amortizable section 197 intangible, is determined under section 167(f)(1).

Section 168(k), prior to amendment by the Act, allowed an additional first year depreciation deduction for the placed-in-service year equal to 50 percent of the adjusted basis of qualified property. Qualified property was defined in part as property the original use of which begins with the taxpayer.

Section 13201 of the Act made several amendments to the allowance for additional first year depreciation deduction in section 168(k). For example, the additional first year depreciation deduction percentage is increased from 50 to 100 percent; the property eligible for the additional first year depreciation deduction is expanded to include certain used depreciable property and certain film, television, or live theatrical productions; the placed-in-service date is extended from before January 1, 2020, to before January 1, 2027 (from before January 1, 2021, to before January 1, 2028, for longer production period property or certain aircraft property described in section 168(k)(2)(B) or (C)); and the date on which a specified plant is planted or grafted by the taxpayer is extended from before January 1, 2020, to before January 1, 2027.

Section 168(k) allows a 100-percent additional first year depreciation deduction for qualified property acquired and placed in service after September 27, 2017, and placed in service before January 1, 2023 (before January 1, 2024, for longer production period property or certain aircraft property described in section 168(k)(2)(B) or (C)). If a taxpayer elects to apply section 168(k)(5), the 100-percent additional first year depreciation deduction also is allowed for a specified plant planted or grafted after September 27, 2017, and before January 1, 2023. The 100-percent additional first year depreciation deduction is decreased by 20 percent annually for qualified property placed in service, or a specified plant planted or grafted, after December 31, 2022 (after December 31, 2023, for longer production period property or certain aircraft property described in section 168(k)(2)(B) or (C)).

Section 168(k)(2)(A), as amended by the Act, defines "qualified property" as meaning, in general, property (1) to which section 168 applies that has a recovery period of 20 years or less, which is computer software as defined in section 167(f)(1)(B) for which a deduction is allowable under section 167(a) without regard to section 168(k), which is water utility property, which is a qualified film or television production as defined in section 181(d) for which a deduction would have been allowable without regard to section 181(a)(2) or (g) or section 168(k), or which is a qualified live theatrical production as defined in section 181(e) for which a deduction would have been allowable without regard to section 181(a)(2) or (g) or section 168(k); (2) the original use of which begins with the taxpayer or the acquisition of which by the taxpayer meets the requirements of section 168(k)(2)(E)(ii); and (3) which is placed in service by the taxpayer before January 1, 2027. Section 168(k)(2)(E)(ii) requires that the acquired property was not used by the taxpayer at any time prior to such acquisition and the acquisition of such property meets the requirements of section 179(d)(2)(A), (B), and (C) and section 179(d)(3).

However, section 168(k)(2)(D) provides that qualified property does not include any property to which the alternative depreciation system under section 168(g) applies, determined without regard to section 168(g)(7) (relating to election to have the alternative depreciation system apply), and after application of section 280F(b) (relating to listed property with limited business use).

Section 13201(h) of the Act provides the effective dates of the amendments to section 168(k) made by section 13201 of the Act. Except as provided in section 13201(h)(2) of the Act, section 13201(h)(1) of the Act provides that these amendments apply to property acquired and placed in service after September 27, 2017. However, property is not treated as acquired after the date on which a written binding contract is entered into for such acquisition. Section 13201(h)(2) provides that the amendments apply to specified plants planted or grafted after September 27, 2017.

Additionally, section 12001(b)(13) of the Act repealed section 168(k)(4) (relating to the election to accelerate alternative minimum tax credits in lieu of the additional first year depreciation deduction) for taxable years beginning after December 31, 2017. Further, section 13204(a)(4)(B)(ii) repealed section 168(k)(3) (relating to qualified improvement property) for property placed in service after December 31, 2017.

Explanation of Provisions

The proposed regulations describe and clarify the statutory requirements that must be met for depreciable property to qualify for the additional first year depreciation deduction provided by section 168(k). Further, the proposed regulations instruct taxpayers how to determine the additional first year depreciation deduction and the amount of depreciation otherwise allowable for this property. Because the Act made substantial amendments to section 168(k), the proposed regulations update existing regulations in § 1.168(k)-1 by providing a new section at § 1.168(k)-2 for property acquired and placed in service after September 27, 2017, and make conforming amendments to the existing regulations.

1. *Eligibility Requirements for Additional First Year Depreciation Deduction*

The proposed regulations follow section 168(k)(2), as amended by the Act, and section 13201(h) of the Act to provide that depreciable property must meet four requirements to be qualified property. These requirements are (1) the depreciable property must be of a specified type; (2) the original use of the depreciable property must commence with the taxpayer or used depreciable property must meet the acquisition requirements of section 168(k)(2)(E)(ii); (3) the depreciable property must be placed in service by the taxpayer within a specified time period or must be planted or grafted by the taxpayer before a specified date; and (4) the depreciable property must be acquired by the taxpayer after September 27, 2017.

2. *Property of a Specified Type*

A. Property Eligible for the Additional First Year Depreciation Deduction

The proposed regulations follow the definition of qualified property in section 168(k)(2)(A)(i) and (k)(5) and provide that qualified property must be one of the following: (1) MACRS property that has a recovery period of 20 years or less; (2) computer software as defined in, and depreciated under, section 167(f)(1); (3) water utility property as defined in section 168(e)(5) and depreciated under section 168; (4) a qualified film or television production as defined in section 181(d) and for which a deduction would have been allowable under section 181 without regard to section 181(a)(2) and (g) or section 168(k); (5) a qualified live theatrical production as defined in section 181(e) and for which a deduction would have been allowable under section 181 without regard to section 181(a)(2) and (g) or section 168(k); or (6) a specified plant as defined in section 168(k)(5)(B) and for which the taxpayer has made an election to apply section 168(k)(5). Qualified improvement property acquired after September 27, 2017, and placed in service after September 27, 2017, and before January 1, 2018, also is qualified property.

For property placed in service after December 31, 2017, section 13204 of the Act amended section 168(e) to eliminate the 15-year MACRS property classification for qualified leasehold improvement property, qualified restaurant property, and qualified retail improvement property, and amended section 168(k) to eliminate qualified improvement property as a specific category of qualified property. Because of the effective date of section 13204 of the Act (property placed in service after December 31, 2017), the proposed regulations provide that MACRS property with a recovery period of 20 years or less includes the following MACRS property that is acquired by the taxpayer after September 27, 2017, and placed in service by the taxpayer after September 27, 2017, and before January 1, 2018: (1) Qualified leasehold improvement property; (2) qualified restaurant property that is qualified improvement property; and (3) qualified retail improvement property. For the same reason, the proposed regulations provide that qualified property includes qualified improvement property that is acquired by the taxpayer after September 27, 2017, and placed in service by the taxpayer after September 27, 2017, and before January 1, 2018. Further, to account for the statutory amendments to the definition of qualified improvement property made by the Act, the proposed regulations define qualified improvement property for purposes of section 168(k)(3) (before amendment by section 13204 of the Act) and section 168(e)(6) (as amended by section 13204 of the Act).

For purposes of determining the eligibility of MACRS property as qualified property, the proposed regulations retain the rule in § 1.168(k)-1(b)(2)(i)(A) that the recovery period applicable for the MACRS property under section 168(c) of the general depreciation system (GDS) is used, regardless of any election made by the taxpayer to depreciate the class of property under the alternative depreciation system of section 168(g) (ADS).

B. Property Not Eligible for the Additional First Year Depreciation Deduction

The proposed regulations provide that qualified property does not include (1) property excluded from the application of section 168 as a result of section 168(f); (2) property that is required to be depreciated under the ADS (as described below); (3) any class of property for which the taxpayer elects not to deduct the additional first year depreciation under section 168(k)(7); (4) a specified plant placed in service by the taxpayer in the taxable year and for which the taxpayer made an election to apply section 168(k)(5) for a prior year under section 168(k)(5)(D); (5) any class of property for which the taxpayer elects to apply section 168(k)(4) (this exclusion applies to property placed in service in any taxable year beginning before January 1, 2018, because section 12001(b)(13) of the Act repealed section 168(k)(4) for taxable years beginning after December 31, 2017); or (6) property described in section 168(k)(9)(A) or (B). Section 168(k)(9) provides that qualified property does not include (A) any property that is primarily used in a trade or business described in section 163(j)(7)(A)(iv), or (B) any property used in a trade or business that has had floor plan financing indebtedness (as defined in section 163(j)(9)) if the floor plan financing interest related to such indebtedness was taken into account under section 163(j)(1)(C). Section 163(j) applies to taxable years beginning after December 31, 2017. Accordingly, the exclusion of property described in section 168(k)(9) from the additional first year depreciation deduction applies to property placed in service in any taxable year beginning after December 31, 2017.

Property is required to be depreciated under the ADS if the property is described under section 168(g)(1)(A), (B), (C), (D), (F), or (G) or if other provisions of the Code require depreciation for the property to be determined under the ADS. Accordingly, MACRS property that is nonresidential real property, residential rental property, and qualified improvement property held by an electing real property trade or business (as defined in section 163(j)(7)(B)), and property with a recovery period of 10 years or more that is held by an electing farming business (as defined in section 163(j)(7)(C)), are not eligible for the additional first year depreciation deduction for taxable years beginning after December 31, 2017. Pursuant to section 168(k)(2)(D), MACRS property for which the taxpayer makes an election under section 168(g)(7) to depreciate the property under the ADS is eligible for the additional first year depreciation deduction (assuming all other requirements are met).

C. Elections

The proposed regulations provide rules for making the election out of the additional first year depreciation deduction pursuant to section 168(k)(7) and for making the election to apply section 168(k)(5) to a specified plant. Additionally, the proposed regulations provide rules for making the election under section 168(k)(10) to deduct 50 percent, instead of 100 percent, additional first year depreciation for qualified property acquired after September 27, 2017, by the taxpayer and placed in service or planted or grafted, as applicable, by the taxpayer during its taxable year that includes September 28, 2017. Because section 168(k)(10) does not state that the election may be made "with respect to any class of property" as stated in section 168(k)(7) for making the election out of the additional first year depreciation deduction, the proposed regulations provide that the election under section 168(k)(10) applies to all qualified property.

3. *New and Used Property*

A. New Property

The proposed regulations generally retain the original use rules in § 1.168(k)-1(b)(3). Pursuant to section 168(k)(2)(A)(ii), the proposed regulations do not provide any date by which the original use of the property must commence with the taxpayer. Because section 13201 of the Act removed the rules regarding sale-leaseback transactions, the proposed regulations also do not retain the original use rules in § 1.168(k)-1(b)(3)(iii)(A) and (C) regarding such transactions, including a sale-leaseback transaction followed by a syndication transaction. The rule in the proposed regulations for syndication transactions involving new or used property is explained later in the preamble.

B. Used Property

Pursuant to section 168(k)(2)(A)(ii) and (k)(2)(E)(ii), the proposed regulations provide that the acquisition of used property is eligible for the additional first year depreciation deduction if such acquisition meets the following requirements: (1) The property was not used by the taxpayer or a predecessor at any time prior to the acquisition; (2) the acquisition of the property meets the related party and carryover basis requirements of section 179(d)(2)(A), (B), and (C) and § 1.179-4(c)(1)(ii), (iii), and (iv), or (c)(2); and (3) the acquisition of the property meets the cost requirements of section 179(d)(3) and § 1.179-4(d).

i. Section 336(e) Election

A section 338 election and a section 336(e) election share many of the same characteristics. Therefore, the proposed regulations modify § 1.179-4(c)(2), which addresses the treatment of a section 338 election, to include property deemed to have been acquired by a new target corporation as a result of a section 336(e) election. Section 1.336-1(a)(1) provides that to the extent not inconsistent with section 336(e) or the regulations under section 336(e), the principles of section 338 and the regulations under section 338 apply for purposes of the regulations under section 336. To the extent that property is deemed to have been acquired by a "new target corporation," the Treasury Department and the IRS read § 1.179-4(c)(2), without modification, as applying to the deemed acquisition of property by a new target corporation as a result of a section 336(e) election, just as it applies as the result of a section 338 election. However, to remove any doubt, the proposed regulations modify § 1.179-4(c)(2) to provide that property deemed to have been acquired by a new target corporation as a result of a section 338 or a section 336(e) election will be considered acquired by purchase for purposes of section 179.

ii. Property Not Previously Used By The Taxpayer

The proposed regulations provide that the property is treated as used by the taxpayer or a predecessor at any time before its acquisition of the property only if the taxpayer or the predecessor had a depreciable interest in the property at any time before the acquisition, whether or not the taxpayer or the predecessor claimed depreciation deductions for the property. If a lessee has a depreciable interest in the improvements made to leased property and subsequently the lessee acquires the leased property of which the improvements are a part, the proposed regulations provide that the unadjusted depreciable basis, as defined in § 1.168(b)-1(a)(3), of the acquired property that is eligible for the additional first year depreciation deduction, assuming all other requirements are met, does not include the unadjusted depreciable basis attributable to the improvements.

Further, if a taxpayer initially acquires a depreciable interest in a portion of the property and subsequently acquires an additional depreciable interest in the same property, the proposed regulations also provide that such additional depreciable interest is not treated as being previously used by the taxpayer. However, if a taxpayer holds a depreciable interest in a portion of the property, sells that portion or a part of that portion, and subsequently acquires a depreciable interest in another portion of the same property, the proposed regulations provide that the taxpayer will be treated as previously having a depreciable interest in the property up to the amount of the portion for which the taxpayer held a depreciable interest in the property before the sale.

The Treasury Department and the IRS request comments on whether a safe harbor should be provided on how many taxable years a taxpayer or a predecessor should look back to determine if the taxpayer or the predecessor previously had a depreciable interest in the property. Such comments should provide the number of taxable years recommended for the look-back period and the reasoning for such number.

iii. Rules Applying to Consolidated Groups

Members of a consolidated group generally are treated as separate taxpayers. See *Woolford Realty Co. v. Rose*, 286 U.S. 319, 328 (1932) ("[a] corporation does not cease to be [a taxpayer] by affiliating with another"). However, the Treasury Department and the IRS believe that the additional first year depreciation deduction should not be permitted to members of a consolidated group when property is disposed of by one member of a consolidated group outside the group and subsequently acquired by another member of the same group because permitting such a deduction would not clearly reflect the group's income tax liability. See section 1502 (permitting consolidated group regulations different from the rules of chapter 1 of subtitle A of the Code otherwise applicable to separate corporations to clearly reflect the income tax liability of a consolidated group or each member of the group). To implement this position, these proposed regulations treat a member of a consolidated group as previously having a depreciable interest in all property in which the consolidated group is treated as previously having a depreciable interest. For purposes of this rule, a consolidated group will be treated as having a depreciable interest in property if any current or previous member of the group had a depreciable interest in the property while a member of the group.

The Treasury Department and the IRS also believe that the additional first year depreciation deduction should not be allowed when, as part of a series of related transactions, one or more members of a consolidated group acquire both the stock of a corporation that previously had a depreciable interest in the property and the property itself. Assume a corporation (the selling corporation) has a depreciable interest in property and sells it to an unrelated party. Subsequently, as part of a series of related transactions, a member of a consolidated group, unrelated to the selling corporation, acquires the property and either that member or a different member of the group acquires the stock of the selling corporation. In substance, the series of transactions is the same as if the selling corporation reacquired the property and then transferred it to another member of the group, in which case the additional first year depreciation deduction would not be allowed. Accordingly, these proposed regulations deny the deduction in such circumstances.

Additionally, if the acquisition of property is part of a series of related transactions that also includes one or more transactions in which the transferee of the property ceases to be a member of a consolidated group, then whether the taxpayer is a member of a consolidated group is tested immediately after the last transaction in the series.

iv. Series of Related Transactions

In determining whether property meets the requirements of section 168(k)(2)(E)(ii), the Treasury Department and the IRS believe that the ordering of steps, or the use of an unrelated intermediary, in a series of related transactions should not control. For example, if a father buys and places equipment in service for use in the father's trade or business and subsequently the father sells the equipment to his daughter for use in her trade or business, the father and daughter are related parties under section 179(d)(2)(A) and § 1.179-4(c)(1)(ii) and therefore, the daughter's acquisition of the equipment is not eligible for the additional first year depreciation deduction. However, if in a series of related transactions, the father sells the equipment to an unrelated party and then the unrelated party sells the equipment to the father's daughter, the daughter's acquisition of the equipment from the unrelated party, absent the rule in the proposed regulations, is eligible for the additional first year depreciation deduction (assuming all other requirements are met). Thus, the proposed regulations provide that in the case of a series of related transactions, the transfer of the property will be treated as directly transferred from the original transferor to the ultimate transferee, and the relation between the original transferor and the ultimate transferee is tested immediately after the last transaction in the series.

C. Application to Partnerships

On September 8, 2003, the Treasury Department and the IRS published temporary regulations (T.D. 9091, 2003-2 C.B. 939) in the **Federal Register** (68 FR 52986) relating to the additional first year depreciation deduction provisions of sections 168(k) and 1400L(b) (before amendment by sections 403 and 408 of the Working Families Tax Relief Act of 2004). Those regulations provided that any increase in the basis of qualified property due to a section 754 election generally is not eligible for the additional first year depreciation deduction. The preamble to those regulations explained that any increase in basis due to a section 754 election does not satisfy the original use requirement. The final regulations (T.D. 9283, 2006-2 C.B. 633, 642-43) published in the **Federal Register** on August 31, 2006 (71 FR 51738) retained the rule for increases in basis due to section 754 elections at § 1.168(k)-1(f)(9). Because the Act amended section 168(k) to allow the additional first year depreciation deduction for certain used property in addition to new property, the Treasury Department and the IRS have reconsidered whether basis adjustments under sections 734(b) and 743(b) now qualify for the additional first year depreciation deduction. The Treasury Department and the IRS also have considered whether certain section 704(c) adjustments as well as the basis of distributed property determined under section 732 should qualify for the additional first year depreciation deduction.

i. Section 704(c) Remedial Allocations

Section 1.704-3(d)(2) provides, in part, that under the remedial allocation method, the portion of a partnership's book basis in contributed property that exceeds its adjusted tax basis is recovered using any recovery period and depreciation (or other cost recovery) method available to the partnership for newly purchased property (of the same type as the contributed property) that is placed in service at the time of contribution. The proposed regulations provide that remedial allocations under section 704(c) do not qualify for the additional first year depreciation deduction under section 168(k).

Notwithstanding the language of § 1.704-3(d)(2) that any method available to the partnership for newly purchased property may be used to recover the portion of the partnership's book basis in contributed property that exceeds its adjusted tax basis, remedial allocations do not meet the requirements of section 168(k)(2)(E)(ii). Because the underlying property is contributed to the partnership in a section 721 transaction, the partnership's basis in the property is determined by reference to the contributing partner's basis in the property, which violates sections 179(d)(2)(C) and 168(k)(2)(E)(ii)(II). In addition, the partnership has already had a depreciable interest in the contributed property at the time the remedial allocation is made, which is in violation of section 168(k)(2)(E)(ii)(I) as well as the original use requirement.

The same rule applies in the case of revaluations of partnership property (reverse section 704(c) allocations).

ii. Zero Basis Property

Section 1.704-1(b)(2)(iv)(*g*)(3) provides that, if partnership property has a zero adjusted tax basis, any reasonable method may be used to determine the book depreciation, depletion, or amortization of the property. The proposed regulations provide that the additional first year depreciation deduction under section 168(k) will not be allowed on property contributed to the partnership with a zero adjusted tax basis because, with the additional first year depreciation deduction, the partners have the potential to shift built-in gain among partners.

iii. Basis Determined Under Section 732

Section 732(a)(1) provides that the basis of property (other than money) distributed by a partnership to a partner other than in liquidation of the partner's interest is its adjusted basis to the partnership immediately before the distribution. Section 732(a)(2) provides that the basis determined under section 732(a)(1) shall not exceed the adjusted basis of the partner's interest in the partnership reduced by any money distributed in the same transaction. Section 732(b) provides that the basis of property (other than money) distributed by a partnership to a partner in liquidation of the partner's interest is equal to the adjusted basis of the partner's interest in the partnership reduced by any money distributed in the same transaction.

Property distributed by a partnership to a partner fails to satisfy the original use requirement because the partnership used the property prior to the distribution. Distributed property also fails to satisfy the acquisition requirements of section 168(k)(2)(E)(ii)(II). Any portion of basis determined by section 732(a)(1) fails to satisfy section 179(d)(2)(C) because it is determined by reference to the partnership's basis in the distributed property. Similarly, any portion of basis determined by section 732(a)(2) or (b) fails to satisfy section 179(d)(3) because it is determined by reference to the distributee partner's basis in its partnership interest (reduced by any money distributed in the same transaction).

iv. Section 734(b) Adjustments

Section 734(b)(1) provides that, in the case of a distribution of property to a partner with respect to which a section 754 election is in effect (or when there is a substantial basis reduction under section 734(d)), the partnership will increase the adjusted basis of partnership property by the sum of (A) the amount of any gain recognized to the distributee partner under section 731(a)(1), and (B) in the case of distributed property to which section 732(a)(2) or (b) applies, the excess of the adjusted basis of the distributed property to the partnership immediately before the distribution (as adjusted by section 732(d)) over the basis of the distributed property to the distributee, as determined under section 732.

Because a section 734(b) basis adjustment is made to the basis of partnership property (i.e., non-partner specific basis) and the partnership used the property prior to the partnership distribution giving rise to the basis adjustment, a section 734(b) basis adjustment fails the original use clause in section 168(k)(2)(A)(ii) and also fails the used property requirement in section 168(k)(2)(E)(ii)(I). The proposed regulations therefore provide that section 734(b) basis adjustments are not eligible for the additional first year depreciation deduction.

v. Section 743(b) Adjustments

Section 743(b)(1) provides that, in the case of a transfer of a partnership interest, either by sale or exchange or as a result of the death of a partner, a partnership that has a section 754 election in effect (or if there is a substantial built-in loss immediately after such partnership interest transfer under section 743(d)), will increase the adjusted basis of partnership property by the excess of the transferee's basis in the transferred partnership interest over the transferee's share of the adjusted basis of partnership's property. This increase is an adjustment to the basis of partnership property with respect to the transferee partner only and, therefore, is a partner specific basis adjustment to partnership property. The section 743(b) basis adjustment is allocated among partnership properties under section 755. As stated above, prior to the Act, a section 743(b) basis adjustment would always fail the original use requirement in section 168(k)(2)(A)(ii) because partnership property to which a section 743(b) basis adjustment relates would have been previously used by the partnership and its partners prior to the transfer that gave rise to the section 743(b) adjustment. After the Act, while a section 743(b) basis adjustment still fails the original use clause in section 168(k)(2)(A)(ii), a transaction giving rise to a section 743(b) basis adjustment may satisfy the used property clause in section 168(k)(2)(A)(ii) because of the used property acquisition requirements of section 168(k)(2)(E)(ii), depending on the facts and circumstances.

Because a section 743(b) basis adjustment is a partner specific basis adjustment to partnership property, the proposed regulations take an aggregate view and provide that, in determining whether a section 743(b) basis adjustment meets the used property acquisition requirements of section 168(k)(2)(E)(ii), each partner is treated as having owned and used the partner's proportionate share of partnership property. In the case of a transfer of a partnership interest, section 168(k)(2)(E)(ii)(I) will be satisfied if the partner acquiring the interest, or a predecessor of such partner, has not used the portion of the partnership property to which the section 743(b) basis adjustment relates at any time prior to the acquisition (that is, the transferee has not used the transferor's portion of partnership property prior to the acquisition), notwithstanding the fact that the partnership itself has previously used the property. Similarly, for purposes of applying section 179(d)(2)(A), (B), and (C), the partner acquiring a partnership interest is treated as acquiring a portion of partnership property, and the partner who is transferring a partnership interest is treated as the person from whom the property is acquired.

For example, the relationship between the transferor partner and the transferee partner must not be a prohibited relationship under section 179(d)(2)(A). Also, the transferor partner and transferee partner may not be part of the same controlled group under section 179(d)(2)(B). Finally, the transferee partner's basis in the transferred partnership interest may not be determined in whole or in part by reference to the transferor's adjusted basis, or under section 1014.

The same result will apply regardless of whether the transferee partner is a new partner or an existing partner purchasing an additional partnership interest from another partner. Assuming that the transferor partner's specific interest in partnership property that is acquired by the transferee partner has not previously been used by the transferee partner or a predecessor, the corresponding section 743(b) basis adjustment will be eligible for the additional first year depreciation deduction in the hands of the transferee partner, provided all other requirements of section 168(k) are satisfied (and assuming § 1.743-1(j)(4)(i)(B)(2) does not apply). This treatment is appropriate notwithstanding the fact that the transferee partner may have an existing interest in the underlying partnership property, because the transferee's existing interest in the underlying partnership property is distinct from the interest being transferred.

Finally, the proposed regulations provide that a section 743(b) basis adjustment in a class of property (not including the property class for section 743(b) basis adjustments) may be recovered using the additional first year depreciation deduction under section 168(k) without regard to whether the partnership elects out of the additional first year depreciation deduction under section 168(k)(7) for all other qualified property in the same class of property and placed in service in the same taxable year. Similarly, a partnership may make the election out of the additional first year depreciation deduction under section 168(k)(7) for a section 743(b) basis adjustment in a class of property (not including the property class for section 743(b) basis adjustments), and this election will not bind the partnership to such election for all other qualified property of the partnership in the same class of property and placed in service in the same taxable year.

D. Syndication Transaction

The syndication transaction rule in the proposed regulations is based on the rules in section 168(k)(2)(E)(iii) for syndication transactions. For new or used property, the proposed regulations provide that if (1) a lessor has a depreciable interest in the property and the lessor and any predecessor did not previously have a depreciable interest in the property, (2) the property is sold by the lessor or any subsequent purchaser within three months after the date the property was originally placed in service by the lessor (or, in the case of multiple units of property subject to the same lease, within three months after the date the final unit is placed in service, so long as the period between the time the first unit is placed in service and the time the last unit is placed in service does not exceed 12 months), and (3) the user (lessee) of the property after the last sale during the three-month period remains the same as when the property was originally placed in service by the lessor, then the purchaser of the property in the last sale during the three-month period is considered the taxpayer that acquired the property and the taxpayer that originally placed the property in service, but not earlier than the date of the last sale. Thus, if a transaction is within the rules described above, the purchaser of the property in the last sale during the three-month period is eligible to claim the additional first year depreciation for the property (assuming all requirements are met), and the earlier purchasers of the property are not.

4. *Placed-in-Service Date*

The proposed regulations generally retain the placed-in-service date rules in § 1.168(k)-1(b)(5). Pursuant to the effective date in section 13201(h) of the Act and section 168(k)(2)(A)(iii) and (k)(2)(B)(i)(II), the proposed regulations provide that qualified property must be placed in service by the taxpayer after September 27, 2017, and before January 1, 2027, or, in the case of property described in section 168(k)(2)(B) or (C), before January 1, 2028. Because section 13201 of the Act removed the rules regarding sale-leaseback transactions, the proposed regulations do not retain the placed-in-service date rules in § 1.168(k)-1(b)(5)(ii)(A) and (C) regarding such transactions, including a sale-leaseback transaction followed by a syndication transaction.

Further, the proposed regulations provide rules for specified plants. Pursuant to section 168(k)(5)(A), if the taxpayer has made an election to apply section 168(k)(5) for a specified plant, the proposed regulations provide that the specified plant must be planted before January 1, 2027, or grafted before January 1, 2027, to a plant that has already been planted, by the taxpayer in the ordinary course of the taxpayer's farming business, as defined in section 263A(e)(4).

Pursuant to section 168(k)(2)(H), the proposed regulations also provide that a qualified film or television production is treated as placed in service at the time of initial release or broadcast as defined under § 1.181-1(a)(7), and a qualified live theatrical production is treated as placed in service at the time of the initial live staged performance. The proposed regulations also provide that the initial live staged performance of a qualified live theatrical production is the first commercial exhibition of a production to an audience. An initial live staged performance does not include limited exhibition, prior to commercial exhibition to general audiences, if the limited exhibition is primarily for purposes of publicity, determining the need for further production activity, or raising funds for the completion of production. For example, the initial live staged performance does not include a preview of the production if the preview is primarily to determine the need for further production activity.

5. *Date of Acquisition*

The proposed regulations provide rules applicable to the acquisition requirements of the effective date under section 13201(h) of the Act. The proposed regulations provide that these rules apply to all property, including self-constructed property or property described in section 168(k)(2)(B) or (C).

A. Written Binding Contract

Pursuant to section 13201(h)(1)(A) of the Act, the proposed regulations provide that the property must be acquired by the taxpayer after September 27, 2017, or, acquired by the taxpayer pursuant to a written binding contract entered into by the taxpayer after September 27, 2017. Because of the clear language of section 13201(h)(1) of the Act regarding written binding contracts, the proposed regulations also provide that property that is manufactured, constructed, or produced for the taxpayer by another person under a written binding contract that is entered into prior to the manufacture, construction, or production of the property for use by the taxpayer in its trade or business or for its production of income is acquired pursuant to a written binding contract. Further, if the written binding contract states the date on which the contract was entered into and a closing date, delivery date, or other similar date, the date on which the contract was entered into is the date the taxpayer acquired the property. The proposed regulations retain the rules in § 1.168(k)-1(b)(4)(ii) defining a binding contract. Additionally, the proposed regulations provide that a letter of intent for an acquisition is not a binding contract.

B. Self-Constructed Property

If a taxpayer manufactures, constructs, or produces property for its own use, the Treasury Department and the IRS recognize that the written binding contract rule in section 13201(h)(1) of the Act does not apply. In such case, the proposed regulations provide that the acquisition rules in section 13201(h)(1) of the Act are treated as met if the taxpayer begins manufacturing, constructing, or producing the property after September 27, 2017. The proposed regulations provide rules similar to those in § 1.168(k)-1(b)(4)(iii)(B) for defining when manufacturing, construction, or production begins, including the safe harbor, and in § 1.168(k)-1(b)(4)(iii)(C) for a contract to acquire, or for the manufacture, construction, or production of, a component of the larger self-constructed property. As stated in the preceding paragraph, these self-constructed rules in the proposed regulations do not apply to property that is manufactured, constructed, or produced for the taxpayer by another person under a written binding contract that is entered into prior to the manufacture, construction, or production of the property.

C. Qualified Film, Television, or Live Theatrical Productions

The proposed regulations also provide rules for qualified film, television, or live theatrical productions. For purposes of section 13201(h)(1)(A) of the Act, the proposed regulations provide that a qualified film or television production is treated as acquired on the date principal photography commences, and a qualified live theatrical production is treated as acquired on the date when all of the necessary elements for producing the live theatrical production are secured. These elements may include a script, financing, actors, set, scenic and costume designs, advertising agents, music, and lighting.

D. Specified Plants

Pursuant to section 13201(h)(2) of the Act, if the taxpayer makes an election to apply section 168(k)(5) for a specified plant, the proposed regulations provide that the specified plant must be planted after September 27, 2017, or grafted after September 27, 2017, to a plant that has already been planted, by the taxpayer in the ordinary course of the taxpayer's farming business, as defined in section 263A(e)(4).

6. *Longer Production Period Property or Certain Aircraft Property*

The proposed regulations provide rules for determining when longer production period property or certain aircraft property described in section 168(k)(2)(B) or (C) meets the acquisition requirements of section 168(k)(2)(B)(i)(III) or (k)(2)(C)(i), as applicable. Pursuant to section 168(k)(2)(B)(i)(III) and (k)(2)(C)(i), the proposed regulations provide that property described in section 168(k)(2)(B) or (C) must be acquired by the taxpayer before January 1, 2027, or acquired by the taxpayer pursuant to a written binding contract that is entered into before January 1, 2027. These acquisition requirements are in addition to those in section 13201(h)(1) of the Act, which require acquisition to occur after September 27, 2017.

The proposed regulations provide that the written binding contract rules for longer production period property and certain aircraft property are the same rules that apply for purposes of determining whether the acquisition requirements of section 13201(h)(1) of the Act are met.

With respect to self-constructed property described in section 168(k)(2)(B) or (C), the proposed regulations follow the acquisition rule in section 168(k)(2)(E)(i) for self-constructed property and provide that the acquisition requirements of section 168(k)(2)(B)(i)(III) or (k)(2)(C)(i), as applicable, are met if a taxpayer manufactures, constructs, or produces the property for its own use and such manufacturing, construction, or productions begins before January 1, 2027. Further, only for purposes of section 168(k)(2)(B)(i)(III) and (k)(2)(C)(i), the proposed regulations provide that property that is manufactured, constructed, or produced for the taxpayer by another person under a written binding contract that is entered into prior to the manufacture, construction, or production of the property for use by the taxpayer in its trade or business or for its production of income is considered to be manufactured, constructed, or produced by the taxpayer. The proposed regulations also provide rules similar to those in § 1.168(k)-1(b)(4)(iii)(B) for defining when manufacturing, construction, or production begins, including the same safe harbor, and in § 1.168(k)-1(b)(4)(iii)(C) for a contract to acquire, or for the manufacture, construction, or production of, a component of the larger self-constructed property.

7. Computation of Additional First Year Depreciation Deduction and Otherwise Allowable Depreciation

Pursuant to section 168(k)(1)(A), the proposed regulations provide that the allowable additional first year depreciation deduction for qualified property is equal to the applicable percentage (as defined in section 168(k)(6)) of the unadjusted depreciable basis (as defined in § 1.168(b)-1(a)(3)) of the property. For qualified property described in section 168(k)(2)(B), the unadjusted depreciable basis (as defined in § 1.168(b)-1(a)(3)) of the property is limited to the property's basis attributable to manufacture, construction, or production of the property before January 1, 2027, as provided in section 168(k)(2)(B)(ii).

Pursuant to section 168(k)(2)(G), the proposed regulations also provide that the additional first year depreciation deduction is allowed for both regular tax and alternative minimum tax (AMT) purposes. However, for AMT purposes, the amount of the additional first year depreciation deduction is based on the unadjusted depreciable basis of the property for AMT purposes. The amount of the additional first year depreciation deduction is not affected by a taxable year of less than 12 months for either regular or AMT purposes.

The proposed regulations provide rules similar to those in § 1.168(k)-1(d)(2) for determining the amount of depreciation otherwise allowable for qualified property. That is, before determining the amount of depreciation otherwise allowable for qualified property, the proposed regulations require the taxpayer to first reduce the unadjusted depreciable basis (as defined in § 1.168(b)-1(a)(3)) of the property by the amount of the additional first year depreciation deduction allowed or allowable, whichever is greater (the remaining adjusted depreciable basis), as provided in section 168(k)(1)(B). Then, the remaining adjusted depreciable basis is depreciated using the applicable depreciation provisions of the Code for the property (for example, section 168 for MACRS property, section 167(f)(1) for computer software, and section 167 for film, television, or theatrical productions). This amount of depreciation is allowed for both regular tax and AMT purposes, and is affected by a taxable year of less than 12 months. However, for AMT purposes, the amount of depreciation allowed is determined by calculating the remaining adjusted depreciable basis of the property for AMT purposes and using the same depreciation method, recovery period, and convention that applies to the property for regular tax purposes. If a taxpayer uses the optional depreciation tables in Rev. Proc. 87-57 (1987-2 C.B. 687) to compute depreciation for qualified property that is MACRS property, the proposed regulations also provide that the remaining adjusted depreciable basis of the property is the basis to which the annual depreciation rates in those tables apply.

8. Special Rules

The proposed regulations also provide rules similar to those in § 1.168(k)-1(f) for certain situations. However, the special rules in § 1.168(k)-1(f)(9) regarding the increase in basis due to a section 754 election are addressed in the proposed regulations regarding the used property acquisition requirements. Further, the special rules in § 1.168(k)-1(f)(1)(iii) regarding property placed in service and transferred in a section 168(i)(7) transaction in the same taxable year, and in § 1.168(k)-1(f)(5) regarding like-kind exchanges or involuntary conversions, are updated to reflect the used property acquisition requirements in section 168(k)(2)(E)(ii). The special rules in the proposed regulations also are updated to reflect the applicable dates under section 168(k), and the changes by the Act to technical terminations of partnerships and the rehabilitation credit.

The proposed regulations provide rules for the following situations: (1) Qualified property placed in service or planted or grafted, as applicable, and disposed of in the same taxable year; (2) redetermination of basis of qualified property; (3) recapture of additional first year depreciation for purposes of section 1245 and section 1250; (4) a certified pollution control facility that is qualified property; (5) like-kind exchanges and involuntary conversions of qualified property; (6) a change in use of qualified property; (7) the computation of earnings and profits; (8) the increase in the limitation of the amount of depreciation for passenger automobiles; (9) the rehabilitation credit under section 47; and (10) computation of depreciation for purposes of section 514(a)(3).

The proposed regulations provide a special rule for qualified property that is placed in service in a taxable year and then contributed to a partnership under section 721(a) in the same taxable year when one of the other partners previously had a depreciable interest in the property. Situation 1 of Rev. Rul. 99-5 (1999-1 C.B. 434) is an example of such a fact pattern. Under § 1.168(k)-1(f)(1)(iii) and its cross-reference to § 1.168(d)-1(b)(7)(ii), the additional first year depreciation deduction associated with the contributed property would be allocated between the contributing partner and the partnership based on the proportionate time the contributing partner and the partnership held the property throughout the taxable year. The partnership could then allocate a portion of the deduction to the partner with a previous depreciable interest in the property. The Treasury Department and the IRS believe that allocating any portion of the deduction to a partner who previously had a depreciable interest in the property would be inconsistent with section 168(k)(2)(E)(ii)(I). Therefore, the proposed regulations provide that, in this situation, the additional first year depreciation deduction with respect to the contributed property is not allocated under the general rules of § 1.168(d)-1(b)(7)(ii). Instead, the additional first year depreciation deduction is allocated entirely to the contributing partner prior to the section 721(a) transaction and not to the partnership.

With respect to like-kind exchanges and involuntary conversions, § 1.168(k)-1(f)(5) provides that the exchanged basis and excess basis, if any, of the replacement property is eligible for the additional first year depreciation deduction if the replacement property is qualified property. The proposed regulations retain this rule if the replacement property also meets the original use requirement. Pursuant to section 168(k)(2)(E)(ii)(II) and its cross-reference to section 179(d)(3), the proposed regulations also provide that only the excess basis, if any, of the replacement property is eligible for the additional first year depreciation deduction if the replacement property is qualified property and also meets the used property acquisition requirements. These rules also apply when a taxpayer makes the election under § 1.168(i)-6(i)(1) to treat, for depreciation purposes only, the total of the exchanged basis and excess basis, if any, in the replacement MACRS property as property placed in service by the taxpayer at the time of replacement and the adjusted depreciable basis of the relinquished MACRS property as disposed of by the taxpayer at the time of disposition. The proposed regulations also retain the other rules in § 1.168(k)-1(f)(5) for like-kind exchanges and involuntary conversions, but update the definitions to be consistent with the definitions in § 1.168(i)-6, which addresses how to compute depreciation of property involved in like-kind exchanges or involuntary conversions.

Proposed Applicability Date

These regulations are proposed to apply to qualified property placed in service or planted or grafted, as applicable, by the taxpayer during or after the taxpayer's taxable year that includes the date of publication of a Treasury decision adopting these rules as final regulations in the **Federal Register**. Pending the issuance of the final regulations, a taxpayer may choose to apply these proposed regulations to qualified property acquired and placed in service or planted or grafted, as applicable, after September 27, 2017, by the taxpayer during taxable years ending on or after September 28, 2017.

Special Analyses

The Administrator of the Office of Information and Regulatory Affairs (OIRA), Office of Management and Budget, has waived review of this proposed rule in accordance with section 6(a)(3)(A) of Executive Order 12866. OIRA will subsequently make a significance determination of the final rule, pursuant to section 3(f) of Executive Order (EO) 12866 and the April 11, 2018, Memorandum of Agreement between the Department of Treasury and the Office of Management and Budget (OMB).

The proposed regulations do not impose a collection of information on small entities and provide clarifying rules for taxpayers to enjoy the tax benefit of 100-percent additional first year depreciation as provided by the amendments to section 168 by the Act. Therefore, a regulatory flexibility analysis is not required under the Regulatory Flexibility Act (5 U.S.C. chapter 6). Pursuant to section 7805(f) of the Code, this notice of proposed rulemaking will be submitted to the Chief Counsel for Advocacy of the Small Business Administration for comment on its impact on small business.

Comments and Requests for a Public Hearing

Before these proposed regulations are adopted as final regulations, consideration will be given to any comments that are submitted timely to the IRS as prescribed in this preamble under the **ADDRESSES** heading. The Treasury Department and the IRS request comments on all aspects of the proposed rules. All comments will be available at *http://www.regulations.gov* or upon request. A public hearing will be scheduled if requested in writing by any person that timely submits written comments. If a public hearing is scheduled, notice of the date, time, and place for the public hearing will be published in the **Federal Register**.

Drafting Information

The principal authors of these proposed regulations are Kathleen Reed and Elizabeth R. Binder of the Office of Associate Chief Counsel (Income Tax and Accounting). However, other personnel from the Treasury Department and the IRS participated in their development.

[¶49,767] **Proposed Amendments of Regulations (REG-136118-15, REG-119337-17, REG-118067-17, REG-120232-17 and REG-120233-17)**, published in the Federal Register on August 17, 2018.

[Code Secs. 704, 705, 706, 6221, 6222, 6225, 6226, 6227, 6231, 6232, 6233, 6234, 6235 and 6241]

Centralized partnership audit regime: Technical Corrections Act of 2018 (TTCA): Partnership items: Partnership-related items: Withdrawal of proposed regulations.—Reg. §§301.6225-4 and 301.6226-4 and amendments of Reg. §§1.704-1, 1.705-1 and 1.706-4, implementing the centralized partnership audit regime, in order to reflect the changes made by the Technical Corrections Act of 2018, contained in Title II of the Consolidated Appropriations Act of 2018 (TTCA), are reproposed. Amendments of Reg. §§301.6221(a)-1, 301.6225-1, 301.6226-2, 301.6226-3 and 301.6227-2 proposed on November 30, 2017, Reg. §§301.6231-1, 301.6232-1, 301.6233(a)-1, 301.6233(b)-1, 301.6234-1 and 301.6235-1 and amendments of Reg. §§301.6221(a)-1, 301.6225-2, 301.6226-1, 301.6226-2, 301.6226-3 and 301.6227-3 proposed on December 19, 2017, Reg. §§301.6225-4 and 301.6226-4 and amendments of Reg. §§1.704-1, 1.705-1, 1.706-4 and 301.6225-3 proposed on February 2, 2018 and Reg. §§301.6221(a)-1, 301.6222-1, 301.6225-1, 301.6225-2, 301.6225-3, 301.6225-4, 301.6226-1, 301.6226-2, 301.6226-3, 301.6226-4, 301.6227-1, 301.6227-2, 301.6227-3, 301.6241-1, 301.6241-2, 301.6241-3, 301.6241-4 and 301.6241-5 proposed on June 14, 2017, are withdrawn. Reg. §§301.6221(a)-1, 301.6222-1, 301.6225-1, 301.6225-2, 301.6225-3, 301.6226-1, 301.6226-2, 301.6226-3, 301.6227-1, 301.6227-2, 301.6227-3, 301.6231-1, 301.6232-1, 301.6233(a)-1, 301.6233(b)-1, 301.6234-1, 301.6235-1, 301.6241-1, 301.6241-2, 301.6241-3, 301.6241-4, 301.6241-5 and 301.6241-6 adopted by T.D. 9844.

AGENCY: Internal Revenue Service (IRS), Treasury.

ACTION: Notice of proposed rulemaking; notice of public hearing; withdrawal and partial withdrawal of notices of proposed rulemaking.

SUMMARY: This document contains proposed regulations implementing the centralized partnership audit regime. This document withdraws and reproposes certain portions of proposed regulations implementing the centralized partnership audit regime that have not been finalized to reflect the changes made by the Technical Corrections Act of 2018, contained in Title II of the Consolidated Appropriations Act of 2018 (TTCA). The proposed regulations affect partnerships with respect to partnership taxable years beginning after December 31, 2017, as well as partnerships that make the election under the Bipartisan Budget Act of 2015 (BBA),to apply the centralized partnership audit regime to partnership taxable years beginning on or after November 2, 2015 and before January 1, 2018.

DATES: Written or electronic comments must be received by October 1, 2018. Outlines of topics to be discussed at the public hearing scheduled for October 9, 2018, at 10 A.M. must be received by October 1, 2018.

ADDRESSES: Send submissions to: CC:PA:LPD:PR (REG-136118-15), room 5207, Internal Revenue Service, P.O. Box 7604, Ben Franklin Station, Washington, DC 20044. Submissions may be hand delivered Monday through Friday between the hours of 8 a.m. and 4 p.m. to CC:PA:LPD:PR (REG-136118-15), Courier's Desk, Internal Revenue Service, 1111 Constitution Avenue NW, Washington, DC 20224, or sent electronically via the Federal eRulemaking Portal at *www.regulations.gov* (IRS REG-136118-15).

FOR FURTHER INFORMATION CONTACT: Concerning the proposed regulations under sections 6221, 6226, 6235, and 6241, Jennifer M. Black of the Office of Associate Chief Counsel (Procedure and Administration), (202) 317-6834; concerning the proposed regulations under sections 6225, 6231, and 6234, Joy E. Gerdy-Zogby of the Office of Associate Chief Counsel (Procedure and Administration), (202) 317-6834; concerning the proposed regulations under sections 6222, 6227, 6232, and 6233, Steven L. Karon of the Office of Associate Chief Counsel (Procedure and Administration), (202) 217-6834; concerning the proposed regulations under section 6225 relating to creditable foreign tax expenditures, Larry R. Pounders, Jr. of the Office of Associate Chief Counsel (International), (202) 317-5465; concerning the proposed regulations relating to chapters 3 and 4 of subtitle A of the Internal Revenue Code (other than section 1446), Subin Seth of the Office of Associate Chief Counsel (International), (202) 317-5003; concerning the proposed regulations relating to section 1446, Ronald M. Gootzeit of the Office of Associate Chief Counsel (International), (202) 317-4953; concerning the proposed regulations under sections 704 through 706 and §§301.6225-4 and 301.6226-4, Allison R. Carmody or Meghan M. Howard of the Office of Associate Chief Counsel (Passthroughs and Special Industries), (202) 317-5279; concerning the submission of comments, the hearing, or to be placed on the building access list to attend the hearing, Regina Johnson, (202) 317-6901 (not toll-free numbers).

SUPPLEMENTARY INFORMATION:

Background

This document contains proposed regulations under sections 704 through 706 to amend the Income Tax Regulations (26 CFR Part 1) under Subpart — Partners and Partnerships and proposed regulations under sections 6221 through 6241 to amend the Procedure and Administration Regulations (26 CFR Part 301) under Subpart - Tax Treatment of Partnership Items to implement the centralized partnership audit regime enacted by section 1101 of the BBA, Public Law 114-74 (BBA), as amended by the Protecting Americans from Tax Hikes Act of 2015, Public Law 114-113 (PATH Act) and sections 201 through 207 of the TTCA, Public Law 115-141. This document also withdraws portions of proposed regulations under sections 704 through 706 and 6221 through 6241 that were published in the **Federal Register** on June 14, 2017 (REG-136118-15, 82 FR 27334), November 30,

2017(REG-119337-17, 82 FR 56765), December 19, 2017(REG-120232-17 and REG-120233-17, 82 FR 27071), and February 2, 2018 (REG-118067-17, 83 FR 4868).

Section 1101(a) of the BBA removed subchapter C of chapter 63 of the Internal Revenue Code (Code) effective for partnership taxable years beginning after December 31, 2017. Subchapter C of chapter 63 of the Code (subchapter C of chapter 63) contained the unified partnership audit and litigation rules that were commonly referred to as the TEFRA partnership procedures or simply TEFRA. Section 1101(b) of the BBA also removed subchapter D of chapter 63 of the Code and part IV of subchapter K of chapter 1 of the Code, rules applicable to electing large partnerships, effective for partnership taxable years beginning after December 31, 2017. Section 1101(c) of the BBA replaced the TEFRA partnership procedures and the rules applicable to electing large partnerships with a centralized partnership audit regime that, in general, determines, assesses, and collects tax at the partnership level.

On December 18, 2015, section 1101 of the BBA was amended by the PATH Act. The amendments under the PATH Act are effective as if included in section 1101 of the BBA, and therefore, subject to the effective dates in section 1101(g) of the BBA.

On June 14, 2017, the Treasury Department and the IRS published in the **Federal Register** (82 FR 27334) a notice of proposed rulemaking (REG-136118-15) (June 2017 NPRM) proposing rules under section 6221 regarding the scope and election out of the centralized partnership audit regime, section 6222 regarding consistent treatment by partners, section 6223 regarding the partnership representative, section 6225 regarding partnership adjustments made by the IRS and determination of the amount of the partnership's liability (referred to as the imputed underpayment), section 6226 regarding the election for partners to take partnership adjustments into account, section 6227 regarding administrative adjustment requests (AARs), and section 6241 regarding definitions and special rules. The Treasury Department and the IRS received written public comments in response to the regulations proposed in the June 2017 NPRM, and a public hearing regarding the proposed regulations was held on September 18, 2017.

On November 30, 2017, the Treasury Department and the IRS published in the **Federal Register** (82 FR 56765) a notice of proposed rulemaking (REG-119337-17) (November 2017 NPRM) proposing rules regarding international provisions under the centralized partnership audit regime, including rules relating to the withholding of tax on foreign persons, the withholding of tax to enforce reporting on certain foreign accounts, and the treatment of creditable foreign tax expenditures of a partnership. No written comments were submitted in response to this NPRM, and no hearing was requested or held.

On December 19, 2017, the Treasury Department and the IRS published in the **Federal Register** (82 FR 27071) a notice of proposed rulemaking (REG-120232-17 and REG-120233-17) (December 2017 NPRM) proposing administrative and procedural rules under the centralized partnership audit regime, including rules addressing assessment and collection, penalties and interest, periods of limitations on making partnership adjustments, and judicial review of partnership adjustments. The regulations proposed in the December 2017 NPRM also provided rules addressing how pass-through partners take into account adjustments under the alternative to payment of the imputed underpayment described in section 6226 and under rules similar to section 6226 when a partnership files an AAR under section 6227. Written comments were received in response to the December 2017 NPRM. However, no hearing was requested or held.

On January 2, 2018, the Treasury Department and the IRS published in the **Federal Register** (82 FR 28398) final regulations under section 6221(b) providing rules for electing out of the centralized partnership audit regime.

On February 2, 2018, the Treasury Department and the IRS published in the **Federal Register** (83 FR 4868) a notice of proposed rulemaking (REG-118067-17) (February 2018 NPRM) proposing rules for adjusting tax attributes under the centralized partnership audit regime. Written comments were received in response to the February 2018 NPRM. However, no hearing was requested or held.

On March 23, 2018, Congress enacted the TTCA, which made a number of technical corrections to the rules under the centralized partnership audit regime. The amendments under the TTCA are effective as if included in section 1101 of the BBA, and therefore, subject to the effective dates in section 1101(g) of the BBA.

On August 9, 2018, the Treasury Department and the IRS published in the **Federal Register** (83 FR 39331) final regulations under section 6223 providing rules relating to partnership representatives and final regulations under § 301.9100-22 providing rules for electing into the centralized partnership audit regime for taxable years beginning on or after November 2, 2015 and before January 1, 2018. Corresponding temporary regulations under § 301.9100-22T were also withdrawn.

In light of the technical corrections made by the TTCA, to the extent regulations have not already been finalized, this document withdraws the regulations proposed in the June 2017 NPRM, the November 2017 NPRM, the December 2017 NPRM, and the February 2018 NPRM (collectively, the prior NPRMs) and proposes regulations reflecting the technical corrections made by the TTCA. The regulations proposed in this document also include clarifications, unrelated to the TTCA as discussed in the Explanation of Provisions section of this preamble. In addition, certain regulations have been reordered and renumbered, typographical errors have been corrected, nonsubstantive editorial changes have been made, and the applicability date provisions in the regulations have been revised to replace references to § 301.9100-22T with references to § 301.9100-22. Finally, the assumed highest rate of tax for corporations in the examples for all applicable periods is now 20 percent to more closely reflect the corporate tax rate in effect under section 11 (as amended by section 13001 of "[a]n Act to provide for the reconciliation pursuant to titles II and V of the concurrent resolution on the budget for fiscal year 2018," Public Law 115-97 (the "Act")).

Although this document withdraws the prior NPRMs, the Explanation of Provisions sections contained in the preambles of the withdrawn NPRMs remain relevant. Therefore, to the extent not inconsistent with the Explanation of Provisions section of this preamble or the preamble to the portions of the proposed regulations that have already been finalized, those Explanation of Provision sections are incorporated by reference in this document. Federal Register citations are provided to assist with locating the relevant section of the preamble in the prior NPRMs. The prior NPRMs are also included in the rulemaking docket for this notice of proposed rulemaking on *www.regulations.gov*.

This document does not address written comments that were submitted in response to the regulations proposed in the prior NPRMs or respond to any statements made during the public hearing held on September 18, 2017. Except to the extent that the written comments relate to the final regulations under section 6221(b) and section 6223, such comments and any comments received in response to this notice of proposed rulemaking will be addressed when the regulations proposed in this document are finalized.

Explanation of Provisions

1. *Scope of the Centralized Partnership Audit Regime and Partnership-Related Item*

Section 6221(a) provides for the determination of certain adjustments at the partnership level under the centralized partnership audit regime. Prior to amendment by the TTCA, section 6221(a) provided that any adjustment to items of income, gain, loss, deduction, or credit of a partnership for a partnership taxable year (and any partner's distributive share thereof) shall be determined, any tax attributable thereto shall be assessed and collected, and the applicability of any penalty, addition to tax, or additional amount which relates to an adjustment to any such item or share shall be determined at the partnership level. Prior to amendment by the TTCA, section 6241(a)(2) provided that the term "partnership adjustment" meant any adjustment in the amount of any item of income, gain, loss, deduction, or credit of a partnership, or any partner's distributive share thereof.

Section 201(c)(2) of the TTCA amended section 6221(a) by replacing the phrase "items of income, gain, loss, deduction, or credit of a partnership for a partnership taxable year (and any partner's distributive share thereof)" with the phrase "a partnership-related item." Section 6221(a) now provides that any adjustment to a partnership-related item and the applicability of any penalty, addition to tax, or additional amount which relates to an adjustment to any partnership-related item shall be determined at the partnership level. Additionally, section 6221(a) provides that any tax attributable to an adjustment to a partnership-related item shall be assessed and collected at the partnership level.

Section 201(a) of the TTCA amended section 6241(2) to provide that the term "partnership adjustment" means any adjustment to a partnership-related item, and the term "partnership-related item" means any item or amount with respect to the partnership (without regard to whether or not such item or amount appears on the partnership's return and including an imputed underpayment and any item or amount relating to any transaction with, basis in, or liability of, the partnership) which is relevant (determined without regard to subchapter C of chapter 63) in determining the tax liability of any person under chapter 1 of the Code (chapter 1) and any partner's distributive share thereof.

By eliminating the reference to items of income, gain, loss, deduction, or credit of a partnership, and instead referring to partnership-related items, which is broadly defined, the amendments by the TTCA clarify that the scope of the centralized partnership audit regime is not narrower than the scope of the partnership audit procedures under TEFRA. Joint Comm. on Taxation, JCX-6-18, *Technical Explanation of the Revenue Provisions of the House Amendment to the Senate Amendment to H.R. 1625 (Rules Committee Print 115-66)*, 37 (2018) (JCX-6-18). Rather, the centralized partnership audit regime is intended to have a scope sufficient to address those items that would have been considered partnership items, affected items, and computational adjustments under TEFRA, including the regulations. *Id.*

A. *Proposed § 301.6221(a)-1*

Proposed rules under § 301.6221(a)-1 were previously published in the **Federal Register** (82 FR 27372-73) in the June 2017 NPRM and the November NPRM (82 FR 56776) (former proposed § 301.6221(a)-1). Former proposed § 301.6221(a)-1(a) provided that the centralized partnership audit regime covers any adjustment to items of income, gain, loss, deduction, or credit of a partnership and any partner's distributive share of those adjusted items. Former proposed § 301.6221(a)-1(b)(1)(i) defined the phrase "items of income, gain, loss, deduction or credit" to mean all items and information required to be shown, or reflected, on a return of the partnership under section 6031, the regulations thereunder, and the forms and instructions prescribed by the IRS for the partnership's taxable year, and any information in the partnership's books and records for the taxable year. In addition, former proposed § 301.6221(a)-1(b)(1)(ii) provided that any factors that needed to be taken into account to determine or allocate the tax treatment of items adjusted under the centralized partnership audit regime were also to be determined at the partnership level. Former proposed § 301.6221(a)-1(b)(2) also addressed items included within the phrase "partner's distributive share." Because the TTCA's amendment of the scope of the centralized partnership audit regime is accomplished by adding a new defined term - "partnership-related item" - the majority of the rules under former proposed § 301.6221(a)-1(b) that addressed the scope of what is adjusted at the partnership level are now incorporated into proposed § 301.6241-6 which defines the term "partnership-related item."

Proposed § 301.6221(a)-1(a) now provides the general rule that, except as otherwise provided under the centralized partnership audit regime, any adjustments to partnership-related items and the applicability of any penalty, addition to tax, or additional amount that relates to an adjustment to any such items are determined at the partnership level. In addition, proposed § 301.6221(a)-1(a) provides that any chapter 1 tax attributable to an adjustment to a partnership-related item is assessed and collected at the partnership level. See section 13 of the preamble for a discussion of special enforcement matters pertaining to partnership-related items that may be adjusted outside of the centralized partnership audit regime.

Proposed § 301.6221(a)-1(a) further provides that any consideration necessary to make a determination at the partnership level under the centralized partnership audit regime is made at the partnership level. This would include the period of limitations on making adjustments under section 6235 as well as any facts necessary to calculate any imputed underpayment under section 6225, except as otherwise provided under the centralized partnership audit regime. These determinations previously constituted factors described under former proposed § 301.6221(a)-1(b)(1)(ii)(F) and (I).

B. *Proposed § 301.6241-6*

Proposed § 301.6241-6 defines the term "partnership-related item." Proposed § 301.6241-6(a) provides the general rule that a partnership-related item is any item or amount with respect to the partnership which is relevant in determining the tax liability of any person under chapter 1 and any partner's distributive share of any such item or amount.

Proposed § 301.6241-6(b) provides that an item or amount is with respect to a partnership without regard to whether or not such item or amount appears on the partnership return. An item or amount is with respect to a partnership if: the item or amount is shown or reflected, or required to be shown, or reflected, on a return of the partnership; the item or amount is in the partnership's books and records; the item or amount is an imputed underpayment; the item or amount relates to any transaction with, basis in, or liability of the partnership; or the item or amount relates to a transaction under section 707(a)(2), 707(b), or 707(c).

Under proposed § 301.6241-6(b)(4) and (7), an item or amount that relates to any transaction with, or liability of, the partnership, is with respect to a partnership only if the item or amount relates to a transaction or liability between the partnership and a partner acting in its capacity as a partner or an indirect partner (as defined in proposed § 301.6241-1(a)(4)) acting in its capacity as an indirect partner. Accordingly, an item or amount that relates to any transaction with or liability of the partnership is not with respect to the partnership if the item or amount is reported (or reportable) solely by a person other than the partnership, a partner not acting in its capacity as a partner, or an indirect partner not acting in its capacity as an indirect partner (except for transactions under section 707). Proposed § 301.6241-6(b)(8) provides that any determination necessary to make an adjustment to an item or amount described in proposed § 301.6241-6(b)(1) through (b)(7) is also an item or amount with respect to the partnership.

Proposed § 301.6241-6(c) provides that the determination of whether an item or amount is relevant in determining the tax liability of any person under chapter 1 is made without regard to the provisions of the centralized partnership audit regime. Proposed § 301.6241-6(c) also clarifies that an item or amount of a partnership is relevant in determining the liability of any person under chapter 1 without regard to whether such item or amount, or adjustment to such item or amount, has an effect on the tax liability of any particular person under chapter 1. Section 6241(2)(B)(i) does not limit whether an item is relevant in determining tax liability under chapter 1 to whether the item is relevant to determining the tax liability of a partner of the partnership under chapter 1. Rather, the statutory language refers to liability under chapter 1 of "any person." An item or amount is a partnership-related item if the item or amount is relevant in determining any person's liability under chapter 1 if the item might have any effect on any person's liability under chapter 1 regardless of whether it actually does have such an effect. Consequently, the IRS is not required to determine if an adjustment would have an actual effect on any person's chapter 1 liability under the Code.

Proposed § 301.6241-6(d) provides a list of examples of partnership-related items. These examples are largely the same as the items described in former proposed § 301.6221(a)-1(b)(1) with a few minor revisions. First, the references to "foreign," "tax," and "§ 1.704-1(b)(4)(viii)(b)" in the example regarding creditable expenditures were removed to clarify that partnership-related item includes any creditable expenditures, not just a creditable foreign tax expenditure. Also, the "including . . ." phrase from each example was removed to be consistent with the broad scope of the centralized partnership audit regime and does not reflect a substantive change. No inference should be drawn from the removal of that language.

Proposed § 301.6241-6(e) provides examples that illustrate the rules under proposed § 301.6241-6.

2. *Partner's Return Must Be Consistent with Partnership Return*

Prior to enactment of the TTCA, section 6222 provided that a partner shall treat on the partner's return "each item of income, gain, loss, deduction, or credit attributable to a partnership" subject to subchapter C of chapter 63 in a manner that is consistent with the treatment of such item on the partnership return. Section 201(c) of the TTCA amended section 6222 to provide that a partner shall treat on the partner's return "any partnership-related item" in a manner which is consistent with the treatment of such item on the partnership return.

A. *Proposed §301.6222-1*

Proposed rules under §301.6222-1 were previously published in the **Federal Register** (82 FR 27375-78) in the June 2017 NPRM (former proposed §301.6222-1). For an explanation of the rules under former proposed 301.6222-1, see 82 FR 27345-46.

Former proposed §301.6222-1(a) provided that a partner's treatment of each item of income, gain, loss, deduction, or credit attributable to a partnership must be consistent with the treatment of those items on the partnership return, including treatment with respect to the amount, timing, and characterization of those items. The reference in former proposed §301.6222-1(a) to "each item of income, gain, loss, deduction, or credit attributable to a partnership" has been replaced with a reference to "any partnership-related item" to reflect the statutory change to section 6222(a). In addition, references throughout former proposed §301.6222-1 to the term "item" have been replaced with references to the term "partnership-related item," as appropriate.

3. *Imputed Underpayment, Modification of Imputed Underpayment, and Adjustments That Do Not Result in an Imputed Underpayment*

Section 6225 provides rules governing the determination of the imputed underpayment, modification of the imputed underpayment, and the treatment of adjustments that do not result in an imputed underpayment. Section 202(c) of the TTCA amended section 6225(a) to reflect the new term "partnership-related item" and to provide that in the case of adjustments to partnership-related items that result in an imputed underpayment the partnership shall pay an amount equal to the imputed underpayment in the adjustment year as provided in section 6232. In the case of adjustments that do not result in an imputed underpayment, such adjustments shall be taken into account by the partnership in the adjustment year.

Section 202(a) of the TTCA amended section 6225(b)(1) to provide that the Secretary shall determine any imputed underpayment with respect to any reviewed year by appropriately netting all partnership adjustments to such reviewed year and applying the highest rate of tax in effect for that year under section 1 or 11. Section 202(a) of the TTCA also amended section 6225(b)(2) to provide that in the case of any adjustment that reallocates the distributive share of any item from one partner to another, such adjustment shall be taken into account by disregarding so much of such adjustment as results in a decrease in the amount of the imputed underpayment.

Section 202(a) of the TTCA also added paragraphs (b)(3) and (b)(4) to section 6225. Section 6225(b)(3) provides that partnership adjustments for any reviewed year shall first be separately determined (and netted as appropriate) within each category of items that are required to be taken into account separately under section 702(a) or other provision of the Code. Section 6225(b)(4) provides if any adjustment would (but for section 6225(b)(4)) result in a decrease in the amount of the imputed underpayment, and could be subject to any additional limitation under the provisions of the Code (or not allowed, in whole or in part, against ordinary income) if such adjustment were taken into account by any person, such adjustment shall not be taken into account when appropriately netting partnership adjustments under section 6225(b)(1)(A) except to the extent otherwise provided by the Secretary.

Section 202(b) of the TTCA amended several provisions relating to modifications of imputed underpayments. Sections 6225(c)(3), (c)(4)(A), and (c)(5)(A)(i), which previously referred to the "portion of the imputed underpayment," were amended to refer to the "portion of the adjustment." This amendment clarifies that modifications under sections 6225(c)(3), (c)(4), and (c)(5) result in disregarding the portion of the partnership adjustment affected by the modification, rather than the portion of the imputed underpayment. Section 202(c) of the TTCA also added section 6225(c)(9), which provides that the Secretary shall establish procedures under which the adjustments described in section 6225(a)(2) - adjustments that do not result in an imputed underpayment - may be modified in such manner as the Secretary determines appropriate.

Section 203 of the TTCA amended section 6225(c)(2) relating to the procedures for partners to take adjustments into account during modification. Section 6225(c)(2)(A) governs the filing of amended returns by partners. Section 6225(c)(2)(B) provides for an alternative procedure to the filing of amended returns. Section 6225(c)(2)(C) provides rules for adjustments that reallocate the distributive share of any item from one partner to another. Section 6225(c)(2)(D) provides that sections 6501 and 6511 shall not apply in certain situations related to amended returns and the alternative procedure to filing amended returns. Section 6225(c)(2)(E) provides that any adjustments to tax attributes that occur as a result of a modification under section 6225(c)(2) are binding on the partners and the partnership. Section 6225(c)(2)(F) provides rules for tiered structures, including defining the term "relevant partner" to mean any partner in the chain of ownership of any partnerships that are partners in the partnership requesting modification.

A. *Proposed §§301.6225-1, 301.6225-2, and 301.6225-3*

Proposed rules under §§301.6225-1, 301.6225-2, and 301.6225-3 were previously published in the **Federal Register** in the June 2017 NPRM (82 FR 27382-91), the November 2017 NPRM (82 FR 56776), and in the December 2017 NPRM (82 FR 60154) (collectively, former proposed §§301.6225-1, 301.6225-2, and 301.6225-3). For an explanation of the rules under former proposed §§301.6225-1, 301.6225-2, and 301.6225-3, see 82 FR 27350-58, 82 FR 56766-75, and 82 FR 60152-53.

Proposed § 301.6225-1 has been reorganized to clarify the process for determining an imputed underpayment. This reorganization, when compared to former proposed § 301.6225-1 (1) more clearly describes the steps necessary to determine an imputed underpayment and adjustments that do not result in an imputed underpayment; (2) consolidates rules regarding adjustments that do not result in an imputed underpayment; and (3) relocates rules regarding creditable expenditures to more clearly explain how to account for creditable expenditures in the determination of the imputed underpayment.

Proposed § 301.6225-1(b) addresses the calculation of the imputed underpayment. Due to the number of adjustments that could be made based on the definition of partnership-related item, the IRS will need to address circumstances in which multiple partnership-related items are adjusted to address a single issue or transaction in the administrative proceeding. Adjusting multiple partnership-related items that relate to the same issue or transaction could result in an imputed underpayment that double-counts some of the adjustments even though, if the partnership and partners had properly reported the item, one or more adjustments would have been subsumed by another item. To prevent double-counting the individual adjustments as inputs into the imputed underpayment, proposed § 301.6225-1(b)(4) provides that the IRS may treat adjustments that would otherwise be double-counted as zero for purposes of determining the imputed underpayment.

Proposed § 301.6225-1(c) describes the different groupings in which adjustments are placed for purposes of determining an imputed underpayment. These groupings are the reallocation grouping, the credit grouping, the creditable expenditure grouping, and the residual grouping. Proposed § 301.6225-1(c)(1) provides authority for the IRS to alter the manner in which adjustments are grouped to appropriately reflect the facts and circumstances.

Proposed § 301.6225-1(c)(2) defines the term "reallocation adjustment" and provides that in general reallocation adjustments are placed in the reallocation grouping. Under proposed § 301.6225-1(c)(3), however, reallocation adjustments to credits are placed in the credit grouping, and under § 301.6225-1(c)(4), reallocation adjustments to creditable expenditures are placed in the creditable expenditure grouping, similar to the rule under former proposed § 301.6225-1(d)(2)(iv). Proposed § 301.6225-1(c)(2)(ii) provides that each reallocation adjustment results in two separate adjustments - one positive adjustment and one negative adjustment. Proposed § 301.6225-1(c)(6) provides similar rules for recharacterization adjustments.

Proposed § 301.6225-1(c)(5)(ii) provides rules for how to account for adjustments to partnership-related items that are not allocated by the partnership to its partners under section 704(b). Proposed § 301.6225-1(d)(2)(iii)(B) provides that adjustments to such items, solely for purposes of determining an imputed underpayment, are treated as a positive adjustment to income to the extent appropriate. The Treasury Department and the IRS request comments regarding how to treat recharacterization and reallocation adjustments related to items that are not allocated under section 704(b).

To incorporate the additions of sections 6225(b)(3) and (b)(4), proposed § 301.6225-1(d)(1) provides that when the IRS determines a negative adjustment (as defined in proposed § 301.6225-1(d)(2)(ii)), all partnership adjustments are placed into subgroupings based on whether the adjusted items are required to be taken into account separately under section 702 and other provisions of the Code. Proposed § 301.6225-1(d)(1) provides authority for the IRS to alter the manner in which adjustments are subgrouped to appropriately reflect the facts and circumstances.

Proposed § 301.6225-1(d)(2) provides for the treatment of certain partnership adjustments and defines the terms negative adjustment and positive adjustment. A negative adjustment is defined as an adjustment that is a decrease in an item of income, treated as a decrease in an item of income, or that is an increase in an item of credit. A positive adjustment is an adjustment that is not a negative adjustment. Proposed § 301.6225-1(d)(3) requires that positive and negative adjustments resulting from reallocation adjustments and recharacterization adjustments be placed into separate subgroupings.

Proposed § 301.6225-1(e) provides rules for appropriately netting adjustments within each grouping or subgrouping and provides that adjustments are not netted between groupings or subgroupings. The statutory changes referencing section 702(a) and other provisions of the Code and the general inability to net negative adjustments result in restrictions on netting in these proposed rules that are broader than the restrictions described in former proposed § 301.6225-1. The examples in the proposed rules have been revised to reflect these broader restrictions on netting.

Proposed § 301.6225-1(f) provides rules related to determining whether adjustments are adjustments that do not result in an imputed underpayment. If the adjustments do not result in an imputed underpayment, such adjustments are taken into account in accordance with § 301.6225-3.

Proposed § 301.6225-1(g) provides the IRS may create multiple imputed underpayments for a particular tax year. Proposed § 301.6225-1(g)(2)(iii)(B) allows a particular adjustment that does not result in an imputed underpayment to be associated with a particular imputed underpayment. This rule ensures that adjustments that are appropriately associated with the imputed underpayment will be taken into account along with the other adjustments underlying the imputed underpayment if an election under section 6226 is made with respect to that imputed underpayment. For example, a reallocation or recharacterization adjustment generally results in more than one adjustment. In the case of a reallocation adjustment, there are adjustments that affect at least two partners. In a recharacterization adjustment, there is an adjustment to correct the characterization and an adjustment disallowing the incorrect characterization. As a result, if an adjustment that does not result in an imputed underpayment is due to a reallocation or recharacterization adjustment and one side of the adjustment is used to calculate a specific imputed underpayment, the other side of the adjustment, which is an adjustment that does not result in an imputed underpayment, is associated with that specific imputed underpayment.

The IRS may also determine that other adjustments that do not result in an imputed underpayment should be associated with a specific imputed underpayment. An adjustment that does not result in an imputed underpayment and that is not associated with a particular specific imputed underpayment is associated with the general imputed underpayment.

Proposed § 301.6225-2 provides guidance on procedures to modify the imputed underpayment. Former § 301.6225-2(b) provided that the effect of modification was determined by considering how the modification changed the relevant portion of the adjustment. This approach to modification is consistent with the amendments to section 6225(c). Accordingly, proposed § 301.6225-2(b) reflects the rule that modification affects the portion of an adjustment.

Proposed § 301.6225-2(b)(3)(iv) provides rules on rate modification in the case of special allocations. Those rules generally mirror the statutory rule under section 6225(c)(4)(B)(ii). The rule in the statute is complex compared with other rate modifications in that they require a valuation analysis. The Treasury Department and the IRS request comments on ways to implement these rules efficiently.

Proposed § 301.6225-2(d)(2) provides rules regarding amended returns and the alternative procedure to filing amended returns. Proposed § 301.6225-2(d)(2) provides that a partnership may satisfy the requirements of amended return modification by submitting all the information required for amended return modification and the partners paying any amount that would be due if the partners had filed amended returns. The Treasury Department and the IRS request comments on how best to implement the alternative procedure to filing amended returns.

Former proposed § 301.6225-2(d)(2)(viii) provided that partners could raise a reasonable cause defense under section 6664(c) (or other partner-level defense as described in former proposed § 301.6226-3(i)(3)) with an amended return in modification. Proposed § 301.6225-(d)(2)(viii) now provides that such partner-level defenses should be raised through a claim for refund that is submitted outside of the modification process. This rule is similar to the current rule regarding partner-level defenses related to adjustments that are taken into account by partners under section 6226. See proposed § 301.6226-3(d)(3).

Section 6225(c)(6) grants the Secretary authority to "by regulations or guidance provide for additional procedures to modify imputed underpayment amounts on the basis of such other factors as the Secretary determines are necessary and appropriate to carry out the purposes of this section." The Treasury Department and the IRS have elected to use this authority in two circumstances that were not included in former proposed § 301.6225-2. First, the Treasury Department and the IRS have concluded that the references to the adjustment year in section 6225(c)(5) make the implementation of section 6225(c)(5) unworkable. No partner would qualify as a specified partner until the adjustment year, but at any time during the administrative proceeding that is relevant to modification, the adjustment year does not yet exist. As a result, the only time this type of modification could be used would be in the case of an AAR because in that case, the adjustment year is the year in which the AAR is filed. In order for modification under section 6225(c)(5) to be administrable, proposed § 301.6225-2(d)(5)(iv) provides that a "qualified relevant partner" is a person that meets the definition of a specified partner but in a year that can be determined at the time modification is requested. The definition of a specified passive activity loss has also been changed to clarify that the years at issue do not have to be the adjustment year.

Second, the Treasury Department and the IRS are also exercising the authority under section 6225(c)(6) to add a modification for partnerships with partners entitled to benefits under an income tax treaty. Proposed § 301.6225-2(d)(9) allows modification if a relevant partner would have qualified for a reduction or exemption from tax with respect to a particular item under an income tax treaty with the United States. The Treasury Department and the IRS request comments on this type of modification.

Proposed § 301.6225-2(e) provides rules for modification of certain types of adjustments that do not result in an imputed underpayment (as defined in proposed § 301.6225-1(f)). Proposed § 301.6225-2(e) limits the ability to modify such adjustments to certain types of modification. The Treasury Department and the IRS request comments on whether the list of allowed modifications under proposed § 301.6225-2(e) is sufficient.

Lastly, proposed § 301.6225-2 adopts the term "relevant partner" to describe any direct or indirect partner in the partnership seeking modification. See section 6225(c)(2)(F) and proposed § 301.6225-2(a).

Proposed § 301.6225-3 provides rules regarding adjustments that do not result in in an imputed underpayment. The changes in the TTCA comport with former proposed § 301.6225-3, which required that the partnership take the adjustments that do not result in an imputed underpayment into account as separately stated or non-separately stated adjustments as appropriate.

B. *Proposed § 301.6225-4*

Proposed rules under § 301.6225-4 were previously published in the **Federal Register** (83 FR 4868-82) in the February 2018 NPRM (former proposed § 301.6225-4). For an explanation of the rules under former proposed § 301.6225-4, see 82 FR 4877.

Proposed § 301.6225-4 sets forth rules under which a partnership and its partners must adjust specified tax attributes to take into account partnership adjustments and the partnership's payment of an imputed underpayment. Changes have been made throughout former proposed § 301.6225-4 to conform to the changes to the definition of "tax attribute" under proposed § 301.6241-1(a)(10). See section 11.A of this preamble regarding the change to the definition of "tax attribute." In addition, the definition of "specified tax attributes" in proposed § 301.6225-4(a)(2) now includes earnings and profits under section 312 in response to comments received concerning the effect of partnership adjustments on a corporate partner's earnings and profits.

4. *Election for the Alternative to Payment of the Imputed Underpayment*

Section 6226 provides an alternative to the general rule under section 6225(a)(1) that the partnership must pay an imputed underpayment. Under section 6226, the partnership may elect to have its reviewed year partners take into account adjustments made by the IRS and pay any tax due as a result of those adjustments. If this election is made, the reviewed year partners must pay any chapter 1 tax resulting from taking into account the adjustments, and the partnership is not required to pay the imputed underpayment.

Section 206(d) of TTCA amended section 6226(a) to clarify that if a partnership makes a valid election under section 6226 with respect to an imputed underpayment, no assessment of such imputed underpayment, levy, or proceeding in any court for the collection of such imputed underpayment shall be made against such partnership.

Section 206(e) of the TTCA amended section 6226(b)(1) to provide that when a partner takes into account the adjustments, the partner's chapter 1 tax is adjusted by the aggregate of the "correction amounts" determined under section 6226(b)(2). After amendment by the TTCA, the correction amounts under section 6226(b)(2) are defined as the amounts by which the partner's chapter 1 tax would increase "or decrease" for the partner's first affected year if the partner's share of the adjustments were taken into account for that year. The correction amounts are also the amount by which the partner's chapter 1 tax would increase "or decrease" by reason of the adjustment to tax attributes for any intervening years. See section 6226(b)(2).

Section 204(a) of the TTCA added to the Code section 6226(b)(4), which provides that a partnership or S corporation that receives a statement under section 6226(a)(2) must file a partnership adjustment tracking report with the IRS and furnish statements under rules similar to the rules of section 6226(a)(2). If the partnership or S corporation fails to furnish such statements, the partnership or S corporation must compute and pay an imputed underpayment under rules similar to the rules of section 6225. A partnership that is a partner must file the partnership adjustment tracking report, and furnish statements or pay an imputed underpayment, notwithstanding any election out of the centralized partnership audit regime under section 6221(b) by the partnership for the tax year that includes the end of the reviewed year of the audited partnership. The term "audited partnership" means the partnership in the chain of ownership that originally made the election under section 6226. See section 6226(b)(4)(D).

A. *Proposed § § 301.6226-1, 301.6226-2, and 301.6226-3*

Proposed rules under § § 301.6226-1, 301.6226-2, and 301.6226-3 were previously published in the **Federal Register** in the June 2017 NPRM (82 FR 27391-97), the November 2017 NPRM (82 FR 56778-79), and the December 2017 NPRM (82 FR 60155-61) (collectively, former proposed § § 301.6226-1, 301.6226-2, and 301.6226-3). For an explanation of the rules under former proposed § § 301.6226-1, 301.6226-2, and 301.6226-3, see 82 FR 27358-66, 82 FR 56769-71, and 82 FR 60148-51.

Former proposed § 301.6226-1(b)(2) provided that if a partnership makes a valid election in accordance with proposed § 301.6226-1, the partnership is not liable for the imputed underpayment to which the election relates. To reflect the statutory change to section 6226(a), language has been added to proposed § 301.6226-1(b)(2) to clarify that if a partnership makes a valid election under section 6226 with respect to an imputed underpayment, the IRS may not assess such imputed underpayment, levy, or bring a proceeding in any court for the collection of that imputed underpayment against such partnership. A similar change has also been made to proposed § 301.6226-1(c)(2) (regarding invalid elections) to clarify that if a final determination is made that a purported election under section 6226 is invalid, the IRS may assess the imputed underpayment with respect to which the election was made against the partnership without regard to the limitations under section 6232(b).

Former proposed § 301.6226-3 provided that a reviewed year partner that is furnished a statement under section 6226(a)(2) is required to pay any additional chapter 1 tax (additional reporting year tax) that results from taking into account the partnership adjustments on that statement. As mentioned above in this section of the preamble, section 206(e) of the TTCA amended section 6226(b) to provide that decreases, as well as increases, in chapter 1 tax that result from taking into account partnership adjustments are used in computing a partner's additional reporting year tax. Section 206(e) of the TTCA also replaced the term "adjustment amount" with "correction amount." Accordingly, proposed § 301.6226-3 now refers to "correction amount" instead of "adjustment amount," as appropriate, and now provides that a reviewed year partner's chapter 1 tax for the reporting year may be increased or decreased by the additional reporting year tax. The additional reporting year tax is the sum of the correction amounts for the first affected year and any correction amounts for the intervening years. Under proposed § 301.6226-3(b)(2) and (3), the correction amounts are the amounts by which the partner's chapter 1 tax for the taxable year would be increased or decreased if the partner's taxable income for that year were recomputed by taking into account, in the case of the first affected year, the partner's share of the partnership adjustments reflected on the statement furnished to the partner or, in the case of any intervening year, any change to tax attributes of the partner resulting from the changes in the first affected year. A correction amount for the first affected year or any intervening year may be less than zero and may be used to offset any correction amounts from any other year in computing the additional reporting year tax. The examples under proposed § 301.6226-3(h) illustrate situations in which a correction amount may be less than zero.

Furthermore, the additional reporting year tax may be less than zero and may offset other taxes owed by the partner on the partner's reporting year return. Accordingly, any references to the additional reporting year tax as a "liability" have been removed from former proposed § 301.6226-3 to account for situations in which the additional reporting year tax is less than zero.

Section 6226(c)(2) provides that interest in the case of a section 6226 election is determined at the partner level, from the due date of the return for the taxable year to which the increase in chapter 1 tax is attributable, and at the underpayment rate under section 6621(a)(2) (substituting 5 percent for 3 percent). As discussed above in this section of the preamble, the TTCA amended section 6226(b) to provide that both increases and decreases in chapter 1 tax are used in computing a partner's additional reporting year tax. However, the TTCA did not similarly amend the reference to "increases" in section 6226(c)(2) with the result that interest only applies to the increases in the chapter 1 tax that would have resulted from taking into account the partnership adjustments under section 6226. No provision under the centralized partnership audit regime provides for interest in the case of a *decrease* in chapter 1 tax that would have resulted in the first affected year or any intervening year if the adjustments were taken into account in those years. Accordingly, proposed § 301.6226-3(c)(1) provides that interest on the correction amounts determined under proposed § 301.6226-3(b) is only calculated for taxable years for which there is a correction amount greater than zero, that is, taxable years for which there would have been an increase in chapter 1 tax if the adjustments were taken into account.

Proposed § 301.6226-3(c)(1) further provides that for purposes of calculating interest on the correction amounts, any correction amount that is less than zero does not offset any correction amount that is greater than zero. Although those amounts may offset when determining the additional reporting year tax (as described in proposed § 301.6226-3(b)), allowing the same offset for purposes of calculating interest is inconsistent with section 6226(c)(2), which provides that interest is determined with respect to any increase determined under section 6226(b)(2).

Proposed § 301.6226-3(d)(3) has also been clarified to provide that if a partner wants to raise a partner-level defense to any penalty, addition to tax, or additional amount, a partner must first pay the penalty, addition to tax, or additional amount and file a claim for refund for the reporting year in order to raise the defense.

As discussed above in this section of the preamble, section 204(a) of the TTCA amended section 6226(b) to provide that partnerships and S corporations that are direct or indirect partners in an audited partnership and that receive statements under 6226(a)(2) must file partnership adjustment tracking reports with the IRS and furnish statements to their owners under rules similar to section 6226. If no statements are furnished, the partnership or S corporation must compute and pay an imputed underpayment.

Former proposed § 301.6226-3(e)(1) provided that a pass-through partner (as defined in proposed § 301.6241-1(a)(5)) that was furnished a statement described in proposed § 301.6226-2 (including a statement as described in former proposed § 301.6226-3(e)(3)) must take into account the adjustments reflected on that statement by either furnishing statements to its partners or by paying an amount calculated like an imputed underpayment. Any statements furnished under those provisions were treated as statements described in proposed § 301.6226-2, and any pass-through partner receiving a statement under former proposed § 301.6226-3(e)(3) was required to also take the adjustments reflected on the statement into account by furnishing statements to its own partners or paying an amount calculated like an imputed underpayment. See former proposed § 301.6226-3(e)(3)(i) and (iv).

Although the rules under former proposed § 301.6226-3(e) were largely consistent with the rules under section 6226(b)(4), some changes were needed to conform the two sets of rules. First, proposed § 301.6226-3(a)(1) now provides that the rules under proposed § 301.6226-3(a)(1) apply to a reviewed year partner except to the extent otherwise provided in proposed § 301.6226-3. Second, proposed § 301.6226-3(e) now includes a requirement that the pass-through partner must file a partnership adjustment tracking report. Third, proposed § 301.6226-3(e) provides a default rule that a pass-through partner must furnish statements to its own partners in accordance with proposed § 301.6226-3(e)(3). If a pass-through partner fails to furnish statements in accordance with proposed § 301.6226-3(e)(3), the pass-through partner must compute and pay an imputed underpayment. Additionally, language referring to a pass-through partner "taking into account" the adjustments under former proposed § 301.6226-3(e) was removed to more closely align with the statutory language in section 6226(b)(4). Fourth, proposed § 301.6226-3(e) defines and refers to the term "audited partnership," which proposed § 301.6226-3(e)(1) defines as the partnership that made the election under § 301.6226-1. See section 6226(b)(4)(D). Lastly, proposed § 301.6226-3(e)(4) provides that the amount a pass-through partner must compute and pay, if it does not furnish statements to its partners, is an "imputed underpayment." See section 6226(b)(4)(A)(ii)(II).

Because under proposed § 301.6226-3(e), pass-through partners compute and pay an "imputed underpayment," rather than calculating correction amounts under proposed § 301.6226-3(b), references in former proposed § 301.6226-3(b) to amended returns filed by indirect partners as part of modification have been deleted. Pass-through partners computing an imputed underpayment under proposed § 301.6226-3(e) may account for modifications submitted by their indirect partners, but non-pass-through partners calculating correction amounts under proposed § 301.6226-3(b) cannot. Accordingly, the references in former proposed § 301.6226-3(b) to amended returns filed by indirect partners were removed.

To reflect the change to the definition of "tax attribute" under proposed § 301.6241-1(a)(10) (see section 11.A. of this preamble), proposed § § 301.6226-2 and 301.6226-3 now only refer to the tax attributes of the partner. For example, proposed § § 301.6226-2(e) and 301.6226-3(e)(3)(iii) no longer require that the audited partnership report any changes to *partnership* tax attributes on the statements furnished to its partners under section 6226(a)(2). Therefore, when a partner computes the partner's correction amount for any intervening year, the partner calculates the amount by which the partner's chapter 1 tax for any intervening year would increase or decrease if any tax attribute of that partner (for example, a net operating loss carryover or capital loss carryover) has been adjusted after taking into account the partner's share of the adjustments in the first affected year.

Finally, references to "items" or "items of income, gain, loss, deduction, or credit" throughout former § § 301.6226-1, 6226-2, and 6226-3 have been replaced with references to "partnership-related items."

B. *Revisions to the regulations under section 6226 unrelated to the TTCA amendments*

In addition to the changes needed to conform to the amendments by the TTCA, some additional changes have been made to former proposed § § 301.6226-1, 6226-2, and 6226-3. First, proposed § 301.6226-1(b)(2) now provides that only those adjustments that do not result in an imputed underpayment which are associated with an imputed underpayment for which an election under section 6226 is made are included in the reviewed year partner's share of the partnership adjustments reported to the partner. Any adjustments that do not result in an imputed underpayment which are not associated with an imputed underpayment for which an election under section 6226 is made are taken into account under section 6225. This change was necessary to clarify which partnership adjustments are pushed out in the case of multiple imputed underpayments where the push out election is not made with respect to all imputed underpayments. See proposed § 301.6225-1(g) for rules regarding the treatment of adjustments that do not result in an imputed underpayment in the context of specific imputed underpayments.

Second, under proposed § 301.6226-1(c)(1), an election under section 6226 is only valid if all the provisions under proposed § 301.6226-1 (regarding making the election) and § 301.6226-2 (regarding the furnishing of statements) are satisfied, and an election made under section 6226 is valid until the IRS determines that the election is invalid. The rule that an election is valid until the IRS determines it is invalid was moved from former proposed § 301.6226-1(c)(2) to proposed § 301.6226-1(c)(1) to clarify that an election that does not fully satisfy the requirements of proposed § § 301.6226-1 and 301.6226-2 is valid unless the IRS determines that the purported election is invalid. For example, if a partnership makes an election in accordance with proposed § 301.6226-1 but fails to furnish statements to its partners, that election is valid until the IRS determines otherwise.

In addition, the word "final" was removed from before the word "determination" in proposed § 301.6226-1(c)(2) when referring to a determination made by the IRS that a purported election under section 6226 is invalid. The removal of the word "final" clarifies that the IRS may determine that an election is invalid and assess and collect the imputed underpayment to which the purported election related without first being required to make a proposed or initial determination of invalidity. Although nothing in the regulations precludes the IRS from first notifying the partnership of a potential problem with an election before determining the election is invalid, proposed § 301.6226-1(c)(2) provides that the IRS may determine that an election is invalid even if the partnership has corrected the statements required to be filed and furnished in accordance with proposed § 301.6226-2(d)(3) and also provides that the IRS is not obligated to require the correction of any errors prior to determining an election is invalid.

Third, several changes were made to clarify that the partnership must provide correct information in order to make a valid election under section 6226 and in order for statements to be properly furnished either under proposed § 301.6226-2 or proposed § 301.6226-3(e)(3). Proposed § 301.6226-1(c)(4)(ii) requires the partnership to provide correct information in its election, and proposed § 301.6226-2(e) and proposed § 301.6226-3(e)(3)(iii) require that the statements filed and furnished with the IRS include correct information. Additionally, proposed § 301.6226-2(d)(3) provides that if the IRS cannot determine whether the statements filed and furnished by the partnership are correct because of a failure by the partnership to comply with any requirements (such as filing a partnership adjustment tracking report), the IRS may, but is not obligated to, require the partnership to provide additional information to substantiate the statements. Proposed § 301.6226-2(d)(2) extends the rules governing corrections of errors in statements to statements furnished by pass-through partners under proposed § 301.6226-3(e)(3) and to provide that, if consent of the IRS is required for a correction, that corrected statements may not be furnished until the IRS provides consent.

Fourth, duplicative language regarding the definition of the extended due date for the adjustment year of the audited partnership was removed from former proposed § 301.6226-3(e)(3)(ii) and (e)(4)(ii).

Fifth, in proposed § 301.6226-3(g), the word "grantor" has been added between the words "wholly-owned" and "trusts" to clarify that "wholly-owned trusts" means "wholly-owned grantor trusts."

Sixth, the phrase "an entity described in § 301.7701-2(c)(2)(i)" in former proposed § 301.6226-3(j) was changed to "a wholly-owned entity disregarded as separate from its owner for Federal tax purposes in the reviewed year" to conform to the definition of disregarded entity under proposed § 301.6241-1(a)(4).

Seventh, proposed § 301.6226-3(c)(2) now provides that interest on any penalties, additions to tax, or additional amounts is calculated from each applicable taxable year until the penalty, addition to tax, or additional amount is paid. Former proposed § 301.6226-3(c)(2) provided that interest was calculated from the first affected year. Under proposed § 301.6226-3(d)(2), partners calculate any penalties, additions to tax, or additional amounts that relate to the partnership adjustments at the partner level. Because the adjustments could create tax effects in more than just the first affected year (for example, as a result of changes to tax attributes in an intervening year), a penalty, addition to tax, or additional amount might likewise result in more than just the first affected year. Accordingly, proposed § 301.6226-3(c)(2) provides that interest on penalties, additions to tax, and additional amounts runs from the applicable taxable year (that is, the particular tax year to which the penalty, addition to tax, or additional amount relates).

Finally, certain errors were corrected in the examples under proposed § 301.6226-3(h). Examples 2 through 4 and 6 through 9 under former proposed § 301.6226-3(h) incorrectly listed the last day to file a petition under section 6234 as the date the adjustments became final, and examples 6 through 9 incorrectly referred to former proposed § 301.6226-1(b) as support for this rule. Under proposed § 301.6226-2(b), partnership adjustments become finally determined on the later of the expiration of the time to file a petition under section 6234 or, if a petition is filed under section 6234, the date when the court's decision becomes final. The examples under proposed § 301.6226-3(h) now reflect that the adjustments become final on the day after the last day to file a petition under section 6234 to be consistent with the rule under § 301.6226-2(b), and incorrect references to § 301.6226-1(b) in Examples 6 through 9 under former proposed § 301.6226-3(h) have been replaced with correct references to § 301.6226-2(b).

Proposed § 301.6226-4

Proposed rules under §§ 301.6226-4 were previously published in the **Federal Register** in the February 2018 NPRM (83 FR 4868) (former proposed § 301.6226-4). For an explanation of the rules under former proposed § 301.6226-4, see 83 FR 4874.

Proposed § 301.6226-4 sets forth rules for adjusting reviewed year partners' tax attributes to take into account partnership adjustments when a partnership makes an election under section 6226. To reflect the addition of section 6226(b)(4), proposed § 301.6226-3(e)(4) now provides that a reviewed year partner that is a pass-through partner must pay an imputed underpayment if the pass-through partner does not furnish statements. In addition, changes have been made throughout former proposed § 301.6226-4 to conform to the change to the definition of "tax attribute" under proposed § 301.6241-1(a)(10). See section 11.A of this preamble. These changes reflect that the adjustments to tax attributes taken into account by a partner should be consistent, regardless of whether the partner files an amended return during modification, participates in the alternative procedure to filing an amended return, or receives a statement under section 6226. Accordingly, the proposed regulations under section 6226 have been revised to refer only to the tax attributes of the partner in the intervening years. Additionally, clarifying changes were made in proposed § 301.6226-4(b) to conform to the terminology used in proposed § 301.6226-3. Lastly, an incorrect cross-reference in former proposed § 301.6226-4(c)(4)(iii) has been replaced with the correct cross-reference.

5. *Administrative Adjustment Requests*

Section 6227 provides a mechanism for a partnership to file an AAR to correct errors on a partnership return for a prior year. Prior to amendment by the TTCA, section 6227(a) provided that a partnership may file a request for administrative adjustment in the amount of one or more items of income, gain, loss, deduction, or credit of the partnership or any partnership taxable year. Section 201(c) of the TTCA amended section 6227(a) by striking "items of income, gain, loss, deduction, or credit of the partnership" and inserting "partnership-related items."

Prior to amendment by the TTCA, section 6227(b) provided that any adjustment requested in an AAR is taken into account for the partnership taxable year in which the AAR is made. Section 206(p) of the TTCA amended section 6227(b) by striking "is made" both places it appears and inserting "is filed."

Prior to amendment by the TTCA, section 6227(b)(1) provided that if an adjustment results in an imputed underpayment, the adjustment may be determined and taken into account by the partnership under rules similar to the rules under section 6225 relating to payment of the imputed underpayment by the partnership, except that the provisions under section 6225 pertaining to modification of the imputed underpayment based on amended returns by partners, the time for submitting information to the Secretary for purposes of modification, and approval by the Secretary of any modification do not apply.

Section 206(p) of the TTCA amended section 6227(b)(1) by striking the reference to "paragraphs (2), (6), and (7)" of section 6225(c) (relating to modification) and inserting "paragraphs (2), (7), and (9)" of section 6225(c). As a result, section 6227(b)(1) provides that adjustments requested in an AAR are taken into account by the partnership under rules similar to section 6225 (except for sections

6225(c)(2), (7), and (9)). As amended by TTCA, section 6225(c)(2) provides rules allowing for amended returns and an alternative procedure to filing amended returns for purposes of modification, section 6225(c)(7) provides that information required to be submitted for purposes of modification be submitted within 270 days from the date on which the notice of a proposed partnership adjustment is mailed under section 6231, and section 6225(c)(9) provides for modification with respect to adjustments that do not result in an imputed underpayment.

Lastly, section 206(f) of the TTCA added section 6227(d) to provide that the Secretary shall issue regulations or other guidance which provide for the proper coordination of section 6227 and section 905(c).

A. *Proposed § § 301.6227-1, 301.6227-2, and 301.6227-3*

Proposed rules under § § 301.6227-1, 301.6227-2, and 301.6227-3 were previously published in the **Federal Register** (82 FR 27397-99) in the June 2017 NPRM, November 2017 NPRM (82 FR 56779), and December 2017 NPRM (82 FR 60161) (collectively, former proposed § § 301.6227-1, 301.6227-2, and 301.6227-3). For an explanation of the rules under former proposed § § 301.6227-1, 301.6227-2, and 301.6227-3, see 82 FR 27366-69, 82 FR 56769, and 82 FR 60151.

Former proposed § 301.6227-1(a) provided that a partner may not file an AAR except if the partner is doing so on behalf of the partnership in the partner's capacity as the partnership representative or if the partner is a partnership-partner filing an AAR under former proposed § 301.6227-3(c). Proposed § 301.6227-3(c), however, does not provide for the filing of an AAR by a partnership-partner. Rather, under proposed § 301.6227-3(c), a partnership-partner takes into account adjustments requested in an AAR by the partnership in which it is a partner by following the rules under proposed § 301.6226-3(e) (except to the extent otherwise provided). Proposed § 301.6227-1(a) therefore is changed to remove the reference to partnership-partners, and now only refers to partners filing AARs in their capacity as a partnership representative.

Proposed § 301.6227-2(a)(1) provides the rules for determining whether an imputed underpayment results from adjustments requested in an AAR by referring to the rules under proposed § 301.6225-1. Under proposed § 301.6227-2(a)(2), in the case of an AAR, a partnership may reduce an imputed underpayment as a result of certain modifications permitted under proposed § 301.6225-2. Under former proposed § 301.6227-2(a)(2), these modifications included modifications that relate to tax-exempt partners (proposed § 301.6225-2(d)(3)), rate modification (proposed § 301.6225-2(d)(4)), modification related to certain passive losses of publicly traded partnerships (proposed § 301.6225-2(d)(5)), modification applicable to qualified investment entities described in section 860 (proposed § 301.6225-2(d)(7)), and other modifications to the extent permitted under future IRS guidance (proposed § 301.6225-2(d)(10)). Proposed § 301.6227-2(a)(2) adopts this same list of modifications and adds modifications related to the composition of the groupings that factor into the calculation of the imputed underpayment (proposed § 301.6225-2(d)(6)(ii)) and modifications related to tax treaties (proposed § 301.6225-2(d)(9)).

Proposed § 301.6227-2(a)(2) provides that other types of modification, such as modification under proposed § 301.6225-2(d)(2) with respect to amended returns, including the alternative procedure to filing amended returns, and modification under proposed § 301.6225-2(d)(8) with respect to closing agreements, are not available in the case of an AAR. Modifications with respect to adjustments that do not result in an imputed underpayment also are also not available in the case of an AAR.

Former proposed § 301.6227-2(a)(2)(i) provided that a partnership did not need to seek IRS approval prior to modifying an imputed underpayment that results from adjustments requested in an AAR. Section 6227(b)(1) does not explicitly carve out section 6225(c)(8),which states that any modification to the imputed underpayment made under section 6225(c) shall be made only upon approval of such modification by the Secretary. Section 6227(b)(1) does provide, however, that partnerships take into account adjustments requested in an AAR under rules similar to the rules under section 6225. In proposing rules similar to the rules under section 6225 for the purposes of requesting an AAR and taking into account adjustments, the Treasury Department and the IRS have determined it is more efficient and beneficial for both the IRS and for partnerships to be able to apply modifications when filing an AAR without first securing approval of permitted modifications. Accordingly, although any modifications in connection with an AAR are subject to IRS approval, the rules under proposed § 301.6227-2(a)(2)(i) provide that the partnership is not required to obtain the approval from the IRS before applying modifications when calculating the amount of the imputed underpayment the partnership needs to pay when filing the AAR. Proposed § 301.6227-2(a)(2)(ii) also provides, however, that modifications to an imputed underpayment resulting from adjustments requested in an AAR may not be applied by the partnership if the AAR that is filed does not include notification to the IRS of the modification, a description of the effect of the modification on the imputed underpayment, an explanation of the basis for such modification, and all necessary documentation to support the partnership's entitlement to such modification.

Under proposed § 301.6227-3, a reviewed year partner that receives a statement described in proposed § 301.6227-1(d) must treat that statement as if it were provided under section 6226(a)(2). Former proposed § 301.6227-3(b)(1) also provided that the restriction in former proposed § 301.6226-3(b)(1) - that the correction amount for the first affected year and any intervening year cannot be less than zero - does not apply in the case of taking into account adjustments requested by the partnership in an AAR. Proposed § 301.6227-3(b)(1) no longer needs to address that restriction because the restriction in former proposed § 301.6226-3(b)(1) no longer exists. Therefore, the exception in former proposed § 301.6227-3(b)(1) has been eliminated. Additionally, the provision in former proposed § 301.6227-3(b)(2), stating that when the additional reporting tax results in being less than zero the partner may reduce his chapter 1 tax for the reporting year, is moved to proposed § 301.6227-3(b)(1).

Former proposed § 301.6227-1 included a reserved paragraph regarding notice of change to amounts of creditable foreign tax expenditures. Proposed § 301.6227-1 also reserves this same paragraph and does not contain rules to coordinate sections 6227 and 905(c). The Treasury Department and the IRS seek comments regarding the coordination of sections 6227 and 905(c) for consideration in future guidance.

Lastly, the reference to "items of income, gain, loss, deduction, or credit of the partnership" in former proposed § 301.6227-1(a) has been replaced with a reference to "partnership-related items."

B. *Revisions to the regulations under section 6227 unrelated to the TTCA amendments*

Proposed § 301.6227-1(a) now coordinates the rules regarding the filing of an AAR and the revocation of a designation of the partnership representative under § 301.6223-1. Former proposed § 301.6227-1(a) provided that the partnership may not file an AAR solely for the purpose of allowing the partnership to change the designation of a partnership representative. Proposed § 301.6227-1(a) now adds that when the partnership changes the designation of the partnership representative or the appointment of a designated individual in conjunction with the filing of an AAR, the change in designation or appointment is treated as occurring prior to the filing of the AAR.

Former proposed § 301.6227-1(b) provided that an AAR may not be filed after a notice of administrative proceeding (NAP) has been mailed. To account for situations in which the IRS mails a NAP, but then withdraws it, proposed § 301.6227-1(b) now provides that an AAR may not be filed after a NAP has been mailed, except when the NAP has been withdrawn under proposed § 301.6231-1(f).

Additions were also made in proposed § 301.6227-3(c) to clarify the rules for pass-through partners, unrelated to the changes made by the TTCA. First, proposed § 301.6227-3(c)(1) provides that when a pass-through partner takes into account adjustments requested in an AAR in accordance with proposed § 301.6226-3(e), the pass-through partner must provide the information described in proposed § 301.6227-3(c)(3) as opposed to the information in described in proposed § 301.6226-3(e)(3)(iii) when furnishing statements to its partners. Second, under proposed § 301.6227-3(c)(1), a pass-through partner that computes and pays an imputed underpayment in accordance with proposed § 301.6226-3(e)(4) may not take into account any modifications. Third, proposed § 301.6227-3(c)(4) provides that when a pass-through partner furnishes a statement to an affected partner under proposed § 301.6227-3(c), the affected partner must treat that statement as if it were a statement described in proposed § 301.6227-3(a) that was furnished to such affected partner.

6. *Notices of Proceedings and Adjustments*

Section 6231(a) provides that the Secretary shall mail to the partnership and to the partnership representative a notice of any administrative proceeding initiated at the partnership level, notice of any proposed partnership adjustment resulting from that proceeding (NOPPA), and notice of any final partnership adjustment (FPA). Prior to amendment by the TTCA, section 6231(a) also provided that any FPA shall be mailed no earlier than 270 days after the date on which the NOPPA is mailed. Such notices shall be sufficient if mailed to the last known address of the partnership and the partnership representative, even if the partnership has terminated its existence. See section 6231(a) flush language (prior to amendment by the TTCA).

Prior to amendment by the TTCA, the statute did not limit the period for the IRS to propose adjustments under the centralized partnership audit regime. Section 206(h) of the TTCA amended section 6231 to address this issue. As amended, section 6231(b)(1) provides that any NOPPA shall not be mailed later than the date determined under section 6235(a)(1), which is generally the date that is 3 years after the later of: (1) the date on which the partnership return for the taxable year was filed, (2) the return due date for the taxable year, or (3) the date on which the partnership filed an AAR with respect to the taxable year.

Section 206(h) of the TTCA makes a conforming amendment to section 6231(a) to reflect the addition of the period of limitations to made partnership adjustments. Prior to amendment, section 6231(a) provided that "Such notices shall be sufficient if mailed to the last known address of the partnership representative or the partnership (even if the partnership has terminated its existence)." The amendment replaced the words "Such notices" with "Any notice of final partnership adjustment."

Section 201(c) of the TTCA also makes a conforming amendment to section 6231(a) by striking the phrase "all items of income, gain, loss, deduction, or credit of the partnership" and inserting "all partnership-related items."

A. *Proposed § 301.6231-1*

Proposed rules under § 301.6231-1 were previously published in the **Federal Register** (82 FR 60161-62) in the December 2017 NPRM (former proposed § 301.6231-1). For an explanation of the rules under former proposed § 301.6231-1, see 82 FR 60151-52.

Although not required by statute, former proposed § 301.6231-1(b)(1) provided a period of limitations for making partnership adjustment. That section provided that a NOPPA may not be mailed after the expiration of the period described in section 6235(a)(1), including any extensions of that period and after applying any of the special rules in section 6235(c) (providing additional time for situations where no return is filed, fraud, and other specified reasons).

Former proposed § 301.6231-1(c) provided that NAPs, NOPPAs, and FPAs are sufficient if mailed to the last known address of the partnership and the partnership representative. As discussed above in this section of the preamble, section 6231(a) now provides that any FPA is sufficient if mailed to the last known address of the partnership and the partnership representative. The Treasury Department and the IRS have determined that while the last known address requirement under section 6231(a) only applies to a notice of final partnership adjustment, the IRS will also mail the NAP and the NOPPA to the last known address of the partnership and the partnership representative.

Accordingly, because the rules under former proposed § 301.6231-1(b)(1) and (c) are consistent with the statutory changes to section 6231(a), those rules are unchanged. The only change to former proposed § 301.6231-1 was to replace references to "item of income, gain, loss, deduction, or credit" and to a "partner's distributive share" in former proposed § 301.6231-1(a)(1) with a reference to "partnership-related item".

7. *Assessment, Collection, and Payment of Imputed Underpayments*

Section 6232(a) provides rules for the assessment, collection, and payment of imputed underpayments. Section 206(g) of the TTCA amended section 6232(a) to clarify that the assessment of any imputed underpayment is not subject to the deficiency procedures under subchapter B of chapter 63 of the Code and to clarify that in the case of an AAR, the underpayment may be assessed when the AAR is filed. See JCX-6-18, at 48.

Section 6232(b) provides limitations on the assessment of an imputed underpayment. Section 206(g) of the TTCA amended section 6232(b) to correct a reference to "assessment of a deficiency" to now refer to "assessment of an imputed underpayment." Section 206(p) of the TTCA also amends section 6232(b) to strike the reference to "this chapter" and replace it with "this subtitle (other than subchapter B of this chapter)."

Section 205 of the TTCA added a new subsection (f) to section 6232 to provide a mechanism for collection of tax due in the case of a failure of a partnership or S corporation to pay an imputed underpayment or specified similar amount. Under section 6232(f)(1), if any amount of any imputed underpayment to which section 6225 applies or any specified similar amount as defined in section 6232(f)(2) has not been paid by the date which is 10 days after the date on which the Secretary provides notice and demand for such payment, the Secretary may assess upon each partner of the partnership a tax equal to such partner's proportionate share of such amount.

Under section 6232(f)(2), the term "specified similar amount" means the amount determined under section 6226(b)(4)(ii)(II) and any amount assessed upon a partner under section 6232(f)(1)(B) that is a partnership or an S corporation. Section 206(g)(2)(B) of the TTCA amended section 6232(b) to provide that the limitations on assessment with respect to an imputed underpayment do not apply in the case of a specified similar amount defined in section 6232(f)(2).

The Treasury Department and the IRS are not proposing rules under section 6232(f) at this time. The Treasury Department and the IRS request comments with respect to section 6232(f), including the determination of a partner's proportionate share of the unpaid amount, for consideration with respect to future guidance.

A. *Proposed § 301.6232-1*

Proposed rules under § 301.6232-1 were previously published in the **Federal Register** (82 FR 60162-63) in the December 2017 NPRM (former proposed § 301.6232-1). For an explanation of the rules under former proposed § § 301.6232-1, see 82 FR 60152.

Former proposed § 301.6232-1(a) provided that because the centralized partnership audit regime under subchapter C of chapter 63 applies to an assessment of an imputed underpayment, the deficiency procedures under subchapter B of chapter 63 do not apply. Former proposed § 301.6232-1(b) provided that the IRS may assess an underpayment reflected on an AAR on the date the AAR is filed. Former proposed § 301.6232-1(c) provided limitations on assessment of the imputed underpayment, except as otherwise provided in § 301.6232-1. Because the rules under former proposed § 301.6232-1(a) and (b) are consistent with the statutory changes to section 6232(a), those rules are unchanged.

Proposed § 301.6232-1(c) is generally the same as former proposed § 301.6232-1(c). However, changes were made to take into account section 206(g)(2)(B) of TTCA, providing that the limitations on assessment do not apply to specified similar amounts, and section 206(p) of TTCA, providing that the limitations on assessments under proposed § 301.6232-1(c) apply except as otherwise provided in subtitle F of the Code (other than deficiency procedures under subchapter B of chapter 63).

With respect to former proposed § 301.6232-1(d), the reference to "items of income, gain, loss, deduction, or credit" in former proposed § 301.6232-1(d)(1)(i) was replaced with a reference to "partnership-related items."

8. *Interest and Penalties Related to Imputed Underpayments*

Section 6233 provides rules related to interest and penalties with respect to imputed underpayments. Section 206(i) of the TTCA amended section 6233 by adding a new subsection (c), which provides a cross-reference to section 6603 for rules allowing deposits to suspend the running of interest on potential underpayments.

A. *Proposed § § 301.6233(a)-1 and 301.6233(b)-1*

Proposed rules under § § 301.6233(a)-1 and 301.6233(b)-1 were previously published in the **Federal Register** (82 FR 60163-65) in the December 2017 NPRM (former proposed § § 301.6233(a)-1 and

301.6233(b)-1). For an explanation of the rules under former proposed §§301.6233(a)-1 and 301.6233(b)-1, see 82 FR 60152-53.

Proposed §301.6233(a)-1 provides rules for determining interest and penalties from the reviewed year, and proposed §301.6233(b)-1 provides rules for determining interest and penalties from the adjustment year. Neither former proposed §301.6233(a)-1 nor former proposed §301.6233(b)-1 provided rules regarding deposits to suspend the running of interest on underpayments. The Treasury Department and the IRS are not proposing rules regarding the interaction of the deposit rules under section 6603 and the interest rules under section 6233. However, the Treasury Department and the IRS request comments for consideration in future guidance regarding the interaction between section 6603 and the interest rules under section 6233.

Former proposed §301.6233(a)-1(c)(2)(ii)(C) provided a definition of "negative adjustment" and defined that term through reference to "items of income, gain, loss, deduction, or credit." Proposed §301.6225-1 now uses the term "negative adjustment" and the phrase "items of income, gain, loss, deduction, or credit" has been removed from subchapter C of chapter 63. To reflect these changes, proposed §301.6233(a)-1(c)(2)(ii)(C) now provides that a "decreasing adjustment" is "an adjustment to a partnership-related item that resulted in a decrease to the imputed underpayment." Example 3 under proposed §301.6233(a)-1(c)(3) also reflects changes to former proposed §§301.6225-1 and 301.6225-2.

Former proposed §301.6233(a)-1(c)(2)(ii), regarding how to calculate the portion of the imputed underpayment to which a penalty applies, referred to "non-credit partnership adjustments" and "credit adjustments." Under proposed §301.6225-1(e)(3)(iii) certain adjustments to creditable expenditures are treated as an adjustment to a credit and may impact the calculation of the imputed underpayment. To properly account for such adjustments when determining the portion of an imputed underpayment subject to a penalty, the term "non-credit partnership adjustment" was changed to "a partnership adjustment that is not an adjustment to a credit or treated as an adjustment to a credit," and the term "credit adjustment" changed to "an adjustment to a credit or treated as an adjustment to a credit."

Former proposed §301.6233(a)-1(c)(2)(iii)(B), regarding the application of the substantial understatement penalty under section 6662(d)(1)(A)(i) to imputed underpayments, provided that taxable income meant the net ordinary business income or loss of the partnership. The reference to "ordinary business" failed to account for other sources of income of the partnership that are appropriate to consider for purposes of the substantial understatement penalty. Therefore, proposed §301.6233(a)-1(c)(2)(iii)(B) now provides that for purposes of determining the amount of tax required to be shown on the return it is the net income or loss of the partnership that is treated as taxable income. See Page 5 of Form 1065, Return of Partnership Income.

Former proposed §301.6233(a)-1(c)(2)(v), pertaining to reasonable cause and good faith defenses, provided that partner-level defenses may not be raised in a proceeding of the partnership except as provided under the modification procedures pertaining to amended returns and partner closing agreements. For clarity, this provision has been moved to proposed §301.6233(a)-1(c)(1). Furthermore, the provision allowing partner-level defenses to penalties to be raised under the modification procedures has been removed. A partner may raise a partner-level defense by filing a claim for refund under procedures existing outside of the centralized partnership audit regime or through an agreement with the IRS regarding an adjustment to a partnership-related item.

9. *Judicial Review of Partnership Adjustments*

Section 6234(a) provides that within 90 days after the date on which an FPA is mailed under section 6231 with respect to any partnership taxable year, the partnership may file a petition for readjustment for such taxable year with the Tax Court, the district court in which the partnership's principal place of business is located, or the Court of Federal Claims. Prior to amendment by the TTCA, section 6234(b)(1) provided that a petition for readjustment under section 6234 may be filed in a district court of the United States or the Court of Federal Claims only if the partnership filing the petition deposits with the Secretary, on or before the date the petition is filed, the amount of the imputed underpayment. Section 206(j) of the TTCA amended section 6234(b)(1) to clarify that the amount of the jurisdictional deposit that the partnership must make in order to file a readjustment petition in a district court or the Court of Federal Claims is the amount of (as of the date of the filing of the petition) the imputed underpayment, penalties, additions to tax, and additional amounts with respect to the imputed underpayment. See JCX-6-18, at 49.

A. *Proposed §301.6234-1*

Proposed rules under §301.6234-1 were previously published in the **Federal Register** (82 FR 60165-66) in the December 2017 NPRM (former proposed §301.6234-1). For a further explanation of the rules under former proposed §301.6234-1, see 82 FR 60153.

Former proposed §301.6234-1(b) provided that a partnership may file a petition for a readjustment of any partnership adjustment in a district court or the Court of Federal Claims "only if the partnership filing the petition deposits with the [IRS], on or before the date the petition is filed, the amount of any imputed underpayment resulting from the partnership adjustment."

To reflect the amendment to section 6234(b)(1) made by section 206(j) of the TTCA regarding the amount of the deposit, proposed §301.6234-1(b) now provides that amount required to be deposited is the amount (as of the date of the filing of the petition) of any imputed underpayment and any penalties, additions to tax, and additional amounts with respect to such imputed underpayment.

To account for the possibility that multiple imputed underpayments may be reflected in an FPA, proposed § 301.6234-1(b) also now provides that the partnership must only deposit the amount of any imputed underpayment to which the petition for readjustment relates and the amount of any penalties, additions to tax, and additional amounts with respect to such imputed underpayment.

10. *Period of Limitations on Making Adjustments*

Section 6235 provides the period of limitations on making adjustments under the centralized partnership audit regime. Under section 6235(a), the general rule is that no adjustment for any partnership taxable year may be made after the later of three specified dates. Section 206(k) of the TTCA amended section 6235(a) by inserting "or section 905(c)" after "Except as otherwise provided in this section." The amendment makes clear that the period of limitations on making adjustments under the centralized partnership audit regime does not limit the period for notification of the Secretary and redetermination of tax under section 905(c) with respect to foreign tax redeterminations.

In addition, section 206(k) of the TTCA amended section 6235 by striking paragraph (d), which provided for a suspension of the period on making adjustments when the Secretary mails an FPA. That provision was similar to a provision that existed under TEFRA, but the provision has no effect on making adjustments under the centralized partnership audit regime. See JCX-6-18, at 49-50.

A. *Proposed § 301.6235-1*

Proposed rules under § 301.6235-1 were previously published in the **Federal Register** (82 FR 60166-67) in the December 2017 NPRM (former proposed § 301.6235-1). For an explanation of the rules under former proposed § 301.6235-1, see 82 FR 60153-54.

Proposed § 301.6235-1(a) now reflects the amendments to section 6235 to provide an exception for section 905(c) and to remove the reference to section 6235(d).

11. *Definitions and Special Rules*

A. *Proposed § 301.6241-1*

Proposed rules under § 301.6241-1 were previously published in the **Federal Register** (82 FR 27399-400) in the June 2017 NPRM (former proposed § 301.6241-1). For an explanation of the rules under former proposed § 301.6241-1, see 82 FR 27369.

Former proposed § 301.6241-1(a)(1) defined the term "adjustment year" to mean the partnership taxable year in which a decision of a court becomes final (if a petition is filed under section 6234), an AAR is made, or, in any other case, when an FPA is mailed (or if the partnership waives its right to an FPA, the year the waiver is executed by the IRS). Section 206(p) of the TTCA amended section 6227 to provide that an AAR is "filed," as opposed to "made." To reflect this amendment, proposed § 301.6241-1(a)(1) now provides that an AAR is "filed" and not "made."

Former proposed § 301.6241-1(a)(3) defined the term "imputed underpayment" as the amount determined under § 301.6225-1. Because an imputed underpayment may also be computed and paid pursuant to proposed § 301.6226-3(e)(4) (relating to pass-through partners) as well as under proposed § 301.6227-2 and § 301.6227-3(c) (relating to AARs), proposed § 301.6241-1(a)(3) now refers to imputed underpayments determined under those provisions. Proposed § 301.6241-1(a)(3) was also clarified to provide that an imputed underpayment calculated under section 6225 is calculated under section 6225 and the regulations thereunder.

Proposed § 301.6241-1(a)(4) now provides that the term "indirect partner" includes a person that holds an interest in the partnership through a wholly owned entity that is disregarded as separate from its owner for Federal income tax purposes, such as a disregarded entity or grantor trust. This change from the language in the former proposed regulations clarifies that a partnership may seek modification under proposed § 301.6225-2 based on indirect partners holding an interest through a disregarded entity or grantor trust.

Proposed § 301.6241-1(a)(6) now provides that the term "partnership adjustment" means any adjustment to a partnership-related item (as defined in proposed § 301.6241-6), and such term includes a portion of a partnership adjustment.

Former proposed § 301.6241-1(a)(10) defined a tax attribute as anything that can affect, with respect to a partnership or partner, the amount or timing of an item of income, gain, loss, deduction, or credit or that can affect the amount of tax due in any taxable year. As discussed in section 4.A. of this preamble, section 203(a) of the TTCA amended section 6225 to provide an alternative procedure to filing amended returns during modification under which a partner agrees to take into account adjustments to the tax attributes "of such partner". Section 6225(c)(2)(B)(ii). To reflect the amendment to section 6225(c)(2)(B) regarding tax attributes of a partner, the phrase "with respect to a partnership or a partner" was removed from the definition of tax attribute under former proposed § 301.6241-1(a)(10). The reference to "items of income, gain, loss, deduction, or credit" in former proposed § 301.6241-1(a)(10) was also replaced with a reference to "partnership-related item."

B. *Proposed § 301.6241-2*

Proposed rules under § 301.6241-2 were previously published in the **Federal Register** (82 FR 27400) in the June 2017 NPRM (former proposed § 301.6241-2). Former proposed § 301.6241-2 provided for coordination between Title 11 of the United States Code, which deals with bankruptcy, and the centralized partnership audit regime. Because the amendments by the TTCA did not affect section 6241(6), the rules under former proposed § 301.6241-2 are unchanged. For an explanation of the rules under former proposed § 301.6241-2, see 82 FR 27369-70.

C. *Proposed § 301.6241-3*

Proposed rules under § 301.6241-3 were previously published in the **Federal Register** (82 FR 27400-02) in the June 2017 NPRM (former proposed § 301.6241-3). For an explanation of the rules under former proposed § 301.6241-3, see 82 FR 27370-71.

Former proposed § 301.6241-3(a)(3) provided that the rules requiring former partners to take into account adjustments of a partnership which the IRS determined had ceased to exist did not apply to the former partners of a partnership that had elected out of the centralized partnership audit regime under section 6221(b). Because under section 6226(b)(4) a partnership-partner that has elected out of the centralized partnership audit regime may be liable for an imputed underpayment in the case of a push out election, proposed § 301.6241-3(a)(3) now provides that the rules under proposed § 301.6241-3 apply to a partnership-partner and its former partners, regardless of whether the partnership-partner has elected out of the centralized partnership audit regime. Accordingly, under proposed § 301.6241-3(a)(3), the former partners of any partnership that may be liable for an imputed underpayment, including a partnership-partner that has elected out of the centralized partnership audit regime, will be required to take into account a partnership adjustment if the IRS determines that such partnership ceased to exist before the partnership adjustment had taken effect. Example 2 under proposed § 301.6241-3(f) illustrates this rule.

Former proposed § 301.6241-3(b)(2)(i) provided that the IRS will not determine that a partnership has ceased to exist solely because: (i) a partnership has technically terminated under section 708(b)(1)(B); (ii) the partnership has made a valid election under section 6226 and the regulations thereunder with respect to any imputed underpayment; or (iii) the partnership has not paid any amount the partnership is liable for under subchapter C of chapter 63. To reflect the amendment to section 708 by the Act to eliminate technical terminations, the reference to section 708(b)(1)(B) was removed from former proposed § 301.6241-3(b)(2)(i). In addition, a rule was added to former proposed § 301.6241-3(b)(2)(i) to provide that a partnership also does not cease to exist solely because it furnished statements in accordance with proposed § 301.6226-3(e)(3). This change clarifies that partnership-partners that properly furnish statements in accordance with proposed § 301.6226-3(e)(3) (and therefore are not liable for an imputed underpayment) are treated the same as an audited partnership who made a valid election under section 6226.

Additional clarifications were made to proposed § 301.6241-3. First, the phrase "any amounts" in former proposed § 301.6241-3(a)(2) was replaced with the phrase "any unpaid amounts." This clarification was made to eliminate the implication that the partnership was not liable for the original amount due and to clarify that if the IRS determines that a partnership has ceased to exist, the partnership is no longer liable for any remaining unpaid amounts due under subchapter C of chapter 63, meaning that if the partnership had made a prior payment, the IRS can retain that payment. Second, former proposed § 301.6241-3(b)(2)(iii) provided that the IRS may not determine that a partnership has ceased to exist after the expiration of the period of limitations on collection. Proposed § 301.6241-3(b)(2)(iii) now provides that the period relevant to this determination is the period of limitations on collection with respect to the imputed underpayment that was assessed against the partnership that ceased to exist. Finally, prior references to section 708(b)(1)(A) in former proposed § 301.6241-3(b)(2), (d)(2), and (f) were changed to refer to section 708(b)(1) to reflect the amendment to section 708 made by the Act.

D. *Proposed § 301.6241-4*

Proposed rules under § 301.6241-4 were previously published in the **Federal Register** (82 FR 27402) in the June 2017 NPRM (former proposed § 301.6241-4). For an explanation of the rules under former proposed § 301.6241-4, see 82 FR 27371.

Former proposed § 301.6241-4 provided that payments made by a partnership under the centralized partnership audit regime, including payment of any imputed underpayment and any amount under proposed § 301.6226-3, were not deductible to the partnership. Because the payment amount for a partnership-partner in the case of a push out election is referred to as an imputed underpayment, reference to any amount under § 301.6226-3 in former proposed § 301.6241-4 became superfluous and thus was removed.

E. *Proposed § 301.6241-5*

Proposed rules under § 301.6241-5 were previously published in the **Federal Register** (82 FR 27402) in the June 2017 NPRM (former proposed § 301.6241-5). For an explanation of the rules under former proposed § 301.6241-5, see 82 FR 27371.

Former proposed § 301.6241-5 provided rules for extending the centralized partnership audit regime to entities filing partnership returns. References in former proposed § 301.6241-5(a) to "items of income, gain, loss, deduction, or credit" and "partner's distributive share" were replaced with a reference to "partnership-related item." Proposed § 301.6241-5(c) now also reflects the fact that certain business arrangements, which may not be classified as entities, can file partnership returns to make an election under section 761(a). Under proposed § 301.6241-5(c), the centralized partnership audit regime does not apply in that case notwithstanding the filing of a partnership return.

12. *Coordination with Other Chapters of the Code*

Section 201(b) of the TTCA added section 6241(9) to the Code regarding the coordination of the centralized partnership audit regime with chapters of the Code other than chapter 1. Section 6241(9)(A) provides that the centralized partnership audit regime shall not apply with respect to any tax imposed (including any amount required to be deducted or withheld) under chapter 2, 2A, 3, or 4 of subtitle A of the Code, except that any partnership adjustment determined under the centralized partnership audit regime for purposes of chapter 1 shall be taken into account for purposes of determining any such tax to the extent that such adjustment is relevant to such determination. Section 6241(9)(B) provides that in the case of any tax imposed (including any amount required to be deducted or withheld) under chapters 3 and 4 of the Code, which is determined with respect to a partnership adjustment, such tax shall be so determined with respect to the reviewed year and shall be so imposed (or so required to be deducted or withheld) with respect to the adjustment year.

Section 201(b) also added section 6501(c)(12) to the Code regarding the statute of limitation on assessment of taxes under chapter 2 or 2A which are attributable to any partnership adjustment. Section 6501(c)(12) provides in the case of any partnership adjustment determined under the centralized partnership audit regime, the period for assessment of any tax imposed under chapter 2 or 2A of the Code which is attributable to such adjustment shall not expire before the date that is one year after one of two events. In the case of an adjustment pursuant to the decision of a court in a proceeding brought under section 6234, the period for assessment shall not expire before the date that is one year after the decision becomes final. In any other case, the period for assessment shall not expire before the date that is one year after 90 days after the date on which the FPA is mailed under section 6231.

A. *Proposed § 301.6241-7*

Former proposed § 301.6221(a)-1(d) provided that nothing in subchapter C of chapter 63 precluded the IRS from making any adjustment to an item of a partnership (as described in the prior version of § 301.6221(a)-1(b)) outside of the centralized partnership audit regime for purposes of determining tax imposed by provisions of the Code other than chapter 1. Accordingly, under former proposed § 301.6221(a)-1(d), the IRS was not precluded from examining a partnership's compliance with its obligations under chapters 3 and 4 (or any other chapter of the Code other than chapter 1) in a proceeding outside of the centralized partnership audit regime. Former proposed § 301.6221(a)-1(f) provided examples to illustrate this concept.

The rules contained in former proposed § 301.6221(a)-1(d), and the examples in former proposed § 301.6221(a)-1(f), are consistent with section 6241(9)(A). However, given that these concepts are now codified in section 6241, the rules and examples under former proposed § 301.6221(a)-1(d) and (f) are now under proposed § 301.6241-7(a)(1) and (2). References to "items of income, gain, loss, deduction, or credit" were replaced with references to "partnership-related item" as defined under proposed § 301.6241-6. Other editorial changes were made to reflect revisions to former proposed § 301.6221(a)-1.

Proposed § 301.6241-7(a)(1) provides that the centralized partnership audit regime does not apply with respect to any tax imposed (including any amount required to be deducted or withheld) under any chapter of the Code other than chapter 1, including chapter 2, 2A, 3, or 4 of the Code. Accordingly, for purposes of determining taxes under chapters of the Code other than chapter 1, the IRS may make adjustments to partnership-related items in proceedings not subject to the centralized partnership audit regime. However, to the extent an adjustment to a partnership-related item or a determination made under the centralized partnership audit regime is relevant in determining tax outside of chapter 1, such adjustment or determination must be taken into account in determining that non-chapter 1 tax. Proposed § 301.6241-7(a)(2) provides examples to illustrate these concepts.

Proposed § 301.6241-7(b) provides rules for coordinating the centralized partnership audit regime with chapters 3 and 4 of the Code. Proposed § 301.6241-7(b)(1) restates the rule in section 6241(9)(B) regarding the timing of withholding for tax imposed under chapters 3 and 4 that is determined with respect to a partnership adjustment. Proposed § 301.6241-7(b)(2) defines the terms chapter 3, chapter 4, and amount subject to withholding.

Former proposed § § 301.6225-1(a)(4) and 301.6226-2(h) provided rules to coordinate the collection of tax in the case of partnership adjustments to amounts subject to withholding under chapters 3 and 4, including rules for when the partnership pays an imputed underpayment resulting from such an adjustment and rules for when the partnership makes the election under section 6226 with respect to such an imputed underpayment. These rules now fall within proposed § 301.6241-7(b)(3) and (b)(4). Proposed § 301.6241-7(b)(4) now provides that a partnership required to pay tax under chapter 3 or chapter 4 when it makes an election under section 6226 is required to pay the tax before the due date of the partnership return for the adjustment year (without regard to extension).

13. *Other Amendments by the TTCA to the Centralized Partnership Audit Regime*

Section 206(l) of the TTCA amended section 6241 by adding a new provision, section 6241(11), providing for the treatment of special enforcement matters. Under section 6241(11), in the case of partnership-related items which involve special enforcement matters, the Secretary may prescribe regulations pursuant to which the centralized partnership audit regime (or any portion thereof) does not apply to such items, and that such items are subject to special rules (including rules related to assessment and collection) as the Secretary determines to be necessary for the effective and efficient enforcement of the Code. For purposes of section 6241(11), the term "special enforcement matters" means: (1) failure to comply with the requirements of section 6226(b)(4)(A)(ii) (regarding the requirement for a pass-through partner to furnish statements or compute and pay an imputed underpayment); (2) assessments under section 6851 (relating to termination assessments of income tax) or section 6861 (relating to jeopardy assessments of income, estate, gift, and certain excise taxes); (3) criminal investigations; (4) indirect methods of proof of income; (5) foreign partners or partnerships;

and (6) other matters that the Secretary determines by regulation present special enforcement considerations. Rules under this provision may be provided in future guidance. The Treasury Department and the IRS are considering proposing rules under section 6241(11)(B)(vi) (dealing with other matters that present special enforcement considerations) which allow certain partnership-related items reported solely by persons other than the partnership to be adjusted outside the centralized partnership audit regime. The Treasury Department and the IRS request comments on this provision, including whether there are any additional special enforcement considerations that should be addressed through regulations.

Section 206(m) of the TTCA amended section 6241 by adding a new provision, section 6241(12), to clarify that a U.S. shareholder of a controlled foreign corporation (CFC) which is a partner of a partnership shall be treated as a partner of such partnership for purposes of the centralized partnership audit regime. The U.S. shareholder's distributive share of the partnership is the U.S. shareholder's pro rata share of the CFC's Subpart F income determined under rules similar to section 951(a)(2). Similarly, a taxpayer that makes a Qualified Electing Fund (QEF) election with respect to a passive foreign investment company (PFIC) that is a partner in a partnership shall be treated as a partner of such partnership. In this case, a taxpayer's distributive share of the partnership is the taxpayer's pro rata share of the PFIC's ordinary earnings and net capital gain determined under rules similar to section 1293(b). Consequently, in both circumstances, the U.S. shareholder of a CFC and the taxpayer of a PFIC will be treated as the adjustment year partner or reviewed year partner under the centralized partnership audit regime, where applicable. Regulatory authority was also given to issue regulations or other guidance as necessary or appropriate to carry out the purpose of the provision, including regulations which apply the rule in similar circumstances or with respect to similarly situated persons. Consequently, in both circumstances, the U.S. shareholder of a CFC and the taxpayer of a PFIC will be treated as the adjustment year partner or reviewed year partner under proposed §§301.6241-1(a)(2) and 301.6241-1(a)(9) where applicable.

Special Analyses

This regulation is not subject to review under section 6(b) of Executive Order 12866 pursuant to the Memorandum of Agreement (April 11, 2018) between the Department of the Treasury and the Office of Management and Budget regarding review of tax regulations.

Because the proposed regulations would not impose a collection of information on small entities, the Regulatory Flexibility Act (5 U.S.C. chapter 6) does not apply.

Pursuant to section 7805(f) of the Code, this notice of proposed rulemaking has been submitted to the Chief Counsel for Advocacy of the Small Business Administration for comment on its impact on small business.

Statement of Availability of IRS Documents

IRS Revenue Procedures, Revenue Rulings, Notices, and other guidance cited in this preamble are published in the Internal Revenue Bulletin (or Cumulative Bulletin) and are available from the Superintendent of Documents, U.S. Government Publishing Office, Washington, DC 20402, or by visiting the IRS website at *www.irs.gov*.

Comments and Public Hearing

Before these proposed regulations are adopted as final regulations, consideration will be given to any electronic and written comments that are submitted timely to the IRS as prescribed in this preamble under the ADDRESSES heading. The Treasury Department and the IRS request comments on all aspects of the proposed rules. All comments will be available at *www.regulations.gov* or upon request.

A public hearing has been scheduled for October 9, 2018, beginning at 10 a.m. in the Auditorium of the Internal Revenue Building, 1111 Constitution Avenue, NW., Washington, DC. Due to building security procedures, visitors must enter at the Constitution Avenue entrance. In addition, all visitors must present photo identification to enter the building. Because of access restrictions, visitors will not be admitted beyond the immediate entrance area more than 30 minutes before the hearing starts. For more information about having your name placed on the building access list to attend the hearing, see the FOR FURTHER INFORMATION CONTACT section of this preamble.

The rules of 26 CFR 601.601(a)(3) apply to the hearing. Persons who wish to present oral comments at the hearing must submit an outline of the topics to be discussed and the time to be devoted to each topic by October 1, 2018. Submit a signed paper or electronic copy of the outline as prescribed in this preamble under the ADDRESSES heading. A period of 10 minutes will be allotted to each person for making comments. An agenda showing the scheduling of the speakers will be prepared after the deadline for receiving outlines has passed. Copies of the agenda will be available free of charge at the hearing.

Drafting Information

The principal authors of these proposed regulations are Jennifer M. Black, Joy E. Gerdy-Zogby, Steven L. Karon, and Brittany Harrison of the Associate Chief Counsel (Procedure and Administration). However, other personnel from the Treasury Department and the IRS participated in their development.

[¶49,768] Proposed Amendments of Regulations (REG-112176-18), published in the Federal Register on August 27, 2018.

[Code Secs. 170 and 642]

Deductions: Charitable contributions: State and local tax credits.—Amendments of Reg. §§1.170A-1, 1.170A-13 and 1.642(c)-3, governing the availability of charitable contribution deductions under section 170 when a taxpayer receives or expects to receive a corresponding state or local tax credit, are proposed.

AGENCY: Internal Revenue Service (IRS), Treasury.

ACTION: Notice of proposed rulemaking and notification of public hearing.

SUMMARY: This document contains proposed amendments to regulations under section 170 of the Internal Revenue Code (Code). The proposed amendments provide rules governing the availability of charitable contribution deductions under section 170 when a taxpayer receives or expects to receive a corresponding state or local tax credit. This document also proposes amendments to the regulations under section 642(c) to apply similar rules to payments made by a trust or decedent's estate. This document provides notification of a public hearing on these proposed regulations.

DATES: Written and electronic comments must be received by October 11, 2018. Requests to speak and outlines of topics to be discussed at the public hearing scheduled for November 5, 2018, must be received by October 11, 2018.

ADDRESSES: Send submissions to Internal Revenue Service, CC:PA:LPD:PR (REG-112176-18), Room 5203, P.O. Box 7604, Ben Franklin Station, Washington, DC 20044. Submissions may be hand-delivered Monday through Friday between the hours of 8:00 a.m. and 4:00 p.m. to CC:PA:LPD:PR (REG-112176-18), Courier's Desk, 1111 Constitution Avenue, N.W., Washington, DC 20224, or sent electronically, via the Federal eRulemaking Portal at www.regulations.gov (indicate IRS and REG-112176-18). The public hearing will be held in the IRS Auditorium, Internal Revenue Building, 1111 Constitution Avenue, N.W., Washington, DC 20224.

FOR FURTHER INFORMATION CONTACT: Concerning the proposed regulations, Merrill D. Feldstein and Mon Lam at (202) 317-4059; concerning submission of comments and requests for a public hearing, Regina Johnson at (202) 317-6901 (not toll-free numbers).

SUPPLEMENTARY INFORMATION:

Background

Section 170(a)(1) generally allows an itemized deduction for any "charitable contribution" paid within the taxable year. Section 170(c) defines "charitable contribution" as a "contribution or gift to or for the use of" any entity listed in that subsection. Section 170(c)(1) includes a contribution or gift to or for the use of a State, a possession of the United States, or any political subdivision of the foregoing, but only if the contribution or gift is made exclusively for public purposes. Section 170(c)(2) includes, in general, a contribution or gift to or for the use of certain corporations, trusts, or community chests, funds, or foundations, organized and operated exclusively for religious, charitable, scientific, literary, or educational purposes, or to foster national or international amateur sports competition, or for the prevention of cruelty to children or animals.

Section 164 generally allows an itemized deduction for the payment of certain taxes, including state and local, and foreign, real property taxes; state and local personal property taxes; and state and local, and foreign, income, war profits, and excess profits taxes. Section 164(b)(6), as added by section 11042 of "An Act to provide for reconciliation pursuant to titles II and V of the concurrent resolution on the budget for fiscal year 2018" (the Act), Pub. L. 115-97, limits an individual's deduction for the aggregate amount of state and local taxes paid during the calendar year to $10,000 ($5,000 in the case of a married individual filing a separate return). This new limitation applies to taxable years beginning after December 31, 2017, and before January 1, 2026.

I. *The Charitable Contribution Deduction*

In 1986, the Supreme Court interpreted the phrase "charitable contribution" in section 170. *See United States v. American Bar Endowment*, 477 U.S. 105, 116-118 (1986). The Court held that the "*sine qua non* of a charitable contribution is a transfer of money or property without adequate consideration"—that is, without the expectation of a *quid pro quo. Id.* at 118. A "payment of money generally cannot constitute a charitable contribution if the contributor expects a substantial benefit in return." *Id.* at 116. The Court recognized that some payments may have a "dual character"—part charitable contribution and part *quid pro* quo—whereby the taxpayer receives some "nominal benefit" of lesser value than the payment. *Id.* at 117. In such cases, the Court reasoned, "it would not serve the purposes of §170 to deny a deduction altogether." *Id.* Instead, the Court held, the charitable contribution deduction is allowed, but only to the extent the amount donated or the fair market value of the property transferred by the taxpayer exceeds the fair market value of the benefit received in return, and only if the excess amount was transferred with the intent of making a gift. *Id.*

For the benefit received in return to reduce the allowable charitable contribution deduction under section 170, the benefits received, or expected to be received, by a donor need only be greater than those benefits that inure to the general public from transfers for charitable purposes. *See, e.g., Singer Co. v. United States*, 449 F.2d 413, 422-423 (Ct. Cl. 1971); *American Bar Endowment*, 477 U.S. at 116-17 (citing *Singer*); *Hernandez v. Commissioner*, 490 U.S. 680 (1989). In addition, the benefits received need not come directly from the donee to reduce the allowable deduction, nor do they need to be specifically quantifiable at the time of transfer. *See, e.g., Singer*, 449 F.2d at 422. The Treasury Department and the IRS have incorporated many of these principles into regulations under section

170. Section 1.170A-1(h)(1) of the Income Tax Regulations provides, for example, that no part of a payment that a taxpayer makes to or for the use of an organization described in section 170(c) that is in consideration for (as defined in § 1.170A-13(f)(6)) goods or services (as defined in § 1.170A-13(f)(5)) is a contribution or gift within the meaning of section 170(c) unless the taxpayer (i) intends to make a payment in an amount that exceeds the fair market value of the goods or services; and (ii) makes a payment in an amount that exceeds the fair market value of the goods or services. Section 1.170A-13(f)(5) defines goods or services to include cash, property, services, benefits, and privileges, and § 1.170A-13(f)(6) provides that a donee provides goods or services in consideration for a taxpayer's payment if, at the time the taxpayer makes the payment to the donee organization, the taxpayer receives or expects to receive goods or services in exchange for that payment.

II. *State and Local Tax Credit Programs*

In recent years, it has become increasingly common for states and localities to provide state or local tax credits in return for contributions by taxpayers to or for the use of certain entities listed in section 170(c). As the use of these tax credit programs by states and localities became more common, the IRS Office of Chief Counsel (IRS Chief Counsel), in multiple Chief Counsel Advice memoranda (CCAs), considered whether the receipt of state tax credits under these programs were *quid pro quo* benefits that would affect the amount of taxpayers' charitable contribution deductions under section 170(a). Although CCAs are released to the public for information purposes, it should be noted that CCAs are not official rulings or positions of the IRS, are not ordinarily reviewed by the Treasury Department, and are not precedential.

In CCAs issued in 2002 and 2004, IRS Chief Counsel reviewed programs involving the issuance of state tax credits in return for the transfer of conservation easements and for payments to certain child care organizations. *See* CCA 200238041 (July 24, 2002); CCA 200435001 (July 28, 2004). In these CCAs, IRS Chief Counsel recognized that these programs raised complex questions and recommended that the tax credit issue be addressed through official published guidance.

In 2010, another CCA explained that published guidance on the issue was not contemplated at that time, but it offered further advice. *See* CCA 201105010 (Oct. 27, 2010) (the 2010 CCA). This 2010 CCA observed that a payment to a state agency or charitable organization in return for a tax credit might be characterized as either a charitable contribution deductible under section 170 or a payment of state tax possibly deductible under section 164. The 2010 CCA advised that taxpayers may take a deduction under section 170 for the full amount of a contribution made in return for a state tax credit, without subtracting the value of the credit received in return. The analysis in the 2010 CCA assumed that after the taxpayer applied the state or local tax credit to reduce the taxpayer's state or local tax liability, the taxpayer would receive a smaller deduction for state and local taxes under section 164. The 2010 CCA cautioned, however, that "there may be unusual circumstances in which it would be appropriate to recharacterize a payment of cash or property that was, in form, a charitable contribution as, in substance, a satisfaction of tax liability."

In addition to the CCAs, IRS Chief Counsel has taken the position in the U.S. Tax Court that the amount of a state or local tax credit that reduces a tax liability is not an accession to wealth under section 61 or an amount realized for purposes of section 1001, and the Tax Court has accepted this view. *See, e.g., Maines v. Commissioner*, 144 T.C. 123, 134 (2015) (holding that the non-refundable portion of a state income tax credit, the amount of which was based on previously-paid property taxes, reduced the current year's tax liability and is not taxable or treated as an item of income); *Tempel v. Commissioner*, 136 T.C. 341, 351-354 (2011) (holding that state income tax credits received by a donor for the transfer of a conservation easement and sold by the donor were capital assets, but that the donor had no adjusted basis in the credits), *aff'd sub nom. Esgar Corp. v. Commissioner*, 744 F.3d 648 (10th Cir. 2014). However, the application of sections 61 and 1001 to state or local tax credits presents different issues than the application of section 170, and none of these cases addressed whether a taxpayer's expectation or receipt of a state or local tax credit may reduce a taxpayer's charitable contribution deduction under section 170. Nor has the Treasury Department or the IRS ever addressed this question in published guidance.

III. *New Limitation in Section 164*

At the time the 2010 CCA was issued, section 164 generally allowed an itemized deduction—unlimited in amount—for the payment of state and local taxes. Accordingly, the question of how to characterize transfers pursuant to state tax credit programs had little practical consequence from a federal income tax perspective because, unless the taxpayer was subject to the alternative minimum tax (AMT) under section 55, a deduction was likely to be available under either section 164 or section 170. Permitting a charitable contribution deduction for a transfer made in exchange for a state or local tax credit generally had no effect on federal income tax liability because any increased deduction under section 170 would be offset by a decreased deduction under section 164.

However, as a result of the new limit on the deductibility of state and local taxes under section 164(b)(6) (as added by the Act), treating a transfer pursuant to a state or local tax credit program as a charitable contribution for federal income tax purposes may reduce a taxpayer's federal income tax liability. When a charitable contribution is made in return for a state or local tax credit and the taxpayer has pre-credit state and local tax liabilities in excess of the $10,000 limitation in section 164(b)(6), a charitable contribution deduction under section 170 would no longer be offset by a reduction in the taxpayer's state and local tax deduction under section 164. Thus, as a consequence, state and local tax credit programs now give taxpayers a potential means to circumvent the $10,000 limitation in section 164(b)(6) by substituting an increased charitable contribution deduction for a disallowed state and local tax deduction. State legislatures are also now considering or have adopted proposals to enact new state and local tax credit programs with the aim of enabling taxpayers to characterize their transfers as fully deductible charitable contributions for federal income tax purposes, while using the same transfers to satisfy or offset their state or local tax liabilities.

In light of the tax consequences of section 164(b)(6) and the resulting increased interest in preexisting and new state tax credit programs, the Treasury Department and the IRS determined that it was appropriate to review the question of whether amounts paid or property transferred in exchange for state or local tax credits are fully deductible as charitable contributions under section 170.

IV. *Notice 2018-54*

Pursuant to this review, in Notice 2018-54, 2018-24 I.R.B. 750, the Treasury Department and the IRS announced on June 11, 2018, their intention to propose regulations addressing the federal income tax treatment of payments made by taxpayers for which the taxpayers receive a credit against their state and local taxes. The notice stated that federal tax law controls the proper characterization of payments for federal income tax purposes and that proposed regulations would assist taxpayers in understanding the relationship between the federal charitable contribution deduction and the new limitation on the deduction for state and local tax payments.

Although Notice 2018-54 was issued in response to state legislation proposed after the enactment of the limitation on state and local tax deductions under section 164(b)(6), the rules in these proposed regulations are based on longstanding federal tax law principles, which apply equally to taxpayers regardless of whether they are participating in a new state and local tax credit program or a preexisting one. Accordingly, the proposed regulations, and the analysis underlying the proposed regulations, are intended to apply to transfers pursuant to state and local tax credit programs established under the recent state legislation as well as to transfers pursuant to state and local tax credit programs that were in existence before the enactment of section 164(b)(6).

V. *Proposed Regulations*

After reviewing the issue, and in light of the longstanding principles of the cases and tax regulations discussed above, the Treasury Department and the IRS believe that when a taxpayer receives or expects to receive a state or local tax credit in return for a payment or transfer to an entity listed in section 170(c), the receipt of this tax benefit constitutes a *quid pro quo* that may preclude a full deduction under section 170(a). In applying section 170 and the *quid pro quo* doctrine, the Treasury Department and the IRS do not believe it is appropriate to categorically exempt state or local tax benefits from the normal rules that apply to other benefits received by a taxpayer in exchange for a contribution. Thus, the Treasury Department and the IRS believe that the amount otherwise deductible as a charitable contribution must generally be reduced by the amount of the state or local tax credit received or expected to be received, just as it is reduced for many other benefits. Accordingly, the Treasury Department and the IRS propose regulations proposing to amend existing regulations under section 170 to clarify this general requirement, to provide for a *de minimis* exception from the general rule, and to make other conforming amendments.

Compelling policy considerations reinforce the interpretation and application of section 170 in this context. Disregarding the value of all state tax benefits received or expected to be received in return for charitable contributions would precipitate significant revenue losses that would undermine and be inconsistent with the limitation on the deduction for state and local taxes adopted by Congress in section 164(b)(6).[1] Such an approach would incentivize and enable taxpayers to characterize payments as fully deductible charitable contributions for federal income tax purposes, while using the same payments to satisfy or offset their state or local tax liabilities. Disregarding the tax benefit would also undermine the intent of Congress in enacting section 170, that is, to provide a deduction for taxpayers' gratuitous payments to qualifying entities, not for transfers that result in economic returns. The Treasury Department and the IRS believe that appropriate application of the *quid pro quo* doctrine to substantial state or local tax benefits is consistent with the Code and sound tax administration.

Explanation of Provisions

The proposed regulations generally provide that if a taxpayer makes a payment or transfers property to or for the use of an entity listed in section 170(c), and the taxpayer receives or expects to receive a state or local tax credit in return for such payment, the tax credit constitutes a return benefit, or *quid pro quo*, to the taxpayer and reduces the charitable contribution deduction.

In addition to credits, the proposed regulations also address state or local tax deductions claimed in connection with a taxpayer's payment or transfer. Although deductions could be considered *quid pro quo* benefits in the same manner as credits, the Treasury Department and the IRS believe that sound policy considerations as well as considerations of efficient tax administration warrant making an

---

[1] The Joint Committee on Taxation estimated that the limitation on state and local tax deductions along with certain other reforms of itemized deductions would raise $668 billion over ten years. A substantial amount of this revenue would be lost if state tax benefits received in exchange for charitable contributions were ignored in determining the charitable contribution deduction. This estimate is not a revenue estimate of the proposed regulations, in part because it includes other reforms of itemized deductions but does not reflect certain other provisions of the Act. *See* Joint Committee on Taxation, "Estimated Budget Effects of the Conference Agreement for H.R. 1, The 'Tax Cuts and Jobs Act,'" JCX-67-17, December 18, 2017 available at https://www.jct.gov/publications.html?func=startdown&id=5053.

exception to *quid pro quo* principles in the case of dollar-for-dollar state or local tax deductions. Because the benefit of a dollar-for-dollar deduction is limited to the taxpayer's state and local marginal rate, the risk of deductions being used to circumvent section 164(b)(6) is comparatively low. In addition, if state and local tax deductions for charitable contributions were treated as *quid pro quo* benefits, it would make the accurate calculation of federal taxes and state and local taxes difficult for both taxpayers and the IRS. For example, the value of a deduction could vary based on the taxpayer's marginal or effective state and local tax rates, making for more complex computations and adding to administrative and taxpayer burden. The proposed regulations thus allow taxpayers to disregard dollar-for-dollar state or local tax deductions. However, the proposed regulations state that, if the taxpayer receives or expects to receive a state or local tax deduction that exceeds the amount of the taxpayer's payment or the fair market value of the property transferred, the taxpayer's charitable contribution deduction must be reduced. The Treasury Department and the IRS request comments on how to determine the amount of this reduction.

To provide consistent treatment for state or local tax deductions and state or local tax credits that provide a benefit that is generally equivalent to a deduction, the proposed regulations include a *de minimis* exception under which a taxpayer may disregard a state or local tax credit if such credit does not exceed 15 percent of the taxpayer's payment or 15 percent of the fair market value of the property transferred by the taxpayer. The *de minimis* exception reflects that the combined value of a state and local tax deduction, that is the combined top marginal state and local tax rate, currently does not exceed 15 percent. Accordingly, under the proposed regulations, a state or local tax credit that does not exceed 15 percent does not reduce the taxpayer's federal deduction for a charitable contribution. The Treasury Department and the IRS request comments on this proposed exception.

In drafting the proposed regulations, the Treasury Department and the IRS also considered whether a taxpayer may decline the receipt or anticipated receipt of a state or local tax credit by taking some affirmative action at the time of the taxpayer's payment or transfer. *See* Rev. Rul. 67-246, 1967-2 C.B. 104 (allowing a full charitable contribution deduction if the taxpayer does not accept or keep any indicia of a return benefit). Because procedures for declining the state or local tax credit would depend on the procedures of each state and locality in administering the tax credits, the Treasury Department and the IRS request comments regarding a rule that would allow taxpayers to decline state or local tax credits and receive full deductions for charitable contributions under section 170.

Trusts and decedents' estates may claim an income tax deduction for charitable contributions under section 642(c). For the same reasons provided above, the proposed regulations amend § 1.642(c)-3 to provide that the proposed rules under § 1.170A-1(h)(3) apply to payments made by a trust or decedent's estate in determining its charitable contribution deduction under section 642(c).

Proposed Applicability Date

The amendments to these regulations are proposed to apply to contributions after August 27, 2018.

Special Analyses

Executive Orders 12866 and 13563 direct agencies to assess costs and benefits of available regulatory alternatives and, if regulation is necessary, to select regulatory approaches that maximize net benefits (including potential economic, environmental, public health and safety effects, distributive impacts, and equity). Executive Order 13563 emphasizes the importance of quantifying both costs and benefits, of reducing costs, of harmonizing rules, and of promoting flexibility. These proposed regulations have been designated as subject to review under Executive Order 12866 pursuant to the Memorandum of Agreement (April 11, 2018) between the Treasury Department and the Office of Management and Budget (OMB) regarding review of tax regulations. OMB has determined that the proposed regulations are subject to review under section 1(b) of the Memorandum of Agreement. These proposed regulations have been reviewed by OMB. These proposed regulations are anticipated to be regulatory actions under EO 13771. The analysis below can provide further detail on this designation.

I. *Need for Regulations*

These proposed regulations provide guidance on the deductibility of charitable contributions when a taxpayer receives or expects to receive a corresponding state or local tax credit. These proposed regulations are intended to clarify the relationship between the federal charitable contribution deduction and the recently-enacted statutory limitation on deductions for state and local taxes paid (the "SALT cap") and to make the federal tax system more neutral with respect to taxpayers' decisions regarding donations. Compelling policy considerations reinforce the interpretation and application of section 170 in this context. Disregarding the value of all state tax benefits received or expected to be received in return for charitable contributions would precipitate revenue losses that would undermine and be inconsistent with the limitation on the deduction for state and local taxes adopted by Congress in section 164(b)(6).

Pursuant to section 6(a)(3)(B) of Executive Order 12866, the following qualitative analysis provides further details regarding the anticipated impact of the proposed regulations. After identifying a baseline in Part II, this analysis provides illustrative scenarios in Part III. Part III.A describes the tax effects of the contributions prior to enactment of the SALT cap in the Act. Part III.B provides examples comparing the enactment of the SALT cap but absent the proposed rule (the baseline) to the proposed rule. Finally, Part IV provides a qualitative assessment of the potential costs and benefits of the proposed rule compared to the baseline.

II. *Baseline*

Prior to this proposed rule, there was no authoritative regulatory guidance on the treatment of state or local tax credits arising from charitable contributions to entities listed in section 170(c), and there was no guidance aside from Notice 2018-54 addressing the interaction between section 170 and the newly enacted SALT cap. As a result, there was a degree of taxpayer uncertainty as to whether state and local tax credits are a return benefit that reduces a taxpayer's charitable contribution deduction. For informational and analytical purposes, however, this analysis assumes as a baseline that state and local tax credits are generally not treated as a return benefit or consideration and therefore do not reduce the taxpayer's charitable contribution deduction under section 170(a).

III. *Illustrative Scenarios*

For the following illustrative scenarios, assume the following facts: Charitable organizations A and B are entities listed in section 170(c) and provide similar public goods. Contributions to charity A are eligible for a dollar-for-dollar state tax credit. Contributions to charity B are ineligible for this credit but are deductible from state taxable income. A taxpayer itemizes deductions, and these itemized deductions in aggregate are at least $1,000 more than the standard deduction. The taxpayer has the choice to contribute $1,000 to charity A, and this $1,000 contribution generates a state tax credit of $1,000,[2] that is, the tax credit is dollar-for-dollar but does not otherwise figure into the calculation of the taxpayer's state tax liability. The taxpayer has more than $1,000 of state tax liability, so that the taxpayer's state tax liability is reduced by the entire $1,000 of the state tax credit. Finally, if the taxpayer makes the $1,000 contribution that generates a state tax credit of $1,000, the taxpayer reduces by $1,000 the withholdings or other payments of state taxes during the taxable year in question. The state taxes paid by the taxpayer are therefore reduced by the full amount of the state tax credit in the same taxable year as the contribution is made.[3] Further assume the taxpayer is in the 24 percent federal tax bracket, itemizes federal tax deductions, and has a state tax rate of 5 percent. If the taxpayer is subject to the AMT, assume an AMT marginal tax rate of 26 percent.

The Act and proposed regulations alter the incentives taxpayers face about whether and how much to give to organizations that receive charitable contributions as well as to which organizations. This is illustrated in the following scenarios, which are also summarized in Table 1 (below).

A. *Prior law: Section 170 charitable contributions prior to the Act*

The tax effects of contributions prior to enactment of the Act are illustrated in the columns labeled "Prior Law" in Table 1.

1. Taxpayer Not Subject to AMT

Prior to enactment of the Act, if the taxpayer made a $1,000 contribution to charity A that generated a state tax credit of $1,000, the deduction for charitable contributions under section 170(a) increased by $1,000, and the deduction for state and local taxes paid under section 164 decreased by $1,000. The taxpayer's itemized deductions, taxable income, and federal tax liability were unchanged from what they would have been in the absence of the contribution.[4] The taxpayer's state tax liability decreased by $1,000 because of the state tax credit. The combined federal and state tax benefits of the $1,000 contribution were therefore $1,000, and the cost to the taxpayer and to the federal government of making the contribution was $0. This is shown in column A under Prior Law for Example 1 in Table 1 and replicated in the same column for Example 2.

2. Taxpayer Subject to AMT

If the taxpayer were subject to the AMT under section 55, however, there was a net benefit to the taxpayer from contributions to charity A, which provided state tax credits. State and local taxes paid are not deductible expenses in determining taxable income under the AMT, but charitable contributions are deductible expenses in determining taxable income under the AMT. If the taxpayer contributed $1,000, taxable income under the AMT was reduced by $1,000 due to the charitable contribution deduction under section 170, but there was no corresponding reduction in the deduction for state and local taxes. Under an AMT marginal tax rate of 26 percent, the federal tax benefit of this $1,000 contribution would be $260. Because of the dollar-for-dollar state tax credit, the taxpayer received a combined federal and state tax benefit of $1,260 for a $1,000 contribution, a net benefit of $260. This is shown in column A under Prior Law for Example 3 in Table 1.

3. Comparison of Contributions to Different Organizations under Prior Law

In combination, state and federal tax laws generally provide a greater incentive to contribute to organizations eligible for state tax credits (charity A) than to other organizations (charity B). The effect of a contribution to charity A are described above.

Prior to enactment of the Act, for a taxpayer not subject to the AMT, a $1,000 contribution to charity B yielded a smaller combined federal and state tax benefit than to charity A. The state tax benefit was $50 ($1,000 times the 5 percent state tax rate). The taxpayer's itemized deductions at the federal level

---

[2] Note that this analysis only addresses state tax credits offering a 100% benefit. The results may differ for credits offering a lower benefit, but the comparative results of the below illustrative examples would be similar.

[3] The results of the examples are generally unchanged if the taxpayer instead receives the credit as a refund of state taxes paid that were deducted from federal taxable income, as such refund would be includible in federal taxable income in the following year.

[4] This assumes the taxpayer was not subject to limitations such as the overall limitation on itemized deductions under section 68 or subject to a percentage limitation for the deduction under section 170, an assumption that is maintained throughout the succeeding discussion.

increased by $950 (the $1,000 charitable contribution deduction less than $50 reduction in state taxes paid). The federal tax benefit of this increase was $228 ($950 times the 24 percent federal tax rate), resulting in a combined federal and state tax benefit of $278. The net cost to the taxpayer of the $1,000 contribution was $722. This is shown in column B under Prior Law for Example 1 in Table 1 and replicated in the same column for Example 2.

For a taxpayer subject to the AMT, a $1,000 contribution to charity B yielded a combined federal and state benefit of $310—the $1,000 contribution multiplied by the taxpayer's marginal tax rate under the AMT of 26 percent, or $260, plus the value of the deduction from state tax, or $50 ($1,000 times the 5 percent state tax rate). The net cost to the taxpayer of the $1,000 contribution was $690. This is shown in column B under Prior Law for Example 3 in Table 1.

Contributing to either charity A or charity B reduced the taxpayer's combined federal and state tax liability, but the existence of the state tax credit for contributions to charity A made contributions to that organization more attractive. This is seen by comparing the Total Tax Benefit in column A under Prior Law to the corresponding value in column B for each of the three examples. For taxpayers not subject to the AMT, contributions to charity A yielded a combined federal and state tax benefit of $1,000, compared to a combined federal and state tax benefit of $278 for a contribution to charity B. The AMT increased the disparity for contributions to charity A versus charity B, resulting in a combined federal and state tax benefit of $1,260 for a contribution to charity A versus $310 for a contribution to charity B.

B. *Examples under baseline (current law and practices under the Act) and proposed rule*

The enactment of the SALT cap in the Act has, in limited circumstances, altered the federal tax effects of charitable contributions as described in the following examples. These are illustrated in the columns labeled "Baseline" and "Proposed Rule" in Table 1.

1. Example 1: Taxpayer Is Above the SALT Cap and Not Subject to the AMT

a. Baseline

If a taxpayer that has a state tax liability of more than $1,000 above the SALT cap and is not subject to the AMT makes a $1,000 contribution to charity A, the deduction for charitable contributions under section 170(a) increases by $1,000, but the deduction for state and local taxes paid under section 164 is unchanged. Consequently, itemized deductions increase by $1,000, and taxable income decreases by $1,000. If the taxpayer is in the 24 percent bracket, federal liability will decrease by $240, and state tax liability will decrease by the $1,000 state tax credit. The combined federal and state tax benefits of the $1,000 contribution are therefore $1,240, and the taxpayer receives a $240 net benefit while the federal government has a loss of $240. This is shown in column A under Baseline for Example 1 in Table 1.

b. Proposed rule

If the same taxpayer makes the $1,000 contribution to charity A under the proposed rule, the entire $1,000 deduction is not deductible under section 170(a), and the deduction for state and local taxes paid under section 164 is unchanged due to the SALT cap. The taxpayer's itemized deductions, taxable income, and federal tax liability are unchanged from what they would be in the absence of the contribution. The taxpayer's state tax liability decreases by $1,000 because of the state tax credit. The combined federal and state tax benefits of the $1,000 contribution are therefore $1,000, or $240 less than under the baseline. This is shown by comparing the Total Tax Benefit in column A under Proposed Rule with the corresponding value in column A under Baseline for Example 1 in Table 1. However, the benefit of the contribution for this taxpayer is the same as the taxpayer faced prior to enactment of the Act. This is shown by comparing the Total Tax Benefit under column A under Proposed Rule with the corresponding value in column A under Prior Law for Example 1 in Table 1.

c. Comparison of contributions to different organizations and proposed rule

Under the baseline and the proposed rule, for a taxpayer with state and local taxes paid over the SALT cap, the value of a contribution to charity B, that is a contribution that results in a one-for-one state income tax deduction and not a state tax credit, is slightly higher than it was pre-Act. This increase is because the state deduction does not reduce the federal deduction for state and local taxes for a taxpayer above the SALT cap. As shown in the Total Tax Benefit row under the B columns for Example 1, under the baseline and the proposed rule, the value of a $1,000 contribution to charity B is $290—the charitable contribution deduction from federal tax ($1,000 times the 24 percent federal tax rate, or $240), plus the value of the deduction from state tax ($1,000 times the 5 percent state tax rate, or $50)—compared to $278 for contributions under prior law (described above). By comparison, as shown in the Total Tax Benefit row under the A columns for Example 1, a contribution to charity A, eligible for a state tax credit, yields a $1,240 tax benefit under the baseline and a $1,000 benefit under the proposed rule.

2. *Example 2: Taxpayer Is Below the SALT Cap and Not Subject to the AMT*

a. Baseline

If a taxpayer that has state and local taxes paid below the SALT cap and is not subject to the AMT makes the $1,000 contribution to charity A, the deduction for charitable contributions under section 170(a) increases by $1,000, and the deduction for state and local taxes paid under section 164 decreases by $1,000. The taxpayer's itemized deductions, taxable income, and federal tax liability are unchanged from what they would be in the absence of the contribution. The taxpayer's state tax liability decreases by $1,000 because of the state tax credit. The combined federal and state tax benefits of the $1,000 contribution are therefore $1,000, and the cost to the taxpayer and to the federal government of making the contribution was $0. This situation is identical to prior law or what taxpayers faced prior to enactment of the Act. This is shown is column A under Baseline and Prior Law for Example 2 in Table 1.

b. Proposed rule

If the same taxpayer makes the $1,000 contribution to charity A under the proposed rule, the entire $1,000 contribution is not deductible under section 170(a), but the deduction for state and local taxes paid under section 164 still decreases by $1,000 because of the $1,000 state tax credit. If the taxpayer is in the 24 percent bracket, the federal tax liability will increase by $240. The taxpayer's state tax liability decreases by the $1,000 state tax credit. The combined federal and state tax benefits of the $1,000 contribution are therefore $760, or $240 less than the baseline. This is shown by comparing the Total Tax Benefit in column A under Proposed Rule with the corresponding value in column A under Baseline for Example 2. In this case, the proposed rule has the effect of increasing the taxpayer's federal taxable income compared to the baseline if the taxpayer makes a contribution to charity A.

c. Comparison of contributions to different organizations, under prior Law, baseline, and proposed rule

Under prior law, and both the baseline scenario and the proposed rule, the tax benefit of charitable contributions to charity B, which are not eligible for a state tax credit but are deductible from both federal and state taxable income, is unchanged from prior law for taxpayers below the SALT cap. Thus, in this example, the benefit of making a contribution to charity B remains $278, as described above for contributions under prior law. This is shown in the Total Tax Benefit row under the B columns for Example 2. By comparison, as shown in the Total Tax Benefit row under the A columns for Example 2, a $1,000 contribution to charity A, eligible for a state tax credit, yields a $1,000 tax benefit under the baseline and a $760 benefit under the proposed rule.

3. *Example 3: Taxpayer is Subject to the AMT*[5]

a. Baseline

If a taxpayer subject to the AMT makes a $1,000 contribution to charity A, the contribution reduces the taxpayer's taxable income under the AMT by $1,000. Under an AMT marginal tax rate of 26 percent, the federal tax benefit of this $1,000 contribution is $260. Because of the dollar-for-dollar state tax credit, the taxpayer would receive a combined federal and state tax benefit of $1,260 for a $1,000 contribution, or a $260 net benefit. This result is identical to the result under prior law (prior to enactment of the Act). This is shown in the A columns under Baseline and Prior Law for Example 3 in Table 1.

b. Proposed rule

If the same taxpayer makes the $1,000 contribution to charity A under the proposed rule, the entire $1,000 is not deductible under section 170(a). Therefore, the taxpayer's taxable income and federal tax liability under the AMT would be unchanged from what they would be in the absence of the contribution. The taxpayer's state tax liability decreases by $1,000 because of the state tax credit. The combined federal and state tax benefits of the $1,000 contribution are therefore $1,000, or $260 less than under the baseline and under the law prior to enactment of the Act. This is shown by comparing the A columns of Example 3 in Table 1. However, under the proposed rule, taxpayers subject to the AMT are in the same position as taxpayers with state and local taxes paid above the SALT cap who are not subject to the AMT. This is shown by comparing the Total Tax Benefit amount under column A for the Proposed Rule for Example 3 to that for Example 1.

c. Comparison of contributions to different organizations, under prior law, baseline and proposed rule

Under the baseline and the proposed rule, the treatment of charitable contributions that are deductible from both federal and state taxable income is unchanged from prior law for taxpayers subject to the AMT. This is shown in the B columns for Example 3 in Table 1. In this example, the benefit of making a contribution to charity B remains $310, as described above for contributions under prior law. By comparison, a contribution to a charity A, eligible for a state tax credit, yields a $1,260 tax benefit under the baseline and a $1,000 benefit under the proposed rule. This is shown in column A under Baseline and Proposed Rule for Example 3 in Table 1.

IV. *Expected Benefits and Costs*

A. *Benefits*

These proposed regulations likely reduce economically inefficient choices motivated by the potential tax benefits described above if these proposed regulations were not promulgated. Under the prior law and baseline scenarios, state and local governments have an incentive to fund governmental activities through independent entities that are eligible to receive deductible contributions and to establish tax credits. This incentive is particularly strong under a SALT cap scenario where state and local governments may do so solely to enable some taxpayers to circumvent the SALT cap. These proposed regulations substantially diminish this incentive to engage in socially wasteful tax-avoidance behavior. As a result, it is expected that fewer such credit programs would be established in the future under the proposed regulations than under the baseline.

---

[5] The Act increased the amount of income exempt from AMT. We estimate that only about 150,000 taxpayers will be subject to the AMT under the Act, compared to more than 4 million under prior law.

To the extent this result occurs, the Treasury Department and IRS estimate that the proposed regulations would reduce overall complexity and paperwork burden for states and for taxpayers who would otherwise engage in charitable contributions solely for the purpose of reducing their state and local tax liability. In addition to reducing paperwork burden, the Treasury Department and IRS anticipate that the proposed regulations will also spare some taxpayers compliance costs associated with complex tax planning designed to avoid the SALT cap.

In addition, these proposed regulations are expected to make the federal tax system more neutral to taxpayers' decisions regarding donations. Under the baseline scenarios, the combined federal and state tax benefits favor contributions to organizations which give rise to a state tax credit for taxpayers, particularly for taxpayers above the SALT cap. Under the proposed regulations, this economic distortion is expected to be reduced. The Treasury Department and the IRS request comments from the public on the potential extent of this expected reduction in economic distortion.

Finally, these proposed regulations provide more certainty to taxpayers by clarifying the rules governing the amount that they can claim as a charitable contribution deduction when they receive a state tax credit or a dollar-for-dollar state tax deduction in exchange for the contribution.

B. *Costs*

The proposed regulations may result in some increase in compliance costs for taxpayers who make contributions that generate state tax credits. Under the baseline, for purposes of the charitable contribution deduction under section 170(a), taxpayers did not need to address state tax credits received for purposes of claiming a charitable contribution; however, they would know the amount of credits received as part of the filing process for state returns. In contrast, under the proposed regulations, taxpayers making a contribution to an organization listed in section 170(c) will need to determine the amount of any state tax credits they will receive or expect to receive in order to reduce their charitable contribution deduction under section 170(a). This additional step will generate some additional compliance costs.

The compliance burden for recipient organizations that directly issue tax credits may increase under the proposed regulations. In order to take a charitable contribution deduction of $250 or more, a taxpayer must have a contemporaneous written acknowledgment (CWA) from the donee entity, usually provided in the form of a letter. The CWA includes the amount received by the entity or a description of property received. The CWA must also disclose whether the donee provided any goods or services in consideration for the contribution and a description and good faith estimate of the value of those goods or services provided. State and local tax credits are not generally provided by the donee entity, but there may be situations in which the entity would be providing the credit and would need to include it in the CWA provided to the donor. The Treasury Department and the IRS request comments on whether additional guidance is needed on substantiation and reporting requirements for donors and donees making or receiving payments or transfers of property in return for state and local tax credits and the extent to which entities do provide tax credits under certain circumstances.

The Treasury Department and the IRS request comments on other potential compliance savings, compliance costs, costs related to increased tax planning and other avoidance behavior, or any effects on charitable contribution decisions that may occur as a result of these proposed regulations. In particular, the Treasury Department and the IRS request comments as to how the proposed regulations might alter incentives regarding contributions to state and local tax credit programs.

Based on an analysis of confidential taxpayer return data and forecasts using that data, the Treasury Department and the IRS note that these proposed regulations will leave charitable giving incentives entirely unchanged for the vast majority of taxpayers. After passage of the Act, which significantly increased the standard deduction, it is estimated that ninety percent of taxpayers will not claim itemized deductions of any kind. Those taxpayers are entirely unaffected by these proposed regulations. It is estimated that approximately five percent of taxpayers will itemize and will have state and local income tax deductions above the SALT cap; these taxpayers will receive the same federal tax benefits under the proposed regulations as they received prior to the Act. See Example 1 above. It is estimated that approximately five percent of taxpayers will itemize but will not have state and local income tax deductions above the SALT cap. The federal tax benefits available to this fraction of taxpayers could be affected by the proposed regulations only if they contribute to programs that entitle them to state tax credits of greater than 15 percent. See Example 2 above. The Treasury Department and the IRS believe that most taxpayers in this third category have never used any state tax credit programs affected by the proposed regulations, and that the proposed regulations will have at most a highly limited, marginal effect on taxpayer decisions to donate to tax credit programs that pre-date TCJA, including educational scholarship programs.[6] The Treasury Department and the IRS request comments on this important consideration and any potential unintended consequences of the proposed regulations not addressed here.

---

[6] The Treasury Department and the IRS are aware of potential concerns about educational scholarship programs in particular. Based on projections for 2018, most taxpayers in the third category described above do not reside in states that offer educational scholarship tax credit programs affected by the proposed regulations, and the vast majority of them have never used such programs.

Table 1: Tax Treatment of $1,000 Contribution to (A) Organization that Gives Rise to $1,000 State Tax Credit and (B) Organization for Which Contribution is Deductible at the State Level

Example 1: Taxpayer Above the SALT Cap, Not Subject to the AMT

	Prior Law		Baseline		Proposed Rule	
Change in	A	B	A	B	A	B
State Income Tax Liability	-1,000	-50	-1,000	-50	-1,000	-50
Federal Income Tax						
Charitable Contribution Deduction	1,000	1,000	1,000	1,000	0	1,000
Deduction for State and Local Taxes	-1,000	-50	0	0	0	0
Itemized Deductions	0	950	1,000	1,000	0	1,000
Taxable Income	0	-950	-1,000	-1,000	0	-1,000
Federal Tax Liability	0	-228	-240	-240	0	-240
Total Tax Benefit (Federal + State)	1,000	278	1,240	290	1,000	290
Net Cost to Taxpayer of $1,000 Contribution	0	722	-240	710	0	710

Example 2: Taxpayer Bel ow the SALT Cap, Not Subject to the AMT

	Prior Law		Baseline		Proposed Rule	
Change in	A	B	A	B	A	B
State Income Tax Liability	-1,000	-50	-1,000	-50	-1,000	-50
Federal Income Tax						
Charitable Contribution Deduction	1,000	1,000	1,000	1,000	0	1,000
Deduction for State and Local Taxes	-1,000	-50	-1,000	-50	-1,000	-50
Itemized Deductions	0	950	0	950	-1,000	950
Taxable Income	0	-950	0	-950	1,000	-950
Federal Tax Liability	0	-228	0	-228	240	-228
Total Tax Benefit (Federal + State)	1,000	278	1,000	278	760	278
Net Cost to Taxpayer of $1,000 Contribution	0	722	0	722	240	722

Example 3: Taxpayer Subject to the AM T

	Prior Law		Baseline		Proposed Rule	
Change in	A	B	A	B	A	B
State Income Tax Liability	-1,000	-50	-1,000	-50	-1,000	-50
Federal Income Tax						
Alternative minimum taxable Income	-1,000	-1,000	-1,000	-1,000	0	-1,000
Federal Tax Liability	-260	-260	-260	-260	0	-260
Total Tax Benefit (Federal + State)	1,260	310	1,260	310	1,000	310
Net Cost to Taxpayer of $1,000 Contribution	-260	690	-260	690	0	690

Assumptions: The taxpayer itemizes deductions and has more than $1,000 of state tax liability. Under prior law, the taxpayer is not subject to the overall limitation on itemized deductions under section 68. The taxpayer faces a 24 percent marginal rate under the federal income tax. If the taxpayer is subject to the AMT, the taxpayer faces a 26 percent marginal rate. A $1,000 contribution to charitable organization A generates a $1,000 state tax credit. A $1,000 contribution to charitable organization B is ineligible for a state tax credit but is deductible under the state's income tax. The taxpayer faces a 5 percent marginal rate under the state's income tax. The baseline assumes continuation of the IRS administrative position that state and local tax credits are not reflected as a return benefit or consideration and therefore do not reduce the taxpayer's charitable contribution deduction under section 170(a). Total Tax Benefit refers to the absolute value of the reduction of the taxpayer's combined federal and state tax liability.

Regulatory Flexibility Act

The Regulatory Flexibility Act (5 U.S.C. chapter 6) does not apply because the proposed regulations primarily affect individuals and do not impose costs, including a collection of information, on small entities. Therefore, a regulatory flexibility analysis is not required. Pursuant to section 7805(f), this notice of proposed rulemaking will be submitted to the Chief Counsel for Advocacy of the Small Business Administration for comment on its impact on small businesses.

Comments and Public Hearing

Before the regulations proposed herein are adopted as final regulations, consideration will be given to any electronic and written comments that are submitted timely to the IRS as prescribed in this preamble under the ADDRESSES heading. The Treasury Department and the IRS request comments on all aspects of the proposed regulations including: (1) Whether there should be recognition of gain or loss when property is transferred in consideration for state or local tax credits that are not *de minimis*; (2) determination of the basis of a transferable tax credit that a taxpayer sells or exchanges; (3) procedures by which a taxpayer may establish that the taxpayer declined receipt of the state or local tax credit; (4) substantiation and reporting requirements for donors and donees making or receiving payments or transfers of property in return for state and local tax credits; (5) for a taxpayer that receives or expects to receive a state or local tax deduction in an amount that exceeds the amount of the taxpayer's payment or the fair market value of the property transferred to an entity listed in section 170(c), suggestions for calculating the reduction to the charitable contribution deduction; and (6) whether and in what manner the regulations should address other state or local tax benefits, such as tax exclusions, that may be provided as consideration for certain payments or transfers to an entity listed in section 170(c). Finally, the Treasury Department and the IRS request comments on alternative regulatory approaches that would effectively prevent circumvention of the new statutory limitation on state and local tax deductions, consistent with applicable law.

All comments submitted will be made available at www.regulations.gov or upon request. A public hearing has been scheduled for November 5, 2018, beginning at 10 a.m. in the Auditorium of the Internal Revenue Building, 1111 Constitution Avenue, N.W., Washington, DC 20224. Due to building security procedures, visitors must enter at the Constitution Avenue entrance. In addition, all visitors must present photo identification to enter the building. Because of access restrictions, visitors will not be admitted beyond the immediate entrance area more than 30 minutes before the hearing starts. For more information about having your name placed on the building access list to attend the hearing, see the "FOR FURTHER INFORMATION CONTACT" section of this preamble.

The rules of 26 CFR 601.601(a)(3) apply to the hearing. Persons who wish to present oral comments at the hearing must submit an outline of the topics to be discussed and the time to be devoted to each topic by October 11, 2018. Submit a signed paper or electronic copy of the outline as prescribed in this preamble under the "Addresses" heading. An agenda showing the scheduling of the speakers will be prepared after the deadline for receiving outlines has passed. Copies of the agenda will be available free of charge at the hearing.

Drafting Information

The principal authors of these proposed regulations are personnel from the Office of the Associate Chief Counsel (Income Tax and Accounting). However, other personnel from the IRS and the Treasury Department participated in their development.

[¶49,769] Proposed Amendments of Regulations (REG-104390-18), published in the Federal Register on September 14, 2018.

[Code Secs. 951, 951A, 1502 and 6038]

Controlled Foreign Corporations (CFCs): Global intangible low-taxed income: U.S. shareholders.—Reg. §§1.951A-0, 1.951A-1, 1.951A-2, 1.951A-3, 1.951A-4, 1.951A-5, 1.951A-6, 1.951A-7, 1.1502-51 and 1.6038-5 and amendments of Reg. §§1.951-1, 1.1502-12, 1.1502-13, 1.1502-32 and 1.6038-2, implementing Code Sec. 951A of the Internal Revenue Code, which was enacted on December 22, 2017, are proposed.

AGENCY: Internal Revenue Service (IRS), Treasury.

ACTION: Notice of proposed rulemaking.

SUMMARY: This document contains proposed regulations implementing section 951A of the Internal Revenue Code. Section 951A was added to the Internal Revenue Code by the Tax Cuts and Jobs Act, which was enacted on December 22, 2017. This document also contains proposed regulations under sections 951, 1502, and 6038. These proposed regulations would affect United States shareholders of controlled foreign corporations.

DATES: Written or electronic comments and requests for a public hearing must be received by November 14, 2018.

ADDRESSES: Send submissions to: Internal Revenue Service, CC:PA:LPD:PR (REG-104390-18), Room 5203, Post Office Box 7604, Ben Franklin Station, Washington, DC 20044. Submissions may be hand-delivered Monday through Friday between the hours of 8 a.m. and 4 p.m. to CC:PA:LPD:PR (indicate REG-104390-18), Courier's Desk, Internal Revenue Service, 1111 Constitution Avenue, N.W., Washington, DC 20224, or sent electronically, via the Federal eRulemaking Portal at *www.regulations.gov* (IRS REG-104390-18).

FOR FURTHER INFORMATION CONTACT: Concerning proposed regulations §§1.951-1, 1.951A-0 through 1.951A-7, 1.6038-2, and 1.6038-5, Melinda E. Harvey or Michael Kaercher at (202) 317-6934; concerning proposed regulations §§1.1502-12, 1.1502-13, 1.1502-32, and 1.1502-51, Austin Diamond-Jones at (202) 317-6847 or Kevin M. Jacobs at (202) 317-5332; concerning submissions of comments or requests for a public hearing, Regina L. Johnson at (202) 317-6901 (not toll free numbers).

SUPPLEMENTARY INFORMATION:

Background

This document contains proposed amendments to 26 CFR part 1 under sections 951, 951A, 1502, and 6038 (the "proposed regulations"). Added to the Internal Revenue Code ("Code") by section 14201(a) of the Tax Cuts and Jobs Act, Pub. L. 115-97 (2017) ("the Act"), section 951A requires a United States shareholder ("U.S. shareholder") of any controlled foreign corporation ("CFC") for any taxable year to include in gross income the shareholder's global intangible low-taxed income ("GILTI") for such taxable year. Section 14201(d) of the Act provides that section 951A applies to taxable years of foreign corporations beginning after December 31, 2017, and to taxable years of U.S. shareholders in which or with which such taxable years of foreign corporations end. The proposed regulations under section 951A provide guidance for U.S. shareholders to determine the amount of GILTI to include in gross income ("GILTI inclusion amount").

Section 14201(b) of the Act added two new foreign tax credit provisions relating to GILTI – section 960(d) provides a foreign tax credit for taxes properly attributable to tested income taken into account by a domestic corporation under section 951A, and section 904(d)(1)(A) provides that any amount included in gross income under section 951A (other than passive category income) is treated as a separate category of income for purposes of section 904. In addition, section 14202(a) of the Act added section 250 to the Code providing domestic corporations a deduction equal to a percentage of their GILTI inclusion amount and foreign-derived intangible income, subject to a taxable income limitation. The proposed regulations do not include any rules relating to foreign tax credits or the deduction under section 250. Rules relating to foreign tax credits and the deduction under section 250 will be included in separate notices of proposed rulemaking. It is anticipated that the proposed regulations relating to foreign tax credits will provide rules for assigning the section 78 gross-up attributable to foreign taxes deemed paid under section 960(d) to the separate category described in section 904(d)(1)(A).

Before the Act, section 951(b) defined a U.S. shareholder of a foreign corporation as a United States person ("U.S. person") that holds at least 10 percent of the total combined voting power of all classes of stock entitled to vote in a foreign corporation. Section 14214(a) of the Act amended this definition to include a U.S. person that holds at least 10 percent of the total value of shares of all classes of stock of the foreign corporation. Section 14215(a) of the Act amended section 951(a)(1) to eliminate the requirement that a foreign corporation must be a CFC for an uninterrupted period of 30 days or more in order to give rise to an inclusion under section 951(a)(1) (the "30-day requirement"). These amendments apply to taxable years of foreign corporations beginning after December 31, 2017, and to taxable years of U.S. shareholders with or within which such taxable years of foreign corporations end. See sections 14214(b) and 14215(b) of the Act. The proposed regulations under section 951 incorporate these amendments into the regulations and provide other guidance necessary for U.S. shareholders to coordinate subpart F and GILTI.

Explanation of Provisions

I. *Section 951A*

A. *Overview*

The Act established a participation exemption system under which certain earnings of a foreign corporation can be repatriated to a corporate U.S. shareholder without U.S. tax. See section 14101(a) of the Act and section 245A. However, Congress recognized that, without any base protection measures, the participation exemption system could incentivize taxpayers to allocate income – in particular, mobile income from intangible property – that would otherwise be subject to the full U.S. corporate tax rate to CFCs operating in low- or zero-tax jurisdictions. See Senate Committee on the Budget, 115th Cong., Reconciliation Recommendations Pursuant to H. Con. Res. 71, at 365 (Comm. Print 2017) ("Senate Explanation"). Therefore, Congress enacted section 951A in order to subject intangible income earned by a CFC to U.S. tax on a current basis, similar to the treatment of a CFC's subpart F income under section 951(a)(1)(A). However, in order to not harm the competitive position of U.S. corporations relative to their foreign peers, GILTI of a corporate U.S. shareholder is taxed at a reduced rate by reason of the deduction under section 250 (with the resulting U.S. tax further reduced by a portion of foreign tax credits under section 960(d)). Id. Also, due to the administrative difficulty in identifying income attributable to intangible assets, in contrast to income from tangible assets, intangible income (and thus GILTI) is determined for purposes of section 951A based on a formulaic approach, under which a 10-percent return is attributed to certain tangible assets ("qualified business asset investment" or "QBAI") and then each dollar of certain income above such "normal return" is effectively treated as intangible income. Id. at 366.

Section 951A(a) provides that a U.S. shareholder of any CFC for a taxable year must include in gross income its GILTI for that year. A GILTI inclusion is treated in a manner similar to a section 951(a)(1)(A) inclusion of a CFC's subpart F income for many purposes of the Code. See section 951A(f)(1). However, a GILTI inclusion is determined in a manner that is fundamentally different from that of an inclusion under section 951(a)(1)(A). Subpart F income is determined at the level of a CFC, and then a U.S. shareholder that owns stock directly or indirectly in the CFC generally includes in gross income its pro rata share of the CFC's subpart F income. The amount of the shareholder's section 951(a)(1)(A) inclusion with respect to one CFC is not taken into account in determining the shareholder's section 951(a)(1)(A) inclusion with respect to another CFC. A U.S. shareholder's pro rata share of a CFC's subpart F income is generally the final step in determining its section 951(a)(1)(A) inclusion.

Similar to an inclusion under section 951(a)(1)(A), the determination of a U.S. shareholder's GILTI inclusion amount begins with the calculation of certain items of each CFC owned by the shareholder, such as tested income, tested loss, or QBAI. A U.S. shareholder then determines its pro rata share of each of these CFC-level items in a manner similar to a shareholder's pro rata share of subpart F income under section 951(a)(2). See section 951A(e)(1). However, in contrast to an inclusion under section 951(a)(1)(A), the U.S. shareholder's pro rata shares of these items are not amounts included in gross income, but rather amounts taken into account by the shareholder in determining the GILTI included in the shareholder's gross income. The U.S. shareholder aggregates (and then nets or multiplies) its pro rata share of each of these items into a single shareholder-level amount – for example, aggregate tested income reduced by aggregate tested loss becomes net CFC tested income and aggregate QBAI multiplied by 10 percent becomes deemed tangible income return. A shareholder's GILTI inclusion amount for a taxable year is then calculated by subtracting one aggregate shareholder-level amount from another – the shareholder's net deemed tangible income return ("net DTIR") is the excess of deemed tangible income return over certain interest expense, and, finally, its GILTI inclusion amount is the excess of its net CFC tested income over its net DTIR.

As explained above, a U.S. shareholder does not compute a separate GILTI inclusion amount with respect to each CFC for a taxable year, but rather computes a single GILTI inclusion amount by reference to all its CFCs. Cf. section 951A(f)(2) (allocating the U.S. shareholder's GILTI inclusion amount to each tested income CFC for purposes of various sections of the Code). Because a U.S. shareholder's GILTI inclusion amount is determined based on the relevant items of all the CFCs of which it is a U.S. shareholder, the effect of the provision is generally to ensure that a U.S. shareholder is taxed on its GILTI wherever (and through whichever CFC) derived. See, for example, Senate Explanation at 366 ("The Committee believes that calculating GILTI on an aggregate basis, instead of on a CFC-by-CFC basis, reflects the interconnected nature of a U.S. corporation's global operations and is a more accurate way of determining a U.S. corporation's global intangible income.").

The proposed regulations under section 951A follow an outline similar to the description in this overview. Proposed §§1.951A-2 through 1.951A-4 provide detailed guidance on items determined at the CFC level – that is, tested income and tested loss, QBAI, and the items necessary to determine the amount of certain interest expense that reduces net DTIR. Proposed §1.951A-1(d) provides rules for determining the U.S. shareholder's pro rata share of these CFC-level items. Finally, proposed §1.951A-1(c) provides rules describing the aggregation of the U.S. shareholder's pro rata share amounts to determine the shareholder's GILTI inclusion amount.

B. *General rules and definitions*

1. Inclusion of GILTI in Gross Income

Proposed §1.951A-1 provides general rules to determine a U.S. shareholder's GILTI inclusion amount and associated definitions. Some of the definitions distinguish between a CFC's taxable year and a U.S. shareholder's taxable year. For example, a "U.S. shareholder inclusion year" refers to the relevant taxable year of the U.S. shareholder and is defined as a taxable year of the U.S. shareholder that includes a CFC inclusion date (as that term is defined in the proposed regulations) of the CFC. See proposed §1.951A-1(e)(4). A "CFC inclusion year" refers to the relevant taxable year of the CFC beginning after December 31, 2017 (the effective date of section 951A for a foreign corporation that is a CFC). See proposed §1.951A-1(e)(2).

2. Determination of Net DTIR

Proposed §1.951A-1(c)(3) defines net DTIR, which is computed at the U.S. shareholder level based on QBAI (as defined in proposed §1.951A-3(b)) held by the shareholder's CFCs and offsets the shareholder's net CFC tested income for purposes of determining the shareholder's GILTI inclusion amount. A CFC's QBAI is equal to its aggregate average adjusted bases in specified tangible property, which is defined as tangible property used in the production of tested income. See section 951A(d)(2)(A) and proposed §1.951A-3(c)(1). Consistent with the statute and the conference report accompanying the Act ("Conference Report"), the proposed regulations clarify that a tested loss CFC does not have specified tangible property. See H.R. Rep. No. 115-466, at 642, fn. 1536 (2017) (Conf. Rep.) and proposed §1.951A-3(b), (c)(1), and (g)(1). Accordingly, for purposes of calculating its GILTI inclusion amount, a U.S. shareholder does not take into account the tangible property of a tested loss CFC in calculating its aggregate pro rata share of QBAI, its deemed tangible income return, or its net DTIR.

3. Determination of Pro Rata Share

Section 951A(e)(1) provides that, for purposes of determining a U.S. shareholder's GILTI inclusion amount, the shareholder's pro rata share of a CFC's tested income, tested loss, and QBAI "shall be determined under the rules of section 951(a)(2) in the same manner as such section applies to subpart F income." Accordingly, the proposed regulations incorporate the pro rata share rules of section 951(a)(2) and §1.951-1(b) and (e), with appropriate modifications to account for the differences between subpart F income, on the one hand, and tested income, tested loss, and QBAI, on the other. Similar to the determination of a U.S. shareholder's pro rata share of subpart F income, proposed §1.951A-1(d)(1) provides that a U.S. shareholder's pro rata share of any CFC item necessary for calculating its GILTI inclusion amount is determined by reference to the stock such shareholder owns (within the meaning of section 958(a)) in the CFC ("section 958(a) stock") as of the close of the CFC's taxable year, including section 958(a) stock treated as owned by the U.S. shareholder through a domestic partnership under proposed §1.951A-5(c). See section I.F of this Explanation of Provisions for an explanation of proposed rules for domestic partnerships and their partners.

In several places, the provisions of proposed §1.951A-1(d) reference section 951(a)(2) and proposed §1.951-1(e), which amends existing §1.951-1(e). See section II.A of this Explanation of Provisions for an explanation of the proposed modifications to §1.951-1(e). Comments requested guidance on how to determine a preferred shareholder's pro rata share of CFC items for purposes of GILTI. Rules relating to the allocation of tested income to preferred stock are included in proposed §1.951A-1(d)(2) by cross-reference to proposed §1.951-1(e). In addition, the proposed regulations provide rules relating to a preferred shareholder's pro rata share of tested loss and QBAI.

A U.S. shareholder's pro rata share of tested income generally is determined in the same manner as its pro rata share of subpart F income under section 951(a)(2) and §1.951-1(b) and (e) (that is, based on the relative amount that would be received by the shareholder in a year-end hypothetical distribution of all the CFC's current year earnings). See proposed § 1.951A-1(d)(2)(i). For purposes of determining a U.S. shareholder's pro rata share of a CFC's QBAI, the amount of QBAI distributed in the hypothetical distribution of section 951(a)(2)(A) and § 1.951-1(e) is generally proportionate to the amount of the CFC's tested income distributed in the hypothetical distribution. See proposed § 1.951A-1(d)(3)(i). However, a special rule in the proposed regulations provides that if a CFC's QBAI exceeds 10 times its tested income, so that the amount of QBAI allocated to preferred stock would exceed 10 times the tested income allocated to the preferred stock under the general proportionate allocation rule, the excess amount of QBAI is allocated solely to the CFC's common stock. See proposed § 1.951A-1(d)(3)(ii). The proposed cap on QBAI allocated to a preferred shareholder (10 times tested income) is derived from the statutory cap on the amount of QBAI that may be used to compute GILTI (10 percent of aggregate QBAI). These rules in the proposed regulations ensure that the notional "normal return" associated with the CFC's QBAI generally flows to the shareholders in a manner consistent with their economic rights in the earnings of the CFC. For illustration, see proposed § 1.951A-1(d)(3)(iii), *Examples 1* and 2.

For purposes of determining a U.S. shareholder's pro rata share of a CFC's tested loss, the amount distributed in the hypothetical distribution is the amount of the tested loss, rather than the CFC's current earnings and profits, and the tested loss is distributed solely with respect to the CFC's common stock, except in certain cases involving dividend arrearages with respect to preferred stock and common stock with no liquidation value. See proposed § 1.951A-1(d)(4)(i) through (iii). In the latter case, the proposed regulations provide that any amount of tested loss that would otherwise be distributed in the hypothetical distribution to a class of common stock that has no liquidation value is instead distributed to the most junior class of equity with a positive liquidation value to the extent of the liquidation value. See proposed § 1.951A-1(d)(4)(iii). In subsequent years, tested income is allocated to any class of stock to the extent that tested loss was allocated to such class in prior years under this special rule. See proposed § 1.951A-1(d)(2)(ii). In addition, the proposed regulations provide that section 951(a)(2)(B) is applied to reduce tested losses, but modified to treat the amount of a dividend received by another person as equal to the amount of the tested loss, without regard to whether an actual dividend is made by the tested loss CFC. See proposed § 1.951A-1(d)(4)(i)(D). The effect of this rule is to reduce a shareholder's pro rata share of tested loss in proportion to the number of days the shareholder did not own the stock of the tested loss CFC within the meaning of section 958(a). Each of these modifications is intended to ensure that the tested loss of a CFC is allocated to each U.S. shareholder in an amount commensurate with the economic loss borne by the shareholder by reason of the tested loss.

Proposed § 1.951A-1(d)(5) and (6) provide rules for determining a shareholder's pro rata share of "tested interest expense" and "tested interest income." Tested interest expense and tested interest income are defined in proposed § 1.951A-4, which is discussed in section I.E of this Explanation of Provisions. A U.S. shareholder's pro rata share of a CFC's tested interest expense for a taxable year equals the amount by which the CFC's tested interest expense reduces the shareholder's pro rata share of tested income, increases the shareholder's pro rata share of tested loss, or both. Conversely, a U.S. shareholder's pro rata share of tested interest income for a taxable year equals the amount by which the CFC's tested interest income increases the shareholder's pro rata share of tested income, reduces the shareholder's pro rata share of tested loss, or both. For example, tested interest income could both increase a U.S. shareholder's pro rata share of tested income and decrease its pro rata share of tested loss if a CFC with tested income for a taxable year would have, without regard to the tested interest income, a tested loss for the taxable year.

The Department of the Treasury ("Treasury Department") and the IRS request comments on the proposed approaches for determining a U.S. shareholder's pro rata share of a CFC's QBAI and tested loss, including how (or whether) to allocate tested loss of a CFC when no class of CFC stock has positive liquidation value.

4. Foreign Currency Translation

Because GILTI is computed at the U.S. shareholder level, the tested income, tested loss, tested interest expense, tested interest income, and QBAI of a CFC that uses a functional currency other than the U.S. dollar must be translated into U.S. dollars. The appropriate exchange rate under section 989(b)(3) for income inclusions under section 951(a)(1)(A) is the average exchange rate for the taxable year of the foreign corporation. GILTI inclusion amounts are similar to section 951(a)(1)(A) inclusions in that both inclusions are determined based on certain income (and, in the case of GILTI, certain losses) of the CFC for the taxable year of the CFC that ends with or within the taxable year of the U.S. shareholder. Therefore, the proposed regulations prescribe the same translation rule that is used for subpart F income for translating a pro rata share of tested income, tested loss, tested interest expense, tested interest income, and QBAI. See proposed § 1.951A-1(d)(1). Similarly, a U.S. shareholder's GILTI inclusion amount that is allocated to a tested income CFC under section 951A(f)(2) is translated from U.S. dollars into the CFC's functional currency using the average exchange rate for the taxable year of the tested income CFC. See proposed § 1.951A-6(b)(2)(iii).

C. *Tested income and tested loss*

1. Determination of Gross Income and Allowable Deductions

Under section 951A(c)(2), tested income and tested loss are determined by beginning with a CFC's gross income, excluding certain items (gross income after exclusions, "gross tested income"), and then subtracting properly allocable deductions determined using rules similar to the rules of section

954(b)(5). While section 951A does not specifically address which expenses of a CFC are allowable as a deduction, existing rules under § 1.952-2 apply to determine the gross income and deductions of a CFC taken into account in determining its subpart F income. The Treasury Department and the IRS have determined that due to the similarities between gross tested income and subpart F income (for example, gross tested income and subpart F income are both determined at the CFC level and taxed to a U.S. shareholder on a current basis), and the overlap between CFCs impacted by GILTI and subpart F (since a CFC can have both tested income and subpart F income), the determinations of gross income and allowable deductions for GILTI should be made in a manner similar to the determination of subpart F income. Accordingly, the proposed regulations require that the gross income and allowable deduction determinations are made under the rules of § 1.952-2. See proposed § 1.951A-2(c)(2). Under § 1.952-2(a)(1) and proposed § 1.951A-2(c)(2), subject to the special rules in § 1.952-2(c), tested income or tested loss of a CFC is determined by treating the CFC as a domestic corporation taxable under section 11 and by applying the principles of section 61 and the regulations thereunder. Therefore, only items of deduction that would be allowable in determining the taxable income of a domestic corporation may be taken into account for purposes of determining a CFC's tested income or tested loss. If an item of a CFC would be disallowed as a deduction in determining the CFC's taxable income if the CFC were a domestic corporation, the item cannot be taken into account for purposes of determining the tested income or tested loss of the CFC even if the item reduces the CFC's earnings and profits.

The Treasury Department and the IRS request comments on the application of the rules under § 1.952-2 for purposes of determining subpart F income, tested income, and tested loss. In particular, comments are requested as to whether these rules should allow a CFC a deduction, or require a CFC to take into account income, that is expressly limited to domestic corporations under the Code. For example, questions have arisen as to whether a CFC could be entitled to a dividends received deduction under section 245A, even though section 245A by its terms applies only to dividends received by a domestic corporation. See Conf. Rep. at 599, fn. 1486. The Treasury Department and the IRS also welcome comments on other approaches to determining tested income or tested loss, including whether additional modifications should be made to § 1.952-2 for purposes of calculating GILTI.

Comments have also requested guidance on the interactions of section 163(j) and section 267A with section 951A. Issues related to sections 163(j), 245A, and 267A will be addressed in future guidance.

2. Income Excluded from Foreign Base Company Income and Insurance Income by Reason of Section 954(b)(4)

As noted in section I.C.1 of this Explanation of Provisions, section 951A(c)(2) requires that the gross income of the CFC for the taxable year be determined without regard to certain items. One of these items is gross income excluded from foreign base company income (as defined in section 954) or insurance income (as defined in section 953) of the CFC by reason of electing the exception under section 954(b)(4) ("high-tax exception"). In response to comments, the proposed regulations clarify that this exclusion applies only to income that is excluded from foreign base company income and insurance income *solely* by reason of an election made to exclude the income under the high-tax exception of section 954(b)(4). Accordingly, the exclusion does not apply to income that would not otherwise be subpart F income or to categories of income that do not constitute subpart F income due to exceptions other than the high-tax exception (for example, as a result of an exception to foreign personal holding company income under section 954(c)(6) or section 954(h)).

3. Gross Income Taken into Account in Determining Subpart F Income

Another item excluded from gross tested income is gross income taken into account in determining a corporation's subpart F income. Comments have requested guidance on the interaction between the earnings and profits limitation to subpart F income under section 952(c), including the recapture rule in section 952(c)(2), and the determination of gross tested income for purposes of section 951A. The Treasury Department and the IRS have determined that any income described in section 952(a) is "taken into account in determining subpart F income" regardless of whether the section 952(c) limitation applies, and therefore should not be included in gross tested income. Conversely, the recapture of subpart F income under section 952(c)(2), even if by reason of earnings and profits attributable to gross tested income, does not result in excluding any amount from gross tested income. Therefore, the proposed regulations provide that tested income and tested loss are determined without regard to the application of section 952(c). See proposed § 1.951A-2(c)(4).

4. Determination of Allowable Deductions Properly Allocable to Gross Tested Income

Section 951A(c)(2)(A)(ii) provides that tested income and tested loss are determined by subtracting from a CFC's gross tested income "the deductions (including taxes) properly allocable to such gross income under rules similar to the rules of section 954(b)(5) (or to which such deductions would be allocable if there were such gross income)." Regulations under section 954(b)(5) require taxpayers to determine net subpart F income by properly allocating and apportioning deductions to the various categories of subpart F income. For this purpose, § 1.954-1(c) provides that taxpayers must first determine the gross amount of each item of income in a category of income (as described in § 1.954-1(c)(1)(iii)) and then allocate and apportion expenses to these categories under the principles of sections 861, 864, and 904(d). Accordingly, in order to apply the principles of section 954(b)(5) to section 951A (as required under section 951A(c)(2)(A)(ii)), the proposed regulations provide that allowable deductions determined under the principles of § 1.952-2 are allocated and apportioned to gross tested income under the principles of section 954(b)(5) and § 1.954-1(c), treating gross tested income that falls within a single separate category (as defined in § 1.904-5(a)(1)) as an additional category of income for this purpose. See proposed § 1.951A-2(c)(3).

Section I.D.5 of this Explanation of Provisions describes a rule that disregards basis in specified tangible property created in certain taxable transfers occurring before the effective date of section 951A for purposes of calculating QBAI. See § 1.951A-3(h)(2). These rules are cross-referenced in proposed § 1.951A-2(c)(5) to disallow any loss or deduction related to such stepped up-basis in any depreciable or amortizable property (including, for example, intangible property) for purposes of calculating tested income or tested loss.

D. *QBAI*

1. QBAI and Specified Tangible Property

Proposed § 1.951A-3(b) provides that a tested income CFC's QBAI for any taxable year is the average of the CFC's aggregate adjusted bases as of the close of each quarter in specified tangible property that is used in a trade or business of the corporation and of a type with respect to which a deduction is allowable under section 167. In general, specified tangible property is tangible property used in the production of tested income. See proposed § 1.951A-3(c)(1). Tangible property is defined as property for which the depreciation deduction provided by section 167(a) is eligible to be determined under section 168 (even if the CFC has elected not to apply section 168). See proposed § 1.951A-3(c)(2). The proposed regulations define tangible property by reference to whether the property can be depreciated under section 168 because, unlike section 167, section 168 applies only to tangible property, and there is a substantial amount of guidance delineating property subject to section 168.

Property that is used in the production of both gross tested income and gross income that is not gross tested income ("dual use property") is proportionately treated as specified tangible property. See proposed § 1.951A-3(d)(1). Generally, the proportion is determined based on the relative amount of gross tested income to income other than gross tested income that the property generates for the taxable year. See proposed § 1.951A-3(d)(2)(i). A special rule is provided for determining the proportion of the property treated as specified tangible property if the property generates no directly identifiable income (for example, because the property is used in general and administrative functions that contribute to the generation of all the income of the CFC). See proposed § 1.951A-3(d)(2)(ii).

Under § 1.167(a)-2, the depreciation allowance for tangible property applies only to that part of the property which is subject to wear and tear, to decay or decline from natural causes, to exhaustion, and to obsolescence. Accordingly, for purposes of section 951A, property that may be in part depreciable qualifies as specified tangible property to the extent it is depreciable. For example, precious metal used in a manufacturing process may be considered specified tangible property in part because it is depreciable in part. See Rev. Rul. 2015-11, 2015-21 I.R.B. 975.

2. Determination of Adjusted Basis of Specified Tangible Property

Proposed § 1.951A-3(e) provides rules to determine the adjusted basis of specified tangible property for purposes of determining QBAI. The general rule in proposed § 1.951A-3(e)(1), like section 951A(d)(3), provides that the adjusted basis in any property is determined by using the alternative depreciation system under section 168(g) ("ADS") and allocating the depreciation deduction with respect to the property ratably to each day during the period in the taxable year to which the depreciation relates. ADS applies for purposes of determining QBAI irrespective of whether the basis of the property is determined using another depreciation method for other purposes of the Code.

The Treasury Department and the IRS recognize that taxpayers may hold specified tangible property that was acquired before December 22, 2017, that was not depreciated using ADS. Section 951A(d) does not distinguish between property acquired before December 22, 2017, and property acquired on or after December 22, 2017. The Treasury Department and the IRS have concluded that, regardless of the date acquired, the adjusted basis in specified tangible property should be determined under ADS in order for the U.S. shareholder's pro rata share of QBAI to be properly determined and not distorted. Therefore, the proposed regulations provide that when determining QBAI, the adjusted basis in property placed in service before December 22, 2017, is determined using ADS as if this system had applied from the date that the property was placed in service. See proposed § 1.951A-3(e)(3).

3. Short Taxable Year

Net DTIR is intended to reduce a U.S. shareholder's GILTI inclusion amount by an annual return on specified tangible property. To ensure that the net DTIR of a CFC with a taxable year of less than 12 months (a "short taxable year") reflects an annual return, the proposed regulations provide a methodology to reduce the QBAI of a CFC with a short taxable year to an amount that, if annualized, would produce an amount equal to the QBAI for a 12-month taxable year. See proposed § 1.951A-3(f).

4. Specified Tangible Property Held Through a Partnership

Section 951A(d)(3)[1] (the "partnership QBAI paragraph") states that if a CFC holds an interest in a partnership at the close of the CFC's taxable year, the CFC takes into account under section 951A(d)(1) its "distributive share of the aggregate of the partnership's adjusted bases (determined as

---

[1] As enacted, section 951A(d) contains two paragraphs designated as paragraph (3).

of such date in the hands of the partnership)" in specified tangible property in computing its QBAI. The partnership QBAI paragraph further provides that a CFC's "distributive share of the adjusted basis of any property shall be the controlled foreign corporation's distributive share of income with respect to such property."

The statutory language "distributive share of the aggregate of the partnership's adjusted basis" is ambiguous because the term "distributive share" is used in subchapter K of the Code with respect to income, gain, loss, and credits of a partnership, but not the bases of assets. A partner of a partnership has a basis in its partnership interest ("outside basis"), while the partnership has a separate basis in the assets of the partnership ("inside basis"). The proposed regulations therefore use the term "share" (rather than "distributive share") when referring to the amount of the inside basis of a partnership asset that a partner that is a CFC may include in its QBAI.

The partnership QBAI paragraph provides that a CFC "shall take into account" under section 951A(d)(1) the CFC's distributive share of the basis in partnership specified tangible property. Because section 951A(d)(1) requires an averaging of basis over the close of each quarter of the taxable year of the CFC, and the term "distributive share" as it pertains to basis is ambiguous, it is unclear based on the statute how a CFC determines its distributive share of the basis of partnership specified tangible property for purposes of determining its QBAI. One interpretation of the partnership QBAI paragraph is that a CFC partner's QBAI is increased by an amount equal to the CFC partner's share of the basis that the partnership has in its specified tangible property as of the close of the CFC partner's taxable year. However, that interpretation would be contrary to the requirement in section 951A(d)(1) that the CFC's bases in specified tangible property be averaged over four quarters. Furthermore, giving the term "distributive share" effect, the amount determined at the end of the CFC partner's taxable year should be reduced for any period during the taxable year when the partnership did not own the property, whereas a CFC partner of a partnership that disposed of property before the close of the CFC's taxable year would receive no QBAI benefit if there were a single measurement date. In addition, a requirement that a partnership's basis in specified tangible property be measured on the last day of a CFC partner's taxable year could be burdensome for partnerships that have one or more CFC partners with taxable years that do not coincide with the partnership's taxable year and, in those cases, would have the effect of decoupling the CFC partner's share of the basis of partnership property used to compute the CFC partner's QBAI from the CFC partner's distributive share of the partnership's income from the property that is taken into account in computing the CFC partner's tested income. Moreover, because depreciation is treated as reducing the adjusted basis of property on each day during the taxable year, calculating a partnership's basis on the final day of the CFC partner's taxable year will generally result in an artificially low basis relative to calculating average adjusted basis over the course of the partnership's taxable year. For the foregoing reasons, the proposed regulations determine a CFC partner's share of the partnership's adjusted basis in specified tangible property by reference to the partnership's average adjusted basis in the property as of the close of each quarter of the partnership's taxable year that ends with or within the CFC's taxable year. See proposed § 1.951A-3(g)(3).

A partner that is a CFC takes into account its share of the adjusted basis of specified tangible property held by a partnership in computing QBAI if, among other things, the property "is used in the production of tested income (determined with respect to such controlled foreign corporation's distributive share of income with respect to such property)." Section 951A(d)(3)(C). Consistent with the general rule for QBAI, only a tested income CFC can increase its QBAI by reason of specified tangible property owned by a partnership. See proposed § 1.951A-3(g)(1). Further, consistent with the parenthetical in the partnership QBAI paragraph, the proposed regulations provide that a CFC partner determines its share of the partnership's average adjusted basis in specified tangible property based on the amount of its distributive share of the gross income produced by the property that is included in the CFC partner's gross tested income relative to the total amount of gross income produced by the property. See proposed § 1.951A-3(g)(2). The proposed regulations incorporate the dual use property rule of section 951A(d)(2)(B) in the context of specified tangible property owned indirectly through a partnership and include similar rules for addressing specified tangible property that does not produce any directly identifiable income. The calculation is performed separately for each item of specified tangible property held by the partnership, taking into account the CFC partner's distributive share of income with respect to such property.

The Treasury Department and the IRS request comments on the proposed approach to specified tangible property held through a partnership, including the rules addressing specified tangible property that does not produce directly identifiable income.

5. Anti-Abuse Provisions

Section 951A(d)(4) provides that "[t]he Secretary shall issue such regulations or other guidance as the Secretary determines appropriate to prevent the avoidance of the purposes of this subsection, including regulations or other guidance which provide for the treatment of property if—(A) such property is transferred, or held, temporarily, or (B) the avoidance of the purposes of this paragraph is a factor in the transfer or holding of such property." The Conference Report describes the scope of section 951A(d)(4), stating that "[t]he conferees intend that non-economic transactions intended to affect tax attributes of CFCs and their U.S. shareholders (including amounts of tested income and tested loss, tested foreign income taxes, net deemed tangible income return, and QBAI) to minimize tax under this provision be disregarded." Conf. Rep. at 645. One specific example illustrated in the

Conference Report is a transaction that occurs after the measurement date of post-1986 earnings and profits under section 965 but before the first taxable year for which section 951A is effective in order to increase a CFC's QBAI. Id.

Consistent with section 951A(d)(4) and the Conference Report, as well as the Secretary's broad authority under section 7805(a) to "prescribe all needful rules and regulations for the enforcement of" the Code, the proposed regulations provide that specified tangible property of a tested income CFC is disregarded for purposes of determining the tested income CFC's average aggregate basis in specified tangible property if the tested income CFC acquires the property with a principal purpose of reducing the GILTI inclusion amount of a U.S. shareholder and holds the property temporarily but over at least one quarter end. See proposed § 1.951A-3(h)(1). For this purpose, property held for less than a twelve month period that includes at least one quarter end during the taxable year of a tested income CFC is treated as temporarily held and acquired with a principal purpose of reducing the GILTI inclusion amount of a U.S. shareholder. Id.

The Treasury Department and the IRS are aware that taxpayers are engaging in transactions like the ones described in the Conference Report involving taxable transfers of property from one CFC to another CFC before the first taxable year of the transferor CFC to which section 951A applies in order to provide the transferee CFC with a stepped-up basis in the transferred property that, for example, may increase a U.S. shareholder's amount of QBAI with respect to the CFC for periods when it is subject to section 951A. See Conf. Rep. at 645. The stepped-up basis may also reduce the transferee CFC's tested income or increase its tested loss (for example, due to increased depreciation or amortization deductions) during periods when it is subject to section 951A. The Treasury Department and the IRS have determined that it would be inappropriate for a taxpayer to reduce its GILTI inclusion amount for any taxable year by reason of a stepped-up basis in CFC assets attributable to transactions between related CFCs during the period after December 31, 2017, but before the effective date of section 951A. Accordingly, the proposed regulations disallow the benefit of a stepped-up basis in specified tangible property transferred between related CFCs during the period before the transferor CFC's first inclusion year for purposes of calculating the transferee CFC's QBAI. See proposed § 1.951A-3(h)(2). As discussed in section I.C.4 of this Explanation of Provisions, these rules are also cross-referenced in proposed § 1.951A-2(c)(5) to disregard a stepped-up basis in any property that is depreciable or amortizable for purposes of calculating tested income and tested loss.

The U.S. tax results claimed with respect to transactions that fall outside the scope of the anti-abuse rules in the proposed regulations may, nonetheless, be challenged under other statutory provisions or judicial doctrines.

E. *Specified interest expense*

To calculate a U.S. shareholder's net DTIR, section 951A(b)(2)(B) provides that 10 percent of the aggregate of the shareholder's pro rata share of the QBAI of each CFC (defined as "deemed tangible income return" in proposed § 1.951A-1(c)(3)(ii)) is reduced by "the amount of interest expense taken into account under subsection (c)(2)(A)(ii) in determining such shareholder's net CFC tested income for the taxable year to the extent the interest income attributable to such expense is not taken into account in determining such shareholder's net CFC tested income." Deductions taken into account under section 951A(c)(2)(A)(ii) are deductions (including taxes) that are properly allocable to gross tested income for purposes of calculating tested income and tested loss. Thus, only a U.S. shareholder's pro rata share of interest expense that is currently deductible and properly allocable to gross tested income is taken into account for purposes of determining the interest expense described in section 951A(b)(2)(B). For purposes of the proposed regulations, interest expense described in section 951A(b)(2)(B) is referred to as "specified interest expense." See proposed § 1.951A-1(c)(3)(iii).

Specified interest expense is a U.S. shareholder-level determination which is net of "attributable" interest income taken into account by the U.S. shareholder. Specifically, specified interest expense of a U.S. shareholder is its pro rata share of interest expense properly allocable to gross tested income reduced by its pro rata share of interest income included in gross tested income to the extent attributable to such interest expense. The effect of this formulation is to count against net DTIR only a U.S. shareholder's pro rata share of interest expense allocable to gross tested income to the extent that the related interest income is not also reflected in the U.S. shareholder's pro rata share of the tested income of another CFC, such as in the case of third-party interest expense or interest expense paid to related U.S. persons.

The amount of interest income "attributable" to interest expense is not defined in section 951A(b)(2)(B). Accordingly, it is necessary to define this concept in the proposed regulations. A definition that incorporates a strict tracing approach would require a U.S. shareholder to determine each item of interest expense with respect to each debt instrument of each of its CFCs to determine whether, and to what extent, the interest income with respect to that debt instrument is taken into account by the U.S. shareholder in determining the shareholder's net CFC tested income. However, the Treasury Department and the IRS have determined that a tracing approach for specified interest expense would be administratively burdensome and difficult to reconcile with the framework of section 951A, which generally requires a determination of CFC-level items followed by a second determination of U.S. shareholder-level aggregate pro rata shares of such items. A tracing approach for specified interest expense would necessitate a hybrid determination, in which the relevant item – "attributable" interest income – could not be determined at the level of the CFC, but rather would require a matching at the U.S. shareholder level of the shareholder's pro rata share of each item of interest expense with its pro rata share of each item of interest income attributable to such interest expense. A tracing approach would create particular complexity with respect to interest paid between CFCs that are owned by different U.S. shareholders in different proportions or with respect to interest for which the accrual of the expense and inclusion of the income occur in separate taxable years.

The Treasury Department and the IRS have instead determined that a netting approach to specified interest expense accomplishes the purpose of the specified interest expense rule in a more administrable manner and is consistent with the requirement that "attributable" interest income be netted against interest expense. Therefore, the proposed regulations provide that a U.S. shareholder's specified interest expense is the excess of its aggregate pro rata share of the tested interest expense of each CFC over its aggregate pro rata share of the tested interest income of each CFC. See proposed § 1.951A-1(c)(3)(iii). Tested interest expense and tested interest income are generally defined by reference to all interest expense and interest income that is taken into account in determining a CFC's tested income or tested loss. See proposed § 1.951A-4(b)(1) and (2).

Comments have questioned whether interest expense of a captive finance CFC must be taken into account for purposes of determining a U.S. shareholder's specified interest expense, or whether the related interest income from unrelated customers may be available to offset such interest expense. Under a netting approach to the computation of specified interest expense, without modifications, whether a CFC's active banking business increases or reduces the specified interest expense of a U.S. shareholder relative to other taxpayers depends on whether the third-party expense related to such business is greater than or less than interest income related to such business. The Treasury Department and the IRS have determined that a U.S. shareholder's specified interest expense, and therefore its net DTIR and its GILTI inclusion amount, should not depend on whether the U.S. shareholder has one or more CFCs engaged in the active conduct of a financing or insurance business, as long as the interest expense of the CFC is incurred exclusively to fund such business with unrelated persons and thus not incurred, for instance, to fund the acquisition of specified tangible property. Therefore, the proposed regulations exclude from the definition of tested interest expense any interest expense of a CFC that is an eligible controlled foreign corporation (within the meaning of section 954(h)(2)) or a qualifying insurance company (within the meaning of section 953(e)(3)) ("qualified CFC"), except to the extent of the qualified CFC's assets unrelated to its financing or insurance business and any interest income received by the qualified CFC from loans to certain related persons (interest expense described in this sentence, "qualified interest expense"). See proposed § 1.951A-4(b)(1)(iii). Further, the proposed regulations exclude from the definition of tested interest income any interest income of a qualified CFC included in the gross tested income of the qualified CFC for the CFC inclusion year that is excluded from subpart F income due to the active financing exception of section 954(h) or the active insurance exception of section 954(i) ("qualified interest income"). See proposed § 1.951A-4(b)(2)(iii).

For purposes of determining specified interest expense, interest income and interest expense are defined broadly to encompass any amount treated as interest under the Code or regulations, and any other amount incurred or recognized in a transaction or series of integrated or related transactions in which the use or forbearance of funds is secured for a period of time if the expense or loss is predominately incurred in consideration of the time value of money. See proposed § 1.951A-4(b)(1)(ii) and (2)(ii).

Comments requested clarification of whether the interest expense of a tested loss CFC is used in the determination of specified interest expense. Regardless of whether interest expense increases tested loss or reduces tested income, the expense is "taken into account . . . in determining the shareholder's net CFC tested income" within the meaning of section 951A(b)(2)(B). In addition, if a tested loss CFC's interest expense were not taken into account for purposes of determining specified interest expense, a taxpayer could easily avoid specified interest expense by incurring offshore debt through a tested loss CFC. Therefore, the proposed regulations confirm that any interest expense taken into account for purposes of determining the tested income or tested loss of a CFC is also taken into account in determining a U.S. shareholder's specified interest expense.

F. *Domestic partnerships and their partners*

Comments requested guidance on the treatment of domestic partnerships that own stock of CFCs. Section 951A itself does not contain any specific rules on domestic partnerships and their partners that directly or indirectly own stock of CFCs. Accordingly, proposed § 1.951A-5 provides this guidance to domestic partnerships and their partners on how to compute their GILTI inclusion amounts. This guidance also applies to S corporations and their shareholders, which are treated as partnerships and partners for purposes of sections 951 through 965. See section 1373.

A domestic partnership is a U.S. person by definition under section 7701(a)(4) and (30) and can therefore be a U.S. shareholder of a CFC under section 951(b). Under current law, a domestic partnership that is a U.S. shareholder includes in gross income its section 951(a)(1)(A) inclusion with respect to a CFC, and its partners include in gross income their distributive share of such inclusion. However, as noted in section I.A of this Explanation of Provisions, there is no analog in section 951(a)(1)(A) to the U.S. shareholder-level determinations required by section 951A, and thus the level at which the section 951(a)(1)(A) determination is made – whether at the level of the partnership or its partners – does not generally affect the amount of the inclusion, if the partnership and its partners are all U.S. shareholders. On the other hand, the GILTI inclusion amount is an aggregation of the U.S. shareholder's pro rata shares of tested income, tested loss, QBAI, tested interest expense, and tested interest income of each of its CFCs. Thus, the level at which the GILTI calculation is made dictates the CFC items to be taken into account by the shareholder, and each of these items can impact the shareholder's GILTI inclusion amount.

The Treasury Department and the IRS considered a number of approaches to applying section 951A with respect to domestic partnerships and their partners. A pure aggregate approach to the treatment of domestic partnerships and their partners would treat the partnership as an aggregate of its partners, so that each partner would calculate its own GILTI inclusion amount taking into account its pro rata share of CFC items through the partnership. However, a pure aggregate approach might also be interpreted by taxpayers to exempt small partners of a domestic partnership from the GILTI regime entirely, a result that is not clearly contemplated in section 951A or its legislative history and is inconsistent with section 951.

The Treasury Department and the IRS also considered a pure entity approach. Under a pure entity approach, the domestic partnership would determine its own GILTI inclusion amount, and each partner would take into gross income its distributive share of such amount. In the case of a partner that is a U.S. shareholder of CFCs owned by the partnership and other CFCs outside the partnership, a pure entity approach would effectively fragment the shareholder's GILTI inclusion amount into multiple GILTI inclusion amounts by separating the items of the CFCs owned by the shareholder through the partnership from the items of the CFCs owned by the shareholder outside the partnership, including through other domestic partnerships. An approach that dramatically alters a U.S. shareholder's inclusion under section 951A for a taxable year depending on the legal structure by which the shareholder owns each CFC presents both an inappropriate planning opportunity as well as a trap for the unwary. Such an approach is also inconsistent with the structure of section 951A, which requires an aggregation of all relevant items of a shareholder's CFCs in order to compute a single GILTI inclusion amount for a U.S. shareholder. As discussed in section III.A of this Explanation of Provisions, the Treasury Department and the IRS relied on similar considerations in concluding that the relevant items of each CFC owned directly or indirectly by members of a consolidated group should be taken into account in determining the GILTI inclusion amount of each member of that group.

In addition, the Treasury Department and the IRS have concluded that other provisions that are related to, and interdependent with, section 951A should apply at the level of a domestic corporate partner. Section 960(d) provides a domestic corporation that is a U.S. shareholder a credit for foreign taxes paid by a CFC that are properly attributable to tested income "taken into account" by the domestic corporation, and determines the amount of that credit by reference to the corporation's aggregate pro rata share of tested income. See section 960(d)(2)(B) and (3). A domestic partnership is not eligible to claim deemed paid credits under section 960(d). Furthermore, under a pure entity approach, a domestic corporate partner of a domestic partnership may not be eligible for a deemed paid credit by reason of its distributive share of the partnership's GILTI inclusion because a partner would not have a pro rata share of the tested income of any CFC owned by the partnership, and thus it would not take into account the tested income of any such CFC. Similarly, only a domestic corporation is eligible for a section 250 deduction. Nonetheless, the Conference Report indicates that the domestic corporate partners of a domestic partnership should get the benefit of a section 250 deduction, which is consistent with an aggregate approach. See Conf. Rep. at 623, fn. 1517.

Based on the foregoing, the Treasury Department and the IRS have determined that the approach that best harmonizes the treatment of domestic partnerships and their partners across all provisions of the GILTI regime (sections 250, 951A, and 960(d)) is neither a pure aggregate nor a pure entity approach. Rather, the most harmonious approach treats a domestic partnership as an entity with respect to partners that are not U.S. shareholders of any CFC owned by the partnership, but treats the partnership as an aggregate for purposes of partners that are themselves U.S. shareholders with respect to one or more CFCs owned by the partnership. This approach ensures that each non-U.S. shareholder partner takes into income its distributive share of the domestic partnership's GILTI inclusion amount (similar to subpart F), while permitting a partner that is itself a U.S. shareholder to determine a single GILTI inclusion amount by reference to all its CFCs, whether owned directly or through a partnership, as well as allowing a corporate U.S. shareholder to calculate a foreign tax credit under section 960(d) with respect to each such CFC and to compute a section 250 deduction with respect to its GILTI inclusion amount determined by reference to each such CFC.

Therefore, the proposed regulations provide that, in general, a domestic partnership that is a U.S. shareholder of one or more CFCs ("U.S. shareholder partnership") computes its own GILTI inclusion amount in the same manner as any other U.S. shareholder, and each partner takes into account its distributive share of the domestic partnership's GILTI inclusion amount under section 702 and § 1.702-1(a)(8)(ii). See proposed § 1.951A-5(b). However, for purposes of section 951A and the proposed regulations, a partner that is itself a U.S. shareholder (within the meaning of section 951(b)) ("U.S. shareholder partner") of one or more CFCs owned directly or indirectly by a domestic partnership ("partnership CFC") is treated as owning proportionately section 958(a) stock in each such partnership CFC as if the partnership were a foreign partnership. See proposed § 1.951A-5(c). As a result, a partner that is itself a U.S. shareholder of a CFC owned by a domestic partnership computes its GILTI inclusion amount for a taxable year by taking into account its proportionate share of the partnership's pro rata share of each of the relevant items – tested income, tested loss, QBAI, tested interest income, and tested interest expense – of such CFC. This rule applies regardless of whether the domestic partnership itself has a GILTI inclusion amount for the taxable year. See proposed § 1.951A-5(g), *Example 6*. In the case that a partner is treated as owning the section 958(a) stock of one or more partnership CFCs, the partner's distributive share of the partnership's GILTI inclusion amount is determined solely by reference to partnership CFCs in which the partner is not a U.S. shareholder. See proposed § 1.951A-5(c) and (g), *Example 3*. A U.S. shareholder partnership is therefore required to provide to its partners their distributive share of the partnership's GILTI inclusion amount, as well as provide to each U.S. shareholder partner the partner's proportionate share of the partnership's pro rata share (if any) of each CFC tested item of each partnership CFC of the partnership, and forms and instructions will be updated accordingly. See proposed § 1.951A-5(f).

To illustrate the differences between the approach taken in the proposed regulations and the pure entity approach, consider a domestic partnership (PRS) with two domestic corporate partners, US1 and US2, owning 5 percent and 95 percent of PRS, respectively. PRS owns 100 percent of the single class of stock of FS1, a CFC with tested income of $100x, and 100 percent of the single class of stock of FS2, a CFC with tested loss of $50x. US2 also owns 100 percent of the single class of stock of FS3, a CFC with tested loss of $20x. Under a pure entity approach, US2's distributive share of PRS's GILTI inclusion amount would be $47.50x (95% x ($100x – $50x)), and US2's pro rata share of FS3's tested loss of $20x would be unused. Under the proposed regulations, US2, because it is a U.S. shareholder partner with respect to FS1 and FS2, aggregates its proportionate share of the tested income and tested loss of FS1 and FS2 with its pro rata share of the tested loss of FS3 in determining its GILTI inclusion amount of $27.50x ((95% x ($100x – $50x)) – $20x). Accordingly, under a pure entity approach, US2 would be incentivized to reorganize its ownership structure (for example, by liquidating PRS or contributing the stock of FS3 to PRS) in order to obtain the full benefit of the tested loss of FS3. Under the proposed regulations, however, US2 has the same GILTI inclusion amount whether it owns its CFCs directly or through one or more partnerships.

The Treasury Department and the IRS request comments as to whether any other approach to the treatment of domestic partnerships and their partners for purposes of section 951A, including a pure entity approach or a pure aggregate approach, would more appropriately harmonize the provisions of the GILTI regime than the approach of the proposed regulations, particularly in light of the administrative and compliance burdens associated with any other approach and the approach of the proposed regulations. In addition, the Treasury Department and the IRS request comments on adjustments required by reason of computing a GILTI inclusion amount, in whole or in part, at the level of the partner of a domestic partnership, including adjustments to the partner's basis in its partnership interest, the partner's section 704(b) capital account, the partnership's basis in CFC stock under section 961, and a CFC's previously taxed earnings and profits with respect to the partner or partnership under section 959.

G. *Treatment of GILTI inclusion amount and adjustments to earnings and profits and basis*

1. Treatment of GILTI as Subpart F Income for Certain Purposes

A U.S. shareholder's GILTI inclusion amount is not an inclusion under section 951(a)(1)(A). Nevertheless, for purposes of some provisions, GILTI inclusion amounts are treated similarly to section 951(a)(1)(A) inclusions. Section 951A(f)(1)(A) provides that any GILTI included in gross income is treated in the same manner as an amount included under section 951(a)(1)(A) for purposes of applying sections 168(h)(2)(B), 535(b)(10), 851(b), 904(h)(1), 959, 961, 962, 993(a)(1)(E), 996(f)(1), 1248(b)(1), 1248(d)(1), 6501(e)(1)(C), 6654(d)(2)(D), and 6655(e)(4).

Section 951A(f)(1)(B) grants the Secretary authority to provide rules applying section 951A(f)(1)(A) to other provisions of the Code. A comment requested clarification as to whether GILTI inclusion amounts are net investment income under section 1411. Pursuant to the authority in section 951A(f)(1)(B), the proposed regulations provide that a GILTI inclusion amount is treated in the same manner as an amount included under section 951(a)(1)(A) for purposes of applying section 1411. See proposed § 1.951A-6(b)(1). Thus, for example, a U.S. shareholder that has made an election pursuant to § 1.1411-10(g) with respect to a CFC to treat amounts included in gross income under section 951(a)(1)(A) as net investment income and to apply the basis adjustment rules of sections 961(a) and (b) with respect to such amounts for section 1411 purposes should also treat the portion of the U.S. shareholder's GILTI inclusion amount treated as being with respect to the CFC under section 951A(f)(2) and proposed § 1.951A-6(b)(2) as net investment income.

Comments have requested that regulations clarify that an inclusion under section 951A is determined before an inclusion under section 951(a)(1)(B). The Treasury Department and the IRS have determined that clarification is unnecessary. Because a GILTI inclusion amount is treated as a section 951(a)(1)(A) inclusion for purposes of section 959, the determination of the amount included under section 951(a)(1)(B) is made after the determination of the amount of a section 951(a)(1)(A) inclusion and the GILTI inclusion amount. See section 959(a)(2) and (f)(1). The Treasury Department and the IRS intend to issue a separate notice of proposed rulemaking to update the regulations under sections 959 and 961 to account for the Act's modifications to the U.S. international tax system, including the enactment of section 245A.

The characterization of GILTI inclusions for purposes of determining the unrelated business taxable income of tax-exempt entities will be addressed in separate guidance. The Treasury Department and the IRS request comments on other areas in which the characterization of a GILTI inclusion amount is relevant, and whether it is appropriate in those areas to treat a GILTI inclusion amount in the same manner as a section 951(a)(1)(A) inclusion or in some other manner (for example, as a dividend).

2. Interaction with Sections 163(e)(3)(B)(i) and 267(a)(3)(B)

Section 267(a)(3)(B) generally provides that a deduction for an item payable to a related CFC is not allowed until paid, except to the extent that an amount attributable to that item is includible (determined without regard to properly allocable deductions and qualified deficits) in the gross income of a U.S. shareholder. Section 163(e)(3)(B)(i) provides a similar rule for original issue discount on a debt instrument held by a related CFC.

The Treasury Department and the IRS have determined that deductions should not be deferred under sections 163(e)(3)(B)(i) and 267(a)(3)(B) to the extent an item is taken into account in determining a U.S. shareholder's GILTI inclusion amount. Accordingly, the proposed regulations provide that a deduction is allowed under sections 163(e)(3)(B)(i) and 267(a)(3)(B) for an item taken into account in determining the net CFC tested income of a U.S. shareholder, including a U.S. shareholder treated under the proposed regulations as owning section 958(a) stock of a CFC owned by a domestic partnership. See proposed § 1.951A-6(c)(1). In the case of a U.S. shareholder that is a domestic partnership, this rule applies only to the extent that one or more U.S. persons (other than domestic partnerships) that are direct or indirect partners of the domestic partnership include in gross income their distributive share of the partnership's GILTI inclusion amount or the item is taken into account by a U.S. shareholder partner of the domestic partnership by reason of § 1.951A-5(c). See proposed § 1.951A-6(c)(2).

3. Basis Adjustments for the Use of Tested Losses

In determining a U.S. shareholder's net CFC tested income, the U.S. shareholder's pro rata share of a tested loss of one CFC may offset the shareholder's pro rata share of tested income of another CFC. Under the statute, such a use of a tested loss does not reduce the U.S. shareholder's basis in the stock of the tested loss CFC, increase the stock basis of the tested income CFC, or affect the earnings and profits of either the tested loss CFC or the tested income CFC.

The Treasury Department and the IRS have determined that in certain cases the lack of adjustments to stock basis of a tested loss CFC can lead to inappropriate results. For example, if the U.S. shareholder's basis in the stock of the tested loss CFC is not reduced to reflect the use of the tested loss to offset tested income taken into account by the U.S. shareholder, the U.S. shareholder would recognize a second and duplicative benefit of the loss – either through the recognition of a loss or the reduction of gain – if the stock of the tested loss CFC is disposed of. See *Charles Ilfeld Co. v. Hernandez*, 292 U.S. 62 (1934) (denying the loss on stock of subsidiaries upon liquidation when operating losses were previously claimed from the subsidiaries' operations because "[i]f allowed, this would be the practical equivalent of double deduction"); *U.S. v. Skelly Oil. Co.*, 394 U.S. 678 (1969) ("the Code should not be interpreted to allow respondent 'the practical equivalent of a double deduction'" (citing *Charles Ilfeld Co.*)); § 1.161-1. On the other hand, in the case of a corporate U.S. shareholder, but not in the case of an individual, gain recognized on the disposition of a CFC attributable to offset tested income would, in most cases, be eliminated as a result of the application of section 964(e) or section 1248(a) and (j), to the extent the gain is recharacterized as a dividend that is eligible for the dividends received deduction under section 245A. Accordingly, proposed § 1.951A-6(e) generally provides that in the case of a corporate U.S. shareholder (excluding regulated investment companies and real estate investment trusts), for purposes of determining the gain, loss, or income on the direct or indirect disposition of stock of a CFC, the basis of the stock is reduced by the amount of tested loss that has been used to offset tested income in calculating net CFC tested income of the U.S. shareholder. The basis reduction is only made at the time of the disposition and therefore does not affect the stock basis prior to a disposition. Requiring the basis reduction only at the time of the disposition prevents the use of tested losses alone from causing the recognition of gain if the reduction exceeds the amount of stock basis.

The basis adjustments apply only to the extent a "net" tested loss of the controlled foreign corporation has been used. This limitation is intended to ensure that the reduction applies only to the extent necessary to eliminate the duplicative loss in the stock. For example, if a $100x tested loss of a CFC (CFC1) offsets $100x of tested income of another CFC (CFC2) in one year in determining a U.S. shareholder's net CFC tested income, and in the next year CFC1 has $20x of tested income that is offset by a $20x tested loss of CFC2, then the $100x used tested loss attributable to the CFC1 stock from the first year is reduced by the $20x of its tested income from the second year that was offset by the tested loss of CFC2, resulting in a "net" used tested loss of $80x. See proposed § 1.951A-6(e)(2).

Similar adjustments apply when the tested loss CFC is treated as owned by the U.S. shareholder through certain intervening foreign entities by reason of section 958(a)(2) to prevent the indirect use of the duplicative loss through the disposition of interests in those intervening entities. The regulations provide an exception to those rules in certain cases when the tested loss CFC and the CFC that generated the tested income that is offset by the tested loss are in the same section 958(a)(2) ownership chain; adjustments are not appropriate in these cases because there is no duplicative loss to the extent the shares of both CFCs are directly or indirectly disposed of. See proposed § 1.951A-6(e)(1)(ii).

A direct disposition of the stock of a CFC can result in the indirect disposition of the stock of one or more lower-tier CFCs. See proposed § 1.951A-6(e)(6)(ii)(B). In such a case, basis adjustments may be made to both the stock of the upper-tier CFC and the stock of the lower-tier CFCs. Accordingly, the proposed regulations provide ordering rules for making these adjustments that, in general, are intended to prevent gain resulting from a basis adjustment attributable to the use of a single tested loss from being taken into account more than once. See proposed § 1.951A-6(e)(1)(iv).

The proposed regulations also include rules that take into account certain nonrecognition transactions involving CFCs, such as the acquisition of CFC stock by a domestic corporation and transactions described in section 381. See proposed § 1.951A-6(e)(4)(ii) and (e)(5). These rules are intended to prevent the elimination or avoidance of the basis adjustments through these types of transactions.

Finally, the proposed regulations provide a special rule to address dispositions of CFC stock by another CFC that is not wholly owned by a single domestic corporation. See proposed § 1.951A-6(e)(7). This rule, which is consistent with proposed § 1.961-3(b) and Revenue Ruling 82-16, 1982-1 C.B. 106, is intended to ensure that the appropriate amount of subpart F income is taken into account by U.S. shareholders of the CFC as a result of the disposition.

The Treasury Department and the IRS request comments on these rules, including whether additional adjustments to stock basis or earnings and profits should be made to account for a used tested loss or offset tested income (for example, whether adjustments should be provided that are consistent with those set forth in proposed § 1.965-2(d) and (f) (REG-104226-18, 83 FR 39514, August 9, 2018)). Comments are also requested on whether similar rules should apply to non-corporate U.S. shareholders, taking into account the fact that non-corporate U.S. shareholders are not entitled to a dividends received deduction under section 245A. Additionally, comments are requested as to whether the definition of "disposition" should be modified. For example, the Treasury Department and the IRS are considering broadening the term to include transactions that do not involve an actual transfer of stock but might result in taxable gain but for the presence of tax basis in CFC stock. Examples of such transactions include distributions subject to section 301(c)(2) or 1059.

II. *Section 951*

A. *Pro rata share rules*

Section 1.951-1(e) was revised in 2005 and 2006 to address certain avoidance structures, such as structures that resulted in non-economic allocations of subpart F income to shareholders of CFCs that are not U.S. shareholders. The Treasury Department and the IRS have become aware of additional avoidance structures. For example, the existing regulations require an allocation of earnings and profits between classes of stock with discretionary distribution rights based on the fair market value of the stock. While this rule appropriately allocates subpart F income in some cases (for example, involving multiple classes of common stock), some taxpayers have attempted to improperly allocate subpart F income by applying these rules to certain structures involving shares with preferred liquidation and distribution rights. Similar avoidance structures involve cumulative preferred stock with dividends that compound less frequently than annually.

This notice of proposed rulemaking proposes to amend § 1.951-1(e) to address these avoidance structures, which implicate section 951A as well as section 951. The proposed regulations clarify that, for purposes of determining a U.S. shareholder's pro rata share of subpart F income, earnings and profits for the taxable year are first hypothetically distributed among the classes of stock and then hypothetically distributed to each share in the class on the hypothetical distribution date, which is the last day of the CFC's taxable year on which it is a CFC. In lieu of prescribing a determination based on fair market value, the proposed regulations provide that the amount of earnings and profits that would be distributed with respect to classes of stock is based on all relevant facts and circumstances. See proposed § 1.951-1(e)(3). In addition, the proposed regulations disregard any transaction or arrangement that is part of a plan a principal purpose of which is to reduce a U.S. shareholder's pro rata share of the subpart F income of a CFC. See proposed § 1.951-1(e)(6). This rule also applies for purposes of determining a U.S. shareholder's pro rata share of amounts for purposes of calculating the shareholder's GILTI inclusion amount. Id. As a result of adding this broader rule, the proposed regulations do not include the specific anti-avoidance rule involving section 304 transactions in existing § 1.951-1(e)(3)(v).

The proposed regulations also modify § 1.951-1(e) in specific ways to take into account section 951A. For example, the proposed regulations provide that a U.S. shareholder's pro rata share of a CFC's subpart F income is determined by reference to the shareholder's proportionate share of the total current earnings and profits that would be distributed in the hypothetical distribution. In addition to determining a U.S. shareholder's pro rata share of a CFC's subpart F income, § 1.951-1(e) also applies for purposes of determining the shareholder's pro rata share of the CFC's tested income. See also proposed § 1.951A-1(d)(2). However, because tested income is not limited to the earnings and profits of a CFC, and because a CFC's tested loss increases its earnings and profits for purposes of determining the subpart F income limitation in section 952(c)(1), the earnings and profits allocated in the hypothetical distribution may exceed the earnings and profits of the CFC computed under section 964. Accordingly, the hypothetical distribution in the proposed regulations is based on the greater of the section 964 earnings and profits or the sum of the subpart F income (increased by reason of any tested loss add-back under section 951A(c)(2)(B)(ii) and proposed § 1.951A-6(d)) and tested income of the CFC.

B. *Partnership blocker structures*

Notice 2010-41, 2010-22 I.R.B. 715, stated that forthcoming regulations would treat a domestic partnership as a foreign partnership for purposes of identifying the U.S. shareholder of a CFC required to include in gross income its pro rata share of the CFC's subpart F income in the circumstances described in the notice. The Treasury Department and the IRS have determined that the same rules should also apply to identify the U.S. shareholder of a CFC for purposes of section 951A. Accordingly, the proposed regulations treat certain controlled domestic partnerships as foreign partnerships for purposes of identifying a U.S. shareholder for purposes of sections 951 through 964. See also proposed § 1.965-1(e) (REG-104226-18, 83 FR 39514, August 9, 2018) (adopting a similar partnership blocker rule for purposes of the section 965 regulations).

C. *Other modifications*

The proposed regulations also update § 1.951-1 consistent with the modification in the Act of the definition of a U.S. shareholder and the elimination in the Act of the 30-day requirement. See proposed § 1.951-1(a) and (g)(1).

III. *Section 1502*

A. *In general*

Section 1502 provides the Secretary authority to

> prescribe such regulations as he may deem necessary in order that the tax liability of any affiliated group of corporations making a consolidated return and of each corporation in the group, both during and after the period of affiliation, may be returned, determined, computed, assessed, collected, and adjusted, in such manner as clearly to reflect the income-tax liability and the various factors necessary for the determination of such liability, and in order to prevent avoidance of such tax liability.

A consolidated group member's inclusion of subpart F income under section 951(a)(1)(A) is determined at the member level. However, as discussed in section I.A of this Explanation of Provisions, a section 951(a)(1)(A) inclusion with respect to a CFC is determined solely by reference to the subpart F income of the CFC, and therefore determining a member's section 951(a)(1)(A) inclusion solely by reference to a CFC the stock of which is owned (within the meaning of section 958(a)) by the member is not distortive of the consolidated group's income tax liability. As a result, the location of the CFC within the group generally has no effect on the consolidated group's income tax liability by reason of section 951(a)(1)(A). In contrast, section 951A requires an aggregate, U.S. shareholder-level calculation, under which a member's pro rata share of the relevant items of one CFC can increase or decrease a member's GILTI inclusion amount otherwise resulting from its ownership of another CFC. Accordingly, a determination of a member's GILTI inclusion amount solely based on its pro rata share of the items of a CFC the stock of which is owned (within the meaning of section 958(a)) by that member may not result in a clear reflection of the consolidated group's income tax liability. For example, a consolidated group could segregate one CFC with tested interest expense under one member and another CFC with QBAI under another member, thereby increasing the net DTIR of the second member relative to the consolidated group's net DTIR if determined at a group level. Alternatively, a strict, separate-entity application of section 951A could inappropriately increase a consolidated group's income tax liability, because one member's excess pro rata share of tested losses or QBAI over tested income would be unavailable to reduce another member's GILTI inclusion amount.

B. *Section 1.1502-51*

In response to comments, the Treasury Department and the IRS have determined that a member's GILTI inclusion amount should be determined by reference to the relevant items of each CFC owned by members of the same consolidated group. As discussed in section I.A of this Explanation of Provisions, a U.S. shareholder includes in gross income its GILTI inclusion amount for any taxable year. GILTI inclusion amount is defined under proposed § 1.951A-1(c)(1) as, with respect to a U.S. shareholder for a taxable year of the shareholder, the excess (if any) of the shareholder's net CFC tested income over the shareholder's net DTIR for the taxable year. Under proposed § 1.1502-51, this definition applies equally to a U.S. shareholder that is a member of a consolidated group. However, consistent with the authority in section 1502, the proposed regulations provide special definitions of net CFC tested income and net DTIR in order to clearly reflect the income tax liability of the consolidated group. Specifically, the proposed regulations provide that, to determine a member's GILTI inclusion amount, the pro rata shares of tested loss, QBAI, tested interest expense, and tested interest income of each member are aggregated, and then a portion of each aggregate amount is allocated to each member of the group that is a U.S. shareholder of a tested income CFC based on the proportion of such member's aggregate pro rata share of tested income to the total tested income of the consolidated group. See proposed § 1.1502-51(e).

As discussed in section I.G.3 of this Explanation of Provisions, proposed § 1.951A-6(e) provides that the adjusted basis of the stock of a CFC is adjusted immediately before its disposition. Proposed § 1.1502-51(c) provides special rules for making these adjustments to the adjusted basis of the stock of a CFC owned by a member in a manner that reflects the special definitions applicable to members.

C. *Section 1.1502-32*

Section 1.1502-32 provides rules for adjusting the basis of the stock of a subsidiary owned by another member to reflect, among other items, the subsidiary's items of income. Accordingly, no new rules are necessary to adjust the basis of the stock of a member because of a GILTI inclusion. However, as previously discussed, proposed §§ 1.951A-6(e) and 1.1502-51(c) provide rules for adjusting the basis of the stock of a CFC immediately before its disposition. As a result, proposed § 1.1502-32(b)(3)(ii)(E) and (iii)(C) provide for adjustments to the basis of the stock of a member to reflect those rules. Specifically, the proposed rules treat a portion of a member's offset tested income amount as tax-exempt income and all of a member's used tested loss amount as a noncapital, nondeductible expense.

As previously discussed, the Treasury Department and the IRS have determined that in the case of a corporate U.S. shareholder, gain recognized on the disposition of stock of a CFC attributable to offset tested income would, in most cases, be eliminated as a result of the application of section 964(e)(4) or section 1248(a) and (j), to the extent the gain or income is eligible for the dividends received deduction under section 245A. In order to not incentivize a sale of the stock of a CFC over a sale of stock of a member, proposed § 1.1502-32(b)(3)(ii)(F) provides that a member is also treated as receiving tax-exempt income immediately before another member recognizes income, gain, deduction, or loss with respect to a share of the first member's stock. The amount of this additional tax-exempt income is the net offset tested income amount allocable to the shares of any CFC owned by the first member to the extent that a distribution of such amount would have been characterized as a dividend eligible for a section 245A deduction and not subject to section 1059.

The Treasury Department and the IRS request comments regarding the coordination of the rules of proposed §§ 1.951A-6(e) and 1.1502-51(c) with the investment adjustment regime of § 1.1502-32. Comments are specifically requested on: (1) whether the amount of the adjustments to the basis of member stock should be limited to the amount of the adjustments to the basis of the stock of a CFC under the rules of proposed § 1.951A-6(e); (2) whether the adjustments to the basis of member stock should all be made on a current basis, made to the extent of the basis adjustments provided in proposed § 1.951A-6(e) on a current basis with any remaining adjustments being made at the time of a disposition of stock of a CFC or of a member, or made only at the time of a disposition of the stock of a CFC or of a member; and (3) whether rules should provide that a deduction under section 245A should not be treated as tax-exempt income to the extent that the underlying dividend is attributable to offset tested income for which basis adjustments have already been made. Additionally, comments are specifically requested as to whether there are any circumstances in which there should be a deemed disposition of the stock of a CFC owned by a member, such that the rules of proposed § 1.951A-6(e) would apply, including, but not limited to, a deconsolidation or taxable disposition of the stock of a member that owns (directly or indirectly) the stock of a CFC to either a person outside of the consolidated group or to another member, and a transfer of the stock of a member in an intercompany transaction that is a nonrecognition transaction. Similarly, comments are specifically requested as to whether there are other transactions that should be described in the definition of transferred shares in proposed § 1.1502-32(b)(3)(ii)(F)(1), such as a deemed disposition pursuant to § 1.1502-19(c)(1)(iii)(B). Lastly, comments are specifically requested as to whether any other adjustments are necessary to prevent the duplication of gain or loss resulting from a member's ownership of a CFC, including situations where a member owning a CFC joins another consolidated group.

In response to comments received, no new rules are being proposed under § 1.1502-33, which provides rules for adjusting the earnings and profits of a subsidiary and any member owning stock of the subsidiary. The Treasury Department and the IRS request comments on whether additional rules under § 1.1502-33 or any other regulations issued under section 1502 are necessary.

IV. *Sections 1.6038-2(a) and 1.6038-5*

Under section 6038(a)(1), U.S. persons that control foreign corporations must file certain information returns with respect to those corporations. Before the Act, a U.S. shareholder would not have had an income inclusion under section 951(a)(1) with respect to a foreign corporation unless the corporation had been a CFC for an uninterrupted period of at least 30 days during the taxable year. While section 6038 does not limit the reporting requirements to foreign corporations that a U.S. person controls for an uninterrupted period of at least 30 days, § 1.6038-2(a) does provide for such a limit. To coordinate with the amendment to section 951(a)(1) that removed the 30-day requirement, this notice of proposed rulemaking proposes to revise § 1.6038-2(a) to provide that certain information reporting is required for U.S. persons that control a foreign corporation at any time during an annual accounting period.

Section 6038(a)(4) allows the Secretary to require any U.S. shareholder of a CFC to provide information required under section 6038(a)(1), which includes information that is similar to the listed information in section 6038(a)(1)(A) through (a)(1)(E), as well as information that "the Secretary determines to be appropriate to carry out the provisions of this title." In order to effectively administer and enforce section 951A, the Treasury Department and the IRS have determined that, in general, U.S. shareholders must file a new Schedule I-1, Information for Global Intangible Low-Taxed Income, to Form 5471, Information Return of U.S. Persons With Respect To Certain Foreign Corporations, as well as new Form 8992, U.S Shareholder Calculation of Global Intangible Low-Taxed Income (GILTI), to provide the information that a U.S. shareholder needs with respect to each of its CFCs to determine the U.S. shareholder's GILTI inclusion amount for a taxable year. Proposed § 1.6038-5 provides the filing requirements for new Form 8992.

V. *Applicability Dates*

Consistent with the applicability date of section 951A, proposed §§ 1.951-1(e)(1)(ii)(B), 1.951A-1 through 1.951A-6, 1.1502-32(b)(3)(ii)(E), (b)(3)(ii)(F), and (b)(3)(iii)(C), and 1.1502-51 are proposed to apply to taxable years of foreign corporations beginning after December 31, 2017, and to taxable years of U.S. shareholders in which or with which such taxable years of foreign corporations end. See section 7805(b)(2). Proposed § 1.951-1(e) (pro rata share of subpart F income) (other than § 1.951-1(e)(1)(ii)(B)) is proposed to apply to taxable years of U.S. shareholders ending on or after

September 13, 2018. See section 7805(b)(1)(B). Consistent with the applicability date of the modification to section 951 in the Act, proposed § 1.951-1(a) (controlled foreign corporations) and § 1.951-1(g) (definition of U.S. shareholder) are proposed to apply to taxable years of foreign corporations beginning after December 31, 2017, and to taxable years of U.S. shareholders with or within which such taxable years of foreign corporations end. See section 7805(b)(2). Proposed § 1.951-1(h) (special rule for partnership blocker structure) is proposed to apply to taxable years of domestic partnerships ending on or after May 14, 2010. See Notice 2010-41 and section 7805(b)(1)(C). Although proposed § 1.951-1(h) applies for purposes of both section 951 and section 951A, the only practical effect of applying this rule to taxable years of domestic partnerships ending on or after May 14, 2010, and before January 1, 2018, concerns the application of section 951. The proposed rule does not have relevance to the application of section 951A until the first taxable year of a CFC owned by a domestic partnership beginning after December 31, 2017 (the effective date of section 951A). Proposed § 1.6038-2(a) (information returns required of U.S. persons with respect to annual accounting periods of certain foreign corporations) and proposed § 1.6038-5 (information returns required of certain U.S. persons to report amounts determined with respect to certain foreign corporations for GILTI purposes) are proposed to apply to taxable years of foreign corporations beginning on or after September 13, 2018. See sections 6038(a)(3) and 7805(b)(1)(B).

Special Analyses

Regulatory Planning and Review – Economic Analysis

Executive Orders 13563 and 12866 direct agencies to assess costs and benefits of available regulatory alternatives and, if regulation is necessary, to select regulatory approaches that maximize net benefits (including potential economic, environmental, public health and safety effects, distributive impacts, and equity). Executive Order 13563 emphasizes the importance of quantifying both costs and benefits, of reducing costs, of harmonizing rules, and of promoting flexibility. The Executive Order 13771 designation for any final rule resulting from these proposed regulations will be informed by comments received.

The proposed regulations have been designated by the Office of Information and Regulatory Affairs (OIRA) as subject to review under Executive Order 12866 pursuant to the Memorandum of Agreement (April 11, 2018) between the Treasury Department and the Office of Management and Budget regarding review of tax regulations. OIRA has determined that the proposed rulemaking is significant. Accordingly, the proposed regulations have been reviewed by OIRA. For more detail on the economic analysis, please refer to the following analysis.

A. *Overview*

The proposed regulations provide taxpayers with computational, definitional, and anti-avoidance guidance regarding the application of section 951A. They provide guidance for U.S. shareholders to determine the amount of GILTI to include in gross income and how to compute the components of GILTI. Among other benefits, this clarity helps ensure that taxpayers all calculate GILTI in a similar manner, which promotes efficiency and equity contingent on the provisions of the overall Code.

The proposed regulations under sections 951A, 1502, and 6038 (proposed §§ 1.951A-1 through 1.951A-7, 1.1502-12, 1.1502-13, 1.1502-32, and 1.1502-51, and 1.6038-5) provide details for taxpayers (including members of a consolidated group) regarding the computation of certain components of GILTI (for example, tested income and tested loss, QBAI, net deemed tangible income return, and specified interest expense), describe the consequences of a GILTI inclusion for purposes of other sections of the Code, and detail the reporting requirements associated with GILTI. These proposed regulations further establish anti-abuse rules to prevent taxpayers from taking measures to inappropriately reduce their GILTI through certain transfers of property. They also disallow certain losses that reduce GILTI from being used a second time.

The proposed regulations under sections 951 and 6038 (proposed §§ 1.951-1 and 1.6038-2) prevent taxpayers from avoiding an inclusion of subpart F income under section 951(a) or the inclusion of GILTI under section 951A through certain artificial arrangements involving the ownership of CFC stock, coordinate the calculation of a U.S. shareholder's subpart F with its GILTI, and conform the regulations to other amendments in the Act, including a modification to the definition of U.S. shareholder for purposes of sections 951(a) and 951A and the elimination of the 30-day CFC status requirement. This economic analysis describes the economic benefits and costs of the proposed regulations.

B. *Economic Analysis of the Proposed Regulations*

1. Background

Because section 951A is a new Code section, many of the details behind the relevant terms and necessary calculations required for the computation of a U.S. shareholder's GILTI inclusion amount would benefit from greater specificity. Thus, as is expected after the passage of major tax reform legislation, the regulations answer open questions and provide detail and specificity for the definitions and concepts described in section 951A, so that U.S. shareholders can readily and accurately determine their GILTI inclusion amounts. For example, the regulations provide definitions of crucial terms, such as tested income, tested loss, specified tangible property, and specified interest expense.

As discussed in section I.A. of the Explanation of Provisions, although a GILTI inclusion is treated similarly to an inclusion of subpart F income for some purposes, it is determined in a manner fundamentally different from that of a subpart F inclusion. Therefore, in some cases it is appropriate for the regulations to rely on subpart F principles, but in other cases different rules are necessary. For example, the regulations apply subpart F rules for purposes of (1) determining a U.S. shareholder's pro rata share of certain items of a CFC, (2) translating foreign currency to U.S. dollars, (3) determining gross income and allowable deductions, and (4) allocating and apportioning allowable deductions to gross tested income. However, it would be inappropriate to rely on subpart F rules for the GILTI computations that are performed at the U.S. shareholder level because subpart F income is determined solely at the level of a CFC. For example, the regulations provide detail on how a U.S. shareholder determines its specified interest expense at the shareholder level based on the interest expense and interest income of each CFC owned by the shareholder.

Additionally, the proposed regulations provide rules regarding the interaction of certain aspects of section 951A with other provisions. For example, they clarify that, regarding the interaction of the earnings and profits limitation (including recapture) for subpart F income and the determination of gross tested income, tested income and tested loss are computed without regard to the earnings and profits limitation in section 952(c). In addition, the proposed regulations provide that GILTI inclusion amounts are considered net investment income under section 1411. Finally, the proposed regulations provide that certain deductions between related parties are not deferred under sections 163(e)(3)(B)(i) and 267(a)(3)(B) to the extent the income is taken into account in determining a U.S. shareholder's GILTI inclusion amount.

Section 951A provides the Secretary of the Treasury the authority to issue regulations and other guidance to prevent the avoidance of the purposes of section 951A(d). As such, regulations under §§1.951A-2 and 1.951A-3 provide that certain transactions that reduce a U.S. shareholder's GILTI inclusion amount, for example, by increasing a CFC's qualified business asset investment (QBAI) or decreasing a CFC's tested income, will be disregarded for purposes of the GILTI computation.

Further, the Treasury Department and the IRS have determined that, in the absence of any adjustment, inappropriate results may arise in cases that a U.S. shareholder's pro rata share of the tested loss of one CFC offsets the shareholder's pro rata share of the tested income of another CFC in determining the shareholder's GILTI inclusion amount. In particular, a U.S. shareholder disposing of the stock of a tested loss CFC could recognize second, duplicative benefits from a single economic loss. Therefore, the proposed regulations provide that, when determining gain or loss on the disposition of the stock of a tested loss CFC, the U.S. shareholder's basis in the stock of the tested loss CFC is reduced by the cumulative amount of tested losses that were used to offset tested income in determining the shareholder's net CFC tested income.

The statute is silent on the computation of GILTI for members of a consolidated group and for domestic partnerships and their partners. Absent these regulations, there would be uncertainty among taxpayers as to whether to calculate a GILTI inclusion amount at the level of a member or its consolidated group, or at the level of a domestic partnership or its partners. Without guidance, different taxpayers would likely take different positions on these matters. The proposed regulations provide clarity by (1) determining the GILTI inclusion amount of each member of a consolidated group by taking into account the relevant items of each CFC owned by members of such group, and (2) providing guidance on the computation of the GILTI inclusion amount of domestic partnerships and their partners.

Finally, these proposed regulations provide reporting requirements necessary to properly administer and enforce section 951A. In particular, the Treasury Department and the IRS have determined that U.S. shareholders must file a new Schedule I-1, Information for Global Intangible Low-Taxed Income, associated with Form 5471, Information Return of U.S. Persons With Respect To Certain Foreign Corporations, as well as new Form 8992, U.S Shareholder Calculation of Global Intangible Low-Taxed Income (GILTI), in order to provide the information that a U.S. shareholder is using with respect to each of its CFCs to determine the U.S. shareholder's GILTI inclusion amount for a taxable year. The proposed regulations also provide that a U.S. shareholder partnership must include on its Schedule K-1, associated with Form 1065, U.S. Return of Partnership Income, certain information necessary for its partners to determine their distributive share of the partnership's GILTI inclusion amount or, in the case of U.S. shareholder partners, to determine their own GILTI inclusion amounts. Finally, to coordinate with the amendment to section 951(a)(1) that removed the 30-day CFC status requirement for subpart F inclusions, the proposed regulations provide that certain information reporting is required for U.S. persons that control a foreign corporation at any time during an annual accounting period.

2. Anticipated benefits and costs of the proposed regulations

a. Baseline

The Treasury Department and the IRS have assessed the benefits and costs of the proposed regulations against a baseline—the way the world would look in the absence of the proposed regulations.

b. Anticipated Benefits

The Treasury Department and the IRS expect that the certainty and clarity provided by these proposed regulations, relative to the baseline, will enhance U.S. economic performance under the statute. Because a tax has not previously been imposed on GILTI and the statute is silent on certain aspects of definitions and calculations, taxpayers can particularly benefit from enhanced specificity regarding the relevant terms and necessary calculations they are required to apply under the statute. In the absence of this enhanced specificity, similarly situated taxpayers might interpret the statutory rules of section 951A differently, potentially resulting in inequitable outcomes. For example, different taxpayers might pursue income-generating activities based on different assumptions about whether that income will be counted as GILTI, and some taxpayers may forego specific investments that other taxpayers deem worthwhile based on different interpretations of the tax consequences alone. The guidance provided in these regulations helps to ensure that taxpayers face more uniform incentives when making economic decisions, a tenet of economic efficiency. Consistent reporting across taxpayers also increases the IRS's ability to consistently enforce the tax rules, thus increasing equity and decreasing opportunities for tax evasion.

For example, the proposed regulations provide a definition of specified interest expense that adopts a netting approach. Alternatives would be to adopt a tracing approach or to remain silent. The Treasury Department and the IRS rejected a tracing approach because it would be more burdensome for taxpayers due to the complexity of matching, at the U.S. shareholder-level, of the shareholder's pro rata share of each item of interest expense with its pro rata share of each item of interest income. The Treasury Department and the IRS also rejected the option of remaining silent because if taxpayers relied on statutory language alone, taxpayers would adopt different approaches because the statute does not define what "attributable" means, leaving it open to differing interpretations.

As discussed above, there are similarities between GILTI and subpart F. Where appropriate, these proposed regulations rely on rules already developed under subpart F. Since taxpayers to whom GILTI applies are already subject to the subpart F regime, it is less costly to them to apply rules they are already familiar with, and they will benefit in reduced time and cost spent learning new rules. For example, the proposed regulations apply existing subpart F rules for determining allowable deductions for GILTI purposes. By relying on existing infrastructure, the proposed regulations allow taxpayers to use the same analysis that they already conduct for subpart F purposes. For additional discussion of the rules for determining allowable deductions, see section I.C.1 of the Explanation of Provisions section.

The Treasury Department and the IRS next considered the benefits and costs of providing these specific proposed terms, calculations, and other details regarding GILTI. In developing these proposed regulations, the Treasury Department and the IRS have generally aimed to apply the principle that an economically efficient tax system would treat income derived from similar economic decisions similarly, to the extent consistent with the statute and considerations of administrability of the tax system. Similar economic decisions, in the context of GILTI, are those that involve property of a similar degree of immobility and that demonstrate active business operations and presence in any particular jurisdiction. See, for example, Senate Explanation, at 366.

An economically efficient tax system would also generally keep the choice among businesses' ownership and organizational structures neutral contingent on the provisions of the corporate income tax and other tax provisions that may affect organizational structure. The Treasury Department and the IRS expect that the proposed regulations, in providing that GILTI be generally calculated on a consolidated group basis and at the partner level in the case of partners that are U.S. shareholders of one or more partnership CFCs, will ensure that shareholders face uniform tax treatment on their GILTI-relevant investments regardless of ownership or organizational structure, thus encouraging market-driven as opposed to tax-driven structuring decisions. If, as an alternative policy approach, GILTI were determined solely at the level of a member (in the case of consolidated groups) or solely at the level of a partnership (in the case of domestic partnerships and their partners), many taxpayers would be compelled to reorganize their ownership structures just to obtain the full aggregation of CFC attributes as envisioned by Congress. Yet other taxpayers would be incentivized to reorganize in an attempt to avoid full aggregation so as to reduce their inclusion below an amount that accurately reflects their GILTI. For an illustration, see section I.F of the Explanation of Provisions. Therefore, the Treasury Department and the IRS propose that GILTI be calculated on a consolidated group basis and at the partner level in the case of partners that are U.S. shareholders of one or more partnership CFCs. The preamble discusses further why those approaches were taken, as well as describing alternative approaches considered. The Treasury Department and the IRS request comments on this proposed approach.

c. Anticipated impacts on administrative and compliance costs

Because the statute requires payment of tax regardless of the issuance of regulations or instructions, the new forms, revisions to existing forms, and proposed regulations can lower the burden on taxpayers of determining their tax liability. The Treasury Department and the IRS expect that the proposed regulations will reduce the costs for taxpayers to comply with the Act, relative to the baseline of no promulgated regulations. The proposed regulations require that each U.S. shareholder partnership provide to each partner its distributive share of the partnership's GILTI inclusion amount and, if the partner is a U.S. shareholder of one or more partnership CFCs, the partner's proportionate share of the partnership's pro rata share of each relevant item of the partnership CFC. Under the baseline, the burden would potentially have fallen on each partner, who would be required to determine its own distributive share of the partnership's GILTI inclusion amount or, if a U.S. shareholder of a partnership CFC, determine its own GILTI inclusion amount by reference to the partnership's pro rata share of items of the partnership CFC. While this latter burden is difficult to assess, because it is unclear how partners would calculate these amounts in the absence of a determination by the partnership and it is similarly unclear what efforts might be made by the partnership to help the partners fulfill this obligation, the Treasury Department and the IRS expect that it would be significantly greater than the burden incurred under the proposed regulations.

Proposed § 1.6038-2(a) increases record-keeping requirements for taxpayers because it requires all taxpayers to file Form 5471 if they held stock in a CFC during the taxable year regardless of the duration of the holding period, rather than only if they held the stock for a 30-day period under the current regulation. The changes in the proposed regulation derive directly from statutory changes to the holding period requirement in the Act.

C. *Paperwork Reduction Act*

The collections of information in these proposed regulations with respect to section 951A are in proposed § § 1.951A-5(f) and 1.6038-5. A separate collection of information applicable to controlling U.S. shareholders of a foreign corporation is in proposed § 1.6038-2(a).

The collection of information in proposed § 1.6038-5 is mandatory for each U.S. shareholder (including a U.S. shareholder partner) that owns (within the meaning of section 958(a)) stock of a CFC. The collection of information in proposed § 1.6038-5 is satisfied by submitting a new reporting form, Form 8992, U.S. Shareholder Calculation of Global Intangible Low-Taxed Income (GILTI), with an income tax return. In addition, for those U.S. shareholders that are required to file Form 5471, Information Return of U.S. Persons with Respect to Certain Foreign Corporations, a new Schedule I-1, Information for Global Intangible Low-Taxed Income, has been added. For purposes of the Paperwork Reduction Act of 1995 (44 U.S.C. 3507(d)) ("PRA"), the reporting burden associated with proposed § 1.6038-5 will be reflected in the IRS Form 14029, Paperwork Reduction Act Submission, associated with Form 5471 (OMB control number 1545-0704) and the new Form 8992 (OMB control number 1545-0123).

The collection of information in proposed § 1.951A-5(f) requires each U.S. shareholder partnership to provide to its partners their distributive share of the partnership's GILTI inclusion amount, as well as provide to each U.S. shareholder partner their proportionate share of the partnership's pro rata share (if any) of each CFC tested item of each partnership CFC of the partnership. The Treasury Department and the IRS anticipate revising Schedule K-1 (Form 1065), Partner's Share of Income, Deductions, Credits, etc., or its instructions to require the provision of this information. For purposes of the PRA, the reporting burden associated with proposed § 1.951A-5(f) will be reflected in the IRS Form 14029, Paperwork Reduction Act Submission, associated with Schedule K-1 (Form 1065, OMB control number 1545-0123).

The collection of information currently required from a U.S. person that controls a foreign corporation is revised by proposed § 1.6038-2(a). Section 1.6038-2(a) presently requires only those U.S. persons with uninterrupted control of a foreign corporation for 30 days or more during the shareholder's annual accounting period to file Form 5471 for that period. Consistent with statutory changes in the Act, the revised collection of information in proposed § 1.6038-2(a) eliminates the 30-day holding period as a precondition to reporting and requires every U.S. person that controls a foreign corporation at any time during an annual accounting period to file Form 5471 for that period. For purposes of the PRA, the reporting burden associated with proposed § 1.6038-2(a) will be reflected in the IRS Form 14029, Paperwork Reduction Act Submission, associated with Form 5471.

When available, drafts of IRS forms are posted for comment at https://apps.irs.gov/app/picklist/list/draftTaxForms.html.

Related New or Revised Tax Forms

	New	Revision of existing form	Number of respondents (estimated)
Schedule I-1 (Form 5471)	✓		25,000 - 35,000
Form 8992	✓		25,000 – 35,000
Form 1065/1120S, Schedule K		✓	8,000 – 12,000
Form 5471 (30 days)		✓	<1,000

D. *Regulatory Flexibility Act*

It is hereby certified that this notice of proposed rulemaking will not have a significant economic impact on a substantial number of small entities within the meaning of section 601(6) of the Regulatory Flexibility Act (5 U.S.C. chapter 6).

The domestic small business entities that are subject to section 951A and this notice of proposed rulemaking are those domestic small business entities that are U.S. shareholders of a CFC.[2] Generally, a U.S. shareholder is any U.S. person that owns 10 percent or more of a foreign corporation's stock, measured either by value or voting power. A CFC is a foreign corporation in which more than 50 percent of its stock is owned by U.S. shareholders, again measured either by value or voting power. Data about the number of domestic small business entities potentially affected by these regulations are not readily available.

The domestic small business entities that are subject to the requirements of proposed § 1.951A-5(f) or 1.6038-5 of this notice of proposed rulemaking are U.S. shareholders of one or more CFCs. The

[2] The Treasury Department and the IRS estimate that there are 25,000-35,000 respondents of all sizes that are likely to file Schedule I-1, Form 5471. Only a small proportion of these are likely to be small businesses. The Treasury Department and the IRS request comments on the number of small businesses that are likely to file Schedule I-1.

Treasury Department and the IRS do not have data to assess the number of small entities potentially affected by § 1.951A-5(f) or 1.6038-5. However, businesses that are U.S. shareholders of CFCs are generally not small businesses because the ownership of sufficient stock in a CFC in order to be a U.S. shareholder generally entails significant resources and investment. Therefore, the Treasury Department and the IRS do not believe that a substantial number of domestic small business entities will be subject to proposed § 1.951A-5(f) or 1.6038-5. Consequently, the Treasury Department and the IRS do not believe that proposed § 1.951A-5(f) or 1.6038-5 will have a significant economic impact on a substantial number of domestic small business entities. Therefore, a Regulatory Flexibility Analysis under the Regulatory Flexibility Act is not required with respect to the collection of information requirements of proposed § 1.951A-5(f) or 1.6038-5.

Existing § 1.6038-2(a) requires only those U.S. persons with uninterrupted control of a foreign corporation for 30 days or more during the shareholder's annual accounting period to file Form 5471 for that period. Proposed § 1.6038-2(a) eliminates the 30-day holding period as a precondition to reporting and requires every U.S. person that controls a foreign corporation at any time during an annual accounting period to file Form 5471 for that period. As a result, those U.S. shareholders that control a foreign corporation for less than 30 days will now be required to file Form 5471 pursuant to proposed § 1.6038-2(a). The domestic small business entities subject to the requirements of proposed § 1.6038-2(a) are those domestic small business entities that control a foreign corporation at any time during a taxable year. For these purposes, a domestic small business entity controls a foreign corporation by owning more than 50 percent of that foreign corporation's stock, measured either by voting power or value. The Treasury Department and the IRS do not believe that a substantial number of domestic small business entities that are controlling shareholders of a foreign corporation will become Form 5471 filers due to the information collection in proposed § 1.6038-2(a) for the following reasons. First, significant resources and investment are required for a U.S. person to own and operate a business in a foreign country as a corporation. Second, the Treasury Department and the IRS believe that satisfying the stock ownership requirement for control for purposes of proposed § 1.6038-2(a) requires a potential outlay of significant resources and investment, including active involvement in managing the foreign corporation due to controlling ownership of the corporation, such that few domestic small business entities are likely to control foreign corporations for purposes of proposed § 1.6038-2(a). For these reasons, the Treasury Department and the IRS do not believe it likely that a domestic small business entity would have controlling ownership of a foreign corporation for less than a 30-day period in a taxable year. As a result, the Treasury Department and the IRS do not believe that a substantial number of domestic small business entities will be affected by the proposed § 1.6038-2(a) eliminating the 30-day holding period as a precondition to filing Form 5471. Consequently, the Treasury Department and the IRS do not believe that proposed § 1.6038-2(a) will have a significant economic impact on a substantial number of domestic small business entities. Therefore, a Regulatory Flexibility Analysis under the Regulatory Flexibility Act is not required with respect to the requirements of proposed § 1.6038-2(a).

Notwithstanding this certification, the Treasury Department and the IRS invite comments from the public about the impact of this proposed rule on small entities.

Pursuant to section 7805(f), this notice of proposed rulemaking has been submitted to the Chief Counsel for Advocacy of the Small Business Administration for comment on its impact on small businesses. The IRS invites the public to comment on this certification.

E. *Unfunded Mandates Reform Act*

Section 202 of the Unfunded Mandates Reform Act of 1995 requires that agencies assess anticipated costs and benefits and take certain other actions before issuing a final rule that includes any Federal mandate that may result in expenditures in any one year by a state, local, or tribal government, in the aggregate, or by the private sector, of $100 million in 1995 dollars, updated annually for inflation. In 2018, that threshold is approximately $150 million. This rule does not include any Federal mandate that may result in expenditures by state, local, or tribal governments, or by the private sector in excess of that threshold.

F. *Executive Order 13132: Federalism*

Executive Order 13132 (entitled "Federalism") prohibits an agency from publishing any rule that has federalism implications if the rule either imposes substantial, direct compliance costs on state and local governments, and is not required by statute, or preempts state law, unless the agency meets the consultation and funding requirements of section 6 of the Executive Order. This proposed rule does not have federalism implications and does not impose substantial direct compliance costs on state and local governments or preempt state law within the meaning of the Executive Order.

Comments and Requests for Public Hearing

Before the proposed regulations are adopted as final regulations, consideration will be given to any comments that are submitted timely to the IRS as prescribed in this preamble under the "ADDRESSES" heading. The Treasury Department and the IRS request comments on all aspects of the proposed regulations, and specifically on the issues identified in sections I.B.3, I.C.1, I.D.4, I.F, I.G.1, I.G.3, and III.C of the Explanations of Provisions. All comments will be available at *www.regulations.gov* or upon request. A public hearing will be scheduled if requested in writing by any person that timely submits written comments. If a public hearing is scheduled, then notice of the date, time, and place for the public hearing will be published in the **Federal Register**.

Drafting Information

The principal authors of the proposed regulations are Melinda E. Harvey and Michael Kaercher of the Office of Associate Chief Counsel (International) and Austin Diamond-Jones and Kevin M. Jacobs of the Office of Associate Chief Counsel (Corporate). However, other personnel from the IRS and the Treasury Department participated in the development of the proposed regulations.

[¶49,770] Proposed Amendments of Regulations (REG-130244-17), published in the Federal Register on September 24, 2018.

[Code Secs. 385 and 1275]

Section 385 regulations: Debt-equity regulations: Section 385 documentation regulations: Minimum documentation requirements: Related-party transaction: Related-party debt.—Amendments of Reg. §§1.385-1, 1.385-2, 1.385-3 and 1.1275-1, removing final regulations setting forth minimum documentation requirements that ordinarily must be satisfied in order for certain related party interests in a corporation to be treated as indebtedness for federal tax purposes (Documentation Regulations), are proposed.

AGENCY: Internal Revenue Service (IRS), Treasury.

ACTION: Notice of proposed rulemaking.

SUMMARY: This document proposes removing final regulations setting forth minimum documentation requirements that ordinarily must be satisfied in order for certain related-party interests in a corporation to be treated as indebtedness for federal tax purposes (Documentation Regulations). This notice of proposed rulemaking also proposes conforming amendments to other final regulations to reflect the proposed removal of the Documentation Regulations. The final regulations to be amended and removed generally affect corporations that issue purported indebtedness to related corporations or partnerships.

DATES: Written or electronic comments and requests for a public hearing must be received by December 24, 2018.

ADDRESSES: Send submissions to: CC:PA:LPD:PR (REG-130244-17), room 5203, Internal Revenue Service, P.O. Box 7604, Ben Franklin Station, Washington, DC 20044. Submissions may be hand-delivered Monday through Friday between the hours of 8 a.m. and 4 p.m. to CC:PA:LPD:PR (REG-130244-17), Courier's Desk, Internal Revenue Service, 1111 Constitution Avenue NW, Washington, DC 20224 or sent electronically via the Federal eRulemaking Portal at *http://www.regulations.gov* (IRS REG-130244-17).

FOR FURTHER INFORMATION CONTACT: Concerning the proposed removal and amendments, Austin Diamond-Jones, (202) 317-6847; concerning submissions of comments or requests for a public hearing, Regina Johnson, (202) 317-6901 (not toll-free numbers).

SUPPLEMENTARY INFORMATION:

Paperwork Reduction Act

In accordance with the Paperwork Reduction Act (44 U.S.C. chapter 35), the information collection included in these regulations under control number 1545-2267 will be discontinued upon the adoption of a final rule.

Background

Overview

Section 385 of the Internal Revenue Code (Code) authorizes the Secretary of the Treasury (Secretary) to prescribe rules to determine whether an interest in a corporation is treated for purposes of the Code as stock or indebtedness (or as in part stock and in part indebtedness) by setting forth factors to be taken into account with respect to particular factual situations.

On April 8, 2016, the Department of the Treasury (Treasury Department) and the IRS published proposed regulations (REG-108060-15) under section 385 of the Code (proposed regulations) in the **Federal Register** (81 FR 20912 (April 8, 2016)) concerning the treatment of certain interests in corporations as stock or indebtedness. A public hearing on the proposed regulations was held on July 14, 2016. The Treasury Department and the IRS also received numerous written comments in response to the proposed regulations, all of which are available at *http://www.regulations.gov*.

On October 21, 2016, the Treasury Department and the IRS published final and temporary regulations under section 385. TD 9790 (I.R.B. 2016-46, 81 FR 72858 (October 21, 2016)). The preamble to TD 9790 describes in detail the comments received on the proposed regulations and the thorough consideration given to each comment. The preamble to TD 9790 also explains the decisions reached by the Treasury Department and the IRS and the revisions that were made to the proposed regulations.

The final and temporary regulations under section 385 are primarily comprised of (i) the Documentation Regulations, which establish minimum documentation requirements that ordinarily must be satisfied in order for purported debt obligations among related parties to be treated as debt for federal tax purposes; and (ii) rules that treat as stock certain debt that is issued by a corporation to a controlling shareholder in a distribution or in another related-party transaction that achieves an economically similar result (together, the Section 385 Regulations).

Under the proposed regulations, the Documentation Regulations would have been applicable with respect to interests issued or deemed issued on or after the date the regulations were finalized. However, when finalized, the Documentation Regulations were made applicable with respect to interests issued or deemed issued on or after January 1, 2018. See § § 1.385-1(f), 1.385-2(d)(2)(iii), and 1.385-2(i). This delayed applicability date responded to taxpayer concerns of inadequate time to begin complying with the Documentation Regulations once they were finalized

Executive Order 13789

Executive Order 13789, issued on April 21, 2017 (E.O. 13789), instructs the Secretary to review all significant tax regulations issued on or after January 1, 2016, and to take concrete action to alleviate the burdens of regulations that (i) impose an undue financial burden on U.S. taxpayers; (ii) add undue complexity to the federal tax laws; or (iii) exceed the statutory authority of the IRS.

E.O. 13789 further instructs the Secretary to submit to the President within 60 days a report (First Report) that identifies regulations that meet these criteria. Notice 2017-38 (2017-30 I.R.B. 147 (July 24, 2017)) included the Section 385 Regulations in a list of eight regulations identified by the Secretary in the First Report as meeting at least one of the first two criteria specified in E.O. 13789. E.O. 13789 further instructs the Secretary to submit to the President a second report (Second Report) that recommends specific actions to mitigate the burden imposed by regulations identified in the First Report.

Notice 2017-36

As previously noted, the final Documentation Regulations were originally promulgated to be applicable with respect to interests issued or deemed issued on or after January 1, 2018. However, in response to continued taxpayer concern with the application of the Documentation Regulations, and in light of contemplated further actions concerning the Section 385 Regulations in connection with the review of those regulations under E.O. 13789, the Treasury Department and the IRS determined that a further delay in the application of the Documentation Regulations would be appropriate. Accordingly, in Notice 2017-36 (2017-33 I.R.B. 208 (August 14, 2017)), the Treasury Department and the IRS announced the intent to amend the Documentation Regulations to delay the applicability of the regulations for 12 months, making the regulations applicable only to interests issued or deemed issued on or after January 1, 2019.

Comments Received in Connection with E.O. 13789

In response to Notice 2017-38 and Notice 2017-36, the Treasury Department and the IRS received approximately 40 comment letters submitted by professional and trade associations, private businesses, public interest groups, and trade unions, as well as over 68,500 comments submitted by individual taxpayers on *http://www.regulations.gov* (website comments) regarding the Section 385 Regulations. The approximately 40 comment letters reflect a wide range of opinions, advocating everything from strengthening to eliminating the Documentation Regulations. The individual taxpayer comments, however, uniformly urged that the Section 385 Regulations as a whole be retained or strengthened.

1. Supporting retaining or strengthening the Documentation Regulations

At one end of the spectrum are comment letters from various public interest groups, trade unions, and other associations that, together, represent almost 500 organizations, comment letters from private citizens, and the 68,502 website comments. These comments strongly urged that the Section 385 Regulations be retained and enforced, if not strengthened. These commenters would not be subject to the Documentation Regulations. However, they are concerned with the possibility of their withdrawal because they view the Section 385 Regulations as an important tool for maintaining the federal income tax base so that small, domestic businesses and working people and families would not be forced to bear an unfair and disproportionate portion of the cost of U.S. society and infrastructure. Further, these commenters view the Section 385 Regulations as an important step in leveling the playing field for small, domestic businesses that cannot take advantage of earnings stripping tax planning, thus allowing such domestic businesses to compete with large multinational companies based solely on their products and services, and not their ability to take advantage of tax planning. In addition, these commenters argued that allowing large multinational corporations to shift earnings offshore does not create jobs or economic growth in the United States and only serves to disadvantage domestic companies.

2. Supporting limiting or withdrawing the Documentation Regulations

All of the remaining commenters raised concerns about the complexity, cost, and burden imposed by the Documentation Regulations. Most of these commenters made various suggestions for modifications that would reduce the scope and burden of the Documentation Regulations in ways they believed would make the rules more reasonable. Few disputed the Treasury Department's authority to promulgate the Documentation Regulations, however.

Among the commenters that made suggestions for modifications to the Documentation Regulations, there was considerable consensus on the modifications being recommended. Most commenters urged that transactions done in the ordinary course of business, including trade payables, be removed from the application of the Documentation Regulations. Many also urged that "market standards" be broadly adopted as the test for determining whether the documentation requirements are satisfied.

Another common concern raised by these commenters was that the consequences of failing to satisfy the Documentation Regulations are too harsh, and commenters suggested expanding the rules to make it easier to cure or avoid noncompliance and to modify the consequences of noncompliance to make these consequences more proportionate to the concerns addressed by the Documentation Regulations. For example, commenters noted that the time for curing defects in documentation could be expanded, the rules for establishing substantial compliance or reasonable cause could be expanded, and an exception could be added to excuse transactions that pose no base-erosion concern. In addition, there were comments suggesting that the consequences of failing to satisfy the regulations could be limited to a denial of interest deductions, which would avoid the collateral effects of re-characterizing the interest as equity.

Most of these commenters also requested that the application of the Documentation Regulations be delayed so that taxpayers would have adequate time to comply with the Documentation Regulations, taking into account any potential additional modifications. Some suggested delaying applicability for an additional year or two, while others suggested delaying applicability until a date that would presumably allow the effects of any tax reform legislation to be taken into account. But many urged that applicability simply be delayed until the Treasury Department and IRS have completed their review, to avoid the expense of putting systems in place that would not satisfy the Documentation Regulations that are ultimately applicable.

There were also various other modifications suggested. Some modifications would apply to taxpayers generally, such as excluding transactions between commonly held consolidated groups, removing the "reserved" sections, and replacing the entire rule with an anti-abuse rule. Other modifications were specific to the industry of the commenter or its constituents, such as raising the threshold amounts for certain businesses with higher gross asset levels and exempting industries that are perceived as less likely to engage in abusive transactions or more likely to engage in activities that further public policy.

While a number of commenters supported the withdrawal of the Documentation Regulations, most of those commenters were among those also offering suggestions for modifications. However, there were a few commenters that argued only for withdrawal.

Explanation of Provisions

On October 16, 2017, the Secretary published the Second Report in the **Federal Register** (82 FR 48013 (October 16, 2017)) stating that the Treasury Department and the IRS are considering revoking the Documentation Regulations and are actively considering developing and proposing streamlined regulations. After careful consideration of the comments received on the Documentation Regulations in connection with E.O. 13789, including with respect to Notice 2017-36 and Notice 2017-38, this notice of proposed rulemaking proposes the removal of the Documentation Regulations.

The Treasury Department and the IRS will continue to study the issues addressed by the Documentation Regulations. When that study is complete, the Treasury Department and the IRS may propose a modified version of the Documentation Regulations. Any such regulations would be substantially simplified and streamlined to reduce the burden on U.S. corporations and yet would still require sufficient documentation and other information for tax administration purposes. Further, they would be proposed with a prospective effective date to allow sufficient lead-time for taxpayers to design and implement systems to comply with those regulations.

Proposed Effective/Applicability Date

The proposed removal of § 1.385-2 and conforming modifications are proposed to be applicable as of the date of publication in the **Federal Register** of a Treasury decision adopting these proposed regulations as final regulations. However, taxpayers may rely on these proposed regulations, in their entirety, until the date a Treasury decision adopting these regulations as final regulations is published in the **Federal Register**.

Statement of Availability of IRS Documents

IRS Revenue Procedures, Revenue Rulings, Notices, and other guidance cited in this document are published in the Internal Revenue Bulletin (or Cumulative Bulletin) and are available from the Superintendent of Documents, U.S. Government Publishing Office, Washington, DC 20402, or by visiting the IRS Web site at *http://www.irs.gov*.

Special Analyses

I. *Regulatory Planning and Review*

Executive Order 13777 directs agencies to alleviate unnecessary regulatory burdens placed on the American people by managing the costs associated with the governmental imposition of private expenditures required to comply with federal regulations. Executive Orders 13771, 13563, and 12866 direct agencies to prudently manage the cost of planned regulations by assessing costs and benefits of available regulatory alternatives and, if regulation is necessary, to select regulatory approaches that maximize net benefits (including potential economic, environmental, public health and safety effects, distributive impacts, and equity). Executive Order 13563 emphasizes the importance of quantifying both costs and benefits, of reducing costs, of harmonizing rules, and of promoting flexibility.

These proposed regulations have been designated as subject to review under Executive Order 12866 pursuant to the Memorandum of Agreement (April 11, 2018) (the "Treasury-OMB MOA") between the Treasury Department and the Office of Management and Budget regarding review of tax regulations. These proposed regulations have been designated a "significant regulatory action" by OIRA under section 3(f) of Executive Order 12866 because they raise novel policy issues. This proposed rule, when final, is expected to be an Executive Order 13771 deregulatory action.

Pursuant to section 6(a)(3)(B) of Executive Order 12866, the following analysis discusses the anticipated economic effects of these proposed regulations. Although not required by that section, the

Treasury Department and the IRS have generally provided monetized estimates in this analysis. These proposed regulations have been reviewed by the Office of Management and Budget.

A. *Affected population*

This analysis uses an expansive definition of the estimated affected population in order to minimize the risk that the analysis will not capture the effects on collateral groups.

1. *Application to C Corporations*

As discussed in TD 9790, this regulatory action affects approximately 6300 large C corporations out of 1.6 million C corporations and 5.8 million corporations of all types. This is because only C corporations that are part of expanded affiliated groups in which one or more members have sufficient assets ($100 million) or revenue ($50 million), or are publicly traded, would have been required to document the relevant transactions.

2. *Documentation of Intercompany Loans and Compliance*

While there is variation across businesses, longer-term intercompany debt would typically be documented, in some form of agreement containing terms and rights, by corporations following good business practices. However, some information that would have been required by the Documentation Regulations, such as a debt capacity analysis, may not typically be prepared in some cases. If applicable, the Documentation Regulations would not have required that a specific type of credit analysis or documentation be prepared in order to establish a related-party debtor's creditworthiness and ability to repay, but merely would have imposed a standard intended to be closer to commercial practice. To the extent that information supporting such analysis is already prepared in accordance with a company's normal business practice, removal of the Documentation Regulations would have a relatively low compliance cost savings. However, where a business has not typically prepared and maintained written debt instruments, term sheets, cash flow, or debt capacity analyses for intercompany debt, compliance cost savings related to the removal of the Documentation Regulations would have been higher. While the level of documentation required is clearly evident in third-party lending, there is little available information on the extent to which related parties document their intercompany loans. Anecdotal evidence and comments received indicate that businesses vary in the extent to which related-party indebtedness is documented.

B. *Description of the Documentation Regulations*

1. *In General*

If applicable, the Documentation Regulations would have prescribed the nature of the documentation necessary to substantiate the federal income tax treatment of related-party interests as indebtedness, including documentation of factors analogous to those found in third-party loans. This generally means that taxpayers would have had to be able to provide such things as: evidence of an unconditional and binding obligation to make interest and principal payments on certain fixed dates; that the holder of the loan has the rights of a creditor, including superior rights to shareholders in the case of dissolution; a reasonable expectation of the borrower's ability to repay the loan; and evidence of conduct consistent with a debtor-creditor relationship. The Documentation Regulations would have applied to relevant intercompany debt issued by U.S. borrowers beginning in 2019 and would have required that the taxpayer's documentation for a given tax year be prepared by the time the borrower's federal income tax return is filed.

The Documentation Regulations would have applied only to related groups of corporations in which the stock of at least one member is publicly traded or the group's financial results report assets exceeding $100 million or annual revenue exceeding $50 million. Because there is no general definition of a small business under the Code, these asset and revenue limits were designed to exceed the maximum receipts threshold used by the Small Business Administration in defining small businesses (U.S. Small Business Administration, *Table of Small Business Size Standards, 2016*). In addition, these thresholds exclude about 99 percent of C corporation taxpayers while retaining 85 percent of economic activity as measured by total income. Approximately 1.5 million out of 1.6 million C corporation tax filers are single entities and therefore have no affiliates with which to engage in tax arbitrage. The intent was to limit the Documentation Regulations to large businesses with highly-related affiliates, which are responsible for most corporate activity. For example, large foreign-controlled domestic C corporations (FCDCs) (those having assets over $100 million or total income over $50 million) make up 3 percent of FCDCs but report 90 percent of FCDC interest deductions and 93 percent of FCDC total income. Similarly, the Documentation Regulations would have exempted most ordinary course transactions.

C. *Assessment of the Documentation Regulations' effects*

The Treasury Department and the IRS estimate that 6,300 or 0.4 percent of C corporation taxpayers would have been affected by the Documentation Regulations, mainly because 95 percent of taxpayers do not have affiliated corporations, and the regulations would have affected only transactions between affiliates.

While only a small fraction of corporate taxpayers will be affected by the removal of the Documentation Regulations, these 6,300 taxpayers tend to be the largest C corporation tax filers, claiming 65 percent of total interest deductions claimed by C corporations, 53 percent of total income claimed by C corporations, 81 percent of total income subject to tax claimed by C corporations, and 75 percent of total income tax after credits claimed by C corporations. Of these C corporations, approximately one-third are FCDCs that report about 20 percent of the affected total income and 20 percent of the affected interest deductions.

1. *Monetized Estimates*

The revenue and compliance burden effects are measured against a no-action baseline, which captures tax-related behavior in the absence of the proposed regulatory action and includes taxpayer behavior the Treasury Department and the IRS expect as a result of the enactment of P.L. 115-97 (TCJA). While this particular regulation does not implement TCJA requirements, it interacts with the TCJA. There are several provisions of the TCJA that reduced the tax advantages of Foreign Controlled Domestic Corporations (FCDCs) over domestically controlled companies (DCCs) and thus may affect the tax revenue and compliance burden consequences of the removal of the Documentation Regulations. First, for taxable years beginning after December 31, 2017, the TCJA reduced the statutory corporate tax rate from 35 percent to 21 percent, which lowers the effective tax rate for DCCs more than for FCDCs. Second, the ability of FCDCs to strip earnings out of the United States using deductions for interest expense was significantly reduced by the TCJA through amendments to section 163(j) of the Code. Specifically, the section 163(j) statutory amendments (1) eliminated the debt-equity ratio safe harbor, (2) reduced the maximum net interest deductions' share of adjusted taxable income from 50 percent to 30 percent, (3) limited all, rather than just related-party, interest deductions, and (4) eliminated the carryforward of excess limitation under pre-TCJA section 163(j). The TCJA's Base Erosion Anti-abuse Tax (BEAT) further reduces this ability. Thus, the benefits of the Documentation Regulations in reducing foreign acquisitions of U.S. assets and interest stripping were reduced by the TCJA.

The vast majority of TCJA provisions are self-executing, which means that they are binding on taxpayers and the IRS without any regulatory action and therefore their applicability and potential taxpayers' responses to such applicability are assumed in the baseline. The Treasury Department and the IRS recognize, however, that the section 163(j) amendments and the BEAT, along with other TCJA provisions, while self-executing, provide interpretive latitude for taxpayers and the IRS and that, without further implementation guidance, those provisions could prompt a variety of potential taxpayer responses. Faced with ambiguous tax provisions that are susceptible to a range of reasonable interpretations, some taxpayers will take conservative filing positions, others will take aggressive filing positions, and still others will simply forego business activity that implicates any uncertain provisions. Accordingly, the Treasury Department and the IRS have included in the baseline their best assessment of taxpayer behavior under current law and regulatory guidance; the baseline does not assume regulatory guidance that has not yet been issued. To the extent that taxpayer responses to any future legislation or rules regarding section 163(j) or the BEAT differ from this assessment, the revenue and compliance burden estimates with respect to the proposed removal of the Documentation Regulations would also be affected.

The Treasury Department and the IRS solicit comments on the revenue and compliance burden estimates with respect to the proposed removal of the Documentation Regulations.

a. *Revenue effects of proposed regulations*

The Treasury Department and the IRS previously addressed revenue effects in the original regulatory impact analysis (RIA) published in the preamble to T.D. 9790 and have received comments that address the revenue effect of the Documentation Regulations. The removal of the Documentation Regulations may slightly increase the ability of some firms to strip earnings out of the United States and so reduce their tax payments. The Treasury Department and the IRS estimate that removal of the Documentation Regulations will reduce revenue by $407 million over the period 2019-2028, using standard revenue reporting conventions (undiscounted nominal total). The net present value of the revenue loss is $302 and $243 ($2018 millions) using real discount rates of 3 and 7 percent, respectively. The annualized amounts are $35.4 and $34.5 ($2018 millions), again based on 3 percent and 7 percent real rates respectively. The revenue effects were estimated using the methodology described in the original RIA published in the preamble to T.D. 9790, although the estimate now covers 2019 to 2028 and includes factors that have changed as a result of TCJA as well as other technical adjustments.

Annualized discounted revenue effects are shown in the following table.

	Fiscal Years 2019 to 2028 (3% real discount rate)	Fiscal Years 2019 to 2028 (7% real discount rate)
Estimated change in annual tax revenue (annualized value, $2018 millions)	-$35.4	-$34.5

b. *Compliance burden effects from proposed regulations*

The Treasury Department and the IRS estimate that removal of the Documentation Regulations will reduce compliance costs by $924 million over the period 2019-2028 (undiscounted nominal total). The net present value of the compliance cost savings is $773 and $685 ($2018 millions) using real discount rates of 3 and 7 percent respectively. These amounts are $90.6 million and $97.5 million on an annualized basis, again based on 3 percent and 7 percent real rates respectively. The methodology for estimating the compliance cost savings also followed the methodology described in the original RIA published in the preamble to T.D. 9790, with analogous adjustments due to the change in the period covered, the effects of TCJA, and other technical adjustments. The Treasury Department and the IRS view the proposed action (removal of § 1.385-2) as reducing both tax revenues and compliance costs but they view the TCJA as primarily affecting the reduction in tax revenue from the action due mainly to reduced allowable interest deductions (163(j)) and to a lesser extent, taxation of certain base eroding payments to related parties (BEAT), including interest. The Treasury Department and the IRS do not expect a significant reduction in the number of relevant related party transactions, only a reduction in the dollar amounts, and therefore see a smaller effect of the TCJA on compliance cost savings than on revenue losses, relative to previous estimates.

In addition, the analysis includes a sensitivity analysis in which the compliance costs were estimated for a 90 percent interval around the central estimate. Annualized discounted ongoing and start-up changes in compliance costs ($2018 millions) are shown in the following table.

Estimated change in annual compliance costs (annualized value, $2018 millions)	Fiscal Years 2019 to 2028 (3% real discount rate)	Fiscal Years 2019 to 2028 (7% real discount rate,)
Central estimate	-$90.6	-$97.5
High estimate	-$113.3	-$121.9
Low estimate	-$68.0	-$73.1

Technical note: In this rulemaking, the Treasury Department made technical adjustments relative to the 2016 rulemaking in calculating the annualized compliance cost estimates. The cost stream in this rulemaking is in 2018 dollars, reflects a two-year delay in effective date (relative to the previous estimates), and applies real discount rates of 3 and 7 percent. Technical adjustments account for part of the difference in the estimates between the rulemakings.

2. *Non-Monetized Effects*

a. *Reduced Tax Compliance*

By slightly increasing the ability of some taxpayers to strip earnings out of the United States through transactions with no meaningful economic or non-tax benefit, and so reducing their tax payments, removal of the Documentation Regulations is likely to slightly reduce the overall perceived legitimacy of the U.S. tax system, and hence reduce voluntary compliance.

b. *Efficiency and growth effects*

By changing the treatment of certain transactions and activities, removal of the Documentation Regulations potentially affects economic efficiency and growth (output). While the removal of the Documentation Regulations may have multiple and to some extent offsetting effects, on net they are likely to slightly reduce economic efficiency. For example, the removal of the Documentation Regulations will likely increase the tax advantage foreign owners have over domestic owners of U.S. assets, and consequently will increase the propensity for foreign acquisitions and ownership of U.S. assets that are motivated by tax considerations rather than economic substance. While these effects will likely be small, they likely reduce efficiency and growth. By increasing the ability to undertake tax-motivated acquisitions or ownership structures, removal of the Documentation Regulations may slightly reduce the incentive for assets to be owned or managed by those most capable of putting the assets to their highest-valued use. Moreover, removal of the Documentation Regulations may put purely domestic U.S. firms on less even tax footing than their foreign-owned competitors operating in the United States. On the other hand, removal of the Documentation Regulations may slightly reduce the effective tax rate and compliance costs on U.S. inbound investment. While the magnitude of this reduction is small, to the extent that it increases new capital investment in the United States, its effects would be efficiency and growth enhancing. Most inbound investment is via acquisition of existing U.S. companies rather than greenfield (new) investment in the United States, however, and thus such investment changes the ownership of existing assets, without necessarily adding to the stock of capital employed in the United States. On balance, the likely effect of the removal of the Documentation Regulations is to reduce the efficiency of the corporate tax system slightly.

c. *Higher Tax Administrative Costs for the IRS.*

The reduced loan documentation required of large corporations as a result of the removal of the Documentation Regulations will reduce the ability of the IRS to more effectively administer the tax laws by making it harder for the IRS to evaluate whether purported debt transactions are legitimate loans. This will raise the cost of auditing and evaluating the tax returns of companies engaged in these transactions.

II. *Regulatory Flexibility Act*

Pursuant to the Regulatory Flexibility Act (5 U.S.C. Chapter 6), it is hereby certified that the proposed regulations will not have a significant economic impact on a substantial number of small entities.

As discussed earlier in this preamble, on October 21, 2016, the Treasury Department and the IRS published final and temporary regulations under section 385. The final and temporary regulations under section 385, among other things, established minimum documentation requirements that must be satisfied in order for purported debt obligations among related parties to be treated as debt for federal tax purposes. When finalized in October 2016, the Documentation Regulations were made applicable with respect to interests issued or deemed issued on or after January 1, 2018. In response to continued taxpayer concern with the application of the Documentation Regulations, the Treasury

Department and the IRS, in Notice 2017-36, further delayed the applicability of the regulations by making the regulations applicable only to interests issued or deemed issued on or after January 1, 2019. This proposed rule, if finalized, would remove these Documentation Regulations that have not yet been made applicable to any interests issued by any taxpayer.

Section 1.385-2, if applicable, would have provided documentation requirements to substantiate the treatment of certain related party instruments as indebtedness. Section 1.385-2 would have applied to large corporate groups (specifically, those that are publically traded, or have assets exceeding $100 million or annual total revenue exceeding $50 million in its expanded group), thus limiting the scope of small entities affected. Section 1.385-2 would have applied to financial institutions, which are considered small entities under the Regulatory Flexibility Act if they have less than $550 million in assets (13 CFR 121). The Treasury Department and the IRS believe that § 1.385-2 would not affect a substantial number of small entities other than small financial institutions. Even if the regulations affected a substantial number of small entities in that sector, the economic impact of this rule would be minimal because the proposed regulations would remove the currently inapplicable documentation requirements in § 1.385-2. Accordingly, a regulatory flexibility analysis is not required.

Pursuant to section 7805(f), this notice of proposed rulemaking has been submitted to the Chief Counsel for Advocacy of the Small Business Administration for comment on its impact on small business.

Unfunded Mandates Reform Act

Section 202 of the Unfunded Mandates Reform Act of 1995 (UMRA) requires that agencies assess anticipated costs and benefits and take certain other actions before issuing a final rule that includes any federal mandate that may result in expenditures in any one year by a state, local, or tribal government, in the aggregate, or by the private sector, of $100 million in 1995 dollars, updated annually for inflation. In 2018, that threshold is approximately $150 million. This proposed rule does not include any mandate that may result in expenditures by state, local, or tribal governments, or by the private sector in excess of that threshold.

Executive Order 13132: Federalism

Executive Order 13132 (entitled "Federalism") prohibits an agency from publishing any rule that has federalism implications if the rule either imposes substantial, direct compliance costs on state and local governments, and is not required by statute, or preempts state law, unless the agency meets the consultation and funding requirements of section 6 of the Executive Order. This proposed rule does not have federalism implications and does not impose substantial direct compliance costs on state and local governments or preempt state law within the meaning of the Executive Order.

Comments and Requests for Public Hearing

Before these proposed regulations are adopted as final regulations, consideration will be given to any comments that are submitted timely to the IRS as prescribed in this preamble under the ADDRESSES heading. All comments will be available at *http://www.regulations.gov* or upon request. A public hearing will be scheduled if requested in writing by any person that timely submits written comments. If a public hearing is scheduled, notice of the date, time, and place of the public hearing will be published in the **Federal Register**.

Drafting Information

The principal author of this notice of proposed rulemaking is Austin Diamond-Jones of the Office of the Associate Chief Counsel (Corporate). However, other personnel from the Treasury Department and the IRS participated in its development.

[¶ 49,771] Proposed Amendments of Regulations (REG-104872-18), published in the Federal Register on October 15, 2018.

[Code Secs. 381, 382, 451, 861, 6655]

Advance payments for goods: Long-term contracts: Gross income: Accrual method.—Amendments of Reg. § 1.381(c)(4)-1, Reg. § 1.382-7, Reg. § 1.451-5, Reg. § 1.861-18, Reg. § 1.6655-0, Reg. § 1.6655-2 and Reg. § 1.6655-6, removing regulations that are no longer necessary after the enactment of recent tax legislation, are proposed.

AGENCY: Internal Revenue Service (IRS), Treasury.

ACTION: Notice of proposed rulemaking.

SUMMARY: This notice of proposed rulemaking proposes to streamline IRS regulations by removing regulations that are no longer necessary after the enactment of recent tax legislation. Specifically, these regulations would remove existing regulations regarding advance payments for goods and long-term contracts. The regulations would affect accrual method taxpayers who receive advance payments for goods, including those for inventoriable goods.

DATES: Written or electronic comments and requests for a public hearing must be received by January 14, 2019.

ADDRESSES: Send submissions to: CC:PA: LPD:PR (REG-104872-18), Room 5205, Internal Revenue Service, P.O. Box 7604, Ben Franklin Station, Washington, DC 20044. Submissions may be hand-delivered Monday through Friday between the hours of 8 a.m. and 4 p.m. to CC:PA:LPD:PR (REG-104872-18), Courier's Desk, Internal Revenue Service, 1111 Constitution Avenue, N.W., Washington, DC, or sent electronically, via the Federal eRulemaking Portal at *www.regulations.gov* (IRS REG-104872-18).

FOR FURTHER INFORMATION CONTACT: Concerning the proposed regulations, Charles Gorham, (202) 317-5091, or Joanna L. Trebat, (202) 317-6890; concerning submissions of comments and requests for a hearing, Regina Johnson, (202) 317-6901 (not toll-free numbers).

SUPPLEMENTARY INFORMATION:

Background and Explanation of Provisions

This document proposes to remove § 1.451-5 of the Income Tax Regulations (26 CFR part 1), and its cross-references, relating to the treatment of advance payments for goods and long-term contracts under section 451 of the Internal Revenue Code (Code).

In general, section 451 provides that the amount of any item of gross income is included in gross income for the taxable year in which it is received by the taxpayer, unless, under the method of accounting used in computing taxable income, the amount is to be properly accounted for as of a different period.

Under § 1.451-1, accrual method taxpayers generally include items of income in the taxable year when all the events have occurred that fix the right to receive the income and the amount of the income can be determined with reasonable accuracy (the "all events" test).

Section 1.451-5 generally allows accrual method taxpayers to defer the inclusion of income for advance payments for goods until the taxable year in which they are properly included in income under the taxpayer's method of accounting for federal income tax purposes if that method results in the advance payments being included in gross income no later than when the advance payments are recognized in gross receipts under the taxpayer's method of accounting for financial reporting purposes.

Section 13221 of "An Act to provide for reconciliation pursuant to titles II and V of the concurrent resolution on the budget for fiscal year 2018," Public Law 115-97 (the "Act"), amended section 451 by redesignating section 451(b) through (i) as (d) through (k) and adding new subsections (b) and (c).

New section 451(b) generally requires that for accrual method taxpayers the all events test with respect to a particular item of gross income must not be treated as met any later than when the item is taken into account as revenue in a taxpayer's applicable financial statement, or such other financial statement as the Secretary may prescribe.

New section 451(c) generally requires an accrual method taxpayer that receives any advance payment described in section 451(c)(4) during the taxable year to include the advance payment in income in the taxable year of receipt or make an election to: (1) include any portion of the advance payment in income in the taxable year of receipt to the extent required under new section 451(b); and (2) include the remaining portion of the advance payment in income in the following taxable year. The election to defer advance payments of goods and services under new section 451(c) is similar to the rules regarding the treatment of advance payments for goods, services, and other specified items provided in Revenue Procedure 2004-34, 2004-1 CB 991. *See* H.R. Rep. No. 115-466, at 429 (2017) (Conf. Rep.).

New section 451(c) and its election to defer advance payments override the deferral method provided by § 1.451-5. *See* H.R. Rep. No. 115-466, at 429 n.880 (2017) (Conf. Rep.). Accordingly, the Treasury Department and the IRS propose to remove § 1.451-5 and its cross references. Removing § 1.451-5 also will ensure that the new deferral rules of section 451(c) apply uniformly and consistently to all taxpayers as well as simplify tax administration.

The rules of section 446 regarding changes in methods of accounting will apply to taxpayers changing a method of accounting for advance payments from a method described in § 1.451-5 to another method. The Treasury Department and the IRS request comments on whether any changes to existing procedural rules under section 446 for changes in methods of accounting are necessary or desirable as a result of removing § 1.451-5.

Proposed Applicability Date

The removal of these regulations would apply as of the date the Treasury decision adopting this notice of proposed rulemaking is published in the **Federal Register**.

Special Analyses

This regulation is not subject to review under section 6(b) of Executive Order 12866 pursuant to the Memorandum of Agreement (April 11, 2018) between the Department of the Treasury and the Office of Management and Budget regarding review of tax regulations. Because the proposed regulations do not impose a collection of information on small entities, the Regulatory Flexibility Act (5 U.S.C. chapter 6) does not apply. Pursuant to section 7805(f) of the Code, this notice of proposed rulemaking has been submitted to the Chief Counsel for Advocacy of the Small Business Administration for comment on its impact on small business.

Comments and Requests for a Public Hearing

Before these proposed regulations are adopted as final regulations, consideration will be given to any comments that are timely submitted to the IRS in the preamble under the "ADDRESSES" section. All comments submitted will be made available at www.regulations.gov for public inspection and copying.

A public hearing will be scheduled, if requested, by any person who timely submits comments. If a public hearing is scheduled, notice of the date, time, and place for the hearing will be published in the **Federal Register**.

Drafting Information

The principal author of this document is Joanna L. Trebat, Office of the Associate Chief Counsel (Income Tax and Accounting). Other personnel from the IRS and Treasury Department participated in its development.

[¶49,772] Proposed Amendments of Regulations (REG-118826-16), published in the Federal Register on October 17, 2018.

[Code Secs. 6045, 6721, 6722 and 6724]

Safe harbor exceptions: Information returns: Penalties: Payee statements.—Amendments of Reg. §§1.6045-1, 301.6721-0, 301.6721-1, 301.6722-1 and 301.6724-1, relating to penalties for failure to file correct information returns or furnish correct payee statements, are proposed.

AGENCY: Internal Revenue Service (IRS), Treasury.

ACTION: Notice of proposed rulemaking.

SUMMARY: This document contains proposed regulations relating to penalties for failure to file correct information returns or furnish correct payee statements. The proposed regulations contain safe harbor rules that, for penalty purposes, generally treat as correct payee statements or corresponding information returns that contain errors relating to de minimis incorrect dollar amounts. They prescribe the time and manner in which a payee may elect not to have the safe harbor rules apply. They also update penalty amounts and update references to information reporting obligations. Finally, they provide rules relating to the reporting of basis of securities by brokers as this reporting relates to the de minimis error safe harbor rules. The proposed regulations affect persons required to either file information returns or to furnish payee statements (filers), and recipients of payee statements (payees).

DATES: Written or electronic comments and requests for a public hearing must be received by December 14, 2018.

ADDRESSES: Send submissions to: CC:PA:LPD:PR (REG-118826-16), Room 5203, Internal Revenue Service, P.O. Box 7604, Ben Franklin Station, Washington, DC 20044. Submissions may be hand-delivered between the hours of 8 a.m. and 4 p.m. to CC:PA:LPD:PR (REG-118826-16), Courier's Desk, Internal Revenue Service, 1111 Constitution Avenue NW., Washington, DC, or sent via the Federal eRulemaking Portal at *www.regulations.gov* (REG-118826-16).

FOR FURTHER INFORMATION CONTACT: Concerning the proposed regulations Mark A. Bond of the Office of Associate Chief Counsel (Procedure and Administration), (202) 317-6844; concerning the submission of comments and a request for a public hearing, Regina L. Johnson, (202) 317-6901 (not toll-free numbers).

SUPPLEMENTARY INFORMATION:

Paperwork Reduction Act

The collection of information contained in this notice of proposed rulemaking has been submitted to the Office of Management and Budget for review in accordance with the Paperwork Reduction Act of 1995 (44 U.S.C. 3507(d)). Comments on the collection of information should be sent to the Office of Management and Budget, Attn: Desk Officer for the Department of the Treasury, Office of Information and Regulatory Affairs, Washington, DC 20503, with copies to the Internal Revenue Service, Attn: IRS Reports Clearance Officer, SE:CAR:MP:T:T:SP, Washington, DC 20224. Comments on the collection of information should be received by December 14, 2018. Comments are specifically requested concerning:

Whether the proposed collection of information is necessary for the proper performance of the Internal Revenue Service, including whether the information will have practical utility;

The accuracy of the estimated burden associated with the proposed collection of information (see below);

How the quality, utility, and clarity of the information to be collected may be enhanced;

How the burden of complying with the proposed collection of information may be minimized, including through the application of automated collection techniques or other forms of information technology; and

Estimates of capital or start-up costs and costs of operation, maintenance, and purchase of service to provide information.

The collection of information in these proposed regulations is in proposed regulations §§301.6722-1(d)(3)(iii) regarding the payee election, 301.6722-1(d)(3)(v)(B) regarding the filer notification, 301.6722-1(d)(3)(vii) regarding the payee revocation, and 301.6722-1(d)(4) regarding record retention. The information in proposed regulations §§301.6722-1(d)(3)(iii) and 301.6722-1(d)(3)(vii) will be used by payees to make and revoke elections and by filers to determine whether they are required to furnish corrected payee statements to payees and file corrected information returns with the IRS to avoid application of penalties under sections 6721 and 6722. The information under proposed regulation §301.6722-1(d)(3)(v)(B) will be used to give filers and payees flexibility in establishing reasonable alternative manners for elections. And the information in proposed regulation §301.6722-1(d)(4) will be used by the IRS to determine whether filers are subject to penalties under sections 6721 and 6722. The collection of information in proposed regulations §§301.6722-1(d)(3)(iii) regarding the payee election, 301.6722-1(d)(3)(v)(B) regarding the filer notification, and 301.6722-1(d)(3)(vii) regarding the payee revocation is voluntary to obtain a benefit. The collection of information in proposed regulation § 301.6722-1(d)(4) regarding record retention is mandatory. The likely respondents are individuals, state or local governments, farms, business or other for-profit institutions, nonprofit institutions, and small businesses or organizations.

Estimated total annual reporting burden: 992,102 hours.

Estimated average annual burden hours per respondent: approximately 0.10 hours.

Estimated number of respondents: 10,057,746.

Estimated annual frequency of responses: 16,123,292.

An agency may not conduct or sponsor, and a person is not required to respond to, a collection of information unless it displays a valid control number assigned by the Office of Management and Budget.

Books or records relating to a collection of information must be retained as long as their contents may become material in the administration of any internal revenue law. Generally, tax returns and tax return information are confidential, as required by 26 U.S.C. 6103.

Background

This document contains proposed amendments to the Income Tax Regulations (26 CFR part 1) under section 6045(g) of the Internal Revenue Code (Code) relating to returns of brokers in the case of securities transactions, as well as proposed amendments to the Procedure and Administration Regulations (26 CFR part 301) under section 6721(c)(3) relating to the safe harbor exception for certain de minimis errors from the penalty for failure to file correct information returns, section 6722(c)(3) relating to the safe harbor exception for certain de minimis errors from the penalty for failure to furnish correct payee statements, and section 6724 relating to the reasonable cause waiver to the section 6721 and section 6722 penalties. It also contains proposed amendments to the regulations under sections 6721, 6722, and 6724 to update penalty amounts and references to specific information reporting obligations.

Section 6045 provides for information reporting by persons doing business as brokers. Section 6045(g) provides for specific rules in the case of reporting of securities transactions, including for the reporting of basis amounts.

Section 6721 imposes a penalty when a person fails to file an information return on or before the prescribed date, fails to include all of the information required to be shown on the information return, or includes incorrect information on the information return. Section 6722 imposes a penalty when a person fails to furnish a payee statement on or before the prescribed date, fails to include all of the information required to be shown on the payee statement, or includes incorrect information on the payee statement. Section 6724 provides definitions, special rules, and a reasonable cause waiver from penalties for a failure relating to an information reporting requirement.

PATH Act Amendments

Section 202(a) of the Protecting Americans from Tax Hikes Act of 2015, Public Law 114-113 (129 Stat. 2242, 3077 (2015)) (PATH Act), added section 6721(c)(3), effective for information returns required to be filed after December 31, 2016. Section 202(b) of the PATH Act added section 6722(c)(3), effective for payee statements required to be furnished after December 31, 2016. Section 202(c) of the PATH Act added section 6045(g)(2)(B)(iii), effective for information returns required to be filed, and payee statements required to be furnished, after December 31, 2016.

Sections 6721(c)(3)(A) and 6722(c)(3)(A) provide that an information return or payee statement that includes one or more de minimis errors in a dollar amount appearing on the information return or payee statement shall be treated as correct for penalty purposes. An error in a dollar amount is de minimis if the difference between any single amount in error and the correct amount does not exceed $100 and, if the difference is with respect to an amount of tax withheld, the difference is not more than $25.

Under section 6722(c)(3)(B), the safe harbor exception does not apply to any payee statement when the person to whom the payee statement is required to be furnished (that is, the payee) makes an election, at the time and in the manner as the Secretary may prescribe, that the safe harbor exception not apply with respect to such statement. Under section 6721(c)(3)(B), an election by the payee with respect to a payee statement operates to make the safe harbor exception for de minimis errors inapplicable to errors on the corresponding information return.

Sections 6721(c)(3)(C) and 6722(c)(3)(C) provide that the Secretary may issue regulations to prevent the abuse of the safe harbor exceptions, including regulations providing that the safe harbor exceptions shall not apply to the extent necessary to prevent abuse.

Section 6045(g)(2)(B)(iii) provides that except as otherwise provided by the Secretary, a customer's adjusted basis for purposes of section 6045 shall be determined by treating any incorrect dollar amount which is not required to be corrected by reason of section 6721(c)(3) or section 6722(c)(3) as the correct amount.

Other Statutory Amendments

Section 1211(b)(2) of the Pension Protection Act of 2006, Public Law 109-280 (120 Stat. 780, 1073 (2006)), added section 6721(e)(2)(D), providing for calculation of the section 6721 penalty for failures due to intentional disregard in the case of a return required to be filed under section 6050V, effective for acquisitions of contracts after August 17, 2006.

Section 2102 of the Creating Small Business Jobs Act of 2010, Public Law 111-240 (124 Stat. 2504, 2561-64 (2010)), increased penalty amounts throughout sections 6721 and 6722 for information returns required to be filed and payee statements required to be furnished on or after January 1, 2011.

Section 208 of the Tax Increase Prevention Act of 2014, Public Law 113-295 (128 Stat. 4010, 4074 (2014)), amended sections 6721(f)(1) and 6722(f)(1) effective for information returns required to be filed and payee statements required to be furnished after December 31, 2014. The amended paragraphs provide for annual inflationary adjustments to the section 6721 and section 6722 penalties.

Section 806 of the Trade Preferences Extension Act of 2015, Public Law 114-27 (129 Stat. 362, 416-18 (2015)), increased the penalty amounts throughout sections 6721 and 6722, effective for returns required to be filed and statements required to be furnished after December 31, 2015.

Section 6724 and the regulations thereunder define the terms "information return" and "payee statement" and provide that the penalties under sections 6721 and 6722 will not be imposed with respect to any failure if it is shown that the failure was due to reasonable cause and not to willful neglect.

Section 2004 of the Surface Transportation and Veterans Health Care Choice Improvement Act of 2015, Public Law 114-41 (129 Stat. 443, 454-55 (2015)), amended section 6724(d)(1) and 6724(d)(2) to add information reporting under section 6035, relating to basis information with respect to property acquired from decedents, to the definitions of information return and payee statement, respectively.

Section 13520(c) of An Act to provide for reconciliation pursuant to titles II and V of the concurrent resolution on the budget for fiscal year 2018, Public Law 115-97 (131 Stat. 2054, 2150 (2017)) (Pub. L. 115-97), amended section 6724(d)(1) and 6724(d)(2) to add information reporting under section 6050Y, regarding returns relating to certain life insurance contract transactions, to the definitions of information return and payee statement, respectively.

Section 206(o) of the Consolidated Appropriations Act of 2018, Public Law 115-141 (132 Stat. 348, 1182 (2018)), amended section 6724(d)(2) to add information reporting under section 6226(a)(2) (regarding statements relating to alternative to payment of imputed underpayment by a partnership) or under any other provision of Title 26 which provides for the application of rules similar to section 6226(a)(2), to the definition of payee statement.

Notice 2017-09, 2017-4 I.R.B. 542, and Comments in Response to the Notice

On January 4, 2017, the Treasury Department and the IRS released Notice 2017-09, 2017-4 I.R.B. 542, "De Minimis Error Safe Harbor to the I.R.C. §§6721 and 6722 Penalties," to provide guidance regarding the de minimis error safe harbor exceptions from information reporting penalties under sections 6721 and 6722. The notice provided requirements for the payee election under section 6722(c)(3)(B), including the time and manner for making the election. The notice clarified that the de minimis error safe harbor exceptions do not apply in the case of an intentional error or if a filer fails to file an information return or furnish a payee statement. The notice required filers to retain certain records. The notice announced the intention of the Treasury Department and the IRS to issue regulations with respect to the de minimis error safe harbor exceptions and the payee election to have the safe harbor exceptions not apply, and stated that to the extent the regulations incorporate the rules contained in the notice, the regulations will be effective for returns required to be filed, and payee statements required to be furnished, after December 31, 2016. The notice solicited comments regarding the rules contained in the notice and regarding any potential abuse of the de minimis error safe harbor exceptions. In response to the notice, the Treasury Department and IRS received 11 comments. The Treasury Department and IRS have considered all of the comments and addressed them in this preamble.

One comment in response to the notice focused on the administrative burden of the election process provided for by Notice 2017-09 and requested that the IRS consider this burden. The comment stated that the framework in Notice 2017-09 misses Congressional intent to reduce the burden of increased penalties as a result of the Trade Preferences Extension Act of 2015 and the costs of correcting information returns for de minimis amounts. Additionally, the comment stated that it could not envision a single reason an individual, financial institution, or the IRS would want a corrected information return issued for a de minimis amount. Congress determined that there was a need for the payee election; therefore, the Treasury Department and the IRS do not propose to deny payees the ability to elect to have a corrected information return filed and payee statement furnished when an error is de minimis, in particular, prior to the issuance of regulations providing the time and manner for how such an election is to be made. The Treasury Department and the IRS have determined that potential administrative burden on filers is one, but not the only, factor that must be considered in implementing these provisions.

The comment requested that the concept of de minimis and the minor dollar amounts subject to the payee election be weighed against the cost and complexity of instituting and monitoring the payee election process described in Notice 2017-09. It stated that a way to ensure reasonability is to integrate the payee election process into existing procedures, systems, and data structures. The Treasury Department and the IRS acknowledge the potential administrative burden on filers inherent to any new rules; however, the Treasury Department and the IRS note that filers are free to integrate the payee election process allowed by the proposed regulations within existing procedures, systems, and data structures. Further, the Treasury Department and the IRS have determined that potential administrative burden on filers is one, but not the only, factor that must be considered in implementing these provisions and that the need to provide an effective framework for payees to make the payee election is an additional factor that must be considered.

The comment further stated that the best framework to satisfy Congressional intent would be one in which a filer could alert a payee at account opening, or on a one-time basis for currently opened accounts, to the fact that the filer will not issue a corrected statement for any errors that fall within the de minimis error limits of $100 and $25. Under the comment's proposal, the notice would specify that the payee could elect to receive corrected payee statements by making an election in a manner prescribed by the filer. The Treasury Department and the IRS note that proposed regulation § 301.6722-1(d)(3)(v) incorporates rules similar to this proposal by providing the option for filers to give notification to every payee to whom the filer furnishes a payee statement of the payee's ability to elect that the safe harbor exception for de minimis errors not apply and by providing the payee reasonable alternative options to make the election, such as by telephone or through a web site. Proposed regulation § 301.6722-1(d)(3)(v)(D)(2) provides that in cases where valid notification has been provided with respect to a particular account, no further notification is required unless the filer wishes to change the reasonable alternative manner. This rule balances the need for payees to have up-to-date information of any reasonable alternative manners proposed by each filer furnishing statements to the payee with the administrative costs to filers who opt to provide notifications.

The comment stated that the payee election should be on an annual basis, applied only to transactions reportable in the year the election is made. Because this suggestion would place considerable burden on payees to make annual elections, either as a precautionary measure or after monitoring payee statements for accuracy, proposed regulation § 301.6722-1(d)(3)(ii) adopts a different rule, providing that the election shall remain in effect until revoked. This rule allows payees to elect to receive corrections whenever they may become necessary, regardless of whether it is the payee or the filer who becomes aware of the de minimis error. In general, the filer will be best positioned to first become aware of any de minimis error. An election with indefinite effect obviates the need for payees to make annual cautionary elections, in case there is an error of which they are not aware.

The comment also stated that an election without the specific account number associated with it should not be valid and that the election should not include the payee's taxpayer identification number (TIN) and address information. The comment raised the issue of fraudulent activity through identity theft, but the comment did not provide details regarding how providing TIN and address information in a payee election raises identify theft concerns. The Treasury Department and the IRS recognize that in some instances the provision of an account number will be expedient for filers, but also recognize that payees, particularly those who have had accounts for extended periods, may not have ready access to their full account numbers. Further, the provision of a payee's TIN and address information ensures that filers will have at their disposal information reasonably sufficient to identify the payee that is making the payee election. Proposed regulation § 301.6722-1(d)(3)(iii) therefore provides that as a default rule a filer shall treat an election as valid regardless of whether the payee provides an account number, and it requires the payee's TIN and address information.

Proposed regulation § 301.6722-1(d)(3)(v), however, also provides that if the filer provides notification to the payee under proposed regulation § 301.6722-1(d)(3)(v)(B), the filer may specify that an election using a reasonable alternative manner under proposed regulation § 301.6722-1(d)(3)(v) need not include the payee's TIN and address information, and must include the payee's account information. These rules would apply only if the payee decides to make use of the alternative election manner proposed by the filer under proposed regulation § 301.6722-1(d)(3)(v) and not the default election manner under proposed regulation § 301.6722-1(d)(3)(iii). The proposed rules thus generally provide for flexibility for filers who choose to send notifications to payees, while maintaining a simple default election option for payees.

The comment also proposed that an election relating to a specific account should apply to all payee statements or to no payee statements in that account. It focused on the burden to filers of elections applied on a statement-by-statement basis, and the potential that an election might apply to payee statements made in composite form. Additionally, the comment requested that the IRS provide some of the reasons it expects a taxpayer will request corrected returns in the de minimis error context on a statement-by-statement basis. The comment's suggested rule is inconsistent with the statutory framework of sections 6721 through 6724, which applies generally on a per statement basis. Section 6722(c)(3)(A) prescribes the de minimis error safe harbor exception "with respect to any payee statement." Additionally, the comment's proposal would significantly limit payees' options for making elections. Further, the Treasury Department and the IRS note that the Code permits filers to provide corrected statements regardless of the de minimis error safe harbor exceptions or payee election. Thus, filers may provide corrections on an account-wide basis once a payee makes an election with respect to a single type of payee statement associated with that account. For example, if a payee submits an election to a filer with respect to the Form 1099-DIV, "Dividends and Distributions," that the filer is required to furnish to the payee, the filer is required under sections 6721(c)(3) and 6722(c)(3) and these proposed regulations to issue corrections even for de minimis errors. Under the proposed regulations, if the filer is also required to furnish a Form 1099-B, "Proceeds From Broker and Barter Exchange Transactions," to the payee, and the payee specifically made the payee's election with respect to the Form 1099-DIV (and not the Form 1099-B), the election under proposed regulation § 301.6722-1(d)(3)(i) does not apply with respect to the Form 1099-B, and the filer is not required to correct Forms 1099-B for de minimis errors. But the filer may decide that it is more administrable for the filer to correct for de minimis errors for every payee statement the filer sends to the payee, including the Form 1099-B. Thus, the per-statement election provides flexibility to filers. In addition, proposed regulation § 301.6722-1(d)(3)(iv) provides that if a payee does not identify the type of payee statement to which the election relates, the filer shall treat the election as applying to all types of payee statements the filer is required to furnish to the payee. Finally, as described above, filers who choose to provide notification and a reasonable alternative manner for the election may provide that as a condition of using the reasonable alternative manner the payee must provide the filer the payee's account number, and the filer may then provide corrections on an account-wide basis. For these reasons, proposed regulation § 301.6722-1(d)(3)(iii) does not adopt the comment's suggested rule.

The comment noted that section 202 of the PATH Act does not contain explicit language regarding a payee's ability to revoke a prior election under section 6722(c)(3)(B). The comment stated that providing for a revocation is unnecessary to accomplish Congress's specific mandate and may prove to be more costly and burdensome than continuing to issue corrections for de minimis errors. The comment further stated that, if revocations are permitted, they should be permitted only on an annual basis applied to the next year after the year in which the revocation was made. The comment's concern is that the language regarding revocations in section 3.02 of Notice 2017-09 could lead to a revocation being applicable to a portion of a calendar year, with an election applicable to a separate portion of that year. The Treasury Department and the IRS do not agree that this will cause significant burden to filers because a revocation does not mandate changes in behavior on behalf of the filer, but rather provides penalty relief for the filer if an information return contains a de minimis error and is not corrected. As a result, proposed regulation § 301.6722-1(d)(3)(vii) provides that a revocation will apply to payee statements that are furnished or are due to be furnished after the revocation is received by the filer.

The Treasury Department and the IRS note that while the revocation may cause the election to apply for only the first part of a calendar year, nothing prevents filers from continuing to issue corrections for the rest of the calendar year (as they had been doing with respect to the portion of the year when the election was in effect). Immediate effect of the revocation provides immediate penalty relief for filers in the case of a de minimis error that is uncorrected and allows filers to stop issuing corrections for de minimis errors as soon after receipt of the revocation as they wish. In the unlikely scenario of an election in a calendar year, followed by a revocation in the same calendar year, followed by another election in the same calendar year, the situation will not be that of various rules for various periods within the calendar year - rather, because the election is effective for the entire calendar year and subsequent years until revoked under proposed regulations §§ 301.6721-1(e)(3) and 301.6722-1(d)(3)(ii), the last, valid election would apply to the same period it would absent the prior election and prior revocation. Because the Treasury Department and the IRS do not view the potential for multiple filings of elections and revocations within a year as a significant concern, the proposed regulations do not complicate the rules in an effort to further address this issue. Regarding the length of the effectiveness of a revocation, an indefinite revocation, rather than an annual revocation system, should impose less administrative burden both on filers and payees given the decreased frequency of filing.

The comment also stated that brokers should be specifically permitted to ignore the use of the de minimis error safe harbor exceptions and continue to issue corrections for de minimis amounts. The Treasury Department and the IRS agree that brokers, like other filers, may do so without specific permission. Because there is no need for the regulations to provide brokers with specific permission, this comment was not adopted.

The comment also commented on the final and temporary regulations under §§ 1.6081-8 and 1.6081-8T contained in TD 9730, stating that the automatic extension to file various information returns should, as a general matter, remain in place. This portion of the comment is beyond the scope of these regulations.

In addition the comment asked for clarification of a filer's reporting obligations under the de minimis error safe harbor exceptions where the threshold reporting obligation is not initially met, but upon a subsequent corrective event, the reportable dollar amount exceeds the threshold amount but does not exceed the de minimis error limit. The de minimis error safe harbor exceptions do not apply to this situation, because they do not apply to a failure to file; the safe harbor exceptions apply only to inadvertent errors on a filed information return or furnished payee statement. This rule is reflected in proposed regulation § 301.6722-1(d)(1). The comment further asked whether an election applies only to payee statements and information returns required to be furnished or filed in the year of the election, or later, or to any corrections made after the election, regardless of when the reporting to which the correction is related is required. Proposed regulation § 301.6722-1(d)(3)(ii) addresses this question by providing that an election under proposed regulation § 301.6722-1(d)(3)(i) applies to payee statements required to be furnished and information returns required to be filed during the calendar year of the election, or later; if a payee statement is required to be furnished or an information return is required to be filed before the beginning of the calendar year of the election, the election would not apply, regardless of when the filer realizes a reporting error was made. The comment asked whether the language in Notice 2017-09 reading "within 30 days of the date of the election" should instead reference 30 days from discovery of the error for purposes of the error being treated as due to reasonable cause and not willful neglect. The "within 30 days of the date of the election" language in the notice is now reflected in proposed regulation § 301.6724-1(h). The Treasury Department and the IRS determined that the election, rather than the discovery of the error, is the appropriate focus because a special rule is needed only in those situations where a payee election causes the de minimis error safe harbor exceptions to not apply. In cases where a payee has made an election under proposed regulation § 301.6722(d)(3)(i) and a filer subsequently discovers an error, whether the error is de minimis or not, the normal reasonable cause rules under section 6724, such as in § 301.6724-1(d)(1) relating to responsible manner, apply. Examples 8 and 9 in proposed regulation § 301.6724-1(k) illustrate these rules.

The comment also requested clarification regarding the following language in section 3.02 of Notice 2017-09:

> Nothing in this notice prevents a payee from requesting that the filer file a corrected information return or furnish a corrected payee statement required to be filed or furnished in a calendar year preceding the calendar year in which the payee makes the election.

The comment asked whether the "or" in the phrase "filed or furnished" should be "and" because, regardless of the payee's request, the filer would both furnish the corrected payee statement and file the corrected information return. The comment also asked whether this language places any obligation upon the filer to oblige the payee's request pursuant to this language. The Treasury Department and the IRS note that the proposed regulations do not include the quoted language, so the comment's inquiries regarding it are not applicable.

Six additional comments concurred with the comments and questions made by the one comment that has been described thus far in this preamble. One of these six additional comments also emphasized the administrative burden needed for financial firms to implement the rules described in Notice 2017-09, and the impact especially on smaller or midsized firms. The comment stated that the increased cost has no tangible benefit or demonstrated revenue-raising impact. The Treasury Department and the IRS note that the statute provides payees with the ability to elect that the de minimis error safe harbor exceptions not apply. The regulations strike a balance between the benefit of the de minimis error safe harbor exceptions for filers and the statutory ability for payees to elect that the de minimis error safe harbor exceptions not apply. The statutory ability for payees to make an election that the de minimis error safe harbor exceptions not apply, rather than any revenue-raising metric, is the benefit to be weighed against administrative burdens to filers.

The comment also stated that the framework set forth in Notice 2017-09 runs contrary to the intent of the notice, existing regulations, and the Trade Preferences Extension Act of 2015, but the comment does not provide details as to how this is the case and we cannot therefore address this portion of the comment.

An additional comment quoted the following language from Notice 2017-09, section 3.01: "This notice does not prohibit a filer from filing corrected information returns and furnishing corrected payee statements if the payee does not make an election." The comment stated that the mitigation of administrative burden of processing corrections under the de minimis error safe harbor exceptions is realized not only by filers but by payees as well, and recommended that guidance discourage corrected statements for de minimis errors. The Treasury Department and the IRS do not agree; accurate reporting is an important goal that should not be discouraged. Thus, the proposed regulations do not adopt the comment's suggestion.

The comment also stated that requiring a filer to provide each payee with written notification of the de minimis error safe harbor exception rules and election out provisions would be unduly burdensome to filers, shifting administrative burden from processing corrected statements to the notification process. The comment recommended that the IRS include a general disclosure regarding the de minimis error safe harbor exceptions in general instructions relating to information returns. The Treasury Department and the IRS decided to not include a notification requirement in the proposed regulations. Rather, the proposed regulations provide only that if filers wish to set up election systems that vary from the default contained in proposed regulation § 301.6722-1(d)(3)(iii), a notification is required for that reasonable alternative manner of election under proposed regulation § 301.6722-1(d)(3)(v). For this reason, the proposed regulations do not reflect this comment. The Treasury Department and the IRS are considering whether to include references to the de minimis error safe harbor exceptions, the election under § 301.6722-1(d)(3)(i), and other information in general instructions or in specific forms or instructions, and note that the current (2018) General Instructions for Certain Information Returns as well as the current (2018) General Instructions for Forms W-2 and W-3 contain discussions of the de minimis error safe harbor exceptions and related information.

The comment also requested clarification regarding whether the de minimis error safe harbor exception is for the cumulative total of multiple errors, or one particular error. The comment noted that the safe harbor exception would be easier to apply if it is calculated on an error-by-error basis. Proposed regulation § 301.6722-1(d)(2) clarifies that the safe harbor exception is calculated on an error-by-error basis.

The comment further stated that if an error is discovered by the filer, the payee should not be able to elect that the de minimis error safe harbor exceptions not apply and that the filer should make the determination of whether a corrected form is needed, in light of the threshold amounts of $100 and $25. The comment stated that the election process does not lead to a reduction in the administrative burden. Because this suggestion is contrary to section 6722(c)(3)(B), which specifically provides for the payee to make the election under section 6722(c)(3)(B), the proposed regulations do not adopt the suggestion.

The comment also stated, regarding any notification requirement, that errors may be identified by the payee and communicated to the filer and then at that point, if the dollar amount is below the applicable threshold, the filer should inform the payee of the de minimis error safe harbor exceptions and the payee's ability to elect that the safe harbor exceptions not apply. As noted above, the proposed regulations do not contain a notification requirement.

The comment stated that additional consideration should be given to allow the payee election to expire, noting that such a rule could reduce administrative burden for filers, given a resulting decrease in required corrections. Because a rule under which the payee election expires after a set amount of time would increase the complexity of the election and revocation framework both for filers (tracking years in which the election is in effect) and for payees (same, and refiling elections after expiration, if desired), proposed regulation § 301.6722-1(d)(3)(ii) does not adopt such a rule.

The comment also requested examples of what a de minimis error correction would look like. A de minimis error correction would be substantially similar to a correction of an error greater than a de minimis error in the context of corrected information reporting -that is, the filing of a corrected information return, and the furnishing of a corrected payee statement (for example, filing a corrected Form 1099-MISC with the IRS, and furnishing a corrected Form 1099-MISC to the payee).

The comment also requested explanation of what "de minimis" is and is not. Proposed regulation § 301.6722-1(d)(2) provides the definition of de minimis error, and proposed regulation § 301.6722-1(d)(5) illustrates this definition with examples.

The comment requested an opt-out provision for filers that, if selected, would remove any responsibility to collect information and keep records under Notice 2017-09. The Treasury Department and the IRS have considered potential expenses that filers might incur in meeting the record retention requirements in proposed regulation § 301.6722-1(d)(4) and have determined that an opt-out provision, while potentially reducing expenses borne by filers, would render the record retention rules ineffective. The record retention requirements facilitate tax administration by providing proof of compliance and assisting filers to avoid penalties under sections 6721 and 6722. The Treasury Department and the IRS note that the notification under proposed regulation § 301.6722-1(d)(3)(v)(B) is a voluntary collection of information because the notification is optional. Therefore, the proposed regulations do not adopt this comment.

Finally, the comment asked whether any notification requirement will be effective for payees receiving their statements in 2016. The effective/applicability date provisions in proposed regulation § 301.6722-1(g) provide that the rules relating to the optional notification by filers under proposed regulation § 301.6722-1(d)(3)(v) are proposed to apply with respect to information returns and payee statements due on or after January 1 of the calendar year immediately following the date of publication of a Treasury decision adopting these rules as final regulations in the **Federal Register**.

An additional comment requested that the payee election provisions under section 6722(c)(3)(B) and proposed regulation § 301.6722-1(d)(3)(i) not apply to Form 8937, "Report of Organizational Actions Affecting Basis of Securities." The comment noted that under section 6045B(e) and regulation § 1.6045B-1(a)(3) a filer need not file and issue individual Forms 8937, but can opt to post a single Form 8937 on its public web site. The comment noted that the Form 8937 is not specific to an individual payee, but instead describes tax basis adjustments in the abstract for use by brokers in determining the basis reporting for their customers. It noted that the individually-focused nature of the payee election is at odds with the public reporting enabled by section 6045B(e) and regulation § 1.6045B-1(a)(3). And it noted that a single election with respect to a posted Form 8937 could lead to inefficiencies for numbers of brokers (including those who did not make the election) once a correction is issued.

The Treasury Department and the IRS acknowledge these concerns. However, Congress presumably was aware of the public reporting option under section 6045B(e) and regulation § 1.6045B-1(a)(3) (enacted October 3, 2008, and published October 18, 2010, respectively) when it enacted the de minimis error safe harbor exceptions. Congress did not provide for authority to exclude information returns or payee statements from the de minimis error safe harbor, or the payee election, based on administrative inconvenience. The proposed regulations therefore do not adopt this comment's suggested rule.

A final comment requested that the payee election be available only as a one-time election and apply prospectively only. The comment stated that nothing in the notice prevents a payee from requesting that the filer file a corrected information return or furnish a corrected payee statement from years preceding the election, and noted that this presents burdens and potential for abuse by payees. The comment may have misconstrued Notice 2017-09, in part, because nothing in the notice provided for an election for a year preceding the year in which the election was made. In like manner, proposed regulation § 301.6722-1(d)(3)(ii) provides that an election made by October 15 of a calendar year -for example, Calendar Year 1 - can apply retrospectively to a Form 1099-MISC required to be furnished in January of Calendar Year 1, but the election would have no validity with respect to any payee statements required to be furnished in any calendar years preceding Calendar Year 1. Thus, the retrospective application is limited to the current calendar year, along with the potential administrative burden and any potential for abuse. The comment does not adequately establish that "cherry picking" the corrections of de minimis dollar amounts poses a significant threat of abuse. Regarding potential administrative burden to filers, while a one-time prospective election might be less burdensome, this is but one factor that must be considered; flexibility for payees in requesting corrected statements is another. As discussed below, proposed regulation § 301.6722-1(d)(3)(ii) balances these factors.

The comment requested the information required for a payee election be streamlined to simplify elections as a matter of customer service. Proposed regulation § 301.6722-1(d)(3)(v) allows filers to provide a reasonable alternative manner that they view as satisfactory to their customers.

The comment also echoed previous comments in requesting the flexibility to issue corrections, despite generally taking advantage of the de minimis error safe harbor exceptions, for purposes of cost basis adjustments under section 6045. To address this and similar comments, proposed regulation § 1.6045-1(d)(6)(vii) provides that when a broker both files a corrected information return and issues a corrected payee statement showing the correct dollar amount, even though not required by section 6721(c)(3) or section 6722(c)(3), the corrected amount is the adjusted basis for section 6045 purposes.

The comment asked that the recordkeeping requirement in section 3.05 of Notice 2017-09, of " . . . as long as that information may be relevant to the administration of any internal revenue law" be reduced from a potentially open-ended length of time to a range of three years (the general statute of limitations on assessment under section 6501) to seven years (the time period used for various Securities and Exchange Commission and Financial Industry Regulatory Authority recordkeeping requirements), stating that the open-ended retention schedule is unnecessary and burdensome. Proposed regulation § 301.6722-1(d)(4) does not adopt this comment, because the records under this section (such as an election, until revoked) may be relevant to tax administration in years beyond the general statute of limitations on assessment under section 6501 for a particular year. For example, if an election is made in 2019 and not revoked until 2025, that election will be relevant with respect to information returns required to be filed and payee statements required to be furnished in 2024. The rules in proposed regulation § 301.6722-1(d)(4) therefore reflect the general record retention rules in section 6001 and § 1.6001-1(e), providing for record retention as long as the contents of an election, revocation, or notification may be material in the administration of any internal revenue law.

Finally, the comment requested guidance regarding how a payee election that the de minimis error safe harbor exceptions not apply would apply to joint accounts, such as when joint account payees submit contrary elections, or one joint account payee submits an election but another does not. Absent contrary provisions under the Internal Revenue Code or Code of Federal Regulations, the rules that typically govern issues of authority over joint accounts should address these matters, and a special rule for purposes of de minimis error reporting is unnecessary. The Treasury Department and the IRS note that filers have the option to ignore the availability of the de minimis error safe harbor exceptions and issue corrections for de minimis amounts as was required to avoid penalties prior to the enactment of the PATH Act. Filers can therefore issue corrections to all joint account payees even if joint account payees submit contrary elections, or one joint account payee submits an election but another does not.

Explanation of Provisions

1. *Safe Harbor Exceptions From Penalties for Certain De Minimis Errors*

In accord with sections 6721(c)(3)(A) and 6722(c)(3)(A), proposed regulations § § 301.6721-1 and 301.6722-1 provide for safe harbor exceptions to the section 6721 and section 6722 penalties. With certain exceptions discussed below, the safe harbor exceptions apply in circumstances when an information return or payee statement is otherwise correct and is timely filed or furnished and includes a de minimis error in a dollar amount reported on the information return or payee statement. When the safe harbor exception applies to an information return or payee statement and the information return or payee statement is otherwise correctly and timely filed or furnished, no correction is required and, for purposes of sections 6721 or 6722, respectively, the information return or payee statement is treated as having been filed or furnished with all of the correct required information.

Pursuant to sections 6721(c)(3)(A) and 6722(c)(3)(A), an error is a de minimis error if the difference between any single amount in error and the correct amount is not more than $100, or, if the difference is with respect to an amount of tax withheld, it is not more than $25. Proposed regulation § 301.6722-1(d)(2) defines tax withheld to include any amount required to be shown on an information return or payee statement (as defined in section 6724(d)(1) and (d)(2), respectively) withheld under section 3402, as well as any such amount that is creditable under sections 27, 31, 33, or 1474. This is not an exclusive definition but is intended to ensure that all amounts giving rise to dollar-for-dollar reductions in tax, including foreign tax credits under section 27, are included as tax withheld.

2. *Errors Due to Intentional Disregard of Information Reporting Requirements*

In accord with sections 6721(e) and 6722(e), proposed regulations § § 301.6721-1(e)(1) and 301.6722-1(d)(1) provide that the safe harbor exceptions for certain de minimis errors do not apply in cases of intentional disregard of the requirements to file correct information returns or furnish correct payee statements. In those cases, higher penalty amounts imposed by sections 6721(e) and 6722(e) and proposed regulations § § 301.6721-1(g) and 301.6722-1(c) apply. For example, a person may not choose to forgo filing information returns or furnishing payee statements that the person is required to file or furnish under the Code and that report amounts less than $100 and tax withheld less than

$25. To do so would be an intentional disregard of the filing requirement and result in higher penalties.

3. *Payee Election to Receive Corrected Payee Statement*

In accord with sections 6721(c)(3)(B) and 6722(c)(3)(B), proposed regulations §§301.6721-1(e)(3) and 301.6722-1(d)(3)(i) allow a payee to elect to have the safe harbor exceptions for certain de minimis errors not apply to the information reporting penalties. The proposed regulations provide that a payee may elect that the safe harbor exception to section 6722 penalties not apply to a payee statement, and that the election will also apply to the safe harbor exception to section 6721 penalties with respect to corresponding information returns. Proposed regulation §301.6722-1(d)(3)(vi) provides that the election is not available with respect to information that may not be altered under specific information reporting rules. For example, §1.6045-4(i)(5) provides special rules for defining gross proceeds in the context of multiple transfers for information reporting on real estate transactions, and prohibits altering information after the due date for filing the Form 1099-S, "Proceeds From Real Estate Transactions." Allowing an election under proposed regulation §301.6722-1(d)(3)(i) with respect to the Form 1099-S would suggest that a correction would or should be made. To resolve any ambiguity between these provisions, proposed regulation §301.6722-1(d)(3)(vi) prohibits an election with respect to information that may not be altered under specific information reporting rules, such as under §1.6045-4(i)(5).

Proposed regulation §301.6722-1(d)(3)(ii) provides that a payee must make any election no later than the later of 30 days after the date on which the payee statement is required to be furnished to the payee, or October 15 of the calendar year, to receive a correct payee statement required to be furnished in that calendar year without having the safe harbor exceptions for certain de minimis errors apply. The October 15 date coincides with the fully-extended due date an individual may have to file an income tax return. In arriving at this date, the Treasury Department and the IRS considered both the needs of persons who furnish payee statements and the needs of payees, who will generally have a filing due date no later than October 15 if their taxable year corresponds to the calendar year referenced on the payee statements they receive. Prior to promulgation of these proposed regulations, the IRS advised payees to request corrected payee statements from filers in cases in which information is incorrect, without time limit on making this request. Imposing a deadline to elect before October 15 could limit a taxpayer's ability to correct errors discovered while the payee is preparing his or her return. The allowance of an election after the due date for most payee statements and through October 15 allows payees to inspect payee statements and make elections for purposes of timely filing their income tax returns. On the other hand, the existence of an election cutoff date of October 15 in the case of most payee statements reduces administrative burden on filers by eliminating elections after October 15. The 30-day rule provides a deadline in cases of payee statements required to be furnished later in the calendar year, such as the Schedule K-1 (Form 1065), "Partner's Share of Income, Deductions, Credits, etc.," required to be furnished to payees by fiscal year partnerships.

To reduce the administrative burden of yearly elections on both payees and filers, an election remains in effect for all subsequent years until revoked under proposed regulation §301.6722-1(d)(3)(vii). The effect of a revocation of a prior election is that the safe harbor exceptions for de minimis errors apply. The revocation will be effective for payee statements furnished or due to be furnished after the revocation is received. Because a revocation makes the safe harbor for certain de minimis errors applicable, potentially reducing the accuracy of information returns and payee statements, payees have no need to be able to make a retroactive revocation after receipt of any payee statements and during the period of preparing individual income tax returns. Likewise, the immediate effect of the revocation is beneficial to the filer, because it immediately applies the de minimis error safe harbor exceptions, eliminating the requirement to issue corrected information returns containing only de minimis errors incurred by an election under proposed regulation §301.6722-1(d)(3)(i). If issuing corrections is easier for the filer, the filer can always do so. A revocation will remain in effect until the payee makes a valid and timely election under proposed regulation §301.6722-1(d)(3)(i).

For determining the "date of receipt" by the filer, paragraphs (ii) and (vii) of proposed regulation §301.6722-1(d)(3), relating to elections and revocations, respectively, provide that for purposes of proposed regulation §301.6722-1 the provisions of section 7502 relating to timely mailing treated as timely delivery apply in determining the date an election under proposed regulation §301.6722-1(d)(3)(ii) or revocation under proposed regulation §301.6722-1(d)(3)(vii) is considered to be received by the filer, treating delivery to the filer as if the filer were an agency, officer, or office under section 7502, so that the date of mailing may control the timeliness of an election or revocation. These rules provide for more clarity regarding the date of an election or revocation.

Under proposed regulation §301.6722-1(d)(3)(iii), the default manner for an election by the payee that the de minimis error safe harbor exceptions not apply is by writing on paper, mailed to the address for the filer appearing on the payee statement the payee received from the filer with respect to which the election is being made, or as provided to them by the filer. Proposed regulation §301.6722-1(d)(3)(iii)(A) through (D) provide the requirements for what information must be included in the written election, such as the payee's name, address, and taxpayer identification number (TIN). This information is necessary for the filer to implement the election.

Proposed regulation § 301.6722-1(d)(3)(v) provides that the payee may make the election under proposed regulation § 301.6722-1(d)(3)(i) in a reasonable alternative manner if the filer provides a valid notification to the payee describing the reasonable alternative manner. The reasonable alternative manner, as described in proposed regulation § 301.6722-1(d)(3)(v)(E), may include electronic elections by e-mail or telephonic elections. For a notification under proposed regulation § 301.6722-1(d)(3)(v) to be valid, and make available the reasonable alternative manner, the notification must be written (paper or electronic), must be timely under the provisions of proposed regulation § 301.6722-1(d)(3)(v)(D), must explain to the payee the payee's ability to make the election under proposed regulation § 301.6722-1(d)(3)(i), must provide an address to which the payee may send a written election under proposed regulation § 301.6722-1(d)(3)(i) and (iii), and must describe the information required for making the election as described by proposed regulation § 301.6722-1(d)(3)(iii)(A) through (D). To be timely under proposed regulation § 301.6722-1(d)(3)(v)(D), a notification must be provided to the payee with, or at the time of, the furnishing of the payee statement, or have previously been timely provided (under the with, or at the time of, rule) to the payee with a payee statement associated with the relevant account. Under proposed regulation § 301.6722-1(d)(3)(v)(D)(2), if a filer wishes to provide for a different reasonable alternative manner than a previous reasonable alternative manner, the applicable timeliness rule is under proposed regulation § 301.6722-1(d)(3)(v)(D)(*1*) (the with, or at the time of, rule) and the filer must accept payee elections under the previous reasonable alternative manner for a period of at least 60 days after the receipt of the new notification by the payee.

To ease the administrative burden on filers, the notification may provide that certain of the information otherwise required under proposed regulation § 301.6722-1(d)(3)(iii)(B) is not required, and that certain of the information (the otherwise optional account number) is required, if the payee decides to use the reasonable alternative manner rather than the default manner.

The combination of the default election under proposed regulation § 301.6722-1(d)(3)(iii) and the reasonable alternative manner, including electronic and telephonic elections, pursuant to a valid notification by the filer, provides a straightforward election process for payees who do not have notification provided them, as well as additional flexibility to filers who wish to provide notification to payees of the election and alternative methods for making the election.

Proposed regulation § 301.6722-1(d)(3)(vii)(A) through (F) provides requirements for a revocation that are similar to the requirements for an election.

4. *Reasonable Cause*

When a payee makes an election under § 301.6722-1(d)(3)(i) by the later of 30 days after the date on which the payee statement is required to be furnished to the payee, or October 15 of the calendar year, the safe harbor exceptions for de minimis errors no longer apply with respect to the payee statement, and corresponding information return, required to be furnished and filed that year. If the payee statement has already been furnished or the information return already been filed, and they contain de minimis errors, the section 6721 and 6722 penalties will apply absent the applicability of an exception other than the safe harbor exceptions for certain de minimis errors. Proposed regulation § 301.6724-1(h) provides special rules to determine whether the exception for reasonable cause applies in this situation. Section 301.6724-1(h) only applies when the safe harbor for certain de minimis errors would have applied, but for an election under § 301.6722-1(d)(3)(i).

Under this provision, a filer may establish that a failure caused by the presence of de minimis errors and an election under § 301.6722-1(d)(3)(i) is due to reasonable cause and not willful neglect by filing a corrected information return or furnishing a corrected payee statement, or both, as applicable, within 30 days of the date of the election. Where specific rules provide for additional time in which to furnish a corrected payee statement and file a corrected information return, for example with Forms W-2C, the 30-day rule does not apply and the specific rules will apply. In the case of filing or furnishing outside of the 30-day period the determination of reasonable cause will be on a case-by-case basis. Examples 8 and 9 in proposed regulation § 301.6724-1(k) illustrate reasonable cause under this provision and when reasonable cause might occur under a separate provision.

5. *Cost Basis*

To encourage correct reporting, and to facilitate brokers with the accurate maintenance of cost basis systems, proposed regulation § 1.6045-1(d)(6)(vii) provides that voluntary corrections by brokers will result in updated adjusted basis under section 6045, even when the incorrect dollar amounts are not "required to be corrected by reason of section 6721(c)(3) or section 6722(c)(3)." See I.R.C. section 6045(g)(2)(B)(iii). This proposed regulation allows brokers who identify a de minimis error in their cost basis systems to fix the mismatch between their systems and the previously-reported (incorrect) dollar amount through voluntary subsequent reporting. The updated adjusted basis under section 6045 has no effect on calculating basis under other basis determination sections, such as section 1012.

6. *Record Retention*

To facilitate proof of compliance, proposed regulation § 301.6722-1(d)(4) provides that filers must retain records of any election, revocation, or notification for as long as the contents of the election, revocation, or notification may be material in the administration of any internal revenue law. Whether an election, revocation, or notification was effectively made under these regulations can affect whether the section 6721 or 6722 penalties apply. Thus, records of any election, revocation, or notification are relevant to determining the tax liability of any person under sections 6721 or 6722. See section 6001 and § 1.6001-1(e).

7. Updates and Conforming Amendments

To reflect increased penalty amounts due to section 2102 of the Creating Small Business Jobs Act of 2010 and section 806 of the Trade Preferences Extension Act of 2015, the proposed regulations update dollar amounts throughout. Additionally, to reflect the provision for annual inflationary adjustments in section 208 of the Tax Increase Prevention Act of 2014, proposed regulations §§301.6721-1(i) and 301.6722-1(f) provide for adjustments for inflation.

To reflect the amendments by section 2004 of the Surface Transportation and Veterans Health Care Choice Improvement Act of 2015, section 13520(c) of Public Law 115-97, and section 206(o) of the Consolidated Appropriations Act of 2018 to sections 6724(d)(1) and 6724(d)(2), proposed regulations §§301.6721-1(h)(2)(xii) and (h)(3)(xxvi) and 301.6722-1(e)(2)(xxxv), (xxxvi), and (xxxvii) are added to update the definitions of information return and payee statement.

To reflect the amendments by section 1211(b)(2) of the Pension Protection Act of 2006 to section 6721(e)(2), proposed regulation §301.6721-1(g)(4)(iv)(D) provides for the calculation of the section 6721 penalty in case of intentional disregard in the case of a return required to be filed under section 6050V.

Proposed regulation §301.6724-1(m) provides for updated procedures for a taxpayer to use to seek an administrative waiver that a failure is due to reasonable cause and not due to willful neglect, as the prior language referencing the district director was out of date.

The proposed regulations remove outdated references to various taxable years, replacing with updated years where necessary, such as in examples.

The proposed regulations make numerous conforming amendments to reflect the addition and renumbering of paragraphs. Proposed regulation §301.6721-0 provides an updated table of contents.

Proposed Effective/Applicability Date

The regulations, as proposed, would generally apply with respect to information returns required to be filed and payee statements required to be furnished on or after January 1 of the calendar year immediately following the date of publication of a Treasury decision adopting these rules as final regulations in the **Federal Register**. Proposed regulation §301.6724-1(h), however, would apply with respect to information returns required to be filed and payee statements required to be furnished on or after January 1, 2017. See I.R.C. section 7805(b)(1)(C) and section 4 of Notice 2017-09, IRB-2017-4 (January 23, 2017).

Effect on Other Documents

Upon the publication of final regulations pursuant to the proposed regulations under sections 6045, 6721, 6722, and 6724 in this notice of proposed rulemaking in the **Federal Register**, Notice 2017-09 will be superseded with respect to information returns required to be filed and payee statements required to be furnished on or after January 1 of the calendar year immediately following the date of publication of a Treasury decision adopting these rules as final regulations in the **Federal Register**.

Special Analyses

These regulations are not subject to review under section 6(b) of Executive Order 12866 pursuant to the Memorandum of Agreement (April 11, 2018) between the Treasury Department and the Office of Management and Budget regarding review of tax regulations.

Pursuant to the Regulatory Flexibility Act (5 U.S.C. chapter 6), it is hereby certified that the collection of information contained in these regulations, if adopted, would not have a significant economic impact on a substantial number of small entities. Accordingly, a regulatory flexibility analysis is not required. As stated in this preamble, the proposed regulations would implement the de minimis error safe harbor exceptions in sections 6721(c)(3) and 6722(c)(3) to the section 6721 and 6722 penalties. Pursuant to section 6722(c)(3)(B), the proposed regulations would also provide for the time and manner for elections by payees that the de minimis error safe harbor exceptions not apply, including optional notifications by filers to provide for an alternative reasonable manner for the election. Finally, the proposed regulations would provide rules for revocations by payees of elections and record retention rules.

Although the proposed regulations may potentially affect a substantial number of small entities, the economic impact on these entities is not expected to be significant. The de minimis error safe harbor exceptions are expected to greatly reduce the burden on filers to file corrected information returns and furnish corrected payee statements because of de minimis errors. In those cases where payees opt to elect that the de minimis error safe harbor exceptions not apply, the expense of making the election will be borne by the payees, which generally will not be small entities.

Filers that are small entities receiving elections may incur costs in processing the elections, including initial costs in implementing systems or modifying existing systems to process elections, and subsequently in time incurred administering these systems. However, because section 6722(c)(3)(B) provides for a payee election, costs flow from the statute regardless of the proposed regulations. Additionally, filers that are small entities generally will have information reporting systems currently in place, and any costs incurred pursuant to the proposed regulations in modifying and implementing these systems are not expected to be significant. The rules in the proposed regulations provide clarity regarding the election process, which is expected to result in a more streamlined process.

Similarly, in those cases where payees opt to revoke a prior election, the expense of making the revocation will be borne by the payees, which generally will not be small entities. Filers that are small entities receiving revocations will benefit from the resulting applicability of the de minimis error safe harbor exceptions, resulting in reduced burden to file corrected information returns and furnish corrected payee statements because of de minimis errors. Filers that are small entities receiving revocations may incur costs in processing the revocations similar to those incurred in processing elections; however, it is expected that systems implementing payee elections can be modified with minimal additional cost to account for revocations in addition to elections. Filers that are small entities opting to provide the optional notification to payees regarding an alternative reasonable manner for making the election may incur costs in providing the notification. However, it is expected that filers will only provide optional notifications when they have determined that any cost in providing the notification is offset by a resulting economic benefit to the filer, such as a more cost-efficient election system. The record retention rules may also increase expenses for filers that are small entities; however, any added expenses are expected to be minimal given existing record retention systems. Pursuant to section 7805(f) of the Code, this notice of proposed rulemaking has been submitted to the Chief Counsel for Advocacy of the Small Business Administration for comment on its impact on small business.

Comments and Requests for Public Hearing

Before these proposed regulations are adopted as final regulations, consideration will be given to any comments that are timely submitted to the IRS as prescribed in the preamble under the **"ADDRESSES"** section. The Treasury Department and the IRS request comments on all aspects of these proposed regulations. All comments submitted will be made available at *www.regulations.gov* or upon request. A public hearing may be scheduled if requested in writing by any person that timely submits written comments. If a public hearing is scheduled, notice of the date, time, and place for the hearing will be published in the **Federal Register**.

Drafting Information

The principal author of these regulations is Mark A. Bond of the Office of the Associate Chief Counsel (Procedure and Administration).

[¶49,773] Proposed Amendments of Regulations (REG-115420-18), published in the Federal Register on October 29, 2018 (corrected 12/31/2018).

[Code Sec. 1400Z-2]

Qualified opportunity zones: Qualified opportunity fund: Buildings and land: Original use and substantial improvement requirements.—Reg. §1.1400Z-2(a)-1, Reg. §1.1400Z-2(c)-1, Reg. §1.1400Z-2(d)-1 and Reg. §1.1400Z-2(e)-1, relating to gains that may be deferred as a result of a taxpayer's investment in a qualified opportunity fund (QOF), are proposed.

AGENCY: Internal Revenue Service (IRS), Treasury.

ACTION: Notice of proposed rulemaking and notice of public hearing.

SUMMARY: This document contains proposed regulations that provide guidance under new section 1400Z-2 of the Internal Revenue Code (Code) relating to gains that may be deferred as a result of a taxpayer's investment in a qualified opportunity fund (QOF). Specifically, the proposed regulations address the type of gains that may be deferred by investors, the time by which corresponding amounts must be invested in QOFs, and the manner in which investors may elect to defer specified gains. This document also contains proposed regulations applicable to QOFs, including rules for self-certification, valuation of QOF assets, and guidance on qualified opportunity zone businesses. The proposed regulations affect QOFs and their investors. This document also provides notice of a public hearing on these proposed regulations.

DATES: Written (including electronic) comments must be received by December 21, 2018. Outlines of topics to be discussed at the public hearing scheduled for January 10, 2019 at 10 a.m. must be received by December 21, 2018.

ADDRESSES: Send submissions to: CC:PA:LPD:PR (REG-115420-18), room 5203, Internal Revenue Service, PO Box 7604, Ben Franklin Station, Washington, DC 20044. Submissions may be hand delivered Monday through Friday between the hours of 8 a.m. and 4 p.m. to CC:PA:LPD:PR (REG-115420-18), Courier's Desk, Internal Revenue Service, 1111 Constitution Avenue, NW., Washington, DC 20224. Alternatively, taxpayers may submit comments electronically via the Federal Rulemaking Portal at *www.regulations.gov* (IRS REG-115420-18). The public hearing will be held in the IRS auditorium, Internal Revenue Building, 1111 Constitution Avenue, NW, Washington, DC.

FOR FURTHER INFORMATION CONTACT: Concerning the proposed regulations, Erika C. Reigle of the Office of Associate Chief Counsel (Income Tax and Accounting), (202) 317-7006 and Kyle C. Griffin of the Office of Associate Chief Counsel (Income Tax and Accounting), (202) 317-4718; concerning the submission of comments, the hearing, or to be placed on the building access list to attend the hearing, Regina L. Johnson, (202) 317-6901 (not toll-free numbers).

SUPPLEMENTARY INFORMATION:

Background

This document contains proposed regulations under section 1400Z-2 of the Code that amend the Income Tax Regulations (26 CFR Part 1). Section 13823 of the Tax Cuts and Jobs Act, Pub. L. No. 115-97, 131 Stat. 2054, 2184 (2017) (TCJA), amended the Code to add sections 1400Z-1 and 1400Z-2. Section 1400Z-1 provides procedural rules for designating qualified opportunity zones and related definitions. Section 1400Z-2 allows a taxpayer to elect to defer certain gains to the extent that corresponding amounts are timely invested in a QOF.

Section 1400Z-2, in conjunction with section 1400Z-1, seeks to encourage economic growth and investment in designated distressed communities (qualified opportunity zones) by providing Federal income tax benefits to taxpayers who invest in businesses located within these zones. Section 1400Z-2 provides two main tax incentives to encourage investment in qualified opportunity zones. First, it allows for the deferral of inclusion in gross income for certain gains to the extent that corresponding amounts are reinvested in a QOF. Second, it excludes from gross income the post-acquisition gains on investments in QOFs that are held for at least 10 years.

As is more fully explained in the Explanation of Provisions, these proposed regulations describe and clarify the requirements that must be met by a taxpayer in order properly to defer the recognition of gains by investing in a QOF. In addition, the proposed regulations provide rules permitting a corporation or partnership to self-certify as a QOF. Finally, the proposed regulations provide initial proposed rules regarding some of the requirements that must be met by a corporation or partnership in order to qualify as a QOF.

Contemporaneous with the issuance of these proposed regulations, the IRS is releasing a revenue ruling addressing the application to real property of the "original use" requirement in section 1400Z-2(d)(2)(D)(i)(II) and the "substantial improvement" requirement in section 1400Z-2(d)(2)(D)(i)(II) and 1400Z-2(d)(2)(D)(ii).

In addition, these proposed regulations address the substantial-improvement requirement with respect to a purchased building located in a qualified opportunity zone. They provide that for purposes of this requirement, the basis attributable to land on which such a building sits is not taken into account in determining whether the building has been substantially improved. Excluding the basis of land from the amount that needs to be doubled under section 1400Z-2(d)(2)(D)(ii) for a building to be substantially improved facilitates repurposing vacant buildings in qualified opportunity zones. Similarly, an absence of a requirement to increase the basis of land itself would address many of the comments that taxpayers have made regarding the need to facilitate repurposing vacant or otherwise unutilized land.

In connection with soliciting comments on these proposed regulations the Department of the Treasury (Treasury Department) and the IRS are soliciting comments on all aspects of the definition of "original use" and "substantial improvement." In particular, they are seeking comments on possible approaches to defining the "original use" requirement, for both real property and other tangible property. For example, what metrics would be appropriate for determining whether tangible property has "original use" in an opportunity zone? Should the use of tangible property be determined based on its physical presence within an opportunity zone, or based on some other measure? What if the tested tangible property is a vehicle or other movable tangible property that was previously used within the opportunity zone but acquired from a person outside the opportunity zone? Should some period of abandonment or under-utilization of tangible property erase the property's history of prior use in the opportunity zone? If so, should such a fallow period enable subsequent productive utilization of the tangible property to qualify as "original use"? Should the rules appropriate for abandonment and underutilization of personal tangible property also apply to vacant real property that is productively utilized after some period? If so, what period of abandonment, underutilization, or vacancy would be consistent with the statute? In addition, comments are requested on whether any additional rules regarding the "substantial improvement" requirement for tangible property are warranted or would be useful.

The Treasury Department and the IRS are working on additional published guidance, including additional proposed regulations expected to be published in the near future. The Treasury Department and the IRS expect the forthcoming proposed regulations to incorporate the guidance contained in the revenue ruling to facilitate additional public comment. The forthcoming proposed regulations are expected to address other issues under section 1400Z-2 that are not addressed in these proposed regulations. Issues expected to be addressed include: the meaning of "substantially all" in each of the various places where it appears in section 1400Z-2; the transactions that may trigger the inclusion of gain that has been deferred under a section 1400Z-2(a) election; the "reasonable period" (see section 1400Z-2(e)(4)(B)) for a QOF to reinvest proceeds from the sale of qualifying assets without paying a penalty; administrative rules applicable under section 1400Z-2(f) when a QOF fails to maintain the required 90 percent investment standard; and information-reporting requirements under section 1400Z-2.

The Treasury Department and the IRS welcome comments on what other additional issues should be addressed in forthcoming proposed regulations or guidance.

Explanation of Provisions

I. *Deferring Tax on Capital Gains by Investing in Opportunity Zones*

A. Gains Eligible for Deferral

The proposed regulations clarify that only capital gains are eligible for deferral under section 1400Z-2(a)(1). In setting forth the gains that are subject to deferral, the text of section 1400Z-2(a)(1) specifies "*gain* from the sale to, or exchange with, an unrelated person of any property held by the taxpayer," to the extent that such gain does not exceed the aggregate amount invested by the taxpayer in a QOF during the 180-day period beginning on the date of the sale or exchange (emphasis added). The statutory text is silent as to whether Congress intended both ordinary and capital gains to be eligible for deferral under section 1400Z-2. (Sections 1221 and 1222 define these two kinds of gains.) However, the statute's legislative history explicitly identifies "capital gains" as the gains that are eligible for deferral. The Treasury Department and the IRS believe, based on the legislative history as well as the text and structure of the statute, that section 1400Z-2 is best interpreted as making deferral available only for capital gains. The proposed regulations provide that a gain is eligible for deferral if it is treated as a capital gain for Federal income tax purposes. Eligible gains, therefore, generally include capital gain from an actual, or deemed, sale or exchange, or any other gain that is required to be included in a taxpayer's computation of capital gain.

The proposed regulations address two additional gain deferral requirements. First, the gain to be deferred must be gain that would be recognized, if deferral under section 1400Z-2(a)(1) were not permitted, not later than December 31, 2026, the final date under section 1400Z-2(a)(2)(B) for the deferral of gain. Second, the gain must not arise from a sale or exchange with a related person as defined in section 1400Z-2(e)(2). Section 1400Z-2(e)(2) incorporates the related person definition in sections 267(b) and 707(b)(1) but substitutes "20 percent" in place of "50 percent" each place it occurs in section 267(b) or section 707(b)(1).

B. Types of Taxpayers Eligible to Elect Gain Deferral

The proposed regulations clarify that taxpayers eligible to elect deferral under section 1400Z-2 are those that recognize capital gain for Federal income tax purposes. These taxpayers include individuals, C corporations (including regulated investment companies (RICs) and real estate investment trusts (REITs)), partnerships, and certain other pass-through entities, including common trust funds described in section 584, as well as, qualified settlement funds, disputed ownership funds, and other entities taxable under § 1.468B of the Income Tax Regulations.

In order to address the numerous issues raised by new section 1400Z-2 for pass-through entities, the proposed regulations include special rules for partnerships and other pass-through entities, and for taxpayers to whom these entities pass through income and other tax items. Under these rules, the entities and taxpayers can invest in a QOF and thus defer recognition of eligible gain. The Treasury Department and the IRS request comments on whether the rules are sufficient and whether more detailed rules are required to provide additional certainty for investors in pass-through entities that are not partnerships.

C. Investments in a QOF

The proposed regulations clarify that, to qualify under section 1400Z-2(a)(1)(A), (that is, to be an eligible interest in a QOF), an investment in the QOF must be an equity interest in the QOF, including preferred stock or a partnership interest with special allocations. Thus, an eligible interest cannot be a debt instrument within the meaning of section 1275(a)(1) and § 1.1275-1(d). Provided that the eligible taxpayer is the owner of the equity interest for Federal income tax purposes, status as an eligible interest is not impaired by the taxpayer's use of the interest as collateral for a loan, whether a purchase-money borrowing or otherwise. The proposed regulations also clarify that deemed contributions of money under section 752(a) do not result in the creation of an investment in a QOF.

D. 180-Day Rule for Deferring Gain by Investing in a QOF

Under section 1400Z-2(a)(1)(A), to be able to elect to defer gain, a taxpayer must generally invest in a QOF during the 180-day period beginning on the date of the sale or exchange giving rise to the gain. Some capital gains, however, are the result of Federal tax rules deeming an amount to be a gain from the sale or exchange of a capital asset, and, in many cases, the statutory language providing capital gain treatment does not provide a specific date for the deemed sale. The proposed regulations address this issue by providing that, except as specifically provided in the proposed regulations, the first day of the 180-day period is the date on which the gain would be recognized for Federal income tax purposes, without regard to the deferral available under section 1400Z-2. The proposed regulations include examples that illustrate the general rule by applying it to capital gains in a variety of situations (including, for example, gains from the sale of exchange-traded stock and capital gain dividend distributions).

If a taxpayer acquires an original interest in a QOF in connection with a gain-deferral election under section 1400Z-2(a)(1)(A), if a later sale or exchange of that interest triggers an inclusion of the deferred gain, and if the taxpayer makes a qualifying new investment in a QOF, then the proposed regulations provide that the taxpayer is eligible to make a section 1400Z-2(a)(2) election to defer the inclusion of the previously deferred gain. Deferring an inclusion otherwise mandated by section 1400Z-2(a)(1)(B) in this situation is permitted only if the taxpayer has disposed of the entire initial investment without which the taxpayer could not have made the previous deferral election under section 1400Z-2. The complete disposition is necessary because section 1400Z-2(a)(2)(A) expressly prohibits the making of a deferral election under section 1400Z-2(a)(1) with respect to a sale or exchange if an election previously made with respect to the same sale or exchange remains in effect. The general 180-day rule described above determines when this second investment must be made to support the second deferral election. Under that rule, the first day of the 180-day period for the new investment in a QOF is the date that section 1400Z-2(b)(1) provides for inclusion of the previously deferred gain.

Comments are requested as to whether the final regulations should contain exceptions to the general 180-day rule and whether it would be helpful for either the final regulations or other guidance to illustrate the application of the general 180-day rule to additional circumstances, and what those circumstances are.

E. Attributes of Included Income When Gain Deferral Ends

Section 1400Z-2(a)(1)(B) and (b) require taxpayers to include in income previously deferred gains. The proposed regulations provide that all of the deferred gain's tax attributes are preserved through the deferral period and are taken into account when the gain is included. The preserved tax attributes include those taken into account under sections 1(h), 1222, 1256, and any other applicable provisions of the Code. Furthermore, the proposed regulations address situations in which separate investments providing indistinguishable property rights (such as serial purchases of common stock in a corporation that is a QOF) are made at different times or are made at the same time with separate gains possessing different attributes (such as different holding periods). If a taxpayer disposes of less than all of its fungible interests in a QOF, the proposed regulations provide that the QOF interests disposed of must be identified using a first-in, first-out (FIFO) method. Where the FIFO method does not provide a complete answer, such as where gains with different attributes are invested in indistinguishable interests at the same time, the proposed regulations provide that a pro-rata method must be used to determine the character, and any other attributes, of the gain recognized. Examples in the proposed regulations illustrate this rule.

Comments are requested as to whether different methods should be used. Any such alternative methods must both provide certainty as to which fungible interest a taxpayer disposes of and allow taxpayers to comply easily with the requirements of section 1400Z-2(a)(1)(B) and (b),which require that certain dispositions of an interest in a QOF cause deferred gain be included in a taxpayer's income.

II. *Special rules*

A. Gain not already subject to an election.

Under section 1400Z-2(a)(2)(A), no election may be made under section 1400Z-2(a)(1) with respect to a sale or exchange if an election previously made with respect to that sale or exchange is in effect. There has been some confusion as to whether this language bars a taxpayer from making multiple elections within 180-days for various parts of the gain from a single sale or exchange of property held by the taxpayer. This rule in section 1400Z-2(a)(2)(A) is meant to exclude from the section 1400Z-2(a)(1) election multiple purported elections with respect to the same gain. (Although the gain itself can be deferred only once, a taxpayer might be seeking to multiply the investments eligible for various increases in basis.) Thus, the proposed regulations clarify that in the case of a taxpayer who has made an election under section 1400Z-2(a) with respect to some but not all of an eligible gain, the term "eligible gain" includes the portion of that eligible gain as to which no election has been made. (All elections with respect to portions of the same gain would, of course, be subject to the same 180-day period.)

B. Section 1256 contracts

The proposed regulations provide rules for capital gains arising from section 1256 contracts. Under section 1256, a taxpayer generally "marks to market" each section 1256 contract at the termination or transfer of the taxpayer's position in the contract or on the last business day of the taxable year if the contract is still held by the taxpayer at that time. The mark causes the taxpayer to take into account in the taxable year any not-yet recognized appreciation or depreciation in the position. This gain or loss, if capital, is treated as 60 percent long-term capital gain or loss and 40 percent short-term capital gain or loss. Currently, for federal income tax purposes, the only relevant information required to be reported by a broker to the IRS and to individuals and certain other taxpayers holding section 1256 contracts, is the taxpayer's net recognized gain or loss from all of the taxpayer's section 1256 contracts held during the taxable year. Some taxpayers holding section 1256 contracts, however, report the gain or loss from section 1256 contracts to the IRS on a per contract basis rather than on an aggregate basis. To minimize the burdens on taxpayers, brokers, and the IRS from tax compliance and tax administration, the proposed regulations allow deferral under section 1400Z-2(a)(1) only for a taxpayer's capital gain net income from section 1256 contracts for a taxable year. In addition, because the capital gain net income from section 1256 contracts for a taxable year is determinable only as of the last day of the taxable year, the proposed regulations provide that the 180-day period for investing capital gain net income from section 1256 contracts in a QOF begins on the last day of the taxable year.

Finally, the proposed regulations do not allow any deferral of gain from a section 1256 contract in a taxable year if, at any time during the taxable year, one of the taxpayer's section 1256 contracts was part of an offsetting-positions transaction (as defined later in the proposed regulations and described later in this preamble) in which any of the other positions was not also a section 1256 contract.

Comments are requested on this limitation and on whether capital gain from a section 1256 contract should be eligible for deferral under section 1400Z-2 on a per contract basis rather than on an aggregate net basis. Reporting on a per contract basis might require a significant increase in the number of information returns that taxpayers would need to file with the IRS as compared to the number of information returns that are currently filed on an aggregate net basis. Comments are requested on how to minimize the burdens and complexity that may be associated with reporting on a per contract basis for section 1256 contracts.

C. Offsetting-positions transactions, including straddles

The Treasury Department and the IRS considered allowing deferral under section 1400Z-2(a)(1) for a net amount of capital gain related to a straddle (as defined in section 1092(c)(1)) after the disposition of all positions in the straddle. However, such a rule would pose significant administrative challenges. For example, additional rules would be needed for a taxpayer to defer such a net amount of capital gain when positions are disposed of in different taxable years (and likely would require affected taxpayers to file amended tax returns). Further, additional rules might be needed to take into account the netting requirements for identified mixed straddles described in § 1.1092(b)-3T or 1.1092(b)-6 and for mixed straddle accounts described in § 1.1092(b)-4T. Accordingly, in the interest of sound tax administration and to provide consistent treatment for transactions involving offsetting positions in personal property, the proposed regulations provide that any capital gain from a position that is or has been part of an offsetting-positions transaction (other than an offsetting-positions transaction in which all of the positions are section 1256 contracts) is not eligible for deferral under section 1400Z-2.

An offsetting-positions transaction is defined in the proposed regulations as a transaction in which a taxpayer has substantially diminished the taxpayer's risk of loss from holding one position with respect to personal property by holding one or more other positions with respect to personal property (whether or not of the same kind). It does not matter whether either of the positions is with respect to actively traded personal property. An offsetting-positions transaction includes a straddle as defined in section 1092 and the regulations thereunder, including section 1092(d)(4), which provides rules for positions held by related persons and certain flow-through entities (for example, a partnership). An offsetting-positions transaction also includes a transaction that would be a straddle (taking into account the principles referred to in the preceding sentence) if the straddle definition did not contain the active trading requirement in section 1092(d)(1).

III. *Gains of Partnerships and Other Pass-Through Entities*

Commenters have requested clarification regarding whether deferral is possible under section 1400Z-2 any time a partnership would otherwise recognize capital gain. The proposed regulations provide rules that permit a partnership to elect deferral under section 1400Z-2 and, to the extent that the partnership does not elect deferral, provide rules that allow a partner to do so. These rules both clarify the circumstances under which each can elect and clarify when the applicable 180-day period begins.

Proposed § 1.1400Z-2(a)-1(c)(1) provides that a partnership may elect to defer all or part of a capital gain to the extent that it makes an eligible investment in a QOF. Because the election provides for deferral, if the election is made, no part of the deferred gain is required to be included in the distributive shares of the partners under section 702, and the gain is not subject to section 705(a)(1). Proposed § 1.1400Z-2(a)-1(c)(2) provides that, to the extent that a partnership does not elect to defer capital gain, the capital gain is included in the distributive shares of the partners under section 702 and is subject to section 705(a)(1). If all or any portion of a partner's distributive share satisfies all of the rules for eligibility under section 1400Z-2(a)(1) (including not arising from a sale or exchange with a person that is related either to the partnership or to the partner), then the partner generally may elect its own deferral with respect to the partner's distributive share. The partner's deferral is potentially available to the extent that the partner makes an eligible investment in a QOF.

Consistent with the general rule for the beginning of the 180-day period, the partner's 180-day period generally begins on the last day of the partnership's taxable year, because that is the day on which the partner would be required to recognize the gain if the gain is not deferred. The proposed regulations, however, provide an alternative for situations in which the partner knows (or receives information) regarding both the date of the partnership's gain and the partnership's decision not to elect deferral under section 1400Z-2. In that case, the partner may choose to begin its own 180-day period on the same date as the start of the partnership's 180-day period.

The proposed regulations state that rules analogous to the rules provided for partnerships and partners apply to other pass-through entities (including S corporations, decedents' estates, and trusts) and to their shareholders and beneficiaries. Comments are requested regarding whether taxpayers need additional details regarding analogous treatment for pass-through entities that are not partnerships.

IV. *How to Elect Deferral*

These proposed regulations require deferral elections to be made at the time and in the manner provided by the Commissioner of Internal Revenue (Commissioner). The Commissioner may prescribe in regulations, revenue procedures, notices, or other guidance published in the Internal Revenue Bulletin or in forms and instructions the time, form, and manner in which an eligible taxpayer may elect to defer eligible gains under section 1400Z-2(a). It is currently anticipated that taxpayers will make deferral elections on Form 8949, which will be attached to their Federal income tax returns for the taxable year in which the gain would have been recognized if it had not been deferred. Form instructions to this effect are expected to be released very shortly after these proposed regulations are published. Comments are requested whether additional proposed regulations or other guidance are needed to clarify the required procedures. In addition IRS releases draft forms for public review and comments. These drafts are posted to *www.IRS.gov/DraftForms* and include a cover sheet that indicates how to submit comments.

V. *Section 1400Z-2(c) Election for Investments Held At Least 10 Years*

A. In General

Under section 1400Z-2(c), a taxpayer that holds a QOF investment for at least ten years may elect to increase the basis of the investment to the fair market value of the investment on the date that the investment is sold or exchanged.

The basis step-up election under section 1400Z-2(c) is available only for gains realized upon investments that were made in connection with a proper deferral election under section 1400Z-2(a). It is possible for a taxpayer to invest in a QOF in part with gains for which a deferral election under section 1400Z-2(a) is made and in part with other funds (for which no section 1400Z-2(a) deferral election is made or for which no such election is available). Section 1400Z-2(e) requires that these two types of QOF investments be treated as separate investments, which receive different treatment for Federal income tax purposes. Pursuant to section 1400Z-2(e)(1)(B), the proposed regulations reiterate that a taxpayer may make the election to step-up basis in an investment in a QOF that was held for 10 years or more only if a proper deferral election under section 1400Z-2(a) was made for the investment.

B. QOF Investments and the 10-Year Zone Designation Period

Section 1400Z-2(c), as stated above, permits a taxpayer to elect to increase the basis in its investment in a QOF if the investment is held for at least ten years from the date of the original investment in the QOF. However, under section 1400Z-1(f), the designations of all qualified opportunity zones now in existence will expire on December 31, 2028. The loss of qualified opportunity zone designation raises numerous issues regarding gain deferral elections that are still in effect when the designation expires. Among the issues that the zone expiration date raises is whether, after the relevant qualified opportunity zone loses its designation, investors may still make basis step-up elections for QOF investments from 2019 and later.

Section 1400Z-2 does not contain specific statutory language like that in some other provisions, such as the D.C. enterprise zones provision in section 1400B(b)(5), that expressly permits a taxpayer to satisfy the requisite holding period after the termination of the designation of a zone. Commenters have raised the question described in the preceding paragraph—whether a taxpayer whose investment in a QOF has its 10-year anniversary after the 2028 calendar year will be able to take advantage of the basis step-up election provided in section 1400Z-2(c). The incentive provided by this benefit is integral to the primary purpose of the provision (*see* H.R. Rept. 115-466, 537, which describes the intent to attract an influx of capital to designated low income communities). For this reason, the proposed regulations permit taxpayers to make the basis step-up election under section 1400Z-2(c) after a qualified opportunity zone designation expires.

The ability to make this election is preserved under these proposed regulations until December 31, 2047, 20$^{1}/_{2}$ years after the latest date that an eligible taxpayer may properly make an investment that is part of an election to defer gain under section 1400Z-2(a). Because the latest gain subject to deferral would be at the end of 2026, the last day of the 180-day period for that gain would be in late June 2027. A taxpayer deferring such a gain would achieve a 10-year holding period in a QOF investment only in late June 2037. Thus, this proposed rule would permit an investor in a QOF that makes an investment as late as the end of June 2027 to hold the investment in the QOF for the entire 10-year holding period described in section 1400Z-2(c), plus another 10 years.

The additional ten year period is provided to avoid situations in which, in order to enjoy the benefits provided by section 1400Z-2(c), a taxpayer would need to dispose of an investment in a QOF shortly after completion of the required 10-year holding period. There may be cases in which disposal shortly after the 10-year holding period would diverge from otherwise desirable business conduct, and, absent the additional time, some taxpayers may lose the statutory benefit.

The Treasury Department and the IRS request comments on this proposed fixed 20$^{1}/_{2}$-year end date for the section 1400Z-2(c) basis step-up election. In particular, whether some other time period would better align with taxpayers' economic interests and the purposes of the statute. Comments may also include an alternative to incentivizing investors to disinvest shortly before any such a fixed end date for the section 1400Z-2(c) basis step-up election. For example, should the regulations provide for a presumed basis step-up election immediately before the ability to elect a step-up upon disposition expires? If such a basis step-up without disposition is allowed, how should a QOF investment be properly valued at the time of the step-up?

VI. *Rules for a Qualified Opportunity Fund*

A. Certification of an Entity as a QOF

Section 1400Z-2(e)(4) allows the Secretary of the Treasury to prescribe regulations for the certification of QOFs for purposes of section 1400Z-2. In order to facilitate the certification process and minimize the information collection burden placed on taxpayers, the proposed regulations generally permit any taxpayer that is a corporation or partnership for tax purposes to self-certify as a QOF, provided that the entity self-certifying is statutorily eligible to do so. The proposed regulations permit the Commissioner to determine the time, form, and manner of the self-certification in IRS forms and instructions or in guidance published in the Internal Revenue Bulletin. It is expected that taxpayers will use Form 8996, Qualified Opportunity Fund, both for initial self-certification and for annual reporting of compliance with the 90-Percent Asset Test in section 1400Z-2(d)(1). It is expected that the Form 8996 would be attached to the taxpayer's Federal income tax return for the relevant tax years. The IRS expects to release this form contemporaneous with the release of these proposed regulations.

B. Designating When a QOF Begins

The proposed regulations allow a QOF both to identify the taxable year in which the entity becomes a QOF and to choose the first month in that year to be treated as a QOF. If an eligible entity fails to specify the first month it is a QOF, then the first month of its initial taxable year as a QOF is treated as the first month that the eligible entity is a QOF. A deferral election under section 1400Z-2(a) may only be made for investments in a QOF. Therefore, a proper deferral election under section 1400Z-2(a) may not be made for an otherwise qualifying investment that is made before an eligible entity is a QOF.

C. Becoming a QOF in a Month Other Than the First Month of the Taxable Year

The proposed regulations provide guidance regarding application of the 90-Percent Asset Test in section 1400Z-2(d)(1) with respect to an entity's first year as a QOF, if the entity chooses to become a QOF beginning with a month other than the first month of its first taxable year. The phrase "first 6-month period of the taxable year of the fund" means the first 6-month period composed entirely of months which are within the taxable year and during which the entity is a QOF. For example, if a calendar-year entity that was created in February chooses April as its first month as a QOF, then the 90-Percent-Asset-Test testing dates for the QOF are the end of September and the end of December. Moreover, if the calendar-year QOF chooses a month after June as its first month as a QOF, then the only testing date for the taxable year is the last day of the QOF's taxable year. Regardless of when an entity becomes a QOF, the last day of the taxable year is a testing date.

The proposed regulations clarify that the penalty in section 1400Z-2(f)(1) does not apply before the first month in which the entity qualifies as a QOF. The Treasury Department and the IRS intend to publish additional proposed regulations that will address, among other issues, the applicability of the section 1400Z-2(f)(1) penalty and conduct that may lead to potential decertification of a QOF.

Section 1400Z-2(e)(4)(B) authorizes regulations to ensure that a QOF has "a reasonable period of time to reinvest the return of capital from investments in qualified opportunity zone stock and qualified opportunity zone partnership interests, and to reinvest proceeds received from the sale or disposition of qualified opportunity zone business property." For example, if a QOF shortly before a testing date sells qualified opportunity zone property, that QOF should have a reasonable amount of time in which to bring itself into compliance with the 90-Percent Asset Test. Soon-to-be-released proposed regulations will provide guidance on these reinvestments by QOFs. Many stakeholders have requested guidance not only on the length of a "reasonable period of time to reinvest" but also on the Federal income tax treatment of any gains that the QOF reinvests during such a period. In the forthcoming notice of proposed rulemaking, the Treasury Department and the IRS will invite additional public comment on the scope of statutorily permissible policy alternatives. The Treasury Department and the IRS will carefully consider those comments in evaluating the widest range of statutorily permissible possibilities.

D. Pre-Existing Entities

Commenters have inquired whether a pre-existing entity may qualify as a QOF or as the issuer of qualified opportunity zone stock or of a qualified opportunity zone partnership. For example, commenters have asked whether a pre-existing entity may self-certify as a QOF or whether, after 2017, a QOF may acquire an equity interest in a pre-existing operating partnership or corporation. The proposed regulations clarify that there is no prohibition to using a pre-existing entity as a QOF or as a subsidiary entity operating a qualified opportunity business, provided that the pre-existing entity satisfies the requirements under section 1400Z-2(d).

As previously discussed, section 1400Z-2(d)(1) requires that a QOF must undergo semi-annual tests to determine whether its assets consist on average of at least 90 percent qualified opportunity zone property. For purposes of these semi-annual tests, section 1400Z-2(d)(2) requires that a tangible asset can be qualified opportunity zone business property by an entity that has self-certified as a QOF or an operating subsidiary entity only if it acquired the asset after 2017 by purchase. The Treasury Department and the IRS request comments on whether there is a statutory basis for additional flexibilities that might facilitate qualification of a greater number of pre-existing entities across broad categories of industries.

E. Valuation Method for Applying the 90-Percent Asset Test

For purposes of the calculation of the 90-Percent Asset Test in section 1400Z-2(d)(1) by the QOF, the proposed regulations require the QOF to use the asset values that are reported on the QOF's applicable financial statement for the taxable year, as defined in § 1.475(a)-4(h) of the Income Tax Regulations. If a QOF does not have an applicable financial statement, the proposed regulations require the QOF to use the cost of its assets. The Treasury Department and the IRS request comments on the suitability of both of these valuation methods, and whether another method, such as tax adjusted basis, would be better for purposes of assurance and administration.

F. Nonqualified Financial Property

Commenters have recommended that the Treasury Department and the IRS adopt a rule that provides that cash be an appropriate QOF property for purposes of the 90-Percent Asset Test, if the cash is held with the intent of investing in qualified opportunity zone property. Specifically, commenters indicated that, because developing a new business or the construction or rehabilitation of real estate may take longer than six months, QOFs should be given longer than the six months provided under section 1400Z-2(d)(1) to invest in qualifying assets.

In response to these comments, the proposed regulations provide a working capital safe harbor for QOF investments in qualified opportunity zone businesses that acquire, construct, or rehabilitate tangible business property, which includes both real property and other tangible property used in a business operating in an opportunity zone. The safe harbor allows qualified opportunity zone businesses to apply the definition of working capital provided in section 1397C(e)(1) to property held by the business for a period of up to 31 months, if there is a written plan that identifies the financial property as property held for the acquisition, construction, or substantial improvement of tangible property in the opportunity zone, there is written schedule consistent with the ordinary business operations of the business that the property will be used within 31-months, and the business substantially complies with the schedule. Taxpayers would be required to retain any written plan in their records.

This expansion of the term "working capital" reflects the fact that section 1400Z-2(d)(iii) anticipates situations in which a QOF or operating subsidiary may need up to 30 months after acquiring a tangible asset in which to improve the asset substantially. In seeking relief, some commenters based their requests on administrative practices that have developed under other sections of the Code that these commenters believe are analogous. The Treasury Department and the IRS request comments on the adequacy of the working-capital safe harbor and of ancillary safe harbors that protect a business during the working capital period, and on whether there is a statutory basis for any additional relief. Comments are also requested about the appropriateness of any further expansion of the "working capital" concept beyond the acquisition, construction, or rehabilitation of tangible business property to the development of business operations in the opportunity zone.

G. Qualified Opportunity Zone Business.

Under section 1400Z-2(d)(1), a QOF is any investment vehicle organized as a corporation or partnership for the purpose of investing in qualified opportunity zone property (other than another QOF). A QOF must hold at least 90 percent of its assets in qualified opportunity zone property. Compliance with the 90 Percent Asset Test is determined by the average of the percentage of the qualified opportunity zone property held in the QOF as measured on the last day of the first 6-month period of the taxable year of the QOF and on the last day of the taxable year of the QOF.

Under section 1400Z-2(d)(2)(A), the term qualified opportunity zone property includes qualified opportunity zone business property. Qualified opportunity zone property may also include certain equity interests in an operating subsidiary entity (either a corporation or a partnership) that qualifies as a qualified opportunity zone business by satisfying certain requirements pursuant to section 1400Z-2(d)(2)(B) and (C).

Consequently, if a QOF operates a trade or business directly and does not hold any equity in a qualified opportunity zone business, at least 90 percent of the QOF's assets must be qualified opportunity zone property.

The definition of qualified opportunity zone business property requires property to be used in a QOZ and also requires new capital to be employed in a QOZ. Under section 1400Z-2(d)(2)(D)(i), qualified opportunity zone business property means tangible property used in a trade or business of a QOF, but only if (1) the property was acquired by purchase after December 31, 2017; (2) the original use of the property in the QOZ commences with the QOF, or the QOF substantially improves the property; and (3) during substantially all of the QOF's holding period for the property, substantially all of the use of the property was in a QOZ.

Under section 1400Z-2(d)(2)(B)(i) and (C), to qualify as a qualified opportunity zone business, an entity must be a qualified opportunity zone business both (a) when the QOF acquires its equity interest in the entity and (b) during substantially all of the QOF's holding period for that interest. The manner of the QOF's acquisition of the equity interest must comply with certain additional requirements.

Under section 1400Z-2(d)(3)(A), for a trade or business to qualify as a qualified opportunity zone business, it must (among other requirements) be one in which *substantially all* of the tangible property owned or leased by the taxpayer is qualified opportunity zone business property.

If an entity qualifies as a qualified opportunity zone business, the value of the QOF's entire interest in the entity counts toward the QOF's satisfaction of the 90 Percent Asset Test. Thus, if a QOF operates a trade or business (or multiple trades or businesses) through one or more entities, then the QOF can satisfy the 90 Percent Asset Test if each of the entities qualifies as a qualified opportunity zone business. The minimum amount of qualified opportunity zone business property owned or leased by a business for it to qualify as a qualified opportunity zone business is controlled by the meaning of the phrase *substantially all* in section 1400Z-2(d)(3)(A)(i).

In determining whether an entity is a qualified opportunity zone business, these proposed regulations propose a threshold to determine whether a trade or business satisfies the *substantially all* requirement in section 1400Z-2(d)(3)(A)(i).

If at least 70 percent of the tangible property owned or leased by a trade or business is qualified opportunity zone business property (as defined section 1400Z-2(d)(3)(A)(i)), the trade or business is treated as satisfying the *substantially all* requirement in section 1400Z-2(d)(3)(A)(i). The 70 percent threshold provided in these proposed regulations is intended to apply only to the term "substantially all" as it is used in section 1400Z-2(d)(3)(A)(i).

The phrase *substantially all* is also used in several other places in section 1400Z-2. That phrase appears in section 1400Z-2(d)(3)(A)(i), in which a qualified opportunity zone business is generally defined as a trade or business "in which substantially all of the tangible property owned or leased by the taxpayer is qualified opportunity zone business property (determined by substituting 'qualified opportunity zone business' for 'qualified opportunity fund' each place it appears in section 1400Z-2(d)(2)(D))." In addition, *substantially all* appears in section 1400Z-2(d)(2)(D)(i)(III), which establishes the conditions for qualifying as an opportunity zone business property "during *substantially all* of the qualified opportunity fund's holding period for such property, *substantially all* of the use of such property was in a qualified opportunity zone" and section 1400Z–2(d)(2)(B)(i)(III) and section 1400Z–2(d)(2)(C)(iii).

Several requirements of section 1400Z-2(d) use *substantially all* multiple times in a row (that is, "substantially all of . . . substantially all of . . . substantially all of . . ."). This compounded use of *substantially all* must be interpreted in a manner that does not result in a fraction that is too small to implement the intent of Congress.

The Treasury Department and the IRS request comments regarding the proposed meaning of the phrase *substantially all* in section1400Z-2(d)(3)(A)(i) as well as in the various other locations in section 1400Z-2(d) where that phrase is used.

H. Eligible Entities.

The proposed regulations clarify that a QOF must be an entity classified as a corporation or partnership for Federal income tax purposes. In addition, it must be created or organized in one of the 50 States, the District of Columbia, or a U.S. possession. In addition, if an entity is organized in a U.S. possession but not in one of the 50 States or in the District of Columbia, then it may be a QOF only if it is organized for the purpose of investing in qualified opportunity zone property that relates to a trade or business operated in the possession in which the entity is organized.

The proposed regulations further clarify that qualified opportunity zone property may include stock or a partnership interest in an entity classified as a corporation or partnership for Federal income tax purposes. In addition, it must be a corporation or partnership created or organized in, or under the laws of, one of the 50 States, the District of Columbia, or a U.S. possession. Specifically, if an entity is organized in a U.S. possession but not in one of the 50 States or the District of Columbia, an equity interest in the entity may be qualified opportunity zone stock or a qualified opportunity zone partnership interest, as the case may be, only if the entity conducts a qualified opportunity zone business in the U.S. possession in which the entity is organized.

The proposed regulations further define a U.S. possession to mean any jurisdiction outside of the 50 States and the District of Columbia in which a designated qualified opportunity zone exists under section 1400Z-1. This definition may include the following U.S. territories: American Samoa, Guam, the Commonwealth of the Northern Mariana Islands, Puerto Rico, and the U.S. Virgin Islands. A complete list of designated qualified opportunity zones is found in Notice 2018-48, 2018-28 I.R.B. 9.

VII. *Section 1400Z-2(e) Investments from Mixed Funds*

If only a portion of a taxpayer's investment in a QOF is subject to the deferral election under section 1400Z-2(a), then section 1400Z-2(e) requires the investment to be treated as two separate investments, which receive different treatment for Federal income tax purposes. Pursuant to section 1400Z-2(e)(1)(B), the proposed regulations reiterate that a taxpayer may make the election to step-up basis in an investment in a QOF that was held for 10 years or more only if a proper deferral election under section 1400Z-2(a) was made for the investment.

Commenters have questioned whether section 752(a) could result in investments with mixed funds under section 1400Z-2(e)(1). Section 1400Z-2(e)(1) requires a taxpayer to treat as two separate investments the combination of an investment to which a section 1400Z-2(a) gain-deferral election applies and an investment of any amount to which such an election does not apply. As previously noted, these proposed regulations clarify that deemed contributions of money under section 752(a) do not constitute an investment in a QOF; therefore, such a deemed contribution does not result in the partner having a separate investment under section 1400Z-2(e)(1). Thus, a partner's increase in outside basis is not taken into account in determining what portion of the partner's interest is subject to the deferral election under section 1400Z-2(a) or what portion is not subject to the deferral election under section 1400Z-2(a). Comments are requested on whether other pass-through entities require similar treatment. Comments are also requested on whether there may be certain circumstances in which not treating the deemed contribution under section 752(a) as creating a separate investment for purposes of section 1400Z-2(e)(1) may be considered abusive or otherwise problematic.

Proposed Effective Date

These regulations generally are proposed to be effective on or after the date of publication in the **Federal Register** of a Treasury decision adopting these proposed rules as final regulations (final regulations publication date). However—

- An eligible taxpayer may rely on the rules of proposed § 1.1400Z-2(a)-1 with respect to eligible gains that would be recognized before the final regulations' date of applicability, but only if the taxpayer applies the rules in their entirety and in a consistent manner.
- A taxpayer may rely on the rules in proposed § 1.1400Z-2(c)-1 with respect to dispositions of investment interests in QOFs in situations where the investment was made in connection with an election under section 1400Z-2(a) that relates to the deferral of a gain such that the first day of 180-day period for the gain was before the final regulations' date of applicability. This reliance is dependent on the taxpayer's applying the rules of § 1.1400Z-2(c)-1 in their entirety and in a consistent manner.
- A QOF may rely on the rules in proposed § 1.1400Z-2(d)-1 with respect to taxable years that begin before the final regulations' date of applicability, but only if the QOF applies the rules in their entirety and in a consistent manner.

- A taxpayer may rely on the rules in proposed § 1.1400Z-2(e)-1 with respect to investments and deemed contributions of money that occur before the final regulations' date of applicability, but only if the taxpayer applies the rules in their entirety and in a consistent manner.

Special Analyses

I. *Regulatory Planning and Review*

Executive Orders 13771, 13563, and 12866 direct agencies to assess costs and benefits of available regulatory alternatives and, if regulation is necessary, to select regulatory approaches that maximize net benefits (including potential economic, environmental, public health and safety effects, distributive impacts, and equity). Executive Order 13563 emphasizes the importance of quantifying both costs and benefits, reducing costs, harmonizing rules, and promoting flexibility.

These proposed regulations have been designated by the Office of Management and Budget's Office of Information and Regulatory Affairs (OIRA) as subject to review under Executive Order 12866 pursuant to the Memorandum of Agreement (April 11, 2018) between the Treasury Department and the Office of Management and Budget regarding review of tax regulations. OIRA has determined that the proposed rulemaking is economically significant and subject to review under EO 12866 and section 1(c) of the Memorandum of Agreement. The Treasury Department and the IRS believe that significant investment will flow into qualified opportunity zones as a result of the TCJA legislation and proposed regulation. This investment is likely to be primarily from other areas of the United States. Accordingly, the proposed regulations have been reviewed by the Office of Management and Budget. In addition, the Treasury Department and the IRS expect the proposed regulation, when final, to be an Executive Order 13771 deregulatory action and request comment on this designation. Details on the costs of the proposed regulations can be found in this economic analysis.

A. *Background and Overview*

Congress enacted section 1400Z-2, in conjunction with section 1400Z-1, as a temporary provision to encourage private sector investment in certain lower-income communities designated as qualified opportunity zones (see Senate Committee on Finance, Explanation of the Bill, at 313 (November 22, 2017)). Taxpayers may elect to defer the recognition of capital gain to the extent of amounts invested in a QOF, provided that the corresponding amounts are invested during the 180-day period beginning on the date such capital gain would have been recognized by the taxpayer. Inclusion of the deferred capital gain in income occurs on the date the investment in the QOF is sold or exchanged, or on December 31, 2026, whichever comes first. For investments in a QOF held longer than five years, taxpayers may exclude 10 percent of the deferred gain from inclusion in income, and for investment held longer than seven years, taxpayers may exclude a total of 15 percent of the deferred gain from inclusion in income. In addition, for investments held longer than 10 years, the post-acquisition gain on the qualifying investment in the QOF may also be excluded from income. In turn, a QOF must hold at least 90 percent of its assets in qualified opportunity zone property, as measured by the average percentage held at the last day of the first 6-month period of the taxable year of the fund and the last day of the taxable year. The statute requires a QOF that fails this 90 percent test to pay a penalty for each month it fails to maintain the 90-percent asset requirement.

The proposed regulations clarify several terms used in the statute, such as what type of gains are eligible for this preferential treatment, what type of taxpayers are eligible, the timing of transactions necessary for satisfying the requirements of the statute, including the time period for which the exclusion on gains for investments held longer than 10 years applies, and certain rules related to the creation and continued qualification of a fund as a QOF.

B. *Need for the Proposed Regulations*

Taxpayers may be unwilling to make investments in QOFs without first having additional clarity on which investments in a QOF would qualify to receive the preferential tax treatment specified by the TCJA. This uncertainty could reduce the amount of investment flowing into lower-income communities designated as qualified opportunity zones below the congressionally intended effect. The lack of additional clarity could also lead to different taxpayers interpreting, and therefore applying, the same statute differently, which could distort the allocation of investment across the qualifying opportunity zones.

C. *Economic Analysis*

1. *Baseline*

The Treasury Department and the IRS have assessed the benefits and costs of the proposed regulations relative to a no-action baseline reflecting anticipated Federal income tax-related behavior in the absence of these proposed regulations.

2. *Anticipated benefits*

a. In general

The Treasury Department and the IRS expect that the certainty and clarity provided by these proposed regulations, relative to the baseline, will enhance U.S. economic performance under the statute. Under the proposed regulations, taxpayers are provided clarity on the type and timing of transactions that would qualify for the beneficial tax treatment provided for investments in QOFs. As a primary benefit, the clarity provided by these proposed regulations would reduce planning costs for taxpayers and make it easier for taxpayers to make investment decisions that more precisely conform to the statutory requirements for QOFs. In addition, the reduction in uncertainty should encourage investment to flow into qualified opportunity zones, consistent with the intent of the TCJA.

The Treasury Department and the IRS considered various alternatives in the promulgation of the proposed regulations, with the major ones described in the following paragraphs. These alternatives included not issuing the proposed regulations under section 1400Z-2. This path was not chosen for several reasons. The TCJA provides both a reward in terms preferential tax treatment of deferred gains, but also a penalty if a QOF does not maintain compliance with the 90-percent asset test. Without the proposed regulations, some taxpayers may have foregone making promising investments within a qualifying opportunity zone out of concern that the investment may later be determined to not be a qualifying investment. As described in the following paragraphs, the proposed regulations help clarify several areas in which the statutory language was either ambiguous or not very specific. Overall, the clarity provided by the proposed regulations should reduce planning costs by taxpayers and enable taxpayers to make economically efficient decisions given the context of the whole Code.

b. Clarity regarding eligible gains

The proposed regulations specify that only capital gains are eligible for deferral and potential exclusion under section 1400Z-2. As discussed in section I.A of the Explanation of Provisions, there is ambiguity that results from the variation between the operative statutory text and the section heading in the statute regarding what type of gains would be eligible for deferral. The Treasury Department and the IRS determined that Congress intended deferral only to be available to capital gains. This clarity provided in the proposed regulations would reduce uncertainty for taxpayers regarding what transactions would qualify for the preferential tax treatment and also reduce administrative and compliance costs.

c. Clarity regarding application to eligible taxpayers

The proposed regulations also clarify which taxpayers are eligible to defer the recognition of capital gain through investing in a QOF and describe how different types of taxpayers may satisfy the requirements for electing to defer capital gain consistent with the rules of section 1400Z-2 and the overall Code. In particular, the proposed regulations describe rules for how partnerships and partners in a partnership may invest in a QOF and elect to defer recognition of capital gains. Partnerships are expected to be a significant source of funds invested in QOFs. Without these proposed rules clarifying how partnerships and partners may satisfy the requirements for the preferential treatment of capital gains, partners may be less willing to invest in a QOF. The proposed regulations help provide a uniform signal to different types of taxpayers of the availability of this preferential treatment of capital gains and provide the mechanics of how these different taxpayers may satisfy the requirements imposed by the statute. Thus these different types of taxpayers may make decisions that are more economically efficient contingent on the overall Code.

d. Clarity regarding electing post-10-year gain exclusion if zone designation expires

Proposed §1.1400Z-2(c)-1 specifies that expiration of a zone designation would not impair the ability of a taxpayer to elect the exclusion from gains for investments held for at least 10 years, provided the disposition of the investment occurs prior to January 1, 2048. The Treasury Department and the IRS considered four alternatives regarding the interaction between the expiration of the designated zones and the election to exclude gain for investments held more than 10 years. A discussion of the economic costs and benefits of the four options follows.

i. Remaining silent on electing post-10-year gain exclusion

The first alternative would be for the proposed regulations to remain silent on this issue. Section 1400Z-2(c) permits a taxpayer to increase the basis in the property held in a QOF longer than 10 years to be equal to the fair market value of that property on the date that the investment is sold or exchanged, thus excluding post-acquisition capital gain on the investment from tax. However, the statutory expiration of the designation of qualified opportunity zones on December 31, 2028, makes it unclear to what extent investments in a QOF made after 2018 would qualify for this exclusion.

Some taxpayers may believe that only investments in a QOF made prior to January 1, 2019, would be eligible for the exclusion from gain if held greater than 10 years. Such taxpayers may rush to complete transactions within 2018, while others may choose to hold off indefinitely from investing in a QOF until they received clarity on the availability of the 10-year exclusion from gain for investments made later than 2018. Other taxpayers may plan to invest in a QOF after 2018 with the expectation that future regulations would be provided or the statute would be amended to make it clear that dispositions of assets within a QOF after 2028 would be eligible for exclusion if held longer than 10 years. The ambiguity of the statute is likely to lead to uneven response by different taxpayers, dependent on the taxpayer's interpretation of the statute, which may lead to an inefficient allocation of investment across qualified opportunity zones.

ii. Providing a clear deadline for electing post-10-year gain exclusion

The alternative adopted by the proposed regulations clarifies that as long as the investment in the QOF was made with funds subject to a proper deferral election under section 1400Z-2(a), which requires the investment to be made prior to June 29, 2027, then the 10-year gain exclusion election is allowed as long as the disposition of the investment occurs before January 1, 2048. This proposed rule would provide certainty to taxpayers regarding the timing of investments eligible for the 10-year gain exclusion. Taxpayers would have a more uniform understanding of what transactions would be eligible for the favorable treatment on capital gains. This would help taxpayers determine which investments provide a sufficient return to compensate for the extra costs and risks of investing in a QOF. This proposed rule would likely lead to an increase in investment within QOFs compared the proposed regulations remaining silent on this issue.

However, setting a fixed date for the disposition of eligible QOFs investments could introduce economic inefficiencies. Some taxpayers may dispose of their investment in a QOF by the deadline in the proposed regulation primarily in order to receive the benefit of the gain exclusion, but that selling date may not be optimal for the taxpayer in terms of the portfolio of assets that the taxpayer could have chosen to invest in were there no deadline. Setting a fixed deadline may also generate an overall decline in asset values in some qualified opportunity zones if many investors in QOFs seek to sell their portion of the fund within the same time period. This decline in asset values may affect the broader level of economic activity within some qualified opportunity zones or affect other investors in such zones that did not invest through a QOF. In anticipation of this fixed deadline, some taxpayers may choose to dispose of QOF assets earlier than the deadline to avoid an anticipated "rush to the exits," but this would seem to conflict with the purpose of the incentives in the statute to encourage "patient" capital investment within qualified opportunity zones. While the proposed regulations may produce these inefficiencies, by providing a long time period for which taxpayers may dispose of their investment within a QOF and still qualify for the exclusion the proposed regulations will lead any such inefficiencies to be minor.

iii. Providing no deadline for electing gain exclusion

As an alternative, the proposed regulations could have provided no deadline for electing the 10-year gain exclusion for investments in a QOF, while still stating that the ability to make the election is not impaired solely because the designation of one or more qualified opportunity zones ceases to be in effect. While this alternative would eliminate the economic inefficiencies associated with a fixed deadline and would likely lead to greater investment in QOFs, it could introduce substantial additional administrative and compliance costs. Taxpayers would also need to maintain records and make efforts to maintain compliance with the rules of section 1400Z-2 on an indefinite basis.

iv. Providing fair market value basis without disposition of investment

Another alternative considered would allow taxpayers to elect to increase the basis in their investment in the QOF if held at least 10 years to the fair market value of the investment without disposing of the property, as long as the election was made prior to January 1, 2048. (Analogously, the proposed regulations could have provided that, at the close of business of the day on which a taxpayer first has the ability to make the 10-year gain exclusion election, the basis in the investment automatically sets to the greater of current basis or the fair market value of the investment.) This alternative would minimize the economic inefficiencies of the proposed regulations resulting from taxpayers needing to dispose of their investment in the opportunity zone at a fixed date not related to any factor other than the lapse of time. However, this approach would require a method of valuing assets that could raise administrative and compliance costs. It may also require the maintenance of records and trained compliance personnel for over two decades.

v. Summary

As discussed in section V.B of the Explanation of Provisions, the Treasury Department and the IRS have determined the ability to exclude gains for investment held at least 10 years in a QOF is integral to the TCJA's purpose of creating qualified opportunity zones. The proposed regulations provide a uniform signal to all taxpayers on the availability of this tax incentive, which should encourage greater investment, and a more efficient distribution of investment, in QOFs than in the absence of these proposed regulations. The relative costs and benefits of the various alternatives are difficult to measure and compare. The proposed regulations would likely produce the lowest compliance and administrative costs among the alternatives and any associated economic inefficiencies are likely to be small.

e. Safe harbors for statutory qualifying property tests

Section 1400Z-2 contains several rules limiting taxpayers from benefitting from the deferral and exclusion of capital gains from income offered by that section without also locating investment within a qualifying opportunity zone. The proposed regulations clarify the rules related to nonqualified financial property and what amounts can be held in cash and cash equivalents as working capital. The statute requires that a QOF must hold 90 percent of its assets in qualified opportunity zone property, such as owning stock or a partnership interest in a qualified opportunity zone business. A qualifying opportunity zone business is subject to the requirements of section 1397C(b)(8), that less than 5 percent of the aggregate adjusted basis of the entity is attributable to nonqualified financial property. The proposed regulations establish a working capital safe harbor consistent with section 1397C(e)(1), under which a qualified opportunity zone business may hold cash or cash equivalents for a period not longer than 31 months and not violate section 1397C(b)(8).

The Treasury Department and the IRS expect that the establishment of safe harbors under these parameters will provide net economic benefits. Without specification of the working capital safe harbor, some taxpayers would not invest in a QOF for fear that the QOF would not be able to deploy the funds soon enough to satisfy the 90-percent asset test. Thus, this part of the proposed regulations would generally encourage investment in QOFs by providing greater specificity to how an entity may consistently satisfy the statutory requirements for maintaining a QOF without penalty. In addition, this part of the proposed regulations minimizes the distortion that may arise between purchasing existing property and sufficiently rehabilitating that property versus constructing new property, as the time frame specified under the statute and proposed regulations are similar (30 months after acquisition for rehabilitating existing property versus 31 months for acquiring and rehabilitating existing property or for constructing new property).

A longer or a shorter period could have been chosen for the working capital safe harbor. A shorter time period would minimize the ability of taxpayers to use the investment in a QOF as a way to lower taxes without actually investing in tangible assets within a qualified opportunity zone, but taxpayers may also forego legitimate investments within an opportunity zone out of concern of not being able to deploy the working capital fast enough to meet the requirements. A longer period would have the opposite effects. Taxpayers could potentially invest in a QOF and receive the benefits of the tax incentive for multiple years before the money is invested into a qualified opportunity zone.

f. Definition of substantially all

The proposed regulations specify that if at least 70 percent of the tangible property owned or leased by a trade or business is qualified opportunity zone business property, then the trade or business is treated as satisfying the substantially all requirement of section 1400Z-2(d)(3)(A)(i). This clarity would provide taxpayers greater certainty when evaluating potential investment opportunities as to whether the potential investment would satisfy the statutory requirements.

However, the 70 percent requirement for a trade or business will give QOFs an incentive to invest in a qualified opportunity zone business rather than owning qualified opportunity zone business property directly. For example, consider a QOF with $10 million in assets that plans to invest 100 percent of its assets in real property. If it held the real property directly, then at least $9 million (90 percent) of the property must be located within an opportunity zone to satisfy the 90 percent asset test for the QOF. If instead, it invests in a subsidiary that then holds real property, then only $7 million (70 percent) of the property must be located within an opportunity zone. In addition, if the QOF only invested $9 million into the subsidiary, which then held 70 percent of its property within an opportunity zone, the investors in the QOF could receive the statutory tax benefits while investing only $6.3 million (63 percent) of its assets within a qualified opportunity zone.

The Treasury Department and the IRS also considered setting this "substantially all" threshold at 90 percent. This would reduce, but not eliminate, the incentive the QOF has to invest in a qualified opportunity zone business rather than directly owning qualified opportunity zone business property compared to the 70 percent threshold. Please see earlier discussion and request for comment regarding this definition for additional detail.

3. *Anticipated impacts on administrative and compliance costs*

The Treasury Department and the IRS anticipate decreased taxpayer compliance costs resulting from the proposed regulations due to the greater taxpayer certainty regarding how to comply with the requirements set forth in the statute. The Treasury Department also anticipates decreased administrative and enforcement costs for the IRS.

D. *Paperwork Reduction Act*

The collection of information in these proposed regulations with respect to QOFs is in proposed § 1.1400Z-2(d)-1. The collection of information in proposed § 1.1400Z-2(d)-1 is satisfied by submitting a new reporting form, Form 8996, Qualified Opportunity Fund, with an income tax return. For purposes of the Paperwork Reduction Act of 1995 (44 U.S.C. 3507(d)) (PRA), the reporting burden associated with proposed § 1.1400Z-2(d)-1 will be reflected in the Paperwork Reduction Act submission associated with new Form 8996 (OMB control number 1545-0123). Notice of the availability of the draft Form 8996 and request for comment will be available at IRS.gov/DraftForms. In addition, the Treasury Department and the IRS request comments on any aspect of this collection in this proposed rulemaking.

The collection of information in proposed § 1.1400Z-2(d)-1 requires each QOF, be it a corporation or partnership, to file a Form 8996 to certify that it is organized to invest in qualified opportunity zone property. In addition, a QOF files Form 8996 annually to certify that the qualified opportunity fund meets the investment standards of section 1400Z-2 or to figure the penalty if it fails to meet the investment standards.

II. *Regulatory Flexibility Act*

Under the Regulatory Flexibility Act (RFA) (5 U.S.C. chapter 6), it is hereby certified that these proposed regulations, if adopted, would not have a significant economic impact on a substantial number of small entities that are directly affected by the proposed regulations. Therefore, a regulatory flexibility analysis under the Regulatory Flexibility Act (5 U.S.C. chapter 6) is not required. Although there is a lack of available data regarding the extent to which small entities invest in QOFs, this certification is based on the belief of the Treasury Department and the IRS that these funds will generally involve investments made by larger entities and investments are entirely voluntary. The Treasury Department and the IRS specifically solicit comment from any party, particularly affected small entities, on the accuracy of this certification.

Pursuant to section 7805(f), this notice of proposed rulemaking has been submitted to the Chief Counsel for Advocacy of the Small Business Administration for comment on its impact on small business.

III. *Unfunded Mandates Reform Act*

Section 202 of the Unfunded Mandates Reform Act of 1995 (UMRA) requires that agencies assess anticipated costs and benefits and take certain other actions before issuing a final rule that includes any Federal mandate that may result in expenditures in any one year by a state, local, or tribal government, in the aggregate, or by the private sector, of $100 million in 1995 dollars, updated annually for inflation. In 2018, that threshold is approximately $150 million. This rule does not include any Federal mandate that may result in expenditures by state, local, or tribal governments, or by the private sector in excess of that threshold.

IV. *Executive Order 13132: Federalism*

Executive Order 13132 (entitled "Federalism") prohibits an agency from publishing any rule that has federalism implications if the rule either imposes substantial, direct compliance costs on state and local governments, and is not required by statute, or preempts state law, unless the agency meets the consultation and funding requirements of section 6 of the Executive Order. This proposed rule does not have federalism implications and does not impose substantial direct compliance costs on state and local governments or preempt state law within the meaning of the Executive Order.

Statement of Availability of IRS Documents

IRS Revenue Procedures, Revenue Rulings, and Notices cited in this preamble are published in the Internal Revenue Bulletin (or Cumulative Bulletin) and are available from the Superintendent of Documents, U.S. Government Publishing Office, Washington, DC 20402, or by visiting the IRS web site at *http://www.irs.gov.*

Comments

Before these proposed regulations are adopted as final regulations, consideration will be given to any electronic and written comments that are submitted timely to the IRS as prescribed in this preamble under the **"ADDRESSES"** heading. The Treasury Department and the IRS request comments on all aspects of the proposed rules. All comments will be available at *http://www.regulations.gov* or upon request.

Drafting Information

The principal author of these proposed regulations is Erika C. Reigle, Office of Associate Chief Counsel (Income Tax & Accounting). However, other personnel from the Treasury Department and the IRS participated in their development.

[¶49,774] Proposed Amendments of Regulations (REG-136724-17), published in the Federal Register on October 29, 2018.

[Code Secs. 36B, 9801, 9802, 9815 and 9831]

Health reimbursement arrangement (HRA): Employee Retirement Income Security Act (ERISA): Insurance.—Reg. §54.9802-4 and amendments of Regs. §§1.36B-2, 54.9801-2, 54.9815-2711 and 54.9831-1, regarding health reimbursement arrangements (HRAs) and other account-based group health plans, are proposed.

AGENCY: Internal Revenue Service, Department of the Treasury; Employee Benefits Security Administration, Department of Labor; Centers for Medicare & Medicaid Services, Department of Health and Human Services.

ACTION: Notice of proposed rulemaking.

SUMMARY: This document sets forth proposed rules to expand opportunities for working men and women and their families to access affordable, quality healthcare through proposed changes to regulations under various provisions of the Public Health Service Act (PHS Act), the Employee Retirement Income Security Act (ERISA), and the Internal Revenue Code (Code) regarding health reimbursement arrangements (HRAs) and other account-based group health plans. (For simplicity, this preamble generally refers only to HRAs, but references to HRAs should also be considered to include other account-based group health plans, unless indicated otherwise.) Specifically, these proposed rules allow integrating HRAs with individual health insurance coverage, if certain conditions are met. The proposed rules also set forth conditions under which certain HRAs would be recognized as limited excepted benefits. Also, the Department of the Treasury (Treasury Department) and the Internal Revenue Service (IRS) propose rules regarding premium tax credit (PTC) eligibility for individuals offered coverage under an HRA integrated with individual health insurance coverage. In addition, the Department of Labor (DOL) proposes a clarification to provide plan sponsors with assurance that the individual health insurance coverage the premiums of which are reimbursed by an HRA or a qualified small employer health reimbursement arrangement (QSEHRA) does not become part of an ERISA plan, provided certain conditions are met. Finally, the Department of Health and Human Services (HHS) proposes rules that would provide a special enrollment period in the individual market for individuals who gain access to an HRA integrated with individual health insurance coverage or who are provided a QSEHRA. The goal of these proposed rules is to expand the flexibility and use of HRAs to provide more Americans with additional options to obtain quality, affordable healthcare. The proposed rules would affect employees and their family members; employers, employee organizations, and other plan sponsors; group health plans; health insurance issuers; and purchasers of individual health insurance coverage. **DATES**: Comments are due on or before [insert date 60 days after date of publication in the **Federal Register**].

ADDRESSES: Written comments may be submitted to the addresses specified below. Any comment that is submitted will be shared with the DOL and HHS. Please do not submit duplicates.

All comments will be made available to the public. **Warning:** Do not include any personally identifiable information (such as name, address, or other contact information) or confidential business information that you do not want publicly disclosed. All comments are posted on the Internet exactly as received, and can be retrieved by most Internet search engines. No deletions, modifications, or redactions will be made to the comments received, as they are public records. Comments may be submitted anonymously.

Comments, identified by REG-136724-17, may be submitted by one of the following methods:

Federal eRulemaking Portal: http://www.regulations.gov. Follow the instructions for submitting comments.

Mail: CC:PA:LPD:PR (REG-136724-17), Room 5205, Internal Revenue Service, P.O. Box 7604, Ben Franklin Station, Washington, DC 20044.

Hand or courier delivery: Monday through Friday between the hours of 8 a.m. and 4 p.m. to CC:PA:LPD:PR (REG-136724-17), Courier's Desk, Internal Revenue Service, 1111 Constitution Avenue NW., Washington, DC 20224.

Comments received will be posted without change to *www.regulations.gov* and available for public inspection.

Inspection of Public Comments: All comments received before the close of the comment period are available for viewing by the public, including any personally identifiable information that is included in a comment. All comments received before the close of the comment period will be posted on the following Web site as soon as possible after they have been received: *https://www.regulations.gov.* Follow the search instructions on that Web site to view public comments.

FOR FURTHER INFORMATION CONTACT: Christopher Dellana, Internal Revenue Service, Department of the Treasury, at (202) 317-5500; Elizabeth Schumacher or Matthew Litton, Employee Benefits Security Administration, Department of Labor, at (202) 693-8335; David Mlawsky or Cam Clemmons, Centers for Medicare & Medicaid Services, Department of Health and Human Services, at (410) 786-1565.

Customer Service Information: Individuals interested in obtaining information from the DOL concerning employment-based health coverage laws may call the EBSA Toll-Free Hotline at 1-866-444-EBSA (3272) or visit the DOL's web site (www.dol.gov/ebsa). In addition, information from HHS on private health insurance coverage and coverage provided by nonfederal governmental group health plans can be found on the Centers for Medicare & Medicaid Services (CMS) web site (www.cms.gov/cciio), and information on healthcare reform can be found at www.HealthCare.gov.

SUPPLEMENTARY INFORMATION:

I. Background

A. *Executive Order 13813*

On October 12, 2017, President Trump issued Executive Order 13813[1], "Promoting Healthcare Choice and Competition Across the United States," stating, in part, that the "Administration will prioritize three areas for improvement in the near term: association health plans (AHPs), short-term, limited-duration insurance (STLDI), and health reimbursement arrangements (HRAs)." With regard to HRAs, the Executive Order directs the Secretaries of the Treasury, Labor, and HHS to "consider proposing regulations or revising guidance, to the extent permitted by law and supported by sound policy, to increase the usability of HRAs, to expand employers' ability to offer HRAs to their employees, and to allow HRAs to be used in conjunction with nongroup coverage." The Executive Order further provides that expanding "the flexibility and use of HRAs would provide many Americans, including employees who work at small businesses, with more options for financing their healthcare." The proposed rules have been developed in response to this Executive Order.[2]

B. *Health Reimbursement Arrangements and Other Account-Based Group Health Plans*

1. *In General*

An account-based group health plan is an employer-provided group health plan that provides for reimbursement of expenses for medical care (as defined under section 213(d) of the Code) (medical care expenses), subject to a maximum fixed-dollar amount of reimbursements for a period (for example, a calendar year). An HRA is a type of account-based group health plan funded solely by employer contributions (with no salary reduction contributions or other contributions by employees) that reimburses an employee solely for medical care expenses incurred by the employee, or the employee's spouse, dependents, and children who, as of the end of the taxable year, have not attained age 27, up to a maximum dollar amount for a coverage period.[3] The reimbursements under these types of arrangements are excludable from the employee's income and wages for Federal income tax

---

[1] 82 FR 48385 (Oct. 17, 2017).

[2] In response to Executive Order 13813, on June 21, 2018, DOL published the Definition of Employer under Section 3(5) of ERISA - Association Health Plans final rule and on August 3, 2018, DOL, HHS and the Treasury Department published the Short-Term, Limited-Duration Insurance final rule. *See* the Association Health Plan final rule at 83 FR 28912 and the Short-Term, Limited-Duration Insurance final rule at 83 FR 38212.

[3] *See* IRS Notice 2002-45, 2002-02 CB 93; Revenue Ruling 2002-41, 2002-2 CB 75; IRS Notice 2013-54, 2013-40 IRB 287.

and employment tax purposes. Amounts that remain in the HRA at the end of the year often may be used to reimburse medical care expenses incurred in later years, depending on the terms of the HRA.

HRAs are not the only type of account-based group health plan. For example, an employer payment plan is also an account-based group health plan. An employer payment plan is an arrangement under which an employer reimburses an employee for some or all of the premium expenses incurred for individual health insurance coverage, or other non-employer sponsored hospital or medical insurance, such as a reimbursement arrangement described in Revenue Ruling 61-146, 1961-2 CB 25, or an arrangement under which the employer uses its funds directly to pay the premium for individual health insurance coverage or other non-employer sponsored hospital or medical insurance covering the employee.[4] Other examples of account-based group health plans include health flexible spending arrangements (health FSAs) and certain other employer-provided medical reimbursement plans that are not HRAs.[5]

2. *Application of the Patient Protection and Affordable Care Act to HRAs and Other Account-Based Group Health Plans*

The Patient Protection and Affordable Care Act, Pub. L. 111-148, was enacted on March 23, 2010; the Health Care and Education Reconciliation Act of 2010, Pub. L. 111-152, was enacted on March 30, 2010 (collectively, PPACA). PPACA reorganized, amended, and added to the provisions of part A of title XXVII of the PHS Act relating to health coverage requirements for group health plans and health insurance issuers in the group and individual markets. The term "group health plan" includes both insured and self-insured group health plans.

PPACA also added section 715 to ERISA and section 9815 to the Code to incorporate the provisions of part A of title XXVII of the PHS Act, PHS Act sections 2701 through 2728 (the market requirements), into ERISA and the Code, making them applicable to group health plans and health insurance issuers providing health insurance coverage in connection with group health plans. In accordance with section 9831(b) and (c) of the Code, section 732(b) and (c) of ERISA, and sections 2722(b), (c) and 2763 of the PHS Act, the market requirements do not apply to a group health plan or health insurance issuers in the group or individual markets in relation to their provision of excepted benefits described in section 9832(c) of the Code, section 733(c) of ERISA, and section 2791(c) of the PHS Act.[6] See the discussion later in this preamble for additional background on excepted benefits. In addition, in accordance with section 9831(a)(2) of the Code and section 732(a) of ERISA, the market requirements do not apply to a group health plan that has fewer than two participants who are current employees on the first day of the plan year.[7]

PHS Act section 2711, as added by PPACA, generally prohibits group health plans and health insurance issuers offering group or individual health insurance coverage[8] from establishing for any individual any lifetime or annual limits on the dollar value of essential health benefits (EHBs), as defined in section 1302(b) of PPACA. PHS Act section 2711, however, does not prevent a group health plan, or a health insurance issuer offering group or individual health insurance coverage, from placing an annual or lifetime dollar limit for any individual on specific covered benefits that are not EHBs, to the extent these limits are otherwise permitted under applicable law.[9]

---

[4] For more information about employer payment plans, *see* IRS Notice 2013-54, Q1 & Q3, and IRS Notice 2015-17, Q4 & Q5, 2015-14 IRB 845.

[5] A QSEHRA, as defined in section 9831(d) of the Code, is not a group health plan for purposes of the market requirements of the Code (except as provided in section 4980I(f)(4) of the Code), parts 6 and 7 of ERISA, and title XXII and XXVII of the PHS Act, and is not included in the definition of HRAs and other account-based group health plans for purposes of these proposed regulations or this preamble. A QSEHRA is, however, considered a group health plan under the PHS Act for purposes of part C of title XI of the Social Security Act (42 USC 1320d, *et seq.*). *See* section 2791(a)(1) of the PHS Act, as amended by section 18001(c) of the Cures Act. As previously noted, the preamble generally refers only to HRAs, but references to HRAs should also be considered to include other account-based group health plans as defined in these proposed rules, unless otherwise specified. This term does not include QSEHRAs, medical savings accounts (MSAs), or health savings accounts (HSAs). In addition, for purposes of these proposed rules, the term "HRA or other account-based group health plan" does not include an employer arrangement that reimburses the cost of individual health insurance coverage in a cafeteria plan under section 125 of the Code (cafeteria plan premium arrangements); however see later in this preamble for a clarification that plan sponsors may offer such an arrangement in addition to an HRA integrated with individual health insurance coverage in certain circumstances and see later in this preamble for a related comment solicitation.

[6] While the PPACA amendments to PHS Act section 2722(b) and (c) (formerly section 2721(c) and (d)) could be read as restricting the exemption for excepted benefits so that it applies only with respect to subpart 2 of part A of title XXVII of the PHS Act, HHS does not intend to use its resources to enforce the market requirements with respect to excepted benefits offered by non-federal governmental plans and encourages States to adopt a similar approach with respect to issuers of excepted benefits. *See* 75 FR 34537 at 34539-34540 (June 17, 2010).

[7] While the PPACA amendments to title XXVII of the PHS Act removed the parallel provision at section 2722(a) (formerly section 2721(a)), HHS follows a similar approach for retiree-only non-federal governmental plans and encourages States to adopt a similar approach with respect to health insurance issuers of retiree-only plans. *See* 75 FR 34537, 34539-34540 (June 17, 2010).

[8] PHS Act section 2711 applies to grandfathered health plans, except that the annual dollar limit prohibition does not apply to grandfathered individual health insurance coverage. Grandfathered health plans are health plans that were in existence as of March 23, 2010, and that are only subject to certain provisions of PPACA, as long as they maintain status as grandfathered health plans under the applicable regulations. *See* 26 CFR 54.9815-1251, 29 CFR 2590.715-1251, and 45 CFR 147.140.

[9] For information regarding EHBs, *see* HHS's February 25, 2013 final regulations addressing EHBs under section 1302 of PPACA (78 FR 12834); *see also* HHS Notice of Benefit and Payment Parameters for 2016 (80 FR 10871, Feb. 27, 2015). In

HRAs are subject to PHS Act section 2711. An HRA generally will fail to comply with PHS Act section 2711 because the arrangement is a group health plan that imposes an annual dollar limit on EHBs that the HRA will reimburse for an individual.

As explained in prior guidance, however, the Treasury Department, DOL, and HHS (collectively, the Departments) have determined that the annual dollar limit prohibition is not applicable to certain account-based group health plans that are subject to other statutory provisions limiting the benefits available under those plans.[10] Specifically, the Departments have explained that the annual dollar limit prohibition does not apply to health FSAs that are offered through a cafeteria plan under section 125 of the Code (cafeteria plan) because section 9005 of PPACA specifically limits salary reduction contributions to health FSAs to $2,500 (indexed for inflation) per year.[11] Similarly, although medical savings accounts (MSAs) under section 220 of the Code and health savings accounts (HSAs) under section 223 of the Code generally are not treated as group health plans subject to the market requirements,[12] the Departments have concluded that the annual dollar limit prohibition would not apply to an MSA or HSA even if a particular arrangement did meet the criteria to be a group health plan because both types of arrangements are subject to specific statutory provisions that limit the contributions.[13] Therefore, the proposed rules do not apply to MSAs, HSAs, or, in certain circumstances, health FSAs.

PHS Act section 2713, as added by PPACA, requires non-grandfathered group health plans, and health insurance issuers offering non-grandfathered group or individual health insurance coverage, to provide coverage for certain preventive services without imposing any cost-sharing requirements for these services.[14] Non-grandfathered HRAs are subject to and fail to comply with PHS Act section 2713 because, while HRAs may be used to reimburse the costs of preventive services, HRAs do not reimburse such costs after the HRAs have reimbursed the maximum dollar amount for a coverage period, and therefore HRAs fail to provide the required coverage, and violate the prohibition on imposing cost-sharing for preventive services.[15]

3. *Prior Regulations and Guidance on Integration of HRAs and Other Account-Based Group Health Plans*

The Departments have previously issued regulations and subregulatory guidance regarding the application of PHS Act sections 2711 and 2713 to HRAs.[16] The regulations and guidance generally

(Footnote Continued)

addition, HHS issued final rules providing States with additional flexibility to define EHBs, starting with plan years beginning on or after January 1, 2020. 45 CFR 156.111 (83 FR 16930, Apr. 17, 2018). The current regulations under PHS Act section 2711 include a definition of EHBs that applies for plans that are not required to provide EHBs. *See* 26 CFR 54.9815-2711(c), 29 CFR 2590.715-2711(c), and 45 CFR 147.126(c). As explained later in this preamble, the proposed rules set forth in this document include proposed amendments to the definition of EHBs under the PHS Act section 2711 regulations to reflect the updated final EHB rules.

[10] *See* 80 FR 72192, 72201 (November 18, 2015).

[11] Notwithstanding this exclusion for certain health FSAs from the application of the annual dollar limit prohibition, regulations under section 125 of the Code provide that health FSAs are not permitted to reimburse employees for premiums for health coverage. *See* proposed 26 CFR 1.125-5(k)(4) (72 FR 43938, 43959 (Aug. 6, 2007)).

[12] *See* 75 FR 37188, 37190 (June 28, 2010) and IRS Notice 2004-2, Q1 & Q3, 2004-2 IRB 269, which defines an HSA as a tax-exempt trust or custodial account and a high-deductible health plan as a health plan; *see also* DOL Field Assistance Bulletins 2004-01 and 2006-02, providing guidance regarding HSAs not constituting "employee welfare benefit plans" covered by title I of ERISA where employer involvement with the HSA is limited.

[13] *See* 75 FR 37188, 37190 (June 28, 2010).

[14] *See also* 26 CFR 54.9815-2713; 29 CFR 2590.715-2713; and 45 CFR 147.130.

[15] Because MSAs and HSAs are generally not treated as group health plans, these arrangements are not subject to PHS Act section 2713. Health FSAs are group health plans and, unless they are excepted benefits, will fail to satisfy the requirements of PHS Act section 2713 unless integrated with other coverage that satisfies these requirements. For more information about the application of PHS Act section 2713 to health FSAs, *see* IRS Notice 2013-54, Q&A 7; DOL Technical Release 2013-03, Q&A-7; and Insurance Standards Bulletin, Application of Affordable Care Act Provisions to Certain Healthcare Arrangements, September 16, 2013, available at https://www.cms.gov/CCIIO/Resources/Regulations-and-Guidance/Downloads/cms-hra-notice-9-16-2013.pdf.

[16] Regulations and subregulatory guidance issued on this topic include: (1) 75 FR 37188 (June 28, 2010); (2) FAQs about Affordable Care Act Implementation (Part XI), available at https://www.dol.gov/sites/default/files/ebsa/about-ebsa/our-activities/resource-center/faqs/aca-part-xi.pdf or http://www.cms.gov/CCIIO/Resources/Fact-Sheets-and-FAQs/aca_implementation_faqs11.html; (3) IRS Notice 2013-54 and DOL Technical Release 2013-03, issued on September 13, 2013, and Insurance Standards Bulletin, Application of Affordable Care Act Provisions to Certain Healthcare Arrangements, September 16, 2013, available at: https://www.cms.gov/CCIIO/Resources/Regulations-and-Guidance/Downloads/cms-hra-notice-9-16-2013.pdf; (4) IRS FAQ on Employer Healthcare Arrangements, available at https://www.irs.gov/affordable-care-act/employer-health-care-arrangements; (5) FAQs about Affordable Care Act Implementation (Part XXII), available at https://www.dol.gov/sites/default/files/ebsa/about-ebsa/our-activities/resource-center/faqs/aca-part-xxii.pdf or https://www.cms.gov/CCIIO/Resources/Fact-Sheets-and-FAQs/Downloads/FAQs-Part-XXII-FINAL.pdf; (6) IRS Notice 2015-17, issued on February 18, 2015, (as detailed in Notice 2015-17, DOL and HHS reviewed and agreed with the guidance in Part II); (7) 80 FR 72192 (November 18, 2015); (8) Notice 2015-87, issued on December 16, 2015; (9) IRS Notice 2016-17, DOL Technical Release No. 2016-01, and Insurance Standards Bulletin, Application of the Market Reforms and Other Provisions of the Affordable Care Act to Student Health Coverage, each issued on February 5, 2016, available at https://www.cms.gov/CCIIO/Resources/Regulations-and-Guidance/Downloads/student-health-bulletin.pdf; (10) FAQs about Affordable Care Act Implementation Part 33, available at https://www.dol.gov/sites/default/files/ebsa/about-ebsa/our-activities/resource-center/faqs/aca-part-33.pdf or https://www.cms.gov/CCIIO/Resources/Fact-Sheets-and-FAQs/Downloads/ACA-FAQ-Set-33-Final.pdf; and (11) FAQs about Affordable Care Act Implementation Part 37, available at https://www.dol.gov/sites/default/files/ebsa/about-ebsa/our-activities/re-

provide that, if an HRA is "integrated" with other group health plan coverage that complies with PHS Act sections 2711 and 2713, the HRA would be considered in compliance because the combined arrangement complies with PHS Act sections 2711 and 2713. The regulations and guidance also provide that HRAs may be integrated with Medicare and TRICARE coverage if certain conditions are met, but may not be integrated with individual health insurance coverage for purposes of complying with PHS Act sections 2711 and 2713.[17]

In the preamble to the 2010 interim final regulations under PHS Act section 2711, the Departments provided that HRAs may be integrated with "other coverage as part of a group health plan" that complies with PHS Act section 2711 in order for the HRAs to be considered to satisfy PHS Act section 2711.[18] The interim final regulations did not, however, set forth rules for implementing integration; the integration methods were set forth in later subregulatory guidance and subsequently included in the final regulations under PHS Act section 2711.

On September 13, 2013, the Treasury Department and the IRS issued Notice 2013-54, the DOL issued Technical Release 2013-03, and HHS issued contemporaneous guidance explaining that HHS concurred with the DOL and Treasury Department guidance.[19] This guidance stated that an HRA may not be integrated with individual health insurance coverage for purposes of PHS Act sections 2711 and 2713, but described methods for integrating an HRA with another group health plan.[20] The provisions in this guidance were later incorporated into the final regulations under PHS Act section 2711, which are summarized later in this section of the preamble.

On November 6, 2014, the Departments issued FAQs about Affordable Care Act Implementation (Part XXII).[21] Q&A-1 reiterated and clarified prior subregulatory guidance by explaining that if an employer offers its employees cash to reimburse the purchase of individual health insurance coverage, the payment arrangement is a group health plan, without regard to whether the employer treats the money as a pre-tax or post-tax benefit to the employee, and may not be integrated with individual health insurance coverage, and therefore will fail to comply with PHS Act sections 2711 and 2713.[22]

On February 18, 2015, the Treasury Department and the IRS issued Notice 2015-17. Q&A-3 of Notice 2015-17 provides that an arrangement under which an employer reimburses (or pays directly) some or all of the medical care expenses for employees covered by TRICARE constitutes an HRA and may not be integrated with TRICARE to comply with PHS Act sections 2711 and 2713 because TRICARE is not a group health plan for integration purposes. However, Q&A-3 states that an HRA that pays for or reimburses medical care expenses for employees covered by TRICARE may be integrated with another group health plan offered by the employer for purposes of PHS Act sections 2711 and 2713 if (1) the employer offers a group health plan (other than the HRA) to the employee that does not consist solely of excepted benefits and that provides minimum value (MV); (2) the employee participating in the HRA is enrolled in TRICARE; (3) the HRA is available only to employees who are enrolled in TRICARE; and (4) the HRA is limited to reimbursement of cost sharing and excepted benefits, including TRICARE supplemental premiums. Notice 2015-17 also included a general reminder that to the extent such an arrangement is available to active employees it may be subject to restrictions under other laws that prohibit offering financial or other incentives for TRICARE-eligible employees to decline employer-provided group health plan coverage, similar to the Medicare secondary payer rules.

Q&A-3 of Notice 2015-17 also provides that an employer payment plan through which an employer reimburses (or pays directly) all or a portion of Medicare part B or D premiums for employees may not be integrated with Medicare coverage to comply with PHS Act sections 2711 and 2713 because Medicare coverage is not a group health plan. But it provides that this type of employer payment plan may be integrated with another group health plan offered by the employer for

---

(Footnote Continued)

source-center/faqs/aca-part-37.pdf or https://www.cms.gov/CCIIO/Resources/Fact-Sheets-and-FAQs/Downloads/FAQs-Part-37.pdf.

[17] 26 CFR 54.9815-2711(d)(4); 29 CFR 2590.715-2711(d)(4) and 45 CFR 147.126(d)(4).

[18] *See* 75 FR 37188, 37190-37191 (June 28, 2010).

[19] *See* Insurance Standards Bulletin, Application of Affordable Care Act Provisions to Certain Healthcare Arrangements, September 16, 2013, available at https://www.cms.gov/CCIIO/Resources/Regulations-and-Guidance/Downloads/cms-hra-notice-9-16-2013.pdf.

[20] In addition to describing the integration methods, IRS Notice 2013-54 and DOL Technical Release 2013-03, in Q&A-5, provided that, whether or not an HRA is integrated with other group health plan coverage, unused amounts that are credited to the HRA while the HRA is integrated with other group health plan coverage may be used to reimburse medical care expenses in accordance with the terms of the HRA after an employee ceases to be covered by the integrated group health plan coverage without causing the HRA to fail to comply with PHS Act sections 2711 and 2713. In IRS Notice 2015-87, Q&A-2, however, the Departments clarified that an HRA that includes terms permitting the purchase of individual health insurance coverage, even if reimbursement is only allowed after the employee ceases to be covered by other integrated group health plan coverage, fails to be integrated with other group health plan coverage and therefore fails to comply with PHS Act sections 2711 and 2713.

[21] *See* FAQs about Affordable Care Act Implementation (Part XXII), available at https://www.dol.gov/sites/default/files/ebsa/about-ebsa/our-activities/resource-center/faqs/aca-part-xxii.pdf or https://www.cms.gov/CCIIO/Resources/Fact-Sheets-and-FAQs/Downloads/FAQs-Part-XXII-FINAL.pdf.

[22] The Treasury Department and the IRS note that the information included in this preamble is not intended to be guidance regarding the proper Federal tax treatment or consequences of any particular arrangement, except to the extent the preamble addresses the application of sections 36B, 9801, 9802, 9815, 9831 and 9832 of the Code and PHS Act sections 2711 and 2713.

purposes of PHS Act sections 2711 and 2713 if: (1) the employer offers a group health plan (other than the employer payment plan) to the employee that does not consist solely of excepted benefits and that provides MV; (2) the employee participating in the employer payment plan is actually enrolled in Medicare parts A and B; (3) the employer payment plan is available only to employees who are enrolled in Medicare part A and part B or D; and (4) the employer payment plan is limited to reimbursement of Medicare part B or D premiums and excepted benefits, including Medigap premiums. Notice 2015-17 also includes a general reminder that to the extent such an arrangement is available to active employees it may be subject to restrictions under other laws, such as the Medicare secondary payer provisions. See later in this preamble for a discussion of the rules provided in the final regulations under PHS Act section 2711 allowing Medicare part B and D reimbursement arrangements to be integrated with Medicare in certain limited circumstances (that is, generally, for HRAs sponsored by employers with fewer than 20 employees).

On November 18, 2015, the Departments finalized the proposed and interim final rules under PHS Act section 2711, incorporating certain subregulatory guidance regarding HRA integration, and making various additional clarifications (the 2015 regulations).[23] Consistent with the initial subregulatory guidance, the final regulations under PHS Act section 2711 provide two methods for integration of HRAs with other group health plan coverage.[24] The first method applies to HRAs integrated with other group health plan coverage that provides MV (the MV Integration Method).[25] The second method applies to HRAs integrated with other group health plan coverage that does not provide MV (the Non-MV Integration Method).[26]

Both the MV Integration Method and the Non-MV Integration Method require that: (1) the HRA plan sponsor offer the employee a group health plan other than the HRA (non-HRA group coverage); (2) the employee receiving the HRA be enrolled in non-HRA group coverage, even if the non-HRA group coverage is not offered by the HRA plan sponsor, such as a group health plan maintained by an employer of the employee's spouse[27] ; and (3) the HRA is made available only to employees who are enrolled in non-HRA group coverage, regardless of whether such coverage is provided by the HRA plan sponsor. For both methods, the non-HRA group coverage may not consist solely of excepted benefits and, for the MV Integration Method, the non-HRA group coverage offered by the employer and in which the employee enrolls must provide MV.

In addition, both the MV Integration Method and the Non-MV Integration Method require that, under the terms of the HRA, an employee (or former employee) be permitted to permanently opt out of and waive future reimbursements at least annually from the HRA. Both integration methods also require that, upon termination of employment, either the funds remaining in the HRA are forfeited or the employee is permitted to permanently opt out of and waive future reimbursements under the HRA. For this purpose, forfeiture of the funds remaining in the HRA, or waiver of future reimbursements under the HRA, occurs even if the forfeited or waived amounts may be reinstated upon a fixed date, the participant's death, or the earlier of the two events.

The two methods differ with respect to the expenses that the HRA may reimburse. Under the MV Integration Method, the HRA may reimburse any medical care expenses, but under the Non-MV Integration Method, the HRA may reimburse only co-payments, co-insurance, deductibles, and premiums under the non-HRA group coverage, as well as medical care that does not constitute EHBs.[28]

The 2015 regulations also include a special integration method for certain arrangements offered by employers that are not required to offer, and do not offer, non-HRA group coverage to employees who are eligible for Medicare coverage (generally, employers with fewer than 20 employees), but that offer non-HRA group coverage that does not consist solely of excepted benefits to employees who are

---

[23] *See* 80 FR 72192 (November 18, 2015). To the extent the final regulations did not incorporate or modify the prior subregulatory guidance, such guidance remains in effect.

[24] These two methods of integration were originally discussed in IRS Notice 2013-54, Q4, and DOL Technical Release 2013-03, available at https://www.dol.gov/agencies/ebsa/employers-and-advisers/guidance/technical-releases/13-03.

[25] *See* 26 CFR 54.9815-2711(d)(2)(ii); 29 CFR 2590.715-2711(d)(2)(ii); 45 CFR 147.126(d)(2)(ii).

[26] *See* 26 CFR 54.9815-2711(d)(2)(i); 29 CFR 2590.715-2711(d)(2)(i); 45 CFR 147.126(d)(2)(i).

[27] In IRS Notice 2015-87, Q&A-4, the Departments clarified that an HRA that may be used to reimburse the medical care expenses of an employee's spouse or dependents (a family HRA) may not be integrated with self-only coverage of the employee under the employer's non-HRA group health plan. On January 12, 2017, the Departments issued guidance to clarify that a family HRA is permitted to be integrated with a combination of coverage under qualifying non-HRA group health plan coverage for purposes of complying with PHS Act sections 2711 and 2713, provided that all of the individuals who are covered under the family HRA are also covered under qualifying non-HRA group coverage. *See* FAQs about Affordable Care Act Implementation Part 37, available at https://www.dol.gov/sites/default/files/ebsa/about-ebsa/our-activities/resource-center/faqs/aca-part-37.pdf or https://www.cms.gov/CCIIO/Resources/Fact-Sheets-and-FAQs/Downloads/FAQs-Part-37.pdf.

[28] Although, in general, an HRA integrated with non-HRA group coverage fails to comply with PHS Act section 2711 if the non-HRA group coverage with which the HRA is integrated does not cover a category of EHB and the HRA is available to cover that category of EHB and limits the coverage to the HRA's maximum benefit, the Departments have provided that if non-HRA group coverage satisfies the MV Integration Method, an HRA will not be treated as failing to comply with PHS Act section 2711, even if the non-HRA group coverage with which the HRA is integrated does not cover a category of EHB and the HRA is available to cover that category of EHB and limits the coverage to the HRA's maximum benefit. *See* IRS Notice 2013-54, Q&A 6.

not eligible for Medicare.[29] For these employers, an HRA that may be used to reimburse premiums under Medicare part B or D may be integrated with Medicare (and deemed to comply with PHS Act sections 2711 and 2713) if the employees who are offered the HRA are enrolled in Medicare part B or D, the HRA is available only to employees who are enrolled in Medicare part B or D, and the HRA complies with the opt-out and forfeiture rules under the MV Integration Method and Non-MV Integration Method. These employers may use either of the non-Medicare-specific integration methods, as applicable, for HRAs offered to employees who are ineligible for Medicare.

The 2015 regulations also incorporate prior subregulatory guidance that HRAs cannot be integrated with individual health insurance coverage for purposes of complying with PHS Act sections 2711 and 2713.[30]

C. *HIPAA Nondiscrimination Provisions*

Prior to the enactment of PPACA, titles I and IV of the Health Insurance Portability and Accountability Act of 1996 (HIPAA), Pub. L. 104-191, added section 9802 of the Code, section 702 of ERISA, and section 2702 of the PHS Act (HIPAA nondiscrimination provisions). The Departments published joint final regulations implementing the HIPAA nondiscrimination provisions on December 13, 2006.[31] Section 1201 of PPACA reorganized and amended the HIPAA nondiscrimination provisions of the PHS Act. (Although section 9802 of the Code and section 702 of ERISA were not amended, the requirements of section 2705 of the PHS Act are also incorporated by reference into section 9815 of the Code and section 715 of ERISA.)[32] As amended by PPACA, the nondiscrimination provisions of section 2705 of the PHS Act largely reflect the 2006 regulations and extend the HIPAA nondiscrimination protections (but not the wellness program exception) to the individual market. These provisions generally prohibit group health plans and health insurance issuers in the group and individual markets from discriminating against individual participants and beneficiaries in eligibility, benefits, or premiums based on a health factor.[33]

Q&A-2 of FAQs about Affordable Care Act Implementation (Part XXII)[34] provided that, if an employer offers employees with high claims risk a choice between enrollment in a traditional group health plan or cash, the arrangement would not comply with the market requirements, citing section 2705 of the PHS Act (which is incorporated by reference into section 9815 of the Code and section 715 of ERISA), as well as the HIPAA nondiscrimination provisions of section 9802 of the Code and section 702 of ERISA. The Q&A explained that such arrangements will violate the nondiscrimination provisions regardless of whether: (1) the cash payment is treated by the employer as pre-tax or post-tax to the employee, (2) the employer is involved in the selection or purchase of any individual market product, or (3) the employee obtains any individual health insurance coverage. The Departments explained that, in the Departments' view, offering cash as an alternative to health coverage for individuals with adverse health factors is an eligibility rule that discourages participation in the traditional group health plan, in contravention of the HIPAA nondiscrimination provisions.

D. *Excepted Benefits*

Section 9831 of the Code, section 732 of ERISA, and sections 2722 and 2763 of the PHS Act provide that the requirements of chapter 100 of the Code, part 7 of ERISA, and title XXVII of the PHS Act, do

---

[29] *See* 26 CFR 54.9815-2711(d)(5); 29 CFR 2590.715-2711(d)(5); 45 CFR 147.126(d)(5). The final regulations did not address the Medicare integration rules that apply to employers with 20 or more employees. For a discussion of those rules, see IRS Notice 2015-17 and the discussion elsewhere in this preamble.

[30] *See* 26 CFR 54.9815-2711(d)(4); 29 CFR 2590.715-2711(d)(4); 45 CFR 147.126(d)(4). *Also see* IRS Notice 2013-54, Q&A-1, and DOL Technical Release 2013-03, Q&A-1. This principle was also reiterated and clarified in the various other pieces of subregulatory guidance summarized elsewhere in this section of the preamble. *See also* IRS Notice 2015-87, Q&A-5, in which the Departments clarified that an HRA that by its terms may only be used to reimburse (or pay directly for) premiums for individual health insurance coverage consisting solely of excepted benefits will not fail to comply with PHS Act sections 2711 and 2713 because those provisions do not apply to a group health plan that is designed to provide only excepted benefits. For guidance on enforcement relief for certain premium reduction arrangements offered by institutions of higher education to students with respect to student health insurance coverage, which is a type of individual health insurance coverage, *see* FAQs about Affordable Care Act Implementation Part 33, available at https://www.dol.gov/sites/default/files/ebsa/about-ebsa/our-activities/resource-center/faqs/aca-part-33.pdf or https://www.cms.gov/CCIIO/Resources/Fact-Sheets-and-FAQs/Downloads/ACA-FAQ-Set-33-Final.pdf. *See also* IRS Notice 2016-17, 2016-9 IRB 358; DOL Technical Release 2016-1, available at http://www.dol.gov/ebsa/newsroom/tr16-01.html; and Insurance Standards Bulletin, Application of the Market Reforms and Other Provisions of the Affordable Care Act to Student Health Coverage, February 5, 2016, available at https://www.cms.gov/CCIIO/Resources/Regulations-and-Guidance/Downloads/student-health-bulletin.pdf. *See* elsewhere in this preamble for additional discussion of student health insurance coverage.

[31] 71 FR 75014.

[32] PPACA section 1201 moved the HIPAA nondiscrimination provisions from PHS Act section 2702 to PHS Act section 2705, with some modification.

[33] The HIPAA nondiscrimination provisions set forth eight health status related factors. The eight health factors are health status, medical condition (including both physical and mental illnesses), claims experience, receipt of health care, medical history, genetic information, evidence of insurability, and disability. These terms are largely overlapping and, in combination, include any factor related to an individual's health. 66 FR 1377, 1379 (January 8, 2001).

[34] *See* FAQs about Affordable Care Act Implementation (Part XXII), available at https://www.dol.gov/sites/default/files/ebsa/about-ebsa/our-activities/resource-center/faqs/aca-part-xxii.pdf or https://www.cms.gov/CCIIO/Resources/Fact-Sheets-and-FAQs/Downloads/FAQs-Part-XXII-FINAL.pdf.

not apply to excepted benefits. Excepted benefits are described in section 9832 of the Code, section 733 of ERISA, and section 2791 of the PHS Act.

There are four statutory categories of excepted benefits. One such category of excepted benefits is limited excepted benefits. Under the statutory provisions, limited excepted benefits may include limited scope vision or dental benefits, benefits for long-term care, nursing home care, home health care, or community-based care, or any combination thereof, and "such other similar, limited benefits as are specified in regulations" by the Departments.[35] To be excepted benefits under this category, the benefits must either: (1) be insured and provided under a separate policy, certificate, or contract of insurance; or (2) otherwise not be an integral part of the plan.[36] The Departments previously exercised the authority to specify additional types of limited excepted benefits with respect to certain health FSAs, certain employee assistance programs, and certain limited wraparound coverage.[37]

Coverage that consists of excepted benefits is not minimum essential coverage (MEC).[38] Therefore, an individual offered or covered by an excepted benefit is not deemed ineligible for the PTC by virtue of the excepted benefit offer or coverage.[39] Further, the offer of an excepted benefit by an employer is not considered to be an offer of MEC under an eligible employer-sponsored plan for purposes of section 4980H of the Code, the employer shared responsibility provisions; thus, an employer will not avoid a payment under section 4980H of the Code by virtue of an offer of an excepted benefit.[40]

E. *Premium Tax Credit*

1. *In General*

Section 36B of the Code allows for the PTC to be available to applicable taxpayers to help with the cost of individual health insurance coverage obtained through an Exchange.[41] Under section 36B(a) and (b)(1) of the Code and 26 CFR 1.36B-3(d), a taxpayer's PTC is the sum of the premium assistance amounts for all coverage months during the taxable year for individuals in the taxpayer's family.

An individual is eligible for the PTC for a month if the individual meets various requirements for the month (a coverage month). Among other things, under section 36B(c)(2) of the Code, a month is not a coverage month for an individual if either: (1) the individual is eligible for coverage under an eligible employer-sponsored plan and the coverage is affordable and provides MV; or (2) the individual is enrolled in an eligible employer-sponsored plan, even if the coverage is not affordable or does not provide MV.[42] An eligible employer-sponsored plan includes coverage under a self-insured (as well as an insured) group health plan[43] and is MEC unless it consists solely of excepted benefits.[44]

An HRA is a self-insured group health plan and therefore is an eligible employer-sponsored plan. Accordingly, an individual currently is ineligible for the PTC for the individual's Exchange coverage for a month if the individual is covered by an HRA or is eligible for an HRA that is affordable and provides MV for the month. Although Treasury Department and IRS guidance provides that an HRA is an eligible employer-sponsored plan and therefore individuals covered by an HRA are ineligible for the PTC[45], to date, the Treasury Department and the IRS have not provided guidance as to the circumstances in which an HRA is considered to be affordable or to provide MV.[46]

2. *Affordability and Minimum Value*

Section 36B(c)(2)(C) of the Code and 26 CFR 1.36B-2(c)(3)(v)(A)(*1*) and (*2*) provide that an eligible employer-sponsored plan is affordable for an employee, or for an individual who may enroll in the coverage because of a relationship to the employee, if the amount the employee must pay for self-only coverage whether by salary reduction or otherwise (the employee's required contribution) does not exceed a specified percentage of the employee's household income. The percentage is adjusted annually. However, 26 CFR 1.36B-2(c)(3)(v)(A)(*3*) provides an employee safe harbor under which an eligible employer-sponsored plan is not considered affordable for an entire plan year if, at the time an individual enrolls in a qualified health plan offered through an Exchange, the Exchange determines that the eligible employer-sponsored plan is not affordable.[47] Thus, the employee safe harbor locks in the Exchange's determination of affordability, which is based on estimated household income, even if

---

[35] *See* section 9832(c)(2) of the Code, section 733(c)(2) of ERISA, and section 2791(c)(2) of the PHS Act.

[36] *See* section 9831(c)(1) of the Code, ERISA section 732(c)(1), and PHS Act section 2722(c)(1) and 2763(b). *See also* the discussion in 2014 final regulations concerning the application of these requirements to benefits such as limited-scope dental and vision benefits and employee assistance programs at 79 FR 59130, 59131-59134 (Oct. 1, 2014).

[37] *See* 26 CFR 54.9831-1(c)(3)(v), (vi) and (vii); 29 CFR 2590.732(c)(3)(v), (vi) and (vii); 45 CFR 146.145(b)(3)(v), (vi) and (vii).

[38] *See* section 5000A(f)(3) of the Code.

[39] *See* section 36B(c)(2)(B) of the Code.

[40] *See* section 4980H(a)(1), (b)(1) of the Code. *See also* 26 CFR 54.4980H-1(a)(14).

[41] Exchanges are entities established under section 1311 of PPACA through which qualified individuals and qualified employers can purchase health insurance coverage.

[42] *See* section 36B(c)(2)(C)(iii) of the Code and 26 CFR 1.36B-2(c)(3)(vii)(A) and 1.36B-3(c).

[43] *See* 26 CFR 1.5000A-2(c).

[44] *See* section 5000A(f)(3) of the Code and 26 CFR 1.5000A-2(g).

[45] *See* IRS Notice 2013-54, Q&A 10.

[46] The Treasury Department and the IRS have provided guidance regarding when amounts newly made available under an HRA count toward the affordability or MV of another group health plan offered by the same employer. *See* 26 CFR 1.36B-2(c)(3)(v)(A)(5) and 26 CFR 1.36B-6(c)(4). *See also* IRS Notice 2015-87, Q&A 7. This document does not make substantive revisions to those rules.

[47] This employee safe harbor does not apply if the individual does not respond to a redetermination notice or, with reckless disregard for the facts, provides incorrect information to the Exchange. *See* 26 CFR 1.36B-2(c)(3)(v)(A)(3).

the eligible employer-sponsored plan ultimately proves to be affordable based on actual household income for the tax year.

Under section 36B(c)(2)(C)(ii) of the Code, a plan provides MV if the plan's share of the total allowed costs of benefits provided under the plan is at least 60 percent of the costs. Section 1302(d)(2)(C) of PPACA provides that, in determining the percentage of the total allowed costs of benefits provided under a group health plan, the regulations promulgated by HHS under that paragraph apply. HHS regulations provide that an employer-sponsored plan provides MV only if the percentage of the total allowed costs of benefits provided under the plan is greater than or equal to 60 percent, and the benefits under the plan include substantial coverage of inpatient hospital services and physician services.[48]

F. *Qualified Small Employer Health Reimbursement Arrangements*

1. *In General*

The 21st Century Cures Act (Cures Act), Pub. L. 114-255, was enacted on December 13, 2016. Section 18001 of the Cures Act amends the Code, ERISA, and the PHS Act to permit an eligible employer to provide a QSEHRA to its eligible employees. The Cures Act provides that a QSEHRA is not a group health plan for purposes of the market requirements, and, as a result, QSEHRAs are not subject to PHS Act sections 2711 and 2713.[49] For purposes of the proposed rules, QSEHRAs are not included in the term "HRA or other account-based group health plans."

Pursuant to section 9831(d) of the Code, a QSEHRA is an arrangement that meets certain conditions, including the following:

- The arrangement provides, after the eligible employee provides proof of coverage[50], for the payment or reimbursement of medical care expenses incurred by the employee or the employee's family members (in accordance with the terms of the arrangement);
- The amount of payments for and reimbursements of medical care expenses incurred by the employee or the employee's family members for any year does not exceed $4,950 ($10,000[51] for an arrangement that also provides for payments or reimbursements of medical care expenses of the eligible employee's family members (family coverage)); and
- The arrangement generally is provided on the same terms to all eligible employees of the eligible employer.[52]

For the purpose of identifying who can provide a QSEHRA, the statute provides that an eligible employer is an employer that is not an applicable large employer (ALE), as defined in section 4980H(c)(2) of the Code and that does not offer a group health plan to any of its employees. The statute also requires that an employer providing a QSEHRA provide a written notice to each eligible employee (as defined in section 9831(d)(3)(A) of the Code) not later than 90 days before the beginning of the plan year (or, in the case of an employee who is not eligible to participate in the arrangement as of the beginning of the plan year, the date on which the employee is first eligible). Section 9831(d)(4) of the Code requires that the notice contain certain content, including information about the maximum dollar amount of payments and reimbursements that may be made under the terms of the QSEHRA for the year to the employee (the permitted benefit), and a statement that the employee should provide the information about the permitted benefit to the applicable Exchange if the employee applies for advance payments of the PTC.

On October 31, 2017, the Treasury Department and the IRS issued Notice 2017-67[53] to provide guidance on the requirements for providing a QSEHRA to eligible employees, the tax consequences of the arrangement, and the requirements for providing written notice of the arrangement to eligible employees.

---

[48] *See* 45 CFR 156.145. *See also* 80 FR 52678 (Sept. 1, 2015).

[49] *See* Section 9831(d)(1) of the Code, section 733(a)(1) of ERISA, and section 2791(a)(1) of the PHS Act. However, QSEHRAs are group health plans under the PHS Act definition for purposes of part C of title XI of the Social Security Act (42 USC 1320d, *et seq.*). *See* section 2791(a)(1) of the PHS Act, as amended by section 18001(c) of the Cures Act. In addition, QSEHRAs were not excluded from ERISA's definition of employee welfare benefit plan under section 3(1) of ERISA and, therefore, remain subject to the requirements for employee welfare benefit plans under ERISA. *See* H. Rept. 114-634 -Small Business Health Care Relief Act of 2016 (the relevant provisions of this bill were passed into law by the Cures Act). Moreover, because QSEHRAs are employee welfare benefit plans, individual health insurance coverage that is reimbursed by a QSEHRA would not become part of an ERISA plan if the conditions of the DOL proposed clarification described later in this preamble are met.

[50] Under section 106(g) of the Code, payments or reimbursements from a QSEHRA are not treated as paid or reimbursed under employer-provided coverage for medical expenses under an accident or health plan for purposes of sections 106 and 105 of the Code if, for the month in which the medical care is provided, the individual does not have minimum essential coverage within the meaning of section 5000A(f) of the Code. *See* IRS Notice 2017-67 for additional discussion of this minimum essential coverage requirement.

[51] Section 9831(d)(2)(D)(ii) of the Code provides that both statutory dollar limits are adjusted for inflation beginning after 2016. The adjusted limits for 2018 are $5,050 for self-only coverage and $10,250 for family coverage.

[52] Section 9831(d)(2)(C) of the Code provides that an arrangement shall not fail to be treated as provided on the same terms merely because the employee's permitted benefit varies in accordance with the variation in price of an insurance policy in the relevant individual health insurance market based on the employee's age or the number of family members whose expenses may be reimbursed under the arrangement. *See* section 9831(d)(2)(C) of the Code and IRS Notice 2017-67 for additional detail.

[53] *See* IRS Notice 2017-67, 2017-47 IRB 517. *See also* IRS Notice 2017-20, 2017-11 IRB 1010, which extended the period for an employer to furnish an initial written notice to its eligible employees regarding a QSEHRA.

If an eligible employer complies with the guidance provided in section 9831(d) of the Code and Notice 2017-67, it may provide a QSEHRA to its eligible employees and the QSEHRA does not have to comply with PHS Act sections 2711 and 2713 because it is not subject to those requirements.

2. *QSEHRAs and the PTC*

The Cures Act also added provisions to section 36B of the Code relating to how a QSEHRA affects a taxpayer's eligibility for the PTC and how a QSEHRA affects a taxpayer's computation of the PTC. Under section 36B(c)(4)(A) of the Code, if an employee is provided a QSEHRA that constitutes affordable coverage for a month, the month is not a coverage month for the employee or the employee's spouse or dependents, meaning that the PTC is not allowed for that month. Section 36B(c)(4)(C) of the Code provides that a QSEHRA constitutes affordable coverage for a month if the excess of the monthly premium for the self-only second lowest cost silver plan in the employee's individual market over 1/12 of the employee's permitted benefit, as defined in section 9831(d)(3)(C) of the Code, does not exceed 1/12 of a percentage of the employee's household income. The percentage, which is adjusted annually, is 9.56 for 2018.[54]

Section 36B(c)(4)(B) of the Code provides that if an employee is provided a QSEHRA that does not constitute affordable coverage for a coverage month the PTC otherwise allowable for the month is reduced by 1/12 of the employee's annual permitted benefit under the QSEHRA.

G. *Individual Market Special Enrollment Periods*

Generally, individuals may enroll in or change to different individual health insurance coverage before the beginning of the calendar year only during the annual open enrollment period described in 45 CFR 155.410. An individual may qualify for a special enrollment period to enroll in or change to a different Exchange plan outside of the annual open enrollment period under a variety of circumstances prescribed by section 1311(c)(6)(C) and (D) of PPACA and as described in 45 CFR 155.420. These special enrollment periods are under the jurisdiction of HHS, and apply to persons seeking individual health insurance coverage through a State or Federal Exchange and, in some cases, to individuals seeking individual health insurance coverage outside an Exchange.[55]

Paragraph (d) of 45 CFR 155.420 describes the special enrollment periods available on the Exchanges to qualified individuals, enrollees, and their dependents. Paragraph (b) of 45 CFR 155.420 describes the coverage effective dates available in connection with each special enrollment period, and paragraph (a)(4) describes the plan changes a qualified individual, enrollee, or dependent may make upon qualifying for a special enrollment period.

With regard to individual health insurance coverage sold outside of the Exchange, 45 CFR 147.104(b)(2) provides that health insurance issuers must provide special enrollment periods for the triggering events described in 45 CFR 155.420(d), except for certain triggering events listed under 45 CFR 147.104(b)(2).

II. Overview of the Proposed Rules on HRA Integration and Excepted Benefits - the Departments of the Treasury, Labor, and Health and Human Services

In developing the proposed rules, the Departments carefully considered how to meet the objectives of Executive Order 13813 in a way that is permitted by law and supported by sound policy. The proposed rules are intended to increase the usability of HRAs to provide more Americans, including employees who work at small businesses, with additional healthcare options. Such changes will facilitate the development and operation of a more efficient healthcare system that provides high-quality care at affordable prices by increasing consumer choice for employees and promoting competition in healthcare markets by adding additional options for employers. In addition, the proposed rules include certain conditions designed to prevent negative consequences that would be inconsistent with certain provisions of HIPAA and PPACA.

The proposed rules would expand the use of HRAs in several ways. First, the proposed rules would remove the current prohibition against integrating an HRA with individual health insurance coverage[56] under the PHS Act section 2711 regulations.[57] The proposed rules would instead permit

---

[54] IRS Notice 2017-67 provides that for purposes of determining whether a QSEHRA constitutes affordable coverage under section 36B(c)(4) of the Code the permitted benefit for self-only coverage is used, regardless of whether the permitted benefit provided to a particular eligible employee is for self-only or family coverage. Further, if the amount of permitted benefit varies based on the age of the employee, the age-applicable self-only coverage amount is used.

[55] Group health plans must provide special enrollment periods under certain circumstances and the Departments have jurisdiction over those provisions. *See* section 9801(f) of the Code, section 701(f) of ERISA, and section 2704(f) of the PHS Act; *see also* 26 CFR 54.9801-6, 29 CFR 2590.701-6, 45 CFR 146.117, and 45 CFR 147.104(b)(3)-(5). The proposed rules do not affect the group health plan special enrollment periods, which continue to apply to group health plans, including HRAs.

[56] For purposes of this preamble and the proposed regulations, "individual health insurance coverage" means health insurance coverage offered to individuals in the individual market, but does not include STLDI. *See* PHS Act section 2791(b)(5), 26 CFR 54.9801-2, 29 CFR 2590.701-2, and 45 CFR 144.103. Individual health insurance coverage can include dependent coverage and therefore can be self-only coverage or other-than-self-only coverage. "Individual market" means the market for health insurance coverage offered to individuals other than in connection with a group health plan. *See* PHS Act section 2791(e)(1), 26 CFR 54.9801-2, 29 CFR 2590.701-2, and 45 CFR 144.103. "Group health insurance coverage" means health insurance coverage offered in connection with a group health plan. *See* ERISA section 733(b)(4), PHS Act section 2791(b)(4), 26 CFR 54.9801-2, 29 CFR 2590.701-2, and 45 CFR 144.103.

[57] These proposed rules would make several non-substantive modifications to language throughout the regula-

an HRA to be integrated with individual health insurance coverage and, therefore, to satisfy PHS Act sections 2711 and 2713, if the provisions of the proposed rules under 26 CFR 54.9802-4, 29 CFR 2590.702-2, and 45 CFR 146.123 are met (hereinafter, "the proposed integration rules").

Second, the proposed rules would expand the definition of limited excepted benefits, under section 9832(c)(2) of the Code, section 733(c)(2) of ERISA, and section 2791(c)(2)(C) of the PHS Act, to recognize certain HRAs limited in amount and that are limited with regard to the types of coverage for which premiums may be reimbursed, as limited excepted benefits if certain other conditions are met (an "excepted benefit HRA").

As discussed later in this preamble, the Treasury Department and the IRS are also proposing regulations under section 36B of the Code that would provide the PTC eligibility rules for individuals who are offered an HRA integrated[58] with individual health insurance coverage.[59] DOL is also proposing a clarification to provide HRA and QSEHRA plan sponsors with assurance that the individual health insurance coverage the premiums of which are reimbursed by the HRA or QSEHRA does not become part of an ERISA plan when certain conditions are met. Finally, HHS is proposing changes to regulations regarding special enrollment periods in the individual market that would provide special enrollment periods for individuals who gain access to HRAs integrated with individual health insurance coverage or who are provided QSEHRAs.

The Departments request comments on all aspects of the proposed rules. The following explanation of the proposed rules also solicits comments on specific topics of particular interest to the Departments.

A. *Integration Rules*

Pursuant to the President's Executive Order to consider proposing regulations to expand and facilitate access to HRAs, the proposed rules would remove the prohibition on integration of an HRA with individual health insurance coverage, if certain conditions are met, and propose requirements that an HRA must meet in order to be integrated with individual health insurance coverage. In order to ensure compliance with PHS Act sections 2711 and 2713, the proposed integration rules provide that to be integrated with individual health insurance coverage, the HRA must require participants[60] and any dependents[61] covered by the HRA to be enrolled in individual health insurance coverage (other than coverage that consists solely of excepted benefits) and to substantiate compliance with this requirement.

Further, in crafting the proposed integration rules, the Departments have considered the possibility that expanding access to HRAs could lead to employers offering coverage options to their employees in a manner that discriminates based on health status and that negatively impacts the individual market for health insurance coverage. In 1996, Congress enacted the HIPAA nondiscrimination provisions, which now generally prohibit group health plans and health insurance issuers in the group and individual markets from discriminating against individual participants and beneficiaries in eligibility, benefits, or premiums based on a health factor. Later, in 2010, Congress enacted PPACA (which included PHS Act sections 2711 and 2713), in part, because individual health insurance coverage was not a viable option for many individuals since issuers in many States could deny coverage or charge higher premiums based on an individual's health risk. To address these issues, PPACA included numerous provisions that were intended to create a competitive individual market that would make affordable coverage available to individuals who do not have access to other health coverage, as described in more detail later in this section of the preamble. In developing these proposed regulations, the Departments have carefully considered how to exercise their rulemaking authority in a manner that is consistent with Congress's overall intent in enacting HIPAA and PPACA. As part of that process, the Departments have considered how to avoid permitting discrimi-

(Footnote Continued)

tions implementing PHS Act section 2711 to account for this change. *See* later in this preamble for a summary of these changes. The proposed regulations do not substantively change the current rules for integration of an HRA with non-HRA group coverage, Medicare or TRICARE. Unless the proposed regulations explicitly conflict with the sub-regulatory guidance that has been issued under PHS Act section 2711, that guidance remains in effect.

[58] References in the preamble to "an offer of an HRA integrated with individual health insurance coverage" or to similar phrases mean an offer of an HRA designed to be integrated with individual health insurance coverage under the proposed integration rules and that will be considered integrated with such individual health insurance coverage for an individual who enrolls in such coverage.

[59] The Treasury Department and the IRS are not proposing regulations under section 36B of the Code related to the excepted benefit HRA because the application of the PTC eligibility rules to excepted benefits is clear under current law. Also, the Treasury Department and the IRS are not proposing regulations under section 4980H of the Code, but see the discussion later in this preamble regarding how an offer of an HRA that is integrated with individual health insurance coverage is treated under section 4980H of the Code.

[60] For this purpose, the definition of participant under 26 CFR 54.9801-2, 29 CFR 2590.701-2, and 45 CFR 144.103 applies, which is defined as a participant within the meaning of section 3(7) of ERISA. Under section 3(7) of ERISA, "the term 'participant' means any employee or former employee of an employer, or any member or former member of an employee organization, who is or may become eligible to receive a benefit of any type from an employee benefit plan which covers employees of such employer or members of such organization, or whose beneficiaries may be eligible to receive any such benefit."

[61] For this purpose, the definition of dependent under 26 CFR 54.9801-2, 29 CFR 2590.701-2, and 45 CFR 144.103 applies, which is defined as "any individual who is or may become eligible for coverage under the terms of a group health plan because of a relationship to a participant."

nation based on health status or similar employer practices with respect to offering HRAs to employees that might have destabilizing effects on the individual market or lead to higher premiums in that market.

The Departments are of the view that allowing HRAs to be integrated with individual health insurance coverage could result in opportunities for employers to encourage higher risk employees (that is, those with high expected medical claims or employees with family members with high expected medical claims) to obtain coverage in the individual market, external to the traditional group health plan sponsored by the employer, in order to reduce the cost of traditional group health plan coverage provided by the employer to lower risk employees.[62] This could happen in a number of ways. For example, if employees are permitted to choose between participating in an employer's traditional group health plan or participating in an HRA integrated with individual health insurance coverage, some higher risk employees may have an incentive to select the HRA and enroll in individual health insurance coverage. This is because most individual health insurance coverage must cover all EHBs and large group market and self-insured group health plans are not required to cover all categories of EHBs. An employer could also deliberately attempt to steer employees with certain medical conditions away from the employer's traditional group health plan. In either case, if HRAs integrated with individual health insurance coverage are used disproportionately by higher risk employees, such arrangements could worsen adverse selection and raise premiums in the individual market.

The Departments also considered the possibility that the market would develop the opposite way. Lower risk employees might choose HRAs integrated with individual health insurance coverage, while higher risk employees might remain with the relative certainty of their employer's traditional group health plan. Such an outcome could result for a host of reasons, including because higher risk employees tend to be more risk averse with respect to changing health benefits and because individual health insurance coverage might have much more restrictive provider networks than traditional group health plans and higher risk employees tend to be more sensitive to the make-up of the provider network than lower risk employees. Also, lower risk employees may prefer an HRA integrated with individual health insurance coverage, as compared to a more generous traditional group health plan, because it could allow them to spend less on premiums and have more funds available to cover cost sharing. Further, employers would have incentives to avoid legal concerns that could be raised by an attempt to steer higher risk employees toward an HRA integrated with individual health insurance coverage.

However, employers will face countervailing incentives to maintain (or improve) the average health risk that they insure. Therefore, the Departments have determined that the risk of market segmentation and health factor discrimination is sufficiently significant to justify including conditions in the proposed regulations intended to address those risks. Accordingly, the proposed regulations would add new regulations at 26 CFR 54.9802-4, 29 CFR 2590.702-2, and 45 CFR 146.123 to prevent a plan sponsor from intentionally or unintentionally, directly or indirectly, steering any participants or dependents with adverse health factors away from the plan sponsor's traditional group health plan and into the individual market. In particular, the proposed integration rules prohibit a plan sponsor from offering the same class of employees both a traditional group health plan and an HRA integrated with individual health insurance coverage. In addition, to the extent a plan sponsor offers an HRA that is integrated with individual health insurance coverage to a class of employees, the proposed integration rules require that the HRA be offered on the same terms to all employees within the class, subject to certain exceptions described later in this preamble.

In the Departments' view, these proposed integration requirements are necessary and appropriate to avoid the risk of market segmentation and to ensure there are protections against discrimination based on health status when HRAs are permitted to integrate with individual health insurance coverage for purposes of compliance with PHS Act sections 2711 and 2713. The Departments also are of the view these requirements are consistent with Congress's intent in enacting both HIPAA and PPACA as well as in granting the Departments the authority to promulgate such regulations as may be necessary or appropriate to carry out the provisions of the Code, ERISA, and the PHS Act that were added as a result of those Acts.[63] More specifically, these proposed integration requirements are intended to mitigate circumstances in which higher risk employees are incentivized (based on the design of the traditional group health plan versus the offer of the HRA) to obtain coverage in the individual market.

These proposed integration conditions avoid creating a high risk of market segmentation. As noted earlier in this preamble, PPACA includes several provisions designed to create a competitive individual market that makes affordable coverage available to individuals who do not have access to other health coverage. *See* PPACA section 1311 (establishing the Exchanges), section 1312(c) (instructing health insurance issuers to consider all enrollees in all health plans in a market - either individual or small group - as members of a single risk pool), section 1401 (establishing the PTC to help qualifying individuals and families pay for individual health insurance coverage), section 1402 (reducing cost-sharing for qualifying individuals enrolled in qualified health plans), and section 1501

---

[62] Amy Monahan and Daniel Schwarcz, "Will Employers Undermine Health Care Reform by Dumping Sick Employees?" *Virginia Law Review*, Vol. 97 (2011).

[63] *See* section 9833 of the Code, section 734 of ERISA, and section 2792 of the PHS Act.

(requiring non-exempt applicable individuals to maintain MEC or be subject to the individual shared responsibility payment).[64] These provisions are intended, in part, to draw more individuals of all risk profiles into the individual market and make premiums for individual market coverage more affordable. In addition, PPACA requires that non-grandfathered individual health insurance coverage cover generally the same categories of EHBs, in part, to prevent health insurance coverage with better benefits from becoming prohibitively expensive as lower-risk individuals gravitate to less expensive individual health insurance coverage with limited benefits while higher risk individuals select more expensive individual health insurance coverage with more generous benefits. PPACA also includes risk adjustment, reinsurance, and risk corridor programs to provide consumers with affordable health insurance coverage, to reduce incentives for issuers to avoid enrolling higher risk individuals, and to stabilize premiums in the individual and small group markets inside and outside of the Exchanges. Taken altogether, these PPACA provisions intend to create a robust and competitive individual market, in part by ensuring that risk pools included both higher risk and lower risk individuals.

If integration of HRAs led to market segmentation, it would result in significant destabilization in the individual market, undermining those provisions of PPACA that are intended to create a robust and competitive individual market. The text of PHS Act sections 2711 and 2713 is ambiguous with regard to whether and how separate plans can integrate to comply with its provisions, and the structural and practical policy concerns discussed earlier in this preamble could, if realized, prompt the Departments to adopt an interpretation of PHS Act sections 2711 and 2713 that prohibits integration of HRAs with individual health insurance coverage. By requiring employers who wish to take advantage of HRA integration with individual health insurance coverage to adhere to the protections described in more detail later in this preamble, in particular the prohibition on offering an HRA integrated with individual health insurance coverage and a traditional group health plan to the same employees, the Departments intend to prevent large-scale destabilization of the individual market, thus allowing the Departments to interpret PHS Act sections 2711 and 2713 to permit integration with individual health insurance coverage. Accordingly, the proposed regulations provide integration rules that are intended to avoid creating a high risk of market segmentation.

Lastly, because eligibility for coverage under an HRA may affect an individual's eligibility for the PTC and enrollment in an HRA affects an individual's eligibility for the PTC, the proposed integration rules allow employees of employers who offer an HRA to opt out of and waive future reimbursements under the HRA. The Departments also propose that HRAs be required to provide a notice to participants eligible for coverage under an HRA integrated with individual health insurance coverage with information regarding how the offer of the HRA or enrollment in the HRA affects their ability to claim the PTC.

The conditions in the proposed integration rules are discussed in detail below.

1. *Requirement that All Individuals Covered by the HRA Are Enrolled in Individual Health Insurance Coverage*

As discussed earlier in this preamble, an HRA is a group health plan that does not comply with PHS Act sections 2711 and 2713 on its own. However, the Departments previously have determined that an HRA can be considered to be in compliance with PHS Act sections 2711 and 2713 if it is integrated with non-HRA group coverage that is subject to and complies with these sections of the PHS Act. In the past, the Departments have made the determination that it is appropriate to treat an HRA as complying with PHS Act sections 2711 and 2713 when integrated with other group health plan coverage because, generally, an individual covered by the combined arrangement has coverage that complies with PHS Act sections 2711 and 2713. (Similarly, as discussed elsewhere in this preamble, other combined arrangements involving Medicare and TRICARE, are also considered to comply with PHS Act sections 2711 and 2713.)

The proposed integration rules similarly provide that an HRA may be integrated with individual health insurance coverage, and will be considered compliant with PHS Act sections 2711 and 2713, if the HRA requires the participant and any dependent(s) to be enrolled in individual health insurance coverage (other than coverage that consists solely of excepted benefits) for each month the individual(s) are covered by the HRA. If the individual covered by the HRA merely has the ability to obtain individual health insurance coverage, but does not actually have that coverage, the HRA would fail to comply with PHS Act sections 2711 and 2713. This proposed requirement would apply with respect to all individuals whose medical care expenses may be reimbursed under the HRA, not just the participant.

For purposes of integrating an HRA with individual health insurance coverage, the Departments are proposing to treat all individual health insurance coverage as subject to and compliant with PHS Act sections 2711 and 2713, except for coverage that consists solely of excepted benefits. While this would allow for integration with grandfathered individual health insurance coverage, which is not subject to and may not be compliant with PHS Act sections 2711 and 2713, only a small number of individuals are currently enrolled in grandfathered individual health insurance coverage and grandfathered coverage may not be sold in the individual market to new enrollees and may only be

---

[64] Section 5000A of the Code, added by PPACA, provides that all non-exempt applicable individuals must maintain MEC or pay an individual shared responsibility payment. On December 22, 2017, the President signed tax reform legislation (Pub. L. 115-97, 131 Stat. 2054) under which the individual shared responsibility payment is reduced to $0 effective as of January 1, 2019.

renewed by current enrollees so long as the coverage meets strict conditions. Additionally, the number of individuals with grandfathered individual health insurance coverage has declined each year since PPACA was enacted, and the already small number of individuals who have retained grandfathered coverage will continue to decline each year. Because it is the Departments' understanding that there are few individuals covered by grandfathered individual health insurance coverage, the Departments are of the view that there will be few instances where such individuals will be offered and accept an HRA that would be integrated with their grandfathered individual health insurance coverage. Moreover, new enrollees cannot enroll in grandfathered individual health insurance coverage, so employers offering traditional group health plans would not be able to shift workers into this coverage. Furthermore, even for non-grandfathered individual health insurance coverage, requiring participants or plan sponsors to substantiate compliance with PHS Act sections 2711 and 2713 for each individual health insurance policy separately is impracticable given that most participants and HRAs are unlikely to be able to reasonably determine the compliance of the individual health insurance policy. An independent assessment of compliance could require the participant or HRA to identify which benefits under each individual health insurance coverage enrolled in by a participant or dependent are considered EHBs for purposes of PHS Act section 2711, and whether all preventive services are covered without cost-sharing under each individual health insurance coverage enrolled in by a participant or dependent. The Departments are of the view that this would be an unwieldy and burdensome task.

The Departments' final rules for grandfathered plans provide that "a plan or health insurance coverage must include a statement that the plan or coverage believes it is a grandfathered health plan . . . in any summary of benefits provided under the plan."[65] The Departments remain concerned, however, that the frequency of this disclosure to participants may be insufficient to substantiate compliance for purposes of these rules. For comparison's sake, ERISA plans must provide a new SPD only every 5 years, and the required disclosure for individual market coverage will differ from state to state. Additionally, other plan materials that provide a summary of benefits that may trigger the grandfathered plan disclosure requirement may not be subject to any specific timing requirements. Furthermore, the Departments have concerns as to whether participants will be able to locate or receive the disclosure materials in the time necessary to allow for a determination of whether the plan with which the HRA will be integrated is grandfathered (and therefore unlikely to comply with sections 2711 and 2713 of the PHS Act) or non-grandfathered (and therefore generally compliant). For example, for ERISA plans, a plan sponsor has 30 days to fulfill a disclosure request. Additionally, despite the fact that individual health insurance coverage may include a disclosure that the policy is grandfathered, there may be instances in which such disclosure is not accurate, or other instances where non-grandfathered individual health insurance coverage does not comply with PHS Act sections 2711 or 2713. For these reasons, the Departments have preliminarily determined that adopting this proxy approach of relying on the sale of the policy in the individual market to deem the policy compliant for purposes of the proposed integration rules strikes an appropriate balance. (See later in this preamble for a discussion of the substantiation requirements that would apply under the proposed integration rules).

The Departments solicit comments on methods by which an HRA could substantiate whether individual health insurance coverage is subject to and complies with PHS Act sections 2711 and 2713, including how an HRA might identify which benefits under the individual health insurance coverage are considered EHBs for purposes of PHS Act section 2711 and how an HRA might determine if all preventive services are covered without cost-sharing. The Departments solicit comments on whether an alternative approach, such as a requirement that an issuer make a representation about compliance and/or grandfather status upon request, would be practical, or whether any other methods might be appropriate as an alternative to the previously outlined proposed proxy approach.

Under the proposed integration rules, the requirement that each individual whose medical care expenses may be reimbursed under the HRA must be enrolled in individual health insurance coverage (other than coverage that consists solely of excepted benefits) would apply for each month that the individual is covered by the HRA. If an individual whose medical care expenses may be reimbursed under an HRA fails to have such individual health insurance coverage for any month, the HRA would fail to comply with PHS Act sections 2711 and 2713 for that month. Accordingly, the proposed rules provide that an HRA may not be integrated with individual health insurance coverage unless the HRA provides that medical care expenses for any individual covered by the HRA will not be reimbursed if the individual ceases to be covered by individual health insurance coverage and, if the individuals covered by the HRA cease to be covered by such individual health insurance coverage, the participant must forfeit the HRA, in accordance with applicable laws (including COBRA and other continuation of coverage requirements).[66]

2. *Prohibition Against Offering Both an HRA Integrated with Individual Health Insurance Coverage and a Traditional Group Health Plan to the Same Class of Employees*

a. In General

To address the previously described concerns about potential adverse selection and health factor discrimination, under the proposed integration rules, a plan sponsor may offer an HRA integrated

---

[65] 26 CFR 54.9815-1251(a)(2); 29 CFR 2590.715-1251(a)(2); 45 CFR 147.140(a)(2).

[66] For an explanation of the application of COBRA to HRAs, see section VII of IRS Notice 2002-45.

with individual health insurance coverage to a class of employees only if the plan sponsor does not also offer a traditional group health plan to the same class of employees.[67] Therefore, a plan sponsor would not be permitted to allow any employee within a class of employees a choice between a traditional group health plan or an HRA integrated with individual health insurance coverage. For this purpose, the term "traditional group health plan" means any group health plan other than either an account-based group health plan or a group health plan that consists solely of excepted benefits. The Departments solicit comments on whether employers should be able to offer employees a choice between a traditional group health plan or an HRA integrated with individual health insurance coverage, and on the definition of "traditional group health plan," including whether an alternate definition or term might be appropriate and whether a definition should be codified as part of these proposed regulations.

b. Classes of Employees

In addition, as described in more detail later in the preamble, the proposed integration rules require a plan sponsor that offers an HRA integrated with individual health insurance coverage to a class of employees to offer the HRA on the same terms to each participant within the class of employees, subject to certain exceptions. The proposed integration rules provide that a plan sponsor may only offer the HRA on different terms to different groups of employees, and may only offer either an HRA integrated with individual health insurance coverage or a traditional group health plan by groups of employees, if those groups are specific classes of employees identified by the proposed rules. The classes are: (1) full-time employees (using either the definition that applies for purposes of section 105(h) or 4980H of the Code, as determined by the plan sponsor); (2) part-time employees (using either the definition that applies for purposes of section 105(h) or 4980H of the Code, as determined by the plan sponsor); (3) seasonal employees (using either the definition that applies for purposes of section 105(h) or 4980H of the Code, as determined by the plan sponsor); (4) employees who are included in a unit of employees covered by a collective bargaining agreement (CBA) in which the plan sponsor participates (as described in 26 CFR 1.105-11(c)(2)(iii)(D)); (5) employees who have not satisfied a waiting period for coverage (if the waiting period complies with the waiting period rules in PHS Act section 2708 and its implementing regulations);[68] (6) employees who have not attained age 25 prior to the beginning of the plan year (as described in 26 CFR 1.105-11(c)(2)(iii)(B)); (7) non-resident aliens with no U.S.-based income (as described in 26 CFR 1.105-11(c)(2)(iii)(E)) (generally, foreign employees who work abroad); and (8) employees whose primary site of employment is in the same rating area, as defined in 45 CFR 147.102(b). In addition, the proposed integration rules allow as additional classes, groups of employees described as a combination of two or more of the enumerated classes. For example, part-time employees included in a unit of employees covered by a CBA might be one class of employees, and full-time employees included in the same unit of employees covered by a CBA might be another class of employees. In that case, for example, the employer could offer an HRA to the part-time employees and not offer (or offer on different terms) an HRA to the full-time employees, but could not differentiate between the part-time employees covered under the CBA except based on any of them being in another class or, if within the same class, except as otherwise allowed under the same-terms requirement as explained later in this preamble. If an HRA is offered to former employees (such as retirees), former employees are considered to be in the same class they were in immediately before separation from service.

The Departments have concluded that it is appropriate to permit plan sponsors to offer different benefits to these classes of employees under the proposed integration rules. First, many employers historically have offered varying benefit packages to members of these different classes of employees clearly for purposes other than inducing higher risk employees to leave the plan sponsor's traditional group health plan. Second, the Departments have determined that it would be burdensome for employers to shift employees from one of these classes of employees to another merely for the purpose of offering different types of health benefits to employees based on a health factor, thereby reducing the risk that a plan sponsor will offer an HRA integrated with individual health insurance coverage only to its higher risk employees. Accordingly, the classes of employees identified in these proposed rules would balance employers' reasonable need to make distinctions among employees with respect to offering health benefits with the public interest in protecting the stability of the individual market risk pools.

Historically, employers have often provided different benefit packages to employees included in a unit of employees covered by a CBA, full-time employees, part-time employees, seasonal employees, employees who work abroad, employees of different ages, employees based on whether they have completed a waiting period, and employees in different locations. This is particularly true in the case of health benefits. For example, unions typically bargain with employers over health benefits provided to employees who are members of that union, and the health benefits that an employer provides pursuant to a CBA are often different than those that it provides to its employees who are not covered by the CBA. Similarly, health benefit packages offered to employees often vary by location, in part because certain healthcare providers or health insurance issuers operate only in some

[67] The Departments note that an employer may not provide a QSEHRA to any employee if it offers any employee a group health plan, including a traditional group health plan or an HRA. *See* section 9831(d)(3)(B)(ii) of the Code.

[68] 26 CFR 54.9815-2708; 29 CFR 2590.715-2708; 45 CFR 147.116.

areas and not in others. A rule that prohibited employers from differentiating between these classes of employees for purposes of offering HRAs integrated with individual health insurance coverage would pose significant costs that might undermine the willingness of employers to offer HRAs in the first place.

The Departments are of the view that these classes of employees are not ones that could be easily manipulated in order to transfer the risks (and perceived higher costs) from the employer's traditional group health plan to the individual market. For example, labor laws generally prevent an employer from classifying an employee as subject to a CBA when the employee traditionally has not been subject to a CBA. Similarly, economic and labor forces generally make it difficult for employers to increase or reduce significantly the number of hours worked by employees in particular positions. In certain situations, ERISA may also prevent an employer from changing employee's hours in order to interfere with an employee's ability to participate in a health plan.[69] The Departments have not proposed permitting plan sponsors to treat salaried and hourly employees as different classes of employees for purposes of these rules, however, as many employers might easily be able to change an employee's status from salaried to hourly (and in certain circumstances, from hourly to salaried) with seemingly minimal economic or other consequences for either the employer or the employees.

To minimize burden and complexity, the Departments do not propose a minimum employer size or employee class size for purposes of applying the proposed integration rules. The Departments recognize that very small employers could manipulate these classes (for example, a very small employer could put someone who is a higher-risk employee in a separate class on his or her own), but note that other economic incentives related to attracting and retaining talent would discourage employers from doing so. The Departments invite comments on whether employer size or employee class size should be considered in determining permissible classes of employees.

In defining certain classes of employees to which different benefits may be offered in the proposed rules, the Departments propose to adopt definitions that are the same as those that apply under sections 105(h) and 4980H of the Code.

Specifically, for purposes of identifying classes of employees for purpose of the proposed integration regulations, an HRA plan sponsor may define "full-time employee," "part-time employee," and "seasonal employee" in accordance with either of those definitions under sections 105(h) and 4980H of the Code, but it must be consistent across these three classes of employees, to the extent it differentiates based on these classes, in using either sections 105(h) or 4980H of the Code to avoid overlapping classes of employees, and the HRA plan document must set forth the applicable definitions prior to the beginning of the plan year in which the definitions will apply. Thus, an HRA plan document may provide that, for the plan year, the term "full-time employee" means a full-time employee under section 4980H of the Code and the regulations thereunder and "part-time employee" means an employee who is not a full-time employee under section 4980H of the Code and the regulations thereunder, for the applicable plan year. But an HRA plan document may not provide that, for the plan year, the term "full-time employee" has the meaning set forth in section 4980H of the Code and the regulations thereunder, and the term "part-time employee" has the meaning set forth in 26 CFR 1.105-11(c)(2)(iii)(C), for the applicable plan year. Nothing would prevent an employer from changing the definitions for a subsequent plan year so long as each class is defined in accordance with the same provision for the applicable plan year and the HRA plan document is updated to reflect the applicable definitions prior to the beginning of the plan year in which the definitions would apply.

For the other classes of employees, the relevant definition under section 105(h) of the Code applies, except for the class of employees based on worksite rating area. The Departments propose to adopt the Code section 105(h) definitions, in part, because they reflect a relatively common understanding of the terms "full-time," "part-time" and "seasonal" employees and because HRAs generally are subject to the nondiscrimination rules of section 105(h) of the Code. The Departments understand that plan sponsors may want to design their employee health plans, which may include offering a traditional group health plan and HRAs (or HRAs in different amounts or under different terms and conditions) to different classes of employees in a manner that complies with the requirements of Code section 105(h) to avoid the inclusion of amounts in income under that section.[70] The Departments have concluded that defining the classes of employees to which different offers of coverage may be made by using the Code section 105(h) definitions may be helpful in accomplishing that result.

As noted earlier, the Departments propose to allow employers to adopt the Code section 4980H definitions as an alternative set of definitions for identifying full-time, part-time, and seasonal employees. The Departments acknowledge that certain employers have already determined how those definitions apply to their workforce and using those same definitions for purposes of applying the proposed integration rules may reduce burden for those employers. Section 4980H of the Code applies to ALEs, which generally includes employers that employed at least 50 full-time employees

---

[69] *See e.g., Marin v. Dave & Buster's, Inc.*, 159 F. Supp. 3d 460 (SDNY 2016).

[70] HRAs generally are subject to the rules under section 105(h) of the Code and its related regulations as self-insured medical reimbursement plans. In general, section 105(h) of the Code provides that certain amounts paid to highly compensated individuals under self-insured medical reimbursement plans are includible in the income of the highly compensated individual. In the near term, the Treasury Department and the IRS intend to issue guidance that addresses the interaction of section 105(h) of the Code and HRAs integrated with individual health insurance coverage.

(including full-time equivalent employees) in the prior calendar year.[71] An employer must classify its employees as either full-time or part-time employees, and in some cases as seasonal employees, in accordance with section 4980H of the Code and the regulations thereunder, in order to determine whether it is an ALE and, if so, to determine which employees it must offer coverage to in order to avoid liabilities under section 4980H of the Code and to complete the associated reporting requirements. Accordingly, ALEs that want to offer HRAs to a particular class of employees, or offer HRAs of differing amounts or under different terms and conditions based on particular classes of employees, may prefer to use the Code section 4980H definitions with which they are familiar and which they have historically communicated to employees through the reporting requirements. The Departments understand, however, that some ALEs may still wish to use the Code section 105(h) definitions, and some non-ALEs may wish to use the Code section 4980H definitions. Therefore, the proposed rules would offer each employer the flexibility to determine which set of definitions are appropriate for its workforce, provided the employer uses the same set of definitions for classifying its full-time, part-time, and seasonal employees to the extent it uses each of these classifications.

The proposed employee classes are intended to provide the flexibility needed to achieve increased HRA usability while establishing parameters sufficient to address the health status discrimination and adverse selection concerns described earlier in this preamble. The Departments considered whether employers should be allowed to offer or vary HRAs integrated with individual health insurance coverage for classes of employees based on a very general standard (like the one that generally applies under the HIPAA nondiscrimination rules, with a broad employment-based classification standard) or a more finite list of classes of employees that have been used in other rules for various employee benefits purposes (for example, under section 105(h) and/or 4980H of the Code). The Departments' view is that a broad and open-ended standard would not be sufficient to mitigate health factor discrimination that could increase adverse selection in the individual market. The classes the Departments propose to permit are ones which, based on the Departments' experience, employers use for other employee benefits and other purposes, with the result that an employer would be unlikely to shift employees between the classes simply for purposes of offering an HRA.

The Departments request comments on the proposed classes of employees, the definitions used, and whether additional classes of employees should be provided (for example, classifications based on form of compensation (hourly versus salaried), employee role or title, occupation, or whether the individual is a former employee). The Departments also seek comment on whether any additional classifications within the proposed classes of employees should be allowed, for example, allowing classifications based on more specific geographic locations, multiple gradations of part-time employees, or gradations based on employee tenure. In addition, the Departments request comments on whether the proposed classes of employees, including the class of employees based on employees having a primary worksite in a particular rating area and the rule allowing combinations of classes of employees, and any potential additional classes, are sufficient to mitigate adverse selection and health status discrimination concerns.

c. Salary Reduction Arrangements

The Departments have been made aware that some employers may wish to allow employees to pay the portion of the premium for individual health insurance coverage that is not covered by an HRA integrated with individual health insurance coverage, if any, by using a salary reduction arrangement under a cafeteria plan. Pursuant to section 125(f)(3) of the Code, an employer may not provide a qualified health plan (as defined in section 1301(a) of PPACA) offered through the Exchange as a benefit under its cafeteria plan.[72] Therefore, an employer may not permit employees to make salary reduction contributions to a cafeteria plan to purchase a qualified health plan (including individual health insurance coverage) offered through an Exchange.

However, section 125(f)(3) of the Code does not apply to individual health insurance coverage that is not purchased on an Exchange. Therefore, for an employee who purchases individual health insurance coverage outside the Exchange, the employer could permit the employee to pay the balance of the premium for the coverage through its cafeteria plan, subject to all applicable guidance.[73] To the extent the arrangement to pay the balance of the premium is a group health plan, such an arrangement would not be considered to be a traditional group health plan for purposes of the proposed integration rules. For a discussion of the application of the same-terms requirement to such an arrangement, see the next section of this preamble. For a general comment solicitation on cafeteria plan premiums arrangements, see later in this preamble.

3. *Same-Terms Requirement*

To address the Departments' concerns about health status discrimination leading to additional adverse selection in the individual market, the proposed integration rules generally require that a plan sponsor that offers an HRA integrated with individual health insurance coverage to a class of employees must offer the HRA on the same terms (that is, both in the same amount and otherwise on the same terms and conditions) to all employees within the class. For this purpose, a class of

[71] Discussion of how section 4980H of the Code would affect an ALE that offers an HRA integrated with individual health insurance coverage is included later in this preamble.

[72] Note that section 125(f)(3)(B) of the Code provides an exception to this prohibition for certain small employers offering employees the opportunity to enroll in the group market through an Exchange.

[73] *See* Prop. Reg. 26 CFR 1.125-1(m); *see also* Rev. Rul. 61-146, 1961-2 CB 25.

employees has the meaning described earlier in this preamble, but see later in this section of the preamble for a discussion of the application of this requirement to former employees. As part of this proposed requirement, the Departments make clear that offering a more generous HRA to individuals based on an adverse health factor violates the integration rules.

The Departments recognize, however, that premiums for individual health insurance coverage obtained by HRA participants and their dependents may vary and thus some variation in amounts made available under an HRA, even within a class of employees, may be appropriate. Therefore, under the proposed integration rules, the maximum dollar amount made available under the HRA for participants within a class of employees may increase as the age of the participant increases, so long as the same maximum dollar amount attributable to that increase in age is made available to all participants of the same age within the same class of employees. In addition, under the proposed integration rules, the maximum dollar amount made available under an HRA within a class of employees may increase as the number of the participant's dependents who are covered under the HRA increases, so long as the same maximum dollar amount attributable to that increase in family size is made available to all participants in that class of employees with the same number of dependents covered by the HRA. Under this exception, a plan sponsor may increase the HRA amount for a class of employees for both age and family size, which would mean, for example, that a plan sponsor could offer two employees in a class of employees of the same age different HRA amounts if the different HRA amounts are attributable to differences in family size. By permitting such variation, the Departments seek to balance the disparate costs of health insurance in the individual market with the need to prevent health status discrimination against HRA participants and their dependents.

Further, although the proposed integration regulations would generally apply to a former employee in the same way that they apply to a current employee (and former employees are considered to be in the same class that they were in immediately before separation from service), the Departments recognize that eligibility for post-employment health coverage, if any, varies widely and may be subject to age, service or other conditions. To avoid undue disruption of employers' practices relating to the provision of post-employment health coverage, the proposed integration rules provide that an HRA may be treated as provided on the same terms even if the plan sponsor offers the HRA to some former employees (for example, to all former employees with a minimum tenure of employment) but fails to offer the HRA to the other former employees within a class of employees. But if a plan sponsor does offer the HRA to one or more former employee(s) within a class of employees, the HRA must be offered to those former employee(s) on the same terms as all other employees within the class.[74] For example, if a plan sponsor offers an HRA to all of its current full-time employees and also to its former employees who were full-time employees immediately prior to separation from service who had at least five years of service, the plan sponsor must provide the HRA on the same terms to the eligible former employees and to the current full-time employees, subject to the generally applicable exceptions to the same terms requirement described elsewhere in this section of the preamble.

The proposed integration rules further provide that if a participant or dependent in an HRA integrated with individual health insurance coverage does not use all of the amounts made available in the HRA to reimburse medical care expenses for a plan year, and the HRA allows for these amounts to be made available to participants and their dependents in later plan years, these carryover amounts would be disregarded for purposes of determining whether the HRA is offered on the same terms, so long as the method for determining whether participants have access to unused amounts in future years, and the methodology and formula for determining the amounts of unused funds that they may access in future years, is the same for all participants in a class of employees. In addition, the proposed rules provide that the ability to pay the portion of the premium for individual health insurance coverage that is not covered by the HRA, if any, by using a salary reduction arrangement under a cafeteria plan[75] is considered to be a term of the HRA for purposes of the proposed integration rules; therefore an HRA shall fail to be treated as provided on the same terms unless such a salary reduction arrangement, if made available to any participant in a class of employees, is made available on the same terms to all participants (other than former employees) in a class of employees.

Further, the Treasury Department and the IRS are aware that an HRA under which the maximum dollar amount varies based on age may face issues regarding the application of section 105(h) of the Code and the regulations thereunder. Accordingly, the Treasury Department and the IRS intend to issue guidance in the near term that describes an anticipated safe harbor that would allow increases in the maximum dollar amount made available under an HRA integrated with individual health

---

[74] Note that the market requirements do not apply to a group health plan that has fewer than two participants who are current employees on the first day of the plan year. *See* section 9831(a)(2) of the Code and section 732(a) of ERISA. HHS follows a similar approach for non-federal governmental retiree-only plans and encourages States to adopt a similar approach with respect to issuers of retiree-only plans. *See* 75 FR 34539 (June 17, 2010). Therefore, a retiree-only HRA need not meet the requirements of any integration test.

[75] As previously noted, pursuant to section 125(f)(3) of the Code, a cafeteria plan may not permit employees to use salary reduction contributions made to a cafeteria plan to purchase individual health insurance coverage offered through an Exchange.

insurance coverage, if certain conditions are met, without a consequence under section 105(h) of the Code.[76]

4. *Opt-out Provision*

As described elsewhere in this preamble, if an individual is covered by an HRA integrated with individual health insurance coverage for a month, regardless of the amount of reimbursement available under the HRA, the individual is not eligible for the PTC for that month. Because in some circumstances an individual may be better off claiming the PTC than receiving reimbursements under an HRA, the Departments' existing rules regarding integration with non-HRA group coverage and with Medicare require plan sponsors that offer HRAs to allow participants to opt out of and waive future reimbursements from the HRA at least annually.[77] These proposed rules include the same requirement. Thus, current employees may be allowed the PTC, if they are otherwise eligible, if they opt out of and waive future reimbursements from the HRA and the HRA is either unaffordable or does not provide MV.[78]

Furthermore, as with the current integration rules, the proposed integration rules require that upon termination of employment, either the remaining amounts in the HRA must be forfeited or the participant must be allowed to permanently opt out of and waive future reimbursements from the HRA to ensure that the HRA participant may choose whether to claim the PTC, if otherwise eligible, or to continue to participate in the HRA after the participant's separation from service.

5. *Substantiation and Verification of Individual Health Insurance Coverage*

As discussed earlier in this preamble, the proposed integration rules would require that the individuals whose medical care expenses may be reimbursed under the HRA must be enrolled in individual health insurance coverage. To facilitate the administration of this requirement, under the proposed integration rules, an HRA must implement, and comply with, reasonable procedures to verify that individuals whose medical care expenses are reimbursable by the HRA are, or will be, enrolled in individual health insurance coverage (other than coverage that consists solely of excepted benefits) during the plan year. The reasonable procedures may include a requirement that a participant substantiate enrollment in individual health insurance coverage by providing either: (1) a document from a third party (for example, the issuer) showing that the participant and any dependent(s) covered by the HRA are, or will be, enrolled in individual health insurance coverage during the plan year (for example, an insurance card or an explanation of benefits pertaining to the relevant time period); or (2) an attestation by the participant stating that the participant and any dependent(s) are or will be enrolled in individual health insurance coverage, the date coverage began or will begin, and the name of the provider of the coverage.[79] For this purpose, an HRA may rely on the documentation or attestation provided by the participant unless the HRA has actual knowledge that any individual covered by the HRA is not, or will not be, enrolled in individual health insurance coverage (other than coverage that consists solely of excepted benefits) for the plan year.

In addition, following the initial substantiation of coverage, with each new request for reimbursement of an incurred medical care expense for the same plan year, the proposed integration rules provide that the HRA may not reimburse a participant for any medical care expenses unless, prior to each reimbursement, the participant provides substantiation (which may be in the form of a written attestation) that the participant and, if applicable, any dependent(s) whose medical care expenses are requested to be reimbursed continue to be enrolled in individual health insurance coverage (other than coverage that consists solely of excepted benefits) for the month during which the medical care expenses were incurred. The attestation may be part of the form used for requesting reimbursement.

---

[76] HRAs generally are subject to the rules under Code section 105(h) and its related regulations as self-insured medical reimbursement plans. In general, Code section 105(h) provides that certain amounts paid to highly compensated individuals under self-insured medical reimbursement plans are includible in the income of the highly compensated individual. The regulations under Code section 105(h) provide that, for purposes of the nondiscriminatory benefits rule under Code section 105(h)(4), "a plan may establish a maximum limit for the amount of reimbursement which may be paid a participant for any single benefit or a combination of benefits. However, any maximum limit attributable to employer contributions must be uniform for all participants and for all dependents of employees who are participants and may not be modified by reason of a participant's age or years of service." *See* 26 CFR 1.105-11(c)(3)(i). The guidance that the Treasury Department and the IRS intend to issue is also anticipated to address the application of the Code section 105(h) uniformity requirement to an HRA integrated with individual health insurance coverage more generally.

[77] *See* 26 CFR 54.9815-2711(d)(2)(i)(E), (d)(2)(ii)(D), (d)(5)(iv), 29 CFR 2590.715-2711(d)(2)(i)(E), (d)(2)(ii)(D), (d)(5)(iv), and 45 CFR 147.126(d)(2)(i)(E), (d)(2)(ii)(D) and (d)(5)(iv)). Note that the rule for integration of an HRA with non-HRA group coverage allows certain HRA amounts that are forfeited to be reinstated in the future, but the proposed rules do not contain a similar provision for HRAs integrated with individual health insurance coverage due to concerns by the Departments about complexity and burden on employers. See 26 CFR 54.9815-2711(d)(3), 29 CFR 2590.715-2711(d)(3), and 45 CFR 147.126(d)(3).

[78] *See* elsewhere in this preamble for a discussion of rules being proposed by the Treasury Department and the IRS regarding the circumstances in which an offer of an HRA integrated with individual health insurance coverage is affordable and provides MV. Also note that a former employee is only rendered ineligible for the PTC if the former employee enrolls in employer-sponsored coverage; an offer of coverage (even if it is affordable and provides MV) does not preclude a former employee from claiming the PTC.

[79] For purposes of the Code provisions affected by the proposed regulations, the otherwise generally applicable substantiation and recordkeeping requirements under section 6001 of the Code apply, including the requirements specified in Rev. Proc. 98-25 (1998-1 CB 689) for records maintained within an Automated Data Processing system.

As with the substantiation of enrollment for the plan year, for this purpose, an HRA may rely on the documentation or attestation provided by the participant unless the HRA has actual knowledge that the participant and any individual seeking reimbursement for the month were not enrolled in individual health insurance coverage (other than coverage that consists solely of excepted benefits) for the month.

6. *Notice Requirement*

Because HRAs are different from traditional employer-provided health coverage in many respects, the Departments are concerned that individuals eligible for HRAs integrated with individual health insurance coverage may not recognize that the offer and/or acceptance of an HRA will have consequences for PTC eligibility, as described elsewhere in this preamble. Therefore, in order to ensure that participants who are eligible to participate in an HRA integrated with individual health insurance coverage understand the potential effect that the offer of and enrollment in the HRA might have on their ability to claim the PTC, these proposed rules include a requirement that an HRA provide written notice to eligible participants. The HRA would be required to provide a written notice to each participant at least 90 days before the beginning of each plan year. For participants who are not yet eligible to participate at the beginning of the plan year (or who are not eligible when the notice is provided at least 90 days prior to the beginning of the plan year), the HRA would be required to provide the notice no later than the date on which the participant is first eligible to participate in the HRA.

The proposed written notice would be required to include certain relevant information, including a description of the terms of the HRA, including the maximum dollar amount made available, as used in the affordability determination under the Code section 36B proposed rules[80] ; a statement of the right of the participant to opt-out of and waive future reimbursement under the HRA; a description of the potential availability of the PTC if the participant opts out of and waives the HRA and the HRA is not affordable under the proposed PTC regulations; a description of the PTC eligibility consequences for a participant who accepts the HRA; a statement that the participant must inform any Exchange to which they apply for advance payments of the PTC of the availability of the HRA, the amount of the HRA, the number of months the HRA is available to participants during the plan year, whether the HRA is available to their dependents and whether they are a current or former employee; a statement that the participant should retain the written notice because it may be needed to determine whether the participant is allowed the PTC; a statement that the HRA may not reimburse any medical care expense unless the substantiation requirements are met; and a statement that it is the responsibility of the participant to inform the HRA if the participant or any dependent whose medical care expenses are reimbursable by the HRA is no longer enrolled in individual health insurance coverage.

This notice would provide some of the information the participant needs in order for the participant to ascertain the consequences of the HRA for PTC eligibility, and would inform them of their responsibilities for the HRA. If the requirements of the Department of Labor's proposed rules at 29 CFR 2510.3-1(l) are met, the notice would be required to also include a statement to advise participants that individual health insurance coverage integrated with the HRA is not subject to ERISA (see section IV of this preamble and the Department of Labor's proposed rules at 29 CFR 2510.3-1(l) for additional explanation regarding this requirement).

The written notice would be required to include the information required by the proposed integration rules, and would be permitted to include other information, as long as the additional information does not conflict with the required information.

The written notice would not need to include information specific to a participant. More specifically, although the notice must contain a description of the potential availability of the PTC for a participant who opts out of and waives an unaffordable HRA and must include the HRA amount that is relevant for determining affordability under the proposed rules at 26 CFR 1.36B-2(c)(5), the proposed rules would not require the HRA to include in the notice a determination of whether the HRA is considered affordable for the participant. The participant would need additional information (that is, their household income and the premium for the lowest cost silver plan in the Exchange for the rating area where they reside) to determine whether the HRA is affordable under the proposed PTC rules, as described in detail in section III of this preamble.

7. *Student Health Insurance Coverage*

Federal regulations under PPACA define student health insurance coverage as a type of individual health insurance coverage.[81] Although those regulations exempt student health insurance coverage

---

[80] The Departments note that in order to comply with the notice requirement, the HRA must determine the amounts that will be newly made available for the plan year prior to the plan year. A similar requirement applies under the proposed premium tax credit regulations. *See* proposed 26 CFR 1.36B-2(c)(5)(v).

[81] Under this definition, student health insurance coverage must be provided pursuant to a written agreement between an institution of higher education (as defined in the Higher Education Act of 1965) and a health insurance issuer, and provided to students enrolled in that institution and their dependents, and does not make health insurance coverage available other than in connection with enrollment as a student (or as a dependent of a student) in the institution, does not condition eligibility for the health insurance coverage on any health status-related factor (as defined in 45 CFR 146.121(a)) relating to a student (or a dependent of a student), and meets any additional requirements that may be imposed under State law. *See* 45 CFR 147.145(a).

from certain provisions of PPACA and HIPAA,[82] they do not exempt such coverage from sections 2711 and 2713 of the PHS Act. Therefore, given that student health insurance coverage is a type of individual health insurance coverage, and is required to comply with sections 2711 and 2713 of the PHS Act, the Departments clarify that under the proposed integration rules an HRA may be integrated with student health insurance coverage that satisfies the requirements in 45 CFR 147.145.[83]

The Departments also wish to confirm that prior guidance,[84] which provided enforcement relief to institutions of higher education for certain healthcare premium reduction arrangements offered in connection with student health coverage (insured or self-insured), remains in effect, pending further guidance.

8. *Comment Solicitation Regarding Various Integration-Related Issues*

In developing the proposed integration rules, the Departments considered whether to allow HRAs intended to satisfy the individual health insurance coverage integration test also to be integrated with group health plan coverage, such as a group health plan maintained by the employer of the participant's spouse, in addition to individual health insurance coverage, because like individual health insurance coverage, group health plan coverage is generally subject to and compliant with PHS Act sections 2711 and 2713. The Departments are not proposing such a rule because allowing such integration would add significant complexity to the individual health insurance coverage integration test.[85] The Departments request comments regarding whether the Departments should allow for such integration and if so, with respect to PHS Act section 2711 compliance, how such an integration test should be designed to take into account that, while most individual health insurance coverage is required to cover all EHBs, large group market and self-insured group health plans are not required to cover all EHBs. The Departments request comments on the demand for such a rule, and any problems such a rule may raise.

The Departments also considered whether to propose a rule to permit HRAs to be integrated with other types of non-group coverage other than individual health insurance coverage, such as STLDI.[86] However, while all individual health insurance coverage that is currently written is non-grandfathered coverage, and therefore is subject to and, presumably, compliant with PHS Act sections 2711 and 2713 (and most individual market coverage that is renewed is also non-grandfathered), other types of non-group coverage, such as STLDI, may not be subject to PHS Act sections 2711 and 2713, in which case, integration would not be sufficient to ensure that the combined benefit package satisfies these requirements. The Departments request comments on whether integration with STLDI (which is not required to, but which may, satisfy PHS Act sections 2711 and 2713) should be permitted, including whether integration should be permitted with any other type of coverage that satisfies PHS Act sections 2711 and 2713, how such integration rules should be structured, as well as comments on what, if any, potential benefits and problems might arise from allowing these types of HRA integration. The Departments also seek comment on whether allowing such integration would raise any concerns about health status discrimination leading to additional adverse selection in the individual market.

The Departments also seek comment on whether the ability to integrate an HRA with individual health insurance coverage has the potential to increase participation in and strengthen the viability of States' individual market risk pools. Further, the Departments invite comment on whether the proposed integration safeguards are appropriate and narrowly tailored to mitigate adverse selection

---

[82] *See* 45 CFR 147.145(b).

[83] Self-insured student health plans are not a form of individual health insurance coverage. Therefore, these proposed integration regulations do not provide for HRA integration with self-insured student health plans.

[84] *See* FAQs About Affordable Care Act Implementation Part 33, available at https://www.dol.gov/sites/default/files/ebsa/about-ebsa/our-activities/resource-center/faqs/aca-part-33.pdf or https://www.cms.gov/CCIIO/Resources/Fact-Sheets-and-FAQs/Downloads/ACA-FAQ-Set-33-Final.pdf. *See also* IRS Notice 2016-17, 2016-9 IRB 358; DOL Technical Release 2016-1, available at http://www.dol.gov/ebsa/newsroom/tr16-01.html; and Insurance Standards Bulletin, Application of the Market Reforms and Other Provisions of the Affordable Care Act to Student Health Coverage, February 5, 2016, available at https://www.cms.gov/CCIIO/Resources/Regulations-and-Guidance/Downloads/student-health-bulletin.pdf.

[85] PHS Act section 2711 applies with respect to the provision of EHBs. Because large group market and self-insured group health plan coverage are not required to provide EHBs, unlike individual health insurance coverage which is generally required to provide all EHBs, in the group health plan integration context, situations may arise where non-HRA group coverage with which the HRA is integrated does not cover every category of EHBs that the HRA covers. In that case, the HRA applies an annual dollar limit to a category of EHBs and the non-HRA group coverage with which it is integrated does not cure that limit by providing unlimited coverage of that category of EHBs. In the 2015 regulations under PHS Act section 2711, and in subregulatory guidance that preceded the Departments final rules, the Departments addressed this issue by providing two tests. Specifically, if the non-HRA group coverage with which an HRA is integrated provides MV, the HRA will not be considered to fail to comply with PHS Act section 2711, even though the HRA might provide reimbursement of an EHB that the plan with which the HRA is integrated does not. If an HRA is integrated with non-HRA group coverage that does not provide MV, the 2015 regulations limit the types of expenses that an HRA may reimburse to reimbursement of co-payments, coinsurance, deductibles, and premiums under the non-HRA group coverage, as well as medical care that does not constitute EHBs. For additional discussion of the final regulations under PHS Act section 2711 see the discussion earlier in this preamble.

[86] *See* the definition of short-term, limited-duration insurance (STLDI) under 26 CFR 54.9801-2, 29 CFR 2590.701-2, 45 CFR 144.103.

and the potential for discrimination based on health status, or whether less restrictive safeguards would suffice.

Further, as noted earlier in this preamble, the proposed integration rules do not address cafeteria plan premium arrangements, other than to provide that plan sponsors may offer such an arrangement in addition to an HRA integrated with individual health insurance coverage in certain circumstances. The Departments invite comments on whether employers may seek to provide cafeteria plan premium arrangements, including as a standalone arrangement, and, if so, what additional guidance is needed in order to facilitate the offering of such arrangements. In particular, the Departments solicit comments on whether the definition of the term "account-based group health plan" should include cafeteria plan premium arrangements in order to permit these arrangements to integrate with individual health insurance coverage subject to the requirements of the rule, including how that treatment would be coordinated with other requirements applicable to employee benefit plans.

9. Revisions to PHS Act Section 2711 Regulations Regarding Integration with Other Group Health Plan Coverage and Medicare

The 2015 regulations under PHS Act section 2711 provide methods for integrating HRAs with coverage under another group health plan, and, in certain circumstances, with Medicare parts B and D. These proposed rules do not substantively change the current group health plan or Medicare integration tests under the existing PHS Act section 2711 regulations. However, these proposed rules include minor proposed revisions to those regulations, including changing the term "account-based plan" to "account-based group health plan" and moving defined terms to a definitions section.

More substantively, these proposed rules would amend the regulations under PHS Act section 2711 to reflect that HRAs may be integrated with individual health insurance coverage subject to the requirements of 26 CFR 54.9802-4, 29 CFR 2590.702-2, and 45 CFR 146.123. Paragraph (d)(4) of 26 CFR 54.9815-2711, 29 CFR 2590.715-2711 and 45 CFR 147.126 is revised accordingly. In addition, for the sake of clarity, the proposed rules add to paragraph (d)(2) in each of the aforementioned PHS Act section 2711 regulations that an HRA integrated with non-HRA group coverage may not be used to purchase individual health insurance coverage (other than coverage that consists solely of excepted benefits), as the Departments previously clarified in Notice 2015-87, Q&A 2.

In addition, the proposed rules update the definition of EHBs set forth in paragraph (c) of the regulations under PHS Act section 2711, which applies for a group health plan or health insurance issuer not required to cover EHBs. The update in the proposed rules reflects the revision to the EHB-benchmark plan selection process that was promulgated in the HHS Notice of Benefit and Payment Parameters for 2019 Final Rule (2019 Payment Notice) and that applies for plan years beginning on or after January 1, 2020.[87] The 2019 Payment Notice revisions provide States with additional choices with respect to the selection of benefits and promote affordable coverage through offering States additional flexibility in their selection of an EHB-benchmark plan for plan years beginning on or after January 1, 2020. The State's existing EHB-benchmark plan will continue to apply for any year for which a State does not select a new EHB-benchmark plan from the available EHB-benchmark plan selection options finalized in the 2019 Payment Notice.[88]

B. *Excepted Benefit HRAs*

There may be scenarios in which an employer wishes to offer an HRA that may not be integrated with non-HRA group coverage, Medicare, TRICARE, or individual health insurance coverage. For example, some employers may wish to offer an HRA without regard to whether its employees have other coverage at all or without regard to whether its employees have coverage that is subject to and satisfies the market requirements. Therefore, these proposed rules would utilize the Departments' discretion under section 9832(c)(2)(C) of the Code, section 733(c)(2)(C) of ERISA, and section 2791(c)(2)(C) of the PHS Act, to recognize HRAs as limited excepted benefits, if certain conditions are met.[89]

As explained earlier in this preamble, the Departments have the authority and discretion to specify in regulations additional limited excepted benefits, that are similar to the limited benefits specified in the statute and that either are insured under a separate policy, certificate, or contract, or are otherwise not an integral part of a plan. The Departments are proposing an excepted benefit HRA that is both consistent with this statutory framework and consistent with the Departments' objective of expanding the availability and usability of HRAs.

The proposed rules provide the following four requirements for an HRA to qualify as an excepted benefit HRA: (1) the HRA must not be an integral part of the plan, (2) the HRA must provide benefits that are limited in amount, (3) the HRA cannot provide reimbursement for premiums for certain health insurance coverage, and (4) the HRA must be made available under the same terms to all similarly situated individuals.

---

[87] *See* 83 FR 16930 (April 17, 2018). The definition of EHB that applies under the PHS Act section 2711 regulations for plan years beginning before January 1, 2020 would not be substantively changed by the proposed rules.

[88] For more information on the revised EHB standard, refer to the preamble to the 2019 Payment Notice, beginning at page 17007.

[89] The proposed rules that recognize certain HRAs as limited excepted benefits do not apply to health FSAs. For a health FSA to qualify as an excepted benefit, the current regulations continue to apply.

1. *Otherwise Not an Integral Part of the Plan*

HRAs are self-insured group health plans and, therefore, are not insurance coverage that can be provided under a separate policy, certificate, or contract of insurance. Accordingly, HRAs must meet the statutory requirement to not be "an integral part of the plan." To satisfy this condition, the proposed rules specify that for an HRA to be an excepted benefit, other group health plan coverage (other than an account-based group health plan or coverage consisting solely of excepted benefits) must be made available by the same plan sponsor for the plan year to the participants offered the HRA. Only individuals who are eligible for participation in the other group health plan would be eligible for participation in the excepted benefit HRA. However, while the plan sponsor would be required to make an offer of other group health plan coverage in order to meet this requirement, HRA participants (and their dependents) would not be required to enroll in the other group health plan in order to be eligible for the excepted benefit HRA.

This provision of the proposed excepted benefit HRA is similar to the requirement that applies under the limited excepted benefits regulations for health FSAs at 26 CFR 54.9831-1(c)(3)(v), 29 CFR 2590.732(c)(3)(v), and 45 CFR 146.145(b)(3)(v).

2. *Limited in Amount*

In creating the excepted benefit HRA, the Departments had to determine what type of HRA would be sufficiently limited to qualify as a limited excepted benefit. Under the statute, limited benefits may include limited scope vision or dental benefits, benefits for long-term care, nursing home care, home health care, or community-based care, or any combination thereof and may include "such other similar, limited benefits as are specified in regulations" by the Departments.

The Departments consistently have applied limiting principles in prior rulemakings under which discretion was exercised to establish additional types of limited excepted benefits. For example, health FSAs constitute excepted benefits only if the arrangement is structured so that the maximum benefit payable to any participant in the class for a year may not exceed two times the participant's salary reduction election under the arrangement for the year (or, if greater, may not exceed $500 plus the amount of the participant's salary reduction election).[90] Additionally, limited wraparound coverage is a limited excepted benefit only if it is limited in amount, such that the cost of coverage per employee (and any covered dependents) under the limited wraparound coverage does not exceed the greater of the maximum permitted annual salary reduction contribution toward a health FSA,[91] or 15 percent of the cost of coverage under the primary plan.[92]

In the proposed rules, the Departments propose that the amounts newly made available for a plan year in an excepted benefit HRA may not exceed $1,800, indexed for inflation for plan years beginning after December 31, 2020. For this purpose, inflation is defined in these proposed rules by reference to the Chained Consumer Price Index for All Urban Consumers, unadjusted (C-CPI-U), published by the Department of Labor. The adjusted limit for plan years beginning in a particular calendar year will be made available early in the fall of the prior calendar year.

In proposing this limit, the Departments considered several factors, including the limits on employer contributions to excepted benefit health FSAs (set at $500 in 1997 if there are no employee contributions to the FSA, although it might be much higher if there are employee contributions[93]). The Departments also considered indexing $500 for medical inflation using the medical care component of the Consumer Price Index for all Urban Consumers (CPI-U). The Departments considered the relationship between $500 and the average cost of insurance in 1997. The Departments also considered a limit of 15 percent-of-the-cost-of-coverage-under-the-primary-plan test, which is the limit used for both supplemental excepted benefits in the group market and limited wraparound coverage, as a benchmark to ensure that the benefits are limited in amount.[94] In considering how such a limit could be an appropriate limit for excepted benefit HRAs, the Departments considered 15 percent of the cost of group coverage for both employee-only and family coverage. However, the Departments also considered how to determine the primary plan in circumstances in which the participant does not enroll in a traditional group health plan, and concluded that such a determination would likely be difficult for employers. The Departments also considered using the cost of coverage for the second-lowest cost silver plan in various markets. These methodologies produced a wide range of possible excepted benefit HRA limits from $1,100 to $2,850. Consistent with the principle of promoting HRA use and availability, rather than proposing a complex test for the limit on amounts newly made available in the excepted benefit HRA, the Departments are proposing a maximum of $1,800 (indexed for inflation) on amounts newly made available for a plan year. This approximates the midpoint amount yielded by the various methodologies considered.

---

[90] 26 CFR 54.9831-1(c)(3)(v); 29 CFR 2590.732(c)(3)(v); 45 CFR 146.145(b)(3)(v).

[91] *See* section 125(i) of the Code.

[92] 26 CFR 54.9831-1(c)(3)(vii); 29 CFR 2590.732(c)(3)(vii); 45 CFR 146.145(b)(3)(vii).

[93] *See* 26 CFR 54.9831-1(c)(3)(v)(B); 29 CFR 2590.732(c)(3)(v)(B); 45 CFR 146.145(b)(3)(v)(B).

[94] *See* 26 CFR 54.9831-1(c)(3)(vii)(B)(2); 29 CFR 2590.732(c)(3)(vii)(B)(2); 45 CFR 146.145(b)(3)(vii)(B)(2). *See also* EBSA Field Assistance Bulletin No. 2007-04 (available at https://www.dol.gov/agencies/ebsa/employers-and-advisers/guidance/field-assistance-bulletins/2007-04); CMS Insurance Standards Bulletin 08-01 (available at http://www.cms.gov/CCIIO/Resources/Files/Downloads/hipaa_08_01_508.pdf); and IRS Notice 2008-23 (2008-07 IRB 433).

In proposing to index the amount by C-CPI-U, the Departments considered several factors, including the difficulties of administering an HRA with a changing amount, and the cost, including the cost to the Departments to publish the amount and provide notice every year, as balanced with the decreasing real value of a set HRA limit and the ability of an employer to maintain the HRA benefit at $1,800, should it choose to do so.

The Departments invite comment on the amount of the proposed maximum dollar limit and whether an alternate amount or formula for determining the maximum dollar limit for an excepted benefit HRA would be more appropriate and, if so, what that alternative would be and why. The Departments specifically request comments on whether the proposed HRA maximum amount of $1,800 should be higher if the HRA covers dependents (or alternatively, whether the $1,800 maximum amount should be lower if the HRA only covers the employee). The Departments also invite comments on the measure of inflation used, including whether the amount should be indexed to inflation (and if there are any administrability concerns associated with indexing), if C-CPI-U is the correct measure of inflation, or whether an alternate measure, such as the overall *medical* care component for CPI-U, or the method specified under section 9831(d)(2)(D) of the Code for QSEHRAs, should be used. The Departments also invite comment on whether the publication of the adjusted limit for plan years beginning in a particular calendar year by early fall of the preceding calendar year will provide employers with sufficient time to adjust the excepted benefit HRA for the upcoming year.

If a participant or dependent in an excepted benefit HRA does not use all of the amounts made available in the excepted benefit HRA to reimburse medical care expenses for a plan year, and the excepted benefit HRA allows for these amounts to be made available to the participant and dependents in later plan years, the Departments propose that these carryover amounts would be disregarded for purposes of determining whether the benefits in the excepted benefit HRA are limited in amount.

Further, the proposed rules provide that if the plan sponsor provides more than one excepted benefit HRA to the participant for the same time period, the amounts made available under such plans are aggregated to determine whether the benefits are limited in amount.

3. *Prohibition on Reimbursement of Premiums for Certain Types of Coverage*

As the third requirement for an HRA to be recognized as a limited excepted benefit, the Departments propose that the HRA would not be permitted to reimburse premiums for individual health insurance coverage, coverage under a group health plan (other than COBRA or other group continuation coverage), or Medicare parts B or D. However, the proposed rules would allow an excepted benefit HRA to reimburse premiums for individual health insurance coverage that consists solely of excepted benefits or coverage under a group health plan that consists solely of excepted benefits, as well as for STLDI premiums, and for COBRA premiums.

The Departments have concluded that this limit is appropriate in light of the requirement that excepted benefits under this statutory provision provide only limited benefits. In addition, the Departments have concluded that this condition is appropriate because under our concurrent proposal to permit HRAs to be integrated with individual health insurance coverage and the current regulations that allow HRAs to be integrated with group health plan coverage and to reimburse premiums for Medicare parts B and D in certain circumstances, an employer that wishes to provide an HRA that reimburses premiums for individual health insurance coverage, coverage under a group health plan, or Medicare parts B or D may do so under the applicable integration rules. Such an approach ensures that excepted benefit HRAs provide limited benefits different from what a traditional group health plan would provide, similar to limited scope dental or vision plans and benefits for long-term care, nursing home care, home health care, and community-based care.

This proposed condition would not limit the ability of an excepted benefit HRA to reimburse premiums for COBRA or other group continuation coverage (premiums for which are generally paid with after-tax funds) or STLDI. Further, the excepted benefit HRA may reimburse premiums other than those listed as specifically excluded. The Departments request comments on this condition, including whether additional clarity is needed regarding whether premiums for certain types of coverage may be reimbursed under the proposed excepted benefit HRA.

4. *Uniform Availability*

To prevent a plan sponsor from intentionally or unintentionally, directly or indirectly, steering any participants or dependents with adverse health factors away from the sponsor's traditional group health plan, the fourth and final requirement for an HRA to be recognized as a limited excepted benefit relates to uniform availability. Specifically, an excepted benefit HRA would be required to be made available under the same terms to all similarly situated individuals (as defined in the HIPAA nondiscrimination regulations) regardless of any health factor. In the Departments' view, this condition is necessary to prevent discrimination based on health status and to preclude opportunities for an employer to offer a more generous excepted benefit HRA to individuals with an adverse health factor, such as an illness or a disability, as an incentive not to enroll in the plan sponsor's traditional group health plan. Therefore, the Departments are proposing a uniform-availability requirement and wish to make it clear that benefits must be provided uniformly, without regard to any health factor. Accordingly, for example, the HRA could not be offered only to employees who have cancer or fail a physical examination, just as the HRA could not be offered only to employees who are cancer-free or who pass a physical examination. Similarly, an employer could not make greater amounts available to an HRA for employees who have cancer or who fail a physical examination, just as an employer could not make greater amounts available to an HRA for employees who are cancer-free or who pass a physical examination. The Departments request comment on whether additional standards are necessary to prevent abuse and discrimination based on a health factor.

C. *Interaction between HRAs Integrated with Individual Health Insurance Coverage and Excepted Benefits HRAs*

Under the proposed rules, an employer would be permitted to offer an HRA integrated with individual health insurance coverage to a class of employees so long as it does not also offer a traditional group health plan to the same class of employees, subject to additional conditions discussed elsewhere in this preamble. However, an employer could only offer an excepted benefit HRA if traditional group health plan coverage is also made available to the employees who are eligible to participate in the excepted benefit HRA. Thus, an employer would not be permitted to offer both an HRA integrated with individual health insurance coverage and an excepted benefit HRA to any employee.[95]

III. Overview of the Proposed Rules Regarding the Premium Tax Credit - Department of the Treasury and IRS

A. *Premium Tax Credit under Section 36B of the Code*

Consistent with the objectives in Executive Order 13813 to expand the use of HRAs, the proposed rules would amend the regulations under section 36B of the Code to provide guidance for individuals who are offered or covered by an HRA integrated with individual health insurance coverage as described in the proposed integration rules and who otherwise may be eligible for the PTC.

An individual who is covered by an HRA integrated with individual health insurance coverage is ineligible for the PTC. However, see the discussion earlier in this preamble of the related requirement under the proposed integration rules that plan sponsors provide participants with the periodic opportunity to opt-out of and waive future reimbursements under an HRA.

The proposed rules under section 36B of the Code describe the PTC eligibility of an individual who is offered, but opts out of, an HRA that is integrated with individual health insurance coverage. Consistent with section 36B of the Code and the existing regulations thereunder, the proposed rules provide that an employee who is offered, but opts out of, an HRA integrated with individual health insurance coverage, and an individual who is offered such an HRA because of a relationship to the employee (a related HRA individual), are eligible for MEC under an eligible employer-sponsored plan for any month the HRA is affordable and provides MV. Thus, these individuals are ineligible for the PTC for their Exchange coverage for months the HRA is affordable and provides MV.

Under the proposed rules, an HRA integrated with individual health insurance coverage is affordable for an employee (and a related HRA individual) for a month if the employee's required HRA contribution does not exceed 1/12 of the product of the employee's household income and the required contribution percentage (defined in 26 CFR 1.36B-2(c)(3)(v)(C)). For this purpose, an employee's required HRA contribution would be the excess of: (1) the monthly premium for the lowest cost silver plan for self-only coverage available to the employee through the Exchange for the rating area in which the employee resides; over (2) the monthly self-only HRA amount provided by the employee's employer, or, if the employer offers an HRA that provides for a single dollar amount regardless of whether an employee has self-only or other-than-self-only coverage, the monthly maximum amount available to the employee. Under the proposed rules, the monthly self-only HRA amount would be the self-only HRA amount newly made available to the employee from the employee's employer under the HRA for the plan year, divided by the number of months in the plan year the HRA is available to the employee. The monthly maximum amount available to the employee under the HRA, which is relevant if the HRA provides one amount regardless of the number of individuals covered, would be the maximum amount newly made available to the employee under the HRA, divided by the number of months in the plan year the HRA is available to the employee.

The affordability rule in the proposed rules uses the lowest cost silver plan for self-only coverage available to the employee through the Exchange for the rating area in which the employee resides, without regard to the type of plan in which the employee actually enrolls. The lowest cost silver plan was chosen because, in the individual market, the lowest cost silver plan is the lowest cost Exchange plan for which the plan's share of the total allowed costs of benefits provided under the plan is certain to be at least 60 percent of such costs, as required by section 36B(c)(2)(C)(ii) of the Code for a plan to provide MV. Specifically, section 36B(c)(2)(C)(ii) of the Code and 26 CFR 1.36B-6 provide that an eligible employer-sponsored plan provides MV only if the plan's share of the total allowed costs of benefits provided to an employee under the plan is at least 60 percent.[96] In selecting the lowest cost plan for which it is certain that the plan's share of the total allowed costs of benefits provided under the plan will be at least 60 percent of such costs, the proposed rules seek to most closely approximate

---

[95] The Departments note that an employer may not provide a QSEHRA to any employee if it offers any employee a group health plan. Accordingly, an employer may not provide a QSEHRA to any employee if it offers any employee an HRA that may be integrated with individual health insurance coverage or an excepted benefit HRA. *See* section 9831(d)(3)(B)(ii) of the Code.

[96] In the individual market, a bronze plan may have an actuarial value of 56 percent, which would not ensure the plan's share of the total allowed costs of benefits provided under the plan is at least 60 percent of such costs, as required by section 36B(c)(2)(C)(ii) of the Code for a plan to provide MV. *See* 45 CFR 156.140.

the PTC eligibility rules that apply to offers of eligible-employer sponsored coverage that is not an HRA.[97] That is, the PTC eligibility rules under the proposed regulations for an HRA offer, as well as under section 36B of the Code for an offer of traditional employer coverage, are both based on the affordability of a plan available to the employee for which the plan's share of the total allowed costs of benefits provided under the plan must be at least 60 percent of such costs. (See the discussion later in this section of when an HRA integrated with individual health insurance coverage is considered to provide MV.) The Treasury Department and the IRS seek comment on whether the silver level plan used for this purpose should be the second lowest cost silver plan,[98] instead of the lowest cost silver plan, for self-only coverage offered in the Exchange for the rating area in which the employee resides or whether another plan should be used, and any operational or other issues that the use of the plan proposed or any alternative plan would entail.

The proposed rules further provide that only amounts that are newly made available for the plan year of the HRA would be taken into account for determining affordability, provided that the amounts are determinable within a reasonable time before the beginning of the plan year of the HRA. Additionally, consistent with the rules for traditional employer coverage, the proposed rules require affordability to be determined separately for each employment period that is less than a full calendar year or for the portions of the plan year of the HRA that fall within different taxable years of the employee. In addition, the proposed rules include examples of affordability calculations.

The proposed rules also address the circumstances in which an HRA is considered to provide MV. As noted earlier in this section of the preamble, section 36B of the Code generally provides that an offer of employer coverage prevents an employee from being allowed the PTC for his or her Exchange coverage only if the employer coverage is both affordable and provides MV. With respect to an offer of an HRA integrated with individual health insurance coverage, the individual health insurance coverage that is proposed to be used for purposes of the affordability test is the lowest cost silver level Exchange coverage for the rating area in which the employee resides, which, as previously noted, will always provide MV. A determination that the integrated arrangement is affordable under the proposed regulations is therefore sufficient to ensure that an employee who is offered an HRA integrated with individual health insurance coverage, and that is determined to be affordable, has the ability to purchase affordable coverage that provides MV. Consequently, the proposed rules provide that an HRA integrated with individual health insurance coverage that is affordable is treated as providing MV.

Determining PTC eligibility in the manner provided under the proposed rules is consistent with current rules for traditional employer coverage. That is, the proposed rules result in consistent treatment for purposes of section 36B of the Code for employees offered an HRA integrated with individual health insurance coverage and employees offered traditional employer coverage. In both instances, the employees may be allowed the PTC if they decline the offer and the coverage is either unaffordable or does not provide MV. Further, in both instances, the employee's required contribution is based on the amount the employee must pay for self-only coverage that provides MV because under the proposed rules affordability would be determined based on the lowest cost silver plan offered in the Exchange for the rating area in which the employee resides (which by definition will always provide MV). If the amount the employee must pay is more than the product of the required contribution percentage and the employee's household income, the employee may be allowed the PTC.

The proposed rules also clarify the ways in which the generally applicable employer-sponsored coverage PTC eligibility rules apply to HRAs integrated with individual health insurance coverage.[100] For example, as with traditional coverage under eligible employer-sponsored plans, the proposed rules provide that an HRA integrated with individual health insurance coverage is not affordable for a month for an employee or related HRA individual if, at the time of enrollment in a qualified health plan, an Exchange determines that the HRA is not affordable. This employee safe harbor locks in an Exchange's determination of unaffordability, which is based on estimated household income, even if the HRA ultimately proves to be affordable based on actual household income for the tax year. Consistent with the existing regulations under section 36B of the Code, the employee safe harbor does not apply (1) to a determination made as part of the redetermination process described in 45 CFR 155.335 unless the individual receiving an Exchange redetermination notification affirmatively responds and provides current information on affordability; or (2) for an individual

---

[97] With regard to an offer of eligible employer-sponsored coverage that is not an HRA, an individual is eligible for the PTC only if the employee's required contribution, which is the portion of the annual premium that would be paid for the lowest cost self-only MV coverage offered by the employer to the employee, exceeds a certain percentage of the employee's household income. *See* section 36B(c)(2)(C) of the Code.

[98] Note that the monthly premium for self-only coverage for the second lowest cost silver plan in the employee's individual health insurance market is used to determine the affordability of a QSEHRA. *See* section 36B(c)(4)(C) of the Code.

[100] The Treasury Department and the IRS have provided guidance regarding when amounts newly made available under an HRA count toward the affordability or MV of another group health plan offered by the same employer. *See* 26 CFR 1.36B-2(c)(3)(v)(A)(5) and 26 CFR 1.36B-6(c)(4). *See also* IRS Notice 2015-87, Q&A 7. This document does not make substantive revisions to those rules but does make clarifying updates to 26 CFR 1.36B-2(c)(3)(v)(A)(5), mainly to incorporate a reference to more recent guidance.

who, with intentional or reckless disregard for the facts, provides incorrect information to an Exchange concerning the relevant HRA amount.

B. *Employer Shared Responsibility Provisions under Section 4980H of the Code*

As part of implementing the objectives of Executive Order 13813, the Treasury Department and the IRS have considered how section 4980H of the Code would apply to an employer offering an HRA integrated with individual health insurance coverage, as set forth in the proposed integration rules and taking into account the proposed rules described previously in this preamble under section 36B of the Code.

Only ALEs are subject to section 4980H of the Code.[101] The Departments anticipate that many employers that would be interested in offering an HRA integrated with individual health insurance coverage, as set forth in the proposed integration rules, may be smaller employers and, therefore, may not need to consider section 4980H of the Code when designing their HRA program.

For an employer that is an ALE, the employer may owe a payment for a month under section 4980H(a) or section 4980H(b) of the Code or neither. In general, an employer will owe a payment under section 4980H(a) of the Code if it fails to offer an eligible employer-sponsored plan to at least 95 percent of its full-time employees and their dependents and at least one full-time employee is allowed the PTC for the month.[102] An HRA is an eligible employer-sponsored plan; therefore, if an ALE offers an eligible employer-sponsored plan (including an HRA) to at least 95 percent of its full-time employees and their dependents, the ALE would not be liable for a payment under section 4980H(a) of the Code for the month.

An employer that is an ALE and which offers an eligible employer-sponsored plan to at least 95 percent of its full-time employees and their dependents (and therefore is not liable for a payment under section 4980H(a) of the Code) may be liable for a payment under section 4980H(b) of the Code if at least one full-time employee is allowed the PTC, which may occur if the eligible employer-sponsored plan offered was not affordable or did not provide MV, or if the employee was not offered coverage. The extent to which a full-time employee who was offered an HRA will be eligible for the PTC depends on the rules proposed under section 36B of the Code. However, in the near term, the Treasury Department and the IRS intend to issue guidance that describes an anticipated safe harbor for purposes of determining whether an employer that has offered an HRA integrated with individual health insurance coverage would be treated as having made an offer of affordable coverage that provides MV for purposes of section 4980H of the Code, regardless of whether the employee who received that offer declines the HRA and claims the PTC.[103]

IV. Individual Health Insurance Coverage and ERISA Plan Status

This document includes a DOL-only proposed regulation that would clarify that the ERISA terms "employee welfare benefit plan," "welfare plan," and, as a direct result, "group health plan" would not include individual health insurance coverage the premiums of which are reimbursed by an HRA and certain other arrangements, provided that the employer, employee organization, or other plan sponsor is not involved in the selection of the individual health insurance coverage, among other criteria. Later, this section of the preamble also describes a related clarification made to regulations of all three Departments. DOL's objective in proposing this regulatory clarification is to provide employees; employers, employee organizations, and other plan sponsors; health insurance issuers; state insurance regulators; and other stakeholders with assurance that insurance policies sold as individual health insurance coverage, and subject to comprehensive Federal (and state) individual market rules for minimum and uniform coverage, standardized pricing, guaranteed availability, and guaranteed renewability, are not part of an HRA or certain other arrangements for purposes of ERISA.[104] Specifically, DOL is proposing an amendment to 29 CFR 2510.3-1 on the definition of "employee welfare benefit plan" in section 3(1) of ERISA.[105] This proposed amendment would also apply to certain existing arrangements that reimburse participants for the purchase of individual health insurance coverage that are not subject to the market requirements (including QSEHRAs and HRAs that have fewer than two participants who are current employees on the first day of the plan year). Further, this proposed amendment would apply to an arrangement under which an employer allows employees to pay the portion of the premium for individual health insurance coverage that is

---

[101] The explanation of section 4980H of the Code provided here is a summary. For a complete explanation of the rules, including for definitions of terms used in this summary, see 26 CFR 54.4980H-1, *et seq.*, published in the Federal Register at 79 FR 8544 (Feb. 12, 2014).

[102] Note that if an ALE offered coverage to all but five of its full-time employees (and their dependents), and five is greater than 5 percent of the employer's full-time employees, the employer will not owe an employer shared responsibility payment under section 4980H(a) of the Code. *See* 26 CFR 54.4980H-4(a).

[103] In addition to setting forth a potential affordability safe harbor, the Treasury Department and the IRS intend to clarify in the upcoming guidance that the affordability safe harbors set forth under 26 CFR 54.4980H-5(e)(2) are available to employers offering an HRA integrated with individual health insurance coverage, subject to the relevant conditions set forth in those regulations.

[104] For examples of other circumstances under which DOL has determined an arrangement is not a plan within the meaning of ERISA, see 29 CFR 2510.3-1(j), 29 CFR 2510.3-2(f), and 29 CFR 2509.99-1. *See also* DOL Field Assistance Bulletins 2004-01 and 2006-02.

[105] In light of the fact that "group health plan" is defined derivatively in ERISA section 733(a)(1), in relevant part, as an "employee welfare benefit plan to the extent that the plan provided medical care . . . directly or through insurance, reimbursement, or otherwise[,]" DOL has concluded that a separate regulation relating to the definition of group health plan is not needed.

not covered by the HRA with which the coverage is integrated or that is not covered by a QSEHRA by using a salary reduction arrangement under a cafeteria plan (supplemental salary reduction arrangement).

Section 3(1) of ERISA specifically defines ERISA-covered welfare plans to include "any plan, fund, or program" "established or maintained by an employer or employee organization" for the provision of health benefits "through the purchase of insurance or otherwise." At the same time, provisions in the PHS Act generally treat individual health insurance and group health insurance as mutually exclusive categories.[106] If individual health insurance coverage were considered to be a group health plan or part of a group health plan, the individual health insurance coverage would likely violate some of the market requirements (for example, the single risk pool requirement). Treatment of such individual health insurance coverage as subject to both individual market and group market requirements thus could result in conflicting requirements, uncertainty and confusion which could inhibit or, in some instances, even preclude, the ability to integrate HRAs with individual health insurance coverage as contemplated by other provisions in the proposed rules.

In light of the PHS Act's treatment of group and individual health insurance coverage policies as mutually exclusive categories and the other provisions in this rulemaking addressing the permissible integration of individual health insurance coverage with HRAs, DOL concluded that the ERISA status of such individual health insurance coverage should be clarified in the context of the proposed rules.[107]

Under the proposed regulatory clarification, the status under ERISA of an HRA, QSEHRA, or supplemental salary reduction arrangement would remain unaffected. However, under the proposal, individual health insurance coverage selected by the employee in the individual market and reimbursed by such a plan would not be treated as part of a group health plan, or as health insurance coverage offered in connection with a group health plan, or as a part of any employee welfare benefit plan for purposes of title I of ERISA, provided all the following conditions are satisfied:

- The purchase of any individual health insurance coverage is completely voluntary for employees.[108]
- The employer, employee organization, or other plan sponsor does not select or endorse any particular issuer or insurance coverage. Providing general contact information regarding availability of health insurance in a state (such as providing information regarding www.healthcare.gov or contact information for a state insurance commissioner's office) or providing general health insurance educational information (such as the uniform glossary of health coverage and medical terms available at: https://www.dol.gov/sites/default/files/ebsa/laws-and-regulations/laws/affordable-care-act/for-employers-and-advisers/sbc-uniform-glossary-of-coverage-and-medical-terms-final.pdf) is permitted.
- Reimbursement for nongroup health insurance premiums is limited solely to individual health insurance coverage.
- The employer, employee organization, or other plan sponsor receives no consideration in the form of cash or otherwise in connection with the employee's selection or renewal of any individual health insurance coverage.
- Each plan participant is notified annually that the individual health insurance coverage is not subject to ERISA. For an HRA integrated with individual health insurance coverage, the notice must meet the requirements set forth in the proposed integration rules at 29 CFR 2590.702-2(c)(6). For a QSEHRA or an HRA that is not subject to 29 CFR 2590.702-2(c)(6), model language is provided in the DOL proposed amendment, which can be used to satisfy the condition.[109] A supplemental salary reduction arrangement need not provide the required notice; the notice will be provided by the HRA or QSEHRA that the salary reduction arrangement supplements.

---

[106] As described earlier, individual health insurance coverage means health insurance coverage offered to individuals in the individual market, but does not include STLDI. *See* PHS Act section 2791(b)(5), 26 CFR 54.9801-2, 29 CFR 2590.701-2, and 45 CFR 144.103. Individual market means the market for health insurance coverage offered to individuals other than in connection with a group health plan. *See* PHS Act section 2791(e)(1), 26 CFR 54.9801-2, 29 CFR 2590.701-2, and 45 CFR 144.103. Group health insurance coverage means health insurance coverage offered in connection with a group health plan. *See* ERISA section 733(b)(4), PHS Act section 2791(b)(4), 26 CFR 54.9801-2, 29 CFR 2590.701-2, and 45 CFR 144.103.

[107] It is the intention of DOL that integration of an HRA with individual health insurance coverage obtained in the individual market, as described in the proposed rules, generally will not result in the individual health insurance coverage being treated as an "employee welfare benefit plan" or a "group health plan" within the meaning of title I of ERISA. However, depending on the particular facts and circumstances surrounding the involvement of an employer, the issue may not be free from doubt. Consequently, DOL proposes the clarification herein.

[108] The fact that a plan sponsor requires such coverage to be purchased as a condition for participation in an HRA or supplemental salary reduction arrangement does not make the purchase involuntary. This issue should not arise in the context of a QSEHRA because in that case, although individuals must be enrolled in MEC, employers may not require employees to enroll in individual health insurance coverage.

[109] In DOL's view, the summary plan description (SPD) for the HRA, QSEHRA, or other ERISA plan would fail to satisfy the style, format, and content requirements in 29 CFR 2520.102-3 and 29 CFR 2520.102-3 unless it contained a discussion of the status of the HRA or QSEHRA and the individual health insurance coverage under ERISA sufficient to apprise the HRA or QSEHRA plan participants and beneficiaries of their rights and obligations under the plan and Title I of ERISA.

DOL invites comments on all aspects of the proposed regulatory clarification. Some of the conditions parallel or are similar to conditions in other existing DOL regulations and related guidance for other types of arrangements, and DOL specifically invites comments on whether all of these conditions are necessary or whether other conditions should be used in place of, or in addition to, those being proposed in this document. DOL has issued guidance describing certain types of employee communications that would not constitute "endorsement" as that condition applies under its regulations on payroll-deduction IRAs, see 29 CFR 2509.99-1, and specifically invites comments on whether similar regulatory or interpretive guidance would be helpful in the context of this proposed regulation. DOL also specifically invites comments on which forms of payment are appropriately treated as "reimbursement" to participants for purposes of this regulatory clarification, consistent with the terms and purposes of ERISA section 3(1). For example, should "reimbursement" be interpreted to include direct payments, individual or aggregate, by the employer, employee organization, or other plan sponsor to the insurance company? DOL also specifically invites comments on whether a better approach would involve providing relief from specified otherwise-applicable obligations under ERISA Title I, rather than carving the policy out as if it were outside of ERISA Title I.

Additionally, existing regulations of all three Departments define "group health insurance coverage" as health insurance coverage offered in connection with a group health plan.[110] The Departments propose to amend that definition by clarifying that individual health insurance coverage the premiums of which are reimbursed by an HRA or a supplemental salary reduction arrangement is not offered in connection with a group health plan, and is not group health insurance coverage, provided all the conditions in proposed 29 CFR 2510.3-1(l) (described earlier in this preamble) are satisfied.[111]

In light of the fact that HRAs are subject to many statutory rules and regulations not specifically addressed in this proposed rulemaking, including various reporting, disclosure, fiduciary, and enforcement provisions under title I of ERISA, DOL also specifically invites comment on whether it would be helpful for DOL to issue additional regulations or guidance addressing the application of ERISA reporting and disclosure requirements to HRAs integrated with such non-ERISA individual health insurance coverage (for example, SPD content and Form 5500 annual reporting requirements). Similarly, the limitation in the proposal on employers, employee organizations, and other plan sponsors receiving consideration from an issuer or person affiliated with an issuer in connection with any participant's purchase or renewal of individual health insurance coverage was not intended to change any ERISA requirements governing the circumstances under which plans, including HRAs, may reimburse employers, employee organizations and other plan sponsors for certain expenses associated with administration of the plan. DOL specifically invites comments on whether there are particular issues in that area related to HRAs, QSEHRAs, or supplemental salary reduction arrangements that would benefit from additional regulatory or interpretive guidance.

V. Overview of the Proposed Rules Regarding Individual Market Special Enrollment Periods - Department of Health and Human Services

As set forth earlier in this preamble, the Departments are proposing regulations to expand the usability of HRAs and to provide flexibility to employers. The proposed rules allowing integration of an HRA with individual health insurance coverage require that the individuals whose medical care expenses may be reimbursed under the HRA must be enrolled in individual health insurance coverage (other than coverage that consists solely of excepted benefits). With the ability to integrate HRAs with individual health insurance coverage, many employees may need access to individual health insurance coverage, on or off Exchange, or may wish to change to another individual health insurance plan in order to take advantage of this employee benefit. Therefore, HHS is proposing a regulation to allow employees and their dependents to enroll in individual health insurance coverage or to change from one individual health insurance coverage plan to another outside of the individual market annual open enrollment period if they gain access to an HRA integrated with individual health insurance coverage.

In addition, because employees and dependents with a QSEHRA generally must be enrolled in MEC,[112] and a significant category of MEC is individual health insurance coverage, HHS has determined that it is also appropriate to apply the new special enrollment period to individuals who are provided QSEHRAs.[113]

More specifically, HHS proposes to add new paragraph 45 CFR 155.420(d)(14) to establish a special enrollment period for when a qualified individual, enrollee, or his or her dependent gains access to and enrolls in an HRA integrated with individual health insurance coverage or is provided a

110 26 CFR 54.9801-2; 29 CFR 2590.701-2, 45 CFR 144.103.

111 Note that the clarification with respect to the meaning of group health insurance coverage is not relevant for QSEHRAs because QSEHRAs are not group health plans.

112 Generally, payments from a QSEHRA to reimburse an eligible employee's medical care expenses are not includible in the employee's gross income if the employee has coverage that provides MEC as defined in section 5000A(f) of the Code, which includes individual health insurance coverage.

113 The Departments note that the new special enrollment period provided in the proposed rules applies only for individuals who gain access to HRAs integrated with individual health insurance coverage or for individuals who are provided QSEHRAs. Therefore, the new special enrollment period provided in the proposed rules would not apply for individuals who gain access to the proposed excepted benefit HRA.

QSEHRA, so that the individual and his or her dependents may enroll in or change his or her enrollment in individual health insurance coverage.

45 CFR 155.420(d)(14) would provide access to coverage in the circumstance in which an employer after the start of the calendar year newly begins offering an HRA to its employees that is integrated with individual health insurance coverage or newly begins providing a QSEHRA to its employees. HHS anticipates that many employers that choose to offer an HRA integrated with individual health insurance coverage or to provide a QSEHRA will do so on a calendar year basis, which will allow employees to enroll in or change individual health insurance coverage during the annual open enrollment period. However, HHS is aware that employers may begin offering HRAs and providing QSEHRAs to their employees at any time during the calendar year and has determined that employers are best suited to determine which twelve-month period to use for their plan year. In addition, the new special enrollment period would apply to individuals who newly gain access to and enroll in an HRA integrated with individual health insurance coverage or who are provided a QSEHRA outside of open enrollment, for example, because the employee is hired after the start of the calendar year.

HHS notes that for some situations in which an employee would newly gain access to an HRA integrated with individual health insurance coverage or would newly be provided a QSEHRA, access to coverage already exists under current authority in 45 CFR 155.410 or 155.420(d). For example, if an employer begins offering an HRA integrated with individual health insurance coverage or begins providing a QSEHRA effective January 1, employees may already enroll in or change individual health insurance coverage during the annual open enrollment period described in 45 CFR 155.410 with such coverage becoming effective January 1 (to coincide with the availability of the HRA or QSEHRA). Similarly, if an employer previously offered another type of group health plan coverage and decides to stop offering that coverage after the start of the calendar year to some or all of its employees (or the plan year ends after the start of the calendar year) and instead begins offering those employees an HRA integrated with individual health insurance coverage or begins providing a QSEHRA to them, the employees might already qualify for a special enrollment period due to a loss of MEC in accordance with 45 CFR 155.420(d)(1). In addition, an employee without a prior offer of employer coverage who is enrolled in Exchange coverage with advance payments of the PTC and cost-sharing reductions (CSRs) currently may qualify for the special enrollment periods in 45 CFR 155.420(d)(6)(i) or (ii) upon gaining access to an HRA integrated with individual health insurance coverage or being provided a QSEHRA after the start of the calendar year, if that results in the loss of eligibility for advance payments of the PTC or a reduction or loss of eligibility for CSRs. However, if this same employee was enrolled in Exchange coverage without advance payments of the PTC or CSRs, he or she would not qualify for this special enrollment period upon gaining access to an HRA integrated with individual health insurance coverage or being provided a QSEHRA after the start of the calendar year, and would instead need the proposed new special enrollment period in 45 CFR 155.420(d)(14) in order to change Exchange coverage.

Because access to and enrollment in health coverage varies by employers and among employees, as does employees' current ability to qualify for a special enrollment period should they gain access to an HRA integrated with individual health insurance coverage or be provided a QSEHRA, HHS has concluded that it is necessary to establish a new special enrollment period as proposed under 45 CFR 155.420(d)(14) so that all employees (and their dependents) who gain access outside of the individual market open enrollment period (for example, after the start of the calendar year) and enroll in HRAs integrated with individual health insurance coverage or are provided QSEHRAs, regardless of their prior coverage situations, may utilize this employee benefit by enrolling in or changing their enrollment in individual health insurance coverage at that time.

HHS proposes to establish a coverage effective date for the special enrollment period in 45 CFR 155.420(d)(14) of the first day of the first month following the individual's plan selection, which is proposed at 45 CFR 155.420(b)(2)(vi). HHS has concluded that a first-of-the-following-month coverage effective date is appropriate for this special enrollment period because it aligns with the coverage effective date option elected by the Federally-facilitated Exchanges (FFEs) for qualified individuals, enrollees, or dependents, including employees, who qualify for a special enrollment period for loss of MEC under 45 CFR 155.420(d)(1). This coverage effective date also aligns with the coverage effective date option elected by the FFEs for the special enrollment period at 45 CFR 155.420(d)(6)(iii), applicable when employees enrolled in employer-sponsored coverage are determined newly eligible for advance payments of the PTC based in part on a finding that they are ineligible for coverage in an eligible-employer sponsored plan in accordance with 26 CFR 1.36B-2(c)(3). HHS has concluded that these existing qualifying events, also known as triggering events, and the new proposed qualifying event are similar to one another and affect potentially overlapping populations and, therefore, should entitle qualifying individuals to the same coverage start dates.

Similarly, HHS proposes to offer the option for advance availability, in addition to subsequent availability, for the proposed special enrollment period in 45 CFR 155.420(d)(14), which would allow qualified individuals, enrollees, and dependents to qualify for this special enrollment period up to 60 days in advance of the qualifying event, as described in paragraph 45 CFR 155.420(c)(2) of the proposed rules. Under this advance availability in combination with 45 CFR 155.420(b)(2)(vi), if an individual's plan selection is made before the date of the qualifying event, then coverage would be effective the first day of the month following the date of the qualifying event, or, if the triggering event is on the first day of a month, on the date of the triggering event. In cases where the qualifying event is the first day of the month, for example, if an individual will gain access to an HRA that can be integrated with individual health insurance coverage on April 1, so long as a plan is selected prior to that date (before or on March 31), the effective date of this new coverage will be the date of the qualifying event (April 1). Advance availability allows individuals who are aware of an upcoming change in eligibility or coverage status to report this change to the Exchanges ahead of time, select a plan, and enroll with a coverage effective date that helps minimize a potential gap in coverage. Because participants whose employers begin offering HRAs integrated with individual health insurance coverage or begin providing QSEHRAs generally must be notified at least 90 days prior to the plan year, participants would have advance knowledge of either benefit. Therefore, HHS has concluded that it makes sense to allow the participant to report this upcoming change to the Exchanges in advance, if desired. Individuals may alternatively elect to report the qualifying event up to 60 days after the date of the qualifying event and qualify for the special enrollment period during the regular special enrollment period window, in accordance with 45 CFR 155.420(c)(1).

In addition, in order to allow participants and their dependents the flexibility to adequately respond to gaining access to an HRA integrated with individual health insurance coverage or to being provided a QSEHRA, HHS also proposes to amend 45 CFR 155.420(a)(4)(iii) to exclude Exchange enrollees who would qualify for the proposed special enrollment period in 45 CFR 155.420(d)(14) from plan enrollment restrictions upon qualifying for this special enrollment period.

Lastly, since these proposed rules would allow for HRAs to be integrated with individual health insurance coverage both on and off Exchange (and because individuals with QSEHRAs may enroll in individual health insurance coverage both on and off Exchange), HHS proposes to include this special enrollment period in the limited open enrollment periods available off Exchange, in accordance with current regulations at 45 CFR 147.104(b)(2). Therefore, an employee or an employee's dependent who gains access to an HRA integrated with individual health insurance coverage or who is provided a QSEHRA may elect to enroll in or change to different Exchange or off-Exchange individual health insurance coverage.

HHS seeks comments on these proposals. If an employer begins offering an HRA or providing a QSEHRA to its employees during the calendar year outside of the Exchange annual open enrollment period, subsequent plan years likely will also begin during the calendar year. Therefore, HHS also seeks comments about whether the proposed new special enrollment period at 45 CFR 155.420(d)(14) should be available to employees who have and are enrolled in an HRA or are provided a QSEHRA each year at the time their new health plan year starts. This would allow employees to enroll in or change to a new plan in response to updated information about their HRA or QSEHRA benefit for each of their group health plan years.

VI. Applicability Date

The proposed HRA integration and HRA excepted benefit provisions described in section II of this preamble, as well as the DOL clarification and the clarification by the Departments described in section IV of this preamble, are proposed to apply to group health plans and health insurance issuers for plan years beginning on or after January 1, 2020. The PTC provisions described in section III of this preamble are proposed to be effective for taxable years beginning on and after January 1, 2020, and the HHS special enrollment period provisions described in section V of this preamble are proposed to be effective January 1, 2020. Taxpayers and others may not rely on these proposed rules. The Departments solicit comments on this proposed applicability date.

VII. Economic Impact and Paperwork Burden

A. *Summary*

The proposed rules would remove the current prohibition on integrating HRAs with individual health insurance coverage, if certain conditions are met. The proposed rules also set forth conditions under which certain HRAs would be recognized as limited excepted benefits. In addition, the Treasury Department and the IRS are proposing rules regarding PTC eligibility for individuals offered coverage under an HRA integrated with individual health insurance coverage. Further, DOL is proposing a clarification to provide HRA, QSEHRA and supplemental salary reduction arrangement plan sponsors with assurance that the individual health insurance coverage the premiums of which are reimbursed by an HRA, QSEHRA or supplemental salary reduction arrangement would not become part of an ERISA plan if certain conditions are met, and the Departments are proposing a related clarification to the definition of group health insurance coverage. Finally, HHS is proposing rules that would provide a special enrollment period in the individual market for individuals who gain access to an HRA integrated with individual health insurance coverage or who are provided a QSEHRA.

The Departments have examined the effects of the proposed rules as required by Executive Order 13563 (76 FR 3821, January 21, 2011, Improving Regulation and Regulatory Review); Executive Order 12866 (58 FR 51735, October 4, 1993, Regulatory Planning and Review); the Regulatory Flexibility Act (September 19, 1980, Pub. L. 96-354); section 1102(b) of the Social Security Act (42 U.S.C. 1102(b)); section 202 of the Unfunded Mandates Reform Act of 1995 (March 22, 1995, Pub. L. 104-4); Executive Order 13132 (64 FR 43255, August 10, 1999, Federalism); the Congressional Review Act (5 U.S.C. 804(2)); and Executive Order 13771 (82 FR 9339, February 3, 2017, Reducing Regulation and Controlling Regulatory Costs).

B. *Executive Orders 12866 and 13563*

Executive Order 12866 directs agencies to assess all costs and benefits of available regulatory alternatives and, if regulation is necessary, to select regulatory approaches that maximize net benefits (including potential economic, environmental, public health and safety effects, distributive impacts, and equity). Executive Order 13563 is supplemental to and reaffirms the principles, structures, and definitions governing regulatory review as established in Executive Order 12866.

Section 3(f) of Executive Order 12866 defines a "significant regulatory action" as an action that is likely to result in a rule: (1) having an annual effect on the economy of $100 million or more in any 1 year, or adversely and materially affecting a sector of the economy, productivity, competition, jobs, the environment, public health or safety, or state, local or tribal governments or communities (also referred to as "economically significant"); (2) creating a serious inconsistency or otherwise interfering with an action taken or planned by another agency; (3) materially altering the budgetary impacts of entitlement grants, user fees, or loan programs or the rights and obligations of recipients thereof; or (4) raising novel legal or policy issues arising out of legal mandates, the President's priorities, or the principles set forth in the Executive Order.

A regulatory impact analysis must be prepared for major rules with economically significant effects (for example, $100 million or more in any 1 year), and a "significant" regulatory action is subject to review by the Office of Management and Budget (OMB). The Departments anticipate that this regulatory action is likely to have economic impacts of $100 million or more in at least 1 year, and thus meets the definition of a "significant rule" under Executive Order 12866. Therefore, the Departments have provided an assessment of the potential costs, benefits, and transfers associated with the proposed rules. In accordance with the provisions of Executive Order 12866, the proposed rules were reviewed by OMB.

1. *Need for Regulatory Action*

This regulatory action is taken in light of Executive Order 13813 directing the Departments to consider proposing regulations or revising guidance to expand the flexibility and use of HRAs. Consistent with Executive Order 13813, the proposed rules are intended to increase the usability of HRAs to provide more Americans, including employees who work at small businesses, with more healthcare options. Such changes will facilitate the development and operation of a healthcare system that provides high-quality care at affordable prices for the American people by increasing consumer choice for employees and promoting competition in healthcare markets by providing additional options for employers.

The Departments are of the view that the benefits of the proposed rules would substantially outweigh the costs of the rules. The proposed rules would increase flexibility and choices of health coverage options for employers and employees. The increased use of HRAs could potentially reduce healthcare spending, particularly less efficient spending,[114] and ultimately result in increased taxable wages for workers currently in firms that offer traditional group health plans. The proposed rules are also expected to increase the number of low- and moderate-wage workers (and their family members) with health insurance coverage.

2. *Summary of Impacts of Proposed HRA Integrated with Individual Health Insurance Coverage*

The expected costs, benefits and transfers of the proposed rules are summarized in Table 1 and discussed in detail later in this section of the preamble.

Table 1: Accounting Table

Costs:
Qualitative: • Loss of health insurance and potentially poorer financial or health outcomes for some individuals who experience premium increases. • Increased administrative costs for employers, employees, and government agencies to learn about and/or use a new health benefits option.
Benefits:
Qualitative: • Gain of health insurance and potentially improved financial or health outcomes for some employees who are newly offered or newly accept benefits. • Increased choice and flexibility for employees and employers around compensation arrangements, potentially resulting in more efficient use of healthcare and more efficient labor markets (including higher taxable wages). • Decreased administrative costs for some employers who no longer offer traditional group health plans for some, or all, employees.

[114] By less efficient healthcare spending, the Departments generally mean spending that is of low value from the consumer's perspective, relative to its cost.

Transfers:	Estimate	Year Dollar	Discount Rate	Period Covered
Annualized Monetized ($/year) (Net tax revenue loss)	$2.7 billion	2020	7 percent	2020 - 2028
	$2.8 billion	2020	3 percent	2020 - 2028

Quantitative:[115]

- Reduced tax revenue as a result of new HRAs offered by employers previously offering no health benefits, less reduced PTC from employees in such firms.
- Increase in average individual market premiums of less than 1 percent and resulting increase in PTC.

Qualitative:

- Increased out-of-pocket costs for some employees who move from traditional group health plans to individual health insurance coverage and decreased costs for other employees who move from traditional group health plans to individual health insurance coverage (i.e., transfers from reduced within-firm cross-subsidization).
- Reduced tax revenue as a result of new excepted benefit HRA.

[115] The monetized estimates are of the net tax revenue loss, including reduced income and payroll tax revenue from employees who would receive HRAs and would not otherwise have a tax exclusion for a traditional group health plan, reduced PTC from individuals who would receive HRAs and would otherwise receive PTC, and increased PTC due to the increase in Exchange premiums. As noted in the text later in this section of the preamble, the quantitative estimates are subject to considerable uncertainty. For example, the rule could cause tax revenue to increase if the adoption of HRAs leads to reduced healthcare spending and higher taxable wages. Or the rule could result in larger premium increases in the individual market, or in premium decreases, if the rule results in more substantial changes in the health of the individual market risk pool. The Departments request comments on the likely costs, benefits and transfers that would result from the proposed rule.

In all cases, the counterfactual baseline for analysis is current law. That is, the analysis assumes as the baseline statutes enacted and regulations that are final as of date of issuance of the proposed rules. This includes PPACA, the reduction of the individual shared responsibility payment to $0, as enacted in Pub. L. 115-97, the AHP final rule[116], the STLDI final rule[117], and all other administrative actions finalized as of the date of issuance of the proposed rules.

Costs

Loss of health insurance coverage. The Departments recognize that some individuals could experience a loss in health insurance coverage and that some of these people would experience worse financial or health outcomes as a result of the proposed rules.[118] Loss of coverage could occur if employers drop traditional group health plans and if some previously covered employees do not accept the HRA and fail to obtain their own coverage. Loss of coverage could also occur if the addition of new enrollees to the individual market causes premiums to rise, resulting in dropping of coverage by current individual market enrollees. In addition, some employees could have fewer choices of plans in the individual market than the number of group health plan choices previously provided by their employer, or might be unable to find new individual health insurance coverage that covers their preferred healthcare providers. As discussed below, the Departments estimate that choice and coverage would, on net, be increased by adoption of the proposed rules. The Departments request comments on this finding and the extent to which the proposed rules could reduce employee choice or cause some individuals to become uninsured.

Increased administrative costs. The proposed rules would also increase some administrative costs for employers, employees, and government entities.

All employers would have a new health benefits option about which to learn. Employers who offer HRAs integrated with individual health insurance coverage but did not offer employer-sponsored health benefits before would face increased costs of administering a health benefit. In addition, all employers that offer HRAs integrated with individual health insurance coverage would be required to establish reasonable procedures to substantiate that individuals covered by the HRA are enrolled in individual health insurance coverage; to provide a notice to all employees who are eligible for the HRA explaining the PTC eligibility consequences of the HRA offer and acceptance and other

[116] *See* 83 FR 28912.

[117] *See* 83 FR 38212.

[118] The Departments note however that increased insurance coverage does not necessarily result in better health. For example, Baicker et al. found that increased Medicaid coverage in Oregon "generated no significant improvements in measured physical health outcomes in the first two years, but it did increase use of health care services, raise rates of diabetes detection and management, lower rates of depression, and reduce financial strain." *See* Baicker, K., S. Taubman, H. Allen, M. Bernstein, J. Gruber, J. Newhouse, E. Schneider, B. Wright, A. Zaslavsky, and A. Finkelstein. 2013. "The Oregon Experiment: Effects of Medicaid on Clinical Outcomes." *New England Journal of Medicine* 368: 1713-22. http://www.nejm.org/doi/full/10.1056/NEJMsa1212321; and survey of the literature in Chapter 6 of *Economic Report of the President*, February 2018, https://www.whitehouse.gov/wp-content/uploads/2018/02/ERP_2018_Final-FINAL.pdf.

information; and to comply with various other generally applicable group health plan requirements, such as maintaining a plan document and complying with various reporting requirements. Employers offering HRAs integrated with individual health insurance coverage would need to establish systems to reimburse premiums and employee out-of-pocket medical care expenses, or hire third-party administrators to do so. In addition, to the extent an employer is subject to section 4980H of the Code, the employer would need to learn about the proposed PTC regulations and any other related guidance under section 4980H of the Code that the Treasury Department and the IRS may issue. As noted later in this preamble, administrative costs associated with HRAs integrated with individual health insurance coverage could be lower than costs for traditional group health plans for some employers. The Departments request comment on the extent to which employer administrative costs would be increased or decreased by the proposed rules.

As to increased administrative burden and costs for employees, employees who previously enrolled in a traditional group health plan and who now receive an HRA integrated with individual health insurance coverage would need to shop for and choose their own insurance and learn new procedures for accessing their HRA benefits. In addition, employees who receive an HRA integrated with individual health insurance coverage would need to substantiate enrollment in individual health insurance coverage once per plan year and in connection with each request for reimbursement.

Further, Exchange enrollees might experience increased compliance burdens, to the extent that they must become familiar with the circumstances in which an offer of an HRA integrated with individual health insurance coverage precludes them from claiming the PTC. For employees who previously did not receive an offer of a traditional group health plan, this would require learning the PTC eligibility rules, and for employees who previously received an offer of a traditional group health plan, this would require learning new and different rules for PTC eligibility. Specifically, an employee who is offered a traditional group health plan is not eligible to claim the PTC for his or her Exchange coverage unless the premium of the lowest cost employer plan providing MV for self-only coverage less the employer contribution for self-only coverage exceeds 9.5 percent (indexed for inflation after 2014) of the employee's household income (assuming the employee meets various other PTC eligibility requirements). In contrast, under the proposed PTC regulations, an employee who is offered an HRA integrated with individual health insurance coverage would not be eligible to claim the PTC for his or her Exchange coverage unless the premium of the lowest cost silver plan for self-only coverage offered by the Exchange for the rating area in which the employee resides less the HRA amount exceeds 9.5 percent (indexed for inflation after 2014) of the employee's household income (assuming the employee meets various other PTC eligibility requirements). However, the Departments note that the proposed rules would require HRA plan sponsors to furnish a notice to participants providing some of the information necessary for an individual to determine if the offer of the HRA could render them ineligible for the PTC.

In addition, if an enrollee in Exchange coverage is eligible for the PTC, the amount of the PTC is based, in part, on the premium for the second lowest cost silver plan for the coverage unit offered in the Exchange for the rating area in which the employee resides. As noted earlier, the proposed PTC rule uses the premium for the lowest cost silver plan offered in the Exchange for the rating area in which the employee resides solely for purposes of PTC eligibility criterion related to an offer of an HRA integrated with individual health insurance coverage. Therefore, Exchange enrollees would need to understand which silver level plan premium applies to them for eligibility purposes and which silver level plan premium applies to their PTC calculation.

Similarly, the Federally-facilitated and State-based Exchanges would incur one-time costs to incorporate the proposed special enrollment period and the PTC regulations, if finalized, into their instructions for enrollees and Exchange employees and in automated calculations. HHS estimates that one-time costs to account for HRAs integrated with individual health insurance coverage for the FFE would be approximately $2.7 million to $3.6 million. In addition, the FFE call center and eligibility support contractors would incur additional annual cost of approximately $255 million annually by 2028 to serve the expanded Exchange population. Assuming that State-based Exchanges (SBEs) would incur costs similar to the FFE, total one-time costs incurred by the 12 SBEs would be $32.4 million to $43.2 million. Total additional ongoing costs incurred by the call centers and eligibility support contractors for the 12 SBEs would be approximately $85 million annually by 2028. The Departments request comments on the implementation and ongoing costs for SBEs. The IRS also would need to add information regarding employees offered HRAs integrated with individual health insurance coverage to instructions for IRS forms for taxpayers, employee training materials, and calculation programs.

The Departments are of the view that the total increase in administrative costs is likely to be modest, and would be significantly outweighed by the benefits of the rule outlined in the next section.

Benefits

Gain of health insurance coverage. Some individuals could experience a gain in health insurance coverage, greater financial security and potentially improved health outcomes, if employees are newly offered and accept HRAs integrated with individual health insurance coverage. As explained in greater detail in the Transfers section later in this preamble, the Departments estimate that on net, the number of insured persons would increase by about 800,000 by 2028, due to the proposed rules.

Most of these newly insured individuals are expected to be low- and moderate-income workers in firms that currently do not offer a traditional group health plan.

Increased choice and flexibility for employees and employers. As a result of the proposed rules, employees would be able to purchase insurance with a tax subsidy by use of an HRA, without being locked into a specific plan or selection of plans chosen by their employer. As noted earlier in this preamble, some employees could have fewer choices of plans in the individual market than the number of group health plan choices previously provided by their employer, or might be unable to find a new individual health insurance coverage that covers their preferred healthcare providers. However, the expansion of enrollment in the individual market due to the proposed rules could also induce additional insurers to provide individual market coverage. The Departments are of the view that on net, the rule would significantly increase choice and flexibility for employees. Employers also would benefit from having another choice of a tax-preferred health benefit to offer their employees, potentially enabling them to attract and retain workers.

Current compensation arrangements can result in less efficient labor markets and inefficient healthcare spending. Employees within a firm (or employees within certain classes within a firm) are generally offered the same set of health benefits. As a result, some employees receive a greater share of compensation in the form of benefits than they would prefer, while others receive less. In addition, some employers offer plans with a wide choice of providers, reflecting the diverse preferences and healthcare needs of their employees. This weakens the ability of employers and insurers to negotiate lower provider prices or otherwise manage employee care.

By expanding the ability of consumers to choose coverage that fits their preferences, the proposed rules would reduce these inefficiencies in labor markets and healthcare spending. Some employees who would be offered HRAs under the proposed rules would choose plans with lower premiums and higher deductibles and copayments (all of which could potentially be paid out of the HRA) and narrower provider networks than they would choose if offered a traditional group health plan. Employees facing higher cost-sharing could become more cost-conscious consumers of healthcare. Narrower provider networks could strengthen the ability of purchasers (through their insurers) to negotiate lower provider prices. Both effects could lead to reduced healthcare spending, which could in turn lead to reductions in amounts made available under HRAs integrated with individual health insurance coverage and corresponding increases in taxable wages. However, these benefits are uncertain and would take some time to occur.[119] Moreover, the provision of a new health benefit that can be used to pay cost-sharing as well as premiums and that is available to employees who were previously uninsured or enrolled in unsubsidized coverage would be expected to increase, rather than decrease, healthcare utilization by some consumers.

Small employers in particular might have little expertise or skill in choosing traditional group health plans or in administering coverage effectively for employees. However, some small employers can already obtain lower-cost coverage in the small group market or through AHPs than they could otherwise provide on their own. Small employers that are not ALEs can also forego offering health benefits and allow their employees to obtain individual health insurance coverage, often with PTC subsidization, without liability under section 4980H of the Code. Qualified small employers can also pursue establishment of QSEHRAs. Thus, small employers whose employees have particularly high healthcare costs or that have little skill or interest in administering health benefits might use these other options to control costs even in the absence of the proposed rules. If so, any increased efficiency gain from providing an additional incentive for small employers to drop traditional group health plans in favor of HRAs integrated with individual health insurance coverage could be modest.

Reduced administrative costs for some employers. Employers that offer an HRA integrated with individual health insurance coverage rather than a traditional group health plan could experience reduced administrative costs. For example, such employers would no longer need to choose health insurance plans or self-insured health benefits for their employees and manage those plans. However, some of these costs would be borne by HRA recipients, as part of their individual market premiums.

Transfers

The Treasury Department performed microsimulation modeling to evaluate the coverage changes and transfers that are likely to be induced by the proposed rules. The Treasury Department's model of health insurance coverage assumes that workers are paid the marginal product of their labor. Employers are assumed to be indifferent between paying wages and paying compensation in the form of benefits (as both expenses are deductible in computing employers' taxable incomes). The model therefore assumes that total compensation paid by a given firm is fixed, and the employer

[119] The proposed HRA integrated with individual health insurance coverage provides an income and payroll tax exclusion that is available only to workers and, unlike the PTC, benefits workers at all income levels, including workers with incomes in excess of 400 percent of the federal poverty level. Thus, it is possible that the proposed rules could encourage individuals to join the labor force or to work more hours or seek higher-paying employment, generating further economic benefits. In addition, the proposed rules could increase labor force mobility (i.e., encourage workers to move more freely to employers where their productivity is highest), because workers enrolled in individual health insurance coverage could find it easier to retain their coverage when they change jobs. However, these effects are highly uncertain, are likely to be relatively small, and might take some time to occur. Labor supply changes are not reflected in the revenue estimates provided in the transfers section below.

allocates this compensation between wages and benefits based on the aggregated preferences of their employees. As a result, employees bear the full cost of employer-sponsored health coverage (net of the value of any tax exclusion), in the form of reduced wages and the employee share of premiums.[120]

The Treasury Department's model assumes that employees' preferences regarding the type of health coverage (or no coverage) are determined by their expected healthcare expenses and the after-tax cost of employer-sponsored insurance, Exchange coverage with the PTC, or Exchange or other individual health insurance coverage integrated with an HRA, and the quality of different types of coverage (including actuarial value).[121] The tax preference for the HRA integrated with individual health insurance coverage is the same as that for a traditional group health plan, and this estimate assumes that employers would contribute the same amount towards an HRA integrated with individual health insurance coverage as they would contribute for a traditional group health plan.[122] Therefore, an employee would prefer an HRA integrated with individual health insurance coverage to a traditional group health plan if the price of individual health insurance coverage is lower than the price of traditional group health plan coverage, as long as the value of the higher quality of the traditional group health plan coverage (if any) does not outweigh the lower cost of individual health insurance coverage. The cost of individual health insurance coverage for an employee could be lower than the cost of the firm's traditional group health plan if the individual health insurance coverage is less generous, if the individual health insurance coverage risk pool is healthier than the firm's risk pool, or if the cost of individual health insurance coverage to a particular employee is lower than the cost of the firm's coverage (because, for example, the employee is younger than the average-age worker in the firm).

When evaluating the choice between an HRA integrated with individual health insurance coverage and the PTC for Exchange coverage, the available coverage is assumed to be the same, but the tax preferences are different. Hence, an employee would prefer the HRA if the value of the income and payroll tax exclusion (including both the employee and employer portion of payroll tax) is greater than the value of the PTC. In modeling this decision, the Departments assume that the employee share of premiums is tax-preferred, either through a salary reduction plan or, for an individual with an HRA integrated with individual health insurance coverage, through reimbursement of premiums from the HRA, with any additional premiums paid through a salary reduction arrangement.[123]

In the Treasury Department's model, employees are aggregated into firms, based on tax data.[124] The expected health expenses of employees in the firm determine the cost of employer-sponsored insurance for the firm.[125] Employees effectively vote for their preferred coverage, and each employer's offered benefit is determined by the preferences of the majority of employees. Employees then decide whether to accept any offered coverage, and the resulting enrollment determines

---

[120] Note that the wage reduction for an employee who is offered a health benefit may be greater or less than the expected cost of coverage for that particular employee. Because employees are generally paid the same regardless of age, health status, family size or acceptance of benefits, the model assumes that each employee bears the same share of the cost of the firm's coverage. The model allows for some limited variation of the wage reduction by wage class and educational status. All costs and benefits of coverage are taken into account and assumed to accrue to employees, including all income and employer and employee payroll tax exclusions and the avoidance of the employer shared responsibility payment under section 4980H of the Code by firms that offer coverage.

[121] Expected health care expenses by type of coverage, age, family size and other characteristics are estimated using the Medical Expenditure Panel Survey - Household Component (MEPS-HC). These predictions are then statistically matched to our tax data. The MEPS-HC is conducted by the United States Census Bureau for the Agency for Healthcare Research and Quality (AHRQ), Department of Health and Human Services.

[122] It is possible that employers that switch from offering traditional group health plans to offering HRAs integrated with individual health insurance coverage will contribute less to HRAs than they pay for group coverage, and increase taxable wages by a corresponding amount. However, it is not clear why an employer that (based on the incomes and preferences of its workforce) wants to substitute contributions to health benefits for wages would not do so today, in the absence of the availability of HRAs integrated with individual health insurance coverage, particularly since the proposed rules generally require that HRAs integrated with individual health insurance coverage be offered on the same terms to all employees in a class of employees, as described earlier in this preamble.

[123] The assumption that coverage subsidized by the PTC is the same as coverage subsidized by an HRA may be incorrect to the extent that coverage on the Exchange differs from off-Exchange individual health insurance coverage. In addition, the assumption that the full premium for an employee with or without an HRA is tax preferred may be incorrect if the employer does not offer a salary reduction plan, if the employee does not elect the salary reduction, or if the employee chooses on-Exchange rather than off-Exchange coverage. Salary reductions may not be used to pay premiums for Exchange coverage. The Departments invite comments on whether these assumptions are important or likely to be incorrect.

[124] A crucial component of the model is the use of Form W-2, Wage and Tax Statement, filed by employers to report wages and other benefits of employees. Forms W-2 with the same employer identification number are grouped together to represent the employees of the firm.

[125] Some small firms are able to purchase community rated coverage in the small group market at lower cost than they could obtain by self-insuring or would pay if they had to purchase coverage in the underwritten large-group market. Firm coverage costs are over-estimated in Treasury's model for these firms. As a result, our model likely over-estimates the extent to which small firms would adopt HRAs integrated with individual health insurance coverage. On the other hand, our assumption that administrative burdens and costs for employees and employers are about the same for HRAs integrated with individual coverage as for traditional group health plans could result in an under-estimate of the extent to which small firms with higher than average administrative costs would adopt HRAs integrated with individual health insurance coverage.

premiums for both employer coverage and individual health insurance coverage. The Treasury Department's model thus predicts enrollment and premiums in each type of coverage.

Transitions from traditional group health plans to HRAs integrated with individual health insurance coverage. Based on microsimulation modeling, the Departments expect that the proposed rules would cause some participants (and their dependents) to move from traditional group health plans to HRAs integrated with individual health insurance coverage. As previously noted, the estimates assume that for this group of firms and employees, employer contributions to HRAs integrated with individual health insurance coverage are the same as contributions to traditional group health plans would have been, and the estimates assume that tax-preferred salary reductions for individual health insurance coverage are the same as salary reductions for traditional group health plan coverage. Thus, by modeling construction there is no change in income or payroll tax revenues for this group of firms and employees (other than the changes in the PTC discussed later in this preamble). The Departments welcome comments on these assumptions.

While the tax preference is assumed to be unchanged for this group, after-tax out-of-pocket costs could increase for some employees (whose premiums or cost-sharing are higher in the individual market than in a traditional group health plan) and decrease for others.

Some employees who are offered a traditional group health plan nonetheless obtain individual health insurance coverage and the PTC, because the traditional group health plan is unaffordable to them or does not provide MV. Some of these employees would no longer be eligible for the PTC for their Exchange coverage when the employer switches from a traditional group health plan to an HRA integrated with individual health insurance coverage because the HRA integrated with individual health insurance coverage is determined to be affordable under the proposed PTC eligibility rules.[126] In addition, some employees who are offered HRAs integrated with individual health insurance coverage would not accept them, and would be newly able to obtain the PTC because the offer of the HRA would be considered to be unaffordable under the proposed PTC rules, even though the traditional group health plan they were previously offered is affordable under current rules.[127]

Transitions from no employer-sponsored health benefit to HRAs integrated with individual health insurance coverage. The Departments expect some employees to be offered HRAs integrated with individual health insurance coverage when they previously received no offer of an employer-sponsored health plan. As a result, taxable wages would fall and nontaxable wages would rise, reducing income tax and payroll tax revenues. In addition, some Exchange enrollees who previously claimed the PTC would be precluded from claiming the PTC as a result of the offer or acceptance of the HRA, reducing PTC transfers. As explained further below, the Departments assume that PTC spending is reduced only among Exchange enrollees with incomes greater than 200 percent of the federal poverty level.

Summary of transfers and coverage changes. The Departments estimate that once employers fully adjust to the proposed rules, roughly 800,000 firms would offer HRAs integrated with individual health insurance coverage. The Departments further estimate that it would take employers and employees about five years to fully adjust to the proposed rules, with about 10 percent of take-up occurring in 2020 and the full effect realized in 2024 and beyond.

This would result in an estimated 1.0 million individuals receiving an HRA integrated with individual health insurance coverage in 2020, growing to 10.7 million in 2028. Conversely, the number of individuals in traditional group health plan coverage would fall by an estimated 0.6 million (0.4 percent) in 2020 and 6.8 million (4.5 percent) in 2028. Similarly, the number of individuals in individual health insurance coverage without an HRA would fall by an estimated 0.3 million (2.2 percent) in 2020 and 3.2 million (23.2 percent) in 2028. The number of uninsured persons would fall by an estimated 0.1 million in 2020 and by an estimated 0.8 million (1.3 percent) in 2028.[128] *See* Table 2 for details.

The modeling suggests that employees in firms that would switch from offering traditional group health plan coverage to offering an HRA integrated with individual health insurance coverage would have, on average, slightly higher expected healthcare expenses than employees in other firms and current individual market enrollees. As a result, premiums in the individual market would be expected to increase by less than 1 percent as a result of the proposed rules, throughout the 2020-2028 period examined. The Treasury Department model is nationally representative and does not necessarily reflect the expected experience for every market. The premium increase resulting from adverse selection could be larger in some markets, and premiums could fall in other markets. The Depart-

[126] As noted below, however, the Departments' estimates assume that individuals with incomes below 200 percent of the federal poverty level are not newly firewalled from the PTC by HRA offers.

[127] The number of persons newly eligible for the PTC is expected to be very small. Under the assumption that employers contribute the same amount towards an HRA as they would for traditional group coverage, employees would become newly eligible for the PTC (if otherwise eligible) only if the lowest cost silver plan premium for self-only individual health insurance coverage is greater than the total cost of the lowest cost MV plan offered by the employer (including the employee and employer share of premiums).

[128] These estimates are annualized counts (e.g., two persons with six months of coverage each count as one covered person), and reflect only coverage for persons under age 65. For more information about Treasury's baseline estimates, see "Treasury's Baseline Estimates of Health Coverage, Fiscal Year 2019 Budget Exercise" June 2018, available at https://www.treasury.gov/resource-center/tax-policy/tax-analysis/Documents/Treasury%27s-Baseline-Estimates-of-Health-Coverage-FY-2019.pdf.

ments invite comments on the extent to which firms with healthy or less healthy risk pools would utilize HRAs integrated with individual health insurance coverage.

Income and payroll tax revenues would be expected to fall by about $500 million in fiscal year 2020 and $13.0 billion in 2028, as firms newly offer tax-preferred health benefits in the form of HRAs integrated with individual health insurance coverage. At the same time, total PTC would be expected to fall by about $100 million in 2020 and by about $6.9 billion in 2028. In total, the proposed rule is estimated to reduce tax revenue by about $400 million in fiscal year 2020, $6 billion in fiscal year 2028, and $29.8 billion over the nine-year period through fiscal year 2028.[129]

Table 2: Estimated Effects of HRAs Integrated with Individual Health Insurance Coverage on Insurance Coverage and Tax Revenues, 2020 - 2028

Calendar Year	**2020**	**2021**	**2022**	**2023**	**2024**	**2025**	**2026**	**2027**	**2028**
Change in Coverage [Millions][a]									
Individual health insurance coverage with HRA	1.0	2.5	5.0	7.7	10.3	10.4	10.6	10.7	10.7
Traditional group health plan	-0.6	-1.6	-3.3	-4.9	-6.6	-6.7	-6.7	-6.8	-6.8
Individual health insurance coverage without HRA	-0.3	-0.7	-1.5	-2.2	-3.0	-3.0	-3.1	-3.2	-3.2
Uninsured	-0.1	-0.2	-0.3	-0.5	-0.7	-0.7	-0.7	-0.7	-0.8
Fiscal Year	**2020**	**2021**	**2022**	**2023**	**2024**	**2025**	**2026**	**2027**	**2028**
Change in Revenue [Billions]									
Premium Tax Credit Reduction	0.1	0.5	1.7	3.2	4.8	5.4	6.0	6.5	6.9
Other Income and Payroll Tax Reduction	0.5	1.5	3.3	5.7	8.3	9.6	11.1	12.2	13.0
Net Revenue Reduction	0.4	1.0	1.5	2.4	3.4	4.2	5.0	5.8	6.0

Notes:

[a] Millions of covered lives, annualized.

The Departments acknowledge that the extent to which firms would offer HRAs integrated with individual health insurance coverage and the results on individual market risk pools and premiums, federal tax revenues, and private costs and benefits are highly uncertain. The Departments invite comment on the estimates and assumptions discussed previously in this preamble.

The Departments particularly emphasize that these estimates assume that every employee in a firm would be offered either an HRA integrated with individual health insurance coverage or a traditional group health plan (but not both and not a choice between the two), or no employer health benefit. The estimates further assume that a firm offering such an HRA would offer the same benefit to each employee in the firm, and would not vary the contribution by location, age, or other permitted factors other than self-only versus non-self-only benefits.[130] In other words, the estimates assume that the proposed rules would be effective in preventing firms from dividing their employees by health status or other factors in a way that would allow firms to capture greater tax subsidies or increase individual market premiums or the PTC.

HRA participation and transfers including individual market premium increases would likely be higher if these assumptions are incorrect. Because the number of individuals in traditional group health plans is large relative to the number of individuals in individual health insurance coverage, relatively small changes in employer offers of coverage can result in large changes in individual market premiums.[131] Consider the following illustrative, simplified example. The Departments

---

[129] These revenue estimates do not account for the possibility that the proposed rules would lead to increased taxable wages.

[130] The Departments imposed two constraints on the microsimulation that could be consistent with allowing the HRA offer to vary across employees within a firm. First, the Departments assume that persons with incomes below 200 percent of the federal poverty level who are enrolled in subsidized individual health insurance coverage in the baseline do not move to an HRA or to uninsured status as a result of the proposed rule. This is consistent with assuming that employers with low-wage workers currently receiving Medicaid or the PTC do not begin to offer HRAs large enough to render such employees ineligible for the PTC or from receiving public coverage. This constraint is also consistent with the assumption that employees who would experience a substantial subsidy loss would move to other jobs that would allow them to retain their current coverage. This assumption reduces the amount of PTC savings generated by the proposal, and also reduces the tax revenue cost of providing HRAs to such employees. Second, the Departments assume that employees with incomes above 400 percent of the federal poverty level who are enrolled in a traditional group health plan do not become uninsured as a result of the proposed rule, even if individual plan premiums are substantially higher than the cost of their traditional group health plan coverage. This is consistent with assuming that employers would provide larger HRAs to older employees or to employees in higher-cost markets than they would provide to other employees in their firms, in order to ensure affordable coverage. It is also consistent with assuming that employees would move to other firms, if they face large premium or cost-sharing increases when their employers switch from traditional group coverage to HRAs integrated with individual health insurance coverage.

[131] The Treasury Department projects that over 150 million persons under age 65 will be enrolled in employer-

estimate that about 80 percent of individuals in employer-sponsored coverage are relatively healthy and 20 percent are relatively unhealthy. Relatively healthy persons in the employer market have health costs equal to about a quarter of average single enrollee costs in the individual market and unhealthy persons in the employer market have health costs that are about three times the cost of the average person in the individual market.[132] Thus, if 5 million individuals moved from the employer market to the individual market, and these 5 million were representative of the average for the employer market with a ratio of healthy to unhealthy of 4 to 1, then individual market premiums would fall by about 3 percent. If, however, a disproportionate number of unhealthy employees enter the individual market, premiums in the individual market would rise. For example, if 3 million healthy and 2 million unhealthy enrollees entered the individual market, premiums would increase by an estimated 14 percent.

The Departments seek comment on the extent to which employers would offer different benefits to different classes of employees, including the classes based on rating area and all other classes, and on combinations of the classes, and the resulting effect on individual market premiums.

The Departments also emphasize that these estimates assume that employers would contribute the same amount to HRAs integrated with individual health insurance coverage as they would to traditional group health plans and that employees would elect the same amount of salary reduction to pay for individual health plans and cost-sharing as they would if they were enrolled in a traditional group health plan. But, as noted above, some employees who would be offered HRAs under the proposed rule would choose plans with lower premiums and higher deductibles and copayments and narrower provider networks than they would choose if offered a traditional group health plan. Higher cost-sharing and narrower provider networks could cause individuals to be more cost-conscious consumers of healthcare.

In addition, the estimates assume that the entire HRA balance is spent on healthcare premiums and cost-sharing each year. However, the Departments are of the view that many employers would allow employees to carry unspent HRA balances over from year to year, and that some employers would allow employees to continue to spend accumulated HRA funds even after separating from their employer. Moreover, HRA benefits are subject to COBRA protections, such that some employees would elect to use accumulated funds for up to 18 months after separation from service. The ability to carry over benefits from year to year could further encourage employees to curtail healthcare spending, particularly less efficient spending. This effect could be modest for several reasons. First, unlike HSA balances, which can be withdrawn for non-health purposes subject to tax but without penalty after age 65 and with a 20 percent penalty before age 65, HRAs may only be used for healthcare. In addition, unlike HSAs, HRAs are not the property of the employee and employers may limit the amount that can be carried over from year-to-year or accessed by the employee after separation. The Departments welcome comment on the extent to which HRA balances would likely be allowed to accumulate over time and accessed after employees separate from employment, and the extent to which employees would be incentivized to become more cost conscious consumers of healthcare.

These estimates further assume that all individual health insurance coverage integrated with an HRA would be treated as subject to and compliant with sections 2711 and 2713 of the PHS Act. The proposed rules prohibit an HRA from being integrated with STLDI and excepted benefits, which are not subject to the market requirements. Grandfathered coverage in the individual market is not subject to the annual dollar prohibition in section 2711 of the PHS Act or to the preventive services requirements in section 2713 of the PHS Act. However, the proposed rules would not require employees or employers to confirm that individual health insurance coverage integrated with an HRA is not grandfathered coverage. Requiring such confirmation would be administratively burdensome and the Departments expect that the number of employees who might use an HRA to buy such coverage would be extremely small, because individuals can only renew and cannot newly enroll in grandfathered individual health insurance coverage.

3. *Impact of Excepted Benefit HRA*

The proposed rules also provide for recognition of a new limited excepted benefit HRA under which amounts newly made available for each plan year are limited to $1,800 (indexed for inflation after 2020). Among other conditions, to offer the excepted benefit HRA, the employer must offer the employee a group health plan that is not limited to excepted benefits and that is not an HRA, but the employee would not need to enroll in this group health plan. The benefit would be funded by the employer, and in the Treasury Department's modeling, this means that it would be paid for by all employees in the firm through an overall reduction in wages. The benefit could be used to pay for any medical expense, other than premiums for individual health insurance coverage, group health plan coverage (other than COBRA, state, or other continuation coverage), or Medicare parts B or D.

(Footnote Continued)

sponsored group health plans in 2020, compared to about 15 million in the individual market.

[132] Estimates are derived from RTI MarketScan claims data for 2014. These data indicate that 80 percent of persons in the employer market have no Hierarchical Condition Codes (HCCs) while 20 percent had one or more HCCs. Persons with no HCCs had costs equal to 24 percent of average single enrollee costs in the individual market and persons with one or more HCCs had costs equal to three times the average individual market enrollee cost.

The excepted benefit HRA could be used to pay premiums for coverage that consists solely of excepted benefits and for other premiums, such as premiums for STLDI.

Due to the availability of other tax preferences for health benefits, including the tax exclusion for employer-sponsored benefits, salary reductions for group and off-Exchange individual health insurance coverage premiums when integrated with an HRA, health FSAs, and non-excepted benefit HRAs, the Departments are of the view that this new excepted benefit would be adopted by a small number of firms. However, it could provide flexibility for firms that want to provide a tax preference to employees that choose STLDI instead of the employer's traditional group health plan. The Departments welcome comments on the costs and benefits of the proposed excepted benefit HRA and the extent to which firms and employees would be likely to adopt such HRAs.

C. *Regulatory Alternatives*

In developing the proposed rules, the Departments considered various alternative approaches.

Retaining prohibition on integration of HRAs with individual health insurance coverage. The Departments considered retaining the existing prohibition on integration of HRAs with individual health insurance coverage. However, the Departments determined that the adverse selection concerns that gave rise to the prohibition could be adequately addressed by including appropriate mitigating conditions in the proposed integration rules. Further, the Departments determined that eliminating the prohibition on integrating HRAs with individual health insurance coverage would increase the usability of HRAs which would provide more Americans, including employees who work at small businesses, with additional healthcare options. Such changes would facilitate the development and operation of a healthcare system that provides high-quality care at affordable prices for the American people by increasing consumer choice for employees and promoting competition in healthcare markets by adding additional options for employers.

Alternative approaches for safeguards intended to prevent health discrimination and adverse selection under the proposed integration rules. In developing the safeguards designed to prevent adverse selection, the Departments considered whether such safeguards are needed and alternatives for the design of such safeguards. As explained in more detail earlier in this preamble, although the Departments considered that it is possible that the consequences of HRA expansion for the individual market could be positive, the Departments determined that allowing HRAs to be integrated with individual health insurance coverage is more likely to result in opportunities for employers to discriminate by encouraging higher risk employees to obtain coverage in the individual market in order to reduce the cost of traditional group health plan coverage provided by the employer to lower risk employees. Such an arrangement could worsen adverse selection and raise premiums in the individual market if HRAs integrated with individual health insurance coverage are used disproportionately by higher risk employees. Thus, there is risk with permitting HRAs to be integrated with individual health insurance coverage without appropriate safeguards.

Accordingly, to significantly temper these concerns, the proposed integration rules prohibit a plan sponsor from offering the same class of employees both a traditional group health plan and an HRA integrated with individual health insurance coverage (or a choice between the two). In addition, to the extent a plan sponsor offers an HRA integrated with individual health insurance coverage to a class of employees, the proposed integration rules require that the HRA be offered on the same terms to all employees within the class, subject to certain exceptions.

In designing these safeguards, the Departments considered various alternatives, including prohibiting an employer that offers an HRA integrated with individual health insurance coverage from offering a traditional group health plan to any of its employees. The Departments instead decided to allow employers to offer either a traditional group health plan or an HRA integrated with individual health insurance coverage (but not a choice between the two) to different classes of employees, based on the determination that such a rule provides an appropriate safeguard against the adverse selection concerns while also providing employers sufficient flexibility, which is intended to allow employers of all sizes to take advantage of the expansion provided in the proposed integration rules.

As explained in more detail earlier in the preamble, the Departments also considered various options for defining the classes of employees that may be used in applying these safeguards. The Departments considered whether employers should be allowed to offer or vary HRAs integrated with individual health insurance coverage for classes of employees based on a very general standard (like the one that applies under the HIPAA nondiscrimination rules, with a broad employment-based classification standard) or a more finite list of classes of employees that have been used in other rules for various employee benefits purposes (for example, under section 105(h) and/or section 4980H of the Code). The Departments' view is that a broad and open-ended standard would not be sufficient to mitigate the risk of adverse selection that more defined categories would help address those concerns. Earlier in the preamble, the Departments solicit comments on all aspects of these classes of employees, including whether these are the appropriate classes of employees, whether alternate classes, such as the categories of similarly situated individuals under the HIPAA nondiscrimination provisions, are preferable, whether additional classes are required and whether allowing benefits to vary based on classes of employees could lead to adverse selection.

Earlier in this preamble, the Departments also seek comment on whether the ability to integrate an HRA with individual health insurance coverage has the potential to increase participation in and strengthen the viability of states' individual market risk pools. Further, the Departments also invite comment on whether the proposed integration safeguards are appropriate and narrowly tailored to prevent adverse selection and health status discrimination or whether less restrictive safeguards would suffice.

Allowing integration with coverage other than individual health insurance coverage under the proposed rules. The Departments considered whether to allow HRAs intended to satisfy the individual health insurance coverage integration test also to be integrated with non-HRA group coverage, such as a group health plan maintained by the employer of the participant's spouse, in addition to individual health insurance coverage, because, like individual health insurance coverage, group health plan coverage is generally subject to and compliant with sections 2711 and 2713 of the PHS Act. The Departments decided against proposing such a rule because allowing such integration would add significant complexity to the individual health insurance coverage integration test, as described earlier in this preamble. However, earlier in this preamble, the Departments request comments regarding whether the Departments should allow for such integration and, if so, with respect to compliance with section 2711 of the PHS Act, how such an integration test should be designed to take into account that, while most individual health insurance coverage is required to cover all EHBs, large group market and self-insured group health plans are not required to cover all EHBs. Earlier in this preamble the Departments also request comments on the demand for such a rule and any problems such a rule may raise.

In addition, the Departments considered whether to propose a rule to permit HRAs to be integrated with other types of non-group coverage other than individual health insurance coverage, such as STLDI. However, while all new individual health insurance coverage that is currently sold is non-grandfathered coverage (and most coverage that is renewed in also non-grandfathered) and is therefore generally subject to and compliant with sections 2711 and 2713 of the PHS Act, other types of coverage, such as STLDI, are not subject to and therefore may not be compliant with sections 2711 and 2713 of the PHS Act, in which case, integration would not be sufficient to ensure that the combined benefit package satisfies these requirements. Earlier in this preamble, the Departments request comments on whether integration with STLDI (which is not required to satisfy sections 2711 and 2713 of the PHS Act) should be permitted, whether integration should be permitted with any other type of coverage that satisfies sections 2711 and 2713 of the PHS Act, how such integration rules should be structured, as well as comments on what, if any, potential benefits and problems might arise from allowing these types of HRA integration. Earlier in this preamble the Departments also seek comments on whether allowing such integration would raise any concerns about health status discrimination leading to additional adverse selection in the individual market.

Alternatives for annual limits on amounts made available under the excepted benefit HRA and alternatives for indexing such amount. With regard to the excepted benefit HRA, in the proposed rules, the Departments propose that the amounts newly made available for a plan year may not exceed $1,800 (indexed for inflation after 2020). For this purpose, inflation is defined in the proposed rules by reference to C-CPI-U, published by the Department of Labor.

In proposing this limit, the Departments considered various alternative amounts, including the limits on employer contributions to excepted benefit health FSAs (set at $500 in 1997 if there are no employee contributions to the health FSA, although it might be much higher if there are employee contributions). The Departments considered the relationship between $500 and the average cost of insurance in 1997. The Departments also considered a limit of 15 percent-of-the-cost-of-coverage-under-the-primary-plan test, which is the limit used for both supplemental excepted benefits in the group market and limited wraparound coverage, as a benchmark to ensure that the benefits are limited in amount. In considering how such a limit could be an appropriate limit for excepted benefit HRAs, the Departments considered 15 percent of the cost of group coverage for both employee-only and family coverage. However, the Departments also considered how to determine the primary plan in circumstances in which the participant does not enroll in a traditional group health plan, and concluded that such a determination would likely be difficult for employers. The Departments also considered using the cost of coverage for the second lowest cost silver plan in various markets.

These methodologies produced a wide range of possible excepted benefit HRA limits from $1,100 to $2,850. Consistent with the principle of promoting HRA use and availability, rather than proposing a complex test for the limit on amounts newly made available in the excepted benefit HRA, the Departments are proposing a maximum of $1,800 (indexed for inflation after 2020) on amounts newly made available for a plan year that approximates the midpoint amount yielded by the various methodologies considered. Earlier in this preamble, the Departments request comments on this amount, and whether an alternate amount or formula for determining the maximum dollar limit for an excepted benefit HRA would be more appropriate and, if so, what that alternative would be and why. Further, earlier in this preamble, the Departments seek comment on whether the maximum dollar limit should be adjusted depending on whether a participant has dependent(s) and, if so, by what amount the maximum dollar limit should be adjusted to in that case.

With regard to indexing the dollar limit on amounts made newly available under the excepted benefit HRA, in proposing to index the amount by C-CPI-U, the Departments considered whether or not to index the amount, including the difficulties of administering an HRA with a changing amount, and the cost, including the cost to the Departments to publish the amount and provide notice every year, as balanced with the decreasing real value of a set HRA limit. The Departments determined that the benefit of indexing the amount outweighs the increased complexity for the Departments and for stakeholders. Earlier in this preamble, the Departments invite comments on the measure of inflation used, including whether the amount should be indexed to inflation (and if there are any administrability concerns associated with indexing), if C-CPI-U is the correct measure of inflation, or whether an alternate measure, such as the overall medical care component for CPI-U, or the method specified under section 9831(d)(2)(D) of the Code for QSEHRAs, should be used.

D. *Paperwork Reduction Act - Department of Health and Human Services*

Under the Paperwork Reduction Act of 1995 (PRA), we are required to provide 60-day notice in the **Federal Register** and solicit public comment before a collection of information requirement is submitted to OMB for review and approval. To fairly evaluate whether an information collection should be approved by OMB, section 3506(c)(2)(A) of the PRA requires that we solicit comment on the following issues:

- The need for the information collection and its usefulness in carrying out the proper functions of our agency.
- The accuracy of our estimate of the information collection burden.
- The quality, utility, and clarity of the information to be collected.
- Recommendations to minimize the information collection burden on the affected public, including automated collection techniques.

1. *Wage Estimates*

To derive wage estimates, the Departments generally used data from the Bureau of Labor Statistics to derive average labor costs (including a 100 percent increase for fringe benefits and overhead) for estimating the burden associated with the ICRs.[133] Table 2 below presents the mean hourly wage, the cost of fringe benefits and overhead, and the adjusted hourly wage.

As indicated, employee hourly wage estimates have been adjusted by a factor of 100 percent. This is necessarily a rough adjustment, both because fringe benefits and overhead costs vary significantly across employers, and because methods of estimating these costs vary widely across studies. Nonetheless, there is no practical alternative, and the Departments are of the view that doubling the hourly wage to estimate total cost is a reasonably accurate estimation method.

TABLE 1: Adjusted Hourly Wages Used in Burden Estimates

Occupation Title	Occupationa l Code	Mean Hourly Wage ($/hour)	Fringe Benefits and Overhead ($/hour)	Adjusted Hourly Wage ($/hour)
Compensation and Benefits Manager	11-3111	$62.50	$62.50	$125.00
Lawyer	23-1011	$68.22	$68.22	$136.44

2. *ICRs Regarding Substantiation of Individual Health Insurance Coverage*

Under the proposed regulations, an HRA must implement reasonable procedures to verify that individuals whose medical care expenses are reimbursable by the HRA are, or will be, enrolled in individual health insurance coverage (other than coverage that consists solely of excepted benefits) for the plan year.

In addition, following the initial substantiation of coverage, with each new request for reimbursement of an incurred medical care expense for the same plan year, the proposed regulations provide that the HRA may not reimburse a participant for any medical care expenses unless, prior to each reimbursement, the participant provides substantiation that the participant and, if applicable, any dependent(s) whose medical care expenses are requested to be reimbursed were enrolled in individual health insurance coverage (other than coverage that consists solely of excepted benefits) for the month during which the medical care expenses were incurred. The attestation may be part of the form used for requesting reimbursement.

To satisfy this requirement, the HRA may require that the participant submit an attestation or a document provided by a third party (for example, an explanation of benefit or insurance card) as substantiation. The associated cost would be negligible and is, therefore, not estimated.

3. *ICRs Regarding Notice Requirement*

These proposed regulations include a requirement that an HRA provide written notice to eligible participants. The HRA would be required to provide a written notice to each participant at least 90 days before the beginning of each plan year. For participants who are not yet eligible to participate at the beginning of the plan year (or who are not eligible when the notice is provided at least 90 days prior to the beginning of the plan year), the HRA must provide the notice no later than the date on which the participant is first eligible to participate in the HRA.

The proposed written notice would be required to include certain relevant information, including a description of the terms of the HRA, including the amount made available that is used in the affordability determination under the Code section 36B proposed rules; a statement of the right of the participant to opt-out of and waive future reimbursement under the HRA; a description of the potential availability of the PTC for a participant who opts out of and waives an HRA if the HRA is not affordable under the proposed PTC regulations; a description of the PTC eligibility consequences for a participant who accepts the HRA; a statement that the participant must inform any Exchange to

[133] *See* May 2017 Bureau of Labor Statistics, Occupational Employment Statistics, National Occupational Employment and Wage Estimates at *https://www.bls.gov/oes/current/oes_nat.htm*.

which they apply for advance payments of the PTC of the availability of the HRA, the amount of the HRA, the number of months the HRA is available to participants during the plan year, whether it is available to their dependents and whether they are a current or former employee; a statement that the participant should retain the written notice because it may be needed to determine whether the participant is allowed the PTC; a statement that the HRA may not reimburse any medical care expense unless the substantiation requirements are met; and a statement that it is the responsibility of the participant to inform the HRA if the participant or any dependent whose medical care expenses are reimbursable by the HRA is no longer enrolled in individual health insurance coverage. The written notice may include other information, as long as the additional information does not conflict with the required information. The written notice would not need to include information specific to a participant.

The Departments estimate that for each HRA plan sponsor, a compensation and benefits manager would need 2 hours (at $125 per hour) and a lawyer would need 1 hour (at $136.44 per hour) to prepare the notices. The total burden for an HRA plan sponsor would be 3 hours with an equivalent cost of approximately $386. This burden would be incurred the first time the plan sponsor provides an HRA that is integrated with individual health insurance coverage. In subsequent years, the burden to update the notice in expected to be minimal and therefore is not estimated.

HHS estimates that in 2020, an estimated 1,203 state and local government entities would offer HRAs that are integrated with individual health insurance coverage.[134] The total burden to prepare notices would be approximately 3,610 hours with an equivalent cost of approximately $464,984. In 2021 approximately 1,805 additional state and local government entities would offer HRAs that are integrated with individual health insurance coverage for the first time and would incur a burden of approximately 5,415 hours with an equivalent cost of approximately $697,476. In 2022, approximately 3,008 additional state and local government entities would offer HRAs that are integrated with individual health insurance coverage for the first time and would incur a burden of approximately 9,024 hours with an equivalent cost of approximately $1.16 million.

HRA plan sponsors would provide the notice to eligible participants every year. HHS estimates that HRA plan sponsors would provide printed notices to approximately 90,162 eligible participants[135] in 2020, 225,405 eligible participants in 2021 and 450,810 eligible participants in 2022. The Departments anticipate that the notices would be approximately 2 pages long and the cost of materials and printing would be $0.05 per page, with a total cost of $0.10 per notice. It is assumed that these notices would be provided along with other benefits information with no additional mailing cost. The Departments assume that approximately 54 percent of notices would be provided electronically and approximately 46 percent would be provided in print along with other benefits information. Therefore, in 2020, state and local government entities providing HRAs that are integrated with individual health insurance coverage would print approximately 41,475 notices at a cost of approximately $4,147. In 2021, approximately 103,686 notices would be printed at a cost of $10,369 and in 2022, approximately 207,373 notices would be printed at a cost of a $20,737.

TABLE 2. Proposed Annual Burden and Costs

Year	Estimated Number of Employers Newly Offering HRAs	Estimated Number of Notices to all Eligible Participants	Total Annual Burden (hours)	Total Estimated Labor Cost	Total Estimated Printing and Materials Cost
2020	1,203	90,162	3,610	$464,984	$4,147
2021	1,805	225,405	5,415	$697,476	$10,369
2022	3,008	450,810	9,024	$1,162,461	$20,737
3 year Average	2,005	255,459	6,016	$774,974	$11,751

[134] U.S. Department of the Treasury, Office of Tax Analysis simulation model suggests that in 2020, approximately 80,000 employers will offer HRAs, with 1.0 million individuals receiving an HRA integrated with individual health insurance coverage. These numbers would increase to 200,000 employers and 2.5 million individuals in 2021 and to 400,000 employers and 5 million individuals in 2022. The Departments estimate that there is, on average, 1 dependent for every policyholder. The Departments also estimate that approximately 2 percent of employers are state and local government entities, accounting for approximately 14 percent of participants.

[135] U.S. Department of the Treasury, Office of Tax Analysis simulation model provides estimates of the number of participants and dependents receiving an HRA integrated with individual health insurance coverage. Number of eligible participants is estimated based on the assumption that 75 percent of eligible participants would enroll in their employers' plans. *See* Section 3 of the Kaiser "2017 Employer Health Benefits Survey". *https://www.kff.org/health-costs/report/2017-employer-health-benefits-survey/*.

TABLE 3. Proposed Recordkeeping and Reporting Requirements

Regulation Section	OMB Control Number	Respondents	Responses	Burden per Response (hours)	Total Annual Burden (hours)	Hourly Labor Cost of Reporting	Total Labor Cost of Reporting	Printing and Materials Cost	Total Cost
§ 146.123(c)(5) § 146.123(c)(6)	0938-0702	2,005	255,459	3	6,016	$128.81	$774,974	$11,751	$786,724

HHS intends to amend the information collection currently approved under OMB control number 0938-0702 "Information Collection Requirements Referenced in HIPAA for the Group Market, Supporting Regulations 45 CFR 146, and forms/instructions" (CMS-10430), to account for this additional burden.

4. *Submission of PRA-Related Comments*

We have submitted a copy of this proposed rule to OMB for its review of the rule's information collection and recordkeeping requirements. The requirements are not effective until they have been approved by OMB.

We invite public comments on these information collection requirements. If you wish to comment, please identify the rule (CMS-9918-P) and, where applicable, the ICR's CFR citation, CMS ID number, and OMB control number.

To obtain copies of a supporting statement and any related forms for the proposed collection(s) summarized in this notice, you may make your request using one of following:

1. Access CMS's website address at *https://www.cms.gov/Regulations-and-Guidance/Legislation/PaperworkReductionActof1995/PRA-Listing.html*.
2. E-mail your request, including your address, phone number, OMB number, and CMS document identifier, to *Paperwork@cms.hhs.gov*.
3. Call the Reports Clearance Office at (410) 786-1326.

See this rule's DATES and ADDRESSES sections for the comment due date and for additional instructions.

E. *Paperwork Reduction Act - Department of Labor and Department of the Treasury*

As part of its continuing effort to reduce paperwork and respondent burden, the Departments conduct a preclearance consultation program to provide the general public and Federal agencies with an opportunity to comment on proposed and continuing collections of information in accordance with the PRA. This helps to ensure that the public understands the Departments' collection instructions, respondents can provide the requested data in the desired format, reporting burden (time and financial resources) is minimized, collection instruments are clearly understood, and the Departments can properly assess the impact of collection requirements on respondents.

Under the PRA, an agency may not conduct or sponsor, and an individual is not required to respond to, a collection of information unless it displays a valid OMB control number. In accordance with the requirements of the PRA, DOL is requesting an OMB control number for three new information collections (ICs) contained in the proposed rules. Two ICs are sponsored jointly by DOL and the Treasury Department: (1) Verification of Enrollment in Individual Health Insurance Coverage (29 CFR 2590.702-2(c)(5)); and (2) HRA Notice to Participants (29 CFR 2590.702-2(c)(6)). A third IC is sponsored solely by DOL (29 CFR 2510.3-1): (3) Notice to Participants that Individual Health Insurance Coverage Policy is Not Subject to Title I of ERISA.

With regard to the Treasury Department, the collection of information contained in these regulations is submitted to OMB for review in accordance with the PRA as follows. The collection of information in these regulations is in 26 CFR 54.9815-2711(d)(4) and 26 CFR 54.9802-4(c)(5) and (c)(6). The burden for the collection of information contained in these regulations is reflected in the burden for OMB Control Number 1545-0123 for the U. S. Business Income Tax Return, 1545-0074 for U.S. Individual Income Tax Return, and 1545-0047 Return of Organizations Exempt From Income Tax. The tax-exempt organization form instructions will be updated in the next revision. The estimated annual burden per respondent, estimated annual burden per recordkeeper, or estimated number of respondents is updated annually.

The Departments have submitted a copy of the proposed rule, Health Reimbursement Arrangements and Other Account-Based Group Health Plans, to OMB in accordance with 44 U.S.C. 3507(d) for review of its information collections. The Departments and OMB are particularly interested in comments that:

• Evaluate whether the collection of information is necessary for the proper performance of the functions of the agency, including whether the information will have practical utility;

• Evaluate the accuracy of the agency's estimate of the burden of the collection of information, including the validity of the methodology and assumptions used;

• Enhance the quality, utility, and clarity of the information to be collected; and

• Minimize the burden of the collection of information on those who are to respond, including through the use of appropriate automated, electronic, mechanical, or other technological collection techniques or other forms of information technology, e.g., permitting electronic submission of responses.

In addition to filing comments on the information collections with the agencies on the same basis as any other aspect of this rule, interested parties may file comments on the information collection requirements with the Office of Management and Budget (OMB). The method for submitting comments to the agencies is explained earlier in the Addresses section of the document. Comments to OMB should be sent to the Office of Information and Regulatory Affairs, Office of Management and Budget, Room 10235, New Executive Office Building, Washington, DC 20503; Attention: Desk Officer for the Employee Benefits Security Administration. Notwithstanding the 60-day comment period to submit comments to the agencies, in order to ensure consideration, OMB requests that comments be submitted within 30 days of publication of this proposed rule. In addition, comments should identify the applicable OMB control number. PRA Addressee: Address requests for copies of the ICR to G. Christopher Cosby, Office of Policy and Research, U.S. Department of Labor, Employee Benefits Security Administration, 200 Constitution Avenue NW, Room N- 5718, Washington, DC 20210. Telephone (202) 693-8410; Fax: (202) 219-5333. These are not toll-free numbers. ICRs submitted to OMB also are available at *http://www.RegInfo.gov*.

Below is a description of the information collections and their burden.

1. *Verification of Enrollment in Individual Health Insurance Coverage*

In order for an HRA to be integrated with individual health insurance, among other requirements, the HRA must implement, and comply with, reasonable procedures to verify that participants and dependents are, or will be, enrolled in individual health insurance coverage during the plan year. This requirement can be satisfied by providing a document from a third party, like an issuer, verifying coverage. As an alternative procedure, this requirement could also be satisfied if the HRA requires participants to provide an attestation of coverage, including the date coverage begins and the provider of the coverage.

In addition, following the initial substantiation of coverage, with each new request for reimbursement of an incurred medical care expense for the same plan year, the HRA may not reimburse participants for any medical care expenses unless, prior to each reimbursement, the participant provides substantiation (which may be in the form of a written attestation) that the participant and, if applicable, the dependent whose medical care expenses are requested to be reimbursed, continue to be enrolled in individual health insurance coverage for the month during which the medical care expenses were incurred. The attestation may be part of the form used for requesting reimbursement.

Documentation, including proof that expenditure of funds is for a medical care expense, is currently universal when seeking reimbursement from an HRA. For the new requirements contained in the proposed regulations regarding verification of enrollment in individual health insurance coverage, the HRA can require proof of coverage or attestations of coverage as part of the processes that already exist for when participants seek reimbursement from HRAs for premiums or other medical care expenses. The additional burden is de minimis, because the attestation can be a part of the information already required when seeking reimbursement. To the extent an HRA develops additional processes for the requirement that individuals verify enrollment in individual health insurance coverage for the plan year, the additional burden is also expected to be de minimis because it involves either attestation or providing documents that already exist.

2. *HRA Notice to Participants*

These proposed regulations require an HRA to provide written notice to eligible participants including, among other things, the following information: (1) a description of the terms of the HRA, including the amounts newly made available as used in the affordability determination under the Code section 36B proposed regulations; (2) a statement of the right of the participant to opt-out of and waive future reimbursement under the HRA; (3) a description of the potential availability of the PTC for a participant who opts out of and waives an HRA if the HRA is not affordable under the proposed PTC regulations; and (4) a description of the PTC eligibility consequences for a participant who accepts the HRA. The written notice may include other information, as long as the additional information does not conflict with the required information. The written notice does not need to include information specific to a participant.

The HRA must provide the written notice to each participant at least 90 days before the beginning of each plan year. For participants who are not yet eligible to participate at the beginning of the plan year (or who are not eligible when the notice is provided at least 90 days prior to the beginning of the plan year), the HRA must provide the notice no later than the date on which the participant is first eligible to participate in the HRA.

The Departments estimate that a compensation and benefits manager would require two hours (at $125 per hour) and a lawyer would require one hour (at $136.44 per hour) to prepare the notice for each HRA. Thus, the total hour burden for each HRA would be 3 hours with an equivalent cost of approximately $386. The Departments estimate that each notice would be two pages, with total materials and printing cost of $0.10 per notice ($0.05 per page). The Departments estimate that 78,797 private employers would[136] newly offer HRAs integrated with individual health insurance coverage

---

[136] U.S. Department of the Treasury, Office of Tax Analysis used a simulation model to obtain these estimates. For 2020 the model estimated that 80,000 employers would offer HRAs integrated with individual health insurance coverage and one million individuals would enroll in those HRAs. Based on DOL estimates about 98 percent of these will be in the private market, and the rest will be though public employers like state and local governments. There are on average one dependent for every policy holder. "Health Insurance Coverage Bulletin", Abstract of the Auxiliary

in 2020[137] as a result of the proposed rules in the first year. Therefore, the Departments estimate for the total hour burden for these HRAs to prepare the notices would be 236,390 hours with an equivalent cost of $30,450,216.

All HRAs integrated with individual health insurance coverage are required to annually send the notice to all eligible participants (those eligible to enroll). The Departments estimate that there would be 576,505 eligible participants at private employers in 2020 that would need to receive the notice.[138] The Departments assume that approximately 54 percent of notices would be provided electronically and approximately 46 percent would be provided in print along with other benefits information. Therefore, a total of 265,192 notices will be printed at a cost of $26,519. Tables 1 and 2 provide estimates for years 2020, 2021 and 2022.

TABLE 1.—*Burden to Prepare HRA Notice for the First Time- Private Sector Employers*

Year	Number of Employers Newly Offering HRAs	Legal Cost Per Hour	Number of Hours for Legal	Benefit Manager Cost per Hour	Number of Hours for Benefit Manager	Total Hour Burden	Total Equivalent Cost
(a)	(b)	(c)	(d)=1*(b)	(e)	(f)=2*(b)	(g)=(d)+(f)	(c)*(d)+(e)*(f)
2020	78,797	$136.44	78,797	$125.00	157,593	236,390	$30,450,216
2021	118,195	$136.44	118,195	$125.00	236,390	354,585	$45,675,324
2022	196,992	$136.44	196,992	$125.00	393,984	590,976	$76,125,539

TABLE 2.—*Burden to Provide Notice to All Eligible Private Sector Participants*

Year	Total # of Notices	# of Notices Sent by Mail	Cost Per Notice	Total Cost Burden
(a)	(b)	(c)	(d)	(e)=(c)*(d)
2020	576,505	265,192	$0.10	$26,519
2021	1,441,262	662,980	$0.10	$66,298
2022	2,882,523	1,325,961	$0.10	$132,596

3. *Notice to Participants that Individual Health Insurance Coverage Policy is not Subject to Title I of ERISA*

In the proposed rules, DOL clarifies that individual health insurance coverage the premiums of which are reimbursed by an HRA, QSEHRA, or supplemental salary reduction arrangement is not considered an "employee welfare benefit plan" with the consumer protections provided under ERISA. HRA plan sponsors are required to notify participants of this fact. For an HRA, this notice requirement is met if annually the notice requirement in 29 CFR 2590.702-2(c)(6) is met, which is part of the HRA Notice to Participants. Therefore, this notice requirement imposes no additional burden. For QSEHRAs and for HRAs not subject to 29 CFR 2590.702-2(c)(6) but that reimburse premiums for individual health insurance coverage, this notice requirement is met if the plan sponsor annually includes language provided in the rule in the Summary Plan Description. DOL estimates that this burden will be de minimis, because the required text is provided by DOL and the required information can be included with other notices.

The information collections are summarized as follows:

Type of Review: New Collection.

Agency: DOL-EBSA, Treasury - IRS

Title: Notice for Health Reimbursement Arrangements integrated with Individual Health Insurance Coverage

OMB Numbers: 1210-new (DOL), 1545-0123, 1545-0074, and 1545-0047 (Treasury).

Affected Public: Private Sector.

Total Respondents: 131,328 three-year average.

Total Responses: 1,633,430 three-year average.

Frequency of Response: Annually.

(Footnote Continued)

Data for the March 2016 Annual Social and Economic Supplement of the Current Population Survey, July 25, 2017. https://www.dol.gov/sites/default/files/ebsa/researchers/data/health-and-welfare/health-insurance-coverage-bulletin-2016.pdf

[137] Comparable numbers for 2021 are 118,195 private employers would newly offer HRAs integrated with individual health insurance coverage and 1,441,262 eligible participants in all HRAs would receive notices, and for 2022 196,992 private employers would newly offer HRAs integrated with individual health insurance coverage and 2,882,523 eligible participants in all HRAs would receive notices.

[138] Number of eligible participants is estimated based on Treasury estimates of the number of individuals enrolled in HRAs integrated with individual coverage, the assumption that there are two enrollees per employee participant, and the assumption that 75 percent of eligible participants would enroll in their employers' plans. *See* Section 3 of the Kaiser "2017 Employer Health Benefits Survey". https://www.kff.org/health-costs/report/2017-employer-health-benefits-survey/.

Estimated Total Annual Burden Hours: 196,992 for each agency (combined total is 393,984 hours). Three year average.

Estimated Total Annual Burden Cost: $37,569 for each agency (combined total is $75,138). Three year average.

F. *Regulatory Flexibility Act*

The Regulatory Flexibility Act (5 U.S.C. 601 *et seq.*) (RFA) imposes certain requirements with respect to Federal rules that are subject to the notice and comment requirements of section 553(b) of the Administrative Procedure Act (5 U.S.C. 551 *et seq.*) and which are likely to have a significant economic impact on a substantial number of small entities. Unless an agency certifies that a proposed rule is not likely to have a significant economic impact on a substantial number of small entities, section 603 of RFA requires that the agency present an initial regulatory flexibility analysis at the time of the publication of the notice of proposed rulemaking describing the impact of the rule on small entities and seeking public comment on such impact. Small entities include small businesses, organizations, and governmental jurisdictions.

The RFA generally defines a "small entity" as (1) a proprietary firm meeting the size standards of the Small Business Administration (SBA) (13 CFR 121.201), (2) a nonprofit organization that is not dominant in its field, or (3) a small government jurisdiction with a population of less than 50,000. (States and individuals are not included in the definition of "small entity.") The Departments use as their measure of significant economic impact on a substantial number of small entities a change in revenues of more than 3 to 5 percent.

The Departments do not expect the proposed rules to produce costs or benefits in excess of 3 to 5 percent of revenues for small entities. Entities that choose to offer an HRA integrated with individual health insurance coverage instead of a traditional group health plan are likely to experience a modest increase or decrease in administrative burden associated with health benefits. Entities that newly offer health benefits in the form of an HRA integrated with individual health insurance coverage would bear modest administrative costs. However, offering an HRA that is integrated with individual health insurance coverage is entirely voluntary on the part of employers, and no employer that would experience substantial costs would be expected to offer an HRA integrated with individual health insurance coverage. In addition, the proposed rules would provide large and small employers with an additional choice of a tax-preferred health benefit to offer their employees, potentially enabling them to attract and retain workers and maintain a healthier workforce.

In addition, section 1102(b) of the Social Security Act requires agencies to prepare a regulatory impact analysis if a rule may have a significant economic impact on the operations of a substantial number of small rural hospitals. This analysis must conform to the provisions of section 603 of the RFA. The proposed rules will not have a direct effect on small rural hospitals though there may be an indirect effect. By reducing the number of uninsured persons, the proposed rules could reduce administrative costs, such as billing costs and the costs of helping patients obtain public health benefits. The proposed rules could also reduce the cost of uncompensated care born by small rural hospitals and other healthcare providers (and shift such costs to insured persons). However, the Departments have determined that the proposed rules will not have a significant impact on the operations of a substantial number of small rural hospitals.

G. *Impact of Regulations on Small Business - Department of the Treasury*

Pursuant to section 7805(f) of the Code, the proposed rules have been submitted to the Chief Counsel for Advocacy of the SBA for comment on its impact on small business.

H. *Unfunded Mandates Reform Act*

Section 202 of the Unfunded Mandates Reform Act of 1995 (UMRA) requires that agencies assess anticipated costs and benefits and take certain other actions before issuing a proposed rule that includes any Federal mandate that may result in expenditures in any 1 year by state, local, or Tribal governments, in the aggregate, or by the private sector, of $100 million in 1995 dollars, updated annually for inflation. In 2018, that threshold is approximately $150 million. The proposed rules do not include any Federal mandate that may result in expenditures by state, local, or tribal governments, or the private sector, that may impose an annual burden that exceeds that threshold.

I. *Federalism*

Executive Order 13132 outlines fundamental principles of federalism. It requires adherence to specific criteria by Federal agencies in formulating and implementing policies that have "substantial direct effects" on the states, the relationship between the national government and states, or on the distribution of power and responsibilities among the various levels of government. Federal agencies promulgating regulations that have these federalism implications must consult with state and local officials, and describe the extent of their consultation and the nature of the concerns of state and local officials in the preamble to the final regulations. In the Departments' view, the proposed rules do not have federalism implications.

J. *Congressional Review Act*

The proposed rules are subject to the Congressional Review Act provisions of the Small Business Regulatory Enforcement Fairness Act of 1996 (5 U.S.C. 801 *et* seq.), and, upon finalization, will be transmitted to the Congress and to the Comptroller General for review in accordance with such provisions.

K. *Reducing Regulation and Controlling Regulatory Cost*

Executive Order 13771, titled Reducing Regulation and Controlling Regulatory Costs, was issued on January 30, 2017 and requires that the costs associated with significant new regulations "shall, to the extent permitted by law, be offset by the elimination of existing costs associated with at least two prior regulations." The proposed rules, if finalized as proposed, are expected to be an Executive Order 13771 deregulatory action.

Statutory Authority

The Department of the Treasury regulations are proposed to be adopted pursuant to the authority contained in sections 7805 and 9833 of the Code.

The Department of Labor regulations are proposed pursuant to the authority contained in 29 U.S.C. 1002, 1135, 1182, 1185d, 1191a, 1191b, and 1191c; Secretary of Labor's Order 1-2011, 77 FR 1088 (Jan. 9, 2012).

The Department of Health and Human Services regulations are proposed to be adopted pursuant to the authority contained in sections 2701 through 2763, 2791, 2792, and 2794 of the PHS Act (42 U.S.C. 300gg–300gg-63, 300gg-91, 300gg-92 and 300gg-94), as amended; sections 1311 and 1321 of PPACA (42 U.S.C. 13031 and 18041).

[¶49,775] Proposed Amendments of Regulations (REG-114540-18), published in the Federal Register on November 5, 2018.

[Code Sec. 956]

Controlled Foreign Corporations (CFCs): Exemptions: Foreign income.—Amendments of Reg. §1.956-1 reducing the amount determined under Section 956 of the Internal Revenue Code with respect to certain domestic corporations, are proposed.

AGENCY: Internal Revenue Service (IRS), Treasury.

ACTION: Notice of proposed rulemaking.

SUMMARY: This document contains proposed regulations that reduce the amount determined under section 956 of the Internal Revenue Code with respect to certain domestic corporations. The proposed regulations affect certain domestic corporations that own (or are treated as owning) stock in foreign corporations.

DATES: Written or electronic comments and requests for a public hearing must be received by December 5, 2018.

ADDRESSES: Send submissions to: CC:PA:LPD:PR (REG-114540-18), Internal Revenue Service, Room 5203, P.O. Box 7604, Ben Franklin Station, Washington, DC 20044. Submissions may be hand-delivered Monday through Friday between the hours of 8 a.m. and 4 p.m. to CC:PA:LPD:PR (REG-114540-18), Courier's Desk, Internal Revenue Service, 1111 Constitution Avenue, NW, Washington, DC 20224, or sent electronically via the Federal eRulemaking Portal at *http://www.regulations.gov* (IRS REG-114540-18).

FOR FURTHER INFORMATION CONTACT: Concerning the proposed regulations, Rose E. Jenkins, (202) 317-6934; concerning submissions of comments or requests for a public hearing, Regina Johnson, (202) 317-6901 (not toll-free numbers).

SUPPLEMENTARY INFORMATION:

Background

I. *Section 956*

The Revenue Act of 1962 (the "1962 Act"), Pub. L. No. 87-834, sec. 12, 76 Stat. at 1006, enacted sections 951 and 956 as part of subpart F of part III, subchapter N, chapter 1 of the 1954 Internal Revenue Code ("subpart F"), as amended. Subpart F was enacted in order to limit the use of low-tax jurisdictions for the purposes of obtaining indefinite deferral of U.S. tax on certain earnings that would otherwise be subject to U.S. federal income tax. H.R. Rep. No. 1447 at 57 (1962). Congress enacted subpart F in part to address taxpayers who had "taken advantage of the multiplicity of foreign tax systems to avoid taxation by the United States on what could ordinarily be expected to be U.S. source income." *Id.* at 58.

Before the 1962 Act, United States shareholders (as defined in section 951(b)) ("U.S. shareholders") of controlled foreign corporations (as defined in section 957) ("CFCs") were not subject to U.S. tax on earnings of the foreign corporations unless and until earnings of the foreign corporations were distributed to the shareholders as a dividend. S. Rep. No. 1881 at 78 (1962). The subpart F regime eliminated deferral for certain - generally passive or highly mobile - earnings of CFCs by subjecting those earnings to immediate U.S. taxation regardless of whether there was an actual distribution. *Id.* at 80. Earnings that were not subject to immediate U.S. taxation under the subpart F regime were generally taxable only upon repatriation, as those earnings did not present the same concerns regarding indefinite tax deferral compared to earnings subject to subpart F.

Section 956 was enacted alongside the subpart F regime in the 1962 Act to ensure that a CFC's earnings not subject to immediate tax when earned (under the subpart F regime) would be taxed when repatriated, either through a dividend or an effective repatriation. Recognizing that repatriation of foreign earnings was possible through means other than a taxable distribution, Congress enacted section 956 "to prevent the repatriation of income to the United States in a manner which does not subject it to U.S. taxation." H.R. Rep. No. 1447 at 58. Congress determined that the investment by a CFC of its earnings in United States property, including obligations of a U.S. person, "is substantially the equivalent of a dividend." *See* S. Rep. No. 1881 at 88 (1962). *See also* S. Rep. No. 94-938 at 226 (1976) ("[S]ince the investment . . . in the stock or debt obligations of a related U.S. person or its domestic affiliates makes funds available for use by the U.S. shareholders, it constitutes an effective repatriation of earnings which should be taxed."). Accordingly, Congress enacted section 956 as an anti-abuse measure to tax a CFC's investment of earnings in United States property in the same manner as if it had distributed those earnings to the United States. *See* JCS-10-87 at 1081-82 (1987) ("In general, two kinds of transactions are repatriations that end deferral and trigger tax. First, an actual dividend payment ends deferral . . . . Second, in the case of a controlled foreign corporation, an investment in U.S. property, such as a loan to the lender's U.S. parent or the purchase of U.S. real estate, is also a repatriation that ends deferral (Code sec. 956)."). Failure to tax CFC investments in United States property would have allowed taxpayers to circumvent the U.S. system of deferral by effectively repatriating earnings without paying U.S. tax on the substantial equivalent of a taxable dividend. Section 956 was thus designed to ensure symmetry between the tax treatment of repatriations through dividends and effective repatriations. *See generally* Notice 2014-52, 2014-42 I.R.B. 712 ("In the absence of section 956, a U.S. shareholder of a CFC could access the CFC's funds (untaxed earnings and profits) in a variety of ways other than by the payment of an actual taxable dividend, such that there would be no reason for the U.S. shareholder to incur the dividend tax. Section 956 eliminates this disincentive to pay a dividend by ensuring parity of treatment for different ways that CFC earnings can be made available for use in the United States or for use by the U.S. shareholder.").

Section 951(a)(1)(B) requires a U.S. shareholder of a CFC to include in gross income the amount determined under section 956 (the "section 956 amount") with respect to the CFC to the extent not excluded from gross income under section 959(a)(2) (the inclusion, a "section 956 inclusion"). *See* sections 951(a)(1)(B), 959(a)(2), and 959(f)(1). Section 951(b) defines a U.S. shareholder as a United States person that owns within the meaning of section 958(a), or is considered as owning by reason of the constructive ownership rules of section 958(b), 10 percent or more of the voting power or value of a foreign corporation. A U.S. shareholder's section 956 amount with respect to a CFC for a taxable year is the lesser of (1) the excess (if any) of such shareholder's pro rata share of the average of the amounts of United States property held (directly or indirectly) by the CFC as of the close of each quarter of such taxable year, over the amount of earnings and profits described in section 959(c)(1)(A) with respect to such shareholder, or (2) such shareholder's pro rata share of the applicable earnings of the CFC. *See* section 956(a). Applicable earnings are defined as the sum of accumulated earnings and profits (not including deficits) described in section 316(a)(1) and current earnings and profits described in section 316(a)(2), reduced by distributions made during the year and earnings and profits described in section 959(c)(1). *See* section 956(b)(1). Under section 956(c), United States property includes tangible property located in the United States, stock of a domestic corporation, an obligation of a United States person, and any right to use in the United States certain intangible property. Enacted as part of the Omnibus Budget Reconciliation Act of 1993, Pub. L. No. 103-66, sec. 13232(b), 107 Stat. 312, section 956(e) grants the Secretary of the Department of Treasury (the "Secretary") the authority to prescribe "such regulations as may be necessary to carry out the purposes of this section, including regulations to prevent the avoidance of the provisions of this section through reorganizations or otherwise."

This regulatory authority is not limited to the adoption of anti-avoidance rules, but rather permits the Secretary to ensure that the application of section 956 is consistent with the "purposes of this section"—chief among them, to ensure symmetry between the treatment of actual dividends and payments which are "substantially the equivalent of a dividend." S. Rep. No. 1881 at 88 (1962). Consistent with this understanding, the Department of Treasury (the "Treasury Department") and the IRS have exercised this regulatory authority to tailor the application of section 956 to the abuse that motivated its adoption, ensuring that the provision applies to the transactions Congress sought to tax, but does not extend to transactions the taxation of which would be inconsistent with the purpose of section 956.[1] For example, in 1964, shortly after section 956 was first enacted, the Treasury Department and the IRS issued regulations containing Treas. Reg. section 1.956-2(d)(2)(ii), providing that any debt collected within one year from the time incurred did not constitute an obligation that could be United States property. *See* T.D. 6704, 29 Fed. Reg. 2599, 2603. This short-term loan exception was removed when the Treasury Department and the IRS issued regulations in 1988 regarding the treatment of factoring receivables as United States property. *See* T.D. 8209, 53 Fed. Reg. 22163, 22169. A one-year debt exception would have been inconsistent with Congress's expansion of section 956 in 1984 to reach factoring receivables, which are often outstanding for less than one year.

---

[1] In addition to authorizing regulations by the Treasury Department and the IRS, Congress has acted on occasion to both expand and contract the scope of section 956 based on an evolving understanding of the potential means by which taxpayers could achieve the abusive results that gave rise to its enactment (that is, the tax-free effective repatriation of earnings through transactions that are economically equivalent to a taxable dividend). Thus, for example, Congress contracted the scope of section 956 in 1976, exempting investments in the stock of unrelated (tested using a 25 percent ownership threshold) U.S. corporations from the definition of United States property. *See* Pub. L. No. 94-455, sec. 1021, 90 Stat. 1520. Conversely, Congress expanded the scope of section 956 in the Deficit Reduction Act of 1984, Pub. L. No. 98-369, sec. 123(b), 98 Stat. 494, by adding certain factoring receivables as a type of United States property because it recognized that certain "corporations based in the United States are using foreign subsidiaries to factor receivables as a device for repatriating foreign earnings tax-free." H.R. Rep. No. 98-432 at 1305 (1984).

Alongside the removal of the 1964 short-term loan exception in the 1988 regulations, the Treasury Department and the IRS issued Notice 88-108, 1988-2 C.B. 466, which indicated that regulations would be issued providing a narrower exception from the definition of obligation for purposes of section 956 for obligations collected within 30 days from the time incurred (the "30-day rule"). However, the notice provided that the exception would not apply to a CFC that holds for 60 or more calendar days during the taxable year obligations which, without regard to the 30-day rule, would constitute United States property. The 30-day rule was expanded to 60 days in order to facilitate the flow of funds from foreign subsidiaries during a financial crisis beginning in 2008, which expansion was also extended to 2009 and 2010. *See* Notice 2008-91, 2008-43 I.R.B. 1001; Notice 2009-10, 2009-5 I.R.B. 419; Notice 2010-12, 2010-4 I.R.B. 326. The 30 day rule was ultimately adopted in final regulations issued on July 12, 2018, as Treas. Reg. section 1.956-2(d)(2)(iv). *See* T.D. 9834, 83 Fed. Reg. 32524, 32537-38.

Since 1964, Congress has modified section 956 several times without addressing Treasury's short-term debt exception; indeed, since then Congress adopted section 956(e) as a positive grant of regulatory authority in 1993, and explicitly validated the short-term debt exception in its legislative history. *See* H.R. Rep. 103-111 at 701 (1993) ("The bill is not intended to change the measurement of U.S. property that may apply, for example, in the case of certain short-term obligations, as provided in IRS Notice 88-108 (1988-2 C.B. 445), interpreting present law.").

Conversely, the Treasury Department and the IRS have at times expanded the scope of section 956 by regulation to ensure that the provision reaches the type of transactions intended by Congress. *See, e.g.*, T.D. 9402, 73 Fed. Reg. 35580, 35582 (adding rules modifying the basis of property transferred to a CFC in certain nonrecognition transactions solely for the purposes of section 956 and providing that "[t]he purpose of this [rule] is to prevent the effective repatriation of earnings and profits of a controlled foreign corporation that acquires United States property in connection with an exchange to which this [rule] applies without a corresponding income inclusion under section 951(a)(1)(B) by claiming a basis in the United States property less than the amount of earnings and profits effectively repatriated"). *See also* T.D. 9834, 83 Fed. Reg. 32524.

II. *Adoption of Participation Exemption System*

On December 22, 2017, Congress enacted the Tax Cuts and Jobs Act, P.L. 115-97 (the "Act"), which established a participation exemption system for the taxation of certain foreign income. Under section 245A(a), in the case of any dividend received from a specified 10-percent owned foreign corporation by a domestic corporation which is a U.S. shareholder with respect to such foreign corporation, there is allowed as a deduction an amount equal to the foreign-source portion of such dividend. A specified 10-percent owned foreign corporation is defined in section 245A(b) as any foreign corporation (other than certain passive foreign investment companies) with respect to which a domestic corporation is a U.S. shareholder. Section 245A(g) grants the Secretary authority to prescribe such regulations or other guidance as may be necessary or appropriate to carry out the provisions of section 245A, including regulations for the treatment of U.S. shareholders owning stock of a specified 10-percent owned foreign corporation through a partnership.

Under section 246(c)(1) and (5), a domestic corporation that is a U.S. shareholder is not permitted a section 245A deduction in respect of any dividend on any share of stock of a specified 10-percent owned foreign corporation that the domestic corporation holds for 365 days or less during the 731-day period beginning on the date that is 365 days before the date on which the share becomes ex-dividend with respect to the dividend. Under section 246(c)(1)(B), a section 245A deduction is also not allowed to the extent the domestic corporation is under an obligation to make related payments with respect to positions in substantially similar or related property.

Explanation of Provisions

The Treasury Department and the IRS have determined that as a result of the enactment of the participation exemption system, the current broad application of section 956 to corporate U.S. shareholders would be inconsistent with the purposes of section 956 and the scope of transactions it is intended to address. Congress determined that certain investments by a CFC of its earnings in United States property are "substantially the equivalent of a dividend" and enacted section 956 to provide similar treatment for dividends and certain investments in United States property constituting effective repatriations. S. Rep. No. 1881 at 88. Before the Act, section 956 applied appropriately to domestic corporations because both dividends from, and investments in United States property by, CFCs were included in income by such domestic corporations. As noted, the purpose of section 956 is generally to create symmetry between the taxation of actual repatriations and the taxation of effective repatriations, by subjecting effective repatriations to tax in the same manner as actual repatriations. Under the participation exemption system, however, earnings of a CFC that are repatriated to a corporate U.S. shareholder as a dividend are typically effectively exempt from tax because the shareholder is generally afforded an equal and offsetting dividends received deduction under section 245A. A section 956 inclusion of a corporate U.S. shareholder, on the other hand, is not eligible for the dividends received deduction under section 245A (because it is not a dividend). As a result, the application of section 956 after the Act to corporate U.S. shareholders of CFCs that would qualify for section 245A deductions would result in disparate treatment of actual dividends and amounts "substantially the equivalent of a dividend"—a result directly at odds with the manifest purpose of section 956.

Accordingly, the proposed regulations continue the Treasury Department and the IRS's longstanding practice of conforming the application of section 956 to its purpose. The proposed regulations exclude corporate U.S. shareholders from the application of section 956 to the extent necessary to maintain symmetry between the taxation of actual repatriations and the taxation of effective repatriations. In general, under section 245A and the proposed regulations, respectively, neither an actual dividend to a corporate U.S. shareholder, nor such a shareholder's amount determined under section 956, will result in additional U.S. tax.

To achieve this result, the proposed regulations provide that the amount otherwise determined under section 956 with respect to a U.S. shareholder for a taxable year of a CFC is reduced to the extent that the U.S. shareholder would be allowed a deduction under section 245A if the U.S. shareholder had received a distribution from the CFC in an amount equal to the amount otherwise determined under section 956. The proposed regulations provide special rules with respect to indirect ownership. Due to the broad applicability of section 245A, in many cases a corporate U.S. shareholder will not have a section 956 inclusion as a result of a CFC holding U.S. property under the proposed regulations.

Section 956 will continue to apply without modification to U.S. shareholders other than corporate U.S. shareholders, such as individuals, to ensure that, consistent with the purposes of section 956, amounts that are substantially the equivalent of a dividend will be treated similarly to actual dividends. This treatment will apply to individuals regardless of whether they make an election under section 962. Because individuals are not eligible for a dividends received deduction under section 245A even if they make an election under section 962, the current application of section 956 to individuals is still necessary to ensure substantial equivalence between an actual repatriation and a deemed repatriation. Similarly, section 956 will continue to apply without reduction to regulated investment companies and real estate investment trusts because they are not allowed the dividends received deduction under section 245A. *See* sections 852(b)(2)(C) and 857(b)(2)(A).

In addition to carrying out the purposes of section 956, the proposed regulations would significantly reduce complexity, costs, and compliance burdens for corporate U.S. shareholders of CFCs. Absent the proposed regulations, corporate U.S. shareholders would need to continue to carefully monitor the application of section 956 to their operations, including provisions related to loans, guarantees, and pledges, to ensure that earnings were repatriated only through actual dividends, and therefore allowed a participation exemption, rather than through a deemed repatriation under section 956 subject to additional U.S. tax. Similarly, in the absence of the proposed regulations, a U.S.-parented group in many cases would need to engage in complex and costly restructuring upon the acquisition of a foreign corporation that owns domestic subsidiaries (since the foreign corporation becomes a CFC and the stock of its domestic subsidiaries represents United States property) solely to avoid a section 956 inclusion. Absent the proposed regulations, section 956 could also serve as a "trap for the unwary" for domestic corporations that fail to recognize that, even though they are entitled to the deduction under section 245A for actual dividends, their section 956 inclusions would continue to be fully subject to U.S. tax.

The proposed regulations also add, in proposed § 1.956-1(g)(5), the effective date for § 1.956-1(e)(6) that was inadvertently deleted in TD 9792, published in the **Federal Register** on November 3, 2016 (81 FR 76497, as corrected at 81 FR 95470 and 95471).

Conforming Amendments

The Treasury Department and the IRS intend to make conforming amendments to the examples throughout the regulations under section 956 upon finalization of the proposed regulations.

Applicability Date

These changes are proposed to apply to taxable years of a CFC beginning on or after the date of publication of the Treasury decision adopting these rules as final regulations in the **Federal Register** (the "finalization date"), and to taxable years of a U.S. shareholder in which or with which such taxable years of the CFC end. With respect to taxable years of a CFC beginning before the finalization date, a taxpayer may rely on the proposed regulations for taxable years of a CFC beginning after December 31, 2017, and for taxable years of a U.S. shareholder in which or with which such taxable years of the CFC end, provided that the taxpayer and United States persons that are related (within the meaning of section 267 or 707) to the taxpayer consistently apply the proposed regulations with respect to all CFCs in which they are U.S. shareholders.

Special Analyses

The Administrator of the Office of Information and Regulatory Affairs (OIRA), Office of Management and Budget, has waived review of this proposed rule in accordance with section 6(a)(3)(A) of Executive Order 12866. OIRA will subsequently make a significance determination of the final rule, pursuant to section 3(f) of Executive Order (E.O.) 12866 and the April 11, 2018, Memorandum of Agreement between the Department of Treasury and the Office of Management and Budget (OMB).

Pursuant to the Regulatory Flexibility Act (5 U.S.C. chapter 6), it is hereby certified that this regulation, if adopted, will not have a significant economic impact on a substantial number of small entities, although some small entities that are domestic corporations could be affected by the regulation and comments are requested on the application of the regulation to domestic partnerships. However, even if a substantial number of small entities were to be affected by this regulation, the Treasury Department and the IRS estimate that the economic impact on such small entities would not be significant as the regulation is expected to marginally reduce compliance costs for smaller entities.

This is because the Treasury Department and the IRS believe that the cost-saving benefits of the proposed regulations with respect to complex third-party borrowing arrangements, internal financial management structures, and restructurings of worldwide operations will generally be available only to large U.S. multinational corporations with 20 or more CFCs. The Treasury Department and the IRS believe that U.S. multinational corporations with less than 20 CFCs generally will not have the types of arrangements in place that would otherwise need to be structured and monitored to avoid section 956. The proposed regulations, if adopted, generally will not affect small entities that are not domestic corporations. The Treasury Department and the IRS invite comments on the impact of this rule on small entities.

Pursuant to section 7805(f), this notice of proposed rulemaking has been submitted to the Chief Counsel for Advocacy of the Small Business Administration for comment on its impact on small businesses.

Comments and Requests for Public Hearing

Before these proposed regulations are adopted as final regulations, consideration will be given to any comments that are submitted timely to the IRS as prescribed in this preamble under the "Addresses" heading. The Treasury Department and the IRS request comments on all aspects of the proposed rules. In particular, comments are requested as to the appropriate application of the proposed regulations to U.S. shareholders that are domestic partnerships, which may have partners that are a combination of domestic corporations, U.S. individuals, or other persons. For example, one approach could be to reduce the amount otherwise determined under section 956 with respect to a domestic partnership to the extent that a domestic corporate partner would be entitled to a section 245A deduction if the partnership received the amount as a distribution. An alternative could be to determine a domestic partnership's section 956 amount and section 956 inclusion without regard to the status of its partners, but then provide that a corporate U.S. shareholder partner's distributive share of the section 956 inclusion is not taxable. Comments are also requested with respect to the maintenance of previously taxed earnings and profits accounts under section 959 and basis adjustments under section 961. Additionally, comments are requested on the interaction between the proposed regulations and section 245A(e). All comments will be available at *http://www.regulations.gov* or upon request.

A public hearing will be scheduled if requested in writing by any person that timely submits written comments. If a public hearing is scheduled, notice of the date, time, and place for the public hearing will be published in the **Federal Register**.

Drafting Information

The principal author of these proposed regulations is Joshua G. Rabon, formerly of the Office of Associate Chief Counsel (International). However, other personnel from the Treasury Department and the IRS participated in their development.

[¶49,776] Proposed Amendments of Regulations (REG-103163-18), published in the Federal Register on November 7, 2018.

[Code Sec. 846]

Insurance companies: Discounting rules: Unpaid losses.—Amendments of Reg. §§1.846-0, 1.846-1, 1.846-2, 1.846-2T, 1.846-3, 1.846-4 and 1.846-4T, providing guidance on new discounting rules for unpaid losses and estimated salvage recoverable of insurance companies for Federal income tax purposes, are proposed.

AGENCY: Internal Revenue Service (IRS), Treasury.

ACTION: Notice of proposed rulemaking; notice of public hearing.

SUMMARY: This document contains proposed regulations providing guidance on new discounting rules for unpaid losses and estimated salvage recoverable of insurance companies for Federal income tax purposes. The proposed regulations implement recent legislative changes to the Internal Revenue Code (Code) and make other technical improvements to the derivation and use of discount factors. The proposed regulations affect entities taxable as insurance companies. This document invites comments and provides notice of a public hearing on these proposed regulations. DATES: Written or electronic comments must be received by December 7, 2018. Requests to speak and outlines of topics to be discussed at the public hearing scheduled for December 20, 2018, at 10 a.m., must be received by December 7, 2018.

ADDRESSES: *Comments:* Send submissions to: CC:PA:LPD:PR (REG-103163-18), Room 5203, Internal Revenue Service, P.O. Box 7604, Ben Franklin Station, Washington, DC 20044. Submissions may be hand-delivered Monday through Friday between the hours of 8 a.m. and 4 p.m. to CC:PA:LPD:PR (REG-103163-18), Courier's Desk, Internal Revenue Service, 1111 Constitution Avenue, NW., Washington, DC 20224, or sent electronically via the Federal eRulemaking Portal at *http://www.regulations.gov* (REG-103163-18).

Public hearing: The public hearing will be held in the IRS Auditorium, Internal Revenue Service, 1111 Constitution Avenue, NW, Washington, DC 20224.

FOR FURTHER INFORMATION CONTACT: Concerning the proposed regulations, Kathryn M. Sneade, (202) 317-6995; concerning submissions of comments and requests to speak at the public hearing, Regina L. Johnson, (202) 317-6901 (not toll-free numbers).

SUPPLEMENTARY INFORMATION:

Background

This document contains proposed amendments to 26 CFR part 1 under section 846 of the Code. Section 846 was added to the Code by section 1023(c) of the Tax Reform Act of 1986, Public Law 99-514 (100 Stat. 2085, 2399). Final regulations under section 846 were published in the **Federal Register** (57 FR 40841) on September 8, 1992 (T.D. 8433). See §§1.846-0 through 1.846-4 (1992 Final Regulations).

This document provides guidance on discounting rules under section 846 of the Code, which were amended on December 22, 2017 by section 13523 of "An Act to provide for reconciliation pursuant to titles II and V of the concurrent resolution on the budget for fiscal year 2018," Public Law 115-97, title 1, 131 Stat. 2152 (2017) (TCJA) for taxable years beginning after December 31, 2017. The discounting rules of section 846, both prior to and after amendment by the TCJA, are used to determine discounted unpaid losses and estimated salvage recoverable of property and casualty insurance companies and discounted unearned premiums of title insurance companies for Federal income tax purposes under section 832, as well as discounted unpaid losses of life insurance companies for Federal income tax purposes under sections 805(a)(1) and 807(c)(2). These rules are discussed in greater detail in parts A and B of this Background section.

Section 13523(a) of the TCJA amended section 846(c) to provide a new definition of the "annual rate" to be used by taxpayers for discounting purposes. Section 13523(b) of the TCJA amended the computational rules for determining loss payment patterns under section 846(d). Section 13523(c) of the TCJA repealed the election under former section 846(e) to use the taxpayer's own historical loss payment pattern instead of the pattern published by the Secretary. These changes are effective for taxable years beginning after December 31, 2017. The proposed regulations implement these changes in the law.

Part C of this Background section discusses smoothing adjustments, and part C of the Explanation of Provisions section of this preamble describes a proposed regulation authorizing the Secretary to adopt a methodology to smooth the loss payment patterns derived from the annual statement loss payment data to avoid negative payment amounts and to otherwise produce a stable pattern of positive discount factors less than one. Part A of the Other Discounting Considerations section of this preamble provides additional detail on the proposed methodology that the Department of the Treasury (Treasury Department) and the IRS anticipate developing under the authority provided in this proposed regulation. The Treasury Department and the IRS intend to describe the methodology used under the rules set forth in the proposed regulations in each revenue procedure that publishes discount factors for a determination year.

Part D of this Background section describes the existing procedures for discounting unpaid losses with respect to accident years not separately reported on the National Association of Insurance Commissioners' (NAIC) annual statement, including the method described in section V of Notice 88-100, 1988-2 C.B. 439 (composite method). Part B of the Other Discounting Considerations section of this preamble describes proposed new procedures for discounting such unpaid losses. These procedures would simplify the discounting of unpaid losses by eliminating the need for a second set of discount factors to be used with respect to accident years not separately reported on the NAIC annual statement.

Part C of the Other Discounting Considerations section of this preamble describes an approach that the Secretary intends to adopt for discounting estimated salvage recoverable by applying the unpaid loss discount factors in each line of business to the estimated salvage recoverable in that line of business.

A. *Discounted Unpaid Losses, Estimated Salvage Recoverable, and Discounted Unearned Premiums*

Under section 832, the taxable income of a property and casualty insurance company (non-life insurance company), including a title insurance company, is the sum of its underwriting income and investment income (as well as gains and other income items), reduced by allowable deductions. Under section 832(b)(3), a non-life insurance company's "losses incurred" is a component of the company's underwriting income. Under section 832(b)(5)(A), the change over a taxable year in the company's "discounted unpaid losses" (as defined in section 846) is a component of its losses incurred for the taxable year. Discounting of unpaid losses is required to take into account the time value of money. See H. Rept. 115-466, at 470 (2017) (Conf. Rep.). Under section 832(b)(3), (4), and (8), a title insurance company's "discounted unearned premiums" is a component of the company's underwriting income. Under section 832(b)(8), a title insurance company must discount its unearned premiums by using the applicable interest rate and the applicable statutory premium recognition pattern. The applicable interest rate for purposes of section 832(b)(8) is the annual rate determined under section 846(c)(2).

Section 832(b)(5)(A) also requires that the change in discounted estimated salvage recoverable be taken into account in computing the losses incurred component of underwriting income. Under section 832(b)(5)(A), the amount of discounted estimated salvage recoverable is determined in accordance with procedures established by the Secretary. Section 1.832-4(c) provides that, except as otherwise provided in guidance published by the Commissioner in the Internal Revenue Bulletin, estimated salvage recoverable must be discounted either (1) by using the applicable discount factors published by the Commissioner for estimated salvage recoverable; or (2) by using the loss payment pattern for a line of business as the salvage recovery pattern for that line of business and by using the applicable interest rate for calculating unpaid losses under section 846(c). In prior years, guidance published by the Commissioner in the Internal Revenue Bulletin has always directed taxpayers to discount estimated salvage recoverable for each line of business using the applicable discount factors published by the Commissioner for estimated salvage recoverable and has not allowed the use of the second option provided for by regulations. These discount factors were determined using the salvage recovery pattern for the line of business and the applicable interest rate for calculating unpaid losses under section 846. See, e.g., Rev. Proc. 2018-13, 2018-7 I.R.B. 356, and Rev. Proc. 2016-59, 2016-51 I.R.B. 849.

The section 846 discounting rules are also relevant for life insurance companies. Section 807(c) provides that, for life insurance companies, the amount of unpaid losses (other than losses on life insurance contracts) is the amount of discounted unpaid losses as defined in section 846 for purposes of both sections 805(a)(1) and 807(c)(2). Section 805(a)(1) provides life insurance companies with a deduction for losses incurred during the taxable year on insurance and annuity contracts. Section 807(c)(2) provides that unpaid losses included in total reserves under section 816(c)(2) are taken into account under section 807(a) and (b) by a life insurance company. In general, section 807(a) provides that a decrease in discounted unpaid losses over the taxable year is included in life insurance company gross income under section 803(a)(2), while section 807(b) provides that an increase in discounted unpaid losses over the taxable year is deductible under section 805(a)(2).

B. *Discounting Rules for Unpaid Losses*

Section 846(a)(1) provides that the amount of discounted unpaid losses as of the end of any taxable year is the sum of the discounted unpaid losses, as of such time, separately computed with respect to unpaid losses in each line of business for each accident year. The amount of discounted unpaid losses in a line of business that is attributable to a specified accident year is calculated by multiplying that accident year's undiscounted unpaid losses at the end of each taxable year by a published discount factor associated with that line of business, accident year, and taxable year. Discount factors are published annually by the IRS. See, e.g., Rev. Proc. 2018-13 and Rev. Proc. 2016-58, 2016-51 I.R.B. 839. These discount factors are derived using the applicable loss payment pattern, determined under section 846(d) using aggregate industry loss payment data, and the applicable interest rate determined by the Secretary under section 846(c).

1. Modification of the Applicable Rate of Interest Used to Discount Unpaid Losses

The "applicable interest rate" used to determine the discount factors associated with any accident year and line of business is the "annual rate" determined under section 846(c)(2).

Before amendment by section 13523(a) of the TCJA, section 846(c)(2) provided that the annual rate for any calendar year was a rate equal to the average of the applicable Federal mid-term rates (as defined in section 1274(d) but based on annual compounding) effective as of the beginning of each of the calendar months in the most recent 60-month period ending before the beginning of the calendar year for which the determination is made. The applicable Federal mid-term rate is determined by the Secretary based on the average market yield on outstanding marketable obligations of the United States with remaining periods of over three years but not over nine years. See section 1274(d)(1).

As amended by section 13523(a) of the TCJA, section 846(c)(2) provides that the annual rate for any calendar year will be determined by the Secretary based on the corporate bond yield curve (as defined in section 430(h)(2)(D)(i), determined by substituting "60-month period" for "24-month period" therein). Section 430, which relates to minimum funding standards for single-employer defined benefit pension plans, includes other rules for determining an "effective interest rate," such as segment rate rules. The term "effective interest rate" along with these other rules, including the segment rate rules, do not apply for purposes of property and casualty insurance reserve discounting. See H. Rept. 115-466, at 471, fn. 979. The corporate bond yield curve is published on a monthly basis by the Treasury Department and consists of spot interest rates for each stated time to maturity. See, e.g., Notice 2018-60, 2018-31 I.R.B. 275. The spot rate for a given time to maturity represents the yield on a bond that gives a single payment at that maturity. For the stated yield curve, times to maturity are specified at half-year intervals from 0.5 year through 100 years. Section 846(c)(2) does not specify how the Secretary is to determine the annual rate for any calendar year based on the corporate bond yield curve.

2. Modification of Computational Rules for Loss Payment Patterns

Under section 846(d)(1), the Secretary determines a loss payment pattern for each line of business by reference to the historical aggregate loss payment data applicable to that line of business for each determination year. Under section 846(d)(4), the determination year is the calendar year 1987 and each fifth calendar year thereafter. Any loss payment pattern determined by the Secretary applies to the accident year ending with the determination year and to each of the four succeeding accident years. Section 846(d)(2)(A) and (B) provide that the determination of a loss payment pattern for any determination year is made using the aggregate experience reported on the annual statements of insurance companies on the basis of the most recent published aggregate data relating to loss payments available on the first day of the determination year. For instance, the payment data used to determine the loss payment patterns for 2017 (the most recent determination year) were reported on annual statements filed for the year 2015.

The loss payment pattern for each line of business is determined in accordance with the computational rules of section 846(d)(3). These rules determine different loss payment patterns for "long-tail" lines of business (any line of business reported in the schedule or schedules of the annual statement relating to auto liability, other liability, medical malpractice, workers' compensation, and multiple peril lines) and "short-tail" lines of business (all lines of business other than long-tail lines of business).

For short-tail lines of business, section 846(d)(3) provides that losses unpaid at the end of the first year following the accident year are treated as paid equally in the second and third years following the accident year. For long-tail lines of business, section 846(d)(3) provides that unpaid losses remaining after ten years are treated as paid in the tenth year following the accident year, except as otherwise provided in that section.

Before amendment by section 13523(b) of the TCJA, section 846(d)(3) provided for the extension of the ten-year payment period specified for long-tail lines by not more than five years provided certain conditions were met.

As amended by section 13523(b) of the TCJA, section 846(d)(3) provides for the extension of the ten-year payment period for a maximum of fourteen additional years if the amount of losses that would have been treated as paid in the tenth year after the accident year exceeds the average of the loss payments treated as paid in the seventh, eighth, and ninth years after the accident year. In that case, the amount of losses that would have been treated as paid in the tenth year after the accident year are treated as paid in such tenth year and each subsequent year in an amount equal to the average of the loss payments treated as paid in the seventh, eighth, and ninth years after the accident year (or, if less, the portion of the unpaid losses not previously taken into account). To the extent such unpaid losses have not been treated as paid before the twenty-fourth year after the accident year, they are to be treated as paid in such twenty-fourth year.

In addition to extending the ten-year payment period, section 13523(b) of the TCJA repealed section 846(d)(3)(E) through (G). Former section 846(d)(3)(G) is discussed in part C of this Background section. Former section 846(d)(3)(F) provided for the Secretary to make appropriate adjustments if annual statement data with respect to payment of losses was available for longer periods after the accident year than the periods assumed under section 846(d). The annual statement requires the reporting of ten years of loss payment data for the international line of business and the three lines of business for non-proportional reinsurance, as it does for long-tail lines of business. Losses from proportional reinsurance are reported in the annual statement schedules related to the underlying line of business, which may be short-tail or long-tail. Under section 846(d)(3), proportional reinsurance unpaid losses are discounted using the discount factors published for the underlying line of business. Former section 846(d)(3)(E) provided special rules for determining loss payment patterns for the international line of business and for reinsurance lines of business based on the combined losses for all long-tail lines of business and provided explicit authority to the Secretary to override these special rules.

The repeal of section 846(d)(3)(E) and (F) means that the statute no longer explicitly provides for the determination of loss payment patterns for non-proportional reinsurance and international lines of business extending beyond three calendar years following the accident year. Non-proportional reinsurance and international lines of business are not included in the list of long-tail lines set forth in section 846(d)(3)(A)(ii). The Treasury Department and the IRS request comments regarding the length of the loss payment patterns for non-proportional reinsurance and international lines of business to be determined under section 846, as amended, and the legal basis for limiting the loss payment patterns for these lines of business to three calendar years following the accident year or extending the loss payment patterns beyond those years.

Section 846(f) (as redesignated by section 13523(c) of the TCJA) provides the Secretary with authority to prescribe such regulations as may be necessary or appropriate to carry out the purposes of section 846, including an explicit grant of authority to prescribe regulations for providing proper treatment of allocated reinsurance. The 1992 Final Regulations provide special rules for the determination of discount factors for proportional and non-proportional reinsurance lines of business and the international line of business. Section 1.846-1(b)(3) of the 1992 Final Regulations provides rules for the determination of discount factors for reinsurance lines of business. Section 1.846-1(b)(3)(i) provides that, with respect to proportional reinsurance lines of business (for accident years after 1987), unpaid losses are discounted using discount factors applicable to the line of business to which those unpaid losses are allocated as required on the annual statement. Section 1.846-1(b)(3)(ii)(A) provides that unpaid losses for non-proportional reinsurance (for accident years after 1991) are discounted using the discount factors published by the IRS for the appropriate reinsurance line of business, subject to an exception set forth in § 1.846-1(b)(3)(iv) (if more than 90 percent of the unallocated losses of a taxpayer for an accident year relate to one underlying line of business, the taxpayer must discount all unallocated reinsurance unpaid losses attributable to that accident year using the discount factors published by the IRS for the underlying line of business). Section 1.846-1(b)(3)(ii)(B) provides rules for unpaid losses for non-proportional reinsurance for accident years 1988 through 1991, and § 1.846-1(b)(3)(iii) provides rules for certain reinsurance unpaid losses for accident years before 1988.

Section 1.846-1(b)(4) of the 1992 Final Regulations provides rules for the determination of discount factors for the international line of business. Section 1.846-1(b)(4) provides that unpaid losses attributable to the international line of business are discounted using the discount factors determined for a "composite" long-tail line of business, unless more than 90 percent of such losses for that accident year are related to a single line of business, in which case the international unpaid losses are discounted using that accident year's published discount factors for the underlying line of business.

3. Repeal of Historical Loss Payment Pattern Election

Before amendment by section 13523(c) of the TCJA, section 846(e) permitted a taxpayer to elect to use its own historical loss payment pattern with respect to all lines of business rather than the industry-wide loss payment pattern determined by the Secretary under section 846(d), provided that applicable requirements were met. Section 13523(c) of the TCJA repealed that election.

4. Transition Rule

The transition rule set forth in section 13523(e) of the TCJA provides that, for the first taxable year beginning after December 31, 2017, the unpaid losses and expenses unpaid (as defined in section 832(b)(5) and (6)) at the end of the preceding taxable year, and the unpaid losses (as defined in sections 805(a)(1) and 807(c)(2)) at the end of the preceding taxable year, are determined as if the amendments made by section 13523 of the TCJA had applied to such unpaid losses and expenses unpaid in the preceding taxable year and by using the interest rate and loss payment patterns applicable to accident years ending with calendar year 2018. Any adjustment resulting from this transition rule is taken into account ratably in such first taxable year and the seven succeeding taxable years. For subsequent taxable years, such amendments are applied with respect to unpaid losses and expenses unpaid for accident years ending with or before calendar year 2018 by using the interest rate and loss payment patterns applicable to accident years ending with calendar year 2018.

C. *Smoothing Adjustments*

As described in part B(2) of this Background section, section 846(d)(1) requires the Secretary to determine, for each determination year, a loss payment pattern for each line of business by reference to the historical aggregate loss payment data applicable to that line of business. The Secretary makes such determination using the aggregate experience reported on the annual statements of insurance companies on the basis of the most recent published aggregate data from such annual statements relating to loss payment patterns available on the first day of the determination year. Because historical loss payment patterns change from accident year to accident year, the annual payment amounts determined on the basis of data taken from a single year's annual statements are not always non-negative and may vary significantly from year to year. Accordingly, use of the annual statement payment data to determine the loss payment pattern without any adjustment to compensate for changes from year to year may produce discount factors that vary widely from one year to the next or discount factors for a particular year or years that are negative or greater than one. See Rev. Proc. 2003-17, 2003-1 C.B. 427.

Former section 846(d)(3)(G), prior to its repeal by section 13523 of the TCJA, provided guidance on one aspect of smoothing. Former section 846(d)(3)(G) provided that, if the amount of losses treated as paid in the ninth year after the accident was negative or zero, the average of the losses treated as paid in the seventh, eighth, and ninth years after the accident year would be used instead to determine the amount of losses treated as paid in the following years. Section 846(d)(3)(B)(ii)(II), as amended by section 13523(b) of the TCJA, provides that the average of the loss payments treated as paid in the seventh, eighth, and ninth years after the accident year is used to determine the amount of losses treated as paid in the following years. Section 846, as amended, provides no additional specific guidance regarding smoothing of the loss payment patterns.

In section 2.03(4) of Rev. Proc. 2003-17 and section 3.04 of Rev. Proc. 2007-9, 2007-3 I.R.B. 278, comments were requested as to whether a methodology should be adopted to smooth the annual statement payment data, and thus produce a more stable pattern of discount factors. The Treasury Department and the IRS received comments that agreed that such a methodology should be adopted and suggested specific methods that could be used.

D. *Composite Method*

Rules for discounting unpaid losses with respect to accident years not separately reported on the NAIC annual statement are described in section V of Notice 88-100 and in Rev. Proc. 2002-74, 2002–2 C.B. 980.

After the enactment of section 846 in 1986, the Treasury Department and the IRS published Notice 88-100 to provide guidance with respect to several issues that were expected to be addressed in then forthcoming regulations under section 846. Section V of Notice 88-100 stated that regulations under section 846 would provide that taxpayers may not use information that does not appear on their NAIC annual statements to allocate aggregate unpaid losses among several accident years, but rather must use a composite discount factor for such aggregated unpaid losses. The notice set forth a method for computing a composite discount factor to be used to compute discounted unpaid losses with respect to accident years not separately reported on the NAIC annual statement, referred to as the "composite method." The notice provided a simplified example to illustrate the operation of this method.

The 1992 Final Regulations provided guidance on several issues addressed in Notice 88-100, rendering portions of Notice 88-100 obsolete. However, the 1992 Final Regulations did not adopt the rule anticipated by section V of Notice 88-100 requiring that taxpayers use a composite discount factor for the aggregate unpaid losses from accident years not separately reported on the NAIC annual statement, and therefore section V of Notice 88-100 was not rendered obsolete.

The 1992 Final Regulations adopted a rule requiring taxpayers to use composite discount factors with respect to any line of business for which the IRS has not published discount factors. See §1.846-1(b)(1)(ii) and (5) of the 1992 Final Regulations. Composite discount factors determined on the basis of the appropriate composite loss payment pattern are published annually by the IRS for use with respect to such lines of business. However, these composite discount factors are unrelated to the composite discount factors of Notice 88-100 that relate to discounting unpaid losses from accident years not separately reported on the NAIC annual statement.

Section 3.01 of Rev. Proc. 2002-74 clarifies that the composite method described in section V of Notice 88-100 is permitted but not required to be used by insurance companies. Section 3.01 also provides that the Secretary will publish composite discount factors annually for use by taxpayers that have not elected under section 846(e) to use their historical loss payment patterns, and such factors have been published annually since 2002, along with the Secretary's tables containing the section 846 loss payment patterns and discount factors and the section 832 salvage discount factors. See, e.g., Rev. Proc. 2016-58. Section 3.02 of Rev. Proc. 2002-74 provides, in part, that taxpayers who do not use a composite method described in section 3.01 of Rev. Proc. 2002-74 should instead use the discount factors for the appropriate year in the Secretary's table for the appropriate line of business. Sections 3.01 and 3.02 of Rev. Proc. 2002-74 also provide instructions for taxpayers that have elected under section 846(e) to use their historical loss payment patterns. However, as discussed in part B(3) of this Background section, section 13523(c) of the TCJA repealed section 846(e).

Explanation of Provisions

A. Modification of the Applicable Rate of Interest Used to Discount Unpaid Losses

Proposed § 1.846-1(c) provides that the applicable interest rate is the annual rate determined by the Secretary for any calendar year on the basis of the corporate bond yield curve (as defined in section 430(h)(2)(D)(i), determined by substituting "60-month period" for "24-month period" therein). The annual rate for any calendar year is the average of the corporate bond yield curve's monthly spot rates with times to maturity of not more than seventeen and one-half years, computed using the most recent 60-month period ending before the beginning of the calendar year for which the determination is made.

Consistent with the text of section 846, as amended by the TCJA, and the statutory structure as a whole, the proposed regulations provide for the use of a single annual rate applicable to all lines of business as was the case under section 846 prior to amendment by the TCJA. Under section 846(c)(2) prior to amendment by section 13523(a) of the TCJA, a single annual rate was used for all lines of business, and the amendments made by the TCJA do not clearly indicate an intent to change from the historical practice of applying a single rate to all loss payment patterns. The change from using the average of the applicable Federal mid-term rates to the averaged corporate bond yield curve, however, indicates that the annual rate should be determined in a manner that more closely matches the investments in bonds used to fund the undiscounted losses to be incurred in the future by insurance companies.

An alternative approach would be the direct application of the corporate bond yield curve to the loss payment pattern for each line of business, which would result in a more accurate measure of the present value of the unpaid losses for each line of business. In light of the investment in corporate bonds to fund the unpaid losses to be paid in the future, the result is a more accurate reflection of the time value of money in the measure of income. Using this approach, for each taxable year, each future loss payment incurred in a line of business for an accident year (as determined by the loss payment pattern determined for that line of business) would be discounted using the spot rate from the corporate bond yield curve with a time to maturity that matches the time between the end of the accident year and the middle of the year of the loss payment.

Although the proposed regulations do not adopt this approach in light of the text of section 846 and the statutory structure as a whole, the maturity range used to determine the single rate applicable to all unpaid losses for all lines of business (times to maturity of not more than seventeen and one-half years) was selected to minimize the differences in taxable income, in the aggregate, resulting from the use of a single discount rate for a given accident year versus the direct application of the corporate bond yield curve for that accident year. For this purpose, losses incurred for the accident year were assumed to be those reported for 2015, and loss payments for each line of business were assumed to follow the loss payment pattern for that line of business determined using aggregate data reported on annual statements filed for 2015. Each maturity range considered had a half-year time to maturity as a lower bound, but had a different upper bound. Discount factors for all lines of business were calculated using the loss payment patterns and the discount rate applicable to the 2018 accident year, and a different discount rate was used for each maturity range being considered. For each maturity range, discounted unpaid losses and taxable income effects were computed for each line of business for the accident year and for each following taxable year. A present value of the taxable income effects for each line of business was calculated and subtracted from the present value of the taxable income effects calculated for that line of business using a direct application of the applicable corporate bond yield curve. Each present-value difference was expressed as a positive number, and these amounts were summed over all lines of business. The selected maturity range was the one that generated the smallest sum of present-value differences in taxable income effects.

In addition to the approach underlying the proposed regulations, the Treasury Department and the IRS considered a number of other options for determining the annual rate on the basis of the corporate bond yield curve. The Treasury Department and the IRS considered other ranges of maturities that could be used to determine a single annual rate applicable to all lines of business, such as the range of maturities used to determine the applicable Federal mid-term rate (over three years but not over nine years), as well as different maturity ranges of the same width (five and one-half years). The Treasury Department and the IRS also considered the use of a variable maturity range.

Under a variable maturity range approach, the annual rate for any calendar year would be the average of the corporate bond yield curve's monthly spot rates with times to maturity contained within the range that would minimize, for that calendar year, the sum of differences in taxable income effects, selected in the same fashion as was the range adopted in the proposed regulations. Additionally, the Treasury Department and the IRS also considered (1) the use of two rates, one for long-tail lines of business, and one for short-tail lines of business; (2) the use of a different annual rate for each line of business; and (3) the direct application of the corporate bond yield curve.

The Treasury Department and the IRS request comments on the method of determining the annual rate on the basis of the corporate bond yield curve, including comments on whether a different option than the one incorporated in the proposed regulations should be adopted in the final regulations and, if so, the legal basis for that alternative option and explanation of how that option would more clearly reflect income.

B. *Proposed Removal of Regulations*

The proposed regulations propose to remove §1.846-1(a)(2) of the 1992 Final Regulations because the examples are no longer relevant. The proposed regulations propose to remove §1.846-1(b)(3)(ii)(B) and (b)(3)(iii) of the 1992 Final Regulations because these provisions apply only to accident years before 1992. The proposed regulations propose to remove §1.846-1(b)(3)(iv) and (b)(4) of the 1992 Final Regulations because section 13523 of the TCJA repealed section 846(d)(3)(E). Section 1.846-1(b)(3)(i) and (b)(3)(ii)(A) of the 1992 Final Regulations are retained (with §1.846-1(b)(3)(ii)(A) being redesignated as §1.846-1(b)(3)(ii)) because these rules continue to provide for the proper treatment of reinsurance unpaid losses. The proposed regulations also propose to make conforming changes to §1.846-1(a) and (b) of the 1992 Final Regulations to reflect the removal of various §1.846-1 provisions, as well as the removal of §§1.846-2 and 1.846-3 of the 1992 Final Regulations.

Section 13523 of the TCJA repealed the section 846(e) election permitting a taxpayer to use its own historical loss payment pattern with respect to all lines of business rather than the industry-wide loss payment pattern determined by the Secretary under section 846(d), provided that applicable requirements were met. Section 1.846-2 of the 1992 Final Regulations, which provides rules for applying the section 846(e) election, is proposed to be removed.

Section 1.846-3 of the 1992 Final Regulations provides "fresh start" and reserve strengthening rules applicable to the last taxable year beginning before January 1, 1987, and the first taxable year beginning after December 31, 1986. Because the rules in §1.846-3 are no longer applicable, §1.846-3 is proposed to be removed.

Section 1.846-4 of the 1992 Final Regulations provides applicability dates for §§1.846-1 through 1.846-3 of the 1992 Final Regulations. Under §1.846-4(a), §1.846-1 applies to taxable years beginning after December 31, 1986. Because §§1.846-2 and 1.846-3 are proposed to be removed, a separate applicability date section for §1.846-1 is no longer needed, and, therefore, §1.846-4 is proposed to be removed. The applicability dates for §1.846-1 are proposed to be included in proposed §1.846-1(e), including the original applicability date for those portions of §1.846-1 that are not proposed to be revised.

Section 1.846-0 of the 1992 Final Regulations, which provides a list of the headings in §§1.846-1 through 1.846-4 of the 1992 Final Regulations, is proposed to be removed.

On April 10, 2006, the Treasury Department and the IRS published in the **Federal Register** (71 FR 17990) a Treasury decision (T.D. 9257) containing §§1.846-2T and 1.846-4T. On January 23, 2008, the Treasury Department and the IRS published in the **Federal Register** (73 FR 3868) a Treasury decision (T.D. 9377) that finalized the rules contained in §1.846-2T in §1.846-2 and finalized the rules contained in §1.846-4T in §1.846-4. T.D. 9377, however, did not remove §§1.846-2T and 1.846-4T from the Code of Federal Regulations (CFR). Because these sections are obsolete, the Treasury Department and the IRS intend to remove §§1.846-2T and 1.846-4T from the CFR when the proposed regulations in this document are finalized.

C. *Smoothing Adjustments*

Section 846(d) instructs the Secretary to determine a loss payment pattern for each line of business for each determination year "by reference to" the historical loss payment pattern applicable to such line of business "on the basis of" the most recent published aggregate data from annual statements of insurance companies available on the first day of the determination year. Section 846 provides broad discretion to the Secretary to make needed adjustments when determining the loss payment patterns for each line of business. Use of loss payment patterns with negative payment amounts may produce discount factors that vary widely from year to year or discount factors that are negative or that exceed one. Commenters responding to prior requests for comments agreed that a methodology should be adopted to smooth the loss payment patterns. Proposed §1.846-1(d)(2) provides that the Secretary may, if necessary to avoid negative payment amounts and otherwise produce a stable pattern of positive discount factors less than one, adjust the loss payment pattern for any line of business using a methodology described by the Secretary in other published guidance.

Part A of the Other Discounting Considerations section of this preamble provides additional detail on the methodology that the Treasury Department and the IRS anticipate using to adjust loss payment patterns.

Proposed Applicability Dates

The rules in proposed § 1.846-1(c) and (d) are proposed to apply to taxable years beginning after December 31, 2017.

Other Discounting Considerations

A. *Smoothing Adjustments*

1. Proposed Methodology

The Treasury Department and the IRS intend to describe the adjustments made to the loss payment patterns produced using annual statement payment data and the methodology used to make such adjustments under the rule set forth in proposed § 1.846-1(d)(2) for each determination year in the revenue procedure publishing discount factors for that determination year. The methodology that the Treasury Department and the IRS anticipate using to make adjustments to loss payment patterns for lines of business described in section 846(d)(3)(A)(ii) is illustrated by the following computational steps.

Step 1. Compute the yearly payment amounts and cumulative payment amounts for the accident year and the nine years following the accident year using the most recent published aggregate data from annual statements relating to loss payment patterns available on the first day of the determination year. If any of the payment amounts for the seventh, eighth, or ninth year following the accident year are negative, or if the sum of these amounts is zero (and the cumulative payment amount for the ninth year following the accident year is not 1 (one)), go to Step 2 of this illustration. Otherwise, compute the average of the payment amounts for these three years for later reference in Step 3 and use in Step 7 of this illustration, and proceed to Step 3 of this illustration.

Step 2. Average the payments for the seventh, eighth, and ninth years after the accident year. If that average is non-positive, include in the average the payment for the immediate prior year (that is, the sixth year following the accident year). If the average payment is still non-positive, continue including payments (from the fifth, fourth, etc. years after the accident year) until a positive average is produced. When a positive average payment amount is achieved, assign this payment amount to all years for which payment amounts were included in the average, and recalculate the cumulative payments for those years.

Step 3. Identify the payment for the year immediately prior to the earliest year included in the average computed in Step 1 or Step 2 of this illustration. Call that year the "current year," and go to Step 4 of this illustration.

Step 4. If the payment for the current year is negative, go to Step 5 of this illustration. If it is non-negative, keep that payment amount for the current year, go to the next prior year, call it the "current year," and repeat this Step 4. Repeat until all payments are non-negative, then go to Step 7 of this illustration.

Step 5. If the payment amount for the current year is negative, average that amount with the payment amounts from an even number of adjacent years, before and after the current year. Choose the minimum number of adjacent years necessary to achieve a non-negative average payment amount. This average may include amounts that were the result of a previous averaging calculation, but may not include any payment amount for a year following the sixth year after the accident year. If including payments for all prior years in the average does not achieve a non-negative average, include as many additional payments from years following the current year as necessary to achieve a non-negative average. Assign the non-negative average payment amount to all years for which payment amounts were included in the calculation of the average, and recalculate the cumulative payments for those years.

Step 6. Identify the payment for the year immediately prior to the earliest year included in the average of Step 5 of this illustration. Call it the "current year," and go to Step 4 of this illustration.

Step 7. Apply the rules of section 846(d)(3)(B)(ii), using the average payment for the seventh, eighth, and ninth year after the accident year, to produce payment amounts for years following the ninth year after the accident year.

For example, using this methodology, if the tentative payment amount for the fifth year following the accident year is negative, that amount is averaged with the tentative payment amounts for the fourth and sixth years following the accident year. If that average is negative, the tentative payment amount for the third year following the accident year is included in the average. If that average is non-negative, it becomes the tentative payment amount for the third through sixth years following the accident year.

2. Comparison to Other Suggested Methods

The methods suggested by commenters responding to the requests for comments in Rev. Proc. 2003-17 and Rev. Proc. 2007-9 can be described in general terms as follows:

(1) Treat a negative estimated loss paid as zero.

(2) Average the negative estimated loss paid with estimated losses from other years to yield a positive result. For instance, commenters suggested two different methods for eliminating a negative estimated loss paid in the ninth year after the accident year: averaging the negative estimated loss with estimated losses from as many earlier years as needed to yield a positive result, and averaging the negative estimated loss with the estimated losses for all later years.

(3) Adjust the negative estimated loss paid to equal the lesser of the value for the next younger year and the amount that brings the cumulative losses paid to 100 percent.

(4) Adjust the negative estimated loss paid using a smoothing calculation that results in younger years having a lower "Estimated Cumulative Losses Paid" than more mature years.

(5) Adjust the negative estimated loss paid by ensuring the percent paid in any year is no higher than the year before.

The Treasury Department and the IRS considered the methods suggested by commenters responding to prior requests for comments, but anticipate using the proposed methodology to adjust loss payment patterns for several reasons. Among other things, the proposed methodology, to the extent possible, centers the average on the negative payment year and therefore should not display a bias towards increasing or decreasing discount factors. The proposed methodology ensures that the amount used to extend the loss payment pattern past the ninth year after the accident year is positive, and preserves the average for the seventh, eighth, and ninth years after the accident year when that average is initially positive.

B. *Discontinuance of Composite Method*

This document proposes to eliminate the need to determine a second set of discount factors to be used with respect to accident years not separately reported on the NAIC annual statement by providing that, effective for taxable years beginning on or after the date the proposed regulations are published as final regulations in the **Federal Register**, a taxpayer that has unpaid losses relating to an accident year not separately reported on the NAIC annual statement must compute discounted unpaid losses with respect to that year using the discount factor published by the Secretary for that year for the appropriate line of business.

The methods described in Rev. Proc. 2002-74, including the composite method described in section 3.01 of Rev. Proc. 2002-74 and section V of Notice 88-100, would not be permitted methods, effective for taxable years beginning on or after the date the proposed regulations are published as final regulations in the **Federal Register**. Section V of Notice 88-100 and Rev. Proc. 2002-74 would be obsolete for taxable years beginning on or after that date. The Treasury Department and the IRS anticipate providing rules applicable to taxpayers that seek to change a method of accounting to comply with these changes. The Treasury Department and the IRS anticipate that these rules will provide that a taxpayer seeking to change to the method of accounting prescribed must follow the applicable procedures for obtaining the Commissioner's automatic consent to a change in accounting method.

C. *Determination of Estimated Discounted Salvage Recoverable*

In prior years, guidance published by the Commissioner in the Internal Revenue Bulletin has directed taxpayers to discount estimated salvage recoverable for each line of business using the applicable discount factors published by the Commissioner for estimated salvage recoverable. See, e.g., Rev. Proc. 2018-13 and Rev. Proc. 2016-59. These discount factors were determined using the salvage recovery pattern for the line of business and the applicable interest rate for calculating unpaid losses under section 846. *Id.* The Treasury Department and the IRS anticipate providing in similar future guidance published in the Internal Revenue Bulletin that estimated salvage recoverable is to be discounted using the published discount factors applicable to unpaid losses. This treatment of estimated salvage recoverable is equivalent to netting undiscounted unpaid losses with estimates of salvage recoverable and discounting the net amount using the unpaid loss discount factors. This method is permitted under section 832(b)(5)(A) and § 1.832-4(c) and should reduce compliance complexity and costs. Separate discount factors for estimated salvage recoverable (including anticipated recoveries on account of subrogation claims) would no longer be published by the IRS. The Treasury Department and the IRS request comments on whether net payment data (loss payments less salvage recovered) and net losses incurred data (losses incurred less salvage recoverable) should be used to compute loss discount factors.

Effect on Other Documents

Section V of Notice 88-100 and Rev. Proc. 2002-74 are proposed to be obsolete for taxable years beginning on or after the date the proposed regulations are published as final regulations in the **Federal Register**.

Special Analyses

This regulation is not subject to review under section 6(b) of Executive Order 12866 pursuant to the Memorandum of Agreement (April 11, 2018) between the Treasury Department and the Office of Management and Budget regarding review of tax regulations. Because these regulations do not impose a collection of information on small entities, the Regulatory Flexibility Act (5 U.S.C. chapter 6) does not apply. Pursuant to section 7805(f) of the Code, this notice of proposed rulemaking will be submitted to the Chief Counsel for Advocacy of the Small Business Administration for comment on its impact on small business.

Comments and Public Hearing

Before these proposed regulations are adopted as final regulations, consideration will be given to any comments that are submitted timely to the IRS as prescribed in this preamble under the **ADDRESSES** heading. The Treasury Department and the IRS request comments on all aspects of the proposed rules. All comments that are submitted by the public will be available for public inspection and copying at *http://www.regulations.gov* or upon request.

A public hearing has been scheduled for December 20, 2018, at 10 a.m., in the IRS Auditorium, Internal Revenue Service, 1111 Constitution Avenue, NW, Washington, DC 20224. Due to building security procedures, visitors must enter at the Constitution Avenue entrance. In addition, all visitors must present photo identification to enter the building. Because of access restrictions, visitors will not be admitted beyond the immediate entrance area more than thirty (30) minutes before the hearing starts. For more information about having your name placed on the building access list to attend the hearing, see the **FOR FURTHER INFORMATION CONTACT** section of this preamble.

The rules of 26 CFR 601.601(a)(3) apply to the hearing. Persons who wish to present oral comments at the hearing must submit written or electronic comments and an outline of the topics to be discussed and the time to be devoted to each topic by December 7, 2018. Such persons should submit a signed paper original and eight (8) copies or an electronic copy. A period of ten (10) minutes will be allotted to each person for making comments. An agenda showing the scheduling of the speakers will be prepared after the deadline for receiving outlines has passed. Copies of the agenda will be available free of charge at the hearing.

Drafting Information

The principal author of these regulations is Kathryn M. Sneade, Office of Associate Chief Counsel (Financial Institutions and Products), IRS. However, other personnel from the Treasury Department and the IRS participated in their development.

Statement of Availability of IRS Documents

The IRS notices and revenue procedures cited in this preamble are published in the Internal Revenue Bulletin (or Cumulative Bulletin) and are available from the Superintendent of Documents, U.S. Government Publishing Office, Washington, DC 20402, or by visiting the IRS website at *http://www.irs.gov.*

[¶49,778] Proposed Amendments of Regulations (REG-107813-18), published in the Federal Register on November 14, 2018.

[Code Sec. 401]

Hardship distributions: Primary beneficiary: Contributions: Financial need.—Amendments of Reg. §§1.401(k)-1, 1.401(k)-3, 1.401(k)-6 and 1.401(m)-3, relating to hardship distributions from section 401(k) plans, are proposed.

AGENCY: Internal Revenue Service (IRS), Treasury.

ACTION: Notice of proposed rulemaking.

SUMMARY: This document contains proposed amendments to the regulations relating to hardship distributions from section 401(k) plans. The amendments reflect statutory changes affecting section 401(k) plans, including recent changes made by the Bipartisan Budget Act of 2018. These regulations would affect participants in, beneficiaries of, employers maintaining, and administrators of plans that contain cash or deferred arrangements or provide for employee or matching contributions.

DATES: Comments and requests for a public hearing must be received by January 14, 2019.

ADDRESSES: Send submissions to CC:PA:LPD:PR (REG-107813-18) Room 5203, Internal Revenue Service, P.O. Box 7604, Ben Franklin Station, Washington, DC 20044. Submissions may be hand-delivered Monday through Friday between the hours of 8 a.m. and 4 p.m. to CC:PA:LPD:PR (REG-107813-18), Courier's Desk, Internal Revenue Service, 1111 Constitution Avenue NW., Washington, DC 20224, or sent electronically via the Federal eRulemaking Portal at www.regulations.gov/ (indicate IRS and REG-107813-18).

FOR FURTHER INFORMATION CONTACT: Concerning the proposed regulations, Roger Kuehnle at (202) 317-6060 or; concerning submissions of comments, the hearing, or to be placed on the building access list to attend the hearing, Regina L. Johnson at (202) 317-6901 (not toll-free numbers).

SUPPLEMENTARY INFORMATION:

Paperwork Reduction Act

The collection of information contained in this notice of proposed rulemaking will be submitted, under approval number 1545-1669, to the Office of Management and Budget in accordance with the Paperwork Reduction Act of 1995 (44 U.S.C. 3507(d)). Comments on the collection of information should be sent to the Office of Management and Budget, Attn: Desk Officer for the Department of the Treasury, Office of Information and Regulatory Affairs, Washington, DC 20503, with copies to the Internal Revenue Service, Attn: IRS Reports Clearance Officer, SE:W:CAR:MP:T:T:SP, Washington, DC 20224. Comments on the collection of information should be received by January 14, 2019. Comments are specifically requested concerning:

Whether the proposed collection of information is necessary for the proper performance of the functions of the IRS, including whether the information will have practical utility;

The accuracy of the estimated burden associated with the proposed collection of information;

How the quality, utility, and clarity of the information to be collected may be enhanced;

How the burden of complying with the proposed collection of information may be minimized, including through the application of automated collection techniques or other forms of information technology; and

Estimates of capital or start-up costs and costs of operation, maintenance, and purchase of services to provide information.

The collection of information in this proposed regulation is in §1.401(k)-1(d)(3)(iii)(B). The collection of information relates to the certification by participants in section 401(k) plans that they have insufficient cash or other liquid assets to cover expenses resulting from a hardship and, thus, will need a distribution from the plan to meet the expenses. The collections of information are required to obtain a benefit.

The likely recordkeepers are individuals.

Estimated total annual reporting burden: 101,250 hours.

Estimated average annual burden per respondent: 45 minutes.

Estimated number of respondents: 135,000.

Estimated frequency of responses: On occasion.

An agency may not conduct or sponsor, and a person is not required to respond to, a collection of information unless it displays a valid control number assigned by the Office of Management and Budget.

Background

Section 401(k)

Section 401(k)(1) of the Internal Revenue Code (Code) provides that a profit-sharing, stock bonus, pre-ERISA money purchase, or rural cooperative plan will not fail to qualify under section 401(a) merely because it contains a cash or deferred arrangement (CODA) that is a qualified CODA. Under section 401(k)(2), a CODA (generally, an arrangement providing for an election by an employee between contributions to a plan or payments directly in cash) constitutes a qualified CODA only if it satisfies certain requirements. Section 401(k)(2)(B) provides that contributions made pursuant to a qualified CODA (referred to as "elective contributions") may be distributed only on or after the occurrence of certain events, including death, disability, severance from employment, termination of the plan, attainment of age 59-1/2, hardship, or, in the case of a qualified reservist distribution, the date a reservist is called to active duty. Section 401(k)(2)(C) requires that elective contributions be nonforfeitable at all times.

Section 401(k)(3)(A)(ii) requires that elective contributions satisfy the actual deferral percentage (ADP) test set forth in section 401(k)(3). Sections 401(k)(11), 401(k)(12), and 401(k)(13) each provide an alternative method of meeting the ADP test. Under section 401(k)(3)(D), qualified nonelective contributions (QNECs) and qualified matching contributions (QMACs), as described in sections 401(m)(4)(C) and 401(k)(3)(D)(ii)(I), respectively, are permitted to be taken into account under the ADP test. Among other requirements, QNECs and QMACs must satisfy the distribution limitations of section 401(k)(2)(B) and the nonforfeitability requirements of section 401(k)(2)(C). Similarly, employer contributions that are made pursuant to the safe harbor plan designs of section 401(k)(12) or (13) must meet the distribution limitations of section 401(k)(2)(B).

Section 401(m)(2)(A) requires that matching contributions and employee contributions satisfy the actual contribution percentage (ACP) test set forth in section 401(m)(2). Sections 401(m)(10), 401(m)(11), and 401(m)(12) each provide an alternative method of meeting the ACP test with respect to matching contributions. As with contributions made to section 401(k) plans pursuant to safe harbor plan designs, employer contributions made pursuant to the safe harbor plan designs of section 401(m)(11) or (12) must meet the distribution limitations of section 401(k)(2)(B).

The Department of the Treasury (Treasury Department) and the IRS issued comprehensive final regulations under sections 401(k) and 401(m) on December 29, 2004 (TD 9169, 69 FR 78143). Since that time, the regulations have been updated to reflect certain subsequent changes to the applicable statute (see TD 9237, 71 FR 6, and TD 9324, 72 FR 21103, providing guidance on designated Roth contributions under section 402A; and TD 9447, 74 FR 8200, providing guidance on section 401(k)(13)). However, the regulations have not been updated to reflect other statutory changes. The regulations have been amended to address other specific issues (see TD 9319, 72 FR 16878, relating to the definition of compensation; TD 9641, 78 FR 68735, relating to mid-year amendments to safe harbor plan designs; and TD 9835, 83 FR 34469, relating to whether QNECs and QMACs must be nonforfeitable when contributed to the plan).

Section 1.401(k)-1(d)(3) provides rules for determining whether a distribution is made on account of an employee's hardship. Under those rules, a distribution is made on account of hardship only if the distribution is made on account of an immediate and heavy financial need and the amount of the distribution is not in excess of the amount necessary to satisfy that need (plus any amounts necessary to pay any taxes or penalties reasonably anticipated to result from the distribution). These determinations must be made on the basis of all the relevant facts and circumstances and in accordance with nondiscriminatory and objective standards set forth in the plan.

Section 1.401(k)-1(d)(3)(iv)(B) provides that a distribution is not treated as necessary to satisfy an immediate and heavy financial need of an employee to the extent the need may be relieved from other resources that are reasonably available to the employee. Under § 1.401(k)-1(d)(3)(iv)(C), in determining whether the need can be relieved from other resources that are reasonably available to an employee, the employer may rely on the employee's representation (unless the employer has actual knowledge to the contrary) that the need cannot reasonably be relieved from resources specified in § 1.401(k)-1(d)(3)(iv)(C).

To simplify administration, the regulations provide certain safe harbors that may be used to determine whether a distribution is made on account of an employee's hardship. Specifically, § 1.401(k)-1(d)(3)(iii)(B) provides a safe harbor under which distributions for six types of expenses are deemed to be made on account of an immediate and heavy financial need. One of the six types is "expenses for the repair of damage to the employee's principal residence that would qualify for the casualty deduction under section 165 (determined without regard to whether the loss exceeds 10% of adjusted gross income)."

In addition, § 1.401(k)-1(d)(3)(iv)(E) provides a safe harbor under which a distribution is deemed necessary to satisfy an immediate and heavy financial need. Under that safe harbor, an employee must first obtain all currently available distributions (including distributions of employee stock ownership plan (ESOP) dividends under section 404(k), but not hardship distributions), and nontaxable plan loans from the plan and any other plan maintained by the employer. Under the safe harbor, an employee's ability to make elective contributions and employee contributions to the plan (and any other plan maintained by the employer) must be suspended for at least 6 months after receipt of the hardship distribution. Pursuant to § 1.401(k)-3(c)(6)(v)(B), in the case of a safe harbor plan described in section 401(k)(12) or (13), the suspension period may not exceed 6 months.

Under § 1.401(k)-1(d)(3)(ii), the maximum amount that may be distributed on account of hardship is the total of the employee's elective contributions that have not previously been distributed (plus earnings, QNECs, and QMACs credited before a specified grandfather date that generally is before 1989). Thus, the maximum amount that may be distributed on account of hardship does not include earnings, QNECs, or QMACs that are not grandfathered.

Section 403(b)

Section 403(b)(7)(A)(ii) provides distribution limitations on amounts contributed to a custodial account that is treated as a section 403(b) annuity contract. Section 403(b)(11) provides that contributions made pursuant to a salary reduction agreement (within the meaning of section 402(g)(3)(C)) (generally referred to in the regulations under section 403(b) as "section 403(b) elective deferrals") may be distributed only on or after the occurrence of certain events, one of which is the employee's hardship. Section 403(b)(11) also provides that no income attributable to these contributions may be distributed on account of hardship.

Section 1.403(b)-6 provides rules for applying these distribution limitations. Section 1.403(b)-6(b) applies to distributions of amounts that are neither attributable to section 403(b) elective deferrals nor made from custodial accounts, § 1.403(b)-6(c) applies to distributions from custodial accounts that are not attributable to section 403(b) elective deferrals, and § 1.403(b)-6(d) applies to distributions of amounts attributable to section 403(b) elective deferrals. Section 1.403(b)-6(d)(2) provides that a hardship distribution of section 403(b) elective deferrals is subject to the rules and restrictions set forth in § 1.401(k)-1(d)(3) and is limited to the aggregate dollar amount of a participant's section 403(b) elective deferrals, without earnings thereon.

Statutory Changes Relating to Section 401(k)

Section 41113 of the Bipartisan Budget Act of 2018, Pub. L. 115-123 (BBA 2018), directs the Secretary of the Treasury to modify § 1.401(k)-1(d)(3)(iv)(E) to (1) delete the 6-month prohibition on contributions following a hardship distribution, and (2) make any other modifications necessary to carry out the purposes of section 401(k)(2)(B)(i)(IV). Section 41114 of BBA 2018 modifies the hardship distribution rules under section 401(k)(2)(B) by adding section 401(k)(14)(A) to the Code, which states that the maximum amount available for distribution upon hardship includes (i) contributions to a profit-sharing or stock bonus plan to which section 402(e)(3) applies, (ii) QNECs, (iii) QMACs, and (iv) earnings on these contributions. Section 41114 of BBA 2018 also adds section 401(k)(14)(B) to the Code, which provides that a distribution is not treated as failing to be made upon the hardship of an employee solely because the employee does not take any available loan under the plan.

Section 11044 of the Tax Cuts and Jobs Act, Pub. L. 115-97 (TCJA), added section 165(h)(5) to the Code. Section 165(h)(5) provides that, for taxable years 2018 through 2025, the deduction for a personal casualty loss generally is available only to the extent the loss is attributable to a federally declared disaster (as defined in section 165(i)(5)).

Section 826 of the Pension Protection Act of 2006, Pub. L. 109-280 (PPA '06), directs the Secretary of the Treasury to modify the rules relating to hardship distributions to permit a section 401(k) plan to treat a participant's beneficiary under the plan the same as the participant's spouse or dependent in determining whether the participant has incurred a hardship. Notice 2007-07, 2007-5 I.R.B. 395, provides guidance for applying this provision.

Section 827(a) of PPA '06 added to the Code section 72(t)(2)(G), which exempts certain distributions from the application of the section 72(t) additional income tax on early distributions. These distributions, referred to as "qualified reservist distributions," include distributions attributable to elective contributions that are made during the period that a reservist has been called to active duty. Section 827(b)(1) of PPA '06 added section 401(k)(2)(B)(i)(V) to the Code, which permits qualified reservist distributions to be made from a section 401(k) plan.[1]

Section 105(b)(1)(A) of the Heroes Earnings Assistance and Relief Tax Act of 2008, Pub. L. 110-245 (HEART Act), added section 414(u)(12) to the Code. Section 414(u)(12)(B)(ii) provides for a 6-month suspension of elective contributions and employee contributions after certain distributions to individuals performing service in the uniformed services.

[1] While section 827(b)(2) and (3) of PPA '06 amended sections 403(b)(7)(A)(ii) and 403(b)(11) to permit qualified reservist distributions to be made from a section 403(b) plan, the regulations under section 403(b) have not yet been updated to reflect these statutory amendments.

Explanation of Provisions

Overview

These proposed regulations update the section 401(k) and (m) regulations to reflect: (1) the enactment of (a) sections 41113 and 41114 of BBA 2018, (b) sections 826 and 827 of PPA '06, and (c) section 105(b)(1)(A) of the HEART Act; and (2) the application of the hardship distribution rules in light of the modification to the casualty loss deduction rules made by section 11044 of the TCJA.

Deemed Immediate and Heavy Financial Need

The proposed regulations modify the safe harbor list of expenses in current § 1.401(k)-1(d)(3)(iii)(B) for which distributions are deemed to be made on account of an immediate and heavy financial need by: (1) adding "primary beneficiary under the plan" as an individual for whom qualifying medical, educational, and funeral expenses may be incurred; (2) modifying the expense listed in § 1.401(k)-1(d)(3)(iii)(B)(*6*) (relating to damage to a principal residence that would qualify for a casualty deduction under section 165) to provide that for this purpose the new limitations in section 165(h)(5) (added by section 11044 of the TCJA) do not apply; and (3) adding a new type of expense to the list, relating to expenses incurred as a result of certain disasters. This new safe harbor expense is similar to relief given by the IRS after certain major federally declared disasters, such as the relief relating to Hurricane Maria and California wildfires provided in Announcement 2017-15, 2017-47 I.R.B. 534, and is intended to eliminate any delay or uncertainty concerning access to plan funds following a disaster that occurs in an area designated by the Federal Emergency Management Agency (FEMA) for individual assistance.

Distribution Necessary to Satisfy Financial Need

Pursuant to BBA 2018 sections 41113 and 41114, the proposed regulations modify the rules for determining whether a distribution is necessary to satisfy an immediate and heavy financial need by eliminating (1) any requirement that an employee be prohibited from making elective contributions and employee contributions after receipt of a hardship distribution, and (2) any requirement to take plan loans prior to obtaining a hardship distribution. In particular, the proposed regulations eliminate the safe harbor in current § 1.401(k)-1(d)(3)(iv)(E), under which a distribution is deemed necessary to satisfy the financial need only if elective contributions and employee contributions are suspended for at least 6 months after a hardship distribution is made and, if available, nontaxable plan loans are taken.

In addition, the proposed regulations eliminate the rules in current § 1.401(k)-1(d)(3)(iv)(B) (under which the determination of whether a distribution is necessary to satisfy a financial need is based on all the relevant facts and circumstances) and provide one general standard for determining whether a distribution is necessary. Under this general standard, a hardship distribution may not exceed the amount of an employee's need (including any amounts necessary to pay any federal, state, or local income taxes or penalties reasonably anticipated to result from the distribution), the employee must have obtained other available distributions under the employer's plans, and the employee must represent that he or she has insufficient cash or other liquid assets to satisfy the financial need. A plan administrator may rely on such a representation unless the plan administrator has actual knowledge to the contrary. In light of the timing of the publication of these proposed regulations, the requirement to obtain this representation would only apply for a distribution that is made on or after January 1, 2020.

The proposed regulations clarify that a plan generally may provide for additional conditions, such as those described in 26 CFR 1.401(k)-1(d)(3)(iv)(B) and (C) (revised as of April 1, 2018) or, for distributions made before January 1, 2020, the representation described in the preceding paragraph, to demonstrate that a distribution is necessary to satisfy an immediate and heavy financial need of an employee. To implement Congress' purpose in enacting section 41113 of BBA 2018 (for example, Congress' concern that a suspension impedes an employee's ability to replace distributed funds), the proposed regulations do not permit a plan to provide for a suspension of elective contributions or employee contributions as a condition of obtaining a hardship distribution. However, in light of the timing of the publication of these proposed regulations, this prohibition would only apply for a distribution that is made on or after January 1, 2020.

Expanded Sources for Hardship Distributions

Pursuant to section 41114 of BBA 2018, the proposed regulations modify § 1.401(k)-1(d)(3) to permit hardship distributions from section 401(k) plans of elective contributions, QNECs, QMACs, and earnings on these amounts, regardless of when contributed or earned. However, plans may limit the type of contributions available for hardship distributions and whether earnings on those contributions are included. Safe harbor contributions made to a plan described in section 401(k)(13) may also be distributed on account of an employee's hardship (because these contributions are subject to the same distribution limitations applicable to QNECs and QMACs). See § 1.401(k)-3(k)(3)(i).

Section 403(b) Plans

Section 1.403(b)-6(d)(2) provides that a hardship distribution of section 403(b) elective deferrals is subject to the rules and restrictions set forth in § 1.401(k)-1(d)(3); thus, the proposed new rules relating to a hardship distribution of elective contributions from a section 401(k) plan generally apply to section 403(b) plans. However, Code section 403(b)(11) was not amended by section 41114 of BBA 2018; therefore, income attributable to section 403(b) elective deferrals continues to be ineligible for distribution on account of hardship.

Amounts attributable to QNECs and QMACs may be distributed from a section 403(b) plan on account of hardship only to the extent that, under §1.403(b)-6(b) and (c), hardship is a permitted distributable event for amounts that are not attributable to section 403(b) elective deferrals. Thus, QNECs and QMACs in a section 403(b) plan that are not in a custodial account may be distributed on account of hardship, but QNECs and QMACs in a section 403(b) plan that are in a custodial account continue to be ineligible for distribution on account of hardship.

Relief for Victims of Hurricanes Florence and Michael

The Treasury Department and the IRS realize that employees adversely affected by Hurricane Florence or Hurricane Michael may need expedited access to plan funds. Accordingly, the relief provided under Announcement 2017-15 is extended to similarly situated victims of Hurricanes Florence and Michael, except that the "Incident Dates" (as defined in that announcement) are as specified by FEMA for these 2018 hurricanes, relief is provided through March 15, 2019, and any necessary amendments must be made no later than the deadline for plan amendments set forth in this preamble under *Plan Amendments*.

Applicability Dates and Reliance

The changes to the hardship distribution rules made by BBA 2018 are effective for plan years beginning after December 31, 2018, and the proposed regulations provide that they generally would apply to distributions made in plan years beginning after December 31, 2018. However, the prohibition on suspending an employee's elective contributions and employee contributions as a condition of obtaining a hardship distribution may be applied as of the first day of the first plan year beginning after December 31, 2018, even if the distribution was made in the prior plan year. Thus, for example, a calendar-year plan that provides for hardship distributions under the pre-2019 safe harbor standards may be amended to provide that an employee who receives a hardship distribution in the second half of the 2018 plan year will be prohibited from making contributions only until January 1, 2019 (or may continue to provide that contributions will be suspended for the originally scheduled 6 months).

In addition, the revised list of safe harbor expenses may be applied to distributions made on or after a date that is as early as January 1, 2018. Thus, for example, a plan that made hardship distributions relating to casualty losses deductible under section 165 without regard to the changes made to section 165 by the TCJA (which, effective in 2018, require that, to be deductible, losses must result from a federally declared disaster) may be amended to apply the revised safe harbor expense relating to casualty losses to distributions made in 2018 so that plan provisions will conform to the plan's operation. Similarly, a plan may be amended to apply the revised safe harbor expense relating to losses (including loss of income) incurred by an employee on account of a disaster that occurs in 2018 (such as Hurricane Florence or Hurricane Michael), provided that the employee's principal residence or principal place of employment at the time of the disaster was located in an area designated by FEMA for individual assistance with respect to the disaster.

Plan Amendments

The Treasury Department and the IRS expect that, if these regulations are finalized as they have been proposed, plan sponsors will need to amend their plans' hardship distribution provisions. The deadline for amending a disqualifying provision is set forth in Rev. Proc. 2016-37, 2016-29 I.R.B. 136. For example, with respect to an individually designed plan that is not a governmental plan, the deadline for amending the plan to reflect a change in qualification requirements is the end of the second calendar year that begins after the issuance of the Required Amendments List described in section 9 of Rev. Proc. 2016-37 that includes the change. A plan provision that is not a disqualifying provision, but is integrally related to a plan provision that is a disqualifying provision, may be amended by the same deadline applicable to a disqualifying provision.

A plan amendment that is related to the final regulations, but does not correct a disqualifying provision, including a plan amendment reflecting (1) the change to section 165 (relating to casualty losses) or (2) the addition of the new safe harbor expense (relating to expenses incurred as a result of certain federally declared disasters), will be treated as integrally related to a disqualifying provision. Therefore all amendments that relate to the final regulations will have the same amendment deadline. This deadline will also apply to an amendment reflecting the extension of the relief under Announcement 2017-15 to victims of Hurricanes Florence and Michael, as provided in this preamble.

Special Analyses

The Administrator of the Office of Information and Regulatory Affairs (OIRA), Office of Management and Budget, has waived review of this proposed rule in accordance with section 6(a)(3)(A) of Executive Order 12866. OIRA will subsequently make a significance determination of the final rule, pursuant to section 3(f) of Executive Order (E.O.) 12866 and the April 11, 2018, Memorandum of Agreement between the Department of the Treasury and the Office of Management and Budget (OMB).

Because these regulations do not impose a collection of information on small entities, the Regulatory Flexibility Act (5 U.S.C. chapter 6) does not apply. Pursuant to section 7805(f) of the Code, these regulations have been submitted to the Chief Counsel for Advocacy of the Small Business Administration for comment on their impact on small business.

Comments and Requests for Public Hearing

Before these proposed regulations are adopted as final regulations, consideration will be given to any comments that are submitted timely to the IRS as prescribed in this preamble under the ADDRESSES heading. The Treasury Department and the IRS request comments on all aspects of the proposed rules. All comments will be available at www.regulations.gov or upon request. A public hearing will be scheduled if requested in writing by any person that timely submits written comments. If a public hearing is scheduled, notice of the date, time, and place for the public hearing will be published in the **Federal Register**.

Drafting Information

The principal author of these regulations is Roger Kuehnle of the Office of Associate Chief Counsel (Tax Exempt and Governmental Entities). However, other personnel from the IRS and Treasury Department participated in their development.

[¶49,779] Proposed Amendments of Regulations (REG-122898-17), published in the Federal Register on November 19, 2018.

[26 CFR Part 300]

Internal Revenue Service: Enrolled agents: Enrolled retirement plan agents: User fees.—Amendments of Regs. §§300.0, 300.5, 300.6, 300.10, 300.11, 300.12 and 300.13, relating to imposing user fees for enrolled agents and enrolled retirement plan agents, are proposed.

AGENCY: Internal Revenue Service (IRS), Treasury.

ACTION: Notice of proposed rulemaking and notice of public hearing.

SUMMARY: This document contains proposed amendments to the regulations relating to imposing user fees for enrolled agents and enrolled retirement plan agents. The proposed regulations remove the initial enrollment user fee for enrolled retirement plan agents because the IRS no longer offers initial enrollment as an enrolled retirement plan agent. The proposed regulations also increase the amount of the renewal user fee for enrolled retirement plan agents from $30 to $67. In addition, the proposed regulations increase the amount of both the enrollment and renewal user fee for enrolled agents from $30 to $67. The proposed regulations affect individuals who are or apply to become enrolled agents and individuals who are enrolled retirement plan agents. The Independent Offices Appropriations Act of 1952 authorizes charging user fees.

DATES: Written or electronic comments must be received by January 18, 2019. Requests to speak and outlines of topics to be discussed at the public hearing scheduled for January 24, 2019, at 10 a.m. must be received by January 18, 2019.

ADDRESSES: Send submissions to: CC:PA:LPD:PR (REG-122898-17), room 5203, Internal Revenue Service, PO Box 7604, Ben Franklin Station, Washington, D.C. 20044. Submissions may be hand-delivered Monday through Friday between the hours of 8 a.m. and 4 p.m. to CC:PA:LPD:PR (REG-122898-17), Courier's Desk, Internal Revenue Service, 1111 Constitution Avenue, NW, Washington, D.C. 20224 or sent electronically via the Federal eRulemaking Portal at *http://www.regulations.gov* (IRS REG-122898-17). The public hearing will be held in the Main Auditorium of the Internal Revenue Service Building, 1111 Constitution Avenue, NW, Washington, D.C. FOR FURTHER INFORMATION CONTACT: Concerning the proposed regulations, Mark Shurtliff at (202) 317-6845; concerning cost methodology, Michael A. Weber at (202) 803-9738; concerning submission of comments, the public hearing, or to be placed on the building access list to attend the public hearing, Regina Johnson at (202) 317-6901 (not toll-free numbers).

SUPPLEMENTARY INFORMATION:

Background and Explanation of Provisions

This document contains proposed amendments to 26 CFR part 300 regarding user fees.

A. *Enrolled Agents and Enrolled Retirement Plan Agents*

Section 330(a)(1) of title 31 of the United States Code authorizes the Secretary of the Treasury to regulate the practice of representatives before the Treasury Department. Before admitting a representative to practice, the Secretary is authorized to "require that the representative demonstrate - (A) good character; (B) good reputation; (C) necessary qualifications to enable the representative to provide to persons valuable service; and (D) competency to advise and assist persons in presenting their cases." 31 U.S.C. 330(a)(2). Pursuant to section 330 of title 31, the Secretary has published regulations governing practice before the IRS in 31 CFR part 10 and reprinted the regulations as Treasury Department Circular No. 230 (Circular 230).

Section 10.4(a) of Circular 230 authorizes the IRS to grant enrollment as enrolled agents to individuals who demonstrate special competence in tax matters by passing a written examination administered by, or under the oversight of, the IRS and who have not engaged in any conduct that would justify suspension or disbarment under Circular 230. Every year, the IRS develops and administers an Enrolled Agent Special Enrollment Examination (EA-SEE) that individuals must pass to become an enrolled agent.

Section 10.4(b) of Circular 230 currently authorizes the IRS to grant enrollment as enrolled retirement plan agents to individuals who demonstrate special competence in qualified retirement plan matters by passing a written examination administered by, or under the oversight of, the IRS and who have not engaged in any conduct that would justify suspension or disbarment under Circular 230. Until February 12, 2016, the IRS annually developed and administered an Enrolled Retirement Plan Agent Special Enrollment Examination (ERPA-SEE) that individuals were required to take and pass to become an enrolled retirement plan agent. After February 12, 2016, however, the IRS stopped offering the ERPA-SEE. Individuals who have already passed the ERPA-SEE may maintain their enrollment as enrolled retirement plan agents, but the IRS is not accepting applications to become new Enrolled Retirement Plan Agents. Accordingly, the proposed regulations propose to remove the user fee for the initial enrollment of an enrolled retirement plan agent currently in Treasury Regulation § 300.10.

Section 10.4(d) also authorizes the IRS to grant enrollment as an enrolled agent or an enrolled retirement plan agent to a qualifying former IRS employee by virtue of past IRS service and technical experience if the former employee has not engaged in any conduct that would justify suspension or disbarment under the provisions of Circular 230 and meets certain other requirements. Application for enrollment as an enrolled agent based on former employment with the IRS must be made within three years from the date of separation from that employment and does not require passing the EA-SEE. When the IRS discontinued offering the ERPA-SEE necessary for enrollment as an enrolled retirement plan agent for individuals without IRS work experience, effective February 12, 2016, the IRS stopped granting individuals enrollment as enrolled retirement plan agents by virtue of past service and technical experience in the IRS.

Once eligible for enrollment as an enrolled agent, whether by examination or former employment with the IRS, an individual must file an application for enrollment with the IRS and currently pay a $30 nonrefundable user fee. To maintain active enrollment and practice before the IRS, an individual who has been enrolled as an enrolled agent or enrolled retirement plan agent must file an application to renew enrollment every three years and currently pay a $30 nonrefundable user fee. 31 CFR 10.6(d).

The IRS Return Preparer Office (RPO) is responsible for certain matters related to authority to practice before the IRS, including acting on applications for enrollment and renewal of enrolled agents and for renewal of enrolled retirement plan agents. 31 CFR 10.1. As a condition for enrollment as an enrolled agent, the RPO may conduct a federal tax-compliance check to determine whether an applicant has filed all required tax returns and has no outstanding federal tax debts and a suitability check to determine whether an applicant has engaged in any conduct that would justify suspending or disbarring any practitioner under Circular 230. 31 CFR 10.5(d). As a condition for renewal, enrolled agents and enrolled retirement plan agents must certify completion of the continuing education requirements. 31 CFR 10.6(e).

As part of its responsibility for administering the enrollment program, RPO determines whether applicants have met the above requirements. 31 CFR 10.6(j)(1). An applicant who is denied enrollment as an enrolled agent for failure to pass a tax-compliance check may reapply if the applicant becomes current with respect to the applicant's tax liabilities. 31 CFR 10.5(d)(2). Applicants who fail to meet the continuing education and fee payment requirements receive from RPO a notice that states the basis for RPO's determination of noncompliance and provides an opportunity to cure the failure. 31 CFR 10.6(j)(1).

B. *User Fee Authority*

The Independent Offices Appropriations Act of 1952 (IOAA) (31 U.S.C. 9701) authorizes each agency to promulgate regulations establishing the charge for services the agency provides (user fees). Under the IOAA, these user-fee regulations are subject to policies prescribed by the President and shall be as uniform as practicable. Those policies are currently set forth in the Office of Management and Budget (OMB) Circular A-25 (OMB Circular), 58 FR 38142 (July 15, 1993).

The IOAA states that the services provided by an agency should be self-sustaining to the extent possible (31 U.S.C. 9701(a)). The OMB Circular states that agencies providing services that confer special benefits on identifiable recipients beyond those accruing to the general public must identify those services, determine whether user fees should be assessed for those services, and, if so, establish user fees that recover the full cost of providing those services. As required by the IOAA and the OMB Circular, agencies are to review user fees biennially and update them as necessary to reflect changes in the cost of providing the underlying services. During these biennial reviews, an agency must calculate the full cost of providing each service, taking into account all direct and indirect costs to any part of the U.S. government. The full cost of providing a service includes, but is not limited to, salaries, retirement benefits, rents, utilities, travel, and management costs, as well as an appropriate allocation of overhead and other support costs associated with providing the service.

An agency should set the user fee at an amount that recovers the full cost of providing the service unless the agency requests, and the OMB grants, an exception to the full-cost requirement. The OMB may grant exceptions only where the cost of collecting the fees would represent an unduly large part of the fee for the activity, or where any other condition exists that, in the opinion of the agency head, justifies an exception. When the OMB grants an exception, the agency does not collect the full cost of providing the service that confers a special benefit on identifiable recipients rather than the public at large, and the agency therefore must fund the remaining cost of providing the service from other available funding sources. When the OMB grants an exception, the agency, and by extension all taxpayers, subsidize the cost of the service to the recipients who would otherwise be required to pay the full cost of providing the service, as the IOAA and the OMB Circular direct.

C. *Enrollment and Renewal User Fees for the Enrolled Agent and Renewal User Fee for the Enrolled Retirement Plan Agent*

As discussed in section A of this preamble, an individual who has been granted enrollment as an enrolled agent or an enrolled retirement plan agent may practice before the IRS. The IRS confers benefits on individuals who are enrolled agents or enrolled retirement plan agents beyond those that accrue to the general public by allowing them to practice before the IRS. Because the ability to practice before the IRS is a special benefit, the IRS charges a user fee to recover the full cost associated with administering the program for enrollment and renewal of enrolled agents and renewal of enrolled retirement plan agents.

On September 30, 2010, the Treasury Department and the IRS published two final regulations in the Federal Register: final regulations (TD 9501, 75 FR 60309) that required tax return preparers who prepare all or substantially all of a tax return or claim for refund for compensation to obtain a preparer tax identification number (PTIN) and final regulations (TD 9503, 75 FR 60316) that required a user fee to apply for or renew a PTIN. Individuals applying for or renewing a PTIN were to be subject to federal tax-compliance and suitability checks and were required to pay a $50 user fee to obtain or renew a PTIN. All enrolled agents and certain enrolled retirement plan agents were required to obtain a PTIN as a condition of enrollment and renewal of enrollment. TD 9527, 76 FR 32286; Notice 2011-91, 2011-47 I.R.B. 792.

On April 19, 2011, the Treasury Department and the IRS published in the Federal Register (76 FR 21805) a final regulation (TD 9523) that reduced the amount of the user fees for the initial enrollment and renewal enrollment for enrolled agents and enrolled retirement plan agents from $125 to $30. Because individuals applying to enroll as an enrolled agent or enrolled retirement plan agent also had to obtain a PTIN, the user fee to enroll or renew enrollment was reduced to reflect that certain review procedures (including federal tax-compliance and suitability checks) would be performed as part of the process to obtain a PTIN. On June 1, 2017, the IRS ceased collecting any user fees related to the PTIN. *See Steele v. United States*, 260 F.Supp.3d 52 (D. D.C. 2017) (holding that the IRS was authorized to require tax return preparers to obtain PTINs, but was not authorized to charge fees for PTINs).

As required by the IOAA and the OMB Circular, the RPO completed its 2017 biennial review of the enrollment and renewal user fees associated with enrolled agents and enrolled retirement plan agents. As discussed in section D of this preamble, during its review the RPO took into account the increase in labor, benefits, and overhead costs incurred in connection with providing services to individuals who enroll or renew enrollment as enrolled agents and enrolled retirement plan agents since the user fee was last changed in 2011. In addition, RPO determined that costs associated with federal tax-compliance checks and suitability checks on enrolled individuals should be recovered as part of the user fee for administering the enrollment and renewal programs. The 2017 biennial review also took into account new costs associated with administering the program for enrolled agents and enrolled retirement plan agents, including the costs of operating a dedicated toll-free helpline in the RPO for enrollment and renewal matters. The RPO determined that the full cost of administering the program for enrolled agents and enrolled retirement plan agents has increased from $30 to $67 per application for enrollment or renewal. The proposed fee complies with the directive in the OMB Circular to recover the full cost of providing a service that confers special benefits on identifiable recipients beyond those accruing to the general public.

D. *Calculation of User Fees Generally*

The IRS follows generally accepted accounting principles (GAAP) in calculating the full cost of processing an application for enrollment or renewal. The Federal Accounting Standards Advisory Board (FASAB) is the body that establishes GAAP that apply for federal reporting entities, such as the IRS. FASAB publishes the FASAB Handbook of Accounting Standards and Other Pronouncements, as Amended (Current Handbook), which is available at *http://files.fasab.gov/pdf-files/2017_fasab_handbook.pdf*. The Current Handbook includes the *Statement of Federal Financial Accounting Standards (SFFAS) No. 4: Managerial Cost Accounting Concepts and Standards for the Federal Government*. *SFFAS No. 4* establishes internal costing standards under GAAP to accurately measure and manage the full cost of federal programs, and the methodology below is in accordance with *SFFAS No. 4*.

1. *Cost Center Allocation*

The IRS determines the cost of its services and the activities involved in producing them through a cost-accounting system that tracks costs to organizational units. The lowest organizational unit in the IRS's cost-accounting system is called a cost center. Cost centers are usually separate offices that are distinguished by subject-matter area of responsibility or geographic region. All costs of operating a cost center are recorded in the IRS's cost-accounting system and allocated to that cost center. The costs allocated to a cost center are the direct costs for the cost center's activities as well as all indirect costs, including overhead, associated with that cost center. Each cost is recorded in only one cost center.

2. *Determining the Per Unit Cost*

To establish the per-unit cost, the total cost of providing the service is divided by the volume of services provided.

3. *Cost Estimation of Direct Labor*

Not all cost centers are fully devoted to one service for which the IRS charges user fees. Some cost centers work on a number of different services across the IRS. In these cases, the IRS uses various cost-measurement techniques to estimate the cost incurred in those cost centers attributable to the program. These techniques include using various timekeeping systems to measure the time required to accomplish activities, or using information provided by subject-matter experts on the time devoted to a program. Once the IRS has estimated the average time required to accomplish an activity, it multiplies that time estimate by the relevant organizational unit's average labor and benefits cost per unit of time to determine the labor and benefits cost incurred to provide the service. To determine the full cost, IRS then adds overhead as discussed below.

4. *Overhead*

Overhead is an indirect cost of operating an organization that cannot be immediately associated with an activity that the organization performs. Overhead includes costs of resources that are jointly or commonly consumed by one or more organizational unit's activities but are not specifically identifiable to a single activity.

These costs can include:

- General management and administrative services of sustaining and supporting organizations.
- Facilities management and ground maintenance services (security, rent, utilities, and building maintenance).
- Procurement and contracting services.
- Financial management and accounting services.
- Information technology services.
- Services to acquire and operate property, plants and equipment.
- Publication, reproduction, and graphics and video services.
- Research, analytical, and statistical services.
- Human resources/personnel services.
- Library and legal services.

To calculate the overhead allocable to a service, the IRS multiplies a Corporate Overhead rate by the labor and benefits costs determined as discussed previously. The IRS calculates the Corporate Overhead rate annually based on cost elements underlying the Statement of Net Cost included in the IRS Annual Financial Statements, which are audited by the Government Accountability Office. The Corporate Overhead rate is the ratio of the sum of the IRS's indirect labor and benefits costs from the supporting and sustaining organizational units—those that do not interact directly with taxpayers—and all non-labor costs to the IRS's labor and benefits costs of its organizational units that interact directly with taxpayers.

The Corporate Overhead rate of 68.00 percent for costs reviewed during FY 2017 was calculated based on FY 2016 costs (which are assumed to be fixed and reoccurring) as follows:

Indirect Labor and Benefits Costs	$1,681,373,747
Non-Labor Costs	+ $2,879,907,032
Total Indirect Costs	$4,561,280,779
Direct Labor and Benefits Costs	÷ $6,708,063,559
Corporate Overhead Rate	68.00%

E. *Calculation of User Fee for Enrolled Agent Enrollment and Renewal and Enrolled Retirement Plan Agent Renewal*

The IRS used projections for fiscal years 2018 through 2020 to determine the direct costs associated with enrolled agent enrollment and renewal and enrolled retirement plan agent renewal. Direct costs are incurred by the RPO and include labor costs for enrollment and renewal submission processing; tax compliance and background checks; continuing education and testing-related activities; and communications, which include the new toll-free helpline.

The labor and benefits for the work performed related to applications for enrolled agent enrollment and renewal and enrolled retirement plan agent renewal is projected to be $2,708,603 in total over fiscal years 2018 through 2020. The labor and benefits costs include the cost to perform background checks and tax compliance checks, which are services that were not included in the previous $30 user fee. The number of enrollment and renewal applications is based on the FY2016 numbers adjusted by the anticipated increase in enrollment. Adding Corporate Overhead expenses to the total labor and benefits results in total costs of $4,550,453 as shown below:

Labor and Benefits	$2,708,603
Corporate Overhead (68%)	$1,841,850
Labor, Benefits, and Overhead	$4,550,453

Dividing this total cost by the projected population of initial enrollment and renewal applications for fiscal years 2018 through 2020 results in a cost per application of $67 as shown below:

Labor, Benefits and Overhead	$4,550,453
Number of Applications	÷ 68,343
Cost Per Application	$ 67

Taking into account the full amount of these costs, the user fee for enrolled agent enrollment or renewal and enrolled retirement plan agent renewal is proposed to be $67 per application. The IRS does not intend to seek an exception from OMB to the full cost requirement.

Special Analyses

OIRA has determined that this regulation is significant and subject to review under section 6(b) of Executive Order 12866.

Pursuant to the Regulatory Flexibility Act (5 U.S.C. chapter 6), it is hereby certified that this regulation will not have a significant economic impact on a substantial number of small entities. The user fee primarily affects individuals who are enrolled agents, apply to become enrolled agents, or are enrolled retirement plan agents. Only individuals, not businesses, can be enrolled agents or enrolled retirement plan agents. Thus, any economic impact of the user fee on small entities generally will occur only when an enrolled agent or enrolled retirement plan agent owns a small business or when a small business employs enrolled agents or enrolled retirement plan agents and reimburses them for their renewal fees. The Treasury Department and IRS estimate that approximately 22,781 individuals will apply annually for enrollment as an enrolled agent, renewal as an enrolled agent, or renewal as an enrolled retirement plan agent. Due to the relatively small number of small businesses that employ enrolled agents or enrolled retirement plan agents, a substantial number of small entities are not likely to be affected. Further, the economic impact on any small entities affected would be limited to paying the $37 difference in cost between the $67 user fee and the previous $30 user fee (for each enrolled agent or enrolled retirement plan agent that a small entity employs and pays for), which is unlikely to present a significant economic impact. The total economic impact of this regulation is thus approximately $842,897 annually, which is the product of the approximately 22,781 individuals and the $37 increase in the fee. Accordingly, the rule is not expected to have a significant economic impact on a substantial number of small entities, and a regulatory flexibility analysis is not required.

It is not anticipated that the increase in user fee that is paid every three years and averages to $12.33 per year will negatively affect enrollment, which has historically remained steady as user fee amounts have changed. Pursuant to section 7805(f), this notice of proposed rulemaking has been submitted to the Chief Counsel for Advocacy of the Small Business Administration for comment on its impact on small business.

Comments and Public Hearing

Before these proposed amendments to the regulations are adopted as final regulations, consideration will be given to any comments that are submitted timely to the IRS as prescribed in the preamble under the "**ADDRESSES**" section. The Treasury Department and the IRS request comments on all aspects of the proposed regulations. All comments submitted will be made available at *www.regulations.gov* or upon request.

A public hearing has been scheduled for January 24, 2019, beginning at 10:00 am in the Main Auditorium of the Internal Revenue Service Building, 1111 Constitution Avenue N.W., Washington, D.C. 20224. Due to building-security procedures, visitors must enter at the Constitution Avenue entrance. All visitors must present photo identification to enter the building. Because of access restrictions, visitors will not be admitted beyond the immediate entrance area more than 30 minutes before the hearing starts. For information about having your name placed on the building access list to attend the hearing, see the "**FOR FURTHER INFORMATION CONTACT**" section of this preamble.

The rules of § 601.601(a)(3) apply to the hearing. Persons who wish to present oral comments at the hearing must submit written or electronic comments and an outline of the topics to be discussed and the time to be devoted to each topic by January 18, 2019. A period of 10 minutes will be allocated to each person for making comments. An agenda showing the scheduling of the speakers will be prepared after the deadline for receiving outlines has passed. Copies of the agenda will be available free of charge at the hearing.

Drafting Information

The principal author of these regulations is Mark Shurtliff, Office of the Associate Chief Counsel (Procedure and Administration). Other personnel from the Treasury Department and the IRS participated in their development.

[¶ 49,780] Proposed Amendments of Regulations (REG-106089-18), published in the Federal Register on December 28, 2018.

[Code Secs. 163, 263A, 382, 383, 446, 469, 860C, 882, 1502 and 1504]

Trade or business: Interest deduction: Real property.—Reg. §§ 1.163(j)-0—1.163(j)-11 and amendments of Reg. §§ 1.263A-9, 1.381(c)(20)-1, 1.382-1, 1.382-2, 1.382-5, 1.382-6, 1.383-0, 1.383-1, 1.446-3, 1.469-9, 1.469-11, 1.860C-2, 1.882-5, 1.1502-13, 1.1502-21, 1.1502-36, 1.1502-79, 1.1502-90, 1.1502-91, 1.1502-95, 1.1502-98, 1.1502-99 and 1.1504-4, regarding the limitation on the deduction for business interest expense after the enactment of recent tax legislation, are proposed. Reg. Reg. §§ 1.163(j)-0—1.163(j)-10, proposed on June 18, 1991, are withdrawn.

AGENCY: Internal Revenue Service (IRS), Treasury.

ACTION: Notice of proposed rulemaking; notification of public hearing; and withdrawal of notice of proposed rulemaking.

SUMMARY: This notice of proposed rulemaking provides rules regarding the limitation on the deduction for business interest expense after the enactment of recent tax legislation. Specifically, these regulations provide general rules and definitions. The regulations also provide rules for calculating the limitation in consolidated group, partnership, and international contexts. The regulations affect taxpayers that have deductible business interest expense, other than certain small businesses, electing real property trades or businesses, electing farming businesses, and certain utility businesses. This document also withdraws a notice of proposed rulemaking relating to the disallowance of a deduction for certain interest paid or accrued by a corporation. This document also provides notice of a public hearing on the proposed regulations. DATES: Written or electronic comments must be received by **[INSERT DATE 60 DAYS AFTER DATE OF PUBLICATION IN THE FEDERAL REGISTER]**. Outlines of topics to be discussed at the public hearing scheduled for February 27, 2019, at 10 a.m. must be received by **[INSERT DATE 60 DAYS AFTER DATE OF PUBLICATION IN THE FEDERAL REGISTER]**. If there is not sufficient time to discuss all of the topics on February 27, 2019, the hearing will continue the following day at 10 a.m. in the same location.

ADDRESSES: Send submissions to: CC:PA:LPD:PR (REG-106089-18), Room 5203, P.O. Box 7604, Ben Franklin Station, Washington, DC 20044. Submissions may be hand-delivered Monday through Friday between the hours of 8 a.m. and 4 p.m. to CC:PA:LPD:PR (REG-106089-18), Courier's Desk, Internal Revenue Service, 1111 Constitution Avenue, NW, Washington, DC, 20224, or sent electronically, via the Federal Rulemaking Portal at http://www.regulations.gov (indicate IRS and REG-106089-18). The public hearing will be held in the Main IRS Auditorium beginning at 10 a.m. in the Internal Revenue Building, 1111 Constitution Avenue, NW, Washington, DC 20224.

FOR FURTHER INFORMATION CONTACT: Concerning § 1.163(j)-1, § 1.163(j)-2, § 1.163(j)-3, § 1.163(j)-9, or § 1.263A-9, Zachary King, (202) 317-4875, Charles Gorham, (202) 317-5091, Susie Bird, (202) 317-4860, Jaime Park, (202) 317-4877, or Sophia Wang, (202) 317-4890; concerning § 1.163(j)-4, § 1.163(j)-5, § 1.163(j)-10, § 1.163(j)-11, § 1.381(c)(20)-1, § 1.382-1, § 1.382-2, § 1.382-5, § 1.382-6, § 1.383-0, § 1.383-1, § 1.1502-13, § 1.1502-21, § 1.1502-36, § 1.1502-79, § 1.1502-91, § 1.1502-95, § 1.1502-98, § 1.1502-99, or § 1.1504-4, Kevin M. Jacobs, (202) 317-5332, Russell Jones, (202) 317-5357, or John Lovelace, (202) 317-5363; concerning § 1.163(j)-6 or § 1.469-9(b)(2), Meghan Howard, (202) 317-5055, William Kostak, (202) 317-6852, Anthony McQuillen, (202) 317-5027, Adrienne Mikolashek, (202) 317-5050, or James Quinn (202) 317-5054; concerning § 1.163(j)-7, § 1.163(j)-8, or § 1.882-5, Angela Holland, (202) 317-5474, Steve Jensen, (202) 317-6938, or Charles Rioux, (202) 317-6842; concerning § 1.446-3, RICs, REITs, REMICs, and the definition of the term "interest", Michael Chin, (202) 317-5846; concerning submissions of comments and outlines of topics for the public hearing, Regina Johnson (202) 317-6901 (not toll-free numbers).

SUPPLEMENTARY INFORMATION:

Background

This document contains proposed amendments to the Income Tax Regulations (26 CFR part 1) under section 163(j) of the Internal Revenue Code (Code). Section 163(j) was amended as part of "An Act to provide for reconciliation pursuant to titles II and V of the concurrent resolution on the budget for fiscal year 2018," Public Law 115-97 (2017) (TCJA). Section 13301(a) of the TCJA amended section 163(j) by removing prior section 163(j)(1) through (9) and adding section 163(j)(1) through (10). The provisions of section 163(j) as amended by section 13301 of the TCJA are effective for tax years beginning after December 31, 2017. Unless otherwise indicated, all references to section 163(j) in this document are references to section 163(j) as amended by the TCJA.

Section 163(j), prior to the amendment by the TCJA (old section 163(j)), disallowed a deduction for "disqualified interest" paid or accrued by a corporation in a taxable year if two threshold tests were satisfied. The first threshold test under old section 163(j) was satisfied if the payor's debt-to-equity ratio exceeded 1.5 to 1.0 (safe harbor ratio). The second threshold test under old section 163(j) was satisfied if the payor's net interest expense exceeded 50 percent of its adjusted taxable income, generally, taxable income computed without regard to deductions for net interest expense, net operating losses, domestic production activities under section 199, depreciation, amortization, and depletion. Disqualified interest for purposes of old section 163(j) included interest paid or accrued to (1) related parties when no Federal income tax was imposed with respect to such interest; (2) unrelated parties in certain instances in which a related party guaranteed the debt; or (3) a real estate investment trust (REIT) by a taxable REIT subsidiary of that REIT. Interest amounts disallowed for any taxable year under old section 163(j) were treated as interest paid or accrued in the succeeding taxable year and could be carried forward indefinitely. In addition, any excess limitation, namely, the excess of 50 percent of the adjusted taxable income of the payor over the payor's net interest expense, could be carried forward three years under old section 163(j)(2)(B). On June 18, 1991, the Department of the Treasury (Treasury Department) and the IRS published in the **Federal Register** (56 FR 27907) a notice of proposed rulemaking (1991-2 C.B. 1040) (Prior Proposed Regulations) to implement the rules under old section 163(j).

In contrast to old section 163(j), for tax years beginning after December 31, 2017, section 163(j) generally limits the amount of business interest expense that can be deducted in the current taxable year (also referred to in this Explanation of Provisions as the current year). Under section 163(j)(1), the amount allowed as a deduction for business interest expense is limited to the sum of (1) the taxpayer's business interest income for the taxable year; (2) 30 percent of the taxpayer's adjusted taxable income (ATI) for the taxable year; and (3) the taxpayer's floor plan financing interest expense for the taxable year. The limitation under section 163(j)(1) applies to all taxpayers, except for certain small businesses that meet the gross receipts test in section 448(c) and certain trades or businesses listed in section 163(j)(7).

Section 163(j)(2) provides that the amount of any business interest not allowed as a deduction for any taxable year as a result of the limitation under section 163(j)(1) is carried forward and treated as business interest paid or accrued in the next taxable year. In contrast to old section 163(j), section 163(j) does not provide for the carryforward of any excess limitation.

Section 163(j)(3) provides that the limitation under section 163(j)(1) does not apply to a taxpayer, other than a tax shelter as defined in section 448(a)(3), with average annual gross receipts of $25 million or less, determined under section 448(c) (including any adjustment for inflation under section 448(c)(4)). For taxpayers other than corporations or partnerships, section 163(j)(3) provides that the gross receipts test is determined for purposes of section 163(j) as if the taxpayer were a corporation or partnership.

Section 163(j)(4) provides special rules for applying section 163(j) in the case of partnerships and S corporations. Section 163(j)(4)(A) requires that the limitation on the deduction for business interest expense be applied at the partnership level, and that a partner's ATI be increased by the partner's share of excess taxable income, as defined in section 163(j)(4)(C), but not by the partner's distributive share of income, gain, deduction, or loss. Section 163(j)(4)(B) provides that the amount of partnership business interest expense limited by section 163(j)(1) is carried forward at the partner-level. Section 163(j)(4)(B)(ii) provides that excess business interest expense allocated to a partner and carried forward is available to be deducted in a subsequent year only if the partnership allocates excess taxable income to the partner. Section 163(j)(4)(B)(iii) provides rules for the adjusted basis in a partnership of a partner that is allocated excess business interest expense. Section 163(j)(4)(D) provides that rules similar to the rules of section 163(j)(4)(A) and (C) apply to S corporations and S corporation shareholders.

Section 163(j)(5) and (6) defines "business interest" and "business interest income," respectively, for purposes of section 163(j). Generally, these terms include interest expense and interest includible in gross income that is properly allocable to a trade or business (as defined in section 163(j)(7)). The legislative history states that "a corporation has neither investment interest nor investment income within the meaning of section 163(d). Thus, interest income and interest expense of a corporation is properly allocable to a trade or business, unless such trade or business is otherwise explicitly excluded from the application of the provision." H. Rept. 115-466, at 386, fn. 688 (2017).

Under section 163(j)(7), the limitation on the deduction for business interest expense in section 163(j)(1) does not apply to certain trades or businesses. The excepted trades or businesses are the trade or business of providing services as an employee, electing real property businesses, electing farming businesses, and certain regulated utility businesses.

Section 163(j)(8) defines ATI as the taxable income of the taxpayer without regard to the following: items not properly allocable to a trade or business; business interest and business interest income; net operating loss deductions; and deductions for qualified business income under section 199A. ATI also generally excludes deductions for depreciation, amortization, and depletion with respect to taxable years beginning before January 1, 2022 and includes other adjustments provided by the Secretary of the Treasury.

Section 163(j)(9) defines "floor plan financing interest" as interest paid or accrued on "floor plan financing indebtedness." These provisions allow taxpayers incurring interest expense for the purpose of securing an inventory of motor vehicles held for sale or lease to deduct the full expense without regard to the limitation under section 163(j)(1).

Section 163(j)(10) provides cross references to provisions requiring that electing farming businesses and electing real property businesses excepted from the limitation under section 163(j)(1) use the alternative depreciation system (ADS), rather than the general depreciation system for certain types of property. The required use of ADS results in the inability of these electing trades or businesses to use the additional first-year depreciation deduction under section 168(k) for those types of property.

The Conference Report states that "[i]n the case of a group of affiliated corporations that file a consolidated return, the limitation applies at the consolidated tax return filing level." H. Rept. 115-466, at 386 (2017). Old section 163(j) treated an affiliated group as one taxpayer, and authorized super-affiliation rules for treating certain other groups as one taxpayer. Both of these provisions were removed by the TCJA, and no equivalent provisions are included in section 163(j).

On April 16, 2018, the Treasury Department and the IRS published Notice 2018-28 (2018-16 I.R.B. 492) to announce an intent to issue proposed regulations that will provide guidance to assist taxpayers in complying with section 163(j). Notice 2018-28 further describes certain rules that those proposed regulations will include to provide taxpayers with interim guidance as more comprehensive guidance is developed. In addition, Notice 2018-28 requested comments from taxpayers about the application of section 163(j). Where relevant to the provisions of these proposed regulations, comments are addressed in the Explanation of Provisions section.

Notice 2018-28 also stated the intent of the Treasury Department and the IRS to withdraw the Prior Proposed Regulations issued under old section 163(j).

Explanation of Provisions

These proposed regulations would withdraw the Prior Proposed Regulations and provide guidance regarding the new limitation on the deduction for business interest expense under section 163(j). These proposed regulations also would add or amend regulations under certain other provisions of the Code where necessary to provide conformity across the Income Tax Regulations. A significant number of the terms used throughout these proposed regulations are defined in proposed § 1.163(j)-1. Some of these terms are discussed in this Explanation of Provisions section as they relate to specific provisions of these proposed regulations.

Consistent with section 163(j)(1), these proposed regulations would limit a taxpayer's deduction for business interest expense to the sum of the taxpayer's current-year business interest income, 30 percent of the taxpayer's ATI, and certain floor plan financing interest expense. These proposed regulations would provide that any amount of business interest expense that cannot be deducted because of the limitation under section 163(j)(1) (section 163(j) limitation) can be carried forward and treated as business interest expense in future years. These proposed regulations also would provide special rules related to the business interest expense carried forward ("disallowed business interest expense carryforwards") by passthrough entities, C corporations, and consolidated groups. Amounts carried forward under old section 163(j) as disallowed disqualified interest are included as disallowed business interest expense carryforwards of a taxpayer to the extent that the amounts otherwise qualify as business interest expense of the taxpayer under these proposed regulations.

These proposed regulations are organized into eleven sections, proposed §§1.163(j)-1 through 1.163(j)-11. Proposed §1.163(j)-1 would provide common definitions used throughout the proposed regulations. Proposed §1.163(j)-2 would provide general rules relating to the computation of a taxpayer's section 163(j) limitation and proposed §1.163(j)-3 would provide ordering and other rules regarding the relationship of the section 163(j) limitation and other provisions of the Code affecting interest. Proposed §1.163(j)-4 would provide rules applicable to C corporations (including REITs, RICs, and consolidated group members) and tax-exempt corporations, whereas proposed §1.163(j)-5 would provide rules governing the disallowed business interest expense carryforwards of C corporations. Proposed §1.163(j)-6 would provide special rules for applying the section 163(j) limitation to partnerships and S corporations. Proposed §1.163(j)-7 would provide rules regarding the application of section 163(j) to foreign corporations and their shareholders, whereas proposed §1.163(j)-8 would provide rules regarding the application of section 163(j) to foreign persons with effectively connected income. Proposed §1.163(j)-9 would provide rules regarding elections for excepted trades or businesses as well as a safe harbor for certain REITs. Proposed §1.163(j)-10 would provide rules to allocate expense and income between non-excepted and excepted trades or businesses. Finally, proposed §1.163(j)-11 would provide certain transition rules relating to the application of the section 163(j) limitation. The remainder of this Explanation of Provisions section discusses these eleven sections, as well as related conforming and coordinating provisions set forth in these proposed regulations.

1. *Proposed §1.163(j)-1: Definitions*

Proposed §1.163(j)-1 would provide definitions of terms used in these proposed regulations. This part 1 of the Explanation of Provisions section briefly discusses the most significant definitions contained in proposed §1.163(j)-1.

A. Adjusted Taxable Income

i. Background

The Prior Proposed Regulations under old section 163(j) defined adjusted taxable income to include a number of adjustments in addition to those set forth in the statutory text of old section 163(j). Some of the additional adjustments resulted in an adjusted taxable income value that approximated cash flow. Two commenters to Notice 2018-28 asked if ATI for purposes of section 163(j) would also attempt to approximate cash flow. Comments on the Prior Proposed Regulations raised a number of administrative concerns with the additions and subtractions to ATI that approximated cash flow in those proposed regulations. The Prior Proposed Regulations were not finalized and therefore did not incorporate the suggestions of these comments to abandon this approach. In addition, because the Prior Proposed Regulations were never finalized, the approach of the Prior Proposed Regulations was never formally required or adopted. Finally, nothing in the Conference Report or the text of section 163(j) requires or suggests that adjustments should be made to ATI in order to approximate cash flow. Such a requirement could have been written into the statutory language or the discussion of section 163(j) contained in the Conference Report if Congress intended ATI to be adjusted in such a manner.

As a result, these proposed regulations would not adopt a cash flow approach to ATI. Instead, proposed §1.163(j)-1(b)(1) would follow the statutory framework of section 163(j)(8) and define ATI to include the adjustments specified in section 163(j)(8)(A), as well as additional adjustments under the authority granted in section 163(j)(8)(B) to prevent double counting and other distortions of items such as floor plan financing interest expense and certain deductions for depreciation, amortization, or depletion upon the sale or disposition of property.

ii. General Application of the Definition of ATI

To compute ATI, taxpayers would first compute taxable income, as defined in proposed §1.163(j)-1(b)(37), in accordance with section 63. In computing taxable income for this purpose, taxpayers would treat all business interest expense as deductible without regard to the section 163(j) limitation. Second, taxpayers would add or subtract, as appropriate, the items specified in these proposed regulations as adjustments to taxable income.

iii. Adjustments to ATI Specifically Referenced in Section 163(j)(8)(A)

Proposed §1.163(j)-1(b)(1) includes as adjustments to taxable income items specifically referenced in section 163(j)(8)(A): any item of income, gain, deduction, or loss which is not properly allocable to a trade or business; business interest and business interest income; net operating loss deductions under section 172; deductions for qualified business income under section 199A; and, deductions for depreciation, amortization, and depletion, but only with respect to taxable years beginning before January 1, 2022. *Net* operating losses under section 172 are added to taxable income in determining ATI, including net operating losses arising in taxable years prior to the effective date of these proposed regulations and carried forward. For purposes of computing ATI, it is intended that deductions for depreciation include special allowances under section 168(k). Additionally, to clarify an issue raised by a commenter in response to Notice 2018-28, the Treasury Department and the IRS note that an amount incurred as depreciation, amortization, or depletion, but capitalized to inventory under section 263A and included in cost of goods sold, is not a deduction for depreciation, amortization, or depletion for purposes of section 163(j).

iv. Other Adjustments to ATI Under Section 163(j)(8)(B)

These proposed regulations would include a number of adjustments under the authority granted in section 163(j)(8)(B). For example, these proposed regulations would include special rules that apply in defining the taxable income of: a regulated investment company (RIC) or REIT in proposed § 1.163(j)-4(b)(4)(ii); a consolidated group in proposed § 1.163(j)-4(d)(2)(iv); a partnership in proposed § 1.163(j)-6(d)(1); an S corporation in proposed § 1.163(j)-6(l)(3); and certain controlled foreign corporations in proposed § 1.163(j)-7(c)(1).

Under the authority granted in section 163(j)(8)(B), proposed § 1.163(j)-1(b)(1) also includes additional adjustments to prevent double counting. Thus, in addition to a subtraction for any floor plan financing interest expense, these proposed regulations include adjustments for sales or dispositions of certain property for taxable years beginning before January 1, 2022. Proposed § 1.163(j)-1(b)(1)(i)(D), (E), and (F) would provide that in determining the amount of a taxpayer's ATI for a taxable year, deductions for depreciation under section 167 or 168, the amortization of intangibles and other amortized expenditures, and depletion under section 611 are added back to a taxpayer's taxable income. As a result, the taxpayer would have increased their taxable income by these amounts for section 163(j) purposes. However, the Treasury Department and the IRS note that a taxpayer could receive a double benefit associated with the depreciation, amortization, and depletion, for ATI calculation purposes if the taxpayer's ATI is increased in respect of a deduction associated with depreciation, amortization, or depletion and then the taxpayer sells or otherwise disposes of the property that was depreciated, amortized, or depleted. This double benefit would result because the amount of the gain that would otherwise be reflected in the ATI in respect of the sale or other disposition would reflect the decreased basis in such assets as a result of the depreciation, amortization, or depletion. Additionally, similar concerns are present if the property was held by either a partnership or a member of a consolidated group and the partnership interest or the stock of the member is sold or otherwise disposed of, because the adjusted basis in the partnership interest or member stock would have been reduced to reflect the depreciation, amortization, or depletion. As a result, these proposed regulations would eliminate the double benefit associated with these sales or other dispositions of property. See proposed § 1.163(j)-1(b)(1)(ii)(C), (D), and (E).

v. Other Rules for Adjusting ATI

Taxpayers can take each adjustment into account only once for purposes of computing ATI; for instance, a deduction for the depreciation of nonbusiness property under section 167 cannot be taken into account as an adjustment to taxable income as both a deduction for depreciation and an item of deduction that is not properly allocable to a trade or business. For purposes of computing ATI, only the adjustments to taxable income that are specified in these proposed regulations may be made. For instance, a deduction under section 243 for dividends received by a C corporation that is neither a RIC nor a REIT reduces the taxable income of the C corporation, and the C corporation cannot add back the amount of such deduction in computing ATI. Proposed § 1.163(j)-4(c)(2) would provide special rules that affect deductions under section 243 for RICs and REITs.

If for a taxable year a taxpayer is allowed a deduction under section 250(a)(1), the taxpayer should take into account the deduction when computing taxable income that is used to calculate ATI, but these proposed regulations would provide that the taxable income limitation in section 250(a)(2) does not apply for this purpose. Taxpayers, however, may be required to make adjustments adding back the section 250(a)(1) deduction to the extent that some or all of the deduction is attributable to an inclusion under section 951A. See proposed § 1.163(j)-7(d).

A separate set of proposed regulations under development will provide general guidance regarding section 250, including the computation of the section 250 deduction and the application of the taxable income limitation in section 250(a)(2).

vi. Comment Request Related to Ordering of Code Provisions

The Treasury Department and the IRS are also aware that various Code provisions in addition to sections 163(j) and 250 (for example, see section 246(b)), affect the amount of taxable income of a taxpayer and are based on, or are limited in some fashion based upon, the taxable income of the taxpayer. As a result, ordering rules are necessary to coordinate application of all of these provisions of the Code with one another. The Treasury Department and the IRS request comments on this matter, which presents broader issues than the ordering of these provisions relative to the application of section 163(j) and may therefore be addressed in guidance unrelated to these proposed regulations.

vii. Comment Request Related to the Computation of ATI

The Treasury Department and the IRS request comments regarding the methodology for computing ATI for purposes of these proposed section 163(j) regulations, including any items that should be included as additional adjustments to taxable income.

B. Interest

There are no generally applicable regulations or statutory provisions addressing when financial instruments are treated as debt for Federal income tax purposes or when a payment is interest. As a result, the proposed regulations draw upon past guidance and case law that address the meaning of interest in the context of Federal tax law. As a general matter, the factors that distinguish debt from equity are described in Notice 94-47, 1994-1 C.B. 357, and interest is defined as compensation for the use or forbearance of money. *Deputy v. Dupont*, 308 U.S. 488 (1940). Using these well-established principles regarding the meaning of interest, these proposed regulations would define interest to include any amount paid or accrued as compensation for the use or forbearance of money under the terms of an instrument or contractual arrangement, including a series of transactions, that is treated as a debt instrument for purposes of section 1275(a) and § 1.1275-1(d) (similar to the definition of interest described in *Deputy v. Dupont*). Thus, these proposed regulations would apply to interest associated with conventional debt instruments, as well as transactions that are indebtedness in substance although not in form. See *Schering-Plough Corp. v. U.S.*, 651 F.Supp. 2d 219 (N.J. Dist. Ct. 2009), aff'd sub nom. *Merck & Co., Inc. v. U.S.*, 652 F.3d 475 (3d Cir. 2011); *Mapco Inc. v. U.S.*, 556 F.2d 1107 (Ct. Cl. 1977). The interest definition in these proposed regulations also would include any amount treated as interest under other provisions of the Code or the regulations thereunder, such as original issue discount, accrued market discount, and amounts with respect to an integrated transaction under § 1.1275-6.

For purposes of section 163(j), these proposed regulations also would treat as interest certain amounts that are closely related to interest and that affect the economic yield or cost of funds of a transaction involving interest, but that may not be compensation for the use or forbearance of money on a stand-alone basis. Income, deduction, gain, or loss from a transaction used to hedge an interest bearing asset or liability, a substitute interest payment made on a debt instrument under the terms of a securities lending or a sale-repurchase transaction, certain commitment fees, and certain debt issuance costs are examples of amounts that would be treated as interest under these proposed regulations. In addition, in order to prevent transactions that are essentially financing transactions from avoiding the application of section 163(j), these proposed regulations contain an anti-avoidance rule that treats as interest expense for purposes of section 163(j) an expense or loss predominantly incurred in consideration of the time value of money in a transaction or series of integrated or related transactions in which a taxpayer secures the use of funds for a period of time.

Treating amounts that are closely related to interest as interest income or expense when appropriate to achieve a statutory purpose is not new; most of the rules treating such payments as interest in these proposed regulations were developed in §§ 1.861-9T and 1.954-2. As a consequence of these rules, however, in some cases certain items could be tested under section 163(j) that are not treated as interest under other provisions that interpret the definition of interest more narrowly. Thus, for example, in certain cases, an amount that was previously deductible under section 162 without limitation could now be tested as business interest expense under section 163(j).

As previously noted, these proposed regulations address the treatment of a commitment fee paid in connection with a lending transaction. This treatment is based on a rule in § 1.954-2(h). The Treasury Department and the IRS request comments on whether other types of fees paid in connection with a lending transaction that are not otherwise treated as interest for Federal income tax purposes should be treated as interest for purposes of section 163(j). As also previously noted, these proposed regulations would treat as interest certain amounts that are closely related to interest and that affect the economic yield or cost of funds of transactions involving interest. The Treasury Department and the IRS request comments on whether additional guidance is needed regarding amounts that are covered or not covered by this rule, specific types of amounts that should or should not be covered, how such amounts are linked to related transactions involving interest, and how such amounts are treated for financial reporting or other nontax purposes. More generally, the Treasury Department and the IRS request comments on whether other types of income and expense should be treated as interest income or interest expense for purposes of section 163(j). For example, should income earned by a taxpayer in a transaction in which the taxpayer provides the use of funds be treated as interest income of the taxpayer if such income is earned predominantly in consideration of the time value of money?

Finally, these proposed regulations generally would treat a swap with significant nonperiodic payments as two separate transactions consisting of an on-market, level payment swap and a loan. The loan would be accounted for by the parties to the contract independently of the swap. The time value component associated with the loan, determined in accordance with § 1.446-3(f)(2)(iii)(A), would be recognized as interest expense to the payor and interest income to the recipient. This provision in these proposed regulations would apply in the same manner as § 1.446-3(g)(4) before it was amended on May 8, 2015, by T.D. 9719 (80 FR 26437, as corrected by 80 FR 61308 (October 13, 2015)), except that this provision would not apply to a collateralized swap that is cleared by a derivatives clearing organization or by a clearing agency. The treatment of such collateralized cleared swaps is reserved, and these proposed regulations would not require testing the assets used for collateralization or condition the exception for collateralized cleared swaps on the extent of collateralization. The Treasury Department and the IRS request comments on the proper treatment of swaps that are cleared by a derivatives clearing organization or by a clearing agency, and any requirements with respect to collateralization that would be necessary or appropriate to identify swaps that could be used to effectively advance funds through the use of nonperiodic payments.

The Treasury Department and the IRS considered three options with respect to the definition of interest. The first option considered was to not provide a definition of interest, and thus rely on general tax principles and case law for purposes of defining interest for purposes of section 163(j). While adopting this option might reduce the compliance burden for some taxpayers, not providing an explicit definition of interest would create its own uncertainty as neither taxpayers nor the IRS might have a clear sense of what types of payments are treated as interest income and interest expense for purposes of section 163(j). Such uncertainty could increase burdens to the IRS and taxpayers including with respect to disputes and litigation about whether particular payments are interest for section 163(j) purposes. Importantly, this option could be distortive as it could result in inappropriate outcomes for taxpayers that earn income that is economically similar to interest income but that has not historically been so treated under general tax principles. For example, in the case of the acquisition of a customer receivable at a discount, existing income tax principles may treat the difference between the acquisition price and the amount ultimately paid on the receivable as ordinary income that is not interest income. In addition, such an approach to the definition of interest would incentivize taxpayers to engage in transactions that provide leverage while generating deductions economically similar to interest but make arguments that such deductions fail to be described by existing principles defining interest expense. If successful, such strategies may greatly limit the application of section 163(j), contrary to the Congressional intent of limiting the deductibility of interest of businesses with the greatest levels of leverage. See House Report, H.R. 115-409 at 248. In addition, such an approach may ignore the statutory language of section 163(j)(1) "[t]he amount allowed as a deduction *under this chapter* for any taxable year for business interest . . . " (emphasis added), which is, on its face, broader than merely deductions under section 163.

The second option considered would have been to adopt a definition of interest but limit the scope of the definition to cover only amounts associated with conventional debt instruments and amounts that are generally treated as interest under the Code or regulations for all purposes prior to the passage of the TCJA. For example, this is similar to the definition of interest proposed in § 1.163(j)-1(b)(20)(i). While this would bring clarity to many transactions regarding what would be deemed interest for the section 163(j) limitation, the Treasury Department and the IRS believe that this approach would potentially distort future financing transactions. Some taxpayers would choose to use financial instruments and transactions that provide a similar economic result to using a conventional debt instrument, but would avoid the label of interest expense under such a definition, potentially enabling these taxpayers to avoid the section 163(j) limitation without a substantive change in capital structure. As a result, the transactions discussed in the prior paragraph would continue to be possible and incentivized under this approach.

In addition, there are certain transactions where under a specific provision of the Code and regulations, amounts could be characterized as ordinary income when in substance the amounts are interest income. For example, in the case of the acquisition of a customer receivable at a discount, existing income tax principles may treat the difference between the acquisition price and the amount ultimately paid on the receivable as ordinary income that is not interest income; however, such income would count as interest income under economic principles. As another example, the receipt of substitute interest paid on a securities loan arrangement may, under existing income tax principles, also be treated as ordinary income rather than interest income despite the fact that such income would also be treated as interest income under economic principles. Prior to the enactment of the section 163(j) interest limitation in TCJA, whether such amounts were labeled as ordinary income or interest income was not often material to the overall tax liability of most taxpayers, but now this distinction may have a significant impact on a large number of taxpayers.

The final option considered and the one ultimately adopted in these proposed regulations is to provide a complete definition of interest that addresses all transactions that are commonly understood to produce interest income and expense, including transactions that may otherwise have been entered into to avoid the application of section 163(j). This approach has the advantage of also providing rules that clearly treat amounts as interest in appropriate cases. Although a comprehensive definition of interest requires an unavoidable degree of detail, the benefits of a detailed definition should decidedly outweigh any complexity that results. The proposed regulations also reduce taxpayer burden by adopting definitions of interest that have already been developed and administered in § § 1.861-9T and 1.954-2, and add several definitions of interest income that were suggested by commenters (such as the rules regarding amounts on contingent payment debt instruments in § 1.163(j)-1(b)(20)(iii)(B)).

The Treasury Department and the IRS invite comments on the definition of interest for purposes of section 163(j) contained in these proposed regulations, whether another definition of interest would be more appropriate in the context of section 163(j), and, generally, what definition of interest would be the most appropriate definition for purposes of section 163(j).

C. Trades or Businesses and Excepted Trades or Businesses

While section 163(j) and the legislative history to section 163(j) provide that certain activities are not treated as trades or businesses, neither section 163(j) nor its legislative history provide a definition of what activities generally constitute a trade or business. The most established and developed definition of trade or business is found under section 162(a), which permits a deduction for ordinary and necessary expenses paid or incurred in carrying on a trade or business. The rules under section 162 for determining the existence of a trade or business are well-established, and there is a large body of case law and administrative guidance interpreting the meaning in section 162 of a trade or business. Therefore, these proposed regulations would define a trade or business as a trade or business within the meaning of section 162, and such definition should aid taxpayers in the proper allocation of interest expense, interest income, and other tax items to a trade or business and an excepted trade or business.

These proposed regulations would also define excepted trades or businesses that are not subject to the limitation of interest expense deduction under section 163(j). These excepted trades or businesses are defined in 163(j)(7)(A), and include (1) the trade or business of providing services as an employee; (2) certain real property businesses that elect to be excepted; (3) certain farming businesses that elect to be excepted; and (4) certain regulated utility businesses. These proposed regulations would provide additional guidance with respect to regulated utility businesses and the allocation of interest expense to such businesses. See proposed §§1.163(j)-1(b)(13) and 1.163(j)-10. Proposed regulations under section 469 would provide additional detail with respect to the definition of a real property trade or business. See proposed §1.469-9(b).

The Treasury Department and the IRS invite comments on whether another definition of trade or business would be preferable or appropriate in the context of section 163(j).

D. Electing Real Property Trade or Business

These proposed regulations would provide that taxpayers can make an election to treat certain trades or businesses as an excepted trade or business if it is a real property trade or business under section 469(c)(7)(C), or certain trades or businesses that are conducted by REITs. Definitions and special rules for REITs would be provided in proposed §1.163(j)-9.

E. Electing Farming Business

These proposed regulations would provide that taxpayers can make an election to treat a trade or business that is a farming business as defined in section 263A(e)(4) or that is a farming business under §1.263A-4(a)(4) for capitalization purposes as an excepted farming business for purposes of section 163(j). These proposed regulations would also provide that a trade or business that is a specified agricultural or horticultural cooperative under section 199A(g)(4) and regulations thereunder can elect to be an excepted farming business for purposes of section 163(j). The Treasury Department and the IRS note that section 163(j)(7)(B) cites section 199A(g)(2) for the definition of a specified agricultural or horticultural cooperative. However, after Public Law 115-141 amended section 199A, the correct citation is section 199A(g)(4). Additionally, the Treasury Department and the IRS are developing separate proposed regulations to provide additional guidance under section 199A(g).

F. Regulated Utility Trade or Business

Consistent with section 163(j)(7)(A)(iv), these proposed regulations would provide that an excepted trade or business includes a regulated utility trade or business that furnishes or sells certain regulated items to the extent the rates for such furnishing or sale have been established or approved by a State or political subdivision thereof, by any agency or instrumentality of the United States, by a public service or public utility commission or other similar body of any State or political subdivision thereof, or by the governing or ratemaking body of an electric cooperative. Certain regulated items are electrical energy, water, or sewage disposal services; gas or steam through a local distribution system; or transportation of gas or steam by pipeline.

Section 163(j) does not define the term "electric cooperative" either directly or by reference to other provisions of the Code. The tax treatment of an electric cooperative is generally governed by section 501(c)(12) of the Code, sections 1381 through 1388 in subchapter T of chapter 1 of subtitle A of the Code (subchapter T), or the common law applicable to cooperatives prior to the enactment of subchapter T. For purposes of section 163(j), the tax treatment of an electric cooperative is not relevant because the statutory language of section 163(j)(7)(A) only requires that rates be set by the ratemaking body of an electric cooperative and does not impose a requirement that the electric cooperative have any particular tax treatment. Accordingly, for purposes of section 163(j), the term electric cooperative includes an electric cooperative that is exempt from income tax under section 501(c)(12), an electric cooperative that is taxable under subchapter T, and an electric cooperative furnishing electric energy to persons in rural areas that is taxable under pre-subchapter T law.

A commenter suggested that rules similar to those that have been used to define public utility property under section 168(i)(10) be used to determine the trade or business that qualifies as a regulated public utility and to distinguish between a regulated and a non-regulated trade or business. The statutory language of section 163(j)(7)(A)(iv) is very similar to that provided under section 168(i)(10) for the definition of a public utility property. Under section 168(i)(10), public utility property is defined as property that is predominately used in one of the enumerated trades or business, which includes the furnishing or sale of certain regulated items listed in section 163(j)(7)(A)(iv), and where the rates for such furnishing or sale are established or approved on a cost of service and rate of return basis.

The Treasury Department and the IRS are aware that such furnishing or sale of the regulated items may not have been established or approved on a cost of service and rate of return basis by a governing or ratemaking body. For example, a public utility may sell some of its electrical energy output at market rates. In this situation, the activity related to the sales at market rates would not be treated as activities related to an excepted regulated utility trade or business under these proposed regulations. Thus, these proposed regulations would provide that to the extent a taxpayer is engaged in both excepted and non-excepted regulated utility trades or businesses, the taxpayer must allocate tax items between the trades or businesses if less than 90 percent of the total output is sold on a cost of service and rate of return basis. Some regulated utility trades or businesses with de minimis market rate sales, rather than pursuant to a cost of service and rate of return basis, are treated as entirely excepted trades or businesses. See proposed § 1.163(j)-10(c)(3)(iii)(C)(3). Guidance related to the allocation methodology for regulated public utility trades or businesses is also provided in proposed § 1.163(j)-10(c)(3)(ii)(C).

G. Floor Plan Financing Interest Expense

These proposed regulations would provide that certain business interest expense paid or accrued on indebtedness used to acquire an inventory of motor vehicles is deductible without regard to the section 163(j) limitation. These proposed regulations would treat all floor plan financing interest expense as business interest expense for purposes of section 163(j), regardless of whether it would otherwise be considered properly allocable to a trade or business that is not excepted under section 163(j).

One commenter to Notice 2018-28 recommended a rule that debt incurred to purchase construction machinery or equipment for sale or lease to farmers should be considered floor plan financing indebtedness for purposes of section 163(j). While H.R. 1, 115th Cong. (as passed by the House of Representatives, November 16, 2017) included construction machinery and equipment in the definition of "motor vehicle" for purposes of floor plan financing indebtedness, the TCJA does not include such machinery and equipment in the statutory definition. The definition of "motor vehicle" for purposes of floor plan financing indebtedness is based on the equipment held for sale or lease, not on the kind of business that the purchaser or lessee is engaged in. Therefore, these proposed regulations do not include the rule suggested by the commenter and merely cross-reference the definition of "motor vehicle" as set forth in section 163(j)(9)(C).

2. *Proposed § 1.163(j)-2: Deduction for Business Interest Expense Limited*

A. General Rules

Consistent with section 163(j)(1), these proposed regulations would provide that the deduction for business interest expense for any taxpayer, other than businesses qualifying for the small business exemption, cannot exceed the sum of current-year business interest income, 30 percent of ATI, and current-year floor plan financing interest expense. See proposed § 1.163(j)-2(b).

To the extent that a taxpayer has business interest expense for the taxable year in excess of the section 163(j) limitation, these proposed regulations would allow the taxpayer a disallowed business interest expense carryforward to the next taxable year. See proposed § 1.163(j)-2(c). The limitation under section 163(j)(1) applies to the total amount of business interest expense of the taxpayer in a taxable year (including disallowed business interest expense carryforwards from prior taxable years) and does not directly trace to interest expense in respect of any particular debt obligation of the taxpayer. Similarly, the disallowed business interest expense carryforward allowed in a taxable year represents the total amount of disallowed business interest expense that is carried forward to the taxable year and does not directly trace to a particular debt obligation of a taxpayer.

B. Exemption for Certain Small Taxpayers; Aggregation; Inherently Personal Items

Consistent with section 163(j)(3), these proposed regulations would provide that taxpayers that meet the gross receipts test of section 448(c) are not subject to the section 163(j) limitation. Eligible taxpayers are those, other than tax shelters under section 448(a)(3), with average annual gross receipts of $25 million or less, tested for the three taxable years immediately preceding the current taxable year. Such a taxpayer is not permitted to make an election under either section 163(j)(7)(B) or (C) because the taxpayer is already not subject to the section 163(j) limitation.

The gross receipts test of section 448(c) is an annual determination based on the prior three taxable years. Thus, a taxpayer's status as an exempt small business under section 163(j) may change from year to year. Because the exemption applies to the taxpayer, any interest paid or accrued in the taxable year in which the taxpayer meets the gross receipts test under section 448(c) is not subject to the section 163(j) limitation. Accordingly, and consistent with section 163(j)(2), these proposed regulations would provide that if a taxpayer who is subject to the limitation under section 163(j)(1) carries disallowed business interest expense forward to a taxable year in which the taxpayer qualifies for the small business exemption, the amount of the carryforward is not subject to the section 163(j) limitation in that taxable year and would be deductible in that taxable year unless disallowed, deferred, or capitalized under another provision of the Code.

Consistent with the regulations under section 448(c), for organizations that are exempt from tax under section 501(a), these proposed regulations would provide that only gross receipts from the activities of such organization that constitute unrelated trades or businesses are taken into account in determining whether the gross receipts test is satisfied. The Treasury Department and the IRS request comments on whether additional guidance is needed in the case of any other exempt organizations with respect to the application of the gross receipts test for purposes of section 163(j).

These proposed regulations would also provide that each partner in a partnership includes a share of partnership gross receipts in proportion to such partner's distributive share of items of gross income that were taken into account by the partnership under section 703. With respect to shareholders in S corporations, these regulations would provide that such shareholders include a pro rata share of the S corporation's gross receipts. The Treasury Department and the IRS request comments on this approach, and also whether other approaches to determining the gross receipts of partners and S corporation shareholders for purposes of section 163(j) would more accurately measure the gross receipts of such partners and shareholders.

These proposed regulations would provide that a taxpayer who is not subject to section 448 is treated as though it were a partnership or corporation when applying the section 448(c) gross receipts test for purposes of the section 163(j) small business exemption. The aggregation rules of sections 52 and 414 would apply to determine whether entities should be aggregated for purposes of the gross receipts test. For an individual taxpayer, it is intended that gross receipts include all items that a business entity could receive, including, but not limited to, business receipts and investment receipts. The only items that an individual taxpayer may exclude from gross receipts for the purpose of the section 163(j) small business exemption are inherently personal items. Inherently personal items include Social Security benefits, personal injury awards and settlements, disability benefits, and wages received as an employee that are reported on Form W-2. Guaranteed payments are not generally equivalent to salaries and wages. See Rev. Rul. 69-187. The Treasury Department and the IRS request comments regarding the scope of inherently personal items.

3. *Proposed § 1.163(j)-3: Relationship of Business Interest Deduction Limitation to Other Provisions Affecting Interest*

These proposed regulations would provide ordering and operating rules to control the interaction of the section 163(j) limitation with other provisions of the Code. The legislative history to the TCJA shows an intent for section 163(j) to apply after other provisions that defer, capitalize, or disallow interest expense. See H. Rept. 115-466, at 387 (2017). Therefore, these proposed regulations generally would apply to interest expense that could be deducted without regard to the section 163(j) limitation; interest expense that has been disallowed, deferred, or capitalized in the current taxable year, or which has not yet been accrued, would not be taken into account for purposes of section 163(j). However, it is intended that, under these proposed regulations, section 163(j) would apply before the operation of the loss limitation rules in sections 465 and 469 and before the application of section 461(l), consistent with how taxpayers apply old section 163(j)(7). In addition, the Treasury Department and the IRS request comments regarding the interaction between section 163(j) and the rules addressing income from discharge of indebtedness under section 108.

The Treasury Department and the IRS have received comments on the interaction of sections 163(j) and 59A, relating to the tax on the base erosion minimum tax amount. These proposed regulations reserve on the interaction of these provisions. The comments previously received, as well as any additional comments received, will be further considered in conjunction with separate guidance under section 59A.

4. *Proposed § 1.163(j)-4: General Rules Applicable to C Corporations (including REITs, RICs, and Members of Consolidated Groups) and Tax-Exempt Corporations*

Proposed § 1.163(j)-4 would provide certain rules regarding the computation of items of income and expense under section 163(j) for taxpayers that are C corporations (including members of a consolidated group, REITs, and RICs) and tax-exempt corporations. Proposed § 1.163(j)-4(b) would provide rules regarding the characterization of items of income, gain, deduction, or loss. Proposed § 1.163(j)-4(c) would provide rules regarding adjustments to earnings and profits. Proposed § 1.163(j)-4(d) would provide special rules applicable to members of a consolidated group.

A. Proposed § 1.163(j)-4(b): Characterization of Items of Income, Gain, Deduction, or Loss

Like other taxpayers, corporations are subject to the limitations on the deductibility of business interest expense in section 163(j). However, unlike other taxpayers, corporations are not subject to the limitations on the deductibility of investment interest expense in section 163(d). In enacting section 163(j), which excludes from the definition of business interest in section 163(j)(5), investment interest within the meaning of section 163(d), and excludes from the definition of business interest income, investment income within the meaning of section 163(d), Congress commented on the interaction between section 163(d) and (j) and the implications thereof for the application of section 163(j) to corporations. More specifically, the legislative history states that—

> [s]ection 163(d) applies in the case of a taxpayer other than a corporation. Thus, a corporation has neither investment interest nor investment income within the meaning of section 163(d). Thus, interest income and interest expense of a corporation is properly allocable to a trade or business, unless such trade or business is otherwise explicitly excluded from the application of the provision.

H. Rept. 115-466, at 386, fn. 688 (2017).

Although the foregoing language could be read to apply to both C corporations and S corporations, it is clear that an S corporation can have investment income and investment expenses within the meaning of section 163(d). These items are separately stated on an S corporation's Schedule K-1, "Partner's Share of Income, Deductions, Credits, etc.," and they are passed through to an S corporation's shareholders. Thus, Congress appears to have made the foregoing statement with C corporations in mind.

Consistent with congressional intent, proposed § 1.163(j)-4(b) would provide that, solely for purposes of section 163(j), and except as otherwise provided in proposed § 1.163(j)-10 (concerning allocations between excepted and non-excepted trades or businesses), all interest paid or accrued by a taxpayer that is a C corporation is treated as business interest expense, and all interest received or accrued by a taxpayer that is a C corporation and that is includible in the taxpayer's gross income is treated as business interest income. Thus, all of a C corporation's interest expense would be subject to limitation under section 163(j), and all of a C corporation's interest income would increase the C corporation's section 163(j) limitation, except to the extent such interest expense or interest income is allocable to an excepted trade or business under proposed § 1.163(j)-10.

To reflect congressional intent, and to achieve consistency with the treatment of interest income and interest expense, proposed § 1.163(j)-4(b) would further provide that, solely for purposes of section 163(j), and except as otherwise provided in proposed § 1.163(j)-10, all other items of income, gain, deduction, or loss of a taxpayer that is a C corporation are properly allocable to a trade or business. As a result, such tax items would be factored into a C corporation's calculation of its ATI (except to the extent such items are allocable to an excepted trade or business).

Although a C corporation cannot have investment interest, investment expenses, or investment income, within the meaning of section 163(d), for purposes of section 163(j), a partnership in which a C corporation is a partner may have such tax items. The partnership will allocate such tax items to its partners, including its C corporation partners, as separately stated items. Thus, the question arises how to treat investment interest, investment expenses, and investment income that is allocated by a partnership to a C corporation partner.

To address this situation, proposed § 1.163(j)-4(b) would recharacterize investment interest expense that a partnership allocates to a C corporation partner as interest expense properly allocable to a trade or business of the C corporation.

Similarly, proposed § 1.163(j)-4(b) would treat investment income and investment expenses that a partnership allocates to a C corporation partner as properly allocable to a trade or business of the C corporation. See the discussion in part 6(G) of this Explanation of Provisions section. However, this rule would not apply to the extent a C corporation partner is allocated a share of a domestic partnership's gross income inclusions under section 951(a) or 951A(a) that are treated as investment income at the partnership level. See § 1.163(j)-7(d)(1)(ii) and the discussion in part 7 of this Explanation of Provisions section.

The recharacterization of investment items at the C corporation partner level under proposed § 1.163(j)-4(b) would not affect the character of these items at the partnership level. It also would not affect the character of the investment interest, investment income, and investment expenses allocated to other (non-C corporation) partners.

Investment interest expense of a partnership that is treated as business interest expense by the C corporation partner would not be treated as excess business interest expense within the meaning of section 163(j)(4)(b)(i) and proposed § 1.163(j)-6. Similarly, investment interest income of a partnership that is treated as business interest income by the C corporation partner would not be treated as excess taxable income within the meaning of section 163(j)(4)(C) and proposed § 1.163(j)-6. This is the case because these items were not treated as business interest expense or factored into the ATI calculation, respectively, at the partnership level. For a discussion of the rules governing excess business interest expense and excess taxable income, see part 6 of this Explanation of Provisions section.

Except as otherwise provided in proposed § 1.163(j)-4(b)(4)(ii) and (iii), the foregoing rules would apply to RICs and REITs. The Treasury Department and the IRS request comments on whether additional special rules are needed for any other entities that are generally taxed as C corporations, including but not limited to cooperatives (as defined in section 1381(a)) and publicly traded partnerships (as defined in section 7704(b)).

These rules also would apply to a corporation that is subject to the unrelated business income tax under section 511, but only with respect to such corporation's items of income, gain, deduction, or loss that are taken into account in computing the corporation's unrelated business taxable income.

B. Proposed § 1.163(j)-4(c): Effect on Earnings and Profits

Distributions by a C corporation to its shareholders out of earnings and profits (E&P) are treated as dividends under section 316(a). Although the Code does not define the term "earnings and profits," the computation of E&P generally is based upon accounting concepts that take into account the economic realities of corporate transactions, in particular, their impact on the corporation's economic ability to pay dividends to its shareholders, and the applicable tax laws.

Proposed § 1.163(j)-4(c) generally would provide that the disallowance and carryforward of a deduction for a C corporation's business interest expense under proposed § 1.163(j)-2 will not affect whether or when such business interest expense reduces the taxpayer's E&P. In other words, C corporations generally should not wait to reduce their E&P for business interest expense until the taxable year in which a deduction for such expense is allowed under section 163(j). This approach, which is the same approach used in the Prior Proposed Regulations under old section 163(j) (see § 1.163(j)-1(e), 56 FR 27907 (June 18, 1991)), reflects the fact that the payment or accrual of business interest expense generally reduces the C corporation's dividend-paying capacity in the year the expense is paid or accrued, without regard to the application of section 163(j). Additionally, disallowed business interest expense carryforwards are somewhat analogous to net operating loss (NOL) carryovers, and taxpayers reduce their E&P in the year the losses that give rise to an NOL are incurred rather than in a subsequent year in which an NOL carryover is absorbed.

However, the section 163(j) regulations would contain several modifications to or clarifications of the general rule regarding E&P. First, if a taxpayer is a RIC or a REIT for the taxable year in which a deduction is disallowed under section 163(j), or in which the RIC or REIT is allocated excess business interest expense from a partnership under section 163(j)(4)(B)(i) and proposed § 1.163(j)-6, then the taxpayer's E&P would not be reduced in the year the expense is paid or accrued without regard to the application of section 163(j). Rather, the taxpayer's E&P would be reduced in the taxable year(s) in which the business interest expense is deductible or, if earlier, in the first taxable year for which the taxpayer no longer is a RIC or a REIT. See proposed § 1.163(j)-4(c)(2) and the discussion of RICs and REITs later in part 4(C) of this Explanation of Provisions section.

Second, a taxpayer would not reduce its E&P in a taxable year beginning after December 31, 2017, to reflect any carryforwards of disallowed disqualified interest (within the meaning of old section 163(j)) to the extent the taxpayer previously reduced its E&P to reflect those interest payments in a prior taxable year. See proposed § 1.163(j)-11(b).

Third, C corporations other than REITs and RICs would make special E&P adjustments with respect to excess business interest expense allocated from a partnership. In general, a C corporation partner must reduce its E&P to reflect expense allocations from the partnership, including allocations of excess business interest expense. However, with respect to excess business interest expense in particular, the C corporation partner also must increase its E&P upon the disposition of the partnership interest to reflect the amount of excess business interest expense that the partner did not take into account while it held the partnership interest.

C. RICs and REITs

RICs and REITs are C corporations and are generally subject to the rules that apply to other C corporations, unless a provision in subchapter M of chapter 1 of the Code makes the rules inapplicable. There are no rules in subchapter M or section 163(j) that make section 163(j) inapplicable to REITs or RICs. Therefore, under these proposed regulations, RICs and REITs would be subject to section 163(j). Some REITs may not have any business interest expense subject to limitation under section 163(j) because they have only electing real property trades or businesses described in section 163(j)(7)(B). Other REITs, however, will have trades or businesses for which the REIT cannot or will not make the election under section 163(j)(7)(B). For example, a mortgage REIT cannot make such an election because real property financing is not an activity described in section 469(c)(7)(C).

RICs and REITs often derive a significant amount (if not all) of their income from property held for investment. However, under these proposed regulations, RICs and REITs would apply the same rules as other C corporations in determining which items are properly allocable to a trade or business. Thus, solely for purposes of 163(j), all of the interest expense and interest income of a RIC or REIT would be treated as business interest expense and business interest income, and all other items of income, gain, deduction, or loss of a RIC or REIT would be treated as properly allocable to a trade or business under proposed § 1.163(j)-4(b), except as otherwise provided in proposed § 1.163(j)-10.

RICs and REITs differ from other taxpayers because the income tax liability of a RIC or REIT is not based directly on its taxable income. Instead, tax is imposed on a RIC's investment company taxable income (ICTI) and a REIT's real estate investment trust taxable income (REITTI), each of which is determined by making certain adjustments to taxable income. These adjustments include the allowance of the deduction for dividends paid and the disallowance of the special corporate deductions in part VIII of subchapter B of chapter 1 of the Code (sections 241 and following) except section 248. The special corporate deductions include the dividends received deduction and the deductions under section 250 in respect of foreign-derived intangible income and global intangible low-taxed income (GILTI).

Under section 163(j)(8), a taxpayer's ATI generally is based on its taxable income, and there is no statutory requirement under which the ATI of a RIC or REIT would be based on ICTI or REITTI. Therefore, unless regulations provide otherwise, the ATI of a RIC or REIT does not reflect the deduction for dividends paid. A RIC or REIT typically pays dividends sufficient to eliminate all or nearly all ICTI or REITTI. As a result, if the ATI of a RIC or REIT took into account the deduction for dividends paid, the ATI of the RIC or REIT typically would be zero, or close to zero. It would be distortive to treat the deduction for dividends paid as reducing ATI because this deduction is merely the mechanism by which RICs and REITs shift the tax liability associated with their income to their shareholders, as intended pursuant to subchapter M of the Code. Therefore, these proposed regulations would not provide a rule that would cause the ATI of a RIC or REIT to take into account the deduction for dividends paid. The deduction for dividends received and the other special corporate deductions previously mentioned, however, are deductions that should reduce the ATI only of taxpayers that benefit from the deductions in determining tax liability. To reduce ATI for such items for taxpayers that cannot in fact utilize these deductions would be distortive. Therefore, under these proposed regulations, the ATI of a RIC or REIT would be increased by the amounts of these special corporate deductions, which decreased the RIC's or REIT's taxable income, because the deductions do not reduce the tax liability of RICs and REITs (or the amounts that RICs or REITs must distribute to eliminate entity-level tax).

RICs and REITs must meet distribution requirements each year in order to be allowed the deduction for dividends paid. If interest expense paid or accrued by a RIC or REIT is disallowed or deferred under section 163(j), or if a RIC or REIT is allocated any excess business interest expense from a partnership, such expense will not reduce the entity's taxable income, the entity's ICTI or REITTI as the case may be, or the amount of dividends that the entity must pay from its earnings and profits. Therefore, the earnings and profits of the RIC or REIT also should not be reduced. Accordingly, these proposed regulations would contain a special rule for RICs and REITs under which their earnings and profits generally would not be reduced by a disallowed business interest expense deduction in the year it is disallowed, or by any excess business interest expense allocated from a partnership.

D. Proposed § 1.163(j)-4(d): Special Rules for Consolidated Groups

Section 1502 provides broad authority for the Secretary of the Treasury to prescribe such regulations as are necessary in order that the tax liability of any affiliated group of corporations filing a consolidated return may be returned, determined, computed, assessed, collected, and adjusted, in order to clearly reflect the income tax liability of the consolidated group and to prevent the avoidance of such tax liability. The legislative history of section 163(j) states that, "[i]n the case of a group of affiliated corporations that file a consolidated return, the limitation applies at the consolidated tax return filing level." H. Rept. 115-466, at 386 (2017). Consistent with legislative intent, proposed § 1.163(j)-4(d) generally would provide that a consolidated group (as defined in § 1.1502-1(h)) has a single section 163(j) limitation. In contrast, members of an affiliated group that does not file a consolidated return would not be aggregated for purposes of applying the section 163(j) limitation. Additionally, partnerships that are wholly owned by members of a consolidated group would not be aggregated with the consolidated group for purposes of applying the section 163(j) limitation. The Treasury Department and the IRS have determined that non-consolidated entities should not be aggregated for purposes of applying the section 163(j) limitation because, whereas old section 163(j)(6)(C) expressly provided that "[a]ll members of the same affiliated group (within the meaning of section 1504(a)) shall be treated as 1 taxpayer," section 163(j) no longer contains such language, and nothing in the legislative history of section 163(j) suggests that Congress intended non-consolidated entities to be treated as a single taxpayer for purposes of section 163(j).

Proposed § 1.163(j)-4(d) would provide specific rules regarding the calculation of the section 163(j) limitation for a consolidated group. In particular, proposed § 1.163(j)-4(d) would provide that the relevant taxable income in computing the group's ATI is the group's consolidated taxable income determined under § 1.1502-11 without regard to any carryforwards or disallowances under section 163(j). Additionally, if for a taxable year a member of a consolidated group is allowed a deduction under section 250(a)(1) that is properly allocable to a non-excepted trade or business, then, for purposes of calculating ATI, consolidated taxable income for the taxable year is determined as if the deduction were not subject to the limitation in section 250(a)(2) and the regulations thereunder. For this purpose, the amount of the deduction allowed under section 250(a)(1) is determined without regard to the application of section 163(j) and the section 163(j) regulations. Moreover, for purposes of calculating the group's section 163(j) limitation, the group's current-year business interest expense and business interest income, respectively, would be the sum of the current-year business interest expense and business interest income of all members of the group. For purposes of this Explanation of Provisions and the proposed section 163(j) regulations, the term "current-year business interest expense" means business interest expense that would be deductible in the current taxable year without regard to section 163(j) and that is not a disallowed business interest expense carryforward from a prior taxable year (see proposed § 1.163(j)-5(a)(2)(i)). Additionally, intercompany obligations (as defined in § 1.1502-13(g)(2)(ii)) would be disregarded for purposes of determining a member's current-year business interest expense and business interest income and for purposes of calculating the consolidated group's ATI, and intercompany items and corresponding items (within the meaning of § 1.1502-13(b)(2)(i) and (b)(3)(i), respectively) would be disregarded for purposes of calculating the group's ATI to the extent those items offset in amount.

Proposed § 1.163(j)-4(d) also cross-references the rules in § 1.1502-32(b), which govern investment adjustments within a consolidated group. Under those rules, if a member has current-year business interest expense for which a deduction is disallowed in the current taxable year under section 163(j), basis in the member's stock would be adjusted in a later taxable year when the expense is absorbed by the group.

Proposed § 1.163(j)-4(d) would further clarify that the transfer of a partnership interest in an intercompany transaction that does not result in the termination of the partnership is treated as a disposition for purposes of the basis adjustment rule in section 163(j)(4)(B)(iii)(II), regardless of whether the transfer is one in which gain or loss is recognized. Several examples would be added to § 1.1502-13(c)(7)(ii) to illustrate the application of these rules. The Treasury Department and the IRS have determined that intercompany transfers of partnership interests should be treated as dispositions for purposes of section 163(j)(4) because dispositions are broadly defined in section 163(j)(4)(B)(iii)(II), and because ignoring intercompany transfers of partnership interests for purposes of section 163(j)(4) would be inconsistent with the view that an entity whose owners are all members of the same consolidated group can be a partnership. In contrast, a change in status of a member, becoming or ceasing to be a member of a consolidated group, would not be treated as a disposition for these purposes.

The Treasury Department and the IRS request comments as to whether the intercompany transfer of a partnership interest in a nonrecognition transaction should constitute a disposition for purposes of section 163(j)(4)(B)(iii)(II) and, if so, how § 1.1502-13(c) should apply to such a transfer if there is excess taxable income in a succeeding taxable year. The Treasury Department and the IRS also request comments as to the treatment of the transfer of a partnership interest in an intercompany transaction that results in the termination of the partnership.

Additionally, proposed § 1.163(j)-4(d) would provide that a member's allocation of excess business interest expense from a partnership and the resulting decrease in basis in the partnership interest under section 163(j)(4)(B) is not a noncapital, nondeductible expense for purposes of § 1.1502-32(b)(3)(iii). Similarly, an increase in a member's basis in a partnership interest under section

163(j)(4)(B)(iii)(II) to reflect excess business interest expense not deducted by the consolidated group is not tax-exempt income for purposes of § 1.1502-32(b)(3)(ii). These special rules are intended to ensure that the allocations and basis adjustments under proposed § 1.163(j)-6 do not result in investment adjustments within the consolidated group. This result is appropriate because the application of the proposed § 1.163(j)-6 rules does not result in a net reduction in the tax attributes of the member partner; rather, there is an exchange of one type of attribute for another (excess business interest expense allocated from the partnership vs. basis in the partnership interest). The Treasury Department and the IRS request comments as to whether additional rules are needed to prevent loss duplication upon the disposition of stock of a member holding partnership interests.

5. *Proposed § 1.163(j)-5: General Rules Governing Disallowed Business Interest Expense Carryforwards for C Corporations*

Proposed § 1.163(j)-5 would provide certain rules regarding disallowed business interest expense carryforwards for taxpayers that are C corporations, including members of a consolidated group. Proposed § 1.163(j)-5(b) would provide rules regarding the treatment of disallowed business interest expense carryforwards. Proposed § 1.163(j)-5(c) would provide cross-references to rules regarding disallowed business interest expense carryforwards in transactions to which section 381(a) applies. Proposed § 1.163(j)-5(d) would provide rules regarding limitations on disallowed business interest expense carryforwards from separate return limitation years (SRLYs). Proposed § 1.163(j)-5(e) would provide cross-references to rules regarding the application of section 382. Proposed § 1.163(j)-5(f) would provide rules regarding the overlap of the SRLY limitation with section 382.

A. Proposed § 1.163(j)-5(b): Treatment of Disallowed Business Interest Expense Carryforwards

Proposed § 1.163(j)-2 limits the amount of business interest expense for which a deduction is allowed in the taxable year. Proposed § 1.163(j)-2 further provides that the amount of any business interest expense not allowed as a deduction for any taxable year as a result of the section 163(j) limitation is carried forward to the succeeding taxable year as a disallowed business interest expense carryforward.

Proposed § 1.163(j)-5(b)(2) generally would provide that, for a C corporation taxpayer that is not a member of a consolidated group, current-year business interest expense is deducted in the current taxable year before any disallowed business interest expense carryforwards from a prior taxable year are deducted in that year. Disallowed business interest expense carryforwards are then deducted in the order of the taxable years in which they arose, beginning with the earliest taxable year, subject to certain limitations (for example, the limitation under section 382). S corporations would be subject to similar rules (see proposed § 1.163(j)-6(l)(5)).

Proposed § 1.163(j)-5(b)(3) would provide similar rules applicable to consolidated groups. In addition, disallowed business interest expense carryforwards from prior separate limitation years (as defined in § 1.1502-1(e)) would be subject to the SRLY limitation. See the discussion of the SRLY rules in part 5(C) of this Explanation of Provisions section.

There are several reasons why the Treasury Department and the IRS have determined that current-year business interest expense and disallowed business interest expense carryforwards should be distinguished for taxpayers that are C corporations and S corporations, and why current-year business interest expense should be deducted before carryforwards from prior taxable years.

First, section 163(j) generally reflects an annual accounting approach. The section 163(j) limitation is calculated anew each year based on the taxpayer's taxable income for that year, and no excess limitation from prior taxable years carries forward to succeeding taxable years. By prioritizing the deduction of current-year business interest expense over disallowed business interest expense carryforwards from prior taxable years, this rule conforms to the annual accounting approach of section 163(j).

Second, if taxpayers were required to deduct disallowed business interest expense carryforwards before or simultaneously with current-year business interest expense, they could end up using some or all of their section 382 limitation on disallowed business interest expense carryforwards rather than on NOLs or other tax items subject to the section 382 limitation. For example, assume that X, a standalone C corporation, has $40x of disallowed business interest expense carryforwards and $30x of NOL carryovers from Year 1, both subject to a section 382 limitation of $35x. In Year 2, X has $50x of current-year business interest expense and a section 163(j) limitation of $45x. If X were required to use its disallowed business interest expense carryforwards before its current-year business interest expense, such carryforwards would absorb all of X's section 382 limitation for the current taxable year, and X would not be able to use any of its NOL carryovers. In contrast, under the rule in proposed § 1.163(j)-5(b), X would use $45x of its current-year business interest expense and none of its disallowed business interest expense carryforwards, thus freeing up its section 382 limitation for its NOL carryovers.

Third, taxpayers that file a consolidated return are required to track their losses by taxable year for purposes of applying the NOL carryover and carryback rules of § 1.1502-21(b) and the NOL SRLY limitation rules of § 1.1502-21(c). As noted in part 5(C) of this Explanation of Provisions section, similar SRLY rules would apply to disallowed business interest expense carryforwards. Thus, a nonconsolidated corporation must track its disallowed business interest expenses by the year in which such expenses are paid or accrued without regard to section 163(j) so that such corporation can comply with the SRLY limitation rules in the event the corporation joins a consolidated group.

Finally, the Treasury Department and the IRS note that, under proposed § 1.163(j)-4(c), C corporations must track their disallowed business interest expense carryforwards by the year in which such items arose (and in which an E&P adjustment was made; see the discussion of proposed § 1.163(j)-4(c) in part 4 of this Explanation of Provisions section) to ensure that E&P is not further reduced in a subsequent year in which the carryforward is deducted. Thus, the Treasury Department and the IRS have determined that these proposed rules should not create an additional administrative burden for C corporations.

Proposed § 1.163(j)-5(b)(3) would further provide rules regarding which member's business interest expense would be deducted by the consolidated group in the current taxable year. If a group's section 163(j) limitation for the taxable year exceeds the aggregate amount of business interest expense, including disallowed business interest expense carryforwards, of all members, then each member's business interest expense, including carryforwards, would be fully deducted in that year, subject to other limitations, such as the section 382 limitation and the SRLY limitation. However, if the aggregate amount of business interest expense, including carryforwards, of all members exceeds the group's section 163(j) limitation for the year, then certain ordering rules would apply:

- *Step 1*: First, the consolidated group would determine whether its section 163(j) limitation for the current year equals or exceeds the members' aggregate current-year business interest expense. If so, then no amount of the consolidated group's current-year business interest expense would be subject to disallowance in the current year under section 163(j), and the consolidated group would skip Steps 2 and 3 of these ordering rules. If not, then the consolidated group must apply Step 2.
- *Step 2*: If the members' aggregate current-year business interest expense exceeds the group's section 163(j) limitation for the current year, each member with current-year business interest expense and either current-year business interest income or floor plan financing interest expense would deduct its current-year business interest expense up to the amount of its business interest income and floor plan financing interest expense for the year.
- *Step 3*: If the consolidated group has any section 163(j) limitation remaining after the application of Step 2 of these ordering rules, each member with remaining current-year business interest expense would deduct its current-year business interest expense pro rata, based on the relative amounts of remaining current-year business interest expense of all members.
- *Step 4*: If the consolidated group has any section 163(j) limitation remaining after the application of Step 1 of these ordering rules, each member's disallowed business interest expense carryforwards from a prior taxable year would be deducted on a pro rata basis, beginning with the earliest year, subject to certain limitations such as the section 382 limitation and the SRLY limitation. For example, assume that P and S are the only members of a consolidated group with a section 163(j) limitation of $200x for the current year (Year 2). Further assume that the amount of current-year business interest expense deducted in Year 2 is $100x, and that P and S, respectively, have $140x and $60x of disallowed business interest expense carryforwards from Year 1 that are not otherwise subject to limitation (for example, under section 382). Under these facts, P would be allowed to deduct $70x of its carryforwards from Year 1 (($140x / ($60x + $140x)) x $100) in Year 2, and S would be allowed to deduct $30x of its carryforwards from Year 1 (($60x / ($60x + $140x)) x $100) in Year 2.
- *Step 5*: Any member with remaining business interest expense after applying Steps 1 through 4 of these ordering rules would carry such expense forward to the succeeding taxable year as a disallowed business interest expense carryforward.

If a corporation ceases to be a member during a consolidated return year, the amount of its business interest expense, including carryforwards from prior taxable years, that is neither deducted by the consolidated group in that year nor reduced under § 1.1502-36(d) would be carried forward to the corporation's first separate return year.

The foregoing rules are intended to roughly mirror the rules in § 1.1502-21 governing the absorption of a consolidated net operating loss (CNOL). However, the Treasury Department and the IRS considered various other approaches to allocating disallowed business interest expense carryforwards among members of a consolidated group. For example, one alternative approach under consideration was a regime whereby disallowed business interest expense carryforwards would be allocated based upon the actual use of externally borrowed funds by each member. Under such an approach, intercompany obligations would be taken into account in allocating disallowed business interest expense carryforwards.

The Treasury Department and the IRS do not propose to adopt such an approach, for several reasons. First, requiring taxpayers to trace externally borrowed funds to the member that ultimately uses such funds would create an administrative burden for taxpayers. Second, because money is fungible, a tracing regime would place undue importance on the location of intercompany obligations. Thus, this approach would permit significant manipulation through the creation of intercompany obligations for the purpose of shifting disallowed business interest expense carryforwards among members. Third, this approach could result in the non-economic allocation of disallowed business interest expense carryforwards to members with no business interest expense to creditors outside the consolidated group. This approach would result in value transfers among consolidated group members and require complex rules to account for those transfers. These proposed regulations implement the statute consistent with legislative intent while avoiding these complications.

The Treasury Department and the IRS request comments on the rules in proposed § 1.163(j)-5(b)(3), including comments on whether these rules should be revised to incorporate additional language or principles from the CNOL allocation rules in § 1.1502-21.

B. Proposed § 1.163(j)-5(c): Disallowed Business Interest Expense Carryforwards in Transactions to Which Section 381(a) Applies

In the case of certain asset acquisitions, section 381(a) generally requires the acquiring corporation to succeed to and take into account the tax items described in section 381(c) of the distributor or transferor corporation. In the TCJA, Congress added disallowed business interest expense carryforwards to the list of items to which the acquiring corporation succeeds in a transaction to which section 381(a) applies (see section 381(c)(20)).

Sections 1.381(c)(1)-1 and 1.381(c)(1)-2 provide rules that, in part, limit the acquiring corporation's ability to use NOL carryforwards in the acquiring corporation's first taxable year ending after the acquisition date. The Treasury Department and the IRS have determined that similar rules should apply to disallowed business interest expense carryforwards. See proposed §§ 1.163(j)-5(c) and 1.381(c)(20)-1.

The Treasury Department and the IRS request comments as to whether section 381(c)(20) and proposed §§ 1.163(j)-5(c) and 1.381(c)(20)-1 should apply to excess business interest expense allocated to a corporate partner.

C. Proposed § 1.163(j)-5(d): Limitations on Disallowed Business Interest Expense Carryforwards From Separate Return Limitation Years

In general, the taxable income of a consolidated group is determined by aggregating the income and losses of each member. Thus, a consolidated group may offset the income earned by profitable members against the losses incurred by other members. However, an exception to this general rule applies to losses incurred by a member in a taxable year in which the member did not join in filing a consolidated return with the current group. The SRLY limitation in § 1.1502-21(c) generally limits the amount of a member's losses arising in a SRLY that may be included in the consolidated group's CNOL to the amount of net income generated by that member. Similar rules in §§ 1.1502-15 and 1.1502-22(c) apply to built-in losses and net capital losses, respectively. Absent a SRLY limitation and other limitations, notably section 382, the consolidated group could reduce its consolidated taxable income simply by acquiring new members with built-in losses, NOLs, net capital losses, or disallowed business interest expense carryforwards.

The Treasury Department and the IRS have determined that rules similar to those in § 1.1502-21(c) should apply to disallowed business interest expense carryforwards. See proposed § 1.163(j)-5(d). However, the calculation of the SRLY limitation for disallowed business interest expense carryforwards would differ from the calculation of the SRLY limitation for NOL carryovers. The SRLY limitation for NOL carryovers is cumulative—in other words, it is based upon a member's aggregate contribution to consolidated taxable income, determined by reference to only the member's tax items, for all consolidated return years of the consolidated group in which the member was included in the group. As a result, a member may carry forward its unused SRLY limitation from one year to the next. In contrast, the SRLY limitation for disallowed business interest expense carryforwards would be calculated annually based upon a member's section 163(j) limitation, determined by reference to only the member's tax items, for any given taxable year. As a result, a member may not carry forward its unused section 163(j) SRLY limitation from one year to the next. The Treasury Department and the IRS have determined that this result is appropriate because Congress did not retain the excess limitation carryforward provisions from old section 163(j). Thus, allowing members to carry forward their unused section 163(j) SRLY limitation would be inconsistent with congressional intent.

Proposed § 1.163(j)-5(d) would provide several additional limitations on a member's ability to use its disallowed business interest expense carryforwards arising in a SRLY. First, such items only may be taken into account by the consolidated group in a taxable year to the extent the group has any remaining section 163(j) limitation for that year after applying the rules in proposed § 1.163(j)-5(b). Second, such items only may be taken into account to the extent the SRLY member's section 163(j) limitation for that year exceeds the amount of the member's business interest expense already taken into account by the group in that year under the rules in proposed § 1.163(j)-5(b). Third, SRLY-limited disallowed business interest expense carryforwards would be deducted on a pro rata basis with non-SRLY limited disallowed business interest expense carryforwards from taxable years ending on the same date.

The Treasury Department and the IRS request comments on the SRLY rules in proposed § 1.163(j)-5(d), including whether a member's SRLY-limited disallowed business interest expense carryforwards should cease to be subject to a SRLY limitation (to the extent of the member's stand-alone section 163(j) limitation) in taxable years in which the member's stand-alone section 163(j) limitation exceeds the consolidated group's section 163(j) limitation.

D. Proposed § 1.163(j)-5(e): Application of Section 382

Like the SRLY limitation, the section 382 limitation limits a taxpayer's ability to reduce its taxable income simply by acquiring a loss corporation. In general, if a loss corporation experiences an ownership change, section 382 limits the amount of the new loss corporation's taxable income that can be offset by pre-change losses to the product of the old loss corporation's value at the time of the ownership change times the long-term tax-exempt rate. For a discussion of the regulations under sections 163(j), 382, and 383 that govern the applicability of section 382 to business interest expense, see parts 11 and 14 through 16 of this Explanation of Provisions section.

E. Proposed § 1.163(j)-5(f): Overlap of SRLY Limitation with Section 382

As noted in parts 5(C) and 5(D) of this Explanation of Provisions section, both the SRLY limitation and the section 382 limitation are intended to prevent taxpayers from trafficking in loss corporations. Moreover, both of these limitations could apply to the same corporation as a result of the same transaction (for example, if a consolidated group acquires a loss corporation in a transaction that is an ownership change for purposes of section 382) or as a result of several transactions that occur within a short period of time.

Section 1.1502-21(g) provides an overlap rule to prevent both the section 382 limitation and the SRLY limitation from applying to NOL carryovers under certain circumstances. The Treasury Department and the IRS have determined that a similar overlap rule should apply with respect to disallowed business interest expense carryforwards. Thus, proposed § 1.163(j)-5(f) would apply the principles of § 1.1502-21(g) to disallowed business interest expense carryforwards when the application of the SRLY limitation would result in an overlap with the application of section 382.

6. *Proposed § 1.163(j)-6: Application of the Business Interest Expense Deduction Limitations to Partnerships and Subchapter S Corporations*

A. In General

Proposed § 1.163(j)-6 would provide guidance regarding partnership and S corporation deductions and carryforwards under section 163(j). To the extent a partnership is subject to the limitations imposed by section 163(j), the section 163(j) limitation shall be applied at the partnership level and any deduction for business interest expense not disallowed under section 163(j) is taken into account in determining the nonseparately stated taxable income or loss of the partnership. Similar rules shall apply to an S corporation. See part 6(H) of this Explanation of Provisions section for a discussion of rules specific to S corporations.

The phrase "nonseparately stated taxable income or loss of the partnership" has not previously been defined by statute. However, section 1366(a)(2) provides a definition of "nonseparately computed income or loss" as applied to S corporations. The legislative history of section 163(j) references "ordinary business income or loss" as reflected on Form 1065, "U.S. Return of Partnership Income," and the partner's distributive share as reflected in Box 1 of Schedule K-1. H. Rept. 115-466, at 387, fn. 690 (2017).

One commenter noted that, in general, an item of income or deduction that is included in nonseparately stated income of a partnership, as determined under section 702(a)(8), loses its tax character in the hands of the partner to whom the item is allocated. The Treasury Department and the IRS agree that for purposes of proposed § 1.163(j)-6(a), to the extent a partnership's business interest expense is less than or equal to the partnership's section 163(j) limitation, such business interest expense loses its character as business interest expense at the partner's level for purposes of the partner's section 163(j) calculation (that is, the business interest expense is not subject to further limitations under section 163(j)). See proposed § 1.163(j)-6(c).

For purposes of the Code other than section 163(j), proposed § 1.163(j)-6(c) would provide that business interest expense and, in the case of a partnership, excess business interest expense, retains its character as business interest expense at the partner and S corporation shareholder-level. For purposes of section 469, such interest retains its characterization as either passive or non-passive when allocated to the partner or shareholder. Additionally, for purposes of section 469, business interest expense from a partnership or S corporation and, in the case of a partnership, excess business interest expense, remains interest derived from a trade or business in the hands of a partner or shareholder, even if the partner or shareholder does not materially participate in the partnership or S corporation's trade or business activity. See proposed § 1.163(j)-3 for additional rules regarding the interaction among sections 461(l), 465, 469, and 163(j).

The Treasury Department and the IRS intend to adopt rules for the proper treatment of business interest income and business interest expense with respect to lending transactions between a passthrough entity and an owner of the entity (self-charged lending transactions). Although reserved in these proposed regulations, the Treasury Department and the IRS intend to adopt certain rules to re-characterize, for both the lender and the borrower, the business interest expense and corresponding business interest income arising from a self-charged lending transaction that may be allocable to the owner, to prevent such business interest income and expense from entering or affecting the section 163(j) limitation calculations for both the lender and the borrower in such situations. One possible approach is to adopt rules similar in scope as those contained in § 1.469-7, dealing with the treatment of self-charged lending transactions for purposes of section 469. The Treasury Department and the IRS request comments with respect to any potential rules that may be considered to achieve this result, as well as comments regarding the potential adverse effects that such rules may have with respect to other Code provisions, such as section 163(d), and any methods for mitigating or eliminating those effects.

Guidance on the treatment of excess business interest expense in tiered partnerships has been reserved in these proposed regulations. Section 163(j)(4) requires the section 163(j) limitation to be taken into account at the entity-level and for business interest expense carryforwards to be allocated to partners. The Treasury Department and the IRS request comments regarding whether, in a tiered partnership arrangement, carryforwards should be allocated through upper-tier partnerships. Additionally, comments are requested regarding how and when an upper-tier partner's basis should be adjusted when a lower-tier partnership is subject to a section 163(j) limitation.

Guidance regarding the application of section 163(j) to a partnership merger or division has been also reserved in these proposed regulations. The Treasury Department and the IRS request comments on the effect of partnership mergers and divisions on excess business interest expense, excess taxable income, and excepted trade or business elections in the context of section 163(j).

B. ATI of a Partnership

i. In General

Proposed § 1.163(j)-6(d) would provide guidance on the ATI of a partnership. Subject to the modifications set forth in proposed § 1.163(j)-6(d) and described in this part 6.B of this Explanation of Provisions section, the ATI of a partnership would be calculated in accordance with proposed § 1.163(j)-1(b)(1). The ATI of the partnership would include any items described in section 703(a)(1), including both separately and nonseparately stated items, to the extent such items are otherwise included under proposed § 1.163(j)-1(b)(1).

ii. Section 743(b), Section 704(c)(1)(C), and Remedial Allocations

The Treasury Department and the IRS considered multiple possible approaches to address the treatment of section 743(b) adjustments to the basis of partnership property upon the transfer of a partnership interest, built-in loss amounts with respect to partnership property under section 704(c)(1)(C), and remedial allocations of income, gain, loss or deduction to a partner pursuant to section 704(c) and § 1.704-3(d) (collectively, partner-level adjustments) under section 163(j). One approach would disregard partner-level adjustments when calculating both the partnership's and the partner's ATI for purposes of section 163(j). This approach is consistent with section 743(b) and the accompanying regulations, which mandate that section 743(b) adjustments are not to be taken into account when determining the partnership's income, gain, deduction, or loss under section 703, and that section 743(b) adjustments are not taken into account until after a partner's distributive share of a deduction is determined.

This approach could, however, lead to odd results. For example, if because of positive section 743(b) adjustments, no current partner includes gain in taxable income on the sale of the partnership property, but the partnership still receives the benefit of the taxable income in its ATI, the partners would be allowed to take a larger amount of business interest expense as a current-year deduction than if the partnership's ATI had included the section 743(b) adjustment. Additionally, when the transferor sells its partnership interest, it generally includes in taxable income the gain resulting from the sale and could possibly include the gain in its own ATI calculation for purposes of its own section 163(j) limitation calculation. This situation could result in the double counting of the income in ATI for section 163(j) purposes, first by the transferor partner on the sale of the partnership interest and again by the partnership on a sale of partnership property.

Under a second approach considered, the partnership would increase or decrease its ATI by the amount of the partner-level adjustments allocated to each partner. Essentially, the partnership would be required to aggregate all partner-level adjustments and take them into account at the partnership level for purposes of section 163(j). The Treasury Department and the IRS viewed taking partner-level adjustments into account at the partnership level as being contrary to the intent of section 743(b), section 704(c)(1)(C), and remedial allocations, and have therefore not adopted this approach.

Under a third approach, (i) partner-level adjustments are not taken into account when computing ATI for purposes of the partnership's section 163(j) limitation; and (ii) each partner's partner-level adjustments are taken into account as items derived directly by the partner in determining its own section 163(j) limitation. This approach takes partner-level adjustments into account at the partner, rather than partnership, level when determining the partner's ATI.

This third approach was recommended by a commenter with respect to section 743(b) adjustments. The commenter argued that if a rule was adopted requiring that a partner's section 743(b) adjustment be included in the computation of a partnership's ATI for purposes of applying section 163(j) at the partnership level, then a particular partner's section 743(b) adjustment could impact the deductibility of partnership interest by other partners, which would be inconsistent with the basic approach taken in the section 743(b) regulations. The Treasury Department and the IRS agree that this approach strikes the best balance between the entity-level calculation under section 163(j) and the aggregate nature of section 743(b) adjustments, as well as other partner-level adjustments. Accordingly, partner-level adjustments are not taken into account when the partnership determines its section 163(j) limitation under proposed § 1.163(j)-6(f). Instead, partner-level adjustments are taken into account by the partner in determining the partner's ATI pursuant to proposed § 1.163(j)-6(e). However, in keeping with the entity approach taken under section 163(j)(4), a partnership shall take adjustments made to the basis of its property pursuant to section 734(b) into account for purposes of calculating its ATI pursuant to proposed § 1.163(j)-6(d).

The commenter acknowledged that this approach would create disparities between the situation where a partnership purchases assets in which, until 2022, depreciation will enter into the partnership's ATI; and a transaction structured as a purchase of partnership interests, where depreciation generated by a section 743(b) basis adjustment or section 704(c) remedial allocation will not enter into a partnership's ATI. The Treasury Department and the IRS are aware of these concerns and request additional comments on the impact of partner-level adjustments on a partnership's ATI calculation under section 163(j), particularly as it relates to publicly traded partnerships.

C. ATI and Business Interest Income of Partners

i. In General

Proposed § 1.163(j)-6(e) would provide that the ATI of a partner shall generally be determined in accordance with proposed § 1.163(j)-1(b)(1) without regard to such partner's distributive share of any items of income, gain, deduction or loss of such partnership, and shall be increased by such partner's share of excess taxable income, as defined in proposed § 1.163(j)-1(b)(13) and determined pursuant to proposed § 1.163(j)-6(f). This provision prohibits the double counting of items in ATI by a partner in its own section 163(j) calculation when a partnership has already taken those items into account under section 163(j). To the extent a partnership has excess taxable income, a partner may include its share of the partnership's excess taxable income, as determined in proposed § 1.163(j)-6(f), in the partner's own ATI for purposes of determining the partner's section 163(j) limitation. For guidance regarding the partner's inclusion of partner-level adjustments, see proposed § 1.163(j)-6(e). For guidance regarding the recharacterization of a partnership's investment interest, investment income, and investment expenses at the C corporation partner-level, see proposed § 1.163(j)-4(b)(3).

ii. Sale of Partnership Interests

Proposed § 1.163(j)-6(e)(3) would provide guidance on the inclusion of the proceeds from the sale of a partnership interest in the selling partner's ATI. In the event a partner sells a partnership interest and the partnership in which the interest is being sold owns only non-excepted trade or business assets, as such term is defined in proposed § 1.163(j)-6(b)(6), the gain or loss on the sale of the partnership interest is included in the partner's ATI. If a partner sells a partnership interest and the partnership in which the interest is being sold owns both excepted assets, as such term is defined in proposed § 1.163(j)-6(b)(7), and non-excepted assets, the partner shall generally use the method set forth in proposed § 1.163(j)-10(c) in order to determine the amount properly allocable to a non-excepted trade or business, and therefore, properly includible in the partner's ATI. Proposed § 1.163(j)-6(e)(4) would also apply to tiered partnerships.

The Treasury Department and the IRS also considered adopting a reasonable method standard by which a partnership could determine the amount properly allocable to a non-excepted trade or business, and therefore, properly includible in the partner's ATI. Such provisions would have adopted tracing rules similar to those set forth in § 1.163-8T, as modified by Notice 88-20, 1988-9 I.R.B. 5 (Feb. 9, 1988), Notice 88-37, 1988-15 I.R.B. 8 (Mar. 16, 1988), and Notice 89-35, 1989-13 I.R.B. 4 (Mar. 9, 1989). The Treasury Department and the IRS request comments on what reasonable methods other than the method set forth in proposed § 1.163(j)-10(c), possibly including a tracing method similar to § 1.163-8T, would be appropriate in order to determine the amount properly allocable to a non-excepted trade or business and under what circumstances such methods would be appropriate.

iii. Double Counting of Business Interest Income Prohibited

Notice 2018-28 stated that for purposes of calculating a partner's annual deduction limitation under section 163(j) for business interest expense paid or accrued by the partner, the partner shall only include business interest income from a partnership in its section 163(j)(1)(A) amount to the extent that business interest income exceeds business interest expense determined at the partnership level under section 163(j). Additionally, a partner shall not include its share of the partnership's floor plan financing for purposes of determining the partner's annual deduction limitation for business interest expense under section 163(j)(1)(C). Proposed § 1.163(j)-6(e)(2) would incorporate these limitations into these proposed regulations.

D. Section 163(j) Partnership Calculation

i. Allocation of Deductible Business Interest Expense and Section 163(j) Excess Items - Made in the Same Manner as the Nonseparately Stated Taxable Income or Loss of the Partnership

Section 163(j)(4)(A)(ii)(II) states that a partner's excess taxable income is determined in the same manner as the nonseparately stated taxable income or loss of the partnership. Section 163(j)(4)(B)(i)(II) states that excess business interest expense is allocated to each partner in the same manner as the nonseparately stated taxable income or loss of the partnership. Similarly, excess business interest income is allocated to each partner in the same manner as the nonseparately stated taxable income or loss of the partnership. The phrase "nonseparately stated taxable income or loss of the partnership" is not defined in section 163(j), and as mentioned in part 6(A) of this Explanation of Provisions section, has not previously been defined by statute or regulations. The phrase "in the same manner as" is also undefined.

Under the proposed regulations, the manner for allocating excess taxable income, excess business interest income, and excess business interest expense (hereinafter "section 163(j) excess items") must be consistent with the Treasury Department and the IRS's resolution of the following three descriptive (1 through 3) and two normative (4 through 5) issues: (1) Section 163(j) is applied at the partnership level; (2) a partnership cannot have both excess taxable income (or excess business interest income) and excess business interest expense in the same taxable year; (3) parity must be preserved between a partnership's deductible business interest expense and section 163(j) excess items and the aggregate of each partner's share of deductible business interest expense and section 163(j) excess items from such partnership; (4) if in a given year a partnership has both deductible business interest expense and excess business interest expense, a partnership should not allocate excess business interest expense to a partner to the extent such partner was allocated the items comprising ATI (or business interest income) that supported the partnership's deductible business interest expense; and (5) if in a given year a partnership has excess taxable income (or excess business interest income), only partners allocated more items comprising ATI (or business interest income) than necessary to support their allocation of business interest expense should be allocated a share of excess taxable income (or excess business interest income).

One commenter proposed a manner for allocating section 163(j) excess items that would require a partnership to allocate each section 163(j) excess item (for example, excess business interest expense) in the same proportion as its underlying section 163(j) item (business interest expense). For example, if partnership AB had $30 of business interest income, which it allocated solely to A, and $40 of business interest expense, which it allocated $20 each to A and B, then A and B would each have $15 of deductible business interest expense and $5 of excess business interest expense. In situations where the partnership does not allocate all of its section 163(j) items pro rata, such as this example, this method could require a partnership to allocate its section 163(j) excess items in a manner inconsistent with the Treasury Department and the IRS's resolution of issues four and five. Because this approach could require a partnership to arguably allocate inappropriate amounts of section 163(j) excess items to its partners, it is not adopted in these proposed regulations.

The calculation adopted in proposed § 1.163(j)-6(f)(2) preserves the entity-level calculation requirement set forth in section 163(j)(4), while also preserving the economics of the partnership and respecting any special allocations made by the partnership in accordance with section 704 and the regulations thereunder. Applying the method in these proposed regulations to the previous example, A would have $20 of deductible business interest expense, and B would have $10 of deductible business interest expense and $10 of excess business interest expense. This result is consistent with the Treasury Department and the IRS's interpretation of section 163(j) as previously discussed.

ii. Allocation of Deductible Business Interest Expense and Section 163(j) Excess Items - General Calculation

Proposed § 1.163(j)-6(f)(2) provides that partnerships must allocate any section 163(j) excess items and any deductible business interest expense in the manner described in paragraphs (f)(2)(i) through (xi). In general, each paragraph (i) through (xi) is a step in a set of instructions that, when completed, provide the partnership with the proper allocation of each of its section 163(j) excess items to each of its partners. This resulting array of allocations is consistent with the Treasury Department and the IRS's resolution of the five key issues described in part 6(D)(i) of this Explanation of Provisions section. Stated otherwise, such prescribed allocations recognize the aggregate nature of partnerships under subchapter K of the Code to the greatest extent possible while remaining consistent with section 163(j) applying at the partnership level.

No rule set forth in proposed § 1.163(j)-6(f)(2) of this section prohibits a partnership from making an allocation to a partner of any section 163(j) item that is otherwise permitted under section 704 and the regulations thereunder. Accordingly, any calculations in proposed § 1.163(j)-6(f)(2)(i) through (xi) are solely for the purpose of determining each partner's deductible business interest expense and section 163(j) excess items, and do not otherwise affect any other provision under the Code, such as section 704(b). Proposed § 1.163(j)-6(f)(2) creates numerous defined terms. These defined terms are solely for the purpose of proposed § 1.163(j)-6(f)(2) and are meant to aid the partnership in its application of proposed § 1.163(j)-6(f)(2) by allowing the calculation to be broken into discrete steps.

Proposed § 1.163(j)-6(f)(2)(i) requires the partnership to calculate its section 163(j) deduction pursuant to proposed § 1.163(j)-2(b). This step is the entity-level calculation required by section 163(j)(4)(A), and it provides the partnership with its total amount of deductible business interest expense, excess business interest income, excess taxable income, and excess business interest expense under section 163(j) for a taxable year. The remaining steps in proposed § 1.163(j)-6(f)(2)(ii) through (xi) determine the allocations a partnership must make of its deductible business interest expense and each section 163(j) excess item to its partners. At the conclusion of the eleven steps set forth in proposed § 1.163(j)-6(f)(2), the total amount of deductible business interest expense and section 163(j) excess items allocated to each partner will equal the partnership's total amount of deductible business interest expense and section 163(j) excess items.

Proposed § 1.163(j)-6(f)(2)(ii) begins the partner-level calculations. It should be noted that the calculations under proposed § 1.163(j)-6(f)(2) do not determine a partner's allocation of business interest expense, business interest income or items comprising ATI, as these allocations are determined under section 704(b) and (c) and the regulations thereunder. Rather, the proposed § 1.163(j)-6(f)(2) partner-level calculations determine each partner's amount of deductible business interest expense and amount of any section 163(j) excess items. This determination provides the starting point for the remainder of the steps in proposed § 1.163(j)-6(f)(2). Only items that were taken into account in the partnership's section 163(j) calculation are taken into account for the proposed § 1.163(j)-6(f)(2) partner-level calculation. Section 743(b) adjustments, built-in loss amounts with respect to partnership property under section 704(c)(1)(C), section 704(c) remedial allocations, allocations of investment income and expense, and amounts determined for the partner under § 1.882-5 are therefore not taken into account for purposes of the proposed § 1.163(j)-6(f)(2) partner-level calculation. To clarify that only section 163(j) items of the partnership are relevant for the calculations under proposed § 1.163(j)-6(f)(2), paragraph (f)(2)(ii) defines "allocable ATI" as a partner's allocable share of the partnership's ATI, "allocable business interest income" as a partner's allocable share of the partnership's business interest income, and "allocable business interest expense" as a partner's allocable share of the partnership's business interest expense that is not floor plan financing interest expense.

As noted previously, the primary goal of proposed § 1.163(j)-6(f)(2) is to provide the partnership with an array of allocations that recognizes the aggregate nature of partnerships under subchapter K of the Code to the greatest extent possible while still remaining consistent with section 163(j) applying at the partnership level. Proposed § 1.163(j)-6(f)(2)(iii) through (v) contain the adjustment mechanism necessary to achieve this goal. Section 163(j) permits taxpayers with a sufficient amount of appropriate income (ATI and business interest income) to deduct their business interest expense. However, section 163(j) applies at the entity level with respect to partnerships under section 163(j)(4). Proposed § 1.163(j)-6(f)(2)(iii) recognizes this normative principle of the statute, and then proposed § 1.163(j)-6(f)(2)(iv) and (v) reconcile the proposed § 1.163(j)-6(f)(2)(iii) partner-level calculation with the proposed § 1.163(j)-6(f)(2)(i) partnership-level result.

To illustrate the mechanism at work in proposed § 1.163(j)-6(f)(2)(iii) through (v), consider the example used above. Partnership AB has $30 of business interest income, which it allocates solely to A, and $40 of business interest expense, which it allocates $20 each to A and B. Upon applying proposed § 1.163(j)-6(f)(2)(iii), AB determines that A has been allocated more allocable business interest income than necessary to deduct its allocable business interest expense ($10 of allocable business interest income excess), and B has not been allocated enough allocable business interest income to deduct its allocable business interest expense ($20 of allocable business interest income deficit). Because AB cannot have both excess business interest income and excess business interest expense in the same year, proposed § 1.163(j)-6(f)(2)(iv) and (v) reconcile the proposed § 1.163(j)-6(f)(2)(iii) partner-level calculation with the proposed § 1.163(j)-6(f)(2)(i) partnership-level result. This process of reallocating allocable business interest income excess to partners with allocable business interest income deficits is broken into two steps; proposed § 1.163(j)-6(f)(2)(iv) first proportionately reduces each partner's excess amount, and then proposed § 1.163(j)-6(f)(2)(v) proportionately reduces each partner's deficit amount to reflect the reallocation of the benefit of the excess amounts.

Proposed § 1.163(j)-6(f)(2)(vii), (ix), and (x) contain the same adjustment mechanism as proposed § 1.163(j)-6(f)(2)(iii) through (v), except for ATI instead of business interest income. To illustrate, if in the previous example AB had $100 of ATI which it allocated solely to A instead of $30 of business interest income, AB would perform the calculations in proposed § 1.163(j)-6(f)(2)(vii), (ix), and (x) - which parallel the calculations in proposed § 1.163(j)-6(f)(2)(iii) through (v) - and arrive at the same result. The partnership must make the adjustments regarding business interest income (proposed § 1.163(j)-6(f)(2)(iii) through (v)) before the adjustments regarding ATI (proposed § 1.163(j)-6(f)(2)(vii), (ix), and (x)) due to section 163(j)(4)(C), which requires partnerships to first fully offset business interest expense using business interest income before turning to ATI.

Finally, proposed § 1.163(j)-6(f)(2)(xi) allocates section 163(j) excess items and deductible business interest expense to the partners. Excess business interest income as determined in proposed § 1.163(j)-6(f)(2)(i) is allocated dollar for dollar to the partners with final allocable excess business interest income determined pursuant to proposed § 1.163(j)-6(f)(2)(iv). After grossing up each partner's final ATI capacity excess amount by ten-thirds (10/3) (the multiplicative inverse of the 30 percent ATI limitation), excess taxable income, as determined in proposed § 1.163(j)-6(f)(2)(i), is allocated dollar for dollar to partners with final ATI capacity excess amounts determined pursuant to proposed § 1.163(j)-6(f)(2)(ix). It is necessary to gross up the ATI capacity excess amount by ten thirds in order to account for the reduction to ATI capacity that occurred in proposed § 1.163(j)-6(f)(2)(vii). Excess business interest expense is allocated dollar for dollar to partners with final ATI capacity deficit amounts determined pursuant to proposed § 1.163(j)-6(f)(2)(x). A partner's allocable business interest expense is deductible business interest expense to the extent it exceeds such partner's share of excess business interest expense.

iii. Allocation of Deductible Business Interest Expense and Section 163(j) Excess Items - Steps 6 and 8

In a given year, if a partnership does not have any partners with a negative allocable ATI under proposed § 1.163(j)-6(f)(2)(vi) (that is, an allocable ATI under proposed § 1.163(j)-6(f)(2)(ii) that is comprised of more items of deduction and loss than income and gain), then the partnership would not have any adjustments under proposed § 1.163(j)-6(f)(2)(vi) and (viii). Thus, the only adjustments and reallocations the partnership would have to perform as part of its proposed § 1.163(j)-6(f)(2) calculation are described in part 6(D)(ii) of this Explanation of Provisions section. However, if a partnership does have a total negative allocable ATI that is greater than zero, then the partnership would have adjustments under proposed § 1.163(j)-6(f)(2)(vi), and may have adjustments under proposed § 1.163(j)-6(f)(2)(viii) as well. Proposed § 1.163(j)-6(f)(2)(vi) and (viii) are closely related. In general, proposed § 1.163(j)-6(f)(2)(viii) corrects distortions that would otherwise occur following certain proposed § 1.163(j)-6(f)(2)(vi) adjustments.

The purpose of proposed § 1.163(j)-6(f)(2)(vi) is to address the situation in which a partner's allocable ATI under proposed § 1.163(j)-6(f)(2)(ii) is comprised of more items of deduction and loss than income and gain - that is, negative allocable ATI. For purposes of the section 163(j) calculation, a partnership that has ATI of less than zero will not be able to deduct business interest expense with respect to ATI under section 163(j)(1). Accordingly, for purposes of the proposed § 1.163(j)-6(f)(2) calculation, the partnership must ensure that each partner has a "final allocable ATI" of at least zero before performing the ATI adjustment calculation described in proposed § 1.163(j)-6(f)(2)(vii), (ix), and (x). This is accomplished by proportionately reallocating positive allocable ATI from partners with positive allocable ATI to partners with negative allocable ATI in order to gross such partners up to zero. Upon completion of the calculation in proposed §1.163(j)-6(f)(2)(vi), the aggregate of the partners' final allocable ATI amounts will equal the partnership's ATI amount used in calculating its section 163(j) limitation under proposed §1.163(j)-6(f)(2)(i), and no partner will have a final allocable ATI amount less than zero.

A partnership must always apply proposed §1.163(j)-6(f)(2)(vi), even if the partnership does not have any numerical adjustment resulting from it. For example, if a partnership has a total negative allocable ATI of $0 in proposed §1.163(j)-6(f)(2)(vi), then even though the partnership will not reallocate any positive allocable ATI in proposed §1.163(j)-6(f)(2)(vi), the partnership must still apply proposed §1.163(j)-6(f)(2)(vi) to convert each partner's positive allocable ATI to final allocable ATI, which is used in subsequent paragraphs as the successor term of allocable ATI.

The purpose of proposed §1.163(j)-6(f)(2)(viii) is to ensure that any adjustments the partnership was required to make under proposed §1.163(j)-6(f)(2)(vi) do not result in proposed §1.163(j)-6(f)(2) requiring the partnership to allocate deductible business interest expense and section 163(j) excess items in an inequitable manner. To illustrate, consider the following example. Partnership ABC has $100 of ATI, comprised of $200 of items of income and gain and $100 of deduction and loss, and $40 of business interest expense. ABC allocates the income and gain $100 each to A and C, and all $100 of the deduction and loss to B. ABC has $40 of business interest expense, which it allocates $20 each to A and B. Upon applying proposed §1.163(j)-6(f)(2)(i), ABC has $30 of deductible business interest expense and $10 of excess business interest expense.

Given these facts and the Treasury Department and the IRS's interpretation of section 163(j), A is clearly entitled to treat all $20 of its allocable business interest expense as deductible business interest expense in the current year, and B should be allocated the $10 of excess business interest expense. However, in the absence of proposed §1.163(j)-6(f)(2)(viii), proposed §1.163(j)-6(f)(2) would require ABC to make different, less equitable, allocations. The issue stems from proposed §1.163(j)-6(f)(2)(vi). Following the application of proposed §1.163(j)-6(f)(2)(vi) and (vii), A has an ATI capacity deficit of $5, B has an ATI capacity deficit of $20, and C has an ATI capacity excess of $15. The calculations in proposed §1.163(j)-6(f)(2)(ix) and (x) reallocate ATI capacity excess to partners with ATI capacity deficits solely based on each partners ATI capacity deficit relative to the total ATI capacity deficit. Because proposed §1.163(j)-6(f)(2)(ix) and (x) only takes each partner's proportionate share of ATI capacity deficit into account when reallocating ATI capacity excess, proposed §1.163(j)-6(f)(2)(ix) and (x) always treat all of partners as though they are on equal footing regardless of any adjustments that may have happened in proposed §1.163(j)-6(f)(2)(vi). As a result, in the absence of proposed §1.163(j)-6(f)(2)(viii), A would be allocated deductible business interest expense of only $18 (instead of $20), and B would be allocated excess business interest expense of only $8 (instead of $10).

The proposed §1.163(j)-6(f)(2)(viii) adjustment begins by filtering out partnerships that do not need to make the adjustment using the criteria listed in proposed §1.163(j)-6(f)(2)(viii)(A). This treatment is possible due to the predictability and limited universe of situations that require a proposed §1.163(j)-6(f)(2)(viii) adjustment. Specifically, a proposed §1.163(j)-6(f)(2)(viii) adjustment is always triggered when a positive allocable ATI partner that helped gross up a negative allocable ATI partner in proposed §1.163(j)-6(f)(2)(vi) is subsequently forced to compete with such partner for a limited amount of ATI capacity excess.

Next, under proposed §1.163(j)-6(f)(2)(viii)(B), a partnership must determine each partner's priority amount. This priority amount represents what a partner's ATI capacity would have been if such partner had not been required under proposed §1.163(j)-6(f)(2)(vi) to offset another partner's negative allocable ATI. For purposes of determining whether to apply proposed §1.163(j)-6(f)(2)(viii)(C) or (D) and performing the calculations under the applicable paragraph, each partner's usable priority amount must be determined. A partner's usable priority amount is the lesser of its priority amount and ATI capacity deficit.

A partnership must use the amounts it determined under proposed §1.163(j)-6(f)(2)(viii)(B) to determine whether it must perform the calculations in proposed §1.163(j)-6(f)(2)(viii)(C) or (D). If the total ATI capacity excess amount, as determined under proposed §1.163(j)-6(f)(2)(vii), is greater than or equal to the total usable priority amount, then the adjustments in proposed §1.163(j)-6(f)(2)(viii)(C) must occur. If the total usable priority amount is greater than the total ATI capacity excess amount, as determined under proposed §1.163(j)-6(f)(2)(vii), then the adjustments in proposed §1.163(j)-6(f)(2)(viii)(D) must occur. The application of proposed §1.163(j)-6(f)(2)(viii)(C) or (D) may result in adjustments to the partner's ATI capacity excess (and deficit) amounts used in proposed §1.163(j)-6(f)(2)(ix) and (x).

The purpose of these adjustments is to ensure that the partners who had a negative allocable ATI do not improperly benefit under proposed §1.163(j)-6(f)(2)(ix) through (xi) to the detriment of the partners who had a positive allocable ATI. In general, proposed §1.163(j)-6(f)(2)(viii)(C) and (D) correct any artificial distortion of the economics between the partners that may have occurred under proposed §1.163(j)-6(f)(2)(vi) by modifying the outputs of proposed §1.163(j)-6(f)(2)(vii) to restore the partners' true economic arrangement before such outputs are used in proposed §1.163(j)-6(f)(2)(ix) and (x). Stated otherwise, proposed §1.163(j)-6(f)(2)(viii)(C) and (D) compensate for the assumption made by proposed §1.163(j)-6(f)(2)(ix) and (x) that all partners are always on equal footing by modifying the outputs of proposed §1.163(j)-6(f)(2)(vii) to put all partners on equal footing before allowing such outputs to reach proposed §1.163(j)-6(f)(2)(ix) and (x).

Turning back to the foregoing example, in accordance with proposed § 1.163(j)-6(f)(2)(viii), ABC would first determine whether it has all three attributes in proposed § 1.163(j)-6(f)(2)(viii)(A)(*1*) through (*3*). Because ABC (1) has excess business interest expense under proposed § 1.163(j)-6(f)(2)(i); (2) has total negative allocable ATI greater than $0 under proposed § 1.163(j)-6(f)(2)(vi); and (3) has a total ATI capacity excess amount greater than $0 under proposed § 1.163(j)-6(f)(2)(vii), ABC must perform the calculations and make the necessary adjustments described under proposed § 1.163(j)-6(f)(2)(viii)(B) and (C) or (D). Given ABC's facts, proposed § 1.163(j)-6(f)(2)(viii)(B) would require ABC to perform the calculations in proposed § 1.163(j)-6(f)(2)(viii)(C). As a result, A would be allocated deductible business interest expense of $20, and B would be allocated excess business interest expense of $10 and deductible business interest expense of $10. This result is consistent with the Treasury Department and the IRS's resolution of the five key issues described in part 6(D)(i) of this Explanation of Provisions section.

The Treasury Department and the IRS request comments on the approach described in this part 6(D). Specifically, comments are requested regarding other reasonable methods to allocate deductible business interest expense, excess taxable income, and excess business interest expense in a manner that permits partners that bear the taxable income supporting the deductible business interest expense to be allocated a disproportionate share of deductible business interest expense and excess taxable income. Finally, comments are requested regarding the fungibility of publicly traded partnership interests with respect to the foregoing approach.

E. Business Interest Expense Carryforwards

i. In General

Proposed § 1.163(j)-6(g) would provide that to the extent a partnership has business interest expense in excess of its section 163(j) limitation, such excess business interest expense shall not be carried forward by the partnership. Instead, such excess business interest expense would be allocated to the partners in accordance with proposed § 1.163(j)-6(f).

A commenter requested guidance regarding whether a partner will be permitted to use its share of the partnership's excess business interest income in the current taxable year to absorb the partner's excess business interest expense allocated from such partnership in prior years. The Treasury Department and the IRS believe that it is consistent with section 163(j) to allow excess business interest income allocated to a partner from a partnership to absorb the partner's excess business interest expenses allocated from that same partnership in an earlier taxable year to the extent of the excess business interest income allocated to the partner. This allowance places partners in a similar position to other taxpayers with carryforwards.

Regarding a partner's allocation of excess taxable income, the Treasury Department and the IRS considered three options when drafting guidance on the deductibility of a partner's excess business interest expense carryforward as it relates to a partner's share of excess taxable income. Section 163(j)(4)(B)(ii)(I) provides that the carryforward "shall be treated as business interest expense paid or accrued by the partner in the next succeeding taxable year in which the partner is allocated excess taxable income from such partnership, but only to the extent of such excess taxable income." The first option would apply a plain reading of the statutory language to treat as paid or accrued by the partner the amount of excess business interest expense carryforward from the partnership equal to the excess taxable income the partner is allocated from the partnership, but it would limit the deductibility of the excess business interest expense by a partner to the partner's business interest income and 30 percent of the partner's ATI for the taxable year. Given this interpretation is the most consistent with the plain meaning of the statute, proposed § 1.163(j)-6(g) would provide that to the extent a partner receives an allocation of excess taxable income from a partnership in a taxable year, such partner's excess business interest expense is treated as paid or accrued in that year in an amount equal to the partner's share of the excess taxable income. To the extent the partner's excess business interest expense exceeds its share of the partnership's excess taxable income in a taxable year, it remains excess business interest expense and is carried over to the following taxable year. When the excess business interest expense is treated as paid or accrued, it becomes business interest paid or accrued by the partner and may be deducted by the partner, subject to any partner-level section 163(j) limitation and any other applicable limitations.

The second option considered would entitle a partner to deduct excess business interest expense only to the extent the partner can deduct that excess business interest expense against the excess taxable income received from the partnership (for example, 30 percent of excess taxable income which increases the partner's ATI under section 163(j)(4)(A)(ii)(II)), regardless of any ATI or business interest income that the partner has from sources other than the partnership. This option would produce the same result as if the partnership had paid or accrued all the relevant income and expense in a single year. The legislative history can be read to suggest this result: "The partner may deduct its share of the partnership's excess business interest in any future year, but only against excess taxable income attributed to the partner by the partnership the activities of which gave rise to the excess business interest carryforward." H. Rept. 115-466, at 391 (2017). However, this interpretation does not appear to be consistent with the plain language of the statute, which states that excess business interest expense is treated as paid or accrued to the extent of the partner's excess taxable income.

The third option considered would entitle a partner to fully deduct excess business interest expense to the extent it receives an allocation of excess taxable income from the same partnership (for example, for every dollar of excess taxable income a partner is allocated, the partner is able to deduct one dollar of excess business interest expense). This interpretation would treat all excess business interest expense, to the extent of excess taxable income, as interest deductible under section 163(a). However, this interpretation ignores the possibility that the partner may be subject to its own section 163(j) limitation and ignores the 30 percent limitation on ATI that a partnership would be subject to had the business interest expense been paid or accrued in the current year. Accordingly, this option is not adopted in the proposed regulations.

ii. Ordering Rule

The ordering rule in proposed § 1.163(j)-6(f)(2)(iii) would clarify that to the extent a partner is allocated excess taxable income or excess business interest income from a partnership in the current taxable year and, in a prior year, that partner was allocated excess business interest expense from that same partnership that has not been previously treated as paid or accrued by the partner, the partner must treat that current-year excess taxable income and excess business interest income as causing the excess business interest expense carried forward from the partnership to be treated as paid or accrued in such year to the extent of the excess taxable income and excess business interest income. In the event a partner receives excess taxable income or excess business interest income from a partnership, it cannot choose to keep excess business interest expense as not paid or accrued in the current taxable year.

F. Basis Adjustments

i. Basis and Capital Account Adjustments for Excess Business Interest Expense Allocations

Generally, a partner's adjusted basis in its partnership interest shall be reduced by allocated items of partnership loss or deduction, but not below zero, pursuant to § 1.704-1(d)(2). Deductible business interest expense and excess business interest expense are subject to section 704(d). If a partner is subject to a limitation on loss under section 704(d) and a partner is allocated losses from a partnership in a taxable year, § 1.704-1(d)(2) requires that the limitation on losses under section 704(d) be apportioned amongst these losses based on the character of each loss (each grouping of losses based on character being a "section 704(d) loss class"). If there are multiple section 704(d) loss classes in a given year, § 1.704-1(d)(2) requires the partner to apportion the limitation on losses under section 704(d) to each section 704(d) loss class proportionately. For purposes of applying this proportionate rule, any deductible business interest expense (whether allocated to the partner in the current taxable year or suspended under section 704(d) in a prior taxable year), any excess business interest expense allocated to the partner in the current taxable year, and any excess business interest expense from a prior taxable year that was suspended under section 704(d) ("negative section 163(j) expense") shall comprise the same section 704(d) loss class. Once the partner determines the amount of limitation on losses apportioned to this section 704(d) loss class, any deductible business interest expense is taken into account before any excess business interest expense or negative section 163(j) expense.

The adjusted basis of a partner in a partnership interest is reduced, but not below zero, by the amount of excess business interest expense allocated to the partner pursuant to proposed § 1.163(j)-6(f)(2). Negative section 163(j) expense is not treated as excess business interest expense in any subsequent year until such negative section 163(j) expense is no longer suspended under section 704(d). Consequently, an allocation of excess taxable income or excess business interest income does not result in the negative section 163(j) expense being treated as business interest expense paid or accrued by the partner. Further, unlike excess business interest expense preventing a partner from including excess taxable income in its ATI as described in section 163(j)(4)(B)(ii) flush language, negative section 163(j) expense does not affect, and is not affected by, any allocation of excess taxable income to the partner. Accordingly, any excess taxable income allocated to a partner from a partnership while the partner still has a negative section 163(j) expense will be included in the partner's ATI. However, once the negative section 163(j) expense is no longer suspended under section 704(d), it becomes excess business interest expense, which is subject to the general rules in proposed § 1.163(j)-6(g). Section 163(j) has no effect on the maintenance of capital accounts (for example, a partner's capital account is reduced in the year such partner is allocated excess business interest expense). See § 1.704-1(b)(2)(iv)(b).

The guidance provided in proposed § 1.163(j)-6(h)(2) is intended to address situations in which a partner is subject to a limitation under section 704(d) and is also allocated excess taxable income. Pursuant to proposed § 1.163(j)-6(g), excess business interest expense would otherwise be treated as paid or accrued by the partner in an amount equal to the excess taxable income, but the partner's basis in the partnership does not increase in an amount equal to the allocated excess taxable income and, therefore, remains subject to the loss limitation in section 704(d). The approach taken in proposed § 1.163(j)-6(h)(2) attempts to reconcile the competing deduction limitations imposed by sections 704(d) and 163(j) along with section 163(j) treating excess business interest expense as paid or accrued by the partner when the partner is allocated excess taxable income. The Treasury Department and the IRS request comments on this issue.

ii. Basis Adjustments Upon Disposition of Partnership Interests Pursuant to Section 163(j)(4)(B)(iii)(II)

Proposed § 1.163(j)-6(h)(3) would provide that if a partner disposes of all or substantially all of its partnership interest, the adjusted basis of the partner in the partnership interest shall be increased immediately before the disposition by the amount of excess, if any, of the amount of the basis reduction under proposed § 1.163(j)-6(h)(1) over the portion of any excess business interest expense allocated to the partner under proposed § 1.163(j)-6(f)(2) which has not been previously treated under proposed § 1.163(j)-6(g) as business interest expense paid or accrued by the partner, regardless of whether the disposition was as a result of a taxable or non-taxable transaction. No deduction under section 163(j) shall be allowed to the transferor or transferee under chapter 1 of the Code for any excess business interest expense resulting in a basis increase under section 163(j) and these proposed regulations or for any negative section 163(j) expense.

In the event a partner disposes of less than substantially all of its interest in a partnership, proposed § 1.163(j)-6(h)(2) would provide that a partner shall not increase its basis in its partnership by the amount of any excess business interest expense that has not yet been treated as paid or accrued by the partner in accordance with proposed § 1.163(j)-6(g). Any such excess business interest expense would remain excess business interest expense in the hands of the transferor partner until such time as the transferor partner is allocated an appropriate amount of excess taxable income or excess business interest income from the partnership or added to the basis of its partnership interest when the partner fully disposes of the partnership interest. Additionally, any negative section 163(j) expense shall remain negative section 163(j) expense of the transferor partner until such negative section 163(j) expense is no longer suspended under section 704(d). These rules are similar to the rules found under section 469 and the regulations thereunder relating to suspended passive activity loss deductions.

The Treasury Department and the IRS considered alternate approaches when analyzing the effect of partial dispositions on a partner's basis. One alternate approach would add excess business interest expense to the partner's basis in the partnership interest to the extent the partner's capital account is reduced by the transfer or redemption. A second approach would increase the partner's remaining basis in the partnership interest by the amount of excess business interest expense that is proportionate to the amount of the partner's adjusted basis in the partnership interest that was transferred or redeemed. This method would require a partner to track its basis in the partnership interest in a manner similar to that set forth in Rev. Rul. 84-53, 1984-15 I.R.B. 17, 1984-1 C.B. 159 (Apr. 9, 1984). The Treasury Department and the IRS request comments on this issue.

G. Investment Items

Proposed § 1.163(j)-6(j) would provide guidance on the treatment of investment income and expense items under section 163(d) allocated by a partnership to its partners. Notice 2018-28 stated that the Treasury Department and the IRS intend to issue regulations clarifying that, solely for purposes of section 163(j), in the case of a taxpayer that is a C corporation, all interest paid or accrued by the C corporation on indebtedness of such C corporation will be business interest expense within the meaning of section 163(j)(5), and all interest on indebtedness held by the C corporation that is includible in gross income of such C corporation will be business interest income within the meaning of section 163(j)(6). Additionally, comments were received requesting guidance on the treatment of investment interest expense and investment interest income, as defined in section 163(d), allocated to a C corporation (corporate partner) by a partnership.

The Treasury Department and the IRS considered two approaches to address this issue. Under the first approach, the investment interest expense would be allocated directly from the partnership to the corporate partner without being subject to the section 163(j) limitations of the partnership. This option is most consistent with a plain reading of the statute. The definition of business interest expense under section 163(j)(5) specifically excludes investment interest. Section 163(j)(4) requires the business interest expense deduction to be calculated with respect to the partnership's specific items of income and expense, and the statute does not require any partner-specific considerations to be taken into account when performing the calculation at the partnership level.

The legislative history of section 163(j) indicates that a corporation can never have investment income and expenses, and instead, those items shall be treated as business interest income and expenses: "Section 163(d) applies in the case of a taxpayer other than a corporation. Thus, a corporation has neither investment interest nor investment income within the meaning of section 163(d). Therefore, interest income and interest expense of a corporation is properly allocable to a trade or business, unless such trade or business is otherwise explicitly excluded from the application of the provision." H. Rept. 115-466, at 386, fn. 688 (2017).

This language suggests a legislative intent to transform any interest that would otherwise be classified as investment interest in the hands of the corporate partner into business interest expense, thereby subjecting that interest to the corporate partner's limitations under section 163(j).

The second approach considered would require a partnership to perform a notional calculation under section 163(j) with respect to the investment interest that is allocated to its corporate partners. Based on the text and legislative history, this provision could arguably be interpreted to mean that investment interest expenses should be classified as business interest expenses at the time they are allocated to a corporate partner, and accordingly, the partnership should perform a section 163(j) calculation with respect to those items because section 163(j) requires a partnership to take the business interest expense deduction into account. Because this calculation would be done at the partnership level, any partnership with both corporate and non-corporate partners would need to make two section 163(j) calculations: one for any corporate partners and one for non-corporate partners.

Proposed § 1.163(j)-6(j) would adopt the first approach. Section 163(j)(4) does not require the partnership to look beyond its own tax attributes to that of its partners when making a determination as to whether a section 163(j) calculation is necessary. Accordingly, a plain reading of the statute does not support the partnership treating investment interest as business interest expense prior to allocating the interest to its partners. Instead, the statute appears to require the corporate partner to calculate its section 163(j) limitation while including this investment interest as it would with all other business and investment interest it receives from all sources.

It should be noted that, with respect to passthrough entities, including S corporations, engaged in trades or businesses that are not passive activities and with respect to which certain owners of the passthrough entities do not materially participate for purposes of section 469, as described in section 163(d)(5)(A)(ii) and as illustrated in Rev. Rul. 2008-12, the rules of section 163(j)(4) will apply to business interest expense allocable to such trades or businesses of those passthrough entities if those entities are otherwise subject to section 163(j). To the extent business interest expense of a passthrough entity is not limited under section 163(j), such business interest expense may still be limited by section 163(d) at the passthrough entity owner level in these situations. With respect to partnerships, to the extent that such business interest expense is limited under section 163(j)(4) and becomes a carryover item of partners who do not materially participate with respect to such trades or businesses, those items will be treated as items of investment interest expense in the hands of those owners for purposes of section 163(d) once those carryover items are treated as paid or accrued in a succeeding taxable year. The Treasury Department and the IRS have concluded that this is the result of the statutory rules contained in section 163(d)(4)(B) and (d)(5)(A)(ii) and, therefore, no additional rules are needed in regulations to reach this result.

H. S Corporations

i. In General

Section 163(j)(4)(D) provides that rules similar to those contained in section 163(j)(4)(A), relating to the entity-level treatment of the section 163(j) deduction, and section 163(j)(4)(C), relating to the definition of excess taxable income, apply to S corporations. Accordingly, proposed § 1.163(j)-6(l) would provide that, in the case of any S corporation, (i) the section 163(j) deduction limitation would be applied at the S corporation level, and (ii) any deduction for business interest expense would be taken into account in determining the nonseparately stated taxable income or loss of the S corporation.

An S corporation would determine its amount allowed as a deduction for business interest expense for the taxable year, that is, its section 163(j) deduction limitation, in the same manner as set forth in proposed § 1.163(j)-2(b). Due to the fact that S corporations generally are required to make pro rata distributions of income, allocations of excess taxable income and excess business interest income would be made in accordance with the shareholders' respective interests in the S corporation after the S corporation determines its section 163(j) deduction limitation pursuant to proposed § 1.163(j)-2(b), in accordance with section 1366(a)(1). See section 1361(b)(1)(D); § 1.1361-1(l) (non-pro rata distributions may create a second class of stock). Because partner-level adjustments are not applicable to S corporation shareholders, the ATI of an S corporation generally would be determined in accordance with proposed § 1.163(j)-1(b)(1) without additional modifications.

ii. Dispositions of S Corporation Stock

Proposed § § 1.163(j)-6(l)(4)(ii) and 1.163(j)-10(b)(4)(ii) would provide guidance regarding the inclusion of the proceeds from the dispositions of S corporation stock in the selling shareholder's ATI. Specifically, proposed § 1.163(j)-6(l)(4)(ii) would provide that, in the event that a shareholder of an S corporation recognizes gain or loss upon the disposition of stock of the S corporation, and the corporation in which the stock is being disposed owns only non-excepted trade or business assets, the gain or loss on the disposition of the stock would be included in the shareholder's ATI. Under proposed § 1.163(j)-10(b)(4)(ii), if a shareholder recognizes gain or loss upon the disposition of stock in an S corporation that owns (1) non-excepted assets and excepted assets, (2) investment assets, or (3) both, the shareholder would determine the proportionate share of the amount properly allocable to a non-excepted trade or business, in accordance with the allocation rules set forth in proposed § 1.163(j)-10(c)(5)(ii)(B)(*3*), and would include such proportionate share of gain or loss in the shareholder's ATI. Proposed § 1.163(j)-10(b)(4)(ii) would also apply to tiered passthrough entities, as defined in proposed § 1.163(j)-7(f)(13), by looking through each passthrough entity tier (for example, an S corporation that is the partner of the highest-tier partnership would look through each lower-tier partnership), subject to proposed § 1.163(j)-10(c)(5)(ii)(D).

iii Double Counting of Business Interest Income Prohibited

Proposed § 1.163(j)-6(l)(4)(iii) would incorporate the limitations set forth in Notice 2018-28, which the Treasury Department and the IRS issued "to prevent the double counting of business interest income and floor plan financing interest expense for purposes of the deduction afforded by section 163(j)." Notice 2018-28, section 7. Consistent with the Notice's statement regarding the application of such limitations to S corporations and their shareholders, proposed § 1.163(j)-6(l)(4)(iii) would provide that, for purposes of calculating an S corporation shareholder's section 163(j) limitation, the shareholder would not include business interest income from an S corporation that is subject to section 163(j) except to the extent it is allocated excess business interest income from that S corporation pursuant to proposed § 1.163(j)-6(l)(1). In addition, proposed § 1.163(j)-6(l)(4)(iii) would provide that an S corporation shareholder could not include its share of the S corporation's floor plan financing interest expense for purposes of calculating a shareholder's section 163(j) limitation because such floor plan financing interest expense would have already have been taken into account by the S corporation in determining its nonseparately stated taxable income or loss for purposes of section 163(j).

iv. Business Interest Expense Carryforwards

Section 163(j)(4) does not indicate the manner by which disallowed business interest expense carryforwards should be treated by an S corporation and its shareholders. However, by virtue of the fact that section 163(j)(4)(D) references both sections 163(j)(4)(A) and (C), but not (B), an inference could be made that Congress intended that disallowed business interest expense carryforwards that arise from an S corporation should be treated differently than excess business interest expense incurred by a partnership. The legislative history appears to support such inference by indicating that the "special rule for carryforward of disallowed partnership interest" in section 163(j)(4)(B) "does not apply to S corporations and their shareholders." H. Rept. 115-466, at 391 (2017).

In light of the statutory language and the legislative history, proposed § 1.163(j)-6(l)(5) provides that the rules set forth in proposed § 1.163(j)-2(c) govern the treatment of S corporation business interest expense carryforwards. Consequently, if an S corporation has a disallowed business interest expense carryforward in the year the S corporation terminates, such item will be carried forward to the succeeding C corporation taxable year. The Treasury Department and the IRS request comments regarding the treatment of disallowed business interest expense carryforwards as an attribute of the S corporation, subject to section 382 limitations, as opposed to the shareholders, and the timing for any adjustments to shareholder basis and the S corporation's accumulated adjustment account. By deferring adjustments to shareholder basis and the S corporation's accumulated adjustments account until any carryforwards are deductible at the corporate level, these proposed regulations generally would match the economics of these adjustments to the shareholders holding stock at the time the S corporation's carryforwards would become deductible.

The Treasury Department and the IRS, however, have considered an alternative option to the rules set forth in proposed § 1.163(j)-6(l)(5). This alternative option would allocate carryforwards from an S corporation to its shareholders in a manner similar to proposed § 1.163(j)-6(g) for partnerships and their partners. This option would require shareholders to receive excess taxable income or excess business interest income from the S corporation in order to treat the disallowed business interest carryforwards as paid or accrued by the shareholder. The shareholder's basis and the S corporation's accumulated adjustment account would be reduced upon an allocation of excess business interest expense to the shareholders.

This alternative option would set forth a framework that would be consistent with the flow-through nature of S corporations. For example, S corporations, similar to partnerships, allocate items of deduction and expense in the year that they occur, even if such items might be suspended at the shareholder-level under section 1366(d). In addition, S corporation shareholders calculate their respective bases in a manner similar to partners, except that S corporation shareholders do not take into account entity-level debt. Thus, corporate attributes generally are suspended at the shareholder-level under the existing subchapter S framework. The Treasury Department and the IRS request comments on this alternative approach and the authoritative support for adopting it.

v. Applicability of Section 382 to S Corporations Regarding Disallowed Business Interest Expense Carryforwards

Although the Treasury Department and the IRS have determined that sections 381(c)(20) and 382(d)(3) and (k)(1) apply to S corporations with respect to disallowed business interest expense carryforwards, the Treasury Department and the IRS continue to consider the extent to which section 382 should apply to S corporations for purposes other than section 163(j). The application of section 382 to S corporations for purposes of section 163(j) should not be construed as creating any inference regarding the application of section 382 to S corporations for other purposes. The Treasury Department and the IRS seek comments regarding the proper integration of these two Code sections and subchapter S of the Code (for example, comments regarding the interaction between sections 382 and 1362(e)(6)(D)).

I. Partnership or S Corporation Not Subject to Section 163(j)

Proposed § 1.163(j)-6(m) would provide guidance regarding partnerships and S corporations not subject to section 163(j). If a partnership or S corporation is not subject to section 163(j) by reason of proposed § 1.163(j)-2(d) (exempt entity), the exempt entity would not be required to perform the business interest expense limitation calculations under proposed § § 1.163(j)-2(b) and 1.163(j)-6. To the extent a partner or shareholder receives business interest expense from an exempt entity, however, that business interest expense will be subject to the partner or shareholder's own section 163(j) deduction. In the event a partner or shareholder is subject to section 163(j) and the S corporation or partnership is not, the partnership or S corporation shall provide the partner or shareholder with the information necessary to inform the partner or shareholder of the partner or shareholder's share of the partnership or S corporation's business interest expense, business interest income, and items of ATI.

To the extent a partnership or S corporation is not subject to section 163(j) by reason of proposed § 1.163(j)-1(b)(38)(ii) because it has an excepted trade or business (excepted entity), the excepted entity would not have to perform the business interest expense limitation calculations under proposed § § 1.163(j)-2(b) and 1.163(j)-6 with respect to the business interest expense that is allocated to such electing trade or business. To the extent a partner or shareholder is allocated any section 163(j) item that is allocated to the partnership's excepted trade or business (excepted 163(j) items), such excepted 163(j) items would be excluded from the partner or shareholder's section 163(j) deduction calculation.

In the event a partnership allocates excess business interest expense to one or more of its partners, and in a later taxable year becomes exempt from the requirements of section 163(j)(4), proposed § 1.163(j)-6(l) would provide that the excess business interest expense from the prior taxable years is treated as paid or accrued by the partner in such later taxable year.

7. Proposed § 1.163(j)-7: Application of Section 163(j) to Foreign Corporations and Their Shareholders

A. Overview

The Treasury Department and the IRS received comments requesting clarification on whether section 163(j) applies to a controlled foreign corporation (as defined in section 957) (CFC) and, if so, the manner in which it applies.

These proposed regulations would provide the general rule that section 163(j) and the section 163(j) regulations apply to determine the deductibility of a CFC's business interest expense in the same manner as those provisions apply to determine the deductibility of a domestic C corporation's business interest expense. See proposed § 1.163(j)-7(b)(2). Thus, a CFC with business interest expense would apply section 163(j) to determine the extent to which that expense is deductible for purposes of computing subpart F income as defined under section 952, tested income as defined under section 951A(c)(2)(A), and income which is effectively connected with the conduct of a U.S. trade or business (ECI), as applicable. Additional guidance for a CFC (and other foreign persons) with ECI is provided in proposed § 1.163(j)-8 and discussed in part 8 of this Explanation of Provisions section.

Notwithstanding the general applicability of section 163(j) to CFCs under these proposed regulations, the Treasury Department and the IRS have determined that it is appropriate in certain cases to modify its application. As discussed in part 7(B) and part 7(C) of this Explanation of Provisions section, these proposed regulations would, in certain cases, limit the amount of a CFC's business interest expense subject to the section 163(j) limitation and modify the computation of a CFC's ATI, respectively.

The Treasury Department and the IRS continue to study whether it would be appropriate to provide additional modifications to the application of section 163(j) to CFCs and whether there are particular circumstances in which it may be appropriate to exempt a CFC from the application of section 163(j). The Treasury Department and the IRS request comments on this matter.

B. Computation of Amount of Business Interest Expense Subject to Section 163(j)

The Treasury Department and the IRS are aware that if business interest expense is paid by one CFC to a related CFC, the application of section 163(j) could result in an inappropriate mismatch of a deduction and payee income item. Such mismatch could inappropriately impact the calculation of the tax liability of a United States shareholder, as defined in section 951(b), under section 951A or the GILTI provision. Consider an example where a United States person (USP) wholly owns two CFCs (CFC1 and CFC2), and CFC1 has made a loan to CFC2 with respect to which CFC1 annually accrues $100x of business interest income that is included in CFC1's tested income, and CFC2 pays or accrues $100x of business interest expense, which absent section 163(j), would be fully deductible in computing CFC2's tested income or tested loss, as applicable. Thus, the intercompany business interest income and business interest expense would fully offset one another for purposes of computing USP's inclusion under section 951A(a). To the extent section 163(j) were to disallow a deduction for business interest expense to CFC2 while the business interest income would be included in CFC1's tested income, the amounts would not fully offset, and USP's inclusion under section 951A(a) may be increased solely due to the use of intercompany debt between CFC1 and CFC2.

The Treasury Department and the IRS considered the possibility of completely disregarding all business interest income and business interest expense with respect to intercompany debt between related CFCs for purposes of computing the section 163(j) limitation of the lender CFC and borrower CFC (the disregard approach). However, the disregard approach was rejected because it could cause inappropriate results where, for example, one CFC (CFC finco) borrows from a third party and on-lends the debt proceeds to one or more other CFCs within a group (funded CFCs). Assume for purposes of simplicity that a CFC finco charges interest on loans to the funded CFCs at the same rate that it is charged by the third party. If intercompany business interest income received by CFC finco and business interest expense paid or accrued by the funded CFCs were disregarded in determining each CFC's section 163(j) limitation, then CFC finco would have no business interest income, and all of CFC finco's business interest expense paid to the third party would be subject to the section 163(j) limitation. Furthermore, all of the funded CFCs would have no business interest expense subject to the section 163(j) limitation. This would be the case, even though the funded CFCs have borrowed from CFC finco and have the use of the funds originally borrowed from the third party.

The Treasury Department and the IRS have determined that an approach that better reflects the reality of borrowings by related CFCs is one that takes into account the principle that money is fungible within a group of highly related CFCs (such a group, a "CFC group" and a CFC that is a member of the group, a "CFC group member"). Accordingly, these proposed regulations would provide for an election to apply an alternative method that would limit the amount of business interest expense of a CFC group member subject to the section 163(j) limitation to the amount of the CFC group member's allocable share of the CFC group's applicable net business interest expense. See proposed § 1.163(j)-7(b)(3). The applicable net business interest expense of a CFC group is the excess, if any, of the sum of the amounts of business interest expense of each CFC group member over the sum of the amounts of business interest income of each CFC group member. See proposed § 1.163(j)-7(f)(3). A CFC group member's allocable share is computed by multiplying the applicable net business interest expense of the CFC group by a fraction, the numerator of which is the CFC group member's net business interest expense (computed on a separate company basis), and the denominator of which is the sum of the amounts of the net business interest expense of each CFC group member with net business interest expense (computed on a separate company basis). See proposed § 1.163(j)-7(f)(1).

Thus, if an election is made to apply the alternative method and if a CFC group has only intercompany debt within the CFC group, then the amount of the CFC group's applicable net business interest expense is zero, and no business interest expense of any CFC group member would be subject to the section 163(j) limitation. As a result, for example, there would be no increase in an inclusion under section 951A(a) solely by reason of the use of intercompany debt within a CFC group. On the other hand, if a CFC group has applicable net business interest expense, then, consistent with the principle that money is fungible, each CFC group member that has net business interest expense, computed on a separate company basis, will determine its allocable share of the applicable net business interest expense, and such allocable share is the amount of business interest expense of the CFC group member that is subject to the section 163(j) limitation. Using its allocable share of the CFC group's applicable net business interest expense, a CFC group member computes its section 163(j) limitation on a separate company basis. However, as discussed in part 7(C) of this Explanation of Provisions section, under these proposed regulations, for purposes of computing a CFC's ATI, an upper-tier CFC group member takes into account a proportionate share of the "excess" ATI of a lower-tier CFC group member.

In general, for purposes of these proposed regulations, a CFC group means two or more CFCs, if at least 80 percent of the stock by value of each CFC is owned, within the meaning of section 958(a), by a single U.S. shareholder or, in aggregate, by related U.S. shareholders that own stock of each member in the same proportion. See proposed § 1.163(j)-7(f)(6). For purposes of identifying a CFC group, members of a consolidated group are treated as a single person, as are individuals filing a joint return, and stock owned by certain passthrough entities is treated as owned by the owners or beneficiaries of the passthrough entity. The Treasury Department and the IRS determined that the alternative method is appropriately limited to situations in which a payor CFC and payee CFC have substantially identical ownership by United States shareholders because the alternative is based on the principle that money is fungible. The alternative is based on the principle that money is fungible, but fungibility should only apply in cases of close relationship where borrowings essentially support the entire group. Furthermore, the mismatch of a deduction and a payee income item is most significant when the payee and payor CFC have substantially identical ownership by United States shareholders. These proposed regulations narrow the scope of foreign corporations that are CFCs for this purpose to those foreign corporations in which at a least one United States shareholder owns stock, within the meaning of section 958. These proposed regulations refer to such a CFC as an "applicable CFC." See proposed § 1.163(j)-7(f)(2).

If one or more CFC group members conduct a financial services business, the alternative method is applied by treating those entities as comprising a separate subgroup (such a subgroup, a "financial services subgroup" and such a member, a "financial services subgroup member"). For this purpose, an entity conducts a financial services business if it is an eligible controlled foreign corporation, as defined in section 954(h)(2)(A), is a qualified insurance company, as defined in section 953(e)(3), or is eligible for the dealer exception in computing foreign personal holding company income as described in section 954(c)(2)(C). The Treasury Department and the IRS determined that it is appropriate to apply the alternative method separately for entities that conduct financial services businesses, because those businesses are typically highly leveraged with significant amounts of business interest income and business interest expense and could reasonably be expected to cause distortion if included in the alternative method with other, non-financial services business CFC group members.

These proposed regulations generally treat a controlled partnership (in general, a partnership in which CFC group members own, in aggregate, at least 80 percent of the interests) as a CFC group member and the interest in the controlled partnership is treated as stock. Thus, for example, if a U.S. person wholly owns two applicable CFCs, which each own a 50-percent interest in a partnership, then, if an election is made to apply the alternative method, the partnership will also apply the alternative method. The Treasury Department and the IRS determined that it is appropriate to extend the relief to partnerships that are substantially owned by CFC group members because the principle that money is fungible is not limited to corporate entities. Furthermore, absent such a rule, a partnership could be used to inappropriately exclude an applicable CFC from the CFC group by having the partnership own the applicable CFC.

These proposed regulations exclude from the definition of a CFC group member an applicable CFC that has ECI. Thus, an applicable CFC with ECI may not compute its section 163(j) limitation under the alternative method, and furthermore, the CFC group, and any financial services subgroup, must exclude such CFC from all group-level computations (for example, in determining the amount of the CFC group's applicable net business interest expense). The Treasury Department and the IRS determined that it is appropriate to exclude an applicable CFC with ECI from application of the alternative method so that section 163(j) applies to a CFC with ECI in the same manner as it does to a domestic C corporation. However, although an applicable CFC with ECI cannot use the alternative method, an applicable CFC with ECI is treated as a CFC group member solely for purposes of determining a CFC group. Thus, for example, if an applicable CFC with ECI is wholly owned by an upper-tier CFC and the applicable CFC with ECI wholly owns a lower-tier CFC, the lower-tier CFC may still qualify as a CFC group member.

If not all CFC group members have the same taxable year, then, if the election is made, these proposed regulations require that all group-level computations be made with respect to a majority U.S. shareholder taxable year. See proposed § 1.163(j)-7(f)(11). Thus, if, for example, USP, a domestic corporation with a calendar taxable year, wholly owns two applicable CFCs, one with a calendar year and one with a November 30 fiscal year, then, with respect to USP's 2019 calendar year, the group-level computations must be determined using amounts for the taxable year ending November 30, 2019, for the one applicable CFC, and amounts for the taxable year ending December 31, 2019, for the other applicable CFC.

Finally, these proposed regulations provide rules concerning the election (referred to as a "CFC group election"), including the requirements for making the CFC group election, the manner for making the CFC group election, and the duration of the CFC group election. See proposed § 1.163(j)-7(b)(5). The Treasury Department and the IRS determined that the alternative method should be elective, rather than required, because for certain situations, the general application of section 163(j) may be preferable to taxpayers.

C. Rules for Computing the ATI of an Applicable CFC

Proposed § 1.163(j)-7(c) would provide rules for computing the ATI of an applicable CFC. The principles of § 1.952-2 for determining the CFC's income and deductions or, for CFCs with ECI, the rules of section 882, apply for purposes of computing the CFC's taxable income. See proposed § 1.163(j)-7(c)(1). The Treasury Department and the IRS request comments on the application of the rules under § 1.952-2 for purposes of determining a CFC's taxable income for purposes of section 163(j). In particular, comments are requested as to whether these rules should allow a CFC a deduction, or require a CFC to take into account income, that is expressly limited to domestic corporations under the Code. For example, questions have arisen as to whether a CFC should be allowed a dividends-received deduction under section 245A, even though section 245A by its terms applies only to dividends received by a domestic corporation.

To mitigate potential double-counting of income in ATI, any dividend received by an applicable CFC from a related person is subtracted from the distributee's taxable income for purposes of computing ATI as the dividend represents income that could be part of the distributing corporation's ATI. See proposed § 1.163(j)-7(c)(2).

If a CFC group election is in effect with respect to a CFC group, then an upper-tier CFC group member takes into account a proportionate share of the "excess" ATI (referred to in these proposed regulations as "CFC excess taxable income") of each lower-tier member in which it directly owns stock for purposes of computing the upper-tier member's ATI. See proposed § 1.163(j)-7(c)(3). The meaning of the term CFC excess taxable income is analogous to the meaning of the term "excess taxable income" in the context of a partnership and S corporation, and, in general, means the amount of a CFC group member's ATI in excess of the amount needed before there would be disallowed business interest expense. See proposed § 1.163(j)-7(f)(5). A CFC group member that is a partnership does not have CFC excess taxable income because under the statute and proposed § 1.163(j)-6, the partnership has excess taxable income and such excess taxable income is allocated to the partners of the partnership. For a discussion of the computation of a partnership's excess taxable income and the treatment of a partner's distributive share of any such excess taxable income, see the discussion in part 6 of this Explanation of Provisions section.

The process of computing and "rolling up" CFC excess taxable income among CFC group members for purposes of computing ATI of each of the CFC group members begins with a lowest-tier member and continues through the chain of ownership to a highest-tier member of the CFC group (referred to in these proposed regulations as a "specified highest-tier member"). Thus, a lowest-tier member computes its section 163(j) limitation, and if the lowest-tier member has CFC excess taxable income, the CFC excess taxable income is taken into account proportionately by one or more higher-tier members that directly own stock of the lower-tier member for purposes of computing ATI; and, if such a higher-tier member has CFC excess taxable income, such CFC excess taxable income is taken into account by a next higher-tier member, and so forth.

A higher-tier member that is a partnership may take into account a pro rata share of the CFC excess taxable income of a lower-tier member, other than a partnership, which does not have CFC excess taxable income, for purposes of computing the higher-tier member partnership's ATI and determining if the higher-tier member partnership has excess taxable income that may be allocated to CFC group members that are partners.

D. Rules for Computing ATI of a United States Shareholder

i. General Rules

In general, a United States shareholder that owns, within the meaning of section 958(a), stock of a CFC is required to include in its gross income each year its pro rata share of the CFC's subpart F income, and investments in U.S. property, as defined in section 956. In addition, a United States shareholder that owns stock of a CFC is required to include in its gross income for each year its GILTI. Thus, these income inclusions are included in the United States shareholder's taxable income, and absent an exercise of regulatory authority, would be included in ATI.

To avoid double counting of the taxable income of a CFC already taken into account to determine the CFC's section 163(j) limitation, proposed § 1.163(j)-7(d)(1)(i) would provide the general rule (the double counting rule) that the ATI of a United States shareholder is computed without regard to any amounts included in gross income under sections 78, 951(a), and 951A(a) that are properly allocable to a non-excepted trade or business of the United States shareholder (each amount, a "specified deemed inclusion" and such amounts, collectively "specified deemed inclusions") and any deduction allowable under section 250(a)(1)(B), without regard to the taxable income limitation in section 250(a)(2), by reason of a specified deemed inclusion (such a deduction, a "specified section 250 deduction").

To the extent a United States shareholder includes amounts in gross income under section 78, 951(a), or 951A(a) that are not properly allocable to a non-excepted trade or business, for example, because such amounts are treated as investment income, within the meaning of section 163(d), of the United States shareholder, then such amounts are not included in ATI (see proposed § 1.163(j)-1(b)(1)(ii)(F)). Thus, for example, if a United States shareholder that is a domestic partnership includes amounts in gross income under section 951(a) or 951A(a) that are treated as investment income with respect to the domestic partnership and therefore are not properly allocable to a trade or business, then such amounts are not included in the ATI of the domestic partnership. However, absent a special rule, to the extent such income inclusions are taken into account as a distributive share of a C corporation partner, the income inclusions would be included in the ATI of the C corporation partner (see proposed § 1.163(j)-4(b)(3)). This result would be contrary to the purpose of the double counting rule. Accordingly, to prevent income inclusions under sections 951(a) and 951A(a) that are treated as investment income with respect to a domestic partnership from being included in the ATI of a corporate partner, these proposed regulations provide that a C corporation partner may not treat such amounts as properly allocable to a trade or business of the C corporation partner. See proposed § 1.163(j)-7(d)(1)(ii).

ii. Rules for a United States Shareholder of a CFC group Member with a CFC Group Election in Effect

If a United States shareholder owns directly or indirectly through one or more foreign partnerships stock of a CFC group member that is a specified highest-tier member for which a CFC group election is in effect, and the specified highest-tier member has CFC excess taxable income that is treated as being attributable to taxable income of the CFC group that resulted in the United States shareholder having specified income inclusions, the United States shareholder may add to its taxable income an amount equal to its proportionate share of the "eligible" CFC excess taxable income of the specified highest-tier member and any other highest-tier members (the addback rule). See proposed § 1.163(j)-7(d)(2). However, the addition to taxable income under the addback rule is limited to the portion of the specified deemed inclusions, all of which are subtracted from taxable income of any United States shareholder under the double-counting rule, that is with respect to CFC group members, reduced by the portion of any specified section 250 deduction that is allowable by reason of such specified deemed inclusions. These proposed regulations refer to the portion described in the preceding sentence as "CFC group inclusions" (see proposed § 1.163(j)-7(d)(2)(iii)). Furthermore, the limitation is computed without regard to amounts included in gross income by reason of section 78 with respect to CFC group members. This result is appropriate because section 78 requires a deemed inclusion only in order to carry out the purposes of the foreign tax credit provisions.

To determine the amount of "eligible" CFC excess taxable income (ETI) of a specified highest-tier member (defined under proposed § 1.163(j)-7(d)(2)(ii) as "eligible CFC group ETI"), the CFC excess taxable income is multiplied by the specified ETI ratio. The specified ETI ratio is a fraction (expressed as a percentage) that compares the amounts of taxable income of each specified highest-tier member and each specified lower-tier member of the specified highest-tier member to the portions of such taxable income that gave rise to inclusions under section 951(a) or 951A(a). The specified ETI ratio includes in the numerator and the denominator of the fraction only taxable income amounts with respect to CFC group members that have CFC excess taxable income without regard to the "roll up" of CFC excess taxable income from a lower-tier member. See proposed § 1.163(j)-7(f)(14). The purpose of the specified ETI ratio is to address the fact that within the CFC group, income of a lower-tier member CFC that is neither subpart F income nor tested income to the extent of GILTI is included in CFC excess taxable income and may be used by an upper-tier CFC group member. It would be distortive for a United States shareholder to obtain an increase in ATI in respect of such income because this income is not taxed in the United States. The specified ETI ratio is intended to provide an estimate of the portion of CFC excess taxable income attributable to this income. The Treasury Department and the IRS determined that this formulaic approach is superior to a tracing approach, because a tracing approach would increase complexity and therefore also generally increase administrative and compliance burdens.

If a United States shareholder of a CFC group member with a CFC group election in effect is a domestic partnership (a U.S. shareholder partnership), the addback rule does not apply to determine the ATI of the U.S. shareholder partnership. See proposed § 1.163(j)-7(d)(3). This is because the Treasury Department and the IRS are of the view that if a U.S. shareholder partnership includes amounts in gross income under section 951(a) or 951A(a) with respect to stock of a CFC group member, then such amounts will, in virtually all fact patterns, be treated as investment income with respect to the partnership, and therefore interest expense of the partnership that is allocable to stock of a CFC group member will be treated as investment interest expense that is not subject to section 163(j) at the partnership-level. In this case, however, if a U.S. shareholder partnership has a domestic C corporation partner (a U.S. corporate partner), the addback rule is applied, with certain modifications, to the U.S. corporate partner for purposes of computing the U.S. corporate partner's ATI. In particular, for purposes of computing the amount of the addition to taxable income of the U.S. corporate partner allowed under the addback rule, the addback rule is modified to provide that the U.S. corporate partner takes into account not only its own specified deemed inclusions with respect to stock of a CFC group member, but for this purpose also its distributive share, if any, of amounts included in gross income under section 951(a) or 951A(a) of the U.S. shareholder partnership with respect to stock of a CFC group member. In addition, the addback rule is modified to provide that for purposes of determining a U.S. corporate partner's pro rata share of eligible CFC excess taxable income of a specified highest-tier member, the U.S. shareholder partnership is treated as if it were a foreign partnership.

E. Effect on Earnings and Profits

Under proposed § 1.163(j)-7(e), and consistent with the rules in proposed § 1.163(j)-4(c), the disallowance and carryforward of a deduction for a foreign corporation's business interest expense does not affect whether and when such business interest expense reduces the corporation's earnings and profits. For example, in the case of a passive foreign investment company (PFIC), the disallowance and carryforward of a deduction will not impact the amount of inclusions of earnings under section 1293 if the PFIC is treated as a qualified electing fund. Similarly, the disallowance and carryforward of a deduction for an applicable CFC's business interest expense will not affect the limitation of subpart F income to earnings and profits under section 952(c).

8. *Proposed § 1.163(j)-8: Application of Section 163(j) to Foreign Persons with Effectively Connected Income*

In general, unlike U.S. citizens or residents that are subject to U.S. tax on their worldwide income, a nonresident alien individual or foreign corporation is subject to net basis income taxation only with respect to its income that is or is treated as effectively connected with a trade or business (ECI) conducted in the United States as provided under section 872 or 882. Deductions are allowed only to the extent that they are connected with such income. In certain circumstances, the tax liability may be reduced or eliminated by the provisions of an income tax treaty entered into by the United States with a foreign country. While a nonresident alien individual or foreign corporation that is not an applicable CFC (hereafter a non-CFC FC) that has ECI is still subject to section 163(j) and the section 163(j) regulations, the rules need to be modified since these foreign persons are only taxed on their ECI. Accordingly, the definitions for ATI, business interest expense, business interest income, and floor plan financing interest expense in § 1.163(j)-1 are modified to limit such amounts to income which is effectively connected income and expenses properly allocable to effectively connected income. See proposed § 1.163(j)-8(b).

As discussed in part 6 of this Explanation of Provisions section, section 163(j)(4) provides that in the case of a partnership, section 163(j) is applied at the partnership level. The partner's ATI is increased by the partnership's excess taxable income, and the partnership's excess business interest expense is allocated to the partner as disallowed business interest expense carryforward that can be deducted when the partners are allocated excess taxable income from the partnership, but only to the extent of such excess. Pursuant to section 163(j)(8)(B), which permits adjustments to the computation of ATI, a nonresident alien individual or non-CFC FC that is a partner in a partnership that is engaged in a U.S. trade or business modifies the application of the general allocation rules in § 1.163(j)-6 with respect to excess taxable income, excess business interest expense, and excess business interest income of the partnership to take into account the limitation of such foreign person's liability for U.S. tax to its ECI. The excess amounts of the partnership, therefore, can be used by the nonresident alien individual or non-CFC FC only to the extent of the partnership's income that would be effectively connected income with respect to the foreign partner. The amount of excess taxable income and excess business interest expense that can be used by such partner is determined by multiplying the amount of the excess taxable income or the excess business interest allocated under § 1.163(j)-6 by a ratio equal to the ATI of the partnership, with the adjustments described previously to limit such amount to only effectively connected income or expense items, over the ATI of the partnership determined under § 1.163(j)-6(d). The amount of excess business interest income that can be used by such partner is limited to ECI business interest income over allocable ECI business interest expense. See proposed § 1.163(j)-8(c).

Proposed § 1.163(j)-8(e) would also include rules coordinating section 163(j) and § 1.882-5. Section 1.882-5 provides rules for determining the amount of a foreign corporation's interest expense that is allocable under section 882(c) to ECI. These proposed regulations require that a foreign corporation that has ECI must first determine its business interest expense allocable to ECI under § 1.882-5 before applying section 163(j). The foreign corporation then applies section 163(j) to its business interest expense to determine if any of that business interest expense is disallowed business interest expense. If the foreign corporation is also a partner in a partnership that has ECI, the foreign corporation must back out that portion of the business interest expense determined under § 1.882-5 which is deemed to have come from the partnership as such business interest expense has already been subject to section 163(j) at the partnership level and the foreign corporation is then left with only the non-partnership business interest expense. If the partnership also had disallowed business interest expense, a portion of the partnership-level interest expense that was backed out of the amount determined under § 1.882-5 will also be disallowed business interest expense. Disallowed business interest expense determined at either the partner-level or partnership level, as appropriate, will not be taken into account for the purpose of determining interest expense under § 1.882-5 in subsequent tax years, but rather will be subject to the limitations of section 163(j).

As provided in proposed § 1.163(j)-8(d), an applicable CFC (as defined in proposed § 1.163(j)-8(g)(1)) that has ECI must first apply the general rules of section 163(j) and the section 163(j) regulations, pursuant to § 1.163(j)-7(b)(2), to determine how section 163(j) applies to the applicable CFC. If, after applying section 163(j) and the section 163(j) regulations, the applicable CFC has disallowed business interest expense, the applicable CFC then must apportion a part of its disallowed business interest expense to interest expense allocable to effectively connected income as determined under § 1.882-5.

These proposed regulations also provide that disallowed business interest expense and disallowed business interest expense carryforwards will not affect the determination of effectively connected earnings and profits or U.S. net equity for purposes of the branch profits tax under section 884. These rules are consistent with the general principles of these proposed regulations with respect to earnings and profits. See proposed § § 1.163(j)-4(c) and 1.163(j)-8(f).

9. Proposed § 1.163(j)-9: Elections for Excepted Trades or Businesses; Safe Harbor for Certain REITs

A. Election Procedure

Proposed § 1.163(j)-9 would provide guidance relating to the election to be treated as an excepted trade or business for real property or farming trades or businesses. These proposed regulations clarify that an election is made for a particular trade or business, not necessarily for a particular entity, and would apply for the taxable year that the election is made and all subsequent years.

Proposed § 1.163(j)-9 would provide the time and manner in which to make the election. Taxpayers making the election should attach an election statement to their timely filed original Federal income tax return, including extensions. The statement should include basic information of the taxpayer and the electing trade or business. Where a taxpayer has multiple trades or businesses that may be eligible for the election, an election must be made for each trade or business, and the election statement must specify or describe the different electing trades or businesses. The election statement is necessary in order for taxpayers and for the IRS to identify each electing trade or business. The Treasury Department and the IRS request comments on whether the information required to be included in the statement is sufficient, or whether additional information should be included to reduce any potential audit controversy.

Because the election applies to the particular trade or business, the election generally terminates automatically if the taxpayer ceases to exist, or ceases the operation of the electing trade or business. However, these proposed regulations would also provide that where a taxpayer transfers all of the assets of an electing trade or business to a related party, the election does not terminate for that trade or business, and transfers to the related party. The purpose of this rule is to disregard a transaction that purports to be a termination or cessation of a trade or business, but is merely a change in the form of conducting the trade or business where the taxpayer (through a related party) retains a relationship to such trade or business. For this purpose, a related party means any person who bears a relationship to the taxpayer which is described in section 267(b) or 707(b)(1). Additional guidance may be provided detailing transactions in which an election might terminate.

Additionally, these proposed regulations would contain an anti-abuse rule to prevent a situation where the taxpayer attempts to terminate the election through a transfer of the assets in the trade or business, but with the intent of resuming a trade or business of a similar nature. These proposed regulations would provide that if a taxpayer re-acquires substantially all of the assets used in the trade or business, or substantially similar assets, and resumes conducting such prior trade or business within 60 months of ceasing the trade or business, the election will be revived with the resumed trade or business.

The Treasury Department and the IRS request comments on the method by which certain taxpayers can make the election under section 163(j)(7)(B) or (C), and the types of transactions in which the election should terminate.

B. Safe Harbor for Certain REITs

Proposed § 1.163(j)-9(g) provides a special safe harbor for REITs. For REITs that take advantage of this safe harbor, the rules applicable to REITs are substantially similar to the general rules provided for other taxpayers. However, these proposed regulations provide certain modifications to take into account the existing rules governing REIT taxation.

If a REIT holds real property, interests in partnerships holding real property, or shares in other REITs holding real property, the safe harbor provides that the REIT is eligible to make an election to be an electing real property trade or business for all or part of its assets. For this purpose, the term "real property" is defined consistently with the definition of real property under section 856, rather than the more restrictive definition set forth under the proposed section 469 regulations.

The term "real property trade or business" in section 469(c)(7)(C) does not include real property financing and, for purposes of the section 163(j) regulations, any assets used in a real property financing trade or business are generally allocated to a non-excepted trade or business. Under proposed § 1.163(j)-9(g), REIT real property financing assets include mortgages, guaranteed mortgage pass-thru certificates, real estate mortgage investment conduit (REMIC) regular interests, and debt instruments issued by publicly offered REITs.

If a REIT makes an election to be an electing real property trade or business, and the value of the REIT's real property financing assets is 10 percent or less of the value of the REIT's total assets, then, under the safe harbor, all of the REIT's assets are treated as assets of an excepted trade or business. This determination is based on the same values used for the REIT asset test under section 856(c)(4) as of the close of the REIT's taxable year. If a REIT makes an election to be an electing real property trade or business, and the value of a REIT's real property financing assets is more than 10 percent of the value of the REIT's total assets, then, under the safe harbor, the REIT's business interest income, business interest expense, and other items of expense and gross income are allocated between excepted and non-excepted trades or businesses under the rules set forth in proposed § 1.163(j)-10, as modified by proposed § 1.163(j)-9(g)(4).

For purposes of valuing a REIT's assets, REIT real property financing assets also include partnership assets that a REIT is deemed to hold under § 1.856-3(g) and the portion of a REIT's interest in another REIT attributable to that other REIT's real property financing assets. The Treasury Department and the IRS request comments on whether the list of real property financing assets in these proposed regulations includes all direct and indirect investments that REITs make to finance real property.

Under the safe harbor, the definition of real property under § 1.856-10 applies to determine whether the assets of a REIT are properly allocable to an excepted trade or business. If a REIT holds an interest in a partnership, in applying the partnership look-through rule described in proposed § 1.163(j)-10(c)(5)(ii)(A)(2), the REIT also applies this definition of real property to determine whether the partnership's assets are allocable to an excepted trade or business.

Under section 856(c)(5)(B), shares in other REITs qualify as real estate assets without regard to the portion of the REIT owned. Under the safe harbor, if a REIT (shareholder REIT) owns shares in another REIT and all of the other REIT's assets are treated as assets of an excepted trade or business, then all of shareholder REIT's adjusted basis in the shares of the other REIT is properly allocable to an excepted trade or business of shareholder REIT. If this is not the case, the safe harbor provides that shareholder REIT applies the partnership look-through rule described in proposed § 1.163(j)-10(c)(5)(ii)(A)(2) (as if the other REIT were a partnership) in determining the extent to which shareholder REIT's adjusted basis in the shares of the other REIT is properly allocable to an excepted trade or business of shareholder REIT. If shareholder REIT does not receive the information from the other REIT that is necessary to apply the look-through rule, then shareholder REIT's shares of the other REIT are properly allocable to a non-excepted trade or business of shareholder REIT.

C. Anti-abuse Rule for Certain Real Property Trades or Businesses

The Treasury Department and the IRS have determined that it would be inappropriate to allow an election to be an excepted real property trade or business for a trade or business that leases substantially all of its real property to the owner of the real property trade or business, or to a related party of the owner. To permit such an election would encourage a taxpayer to enter into non-economic structures where the real estate components of non-real estate businesses are separated from the rest of such businesses in order to artificially reduce the application of section 163(j) by leasing the real property to the taxpayer or a related party of the taxpayer and electing for this "business" to be an excepted real property trade or business. As a result, these proposed regulations would also contain an anti-abuse rule. If at least 80 percent of the business's real property, determined by fair market value, is leased to a trade or business under common control with the real property trade or business, the trade or business will not be eligible for the election. Common control in this case means that 50 percent of the direct and indirect ownership interests in both businesses are held by related parties within the meaning of sections 267(b) and 707(b). REITs that lease qualified lodging facilities, as defined in section 856(d)(9)(D), and qualified healthcare properties, as defined in section 856(e)(6)(D), are generally permitted pursuant to section 856(d)(8)(B) to lease these properties to a taxable REIT subsidiary; thus, this anti-abuse rule does not apply to these types of REITs. The Treasury Department and the IRS request comments on whether other exceptions to the anti-abuse rule (such as, for example, an exception for certain fact patterns where real property that is leased from a related party is ultimately sub-leased to a third party) would be appropriate.

10. *Proposed § 1.163(j)-10: Allocation of Expense and Income to an Excepted Trade or Business*

As provided in section 163(j)(7) and proposed § 1.163(j)-2, certain trades or businesses are excepted from the application of section 163(j), including electing real property trades or businesses, electing farming businesses, regulated utility trades or businesses, and the trade or business of performing services as an employee. Section 1.163(j)-10 would provide rules for determining the amount of a taxpayer's interest expense, interest income, and other tax items that is properly allocable to excepted and non-excepted trades or businesses for purposes of section 163(j). It is not necessary for a taxpayer to undertake any allocations under proposed § 1.163(j)-10 if all of the taxpayer's items are properly allocable to non-excepted trades or businesses, or if all of the taxpayer's items are properly allocable to excepted trades or businesses.

Proposed § 1.163(j)-10(a) would provide an overview of the section and certain general rules, including rules regarding the application of the allocation rules to members of a consolidated group. Proposed § 1.163(j)-10(b) would provide rules regarding the allocation of tax items other than interest expense and interest income between excepted and non-excepted trades or businesses. Proposed § 1.163(j)-10(c) would provide the general method of allocating interest expense and interest income between excepted and non-excepted trades or businesses using asset basis, as well as various special rules that would apply under this general method. Proposed § 1.163(j)-10(d) would describe several limited situations in which tracing rather than asset-based allocation is required.

Organizations subject to tax under section 511 are required to compute their unrelated business taxable income separately with respect to each trade or business, resulting in a more granular allocation than is required for purposes of the section 163(j) regulations. Accordingly, proposed § 1.163(j)-10(a)(5) would provide that such organizations would apply the allocation rules under section 512 and the regulations thereunder in determining whether items of income or expense are allocable to an excepted trade or business. The Treasury Department and the IRS request comments as to whether additional guidance is needed regarding the allocation of income and expenses of an organization subject to tax under section 511 to an excepted trade or business for purposes of section 163(j).

A. Proposed § 1.163(j)-10(a): Overview

Before applying the allocation rules in proposed § 1.163(j)-10, a taxpayer first must determine whether any interest paid or accrued is properly allocable to a trade or business. If so, and if the taxpayer does not qualify for the small business exemption under section 163(j)(3) and proposed § 1.163(j)-2, the taxpayer must apply the allocation rules of proposed § 1.163(j)-10 if the taxpayer has tax items from both excepted and non-excepted trades or businesses. The taxpayer must do so in order to determine the amount of interest expense that is business interest expense subject to limitation under section 163(j) and to determine which items are included or excluded in computing its section 163(j) limitation.

For purposes of the allocation rules in proposed § 1.163(j)-10, a taxpayer's activities are not treated as a trade or business if those activities do not involve the provision of services or products to a person other than the taxpayer. For example, if a taxpayer engaged in a manufacturing trade or business has in-house legal personnel that provide legal services solely to the taxpayer, the taxpayer is not treated as also engaged in the trade or business of providing legal services.

Additionally, for purposes of the allocation rules in proposed § 1.163(j)-10, a consolidated group would be treated as a single corporation. Thus, stock of a member that is owned by another member of the same group would not be treated as an asset for purposes of proposed § 1.163(j)-10, and the transfer of member stock to a nonmember would be treated by the group as the transfer of the member's assets. Additionally, the group, rather than a particular member, would be treated as engaged in excepted or non-excepted trades or businesses. Intercompany obligations issued by a member borrower would not be considered an asset of the creditor member for purposes of allocating asset basis between excepted and non-excepted trades or businesses. Moreover, intercompany transactions would be disregarded for purposes of proposed § 1.163(j)-10, along with the resulting offsetting items.

The Treasury Department and the IRS have determined that this approach to consolidated groups is necessary for purposes of proposed § 1.163(j)-10 because a particular trade or business may be conducted by multiple group members that also are engaged in other trades or businesses. Under these proposed regulations, the distinction between excepted and non-excepted trades or businesses applies at the level of the trade or business, not at the level of the group member; thus, the allocation rules in this section apply without regard to which member conducts a trade or business or possesses assets used in a trade or business.

The Treasury Department and the IRS considered an approach to the allocation rules in proposed § 1.163(j)-10 that would have taken into account intercompany transactions between consolidated group members engaged in excepted trades or businesses and members engaged in non-excepted trades or businesses. However, this approach would have resulted in different treatment for consolidated groups in which each member conducts a single trade or business and consolidated groups in which a single member engages in multiple trades or businesses. Moreover, if intercompany transactions were taken into account for purposes of proposed § 1.163(j)-10, then taxpayers potentially could increase the amount of interest allocable to an excepted trade or business or increase their section 163(j) limitation by engaging in intercompany transactions. Thus, the Treasury Department and the IRS have determined that intercompany transactions should be disregarded for purposes of proposed § 1.163(j)-10.

After a consolidated group has determined the percentage of the group's interest expense that is allocable to an excepted trade or business and thus is not subject to limitation under section 163(j), this exempt percentage would be applied proportionally to each member that has paid or accrued interest to a person other than a group member during the taxable year. Thus, in general, each member with interest paid or accrued to a lender that is not a group member will have the same percentage of interest allocable to excepted trades or businesses, regardless of whether any particular member actually engaged in an excepted trade or business. For rules regarding the deduction of interest expense paid or accrued by group members, see the discussion of proposed § 1.163(j)-5(b) in part 5 of this Explanation of Provisions section.

B. Proposed § 1.163(j)-10(b): Allocating Tax Items Other Than Interest Income and Interest Expense

In general, gross income other than dividends and interest income would be allocated to the trade or business that generated such gross income. The Treasury Department and the IRS request comments regarding this method of allocating items of income other than dividends and interest, including comments as to how this rule should be expanded or clarified.

With regard to dividend income, the Treasury Department and the IRS have determined that, if a taxpayer's ownership interest in a corporation equals or exceeds a certain threshold, the taxpayer generally should look through to the business activities of the corporation that paid the dividend.

More specifically, if a taxpayer owns at least 80 percent of the stock of a domestic C corporation or a CFC (by vote and value; see section 1504(a)(2)) that is not eligible for the small business exemption under section 163(j)(3) and proposed § 1.163(j)-2(d)(1), then the taxpayer's dividend income would be treated as allocable to excepted or non-excepted trades or businesses based upon the relative amounts of the payor corporation's adjusted basis in the assets used in such trades or businesses. Additionally, if at least 90 percent of the payor corporation's adjusted basis in its assets is allocable to either excepted trades or businesses or non-excepted trades or businesses, then all of the taxpayer's dividend income from such corporation for the taxable year would be treated as allocable to either excepted or non-excepted trades or businesses, respectively.

If a shareholder in an S corporation looks through to the S corporation's basis in its assets for purposes of the basis allocation rules in proposed § 1.163(j)-10(c), the shareholder also would be required to look through to the S corporation's basis in its assets for purposes of characterizing any dividends received from the S corporation.

If a taxpayer receives a dividend that is not investment income, and if the dividend look-through rule is inapplicable to the taxpayer, then the taxpayer would treat the dividend income as allocable to a non-excepted trade or business. The Treasury Department and the IRS request comments on this proposed rule, including whether taxpayers that are C corporations or tax-exempt corporations should treat dividend income as allocable to a non-excepted trade or business if they fail to meet the minimum ownership threshold for dividends from domestic C corporations and CFCs.

With regard to dispositions of stock in a corporation or interests in a partnership, if a taxpayer recognizes gain or loss upon the disposition of stock in a non-consolidated C corporation that is not property held for investment, within the meaning of section 163(d)(5), and if the taxpayer looks through to the corporation's basis in its assets for purposes of the basis allocation rules in proposed § 1.163(j)-10(c), then the taxpayer would allocate the gain or loss to excepted or non-excepted trades or businesses based upon the relative amounts of the corporation's adjusted basis in the assets used in its trades or businesses, determined pursuant to proposed § 1.163(j)-10(c). If the taxpayer does not look through to the corporation's basis in its assets, the taxpayer would treat the gain or loss as allocable to a non-excepted trade or business. If a taxpayer recognizes gain or loss upon the disposition of interests in a partnership or stock in an S corporation that owns (1) non-excepted assets and excepted assets, (2) investment assets, or (3) both, the taxpayer would determine the proportionate share of the amount of basis properly allocable to a non-excepted trade or business in accordance with the allocation rules set forth in proposed § 1.163(j)-10(c)(5)(ii)(A) or proposed § 1.163(j)-10(c)(5)(ii)(B)(3), as appropriate, and include such proportionate amount of gain or loss in the taxpayer's ATI.

With regard to expenses, losses, and deductions other than interest, any such items that are definitely related to a trade or business, within the meaning of § 1.861-8(b), would be allocable to that trade or business. All other expenses would be ratably apportioned to gross income. The Treasury Department and the IRS request comments on this proposed method of allocating expenses other than interest expense, including whether this proposed rule should incorporate any of the special allocation rules in § 1.861-8(e).

C. Proposed § 1.163(j)-10(c): Allocating Interest Expense and Interest Income

Proposed § 1.163(j)-10(c) would set forth the general rule for allocating interest expense and interest income between excepted and non-excepted trades or businesses. Under this general rule, interest expense and interest income would be allocated between excepted and non-excepted trades or businesses based upon the relative amounts of the taxpayer's adjusted basis in the assets used in its excepted and non-excepted trades or businesses. This general method of allocation reflects the fact that money is fungible and the view that interest expense is attributable to all activities and property, regardless of any specific purpose for incurring an obligation on which interest is paid.

Under proposed § 1.163(j)-10(c), a taxpayer would determine the adjusted basis in its assets on a quarterly basis (each such quarterly period, a "determination period") and average those amounts to determine the relative amounts of asset basis for its excepted and non-excepted trades or businesses for a taxable year. The Treasury Department and the IRS request comments on the frequency of asset basis determinations required under proposed § 1.163(j)-10(c).

Proposed § 1.163(j)-10(c)(1) contains a general de minimis rule. Under this rule, if at least 90 percent of a taxpayer's basis in its assets for the taxable year is allocable to either excepted or non-excepted trades or businesses, determined under proposed § 1.163(j)-10(c), then all of the taxpayer's interest expense and interest income for that year that is properly allocable to a trade or business would be treated as allocable to excepted or non-excepted trades or businesses, respectively. The Treasury Department and the IRS request comments as to whether the application of this de minimis rule should be elective.

If an asset is used in more than one trade or business during a determination period, the taxpayer's basis in such asset would be allocated to each trade or business using the permissible methodology (see the following paragraph) that most reasonably reflects the use of the asset in each trade or business during the determination period. An allocation methodology most reasonably reflects the use of the asset in each trade or business if the methodology most properly reflects the proportionate benefit derived from the use of the asset in each trade or business.

Proposed § 1.163(j)-10(c) would provide several permissible methodologies for allocating basis in an asset used in more than one trade or business during a determination period, including the following: the relative amounts of gross income that an asset generates, has generated, or may reasonably be expected to generate with respect to the trades or businesses; the relative amounts of physical space used by each trade or business if the asset is land or an inherently permanent structure; and the relative amounts of output of each trade or business if each trade or business generates the same unit of output. The choice of method would be subject to de minimis exceptions, and taxpayers generally would not be permitted to vary their allocation methodology across determination periods within a taxable year or from one year to the next. Additionally, if none of the permissible methodologies reasonably reflects the use of an asset in each trade or business, the taxpayer's basis in the asset would not be taken into account for purposes of proposed § 1.163(j)-10(c). The Treasury Department and the IRS request comments on these proposed methods of allocating basis in an asset used in more than one trade or business.

Proposed § 1.163(j)-10(c)(3)(iii) would provide that for utility trades or businesses, the only permissible method for allocating asset basis between excepted and non-excepted utility activities is the relative amounts of output of the trades or businesses. For example, if an asset is used to furnish or sell electric energy, and a portion of the energy is sold to wholesale customers where rates are not set on a cost of service and rate of return basis while the remaining portion is sold at a rate established by a ratemaking body described in proposed § 1.163(j)-1(b)(13), the taxpayer must allocate the basis in the asset between the taxpayer's excepted and non-excepted trades or businesses. The Treasury Department and the IRS believe that other methods listed in proposed § 1.163(j)-10(c) that do not take into account the relative amounts of regulated and unregulated utility activities do not properly reflect the proportionate benefit derived from the use of the asset in each trade or business. The Treasury Department and the IRS request comments on this allocation methodology, including whether another methodology would more accurately reflect the extent to which a trade or business is an excepted utility business for this purpose.

These proposed regulations also would provide a de minimis rule for utility trades or businesses. Under the proposed de minimis rule, if more than 90 percent of the output of a trade or business is sold at rates described in the exception for regulated utility trades or businesses, the taxpayer would treat the entire trade or business as an excepted trade or business. The Treasury Department and the IRS request comments with respect to the de minimis rule for assets used in a utility trade or business, including whether another percentage threshold with respect to the de minimis rule would be more appropriate.

The allocation of asset basis between excepted and non-excepted trades or businesses under proposed § 1.163(j)-10(c) would be subject to numerous additional special rules. First, a taxpayer's adjusted basis in tangible depreciable property other than inherently permanent structures for which a deduction is allowable under section 167 would be determined using the alternative depreciation system under section 168(g). Additional first year depreciation, for example under section 168(k), would not be taken into account for purposes of the basis allocation rule in proposed § 1.163(j)-10(c) due to the distortive effects that such depreciation would have upon the relative adjusted basis of assets. Further, a taxpayer's adjusted basis in tangible depreciable property other than inherently permanent structures for which a deduction is allowable under section 168 of the 1954 Code (former section 168) would be determined using the taxpayer's method of computing depreciation for the property under former section 168. Additionally, a taxpayer's adjusted basis in any intangible asset with respect to which a deduction is allowable under section 167 or section 197 would be determined in accordance with section 167 or section 197, as applicable. Self-created intangibles would not be taken into account for purposes of the allocation rules in proposed § 1.163(j)-10(c). The Treasury Department and the IRS request comments on these proposed rules regarding asset basis in depreciable property, including whether taxpayers should be permitted to use other methods of depreciation, such as the general depreciation system under section 168(a), for purposes of proposed § 1.163(j)-10(c).

Second, the adjusted basis of any asset that is land, including nondepreciable improvements to land, or an inherently permanent structure used in a trade or business generally would be its unadjusted basis rather than its adjusted basis. This special rule, which would not apply to land or inherently permanent structures that fall within the special rule described in the following paragraph, is intended to provide taxpayers with a readily ascertainable figure that better reflects the relative underlying value of this limited class of assets—which, in some cases, are held for many years—than adjusted basis. The Treasury Department and the IRS request comments regarding this approach to allocating basis to land and inherently permanent structures, including whether this rule should be elective, and whether taxpayers should be able to use fair market value rather than acquisition basis for land or inherently permanent structures used in a trade or business.

Third, assets that have been acquired or that are under development but that are not yet used in a trade or business would not be taken into account for purposes of proposed § 1.163(j)-10(c). Such assets would include (but would not be limited to) construction works in progress, such as buildings, airplanes, or ships, prior to their completion, and land that was acquired by a taxpayer for construction of a building by the taxpayer to be used in a trade or business if the building is not yet placed in service. This rule would not apply to stock in a corporation or interests in a partnership. The Treasury Department and the IRS request comments on this special rule, including whether and to what extent exceptions are needed (for example, with respect to start-up businesses).

Fourth, trusts required by law to fund specific liabilities (for example, pension trusts and plant decommissioning trusts) would not be taken into account for purposes of proposed § 1.163(j)-10(c).

Fifth, taxpayers generally would be permitted to look through their interests in partnerships or S corporations, and taxpayers that satisfy a minimum ownership threshold in non-consolidated domestic C corporations and CFCs would be required to look through their interests in such corporations, in determining the extent to which their basis in a partnership interest or corporate stock is allocable to excepted or non-excepted trades or businesses. For domestic C corporations and CFCs, the minimum ownership threshold would be 80 percent by vote and value (see section 1504(a)(2)). Partners that own 80 percent or more of the capital or profits interests in a partnership, and shareholders that own 80 percent or more of S corporation stock by vote and value, generally would be required, rather than merely permitted, to look through their interests in the partnership or S corporation for this purpose.

These look-through rules would not apply to a taxpayer with an interest in a partnership or non-consolidated subsidiary that is eligible for the small business exemption under section 163(j)(3) and proposed § 1.163(j)-2(d)(1). The Treasury Department and the IRS have determined that the look-through rules should not be available in these cases because of the administrative burden that would be imposed on small businesses from collecting and providing information to their shareholders or partners regarding inside asset basis when those small businesses are themselves exempt from the application of section 163(j). The Treasury Department and the IRS also have determined that small businesses that are exempt under section 163(j)(3) and proposed § 1.163(j)-2(d)(1) may not make an election under proposed § 1.163(j)-9.

If a taxpayer does not look through a C corporation for purposes of the allocation rules in § 1.163(j)-10(c), and if the taxpayer is not a C corporation or tax-exempt corporation, the taxpayer generally would treat its basis in the stock as an asset held for investment; if the taxpayer is a C corporation or tax-exempt corporation, the taxpayer would treat its entire basis in the C corporation stock as allocable to a non-excepted trade or business. If a taxpayer does not look through a partnership or S corporation, and if the taxpayer is not a C corporation or tax-exempt corporation, the taxpayer would generally treat its basis in a partnership interest or S corporation stock as either an investment asset or a non-excepted trade or business asset. If the taxpayer does not look through a partnership or S corporation, and if the taxpayer is a C corporation or a tax-exempt corporation, the taxpayer would treat its entire basis in the partnership interest or S corporation stock as allocable to a non-excepted trade or business.

The Treasury Department and the IRS request comments on these proposed look-through rules, including whether any further adjustments should be made to the taxpayer's basis in its partnership interest or corporate stock (for example, under § 1.861-12(c)(2)) and whether the minimum ownership threshold for nonconsolidated domestic C corporations and CFCs should be modified.

Sixth, a taxpayer's basis in its customer receivables and cash and cash equivalents would be disregarded for purposes of proposed § 1.163(j)-10(c). This rule is intended to discourage taxpayers from moving cash to excepted trades or businesses to increase the amount of asset basis therein. For these purposes, the term "cash and cash equivalents" would include cash, foreign currency, commercial paper, interests in certain investment companies, government obligations, derivatives that are substantially secured by an obligation of a government, and similar assets. The Treasury Department and the IRS request comments on this special rule, including the list of assets to which it would apply, and whether any exceptions should apply, such as for working capital.

Seventh, solely for purposes of determining the amount of basis allocable to excepted and non-excepted trades or businesses under proposed § 1.163(j)-10(c), an election under section 336, 338, or 754, as applicable, would be deemed to have been made for any acquisition of corporate stock or partnership interests with respect to which the taxpayer demonstrates to the satisfaction of the Commissioner of the Internal Revenue Service (the Commissioner) that the taxpayer was eligible to make such an election but was actually or effectively precluded from doing so by a regulatory agency with respect to a regulated utility trade or business. The Treasury Department and the IRS have determined that such a rule is necessary to place taxpayers that are actually or effectively precluded from making an election under section 336, 338, or 754 on the same footing for purposes of the basis allocation rules in proposed § 1.163(j)-10(c) as taxpayers that are not subject to such limitations. The Treasury Department and the IRS request comments on this special rule.

Eighth, taxpayers would be required to comply with certain reporting requirements regarding their asset basis allocation under proposed § 1.163(j)-10(c). Additionally, taxpayers would be required to keep books of account and other records and data as necessary to substantiate the taxpayer's use of an asset in an excepted trade or business (see § 1.6001-1). If the taxpayer fails to provide the required information, proposed § 1.163(j)-10(c) would permit the Commissioner to treat all of the taxpayer's interest expense as properly allocable to a non-excepted trade or business, unless the taxpayer shows that there was reasonable cause for failing to comply with, and the taxpayer acted in good faith with respect to, these reporting requirements. The Treasury Department and the IRS request comments on these proposed reporting requirements and the consequences of failing to satisfy these requirements.

Finally, proposed § 1.163(j)-10(c) would provide that a taxpayer's adjusted basis in an asset will not be taken into account for purposes of this section if one of the principal purposes for the acquisition, disposition, or change in use of that asset is to increase artificially the amount of basis allocable to excepted or non-excepted trades or businesses.

The foregoing basis allocation rules would not apply to disallowed business interest expense carryforwards, with the exception of disallowed disqualified interest. Disallowed business interest expense carryforwards other than disallowed disqualified interest would have been allocated during the year in which they were first disallowed under section 163(j). On becoming carryforwards, these disallowed expenses would retain their allocation from prior taxable years and would not be reallocated in a subsequent taxable year. The Treasury Department and the IRS request comments as to how the allocation rules in proposed § 1.163(j)-10 should apply to disallowed disqualified interest.

These basis allocation rules also would not apply to floor plan financing interest expense. As provided in section 163(j)(1)(C) and proposed § 1.163(j)-2, taxpayers are entitled to deduct their business interest expense to the full extent of their floor plan financing interest expense.

The Treasury Department and the IRS considered various alternatives to asset basis in determining how interest expense should be allocated between excepted and non-excepted trades or businesses. One such alternative was a tracing regime whereby taxpayers would be required to trace disbursements of debt proceeds to specific expenditures. However, tracing would impose a significant administrative burden upon taxpayers. Further, it is not clear how taxpayers would retroactively apply a tracing regime to existing debt. In particular, because C corporations would have had no reason to trace the proceeds of any existing indebtedness, imposing a tracing regime on existing indebtedness would require corporations to reconstruct the use of funds within their treasury operations at the time such indebtedness was issued, even if the issuance occurred many years ago, and even if the funds were used for a myriad of purposes across a large number of entities. Such an approach would involve a great deal of administrative cost and may be impractical or even impossible for indebtedness issued years ago.

Moreover, because money is fungible, the Treasury Department and the IRS have determined that a tracing regime would be distortive and subject to manipulation, and thus would not be appropriate. Although taxpayers are impacted from both a commercial and tax perspective by the amount of capital raised through the issuance of equity and indebtedness, any trade or business conducted by a taxpayer is generally indifferent to the source of funds. As a result, if taxpayers were allowed to use a tracing regime to allocate indebtedness to excepted trades or businesses, there would be an incentive to treat excepted trades or businesses as funded largely from indebtedness, and to treat non-excepted trades or businesses as funded largely from other types of funding, such as equity funding, despite the fact that, as an economic matter, all of a taxpayer's trades or businesses are funded based on the taxpayer's overall capital structure.

The assumption that a trade or business is indifferent to its source of funds may not be appropriate in cases in which certain indebtedness is secured by the assets of the trade or business and cash flow from those assets is expected to support the payments required on the indebtedness. These proposed regulations would provide for a limited tracing rule in those cases. See the discussion of qualified non-recourse indebtedness in proposed § 1.163(j)-10(d) in part 10(D) of this Explanation of Provisions section.

The Treasury Department and the IRS also considered allocating interest expense based upon the relative fair market value of the assets used in excepted and non-excepted trades or businesses. However, determinations of fair market value frequently are burdensome for taxpayers, which may have numerous assets without a readily established market price, and for the IRS. For this reason, disputes between taxpayers and the IRS over the fair market value of an asset are a common and costly occurrence. In the TCJA, Congress repealed the use of fair market value in the apportionment of interest expense under section 864 of the Code (see section 14502(a) of the TCJA). Thus, the Treasury Department and the IRS have determined that allocating interest expense based upon the relative fair market value of assets is a less viable approach than a regime based upon relative amounts of asset basis.

The Treasury Department and the IRS also considered allocating interest expense to excepted and non-excepted trades or businesses based on the relative amounts of gross income generated by such trades or businesses. However, gross income is more variable and volatile than asset basis, in part because it is based on an annual measurement. Methods could be developed to look at multiple years of gross income through an averaging or other smoothing methodology, but any such approach would necessarily create a number of difficult technical questions because the income of different trades or businesses may be subject to differing business cycles and the timing of income items may be within taxpayers' control. In the TCJA, Congress also repealed the use of gross income in the apportionment of interest expense under section 864 of the Code (see section 14502(a) of the TCJA).

Thus, although allocating interest expense between excepted and non-excepted trades or businesses using asset basis is not without its shortcomings, the Treasury Department and the IRS have determined that this approach represents the most viable option. The Treasury Department and the IRS also note that various commenters recommended using this approach to allocate interest expense between excepted and non-excepted trades or businesses.

The Treasury Department and the IRS have determined that the same approach should be used to allocate interest income, for several reasons. Such an approach is simpler to administer than applying a separate regime to interest income. Additionally, using the same regime for both interest expense and interest income reduces the likelihood that the IRS or taxpayers will be whipsawed. Under this rule, the greater the amount of basis in assets used in excepted trades or businesses, the greater the amount of both interest expense that is not subject to the section 163(j) limitation and interest income that is not properly allocable to a trade or business and that, as a result, is not factored into the taxpayer's calculation of ATI, which reduces the amount of interest expense that may be deducted.

The Treasury Department and the IRS request comments on the use of asset basis to allocate interest expense and interest income between excepted and non-excepted trades or businesses, including whether other measures, such as gross income, should be used in addition to, or instead of, asset basis. The Treasury Department and the IRS also request comments on the special rules contained in proposed § 1.163(j)-10(c), including whether additional special rules are needed (for example, for financial instruments that are marked to market within the meaning of section 475, or additional rules contained in § 1.861-12T).

D. Proposed § 1.163(j)-10(d): Direct Allocations

The basis allocation rules in proposed § 1.163(j)-10(c) would not apply to interest expense and interest income in several circumstances. First, a taxpayer with qualified nonrecourse indebtedness would be required to directly allocate interest expense from such indebtedness to the taxpayer's assets, as provided in § 1.861-10T(b). Second, a taxpayer that is engaged in the trade or business of banking, insurance, financing, or a similar business would be required to directly allocate interest expense and interest income from such business to the taxpayer's assets used in that business. The special rule for cash and cash equivalents under proposed § 1.163(j)-10(c) would not apply to such taxpayers.

A taxpayer to which both proposed § 1.163(j)-10(c) and (d) apply would be required to reduce its asset basis for purposes of proposed § 1.163(j)-10(c) to reflect assets to which interest expense is directly allocated under proposed § 1.163(j)-10(d).

The Treasury Department and the IRS request comments as to whether direct allocation should be required in any other circumstances, including but not limited to circumstances in which a taxpayer with both excepted and non-excepted trades or businesses is subject to significant limitations on transferring borrowed funds outside the excepted trade or business. The Treasury Department and the IRS also request comments on whether a taxpayer should be permitted to elect to treat all of its interest expense and interest income as properly allocable to non-excepted trades or businesses for purposes of section 163(j), in lieu of applying the allocation rules in proposed § 1.163(j)-10(c) and (d).

11. *Proposed § 1.163(j)-11: Transition Rules*

Proposed § 1.163(j)-11 would provide certain transition rules. Proposed § 1.163(j)-11(a) would provide rules that apply if a corporation (S) that is subject to the section 163(j) limitation joins a consolidated group whose taxable year began before January 1, 2018, and thus is not currently subject to the section 163(j) limitation. For example, assume that S is a calendar-year, stand-alone C corporation, and that S is acquired by Acquiring Group (with a November 30 fiscal year) on May 31, 2018. Acquiring Group is not subject to the section 163(j) limitation during its taxable year beginning December 1, 2017, but S is subject to the section 163(j) limitation for its short taxable year beginning January 1, 2018. Is S subject to the section 163(j) limitation for the taxable period beginning June 1, 2018? What happens to any disallowed business interest expense carryforwards from S's short taxable year ending May 31, 2018?

Proposed § 1.163(j)-11(a) would provide that, in those situations to which proposed § 1.163(j)-11(a) applies, the status of the acquiring group will control the application of section 163(j) to a target during the period that the target is included in the group. Therefore, if S is subject to the section 163(j) limitation at the time of its acquisition by a consolidated group with a taxable year beginning before January 1, 2018, then S will not be subject to the section 163(j) limitation for the portion of the acquiring group's taxable year in which S is a member. Additionally, any disallowed business interest expense carryforwards from S's taxable year that ended on the date of S's change in status will be carried forward to the acquiring group's first taxable year beginning after December 31, 2017.

Proposed § 1.163(j)-11(b) of this section would provide special rules for taxpayers with carryforwards under old section 163(j). Old section 163(j)(1)(A) disallowed a deduction to a corporation for disqualified interest (within the meaning of old section 163(j)(3)) paid or accrued by the corporation during the taxable year if old section 163(j) applied to such year. Old section 163(j)(1)(B) provided that any amount disallowed under old section 163(j)(1)(A) for any taxable year would be treated as disqualified interest paid or accrued in the succeeding taxable year.

Proposed § 1.163(j)-11(b) would provide that a taxpayer's interest expense for which a deduction was disallowed under old section 163(j) is carried forward to the taxpayer's first taxable year beginning after December 31, 2017, and is subject to disallowance under section 163(j) and proposed § 1.163(j)-2, except to the extent such interest is allocable to an excepted trade or business under proposed § 1.163(j)-10.

As noted in part 4(D) of this Explanation of Provisions section, old section 163(j) treated all members of the same affiliated group as a single taxpayer regardless of whether such members filed a consolidated return, but the section 163(j) regulations would treat members of the same affiliated group as one taxpayer only if such members file a consolidated return. Proposed § 1.163(j)-11(b) would provide rules based upon the rules in § 1.163(j)-5(c)(2) of the Prior Proposed Regulations for allocating disallowed disqualified interest carryforwards among members of an affiliated group that was treated as a single taxpayer under old section 163(j).

Proposed § 1.163(j)-11(b) also would clarify the application of section 382 to disallowed disqualified interest carryforwards. For example, disallowed disqualified interest would not be treated as a pre-change loss subject to a section 382 limitation under section 382(d)(3) with regard to an ownership change on a change date occurring before the date the Treasury decision adopting these regulations as final regulations is published in the **Federal Register**, unless the disallowed disqualified interest is carried forward under section 163(j)(2). But see section 382(h)(6)(B) regarding built-in deduction items.

Similarly, for purposes of section 382(k)(1), regarding determination of status as a loss corporation, disallowed disqualified interest would not be treated as a carryforward of disallowed interest described in section 381(c)(20) with regard to an ownership change on a change date occurring before the date the Treasury decision adopting these regulations as final regulations is published in the **Federal Register**, unless the disallowed disqualified interest is carried forward under section 163(j)(2). But see section 382(h)(6) regarding built-in deductions. For a description of changes to regulations under section 382, see the discussion of proposed §§1.382-2 and 1.382-6 in parts 14 and 15 of this Explanation of Provisions section.

Finally, whereas old section 163(j)(2)(B)(ii) permitted taxpayers with excess limitation, within the meaning of old section 163(j)(2)(B)(iii), to carry such limitation forward, section 163(j) contains no such language. Thus, the Treasury Department and the IRS have determined that no amount of excess limitation under old section 163(j)(2)(B) may be carried forward to taxable years beginning after December 31, 2017.

12. *Proposed §1.263A-9*

Because of the amendments to section 163(j), a conforming amendment to §1.263A-9(g) is required. Proposed §1.263A-9 would update references to section 163(j) to reflect current law.

13. *Proposed §1.381(c)(20)-1*

As noted in part 5 of this Explanation of Provisions section, Congress added disallowed business interest expense carryforwards to the list of items to which the acquiring corporation succeeds in a transaction to which section 381(a) applies. See section 381(c)(20). Sections 1.381(c)(1)-1 and 1.381(c)(1)-2 provide rules that, in part, limit the acquiring corporation's ability to use NOL carryforwards in the acquiring corporation's first taxable year ending after the acquisition date. The Treasury Department and the IRS have determined that similar rules should apply to disallowed business interest expense carryforwards.

Proposed §1.381(c)(20)-1 also would provide that, for purposes of section 381(c)(20), the term "carryover of disallowed business interest described in section 163(j)(2)" includes disallowed disqualified interest.

14. *Proposed §1.382-2*

In the TCJA, Congress added section 382(d)(3) and a new sentence to section 382(k)(1) for taxable years beginning after December 31, 2017. Section 1.382-2 contains certain definitions for purposes of sections 382 and 383 and the regulations thereunder, including definitions of the terms "pre-change loss" and "loss corporation."

Section 382(d)(3) provides that, for purposes of section 382, the term "pre-change loss" includes carryovers of disallowed interest described in section 163(j)(2) "under rules similar to the rules" in section 382(d)(1). Section 163(j)(2) provides that interest expense paid or accrued in a taxable year that is not allowed as a deduction pursuant to section 163(j)(1) is carried forward to the succeeding taxable year. Section 382(d)(1) treats as a "pre-change loss" both (i) net operating loss carryforwards to the taxable year in which the change date occurs (change year), and (ii) the net operating loss carryforward for the change year, to the extent such loss is allocable to the pre-change period. Proposed §1.382-2 would clarify the equivalent treatment of items under section 382(d)(1) and (3) by providing that a "pre-change loss" includes the portion of any disallowed business interest expense of the old loss corporation paid or accrued in the taxable year of the testing date that is attributable to the pre-change period.

For purposes of determining the portion of disallowed business interest expense that is attributable to the pre-change period, proposed §1.382-2 would require that disallowed business interest expense be ratably allocated to each day in the year, regardless of whether the loss corporation makes a closing-of-the-books election under §1.382-6(b)(2) with regard to allocating its other taxable items to the pre-change period and the post-change period within the change year. This ratable allocation of disallowed business interest expense is consistent with the allocation of the loss corporation's deduction for business interest expense in the taxable year of the ownership change (see proposed §1.382-6). Ratable allocation also is consistent with the general application of the section 163(j) regulations, which apply without regard to any particular debt instrument or particular date of payment or accrual of interest. See the discussion in part 2(A) of this Explanation of Provisions section.

The TCJA also modified section 382(k)(1) to provide that the term "loss corporation" includes a corporation entitled to use a disallowed business interest expense carryforward. These proposed regulations would revise §1.382-2 to reflect the changes to the definitions of the terms "pre-change loss" and "loss corporation." These provisions would be applicable with regard to ownership changes occurring on or after the date on which the Treasury decision adopting these regulations as final regulations is published in the **Federal Register**.

15. *Proposed §1.382-6*

When a loss corporation experiences an ownership change, §1.382-6(a) provides that, in general, the loss corporation must allocate its NOL or taxable income and its net capital loss or modified capital gain net income for the change year between the pre-change period and the post-change period by ratably allocating an equal portion to each day in the year. However, instead of using ratable allocation, a loss corporation may elect to use the closing-of-the-books method in § 1.382-6(b). A closing-of-the-books election applies only for purposes of certain allocations, such as NOL or taxable income allocations, and does not terminate the loss corporation's taxable year as of the change date.

Proposed § 1.382-6 would clarify that, for purposes of section 163(j), a loss corporation's current-year business interest expense may not be allocated under the closing-of-the-books method. Thus, even if a taxpayer generally has a closing-of-the-books election in effect for the change year, the taxpayer would be required to ratably allocate its current-year business interest expense for which a deduction is allowable under section 163(j) in that year between the pre-change period and the post-change period. For example, if X, a calendar-year loss corporation, experiences an ownership change on May 26, 2019, and if X has $100x of current-year business interest expense for which a deduction is allowable under section 163(j) for that year, $40x of X's business interest expense deduction would be allocated to the pre-change period, and $60x of X's business interest expense deduction would be allocated to the post-change period, regardless of which of the two general allocation methods - ratable allocation or closing-of-the-books - X uses. Under this approach, taxpayers would not need to compute ATI separately for the pre-change and post-change periods.

The Treasury Department and the IRS are considering publishing a separate notice of proposed rulemaking to address, among other issues, the treatment of a corporate partner's excess business interest expense (including negative section 163(j) expense) under section 382.

16. *Proposed § 1.383-1*

Section 1.383-1(d) provides ordering rules for the utilization of pre-change losses and pre-change credits and for the absorption of the section 382 limitation and the section 383 credit limitation. Generally, pre-change capital losses are absorbed first for these purposes, followed by NOLs and recognized built-in losses, other pre-change losses and, finally, pre-change credits.

The Treasury Department and the IRS have determined that disallowed business interest expense carryforwards should be absorbed after pre-change capital losses and all recognized built-in losses, but before NOLs. Disallowed business interest expense carryforwards should be absorbed before NOLs because taxpayers must calculate their current-year income or loss in order to determine whether and to what extent they can use an NOL in that year, and deductions for business interest expense, including carryforwards from prior taxable years, factor into the calculation of current-year income or loss.

Proposed § 1.383-1 would reflect the addition of disallowed business interest expense to the ordering rules, would make conforming changes to other provisions, and would update other provisions to reflect additional changes effectuated by the TCJA. The ordering rules in proposed § 1.383-1 include alternative rules that reflect the fact that certain regulations pertaining to the interaction between sections 163(j) and 382 may not be applicable to all ownership changes.

17. *Proposed § 1.469-9(b)*

These proposed regulations would also propose amendments to § 1.469-9(b) to provide rules relating to the definition of real property trade or business under section 469(c)(7)(C). Specifically, these proposed regulations would provide guidance on the meaning of real property and on the types of trades or businesses that qualify as "real property trades or businesses" for purposes of section 469(c)(7).

Section 469(a) of the Code disallows passive activity losses or credits. In general, a passive activity loss is the excess of the aggregate losses over the aggregate income from all passive activities in a taxable year. A passive activity is defined as any trade or business activity in which the taxpayer does not materially participate, and any rental activity subject to the exception for rental real estate under section 469(c)(7). Generally, under section 469(c)(2), a rental activity is treated as a per se passive activity regardless of whether the taxpayer materially participates in the activity.

The Omnibus Budget Reconciliation Act of 1993, Public Law 103-66, sec. 13143(a), added section 469(c)(7) to the Code effective for tax years beginning after December 31, 1993. In doing so, Congress expressed the belief that applying the "per se" passive rule to all rental real estate activities disadvantaged taxpayers who were otherwise actively engaged in real estate businesses and who also owned rental real estate. According to H. Rept. 103-111, 103rd Cong., 1st sess. (May 25, 1993), "[t]he committee considers it unfair that a person who performs personal services in a real estate trade or business in which he materially participates may not offset losses from rental real estate activities against income from nonrental real estate activities or against other types of income such as portfolio investment income." Section 469(c)(7) was added to alleviate this unfair treatment.

Section 469(c)(7) provides that the rental real estate activities of qualifying taxpayers who are actively engaged in real property trades or businesses are not subject to the "per se" passive rule in section 469(c)(2). Instead, under section 469(c)(7), a rental real estate activity of a qualifying taxpayer will not be a passive activity if the taxpayer materially participates in the rental real estate activity.

In section 469(c)(7)(C), Congress defined "real property trade or business" as "any real property development, redevelopment, construction, reconstruction, acquisition, conversion, rental, operation, management, leasing, or brokerage trade or business." However, neither section 469 nor the legislative history defines any of the terms contained in section 469(c)(7)(C).

These proposed regulations would amend the regulations under section 469 to provide a definition of the term "real property" along with certain other terms contained in section 469(c)(7)(C). Consistent with ordinary usage, these proposed regulations would define "real property" to include land, buildings, and other inherently permanent structures that are permanently affixed to land, and exclude from the definition certain other items, such as machines and equipment that serve an active function, which may be permanently affixed to real property.

Given Congress's focus in enacting section 469(c)(7) to provide relief to entrepreneurs in real property trades or businesses with some nexus to or involvement with rental real estate, these proposed regulations would not include trades or businesses that generally do not play a significant or substantial role in the creation, acquisition, or management of rental real estate in the definition of real property trade or business under section 469(c)(7)(C). Therefore, taxpayers engaged in trades or businesses that are not directly or substantially involved in the creation, acquisition, or management of rental real estate, or that provide personal services which are merely ancillary to a real property trade or business, will generally not be treated as engaged in real property trades or businesses for this purpose. In addition, machinery, equipment, and other assets or items that are not generally viewed as items of real property until after their installation or permanent affixation to real property (for example, HVAC systems, elevators, escalators, solar panels, glass fixtures, doors, windows, tiling, etc.) will not be treated as real property for these purposes and, accordingly, taxpayers engaged in trades or businesses of manufacturing, installing, operating, maintaining, or repairing such items generally will not be treated as engaged in real property trades or businesses within the meaning of section 469(c)(7)(C).

As the Treasury Department and the IRS have previously recognized (see Notice of Proposed Rulemaking, "Definition of Real Estate Investment Trust Real Property," published in the **Federal Register** (79 FR 27508, 27510) on May 14, 2014), the term "real property" appears in numerous Code provisions, which could ordinarily imply that, absent specific statutory modifications, the term "real property" should have the same meaning throughout the Code. However, the context and legislative purpose underlying a specific Code provision may necessitate a broader or narrower definition of the term "real property" than may be applied for other Code provisions. These proposed regulations under section 469 provide a definition of real property that is, for example, narrower than the one provided in the REIT context. The definition provided in these proposed regulations would apply solely for purposes of section 469(c)(7), and these regulations should not be construed in any way as applying to, or changing, the definitions in other Code provisions.

These proposed regulations would also define "real property operation" to mean the work done on a day-to-day basis by a direct, or indirect, owner of the real property, in a trade or business relating to the maintenance and occupancy of the real property to make the property available to be used, or held out for use, by customers. Similarly, these proposed regulations would define "real property management" to mean work performed by third party managers on behalf of owners in a trade or business relating to the day-to-day maintenance and occupancy of the real property to make it available to be used, or held out for use, by customers. In both instances, the principal purpose of the trade or business must be the provision of the use of the real property (or physical space accorded by or within the real property) to one or more customers, and not the provision of other significant or extraordinary services to customers in conjunction with the customers' incidental use of the real property or physical space accorded by or within the real property.

These proposed regulations would reserve on the remaining terms in section 469(c)(7)(C). Comments are requested as to whether further definitions are needed.

18. *Proposed § 1.860C-2*

Because REMICs are not treated as carrying on a trade or business for purposes of section 162 and are not C corporations, the Treasury Department and the IRS have determined that section 163(j) should not apply to REMICs, and these proposed regulations would amend § 1.860C-2 to provide that a REMIC is allowed a deduction, determined without regard to section 163(j), for any interest expense accrued during the taxable year. Section 1.860C-2(b)(2)(ii) of these proposed regulations would apply for taxable years beginning after December 31, 2017. However, taxpayers may rely on proposed § 1.860C-2(b)(2)(ii) prior to the date final regulations are published in the **Federal Register**.

19. *Proposed § 1.1502-36*

Section 1.1502-36 contains the unified loss rule, which limits the ability of a consolidated group to recognize non-economic or duplicated losses on subsidiary stock. The rule applies when a consolidated group member transfers subsidiary (S) stock that has a loss. If § 1.1502-36(d) applies to the transfer of a loss share, the attributes of S and its lower-tier subsidiaries are reduced as needed to prevent the duplication of any loss recognized on the transferred stock. Such attributes include capital loss carryovers, NOL carryovers, deferred deductions, and basis of assets other than cash and general deposit accounts. See § 1.1502-36(d)(4).

The Treasury Department and the IRS have determined that, for purposes of § 1.1502-36(d), disallowed business interest expenses should be treated as deferred deductions. Section 1.1502-36 would be modified accordingly.

20. *Proposed § § 1.1502-91 through 1.1502-99*

As discussed in parts 11 and 14 through 16 of this Explanation of Provisions section, the section 163(j) regulations and § § 1.382-2, 1.382-6, and 1.383-1 of these proposed regulations would address the application of section 382 to business interest expense, including disallowed business interest expense carryforwards. Sections 1.1502-90 through 1.1502-99 contain rules applying section 382 to a consolidated group. These proposed regulations would add a new coordination rule in § 1.1502-98(b) pursuant to which the rules in § § 1.1502-91 through 1.1502-96 would apply to business interest expense, including disallowed business interest expense carryforwards, of members of a consolidated group (or corporations that join or leave a consolidated group), with appropriate adjustments.

The Treasury Department and the IRS request comments on the new coordination rule in § 1.1502-98(b), including whether additional examples should be added to clarify the application of this rule.

21. *Areas Where the Proposed Regulations Have Reserved on Issues*

The proposed regulations reserve on a number of issues, either where the reserved issue is expected to be addressed in other guidance, where comments would be helpful in determining the best manner of addressing an issue, or where the Treasury Department and the IRS are unsure whether additional guidance would be helpful.

A. Reservations Made Because Other Guidance May Address the Reserved Issue

The proposed regulations reserve on the interaction of sections 163(j) and 59A because separate guidance under section 59A is expected to address these issues.

The proposed regulations under sections 382 and 383 also reserve on a number of paragraphs related to the treatment of a corporate partner's excess business interest expense (including negative section 163(j) expense) under section 382. The Treasury Department and the IRS are considering publishing a separate notice of proposed rulemaking to address these and other issues related to section 382.

B. Reservations Made Where Comments Would Be Helpful in Determining the Best Manner of Addressing an Issue

The proposed regulations reserve on the treatment of collateralized cleared swaps and the types of fees that should be treated as interest for purposes of the interest definition because comments would be helpful in determining the best manner of addressing these issues. The proposed regulations also reserve on the coordination with certain other statutory provisions based on or limited by the income of taxpayers because determining the best approach for ordering such provisions would benefit from comments.

For similar reasons, the proposed regulations also reserve on the proper treatment of business interest income and business interest expense with respect to lending transactions between a passthrough entity and an owner of the entity (self-charged lending transactions), the treatment of excess business interest expense in tiered partnerships has been reserved in these proposed regulations, and the application of section 163(j) to a partnership merger or division.

C. *Reservations Made Where the Treasury Department and the IRS are Unsure Whether Additional Guidance Would Be Helpful*

The proposed regulations reserve on nine of the eleven terms listed in section 469(c)(7)(C). Comments are requested as to whether further definitions are needed. However, in the absence of comments requesting additional guidance with respect to these terms, it is unclear whether such additional guidance would be helpful.

Finally, the proposed regulations also reserve on additional guidance in the case of certain exempt organizations with respect to the application of the gross receipts test for purposes of section 163(j) because in the absence of comments it is unclear whether any such rules are necessary.

Statement of Availability of IRS Documents

The IRS Notices and Revenue Procedures cited in this document are published in the Internal Revenue Bulletin (or Cumulative Bulletin) and are available from the Superintendent of Documents, U.S. Government Printing Office, Washington, DC 20402, or by visiting the IRS website at *http://www.irs.gov*.

Proposed Applicability/Effective Dates

Except as otherwise provided in this section, the regulations are proposed to be effective for taxable years ending after the date the Treasury decision adopting these regulations as final is published in the **Federal Register**. However, taxpayers and their related parties, within the meaning of sections 267(b) and 707(b)(1), may apply the rules of these regulations to a taxable year beginning after December 31, 2017, so long as the taxpayers and their related parties consistently apply the rules of § § 1.163(j)-1, 1.163(j)-2, 1.163(j)-3, 1.163(j)-4, 1.163(j)-5, 1.163(j)-6, 1.163(j)-7, 1.163(j)-8, 1.163(j)-9, 1.163(j)-10, and 1.163(j)-11, and if applicable, § § 1.263A-9, 1.381(c)(20)-1, 1.382-6, 1.383-1, 1.469-9, 1.882-5, 1.1502-13, 1.1502-21, 1.1502-36, 1.1502-79, 1.1502-91 through 1.1502-99 (to the extent they effectuate the rules of § § 1.382-6 and 1.383-1), and 1.1504-4 to those taxable years.

With respect to proposed § § 1.382-2, 1.382-5, and 1.1502-91 through 1.1502-99 (to the extent they effectuate the rules of § § 1.382-2 and 1.382-5), if applicable, the regulations are proposed to be effective for ownership changes occurring on or after the date the Treasury decision adopting these regulations as final regulations is published in the **Federal Register**. However, taxpayers and their related parties, within the meaning of sections 267(b) and 707(b)(1), may apply the rules of § § 1.382-2 and 1.382-5, and 1.1502-91 through 1.1502-99 (to the extent they effectuate the rules of § § 1.382-2 and 1.382-5), if applicable, to an ownership change that occurs in a taxable year beginning after December 31, 2017, so long as the taxpayers and their related parties consistently apply the rules of § § 1.163(j)-1, 1.163(j)-2, 1.163(j)-3, 1.163(j)-4, 1.163(j)-5, 1.163(j)-6, 1.163(j)-7, 1.163(j)-8, 1.163(j)-9, 1.163(j)-10, and

1.163(j)-11, and if applicable, §§1.263A-9, 1.381(c)(20)-1, 1.382-6, 1.383-1, 1.469-9, 1.882-5, 1.1502-13, 1.1502-21, 1.1502-36, 1.1502-79, and 1.1504-4 to taxable years beginning after Decembers 31, 2017.

Special Analyses

I. *Regulatory Planning and Review - Economic Analysis*

Executive Orders 13771, 13563 and 12866 direct agencies to assess costs and benefits of available regulatory alternatives and, if regulation is necessary, to select regulatory approaches that maximize net benefits (including potential economic, environmental, public health and safety effects, distributive impacts, and equity). Executive Order 13563 emphasizes the importance of quantifying both costs and benefits, of reducing costs, of harmonizing rules, and of promoting flexibility.

These proposed regulations have been designated by the Office of Information and Regulatory Affairs (OIRA) as Economically Significant under section 1(c) of the Memorandum of Agreement (April 11, 2018) between the Treasury Department and the Office of Management and Budget (OMB) regarding review of tax regulations and thereby subject to review under Executive Order 12866. Accordingly, these proposed regulations have been reviewed by OIRA. In addition, the Treasury Department and the IRS expect the proposed regulations, when final, to be an Executive Order 13771 regulatory action and request comment on this designation. For more detail on the economic analysis, please refer to the following analysis.

A. Background and Overview

The TCJA substantially modified the statutory rules of section 163(j) to limit the amount of net business interest expense that can be deducted in the current taxable year of any taxpayer with only limited exceptions. As previously described in this preamble, section 163(j) prior to TCJA generally applied to domestic corporations with interest paid or accrued to related persons that were not subject to Federal income tax. As described in the Explanation of Provisions section, the amount allowed under section 163(j)(1) as a deduction for business interest expense is limited to the sum of (1) the taxpayer's business interest income for the taxable year; (2) 30 percent of the taxpayer's ATI for the taxable year; and (3) the taxpayer's floor plan financing interest expense for the taxable year. The section 163(j) limitation applies to all taxpayers, except for certain small businesses with average annual gross receipts of $25 million or less and certain trades or businesses. Any amount of business interest not allowed as a deduction for any taxable year as a result of the limitation under section 163(j)(1) is carried forward and treated as business interest paid or accrued in the next taxable year under section 163(j)(2).

Congress modified section 163(j) under TCJA, in part, out of concern that prior law treated debt-financed investment more favorably than equity-financed investment. This debt bias generally encouraged taxpayers to utilize more leverage than would occur in the absence of the Code. Limiting the deduction of business interest is meant to reduce the relative favorability of debt and hence encourage a more efficient capital structure for firms. Congress also believed it necessary to apply the limit broadly across different types of taxpayers so as not to distort the choice of entity (see H. Rept. 115-409, at 247 (2017)).

B. Need for the Proposed Regulations

Because the section 163(j) limitation has been substantially modified, a large number of the relevant terms and necessary calculations that taxpayers are currently required to apply under the statute can benefit from greater specificity. Among other benefits, the clarity provided by the proposed regulations generally helps ensure that all taxpayers calculate the business interest expense limitation in a similar manner.

For example, there is no universal definition for the term "interest" under the Code. In general, because section 163(j) applies to limit certain deductions for interest under chapter A of the Code, the proposed regulations' definition of the term "interest" is relatively broad to create a balanced application of section 163(j). This definition limits tax-avoidance incentives for taxpayers to, in form, label payments as something other than interest that, in substance, are economically interest. At the same time, this definition allows taxpayers to treat certain amounts of income as business interest income for purposes of calculating the section 163(j) limitation that they may be required to, for non-tax reasons, label as something other than interest, so that taxpayers with such income are not unduly impacted by the section 163(j) limitation.

Pursuant to section 163(j)(8)(B), the proposed regulations prescribe adjustments to the calculation of ATI to prevent double counting of deductions and to provide relief for particular types of taxpayers or taxpayers in particular circumstances to ensure that such taxpayers are treated similarly to other taxpayers when calculating ATI.

The statute applies broadly to different types of entities, including passthrough entities such as partnerships and S corporations. The statute specifies that the section 163(j) limitation applies at the entity level for a partnership but that items such as excess business interest expense and excess taxable income must be allocated to partners for a variety of reasons including to compute their own 163(j) limitation. The statute further specifies that the items should be allocated in the same manner as "nonseparately stated taxable income or loss of the partnership"; however, this concept has not previously been defined by statute or regulations. Without the specified method of allocating these excess items provided by the proposed regulations, partnerships would likely have both significant flexibility but also uncertainty in determining which partners receive excess items. This flexibility could potentially lead partnerships to specially allocate items of income or expense such that they are separately stated to change the partner's allocation of excess interest expense or excess taxable income.

There are a number of potential uncertainties in how taxpayers should apply the section 163(j) limitation to CFCs in a manner consistent with other provisions of the Code. For example, interest deductions of individual CFCs may be limited by section 163(j) but might not be if the interest deductions of CFCs were computed on a group basis. The proposed regulations provide an election for treating related CFCs similarly to a consolidated group for the purpose of calculating the amount of business interest expense for purposes of the section 163(j) limitation. This election also provides clarity that in performing a CFC group calculation, finance and non-finance businesses are largely treated as separate groups (because of the dual role of interest payments as a cost of goods or services sold as well as a payment for debt finance and because of possible distortions in the case of conglomerate companies with financial and nonfinancial businesses in their CFCs, due to financial businesses' outsize amounts of interest expense and income). The proposed regulations also provide clarity by permitting the bottom-up transfer within chains of CFCs of excess taxable income for electing groups of CFCs.

Other areas where clarity is provided under the proposed regulations for CFCs include adjustments for partnerships held by CFCs, the treatment of CFCs with effectively connected income (ECI), the treatment of intergroup dividends (to avoid double counting of ATI), the effect of deemed inclusions (from branch income, Subpart F income, and GILTI) (also to avoid double counting of ATI), and the effect foreign derived intangible income (FDII) on ATI.

For purposes of section 163(j), the statute states in section 163(j)(7) that the term "trade or business" does not include certain regulated utilities, or an electing real property trade or business or an electing farming business. While the statute does reference other places in the Code where a farming business and a real property trade or business are described or defined, regulations have not previously been issued under section 469(c)(7)(C), the rule that section 163(j) refers to in order to define a real property trade or business. The proposed regulations provide such a definition, which clarifies whether a trade or business could elect as a real property trade or business to be excepted from section 163(j). In addition, the proposed regulations describe procedures for allocating income and business interest income and expense between excepted and non-excepted trades or businesses of the taxpayer. The proposed regulations provide a uniform method for allocating income and business interest income and expense which should lower administrative and compliance costs relative to no guidance being provided.

C. Economic Analysis

1. Baseline

The analysis in this section compares the proposed regulations to a no-action baseline reflecting anticipated Federal income tax-related and other economic behavior in the absence of these proposed regulations.

2. Anticipated Benefits

a. In General

The Treasury Department and the IRS expect that the definitions and guidance provided in the proposed regulations will enhance U.S. economic performance relative to the baseline. An economically efficient tax system generally aims to treat income and expense derived from similar economic decisions similarly in order to reduce incentives to make choices based on tax rather than market incentives. In this context, an important benefit of this part of the proposed regulations is to reduce taxpayer uncertainty regarding the calculation of the section 163(j) limitation relative to an alternative scenario in which no such regulations were issued and thus to help ensure that all taxpayers interpret the statutory rules of section 163(j) in a similar manner, a tenet of economic efficiency.

b. Proposed §§1.163(j)-1 through 1.163(j)-5

The proposed regulations make several adjustments to the calculation of ATI. One of these adjustments prevents the double counting of depreciation deductions when a depreciable asset is sold (only relevant for taxable years beginning before January 1, 2022). Other adjustments apply to particular types of taxpayers, such as RICs, REITs, or consolidated groups. These adjustments ensure that the section 163(j) limitation is applied evenly across different types of taxpayers in a manner consistent with the Code. Without such adjustments, certain taxpayers may be disadvantaged relative to otherwise similar taxpayers. For example, if RICs and REITs included the dividends paid deduction when calculating ATI, then these taxpayers would almost always have ATI of zero or close to zero, which would limit the ability of such taxpayers to ever deduct business interest expense for Federal income tax purposes.

In addition, the proposed regulations define the term "interest." There are several places in the Code and regulations where interest expense or interest income is defined, such as in the regulations that allocate and apportion interest expense (§1.861-9T) and in the subpart F regulations (§1.954-2). However, these rules only apply to particular taxpayers in particular situations. As described in the Explanation of Provisions section, there are no generally applicable statutory provisions or regulations addressing when financial instruments are treated as debt for Federal income tax purposes or when a payment is interest. The approach taken to defining interest for the section 163(j) limitation in these proposed regulations is to (1) include amounts associated with conventional debt instruments and amounts already treated as interest for all purposes under existing statutory provisions or regulations; (2) add some additional amounts that are functionally similar to interest, such as the rules regarding amounts on contingent payment debt instruments in § 1.163(j)-1(b)(20)(iii)(B), which was drafted in response to comments, or amounts treated as interest for certain purposes, such as amounts described in §§ 1.861-9T and 1.954-2; and (3) provide an anti-avoidance rule based on the economic principle that any expense or loss predominantly incurred in consideration of the time value of money is treated as an interest expense for section 163(j). Thus, the proposed regulations would apply to interest associated with conventional debt instruments, as well as transactions that are indebtedness in substance even if not in form.

Other options for defining interest were considered by the Treasury Department and the IRS but were determined to be less beneficial and not chosen. The first option considered would be to not provide a definition of interest in the proposed regulations, and thus rely on general tax principles and case law for purposes of defining interest for purposes of section 163(j). While adopting this option might reduce the compliance burden for some taxpayers, not providing an explicit definition of interest would create its own uncertainty (as neither taxpayers nor the IRS might have a clear sense of what types of payments are treated as interest income and interest expense for purposes of section 163(j)). Such uncertainty could increase burdens to the IRS and taxpayers including with respect to disputes and litigation about whether particular payments are interest for section 163(j) purposes.

In addition, such an approach to the definition of interest could encourage taxpayers to engage in transactions that provide financing while generating deductions economically similar to interest but make arguments that such deductions fail to be described by existing principles defining interest expense. There are several reasons why curbing such taxpayer behavior would be beneficial. First, taxpayer use of such transactions is likely to be uneven and dependent in part on the subjective understanding of taxpayers regarding whether such transactions would be allowable under the statute. Second, the ability of taxpayers to engage in such transactions would likely be correlated with size of the trade or business, with large businesses more likely to benefit from such avoidance strategies than small businesses. Third, when the deciding factor for using such transactions is the tax benefit of avoiding a section 163(j) limitation, then such transactions would impose more cost or risk on the taxpayer than using a traditional debt instrument. Engaging in such transactions is an inefficient use of resources. Fourth, such avoidance strategies may also discourage taxpayers from shifting to a less leveraged capital structure, and thus would counteract the intention of the statute to reduce the prevalence of highly-leveraged firms and the probability of systemic financial distress. Fifth, greater use of financing outside of conventional debt instruments may make it more difficult for financial institutions to determine the overall level of leverage and credit risk of firms seeking financing, which may distort the allocation of capital across businesses away from firms and investments with less credit risk.

The second option considered would have been to adopt a definition of interest but limit it to amounts associated with conventional debt instruments and amounts that were already treated as interest under the Code or regulations for all purposes prior to the passage of the TCJA. For example, this is similar to the definition of interest proposed in § 1.163(j)-1(b)(20)(i). While this would bring clarity to many transactions regarding what would be deemed interest for the section 163(j) limitation, it would potentially distort future financing transactions. Some taxpayers would choose to use financial instruments and transactions that provide a similar economic result of using a conventional debt instrument, but would avoid the label of business interest expense, potentially enabling these taxpayers to avoid the section 163(j) limitation without a substantive change in capital structure. The arguments discussed above regarding the costs of this situation would continue to apply.

In addition, there are certain transactions where under a specific provision of the Code and regulations, amounts could be deemed ordinary income when in substance the amounts are interest income. For example, the receipt of substitute interest paid on a securities loan arrangement may, under existing income tax principles, be treated as ordinary income rather than interest income despite the fact that such income is economically equivalent to interest income. Prior to the enactment of the 163(j) interest limitation, whether the amount was labeled as ordinary income or interest was not material to the overall tax liability of the taxpayer, but now this distinction matters.

Because of the tax-motivated financing distortions that would arise from a less comprehensive definition of interest, the Treasury Department and the IRS consider the best approach to the definition of interest is to expand the definition beyond § 1.163(j)-1(b)(20)(i). Under § 1.163(j)-1(b)(20)(ii) and (iii), the Treasury Department and the IRS identified existing financial transactions that have the economic substance of debt and interest, but under the existing Code and regulations may have been deemed ordinary income or gain or may have been treated as interest for limited purposes, and clarifies that such amounts would be considered interest income or expense for the purpose of the new section 163(j) limitation.

In addition, it is difficult for the Treasury Department and the IRS to specifically identify every type of transaction already in practice or to anticipate future innovations in financial transactions, therefore, proposed § 1.163(j)-1(b)(20)(iv) provides an anti-avoidance rule that any expense or loss predominately incurred in consideration of the time value of money is treated as an interest expense for purposes of section 163(j). This should help limit the ability of taxpayers to structure transactions in such a way that would allow deductible expenses that are economically similar to interest and frustrate the application of the statute.

In summary, the definition of interest in these proposed regulations provides clarity to taxpayers and the IRS regarding which specific transactions and types of transactions generate interest subject to the section 163(j) limitation, which should lower compliance and administrative costs relative to providing no definition or a more limited definition of interest. Also, the proposed definition should encourage a more efficient allocation of capital and use of financing across taxpayers.

c. Proposed § 1.163(j)-6

The proposed regulations § 1.163(j)-6 provide guidance on how to allocate partnership excess business interest expense, excess business interest income, and excess taxable income to partners. The statute specifies that the limitation applies at the partnership level but that these items must be allocated to partners for their own 163(j) limitation and because carryforwards of these items occurs at the partner level. Without a specified method of allocating these excess items, partnerships would likely have significant freedom to determine which partners receive excess items. While the statute specifies that the items should be allocated in the same manner as "nonseparately stated taxable income or loss of the partnership", this concept has not previously been defined by statute or regulations. Partnerships have significant control over what items are separately and nonseparately stated for each partner and could potentially reclassify income to be separately stated to favorably change the partner's allocation of excess interest expense or excess taxable income.

The allocation method detailed in the proposed regulations follows a number of principles. First, it ensures that the sum of the excess items at the partner level is equal to the partnership level. Second, it ensures that the partnership does not allocate excess business interest expense to a partner that was allocated items comprising ATI and business interest income that supported the partnership's deductible business interest expense (unless the partner was allocated more interest expense than its share of deductible business interest expense). Finally, it ensures that the partnership allocates any excess taxable income or excess business interest income to partners that are allocated more items comprising ATI or business interest income than necessary to support their allocation of business interest expense. The proposed regulations provide a method to ensure that all partnerships allocate these items consistently and in a way that matches income and interest expense, thus promoting economically efficient investment decisions. Equivalently, they address tax motivated allocations of excess items to avoid the section 163(j) limitation.

The proposed regulations also ensure that, for owners of partnerships and S corporations, business interest income is used only once, at the entity level, in offsetting business interest expenses. This eliminates the incentive to create tiered partnerships purely to double-count interest income in order to avoid the Section 163(j) limitation. It also avoids exacerbating the incentive to seek out interest income relative to other forms of income in order to avoid the Section 163(j) limitation. By avoiding these incentives, the proposed regulations would reduce economically inefficient uses of resources.

d. Proposed § § 1.163(j)-7 through 1.163(j)-8

The Treasury Department and the IRS expect that proposed § § 1.163(j)-7 through 1.163(j)-8 will implement the section 163(j) limitation consistent with preserving the integrity of the international tax system reflected in the Code after TCJA. As described in the Explanation of Provisions section, business interest deductions of individual CFCs may be limited by section 163(j) even when, if calculated on a group basis, business interest deductions would not be limited. The application of section 163(j) to CFCs on an individual basis can result in inappropriate results in certain cases. In particular, to the extent section 163(j) were to disallow a deduction for business interest expense to a CFC that has borrowed from a related CFC, the interest paid to the lender CFC would be included in the income of the lender CFC, the amounts would not fully offset, and the United States shareholder's inclusion under subpart F and GILTI may be increased solely due to the use of intercompany debt between these CFCs. Taxpayers could restructure or "self-help" to reduce this problem, but that option involves economically wasteful restructuring costs to the taxpayer. Another option is to ignore within-group interest payments (the "disregard approach"), but that could lead to inappropriate results, for example, a CFC group member borrowing from a third party and using the loan proceeds to lend to related CFCs (borrowing CFCs) would not be able to have interest income from the loans to the borrowing CFCs offset the interest expense to the third party lender for purposes of the section 163(j) limitation while the borrowing CFCs would not have any interest expense subject to the section 163(j) limitation, even though they are benefiting from the capital provided by the third party loan. The Treasury Department and the IRS consider a preferable option within the authority of the Treasury Department and the IRS to be to allow an election to treat related CFCs and their U.S. shareholders as a group for purposes of calculating the amount of business interest expense subject to the section 163(j) limitation (the "alternative method").

e. Proposed § § 1.163(j)-9 through 1.163(j)-11

Proposed § 1.163(j)-9 provides (1) guidance in applying the rules for farming and real property trade or business elections and (2) guidance in use of a safe harbor for REITs. For electing real property trade or business and electing farming business, the statue specifies that "any such election shall be made at such time and in such manner as the Secretary shall prescribe, and once made, shall be irrevocable." Therefore proposed § 1.163(j)-9 provides taxpayers with the time and manner for electing real property trades or businesses and electing farming businesses. In addition, proposed § 1.163(j)-9 defines the conditions under which an election terminates. Without these conditions specified, taxpayers may engage in behavior which counteracts the intention of the statute and would not otherwise be taken except to game the irrevocable nature of the election the statute specified. The conditions specified increase the likelihood that all similarly situated taxpayers interpret the 'irrevocable' designation similarly and will not engage in tax-motivated behavior to appear to cease operations in an effort to change an irrevocable designation.

Proposed § 1.163(j)-9(g) provides a safe harbor for certain REITs to elect to be electing real property trades or businesses. In addition, a special rule applies to REITs for which 10 percent or less of the value of the REIT's assets are real property financing assets. Under this rule, all of the assets of the REIT are treated as real property trade or business assets. The benefit of the safe harbor is to provide REITs the same tax treatment and apply the same general rules as apply to other taxpayers, an economically efficient approach. The special rule threshold of 10 percent for real property financing assets has the benefit of maintaining consistency with section 856(c)(4), which uses the same values for the REIT asset test at the close of the REIT's taxable year. Taxpayers will benefit in reduced time and cost applying new rules if they are familiar and consistent with other rules that they must comply with under the Code.

Proposed § 1.163(j)-9 provides a rule that stipulates that if at least 80 percent of a trade or business's real property (by fair market value) is leased to a trade or business under common control with the real property trade or business, the trade or business cannot make an election to be an electing real trade or business. In the absence of such a rule, taxpayers could restructure their business such that real estate components of non-real estate businesses are separated from the rest of their business to artificially reduce the application of section 163(j) by leasing the real property to the taxpayer and electing this "business" to be an excepted real property trade or business. Therefore, the prime benefit of this rule is to preserve the intent of the statute of allowing elections in the real property sector without incentivizing other sectors of the economy to restructure their business for the sole intent of avoiding the section 163(j) limitation. This guidance ensures that taxpayers face more uniform incentives when making economic decisions, a tenet of economic efficiency. Rules that maintain consistent structuring activity across taxpayers also increases IRS's ability to consistently enforce the tax rules, thus decreasing opportunities for tax evasion.

Proposed § 1.163(j)-10 provides rules for allocations of ATI and interest expense and interest income between excepted and non-excepted trades or businesses. The proposed regulations allocate interest expense and interest income between the related excepted and non-excepted trades or businesses based upon the relative amounts of the taxpayer's adjusted tax basis in the assets used in its excepted and non-excepted trades or businesses. As discussed in the Explanation of Provisions section, this general method of allocation reflects the fact that money is fungible and the view that interest expense is attributable to all activities and property, regardless of any specific purpose for incurring an obligation on which interest is paid. Since any allocation method will require an increase in compliance costs for taxpayers, an allocation is only required when the share of the asset tax basis in the excepted or non-excepted business exceeds 10 percent. Finally, this asset basis approach provides consistency with the regulations under section 861. By providing taxpayer guidance that is already familiar to them and consistent with other parts of the Code, taxpayers benefit in reduced time and cost spent learning and applying new rules.

The Treasury Department and the IRS considered several alternatives to this asset basis approach for allocating interest income and expense. First, a tracing approach was considered whereby taxpayers would be required to trace disbursements of debt proceeds to specific expenditures. However, tracing would impose a significant administrative burden upon taxpayers due to the complexity of matching interest income and expense among related companies. Further, it is not clear how taxpayers would retroactively apply a tracing regime to existing debt. In particular, because C corporations would have had no reason to trace the proceeds of any existing indebtedness, imposing a tracing regime on existing indebtedness would require corporations to reconstruct the use of funds within their treasury operations at the time such indebtedness was issued, even if the issuance occurred many years ago, and even if the funds were used for a myriad of purposes across a large number of entities. Such an approach would involve a great deal of administrative cost and may be impractical or even impossible for indebtedness issued years ago.

Moreover, because money is fungible, a tracing regime would be distortive and subject to manipulation. Although taxpayers are impacted from both a commercial and tax perspective by the amount of capital raised through the issuance of equity and indebtedness, any trade or business conducted by a taxpayer is generally indifferent to the source of funds. As a result, if taxpayers were allowed to use a tracing regime to allocate indebtedness to excepted trades or businesses, there would be an incentive to treat excepted trades or businesses as funded largely from indebtedness, and to treat non-excepted trades or businesses as funded largely from other types of funding, such as equity funding, despite the fact that, as an economic matter, all of a taxpayer's trades or businesses are funded based on the taxpayer's overall capital structure.

The Treasury Department and the IRS rejected a tracing approach because the complexity of such an approach could be more difficult for taxpayers and the IRS to administer and would create too great an incentive to structure financing with the sole purpose of avoiding the application of the statute. The assumption that a trade or business is indifferent to its source of funds may not be appropriate in cases in which certain indebtedness is secured by the assets of the trade or business and cash flow from those assets is expected to support the payments required on the indebtedness. These proposed regulations would provide for a limited tracing rule in those cases. See the discussion of qualified non-recourse indebtedness in proposed § 1.163(j)-10(d) in part 10(D) of the Explanation of Provisions section.

Second, the Treasury Department and the IRS also considered allocating interest expense based upon the relative fair market value of the assets used in excepted and non-excepted trades or businesses. However, determinations of fair market value frequently are burdensome for taxpayers, which may have numerous assets without a readily established market price, and for the IRS. For this reason, disputes between taxpayers and the IRS over the fair market value of an asset are a common and costly occurrence. In the TCJA, Congress repealed the use of fair market value in the apportionment of interest expense under section 864 of the Code (see section 14502(a) of the TCJA). Thus, the Treasury Department and the IRS have determined that allocating interest expense based upon the relative fair market value of assets is a less viable approach than a regime based upon relative amounts of asset basis.

Third, the Treasury Department and the IRS also considered allocating interest expense to excepted and non-excepted trades or businesses based on the relative amounts of gross income generated by such trades or businesses. However, gross income is more variable and volatile than asset basis, in part because it is based on an annual measurement. Methods could be developed to look at multiple years of gross income through an averaging or other smoothing methodology, but any such approach would necessarily create a number of difficult technical questions because the income of different trades or businesses may be subject to differing business cycles and the timing of income items may be within taxpayers' control. In the TCJA, Congress also repealed the use of gross income in the apportionment of interest expense under section 864 of the Code (see section 14502(a) of the TCJA). The Treasury Department and the IRS request comment on the approaches and decisions discussed in this section.

3. *Anticipated Impacts on Administrative and Compliance Costs*

The proposed regulations include requirements about how excess interest income, interest expense, and taxable income should be allocated to partners. This allocation method will require some partnerships to do a number of calculations to figure out the appropriate allocations.

The proposed regulations as applied to CFCs involve additional tax calculations, such as aggregating CFC income, separating finance from non-finance businesses, and eliminating intra-group dividends, but these calculations are relatively simple and involve data that are already collected. Hence, the increase in compliance costs should not be substantial. Furthermore, because the alternative method is elective, the associated compliance costs would be avoided if the election is not made.

As the compliance costs in both of these cases would be part of the cost of filing tax Form 8990, "Limitation on Business Interest Expense," the estimate of the cost of these calculations will be included as part of the overall reporting burden of Form 8990, as is further discussed in the next section.

D. *Paperwork Reduction Act*

The collection of information contained in this notice of proposed rulemaking has been submitted to the Office of Management and Budget for review in accordance with the Paperwork Reduction Act of 1995 (44 U.S.C. 3507(d)). An agency may not conduct or sponsor, and a person is not required to respond to, a collection of information unless it displays a valid control number assigned by the Office of Management and Budget.

Books or records relating to a collection of information must be retained as long as their contents may become material in the administration of any internal revenue law. Generally, tax returns and return information are confidential, as required by section 6103.

1. Collections of Information

The collection of information in these proposed regulations is in §§ 1.163(j)-9 and 1.163(j)-10. The collection of information in proposed § 1.163(j)-9 is required for taxpayers to make a one-time election to treat their real property or farming trade or business as an electing real property trade or business or an electing farming trade or business under section 163(j)(7)(B) and (C). The collection of information in proposed § 1.163(j)-10 is required for taxpayers to demonstrate how they allocated their interest expense, interest income, and other items of income and deduction between excepted and non-excepted trades or businesses. It is necessary to report this information to the IRS to ensure that taxpayers properly report the amount of interest that is potentially subject to the limitation.

The collection of information is necessary to ensure tax compliance but is not expected to be available as a finalized IRS form by the end of the calendar year. When available, draft revised versions of the affected IRS forms will be posted for comment at *https://apps.irs.gov/app/picklist/list/draftTaxForms.html*. All of the information collections mentioned in §§ 1.163(j)-9 and 1.163(j)-10 may eventually be reported on a form. The specific forms that are expected to change as a result of these proposed regulations are described in more detail in the next section.

2. Future Expected Modifications to Forms to Collect Information

In order to collect necessary information, we are modifying four forms (Forms 1120, 1120S, 1065, and 1120-REIT) and creating one new form (Form 8990). We are modifying Forms 1120, 1120S, 1065, and 1120-REIT to ask filers about the applicability of section 163(j) and the need to file the new Form 8990, as well as the related one-time election statement. When the changes to the IRS forms are finalized, every taxpayer who deducts business interest beginning in tax year 2018 generally will be required to file a new tax Form 8990, "Limitation on Business Interest Expense IRC 163(j)," except for taxpayers with average annual gross receipts of $25 million or less for the three prior tax years (as determined under section 448(c) principles, and as adjusted for inflation starting in 2019). For purposes of the Paperwork Reduction Act of 1995 (44 U.S.C. 3507(d)), the reporting burden of tax form 8990 is associated with OMB control number 1545-0123. Tax form 8990 is estimated to be required by fewer than 92,500 taxpayers in 2018.

The draft forms are available on the IRS website at:

Draft Form	IRS Website Link
Form 1120	https://www.irs.gov/pub/irs-dft/f1120—dft.pdf (Draft instructions: https://www.irs.gov/pub/irs-dft/i1120—dft.pdf)
Form 1120S	https://www.irs.gov/pub/irs-dft/f1120s—dft.pdf (Draft instructions: https://www.irs.gov/pub/irs-dft/i1120s—dft.pdf)
Form 1065	https://www.irs.gov/pub/irs-dft/f1065—dft.pdf (Draft instructions: https://www.irs.gov/pub/irs-dft/i1065—dft.pdf)
Form 1120-REIT	https://www.irs.gov/pub/irs-dft/f1120rei—dft.pdf (Draft instructions: https://www.irs.gov/pub/irs-dft/i1120rei—dft.pdf)
Form 8990	https://www.irs.gov/pub/irs-dft/f8990—dft.pdf

A draft of the Form 8990 instructions is not available at the time of the proposed rule-making. When available, a draft of the IRS Form 8990 instructions will be posted for comment at https://www.irs.gov/pub/irs-dft/f8990—dft.pdf.

3. Burden Estimates

The following estimates are based on the information that is available to the IRS. The most recently available 2015 Statistics of Income (SOI) tax data indicates that 80,702 firms would have contemplated a one-time election to opt out of the section 163(j) limitation as an electing real property trade or business or as an electing farming business were the statute then in effect. The Treasury Department and the IRS anticipate that these proposed regulations will apply to a similar proportion of taxpayers going forward. This estimate is based on a count of filers of Forms 1120, 1120S, 1065, and 1120-REIT in the real estate and farming industries that had over $25 million in gross receipts in taxable year 2015. Each of these forms for taxable years after 2017 will ask filers about the applicability of 163(j) and the need to file Form 8890 as well as the related one-time election. Similarly, using the 2015 SOI tax data, we estimate that 82,755 firms would have allocated interest income and expenses among multiple trades or businesses, some of which are excepted from the section 163(j) limitation and some that are not. This estimate is a count of all tax Forms 1120, 1120S, and 1065 in real estate, farming, and public utilities industries that had over $25 million in gross receipts. While the number of affected taxpayers will increase with growth in the economy, the Treasury Department and the IRS expect that the portion of affected taxpayers will remain approximately the same over the foreseeable future.

The time and dollar compliance burden are derived from the Business Taxpayers Burden model provided by the IRS's Office of Research, Applied Analytics, and Statistics (RAAS). This model relates the time and out-of-pocket costs of business tax preparation, derived from survey data, to assets and receipts of affected taxpayers along with other relevant variables. See Tax Compliance Burden (John Guyton et al, July 2018) at https://www.irs.gov/pub/irs-soi/d13315.pdf. A respondent may require more or less time than the estimated burden, depending on the circumstances.

The burden estimates listed in the below table attempt to capture only those discretionary changes made in these proposed regulations, and may not include burden estimates for forms associated with the statute. Changes made by the Act or through new information collections are captured separately in forthcoming published Supporting Statements for each of these forms and will be aggregated with the estimates provided below to summarize the total burden estimates for each information collection listed below. Those total burden estimates will be available for review and public comment at https://www.reginfo.gov/public/Forward?SearchTarget=PRA&textfield. The Treasury Department and the IRS request comment on these estimates.

	Likely Respondents	Estimated number of respondents (2015 levels)	Estimated average annual burden hours per respondent	Estimated total annual reporting burden (hours) (2015 levels)	Estimated monetized burden @ $95/hour ($2017 millions)	Estimated frequency of responses
§ 1.163(j)-9 (one-time election statement)	Individuals, corporations, and partnerships with real property or farming trades or businesses with gross receipts exceeding the statutory threshold of $25 million	80,702 business respondents (including Forms 1120, 1120-REIT, 1120-S, and 1065 filers)	0 to 30 minutes (estimated average:15 minutes)	20,176	$1.9	One-time
§ 1.163(j)-10 (annual allocation statement)	Individuals, corporations, and partnerships (1) with more than one trade or business (at least one of which is a real property or farming trade or business), and (2) public utilities, with gross receipts exceeding the statutory threshold of $25 million	82,755 business respondents (including Forms 1120, 1120-S, and 1065 filers)	15 minutes to 2 hours (estimated average: 1 hour)	82,755	$7.9	Annually
§ 1.163(j)-10 (one-time start-up cost to develop procedures for filing an annual allocation statement)	Same as above	82,755	4 hours (start-up burden)	331,020	$31.4	One-time
Three year monetized burden estimate					$19.0	Three year annual average

The three-year annual average of the monetized burden for the information collection and resulting from discretionary requirements contained in this rulemaking is estimated to be19.0 million ($2017) ([($1.9 million+ $31.4 million) + ($7.9 million x 3)]/3). To ensure more accuracy and consistency across its information collections, the IRS is currently in the process of revising the methodology it uses to estimate burden and costs. Once this methodology is complete, the IRS will provide this information to reflect a more precise estimate of burdens and costs.

The Treasury Department and the IRS request comment on the assumptions, methodology, and burden estimates related to this information collection. Comments on the collection of information should be sent to the Office of Management and Budget, Attn: Desk Officer for the Department of the Treasury, Office of Information and Regulatory Affairs, Washington, DC 20503, with copies to the Internal Revenue Service, Attn: IRS Reports Clearance Officer, SE:W:CAR:MP:T:T:SP, Washington, DC 20224. Comments on the collection of information should be received by **[INSERT DATE 60 DAYS AFTER DATE OF PUBLICATION IN THE FEDERAL REGISTER]**.

Comments are specifically requested concerning—

Whether the proposed collection of information is necessary for the proper performance of the functions of the IRS, including whether the information will have practical utility;

The accuracy of the estimated burden associated with the proposed collection of information;

How the quality, utility, and clarity of the information to be collected may be enhanced;

How the burden of complying with the proposed collection of information may be minimized, including through the application of automated collection techniques or other forms of information technology; and

Estimates of capital or start-up costs and costs of operation, maintenance, and purchase of services to provide information.

II. *Regulatory Flexibility Act*

It is hereby certified that these proposed regulations, if adopted as final, will not have a significant economic impact on a substantial number of small entities. Although the Treasury Department and the IRS believe that the proposed regulations may impact small entities, the number of small entities impacted is low.

Section 163(j) provides exceptions for which many small entities will qualify. First, under section 163(j)(3), the limitation does not apply to any taxpayer, other than a tax shelter under section 448(a)(3), which meets the gross receipts test under section 448(c) for any taxable year. A taxpayer meets the gross receipts test under section 448(c) if the taxpayer has average annual gross receipts for the 3-taxable year period ending with the taxable year that precedes the current taxable year that do not exceed $25,000,000. Second, section 163(j) provides that certain trades or businesses are not subject to the limitation, including the trade or business of performing services as an employee, electing real property trades or businesses, electing farming businesses, and certain utilities as defined in section 163(j)(7)(A)(iv). Lastly, certain REITs, as described in proposed § 1.163(j)-9(g), are eligible to make the election out of the limitation as a real property trades or businesses.

Any economic impact on any small entities as a result of the requirements in this notice of proposed rulemaking are not expected to be significant. The small entities potentially subject to the provision in proposed § 1.163(j)-9 are individuals, corporations, including S corporations, and partnerships that (1) have average annual gross receipts for the 3-taxable year period ending with the taxable year that precedes the current taxable year exceeding $25,000,000, and (2) want to make the election out of the limitation as an electing real property trade or business under section 163(j)(7)(B) or electing farming business under section 163(j)(7)(C). Proposed § 1.163(j)-9 requires such taxpayers to attach a one-time statement to their return providing the taxpayer's name, address, social security number (SSN) or employer identification number (EIN), a description of the taxpayer's electing trade or business, including the principal business activity code, a statement that the taxpayer acknowledges the election is irrevocable, and a statement that the taxpayer is making an election under section 163(j)(7)(B) or (C), as applicable.

The small entities potentially subject to the requirements in proposed § 1.163(j)-10 are individuals, corporations (including S corporations), and partnerships that (1) have average annual gross receipts for the 3-taxable year period ending with the taxable year that precedes the current taxable year exceeding $25,000,000, and (2) have multiple trades or businesses, some of which are excepted from the limitation and some of which are not excepted from the limitation, for which the taxpayer must properly allocate business interest expense. Proposed § 1.163(j)-10 requires such taxpayers to attach an annual statement to their return demonstrating the following: (1) The taxpayer's adjusted basis in the aggregated assets used in its excepted and non-excepted businesses, (2) the determination dates on which asset basis was measured during the taxable year, (3) the names and TINs of all entities for which basis information is being provided, (4) asset basis information for corporations or partnerships if the taxpayer looks through to the corporation's or partnership's basis in the corporation's or partnership's assets under proposed § 1.163(j)-10(c)(5)(ii), and (5) a summary of the method or methods used to determine asset basis in property used in both excepted and non-excepted businesses.

As discussed elsewhere in this preamble, the reporting burden for the one-time election statement is estimated at 0 to 30 minutes, depending on individual circumstances, with an estimated average of 15 minutes for all affected entities, regardless of size. The reporting burden for the annual allocation statement is estimated at 15 minutes to 2 hours, depending on individual circumstances, with an estimated average of 1 hour. The estimated monetized burden for compliance is $95 per hour.

For these reasons, the Treasury Department and the IRS have determined that the collections of information in this notice of proposed rulemaking will not have a significant economic impact. Accordingly, a regulatory flexibility analysis under the Regulatory Flexibility Act (5 U.S.C. chapter 6) is not required. Notwithstanding this certification, the Treasury Department and the IRS invite comments from interested members of the public on both the number of entities affected and the economic impact on small entities.

It is hereby certified that proposed § § 1.163(j)-4, 1.163(j)-5, and 1.163(j)-6 will not have a significant economic impact on a substantial number of small entities. Although the Treasury Department and the IRS believe that the proposed regulations may affect small entities, the economic impact on small entities as a result of the notice of proposed rulemaking is not expected to be significant. In particular, only firms with more than $25 million in gross receipts are required to file a tax Form 8990. Accordingly, a regulatory flexibility analysis under the Regulatory Flexibility Act (5 U.S.C. chapter 6) is not required. Notwithstanding this certification, the Treasury Department and the IRS invite comments from interested members of the public on both the number of entities affected and the economic impact on small entities.

Pursuant to section 7805(f) of the Code, this notice of proposed rulemaking has been submitted to the Chief Counsel for Advocacy of the Small Business Administration for comment on its impact on small business.

Comments and Public Hearing

Before these proposed regulations are adopted as final regulations, consideration will be given to any comments that are submitted timely to the IRS in the preamble under the **ADDRESSES** section. The Treasury Department and the IRS request comments on all aspects of the proposed rules.

All comments submitted will be made available at *http://www.regulations.gov* for public inspection and copying. A public hearing has been scheduled for February 27, 2019, beginning at 10 a.m. in the Auditorium of the Internal Revenue Building, 1111 Constitution Avenue NW, Washington, DC 20224. If there is not sufficient time to discuss all of the topics on February 27, 2019, the hearing will continue the following day at 10 a.m. in the same location. Due to building security procedures, visitors must enter at the Constitution Avenue entrance. In addition, all visitors must present photo identification to enter the building. Because of access restrictions, visitors will not be admitted beyond the immediate entrance area more than 30 minutes before the hearing starts. For more information about having your name placed on the building access list to attend the hearing, see the **FOR FURTHER INFORMATION CONTACT** section of this preamble.

The rules of 26 CFR 601.601(a)(3) apply to the hearing. Persons who wish to present oral comments at the hearing must submit an outline of the topics to be discussed and the time to be devoted to each topic by [**INSERT DATE 60 DAYS AFTER DATE OF PUBLICATION IN THE FEDERAL REGISTER**]. Submit a signed paper or electronic copy of the outline as prescribed in this preamble under the **ADDRESSES** heading. An agenda showing the scheduling of the speakers will be prepared after the deadline for receiving outlines has passed. Copies of the agenda will be available free of charge at the hearing.

Drafting Information

The principal authors of these regulations are Susie Bird, Charles Gorham, Zachary King, Jaime Park, Kathy Reed, and Sophia Wang, Office of the Associate Chief Counsel (Income Tax and Accounting); Kevin M. Jacobs, Russell Jones, and John Lovelace, Office of the Associate Chief Counsel (Corporate); Meghan Howard, William Kostak, Anthony McQuillen, Adrienne Mikolashek, and James Quinn, Office of the Associate Chief Counsel (Passthroughs and Special Industries); Angela Holland, Steve Jensen, and Charles Rioux, Office of the Associate Chief Counsel (International); William E. Blanchard, Michael Chin, Steven Harrison, Andrea Hoffenson, and Diana Imholtz, Office of the Associate Chief Counsel (Financial Institutions and Products). Other personnel from the Treasury Department and the IRS participated in their development.

[¶49,781] Proposed Amendments of Regulations (REG-105600-18), published in the Federal Register on December 7, 2018 (corrected 3/6/2019).

[Code Secs. 78, 861, 901, 904, 952, 954, 960, 965]

Foreign Tax Credit: Dividends: Foreign subsidiaries.—Reg. §§1.861-13, 1.901(j)-1, 1.904(b)-3 and amendments of Reg. §§1.78-1, 1.861-8, 1.861-9, 1.861-10, 1.861-11, 1.861-12, 1.861-14, 1.861-17, 1.904-1, 1.904-2, 1.904-3, 1.904-4, 1.904-5, 1.904-6, 1.904(f)-12, 1.952-1, 1.954-1, 1.960-1, 1.960-2, 1.960-3, 1.960-4, 1.960-5, 1.960-6, 1.960-7, 1.965-5 and 1.965-7, relating to the determination of the foreign tax credit under the Internal Revenue Code (the "Code"), are proposed.

AGENCY: Internal Revenue Service (IRS), Treasury.

ACTION: Notice of proposed rulemaking.

SUMMARY: This document contains proposed regulations that provide guidance relating to the determination of the foreign tax credit under the Internal Revenue Code (the "Code"). The guidance relates to changes made to the applicable law by the Tax Cuts and Jobs Act (the "Act"), which was enacted on December 22, 2017. Guidance on other foreign tax credit issues, including in relation to pre-Act statutory amendments, is also included in this document. The proposed regulations provide guidance needed to comply with statutory changes and affect individuals and corporations claiming foreign tax credits.

DATES: Written or electronic comments and requests for a public hearing must be received by February 5, 2018.

ADDRESSES: Send submissions to CC:PA:LPD:PR (REG-105600-18), room 5203, Internal Revenue Service, PO Box 7604, Ben Franklin Station, Washington, DC 20224. Submissions may be hand delivered Monday through Friday between the hours of 8 a.m. and 4 p.m. to CC:PA:LPD:PR (REG-105600-18), Courier's desk, Internal Revenue Service, 1111 Constitution Avenue, NW., Washington, DC 20044, or sent electronically, via the Federal eRulemaking Portal at *www.regulations.gov* (indicate IRS and REG-105600-18).

FOR FURTHER INFORMATION CONTACT: Concerning the proposed regulations under §§1.861-8 through 1.861-13, 1.861-17, and 1.904(b)-3, Jeffrey P. Cowan, (202) 317-4924; concerning the proposed regulations under §§1.901(j)-1, 1.904-1 through 1.904-6, 1.904(f)-12, and 1.954-1, Jeffrey L. Parry, (202) 317-4916, and Larry R. Pounders, (202) 317-5465; concerning §§1.78-1 and 1.960-1 through 1.960-7, Suzanne M. Walsh, (202) 317-4908; concerning §§1.965-5 and 1.965-7, Karen J. Cate, (202) 317-4667; concerning submissions of comments and requests for a public hearing, Regina Johnson, (202) 317-6901 (not toll-free numbers).

SUPPLEMENTARY INFORMATION:

Background

The Act made several significant changes to the Internal Revenue Code with respect to the foreign tax credit rules and related rules for allocating and apportioning expenses for purposes of determining the foreign tax credit limitation. In particular, the Act repealed the fair market value method of asset valuation for purposes of allocating and apportioning interest expense under section 864(e)(2), added section 904(b)(4), added two foreign tax credit limitation categories in section 904(d), amended section 960(a) through (c), added section 960(d) through (f), and repealed section 902 along with making other conforming changes. The Act also added section 951A, which requires a United States shareholder of a controlled foreign corporation ("CFC") to include certain amounts in income (a "global intangible low-taxed income inclusion" or "GILTI inclusion").

This document contains proposed regulations (the "proposed regulations") addressing (1) the allocation and apportionment of deductions under sections 861 through 865 and adjustments to the foreign tax credit limitation under section 904(b)(4); (2) transition rules for overall foreign loss, separate limitation loss, and overall domestic loss accounts under section 904(f) and (g), and for the carryover and carryback of unused foreign taxes under section 904(c); (3) the addition of separate categories under section 904(d) and other necessary updates to the regulations under section 904, including revisions to the look-through rules and other updates to reflect pre-Act statutory amendments; (4) the calculation of the exception from subpart F income for high-taxed income under section 954(b)(4); (5) the determination of deemed paid credits under section 960 and the gross up under section 78; and (6) the application of the election under section 965(n).

Explanation of Provisions

I. *Allocation and Apportionment of Deductions and the Calculation of Taxable Income for Purposes of Section 904(a)*

The foreign tax credit limitation under section 904 is determined, in part, based on a taxpayer's taxable income from sources without the United States. Regulations under sections 861 through 865 provide rules for allocating and apportioning deductions to determine, among other things, a taxpayer's taxable income from sources without the United States for purposes of applying section 904. Section 904(b)(4) makes certain adjustments to both the taxpayer's taxable income from sources without the United States and the taxpayer's entire taxable income for purposes of computing the applicable foreign tax credit limitation. Proposed §§1.861-8 through 1.861-13 and 1.861-17 amend existing regulations to clarify how deductions are allocated and apportioned in general, and provide new rules to account for the specific changes made to sections 864(e) and 904 by the Act. Proposed §1.904(b)-3 provides rules regarding the application of section 904(b)(4) for purposes of determining a taxpayer's foreign tax credit limitation.

The Department of the Treasury ("Treasury Department") and the Internal Revenue Service ("IRS") have received comments suggesting that section 951A, in combination with section 904(d)(1)(A) (the "section 951A category"), was intended to provide that the income of a United States shareholder derived through the CFC would be subject to additional U.S. tax if the foreign effective tax rate is below a particular rate, and should be effectively exempt from U.S. tax if the foreign effective tax rate is at or above that rate. These comments generally cite language in H.R. Rep. 115-466 (2017) (the "Conference Report") illustrating that no U.S. "residual tax" applies to foreign earnings subject to a foreign effective tax rate of 13.125 percent or more.

Allocated expenses may reduce the amount of section 951A category income included in U.S. taxable income below the amount of the foreign base on which the CFC paid at least a 13.125 percent foreign effective tax rate, with the effect that the United States shareholder's foreign taxes deemed paid may exceed the pre-credit U.S. tax on its section 951A category income, resulting in excess credits that may not offset U.S. tax on other income. This result flows from the fact that the foreign tax credit limitation under section 904 is calculated with respect to the pre-credit U.S. tax on the shareholder's net foreign source taxable income in each separate category. The comments nevertheless suggest that taxpayers' inability to reduce U.S. tax on non-section 951A category income (such as U.S. source income) with the excess credits is tantamount to imposing U.S. "residual tax" on section 951A category income, even though the actual U.S. tax liability on that income, as reduced by foreign tax credits, is zero. The comments suggest that in order to assure full utilization of foreign tax credits associated with section 951A category income that is subject to a foreign effective tax rate of 13.125 percent or greater, no expenses should be allocated and apportioned to the section 951A category income.

The Treasury Department and the IRS have determined that the Act is not consistent with this view of how the section 904 limitation should apply to the section 951A category. Congress added a new separate category under section 904(d)(1) for amounts includible under section 951A and amended section 904(c) to disallow carryovers of excess foreign tax credits in that category, but did not modify the existing rules under section 904 or sections 861 through 865 to provide for special treatment of expenses allocable to the section 951A category. Other provisions added in the Act are inconsistent with the notion described by comments that Congress intended effectively to exempt section 951A category income that was subject to a certain foreign effective tax rate from U.S. tax, since those provisions may result in U.S. tax being imposed on income derived through a CFC even if the foreign effective tax rate on the income exceeds 13.125 percent. See, for example, sections 59A (limiting the benefits of foreign tax credits) and 250(a)(2)(B)(ii) (limiting the deduction under section 250 in certain cases). In addition, numerous provisions in the Code that were unamended by the Act apply by their terms to section 951A category income, also indicating that Congress did not intend to eliminate generally-applicable limitations on foreign tax credits associated with foreign earnings of a CFC even if such earnings were subject to a certain foreign effective tax rate. For example, the Act did not amend provisions that limit the availability of foreign tax credits (such as sections 901(j), (k), (l), or (m)) or that reduce (or increase) the foreign tax credit limitation in the section 951A category based on U.S. or foreign losses in other separate categories or losses in other years (sections 904(f) and (g)). These provisions apply to a GILTI inclusion and related taxes under section 960(d), and as applied the provisions are not consistent with the policy of determining allowable foreign tax credits based solely on a CFC's foreign effective tax rate because they may reduce the amount of taxes that may be credited without regard to the foreign effective tax rate of the CFC. The Act did, however, add section 904(b)(4)(B), which disregards certain deductions other than those that are "properly allocable or apportioned to" amounts includible under sections 951A(a) or 951(a)(1) and stock that produces amounts includible under section 951A(a) or 951(a)(1). This new provision plainly contemplates that deductions will be allocated and apportioned to the section 951A category.

Accordingly, the proposed regulations generally apply the existing approach of the expense allocation rules to determine taxable income in the section 951A category, as well as the new foreign branch category described in section 904(d)(1)(B). However, as discussed in Part I.A of this Explanation of Provisions, the proposed regulations also provide for exempt income and exempt asset treatment with respect to income in the section 951A category that is offset by the deduction allowed under section 250(a)(1) for inclusions under section 951A(a) and a corresponding percentage of the stock of CFCs that generates such income. This will generally have the effect of reducing the amount of expenses apportioned to the section 951A category.

The Treasury Department and the IRS recognize that in light of the significant reduction in the corporate tax rate and the enactment of section 951A, the foreign tax credit limitation and the related expense allocation rules will have a broader impact on taxpayers than before the Act. In particular, although all U.S. taxpayers claiming foreign tax credits were subject to the foreign tax credit limitation under section 904, many taxpayers were not significantly affected by the limitation so long as the U.S. corporate tax rate was higher than the effective foreign tax rate. In addition, the pre-Act deferral system that taxed non-passive income earned through foreign subsidiaries (and allowed deemed paid foreign tax credits) only upon repatriation allowed taxpayers to manage their foreign tax credit limitation by timing repatriations. However, the Act's reduction in the U.S. corporate tax rate, limitations on deferral, and introduction of a participation exemption regime without deemed paid credits has limited the benefits of this type of planning. The Treasury Department and the IRS welcome comments on the proposed approach and anticipated impacts.

Many of the existing expense allocation rules have not been significantly modified since 1988. Furthermore, for taxable years beginning after December 31, 2020, a worldwide affiliated group will be able to elect to allocate and apportion interest expense on a worldwide basis. *See* section 864(f). The Treasury Department and the IRS expect the implementation of section 864(f) will have a significant impact on the effect of interest expense apportionment and will necessitate a reexamination of the existing expense allocation rules.

Therefore, the Treasury Department and the IRS expect to reexamine the existing approaches for allocating and apportioning expenses, including in particular the apportionment of interest, research and experimentation ("R&E"), stewardship, and general & administrative expenses, as well as to reexamine the "CFC netting rule" in § 1.861-10(e). The Treasury Department and the IRS request comments with respect to specific revisions to the regulations that should be made in connection with this review.

Part I.A of this Explanation of Provisions describes proposed changes to the rules addressing exempt income and assets, including the application of those rules in the context of the deduction under section 250. Part I.B of this Explanation of Provisions describes rules to address the allocation and apportionment of the deduction under section 250 and clarifying changes to the allocation and apportionment of certain other deductions. Part I.C of this Explanation of Provisions describes a new rule addressing loans to partnerships by certain partners and their affiliates. Part I.D of this Explanation of Provisions describes a revision to the CFC netting rule. Part I.E of this Explanation of Provisions describes rules for the valuation of assets, including stock, for purposes of allocating and apportioning deductions. Part I.F of this Explanation of Provisions describes rules for characterizing the stock of certain foreign corporations for purposes of allocating and apportioning deductions. Part I.G of this Explanation of Provisions describes rules for certain elections relating to the allocation and apportionment of R&E expenditures. Part I.H of this Explanation of Provisions describes rules for applying section 904(b)(4).

A. *Changes and clarifications to definitions of exempt income and exempt asset*

Section 864(e)(3) provides that, for purposes of allocating and apportioning any deductible expense, any tax-exempt asset (and any income from the asset) is not taken into account. Section 864(e)(3) also provides that a similar rule applies for the portion of any dividend equal to the deduction allowable under section 243 or 245(a) with respect to the dividend and the like portion of any stock the dividends on which would be so deductible. Section 864(e)(3) was not modified by the Act.

The Treasury Department and the IRS are aware that some taxpayers have taken the position that under § 1.861-8T(d)(2)(ii) assets or income that are partially exempt, excluded, or eliminated may be treated as entirely exempt. This interpretation is inconsistent with section 864(e)(3). The proposed regulations revise the definitions of exempt income and exempt asset to clarify that income or assets are treated as exempt (or partially exempt) under section 864(e)(3) only to the extent that the income or the income from the assets are, or are treated as, exempt, excluded, or eliminated. Proposed § 1.861-8(d)(2)(ii)(A).

New section 250(a)(1) allows a domestic corporate shareholder a deduction (the "section 250 deduction") equal to portions of its foreign-derived intangible income ("FDII"), GILTI inclusion, and the amount treated as a dividend under section 78 that is attributable to its GILTI inclusion. Because the section 250 deduction effectively exempts a portion of certain income, the proposed regulations provide that for purposes of applying the expense allocation and apportionment rules, the gross income offset by the section 250 deduction is treated as exempt income, and the stock or other asset giving rise to that income is treated as a partially exempt asset. *See* Senate Committee on Finance, Explanation of the Bill, S. Prt. 115-20, at 376 n.1210 (November 22, 2017) ("The Committee intends that the deduction allowed by new Code section 250 be treated as exempting the deducted income from tax."). This rule does not apply for purposes of determining the amount of the foreign derived intangible income in applying section 250 as the operative section. No inference is intended regarding whether the section 250 deduction is treated as giving rise to exempt income or assets for any other purpose of the Code other than for purposes of the allocation and apportionment of deductions under § § 1.861-8 through 1.861-17.

Under proposed § 1.861-8(d)(2)(ii)(C)(*1*), a portion of a domestic corporation's gross income that is FDII or results from a GILTI inclusion (and the corresponding section 78 gross up) is treated as exempt income based on the amount of the section 250 deduction allowed to the United States shareholder under section 250(a)(1). Similarly, the value of a domestic corporation's assets that produce FDII or GILTI is reduced to reflect the fact that the income from the assets is treated in part as exempt. Proposed § 1.861-8(d)(2)(ii)(C)(2).

The amount of the section 250 deduction used to determine the amount of gross income that is exempt is reduced to the extent section 250(a)(2)(B) requires a reduction to the amount of the deduction. Therefore, proposed § 1.861-8(d)(2)(ii)(C) does not apply to treat income or assets as exempt if the domestic corporation is not allowed a deduction under section 250(a)(2), even though the domestic corporation may have FDII or a GILTI inclusion.

A special rule is provided in proposed § 1.861-8(d)(2)(ii)(C)(*2*)(*ii*) to determine the portion of CFC stock that gives rise to a GILTI inclusion that is treated as exempt. The rule provides that a portion of CFC stock owned by a domestic corporation that is a United States shareholder of the CFC is treated as exempt based on a fraction equal to the amount of the section 250 deduction allowed to the domestic corporation under section 250(a)(1)(B)(i) (taking into account the reduction, if any, required under section 250(a)(2)(B)(ii)), divided by the domestic corporation's GILTI inclusion. In general, the fraction is applied to the portion of the CFC stock that is treated as giving rise to a GILTI inclusion and that is not assigned to a section 245A subgroup, as determined under the rules in proposed § 1.861-13. *See* Part I.F.1 and I.H of this Explanation of Provisions. To the extent the domestic corporation is allowed a section 250 deduction for an amount under section 250(a)(1)(B) (because the domestic corporation has a GILTI inclusion), the proposed regulations treat a portion of the stock of a CFC with respect to which the domestic corporation is a United States shareholder as exempt even if the CFC has a tested loss for the taxable year.

Section 245A(a) allows domestic corporate shareholders a deduction equal to the foreign-source portion of dividends received from certain foreign corporations (the "section 245A deduction"), subject to certain limitations described in section 246. Although section 864(e)(3) contemplates that dividends described in sections 243 and 245(a) are treated similarly to exempt income to the extent of the deductions allowed under those sections, section 864(e)(3) does not apply to the dividend income reduced by the section 245A deduction. Instead, section 904(b)(4) provides for alternative adjustments. *See* Part I.H.2 of this Explanation of Provisions for a discussion of the different approaches under section 864(e)(3) and 904(b)(4). Proposed § 1.861-8(d)(2)(iii)(C) clarifies that the section 245A deduction does not give rise to exempt income. Similarly, no asset is treated as an exempt asset by reason of the section 245A deduction. Different treatment is provided under § 1.861-8T(d)(2)(ii)(B) for dividends received deductions under sections 243 and 245 because section 864(e)(3) specifically provides that similar rules to the exempt asset and income rules apply to those deductions.

Finally, the proposed regulations confirm in proposed § 1.861-8(d)(2)(iv) that earnings and profits excluded from income under section 959 ("previously taxed earnings and profits") do not result in any portion of the stock in a CFC being treated as an exempt asset. Under § § 1.861-12 and 1.861-12T, stock in a CFC is characterized by reference to the income generated each year by the CFC's assets. Previously taxed earnings and profits are not a type of income that is generated during the taxable year by a CFC's assets; rather, the CFC's assets, whether acquired with previously taxed or non-previously taxed earnings and profits or with another source of funds, generate income used to characterize the stock. For the avoidance of doubt, proposed § 1.861-8(d)(2)(iv) confirms that the fact that a CFC has previously taxed earnings and profits does not result in any portion of the CFC's stock being treated as an exempt asset under section 864(e)(3).

B. *Allocation and apportionment of foreign income taxes, the section 250 deduction, and a distributive share of partnership deductions*

Section 1.861-8(e) provides rules for allocating and apportioning certain deductions. Section 1.861-8(e)(6) provides rules for the allocation and apportionment of deductions for state, local, and foreign income, war profits and excess profits taxes. In the case of deductions for foreign income, war profits and excess profits taxes, the allocation and apportionment rules under § 1.861-8(e) are intended to be consistent with the principles of § 1.904-6. The proposed regulations clarify this result by expressly incorporating the principles of § 1.904-6(a)(1)(i), (ii), and (iv) in allocating and apportioning taxes to the relevant statutory and residual groupings (and not just to separate categories of income for purposes of determining the foreign tax credit limitation).

The proposed regulations include rules for allocating and apportioning the section 250 deduction. For these purposes, although the section 250 deduction is a single deduction that equals the sum of the amounts specified in section 250(a)(1)(A) and (B), the proposed regulations provide separate rules with respect to (i) the portion of the section 250 deduction for FDII and (ii) the portion of the section 250 deduction for the GILTI inclusion and the amount of the section 78 gross up attributable to foreign taxes deemed paid with respect to the GILTI inclusion. The amount of each portion of the section 250 deduction to be allocated and apportioned takes into account any reductions required under section 250(a)(2)(B).

Under proposed § 1.861-8(e)(13), the portion of the section 250 deduction for FDII is treated as definitely related and allocable to the specific class of gross income that is included in the taxpayer's foreign-derived deduction eligible income (as defined in section 250(b)(4)). Although foreign-derived deduction eligible income is an amount net of expenses, the class is determined based solely on the gross income that is used to calculate foreign-derived deduction eligible income. In cases where the income is allocated to a class that contains multiple categories under section 904(d) or U.S. source income, the deduction is apportioned ratably based on the relative amounts of gross income in the different income groupings.

Proposed § 1.861-8(e)(14) provides a similar rule for the portion of the section 250 deduction allowed for the GILTI inclusion and the corresponding section 78 gross up. In certain cases, gross income from the GILTI inclusion could be in a grouping other than the grouping for section 951A category income (for example, because it is U.S. source or passive category income). In such cases, the deduction for the GILTI inclusion and the section 78 gross up is apportioned ratably based on the relative amounts of gross income in the different income groupings.

The proposed regulations also clarify the general rule for allocating and apportioning a taxpayer's distributive share of partnership deductions. Proposed § 1.861-8(e)(15) provides that if a taxpayer is a partner in a partnership, the taxpayer's deductions that are allocated and apportioned include the taxpayer's distributive share of the partnership's deductions.

C. *Special rule for specified partnership loans*

The Treasury Department and the IRS are aware that certain loans made to a partnership by a United States person, or a member of its affiliated group, that owns an interest (directly or indirectly) in the partnership can result in a distortion in the determination of the foreign tax credit limitation under section 904 when the same person takes into account both a distributive share of the interest expense and the interest income with respect to the same loan. This result occurs due to differences in the rules that govern the source and separate category of the interest income and those that govern the allocation and apportionment of interest expense. To prevent the distortive effect of these differences, proposed § 1.861-9(e)(8)(ii) generally provides that, to the extent the lender in a specified partnership loan transaction takes into account both interest expense and interest income with respect to the same loan, the interest income is assigned to the same statutory and residual groupings as those groupings from which the interest expense is deducted, as determined under the allocation and apportionment rules in §§ 1.861-9 through 1.861-13. Additionally, proposed § 1.861-9(e)(8)(i) provides that, for purposes of applying the allocation and apportionment rules, a portion of the loan is not taken into account as an asset of the lender based on the ratio of the portion of the interest income included by the lender that is subject to this matching rule to the total amount of interest income included by the lender with respect to the loan in the taxable year. The proposed regulations include anti-avoidance rules to extend these provisions to certain back-to-back loans or loans made through CFCs. *See* proposed § 1.861-9(e)(8)(iii) and (iv). The proposed regulations also apply the specified partnership loan rules to transactions that are not loans but that give rise to deductions that are allocated and apportioned in the same manner as interest expense under § 1.861-9T(b). Proposed § 1.861-9(e)(8)(v).

D. *Revision to CFC netting rule relating to hybrid debt*

Section 1.861-10(e)(8)(vi) provides that for purposes of applying the CFC netting rule of § 1.861-10(e), certain related party hybrid debt is treated as related group indebtedness, but the income derived from the hybrid debt is not treated as interest income derived from related group indebtedness. As a result, no interest expense is generally allocated to income from the hybrid debt, but the debt may nevertheless increase the amount of allocable related group indebtedness for which a reduction in assets is required under § 1.861-10(e)(7). This has a distortive effect on the general allocation and apportionment of other interest expense under § 1.861-9. The proposed regulations revise § 1.861-10(e)(8)(vi) to provide that hybrid debt is not treated as related group indebtedness for purposes of the CFC netting rule. Proposed § 1.861-10(e)(8)(vi) also provides that hybrid debt is not treated as related group indebtedness for purposes of determining the foreign base period ratio, which is based on the average of related group debt-to-asset ratios in the five prior taxable years, even if the hybrid debt was otherwise properly treated as related group indebtedness in a prior year. This is necessary to prevent distortions that would otherwise arise in comparing the ratio in a year in which the hybrid debt was treated as related group indebtedness to the ratio in a year in which the hybrid debt is not treated as related group indebtedness.

E. *Valuation of assets for purposes of apportioning interest expense and other deductions*

1. Repeal of Fair Market Value Method and Transition Relief

Section 864(e)(2) requires taxpayers to apportion interest expense on the basis of assets rather than income. Under the asset method, a taxpayer apportions interest expense to the various statutory groupings based on the average total value of assets within each grouping for the taxable year as determined under the asset valuation rules of § 1.861-9T(g). Before the Act, taxpayers could elect to determine the value of their assets under the tax book value, alternative tax book value, or the fair market value method, and were required to obtain the Commissioner's approval to switch from the fair market value method to the tax book or alternative tax book value methods. *See* § 1.861-8T(c)(2). In light of the Act's repeal of the fair market value method for apportioning interest for taxable years beginning after December 31, 2017, taxpayers using the fair market value method must switch to the tax book or alternative tax book value method for purposes of apportioning interest expense for the taxpayer's first taxable year beginning after December 31, 2017. Proposed §§ 1.861-8(c)(2) and 1.861-9(i)(2) provide that the Commissioner's approval is not required for this change.

For purposes of determining asset values, an average of values within each statutory grouping is computed for the year on the basis of the values of assets at the beginning and end of the year. *See* § 1.861-9T(g)(2)(i)(A). The Treasury Department and the IRS understand that taxpayers previously using the fair market value method may not have had an independent reason to calculate the adjusted tax basis of their assets as of the beginning of their first post-2017 taxable year as required by the tax book value and alternative tax book value methods. To provide transitional relief, the proposed regulations provide in § 1.861-9(g)(2)(i) that for the first taxable year beginning after December 31, 2017, a taxpayer that had been using the fair market value method may choose to determine asset values using an average of the end of the first quarter and the year-end values of its assets, provided that all the members of an affiliated group (as defined in § 1.861-11T(d)) make the same choice and no substantial distortion would result.

The amendments made to section 864(e)(2) by the Act repealed the fair market value method only for purposes of allocating and apportioning interest expense. Accordingly, the fair market value method and the rules in § 1.861-9(h) remain applicable for non-interest expenses that are properly apportioned on the basis of the relative fair market values of assets.

2. Clarification of Rules for Adjusting Stock Basis in Nonaffiliated 10 percent Owned Corporations for Earnings and Profits

Under section 864(e)(4)(A) and § 1.861-12(c)(2)(i)(A), for purposes of apportioning expenses on the basis of the tax book value of assets, certain adjustments are made to the adjusted basis of stock in a 10 percent owned corporation based on the earnings and profits (or deficits in earnings and profits) of the corporation attributable to the stock. The Treasury Department and the IRS are aware that some taxpayers have taken the position that the adjustment to basis for earnings and profits under § 1.861-12T(c)(2) does not include previously taxed earnings and profits. This interpretation is inconsistent with the text and purpose of section 864(e)(4) and § 1.861-12(c)(2). The adjustment under section 864(e)(4) is intended to better approximate the value of stock. *See* Joint Committee on Tax'n, General Explanation of the Tax Reform Act of 1986 (P.L. 99-514) (May 4, 1987), JCS-10-87, at p.87. Whether or not certain earnings and profits are reclassified from earnings described in section 959(c)(3) to previously taxed earnings and profits has no bearing on the value of the stock. Therefore, the proposed regulations confirm that previously taxed earnings and profits are taken into account for purposes of the adjustment described in § 1.861-12(c)(2). In addition, the proposed regulations clarify that the reference to the "rules of section 1248" in § 1.861-12T(c)(2)(i)(B) is intended to provide rules for determining the pro rata share of earnings and profits attributable to the taxpayer's shares, and is not relevant to determining the amount of the foreign corporation's earnings and profits subject to the adjustment, which is governed by the rules in sections 964(a) and 986. Proposed § 1.861-12(c)(2)(i)(B)(2).

The Treasury Department and the IRS are also aware that taxpayers have expressed uncertainty as to which values are used for averaging beginning and year-end values in the case of 10 percent owned corporations whose stock basis is adjusted under § 1.861-12(c)(2) (including rules described in § 1.861-12T(c)(2)), which, in general, first eliminates any additions to basis on account of previously taxed earnings and profits made under sections 961 and 1293(d), and then increases or decreases adjusted basis by the shareholder's pro rata share of total earnings and profits. The proposed regulations clarify in proposed § 1.861-9(g)(2)(i)(B) that the beginning and end-of-year values of stock are determined without regard to any adjustments under section 961(a) or 1293(d), and before making the adjustment for earnings and profits provided in § 1.861-12(c)(1)(i)(A). The adjustment for total earnings and profits provided in § 1.861-12(c)(1)(i)(A) is only made after the average of the beginning and end of year values has been determined.

3. Determination of Stock Basis in Connection with Section 965(b)

In Part VII.D of the Explanation of Provisions of the notice of proposed rulemaking for the regulations under section 965, *see* 83 FR 39,531, the Treasury Department and the IRS acknowledged that the application of section 965(b)(4)(A) and (B) may warrant the issuance of special rules for the determination of adjusted basis. For example, if the increase in earnings and profits under section 965(b)(4)(B) and § 1.965-2(d)(2) is taken into account for purposes of determining the increase to adjusted basis under § 1.861-12(c)(2)(i)(A), and there is no corresponding reduction to the adjusted basis in the stock of the foreign corporation, the tax book value of the stock would be overstated by the amount of the increase.

If a shareholder elects to make the basis adjustments under proposed § 1.965-2(f)(2)(i), the tax book value of the stock of its foreign corporations that were specified foreign corporations (as defined in § 1.965-1(f)(45)) will generally reflect the proper adjusted basis amounts as long as any amounts included in basis under proposed § 1.965-2(f)(2)(ii)(A) are treated similarly to adjustments under section 961 and not included in the taxpayer's basis in stock under § 1.861-12T(c)(2)(i)(B). Accordingly, proposed § 1.861-12(c)(2)(i)(B)(*1*)(*ii*) provides that, for purposes of § 1.861-12(c)(2), a taxpayer determines the basis in the stock of a specified foreign corporation as if it had made the election under § 1.965-2(f)(2)(i), even if the taxpayer did not in fact make the election, but does not include the amount included in basis under § 1.965-2(f)(2)(ii)(A) (because the amount of that increase would not be included if the increase was by operation of section 961). For this purpose, the amount included in basis under proposed § 1.965-2(f)(2)(ii)(A) is determined without regard to whether any portion of the amount is netted against other basis adjustments under proposed § 1.965-2(h)(2). Proposed § 1.861-12(c)(2)(i)(B)(*1*)(*ii*) applies to the taxable year of the inclusion under section 965 as well as to future taxable years.

The Treasury Department and the IRS request comments on alternative ways to account for section 965(b) that minimize taxpayer burdens without distorting the measurement of a CFC's tax book value.

F. *Characterization of stock of certain foreign corporations under § 1.861-12*

1. Characterization of CFC Stock to Account for Section 951A Category, Treaty Categories, and Section 904(b)(4)

Section 1.861-12 provides special rules for applying the asset method in order to apportion expenses to the separate categories in computing the foreign tax credit limitation. The proposed regulations clarify in § 1.861-12(a) that § 1.861-12 also applies in apportioning expenses among statutory and residual groupings for operative sections other than section 904.

Special rules are provided in § 1.861-12T(c) regarding the treatment of stock, including stock in 10 percent owned corporations (as defined in § 1.861-12T(c)(2)(ii)) and stock in CFCs. The purpose of the stock characterization rules of § 1.861-12T(c) is to characterize the stock by reference to the income which the stock generates to its owner. With respect to CFCs, the rules generally look through to the income generated by the assets of the CFC for purposes of characterizing the stock of the CFC. Before the Act, the income earned by the CFC was generally assigned to the same separate category to which that income would be assigned if earned directly by the United States shareholder because the categories of income of a CFC and U.S. person were the same, and the look-through rules under section 904(d)(3) generally applied to ensure that once income was assigned to a separate category, the category of the income was maintained when the income was paid or distributed by the CFC to its owner or taken into account as an inclusion by the owner.

As described in Part II.B.3 of this Explanation of Provisions, the new separate category for section 951A category income applies only to an inclusion by a United States person of gross income under section 951A(a). Accordingly, gross tested income of a CFC is generally assigned to the general category, even though the stock of the CFC may give rise to a GILTI inclusion that is section 951A category income in the hands of a United States shareholder. Therefore, § 1.861-12T(c) would not result in characterizing any of the stock of the CFC as a section 951A category asset because the tested income of the CFC is assigned to the general category, even though the related income included by the United States shareholder is assigned to the section 951A category. Accordingly, the proposed regulations in § 1.861-13 provide special rules to account for the fact that, with respect to the section 951A category, the application of § 1.861-12T(c) to determine the income of the CFC or the income generated by the assets of the CFC does not, on its own, reflect the separate category of the income generated by the stock of the CFC to the United States shareholder. The proposed regulations also address a similar issue that arises when a CFC earns U.S. source income that is included under section 951(a) or 951A(a) in gross income of a United States shareholder who elects under an income tax treaty to treat the inclusion as foreign source income, resulting in separate category treatment for income resourced under a tax treaty (a "treaty category"). *See* section 904(h). Proposed § 1.861-13 applies solely for purposes of characterizing stock when section 904 is the operative section.

Under proposed § 1.861-13, a taxpayer first determines the amount of the stock of a CFC that is characterized in each of the statutory groupings described in § 1.861-13(a)(1) under the asset method or the modified gross income method. Under the modified gross income method, stock of a CFC may be characterized as producing general category gross tested income even though the CFC has a tested loss. *See* proposed § 1.861-13(a)(1)(ii).

Next, a portion of the stock characterized as producing general category gross tested income is assigned to the section 951A category. Only a portion of the stock so characterized is assigned to the section 951A category because the amount of the GILTI inclusion by the United States shareholder may be less than the aggregate tested income of its CFCs because of offsets from another CFC's tested loss or because of a reduction for net deemed tangible income return described in section 951A(b)(2). The inclusion percentage, as defined in section 960(d)(2), takes into account the percentage of net CFC tested income that is not included under section 951A(a) due to tested losses or the net deemed tangible income return. Accordingly, proposed § 1.861-13(a)(2) assigns a United States shareholder's stock in a CFC generating gross tested income to the section 951A category based on the United States shareholder's inclusion percentage as determined under § 1.960-2(c)(2). In general, earnings and profits related to the gross tested income that is not included under section 951A(a), when distributed, result in dividend income that is assigned to the general category.

The use of the inclusion percentage to assign stock to the section 951A category applies regardless of whether the stock of the CFC produces tested income or a tested loss for the year, in order to reflect the aggregate nature of the calculation of a United States shareholder's GILTI inclusion. Stock of a CFC is generally assigned to the statutory grouping for gross tested income, under either the asset or modified gross income methods described in proposed § 1.861-12(c)(3), if the CFC's assets generate gross tested income or if the CFC earns gross tested income, even if the CFC ultimately produces a tested loss for the taxable year. However, a United States shareholder with no GILTI inclusion for a taxable year has an inclusion percentage of zero, and therefore none of the stock of its CFCs is assigned to the section 951A category in that year.

Under proposed § 1.861-13(a)(3), a similar rule applies for characterizing stock as a treaty category asset if stock of a CFC is assigned to the statutory grouping for gross tested income that was resourced under a treaty. The portion of the stock of the CFC that is assigned to a treaty category is based on the United States shareholder's inclusion percentage. In the case of stock of a CFC initially assigned to the statutory groupings for gross subpart F income that is resourced under a treaty, all of that stock is assigned to a treaty category.

Finally, in the case of stock of a CFC assigned to the general and passive categories or the residual grouping for U.S. source income, proposed § 1.861-13(a)(5) provides rules for subdividing the categories or groupings into a section 245A subgroup and non-section 245A subgroup for purposes of applying section 904(b)(4). See Part I.H of this Explanation of Provisions for a description of the regulations under section 904(b)(4). In general, these rules provide that the portion of stock that does not generate income that is included under section 951A(a) or 951(a)(1) and does not represent income described in section 245(a)(5) (which gives rise to a dividends received deduction under section 245 instead of section 245A) is assigned to the section 245A subgroup.

2. Treatment of Gross Tested Income for Tiers of CFCs

Both the asset method and modified gross income method described in § 1.861-12T(c)(3) provide rules to characterize stock in a CFC when there are tiers of CFCs. Under the modified gross income method in § 1.861-12T(c)(3)(iii), a taxpayer characterizes the value of the first-tier CFC based on the gross income net of interest expense of the CFC within each relevant separate category. In the case of vertically-owned CFCs, gross income of any higher-tier CFC includes the gross income net of interest expense of any lower-tier CFC, but does not include subpart F income of any lower-tier CFC. *See* § 1.861-9T(j)(2). However, § 1.861-12T(c)(3)(iii) provides that for purposes of applying the modified gross income method to characterize CFC stock, the gross income of the first-tier CFC includes the total amount of subpart F income (net of interest expense apportioned at the level of the CFC that earned the income) of any lower-tier CFC.

The proposed regulations add similar rules for GILTI inclusions. In particular, the proposed regulations provide in § § 1.861-9(j)(2)(ii)(C) and 1.861-12(c)(3)(iii) that for purposes of characterizing CFC stock under the modified gross income method, the gross tested income of lower-tier CFCs, net of interest expense apportioned to the tested income, is excluded from the gross income of intermediate-tier CFCs but is included in the gross income of the first-tier CFC. The Treasury Department and the IRS request comments on whether additional rules are required to account for gross tested income earned in lower-tier CFCs, including gross tested income of lower-tier CFCs that produce tested losses.

3. Characterization of Stock of a Noncontrolled 10-Percent Owned Foreign Corporation

To reflect the repeal of section 902, the Act modifies section 904(d)(2)(E) to provide a new definition for a noncontrolled 10-percent owned foreign corporation. The proposed regulations modify § 1.861-12(c)(4) to provide that stock in a noncontrolled 10-percent owned foreign corporation is generally characterized under the same rules previously used for noncontrolled section 902 corporations.

G. *Allocation and apportionment of research and experimental expenditures*

In general, R&E expenditures are apportioned between groupings within product categories according to either a sales or gross income method of apportionment at the taxpayer's election. § 1.861-17(c) and (d). Under § 1.861-17(e)(1), a taxpayer may choose to use either the sales method or gross income method for its original return for its first taxable year. The taxpayer's use of either method constitutes a binding election to use the method chosen for that year and for the subsequent four years. Within this five-year period, the election can only be revoked with the Commissioner's consent. A taxpayer may change the election at any time after five years, but the new election is binding for a new five-year period. § 1.861-17(e)(2).

In light of the numerous amendments to the foreign tax credit rules made by the Act, the proposed regulations provide a one-time exception to the five-year binding election period. Accordingly, under proposed §1.861-17(e)(3), even if a taxpayer is subject to the binding election period, for the taxpayer's first taxable year beginning after December 31, 2017, the taxpayer may change its apportionment method without obtaining the Commissioner's consent. This one-time change of method constitutes a binding election to use the method chosen for that year and for the next four taxable years.

The Treasury Department and the IRS request comments on whether other aspects of §1.861-17 should be revised in light of the changes to section 904(d), in particular the addition of the section 951A category. For example, because the look-through rules in section 904(d)(3)(C) do not assign interest, rents, or royalties that reduce tested income to the section 951A category, royalties paid by a CFC to a United States shareholder are generally general category income even though the sales by the CFC to which the royalties relate may generate income in the section 951A category to the United States shareholder. This could result in R&E expenditures being apportioned under the sales method solely to the section 951A category, even though the royalty income is assigned to the general category. However, under the gross income method, R&E expenditures would be apportioned to both the general and section 951A category. Comments are requested on whether and how the regulations governing either or both methods should be revised to account for the addition of the section 951A category.

H. *Section 904(b)(4)*

1. Effect of Section 904(b)(4) on the Foreign Tax Credit Limitation

Under new section 904(b)(4), for purposes of the foreign tax credit limitation in section 904(a), a domestic corporation that is a United States shareholder with respect to a specified 10-percent owned foreign corporation disregards the "foreign-source portion" of any dividend received from the foreign corporation and any deductions properly allocable or apportioned to income (other than amounts includible under section 951(a)(1) or 951A(a)) with respect to the stock of the foreign corporation or to the stock itself (to the extent income with respect to the stock is other than amounts includible under section 951(a)(1) or 951A(a)). Dividends and deductions that are disregarded under section 904(b)(4) result in an adjustment to both the taxpayer's foreign source taxable income in the relevant separate category (the numerator of the fraction under section 904(a)) and its worldwide taxable income (the denominator of the fraction under section 904(a)) in all separate categories.

In general, under section 904(b)(4), disregarding both the dividend income eligible for a deduction under section 245A as well as the associated deduction under section 245A has no effect on the foreign tax credit limitation in any separate category because they generally net to zero. However, additional deductions that are disregarded under section 904(b)(4)(B) generally have the effect of increasing the foreign tax credit limitation with respect to the separate category to which the deductions are allocated and apportioned, because both the numerator (foreign source taxable income in the category) and the denominator (worldwide taxable income) of the fraction under section 904(a) are increased by the same amount. In contrast, the limitation in other categories will generally decrease because the numerator (foreign source taxable income in the category) is unchanged but the denominator (worldwide taxable income) of the fraction is increased.

2. Income Other Than Amounts Includible Under Section 951(a)(1) or 951A(a)

Section 904(b)(4)(B) requires determining what income with respect to stock of a specified 10-percent owned foreign corporation is income "other than amounts includible under section 951(a)(1) or 951A(a)." The terms used in section 904(b)(4) are defined by reference to definitions provided in section 245A.

As discussed in Part I.A of this Explanation of Provisions, with respect to other dividends received deductions, section 864(e)(3) provides that rules similar to the exempt income and exempt asset rules apply to the dividends and stock on which the dividends are paid. The Act did not extend this treatment to the section 245A deduction but instead added section 904(b)(4). In contrast to section 864(e)(3), which removes the exempt income and assets from the determination before deductions are allocated and apportioned under the rules of §§1.861-8 through 1.861-17, section 904(b)(4) provides that the deductions are disregarded after they have been allocated and apportioned. Disregarding the deductions after they have been allocated and apportioned is consistent with a policy that the deductions are properly allocable and apportioned to income eligible for a section 245A deduction and, therefore, should not be apportioned to income in other separate categories or U.S. source income. By disregarding these deductions, section 904(b)(4) has the effect of computing the foreign tax credit limitation fraction in section 904(a) (but not the pre-credit U.S. tax) as if the deductions had not been allowed.

The proposed regulations provide that income "other than amounts includible under section 951(a)(1) or 951A(a)" refers to income for which a section 245A deduction is allowed. Thus, in the case of section 904(b)(4)(B)(i), proposed §1.904(b)-3(c)(1) provides that income for which a section 245A deduction is allowed means dividends for which a section 245A deduction is allowed. In the case of section 904(b)(4)(B)(ii), proposed §1.904(b)-3(c)(1) and (2) provide rules for determining what amount of stock of the foreign corporation corresponds to income that, if distributed, is generally eligible for a section 245A deduction, by subdividing a portion of the stock into a section 245A subgroup and a non-section 245A subgroup within each separate category.

3. Expenses Properly Allocable to Dividend Income

Proposed § 1.904(b)-3(a)(1)(ii) provides that deductions "properly allocable" to dividends for which a section 245A deduction is allowed are disregarded. The amount of properly allocable deductions is determined by treating each section 245A subgroup for each separate category as a statutory grouping under § 1.861-8(a)(4) for purposes of allocating and apportioning deductions. Only dividend income for which a section 245A deduction is allowed is included in a section 245A subgroup. *See* § 1.904(b)-3(b) and (c)(1). Because hybrid dividends described in section 245A(e)(4), and dividends on stock with respect to which the holding period requirements of section 246(c) are not met, are ineligible for a deduction under section 245A, the dividends and the deductions allocable or apportioned to them are not disregarded under section 904(b)(4).

The deductions allocated and apportioned to the section 245A subgroup within each separate category are disregarded for purposes of determining the foreign source taxable income in the separate category and the entire taxable income included in the fraction under section 904(a) for all separate categories. Deductions allocated and apportioned to the section 245A subgroup within the residual grouping for U.S. source income are disregarded solely for purposes of determining the denominator of the limitation fraction (worldwide taxable income) in the separate categories that have foreign source taxable income. Proposed § 1.904(b)-3(a)(2). Dividends in the residual grouping for which a section 245A deduction is allowed could include, for example, dividends from a United States-owned foreign corporation (as defined in section 904(h)(6)) paid out of U.S. source income that is neither effectively connected income nor dividend income received from a domestic corporation. *See* sections 245A(c)(3) and 245(a)(5).

Proposed § 1.904(b)-3(b) also provides that the section 245A deduction is always allocated solely to a section 245A subgroup and therefore is always disregarded under section 904(b)(4).

4. Expenses Properly Allocable to Stock

In order to determine the deductions "properly allocable" to stock of a specified 10-percent owned foreign corporation that is in the section 245A subgroup, the stock is first characterized for purposes of allocating and apportioning expenses under § 1.861-12 and, if applicable, § 1.861-13. In the case of a specified 10-percent owned foreign corporation that is not a CFC, all of the value of its stock is generally in a section 245A subgroup because the stock cannot generate an inclusion under section 951(a)(1) or 951A(a). Proposed § 1.904(b)-3(c)(2). If the specified 10-percent owned foreign corporation is a CFC, a portion of the value of stock in each separate category and in the residual grouping for U.S. source income is subdivided between a section 245A and non-section 245A subgroup under the rules described in § 1.861-13(a)(5). *See* Part I.F.1 of this Explanation of Provisions. The amount of properly allocable deductions is determined by treating the section 245A subgroup for each separate category as a statutory grouping under § 1.861-8(a)(4) for purposes of allocating and apportioning deductions on the basis of assets, which include the stock.

Previously taxed earnings and profits do not affect the amount of expenses that are disregarded under section 904(b)(4). The characterization of stock in a specified 10-percent owned foreign corporation for purposes of section 904(b)(4)(B)(ii) is determined on an annual basis by applying the rules in § 1.861-12(c), which generally requires applying either the asset method or the modified gross income method. Whether or not the CFC has previously taxed earnings and profits, including from prior years or due to section 965, has no bearing on how either method is applied to characterize stock. *See also* proposed § 1.861-12(c)(2)(i)(B)(2).

5. Coordination with OFL/ODL rules

Because the section 904(b)(4) adjustments apply in computing the foreign tax credit limitation under section 904(a), proposed § 1.904(b)-3(d) provides that the adjustments under section 904(b)(4), like the adjustments under section 904(b)(2) to account for foreign source capital gain net income and rate differentials, apply before the operation of both the separate limitation loss and overall foreign loss rules in section 904(f) and the overall domestic loss rules in section 904(g). This rule permits loss accounts to be recaptured out of income that is added to the foreign tax credit limitation calculation by reason of the section 904(b)(4) adjustments.

II. *Foreign Tax Credit Limitation Under Section 904*

The proposed regulations update §§ 1.904-1 through 1.904-6 (the "section 904 regulations") to eliminate deadwood and reflect statutory amendments made to section 904 before the Act. For example, proposed §§ 1.904-1 through 1.904-3 reflect the repeal of the overall limitation and per-country limitation. Proposed § 1.904-4 reflects statutory amendments made before the Act eliminating various separate categories described in section 904(d)(1).

The proposed regulations also propose revisions and additions to the section 904 regulations to reflect the changes made under the Act. Part II.A of this Explanation of Provisions describes proposed transition rules to account for the addition of separate categories for section 951A category income and foreign branch category income. Part II.B of this Explanation of Provisions describes (1) proposed amendments to the rules relating to the passive category with respect to high-taxed income, export financing interest, and financial services income; (2) rules relating to the foreign branch category, section 951A category, and separate category described in section 904(d)(6) for items resourced under a treaty; and (3) rules for assigning the section 78 gross up and section 986(c) gain or loss to a separate category. Part II.C of this Explanation of Provisions describes updates relating to amendments made by the Act replacing references to "noncontrolled section 902 corporations" with "non-controlled 10 percent owned foreign corporations." Part II.D of this Explanation of Provisions describes proposed amendments to the look-through rules under sections 904(d)(3) and (d)(4) to account for the addition of the foreign branch category and section 951A category under the Act. Part II.E of this Explanation of Provisions describes the proposed changes to the rules for allocating and apportioning foreign taxes to separate categories.

A. *Transition rules in proposed § § 1.904-2(j) and 1.904(f)-12(j) accounting for the increase in section 904(d)(1) separate categories*

1. Carryovers and Carrybacks of Unused Foreign Taxes under Section 904(c)

The Act does not provide any transition rules for assigning carryforwards of unused foreign taxes earned in pre-2018 taxable years to a different separate category, including the new post-2017 separate categories for section 951A category income and foreign branch category income. Therefore, proposed § 1.904-2(j)(1)(ii) provides that if unused foreign taxes paid or accrued or deemed paid with respect to a separate category of income are carried forward to a taxable year beginning after December 31, 2017, those taxes are allocated to the same post-2017 separate category as the pre-2018 separate category from which the unused foreign taxes are carried.

However, double taxation may result if unused foreign taxes paid, accrued, or deemed paid in a pre-2018 taxable year are not assigned to the separate category to which the taxes would have been assigned if the new post-2017 separate categories had existed in the pre-2018 taxable year. This could arise, for example, if unused foreign taxes imposed on income derived through foreign branches in a pre-2018 taxable year are not associated with foreign branch category income. Matching the unused foreign taxes to the separate category that includes income of the same type as the income on which the taxes were imposed furthers the purpose of the section 904(c) foreign tax credit carryover rules to mitigate the effect of timing differences in the recognition of income for U.S. and foreign tax purposes that could otherwise result in double taxation. *See* H.R. Rep. No. 85-775, at 27 (1957).

Therefore, proposed § 1.904-2(j)(1)(iii) provides an exception that permits taxpayers to assign unused foreign taxes in the pre-2018 separate category for general category income to the post-2017 separate category for foreign branch category income to the extent they would have been assigned to that separate category if the taxes had been paid or accrued in a post-2017 taxable year. Any remaining unused taxes are assigned to the post-2017 separate category for general category income. The exception applies only to unused taxes that were paid or accrued, and not taxes that were deemed paid with respect to dividends or inclusions from foreign corporations, because income derived through foreign corporations cannot be foreign branch category income. *See* Part II.B.2 of this Explanation of Provisions.

Because the new post-2017 separate category for foreign branch category income does not include income that would have been passive category income or income in a separate category described in proposed § 1.904-4(m) that is not listed in section 904(d)(1) (a "specified separate category") if earned in a pre-2018 taxable year, the exception in proposed § 1.904-2(j)(1)(iii) applies only to unused foreign taxes that were paid or accrued with respect to income in the pre-2018 separate category for general category income. Furthermore, because the determination of taxable income in the section 951A category is intertwined with numerous other new provisions in the Code outside of section 904 that contain novel elements (such as the section 250 deduction and the new inclusion rules in section 951A that permit the sharing of tested losses among CFCs) that did not exist under prior law, it is not possible to reconstruct the amount of unused foreign taxes in a pre-2018 taxable year that would have been assigned to section 951A category income. Therefore, the reallocation exception in the proposed regulations does not require or allow taxpayers to assign any unused foreign taxes to the post-2017 separate category for section 951A category income, which is not eligible to be sheltered from U.S. tax by foreign tax credit carryovers. *See* section 904(c).

The proposed regulations require taxpayers applying the exception in § 1.904-2(j)(1)(iii) to analyze general category income earned in prior years in order to determine the extent to which the income would have been foreign branch category income under the rules described in proposed § 1.904-4(f). Unused foreign taxes in the general category arising in those prior years are then allocated and apportioned under § 1.904-6 between the general category and the foreign branch category. This analysis does not require applying any other post-Act provisions to prior years (for example, the new expense allocation rules described in the proposed regulations would not be relevant to the analysis).

The Treasury Department and the IRS recognize that taxpayers may face difficulties in reconstructing the allocation of unused foreign taxes. Therefore, the Treasury Department and the IRS request comments on whether the final regulations should include a simplified rule for taxpayers that choose to reconstruct the allocation of general category unused foreign taxes (for example, by looking to the relative amounts of foreign branch category and general category income or assets in the first post-2017 taxable year to which the unused foreign taxes are carried), what form such a rule should take, and whether there are any special concerns regarding members that have left a consolidated group. See, for example, § 1.904-7(f)(4)(ii).

All income included in the post-2017 separate category for foreign branch category income would have been general category income if earned in a pre-2018 taxable year. All income included in the post-2017 separate categories for general category income, passive category income, or income in a specified separate category would have been treated as general category income, passive category income, or income in a specified separate category, respectively, if earned in a pre-2018 taxable year. Accordingly, proposed § 1.904-2(j)(2)(ii) and (iii) provides that any unused foreign taxes with respect to general category income or foreign branch category income in a post-2017 taxable year that are carried back to a pre-2018 taxable year are allocated to the pre-2018 separate category for general category income, and any excess foreign taxes with respect to passive category income or income in a specified separate category in a post-2017 taxable year that are carried back to a pre-2018 taxable year are allocated to the same pre-2018 separate category. No rule is included with respect to the post-2017 separate category for section 951A category income (including a separate category for a GILTI inclusion that is resourced under a tax treaty), because carrybacks are not allowed for unused foreign taxes in that separate category.

2. Separate Limitation Losses, Overall Foreign Losses, and Overall Domestic Losses

Similar to the transition rules for carryovers and carrybacks of unused foreign taxes, the proposed regulations provide transition rules for recapture in a post-2017 taxable year of an overall foreign loss (OFL) or separate limitation loss (SLL) in a pre-2018 separate category that offset U.S. source income or income in another pre-2018 separate category, respectively, in a pre-2018 taxable year, as well as for recapture of an overall domestic loss (ODL) that offset income in a pre-2018 separate category in a pre-2018 taxable year.

Proposed § 1.904(f)-12(j) provides that any SLL or OFL accounts in the pre-2018 separate category for passive category income or income in a specified separate category remain in the same post-2017 separate category. Any SLL or OFL account in the pre-2018 separate category for general category income is allocated between the post-2017 separate categories for general category income and foreign branch category income in the same proportion that any unused foreign taxes with respect to the pre-2018 separate category for general category income are allocated to those post-2017 separate categories. Therefore, in the case of a taxpayer that does not apply the exception described in proposed § 1.904-2(j)(1)(iii), all of its SLL or OFL accounts in the pre-2018 separate category for general category income remain in the general category. In addition, if there were no unused foreign taxes in the pre-2018 general category to be allocated, proposed § 1.904(f)-12(j)(3)(i) provides that all SLL or OFL accounts in the pre-2018 separate category for general category income remain in the general category. Similar rules are provided with respect to the recapture of SLLs or ODLs that reduced income in a separate category in a pre-2018 taxable year, as well as for foreign losses that are part of a net operating loss that is incurred in a pre-2018 taxable year and carried forward to post-2017 taxable years.

B. *Separate categories of income*

1. Treatment of Export Financing Interest, High-taxed Income, and Financial Services Income

Under section 904(d)(2)(B)(iii), passive income does not include export financing interest and high-taxed income. Before the Act, the only separate category described in section 904(d)(1) aside from passive category income was general category income, and therefore § § 1.904-4(c) and (h)(2) treated export financing interest and high-taxed income as general category income.

Given the expansion of categories under section 904(d)(1) to include foreign branch category and section 951A category income, and the fact that section 904(d)(2)(B)(iii) only provides that export financing interest and high-taxed income are not passive income, the proposed regulations provide that export financing interest and high-taxed income should be categorized based on whether the income otherwise meets the definition of foreign branch category income, section 951A category income, or general category income. Therefore, the proposed regulations revise § 1.904-4(c) and (h)(2) to provide that export financing interest and high-taxed income are assigned to separate categories other than passive category income based on the general rules in § 1.904-4.

To coordinate the high-taxed income rules of section 904(d)(2)(F) with the new rules for computing foreign income taxes deemed paid under section 960 described in Part IV of this Explanation of Provisions, the proposed regulations revise the grouping rules of § 1.904-4(c)(4) to group passive category income from dividends, subpart F and GILTI inclusions from each foreign corporation, and passive category income derived from each foreign qualified business unit (QBU), under the grouping rules in § 1.904-4(c)(3) rather than by reference to the source of the corporation's or QBU's income. The Treasury Department and the IRS request comments on whether additional changes should be made to the high-taxed income rules in § 1.904-4(c) in light of changes to section 904(d) made by the Act.

Both before and after the Act, section 904(d)(2)(C)(i) provides that certain financial services income is treated as general category income. However, the Act's addition of foreign branch category and section 951A category income, which are new and more specific categories, take precedence over the treatment of financial services income as general category income. Therefore, the proposed regulations provide that any financial services income not treated as foreign branch category income or section 951A category income is generally treated as general category income. *See* proposed § 1.904-4(e).

The proposed regulations do not include any substantive changes to the definition of financial services entity in § 1.904-4(e)(3). It is intended that the current classification of an entity as a financial services entity is generally unaffected by the changes made by the proposed regulations to the look-through rules in § 1.904-5. However, the Treasury Department and the IRS are considering modifications to the gross income-based test for determining financial services entity status and request comments in this regard, particularly with respect to the appropriate treatment of related party payments.

2. Foreign Branch Category Income

i. Gross income in the category

Section 904(d)(1)(B) provides a new separate category for foreign branch category income, which is defined in section 904(d)(2)(J) as the business profits of a United States person attributable to a qualified business unit (QBU) in a foreign country (excluding passive category income). Section 904(d)(1)(B) further provides that the amount of business profits attributable to a QBU is determined under rules established by the Secretary.

Section 904(d)(2)(J) limits foreign branch income to income of a United States person. Therefore, foreign persons (including CFCs) cannot have foreign branch category income. While a domestic partnership (or other pass-through entity) that is a United States person may earn income that is attributable to a foreign branch of such partnership, a distributive share of income earned by a domestic partnership cannot be foreign branch category income to foreign partners of the partnership. To avoid any conflict, the proposed regulations define foreign branch category income as the gross income of a United States person (other than a pass-through entity).

Specifically, proposed § 1.904-4(f)(1)(i) provides that foreign branch category income means the gross income of a United States person (other than a pass-through entity) that is attributable to foreign branches held directly or indirectly through disregarded entities by the United States person. Foreign branch category income also includes a United States person's (other than a pass-through entity) distributive share of partnership income that is attributable to a foreign branch held by the partnership directly or indirectly through another partnership or other pass-through entity. Similar principles apply for income of any other type of pass-through entity that is attributable to a foreign branch. All the income described is aggregated in a single foreign branch category; there are not separate categories for each foreign branch. Conforming changes are made to the rules for allocating and apportioning partnership deductions and creditable foreign tax expenditures. *See* proposed §§ 1.861-9(e)(9) and 1.904-6(b)(4)(ii).

In general, gross income is attributable to a foreign branch to the extent it is reflected on a foreign branch's separate set of books and records. For this purpose, items of gross income must be adjusted to conform to Federal income tax principles. In addition, the proposed regulations provide several rules adjusting the gross income attributable to a foreign branch from what is reflected on the foreign branch's separate set of books and records.

First, the proposed regulations provide that gross income attributable to a foreign branch does not include items arising from activities carried out in the United States. Proposed § 1.904-4(f)(2)(ii).

Second, the regulations provide that gross income attributable to a foreign branch does not include items of gross income arising from stock, including dividend income, income included under section 951(a)(1), 951A(a), or 1293(a) or gain from the disposition of stock. Proposed § 1.904-4(f)(2)(iii)(A); *cf.* § 1.987-2(b)(2) (providing a similar rule in connection with attribution of items of income, gain, deduction, or loss to a section 987 QBU). An exception is provided for gain from the disposition of stock, where the stock would be dealer property. Proposed § 1.904-4(f)(2)(iii)(B).

Third, the proposed regulations provide that foreign branch category income does not include gain realized by a foreign branch owner on the disposition of an interest in a disregarded entity or an interest in a partnership or other pass-through entity. Proposed § 1.904-4(f)(2)(iv)(A). However, an exception is provided for the sale of a partnership interest if the gain is reflected on the books and records of a foreign branch and the interest is held in the ordinary course of the foreign branch owner's trade or business. Proposed § 1.904-4(f)(2)(iv)(B).

Fourth, the proposed regulations provide anti-abuse rules relating to the reflection of income on the books and records of a branch. The Treasury Department and the IRS are concerned that in certain cases gross income items could be inappropriately recorded on the books and records of a foreign branch or a foreign branch owner. Therefore, the proposed regulations include an anti-abuse rule providing for the reattribution of gross income if a principal purpose of recording, or failing to record, an item on the books and records of a foreign branch is the avoidance of Federal income tax or avoiding the purposes of section 904 or section 250. Proposed § 1.904-4(f)(2)(v). The rule further provides a presumption that interest income received by a foreign branch from a related party is not gross income attributable to the foreign branch unless the interest income meets the definition of financial services income.

Finally, in order to accurately reflect the gross income attributable to a foreign branch, a determination that affects not only the application of section 904(a) but also the determination of deduction eligible income under section 250(b)(3)(A), the proposed regulations provide that gross income attributable to a foreign branch that is not passive category income must be adjusted to reflect certain transactions that are disregarded for Federal income tax purposes. Proposed § 1.904-4(f)(2)(vi). This rule applies to transactions between a foreign branch and its foreign branch owner, as well as transactions between or among foreign branches, involving payments that would be deductible or capitalized if the payment were regarded for Federal income tax purposes. For example, a payment made by a foreign branch to its foreign branch owner may, to the extent allocable to non-passive category income, result in a downward adjustment to the gross income attributable to the foreign branch and an increase in the general category gross income of the United States person. Each payment in a series of disregarded back-to-back payments, for example, a payment from one foreign branch to another foreign branch followed by a payment to the foreign branch owner, must be accounted for separately under these rules. Comments are requested on whether special rules are required in the case of a true branch (generally, a branch that is taxable solely on profits from a business conducted in the country and not taxable as a resident of that country) with respect to amounts that are deemed to be made to or from the home office of the branch under the foreign jurisdiction's rules for attributing profits to the branch.

In general, the proposed regulations do not treat disregarded transactions as "regarded" for Federal income tax purposes; rather, they provide that certain disregarded transactions result in a redetermination of whether gross income of the United States person is attributable to its foreign branch or to the foreign branch owner. Thus, while disregarded transactions may allocate income between the foreign branch category and the general category, those transactions have no effect on the amount, character, or source of a United States person's gross income. U.S. source gross income that is reallocated from the general category to the foreign branch category and that is properly subject to foreign tax may be eligible to be treated as foreign source income under the terms of an income tax treaty, in which case the resourced income would be subject to a separate foreign tax credit limitation for income resourced under a tax treaty. *See* section 904(d)(6).

The proposed regulations provide an exception from the special rules regarding disregarded transactions that applies to contributions, remittances, and payments of interest (including certain interest equivalents). Proposed § 1.904-4(f)(2)(vi)(C). Generally, contributions, remittances, and interest payments to or from a foreign branch reflect a shift of, or return on, capital rather than a payment for goods and services. However, the different treatment of contributions and remittances, on the one hand, and other disregarded transactions, on the other, could allow for non-economic reallocations of the amount of gross income attributable to the foreign branch category. To prevent this in connection with certain transactions, the proposed regulations require the amount of gross income attributable to a foreign branch (and the amount attributable to the foreign branch owner) to be adjusted to account for consideration that would be due in any disregarded transactions in which property described in section 367(d)(4) is transferred to or from a foreign branch if the transactions were regarded, whether or not a disregarded payment is made in connection with the transfer. Proposed § 1.904-4(f)(2)(vi)(D). The proposed regulations further require that the amount of any adjustment under the disregarded payment provisions must be determined under the arm's length principle of section 482 and the regulations under that section. Proposed § 1.904-4(f)(2)(vi)(E).

The Treasury Department and the IRS request comments on how adjustments relating to these transactions could be limited or simplified to reduce administrative and compliance burdens while still providing for an accurate categorization of gross income, consistent with the purpose of both sections 904 and 250(b)(3)(A). For example, comments are requested on whether these rules should be narrowed to cover a more limited set of transactions or whether disregarded payments should be netted before determining the amount of reallocation.

The proposed regulations do not propose any special rules for determining the amount of deductions allocated and apportioned to foreign branch category income, including deductions reflected on the books and records of foreign branches. Therefore, the proposed regulations provide that the rules for allocating and apportioning deductions in § § 1.861-8 through 1.861-17 that apply with respect to the other separate categories also apply to the foreign branch category. The Treasury Department and the IRS request comments on whether any special rules should be issued for determining the allocation and apportionment of deductions between the foreign branch category and the general category. In addition, the Treasury Department and the IRS request comments on whether special rules should be provided for financial institutions with branches subject to regulatory capital requirements, including for example, rules similar to those in § 1.882-5.

ii. Definition of a foreign branch

The proposed regulations define a foreign branch by reference to the regulations under section 989 ("section 989 regulations") by providing that a foreign branch is a QBU described in § 1.989(a)-1(b)(2)(ii) and (b)(3) that carries on a trade or business outside the United States. Proposed § 1.904-4(f)(3)(iii). In general, § 1.989(a)-1(b)(2)(ii) provides rules for treating activities of a branch of a taxpayer as a QBU. Specifically, it provides that the activities of a corporation, partnership, trust, estate, or individual qualify as a separate QBU if the activities constitute a trade or business, and a separate set of books and records is maintained with respect to the activities. Section 1.989(a)-1(b)(3) includes a special rule treating activities generating income effectively connected with the conduct of a trade or business as a separate QBU.

The section 989 regulations treat partnerships and trusts as *per se* QBUs. *See* § 1.989(a)-1(b)(2)(i). As a result, they do not include a rule treating the activities of a partnership or trust that constitute a trade or business, but for which a separate set of books and records is not maintained, as a QBU. For example, § 1.989(a)-1(b)(2)(ii) would not treat the activities of a partnership QBU as a QBU if no separate set of books is maintained with respect to the activities.

In order to ensure that foreign branch category income does not include income reflected on the books and records of a QBU unless the QBU conducts a trade or business, the proposed regulations' definition of foreign branch does not incorporate the section 989 regulations' *per se* QBU rules, and instead requires that a foreign branch carry on a trade or business. In addition, the proposed regulations include a special rule, as illustrated by an example, providing that a foreign branch may consist of activities conducted through a partnership or trust that constitute a trade or business conducted outside the United States, but for which no separate set of books and records is maintained. *See* § 1.904-4(f)(4)(i), *Example 1*.

The proposed regulations also modify the trade or business requirements in the section 989 regulations for purposes of the foreign branch definition. Specifically, to constitute a foreign branch, a QBU must carry on a trade or business outside the United States. For this purpose, activities that constitute a permanent establishment in a foreign country under a bilateral U.S. tax treaty, whether or not the activities also rise to the level of a separate trade or business, are presumed to constitute a trade or business. *See* proposed § 1.904-4(f)(3)(iii)(B).

Under § 1.989(a)-1(c), for activities to constitute a trade or business, they must ordinarily include the collection of income and the payment of expenses. The proposed regulations provide that, for purposes of determining whether a set of activities satisfy the trade or business requirement of § 1.989(a)-1(c) in the context of the definition of a foreign branch, activities that relate to disregarded transactions are taken into account and may give rise to a trade or business for this purpose. *See* proposed § 1.904-4(f)(3)(iii)(B).

3. Section 951A Category Income

Section 904(d)(1)(A) defines a new separate category as "any amount includible in gross income under section 951A (other than passive category income)." Consistent with that language, proposed § 1.904-4(g) provides that the gross income included in the section 951A category is generally the gross income of a United States shareholder from a GILTI inclusion. However, a GILTI inclusion that is allocable to passive category income under the look-through rules in § 1.904-5(c)(6) is excluded from section 951A category income. A passive category GILTI inclusion could arise, for example, from a CFC's distributive share of partnership income in which the CFC owns less than 10 percent of the value in the partnership. *See* proposed § 1.904-4(n)(1)(ii). Comments are requested on whether the rules treating a less than 10 percent partner's distributive share of partnership income as passive category income should be modified.

In addition, the proposed regulations amend § 1.904-2(a) to reflect the exclusion of foreign tax credit carryovers under section 904(c) for foreign taxes paid or accrued with respect to section 951A category income or with respect to section 951A category income that is treated as income in a separate category for income resourced under a tax treaty.

4. Items Resourced Under a Treaty

Legislation commonly referred to as the Education Jobs and Medicaid Assistance Act (EJMAA), enacted on August 10, 2010, added section 904(d)(6), which, as amended by the Tax Cuts and Jobs Act, provides that if, without regard to any treaty obligation of the United States, any item of income would be treated as derived from sources within the United States, under a treaty obligation of the United States the item of income would be treated as arising from sources outside the United States, and the taxpayer chooses the benefits of the treaty obligation to treat the income as arising from sources outside the United States, then subsections 904(a), (b), and (c) and sections 907 and 960 shall be applied separately with respect to each item. Thus, section 904(d)(6)(A) applies a separate foreign tax credit limitation to each item of resourced income, without regard to the separate category to which the item would otherwise be assigned.

i. Grouping methodology

Proposed § 1.904-4(k)(2) adopts a grouping methodology similar to that employed in § 1.904-5(m)(7) with respect to income treated as in a separate category under the separate treaty resourcing rules of section 904(h)(10). Under the proposed regulations, the taxpayer must segregate income treated as foreign source under each treaty and then compute a separate foreign tax credit limitation for income in each separate category that is resourced under that treaty.

For purposes of allocating foreign taxes to each grouping of section 904(d)(6) income, the principles of § 1.904-6 apply to allocate to the section 904(d)(6) separate category all foreign income taxes related to the income included in that group, including taxes imposed by a third country. The Treasury Department and the IRS are considering whether the regulations should provide a special rule limiting the tax assigned to a section 904(d)(6) separate category to tax paid to the foreign country that is a party to the income tax treaty pursuant to which the income is resourced, and request comments on this issue.

ii. Coordination with certain treaty and Code provisions

Some U.S. income tax treaties contain provisions for the tax treatment in both Contracting States of certain types of income derived from sources within the United States by U.S. citizens who are residents of the other Contracting State. See, for example, paragraph 3 of Article 24 (Relief from Double Taxation) of the income tax convention between the United States and Ireland, signed on July 28, 1997. These rules generally use a three-step approach to determine the U.S. citizen's ultimate U.S. income tax liability with respect to an applicable item of income. First, the other Contracting State provides a credit against its tax for the notional U.S. tax that would apply under the treaty to a resident of the other Contracting State who is not a U.S. citizen. Second, the United States provides a credit against U.S. tax for the income tax paid or accrued to the other Contracting State after the application of the credit for notional U.S. tax by the other Contracting State. Finally, the income is deemed to arise in the other Contracting State to the extent necessary to avoid double taxation under these rules.

These treaty rules are generally designed to preserve the United States' primary right to tax U.S. source income and to resource only enough income to allow a taxpayer to claim a credit for the related foreign taxes, as reduced by the notional credit for U.S. source-based tax. Although excess foreign tax credits may arise from the operation of these rules, excess limitation permitting the use of unrelated foreign tax credits to offset the U.S. tax on the resourced income generally cannot. Since U.S. citizens subject to these provisions generally cannot generate excess limitation, and it would be burdensome to subject individuals to the operation of section 904(d)(6) when they are already subject to the three-step treaty rule, the proposed regulations exclude the income of these individuals from the operation of section 904(d)(6). Accordingly, proposed § 1.904-4(k)(4)(i) provides that income resourced under the relief from double taxation provisions in U.S. income tax treaties that are solely applicable to U.S. citizens who are residents of the other Contracting State is not subject to section 904(d)(6)(A) and § 1.904-4(k)(1).

In addition, under the mutual agreement procedures of U.S. income tax treaties, U.S. taxpayers may request assistance from the U.S. competent authority, such as for the relief of double taxation in cases not provided for in the treaty. Where the U.S. competent authority agrees to grant relief to a taxpayer that involves resourcing, the taxpayer has effectively chosen the benefit of a treaty obligation of the United States to treat the item of income as foreign source. Accordingly, proposed § 1.904-4(k)(4)(ii) clarifies that section 904(d)(6) separate category treatment applies to items of income resourced pursuant to a competent authority agreement.

5. Section 78 Gross Up and Section 986(c) Gain or Loss

Numerous comments were received requesting guidance on the appropriate separate category to which the gross up described in section 78 attributable to foreign taxes deemed paid under section 960(d) should be assigned. Proposed § 1.904-4(o) provides a rule consistent with existing § 1.904-6(b)(3) that assigns the gross up to the same separate category as the deemed paid taxes. See Part II.E.3 of this Explanation of Provisions for a description of rules for allocating and apportioning deemed paid taxes to separate categories.

Proposed § 1.904-4(p) also provides a rule assigning gain or loss under section 986(c) with respect to a distribution of previously taxed earnings and profits to the separate category from which the distribution was made.

C. *Noncontrolled 10-percent foreign corporation*

Under section 904(d)(2)(E) as amended by the Act, the term “noncontrolled section 902 corporation” has been revised to “noncontrolled 10-percent owned foreign corporation.” The definition has also been amended to reflect the repeal of section 902, but maintains pre-Act rules for when a taxpayer meets the requisite stock ownership with respect to a passive foreign investment company (“PFIC”). The proposed regulations update the references in the section 904 regulations to noncontrolled section 902 corporations to reflect the revised statutory term and definition.

The ownership requirement for PFICs differs from the United States shareholder requirement that generally applies to a noncontrolled 10-percent owned foreign corporation described in section 904(d)(2)(E)(i)(I). The proposed regulations in § 1.904-5(a)(4)(vi) provide that for purposes of the regulations under section 904, any reference to a United States shareholder in the context of a noncontrolled 10-percent owned foreign corporation also includes a taxpayer that meets the stock ownership requirements described in section 904(d)(2)(E)(i)(II), even if the taxpayer is not a United States shareholder within the meaning of section 951(b).

D. *Look-through rules*

Before amendments made by the American Jobs Creation Act of 2004 (AJCA), section 904(d)(3) generally provided that dividends, interest, rents, and royalties (“look-through payments”) received or accrued by a taxpayer from a CFC in which the taxpayer is a United States shareholder were treated as income in the separate category to which the payment was allocable. Section 904(d)(4) provided similar look-through rules for dividends from noncontrolled section 902 corporations. The AJCA reduced the number of separate categories from nine to two, and revised section 904(d)(3). Under section 904(d)(3)(A) as amended by the AJCA, except as otherwise provided by section 904(d)(3), dividends, interest, rents, and royalties received or accrued by a taxpayer from a CFC in which the taxpayer is a United States shareholder are not treated as passive category income. Exceptions are provided, generally, when the payment is allocable to passive category income. However, the existing regulations under § 1.904-5 were largely unchanged after the AJCA amendments and retained the pre-AJCA approach to assigning dividends, interest, rents, and royalties based on the separate category of the income to which the payment was allocable, rather than excluding the income from the passive category to the extent not allocable to the passive category. In practice, because there were generally only two separate categories after the AJCA and because the general category was a residual category, the approach under the existing regulations of assigning payments to a separate category based on the separate category to which they were allocable resulted in payments that were not allocable to passive category income being assigned to the general category.

The Act added two new separate categories to section 904(d)(1) but made no changes to the look-through rules in section 904(d)(3) and (4). In addition, the legislative history does not provide any indication of how the look-through rules were intended to operate with the addition of the new separate categories.

The proposed regulations provide that the look-through rules under section 904(d)(3) provide look-through treatment solely for payments allocable to the passive category. Any other payments described in section 904(d)(3) are assigned to a separate category other than the passive category based on the general rules in § 1.904-4. Therefore, proposed § 1.904-5 revises the various look-through rules to reflect the application of look-through rules solely with respect to payments allocable to passive category income. Dividends, interest, rents, or royalties paid from a CFC to a United States shareholder thus are not assigned to a separate category (other than the passive category) under the look-through rules, but are assigned to the foreign branch category, a specified separate category described in proposed § 1.904-4(m), or the general category under the rules of proposed § 1.904-4(d).

Consistent with the general rule for look-through payments, section 904(d)(3)(B) assigns amounts included under section 951(a)(1)(A) ("subpart F inclusions") to the passive category to the extent the inclusion is attributable to passive category income. Under the authority of section 951A(f)(1)(B), the proposed regulations treat GILTI inclusions in the same manner as subpart F inclusions for purposes of section 904(d)(3)(B). Therefore, proposed § 1.904-5(c)(6) provides that GILTI inclusions are treated as passive category income to the extent the amount so included is attributable to income received or accrued by the CFC that is passive category income.

Under the proposed regulations, the look-through rules also do not apply to treat deductible payments made by a foreign branch that are allocable to foreign branch category income (for example, payments made by a foreign disregarded entity that constitutes a foreign branch to a related look-through entity) as foreign branch category income. Instead, the rules of § 1.904-4 apply to characterize the income in the hands of the recipient.

Finally, as a result of the proposed revisions to § 1.904-5 that limit the look-through rules generally to passive category income, the proposed regulations include a rule addressing income subject to the separate category required under section 901(j)(1)(B). These rules ensure that income from sources within countries described in section 901(j)(2) that is paid or accrued through one or more entities retains its source and therefore continues to be subject to the separate category described in section 901(j)(1)(B). *See* proposed § 1.901(j)-1(a).

E. *Allocation and apportionment of foreign taxes*

1. Special Rule for Base and Timing Differences

Section 904(d)(2)(H)(i) and § 1.904-6(a)(1)(iv) provide a special rule for allocating foreign tax that is imposed on an amount that does not constitute income under Federal income tax principles (a "base difference"). Section 1.904-6(a)(1)(iv) also provides special rules for timing differences.

The proposed regulations clarify that base differences arise only in limited circumstances, such as in the case of categories of items such as life insurance proceeds or gifts, which are excluded from income for Federal income tax purposes but may be taxed as income under foreign law. In contrast, a computational difference attributable to differences in the amounts, as opposed to the types, of items included in U.S. taxable income and the foreign tax base does not give rise to a base difference. *See* proposed § 1.904-6(a)(1)(iv). For example, a difference between U.S. and foreign tax law in the amount of deductions that are allowed to reduce gross income, like a difference in depreciation conventions or in the timing of recognition of gross income, is not considered to give rise to a base difference.

In addition, the proposed regulations clarify that the fact that a distribution of previously taxed earnings and profits is exempt from Federal income tax does not mean that a tax imposed on the distribution is attributable to a base difference. Instead, because the previously taxed earnings and profits were included in U.S. taxable income in a prior year, the tax imposed on the distribution is treated as attributable to a timing difference and is allocated to the separate category to which the earnings and profits from which the distribution was paid are attributable.

2. Taxes Imposed in Connection with Foreign Branches

The regulations in § 1.904-6(a) generally provide that foreign taxes are allocated and apportioned to separate categories by reference to the separate category of the income to which the foreign tax relates. Disregarded transactions between a foreign branch and the United States owner of the foreign branch (or between two foreign branches of the same United States person) may involve disregarded payments that are subject to foreign tax, including disregarded payments that result in the reallocation of gross income between the foreign branch category and the general category under the proposed regulations in § 1.904-4(f)(2)(vi). *See* proposed § 1.904-4(f) and Part II.B.2 of this Explanation of Provisions. While existing regulations under § 1.904-6(a) provide general rules for allocating and apportioning foreign taxes imposed with respect to income of a foreign branch, proposed § 1.904-6(a)(2) provides special rules to coordinate the existing regulations under § 1.904-6(a)(1) with the computation of foreign branch category income in proposed § 1.904-4(f).

The proposed regulations are consistent with the general principles and purpose of § 1.904-6(a)(1) and are intended to provide clarity where the application of these principles would be difficult or uncertain. The Treasury Department and the IRS recognize that there may be additional circumstances where the application of these rules may be ambiguous and request comments on whether further guidance is needed to clarify how foreign taxes should be allocated and apportioned between the foreign branch category and other separate categories.

3. Taxes Deemed Paid Under Section 960

The proposed regulations propose modifications to § 1.904-6(b) to reflect the Act's repeal of section 902 and revisions to section 960. In general, the proposed regulations provide that foreign income taxes deemed paid under section 960(a) or (d) are allocated to the same separate category to which the related section 951(a)(1) or 951A(a) inclusion is assigned. Similarly, in the case of a distribution of previously taxed earnings and profits described in section 960(b)(1) or (2), any foreign tax deemed paid with respect to the distribution under section 960(b) is allocated to the separate category to which the distribution is attributable.

4. Creditable Foreign Tax Expenditures

As discussed in Part II.B.2 of this Explanation of Provisions, a U.S. or foreign partnership does not characterize any of its income as foreign branch category income. Instead, a distributive share of a partnership's income may be characterized as foreign branch category income in the hands of certain U.S. partners. In order to ensure that creditable foreign tax expenditures (CFTEs) that are allocated to a partner that has a distributive share of income that is assigned to the foreign branch category are appropriately assigned, proposed § 1.904-6(b)(4) provides rules for allocating and apportioning CFTEs to the foreign branch category.

III. *Treatment of Subsequent Reductions in Tax In Applying Section 954(b)(4)*

The Treasury Department and the IRS are aware that certain taxpayers have formed CFCs in certain jurisdictions that purport to have a type of integration regime whereby all or substantially all of the corporate income tax paid by the CFC on its earnings is refunded to its shareholder when the earnings are distributed, even though the shareholder is not subject to any foreign tax on the distribution. These taxpayers rely on the rules in § 1.954-1(d)(3), which provide that a subsequent reduction in corporate foreign income taxes when earnings are later distributed to a shareholder does not affect the amount of foreign income taxes used to compute the effective tax rate on an item of income unless the reduction requires a redetermination of the United States shareholder's U.S. tax under section 905(c). These taxpayers claim that the high-tax exception from foreign base company income under section 954(b)(4) allows them to exclude the CFC's income from current taxation under subpart F, despite the fact that all or substantially all of the foreign corporate income tax is later refunded to the shareholder.

The proposed regulations modify § 1.954-1(d)(3) to provide that to the extent the foreign income taxes paid or accrued by a CFC are reasonably certain to be returned to a shareholder upon a subsequent distribution to the shareholder, the foreign income taxes are not treated as paid or accrued for purposes of the high-tax exception under section 954(b)(4). The IRS may also challenge these arrangements under existing law, for example, on the ground that the payment to the shareholder constitutes a refund under § 1.901-2(e)(2) or a subsidy under section 901(i) and § 1.901-2(e)(3) that reduces the amount of tax the CFC is considered to have paid.

Comments are requested on what special rules under § 1.954-1(d)(3), § 1.901-2, and section 905(c) should be considered to account for genuine integration regimes that do not have the effect of exempting resident corporations and their shareholders from all or substantially all tax.

IV. *Deemed Paid Taxes Under New Section 960 and New Section 78*

Section 960(a) and (d), as revised by the Act, deems a domestic corporation that is a United States shareholder of a CFC to pay the portion of the foreign income taxes paid or accrued by the CFC that is properly attributable to income of the CFC that the United States shareholder takes into account in computing its subpart F or GILTI inclusion, subject to certain limitations. Section 960(b), as revised by the Act, provides rules for taxes that are deemed paid in connection with distributions by a CFC of previously taxed earnings and profits to either a United States shareholder that is a domestic corporation or to a shareholder that is a CFC. *Cf.* section 960(a)(3) (as in effect on December 21, 2017). Proposed § § 1.960-1 through 1.960-3 provide rules for determining a domestic corporation's deemed paid taxes under section 960(a), (b), and (d).

Additionally, the Act redesignated former section 960(b), relating to excess limitation accounts, without change, as section 960(c). The proposed regulations treat a GILTI inclusion amount as a subpart F inclusion for purposes of section 960(c). *See* section 951A(f)(1)(B). Therefore, the proposed regulations modify § § 1.960-4 and 1.960-5 to reflect the additional application of section 960(c) to GILTI inclusion amounts. Comments are requested on whether additional amendments to the proposed regulations are appropriate, including additional rules in § 1.960-4 to account for unique aspects of the section 951A category.

Finally, § 1.960-7 includes updated applicability dates for § § 1.960-1 through 1.960-6, which are consistent with the effective dates of the Act.

The Act also amended section 78 to, among other things, reflect the addition of deemed paid credits under section 960(d) and to provide that any amount of taxes deemed paid under section 960 that is treated as a dividend under section 78 (a "section 78 dividend") is not eligible for a section 245A deduction. The proposed regulations revise § 1.78-1 to reflect changes made to section 78.

Part IV.A of this Explanation of Provisions describes computational and grouping rules relating to the calculation of deemed paid taxes under section 960(a), (b), and (d). Part IV.B of this Explanation of Provisions describes specific rules for the calculation of deemed paid taxes under section 960(a) and (d). Part IV.C of this Explanation of Provisions describes specific rules for the calculation of deemed paid taxes under section 960(b). Part IV.D of this Explanation of Provisions describes the application of the rules under section 960(a), (b), and (d) when the domestic corporation owns the CFC through a domestic partnership. Part IV.E of this Explanation of Provisions describes revisions to § 1.78-1.

A. *Computational and grouping rules for purposes of calculating taxes deemed paid under section 960*

1. Current Year Taxes

For a particular taxable year, a CFC may have subpart F income or tested income that is taken into account by a domestic corporation that is a United States shareholder of the CFC under sections 951(a)(1)(A) or 951A(a), and may incur foreign income taxes related to that income that may be treated as deemed paid by the United States shareholder under sections 960(a) or (d). Additionally, a

CFC may receive distributions of previously taxed earnings and profits and incur foreign income taxes with respect to those distributions that may subsequently be treated as deemed paid by the United States shareholder or an upper-tier CFC under section 960(b).

Proposed § 1.960-1 provides definitions as well as computational and grouping rules that associate the current year foreign income taxes ("current year taxes") of the CFC with current year income of the CFC or a distribution of previously taxed earnings and profits received by the CFC. These taxes, in turn, may be deemed paid by the United States shareholder or upper-tier CFC under section 960. Foreign income taxes generally include income, war profits, and excess profits taxes that are imposed by a foreign country or a possession of the United States. *See* proposed § 1.960-1(b)(5). The term "possession of the United States" means American Samoa, Guam, the Commonwealth of the Northern Mariana Islands, Puerto Rico, or the U.S. Virgin Islands.

Current year taxes of a CFC are foreign income taxes paid or accrued by the CFC in its current taxable year, and the rules of section 461 and the "relation-back" doctrine apply to determine the timing of the accrual of foreign income taxes and the year for which they are taken into account. *See* proposed § 1.960-1(b)(4). Thus, for example, foreign income taxes calculated on the basis of net income accrue in the U.S. taxable year of the CFC with or within which its foreign taxable year ends, and are eligible to be deemed paid in the taxable year of the United States shareholder with or within which the U.S. taxable year of the CFC ends, even if a portion of the foreign taxable year of the CFC falls within an earlier or later U.S. taxable year of the CFC or its United States shareholder. Current year taxes of a CFC that are imposed on an amount under foreign law that would be income under U.S. law in a different taxable year are eligible to be deemed paid in the year in which the foreign tax accrues, and not in the earlier or later year when the related income is recognized for U.S. tax purposes. The current taxable year of the CFC is its U.S. taxable year for which a domestic corporation that is a United States shareholder of the CFC has a subpart F or GILTI inclusion with respect to the CFC, or during which the CFC receives a section 959(b) distribution or makes a section 959(a) distribution or a section 959(b) distribution.

2. Computational Rules

Proposed § 1.960-1(c)(1) describes and orders the computations involved in calculating the foreign income taxes deemed paid by either a domestic corporation that is a United States shareholder of a CFC or by a CFC that is a shareholder of another CFC. These steps are applied by each CFC in a chain of ownership beginning with the lowest-tier CFC with respect to which the domestic corporation is a United States shareholder.

Under these computational rules, a United States shareholder first applies the grouping rules described in Part IV.A.3 of this Explanation of Provisions to assign the income of the CFC to separate categories of income described in proposed § 1.904-5(a)(4)(v) (each a "section 904 category") and then to groups that correspond to certain types of income (each, an "income group") in a section 904 category. If the CFC receives a distribution of previously taxed earnings and profits ("PTEP"), it increases the group or groups (each, a "PTEP group") within an annual PTEP account that corresponds both to the taxable year for which a CFC took into account the income from which the previously taxed earnings and profits arose, and to the separate category of the United States shareholder to which the amount of the resulting inclusion under sections 951(a)(1)(A) or 951A was assigned. The rules for grouping previously taxed earnings and profits within an annual PTEP account are described in Part IV.C.1 of this Explanation of Provisions. The income and PTEP groups, which are discussed in more detail below, are the mechanism for computing taxes deemed paid under section 960.

Second, deductions of the CFC, including for expenses attributable to current year taxes, are allocated and apportioned to the income groups. Current year taxes are also allocated and apportioned to a PTEP group that was increased in the first step. Third, taxes deemed paid by the United States shareholder under section 960(a) and (d), and taxes deemed paid by the CFC under section 960(b)(2) in connection with its receipt of a section 959(b) distribution, are calculated. Fourth, the previously taxed earnings and profits resulting from the subpart F inclusion or GILTI inclusion of the United States shareholder are added to an annual PTEP account and further assigned to the relevant PTEP groups within the account. Fifth, the first four steps are repeated for each higher-tier CFC. Sixth, with respect to the highest-tier CFC, the United States shareholder computes its taxes deemed paid under section 960(b)(1).

Proposed § 1.960-1(c)(2) provides that only items that the CFC takes into account during its current taxable year are used in the computational rules of § 1.960-1(c)(1). The items of gross income and expense that are in a section 904 category and income group within a section 904 category are therefore items that the CFC accrues and takes into account in its current taxable year, and the foreign income taxes that are eligible to be deemed paid are foreign income taxes that the CFC pays or accrues in its current taxable year. Proposed § 1.960-1(c)(3) provides rules relating to foreign currency and translation.

3. Associating Current Year Taxes with Income Groups

In order to determine the foreign income taxes paid or accrued by the CFC that are properly attributable to amounts that a domestic corporation that is a United States shareholder of the CFC takes into account in determining its subpart F or GILTI inclusions, proposed § 1.960-1(d) provides rules associating current year taxes of the CFC with the types of income earned by the CFC from which the inclusions arise. Proposed § 1.960-1(d) requires a CFC to assign its income to one or more income groups within each section 904 category. Deductions of the CFC, including for current year taxes, are allocated and apportioned to the income groups in order to determine net income (or loss) in each income group and to identify the current year foreign income taxes that relate to the income in each income group for section 960 purposes.

i. Income Group Definitions

Proposed § 1.960-1(d)(2)(ii) defines several separate income groups with respect to the subpart F income of the CFC ("subpart F income groups") within each applicable section 904 category. Each single item of foreign base company income as defined in § 1.954-1(c)(1)(iii) is a separate subpart F income group. For example, with respect to a CFC, § 1.954-1(c)(1)(iii)(A)(2) identifies as a single item of income all foreign base company income (other than foreign personal holding company income) that falls within both a single separate category (typically, general category income) and a single category of foreign base company income described in each of § 1.954-1(c)(1)(iii)(A)(2)(*i*) through (*v*). Therefore, there is a single subpart F income group within the general category that consists of all of a CFC's foreign base company sales income. Section 1.954-1(c)(1)(iii)(B) provides grouping rules for items of passive category foreign personal holding company income, each of which is also treated as a separate subpart F income group under § 1.960-1. Proposed § 1.960-1(d)(2)(ii)(B)(2) also defines a separate subpart F income group for the CFC's insurance income described in section 952(a)(1), for its international boycott income described in section 952(a)(3), for the sum of its illegal bribes and kickbacks described in section 952(a)(4), and for income included in a section 901(j) separate category described in section 952(a)(5).

Proposed § 1.960-1(d)(2)(ii)(C) also defines separate income groups for tested income (each, a "tested income group") in each section 904 category. In general, tested income will be in a single tested income group within the general category. Because a CFC cannot earn section 951A category income or foreign branch category income at the CFC level, there is no tested income group within either section 904 category. With respect to the CFC's general category tested income group, GILTI inclusion amounts and taxes with respect to the tested income group will generally be treated as income and deemed paid taxes in the section 951A category. *See* §§ 1.904-4(g), 1.904-6(b)(1).

Income in a section 904 category that is not of a type that is included in one of the subpart F income groups or tested income groups is assigned to the residual income group. *See* proposed § 1.960-1(d)(2)(ii)(D).

ii. Computing Net Income in an Income Group and Assigning Current Year Taxes to an Income Group

In order to determine its net income in each income group, a CFC first assigns its items of gross income to a section 904 category and to the appropriate income group within the category, and then allocates and apportions its deductions and expenses, including current year taxes, to the categories and to the income groups within the categories under the rules of sections 861 through 865 and 904(d) and the regulations under those sections.

Current year taxes are allocated and apportioned to income groups for two purposes. The first purpose is to deduct current year taxes (in functional currency) from gross income in the income group in computing the net income in the income group. The second purpose is to associate an amount of current year taxes (in U.S. dollars) with an income group. These current year taxes associated with an income group are eligible to be deemed paid by a United States shareholder that has a subpart F or GILTI inclusion that is attributable to that income group. The rules for allocating and apportioning current year taxes are the same for both purposes. *See also* proposed § 1.861-8(e)(6) (clarifying that the rules for allocating and apportioning deductions for foreign income tax expense are the same as the rules for allocating and apportioning foreign income taxes to separate categories under § 1.904-6).

Proposed § 1.960-1(d)(3)(ii) applies the rules of § 1.904-6 to allocate and apportion current year taxes to and among the section 904 categories based upon the amount of taxable income, as calculated under foreign law, of the CFC that is in each section 904 category. Proposed § 1.960-1(d)(3)(ii) then applies the principles of § 1.904-6 to allocate and apportion current year taxes to and among the income groups. If a PTEP group of the CFC is increased as a result of a section 959(b) distribution that it receives in the current taxable year, then for purposes of allocating and apportioning current year taxes that are imposed solely by reason of the section 959(b) distribution, the PTEP group is treated as an income group within the section 904 category. Part IV.C of this Explanation of Provisions discusses the rules for tracking amounts in PTEP groups and for computing deemed paid credits with respect to distributions of previously taxed earnings and profits from a PTEP group. Current year taxes that are not allocated and apportioned to a subpart F or tested income group, or to a PTEP group that is treated as an income group, are allocated and apportioned to a residual income group. Current year taxes allocated and apportioned to a residual income group cannot be deemed paid under section 960 for any taxable year. Proposed § 1.960-1(e).

Under § 1.904-6, Federal income tax principles apply to determine the separate category, income group, or PTEP group of the CFC's gross items of income and expense, the amounts of which are computed under foreign law, that are included in the foreign tax base. For example, if the United States treats a distribution as resulting in capital gain that is passive category income, but foreign law treats the item as a dividend that would be general category income, the item is assigned to the passive category for purposes of allocating and apportioning current year taxes of the CFC to the item. *See also* proposed § 1.904-6(a)(1)(i). The amount of the item, however, is determined under foreign law, and expenses (also determined under foreign law) are allocated and apportioned to the income under foreign law principles or as otherwise provided in § 1.904-6(a)(1)(ii).

Proposed § 1.960-1(d)(3)(ii)(B) also provides a rule for addressing base and timing differences (within the meaning of proposed § 1.904-6(a)(1)(iv)) for purposes of allocating and apportioning current year taxes of a CFC to income groups and PTEP groups. Current year taxes that are attributable to a base difference are allocated to the residual income group, and therefore are ineligible to be deemed paid. Current year taxes that are attributable to a timing difference — namely, current year tax imposed on an amount that is income of the CFC in a different taxable year under Federal income tax law — are allocated and apportioned to a section 904 category and income group as though the income that foreign law recognizes in the CFC's current taxable year were also recognized for Federal income tax purposes in that year. Proposed § 1.960-1(d)(3)(ii)(B) includes a special rule, which is discussed in Part IV.C.2 of this Explanation of Provisions, for current year taxes that are attributable to a timing difference resulting from a section 959(b) distribution.

B. *Taxes deemed paid under section 960(a) and (d) for subpart F inclusions and GILTI inclusion amounts*

Section 960(a) provides that a domestic corporation that is a United States shareholder of a CFC is deemed to have paid the CFC's foreign income taxes that are properly attributable to the item of income of the CFC that the United States shareholder includes in gross income under section 951(a)(1) as a subpart F inclusion.

Section 960(d) provides that a domestic corporation that is a United States shareholder is deemed to have paid 80 percent of an amount that is equal to the product of the United States shareholder's inclusion percentage and the aggregate of the tested foreign income taxes paid or accrued by the CFCs of the United States shareholder. The inclusion percentage of the United States shareholder is the ratio of the United States shareholder's GILTI inclusion amount with respect to its CFCs to the aggregate amount of the United States shareholder's pro rata share of tested income of those CFCs. Section 960(d)(3) defines tested foreign income taxes as the foreign income taxes paid or accrued by a CFC of a United States shareholder that are properly attributable to the tested income of the CFC that the United States shareholder takes into account in computing its GILTI inclusion amount.

1. Subpart F Inclusions

Under proposed § 1.960-2(b), the amount of the foreign income taxes of a CFC that its United States shareholder that is a domestic corporation is deemed to pay under section 960(a) is computed with respect to the income of the CFC, determined under Federal income tax principles in each subpart F income group within a section 904 category. A domestic corporate shareholder that has a subpart F inclusion with respect to its CFC is deemed to pay the CFC's foreign income taxes that are properly attributable to the items of income of the CFC that give rise to the subpart F inclusion of that shareholder. The amount of taxes that are properly attributable to an item of income for this purpose is equal to the domestic corporate shareholder's proportionate share of the current year taxes of the CFC that are allocated and apportioned to the subpart F income group within a section 904 category of the CFC to which the item of income is attributable. The proportionate share for each subpart F income group is equal to the current year taxes that are allocated and apportioned to a subpart F income group within a section 904 category multiplied by a fraction equal to the portion of the subpart F inclusion that is attributable to that subpart F income group to the total income in that subpart F income group. Therefore, no tax is deemed paid by a corporate United States shareholder of a CFC with respect to a subpart F income group to which current year taxes of the CFC are allocated and apportioned (including by reason of the rule for timing differences) but with respect to which no portion of a subpart F inclusion is attributable.

The denominator of the fraction, the net income in the subpart F income group, is not reduced to reflect any prior year deficits because those deficits do not reduce the subpart F income of the CFC in the current year. A pro rata share of a prior year qualified deficit reduces the amount of a United States shareholder's subpart F inclusion, and therefore by its own account reduces the numerator of the fraction. Proposed § 1.960-2(b)(3)(ii). The denominator of the fraction is, however, reduced to reflect the limitation in section 952(c)(1)(A) of the subpart F income of the CFC to its current year earnings and profits. The denominator is also reduced to reflect any reduction in the subpart F income of a CFC under section 952(c)(1)(C), which allows a CFC to reduce certain of its subpart F income by an amount of certain current year deficits of certain CFCs in the same chain of ownership. Proposed § 1.960-2(b)(3)(iii).

Section 960(a) treats foreign income taxes of a CFC as deemed paid by a United States shareholder only with respect to an item of income of a CFC that is included in the gross income of the United States shareholder under section 951(a)(1). Proposed § 1.960-2(b)(1) treats taxes as deemed paid under section 960(a) specifically with respect to subpart F inclusions because the inclusions are with respect to items of income of the CFC. In contrast, an inclusion under section 951(a)(1)(B) is not an inclusion of an "item of income" of the CFC but instead is an inclusion equal to an amount that is determined under the formula in section 956(a). Therefore, proposed § 1.960-2(b)(1) provides that no foreign income taxes are deemed paid under section 960(a) with respect to an inclusion under section 951(a)(1)(B).

2. GILTI Inclusion Amounts

Proposed § 1.960-2(c) provides that the amount of the tested foreign income taxes that a United States shareholder is deemed to pay under section 960(d) is computed with respect to the income of the CFC in each tested income group within a section 904 category. For purposes of determining a

United States shareholder's tested foreign income taxes, the CFC's current year taxes are first allocated and apportioned to the tested income group within a section 904 category in order to determine the foreign income taxes "properly attributable" to the tested income group. The United States shareholder's tested foreign income taxes for a tested income group within a section 904 category is equal to its proportionate share of the CFC's current year taxes, determined by multiplying the CFC's current year taxes that are allocated and apportioned to a tested income group within a section 904 category by a fraction that is equal to the tested income of the CFC in the tested income group that is included in computing the domestic corporation's aggregate amount described in section 951A(c)(1)(A) and proposed § 1.951A-1(c)(2)(i), divided by the total income in the tested income group.

The United States shareholder's inclusion percentage is required to determine the amount of taxes deemed paid by the United States shareholder. In general, current year taxes allocated and apportioned to a tested income group will be in the general category at the level of the CFC, although in limited cases involving passive category tested income, current year taxes may be allocated and apportioned to the passive category. However, the domestic corporation computes only a single inclusion percentage with respect to all of its tested income, regardless of the section 904 category to which the tested income is assigned.

In the case of a United States shareholder that is a member of a consolidated group, the numerator of the inclusion percentage is computed using the GILTI inclusion amount of a United States shareholder as determined under § 1.1502-51. *See* § 1.951A-1(c)(4).

C. *Taxes deemed paid under section 960(b) with respect to section 959 distributions*

Section 960(b)(1) provides that a United States shareholder of a CFC is deemed to have paid the CFC's foreign income taxes that the United States shareholder has not been previously deemed to pay and that are properly attributable to a distribution from the CFC that the United States shareholder excludes from its income under section 959(a) (a "section 959(a) distribution"). Section 960(b)(2) provides that a CFC is deemed to have paid the foreign income taxes of another CFC that have not previously been deemed paid by a United States shareholder and that are properly attributable to a distribution from the other CFC to which section 959(b) applies (a "section 959(b) distribution," and together with a section 959(a) distribution, a "section 959 distribution").

1. PTEP Groups in Annual PTEP Accounts and Associated Taxes

Proposed § 1.960-3(c)(1) requires a CFC to establish a separate, annual account ("annual PTEP account") for its earnings and profits for its current taxable year to which subpart F or GILTI inclusions of United States shareholders of the CFC are attributable. Each account must correspond to the inclusion year of the previously taxed earnings and profits and to the section 904 category of the inclusions at the United States shareholder level. Accordingly, a CFC may have an annual PTEP account in the section 951A category or a treaty category (as defined in § 1.861-13(b)(6)), even though income of the controlled foreign corporation cannot initially be assigned to the section 951A category or a treaty category. The previously taxed earnings and profits in each annual account are then assigned to one of ten possible groups of previously taxed earnings and profits described in proposed § 1.960-3(c)(2) (each, a "PTEP group"). The PTEP groups serve a similar function to the subpart F income groups and tested income groups — they are the mechanism for associating foreign taxes paid or accrued, or deemed paid, by a CFC with section 959 distributions of previously taxed earnings and profits. If, following the issuance of new guidance under section 959 (which will be addressed in a separate guidance project), it is determined that maintaining all ten of the PTEP groups is unnecessary, or that grouping of annual accounts into multi-year accounts is permissible, the Treasury Department and the IRS will consider consolidating PTEP groups as part of finalizing the proposed regulations.

A CFC accounts for a section 959(b) distribution that it receives by adding the distribution amount to an annual PTEP account and PTEP group that corresponds to the annual PTEP account and PTEP group from which the distributing CFC made the distribution. Proposed § 1.960-3(c)(3). A CFC that makes a section 959 distribution must similarly reduce the annual PTEP account and PTEP group within the account from which the distribution is made by the distribution amount. A CFC must also reduce PTEP groups that relate to previously taxed earnings and profits described in section 959(c)(2) ("section 959(c)(2) PTEP") to account for reclassification of amounts into those groups as previously taxed earnings and profits described in section 959(c)(1) ("reclassified PTEP"), and increase the PTEP group that corresponds to the reclassified amount. Proposed § 1.960-3(c)(4).

2. Associating Foreign Income Taxes with PTEP Groups

A CFC must also account for the foreign income taxes that it pays, accrues or is deemed to pay with respect to the amount in each PTEP group ("PTEP group taxes"). PTEP group taxes are accounted for with respect to previously taxed earnings and profits assigned to a PTEP group within an annual PTEP account. PTEP group taxes consist of (1) the current year taxes paid or accrued by the CFC as the result of its receipt of a section 959(b) distribution that are allocated and apportioned to the PTEP group; (2) foreign income taxes that are deemed paid by the CFC with respect to an amount in a PTEP group; and (3) in the case of a reclassified PTEP group, foreign income taxes that were paid, accrued or deemed paid with respect to an amount that was initially included in a section 959(c)(2) PTEP group and subsequently added to a corresponding reclassified PTEP group. Proposed § 1.960-3(d)(1). PTEP group taxes are reduced by the amount of foreign income taxes in the group that are deemed paid by a United States shareholder under section 960(b)(1) or by another CFC under section

960(b)(2), and foreign income taxes relating to a PTEP group that is reclassified to a section 959(c)(1) PTEP group. Proposed § 1.960-3(d)(2).

As discussed in Part IV.A.3.ii of this Explanation of Provisions, proposed § 1.960-1(d)(3)(ii)(A) associates current year taxes of a CFC with a PTEP group for purposes of section 960(b) only in the case of an increase in a PTEP group as a result of the receipt of a section 959(b) distribution. The increased PTEP group is treated as an income group to which current year taxes that are imposed solely by reason of that section 959(b) distribution are allocated and apportioned. For example, a withholding tax imposed on a section 959(b) distribution received by an upper-tier CFC is allocated and apportioned to the PTEP group that is increased by the section 959(b) distribution. The withholding tax also reduces (as a deduction) the amount in that same PTEP group.

Proposed § 1.960-1(d)(3)(ii)(B) generally applies the timing difference rule of § 1.904-6(a)(1)(iv) to allocate and apportion current year taxes that are attributable to a timing difference to a section 904 category and income group as if the CFC recognized the related income under Federal income tax principles in its current taxable year. Proposed § 1.960-1(d)(3)(ii)(B) also clarifies the rule for previously taxed earnings and profits by providing that if current year taxes are attributable to a timing difference, the taxes are only treated as related to a PTEP group if the taxes are imposed solely by reason of a section 959(b) distribution that increases the PTEP group. For example, a timing difference described in proposed § 1.904-6(a)(1)(iv) could include a situation in which Federal income tax principles require marking-to-market gain on an asset, resulting in an inclusion under section 951A(a), but the foreign jurisdiction only imposes tax when the asset is disposed of in a later year. Under proposed § 1.960-1(d)(3)(ii)(B), the later-imposed foreign income tax is treated as related to the tested income group (if any) for the year in which the tax is imposed, and not to a PTEP group in an annual PTEP account for the earlier year in which the gain was recognized for Federal income tax purposes. In addition, an income tax imposed on a distributing CFC (in contrast to a tax, such as a withholding tax, imposed on the recipient of the distribution) by reason of a section 959 distribution is treated as a timing difference and is treated as related to the subpart F income group or tested income group for the current taxable year (if any) in which the distribution is made, and not to a PTEP group in an annual PTEP account for the earlier year in which the distributed earnings and profits were recognized for Federal income tax purposes.

Therefore, under proposed § 1.960-1(d)(3)(ii)(B), the only taxes that are allocated and apportioned to a PTEP group are taxes that are imposed solely by reason of a CFC's receipt of a section 959(b) distribution and that are otherwise allocated and apportioned to the PTEP group under § 1.904-6 principles. For example, a net basis tax imposed on a CFC's receipt of a section 959(b) distribution by the CFC's country of residence is treated as related to a PTEP group. Similarly, a withholding tax imposed with respect to a CFC's receipt of a section 959(b) distribution is allocated and apportioned to a PTEP group. In contrast, a withholding tax imposed on a disregarded payment from a disregarded entity to a CFC owner is treated as a timing difference and is never treated as related to a PTEP group (even if all of the CFC's earnings and profits are previously taxed earnings and profits from income earned by the disregarded entity), because the tax is not imposed solely by reason of a section 959(b) distribution. The withholding tax, however, may be treated as related to a subpart F income group or tested income group under the rule for timing differences.

3. Computational Rules

Proposed § 1.960-3(b) provides rules for determining the amount of taxes deemed paid with respect to a section 959(a) distribution. A domestic corporation that receives a section 959(a) distribution is deemed to have paid the foreign income taxes that are properly attributable to the section 959(a) distribution from the PTEP group of the distributing CFC, to the extent the PTEP group taxes have not already been deemed to have been paid in the current taxable year or any prior taxable year. Proposed § 1.960-3(b)(1). The amount of foreign income taxes that are properly attributable to a domestic corporation's receipt of a section 959(a) distribution from a PTEP group within a section 904 category are its proportionate share of PTEP group taxes associated with the PTEP group. The domestic corporation's proportionate share of foreign income taxes associated with a section 959(a) distribution from a PTEP group is determined by a fraction equal to the amount of the section 959(a) distribution attributable to the PTEP group over the total amount of previously taxed earnings and profits in the PTEP group.

A single section 959(a) distribution could be attributable to multiple PTEP groups, with respect to multiple different inclusion years, of the distributing CFC. The proposed regulations, including the order of the list of PTEP groups in § 1.960-3(c)(2), do not provide rules for the allocation of distributions among different kinds of previously taxed earnings and profits under section 959(c). The Treasury Department and the IRS anticipate that future regulations under section 959 will provide ordering rules for determining the annual PTEP account and PTEP group to which a section 959 distribution is attributable.

Proposed § 1.960-3(b)(2) provides similar rules to those in proposed § 1.960-3(b)(1) for taxes deemed paid under section 960(b)(2) with respect to a CFC's receipt of a section 959(b) distribution.

Proposed § 1.960-3(d)(3) provides a rule relating to foreign income taxes paid or accrued in a taxable year of a CFC that began before January 1, 2018, with respect to an annual PTEP account, and a PTEP group within such account, that was established for an inclusion year of a CFC that began before January 1, 2018. Specifically, in certain cases, the foreign income taxes may be deemed paid under section 960(b) with respect to a section 959 distribution in a year of the CFC that begins after December 31, 2017.

However, the Treasury Department and the IRS recognize that with respect to CFC taxable years beginning before January 1, 2018, the application of section 960(a)(3) was uncertain and some taxpayers may have added taxes paid or accrued with respect to a section 959 distribution to post-1986 foreign income taxes described in section 902(c)(2) (as in effect on December 21, 2017). In that case, those foreign income taxes could have been included in computing foreign taxes deemed paid under section 902 with respect to a distribution or inclusion of post-1986 undistributed earnings (including by reason of sections 960 and 965) in taxable years of CFCs beginning before January 1, 2018, in which case the taxes are not available to be deemed paid under section 960(b).

The proposed regulations under section 965, see 83 Fed. Reg. 39,514, reserved on the application of section 965(g) to taxes deemed paid under new section 960(b). The preamble to the regulations under section 965 indicated that future regulations would provide rules for new section 960(b) similar to the rules that apply for section 960(a)(3) (as in effect on December 21, 2017).

The proposed regulations in this document provide a rule in proposed § 1.965-5(c)(1)(iii) similar to the rule that applies to taxes deemed paid under section 960(a)(3) that is in proposed § 1.965-5(c)(1)(i) and (ii). In particular, no credit is allowed for the applicable percentage of taxes deemed paid under section 960(b) that are attributable to the PTEP groups described in § 1.960-3(c)(2) that relate to section 965.

In order to ensure that the disallowance under section 965(g) only applies once, the rule in proposed § 1.965-5(c)(1)(iii) does not apply to taxes deemed paid under section 960(b)(2) with respect to a section 959(b) distribution, but only applies when previously taxed earnings and profits are distributed to a domestic corporate shareholder.

D. *Domestic partnerships*

If a domestic corporation owns an interest in a CFC through a domestic partnership, to the extent the domestic corporation is a United States shareholder with respect to the CFC, the proposed regulations provide that the domestic corporation is deemed to have paid foreign income taxes as if the domestic corporation had included the income from the CFC directly rather than as a distributive share of the partnership's income. Proposed § 1.960-2(b)(4) provides that a domestic corporation that has a distributive share of a domestic partnership's subpart F inclusion and is also a United States shareholder with respect to the CFC that gives rise to a subpart F inclusion is treated as a subpart F inclusion of the domestic corporation for purposes of section 960(a). Similarly, the domestic corporation's distributive share of a domestic partnership's receipt of a section 959(a) distribution is treated as a receipt by the domestic corporation directly for purposes of proposed § 1.960-3(b)(1). *See* proposed § 1.960-3(b)(5). In the case of section 960(d), the GILTI inclusion amount of a domestic corporation that is also a United States shareholder of a CFC through its interest in a domestic partnership is generally determined at the partner level and therefore the rules in proposed § 1.960-2(c) apply in the same manner as if the domestic corporation included the GILTI inclusion amount directly. *See* proposed § 1.951A-5(c).

E. Section 78 dividend

The proposed regulations revise § 1.78-1 to reflect the amended section 78, as well as make conforming changes to reflect pre-Act statutory amendments. In addition, the proposed regulations provide that section 78 dividends that relate to taxable years of foreign corporations that begin before January 1, 2018, are not treated as dividends for purposes of section 245A. This rule is necessary by reason of the enactment of section 245A to ensure that similarly situated taxpayers do not have different tax consequences under section 245A with respect to section 78 dividends. Absent this rule, a United States shareholder of a CFC using a fiscal year beginning in 2017 as its U.S. taxable year (a "fiscal year CFC") could potentially claim a section 245A deduction with respect to its section 78 dividend attributable to the United States shareholder's inclusion under section 951 (including by reason of section 965) for the CFC's fiscal year ending in 2018, whereas a United States shareholder of a CFC using the calendar year as its U.S. taxable year could not claim a section 245A deduction with respect to any section 78 dividend for any taxable year. There is no indication that Congress intended to treat these similarly situated taxpayers differently with respect to the section 78 dividend given that the purpose of the section 78 dividend — to prevent a taxpayer from obtaining the benefit of both a credit under section 901 and a deduction with respect to the same foreign tax — is unrelated to the CFC's U.S. taxable year. Accordingly, proposed § 1.78-1(c) includes a special applicability date to prevent this potential disparate treatment and double benefit to taxpayers with fiscal year CFCs.

V. *Effect of Section 965(n) Election*

Section 965(n) allows a taxpayer to exclude section 965(a) inclusions (reduced by section 965(c) deductions) and associated section 78 gross ups in determining the amount of the net operating loss carryover or carryback that is absorbed in the taxable year of the inclusions. Proposed § 1.965-7(e)(1), as proposed to be added at 83 FR 39,514 (August 9, 2018), provides that the election also applies to the determination of the amount of the net operating loss for the taxable year.

These proposed regulations at § 1.965-7(e)(1)(i) clarify that if the section 965(n) election creates or increases a net operating loss under section 172 for the taxable year, then the taxable income of the person for the taxable year cannot be less than the amount described in proposed § 1.965-7(e)(1)(ii). This rule is necessary to prevent the same deduction from being taken into account in the taxable year and also used again to create a net operating loss that is deducted in a different taxable year. The amount of the deductions that create or increase a net operating loss for the taxable year in each separate category and the U.S. source residual category by reason of the section 965(n) election is determined under proposed § 1.965-7(e)(1)(iv), and those amounts are not also taken into account in computing taxable income or the foreign tax credit limitations under section 904 for that year.

Proposed § 1.965-7(e)(1)(iv)(A) clarifies that the election under section 965(n) applies solely for purposes of determining the amount of the net operating loss for the election year and the amount of net operating loss carryover or carryback to that year. The proposed regulations provide ordering rules to coordinate the election's effect on section 172 with the computation of the foreign tax credit limitations under section 904.

First, deductions that would have been allowed for the taxable year but for the section 965(n) election, other than the amount of any net operating loss carryover or carryback to the election year that is not allowed by reason of the election, are allocated and apportioned under §§ 1.861-8 through 1.861-17 in the taxable year for which the section 965(n) election is made. The section 965(a) inclusions and associated section 78 gross ups are taken into account for this purpose, and also in applying the rules under § 1.904(g)-3(b)(3) to determine the source components of a partial net operating loss carryover to the taxable year for which the section 965(n) election is made, if any, including when the amount deducted under section 172 in that year is reduced by reason of the section 965(n) election. Proposed § 1.965-7(e)(1)(iv)(B)(*1*).

Second, the proposed regulations provide that the amount by which a net operating loss is created or increased by reason of the section 965(n) election, if any, is considered to comprise a ratable portion of all of the taxpayer's deductions (other than the section 965(c) deduction) that are allocated and apportioned to each statutory and residual grouping for the taxable year under the rules in proposed § 1.965-7(e)(1)(iv)(B)(*1*). Proposed § 1.965-7(e)(1)(iv)(B)(2).

Third, deductions allocated and apportioned to the statutory and residual groupings, to the extent deducted in the election year rather than deferred to create or increase a net operating loss, are combined with income in those groupings to determine the foreign tax credit limitations for the year. Deductions allocated and apportioned to the section 965(a) inclusions and associated section 78 gross ups therefore reduce income in the separate category or categories (or U.S. source residual category) to which those section 965 amounts are assigned, and are not re-allocated to reduce other income, other than by operation of the separate limitation loss and overall domestic loss allocation rules of section 904(f) and (g). *See* proposed § 1.965-7(e)(1)(iv)(B)(*3*). Accordingly, the section 965(a) inclusions and associated section 78 gross ups may both attract and absorb deductions in the election year in calculating the separate foreign tax credit limitations under section 904.

VI. *Applicability Dates*

In general, the portions of the proposed regulations that relate to statutory amendments made by the Act apply to taxable years beginning after December 22, 2017. *See* section 7805(b)(2). Other portions of the proposed regulations that do not relate to the Act apply for taxable years ending on or after December 7, 2018. Certain portions of the proposed regulations contain rules that relate to the Act as well as rules that do not relate to the Act. These regulations generally apply to taxable years that satisfy both of the following two conditions: (1) the taxable year begins after December 22, 2017, and (2) ends on or after December 7, 2018. *See* section 7805(b)(1)(B).

A special applicability date is provided is provided in § 1.861-12(k) in order to apply § 1.861-12(c)(2)(i)(*B*)(*1*)(*ii*) to the last taxable year of a foreign corporation beginning before January 1, 2018, since there may be an inclusion under section 965 for that taxable year. A special applicability date is also provided in § 1.904(b)-3(f) with respect to that section because section 904(b)(4) applies to deductions with respect to taxable years ending after December 31, 2017. Finally, a special applicability date is provided in § 1.78-1(c) in order to apply the second sentence of § 1.78-1(a) to section 78 dividends received after December 31, 2017, with respect to a taxable year of a foreign corporation beginning before January 1, 2018. *See* Part IV.E of this Explanation of Provisions.

Proposed §§ 1.965-5(c)(1)(iii) and 1.965-7(e)(1)(i) and (iv) have the applicability dates provided in proposed § 1.965-9 (contained in 83 Fed. Reg. 39,514).

VII. *Conforming Amendments*

Sections 1.902-0 through 1.902-4 will be withdrawn as part of finalizing the proposed regulations. With respect to portions of the temporary regulations under sections 861 through 865 that are being reproposed under the proposed regulations, the Treasury Department and the IRS will remove the corresponding temporary regulations upon finalization of the proposed regulations. In addition, the Treasury Department and the IRS intend to make conforming amendments to the examples throughout the foreign tax credit regulations upon finalization of the proposed regulations. In light of the numerous changes made under the Act to various defined terms and statutory cross references, the Treasury Department and the IRS also request comments on other regulations that require updating to conform to changes made by the Act.

Special Analyses

I. *Regulatory Planning and Review*

Executive Orders 13563 and 12866 direct agencies to assess costs and benefits of available regulatory alternatives and, if regulation is necessary, to select regulatory approaches that maximize net benefits (including potential economic, environmental, public health and safety effects, distributive impacts, and equity). Executive Order 13563 emphasizes the importance of quantifying both costs and benefits, reducing costs, harmonizing rules, and promoting flexibility. The Executive Order 13771 designation for any final rule resulting from these proposed regulations will be informed by comments received. The preliminary EO 13771 designation for this proposed rule is regulatory.

The proposed regulations have been designated by the Office of Information and Regulatory Affairs (OIRA) as subject to review under Executive Order 12866 pursuant to the Memorandum of Agreement (MOA, April 11, 2018) between the Treasury Department and the Office of Management and Budget regarding review of tax regulations. OIRA has designated this rule as a significant regulatory action, under Executive Order 12866, and as economically significant under EO 12866 and section 1(c) of the MOA. Accordingly, the proposed regulations have been reviewed by the Office of Information and Regulatory Affairs. For more detail on the economic analysis, please refer to the following analysis.

A. *Background*

Before the Act, the United States taxed its citizens, residents, and domestic corporations on their worldwide income. However, to the extent that both the foreign jurisdiction and the U.S. taxed the same income, this would have resulted in double taxation. The U.S. foreign tax credit (FTC) regime alleviated the double taxation issue by allowing a non-refundable credit for foreign income taxes paid or accrued to reduce U.S. tax on foreign source income.

Under the Code, the FTC calculation is applied separately to different categories of income (a "separate category"). For example, suppose a domestic corporate taxpayer has $100 of active foreign source income in the "general category," $100 of passive foreign source income in the "passive category," $50 of foreign taxes associated with the "general category" income, and $0 of foreign taxes associated with the "passive category" income. The allowable FTC is determined separately for the different categories of income (general and passive). Therefore, none of the $50 of "general category" FTCs can be used to offset U.S. tax on the "passive category" income. This taxpayer has a pre-FTC U.S. tax liability of $42 (21 percent of $200) but can claim a FTC for only $21 (21 percent of $100) of this liability, which is with respect to active foreign source income in the general category. The taxpayer carries over the remaining $29 of foreign taxes ($50 minus $21) and can generally apply the taxes as a credit in the prior taxable year or over the next 10 years against U.S. tax on general category foreign source income, subject to certain restrictions.

Further, certain expenses borne by U.S. parents and domestic affiliates that support foreign operations are allocated to separate categories based, for example, on gross income or assets. These allocations reduce foreign source taxable income and therefore reduce the allowable FTCs for the separate category, since FTCs are limited to the U.S. income tax on the foreign source taxable income (i.e., foreign source income less allocated expenses) in that separate category. The foreign income and related taxes from one separate category generally cannot be combined with another category. Prior to 2007, there were generally nine separate categories. In general, the American Jobs Creation Act of 2004 reduced the number of separate categories to two — the passive and general categories of income. These two separate categories generally prevailed until passage of the Act.[1]

The 2017 Act made several significant changes to the FTC rules and related rules for allocating expenses to foreign income for the purpose of calculating the allowable FTCs. In particular, the Act repealed the fair market value method of asset valuation used to apportion interest expense to separate categories based on the fair market value of assets, added new separate categories for global intangible low-taxed income (the section 951A category) and foreign branch income, and amended Code sections which address deemed paid credits for subpart F income, global intangible low-taxed income (GILTI), and distributions of previously taxed earnings and profits. Further, because repatriated dividends are no longer taxable, the Act also repealed section 902 (which allowed a domestic corporation to claim FTCs with respect to dividends paid from a foreign corporation) and made other conforming changes.

These regulations provide the detail, structure and language required to implement the changes made by the statute. The following analysis describes the need for the proposed regulations, as well as provides an overview of the regulations, discussion of the costs and benefits of these regulations as compared with the baseline, and a discussion of alternative policy choices that were considered.

B. *The need for proposed regulations*

The numerous changes to the FTC rules in the Act require practical guidance for implementation. The proposed regulations provide the details, methodology, and approaches necessary to conform the existing FTC regulations to the many changes specified in the Act; for example, they provide structure and detail concerning how to incorporate the new separate categories of income into the foreign tax credit calculation, including how expenses will be allocated to separate categories. The regulations also update outdated portions of the existing regulations to help conform the existing regulations to the post-Act world. Thus, the guidance provides certainty, clarity, and consistency regarding FTC computations, which promotes efficiency and equity, contingent on the overall Code.

C. *Baseline*

The economic analysis that follows compares the proposed regulations to a no-action baseline reflecting anticipated federal income tax-related behavior in the absence of these proposed regula-

---

[1] Although there are several other separate categories that may apply, such as under sections 901(j) and 904(h)(10), these separate categories generally arise only in rare circumstances.

tions. A no-action baseline reflects the current environment including the existing FTC regulations, prior to any amendment by the proposed regulations.

D. *Overview of the proposed regulations*

As noted above, the proposed regulations specify the methodologies and approaches necessary to conform the existing regulations to the many changes specified in the Act. Several aspects of the proposed regulations are particularly noteworthy, as they involve more discretion on the part of the Treasury Department and the IRS. These are the aspect of the regulations governing expense allocation, the aspect of the regulations governing FTC carryovers to the new foreign income categories, the special applicability date regarding the section 78 gross up, and the anti-abuse rules addressing certain loans made to partnerships. The ultimate rules proposed, as well as the alternatives that were considered are discussed below.

Most notably, in response to taxpayer requests for guidance, these regulations help interpret the statute by providing details regarding how expenses must be apportioned to the new separate categories created by the Act. In particular, the proposed regulations specify that, for purposes of applying the expense allocation and apportionment rules, the gross income offset by the section 250 deduction is treated as exempt income, and the stock giving rise to GILTI that is offset by the section 250 deduction is treated as an exempt asset (see Part I.A of the Explanation of Provisions). Such treatment implies that fewer expenses will be allocated to the section 951A category as a result of this rule, leading to higher computed foreign source taxable income, a larger foreign tax credit limitation, and a larger foreign tax credit offset with respect to GILTI income. Because these expenses are now allocated to another separate category (where they may be less likely to displace FTCs) or to U.S. source income, this rule will in general reduce the tax burden of U.S. multinational corporations with GILTI income and allocable expenses.

The regulations also address how FTC carryovers are to be allocated across the new separate categories. The formation of two new separate categories requires a determination regarding how pre-Act FTC carryovers must be allocated across new and existing separate categories. The Treasury Department and the IRS determined that, because continuity in the definition of income and assignment of tax attributes is appropriate, taxpayers should be able to analyze their general category income earned in prior years to determine the extent to which it would have been considered to belong in the new separate category for foreign branch income under the rules described here (see Part II.A of the Explanation of Provisions). However, because allocation of pre-Act income to hypothetical post-Act separate categories has the potential to be administratively burdensome, the regulation provides that the allocation of FTC carryovers to the new foreign branch category is optional, which allows for continuity of income treatment while minimizing administrative and compliance burdens during the transition. For taxpayers that do not choose to allocate FTC carryovers to the new foreign branch category, their FTC carryovers will remain in the general category. See Part I.E.2 of this Special Analyses for a discussion of alternatives considered and additional reasoning regarding the approach taken under the proposed regulations.

Further, as described in section IV.E of the Explanation of Provisions, the proposed regulations include an updated applicability date for the new section 78 provisions. In particular, the proposed regulations provide that section 78 dividends relating to taxable years of foreign corporations beginning before January 1, 2018, are not treated as dividends for purposes of the section 245A deduction. As further noted in section IV.E of the Explanation of Provisions, absent this rule, taxpayers that have calendar year CFCs instead of fiscal year CFCs would be treated differently with respect to their section 78 dividends solely on the basis of this difference in tax year status; and taxpayers with fiscal year CFCs could receive the double benefit of a section 245A deduction and a FTC under section 960 with respect to the same foreign taxes. Allowing a double benefit for a single expense erodes the U.S. tax base and treats otherwise similar taxpayers (those who have different CFC tax years) inequitably. Based on these equity considerations, the Treasury Department and the IRS expect that the proposed regulation will provide greater net benefits than the alternative of not issuing a regulation on this issue.

The regulations also address certain potentially abusive borrowing arrangements, such as when a U.S. person lends money to a foreign partnership in order to artificially increase foreign source income (and therefore the FTC limitation) without affecting U.S. taxable income (see Part I.C. of the Explanation of Provisions). This is accomplished, for example, by lending to a controlled partnership, which has no effect on U.S. taxable income, because the interest income received from the partnership is offset by the lender's share of the interest expense incurred by the partnership. However, the transaction can increase foreign source income and allowable foreign tax credits, because the existing interest expense allocation rules do not generally allocate interest income and interest expenses similarly. To prevent such artificial inflation of foreign tax credits, the regulations specify that interest income attributable to borrowing through a partnership will be allocated across foreign tax credit separate categories in the same manner as the associated interest expense. See Part I.E.2 of this Special Analyses for a discussion of alternatives considered and additional reasoning regarding the approach taken under the proposed regulations.

In addition, the regulations clarify and provide guidance on numerous other technical issues. For example, they clarify the regulatory environment by updating inoperative language in §§1.904-1 through 1.904-3; parts of the regulations have not previously been updated to reflect changes to section 904 made in 1978. They also ease transitional administrative burdens associated with the implementation of the Act; for example, allowing a one-time exception to the 5 year waiting period for the election of the gross income or sales method for R&D expense allocation (See Part I.G of the Explanation of Provisions), or by allowing a simplified definition of average basis for the first year taxpayers are required to use the tax book method of valuation (See Part I.E.1 of the Explanation of Provisions).

The regulations further clarify the § 1.904-6 rules concerning how allocation of taxes across separate categories should be calculated in the presence of base and timing differences. A base difference occurs, for example, if the foreign jurisdiction taxes income, such as life insurance proceeds or gifts, which are excluded from income for U.S. tax purposes. A timing difference occurs, for example, if the U.S. tax rules define income as being earned by marking an asset to market, but a domestic corporation operates a CFC in a foreign jurisdiction that defines income as being earned by realization upon sale. Regulatory guidance instructs taxpayers how to appropriately navigate these cross jurisdictional base and timing differences in the assignment of taxes to FTC separate categories. They also fill technical gaps in how to implement the statute in practice, for example, by providing a clear rule for how to characterize the value of stock in each separate category in the context of the new separate categories.

The guidance, clarity, and specificity provided by the regulations help ensure that all taxpayers calculate foreign income and the foreign tax credit in a similar manner. The economic analysis that follows discusses the costs and benefits of these regulations, and the alternative choices that could have been made, in greater detail.

E. *Economic analysis*

1. Anticipated benefits and costs of the proposed regulations

The Treasury Department and the IRS have assessed the benefits and costs of the proposed regulations against a no-action baseline — which, as explained above, is the *status quo* in the absence of the proposed regulations. The Treasury Department and IRS expect that the certainty and clarity provided by these proposed regulations, relative to the no-action baseline, will improve U.S. economic efficiency. For example, because separate categories for GILTI and foreign branch income did not previously exist, taxpayers can benefit from the enhanced specificity regarding how income, expenses, and carryover foreign tax credits should be allocated across these separate categories. In the absence of this enhanced clarity, similarly situated taxpayers might interpret the statute differently, potentially resulting in inequitable outcomes. For example, some taxpayers may forego specific investments that other taxpayers deem worthwhile based on different interpretations of the tax consequences alone. The guidance provided in these regulations helps to ensure that taxpayers face more uniform incentives when making economic decisions, which will generally improve economic efficiency. In order to give a rough sense of the population potentially affected by these regulations, a table reporting the number of affected filers is provided in Part II of this Special Analyses.

In the absence of the enhanced specificity provided by the regulations described above, similarly situated taxpayers might interpret the statutory rules differently, and different taxpayers might then pursue or forego economic activities based on different interpretations of the tax consequences alone. By providing clear rules to eliminate ambiguity and to fill in technical gaps, the guidance provided in these regulations helps to ensure that taxpayers face more uniform incentives. Such uniformity across economic decision-makers is a tenet of economic efficiency. Clear and consistent rules also increase transparency and decrease the incentives and opportunities for tax evasion. Rules to combat abusive transactions also help to ensure that taxpayers make decisions based on market conditions rather than on tax considerations.

Further, because the changes introduced in the Act are substantial, the start-up costs and learning curves involved in complying with the Act will also be substantial. In particular, the Act's elimination of tax imposed on repatriations going forward, the creation of the tax on global intangible low taxed income (and the corresponding section 951A category), and the creation of a deduction for foreign-derived intangible income each embody a completely new component of U.S. international tax law, and together restructure a U.S. international tax system that had remained relatively constant since 1987. By definition, transitioning to such a completely new system will involve substantial start-up costs in terms of learning the nuances of the new rules, and revamping record keeping, documentation, and software systems to aid in filling out the new tax forms and to ensure the availability of all the records required to benefit from new exclusions and deductions (such as the section 250 deduction). The proposed regulations assist taxpayers in this process by providing definitional clarity in order to minimize the disruption caused by the move to the new system. When possible and appropriate, they further provide significant transitional flexibility in order to help relieve compliance burdens and reduce transition administrative costs. Additional details, including the types of cost savings and benefits expected, are discussed below, as well as in Part I.E.2 of this Special Analyses.

Notably, as mentioned in Part I of the Explanation of Provisions, taxpayers have repeatedly requested regulatory guidance concerning appropriate expense allocation in light of the new separate categories for GILTI and foreign branch income; in the absence of new regulations, the correct approach for allocating expenses is subject to interpretation. Therefore, the proposed regulations seek to clarify the allowable expense allocation rules that are consistent with legislative history's description of the section 250 deduction as effectively exempting income, by specifying that the income associated with the section 250 deduction is, for foreign tax credit purposes, treated as partially exempt. The regulations therefore potentially increase the competitiveness of U.S. corporations relative to the no-action baseline, which includes proposed though not yet final regulations under section 951A, by generally reducing the amount of U.S. parent expenses that are allocated to the section 951A category. They also provide certainty and clarity for taxpayers, which, as noted above, increases efficiency and transparency, and reduces the incentive for evasion, relative to the no-action baseline.

However, the reduced expense allocation to the section 951A category resulting from these proposed regulations has the potential to reduce Federal tax revenue relative to the statute and in consideration of proposed though not yet final regulations related to section 951A. In addition, it could also provide some taxpayers with the incentive to locate more of their worldwide expenses in the United States, because U.S. expenses will have the potential to reduce U.S. taxable income, and also increase allowable foreign tax credits relative to the no-action baseline. However, the post-Act U.S. interest expense limitation rules under section 163(j) make it more difficult to use excessive interest expense to reduce U.S. taxable income, and the significantly lower U.S. statutory corporate rate reduces the (previously strong) incentive to locate "fungible" deductions such as interest expense in the United States. Therefore, any increase in the incentive to report interest expense in the United States resulting from the reduced expense allocation to the section 951A category is likely to be relatively minor. The Treasury Department and the IRS welcome comments on this estimated impact of the reduced expense allocation.

In addition to the provisions described in the overview section above, the look-through rules provide an example of a proposed rule that fills a technical gap left by the implementation of the Act that if left unaddressed would impose significant tax uncertainty on taxpayers and negatively impact taxpayers' economic decision making. Before the Act, dividends, interest, rents and royalties ("look-through payments") paid to a United States shareholder by its CFC were generally allocated to the general category to the extent that they were not treated as passive category income. The Act split the general category income into three categories: general category, section 951A category, and foreign branch category, creating a question of how to assign non-passive category look-through payments to the two new separate categories. The Treasury Department and the IRS studied this issue and propose to revise the look-through rules to clarify that non-passive look-through payments cannot be assigned to the section 951A category but instead are generally assigned to the general category or foreign branch category. This treatment is consistent with the fact that the new section 951A category by definition cannot include payments of dividends, interest, rents, and royalties made directly to a United States shareholder. On the other hand, certain interest, rents, and royalties earned by a foreign branch can meet the definition of foreign branch category income, and the general category is a residual category that encompasses all income that is not specifically assigned to any other category.

Whether a deduction is disallowed under section 267A with respect to a payment of interest or royalties does not affect the treatment of such payment in the hands of the recipient for purposes of section 904(d)(3). Furthermore, future regulations issued under section 267A will address whether such payments that are subject to U.S. tax are subject to the disallowance under section 267A.

2. Alternatives Considered

The Treasury Department and the IRS next considered the benefits and costs of providing these specific methodologies and definitions regarding FTC calculations relative to possible alternatives. In choosing among alternatives, the Treasury Department and the IRS strive to adhere to Congressional intent and consistency with existing law, while minimizing economic distortions and compliance burdens imposed on taxpayers, and promoting market-driven decision making and administrative feasibility.

The Act created two new separate categories with respect to FTCs, splitting the existing general category into general, section 951A, and foreign branch categories. The Act did not, however, specify how FTC carryovers were to be treated. The Treasury Department and the IRS considered alternative methods of allocating FTC carryovers originally associated with the general category to the new section 951A and foreign branch categories. One option that was considered would have required taxpayers to reassign existing general category FTC carryovers to the section 951A category as if that category existed prior to the adoption of the statute. Allocating carryovers to the section 951A category was deemed infeasible because it would be extraordinarily burdensome on taxpayers to attempt to recreate historical GILTI and would present numerous technical challenges. Such an approach would also result in eliminating the ability of taxpayers to credit those FTC carryovers since no carryovers are allowed for FTCs attributable to the section 951A category. This outcome would negatively impact taxpayers that had potentially structured their prior decisions on their presumed ability to use these FTC carryovers against U.S. tax on general category income and could result in costly and undesirable financial statement adjustments for some companies without providing any corresponding economic efficiency gains.

By contrast, allocating carryovers to the foreign branch category would be technically feasible and therefore does not present the same technical challenges as allocating FTC carryovers to the section 951A category would. However, with respect to FTC carryovers and the foreign branch category, the Treasury Department and the IRS first considered providing no additional guidance beyond the existing statutory language, which would mean that FTC carryovers would remain in the general category and none would be reassigned to the foreign branch category. However, requiring FTC carryovers to remain in the general category would potentially prevent taxpayers with substantial historic and continuing branch operations and who previously incurred taxes on their branch income from being able to utilize FTC carryovers in future years because general category carryovers would not be available to offset U.S. tax on future foreign branch category income. This outcome would negatively impact taxpayers that had potentially structured their prior decisions on their presumed ability to use these FTC carryovers to reduce U.S. tax on what became their future foreign branch category income.

As an alternative, the Treasury Department and the IRS considered requiring that all taxpayers do a computation to assign general category FTC carryovers to the foreign branch category. The concept of branch income existed prior to TCJA, and thus there would have been continuity in the assignment of pre- and post-TCJA FTCs associated with foreign branch category income. However, these FTC carryovers had previously been allocated to the general category and hence some taxpayers had potentially structured their prior decisions on their presumed ability to use these taxes against U.S. tax on general category income. Therefore, reassigning such FTC carryovers after the fact could create perverse incentives for some taxpayers to restructure their ongoing operations into branch form in order to generate foreign branch category income that can absorb FTC carryovers that were reassigned to the foreign branch category. Furthermore, requiring taxpayers to reconstruct prior year events in order to determine what income and FTCs would have been associated with the foreign branch category would be burdensome for taxpayers, again with no corresponding efficiency gains. The benefit of matching income and FTCs which applies more generally as a principle of economically efficient taxation is less relevant in this context because the foreign taxes have already been incurred.

On the basis of these considerations of compliance burden and efficiency gains (or lack thereof), the proposed regulations settled on an approach whereby FTC carryovers would by default remain in the general category but the regulations also provide an option to allow taxpayers to allocate transitional FTC carryovers to the foreign branch category. The Treasury Department and the IRS chose this approach in response to some taxpayers' concerns that their business and investment plans were based on the presumption that FTC carryovers could be used against U.S. tax on general category income and precluding them from using FTCs in this way would have negative economic implications. On the other hand, taxpayers whose foreign branch category income could absorb greater levels of FTCs can self-select into reconstructing what income and FTCs would have been associated with the foreign branch category income. Thus, taxpayers for whom the costs exceed the benefits would choose to retain the FTCs in the general category, while taxpayers for whom the benefits exceed the costs would choose to incur the costs of doing the computation. This rule provides the most flexibility, continuity, and compliance cost savings to taxpayers with respect to these transitional FTC carryovers.

The Treasury Department and the IRS also faced the question of how to align interest income and interest expenses related to loans to a partnership from a U.S. partner. The Treasury Department and the IRS chose to match interest income allocation to interest expense allocation, rather than the reverse, because this minimizes distortions that could arise in the apportionment of other types of expenses. Under the matching rule in the proposed regulations, the gross interest income is apportioned between U.S. and foreign sources in each separate category based on a taxpayer's interest expense apportionment ratios. The Treasury Department and the IRS considered an alternative approach of tracing expenses to gross income under which the gross interest income would, under the general rules for sourcing interest income, be 100 percent foreign source income if paid by a foreign partnership not engaged in a U.S. trade or business. Some deductions, such as general and administrative expenses, can be apportioned on the basis of gross income to foreign sources. A rule that did not alter the source of the gross interest income would affect the allocation and apportionment of these other expenses, such as general and administrative expenses, that can be allocated on the basis of gross income to foreign sources. The matching rule limits these distortions because it minimizes the artificial increase in gross foreign source income based solely on a related party loan to a partnership. Accordingly, the proposed matching rule achieves a more neutral foreign tax credit limitation result and better minimizes the impact of related party loans on a taxpayer's foreign tax credit limitation.

The Treasury Department and the IRS considered two options with respect to the application of the section 245A deduction to section 78 dividends. The first option considered was to do nothing and allow taxpayers with fiscal year CFCs to get a double benefit, leaving taxpayers with calendar year CFCs at a relative disadvantage. An additional drawback of this approach is that taxpayers with fiscal year CFCs would likely face uncertainty with respect to their tax positions, as the availability of a section 245A deduction to a section 78 dividend may be anticipated to be deemed inappropriate and ultimately be reversed. Such delayed changes would force taxpayers that are publicly traded companies to issue costly restatements of their financial accounts, which could result in stock market volatility. The second option considered was to eliminate this inequity of tax treatment between taxpayers with calendar year CFCs versus fiscal year CFCs by providing that section 78 dividends relating to taxable years beginning before January 1, 2018, are not treated as dividends for purposes of the section 245A deduction. The advantage of this approach is that it eliminates the disparate tax treatment of otherwise similarly situated taxpayers because it removes the unintended benefit for taxpayers with fiscal year CFCs. This approach also promotes economic efficiency by resolving the uncertainty related to the availability of a section 245A deduction to a section 78 dividend. The latter option is the approach adopted in the proposed regulations.

II. *Paperwork Reduction Act*

The rules relating to foreign tax credits that were modified by the Act are reflected in several revised and new schedules added to existing forms. For purposes of the Paperwork Reduction Act of 1995 (44 U.S.C. 3507(d)) ("PRA"), the reporting burden associated with the revised and new schedules will be reflected in the IRS Forms 14029, Paperwork Reduction Act Submission, associated with the forms described in this Part II.

Form 1118, Foreign Tax Credit - Corporations, has been revised to add new Schedule C (Tax Deemed Paid With Respect to Section 951(a)(1) Inclusions by Domestic Corporation Filing Return (Section 960(a)), Schedule D (Tax Deemed Paid With Respect to Section 951A Income by Domestic Corporation Filing the Return (Section 960(d)), and Schedule E (Tax Deemed Paid With Respect to Previously Taxed Income by Domestic Corporation Filing the Return (Section 960(b)). In addition, the existing schedules of Form 1118 have been modified to account for the two new separate categories of income under section 904(d); the repeal of section 902 indirect credits for foreign taxes deemed paid with respect to dividends from foreign corporations; modified indirect credits under section 960 for inclusions under sections 951(a)(1) and 951A; modified section 78 gross up with respect to inclusions under sections 951(a)(1) and 951A; the revised sourcing rule for certain income from the sale of inventory under section 863(b); the repeal of the fair market value method for apportioning interest expense under 864(e); new adjustments for purposes of section 904 with respect to expenses allocable to certain stock or dividends for which a dividends received deduction is allowed under section 245A; the election to increase pre-2018 section 904(g) Overall Domestic Loss (ODL) recapture; and limited foreign tax credits with respect to inclusions under section 965. For purposes of the PRA, the reporting burden associated with these changes is reflected in the IRS Form 14029, Paperwork Reduction Act Submission, associated with Form 1118 (OMB control number 1545-0123, which represents a total estimated burden time, including all other related forms and schedules, of 3.157 billion hours and total estimated monetized costs of $58.148 billion).

Form 5471, Information Return of U.S. Persons With Respect to Certain Foreign Corporations, has also been revised to add Schedule E-1 (Taxes Paid, Accrued, or Deemed Paid on Accumulated Earnings and Profits (E&P) of Foreign Corporation) and Schedule P (Previously Taxed Earnings and Profits of U.S. Shareholder of Certain Foreign Corporations) and to amend Schedule E (Income, War Profits, and Excess Profits Taxes Paid or Accrued) and Schedule J (Accumulated Earnings & Profits (E&P) of Controlled Foreign Corporations). These changes to the Form 5471 reflect the two new separate categories of income under section 904(d); the repeal of section 902 indirect credits for foreign taxes deemed paid with respect to dividends from foreign corporations; modified indirect credits under section 960 for inclusions under sections 951(a)(1) and 951A; and limited foreign tax credits with respect to inclusions under section 965. For purposes of the PRA, the reporting burden associated with these changes is reflected in the IRS Form 14029, Paperwork Reduction Act Submission, associated with Schedules E, E-1, J, and P of Form 5471 (OMB control number 1545-0123).

Schedule B (Specifically Attributable Taxes and Income (Section 999(c)(2)) of the Form 5713, International Boycott Report, has also been revised to reflect the repeal of section 902. Schedule C (Tax Effect of the International Boycott Provisions) of the Form 5713 has been revised to account for the new section 904(d) categories of income. For purposes of the PRA, the reporting burden associated with these changes is reflected in the IRS Form 14029, Paperwork Reduction Act Submission, associated with Schedules B and C of Form 5713 (OMB control number 1545-0216, which represents a total estimated burden time, including all other related forms and schedules, of 143,498 hours).

Schedules K and K-1 of the following forms have been revised to account for the new section 904(d) categories of income: Form 1065, U.S. Return of Partnership Income, Form 1120-S, U.S. Income Tax Return for an S Corporation, and Form 8865, Return of U.S. Persons With Respect to Certain Foreign Partnerships. Form 1116, Foreign Tax Credit (Individual, Estate, or Trust), has also been revised to account for the new section 904(d) categories of income. For purposes of the PRA, the reporting burden associated with these changes is reflected in the IRS Form 14029, Paperwork Reduction Act Submission, associated with Forms 1065 and 1120S (OMB control number 1545-0123), associated with Form 8865 (OMB control number 1545-1668, which represents a total estimated burden time, including all other related forms and schedules, of 289,354 hours), and associated with Form 1116 (OMB control numbers 1545-0121, which represents a total estimated burden time, including all other related forms and schedules, of 25,066,693 hours; and 1545-0074, which represents a total estimated burden time, including all other related forms and schedules, of 1.784 billion hours and total estimated monetized costs of $31.764 billion).

The IRS estimates the number of affected filers for the aforementioned forms to be the following:

Form	Number of Respondents* (estimated)
Form 1116	8,000,000
Form 1118	15,000
Form 1065	4,000,000
Form 1065 Schedule K-1	24,750,000
Form 1120-S	4,750,000

Form	Number of Respondents* (estimated)
Form 1120-S Schedule K-1	7,500,000
Form 5471	28,000
Form 5471 Schedule E	10,000
Form 5471 Schedule J	25,500
Form 5713 Schedule B	<1,000
Form 5713 Schedule C	<1,000
Form 8865	14,500

Data tabulated from 2015 and 2016 Business Return Transaction File and E-file data.

* Except for K-1 filings, which count the total number of K-1s received; same issuer K-1s are aggregated at the recipient level.

The current status of the Paperwork Reduction Act submissions related to foreign tax credits is provided in the following table. The burden estimates provided in the above narrative are aggregate amounts that relate to the entire package of forms associated with the OMB control number, and include but do not isolate the estimated burden of only the foreign tax credit-related forms that are included in the tables in this Part II. The Treasury Department and the IRS have assumed that any burden estimates and forms, including new information collections, related to foreign tax credits capture changes made by the Act and that no additional information collection burdens arise out of discretionary authority exercised in these regulations. The Treasury Department and the IRS welcome comments on all aspects of information collection burdens related to the foreign tax credit. In addition, the IRS forms will be posted and available for comment at https://apps.irs.gov/app/picklist/list/draftTaxForms.html.

Form	Type of Filer	OMB Number(s)	Status
Form 1116	All other Filers (mainly trusts and estates) (Legacy system)	1545-0121	Approved by OMB through 10/30/2020.
	Link: https://www.reginfo.gov/public/do/PRAViewICR?ref_nbr=201704-1545-023		
	Business (NEW Model)	1545-0123	Published in the Federal Register Notice (FRN) on 10/8/18. Public Comment period closes on 12/10/18.
	Link: https://www.federalregister.gov/documents/2018/10/09/2018-21846/proposed-collection-comment-request-for-forms-1065-1065-b-1066-1120-1120-c-1120-f-1120-h-1120-nd		
	Individual (NEW Model)	1545-0074	Limited Scope submission (1040 only) on 10/11/18 at OIRA for review. Full ICR submission (all forms) scheduled in 3-2019. 60 Day FRN not published yet for full collection.
	Link: https://www.reginfo.gov/public/do/PRAViewICR?ref_nbr=201808-1545-031		
Form 1118	Business (NEW Model)	1545-0123	Published in the FRN on 10/8/18. Public Comment period closes on 12/10/18.
	Link https://www.federalregister.gov/documents/2018/10/09/2018-21846/proposed-collection-comment-request-for-forms-1065-1065-b-1066-1120-1120-c-1120-f-1120-h-1120-nd		
Form 1065 (including Schedule K-1)	Same as above	Same as above	Same as above
	Link: Same as above.		
Form 1120-S (including Schedule K-1)	Same as above	Same as above	Same as above

Form	Type of Filer	OMB Number(s)	Status
	Link: Same as above.		
	Business (NEW Model)	1545-0123	Published in the FRN on 10/8/18. Public Comment period closes on 12/10/18.
Form 5471 (including Schedules E, J)	Link: https://www.federalregister.gov/documents/2018/10/09/2018-21846/proposed-collection-comment-request-for-forms-1065-1065-b-1066-1120-1120-c-1120-f-1120-h-1120-nd		
	Individual (NEW Model)	1545-0074	Limited Scope submission (1040 only) on 10/11/18 at OIRA for review. Full ICR submission for all forms in 3-2019. 60 Day FRN not published yet for full collection.
	Link: https://www.reginfo.gov/public/do/PRAViewICR?ref_nbr=201808-1545-031		
	All other Filers (mainly trusts and estates) (Legacy system)	1545-0216	Published in the FRN on 3/28/18. Public Comment period closed 5/29/18. Renewal submitted on 10/11/18 for review to OIRA. New 2018 Forms not included in renewal to OIRA due to timing of submission.
Form 5713 Schedules B, C	Link: https://www.federalregister.gov/documents/2018/10/29/2018-23515/agency-information-collection-activities-submission-for-omb-review-comment-request-multiple-internal https://www.reginfo.gov/public/do/PRAViewICR?ref_nbr=201807-1545-001		
	Business (NEW Model)	1545-0123	Published in the FRN on 10/11/18. Public Comment period closes on 12/10/18.
	Link: https://www.federalregister.gov/documents/2018/10/09/2018-21846/proposed-collection-comment-request-for-forms-1065-1065-b-1066-1120-1120-c-1120-f-1120-h-1120-nd		
	Individual (NEW Model)	1545-0074	Limited Scope submission (1040 only) on 10/11/18 at OIRA for review. Full ICR submission for all forms in 3-2019. 60 Day FRN not published yet for full collection.
	Link: https://www.reginfo.gov/public/do/PRAViewICR?ref_nbr=201808-1545-031		
	All other Filers (mainly trusts and estates) (Legacy system)	1545-1668	Published in the FRN on 10/1/18. Public Comment period closes on 11/30/18. ICR in process by Treasury as of 10/17/18.
Form 8865	Link: https://www.federalregister.gov/documents/2018/10/01/2018-21288/proposed-collection-comment-request-for-regulation-project		
	Business (NEW Model)	1545-0123	Published in the FRN on 10/8/18. Public Comment period closes on 12/10/18.
	Link: https://www.federalregister.gov/documents/2018/10/09/2018-21846/proposed-collection-comment-request-for-forms-1065-1065-b-1066-1120-1120-c-1120-f-1120-h-1120-nd		

Form	Type of Filer	OMB Number(s)	Status
	Individual (NEW Model)	1545-0074	Limited Scope submission (1040 only) on 10/11/18 at OIRA for review. Full ICR submission for all forms in 3-2019. 60 Day FRN not published yet for full collection.
	Link: https://www.reginfo.gov/public/do/PRAViewICR?ref_nbr=201808-1545-031		

III. *Regulatory Flexibility Act*

Pursuant to the Regulatory Flexibility Act (5 U.S.C. chapter 6), it is hereby certified that this regulation, if adopted, will not have a significant economic impact on a substantial number of small entities within the meaning of section 601(6) of the Regulatory Flexibility Act.

The proposed regulations provide guidance needed to comply with statutory changes and affect individuals and corporations claiming foreign tax credits. The domestic small business entities that are subject to the foreign tax credit rules in the Code and this notice of proposed rulemaking are generally those domestic small business entities that are at least 10 percent corporate shareholders of foreign corporations, and so are eligible to claim dividends-received deductions or compute foreign taxes deemed paid under section 960 with respect to inclusions under subpart F and section 951A from controlled foreign corporations. Other provisions of the Act, such as the new separate foreign tax credit limitation category for foreign branch income and the repeal of the option to allocate and apportion interest expense on the basis of the fair market value (rather than tax basis) of a taxpayer's assets, might also affect domestic small business entities that operate in foreign jurisdictions. Data about the number of domestic small business entities potentially affected by these aspects of the Act, and therefore potentially by these proposed regulations, is not readily available.

However, the Treasury Department and IRS do not believe a substantial number of domestic small business entities will be affected by this notice of proposed rulemaking. Many of the more significant aspects of the proposed regulations, including all of the rules in proposed §§1.861-8(d)(2)(C), 1.861-10, 1.861-12, 1.861-13, 1.901(j)-1, 1.904-5, 1.904(b)-3, 1.954-1, 1.960-1 through 1.960-3, and 1.965-7 apply only to United States persons that operate a foreign business in corporate form, and, in most cases, only if the foreign corporation is a CFC. Because it takes significant resources and investment for a foreign business to operate outside of the United States in corporate form, and in particular to own a CFC, the owners of such businesses will infrequently be domestic small business entities. Consequently, the Treasury Department and the IRS do not believe that the proposed regulations will affect a substantial number of domestic small business entities. The Treasury Department and the IRS welcome comments regarding the amount and types of domestic small business entities that may be affected by this rule.

The Treasury Department and the IRS also do not believe that the proposed regulations will have a substantial economic effect on domestic small business entities. See Table below. Based on published information from 2013, foreign tax credits as a percentage of three different tax-related measures of annual receipts (see Table for variables) by corporations are substantially less than the 3 to 5 percent threshold for significant economic impact. The amount of foreign tax credits in 2013 is an upper bound on the change in foreign tax credits resulting from the proposed regulations.

Size (by Business Receipts)	under $500,000	$500,000 under $1,000,000	$1,000,000 under $5,000,000	$5,000,000 under $10,000,000	$10,000,000 under $50,000,000	$50,000,000 under $100,000,000	$100,000,000 under $250,000,000	$250,000,000 or more
FTC/Total Receipts	0.03%	0.00%	0.00%	0.01%	0.01%	0.03%	0.09%	0.56%
FTC/(Total Receipts-Total Deductions)	0.48%	0.03%	0.04%	0.26%	0.22%	0.51%	1.20%	9.00%
FTC/Business Receipts	0.05%	0.00%	0.00%	0.01%	0.01%	0.04%	0.10%	0.64%

Source: Statistics of Income (2013) Form 1120 available at https://www.irs.gov/statistics

To the extent a domestic small business entity is affected by the Act, the proposed regulations help reduce their compliance costs by providing clarity, certainty, and flexibility to the taxpayer regarding how to take into account the changes made by the Act in claiming foreign tax credits. Therefore, a Regulatory Flexibility Analysis under the Regulatory Flexibility Act is not required with respect to the proposed regulations.

Notwithstanding this certification, the Treasury Department and the IRS invite comments on the impact of this rule on small entities.

Pursuant to section 7805(f), this notice of proposed rulemaking has been submitted to the Chief Counsel for Advocacy of the Small Business Administration for comment on its impact on small businesses. The Treasury Department and the IRS invites the public to comment on this certification.

IV. *Unfunded Mandates Reform Act*

Section 202 of the Unfunded Mandates Reform Act of 1995 (UMRA) requires that agencies assess anticipated costs and benefits and take certain other actions before issuing a final rule that includes any Federal mandate that may result in expenditures in any one year by a state, local, or tribal government, in the aggregate, or by the private sector, of $100 million in 1995 dollars, updated annually for inflation. In 2018, that threshold is approximately $150 million. This rule does not include any Federal mandate that may result in expenditures by state, local, or tribal governments, or by the private sector in excess of that threshold.

V. *Executive Order 13132: Federalism*

Executive Order 13132 (entitled "Federalism") prohibits an agency from publishing any rule that has federalism implications if the rule either imposes substantial, direct compliance costs on state and local governments, and is not required by statute, or preempts state law, unless the agency meets the consultation and funding requirements of section 6 of the Executive Order. This proposed rule does not have federalism implications and does not impose substantial direct compliance costs on state and local governments or preempt state law within the meaning of the Executive Order.

Comments and Requests for Public Hearing

Before the proposed regulations are adopted as final regulations, consideration will be given to any comments that are submitted timely to the IRS as prescribed in this preamble under "Addresses." The Treasury Department and the IRS request comments on all aspects of the proposed rules. All comments will be available at www.regulations.gov or upon request. A public hearing will be scheduled if requested in writing by any person that timely submits comments. If a public hearing is scheduled, notice of the date, time, and place for the public hearing will be published in the **Federal Register**.

Drafting Information

The principal authors of the proposed regulations are Karen J. Cate, Jeffrey P. Cowan, Jeffrey L. Parry, Larry R. Pounders, and Suzanne M. Walsh of the Office of Associate Chief Counsel (International). However, other personnel from the Treasury Department and the IRS participated in their development.

[¶49,782] Proposed Amendments of Regulations (REG-132881-17), published in the Federal Register on December 18, 2018.

[Code Secs. 1441, 1461, 1471, 1473 and 1474]

Withholding: Nonresident aliens: Foreign financial institutions (FFIs): Non-financial foreign entities (NFFEs): Foreign Account Tax Compliance Act (FATCA): Foreign passthru payments.—Amendments of Reg. §§1.1441-1, 1.1441-6, 1.1461-1, 1.1461-2, 1.1471-1—1.1471-5, 1.1473-1, 1.1474-1 and 1.1474-2, eliminating withholding on payments of gross proceeds, deferring withholding on foreign passthru payments, eliminating withholding on certain insurance premiums, and clarifying the definition of investment entity, are proposed.

AGENCY: Internal Revenue Service (IRS), Treasury.

ACTION: Notice of proposed rulemaking.

SUMMARY: This document contains proposed regulations eliminating withholding on payments of gross proceeds, deferring withholding on foreign passthru payments, eliminating withholding on certain insurance premiums, and clarifying the definition of investment entity. This notice of proposed rulemaking also includes guidance concerning certain due diligence requirements of withholding agents and guidance on refunds and credits of amounts withheld.

DATES: Written or electronic comments and requests for a public hearing must be received by February 16, 2019.

ADDRESSES: Send submissions to: CC:PA:LPD:PR (REG-132881-17), Internal Revenue Service, Room 5203, PO Box 7604, Ben Franklin Station, Washington, DC 20044. Submissions may also be hand-delivered Monday through Friday between the hours of 8 a.m. and 4 p.m. to CC:PA:LPD:PR (REG-132881-17), Courier's Desk, Internal Revenue Service, 1111 Constitution Avenue, NW, Washington, DC 20224; or sent electronically via the Federal eRulemaking Portal at *http://www.regulations.gov* (IRS REG-132881-17).

FOR FURTHER INFORMATION CONTACT: Concerning the proposed regulations, John Sweeney, Nancy Lee, or Subin Seth, (202) 317-6942; concerning submissions of comments and/or requests for a public hearing, Regina Johnson, (202) 317-6901 (not toll free numbers).

SUPPLEMENTARY INFORMATION:

Background

This document contains amendments to the Income Tax Regulations (26 CFR part 1) under chapter 4 (sections 1471 through 1474) commonly known as the Foreign Account Tax Compliance Act (FATCA). This document also contains amendments to the Income Tax Regulations (26 CFR part 1) under sections 1441 and 1461.

On January 28, 2013, the Department of the Treasury (Treasury Department) and the IRS published final regulations under chapter 4 in the **Federal Register** (TD 9610, 78 FR 5873), and on September 10,

2013, corrections to the final regulations were published in the **Federal Register** (78 FR 55202). The regulations in TD 9610 and the corrections thereto are collectively referred to in this preamble as the 2013 final chapter 4 regulations. On March 6, 2014, the Treasury Department and the IRS published temporary regulations under chapter 4 (TD 9657, 79 FR 12812) that clarify and modify certain provisions of the 2013 final chapter 4 regulations, and corrections to the temporary regulations were published in the **Federal Register** on July 1, 2014, and November 18, 2014 (79 FR 37175 and 78 FR 68619, respectively). The regulations in TD 9657 and the corrections thereto are referred to in this preamble as the 2014 temporary chapter 4 regulations. A notice of proposed rulemaking cross-referencing the 2014 temporary chapter 4 regulations was published in the **Federal Register** on March 6, 2014 (79 FR 12868).

On March 6, 2014, the Treasury Department and the IRS published temporary regulations under chapters 3 and 61 in the **Federal Register** (TD 9658, 79 FR 12726) to coordinate with the regulations under chapter 4, and corrections to those temporary regulations were published in the **Federal Register** (79 FR 37181) on July 1, 2014. Collectively, the regulations in TD 9657 and the corrections thereto are referred to in this preamble as the 2014 temporary coordination regulations. A notice of proposed rulemaking cross-referencing the 2014 temporary coordination regulations was published in the **Federal Register** on March 6, 2014 (79 FR 12880).

On January 6, 2017, the Treasury Department and the IRS published final and temporary regulations under chapter 4 in the **Federal Register** (TD 9809, 82 FR 2124), and corrections to those final regulations were published on June 30, 2017 in the **Federal Register** (82 FR 27928). Collectively, the regulations in TD 9809 and the corrections thereto are referred to in this preamble as the 2017 chapter 4 regulations. A notice of proposed rulemaking cross-referencing the temporary regulations in TD 9809 and proposing regulations under chapter 4 relating to verification requirements for certain entities was published in the **Federal Register** on January 6, 2017 (82 FR 1629). Also on January 6, 2017, the Treasury Department and the IRS published final and temporary regulations under chapters 3 and 61 in the **Federal Register** (TD 9808, 82 FR 2046), and corrections to those final regulations were published on June 30, 2017 in the **Federal Register** (82 FR 29719). Collectively, the regulations in TD 9808 and the corrections thereto are referred to in this preamble as the 2017 coordination regulations. A notice of proposed rulemaking cross-referencing the temporary regulations in TD 9808 was published in the **Federal Register** on January 6, 2017 (82 FR 1645).

Pursuant to Executive Order 13777, Presidential Executive Order on Enforcing the Regulatory Reform Agenda (82 FR 9339), the Treasury Department is responsible for conducting a broad review of existing regulations. In a Request for Information published on June 14, 2017 (82 FR 27217), the Treasury Department invited public comment concerning regulations that should be modified or eliminated in order to reduce unnecessary burdens. In addition, in Notice 2017-28 (2017-19 I.R.B. 1235), the Treasury Department and the IRS invited public comment on recommendations for the 2017–2018 Priority Guidance Plan for tax guidance, including recommendations relating to Executive Order 13777. In response to the invitations for comments in the Request for Information and Notice 2017-28, the Treasury Department and the IRS received comments suggesting modifications to the regulations under chapters 3 and 4. See also Executive Order 13789, Identifying and Reducing Tax Regulatory Burdens, issued on April 21, 2017 (82 FR 19317) and the second report issued in response (82 FR 48013) (stating that the Treasury Department continues to analyze all recently issued significant regulations and is considering possible reforms of recent regulations, which include regulations under chapter 4).

Based on public input, and taking into account the burden-reducing policies described in Executive Orders 13777 and 13789, these regulations propose certain amendments to the regulations under chapters 3 and 4, including certain refund related issues for which comments were received. The Explanation of Provisions section of this preamble describes these proposed amendments and addresses public comments received in response to the Request for Information and Notice 2017-28, other than comments that would require a statutory change or were addressed in prior Treasury decisions. The Explanation of Provisions section of this preamble also discusses comments to the 2017 chapter 4 regulations and 2017 coordination regulations to the extent the comments relate to amendments that are included in these proposed regulations. The Treasury Department and the IRS continue to study other public comments.

Explanation of Provisions

I. *Elimination of Withholding on Payments of Gross Proceeds from the Sale or Other Disposition of Any Property of a Type Which Can Produce Interest or Dividends from Sources Within the United States*

Under sections 1471(a) and 1472, withholdable payments made to certain foreign financial institutions (FFIs) and certain non-financial foreign entities (NFFEs) are subject to withholding under chapter 4. Section 1473(1) states that, except as otherwise provided by the Secretary, the term "withholdable payment" means: (i) Any payment of interest (including any original issue discount), dividends, rents, salaries, wages, premiums, annuities, compensations, remunerations, emoluments, and other fixed or determinable annual or periodical gains, profits, and income, if such payment is from sources within the United States; and (ii) any gross proceeds from the sale or other disposition of any property of a type which can produce interest or dividends from sources within the United States.

Since the enactment of chapter 4, the Treasury Department and the IRS have received comments from withholding agents on the burden of implementing a requirement to withhold on gross proceeds. The comments have noted in particular the lead time required to implement such a requirement and the potential complexity of a sufficient regulatory framework. The comments assert that withholding on gross proceeds would require significant efforts by withholding agents, including executing brokers that do not obtain tax documentation. The comments assert that adding this withholding requirement is of limited incremental benefit in supporting the objectives of chapter 4 with respect to foreign entities investing in U.S. securities. In response to these comments, the Treasury Department and the IRS have repeatedly issued guidance deferring the date when withholding on gross proceeds would begin. The 2017 chapter 4 regulations provide that such withholding will begin on January 1, 2019.

Many U.S. and foreign financial institutions, foreign governments, the Treasury Department, the IRS, and other stakeholders have devoted substantial resources to implementing FATCA withholding on withholdable payments. At the same time, 87 jurisdictions have an IGA in force or in effect and 26 jurisdictions are treated as having an IGA in effect because they have an IGA signed or agreed in substance, which allows for international cooperation to facilitate FATCA implementation. The Treasury Department and the IRS have determined that the current withholding requirements under chapter 4 on U.S. investments already serve as a significant incentive for FFIs investing in U.S. securities to avoid status as nonparticipating FFIs, and that withholding on gross proceeds is no longer necessary in light of the current compliance with FATCA. For these reasons, under the authority provided under section 1473(1) these proposed regulations would eliminate withholding on gross proceeds by removing gross proceeds from the definition of the term "withholdable payment" in § 1.1473-1(a)(1) and by removing certain other provisions in the chapter 4 regulations that relate to withholding on gross proceeds. As a result of these proposed changes to the chapter 4 regulations, only payments of U.S. source FDAP that are withholdable payments under § 1.1473-1(a) and that are not otherwise excepted from withholding under § 1.1471-2(a) or (b) would be subject to withholding under sections 1471(a) and 1472.

II. *Deferral of Withholding on Foreign Passthru Payments*

An FFI that has an agreement described in section 1471(b) in effect with the IRS is required to withhold on any passthru payments made to its recalcitrant account holders and to FFIs that are not compliant with chapter 4 (nonparticipating FFIs). Section 1471(d)(7) defines a "passthru payment" as any withholdable payment or other payment to the extent attributable to a withholdable payment.

In Notice 2010-60 (2010-37 I.R.B. 329), the Treasury Department and the IRS requested comments on methods a participating FFI could use to determine whether payments it makes are attributable to withholdable payments. In Notice 2011-34 (2011-19 I.R.B. 765), the Treasury Department and the IRS set forth a proposed framework for participating FFIs to withhold on such payments based on a methodology for determining a "passthru payment percentage" to be applied to certain payments made by FFIs. After the publication of Notice 2011-34, stakeholders noted the burdens and complexities in implementing a system for withholding on these payments along the lines of that described in the notice. In light of those comments, the framework outlined in Notice 2011-34 was not incorporated into the 2013 final chapter 4 regulations. In addition, the Treasury Department and the IRS have repeatedly issued guidance deferring the date when withholding on these payments would begin (referred to in guidance as "foreign passthru payments"). The 2017 chapter 4 regulations provide that such withholding will not begin until the later of January 1, 2019, or the date of publication in the **Federal Register** of final regulations defining the term "foreign passthru payment."

The Treasury Department and the IRS have received comments noting that withholding on foreign passthru payments may not be needed given the number of IGAs in effect. One comment also recommended that if the Treasury Department and the IRS determine, based on an evaluation of the data received from FFIs on payments to nonparticipating FFIs in 2015 and 2016, that withholding on foreign passthru payments is necessary, the Treasury Department and the IRS should develop a more targeted solution.

Both in recognition of the time necessary to implement a system for withholding on foreign passthru payments and in recognition of the successful engagement of Treasury and partner jurisdictions to conclude intergovernmental agreements to implement FATCA, these proposed regulations further extend the time for withholding on foreign passthru payments. Accordingly, under proposed regulation § 1.1471-4(b)(4), a participating FFI will not be required to withhold tax on a foreign passthru payment made to a recalcitrant account holder or nonparticipating FFI before the date that is two years after the date of publication in the **Federal Register** of final regulations defining the term "foreign passthru payment." The proposed regulations also make conforming changes to other provisions in the chapter 4 regulations that relate to foreign passthru payment withholding.

Notwithstanding these proposed amendments, the Treasury Department and the IRS remain concerned about the long-term omission of withholding on foreign passthru payments. The Treasury Department and the IRS acknowledge the progress made in implementing FATCA. Nevertheless, concerns remain regarding account holders of participating FFIs that remain recalcitrant account holders or nonparticipating FFIs and regarding payments made to nonparticipating FFIs. Withholding on foreign passthru payments serves important purposes. First, it provides one way for an FFI that has entered into an FFI agreement to continue to remain in compliance with its agreement, even if some of its account holders have failed to provide the FFI with the information necessary for the FFI to properly determine whether the accounts are U.S. accounts and perform the required reporting, or, in the case of account holders that are FFIs, have failed to enter into an FFI agreement. Second, withholding on foreign passthru payments prevents nonparticipating FFIs from avoiding FATCA by investing in the United States through a participating FFI "blocker." For example, a participating FFI that is an investment entity could receive U.S. source FDAP income free of withholding under chapter 4 and then effectively pay the amount over to a nonparticipating FFI as a corporate distribution. Despite being attributable to the U.S. source payment, the payment made to the nonparticipating FFI may be treated as foreign source income and therefore not a withholdable payment subject to chapter 4 withholding.

Accordingly, the Treasury Department and the IRS continue to consider the feasibility of a system for implementing withholding on foreign passthru payments. The Treasury Department and the IRS request additional comments from stakeholders on alternative approaches that would serve the same compliance objectives as would foreign passthru payment withholding and that could be more efficiently implemented by FFIs.

III. *Elimination of Withholding on Non-Cash Value Insurance Premiums Under Chapter 4*

Under § 1.1473-1(a)(1), a withholdable payment generally includes any payment of U.S. source FDAP income, subject to certain exclusions, such as for "excluded nonfinancial payments." Excluded nonfinancial payments do not include premiums for insurance contracts. The 2013 final chapter 4 regulations included, however, a transitional rule that deferred withholding on payments with respect to offshore obligations until January 1, 2017, which was extended in the 2014 chapter 4 regulations to include premiums paid by persons acting as insurance brokers with respect to offshore obligations. Additionally, in response to comments noting the burden of providing to withholding agents withholding certificates and withholding statements for payments of insurance premiums, the chapter 4 regulations provide a rule generally allowing a withholding agent to treat as a U.S. payee a U.S. broker receiving a payment of an insurance premium in its capacity as an intermediary or an agent of a foreign insurer. The IRS also generally permits non-U.S. insurance brokers that are NFFEs to become qualified intermediaries in order to alleviate burden on the foreign brokers and U.S. withholding agents.

Notwithstanding these allowances, the Treasury Department and the IRS continued to receive comments requesting elimination of withholding under chapter 4 on premiums for insurance contracts that do not have cash value (non-cash value insurance premiums). The comments cited the burden on insurance brokers of documenting insurance carriers, intermediaries, and syndicates of insurers for chapter 4 purposes, noting examples to demonstrate the volume and complexity of placements with insurers of the insurance policies typically arranged by the brokers for their clients. The comments argued that withholding on non-cash value insurance premiums is not necessary to further the purposes of chapter 4.

At the same time, certain foreign entities that conducted a relatively small amount of insurance business had taken the position that they were not passive foreign investment companies (PFICs) under section 1297(a). Section 1297(a) generally defines a PFIC as a foreign corporation if 75 percent or more of the corporation's gross income for the taxable year is passive income or 50 percent or more of its assets produce, or are held for the production of, passive income. Section 1297(b)(2)(B), prior to a recent change in law (described below), provided an exception from the U.S. owner reporting and anti-deferral rules applicable to PFICs for corporations "predominantly engaged" in an insurance business. Withholding under chapter 4 on non-cash value insurance premiums strengthened the IRS's enforcement efforts, with respect to the use of the exception in section 1297(b)(2)(B) by U.S. owners of foreign corporations for tax avoidance and evasion, by facilitating reporting of the U.S. owners to avoid withholding on premiums received by the entity.

The preamble to the 2017 chapter 4 regulations noted that future changes to the PFIC rules may create an opportunity to revise the treatment of foreign insurance companies under chapter 4. 82 FR 2140. On December 22, 2017, the Tax Cuts and Jobs Act, Pub.L. No. 115-97 (2017) amended section 1297(b)(2)(B) to provide a more limited exception to PFIC status by replacing the exception for corporations predominantly engaged in an insurance business with a more stringent test based generally on a comparison of the corporation's insurance liabilities and its total assets. This amendment is expected to mitigate the need for reporting on the U.S. owners of these companies under chapter 4 because the Treasury Department and the IRS anticipate that these entities will either amend their business models on account of the change in law or will otherwise comply with the PFIC reporting requirements.

In light of the aforementioned change in law and in furtherance of the burden-reducing policies in Executive Orders 13777 and 13789, these proposed regulations provide that premiums for insurance contracts that do not have cash value (as defined in § 1.1471-5(b)(3)(vii)(B)) are excluded nonfinancial payments and, therefore, not withholdable payments.

IV. *Clarification of Definition of Investment Entity*

Under § 1.1471-5(e)(4)(i)(B), an entity is an investment entity (and therefore a financial institution) if the entity's gross income is primarily attributable to investing, reinvesting, or trading in financial assets and the entity is "managed by" another entity that is a depository institution, custodial institution, insurance company, or an investment entity described in § 1.1471-5(e)(4)(i)(A). Section 1.1471-5(e)(4)(v), *Example 2*, illustrates this rule with an example in which a fund is an investment entity because another financial institution (an investment advisor) provides investment advice to the fund and has discretionary management of the assets held by a fund and the fund meets the gross income test. In *Example 6* of § 1.1471-5(e)(4)(v), a trust is an investment entity because the trustee (an

FFI) manages and administers the assets of the trust in accordance with the terms of the trust instrument and the trust meets the gross income test. Section 1.1471-5(e)(4)(v), *Example 8*, provides an example in which an entity is an investment entity because an introducing broker (that is, a broker using another broker to clear and settle its trades) has discretionary authority to manage the entity's assets and provides services as an investment advisor and manager to the entity and the entity meets the gross income test.

The Treasury Department and the IRS received a comment requesting that "discretionary authority" be more narrowly construed for purposes of treating an entity as an investment entity described in § 1.1471-5(e)(4)(i)(B). The comment suggested that an entity should not be treated as an investment entity solely because the entity invests in a mutual fund or similar vehicle because the investments made by the mutual fund are not tailored to the entity that invests in it. The comment requested the same result for a variety of other types of investment products and solutions with varying degrees of investor involvement and standardization, including an investment in a "discretionary mandate." According to the comment, a "discretionary mandate" is an investment product or solution offered by a financial institution to certain clients where the financial institution manages and invests the client's funds directly (rather than the client investing in a separate entity) in accordance with the client's investment goals. The comment noted that some discretionary mandate clients claim to be passive NFFEs rather than FFIs.

As described in the examples, the "managed by" category of investment entities generally covers entities that receive specific professional management advice from an advisor that is tailored to the investment needs of the entity. A financial institution does not have discretionary authority over an entity merely because it sells the entity shares in a widely-held fund that employs a predetermined investment strategy. These proposed regulations clarify that an entity is not "managed by" another entity for purposes of § 1.1471-5(e)(4)(i)(B) solely because the first-mentioned entity invests all or a portion of its assets in such other entity, and such other entity is a mutual fund, an exchange traded fund, or a collective investment entity that is widely held and is subject to investor-protection regulation. In contrast, an investor in a discretionary mandate described above is "managed by" the financial institution under § 1.1471-5(e)(4)(i)(B).

The clarification in these proposed regulations is similar to the guidance published by the OECD interpreting the definition of a "managed by" investment entity under the Common Reporting Standard.

V. *Modifications to Due Diligence Requirements of Withholding Agents Under Chapters 3 and 4*

A. *Treaty statements provided with documentary evidence for chapter 3*

Under chapter 3, a withholding agent must generally obtain either a withholding certificate or documentary evidence and a treaty statement in order to apply a reduced rate of withholding based on a payee's claim for benefits under a tax treaty. The 2017 coordination regulations added a requirement that when a treaty statement is provided with documentary evidence by an entity beneficial owner to claim treaty benefits, the statement must identify the specific limitation on benefits (LOB) provision relied upon in the treaty. In addition, the 2017 coordination regulations added a three-year validity period applicable to treaty statements provided with documentary evidence and a transition period that expires January 1, 2019, for withholding agents to obtain new treaty statements that comply with the new LOB requirement for accounts that were documented with documentary evidence before January 6, 2017 (preexisting accounts). The QI agreement in Revenue Procedure 2017-15, 2017-3 I.R.B. 437 (2017 QI agreement) cross-references the 2017 coordination regulations for the three-year validity period for treaty statements provided with documentary evidence and provides a two-year transition rule for accounts documented before January 1, 2017. Similar provisions are included in the WP and WT agreements in Revenue Procedure 2017-21, 2017-6 I.R.B. 791 (2017 WP and WT agreements).

Comments have noted the burden of complying with the new treaty statement requirements, including difficulties in obtaining new treaty statements for preexisting accounts within the transitional period given the large number of account holders impacted by this requirement. The comments requested an additional one-year period for withholding agents to obtain new treaty statements for preexisting accounts, and the removal of the three-year validity period for a treaty statement that meets the LOB requirement. A comment also noted that a three-year validity period for a treaty statement is not needed for certain categories of entities whose treaty status is unlikely to change, such as publicly traded corporations and government entities.

In response to these comments, these proposed regulations include several changes to the rules on treaty statements provided with documentary evidence. First, these proposed regulations extend the time for withholding agents to obtain treaty statements with the specific LOB provision identified for preexisting accounts until January 1, 2020 (rather than January 1, 2019). Second, these proposed regulations add exceptions to the three-year validity period for treaty statements provided by tax exempt organizations (other than tax-exempt pension trusts or pension funds), governments, and publicly traded corporations, entities whose qualification under an applicable treaty is unlikely to change. See proposed § 1.1441-1(e)(4)(ii)(A)(2). In addition, these proposed regulations correct an inadvertent omission of the actual knowledge standard for a withholding agent's reliance on the beneficial owner's identification of an LOB provision on a treaty statement provided with documentary evidence, the same as the standard that applies to a withholding certificate used to make a treaty claim. See proposed § 1.1441-6(c)(5)(i). The proposed amendments described in this section V.A. will also be incorporated into the 2017 QI agreement and 2017 WP and WT agreements, and a QI, WP, or WT may rely upon these proposed modifications until such time.

B. *Permanent residence address subject to hold mail instruction for chapters 3 and 4*

In response to comments received on the 2014 temporary coordination regulations and the 2014 QI agreement regarding the definition of a "permanent residence address," the 2017 coordination regulations (and the 2017 chapter 4 regulations by cross-reference) allow an address to be treated as a permanent residence address despite being subject to a hold mail instruction when a person provides documentary evidence establishing residence in the country in which the person claims to be a resident for tax purposes. Comments noted that the allowance to obtain documentary evidence establishing residence in a particular country is unnecessarily strict when the person is not claiming treaty benefits, and that it is unclear what documentary evidence may be used to establish residence for purposes of this allowance.

These proposed regulations provide that the documentary evidence required in order to treat an address that is provided subject to a hold mail instruction as a permanent residence address is documentary evidence that supports the person's claim of foreign status or, for a person claiming treaty benefits, documentary evidence that supports the person's residence in the country where the person claims treaty benefits. Regardless of whether the person claims treaty benefits, the documentary evidence on which a withholding agent may rely is the documentary evidence described in § 1.1471-3(c)(5)(i), without regard to the requirement that the documentation contain a permanent residence address.

A comment also requested the removal of any limitation on reliance on a permanent residence address subject to a hold mail instruction because many account holders prefer to receive electronic correspondence rather than paper mail. In response to this comment, proposed § 1.1471-1(b)(62) adds a definition of a hold mail instruction to clarify that a hold mail instruction does not include a request to receive all correspondence (including account statements) electronically.

These proposed regulations apply for purposes of chapters 3 and 4. A QI, WP, or WT may rely upon these proposed modifications until they are incorporated into the 2017 QI agreement and 2017 WP and WT agreements.

VI. *Revisions Related to Credits and Refunds of Overwithheld Tax*

A. *Withholding and reporting in a subsequent year*

Under § 1.1441-5(b)(2)(i)(A), a U.S. partnership is required to withhold on an amount subject to chapter 3 withholding (as defined in § 1.1441-2(a)) that is includible in the gross income of a partner that is a foreign person. A U.S. partnership satisfies this requirement by withholding on distributions to the foreign partner that include an amount subject to chapter 3 withholding. To the extent a foreign partner's distributive share of income subject to chapter 3 withholding is not actually distributed to the partner, the U.S. partnership must withhold on the partner's distributive share of the income on the earlier of the date that the statement required under section 6031(b) (Schedule K-1, Partner's Share of Income, Deductions, Credits, etc.) is mailed or otherwise provided to the partner or the due date for furnishing the statement. Under section 6031(b), a partnership that files its return for a calendar year (calendar-year partnership) must generally furnish to each partner a Schedule K-1 on or before March 15 following the close of the taxable year, a due date that may be extended up to six months. See § § 1.6031(b)-1T(b) and 1.6081-2T(a). Similar requirements apply to a foreign partnership that has entered into an agreement with the IRS to act as a WP. See the 2017 WP agreement. A foreign partnership other than a WP generally satisfies its withholding requirement in the same manner for amounts received from a withholding agent that failed to withhold to the extent required. See § 1.1441-5(c)(2) and (c)(3)(v). For purposes of chapter 4, similar withholding rules apply to a partnership that receives a withholdable payment allocable to a foreign partner. See § 1.1473-1(a)(5)(ii) and (vi).

Under § 1.1461-1(c)(1) and (2), a partnership is required to report on Form 1042-S, Foreign Person's U.S. Source Income Subject to Withholding, any amount subject to withholding that is allocable to a foreign partner for a calendar year. The partnership must file Form 1042-S (and furnish a copy to the partner) by March 15 of the calendar year following the year in which it receives the amount subject to withholding. The due date for filing a Form 1042-S may be automatically extended by 30 days (and an additional 30 days at the discretion of the IRS). See § 1.6081-8T(a). Amounts that are reportable on Forms 1042-S are also required to be reported on a withholding agent's income tax return, Form 1042, Annual Withholding Tax Return for U.S. Source Income of Foreign Persons. The due date for Form 1042 is March 15, which may be automatically extended for six months. See § 1.6081-10. Similar reporting rules apply to a partnership that receives a withholdable payment and withholds under chapter 4. See § 1.1474-1(c) and (d)(1).

Because the extended due date for filing a Form 1042-S generally occurs before the extended due date for furnishing a Schedule K-1 to a foreign partner, a partnership may be required to report an amount subject to withholding on a Form 1042-S before it performs all of the withholding required on such amount under § 1.1441-5(b)(2)(i)(A) or § 1.1473-1(a)(5)(ii) and (vi). To address this case, the Instructions for Form 1042 require a domestic partnership to report any withholding that occurs with respect to an amount that a partnership received but did not distribute to a partner in a calendar year (preceding year) on the partnership's Form 1042 for the following calendar year (subsequent year) (referred to as the "lag method" of reporting). In this case, the partnership would deposit the amount in the subsequent year and designate the deposit as made for that year for reporting on Form 1042. To correspond to the timing of the reporting on Form 1042, the partnership must also report this withholding on Forms 1042-S filed and issued for the subsequent year. For example, a calendar year domestic partnership that receives U.S. source dividends in 2017 (but does not make a distribution to its foreign partners), must withhold on the foreign partners' share of the dividend income by the time the partnership issues Schedules K-1 to the foreign partners, which could be as late as September 15, 2018. The lag method of reporting requires the partnership to report the withholding on the Forms 1042-S and 1042 for the 2018 year (which are issued and filed in 2019). The WP agreement includes a similar requirement to that described in this paragraph when a WP withholds after the due date for Form 1042-S (including extensions). The Instructions for Form 1042 provide a similar reporting rule for a domestic trust that withholds in a subsequent year on income of the trust that it is required to distribute but has not actually distributed to a foreign beneficiary. See § 1.1441-5(b)(2)(ii) and (iii). The WT agreement includes a similar requirement for a WT.

Apart from the cases described in the preceding paragraph, in certain other cases, a withholding agent is permitted to withhold an amount in a subsequent year that relates to the preceding year. For example, a withholding agent adjusting underwithholding under § 1.1461-2(b) or § 1.1474-2(b) may withhold the additional amount by the due date (without extensions) of Form 1042. In these cases, the Instructions for Form 1042 provide that, in contrast to the reporting required by partnerships and certain trusts described in the preceding paragraph, a withholding agent withholding in a subsequent year must designate the deposit and report the tax for the preceding year.

Comments have noted issues that arise under the lag method when a partner files an income tax return to report the partnership income allocated to the partner and to claim credit under section 33 (or a refund) based on the partnership's withholding. When a partnership applies the lag method, it issues a Form 1042-S for the subsequent year (and the related withholding) that generally reflects the income received by the partnership in the preceding year. However, the income is reported to the partner on Schedule K-1 for the preceding year, thus resulting in a mismatch between the income allocated to the partner and the withholding on that income. Because a partner must attach to its income tax return a Form 1042-S that it receives from a partnership to claim a credit or refund of overwithholding under § 301.6402-3(e), the partner cannot support the claim with the Form 1042-S until after the year in which the partner is required to report the income shown on the Schedule K-1.

These proposed regulations generally require a withholding agent (including a partnership or trust) that withholds in a subsequent year to designate the deposit as attributable to the preceding year and report the amount on Forms 1042 and 1042-S for the preceding year. This proposed rule incorporates the existing rule for withholding agents (other than partnerships and trusts) from the form instructions, and extends the rule to partnerships and trusts. An exception to this requirement for a partnership that is not a calendar-year partnership (a fiscal-year partnership) provides that such partnership may designate a deposit as made for the subsequent year and report the amount on Forms 1042 and 1042-S for the subsequent year. This exception allows a fiscal-year partnership flexibility to determine the year for reporting that will result in the best matching of the income and the related withholding.

These proposed regulations also provide a revised due date for a partnership to file and furnish Form 1042-S when it withholds the tax after March 15 of the subsequent year that it designates as deposited for the preceding year. Under this new rule, the due date for a partnership to file and furnish a Form 1042-S in such a case will be September 15 of the subsequent year. This revised due date corresponds to the due date for a partnership to file Form 1042 with an extension and the due date for a calendar-year partnership to furnish a Schedule K-1 to a partner with an extension so that the partnership has sufficient time to determine the amount of withholding due and to coordinate with the extended due date for furnishing the Schedule K-1.

Based on the revisions included in these proposed regulations, the IRS intends to amend the Instructions for the 2019 Form 1042 to remove the requirement that a partnership or trust apply the lag method and to incorporate these proposed regulations. The IRS also intends to amend the Instructions to the 2019 Form 1042-S to require that in a case when a partnership is filing Form 1042-S after March 15 for a partner's distributive share of an amount received by the partnership in the preceding year, the partnership must file and issue a separate Form 1042-S for such amount for the preceding year (in addition to any Forms 1042-S filed and issued to the partner for amounts that are withheld when distributed to the partner before March 15 and reported for the preceding year).

The Treasury Department and the IRS intend to amend the WP and WT agreements to the extent necessary to incorporate the proposed regulations, and until such time a WP or WT may rely on these proposed modifications for purposes of its filing and deposit requirements.

B. *Adjustments to overwithholding under the reimbursement and set-off procedures*

Under § 1.1461-2(a), a withholding agent that has overwithheld and deposited the tax may adjust the overwithheld amount under either the reimbursement procedure or the set-off procedure. Under the reimbursement procedure, a withholding agent may repay the beneficial owner or payee the amount of tax overwithheld and then reimburse itself by reducing, by the amount of such repayment, any deposit of withholding tax otherwise required to be made before the end of the calendar year following the year of overwithholding. The withholding agent must make any repayment to the beneficial owner or payee before the earlier of the due date for filing Form 1042-S (without extensions) for the calendar year of overwithholding or the date on which the Form 1042-S is actually filed with the IRS, and must state on a timely filed Form 1042 (without extensions) for the calendar year of overwithholding that the filing constitutes a claim for credit in accordance with § 1.6414-1.

Under the set-off procedure, a withholding agent may apply the overwithheld amount against any amount which would otherwise be subject to withholding that is paid to the beneficial owner or payee before the earlier of the due date for filing Form 1042-S (without extensions) for the calendar year of overwithholding or the date that the Form 1042-S is actually filed with the IRS. Similar rules for adjusting overwithholding apply for purposes of chapter 4. See § 1.1474-2(a)(3) and (4).

If a withholding agent cannot apply the reimbursement or set-off procedure, a beneficial owner or payee must file a claim for credit or refund with the IRS in order to recover the overwithheld tax. Informal comments have requested to expand the cases in which a withholding agent may apply the reimbursement and set-off procedures in order to limit the need for a beneficial owner or payee to claim a credit or refund. These proposed regulations respond to these comments by modifying the reimbursement procedure to allow a withholding agent to use the extended due date for filing Forms 1042 and 1042-S to make a repayment and claim a credit. These proposed regulations also include revisions to conform the requirements for the set-off procedures to those that apply to the reimbursement procedures. In addition, these proposed regulations remove the requirement that a withholding agent include with its Form 1042 a statement that the filing constitutes a claim for credit when it applies reimbursement in the year following the year of the overwithholding. This statement is no longer necessary because Form 1042 was revised in 2016 to provide separate fields for adjustments to overwithholding and underwithholding.

These proposed regulations also provide that a withholding agent may not apply the reimbursement and set-off procedures after the date on which Form 1042-S has been furnished to the beneficial owner or payee (in addition to, under the current regulations, after the date a Form 1042-S has been filed). Because of the liberalizing amendments described in the preceding paragraph, this change is needed to ensure that a Form 1042-S furnished to a beneficial owner or payee reflects any repayments made pursuant to these adjustment procedures and is consistent with the associated Form 1042-S that is filed with the IRS. A QI, WP, or WT may rely upon the proposed modifications described in this section VI.B until they are incorporated into the 2017 QI agreement and 2017 WP and WT agreements.

C. *Reporting of withholding by nonqualified intermediaries*

A withholding agent that makes a payment subject to chapter 3 withholding to a nonqualified intermediary (as defined in § 1.1441-1(c)(14)) can reliably associate the payment with documentation when it obtains a valid intermediary withholding certificate (that is, Form W-8IMY, Certificate of Foreign Intermediary, Foreign Flow-Through Entity, or Certain U.S. Branches for United States Tax Withholding) from the nonqualified intermediary and a withholding statement that allocates the payment among the payees and includes the documentation for each payee as described in § 1441-1(b)(2)(vii)(B) and (e)(3)(iii). For purposes of chapter 4, a withholding agent making a withholdable payment to a nonqualified intermediary that is a participating FFI or a registered deemed-compliant FFI may rely on a withholding statement that includes an allocation of the payment to a chapter 4 withholding rate pool of payees, and must obtain payee-specific documentation for payees that are not includible in a chapter 4 withholding rate pool to permit any reduced rate of withholding. See § 1.1471-3(c)(3)(iii)(B).

To the extent that a withholding agent cannot reliably associate a withholdable payment made to a nonqualified intermediary with valid documentation under § 1.1471-3(c), the withholding agent must presume that the payment is made to a nonparticipating FFI and withhold 30 percent of the payment. See § 1.1471-3(f)(5). In such a case, the withholding agent is required to report the payment as a chapter 4 reportable amount made to an unknown recipient on a Form 1042-S that reports the nonqualified intermediary as an intermediary and the amount withheld as chapter 4 withholding. See the Instructions for Form 1042-S. If the amount withheld upon under chapter 4 is an amount subject to withholding under chapter 3, the withholding agent is relieved from its obligation to also withhold under chapter 3 on the payment. § 1.1441-3(a)(2). To the extent that a nonqualified intermediary is required to report the same payments to its account holders on Forms 1042 and 1042-S under the chapter 3 or 4 regulations, the nonqualified intermediary need not withhold when chapter 3 or 4 withholding has already been applied by its withholding agent, and it substantiates the withholding by attaching to its Form 1042 a copy of the Form 1042-S furnished by the withholding agent.

Comments have noted that some U.S. withholding agents charge fees for the administrative burden associated with reviewing underlying documentation that is included with a withholding statement provided by a nonqualified intermediary. In other cases, nonqualified intermediaries may not be able to obtain such documentation from account holders. For these reasons, some nonqualified intermediaries provide withholding agents with valid Forms W-8IMY to establish their chapter 4 statuses but do not provide any underlying payee documentation or withholding rate pool information to substantiate the allocations to payees shown on a withholding statement. Comments have stated that the requirement for withholding agents to report the withholding applied to withholdable payments as chapter 4 withholding in these cases (because the payees are presumed to be nonparticipating FFIs) has made it difficult for account holders to claim foreign tax credits from foreign jurisdictions that do not view the chapter 4 withholding tax as a creditable income tax. These comments recommended various proposals to allow a nonqualified intermediary to report the withholding as chapter 3 withholding applied to its account holders.

In response to the comments described in the preceding paragraph, these proposed regulations modify the rules for reporting by a nonqualified intermediary under §§1.1461-1(c)(4)(iv) and 1.1474-1(d)(2)(ii) to address a case in which a nonqualified intermediary receives a payment for which a withholding agent has withheld at the 30-percent rate under chapter 4 and reported the payment on Form 1042-S as made to an unknown recipient. In such a case, these proposed regulations permit a nonqualified intermediary that is a participating FFI or registered deemed-compliant FFI to report the withholding applied to the nonqualified intermediary on a Form 1042-S as chapter 3 withholding to the extent that the nonqualified intermediary determines that the payment is not an amount for which withholding is required under chapter 4 based on the payee's chapter 4 status. Under the existing reporting requirements, the nonqualified intermediary would be required to file a Form 1042 and would need to be furnished a copy of the Form 1042-S filed by the withholding agent to substantiate the credit against its withholding tax liability for the withholding applied by its withholding agent. Under the modified requirement, the nonqualified intermediary would be permitted to substantiate the credit even though the Form 1042-S furnished to it reports chapter 4 withholding and the corresponding Forms 1042-S that the nonqualified intermediary issues reports chapter 3 withholding. This change should assist account holders using Form 1042-S to claim foreign tax credits in their jurisdictions of residence in these cases. The Treasury Department and the IRS are of the view that this determination should be limited to a nonqualified intermediary that is a participating FFI or registered deemed-compliant FFI given the role of these FFIs in documenting their account holders for chapter 4 purposes and their compliance requirements under the chapter 4 regulations or an applicable IGA jurisdiction.

Reliance on Proposed Regulations

Under section 7805(b)(1)(C), taxpayers may rely on the proposed regulations until final regulations are issued, except as otherwise provided in this paragraph. With respect to the elimination of withholding on non-cash value insurance premiums under proposed §1.1473-1(a)(3)(iii), the clarification of the definition of a "managed by" investment entity under proposed §1.1471-5(e)(4)(i)(B), and the revised allowance for a permanent residence address subject to a hold mail instruction under proposed §§1.1441-1(c)(38) and 1.1471-1(b)(99), taxpayers may apply the modifications in these proposed regulations for all open tax years until final regulations are issued. For the revisions included in these proposed regulations that relate to credits and refunds of withheld tax, taxpayers may not rely on these proposed regulations until Form 1042 and Form 1042-S are updated for the 2019 calendar year.

Special Analyses

The Administrator of the Office of Information and Regulatory Affairs (OIRA), Office of Management and Budget (OMB), has waived review of this proposed rule in accordance with section 6(a)(3)(A) of Executive Order 12866. OIRA will subsequently make a significance determination of the final rule, pursuant to section 3(f) of Executive Order 12866 and the April 11, 2018, Memorandum of Agreement between the Treasury Department and the OMB.

The Treasury Department and the IRS expect the proposed regulation, when final, to be an Executive Order 13771 deregulatory action and request comment on this designation.

Paperwork Reduction Act

The collection of information contained in these proposed regulations is in a number of provisions, including §§1.1441-1, 1.1461-1, 1.1461-2, 1.1474-1, and 1.1474-2. The IRS intends that the information collection requirements of these regulations will be implemented through the use of Forms 1042 and 1042-S. As a result, for purposes of the Paperwork Reduction Act (44 U.S.C. 3507), the reporting burden associated with the collection of information in these regulations will be reflected in the information burden and OMB control number of the appropriate IRS form.

An agency may not conduct or sponsor, and a person is not required to respond to, a collection of information unless the collection of information displays a valid control number.

The proposed regulations will not increase the number of taxpayers required to file a return. Current filers may have to modify slightly how they report, but the burden of reporting should not increase.

As described in section VI.A of the Explanations of Provisions, the proposed regulations allow a partnership that withholds in a subsequent year to designate the deposit as attributable to the preceding year and report the withholding on Forms 1042 and 1042-S for the preceding year (rather than the subsequent year). In addition, the proposed regulations allow a partnership that withholds after March 15 of the subsequent year to file Form 1042-S on or before September 15 of such year. The IRS intends to modify Form 1042-S to add a check box to the form so that a partnership filer can indicate that it qualifies for the September 15 due date for filing the form. A partnership that relies on the September 15 due date may need to file an additional Form 1042-S if it is filing to report a partner's distributive share of an amount received by the partnership in the preceding year and it has already filed a Form 1042-S for such partner for the same year. Information on the number of partnerships that withhold in a year subsequent to the year in which the amount was received is not available. However, as an upper bound, table 1 shows the estimated number of partnerships that file Form 1042.

As explained in section IV.B of the Explanation of Provisions, the proposed regulations provide additional time for withholding agents to apply the reimbursement or set-off procedure to adjust overwithholding. The proposed revision may increase the amounts reported by filers of Forms 1042 and 1042-S, but should not affect the number of filers. It is unknown how many withholding agents will use the reimbursement and set-off procedures as a result of the modifications to those procedures in the proposed regulations. However, as an upper bound, table 1 shows the estimated number of withholding agents that report non-zero amounts as adjustments to overwithholding.

Finally, as described in section IV.C of the Explanation of Provisions, the proposed regulations permit certain nonqualified intermediaries to report on certain payments on Form 1042-S using the code for chapter 3 withholding rather than the code for chapter 4 withholding in certain cases in which chapter 4 withholding is applied on payments made to the nonqualified intermediaries. This modification in the proposed regulations should not affect the number of filers or increase any burdens, but rather change how nonqualified intermediaries report to certain recipients. It is not possible to estimate the number of nonqualified intermediaries that may change the code from chapter 4 to chapter 3, so as an upper bound, table 1 shows the estimated number of withholding agents that are nonqualified intermediaries that file Form 1042-S.

Table 1: Related Tax Form Counts

	Number of respondents (estimated)
Total number of Form 1042 filers	45,000 - 50,000
Partnership filers of Form 1042	2,000 – 3,000
Form 1042 filers reporting adjustments to overwithholding	4,000 – 5,000
Nonqualified intermediaries filers of Form 1042-S	500

Tax Form 1042 data are from administrative tax files while the Form 1042-S information is from a 2016 data file on foreign tax withholding.

Books and records relating to a collection of information must be retained as long as their contents may be material in the administration of any internal revenue law. Generally, tax returns and tax return information are confidential, as required by 26 U.S.C. 6103.

Regulatory Flexibility Act

It is hereby certified that the collection of information requirements in this notice of proposed rulemaking will not have a significant economic impact on a substantial number of small business entities within the meaning of section 601(6) of the Regulatory Flexibility Act (5 U.S.C. chapter 6). This notice of proposed rulemaking reduces the information required to be reported under chapters 3 and 4 as required by TDs 9610, 9657, 9658, 9808, and 9809, information collections that were certified by the Treasury Department and the IRS as not resulting in a significant economic impact on a substantial number of small business entities. The burden-reducing information collections of this notice of proposed rulemaking provide benefits for small business entities consistent with the Regulatory Flexibility Act's objective that information collections achieve statutory objectives while minimizing any significant impact on small business entities. Therefore, a Regulatory Flexibility Analysis is not required.

Pursuant to section 7805(f), this regulation has been submitted to the Chief Counsel for Advocacy of the Small Business Administration for comment on its impact on small businesses.

Statement of Availability of IRS Documents

IRS Revenue Procedures, Revenue Rulings, Notices, and other guidance cited in this preamble are published in the Internal Revenue Bulletin (or Cumulative Bulletin) and are available from the Superintendent of Documents, U.S. Government Publishing Office, Washington, DC 20402, or by visiting the IRS website at *www.irs.gov*.

Comments and Requests for Public Hearing

Before these proposed regulations are adopted as final regulations, consideration will be given to any comments that are submitted timely to the IRS as prescribed in this preamble under the "Addresses" heading. The Treasury Department and the IRS request comments on all aspects of the proposed rules but specifically on foreign passthru payment withholding and the definition of investment entity, as discussed in section II of the Explanation of Provisions. All comments will be available for public inspection and copying. A public hearing will be scheduled if requested in writing by any person that timely submits written comments. If a public hearing is scheduled, notice of the date, time, and place for the public hearing will be published in the **Federal Register**.

Drafting Information

The principal authors of these proposed regulations are John Sweeney, Nancy Lee, and Subin Seth, Office of Associate Chief Counsel (International). However, other personnel from the IRS and the Treasury Department participated in their development.

[¶49,783] Proposed Amendments of Regulations (REG-104259-18), published in the Federal Register on December 21, 2018.

[Code Secs. 59A, 383, 1502, 6038A and 6655]

Tax Cuts and Jobs Act (TCJA): Base erosion: Anti-abuse tax.—Reg. §§1.59A-1—1.59A-10, 1.1502.59A and amendments of Reg. §§1.383-1, 1.1502-2, 1.1502-4, 1.1502-43, 1.1502-47, 1.1502-100, 1.6038A-1, 1.6038A-2, 1.6038A-4 and 1.6655-5 regarding the tax on base erosion payments of

taxpayers with substantial gross receipts and reporting requirements thereunder, are proposed. Proposed Reg. § 1.1502-2 proposed on December 30, 1992, is withdrawn.

AGENCY: Internal Revenue Service (IRS), Treasury.

ACTION: Notice of proposed rulemaking.

SUMMARY: This document contains proposed regulations that provide guidance regarding the tax on base erosion payments of taxpayers with substantial gross receipts and reporting requirements thereunder. The proposed regulations would affect corporations with substantial gross receipts that make payments to foreign related parties. The proposed regulations under section 6038A would affect any reporting corporations within the meaning of section 6038A or 6038C.

DATES: Written or electronic comments and requests for a public hearing must be received by February 9, 2019.

ADDRESSES: Send submissions to CC:PA:LPD:PR (REG-104259-18), room 5203, Internal Revenue Service, PO Box 7604, Ben Franklin Station, Washington, DC 20044. Submissions may be hand delivered Monday through Friday between the hours of 8 a.m. and 4 p.m. to CC:PA:LPD:PR (REG-104259-18), Courier's desk, Internal Revenue Service, 1111 Constitution Avenue, NW., Washington, DC 20224, or sent electronically, via the Federal eRulemaking Portal at www.regulations.gov (IRS REG-104259-18).

FOR FURTHER INFORMATION CONTACT: Concerning §§ 1.59A-1 through -10 of the proposed regulations, Sheila Ramaswamy or Karen Walny at (202) 317-6938; concerning the services cost method exception, L. Ulysses Chatman at (202) 317-6939; concerning §§ 1.383-1, 1.1502-2, 1.1502-4, 1.1502-43, 1.1502-47, 1.1502-59A, 1.1502-100, and 1.6655-5 of the proposed regulations, Julie Wang at (202) 317-6975 or John P. Stemwedel at (202) 317-5024; concerning §§ 1.6038A-1, 1.6038A-2, and 1.6038A-4 of the proposed regulations, Brad McCormack or Anand Desai at (202) 317-6939; concerning submissions of comments and requests for a public hearing, Regina Johnson at (202) 317-6901 (not toll-free numbers).

SUPPLEMENTARY INFORMATION:

Background

This document contains proposed amendments to 26 CFR part 1 under sections 59A, 383, 1502, 6038A, 6038C, and 6655 of the Internal Revenue Code (the "Code"). The Tax Cuts and Jobs Act, Pub. L. 115-97 (2017) (the "Act"), which was enacted on December 22, 2017, added section 59A to the Code. Section 59A imposes on each applicable taxpayer a tax equal to the base erosion minimum tax amount for the taxable year (the "base erosion and anti-abuse tax" or "BEAT").

The Act also added reporting obligations regarding this tax for 25-percent foreign-owned corporations subject to section 6038A and foreign corporations subject to section 6038C and addressed other issues for which information reporting under those sections is important to tax administration.

Explanation of Provisions

I. *Overview*

These proposed regulations provide guidance under section 59A regarding the determination of the tax on base erosion payments for certain taxpayers with substantial gross receipts. In general, the proposed regulations provide rules for determining whether a taxpayer is an applicable taxpayer on which the BEAT may be imposed and rules for computing the taxpayer's BEAT liability.

Part II of this Explanation of Provisions section describes the rules in proposed § 1.59A-2 for determining whether a taxpayer is an applicable taxpayer on which the BEAT may be imposed. Part III of this Explanation of Provisions section describes the rules in proposed § 1.59A-3(b) for determining the amount of base erosion payments. Part IV of this Explanation of Provisions section describes the rules in proposed § 1.59A-3(c) for determining base erosion tax benefits arising from base erosion payments. Part V of this Explanation of Provisions section describes the rules in proposed § 1.59A-4 for determining the amount of modified taxable income, which is computed in part by reference to a taxpayer's base erosion tax benefits and base erosion percentage of any net operating loss deduction. Part VI of this Explanation of Provisions section describes the rules in proposed § 1.59A-5 for computing the base erosion minimum tax amount, which is computed by reference to modified taxable income. Part VII of this Explanation of Provisions section describes general rules in proposed § 1.59A-7 for applying the proposed regulations to partnerships. Part VIII of this Explanation of Provisions section describes certain rules in the proposed regulations that are specific to banks and registered securities dealers. Part IX of this Explanation of Provisions section describes certain rules in the proposed regulations that are specific to insurance companies. Part X of this Explanation of Provisions section describes the anti-abuse rules in proposed § 1.59A-9.

Parts XI-XIII of this Explanation of Provisions section address rules in proposed § 1.1502-59A regarding the general application of the BEAT to consolidated groups. Part XIV of this Explanation of Provisions section addresses proposed amendments to § 1.383-1 to address limitations on a loss corporation's items under section 382 and 383 in the context of the BEAT. Part XV of this Explanation of Provisions section describes reporting and record keeping requirements.

II. *Applicable Taxpayer*

The BEAT applies only to a taxpayer that is an applicable taxpayer. Proposed § 1.59A-2 provides rules for determining if a taxpayer is an applicable taxpayer.

Generally, an applicable taxpayer is a corporation (other than (1) a regulated investment company ("RIC"), (2) a real estate investment trust ("REIT"), or (3) an S corporation) that satisfies the gross receipts test and the base erosion percentage test. Section 59A and the proposed regulations provide that the taxpayer and certain other corporations that are related to the taxpayer are treated as one person for purposes of determining whether a taxpayer satisfies these tests.

Part II.A of this Explanation of Provisions section describes the proposed rules for determining the aggregate group for applying the gross receipts test and the base erosion percentage test. Part II.B of this Explanation of Provisions section describes the proposed rules for applying the gross receipts test. Part II.C of this Explanation of Provisions section describes the proposed rules for applying the base erosion percentage test. Part II.D of this Explanation of Provisions section describes the proposed rules for applying these tests on an aggregate group basis when members of the aggregate group have different taxable years. Part II.E of this Explanation of Provisions section describes proposed rules for computing the base erosion percentage for a taxpayer with deductions taken into account under a mark-to-market method of accounting.

A. *Determining the Aggregate Group for Purposes of Applying the Gross Receipts Test and the Base Erosion Percentage Test*

Section 59A(e)(3) aggregates corporations ("aggregate group") on the basis of persons treated as a single employer under section 52(a), which treats members of the "same controlled group of corporations" (as defined in section 1563(a) with certain modifications) as one person. Although a section 1563(a) controlled group can include both foreign and domestic corporations, the proposed regulations treat foreign corporations as outside of the controlled group for purposes of applying the aggregation rules, except to the extent that the foreign corporation has effectively connected income. This limitation on the extent to which foreign corporations are included in the aggregate group ensures that payments made by a domestic corporation, or a foreign corporation with respect to its effectively connected income, to a foreign related corporation are not inappropriately excluded from the base erosion percentage test. Accordingly, the proposed regulations provide that a taxpayer must apply the gross receipts test and the base erosion percentage test using the aggregate group consisting of members of the same controlled group of corporations for purposes of section 52(a) that are (i) domestic corporations and (ii) foreign corporations, but only with regard to gross receipts taken into account in determining income which is effectively connected with the conduct of a trade or business in the United States and subject to tax under section 882(a). The proposed regulations limit the aggregate group to corporations that benefit from deductions, and accordingly may have base erosion tax benefits, while excluding foreign corporations that are not subject to U.S. income tax (except on a gross basis under section 881, with respect to income that is not effectively connected with a trade or business in the United States) and do not benefit from deductions. In the case of a foreign corporation that determines its net taxable income under an applicable income tax treaty of the United States, the foreign corporation is a member of the aggregate group with regard to gross receipts taken into account in determining its net taxable income.

The proposed regulations generally provide that payments between members of the aggregate group are not included in the gross receipts of the aggregate group, consistent with the single entity concept in section 59A(e)(3). Similarly, the proposed regulations generally provide that payments between members of the aggregate group are also not taken into account for purposes of the numerator or the denominator in the base erosion percentage calculation.

Payments between the aggregate group and any foreign corporation that is not within the aggregate group with respect to the payment are taken into account in applying both the gross receipts test and the base erosion percentage test. However, because a foreign corporation is considered within the aggregate group to the extent it is subject to net income tax in the United States, payments to a foreign corporation from within the aggregate group that are subject to net income tax in the United States are eliminated and not taken into account in applying the gross receipts test and the base erosion percentage test. Thus, it may be the case that a payment by a domestic corporation to a foreign corporation is not taken into account in determining applicable taxpayer status because the payee is subject to net income tax in the United States on that payment, while another payment by the same domestic corporation to the same foreign corporation is taken into account in determining applicable taxpayer status because the payee is not subject to net income tax in the United States on that payment. The Treasury Department and the IRS welcome comments on the proposed regulations addressing the aggregate group for purposes of the gross receipts test and the base erosion percentage test.

B. *Gross Receipts Test*

A taxpayer satisfies the gross receipts test if the taxpayer, or the aggregate group of which the taxpayer is a member, has $500 million or more of average annual gross receipts during the three prior taxable years. In the case of a foreign corporation, the gross receipts test only takes into account gross receipts that are taken into account in determining income that is subject to net income tax as income effectively connected with the conduct of a trade or business within the United States, or taken into account in determining net taxable income under an applicable U.S. income tax treaty.

In the case of an aggregate group, the proposed regulations measure gross receipts of a taxpayer by reference to the taxpayer's aggregate group determined as of the end of the taxpayer's taxable year for which BEAT liability is being computed, and takes into account gross receipts of those aggregate group members during the three-year period preceding that taxable year.

The proposed regulations further clarify how a taxpayer computes gross receipts, including providing rules for corporations that have been in existence for fewer than three years or have short years. These proposed rules are generally consistent with rules set forth in section 448(c). See section 59A(e)(2)(B) (providing that rules similar to the rules of section 448(c)(3)(B) through (D) apply in determining gross receipts for purposes of section 59A). The proposed regulations also clarify how gross receipts are determined if members of the aggregate group have different taxable years, as discussed in Part II.D of this Explanation of Provisions section.

In addition, the proposed regulations clarify how gross receipts are determined for corporations subject to tax under subchapter L (including a foreign corporation subject to tax under section 842(a)).

If a member of an aggregate group owns an interest in a partnership, the proposed regulations provide that the group includes its share of the gross receipts of the partnership in its gross receipts computation. The aggregate group's share of the gross receipts of the partnership is proportionate to its distributive share of items of gross income from the partnership. See Part VII of this Explanation of Provisions section for a more detailed description of the application of section 59A to partnerships.

C. *Base Erosion Percentage Test*

The base erosion percentage test is satisfied with respect to a taxpayer if the taxpayer (or if the taxpayer is a member of an aggregate group, the aggregate group of which the taxpayer is a member) has a base erosion percentage of three percent or more. Generally, a lower threshold of two percent applies if the taxpayer, or a member of the taxpayer's aggregate group, is a member of an affiliated group (as defined in section 1504(a)(1)) that includes a domestic bank or registered securities dealer. The proposed regulations provide that the lower two percent threshold does not apply, however, in the case of an aggregate group or consolidated group that has de minimis bank or registered securities dealer activities. See Part VIII of this Explanation of Provisions section for a more detailed description of these rules.

The proposed regulations provide that the base erosion percentage for a taxable year is computed by dividing (1) the aggregate amount of base erosion tax benefits (the "numerator") by (2) the sum of the aggregate amount of deductions plus certain other base erosion tax benefits (the "denominator"). As described in Part II.A of this Explanation of Provisions section, in the case of a taxpayer that is a member of an aggregate group, the base erosion percentage is measured by reference to the deductions or certain reductions in gross income of the taxpayer and members of the taxpayer's aggregate group as of the end of the taxpayer's taxable year. Base erosion tax benefits are generally the deductions or reductions in gross income that result from base erosion payments. Part III of this Explanation of Provisions section describes the proposed rules for determining the amount of base erosion payments, and Part IV of this Explanation of Provisions section describes the proposed rules for determining the base erosion payments that give rise to base erosion tax benefits.

The numerator of the base erosion percentage excludes deductions for (i) amounts paid or accrued to foreign related parties for services qualifying for the exception in proposed § 1.59A-3(b)(3)(i) (the "services cost method ("SCM") exception"), (ii) payments covered by the qualified derivatives payments ("QDP") exception in proposed § 1.59A-3(b)(3)(ii), and (iii) amounts excluded pursuant to the total loss-absorbing capacity ("TLAC") exception in proposed § 1.59A-3(b)(3)(v). See Parts III.B.1, III.B.2, and III.B.5 of this Explanation of Provisions section, for discussions of the SCM exception, QDP exception, and TLAC exception, respectively. Generally, these deductions are also excluded from the denominator of the base erosion percentage.

An applicable taxpayer may make a payment to a foreign related party that is not a member of the aggregate group, if, for example, the recipient of the payment is a 25-percent owner as described in proposed § 1.59A-1(b)(17) who does not own more than 50 percent of the applicable taxpayer, and that payment may qualify for the ECI exception described in proposed § 1.59A-3(b)(3)(iii). If so, and if that payment also qualifies for either the SCM exception described in proposed § 1.59A-3(b)(3)(i), the QDP exception described in proposed § 1.59A-3(b)(3)(ii), or the TLAC exception described in proposed § 1.59A-3(b)(3)(v), the payment will be included in the denominator for purposes of the base erosion percentage. For example, if an applicable taxpayer makes a deductible payment to a foreign related person who is a 25-percent owner and that payment is both a QDP and subject to federal income taxation as income that is, or is treated as, effectively connected with the conduct of a trade or business in the United States under an applicable provision of the Internal Revenue Code or regulations, that deductible payment is included in the denominator of the base erosion percentage. However, if the applicable taxpayer makes a deductible payment to a foreign related person and that payment is a QDP, but not otherwise subject to federal income taxation, that deductible payment is excluded from the denominator of the base erosion percentage.

The proposed regulations also exclude any section 988 losses from the numerator and the denominator in determining the base erosion percentage. See Part III.B.4 of this Explanation of Provisions section, describing the exception for section 988 losses from the definition of base erosion payments.

The numerator of the base erosion percentage only takes into account base erosion tax benefits, which generally are base erosion payments for which a deduction is allowed under the Code for a taxable year. See Part IV of this Explanation of Provisions section. Similarly, the proposed regulations ensure that the denominator of the base erosion percentage only takes into account deductions allowed under the Code by providing that the denominator of the base erosion percentage does not include deductions that are not allowed in determining taxable income for the taxable year.

Finally, because a deduction allowed under section 965(c) to a United States shareholder of a deferred foreign income corporation is not one of the categories of deductions specifically excluded from the denominator under section 59A(c)(4)(B), that deduction is included in the denominator.

In general, as discussed in more detail in Part IV.A of this Explanation of Provisions section, if tax is imposed by section 871 or 881 and that tax has been deducted and withheld under section 1441 or 1442 on a base erosion payment, the base erosion payment is not treated as a base erosion tax benefit for purposes of calculating a taxpayer's modified taxable income. If an income tax treaty reduces the amount of withholding imposed on the base erosion payment, the base erosion payment is treated as a base erosion tax benefit to the extent of the reduction in withholding under rules similar to those in section 163(j)(5)(B) as in effect before the Act.

The proposed regulations apply the same rule concerning withholding taxes for purposes of the base erosion percentage computation. Accordingly, a base erosion tax benefit is not included in the numerator when the payment was subject to tax under section 871 or 881 and that tax has been deducted and withheld under section 1441 or 1442. In addition, the proposed regulations provide that for any base erosion payment subject to a reduced rate of withholding tax under an income tax treaty, the associated amount of base erosion tax benefits eliminated from the numerator of the base erosion percentage calculation is determined using rules similar to those in section 163(j)(5)(B) as in effect before the Act.

The base erosion percentage also takes into account the two categories of base erosion tax benefits that result from reductions in gross income rather than deductions allowed under the Code (that is, (1) certain premium or other consideration paid to a foreign related party for reinsurance, and (2) amounts paid or accrued by the taxpayer to certain surrogate foreign corporations that result in a reduction in gross receipts to the taxpayer). Section 59A(c)(4)(A)(ii)(II) provides that those base erosion tax benefits that result from reductions in gross income are included in the both the numerator and the denominator in the same amount. Other payments that reduce gross income but that are not base erosion payments are not included in the denominator of the base erosion percentage.

D. *Taxpayers in an Aggregate Group with Different Taxable Years*

Section 59A determines the status of a corporation as an applicable taxpayer on the basis of the aggregate group rules by taking into account the gross receipts and base erosion payments of each member of the aggregate group. However, each member must compute the aggregate group amount of gross receipts and base erosion payments based on its own taxable year and based on those corporations that are members of the aggregate group at the end of such taxable year. Therefore, members with different taxable years may have different base erosion percentages.

However, each corporation that is an applicable taxpayer computes its modified taxable income and base erosion minimum tax amount on a separate taxpayer basis. In the case of a group of affiliated corporations filing a consolidated tax return, the consolidated group is treated as a single taxpayer for purposes of section 59A, and its modified taxable income and base erosion minimum tax amount are determined on a consolidated group basis.

The proposed regulations provide rules for determining whether the gross receipts test and base erosion percentage test are satisfied with respect to a specific taxpayer when other members of its aggregate group have different taxable years. See proposed § 1.59A-2(e)(3)(vii). In general, the proposed regulations provide that each taxpayer determines its gross receipts and base erosion percentage by reference to its own taxable year, taking into account the results of other members of its aggregate group during that taxable year. In other words, for purposes of determining the gross receipts, base erosion tax benefits, and deductions of the aggregate group, the taxpayer must include those amounts that occur during the course of the taxpayer's own taxable year, not another member of the aggregate group's taxable year, if different. The proposed regulations adopt this approach to provide certainty for taxpayers and avoid the complexity of a rule that identifies a single taxable year for an aggregate group for purposes of section 59A that may differ from a particular member of the aggregate group's taxable year. As a result of this rule, two related taxpayers with different taxable years will compute their applicable gross receipts and base erosion percentage by reference to different periods, even though in each case the calculations are done on an aggregate group basis that takes into account other members of the controlled group. Taxpayers may use a reasonable method to determine the gross receipts and base erosion percentage information for the time period of the member of the aggregate group with a different taxable year. For an illustration of this rule, see proposed § 1.59A-2(f)(2) (*Example 2*).

The proposed regulations also provide that when determining the base erosion percentage for a taxpayer that is a member of an aggregate group with other members that have a different taxable year, the effective date in section 14401(e) of the Act, as it applies to the taxpayer making the return, controls whether that taxpayer takes into account transactions of other members of its aggregate group. (Section 14401(e) of the Act provides that section 59A applies only to base erosion payments paid or accrued in taxable years beginning after December 31, 2017.)

Thus, if one corporation (US1) that has a calendar year is a member of an aggregate group with another corporation (US2) that has a taxable year ending November 30, when US1 computes its base erosion percentage for its calendar year ending December 31, 2018, the base erosion payments made by US2 during the period from January 1, 2018, through December 31, 2018, are taken into account with respect to US1 for its computations even though US2's base erosion payments in its taxable year ending November 30, 2018, are not base erosion payments with respect to US2 because of section 14401(e) of the Act. Correspondingly, US2's taxable year beginning December 1, 2017, and ending November 30, 2018, is not subject to section 59A because US2's base erosion payments occur in a year beginning before January 1, 2018, and base erosion payments made by US1 during the period from December 1, 2017 through November 30, 2018, do not change that result. For a general discussion of the Act's effective date for section 59A, see Part III.C of this Explanation of Provisions section.

E. *Mark-to-Market Deductions*

As discussed in Part II.C of this Explanation of Provisions section, the taxpayer (or in the case of a taxpayer that is a member of an aggregate group, the aggregate group) must determine the amount of base erosion tax benefits in the numerator and the total amount of certain deductions, including base erosion tax benefits, in the denominator to determine the base erosion percentage for the year. The proposed regulations provide rules for determining the amount of base erosion tax benefits in the case of transactions that are marked to market. These proposed rules also apply for determining the total amount of the deductions that are included in the denominator of the base erosion percentage computation.

Specifically, to ensure that only a single deduction is claimed with respect to each transaction, the proposed regulations combine all income, deduction, gain, or loss on each transaction for the year to determine the amount of the deduction that is used for purposes of the base erosion percentage test. This rule does not modify the net amount allowed as a deduction pursuant to the Code and regulations. This rule is intended to prevent distortions in deductions from being included in the denominator of the base erosion percentage, including as a result of the use of an accounting method that values a position more frequently than annually.

III. *Base Erosion Payments*

The proposed regulations define a base erosion payment as a payment or accrual by the taxpayer to a foreign related party (as defined in § 1.59A-1(b)(12)) that is described in one of four categories: (1) a payment with respect to which a deduction is allowable; (2) a payment made in connection with the acquisition of depreciable or amortizable property; (3) premiums or other consideration paid or accrued for reinsurance that is taken into account under section 803(a)(1)(B) or 832(b)(4)(A); or (4) a payment resulting in a reduction of the gross receipts of the taxpayer that is with respect to certain surrogate foreign corporations or related foreign persons.

A payment or accrual that is not within one of the categories may be a base erosion payment described in one of the other categories. For example, a deductible payment related to reinsurance that does not meet the requirements for the third category of base erosion payments may still be a base erosion payment under the first category because the payment is deductible. Nonetheless, to the extent all or a portion of a payment or accrual is described in more than one of these categories, the amount is only taken into account once as a base erosion payment.

Except as otherwise provided in the proposed regulations, the determination of whether a payment or accrual by the taxpayer to a foreign related party is described in one of these four categories is made under general U.S. federal income tax law. For example, the proposed regulations do not explicitly address whether a royalty payment is classified as deductible under section 162 or as a cost includible in inventory under sections 471 and 263A resulting in a reduction in gross income under section 61.

In general, the treatment of a payment as deductible, or as other than deductible, such as an amount that reduces gross income or is excluded from gross income because it is beneficially owned by another person, generally will have federal income tax consequences that will affect the application of section 59A and will also have consequences for other provisions of the Code. In light of existing tax law dealing with identifying who is the beneficial owner of income, who owns an asset, and the related tax consequences (including under principal-agent principles, reimbursement doctrine, case law conduit principles, assignment of income or other principles of generally applicable tax law), the proposed regulations do not establish any specific rules for purposes of section 59A for determining whether a payment is treated as a deductible payment or, when viewed as part of a series of transactions, should be characterized in a different manner.

Part III.A of this Explanation of Provisions section discusses the operating rules for certain specific types of base erosion payments and Part III.B of this Explanation of Provisions section describes certain exceptions to the definition of base erosion payments.

A. *Certain Specific Types of Base Erosion Payments*

This Part III.A of this Explanation of Provisions describes proposed operating rules for determining whether there is a payment or accrual that can give rise to a base erosion payment. This part also discusses proposed rules coordinating the definition of base erosion payment with rules that allocate deductions for purposes of determining a foreign corporation's effectively connected income.

1. Payments or Accruals That Consist of Non-Cash Consideration

The proposed regulations clarify that a payment or accrual by a taxpayer to a foreign related party may be a base erosion payment regardless of whether the payment is in cash or in any form of non-cash consideration. See proposed § 1.59A-3(b)(2)(i). There may be situations where a taxpayer incurs a non-cash payment or accrual to a foreign related party in a transaction that meets one of the definitions of a base erosion payment, and that transaction may also qualify under certain nonrecognition provisions of the Code. Examples of these transactions include a domestic corporation's acquisition of depreciable assets from a foreign related party in an exchange described in section 351, a liquidation described in section 332, and a reorganization described in section 368.

The proposed regulations do not include any specific exceptions for these types of transactions even though (a) the transferor of the assets acquired by the domestic corporation may not recognize gain or loss, (b) the acquiring domestic corporation may take a carryover basis in the depreciable or amortizable assets, and (c) the importation of depreciable or amortizable assets into the United States in these transactions may increase the regular income tax base as compared to the non-importation of those assets. The Treasury Department and the IRS have determined that neither the nonrecognition of gain or loss to the transferor nor the absence of a step-up in basis to the transferee establishes a basis to create a separate exclusion from the definition of a base erosion payment. The statutory definition of this type of base erosion payment that results from the acquisition of depreciable or amortizable assets in exchange for a payment or accrual to a foreign related party is based on the amount of imported basis in the asset. That amount of basis is imported regardless of whether the transaction is a recognition transaction or a transaction subject to rules in subchapter C or elsewhere in the Code.

In contrast, for transactions in which a taxpayer that owns stock in a foreign related party receives depreciable property from the foreign related party as an in-kind distribution subject to section 301, there is no base erosion payment because there is no consideration provided by the taxpayer to the foreign related party in exchange for the property. Thus, there is no payment or accrual.

In addition, because section 59A(d)(1) defines the first category of base erosion payment as "any amount paid or accrued by the taxpayer to a foreign person which is a related party of the taxpayer and with respect to which a deduction is allowable under this chapter," a base erosion payment also includes a payment to a foreign related party resulting in a recognized loss; for example, a loss recognized on the transfer of property to a foreign related party. The Treasury Department and the IRS welcome comments about the treatment of payments or accruals that consist of non-cash consideration. See Part III.B.4 of this Explanation of Provisions section for a specific exception from the base erosion payment definition for exchange loss from a section 988 transaction.

2. Interest Expense Allocable to a Foreign Corporation's Effectively Connected Income

Section 59A applies to foreign corporations that have income that is subject to net income taxation as effectively connected with the conduct of a trade or business in the United States, taking into account any applicable income tax treaty of the United States. These proposed regulations generally provide that a foreign corporation that has interest expense allocable under section 882(c) to income that is effectively connected with the conduct of a trade or business within the United States will have a base erosion payment to the extent the interest expense results from a payment or accrual to a foreign related party. The amount of interest that will be treated as a base erosion payment depends on the method used under § 1.882-5.

If a foreign corporation uses the method described in § 1.882-5(b) through (d), interest on direct allocations and on U.S.-booked liabilities that is paid or accrued to a foreign related party will be a base erosion payment. If U.S.-booked liabilities exceed U.S.-connected liabilities, a foreign corporation computing its interest expense under this method must apply the scaling ratio to all of its interest expense on a pro-rata basis to determine the amount that is a base erosion payment. Interest on excess U.S.-connected liabilities also may be a base erosion payment if the foreign corporation has liabilities with a foreign related party.

If a foreign corporation determines its interest expense under the separate currency pools method described in § 1.882-5(e), the amount of interest expense that is a base erosion payment is equal to the sum of (1) the interest expense on direct allocations paid or accrued to a foreign related party and (2) the interest expense in each currency pool multiplied by the ratio of average foreign related party liabilities over average total liabilities for that pool. The base erosion payment exceptions discussed in Part III.B of this Explanation of Provisions section may apply and may lower the amount of interest expense that is a base erosion payment.

The Treasury Department and the IRS recognize that § 1.882-5 provides certain simplifying elections for determining the interest deduction of a foreign corporation. In particular, § 1.882-5(c) generally provides that the amount of U.S.-connected liabilities equals the total value of U.S. assets multiplied by the taxpayer's worldwide leverage ratio. However, § 1.882-5(c)(4) allows a taxpayer to elect to use a fixed ratio instead of its actual worldwide leverage ratio. Similarly, § 1.882-5(d)(5)(ii)(A) provides a general rule that the deduction for interest on excess U.S.-connected liabilities is determined by reference to the average rate of interest on U.S.-dollar liabilities that are not U.S.-booked liabilities. However, § 1.882-5(d)(5)(ii)(B) allows certain taxpayers to elect to determine the deduction by reference to the 30-day London Interbank Offering Rate. The Treasury Department and the IRS request comments about similar simplifying elections for determining the portion of U.S.-connected liabilities that are paid to a foreign related party.

3. Other Deductions Allowed with Respect to Effectively Connected Income

Like excess interest expense, the proposed regulations provide that the amount of a foreign corporation's other deductions properly allocated and apportioned to effectively connected gross income under § 1.882-4 are base erosion payments to the extent that those deductions are paid or accrued to a foreign related party. Section 1.882-4(a)(1) generally provides that a foreign corporation engaged in a trade or business within the United States is allowed the deductions which are properly allocated and apportioned to the foreign corporation's gross income which is effectively connected its conduct of a trade or business within the United States. The proposed regulations follow the approach under § 1.882-4. Accordingly, the regulations identify base erosion payments by tracing each item of deduction, and determining whether the deduction arises from a payment to a foreign related party.

If a foreign corporation engaged in a trade or business within the United States acquires property of a character subject to the allowance for depreciation (or amortization in lieu of depreciation) from a foreign related party, the amount paid or accrued by the taxpayer to the foreign related party is a base erosion payment to the extent the property is used, or held for use, in the conduct of a trade or business within the United States.

4. Income Tax Treaties

Certain U.S. income tax treaties provide alternative approaches for the allocation or attribution of business profits of an enterprise of one contracting state to its permanent establishment in the other contracting state on the basis of assets used, risks assumed, and functions performed by the permanent establishment. The use of a treaty-based expense allocation or attribution method does not, in and of itself, create legal obligations between the U.S. permanent establishment and the rest of the enterprise. These proposed regulations recognize that as a result of a treaty-based expense allocation or attribution method, amounts equivalent to deductible payments may be allowed in computing the business profits of an enterprise with respect to transactions between the permanent establishment and the home office or other branches of the foreign corporation ("internal dealings"). The deductions from internal dealings would not be allowed under the Code and regulations, which generally allow deductions only for allocable and apportioned costs incurred by the enterprise as a whole. The proposed regulations require that these deductions from internal dealings allowed in computing the business profits of the permanent establishment be treated in a manner consistent with their treatment under the treaty-based position and be included as base erosion payments.

The proposed regulations include rules to recognize the distinction between the allocations of expenses that are addressed in Parts III.A.2 and 3 of this Explanation of Provisions section, and internal dealings. In the first instance, the allocation and apportionment of expenses of the enterprise to the branch or permanent establishment is not itself a base erosion payment because the allocation represents a division of the expenses of the enterprise, rather than a payment between the branch or permanent establishment and the rest of the enterprise. In the second instance, internal dealings are not mere divisions of enterprise expenses, but rather are priced on the basis of assets used, risks assumed, and functions performed by the permanent establishment in a manner consistent with the arm's length principle. The approach in the proposed regulations creates parity between deductions for actual regarded payments between two separate corporations (which are subject to section 482), and internal dealings (which are generally priced in a manner consistent with the applicable treaty and, if applicable, the OECD Transfer Pricing Guidelines). The rules in the proposed regulations applicable to foreign corporations using this approach apply only to deductions attributable to internal dealings, and not to payments to entities outside of the enterprise, which are subject to the general base erosion payment rules as provided in proposed § 1.59A-3(b)(4)(v)(A).

5. Certain Payments to Domestic Passthrough Entities with Foreign Owners or to Another Aggregate Group Member

The proposed regulations also provide rules for certain payments to a domestic trust, REIT or RIC, and for certain payments to a related domestic corporation that is not part of a consolidated group. Proposed § 1.59A-3(b)(2)(v) provides a rule that applies when a domestic trust, REIT or RIC receives a payment that otherwise would be a base erosion payment. Proposed § 1.59A-3(b)(2)(vi) applies when a taxpayer transfers certain property to a member of an aggregate group that includes the taxpayer, to ensure that any deduction for depreciation (or amortization in lieu of deprecation) by the transferee taxpayer remains a base erosion tax benefit to the same extent as the amount that would have been a base erosion tax benefit in the hands of the transferor.

B. *Exceptions from the Base Erosion Payment Definition*

1. Exception for Certain Amounts with Respect to Services

The SCM exception described in section 59A(d)(5) provides that section 59A(d)(1) (which sets forth the general definition of a base erosion payment) does not apply to any amount paid or accrued by a taxpayer for services if (A) the services are eligible for the services cost method under section 482 (determined without regard to the requirement that the services not contribute significantly to fundamental risks of business success or failure) and (B) the amount constitutes the total services cost with no markup component. The Treasury Department and the IRS interpret "services cost method" to refer to the services cost method described in § 1.482-9(b), interpret the requirement regarding "fundamental risks of business success or failure" to refer to the test in § 1.482-9(b)(5) commonly called the business judgment rule, and interpret "total services cost" to refer to the definition of "total services costs" in § 1.482-9(j).

Section 59A(d)(5) is ambiguous as to whether the SCM exception applies when an amount paid or accrued for services exceeds the total services cost, but the payment otherwise meets the other requirements for the SCM exception set forth in section 59A(d)(5). Under one interpretation of section 59A(d)(5), the SCM exception does not apply to any portion of a payment that includes any mark-up component. Under another interpretation of section 59A(d)(5), the SCM exception is available if there is a markup, but only to the extent of the total services costs. Under the former interpretation, any amount of markup would disqualify a payment, in some cases resulting in dramatically different tax effects based on a small difference in charged costs. In addition, if any markup were required, for example because of a foreign tax law or non-tax reason, a payment would not qualify for the SCM exception. Under the latter approach, the services cost would continue to qualify for the SCM exception provided the other requirements of the SCM exception are met. The latter approach to the SCM exception is more expansive because it does not limit qualification to payments made exactly at cost.

The proposed regulations provide that the SCM exception is available if there is a markup (and if other requirements are satisfied), but that the portion of any payment that exceeds the total cost of services is not eligible for the SCM exception and is a base erosion payment. The Treasury Department and the IRS have determined that this interpretation is more consistent with the text of section 59A(d)(5). Rather than require an all-or-nothing approach to service payments, section 59A(d)(5) provides an exception for "any amount" that meets the specified test. This language suggests that a service payment may be disaggregated into its component amounts, just as the general definition of base erosion payment applies to the deductible amount of a foreign related party payment even if the entire payment is not deductible. See section 59A(d)(1). The most logical interpretation is that a payment for a service that satisfies subparagraph (A) is excepted up to the qualifying amount under subparagraph (B), but amounts that do not qualify (i.e., the markup component) are not excepted. This interpretation is reinforced by the fact that section 59A(d)(5)(A) makes the SCM exception available to taxpayers that cannot apply the services cost method described in § 1.482-9(b) (which permits pricing a services transaction at cost for section 482 purposes) because the taxpayer cannot satisfy the business judgment rule in § 1.482-9(b)(5). Because a taxpayer in that situation cannot ordinarily charge cost, without a mark-up, for transfer pricing purposes, failing to adopt this approach would render the parenthetical reference in section 59A(d)(5)(A) a nullity. The interpretation the proposed regulations adopt gives effect to the reference to the business judgment rule in section 59A(d)(5). The Treasury Department and the IRS welcome comments on whether the regulations should instead adopt the interpretation of section 59A(d)(5) whereby the SCM exception is unavailable to a payment that includes any mark-up component.

To be eligible for the SCM exception, the proposed regulations require that all of the requirements of § 1.482-9(b) must be satisfied, except as modified by the proposed regulations. Therefore, a taxpayer's determination that a service qualifies for the SCM exception is subject to review under the requirements of § 1.482-9(b)(3) and (b)(4), and its determination of the amount of total services cost and allocation and apportionment of costs to a particular service is subject to review under the rules of § 1.482-9(j) and § 1.482-9(k), respectively.

Although the proposed regulations do not require a taxpayer to maintain separate accounts to bifurcate the cost and markup components of its services charges to qualify for the SCM exception, the proposed regulations do require that taxpayers maintain books and records adequate to permit verification of, among other things, the amount paid for services, the total services cost incurred by the renderer, and the allocation and apportionment of costs to services in accordance with § 1.482-9(k). Because payments for certain services that are not eligible for the SCM due to the business judgment rule or for which taxpayers select another transfer pricing method may still be eligible for the SCM exception to the extent of total services cost, the record-keeping requirements in the proposed regulations differ from the requirements in § 1.482-9(b)(6). See § 1.59A-3(b)(3)(i)(B)(2). Unlike § 1.482-9(b)(6), the proposed regulations do not require that taxpayers "include a statement evidencing [their] intention to apply the services cost method to evaluate the arm's length charge for such services," but the proposed regulations do require that taxpayers include a calculation of the amount of profit mark-up (if any) paid for the services. For purposes of qualifying for the SCM exception under section 59A(d)(5), taxpayers are required to comply with the books and records requirements under these proposed regulations but not § 1.482-9(b)(6).

The proposed regulations also clarify that the parenthetical reference in section 59A(d)(5) to the business judgment rule prerequisite for applicability of the services cost method — "(determined without regard to the requirement that the services not contribute significantly to fundamental risks of business success or failure)" — disregards the entire requirement set forth in § 1.482-9(b)(5) solely for purposes of section 59A(d)(5).

2. Qualified Derivative Payments

Section 59A(h) provides that a qualified derivative payment (QDP) is not a base erosion payment. Proposed § 1.59A-6 defines a QDP as any payment made by a taxpayer to a foreign related party pursuant to a derivative for which the taxpayer recognizes gain or loss on the derivative on a mark-to-market basis (treats the derivative as sold on the last business day of the taxable year), the gain or loss is ordinary, and any gain, loss, income or deduction on a payment made pursuant to the derivative is also treated as ordinary.

The QDP exception applies only if the taxpayer satisfies reporting requirements in proposed § 1.6038A-2(b)(7)(ix). If a taxpayer satisfies the reporting requirements for some QDPs, but not all, then only the payments for which the taxpayer fails to satisfy the reporting requirements will be ineligible for the QDP exception. Section 1.6038A-2(b)(7)(ix) will first apply to taxable years beginning after final regulations are published, which provides taxpayers additional time to meet those reporting requirements. The proposed regulations provide that before final regulations are published, taxpayers satisfy the reporting requirements for QDPs by reporting the aggregate amount of QDPs for the taxable year on Form 8991, *Tax on Base Erosion Payments of Taxpayers With Substantial Gross Receipts*.

Section 59A(h)(3) provides two exceptions to the QDP exception. Specifically, the QDP exception does not apply (1) to a payment that would be treated as a base erosion payment if it were not made pursuant to a derivative or (2) with respect to a contract that has derivative and nonderivative components, to a payment that is properly allocable to the nonderivative component. The proposed regulations do not specifically address or modify these statutory provisions. For the avoidance of doubt, the Treasury Department and the IRS observe that these rules in section 59A(h)(3) are self-executing; thus, taxpayers must apply these two rules to determine whether any of their payments pursuant to derivatives fail to qualify for the QDP exception. The Treasury Department and the IRS request comments on whether regulations should further clarify the statutory provisions in section 59A(h)(3).

Proposed § 1.59A-6(d) defines a derivative as any contract, the value of which, or any payment with respect to which, is determined by reference to any stock, evidence of indebtedness, actively traded commodity, currency, or any rate, price, amount, index, formula or algorithm. However, direct ownership of any of these items is not ownership of a derivative. The proposed regulations clarify that for purposes of section 59A(h)(4), a derivative does not include an insurance contract, a securities lending transaction, a sale-repurchase transaction, or any substantially similar transaction.

For federal tax purposes, a sale-repurchase transaction satisfying certain conditions is treated as a secured loan. Sections 59A(h)(3) and 59A(h)(4) explicitly exclude from qualified derivatives payment status any payment that would be treated as a base erosion payment if it were not made pursuant to a derivative, such as a payment of interest on a debt instrument. Accordingly, for purposes of section 59A(h), the proposed regulations provide that sale-repurchase transactions are not treated as derivatives. Because sale-repurchase transactions and securities lending transactions are economically similar to each other, the Treasury Department and the IRS have determined that these transactions should be treated similarly for purposes of section 59A(h)(4), and therefore payments on those transactions are not treated as QDPs. The Treasury Department and the IRS request comments on whether securities lending transactions and sale-repurchase transactions have been properly excluded from the definition of a derivative, including whether certain transactions lack a significant financing component such that those transactions should be treated as derivatives for purposes of section 59A(h). The Treasury Department and the IRS also request comments regarding whether any additional transactions or financial instruments should be explicitly excluded from the definition of a derivative.

3. Exception to Base Erosion Payment Status for Payments the Recipient of which is Subject to U.S. Tax

In general, for a payment or accrual to be treated as a base erosion payment, the recipient must be a foreign person (within the meaning of section 6038A(c)(3)) that is a related party with respect to the taxpayer, and a deduction must be allowable with respect to the payment or accrual. See section 59A(f). Section 6038A(c)(3) defines "foreign person" as any person that is not a United States person within the meaning of section 7701(a)(30), but for this purpose the term "United States person" does not include any individual who is a citizen of any U.S. territory (but not otherwise a citizen of the United States) and who is not a resident of the United States. See proposed § 1.59A-1(b)(10). The Treasury Department and the IRS have determined that it is appropriate in defining a base erosion payment to consider the U.S. tax treatment of the foreign recipient. In particular, the Treasury Department and the IRS have determined that a payment to a foreign person should not be taxed as a base erosion payment to the extent that payments to the foreign related party are effectively connected income. Those amounts are subject to tax under sections 871(b) and 882(a) on a net basis in substantially the same manner as amounts paid to a United States citizen or resident or a domestic corporation. Accordingly, the proposed regulations include an exception from the definition of base erosion payment for amounts that are subject to tax as income effectively connected with the conduct of a U.S. trade or business. In the case of a foreign recipient that determines its net taxable income under an applicable income tax treaty, the exception from the definition of base erosion payment applies to payments taken into account in determining net taxable income under the treaty.

4. Exchange Loss from a Section 988 Transaction

Proposed § 1.59A-3(b)(3)(iv) provides that exchange losses from section 988 transactions described in § 1.988-1(a)(1) are not base erosion payments. The Treasury Department and the IRS have determined that these losses do not present the same base erosion concerns as other types of losses that arise in connection with payments to a foreign related party. Accordingly, under these proposed regulations, section 988 losses are excluded from the numerator.

The proposed regulations also provide that section 988 losses are excluded from the denominator of the base erosion percentage. Specifically, proposed § 1.59A-2(e)(3)(ii)(D) provides that an exchange loss from a section 988 transaction (including with respect to persons other than foreign related parties) is not included in the denominator when calculating the base erosion percentage. Exchange gain from a section 988 transaction, however, is included as a gross receipt for purposes of the gross receipts test under proposed § 1.59A-2(d).

The Treasury Department and the IRS request comments on the treatment of section 988 losses in the context of section 59A, including whether the rule relating to section 988 losses in the denominator of the base erosion percentage calculation should be limited to transactions with a foreign related party.

5. Exception for Interest on Certain Instruments Issued by Globally Systemically Important Banking Organizations.

The Federal Reserve requires that certain global systemically important banking organizations (GSIBs) issue TLAC securities as part of a global framework for bank capital that has sought to minimize the risk of insolvency. In particular, the Board of Governors of the Federal Reserve (the Board) has issued regulations that prescribe the amount and form of external TLAC securities that domestic GSIBs must issue and internal TLAC securities that certain foreign GSIBs must issue. In the case of internal TLAC securities, the Board regulations require the domestic intermediate holding company of a foreign GSIB to issue a specified minimum amount of TLAC to its foreign parent. Section 59A(i) provides that the Secretary shall prescribe such regulations or other guidance as may be necessary or appropriate to carry out the provisions of section 59A, including regulations addressing specifically enumerated situations. The Treasury Department and the IRS have determined that because of the special status of TLAC as part of a global system to address bank solvency and the precise limits that Board regulations place on the terms of TLAC securities and structure of intragroup TLAC funding, it is necessary and appropriate to include an exception to base erosion payment status for interest paid or accrued on TLAC securities required by the Federal Reserve.

Specifically, the proposed regulations include a TLAC exception that applies only to the extent of the amount of TLAC securities required by the Federal Reserve under subpart P of part 252 of 12 C.F.R. As a result, the exception is scaled back if the adjusted issue price of the average amount of TLAC securities issued and outstanding exceeds the average amount of TLAC long-term debt required by the Federal Reserve for the taxable year. The TLAC exception applies only to securities required by the Federal Reserve, and as a result generally does not apply to securities issued by a foreign corporation engaged in a U.S. trade or business because the applicable Federal Reserve requirement applies only to domestic institutions. However, the Treasury Department and the IRS acknowledge that foreign regulators may impose similar requirements on the financial institutions they regulate. The Treasury Department and the IRS request comments regarding a similar exception for foreign corporations that are required by law to issue a similar type of loss-absorbing instrument, including the appropriate scope of an exception that would provide parity between the treatment of domestic corporations and foreign corporations engaged in a U.S. trade or business.

C. *Base Erosion Payments Occurring Before the Effective Date and Pre-2018 Disallowed Business Interest*

Section 14401(e) of the Act provides that section 59A applies only to base erosion payments paid or accrued in taxable years beginning after December 31, 2017. The statutory definition of a base erosion tax benefit is based upon the definition of a base erosion payment. Accordingly, the proposed regulations confirm the exclusion of a deduction described in section 59A(c)(2)(A)(i) (deduction allowed under Chapter 1 for the taxable year with respect to any base erosion payment) or section 59A(c)(2)(A)(ii) (deduction allowed under Chapter 1 for the taxable year for depreciation or amortization with respect to any property acquired with such payment) that is allowed in a taxable year beginning after December 31, 2017, if it relates to a base erosion payment that occurred in a taxable year beginning before January 1, 2018.

For example, if in 2015, a calendar year taxpayer makes a payment or accrual to a foreign related party to acquire depreciable property, the 2015 payment is excluded from the definition of a base erosion payment because of section 14401(e) of the Act. As a result, the taxpayer's depreciation deduction allowed in 2018 with respect to this property is not a base erosion tax benefit.

Similarly, if in 2016, a taxpayer with a calendar year had paid or accrued interest on an obligation to a foreign related party, but the interest was not deductible in 2016 due to the application of section 267(a), the 2016 accrual of the interest amount is excluded from the definition of a base erosion payment because of section 14401(e) of the Act. As a result, if the interest amount becomes deductible in 2018, the taxpayer's deduction allowed in 2018 with respect to this item is not a base erosion tax benefit.

In the case of business interest expense that is not allowed as a deduction under section 163(j)(1), the proposed regulations provide a rule that clarifies that the effective date rules apply in a similar manner as with other base erosion payments that initially arose before the effective date in section 14401(e) of the Act. Section 163(j), as modified by the Act, provides that the deduction for business interest expense is limited to the sum of business interest income, 30 percent of adjusted taxable income ("ATI"), and the amount of any floor plan financing interest. Section 163(j)(2) further provides that any disallowed business interest is carried forward to the succeeding year, and that the carryforward amount is treated as "paid or accrued" in the succeeding taxable year.

In Notice 2018-28, 2018-16 I.R.B. 492, Section 3, the Treasury Department and the IRS stated that business interest carried forward from a taxable year beginning before January 1, 2018, will be treated in the same manner as interest paid or accrued in a taxable year beginning after December 31, 2017, for purposes of section 59A. Under this approach, business interest expense that was initially paid or accrued in a taxable year beginning before January 1, 2018, could nonetheless be a base erosion payment in a taxable year beginning after December 31, 2017, because section 163(j)(2) deems a recurring "payment or accrual" for such item in each carryforward year. Comments requested that the Treasury Department and the IRS reconsider the position taken in Notice 2018-28, on the basis that the determination of whether a payment is a base erosion payment should be made as of the date of the actual payment of interest rather than the date that a deduction is allowed under section 163(j).

The Treasury Department and the IRS agree and have determined that the approach described in Notice 2018-28 is not consistent with the general effective date provision in Section 14401(e) of the Act because the language in section 163(j)(2) deeming a recurring "payment or accrual" is primarily to implement the carryforward mechanism in section 163(j), rather than to treat interest that is carried forward to a subsequent taxable year as paid or accrued for all tax purposes in that subsequent taxable year. Accordingly, the proposed regulations do not follow the approach described in Notice 2018-28. Instead, the proposed regulations provide that any disallowed disqualified interest under section 163(j) that resulted from a payment or accrual to a foreign related party and that is carried forward from a taxable year beginning before January 1, 2018, is not a base erosion payment. The proposed regulations also clarify that any disallowed business interest carryforward under section 163(j) that resulted from a payment or accrual to a foreign related party is treated as a base erosion payment in the year that the interest was paid or accrued even though the interest may be deemed to be paid or accrued again in the year in which it is actually deducted. The rule in the proposed regulations generally is consistent with excluding interest paid or accrued before January 1, 2018 (generally under financing arranged prior to the Act) from treatment as a base erosion payment. The Treasury Department and the IRS welcome comments with respect to the treatment of disallowed disqualified interest under section 163(j) from a taxable year beginning before January 1, 2018. See Part IV.B of this Explanation of Provisions section for proposed rules determining the amount of business interest expense for which a deduction is allowed when section 163(j) applies to limit interest deductions.

IV. *Base Erosion Tax Benefits*

The amount of base erosion tax benefits is an input in (i) the computation of the base erosion percentage test (discussed in Part II.C of this Explanation of Provisions section) and (ii) the determination of modified taxable income (discussed in Part V of this Explanation of Provisions section). Generally, a base erosion tax benefit is the amount of any deduction relating to a base erosion payment that is allowed under the Code for the taxable year. Base erosion tax benefits are defined in proposed § 1.59A-3(c).

A. *Withholding Tax on Payments*

As discussed in Part II.C of this Explanation of Provisions section, if tax is imposed by section 871 or 881 and the tax is deducted and withheld under section 1441 or 1442 without reduction by an applicable income tax treaty on a base erosion payment, the base erosion payment is treated as having a base erosion tax benefit of zero for purposes of calculating a taxpayer's modified taxable income. If an income tax treaty reduces the amount of withholding imposed on the base erosion payment, the base erosion payment is treated as a base erosion tax benefit to the extent of the reduction in withholding under rules similar to those in section 163(j)(5)(B) as in effect before the Act.

B. *Rules for Classifying Interest for which a Deduction is Allowed when Section 163(j) Limits Deductions*

Section 59A(c)(3) provides a stacking rule in cases in which section 163(j) applies to a taxpayer, under which the reduction in the amount of deductible interest is treated as allocable first to interest paid or accrued to persons who are not related parties with respect to the taxpayer and then to related parties. The statute does not provide a rule for determining which portion of the interest treated as paid to related parties (and thus potentially treated as a base erosion payment) is treated as paid to a foreign related person as opposed to a domestic related person. Proposed § 1.59A-3(c)(4) provides rules coordinating section 163(j) with the determination of the amount of base erosion tax benefits. This rule provides, consistent with section 59A(c)(3), that where section 163(j) applies to limit the amount of a taxpayer's business interest expense that is deductible in the taxable year, a taxpayer is required to treat all disallowed business interest first as interest paid or accrued to persons who are not related parties, and then as interest paid or accrued to related parties for purposes of section 59A. More specifically, the proposed regulations provide that when a corporation has business interest expense paid or accrued to both unrelated parties and related parties, the amount of allowed business interest expense is treated first as the business interest expense paid to related parties, proportionately between foreign and domestic related parties, and then as business interest expense paid to unrelated parties. Conversely, the amount of a disallowed business interest expense carryforward is treated first as business interest expense paid to unrelated parties, and then as business interest expense paid to related parties, proportionately between foreign and domestic related party business interest expense.

Because section 163(j) and the proposed regulations thereunder provide an ordering rule that allocates business interest expense deductions first to business interest expense incurred in the current year and then to business interest expense carryforwards from prior years (starting with the earliest year) in order to separately track the attributes on a year-by-year layered approach for subchapter C purposes, these proposed regulations follow that convention. Accordingly, the proposed regulations also follow a year-by-year convention in the allocation of business interest expense and carryovers among the related and unrelated party classifications. See also the discussion of singular tax attributes in Part V.A of this Explanation of Provisions section. The proposed regulations adopt a similar approach for business interest expense and excess business interest of a partnership that is allocated to a corporate partner by separately tracking and ordering items allocated from a partnership.

V. *Modified Taxable Income*

For any taxable year, section 59A imposes a tax on each applicable taxpayer equal to the base erosion minimum tax amount for that year. Section 59A(b)(1) provides that the base erosion minimum tax amount is determined based on an applicable taxpayer's modified taxable income for the taxable year. Part V.A of this Explanation of Provisions section discusses how an applicable taxpayer computes its modified taxable income. Part V.B of this Explanation of Provisions section describes how modified taxable income is calculated if an applicable taxpayer has an overall taxable loss for a taxable year. Finally, Part V.C of this Explanation of Provisions section describes the base erosion percentage that is used when the base erosion percentage of a net operating loss deduction ("NOL deduction") is added back to taxable income for purposes of the modified taxable income calculation.

A. *Method of Computation*

Section 59A(c)(1) provides that the term modified taxable income means the taxable income of the taxpayer computed under Chapter 1 for the taxable year, determined without regard to base erosion tax benefits and the base erosion percentage of any NOL deduction under section 172 for the taxable year. The proposed regulations clarify that the computation of modified taxable income and the computation of the base erosion minimum tax amount (which is discussed in Part VI of this Explanation of Provisions section) are made on a taxpayer-by-taxpayer basis. That is, under the proposed regulations, the aggregate group concept is used solely for determining whether a taxpayer is an applicable taxpayer and the base erosion percentage of any NOL deduction. This approach is consistent with section 59A(a)'s imposition of a tax equal to the base erosion minimum tax amount, which is in addition to the regular tax liability of a taxpayer.

The proposed regulations also provide that the computation of modified taxable income is done on an add-back basis. The computation starts with taxable income (or taxable loss) of the taxpayer as computed for regular tax purposes, and adds to that amount (a) the gross amount of base erosion tax benefits for the taxable year and (b) the base erosion percentage of any NOL deduction under section 172 for the taxable year.

The proposed regulations do not provide for the recomputation of income under an approach similar to the alternative minimum tax, which the Act repealed for corporations. See section 12001(a) of the Act. Under a recomputation approach, attributes that are limited based on taxable income would be subject to different annual limitations, and those attributes would have to be re-computed for purposes of section 59A. Applying this approach in a manner that reflects the results of the BEAT-basis recomputation to subsequent years would lead to parallel attributes that are maintained separately in a manner similar to the pre-Act corporate alternative minimum tax. For example, the amount of the net operating loss used to reduce modified taxable income would differ from the amount used in computing regular tax liability, and the carryforward of unused net operating loss that is used to compute regular tax liability would not reflect the net operating loss amount used to reduce modified taxable income (absent a separate BEAT-basis carryover). The annual limitation under section 163(j)(1), which generally limits a corporation's annual deduction for business interest expense, would present similar issues under a recomputation approach. Consequently, the add-back approach also provides simplification relative to the recomputation approach because the add-back approach eliminates the need to engage in the more complex tracking of separate attributes on a BEAT basis in a manner similar to the repealed corporate AMT. The Treasury Department and the IRS welcome comments on the add-back approach provided in the proposed regulations, and the practical effects of an alternative recomputation-based approach.

B. *Conventions for Computing Modified Taxable Income - Current Year Losses and Excess Net Operating Loss Carryovers*

If a taxpayer has an excess of deductions allowed by Chapter 1 over gross income, computed without regard to the NOL deduction, the taxpayer has negative taxable income for the taxable year. Generally, the proposed regulations provide that a negative amount is the starting point for computing modified taxable income when there is no NOL deduction from net operating loss carryovers and carrybacks.

The proposed regulations further provide a rule applicable to situations in which there is a NOL deduction from a net operating loss carryover or carryback to the taxable year and that NOL deduction exceeds the amount of positive taxable income before that deduction (because, for example, the loss arose in a year beginning before January 1, 2018). The proposed regulations provide that the excess amount of NOL deduction does not reduce taxable income below zero for determining the starting point for computing modified taxable income. The Treasury Department and the IRS have determined that this rule is necessary because section 172(a) could be read to provide that, for example, if a taxpayer has a net operating loss of $100x that arose in a taxable year beginning before January 1, 2018, that is carried forward, and in a subsequent year the taxpayer has taxable income of $5x before taking into account the $100x net operating loss carryover deduction, the taxpayer may nonetheless have a $100x NOL deduction in that year or a $95x taxable loss (even though $95x of the net operating loss would remain as a carryforward to future years, as well). Because the proposed regulations recognize the notion of a taxable loss when deductions other than the NOL deduction exceed gross income (as discussed earlier in this Part V), this rule clarifies that the taxpayer's starting point for computing modified taxable income in this situation is zero, rather than negative $95x.

The proposed regulations further clarify that the NOL deduction taken into account for purposes of adding the base erosion percentage of the NOL deduction to taxable income under section

59A(c)(1)(B) is determined in the same manner. Accordingly, in the example above, the base erosion percentage of the NOL deduction added to taxable income is computed based on the $5x NOL deduction that reduces regular taxable income to zero, rather than the entire $100x of net operating loss carryforward, $95x of which is not absorbed in the current taxable year.

Finally, the proposed regulations provide that an applicable taxpayer's taxable income is determined according to section 63(a) without regard to the rule in section 860E(a)(1). That rule generally provides that a holder of a residual interest in a real estate mortgage investment conduit ("REMIC") may not have taxable income less than its excess inclusion amount. As a result of section 860E(a)(1), a holder of a REMIC residual interest may have taxable income for purposes of computing its regular tax liability even though it has a current year loss. The proposed regulations provide that the limitation in section 860E(a)(1) is disregarded for purposes of calculating modified taxable income under section 59A. The rule described in this paragraph is relevant, for example, in situations when the taxpayer would have negative taxable income attributable to a current year loss, as described in this Part V.B, or no taxable income as a result of a net operating loss. Because section 860E(a)(1) ensures that the excess inclusion is subject to tax under section 11, the Treasury Department and the IRS have determined that it is not appropriate to apply the rule in section 860E(a)(1) for the purpose of calculating modified taxable income under section 59A.

C. *Conventions for Computing Modified Taxable Income - Determining the Base Erosion Percentage of NOL Deductions*

Section 59A(c)(1)(B) provides that modified taxable income includes the base erosion percentage of any NOL deduction allowed under section 172 for the taxable year. In this context, the relevant base erosion percentage could be either the base erosion percentage in the year that the net operating loss arose, or alternatively, the base erosion percentage in the year in which the taxpayer takes the NOL deduction. Proposed § 1.59A-4(b)(2)(ii) applies the base erosion percentage of the year in which the loss arose, or vintage year, because the base erosion percentage of the vintage year reflects the portion of base eroding payments that are reflected in the net operating loss carryover. In addition, because the vintage-year base erosion percentage is a fixed percentage, taxpayers will have greater certainty as to the amount of the future add-back to modified taxable income (as compared to using the utilization-year base erosion percentage).

Based on this approach, the proposed regulations also provide that in the case of net operating losses that arose in taxable years beginning before January 1, 2018, and that are deducted as carryovers in taxable years beginning after December 31, 2017, the base erosion percentage is zero because section 59A applies only to base erosion payments that are paid or accrued in taxable years beginning after December 31, 2017. See section 14401(e) of the Act. As a result, there is no add-back to modified taxable income for the use of those net operating loss carryovers. The Treasury Department and the IRS welcome comments on the vintage-year approach as well as the alternative utilization-year approach.

The proposed regulations also clarify that in computing the add-back for NOL deductions for purposes of the modified taxable income calculation, the relevant base erosion percentage is the base erosion percentage for the aggregate group that is used to determine whether the taxpayer is an applicable taxpayer, rather than a separate computation of base erosion percentage computed solely by reference to the single taxpayer.

VI. *Base Erosion Minimum Tax Amount*

An applicable taxpayer computes its base erosion minimum tax amount ("BEMTA") for the taxable year to determine its liability under section 59A(a). Proposed § 1.59A-5 describes the calculation of the BEMTA. Generally, the taxpayer's BEMTA equals the excess of (1) the applicable tax rate for the taxable year ("BEAT rate") multiplied by the taxpayer's modified taxable income for the taxable year over (2) the taxpayer's adjusted regular tax liability for that year. See Part VIII of this Explanation of Provisions section for a discussion of the higher BEAT rate for certain banks and registered securities dealers.

In determining the taxpayer's adjusted regular tax liability for the taxable year, credits (including the foreign tax credit) are generally subtracted from the regular tax liability amount. To prevent an inappropriate understatement of a taxpayer's adjusted regular tax liability, the proposed regulations provide that credits for overpayment of taxes and for taxes withheld at source are not subtracted from the taxpayer's regular tax liability because these credits relate to federal income tax paid for the current or previous year.

For taxable years beginning before January 1, 2026, under section 59A(b)(1)(B), the credits allowed against regular tax liability (which reduce the amount of regular tax liability for purposes of calculating BEMTA) are not reduced by the research credit determined under section 41(a) or by a portion of applicable section 38 credits. For taxable years beginning after December 31, 2025, this special treatment of the research credit and applicable section 38 credits no longer applies. As a result, an applicable taxpayer may have a greater BEMTA than would be the case in taxable years beginning before January 1, 2026. In general, foreign tax credits are taken into account in computing a taxpayer's regular tax liability before other credits. See section 26(a). As a result, a taxpayer with foreign tax credits that reduce its regular tax liability to, or close to, zero may not use its section 41(a) credits or its applicable section 38 credits in computing its regular tax liability. In these situations, those credits will not be taken into account in computing the taxpayer's BEMTA even in a pre-2026 year. Instead, those credits will reduce (or, put differently, will prevent an increase in) the BEMTA in the year when those credits are used for regular tax purposes (provided that the taxable year begins before January 1, 2026).

VII. *Application of Section 59A to Partnerships*

A partnership is not an "applicable taxpayer" as defined in Section 59A; only corporations can be applicable taxpayers. In general, however, a partnership also is not subject to the income tax imposed by Chapter 1 of Subtitle A of the Code. Instead, partners are liable for income tax only in their separate capacities. Each taxpayer that is a partner in a partnership takes into account separately the partner's distributive share of the partner's income or loss in determining its taxable income. Accordingly, an item of income is subject to federal income taxation based on the status of the partners, and not the partnership as an entity. Similarly, a partnership does not itself benefit from a deduction. Instead, the tax benefit from a deduction is taken by the taxpayer that is allocated the deduction under section 704. Section 702(b) provides that the character of any item be taken into account as if such item were realized directly from the source from which realized by the partnership, or incurred in the same manner as incurred by the partnership. Section 702(b) acknowledges that differences in partner tax characteristics (for example, whether the partner is a corporation or an individual, or domestic or foreign) may result in differences in the tax consequences of items the partnership allocates to its partners.

The proposed regulations generally apply an aggregate approach in conjunction with the gross receipts test for evaluating whether a corporation is an applicable taxpayer and in addressing the treatment of payments made by a partnership or received by a partnership for purposes of section 59A. The proposed regulations generally provide that partnerships are treated as an aggregate of the partners in determining whether payments to or payments from a partnership are base erosion payments consistent with the approach described in subchapter K as well as the authority provided in section 59A(i)(1) to prescribe such regulations that are necessary or appropriate to carry out the provisions of section 59A, including through the use of intermediaries or by characterizing payments otherwise subject to section 59A as payments not subject to 59A. Thus, when determining whether a corporate partner that is an applicable taxpayer has made a base erosion payment, amounts paid or accrued by a partnership are treated as paid by each partner to the extent an item of expense is allocated to the partner under section 704. Similarly, any amounts received by or accrued to a partnership are treated as received by each partner to the extent the item of income or gain is allocated to each partner under section 704. The rules and exceptions for base erosion payments and base erosion tax benefits then apply accordingly on an aggregate basis.

The Treasury Department and the IRS have determined that a rule that applies the aggregate principle consistently is necessary to align the treatment of economically similar transactions. The proposed rule prevents an applicable taxpayer from (a) paying a domestic partnership that is owned by foreign related parties, rather than paying those foreign partners directly, to circumvent the BEAT and (b) causing a partnership in which an applicable taxpayer is a partner to make a payment to a foreign related party, rather than paying that foreign related party directly. The rule applies consistently when a payment is to a foreign partnership that is owned, for example, by domestic corporations. This rule also addresses situations in which a partnership with an applicable taxpayer partner makes a payment to a foreign related party. Partners with certain small ownership interests are excluded from this aggregate approach for purposes of determining base erosion tax benefits from the partnership. This small ownership interests exclusion generally applies to partnership interests that represent less than ten percent of the capital and profits of the partnership and less than ten percent of each item of income, gain, loss, deduction, and credit; and that have a fair market value of less than $25 million. See proposed § 1.59A-7(b)(4). The Treasury Department and the IRS determined that a threshold of ten percent appropriately balanced the administrative burdens of determining whether deductions allocated to a partner with a small ownership interest in a partnership are base erosion payments with the Treasury Department and IRS's interest in maintaining a consistent aggregate approach to partnerships in applying to the BEAT. In determining the appropriate threshold for a small ownership interest, the Treasury Department and the IRS considered the treatment of small ownership interests in partnerships in analogous situations in other Treasury regulations. The Treasury Department and the IRS welcome comments on the aggregate approach to partnerships as well as the exception for small ownership interests, including the specific thresholds for the exception.

The proposed regulations do not provide for special treatment of base erosion tax benefits attributable to a partnership or to partnership nonrecognition transactions. Instead, the aggregate principle generally applies to these situations. For example, if a partnership acquires property from a foreign related party of a taxpayer that is a partner in the partnership, deductions for depreciation of the property allocated to the taxpayer generally are base erosion tax benefits. Similarly, if a foreign related party and a taxpayer form a partnership, and the foreign related party contributes depreciable property, deductions for depreciation of the property generally are base erosion tax benefits, in part, because the partnership is treated as acquiring the property in exchange for an interest in the partnership under section 721. This approach is consistent with the approach taken with respect to subchapter C transactions, as described in Part III.A.1 of this Explanation of Provisions section.

The proposed regulations provide that with respect to any person that owns an interest in a partnership, the related party determination under section 59A(g) applies at the partner level.

VIII. *Rules Relating to Banks and Dealers for Purposes of Computing the Base Erosion Percentage and Determining the BEAT Rate for Computing BEMTA*

Section 59A modifies two general rules in the case of certain banks or registered securities dealers. First, section 59A(e)(1)(C) lowers the base erosion percentage threshold for certain banks and registered securities dealers from three percent or more to two percent or more. See Part II.C of this Explanation of Provisions section for additional discussion of this rule. Second, section 59A(b)(3) provides that the BEAT rate is one percentage point higher for those banks or registered securities dealers.

The proposed regulations do not modify the statutory definition of the term "bank" for these purposes from its reference to section 581, which defines a bank by reference to a bank or trust company incorporated and doing business under the laws of United States (including laws related to the District of Columbia) or of any state. Thus, a foreign corporation licensed to conduct a banking business in the United States and subject to taxation with respect to income that is, or is treated as, effectively connected with the conduct of a trade or business in the United States is not included in this definition.

The proposed regulations clarify that the term "registered securities dealer" is limited to a dealer as defined in section 3(a)(5) of the Securities Exchange Act of 1934 that is registered, or required to be registered, under section 15 of the Securities Exchange Act of 1934.

The proposed regulations also confirm that the operative rules that lower the base erosion percentage threshold and that increase the BEAT rate apply only to a taxpayer that is a member of an affiliated group as defined in section 1504(a)(1), and thus do not apply, for example, if the taxpayer is not affiliated with another includible corporation (within the meaning of section 1504(b)(1)), or if the taxpayer is not itself an includible corporation (for example, a foreign corporation that is an applicable taxpayer).

For purposes of applying the lower base erosion percentage threshold to banks and registered securities dealers, the proposed regulations clarify that because the base erosion percentage is determined on an aggregate group basis, the lower threshold applies if any member of the aggregate group is a member of an affiliated group that includes a bank or registered securities dealer. The proposed regulations provide a limited exception for members of an affiliated group that includes a bank or registered securities dealer where the bank or registered securities dealer activities are de minimis. This de minimis rule provides that a consolidated group, or a member of the aggregate group of which the taxpayer is a member, is not subject to the lower base erosion percentage threshold if its gross receipts attributable to the bank or the registered securities dealer are less than two percent of the aggregate group's total gross revenue. This de minimis rule uses the same threshold measurement for exclusion from the special rule for banks and registered securities dealers (two percent) that is used as the base erosion percentage threshold for banks or registered securities dealers to determine whether such taxpayers are applicable taxpayers that are subject to the BEAT, with the latter test functioning in a manner similar to a de minimis threshold for the application of the BEAT. See Part II.C of this Explanation of Provisions section. The Treasury Department and the IRS welcome comments on the scope of the de minimis rule for banks and registered securities dealers. See also Part III.B.5 of this Explanation of Provisions section for a discussion of an exception to base erosion payment status for interest on TLAC securities.

IX. *Rules Relating to Insurance Companies*

The definition of a base erosion payment in section 59A(d) includes any premiums or other consideration paid or accrued by a taxpayer to a foreign related party for any reinsurance payments taken into account under section 803(a)(1)(B) or 832(b)(4)(A). Generally, section 803(a)(1) defines gross income for a life insurance company to include the gross amount of premiums and other consideration on insurance and annuity contracts less return premiums and premiums and other consideration arising out of indemnity reinsurance. For an insurance company other than a life insurance company, under section 832(b), gross income generally includes underwriting income, which is comprised of premiums earned during the taxable year less losses incurred and expenses incurred. Section 832(b)(4)(A) provides that the amount of premiums earned on insurance contracts is the amount of gross premiums written on insurance contracts during the taxable year less return premiums and premiums paid for reinsurance.

The Treasury Department and the IRS are aware that certain reinsurance agreements provide that amounts paid to and from a reinsurer are settled on a net basis or netted under the terms of the agreement. The Treasury Department and the IRS are also aware that other commercial agreements with reciprocal payments may be settled on a net basis or netted under the terms of those agreements. The proposed regulations do not provide a rule permitting netting in any of these circumstances because the BEAT statutory framework is based on including the gross amount of deductible and certain other payments (base erosion payments) in the BEAT's expanded modified taxable income base without regard to reciprocal obligations or payments that are taken into account in the regular income tax base, but not the BEAT's modified taxable income base. Generally, the amounts of income and deduction are determined on a gross basis under the Code; however, as discussed in Part III of this Explanation of Provisions section, if there are situations where an application of otherwise generally applicable tax law would provide that a deduction is computed on a net basis (because an item received reduces the item of deduction rather than increasing gross income), the proposed regulations do not change that result. The Treasury Department and the IRS request comments addressing whether a distinction should be made between reinsurance contracts entered into by an applicable taxpayer and a foreign related party that provide for settlement of amounts owed on a net basis and other commercial contracts entered into by an applicable taxpayer and a foreign related party that provide for netting of items payable by one party against items payable by the other party in determining that net amount to be paid between the parties.

The proposed regulations also do not provide any specific rules for payments by a domestic reinsurance company to a foreign related insurance company. In the case of a domestic reinsurance company, claims payments for losses incurred and other payments are deductible and are thus potentially within the scope of section 59A(d)(1). See sections 803(c) and 832(c). In the case of an insurance company other than a life insurance company (non-life insurance company) that reinsures foreign risk, certain of these payments may also be treated as reductions in gross income under section 832(b)(3), which are not deductions and also not the type of reductions in gross income described in sections 59A(d)(3). The Treasury Department and the IRS request comments on the appropriate treatment of these items under subchapter L. The Treasury Department and the IRS also recognize that to the extent that the items are not treated as deductions for non-life insurance companies this may lead to asymmetric treatment for life insurance companies that reinsure foreign risk because part I of subchapter L (the rules for life insurance companies) refers to these costs only as deductions (that is, does not also refer to the costs as reductions in gross income in a manner similar to section 832(b)(3)). The Treasury Department and the IRS request comments on whether the regulations should provide that a life insurance company that reinsures foreign risk is treated in the same manner as a non-life insurance company that reinsures foreign risk.

The proposed regulations do not address a foreign insurance company that has in effect an election to be treated as a domestic corporation for purposes of the Code. Amounts paid or accrued to such a company are not base erosion payments because the corporation is treated as a domestic corporation for purposes of the Code.

X. *Anti-Abuse and Recharacterization Rules*

Proposed § 1.59A-9(b) provides that certain transactions that have a principal purpose of avoiding section 59A will be disregarded or deemed to result in a base erosion payment. This proposed anti-abuse rule addresses the following types of transactions: (a) transactions involving intermediaries acting as a conduit to avoid a base erosion payment; (b) transactions entered into to increase the deductions taken into account in the denominator of the base erosion percentage; and (c) transactions among related parties entered into to avoid the application of rules applicable to banks and registered securities dealers (for example, causing a bank or registered securities dealer to disaffiliate from an affiliated group so as to avoid the requirement that it be a member of such a group).

XI. *Consolidated Groups as Taxpayers*

Affiliated groups of domestic corporations that elect to file a consolidated income tax return generally compute their income tax liability on a "single-entity" basis. Because the regular tax liability is computed on a single entity basis, the additional tax imposed by section 59A must also be imposed on the same basis (because it is an addition to that regular tax liability). Accordingly, the proposed regulations provide that for affiliated corporations electing to file a consolidated income tax return, the tax under section 59A is determined at the consolidated group level, rather than determined separately for each member of the group. The BEAT is an addition to the regular corporate income tax under section 11, and the regular corporate income tax is applied to a consolidated group on a consolidated basis. Further, application of the BEAT on a group level eliminates the differences in the aggregate amount of taxation to a consolidated group that would otherwise occur, based on the location of deductions, including, for example, the location of related party interest payments within the group. Accordingly, the BEAT is also applied on a consolidated basis. This single taxpayer treatment for members of a consolidated group applies separately from the aggregate group concept in proposed § 1.59A-2(c), which also treats all members of the aggregate group as a single entity, but in that case, only for purposes of applying the gross receipts test and base erosion percentage test for determining whether a particular taxpayer is an applicable taxpayer. See generally, Part II of this Explanation of Provisions section.

To properly reflect the taxable income of the group, consolidated return regulations generally determine the tax treatment of items resulting from intercompany transactions (as defined in § 1.1502-13(b)(1)(i)) by treating members of the consolidated group as divisions of a single corporation (single entity treatment). In general, the existence of an intercompany transaction should not change the consolidated taxable income or consolidated tax liability of a consolidated group. Consistent with single entity treatment, items from intercompany transactions are not taken into account for purposes of making the computations under section 59A. For example, any increase in depreciation deductions resulting from intercompany sales of property are disregarded for purposes of determining the taxpayer's base erosion percentage. Similarly, interest payments on intercompany obligations (as defined in § 1.1502-13(g)(2)(ii)) are not taken into account in making the computations under section 59A.

XII. *Coordinating Consolidated Group Rules for Sections 59A(c)(3) and 163(j)*

Section 59A(c)(3) and proposed § 1.59A-3(c)(4) coordinate the application of section 163(j) with the determination of the amount of base erosion tax benefits when a taxpayer has business interest expense paid to both unrelated parties and related parties. Those rules provide that, where section 163(j) applies to limit the amount of a taxpayer's business interest that is deductible in a taxable year, the taxpayer is required to treat all disallowed business interest as allocable first to interest paid or accrued to persons who are not related parties, and then to related parties. See Part IV.B of this Explanation of Provisions section.

Proposed § 1.1502-59A provides rules regarding application of section 59A(c)(3) to consolidated groups. These rules are required for the allocation of the BEMTA among members of the group under section 1552. In addition, apportionment of the domestic related party status and foreign related party status (defined later in this Part XII) of section 163(j) carryforwards among members of the group is necessary when a member deconsolidates from the group.

The proposed regulations implement the classification approach of proposed § 1.59A-3(c)(4) on a consolidated basis (the "classification rule"), to identify which interest deductions are allocable to domestic related party payments, foreign related party payments, and unrelated party payments. Slightly different rules apply to the deduction of current year business interest expense than to the deduction of section 163(j) carryforwards. A consolidated group applies these rules to the amount of business interest expense (either from current year business interest expense or from carryforward amounts) that is actually deducted pursuant to section 163(j) and proposed § § 1.163(j)-4(d) and 1.163(j)-5(b)(3). If the group deducts business interest expense paid or accrued in different taxable years (for example, both current year business interest expense and section 163(j) carryforwards), the classification rule applies separately to business interest expense incurred in each taxable year. For purposes of the proposed regulations, a member's current year business interest expense is the member's business interest expense that would be deductible in the current taxable year without regard to section 163(j) and that is not a disallowed business interest expense carryforward from a prior taxable year.

The classification rule applies on a single-entity basis to deductions of current year business interest expense. The consolidated group classifies its aggregate business interest deduction from current year business interest expense based on the aggregate current year business interest expense of all types (related or unrelated) paid by members of the group to nonmembers. Business interest deductions are treated as from payments or accruals to related parties first, and then from payments or accruals to unrelated parties. If there are payments to both foreign related parties and domestic related parties, the deductions are classified as to the related parties on a pro-rata basis.

Recognizing the flexibility of related-party financing, these proposed regulations provide that, if the group has aggregate business interest deductions classified as payments or accruals to a domestic related party (domestic related party status) or foreign related party (foreign related party status), the status of such payments or accruals is spread among members of the group (the allocation rule). Specifically, the domestic related party status and foreign related party status of the deduction is allocated among members of the group in proportion to the amount of each member's deduction of its current year business interest expense. Similarly, if any part of a section 163(j) carryforward is from a payment or accrual to a domestic related party or a foreign related party, the related party status of the section 163(j) carryforwards for the year will be allocated among members of the group. The allocation is in proportion to the relative amount of each member's section 163(j) carryforward from that year. Members' additional section 163(j) carryforward amounts are treated as payments or accruals to unrelated parties. The allocation rule applies separately to each carryforward year.

With regard to the deduction of any member's section 163(j) carryforward, the classification rule applies on an entity-by-entity basis. As discussed, before a member's section 163(j) carryforward moves forward into subsequent years, it is allocated a domestic related party status, foreign related party status, or unrelated party status. This allocation ensures that business interest deductions drawn from any carryforward originating in the same consolidated return year bear the same ratio of domestic related, foreign related, and unrelated statuses. When a member deducts any portion of its section 163(j) carryforward, the member applies section 59A(c)(3) and proposed § 1.59A-3(c)(4) to determine the status of the deducted carryforward, based on the status previously allocated to the member's section 163(j) carryforward for the relevant tax year. The tax liability imposed under section 59A on the consolidated group is allocated among the members of the consolidated group pursuant to the consolidated group's tax allocation method, taking into account these allocations. See section 1552.

If a member that is allocated a foreign related party status or domestic related party status to its section 163(j) carryforward deconsolidates from the group, the departing member's carryforward retains the allocated status. The departing member (and not the original consolidated group) takes into account the status of that carryforward for purposes of computing the BEAT in future years.

XIII. *Consolidated Tax Liability*

In § 1.1502-2, a reference is added to the base erosion anti-abuse tax as a tax included in the computation of consolidated tax liability. Additionally, the proposed regulations make the following changes: (1) remove paragraph (j) of this regulation section because section 1333, relating to war loss recoveries, was repealed by section 1901(a)(145)(A) of the Tax Reform Act of 1976, Pub. L. 94-455, (2) remove paragraph (h) of this regulation section because section 1201, relating to the alternative tax for corporations, was repealed by section 13001(b)(2)(A) of the Act, and (3) update the cross reference to life insurance taxable income to section 801, following the revision of subchapter L of chapter 1 of the code in section 211 of the Deficit Reduction Act of 1984, Pub. L. 98-369.

In addition, the proposed regulations also make nonsubstantive changes to reorganize the structure of current § 1.1502-2. Specifically, the proposed regulations reorganize the current § 1.1502-2 to properly designate the unnumbered paragraphs. The proposed regulations also update other regulation sections that reference § 1.1502-2.

Finally, the proposed regulations correct an error in § 1.6655-5(e) *Example 10*. The proposed regulations replace the reference to "§ 1.1502-2(h)" with a reference to "1.1502-1(h)" because the context of *Example 10* demonstrates that the intended reference was to the definition of a consolidated group.

XIV. *Sections 382 and 383*

Section 1.383-1 provides that only otherwise currently allowable pre-change losses and pre-change credits will result in the absorption of the section 382 limitation and the section 383 credit limitation. The limitations under sections 382 and 383 are applied after the application of all other limitations contained in subtitle A of the Code. If the pre-change losses or pre-change credits cannot be deducted or otherwise used, they are carried forward to the next taxable year. The BEAT is not a modification to the normal computation of income tax under Subtitle A of the Code but an addition to that income tax. Therefore, these proposed regulations clarify that additions to tax under section 59A do not affect whether a loss, deduction, or credit is absorbed under section 382 or section 383.

XV. *Reporting and Recordkeeping Requirements Pursuant to Section 6038A*

Section 6038A imposes reporting and recordkeeping requirements on domestic corporations that are 25-percent foreign-owned. Section 6038C imposes the same reporting and recordkeeping requirements on certain foreign corporations engaged in a U.S. trade or business. These corporations are collectively known as "reporting corporations."

Reporting corporations are required to file an annual return on Form 5472, *Information Return of a 25% Foreign-Owned U.S. Corporation or a Foreign Corporation Engaged in a U.S. Trade or Business (Under Sections 6038A and 6038C of the Internal Revenue Code)*, with respect to each related party with which the reporting corporation has had any "reportable transactions." See § 1.6038A-2. Reporting corporations are also subject to specific requirements under sections 6038A and 6038C to maintain and make available the permanent books of account or records as required by section 6001 that are sufficient to establish the accuracy of the federal income tax return of the corporation, including information, documents, or records to the extent they may be relevant to determine the correct U.S. tax treatment of transactions with related parties. See § 1.6038A-3.

The Act amended section 6038A by adding paragraph (b)(2), which authorizes regulations requiring information from a reporting corporation that is also a section 59A "applicable taxpayer" for purposes of administering section 59A. Section 6038A(b)(2) applies to taxable years beginning after December 31, 2017. These proposed regulations identify certain types of information that will be required to be reported on Form 5472 and Form 8991, *Tax on Base Erosion Payments of Taxpayers With Substantial Gross Receipts*, and also provide the time and manner for reporting. While an applicable taxpayer that is not a reporting corporation would not be subject to monetary penalties and collateral provisions specific to sections 6038A and 6038C, the taxpayer remains subject to BEAT-related reporting obligations, including Form 8991, and applicable consequences for noncompliance.

Under section 59A(d)(4), the status of a foreign shareholder as a surrogate foreign corporation as defined in section 7874(a)(2)(B) or as a member of the same expanded affiliated group, as defined in section 7874(c)(1), as the surrogate foreign corporation can affect the treatment of payments from a taxpayer to that corporation under section 59A(d). If the reporting corporation is an expatriated entity as defined in section 7874(a)(2), the taxation of certain transactions between it and its foreign related persons as defined in section 7874(d)(3) may be affected. Consequently, the proposed regulations require all reporting corporations to state whether a foreign shareholder required to be listed on Form 5472 is a surrogate foreign corporation. The form may provide for reporting of whether the shareholder is a member of an expanded affiliated group including the surrogate foreign corporation.

In addition, to facilitate screening for important tax compliance concerns under section 59A as well as other provisions at the return filing stage, these proposed regulations clarify that the IRS may require by form or by form instructions the following information: (1) reporting of particular details of the reporting corporation's relationships with related parties in regard to which it is required to file a Form 5472, (2) reporting of transactions within certain categories on a more detailed basis, (3) reporting of the manner (such as type of transfer pricing method used) in which the reporting corporation determined the amount of particular reportable transactions and items, and (4) summarization of a reporting corporation's reportable transactions and items with all foreign related parties on a schedule to its annual Form 5472 filing.

XVI. *Partial withdrawal of proposed regulations*

The proposed regulations also withdraw, in part, a notice of proposed rulemaking. Because of statutory changes in section 12001 of the Act, the proposed regulations would not incorporate the substance of § 1.1502-2, relating to the computation of a consolidated group's alternative minimum tax, of the notice of proposed rulemaking (IA-57-89) published in the **Federal Register** on December 30, 1992 (57 FR 62251). Accordingly, the Partial Withdrawal of Proposed Regulations section in this document withdraws that section of the notice of proposed rulemaking.

Proposed Applicability Date

Under section 7805(b)(2), and consistent with the applicability date of section 59A, these regulations (other than the proposed reporting requirements for QDPs in proposed § 1.6038A-2(b)(7)) are proposed to apply to taxable years beginning after December 31, 2017. Until finalization, a taxpayer may rely on these proposed regulations for taxable years beginning after December 31, 2017, provided the taxpayer and all related parties of the taxpayer (as defined in proposed § 1.59A-1(b)(17)) consistently apply the proposed regulations for all those taxable years that end before the finalization date.

With respect to the reporting requirements for QDPs, proposed § 1.6038A-2(b)(7)(ix) applies to taxable years beginning one year after final regulations are published in the **Federal Register**, although simplified QDP reporting requirements provided in § 1.6038A-2(g) are also proposed to apply to taxable years beginning after December 31, 2017.

If any provision is finalized after June 22, 2019, the Treasury Department and the IRS generally expect that such provision will apply only to taxable years ending on or after December 17, 2018. *See* section 7805(b)(1)(B).

Special Analyses

Regulatory Planning and Review - Economic Analysis

Executive Orders 13563 and 12866 direct agencies to assess costs and benefits of available regulatory alternatives and, if regulation is necessary, to select regulatory approaches that maximize net benefits (including potential economic, environmental, public health and safety effects, distributive impacts, and equity). Executive Order 13563 emphasizes the importance of quantifying both costs and benefits, of reducing costs, of harmonizing rules, and of promoting flexibility. The preliminary Executive Order 13771 designation for this proposed rule is regulatory.

The proposed regulations have been designated by the Office of Management and Budget's ("OMB") Office of Information and Regulatory Affairs ("OIRA") as subject to review under Executive Order 12866 pursuant to the Memorandum of Agreement (April 11, 2018) between the Treasury Department and OMB regarding review of tax regulations. OIRA has determined that the proposed rulemaking is economically significant under section 1(c) of the Memorandum of Agreement and thereby subject to review. Accordingly, the proposed regulations have been reviewed by OMB.

A. *Overview*

The proposed regulations provide guidance under section 59A regarding the determination of the tax on base erosion payments for certain taxpayers with substantial gross receipts. They provide guidance for applicable taxpayers to determine the amount of BEAT liability and how to compute the components of the tax calculation. Among other benefits, this clarity helps ensure that all taxpayers apply section 59A in a similar manner, which promotes efficiency and equity with respect to the provisions of the overall Code.

The proposed regulations under sections 59A (proposed §§ 1.59A-1 through 1.59A-10) provide details for taxpayers regarding whether a taxpayer is an applicable taxpayer and the computation of certain components of the base erosion minimum tax, including the amount of base erosion payments, the amount of base erosion tax benefits arising from base erosion payments, and modified taxable income. The proposed regulations also provide guidance for banks, registered securities dealers, and insurance companies and provide guidance attributing partnership income and deductions involving partnerships to the owners of the partnerships (amounts paid by and to partnerships). These proposed regulations also establish anti-abuse rules to prevent taxpayers from taking measures to inappropriately avoid section 59A.

The proposed regulations under sections 383, 1502 and 6038A (proposed §§ 1.383-1, 1.502-2, 1.502-59A, 1.6038A-1, 1.6038A-2, and 1.6038-4) provide rules for the application of section 59A with respect to limitations on certain capital losses and excess credits, consolidated groups and their members, and reporting requirements, which include submitting, in certain cases, new Form 8991, Tax on Base Erosion Payments of Taxpayers With Substantial Gross Receipts. This economic analysis describes the economic benefits and costs of the proposed regulations. The Treasury Department and the IRS anticipate that any final rule will contain the analysis prescribed by the Memorandum of Agreement (April 11, 2018) between the Treasury Department and OMB.

B. *Economic Analysis of the Proposed Regulations*

1. *Background*

Congress was concerned, in part, that foreign-owned U.S. subsidiaries are able to reduce their U.S. tax liability by making deductible payments to a foreign parent or foreign affiliates, eroding the U.S tax base if the payments are subject to little or no U.S. withholding tax. This result may favor foreign-headquartered companies over U.S. headquartered companies, creating a tax-driven incentive for foreign takeovers of U.S. firms and enhancing the pressure for U.S headquartered companies to re-domicile abroad and shift income to low-tax jurisdictions. Senate Committee on Finance, Explanation of the Bill, S. Rpt. 115-20, at 391. Section 59A was introduced, in part, as a minimum tax to prevent excessive reduction in corporate tax liability using deductible and certain other payments to foreign related parties.

The Treasury Department views section 59A as largely self-executing, which means that it is binding on taxpayers and the IRS without any regulatory action. The Treasury Department and the IRS recognize, however, that section 59A, while self-executing, provides interpretive latitude for taxpayers and the IRS that could, without further implementation guidance, prompt a variety of responses. Consequently, many of the details behind the relevant terms and necessary calculations required for the computation of an applicable taxpayer's BEAT liability would benefit from greater specificity. As is expected after the passage of major tax reform legislation, the proposed regulations answer unresolved questions and provide detail and specificity for the definitions and concepts described in section 59A, so that taxpayers can readily and accurately determine if they are applicable taxpayers and, if so, compute their BEMTA. For example, the proposed regulations define the scope of crucial terms such as applicable taxpayer, base erosion payments, base erosion tax benefits, de minimis exemptions, and modified taxable income. Specific examples of where these proposed regulations provide clarification of the statute are discussed in this Part B of the Special Analyses section.

As explained in Part VI of the Explanation of Provisions section, an applicable taxpayer computes its BEMTA for the taxable year to determine its liability under section 59A(a). In general, the taxpayer's BEMTA is equal to the excess of (1) the applicable tax rate for the year at issue multiplied by the taxpayer's modified taxable income over (2) the taxpayer's adjusted regular tax liability for that year. Modified taxable income is a taxpayer's taxable income for the year calculated without regard to any base erosion tax benefit or the base erosion percentage of any allowable net operating loss deductions.

In general, the proposed regulations interpret the statute by answering two important questions: (1) to which taxpayers does the BEAT apply, and (2) how do the rules apply to those taxpayers?

a. Applicable Taxpayer

In order for the BEAT to apply, a taxpayer must be an applicable taxpayer, as described in Part II of the Explanation of Provisions section. In general, an applicable taxpayer is a corporation, other than a RIC, REIT, or an S corporation, that satisfies the gross receipts test and the base erosion percentage test. For purposes of these tests, members of a group of corporations related by stock ownership are aggregated. Section 59A(e)(3) refers to aggregation on the basis of persons treated as a single taxpayer under section 52(a) (controlled group of corporations), which includes both domestic and foreign persons. As discussed in Part II.A of the Explanation of Provisions section, the Treasury Department and the IRS determined that to implement the provisions of section 59A, it was necessary to treat foreign corporations as outside of the controlled group for purposes of applying the aggregation rules, except to the extent that the foreign corporation is subject to net income tax under section 882(a) (tax on income of foreign corporations connected with U.S. business). Upon aggregation of domestic and foreign controlled groups of corporations, intra-aggregate group transactions are eliminated. If aggregation were defined to include both domestic and all foreign persons (i.e., a "single employer" under section 52(a)), this elimination would include most base erosion payments, which are defined by section 59A(d)(1) as "any amount paid or accrued by the taxpayer to a foreign person which is a related party of the taxpayer and with respect to which a deduction is allowed under this chapter." Without these base erosion payments, virtually no taxpayer or aggregated group would satisfy the base erosion percentage test; thus substantially all taxpayers (or the aggregate group of which the taxpayer was a member) would be excluded from the requirement to pay a tax equal to the BEMTA.

A taxpayer, or the aggregate group of which the taxpayer is a member, satisfies the gross receipts test if it has average annual gross receipts of at least $500 million for the three taxable years ending with the preceding taxable year.

The base erosion percentage test is satisfied if the taxpayer (or aggregated group) has a base erosion percentage of three percent or more. A lower two percent base erosion percentage applies for banks and registered securities dealers. As explained in proposed § 1.52A-2(e), the base erosion percentage is computed by dividing (1) the aggregate amount of base erosion tax benefits by (2) the sum of the aggregate amount of deductions plus certain other base erosion tax benefits.

The statute is ambiguous or silent on certain details for determining whether a taxpayer is an applicable taxpayer, including the aggregation rule described in Part II.A. of the Explanation of Provisions section. Absent these proposed regulations, there would be uncertainty among taxpayers as to whether the tax equal to the BEMTA would apply to them. Without guidance, different taxpayers would likely take different positions regarding the determination of their status as an applicable taxpayer, which would result in inefficient decision-making and inconsistent application of the statute as taxpayers engage in corporate restructurings, or adjust investment and spending policies based on tax planning strategies to manage BEAT liability (as discussed in this Part B.2.b. of the Special Analyses section). The proposed regulations provide clarity by (1) defining the aggregate group to which the gross receipts and base erosion percentage tests apply, and (2) providing guidance on the definitions and computations necessary to apply those tests.

b. *BEAT Calculation*

Part III of the Explanation of Provisions section discusses the rules regarding the types of payments that are base erosion payments (as defined in proposed § 1.52A-3(b)). Section 59A(d)(5) provides an exception from the definition of a base erosion payment for an amount paid or accrued by a taxpayer for services if the services are eligible for the services cost method under section 482 (without regard to certain requirements under the section 482 regulations) and the amount constitutes the total services cost with no markup component. The statute is ambiguous as to whether the SCM exception (1) does not apply to a payment or accrual that includes a markup component, or (2) does apply to such a payment or accrual that includes a markup component, but only to the extent of the total services costs. The proposed regulations follow the latter approach as discussed in Part B.2.b. of this Special Analyses section.

As discussed in Part III.B.3 of the Explanation of Provisions section, the proposed regulations provide an exception from the definition of base erosion payment for payments to the U.S. branch of a foreign person to the extent that payments to the foreign related party are treated as effectively connected income. In general, whether a payment is a base erosion payment is determined based on whether the recipient is a foreign person (as defined in section 6038A(c)(3)) and a related party, and whether the payment is deductible to the payor. See section 59A(f). A foreign person means any person who is not a United States person. However, as discussed in Part III.B.3. of the Explanation of Provisions section, the Treasury Department and the IRS determined that establishing whether a payment is a base erosion payment based solely on the status of the recipient as a foreign person is inconsistent with the statute's intent of eliminating base erosion. Deductible payments to a foreign person that are treated as effectively connected income are subject to tax under section 871(b) and 882(a) in substantially the same manner as payments to a U.S. citizen or resident, or a domestic corporation, and, thus, such payments do not result in base erosion. Proposed § 1.52A-3(b)(3)(iii) adopts an exception for such amounts.

As described in this Part B.1. of the Special Analyses section, modified taxable income is a taxpayer's taxable income for the year calculated without regard to any base erosion tax benefit or the base erosion percentage of any allowable net operating loss deductions under section 172 (net operating loss deduction). As discussed in Part V.A. of the Explanation of Provisions section, modified taxable income is not calculated by recomputing the tax base without base erosion tax benefits under an approach similar to the alternative minimum tax, which the Act repealed for corporations. To do so would require taxpayers to maintain records for separate carryforward balances for attributes, such as net operating loss deductions and business interest expense carryovers. These items are limited based on taxable income, so under the recomputation or alternative minimum tax-approach, there would most likely be different annual limitations and other computational differences for regular tax purposes and section 59A purposes.

As discussed in Part VII of the Explanation of Provisions section, the proposed regulations apply the aggregate approach to base erosion payments involving partnerships because partnerships are pass-through entities that are not themselves subject to U.S. income tax, but rather the income of the partnership is taxed to the partners in the partnership. Accordingly, the proposed regulations provide that payments by a corporation to a partnership, and payments by a partnership to a corporation, are treated in the first instance as payments to the partners in the partnership and in second instance as payments by the partners in the partnership. For example, in the absence of this aggregate approach rule, a payment by an applicable taxpayer (corporation) to a related foreign partnership could be a base erosion payment even if all of the partners in the partnership are domestic persons. Under this rule, which applies an aggregate approach to partnerships, the payment by the applicable taxpayer (corporation) to a related foreign partnership is only treated as a base erosion payment to the extent that the partners in the foreign partnership are themselves foreign related parties. Conversely, also in the absence of this aggregate approach rule, a payment by an applicable taxpayer (corporation) to a related domestic partnership could not be a base erosion payment even if some or all of the partners in the partnership are foreign related parties. Under the aggregate approach, the payment by an applicable taxpayer (corporation) to a related domestic partnership is treated as a base erosion payment to the extent that the partners in the domestic partnership are foreign related parties. This approach is thus neutral in both preventing potential abuse and preventing potential over breadth. The regulations thus eliminate a distortion that would otherwise be present if the status of base erosion payments is made by reference to the partnership, rather than by reference to the partners. For example, in the absence of the proposed regulations, taxpayers might be incentivized to route payments through a domestic partnership that is formed by foreign persons as an intermediary to avoid the BEAT. Conversely, in the absence of the proposed regulations, taxpayers would be incentivized to restructure to avoid making any payments to a foreign partnership that has partners that are solely domestic because such payment could be inappropriately classified as a base erosion payment. The Treasury Department requests comments on the approach to partnerships in the proposed regulations.

c. *Anti-abuse and Reporting Requirements*

Section 59A(i) provides the Secretary authority to issue regulations and other guidance to prevent the avoidance of the purposes of section 59A. As such, proposed § 1.59A-9 provides rules recharacterizing certain specified transactions as necessary to prevent the avoidance of section 59A, and provides examples.

The proposed regulations also provide reporting requirements necessary to properly administer and enforce section 59A. In particular, the Treasury Department and the IRS have identified certain types of information from taxpayers who are applicable taxpayers for purposes of section 59A that will be required to be reported on Form 5472, Information Return of a 25% Foreign-Owned U.S. Corporation or a Foreign Corporation Engaged in a U.S. Trade or Business (Under Sections 6038A and 6038C of the Internal Revenue Code), and a new Form 8991, Tax on Base Erosion Payments of Taxpayers With Substantial Gross Receipts. Further detail regarding anticipated paperwork burdens can be found in Part C (Paperwork Reduction Act) of this Special Analyses section, which includes a link to draft forms and guidance for providing comment on the proposed forms.

2. *Anticipated Benefits and Costs of the Proposed Regulations*

a. *Baseline*

The Treasury Department and the IRS have assessed the impacts, benefits, and costs of the proposed regulations against a "no action" baseline that reflects projected tax-related and other behavior in the absence of the proposed regulations.

The Treasury Department projects that the proposed regulations will have a non-revenue effect on the economy of at least $100 million per year ($2018) measured against this baseline. The Treasury Department requests comments on this conclusion.

b. *Anticipated Benefits*

The Treasury Department and IRS expect that the certainty and clarity provided by these proposed regulations, relative to the baseline, will enhance U.S. economic performance under the statute. Because a tax has not previously been imposed on base-eroding payments in this manner and the statute is silent on certain aspects of definitions and calculations, taxpayers can particularly benefit from enhanced specificity regarding the relevant terms and necessary calculations they are required to apply under the statute. In the absence of this enhanced specificity, similarly situated taxpayers might interpret the statutory rules of section 59A differently. For example, different taxpayers might pursue intercompany investment and payment policies based on different assumptions about whether such investments and payments are base eroding payments subject to section 59A, and some taxpayers may forego specific investments and payments that other taxpayers deem worthwhile based on different interpretations of the tax consequences alone. The guidance provided in these proposed regulations helps to ensure that taxpayers face more uniform incentives when making economic decisions, a tenet of economic efficiency. Consistent reporting across taxpayers also increases the IRS's ability to consistently enforce the tax rules, thus increasing equity and decreasing opportunities for tax evasion.

For example, as described in Part III.B.3 of the Explanation of Provisions section, the proposed regulations exclude from base erosion payments those payments made to a foreign related party that are treated as effectively connected income of the foreign payee. Such payments are treated as income to the recipient and subject to U.S. tax, substantially similar to any payment between related U.S. corporations. The payments are not base eroding because their receipt is taxable by the United States. Further, treatment of effectively connected income payments to a foreign related party would produce different tax results for two similarly situated U.S. taxpayers. That is, if the taxpayer were to make a payment to a related U.S. corporation, the payment generally would not be subject to the BEAT, but if a taxpayer were to make a payment to a foreign person with respect to its effectively connected income, it would give rise to BEAT liability, despite the fact that in both cases the recipients include the payment in U.S. taxable income.

The Treasury Department and the IRS also considered the benefits and costs of providing the specific proposed terms, calculations, and other details regarding the BEAT. In developing these proposed regulations, the Treasury Department and the IRS have generally aimed to apply the principle that an economically efficient tax system would treat income derived from similar economic decisions similarly, to the extent consistent with the statute and considerations of administrability of the tax system. For example, as noted in Part B.1.b. of this Special Analyses section, section 59A(d)(5) provides an exception to the definition of a base erosion payment for certain payments made to foreign related parties for services that meet the eligibility requirements for use of the SCM (under section 482). The proposed regulations adopt an approach that allows an SCM exception for the total cost of services even if there is a profit markup so long as a transaction meets certain other requirements for using the SCM (under section 482). The proposed regulations provide that the portion of any payment that exceeds the total cost of services is not eligible for the SCM exception and is a base eroding payment.

Alternatives would have been to disallow the SCM exception for the entire amount of any payment that includes a markup component, or to not provide any guidance at all regarding the SCM exception. The Treasury Department and the IRS rejected the former approach. The section 482 regulations mandate intercompany pricing under an "arm's length standard." Under specific circumstances, the section 482 regulations provide that intercompany payments for services can be set by a taxpayer at the cost of providing the service with no profit markup. However, the section 482 regulations prohibit use of this cost-only SCM approach for services "that contribute significantly to fundamental risks of business success or failure" (the "business judgment rule"). See § 1.482-9(b)(5). At arm's length, such services would generally be priced to include a profit element to satisfy the market's demand for, and supply of, services among recipients and providers. Section 59A(d)(5)(A) explicitly allows an exception from the BEAT for services that would be eligible for the SCM, "determined without regard to [the business judgment rule]." By allowing an exception from the BEAT for intercompany service payments that do not include a profit markup (i.e., under the SCM transfer pricing method), but also for intercompany service payments that must apply a different transfer pricing method, and therefore generally would include a profit markup at arm's length (i.e., those subject to the business judgment rule), the statute creates ambiguity about the SCM exception's application with respect to the portion of intercompany prices paid for services reflecting the cost of providing the services when there is also a mark-up component.

To promote the consistent application by taxpayers of a SCM exception to the BEAT, and to provide greater clarity, the proposed regulations provide that the SCM exception is available if there is a profit markup (provided that other requirements are satisfied), but the portion of any payment exceeding cost is not eligible for the SCM exception. The Treasury Department and the IRS also rejected the option of not providing any guidance at all regarding the SCM exception because if taxpayers relied on statutory language alone, taxpayers would adopt different approaches due to ambiguity in the statute, leaving it open to differing statutory interpretations and an inconsistent application of the statute. The Treasury Department and IRS expect that approximately one-half of taxpayers filing Form 8891 would avail themselves of the SCM exception. The Treasury Department and the IRS request comments about application of the SCM exception.

As discussed in Part V.A of the Explanation of Provisions section, the Treasury Department and the IRS also considered alternatives regarding the method by which modified taxable income could be calculated for purposes of the BEAT. The proposed regulations could have followed an add-back approach or an approach more similar to that used for the alternative minimum tax. As noted in Part B.1.b. of this Special Analyses section, the proposed regulations adopt the former approach, which is expected to be less costly for taxpayers to apply since taxpayers will not have to recompute their entire tax return on a different basis, or maintain separate sets of records to track annual limitations on attributes such as net operating loss carryforwards or business interest expense carryforwards.

In addition, the proposed regulations clarify that the computations of modified taxable income and BEMTA are done on a taxpayer-by-taxpayer basis. That is, the aggregate group concept is used solely for determining whether a taxpayer is an applicable taxpayer, and does not apply to the computations of modified taxable income and the BEMTA. In the absence of these clarifying definitions, taxpayers could calculate the BEMTA differently depending on their differing views of the base on which the BEAT should be calculated (i.e., aggregated group, consolidated group, individual company), leading to inequitable results across otherwise similar taxpayers. Under the proposed regulations' approach for the calculation of modified taxable income and BEMTA, it is also expected to be less costly for taxpayers to calculate BEMTA since the statutory framework of section 59A applies in addition to the regular tax liability of a taxpayer. Calculation of BEAT liability at an aggregate level, for example, would require taxpayers to first aggregate regular taxable liabilities of the different taxpayers, calculate the BEMTA on an aggregated basis, and then reallocate any BEAT liability among the separate taxpayers. The approach of the proposed regulations, which clarify that the tax should be calculated on a separate taxpayer basis, simplifies these calculations.

The proposed regulations also include de minimis thresholds for partnerships and for registered securities dealers. In general, such thresholds reduce compliance costs for the large number of small taxpayers that would fall below such threshold without substantially affecting the BEAT base. For the de minimis exception for banks and registered securities dealers, in the absence of an exception, affiliated groups that are not principally engaged in banking or securities dealing would be incentivized to alter their business structure to eliminate minimal banks or registered securities dealers from their aggregate groups. These changes would give rise to tax-motivated, inefficient restructuring costs. A de minimis threshold reduces this potential inefficiency again without substantially affecting the BEAT base. In both cases, the thresholds were chosen to balance these competing concerns and to adhere to generally similar standards elsewhere in the Code. The Treasury Department and IRS request comment on the impact of this approach.

3. *Anticipated impacts on administrative and compliance costs*

Because the statute requires payment of tax regardless of the issuance of regulations or instructions, the new forms, revisions to existing forms, and other proposed regulations can lower the burden on taxpayers of determining their tax liability. The Treasury Department and the IRS expect that the proposed regulations will reduce the costs for taxpayers to comply with the Act, on balance, relative to the baseline of no promulgated regulations.

Certain record-keeping requirements added by the proposed regulations derive directly from statutory changes that require information from a reporting corporation that is also a section 59A applicable taxpayer. Proposed § 1.6038A-2 increases record-keeping requirements for taxpayers because additional information is to be reported on Form 5472 and Form 8991.

Proposed § 1.59A-3(b)(3) also increases record-keeping requirements for taxpayers because additional information is required for taxpayers to satisfy a regulatory requirement of the SCM exception. The requirement added by these proposed regulations is consistent with the requirements for eligibility for the services cost method under section 482, including the existing requirements of § 1.482-9(b).

C. *Paperwork Reduction Act*

1. *Collections of Information - Forms 8891, 5471, 5472, and 8858*

The collections of information in these proposed regulations with respect to section 59A are in proposed §§ 1.59-3(b)(3) and 1.6038A-2. The information collection requirements pursuant to proposed § 1.59A-3(b)(3)(i)(C) are discussed further below. The IRS intends that the collections of information pursuant to section 59A, except with respect to information collected under proposed § 1.59A-3(b)(3), will be conducted by way of the following:

- Form 8991, Tax on Base Erosion Payments of Taxpayers With Substantial Gross Receipts;
- Schedule G to the Form 5471, Information Return of U.S. Persons With Respect to Certain Foreign Corporations;
- Part VIII of the updated Form 5472, Information Return of a 25% Foreign-Owned U.S. Corporation or a Foreign Corporation Engaged in a U.S. Trade or Business;
- Revised Form 8858, Information Return of U.S. Persons With Respect to Foreign Disregarded Entities.

For purposes of the Paperwork Reduction Act, the reporting burden associated with the collections of information with respect to section 59A, other than with respect to proposed § 1.59A-3(b)(3), will be reflected in the IRS Forms 14029 Paperwork Reduction Act Submission, associated with Forms 5471 (OMB control numbers 1545-0123, and 1545-0074), 5472 (OMB control number 1545-0123), 8858 (OMB control numbers 1545-0123, 1545-0074, and 1545-1910), and 8991 (OMB control number 1545-0123).

The current status of the Paperwork Reduction Act submissions related to BEAT is provided in the following table. The BEAT provisions are included in aggregated burden estimates for the OMB control numbers listed below which, in the case of 1545-0123, represents a total estimated burden time, including all other related forms and schedules for corporations, of 3.157 billion hours and total estimated monetized costs of $58.148 billion ($2017) and, in the case of 1545-0074, a total estimated burden time, including all other related forms and schedules for individuals, of 1.784 billion hours and total estimated monetized costs of $31.764 billion ($2017). The burden estimates provided in the OMB control numbers below are aggregate amounts that relate to the entire package of forms associated with the OMB control number, and will in the future include but not isolate the estimated burden of only the BEAT requirements. These numbers are therefore unrelated to the future calculations needed to assess the burden imposed by the proposed regulations. The Treasury Department and IRS urge readers to recognize that these numbers are duplicates and to guard against overcounting the burden that international tax provisions imposed prior to TCJA. No burden estimates specific to the proposed regulations are currently available. The Treasury Department has not estimated the burden, including that of any new information collections, related to the requirements under the proposed regulations. Those estimates would capture both changes made by the Act and those that arise out of discretionary authority exercised in the proposed regulations. The Treasury Department and the IRS request comment on all aspects of information collection burdens related to the proposed regulations. In addition, when available, drafts of IRS forms are posted for comment at *https://apps.irs.gov/app/picklist/list/draftTaxForms.htm*.

Form	Type of Filer	OMB Number(s)	Status
Form 5471 (including Schedule G)	Business (NEW Model)	1545-0123	Published in the FRN on 10/8/18. Public Comment period closes on 12/10/18.
	Link: *https://www.federalregister.gov/documents/2018/10/09/2018-21846/proposed-collection-comment-request-for-forms-1065-1065-b-1066-1120-1120-c-1120-f-1120-h-1120-nd*		
	Individual (NEW Model)	1545-0074	Limited Scope submission (1040 only) on 10/11/18 at OIRA for review. Full ICR submission for all forms in 3/2019. 60 Day FRN not published yet for full collection.
	Link: https://www.reginfo.gov/public/do/PRAViewICR?ref_nbr=201808-1545-031		
Form 5472 (including Part VIII)	Business (NEW Model)	1545-0123	Published in the FRN on 10/11/18. Public Comment period closes on 12/10/18.
	Link: *https://www.federalregister.gov/documents/2018/10/09/2018-21846/proposed-collection-comment-request-for-forms-1065-1065-b-1066-1120-1120-c-1120-f-1120-h-1120-nd*		
	All other Filers (mainly trusts and estates) (Legacy system)	1545-1910	Published in the FRN on 10/30/18. Public Comment period closes on11/30/18. ICR in process by the Treasury Department as of 9/6/18.
Form 8858	Link: *https://www.federalregister.gov/documents/2018/10/30/2018-23644/agency-information-collection-activities-submission-for-omb-review-comment-request-multiple-irs*		
	Business (NEW Model)	1545-0123	Published in the FRN on 10/8/18. Public Comment period closes on 12/10/18.
	Link: https://www.federalregister.gov/documents/2018/10/09/2018-21846/proposed-collection-comment-request-for-forms-1065-1065-b-1066-1120-1120-c-1120-f-1120-h-1120-nd		
	Individual (NEW Model)	1545-0074	Limited Scope submission (1040 only) on 10/11/18 at OIRA for review. Full ICR submission for all forms in 3-2019. 60 Day FRN not published yet for full collection.
	Link: *https://www.reginfo.gov/public/do/PRAViewICR?ref_nbr=201808-1545-031*		

Form	Type of Filer	OMB Number(s)	Status
Form 8991	Business (NEW Model)	1545-0123	Published in the FRN on 10/11/18. Public Comment period closes on 12/10/18.
	Link: *https://www.federalregister.gov/documents/2018/10/09/2018-21846/proposed-collection-comment-request-for-forms-1065-1065-b-1066-1120-1120-c-1120-f-1120-h-1120-nd*		

Related New or Revised Tax Forms

	New	Revision of existing form	Number of respondents (2018, estimated)
Form 8991	✓		3,500 - 4,500
Form 5471, Schedule G		✓	15,000 - 25,000
Form 5472, Part VIII	✓		80,000 - 100,000
Form 8858		✓	15,000 - 25,000

The numbers of respondents in the Related New or Revised Tax Forms table were estimated by Treasury's Office of Tax Analysis based on data from IRS Compliance Planning and Analytics using tax return data for tax years 2015 and 2016. Data for Form 8991 represent preliminary estimates of the total number of taxpayers which may be required to file the new Form 8991. Only certain large corporate taxpayers with gross receipts of at least $500 million are expected to file this form. Data for each of the Forms 5471, 5472, and 8858 represent preliminary estimates of the total number of taxpayers that are expected to file these information returns regardless of whether that taxpayer must also file Form 8991.

2. Collection of Information - Proposed § 1.59A-3(b)(3)

In contrast to the collections of information pursuant to other provisions of section 59A (as discussed above), the IRS intends that the information collection requirements pursuant to proposed § 1.59A-3(b)(3)(i)(C) will be satisfied by the taxpayer maintaining permanent books and records that are adequate to verify the amount charged for the services and the total services costs incurred by the renderer, including a description of the services in question, identification of the renderer and the recipient of the services, calculation of the amount of profit mark-up (if any) paid for the services, and sufficient documentation to allow verification of the methods used to allocate and apportion the costs to the services.

The collection of information contained in proposed § 1.59A-3(b)(3) has been submitted to the Office of Management and Budget for review in accordance with the Paperwork Reduction Act of 1994 (44 U.S.C. 3507(d)). Comments on the collection of information should be sent to the Office of Management and Budget, Attn: Desk Officer for the Department of the Treasury, Office of Information and Regulatory Affairs, Washington, DC 20503, with copies to the Internal Revenue Service, Attn: IRS Reports Clearance Officer, SE:W:CAR:MP:T:T:SP, Washington, DC 20224. Comments on the collection of information should be received by February 9, 2019.

Comments are specifically requested concerning:

Whether the proposed collection of information is necessary for the proper performance of the duties of the IRS, including whether the information will have practical utility;

The accuracy of the estimated burden associated with the proposed collection of information (including underlying assumptions and methodology);

How the quality, utility, and clarity of the information to be collected may be enhanced;

How the burden of complying with the proposed collection of information may be minimized, including through the application of automated collection techniques or other forms of information technology; and

Estimates of capital or start-up costs and costs of operation, maintenance, and purchases of services to provide information.

The collection of information in proposed § 1.59A-3(b)(3) is mandatory for taxpayers seeking to exclude certain amounts paid or accrued to a foreign related party for services from treatment as base erosion payments for purposes of section 59A (the "SCM exception to the BEAT", as discussed this Part B.2.b. of the Special Analyses section). Taxpayers seeking to rely on the SCM exception to the BEAT are aggregate groups of corporations with average annual gross receipts of at least $500 million and that make payments to foreign related parties. The information required to be maintained will be used by the IRS for tax compliance purposes.

Estimated total annual reporting burden: 5,000 hours.

Estimated average annual burden hours per respondent: 2.5 hours.

Estimated average cost per respondent ($2017): $238.00.

Estimated number of respondents: 2,000. This estimate is based on the assumption that only a portion of taxpayers will qualify for the SCM exception, multiplied by the number of respondents shown above.

Estimated annual frequency of responses: Once.

Based on these estimates, the annual three-year reporting burden for those electing the SCM exemption is $0.16 mn/yr ($2017) ($238 x 2000/3, converted to millions).

An agency may not conduct or sponsor, and a person is not required to respond to, a collection of information unless it displays a valid control number assigned by the Office of Management and Budget.

Books or records relating to a collection of information must be retained as long as their contents may become material in the administration of any internal revenue law. Generally, tax returns and tax return information are confidential, as required by 26 U.S.C. 6103.

D. *Regulatory Flexibility Act*

It is hereby certified that these regulations will not have a significant economic impact on a substantial number of small entities within the meaning of section 601(6) of the Regulatory Flexibility Act (5 U.S.C. chapter 6). Accordingly, a regulatory flexibility analysis is not required. This certification is based on the fact that these regulations will primarily affect aggregate groups of corporations with average annual gross receipts of at least $500 million and that make payments to foreign related parties. Generally only large businesses both have substantial gross receipts and make payments to foreign related parties.

Notwithstanding this certification, the Treasury Department and the IRS invite comments from the public about the impact of this proposed rule on small entities.

Pursuant to section 7805(f), these regulations will be submitted to the Chief Counsel for Advocacy of the Small Business Administration for comment on their impact on small business.

E. *Unfunded Mandates Reform Act*

Section 202 of the Unfunded Mandates Reform Act of 1995 (UMRA) requires that agencies assess anticipated costs and benefits and take certain other actions before issuing a final rule that includes any Federal mandate that may result in expenditures in any one year by a state, local, or tribal government, in the aggregate, or by the private sector, of $100 million in 1995 dollars, updated annually for inflation. In 2018, that threshold is approximately $150 million. This rule does not include any Federal mandate that may result in expenditures by state, local, or tribal governments, or by the private sector in excess of that threshold.

F. *Executive Order 13132: Federalism*

Executive Order 13132 (entitled "Federalism") prohibits an agency from publishing any rule that has federalism implications if the rule either imposes substantial, direct compliance costs on state and local governments, and is not required by statute, or preempts state law, unless the agency meets the consultation and funding requirements of section 6 of the Executive Order. This proposed rule does not have federalism implications and does not impose substantial direct compliance costs on state and local governments or preempt state law within the meaning of the Executive Order.

Comments and Request for Public Hearing

Before these proposed regulations are adopted as final regulations, consideration will be given to any comments that are submitted timely to the IRS as prescribed in this preamble under the "Addresses" heading. The Treasury Department and the IRS request comments on all aspects of the proposed rules.

All comments will be available at *www.regulations.gov* or upon request. A public hearing will be scheduled if requested in writing by any person that timely submits written comments. If a public hearing is scheduled, notice of the date, time, and place for the public hearing will be published in the **Federal Register**.

Statement of Availability of IRS Documents

IRS revenue procedures, revenue rulings, notices, and other guidance cited in this preamble are published in the Internal Revenue Bulletin and are available from the Superintendent of Documents, U.S. Government Publishing Office, Washington, DC 20402, or by visiting the IRS website at *http://www.irs.gov*.

Drafting Information

The principal authors of the proposed regulations are Sheila Ramaswamy and Karen Walny of the Office of Associate Chief Counsel (International) and Julie Wang and John P. Stemwedel of the Office of Associate Chief Counsel (Corporate). However, other personnel from the Treasury Department and the IRS participated in their development.

Partial Withdrawal of Proposed Regulations

Accordingly, under the authority of 26 U.S.C. 7805 and 26 U.S.C. 1502, § 1.1502-2 of the notice of proposed rulemaking (IA-57-89) published in the **Federal Register** on December 30, 1992 (57 FR 62251) is withdrawn.

[¶ 49,784] Proposed Amendments of Regulations (REG-113604-18), published in the Federal Register on December 27, 2018.

[Code Secs. 864 and 897]

Source of income: Foreign income: Nonresident aliens: Foreign corporations: US real property.Reg. § § 1.864(c)(8)-1 and 1.897-7 and amendments of Reg. § 1.897-7T, implementing section 864(c)(8) of the Internal Revenue Code, are proposed.

AGENCY: Internal Revenue Service (IRS), Treasury.

ACTION: Notice of proposed rulemaking.

SUMMARY: This document contains proposed regulations implementing section 864(c)(8) of the Internal Revenue Code. The proposed regulations affect certain foreign persons that recognize gain or loss from the sale or exchange of an interest in a partnership that is engaged in a trade or business within the United States. The proposed regulations also affect partnerships that, directly or indirectly, have foreign persons as partners.

DATES: Written or electronic comments and requests for a public hearing must be received by February 25, 2019.

ADDRESSES: Send submissions to: CC:PA:LPD:PR (REG-113604-18), Internal Revenue Service, Room 5203, P.O. Box 7604, Ben Franklin Station, Washington, DC 20044. Submissions may be hand-delivered Monday through Friday between the hours of 8 a.m. and 4 p.m. to CC:PA:LPD:PR (REG-113604-18), Courier's Desk, Internal Revenue Service, 1111 Constitution Avenue, NW., Washington, DC 20224, or sent electronically via the Federal eRulemaking Portal at *http://www.regulations.gov* (IRS REG-113604-18).

FOR FURTHER INFORMATION CONTACT: Concerning the proposed regulations, Ronald M. Gootzeit or Chadwick Rowland, (202) 317-6937; concerning submissions of comments or requests for a public hearing, Regina L. Johnson, (202) 317-6901 (not toll-free numbers).

SUPPLEMENTARY INFORMATION:

Background

A foreign partner in a partnership that is engaged in the conduct of a trade or business within the United States is itself considered to be so engaged. *See* section 875. Under a 1991 revenue ruling, in determining the tax consequences of the sale or exchange of a foreign partner's interest in a partnership engaged in the conduct of a trade or business within the United States, the IRS held that the partnership's property located in the United States that is used or held for use in the partnership's trade or business within the United States is used to determine the extent to which income derived from the sale or exchange of the partnership interest is effectively connected with the conduct of the partner's trade or business within the United States. Rev. Rul. 91-32, 1991-1 C.B. 107. Under the ruling, if there is unrealized gain or loss in partnership assets that would be treated as effectively connected with the conduct of the partnership's trade or business within the United States if those assets were sold by the partnership, some or all of the foreign person's gain or loss from the sale or exchange of a partnership interest may be treated as effectively connected with the partner's conduct of a trade or business within the United States. However, a 2017 Tax Court case held instead that, generally, gain or loss on the sale or exchange by a foreign person of an interest in such a partnership is foreign source gain or loss based on the residence of the selling partner because gain on the sale of the partnership interest is not attributable to the partnership's assets and activities. As a result, such gain or loss generally would not be treated as effectively connected with the conduct of a trade or business. *Grecian Magnesite Mining v. Commissioner*, 149 T.C. No. 3 (2017), *appeal argued*, No. 17-1268 (D.C. Cir. Oct. 9, 2018).

Section 864(c)(8), which was added to the Internal Revenue Code (the "Code") by section 13501 of the Tax Cuts and Jobs Act, Public Law 115-97 (2017) (the "Act"), generally overturns the result of *Grecian Magnesite Mining v. Commissioner* by providing that gain or loss of a nonresident alien individual or foreign corporation (a "foreign transferor") from the sale, exchange, or other disposition ("transfer") of a partnership interest is treated as effectively connected with the conduct of a trade or business within the United States ("effectively connected gain" or "effectively connected loss") to the extent that the transferor would have had effectively connected gain or loss if the partnership had sold all of its assets at fair market value as of the date of the sale or exchange ("deemed sale").

Section 864(c)(8)(E) generally provides that the Secretary shall prescribe such regulations or other guidance as the Secretary determines appropriate for the application of section 864(c)(8). Section 864(c)(8) is effective for sales, exchanges, and dispositions on or after November 27, 2017.

New section 1446(f) was also added to the Code by section 13501 of the Act. Section 1446(f)(1) requires that the transferee of a partnership interest withhold 10 percent of the amount realized on the transferor's disposition of the partnership interest (if any portion of the gain would be treated as effectively connected gain) unless the transferor certifies that the transferor is not a foreign person. Section 1446(f) is effective for sales, exchanges, and dispositions after December 31, 2017.

On December 29, 2017, the Department of the Treasury (the "Treasury Department") and the IRS released Notice 2018-08, 2018-7 I.R.B. 352 (the "PTP Notice"). The PTP Notice temporarily suspends the requirement to withhold on amounts realized in connection with the sale, exchange, or disposition of certain interests in publicly traded partnerships ("PTPs") in response to stakeholder concerns that applying section 1446(f) to dispositions of interests in PTPs without guidance presented significant practical problems. On April 2, 2018, the Treasury Department and the IRS released Notice 2018-29, 2018-16 I.R.B. 495, which announced an intent to issue proposed regulations under section 1446(f) that apply in the case of a disposition of a partnership interest that is not publicly traded and provided temporary guidance.

Explanation of Provisions

I. *Gain or Loss on the Transfer of a Partnership Interest*

Section 864(c)(8)(A) provides that gain or loss of a foreign transferor from the transfer of an interest, owned directly or indirectly, in a partnership that is engaged in any trade or business within the United States is treated as effectively connected gain or loss to the extent such gain or loss does not exceed the amount determined under section 864(c)(8)(B). In general, section 864(c)(8)(B) limits the amount of effectively connected gain or loss to the portion of the foreign transferor's distributive share of gain or loss that would have been effectively connected gain or loss if the partnership had sold all of its assets at fair market value. The proposed regulations set forth rules for determining gain or loss described in section 864(c)(8)(A) and the limitation described in section 864(c)(8)(B), each of which is discussed in this section I of this Explanation of Provisions.

A. *Determination of Gain or Loss Described in Section 864(c)(8)(A)*

To determine the amount of gain or loss described in section 864(c)(8)(A), generally, the proposed regulations require that a foreign transferor first determine its gain or loss on the transfer of a partnership interest ("outside gain" and "outside loss"). For this purpose, the proposed regulations provide that outside gain or loss is determined under all relevant provisions of the Code and the regulations thereunder. As described in section I.A.1 of this Explanation of Provisions, a foreign transferor may recognize capital gain or loss ("outside capital gain" or "outside capital loss") and ordinary gain or loss ("outside ordinary gain" or "outside ordinary loss") on the transfer of its partnership interest and must separately apply section 864(c)(8) with respect to its capital gain or loss and its ordinary gain or loss.

1. Interaction with Sections 741 and 751

Section 864(c)(8) provides rules regarding the treatment of gain or loss on the transfer of a partnership interest as effectively connected gain or loss, but it does not address the computation of the amount of gain or loss to a partner upon the transfer. Rather, applicable tax law, including subchapter K, determines the amount and character of outside gain or loss on the transfer of a partnership interest. For example, the reduction in a transferor's share of partnership liabilities is treated as an amount realized on the transfer of the partnership interest under section 1001 and the regulations thereunder. See section 752(d) and § 1.752-1(h).

Section 741 provides that on a sale or exchange of an interest in a partnership, gain or loss is recognized by the transferor, and shall be considered capital gain or loss except as otherwise provided in section 751. Section 751 provides that an amount received by a transferor of a partnership interest that is attributable to unrealized receivables or inventory items of the partnership ("section 751 property") is considered ordinary income or loss. As a result of sections 741 and 751 and the regulations thereunder, gain or loss on a sale or exchange of a partnership interest can comprise capital gain, capital loss, ordinary income, or ordinary loss (or a combination thereof). See §§ 1.741-1(a) and 1.751-1(a).

In general, the proposed regulations provide that a foreign transferor must determine the portion of its capital gain or loss, and the portion of its ordinary income or loss from section 751 property, that must each be characterized as effectively connected gain or loss under section 864(c)(8). See proposed § 1.864(c)(8)-1(b). As provided in section 864(c)(8)(A) and further described in section I.B of this Explanation of Provisions, the proposed regulations provide that a foreign partner's effectively connected gain or loss will not exceed its outside gain or loss on the sale of the interest as determined under sections 741 and 751 and the regulations thereunder. Thus, the amount of gain or loss determined under section 741 (before application of section 751) is not a limitation on the amount of gain or loss characterized as effectively connected with the conduct of a trade or business within the United States under the proposed regulations.

2. Nonrecognition Transactions

The proposed regulations provide that the gain or loss on the transfer of a partnership interest that is subject to tax as effectively connected gain or loss is limited to gain or loss otherwise recognized under the Code. See proposed § 1.864(c)(8)-1(b)(2)(ii). When a nonrecognition provision results in a foreign transferor recognizing only a portion of its gain or loss on the transfer of an interest in a partnership, section 864(c)(8) may apply with respect to the portion of the gain or loss recognized.

Although section 864(c)(8)(E) authorizes regulations or other guidance with respect to the application of section 864(c)(8) to nonrecognition transactions, the proposed regulations do not contain special rules applicable to nonrecognition transactions. The Treasury Department and the IRS recognize, however, that certain nonrecognition transactions may have the effect of reducing gain or loss that would be taken into account for U.S. federal income tax purposes. For example, if a partnership that conducts a trade or business within the United States owns property not subject to tax under section 871(b) or 882(a) in the hands of a foreign partner, the partnership may distribute that property to the foreign partner rather than a U.S. partner. The Treasury Department and the IRS continue to consider, and comments are requested regarding, whether other Code provisions adequately address transactions that rely on section 731 distributions to reduce the scope of assets subject to U.S. federal income taxation, and may propose rules addressing these types of transactions.

B. *Determination of Deemed Sale Gain or Loss*

1. In General

After outside gain and loss are determined under proposed § 1.864(c)(8)-1(b), the proposed regulations set forth three amounts that a foreign transferor must determine to derive the limitation in section 864(c)(8)(B) against which the outside gain or loss is compared: (1) With respect to each asset held by the partnership, the amount of gain or loss that the partnership would recognize in connection with a deemed sale to an unrelated party in a fully taxable transaction for cash equal to the asset's fair market value immediately before the partner's transfer of its partnership interest; (2) the amount of that gain or loss that would be treated as effectively connected gain or loss ("deemed sale EC gain" and "deemed sale EC loss"); and (3) the foreign transferor's distributive share of the ordinary and capital components of any deemed sale EC gain and deemed sale EC loss. The proposed regulations refer to the separate sums of the foreign transferor's distributive shares of the ordinary and capital components of deemed sale EC gain and deemed sale EC loss items for all assets, determined at the level of the foreign transferor, as "aggregate deemed sale EC capital gain," "aggregate deemed sale EC capital loss," "aggregate deemed sale EC ordinary gain," and "aggregate deemed sale EC ordinary loss."

After each of these aggregate amounts is determined, the proposed regulations implement the limitation described in section 864(c)(8)(B), generally, by comparing the foreign transferor's outside gain or loss amounts with the relevant aggregate deemed sale EC gain or loss. This determination is made separately with respect to capital gain or capital loss and gain or loss treated as ordinary income or ordinary loss. Thus, for example, a foreign transferor would compare its outside capital gain to its aggregate deemed sale EC capital gain, treating the former as effectively connected gain only to the extent it does not exceed the latter. See proposed § 1.864(c)(8)-1(b)(3).

2. Treatment of Deemed Sale Gain or Loss as Effectively Connected Gain or Loss

As described in Part I.B.1 of this Explanation of Provisions, the proposed regulations require a foreign transferor to determine the amount of gain or loss that would arise in a deemed asset sale that would be treated as effectively connected gain or loss. In general, gain or loss on the sale of personal property is effectively connected with the conduct of a trade or business within the United States if the gain is from sources within the United States and it satisfies the requirements of section 864(c) and the regulations thereunder. Accordingly, the proposed regulations provide that section 864 and the regulations thereunder apply for purposes of determining whether gain or loss that would arise in a deemed asset sale would be treated as effectively connected gain or loss. See proposed § 1.864(c)(8)-1(c)(2)(i).

The determination as to whether gain or loss from a deemed asset sale by the partnership would be from sources within or without the United States, and whether that income would be treated as effectively connected gain or loss, is based on certain factual determinations, including whether the gain or loss results from a sale that is attributable to an office or other fixed place of business in the United States. The proposed regulations provide that, for purposes of determining whether gain or loss recognized in connection with a deemed asset sale by the partnership would be from sources within or without the United States, and thus whether that income would be treated as effectively connected gain or loss, the deemed asset sale is treated as attributable to an office or fixed place of business in the United States maintained by the partnership. As a result, deemed sale gain or loss generally would be treated as from sources within the United States. To prevent this rule from potentially converting gain or loss from assets with no connection to the partnership's trade or business within the United States into effectively connected gain or loss, the proposed regulations provide that gain or loss from the deemed sale of a partnership asset is not treated as effectively connected gain or loss if (1) no income or gain previously produced by the asset was taxable as effectively connected with the conduct of a trade or business within the United States by the partnership (or a predecessor of the partnership) during the ten-year period ending on the date of the transfer, and (2) the asset was not used, or held for use, in the conduct of a trade or business within the United States by the partnership (or a predecessor of the partnership) during the ten-year period ending on the date of transfer. See proposed § 1.864(c)(8)-1(c)(2)(ii). Comments are requested as to whether additional guidance is needed regarding the source of gain or loss resulting from a deemed sale by the partnership, including rules coordinating this rule with section 865(e)(2)(B).

3. Determining Distributive Share of Deemed Sale EC Gain and Deemed Sale EC Loss

The flush language of section 864(c)(8)(B) provides that a transferor partner's distributive share of gain or loss on the deemed sale is determined in the same manner as the transferor partner's distributive share of the non-separately stated taxable income or loss of the partnership. The term "non-separately stated taxable income or loss of the partnership" is not defined in the Code or regulations. The proposed regulations provide that a partner's distributive share of gain or loss from the deemed sale is determined under all applicable Code sections (including section 704), taking into account allocations of tax items applying the principles of section 704(c), including any remedial allocations under § 1.704-3(d), and any section 743 basis adjustment pursuant to § 1.743-1(j)(3). The Treasury Department and IRS propose this approach because applying section 704 more closely ties the results of the deemed sale with regard to the selling foreign partner to the economic results of an actual sale, as compared (for example) to an approach that did not consider special allocations or considered only a partner's share of ordinary business income, which would distort the economic agreement among the partners. See proposed § 1.864(c)(8)-1(c)(3)(i).

The Treasury Department and the IRS are considering whether section 704 and the regulations thereunder adequately prevent the avoidance of the purposes of section 864(c)(8) through allocations of effectively connected gain or loss to specific partners. For example, immediately before a foreign transferor sells its interest in a partnership, adjustments could be made to partnership allocations that would result in the foreign transferor recognizing less effectively connected gain from the deemed sale by the partnership. While statutory and regulatory provisions, as well as judicial doctrines, may limit the extent to which inappropriate results may be obtained in that transaction or similar transactions, the Treasury Department and the IRS are considering whether additional guidance is necessary to prevent abuse. Comments are requested as to whether there are specific situations in which the purposes of section 864(c)(8) may be avoided and specific suggestions for additional guidance to address those situations.

C. *Source*

Neither section 864(c)(8) nor the proposed regulations address the source of gain or loss from the transfer of a partnership interest. Section 864(c)(4) provides that, except as enumerated in section 864(c)(4)(B) and (C), no income, gain, or loss from sources without the United States is treated as effectively connected gain or loss. Section 864(c)(8)(A) and the proposed regulations, however, apply "[n]otwithstanding any other provision of [subtitle A of the Code]," such that gain or loss recognized on the transfer of an interest in a partnership that is engaged in a trade or business within the United States may be treated as effectively connected gain or loss even if it is from sources without the United States. Comments are requested as to whether, and what, additional guidance is necessary regarding the source of gain or loss subject to section 864(c)(8).

D. *Provision is Non-Exclusive*

The proposed regulations clarify that they do not apply to prevent any portion of gain or loss recognized on the transfer of a partnership interest from being treated as effectively connected gain or loss under other provisions of the Code (subject to a special rule coordinating the application of section 864(c)(8) and section 897). Thus, if a foreign transferor maintains an office or fixed place of business in the United States, and sells a partnership interest in a transaction that generates gain or loss attributable to that office, gain or loss recognized in connection with that transfer may be United States source income under section 865(e)(2), and may be treated as effectively connected income under section 864(c)(2). If the amount of gain or loss recognized that would be treated as effectively connected gain or loss under section 864(c)(2) exceeds the amount of gain that would be treated as effectively connected gain under section 864(c)(8), then the larger amount would be treated as effectively connected gain. See proposed § 1.864(c)(8)-1(b)(1).

II. *Coordination with Section 897*

Section 897(g) generally provides that, under regulations prescribed by the Secretary, the amount realized by a nonresident alien individual or foreign corporation in exchange for all or part of its interest in a partnership is, to the extent attributable to United States real property interests (as defined in section 897(c)), considered as an amount received from the sale or exchange in the United States of such property. Accordingly, section 897(g) generally provides the same result for United States real property interests as Revenue Ruling 91-32 provides for property used, or held for use, in a trade or business in the United States. In general, section 864(c)(8)(C) provides that if a partnership described in section 864(c)(8)(A) holds any United States real property interest at the time of the transfer of the partnership interest, then the gain or loss treated as effectively connected gain or loss under section 864(c)(8)(A) is reduced by the amount treated as effectively connected gain or loss with respect to that United States real property interest under section 897. The effect of section 864(c)(8)(C) is to prevent gain or loss from a United States real property interest that is taxed under section 897 from being taken into account a second time under section 864(c)(8).

In the proposed regulations, the limitation on effectively connected gain or loss in section 864(c)(8)(B) is based on a deemed sale by the partnership of all of its assets, including all United States real property interests held by the partnership, which are treated as effectively connected assets under section 897. See proposed § 1.864(c)(8)-1(c)(2)(i). To coordinate the taxation of United States real property interests under sections 897(g) and 864(c)(8), the proposed regulations provide that when a partnership holds United States real property interests and is also subject to section 864(c)(8) because it is engaged in the conduct of a trade or business within the United States without regard to section 897, the amount of the foreign transferor's effectively connected gain or loss will be determined under section 864(c)(8) and not under section 897(g). Therefore, the reduction called for by section 864(c)(8)(C) is not necessary. See proposed § 1.864(c)(8)-1(d).

The regulations include a proposed rule in regulations under section 897, which serves as a cross-reference to this coordination rule. See section V of this Explanation of Provisions for a discussion of a proposed anti-stuffing rule that also applies in the context of section 897. Further, comments are requested as to the interaction of this rule with other rules in the regulations under section 897, including the special rule for publicly traded partnerships in § 1.897-1(c)(2)(iv).

III. *Tiered Partnerships*

Section 864(c)(8) applies to a foreign nonresident alien individual or foreign corporation that owns an interest in a partnership directly or indirectly. Consistent with section 12 of Notice 2018-29, the proposed regulations provide that if a foreign transferor transfers an interest in an upper-tier partnership that owns, directly or indirectly, an interest in one or more lower-tier partnerships that are engaged in the conduct of a trade or business within the United States, then the deemed sale gain or loss must be computed with respect to each lower-tier partnership, the amount of effectively connected gain or loss that would be allocated to the upper-tier partnership must be determined, and the amount of gain or loss recognized by a foreign transferor that is treated as effectively connected gain or loss under proposed § 1.864(c)(8)-1(c) must be determined by reference to the transferor's distributive share of effectively connected gain or loss arising from each lower-tier partnership. See proposed § 1.864(c)(8)-1(e)(1).

The proposed regulations also clarify that when a foreign transferor is a partner in an upper-tier partnership and the upper-tier partnership transfers an interest in a lower-tier partnership that is engaged in the conduct of a trade or business within the United States, the upper-tier partnership must determine its effectively connected gain or loss by applying the principles of the proposed regulations, including the tiered partnership rules described in proposed § 1.864(c)(8)-1(e)(1).

IV. *Treaties*

The business profits articles of many U.S. income tax treaties limit the taxation of income that is otherwise treated as effectively connected with the conduct of a trade or business within the United States under the Code to income and gain attributable to a permanent establishment in the United States. The applicable gains articles of many U.S. income tax treaties allow the country in which a permanent establishment is located to tax gains from the alienation of movable property forming part of the business property of a permanent establishment, including gains from the alienation of a permanent establishment, alone or with the whole enterprise of which it is a part. In general, the permanent establishment of a partnership in the United States is considered a permanent establishment of the partners of the partnership. See *Donroy, Ltd. v. United States*, 196 F.Supp. 54 (N.D. Cal. 1961), *aff'd* 301 F.2d 200 (9th Cir. 1962), and *Unger v. Comm'r*, T.C. Memo. 1990-15, 58 TCM 1157, *aff'd* 936 F.2d 1316 (D.C. Cir. 1991).

The proposed regulations provide that the disposition of a foreign partner's interest in a partnership, in whole or in part, is a disposition of all or part of a partner's permanent establishment. Thus, to the extent the partnership's assets form part of a foreign partner's permanent establishment in the United States, the permanent establishment paragraph of the gains article would generally preserve the United States' taxing jurisdiction over the gain on the transfer of a partnership interest that is subject to tax under section 864(c)(8). In addition, if an income tax treaty has a gains article that permits the United States to apply its domestic laws to tax gains or does not have a gains article, the treaty does not prevent the application of section 864(c)(8).

Gains articles of treaties also frequently have special provisions covering certain assets, regardless of whether the assets form part of a permanent establishment, such as gains from dispositions of United States real property interests and ships and aircraft used in international traffic. If a gains article of an income tax treaty prohibits taxation of the gain from the disposition of any asset, such as ships or aircraft used in international traffic, the gains and losses from those assets will not be considered assets that form part of the permanent establishment, nor will they be taken into account in determining deemed sale EC gain or deemed sale EC loss, for purposes of computing the section 864(c)(8)(B) limitation. If the gains article of an applicable income tax treaty allows the taxation of gain from the disposition of a United States real property interest, the transfer of an interest in a partnership that holds a United States real property interest remains subject to section 897(g) even if the transfer is not subject to section 864(c)(8) (because the partnership's assets are not treated as forming part of a permanent establishment in the United States). See proposed § 1.864(c)(8)-1(d).

V. *Anti-Stuffing Rule*

The proposed regulations include an anti-stuffing rule applicable to both these regulations and section 897. This rule is included to prevent inappropriate reductions in amounts characterized as effectively connected with the conduct of a trade or business within the United States under section 864(c)(8) or section 897. A cross-reference to this rule is also included in the proposed regulation under section 897.

VI. *Section 1446(f) Guidance*

The proposed regulations do not provide guidance under section 1446(f). The Treasury Department and the IRS intend to issue guidance under section 1446(f) expeditiously.

Applicability Dates

The proposed regulations apply to transfers occurring on or after November 27, 2017, the effective date of section 864(c)(8). See section 7805(b)(2). If any provision is finalized after June 22, 2019, the Treasury Department and the IRS expect that such provision will apply only to transfers occurring on or after December 26, 2018. *See* section 7805(b)(1)(B).

Special Analyses

Executive Orders 13771, 13563, and 12866 direct agencies to assess costs and benefits of available regulatory alternatives and, if regulation is necessary, to select regulatory approaches that maximize net benefits, including potential economic, environmental, public health and safety effects, distributive impacts, and equity. Executive Order 13563 emphasizes the importance of quantifying both costs and benefits, reducing costs, harmonizing rules, and promoting flexibility.

These proposed regulations have been designated by the Office of Management and Budget's Office of Information and Regulatory Affairs (OIRA) as subject to review under Executive Order 12866 pursuant to the Memorandum of Agreement (April 11, 2018) between the Treasury Department and the Office of Management and Budget regarding review of tax regulations. OIRA has determined that the proposed rulemaking is significant and subject to review under EO 12866 and section 1(b) of the Memorandum of Agreement. Accordingly, the proposed regulations have been reviewed by the Office of Management and Budget.

The Treasury Department and the IRS have assessed the benefits and costs of the proposed regulations relative to a no-action baseline reflecting anticipated tax-related behavior and other economic behavior in the absence of these proposed regulations. Because the proposed regulations generally provide taxpayers with additional certainty on the amount and character of gain or loss treated as effectively connected income as a result of section 864(c)(8) and concurrently coordinate section 864(c)(8) with other provisions in the Code, the Treasury Department and the IRS anticipate only minimal economic or revenue effects from the proposed regulations. The Treasury Department and the IRS estimate that between 5,000 and 10,000 taxpayers are potentially affected by section 864(c)(8), with only a fraction of these taxpayers having gain or loss from disposition of a partnership in any one year. The Treasury Department and the IRS estimate that the affected taxpayers would see a minimal difference in treatment between these proposed regulations and Revenue Ruling 91-32. Comments are requested regarding these assessments. The Treasury Department and the IRS have assessed that the proposed regulations do not establish a new collection of information nor modify an existing collection that requires the approval of the Office of Management and Budget under the Paperwork Reduction Act (44 U.S.C. chapter 35). The Treasury Department and the IRS seek comments on this assessment.

Section 864(c)(8) and the proposed regulations generally apply to nonresident alien individuals and foreign corporations on the transfer of an interest in a partnership that is engaged in a trade or business within the United States, and not directly to the trade or business the partnership conducts in the United States. Under section 605 of the Regulatory Flexibility Act (5 U.S.C. chapter 6), the Treasury Department and the IRS certify that the proposed regulations will not have a significant economic impact on a substantial number of small entities. The reason is that the proposed regulations generally apply to nonresident alien individuals and foreign corporations on the transfer of an interest in a partnership and not directly to a domestic small business. Pursuant to section 7805(f), this notice of proposed rulemaking has been submitted to the Chief Counsel for Advocacy of the Small Business Administration for comment on their impact on small business.

Comments and Requests for Public Hearing

Before the proposed regulations are adopted as final regulations, consideration will be given to any comments that are submitted timely to the IRS as prescribed in this preamble under the "**ADDRESSES**" heading. The Treasury Department and the IRS request comments on all aspects of the proposed regulations, and specifically on the issues identified in sections I.A.2, I.B, and I.C of the Explanations of Provisions. All comments will be available at *www.regulations.gov* or upon request. A public hearing will be scheduled if requested in writing by any person that timely submits written comments. If a public hearing is scheduled, then notice of the date, time, and place for the public hearing will be published in the **Federal Register**.

Drafting Information

The principal authors of the proposed regulations are Ronald M. Gootzeit and Chadwick Rowland, Office of Associate Chief Counsel (International). However, other personnel from the Treasury Department and the IRS participated in their development.

Statement of Availability of IRS Documents

IRS Revenue Procedures, Revenue Rulings, notices, and other guidance cited in this document are published in the Internal Revenue Bulletin (or Cumulative Bulletin) and are available from the Superintendent of Documents, U.S. Government Printing Office, Washington, DC 20402, or by visiting the IRS website at *http://www.irs.gov*.

[¶49,785] Proposed Amendments of Regulations (REG-104352-18), published in the Federal Register on December 28, 2018.

[Code Secs. 245, 267, 1503, 6038 and 7701]

Foreign corporations: Transactions between related taxpayers: Consolidated returns: Computation of tax.Reg. §§1.245A(e)-1, 1.267A-1—1.267A-7 and amendments of Reg. §§1.1503(d)-1, 1.1503(d)-3, 1.1503(d)-6, 1.1503(d)-7, 1.1503(d)-8, 1.6038-2, 1.6038-3, 1.6038A-2 and 301.7701-3 implementing sections 245A(e) and 267A of the Internal Revenue Code ("Code") regarding hybrid dividends and certain amounts paid or accrued in hybrid transactions or with hybrid entities, are proposed.

AGENCY: Internal Revenue Service (IRS), Treasury.

ACTION: Notice of proposed rulemaking.

SUMMARY: This document contains proposed regulations implementing sections 245A(e) and 267A of the Internal Revenue Code ("Code") regarding hybrid dividends and certain amounts paid or accrued in hybrid transactions or with hybrid entities. Sections 245A(e) and 267A were added to the Code by the Tax Cuts and Jobs Act, Pub. L. No. 115-97 (2017) (the "Act"), which was enacted on December 22, 2017. This document also contains proposed regulations under sections 1503(d) and 7701 to prevent the same deduction from being claimed under the tax laws of both the United States and a foreign country. Further, this document contains proposed regulations under sections 6038, 6038A, and 6038C to facilitate administration of certain rules in the proposed regulations. The proposed regulations affect taxpayers that would otherwise claim a deduction related to such amounts and certain shareholders of foreign corporations that pay or receive hybrid dividends.

DATES: Written or electronic comments and requests for a public hearing must be received by February 26, 2019.

ADDRESSES: Send submissions to: Internal Revenue Service, CC:PA:LPD:PR (REG-104352-18), Room 5203, Post Office Box 7604, Ben Franklin Station, Washington, DC 20044. Submissions may be hand-delivered Monday through Friday between the hours of 8 a.m. and 4 p.m. to CC:PA:LPD:PR (indicate REG-104352-18), Courier's Desk, Internal Revenue Service, 1111 Constitution Avenue, N.W., Washington, DC 20224, or sent electronically, via the Federal eRulemaking Portal at *www.regulations.gov* (IRS REG-104352-18).

FOR FURTHER INFORMATION CONTACT: Concerning the proposed regulations, contact Tracy Villecco at (202) 317-3800; concerning submissions of comments or requests for a public hearing, Regina L. Johnson at (202) 317-6901 (not toll free numbers).

SUPPLEMENTARY INFORMATION:

Background

I. *In General*

This document contains proposed amendments to 26 CFR parts 1 and 301 under sections 245A(e), 267A, 1503(d), 6038, 6038A, 6038C, and 7701 (the "proposed regulations"). Added to the Code by sections 14101(a) and 14222(a) of the Act, section 245A(e) denies the dividends received deduction under section 245A with respect to hybrid dividends, and section 267A denies certain interest or royalty deductions involving hybrid transactions or hybrid entities. The proposed regulations only include rules under section 245A(e); rules addressing other aspects of section 245A, including the general eligibility requirements for the dividends received deduction under section 245A(a), will be addressed in a separate notice of proposed rulemaking. Section 14101(f) of the Act provides that section 245A, including section 245A(e), applies to distributions made after December 31, 2017. Section 14222(c) of the Act provides that section 267A applies to taxable years beginning after December 31, 2017. Other provisions of the Code, such as sections 894(c) and 1503(d), also address certain hybrid arrangements.

II. *Purpose of Anti-Hybrid Rules*

A cross-border transaction may be treated differently for U.S. and foreign tax purposes because of differences in the tax law of each country. In general, the U.S. tax treatment of a transaction does not take into account foreign tax law. However, in specific cases, foreign tax law is taken into account - for example, in the context of withholdable payments to hybrid entities for which treaty benefits are claimed under section 894(c) and for dual consolidated losses subject to section 1503(d) - in order to address policy concerns resulting from the different treatment of the same transaction or arrangement under U.S. and foreign tax law.

In response to international concerns regarding hybrid arrangements used to achieve double non-taxation, Action 2 of the OECD's Base Erosion and Profit Shifting ("BEPS") project, and two final reports thereunder, address hybrid and branch mismatch arrangements. *See* OECD/G20, *Neutralising the Effects of Hybrid Mismatch Arrangements, Action 2: 2015 Final Report* (October 2015) (the "Hybrid Mismatch Report"); OECD/G20, *Neutralising the Effects of Branch Mismatch Arrangements, Action 2: Inclusive Framework on BEPS* (July 2017) (the "Branch Mismatch Report"). The Hybrid Mismatch Report sets forth recommendations to neutralize the tax effects of hybrid arrangements that exploit differences in the tax treatment of an entity or instrument under the laws of two or more countries (such arrangements, "hybrid mismatches"). The Branch Mismatch Report sets forth recommendations to neutralize the tax effects of certain arrangements involving branches that result in mismatches similar to hybrid mismatches (such arrangements, "branch mismatches"). Given the similarity between hybrid mismatches and branch mismatches, the Branch Mismatch Report recommends that a jurisdiction adopting rules to address hybrid mismatches adopt, at the same time, rules to address branch mismatches. *See* Branch Mismatch Report, at p. 11, Executive Summary. Otherwise, taxpayers might "shift[] from hybrid mismatch to branch mismatch arrangements in order to secure the same tax advantages." *Id.*

The Act's legislative history explains that section 267A is intended to be "consistent with many of the approaches to the same or similar problems [regarding hybrid arrangements] taken in the Code, the OECD base erosion and profit shifting project ("BEPS"), bilateral income tax treaties, and provisions or rules of other countries." *See* Senate Committee on Finance, Explanation of the Bill, at 384 (November 22, 2017). The types of hybrid arrangements of concern are arrangements that "exploit differences in the tax treatment of a transaction or entity under the laws of two or more tax jurisdictions to achieve double non-taxation, including long-term deferral." *Id.* Hybrid arrangements targeted by these provisions are those that rely on a hybrid element to produce such outcomes.

These concerns also arise in the context of section 245A as a result of the enactment of a participation exemption system for taxing foreign income. Under this system, section 245A(e) generally prevents double non-taxation by disallowing the 100 percent dividends received deduction for dividends received from a controlled foreign corporation ("CFC"), or by mandating subpart F inclusions for dividends received from a CFC by another CFC, if there is a corresponding deduction or other tax benefit in the foreign country.

Explanation of Provisions

I. *Section 245A(e) - Hybrid Dividends*

A. *Overview*

The proposed regulations under section 245A(e) address certain dividends involving hybrid arrangements. The proposed regulations neutralize the double non-taxation effects of these dividends by either denying the section 245A(a) dividends received deduction with respect to the dividend or requiring an inclusion under section 951(a) with respect to the dividend, depending on whether the dividend is received by a domestic corporation or a CFC.

The proposed regulations provide that if a domestic corporation that is a United States shareholder within the meaning of section 951(b) ("U.S. shareholder") of a CFC receives a "hybrid dividend" from the CFC, then the U.S. shareholder is not allowed the section 245A(a) deduction for the hybrid dividend, and the rules of section 245A(d) (denial of foreign tax credits and deductions) apply. *See* proposed § 1.245A(e)-1(b). In general, a dividend is a hybrid dividend if it satisfies two conditions: (i) but for section 245A(e), the section 245A(a) deduction would be allowed, and (ii) the dividend is one for which the CFC (or a related person) is or was allowed a deduction or other tax benefit under a "relevant foreign tax law" (such a deduction or other tax benefit, a "hybrid deduction"). *See* proposed § 1.245A(e)-1(b) and (d). The proposed regulations take into account certain deductions or other tax benefits allowed to a person related to a CFC (such as a shareholder) because, for example, certain tax benefits allowed to a shareholder of a CFC are economically equivalent to the CFC having been allowed a deduction.

B. *Relevant foreign tax law*

The proposed regulations define a relevant foreign tax law as, with respect to a CFC, any regime of any foreign country or possession of the United States that imposes an income, war profits, or excess profits tax with respect to income of the CFC, other than a foreign anti-deferral regime under which an owner of the CFC is liable to tax. *See* proposed § 1.245A(e)-1(f). Thus, for example, a relevant foreign tax law includes the tax law of a foreign country of which the CFC is a tax resident, as well as the tax law applicable to a foreign branch of the CFC.

C. *Deduction or other tax benefit*

1. In General

Under the proposed regulations, only deductions or other tax benefits that are "allowed" under the relevant foreign tax law may constitute a hybrid deduction. *See* proposed § 1.245A(e)-1(d). Thus, for example, if the relevant foreign tax law contains hybrid mismatch rules under which a CFC is denied a deduction for an amount of interest paid with respect to a hybrid instrument to prevent a deduction/no-inclusion ("D/NI") outcome, then the payment of the interest does not give rise to a hybrid deduction, because the deduction is not "allowed." This prevents double-taxation that could arise if a hybrid dividend were subject to both section 245A(e) and a hybrid mismatch rule under a relevant foreign tax law.

For a deduction or other tax benefit to be a hybrid deduction, it must relate to or result from an amount paid, accrued, or distributed with respect to an instrument of the CFC that is treated as stock for U.S. tax purposes. That is, there must be a connection between the deduction or other tax benefit under the relevant foreign tax law and the instrument that is stock for U.S. tax purposes. Thus, a hybrid deduction includes an interest deduction under a relevant foreign tax law with respect to a hybrid instrument (stock for U.S. tax purposes, indebtedness for foreign tax purposes). It also includes dividends paid deductions and other deductions allowed on equity under a relevant foreign tax law, such as notional interest deductions ("NIDs"), which raise similar concerns as traditional hybrid instruments. However, it does not, for example, include an exemption provided to a CFC under its tax law for certain types of income (such as income attributable to a foreign branch), because there is not a connection between the tax benefit and the instrument that is stock for U.S. tax purposes.

The proposed regulations provide that deductions or other tax benefits allowed pursuant to certain integration or imputation systems do not constitute hybrid deductions. *See* proposed § 1.245A(e)-1(d)(2)(i)(B). However, a system that has the effect of exempting earnings that fund a distribution from foreign tax at both the CFC and shareholder level gives rise to a hybrid deduction. *See id.; see also* proposed § 1.245A(e)-1(g)(2), *Example* 2.

2. Effect of Foreign Currency Gain or Loss

The payment of an amount by a CFC may, under a provision of foreign tax law comparable to section 988, give rise to gain or loss to the CFC that is attributable to foreign currency. The proposed regulations provide that such foreign currency gain or loss recognized with respect to such deduction or other tax benefit is taken into account for purposes of determining hybrid deductions. *See* proposed § 1.245A(e)-1(d)(6); *see also* section II.K.1 of this Explanation of Provisions (requesting comments on foreign currency rules).

D. *Tiered hybrid dividends*

Proposed § 1.245A(e)-1(c) sets forth rules related to hybrid dividends of tiered corporations ("tiered hybrid dividends"), as provided under section 245A(e)(2). A tiered hybrid dividend means an amount received by a CFC from another CFC to the extent that the amount would be a hybrid dividend under proposed § 1.245A(e)-1(b) if the receiving CFC were a domestic corporation. Accordingly, the amount must be treated as a dividend under U.S. tax law to be treated as a tiered hybrid dividend; the treatment of the amount under the tax law in which the receiving CFC is a tax resident (or under any other foreign tax law) is irrelevant for this purpose.

If a CFC receives a tiered hybrid dividend from another CFC, and a domestic corporation is a U.S. shareholder of both CFCs, then (i) the tiered hybrid dividend is treated as subpart F income of the receiving CFC, (ii) the U.S. shareholder must include in gross income its pro rata share of the subpart F income, and (iii) the rules of section 245A(d) apply to the amount included in the U.S. shareholder's gross income. *See* proposed § 1.245A(e)-1(c)(1). This treatment applies notwithstanding any other provision of the Code. Thus, for example, exceptions to subpart F income such as those provided under section 954(c)(3) ("same country" exception for income received from related persons) and section 954(c)(6) (look-through rule for related CFCs) do not apply. As additional examples, the gross amount of subpart F income cannot be reduced by deductions taken into account under section 954(b)(5) and § 1.954-1(c), and is not subject to the current earnings and profits limitation under section 952(c).

E. *Interaction with section 959*

Distributions of previously taxed earnings and profits ("PTEP") attributable to amounts that have been taken into account by a U.S. shareholder under section 951(a) are, in general, excluded from the gross income of the U.S. shareholder when distributed under section 959(a), and under section 959(d) are not treated as a dividend (other than to reduce earnings and profits). As a result, distributions from a CFC to its U.S. shareholder out of PTEP are not eligible for the dividends received deduction under section 245A(a), and section 245A(e) does not apply. Similarly, distributions of PTEP from a CFC to an upper-tier CFC are excluded from the gross income of the upper-tier CFC under section 959(b), but only for the limited purpose of applying section 951(a). In addition, such amounts continue to be treated as dividends because section 959(d) does not apply to such amounts. Accordingly, distributions out of PTEP could qualify as tiered hybrid dividends that would result in an income inclusion to a U.S. shareholder. To prevent this result, the proposed regulations provide that a tiered hybrid dividend does not include amounts described in section 959(b). *See* proposed § 1.245A(e)-1(c)(2).

F. *Interaction with section 964(e)*

Under section 964(e)(1), gain recognized by a CFC on the sale or exchange of stock in another foreign corporation may be treated as a dividend. In certain cases, section 964(e)(4): (i) treats the dividend as subpart F income of the selling CFC; (ii) requires a U.S. shareholder of the CFC to include in its gross income its pro rata share of the subpart F income; and (iii) allows the U.S. shareholder the section 245A(a) deduction for its inclusion in gross income. As is the case with the treatment of tiered hybrid dividends, the treatment of dividends under section 964(e)(4) applies notwithstanding any other provision of the Code.

The proposed regulations coordinate the tiered hybrid dividend rules and the rules of section 964(e) by providing that, to the extent a dividend arising under section 964(e)(1) is a tiered hybrid dividend, the tiered hybrid dividend rules, rather than the rules of section 964(e)(4), apply. Thus, in such a case, a U.S. shareholder that includes an amount in its gross income under the tiered hybrid dividend rule is not allowed the section 245A(a) deduction, or foreign tax credits or deductions, for the amount. *See* proposed § 1.245A(e)-1(c)(1) and (4).

G. *Hybrid deduction accounts*

1. In General

In some cases, the actual payment by a CFC of an amount that is treated as a dividend for U.S. tax purposes will result in a corresponding hybrid deduction. In many cases, however, the dividend and the hybrid deduction may not arise pursuant to the same payment and may be recognized in different taxable years. This may occur in the case of a hybrid instrument for which under a relevant foreign tax law the CFC is allowed deductions for accrued (but not yet paid) interest. In such a case, to the extent that an actual payment has not yet been made on the instrument, there generally would not be a dividend for U.S. tax purposes for which the section 245A(a) deduction could be disallowed under section 245A(e). Nevertheless, because the earnings and profits of the CFC would not be reduced by the accrued interest deduction, the earnings and profits may give rise to a dividend when subsequently distributed to the U.S. shareholder. This same result could occur in other cases, such as when a relevant foreign tax law allows deductions on equity, such as NIDs.

The disallowance of the section 245A(a) deduction under section 245A(e) should not be limited to cases in which the dividend and the hybrid deduction arise pursuant to the same payment (or in the same taxable year for U.S. tax purposes and for purposes of the relevant foreign tax law). Interpreting the provision in such a manner would result in disparate treatment for hybrid arrangements that produce the same D/NI outcome. Accordingly, the proposed regulations define a hybrid dividend (or tiered hybrid dividend) based, in part, on the extent of the balance of the "hybrid deduction accounts" of the domestic corporation (or CFC) receiving the dividend. *See* proposed § 1.245A(e)-1(b) and (d). This ensures that dividends are subject to section 245A(e) regardless of whether the same payment gives rise to the dividend and the hybrid deduction.

A hybrid deduction account must be maintained with respect to each share of stock of a CFC held by a person that, given its ownership of the CFC and the share, could be subject to section 245A upon a dividend paid by the CFC on the share. *See* proposed § 1.245A(e)-1(d) and (f). The account, which is maintained in the functional currency of the CFC, reflects the amount of hybrid deductions of the CFC (allowed in taxable years beginning after December 31, 2017) that have been allocated to the share. A dividend paid by a CFC to a shareholder that has a hybrid deduction account with respect to the CFC is generally treated as a hybrid dividend or tiered hybrid dividend to the extent of the shareholder's balance in all of its hybrid deduction accounts with respect to the CFC, even if the dividend is paid on a share that has not had any hybrid deductions allocated to it. Absent such an approach, the purposes of section 245A(e) might be avoided by, for example, structuring dividend payments such that they are generally made on shares of stock to which a hybrid deduction has not been allocated (rather than on shares of stock to which a hybrid deduction has been allocated, such as a share that is a hybrid instrument).

Once an amount in a hybrid deduction account gives rise to a hybrid dividend or a tiered hybrid dividend, the account is correspondingly reduced. *See* proposed § 1.245A(e)-1(d). The Treasury Department and the IRS request comments on whether hybrid deductions attributable to amounts included in income under section 951(a) or section 951A should not increase the hybrid deduction account, or, alternatively, the hybrid deduction account should be reduced by distributions of PTEP, and on whether the effect of any deemed paid foreign tax credits associated with such inclusions or distributions should be considered.

2. Transfers of Stock

Because hybrid deduction accounts are with respect to stock of a CFC, the proposed regulations include rules that take into account transfers of the stock. *See* proposed § 1.245A(e)-1(d)(4)(ii)(A). These rules, which are similar to the "successor" PTEP rules under section 959 (*see* § 1.959-1(d)), ensure that section 245A(e) properly applies to dividends that give rise to a D/NI outcome in cases where the shareholder that receives the dividend is not the same shareholder that held the stock when the hybrid deduction was incurred. These rules only apply when the stock is transferred among persons that are required to keep hybrid deduction accounts. Thus, if the stock is transferred to a person that is not required to keep a hybrid deduction account - such as an individual or a foreign corporation that is not a CFC - the account terminates (subject to the anti-avoidance rule, discussed in section I.H of this Explanation of Provisions). Finally, the proposed regulations include rules that take into account certain non-recognition exchanges of the stock, such as exchanges in connection with asset reorganizations, recapitalizations, and liquidations, as well as transfers and exchanges that occur mid-way through a CFC's taxable year. *See* proposed § 1.245A(e)-1(d)(4)(ii)(B) and (d)(5). The Treasury Department and the IRS request comments on these rules.

3. Dividends from Lower-Tier CFCs

The proposed regulations provide a special rule to address earnings and profits of a lower-tier CFC that are included in a domestic corporation's income as a dividend by virtue of section 1248(c)(2). In these cases, the proposed regulations treat the domestic corporation as having certain hybrid deduction accounts with respect to the lower-tier CFC that are held and maintained by other CFCs. *See* proposed § 1.245A(e)-1(b)(3). This ensures that, to the extent the earnings and profits of the lower-tier CFC give rise to the dividend, hybrid deduction accounts with respect to the lower-tier CFC are taken into account for purposes of the determinations under section 245A(e), even though the accounts are held indirectly by the domestic corporation. A similar rule applies with respect to gains on stock sales treated as dividends under section 964(e)(1). *See* proposed § 1.245A(e)-1(c)(3).

H. *Anti-avoidance rule*

The proposed regulations include an anti-avoidance rule. This rule provides that appropriate adjustments are made, including adjustments that would disregard a transaction or arrangement, if a transaction or arrangement is engaged in with a principal purpose of avoiding the purposes of proposed § 1.245A(e)-1.

II. *Section 267A - Related Party Amounts Involving Hybrid Transactions and Hybrid Entities*

A. *Overview*

As indicated in the Senate Finance Committee's Explanation of the Bill, hybrid arrangements may exploit differences under U.S. and foreign tax law between the tax characterization of an entity as transparent or opaque or differences in the treatment of financial instruments or other transactions. The proposed regulations under section 267A address certain payments or accruals of interest or royalties for U.S. tax purposes (the amount of such interest or royalty, a "specified payment") that involve hybrid arrangements, or similar arrangements involving branches, that produce D/NI (deduction/no inclusion) outcomes or indirect D/NI outcomes. *See also* section II.J.1 of this Explanation of Provisions (discussing certain amounts that are treated as specified payments). The proposed regulations neutralize the double non-taxation effects of the arrangements by denying a deduction for the specified payment to the extent of the D/NI outcome.

B. *Scope*

1. Disallowed Deductions

The proposed regulations generally disallow a deduction for a specified payment if and only if the payment is (i) a "disqualified hybrid amount," meaning that it produces a D/NI outcome as a result of a hybrid or branch arrangement; (ii) a "disqualified imported mismatch amount," meaning that it produces an indirect D/NI outcome as a result of the effects of an offshore hybrid or branch arrangement being imported into the U.S. tax system; or (iii) made pursuant to a transaction a principal purpose of which is to avoid the purposes of the regulations under section 267A and it produces a D/NI outcome. *See* proposed § 1.267A-1(b). Thus, the proposed regulations do not address D/NI outcomes that are not the result of hybridity. *See also* section II.E of this Explanation of

Provisions (discussing the link between hybridity and a D/NI outcome). In addition, the proposed regulations do not address double-deduction outcomes. Section 267A is intended to address D/NI outcomes; transactions that produce double-deduction outcomes are addressed through other provisions (or doctrines), such as the dual consolidated loss rules under section 1503(d). *See also* section IV.A.1 of this Explanation of Provisions (discussing the dual consolidated loss rules).

2. Parties Subject to Section 267A

The application of section 267A by its terms is not limited to any particular category of persons. The proposed regulations, however, narrow the scope of section 267A so that it applies only to deductions of "specified parties." Deductions of persons other than specified parties are not subject to disallowance under section 267A because the deductions of such other persons generally do not have significant U.S. tax consequences.

A specified party means any of (i) a tax resident of the United States, (ii) a CFC for which there is one or more United States shareholders that own (within the meaning of section 958(a)) at least ten percent of the stock of the CFC, and (iii) a U.S. taxable branch (which includes a U.S. permanent establishment of a tax treaty resident). *See* proposed § 1.267A-5(a). The term generally includes a CFC because, for example, a specified payment made by a CFC to the foreign parent of the CFC's U.S. shareholder, or a specified payment by the CFC to an unrelated party pursuant to a structured arrangement, may indirectly reduce income subject to U.S. tax. Specified payments made by a CFC to other related CFCs or to U.S. shareholders of the CFC, however, typically will not be subject to section 267A because of the rules in proposed § 1.267A-3(b) that exempt certain payments included in income of a U.S. tax resident or taken into account under the subpart F or global intangible low-tax income ("GILTI") rules. *See also* section II.F of this Explanation of Provisions (discussing the relatedness or structured arrangement limitation); section II.H of this Explanation of Provisions (discussing exceptions for amounts included or includible in income). Similarly, the term includes a U.S. taxable branch because a payment made by the home office may be allocable to and thus reduce income subject to U.S. tax under sections 871(b) or 882. *See also* section II.K.2 of this Explanation of Provisions (discussing amounts considered paid or accrued by a U.S. taxable branch for section 267A purposes).

The term specified party does not include a partnership because a partnership generally is not liable to tax and therefore is not the person allowed a deduction. However, a partner of a partnership may be a specified party. For example, in the case of a payment made by a partnership a partner of which is a domestic corporation, the domestic corporation is a specified party and its allocable share of the deduction for the payment is subject to disallowance under section 267A.

C. *Amount of a D/NI outcome*

1. In General

Proposed § 1.267A-3(a) provides rules for determining the "no-inclusion" aspect of a D/NI outcome - that is, the amount of a specified payment that is or is not included in income under foreign tax law. The proposed regulations provide that only "tax residents" or "taxable branches" are considered to include an amount in income. Parties other than tax residents or taxable branches, for example, an entity that is fiscally transparent for purposes of the relevant tax laws, do not include an amount in income because such parties are not liable to tax.

In general, a tax resident or taxable branch includes a specified payment in income for this purpose to the extent that, under its tax law, it includes the payment in its income or tax base at the full marginal rate imposed on ordinary income, and the payment is not reduced or offset by certain items (such as an exemption or credit) particular to that type of payment. *See* proposed § 1.267A-3(a)(1).

Whether a tax resident or taxable branch includes a specified payment in income is determined without regard to any defensive or secondary rule in hybrid mismatch rules (which generally requires the payee to include certain amounts in income, if the payer is not denied a deduction for the amount), if any, under the tax resident's or taxable branch's tax law. Otherwise, in cases in which such tax law contains a secondary response, the analysis of whether the specified payment is included in income could become circular: for example, whether the United States denies a deduction under section 267A may depend on whether the payee includes the specified payment in income, and whether the payee includes it in income (under a secondary response) may depend on whether the United States denies the deduction.

A specified payment may be considered included in income even though offset by a generally applicable deduction or other tax attribute, such as a deduction for depreciation or a net operating loss. For this purpose, a deduction may be treated as being generally applicable even if closely related to the specified payment (for example, if the deduction and payment are in connection with a back-to-back financing arrangement).

If a specified payment is taxed at a preferential rate, or if there is a partial reduction or offset particular to the type of payment, a portion of the payment is considered included in income. The portion included in income is the amount that, taking into account the preferential rate or reduction or offset, is subject to tax at the full marginal rate applicable to ordinary income. *See* proposed § 1.267A-3(a)(1); *see also* proposed § 1.267A-6(c), *Example* 2 and *Example 7*.

2. Timing Differences

Some specified payments may never be included in income. For example, a specified payment treated as a dividend under a tax resident's tax laws may be permanently excluded from its income under a participation exemption. Permanent exclusions are always treated as giving rise to a no-inclusion. *See* proposed § 1.267A-3(a)(1).

Other specified payments, however, may be included in income but on a deferred basis. Some of these timing differences result from different methods of accounting between U.S. tax law and foreign tax law. For example, and subject to certain limitations such as those under sections 163(e)(3) and 267(a) (generally applicable to payments involving related parties, but not to payments involving structured arrangements), a specified payment may be deductible for U.S. tax purposes when accrued and later included in a foreign tax resident's income when actually paid. *See also* section II.K.3 of this Explanation of Provisions (discussing the coordination of section 267A with rules such as sections 163(e)(3) and 267(a)). Timing differences may also occur in cases in which all or a portion of a specified payment that is treated as interest for U.S. tax purposes is treated as a return of principal for purposes of the foreign tax law.

In some cases, timing differences reverse after a short period of time and therefore do not provide a meaningful deferral benefit. The Treasury Department and the IRS have determined that routine, short-term deferral does not give rise to the policy concerns that section 267A is intended to address. In addition, subjecting such short-term deferral to section 267A could give rise to administrability issues for both taxpayers and the IRS, because it may be challenging to determine whether the taxable period in which a specified payment is included in income matches the taxable period in which the payment is deductible.

Other timing differences, though, may provide a significant and long-term deferral benefit. Moreover, taxpayers may structure transactions that exploit these differences to achieve long-term deferral benefits. Timing differences that result in long-term deferral have an economic effect similar to a permanent exclusion and therefore give rise to policy concerns that section 267A is intended to address. *See* Senate Explanation, at 384 (expressing concern with hybrid arrangements that "achieve double non-taxation, including long-term deferral."). Accordingly, proposed § 1.267A-3(a)(1) provides that short-term deferral, meaning inclusion during a taxable year that ends no more than 36 months after the end of the specified party's taxable year, does not give rise to a D/NI outcome; inclusions outside of the 36-month timeframe, however, are treated as giving rise to a D/NI outcome.

D. *Hybrid and branch arrangements giving rise to disqualified hybrid amounts*

1. Hybrid Transactions

Proposed § 1.267A-2(a) addresses hybrid financial instruments and similar arrangements (collectively, "hybrid transactions") that result in a D/NI outcome. For example, in the case of an instrument that is treated as indebtedness for purposes of the payer's tax law and stock for purposes of the payee's tax law, a payment on the instrument may constitute deductible interest expense of the payer and excludible dividend income of the payee (for instance, under a participation exemption).

In general, the proposed regulations provide that a specified payment is made pursuant to a hybrid transaction if there is a mismatch in the character of the instrument or arrangement such that the payment is not treated as interest or a royalty, as applicable, under the tax law of a "specified recipient." Examples of such a specified payment include a payment that is treated as interest for U.S. tax purposes but, for purposes of a specified recipient's tax law, is treated as a distribution on equity or a return of principal. When a specified payment is made pursuant to a hybrid transaction, it generally is a disqualified hybrid amount to the extent that the specified recipient does not include the payment in income.

The proposed regulations broadly define specified recipient as (i) any tax resident that under its tax law derives the specified payment, and (ii) any taxable branch to which under its tax law the specified payment is attributable. *See* proposed § 1.267A-5(a)(19). In other words, a specified recipient is any party that may be subject to tax on the specified payment under its tax law. There may be more than one specified recipient of a specified payment. For example, in the case of a specified payment to an entity that is fiscally transparent for purposes of the tax law of its tax resident owners, each of the owners is a specified recipient of a share of the payment. In addition, if the entity is a tax resident of the country in which it is established or managed and controlled, then the entity is also a specified recipient. Moreover, in the case of a specified payment attributable to a taxable branch, both the taxable branch and the home office are specified recipients.

The proposed regulations deem a specified payment as made pursuant to a hybrid transaction if there is a long-term mismatch between when the specified party is allowed a deduction for the payment under U.S. tax law and when a specified recipient includes the payment in income under its tax law. This rule applies, for example, when a specified payment is made pursuant to an instrument viewed as indebtedness under both U.S. and foreign tax law and, due to a mismatch in tax accounting treatment between the U.S. and foreign tax law, results in long-term deferral. In these cases, this rule treats the long-term deferral as giving rise to a hybrid transaction; the rules in proposed § 1.267A-3(a)(1) (discussed in section II.C.2 of this Explanation of Provisions) treat the long-term deferral as creating a D/NI outcome.

Lastly, proposed § 1.267A-2(a)(3) provides special rules to address securities lending transactions, sale-repurchase transactions, and similar transactions. In these cases, a specified payment (that is, interest consistent with the substance of the transaction) might not be regarded under a foreign tax law. As a result, there might not be a specified recipient of the specified payment under such foreign tax law, absent a special rule. To address this scenario, the proposed regulations provide that the determination of the identity of a specified recipient under the foreign tax law is made with respect to an amount connected to the specified payment and regarded under the foreign tax law - for example, a dividend consistent with the form of the transaction. The Treasury Department and the IRS request comments on whether similar rules should be extended to other specific transactions.

2. Disregarded Payments

Proposed § 1.267A-2(b) addresses disregarded payments. Disregarded payments generally give rise to a D/NI outcome because they are regarded under the payer's tax law and are therefore available to offset income not taxable to the payee, but are disregarded under the payee's tax law and therefore are not included in income.

In general, the proposed regulations define a disregarded payment as a specified payment that, under a foreign tax law, is not regarded because, for example, it is a disregarded transaction involving a single taxpayer or between consolidated group members. For example, a disregarded payment includes a specified payment made by a domestic corporation to its foreign owner if, under the foreign tax law, the domestic corporation is a disregarded entity and therefore the payment is not regarded. It also includes a specified payment between related foreign corporations that are members of the same foreign consolidated group (or can otherwise share income or loss) if, under the foreign tax law, payments between group members are not regarded, or give rise to a deduction or similar offset to the payer member that is available to offset the corresponding income of the recipient member.

In general, a disregarded payment is a disqualified hybrid amount only to the extent it exceeds dual inclusion income. For example, if a domestic corporation that for foreign tax purposes is a disregarded entity of its foreign owner makes a disregarded payment to its foreign owner, the payment is a disqualified hybrid amount only to the extent it exceeds the net of the items of gross income and deductible expense taken into account in determining the domestic corporation's income for U.S. tax purposes and the foreign owner's income for foreign tax purposes. This prevents the excess of the disregarded payment over dual inclusion income from offsetting non-dual inclusion income. Such an offset could otherwise occur, for example, through the U.S. consolidation regime, or a sale, merger, or similar transaction.

A disregarded payment could also be viewed as being made pursuant to a hybrid transaction because the payment of interest or royalty would not be viewed as interest or royalty under the foreign tax law (since the payment is disregarded). The proposed regulations address disregarded payments separately from hybrid transactions, however, because disregarded payments are more likely to offset dual inclusion income and therefore are treated as disqualified hybrid amounts only to the extent they offset non-dual inclusion income.

3. Deemed Branch Payments

Proposed § 1.267A-2(c) addresses deemed branch payments. These payments result in a D/NI outcome when, under an income tax treaty, a deductible payment is deemed to be made by a permanent establishment to its home office and offsets income not taxable to the home office, but the payment is not taken into account under the home office's tax law.

In general, the proposed regulations define a deemed branch payment as interest or royalty considered paid by a U.S. permanent establishment to its home office under an income tax treaty between the United States and the home office country. *See* proposed § 1.267A-2(c)(2). Thus, for example, a deemed branch payment includes an amount allowed as a deduction in computing the business profits of a U.S. permanent establishment with respect to the use of intellectual property developed by the home office. *See*, for example, the U.S. Treasury Department Technical Explanation to the income tax convention between the United States and Belgium, signed November 27, 2006 ("[T]he OECD Transfer Pricing Guidelines apply, by analogy, in determining the profits attributable to a permanent establishment.").

When a specified payment is a deemed branch payment, it is a disqualified hybrid amount if the home office's tax law provides an exclusion or exemption for income attributable to the branch. In these cases, a deduction for the deemed branch payment would offset non-dual inclusion income and therefore give rise to a D/NI outcome. If the home office's tax law does not have an exclusion or exemption for income attributable to the branch, then, because U.S. permanent establishments cannot consolidate or otherwise share losses with U.S. taxpayers, there would generally not be an opportunity for a deduction for the deemed branch payment to offset non-dual inclusion income.

4. Reverse Hybrids

Proposed § 1.267A-2(d) addresses payments to reverse hybrids. In general, and as discussed below, a reverse hybrid is an entity that is fiscally transparent for purposes of the tax law of the country in which it is established but not for purposes of the tax law of its owner. Thus, payments to a reverse hybrid may result in a D/NI outcome because the reverse hybrid is not a tax resident of the country in which it is established, and the owner does not derive the payment under its tax law. Because this D/NI outcome may occur regardless of whether the establishment country is a foreign country or the United States, the proposed regulations provide that both foreign and domestic entities may be reverse hybrids. A domestic entity that is a reverse hybrid for this purpose therefore differs from a "domestic reverse hybrid entity" under § 1.894-1(d)(2)(i), which is defined as "a domestic entity that is treated as not fiscally transparent for U.S. tax purposes and as fiscally transparent under the laws of an interest holder's jurisdiction[.]"

For an entity to be a reverse hybrid under the proposed regulations, two requirements must be satisfied. These requirements generally implement the definition of hybrid entity in section 267A(d)(2), with certain modifications. First, the entity must be fiscally transparent under the tax law of the country in which it is established, whether or not it is a tax resident of another country. For this purpose, the determination of whether an entity is fiscally transparent with respect to an item of income is made using the principles of § 1.894-1(d)(3)(ii) (but without regard to whether there is an income tax treaty in effect between the entity's jurisdiction and the United States).

Second, the entity must not be fiscally transparent under the tax law of an "investor." An investor means a tax resident or taxable branch that directly or indirectly owns an interest in the entity. For this purpose, the determination of whether an investor's tax law treats the entity as fiscally transparent with respect to an item of income is made under the principles of § 1.894-1(d)(3)(iii) (but without regard to whether there is an income tax treaty in effect between the investor's jurisdiction and the United States). If an investor views the entity as not fiscally transparent, the investor generally will not be currently taxed under its tax law on payments to the entity. Thus, the non-fiscally-transparent status of the entity is determined on an investor-by-investor basis, based on the tax law of each investor. In addition, a tax resident or a taxable branch may be an investor of a reverse hybrid even if the tax resident or taxable branch indirectly owns the reverse hybrid through one or more intermediary entities that, under the tax law of the tax resident or taxable branch, are not fiscally transparent. In such a case, however, the investor's no-inclusion would not be a result of the payment being made to the reverse hybrid and therefore would not be a disqualified hybrid amount. *See also* section II.E of this Explanation of Provisions (explaining that the D/NI outcome must be a result of hybridity); proposed § 1.267A-6(c), *Example 5* (analyzing whether a D/NI outcome with respect to an upper-tier investor is a result of the specified payment being made to the reverse hybrid).

When a specified payment is made to a reverse hybrid, it is generally a disqualified hybrid amount to the extent that an investor does not include the payment in income. For this purpose, whether an investor includes the specified payment in income is determined without regard to a subsequent distribution by the reverse hybrid. Although a subsequent distribution may be included in the investor's income, the distribution may not occur for an extended period and, when it does occur, it may be difficult to determine whether the distribution is funded from an amount comprising the specified payment.

In addition, if an investor takes a specified payment into account under an anti-deferral regime, then the investor is considered to include the payment in income to the extent provided under the general rules of proposed § 1.267A-3(a). *See* proposed § 1.267A-6(c), *Example 5*. Thus, for example, if the investor's inclusion under the anti-deferral regime is subject to tax at a preferential rate, the investor is considered to include only a portion of the specified payment in income.

5. Branch Mismatch Payments

Proposed § 1.267A-2(e) addresses branch mismatch payments. These payments give rise to a D/NI outcome due to differences between the home office's tax law and the branch's tax law regarding the allocation of items of income or the treatment of the branch. This could occur, for example, if the home office's tax law views a payment as attributable to the branch and exempts the branch's income, but the branch's tax law does not tax the payment.

Under the proposed regulations, a specified payment is a branch mismatch payment when two requirements are satisfied. First, under a home office's tax law, the specified payment is treated as attributable to a branch of the home office. Second, under the tax law of the branch country, either (i) the home office does not have a taxable presence in the country, or (ii) the specified payment is treated as attributable to the home office and not the branch. When a specified payment is a branch mismatch payment, it is generally a disqualified hybrid amount to the extent that the home office does not include the payment in income.

E. *Link between hybridity and D/NI outcome*

Under section 267A(a), a deduction for a payment is generally disallowed if (i) the payment involves a hybrid arrangement, and (ii) a D/NI outcome occurs. In certain cases, although both of these conditions are satisfied, the D/NI outcome is not a result of the hybridity. For example, in the hybrid transaction context, the D/NI outcome may be a result of the specified recipient's tax law containing a pure territorial system (and thus exempting from taxation all foreign source income) or not having a corporate income tax, or a result of the specified recipient's status as a tax-exempt entity under its tax law.

The proposed regulations provide that a D/NI outcome gives rise to a disqualified hybrid amount only to the extent that the D/NI outcome is a result of hybridity. *See*, for example, proposed § 1.267A-2(a)(1)(ii); *see also* Senate Explanation, at 384 ("[T]he Committee believes that hybrid arrangements exploit differences in the tax treatment of a transaction or entity under the laws of two or more jurisdictions *to achieve* double non-taxation . . .") (emphasis added).

To determine whether a D/NI outcome is a result of hybridity, the proposed regulations generally apply a test based on facts that are counter to the hybridity at issue. For example, in the hybrid transaction context, a specified recipient's no-inclusion is a result of the specified payment being made pursuant to the hybrid transaction to the extent that the no-inclusion would not occur were the payment to be treated as interest or a royalty for purposes of the specified recipient's tax law.

This test also addresses cases in which, for example, a specified payment is made to a fiscally transparent entity (such as a partnership) and owners of the entity that are specified recipients of the payment each derive only a portion of the payment under its tax law. The test ensures that, with respect to each specified recipient, only the no-inclusion that occurs for the portion of the specified payment that it derives may give rise to a disqualified hybrid amount. In addition, as a result of the relatedness or structured arrangement limitation discussed in section II.F of this Explanation of Provisions, the no-inclusion with respect to the specified recipient is taken into account under the proposed regulations only if the specified recipient is related to the specified party or is a party to a structured arrangement pursuant to which the specified payment is made.

F. *Relatedness or structured arrangement limitation*

In determining whether a specified payment is made pursuant to a hybrid or branch mismatch arrangement, the proposed regulations generally only consider the tax laws of tax residents or taxable branches that are related to the specified party. *See* proposed § 1.267A-2(f). For example, in general, only the tax law of a specified recipient that is related to the specified party is taken into account for purposes of determining whether the specified payment is made pursuant to a hybrid transaction. Because a deemed branch payment by its terms involves a related home office, the relatedness limitation in proposed § 1.267A-2(f) does not apply to proposed § 1.267A-2(c).

The proposed regulations provide that related status is determined under the rules of section 954(d)(3) (involving ownership of more than 50 percent of interests) but without regard to downward attribution. *See* proposed § 1.267A-5(a)(14). In addition, to ensure that a tax resident may be considered related to a specified party even though the tax resident is a disregarded entity for U.S. tax purposes, the proposed regulations provide that such a tax resident is treated as a corporation for purposes of the relatedness test. A similar rule applies with respect to a taxable branch.

However, the Treasury Department and the IRS are aware that some hybrid arrangements involving unrelated parties are designed to give rise to a D/NI outcome and therefore present the policy concerns underlying section 267A. Furthermore, it is likely that in such cases the specified party will have, or can reasonably obtain, the information necessary to comply with section 267A. Accordingly, the proposed regulations generally provide that the tax law of an unrelated tax resident or taxable branch is taken into account for purposes of section 267A if the tax resident or taxable branch is a party to a structured arrangement. *See* proposed § 1.267A-2(f). The proposed regulations set forth a test for when a transaction is a structured arrangement. *See* proposed § 1.267A-5(a)(20). In addition, the proposed regulations impute an entity's participation in a structured arrangement to its investors. *See id.* Thus, for example, in the case of a specified payment to a partnership that is a party to a structured arrangement pursuant to which the payment is made, a tax resident that is a partner of the partnership is also a party to the structured arrangement, even though the tax resident may not have actual knowledge of the structured arrangement.

G. *Effect of inclusion in another jurisdiction*

The proposed regulations provide that a specified payment is a disqualified hybrid amount if a D/NI outcome occurs as a result of hybridity in any foreign jurisdiction, even if the payment is included in income in another foreign jurisdiction. *See* proposed § 1.267A-6(c), *Example 1.* Absent such a rule, an inclusion of a specified payment in income in a jurisdiction with a (generally applicable) low rate might discharge the application of section 267A even though a D/NI outcome occurs in another jurisdiction as a result of hybridity.

For example, assume FX, a tax resident of Country X, owns US1, a domestic corporation, and FZ, a tax resident of Country Z that is fiscally transparent for Country X tax purposes. Also, assume that Country Z has a single, low-tax rate applicable to all income. Further, assume that FX holds an instrument issued by US1, a $100x payment with respect to which is treated as interest for U.S. tax purposes and an excludible dividend for Country X tax purposes. In an attempt to avoid US1's deduction for the $100x payment being denied under the hybrid transaction rule, FX contributes the instrument to FZ, and, upon US1's $100x payment, US1 asserts that, although a $100x no-inclusion occurs with respect to FX as a result of the payment being made pursuant to the hybrid transaction, the payment is not a disqualified hybrid amount because FZ fully includes the payment in income (albeit at a low-tax rate). The proposed regulations treat the payment as a disqualified hybrid amount.

This rule only applies for inclusions under the laws of foreign jurisdictions. See proposed § 1.267A-3(b), and section II.H of this Explanation of Provisions, for exceptions that apply when the payment is included or includible in a U.S. tax resident's or U.S. taxable branch's income.

The Treasury Department and IRS request comments on whether an exception should apply if the specified payment is included in income in any foreign jurisdiction, taking into account accommodation transactions involving low-tax entities.

H. *Exceptions for certain amounts included or includible in a U.S. tax resident's or U.S. taxable branch's income*

Proposed § 1.267A-3(b) provides rules that reduce disqualified hybrid amounts to the extent the amounts are included or includible in a U.S. tax resident's or U.S. taxable branch's income. In general, these rules ensure that a specified payment is not a disqualified hybrid amount to the extent included in the income of a tax resident of the United States or a U.S. taxable branch, or taken into account by a U.S. shareholder under the subpart F or GILTI rules.

Source-based withholding tax imposed by the United States (or any other country) on disqualified hybrid amounts does not neutralize the D/NI outcome and therefore does not reduce or otherwise affect disqualified hybrid amounts. Withholding tax policies are unrelated to the policies underlying hybrid arrangements - for example, withholding tax can be imposed on non-hybrid payments - and, accordingly, withholding tax is not a substitute for a specified payment being included in income by a tax resident or taxable branch. *See also* section II.L of this Explanation of Provisions (interaction with withholding taxes and income tax treaties). Furthermore, other jurisdictions applying the defensive or secondary rule to a payment (which generally requires the payee to include the payment in income, if the payer is not denied a deduction for the payment under the primary rule) may not treat withholding taxes as satisfying the primary rule and may therefore require the payee to include the payment in income if a deduction for the payment is not disallowed (regardless of whether withholding tax has been imposed).

Thus, the proposed regulations do not treat amounts subject to U.S. withholding taxes as reducing disqualified hybrid amounts. Nevertheless, the Treasury Department and the IRS request comments on the interaction of the proposed regulations with withholding taxes and whether, and the extent to which, there should be special rules under section 267A when withholding taxes are imposed in connection with a specified payment, taking into account how such a rule could be coordinated with the hybrid mismatch rules of other jurisdictions.

I. *Disqualified imported mismatch amounts*

Proposed § 1.267A-4 sets forth a rule to address "imported" hybrid and branch arrangements. This rule is generally intended to prevent the effects of an "offshore" hybrid arrangement (for example, a hybrid arrangement between two foreign corporations completely outside the U.S. taxing jurisdiction) from being shifted, or "imported," into the U.S. taxing jurisdiction through the use of a non-hybrid arrangement.

Accordingly, the proposed regulations disallow deductions for specified payments that are "disqualified imported mismatch amounts." In general, a disqualified imported mismatch amount is a specified payment: (i) that is non-hybrid in nature, such as interest paid on an instrument that is treated as indebtedness for both U.S. and foreign tax purposes, and (ii) for which the income attributable to the payment is directly or indirectly offset by a hybrid deduction of a foreign tax resident or taxable branch. The rule addresses "indirect" offsets in order to take into account, for example, structures involving intermediaries where the foreign tax resident that receives the specified payment is different from the foreign tax resident that incurs the hybrid deduction. *See* proposed § 1.267A-6(c), *Example 8, Example 9,* and *Example 10*.

In general, a hybrid deduction for purposes of the imported mismatch rule is an amount for which a foreign tax resident or taxable branch is allowed an interest or royalty deduction under its tax law, to the extent the deduction would be disallowed if such tax law were to contain rules substantially similar to the section 267A proposed regulations. For this purpose, it is not relevant whether the amount is recognized as interest or a royalty under U.S. law, or whether the amount would be allowed as a deduction under U.S. law. Thus, for example, a deduction with respect to equity (such as a notional interest deduction) constitutes a hybrid deduction even though such a deduction would not be recognized (or allowed) under U.S. tax law. As another example, a royalty deduction under foreign tax law may constitute a hybrid deduction even though for U.S. tax purposes the royalty is viewed as made from a disregarded entity to its owner and therefore is not regarded.

The requirement that the deduction would be disallowed if the foreign tax law were to contain rules substantially similar to those under section 267A is intended to limit the application of the imported mismatch rule to cases in which, had the foreign-to-foreign hybrid arrangement instead involved a specified party, section 267A would have applied to disallow the deduction. In other words, this requirement prevents the imported mismatch rule from applying to arrangements outside the general scope of section 267A, even if the arrangements are hybrid in nature and result in a D/NI (or similar) outcome. For example, in the case of a deductible payment of a foreign tax resident to a tax resident of a foreign country that does not impose an income tax, the deduction would generally not be a hybrid deduction - even though it may be made pursuant to a hybrid instrument - because the D/NI outcome would not be a result of hybridity. *See* section II.E of this Explanation of Provisions (requiring a link between hybridity and the D/NI outcome, for a specified payment to be a disqualified hybrid amount).

Further, the proposed regulations include "ordering" and "funding" rules to determine the extent that a hybrid deduction directly or indirectly offsets income attributable to a specified payment. In addition, the proposed regulations provide that certain payments made by non-specified parties the tax laws of which contain hybrid mismatch rules are taken into account when applying the ordering and funding rules. Together, these provisions are intended to coordinate proposed § 1.267A-4 with foreign imported mismatch rules, in order to prevent the same hybrid deduction from resulting in deductions for non-hybrid payments being disallowed under imported mismatch rules in more than one jurisdiction.

J. *Definitions of interest and royalty*

1. Interest

There are no generally applicable regulations or statutory provisions addressing when financial instruments are treated as debt for U.S. tax purposes or when a payment is interest. As a general matter, however, the factors that distinguish debt from equity are described in Notice 94-47, 1994-1 C.B. 357, and interest is defined as compensation for the use or forbearance of money. *Deputy v. Dupont*, 308 U.S. 488 (1940).

Using these principles, the proposed regulations define interest broadly to include interest associated with conventional debt instruments, other amounts treated as interest under the Code, as well as transactions that are indebtedness in substance although not in form. *See* proposed § 1.267A-5(a)(12).

In addition, in order to address certain structured transactions, the proposed regulations apply equally to "structured payments." Proposed § 1.267A-5(b)(5) defines structured payments to include a number of items such as an expense or loss predominately incurred in consideration of the time value of money in a transaction or series of integrated or related transactions in which a taxpayer secures the use of funds for a period of time. This approach is consistent with the rules treating such payments similarly to interest under § § 1.861-9T and 1.954-2.

The definitions of interest and structured payments also provide for adjustments to the amount of interest expense or structured payments, as applicable, to reflect the impact of derivatives that affect the economic yield or cost of funds of a transaction involving interest or structured payments. The definitions of interest and structured payments contained in the proposed regulations apply only for purposes of section 267A. However, solely for purposes of certain other provisions, similar definitions apply. For example, the definition of interest and structured payments under the proposed regulations is similar in scope to the definition of items treated similarly to interest under § 1.861-9T for purposes of allocating and apportioning deductions under section 861 and similar to the items treated as interest expense for purposes of section 163(j) in proposed regulations under section 163(j).

The Treasury Department and the IRS considered three options with respect to the definition of interest for purposes of section 267A. The first option considered was to not provide a definition of interest, and thus rely on general tax principles and case law to define interest for purposes of section 267A. While adopting this option might reduce complexity for some taxpayers, not providing an explicit definition of interest would create its own uncertainty as neither taxpayers nor the IRS might have a clear sense of what types of payments are treated as interest expense subject to disallowance under section 267A. Such uncertainty could increase burdens to the IRS and taxpayers by increasing the number of disputes about whether particular payments are interest for section 267A purposes. Moreover, this option could be distortive as it would provide an incentive to taxpayers to engage in transactions generating deductions economically similar to interest while asserting that such deductions are not described by existing principles defining interest expense. If successful, such strategies could allow taxpayers to avoid the application of section 267A through transactions that are similar to transactions involving interest.

The second option considered would have been to adopt a definition of interest but limit the scope of the definition to cover only amounts associated with conventional debt instruments and amounts that are generally treated as interest for all purposes under the Code or regulations prior to the passage of the Act. This would be equivalent to only adopting the rule that is proposed in § 1.267A-5(a)(12)(i) without also addressing structured payments, which are described in proposed § 1.267A-5(b)(5). While this would clarify what would be deemed interest for purposes of section 267A, the Treasury Department and the IRS have determined that this approach would potentially distort future financing transactions. Some taxpayers would choose to use financial instruments and transactions that provide a similar economic result of using a conventional debt instrument, but would avoid the label of interest expense under such a definition, potentially enabling these taxpayers to avoid the application of section 267A. As a result, under this second approach, there would still be an incentive for taxpayers to engage in the type of avoidance transactions discussed in the first alternative.

The final option considered and the one ultimately adopted in the proposed regulations is to provide a complete definition of interest that addresses all transactions that are commonly understood to produce interest expense, as well as structured payments that may have been entered into to avoid the application of section 267A. The proposed regulations also reduce taxpayer burden by adopting definitions of interest that have already been developed and administered in § § 1.861-9T and 1.954-2 and that have been proposed for purposes of section 163(j). The definition of interest provided in the proposed regulations applies only for purposes of section 267A and not for other purposes of the Code, such as section 904(d)(3).

The Treasury Department and the IRS welcome comments on the definition of interest for purposes of section 267A contained in the proposed regulations.

2. Royalty

Section 267A does not define the term royalty and there is no universal definition of royalty under the Code. The Treasury Department and the IRS considered providing no definition for royalties. However, similar to the discussion in Section II.J.1 of this Explanation of Provisions with respect to the definition of interest, not providing a definition for royalties and relying instead on general tax principles could create uncertainty as neither taxpayers nor the IRS might have a clear sense of what types of payments are treated as royalties subject to disallowance under section 267A. Such uncertainty could increase burdens to the IRS and taxpayers with respect to disputes about whether particular payments are royalties for section 267A purposes.

Instead, the Treasury Department and the IRS have determined that providing a definition of royalties would increase certainty, and therefore the proposed regulations define the term royalty for purposes of section 267A to include amounts paid or accrued as consideration for the use of, or the right to use, certain intellectual property and certain information concerning industrial, commercial or scientific experience. *See* proposed § 1.267A-5(a)(16). The term does not include amounts paid or accrued for after-sales services, for services rendered by a seller to the purchaser under a warranty, for pure technical assistance, or for an opinion given by an engineer, lawyer or accountant. The definition of royalty provided in the proposed regulations applies only for purposes of section 267A and not for other purposes of the Code, such as section 904(d)(3).

The definition of royalty is generally based on the definition used in tax treaties and, in particular, the definition incorporated into Article 12 of the 2006 U.S. Model Income Tax Treaty. This definition is also generally consistent with the language of section 861(a)(4). In addition, similar to the approach in the technical explanation to Article 12 of the 2006 U.S. Model Income Tax Treaty, the proposed regulations provide certain circumstances where payments are not treated as paid or accrued in consideration for the use of information concerning industrial, commercial or scientific experience. By using definitions that have already been developed and administered in other contexts, the proposed regulations provide an approach that reduces taxpayer burdens and uncertainty. The Treasury Department and the IRS welcome comments on the definition of royalty for purposes of section 267A contained in the proposed regulations.

K. *Miscellaneous issues*

1. Effect of Foreign Currency Gain or Loss

The proposed regulations provide that foreign currency gain or loss recognized under section 988 is not separately taken into account under section 267A. *See* proposed § 1.267A-5(b)(2). Rather, foreign currency gain or loss recognized with respect to a specified payment is taken into account under section 267A only to the extent that the specified payment is in respect of accrued interest or an accrued royalty for which a deduction is disallowed under section 267A. Thus, for example, a section 988 loss recognized with respect to a specified payment of interest is not separately taken into account under section 267A (even though under the tax law of the tax resident to which the specified payment is made the tax resident does not include in income an amount corresponding to the section 988 loss, as the specified payment is made in the tax resident's functional currency).

The Treasury Department and the IRS recognize that additional rules addressing the effect of different foreign currencies may be necessary. For example, a hybrid deduction for purposes of the imported mismatch rule may be denominated in a different currency than a specified payment, in which case a translation rule may be necessary to determine the amount of the specified payment that is subject to the imported mismatch rule. The Treasury Department and the IRS request comments on foreign currency rules, including any rules regarding the translation of amounts between currencies, for purposes of the proposed regulations under sections 245A and 267A. 2. Payments by U.S. Taxable Branches

Certain expenses incurred by a nonresident alien or foreign corporation are allowed as deductions under sections 873(a) and 882(c) in determining that person's effectively connected income. To the extent the deductions arise from transactions involving certain hybrid or branch arrangements, the deductions should be disallowed under section 267A, as discussed in section II.B of this Explanation of Provisions. The proposed regulations do so by (i) treating a U.S. taxable branch (which includes a permanent establishment of a foreign person) as a specified party, and (ii) providing rules regarding interest or royalties considered paid or accrued by a U.S. taxable branch, solely for purposes of section 267A (and thus not for other purposes, such as chapter 3 of the Code). *See* proposed § 1.267A-5(b)(3). The effect of this approach is that interest or royalties considered paid or accrued by a U.S. taxable branch are specified payments that are subject to the rules of proposed §§ 1.267A-1 through 1.267A-4. *See also* proposed § 1.267A-6(c), *Example 4*.

In general, a U.S. taxable branch is considered to pay or accrue any interest or royalties allocated or apportioned to effectively connected income of the U.S. taxable branch. *See* proposed § 1.267A-5(b)(3)(i). However, if a U.S. taxable branch constitutes a U.S. permanent establishment of a treaty resident, then the U.S. permanent establishment is considered to pay or accrue the interest or royalties deductible in computing its business profits. Although interest paid by a U.S. taxable branch may be subject to withholding tax as determined under section 884(f)(1)(A) and § 1.884-4, those rules are not relevant for purposes of section 267A.

The proposed regulations also provide rules to identify the manner in which a specified payment of a U.S. taxable branch is considered made. *See* proposed § 1.267A-5(b)(3)(ii). Absent such rules, it might be difficult to determine whether the specified payment is made pursuant to a hybrid or branch arrangement (for example, made pursuant to a hybrid transaction or to a reverse hybrid). However, these rules regarding the manner in which a specified payment is made do not apply to interest or royalties deemed paid by a U.S. permanent establishment in connection with inter-branch transactions that are permitted to be taken into account under certain U.S. tax treaties - such payments, by definition, constitute deemed branch payments (subject to disallowance under proposed § 1.267A-2(c)) and are therefore made pursuant to a branch arrangement.

3. Coordination with Other Provisions

Proposed § 1.267A-5(b)(1) coordinates the application of section 267A with other provisions of the Code and regulations that affect the deductibility of interest and royalties. This rule provides that, in general, section 267A applies after the application of other provisions of the Code and regulations. For example, a specified payment is subject to section 267A for the taxable year for which a deduction for the payment would otherwise be allowed. Thus, if a deduction for an accrued amount is deferred under section 267(a) (in certain cases, deferring a deduction for an amount accrued to a related foreign person until paid), then the deduction is tested for disallowance under section 267A for the taxable year in which the amount is paid. Absent such a rule, an accrued amount for which a deduction is deferred under section 267(a) could constitute a disqualified hybrid amount even though the amount will be included in the specified recipient's income when actually paid. This coordination rule also provides that section 267A applies to interest or royalties after taking into account provisions that could otherwise recharacterize such amounts, such as § 1.894-1(d)(2).

4. E&P Reduction

Proposed § 1.267A-5(b)(4) provides that the disallowance of a deduction under section 267A does not affect whether or when the amount paid or accrued that gave rise to the deduction reduces earnings and profits of a corporation. Thus, a corporation's earnings and profits may be reduced as a result of a specified payment for which a deduction is disallowed under section 267A. This is consistent with the approach in the context of other disallowance rules. *See* § 1.312-7(b)(1) ("A loss . . . may be recognized though not allowed as a deduction (by reason, for example, of the operation of sections 267 and 1211 . . .) but the mere fact that it is not allowed does not prevent a decrease in earnings and profits by the amount of such disallowed loss."); *Luckman v. Comm'r*, 418 F.2d 381, 383-84 (7th Cir. 1969) ("[T]rue expenses incurred by the corporation reduce earnings and profits despite their nondeductibility from current income for tax purposes.").

5. De Minimis Exception

The proposed regulations provide a de minimis exception to make the rules more administrable. *See* proposed § 1.267A-1(c). As a result of this exception, a specified party is excepted from the application of section 267A for any taxable year for which the sum of its interest and royalty deductions (plus interest and royalty deductions of any related specified parties) is below $50,000. This rule applies based on any interest or royalty deductions, regardless of whether the deductions would be disallowed under section 267A. In addition, for purposes of this rule, specified parties that are related are treated as a single specified party.

The Treasury Department and the IRS welcome comments on the de minimis exception and whether another threshold would be more appropriate to implement the purposes of section 267A.

L. *Interaction with withholding taxes and income tax treaties*

The determination of whether a deduction for a specified payment is disallowed under section 267A is made without regard to whether the payment is subject to withholding under section 1441 or 1442 or is eligible for a reduced rate of tax under an income tax treaty. Since the U.S. tax characterization of the payment prevails in determining the treaty rate for interest or royalties, regardless of whether the payment is made pursuant to a hybrid transaction, the proposed regulations will generally result in the disallowance of a deduction but treaty benefits may still be claimed, as long as the recipient is the beneficial owner of the payment and otherwise eligible for treaty benefits. On the other hand, if interest or royalties are paid to a fiscally transparent entity that is a reverse hybrid, as defined in proposed § 1.267A-2(d), the payment generally will not be deductible under the proposed regulations if the investor does not derive the payment, and will not be eligible for treaty benefits if the interest holder under § 1.894-1(d) does not derive the payment. The proposed regulations will only apply, however, if the investor is related to the specified party, whereas the reduced rate under the treaty may be denied without regard to whether the interest holder is related to the payer of the interest or royalties.

Certain U.S. income tax treaties also address indirectly the branch mismatch rules under proposed § 1.267A-2(e). Special rules, generally in the limitation on benefits articles of income tax treaties, increase the tax treaty rate for interest and royalties to 15 percent (even if otherwise not taxable under the relevant treaty article) if the amount paid to a permanent establishment of the treaty resident is subject to minimal tax, and the foreign corporation that derives and beneficially owns the payment is a resident of a treaty country that excludes or otherwise exempts from gross income the profits attributable to the permanent establishment to which the payment was made.

III. *Information Reporting under Sections 6038, 6038A, and 6038C*

Under section 6038(a)(1), U.S. persons that control foreign business entities must file certain information returns with respect to those entities, which includes information listed in section 6038(a)(1)(A) through (a)(1)(E), as well as information that "the Secretary determines to be appropriate to carry out the provisions of this title." Section 6038A similarly requires 25-percent foreign-owned domestic corporations (reporting corporations) to file certain information returns with respect to those corporations, including information related to transactions between the reporting corporation and each foreign person which is a related party to the reporting corporation. Section 6038C imposes the same reporting requirements on certain foreign corporations engaged in a U.S. trade or business (also, a reporting corporation).

The proposed regulations provide that a specified payment for which a deduction is disallowed under section 267A, as well as hybrid dividends and tiered hybrid dividends under section 245A, must be reported on the appropriate information reporting form in accordance with sections 6038 and 6038A. *See* proposed § § 1.6038-2(f)(13) and (14), 1.6038-3(g)(3), and 1.6038A-2(b)(5)(iii).

IV. *Sections 1503(d) and 7701 - Application to Domestic Reverse Hybrids*

A. *Overview*

1. Dual Consolidated Loss Rules

Congress enacted section 1503(d) to prevent the "double dipping" of losses. *See* S. Rep. 313, 99th Cong., 2d Sess., at 419-20 (1986). The Senate Report explains that "losses that a corporation uses to offset foreign tax on income that the United States does not subject to tax should not also be used to reduce any other corporation's U.S. tax." *Id.* Section 1503(d) and the regulations thereunder generally provide that, subject to certain exceptions, a dual consolidated loss of a corporation cannot reduce the taxable income of a domestic affiliate (a "domestic use"). *See* §§1.1503(d)-2 and 1.1503-4(b). Section 1.1503(d)-1(b)(5) defines a dual consolidated loss as a net operating loss of a dual resident corporation or the net loss attributable to a separate unit (generally defined as either a foreign branch or an interest in a hybrid entity). *See* §1.1503(d)-1(b)(4).

The general prohibition against the domestic use of a dual consolidated loss does not apply if, pursuant to a "domestic use election," the taxpayer certifies that there has not been and will not be a "foreign use" of the dual consolidated loss during a certification period. *See* §1.1503(d)-6(d). If a foreign use or other triggering event occurs during the certification period, the dual consolidated loss is recaptured. A foreign use occurs when any portion of the dual consolidated loss is made available to offset the income of a foreign corporation or the direct or indirect owner of a hybrid entity (generally non-dual inclusion income). *See* §1.1503(d)-3(a)(1). Other triggering events include certain transfers of the stock or assets of a dual resident corporation, or the interests in or assets of a separate unit. *See* §1.1503(d)-6(e).

The regulations include a "mirror legislation" rule that, in general, prevents a domestic use election when a foreign jurisdiction has enacted legislation similar to section 1503(d) that denies any opportunity for a foreign use of the dual consolidated loss. *See* §1.1503(d)-3(e). As a result, the existence of mirror legislation may prevent the dual consolidated loss from being put to a domestic use (due to the domestic use limitation) or to a foreign use (due to the foreign "mirror legislation") such that the loss becomes "stranded." In such a case, the regulations contemplate that the taxpayer may enter into an agreement with the United States and the foreign country (for example, through the competent authorities) pursuant to which the losses are used in only one country. *See* §1.1503(d)-6(b).

2. Entity Classification Rules

Sections 301.7701-1 through 301.7701-3 classify a business entity with two or more members as either a corporation or a partnership, and a business entity with a single owner as either a corporation or a disregarded entity. Certain domestic business entities, such as limited liability companies, are classified by default as partnerships (if they have more than one member) or as disregarded entities (if they have only one owner) but are eligible to elect for federal tax purposes to be classified as corporations. *See* §301.7701-3(b)(1).

B. *Domestic reverse hybrids*

The Treasury Department and the IRS are aware that structures involving domestic reverse hybrids have been used to obtain double-deduction outcomes because they were not subject to limitation under current section 1503(d) regulations. A domestic reverse hybrid generally refers to a domestic business entity that elects under §301.7701-3(c) to be treated as a corporation for U.S. tax purposes, but is treated as fiscally transparent under the tax law of its investors. In these structures, a foreign parent corporation typically owns the majority of the interests in the domestic reverse hybrid. Domestic reverse hybrid structures can lead to double-deduction outcomes because, for example, deductions incurred by the domestic reverse hybrid can be used (i) under U.S. tax law to offset income that is not subject to tax in the foreign parent's country, such as income of domestic corporations with which the domestic reverse hybrid files a U.S. consolidated return, and (ii) under the foreign parent's tax law to offset income not subject to U.S. tax, such as income of the foreign parent other than the income (if any) of the domestic reverse hybrid. Taxpayers take the position that these structures are not subject to the current section 1503(d) regulations because the domestic reverse hybrid is neither a dual resident corporation (because it is not subject to tax on a residence basis or on its worldwide income in the foreign parent country) nor a separate unit of a domestic corporation.

A comment on regulations under section 1503(d) that were proposed in 2005 asserted that this result is inconsistent with the policies underlying section 1503(d), which was adopted, in part, to ensure that domestic corporations were not put at a competitive disadvantage as compared to foreign corporations through the use of certain inbound acquisition structures. *See* TD 9315. The comment suggested that the scope of the final regulations be broadened to treat such entities as separate units, the losses of which are subject to the restrictions of section 1503(d). *Id.*

In response to this comment, the preamble to the 2007 final dual consolidated loss regulations stated that the Treasury Department and the IRS acknowledged that this type of structure results in a double dip similar to that which Congress intended to prevent through the adoption of section 1503(d). The final regulations did not address these structures, however, because the Treasury Department and the IRS determined at that time that a domestic reverse hybrid was neither a dual resident corporation nor a separate unit and, therefore, was not subject to section 1503(d). *See* TD 9315. The preamble noted, however, that the Treasury Department and the IRS would continue to study these and similar structures.

The Treasury Department and the IRS have determined that these structures are inconsistent with the principles of section 1503(d) and, as a result, raise significant policy concerns. Accordingly, the proposed regulations include rules under sections 1503(d) and 7701 to prevent the use of these structures to obtain a double-deduction outcome. The proposed regulations require, as a condition to a domestic entity electing to be treated as a corporation under §301.7701-3(c), that the domestic entity consent to be treated as a dual resident corporation for purposes of section 1503(d) (such an entity, a "domestic consenting corporation") for taxable years in which two requirements are satisfied. *See* proposed §301.7701-3(c)(3). The requirements are intended to restrict the application of section

1503(d) to cases in which it is likely that losses of the domestic consenting corporation could result in a double-deduction outcome.

The requirements are satisfied if (i) a "specified foreign tax resident" (generally, a body corporate that is a tax resident of a foreign country) under its tax law derives or incurs items of income, gain, deduction, or loss of the domestic consenting corporation, and (ii) the specified foreign tax resident is related to the domestic consenting corporation (as determined under section 267(b) or 707(b)). *See* proposed § 1.1503(d)-1(c). For example, the requirements are satisfied if a specified foreign tax resident directly owns all the interests in the domestic consenting corporation and the domestic consenting corporation is fiscally transparent under the specified foreign tax resident's tax law. In addition, an item of the domestic consenting corporation for a particular taxable year is considered derived or incurred by the specified tax resident during that year even if, under the specified foreign tax resident's tax law, the item is recognized in, and derived or incurred by the specified foreign tax resident in, a different taxable year.

Further, if a domestic entity filed an election to be treated as a corporation before December 28, 2018 such that the entity was not required to consent to be treated as a dual resident corporation, then the entity is deemed to consent to being treated as a dual resident corporation as of its first taxable year beginning on or after the end of a 12-month transition period. This deemed consent can be avoided if the entity elects, effective before its first taxable year beginning on or after the end of the transition period, to be treated as a partnership or disregarded entity such that it ceases to be a corporation for U.S. tax purposes. For purposes of such an election, the 60 month limitation under § 301.7701-3(c)(1)(iv) is waived.

Finally, the proposed regulations provide that the mirror legislation rule does not apply to dual consolidated losses of a domestic consenting corporation. *See* proposed § 1.1503(d)-3(e)(3). This exception is intended to minimize cases in which dual consolidated losses could be "stranded" when, for example, the foreign parent jurisdiction has adopted rules similar to the recommendations in Chapter 6 of the Hybrid Mismatch Report. The exception does not apply to dual consolidated losses attributable to separate units because, in such cases, the United States is the parent jurisdiction and the dual consolidated loss rules should neutralize the double-deduction outcome.

V. *Triggering Event Exception for Compulsory Transfers*

As noted in section IV.A.1 of this Explanation of Provisions, certain triggering events require a dual consolidated loss that is subject to a domestic use election to be recaptured and included in income. The dual consolidated loss regulations also include various exceptions to these triggering events, including an exception for compulsory transfers involving foreign governments. *See* § 1.1503(d)-6(f)(5).

A comment on the 2007 final dual consolidated loss regulations stated that the policies underlying the triggering event exception for compulsory transfers involving foreign governments apply equally to compulsory transfers involving the United States government. Accordingly, the comment requested guidance under § 1.1503(d)-3(c)(9) to provide that the exception is not limited to foreign governments. The comment suggested, as an example, that the exception should apply to a divestiture of a hybrid entity engaged in proprietary trading pursuant to the "Volcker Rule" contained in the Dodd-Frank Wall Street Reform and Consumer Protection Act, Pub. L. No. 111-203 (2010).

The Treasury Department and the IRS agree with this comment and, accordingly, the proposed regulations modify the compulsory transfer triggering event exception such that it will also apply with respect to the United States government.

VI. *Disregarded Payments Made to Domestic Corporations*

As discussed in sections II.D.2 and 3 of this Explanation of Provisions, the proposed regulations under section 267A address D/NI outcomes resulting from actual and deemed payments of interest and royalties that are regarded for U.S. tax purposes but disregarded for foreign tax purposes. The proposed regulations under section 267A do not, however, address similar structures involving payments to domestic corporations that are regarded for foreign tax purposes but disregarded for U.S. tax purposes.

For example, USP, a domestic corporation that is the parent of a consolidated group, borrows from a bank to fund the acquisition of the stock of FT, a foreign corporation that is tax resident of Country X. USP contributes the loan proceeds to USS, a newly formed domestic corporation that is a member of the USP consolidated group, in exchange for all the stock of USS. USS then forms FDE, a disregarded entity that is tax resident of Country X, USS lends the loan proceeds to FDE, and FDE uses the proceeds to acquire the stock of FT. For U.S. tax purposes, USP claims a deduction for interest paid on the bank loan, and USS does not recognize interest income on interest payments made to it from FDE because the payments are disregarded. For Country X tax purposes, the interest paid from FDE to USS is regarded and gives rise to a loss that can be surrendered (or otherwise used, such as through a consolidation regime) to offset the operating income of FT.

Under the current section 1503(d) regulations, the loan from USS to FDE does not result in a dual consolidated loss attributable to USS's interest in FDE because interest paid on the loan is not regarded for U.S. tax purposes; only items that are regarded for U.S. tax purposes are taken into account for purposes of determining a dual consolidated loss. *See* § 1.1503(d)-5(c)(1)(ii). In addition, the regarded interest expense of USP is not attributed to USS's interest in FDE because only regarded items of USS, the domestic owner of FDE, are taken into account for purposes of determining a dual consolidated loss. *Id*. The result would generally be the same, however, even if USS, rather than USP, were the borrower on the bank loan. *See* § 1.1503(d)-7(c), *Example 23*.

The Treasury Department and the IRS have determined that these transactions raise significant policy concerns that are similar to those relating to the D/NI outcomes addressed by sections 245A(e) and 267A, and the double-deduction outcomes addressed by section 1503(d). The Treasury Department and the IRS are studying these transactions and request comments.

VII. *Applicability Dates*

Under section 7805(b)(2), and consistent with the applicability date of section 245A, proposed § 1.245A(e)-1 applies to distributions made after December 31, 2017. Under section 7805(b)(2), proposed § § 1.267A-1 through 1.267A-6 generally apply to specified payments made in taxable years beginning after December 31, 2017. This applicability date is consistent with the applicability date of section 267A. The Treasury Department and the IRS therefore expect to finalize such provisions by June 22, 2019. *See* section 7805(b)(2). However if such provisions are finalized after June 22, 2019, then the Treasury Department and the IRS expect that such provisions will apply only to taxable years ending on or after December 28, 2018. *See* section 7805(b)(1)(B).

As provided in proposed § 1.267A-7(b), certain rules, such as the disregarded payment and deemed branch payment rules as well as the imported mismatch rule, apply to specified payments made in taxable years beginning on or after December 28, 2018. *See* section 7805(b)(1)(B).

Proposed § § 1.6038-2, 1.6038-3, and 1.6038A-2, which require certain reporting regarding deductions disallowed under section 267A, as well as hybrid dividends and tiered hybrid dividends under section 245A, apply with respect to information for annual accounting periods or tax years, as applicable, beginning on or after December 28, 2018. *See* section 7805(b)(1)(B).

Proposed § § 1.1503(d)-1 and -3, treating domestic consenting corporations as dual resident corporations, apply to taxable years ending on or after December 28, 2018. *See* section 7805(b)(1)(B).

Proposed § 1.1503(d)-6, amending the compulsory transfer triggering event exception, applies to transfers that occur on or after December 28, 2018, but taxpayers may apply the rules to earlier transfers. *See* section 7805(b)(1)(B).

Proposed § 301.7701-3(a) and (c)(3) apply to a domestic eligible entity that on or after December 28, 2018 files an election to be classified as an association (regardless of whether the election is effective before December 28, 2018). These provisions also apply to certain domestic eligible entities the interests in which are transferred or issued on or after December 28, 2018. *See* section 7805(b)(1)(B).

Special Analyses

I. *Regulatory Planning and Review*

Executive Orders 13771, 13563, and 12866 direct agencies to assess costs and benefits of available regulatory alternatives and, if regulation is necessary, to select regulatory approaches that maximize net benefits, including potential economic, environmental, public health and safety effects, distributive impacts, and equity. Executive Order 13563 emphasizes the importance of quantifying both costs and benefits, reducing costs, harmonizing rules, and promoting flexibility. The preliminary EO 13771 designation for this proposed rulemaking is regulatory.

The proposed regulations have been designated by the Office of Management and Budget's Office of Information and Regulatory Affairs (OIRA) as subject to review under Executive Order 12866 pursuant to the Memorandum of Agreement (April 11, 2018) between the Treasury Department and the Office of Management and Budget regarding review of tax regulations ("MOA"). OIRA has determined that the proposed rulemaking is economically significant and subject to review under EO 12866 and section 1(c) of the Memorandum of Agreement. Accordingly, the proposed regulations have been reviewed by the Office of Management and Budget.

A. *Background*

Hybrid arrangements include both "hybrid entities" and "hybrid instruments." A hybrid entity is generally an entity which is treated as a flow-through or disregarded entity for U.S. tax purposes but as a corporation for foreign tax purposes or vice versa. Hybrid instruments are financial instruments that share characteristics of both debt and equity and are treated as debt for U.S. tax purposes and equity in the foreign jurisdiction or vice versa.

Before the Act, U.S. subsidiaries of foreign-based multinational enterprises could employ cross-border hybrid arrangements as legal tax-avoidance techniques by exploiting differences in tax treatment across jurisdictions. These arrangements allowed taxpayers to claim tax deductions in the United States without a corresponding inclusion in another jurisdiction.

The United States has a check-the-box regulatory provision, under which some taxpayers can choose whether they are treated as corporations, where they may face a separate entity level tax, or as partnerships, where there is no such separate entity tax (but rather only owner-level tax), under the U.S. tax code. This choice allows taxpayers the ability to become hybrid entities that are viewed as corporations in one jurisdiction, but not in another. For example, a foreign parent could own a domestic subsidiary limited liability partnership (LLP) that, under the check-the-box rules, elects to be treated as a corporation under U.S. tax law. However, this subsidiary could be viewed as a partnership under foreign tax law. The result is that the domestic subsidiary could be entitled to a deduction for U.S. tax purposes for making interest payments to the foreign parent, but the foreign country would see a payment between a partnership and a partner, and therefore would not tax the interest income. That is, the corporate structure would enable the business entity to avoid paying U.S.

tax on the interest by allowing a deduction attributable to an intra-group loan, despite the interest income never being included under foreign tax law.

In addition, there are hybrid instruments, which share characteristics of both debt and equity. Because of these shared characteristics, countries may be inconsistent in their treatment of such instruments. One example is perpetual debt, which many countries treat as debt, but the United States treats as equity. If a foreign affiliate of a U.S.-based multinational issued perpetual debt to a U.S. holder, the interest payments would be tax deductible in a foreign jurisdiction that treats the instrument as debt, while the payments are treated as dividends in the United States and potentially eligible for a dividends received deduction (DRD).

The Act adds section 245A(e) to the Code to address issues of hybridity by introducing a hybrid dividends provision, which disallows the DRD for any dividend received by a U.S. shareholder from a controlled foreign corporation if the dividend is a hybrid dividend. The statute defines a hybrid dividend as an amount received from a controlled foreign corporation for which a deduction would be allowed under section 245A(a) and for which the controlled foreign corporation received a deduction or other tax benefit in a foreign country. Hybrid dividends between controlled foreign corporations with a common U.S. shareholder are treated as subpart F income.

The Act also adds section 267A of the Code to deny a deduction for any disqualified related party amount paid or accrued as a result of a hybrid transaction or by, or to, a hybrid entity. The statute defines a disqualified related party amount as any interest or royalty paid or accrued to a related party where there is no corresponding inclusion to the related party in the other tax jurisdiction or the related party is allowed a deduction with respect to such amount in the other tax jurisdiction. The statute's definition of a hybrid transaction is any transaction where there is a mismatch in tax treatment between the U.S. and the other foreign jurisdiction. Similarly, a hybrid entity is any entity which is treated as fiscally transparent for U.S. tax purposes but not for purposes of the foreign tax jurisdiction, or vice versa.

B. *Overview*

The hybrids provisions in the Act and the proposed regulations are anti-abuse measures. Taxpayers have been taking aggressive tax positions to take advantage of tax treatment mismatches between jurisdictions in order to achieve favorable tax outcomes at the detriment of tax revenues (see OECD/G20 Hybrid Mismatch Report, October 2015 and OECD/G20 Branch Mismatch Report, July 2017). The statute and the proposed regulations serve to conform the U.S. tax system to recently agreed-upon international tax principles (see OECD/G20 Hybrids Mismatch Report, October 2015 and OECD/G20 Branch Mismatch Report, July 2017), consistent with statutory intent, while protecting U.S. interests and the U.S. tax base. International tax coordination is particularly advantageous in the context of hybrids as it has the potential to greatly curb opportunities for hybrid arrangements, while avoiding double taxation. The anticipated effect of the statute and proposed regulations is a reduction in tax revenue loss due to hybrid arrangements, at the cost of an increase in compliance burden for a limited number of sophisticated taxpayers, as explained below.

C. *Need for the proposed regulations*

Because the Act introduced new sections to the Code to address hybrid entities and hybrid instruments, a large number of the relevant terms and necessary calculations that taxpayers are currently required to apply under the statute can benefit from greater specificity. Taxpayers will lack clarity on which types of arrangements are subject to the statute without the additional interpretive guidance and clarifications contained in the proposed regulations. This lack of clarity could lead to a shifting of corporate income overseas through hybrid arrangements, further eroding U.S. tax revenues. Without accompanying rules to cover branches, structured arrangements, imported mismatches, and similar structures, the statute would be extremely easy to avoid, a pathway that is contrary to Congressional intent. It could also lead to otherwise similar taxpayers interpreting the statute differently, distorting the equity of tax treatment for otherwise similarly situated taxpayers. Finally, the lack of clarity could cause some taxpayers unnecessary compliance burden if they misinterpret the statute.

D. *Economic analysis*

1. Baseline

The Treasury Department and the IRS have assessed the benefits and costs of the proposed regulations relative to a no-action baseline reflecting anticipated tax-related behavior and other economic behavior in the absence of the proposed regulations.

The baseline includes the Act, which effectively cut the top statutory corporate income tax rate from 35 to 21 percent. This change lowered the value of using hybrid arrangements for multinational corporations, because the value of such arrangements is proportional to the tax they allow the corporation to avoid. As such, some firms with an incentive to set up hybrid arrangements prior to the Act would no longer find it profitable to maintain these arrangements. The Act also modified section 163(j), and regulations interpreting this provision are expected to be finalized soon, which together further limit the deductibility of interest payments. These statutory and regulatory changes further curb the incentive to set up and maintain hybrid arrangements for multinational corporations, since interest payments are a primary vehicle through which hybrid arrangements generated deductions prior to the Act. Further, prior to the Act, the Treasury Department and the IRS issued a series of regulations that reduced or eliminated the incentive for multinational corporations to invert, or change their tax residence to avoid U.S. taxes (including setting up some hybrid arrangements). As a result, under the baseline, the value of hybrid arrangements reflects the existing regulatory framework and the Act and its associated soon-to-be-finalized regulations, all of which strongly affect the value of hybrid arrangements as a tax avoidance technique.

2. Anticipated Costs and Benefits

i. Economic Effects

The Treasury Department has determined that the discretionary non-revenue impacts of the proposed hybrid regulations will reduce U.S. Gross Domestic Product (GDP) by less than $100 million per year ($2018).

To evaluate this effect, the Treasury Department considered the share of interest deductions that would be disallowed by the proposed regulations. Using Treasury Department models applied to confidential 2016 tax data, the Treasury Department calculated the average effective tax rate for potentially affected taxpayers under a range of levels of interest payment deductibility, including the level of deductibility under the Act without the proposed regulations. The difference between the estimated effective tax rate under the Act and without the discretionary elements of the proposed regulations and the range of estimated effective tax rates that include the proposed regulations provides a range of estimates of the net increase in the effective tax rate due to the discretion exercised in the proposed regulations. The Treasury Department next applied an elasticity of taxable income to the range of estimated increases in the effective tax rate to estimate the reduction in taxable income for each of the affected taxpayers in the sample. The Treasury Department then examined a range of estimates of the relationship between the change in taxable income and the real change in economic activity. Finally, the Treasury Department extrapolated the results through 2027.

The Treasury Department concludes from this evaluation that the discretionary aspects of the proposed rules will reduce GDP annually by less than $100 million ($2018). The projected effects reflect the proposed regulations alone and do not include non-revenue economic effects stemming from the Act in the absence of the proposed regulations. More specifically, the analysis did not estimate the impacts of the statutory requirement that hybrid dividends shall be treated as subpart F income of the receiving controlled foreign corporations for purposes of section 951(a)(1)(A) for the taxable year and shall not be permitted a foreign tax credit. *See* section 245A(e).

The Treasury Department solicits comments on the methodology used to evaluate the non-revenue economic effects of the proposed regulations and anticipates that further analysis will be provided at the final rule stage.

ii. Anticipated Costs and Benefits of Specific Provisions

a. Section 245A(e)

Section 245A(e) applies in certain cases in which a CFC pays a hybrid dividend, which is a dividend paid by the CFC for which the CFC received a deduction or other tax benefit under foreign tax law (a hybrid deduction). The proposed regulations provide rules for identifying and tracking such hybrid deductions. These rules set forth common standards for identifying hybrid deductions and therefore clarify what is deemed a hybrid dividend by the statute and ensure equitable tax treatment of otherwise similar taxpayers.

The proposed regulations also address timing differences to ensure that there is parity between economically similar transactions. Absent such rules, similar transactions may be treated differently due to timing differences. For example, if a CFC paid out a dividend in a given taxable year for which it received a deduction or other tax benefit in a prior taxable year, the taxpayer might claim the dividend is not a hybrid dividend, since the taxable year in which the dividend is paid for U.S. tax purposes and the year in which the tax benefit is received do not overlap. Absent rules, such as the proposed regulations, the purpose of section 245A(e) might be avoided and economically similar transactions might be treated differently.

Finally, these rules excuse certain taxpayers from having to track hybrid deductions (namely taxpayers without a sufficient connection to a section 245A(a) dividends received deduction). The utility of requiring these taxpayers to track hybrid deductions would be outweighed by the burdens of doing so. The proposed regulations reduce the compliance burden on taxpayers that are not directly dealing with hybrid dividends.

b. Section 267A

Section 267A disallows a deduction for interest or royalties paid or accrued in certain transactions involving a hybrid arrangement. Congress intended this provision to address cases in which the taxpayer is provided a deduction under U.S. tax law, but the payee does not have a corresponding income inclusion under foreign tax law, dubbed a "deduction/no-inclusion outcome" (D/NI outcome). See Senate Explanation, at 384. This affects taxpayers that attempt to use hybrid arrangements to strip income out of the United States taxing jurisdiction.

The proposed regulations disallow a deduction under section 267A only to the extent that the D/NI outcome is a result of a hybrid arrangement. Note that under the statute but without the proposed regulations, a deduction would be disallowed simply if a D/NI outcome occurs and a hybrid arrangement exists (see section II.E of the Explanation of Provisions). For example, a royalty payment made to a hybrid entity in the U.K. qualifying for a low tax rate under the U.K. patent box regime could be denied a deduction in the U.S. under the statute. However, the low U.K. rate is a result of the lower tax rate on patent box income and not a result of any hybrid arrangement. In this example, there is no link between hybridity and the D/NI outcome, since it is the U.K. patent box regime that yields the D/NI outcome and the low U.K. patent box rate is available to taxpayers regardless of whether they are organized as hybrid entities or not. The proposed regulations limit the application of section 267A to cases where the D/NI outcome occurs as a result of hybrid arrangements and not due to a generally applicable feature of the jurisdiction's tax system.

The proposed regulations also provide several exceptions to section 267A in order to refine the scope of the provision and minimize burdens on taxpayers. First, the proposed regulations generally exclude from section 267A payments that are included in a U.S. tax resident's or U.S. taxable branch's income or are taken into account for purposes of the subpart F or global intangible low-taxed income (GILTI) provisions. While the exception for income taken into account for purposes of subpart F is in the statute, the proposed regulations expand the exception to cover GILTI. This avoids potential double taxation on that income. In addition, as a refinement compared with the statute, the extent to which a payment is taken into account under subpart F is determined without regard to allocable deductions or qualified deficits. The proposed regulations also provide a de minimis rule that excepts small taxpayers from section 267A, minimizing the burden on small taxpayers.

Finally, the proposed regulations address a comprehensive set of transactions that give rise to D/NI outcomes. The statute, as written, does not apply to certain hybrid arrangements, including branch arrangements and certain reverse hybrids, as described above (see section II.D of the Explanation of Provisions). The exclusion of these arrangements could have large economic and fiscal consequences due to taxpayers shifting tax planning towards these arrangements to avoid the new anti-abuse statute. The proposed regulations close off this potential avenue for additional tax avoidance by applying the rules of section 267A to branch mismatches, reverse hybrids, certain transactions with unrelated parties that are structured to achieve D/NI outcomes, certain structured transactions involving amounts similar to interest, and imported mismatches.

3. Alternatives Considered

i. Addressing conduit arrangements/imported mismatches

Section 267A(e)(1) provides regulatory authority to apply the rules of section 267A to conduit arrangements and thus to disallow a deduction in cases in which income attributable to a payment is directly or indirectly offset by an offshore hybrid deduction. The Treasury Department and the IRS considered four options with regards to conduit arrangement rules.

The first option was to not implement any conduit rules, and thus rely on existing and established judicial doctrines (such as conduit principles and substance-over-form principles) to police these transactions. A second option considered was to address conduit arrangement concerns through a broad anti-abuse rule. On the one hand, both of these approaches might reduce complexity by eliminating the need for detailed regulatory rules addressing conduit arrangements. On the other hand, such approaches could create uncertainty (as neither taxpayers nor the IRS might have a clear sense of what types of transactions might be challenged under the judicial doctrines or anti-abuse rule) and could increase burdens to the IRS (as challenging under judicial doctrines or anti-abuse rules are generally difficult and resource intensive). Significantly, such approaches could result in double non-taxation (if judicial doctrines or anti-abuse rules were to not be successfully asserted) or double-taxation (if judicial doctrines or anti-abuse rules were to not take into account the application of foreign tax law, such as a foreign imported mismatch rule).

A third option considered was to implement rules modeled off existing U.S. anti-conduit rules under § 1.881-3. On the positive side, such an approach would rely on an established and existing framework that taxpayers are already familiar with and thus there would be a lesser need to create and apply a new framework or set of rules. On the negative side, existing anti-conduit rules are limited in certain respects as they apply only to certain financing arrangements, which exclude certain stock, and they address only withholding tax policies, which pose separate concerns from section 267A policies (D/NI policies). Furthermore, taxpayers have implemented structures that attempt to avoid the application of the existing anti-conduit rules. Detrimental to tax equity, such an approach could also lead to double-taxation, as the existing anti-conduit rules do not take into account the application of foreign tax law, such as a foreign imported mismatch rule.

The final option considered was to implement rules that are generally consistent with the BEPS imported mismatch rule. The first advantage of such an approach is that it provides certainty about when a deduction will or will not be disallowed under the rule. The second advantage of this approach is that it neutralizes the risk of double non-taxation, while also neutralizing the risk of double taxation. This is because this option is modeled off the BEPS approach, which is being implemented by other countries, and also contains explicit rules to coordinate with foreign tax law. Coordinating with the global tax community reduces opportunities for economic distortions. Although such an approach involves greater complexity than the alternatives, the Treasury Department and IRS expect the benefits of this approach's comprehensiveness, administrability, and conduciveness to taxpayer certainty, to be substantially greater than the complexity burden in comparison with the available alternative approaches. Thus, this is the approach adopted in the proposed regulations.

ii. De minimis rules

The proposed regulations provide a de minimis exception that exempts taxpayers from the application of section 267A for any taxable year for which the sum of the taxpayer's interest and royalty deductions (plus interest and royalty deductions of any related specified parties) is below $50,000. The exception's $50,000 threshold looks to a taxpayer's amount of interest or royalty deductions without regard to whether the deductions involve hybrid arrangements and therefore, absent the de minimis exception, would be disallowed under section 267A.

The Treasury Department and the IRS considered not providing a de minimis exception because hybrid arrangements are highly likely to be tax-motivated structures undertaken only by mostly sophisticated investors. However, it is possible that, in limited cases, small taxpayers could be subject to these rules, for example, as a result of timing differences or a lack of familiarity with foreign law. Furthermore, section 267A is intended to stop base erosion and tax avoidance, and in the case of small taxpayers, it is expected that the revenue gains from applying these rules would be minimal since few small taxpayers are expected to engage in hybrid arrangements.

The Treasury Department and IRS also considered a de minimis exception based on a dollar threshold with respect to the amount of interest or royalties involving hybrid arrangements. However, such an approach would require a taxpayer to first apply the rules of section 267A to identify its interest or royalty deductions involving hybrid arrangements in order to determine whether the de minimis threshold is satisfied and thus whether it is subject to section 267A for the taxable year. This would therefore not significantly reduce burdens on taxpayers with respect to applying the rules of section 267A.

Therefore, the proposed regulations adopt a rule that looks to the overall amount of interest and royalty payments, whether or not such payments involve hybrid arrangements. This has the effect of exempting, in an efficient manner, small taxpayers that are unlikely to engage in hybrid arrangements, and therefore such taxpayers do not need to consider the application of these rules.

iii. Deemed branch payments and branch mismatch payments

The proposed regulations expand the application of section 267A to certain transactions involving branches. This was necessary in order to ensure that taxpayers could not avoid section 267A by engaging in transactions that were economically similar to the hybrid arrangements that are covered by the statute. For example, assume that a related party payment is made to a foreign entity in Country X that is owned by a parent company in Country Y. Further assume that there is a mismatch between how Country X views the entity (fiscally transparent) versus how Country Y views it (not fiscally transparent). In general, section 267A's hybrid entity rules prevent a D/NI outcome in this case. However, assume instead that the parent company forms a branch in Country X instead of a foreign entity, and Country Y (the parent company's jurisdiction) exempts all branch income under its territorial system. On the other hand, due to a mismatch in laws governing whether a branch exists, Country X does not view the branch as existing and therefore does not tax payments made to the branch. Absent regulations, taxpayers could easily avoid section 267A through use of branch structures, which are economically similar to the foreign entity structure in the first example.

In the absence of the proposed regulations, taxpayers may have found it valuable to engage in transactions that are economically similar to hybrid arrangements but that avoided the application of 267A. Such transactions would have resulted in a loss in U.S. tax revenue without any accompanying efficiency gain. Furthermore, to the extent that these transactions were structured specifically to avoid the application of section 267A and were not available to all taxpayers, they would generally have led to an efficiency loss in addition to the loss in U.S. tax revenue.

iv. Exceptions for income included in U.S. tax and GILTI inclusions

Section 267A(b)(1) provides that deductions for interest and royalties that are paid to a CFC and included under section 951(a) in income (as subpart F income) by a United States shareholder of such CFC are not subject to disallowance under section 267A. The statute does not state whether section 267A applies to a payment that is included directly in the U.S. tax base (for example, because the payment is made directly to a U.S. taxpayer or a U.S. taxable branch), or a payment made to a CFC that is taken into account under GILTI (as opposed to being included as subpart F income) by such CFC's United States shareholders. However, the grant of regulatory authority in section 267A(e) includes a specific mention of exceptions in "cases which the Secretary determines do not present a risk of eroding the Federal tax base." *See* section 267A(e)(7)(B).

The Treasury Department and the IRS considered providing no additional exception for payments included in the U.S. tax base (either directly or under GILTI), therefore the only exception available would be the exception provided in the statute for payments included in the U.S tax base by subpart F inclusions. This approach was rejected in the case of a payment to a U.S. taxpayer since it would result in double taxation by the United States, as the United States would both deny a deduction for a payment as well as fully include such payment in income for U.S. tax purposes. Similarly, in the case of hybrid payments made by one CFC to another CFC with the same United States shareholders, a payment would be included in tested income of the recipient CFC and therefore taken into account under GILTI. If section 267A were to apply to also disallow the deduction by the payor CFC, this could also lead to the same amount being subject to section 951A twice because the payor CFC's tested income would increase as a result of the denial of deduction, and the payee would have additional tested income for the same payment.

Payments that are included directly in the U.S. tax base or that are included in GILTI do not give rise to a D/NI outcome and, therefore, it is consistent with the policy of section 267A and the grant of authority in section 267A(e) to exempt them from disallowance under section 267A. Therefore, the proposed regulations provide that such payments are not subject to disallowance under section 267A.

v. Link between hybridity and D/NI

As discussed in section II.E of the Explanation of Provisions and section I.D.2.ii of this Special Analyses, the proposed regulations limit disallowance to cases in which the no-inclusion portion of the D/NI outcome is a result of hybridity as opposed to a different feature of foreign tax law, such as a general preference for royalty income.

Under the language of the statute, no link between hybridity and the no-inclusion outcome appears to be required. The Treasury Department and the IRS considered following this approach, which would have resulted in a deduction being disallowed even though if the transaction had been a non-hybrid transaction, the same no-inclusion outcome would have resulted. However, the Treasury Department and the IRS rejected this option because it would lead to inconsistent and arbitrary results. In particular, such an approach would incentivize taxpayers to restructure to eliminate hybridity in order to avoid the application of section 267A in cases where hybridity does not cause a D/NI outcome. Such restructuring would eliminate the hybridity without actually eliminating the D/NI outcome since the hybridity did not cause the D/NI outcome. Interpreting section 267A in a manner that incentivizes taxpayers to engage in restructurings of this type would generally impose costs on taxpayers to retain deductions where hybridity is irrelevant to a D/NI outcome, without furthering the statutory purpose of section 267A to neutralize hybrid arrangements.

Furthermore, the policy of section 267A is not to address all situations that give rise to no-inclusion outcomes, but to only address a subset of such situations where they arise due to hybrid arrangements. When base erosion or double non-taxation arises due to other features of the international tax system (such as the existence of low-tax jurisdictions or preferential regimes for certain types of income), there are other types of rules that are better suited to address these concerns (for example, through statutory impositions of withholding taxes, revisions to tax treaties, or new statutory provisions such as the base erosion and anti-abuse tax under section 59A). Moreover, the legislative history to section 267A makes clear that the policy of the provision is to eliminate the tax-motivated hybrid structures that lead to D/NI outcomes, and was not a general provision for eliminating all cases of D/NI outcomes. *See* Senate Explanation, at 384 ("[T]he Committee believes that hybrid arrangements exploit differences in the tax treatment of a transaction or entity under the laws of two or more jurisdictions to *achieve* double non-taxation . . .") (emphasis added). In addition, to the extent that regulations limit disallowance to those cases in which the no-inclusion portion of the D/NI outcome is a result of hybridity, the scope of section 267A is limited and the burden on taxpayers is reduced without impacting the core policy underlying section 267A. Therefore, the proposed regulations provide that a deduction is disallowed under section 267A only to the extent that the no-inclusion portion of the D/NI outcome is a result of hybridity.

vi. Timing differences under section 245A

In some cases, there may be a timing difference between when a CFC pays an amount constituting a dividend for U.S. tax purposes and when the CFC receives a deduction for the amount in a foreign jurisdiction. Timing differences may raise issues about whether a deduction is a hybrid deduction and thus whether a dividend is considered a hybrid dividend. The Treasury Department and the IRS considered three options with respect to this timing issue.

The first option considered was to not address timing differences, and thus not treat such transactions as giving rise to hybrid dividends. Not addressing the timing differences would raise policy concerns, since failure to treat the deduction as giving rise to a hybrid dividend would result in the section 245A(a) DRD applying to the dividend, allowing the amount to permanently escape both foreign tax (through the deduction) and U.S. tax (through the DRD).

The second option considered was to not address the timing difference directly under section 245A(e), but instead address it under another Code section or regime. For example, one method that would be consistent with the BEPS Report would be to mandate an income inclusion to the U.S. parent corporation at the time the deduction is permitted under foreign law. This would rely on a novel approach that deems an inclusion at a particular point in time despite the fact that the income has otherwise not been recognized for U.S. tax purposes.

The final option was to address the timing difference by providing rules requiring the establishment of hybrid deduction accounts. These hybrid deduction accounts will be maintained across years so that deductions that accrue in one year will be matched up with income arising in a different year, thus addressing the timing differences issue. This approach appropriately addresses the timing differences under section 245A of the Code. The Treasury Department and IRS expect the benefits of this option's comprehensiveness and clarity to be substantially greater than the tax administration and compliance costs it imposes, relative to the alternative options. This is the approach adopted by the proposed regulations.

vii. Timing differences under section 267A

A similar timing issue arises under section 267A. Here, there is a timing difference between when the deduction is otherwise permitted under U.S. tax law and when the payment is included in the payee's income under foreign tax law. The legislative history to section 267A indicates that in certain cases such timing differences can lead to "long term deferral" and that such long-term deferral should be treated as giving rise to a D/NI outcome. In the context of section 267A, the Treasury Department and the IRS considered three options with respect to this timing issue.

The first option considered was to not address timing differences, because they will eventually reverse over time. Although such an approach would result in a relatively simple rule, it would raise significant policy concerns because, as indicated in the legislative history, long-term deferral can be equivalent to a permanent exclusion.

The second option considered was to address all timing differences, because even a timing difference that reverses within a short period of time provides a tax benefit during the short term. Although such an approach might be conceptually pure, it would raise significant practical and administrative difficulties. It could also lead to some double-tax, absent complicated rules to calibrate the disallowed amount to the amount of tax benefit arising from the timing mismatch.

The final option considered was to address only certain timing differences-namely, long-term timing differences, such as timing differences that do not reverse within a 3 taxable year period. The Treasury Department and IRS expect that the net benefits of this option's comprehensiveness, clarity, and tax administrability and compliance burden are substantially higher than those of the available alternatives. Thus, this option is adopted in the proposed regulations.

4. Anticipated impacts on administrative and compliance costs

The Treasury Department and the IRS estimate that there are approximately 10,000 taxpayers in the current population of taxpayers affected by the proposed regulations or about 0.5% of all corporate filers. This is the best estimate of the number of sophisticated taxpayers with capabilities to structure a hybrid arrangement. However, the Treasury Department and the IRS anticipate that fewer taxpayers would engage in hybrid arrangements going forward as the statute and the proposed regulations would make such arrangements less beneficial to taxpayers. As such, the taxpayer counts provided in section II of this Special Analyses are an upper bound of the number of affected taxpayers by the proposed regulations.

It is important to note that the population of taxpayers affected by section 267A and the proposed regulations under section 267A will seldom include U.S.-based companies as these companies are taxed under the new GILTI regime as well as subpart F. Instead, section 267A and the proposed regulations apply predominantly to foreign-headquartered companies that employ hybrid arrangements to strip income out of the U.S., undermining the collection of U.S. tax revenue. In addition, although section 245A(e) applies primarily to U.S.-based companies, the amounts of dividends affected are limited because a large portion of distributions will be treated as previously taxed earnings and profits due to the operation of both the GILTI regime and the transition tax under section 965, and such distributions are not subject to section 245A(e).

II. *Paperwork Reduction Act*

The collections of information in the proposed regulations are in proposed §§1.6038-2(f)(13) and (14), 1.6038-3(g)(3), and 1.6038A-2(b)(5)(iii).

The collection of information in proposed §1.6038-2(f)(13) and (14) is mandatory for every U.S. person that controls a foreign corporation that has a deduction disallowed under section 267A, or that pays or receives a hybrid dividend or tiered hybrid dividend under section 245A, respectively, during an annual accounting period and files Form 5471 for that period (OMB control number 1545-0123, formerly, OMB control number 1545-0704). The collection of information in proposed §1.6038-2(f)(13) is satisfied by providing information about the disallowance of the deduction for any interest or royalty under section 267A for the corporation's accounting period as Form 5471 and its instructions may prescribe, and the collection of information in proposed §1.6038-2(f)(14) is satisfied by providing information about hybrid dividends or tiered hybrid dividends under section 245A(e) for the corporation's accounting period as Form 5471 and its instructions may prescribe. For purposes of the PRA, the reporting burden associated with proposed §1.6038-2(f)(13) and (14) will be reflected in the IRS Form 14029, Paperwork Reduction Act Submission, associated with Form 5471. As provided below, the estimated number of respondents for the reporting burden associated with proposed §1.6038-2(f)(13) and (14) is 1,000 and 2,000, respectively.

The collection of information in proposed §1.6038-3(g)(3) is mandatory for every U.S. person that controls a foreign partnership that paid or accrued any interest or royalty for which a deduction is disallowed under section 267A during the partnership tax year and files Form 8865 for that period (OMB control number 1545-1668). The collection of information in proposed §1.6038-3(g)(3) is satisfied by providing information about the disallowance of the deduction for any interest or royalty under section 267A for the partnership's tax year as Form 8865 and its instructions may prescribe. For purposes of the PRA, the reporting burden associated with proposed §1.6038-3(g)(3) will be reflected in the IRS Form 14029, Paperwork Reduction Act submission, associated with Form 8865. As provided below, the estimated number of respondents for the reporting burden associated with proposed §1.6038-3(g)(3) is less than 1,000.

The collection of information in proposed §1.6038A-2(b)(5)(iii) is mandatory for every reporting corporation that has a deduction disallowed under section 267A and files Form 5472 (OMB control number 1545-0123, formerly, OMB control number 1545-0805) for the tax year. The collection of information in proposed §1.6038A-2(b)(5)(iii) is satisfied by providing information about the disallowance of the reporting corporation's deduction for any interest or royalty under section 267A for the tax year as Form 5472 and its instructions may prescribe. For purposes of the PRA, the reporting burden associated with proposed §1.6038A-2(b)(5)(iii) will be reflected in the IRS Form 14029, Paperwork Reduction Act submission, associated with Form 5472. As provided below, the estimated number of respondents for the reporting burden associated with proposed §1.6038A-2(b)(5)(iii) is 7,000.

The revised tax forms are as follows:

	New	Revision of existing form	Number of respondents (estimated, rounded to nearest 1,000)
Schedule G (Form 5471)		✓	1,000
Schedule I (Form 5471)		✓	2,000
Form 5472		✓	7,000
Form 8865		✓	<1,000

The current status of the Paperwork Reduction Act submissions related to the tax forms that will be revised as a result of the information collections in the proposed regulations is provided in the accompanying table. As described above, the reporting burdens associated with the information collections in proposed § § 1.6038-2(f)(13) and (14) and 1.6038A-2(b)(5)(iii) are included in the aggregated burden estimates for OMB control number 1545-0123, which represents a total estimated burden time for all forms and schedules for corporations of 3.157 billion hours and total estimated monetized costs of $58.148 billion ($2017). The overall burden estimates provided in 1545-0123 are aggregate amounts that relate to the entire package of forms associated with the OMB control number and will in the future include but not isolate the estimated burden of the tax forms that will be revised as a result of the information collections in the proposed regulations. These numbers are therefore unrelated to the future calculations needed to assess the burden imposed by the proposed regulations. They are further identical to numbers provided for the proposed regulations relating to foreign tax credits (83 FR 63200). The Treasury Department and IRS urge readers to recognize that these numbers are duplicates and to guard against overcounting the burden that international tax provisions imposed prior to the Act. No burden estimates specific to the proposed regulations are currently available. The Treasury Department has not identified any burden estimates, including those for new information collections, related to the requirements under the proposed regulations. Those estimates would capture both changes made by the Act and those that arise out of discretionary authority exercised in the proposed regulations. The Treasury Department and the IRS request comments on all aspects of information collection burdens related to the proposed regulations. In addition, when available, drafts of IRS forms are posted for comment at *https://apps.irs.gov/app/picklist/list/draftTaxForms.htm.*

Form	Type of Filer	OMB Number(s)	Status
Form 5471	All other Filers (mainly trusts and estates) (Legacy system)	1545-0121	Approved by OMB through 10/30/2020.
	Link: https://www.reginfo.gov/public/do/PRAViewICR?ref_nbr=201704-1545-023		
	Business (NEW Model)	1545-0123	Published in the Federal Register Notice (FRN) on 10/8/18. Public Comment period closed on 12/10/18.
	Link: https://www.federalregister.gov/documents/2018/10/09/2018-21846/proposed-collection-comment-request-for-forms-1065-1065-b-1066-1120-1120-c-1120-f-1120-h-1120-nd		
	Individual (NEW Model)	1545-0074	Limited Scope submission (1040 only) on 10/11/18 at OIRA for review. Full ICR submission (all forms) scheduled in 3/2019. 60 Day FRN not published yet for full collection.
	Link: https://www.reginfo.gov/public/do/PRAViewICR?ref_nbr=201808-1545-031		
Form 5472	Business (NEW Model)	1545-0123	Published in the FRN on 10/8/18. Public Comment period closed on 12/10/18.
	Link: https://www.federalregister.gov/documents/2018/10/09/2018-21846/proposed-collection-comment-request-for-forms-1065-1065-b-1066-1120-1120-c-1120-f-1120-h-1120-nd		
	Individual (NEW Model)	1545-0074	Limited Scope submission (1040 only) on 10/11/18 at OIRA for review. Full ICR submission for all forms in 3/2019. 60 Day FRN not published yet for full collection.

Form	Type of Filer	OMB Number(s)	Status
	Link: https://www.reginfo.gov/public/do/PRAViewICR?ref_nbr=201808-1545-031		
Form 8865	All other Filers (mainly trusts and estates) (Legacy system)	1545-1668	Published in the FRN on 10/1/18. Public Comment period closed on 11/30/18. ICR in process by Treasury as of 10/17/18.
	Link: https://www.federalregister.gov/documents/2018/10/01/2018-21288/proposed-collection-comment-request-for-regulation-project		
	Business (NEW Model)	1545-0123	Published in the FRN on 10/8/18. Public Comment period closed on 12/10/18.
	Link: https://www.federalregister.gov/documents/2018/10/09/2018-21846/proposed-collection-comment-request-for-forms-1065-1065-b-1066-1120-1120-c-1120-f-1120-h-1120-nd		
	Individual (NEW Model)	1545-0074	Limited Scope submission (1040 only) on 10/11/18 at OIRA for review. Full ICR submission for all forms in 3/2019. 60 Day FRN not published yet for full collection.
	Link: https://www.reginfo.gov/public/do/PRAViewICR?ref_nbr=201808-1545-031		

III. *Regulatory Flexibility Act*

It is hereby certified that this notice of proposed rulemaking will not have a significant economic impact on a substantial number of small entities within the meaning of section 601(6) of the Regulatory Flexibility Act (5 U.S.C. chapter 6).

The small entities that are subject to proposed §§1.6038-2(f)(13), 1.6038-3(g)(3), and 1.6038A-2(b)(5)(iii) are small entities that are controlling U.S. shareholders of a CFC that is disallowed a deduction under section 267A, small entities that are controlling fifty-percent partners of a foreign partnership that makes a payment for which a deduction is disallowed under section 267A, and small entities that are 25 percent foreign-owned domestic corporations and disallowed a deduction under section 267A, respectively. In addition, the small entities that are subject to proposed §1.6038-2(f)(14) are controlling U.S. shareholders of a CFC that pays or received a hybrid dividend or a tiered hybrid dividend.

A controlling U.S. shareholder of a CFC is a U.S. person that owns more than 50 percent of the CFC's stock. A controlling fifty-percent partner is a U.S. person that owns more than a fifty-percent interest in the foreign partnership. A 25 percent foreign-owned domestic corporation is a domestic corporation at least 25 percent of the stock of which is owned by a foreign person.

The Treasury Department and the IRS do not have data readily available to assess the number of small entities potentially affected by proposed §§1.6038-2(f)(13) or (14), 1.6038-3(g)(3), or 1.6038A-2(b)(5)(iii). However, entities potentially affected by these sections are generally not small businesses, because the resources and investment necessary for an entity to be a controlling U.S. shareholder, a controlling fifty-percent partner, or a 25 percent foreign-owned domestic corporation are generally significant. Moreover, the de minimis exception under section 267A excepts many small entities from the application of section 267A for any taxable year for which the sum of its interest and royalty deductions (plus interest and royalty deductions of certain related persons) is below $50,000. Therefore, the Treasury Department and the IRS do not believe that a substantial number of domestic small business entities will be subject to proposed §§1.6038-2(f)(13) or (14), 1.6038-3(g)(3), or 1.6038A-2(b)(5)(iii). Accordingly, the Treasury Department and the IRS do not believe that proposed §§1.6038-2(f)(13) or (14), 1.6038-3(g)(3), or 1.6038A-2(b)(5)(iii) will have a significant economic impact on a substantial number of small entities. Therefore, a Regulatory Flexibility Analysis under the Regulatory Flexibility Act is not required.

The Treasury Department and the IRS do not believe that the proposed regulations have a significant economic impact on domestic small business entities. Based on published information from 2012 from form 5472, interest and royalty amounts paid to related foreign entities by foreign-owned U.S. corporations over total receipts is 1.6 percent. (https://www.irs.gov/statistics/soi-tax-stats-transactions-of-foreign-owned-domestic-corporations#_2, Classified by Industry 2012) This is substantially less than the 3 to 5 percent threshold for significant economic impact. The calculated percentage is likely to be an upper bound of the related party payments affected by the proposed hybrid regulations. In particular, this is the ratio of the potential income affected and not the tax revenues, which would be less than half this amount. While 1.6 percent is only for foreign-owned domestic corporations with total receipts of $500 million or more, these are entities that are more likely to have related party payments and so the percentage would be higher. Moreover, hybrid arrangements are only a subset of these related party payments; therefore this percentage is higher than what it would be if only considering hybrid arrangements,

Notwithstanding this certification, Treasury and IRS invite comments about the impact this proposal may have on small entities.

Pursuant to section 7805(f) of the Code, this notice of proposed rulemaking has been submitted to the Chief Counsel for Advocacy of the Small Business Administration for comment on its impact on small business.

Comments and Requests for a Public Hearing

Before the proposed regulations are adopted as final regulations, consideration will be given to any comments that are submitted timely to the IRS as prescribed in this preamble under the "ADDRESSES" heading. The Treasury Department and the IRS request comments on all aspects of the proposed rules. All comments will be available at *www.regulations.gov* or upon request. A public hearing will be scheduled if requested in writing by any person that timely submits written comments. If a public hearing is scheduled, notice of the date, time, and place for the public hearing will be published in the **Federal Register**.

Drafting Information

The principal authors of the proposed regulations are Shane M. McCarrick and Tracy M. Villecco of the Office of Associate Chief Counsel (International). However, other personnel from the Treasury Department and the IRS participated in the development of the proposed regulations.

[¶49,786] Proposed Amendments of Regulations (REG-141739-08), published in the Federal Register on December 28, 2018.

[Code Secs. 150 and 1001]

Closing agreement programs: Tax-exempt bonds: Reissuance of bonds: State and local bonds: Computation of gain and loss.—Reg. §1.150-3 and amendments of Reg. §1.1001-3, addressing when tax-exempt bonds are treated as retired for purposes of section 103 and sections 141 through Code Sec. 150 of the Internal Revenue Code (Code), are proposed.

AGENCY: Internal Revenue Service (IRS), Treasury.

ACTION: Notice of proposed rulemaking.

SUMMARY: This document contains proposed regulations that address when tax-exempt bonds are treated as retired for purposes of section 103 and sections 141 through 150 of the Internal Revenue Code (Code). The proposed regulations are necessary to unify and to clarify existing guidance on this subject. The proposed regulations affect State and local governments that issue tax-exempt bonds.

DATES: Comments and requests for a public hearing must be received by March 1, 2019.

ADDRESSES: Send submissions to: CC:PA:LPD:PR (REG-141739-08), Room 5203, Internal Revenue Service, P.O. Box 7604, Ben Franklin Station, Washington, DC 20044. Submissions may be hand-delivered Monday through Friday between the hours of 8 a.m. and 4 p.m. to CC:PA:LPD:PR (REG-141739-08), Courier's Desk, Internal Revenue Service, 1111 Constitution Avenue, NW., Washington, DC 20224, or sent electronically via the Federal eRulemaking Portal at *www.regulations.gov* (REG-141739-08).

FOR FURTHER INFORMATION CONTACT: Concerning the proposed regulations, Spence Hanemann, (202) 317-6980; concerning submissions of comments and requesting a hearing, Regina Johnson, (202) 317-6901 (not toll-free numbers). SUPPLEMENTARY INFORMATION:

Background

This document contains proposed amendments to 26 CFR part 1 under sections 150 and 1001 of the Code (Proposed Regulations).

1. In general

In general, under section 103, interest received by the holders of certain bonds issued by State and local governments is exempt from Federal income tax. To qualify for the tax exemption, a bond issued by a State or local government must satisfy various eligibility requirements under sections 141 through 150 at the time of issuance of the bond. If the issuer and holder agree after issuance to modify the terms of a tax-exempt bond significantly, the original bond may be treated as having been retired and exchanged for a newly issued, modified bond. Similarly, if the issuer or its agent acquires and resells the bond, the bond may be treated as having been retired upon acquisition and replaced upon resale with a newly issued bond.

The term "reissuance" commonly refers to the effect of a transaction in which a new debt instrument replaces an old debt instrument as a result of retirement of the old debt instrument pursuant to such an exchange or extinguishment. In the case of a reissuance, the reissued bond must be retested for qualification under sections 103 and 141 through 150. The reissuance of an issue of tax-exempt bonds may result in various negative consequences to the issuer, such as changes in yield for purposes of the arbitrage investment yield restrictions under section 148(a), acceleration of arbitrage rebate payment obligations under section 148(f), and change-in-law risk.

2. Tender Option Bonds

Tender option bonds and variable rate demand bonds (collectively, tender option bonds) have special features that present reissuance questions. Specifically, tender option bonds have original terms that provide for a tender option interest rate mode, as described in this paragraph. Issuers of tax-exempt bonds often preauthorize several different interest rate modes in the bond documents and retain an option to switch interest rate modes under parameters set forth in the bond documents. During a tender option mode, tender option bonds have short-term interest rates that are reset periodically at various short-term intervals (typically, every seven days) based on the current market rate necessary to remarket the bonds at par. In connection with each resetting of the interest rate, the holder of a tender option bond has a right or requirement to tender the bond back to the issuer or its agent for purchase at par. Tender option bonds also may have interest rate mode conversion options that permit the issuer or conduit borrower to change the interest rate mode on the bonds from a tender option mode to another short-term interest rate mode or to a fixed interest rate to maturity. At the time of a conversion to another interest rate mode, the holder of a tender option bond typically has the right or requirement to tender the bond for purchase at par.

Tender option bonds generally have third-party liquidity facilities from banks or other liquidity providers to ensure that there is sufficient cash to repurchase the bonds upon a holder's tender, and they also commonly have credit enhancement from bond insurers or other third-party guarantors. Upon a holder's exercise of its tender rights in connection with either a resetting of the interest rate during a tender option mode or a conversion to another interest rate mode, a remarketing agent or a liquidity provider typically will acquire the bonds subject to the tender and resell the bonds either to the same bondholders or to others willing to purchase such bonds.

3. *Existing Guidance*

To address reissuance questions related to tax-exempt bonds, on December 27, 1988, the IRS published Notice 88-130, 1988-2 CB 543, which provides rules for determining when a tax-exempt bond is retired for purposes of sections 103 and 141 through 150. Notice 88-130 provides in part that a tax-exempt bond is retired when there is a change to the terms of the bond that results in a disposition of the bond for purposes of section 1001. In addition, Notice 88-130 provides special rules for retirement of certain tender option bonds that meet a definition of the term "qualified tender bond."

On June 26, 1996, the Department of the Treasury (Treasury Department) and the IRS published final regulations under § 1.1001-3 (1996 Final Regulations) in the **Federal Register** (61 FR 32926). These regulations provide rules for determining whether a modification of the terms of a debt instrument, including a tax-exempt bond, results in an exchange for purposes of section 1001. In recognition of a need to coordinate the interaction of the prior guidance in Notice 88-130 with the subsequent final regulations under § 1.1001-3 for particular tax-exempt bond purposes, the Treasury Department and the IRS stated their intention to issue regulations under section 150 on this subject in the **Federal Register** (61 FR 32930).

On April 14, 2008, the IRS published Notice 2008-41, 2008-1 CB 742. Like Notice 88-130, Notice 2008-41 provides rules for determining when a tax-exempt bond is retired for purposes of sections 103 and 141 through 150 and includes special rules for qualified tender bonds. While the retirement standards provided in these two notices are similar, Notice 2008-41 was intended to coordinate the retirement standards for tax-exempt bond purposes with the 1996 Final Regulations on modifications of debt instruments under § 1.1001-3 and to be more administrable than Notice 88-130. In order to preserve flexibility and to limit potential unintended consequences during the 2008 financial crisis, Notice 2008-41 permitted issuers to apply either notice. Generally, under Notice 2008-41, a tax-exempt bond is retired when a significant modification to the terms of the bond occurs under § 1.1001-3, the bond is acquired by or on behalf of its issuer, or the bond is otherwise redeemed or retired. The notice clarifies that, for purposes of these retirement standards, the purchase of a tax-exempt bond by a third-party guarantor or third-party liquidity facility provider pursuant to the terms of the guarantee or liquidity facility is not treated as a purchase or other acquisition by or on behalf of a governmental issuer. Although these general rules apply to a qualified tender bond, Notice 2008-41 also provides that certain features of qualified tender bonds will not result in a retirement. In Notice 2008-41, the Treasury Department and the IRS reiterated their intention to provide guidance on the retirement of tax-exempt bonds in regulations under section 150.

The Proposed Regulations provide rules for determining when tax-exempt bonds are treated as retired for purposes of sections 103 and 141 through 150. The Proposed Regulations also amend § 1.1001-3(a)(2) to conform that section to the special rules in the Proposed Regulations for retirement of qualified tender bonds.

Explanation of provisions

1. *Section 1.150-3: Retirement of Tax-Exempt Bonds*

A. General Rules for Retirement of a Tax-Exempt Bond

The Proposed Regulations generally provide retirement standards that apply to tax-exempt bonds for purposes of sections 103 and 141 through 150. These retirement standards follow the guidance in Notice 2008-41 with technical refinements. The Proposed Regulations provide that a tax-exempt bond is retired if a significant modification to the terms of the bond occurs under § 1.1001-3, if the issuer or an agent acting on its behalf acquires the bond in a manner that liquidates or extinguishes the bondholder's investment in the bond, or if the bond is otherwise redeemed (for example, redeemed at maturity).

For this purpose, the Proposed Regulations define the term "issuer" to mean the State or local governmental unit that actually issues the bonds and any related party (as defined in § 1.150-1(b)) to that actual issuer. In the case of a governmental unit, the applicable related party definition under § 1.150-1(b) applies a controlled group test under § 1.150-1(e) to determine related party status, based generally on all of the facts and circumstances. This controlled group test includes special rules which specifically treat control over the governing board of a governmental unit and control over use of funds or assets of a governmental unit as giving rise to controlled group status.

By focusing on the actual issuer rather than on a conduit borrower, this definition of issuer maintains and respects the essential legal construct necessary for issuance of many tax-exempt bonds, such as qualified private activity bonds under section 141(e), that the actual issuer be treated as the obligor in conduit financings. Thus, under the Proposed Regulations, the acquisition of a tax-exempt bond by a conduit borrower that is not a related party to the actual issuer does not result in the retirement of that bond.

The Proposed Regulations also prescribe certain consequences for a bond that is retired pursuant to a deemed exchange under § 1.1001-3 or following the acquisition of the bond by the issuer or the issuer's agent. In the former case, the bond is treated as a new bond issued at the time of the modification as determined under § 1.1001-3. In the latter case, if the issuer resells the bond, the bond is treated as a new bond issued at the time of resale. If the issuer does not resell the acquired bond, the acquired bond is simply retired. In either case in which a retired bond is treated as a newly issued bond, the issuer must consider whether the new bond refunds the retired bond. For this purpose, the rules regarding the definition of a refunding issue under § 1.150-1(d) apply. For example, if the issuer of the bond retired pursuant to § 1.1001-3 is the same as the issuer (or a related party to the issuer) of the newly issued bond, the newly issued bond will be part of a current refunding issue that refunds the retired bond.

B. Exceptions to Retirement of a Tax-Exempt Bond

The Proposed Regulations provide three exceptions that limit retirements resulting from the operation of the general rules. Two of these exceptions are intended to prevent the special features of tender option bonds from resulting in a retirement. A third exception applies to all tax-exempt bonds.

The first two exceptions in the Proposed Regulations apply to qualified tender bonds, a defined term that is essentially a tender option bond meeting certain requirements. Specifically, a qualified tender bond is a tax-exempt bond that, pursuant to the terms of its governing contract, bears interest during each interest rate mode at a fixed rate, a qualified floating rate under § 1.1275-5, or an objective rate that is permitted for a tax-exempt bond under § 1.1275-5(c)(5). Furthermore, interest on a qualified tender bond must be unconditionally payable at periodic intervals of no more than a year. Finally, a qualified tender bond may not have a stated maturity date later than 40 years after its issue date and must include a qualified tender right. This definition is similar to the definition of qualified tender bond provided in Notice 2008-41.

The Proposed Regulations define a qualified tender right required for a qualified tender bond in terms of the mechanics by which the tender right operates. The Proposed Regulations define a qualified tender right to include either a tender right that arises periodically during a tender option mode or a tender right that arises upon the exercise of the issuer's option under the original terms of the bond to change the interest rate mode.

A qualified tender bond has two features that otherwise could result in retirement of the bond under the general rules for retirement in the Proposed Regulations. First, when accompanied by a qualified tender right, an exercise of the issuer's option to change the interest rate mode might, in some circumstances, qualify as a modification under the rule in § 1.1001-3(c)(2)(iii) for alterations that result from the exercise of an option. Thus, absent the exception in the Proposed Regulations, a qualified tender right might result in a modification that, if significant, would cause the qualified tender bond to be retired. To address this circumstance, the Proposed Regulations provide an exception that avoids retirement by disregarding a qualified tender right for purposes of determining whether a significant modification of a qualified tender bond under § 1.1001-3 results in retirement of the bond. Consequently, the issuer's option to change the interest rate mode typically would qualify as a unilateral option and the change of interest rate mode resulting from exercise of that option would not be a modification of the qualified tender bond.

The second feature of a qualified tender bond that could result in retirement of the bond under the general rules for retirement in the Proposed Regulations is the financing structure feature that may require the issuer or its agent to acquire the bond upon exercise of the qualified tender right. To address this circumstance, the Proposed Regulations provide another exception under which an acquisition of a qualified tender bond pursuant to the exercise of a qualified tender right will not result in retirement, provided that neither the issuer nor its agent holds the bond for longer than 90 days. This 90-day period is intended to provide the issuer or its remarketing agent with sufficient time to resell a tendered bond to a new holder.

The Proposed Regulations also provide an exception to the general rules of retirement for all tax-exempt bonds. This exception, carried forward from Notice 2008-41, provides that acquisition of a tax-exempt bond by a guarantor or liquidity facility provider acting as the issuer's agent does not result in retirement of the bond if the acquisition is pursuant to the terms of the guarantee or liquidity facility and the guarantor or liquidity facility provider is not a related party (as defined in § 1.150-1(b)) to the issuer.

2. *Applicability Dates*

The rules in §1.150-3 of the Proposed Regulations are proposed to apply to events and actions taken with respect to bonds that occur on or after the date that is 90 days after the date of publication of the Treasury decision adopting these rules as final regulations in the **Federal Register**. Issuers may apply these regulations to events and actions taken with respect to bonds that occur before that date. The Treasury Department and the IRS expect that the final regulations will obsolete Notice 88-130 and Notice 2008-41.

Special Analyses

This regulation is not subject to review under section 6(b) of Executive Order 12866 pursuant to the Memorandum of Agreement (April 11, 2018) between the Department of the Treasury and the Office of Management and Budget regarding review of tax regulations. Because these regulations do not impose a collection of information on small entities, the Regulatory Flexibility Act (5 U.S.C. chapter 6) does not apply. Pursuant to section 7805(f) of the Code, this notice of proposed rulemaking will be submitted to the Chief Counsel for Advocacy of the Small Business Administration for comment on its impact on small entities.

Comments and Requests for Public Hearing

Before the Proposed Regulations are adopted as final regulations, consideration will be given to any comments that are submitted timely to the IRS as prescribed in this preamble under the ADDRESSES heading. The Treasury Department and the IRS request comments on all aspects of the proposed rules. All comments will be available at *www.regulations.gov* or upon request. A public hearing will be scheduled if requested in writing by any person that timely submits written comments. If a public hearing is scheduled, notice of the date, time, and place for the hearing will be published in the **Federal Register**.

Drafting Information

The principal authors of these regulations are Spence Hanemann of the Office of Associate Chief Counsel (Financial Institutions and Products) and Vicky Tsilas, formerly of the Office of Associate Chief Counsel (Financial Institutions and Products). However, other personnel from the Treasury Department and the IRS participated in their development.

Availability of IRS Documents

The IRS notices cited in this preamble are published in the Internal Revenue Bulletin (or Cumulative Bulletin) and are available from the Superintendent of Documents, U.S. Government Publishing Office, Washington, DC 20402, or by visiting the IRS website at www.irs.gov.

[¶49,787] Proposed Amendments of Regulations (REG-134652-18), published in the Federal Register on February 8, 2019.

[Code Sec. 199A]

Qualified business income: Deduction.—Regs. §§1.199A-0, 1.199A-3 and 1.199A-6 concerning the deduction for qualified business income under section 199A of the Internal Revenue Code (Code), are proposed.

AGENCY: Internal Revenue Service (IRS), Treasury.

ACTION: Notice of proposed rulemaking.

SUMMARY: This document contains proposed regulations concerning the deduction for qualified business income under section 199A of the Internal Revenue Code (Code). The proposed regulations will affect certain individuals, partnerships, S corporations, trusts, and estates. The proposed regulations provide guidance on the treatment of previously suspended losses that constitute qualified business income. The proposed regulations also provide guidance on the determination of the section 199A deduction for taxpayers that hold interests in regulated investment companies, charitable remainder trusts, and split-interest trusts.

DATES: Written or electronic comments and requests for a public hearing must be received by April 9, 2019.

ADDRESSES: Submit electronic submissions to the Federal eRulemaking Portal at *www.regulations.gov* (indicate IRS and REG-134652-18) by following the online instructions for submitting comments. Once submitted to the Federal eRulemaking Portal, comments cannot be edited or withdrawn. The Department of the Treasury (Treasury Department) and the IRS will publish for public availability any comment received to its public docket, whether submitted electronically or in hard copy. Send hard copy submissions to CC:PA:LPD:PR (REG-134652-18), Room 5203, Internal Revenue Service, P.O. Box 7604, Ben Franklin Station, Washington, D.C., 20044. Submissions may be hand-delivered Monday through Friday between the hours of 8 a.m. and 4 p.m. to CC:PA:LPD:PR (REG-134652-18), Courier's Desk, Internal Revenue Service, 1111 Constitution Avenue, N.W., Washington, D.C., 20224.

FOR FURTHER INFORMATION CONTACT: Concerning §1.199A-3(d), Michael Y. Chin or Steven Harrison at (202) 317-6842; concerning §§1.199A-3(b) and 1.199A-6, Vishal R. Amin or Frank J. Fisher at (202) 317-6850 or Robert D. Alinsky or Margaret Burow at 202-317-5279; concerning submissions of comments or requests for a public hearing, Regina Johnson at (202) 317-6901 (not toll-free numbers).

SUPPLEMENTARY INFORMATION:

Background

This document contains proposed amendments to the Income Tax Regulations (26 CFR part 1) under section 199A of the Code.

Section 199A was enacted on December 22, 2017, by section 11011 of "An Act to provide for reconciliation pursuant to titles II and V of the concurrent resolution on the budget for fiscal year 2018," Pub.L. 115-97 (TCJA), and was amended on March 23, 2018, retroactively to January 1, 2018, by section 101 of Division T of the Consolidated Appropriations Act, 2018, Pub.L. 115-141, (2018 Act). Section 199A applies to taxable years beginning after 2017 and before 2026.

Section 199A provides a deduction of up to 20 percent of qualified business income from a U.S. trade or business operated as a sole proprietorship or through a partnership, S corporation, trust, or estate (section 199A deduction). The section 199A deduction may be taken by individuals and by some estates and trusts. A section 199A deduction is not available for wage income or for income earned by a C corporation. For taxpayers whose taxable income exceeds a statutorily-defined amount (threshold amount), section 199A may limit the taxpayer's section 199A deduction based on (i) the type of trade or business engaged in by the taxpayer, (ii) the amount of W-2 wages paid with respect to the trade or business (W-2 wages), and/or (iii) the unadjusted basis immediately after acquisition (UBIA) of qualified property held for use in the trade or business (UBIA of qualified property). These statutory limitations are subject to phase-in rules based upon taxable income above the threshold amount.

Section 199A also allows individuals and some trusts and estates (but not corporations) a deduction of up to 20 percent of their combined qualified real estate investment trust (REIT) dividends and qualified publicly traded partnership (PTP) income, including qualified REIT dividends and qualified PTP income earned through passthrough entities. This component of the section 199A deduction is not limited by W-2 wages or UBIA of qualified property.

The section 199A deduction is the lesser of (1) the sum of the combined amounts described in the prior two paragraphs or (2) an amount equal to 20 percent of the excess (if any) of taxable income of the taxpayer for the taxable year over the net capital gain of the taxpayer for the taxable year.

Additionally, section 199A(g) provides that specified agricultural or horticultural cooperatives may claim a special entity-level deduction that is substantially similar to the domestic production activities deduction under former section 199.

The statute expressly grants the Secretary authority to prescribe such regulations as are necessary to carry out the purposes of section 199A (section 199A(f)(4)), and also provides specific grants of authority with respect to certain issues: the treatment of acquisitions, dispositions, and short-tax years (section 199A(b)(5)); certain payments to partners for services rendered in a non-partner capacity (section 199A(c)(4)(C)); the allocation of W-2 wages and UBIA of qualified property (section 199A(f)(1)(A)(iii)); restricting the allocation of items and wages under section 199A and such reporting requirements as the Secretary determines appropriate (section 199A(f)(4)(A)); the application of section 199A in the case of tiered entities (section 199A(f)(4)(B); preventing the manipulation of the depreciable period of qualified property using transactions between related parties (section 199A(h)(1)); and determining the UBIA of qualified property acquired in like-kind exchanges or involuntary conversions (section 199A(h)(2)).

The Treasury Department and the Internal Revenue Service published proposed regulations interpreting section 199A on August 16, 2018 (the August Proposed Regulations) (83 FR 40884). The August Proposed Regulations contain six substantive sections, §§1.199A-1 through 1.199A-6, each of which provides rules relevant to the calculation of the section 199A deduction. The August Proposed Regulations, with modifications in response to comments and testimony received, were adopted as final regulations in TD 9847, issued concurrently with this notice of proposed rulemaking and published elsewhere in this issue of the Federal Register.

Explanation of Provisions

These proposed regulations propose rules addressing issues not addressed in the August Proposed Regulations that are necessary to provide taxpayers with computational, definitional, and anti-avoidance guidance regarding the application of section 199A. Specifically, these proposed regulations contain amendments to two substantive sections of the August Proposed Regulations, §§1.199A-3 and 1.199A-6, each of which provides rules relevant to the calculation of the section 199A deduction. These additional proposed rules respond to comments received on the August Proposed Regulations as well as address certain issues identified after additional study. This Explanation of Provisions describes each of the proposed rules contained in this document in turn. The Treasury Department and the IRS request comments on all aspects of these proposed regulations.

I. *Treatment of Previously Suspended Losses That Constitute QBI.*

Section 1.199A-3(b)(1)(iv) of the final regulations provides that previously disallowed losses or deductions (including under sections 465, 469, 704(d), and 1366(d)) allowed in the taxable year are generally taken into account for purposes of computing QBI except to the extent the losses or deductions were disallowed, suspended, limited, or carried over from taxable years ending before January 1, 2018. The final regulations also provide a first-in-first-out ordering rule. One commenter on the August Proposed Regulations suggested that a special rule should be provided to identify the section 469 trade or business losses that are used to offset income if the taxpayer's section 469 groupings differ from the taxpayer's section 199A aggregations. The commenter recommended that any section 469 loss carryforward that is later used should be allocated across the taxpayer's section

199A aggregations based on income with respect to such aggregations in the year the loss was generated.

The Treasury Department and the IRS believe that that previously disallowed losses should be treated as losses from a separate trade or business for both the reasons stated by the commenter and because the losses may relate to a trade or business that is no longer in existence. Accordingly, these proposed regulations amend § 1.199A-3(b)(1)(iv) to provide that such losses are treated as loss from a separate trade or business. To the extent that losses relate to a PTP, they must be treated as losses from a separate PTP. Section 1.199A-3(b)(1)(iv)(B) provides that attributes of the disallowed loss are determined in the year the loss is incurred.

II. *Regulated Investment Companies with Interests in REITs and PTPs*

A. *REITs*

Section 1.199A-3 restates the definitions in section 199A(c) and provides additional guidance on the determination of QBI, qualified REIT dividends, and qualified PTP income. For simplicity, the regulations use the term *individual* when referring to an individual, trust, estate, or other person eligible to claim the section 199A deduction. *See* § 1.199A-1(a)(2). The term *relevant passthrough entity (RPE)* is used to describe passthrough entities that directly operate the trade or business or pass through the trade or business' items of income, gain, loss, or deduction from lower-tier RPEs to the individual. *See* § 1.199A-1(b)(10).

A number of commenters on the August Proposed Regulations requested guidance that would allow a shareholder in a regulated investment company within the meaning of section 851(a) (RIC) to take a section 199A deduction with respect to certain income of, or distributions from, the RIC. Because a RIC is a subchapter C corporation, a shareholder in a RIC generally does not take into account a share of the RIC's items of income, deduction, gain, or loss. Part 1 of subchapter M, however, has features that allow the tax consequences of investing in a RIC to approximate those of a direct investment in the assets of the RIC. The principal feature is the allowance of the deduction for dividends paid under section 852(b)(2)(D). If a corporation qualifies as a RIC under section 851 and meets the distribution requirements and other requirements in section 852(a), the RIC's income tax is computed on its investment company taxable income (ICTI), which is its taxable income with certain adjustments, including the allowance of the deduction for dividends paid. *See* section 852(b)(2). ICTI also excludes the amount of the RIC's net capital gain, but tax is separately imposed on that amount to the extent it exceeds the deduction for dividends paid, taking into account only capital gain dividends. *See* section 852(b)(3)(A). The deduction for dividends paid allows RICs to eliminate all or most of their corporate income tax liability.

If a RIC has certain items of income or gain, subchapter M also provides rules under which a RIC may pay dividends that a shareholder in the RIC may treat in the same manner (or a similar manner) as the shareholder would treat the underlying item of income or gain if the shareholder realized it directly. Although this treatment differs fundamentally from the pass-through treatment of partners or trust beneficiaries, this preamble refers to is as "conduit treatment." For example, under section 852(b)(3), a RIC that has net capital gain for a taxable year generally may pay capital gain dividends, and shareholders receiving the capital gain dividends treat them as gain from the sale or exchange of a capital asset held for more than one year. Section 852(b)(3) provides necessary limits and procedures that apply to capital gain dividends. There are similar statutory provisions for exempt-interest dividends under section 852(b)(5), interest-related dividends under section 871(k)(1), short-term capital gain dividends under section 871(k)(2), dividends eligible for the dividends received deduction under section 854(b)(1)(A), and qualified dividend income under section 854(b)(1)(B). Rules for paying dividends corresponding to different types of long-term capital gain have been provided in guidance under regulatory authority granted in section 1(h). *See* Notice 2015-41, 2015-24 I.R.B. 1058, modifying Notice 2004-39, 2004-1 C.B. 982 and Notice 97-64, 1997-2 C.B. 323.

Investing in RICs enables small investors to gain benefits, such as professional management and broad diversification, that otherwise would be available only to investors with more resources. The House Report for the enactment of the Internal Revenue Code of 1954 explained that the RIC regime "permits investors to pool their funds through the use of a corporation in order to obtain skilled, diversified investment in corporate securities without having to pay an additional layer of corporate tax." H.R. Rep. No. 83-1337, p. 73 (1954). The ability to elect to be taxed as a RIC is available typically only to domestic corporations that, at all times during the taxable year, are registered under the Investment Company Act of 1940, as amended (15 U.S.C. 80a-1 to 80b–2). *See* section 851(a)(1)(A).

Section 199A(f)(4) directs the Secretary to prescribe such regulations as are necessary to carry out the purposes of section 199A, including regulations for its application in the case of tiered entities. The Treasury Department and the IRS have determined that it is consistent with the grant of authority under section 199A and the purposes of part 1 of subchapter M of chapter 1 of the Code to provide for conduit treatment of qualified REIT dividends. The Treasury Department and the IRS continue to consider whether it is appropriate to provide for conduit treatment of qualified PTP income.

These proposed regulations provide rules under which a RIC that receives qualified REIT dividends may pay section 199A dividends. Non-corporate shareholders receiving section 199A dividends would treat them as qualified REIT dividends under section 199A(e)(3), provided the shareholder meets the holding period requirements for its shares in the RIC.

The rules under which a RIC would compute and report section 199A dividends are based on the rules for capital gain dividends in section 852(b)(3) and exempt-interest dividends in section 852(b)(5). The amount of a RIC's section 199A dividends for a taxable year would be limited to the excess of the RIC's qualified REIT dividends for the taxable year over allocable expenses. Section 199A dividends generally are also subject to the principles that apply to other RIC dividends. *See, e.g.*, Rev. Rul. 2005-31, 2005-1 C.B. 1084; Rev. Rul. 89-81, 1989-1 C.B. 226.

B. *PTPs*

One of the commenters recommending that the regulations permit conduit treatment for qualified REIT dividends received by a RIC also recommended that the regulations permit conduit treatment for qualified PTP income received by a RIC. In response to this comment, the Treasury Department and the IRS have given significant consideration to including in this notice of proposed rulemaking regulations that would provide conduit treatment for qualified PTP income. However, unlike conduit treatment for qualified REIT dividends received by a RIC, conduit treatment of qualified PTP income received by a RIC presents several novel issues. The commenter recommending this conduit treatment did not address these issues or make any suggestions as to how they should be resolved. The need to resolve these issues in a way that would afford RIC shareholders treatment that is similar to the treatment they would receive if they held the PTP interests directly while preserving the relative simplicity of the tax treatment of RIC investors has prevented the Treasury Department and the IRS from crafting and including appropriate rules in these proposed regulations. As noted later in this part of the Explanation of Provisions, the Treasury Department and the IRS continue to consider permitting conduit treatment for qualified PTP income received by a RIC to further the purposes of section 199A(b)(1)(B) and seek public comment to assist in resolving these novel issues with a view to developing regulations permitting conduit treatment for qualified PTP income.

These issues arise in part from the fact that income attributable to a specified service trade or business within the meaning of section 199A(d)(2) (SSTB) of a PTP may be qualified PTP income for taxpayers with taxable income below the threshold amount, but not for taxpayers with taxable income above the top of the phase-out range. For taxpayers with taxable income in the phase-out range, a portion of PTP income attributable to an SSTB is qualified PTP income. There is no precedent for providing conduit treatment for a RIC (or any other C corporation) with respect to income of a PTP or other partnership taxed in this manner, and the complexity and potential confusion such treatment might create for RIC investors is arguably inconsistent with the relative simplicity that the tax system has historically provided for RIC investors. This is particularly true given the limitation on the portion of a RIC's assets that can be invested in qualified PTPs as defined in section 851(h) (the type of PTP likely to be engaged in a trade or business) and the limited portion of the RIC's dividends that would likely be attributable to income from such PTPs.

Another novel issue is presented by the rules relating to the treatment of losses for purposes of section 199A. First, a PTP may not net losses from an SSTB against income from a non-SSTB, and vice versa, in determining the amounts that it reports to its partners. Thus, PTPs are required to separately calculate income and deductions from SSTBs and non-SSTBs and report that information to their partners. Second, if a taxpayer has a net loss from an SSTB or a non-SSTB that is allowed in determining taxable income for a taxable year, that loss may be required to be carried over to the subsequent year for section 199A attribute purposes. In the case of a RIC, it is not clear to what extent these requirements can be implemented by permitting RIC dividends to reflect attributes of the RIC's investment experiences in PTPs. For example, it is difficult to conceive how losses of a RIC can be passed through to shareholders upon the payment of a dividend, which would be inconsistent with the status of a RIC as a C corporation. *See* section 311(a). In addition, RICs and RIC shareholders would experience complexity inconsistent with the longstanding tax policy of providing simplified reporting for RIC investors.

Consistent with RICs' status as C corporations, RICs could instead offset losses from PTPs against qualified REIT dividends received, with any excess PTP losses carried forward as negative qualified PTP income for section 199A attribute purposes at the RIC level. To the extent RICs would be required to carry forward PTP losses, it would appear that RICs would need to track separate loss carryforwards for SSTB PTP losses and non-SSTB PTP losses. While netting qualified non-SSTB losses from PTPs against larger amounts of qualified REIT dividends would support RIC dividends that could be treated as eligible for the section 199A deduction by the RICs' shareholders regardless of income level, SSTB losses from PTPs would complicate the offset of qualified PTP losses against qualified REIT dividends by RICs because SSTB losses from a PTP do not offset qualified REIT dividends for taxpayers with taxable income above the phase-out range. Such losses do, however, offset qualified REIT dividends for taxpayers with income below the threshold amount. For taxpayers with income in the phase-out range, these losses partially offset qualified REIT dividends to a greater or lesser extent depending on where the taxpayer's income falls in the phase-out range. It is not clear how a conduit regime for qualified PTP income could work in terms of treating RIC shareholders in the phase-out range in a manner that is consistent with the treatment they would receive if they received the qualified REIT dividend and the qualified PTP loss from an SSTB directly rather than through a RIC.

Providing conduit treatment for qualified PTP income would also raise potentially significant issues with respect to the treatment of RIC shareholders that are non-U.S. persons, tax-exempt organizations, and trusts underlying individual retirement accounts (IRAs) and qualified retirement plans. In order to be qualified PTP income, section 199A(c)(3)(A)(i) requires that the income must be effectively connected with a U.S. trade or business. If conduit treatment is afforded to RIC dividends attributable to such PTP income for section 199A purposes, it is not clear that a RIC dividend attributable to such income could be disregarded for purposes of calculating effectively connected income of a non-U.S. shareholder or unrelated business taxable income of a tax-exempt organization or trust underlying an IRA or qualified retirement plan. Given that such investors typically do not hold directly interests in PTPs intentionally, but do so through corporate "blockers," allowing conduit treatment for qualified PTP income through RICs could cause unwelcome results for non-U.S. shareholders, tax-exempt organizations, and trusts underlying IRAs and qualified retirement plans holding RIC stock.

The Treasury Department and the IRS continue to evaluate whether it is appropriate to provide conduit treatment for qualified PTP income through RICs, and request detailed comments on these novel issues. In particular, comments are requested concerning: (1) Whether RICs have sufficient qualified items of PTP income, gain, deduction, or loss to warrant a conduit regime that would permit RICs to pay qualified PTP dividends to shareholders; (2) How to provide conduit treatment for qualified PTP income for taxpayers with income below the threshold amount or within the phase-out range, particularly where a RIC has qualified REIT dividends and a qualified PTP loss from an SSTB; (3) How to treat losses of PTPs arising from SSTBs and non-SSTBs; (4) Whether conduit treatment for qualified PTP income can be disregarded for purposes of determining the effectively connected income or unrelated business taxable income of certain RIC shareholders; (5) Whether SSTB items are sufficiently rare or incidental for PTPs that a conduit regime for PTP dividends should exclude all SSTB items; and (6) How to implement conduit treatment for qualified PTP income in a way that is consistent with the policy goal of preserving the overall relative simplicity of the tax treatment of investors in RICs while still achieving the policy goals of section 199A and section 199A(b)(1)(B) in particular.

III. *Special Rules for Trusts and Estates*

Section 1.199A-6 provides guidance that certain specified entities (for example, trusts and estates) may need to follow to enable the computation of the section 199A deduction of the entity and each of its owners. Section 1.199A-6(d) contains special rules for applying section 199A to trusts and decedents' estates. The August Proposed Regulations expressly requested comments, and comments were submitted, on whether and how certain trusts and other entities would be able to take a deduction under section 199A. These proposed regulations take those suggestions into consideration in proposing rules applicable to those particular situations identified by commenters.

In the case of a section 199A deduction claimed by a non-grantor trust or estate, section 199A(f)(1)(B) applies rules similar to the rules under former section 199(d)(1)(B)(i) for the apportionment of W–2 wages and the apportionment of UBIA of qualified property. In the case of a non-grantor trust or estate, the QBI and expenses properly allocable to the business, including the W-2 wages relevant to the computation of the wage limitation, and relevant UBIA of depreciable property must be allocated among the trust or estate and its various beneficiaries. Specifically, § 1.199A-6(d)(3)(ii) provides that each beneficiary's share of the trust's or estate's QBI and W-2 wages is determined based on the proportion of the trust's or estate's DNI that is deemed to be distributed to that beneficiary for that taxable year. Similarly, the proportion of the entity's DNI that is not deemed distributed by the trust or estate will determine the entity's share of the QBI and W-2 wages. In addition, if the trust or estate has no DNI in a particular taxable year, any QBI and W-2 wages are allocated to the trust or estate, and not to any beneficiary.

In addition, § 1.199A-6(d)(3)(ii) provides that, to the extent the trust's or estate's UBIA of qualified property is relevant to a trust or estate and any beneficiary, the trust's or estate's UBIA of qualified property will be allocated among the trust or estate and its beneficiaries in the same proportions as is the DNI of the trust or estate. This is the case regardless of how any depreciation or depletion deductions resulting from the same property may be allocated under section 643(c) among the trust or estate and its beneficiaries for purposes other than section 199A.

Under § 1.199A-6(d)(3)(iv), the threshold amount is determined at the trust level after taking into account any distribution deductions. Commenters have noted that taxpayers could circumvent the threshold amount by dividing assets among multiple trusts, each of which would claim its own threshold amount. This result is inappropriate and inconsistent with the purpose of section 199A. Therefore, § 1.199A-6(d)(3)(vii) provides that a trust formed or funded with a principal purpose of receiving a deduction under section 199A will not be respected for purposes of determining the threshold amount under section 199A.

In the August Proposed Regulations, the Treasury Department and the IRS requested comments with respect to whether taxable recipients of annuity and unitrust interests in charitable remainder trusts and taxable beneficiaries of other split-interest trusts may be eligible for the section 199A deduction to the extent that the amounts received by such recipients include amounts that may give rise to the deduction. The request for such comments indicated that such comments should include explanations of how amounts that may give rise to the section 199A deduction would be identified and reported in the various classes of income of the trusts received by such recipients and how the excise tax rules in section 664(c) would apply to such amounts.

A. *Charitable remainder trust beneficiary's eligibility for the deduction*

A few commenters suggested that a charitable remainder trust under section 664 should be allowed to calculate the deduction at the trust level and that the charitable remainder trust should be treated as a single taxpayer for purposes of the thresholds for taxable income, W-2 wages, and UBIA of qualified property.

Several commenters recommended that, if unrelated business taxable income (UBTI) is qualified business income, the section 199A deduction should be allowed before the UBTI excise tax is imposed. However, other commenters disagreed. Another commenter stated that the section 199A deduction should not be allowed when calculating UBTI because it is not a deduction directly connected with carrying on the trade or business and is allowable only for purposes of chapter 1, while the excise tax on UBTI is imposed under chapter 42 (that is, it is not an income tax). Another commenter said the UBTI excise tax under section 664(c) should not affect QBI because that tax is charged to principal.

One commenter recommended that QBI should be allocated to the ordinary income tier. Another recommended that QBI should be the bottom of the first tier (last to be distributed) and section 199A items should be reported on the Schedule K-1 when QBI is deemed distributed. Another commenter stated that a charitable remainder trust has no taxable income and no DNI, so the allocation of QBI, W-2 wages, and UBIA of qualified property should be allocated to beneficiaries based on the percentage of distributions from the ordinary income tier, with QBI allocated to the charitable remainder trust remaining a tier one item. Another commenter stated that QBI cannot be a separate tier because it is a deduction, rather than a rate difference.

The Treasury Department and the IRS believe that, because a charitable remainder trust described in section 664 is not subject to income tax, and because the excise tax imposed by section 664(c) is treated as imposed under chapter 42, the trust does not either have or calculate a section 199A deduction and the threshold amount described in section 199A(e)(2) does not apply to the trust. Furthermore, application of section 199A to effectively reduce the 100 percent rate of tax imposed by section 664(c) on any UBTI would be inconsistent with the intent of section 664(c) to deter trusts from making investments that generate significant UBTI. However, any taxable recipient of a unitrust or annuity amount from the trust must determine and apply the recipient's own threshold amount for purposes of section 199A, taking into account any annuity or unitrust amounts received from the trust. Therefore, a taxable recipient of a unitrust or annuity amount from a charitable remainder trust may take into account QBI, qualified REIT dividends, and qualified PTP income for purposes of determining the recipient's section 199A deduction for the taxable year to the extent that the unitrust or annuity amount distributed to such recipient consists of such section 199A items under § 1.664-1(d).

In order to determine the order of distribution of the various classes of income of the trust for purposes of applying § 1.664-1(d), QBI, qualified REIT dividends, and qualified PTP income of a charitable remainder trust will be allocated to the classes of income within the category of income described in § 1.664-1(d)(1)(i)(a)(1) based on the rate of tax that normally would apply to that type of income, not taking into account the characterization of that income as QBI, qualified REIT dividends, or qualified PTP income for purposes of section 199A. Accordingly, any QBI, qualified REIT dividends, and qualified PTP income will be treated as distributed from the trust to a unitrust or annuity recipient only when all other classes of income within the ordinary income category subject to a higher rate of tax (not taking into account section 199A) have been exhausted. The unitrust or annuity recipient will be treated as receiving a proportionate amount of any QBI, qualified REIT dividends, and qualified PTP income that is distributed along with other income in the same class within the ordinary income category. To the extent that a trust is treated as distributing QBI, qualified REIT dividends, or qualified PTP income to more than one unitrust or annuity recipient in the taxable year, the distribution of such income will be treated as made to the recipients proportionately, based on their respective shares of the total of QBI, qualified REIT dividends, and qualified PTP income distributed for that year. The amount of any W-2 wages or UBIA of qualified property of the charitable remainder trust in a taxable year will be allocable to unitrust or annuity recipients based on each recipient's share of the trust's total QBI (whether or not distributed) for that taxable year.

Any QBI, qualified REIT dividends, or qualified PTP income of the trust that is unrelated business taxable income is subject to excise tax and § 1.664-1(c) requires that tax to be allocated to the corpus of the trust. Certain other rules relating to charitable remainder trusts are provided.

B. *Split-interest trusts*

The August Proposed Regulations requested comments on whether any special rules were necessary with respect to split-interest trusts. One commenter suggested that additional rules may be necessary for split-interest trusts other than charitable reminder trusts. After considering the comment and studying other split-interest trusts in more depth after the publication of the August Proposed Regulations, the Treasury Department and the IRS have determined that special rules for other split-interest trusts, such as non-grantor charitable lead trusts or pooled income funds, are not necessary because such trusts are taxable under part I, subchapter J, chapter 1 of the Code, except subpart E. Such split-interest trusts would apply the rules for non-grantor trusts and estates set forth in § 1.199A-6(d)(3) to determine any applicable section 199A deduction for the trust or its taxable beneficiaries.

C. *Separate shares*

Although no comments were received with respect the application of the threshold amount to separate shares, the Treasury Department and the IRS believe that clarification with respect to this issue may be necessary. These proposed regulations provide that, in the case of a trust described in section 663(c) with substantially separate and independent shares for multiple beneficiaries, such separate shares will not be treated as separate trusts for purposes of applying the threshold amount. Instead, the trust will be treated as a single trust for purposes of determining whether the taxable income of the trust exceeds the threshold amount. The purpose of the separate share rule in section 663(c) is to treat distributions of trust DNI to trust beneficiaries as independent taxable events solely for purposes of applying sections 661 and 662 with respect to each beneficiary's separate share. The rule determines each beneficiary's share of DNI based on the amount of DNI from that beneficiary's separate share, rather than as a percentage of the trust's DNI.

Nevertheless, under the separate share rule, if a trust retains any portion of DNI, the trust will be subject to tax as a single trust with respect to the retained DNI. Only trusts with retained DNI will be eligible for the section 199A deduction, because a trust will be allocated QBI, qualified REIT dividends, and qualified PTP income only in proportion to the amount of DNI retained by the trust for the taxable year. For this reason, a trust, regardless of the number of separate shares it has for its beneficiaries under the separate share rule of section 663(c), will be treated as a single trust for purposes of applying the threshold amount under section 199A. To the extent that a taxable beneficiary of a trust receives a distribution of DNI from the beneficiary's separate share of the trust which includes section 199A items, the beneficiary would apply its own threshold amount to those section 199A items in computing its section 199A deduction in accordance with the rules of § 1.199A-6(d).

Availability of IRS Documents

IRS notices cited in this preamble are made available by the Superintendent of Documents, U.S. Government Printing Office, Washington, DC 20402.

Proposed Effective/Applicability Date

Section 7805(b)(1)(A) and (B) of the Code generally provide that no temporary, proposed, or final regulation relating to the internal revenue laws may apply to any taxable period ending before the earliest of (A) the date on which such regulation is filed with the **Federal Register**, or (B) in the case of a final regulation, the date on which a proposed or temporary regulation to which the final regulation relates was filed with the **Federal Register**.

The amendments to §§ 1.199A-3 and 1.199A-6 set forth in this notice of proposed rulemaking generally are proposed to apply to taxable years ending after the date of publication of a Treasury decision adopting these rules as final regulations in the **Federal Register**. However, taxpayers may rely on the rules in the amendments to §§ 1.199A-3 and 1.199A-6 set forth in this notice of proposed rulemaking, in their entirety, until the date a Treasury decision adopting these regulations as final regulations is published in the **Federal Register**.

Special Analyses

I. *Regulatory Planning and Review - Economic Analysis*

Executive Orders 13563 and 12866 direct agencies to assess costs and benefits of available regulatory alternatives and, if regulation is necessary, to select regulatory approaches that maximize net benefits (including potential economic, environmental, public health and safety effects, distributive impacts, and equity). Executive Order 13563 emphasizes the importance of quantifying both costs and benefits, of reducing costs, of harmonizing rules, and of promoting flexibility.

The proposed regulations have been designated by the Office of Management and Budget's ("OMB") Office of Information and Regulatory Affairs ("OIRA") as subject to review under Executive Order 12866 pursuant to the Memorandum of Agreement (April 11, 2018) between the Treasury Department and OMB regarding review of tax regulations. It has been determined that the proposed rulemaking is economically significant under section 1(c) of the Memorandum of Agreement and thereby subject to review. Accordingly, the proposed regulations have been reviewed by OMB.

A. *Overview*

Congress enacted section 199A to provide taxpayers other than corporations a deduction of up to 20 percent of QBI from domestic businesses plus up to 20 percent of their combined qualified REIT dividends and qualified PTP income. As stated in the Explanation of Provisions, these regulations are necessary to provide taxpayers with computational, definitional, and anti-avoidance guidance regarding the application of section 199A. These proposed regulations contain amendments to § 1.199A-3, providing further guidance to taxpayers for purposes of calculating the section 199A deduction. They provide clarity for taxpayers in determining their eligibility for the deduction and the amount of the allowed deduction. Among other benefits, this clarity helps ensure that taxpayers all calculate the deduction in a similar manner, which encourages decision-making that is economically efficient contingent on the provisions of the overall Code.

B. *Baseline*

The analysis in this section compares the proposed regulation to a no-action baseline reflecting anticipated Federal income tax-related behavior in the absence of these regulations.

C. *Economic Analysis of the Proposed Amendments to §1.199A-3*

1. *Background*

Because the section 199A deduction has not previously been available, §§1.199A-1 through 1.199A-6 provide greater specificity for a large number of the relevant terms and necessary calculations taxpayers are currently required to apply under the statute. However, one subject not covered by the August 2018 Proposed Regulations is the treatment of REIT dividends received by RICs. Because RICs are taxed as C corporations, they are ineligible for the section 199A deduction under the statute, which generally does not apply to C corporations. However, the statute also directs the Secretary to prescribe such regulations as are necessary to carry out the purposes of section 199A, including regulations for its application in the case of tiered entities. Thus these proposed regulations establish rules under which a RIC that earns qualified REIT dividends may pay section 199A dividends to its shareholders.

An alternative approach the Treasury Department and the IRS could have taken would be to remain silent on this issue. For reasons given below, the Treasury Department and the IRS concluded such an approach would likely give rise to less economically efficient decisions than the approach taken in these proposed regulations.

2. *Anticipated benefits of the Proposed Amendments to §1.199A-3*

The Treasury Department and the IRS expect that the definitions and guidance provided in the proposed amendments to §1.199A-3 will implement the section 199A deduction in an economically efficient manner. An economically efficient tax system generally aims to treat income derived from similar economic decisions similarly in order to reduce incentives to make choices based on tax rather than market incentives. In absence of these proposed regulations, the section 199A statute would not accomplish this in the case of REIT dividends. Under the statute and the section 199A final regulations, individuals who directly hold ownership interests in a REIT would generally qualify for the section 199A deduction on their qualified REIT dividends. However, individuals who are shareholders of a RIC that has an ownership interest in a REIT would not receive any benefit from section 199A on REIT dividends received by the RIC, even if the RIC pays dividends to the individual. Thus, in the absence of these supplemental proposed regulations, a market distortion is introduced by section 199A whereby direct ownership of REITs is tax-advantaged relative to indirect ownership of REITs through RICs.

These proposed regulations remove this distortion. The proposed amendments to §1.199A-3 establish rules under which a RIC that earns qualified REIT dividends may pay section 199A dividends to its shareholders, such that the effective tax treatment of qualified REIT dividends is similar under the proposed regulations regardless of whether a taxpayer invests in a REIT directly or through a RIC.

3. *Anticipated costs of the Proposed Amendments to §1.199A-3*

The Treasury Department and the IRS do not anticipate any meaningful economic distortions to be induced by the proposed amendments to §1.199A-3 because the proposed amendments seek to continue to provide similar tax treatment to REIT income regardless of whether it is held directly or through a RIC. Prior to TCJA, the tax treatment was similar, but TCJA made REIT dividends eligible for the section 199A deduction, and the section 199A final regulations did not address this uncertainty. This proposed amendment ensures that REIT income earned through a RIC is also eligible for the same deduction. RICs are financial intermediaries, and, as a general rule, economic distortion is minimized to the extent that the tax consequences of investment through an intermediary correspond to the tax consequences of direct investment. The Treasury Department and the IRS request comments regarding any anticipated economic costs. Changes to the collective paperwork burden arising from this and other sections of these regulations are discussed in section D, *Anticipated impacts on administrative and compliance costs*, of this analysis.

D. *Anticipated impacts on administrative and compliance costs*

The proposed regulations add to the compliance costs of RICs and intermediaries such as brokerage firms that hold RIC shares. In order for a RIC's shareholders to benefit from the section 199A deduction on qualified REIT dividends earned by the RIC, the proposed regulations require the RIC to compute and report section 199A dividends to its shareholders. Though many RICs keep detailed records of their investment portfolios, this action nonetheless creates non-trivial administrative costs for any RICs and intermediaries that wish to provide section 199A dividends to their shareholders. These costs and the associated impacted tax forms are described in the Paperwork Reduction Act section of this proposed amendment.

E. *Executive Order 13771.*

These regulations have been designated as regulatory under E.O. 13771.

II. **Paperwork Reduction Act**

The collection of information required by this proposed regulation is in proposed §1.199A-3. The collection of information in proposed §1.199A-3 is required for RICs that choose to report information regarding qualified REIT dividends to their shareholders. It is necessary to report the information to the IRS and relevant taxpayers in order to ensure that taxpayers properly report in accordance with the rules of the proposed regulations the correct amount of deduction under section 199A. The collection of information in proposed §1.199A-3 is satisfied by providing information about section 199A dividends as Form 1099-DIV and its instructions may prescribe.

For purpose of the PRA, the reporting burden associated with § 1.199A-3 will be reflected in the IRS Form 14029, Paperwork Reduction Act Submission, associated with Form 1099-DIV (OMB control number 1545-0110). The burden associated with the information collection in the proposed regulations represents 1.567 million hours and $149 million ($2018) annually to comply with the information collection requirement in the proposed regulations. The burden hours estimate was derived from IRS's legacy burden model and is discussed in further detail on 1545-0110. The hourly rate is derived from RAAS's Business Taxpayer Burden model that relates time and out-of-pocket costs of business tax preparation, derived from survey data, to assets and receipts of affected taxpayers along with other relevant variables, and converted by the Treasury Department to $2017. The Treasury Department and the IRS request comments on all aspects of information collection burdens related to the proposed regulations. In addition, when available, drafts of the applicable IRS forms are posted for comment at https://www.irs.gov/pub/irs-pdf/f1099div.pdf.

III. *Regulatory Flexibility Act*

It is hereby certified that the collections of information in proposed § 1.199A-3 will not have a significant economic impact on a substantial number of small entities.

The collection in proposed § 1.199A-3 applies only to RICs that pay section 199A dividends. As described above, Congress created RICs to give small investors access to the professional management and asset diversification that are available only with very large investment portfolios. To insure appropriate non-tax regulation of these substantial investment portfolios, subchapter M of chapter 1 of subtitle A the Code requires that such RICs must be eligible for registration, and must actually be registered, with the Securities and Exchange Commission under the Investment Company Act of 1940. There are some small businesses that are publicly traded, but most publicly traded businesses are not small entities as defined by the Regulatory Flexibility Act. Thus, the Treasury Department and IRS expect that most RICs are not small entities for purposes of the Regulatory Flexibility Act. Accordingly, the Treasury Department and the IRS have determined that the collection of information in this notice of proposed rulemaking will not have a significant economic impact. Accordingly, a regulatory flexibility analysis under the Regulatory Flexibility Act (5 U.S.C. chapter 6) is not required. Notwithstanding this certification, the Treasury Department and the IRS invite comments from interested members of the public on both the number of entities affected and the economic impact on small entities.

Pursuant to section 7805(f) of the Code, this notice of proposed rulemaking has been submitted to the Chief Counsel for Advocacy of the Small Business Administration for comment on its impact on small business.

Pursuant to section 7805(f) of the Code, this notice of proposed rulemaking has been submitted to the Chief Counsel for Advocacy of the Small Business Administration for comment on its impact on small business.

Comments and Requests for Public Hearing

The Treasury Department and the IRS request comments on all aspects of the proposed rules.

Before these proposed regulations are adopted as final regulations, consideration will be given to any comments that are submitted timely to the IRS as prescribed in this preamble under the "Addresses" heading. All comments will be available at *www.regulations.gov* or upon request. A public hearing will be scheduled if requested in writing by any person that timely submits written comments. If a public hearing is scheduled, then notice of the date, time, and place for the public hearing will be published in the **Federal Register**.

Drafting Information

The principal authors of these regulations are Michael Y. Chin and Steven Harrison, Office of the Associate Chief Counsel (Financial Institutions and Products) and Robert Alinsky, Vishal R. Amin, Margaret Burow, and Frank J. Fisher, Office of the Associate Chief Counsel (Passthroughs and Special Industries). However, other personnel from the Treasury Department and the IRS participated in their development.

[¶ 49,788] Proposed Amendments of Regulations (REG-104464-18), published in the Federal Register on March 6, 2019 (corrected 4/11/2019 and 4/12/2019).

[Code Secs. 250, 962, 1502, 6038, 6038A]

Deductions: Foreign-derived intangible income: Global intangible low-taxed income.—Reg. §§ 1.250-0, 1.250-1, 1.250(a)-1, 1.250(b)-1—1.250(b)-6 and 1.1502-50 and amendments of Reg. §§ 1.962-1, 1.1502-12, 1.1502-13, 1.6038-2, 1.6038-3 and 1.6038A-2, providing guidance to determine the amount of the deduction for foreign-derived intangible income and global intangible low-taxed income.

AGENCY: Internal Revenue Service (IRS), Treasury.

ACTION: Notice of proposed rulemaking.

SUMMARY: This document contains proposed regulations that provide guidance to determine the amount of the deduction for foreign-derived intangible income and global intangible low-taxed income. This document also contains proposed regulations coordinating the deduction for foreign-derived intangible income and global intangible low-taxed income with other provisions in the Internal Revenue Code.

DATES: Written or electronic comments and requests for a public hearing must be received by May 6, 2019.

ADDRESSES: Send submissions to: CC:PA:LPD:PR (REG-104464-18), Room 5203, Internal Revenue Service, P.O. Box 7604, Ben Franklin Station, Washington, DC 20044. Submissions may be hand-delivered Monday through Friday between the hours of 8 a.m. and 4 p.m. to: CC:PA:LPD:PR (REG-104464-18), Courier's Desk, Internal Revenue Service, 1111 Constitution Avenue NW, Washington, DC 20224. Alternatively, taxpayers may submit comments electronically via the Federal eRulemaking Portal at *http://www.regulations.gov* (REG-104464-18).

FOR FURTHER INFORMATION CONTACT: Concerning proposed § § 1.250(a)-1 through 1.250(b)-6, 1.962-1, 1.6038-2, 1.6038-3, and 1.6038A-2, Kenneth Jeruchim at (202) 317-6939; concerning proposed § § 1.1502-12, 1.1502-13 and 1.1502-50, Michelle A. Monroy at (202) 317-5363 or Austin Diamond-Jones at (202) 317-6847; concerning submissions of comments and requests for a public hearing, Regina L. Johnson, (202) 317-6901 (not toll free numbers).

SUPPLEMENTARY INFORMATION:

Background

This document contains proposed amendments to 26 CFR part 1 under sections 250, 962, 1502, 6038, and 6038A ("proposed regulations"). Section 14202(a) of the Tax Cuts and Jobs Act, Public Law 115-97 (2017) (the "Act"), added section 250 to the Internal Revenue Code (the "Code").[1] The new section provides a domestic corporation with a deduction ("section 250 deduction") for its foreign-derived intangible income ("FDII") and its global intangible low-taxed income ("GILTI") and the amount treated as a dividend under section 78 which is attributable to its GILTI. Section 14202(c) of the Act provides that section 250 and the conforming amendments in section 14202(b) apply to taxable years beginning after December 31, 2017.

Section 14201(a) of the Act (codified in section 951A) requires a United States shareholder ("U.S. shareholder") of any controlled foreign corporation ("CFC") for any taxable year to include in gross income the shareholder's GILTI for the year. The Department of the Treasury ("Treasury Department") and the IRS published a separate notice of proposed rulemaking that provides guidance to U.S. shareholders on how to determine the amount of GILTI to include in gross income. See 83 FR 51072 (Oct. 10, 2018).

Section 14302(a) of the Act also added a new foreign tax credit category for foreign branch income (defined in section 904(d)(2)(J)), which is cross-referenced in section 250(b)(3)(A)(i)(VI). The Treasury Department and the IRS published a separate notice of proposed rulemaking that provides rules for determining a corporation's foreign branch income for purposes of section 904. See 83 FR 63200 (Dec. 7, 2018).

Explanation of Provisions

I. *Overview of Proposed Regulations*

In general, income earned directly by a U.S. person on foreign business income is subject to U.S. tax on a current basis. Before the Act, foreign business income earned indirectly by a U.S. person through a foreign corporation was not generally subject to U.S. tax until such income was distributed as a dividend to the U.S. person. Certain anti-deferral regimes could cause the U.S. owner to be taxed on a current basis in the United States regardless of whether the income had been distributed as a dividend to the U.S. owner. Sections 951 through 965 of the Code (generally referred to as the "subpart F" provisions), applicable to certain passive and mobile categories of income earned by CFCs, is the main anti-deferral regime of relevance to U.S.-based corporate groups. However, because subpart F does not generally apply to active foreign business income of a CFC (as defined in section 957(a)), U.S. shareholders before the Act could indefinitely defer U.S. taxation with respect to their foreign business income — in particular, mobile income arising from the exploitation of intangible property — by allocating such income to its CFCs operating in low- or zero-tax jurisdictions. This system of deferral, in turn, resulted in a "lock-out effect," whereby U.S. shareholders that had allocated income to CFCs formed in low- or zero-tax jurisdictions could not repatriate such income to the United States without incurring significant U.S. tax.

In order to facilitate the efficient redeployment of foreign earnings in the United States, the Act established a participation exemption system under which certain earnings of a foreign corporation can be repatriated to a corporate U.S. shareholder without U.S. tax. See section 14101(a) of the Act and section 245A. However, Congress recognized that, without any base protection measures, the participation exemption system could further incentivize taxpayers to allocate intangible income to CFCs formed in low- or zero-tax jurisdictions because the earnings related to such intangible income could now be repatriated to the United States without incurring any U.S. tax. See Senate Committee on the Budget, 115th Cong., "Reconciliation Recommendations Pursuant to H. Con. Res. 71," at 370 (Comm. Print 2017) ("Senate Explanation"). Therefore, Congress enacted section 951A, which subjects a U.S. shareholder's "global intangible low-taxed income" or "GILTI" (a new term created by the Act) derived through its CFCs to U.S. tax on a current basis, similar to the taxation of such CFCs' subpart F income under section 951(a)(1)(A).

---

[1] Except as otherwise stated, all section references in this preamble are to the Internal Revenue Code.

Most member countries of the Organisation for Economic Co-operation and Development ("OECD") provide a full or partial (e.g., 95 percent) participation exemption with respect to income of foreign subsidiaries distributed to domestic shareholders. See OECD (2018), *Tax Policy Reforms 2018: OECD and Selected Partner Economies*, at 73, OECD Publishing, Paris (Sept. 2018). While some countries also have CFC inclusion regimes similar to subpart F that subject certain narrow classes of income of foreign subsidiaries to current tax in the home country, many countries do not subject active foreign business income of foreign subsidiaries to current tax. Congress recognized that taxing such income at the full U.S. corporate tax rate could hurt the competitive position of U.S. corporations relative to their foreign peers, and therefore determined that GILTI earned by such corporations should be subject to a reduced effective U.S. tax rate. See Senate Explanation, at 370. Accordingly, Congress enacted section 250, which provides corporate U.S. shareholders a deduction of 50 percent for taxable years beginning after December 31, 2017, and before January 1, 2026, with respect to their GILTI, and the amount treated as a dividend under section 78 which is attributable to their GILTI ("section 78 gross-up"). In contrast, a domestic corporation's inclusion of its CFCs' subpart F income is not eligible for the section 250 deduction, and is therefore generally subject to U.S. tax at the full corporate rate.

After the Act, income earned directly by a domestic corporation is subject to a 21 percent rate. Absent a deduction with respect to intangible income attributable to foreign market activity earned directly by a domestic corporation, the lower effective tax rate applicable to GILTI by reason of the section 250 deduction would perpetuate the pre-Act incentive for domestic corporations to allocate intangible income to CFCs formed in low- or zero-tax jurisdictions. Therefore, to neutralize the effect of providing a lower U.S. effective tax rate with respect to the active earnings of a CFC of a domestic corporation through a deduction for GILTI, section 250 provides a lower effective U.S. tax rate with respect to "foreign-derived intangible income" or "FDII" (a new term created by the Act) earned directly by the domestic corporation through a deduction of 37.5 percent for taxable years beginning after December 31, 2017, and before January 1, 2026. The result of the section 250 deduction for both GILTI and FDII is to help neutralize the role that tax considerations play when a domestic corporation chooses the location of intangible income attributable to foreign-market activity, that is, whether to earn such income through its U.S.-based operations or through its CFCs.

The proposed regulations provide guidance for determining the amount of the section 250 deduction allowed to a domestic corporation for its FDII and GILTI. Proposed § 1.250(a)-1 provides rules for determining the amount of the deduction, including rules for applying the taxable income limitation of section 250(a)(2). Proposed § 1.250(b)-1 provides general rules for computing a domestic corporation's FDII. Proposed § 1.250(b)-2 provides rules for determining a domestic corporation's qualified business asset investment ("QBAI"), which is a component of the computation of FDII. Proposed § 1.250(b)-3 provides general rules for determining gross income included in gross foreign-derived deduction eligible income ("gross FDDEI"), which is a component of the computation of FDII. Proposed § 1.250(b)-4 provides rules for determining gross FDDEI from sales of property. Proposed § 1.250(b)-5 provides rules for determining gross FDDEI from the provision of a service. Proposed § 1.250(b)-6 provides rules relating to the sale of property or the provision of a service to a related party.

II. *Amount of Deduction Allowed Under Section 250(a)*

Proposed § 1.250(a)-1 provides general rules to determine the amount of a domestic corporation's section 250 deduction and associated definitions that apply for purposes of the proposed regulations. The section 250 deduction is available only to domestic corporations. See section 250(a)(1) and proposed § 1.250(a)-1(b)(1). For this purpose, the term "domestic corporation" has the meaning set forth in section 7701(a) — an association, joint-stock company, or insurance company created or organized in the United States or under the law of the United States or of any State — but does not include a regulated investment company (as defined in section 851), a real estate investment trust (as defined in section 856), or an S corporation (as defined in section 1361). See proposed § 1.250(a)-1(c)(1). The section 250 deduction is not available to individuals except in certain cases where an individual makes an election under section 962. See part IV of this Explanation of Provisions section for more information about that provision.

As discussed in part I of this Explanation of Provisions section, the deduction under section 250 is generally intended to reduce the effective rate of U.S. income tax on FDII and GILTI in order to help neutralize the role that tax considerations play when a domestic corporation chooses the location of intangible income attributable to foreign-market activity. There is no indication that Congress intended the section 250 deduction to reduce the effective rate of tax imposed by non-income tax provisions outside of chapter 1 of the Internal Revenue Code. Accordingly, for purposes of the excise tax imposed by section 4940(a), the proposed regulations provide that a section 250 deduction is not treated as an ordinary and necessary expense paid or incurred for the production or collection of gross investment income within the meaning of section 4940(c)(3)(A). See proposed § 1.250(a)-1(b)(4).

The section 250 deduction is subject to a taxable income limitation. If, for any taxable year, the sum of a domestic corporation's FDII and GILTI exceeds its taxable income, the excess is allocated pro rata to reduce the corporation's FDII and GILTI solely for purposes of computing the amount of the section 250 deduction. See section 250(a)(2) and proposed § 1.250(a)-1(b)(2). For this purpose, a domestic corporation's taxable income is determined without regard to the section 250 deduction. See section 250(a)(2)(A)(ii) and proposed § 1.250(a)-1(c)(4). The Code does not otherwise define "taxable income" for purposes of applying the taxable income limitation of section 250(a)(2).

In general, a taxpayer's taxable income is based, in part, upon the availability, and proper calculation, of deductions. However, multiple Code provisions simultaneously limit the availability of a deduction based, directly or indirectly, upon a taxpayer's taxable income, including sections 163(j)(1) (limiting a deduction for business interest) and 172(a)(2) (limiting a net operating loss deduction). Sections 163(j)(2) and 172(b) also provide that any deduction not allowed to a taxpayer for a taxable year by reason of the limitation in section 163(j)(1) or 172(a)(2), respectively, may be allowed to the taxpayer, subject to the same limitation, in its succeeding taxable year. A taxpayer's net operating loss for a taxable year is determined without regard to the section 250 deduction (see section 172(d)(9)), and a taxpayer's adjusted taxable income is determined without regard to section 172. See section 163(j)(8)(A)(iii). However, neither section 163(j) nor section 250 prescribes an ordering rule with respect to the other provision.

The Treasury Department and the IRS considered proposing computations requiring the use of simultaneous equations in lieu of an ordering rule but determined that an approach that requires such computations would result in undue administrative and compliance burdens. Therefore, the proposed regulations provide an ordering rule for applying sections 163(j) and 172 in conjunction with section 250 that the Treasury Department and the IRS have determined is consistent with the statutory language for each provision. Specifically, the proposed regulations provide that a domestic corporation's taxable income for purposes of applying the taxable income limitation of section 250(a)(2) is determined after all of the corporation's other deductions are taken into account. See proposed § 1.250(a)-1(c)(4). Accordingly, a domestic corporation's taxable income for purposes of section 250(a)(2) is its taxable income determined without regard to section 250, but taking into account the application of sections 163(j) and 172(a), including amounts permitted to be carried forward to such taxable year by reason of sections 163(j)(2) and 172(b).

Proposed regulations issued under section 163(j) provide guidance on the interaction of sections 163(j) and 250 that the Treasury Department and the IRS consider to be consistent with these proposed regulations under section 250. See 83 FR 67490 (Dec. 28, 2018). Specifically, the proposed regulations under section 163(j) provide that, for purposes of determining the limitation under section 163(j), a deduction under section 250(a)(1) that is properly allocable to a non-excepted trade or business is taken into account in determining a taxpayer's taxable income and thus its adjusted taxable income. See proposed § 1.163(j)-1(b)(37)(ii). However, for this purpose, the taxpayer's deduction under section 250(a)(1) is determined without regard to the limitations under sections 250(a)(2) and 163(j). See id.

As a result of these proposed regulations under section 250 and the proposed regulations under section 163(j), a domestic corporation's allowable business interest under section 163(j), its net operating loss deduction under section 172(a), and its section 250 deduction are determined in the following manner: First, a domestic corporation computes the tentative amount of its FDII and the tentative amount of its section 250 deduction ("tentative section 250 deduction") taking into account all deductions, but without regard to any carryforwards or disallowances under section 163(j), the amount of any net operating loss deduction under section 172(a), or the taxable income limitation of section 250(a)(2) and proposed § 1.250(a)-1(b)(2). Second, the corporation computes the amount of its business interest allowed after the application of section 163(j), for this purpose taking into account the amount of its tentative section 250 deduction but without regard to the amount of any net operating loss deduction under section 172(a). See section 163(j)(8)(A)(iii) and proposed § 1.163(j)-1(b)(1)(i)(B) and (b)(37)(ii). Third, the corporation computes the amount of its net operating loss deduction under section 172(a), for this purpose taking into account the amount of its business interest allowed after application of section 163(j) and the taxable income limitation of section 172(a)(2), but without regard to the amount of its section 250 deduction (including its tentative section 250 deduction). See section 172(d)(9). Fourth, the corporation computes the amount of its FDII, for this purpose taking into account the amount of its business interest allowed after application of section 163(j) and the amount of its net operating loss deduction under section 172(a) (determined in steps two and three, respectively). See part III(A)(2) of this Explanation of Provisions section for a discussion on the allocation of deductions to gross DEI and gross FDDEI. Fifth, the corporation computes the amount of its section 250 deduction after the application of the taxable income limitation of section 250(a)(2) and proposed § 1.250(a)-1(b)(2), for this purpose taking into account the amount of its business interest allowed after application of section 163(j) and the amount of its net operating loss deduction under section 172(a). See proposed § 1.250(a)-1(f)(2) (*Example 2*), which illustrates the interaction of sections 163(j), 172, and 250.

The Treasury Department and the IRS request comments on the proposed ordering rule, as well as how the section 250 deduction should be accounted for in determining adjusted taxable income at the partnership level under section 163(j)(4)(A).

III. *Determination of FDII*

A. General Computational Rules

1. In General

A domestic corporation's FDII is the corporation's deemed intangible income ("DII") multiplied by the corporation's foreign-derived ratio. Proposed § 1.250(b)-1(b). A domestic corporation's DII is the excess (if any) of the corporation's deduction eligible income ("DEI") over its deemed tangible income return ("DTIR"). Proposed § 1.250(b)-1(c)(3). A domestic corporation's DTIR is 10 percent of the corporation's QBAI. Proposed § 1.250(b)-1(c)(4). The foreign-derived ratio is the domestic corporation's ratio of foreign-derived deduction eligible income ("FDDEI") to DEI. Proposed § 1.250(b)-1(c)(13).

2. Determination of DEI and FDDEI

A domestic corporation's DEI is the excess of its gross income without regard to certain excluded items ("gross DEI") over the deductions properly allocable to gross DEI. See proposed § 1.250(b)-1(c)(2). Gross DEI excludes six categories of gross income: any amount included in gross income under section 951(a), GILTI, financial services income, dividends from CFCs, domestic oil and gas extraction income, and foreign branch income. See proposed § 1.250(b)-1(c)(14). The proposed regulations clarify that, for this purpose, a dividend includes any amount treated as a dividend under any other provision of subtitle A of the Internal Revenue Code, including the section 78 gross-up attributable to inclusions under sections 951(a) and 951A(a). See proposed § 1.250(b)-1(c)(5). In addition, the proposed regulations define foreign branch income by reference to proposed § 1.904-4(f), except that it also includes the sale, directly or indirectly, of any asset (other than stock) that produces gross income attributable to a foreign branch, including by reason of the sale of a disregarded entity or partnership interest. See proposed § 1.250(b)-1(c)(11). The result is that income from the sale of any such asset is not included in gross DEI. Finally, the proposed regulations define financial services income by reference to section 904(d)(2)(D) and proposed § 1.904-4(e)(1)(ii).

For purposes of calculating the foreign-derived ratio, FDDEI is the excess of gross FDDEI over deductions properly allocable to gross FDDEI. See proposed § 1.250(b)-1(c)(12). The proposed regulations define gross FDDEI as the portion of a corporation's gross DEI that is derived from all of its "FDDEI sales" and "FDDEI services" (collectively, "FDDEI transactions"). See proposed § 1.250(b)-1(c)(8), (9), (10), and (15). The determination of whether a sale of property or a provision of a service is a FDDEI sale or a FDDEI service, respectively, is made under the provisions of proposed § § 1.250(b)-3 through 1.250(b)-6. See part III(B) through (F) of this Explanation of Provisions section. The portion of a corporation's gross DEI that is not gross FDDEI is referred to as gross non-FDDEI. See proposed § 1.250(b)-1(c)(16). Therefore, all income included in gross DEI is included in either gross FDDEI or gross non-FDDEI, and all income included in either gross FDDEI or gross non-FDDEI is included in gross DEI.

In the case of property produced or acquired for resale, gross income is generally determined by subtracting cost of goods sold from gross sales receipts. In determining the amount of gross income included in gross DEI or gross FDDEI, cost of goods sold is attributed to gross receipts with respect to gross DEI and gross FDDEI using any reasonable method. See proposed § 1.250(b)-1(d)(1). The proposed regulations clarify that cost of goods sold that is associated with activities undertaken in an earlier taxable year cannot be segregated into component costs and attributed disproportionately to amounts excluded from gross FDDEI or to amounts excluded from gross DEI. See id. This is similar to the clarification in proposed § 1.199-4(b)(2)(iii)(A) and is intended to preclude a method that attributes cost of goods sold of an inventory item to gross receipts other than gross receipts included in the computation of gross DEI or gross FDDEI if the gross receipts from the sale of that item are included in the computation of amounts included in the computation of gross DEI or gross FDDEI, respectively. See 80 FR 51978, 51990 (Aug. 27, 2015). The Treasury Department and the IRS request comments on whether there are alternative approaches for dealing with timing issues, and whether additional rules should be provided for attributing cost of goods sold in determining gross DEI and gross FDDEI. Cf. § 1.199-4(b)(2) through (6).

Section 250(b)(3)(A) defines DEI as the excess of a domestic corporation's gross income (excluding certain items) over "the deductions (including taxes) properly allocable to such gross income." FDDEI is defined as "any deduction eligible income" of the taxpayer generated through foreign-market sales and services. See section 250(b)(4). Therefore, a taxpayer's deductions that are "properly allocable" to gross DEI and gross FDDEI must be determined for purposes of calculating its DEI and FDDEI. The statute does not specify how deductions should be allocated for purposes of determining DEI and FDDEI. However, the rules set forth in § § 1.861-8 through 1.861-14T and 1.861-17 apply for purposes of several other provisions in the Code which require the determination of taxable income from specific sources or activities, for example, for purposes of determining the foreign tax credit limitation under section 904 or qualified production activities income under former section 199. See generally § § 1.199-4 and 1.861-8(f)(1). Accordingly, the proposed regulations provide that the rules set forth in § § 1.861-8 through 1.861-14T and 1.861-17 apply for purposes of determining DEI and FDDEI. See proposed § 1.250(b)-1(d)(2)(i). In order to avoid circularity, in applying those rules for purposes of determining DEI and FDDEI, the section 250 deduction is not treated as giving rise to exempt income or assets. See proposed § 1.861-8(d)(2)(ii)(C)(4). Comments are requested on whether alternative approaches should be considered or additional rules are needed for purposes of allocating and apportioning a net operating loss deduction to gross DEI and gross FDDEI.

In certain circumstances, as a result of expense apportionment or attribution of cost of goods sold, a domestic corporation's FDDEI could exceed its DEI. For example, a domestic corporation could have $80x of DEI and $100x of FDDEI, with losses attributable to domestic market sales accounting for the $20x difference between DEI and FDDEI. However, it would be inconsistent with the statutory language to treat a domestic corporation as having a foreign-derived ratio in excess of one, and therefore FDII in excess of DII. In particular, section 250(b)(4) defines FDDEI as a subset of DEI, that is, "any deduction eligible income of such taxpayer which is derived in connection with" certain transactions. Therefore, the proposed regulations clarify that the foreign-derived ratio cannot exceed one. See proposed § 1.250(b)-1(c)(13).

3. Treatment of Partnerships

Section 250(a)(1) allows a deduction to a domestic corporation, but does not provide any rules for domestic corporations that are partners in a partnership. However, the conference report accompanying the Act ("Conference Report") suggests that Congress intended that a domestic corporate partner of a partnership receive the benefit of a section 250 deduction for its FDII and GILTI. See H. Rept. 115-466, at 623, fn. 1517 (2017) (Conf. Rep.) ("The Committee intends that the deduction allowed by new Code section 250 be treated as exempting the deducted income from tax. Thus, for example, the deduction for global intangible low-taxed income could give rise to an increase in a domestic corporate partner's basis in a domestic partnership under section 705(a)(1)(B).").

The proposed regulations give effect to this legislative intent by adopting an aggregate approach to partnerships for determining a domestic corporate partner's FDII attributable to the income and assets of a partnership. Specifically, the proposed regulations provide that a domestic corporate partner of a partnership takes into account its distributive share of a partnership's gross DEI, gross FDDEI, and deductions in order to calculate the partner's FDII. See proposed § 1.250(b)-1(e)(1). In addition, for purposes of determining a domestic corporate partner's DTIR, a domestic corporation's QBAI is increased by its share of the partnership's adjusted basis in partnership specified tangible property. See proposed § 1.250(b)-2(g).

Under the proposed regulations, the section 250 deduction is computed and allowed solely at the level of a domestic corporate partner. The Conference Report in footnote 1517 suggests that the section 250 deduction could give rise to an increase in a domestic corporate partner's basis in a domestic partnership under section 705(a)(1)(B) because some of the partnership's income may be treated as exempt income by reason of section 250. However, regardless of whether the deduction gives rise to exempt income in other contexts, because the section 250 deduction is computed and allowed solely at the level of a domestic corporate partner, the section 250 deduction does not exempt the deducted income from tax for purposes of applying section 705(a)(1)(B). As a result, a basis adjustment to a domestic corporate partner's interest in a domestic partnership is not appropriate to account for a section 250 deduction.

4. Treatment of Tax-Exempt Corporations

A domestic corporation that is subject to the unrelated business income tax under section 511 may claim a section 250 deduction. However, the proposed regulations clarify that such corporation's FDII for this purpose is determined only with respect to the corporation's items of income, gain, deduction, or loss, and adjusted bases in property, that are taken into account in computing its unrelated business taxable income. See proposed § 1.250(b)-1(g). The proposed regulations also clarify how a tax-exempt corporation subject to the unrelated business income tax under section 511 computes the dual use ratio with respect to property used in the production of gross DEI and income that is not gross DEI for purposes of determining its QBAI. See id.

5. Determination of QBAI

Section 250(b)(2)(B) provides that QBAI for purposes of section 250 is defined under section 951A(d), and is determined by substituting "deduction eligible income" for "tested income" and without regard to whether the corporation is a CFC. Accordingly, the determination of QBAI for purposes of FDII is similar to the determination of QBAI for purposes of GILTI. Compare proposed § 1.951A-3 with proposed § 1.250(b)-2. A domestic corporation's QBAI for FDII is equal to its aggregate average adjusted bases in specified tangible property, which is defined as tangible property used in the production of gross DEI. See proposed § 1.250(b)-2(b) and (c). The proposed regulations also provide rules for dual use property, calculating QBAI in a short taxable year, and calculating a domestic corporate partner's share of partnership QBAI. See proposed § 1.250(b)-2(d), (f), and (g).

In order to prevent the avoidance of the purposes of QBAI, the proposed regulations disregard certain transfers of specified tangible property by a domestic corporation to a related party where the corporation continues to use the property in production of gross DEI. See sections 250(c) and 951A(d)(4). Specifically, for purposes of calculating a domestic corporation's QBAI, the proposed regulations disregard a transfer of specified tangible property by the domestic corporation to a related party (whose QBAI would not be taken into account in calculating the corporation's DTIR) if, within a two-year period beginning one year before the transfer, the domestic corporation (or a related party whose QBAI would be taken into account in calculating the corporation's DTIR) leases the same or substantially similar property from a related party and such transfer and lease occur pursuant to a principal purpose of reducing the domestic corporation's DTIR. See proposed § 1.250(b)-2(h)(1) and (h)(4)(i) through (iv). A transfer and lease described in the preceding sentence is treated per se as occurring pursuant to a principal purpose of reducing a domestic corporation's DTIR if both the transfer and the lease occur within the same six-month period. See proposed § 1.250(b)-2(h)(3). If the anti-avoidance rule applies, the domestic corporation that transferred the property is treated as owning such property from the later of the beginning of the term of the lease or date of the transfer until the earlier of the end of the term of the lease or the end of the recovery period of the transferred property. See proposed § 1.250(b)-2(h)(1).

The anti-avoidance rule does not apply to a transfer to and lease from an unrelated party, unless the transfer to and lease from the unrelated party is pursuant to a structured arrangement. See proposed § 1.250(b)-2(h)(2). A structured arrangement exists only if either a reduction in the domestic corporation's DTIR is a material factor in the pricing of the arrangement with the transferee or, based on all the facts and circumstances, the reduction in the domestic corporation's DTIR is a principal purpose of the arrangement. See id. The proposed regulations provide a non-inclusive list of facts and circumstances indicating that a principal purpose of an arrangement is the reduction of DTIR. See proposed § 1.250(b)-2(h)(2)(ii)(A) through (D). The Treasury Department and the IRS welcome comments on alternative approaches to identifying a structured arrangement involving unrelated parties.

No inference is intended regarding the application of any other Code section or judicial doctrine that may apply to affect the determination of FDII and its components.

B. General Rules for FDDEI Transactions

1. Definitions of Sale, Foreign Person, and United States

Proposed § 1.250(b)-3 provides rules relevant to determining whether a sale of property is a FDDEI sale and whether a provision of a service is a FDDEI service.

Section 250(b)(5)(E) provides that for purposes of section 250(b), the term "sale" includes any lease, license, exchange, or other disposition. Accordingly, for purposes of determining whether a sale of property is a FDDEI sale, the proposed regulations define "sale" to include a lease, license, exchange, or other disposition of property, including a transfer of property resulting in gain or an income inclusion under section 367. See proposed § 1.250(b)-3(b)(7).

The proposed regulations define a foreign person as a person that is not a United States person, which includes a foreign government or international organization for purposes of the proposed regulations. See proposed § 1.250(b)-3(b)(2). A United States person ("U.S. person") has the same meaning as under section 7701(a)(30), except that an individual that is a bona fide resident of a U.S. territory within the meaning of section 937(a) is excluded. See proposed § 1.250(b)-3(b)(10). While corporations formed in U.S. territories are generally treated as foreign corporations, under section 7701(a)(30), U.S. persons include all U.S. citizens or residents, regardless of whether they reside in a U.S. territory. However, a bona fide resident of a U.S. territory is generally exempt from U.S. tax on income sourced in that territory. See sections 931(a), 932(c)(4), 933(1), and 935. Therefore, to prevent the disparate treatment of sales to entities in a U.S. territory (potentially qualifying as a FDDEI sale) and sales to individuals in a U.S. territory (not qualifying as a FDDEI sale), the proposed regulations exclude bona fide residents of a U.S. territory from the definition of U.S. person.

A partnership is generally a "person" for purposes of the Code. See section 7701(a)(1). Accordingly, in determining whether a sale of property to or by a partnership qualifies as a FDDEI sale, or the provision of a service to or by a partnership qualifies as a FDDEI service, the proposed regulations treat a partnership as a person. See proposed § 1.250(b)-3(g). Therefore, for example, a sale of property to a foreign partnership for a foreign use may constitute a FDDEI sale because such sale is to a foreign person, whereas a sale of property to a domestic partnership, even if for a foreign use, will not constitute a FDDEI sale because such sale is to a domestic person. The Treasury Department and the IRS request comments on whether there are circumstances where it would be appropriate to treat a partnership as an aggregate of its partners for purposes of determining whether a sale of property or a provision of a service to a partnership is a sale or service to a foreign person.

The proposed regulations provide that the term "United States" generally has the meaning described in section 7701(a)(9). See proposed § 1.250(b)-3(b)(9). However, with respect to mines, oil and gas wells, and other natural deposits, the term United States includes certain seabed and subsoil of submarine areas adjacent to the territorial waters of the United States, as described in section 638(1). See id.

2. Foreign Military Sales

The Treasury Department and the IRS recognize that the statute is unclear as to whether a sale of property or the provision of a service to the U.S. government for resale or on-service to a foreign government under the Arms Export Control Act of 1976, as amended (22 U.S.C. 2751 et seq.), may qualify for the section 250 deduction. In general, the Arms Export Control Act governs the export of certain sales and services to foreign governments. Under the Arms Export Control Act, a seller or service provider provides sales or services to the U.S. government that are for the ultimate benefit of a foreign government. The concern is that such sale or service to the U.S. government governed by the Arms Export Control Act is not a sale to a "person who is not a United States person" within the meaning of section 250(b)(4)(A) or a service to a "person not located within the United States" within the meaning of section 250(b)(4)(B), notwithstanding that such a sale or service is ultimately provided to the foreign government.

The proposed regulations provide that, for purposes of section 250, a sale of property or the provision of a service to the U.S. government under the Arms Export Control Act of 1976 is treated as a sale of property or provision of a service to a foreign government. See proposed § 1.250(b)-3(c). See part I(D)(3) of the Special Analyses section for additional discussion regarding the analysis for the adoption of this rule. As discussed in part III(B)(1) of this Explanation of Provisions section, a foreign government or international organization is a foreign person for purposes of section 250 and the proposed regulations. See proposed § 1.250(b)-3(b)(2). Therefore, a sale of property or provision of a service to the U.S. government under the Arms Export Control Act may qualify as a FDDEI transaction if the other requirements under proposed §§ 1.250(b)-3 through 1.250(b)-6 are satisfied. To the extent other requirements under proposed §§ 1.250(b)-3 through 1.250(b)-6 are not satisfied, a sale or service will not qualify as a FDDEI transaction regardless of whether such sale or service is pursuant to the Arms Export Control Act.

The Treasury Department and the IRS have not currently identified readily available documentation sufficient to demonstrate that a particular sale or service was made pursuant to the Arms Export Control Act. Comments are requested on whether final regulations should provide guidance on how taxpayers can demonstrate that a sale or service has been made pursuant to the Arms Export Control Act.

3. Knowledge and Reason to Know

As discussed in part III(C) of this Explanation of Provisions section, the proposed regulations provide that a sale of property qualifies as a FDDEI sale only if the seller or renderer does not know or have reason to know that the recipient is not a foreign person or that the property will not be for a foreign use. See proposed §1.250(b)-4(c), (d), and (e). In addition, as discussed in part III(D) of this Explanation of Provisions section, the proposed regulations provide that the provision of a general service (as defined in proposed §1.250(b)-5(c)(4)) qualifies as a FDDEI service only if the renderer of the service does not know or have reason to know that the recipient is located within the United States. See proposed §1.250(b)-5(d)(1) and (e)(1). The terms "know" and "reason to know" are used throughout the Code and Treasury regulations. The Treasury Department and the IRS request comments regarding whether definitions of "know" and "reason to know" are necessary for purposes of the section 250 regulations.

4. Reliability of Documentation

In order for a transaction to constitute a FDDEI transaction, the proposed regulations prescribe different types of documentation that are required to be obtained for each type of transaction. For example, in the case of a sale of property, the seller must obtain documentation that establishes the recipient's status as a foreign person. See proposed §1.250(b)-4(c)(2). See parts III(C) and III(D) of this Explanation of Provisions section for an explanation of the documentation requirements in these proposed regulations; see also part II of the Special Analyses section for a discussion of the Paperwork Reduction Act.

The proposed regulations provide that, for any documentation described in the proposed regulations to be relied upon, the seller or renderer must obtain the documentation by the FDII filing date, the documentation must be obtained no earlier than one year before the sale or service, and the seller or renderer must not know or have reason to know that the documentation is incorrect or unreliable. See proposed §1.250(b)-3(d); see also proposed §1.250(b)-3(b)(1) (defining the term "FDII filing date"). For this purpose, a seller or renderer has reason to know that documentation is unreliable or incorrect if its knowledge of all the relevant facts or statements contained in the documentation is such that a reasonably prudent person in the position of the seller or renderer would question the accuracy of the documentation. See proposed §1.250(b)-3(d)(1).

The Treasury Department and the IRS welcome comments on the documentation requirements in the proposed regulations.

5. Transactions Consisting of Both Sales and Services

Under section 250(b)(4) and (5) and these proposed regulations, the criteria for establishing that a transaction is foreign-derived is different for sales and services. For example, a transaction with a U.S. person that is located outside of the United States may qualify as a FDDEI service, but cannot qualify as a FDDEI sale. Because a transaction might include elements of both a sale and a service, the proposed regulations clarify that a transaction is classified according to the overall predominant character of the transaction. See proposed §1.250(b)-3(e). For example, a sale of equipment that includes incidental support services from the seller at no additional cost would be classified as a sale, and therefore the provisions of proposed §1.250(b)-4 would apply to determine whether gross income from the transaction is included in gross FDDEI.

6. Special Rule for Certain Loss Transactions

A domestic corporation's FDDEI includes all gross income included in gross DEI that is derived from FDDEI sales and FDDEI services in a taxable year, reduced by the amount of deductions properly allocable to such income. See proposed §1.250(b)-1(c)(12) and part III(A)(2) of this Explanation of Provisions section. In most cases, a FDDEI sale or FDDEI service will increase a domestic corporation's section 250 deduction, because the income from such sale or service will increase the corporation's FDDEI and thus its foreign-derived ratio. However, in some cases, a FDDEI sale or a FDDEI service could have the effect of reducing FDDEI and thus a domestic corporation's section 250 deduction for the year. This could happen where, for instance, the domestic corporation's cost of goods sold attributed to property sold in a FDDEI sale exceeds its gross receipts from the sale, or the expenses allocated to the gross income from a FDDEI sale or FDDEI service exceed the gross income arising from the sale or service. In such a case, absent a rule to the contrary, a domestic corporation could intentionally fail to satisfy the documentation requirements with respect to a transaction that would otherwise qualify as a FDDEI sale or FDDEI service in order to prevent the transaction from reducing its FDDEI and thereby its section 250 deduction.

Section 250(b) does not contemplate a transaction-by-transaction determination of FDII, but rather an aggregate calculation based on all gross income "which is derived in connection with" sales and services described in section 250(b)(4). Therefore, it would be inappropriate to permit taxpayers to elect to exclude losses related to sales to foreign persons for a foreign use and services to persons located outside the United States by merely failing the documentation requirements. Accordingly, the proposed regulations provide that if a seller or renderer knows or has reason to know that property is sold to a foreign person for a foreign use or a general service is provided to a person located outside the United States, but the seller or renderer does not satisfy the documentation requirements applicable to such sale or service, the sale of property or provision of a service is nonetheless deemed a FDDEI transaction if treating the sale or service as a FDDEI transaction would reduce a domestic corporation's FDDEI. See proposed § 1.250(b)-3(f).

The special loss transaction rule in proposed § 1.250(b)-3(f) does not apply to proximate services, property services, and transportation services, each of which is defined and discussed in part III(D)(3) through (5) of this Explanation of Provisions section, because the proposed regulations do not require documentation with respect to such services. Therefore, a proximate service, property service, or transportation service is a FDDEI service if it meets the applicable substantive requirements for a FDDEI service described in § 1.250(b)-5(f), (g), and (h), respectively.

C. FDDEI Sales

1. In General

Section 250(b)(4)(A) provides that FDDEI includes income from property the taxpayer sells to any person who is not a U.S. person, and which the taxpayer establishes to the satisfaction of the Secretary is for a foreign use. Accordingly, the proposed regulations define a FDDEI sale as a sale of property to a foreign person for a foreign use. See proposed § 1.250(b)-4(b).

2. Foreign Person

The proposed regulations provide that a recipient is treated as a foreign person only if the seller obtains documentation of the recipient's foreign status and does not know or have reason to know that the recipient is not a foreign person. See proposed § 1.250(b)-4(c)(1). The proposed regulations provide several types of permissible documentation for this purpose, such as a written statement by the recipient indicating that the recipient is a foreign person. See proposed § 1.250(b)-4(c)(2)(i). To alleviate the burden of documentation on small businesses and small transactions, the proposed regulations allow a seller that has less than $10,000,000 of gross receipts in the prior taxable year, or less than $5,000 in gross receipts from a single recipient during the current taxable year, to treat a recipient as a foreign person if the seller has a shipping address for the recipient that is outside the United States. See proposed § 1.250(b)-4(c)(2)(ii). The $10,000,000 and $5,000 thresholds were chosen based on the experience of the Treasury Department and the IRS and not based on any specific quantitative analysis. The Treasury Department and the IRS request comments regarding whether the $10,000,000 and $5,000 thresholds are appropriate and especially solicit comments that provide data, other evidence, and models that can enhance the rigor of the process by which such thresholds are determined.

3. Foreign Use

Under the proposed regulations, the rules applicable to the determination of whether a sale of property is for a foreign use depends on whether the property sold is "general property" or "intangible property." See proposed § 1.250(b)-4(d) and (e). The proposed regulations define general property as property other than intangible property, a security (as defined in section 475(c)(2)), or a commodity (as defined in section 475(e)(2)(B) through (D)). See proposed § 1.250(b)-3(b)(3). The proposed regulations define intangible property by cross-reference to section 367(d)(4). See proposed § 1.250(b)-3(b)(4).

The proposed regulations provide that a sale of a security (as defined in section 475(c)(2)) or a commodity (as defined in section 475(e)(2)(B) through (D)) is not a FDDEI sale because such financial instruments are not subject to "any use, consumption, or disposition" outside the United States within the meaning of section 250(b)(5)(A). See proposed § 1.250(b)-4(f).

The proposed regulations provide that a sale of property (whether general property or intangible property) is treated as for a foreign use only if the seller obtains documentation that the property is for a foreign use and does not know or have reason to know, as of the FDII filing date, that the property is not for a foreign use (or, in the case of intangible property, that the portion of the sale of the intangible property for which the seller establishes foreign use is not for a foreign use). See proposed § 1.250(b)-4(d)(1) and (e)(1). Accordingly, if, as of the FDII filing date, the seller does not know or have reason to know that either the documentation obtained with respect to the sale is not reliable or that the property is not for a foreign use within the meaning of § 1.250(b)-4(d)(2) or (e)(2), then the sale of the property is treated as for a foreign use under § 1.250(b)-4(d)(1) or (e)(1) even if, in fact, the sale of such property is not for a foreign use within the meaning of § 1.250(b)-4(d)(2) or (e)(2).

a. Foreign Use for General Property

The sale of general property is for a foreign use if either the property is not subject to domestic use within three years of delivery of the property or the property is subject to manufacture, assembly, or other processing outside the United States before any domestic use of the property. See proposed § 1.250(b)-4(d)(2)(i) and Conf. Rep. at 625, fn. 1522 ("If property is sold by a taxpayer to a person who is not a U.S. person, and after such sale the property is subject to manufacture, assembly, or other processing (including the incorporation of such property, as a component, into a second product by means of production, manufacture, or assembly) outside the United States by such person, then the property is for a foreign use."). Domestic use is defined as the use, consumption, or disposition of property within the United States, including manufacture, assembly, or other processing within the United States. See proposed § 1.250(b)-4(d)(2)(ii). Comments are requested on the supply chain implications of these rules.

General property is subject to manufacturing, assembly, or other processing only if it meets either of the following two tests: (1) there is a physical and material change to the property, or (2) the property is incorporated as a component into a second product. See proposed § 1.250(b)-4(d)(2)(iii)(A). The proposed regulations clarify that a physical and material change does not include "minor assembly, packaging, or labeling." See proposed § 1.250(b)-4(d)(2)(iii)(B). However, whether property has undergone a physical and material change (as opposed to minor assembly, packaging, or labeling) is determined based on all the relevant facts and circumstances. The Treasury Department and the IRS request comments regarding whether additional guidance should be provided for determining whether property has undergone a physical and material change.

General property is incorporated as a component into a second product only if the fair market value of the property when it is delivered to the recipient constitutes no more than 20 percent of the fair market value of the second product, determined when the second product is completed. See proposed § 1.250(b)-4(d)(2)(iii)(C). If the seller sells multiple items of property that are incorporated into the second product, an aggregation rule treats all of the property sold by the seller that is incorporated into the second product as a single item of property for purposes of determining whether the property constitutes more than 20 percent of the fair market value of the second product. See id.

In order to establish that general property is for a foreign use, the seller must generally obtain documentation with respect to the sale. See proposed § 1.250(b)-4(d)(3). Such documentation could include, for example, proof of shipment of the property to a foreign address. See proposed § 1.250(b)-4(d)(3)(i). However, in the case of certain small businesses and small transactions, the seller may rely on a foreign shipping address for the recipient instead of obtaining documentation. See proposed § 1.250(b)-4(d)(3)(ii).

In lieu of the general documentation requirements for determining foreign use for sales of general property, in the case of a sale of multiple items of general property, which because of their fungible nature cannot reasonably be specifically traced to the location of use ("fungible mass"), a seller may establish that some, but not all, of the property is for a foreign use through market research, including statistical sampling, economic modeling, and other similar methods. See proposed § 1.250(b)-4(d)(3)(iii). A de minimis rule applies to treat the entire fungible mass as for a foreign use if a seller obtains documentation establishing that 90 percent or more of the fungible mass is for a foreign use. See id. Conversely, no portion of the fungible mass is treated as for a foreign use if the seller does not obtain documentation establishing that 10 percent or more of the fungible mass is for a foreign use. Id.

A special rule applies for purposes of determining whether the sale of certain transportation property is for a foreign use, which takes into account the special nature of property used for international transportation. Specifically, the sale of aircraft, railroad rolling stock, vessel, motor vehicle, or similar property that provides a mode of transportation and is capable of traveling internationally is for a foreign use only if, during the three-year period from the date of delivery of the property, the property is located outside the United States more than 50 percent of the time and more than 50 percent of the miles traversed in the use of such property will be traversed outside the United States. See proposed § 1.250(b)-4(d)(2)(iv). The seller can establish that a sale of general property used for international transportation is for a foreign use through, for example, a written statement from the recipient that the property is anticipated to satisfy the test described in the preceding sentence. See proposed § 1.250(b)-4(d)(3)(i)(A).

b. Foreign Use for Intangible Property

As discussed in part III(B) of this Explanation of Provisions section, a sale includes a license and any transfer of property in which gain or income is recognized under section 367, including a transfer of intangible property subject to section 367(d). See proposed § 1.250(b)-3(b)(7). The proposed regulations provide that a sale of intangible property is for a foreign use to the extent revenue is earned from exploiting the intangible property outside the United States, the documentation requirements are satisfied, and the seller does not know or have reason to know that the portion of the sale of the intangible property for which the seller establishes foreign use is not for a foreign use. See proposed § 1.250(b)-4(e)(1). Unlike a sale of general property (other than a sale of a fungible mass), a seller may establish foreign use for a portion of the income from the sale of intangible property. For purposes of determining whether a sale of intangible property is for a foreign use, the location where revenue is earned is generally determined based on the location of end-user customers licensing the intangible property or purchasing products for which the intangible property was used in development, manufacture, sale, or distribution. See proposed § 1.250(b)-4(e)(2). This determination is generally made on an annual basis based on the actual revenue earned by the recipient. Id.

Special rules apply to lump sum sales because, in these cases, it may be difficult or impossible to know the location where revenue will be generated when the sale occurs. The determination of foreign use in these cases is made based on the net present value of revenue the seller would have reasonably expected to earn from the exploitation of the intangible property. See proposed § 1.250(b)-4(e)(2)(iii). For sales of rights to intangible property for use both within and outside the United States, the seller must establish the proportionate amount of revenue earned within and outside the United States from use of the intangible property to establish foreign use. The proposed regulations describe documentation that can be used to establish where revenue is earned from use of the intangible property. See proposed § 1.250(b)-4(e)(3)(i). For example, if a domestic corporation licenses to a foreign person the worldwide rights to market and sell an item protected by a copyright, the domestic corporation would need to obtain documentation, as provided in the proposed regulations, establishing where revenue is earned from sales of the copyright-protected item.

A seller may establish the extent to which a sale of intangible property for a lump sum is for a foreign use through documentation containing reasonable projections of the amount and location of revenue that the seller would have reasonably expected to earn from the use of intangible property. See proposed § 1.250(b)-4(e)(3)(iii). To be considered reasonable, the net present value must be consistent with the financial data and projections used by the seller to determine the sales price to the foreign person. See id. The same rule for documentation applies to a sale to a foreign person (other than a related party of the seller) for annual payments that are not contingent on revenue or profit unless the seller has access to reliable information to determine the actual revenue earned by the foreign unrelated party from the exploitation of the intangible property. See proposed § 1.250(b)-4(e)(3)(ii).

As discussed in part III(C)(3)(a) of this Explanation of Provisions section, a sale of general property is treated as for a foreign use if the property is subject to manufacturing, assembly, or other processing outside the United States. See proposed § 1.250(b)-4(d)(2)(i)(B). This rule is based on footnote 1522 of the Conference Report, which provides that "[i]f property is sold by a taxpayer to a person who is not a U.S. person, and after such sale the property is subject to manufacture, assembly, or other processing (including the incorporation of such property, as a component, into a second product by means of production, manufacture, or assembly) outside the United States by such person, then the property is for a foreign use." Intangible property is not "subject to" manufacture, assembly, or processing, and there is no other discussion in the Conference Report that indicates an intent to provide an analogous rule for intangible property otherwise used in the manufacturing process. However, comments are requested on whether a rule for intangible property similar to proposed § 1.250(b)-4(d)(2)(i)(B) is appropriate. Comments are also requested on what additional rules may be needed for determining the location of revenue generation from end-users and what types of documentation should be accepted to document the location of revenue generation with respect to intangible property.

D. FDDEI Services

1. In General

Section 250(b)(4)(B) provides that FDDEI includes income from services provided by a domestic corporation to any person, or with respect to property, not located within the United States. Section 250 does not prescribe rules for determining whether a person or property is "not located within the United States." Proposed § 1.250(b)-5 provides rules for determining whether a service is provided to a person, or with respect to property, located outside the United States.

Under the proposed regulations, whether a service is provided to a person, or with respect to property, located outside the United States, depends on the type of service provided and, in the case of a general service (defined below), the type of recipient of the service. The proposed regulations distinguish between services where the service provider (the "renderer") and the recipient are in physical proximity when the service is performed ("proximate services"), services with respect to tangible property ("property services"), services to transport people or property ("transportation services"), and all other services ("general services"). See proposed § 1.250(b)-5(b) and (c)(4) through (7). For purposes of determining whether a service constitutes a FDDEI service, the proposed regulations look to the location of the performance of the service for proximate services, the location of the property for property services, the origin and destination of transportation services, and the location of the recipient for general services. See proposed § 1.250(b)-5(d) through (h).

Each category of service described in § 1.250(b)-5 is mutually exclusive of each other category, and every possible service is described in a single category. Therefore, whether a service is a FDDEI service is determined under the rules relevant to one, and only one, category of service described in § 1.250(b)-5. For example, a general service that is provided to a recipient located within the United States is not a FDDEI service, even if the service is performed outside the United States, whereas a property service that is performed outside the United States is a FDDEI service, even if the recipient of the service is located within the United States. See parts III(D)(2) and (4) of this Explanation of Provisions section.

2. General Services to Persons Located Outside the United States

A general service is a service other than a proximate service, a property service, or a transportation service. See proposed § 1.250(b)-5(c)(4). General services is the residual category of services. Accordingly, a service that is not a property service, a transportation service, or a proximate service is analyzed as a general service.

For general services, the proposed regulations distinguish between services provided to "consumers" and services provided to "business recipients." A consumer is defined as an individual that purchases a service for personal consumption. See proposed § 1.250(b)-5(c)(3). A business recipient is defined as any recipient other than a consumer. See proposed § 1.250(b)-5(c)(2). In both cases, general services are treated as provided to a person located outside the United States if the renderer does not know or have reason to know that the consumer or business recipient is located within the United States and obtains appropriate documentation. See proposed § 1.250(b)-5(d)(1) and (e)(1).

a. General Services to Consumers

The provision of a general service to a consumer located outside the United States is a FDDEI service. See proposed § 1.250(b)-5(b)(1). The proposed regulations provide that the consumer is located where a consumer resides when the service is provided. See proposed § 1.250(b)-5(d)(2).

The proposed regulations require a domestic corporation to document the location of the consumer. See proposed § 1.250(b)-5(d)(1) and (3). The proposed regulations provide several types of permissible documentation for this purpose, including a written statement by the consumer indicating the residence of the consumer when the service is provided. See proposed § 1.250(b)-5(d)(3)(i). However, in the case of certain small businesses and small transactions, the renderer may rely on a foreign billing address for the consumer instead of obtaining documentation. See proposed § 1.250(b)-5(d)(3)(ii).

b. General Services to Business Recipients

The provision of a general service to a business recipient located outside the United States is a FDDEI service. See proposed § 1.250(b)-5(b)(2). Under the proposed regulations, all general services that are not provided to consumers are treated as services provided to business recipients, regardless of whether the recipient is engaged in a trade or business. See proposed § 1.250(b)-5(c)(2).

The proposed regulations determine the location of a business recipient based on the location of the business recipient's operations, and the operations of any related party of the recipient, that receive a benefit (as defined in § 1.482-9(l)(3)) from such service. See proposed § 1.250(b)-5(e)(2) and (4). For purposes of this determination, the location of residence, incorporation, or formation of a business recipient is not relevant. For example, a general service that confers a benefit only on the U.S. operations of a foreign person will generally not qualify as a FDDEI service, whereas a service that confers a benefit only on the foreign operations of a U.S. person will generally qualify as a FDDEI service. For purposes of this rule, a business recipient is treated as having operations in any location where it maintains an office or other fixed place of business. See proposed § 1.250(b)-5(e)(2)(ii).

The proposed regulations provide that a service is generally provided to a business recipient located outside the United States to the extent that the renderer's gross income from providing the service is allocated to the business recipient's operations outside the United States. See proposed § 1.250(b)-5(e)(2)(i). To make this allocation, the renderer must first determine which of the business recipient's operations receive a benefit from the service. See proposed § 1.250(b)-5(e)(2)(i)(A). Where the service confers a benefit on the operations of the business recipient in specific locations, gross income of the renderer is allocated based on the location of the operations in specific locations that receive the benefit. See id. Where a service confers a benefit on the recipient's business as a whole, or where reliable information about the particular portion of the operations that specifically receive a benefit from the service is unavailable, the proposed regulations provide that the service is deemed to confer a benefit on all of the business recipient's operations. See id. The renderer then must allocate its gross income from providing the service between the operations that receive a benefit from the service that are located within and outside the United States. See proposed § 1.250(b)-5(e)(2)(i)(B). For this purpose, any reasonable method may be used, and the principles of § 1.482-9(k) apply to determine whether a method is reasonable. See id. A reasonable method may include, for example, an allocation based on the renderer's time spent working with different offices of the business recipient or publicly available information about the business recipient's revenue from different markets. See id. The Treasury Department and the IRS request comments on this approach for determining the location of a business recipient that operates both within and outside of the United States.

The proposed regulations also require a domestic corporation to obtain documentation sufficient to establish the location of a business recipient's operations that benefit from the service. See proposed § 1.250(b)-5(e)(1) and (3). A domestic corporation may obtain a statement from the recipient specifying the location of the operations that will benefit from the service or include a similar statement in a binding contract. See proposed § 1.250(b)-5(e)(3)(i)(A) and (B). A domestic corporation may also establish the location of the business recipient using information provided in the ordinary course of the provision of a service or publicly available information. See proposed § 1.250(b)-5(e)(3)(i)(C) and (D). However, in the case of certain small businesses and small transactions, the renderer may rely on a foreign billing address for the business recipient instead of obtaining documentation. See proposed § 1.250(b)-5(e)(3)(ii).

3. Proximate Services

The provision of a proximate service to a recipient located outside the United States is a FDDEI service. See proposed § 1.250(b)-5(b)(3). A proximate service is defined as a service, other than a property service or a transportation service, substantially all of which is performed in the physical presence of the recipient or, in the case of a business recipient, its employees. See proposed § 1.250(b)-5(c)(6). For example, a training, consulting, or auditing service that is performed on-site would generally constitute a proximate service. Substantially all of a service is performed in the physical presence of the recipient or its employees if the renderer spends more than 80 percent of the time providing the service in the physical presence of the recipient or its employees. See proposed § 1.250(b)-5(c)(6). The recipient of a proximate service is treated as located where the service is performed. See proposed § 1.250(b)-5(f). If a proximate service is performed partly within and partly outside the United States, a proportionate amount of the service is treated as rendered to a person located outside the United States corresponding to the portion of time spent providing the proximate service outside the United States. See id.

4. Property Services

The provision of a property service with respect to tangible property located outside the United States is a FDDEI service. See proposed § 1.250(b)-5(b)(4). A property service is defined as a service, other than a transportation service, provided with respect to tangible property, but only if substantially all of the service is performed at the location of the property and results in physical manipulation of the property such as through assembly, maintenance, or repair. See proposed § 1.250(b)-5(c)(5). The proposed regulations provide that substantially all of a service is performed at the location of property if the renderer spends more than 80 percent of the time providing the service at or near the location of the property. See id. A property service is a FDDEI service only if the tangible property with respect to which the service is performed is located outside the United States for the duration of the period of performance. See proposed § 1.250(b)-5(g). The Treasury Department and the IRS request comments on whether to consider an exception for property that is located in the United States temporarily solely for purposes of the performance of certain services, such as maintenance or repairs. As discussed in part III(E) of this Explanation of Provisions section, a property service may qualify as a FDDEI service even if it is performed for a person located within the United States.

Other services that relate to property but may not necessarily be provided in close proximity to tangible property or do not result in the physical manipulation of such property such as through assembly, maintenance, or repair may be subject to the rules for proximate services, transportation services, or general services. For example, an architectural or engineering service that is not performed in physical proximity to the property or the recipient will be evaluated as a general service even if the service relates to property located outside the United States, and thus whether such a service is a FDDEI service will be determined based on the location of the recipient rather than the location of the property.

5. Transportation Services

The provision of a transportation service to a recipient, or with respect to property, located outside the United States is a FDDEI service. See proposed § 1.250(b)-5(b)(5). A transportation service is defined as a service to transport a person or property using any mode of transportation (such as an airplane). See proposed § 1.250(b)-5(c)(7).

Basing the location of a transportation service on the residence of the recipient of the transportation service could provide inconsistent results with respect to similar services. Similarly, providing different rules for the transportation of a person or property could provide inconsistent results with respect to similar services. Therefore, the proposed regulations provide that whether a "transportation service" is provided to a recipient, or with respect to property, located outside the United States is determined based on the origin and destination of the service. See proposed § 1.250(b)-5(h). If both the origin and destination of a transportation service are outside of the United States, then the service is a FDDEI service. See id. If either the origin or the destination of the transportation service is outside of the United States, but not both, then 50 percent of the service is a FDDEI service and thus 50 percent of the gross income from the provision of the service is included in the renderer's gross FDDEI. See id.

E. Domestic Intermediary Rules

Section 250(b)(5)(B) describes special rules for "domestic intermediaries" (the "domestic intermediary rules"). Section 250(b)(5)(B)(i) provides that if a seller sells property to another person (other than a related party) for further manufacture or other modification within the United States, the property is not treated as sold for a foreign use even if such other person subsequently uses such property for a foreign use. Section 250(b)(5)(B)(ii) provides that services provided to a person (other than a related party) located within the United States are not treated as services described in section 250(b)(4)(B) even if such other person uses such services in providing services that are described in section 250(b)(4)(B).

The proposed regulations do not contain specific rules corresponding to the domestic intermediary rules because those rules are encompassed within the general rules relating to FDDEI sales and FDDEI services in the proposed regulations. With respect to sales of property, the proposed regulations provide that general property is not for a foreign use if, before being subject to manufacture, assembly, or other processing outside the United States, the property is subject to a domestic use. See proposed § 1.250(b)-4(d)(2)(i). For this purpose, domestic use includes manufacture, assembly, or other processing within the United States. See proposed § 1.250(b)-4(d)(2)(ii)(B). In addition, a sale of property to a U.S. person cannot qualify as a FDDEI sale under any circumstance. See section 250(b)(4)(A) and proposed § 1.250(b)-4(b). Therefore, a sale of property to a foreign person for further manufacture in the United States or to a U.S. person does not qualify for a FDDEI sale, regardless of the ultimate use of the property by the recipient.

With respect to the provision of services, the proposed regulations provide that a service is a FDDEI service only if the recipient of the service, or the property to which the service relates, is located outside the United States. See proposed § 1.250(b)-5(b)(1) through (5). Therefore, a service provided to a person, or with respect to property, located within the United States is not a FDDEI service, regardless of the ultimate use of the service by the recipient.

Section 250(b)(5)(B)(ii) could be read literally to provide that a FDDEI service includes only services provided to a person not located within the United States, in which case a service provided "with respect to property located outside the United States" would not qualify as a FDDEI service if the recipient of such service was located within the United States. As discussed in part III(D) of this

Explanation of Provisions section, consistent with the general rule of section 250(b)(4)(B), the proposed regulations clarify that a service qualifies as a FDDEI service if it is provided either to a person located outside the United States or with respect to property located outside the United States. The Treasury Department and the IRS have determined that an interpretation of section 250(b)(5)(B)(ii) that effectively eliminates the disjunctive test of section 250(b)(4)(B) would not be reasonable. Therefore, under the proposed regulations, whether a service that is treated as with respect to property — a property service or a transportation service — is a FDDEI service is determined solely by reference to the location of the property, and not the location of the recipient. See proposed § 1.250(b)-5(g) and (h).

Finally, the parenthetical references to related parties in the domestic intermediary rules could be read to imply the existence of an exception for further manufacture or modification in the United States by a related party or a service provided to a related party located within the United States. However, the general rules of section 250(b)(4)(A) and (B) do not authorize such exceptions, and the domestic intermediary rules do not purport to expand these general rules, but rather to limit the transactions that qualify under them. Therefore, with respect to related party domestic intermediaries, the proposed regulations do not provide an exception to the general rule that property must be sold to a foreign person to qualify as a FDDEI sale or that a service must be provided to a person located outside the United States to qualify as a FDDEI service. Cf. part V of this Explanation of Provisions section regarding the applicability of the attribute redetermination rule of § 1.1502-13(c)(1)(i) to the determination of FDDEI of a member of a consolidated group.

F. Related Party Transactions

A sale of property or a provision of a service may qualify as a FDDEI transaction, regardless of whether the recipient of such service is a related party of the seller or renderer. However, in the case of a sale of general property or a provision of a general service to a related party, section 250(b)(5)(C) and proposed § 1.250(b)-6 provide additional requirements that must be satisfied for the transaction to qualify as a FDDEI sale or FDDEI service. These requirements must be satisfied in addition to the general requirements that apply to such sales and services as provided in proposed §§ 1.250(b)-3 through 1.250(b)-5.

The proposed regulations define a related party with respect to any person as any member of a modified affiliated group that includes such person. Proposed § 1.250(b)-1(c)(19). A modified affiliated group is defined as an affiliated group as provided in section 1504(a) by substituting "more than 50 percent" for "at least 80 percent" each place it appears, and without regard to section 1504(b)(2) and (3). Proposed § 1.250(b)-1(c)(17)(i). A modified affiliated group also includes any person other than a corporation that is controlled by one or more members of a modified affiliated group or that controls such a member. Proposed § 1.250(b)-1(c)(17)(ii). For this purpose, "control" is defined as provided in section 954(d)(3), meaning direct, indirect, or constructive ownership under section 958 of more than 50 percent of the value of the beneficial interests in such person. Proposed § 1.250(b)-1(c)(17)(iii).

1. Related Party Sales

Section 250(b)(5)(C)(i) provides that property sold to a related party that is not a U.S. person "shall not be treated as for a foreign use unless (I) such property is ultimately sold by a related party, or used by a related party in connection with property which is sold or the provision of services, to another person who is an unrelated party who is not a United States person, and (II) the taxpayer establishes to the satisfaction of the Secretary that such property is for a foreign use." Accordingly, the proposed regulations provide that a sale of general property to a foreign related party (a "related party sale") qualifies as a FDDEI sale only if certain additional requirements described in § 1.250(b)-6(c)(1)(i) or (ii) are satisfied. See proposed § 1.250(b)-6(c)(1).

If a foreign related party resells the purchased property (such as where the foreign related party is a distributor or a manufacturer of a product that incorporates the purchased property as a component), the sale to the foreign related party qualifies as a FDDEI sale only if an unrelated party transaction with respect to such sale occurs and the unrelated party transaction is a FDDEI sale. An unrelated party transaction is generally a transaction between the foreign related party and an unrelated foreign person in which the property purchased by the foreign related party is sold or used. See proposed § 1.250(b)-6(b)(5). For purposes of this rule, whether property is a component of another property that is subsequently sold in an unrelated party transaction is determined without regard to the rule defining a "component" for purposes of determining whether general property is subject to manufacturing, assembly, or other processing, as described in part III(C)(3)(a) of this Explanation of Provisions section. The unrelated party sale generally must occur on or before the FDII filing date; otherwise the gross income from the related party sale is included in the domestic corporation's gross DEI for the taxable year of the related party sale, but is not included in its gross FDDEI. See proposed § 1.250(b)-6(c)(1)(i). However, if an unrelated party transaction occurs after the FDII filing date but within the period of limitations provided by section 6511, the proposed regulations provide that the domestic corporation may file an amended return for the taxable year in which the related party sale occurred claiming the related party sale as a FDDEI sale for purposes of determining the taxpayer's foreign-derived intangible income for that taxable year, provided that the sale otherwise meets the requirements in proposed § 1.250(b)-6(c)(1)(i). See id. The Treasury Department and the IRS welcome comments on whether alternatives should be considered in lieu of requiring the filing of an amended return.

For transactions other than the resale of purchased property, such as where the foreign related party uses the purchased property to produce other property that is sold in unrelated party transactions, or where the foreign related party uses the property in the provision of a service in an unrelated party transaction, the sale of property does not qualify as a FDDEI sale unless, as of the FDII filing date, the seller reasonably expects that more than 80 percent of the revenue earned by the foreign related party from the use of the property in all transactions will be earned from unrelated party transactions that are FDDEI transactions (determined without regard to the documentation requirements in § 1.250(b)-4 or § 1.250(b)-5). See proposed § 1.250(b)-6(c)(1)(ii).

The rules applicable to related party sales apply only to determine whether sales of general property qualify as a FDDEI sale. See proposed § 1.250(b)-6(c)(1). Sales of intangible property, whether to a related or an unrelated party, are for a foreign use only to the extent that the intangible property generated revenue from exploitation outside the United States. See proposed § 1.250(b)-4(e)(2) and part III(C)(3)(b) of this Explanation of Provisions section. Thus, additional rules with respect to related party sales of intangible property are unnecessary to ensure that such sales are ultimately for a foreign use.

2. Related Party Services

Section 250(b)(5)(C)(ii) provides that a service provided to a related party not located in the United States "shall not be treated [as a FDDEI service] unless the taxpayer establishe[s] to the satisfaction of the Secretary that such service is not substantially similar to services provided by such related party to persons located within the United States." Accordingly, the proposed regulations generally provide that a provision of a general service to a business recipient that is a related party qualifies as a FDDEI service only if the service is not substantially similar to a service provided by the related party to persons located within the United States. See proposed § 1.250(b)-6(d)(1).

Absent section 250(b)(5)(C)(ii) and proposed § 1.250(b)-6(d)(1) (the "related party services rule"), a domestic corporation could generate gross FDDEI from the provision of services that primarily benefit persons within the United States by using a related party located outside the United States as a conduit. The related party services rule prevents taxpayers from claiming gross FDDEI derived from such "round tripping" arrangements. In contrast, proximate services, property services, and transportation services by their nature present minimal risk for "round tripping," because the location of the recipient or property, as applicable, for purposes of such services is generally determined based on the place of performance. See proposed § 1.250(b)-5(f), (g), and (h), and parts III(D)(3), (4), and (5) of this Explanation of Provisions section. Further, a general service provided to a consumer that is a related party cannot be substantially similar to a service provided by a consumer to a person located within the United States, because a consumer, by definition, is an individual that purchases the service for personal use. See proposed § 1.250(b)-5(c)(3). Accordingly, the proposed regulations provide that the related party services rule applies only to determine whether a general service provided to a business recipient that is a related party is a FDDEI service. See proposed § 1.250(b)-6(d)(1).

A service provided by a renderer to a related party is "substantially similar" to a service provided by the related party to a person located within the United States if the renderer's service (or "related party service") is used by the related party to provide a service to a person located within the United States and either the "benefit test" of proposed § 1.250(b)-6(d)(2)(i) or the "price test" of proposed § 1.250(b)-6(d)(2)(ii) is satisfied. The rules to determine the location of a recipient of a service provided by a related party are generally the same as the rules for determining the location of a recipient of a service provided by the renderer.

The benefit test is satisfied if 60 percent or more of the benefits conferred by the related party service are to persons located within the United States. See proposed § 1.250(b)-6(d)(2)(i). For this purpose, the term "benefit" has the meaning provided in § 1.482-9(l)(3). See proposed § 1.250(b)-5(c)(1). Therefore, a related party service provides a benefit to a customer of the related party if it provides "a reasonably identifiable increment of economic or commercial value" to the customer, rather than an indirect or remote benefit. See § 1.482-9(l)(3)(i) and (ii). Because the benefit test compares the benefits from the service provided to persons located in the United States to the total benefits from the service provided by the renderer (rather than to the total benefits of the service provided by the related party), a service provided to a related party is "substantially similar" to a service provided by the related party to persons located within the United States if 60 percent or more of the benefits of the service are conferred on persons located within the United States, even if the related party adds significant value to the service through, for instance, bundling the related party service with other high value services.

Under the price test, a service provided by a renderer to a related party is "substantially similar" to a service provided by the related party to a person located within the United States if the renderer's service is used by the related party to provide a service to a person located within the United States and 60 percent or more of the price that persons located within the United States pay for the service provided by the related party is attributable to the renderer's service. See proposed § 1.250(b)-6(d)(2)(ii). Therefore, the price test compares the value of the service that is provided by the renderer to the related party to the value of the service that is provided by the related party to its customers. Consequently, a related party service that is not treated as substantially similar to a service provided by the related party to persons located in the United States under the benefit test, because more than 40 percent of the benefits from the service are conferred to persons located outside the United States, is nonetheless treated as "substantially similar" under the price test if the related party service accounts for 60 percent or more of the total price that is charged to customers located within the United States.

If a related party service is treated as substantially similar to a service provided by the related party to a person located within the United States solely by reason of the price test, the general rule that wholly disqualifies the related party service as a FDDEI service does not apply. Rather, in such case, a portion of the gross income from the related party service will be treated as a FDDEI service corresponding to the ratio of benefits conferred by the related party service to persons not located within the United States to the sum of all benefits conferred by the related party service. See proposed § 1.250(b)-6(d)(1).

IV. *Section 250 Deduction for Individuals Making a Section 962 Election*

As discussed in part II of this Explanation of Provisions section, the section 250 deduction for FDII and GILTI is available only to domestic corporations. However, section 962(a)(1) provides that an individual that is a U.S. shareholder may generally elect to be taxed on amounts included in the individual's gross income under section 951(a) in "an amount equal to the tax that would be imposed under section 11 if such amounts were received by a domestic corporation." GILTI is treated as an amount included under section 951(a) for purposes of section 962. See section 951A(f)(1)(A) and proposed § 1.951A-6(b)(1). A section 962 election can be made by an individual U.S. shareholder who is considered, by reason of section 958(b), to own stock of a foreign corporation owned (within the meaning of section 958(a)) by a domestic pass-through entity, including a partnership or an S corporation. See § 1.962-2(a).

Congress enacted section 962 to ensure that individuals' tax burdens with respect to undistributed foreign earnings of their CFCs "will be no heavier than they would have been had they invested in an American corporation doing business abroad." S. Rept. 1881, 1962-3 C.B. 784, at 798. Existing § 1.962-1(b)(1)(i) provides that a deduction of a U.S. shareholder does not reduce the amount included in gross income under section 951(a) for purposes of computing the amount of tax that would be imposed under section 11. However, allowing a section 250 deduction with respect to GILTI of an individual (including an individual that is a shareholder of an S corporation or a partner in a partnership) that makes an election under section 962 is consistent with the purpose of that provision of ensuring that such individual's tax burden with respect to its CFC's undistributed foreign earnings is no greater than if the individual owned such CFC through a domestic corporation. Accordingly, the proposed regulations provide that, for purposes of section 962, "taxable income" as used in section 11 of an electing individual is reduced by the portion of the section 250 deduction that would be allowed to a domestic corporation with respect to the individual's GILTI and the section 78 gross-up attributable to the shareholder's GILTI. See proposed § 1.962-1(b)(1)(i)(B)(*3*).

V. *Application of Section 250 to Consolidated Groups*

As discussed in the Background section of this preamble, section 250 provides a domestic corporation a deduction for its FDII, GILTI, and the section 78 gross-up attributable to its GILTI. The section 250 deduction is available to a member of a consolidated group ("member") in the same manner as the deduction is available to any domestic corporation. However, a computation of a member's section 250 deduction based solely on its items of income and QBAI may not result in a clear reflection of the consolidated group's income tax liability. For example, a consolidated group could segregate all of its QBAI in one member, thereby decreasing the DTIR of other members relative to the consolidated group's DTIR if determined at a group level. Alternatively, a strict, separate-entity application of section 250 could inappropriately decrease a consolidated group's aggregate amount of deduction for its FDII, for instance, because one member's DII (which is the excess of DEI over DTIR) would not be taken into account in calculating the FDII of another member that has FDDEI in excess of its DEI.

Based on the foregoing, the proposed regulations provide that a member's section 250 deduction is determined by reference to the relevant items of all members of the same consolidated group. Consistent with the authority provided by section 1502, the proposed regulations ensure that the aggregate amount of section 250 deductions allowed to members appropriately reflects the income, expenses, gains, losses, and property of all members. Definitions in proposed § 1.1502-50(f) result in the aggregation of the DEI, FDDEI, DTIR, and GILTI of all members. These aggregate numbers and the consolidated group's consolidated taxable income are then used to calculate an overall deduction amount for the group. Proposed § 1.1502-50(b) then allocates this overall deduction amount among the members on the basis of their respective contributions to the consolidated group's aggregate amount of FDDEI and the consolidated group's aggregate amount of GILTI.

The proposed regulations also address two issues relating to intercompany transactions. First, the proposed regulations add an example to § 1.1502-13 demonstrating the applicability of the attribute redetermination rule of § 1.1502-13(c)(1)(i) to the determination of FDDEI. This example applies the intercompany transaction rules to clearly reflect consolidated taxable income. It does not indicate a change in the law. In this example, the attribute redetermination rule applies to gross DEI and gross FDDEI, which are attributes of an intercompany or corresponding item. The Treasury Department and the IRS were concerned that applying § 1.1502-13(c) to DEI and FDDEI directly could result in circular computations due to the apportionment of certain expenses on a gross income basis. In addition, the example illustrates the applicability of the attribute redetermination rule in the context of an intercompany loss. In such circumstances, the application of the allocation and apportionment rules of § § 1.861-8 through 1.861-14T and 1.861-17 may be modified in order to achieve the same overall result within the consolidated group that would occur if the members were divisions of a single corporation.

Second, the proposed regulations provide that, for purposes of determining a member's QBAI, the basis of specified tangible property will not be affected by an intercompany transaction. See proposed § 1.1502-50(c)(1). Accordingly, an intercompany transaction cannot result in the increase or decrease of a consolidated group's aggregate amount of DTIR or, in turn, aggregate amount of deduction.

VI. *Reporting Requirements*

To claim a deduction under section 250 by reason of having FDII, a taxpayer must calculate its deemed intangible income, deduction eligible income, and foreign-derived deduction eligible income. None of these terms are used in other provisions of the Code, and thus pre-existing forms do not collect data relevant to determining these amounts. In addition, when calculating its deduction under section 250, a taxpayer must determine the application of the taxable income limitation of section 250(a)(2). In order to effectively administer and enforce section 250, the proposed regulations require the collection of relevant information on new or existing forms.

A domestic corporation or an individual making an election under section 962 that claims a deduction under section 250 for a taxable year must make an annual return on Form 8993, "Section 250 Deduction for Foreign-Derived Intangible Income (FDII) and Global Intangible Low-Taxed Income (GILTI)" (or any successor form) for such year, providing the information required by the form. See proposed § 1.250(a)-1(d).

Certain related party transactions are reported on various information returns under sections 6038 and 6038A. Under section 6038(a)(1), U.S. persons that control foreign business entities ("controlling U.S. persons") must report certain information with respect to those entities, which includes information listed in section 6038(a)(1)(A) through (E), as well as information that "the Secretary determines to be appropriate to carry out the provisions of this title." This information is reported on Form 5471, "Information Return of U.S. Persons With Respect To Certain Foreign Corporations," or Form 8865, "Return of U.S. Persons With Respect to Certain Foreign Partnerships," as applicable. Section 6038A requires 25-percent foreign-owned domestic corporations ("reporting corporations") to file certain information returns with respect to those corporations, including information related to transactions between the reporting corporation and each foreign person which is a related party to the reporting corporation. This information is reported on Form 5472, "Information Return of a 25% Foreign-Owned U.S. Corporation or a Foreign Corporation Engaged in a U.S. Trade or Business." In order to effectively administer and enforce section 250, the proposed regulations provide that controlling U.S. persons or reporting corporations, as described above, that claim a deduction under section 250 determined by reference to FDII with respect to amounts reported on Form 5471, 5472, or 8865 must report certain information relating to transactions with foreign business entities or related parties in accordance with sections 6038 and 6038A. See proposed § § 1.6038-2(f)(15), 1.6038-3(g)(4), and 1.6038A-2(b)(5)(iv).

Certain partnerships and their partners also have reporting requirements under sections 6031 and 6038 with respect to partnership income. A domestic partnership is generally required to file an annual information return (Form 1065, "U.S. Return of Partnership Income") and provide information to its partners on Schedule K-1 (Form 1065), "Partner's Share of Income, Deductions, Credits, etc.," with respect to each partner's distributive share of partnership items and other information. See section 6031 and § 1.6031(b)-1T. The proposed regulations provide that a partnership that has one or more direct or indirect partners that are domestic corporations and that is required to file a return under section 6031 must furnish on Schedule K-1 (Form 1065) the partner's share of the partnership's gross DEI, gross FDDEI, deductions that are definitely related to the partnership's gross DEI and gross FDDEI, and partnership QBAI for each taxable year in which the partnership has gross DEI, gross FDDEI, or partnership specified tangible property. See proposed § 1.250(b)-1(e)(2). Although a foreign partnership that does not have income effectively connected with a trade or business within the United States or U.S. source income is not required to file Form 1065, a U.S. person who owns a ten-percent interest or a fifty-percent interest of a foreign partnership controlled by U.S. persons is required to report certain information under section 6038. Similar to the requirements for partnership reporting on Form 1065, the proposed regulations require controlling ten-percent partners and controlling fifty-percent partners (as defined in § 1.6038-3(a)(1) and (2)) of certain foreign partnerships controlled by U.S. persons to report on Schedule K-1 (Form 8865), "Partner's Share of Income, Deductions, Credits, etc.," the partner's share of the partnership's gross DEI, gross FDDEI, deductions that are definitely related to the partnership's gross DEI and gross FDDEI, and partnership QBAI. See proposed § 1.6038-3(g)(4).

VII. *Applicability Dates*

Proposed § § 1.250(a)-1 through 1.250(b)-6 are proposed to apply to taxable years ending on or after March 4, 2019. See section 7805(b)(1)(B). However, the Treasury Department and the IRS recognize that these rules may apply to transactions that have occurred before the filing of these proposed regulations and that taxpayers may not be able to obtain the documentation required for transactions that have already been completed. Accordingly, for taxable years beginning on or before March 4, 2019, taxpayers may use any reasonable documentation maintained in the ordinary course of the taxpayer's business that establishes that a recipient is a foreign person, property is for a foreign use (within the meaning of proposed § 1.250(b)-4(d) and (e)), or a recipient of a general service is located outside the United States (within the meaning of proposed § 1.250(b)-5(d)(2) and (e)(2)), as applicable, in lieu of the documentation required in proposed § § 1.250(b)-4(c)(2), (d)(3), and (e)(3) and 1.250(b)-5(d)(3) and (e)(3), provided that such documentation meets the reliability requirements described in proposed § 1.250(b)-3(d). Reasonable documentation includes, but is not limited to, documents described in or similar to the documents described in proposed § § 1.250(b)-4(c)(2), (d)(3), and (e)(3) and 1.250(b)-5(d)(3) and (e)(3). For this purpose, reasonable documentation also includes the documentation described in the special rules for small businesses and small transactions in proposed § § 1.250(b)-4(c)(2)(ii) and (d)(3)(ii) and 1.250(b)-5(d)(3)(ii) and (e)(3)(ii), even if the taxpayer would not otherwise qualify for the special rules. The Treasury Department and the IRS welcome comments on this special applicability date rule.

Proposed § 1.962-1(b)(1)(i)(B)(3), which allows individuals making an election under section 962 to take into account the section 250 deduction, is proposed to apply to taxable years of a foreign corporation ending on or after March 4, 2019, and with respect to a U.S. person, for the taxable year in which or with which such taxable year of the foreign corporations ends. See id. Taxpayers may rely on proposed § § 1.250(a)-1 through 1.250(b)-6 and § 1.962-1(b)(1)(i)(B)(3) for taxable years ending before March 4, 2019.

Proposed § 1.1502-50 is proposed to apply to consolidated return years ending on or after the date of publication of the Treasury decision adopting these rules as final regulations in the **Federal Register**. See sections 1503(a) and 7805(b)(1)(A). Taxpayers may rely on proposed § 1.1502-50 for taxable years ending before the date of publication of the Treasury decision adopting these rules as final regulations in the **Federal Register**.

Proposed § § 1.6038-2(f)(15) and 1.6038A-2(b)(5)(iv) are proposed to apply with respect to information for annual accounting periods beginning on or after March 4, 2019. See sections 6038(a)(3) and 7805(b)(1)(B). Proposed § 1.6038-3(g)(4) is proposed to apply to taxable years of a foreign partnership beginning on or after March 4, 2019. See section 7805(b)(1)(B).

Special Analyses

I. *Regulatory Planning and Review — Economic Analysis*

Executive Orders 13563 and 12866 direct agencies to assess costs and benefits of available regulatory alternatives and, if regulation is necessary, to select regulatory approaches that maximize net benefits (including potential economic, environmental, public health and safety effects, distributive impacts, and equity). Executive Order 13563 emphasizes the importance of quantifying both costs and benefits, of reducing costs, of harmonizing rules, and of promoting flexibility.

These proposed regulations have been designated as economically significant by the Office of Management and Budget's Office of Information and Regulatory Affairs (OIRA) and subject to review under Executive Order 12866 pursuant to the Memorandum of Agreement (April 11, 2018) between the Treasury Department and the Office of Management and Budget regarding review of tax regulations.

A. Background

As described in part I of the Explanation of Provisions section, the section 250 deduction is an important component of the changes to the U.S. international tax system included in the Act. The purpose of the section 250 deduction is to minimize the role that U.S. tax considerations play in a domestic corporation's decision whether to service foreign markets directly or through a controlled foreign corporation ("CFC"). See Senate Explanation, at 370 ("[O]ffering similar, preferential rates for intangible income derived from serving foreign markets, whether through U.S.-based operations or through CFCs, reduces or eliminates the tax incentive to locate or move intangible income abroad, thereby limiting one margin where the Code distorts business investment decisions."). Further, the section 250 deduction protects the U.S. tax base against base erosion incentives created by the new participation exemption system established under section 245A, discussed in part I of the Explanation of Provisions section. At the most basic level, the section 250 deduction is allowed to a domestic corporation with respect to its intangible income derived from foreign markets, resulting in a lower effective rate of U.S. tax on its global intangible low-taxed income ("GILTI") and foreign-derived intangible income ("FDII").

The Act defines a corporation's FDII as the portion of its return in excess of a return on tangible assets that is derived from serving foreign markets, while it defines a corporation's GILTI as the portion of its return in excess of a return on tangible assets that is derived through its foreign affiliates. FDII and GILTI are calculated through formulas set out in sections 250 and 951A, respectively. For taxable years between 2018 and 2026, section 250 generally allows a deduction equal to the sum of 37.5 percent of the corporation's FDII plus 50 percent of its GILTI (thereafter, these deductions are reduced to 21.875 percent and 37.5 percent, respectively). These deduction rates produce comparable tax rates on income earned from serving foreign markets, regardless of where such income is earned. Different percentages are required by the Act to achieve approximate parity, given that the 80 percent limitation on foreign tax credits in section 960(d) results in additional U.S. tax.[2] More

[2] At the most basic level, abstracting from various complexities of the GILTI regime, the 21 percent U.S. statutory rate with a 50 percent deduction for GILTI implies that at foreign effective rates in excess of 10.5 percent (assuming no U.S. expenses), foreign tax credits are sufficient to fully offset U.S. tax on GILTI income. However, the GILTI regime limits foreign tax credits to 80 percent of their total value, so a "baseline" GILTI scenario, with zero expense allocations,

specifically, the Act defines a domestic corporation's FDII as its deemed intangible income ("DII") multiplied by the percentage of its deduction eligible income ("DEI") that is foreign-derived deduction eligible income ("FDDEI"). The Act defines DEI as the excess of the corporation's gross income (with certain exclusions[3]) over deductions (including taxes) properly allocable to the income. The Act defines DII as the excess (if any) of its DEI over 10 percent of its qualified business asset investment ("QBAI"), or tangible asset base. The Act defines FDDEI as DEI derived from sales of property to foreign persons for foreign use and from the provision of services to persons, or with respect to property, located outside the United States. Finally, if the sum of a corporation's FDII and GILTI exceeds its taxable income (determined without regard to section 250), then the Act requires that the amount of FDII and GILTI for which a deduction is allowed is reduced pro rata by the excess. While the Act provides the framework for determining a domestic corporation's FDII, it grants discretion to the Secretary to establish how certain requirements, such as whether sales are for a foreign use, are satisfied. See sections 250(b)(4)(A) and (B), (b)(5)(C)(i)(II), and (b)(5)(C)(ii). In addition, the Act does not address all of the details necessary to calculate FDII, such as the allocation of expenses. Further, the Act is unclear regarding whether the section 250 deduction for FDII is available for certain foreign military sales or services and whether a section 250 deduction for GILTI is available for an individual taxpayer making a section 962 election. The following analysis describes the need for the proposed regulations and discusses the costs and benefits relative to the baseline, as well as the important alternative regulatory choices that were considered.

B. The Need for Proposed Regulations

The purpose of the proposed regulations is to provide guidance to taxpayers in determining the amount of their deduction under section 250. Section 250(c) states that "[t]he Secretary shall prescribe such regulations or other guidance as may be necessary or appropriate to carry out the provisions of [section 250]." Therefore, the proposed regulations seek to provide the detail, structure, and language required to implement section 250.

The proposed regulations seek to assist taxpayers in calculating the allowable section 250 deduction, for example, by providing details on how to compute FDII, and the components of FDII such as QBAI, DEI, and FDDEI. In particular, with respect to FDDEI, the proposed regulations provide guidance on which sales of property and which provisions of services generate gross income included in FDDEI, and on how to allocate expenses to such gross income to determine FDDEI.

In addition, the proposed regulations provide an ordering rule to coordinate the computation of the section 250 taxable income limitation with the taxable income limitations across other provisions of the Code.

The proposed regulations also seek to clarify that the section 250 deduction for FDII is available for certain foreign military sales and services. In addition, the proposed regulations allow a section 250 deduction to individual taxpayers with respect to GILTI if they make an election under section 962.

Finally and importantly, the proposed regulations also seek to provide clarity and guidance regarding the types of documentation required to substantiate that, in fact, sales of property are to foreign persons for a foreign use and provisions of services are to persons, or with respect to property, located outside the United States. In developing the proposed regulations, the Treasury Department and the IRS sought to balance the need for rigorous documentation to ensure compliance with the desire to minimize administrative burden and costs to taxpayers.

C. Baseline

The economic analysis that follows compares the proposed regulations to a no-action baseline reflecting anticipated Federal income tax-related behavior in the absence of the proposed regulations. A no-action baseline reflects the current environment including the existing international tax regulations, prior to any amendment by the proposed regulations.

D. Cost and Benefits of the Proposed Regulations and Potential Alternatives

The proposed regulations provide certainty, clarity, and consistency in the application of the section 250 deduction by unambiguously defining terms, calculations, and acceptable forms of documentation, and also by making clear the conditions under which military sales are eligible to claim the deduction. In the absence of such guidance, the chance that different taxpayers would interpret the statute differently would be exacerbated. Similarly situated taxpayers might interpret the statutory rules pertaining to particular sales or services differently, with one taxpayer pursuing a sale that another taxpayer might decline to make, because of different interpretations of how the income would be treated under section 250. If this second taxpayer's activity were more profitable, an economic loss arises. Such situations are more likely to arise in the absence of guidance. While no guidance can curtail all differential or inaccurate interpretations of the statute, the proposed regula-

(Footnote Continued)

implies that foreign tax credits can fully offset U.S. tax on GILTI at foreign effective tax rates in excess of 13.125 percent (i.e., 10.5 / 0.8). The section 250 deduction for FDII is also intended to have a "baseline rate" of 13.125 percent (i.e., 0.21 x (1 - 0.375)); typically foreign tax credits are not relevant for FDII, and there is no 80 percent limitation applied to foreign tax credits with respect to FDII.

[3] The exclusions are: (1) subpart F inclusions (section 951); (2) GILTI; (3) financial services income (as defined in section 904(d)(2)(D)); (4) dividends received from the corporation's CFCs; (5) domestic oil and gas extraction income; and (6) foreign branch income (as defined in section 904(d)(2)(J)).

tions will significantly mitigate the chance for such interpretations and thereby increase economic efficiency.

In general, the Treasury Department and the IRS expect that in the absence of this guidance, taxpayers would undertake fewer eligible sales and services. Thus, the proposed regulation will generally enhance U.S. sales and services across all eligible activities. The Treasury Department and the IRS have not made quantitative estimates of these effects.

The benefits and costs of major, specific provisions of these proposed regulations relative to the no-action baseline and alternatives to these proposed rules considered by the Treasury Department and the IRS are discussed in further detail below.

1. Documentation Requirements

The proposed regulations set forth what forms of documentation can be used to substantiate that receipts qualify as "foreign-derived" for purposes of FDII and the section 250 deduction. In general, the Treasury Department and the IRS weighed the compliance burden imposed on taxpayers from documentation requirements against the need for documentation to be sufficiently rigorous in establishing foreign use or the location of a person that receives a service. Because the statute provides different requirements for sales or services to qualify for a section 250 deduction and the proposed regulations provide different requirements depending on the type of sale or the type of service, and because documentation needs to be tailored to the applicable requirement, the proposed regulations specify different types of acceptable documentation for different types of transactions. In particular, documentation requirements vary with respect to the determination of whether a sale of property is to a foreign person, whether a sale of general property is for a foreign use, whether a sale of intangible property is for a foreign use, whether an individual consumer of a general service is located outside the United States, and whether a business recipient of a general service is located outside the United States.

In each case, the proposed regulations provide that the list of acceptable documentation constitutes reasonable proof that a transaction is a FDDEI transaction. In general, the types of documentation listed are readily accessible to most taxpayers. For example, with respect to demonstrating foreign use for general property, taxpayers can show evidence of shipment to a location outside the United States (presuming that the seller has no knowledge or reason to know that that information is unreliable or incorrect).

To further reduce compliance burdens, the proposed regulations allow additional flexibility for particular types of taxpayers or transactions. For example, throughout the proposed regulations, small businesses (defined in the proposed regulations as taxpayers with less than $10 million of gross receipts annually) are subject to less stringent documentation requirements because their smaller scale makes compliance more burdensome for them and makes the sophisticated tax minimization planning that can sometimes characterize abuse unlikely. Small transactions (defined in the proposed regulations as less than $5,000 of gross receipts from a single recipient) are also subject to less stringent documentation requirements, because the fixed costs of compliance likely account for a larger fraction of the profit on small transactions, and large scale abuse is less likely. The Treasury Department and the IRS request comments on whether the thresholds in the proposed regulations for small businesses and small transactions are appropriate and especially solicit comments that provide data, other evidence, and models that can enhance the rigor of the process by which such thresholds are determined. Further, the proposed regulations allow a more flexible approach for the documentation of sales of fungible general property because it is burdensome and unnecessary to track each sale of a fungible item as long as the taxpayer can establish by documentation that a certain percentage of the fungible property is for a foreign use.

In determining appropriate documentation requirements, the Treasury Department and the IRS balanced the rigor and reliability of the proof that transactions are foreign-derived with the cost to taxpayers of obtaining such documentation. The Treasury Department and the IRS considered a spectrum of trade-offs between the rigor of proof of foreign use and the burden such proof would impose on taxpayers. One option considered was allowing only the most stringent form of documentation in each case (for example, a written statement of foreign use made under penalties of perjury, plus evidence of such use) without any flexibility, but this was deemed overly burdensome for taxpayers and foreign buyers. Overly burdensome documentation requirements might shift transactions to sellers that do not need or cannot use the FDII deduction, or it may discourage foreign persons from transacting with a U.S. seller or renderer. The Treasury Department and the IRS aimed to propose rules that would not alter economic decisions because of these concerns. In addition, highly burdensome rules may lead to abuse. For example, a foreign buyer that falsifies documentation provided to a domestic corporation to allow the corporation to obtain a deduction would not be subject to penalties by the IRS. Because the incentives for compliance by foreign buyers are limited (for example, contractual liability between the parties), the burden should also be limited. In comparison, chapters 3 and 4 of subtitle A of the Code require U.S. financial institutions to withhold on certain payments to foreign persons if they do not provide documentation. Because of the enforcement mechanism built into the statutes in chapters 3 and 4 (i.e., withholding), the IRS can require stricter documentation (for example, most foreign persons have to provide to the financial institution a specific IRS form, completed and signed under penalties of perjury, and in some cases must attach additional documentation on underlying payees).

The Treasury Department and the IRS also considered a system in which taxpayers submitted documentation in advance of a potential FDDEI transaction for the IRS to review and determine whether the documentation is sufficient. This option was rejected because the time involved would delay normal business transactions.

A third option that the Treasury Department and the IRS considered was to allow a taxpayer to use its discretion to determine what type of documentation is appropriate, but this would not provide sufficient clarity and assurance to taxpayers and is potentially open to abuse. For each type of transaction, the Treasury Department and the IRS chose to allow a menu of acceptable documentation options that vary according to the type of transaction, and selected documentation options that would be readily available to the taxpayer whenever possible. By allowing taxpayers to, in some cases, rely on documents already obtained in the normal course of business, the proposed regulations impose essentially zero documentation cost in such cases. The Treasury Department and the IRS request comments on the approaches and decisions relating to documentation requirements discussed in this part I(D)(1) of this Special Analyses section. See part II of this Special Analyses section regarding the Paperwork Reduction Act for additional discussion on the expected paperwork burden of these documentation requirements.

2. Computation of the Ratio of FDDEI to DEI

The proposed regulations provide guidance on the computation of the foreign-derived ratio. As noted in part I(A) of this Special Analyses section, the Act defines a corporation's FDII as its DII multiplied by the corporation's foreign-derived ratio, which is the ratio of its DEI to its FDDEI. The proposed regulations specify that, for purposes of determining the numerator of the foreign-derived ratio, the domestic corporation must allocate expenses to its gross FDDEI. The Treasury Department and the IRS deemed this approach the most consistent with the statute by providing what the Treasury Department and the IRS have determined to be the most accurate measure of the corporation's income that is "foreign-derived," through matching of expenses to gross income.

The Treasury Department and the IRS considered two other approaches; one, in which the foreign-derived ratio would be computed as the ratio of foreign versus U.S. gross receipts and another in which the ratio would be computed as foreign versus U.S. gross income. The Treasury Department and the IRS have determined that both of these approaches would result in a less accurate measure of foreign-derived net income. The Treasury Department and the IRS have determined that these alternative approaches could also reward low margin (or even loss-leading) sales or services to foreign markets by allowing a section 250 deduction due to positive gross receipts or income from foreign sources, even if the net income from foreign sources after allocated expenses is zero or negative. The Treasury Department and the IRS have determined that the chosen alternative generally provides the most accurate computation of FDII but solicit comments on whether an alternative method would be more appropriate.

3. Military Sales

Section 250 requires sales to be made to a foreign person and services to be provided to a person located outside the United States but does not include specific rules applicable to foreign military sales or services. For example, many sales of military equipment and services by a U.S. defense contractor to a foreign government are structured, pursuant to the Arms Export Control Act, as sales and services provided to the U.S. government for resale or on-service to the foreign government. See part III(B)(2) of the Explanation of Provisions section for additional discussion of the Arms Export Control Act. In effect, the contractor is selling goods and services to a foreign person, but the sale is technically made to the U.S. government. The Treasury Department and the IRS recognize that the statute is unclear as to whether certain foreign military sales and services can qualify for the section 250 deduction, due to the concern that a foreign military sale or service pursuant to the Arms Export Control Act would not qualify as a sale or service to a foreign person since the sale is actually made to the U.S. government and not to a foreign person or a person located outside the United States.

The Treasury Department and the IRS considered several options for addressing this issue. One option was not addressing this issue in the proposed regulations. This option was rejected because the Treasury Department and the IRS determined that it would perpetuate uncertainty about the application of section 250 to foreign military sales and services and could result in economic inequities if some taxpayers took the position that foreign military sales and services qualify for a section 250 deduction but other similarly-situated taxpayers took the position that such sales and services do not qualify. A second option the Treasury Department and the IRS considered was to clarify that a foreign military sale or service through the U.S. government can never qualify for a section 250 deduction. However, this option was rejected because the Treasury Department and the IRS determined that it would treat taxpayers in the defense industry inequitably relative to other industries by denying them a section 250 deduction with respect to a significant amount of their foreign market sales or services. A third option the Treasury Department and the IRS considered was to allow any sale or service to a U.S. person that acts as an intermediary and does not take on the benefits and burdens of ownership to potentially qualify for a section 250 deduction if there is an ultimate foreign recipient. This option was rejected because the Treasury Department and the IRS determined that such a broad exception would allow multiple deductions in instances where both the seller and the intermediary buyer are U.S. taxpayers, because both the seller and the intermediary could potentially qualify for a section 250 deduction. In contrast, the U.S. government is not a taxpayer eligible for a section 250 deduction so only the seller would benefit from a special rule for military exports. Furthermore, determining whether a party is an "intermediary" for this purpose would require a complex facts and circumstances analysis of whether the party had the benefits and burdens of ownership, which could create uncertainty in the application of section 250 with respect to any transaction in which property or services are sold for resale or on-service.

The proposed regulations provide uniform tax treatment across the economy by generally allowing all sectors to claim the section 250 deduction, subject to other applicable rules. Otherwise, certain sales and services by the defense industry that are clearly intended for a foreign use, and that satisfy all other requirements under section 250, would be denied the benefit solely as a result of such sales or services being first made to the U.S. government under the Arms Export Control Act, whereas other industries that are not subject to the Arms Export Control Act would not have this concern. Therefore, the proposed regulations provide that foreign military sales or services to the U.S. government under the Arms Export Control Act would be treated as a sale of property or provision of a service to a foreign person. This rule seeks to provide uniform tax treatment between the defense sector and other sectors of the U.S. economy with respect to sales and services that are clearly meant for a foreign use.

4. Section 962

The section 250 deduction for FDII and GILTI is available only to domestic corporations. However, Congress enacted section 962 in Public Law 89-834 (1962) to ensure that individuals' tax burdens with respect to undistributed foreign earnings of their CFCs are comparable with their tax burdens if they had held their CFCs through a domestic corporation. See S. Rept. 1881, 87th Cong., 2d Sess. 92 (1962). Allowing a section 250 deduction with respect to GILTI of an individual (including an individual that is a shareholder of an S corporation or a partner in a partnership) that makes an election under section 962 provides comparable treatment for this income.

The Treasury Department and the IRS considered two options with respect to extending the section 250 deduction to individuals (which include, for this purpose, individual partners in partnerships and individual shareholders in S corporations) that make an election under section 962. The first option considered was to not allow the deduction for individuals. Not allowing the section 250 deduction would require that individuals that own their CFCs directly (or indirectly through a partnership or S corporation) transfer the stock of their CFCs to new U.S. corporations in order to obtain the benefit of the section 250 deduction. The Treasury Department and the IRS determined that such reorganization would be economically costly, both in terms of legal fees and substantive economic costs related to organizing and operating new corporate entities. The second option considered was to give individuals the section 250 deduction with respect to their GILTI if they make the section 962 election. The Treasury Department and the IRS determined that allowing individuals the section 250 deduction would improve economic efficiency by preventing the need for costly restructuring solely for the purpose of tax savings. This is the option adopted by the Treasury Department and the IRS in the proposed regulations. The Treasury Department and the IRS welcome comments on whether an alternative approach would be more appropriate.

II. *Paperwork Reduction Act*

The proposed regulations provide the authority for the IRS to require taxpayers to file certain forms (identified and discussed in further detail below) with the IRS to obtain the benefit of the section 250 deduction. In order to provide advance notice and solicit public comment, the IRS released drafts of the relevant forms in 2018 based on the statutory language and requested comments. The IRS received no comments on the forms during the comment period. The 2018 versions of the forms that were released in 2018 are available at *https://www.irs.gov/forms-instructions*. The Treasury Department and the IRS are not proposing to make any changes to those forms through these regulations. The Treasury Department and the IRS are also soliciting public comment on the forms and paperwork requirements in general discussed in the proposed regulations. The Treasury Department and the IRS specifically request comments on whether there are (1) ways to reduce the burdens associated with the forms, (2) opportunities to clarify the forms or associated instructions, or (3) ways to improve the quality of the collections in general.

The proposed regulations require all taxpayers with a section 250 deduction to file one new form (Form 8993). The proposed regulations also authorize the IRS to request additional information on several existing forms (Forms 1065 (Schedule K-1), 5471, 5472, and 8865) if the filer of the form has a deduction under section 250. With respect to Forms 5471, 5472, and 8993, the proposed regulations do not specify the information that will be required from taxpayers that have a section 250 deduction, but instead provide that this information will be prescribed by the forms and instructions. With respect to Forms 1065 (Schedule K-1) and 8865, the proposed regulations specify the additional information that must be provided. For additional explanation of the reporting requirements contained in these proposed regulations, see part VI of the Explanation of Provisions section. The rest of this part II of the Special Analyses section provides additional details on forms and information about the paperwork burden.

The information collection burdens under the Paperwork Reduction Act, 44 U.S.C. 3501 et seq. ("PRA") from the proposed regulations are in proposed §§1.250(a)-1(d), 1.250(b)-1(e)(2), 1.6038-2(f)(15), 1.6038-3(g)(4), and 1.6038A-2(b)(5)(iv).

The collection of information in proposed §1.250(a)-1(d) would be mandatory for each domestic corporation claiming a deduction under section 250 as well as for any individual making an election under section 962 that claims a deduction under section 250 attributable to the individual's GILTI.

The collection of information in proposed § 1.250(a)-1(d) is pursuant to sections 6001 and 6011 and would be satisfied by submitting a new reporting form, Form 8993, "Section 250 Deduction for Foreign-Derived Intangible Income (FDII) and Global Intangible Low-Taxed Income (GILTI)," with an income tax return. For purposes of the PRA, the reporting burden associated with proposed § 1.250(a)-1(d) will be reflected in the PRA submission for new Form 8993 (OMB control numbers 1545-0123 in the case of business taxpayers, and 1545-0074 in the case of individual taxpayers).

The collection of information in proposed § 1.250(b)-1(e)(2) would require each partnership to provide to each of its partners the partner's distributive share of gross DEI, gross FDDEI, deductions that are definitely related to the partnership's gross DEI and gross FDDEI, and partnership QBAI. For purposes of the PRA, the reporting burden associated with proposed § 1.250(b)-1(e)(2) would be reflected in the PRA submission for Form 1065 (OMB control number 1545-0123).

The collection of information in proposed § 1.6038-2(f)(15) would require every U.S. person that controls a foreign corporation during an annual accounting period and files Form 5471, "Information Return of U.S. Persons With Respect to Certain Foreign Corporations," for that period. The collection of information in proposed § 1.6038-2(f)(15) would be satisfied by providing information about the section 250 deduction for the corporation's accounting period as Form 5471 and its instructions may prescribe. For purposes of the PRA, the reporting burden on the applicable business taxpayers associated with proposed § 1.6038-2(f)(15) will be reflected in the PRA submission for Form 5471 (OMB control number 1545-0123).

The collection of information in proposed § 1.6038-3(g)(4) would be mandatory for every U.S. person that controls a foreign partnership during the partnership tax year and files Form 8865, "Return of U.S. Persons With Respect to Certain Foreign Partnerships," for that period. The collection of information in proposed § 1.6038-3(g)(4) would require a controlling ten-percent partner or controlling fifty-percent partner to provide to the IRS on Form 8865 its share of the partnership's gross DEI, gross FDDEI, deductions that are definitely related to the partnership's gross DEI and gross FDDEI, and partnership QBAI. For purposes of the PRA, the reporting burden associated with proposed § 1.6038-3(g)(4) will be reflected in the PRA submission for Form 8865 (OMB control number 1545-1668).

The collection of information in proposed § 1.6038A-2(b)(5)(iv) would be mandatory for every reporting corporation that files Form 5472, "Information Return of a 25% Foreign-Owned U.S. Corporation or a Foreign Corporation Engaged in a U.S. Trade or Business," for the tax year. The collection of information in proposed § 1.6038A-2(b)(5)(iv) would be satisfied by providing information about the section 250 deduction for the tax year as Form 5472 and its instructions may prescribe. For purposes of the PRA, the reporting burden associated with proposed § 1.6038A-2(b)(5)(iv) will be reflected in the PRA submission for Form 5472 (OMB control number 1545-0123).

The tax forms that will be created or revised as a result of the information collections in the proposed regulations, as well as the estimated number of respondents, are as follows:

Related New or Revised Tax Forms

	New	Revision of existing form	Number of respondents (estimated)
Form 8993	✓		75,000 - 350,000
Form 1065, Schedule K-1 (for corporate partners only, revision starting TY2020)		✓	15,000 - 45,000
Form 5471		✓	10,000 - 20,000
Form 8865		✓	<10,000
Form 5472		✓	50,000 - 80,000

Source: RAAS:CDW and ITA

The numbers of respondents in the Related New or Revised Tax Forms table were estimated by the Research, Applied Analytics and Statistics Division ("RAAS") of the IRS from the Compliance Data Warehouse ("CDW"), using tax years 2014 through 2016; as well as based on export data from the International Trade Administration ("ITA") for 2015 and 2016. Tax data for 2017 are not yet available due to extended filing dates. Data for Form 8993 represent preliminary estimates of the total number of taxpayers that may be required to file the new Form 8993. The upper bound estimate reflects the total number of exporting companies reported in the ITA data, as well as the CDW-based counts of individuals reporting related party transactions. The lower bound estimate reflects the CDW-based counts of individual and corporate taxpayers reporting related party transactions. Data for each of the Forms 1065, 5471, 5472, and 8865 represent preliminary estimates of the total number of taxpayers that are expected to file these revised forms regardless of whether that taxpayer must also file Form 8993.

The current status of the Paperwork Reduction Act submissions related to the tax forms that will be revised as a result of the information collections in the proposed regulations is provided in the accompanying table. As described above, the reporting burdens associated with the information collections in the proposed regulations are included in the aggregated burden estimates for OMB control numbers 1545-0123 (which represents a total estimated burden time for all forms and schedules for corporations of 3.157 billion hours and total estimated monetized costs of $58.148 billion ($2017)), 1545-0074 (which represents a total estimated burden time, including all other related forms and schedules for individuals, of 1.784 billion hours and total estimated monetized costs of $31.764 billion ($2017)), and 1545-1668 (which represents a total estimated burden time for all related forms and schedules for other filers, in particular trusts and estates, of 281,974 hours and total estimated monetized costs of $25.107 million ($2017)). The overall burden estimates provided for the OMB control numbers below are aggregate amounts that relate to the entire package of forms associated with the applicable OMB control number and will in the future include, but not isolate, the estimated burden of the tax forms that will be created or revised as a result of the information collections in the proposed regulations. These numbers are therefore unrelated to the future calculations needed to assess the burden imposed by the proposed regulations. These burdens have been reported for other regulations related to the taxation of cross-border income and the Treasury Department and the IRS urge readers to recognize that these numbers are duplicates and to guard against overcounting the burden that international tax provisions imposed prior to the Act. No burden estimates specific to the forms affected by the proposed regulations are currently available. The Treasury Department and the IRS have not estimated the burden, including that of any new information collections, related to the requirements under the proposed regulations. The Treasury Department and the IRS request comments on all aspects of information collection burdens related to the proposed regulations, including estimates for how much time it would take to comply with the paperwork burdens described above for each relevant form and ways for the IRS to minimize the paperwork burden.

Form	Type of Filer	OMB Number(s)	Status
Form 8993 (NEW)	Business (NEW Model)	1545-0123	Published in the **Federal Register** Notice (FRN) on 10/11/18. Public Comment period closed on 12/10/18.
	Link: https://www.federalregister.gov/documents/2018/10/09/2018-21846/proposed-collection-comment-request-for-forms-1065-1065-b-1066-1120-1120-c-1120-f-1120-h-1120-nd		
	Individual (NEW Model)	1545-0074	Limited Scope submission (1040 only). Full ICR submission for 2019 for all forms in 3/2019. 60 Day FRN not published yet for full collection for 2019.
	Link: https://www.reginfo.gov/public/do/PRAViewICR?ref_nbr=201808-1545-031		
Form 1065, Schedule K-1	Business (NEW Model)	1545-0123	Published in the FRN on 10/11/18. Public Comment period closed on 12/10/18.
	Link: https://www.federalregister.gov/documents/2018/10/09/2018-21846/proposed-collection-comment-request-for-forms-1065-1065-b-1066-1120-1120-c-1120-f-1120-h-1120-nd		
Form 5471	Business (NEW Model)	1545-0123	Published in the FRN on 10/11/18. Public Comment period closed on 12/10/18.
	Link: https://www.federalregister.gov/documents/2018/10/09/2018-21846/proposed-collection-comment-request-for-forms-1065-1065-b-1066-1120-1120-c-1120-f-1120-h-1120-nd		
Form 8865	All other filers (mainly trusts and estates) (Legacy system)	1545-1668	Published in the FRN on 10/01/18. Public Comment period closed on 11/30/18.
	Link: *https://www.federalregister.gov/documents/2018/10/01/2018-21288/proposed-collection-comment-request-for-regulation-project*		
Form 5472	Business (NEW Model)	1545-0123	Published in the FRN on 10/11/18. Public Comment period closed on 12/10/18.
	Link: https://www.federalregister.gov/documents/2018/10/09/2018-21846/proposed-collection-comment-request-for-forms-1065-1065-b-1066-1120-1120-c-1120-f-1120-h-1120-nd		

III. *Regulatory Flexibility Act*

It is hereby certified that this notice of proposed rulemaking will not have a significant economic impact on a substantial number of small entities within the meaning of section 601(6) of the Regulatory Flexibility Act (5 U.S.C. chapter 6). Although the Treasury Department and the IRS project that the proposed regulations may affect a substantial number of small entities, the economic impact on small entities as a result of this notice of proposed rulemaking is not expected to be significant.

The small business entities that are subject to section 250 and this notice of proposed rulemaking are small domestic corporations claiming a deduction under section 250 based on their FDII and GILTI. Pursuant to proposed § 1.250(a)-1(d), taxpayers are required to file new Form 8993 to compute the amount of the eligible deduction for FDII and GILTI under section 250. The Treasury Department and the IRS estimate that there are between 75,000 and 350,000 respondents of all sizes that are likely to file Form 8993. The lower end estimate comes from IRS-collected data on related party transactions that are indicative of exports to related parties. These data provide a lower bound for the number of taxpayers that export since related party exports are only a part of total exports. The IRS does not collect information on exports to third parties; therefore, International Trade Administration ("ITA") statistics of the number of companies engaged in export activities are used.[4] The ITA data provide the upper bound of the estimate of affected taxpayers. The Treasury Department and the IRS welcome comments on the analysis of number of entities affected, particularly on how such analysis should take into account different industries. Additionally, under proposed § 1.250(b)-1(e), a partnership that has one or more direct or indirect partners that are domestic corporations and that is required to file a return under section 6031 must furnish on Schedule K-1 (Form 1065) certain information that would allow the partner to accurately calculate its FDII. The Treasury Department and the IRS estimate the number of domestic corporations that are direct or indirect partners in a partnership affected by proposed § 1.250(a)-1(e) is between 15,000 and 45,000.

In order to substantiate the amount of the section 250 deduction on Form 8993 related to the calculation of FDII for the sale of property or the provision of a service, the proposed regulations in §§ 1.250(b)-3 through 1.250(b)-5 prescribe different types of documentation that should be obtained for each transaction. As discussed in the Explanation of Provisions section of the preamble, the proposed regulations provide several types of permissible documentation for the purpose of determining the amount of a domestic corporation's income that is considered foreign-derived. For example, in the case of a sale of general property, the seller must (1) obtain documentation that establishes the recipient's status as a foreign person, such as a written statement by the recipient indicating that the recipient is a foreign person; and (2) obtain documentation that the property is for foreign use, such as proof of shipment of the property to a foreign address.

To alleviate the burden of documentation on many small businesses and small transactions, the proposed regulations allow a seller that has less than $10,000,000 of gross receipts in the prior taxable year, or less than $5,000 in gross receipts from a single recipient during the current taxable year, to treat a recipient as a foreign person if the seller has a shipping address for the recipient that is outside the United States. The small business and small transaction exceptions to establish foreign person status are applicable to sales of both general property and intangible property. Furthermore, to establish that general property is for a foreign use, certain small businesses and businesses with small transactions may rely on the existence of a foreign shipping address for the recipient instead of obtaining documentation. The proposed regulations also contain small business and small transaction exceptions related to general services provided to consumers and business recipients. The Treasury Department and the IRS anticipate that a substantial share of small entities claiming a section 250 deduction will qualify for the small business and small transactions exceptions described above, thereby significantly reducing the overall burden of the proposed regulations on small entities. The Treasury Department and the IRS solicit comments on this issue.

The reporting burden for completing Form 8993 is estimated to average 24 hours for all affected entities, regardless of size. The reporting burden on small entities (those with receipts below $10 million in RAAS calculations) is estimated to average 15 hours. Based on the monetized hourly burden reported below, the annual per-entity reporting burden will be $1,067. The Treasury Department and the IRS project that compliance with the documentation requirements in the proposed regulations will have a de minimis or limited impact on all affected entities, regardless of size, as the majority of taxpayers will be able to use records that are maintained in the normal course of business. Small business entities that have less than $10 million of gross receipts in the prior taxable year, or less than $5,000 in gross receipts from a single recipient during the current taxable year, are expected to experience 0 to 5 minutes, with an average of 2.5 minutes, of recordkeeping per transaction recipient. Taxpayers ineligible to qualify for either exception are expected to experience 0 to 30 minutes, with an average of 15 minutes, of recordkeeping per transaction recipient. These hourly estimates were derived by RAAS based the existence of exceptions available to small businesses, as well as based on the previously noted overlap between acceptable documentation and records kept in the normal course of business, suggesting limited impact. The hourly estimates include all associated activities: recordkeeping, tax planning, learning about the law, gathering tax materials, form completion and submissions, and time with a tax preparer or use of tax software. The estimated monetized

---

[4] ITA data was accessed at *http://tse.export.gov/EDB/SelectReports.aspx?DATA=ExporterDB* in December, 2018.

burden for compliance is $71.14 per hour, a figure computed from the IRS Business Taxpayer Burden model which assigns each firm in the micro data a monetization rate based on total revenue and assets reported on their tax return. See Tax Compliance Burden (John Guyton et al., July 2018) at *https://www.irs.gov/pub/irs-soi/d13315.pdf*. The assigned monetization rates include, in addition to wages, employer non-wage costs such as employment taxes, benefits, and overhead. For these reasons, the Treasury Department and the IRS have determined that the requirements in proposed §§1.250(a)-1 and 1.250(b)-3 through 1.250(b)-6 will not have a significant economic impact on a substantial number of small entities. Therefore, a Regulatory Flexibility Analysis under the Regulatory Flexibility Act is not required with respect to proposed §§1.250(a)-1 and 1.250(b)-3 through 1.250(b)-6.

The small business entities that are subject to proposed §1.6038-2(f)(15) are domestic small business entities that are controlling U.S. shareholders of a foreign corporation and that claim a deduction under section 250 by reason of having FDII. For these purposes, a domestic small business entity controls a foreign corporation by owning more than 50 percent of that foreign corporation's stock, measured either by value or voting power. The data to assess the number of small entities potentially affected by §1.6038-2(f)(15) are not readily available. However, businesses that are controlling U.S. shareholders of a foreign corporation are generally not small businesses because the ownership of sufficient stock in a foreign corporation in order to be a controlling U.S. shareholder generally entails significant resources and investment. Therefore, the Treasury Department and the IRS project that a substantial number of domestic small business entities will not be subject to proposed §1.6038-2(f)(15). Consequently, the Treasury Department and the IRS have determined that proposed §1.6038-2(f)(15) will not have a significant economic impact on a substantial number of small entities. Therefore, a Regulatory Flexibility Analysis under the Regulatory Flexibility Act is not required with respect to the collection of information requirements of proposed §1.6038-2(f)(15).

The small business entities that are subject to proposed §1.6038-3(g)(4) are domestic small entities that are controlling fifty-percent partners or controlling ten-percent partners of a foreign partnership and that claim a deduction under section 250 by reason of having FDII. A controlling fifty-percent partner is a U.S. person that owns more than a fifty-percent interest in a foreign partnership. A controlling ten-percent partner is a U.S. person that owns a ten-percent or greater interest in a foreign partnership that is controlled by U.S. persons owning at least a ten-percent interest. For these purposes, a fifty percent interest or ten percent interest in a partnership is an interest equal to fifty percent or ten percent of the capital or profits interest in a partnership, or an interest to which fifty percent or ten percent of the deductions or losses of the partnership are allocated, respectively. The data to assess the number of small entities potentially affected by proposed §1.6038-3(g)(4) are not readily available. However, businesses that are controlling fifty-percent partners or controlling ten-percent partners of a foreign partnership are generally not small businesses because the ownership of a sufficient interest in a foreign partnership in order to be a controlling fifty-percent partner or a controlling ten-percent partner generally entails significant resources and investment. Therefore, the Treasury Department and the IRS have determined that proposed §1.6038-3(g)(4) will not affect a substantial number of domestic small business entities. Moreover, any increase in costs imposed by the rule is likely to be small, relative to total costs, for any entity. Consequently, the Treasury Department and the IRS have determined that proposed §1.6038-3(g)(4) will not have a significant economic impact on a substantial number of small entities. Therefore, a Regulatory Flexibility Analysis under the Regulatory Flexibility Act is not required with respect to the collection of information requirements of proposed §1.6038-3(g)(4).

The small business entities that are subject to proposed §1.6038A-2(b)(5)(iv) are domestic small entities that are at least 25-percent foreign-owned, by vote or value, that claim a deduction under section 250 by reason of having FDII. The data to assess the number of small entities potentially affected by proposed §1.6038A-2(b)(5)(iv) is not readily available. However, domestic corporations that are at least 25-percent foreign-owned are generally not small businesses because a foreign person's ownership of at least 25 percent of a domestic corporation, whether by vote or value, generally entails significant resources and investment, and a foreign person is unlikely to expend such resources to invest in a small domestic entity. Therefore, the Treasury Department and the IRS project that a substantial number of domestic small business entities will not be subject to proposed §1.6038A-2(b)(5)(iv). Consequently, the Treasury Department and the IRS have determined that that proposed §1.6038A-2(b)(5)(iv) will not have a significant economic impact on a substantial number of small entities. Therefore, a Regulatory Flexibility Analysis under the Regulatory Flexibility Act is not required with respect to the collection of information requirements of proposed §1.6038A-2(b)(5)(iv).

Notwithstanding this certification, the Treasury Department and the IRS invite comments from the public on both the number of entities affected and the economic impact of this proposed rule on small entities.

Pursuant to section 7805(f) of the Code, this notice of proposed rulemaking has been submitted to the Chief Counsel for Advocacy of the Small Business Administration for comment on its impact on small businesses.

IV. *Unfunded Mandates Reform Act*

Section 202 of the Unfunded Mandates Reform Act of 1995 requires that agencies assess anticipated costs and benefits and take certain other actions before issuing a final rule that includes any Federal mandate that may result in expenditures in any one year by a state, local, or tribal government, in the aggregate, or by the private sector, of $100 million in 1995 dollars, updated annually for inflation. In 2018, that threshold is approximately $150 million. This rule does not include any Federal mandate that may result in expenditures by state, local, or tribal governments, or by the private sector in excess of that threshold.

V. *Executive Order 13132: Federalism*

Executive Order 13132 (entitled "Federalism") prohibits an agency from publishing any rule that has federalism implications if the rule either imposes substantial, direct compliance costs on state and local governments, and is not required by statute, or preempts state law, unless the agency meets the consultation and funding requirements of section 6 of the Executive Order. This proposed rule does not have federalism implications, does not impose substantial direct compliance costs on state and local governments, and does not preempt state law within the meaning of the Executive Order.

Comments and Requests for Public Hearing

Before these proposed regulations are adopted as final regulations, consideration will be given to any written or electronic comments that are submitted timely to the IRS as prescribed in this preamble under the **ADDRESSES** section. Comments are requested on all aspects of the proposed regulations. In addition, the Treasury Department and the IRS solicit comments regarding the appropriateness of the numerical thresholds in the following provisions, along with data, other evidence, and models that can enhance the rigor of the process by which such thresholds are determined: proposed § 1.250(b)-4(c)(2)(ii), (d)(2)(iii)(C), (d)(2)(iv), (d)(3)(ii) and (iii); proposed § 1.250(b)-5(c)(5), (c)(6), (d)(3)(ii), (e)(3)(ii), and (h); and proposed § 1.250(b)-6(c)(1)(ii) and (d)(2).

All comments will be available at *http://www.regulations.gov* or upon request. A public hearing will be scheduled if requested in writing by any person that timely submits written comments. If a public hearing is scheduled, notice of the date, time, and place for the public hearing will be published in the **Federal Register**.

Drafting Information

The principal authors of these proposed regulations are Kenneth Jeruchim of the Office of the Associate Chief Counsel (International) and Michelle A. Monroy and Austin Diamond-Jones of the Office of Associate Chief Counsel (Corporate). However, other personnel from the Treasury Department and the IRS participated in their development.

Statement of Availability of IRS Documents

IRS Revenue Procedures, Revenue Rulings, Notices, and other guidance cited in this document are published in the Internal Revenue Bulletin and are available from the Superintendent of Documents, U.S. Government Printing Office, Washington, DC 20402, or by visiting the IRS website at *http://www.irs.gov*.

[¶ 49,789] Proposed Amendments of Regulations (REG-103083-18) , published in the Federal Register on March 25, 2019.

[Code Secs. 101 and 6050Y]

Information returns: Life insurance contract transactions: Reporting requirements.—Reg. §§ 1.6050Y-1 —1.6050Y-4 and amendments of Reg. §§ 1.101-1 and 1.101-6, providing guidance on new information reporting obligations under section 6050Y related to reportable policy sales of life insurance contracts and payments of reportable death benefits, are proposed.

AGENCY: Internal Revenue Service (IRS), Treasury.

ACTION: Notice of proposed rulemaking; notification of public hearing.

SUMMARY: This document contains proposed regulations providing guidance on new information reporting obligations under section 6050Y related to reportable policy sales of life insurance contracts and payments of reportable death benefits. The proposed regulations also provide guidance on the amount of death benefits excluded from gross income under section 101 following a reportable policy sale. The proposed regulations affect parties involved in certain life insurance contract transactions, including reportable policy sales, transfers of life insurance contracts to foreign persons, and payments of reportable death benefits. This document invites comments and provides a notice of a public hearing on these proposed regulations.

DATES: Written or electronic comments must be received by May 9, 2019. Requests to speak and outlines of topics to be discussed at the public hearing scheduled for June 5, 2019, at 10 a.m. must be received by May 9, 2019.

ADDRESSES: Send submissions to: CC:PA:LPD:PR (REG-103083-18), Room 5203, Internal Revenue Service, P.O. Box 7604, Ben Franklin Station, Washington, DC 20044. Submissions may be hand-delivered Monday through Friday between the hours of 8 a.m. and 4 p.m. to CC:PA:LPD:PR (REG-103083-18), Courier's Desk, Internal Revenue Service, 1111 Constitution Avenue, NW., Washington, DC 20224, or sent electronically via the Federal eRulemaking Portal at *www.regulations.gov* (IRS REG-103083-18).

FOR FURTHER INFORMATION CONTACT: Concerning the proposed regulations, Kathryn M. Sneade, (202) 317-6995; concerning submissions of comments and requests to speak at the public hearing, Regina Johnson, (202) 317-6901 (not toll-free numbers).

SUPPLEMENTARY INFORMATION:

Paperwork Reduction Act

The collection of information contained in this notice of proposed rulemaking has been submitted to the Office of Management and Budget for review under OMB Control Numbers 1545-0119, 1545-1621, and 1545-2281 in accordance with the Paperwork Reduction Act of 1995 (44 U.S.C. 3507(d)). In general, the collection of information in the proposed regulations is required under section 6050Y of the Internal Revenue Code (Code): (1) The requirement under §1.6050Y-2 of the proposed regulations for an acquirer to report certain information about payments made in reportable policy sales is required under section 6050Y(a); (2) the requirement under §1.6050Y-3 of the proposed regulations for an issuer to report certain information about transferors of life insurance contracts is required under section 6050Y(b); and (3) the requirement under §1.6050Y-4 of the proposed regulations for a payor to report certain information about payments of reportable death benefits is required under section 6050Y(c). Section 1.6050Y-3(a)(3) of the proposed regulations would require the issuer to report to the seller and the IRS the amount the seller would have received if the seller had surrendered the life insurance contract on the date of the reportable policy sale. This information is necessary to allow the seller and the IRS to determine the character of all or a portion of the seller's taxable income from the sale of the life insurance contract (capital or ordinary). Sections 1.6050Y-3(f)(1) and 1.6050Y-4(e)(1) of the proposed regulations contain reporting exceptions for certain foreign beneficial owners. To determine qualification for these reporting exceptions, §§1.6050Y-3(f)(1) and 1.6050Y-4(e)(1) would require that certain foreign beneficial owners provide a Form W-8ECI, "Certificate of Foreign Person's Claim that Income is Effectively Connected with the Conduct of a Trade or Business in the United States," to certain persons. This information is necessary to document whether the reporting exception in either §1.6050Y-3(f)(1) or §1.6050Y-4(e)(1) applies in a particular situation.

The likely respondents to the collection of information are (1) Entities acquiring life insurance contracts in reportable policy sales; (2) life insurance companies; (3) life insurance companies and other entities making payments of reportable death benefits; and (4) entities receiving payments of reportable death benefits.

The burden for the collection of information contained in §1.6050Y-2 of the proposed regulations will be reflected in the burden on the form that the IRS created to request the information in section 6050Y(a) and §1.6050Y-2 of the proposed regulations (Form 1099-LS, "Reportable Life Insurance Sale"). The burden for the collection of information contained in §1.6050Y-3 of the proposed regulations will be reflected in the burden on the form that the IRS created to request the information in section 6050Y(b) and §1.6050Y-3 of the proposed regulations (Form 1099-SB, "Seller's Investment in Life Insurance Contract"). The OMB Control Number for both of these forms is 1545-2281. The burden for the collection of information contained in §1.6050Y-4 of the proposed regulations will be reflected in the burden on the Form 1099-R, "Distributions From Pensions, Annuities, Retirement or Profit-Sharing Plans, IRAs, Insurance Contracts, etc." (OMB Control Number 1545-0119). The burden for the collection of information contained in §§1.6050Y-3(f)(1) and 1.6050Y-4(e)(1) of the proposed regulations will be reflected in the burden on the Form W-8ECI (OMB Control Number 1545-1621), when the burden is revised to reflect the additional collection of information in §§1.6050Y-3(f)(1) and 1.6050Y-4(e)(1) of the proposed regulations.

Comments on the collection of information should be sent to the Office of Management and Budget, Attn: Desk Officer for the Department of the Treasury, Office of Information and Regulatory Affairs, Washington, DC 20503, with copies to the Internal Revenue Service, Attn: IRS Reports Clearance Officer, SE:CAR:MP:T:T:SP, Washington, DC 20224. Comments on the collection of information should be received by [***INSERT DATE 60 DAYS AFTER THE DATE OF PUBLICATION IN THE FEDERAL REGISTER***].

Comments are specifically requested concerning:

Whether the proposed collection of information is necessary for the proper performance of the functions of the IRS, including whether the information will have practical utility;

The accuracy of the estimated burden associated with the proposed collection of information;

How the quality, utility, and clarity of the information to be collected may be enhanced;

How the burden of complying with the proposed collection of information may be minimized, including through the application of automated collection techniques or other forms of information technology; and

Estimates of capital or start-up costs and costs of operation, maintenance, and purchase of services to provide information.

An agency may not conduct or sponsor, and a person is not required to respond to, a collection of information unless it displays a valid control number assigned by the Office of Management and Budget.

Background

This document contains proposed amendments to 26 CFR part 1 under sections 101 and 6050Y of the Code (proposed regulations). The proposed regulations implement recent legislative changes to sections 101 and 6050Y by sections 13520 and 13522 of "[a]n Act to provide for reconciliation pursuant to titles II and V of the concurrent resolution on the budget for fiscal year 2018," Pub. L. 115-97, 131 Stat. 2054, 2149 (Act). The proposed regulations under section 101 amend final regulations under section 101 published in the **Federal Register** on November 26, 1960 (25 FR 11402), as subsequently amended on December 24, 1964 (29 FR 18356), September 27, 1982 (47 FR 42337), and July 26, 2007 (72 FR 41159) (existing regulations).

Section 13520 of the Act added section 6050Y to chapter 61 (Information and Returns) of subtitle A of the Code (chapter 61). Section 6050Y imposes information reporting obligations related to certain life insurance contract transactions, including reportable policy sales and payments of reportable death benefits. Section 6050Y provides that each of the returns required by section 6050Y is to be made "at such time and in such manner as the Secretary shall prescribe." The proposed regulations under section 6050Y implement section 6050Y. The proposed regulations specify the manner in which and time at which the information reporting obligations must be satisfied. The proposed regulations also provide definitions and rules that govern the application of the information reporting obligations.

Section 13522 of the Act amended section 101. New section 101(a)(3) defines the term "reportable policy sale" and provides rules for determining the amount of death benefits excluded from gross income following a reportable policy sale. The proposed regulations under section 101 provide definitions applicable under sections 101 and 6050Y and guidance for determining the amount of death benefits excluded from gross income following a reportable policy sale.

Notice 2018-41, 2018-20 I.R.B. 584, described sections 13520 and 13522 of the Act and the regulations the Department of the Treasury (Treasury Department) and the IRS expected to propose under sections 101 and 6050Y. The Treasury Department and the IRS received comments in response to the notice and considered these comments in developing these proposed regulations.

Explanation of Provisions

Section 6050Y imposes information reporting obligations related to reportable policy sales of life insurance contracts and payments of reportable death benefits. Section 1.6050Y-1 of the proposed regulations contains definitional provisions. Sections 1.6050Y-2, 1.6050Y-3, and 1.6050Y-4 of the proposed regulations provide guidance on the reporting obligations imposed by section 6050Y(a), (b), and (c), respectively.

1. *Section 1.6050Y-1: Definitions*

The definitions set forth in § 1.6050Y-1 of the proposed regulations apply for purposes of §§ 1.6050Y-1 through -4 of the proposed regulations.

Under the proposed regulations, "life insurance contract," also referred to as a life insurance policy, is defined by reference to section 7702(a). *See* § 1.6050Y-1(a)(9) of the proposed regulations. "Interest in a life insurance contract," "transfer of an interest in a life insurance contract," "direct acquisition of an interest in a life insurance contract," "indirect acquisition of an interest in a life insurance contract," and "reportable policy sale" are defined by reference to the proposed regulations under section 101. *See* § 1.6050Y-1(a)(3), (5), (6), (14), and (19) of the proposed regulations. "Foreign person" means a person that is not a "United States person," as defined in section 7701(a)(30). *See* § 1.6050Y-1(a)(4) of the proposed regulations.

Section 6050Y(a) requires any person that acquires a life insurance contract or any interest in a life insurance contract in a reportable policy sale during any taxable year to report certain information regarding the transaction, including information about each recipient of payment in the reportable policy sale. Under the proposed regulations, "acquirer" means any person that, directly or indirectly, acquires an interest in a life insurance contract in a reportable policy sale. *See* § 1.6050Y-1(a)(1) of the proposed regulations.

Section 6050Y(d)(1) defines "payment," with respect to any reportable policy sale, to mean the amount of cash and the fair market value of any other consideration transferred in the sale. Under the proposed regulations, "reportable policy sale payment" means the total amount of cash and the fair market value of any other consideration transferred, or to be transferred, in a reportable policy sale, including any amount of a reportable policy sale payment recipient's debt assumed by the acquirer in a reportable policy sale. *See* § 1.6050Y-1(a)(15) of the proposed regulations. An interest in a life insurance contract may be acquired directly, from the direct holder of the interest, or indirectly, through the acquisition of an ownership interest in an entity that holds an interest in a life insurance contract. *See* §§ 1.101-1(e)(3)(i) and (ii) and 1.6050Y-1(a)(3) and (5) of the proposed regulations. In the case of an indirect acquisition of an interest in a life insurance contract that is a reportable policy sale, the reportable policy sale payment is the amount of cash and the fair market value of any other consideration transferred for the ownership interest in the entity that is appropriately allocable to the interest in the life insurance contract held by the entity. *See* § 1.6050Y-1(a)(15) of the proposed regulations. The proposed regulations require the acquirer to report the aggregate amount of reportable policy sale payments made, or to be made, with respect to a reportable policy sale. *See* § 1.6050Y-2(a)(5) of the proposed regulations. Accordingly, when an acquirer makes payments in installments in more than one year, the acquirer reports the total amount of all payments in the year of the policy sale.

"Reportable policy sale payment recipient" means any person that receives a reportable policy sale payment in a reportable policy sale. *See* § 1.6050Y-1(a)(16) of the proposed regulations. The seller in a reportable policy sale is a reportable policy sale payment recipient if the seller receives a reportable policy sale payment. A broker or other intermediary that retains a portion of the cash or other consideration transferred in a reportable policy sale is also a reportable policy sale payment recipient. Id. The aggregate amount of all reportable policy sale payments made with respect to a reportable policy sale must be reported under section 6050Y(a). The objective of the proposed regulations is for the acquirer to report the net payment, if any, made to each person involved in a reportable policy sale. Accordingly, if the acquirer transfers cash or other consideration to a broker in a reportable policy sale, the broker is a reportable policy sale payment recipient, and the reportable policy sale payment made to the broker is the amount of cash and the fair market value of any other consideration retained by the broker. The reportable policy sale payment made to the seller would be the amount of cash and fair market value of any other consideration transferred to the seller, including any amount of the seller's debt assumed by the acquirer in a reportable policy sale, and it would not include the amount of the reportable policy sale payment made to the broker.

Comments received on Notice 2018-41 suggested that the amount of the payment to a seller in a reportable policy sale that should be reported under section 6050Y(a) should be the amount actually paid to the seller. These comments were taken into consideration in developing the definition of "reportable policy sale payment recipient" in the proposed regulations, as well as the reporting requirements in the proposed regulations, which require the acquirer in a reportable policy sale to report, with respect to each reportable policy sale payment recipient, the aggregate amount of reportable policy sale payments made to that person. *See* § 1.6050Y-2(a)(5) of the proposed regulations.

Comments received on Notice 2018-41 suggested that no reporting should be required for payments of ancillary costs and expenses in a reportable policy sale, including broker fees, securities intermediary fees, and other fees and expenses. Comments noted that the person paying these expenses is normally paying them in connection with the conduct of a trade or business, and is therefore required to report these amounts to payees in accordance with applicable rules. The proposed regulations require the acquirer in a reportable policy sale to report all reportable policy sale payments made with respect to the reportable policy sale, meaning all amounts of cash and the fair market value of any other consideration transferred in the reportable policy sale, including any amount of a reportable policy sale payment recipient's debt assumed by the acquirer in a reportable policy sale. The Treasury Department and the IRS are considering whether reportable policy sale payments should be defined to exclude payments of any ancillary costs and expenses and request comments regarding the types of payments made by acquirers in reportable policy sales, the recipients of those payments, and existing reporting requirements applicable to those payments.

Section 6050Y(b) requires issuers of life insurance contracts receiving a written statement furnished by an acquirer under section 6050Y(a) and § 1.6050Y-2 of the proposed regulations (a "reportable policy sale statement" or "RPSS," under § 1.6050Y-1(a)(17) of the proposed regulations) or notice of a transfer to a foreign person to report certain information regarding sellers. Under the proposed regulations, "seller" means any person that holds an interest in a life insurance contract and transfers that interest, or any part of that interest, to an acquirer in a reportable policy sale or any person that owns a life insurance contract and transfers title to, possession of, or legal ownership of that life insurance contract to a foreign person. *See* § 1.6050Y-1(a)(18) of the proposed regulations. "Notice of a transfer to a foreign person" means any notice of a transfer of a life insurance contract (*i.e.*, a transfer of title to, possession of, or legal ownership of the life insurance contract) received by a 6050Y(b) issuer (as that term is defined in § 1.6050Y-1(a)(8)(iii)(B) of the proposed regulations). *See* § 1.6050Y-1(a)(10) of the proposed regulations. Notice of a transfer to a foreign person includes information provided for nontax purposes such as a change of address notice for purposes of sending statements or for other purposes, and information relating to loans, premiums, or death benefits with respect to the contract, unless the 6050Y(b) issuer knows that no transfer of the life insurance contract has occurred or knows the transferee is a United States person. Id. For this purpose, a 6050Y(b) issuer may rely on a Form W-9, Request for Taxpayer Identification Number and Certification, or a valid substitute form, that meets the requirements of § 1.1441-1(d)(2) (substituting "6050Y(b) issuer" for "withholding agent"), that indicates the transferee is a United States person.

The definition of "issuer" under the proposed regulations depends on the context in which the term is used. In general, the term "issuer" means, on any date, with respect to any interest in a life insurance contract, any person that bears any part of the risk with respect to the life insurance contract on that date and any person responsible on that date for administering the contract, including collecting premiums and paying death benefits. *See* § 1.6050Y-1(a)(8)(i) of the proposed regulations. For instance, if a reinsurer reinsures on an indemnity basis all or a portion of the risks that the original issuer (and continuing contract administrator) might otherwise have incurred with respect to a life insurance contract, both the reinsurer and the original issuer of the contract are issuers of the life insurance contract. Id.

Additionally, any designee of an issuer for purposes of section 6050Y reporting purposes is generally also considered an issuer. *See* § 1.6050Y-1(a)(8)(i) of the proposed regulations. Under § 1.6050Y-1(a)(8)(iv) of the proposed regulations, a person is the designee of an issuer for purposes of section 6050Y reporting under § 1.6050Y-1(a)(8) only if so designated in writing, including electronically. The designation must be signed and acknowledged, in writing or electronically, by the person named as designee, or that person's representative, and by the issuer making the designation, or a representative of that issuer.

For purposes of information reporting by the acquirer under section 6050Y(a) and § 1.6050Y-2 of the proposed regulations, the "6050Y(a) issuer" is the issuer that is responsible for administering the life insurance contract, including collecting premiums and paying death benefits under the contract, on the date of the reportable policy sale. *See* § 1.6050Y-1(a)(8)(ii) of the proposed regulations.

For purposes of information reporting by the issuer under section 6050Y(b) and § 1.6050Y-3 of the proposed regulations, the definition of "6050Y(b) issuer" depends on whether the reporting obligation results from a reportable policy sale and the receipt of a RPSS, or by a transfer to a foreign person and the receipt of notice of a transfer to a foreign person. *See* § 1.6050Y-1(a)(8)(iii)(A) of the proposed regulations (applicable to reportable policy sales) and § 1.6050Y-1(a)(8)(iii)(B) of the proposed regulations (applicable to transfers to foreign persons).

With respect to a life insurance contract, or an interest therein, that is transferred in a reportable policy sale, the 6050Y(b) issuer is any person that (1) Receives a RPSS with respect to the life insurance contract or interest therein (or, in the case of a designee, receives notice that the issuer for whom it serves as designee received a RPSS), and (2) is or was, on or before the date of receipt of the RPSS, an issuer (as defined in § 1.6050Y-1(a)(8)(i) of the proposed regulations) with respect to the life insurance contract. *See* § 1.6050Y-1(a)(8)(iii)(A) of the proposed regulations. More than one person may meet this definition, but a 6050Y(b) issuer's reporting obligation is deemed satisfied if the information required by section 6050Y(b) and § 1.6050Y-3 is timely reported by any other 6050Y(b) issuer. *See* § 1.6050Y-3(b) of the proposed regulations.

With respect to a life insurance contract transferred to a foreign person, the 6050Y(b) issuer generally is any person that (1) Receives notice of the transfer of the life insurance contract to a foreign person, and (2) is or was, on the date of transfer or on the date of receipt of the notice, an issuer (as defined in § 1.6050Y-1(a)(8)(i) of the proposed regulations), with respect to the life insurance contract. *See* § 1.6050Y-1(a)(8)(iii)(B) of the proposed regulations. However, a person is not a 6050Y(b) issuer under § 1.6050Y-1(a)(8)(iii)(B) of the proposed regulations if (1) That person (or, in the case of a designee, the issuer for whom it serves as designee) is not responsible for administering the life insurance contract, including collecting premiums and paying death benefits under the contract, on the date the notice of a transfer to a foreign person of a life insurance contract is received, and (2) that person, or its designee, provides the 6050Y(b) issuer that is responsible for administering the life insurance contract, including collecting premiums and paying death benefits under the contract, on that date with such notice and any available information necessary to accomplish reporting under section 6050Y(b) and § 1.6050Y-3 of the proposed regulations. *See* § 1.6050Y-1(a)(8)(iii)(B) of the proposed regulations.

Section 6050Y(c) imposes reporting requirements on any person that makes a payment of reportable death benefits during any taxable year. Section 6050Y(d)(4) defines the term "reportable death benefits" to mean amounts paid by reason of the death of the insured under a life insurance contract that has been transferred in a reportable policy sale. The proposed regulations clarify that the amounts must be attributable to an interest in the life insurance contract that was transferred in a reportable policy sale. *See* § 1.6050Y-1(a)(12) of the proposed regulations. For instance, if the original policyholder of a life insurance contract transfers a 50 percent interest in the life insurance contract in a reportable policy sale, amounts paid by reason of the death of the insured that are attributable to the 50 percent interest retained by the original policyholder are not reportable death benefits.

The proposed regulations define "payor" to mean any person making a payment of reportable death benefits and "reportable death benefits payment recipient" to mean any person that receives reportable death benefits as a beneficiary under the life insurance contract or as the holder of an interest in the life insurance contract. *See* § 1.6050Y-1(a)(11) and (13) of the proposed regulations. Comments received on Notice 2018-41 suggested that "payor" be defined the same as "issuer" for purposes of section 6050Y. The proposed regulations do not adopt this suggestion, but comments are requested as to whether payor should be so narrowly defined, or should also include any holder of an interest in a life insurance contract that receives reportable death benefits attributable to that interest and is contractually obligated to pay part or all of the proceeds to the beneficial owner of the interest. Comments are also requested as to whether, for purposes of reporting under section 6050Y(c), reportable death benefits payment recipients should include, in addition to any person that receives reportable death benefits as a beneficiary under the life insurance contract, any person that receives reportable death benefits as the holder of an interest in the life insurance contract.

Section 6050Y(b) and § 1.6050Y-3 of the proposed regulations require issuers to report the seller's investment in the contract to the seller, and section 6050Y(c) and § 1.6050Y-4 of the proposed regulations require payors to report the payor's estimate of the buyer's investment in the contract to the reportable death benefits payment recipient. The "buyer," with respect to any interest in a life insurance contract that has been transferred in a reportable policy sale, is the person that was the most recent acquirer of that interest in a reportable policy sale as of the date reportable death benefits are paid under the contract. *See* § 1.6050Y-1(a)(2) of the proposed regulations.

Under the proposed regulations, the meaning of "investment in the contract" depends on whose investment in the contract is being determined. With respect to the original policyholder of a life insurance contract, § 1.6050Y-1(a)(7)(i) of the proposed regulations provides that "investment in the contract" has the same meaning as under section 72(e)(6). With respect to the original policyholder, the issuer will have all of the information required to determine that amount.

With respect to anyone other than the original policyholder, the issuer or payor may lack information required to determine the seller's or buyer's investment in the contract as defined in section 72(e)(6), such as the aggregate amount of consideration paid for the contract and the extent to which amounts received under the contract were excludable from gross income. In this context, § 1.6050Y-1(a)(7)(i) of the proposed regulations provides that "investment in the contract" has the same meaning as "estimate of investment in the contract." Section 1.6050Y-1(a)(7)(ii) of the proposed regulations defines "estimate of investment in the contract" with respect to any person other than the original policyholder to mean, on any date, the aggregate amount of premiums paid for the contract by that person before that date, less the aggregate amount received under the contract by that person before that date to the extent such information is known to or can reasonably be estimated by the issuer or payor.

2. *Section 1.6050Y-2: Reporting of Payments by Acquirer in a Reportable Policy Sale*

Section 6050Y(a) requires reporting of payments made by an acquirer in a reportable policy sale. Section 1.6050Y-2(a) of the proposed regulations sets forth the requirement of information reporting applicable to acquirers in reportable policy sales under section 6050Y(a)(1) and describes the information that must be reported.

The proposed regulations allow for unified reporting by the acquirers in a series of prearranged transfers of any interest in a life insurance contract. *See* §1.6050Y-2(b) and (d)(3) of the proposed regulations. A series of prearranged transfers of an interest in a life insurance contract may include transfers in which one or more persons serve as intermediaries. Such intermediaries may acquire title or possession of an interest in a life insurance contract for state law purposes as nominee on behalf of another person or persons. Comments received on Notice 2018-41 suggested that a rule allowing unified reporting be adopted with respect to acquirers in a series of prearranged transfers, and these comments were taken into consideration in developing the rules in the proposed regulations.

Section 1.6050Y-2(c) of the proposed regulations sets forth the time and place for filing returns required under section 6050Y(a)(1).

Section 1.6050Y-2(d) of the proposed regulations sets forth the requirement under section 6050Y(a)(2) for the acquirer in a reportable policy sale to furnish a written statement to certain persons with respect to whom information is required on the return required by section 6050Y(a)(1). These persons are the recipients of payments in reportable policy sales (reportable policy sale payment recipients) and the 6050Y(a) issuers.

A written statement provided to a reportable policy sale payment recipient is not required to include information with respect to any other reportable policy sale payment recipient in the reportable policy sale. *See* §1.6050Y-2(d)(1)(i) of the proposed regulations. For instance, the statement is not required to provide information about reportable policy sale payments to any other reportable policy sale payment recipient. Id. The contact information of the person furnishing the written statement must provide direct access to a person that can answer questions about the statement. Id.

Reportable policy sale payment recipients may use the information in the written statements furnished by acquirers to determine their taxable income. To facilitate proper tax reporting, the proposed regulations provide that an acquirer must furnish any written statement required to be provided to a reportable policy sale payment recipient no later than February 15 of the year following the calendar year in which the reportable policy sale occurs. *See* §1.6050Y-2(d)(1)(ii) of the proposed regulations. The proposed regulations adopt this deadline because a person may be both a reportable policy sale payment recipient and a seller with respect to a reportable policy sale, and this deadline for an acquirer to furnish a written statement to a reportable policy sale payment recipient coordinates with the deadline in §1.6050Y-3(d)(2) of the proposed regulations for a 6050Y(b) issuer that receives a RPSS to furnish a written statement to a seller.

Generally, a 6050Y(a) issuer that receives a RPSS from an acquirer becomes a 6050Y(b) issuer subject to reporting obligations under section 6050Y(b), including the obligation under section 6050Y(b)(2) to furnish a written statement to the seller in a reportable policy sale. Because 6050Y(b) issuers' reporting obligation is with respect to sellers, the proposed regulations provide that acquirers must furnish the 6050Y(a) issuer with a RPSS with respect to each reportable policy sale payment recipient that is also a seller. *See* §1.6050Y-2(d)(2)(i)(A) of the proposed regulations. However, an acquirer acquiring an interest in a life insurance contract in an indirect acquisition is not required to furnish a RPSS to the 6050Y(a) issuer. *See* §1.6050Y-2(d)(2)(i)(B) of the proposed regulations. As provided in section 6050Y(a)(2)(B), the proposed regulations provide that acquirers are not required to set forth the amount of any reportable policy sale payment in a RPSS furnished to a 6050Y(a) issuer. *See* §1.6050Y-2(d)(2)(i)(A) of the proposed regulations. Sellers may need the information in the written statements furnished by 6050Y(b) issuers that have received a RPSS to determine their taxable income. To facilitate proper tax reporting, the proposed regulations therefore provide that an acquirer must furnish a RPSS to the 6050Y(a) issuer by the later of (1) 20 days after the reportable policy sale, or (2) 5 days after the end of the applicable state law rescission period. *See* §1.6050Y-2(d)(2)(ii) of the proposed regulations. However, if the later date is after January 15 of the year following the calendar year in which the reportable policy sale occurred, the RPSS must be furnished by January 15 of the year following the calendar year in which the reportable policy sale occurred. Id. Section 1.6050Y-3(d)(2) of the proposed regulations generally requires that the 6050Y(b) issuer furnish any written statement required by section 6050Y(b)(2) to the seller no later than February 15 of the year following the calendar year in which the reportable policy sale occurs.

Section 1.6050Y-2(e) of the proposed regulations requires the acquirer to correct returns filed under section 6050Y(a)(1) and written statements furnished under section 6050Y(a)(2) within 15 days of the acquirer's receipt of notice of the rescission of the related reportable policy sale.

Section 1.6050Y-2(f) of the proposed regulations sets forth exceptions to reporting under section 6050Y(a) that may apply to an acquirer that is a foreign person. These exceptions are described in section 5 of this Explanation of Provisions.

Section 1.6050Y-2(g) of the proposed regulations describes the penalty provisions applicable when a person is required under section 6050Y(a) to file an information return, or furnish a written statement, but fails to do so on or before the prescribed date, fails to include all of the information required to be shown, or includes incorrect information.

3. *Section 1.6050Y-3: Reporting of Transferor's Investment in the Contract by 6050Y(b) Issuer (Reportable Policy Sale or Transfer to a Foreign Person)*

Section 6050Y(b) requires the issuer to report certain information to the seller, including the seller's investment in the contract. Section 1.6050Y-3(a) of the proposed regulations sets forth the information reporting requirement applicable to 6050Y(b) issuers under section 6050Y(b)(1). In addition to the specific information required to be reported under section 6050Y(b)(1), Notice 2018-41 indicated that the proposed regulations would require the issuer to report the amount that would have been received by the policyholder upon surrender of the contract. A comment received on Notice 2018-41 suggested that an issuer should not be required to report this amount because the information may be provided directly by the issuer to the seller upon request.

A purpose of section 6050Y is to provide the seller in a reportable policy sale and the IRS with the information needed to determine the seller's taxable income from the sale. In the case of a sale of a cash value life insurance contract, the gain is ordinary income to the extent of the amount that would be recognized as ordinary income if the contract were surrendered, and any excess is capital gain. *See* Rev. Rul. 2009-13, 2009-21 I.R.B. 1029. To ensure that the seller and the IRS have the relevant information needed to calculate the seller's gain from the sale, including the amount of any capital or ordinary gain, the proposed regulations do not adopt the suggestion and would require the 6050Y(b) issuer to report to the seller and the IRS the amount that would have been received by the policyholder upon surrender of the contract. The Treasury Department and the IRS have determined that requiring the reporting of this information is authorized under section 6050Y(b)(1), as well as under sections 6011(a) and 7805.

Section 1.6050Y-3(b) of the proposed regulations provides that a 6050Y(b) issuer's reporting obligation under section 6050Y(b) and § 1.6050Y-3(a) is deemed satisfied if the information required by section 6050Y(b) and § 1.6050Y-3 is timely reported by any other 6050Y(b) issuer or a third party information reporting contractor.

Section 1.6050Y-3(c) of the proposed regulations sets forth the time and place for filing returns required under section 6050Y(b)(1).

Section 1.6050Y-3(d)(1) of the proposed regulations sets forth the requirement under section 6050Y(b)(2) to furnish statements to certain persons with respect to whom information is required on the return required by section 6050Y(b)(1). These persons are the sellers that (1) Transfer interests in life insurance contracts in reportable policy sales and are reportable policy sale payment recipients, or (2) transfer life insurance contracts to foreign persons. The sellers may use the information in the written statements furnished under section 6050Y(b)(2) to determine their taxable income.

To facilitate proper tax reporting, § 1.6050Y-2(d)(2)(ii) of the proposed regulations requires acquirers to furnish a RPSS to the 6050Y(a) issuer by January 15 of the year following the calendar year in which the reportable policy sale occurred, if not earlier, and § 1.6050Y-3(d)(2) of the proposed regulations provides that a 6050Y(b) issuer generally must furnish any written statement required to be provided to a seller no later than February 15 of the year following the calendar year in which the reportable policy sale or transfer to a foreign person occurs. Comments received on Notice 2018-41 suggested that issuers be required to furnish written statements required by section 6050Y(b)(2) to the seller no later than February 15 of the year following the calendar year in which the reportable policy sale occurs, noting that this is currently the due date for section 6045 broker returns and consolidated statements, and brokers also rely on third party information (e.g., dividend reclassifications). The Treasury Department and the IRS propose to adopt this suggestion. *See* § 1.6050Y-3(d)(2) of the proposed regulations. Section 1.6050Y-3(d)(3) of the proposed regulations provides that a 6050Y(b) issuer's reporting obligation is deemed satisfied if the information required by § 1.6050Y-3(d)(1) of the proposed regulations with respect to that 6050Y(b) issuer is timely reported on behalf of that 6050Y(b) issuer consistent with forms, instructions, and other IRS guidance by one or more other 6050Y(b) issuers or by a third party information reporting contractor.

Section 1.6050Y-3(e) of the proposed regulations requires the 6050Y(b) issuer to correct returns filed under section 6050Y(b)(1) and written statements furnished under section 6050Y(b)(2) within 15 days of the 6050Y(b) issuer's receipt of notice of the rescission of the related reportable policy sale or transfer to a foreign person.

Section 1.6050Y-3(f) of the proposed regulations sets forth exceptions to reporting under section 6050Y(b) that may apply to 6050Y(b) issuers. These exceptions are described in section 5 of this Explanation of Provisions.

Section 1.6050Y-3(g) of the proposed regulations describes the penalty provisions applicable when a person is required under section 6050Y(b) to file an information return, or furnish a written statement, but fails to do so on or before the prescribed date, fails to include all of the information required to be shown, or includes incorrect information.

4. *Section 1.6050Y-4: Reporting of Reportable Death Benefits by Payor*

Section 6050Y(c) requires payors to report payments of reportable death benefits. Section 1.6050Y-4(a) of the proposed regulations sets forth the requirement of information reporting applicable to payors under section 6050Y(c)(1).

Section 1.6050Y-4(b) of the proposed regulations sets forth the time and place for filing returns required under section 6050Y(c)(1).

Section 1.6050Y-4(c)(1) of the proposed regulations sets forth the requirement under section 6050Y(c)(2) to furnish statements to persons with respect to whom information is required on the return required by section 6050Y(c)(1). These persons are the recipients of reportable death benefits (reportable death benefits payment recipients). The reportable death benefits payment recipients may use the information in the written statements furnished under section 6050Y(c)(2) to determine their taxable income. To facilitate proper tax reporting, § 1.6050Y-4(c)(2) of the proposed regulations provides that a payor must furnish any written statement required to be provided to a reportable death benefits payment recipient no later than January 31 of the year following the calendar year in which the reportable policy sale occurs. The proposed regulations use January 31 because it is generally the deadline for furnishing copies of Form 1099-R to recipients.

Section 1.6050Y-4(d) of the proposed regulations requires the payor to correct returns filed under section 6050Y(c)(1) and written statements furnished under section 6050Y(c)(2) within 15 days of the payor's receipt of notice of the rescission of the related reportable policy sale.

Section 1.6050Y-4(e) of the proposed regulations sets forth exceptions to reporting under section 6050Y(c) that may apply to payors. These exceptions are described in the next section of this Explanation of Provisions.

Section 1.6050Y-4(f) of the proposed regulations describes the penalty provisions applicable when a person is required under section 6050Y(c) to file an information return, or furnish a written statement, but fails to do so on or before the prescribed date, fails to include all of the information required to be shown, or includes incorrect information.

5. *Exceptions to Reporting under Section 6050Y*

The proposed regulations include certain exceptions to the reporting requirements otherwise imposed on acquirers, 6050Y(b) issuers, and payors under §§ 1.6050Y-2, -3, and -4 of the proposed regulations, respectively. These exceptions to reporting are similar in their intended purposes to exceptions included in regulations issued under other sections in chapter 61 that except reporting by certain payors and brokers (as applicable based on the section) with respect to a transaction occurring outside the United States when no nexus of the transaction to the United States is identified (under criteria specified in each of the regulations). For example, § 1.6045-1 generally requires brokers to report the proceeds of certain sales (such as sales of securities) on a Form 1099-B, Proceeds from Broker and Barter Exchange Transactions, but includes an exception to the term "broker" that applies to most non-U.S. securities brokers for sales that are effected outside of the United States within the meaning provided in those regulations. *See* § 1.6045-1(a) and (g)(3)(iii). Reporting of payments under several of the sections in chapter 61 is also excepted when a payor or broker is permitted to treat the person receiving the payments as a foreign person. For certain of those excepted payments, withholding and reporting requirements may instead apply under chapter 3 of subtitle A of the Code.

Sections 1.6050Y-2(f) and 1.6050Y-3(f)(2) of the proposed regulations describe exceptions to the reporting otherwise required of an acquirer and 6050Y(b) issuer under section 6050Y(a) or (b), respectively, for cases in which the Treasury Department and the IRS are of the view that a nexus of the sale or life insurance contract to the United States is insufficient for applying the reporting provisions of those sections.

Sections 1.6050Y-3(f)(1) and 1.6050Y-4(e)(1) of the proposed regulations provide that reporting under section 6050Y(b) or (c) is not required by 6050Y(b) issuers and payors with respect to sellers or reportable death benefits payment recipients, respectively, documented as foreign beneficial owners under the requirements of the regulations under section 1441. The proposed regulations include, however, two modifications to those requirements. First, §§ 1.6050Y-3(f)(1) and 1.6050Y-4(e)(1) of the proposed regulations permit a 6050Y(b) issuer or payor to treat a partnership or trust as a foreign beneficial owner provided that the 6050Y(b) issuer or payor obtains a written certification from the partnership or trust that no beneficial owner (within the meaning of § 1.1441-1(c)(6)(ii)) of any portion of the sales proceeds or reportable death benefits payment (as applicable based on the section) received by the partnership or trust is a United States person, as well as documentation establishing the partnership's or trust's foreign status. The treatment described in the preceding sentence does not apply, however, when the issuer or payor has actual knowledge that a United States person is a beneficial owner of all or a portion of the sale proceeds or reportable death benefit payment. Second, § 1.6050Y-3(f)(1) of the proposed regulations provides that this exception does not apply to a foreign beneficial owner for which the sale of the insurance contract (or interest therein) results in a requirement to report any of the income from the sale as effectively connected with a U.S. trade or business. To address those cases, the proposed regulations provide that a seller required to report any of the income from the sale of an insurance contract (or interest therein) as effectively connected with the conduct of a trade or business in the United States under section 864(b) must provide to the 6050Y(b) issuer a Form W-8ECI, Certificate of Foreign Person's Claim that Income is Effectively Connected with the Conduct of a Trade or Business in the United States. The proposed regulations do not permit a 6050Y(b) issuer to apply the exception when it receives a Form W-8ECI from a seller or has reason to know that the seller is required to report any of the sale proceeds as income effectively connected with a U.S. trade or business. Similar provisions apply with respect to foreign beneficial owners of reportable death benefits under § 1.6050Y-4(e)(1) of the proposed regulations. However, in response to comments received on Notice 2018-41, the Treasury Department and the IRS are considering whether payors required under section 6050Y(c) and § 1.6050Y-4(e)(1) of the proposed regulations to report payments of reportable death benefits that are income effectively connected with a U.S. trade or business may satisfy their reporting obligation under section 6050Y(c) by filing a Form 1042-S, Foreign Person's U.S. Source Income Subject to Withholding, or if such payors may be relieved from the obligation to report some of the information required to be reported under section 6050Y(c).

Section 1.6050Y-4(e)(2) of the proposed regulations also includes a reporting exception for death benefits paid under an insurance contract (or interest therein) held by a buyer that obtained the contract or interest in a reportable policy sale that was within an exception to reporting described in § 1.6050Y-3(f)(2) of the proposed regulations. The exception to reporting described in § 1.6050Y-3(f)(2) of the proposed regulations applies in those cases in which a 6050Y(b) issuer received only a notice of transfer to a foreign person and, because the requirements set forth in § 1.6050Y-3(f)(2)(i) through (iii) of the proposed regulations were met, was not required to treat the transfer as reportable for purposes of section 6050Y(b).

6. *Section 1.101-1: Exclusion from Gross Income of Proceeds of Life Insurance Contracts Payable by Reason of Death*

Generally, amounts received under a life insurance contract that are paid by reason of the death of the insured are excluded from federal income tax under section 101(a)(1). However, if a life insurance contract is sold or otherwise transferred for valuable consideration, the "transfer for value rule" set forth in section 101(a)(2) limits the excludable portion of the amount paid by reason of the death of the insured. Section 101(a)(2) provides that the excludable amount following a transfer for valuable consideration generally may not exceed the sum of (1) The actual value of the consideration paid by the transferee to acquire the life insurance contract and (2) the premiums and other amounts subsequently paid by the transferee. Section 101(a)(2) provides two exceptions to this transfer for value rule. Specifically, the limitation set forth in section 101(a)(2) does not apply if (1) The transferee's basis in the contract is determined in whole or in part by reference to the transferor's basis in the contract or (2) the transfer is to the insured, to a partner of the insured, to a partnership in which the insured is a partner, or to a corporation in which the insured is a shareholder or officer.

Section 13522 of the Act added section 101(a)(3) to the Code. Section 101(a)(3)(A) provides that these two exceptions shall not apply in the case of a transfer of a life insurance contract, or any interest therein, that is a reportable policy sale. Section 101(a)(3)(B) defines the term "reportable policy sale" to mean the acquisition of an interest in a life insurance contract, directly or indirectly, if the acquirer has no substantial family, business, or financial relationship with the insured apart from the acquirer's interest in such life insurance contract. For purposes of the preceding sentence, the term "indirectly" applies to the acquisition of an interest in a partnership, trust, or other entity that holds an interest in the life insurance contract.

The proposed regulations update § 1.101-1(a)(1) of the existing regulations to reflect the repeal of section 101(b) (treatment of employees' death benefits) in 1996, and the addition of section 7702 (definition of life insurance contract) in 1984, section 101(j) (treatment of certain employer-owned life insurance contracts) in 2006, and section 101(a)(3) (exception to valuable consideration rules for reportable policy sales) in 2017. The proposed regulations remove the second and third sentences of § 1.101-1(a)(1) of the existing regulations and add a sentence at the end of § 1.101-1(a)(1) to address the earlier changes in law. To address the changes in law made by the Act, the proposed regulations under section 101 provide updated rules for determining the amount of death benefits excluded from gross income following a transfer for value or gratuitous transfer, including a reportable policy sale, and provide definitions applicable under section 101. The proposed regulations under section 6050Y adopt the relevant definitions by cross-reference.

The proposed regulations provide that any transfer of an interest in a life insurance contract for cash or other consideration reducible to a money value is a transfer for valuable consideration. *See* § 1.101-1(f)(5) of the proposed regulations; *see also* § 25.2512-8 ("[a] consideration not reducible to a value in money or money's worth, as love and affection, promise of marriage, etc., is to be wholly disregarded"). An interest in a life insurance contract (also referred to as a life insurance policy) is held by any person that has taken title to or possession of the life insurance contract, in whole or part, for state law purposes, including any person that has taken title or possession as nominee for another person, or by any person that has an enforceable right to receive all or a part of the proceeds of the life insurance contract or to any other economic benefits of the insurance policy as described in § 20.2042-1(c)(2). *See* § 1.101-1(e)(1) of the proposed regulations. The enforceable right to designate a contract beneficiary is an interest in a life insurance contract. Id. Any person named as the owner in a life insurance contract generally is the owner (or an owner) of the contract and holds an interest in the contract. Id.

The transfer of an interest in a life insurance contract includes the transfer of any interest in the life insurance contract as well as any transfer of the life insurance contract itself (meaning a transfer of title to, possession of, or legal or beneficial ownership of the life insurance contract). *See* § 1.101-1(e)(2) of the proposed regulations. For instance, the creation of an enforceable right to receive all or a part of the proceeds of a life insurance contract constitutes the transfer of an interest in the life insurance contract. Id. However, the revocable designation of a beneficiary of the policy proceeds does not constitute a transfer of an interest in a life insurance contract to the beneficiary until the designation becomes irrevocable other than by reason of the death of the insured. Id. For purposes of this rule, a beneficiary designation is not revocable if the person with the right to designate the beneficiary of the contract has an enforceable contractual obligation to designate a particular contract beneficiary. The pledging or assignment of a policy as collateral security also is not a transfer of an interest in a life insurance contract. Id. In response to comments received on Notice 2018-41 suggesting that the initial owner of a life insurance contract should not be considered an "acquirer" for purposes of section 6050Y(a), § 1.101-1(e)(2) of the proposed regulations clarifies that the issuance of a life insurance contract to a policyholder, other than the issuance of a policy in an exchange pursuant to section 1035, is not a transfer of an interest in a life insurance contract.

Section 1.101-1(b)(1)(i) of the proposed regulations provides that, in the case of a transfer of an interest in a life insurance contract for valuable consideration, the amount of the proceeds attributable to the interest that is excludable from gross income under section 101(a)(1) is limited under section 101(a)(2) to the sum of the actual value of the consideration for the transfer paid by the transferee and the premiums and other amounts subsequently paid by the transferee with respect to that interest. Consistent with section 101(a)(3), this general rule applies to all transfers of interests in life insurance contracts for valuable consideration that are reportable policy sales. Consistent with section 101(a)(2), this general rule also continues to apply to transfers of interests in life insurance contracts for valuable consideration that are not reportable policy sales, unless an exception set forth in section 101(a)(2) applies. *See* § 1.101-1(b)(1)(i) and (ii) of the proposed regulations. Section 1.101-1(b)(1)(ii)(A) of the proposed regulations applies to carryover basis transfers that are not also subject to § 1.101-1(b)(1)(ii)(B) of the proposed regulations. Section 1.101-1(b)(1)(ii)(B) of the proposed regulations applies to transfers to certain persons.

Under § 1.101-1(b)(1)(ii)(A) of the proposed regulations, the limitation described in section 101(a)(2) and § 1.101-1(b)(1)(i) of the proposed regulations does not apply to the transfer of an interest in a life insurance contract for valuable consideration if (1) The transfer is not a reportable policy sale, (2) the basis of the interest transferred, for the purpose of determining gain or loss with respect to the transferee, is determinable in whole or in part by reference to the basis of that interest in the hands of the transferor, and (3) § 1.101-1(b)(1)(ii)(B) of the proposed regulations does not apply to the transfer. The amount of the proceeds attributable to the interest that is excludable from gross income under section 101(a)(1) is, however, limited to the sum of (1) The amount that would have been excludable by the transferor, and (2) the premiums and other amounts subsequently paid by the transferee.

This limitation applies without regard to whether the interest previously has been transferred or to the nature of any prior transfer of the interest. For instance, it is irrelevant whether a prior transfer was gratuitous or for value, whether section 101(a)(2)(A) or (B) applied to a prior transfer, whether any prior transfer was a reportable policy sale, or whether the prior transfer was of the same interest or a larger interest in a life insurance contract that included the same interest. If the full amount of the proceeds would have been excludable by the transferor, as would generally be the case if the original policyholder is the transferor, § 1.101-1(b)(1)(ii)(A) of the proposed regulations will, as a practical matter, impose no limitation on the amount of the proceeds attributable to the interest that is excludable from gross income under section 101(a)(1).

Under § 1.101-1(b)(1)(ii)(B)(*1*) of the proposed regulations, the limitation on the excludable amount of the proceeds described in section 101(a)(2) and § 1.101-1(b)(1)(i) of the proposed regulations will not apply to an interest in a life insurance contract that is transferred for valuable consideration if (1) The transfer is not a reportable policy sale and the interest was not previously transferred for valuable consideration in a reportable policy sale, and (2) the transfer is to the insured, a partner of the insured, a partnership in which the insured is a partner, or a corporation in which the insured is a shareholder or officer (a (B)(*1*) person).

Under § 1.101-1(b)(1)(ii)(B)(*2*) of the proposed regulations, if a transfer of an interest in a life insurance contract to a (B)(*1*) person follows a transfer for valuable consideration in a reportable policy sale (whether in the immediately preceding transfer or an earlier transfer), the amount of the proceeds attributable to that interest that is excludable from gross income under section 101(a)(1) is limited to the sum of (1) The higher of the amount that would have been excludable by the transferor if the transfer to the (B)(*1*) person had not occurred or the actual value of the consideration for the transfer to the (B)(*1*) person paid by the (B)(*1*) person, and (2) the premiums and other amounts subsequently paid by the transferee. Thus, in determining the excludable amount of the proceeds attributable to an interest in a life insurance contract that is transferred to a (B)(*1*) person in a transfer that is not a reportable policy sale, the limitation described in section 101(a)(2) and § 1.101-1(b)(1)(i) of the proposed regulations is inapplicable unless the interest previously had been transferred in a reportable policy sale. Additionally, because of the alternative in the formula for computing the limitation, a (B)(*1*) person will not be subject to a less favorable limitation than the limitation applicable to a transferee in a carryover basis transfer eligible for the exception set forth in § 1.101-1(b)(1)(ii)(A) of the proposed regulations.

The proposed regulations provide a single rule applicable to all gratuitous transfers of interests in life insurance contracts, including reportable policy sales that are not for valuable consideration: the amount of the proceeds attributable to the interest that is excludable from gross income under section

101(a)(1) is limited to the sum of (1) The amount of the proceeds attributable to the gratuitously transferred interest that would have been excludable by the transferor if the transfer had not occurred, and (2) the premiums and other amounts subsequently paid by the transferee. *See* § 1.101-1(b)(2)(i) of the proposed regulations. Although § 1.101-1(b)(2) of the existing regulations provides a special rule for gratuitous transfers made by or to the insured, a partner of the insured, a partnership in which the insured is a partner, or a corporation in which the insured is a shareholder or officer, such a rule is not required by section 101(a), and the proposed regulations do not contain a special rule for these transfers because it could be subject to abuse.

Section 1.101-1(b)(3) of the proposed regulations clarifies that, for purposes of § 1.101-1(b)(1) and (2) of the proposed regulations, in determining the amounts, if any, of consideration paid by the transferee for the transfer of an interest in a life insurance contract and premiums and other amounts subsequently paid by the transferee with respect to that interest, the amounts paid by the transferee are reduced, but not below zero, by amounts received by the transferee under the life insurance contract that are not received as an annuity, to the extent excludable from gross income under section 72(e). This provision is necessary to prevent an exclusion from gross income based on a double-counting of consideration paid.

Section 1.101-1(c) of the proposed regulations defines the term "reportable policy sale," which was introduced in section 101(a)(3). The proposed regulations provide that, as a general matter, any direct or indirect acquisition of an interest in a life insurance contract is a "reportable policy sale" if the acquirer has, at the time of the acquisition, no substantial family, business, or financial relationship with the insured apart from the acquirer's interest in that life insurance contract. *See* § 1.101-1(c)(1) of the proposed regulations.

Under § 1.101-1(e)(3)(i) of the proposed regulations, the transfer of an interest in a life insurance contract results in the direct acquisition of the interest by the transferee (acquirer). Under § 1.101-1(e)(3)(ii) of the proposed regulations, an indirect acquisition of an interest in a life insurance contract occurs when a person (acquirer) becomes a beneficial owner of a partnership, trust, or other entity that holds (directly or indirectly) an interest in the life insurance contract. For this purpose, the term "other entity" does not include a C corporation (as that term is defined in section 1361(a)(2)), unless more than 50 percent of the gross value of the assets of the C corporation (as determined under § 1.101-1(f)(4)) consists of life insurance contracts immediately before the indirect acquisition. Under § 1.101-1(f)(1) of the proposed regulations, a "beneficial owner" of a partnership, trust, or other entity is an individual or C corporation with an ownership interest in that partnership, trust, or other entity. The beneficial owner's interest may be held directly or indirectly, through one or more other partnerships, trusts, or other entities.

Accordingly, under § 1.101-1(e)(3)(ii) of the proposed regulations, persons that acquire shares in a C corporation that holds an interest in a life insurance contract generally will not be considered to have an indirect acquisition of an interest in such contract. However, if the C corporation primarily owns life insurance contracts (or interests therein), any person that acquires shares in the C corporation will be considered to have an indirect acquisition of an interest in any life insurance contract held by the C corporation.

Section 1.101-1(d) of the proposed regulations defines the terms "substantial family relationship," "substantial business relationship," and "substantial financial relationship." Under section 1.101-1(d)(1) of the proposed regulations, a "substantial family relationship" is the relationship between an individual and any family member of that individual as defined in § 1.101-1(f)(3) of the proposed regulations. A substantial family relationship also exists between an individual and his or her former spouse with regard to a transfer of an interest in a life insurance contract to (or in trust for the benefit of) that former spouse incident to divorce. *See* § 1.101-1(d)(1) of the proposed regulations. Additionally, a substantial family relationship exists between the insured and an entity if all of the entity's beneficial owners have a substantial family relationship with the insured. Id.

Section 1.101-1(d)(2) describes the two situations in which a substantial business relationship exists between the acquirer and insured: (1) The insured is a key person (as defined in section 264) of, or materially participates (as defined in section 469 and the corresponding regulations) in, an active trade or business as an owner, employee, or contractor, and at least 80% of that trade or business is owned (directly or indirectly, through one or more partnerships, trusts, or other entities) by the acquirer or the beneficial owners of the acquirer, and (2) the acquirer acquires an active trade or business and acquires the interest in the life insurance contract either as part of that acquisition or from a person owning significant property leased to the acquired trade or business or life insurance policies held to facilitate the succession of the ownership of the business, if certain requirements are met. *See* § 1.101-1(d)(2)(i) and (ii) of the proposed regulations.

Comments received on Notice 2018-41 suggested that acquisitions of life insurance contracts, or interests therein, in certain ordinary course business transactions involving the acquisition of a trade or business should not be considered reportable policy sales, including ordinary course business transactions whereby one trade or business acquires another trade or business that owns life insurance on the lives of former employees or directors. The definition of substantial business relationship in § 1.101-1(d)(2) of the proposed regulations, as well as certain other provisions in the proposed regulations, are intended to exclude certain of these transactions from the definition of reportable policy sales.

Section 1.101-1(d)(3) of the proposed regulations describes the three situations in which a substantial financial relationship exists between the insured and the acquirer: (1) The acquirer (directly or indirectly, through one or more partnerships, trusts, or other entities of which it is a beneficial owner) has, or the beneficial owners of the acquirer have, a common investment (other than the interest in the life insurance contract) with the insured and a buy-out of the insured's interest in the common investment by the co-investor(s) after the insured's death is reasonably foreseeable; (2) the acquirer maintains the life insurance contract on the life of the insured to provide funds to purchase assets or satisfy liabilities following the death of the insured; or (3) the acquirer is an organization described in sections 170(c), 2055(a), and 2522(a) that previously received financial support in a substantial amount or significant volunteer support from the insured. *See* § 1.101-1(d)(3)(i) through (iii) of the proposed regulations.

The proposed regulations also specify that the fact that an acquirer is a partner of the insured, a partnership in which the insured is a partner, or a corporation in which the insured is a shareholder or officer (all relationships that are covered by an exception from the transfer for value rule) is not sufficient to establish a substantial business or financial relationship, nor is such status required to establish a substantial business or financial relationship. *See* § 1.101-1(d)(4)(ii) of the proposed regulations. The proposed regulations also clarify that, for purposes of determining whether the acquirer in an indirect acquisition of an interest in a life insurance contract has a substantial business or financial relationship with the insured, the acquirer will be deemed to have a substantial business or financial relationship with the insured if the direct holder of the interest in the life insurance contract has a substantial business or financial relationship with the insured immediately before and after the date the acquirer acquires its interest. *See* § 1.101-1(d)(4)(i) of the proposed regulations. Accordingly, the acquirer in an indirect acquisition may establish a substantial business or financial relationship with the insured based on the acquirer's own relationship with the insured or the relationship between the insured and the direct holder of the interest in the life insurance contract.

The proposed regulations also provide several exceptions from the definition of reportable policy sale. The proposed regulations provide that the transfer of an interest in a life insurance contract between certain related entities is not a reportable policy sale. Specifically, a transfer between entities with the same beneficial owners is not a reportable policy sale if the ownership interest of each beneficial owner in each entity does not vary by more than a 20 percent ownership interest. *See* § 1.101-1(c)(2)(i) and (g)(10) of the proposed regulations. Also, a transfer between corporations that are members of an affiliated group (as defined in section 1504(a)) that files a consolidated U.S. tax return for the taxable year in which the transfer occurs is not a reportable policy sale. *See* § 1.101-1(c)(2)(ii) of the proposed regulations.

Finally, in response to comments received on Notice 2018-41, certain indirect acquisitions of life insurance contracts, or interests in life insurance contracts, are excepted from the definition of a reportable policy sale. The limited definition of "indirect acquisition" under § 1.101-1(e)(3)(ii) of the proposed regulations means that shareholders acquiring an interest in a C corporation that holds an interest in one or more life insurance contracts will not be considered to have an indirect acquisition or reportable policy sale unless the C corporation primarily owns life insurance contracts (or interests therein). The proposed regulations also provide an exception from the definition of a reportable policy sale for an indirect acquisition of an interest in a life insurance contract if the direct holder of the interest acquired the interest in a reportable policy sale and reported the acquisition in compliance with section 6050Y(a) and § 1.6050Y-2 of the proposed regulations. *See* § 1.101-1(c)(2)(iii)(A) of the proposed regulations. Also, the indirect acquisition of an interest in a life insurance contract is not a reportable policy sale if (1) Immediately before the acquisition, no more than 50 percent of the gross value of the assets of the entity that directly holds the interest in the life insurance contract consists of life insurance contracts, and (2) the acquirer and his or her family members own five percent or less of the ownership interests in the entity that directly holds the interest in the life insurance contract. *See* § 1.101-1(c)(2)(iii)(B) of the proposed regulations. Section 1.101-1(f)(4) of the proposed regulations provides rules regarding the determination of the gross value of assets for this purpose.

Applicability Dates

The rules in § 1.101-1(b) through (g) of the proposed regulations are proposed to apply, for purposes of section 6050Y, to reportable policy sales made after December 31, 2017, and to reportable death benefits paid after December 31, 2017. For any other purpose, § 1.101-1(b) through (g) of the proposed regulations apply to transfers of life insurance contracts, or interests therein, made after the date the Treasury decision adopting these regulations as final regulations is published in the **Federal Register**.

The rules in § 1.6050Y-1 of the proposed regulations are proposed to apply to reportable policy sales made and reportable death benefits paid after December 31, 2017. The rules in § § 1.6050Y-2 and 1.6050Y-3 are proposed to apply to reportable policy sales made after December 31, 2017. The rules in § 1.6050Y-4 are proposed to apply to reportable death benefits paid after December 31, 2017. *See* § 1.6050Y-1(b) of the proposed regulations.

For reportable policy sales and payments of reportable death benefits occurring after December 31, 2017, and before the date final regulations are published in the **Federal Register**, § 1.6050Y-1(b) of the proposed regulations would provide transition relief as follows:

1. With respect to reportable policy sales occurring after December 31, 2017, and before the date final regulations are published in the **Federal Register**, statements required to be furnished to issuers

under section 6050Y(a)(2) must be furnished by the later of the applicable deadline set forth in final regulations or 60 days after the date final regulations are published in the **Federal Register**;

2. With respect to reportable policy sales occurring after December 31, 2017, and before the date final regulations are published in the **Federal Register**, returns required to be filed under section 6050Y(a)(1) and (b)(1) and statements required to be furnished to payment recipients and sellers under section 6050Y(a)(2) and (b)(2) must be filed or furnished by the later of the applicable deadline set forth in final regulations or 90 days after the date final regulations are published in the **Federal Register**; and

3. With respect to payments of reportable death benefits paid after December 31, 2017, and before the date final regulations are published in the **Federal Register**, returns required to be filed under section 6050Y(c)(1) and statements required to be furnished to payment recipients under section 6050Y(c)(2) must be filed or furnished by the later of the applicable deadline set forth in final regulations or 90 days after the date final regulations are published in the **Federal Register**.

Special Analyses

The proposed regulations are not subject to review under section 6(b) of Executive Order 12866 pursuant to the Memorandum of Agreement (April 11, 2018) between the Treasury Department and the Office of Management and Budget regarding review of tax regulations.

When the IRS issues a proposed rulemaking imposing a requirement on small entities, the Regulatory Flexibility Act (RFA) requires the agency to "prepare and make available for public comment an initial regulatory flexibility analysis," which will "describe the impact of the proposed rule on small entities." 5 U.S.C. 603(a). Section 605(b) of the RFA allows an agency to certify a rule, in lieu of preparing an analysis, if the proposed rulemaking is not expected to have a significant economic impact on a substantial number of small entities.

Pursuant to the RFA, it is hereby certified that the proposed regulations will not have a significant economic impact on a substantial number of small entities. Section 13520 of the Act added section 6050Y to chapter 61 (Information and Returns) of the Code. Section 6050Y imposes information reporting obligations related to certain life insurance contract transactions, including reportable policy sales and payments of reportable death benefits. Section 6050Y provides that each of the returns required by section 6050Y is to be made "at such time and in such manner as the Secretary shall prescribe." The proposed regulations under section 6050Y would implement section 6050Y by specifying the manner in which and time at which the information reporting obligations must be satisfied. Accordingly, because the regulations are limited in scope to time and manner of information reporting and definitional information, the economic impact of the proposal is expected to be minimal. In addition, the IRS and Treasury expect that the reporting burden will fall primarily on financial and insurance firms with annual receipts greater than $38.5 million (see 13 CFR 121.201, sector 52 (finance and insurance)). Therefore, because the Commissioner of the IRS hereby certifies that the proposed regulations will not have a significant economic impact on a substantial number of small entities, a regulatory flexibility analysis is not required. The Treasury Department and the IRS request comments on the accuracy of this statement. Pursuant to section 7805(f) of the Code, this notice of proposed rulemaking will be submitted to the Chief Counsel for Advocacy of the Small Business Administration for comment on its impact on small entities.

Comments and Public Hearing

Before these proposed regulations are adopted as final regulations, consideration will be given to any comments that are submitted timely to the IRS as prescribed in this preamble under the "Addresses" heading. The Treasury Department and the IRS request comments on all aspects of the proposed rules. The Treasury Department and the IRS specifically request comments on the following:

1. Whether the proposed regulations should provide rules regarding the electronic furnishing of statements that differ in any way from the rules regarding the electronic furnishing of statements that are set forth in § 31.6051-1(j).

2. Information about the types and timing of payments made by acquirers in reportable policy sales, including the types of ancillary costs and expenses paid in reportable policy sales, the recipients of those payments, and existing reporting requirements applicable to those payments.

3. Whether, for purposes of reporting under section 6050Y(c), only issuers should be considered payors of reportable death benefits or whether payors should be more broadly defined to include any holder of an interest in a life insurance contract that receives reportable death benefits attributable to that interest and is contractually obligated to pay them to the beneficial owner of the interest.

4. Whether a substantial business relationship or substantial financial relationship should be considered to exist between the acquirer and insured for purposes of section 101(a)(3) in any situation not included in the definition of "substantial business relationship" in § 1.101-1(d)(2) of the proposed regulations or the definition of "substantial financial relationship" in § 1.101-1(d)(3) of the proposed regulations.

5. Whether the proposed regulations should include additional provisions regarding the treatment of section 1035 exchanges of life insurance contracts.

6. Whether the exceptions to reporting by 6050Y(b) issuers and payors under § § 1.6050Y-3(f)(1) and 1.6050Y-4(e)(1) of the proposed regulations (covering sellers and reportable death benefit payment recipients documented as foreign beneficial owners) are appropriate, including for cases in which a foreign partnership or a foreign trust is the seller or reportable death benefit payment recipient, and

also whether the proposed reporting requirements are duplicative or could be combined with other reporting requirements.

All comments that are submitted by the public will be available for public inspection and copying at www.regulations.gov or upon request.

A public hearing has been scheduled for June 5, 2019, at 10 a.m., in the IRS Auditorium, Internal Revenue Service, 1111 Constitution Avenue, NW, Washington, DC. Due to building security procedures, visitors must enter at the Constitution Avenue entrance. In addition, all visitors must present photo identification to enter the building. Because of access restrictions, visitors will not be admitted beyond the immediate entrance area more than 15 minutes before the hearing starts. For more information about having your name placed on the building access list to attend the hearing, see the "FOR FURTHER INFORMATION CONTACT" section of this preamble.

The rules of 26 CFR 601.601(a)(3) apply to the hearing. Persons who wish to present oral comments at the hearing must submit written or electronic comments and an outline of the topics to be discussed and the time to be devoted to each topic by May 9, 2019. Such persons should submit a signed paper original and eight (8) copies or an electronic copy. A period of 10 minutes will be allotted to each person for making comments. An agenda showing the scheduling of the speakers will be prepared after the deadline for receiving outlines has passed. Copies of the agenda will be available free of charge at the hearing.

Drafting Information

The principal author of these regulations is Kathryn M. Sneade, Office of Associate Chief Counsel (Financial Institutions and Products), IRS. However, other personnel from the Treasury Department and the IRS participated in their development.

Availability of IRS Documents

The IRS notice cited in this preamble is published in the Internal Revenue Bulletin (or Cumulative Bulletin) and is available from the Superintendent of Documents, U.S. Government Publishing Office, Washington, DC 20402, or by visiting the IRS website at www.irs.gov.

[¶49,790] Proposed Amendments of Regulations (REG-135671-17) , published in the Federal Register on March 25, 2019.

[Code Sec. 337]

Corporate partner: Corporate-level gain: Equity interests.—Amendments of Reg. §1.337(d)-3, amending final regulations that prevent a corporate partner from avoiding corporate-level gain through transactions with a partnership involving equity interests of the partner or certain related entities, are proposed.

AGENCY: Internal Revenue Service (IRS), Treasury.

ACTION: Notice of proposed rulemaking.

SUMMARY: This document contains proposed regulations to amend final regulations that prevent a corporate partner from avoiding corporate-level gain through transactions with a partnership involving equity interests of the partner or certain related entities. These regulations affect partnerships and their partners.

DATES: Comments and requests for a public hearing must be received by June 24, 2019. ADDRESSES: Send submissions to: CC:PA:LPD:PR (REG-135671-17), Room 5203, Internal Revenue Service, P.O. Box 7604, Ben Franklin Station, Washington, DC 20044. Submissions may be hand-delivered Monday through Friday between the hours of 8 a.m. and 4 p.m. to CC:PA:LPD:PR (REG-135671-17), Courier's Desk, Internal Revenue Service, 1111 Constitution Avenue, NW, Washington, DC 20224, or sent electronically, via the Federal eRulemaking Portal at *http://www.regulations.gov* (IRS REG-135671-17).

FOR FURTHER INFORMATION CONTACT: Concerning the proposed regulations, Kevin I. Babitz, (202) 317-6852, or Mary Brewer, (202) 317-6975; concerning submission of comments or to request a public hearing, Regina L. Johnson at (202) 317-6901.

SUPPLEMENTARY INFORMATION:

Background and Explanation of Provisions

This notice of proposed rulemaking contains amendments to the Income Tax Regulations (26 CFR part 1) under section 337(d) of the Internal Revenue Code (Code) set forth in §1.337(d)-3 (final regulations) that prevent a corporate partner from using a partnership to avoid recognition of corporate-level gain. The final regulations largely adopted proposed regulations (REG-149518-03) published in the **Federal Register** (80 FR 33451) on June 12, 2015 (2015 regulations) with minor, nonsubstantive clarifying changes in response to requests for further certainty in the single comment letter received on the proposed regulations. See the Explanation of Provisions section of the preamble to TD 9833 (83 FR 26580 (June 8, 2018)) for a detailed discussion of each of the specific points raised in the comment letter received on the 2015 regulations.

The rules set forth in this notice of proposed rulemaking contain substantive modifications to the final regulations relating to the definition of Stock of the Corporate Partner. Accordingly, the Treasury Department and the IRS determined it appropriate to publish these modifications in the form of new proposed regulations to afford the public the opportunity to submit additional comments.

1. Stock of the Corporate Partner: Attribution

The final regulations apply to certain partnerships that hold stock of a Corporate Partner. For this purpose, a *Corporate Partner* is defined as a person that holds or acquires an interest in a partnership and that is classified as a corporation for federal income tax purposes. The final regulations define *Stock of the Corporate Partner* expansively to include stock and other equity interests, including warrants, other options, and similar interests, either in the Corporate Partner or in a corporation (referred to in this Background and Explanation of Provisions section as a Controlling Corporation) that controls the Corporate Partner within the meaning of section 304(c), except that section 318(a)(1) and (3) would not apply. Stock of the Corporate Partner also includes an interest in any entity to the extent that the value of the interest is attributable to Stock of the Corporate Partner.

The final regulations adopted a definition of Stock of the Corporate Partner that was modified as compared to the definition in the regulations that the Treasury Department and the IRS proposed on December 15, 1992 (PS-91-90, REG-208989-90, 1993-1 CB 919) (1992 proposed regulations). The final regulations broadened the definition of Stock of the Corporate Partner with respect to the relationship needed for a Controlling Corporation to be treated as controlling the Corporate Partner (using a modified section 304(c) standard instead of section 1504(a)) but also narrowed the definition, generally excluding sister corporations and subsidiary corporations of the Corporate Partner from being treated as Controlling Corporations.

More specifically, the final regulations define Stock of a Corporate Partner by including stock and other equity interests of any corporation that controls the Corporate Partner within the meaning of section 304(c), except that section 318(a)(1) and (3) shall not apply (section 304(c) control). In contrast, the 1992 proposed regulation's definition was limited to stock or other equity interests issued by the Corporate Partner and its "section 337(d) affiliates" – that is any corporation that is a member of an affiliated group as defined in section 1504(a) of the Code without regard to section 1504(b).

Section 304(c) control generally exists when there is ownership of stock of a corporation possessing at least 50 percent of the total combined voting power of all classes of the corporation's stock entitled to vote or at least 50 percent of the value of the shares of all classes of stock of the corporation, while control of a corporation under section 1504(a)(2) requires ownership of stock of the corporation possessing at least 80 percent of the total voting power of the stock of the corporation and at least 80 percent of the total value of the stock of the corporation. The Treasury Department and the IRS adopted this lower ownership threshold for determining control in the final regulations as a more appropriate standard for this purpose because General Utilities repeal could more easily be avoided by acquiring stock of a corporation that owns less than 80 percent of the vote and value of the Corporate Partner's stock. See *General Utilities & Operating Co. v. Helvering*, 296 U.S. 200 (1935).

While section 304(c) incorporates the constructive ownership rules of section 318(a) with some modifications, the 2015 regulations excluded the application of section 318(a)(1) and (3) from their definition of control.

The commenter that submitted the only comment on the 2015 regulations demonstrated that families could use the exclusion of section 318(a)(1) attribution from the determination of section 304(c) control to structure transactions using partnerships to eliminate gain on appreciated assets or contravene the purposes of section 337(d) in other ways. For example—

Husband owns 90 percent of corporation A, which owns 49 percent of Corporate Partner (CP). Wife owns 90 percent of corporation B, which also owns 49 percent of CP. CP owns an interest in partnership PRS. Under these facts, because the 2015 regulations determined section 304(c) control without applying the section 318(a)(1) family attribution rule, neither A nor B control CP. Accordingly, other partners in Partnership could contribute stock of A and B to PRS in exchange for an interest in PRS without triggering gain to A or B.

The Treasury Department and the IRS agree with the commenter that excluding section 318(a)(1) attribution from the determination of section 304(c) control could produce unintended results. In addition, the Treasury Department and the IRS have determined that taxpayers can structure transactions to take advantage of the exclusion of section 318(a)(3) attribution from the determination of section 304(c) control. For example, in the preceding fact pattern, if the interests held by Husband and Wife were instead held by a single corporation, X, neither A nor B would control CP without the application of section 318(a)(3) attribution.

As a result, the Treasury Department and the IRS propose to modify the definition of Stock of the Corporate Partner to eliminate the exclusion of section 318(a)(1) and (3) attribution from the determination of section 304(c) control. However, as explained below, the Treasury Department and the IRS propose to limit this expanded definition of Stock of the Corporate Partner to entities that own a direct or indirect interest in the Corporate Partner.

The exclusion of attribution under sections 318(a)(1) and 318(a)(3) in the 2015 regulations and the final regulations was intended to limit section 304(c) control to entities that own a direct or indirect interest in the Corporate Partner, while excluding entities that do not own a direct or indirect interest in the Corporate Partner. To implement this intent more precisely, the Treasury Department and the IRS propose to limit the proposed scope of section 304(c) control to ownership, direct or indirect, of an interest in the Corporate Partner. For the purpose of testing direct or indirect ownership of an interest in the Corporate Partner, ownership of Stock of the Corporate Partner would be attributed to an entity under section 318(a)(2) (except that the 50-percent ownership limitation in section 318(a)(2)(C) would not apply) and under section 318(a)(4), but otherwise without regard to section 318. Thus, sections 318(a)(1), 318(a)(3), and 318(a)(5) would not apply for determining whether an entity directly or indirectly owns an interest in Stock of the Corporate Partner, but once an entity is found to directly or indirectly own an interest in such stock, then the section 304(c) control definition would apply in its entirety to determine whether the tested entity is a Controlling Corporation. The Treasury Department and the IRS continue to study the appropriate scope of the definition of Stock of the Corporate Partner, and request comments regarding these provisions.

2. Definition of Stock of the Corporate Partner: Affiliated Groups

These proposed regulations, if finalized, would make a second change to the definition of Stock of the Corporate Partner. The final regulations provide that the term Stock of the Corporate Partner does not include any stock or other equity interests held or acquired by a partnership if all interests in the partnership's capital and profits are held by members of an affiliated group as defined in section 1504(a) that includes the Corporate Partner (Affiliated Group Exception). The 1992 proposed regulations included affiliate stock within its definition of the Stock of a Corporate Partner, but the 2015 proposed regulations instead set forth this Affiliated Group Exception, which the final regulations adopted. Thus, the final regulations do not apply if a domestic corporation and its wholly owned domestic subsidiaries (each of which is an includible corporation under section 1504(b)) are the only partners in a partnership and any of these corporations contributes stock of another affiliate to a partnership. The preamble to T.D. 9722 (80 FR 33402 (June 12, 2015)), which contained temporary regulations that accompanied the 2015 regulations, stated that the Treasury Department and the IRS had determined that the Affiliated Group Exception is appropriate because "the purpose of these regulations is not implicated if a partnership is owned entirely by affiliated corporations."

After further study, the Treasury Department and the IRS have determined that the Affiliated Group Exception may result in abuse and therefore is not appropriate. Specifically, the Treasury Department and the IRS believe that a partnership held entirely by members of an affiliated group could enter into transactions that permanently eliminate the built-in gain on an appreciated asset that one partner contributes to the partnership. For example—

Assume that P, a corporation, owns all of the stock of S1, and S1 owns all of the stock of CP. P, S1, and CP are members of an affiliated group. P and CP form a 50-50 partnership; CP contributes an appreciated asset to the partnership; and P contributes S1 stock with basis equal to fair market value. After seven years, the partnership liquidates and distributes the S1 stock to CP and the appreciated asset to P. At that time, the asset may be sold outside of the group with an artificially increased basis. The built-in gain that was in the asset is now preserved in the S1 stock held by CP. The group may permanently eliminate the gain without tax by liquidating CP under section 332. CP would receive nonrecognition treatment on distribution of the S1 stock to S1 under section 332, and S1 would receive nonrecognition treatment on the receipt of its own stock under section 1032. Thus, the liquidation of CP permanently eliminates the built-in gain on the appreciated asset that attached to the hook stock CP held in S1 after the liquidation of the partnership.

This ability to increase the basis of an appreciated asset artificially and to eliminate the built-in gain permanently contravenes the purposes of section 337(d) and these regulations. The Treasury Department and the IRS are also aware that practitioners have observed that the Affiliated Group Exception runs counter to the general rule that related-party transactions are subject to greater scrutiny. In light of these concerns, these proposed regulations would remove the Affiliated Group Exception contained in the final regulations.

However, because there may be specific circumstances under which the elimination of the Affiliated Group Exception could adversely impact ordinary business transactions between affiliated group members and group-owned partnerships, the Treasury Department and the IRS request comments describing situations in which a more tailored version of the Affiliated Group Exception would be warranted.

3. Definition of Stock of the Corporate Partner: Value of an interest attributable to Stock of the Corporate Partner

These proposed regulations would modify the scope of the rule in the final regulations that Stock of the Corporate Partner includes interests in any entity to the extent that the value of the interest is attributable to Stock of the Corporate Partner (Value Rule). Under the final regulations, the Value Rule applies to all interests in an entity regardless of whether the entity is controlled by the Corporate Partner. The sole commenter responding to the 2015 regulations agreed that the scope of the Value Rule was appropriate if the entity was controlled by the Corporate Partner. However, for entities that are not controlled by the Corporate Partner, the commenter asked that the scope of the Value Rule be narrowed to apply only if 20 percent or more of the assets of an entity were Stock of the Corporate Partner.

The Treasury Department and the IRS agree that the Value Rule in the 2015 regulations and the final regulations could be overbroad in certain circumstances. For example—

Assume X, a publicly traded corporation, owns a portfolio investment in P, a publicly traded corporation. P controls CP, a Corporate Partner under the final regulations, within the meaning of section 304(c); thus, P's stock is Stock of the Corporate Partner under the final regulations. Under the Value Rule, X's stock would be Stock of the Corporate Partner to the extent that the value of X is attributable to Stock of the Corporate Partner. If CP contributed appreciated property to a partnership, and another party contributed X stock to the partnership, CP would be unable to determine whether it had engaged in a Section 337(d) Transaction (within the meaning of § 1.337(d)-3(c)(3)) or otherwise apply the rules of the final regulations because CP (through P) might have no way to determine that the X stock used in the transaction could be Stock of the Corporate Partner. Alternatively, if CP were aware that X owned a portfolio investment in P, it would have no ability to determine the amount of X stock that is Stock of the Corporate Partner under the Value Rule. This is because, absent actual or constructive knowledge (for example through required disclosures such as filings with the Securities and Exchange Commission), a widely held corporation might not know or have the ability to know who owns its stock.

For this reason, the Treasury Department and the IRS have determined that narrowing the scope of the Value Rule is appropriate. However, the Treasury Department and the IRS decline to adopt the commenter's specific suggestion that interests in an entity not be subject to the Value Rule unless 20 percent or more of the assets of the entity consisted of Stock of the Corporate Partner. Such a rule would cause the Value Rule to be overly narrow and could permit taxpayers to structure transactions that would contravene the purpose of section 337(d) and these regulations. Instead, the Treasury Department and the IRS propose to narrow the scope of the Value Rule through an alternate measure. Under the proposed regulations, if an entity is not controlled by the Corporate Partner and is not a Controlling Corporation, the Value Rule would apply to treat interests in the entity as Stock of the Corporate Partner only if the entity owns, directly or indirectly, 5 percent or more of the stock, by vote or value, of the Corporate Partner. For this purpose, direct or indirect ownership would mean ownership of stock that would be attributed to a person under section 318(a)(2) (except that the 50-percent ownership limitation in section 318(a)(2)(C) would not apply) and under section 318(a)(4), but otherwise without regard to section 318. The Treasury Department and the IRS believe that using a 5-percent ownership threshold is appropriate because entities have the ability to determine whether they have 5-percent or greater owners, and corporations may track their 5-percent shareholders for other reasons (such as for section 382 purposes). Further, the Treasury Department and the IRS propose to apply this 5-percent threshold to direct or indirect stock ownership, rather than all equity interests, in the Corporate Partner in order to make the Value Rule more readily administrable.

The proposed regulations also would clarify how taxpayers should apply the Value Rule to determine the extent to which the value of an equity interest is attributable to Stock of the Corporate Partner. The proposed regulations would provide that taxpayers would multiply the value of the equity interest in an entity by a ratio, the numerator of which is the fair market value of the Stock of the Corporate Partner owned directly or indirectly by the entity and the denominator of which is the fair market value of all of the equity interests in the entity. For this purpose, direct or indirect ownership would mean ownership of stock that would be attributed to a person under section 318(a)(2) (except that the 50-percent ownership limitation in section 318(a)(2)(C) would not apply) and under section 318(a)(4), but otherwise without regard to section 318. The proposed regulations would also provide that the ratio may not exceed one. The Treasury Department and the IRS determined that the fair market value of all of the equity interests in the entity is the most appropriate measure to determine the value of the entity because the Value Rule seeks to determine what portion of the value of an equity interest in an entity reflects the value of Stock of the Corporate Partner owned by that entity.

Additionally, the proposed regulations would clarify that, if an equity interest is Stock of the Corporate Partner because it is an interest in the Corporate Partner or in an entity with a direct or indirect ownership interest that controls the Corporate Partner within the meaning of section 304(c), then the Value Rule will not apply. The Treasury Department and the IRS request comments on all aspects of the proposed changes to the scope of the Value Rule, including the appropriate measure of the value of the entity.

4. Exception for Certain Dispositions of Stock

Finally, these proposed regulations would make a modification to the exception for certain dispositions of stock in § 1.337(d)-3(f)(2) to make its language consistent with the modified definition of Stock of the Corporate Partner. Under this exception, the final regulations do not apply to Stock of the Corporate Partner that (i) is disposed of (by sale or distribution) by the partnership before the due date (including extensions) of its federal income tax return for the taxable year of the relevant transaction; and (ii) is not distributed to the Corporate Partner or a corporation that controls the Corporate Partner. With respect to the second requirement, the final regulations refer to a corporation that controls the Corporate Partner within the meaning of section 304(c), except that section 318(a)(1) and (3) shall not apply. For the same reasons that these proposed regulations modify the definition of Stock of the Corporate Partner, these proposed regulations also modify the second requirement of this exception to refer to a corporation that controls the Corporate Partner within the meaning of section 304(c), but only if the controlling corporation owns directly or indirectly stock or another equity interest in the Corporate Partner, in order to conform the second requirement with the modified definition of Stock of the Corporate Partner.

Proposed Effective Date

These regulations are proposed to be effective as of the date of their publication as final regulations in the **Federal Register**. Taxpayers may rely on these proposed regulations for transactions occurring on or after June 12, 2015 and prior to the date that these regulations are published as final regulations in the **Federal Register**, provided that the taxpayer consistently applies all of the proposed regulations to such transactions.

Special Analyses

These proposed regulations are not subject to review under section 6(b) of Executive Order 12866 pursuant to the Memorandum of Agreement (April 11, 2018) between the Treasury Department and the Office of Management and Budget regarding review of tax regulations.

These proposed regulations do not impose a collection of information on small entities. Further, pursuant to the Regulatory Flexibility Act (5 U.S.C. chapter 6), it is hereby certified that these proposed regulations would not have a significant economic impact on a substantial number of small entities. This certification is based on the fact that these proposed regulations would primarily affect sophisticated ownership structures with interlocking ownership of corporations, partnerships and corporate stock. Accordingly, a regulatory flexibility analysis is not required. Pursuant to section 7805(f) of the Internal Revenue Code, these regulations have been submitted to the Chief Counsel for Advocacy of the Small Business Administration for comment on its impact on small business.

Comments and Requests for a Public Hearing

Before these proposed regulations are adopted as final regulations, consideration will be given to comments that are submitted timely to the IRS as prescribed in this preamble under the **ADDRESSES** heading. The Treasury Department and the IRS request comments on all aspects of the proposed rules. All comments will be available at *http://www.regulations.gov* or upon request. A public hearing will be scheduled if requested in writing by any person that timely submits written or electronic comments. If a public hearing is scheduled, notice of the date, time, and place for the public hearing will be published in the **Federal Register**. **Drafting Information**

The principal authors of these regulations are Kevin I. Babitz, Office of the Associate Chief Counsel (Passthroughs and Special Industries) and Mary Brewer, Office of the Associate Chief Counsel (Corporate). However, other personnel from the Treasury Department and the IRS participated in their development.

[¶49,791] Proposed Amendments of Regulations (REG-113943-17), published in the Federal Register on March 26, 2019.

[Code Sec. 337]

Property: C corporation: Real Estate Investment Trusts (REITs).—Amendments of Reg. §1.337(d)-7, providing guidance for transactions in which property of a C corporation becomes the property of a REIT following certain corporate distributions of controlled corporation stock, are proposed. Amendments to Reg. §1.337(d)-7(c)(6), (f), (g)(2)(ii) and (iv), proposed on June 8, 2016, are withdrawn.

AGENCY: Internal Revenue Service (IRS), Treasury.

ACTION: Partial withdrawal of notice of proposed rulemaking and notice of proposed rulemaking.

SUMMARY: This document withdraws a portion of a notice of proposed rulemaking published in the Proposed Rules section of the **Federal Register** on June 8, 2016. If adopted, the proposed rules would have provided guidance for transactions in which property of a C corporation becomes the property of a REIT following certain corporate distributions of controlled corporation stock. This document also contains a notice of proposed rulemaking that provides revised guidance on the same subject. These proposed regulations would affect REITs, C corporations the property of which becomes property of a REIT, and their respective shareholders.

DATES: Comments and requests for a public hearing must be received by May 10, 2019. ADDRESSES: Send submissions to: CC:PA:LPD:PR (REG-113943-17), room 5203, Internal Revenue Service, PO Box 7604, Ben Franklin Station, Washington, DC 20044. Submissions may be hand-delivered Monday through Friday between the hours of 8 a.m. and 4 p.m. to CC:PA:LPD:PR (REG-113943-17), Courier's Desk, Internal Revenue Service, 1111 Constitution Avenue, N.W., Washington, DC 20224 or sent electronically via the Federal eRulemaking Portal at http://www.regulations.gov/ (IRS REG-113943-17).

FOR FURTHER INFORMATION CONTACT: Concerning the proposed regulations, Austin Diamond-Jones, (202) 317-5363; concerning the submission of comments or to request a public hearing, Regina Johnson, (202) 317-6901 (not toll-free numbers). SUPPLEMENTARY INFORMATION

Background

This document contains proposed amendments to 26 CFR part 1 under section 337(d) of the Internal Revenue Code (Code).

On June 8, 2016, the Department of the Treasury (Treasury Department) and the IRS published temporary regulations (TD 9770) under section 337(d) (Temporary Regulations) in the **Federal Register** (81 FR 36793) concerning certain transfers of property to regulated investment companies (RICs) and real estate investment trusts (REITs). A notice of proposed rulemaking (REG-126452-15) was published in the **Federal Register** (81 FR 36816) on the same day (2016 Proposed Regulations). The text of the Temporary Regulations served as the text for part of the 2016 Proposed Regulations, which also included an amendment not addressed in the Temporary Regulations. A correction to the Temporary Regulations was published in the **Federal Register** (81 FR 41800) on June 28, 2016.

The Treasury Department and the IRS received one written comment and a letter addressed to the Secretary of the Treasury (Secretary) by the Chairmen and Ranking Members of the Ways and Means Committee of the U.S. House of Representatives and the Finance Committee of the U.S. Senate in response to the 2016 Proposed Regulations. The comment requested a public hearing, and a hearing was held on November 9, 2016.

After consideration of the letter, the written comment, and the comments made at the public hearing, the Treasury Department and the IRS adopted the 2016 Proposed Regulations, in part, in final regulations (TD 9810) published in the **Federal Register** (82 FR 5387) on January 18, 2017 (Final Regulations). The Final Regulations adopted a definition of the term "recognition period" that is consistent with that used in section 1374(d) relating to S corporations. The Final Regulations amended and removed the corresponding provisions in the Temporary Regulations and indicated that the Treasury Department and the IRS would continue to study other issues addressed in the Temporary Regulations and the 2016 Proposed Regulations.

Executive Order 13789 (E.O. 13789), issued on April 21, 2017, instructed the Secretary to review all significant tax regulations issued on or after January 1, 2016, and to take concrete action to alleviate the burdens of regulations that (i) impose an undue financial burden on U.S. taxpayers; (ii) add undue complexity to the federal tax laws; or (iii) exceed the statutory authority of the IRS. E.O. 13789 further instructed the Secretary to submit to the President within 60 days an interim report identifying regulations that meet these criteria.

Notice 2017-38 (2017-30 I.R.B. 147 (July 24, 2017)) included the Temporary Regulations in a list of eight regulations identified by the Secretary in the interim report as meeting at least one of the first two criteria specified in E.O. 13789. In particular, Notice 2017-38 mentioned a concern raised by commenters that the Temporary Regulations "could result in over-inclusion of gain in some cases, particularly where a large corporation acquires a small corporation that engaged in a Section 355 spinoff and the large corporation subsequently makes a REIT election." *See also* Executive Order 13789—Second Report to the President on Identifying and Reducing Tax Regulatory Burdens (Second Report), 82 FR 48013 (October 16, 2017) (stating that the Treasury Department and the IRS "agree that the temporary regulations may produce inappropriate results in some cases"). The Treasury Department and the IRS received three written comments in response to Notice 2017-38 and the Second Report that addressed the Temporary Regulations and the 2016 Proposed Regulations.

Explanation of Provisions

I. *Gain Recognized by Successor Corporations*

Pursuant to § 1.337(d)-7(c)(6) of the 2016 Proposed Regulations, if a C corporation is the distributing corporation or the controlled corporation in a "related section 355 distribution" (within the meaning of proposed § 1.337(d)-7(f)(1)(i)), and the C corporation or its successor (within the meaning of proposed § 1.337(d)-7(f)(2)) engages in a conversion transaction (as defined in § 1.337(d)-7(a)(2)(ii)) involving a REIT, the C corporation or its successor will be treated as making a deemed sale election (within the meaning of proposed § 1.337(d)-7(c)). Commenters suggested that application of proposed § 1.337(d)-7(c)(6) to successors (within the meaning of proposed § 1.337(d)-7(f)(2)) could result in recognition of gain greatly in excess of the amount that would have been recognized if the distributing corporation or the controlled corporation had directly engaged in a conversion transaction.

To illustrate the issue, consider the following example (Example One): Each of Distributing and Acquiring is a C corporation, and each holds real estate assets with $1 billion fair market value and $0 adjusted basis. Distributing and Acquiring are unrelated. Distributing owns 100 percent of the stock of Controlled, which holds assets with $20 million fair market value and $0 adjusted basis. In Year 1, Distributing distributes the stock of Controlled in a section 355 distribution (as defined in proposed § 1.337(d)-7(a)(2)(vi)). In Year 3, Acquiring acquires Controlled in a transaction in which Acquiring becomes a successor of Controlled (within the meaning of proposed § 1.337(d)-7(f)(2)). At that time, Acquiring has no plan to convert to a REIT. No asset held by Distributing, Controlled, or Acquiring appreciates or depreciates in value between Year 1 and Year 9. In Year 9, Acquiring merges into a REIT and does not make a deemed sale election under § 1.337(d)-7(c)(5).

As a successor to Controlled, Acquiring itself was ineligible to make a REIT election until Year 11. Section 856(c)(8). However, the merger of Acquiring into a REIT is not addressed by section 856(c)(8). On the other hand, if Acquiring were not a successor to a distributing corporation or a controlled corporation, its assets would be subject to section 1374 treatment upon the merger (unless Acquiring actually made a deemed sale election).

Because Acquiring is a successor to a controlled corporation and engages in a conversion transaction within ten years of a related section 355 distribution, the 2016 Proposed Regulations would treat Acquiring as making a deemed sale election and require Acquiring to recognize $1.02 billion gain ($1.02 billion fair market value less $0 adjusted bases of all its property at the time of the merger). This gain would greatly exceed the $20 million gain ($20 million fair market value less $0 adjusted basis) Controlled would have recognized if Acquiring had been a REIT when it acquired Controlled's converted property. The Treasury Department and the IRS agree with the commenters that this result is inappropriate.

To address the concern described in the previous paragraph, the Treasury Department and the IRS propose adopting a new limitation to the general rule in newly proposed § 1.337(d)-7(c)(6)(i) (the general rule) (which is the same as the general rule in the 2016 Proposed Regulations). As a result of the limitation, gain immediately recognized by a C corporation engaging in a section 355 distribution and a later conversion transaction will be limited to gain on property traceable to the section 355 distribution.

The limitation is based on a comment received and would be available to a distributing corporation or a controlled corporation (and a successor) that engages in a conversion transaction within the ten-year period following a related section 355 distribution. The limitation would provide that, if a C corporation is treated as making a deemed sale election but has not actually made such an election, the C corporation would be treated as making the election only with respect to its distribution property. "Distribution property" would be defined as property owned by a distributing corporation or a controlled corporation or a member of the separate affiliated group of the distributing corporation or the controlled corporation (SAG member) immediately after a section 355 distribution, and other property the basis of which is determined, directly or indirectly, in whole or in part, by reference to that property. However, no formulation of the step transaction doctrine will be used to determine whether property acquired after the distribution is distribution property. The C corporation's property that is not distribution property would be subject to section 1374 treatment under § 1.337(d)-7(b) instead of deemed sale treatment under § 1.337(d)-7(c)(6). In general, the C corporation must establish that any particular property is not distribution property. However, property with built-in loss as of the date of the conversion transaction will be presumed to not be distribution property unless the C corporation establishes that it owned such property immediately after the related section 355 distribution.

To illustrate the limitation, consider the following example (Example Two): Distributing is a C corporation that owns 100 percent of the stock of Controlled. In Year 1, Distributing distributes the stock of Controlled in a section 355 distribution. At the time of the section 355 distribution, Controlled has one asset (Asset 1) with $5 million fair market value and $0 adjusted basis. In Year 2, Controlled purchases a second asset (Asset 2), which has $1 million fair market value and $1 million adjusted basis. In Year 5, Controlled engages in a conversion transaction when it merges into a REIT in a transaction described in section 368(a)(1). At the time of the merger, Asset 1 has $5.5 million fair market value, and Asset 2 has $1.1 million fair market value. The adjusted bases of Asset 1 and Asset 2 are both unchanged.

If the limitation is available and Controlled does not make a deemed sale election, Controlled would be treated as making a deemed sale election only with respect to Asset 1 (and not Asset 2) because Asset 1 was held by Controlled immediately after the related section 355 distribution and is therefore distribution property. Because Controlled can establish that it did not own Asset 2 immediately after the related section 355 distribution (and the basis of Asset 2 was not determined, directly or indirectly, in whole or in part, by reference to the basis of an asset held by Controlled immediately after the related section 355 distribution in Year 1), Asset 2 is not distribution property, and Controlled will not be treated as electing deemed sale treatment with respect to Asset 2. Accordingly, Controlled would recognize $5.5 million gain on Asset 1 ($5.5 million fair market value less $0 adjusted basis), and the REIT would be subject to section 1374 treatment with respect to Asset 2 and its $0.1 million built-in gain.

However, if Controlled had elected deemed sale treatment or was unable to establish that Asset 2 was not distribution property, then all of its assets that became converted property, rather than only the distribution property, would be treated as sold upon Controlled's merger into a REIT in Year 5. Controlled would recognize $5.6 million gain ($5.5 million gain on Asset 1 ($5.5 million fair market value less $0 adjusted basis at the time of the merger) and $0.1 million gain on Asset 2 ($1.1 million fair market value less $1 million adjusted basis at the time of the merger)). Neither Asset 1 nor Asset 2 would be subject to section 1374 treatment.

As a result of the combination of the general rule and the limitation, a C corporation that engages in a section 355 distribution and a later conversion transaction recognizes immediate gain only on property that is traceable to the section 355 distribution. Application of the limitation could cause a single conversion transaction to result in some property being subject to deemed sale treatment and other property being subject to section1374 treatment. However, the Treasury Department and the IRS have determined that this approach is administrable by both taxpayers and the IRS and that it satisfies the concerns expressed by E.O. 13789, Notice 2017-38, and the Second Report. Because application of the limitation results in only property held immediately after the related section 355 distribution being subject to deemed sale treatment, the property of a successor to the distributing corporation, the controlled corporation, or a SAG member will not be subject to deemed sale treatment unless such property is distribution property from a related section 355 distribution involving the successor.

A commenter suggested an approach pursuant to which distribution property subject to deemed sale treatment as a result of the general rule could be deemed to be sold for its fair market value at the time of the related section 355 distribution. However, the commenter stated that this approach "may be objectionable given [E.O. 13789's] focus on reducing complexity and taxpayer burdens in Treasury regulations," because it would require taxpayers to perform a valuation of their assets at the time of a related section 355 distribution and to keep records of the valuation in case the taxpayer engages in a later conversion transaction. In the commenter's view, this valuation and record keeping would be burdensome and result in administrative difficulties for both taxpayers and the IRS. The Treasury Department and the IRS agree.

In addition, section 1374 treatment would need to be applied to post-distribution appreciation to prevent it from inappropriately escaping corporate-level taxation. As a result, an individual asset that is distribution property would be subject to deemed sale treatment on the gain inherent in the asset at the time of the related section 355 distribution, and to section 1374 treatment on the appreciation in such asset after the post-distribution period. This result further increases the burdens and administrative difficulties imposed by the alternative approach. Because this approach is inconsistent with the goal of reducing administrative burdens described in E.O. 13789 and reflected in Notice 2017-38 and the Second Report, the Treasury Department and the IRS decline to adopt this approach.

II. *Predecessors and Successors of SAG Members*

The Treasury Department and the IRS are aware of certain situations in which the predecessor or successor to a SAG member would not itself be a SAG member immediately before or after, respectively, the transaction giving rise to the predecessor-successor relationship. To prevent avoidance, the proposed regulations would expand the rule of proposed § 1.337(d)-7(f)(2) so that references to a member of the separate affiliated group of the distributing corporation or the controlled corporation include references to any successor of such member.

III. *Additional Comments*

A commenter described an example similar to the following example (Example Three): Distributing is a C corporation that holds real estate assets with $1 billion fair market value and $0 adjusted basis. Distributing owns 100 percent of the stock of Controlled, which holds assets with $100,000 fair market value and $0 adjusted basis. In Year 1, Distributing distributes the stock of Controlled in a section 355 distribution. In Year 10, Distributing merges into a REIT.

Under the 2016 Proposed Regulations, Distributing would have been treated as making a deemed sale election as a result of engaging in a conversion transaction (the merger) during the ten-year period following a section 355 distribution. Accordingly, Distributing would have recognized $1 billion gain as a result of being treated as selling all of its real estate assets. The commenter argued that requiring a C corporation to recognize the built-in gain on assets worth $1 billion because of a distribution of assets worth $100,000 in an earlier year "seems absurd." The Treasury Department and the IRS disagree. Section 856(c)(8), which was added by section 311 of the Protecting Americans Against Tax Hikes Act of 2015 (PATH Act), enacted as Division Q of the Consolidated Appropriations Act, 2016, Public Law 114-113, 129 Stat. 2422, prevents the distributing corporation, the controlled corporation, and any successor to the distributing corporation or the controlled corporation from electing REIT status for ten years following a section 355 distribution. Section 856(c)(8) applies regardless of any disparity in size between the distributing corporation and the controlled corporation. The commenter did not identify any reason a merger into a REIT should be treated more favorably than a conversion to a REIT. Accordingly, the Treasury Department and the IRS have determined that application of the 2016 Proposed Regulations in the hypothetical presented by the commenter is consistent with the intent of Congress expressed by the PATH Act. The newly proposed regulations would not change this rule.

The Treasury Department and the IRS continue to study the Temporary Regulations and the 2016 Proposed Regulations, including issues raised by the comments, and welcome further comments on those issues.

Special Analyses

This regulation is not subject to review under section 6(b) of Executive Order 12866 pursuant to the Memorandum of Agreement (April 11, 2018) between the Department of the Treasury and the Office of Management and Budget regarding review of tax regulations. Pursuant to the Regulatory Flexibility Act (5 U.S.C. chapter 6), it is hereby certified that these proposed regulations will not have a significant economic impact on a substantial number of small entities. These proposed regulations would affect transactions in which property of a C corporation becomes the property of a REIT following a section 355 distribution of controlled C corporation stock. Generally, these section 355 distributions involve publicly traded C corporations, which typically are not small entities as defined by the Regulatory Flexibility Act. Transactions in which the property of such C corporation becomes the property of a REIT generally involve the transfer of all of the assets of the C corporation. Therefore, the transferee REIT likely also would not be a small entity, as defined by the Regulatory Flexibility Act. As a result, this certification is based on the conclusion that these proposed regulations would primarily affect large C corporations and REITs that have substantial numbers of shareholders. Therefore, a regulatory flexibility analysis is not required. Pursuant to section 7805(f) of the Code, this regulation has been submitted to the Chief Counsel for Advocacy of the Small Business Administration for comment on its impact on small business.

Statement of Availability of IRS Documents

IRS Revenue Procedures, Revenue Rulings, Notices, and other guidance cited in this preamble are published in the Internal Revenue (or Cumulative Bulletin) and are available from the Superintendent of Documents, U.S. Government Publishing Office, Washington, DC 20402, or by visiting the IRS website at http://www.irs.gov.

Comments and Requests for Public Hearing

Before these proposed regulations are adopted as final regulations, consideration will be given to any comments that are submitted timely to the IRS as prescribed in this preamble under the "Addresses" heading. The Treasury Department and the IRS request comments on all aspect of the proposed rules. In particular, the Treasury Department and the IRS are requesting comments whether further guidance is necessary regarding how taxpayers should be permitted to establish whether property is or is not distribution property. All comments will be available at http://www.regulations.gov or upon request. A public hearing will be scheduled in writing by any person that timely submits written comments. If a public hearing is scheduled, notice of the date, time, and place of the public hearing will be published in the **Federal Register**.

Drafting Information

The principal author of these regulations is Austin Diamond-Jones, Office of Associate Chief Counsel (Corporate). However, other personnel from the Treasury Department and the IRS participated in their development.

[¶ 49,792] Proposed Amendments of Regulations (REG-121694-16), published in the Federal Register on March 26, 2019 (corrected 4/23/2019).

[Code Secs. 301, 356, 368 and 902]

Distribution: Stock ownership: Shareholder.—Amendments of Reg. §§1.301-1, 1.356-1, 1.368-2, 1.902-1 and 1.902-3, containing proposed regulations under section 301 of the Internal Revenue Code of 1986 (Code), are proposed.

AGENCY: Internal Revenue Service (IRS), Treasury.

ACTION: Notice of proposed rulemaking.

SUMMARY: This document contains proposed regulations under section 301 of the Internal Revenue Code of 1986 (Code). The proposed regulations would update existing regulations under section 301 to reflect statutory changes made by the Technical and Miscellaneous Revenue Act of 1988, which changes provide that the amount of a distribution of property made by a corporation to its shareholder is the fair market value of the distributed property. The proposed regulations would affect any shareholder who receives a distribution of property from a corporation.

DATES: Written or electronic comments and requests for a public hearing must be received by June 24, 2019.

ADDRESSES: Send submissions to: CC:PA:LPD:PR (REG-121694-16), Room 5203, Internal Revenue Service, PO Box 7604, Ben Franklin Station, Washington, DC 20044. Submissions may be hand-delivered Monday through Friday between the hours of 8 a.m. and 4 p.m. to CC:PA:LPD:PR (REG-121694-16), Courier's Desk, Internal Revenue Service, 1111 Constitution Avenue, NW, Washington, DC 20224, or sent electronically, via the Federal eRulemaking Portal at www.regulations.gov (indicate IRS and REG-121694-16).

FOR FURTHER INFORMATION CONTACT: Concerning the proposed regulations, Grid R. Glyer, (202) 317-6847; concerning submission of comments, Regina Johnson, (202) 317-6901 (not toll-free numbers).

SUPPLEMENTARY INFORMATION:

Background

Section 301 of the Code originally was enacted as part of the Internal Revenue Code of 1954. Section 301 provides rules for the treatment of a distribution of property, including money, made by a corporation to its shareholder with respect to that shareholder's stock ownership in that corporation (distribution).

Section 301(b)(1) provides general rules for determining the amount of a distribution. As enacted in 1954, section 301(b)(1) provided rules for determining the amount of a distribution that differed depending on whether the shareholder receiving the distribution (distributee) was a corporation. Pre-1986 amendments to section 301(b)(1) added special rules to determine the amount of distributions received from foreign distributing corporations and by foreign corporate distributees. Similarly, section 301(d), as enacted in 1954, provided rules for determining the basis of property received in a distribution that differed depending on whether the distributee was a corporation. As with section 301(b)(1), pre-1986 amendments to section 301(d) added special rules to determine the basis of property received from foreign distributing corporations and by foreign corporate distributees.

Section 1006(e)(10) of the Technical and Miscellaneous Revenue Act of 1988, Pub. L. No. 100-647, 102 Stat. 3342 (1988) (the Act), amended section 301(b)(1) to eliminate the distinction between corporate and noncorporate distributees as well as the special rules relating to foreign corporations. Similarly, section 1006(e)(11) of the Act amended section 301(d) to eliminate the distinction between corporate and noncorporate distributees. (These amendments to section 301(b)(1) and (d) are referred to as the 1988 Amendments.) Section 1019(a) of the Act provided that, in general, the 1988 Amendments were effective as if included in the Tax Reform Act of 1986, Pub. L. No. 99-514, 100 Stat. 2085 (1986).

As a result of the 1988 Amendments, effective for taxable years beginning after December 31, 1986, section 301(b)(1) provides that, for purposes of section 301, the amount of any distribution shall be the amount of money received plus the fair market value of the other property received. Section 301(d), as amended by the 1988 Amendments and effective for taxable years beginning after December 31, 1986, provides that the basis of property received in a distribution to which section 301(a) applies shall be the fair market value of such property.

The current regulations issued under section 301 reflect the rules of sections 301(b)(1) and 301(d) as they existed prior to the 1988 Amendments. Accordingly, to the extent preempted by statute, the current regulations have no application.

Explanation of Provisions.

The proposed regulations update § 1.301-1 to reflect the statutory changes made to section 301(b)(1) and (d) by the 1988 Amendments. The scope of the changes to the current regulations issued under section 301 made by these proposed regulations is limited to (1) deleting regulatory provisions made obsolete by statutory changes, (2) making minor additions and revisions to regulatory provisions to reflect current statutory text, and (3) making certain non-substantive changes for purposes of clarity and readability, including reordering and redesignating paragraphs of the current regulations. The proposed regulations also update cross-references in §§1.356-1(f), 1.368-2(m)(3)(iii), 1.902-1(a)(12), and 1.902-3(a)(7) to reflect the proposed reordering and redesignating of paragraphs in §1.301-1.

Specifically, some of the provisions of current §1.301-1(b) are now found in proposed §1.301-1(c). Thus, the definition of the amount of a distribution subject to section 301 and the determination of the fair market value of a distribution remain in §1.301-1(b), while the determination of when to include a distribution in gross income, and its fair market value, is now found in proposed §1.301-1(c).

In addition, current §1.301-1(g) is redesignated as proposed §1.301-1(f) and is revised to clarify the application of the principles of section 357(d) to the limitation on the amount of a distribution provided by section 301(b)(2). Section 357(d) was added to the Code by section 3001(b)(1) of the Miscellaneous Trade and Technical Corrections Act of 1999, Pub.L. No. 106-36, 113 Stat. 127. On January 4, 2001, the Treasury Department and the IRS published a temporary regulation (T.D. 8924) in the **Federal Register** (66 FR 723) to address this interaction. Current §1.301-1(g), published in the **Federal Register** (66 FR 49278) on September 27, 2001 as T.D. 8964, provides that no reduction shall be made for the amount of any liability, unless the liability is assumed by the shareholder within the meaning of section 357(d). Proposed §1.301-1(f) would clarify the language of current §1.301-1(g) by providing that no reduction in the amount of a distribution is made for the amount of any liability except to the extent the liability is assumed by the shareholder within the meaning of section 357(d).

The specific changes to §1.301-1 are shown in the following table:

Paragraph Designation in §1.301-1	Change
(a)	Updated to reflect current law
(b)	Updated to reflect current law, with the definition of the amount of a distribution subject to section 301 and the determination of the fair market value of a distribution remaining in paragraph (b) and the determination of when to include a distribution in gross income, and its fair market value, redesignated as paragraph (c)
(c)	Redesignated as paragraph (d)
(d)	Deleted as obsolete
(e)	Deleted as obsolete
(f)	Updated to reflect current law and redesignated as paragraph (e)
(g)	Redesignated as paragraph (f) and revised to clarify that no reduction in the amount of a distribution is made for the amount of any liability except to the extent the liability is assumed by the shareholder within the meaning of section 357(d).
(h)	Updated to reflect current law and redesignated as paragraph (g)
(i)	No change
(j)	Updated to reflect current law and redesignated as paragraph (h)
(k)	Deleted as obsolete
(l)	Redesignated as paragraph (j)
(m)	Redesignated as paragraph (k)
(n)	Deleted as obsolete
(o)	Deleted as obsolete
(p)	Redesignated as paragraph (l)
(q)	Redesignated as paragraph (m)
(n)	New effective date paragraph

Proposed Effective/Applicability Date

The proposed regulations would apply to distributions made after the date of publication of the Treasury decision adopting these rules as final regulations in the **Federal Register**. However, these proposed regulations would update current regulations under section 301 to reflect statutory changes made by the 1988 Amendments, which statutory changes apply to distributions made in taxable years beginning after December 31, 1986.

Special Analyses

This regulation is not subject to review under section 6(b) of Executive Order 12866 pursuant to the Memorandum of Agreement (April 11, 2018) between the Department of the Treasury and the Office of Management and Budget regarding review of tax regulations. Because these regulations do not impose a collection of information on small entities, the Regulatory Flexibility Act (5 U.S.C. chapter 6) does not apply.

Pursuant to section 7805(f), this notice of proposed rulemaking has been submitted to the Chief Counsel for Advocacy of the Small Business Administration for comment on its impact on small business.

Comments and Requests for Public Hearing

Before these proposed regulations are adopted as final regulations, consideration will be given to any comments that are submitted timely to the IRS as prescribed in this preamble under the "Addresses" heading. The Treasury Department and the IRS request comments on all aspects of the proposed rules. All comments will be available at *www.regulations.gov* or upon request. A public hearing will be scheduled if requested in writing by any person that timely submits written comments. If a public hearing is scheduled, notice of the date, time, and place for the public hearing will be published in the **Federal Register**.

Drafting Information

The principal author of these regulations is Grid R. Glyer of the Office of Associate Chief Counsel (Corporate). Other personnel from the Treasury Department and the IRS participated in developing these regulations.

[¶49,793] Proposed Amendments of Regulations (REG-143686-07), published in the Federal Register on March 28, 2019.

[Code Secs. 301, 302, 304, 351, 354, 355, 356, 358, 368, 861, 1002, 1016 and 1374]

Withdrawal: Stock basis: Distributions of property: Dividend.—Regs. §§1.301-2, 1.302-5 and 1.861-12 and amendments of Regs. §§1.302-2, 1.304-1, 1.304-2, 1.304-3, 1.304-5, 1.351-2, 1.354-1, 1.355-1, 1.356-1, 1.358-1, 1.358-2, 1.358-6, 1.368-1, 1.1002-1, 1.1016-2 and 1.1374-10, proposed on January 21, 2009, withdrawing a notice of proposed rulemaking containing proposed regulations under numerous sections of the Internal Revenue Code (Code), are withdrawn.

AGENCY: Internal Revenue Service (IRS), Treasury.

ACTION: Proposed rule; withdrawal.

SUMMARY: This document withdraws a notice of proposed rulemaking containing proposed regulations under numerous sections of the Internal Revenue Code (Code). The proposed regulations being withdrawn would have provided guidance on the recovery of stock basis in distributions of property made by a corporation to a shareholder and certain transactions treated as dividend-equivalents, as well as guidance regarding the determination of gain and the basis of stock or securities received in certain transactions. The proposed regulations being withdrawn would have affected shareholders and security holders of corporations.

DATES: As of March 28, 2019, the notice of proposed rulemaking that was published in the **Federal Register** (74 FR 3509) on January 21, 2009, with corrections published in the **Federal Register** (74 FR 9575) on March 5, 2009, is withdrawn.

FOR FURTHER INFORMATION CONTACT: Kevin M. Jacobs at (202) 317-5332 or Aglaia Ovtchinnikova at (202) 317-6975 (neither a toll-free number).

SUPPLEMENTARY INFORMATION:

Background

On January 21, 2009, the Department of the Treasury (Treasury Department) and the IRS published a notice of proposed rulemaking (REG-143686-07) in the **Federal Register** (74 FR 3509) containing proposed regulations under sections 301, 302, 304, 351, 354, 355, 356, 358, 368, 861, 1001, and 1016 of the Code. On March 5, 2009, the Treasury Department and the IRS published corrections to the notice of proposed rulemaking in the **Federal Register** (74 FR 9575) (collectively, the 2009 Proposed Regulations).

The 2009 Proposed Regulations generally would have provided a single model for stock basis recovery by a shareholder that receives a distribution to which section 301 applies and a single model for sale and exchange transactions to which section 302(a) applies, including certain elements of an exchange in pursuance of a plan of reorganization under section 368. The 2009 Proposed Regulations also would have defined the scope of the exchange that must be analyzed under particular Code provisions and provided a methodology for determining gain under section 356 and stock basis under section 358.

The 2009 Proposed Regulations responded to comments received by the Treasury Department and the IRS regarding the then-recently published section 358 regulations. These comments included suggestions to expand the tracing rules of the section 358 regulations to stock transfers that are subject to section 351 but do not qualify as reorganizations, as well as questions regarding whether (and, if so, to what extent) shareholder elections constitute terms of an exchange and whether the terms of an exchange control for purposes of qualifying a transaction as a reorganization under section 368.

Finally, the 2009 Proposed Regulations included amendments to the current regulations under section 304 that would have updated those regulations to reflect statutory amendments to that section. See section 226 of the Tax Equity and Fiscal Responsibility Act of 1982, Pub. L. 97-248 (96 Stat. 325, 490) (September 3, 1982), section 712(l) of the Deficit Reduction Act of 1984, Pub. L. 98-369 (98 Stat. 494, 953-55) (July 18, 1984), section 1875(b) of the Tax Reform Act of 1986, Pub. L. 99-514 (100 Stat. 2085, 2894) (October 22, 1986), and section 1013 of the Taxpayer Relief Act of 1997, Pub. L. 105-34 (111 Stat. 788, 918) (August 5, 1997).

The Treasury Department and the IRS received many comments regarding the 2009 Proposed Regulations. The chief concern raised by commenters was that the approach taken in the 2009 Proposed Regulations represented an unwarranted departure from current law as a result of which minor changes to an overall business transaction could cause meaningful changes to the tax consequences, thereby elevating the form of the transaction over its substance.

After thoroughly considering the comments received, the Treasury Department and the IRS have determined that it is unlikely that the approach of the 2009 Proposed Regulations can be implemented in comprehensive final regulations without significant modifications. As a result, the Treasury Department and the IRS have decided to withdraw the 2009 Proposed Regulations. The Treasury Department and the IRS are continuing to study the issues addressed in the 2009 Proposed Regulations, with a particular focus on issues surrounding sections 301(c)(2) and 304, and § 1.302-2(c) of the Income Tax Regulations.

The Treasury Department and the IRS continue to believe that under current law, the results of a section 301 distribution should derive from the consideration received by a shareholder in respect of each share of stock, notwithstanding designations otherwise. See *Johnson v. United States*, 435 F.2d 1257 (4th Cir. 1971). The Treasury Department and the IRS also continue to believe that, under current law, with respect to redemptions governed by section 302(d), any unrecovered basis in the redeemed stock of a shareholder may be shifted to other stock only if such an adjustment is a proper adjustment within the meaning of § 1.302-2(c). Not all shifts of a redeemed shareholder's unrecovered basis result in proper adjustments, and certain basis adjustments can lead to inappropriate results. See, *e.g.*, Notice 2001-45, 2001-33 I.R.B. 129.

Drafting Information

The principal author of this withdrawal notice is Aglaia Ovtchinnikova of the Office of Associate Chief Counsel (Corporate). However, other personnel from the Treasury Department and the IRS participated in its development.

[¶ 49,794] Proposed Amendments of Regulations (REG-124627-11), published in the Federal Register on April 1, 2019.

[Code Sec. 368]

Corporations: Reorganizations: Continuity of interest: Measuring continuity of interest.—Amendments of Reg. § 1.368-1, proposed on December 19, 2011, withdrawing a notice of proposed rulemaking that would have provided guidance on how to determine whether certain transactions satisfy the continuity of interest (COI) requirement under § 1.368-1(e), applicable to certain corporate reorganizations described in section 368 of the Internal Revenue Code of 1986 (Code), are withdrawn.

AGENCY: Internal Revenue Service (IRS), Treasury.

ACTION: Withdrawal of notice of proposed rulemaking.

SUMMARY: This document withdraws a notice of proposed rulemaking that would have provided guidance on how to determine whether certain transactions satisfy the continuity of interest (COI) requirement under § 1.368-1(e), applicable to certain corporate reorganizations described in section 368 of the Internal Revenue Code of 1986 (Code). The proposed regulations being withdrawn would have affected corporations and their shareholders.

DATES: As of April 1, 2019, the

proposed amendment to § 1.368-1 in the notice of proposed rulemaking (REG-124627-11) that was published in the **Federal Register** (76 FR 78591) on December 19, 2011, is withdrawn.

FOR FURTHER INFORMATION CONTACT: Jean R. Broderick at (202) 317-6848 (not a toll-free number).

SUPPLEMENTARY INFORMATION:

Background

The provisions of subchapter C, chapter 1, of the Code generally provide nonrecognition treatment for corporate transactions that are described as reorganizations in section 368. The COI requirement is one of a number of requirements that a transaction must satisfy in order to qualify as a reorganization. The COI requirement prevents transactions that resemble sales from qualifying as reorganizations. *Pinellas Ice & Cold Storage Co. v. Commissioner*, 287 U.S. 462 (1933).

The COI requirement requires that, in substance, a substantial part of the value of the target corporation (Target) shareholders' proprietary interests (*i.e.*, stock) in Target be preserved. Section 1.368-1(e)(1)(i); *John A. Nelson Co. v. Helvering*, 296 U.S. 374 (1935). A Target shareholder's proprietary interest in Target is preserved to the extent it is exchanged for either the stock of the acquiring corporation (Acquiror) or, in the case of a triangular reorganization (as defined in § 1.358-6(b)(2)), the stock of a corporation in control (within the meaning of section 368(c)) of Acquiror (in either case, Issuing Corporation stock). To the extent the Target shareholders' proprietary interests are exchanged for money or other property, their proprietary interests are not preserved. Section 1.368-1(e)(1)(i).

To determine whether a substantial part of the Target shareholders' proprietary interests has been preserved, the value of the Issuing Corporation stock the Target shareholders received is compared to the aggregate value of the consideration the Target shareholders received. Prior to 2011, the determination of whether the COI requirement is satisfied had been based on the value of the Issuing Corporation stock "as of the effective date of the reorganization" (Closing Date). Rev. Proc. 77-37 (1977-2 C.B. 568).

On December 19, 2011, the Department of the Treasury (Treasury Department) and the IRS issued final regulations (TD 9565, 76 FR 78540) that include a special rule (Signing Date Rule) that applies if a binding contract to effect a potential reorganization provides for fixed consideration (as defined in § 1.368-1(e)(2)(iii)(A)) to be exchanged for the Target shareholders' proprietary interests. Section 1.368-1(e)(2)(i). If the Signing Date Rule applies, the consideration is valued as of the end of the last business day before the first date there is a binding contract (Pre-signing Date), rather than on the Closing Date.

On the same date, the Treasury Department and the IRS published proposed regulations (2011 Proposed Regulations) (REG-124627-11, 76 FR 78591) that identified situations, other than those covered by the Signing Date Rule, in which the value of Issuing Corporation stock could be determined based on a value other than its actual trading price on the Closing Date. In one of these situations, the 2011 Proposed Regulations would have allowed the parties to use an average of the trading prices of Issuing Corporation stock over a number of days, in lieu of its actual trading price on the Closing Date, for purposes of determining whether the COI requirement is satisfied.

The Treasury Department and the IRS have determined that current law generally provides sufficient guidance to taxpayers with respect to the COI requirement. Therefore, the Treasury Department and the IRS have decided to withdraw the 2011 Proposed Regulations. However, after considering comments received on the 2011 Proposed Regulations, the IRS has concluded that, in certain circumstances, taxpayers should be able to rely on certain average stock valuation methods for purposes of measuring COI. Accordingly, the IRS issued a revenue procedure effective January 23, 2018, that provides the circumstances under which the IRS will not challenge a taxpayer's use of certain stock valuation methods to value certain Issuing Corporation stock for purposes of determining whether the COI requirement is satisfied. *See* Rev. Proc. 2018-12, I.R.B. 2018-6.

Statement of Availability of IRS Documents

Rev. Proc. 2018-12 is published in the Internal Revenue Bulletin and is available from the Superintendent of Documents, U.S. Government Publishing Office, Washington, DC 20402, or by visiting the IRS website at http://www.irs.gov.

Drafting Information

The principal author of this withdrawal notice is Jean Broderick of the Office of Associate Chief Counsel (Corporate). However, other personnel from the Treasury Department and the IRS participated in its development.

[¶ 49,795] Proposed Amendments of Regulations (REG-120186-18) and partial withdrawal of **Notice of Proposed Regulations, NPRM REG-120186-18**, published in the Federal Register on May 1, 2019.

[Code Sec. 1400Z-2]

Qualified opportunity fund: Capital gains: Opportunity zones.—Reg. §§ 1.1400Z-2(b)(1), 1.1400Z-2(f)(1) and 1.1400Z-2(g)(1) and amendments of Reg. §§ 1.1400Z-2(a)(1), 1.1400Z-2(c)(1) and 1.1400Z-2(d)(1), relating to gains that may be deferred as a result of a taxpayer's investment in a qualified opportunity fund (QOF), as well as special rules for an investment in a QOF held by a taxpayer for at least 10 years, are proposed. Reg. § 1.1400Z-2(d)-1(c)(4)(i), (c)(5), (c)(6), (c)(7), (d)(2)(i)(A), (d)(2)(ii), (d)(2)(iii), (d)(5)(i), and (d)(5)(ii)(B), proposed on October 29, 2018, are withdrawn.

AGENCY: Internal Revenue Service (IRS), Treasury.

ACTION: Notice of proposed rulemaking; partial withdrawal of a notice of proposed rulemaking.

SUMMARY: This document contains proposed regulations that provide guidance under new section 1400Z-2 of the Internal Revenue Code (Code) relating to gains that may be deferred as a result of a taxpayer's investment in a qualified opportunity fund (QOF), as well as special rules for an investment in a QOF held by a taxpayer for at least 10 years. This document also contains proposed regulations that update portions of previously proposed regulations under section 1400Z-2 to address various issues, including: the definition of "substantially all" in each of the various places it appears in section 1400Z-2; the transactions that may trigger the inclusion of gain that a taxpayer has elected to defer under section 1400Z-2; the timing and amount of the deferred gain that is included; the treatment of leased property used by a qualified opportunity zone business; the use of qualified opportunity zone business property in the qualified opportunity zone; the sourcing of gross income to the qualified opportunity zone business; and the "reasonable period" for a QOF to reinvest proceeds from the sale of qualifying assets without paying a penalty. These proposed regulations will affect QOFs and taxpayers that invest in QOFs.

DATES: Written (including electronic) comments must be received by **[INSERT DATE 60 DAYS AFTER DATE OF PUBLICATION IN THE FEDERAL REGISTER]**. Outlines of topics to be discussed at the public hearing scheduled for July 9, 2019, at 10 a.m. must be received by **[INSERT DATE 60 DAYS AFTER DATE OF PUBLICATION OF THIS DOCUMENT IN THE FEDERAL REGISTER]**. The public hearing will be held at the New Carrollton Federal Building at 5000 Ellin Road in Lanham, Maryland 20706.

ADDRESSES: Submit electronic submissions via the Federal eRulemaking Portal at *www.regulations.gov* (indicate IRS and REG-120186-18) by following the online instructions for submitting comments. Once submitted to the Federal eRulemaking Portal, comments cannot be edited or withdrawn. The Department of the Treasury (Treasury Department) and the IRS will publish for public availability any comment received to its public docket, whether submitted electronically or in hard copy. Send hard copy submissions to: CC:PA:LPD:PR (REG-120186-18), room 5203, Internal Revenue Service, PO Box 7604, Ben Franklin Station, Washington, DC 20044. Submissions may be hand-delivered Monday through Friday between the hours of 8 a.m. and 4 p.m. to CC:PA:LPD:PR (REG-120186-18), Courier's Desk, Internal Revenue Service, 1111 Constitution Avenue, NW, Washington, DC 20224.

FOR FURTHER INFORMATION CONTACT: Concerning the proposed regulations, Erika C. Reigle of the Office of Associate Chief Counsel (Income Tax and Accounting), (202) 317-7006, and Kyle C. Griffin of the Office of Associate Chief Counsel (Income Tax and Accounting), (202) 317-4718; concerning the submission of comments, the hearing, or to be placed on the building access list to attend the hearing, Regina L. Johnson, (202) 317-6901 (not toll-free numbers).

SUPPLEMENTARY INFORMATION:

Background

This document contains proposed regulations under section 1400Z-2 of the Code that amend the Income Tax Regulations (26 CFR part 1). Section 13823 of the Tax Cuts and Jobs Act, Public Law 115-97, 131 Stat. 2054, 2184 (2017) (TCJA), amended the Code to add sections 1400Z-1 and 1400Z-2. Sections 1400Z-1 and 1400Z-2 seek to encourage economic growth and investment in designated distressed communities (qualified opportunity zones) by providing Federal income tax benefits to taxpayers who invest new capital in businesses located within qualified opportunity zones through a QOF.

Section 1400Z-1 provides the procedural rules for designating qualified opportunity zones and related definitions. Section 1400Z-2 provides two main tax incentives to encourage investment in qualified opportunity zones. First, it allows for the deferral of inclusion in gross income of certain gain to the extent that a taxpayer elects to invest a corresponding amount in a QOF. Second, it allows for the taxpayer to elect to exclude from gross income the post-acquisition gain on investments in the QOF held for at least 10 years. Additionally, with respect to the deferral of inclusion in gross income of certain gain invested in a QOF, section 1400Z-2 permanently excludes a portion of such deferred gain if the corresponding investment in the QOF is held for five or seven years.

On October 29, 2018, the Department of the Treasury (Treasury Department) and the IRS published in the **Federal Register** (83 FR 54279) a notice of proposed rulemaking (REG-115420-18) providing guidance under section 1400Z-2 of the Code for investing in qualified opportunity funds (83 FR 54279 (October 29, 2018)). A public hearing on 83 FR 54279 (October 29, 2018) was held on February 14, 2019. The Treasury Department and the IRS continue to consider the comments received on 83 FR 54279 (October 29, 2018), including those provided at the public hearing.

As is more fully explained in the Explanation of Provisions, the proposed regulations contained in this notice of proposed rulemaking describe and clarify requirements relating to investing in QOFs not addressed in 83 FR 54279 (October 29, 2018). Specifically, and as was indicated in 83 FR 54279 (October 29, 2018), these proposed regulations address the meaning of "substantially all" in each of the various places where it appears in section 1400Z-2; the reasonable period for a QOF to reinvest proceeds from the sale of qualifying assets without paying a penalty pursuant to section 1400Z-2(e)(4)(B); the transactions that may trigger the inclusion of gain that has been deferred under a section 1400Z-2(a) election; and other technical issues with regard to investing in a QOF. Because portions of 83 FR 54279 (October 29, 2018) contained certain placeholder text, included less detailed guidance in certain areas that merely cross-referenced statutory rules, or lacked sufficient detail to address these issues, this notice of proposed rulemaking withdraws paragraphs (c)(4)(i), (c)(5) and (6), (d)(2)(i)(A), (d)(2)(ii) and (iii), (d)(5)(i), and (d)(5)(ii)(B) of proposed § 1.1400Z2(d)-1 of 83 FR 54279 (October 29, 2018), and proposes in their place new paragraphs (c)(4)(i), (c)(5) and (6), (d)(2)(i)(A), (d)(2)(ii) and (iii), (d)(5)(i), and (d)(5)(ii)(B) of proposed § 1.1400Z2(d)-1.

The Treasury Department and the IRS welcome suggestions as to other issues that should be addressed to further clarify the rules under section 1400Z-2, as well as comments on all aspects of these proposed regulations.

Within a few months of the publication of these proposed regulations, the Treasury Department and the IRS expect to address the administrative rules under section 1400Z-2(f) applicable to a QOF that fails to maintain the required 90 percent investment standard of section 1400Z-2(d)(1), as well as information-reporting requirements for an eligible taxpayer under section 1400Z-2, in separate regulations, forms, or publications.

In addition, the Treasury Department and the IRS anticipate revising the Form 8996 (OMB Control number 1545-0123) for tax years 2019 and following. As provided for under the rules set forth in 83 FR 54279 (October 29, 2018), a QOF must file a Form 8996 with its Federal income tax return for initial self-certification and for annual reporting of compliance with the 90-Percent Asset Test in section 1400Z-2(d)(1). Subject to tax administration limitations, the Paperwork Reduction Act of 1995 (44 U.S.C. 3507(d)), and other requirements under law, it is expected that proposed revisions to the Form 8996 could require additional information such as (1) the employer identification number (EIN) of the qualified opportunity zone businesses owned by a QOF and (2) the amount invested by QOFs and qualified opportunity zone businesses located in particular Census tracts designated as qualified opportunity zones. In that regard, consistent with Executive Order 13853 of December 12, 2018, *Establishing the White House Opportunity and Revitalization Council* (EO 13853), published in the **Federal Register** (83 FR 65071) on December 18, 2018, and concurrent with the publication of these proposed regulations, the Treasury Department and the IRS are publishing a request for information (RFI) under this subject in the Notices section of this edition of the **Federal Register**, with a docket for comments on www.regulations.gov separate from that for this notice of proposed rulemaking, requesting detailed comments with respect to methodologies for assessing relevant aspects of investments held by QOFs throughout the United States and at the State, Territorial, and Tribal levels, including the composition of QOF investments by asset class, the identification of designated qualified opportunity zone Census tracts that have received QOF investments, and the impacts and outcomes of the investments in those areas on economic indicators, including job creation, poverty reduction, and new business starts. EO 13853 charges the White House Opportunity and Revitalization Council, of which the Treasury Department is a member, to determine "what data, metrics, and methodologies can be used to measure the effectiveness of public and private investments in urban and economically distressed communities, including qualified opportunity zones." See the requests for comments in the RFI regarding these or other topics regarding methodologies for assessing the impacts of sections 1400Z-1 and 1400Z-2 on qualified opportunity zones throughout the Nation.

Explanation of Provisions

I. *Qualified Opportunity Zone Business Property*

A. Definition of Substantially All for Purposes of Sections 1400Z-2(d)(2) and (d)(3)

The proposed rule published at 83 FR 54279 (October 29, 2018) clarified that, for purposes of section 1400Z-2(d)(3)(A)(i), for determining whether an entity is a qualified opportunity zone business, the threshold to determine whether a trade or business satisfies the *substantially all* test is 70 percent. *See* 83 FR 54279, 54294 (October 29, 2018). If at least 70 percent of the tangible property owned or leased by a trade or business is qualified opportunity zone business property (as defined in section 1400Z-2(d)(3)(A)(i)), proposed § 1.1400Z2(d)-1(d)(3)(i) in 83 FR 54279 (October 29, 2018) provides that the trade or business is treated as satisfying the *substantially all* requirement in section 1400Z-2(d)(3)(A)(i).

The phrase *substantially all* is also used throughout section 1400Z-2(d)(2). The phrase appears in section 1400Z-2(d)(2)(D)(i)(III), which establishes the conditions for property to be treated as qualified opportunity zone business property ("during *substantially all* of the qualified opportunity fund's holding period for such property, *substantially all* of the use of such property was in a qualified opportunity zone"). The phrase also appears in sections 1400Z-2(d)(2)(B)(i)(III) and 1400Z-2(d)(2)(C)(iii), which require that during *substantially all* of the QOF's holding period for qualified opportunity zone stock or qualified opportunity zone partnership interests, such corporation or partnership qualified as a qualified opportunity zone business.

The proposed rule published at 83 FR 54279 (October 29, 2018) reserved the proposed meaning of the phrase *substantially all* as used in section 1400Z-2(d)(2). The statute neither defines the meaning of *substantially all* for the QOF's holding period for qualified opportunity zone stock, qualified opportunity zone partnership interests, and qualified opportunity zone business property, nor defines it for purposes of testing the use of qualified opportunity zone business property in a qualified opportunity zone. The Treasury Department and the IRS have received numerous questions and comments on the threshold limits of *substantially all* for purposes of section 1400Z-2(d)(2). Many commenters suggested that a lower threshold for the use requirement of section 1400Z-2(d)(2)(D)(i)(III) would allow a variety of businesses to benefit from qualifying investments in QOFs. Other commentators suggested that too low a threshold would negatively impact the low-income communities that section 1400Z-2 is intended to benefit, because the tax-incentivized investment would not be focused sufficiently on these communities.

Consistent with 83 FR 54279 (October 29, 2018) these proposed regulations provide that, in testing the use of qualified opportunity zone business property in a qualified opportunity zone, as required in section 1400Z-2(d)(2)(D)(i)(III), the term *substantially all* in the context of "use" is 70 percent. With respect to owned or leased tangible property, these proposed regulations provide identical requirements for determining whether a QOF or qualified opportunity zone business has used substantially all of such tangible property within the qualified opportunity zone within the meaning of section 1400Z-2(d)(2)(D)(i)(III). Whether such tangible property is owned or leased, these proposed regulations propose that the substantially all requirement regarding "use" is satisfied if at least 70 percent of the use of such tangible property is in a qualified opportunity zone.

As discussed in the preamble to 83 FR 54279 (October 29, 2018) a compounded use of *substantially all* must be interpreted in a manner consistent with the intent of Congress. Consequently, the

Treasury Department and the IRS have determined that a higher threshold is necessary in the holding period context to preserve the integrity of the statute and for the purpose of focusing investment in designated qualified opportunity zones. Thus, the proposed regulations provide that the term *substantially all* as used in the holding period context in sections 1400Z-2(d)(2)(B)(i)(III), 1400Z-2(d)(2)(C)(iii), and 1400Z-2(d)(2)(D)(i)(III) is defined as 90 percent. Using a percentage threshold that is higher than 70-percent in the holding period context is warranted as taxpayers are more easily able to control and determine the period for which they hold property. In addition, given the lower 70-percent thresholds for testing both the use of tangible property in the qualified opportunity zone and the amount of owned and leased tangible property of a qualified opportunity zone business that must be qualified opportunity zone business property, applying a 70-percent threshold in the holding period context can result in much less than half of a qualified opportunity zone business's tangible property being used in a qualified opportunity zone. Accordingly, the Treasury Department and the IRS have determined that using a threshold lower than 90 percent in the holding period context would reduce the amount of investment in qualified opportunity zones to levels inconsistent with the purposes of section 1400Z-2.

The Treasury Department and the IRS request comments on these proposed definitions of *substantially all* for purposes of section 1400Z-2(d)(2).

B. Original Use of Tangible Property Acquired by Purchase

In 83 FR 54279 (October 29, 2018) the Treasury Department and the IRS specifically solicited comments on the definition of the "original use" requirement in section 1400Z-2(d)(2)(D)(i)(II) for both real property and tangible personal property and reserved a section of the proposed regulations to define the phrase *original use*. The requirement that tangible property acquired by purchase have its "original use" in a qualified opportunity zone commencing with a qualified opportunity fund or qualified opportunity zone business, or be substantially improved, in order to qualify for tax benefits is also found in other sections of the Code. Under the now-repealed statutory frameworks of both section 1400B (related to the DC Zone) and section 1400F (related to Renewal Communities), qualified property for purposes of those provisions was required to have its original use in a zone or to meet the requirements of substantial improvement as defined under those provisions. The Treasury Department and the IRS have received numerous questions on the meaning of "original use." Examples of these questions include: May tangible property be previously used property, or must it be new property? Does property previously placed in service in the qualified opportunity zone for one use, but now placed in service for a different use, qualify? May property used in the qualified opportunity zone be placed in service in the same qualified opportunity zone by an acquiring, unrelated taxpayer?

After carefully considering the comments and questions received, the proposed regulations generally provide that the "original use" of tangible property acquired by purchase by any person commences on the date when that person or a prior person first places the property in service in the qualified opportunity zone for purposes of depreciation or amortization (or first uses the property in the qualified opportunity zone in a manner that would allow depreciation or amortization if that person were the property's owner). Thus, tangible property located in the qualified opportunity zone that is depreciated or amortized by a taxpayer other than the QOF or qualified opportunity zone business would not satisfy the original use requirement of section 1400Z-2(d)(2)(D)(i)(II) under these proposed regulations. Conversely, tangible property (other than land) located in the qualified opportunity zone that has not yet been depreciated or amortized by a taxpayer other than the QOF or qualified opportunity zone business would satisfy the original use requirement of section 1400Z-2(d)(2)(D)(i)(II) under these proposed regulations. However, the proposed regulations clarify that used tangible property will satisfy the original use requirement with respect to a qualified opportunity zone so long as the property has not been previously used (that is, has not previously been used within that qualified opportunity zone in a manner that would have allowed it to depreciated or amortized) by any taxpayer. (For special rules concerning the original use requirement for assets acquired in certain transactions to which section 355 or section 381 applies, *see* proposed § 1.1400Z2(b)-1(d)(2) in this notice of proposed rulemaking.)

The Treasury Department and the IRS have also studied the extent to which usage history of vacant structures or other tangible property (other than land) purchased after 2017 but previously placed in service within the qualified opportunity zone may be disregarded for purposes of the original use requirement if the structure or other property has not been utilized or has been abandoned for some minimum period of time and received multiple public comments regarding this issue. Several commenters suggested establishing an "at least one-year" vacancy period threshold similar to that employed in § 1.1394-1(h) to determine whether property meets the original use requirement within the meaning of section 1397D (defining qualified zone property) for purposes of section 1394 (relating to the issuance of enterprise zone facility bonds). Given the different operation of those provisions and the potential for owners of property already situated in a qualified opportunity zone to intentionally cease occupying property for 12 months in order to increase its marketability to potential purchasers after 2017, other commenters proposed longer vacancy thresholds ranging to five years. The Treasury Department and the IRS are proposing that where a building or other structure has been vacant for at least five years prior to being purchased by a QOF or qualified opportunity zone business, the purchased building or structure will satisfy the original use requirement. Comments are requested on this proposed approach, including the length of the vacancy period and how such a standard might be administered and enforced.

In addition, in response to questions about a taxpayer's improvements to leased property, the proposed regulations provide that improvements made by a lessee to leased property satisfy the original use requirement and are considered purchased property for the amount of the unadjusted cost basis of such improvements as determined in accordance with section 1012.

As provided in Rev. Rul. 2018-29, 2018 I.R.B 45, and these proposed regulations, if land that is within a qualified opportunity zone is acquired by purchase in accordance with section 1400Z-2(d)(2)(D)(i)(I), the requirement under section 1400Z-2(d)(2)(D)(i)(II) that the original use of tangible property in the qualified opportunity zone commence with a QOF is not applicable to the land, whether the land is improved or unimproved. Likewise, unimproved land that is within a qualified opportunity zone and acquired by purchase in accordance with section 1400Z-2(d)(2)(D)(i)(I) is not required to be substantially improved within the meaning of section 1400Z-2(d)(2)(D)(i)(II) and (d)(2)(D)(ii). Multiple public comments were received suggesting that not requiring the basis of land itself to be substantially improved within the meaning of section 1400Z-2(d)(2)(D)(i)(II) and (d)(2)(D)(ii) would lead to speculative land purchasing and potential abuse of section 1400Z-2.

The Treasury Department and the IRS have considered these comments. Under section 1400Z-2(d)(2)(D)(i)(II) and these proposed regulations, land can be treated as qualified opportunity zone business property for purposes of section 1400Z-2 only if it is used in a trade or business of a QOF or qualified opportunity zone business. As described in part III.D. of this Explanation of Provisions, only activities giving rise to a trade or business within the meaning of section 162 may qualify as a trade or business for purposes of section 1400Z-2; the holding of land for investment does not give rise to a trade or business and such land could not be qualified opportunity zone business property. Moreover, land is a crucial business asset for numerous types of operating trades or businesses aside from real estate development, and the degree to which it is necessary or useful for taxpayers seeking to grow their businesses to improve the land that their businesses depend on will vary greatly by region, industry, and particular business. In many cases, regulations that imposed a requirement on all types of trades or businesses to substantially improve (within the meaning of section 1400Z-2(d)(2)(D)(i)(II) and (d)(2)(D)(ii)) land that is used by them may encourage noneconomic, tax-motivated business decisions, or otherwise effectively prevent many businesses from benefitting under the opportunity zone provisions. Such rules also would inject a significant degree of additional complexity into these proposed regulations.

Nevertheless, the Treasury Department and the IRS recognize that, in certain instances, the treatment of unimproved land as qualified opportunity zone business property could lead to tax results that are inconsistent with the purposes of section 1400Z-2. For example, a QOF's acquisition of a parcel of land currently utilized entirely by a business for the production of an agricultural crop, whether active or fallow at that time, potentially could be treated as qualified opportunity zone business property without the QOF investing any new capital investment in, or increasing any economic activity or output of, that parcel. In such instances, the Treasury Department and the IRS have determined that the purposes of section 1400Z-2 would not be realized, and therefore the tax incentives otherwise provided under section 1400Z-2 should not be available. If a significant purpose for acquiring such unimproved land was to achieve that inappropriate tax result, the general anti-abuse rule set forth in proposed § 1.1400Z2(f)-1(c) (and described further in part X of this Explanation of Provisions) would apply to treat the acquisition of the unimproved land as an acquisition of non-qualifying property for section 1400Z-2 purposes. The Treasury Department and the IRS request comments on whether anti-abuse rules under section 1400Z-2(e)(4)(c), in addition to the general anti-abuse rule, are needed to prevent such transactions or "land banking" by QOFs or qualified opportunity zone businesses, and on possible approaches to prevent such abuse.

Conversely, if real property, other than land, that is acquired by purchase in accordance with section 1400Z-2(d)(2)(D)(i)(I) had been placed in service in the qualified opportunity zone by a person other than the QOF or qualified opportunity zone business (or first used in a manner that would allow depreciation or amortization if that person were the property's owner), it must be substantially improved to be considered qualified opportunity zone business property. Substantial improvement by the QOF or qualified opportunity zone business for real property, other than land, is determined by applying the requirements for substantial improvement of tangible property acquired by purchase set forth in section 1400Z-2(d)(2)(D)(ii).

The Treasury Department and the IRS request comments on these proposed rules regarding the original use requirement generally, including whether certain cases may warrant additional consideration. Comments are also requested as to whether the ability to treat such prior use as disregarded for purposes of the original use requirement should depend on whether the property has been fully depreciated for Federal income tax purposes, or whether other adjustments for any undepreciated or unamortized basis of such property would be appropriate. The Treasury Department and the IRS are also studying the circumstances under which tangible property that had not been purchased but has been overwhelmingly improved by a QOF or a qualified opportunity zone business may be considered as satisfying the original use requirement and request comment regarding possible approaches.

Under these proposed regulations, the determination of whether the substantial improvement requirement of section 1400Z-2(d)(2)(D)(ii) is satisfied for tangible property that is purchased is made on an asset-by-asset basis. The Treasury Department and the IRS have considered the possibility, however, that an asset-by-asset approach might be onerous for certain types of businesses. For example, the granular nature of an asset-by-asset approach might cause operating businesses with significant numbers of diverse assets to encounter administratively difficult asset segregation and tracking burdens, potentially creating traps for the unwary. As an alternative, the Treasury Department and the IRS have contemplated the possibility of applying an aggregate standard for determining compliance with the substantial improvement requirement, potentially allowing tangible property to be grouped by location in the same, or contiguous, qualified opportunity zones. Given that an aggregate approach could provide additional compliance flexibility, while continuing to incentivize high-quality investments in qualified opportunity zones, the Treasury Department and the IRS request comments on the potential advantages, as well as disadvantages, of adopting an aggregate approach for substantial improvement.

Additional comments are requested regarding the application of the substantial improvement requirement with respect to tangible personal property acquired by purchase that is not capable of being substantially improved (for example, equipment that is nearly new but was previously used in the qualified opportunity zone and the cost of fully refurbishing the equipment would not result in a doubling of the basis of such property). Specifically, comments are requested regarding whether the term "property" in section 1400Z-2(d)(2)(D)(ii) should be interpreted in the aggregate to permit the purchase of items of non-original use property together with items of original use property that do not directly improve such non-original use property to satisfy the substantial improvement requirement. In that regard, comments are requested as to the extent to which such treatment may be appropriate given that such treatment could cause a conflict between the independent original use requirement of section 1400Z-2(d)(2)(D)(i)(II) and the independent substantial improvement requirement of section 1400Z-2(d)(2)(D)(i)(II) by reason of the definition of substantial improvement under section 1400Z-2(d)(2)(D)(ii). Comments are also requested regarding the treatment of purchases of multiple items of separate tangible personal property for purposes of section 1400Z-2(d)(2)(D)(i)(II) that have the same applicable depreciation method, applicable recovery period, and applicable convention, and which are placed in service in the same year by a QOF or qualified opportunity zone business in one or more general asset accounts within the meaning of section 168(i) and § 1.168(i)-1.

C. Safe Harbor for Testing Use of Inventory in Transit

Section 1400Z-2(d)(2)(D)(i)(III) provides that qualified opportunity zone business property means tangible property used in a trade or business of the QOF if, during substantially all of the QOF's holding period for such property, substantially all of the use of such property was in a qualified opportunity zone. Commentators have inquired how inventory will be treated for purposes of determining whether substantially all of the tangible property is used in the qualified opportunity zone. Commentators expressed concern that inventory in transit on the last day of the taxable year of a QOF would be counted against the QOF when determining whether the QOF has met the 90-percent ownership requirement found in section 1400Z-2(d)(1) (90-percent asset test).

The proposed regulations clarify that inventory (including raw materials) of a trade or business does not fail to be used in a qualified opportunity zone solely because the inventory is in transit from a vendor to a facility of the trade or business that is in a qualified opportunity zone, or from a facility of the trade or business that is in a qualified opportunity zone to customers of the trade or business that are not located in a qualified opportunity zone. Comments are requested as to whether the location of where inventory is warehoused should be relevant and whether inventory (including raw materials) should be excluded from both the numerator and denominator of the 70-percent test for QOZBs.

The Treasury Department and the IRS request comments on the proposed rules regarding the determination of whether inventory, as well as other property, is used in a qualified opportunity zone, including whether certain cases or types of property may warrant additional consideration.

II. *Treatment of Leased Tangible Property*

As noted previously, section 1400Z-2(d)(3)(A)(i) provides that a qualified opportunity zone business is a trade or business in which, among other things, substantially all (that is, at least 70 percent) of the tangible property owned or leased by the taxpayer is "qualified opportunity zone business property" within the meaning of section 1400Z-2(d)(2)(D), determined by substituting "qualified opportunity fund" with "qualified opportunity zone business" each place that such term appears. Taking into account this substitution, section 1400Z-2(d)(2)(D)(i) provides that qualified opportunity zone business property is tangible property that meets the following requirements: (1) the tangible property was acquired by the trade or business by purchase (as defined in section 179(d)(2)) after December 31, 2017; (2) the original use of such property in the qualified opportunity zone commences with the qualified opportunity zone business, or the qualified opportunity zone business substantially improves the property; and (3) for substantially all of the qualified opportunity zone business's holding period of the tangible property, substantially all of the use of such property is in the qualified opportunity zone. Commenters have expressed concern as to whether tangible property that is leased by a qualified opportunity zone business can be treated as satisfying these requirements. Similar questions have arisen with respect to whether tangible property leased by a QOF could be treated as satisfying the 90-percent asset test under section 1400Z-2(d)(1).

A. Status as Qualified Opportunity Zone Business Property

The purposes of sections 1400Z-1 and 1400Z-2 are to increase business activity and economic investment in qualified opportunity zones. As a proxy for evaluating increases in business activity and economic investment in a qualified opportunity zone, these sections of the Code generally measure increases in tangible business property used in that qualified opportunity zone. The general approach of the statute in evaluating the achievement of those purposes inform the proposed regulations' treatment of tangible property that is leased rather than owned. The Treasury Department and the IRS also recognize that not treating leased property as qualified opportunity zone business property may have an unintended consequence of excluding investments on tribal lands designated as qualified opportunity zones because tribal governments occupy Federal trust lands and these lands are, more often than not, leased for economic development purposes.

Given the purpose of sections 1400Z-1 and 1400Z-2 to facilitate increased business activity and economic investment in qualified opportunity zones, these proposed regulations would provide greater parity among diverse types of business models. If a taxpayer uses tangible property located in a qualified opportunity zone in its business, the benefits of such use on the qualified opportunity zone's economy would not generally be expected to vary greatly depending on whether the business pays cash for the property, borrows in order to purchase the property, or leases the property. Not recognizing that benefits can accrue to a qualified opportunity zone regardless of the manner in which a QOF or qualified opportunity zone business acquires rights to use tangible property in the qualified opportunity zone could result in preferences solely based on whether businesses choose to own or lease tangible property, an anomalous result inconsistent with the purpose of sections 1400Z-1 and 1400Z-2.

Accordingly, leased tangible property meeting certain criteria may be treated as qualified opportunity zone business property for purposes of satisfying the 90-percent asset test under section 1400Z-2(d)(1) and the substantially all requirement under section 1400Z-2(d)(3)(A)(i). The following two general criteria must be satisfied. First, analogous to owned tangible property, leased tangible property must be acquired under a lease entered into after December 31, 2017. Second, as with owned tangible property, substantially all of the use of the leased tangible property must be in a qualified opportunity zone during substantially all of the period for which the business leases the property.

These proposed regulations, however, do not impose an original use requirement with respect to leased tangible property for, among others, the following reasons. Unlike owned tangible property, in most circumstances, leased tangible property held by a lessee cannot be placed in service for depreciation or amortization purposes because the lessee does not own such tangible property for Federal income tax purposes. In addition, in many instances, leased tangible property may have been previously leased to other lessees or previously used in the qualified opportunity zone. Furthermore, taxpayers generally do not have a basis in leased property that can be depreciated, again, because they are not the owner of such property for Federal income tax purposes. Therefore, the proposed regulations do not impose a requirement for a lessee to "substantially improve" leased tangible property within the meaning of section 1400Z-2(d)(2)(D)(ii).

Unlike tangible property that is purchased by a QOF or qualified opportunity zone business, the proposed regulations do not require leased tangible property to be acquired from a lessor that is unrelated (within the meaning of section 1400Z-2(e)(2)) to the QOF or qualified opportunity zone business that is the lessee under the lease. However, in order to maintain greater parity between decisions to lease or own tangible property, while also limiting abuse, the proposed regulations provide one limitation as an alternative to imposing a related person rule or a substantial improvement rule and two further limitations that apply when the lessor and lessee are related.

First, the proposed regulations require in all cases, that the lease under which a QOF or qualified opportunity zone business acquires rights with respect to any leased tangible property must be a "market rate lease." For this purpose, whether a lease is market rate (that is, whether the terms of the lease reflect common, arms-length market practice in the locale that includes the qualified opportunity zone) is determined under the regulations under section 482. This limitation operates to ensure that all of the terms of the lease are market rate.

Second, if the lessor and lessee are related, the proposed regulations do not permit leased tangible property to be treated as qualified opportunity zone business property if, in connection with the lease, a QOF or qualified opportunity zone business at any time makes a prepayment to the lessor (or a person related to the lessor within the meaning of section 1400Z-2(e)(2)) relating to a period of use of the leased tangible property that exceeds 12 months. This requirement operates to prevent inappropriate allocations of investment capital to prepayments of rent, as well as other payments exchanged for the use of the leased property.

Third, also applicable when the lessor and lessee are related, the proposed regulations do not permit leased tangible personal property to be treated as qualified opportunity zone business property unless the lessee becomes the owner of tangible property that is qualified opportunity zone business property and that has a value not less than the value of the leased personal property. This acquisition of this property must occur during a period that begins on the date that the lessee receives possession of the property under the lease and ends on the earlier of the last day of the lease or the end of the 30-month period beginning on the date that the lessee receives possession of the property under the lease. There must be substantial overlap of zone(s) in which the owner of the property so acquired uses it and the zone(s) in which that person uses the leased property.

Finally, the proposed regulations include an anti-abuse rule to prevent the use of leases to circumvent the substantial improvement requirement for purchases of real property (other than unimproved land). In the case of real property (other than unimproved land) that is leased by a QOF, if, at the time the lease is entered into, there was a plan, intent, or expectation for the real property to be purchased by the QOF for an amount of consideration other than the fair market value of the real property determined at the time of the purchase without regard to any prior lease payments, the leased real property is not qualified opportunity zone business property at any time.

The Treasury Department and the IRS request comments on all aspects of the proposed treatment of leased tangible property. In particular, a determination under section 482 of whether the terms of the lease reflect common, arms-length market practice in the locale that includes the qualified opportunity zone takes into account the simultaneous combination of all terms of the lease, including rent, term, possibility of extension, presence of an option to purchase the leased asset, and (if there is such an option) the terms of purchase. Comments are requested on whether taxpayers and the IRS may encounter undue burden or difficulty in determining whether a lease is market rate. If so, how should the final regulations reduce that burden? For example, should the final regulations describe one or more conditions whose presence would create a presumption that a lease is (or is not) a market rate lease? Comments are also requested on whether the limitations intended to prevent abusive situations through the use of leased property are appropriate, or whether modifications are warranted.

B. Valuation of Leased Tangible Property

Based on the foregoing, these proposed regulations provide methodologies for valuing leased tangible property for purposes of satisfying the 90-percent asset test under section 1400Z-2(d)(1) and the substantially all requirement under section 1400Z-2(d)(3)(A)(i). Under these proposed regulations, on an annual basis, leased tangible property may be valued using either an applicable financial statement valuation method or an alternative valuation method, each described further below. A QOF or qualified opportunity zone business, as applicable, may select the applicable financial statement valuation method if they actually have an applicable financial statement (within the meaning of § 1.475(a)-4(h)). Once a QOF or qualified opportunity zone business selects one of those valuation methods for the taxable year, it must apply such method consistently to all leased tangible property valued with respect to the taxable year.

Financial statement valuation method

Under the applicable financial statement valuation method, the value of leased tangible property of a QOF or qualified opportunity zone business is the value of that property as reported on the applicable financial statement for the relevant reporting period. These proposed regulations require that a QOF or qualified opportunity zone business may select this applicable financial statement valuation only if the applicable financial statement is prepared according to U.S. generally accepted accounting principles (GAAP) and requires recognition of the lease of the tangible property.

Alternative valuation method

Under the alternative valuation method, the value of tangible property that is leased by a QOF or qualified opportunity zone business is determined based on a calculation of the "present value" of the leased tangible property. Specifically, the value of such leased tangible property under these proposed regulations is equal to the sum of the present values of the payments to be made under the lease for such tangible property. For purposes of calculating present value, the discount rate is the applicable Federal rate under section 1274(d)(1), determined by substituting the term "lease" for "debt instrument."

These proposed regulations require that a QOF or qualified opportunity zone business using the alternative valuation method calculate the value of leased tangible property under this alternative valuation method at the time the lease for such property is entered into. Once calculated, these proposed regulations require that such calculated value be used as the value for such asset for all testing dates for purposes of the "substantially all of the use" requirement and the 90-percent asset test.

The Treasury Department and the IRS request comments on these proposed rules regarding the treatment and valuation of leased tangible property, including whether other alternative valuation methods may be appropriate, or whether certain modifications to the proposed valuation methods are warranted.

III. *Qualified Opportunity Zone Businesses*

A. Real Property Straddling a Qualified Opportunity Zone

Section 1400Z-2(d)(3)(A)(ii) incorporates the requirements of section 1397C(b)(2), (4), and (8) related to Empowerment Zones. The Treasury Department and the IRS have received numerous comments on the ability of a business that holds real property straddling multiple Census tracts, where not all of the tracts are designated as a qualified opportunity zone under section 1400Z-1, to satisfy the requirements under sections 1400Z-2 and 1397C(b)(2), (4), and (8). Commenters have suggested that the proposed regulations adopt a rule that is similar to the rule used for purposes of other place-based tax incentives (that is, the Empowerment Zones) enshrined in section 1397C(f). Section 1397C(f) provides that if the amount of real property based on square footage located within the qualified opportunity zone is substantial as compared to the amount of real property based on square footage outside of the zone, and the real property outside of the zone is contiguous to part or all of the real property located inside the zone, then all of the property would be deemed to be located within a qualified zone.

These proposed regulations provide that in satisfying the requirements of section 1400Z-2(d)(3)(A)(ii), section 1397C(f) applies in the determination of whether a qualified opportunity zone is the location of services, tangible property, or business functions (substituting "qualified opportunity zone" for "empowerment zone"). Real property located within the qualified opportunity zone should be considered substantial if the unadjusted cost of the real property inside a qualified opportunity zone is greater than the unadjusted cost of real property outside of the qualified opportunity zone.

Comments are requested as to whether there exist circumstances under which the Treasury Department and the IRS could apply principles similar to those of section 1397C(f) in the case of other requirements of section 1400Z-2.

B. 50 Percent of Gross Income of a Qualified Opportunity Zone Business

Section 1397C(b)(2) provides that, in order to be a "qualified business entity" (in addition to other requirements found in section 1397C(b)) with respect to any taxable year, a corporation or partnership must derive at least 50 percent of its total gross income "from the active conduct of such business." The phrase *such* business refers to a business mentioned in the preceding sentence, which discusses "a qualified business within an empowerment zone." For purposes of application to section 1400Z-2, references in section 1397C to "an empowerment zone" are treated as meaning a qualified opportunity zone. Thus, the corporation or partnership must derive at least 50 percent of its total gross income from the active conduct of a business within a qualified opportunity zone.

An area of concern for commenters is how the Treasury Department and the IRS will determine whether this 50-percent gross income requirement is satisfied. Commenters recommended that the Treasury Department and the IRS provide guidance to clarify the requirements of sections 1400Z-2(d)(3)(A)(ii) and 1397C(b)(2).

The proposed regulations provide three safe harbors and a facts and circumstances test for determining whether sufficient income is derived from a trade or business in a qualified opportunity zone for purposes of the 50-percent test in section 1397C(b)(2). Businesses only need to meet one of these safe harbors to satisfy that test. The first safe harbor in the proposed regulations requires that at least 50 percent of the services performed (based on hours) for such business by its employees and independent contractors (and employees of independent contractors) are performed within the qualified opportunity zone. This test is intended to address businesses located in a qualified opportunity zone that primarily provide services. The percentage is based on a fraction, the numerator of which is the total number of hours spent by employees and independent contractors (and employees of independent contractors) performing services in a qualified opportunity zone during the taxable year, and the denominator of which is the total number of hours spent by employees and independent contractors (and employees of independent contractors) in performing services during the taxable year.

For example, consider a startup business that develops software applications for global sale in a campus located in a qualified opportunity zone. Because the business' global consumer base purchases such applications through internet download, the business' employees and independent contractors are able to devote the majority of their total number of hours to developing such applications on the business' qualified opportunity zone campus. As a result, this startup business would satisfy the first safe harbor, even though the business makes the vast majority of its sales to consumers located outside of the qualified opportunity zone in which its campus is located.

The second safe harbor is based upon amounts paid by the trade or business for services performed in the qualified opportunity zone by employees and independent contractors (and employees of independent contractors). Under this test, if at least 50 percent of the services performed for the business by its employees and independent contractors (and employees of independent contractors) are performed in the qualified opportunity zone, based on amounts paid for the services performed, the business meets the 50-percent gross income test found in section 1397C(b)(2). This test is determined by a fraction, the numerator of which is the total amount paid by the entity for employee and independent contractor (and employees of independent contractors) services performed in a qualified opportunity zone during the taxable year, and the denominator of which is the total amount paid by the entity for employee and independent contractor (and employees of independent contractors) services performed during the taxable year.

For illustration, assume that the startup business described above also utilizes a service center located outside of the qualified opportunity zone and that more employees and independent contractor working hours are performed at the service center than the hours worked at the business' opportunity zone campus. While the majority of the total hours spent by employees and independent contractors of the startup business occur at the service center, the business pays 50 percent of its total compensation for software development services performed by employees and independent contractors on the business' opportunity zone campus. As a result, the startup business satisfies the second safe harbor.

The third safe harbor is a conjunctive test concerning tangible property and management or operational functions performed in a qualified opportunity zone, permitting a trade or business to use the totality of its situation to meet the requirements of sections 1400Z-2(d)(3)(A)(i) and 1397C(b)(2). The proposed regulations provide that a trade or business may satisfy the 50-percent gross income requirement if (1) the tangible property of the business that is in a qualified opportunity zone and (2) the management or operational functions performed for the business in the qualified opportunity zone are each necessary to generate 50 percent of the gross income of the trade or business. Thus, for example, if a landscaper's headquarters are in a qualified opportunity zone, its officers and employees manage the daily operations of the business (occurring within and outside the qualified opportunity zone) from its headquarters, and all of its equipment and supplies are stored within the headquarters facilities or elsewhere in the qualified opportunity zone, then the management activity and the storage of equipment and supplies in the qualified opportunity zone are each necessary to generate 50 percent of the gross income of the trade or business. Conversely, the proposed regulations provide that if a trade or business only has a PO Box or other delivery address located in the qualified opportunity zone, the presence of the PO Box or other delivery address does not constitute a factor necessary to generate gross income by such business.

Finally, taxpayers not meeting any of the other safe harbor tests may meet the 50-percent requirement based on a facts and circumstances test if, based on all the facts and circumstances, at least 50 percent of the gross income of a trade or business is derived from the active conduct of a trade or business in the qualified opportunity zone.

The Treasury Department and the IRS request comments on the proposed safe harbor rules regarding the 50-percent gross income requirement, including comments offering possible additional safe harbors, such as one based on headcount of certain types of service providers, and whether certain modifications would be warranted to prevent potential abuses.

C. Use of Intangibles

As provided in 83 FR 54279 (October 29, 2018) and section 1400Z-2(d)(3), a qualified opportunity zone trade or business must satisfy section 1397C(b)(4). Section 1397C(b)(4) requires that, with respect to any taxable year, a substantial portion of the intangible property of a qualified business entity must be used in the active conduct of a trade or business in the qualified opportunity zone, but section 1397C does not provide a definition of "substantial portion." The IRS and the Treasury Department have received comments asking for the definition of substantial portion. Accordingly, the proposed regulations provide that, for purposes of determining whether a substantial portion of intangible property of a qualified opportunity zone is used in the active conduct of a trade or business, the term *substantial portion* means at least 40 percent.

D. Active Conduct of a Trade or Business

Section 1400Z-2(d)(3)(A)(ii) also incorporates requirement (2) of section 1397C(b), which requires at least 50 percent of the total gross income of a qualified business entity to be derived from the active conduct of a trade or business within a zone. The IRS has received comments asking if the active conduct of a trade or business will be defined for purposes of section 1400Z-2. Other commentators have expressed concern that the leasing of real property by a qualified opportunity zone business may not amount to the active conduct of a trade or business if the business has limited leasing activity.

Section 162(a) permits a deduction for ordinary and necessary expenses paid or incurred in carrying on a trade or business. The rules under section 162 for determining the existence of a trade or business are well-established, and there is a large body of case law and administrative guidance interpreting the meaning of a trade or business for that purpose. Therefore, these proposed regulations define a trade or business for purposes of section 1400Z-2 as a trade or business within the meaning of section 162. However, these proposed regulations provide that the ownership and operation (including leasing) of real property used in a trade or business is treated as the active conduct of a trade or business for purposes of section 1400Z-2(d)(3). No inference should be drawn from the preceding sentence as to the meaning of the "active conduct of a trade or business" for purposes of other provisions of the Code, including section 355.

The Treasury Department and the IRS request comments on the proposed definition of a trade or business for purposes of section 1400Z-2(d)(3). In addition, comments are requested on whether additional rules are needed in determining if a trade or business is actively conducted. The Treasury Department and the IRS further request comments on whether it would be appropriate or useful to extend the requirements of section 1397C applicable to qualified opportunity zone businesses to QOFs.

E. Working Capital Safe Harbor

Responding to comments received on 83 FR 54279 (October 29, 2018) the proposed regulations make two changes to the safe harbor for working capital. First, the written designation for planned use of working capital now includes the development of a trade or business in the qualified opportunity zone as well as acquisition, construction, and/or substantial improvement of tangible property. Second, exceeding the 31-month period does not violate the safe harbor if the delay is attributable to waiting for government action the application for which is completed during the 31-month period.

IV. *Special Rule for Section 1231 Gains*

In 83 FR 54279 (October 29, 2018) the proposed regulations clarified that only capital gains are eligible for deferral under section 1400Z-2(a)(1). Section 1231(a)(1) provides that, if the section 1231 gains for any taxable year exceed the section 1231 losses, such gain shall be treated as long-term capital gain. Thus, the proposed regulations provide that only this gain shall be treated as an eligible gain for purposes of section 1400Z-2.

In addition, the preamble in 83 FR 54279 (October 29, 2018) stated that some capital gains are the result of Federal tax rules deeming an amount to be a gain from the sale or exchange of a capital asset, and, in many cases, the statutory language providing capital gain treatment does not provide a specific date for the deemed sale. Thus, 83 FR 54279 (October 29, 2018) addressed this issue by providing that, except as specifically provided in the proposed regulations, the first day of the 180-day period set forth in section 1400Z-2(a)(1)(A) and the regulations thereunder is the date on which the gain would be recognized for Federal income tax purposes, without regard to the deferral available under section 1400Z-2. Consistent with 83 FR 54279 (October 29, 2018) and because the capital gain income from section 1231 property is determinable only as of the last day of the taxable year, these proposed regulations provide that the 180-day period for investing such capital gain income from section 1231 property in a QOF begins on the last day of the taxable year.

The Treasury Department and the IRS request comments on the proposed treatment of section 1231 gains.

V. *Relief with Respect to the 90-Percent Asset Test*

A. *Relief for Newly Contributed Assets*

A new QOF's ability to delay the start of its status as a QOF (and thus the start of its 90-percent asset tests) provides the QOF the ability to prepare to deploy new capital before that capital is received and must be tested. Failure to satisfy the 90-percent asset test on a testing date does not by itself cause an entity to fail to be a QOF within the meaning of section 1400Z-2(d)(1) (this is the case even if it is the QOF's first testing date). Some commentators on 83 FR 54279 (October 29, 2018) pointed out that this start-up rule does not help an existing QOF that receives new capital from an equity investor shortly before the next semi-annual test. The proposed regulations, therefore, allow a QOF to apply the test without taking into account any investments received in the preceding 6 months. The QOF's ability to do this, however, is dependent on those new assets being held in cash, cash equivalents, or debt instruments with term 18 months or less.

B. *QOF Reinvestment Rule*

Section 1400Z-2(e)(4)(B) authorizes regulations to ensure a QOF has "a reasonable period of time to reinvest the return of capital from investments in qualified opportunity zone stock and qualified opportunity zone partnership interests, and to reinvest proceeds received from the sale or disposition of qualified opportunity zone property." For example, if a QOF, shortly before a testing date, sells qualified opportunity zone property, that QOF should have a reasonable amount of time in which to bring itself into compliance with the 90-percent asset test. Many stakeholders have requested guidance not only on the length of a "reasonable period of time to reinvest," but also on the Federal income tax treatment of any gains that the QOF reinvests during such a period.

The proposed regulations provide that proceeds received by the QOF from the sale or disposition of (1) qualified opportunity zone business property, (2) qualified opportunity zone stock, and (3) qualified opportunity zone partnership interests are treated as qualified opportunity zone property for purposes of the 90-percent investment requirement described in 1400Z-1(d)(1) and (f), so long as the QOF reinvests the proceeds received by the QOF from the distribution, sale, or disposition of such property during the 12-month period beginning on the date of such distribution, sale, or disposition. The one-year rule is intended to allow QOFs adequate time in which to reinvest proceeds from qualified opportunity zone property. Further, in order for the reinvested proceeds to be counted as qualified opportunity zone business property, from the date of a distribution, sale, or disposition until the date proceeds are invested in other qualified opportunity zone property, the proceeds must be continuously held in cash, cash equivalents, and debt instruments with a term of 18 months or less. Finally, a QOF may reinvest proceeds from the sale of an investment into another type of qualifying investment. For example, a QOF may reinvest proceeds from a sale of an investment in qualified opportunity stock into qualified opportunity zone business property. Analogous to the flexibility in the safe harbor for working capital, the proposed regulations extend QOF reinvestment relief from application of the 90-percent asset test if failure to meet the 12-month deadline is attributable to delay in government action the application for which is complete.

The Treasury Department and the IRS request comments on whether an analogous rule for QOF subsidiaries to reinvest proceeds from the disposition of qualified opportunity zone property would be beneficial.

Additionally, commenters have requested that the grant of authority in section 1400Z-2(e)(4)(B) be used to exempt QOFs and investors in QOFs from the Federal income tax consequences of dispositions of qualified opportunity zone property by QOFs or qualified opportunity zone businesses if the proceeds from such dispositions are reinvested within a reasonable timeframe. The Treasury Department and the IRS believe that the grant of this regulatory authority permits QOFs a reasonable time to reinvest such proceeds without the QOF being harmed (that is, without the QOF incurring the penalty set forth in section 1400Z-2(f) because the proceeds would not be qualified opportunity zone property). However, the statutory language granting this regulatory authority does not specifically authorize the Secretary to prescribe rules for QOFs departing from the otherwise operative recognition provisions of sections 1001(c) and 61(a)(3).

Regarding the tax benefits provided to investors in QOFs under section 1400Z-2(b) and (c), as stated earlier, sections 1400Z-1 and 1400Z-2 seek to encourage economic growth and investment in designated distressed communities (qualified opportunity zones) by providing Federal income tax benefits to taxpayers who invest in businesses located within these zones through a QOF. Congress tied these tax incentives to the longevity of an investor's stake in a QOF, not to a QOF's stake in any specific portfolio investment. Further, Congress expressly recognized that many QOFs would experience investment "churn" over the lifespan of the QOF and anticipated this by providing the Secretary the regulatory latitude for permitting QOFs a reasonable time to reinvest capital. Consistent with this regulatory authority, the Treasury Department and the IRS clarify that sales or dispositions of assets by a QOF do not impact in any way investors' holding periods in their qualifying investments or trigger the inclusion of any deferred gain reflected in such qualifying investments so long as they do not sell or otherwise dispose of their qualifying investment for purposes of section 1400Z-2(b). However, the Treasury Department and the IRS are not able to find precedent for the grant of authority in section 1400Z-2(e)(4)(B) to permit QOFs a reasonable time to reinvest capital and allow the Secretary to prescribe regulations permitting QOFs or their investors to avoid recognizing gain on the sale or disposition of assets under sections 1001(c) and 61(a)(3), and notes that examples of provisions in subtitle A of the Code that provide for nonrecognition treatment or exclusion from income can be found in sections 351(a), 354(a), 402(c), 501(a), 721(a), 1031(a), 1032(a), and 1036(a), among others, some of which are applied in the proposed rules and described as selected examples in this preamble. In this regard, the Treasury Department and the IRS are requesting commenters to provide prior examples of tax regulations that exempt realized gain from being recognized under sections 1001(c) or 61(a)(3) by a taxpayer (either a QOF or qualified opportunity zone business, or in the case of QOF partnerships or QOF S corporations, the investors that own qualifying investments in such QOFs) without an operative provision of subtitle A of the Code expressly providing for nonrecognition treatment; as well as to provide any comments on the possible burdens imposed if these organizations are required to reset the holding period for reinvested realized gains, including administrative burdens and the potential chilling effect on investment incentives that may result from these possible burdens, and whether specific organizational forms could be disproportionately burdened by this proposed policy.

VI. *Amount of an Investment for Purposes of Making a Deferral Election*

A taxpayer may make an investment for purposes of an election under section 1400Z-2(a) by transferring cash or other property to a QOF, regardless of whether the transfer is taxable to the transferor (such as where the transferor is not in control of the transferee corporation), provided the transfer is not re-characterized as a transaction other than an investment in the QOF (as would be the case where a purported contribution to a partnership is treated as a disguised sale). These proposed regulations provide special rules for determining the amount of an investment for purposes of this election if a taxpayer transfers property other than cash to a QOF in a carryover basis transaction. In that case, the amount of the investment equals the lesser of the taxpayer's adjusted basis in the equity received in the transaction (determined without regard to section 1400Z-2(b)(2)(B)) or the fair market value of the equity received in the transaction (both as determined immediately after the transaction). In the case of a contribution to a partnership that is a QOF (QOF partnership), the basis in the equity to which section 1400Z-2(b)(2)(B)(i) applies is calculated without regard to any liability that is allocated to the contributor under section 752(a). These rules apply separately to each item of property contributed to a QOF, but the total amount of the investment for purposes of the election is limited to the amount of the gain described in section 1400Z-2(a)(1).

The proposed regulations set forth two special rules that treat a taxpayer as having created a mixed-funds investment (within the meaning of proposed § 1.1400Z2(b)-1(a)(2)(v)). First, a mixed-funds investment will result if a taxpayer contributes to a QOF, in a nonrecognition transaction, property that has a fair market value in excess of the property's adjusted basis. Second, a mixed-funds investment will result if the amount of the investment that might otherwise support an election exceeds the amount of the taxpayer's eligible gain described in section 1400Z-2(a)(1). In each instance, that excess (that is, the excess of fair market value over adjusted basis, or the excess of the investment amount over eligible gain, as appropriate) is treated as an investment described in section 1400Z-2(e)(1)(A)(ii) (that is, the portion of the contribution to which a deferral election does not apply).

If a taxpayer acquires a direct investment in a QOF from a direct owner of the QOF, these proposed regulations also provide that, for purposes of making an election under section 1400Z-2(a), the taxpayer is treated as making an investment in an amount equal to the amount paid for the eligible interest.

The Treasury Department and the IRS request comments on the proposed rules regarding the amount with respect to which a taxpayer may make a deferral election under section 1400Z-2(a).

VII. *Events That Cause Inclusion of Deferred Gain (Inclusion Events)*

A. In General

Section 1400Z-2(b)(1) provides that the amount of gain that is deferred if a taxpayer makes an equity investment in a QOF described in section 1400Z-2(e)(1)(A)(i) (qualifying investment) will be included in the taxpayer's income in the taxable year that includes the earlier of (A) the date on which the qualifying investment is sold or exchanged, or (B) December 31, 2026. By using the terms "sold or exchanged," section 1400Z-2(b)(1) does not directly address non-sale or exchange dispositions, such as gifts, bequests, devises, charitable contributions, and abandonments of qualifying investments. However, the Conference Report to accompany H.R. 1, Report 115-466 (Dec. 15, 2017) provides that, under section 1400Z-2(b)(1), the "deferred gain is recognized on the earlier of the date on which the [qualifying] investment is disposed of or December 31, 2026." *See* Conference Report at 539.

The proposed regulations track the disposition language set forth in the Conference Report and clarify that, subject to enumerated exceptions, an inclusion event results from a transfer of a qualifying investment in a transaction to the extent the transfer reduces the taxpayer's equity interest in the qualifying investment for Federal income tax purposes. Notwithstanding that general principle, and except as otherwise provided in the proposed regulations, a transaction that does not reduce a taxpayer's equity interest in the taxpayer's qualifying investment is also an inclusion event under the proposed regulations to the extent the taxpayer receives property from a QOF in a transaction treated as a distribution for Federal income tax purposes. For this purpose, property generally is defined as money, securities, or any other property, other than stock (or rights to acquire stock) in the corporation that is a QOF (QOF corporation) that is making the distribution. The Treasury Department and the IRS have determined that it is necessary to treat such transactions as inclusion events to prevent taxpayers from "cashing out" a qualifying investment in a QOF without including in gross income any amount of their deferred gain.

Based upon the guidance set forth in the Conference Report and the principles underlying the "inclusion event" concept described in the preceding paragraphs, the proposed regulations provide taxpayers with a nonexclusive list of inclusion events, which include:

(1) A taxable disposition (for example, a sale) of all or a part of a qualifying investment (qualifying QOF partnership interest) in a QOF partnership or of a qualifying investment (qualifying QOF stock) in a QOF corporation;

(2) A taxable disposition (for example, a sale) of interests in an S corporation which itself is the direct investor in a QOF corporation or QOF partnership if, immediately after the disposition, the aggregate percentage of the S corporation interests owned by the S corporation shareholders at the time of its deferral election has changed by more than 25 percent. When the threshold is exceeded, any deferred gains recognized would be reported under the provisions of subchapter S of chapter 1 of subtitle A of the Code (subchapter S);

(3) In certain cases, a transfer by a partner of an interest in a partnership that itself directly or indirectly holds a qualifying investment;

(4) A transfer by gift of a qualifying investment;

(5) The distribution to a partner of a QOF partnership of property that has a value in excess of basis of the partner's qualifying QOF partnership interest;

(6) A distribution of property with respect to qualifying QOF stock under section 301 to the extent it is treated as gain from the sale or exchange of property under section 301(c)(3);

(7) A distribution of property with respect to qualifying QOF stock under section 1368 to the extent it is treated as gain from the sale or exchange of property under section 1368(b)(2) and (c);

(8) A redemption of qualifying QOF stock that is treated as an exchange of property for the redeemed qualifying QOF stock under section 302;

(9) A disposition of qualifying QOF stock in a transaction to which section 304 applies;

(10) A liquidation of a QOF corporation in a transaction to which section 331 applies; and

(11) Certain nonrecognition transactions, including:

a. A liquidation of a QOF corporation in a transaction to which section 332 applies;

b. A transfer of all or part of a taxpayer's qualifying QOF stock in a transaction to which section 351 applies;

c. A stock-for-stock exchange of qualifying QOF stock in a transaction to which section 368(a)(1)(B) applies;

d. A triangular reorganization of a QOF corporation within the meaning of § 1.358-6(b)(2);

e. An acquisitive asset reorganization in which a QOF corporation transfers its assets to its shareholder and terminates (or is deemed to terminate) for Federal income tax purposes;

f. An acquisitive asset reorganization in which a corporate taxpayer that made the qualifying investment in the QOF corporation (QOF shareholder) transfers its assets to the QOF corporation and terminates (or is deemed to terminate) for Federal income tax purposes;

g. An acquisitive asset reorganization in which a QOF corporation transfers its assets to an acquiring corporation that is not a QOF corporation within a prescribed period after the transaction;

h. A recapitalization of a QOF corporation, or a contribution by a QOF shareholder of a portion of its qualifying QOF stock to the QOF corporation, if the transaction has the result of reducing the taxpayer's equity interest in the QOF corporation;

i. A distribution by a QOF shareholder of its qualifying QOF stock to its shareholders in a transaction to which section 355 applies;

j. A transfer by a QOF corporation of subsidiary stock to QOF shareholders in a transaction to which section 355 applies if, after a prescribed period following the transaction, either the distributing corporation or the controlled corporation is not a QOF; and

k. A transfer to, or an acquisitive asset reorganization of, an S corporation which itself is the direct investor in a QOF corporation or QOF partnership if, immediately after the transfer or reorganization, the percentage of the S corporation interests owned by the S corporation shareholders at the time of its deferral election has decreased by more than 25 percent.

Each of the previously described transactions would be an inclusion event because each would reduce or terminate the QOF investor's direct (or, in the case of partnerships, indirect) qualifying investment for Federal income tax purposes or (in the case of distributions) would constitute a "cashing out" of the QOF investor's qualifying investment. As a result, the QOF investor would recognize all, or a corresponding portion, of its deferred gain under section 1400Z-2(a)(1)(B) and (b).

The Treasury Department and the IRS request comments on the proposed rules regarding the inclusion events that would result in a QOF investor recognizing an amount of deferred gain under section 1400Z-2(a)(1)(B) and (b), including the pledging of qualifying investments as collateral for nonrecourse loans.

B. Timing of Basis Adjustments

Under section 1400Z-2(b)(2)(B)(i), an electing taxpayer's initial basis in a qualifying investment is zero. Under section 1400Z-2(b)(2)(B)(iii) and (iv), a taxpayer's basis in its qualifying investment is increased automatically after the investment has been held for five years by an amount equal to 10 percent of the amount of deferred gain, and then again after the investment has been held for seven years by an amount equal to an additional five percent of the amount of deferred gain. The proposed regulations clarify that such basis is basis for all purposes and, for example, losses suspended under section 704(d) would be available to the extent of the basis step-up.

The proposed regulations also clarify that basis adjustments under section 1400Z-2(b)(2)(B)(ii), which reflect the recognition of deferred gain upon the earlier of December 31, 2026, or an inclusion event, are made immediately after the amount of deferred capital gain is taken into income. If a basis adjustment is made under section 1400Z-2(b)(2)(B)(ii) as a result of a reduction in direct tax ownership of a qualifying investment, a redemption, a distribution treated as gain from the sale or exchange of property under section 301(c)(3) or section 1368(b)(2) and (c), or a distribution to a partner of property with a value in excess of the partner's basis in the qualifying QOF partnership interest, the basis adjustment is made before determining the tax consequences of the inclusion event with respect to the qualifying investment (for example, before determining the recovery of basis under section 301(c)(2) or the amount of gain the taxpayer must take into account under section 301, section 1368, or the provisions of subchapter K of chapter 1 of subtitle A of the Code (subchapter K), as applicable). For a discussion of distributions as inclusion events, *see* part VII.G of this Explanation of Provisions.

The proposed regulations further clarify that, if the taxpayer makes an election under section 1400Z-2(c), the basis adjustment under section 1400Z-2(c) is made immediately before the taxpayer disposes of its QOF investment. For dispositions of qualifying QOF partnership interests, the bases of the QOF partnership's assets are also adjusted with respect to the transferred qualifying QOF partnership interest, with such adjustments calculated in a manner similar to the adjustments that would have been made to the partnership's assets if the partner had purchased the interest for cash immediately prior to the transaction and the partnership had a valid section 754 election in effect. This will permit basis adjustments to the QOF partnership's assets, including its inventory and unrealized receivables, and avoid the creation of capital losses and ordinary income on the sale. See part VII.D.4 of this Explanation of Provisions for a special election for direct investors in QOF partnerships and S corporations that are QOFs (QOF S corporations) for the application of section 1400Z-2(c) to certain sales of assets of a QOF partnership or QOF S corporation. With respect to that special election, the Treasury Department and the IRS intend to implement targeted anti-abuse provisions (for example, provisions addressing straddles). The Treasury Department and IRS request comments on whether one or more such provisions are appropriate to carry out the purposes of section 1400Z-2.

More generally, the Treasury Department and the IRS request comments on the proposed rules regarding the timing of basis adjustments under section 1400Z-2(b) and (c).

C. Amount Includible

In general, other than with respect to partnerships, if a taxpayer has an inclusion event with regard to its qualifying investment in a QOF, the taxpayer includes in gross income the lesser of two amounts, less the taxpayer's basis. The first amount is the fair market value of the portion of the qualifying investment that is disposed of in the inclusion event. For purposes of this section, the fair market value of that portion is determined by multiplying the fair market value of the taxpayer's entire qualifying investment in the QOF, valued as of the date of the inclusion event, by the percentage of the taxpayer's qualifying investment that is represented by the portion disposed of in the inclusion event. The second amount is the amount that bears the same ratio to the remaining deferred gain as the first amount bears to the total fair market value of the qualifying investment in the QOF immediately before the transaction.

For inclusion events involving partnerships, the amount includible is equal to the percentage of the qualifying QOF partnership interest disposed of, multiplied by the lesser of: (1) the remaining deferred gain less any basis adjustments pursuant to section 1400Z-2(b)(2)(B)(iii) and (iv) or (2) the gain that would be recognized by the partner if the interest were sold in a fully taxable transaction for its then fair market value.

For inclusion events involving a QOF shareholder that is an S corporation, if the S corporation undergoes an aggregate change in ownership of more than 25 percent, there is an inclusion event with respect to all of the S corporation's remaining deferred gain (*see* part VII.D.3 of this Explanation of Provisions).

A special "dollar-for-dollar" rule applies in certain circumstances if a QOF owner receives property from a QOF that gives rise to an inclusion event. These circumstances include actual distributions with respect to qualifying QOF stock that do not reduce a taxpayer's direct interest in qualifying QOF stock, stock redemptions to which section 302(d) applies, and the receipt of boot in certain corporate reorganizations, as well as actual or deemed distributions with respect to qualifying QOF partnership interests. This dollar-for-dollar rule would be simpler to administer than a rule that would require taxpayers to undertake valuations of QOF investments each time a QOF owner received a distribution with respect to the qualifying investment or received boot in a corporate reorganization. If this dollar-for-dollar rule applies, the taxpayer includes in gross income an amount of the taxpayer's remaining deferred gain equal to the lesser of (1) the remaining deferred gain, or (2) the amount that gave rise to the inclusion event. The Treasury Department and the IRS request comments on the dollar-for-dollar rule and the circumstances in which this rule would apply under these proposed regulations.

D. Partnership and S Corporation Provisions

1. Partnership Provisions in General

With respect to property contributed to a QOF partnership in exchange for a qualifying investment, the partner's basis in the qualifying interest is zero under section 1400Z-2(b)(2)(B)(i), increased by the partner's share of liabilities under section 752(a). However, the carryover basis rules of section 723 apply in determining the basis to the partnership of property contributed. The Treasury Department and the IRS are aware that, where inside-outside basis disparities exist in a partnership, taxpayers could manipulate the rules of subchapter K to create non-economic gains and losses. Accordingly, the Treasury Department and the IRS request comments on rules that would limit abusive transactions that could be undertaken as a result of these disparities.

The proposed regulations provide that the transfer by a partner of all or a portion of its interest in a QOF partnership or in a partnership that directly or indirectly holds a qualifying investment generally will be an inclusion event. However, a transfer in a transaction governed by section 721 (partnership contributions) or section 708(b)(2)(A) (partnership mergers) is generally not an inclusion event, provided there is no reduction in the amount of the remaining deferred gain that would be recognized under section 1400Z-2 by the transferring partners on a later inclusion event. Similar rules apply in the case of tiered partnerships. However, the resulting partnership or new partnership becomes subject to section 1400Z-2 to the same extent as the original taxpayer that made the qualifying investment in the QOF.

Partnership distributions in the ordinary course of partnership operations may, in certain instances, also be considered inclusion events. Under the proposed regulations, the actual or deemed distribution of cash or other property with a fair market value in excess of the partner's basis in its qualifying QOF partnership interest is also an inclusion event.

2. Partnership Mixed-Funds Investments

Rules specific to section 1400Z-2 are needed for mixed-funds investments where a partner contributes to a QOF property with a value in excess of its basis, or cash in excess of the partner's eligible section 1400Z-2 gain, or where a partner receives a partnership interest in exchange for services (for example, a carried interest). Section 1400Z-2(e)(1) provides that only the portion of the investment in a QOF to which an election under section 1400Z-2(a) is in effect is treated as a qualifying investment. Under this rule, the share of gain attributable to the excess investment and/or the service component of the interest in the QOF partnership is not eligible for the various benefits afforded qualifying investments under section 1400Z-2 and is not subject to the inclusion rules of section 1400Z-2. This is the case with respect to a carried interest, despite the fact that all of the partnership's investments might be qualifying investments.

The Treasury Department and the IRS considered various approaches to accounting for a partner holding a mixed-funds investment in a QOF partnership and request comments on the approach adopted by the proposed regulations. For example, a partner could be considered to own two separate investments and separately track the basis and value of the investments, similar to a shareholder tracking two separate blocks of stock. However, that approach is inconsistent with the subchapter K principle that a partner has a unitary basis and capital account in its partnership interest. Thus, the proposed regulations adopt the approach that a partner holding a mixed-funds investment will be treated as holding a single partnership interest with a single basis and capital account for all purposes of subchapter K, but not for purposes of section 1400Z-2. Under the proposed regulations, solely for purposes of section 1400Z-2, the mixed-funds partner will be treated as holding two interests, and all partnership items, such as income and debt allocations and property distributions, would affect qualifying and non-qualifying investments proportionately, based on the relative allocation percentages of each interest. Allocation percentages would generally be based on relative capital contributions for qualifying investments and other investments.

However, section 704(c) principles apply to partnership allocations attributable to property with value-basis disparities to prevent inappropriate shifts of built-in gains or losses between qualifying investments and non-qualifying investments. Additionally, special rules apply in calculating the allocation percentages in the case of a partner who receives a profits interest for services, with the percent attributable to the profits interest being treated as a non-qualifying investment to the extent of the highest percentage interest in residual profits attributable to the interest.

In the event of an additional contribution of qualifying or non-qualifying amounts, a revaluation of the relative partnership investments is required immediately before the contribution in order to adequately account for the two components.

Consistent with the unitary basis rules of subchapter K, a distribution of money would not give rise to section 731 gain unless the distribution exceeded the partner's total outside basis. For example, if a partner contributed $200 to a QOF partnership, half of which related to deferred section 1400Z-2 gain, and $20 of partnership debt was allocated to the partner, the partner's outside basis would be $120 (zero for the qualifying investment contribution, plus $100 for the non-qualifying investment contribution, plus $20 under section 752(a)), and only a distribution of money in excess of that amount would trigger gain under subchapter K. However, for purposes of calculating the section 1400Z-2 gain, the qualifying investment portion of the interest would have a basis of $10, with the remaining $110 attributable to the non-qualifying investment. A distribution of $40 would be divided between the two investments and would not result in gain under section 731; however, the distribution would constitute an inclusion event under section 1400Z-2, and the partner would be required to recognize gain in the amount of $10 (the excess of the $20 distribution attributable to the qualifying investment over the $10 basis in the interest).

The Treasury Department and the IRS are concerned with the potential complexity associated with this approach and request comments on alternative ways to account for distributions in the case of a mixed-funds investment in a QOF partnership. The Treasury Department and the IRS also request comments on whether an ordering rule treating the distribution as attributable to the qualifying or non-qualifying investment portion first is appropriate, and how any alternative approach would simplify the calculations.

3. Application to S Corporations

Under section 1371(a), and for purposes of these proposed regulations, the rules of subchapter C of chapter 1 of subtitle A of the Code (subchapter C) applicable to C corporations and their shareholders apply to S corporations and their shareholders, except to the extent inconsistent with the provisions of subchapter S. In such instances, S corporations and their shareholders are subject to the specific rules of subchapter S. For example, similar to rules applicable to QOF partnerships, a distribution of property to which section 1368 applies by a QOF S corporation is an inclusion event to the extent that the distributed property has a fair market value in excess of the shareholder's basis, including any basis adjustments under section 1400Z-2(b)(2)(B)(iii) and (iv). In addition, the rules set forth in these proposed regulations regarding liquidations and reorganizations of QOF C corporations and QOF C corporation shareholders apply equally to QOF S corporations and QOF S corporation shareholders.

However, flow-through principles under subchapter S apply to S corporations when the application of subchapter C would be inconsistent with subchapter S. For example, if an inclusion event were to occur with respect to deferred gain of an S corporation that is an investor in a QOF, the shareholders of such S corporation would include such gain pro rata in their respective taxable incomes. Consequently, those S corporation shareholders would increase their bases in their S corporation stock at the end of the taxable year during which the inclusion event occurred. Pursuant to the S corporation distribution rules set forth in section 1368, the S corporation shareholders would receive future distributions from the S corporation tax-free to the extent of the deferred tax amount included in income and included in stock basis.

In addition, these proposed regulations set forth specific rules for S corporations to provide certainty to taxpayers regarding the application of particular provisions under section 1400Z-2. Regarding section 1400Z-2(b)(1)(A), these proposed regulations clarify that a conversion of an S corporation that holds a qualifying investment in a QOF to a C corporation (or a C corporation to an S corporation) is not an inclusion event because the interests held by each shareholder of the C corporation or S corporation, as appropriate, would remain unchanged with respect to the corporation's qualifying investment in a QOF. With regard to mixed-funds investments in a QOF S corporation described in section 1400Z-2(e)(1), if different blocks of stock are created for otherwise qualifying investments to track basis in these qualifying investments, the proposed regulations make clear that the separate blocks will not be treated as different classes of stock for purposes of S corporation eligibility under section 1361(b)(1).

The proposed regulations also provide that, if an S corporation is an investor in a QOF, the S corporation must adjust the basis of its qualifying investment in the manner set forth for C corporations in proposed § 1.1400Z2(b)-1(g), except as otherwise provided in these rules. This rule does not affect adjustments to the basis of any other asset of the S corporation. The S corporation shareholder's pro-rata share of any recognized deferred capital gain at the S corporation level will be separately stated under section 1366 and will adjust the shareholders' stock basis under section 1367. In addition, the proposed regulations make clear that any adjustment made to the basis of an S corporation's qualifying investment under section 1400Z-2(b)(2)(B)(iii) or (iv) or section 1400Z-2(c) will not (1) be separately stated under section 1366, and (2) until the date on which an inclusion event with respect to the S corporation's qualifying investment occurs, adjust the shareholders' stock basis under section 1367. If a basis adjustment under section 1400Z-2(b)(2)(B)(ii) is made as a result of an inclusion event, then the basis adjustment will be made before determining the other tax consequences of the inclusion event.

Finally, under these proposed regulations, special rules would apply in the case of certain ownership shifts in S corporations that are QOF owners. Under these rules, solely for purposes of section 1400Z-2, the S corporation's qualifying investment in the QOF would be treated as disposed of if there is a greater-than-25 percent change in ownership of the S corporation (aggregate change in ownership). If an aggregate change in ownership has occurred, the S corporation would have an inclusion event with respect to all of the S corporation's remaining deferred gain, and neither section 1400Z-2(b)(2)(B)(iii) or (iv), nor section 1400Z-2(c), would apply to the S corporation's qualifying investment after that date. This proposed rule attempts to balance the status of the S corporation as the owner of the qualifying investment with the desire to preserve the incidence of the capital gain inclusion and income exclusion benefits under section 1400Z-2. The Treasury Department and the IRS request comments on the proposed rules regarding ownership changes in S corporations that are QOF owners.

4. Special Election for Direct Investors in QOF Partnerships and QOF S Corporations

For purposes of section 1400Z-2(c), which applies to investments held for at least 10-years, a taxpayer that is the holder of a direct qualifying QOF partnership interest or qualifying QOF stock of a QOF S corporation may make an election to exclude from gross income some or all of the capital gain from the disposition of qualified opportunity zone property reported on Schedule K-1 of such entity, provided the disposition occurs after the taxpayer's 10-year holding period. To the extent that such Schedule K-1 separately states capital gains arising from the sale or exchange of any particular capital asset, the taxpayer may make an election under section 1400Z-2(c) with respect to such separately stated item. To be valid, the taxpayer must make such election for the taxable year in which the capital gain from the sale or exchange of QOF property recognized by the QOF partnership or QOF S corporation would be included in the taxpayer's gross income, in accordance with applicable forms and instructions. If a taxpayer makes this election with respect to some or all of the capital gain reported on such Schedule K-1, the amount of such capital gain that the taxpayer elects to exclude from gross income is excluded from income for purposes of the Internal Revenue Code and the regulations thereunder. For basis purposes, such excluded amount is treated as an item of income described in sections 705(a)(1) or 1366 thereby increasing the partners or shareholders' bases by their shares of such amount. These proposed regulations provide no similar election to holders of qualifying QOF stock of a QOF C corporation that is not a QOF REIT.

The Treasury Department and the IRS request comments on the eligibility for, and the operational mechanics of, the proposed rules regarding this special election.

5. Ability of QOF REITs to pay tax-free capital gain dividends to 10-plus-year investors

The proposed rules authorize QOF real estate investment trusts (QOF REITs) to designate special capital gain dividends, not to exceed the QOF REIT's long-term gains on sales of Qualified Opportunity Zone property. If some QOF REIT shares are qualified investments in the hands of some shareholders, those special capital gain dividends are tax free to shareholders who could have elected a basis increase in case of a sale of the QOF REIT shares. The Treasury Department and the IRS request comments on the eligibility for, and the operational mechanics of, the proposed rules regarding this special treatment.

E. Transfers of Property by Gift or by Reason of Death

For purposes of sections 1400Z-2(b) and (c), any disposition of the owner's qualifying investment is an inclusion event for purposes of section 1400Z-2(b)(1) and proposed § 1.1400Z2(b)-1(a), except as provided in these proposed regulations. Generally, transfers of property by gift, in part or in whole, either will reduce or terminate the owner's qualifying investment. Accordingly, except as provided in these proposed regulations, transfers by gift will be inclusion events for purposes of section 1400Z-2(b)(1) and proposed § 1.1400Z2(b)-1(c).

For example, a transfer of a qualifying investment by gift from the donor, in this case the owner, to the donee either will reduce or will terminate the owner's qualifying investment, depending upon whether the owner transfers part or all of the owner's qualifying investment. A charitable contribution, as defined in section 170(c), of a qualifying interest is also an inclusion event because, again, the owner's qualifying investment is terminated upon the transfer. However, a transfer of a qualifying investment by gift by the taxpayer to a trust that is treated as a grantor trust of which the taxpayer is the deemed owner is not an inclusion event. The rationale for this exception is that, for Federal income tax purposes, the owner of the grantor trust is treated as the owner of the property in the trust until such time that the owner releases certain powers that cause the trust to be treated as a grantor trust. Accordingly, the owner's qualifying investment is not reduced or eliminated for Federal income tax purposes upon the transfer to such a grantor trust. However, any change in the grantor trust status of the trust (except by reason of the grantor's death) is an inclusion event because the owner of the trust property for Federal income tax purposes is changing.

Most transfers by reason of death will terminate the owner's qualifying investment. For example, the qualifying investment may be distributed to a beneficiary of the owner's estate or may pass by operation of law to a named beneficiary. In each case, the owner's qualifying investment is terminated. Nevertheless, in part because of the statutory direction that amounts recognized that were not properly includible in the gross income of the deceased owner are to be includible in gross income as provided in section 691, the Treasury Department and the IRS have concluded that the distribution of the qualifying investment to the beneficiary by the estate or by operation of law is not an inclusion event for purposes of section 1400Z-2(b). Thus, the proposed regulations would provide that neither a transfer of the qualifying investment to the deceased owner's estate nor the distribution by the estate to the decedent's legatee or heir is an inclusion event for purposes of section 1400Z-2(b). Similarly, neither the termination of grantor trust status by reason of the grantor's death nor the distribution by that trust to a trust beneficiary by reason of the grantor's death is an inclusion event for purposes of section 1400Z-2(b). In each case, the recipient of the qualifying investment has the obligation, as under section 691, to include the deferred gain in gross income in the event of any subsequent inclusion event, including for example, any further disposition by that recipient.

F. *Exceptions for Disregarded Transfers and Certain Types of Nonrecognition Transactions*

1. In general

Proposed § 1.1400Z2(b)-1(c) describes certain transfers that are not inclusion events with regard to a taxpayer's qualifying investment for purposes of section 1400Z-2(b)(1). For example, a taxpayer's transfer of its qualifying investment to an entity that is disregarded as separate from the taxpayer for Federal income tax purposes is not an inclusion event because the transfer is disregarded for Federal income tax purposes. The same rationale applies here as in the case of a taxpayer's transfer of its qualifying investment to a grantor trust of which the taxpayer is the deemed owner. However, a change in the entity's status as disregarded would be an inclusion event.

Additionally, a transfer of a QOF's assets in an acquisitive asset reorganization described in section 381(a)(2) (qualifying section 381 transaction) generally is not an inclusion event if the acquiring corporation is a QOF within a prescribed period of time after the transaction. Following such a qualifying section 381 transaction, the taxpayer retains a direct qualifying investment in a QOF with an exchanged basis. However, the proposed regulations provide that a qualifying section 381 transaction generally is an inclusion event, even if the acquiring corporation qualifies as a QOF within the prescribed post-transaction period, to the extent the taxpayer receives boot in the reorganization (other than boot that is treated as a dividend under section 356(a)(2)) because, in those situations, the taxpayer reduces its direct qualifying investment in the QOF (*see* part VII.F.2 of this Explanation of Provisions).

A transfer of a QOF shareholder's assets in a qualifying section 381 transaction also is not an inclusion event, except to the extent the QOF shareholder transfers less than all of its qualifying investment in the transaction, because the successor to the QOF shareholder will retain a direct qualifying investment in the QOF. Similar reasoning extends to a transfer of a QOF shareholder's assets in a liquidation to which section 332 applies, to the extent that no gain or loss is recognized by the QOF shareholder on the distribution of the QOF interest to the 80-percent distributee, pursuant to section 337(a). This rule does not apply if the QOF shareholder is an S corporation and if the qualifying section 381 transaction causes the S corporation to have an aggregate ownership change of more than 25 percent (as discussed in part VII.D.2 of this Explanation of Provisions).

Moreover, the distribution by a QOF of a subsidiary in a transaction to which section 355 (or so much of section 356 as relates to section 355) applies is not an inclusion event if both the distributing corporation and the controlled corporation qualify as QOFs immediately after the distribution (qualifying section 355 transaction), except to the extent the taxpayer receives boot. The Treasury Department and the IRS have determined that continued deferral under section 1400Z-2(a)(1)(A) is appropriate in the case of a qualifying section 355 transaction because the QOF shareholder continues its original direct qualifying investment, albeit reflected in investments in two QOF corporations.

Finally, a recapitalization (within the meaning of section 368(a)(1)(E)) of a QOF is not an inclusion event, as long as the QOF shareholder does not receive boot in the transaction and the transaction does not reduce the QOF shareholder's proportionate interest in the QOF corporation. Similar rules apply to a transaction described in section 1036.

2. Boot in a reorganization

An inclusion event generally will occur if a QOF shareholder receives boot in a qualifying section 381 transaction in which a QOF's assets are acquired by another QOF corporation. Under proposed § 1.1400Z2(b)-1(c), if the taxpayer realizes a gain on the transaction, the amount that gives rise to the inclusion event is the amount of gain under section 356 that is not treated as a dividend (*see* section 356(a)(2)). A similar rule applies to boot received by a QOF shareholder in a qualifying section 355 transaction to which section 356(a) applies. If the taxpayer in a qualifying section 381 transaction realizes a loss on the transaction, the amount that gives rise to the inclusion event is an amount equal to the fair market value of the boot received.

However, if both the target QOF and the acquiring corporation are wholly and directly owned by a single shareholder (or by members of the same consolidated group), and if the shareholder receives (or the group members receive) boot with respect to a qualifying investment, proposed § 1.1400Z2(b)-1(c)(8) (applicable to distributions by QOF corporations) applies to the boot as if it were distributed in a separate transaction to which section 301 applies.

Similarly, the corporate distribution rules of proposed § 1.1400Z2(b)-1(c)(8) would apply to a QOF shareholder's receipt of boot in a qualifying section 355 transaction to which section 356(b) applies. By its terms, section 356(b) states that the corporate distribution rules of section 301 apply if a distributing corporation distributes both stock of its controlled corporation and boot. As a result, under these proposed regulations, there would be an inclusion event to the extent section 301(c)(3) would apply to the distribution. The Treasury Department and the IRS request comments on the proposed treatment of the receipt of boot as an inclusion event.

If the qualifying section 381 transaction is an intercompany transaction, the rules in § 1.1502-13(f)(3) regarding boot in a reorganization apply to treat the boot as received in a separate distribution. These rules do not apply in cases in which either party to the distribution becomes a member or nonmember as part of the same plan or arrangement. However, as noted in part VIII of this Explanation of Provisions, a qualifying section 355 transaction cannot be an intercompany transaction.

G. Distributions and Contributions

Under the proposed regulations, and subject to certain exceptions, distributions made with respect to qualifying QOF stock (including redemptions of qualifying QOF stock that are treated as distributions to which section 301 applies) and certain distributions with respect to direct or indirect investments in a QOF partnership are treated as inclusion events. In the case of a QOF corporation, an actual distribution with respect to a qualifying investment results in inclusion only to the extent it is treated as gain from a sale or exchange under section 301(c)(3). A distribution to which section 301(c)(3) applies results in inclusion because that portion of the distribution is treated as gain from the sale or exchange of property. Actual distributions treated as dividends under section 301(c)(1) are not inclusion events because such distributions neither reduce a QOF shareholder's direct equity investment in the QOF nor constitute a "cashing out" of the QOF shareholder's equity investment in the QOF. In turn, actual distributions to which section 301(c)(2) applies are not inclusion events because the reduction of basis under that statutory provision is not treated as gain from the sale or exchange of property.

For these purposes, a distribution of property also includes a distribution of stock by a QOF that is treated as a distribution of property to which section 301 applies under section 305(b). The Treasury Department and the IRS have determined that this type of distribution should be an inclusion event, even though it does not reduce the recipient's interest in the QOF, because it results in an increase in the basis of QOF stock. The Treasury Department and the IRS request comments on the proposed treatment of distributions to which section 305(b) applies.

In the case of a redemption that is treated as a distribution to which section 301 applies, the Treasury Department and the IRS have determined that the full amount of the redemption generally should be an inclusion event, regardless of whether a portion of the redemption proceeds are characterized as a dividend under section 301(c)(1) or as the recovery of basis under section 301(c)(2). Otherwise, such a redemption could reduce a shareholder's direct equity investment without triggering an inclusion event (if the full amount of the redemption proceeds is characterized as either a dividend or as the recovery of basis). However, there are circumstances in which the shareholder's interest in the QOF is not reduced by a redemption (for example, if the shareholder wholly owns the distributing corporation). Thus, if a QOF redeems stock wholly and directly held by its sole QOF shareholder (or by members of the same consolidated group), the proposed regulations do not treat the redemption as an inclusion event to the extent the proceeds are characterized as a dividend under section 301(c)(1) or as a recovery of basis under section 301(c)(2). The Treasury Department and the IRS request comments on the proposed treatment of redemptions that are treated as distributions to which section 301 applies.

In the case of a QOF partnership, interests in which are directly or indirectly held by one or more partnerships, a distribution by one of the partnerships (including the QOF partnership) of property with a value in excess of the basis of the distributee's partnership interest is also an inclusion event. In the absence of this rule, a direct or indirect partner in a QOF partnership could dilute the value of its qualifying investment and thereby reduce the amount of deferred gain that would be recognized in a subsequent transaction.

The transfer by a QOF owner of its qualifying QOF stock or qualifying QOF partnership interest in a section 351 exchange generally would be an inclusion event under the proposed regulations, because the contribution would reduce the QOF owner's direct interest in the QOF. However, the contribution by a QOF shareholder of a portion (but not all) of its qualifying QOF stock to the QOF itself in a section 351 exchange would not be so treated, as long as the contribution does not reduce the taxpayer's equity interest in the qualifying investment (for example, if the QOF shareholders made pro rata contributions of qualifying QOF stock).

The Treasury Department and the IRS request comments on the proposed rules governing inclusion events, including whether additional rules are needed to prevent abuse.

VIII. *Consolidated Return Provisions*

A. QOF Stock is Not Stock for Purposes of Affiliation

The framework of section 1400Z-2 and the consolidated return regulations are incompatible in many respects. If a QOF corporation could be a subsidiary member of a consolidated group, extensive rules altering the application of many consolidated return provisions would be necessary to carry out simultaneously the policy objectives of section 1400Z-2 and the consolidated return regulations. For example, special rules would be required to take into account the interaction of section 1400Z-2 with §§1.1502-13 (relating to intercompany transactions), 1.1502-32 (relating to the consolidated return investment adjustment regime), and 1.1502-19 (relating to excess loss accounts).

Section 1400Z-2 is inconsistent with the intercompany transaction regulations under §1.1502-13. The stated purpose of the regulations under §1.1502-13 is to ensure that the existence of an intercompany transaction (a transaction between two members of a consolidated group) does not result in the creation, prevention, acceleration, or deferral of consolidated taxable income or tax liability. In other words, the existence of the intercompany transaction must not affect the consolidated taxable income or tax liability of the group as a whole. Therefore, §1.1502-13 generally determines the tax treatment of items resulting from intercompany transactions by treating members of the consolidated group as divisions of a single corporation (single-entity treatment).

The deferral of gain permitted under section 1400Z-2 would conflict with the purposes of § 1.1502-13 if the QOF shareholder and QOF corporation were members of the same consolidated group. Under section 1400Z-2, a qualifying investment in a QOF results in the deferral of the recognition of gain that would otherwise be recognized. However, allowing a transfer by a member investor to a member QOF to result in the deferral of gain recognition directly contradicts the express purpose of the intercompany transaction regulations. Therefore, consolidation of a QOF corporation with a corporation that otherwise would be a QOF shareholder not only would violate a basic tenet of single-entity treatment, but also would necessitate the creation of an elaborate system of additional consolidated return rules to establish the proper tax treatment of intercompany transactions involving a group member that is a QOF (QOF member). For the same reasons, special rules would be necessary to address the consequences under section 1400Z-2 of distributions from QOF members to other group members. In addition, special rules would be required to determine if and how § 1.1502-13 would apply for purposes of testing whether a member of the group (tested member) met the requirements of section 1400Z-2(d) to continue to be treated as a QOF following an intercompany transaction. For example, such rules would need to address whether satisfaction of the requirements should be tested by taking into account not only property held by the tested member, but also property held by other members that have been counterparties in an intercompany transaction.

Section 1400Z-2 is also inconsistent with the consolidated return investment adjustment regime. Section 1.1502-32 requires unique adjustments to the basis of member stock to reflect income, gain, deduction, and loss items of group members. These rules apply only to members of consolidated groups, and they cause stock basis in subsidiary members of consolidated groups to be drastically different from the stock basis that would exist outside of a group. These investment adjustment rules would affect the timing and amount of inclusion of the deferred capital gain under section 1400Z-2, because the governing rules under section 1400Z-2 depend on the observance of very particular stock basis adjustments. Therefore, significant modifications to the application of the investment adjustment rules under § 1.1502-32 would be required to implement section 1400Z-2 if the QOF shareholder and QOF corporation were members of the same group. Further, the rules of § 1.1502-32 are integral to the application of the consolidated return system, and it would be virtually impossible to accurately anticipate all of the instances in which the special basis rules should be applied to the QOF member, as well as to any includible corporations owned by the QOF member (such corporations also would be included in the group).

As a final example, special rules would also be needed to harmonize the excess loss account (ELA) concept established by the rules in § 1.1502-19 with the operation of section 1400Z-2. The consolidated return regulations provide for downward stock basis adjustments that take into account distributions by lower-tier members to higher-tier members and the absorption of member losses by other members of the group. As a result of these adjustments, a member of a group may have negative basis (that is, an ELA) in its stock in another member. The existence of negative stock basis is not contemplated under section 1400Z-2, and it is unique to the consolidated return regulations. Harmonizing rules would be required to ensure the special QOF basis election under section 1400Z-2(c) would not eliminate an ELA in the stock of the QOF member and provide a benefit beyond what was intended by section 1400Z-2. In other words, the basis adjustment under section 1400Z-2(c) should exclude from income no more than the appreciation in the QOF investment.

In summary, section 1400Z-2 and the consolidated return system are based on incompatible principles and rules. To enable the two systems to interact in a manner that effectuates the purposes of each, complicated additional regulations would be required. However, it is not possible to anticipate all possible points of conflict. Therefore, rather than trying to forcibly harmonize the two frameworks, these proposed regulations treat QOF stock as not stock for purposes of section 1504, which sets forth the requirements for corporate affiliation. Consequently, a QOF C corporation can be the common parent of a consolidated group, but it cannot be a subsidiary member of a consolidated group. In other words, a QOF C corporation owned by members of a consolidated group is not a member of that consolidated group. These proposed regulations treat QOF stock as not stock for the broad purpose of section 1504 affiliation.

The Treasury Department and the IRS request comments on whether this rule should be limited to treat QOF stock as not stock only for the purposes of consolidation, as well as whether the burden of potentially applying two different sets of consolidated return rules would be outweighed by benefits of permitting QOF C corporations to be subsidiary members of consolidated groups.

B. Separate Entity Treatment for Members of a Consolidated Group Qualifying for Deferral under Section 1400Z-2

The proposed regulations clarify that section 1400Z-2 applies separately to each member of a consolidated group. Accordingly, to qualify for gain deferral, the same member of the consolidated group must: (i) Sell a capital asset to an unrelated person, the gain of which the member elects to be deferred under section 1400Z-2; and (ii) invest an amount of such deferred gain from the original sale into a QOF.

C. Basis Increases in Qualifying Investment "Tier Up" the Consolidated Group

Sections 1400Z-2(b)(2)(B)(iii) and (iv) and 1400Z-2(c) provide special basis adjustments applicable to qualifying investments held for five years, seven years, and at least 10 years. If the QOF owner is a member of a consolidated group, proposed § 1.1400Z2(g)-1(c) would treat these basis adjustments to the qualifying investment as meeting the requirements of § 1.1502-32(b)(3)(ii)(D), and thus as tax-exempt income to the QOF owner. Consequently, upper-tier members that own stock in the QOF owner would increase their basis in the stock of the QOF owner by the amount of the resulting tax-exempt income. The basis increase under section 1400Z-2(c) would be treated as tax-exempt income only if the qualifying investment were sold or exchanged and the QOF owner elected to apply the special rule in section 1400Z-2(c). Treating these special basis adjustments under section 1400Z-2 as tax-exempt income to the QOF owner is necessary to ensure that the amounts at issue remain tax-free at all levels within the consolidated group. For example, this treatment would prevent an unintended income inclusion upon a member's sale of the QOF owner's stock.

D. The Attribute Reduction Rule in § 1.1502-36(d)

These proposed regulations clarify how a member's basis in a qualifying investment is taken into account for purposes of applying the attribute reduction rule in § 1.1502-36(d). When a member (M) transfers a loss share of subsidiary (S) stock, the rules in § 1.1502-36 apply. If the transferred S share is a loss share after the application of § 1.1502-36(b) and (c), the attribute reduction rule in § 1.1502-36(d) applies to prevent duplication of a single economic loss. In simple terms, § 1.1502-36(d) compares M's basis in the loss S share to the amount of S's tax attributes that are allocable to the loss share. If loss duplication exists on the transfer of the S share (as determined under the mechanics of § 1.1502-36(d)), S must reduce its tax attributes by its attribute reduction amount (ARA). In certain cases, M instead may elect to reduce its basis in the loss S share. To ensure that the purposes of both section 1400Z-2 and § 1.1502-36(d) are effectuated, the proposed regulations provide special rules regarding the application of § 1.1502-36(d) when S owns a qualifying investment.

In applying the anti-loss duplication rule discussed in the preceding paragraph, S includes its basis in a qualifying investment in determining whether there is loss duplication and, if so, the amount of the duplicated loss. However, if loss duplication exists, S cannot cure the loss duplication by reducing its basis in the qualifying investment under § 1.1502-36(d). Because of the special QOF basis election available under section 1400Z-2(c), reducing S's basis in the qualifying investment would not achieve the anti-loss duplication purpose of § 1.1502-36(d) if the special QOF basis election were made at a later date. This is because any basis reduced under § 1.1502-36(d) would be restored on the sale of the qualifying investment. Therefore, S must reduce its other attributes. If S's attribute reduction amount exceeds S's attributes available for reduction, then the parent of the group is deemed to elect under § 1.1502-36(d)(6) to reduce M's basis in S to the extent of S's basis in the qualifying investment. The reduction of M's basis in S is limited to the remaining ARA.

IX. *Holding Periods and Other Tacking Rules*

Under section 1400Z-2(b)(2)(B) and (c), increases in basis in a qualifying investment held by an investor in a QOF are, in part, dependent upon the QOF investor's holding period for that qualifying investment. The proposed regulations generally provide that, for purposes of section 1400Z-2(b)(2)(B) and (c), a QOF investor's holding period for its qualifying investment does not include the period during which the QOF investor held property that was transferred to the QOF in exchange for the qualifying investment. For example, if an investor transfers a building that it has owned for 10 years to a QOF corporation in exchange for qualifying QOF stock, the investor's holding period for the qualifying QOF stock for purposes of section 1400Z-2 begins on the date of the transfer, not the date the investor acquired the building.

Similarly, if an investor disposes of its entire qualifying investment in QOF 1 and reinvests in QOF 2 within 180 days, the investor's holding period for its qualifying investment in QOF 2 begins on the date of its qualifying investment in QOF 2, not on the date of its qualifying investment in QOF 1.

However, a QOF shareholder's holding period for qualifying QOF stock received in a qualifying section 381 transaction in which the acquiring corporation is a QOF immediately thereafter, or received in a recapitalization of a QOF, includes the holding period of the QOF shareholder's qualifying QOF stock exchanged therefor. Similar rules apply to QOF stock received in a qualifying section 355 transaction. The Treasury Department and the IRS have determined that, in these situations, a QOF shareholder should be permitted to tack its holding period for its initial qualifying investment because the investor's direct equity investment in a QOF continues. In the case of a qualifying section 381 transaction in which the acquiring corporation is a QOF immediately thereafter, the investor's continuing direct equity investment in a QOF is further reflected in the investor's exchanged basis in the stock of the acquiring corporation. Tacked holding period rules apply in the same manner with respect to a QOF partner's interest in a QOF partnership, for example, in the case of a partnership merger where the QOF partner's resulting investment in the QOF partnership continues. Finally, the recipient of a qualifying investment by gift that is not an inclusion event, or by reason of the death of the owner, may tack the donor's or decedent's holding period, respectively.

Similar rules apply for purposes of determining whether the "original use" requirement in section 1400Z-2(d)(2)(D) commences with the acquiring corporation (after a qualifying section 381 transaction in which the acquiring corporation is a QOF immediately thereafter) or the controlled corporation (after a qualifying section 355 transaction). In each case, the acquiring corporation or the controlled corporation satisfies the original use requirement if the target corporation or the distributing corporation, respectively, did so before the transaction. Thus, the acquiring corporation and the controlled corporation may continue to treat the historic qualified opportunity zone business property received from the target corporation and the distributing corporation, respectively, as qualified opportunity zone business property.

X. *General Anti-Abuse Rule*

Proposed § 1.1400Z2(f)-1(c) provides a general anti-abuse rule pursuant to section 1400Z-2(e)(4)(C), which provides that "the Secretary shall prescribe such regulations as may be necessary or appropriate to carry out the purposes of this section, including * * * rules to prevent abuse." The Treasury Department and the IRS expect that most taxpayers will apply the rules in section 1400Z-2 and § § 1.1400Z2(a)-1 through 1.1400Z2(g)-1 in a manner consistent with the purposes of section 1400Z-2. However, to prevent abuse, proposed § 1.1400Z2(f)-1(c) provides that if a significant purpose of a transaction is to achieve a tax result that is inconsistent with the purposes of section 1400Z-2, the Commissioner can recast a transaction (or series of transactions) for Federal tax purposes as appropriate to achieve tax results that are consistent with the purposes of section 1400Z-2. Whether a tax result is inconsistent with the purposes of section 1400Z-2 must be determined based on all the facts and circumstances. For example, this general anti-abuse rule could apply to a treat a purchase of agricultural land that otherwise would be qualified opportunity zone business property as a purchase of non-qualified opportunity zone business property if a significant purpose for that purchase were to achieve a tax result inconsistent with the purposes of section 1400Z-2 (see part I.B of this Explanation of Provisions).

The Treasury Department and the IRS request comments on this proposed anti-abuse rule, including whether additional details regarding what tax results are inconsistent with the purposes of section 1400Z-2 is required or whether examples of particular types of abusive transactions would be helpful.

XI. *Entities Organized under a Statute of a Federally Recognized Indian Tribe and Issues Particular to Tribally Leased Property*

Commenters have asked whether Indian tribal governments, like state and territorial governments, can charter a partnership or corporation that is eligible to be a QOF. Proposed § 1.1400Z2(d)-1(e)(1) provides that, if an entity is not organized in one of the 50 states, the District of Columbia, or the U.S. possessions, it is ineligible to be a QOF. Similarly, proposed § 1.1400Z2(d)-1(e)(2) provides that, if an entity is not organized in one of the 50 states, the District of Columbia, or the U.S. possessions, an equity interest in the entity is neither qualified opportunity zone stock nor a qualified opportunity zone partnership interest. The Treasury Department and the IRS have determined that, for purposes of both proposed § 1.1400Z2(d)-1(e)(1) and (2), an entity "organized in" one of the 50 states includes an entity organized under the law of a Federally recognized Indian tribe if the entity's domicile is located in one of the 50 states. Such entity satisfies the requirement in section 1400Z-2(d)(2)(B)(i) and (C) that qualified opportunity zone stock is stock in a domestic corporation and a qualified opportunity zone partnership interest is an interest in a domestic partnership. See section 7701(a)(4). The Treasury Department and the IRS, while acknowledging the sovereignty of federally recognized Indian tribes, note that an entity that is eligible to be a QOF will be subject to Federal income tax under the Code, regardless of the laws under which it is established or organized.

Commenters also noted that Indian tribal governments occupy Federal trust lands, and that these lands are often leased for economic development purposes. According to these commenters, the right to use Indian tribal government reservation land managed by the Secretary of the Interior can raise unique issues with respect to lease valuations. As discussed in part II of this Explanation of Provisions, these proposed regulations address the treatment of leased tangible property in general.

In order to obtain tribal input in accordance with Executive Order 13175, "Consultation and Coordination with Indian Tribal Governments," and consistent with Treasury's Tribal Consultation Policy (80 FR 57434, September 23, 2015), the Treasury Department and the IRS will schedule Tribal Consultation with Tribal Officials before finalizing these regulations to obtain additional input, within the meaning of the Tribal Consultation Policy, on QOF entities organized under the law of a Federally recognized Indian tribe and whether any additional guidance may be needed regarding QOFs leasing tribal government Federal trust lands or regarding leased real property located on such lands, as well as other Tribal implications of the proposed regulations. Such Tribal Consultation will also seek input on questions regarding the tax status of certain tribally chartered corporations other than QOFs.

Proposed Effective/Applicability Dates

Section 7805(b)(1)(A) and (B) of the Code generally provides that no temporary, proposed, or final regulation relating to the internal revenue laws may apply to any taxable period ending before the earliest of (A) The date on which such regulation is filed with the **Federal Register**; or (B) in the case of a final regulation, the date on which a proposed or temporary regulation to which the final regulation relates was filed with the **Federal Register**. However, section 7805(b)(2) provides that regulations filed or issued within 18 months of the date of the enactment of the statutory provision to which they relate are not prohibited from applying to taxable periods prior to those described in section 7805(b)(1). Furthermore, section 7805(b)(3) provides that the Secretary may provide that any regulation may take effect or apply retroactively to prevent abuse.

Consistent with authority provided by section 7805(b)(1)(A), the rules of proposed § § 1.1400Z2(a)-1, 1.1400Z2(b)-1, 1.1400Z2(c)-1, 1.1400Z2(d)-1, 1.1400Z2(e)-1, 1.1400Z2(f)-1, and 1.1400Z2(g)-1 generally apply to taxable years ending after **[INSERT DATE OF PUBLICATION IN FEDERAL REGISTER]**. However, taxpayers may generally rely on the rules of proposed

§§1.1400Z2(a)-1, 1.1400Z2(b)-1, 1.1400Z2(d)-1, 1.1400Z2(e)-1, 1.1400Z2(f)-1, and 1.1400Z2(g)-1 set forth in this notice of proposed rulemaking for periods prior to the finalization of those sections if they apply these proposed rules consistently and in their entirety. This pre-finalization reliance does not apply to the rules of proposed §1.1400Z2(c)-1 set forth in this notice of proposed rulemaking as these rules do not apply until January 1, 2028.

Special Analyses

I. *Regulatory Planning and Review*

Executive Orders 13771, 13563, and 12866 direct agencies to assess the costs and benefits of available regulatory alternatives and, if regulation is necessary, to select regulatory approaches that maximize net benefits (including potential economic, environmental, public health and safety effects, distributive impacts, and equity). Executive Order 13563 emphasizes the importance of quantifying both costs and benefits, reducing costs, harmonizing rules, and promoting flexibility.

These proposed regulations have been designated by the Office of Management and Budget's Office of Information and Regulatory Affairs (OIRA) as economically significant under Executive Order 12866 pursuant to the Memorandum of Agreement (April 11, 2018) between the Treasury Department and the Office of Management and Budget regarding the review of tax regulations. Accordingly, the proposed regulations have been reviewed by the Office of Management and Budget. In addition, the Treasury Department and the IRS expect the proposed regulations, when final, to be an Executive Order 13771 deregulatory action and request comment on this designation.

A. *Background and Overview*

Congress enacted section 1400Z-2, in conjunction with section 1400Z-1, as a temporary provision to encourage private sector investment in certain lower-income communities designated as qualified opportunity zones (see Senate Committee on Finance, Explanation of the Bill, at 313 (November 22, 2017)). Taxpayers may elect to defer the recognition of capital gain to the extent of amounts invested in a QOF, provided that such amounts are invested during the 180-day period beginning on the date such capital gain would have been recognized by the taxpayer. Inclusion of the deferred capital gain in income occurs on the date the investment in the QOF is sold or exchanged or on December 31, 2026, whichever comes first. For investments in a QOF held longer than five years, taxpayers may exclude 10 percent of the deferred gain from inclusion in income, and for investments held longer than seven years, taxpayers may exclude a total of 15 percent of the deferred gain from inclusion in income. In addition, for investments held longer than 10 years, the post-acquisition gain on the qualifying investment in the QOF also may be excluded from income through a step-up in basis in the qualifying investment. In turn, a QOF must hold at least 90 percent of its assets in qualified opportunity zone property, as measured by the average percentage of assets held on the last day of the first 6-month period of the taxable year of the fund and on the last day of the taxable year. The statute requires a QOF that fails this 90-percent test to pay a penalty for each month it fails to satisfy this requirement.

The proposed regulations clarify several terms used in the statute, such as what constitutes "substantially all" in each of the different places that phrase is used in section 1400Z-2, the use of qualified opportunity zone business property (including leased property) in a qualified opportunity zone, the sourcing of income to a qualified opportunity zone business, the "reasonable period" for a QOF to reinvest proceeds from the sale of qualifying assets without paying a penalty, and what transactions comprise an inclusion event that would lead to the inclusion of deferred gain in gross income. In part, the proposed regulations amend portions of previously proposed regulations related to section 1400Z-2.

B. *Need for the Proposed Regulations*

The Treasury Department and the IRS are aware of concerns raised by commenters that investors have been reticent to make substantial investments in QOFs without first having additional clarity on which investments in a QOF would qualify to receive the preferential tax treatment specified by the TCJA. This uncertainty could reduce the amount of investment flowing into lower-income communities designated as qualified opportunity zones. The lack of additional clarity could also lead to different taxpayers interpreting, and therefore applying, the same statute differently, which could distort the allocation of investment across the qualified opportunity zones.

C. *Economic Analysis*

1. Baseline

The Treasury Department and the IRS have assessed the benefits and costs of the proposed regulations relative to a no-action baseline reflecting anticipated Federal income tax-related behavior in the absence of these proposed regulations.

2. Economic Effects of the Proposed Regulation

a. Summary of Economic Effects

The proposed regulations provide certainty and clarity to taxpayers regarding utilization of the tax preference for capital gains provided in section 1400Z-2 by defining terms, calculations, and acceptable forms of documentation. The Treasury Department and the IRS project that this added clarity generally will encourage taxpayers to invest in QOFs and will increase the amount of investment located in qualified opportunity zones. The Treasury Department and the IRS have not made quantitative estimates of these effects.

The benefits and costs of major, specific provisions of these proposed regulations relative to the no-action baseline and alternatives to these proposed rules considered by the Treasury Department and the IRS are discussed in further detail below.

b. Qualified Opportunity Zone Business Property and Definition of Substantially All

The proposed regulations establish the threshold for satisfying the *substantially all* requirements for four out of the five uses of the term in section 1400Z-2. The other *substantially all* test in section 1400Z-2(d)(3)(A)(i) already had been set at 70 percent by prior proposed regulations (83 FR 54279, October 29, 2018). The proposed regulations provide that the term *substantially all* means at least 90 percent with regard to the three holding period requirements in section 1400Z-2(d)(2). The other *substantially all* term in section 1400Z-2(d)(2)(D)(i)(III) in the context of "use" is set to 70 percent, the same as the threshold established under the prior proposed rulemaking. The clarity provided in the proposed regulations reduces uncertainty for prospective investors regarding which investments would satisfy the requirements of section 1400Z-2. This clarity likely would lead to a greater level of investment in QOFs.

In choosing what values to assign to the substantially all terms, the Treasury Department and the IRS considered the costs and benefits of setting the threshold higher or lower. Setting the threshold higher would limit the type of businesses and investments that would be able to meet the proposed requirements and possibly distort the industry concentration within some opportunity zones. Setting the threshold lower would allow investors in certain QOFs to receive capital gains tax relief while placing a relatively small portion of its investment within a qualified opportunity zone. A lower threshold would increase the likelihood that a taxpayer may receive the benefit of the preferential treatment on capital gains without placing in service more tangible property within a qualified opportunity zone than would have occurred in the absence of section 1400Z-2. This latter concern is magnified by the way the different requirements in section 1400Z-2 interact.

For example, these regulations imply that a QOF could satisfy the substantially all standards with as little as 40 percent of the tangible property effectively owned by the fund being used within a qualified opportunity zone. This could occur if 90 percent of QOF assets are invested in a qualified opportunity zone business, in which 70 percent of the tangible assets of that business are qualified opportunity zone business property; and if, in addition, the qualified opportunity zone business property is only 70 percent in use within a qualified opportunity zone, and for 90 percent of the holding period for such property. Multiplying these shares together (0.9 x 0.7 x 0.7 x 0.9 = 0.4) generates the result that a QOF could satisfy the requirements of section 1400Z-2 under the proposed regulations with just 40 percent of its assets effectively in use within a qualified opportunity zone.

The Treasury Department and the IRS recognize that the operations of certain types of businesses may extend beyond the Census tract boundaries that define qualified opportunity zones. The substantially all thresholds provided in the proposed regulations are set at levels so as to limit the ability of investors in QOFs to receive preferential capital gains treatment, unless a consequential amount of tangible property used in the underlying business is located within a qualified opportunity zone, while also allowing flexibility to business operations so as not to significantly distort the types of businesses that can qualify for opportunity zone funds.

c. Valuation of Leased Property

The proposed regulations provide two methods for determining the asset values for purposes of the 90-percent asset test in section 1400Z-2(d)(1) for QOFs or the value of tangible property for the substantially all test in section 1400Z-2(d)(3)(A)(i) for qualified opportunity zone businesses. Under the first method, a taxpayer may value owned or leased property as reported on its applicable financial statement for the reporting period. Alternatively, the taxpayer may set the value of owned property equal to the unadjusted cost basis of the property under section 1012. The value of leased property under the alternative method equals the present value of total lease payments at the beginning of the lease. The value of the property under the alternative method for the 90-percent asset test and substantially all test does not change over time as long as the taxpayer continues to own or lease the property.

The two methods should provide similar values for leased property at the time that the lease begins, as beginning in 2019, generally accepted accounting principles (GAAP) require public companies to calculate the present value of lease payments in order to recognize the value of leased assets on the balance sheet. However, there are differences. On financial statements, the value of the leased property declines over the term of the lease. Under the alternative method, the value of the leased asset is calculated once at the beginning of the lease term and remains constant while the term of the lease is still in effect. This difference in valuation of property over time between using financial statements and the alternative method also exist in the case of owned property. In addition, the two approaches would generally apply different discount rates, thus leading to some difference in the calculated present value under the two methods.

The Treasury Department and the IRS provide the alternative method to allow for taxpayers that either do not have applicable financial statements or do not have them available in time for the asset test. In addition, the alternative method is simpler, thus reducing compliance costs, and would provide greater certainty in projecting future compliance with the 90-percent asset and substantially all tests. Thus, some taxpayers with applicable financial statements may elect to use the alternative method. The drawback to the alternative method is that it does not account for depreciation, and, over time, the values used for the sake of the 90-percent asset test and the substantially all test may diverge from the actual value of the property.

The Treasury Department and the IRS have determined that the value of leased property should be included in both the numerator and the denominator of the 90-percent asset test and the substantially all test, as this would be less distortive to business decisions compared to other available options. Leasing is a common business practice, and treating leased property differently than owned property could lead to economic distortions. If the value of leased property were not included in the tests at all, then it would be relatively easy for taxpayers to choose where to locate owned and leased property so as to technically meet the standards of the test, while maintaining substantial business operations outside of a qualified opportunity zone.

The Treasury Department and the IRS considered a third option for how leased property should be included in the 90-percent asset and substantially all tests. Under this option, leased property of the taxpayer would be included only in the denominator of the fraction. The reason for this is that leased property generally would not satisfy the purchase and original use requirements of section 1400Z-2(d)(2)(D)(i) and thus would not be deemed as qualified opportunity zone business property. However, not allowing leased property located within a qualified opportunity zone to be treated as qualified opportunity zone business property could distort business decisions of taxpayers and also could make it difficult for some businesses to satisfy the substantially all test in section 1400Z-2(d)(3)(A)(i), despite bringing new economic activity to a qualified opportunity zone.

For example, a start-up business that rented office space within a qualified opportunity zone and owned tangible property in the form of computers and other office equipment likely would fail the substantially all test if leased property only were included in the denominator of the substantially all fraction, despite all of its operations being located within a qualified opportunity zone. This may lead businesses to take on extra debt in order to purchase property located within a qualified opportunity zone, thus increasing the risk of financial distress, including bankruptcy.

One potential disadvantage of including leased property in both the numerator and denominator of the substantially all test is that it may weaken the incentive to construct new real property or renovate existing real property within a qualified opportunity zone, as taxpayers would be able to lease existing real property in a zone without improving it and become a qualified opportunity zone business. However, allowing the leasing of existing real property within a zone may encourage fuller utilization and improvement of such property and limit the abandonment or destruction of existing productive property within a qualified opportunity zone when new tax-favored real property becomes available.

Hence, including leased property in both the numerator and the denominator of the 90-percent asset test and substantially all test encourages economic activity within qualified opportunity zones while reducing the potential distortions between owned and leased property that may occur under other options.

d. Qualified Opportunity Zone Business

Section 1400Z-2(d)(3)(A)(ii) incorporates the requirement of section 1397C(b)(2) that a qualified business entity must derive at least 50 percent of its total gross income during a taxable year from the active conduct of a qualified business in a zone. The proposed regulations provide multiple safe harbors for determining whether this standard has been satisfied.

Two of these safe harbors provide different methods for measuring the labor input of the entity. The labor input can be measured in terms of hours or compensation paid. The proposed regulations provide that if at least 50 percent of the labor input of the entity is located within a zone (as measured by one of the two provided approaches), then the section 1397C(b)(2) requirement is satisfied.

In addition, a third safe harbor provides that the 50 percent gross income requirement is met if the tangible property of the trade or business located in a qualified opportunity zone and the management or operational functions performed in the qualified opportunity zone are each necessary for the generation of at least 50 percent of the gross income of the trade or business.

The determination of the location of income for businesses that operate in multiple jurisdictions can be complex, and the rules promulgated by taxing authorities to determine the location of income are often burdensome and may distort economic activity. The provision of alternative safe harbors in these proposed regulations should reduce the compliance and administrative burdens associated with determining whether this statutory requirement has been met. In the absence of such safe harbors, some taxpayers may interpret the 50 percent of gross income standard to require that a majority of the sales of the entity must be located within a zone. The Treasury Department and the IRS have determined that a standard based strictly on sales would discriminate against some types of businesses (for example, manufacturing) in which the location of sales is often different from the location of the production, and thus would preclude such businesses from benefitting from the incentives provided in section 1400Z-2. Furthermore, the potential distortions introduced by the provided safe harbors would increase incentives to locate labor inputs within a qualified opportunity zone. To the extent that such distortions exist, they further the statutory goal of encouraging economic activity within qualified opportunity zones. Given the flexibility provided to taxpayers in choosing a safe harbor, other distortions, such as to business organizational structuring, are likely to be minimal.

e. QOF Reinvestment Rule

The proposed regulations provide that a QOF has 12 months from the time of the sale or disposition of qualified opportunity zone property or the return of capital from investments in qualified opportunity zone stock or qualified opportunity zone partnership interests to reinvest the proceeds in other qualified opportunity zone property before the proceeds would not be considered qualified opportunity zone property with regards to the 90-percent asset test. This proposed rule provides clarity and gives substantial flexibility to taxpayers in satisfying the 90-percent asset test, which should encourage greater investment within QOFs compared to the baseline.

f. Other Topics

The proposed regulations clarify several other areas where there is uncertainty in how to apply the statute in practice. For example, the proposed regulations clarify what events cause the inclusion of deferred gain, that a QOF may not be a subsidiary member of a consolidated group, and how to determine the length of holding periods in a qualifying investment. These proposed regulations provide greater certainty to taxpayers regarding how to structure investments so as to comply with the statutory requirements of the opportunity zone incentive. This should reduce administration and compliance costs and encourage greater investment in QOFs.

D. *Paperwork Reduction Act*

The proposed regulation establishes a new collection of information in § 1.1400Z2(b)-1(h). In proposed § 1.1400Z2(b)-1(h)(1), the collection of information requires (i) a partnership that makes a deferral election to notify all of its partners of the deferral election, and (ii) a partner that makes a deferral election to notify the partnership in writing of its deferral election, including the amount of the eligible gain deferred. Similar requirements are set forth in proposed § 1.1400Z2(b)-1(h)(4) regarding S corporations and S corporation shareholders. The collection of information in proposed § 1.1400Z2(b)-1(h)(2) requires direct and indirect owners of a QOF partnership to provide the QOF partnership with a written statement containing information requested by the QOF partnership that is necessary to determine the direct and indirect owners' shares of deferred gain. Lastly, the collection of information in proposed § 1.1400Z2(b)-1(h)(3) requires a QOF partner to notify the QOF partnership of an election under section 1400Z-2(c) to adjust the basis of the qualifying QOF partnership interest that is disposed of in a taxable transaction. Similar requirements again are set forth in proposed § 1.1400Z2(b)-1(h)(4) regarding QOF S corporations and QOF S corporation shareholders. The collection of information contained in this proposed regulation will not be conducted using a new or existing IRS form.

The likely respondents are partnerships and partners, and S corporations and S corporation shareholders.

Estimated total annual reporting burden: 8,500 hours.

Estimated average annual burden per respondent: 1 hour.

Estimated number of respondents: 8,500.

Estimated frequency of responses: 8,500.

The collections of information contained in this notice of proposed rulemaking will be submitted to the Office of Management and Budget in accordance with the Paperwork Reduction Act of 1995 (44 U.S.C. 3507(d)). Comments on the collection of information should be sent to the Office of Management and Budget, Attn: Desk Officer for the Department of the Treasury, Office of Information and Regulatory Affairs, Washington, DC 20503, with copies to the Internal Revenue Service, Attn: IRS Reports Clearance Officer, SE:W:CAR:MP:T:T:SP, Washington, DC 20224. Comments on the collection of information should be received by **[*INSERT DATE 60 DAYS AFTER PUBLICATION IN THE FEDERAL REGISTER*]**. Comments are specifically requested concerning:

Whether the proposed collection of information is necessary for the proper performance of the functions of the IRS, including whether the information will have practical utility;

The accuracy of the estimated burden associated with the proposed collection of information;

How the quality, utility, and clarity of the information to be collected may be enhanced;

How the burden of complying with the proposed collection of information may be minimized, including through the application of automated collection techniques or other forms of information technology; and

Estimates of capital or start-up costs and costs of operation, maintenance, and purchase of services to provide information.

An agency may not conduct or sponsor, and a person is not required to respond to, a collection of information unless it displays a valid control number assigned by the Office of Management and Budget.

II. *Regulatory Flexibility Act*

Under the Regulatory Flexibility Act (RFA) (5 U.S.C. chapter 6), it is hereby certified that these proposed regulations, if adopted, would not have a significant economic impact on a substantial number of small entities that are directly affected by the proposed regulations.

As discussed elsewhere in this preamble, the proposed regulations would provide certainty and clarity to taxpayers regarding utilization of the tax preference for capital gains provided in section 1400Z-2 by defining terms, calculations, and acceptable forms of documentation. The Treasury Department and the IRS anticipate that this added clarity generally will encourage taxpayers to invest in QOFs and will increase the amount of investment located in qualified opportunity zones.

Investment in QOFs is entirely voluntary, and the certainty that would be provided in the proposed regulations is anticipated to minimize any compliance or administrative costs, such as the estimated average annual burden (1 hour) under the Paperwork Reduction Act. For example, the proposed regulations provide multiple safe harbors for purpose of determining whether the 50-percent gross income test has been met as required by section 1400Z-2(d)(3)(A)(ii) for a qualified opportunity zone business.

Taxpayers affected by these proposed regulations include QOFs, investors in QOFs, and qualified opportunity zone businesses in which a QOF holds an ownership interest. The proposed regulations will not directly affect the taxable incomes and liabilities of qualified opportunity zone businesses; they will affect only the taxable incomes and tax liabilities of QOFs (and owners of QOFs) that invest in such businesses. Although there is a lack of available data regarding the extent to which small entities invest in QOFs, will certify as QOFs, or receive equity investments from QOFs, the Treasury Department and the IRS project that most of the investment flowing into QOFs will come from large corporations and wealthy individuals, though some of these funds would likely flow through an intermediary investment partnership. It is expected that some QOFs and qualified opportunity zone businesses would be classified as small entities; however, the number of small entities significantly affected is not likely to be substantial.

Accordingly, it is hereby certified that this rule would not have a significant economic impact on a substantial number of small entities. The Treasury Department and the IRS specifically invite comments from any party, particularly affected small entities, on the accuracy of this certification.

Pursuant to section 7805(f), this notice of proposed rulemaking has been submitted to the Chief Counsel for Advocacy of the Small Business Administration for comment on its impact on small business.

III. *Unfunded Mandates Reform Act*

Section 202 of the Unfunded Mandates Reform Act of 1995 (UMRA) requires that agencies assess anticipated costs and benefits and take certain other actions before issuing a final rule that includes any Federal mandate that may result in expenditures in any one year by a state, local, or tribal government, in the aggregate, or by the private sector, of $100 million in 1995 dollars, updated annually for inflation. In 2018, that threshold is approximately $150 million. This rule does not include any Federal mandate that may result in expenditures by state, local, or tribal governments, or by the private sector in excess of that threshold.

IV. *Executive Order 13132: Federalism*

Executive Order 13132 (entitled "Federalism") prohibits an agency from publishing any rule that has federalism implications if the rule either imposes substantial, direct compliance costs on state and local governments, and is not required by statute, or preempts state law, unless the agency meets the consultation and funding requirements of section 6 of the Executive Order. This proposed rule does not have federalism implications and does not impose substantial direct compliance costs on state and local governments or preempt state law within the meaning of the Executive Order.

Statement of Availability of IRS Documents

IRS Revenue Procedures, Revenue Rulings, and Notices cited in this preamble are published in the Internal Revenue Bulletin (or Cumulative Bulletin) and are available from the Superintendent of Documents, U.S. Government Publishing Office, Washington, DC 20402, or by visiting the IRS web site at *http://www.irs.gov*.

Comments

Before these proposed regulations are adopted as final regulations, consideration will be given to any electronic and written comments that are submitted timely to the IRS as prescribed in this preamble under the **"ADDRESSES"** heading. The Treasury Department and the IRS request comments on all aspects of the proposed rules. All comments will be available at *http://www.regulations.gov* or upon request.

Drafting Information

The principal authors of these proposed regulations are Erika C. Reigle and Kyle Griffin, Office of the Associate Chief Counsel (Income Tax & Accounting); Jeremy Aron-Dine and Sarah Hoyt, Office of the Associate Chief Counsel (Corporate); and Marla Borkson and Sonia Kothari, Office of the Associate Chief Counsel (Passthroughs and Special Industries). Other personnel from the Treasury Department and the IRS participated in their development.

List of Subjects in 26 CFR Part 1

Income Taxes, Reporting and recordkeeping requirements.

Partial Withdrawal of a Notice of Proposed Rulemaking

Accordingly, under the authority of 26 U.S.C. 1400Z-2(e)(4) and 7805, § 1.1400Z2(d)-1(c)(4)(i), (c)(5), (6), and (7), (d)(2)(i)(A), (d)(2)(ii) and (iii), (d)(5)(i), and (d)(5)(ii)(B), of the notice of proposed rulemaking (REG-115420-18) published in the **Federal Register** on October 29, 2018 (83 FR 54279) are withdrawn.

[¶49,796] Proposed Amendments of Regulations (REG-117062-18), published in the Federal Register on April 19, 2019.

[Code Secs. 641 and 1361]

Potential current beneficiaries: Electing small business trust: S corporation: Nonresident aliens.—Amendments of Reg. §§1.641(c)-1 and 1.1361-1, regarding the recent statutory expansion of the class of permissible potential current beneficiaries (PCBs) of an electing small business trust (ESBT) to include nonresident aliens (NRAs), are proposed.

AGENCY: Internal Revenue Service (IRS), Treasury.

ACTION: Notice of proposed rulemaking.

SUMMARY: This notice of proposed rulemaking provides rules regarding the recent statutory expansion of the class of permissible potential current beneficiaries (PCBs) of an electing small business trust (ESBT) to include nonresident aliens (NRAs). In particular, these proposed regulations would ensure that the income of an S corporation will continue to be subject to U.S. Federal income tax when an NRA is a deemed owner of a grantor trust that elects to be an ESBT.

DATES: Comments and requests for a public hearing must be received by June 3, 2019. ADDRESSES: Submit electronic submissions via the Federal Rulemaking Portal at *www.regulations.gov* (indicate IRS and REG-117062-18) by following the online instructions for submitting comments. The Department of the Treasury (Treasury Department) and the IRS will publish for public availability any comment received to its public docket, whether submitted electronically or in hard copy. Send hard copy submissions to: CC:PA:LPD:PR (REG-117062-18), Room 5203, Internal Revenue Service, P.O. Box 7604, Ben Franklin Station, Washington, DC 20044. Submissions may be hand-delivered Monday through Friday between the hours of 8 a.m. and 4 p.m. to CC:PA:LPD:PR (REG-117062-18), Courier's Desk, Internal Revenue Service, 1111 Constitution Avenue NW, Washington, DC, 20224.

FOR FURTHER INFORMATION CONTACT: Concerning the proposed regulations, Cynthia Morton, (202) 317-5279; concerning submissions and the hearing, Regina Johnson, (202) 317-6901(not toll-free numbers).

SUPPLEMENTARY INFORMATION:

Background

1. *Overview*

This document contains proposed amendments to the Income Tax Regulations (26 CFR part 1) under sections 641 and 1361 of the Internal Revenue Code (Code).

Section 13541(a) of "An Act to provide for reconciliation pursuant to titles II and V of the concurrent resolution on the budget for fiscal year 2018," Public Law 115-97,131 Stat. 2054, 2154 (TCJA) amended section 1361(c)(2)(B)(v) of the Code to allow NRAs to be PCBs of ESBTs. As amended, section 1361(c)(2)(B)(v) provides that NRA PCBs will not be taken into account for purposes of the S corporation shareholder-eligibility requirement that otherwise prohibits NRA shareholders. See section 1361(b)(1)(C).

A. S Corporations and NRAs

An S corporation is a "small business corporation" for which an election, made under section 1362(a), is in effect. Section 1361(b)(1) defines the term "small business corporation" as a domestic corporation that (i) is not an ineligible corporation (as defined in section 1361(b)(2)); (ii) does not have more than 100 shareholders; (iii) does not have a shareholder who is not an individual, estate, a certain type of trust, or a certain type of tax-exempt organization; (iv) does not have more than one class of stock; and (v) as relevant to these proposed regulations, does not have an NRA as a shareholder.

Section 7701(b)(1)(B) defines an NRA as an individual who is neither a citizen of the United States nor a resident of the United States, within the meaning of section 7701(b)(1)(A). Section 7701(b)(1)(A) provides that an alien individual is treated as a resident of the United States with respect to any calendar year if (and only if) such individual (i) is a lawful permanent resident of the United States at any time during such calendar year; (ii) meets the substantial presence test of section 7701(b)(3); or (iii) makes the first-year election provided in section 7701(b)(4).

B. Categories of Trusts Permitted to be S Corporation Shareholders

Only certain trusts are permitted to be an S corporation shareholder. Specifically, sections 1361(c)(2) and (d)(1)(A) provide that the following trusts may be an S corporation shareholder: (i) A grantor trust wholly owned by an individual who is a citizen or resident of the United States; (ii) a voting trust; (iii) certain grantor trusts that continue to exist for a period generally not longer than two years after the grantor's death; (iv) certain testamentary trusts for two years after the S corporation stock is transferred to it; (v) a qualified subchapter S trust; (vi) certain individual retirement accounts under section 408(a) that hold certain bank or company stock; and (vii) as relevant to these proposed regulations, a domestic trust that qualifies as an ESBT.

C. Overview of ESBTs

To expand the categories of trusts permitted to be S corporation shareholders under section 1361(c)(2) and thereby, in particular, to facilitate family financial planning, Congress added ESBTs to the list of permitted categories of S corporation shareholders over two decades ago. See H. Rept. 104-586, at 82 (1996); S. Rept. 104-281, at 46 (1996). An ESBT must be a domestic trust based on the flush language under section 1361(c)(2)(A), which provides that a foreign trust cannot be an eligible S corporation shareholder. Read together with section 1361(e)(1), an ESBT is any domestic trust that satisfies the following requirements: (i) The trust does not have as a beneficiary any person other than an individual, an estate, or an organization described in section 170(c)(2) through (5), or an organization described in section 170(c)(1) that holds a contingent interest in such trust and is not a PCB; (ii) no interest in the trust was acquired by purchase; and (iii) an election has been made under section 1361(e) with respect to the trust. An ESBT may hold S corporation stock as well as other property, and may accumulate trust income. In addition, and as relevant to these proposed regulations, (i) a PCB may be one of multiple beneficiaries of an ESBT, and (ii) a grantor trust may elect to be an ESBT.

i. PCB as an ESBT Beneficiary

For purposes of determining whether a corporation is an S corporation, each PCB of an ESBT is treated as a separate S corporation shareholder. See section 1361(c)(2)(B)(v). A PCB, with respect to any period, is any person who at any time during such period is entitled to, or at the discretion of any person may receive, a distribution from the principal or income of the ESBT (determined without regard to any power of appointment to the extent such power remains unexercised). See section 1361(e)(2). As relevant to these proposed regulations, a PCB also can be the deemed owner of a grantor trust that elects to be an ESBT.

ii. ESBTs Divided into Portions for Tax Liability Determinations

An ESBT that owns stock of an S corporation, as well as other property, is treated as two separate trusts (S portion and non-S portion, respectively) for purposes of chapter 1 of subtitle A of the Code (chapter 1), even though the ESBT is treated as a single trust for administrative purposes. See § 1.641(c)-1(a). Specifically, section 641(c)(1)(A) provides that the S portion, which consists solely of S corporation stock, is (i) treated as a separate trust for purposes of chapter 1, and (ii) taxed in accordance with section 641(c)(2). The non-S portion of the ESBT remains subject to the normal trust income taxation rules of subparts A through D of subchapter J of chapter 1 (subchapter J) that govern simple and complex trusts. In addition, the S portion or non-S portion (or both) can be treated as owned by a grantor under § 1.641(c)-1(b)(1), referred to as the "grantor portion," and is subject to the rules under subpart E of subchapter J.

iii. Effect of ESBT Election by a Grantor Trust

A grantor trust generally is a trust over which the grantor or other deemed owner retains the power to control or direct the trust's income or assets. If a trust is a grantor trust, then (i) the deemed owner is treated as the owner of the assets, (ii) the trust is disregarded as a separate entity for Federal income tax purposes, and (iii) all items of income, deduction, and credit are taxed to the deemed owner. Wholly or partially-owned grantor trusts can make an ESBT election but the grantor trust taxation rules of the Code override the ESBT provisions. Therefore, an ESBT pays tax directly at the trust level on its S corporation income and that income is not passed through to the beneficiaries, except for the amount that is taxed to the owner of the grantor trust portion.

The Department of the Treasury (Treasury Department) and the IRS promulgated regulations in 2002 to clarify that the items of income, deduction, and credit of the portion of an ESBT treated as owned by a grantor or other person under the grantor trust rules are taken into account by the deemed owner (rather than the ESBT) under section 671 in computing the deemed owner's taxable income. See § 1.641(c)-1(c). Therefore, under those regulations, a wholly-owned grantor trust can be an ESBT, but with no immediate change to the grantor trust's taxation. While an ESBT may be divided into a non-S portion, an S portion, and a grantor trust portion, the statutory definitions of an ESBT and of a PCB focus on all the persons who are beneficiaries or PCBs of the entire trust, rather than beneficiaries of only the S portion. As relevant to these proposed regulations, the deemed owner of the grantor trust portion is treated as a PCB of the ESBT.

2. *TCJA Expansion of Qualifying Beneficiaries of ESBTs*

A. Prior Law and TCJA Change

Prior to the enactment of the TCJA, a change in the immigration status of a PCB of an ESBT that owns S corporation stock from resident alien to NRA would have terminated an ESBT election, and therefore also terminated the corporation's election as an S corporation. This result would have occurred because, prior to the TCJA-enacted exception to the section 1361(b)(1)(C) eligible-shareholder requirement, section 1361(c)(2)(B)(v) provided, in relevant part, that each PCB of an ESBT must be treated as a shareholder of the S corporation. As discussed in part 1(A) of this Background section, if a purported S corporation has an NRA shareholder, such S corporation would fail the qualification requirements listed in section 1361(b)(1), resulting in the termination of its status as an S corporation.

Section 13541(a) of the TCJA amended section 1361(c)(2)(B)(v) to provide that the rule treating each PCB of an ESBT as a shareholder does not apply for purposes of the eligible-shareholder requirement of section 1361(b)(1)(C). As a result of that TCJA amendment, if a resident alien PCB of an ESBT becomes an NRA, the status of that PCB as an NRA will not cause the S corporation of which the ESBT is a shareholder to fail the requirement in section 1361(b)(1)(C), which otherwise would terminate its S election. While Congress amended section 1361(c)(2)(B)(v) to expand the scope of qualifying beneficiaries of ESBTs, Congress left unaltered the rule under section 1361(b)(1)(C) that an S corporation cannot have an NRA as a shareholder.

B. TCJA Expansion

Prior to the TCJA, only individuals subject to Federal income taxation could receive an ESBT's share of S corporation income because a grantor trust that elected ESBT status could not have had a deemed owner who was an NRA. Without these proposed regulations, the TCJA's expansion of an ESBT's permissible PCBs to include an NRA would allow S corporation income attributed to the grantor portion of an ESBT that is received by a NRA deemed owner of that portion, to escape Federal income taxation, contrary to Congressional intent. For example, if an NRA were to be a deemed owner of a grantor trust that elected to be an ESBT, and thus were to be allocated foreign source income of the S corporation or income not effectively connected with the conduct of a U.S. trade or business under section 864(c)(4)(B), that NRA would not be required to include such S corporation items in income under section 671 because the NRA would not be liable for Federal income tax on such income under section 871(a) or (b). Additionally, if that NRA is a resident of a country with which the United States has an income tax treaty, U.S. source income of the S corporation also might be exempt from tax or subject to a lower rate of Federal income tax in the hands of that NRA.

Under section 672(f)(2)(A)(ii), trust income, deductions, and credits are taxed to NRA grantors if the only amounts distributable from such portion (whether income or corpus) during the lifetime of the grantor are amounts distributable to the grantor or the spouse of the grantor. Such a trust would not be a foreign trust solely because the grantor retained this right, provided that (1) a U.S. court had primary jurisdiction over the trust, as required by section 7701(a)(30)(E)(i), and (2) U.S. persons controlled substantial trust decisions, as required by section 7701(a)(30)(E)(ii). Accordingly, a domestic trust described in section 672(f)(2)(A)(ii) that elects ESBT status would be a grantor trust, and the income from the trust would be taxed to the NRA grantor-owner(s) (that is, the grantor and the grantor's spouse) during the grantor's lifetime. These NRA deemed owners would not be subject to U.S. Federal income tax on the S corporation income unless this income was U.S. source fixed or determinable income or income effectively connected with a U.S. trade or business.

C. Income from S Portion of ESBT Should Not Escape U.S. Federal Income Taxation

In discussing the amendment to section 1361(c)(2)(B)(v) allowing an NRA to be a PCB of an ESBT, the Conference Report made the following two observations regarding present S corporation law: First, the portion of an ESBT that consists of S corporation stock "is treated as a separate trust" and generally (that is, not taking into account capital gains) is "taxed on its share of the S corporation's income at the highest rate of tax imposed on individual taxpayers." H. Rept. 115-466, at 517 (2017). See also § 1.641(c)-1(e)(1) (articulating the capital gains exception regarding Congress' use of the word "generally"). Second, Congress noted that an "[ESBT's share of S corporation] income (whether or not distributed by the ESBT) is not taxed to the beneficiaries of the ESBT." Id. These observations reflect the general rule of ESBT taxation that (i) subjects the ESBT to tax on its S corporation income at the trust level, rather than the beneficiary level, and accordingly (ii) is indifferent to the citizenship or residence status of the ESBT's beneficiaries because the ESBT must be domestic. The observations do not take into account the interaction between the ESBT and grantor trust tax regimes, which allows a trust to be an ESBT for S corporation qualification purposes while permitting all or a portion of the trust subject to the grantor trust provisions to be taxed as a grantor trust, rather than as an ESBT. As described earlier, § 1.641(c)-1(c) provides that the taxable income of a grantor trust that elects to be an ESBT is treated as the taxable income of the deemed owner of the trust (including a deemed owner who is an NRA), regardless of whether the ESBT distributes the income.

The report accompanying the Senate bill (Senate Report) similarly indicates that Congress assumed that the taxation of income at the ESBT level would protect against potential tax avoidance that might otherwise result from permitting an NRA to be a PCB of an ESBT: "An ESBT that is an S corporation shareholder is taxed on its share of the S corporation's income at the highest rate of tax imposed on individual taxpayers. For that reason, the Committee believes that allowing a nonresident alien individual to be a potential current beneficiary of an ESBT presents little risk of tax avoidance." S. Comm. on the Budget, Reconciliation Recommendations Pursuant to H. Con. Res. 71, S. Print No. 115-20, at 235-236 (2017).

Based on this legislative history of section 1361(c)(2)(B)(v), the Treasury Department and the IRS have determined that the expansion of that clause to allow an NRA to be an ESBT PCB was not intended to override longstanding statutory provisions that have operated to ensure that all of the S corporation income remains subject to Federal income tax. In the absence of regulations, the post-TCJA ability of an NRA to be a PCB of an ESBT, in combination with the potential for a grantor trust portion of an ESBT to be owned by an NRA under section 672(f)(2)(A)(1)(ii), could result in S corporation income passing without tax from the domestic ESBT to the NRA and escaping Federal income taxation.

Explanation of Provisions

These proposed regulations would ensure that, with respect to situations in which an NRA is a deemed owner of a grantor trust that has elected to be an ESBT, the S corporation income of the ESBT would continue to be subject to U.S. Federal income tax. Specifically, the proposed regulations would modify the allocation rules under § 1.641(c)-1 to require that the S corporation income of the ESBT be included in the S portion of the ESBT if that income otherwise would have been allocated to an NRA deemed owner under the grantor trust rules. Accordingly, such income would be taxed to the domestic ESBT by providing that, if the deemed owner is an NRA, the grantor portion of net income must be reallocated from the grantor portion of the ESBT to the ESBT's S portion.

The proposed regulations also would implement Congress' amendment to section 1361(c)(2)(B)(v) by making conforming revisions to § 1.1361-1(m). For example, the proposed regulations would update the description of PCBs in § 1.1361-1(m)(4)(i) to reflect the ability of NRAs to be PCBs of ESBTs. The proposed regulations similarly would update other provisions in § 1.1361-1(m) to reflect that ability.

Proposed Effective/Applicability Date

Section 7805(b)(1)(A) and (B) of the Code generally provide that no temporary, proposed, or final regulation relating to the internal revenue laws may apply to any taxable period ending before the earliest of (A) the date on which such regulation is filed with the **Federal Register**, or (B) in the case of a final regulation, the date on which a proposed or temporary regulation to which the final regulation relates was filed with the **Federal Register**. However, section 7805(b)(2) provides that regulations filed or issued within 18 months of the date of the enactment of the statutory provision to which they relate are not prohibited from applying to taxable periods prior to those described in section 7805(b)(1). Furthermore, section 7805(b)(3) provides that the Secretary may provide that any regulation may take effect or apply retroactively to prevent abuse.

Accordingly, to prevent abuse of sections 641 and 1361 and the regulations thereunder, these proposed regulations are proposed to apply to all ESBTs after December 31, 2017.

Special Analyses

This regulation is not subject to review under section 6(b) of Executive Order 12866 pursuant to the Memorandum of Agreement (April 11, 2018) between the Department of the Treasury and the Office of Management and Budget regarding review of tax regulations.

This notice of proposed rulemaking does not impose a collection of information on any small entities. Accordingly, a regulatory flexibility analysis under the Regulatory Flexibility Act (5 U.S.C. chapter 6) is not required. Notwithstanding this certification, the Treasury Department and the IRS invite comments from interested members of the public on both the number of entities affected and the economic impact on small entities.

Pursuant to section 7805(f) of the Code, this notice of proposed rulemaking has been submitted to the Chief Counsel for Advocacy of the Small Business Administration for comment on its impact on small business.

Comments and Requests for Public Hearing

Before these proposed regulations are adopted as final regulations, consideration will be given to any comments that are submitted timely to the IRS as prescribed in this preamble under the **ADDRESSES** heading.

All comments will be available at http://www.regulations.gov or upon request. A public hearing may be scheduled if requested in writing by any person that timely submits written comments. If a public hearing is scheduled, notice of the date, time, and place for the public hearing will be published in the **Federal Register**.

Drafting Information

The principal author of these proposed regulations is Cynthia Morton of the Office of Associate Chief Counsel (Passthroughs and Special Industries). However, other personnel from the IRS and the Treasury Department participated in their development.
